Y0-BDU-768

THE FAR EAST AND AUSTRALASIA
1982-83

THE FAR EAST AND AUSTRALASIA

1982-83

A Survey and Directory of Asia and the Pacific

EUROPA PUBLICATIONS LIMITED

18 BEDFORD SQUARE LONDON WC1B 3JN

Fourteenth Edition 1982–83

18 Bedford Square, London, WC1B 3JN

Library of Congress Catalog Card Number 74 - 417170

AUSTRALIA AND NEW ZEALAND
James Bennett (Collaroy) Pty. Ltd.,
4 Collaroy Street, Collaroy, N.S.W. 2097, Australia

INDIA
UBS Publishers Distributors Ltd.,
P.O.B. 7015, 5 Ansari Road, New Delhi 110002

JAPAN
Maruzen Co. Ltd., P.O.B. 5050, Tokyo International 100–31

British Library Cataloguing in Publication Data
The Far East and Australasia—14th ed.
(1982–83)
1. Asia—Periodicals
950'.428'05 DS1
ISBN 0-905118-76-6
ISSN 0071-3791

Printed and bound in England by
Staples Printers Rochester Limited
at The Stanhope Press.

Foreword

THE FAR EAST AND AUSTRALASIA is an annual reference book on the countries of Asia, including the Soviet Union in Asia, Australia and New Zealand and the Pacific Islands.

The first part of the book deals with topics relevant to the entire area such as development and population problems, recent political developments, commodities and religion. The section on commodities includes not only major agricultural products but also the most important minerals of the region. A survey (with index) of the major international organizations concerned with the area is also included. A calendar of the most important events which have taken place in the region in the past year is included at the very beginning of the book.

Information on individual countries is contained in Part Two. For each country or territory there are essays on its geography, history and economy, a statistical survey and detailed information on its constitution, government, legislature and other political, economic and commercial institutions. The information is revised annually by a variety of methods, including direct mailing to the institutions listed. Finally, a general reference section includes a Who's Who of prominent and distinguished personalities in the area, and sections on weights and measures, calendars and time reckoning, research institutes and a select bibliography of periodicals.

August 1982

Acknowledgements

The co-operation, interest and advice of all the authors who have contributed to this volume have been invaluable and greatly appreciated. We are also, of course, greatly in the debt of innumerable organizations connected with the Asian and Pacific region, especially the national statistical and information offices, whose co-operation in providing information we gratefully acknowledge. We are particularly grateful for permission to make extensive use of material from the following sources: the UN *Statistical Yearbook, Demographic Yearbook, Yearbook of Industrial Statistics* and *Yearbook of National Accounts Statistics*; the FAO *Production Yearbook, Yearbook of Forest Products* and *Yearbook of Fishery Statistics*; the ILO *Year Book of Labour Statistics*; and the IMF's monthly *International Financial Statistics*. We are also indebted to the International Institute for Strategic Studies, 23 Tavistock Street, London, WC2E 7NQ, for the use of defence statistics from *The Military Balance*.

We must also acknowledge our debt to other publications. The following in particular, have been of immense value in providing regular coverage of the affairs of the Asian and Pacific region: *Asia Research Bulletin*, Singapore; *Asiaweek*, Hong Kong; *The Far Eastern Economic Review*, and its *Asia Yearbook*, Hong Kong; *The Economist*, London; *IMF Survey*, Washington; *Keesing's Contemporary Archives*, Bath; and *Summary of World Broadcasts: Part 3, The Far East*, BBC, Reading.

Contents

Page

INDEX OF TERRITORIES ix
CONTRIBUTORS x
ABBREVIATIONS xii
CALENDAR OF EVENTS xviii

Part One
General Survey

ASIA AND THE PACIFIC: RECENT TRENDS 3
POPULATION IN ASIA AND THE PACIFIC 27
THE RELIGIONS OF ASIA 44
DEVELOPMENT PROBLEMS OF ASIA 56
MAJOR COMMODITIES OF ASIA AND THE PACIFIC 65

Part Two
Regional Organizations

THE UNITED NATIONS IN ASIA AND THE PACIFIC 99
- Members' Contributions, Year of Admission 99
- Permanent Missions 99
- The Trusteeship Council 100
- Economic and Social Commission for Asia and the Pacific—ESCAP 101
- Food and Agriculture Organization—FAO 105
- International Bank for Reconstruction and Development—IBRD (World Bank) 106
- International Development Association—IDA 107
- International Finance Corporation—IFC 108
- United Nations Development Programme—UNDP 108
- United Nations Educational, Scientific and Cultural Organization—UNESCO 110
- United Nations High Commissioner for Refugees—UNHCR 111
- World Health Organization—WHO 112
- Other Regional Offices of the UN System 113
- UN Information Centres 114

ANZUS 115
ASIAN DEVELOPMENT BANK—ADB 116
ASIAN PRODUCTIVITY ORGANIZATION—APO 120
ASSOCIATION OF SOUTH EAST ASIAN NATIONS—ASEAN 121
THE COLOMBO PLAN FOR CO-OPERATIVE ECONOMIC AND SOCIAL DEVELOPMENT IN ASIA AND THE PACIFIC 125
THE COMMONWEALTH 128
EUROPEAN COMMUNITY 130
SOUTH PACIFIC COMMISSION—SPC 131
SOUTH PACIFIC FORUM 134
- South Pacific Bureau for Economic Co-operation—SPEC 134

DIRECTORY OF OTHER REGIONAL ORGANIZATIONS 136
INDEX OF REGIONAL ORGANIZATIONS 142

CONTENTS

Part Three

Country Surveys

	Page
Afghanistan	145
Australia	179
Australian Dependencies in the Indian Ocean	237
Bangladesh	238
Bhutan	269
Brunei	277
Burma	290
China (including Taiwan)	325
Hong Kong	405
India	433
Indonesia	506
Japan	553
Kampuchea	619
Korea	634
Laos	700
Macau	720
Malaysia	732
Maldives	779
Mongolia	786
Nepal	807
New Zealand	826
Pacific Islands	865
Pakistan	959
The Philippines	1008
Singapore	1052
Sri Lanka	1090
Thailand	1124
U.S.S.R. in Asia	1161
Viet-Nam	1194

Other Reference Material

	Page
Who's Who in the Far East and Australasia	1230
Weights and Measures	1385
Calendars and Time Reckoning	1391
Research Institutes	1394
Select Bibliography (Periodicals)	1405

Index of Territories

Afghanistan, 145
American Samoa, 871
Australia, 179
Bangladesh, 238
Bhutan, 269
Brunei, 277
Burma, 290
Cambodia (*see* Kampuchea)
Caroline Islands, 940
Ceylon (*see* Sri Lanka)
China, 325
Christmas Island, 237
Cocos (Keeling) Islands, 237
Cook Islands, 873
Coral Sea Islands Territory, 876
Federated States of Micronesia (*see* Trust Territory of the Pacific Islands)
Fiji, 877
Formosa (*see* Taiwan)
French Polynesia, 888
Gilbert Islands (*see* Kiribati)
Guam, 891
Hawaii, 894
Hong Kong, 405
India, 433
Indonesia, 506
Japan, 553
Johnston Island, 896
Kampuchea, 634
Kazakh S.S.R., 1165
Kirghiz S.S.R., 1169
Kiribati, 897
Korea, Democratic People's Republic of (North Korea), 634, 635, 646, 651, 664
Korea, Republic of (South Korea), 634, 635, 640, 655, 676
Laos, 700
Macau, 720
Malaysia, 732
Maldives, 779
Marshall Islands, 940
Micronesia, Federated States of (*see* Trust Territory of the Pacific Islands)
Midway Islands, 900
Mongolia, 786
Nauru, 901
Nepal, 807
New Caledonia, 904
New Hebrides (*see* Vanuatu)
New Zealand, 826
Niue, 908
Norfolk Island, 910
Northern Mariana Islands, 912
Pacific Islands, Trust Territory of, 940
Pakistan, 959
Papua New Guinea, 914
The Philippines, 1008
Pitcairn Islands, 927
Samoa, American (*see* American Samoa)
Samoa, Western (*see* Western Samoa)
Siberia, 1181
Singapore, 1052
Solomon Islands, 928
Soviet Far East, 1181
Sri Lanka, 1090
Tadzhik S.S.R., 1172
Tahiti (*see* French Polynesia)
Taiwan, 327, 340, 350, 387
Thailand, 1124
Tokelau, 935
Tonga, 937
Trust Territory of the Pacific Islands, 940
Turkmen S.S.R., 1175
Tuvalu, 944
Uzbek S.S.R., 1178
Vanuatu, 947
Viet-Nam, 1194
Wake Island, 951
Wallis and Futuna Islands, 951
Western Samoa, 952

Contributors

Bryant J. Allen, Department of Human Geography, Research School of Pacific Studies, The Australian National University, Canberra.
(The Pacific Islands, p. 865.)

Iain Buchanan, Lecturer in Geography, University of Leicester, England.
(Petroleum, p. 77, Economic Survey of Indonesia, p. 514.)

T. M. Burley, Manager, Economist Intelligence Unit, London, England.
(History and Economic Survey of Brunei, pp. 277, 279, Economic Survey of North Korea, p. 651, South Korea, p. 655, Laos, p. 705, the Philippines, p. 1017.)

Renato Constantino, Professorial Lecturer, Department of Political Science, University of the Philippines.
(History of the Philippines, p. 1009.)

Harvey Demaine, Department of Geography, School of Oriental and African Studies, University of London.
(Physical and Social Geography of Brunei, p. 277, Burma, p. 290, Indonesia, p. 506, Kampuchea, p. 619, Laos, p. 700, Malaysia, p. 732, the Philippines, p. 1008, Singapore, p. 1052, Thailand, p. 1124, Viet-Nam, p. 1194; Economic Survey of Viet-Nam, p. 1204).

Christopher Dixon, Lecturer in Geography, City of London Polytechnic, London, England.
(Economic Survey of Indonesia, p. 514, Thailand, p. 1130.)

B. H. Farmer, Director, Centre of South Asian Studies, University of Cambridge, England.
(Physical and Social Geography of Bangladesh, p. 238, Bhutan, p. 269, India, p. 433, Maldives, p. 779, Nepal, p. 807, Pakistan, p. 959, Sri Lanka, p. 1090.)

Charles A. Fisher, late Professor of Geography, School of Oriental and African Studies, University of London, England.
(Physical and Social Geography of Brunei, p. 277, Burma, p. 290, Indonesia, p. 506, Kampuchea, p. 619, Laos, p. 700, Malaysia, p. 732, the Philippines, p. 1008, Singapore, p. 1052, Thailand, p. 1124, Viet-Nam, p. 1194.)

W. B. Fisher, former Professor of Geography, University of Durham, England.
(Physical and Social Geography of Afghanistan, p. 145.)

C. P. FitzGerald, Emeritus Professor, Australian National University, Canberra, Australia.
(History of China, p. 328, Taiwan, p. 340.)

Michael Freeberne, Lecturer in Geography, School of Oriental and African Studies, University of London, England.
(Physical and Social Geography of China, p. 357, Hong Kong, p. 405.)

J. M. Gullick, former Malaysian Civil Servant.
(History of Malaysia, p. 732.)

Hisao Kanamori, President, Japan Economic Research Center (Nihon Keizai Kenkyū Center), Tokyo, Japan.
(Economic Survey of Japan, p. 564.)

Frank H. H. King, Professor of Economic History, University of Hong Kong.
(Economic Survey of Hong Kong, p. 409 and Geography, History and Economic Survey of Macau, pp. 720, 722.)

E. Stuart Kirby, Professor Emeritus (International Economics), University of Aston, Birmingham, England; Senior Associate, St. Antony's College, Oxford, England; Visiting Professor, Slavic Research Institute, Hokkaido University, Japan, 1978–79.
(The Soviet Far East and Siberia, p. 1181.)

Jean-Pierre Lehmann, Director, Centre for Japanese Studies, University of Stirling.
(History of Japan, p. 555.)

Michael Leifer, Reader in International Relations, The London School of Economics and Political Science, University of London, England.
(History and Economic Survey of Kampuchea, pp. 619, 623.)

David H. B. Lim, formerly of the Economic Research Centre, University of Singapore.
(Economic Survey of Singapore, p. 1058.)

A. E. McQueen, Assistant General Manager, New Zealand Government Railways.
(Physical and Social Geography of Australia, p. 179, New Zealand, p. 826.)

W. J. Merrilees, Department of Economics, The University of Sydney.
(Economic Survey of Australia, p. 190.)

Norman Miners, Senior Lecturer in Political Science, University of Hong Kong.
(History of Hong Kong, p. 406.)

Sharif al Mujahid, Director, Quaid-i-Azam Academy, Karachi, Pakistan.
(History of Pakistan, p. 960.)

Ramon H. Myers, Curator, East Asian Collection, and Senior Fellow in the Hoover Institution, Stanford, Calif., U.S.A.
(Economic Survey of Taiwan, p. 350.)

Andrew C. Nahm, Professor of Asian History and Director, Center for Korean Studies, Western Michigan University, Kalamazoo, Mich., U.S.A.
(History of Korea, p.635.)

CONTRIBUTORS

Geoffrey Parrinder, Emeritus Professor of the Comparative Study of Religions, University of London, England.

(The Religions of Asia, p. 44).

Jan M. Pluvier, Institute for Modern Asiatic History, University of Amsterdam, The Netherlands.

(History of Indonesia, p. 508.)

Kevin Rafferty, Correspondent for various newspapers and journals in and about Asia; former editor *Business Times*, Kuala Lumpur, Malaysia; Consultant Editor, The Indian Express Group, Delhi and Bombay, India.

(Asia and the Pacific, p. 3, Economic Survey of Afghanistan, p. 155, Economic Survey of Bangladesh, p. 243, of India, p. 444, of Pakistan, p. 973.)

Carla on Rapoport, staff of *Financial Times*, London.

(Economic Survey of Hong Kong, p. 409).

Peter Robb, Lecturer in History, School of Oriental and African Studies, University of London, England.

(History of Bangladesh, p. 239, of India, p. 436.)

J. W. Rowe, Executive Director, New Zealand Employers' Federation; former Professor of Economics, Massey University, New Zealand.

(Economic Survey of New Zealand, p. 834.)

S. W. R. de A. Samarasinghe, Lecturer in Economics, University of Peradeniya, Peradeniya, Sri Lanka.

(Economic Survey of Sri Lanka, p. 1098).

A. J. K. Sanders, Fellow of the Institute of Linguists, London, England; BBC writer and broadcaster on Asian Affairs.

(Physical and Social Geography, History, Economic Survey and Statistical Survey of Mongolia, pp. 786, 787, 790 and 793, Mongolian biographies.)

John Sargent, Reader in Geography, School of Oriental and African Studies, University of London, England.

(Physical and Social Geography of Japan, p. 553, Korea, p. 634.)

Linda Seah, Lecturer, Department of Economics and Statistics, National University of Singapore.

(Economic Survey of Malaysia, p. 740, of Singapore, p. 1058).

Ann Sheehy, Senior Research Analyst, Radio Free Europe-Radio Liberty (Radio Liberty Division), Munich, Federal Republic of Germany.

(Soviet Central Asia, p. 1161.)

Kingsley M. de Silva, Professor of Ceylon History, University of Sri Lanka.

(History of Sri Lanka, p. 1091.)

Josef Silverstein, Professor of Political Science, Rutgers College, U.S.A.

(History of Burma, p. 292.)

Ralph Smith, Reader, History of South-East Asia, School of Oriental and African Studies, University of London, England.

(History of Laos, p. 700, History of Viet-Nam, p. 1195).

Philip A. Snow, M.B.E., J.P., Fellow of the Royal Anthropological Institute; former administrator, Fiji and the Western Pacific.

(Bibliography of the Pacific Territories, p. 957, Pacific biographies.)

David I. Steinberg, Office of Evaluation, Bureau for Program and Policy Coordination, Agency for International Development, Washington, D.C., U.S.A.

(Economic Survey of Burma, p. 300.)

Richard Storry, late Director of the Far East Centre and Fellow, St. Antony's College, Oxford, England.

(History of Japan, p. 555.)

E. J. Tapp, Visiting Lecturer in History, University of Waikato, New Zealand.

(History of Australia, p. 181, New Zealand, p. 828.)

C. Mary Turnbull, Department of History, University of Hong Kong.

(History of Singapore, p. 1052.)

Michael Williams, Fellow and Tutor in Geography, Oriel College, Oxford; University Lecturer, University of Oxford, England.

(Population in Asia and the Pacific, p. 22.)

Dick Wilson, formerly Editor, *The China Quarterly* and *Far Eastern Economic Review*, Hong Kong.

(Development Problems of Asia, p. 56.)

David K. Wyatt, Professor of South-East Asian History, Cornell University, Ithaca, N.Y., U.S.A.

(History of Thailand, p. 1125.)

Malcolm E. Yapp, Senior Lecturer in the History of the Near and Middle East, School of Oriental and African Studies, University of London, England.

(History of Afghanistan, p. 148.)

Abbreviations

A.A.S.A.	Associate of the Australian Society of Accountants
A.B.	Bachelor of Arts
A.B.C.	Australian Broadcasting Commission
A.C.	Companion of the Order of Australia
A.C.A.	Associate of the Institute of Chartered Accountants
Acad.	Academy; Academician
accred.	accredited
A.C.T.	Australian Capital Territory
ADB	Asian Development Bank
A.D.C.	Aide-de-camp
Adm.	Admiral
admin.	Administration, Administrative, Administrator
Af.	Afghani
A.F.C.	Air Force Cross
A.F.I.A.	Associate of the Federal Institute of Accountants (Australia)
Agric.	Agriculture
a.i.	ad interim
A.I.A.	Associate of the Institute of Actuaries
A.I.B.	Associate of the Institute of Bankers
A.I.C.C.	All-India Congress Committee
AID	Agency for International Development (U.S.A.)
A.I.F.	Australian Imperial Forces
AIR	All India Radio
A.K.	Knight of the Order of Australia
Alt.	Alternate
A.M.	Master of Arts; Member of the Order of Australia; Amplitude Modulation
Amb.	Ambassador
AMN	Ahli Mangku Negara (Malaysia)
A.M.N.Z.I.E.	Associate Member New Zealand Institute of Engineers
anon.	anonymous
ANSA	Agenzia Nazionale Stampa Associata (Italian News Agency)
ANU	Australian National University
ANZAC	Australian and New Zealand Army Corps
A.N.Z.I.C.	Associate New Zealand Institute of Chemists
ANZUS	Australia, New Zealand and the United States
A.O.	Officer of the Order of Australia
A.P.	Andhra Pradesh; Associated Press
approx.	approximately
apptd.	appointed
A.R.	Autonomous Region
Ariz.	Arizona
ASEAN	Association of South East Asian Nations
ASPAC	Asian and Pacific Council
asscn.	association
assoc.	associate, associated
A.S.S.R.	Autonomous Soviet Socialist Republic (U.S.S.R.)
asst.	assistant
Aug.	August
Aust.	Australia
auth.	authorized
avda.	avenida (avenue)
ave.	avenue
b.	born
B.A.	Bachelor of Arts
B.Admin.	Bachelor of Administration
B.Agr.	Bachelor of Agriculture
B.A.Sc.	Bachelor of Applied Sciences
B.B.A.	Bachelor of Business Administration
B.B.C.	British Broadcasting Corporation
B.Ch., B.Chir.	Bachelor of Surgery
B.C.L.	Bachelor of Civil Law; Bachelor of Canon Law
B.Com.	Bachelor of Commerce
B.D.	Bachelor of Divinity
Bd.	Board
B.E.	Bachelor of Engineering; Bachelor of Education
B.Ec., B.Econ	Bachelor of Economics
B.E.E.	Bachelor of Electrical Engineering
B.E.M.	British Empire Medal
B.Eng.	Bachelor of Engineering
Bhd.	Berhad (Public Limited Company)
Bldg.	Building
B.Litt.	Bachelor of Letters
B.LL.	Bachelor of Laws
B.L.S.	Bachelor of Library Sciences
Blvd.	Boulevard
B.Mus.	Bachelor of Music
Bn.	Battalion
B.O.C.	British Oxygen Company Ltd.
B.P.	British Petroleum; Boîte Postale (Postbox)
B.Paed.	Bachelor of Pædiatrics
b.p.d.	barrels per day
br.(s)	branch(es)
Brig.	Brigadier
B.S.	Bachelor of Surgery
B.S., B.Sc.	Bachelor of Science
B.S.A.	Bachelor of Scientific Agriculture
Bt.	Baronet
BTN	Brussels Tariff Nomenclature
C.	Centigrade
c.	circa
C.A.	Chartered Accountant
Calif.	California
Cantt.	Cantonment
cap.	capital
Capt.	Captain
C.B.	Companion of the (Order of the) Bath
C.B.E.	Commander of the (Order of the) British Empire
CCP	Chinese Communist Party
C.D.F.C.	Commonwealth Development Finance Company Ltd.
C.E.	Civil Engineer; Chartered Engineer
Cen.	Central
C.Eng.	Chartered Engineer
CENTO	Central Treaty Organization
CFP	Communauté française du pacifique
C.H.	Companion of Honour
Chair.	Chairman
Ch.B.	Bachelor of Surgery
Ch.M.	Master of Surgery
CIA	Central Intelligence Agency
C.I.E.	Companion of (the Order of) the Indian Empire
Cie.	Company
c.i.f.	cost, insurance and freight
circ.	circulation
C.-in-C.	Commander-in-Chief
cm.	centimetre(s)
C.M.	Master in Surgery
CMEA	Council for Mutual Economic Assistance (COMECON)

C.M.G. .. .. Companion of (the Order of) St. Michael and St. George
cnr. .. .. corner
CNRRA .. Chinese National Relief and Rehabilitation Administration
Co. .. .. Company; County
C.O. .. .. Commanding Officer
Col. .. .. Colonel
Coll. .. .. College
COMECON .. *see* CMEA
Comm. .. .. Commission
Commdg. .. Commanding
Commdr. .. Commander
Commr. .. Commissioner
Conf. .. .. Conference
Confed. .. .. Confederation
Conn. .. .. Connecticut
Co-op. .. .. Co-operative
Corpn. .. .. Corporation
Corr. .. .. Corresponding
Corresp. .. Correspondent; Corresponding
CP .. .. Communist Party
C.P.I. .. .. Communist Party of India
C.P.O. .. .. Central Post Office
CPPCC .. .. Chinese People's Political Consultative Conference
C.P.S.U. .. Communist Party of the Soviet Union
Cres. .. .. Crescent
C.S.C. .. .. Conspicuous Service Cross
C.S.I. .. .. Companion of (the Order of) the Star of India
CSIRO .. .. Commonwealth Scientific and Industrial Research Organization
C.St.J. .. .. Commander of (the Order of) St. John of Jerusalem
Cttee. .. .. Committee
cu. .. .. cubic
C.V.O. .. .. Commander of the (Royal) Victorian Order

D.Agr. .. .. Doctor of Agriculture
D.B. .. .. Bachelor of Divinity
D.B.A. .. .. Doctor of Business Administration
D.B.E. .. .. Dame Commander of (the Order of) the British Empire
D.C.L. .. .. Doctor of Civil Law
D.D., D.Dr. .. Doctor of Divinity
D. de l'Univ. .. Docteur de l'Université
D.D.S. .. .. Doctor of Dental Surgery
D.D.Sc.. .. Doctor of Dental Science (Melbourne)
Dec. .. .. December
D.Econ. .. Doctor of Economics
del. .. .. delegate, delegation
D. en D. .. Docteur en Droit (Doctor of Law)
D. en Fil. y Let. .. Doctor of Philosophy and Letters
D.Eng. .. .. Doctor of Engineering
Dem. .. .. Democratic
dep. .. .. deposit(s)
Dept. .. .. Department
devt. .. .. development
D.F.A. .. .. Diploma of Fine Arts
D.F.C. .. .. Distinguished Flying Cross
D.H. .. .. Doctor of Humanities
Dip.N.Z.L.S. .. Diploma of the New Zealand Library Society
Dipl. .. .. Diploma
Dir. .. .. Director
Div. .. .. Division(al)
D.K. .. .. Darjah Kerabat (Malaysia)
D.K.M. .. .. Darjah Kerabat Di Rajah Malaysia
D.L. .. .. Doctor of Laws
D.Lit(t). .. Doctor of Letters; Doctor of Literature
D.Met. .. .. Diploma of Meteorology
D.M.N. .. .. Darjah Utama Seri Mahkota Negara (Malaysia)
D.Mus. .. .. Doctor of Music
D.P.A. .. .. Diploma in Public Administration
D.P.H. .. .. Diploma in Public Health
D.Phil. .. .. Doctor of Philosophy
D.Phil.Nat. .. Doctor of Natural Philosophy
D.P.M. .. .. Dato Paduka Mahkota (Most Honourable Order of the Crown)
D.P.M.T. .. Datuk Paduka Mahkota Trengganu (Malaysia)
D.P.R. .. .. Democratic People's Republic
Dr. .. .. Doctor
Dr.Ec. .. .. Doctor of Economics
Dr.Jur. .. .. Doctor of Laws
D.S.C. .. .. Distinguished Service Cross
D.Sc. .. .. Doctor of Science
D.S.O. .. .. Distinguished Service Order
D.T.M. .. .. Diploma of Tropical Medicine
D.T.M. and H. .. Diploma of Tropical Medicine and Hygiene
D.V.M. .. .. Doctor of Veterinary Medicine
D.V.Sc. .. .. Doctor of Veterinary Science
d.w.t. .. .. dead weight tons

E. .. .. East, Eastern, Evening, Embassy
ECAFE .. .. Economic Commission for Asia and the Far East (UN) (*see* ESCAP)
Econ. .. .. Economist, Economics
ECOSOC .. Economic and Social Council (UN)
E.D. .. .. Doctor of Engineering; Efficiency Decoration
ed. .. .. educated; editor
Ed.B. .. .. Bachelor of Education
Ed.M. .. .. Master of Education
edn. .. .. edition
Educ. .. .. Education
EEC .. .. European Economic Community
EFTA .. .. European Free Trade Association
e.g. .. .. exempli gratia (for example)
Elec. .. .. Electrical
Emer. .. .. Emeritus
Eng. .. .. Engineer, Engineering
Eng.D. .. .. Doctor of Engineering
ESCAP .. .. Economic and Social Commission for Asia and the Pacific (UN)
est. .. .. established; estimate; estimated
etc. .. .. etcetera
excl. .. .. excluding
Exec. .. .. Executive
exhbn. .. .. exhibition
Ext. .. .. External, Externas, Extension

F. .. .. Fahrenheit; Franc
f. .. .. founded
F.A.A. .. .. Fellow Australian Academy of Sciences
F.A.A.S. .. Fellow of the American Academy for the Advancement of Science
F.A.C.E. .. Fellow of the Australian College of Education
F.A.C.P. .. Fellow of the American College of Physicians
F.A.C.S. .. Fellow of the American College of Surgeons
F.A.H.A. .. Fellow of the Australian Academy of the Humanities
F.A.I.A.S. .. Fellow of the Australian Institute of Agricultural Science
F.A.I.I. .. Fellow of the Australian Insurance Institute

F.A.I.M. .. Fellow of the Australian Institute of Management
F.A.I.P. .. Fellow of the Australian Institute of Physics
F.A.M.S. .. Fellow Indian Academy of Medical Sciences
FAO .. .. Food and Agriculture Organization
F.A.S.A. .. Fellow of the Australian Society of Accountants
F.A.S.S.A. .. Fellow of the Academy of Social Sciences in Australia
F.C.A. .. .. Fellow of the Institute of Chartered Accountants
F.C.I.S... .. Fellow of the Chartered Institute of Secretaries
F.C.O. .. .. Foreign and Commonwealth Office
Feb. .. .. February
Fed. .. .. Federation, Federal
FIDES .. .. Fonds d'Investissement pour le Développement Economique et Social (Investment Fund for Economic and Social Development)
FIDOM .. .. Fonds d'Investissement des Départements d'Outre-Mer (Investment Fund of the Overseas Territories)
F.I.E. .. .. Fellow of the Institution of Engineers
F.I.E.A. .. Fellow of the Institute of Education Administration
F.I.E.E. .. Fellow of the Institution of Electrical Engineers
Fin. .. .. Financial
F.Inst.P. .. Fellow of the Institute of Physics
FM .. .. Frequency Modulation
fmr.(ly) .. .. former(ly)
F.N.I. .. .. Fellow of the National Institute of Sciences of India
F.N.Z.I. .. Fellow of the New Zealand Institute
f.o.b. .. .. free on board
F.P.A.N.Z. .. Fellow, Public Accountant, New Zealand
F.R.A.C.I. .. Fellow of the Royal Australian Chemical Institute
F.R.A.C.P. .. Fellow Royal Australasian College of Physicians
F.R.A.C.S. .. Fellow of the Royal Australasian College of Surgeons
F.R.A.I.A. .. Fellow of the Royal Australian Institute of Architects
F.R.A.S. .. Fellow of the Royal Astronomical Society; Fellow of the Royal Asiatic Society
F.R.C.M. .. Fellow of the Royal College of Music
F.R.C.O.G. .. Fellow of the Royal College of Obstetricians and Gynaecologists
F.R.C.P. .. Fellow of the Royal College of Physicians
F.R.C.S. .. Fellow of the Royal College of Surgeons
Fri. .. .. Friday
F.R.Met.Soc. .. Fellow of the Royal Meteorological Society
F.R.M.S. .. Fellow of the Royal Microscopical Society
F.R.S. .. .. Fellow of the Royal Society
F.R.S.A. .. Fellow of the Royal Society of Arts
F.R.S.N.Z. .. Fellow of the Royal Society of New Zealand
F.S.S. .. .. Fellow of the Royal Statistical Society
ft. .. .. foot (feet)
F.T.S. .. .. Fellow of the Australian Academy of Technological Sciences
FUNC/K .. Front uni national du Kampuchea (United National Front of Cambodia)
F.Z.S. .. .. Fellow of the Zoological Society

Ga. .. .. Georgia
GATT .. .. General Agreement on Tariffs and Trade
G.B.E. .. Knight (or Dame) Grand Cross of (the Order of) the British Empire
G.C. .. .. George Cross
G.C.B. .. .. Knight Grand Cross of (the Order of) the Bath
G.C.I.E. .. (Knight) Grand Commander of the Indian Empire
G.C.M.G. .. Knight Grand Cross of (the Order of) St. Michael and St. George
G.C.S.I. .. Knight Grand Commander of the Star of India
G.C.V.O. .. Knight Grand Cross of the (Royal) Victorian Order
G.D.P. .. Gross Domestic Product
Gen. .. .. General
G.M.B.E. .. Grand Master of the Order of the British Empire
G.N.P. .. Gross National Product
GOC (in C) .. General Officer Commanding (in Chief)
Gov. .. .. Governor
Govt. .. .. Government
G.P.O. .. General Post Office
Grp. Capt. .. Group Captain
g.r.t. .. .. gross registered tons
GRUNC/K .. Gouvernement royal d'union nationale du Kampuchea (Royal Government of National Union of Cambodia)

ha. .. .. hectare(s)
h.c. .. .. honoris causa
HC .. .. High Commission(er)
H.E. .. .. His (or Her) Eminence; His (or Her) Excellency
H.H. .. .. His (or Her) Highness
H.I.H. .. .. His (or Her) Imperial Highness
hl. .. .. hectolitre(s)
H.M. .. .. His (or Her) Majesty
H.M.S. .. .. His (or Her) Majesty's Ship
Hon. .. .. Honorary; Honourable
Hosp. .. .. Hospital
H.Pk. .. .. Hilal-e-Pakistan
H.Q. .. .. Headquarters
H.R.H. .. .. His (or Her) Royal Highness
H.S.H. .. .. His (or Her) Serene Highness
Hum.D. .. Doctor of Humanities

IAEA .. .. International Atomic Energy Agency
IAS .. .. Indian Administrative Service
IBRD .. .. International Bank for Reconstruction and Development (World Bank)
ICAO .. .. International Civil Aviation Organization
ICC .. .. International Chamber of Commerce
ICFTU .. International Confederation of Free Trade Unions
ICOM .. .. International Council of Museums
I.C.S. .. .. Indian Civil Service
ICSU .. International Council for Scientific Unions
IDA .. .. International Development Association
I.E.E. .. .. Institution of Electrical Engineers
I.E.S. .. .. Indian Educational Service
IFC .. .. International Finance Corporation
I.F.S. .. .. Indian Forest Service

ABBREVIATIONS

IGC .. .. International Geophysical Committee
Ill. .. .. Illinois
ILO .. .. International Labour Organisation
IMCO .. .. Inter-Governmental Maritime Consultative Organization
IMF .. .. International Monetary Fund
I.M.S. .. .. Indian Medical Service
in. (ins.) .. inch (inches)
Inc. .. .. Incorporated
incl. .. .. including
Ind. .. .. Independent
Ing. .. .. Engineer
Insp. .. .. Inspector
Inst. .. .. Institute
Int. .. .. International
IPU .. .. Inter-Parliamentary Union
Ir. .. .. Engineer
Is. .. .. Island(s)
I.S.E. .. .. Indian Service of Engineers
ITU .. .. International Telecommunications Union
I.U.P.A.C. .. International Union of Pure and Applied Chemistry

JAL .. .. Japan Airlines
Jan. .. .. January
J.C.D. .. .. Dr. Canon Law
J.D. .. .. Doctor of Jurisprudence
J.M.K. .. Setia Jiwa Mahkota Kelantan
J.M.N. .. Johan Mangku Negara (Malaysia)
Jnr., Jr. .. Junior
J.P. .. .. Justice of the Peace
J.S.D. .. .. Doctor of Juristic Science
J.S.M. .. .. Johan Setia Mahkota (Malaysia)
Jt. .. .. Joint
J.U.D. .. .. Doctor of Canon or Civil Law

K .. .. kina
K.B.E. .. .. Knight Commander of (the Order of) the British Empire
K.C.B. .. .. Knight Commander of (the Order of) the Bath
K.C.I.E. .. Knight Commander of (the Order of) the Indian Empire
K.C.M.G. .. Knight Commander of (the Order of) St. Michael and St. George
K.C.S.I. .. Knight Commander of the Star of India
K.C.V.O. .. Knight Commander of the (Royal) Victorian Order
kg. .. .. kilogramme(s)
K.G. .. .. Knight of (the Order of) the Garter
K.K. .. .. Kaien Kaisha (Limited Company) (Japan)
KLM .. .. Koninklijke Luchtvaart Maatschappij (Royal Dutch Airlines)
km. .. .. kilometre(s)
K.M.N. .. .. Kesatria Mangku Negara (Malaysian decoration)
KNUFNS .. Kampuchean National United Front for National Salvation
K.St.J. .. .. Knight of (the Order of) St. John
K.T. .. .. Knight of (the Order of) the Thistle
Kt. .. .. Knight
kW. .. .. kilowatt(s)
kWh. .. .. kilowatt hours

lb. .. .. pound(s)
Legis. .. .. Legislative, Legislature
L. en D. .. Licencié en Droit
Lib.Dip. .. Librarian Diploma
Libr. .. .. Librarian
Lic. .. .. Licenciado (Licenciate of law)
L.H.D. .. .. Doctor of Literature
Litt.D. .. .. Doctor of Letters
LL.B. .. .. Bachelor of Laws
LL.D. .. .. Doctor of Laws
LL.M. .. .. Master of Laws
L.M.S. .. .. London Missionary Society
LN .. .. League of Nations
LNG .. .. liquefied natural gas
LPG .. .. liquefied petroleum gas
L.R.C.P. .. Licentiate of the Royal College of Physicians
Lt., Lieut. .. Lieutenant
Ltd. .. .. Limited

m. .. .. million
M.A. .. .. Master of Arts
M.Agr.Sc. .. Master of Agricultural Science
Maj. .. .. Major
Man. .. .. Manager; Managing; Management
MAPHILINDO Malaya, Philippines, Indonesia
Mar. .. .. March
M.Arch. .. Master of Architecture
Mass. .. .. Massachusetts
Math. .. .. Mathematics, Mathematical
M.B. .. .. Bachelor of Medicine
M.B.A. .. .. Master of Business Administration
M.B.E. .. .. Member of (the Order of) the British Empire
M.C. .. .. Military Cross
M.C.A. .. .. Malay Chinese Association
M.Ch. .. .. Master of Surgery
M.Com. .. .. Master of Commerce
M.D. .. .. Doctor of Medicine
M.D.S. .. .. Master of Dental Surgery
MEA .. .. Middle East Airlines
M.Ec. .. .. Master of Economics
Mech. .. .. Mechanics, Mechanical
Med. .. .. Medical
mem. .. .. member
Mfg. .. .. Manufacturing
Mfr.(s) .. .. Manufacturer(s)
Mgr. .. .. Monsignor, Monseigneur
M.H.A. .. .. Member of the House of Assembly
M.I.C. .. .. Malay Indian Congress
Mich. .. .. Michigan
M.I.E.Aust. .. Member of the Institution of Engineers of Australia
Mil. .. .. Military
M.L. .. .. Master of Laws
M.L.A. .. .. Member of the Legislative Assembly
M.L.C. .. .. Member of the Legislative Council
M.M. .. .. Military Medal
Mon. .. .. Monday
M.P. .. .. Member of Parliament; Madhya Pradesh
M.P.H. .. .. Master of Public Health
M.Pharm. .. Master of Pharmacy
M.R.C.P. .. Member of the Royal College of Physicians
M.R.C.S. .. Member of the Royal College of Surgeons
M.R.C.V.S. .. Member of the Royal College of Veterinary Surgeons
M.R.S.H. .. Member of the Royal Society for the Promotion of Health
M.R.S.L. .. Member of the Royal Society of Literature
M.S. .. .. Master of Science; Master of Surgery
M.Sc. .. .. Master of Science
M.Sc.Tech. .. Master of Technical Science
MSS. .. .. Manuscripts
Mt. .. .. Mount, Mountain

m.t. .. .. metric ton(s)
M.Th. .. .. Master of Theology
M.V.O. .. .. Member of the (Royal) Victorian Order
MW. .. .. Megawatt(s)
MWh. .. .. Megawatt hour(s)

N. .. .. North, Northern
n.a. .. .. not available
Nat. .. .. National
NATO .. .. North Atlantic Treaty Organization
n.e.s. .. .. not elsewhere specified
NH .. .. néo-hébridais
N.I. .. .. North Island
N.J. .. .. New Jersey
NLF .. .. National Liberation Front (of South Viet-Nam)
no. .. .. number
Nov. .. .. November
N.P.C. .. .. National People's Congress
N.R. .. .. Nepalese Rupee(s)
n.r.t. .. .. net registered tons
N.S.W. .. .. New South Wales
NT .. .. New Taiwan
N.V. .. .. Naamloze Vennootschap (Limited Company)
N.W.F.P. .. North-West Frontier Province
N.Y. .. .. New York
N.Z. .. .. New Zealand

O.B.E. .. .. Officer of (the Order of) the British Empire
O.C. .. .. Officer Commanding
Oct. .. .. October
O.D.I. .. .. Overseas Development Institute
OECD .. .. Organisation for Economic Co-operation and Development
O.F.M. .. .. Order of Friars Minor
O.M. .. .. Member of the Order of Merit
O.P. .. .. Order of Preachers (Dominicans)
OPEC .. .. Organization of Petroleum Exporting Countries
Org. .. .. Organization, organizing
O.S.B. .. .. Order of St. Benedict
oz. .. .. ounce(s)

p.a. .. per annum
Pa. .. .. Pennsylvania
P.A.F. .. .. Philippines Air Force
PAL .. .. Philippines Air Lines, Inc.
Parl. .. .. Parliament, Parliamentary
Path. .. .. Pathology
P.C. .. .. Privy Counsellor
P.C.C. .. .. Provincial Congress Committee
P.D.K. .. .. Panglima Darjah Kinabalu
Perm. .. .. Permanent
Phar.D. .. .. Doctor of Pharmacy
Ph.D. .. .. Doctor of Philosophy
Ph.L. .. .. Licentiate of Philosophy
PIA .. .. Pakistan International Airlines
P.I.S. .. .. Pingat Sultan Ibrahim (Malaysia)
P.J.K. .. .. Pingat Jasa Kebaktian (Malaysia)
P.K.T. .. .. Pingat Kalakuan Terpuji (Malaysia)
pl. .. .. place, platz, ploschad (square)
PLA .. .. People's Liberation Army (China)
P.M.K. .. .. Paduka Mahkota Kelantan (Malaysia)
P.M.N. .. .. Panglima Mangku Negara (Malaysia)
P.M.P. .. .. Paduka Mahkota Perak (Malaysia)
P.N. .. .. Pakistan Navy
P.N.B.S. .. Panglima Negara Bintang Sarawak (Malaysia)
P.N.G. .. .. Papua New Guinea
P.O. .. .. Post Office
P.O.B. .. .. Post Office Box
Pol., Polit. .. Political
P.P.T. .. .. Pingat Pekerti Terpileh (Malaysia)
P.R. .. .. People's Republic; Public Relations
pr. .. .. prospekt (avenue)
Pref. .. .. Prefecture
Pres. .. .. President
PRG .. .. Provisional Revolutionary Government (of South Viet-Nam)
Prof. .. .. Professor
Propr. .. .. Proprietor
Prov. .. .. Province; provincial; provisional
P.S.D. .. .. Panglima Setia Di Raja (Malaysia)
P.S.M. .. .. Panglima Setia Mahkota (Malaysia)
PTT .. .. Post, Telegraphs, Telephones
Pte. .. .. Private
Pty. .. .. Proprietary
p.u. .. .. paid up
publ. .. .. publication
Publr. .. .. Publisher
P.Y.G.P. .. Darjah Pahlawan Yang Amat Gagah Perkasa Kelantan (Malaysia)

Q.C. .. .. Queen's Counsel
Qld. .. .. Queensland
q.v. .. .. quod vide (to which refer)

R(s). .. .. Rupee(s)
R.A.A.F. .. Royal Australian Air Force
R.A.F. .. .. Royal Air Force
R.A.M.C. .. Royal Army Medical Corps
R.A.N. .. .. Royal Australian Navy
Rd. .. .. Road
Ref. .. .. Reference
reg. .. .. registered
Regt. .. .. Regiment
Rep., rep. .. Republican, representative
Repub. .. .. Republic
res. .. .. reserve(s)
resgnd. .. .. resigned
retd. .. .. retired
rev. .. .. revised
Rev. .. .. Reverend
R.I. .. .. Royal Institute
Rm. .. .. Room
RMB .. .. Renminbi ("People's Currency" in China)
R.N. .. .. Royal Navy
R.N.V.R. .. Royal Navy Volunteer Reserve
R.N.Z.A.F. .. Royal New Zealand Air Force
Rp(s). .. .. Rupiah(s)
R.S.F.S.R. .. Russian Soviet Federative Socialist Republic
Rt. .. .. Right
R.T.A. .. .. Royal Thai Army
R.T.A.F. .. Royal Thai Air Force

S. .. .. South, Southern
S.A. .. .. South Africa; South Australia; Société Anonyme; Sociedad Anónima (limited company)
SAS .. .. Scandinavian Airlines System
S.B. .. .. Bachelor of Science
Sc.D. .. .. Doctor of Science
Sdn. Bhd. .. Sendirian Berhad (Private Limited Company)
SDR(s) .. .. Special Drawing Right(s)
SEATO .. .. South-East Asia Treaty Organization
Sec. .. .. Secretary; section
Secr. .. .. Secretariat
Sept. .. .. September
SIA .. .. Singapore Airlines Ltd.

S.I.M.P. .. Seri Indera Mahkota Pahang (Malaysia)
Sir J. J. .. Sir Jamsetjee Jeejeebhoy
SITC .. .. Standard International Trade Classification
S.J. .. .. Society of Jesus (Jesuits)
S.J.D. .. .. Doctor of Juristic Science
S.J.M.K. .. Seri Paduka Jiwa Mahkota Kelantan (Malaysia)
S.M. .. .. Master of Science
S.M.N. .. .. Seri Maharaja Mangku Negara (Malaysia)
S.M.R. .. Standard Malaysian Rubber Scheme
S.O.A.S. .. School of Oriental and African Studies, University of London
Soc. .. .. Society
SPC .. .. South Pacific Commission
S.Pk. .. .. Sitara-e-Pakistan
S.P.M.K. .. Seri Paduka Mahkota Kelantan (Kedah) (Malaysia)
S.P.M.P. .. Seri Paduka Mahkota Perak (Perlis) (Malaysia)
S.P.M.S. .. Seri Paduka Mahkota Selangor (Malaysia)
sq. .. .. square
Sqn. .. .. Squadron
Sr., Snr. .. Senior
S.S.R. .. .. Soviet Socialist Republic
St. .. .. Saint; San; Santo; Street
Sta. .. .. Santa
S.T.D. .. .. Sacrae Theologiæ Doctor (Doctor of Sacred Theology)
Supt. .. .. Superintendent

TAB .. .. Technical Assistance Board (UN)
T.A.C. .. .. Technical Assistance Committee
Tas. .. .. Tasmania
TASS .. .. Telegrafnoye Agenstvo Sovietskovo Soyuza (Soviet News Agency)
T.D. .. .. Territorial Decoration
tech., techn. .. technical, technology, technological
Th.D. .. .. Doctor of Theology
Th.L. .. .. Theological Licentiate
Th.M. .. .. Master of Theology
Thurs. .. .. Thursday
T.N.I. .. .. Tintara Nasional Indonesia
trans. .. .. translator, translated
Treas. .. .. Treasurer
T.U. .. .. Trade Union
T.U.C. .. .. Trades Union Congress
Tues. .. .. Tuesday
TV .. .. television
TWA .. .. Trans World Airlines, Inc.

Ul. .. .. ulitsa (street)
U.K. .. .. United Kingdom
UN .. .. United Nations
UNCDF .. United Nations Capital Development Fund
UNCTAD .. United Nations Conference on Trade and Development
UNCURK .. United Nations Commission for the Unification and Rehabilitation of Korea
UNDP .. United Nations Development Programme
UNEF .. United Nations Emergency Force
UNESCO .. United Nations Educational, Scientific and Cultural Organization
UNHCR .. United Nations High Commission for Refugees
UNICEF .. United Nations Children's Fund
UNIDO .. United Nations Industrial Development Organization
UNITAR .. United Nations Institute for Training and Research
Univ. .. .. University
UNKRA .. United Nations Korean Reconstruction Agency
UNMOGIP .. United Nations Military Observer Group for India and Pakistan
UNROB .. United Nations Relief Office, Bangladesh
UNROD .. United Nations Relief Operation, Dacca
UNRRA .. United Nations Relief and Rehabilitation Administration
UNRWA .. United Nations Relief and Works Agency
U.P. .. .. Uttar Pradesh
UPI .. .. United Press International
UPU .. .. Universal Postal Union
U.S.A. .. .. United States of America
U.S.S.R. .. Union of Soviet Socialist Republics
UTA .. .. Union des Transports Aériens

V.C. .. .. Victoria Cross
V.D. .. .. Volunteer Officers' Decoration; Victorian Decoration
Ven. .. .. Venerable
VHF .. .. Very High Frequency
Vic. .. .. Victoria
vol.(s) .. .. volume(s)

W. .. .. West, Western
W.A. .. .. Western Australia
Wash. .. .. Washington (state)
Wed. .. .. Wednesday
WFTU .. .. World Federation of Trade Unions
WHO .. .. World Health Organization
WMO .. .. World Meteorological Organization

Y.M.C.A. .. Young Men's Christian Association
yr. .. .. year
Y.W.C.A. .. Young Women's Christian Association

Calendar of Events

1981

AUGUST

9 *Thailand:* former Prime Minister, Gen. Kriangsak Chomanan, won by-election in north-eastern province of Roi Et.
11 *Thailand:* Gen. Prayuth Churumanee appointed army Commander-in-Chief in place of Premier Prem. Tinsulamond.
12 *Sri Lanka:* former Prime Minister, Mrs. Sirimavo Bandaranaike, escaped injury when bombs were thrown at a platform from which she was addressing a political meeting in Gampaha; 70 people hurt.
China: Taiwanese air force officer, Major Huang Zhicheng, who defected to the People's Republic on August 11th, given reward worth U.S. $400,000 by the PLA.
13 *New Zealand:* fire destroyed the grandstand at the Christchurch rugby ground where the first Test match between New Zealand and the touring South African Springboks was due to be played; arson suspected.
14 *India:* Government banned strikes in certain essential services for six months in Assam following 24-hour general strike.
15 *Sri Lanka:* troops opened fire on rioters in Gampaha.
Pakistan: main leftist opposition leaders released from prison.
17 *Afghanistan:* President Babrak Karmal announced establishment of Defence Council to co-ordinate all state and military departments in fight against rebels.
21 *Sri Lanka:* press censorship imposed by Government.
25 *Sri Lanka:* death penalty introduced for unlawful possession and transport of weapons and explosives.
Democratic People's Republic of Korea: thought to have fired a missile at U.S. Air Force SR71 reconnaissance aircraft flying in Republic of Korea and international air space.
27 *New Zealand:* M.P.s unanimously rejected proposal for referendum on New Zealand's sporting links with South Africa, prompted by controversial Springbok rugby tour.
31 *Sri Lanka:* President Jayawardene, the Prime Minister, eight Cabinet ministers and opposition Tamil United Liberation Front leaders agreed to set up a joint committee, with the President as Chairman, to discuss their differences.
Solomon Islands: Parliament elected new Prime Minister, Solomon Mamaloni.

SEPTEMBER

1 *U.S.A.:* agreed to pay about £600,000 compensation to the insurer, owner and charterer of Japanese cargo ship sunk in collision with U.S. Navy nuclear submarine *George Washington* on April 9th.
2 *India:* rejected credentials of George Griffin, prospective political counsellor in U.S. Embassy in Delhi; he was accused in India and on Soviet radio of being a CIA agent.
4 *Kampuchea:* three resistance leaders, Norodom Sihanouk, Son Sann and Khieu Samphan, agreed in Singapore on joint political and military action against Vietnamese-backed Phnom-Penh regime.
6 *Bangladesh:* general strike called, then cancelled by opposition groups after Government announced deferral of presidential election to November 15th; opposition parties wanted more time to campaign.
8 *Tuvalu:* first general election since independence.
11 *China:* Cabinet reshuffle announced; Li Qiang resigned as Minister of Foreign Trade.
16 *India:* bill prohibiting strikes in essential services approved by Lok Sabha (Lower House).
17 *Malaysia:* Foreign Minister, Muhammad Ghazalie bin Shafie, said that diplomatic relations would be accorded the PLO.
Tuvalu: Parliament elected new Prime Minister, Dr. Tomasi Puapua.
18 *India:* vote of "no confidence" in Mrs. Gandhi's Government defeated in Lok Sabha by 294 votes to 83.
Kampuchea: ousted Khmer Rouge regime retained right to represent the country at UN by vote of 77–37 (31 abstentions) in General Assembly.
21 *Bangladesh:* state of emergency, imposed after assassination of President Ziaur Rahman, officially terminated.

23 *Bangladesh:* violent protests against execution in Dacca of 12 army officers convicted of complicity in assassination of President Ziaur Rahman.

24 *Kampuchea:* mass graves of more than 65,000 people, killed in Pol Pot era, discovered by Vietnamese.

30 *Australia:* conference of Commonwealth Heads of Government began in Melbourne; Malaysia's Prime Minister declined to attend.

China: Marshal Ye Jianying, in interview with Xinhua news agency, made further overtures to Taiwan on the subject of ultimate political union with the mainland.

Republic of Korea: Seoul chosen as venue for 1988 Olympic Games by International Olympic Committee.

Pakistan: commandos overpowered five Sikh extremists who had hijacked an India Airlines aircraft and 45 passengers and taken them to Lahore.

OCTOBER

1 *Thailand:* fifth five-year economic and social development plan launched.

3 *Malaysia:* Prime Minister Mahathir Mohamad said that all future Government purchases of British goods and services would first have to be cleared by his office; seen as retaliation against British measures to tighten rules on corporate takeovers by Malaysia and other countries.

4 *Burma:* voting began in two-week long general election.

10 *China:* on anniversary of 1911 revolution, Hu Yaobang, Communist Party Chairman, invited President Chiang Ching-kuo and Prime Minister Sun Yun-suan of Taiwan to visit the mainland, irrespective of their views on holding reunification talks.

14 *Japan:* Yasser Arafat, leader of PLO, held talks with Prime Minister Suzuki and Foreign Minister Sonoda.

China: diplomatic sources in Beijing said that 100 men died when the submarine they were in exploded during ballistic missile tests in September.

15 *Viet-Nam:* Yasser Arafat arrived on official visit.

China: launched its second nuclear-powered submarine in May, according to diplomatic sources.

16 *Japan:* nearly 100 people killed in colliery disaster at Yubari, Hokkaido.

23 *Singapore:* C. V. Devan Nair named third President of Singapore and formally voted in by Parliament.

30 *India:* England cricket team's tour, which had been put in jeopardy by sporting links with South Africa of two of its members, approved by Indian Cabinet.

30 *Singapore:* J. B. Jeyaretnam, of opposition Workers' Party, became first opposition M.P. for 15 years by winning a by-election.

NOVEMBER

8 *Burma:* U Thaung Kyi, Secretary-General of ruling Burma Socialist Programme Party, died.

9 *Sri Lanka:* pacts of 1964 and 1974 with India, to settle about 1 million stateless people of Indian origin from tea plantations, lapsed this month with the future of half this number still undecided; India was to take back 600,000 (has taken 365,000) and Sri Lanka to give citizenship to 400,000 (has granted it to 160,000).

Burma: U Ne Win stood down as President (remaining leader of Burma Socialist Programme Party for a further four years), to be replaced by U San Yu.

12 *France:* Mrs. Gandhi began first state visit for 10 years.

14 *Kampuchea:* three main resistance groups agreed in Bangkok the principles and political programme of a coalition government in exile.

China: agreed to pay its contribution of U.S. $59 million, outstanding for 10 years, to UN budget.

15 *Bangladesh:* Abdus Sattar elected by overwhelming majority in presidential election.

17 *Sri Lanka:* state of emergency, in force since August 17th, extended for a further month.

18 *Afghanistan:* UN General Assembly voted 116–23 (12 abstentions) for immediate withdrawal of Soviet troops.

19 *Taiwan:* Gen. Kao Kuei-yuan resigned as Defence Minister for health reasons.

23 *India:* expelled three Pakistani diplomats accused of spying.

24 *Pakistan:* expelled four Indian diplomats.

Bangladesh: Dr. Mirza Nurul Huda appointed Vice-President.

25 *Taiwan:* Cabinet reshuffle.

26 *Taiwan:* Gen. Hua Pei-tsun appointed Chief of General Staff.
China: formally postponed scheduled revision of its constitution.
28 *Bangladesh:* President Sattar appointed 42-member Council of Ministers, taking Defence and Planning portfolios himself.
New Zealand: general election thought to have resulted in first ever "hung" Parliament.
30 *Japan:* Cabinet reshuffle; Yoshio Sakurauchi became Foreign Minister and was replaced by Susumu Nikaido as Secretary-General of the ruling Liberal-Democratic Party.

DECEMBER

1 *New Zealand:* recount in marginal seat of Gisborne revealed win for ruling National Party, not Labour Party as first thought, giving it clear two-seat overall majority; National Party 47 seats, Labour Party 43, Social Credit Party 2.
2 *Pakistan:* five Pakistanis killed and three wounded by two Afghan helicopter gunships intruding into Pakistan air space, according to official statement.
4 *Kampuchea:* Pen Sovan replaced by Heng Samrin as Secretary-General of People's Revolutionary Party
8 *Kampuchea:* communiqué issued by Khmer Rouge regime announced dissolution of its Communist Party.
Kampuchea: Chan Si appointed acting Premier.
Laos: diplomatic relations with France, severed in 1978, were restored.
10 *China:* Indian delegation began talks in Beijing intended to improve relations between the two countries; first since border war of 1962.
11 *New Zealand:* Prime Minister Muldoon named his Cabinet.
17 *Sri Lanka:* state of emergency extended for a further month.
18 *Sri Lanka:* Freedom Party Leader, Mrs. Sirimavo Bandaranaike, dismissed Deputy Leader, Maithripala Senanayake, her son, and 15 other leading party members who had formed breakaway group, the Authentic Freedom Party.
19 *Thailand:* Prime Minister, Gen. Prem Tinsulanond, dismissed three senior military officers from Cabinet and brought Social Action Party into his coalition Government, giving it nine portfolios.
22 *Hong Kong:* Sir Edward Youde appointed new Governor.
26 *Pakistan:* President Zia named 287 of 350-member Federal Advisory Council (*Majlis-e-Shoora*) expected to be convened in February 1982 as interim body for consultation on Government affairs.
Indonesia: President Suharto commuted death sentence on former Foreign Minister, Dr. Subandrio, and former Air Force Chief, Umar Dhani, to life imprisonment.

1982

JANUARY

1 *Bangladesh:* President Sattar set up National Security Council to explore how armed forces could contribute to nation's development; replaced National Defence Council.
3 *Republic of Korea:* President Chun Doo-Hwan replaced Prime Minister Nam Duck-Woo with Yoo Chang-Soon and made five other Cabinet changes.
5 *Republic of Korea:* midnight—4 a.m. curfew lifted (except for sensitive regions near border with Democratic People's Republic) for first time in 30 years.
7 *Bangladesh:* President Abdus Sattar, the sole candidate, elected President of National Party.
10 *Malaysia:* Foreign Minister Ghazalie bin Shafie survived air crash.
Singapore: 10 alleged members of Organisasi Pembebasan Rakyat Singapura (People's Liberation Organization of Singapore) arrested and charged with plotting to overthrow Government.
11 *Pakistan:* Federal Advisory Council inaugurated; press censorship relaxed, excepting reports on military and judicial matters.
12 *Kampuchea:* Khmer Rouge suffered severe defeat at hands of Vietnamese in attack on forward supply base near Laos, Kampuchea and Thailand borders.
India: A. R. Antulay, Chief Minister of Maharashtra, indicted by state High Court for malpractices and abuse of power; he resigned later that day.
Indonesia: recalled its Ambassador to Philippines, Lieut.-Gen. Leo Lopulisa, for consultations after repetition of remarks suggesting that President Marcos should take formal steps to renounce his claim to Malaysian state of Sabah.

13 *Australia:* Sir Ninian Stephen appointed new Governor-General
15 *India:* Cabinet reshuffle; Mrs. Gandhi handed over Defence portfolio to Finance Minister Ramaswamy Venkataraman; Jaganath Kaushal, former Governor of Bihar, only new minister.
Mongolia: President of Academy of Sciences, Badzaryn Shirendev, dismissed.
17 *Sri Lanka:* state of emergency, imposed in August 1981, lifted.
18 *India:* over 2,000 union officials and strike organizers arrested on eve of one-day general strike.
Philippines: President Marcos admitted that Philippine fighter aircraft had strafed Japanese chemical tanker off Mindanao Island on January 15th.
19 *India:* one-day general strike; 6,000 union officials and strike organizers arrested before it began.
22 *Republic of Korea:* President Chun proposed formula for reunification with Democratic People's Republic, beginning with summit meeting and agreement on basic relations.
25 *Kampuchea:* in letter to ASEAN, Ieng Sary, Khmer Rouge Foreign Minister, rejected Singapore's proposal of November 1981 that loose coalition of Kampuchean interests be set up to oppose Vietnamese presence in their country.
26 *Democratic People's Republic of Korea:* President Kim Il Sung rejected President Chun's proposal for united Korea under common constitution.
29 *India:* Pakistan Foreign Minister, Agha Shahi, arrived for talks on proposed "no war" pact.

FEBRUARY

6 *Indonesia:* expelled Soviet Assistant Military Attaché, Lieut.-Col. S. P. Yegorov, for spying; Aeroflot representative in Jakarta, Aleksandr Finenko (alleged KGB agent), also arrested.
9 *Japan:* DC8 airliner crashed in Tokyo Bay before landing, killing 24 people and injuring 150.
10 *Indonesia:* Soviet diplomat, Gregor Odariouk, asked to leave country by Government, official sources said.
11 *Bangladesh:* President Adbus Sattar dismissed entire Cabinet.
12 *Bangladesh:* new Cabinet sworn in.
16 *Sri Lanka:* began inaugural cricket Test match against England.
Pakistan: Gen. Sahibzada Yaqub Khan became first General to be Foreign Minister, replacing Agha Shahi.
19 *India:* Crown Prince Namgyal Wangchuk named new Chogyal of Sikkim after death of his father on January 29th.
22 *Singapore:* Soviet diplomat, Anatoly Larkin, and marine engineer, Aleksandr Bondarev, expelled for spying.
28 *Democratic People's Republic of Korea:* general elections.

MARCH

2 *Republic of Korea:* jailed dissident Kim Dae Jung's sentence reduced from life imprisonment to 20 years and more than 2,850 prisoners given amnesty or reduced sentences to mark anniversary of Fifth Republic.
5 *Bangladesh:* President Sattar added two ministers to Cabinet and named two new state ministers.
8 *China:* four Government ministers dismissed; Miss Chen Muhua appointed to head new Ministry of Foreign Trade and Economic Relations; Liu Yi made Minister of Commerce, Qin Zhongha Minister of Chemical Industry.
13 *Australia:* opposition Labor Party candidate, Michael Maher, won by-election in Sydney suburb of Lowe; first defeat for ruling Liberal-Country Party coalition since 1975.
15 *India:* Soviet Defence Minister, Dmitriy Ustinov, arrived with high-level military delegation.
21 *Bangladesh:* Vice-President, Dr. Mirza Nurul Huda, resigned, claiming that he was a victim of a campaign by ruling Nationalist Party.
24 *Bangladesh:* Lieut.-Gen. Hossain Mohammad Ershad, Chief of Army Staff, led military coup and proclaimed himself Chief Martial Law Administrator.
27 *Bangladesh:* Abdul Fazal Mohammad Ashanuddin Chowdhury, a retired judge, sworn in as President.

31 *Viet-Nam:* Gen. Vo Nguyen Giap removed from Communist Party Politburo by Fifth National Congress.

APRIL

3 *Australia:* Liberal Party lost state election in Victoria, having been in power there since 1955.
5 *Thailand:* Bangkok's bicentenary celebrations.
8 *Australia:* Prime Minister Malcolm Fraser retained Liberal Party leadership, defeating former Cabinet minister Andrew Peacock in election.
19 *Australia:* Michael MacKellar, Minister of Health, and John Moore, Minister of Business and Consumer Affairs, resigned over former's illegal importation of colour TV.
21 *Korea:* troops of North and South fought four-hour gun battle across demilitarized zone.
22 *Malaysia:* Mahathir Mohamad's National Front coalition won 133 seats in general election to House of Representatives, compared with opposition parties' 21.
25 *Viet-Nam:* Government reshuffle.
28 *Republic of Korea:* Interior Minister, Suh Chung Hwa, resigned to be replaced by Gen. Roh Tae Woo, after authorities failure to prevent killing of 56 people by deranged policeman.

MAY

4 *Indonesia:* ruling Golkar Party won 244 of 364 seats contested in general election.
7 *Australia:* Cabinet reshuffle; Ian Sinclair became Defence Minister, replacing Jim Killen who became Vice-President of the Executive Council and Government Leader in House of Representatives.
10 *Philippines:* all Supreme Court Judges resigned; all but two reinstated in new Supreme Court Judiciary.
15 *Australia:* Labor Party lost control of Tasmania, having governed there since 1972.
20 *Hong Kong:* new Governor, Sir Edward Youde, sworn in.
Republic of Korea: entire Cabinet tendered resignations; that of Democratic Justice Party Secretary-General, Kwon Jung-Dal, accepted over multi-million dollar loan scandal.
New Zealand: Prime Minister Muldoon offered his country's only operational frigate to Britain for duration of Falklands conflict.
21 *Republic of Korea:* 11 more resignations accepted and 11 new Cabinet appointments made; Prime Minister, Deputy Premier, Economic Planning and Finance Ministers retained their Posts.
29 *China:* State Economic Commission, organ of State Council, inaugurated.
31 *Japan:* People's Republic of China Premier, Zhao Zhiyang, began official visit.

JUNE

1 *Singapore:* Goh Chok Tong appointed Defence Minister in place of Howe Yoon Chong, who became Health Minister.
2 *Republic of Korea:* Lho Shin Yong became Head of Agency for National Security Planning (formerly Korean CIA) and was replaced as Foreign Minister by Lee Bum Suk.
5 *Papua New Guinea:* three-week long general election began.
6 *Republic of Korea:* Ham Pyong Choon appointed presidential Secretary-General.
9 *Philippines:* Government won all 34 seats in southern Philippines autonomous regional assembly elections.
14 *New Zealand:* Derek Quigley, Minister of Works and Housing, resigned after criticizing Government's economic strategy.
18 *Viet-Nam:* Huynh Tan Phat resigned as Vice-Chairman of Council of Ministers.
22 *Kampuchea:* two anti-communist Kampuchean resistance groups and Khmer Rouge signed agreement in Kuala Lumpur establishing a Kampuchean coalition Government in exile; leading figures: President—Norodom Sihanouk (Moulinaka group); Vice-President—Khieu Samphan (Khmer Rouge); Prime Minister—Son Sann (Khmer People's National Liberation Front).
24 *Republic of Korea:* Cabinet reshuffle; Kim Sang Hyup made Prime Minister.
28 *Papua New Guinea:* former Premier Michael Somare's Pangu Party won most seats in general election.

JULY

7 *Viet-Nam:* Foreign Minister, Nguyen Co Thach, said that significant numbers of Vietnamese troops would be withdrawn from Kampuchea during July.

9 *Singapore:* J. B. Jeyaretnam, sole opposition M.P., appeared before House privileges committee to answer charges of corruption.
Maldives: became 47th member of Commonwealth.

10 *Malaysia:* Datuk Mokhtar Hashim, Minister for Culture, Youth and Sports, remanded in custody, charged with murder of Mohamed Taha Talib, Speaker of Negri Sembilan State Assembly.

11–17 *Fiji:* general election; Ratu Sir Kamisese K.T. Mara's Alliance Party returned to power with reduced majority.

16 *India:* Home Affairs Minister, Giani Zail Singh, elected first Sikh President of India.
Australia: Bill Hayden re-elected Leader of opposition Labor Party by 42 votes to 37 over Robert Hawke.

23 *New Caledonia:* about 250 right-wing demonstrators, protesting the takeover of the administration by a coalition dominated by pro-independence parties, were dispersed by police with tear gas.

24–27 *Japan:* torrential rain caused flooding and landslides in which more than 250 people died and thousands were made homeless.

26 *Viet-Nam:* IMF refused Viet-Nam's request for U.S. $150 million (£87 million) loan in SDRs for balance of payments assistance, until there were fundamental reforms in the economy; $80 million had been granted earlier.

27 *Singapore:* charges of corruption against J. B. Jeyaretnam withdrawn.

29 *Australia:* new Governor-General, Sir Ninian Stephen, sworn in.

AUGUST

2 *Papua New Guinea:* Parliament elected a new Prime Minister, Michael Somare.

7 *Philippines:* Imelda Marcos, wife of President Marcos, and Roberto Benedicto, Chairman of Philippine Sugar Commission, appointed members of Cabinet Executive Committee.

16 *India:* vote of "no confidence" in Mrs. Gandhi's Government defeated by 327 votes to 110.

18 *India:* police revolt in Bombay led to rioting and looting; army called in.

PART ONE

General Survey

Asia and the Pacific: Recent Trends

Kevin Rafferty

Ronald Reagan entered the White House in 1981, pledged to uphold the values of western freedom and check the advance of Soviet-style communism. In Asia and the Pacific region there were many places where he seemed assured of a warm welcome. As his key adviser and Secretary of State, the new President chose a general and former North Atlantic Treaty Organization (NATO) commander, Alexander M. Haig, Jr. On his first visit to Asia as Secretary in mid-1981, Haig used strong words to lay down the challenge. In Manila, in front of foreign ministers from South East Asia, Japan, the EEC, Australia, Canada and New Zealand, he pledged to "challenge blatant Soviet interventionism wherever it occurs." He also promised: "Let there be no doubt that the United States will maintain and strengthen its own military capability in the Pacific and Asia as a contribution to the security of the area in the face of the Soviet military build-up."

Experience proved that, in hard reality, it was harder to put right the wrongs. The U.S.S.R. was still ensconced firmly in Afghanistan; it was increasingly using military facilities provided by Viet-Nam, its ally and partner in the Council for Mutual Economic Assistance (CMEA). Of more serious moment, Asian hopes in the Reagan administration began to turn sour with the prolonged recession. By 1982 even the richest and most promising countries, such as Malaysia, began to experience falling growth rates. Other countries, such as South Korea and Hong Kong, began to be hurt by the deliberately damaging trade policies which were increasingly pursued by the rich Western countries. There was a growing feeling of being let down.

The threat of a changed world order, in which arms would again play a major part, burst on to the scene at the end of 1979 when the Western world was still recovering from Christmas celebrations. The Soviet Union poured troops, tanks, aircraft, artillery and armour into Afghanistan, supposedly at the request of President Hafizullah Amin who was promptly overthrown, killed and replaced by Babrak Karmal, whom the Russians had conveniently helped across the border from exile. By 1982 the U.S.S.R. had probably 100,000 soldiers in the country and a fierce struggle dragged on. Tiny, tribal, sparsely-populated Afghanistan, the country left over after the nineteenth-century imperial powers had chewed territories like dogs gnawing bones, was once more thrust to the centre of the Asian stage.

Because of the size of the Soviet Union, the last and greatest of the old imperial powers and still clinging to its empire, the repercussions rippled far and wide. There was not a country in Asia nor in the Pacific that could feel safe and unaffected by what was going on in the remote mountain fastnesses of Afghanistan. With its thrust into Kabul the Kremlin was well poised to keep a watchful eye on the uncertainty in Ayatollah Khomeini's Iran and from there could survey the oil-rich and troubled Gulf; to the east, it was at the doorstep of the Indian subcontinent. The struggle for Afghanistan as well as the conflict still flaring in Indochina raised again the Great Power struggle. But it was not just a struggle for possession of territory. After all Afghanistan is a barren difficult terrain. Also at stake was the possibility of interdiction of oil supplies from the Gulf. And equally important was prestige and the very Asian idea of "face": if the Soviet Union absorbed Afghanistan, faith in America would fall further.

Afghanistan was not the only uncertainty of the new decade of the 1980s. Fighting in Indochina spilled over to Thailand. Burma, India, Japan, Malaysia, Thailand, Bangladesh and South Korea all changed rulers, and only the first four did it peacefully. There was an abortive military coup in Thailand. The Bangladesh President was assassinated by former army colleagues. There were rallies on the streets against strong-men regimes in Pakistan, Bangladesh and Taiwan as well as South Korea. There were open grumbles against the rulers in China, Indonesia and the Philippines. The Pacific islands looked as if they might be victims of another scramble for power. Almost every country began to feel the chill winds of recession blowing from the U.S.A. through the industrialized world. It was not just that the U.S.A., and hence the rest of the industrialized world, was experiencing hard times. There was the conviction that Reagan's policies were deliberately prolonging the recession and were doing nothing to restore the international economy to health. On top of that, there was the feeling that the West selfishly did not care about what was happening in Asia.

The area of Asia and the Pacific is vitally important for many reasons. Asia is the largest of the five continents, and the mass of land and water of Asia and the Pacific covers vast stretches of the globe. Most obviously the whole arena is the stage of the Great Powers. Given the vastness of the Soviet Union, stretching from its European borders through Asia, making Turkey, Iran, Afghanistan, China and Japan its neighbours and India and Pakistan its near-neighbours; given the Pacific coasts of both the Soviet Union and the United States; given the worldwide maritime interests of both Moscow and Washington; given the importance of Japan to the U.S.A. yet its closeness to the Soviet eastern outposts; given the recent emergence of China; given the use of smaller countries almost as proxies by Moscow, Washington and Beijing (Peking), no country in the region, least of all the tiny Pacific Ocean islands, can ignore the policies of the Soviet Union, the U.S.A. and even China within Asia. Yet the region is important for other reasons too.

It contains about 56 per cent of the world's population: more than 2,500 million people by mid-1981. These people belong to every creed and colour. They include white men in Australia and New Zealand, Indians, Chinese, Japanese, Koreans, Thais, Vietnamese, Mongolians, Melanesians, Polynesians, Micronesians, Aborigines, Christians, Buddhists, Hindus, Muslims, Confucians, Taoists, Shintoists, animists, ancestor worshippers, believers in strange cargo cults, professors of many gods and of none. Asia and the Pacific contain the fastest growing countries in the world in terms of both economic growth and population growth, the richest country in per caput terms—the tiny island of Nauru with annual phosphate income of $123 million or $27,000 per Nauruan—and one of the economic giants—Japan. Yet Asia also has the largest number of absolutely poor people in the world: 600 million out of a total of 800 million according to the World Bank's 1978 *World Development Report*. While Japanese were beginning to approach American standards of prosperity, and Korean, Hong Kong, Taiwanese and Singaporean companies began to dream of taking on the Japanese giants, many poor peasants in Bangladesh, India, Indonesia and Pakistan, and indeed Afghanistan, could not imagine the security of even a regular job or a single square meal a day. In the shanty towns of Asia millions of people lived crammed into hovels that would cause a national outcry if they housed dogs in the West. This is the scene on which the winds and tides of gloom began to spread as the 1980s continued.

The events in Afghanistan which culminated in the Soviet invasion had their origins years earlier. By the mid to late-1950s the Western powers had allowed Moscow to make most of the running in Afghanistan. With the appearance of Muhammad Daud, the cousin of King Zahir Shah, as Prime Minister, Moscow began giving large amounts of aid. When Daud deposed the King, the Kremlin moved into a controlling position, especially as Daud pursued a policy of hostility to Pakistan and relied upon the Soviet Union to arm and train his troops. By 1978 it was said that Moscow was the dominant power in Afghanistan and Daud would not be able to follow any policy of which the Soviet Union disapproved. But Daud began to feel that his staunch Afghan nationalist inclinations were being cramped by pressure from Moscow and he tried to edge away without really infringing on the Soviet Union's preeminence. Then Daud was bloodily overthrown in April 1978 and the Russians really entered the "cockpit of Asia". It will long be a matter of argument whether the Kremlin helped to plan the Taraki coup that overthrew Daud or whether it was merely the main beneficiary. At any rate, before the end of 1978 there were hundreds of Soviet military and civil advisers upon whom the new Afghan Government depended. But the wings and factions of the People's Democratic Party led by Nur Muhammad Taraki continued to squabble among themselves. At the same time a considerable pro-Muslim tribal rebellion had begun against the new godless regime and their fair-skinned advisers from the north.

When the quarrel between Taraki, the self-styled "writer, journalist and poet", and Hafizullah Amin, the hard-line Marxist, burst into the open with the October 1979 "resignation" of Taraki supposedly because of ill-health (possibly caused by a bullet in the head), events began to move rapidly. Amin had been responsible for the tough land reforms, abolitions of dowries and other radical measures which had angered the mullahs and tribesmen. Possibly because they feared a spillover of the rebellion to the Muslim tribes of their own border regions, the Soviet leaders decided that they could not tolerate Amin and invaded to place Babrak Karmal in the position of power in Kabul.

Under more ordinary circumstances Karmal might have been a good choice. He had been a popular student leader and had sat as a member of Parliament for years before Daud abolished Parliament. He had been a deputy to Taraki before Amin ousted and exiled him. But riding to power with the Russians simply increased the rebellion. Karmal by mid-1980 was a puppet and prisoner of the Russians. The Russians faced armed rebellion in the hillsides and sullen resentment in the towns. Ambushes, back-street killings were as common as sniping raids and full-blooded Soviet bombing missions against the hillside villages as the two sides fought a mixture of a tribal "eye for an eye, tooth for a tooth" struggle and modern warfare. The tribesmen appeared to have no hope of expelling the Soviet forces, but nor did the Russians look like taking a grip on the whole country without massive slaughter. Once again, innocent people suffered and several million refugees scattered and fled. Some of them were guerrilla fighters, using the safety of Pakistan for their training and base camps, but a lot more were pathetic huddles of women and children who had gathered what possessions they could and departed. The Russians stayed. The Olympic boycott in 1980 did not prevent the games from being held in Moscow with many major countries participating.

By the middle of 1982, the number of refugees had exceeded 3 million. Accusations from Kabul and the U.S.S.R. of American supplies to the rebels gained some credence from statements by President Anwar Sadat of Egypt just before he was assassinated, but any such supplies were on a small scale. The rebels were hard pressed to obtain weapons except mainly small arms of Second World War or even earlier vintage. These were little match for the modern Soviet armoury, including huge helicopter gunships, especially as the Soviet forces were not afraid of public opinion, either at home or abroad, and were prepared to resort to "overkill" techniques such as bombing whole villages. The net result was that the large claims by rebels of their great victories became less triumphal. Pakistan was afraid to antagonize the U.S.S.R. by encouraging large-scale arms supplies. India, in many issues the leader of the non-aligned conscience, was even more careful and wanted the good offices of Moscow as an arms supplier. With the increasing Middle East conflicts and the Falklands fighting, the Western press and Western Governments were diverted and turned to other things. With its ally Viet-Nam holding sway in

Indochina, the active Soviet foreign policy still seemed to have paid dividends.

The troubles between Kampuchea and Viet-Nam had been rumbling ever since the two very different communist regimes took over in Phnom-Penh and over all Viet-Nam. Pol Pot inclined towards China; the Vietnamese communists towards the Soviet Union. Viet-Nam blamed the Pol Pot regime in Phnom-Penh for incursions into its territory and Kampuchea complained that Hanoi would not discuss border disputes. By late 1977 Hanoi had decided that it could tolerate Pol Pot no longer. An initial large-scale Vietnamese incursion in late 1977 was successfully repulsed by the Kampucheans, or so they thought. However, as soon as the monsoon had finished in late 1978 Hanoi went into action. It announced the formation of a Kampuchean liberation movement in early December, declaring "Decidedly, the crimes of the Pol Pot-Ieng Sary gang can no longer be counted. Everywhere our people have witnessed massacres, more atrocious, more barbarous, than those committed in the Middle Ages or perpetrated by the Hitlerite fascists. Those who stay in the country live in constant fear—like fish caught in a net not knowing when their turn will come to be massacred."

By early December the "liberators" had assembled a force of 14 divisions: 120,000 men, backed by tanks, heavy artillery and Soviet-built MiG aircraft; and on December 25th, 1978, the attack began. It was a classic *blitzkrieg* which will go down in the history books: within two weeks Phnom-Penh had fallen, deserted by Pol Pot's men, and within three weeks the invaders had swept across Kampuchea. But such swift victory invited scepticism. Prince Norodom Sihanouk, the former ruler of Kampuchea, expressed it best. He said "Even the Vietnamese confess that the so-called front (the "liberators") was founded one month ago. How can you have such a terrible army, with big artillery, in only one month? You must be good mathematicians to be able to use such guns. The Vietnamese are poor, desperately poor; they have no rice to eat. They went to Japan, Asian countries and many other countries to beg for money, rice and everything. They accepted everything, even a piece of bread and an egg for breakfast. How could they possibly have such tanks and weapons?"

The action of the Vietnamese in invading Kampuchea—for few people outside Viet-Nam believed the claim that the "liberators" were Kampucheans—brought condemnation from outside, but no action except the steady mopping up of Pol Pot's troublesome resistance fighters. Hanoi effectively controlled all Indochina. A United Nations Security Council resolution against Viet-Nam was avoided only by a Soviet veto, but China acted by attacking Viet-Nam in February 1979. It was a short campaign in which China withdrew its forces after capturing three Vietnamese border towns. The wars were short, but the hostility continued and the repercussion rippled not just through Indochina but right round Asia and the Pacific.

Bigger neighbours were watching. A French newspaper carried a cartoon of a Kampuchean minnow being swallowed by a Vietnamese fish which was itself about to be devoured by a Chinese shark, again about to be eaten by a huge Soviet whale. Even the countries of the Association of South East Asian Nations (Indonesia, Malaysia, the Philippines, Singapore and Thailand), all neighbours of communist Indochina, felt betrayed, because, immediately before Hanoi invaded Kampuchea, Viet-Nam's Prime Minister, Pham Van Dong, had assured ASEAN that his country had no territorial ambitions. They probably wondered who would be next. China saw a Soviet plot behind all these events, as Viet-Nam had just signed a 25-year friendship pact with Moscow and had joined the CMEA before unleashing its forces. Hanoi claimed that the hand of Beijing (Peking) was behind Pol Pot. Such events and cross-currents meant that other countries in the area began to review their relations with others to see just how they would be affected by whose grand designs.

The struggle in Indochina goes on. The 200,000 Vietnamese troops continued to consolidate in Kampuchea and were able to restore some peace and order to Phnom-Penh, once a city of wide boulevards and great charm. Sufficient stability was brought back for the Vietnamese-backed regime to hold a general election in 1981—won, of course, by Heng Samrin in overwhelming communist fashion. However, the 30,000 Khmer Rouge guerrillas owing allegiance to Pol Pot continued to fight and harry the Vietnamese regulars, using the cover of the mountains and fleeing, from time to time, to Thailand to rest and re-equip themselves. Hanoi waved both an olive branch and a stick. In June 1980 the Vietnamese Foreign Minister, Nguyen Co Thach, visited South-East Asia and tried to persuade Malaysia and Indonesia, worried about China's intentions, that Hanoi was peaceable. On the eve of the ASEAN Foreign Ministers' meeting in Kuala Lumpur, however, two Vietnamese infantry companies crossed into Thailand through the sprawling shanties full of Kampuchean refugees. The message was that Thailand should not repatriate the refugees, including the refreshed Pol Pot guerrillas. Yet the Vietnamese act stiffened the resistance of Indonesia and Malaysia against Hanoi. The same thing happened in 1981, with Hanoi suggesting that the communist and non-communist countries should meet for regional talks, while its ministers were telling Thailand that they would have no hesitation in sending troops across again if refugees were resettled across the border.

A much wider circle of countries were affected by the Indochina conflict, with boatloads of refugees being washed up on their shores after the perilous journey across the seas from Viet-Nam. Thousands of people, many of them in small leaky boats, landed on the coasts of Thailand, Malaysia, Indonesia, Hong Kong and Taiwan, having travelled hundreds of miles across the South China Sea. Because most of the refugees were of Chinese origin it was claimed that they were fleeing from Vietnamese genocide. Of course, Hanoi was undoubtedly worried by the presence of hostile Chinese, but there was another factor: the hard-liners in Hanoi were determined to root out the old ways and to introduce true "socialism". Again, it was mainly, but not solely, the Chinese traders and middle classes who stood in their way. When Hanoi pressed ahead with the collectivization of agriculture and talked of the subordination of the peasants to the working classes there was the prospect of a much wider and bigger exodus.

One could only guess at the number of refugees involved especially as many had undoubtedly perished at sea. Some diplomats thought that the exodus would exceed one million and could go as high as five million. Another aspect of this problem which was upsetting the countries that had to bear the burden of the refugees was that Viet-Nam was extracting a toll of their savings before allowing them to leave. In June 1979 a Hong Kong official accused Viet-Nam of having made U.S. $3,000 million from the refugees. By 1981, pressures on Viet-Nam had reduced the refugee flow, though some people continued to come out of the country at great peril, and Hanoi showed no inclination in spite of the costs of war and its own economic plight to soften its hard line. Though thousands of refugees had found homes in the rich industrialized countries, thousands still remained in places like Hong Kong, squatting in only temporary havens. Throughout 1981 and into 1982, small numbers of leaky boats continued to set sail and from time to time there were rumours that hundreds more were still willing to face the risks of the seas and the storms and the pirates. Continuing economic deprivation in Viet-Nam was one of the most powerful reasons propelling them.

In his opening speech to the ASEAN Foreign Ministers' meeting in Manila in June 1981, Singapore's Foreign Minister, Suppiah Dhanabalan, estimated that Viet-Nam's economic growth rate had been zero in 1979 and in 1980, and said that the Vietnamese faced shortages of most essentials and monthly food rations of only 13 kg. per person. He contrasted this with the steady 8 per cent annual growth rates and independence of the ASEAN countries. Viet-Nam was increasingly under the shadow of the Soviet Union. He and the other ASEAN ministers urged Viet-Nam, in its own interest, to talk peace with ASEAN. However, they rejected Hanoi's suggestion of a regional meeting precisely because they said that the Kampuchea and Indochina problems had international implications because of the indirect involvement of the external powers. The ministers put forward the essential elements in a peace package: withdrawal of Vietnamese forces; a United Nations force to keep law and order; disarming of all Kampuchean factions; a free UN-supervised election, in which the Heng Samrin regime could participate; guarantees that Kampuchea would pose no threat to its neighbours, ASEAN and Viet-Nam included. Such guarantees would have to include the external powers which are indirect parties to the conflict.

The ASEAN ministers could not, however, decide on a package of inducements—other than the promise that peaceful co-operation was better than tension and conflict—to tempt Viet-Nam to talk. Nor could they agree to use a stick against Hanoi by arming the guerrilla fighters. The non-communist states were backing the attempt to stitch together a United Front of Kampuchean patriots in which the Pol Pot regime would be reduced to a less prominent role. However, Gen. Carlos Romulo, the Philippines Foreign Minister and chairman of the meeting, said that ASEAN would give only diplomatic and not military backing to the United Front. Hanoi, however, repeated its insistence that it would not have anything to do with the international conference scheduled for New York in mid-July 1981, under the auspices of the United Nations.

In the event, the Vietnamese did not attend and by 1982, in spite of increasing domestic hardships, Hanoi stood firm. The ASEAN countries, gently helped by encouraging noises from outside, tried to encourage the formation of a three-sided Kampuchean coalition of anti-Hanoi forces. This would have consisted of the Khmers Rouges, Prince Sihanouk and the groups loyal to Son Sann, a former Prime Minister. The idea was to present a realistic alternative government to the Hanoi-backed regime. Only China was prepared to lend unqualified and open support to the bloodthirsty Pol Pot regime. Other countries were embarrassed. However, the Kampucheans could not be persuaded to come together. The problem then was that the Beijing-aided Khmers Rouges were the only real fighting force which was able to challenge the Vietnamese troops. Even so, they were being worn down and the Vietnamese extended their control. Some diplomats believe that, unless a diplomatic breakthrough occurs in 1982, Hanoi's grip on Kampuchea will be impossible to break.

Conflicts in Afghanistan and Indochina were merely the most immediate of the problems in Asia; the rest of the region was not lacking in potential flashpoints. The most obvious was the long frontier between the Soviet Union and China. Vigilance in this area was not relaxed in spite of Beijing's agreement to talk to Moscow in mid-1979. This was an obvious ploy to try to isolate Viet-Nam.

The U.S.S.R. has shown its concern about the frontier by quadrupling its forces since 1968. In 1978 it had 45 divisions spread across the territory around Manzhou (Manchuria) between Outer Mongolia and the Pacific. In any open confrontation the odds would strongly favour the Russians. They have nuclear tactical missiles around Vladivostok, Khabarovsk and Chita. The Trans-Siberian railway is protected by 200 intermediate-range ballistic missiles with one-megaton warheads. Further west along the railway there are another 200 intercontinental ballistic missiles which are equipped with 25-megaton warheads. In addition, other Soviet intercontinental ballistic missiles, now aimed at the U.S.A., could be reprogrammed to face China. On top of this the Soviet Far East command has about 2,500 warheads for tactical ground and aerial delivery (about half the number deployed for use against NATO). There are also 1,200 Soviet aircraft including Sukhoi Su-19s, MiG-23s and the MiG-25 known as the Foxbat. The TU V-G Backfire aircraft which could drop nuclear bombs have been seen by satellites on airfields within range of China. All the troops and hardware are protected by a sophisticated radar curtain in three tiers. China by comparison has fewer defence forces close to the Soviet frontier and only a handful of divisions based at Harbin. Beijing is known to be worried about the Soviet strength. Indeed when the former U.S. Defence Secretary, James Schlesinger, was in Beijing, the Chinese faced him with exasperated questions about why the Americans only complained about the Soviet Union's defence build-up, but did not do anything to counter it.

The Chinese have always placed greater faith in men rather than machines. There were signs in the late 1970s, however, that they were getting sufficiently worried about the obsolescence of their equipment to begin to search abroad. A deal was made with Rolls-Royce for Spey engines in 1975 and subsequently there were visits both by Chinese salesmen to Europe in 1977 and by westerners to China, including Marshal of the Royal Air Force Sir Neil Cameron, who suggested co-operation with China over tanks against the "common enemy", the Soviet Union. One good chance the Chinese have is that in the early 1980s new breakthroughs are expected in military technology and they would be in a good position to benefit. However, they would still face the dilemma of whether to spend heavily on military equipment and forego the programme of economic development. If the Russians crossed the border in force, China's best hope would be that the forces close to the frontier would act as a tripwire and that any invader would fall foul of regular forces on the road to Beijing. This argument is supported by the old saying that anyone who tries to capture Moscow or Beijing would be a fool. He would be sucked like a fly into a spider's web.

When U.S. Secretary of State Alexander Haig was in Beijing in 1981 he opened the way for the Chinese to buy lethal weapons from Washington. There was some confusion in the banner headlines that greeted the change of American policy. There were some claims that China would immediately go on a buying spree, especially for weapons that could be used in Indochina by the Pol Pot guerrillas fighting the Heng Samrin regime. Mr. Haig denied that any arms sale agreement had been reached. He said that the decision meant that China had been taken off the list of countries, like the Soviet Union, to which lethal arms sales were completely banned and had been placed on a list "in the category of a country like Yugoslavia, a friendly non-aligned country". The U.S.A. would consult with its allies before giving arms to China and requests would be considered on a case-by-case basis. He added: "I did not sense an appetite for U.S. arms. European markets have been open to China for a long time, but there has not been much buying."

By 1982 the issue which exploded in the face of Washington was not arms for China but arms sales to Taiwan, the offshore island of 18 million people ruled by the Kuomintang (Nationalists), who claim to be the inheritors of Sun Yat-sen's mantle and the rightful rulers of all China. Beijing objected to American arms sales to Taiwan. Premier Zhao Ziyang warned: "If the U.S.A. persists in selling arms to Taiwan, it would have a very serious negative effect on relations between China and the U.S.A." In the U.S. Congress, however, Taiwan had its supporters. Senator Barry Goldwater accused China of trying to bully the U.S.A. into abandoning Taiwan and of planning to take military action against the island. The American Taiwan Relations Act provides security guarantees to the offshore island against infringement of its sovereignty. The Act was the price of the American withdrawal of troops from Taiwan to normalize relations with Beijing. Although China has denounced the Act, Taiwan has supporters in Congress who would not tolerate the U.S.A.'s letting down the Nationalists.

It is not only the Soviet military build-up within its own borders which has caused concern among Western analysts and non-communist governments of the region; attention has also been paid to the increase in the Soviet fleet's activities in both the Indian and Pacific Oceans. There are now about 100 Soviet submarines in the Pacific, 40 of them nuclear and 20 armed with long-range missiles aimed at the United States. However, the American Pacific fleet is almost certainly more than a match for the Russian one. It is unlikely that the Russians would revert to overt action such as threatening merchant marine shipping because of the international implications involved, but Washington and Tokyo are still concerned with the problem of submarine surveillance in the shallow Japan Sea.

Soviet naval activity in the Indian Ocean also flared into the headlines for a short while in the 1970s. The Russians normally have about 20 ships, though at times the number has risen to 25. What of course is not so easy to assess is how many of the Soviet merchant marine vessels do double-duty. In the mid-1970s the U.S. Congress granted extra funds for the Diego Garcia base on an atoll in the Indian Ocean. However, most of these were for communication protection systems, to keep track of what the Russians were up to, rather than for a fully equipped base. The runway was to be lengthened, but not enough to take B-52 bombers. In July 1980 Mauritius and other African States demanded the return of Diego Garcia to Mauritius, which had ceded it to Britain for a communications centre before independence.

The new Reagan administration began work on a five-year plan to construct or expand military bases across the Middle East and Indian Ocean area to support its forces in the area. The total cost was secret, but could amount to $2,000 million. The Republican President immediately raised the sums earmarked by his Democratic predecessor, Jimmy Carter, and showed that the words of challenge to Soviet expansionism would be matched by higher spending. In mid-1982 Richard Armitage, a U.S. Defence Department official responsible for the Asia-Pacific region, accused the U.S.S.R. of trying to choke off the sea lanes between the Pacific and Indian Oceans through Singapore and the Strait of Malacca. He claimed that Soviet use of bases in Viet-Nam was becoming more frequent.

The Great Power presence question which came to the surface with the accession of a new American

President was that of U.S. troops in South Korea. President Carter proposed to withdraw 32,000 men in stages, over the next four or five years, a move which alarmed most of the American top military brass as well as most of Korean opinion both Government and opposition, upset the Japanese leaders, and the non-communists of South-East Asia. Major-General John Singlaub risked, and received, a public rebuke from the President when he called the policy into question in 1977. The Koreans and the American military argued that the removal of the troops could lead to a North Korean invasion and might possibly trigger off the start of the Third World War. But President Carter was initially unmoved, though he did promise that compensatory measures would be taken so that South Korea would not be left unprotected. In 1978 President Carter made further concessions by postponing some troop withdrawals, and in 1979 further withdrawals were halted while evidence of stronger North Korean forces was studied. The CIA believed that the strength of Pyongyang's troops was 25 to 30 per cent more than previously estimated. Some Asian countries began to show concern that the U.S.A. did not care about Asia. The new Reagan administration cancelled plans to withdraw troops, and President Chun Doo Hwan was the first Head of State to visit the new President. Suddenly relations between Seoul and Washington became warm, though by this time the difference in policy with the new administration was negligible.

The other question of direct American involvement in the region concerned the base at Subic Bay in the Philippines. President Marcos, in an interesting and at first sight contradictory approach, seemed anxious to have American protection, but he insisted that the Filipinos themselves must control the bases. In fact the demand was not contradictory but merely reflected the increasing nationalism of most of the countries of the area. In late 1978 a fresh agreement was made, giving Manila control of the bases.

In mid-1982, however, there was a rumour in various Asian capitals that Washington was re-thinking its defence strategy in the region. Nevertheless, John Holdridge, Assistant Secretary of State for East Asian and Pacific Affairs, claimed: "There is no change in the military posture maintained by America in Asia and the Pacific." He added: "our intention to provide military security support in the region remains unchanged." He said that there would be an increase in U.S. strength in the region, though only "commensurate" with worldwide increases in U.S. strength.

An isolated event of the mid-1970s which caused a major flutter was the defection of the Soviet MiG-25 pilot, Lieut. Belenko, which exposed a number of important questions. There were two ways of looking at this. One was to argue that Japan's fears about the need to build up its defence forces in the wake of the American withdrawal from South Korea were pointless because the Japanese did not react quickly enough to the radar warning, and any four such aircraft could have destroyed all the important Japanese military installations; the other claim was that the aircraft had only enough fuel left for two minutes more flying when it landed, so that in actual combat the Russians would be less well off.

On the western fringes of the region, the downfall of the Shah of Iran and the coming to power of an Islamic fundamentalist leader, Ayatollah Khomeini, posed new problems. Beneath Khomeini's dogmatic umbrella there were so many squabbling groups that the great powers stayed on the sidelines, watching, waiting and worrying. In 1982 the Iranian successes against the Iraqis gave a new twist and boosted Iran's confidence. The invasion of Lebanon by Israel added an extra dimension which threatened to unite Iran and the Arabs. The flight and death of the Shah had shown yet again that lavish spending on arms and sophisticated weapons cannot guarantee a regime. At the height of the first oil boom, he had spent heavily on arms and defence and dreamed of patrolling the seas between the Gulf and Australia.

To add to these uncertainties in the west, the hanging of Zulfiqar Ali Bhutto, former President and Prime Minister of Pakistan, in April 1979 caused upheaval there, but the country's military rulers kept a tight grip on the population, although widespread dissent remained only just below the surface. Pakistan also caused anxiety within Asia in 1979 when it was feared that it was well on the road to building an atomic bomb. Mr. Bhutto had spoken of "an Islamic bomb" to match the "Christian bomb" of the West and the "Hindu bomb" of India (despite the fact that the Indian Government has said that its nuclear capability would be for peaceful purposes only). There was speculation that certain Islamic countries were financing Pakistan's nuclear research and there has been evidence that Pakistanis working in the West had had access to knowledge and supplies essential to the construction of an atom bomb. The fear was that, if Pakistan developed an atomic bomb, other countries, both within Asia and outside it, would also devote precious time and resources to the atomic quest. India especially was concerned about Pakistan's nuclear progress.

DEFENCE EXPENDITURE

For whatever the reasons, hopes of self-aggrandisement or hegemony over others or just plain fear, all the countries of the Asian-Pacific region are spending millions of dollars on weapons and armaments which could be spent better on social services and attempting to solve the problems of poverty. It is a sad indication of the order of priorities that an average of U.S. $220 is spent on each schoolchild throughout the world annually, whereas every serviceman has $12,239 lavished on him. Between 1960 and 1974, the developing countries of the world more than doubled their outlay in real terms on weapons. According to the Stockholm International Peace Research Institute in 1978, about 75 per cent of the current world arms trade is with the Third World.

None of the Asian or Pacific countries spends as heavily as did the Shah in Iran. His annual defence budget reached $10,000 million or probably the same as China's. Asia does, however, have several countries which spend over $1,000 million per year on defence.

Some of the larger countries, such as India, Pakistan and the two Koreas, have been stepping up the money going to defence. Indian defence spending reached a record Rs. 53,380 million ($5,680 million), or nearly 4 per cent of G.N.P., in the 1982/83 budget. Even Japan, which has no army but only self-defence forces, spends thousands of millions of dollars. Malaysia pushed up defence spending sharply in the 1981–86 plan. Singapore, with only 2.5 million people, is the second biggest spender in per caput terms, following hard on the heels of Australia. (Exact comparisons are difficult to make because a number of countries' budgets do not give the true cost of military expenditure.)

In 1980 India, modernizing its defence forces, took delivery of its first Anglo-French Jaguar strike aircraft and signed a U.S. $1,600 million deal with the Soviet Union for tanks, missiles and arms. Worried Pakistani experts calculated the true cost of the Indo-Soviet deal at $5,000 to $7,000 million. Islamabad began to look around for its own renewed defences, and the new Reagan team promised a five-year $2,500 million aid package, much of which would go to upgrading the obsolete Pakistan military machine. Each extra notch invited a response from the other side. India claimed that the new F-16 aircraft which Pakistan was obtaining from the U.S.A. would tip the balance against it as it gave Islamabad strike aircraft that could reach important Indian military installations. New Delhi's response was to seek the latest generation of French Mirage 2000 aircraft and the MiG 27 from the U.S.S.R.

DISPUTES WITHIN ASIA

What is much more important, the Asian countries themselves can hardly be said to be at peace with one another. In each of the major areas, whether the Indian sub-continent, South-East Asia or even the South Pacific, there are disputes between neighbouring countries which add to the tension and costs of maintaining the status quo, without even beginning to tackle the problems of the area.

The disputes on the Indian sub-continent are probably the most long-standing, stretching back to the foundation of independent India and Pakistan in 1947. They have caused three wars, thousands killed and many refugees, and have helped in the break-up of Pakistan as well as resulting in the expenditure of millions of dollars on armaments. Although accepted by India and Pakistan, the boundaries of Independence laid out by the British were untidy and left too many jagged edges. In the west, Afghanistan did not accept the old Durand line boundary of the British Empire and continues to regard the disputed boundary as a source of political difference with Pakistan although relations improved in the mid-1970s. But the changes of government in Afghanistan and Pakistan threatened to shake the whole sub-continent. India, though carefully keeping its own counsel on the matter, was unsettled by the coming of a more pro-Islamic government in Pakistan and the dangers following the hanging of Mr. Bhutto. Then came the new Government of President Taraki in Afghanistan reopening the possibility of a resurgence of the Pakhtunistan issue. By the 1980s there was some danger of conflict between Afghanistan and Pakistan. There were several camps of Afghan rebels and refugees across the border in Pakistan's North-West Frontier Province. Had Soviet forces not been tied down by the Muslim rebels, there were fears in Pakistan that the Kremlin might encourage Kabul to renew its claims to the lands as far as the Indus, including Peshawar.

Relations between India and Pakistan, more intense than the long smouldering problem between Pakistan and Afghanistan, appeared calmer. Some leading officials party to the negotiations told the author that there were unwritten agreements between India and Pakistan to accept the present disputed ceasefire line across Kashmir as the international boundary between the two countries. Officially, however, any such treaty, secret clause or private agreement was denied. To outsiders it seemed unthinkable that it would be in the interest of either India or Pakistan to go to war again over Kashmir, given the time that the people had lived as part of India or Pakistan, and the imbalance in forces, with India having a million men under arms and Pakistan only half that number. There remained, however, the dangers of religious antagonism or unscrupulous politicians using the "enemy at the gate" as a rallying cry to divert attention from problems at home; and, of course, the tensions raised by the issue of Pakistan's bomb. The new military deal between Washington and Islamabad also soured improving relationships, even though India had a much bigger deal with the Soviet Union. Pakistan, even a rearmed Pakistan, seemed in no position to challenge a bigger and mightier India. Yet such is the mistrust that an improving atmosphere, with friendly talks, quickly froze when the U.S.-Pakistan deal became public. Talks between India and Pakistan stuttered in stop-start fashion, with both sides nervous of suggestions of a no-war pact and the implications which that would have for the status of Kashmir.

Long-strained relations between China and India had taken a turn for the better in 1976 when India announced the sending of an Ambassador to Beijing after a gap of almost 14 years. When China invaded Viet-Nam after Hanoi's conquest of Kampuchea, India tried hard to maintain an even hand, but Beijing did not help its case by invading precisely when the Indian Foreign Minister, A. B. Vajpayee, was visiting the Chinese capital. He cut short the visit because of the outcry in New Delhi. Only in 1981 were renewed attempts made to improve ties. Huang Hua, China's Foreign Minister, went at the end of June on an extended visit to India, signalling Beijing's attempt to repair past damage. It was the first visit by a ranking Chinese to India since Zhou Enlai in the early 1960s.

In the early 1980s, old sores between India and Bangladesh threatened to become inflamed again. The problems concerned the long open border between the two countries and the water resources of the Himalayas which are shared between the two. Troubles in north-east India over the influx of non-locals provided one flashpoint. The native-born people of the region claimed that the newcomers—mainly Muslims but also Bengalis from Calcutta who had been coming in since long before Bangladesh was formed—were taking the best jobs. The other issue of the waters of the Ganga (Ganges)–Brahmaputra delta system is even more complicated. The headwaters of the great river system lie in the mountains, far away from Bangladesh, but most of the tributaries reach the sea through Bangladesh. India has already built a barrage on the Ganga at Farakka in West Bengal. The object is to supply enough water to help flush Calcutta port, which has been silting up. However, the barrage also deprives Bangladesh of the lower waters. Under agreements made in the late 1970s, the two countries agreed to share the Farakka waters, but these agreements were due to expire in late 1982. In addition, India was talking again about building a "link canal" which would run for 200 miles (320 km.) and join the Ganga to the Brahmaputra river, allowing the larger waters of the Brahmaputra to flow to the Ganga and India. Of the minimum flow of 120,000 cubic feet per second (cusecs), the Indian Government proposed to take 100,000 cusecs for India's use.

The problem was that the canal would run for 70 miles (113 km.) across Bangladesh, and Bangladesh was opposed to the canal. New talks were started in mid-1982 under Gen. Hossain Ershad's military-backed Government. In the Bay of Bengal, the changing course of the rivers also led to trouble about the land formed out of the silt. In 1981 India sent a gunboat to reinforce its claims to one small island in the bay.

ASEAN

Further east, all the non-communist countries of South-East Asia were preoccupied by what they saw as a monolithic communist menace. One of the noteworthy features of the 1970s, immediately after the end of the Viet-Nam war, was the impetus given to closer association between the five countries of the Association of South East Asian Nations (ASEAN): Indonesia, Malaysia, the Philippines, Singapore and Thailand. The Association had been founded in 1967 and was not noted for any great achievements in concert. In fact it was not until 1976 that all the Heads of Government met together in Bali, Indonesia, less than a year after the end of the Viet-Nam war. Sinnathamby Rajaratnam, Foreign Minister of Singapore, declared at the meeting of Foreign Ministers in Manila in 1976 that "We in ASEAN are the only working and coherent association of states, not merely in South-East Asia but in Asia as well." That might not be disputed, but only because of the lack of rival contenders who had bothered to form relationships across the continent.

But even in 1981, if asked to name the achievements of ASEAN as a body, the first comment would be to point to its opposition to Hanoi's policy in Kampuchea, and even this unity looked as if it might be upset if Hanoi behaved more diplomatically. In the course of 1981, however, the ASEAN states worked hard to forge greater unity. On the Kampuchean question they preserved their common front in spite of the pressures and their diverse interests, especially their varying suspicions of China, the other party hovering in the wings and determined to "fight to the last drops of blood of the last Kampuchean", as one observer put it.

Some economic progress was also made. In addition to the earlier treaty of concord and the treaty of amity and friendship signed at the Bali summit, in 1981 the economic ministers worked out and the foreign ministers signed a basic agreement on ASEAN industrial "complementation", which envisaged a greater role for the ASEAN-wide private sector. How this will evolve will depend on the governments' resolve in the next few years. In the past it has been easier to make joint programmes or laws than to achieve effective co-operation. At the 1981 meetings the ministers agreed on a further range of tariff cuts on intra-ASEAN trade but, for all that, the largest share of ASEAN trade is with western industrial countries, including Japan, rather than between the countries of the association. Some economists characterized the ASEAN approach to trade cuts as timid. In addition, the ministers agreed that three projects could be considered at any one time from any one country for joint ASEAN projects.

Harder economic times also placed pressure on ASEAN to make a joint stand. At meetings in 1982 there was unity among the five members on the need to act together to force the industrialized countries to be less protective and to consider the interests of developing countries on commodity prices. Cesar Virata, the Philippines Prime Minister, said the aim "is to act more like an economic community. We have to trade more." How successful they will be remains to be tested. When, shortly before, Malaysia tried to persuade Indonesia and Thailand, two of the other big tin producers, to joint action to cut production and thus set up an OPEC-style tin cartel—or "TINPEC"—Indonesia was reluctant to join in. In addition, the first joint industrial schemes, agreed as long ago as the 1976 Bali summit, were still making slow progress.

The work on the five "ASEAN" industrial projects decided at Bali is proceeding, although the original timetable of setting them up "within three years" went completely by the board. Singapore dropped out and several projects were revised with Indonesia and Malaysia taking urea, Thailand rock salt and soda ash, and the Philippines a copper fabricating plant. Although at the time of the Bali summit the "ASEAN projects" were hailed as a breakthrough, the plans of 1976 fell short of the suggestions made in a 1972 UN study on industrial co-operation. The UN experts suggested three possible approaches: selective trade liberalism on an item-by-item basis, which would encourage specialization and better use of capacity; complementary agreements in which different parts of industries in each country would specialize in different products and thus encourage cheaper and more efficient production across ASEAN; and package deals under which new and large-scale projects of industries not already in the region could be established.

It was estimated that package deals could reduce investment costs by up to 30 per cent, but the ASEAN projects agreed at Bali would hardly count as they are on a small scale. They are merely testing the water, yet they are still taking a long time to get under way.

Anyone wishing to promote ASEAN as an organization has to try to cross a threshold which the majority of political leaders feel they cannot cross. National and nationalistic interests are too strong for anyone to put forward the idea of a political ASEAN along the lines towards which the European Economic Community is supposed to aspire. Even in their attitudes towards Viet-Nam, the ASEAN countries were not of one mind. Malaysia, with a large Chinese minority and with communist terrorists of Chinese origin continuing their jungle struggle, and Indonesia, with Chinese industrialists and traders dominating its business life, were just as anti-communist. But they were equally nervous of Beijing's role in Indochina and its use of Pol Pot as a proxy. Both countries were markedly less hostile towards Hanoi, but Hanoi's intransigence prevented it from capitalizing on this potential split.

It might be nice to dream of overstepping more than a generation of problems by creating with ASEAN a community in which individuals count more than nationality or any other consideration. But it would be naive to think that Indonesia could consider surrendering sovereignty; or that Malays, conscious of their own struggle to reach parity in Malaysia, would make grand gestures. There are paradoxes here. In Europe, the French, German and British struggled with one another for centuries until passions were spent and some Europeans could recognize a common ideal. The ASEAN countries, separated by millions of miles of sea and by different European colonial empires, were never really distant enough to recognize a strong affinity today, other than that of common fear of the "Red menace".

"THE RED MENACE"

The end of the Viet-Nam war gave a new impetus to fear. There were frequent meetings between the government leaders on a bilateral basis, ministerial meetings galore, and a Second ASEAN Summit held in Kuala Lumpur in August 1977 at which Japan promised to give greater assistance to the ASEAN countries. Following the coup in Thailand there was strong co-operation between Malaysia and Thailand in trying to combat the common communist guerrilla problem faced by both countries.

In fact, so strong is the anti-communist feeling that an outsider can only wonder if it is too strong and could become counter-productive. Malaysia showed itself to be the most prepared to deal with communism on an international basis. It had opened diplomatic relations with China in 1972, and Malaysian Government ministers had travelled to China to boost trade links and had held discussions with Soviet shipping interests to try to undercut western freight conferences. However, this tolerance stopped at the international boundary line and, as in Singapore, anyone caught as a communist or professing the communist cause would be put in prison under the Internal Security Act (ISA), allowing for imprisonment for periods of two years without any need for a trial or appeal to habeas corpus.

Singapore also has the same kind of internal security laws and has been freer to use them. When Datuk Seri Dr Mahathir bin Mohamad and Datuk Musa Hitam became Prime Minister and Deputy Prime Minister in 1981, they released a number of people who had been held under the special security laws, and the new leaders seemed more reluctant to use such powers.

Malaysia and Thailand conducted several joint operations against the communists operating from Thailand, which gained a great deal of attention in the local press with the suggestion that this was the way that the "Red menace" was being defeated. In reality, however, the best successes against the communists were made by improving police intelligence work, which allowed the Malaysians particularly to pick up important communist figures.

The most surprising leader was President Ferdinand Marcos of the Philippines. In the uncertainty after the death of Chairman Mao Zedong (Mao Tse-tung) he showed great diplomatic flexibility, journeying to all the major powers or using his wife or daughter as special envoy. In the event, nervous fears of open Chinese hostility towards the non-communist countries or of moves to renew friendship with the Soviet Union were misplaced. China kept up its tirade against Moscow, and seemed intent on solving domestic problems after the downfall of the "Gang of Four". Mr. Marcos's ability and willingness to respond quickly to new situations was illustrated by his handling of the insurgent Muslims in Mindanao who wanted autonomy. Fearing that failure to reach a compromise with the Muslims would endanger oil supplies from the Middle East, President Marcos held long negotiations with the Mindanao Muslims, using Colonel Gaddafi, the Libyan leader, as mediator. Partial agreements were twice reached in 1977 but not properly kept, as each side accused the other of bad faith. In 1978 and 1979 the fighting flared again and opponents of President Marcos, who also faced disturbances in Manila, claimed that it was the penalty of dictatorship. In 1981 a newly-elected President Marcos, under a French-style constitution giving him enormous powers, still faced rebellion, with reports that the Muslims and the left-wing New People's Army had joined forces.

In the Pacific there were signs of the beginning of a new scramble for power. More islands, including the New Hebrides and the UN Trust Territory of Micronesia, were on the brink of independence. New advances in technology made the waters of the Pacific Ocean a potential source of valuable minerals. The fishing fleets of bigger countries already sailed the vast ocean, but by 1980, according to Mr. A. V. Hughes, then Permanent Secretary at the Finance Ministry in Solomon Islands, "We are probably witnessing the start of the second 'scramble for the Pacific' just a hundred years after the first such carve-up. This time populous and powerful Asian nations will join those of America and Europe, together with multinational corporations based round the world, and themselves as powerful as medium-sized nations, targeted on natural resource exploitation." France seemed reluctant to see the New Hebrides, the condominium which it ruled jointly with Britain, gain its independence. When secession troubles broke out on the northern island of Espiritu Santo, French settlers played a leading role and the French Government was reluctant to use force to stop the secession movement. Critics of France said it was because Paris feared a similar independence move in nickel-rich New Caledonia, and that it did not want to give up its nuclear test sites in Polynesia nor the opportunity of commanding miles and miles of ocean resources from its tiny Pacific possessions. In the end, the New Hebrides became independent as Vanuatu, with the rebellion still festering. British Royal Marines despatched to Vila more or less had a holiday as the French would not allow their use. In the end a small force from Papua New Guinea quickly put down the rebellion in an important display of Pacific partnership.

DEMOCRACY OR DICTATORSHIP

In terms of political styles and systems of government, the past thirty years have seen a common changing pattern in Asia. At the outset, most territories apart from Thailand and Afghanistan were under colonial rule. Then they achieved freedom under Westminster or American Congress style democracy, but saw its gradual erosion and a drift to dictatorship or a one-party state. Only India, one of the poorest countries in the area, and Japan, Australia and New Zealand, among the richest, stand out as countries that would be easily recognized in the West as democratic. Many of the rest claim to be democratic and go through the motions of holding elections, but in all of them there are restrictions and trammels which their leaders justify in terms of economic progress, the stability of the state or fighting against the communist (or capitalist) menace threatening from without. Of the rest, Malaysia comes the closest to being a complete democracy with free elections, a multi-party system, and a working parliament. What detracts from Malaysia's democracy is the system of arrests without trial under the Internal Security Act, and the large number of forbidden, sensitive issues. Singapore's Government could also claim that its measures had the overwhelming support of the populace. Until 1981 Mr. Lee Kuan Yew's People's Action Party had swept all before it and demolished the opposition at successive general elections. In a by-election in 1981 Mr. J. B. Jeyaretnam, the Workers' Party candidate, defeated the PAP man to give the opposition its first seat in Parliament since the 1960s. The vote was a rude blow to the ruling party, and the Second Deputy Prime Minister, Sinnathamby Rajaratnam (the PAP's leading philosopher), began to question the need for an opposition to a good government.

Several Asian Government leaders have claimed in recent years that a western style democracy is not appropriate to the needs of developing countries of Asia. It is far better, they have argued, that the people are well-fed, and have homes and jobs, than that they have freedom to express opinions which may lead to disruption. The actual experiences of some of the countries are worth examining.

India had recent experience of the increasingly typical Asian-style government: a controlled democracy or supposedly benevolent dictatorship. There is little evidence that the authoritarian period of Mrs. Gandhi allowed India to begin to tackle any of its huge outstanding problems. It created enormous resentment among the people, and concentrated power in the hands of a small number of people who had no idea how to exercise it other than to stay in power. In 1977 the Indian electorate showed their wish to return to democracy, even though the Government of Mrs. Gandhi had the huge advantage of the government propaganda machine on its side. Mrs. Gandhi lost heavily to a hotchpotch of opposition groups which had come together under the label of Janata Party. However, squabbling among the various Janata Party factions prevented the Government from implementing any of its promises about giving the Indian masses a new deal. In August 1979 the fights by the Janata factions broke the party, and in the January elections that followed Mrs. Indira Gandhi swept back to power. "The people wanted a firm ruler, and the Janata failed, so Mrs. Gandhi was given another opportunity," said Prabhash Joshi, editor of the *Indian Express*, Chandigarh. This time Mrs. Gandhi was faithfully guided by her young son Sanjay, and the two were accused of planning a dynasty. Though Sanjay Gandhi had no formal claim to power other than as an ordinary member of parliament, he acted as an alternative Prime Minister superintending many important decisions. But any plans for a dynasty came crashing down in June 1980 when Sanjay Gandhi was killed in trying to loop the loop in a light aircraft over New Delhi. Hopes and fears of an Indian dynasty were revived when Rajiv Gandhi, the elder brother, entered politics and Parliament and soon had a score of admirers, simply because he was Mrs. Gandhi's son and had her ear. She, for that reason, trusted him where she would not trust others. Rajiv Gandhi entered politics with reluctance and modesty but was being thrust to the centre stage. He did not enjoy the same degree of close political trust that his brother had with Mrs. Gandhi. Nor did he appear to know what to do with, or how to lead, the fawning supporters who flocked to him. Sanjay Gandhi's young widow, Maneka, appeared more ambitious, so ambitious that her mother-in-law perceived a threat and thrust her out of the prime ministerial home.

Some critics of western democratic styles, including Lee Kuan Yew, have more or less pointed to India and said: "But look where unrestrained democracy gets you". India, though, has peculiar problems of both government and economic development, which only an unwary commentator would sweep aside with easy generalizations. And democracy has its champions in the eastern half of the Asia/Australasia area. One might well object to Australia and New Zealand on the grounds that they are largely peopled by white men with white men's standards and European prosperity—though it might be considered racialist to claim that only white men are suited to or fitted to uphold democracy. However, there remains the example of Japan, which was a poor country and one humbled by war in 1945. Even as late as 1960, its G.N.P. per head was only $380. In 1977, per caput G.N.P. rose to over $5,000, and Japan overtook the United Kingdom and began to chase American living standards. Japan's economy grew steadily at rates of more than 10 per cent a year during the 1960s and early 1970s, until the oil crisis overtook it. Then it was the most severely affected of all the industrialized countries in terms of the burden of the extra oil bill. But it has recovered quickly. Throughout, Japan has retained its democratic system. Since the mid-1950s, it has admittedly had the advantage of a stable Liberal-Democratic Party Government. To the objections of those who say that this gave it stability over, for example India, it should be pointed out that India also had a one-party government, and that the Japanese Liberal-Democratic Party is no less a coalition of uneasy bedfellows than was the Congress in India until its defeat.

A DIVIDED CONTINENT

One of the greatest political problems—and this has far-reaching economic and development implications—of Asia and the Pacific, is that the countries have not learnt to live with themselves. Everything in Asia is overshadowed by Great Power play. Countries are split between the communist and non-communist camps, wary of each other, issuing hostile propaganda, and rarely think of putting their weight together against the more powerful industrialized world, which includes the Soviet Communist bloc. Even India, which is the biggest of the countries apart from China, although it would like to think that it is a power in itself, is constantly checking to see that it does not swing too far towards the Soviet Union or the West. India is so big that it has its own ambitions, and has not been able to establish easy relations which would have permitted a more relaxed attitude towards its immediate and smaller neighbours. The neighbours in turn have retained hostility toward India, although sometimes as a matter of form rather than on the merits of a particular case.

In South-East Asia, the antipathies are more sharply drawn because of the all-pervading fear of communism on the one hand and imperialist plots on the other. It should be said, for the benefit of left-leaning academics who tend to pour scorn on the behaviour of Lee Kuan Yew and other South-East Asian anti-communist leaders, that the propaganda issued by communist Indochina is, if anything, rather more frightening. Hanoi's broadcasts, for example, magnify the mildest activity by the South-East Asian Governments and depict it as part of a capitalist-imperialist conspiracy, even when there is no question of United States or other Western Power involvement.

It can be argued that communist Indochina has reason to be suspicious. After all, Thailand and South Viet-Nam were used by the Americans as jumping-off grounds for raids on Indochina, so that it is the responsibility of the non-communist states to prove their goodwill. Invitations have been issued to communist Indochina about the possibility of their joining ASEAN, but the communists have so far rejected the Association as part of the "imperialist" conspiracy. Beijing, of course, had a different attitude and was prepared to use ASEAN in its rivalry with Vietnamese-led Indochina. However, it was not prepared to give up its solid support for the Khmers Rouges, hated elsewhere in the world.

The territories in the Pacific are, generally speaking, tiny areas and not unnaturally fall under the shadow of Australia or New Zealand. The exceptions are the French dependencies (mainly New Caledonia and French Polynesia) and the American Pacific territories. New Caledonia is a French territory dominated by the mining company Société le Nickel, half populated with Frenchmen; so very rich that per caput income is equivalent to that in Japan or the United Kingdom and so French that it is impossible to obtain Australian wines there.

The rest of South-East Asia has not been properly proved. In Thailand the politicians are under serious strain, not so much because of communist pressures but because of cracks in the underlying system. The communist guerrillas are merely leaning on and exposing the flaws of the underlying framework, where so much is concentrated on the élite in Bangkok. It is inconceivable for anyone who knows the Thais to imagine that a non-Thai would be welcomed as ruler or be able to survive for long. Other countries of the region are not under such serious pressure, because they have better resources (in the case of Malaysia) or have had bad experiences with a communist-leaning regime (Indonesia) or have a government which is preoccupied with trying to do something about the problems honestly (Indonesia again). If the western industrial countries wish to foster concepts of freedom and democracy they would be better advised to make sure that the Asian and Pacific ring of countries are given the best opportunities to fulfil their own potential.

On the dogmatic question of whether communism or capitalism is better suited to the peoples of Asia and the Pacific, the probable answer is that they want a system which works. Where the system has manifestly failed, as it did in China years ago and as it did in South Viet-Nam, the established regime may be in danger. Force of arms of course may be a powerful persuader—and this is what finally toppled South Viet-Nam. America's mistake was in propping up a decaying élite in South Viet-Nam rather than giving help which would go to the masses of people. Alien power will always meet with suspicion. Indeed, the Vietnamese are remembering old antipathies against the Chinese.

In parenthesis, no communist state of Asia has distinguished itself in solving its underlying economic problems. China has certainly made a better job than before the communists took over. But Taiwan has done better than mainland China and the overtures of the latter to the West for assistance speak volumes about the limitations of Chinese autonomous growth. It may not be fair to judge Viet-Nam, which was preoccupied for so long with a costly war but the hardliners in Hanoi appear to be prepared to put pure ideology before anything else, even if it results in misery or drives people out of the country. Kampuchea under Pol Pot told its own tale of wretchedness, though the policy of emptying the towns, done more gently, would commend itself to radicals. By comparison, North Korea is a success, but not as successful as capitalist South Korea. The per caput income of the Asian communist countries is mostly the same as poor South Asia, except for North Korea and Mongolia, but South-East and East Asian countries like Singapore, Hong Kong, South Korea, Taiwan, and Malaysia are a long way ahead. Per caput income, of course, is not an especially reliable guide to economic development, but that will be examined later. Nor is economic development a guarantee of smooth political succession. In Japan Prime Minister Masayoshi Ohira died, yet his party won an even bigger majority in the general elections to assure continued Liberal Democratic rule of the country. But throughout 1980 South Korea struggled with the consequences of the sudden death of a strong man. President Park Chung Hee was assassinated in October 1979 by the head of the Korean Central Intelligence Agency. The remaining generals fought among themselves and struggled to quash the outbursts of popular demand led by students for more civil liberties. The display of public disunity was probably more encouraging than anything else to Kim Il Sung's forces marshalled to the north of the 38th parallel that marks the world's longest running truce-line. By 1981 South Korea's new leader, Chun Doo Hwan (another retired general), had looked secure enough in Seoul's Blue House—the presidential palace. In 1982, however, he was shaken by a major corruption scandal involving a relative of Chun's wife among the accused. Half the Cabinet lost their jobs in the repercussions.

ECONOMIC DEVELOPMENT

Asia undoubtedly exhibits all the problems of economic development. The twentieth century saw a post-war era of unparalleled growth and technical and economic progress. Man travelled to the moon and beyond, and people in the West became accustomed to social and economic advances in their homes, such as refrigerators, colour televisions, fitted carpets, and other utilities. In Asia they are not so common. A few extracts from the 1976 *Annual Report* of the Asian Development Bank issued in 1977 will suffice: "For the first time in three decades, the region is free from major conflicts; but for millions of people, insecurity persists at the economic and social level. . . .

"The second half of the decade (1970s) brought a new set of problems for DMCs (developing member countries) of the region—problems largely beyond their control. Just as many of these countries were showing encouraging progress in economic growth and production, they experienced a severe setback through a train of adverse developments on the international economic front. Worldwide inflation, sharp increases in oil prices, a persistent economic recession in industrialized countries and worsening terms of trade over the past few years combined to retard economic and social progress and to reduce the earlier momentum of growth. War and natural disasters also took a heavy toll. It is a tribute to the resilience and growing sense of self-reliance and economic discipline among the developing nations of the Bank's region that they have not only survived the adversities, but in some cases have still managed to record substantial progress."

Whereas per caput income in the West is $5,000 or more, even in the relatively backward countries, in Asia there are many countries with per caput incomes of only $250 and a majority below $500. A citizen of the United Kingdom or the U.S.A. consumes more protein and calories than he needs; one of India, Bangladesh or Indonesia is lucky to get two-thirds of his basic needs (*see* Table 1). The same shortfall occurs in other aspects of life.

In its 1977 report (published in 1978), the Asian Development Bank outlined the problem: "Unless higher rates of growth are achieved by major industrial countries, not only will they continue to experience unsatisfactory levels of unemployment but also the growth of world trade will be retarded, and many developing countries, especially those that are highly export-oriented, will suffer as a result. Increased restraints on imports by industrial countries could further affect exports of manufactured goods by developing countries, resulting in larger deficits in their external accounts." The vulnerability of the countries of the Asia and Pacific region began to be exposed in 1977 and in the years that followed life became more difficult. By 1979 the developing countries were facing higher import bills for essential energy, together with the effects of both recession and protectionism in the West. By 1981 some of those energy bills had doubled in spite of frugal use. Protection was on the march in the West, too. In 1982 the oil glut eased some of the pressure. At least oil bills did not go higher. Yet new problems were created as Western markets closed, commodity prices fell and the terms of trade dropped sharply.

The susceptibility of the Asian and Pacific countries to what is happening in the West is shown by the fact that more than 60 per cent of their exports go to the three big trading groups, the U.S.A., Japan and Western Europe. Trade within the developing countries of the region (which account for almost half of the world's population) is less than 20 per cent of total trade. The developing countries have made sterling efforts to diversify but they find that the lucrative Middle East markets prefer goods made in the West. Some countries, like India, Pakistan and South Korea, have made an impression by exporting labour but, in the case of the poorer countries, this means sacrificing skilled labour. Despite all these problems the rich countries favoured a policy of protectionism. Even though the poor countries were worse off both relatively and absolutely, senior officials in western trade ministries told the author that they were thinking more intently of their own problems, so the trend would be towards protectionism—even if it could bankrupt some of the developing countries. This is a point which will recur in looking at the potential for economic development.

In 1973 the oil-exporting countries quadrupled their prices. The rich countries were hit. The developing countries of Asia were doubly hit; firstly because as they already had balance of payments problems, they were less able to cope with higher oil bills and secondly because, with the recession, the industrialized world cut back its own growth prospects. By the late 1970s there had been some recovery. The poorest of the non-oil developing countries had survived the oil crisis and some of them had even prospered. This was largely because of higher rainfall and better harvests which, for example, helped to make India virtually self-sufficient in food grain production for the first time. However, between 1979 and 1981, as oil prices were raised again, the whole fragile world economic structure threatened to tumble down, again with the developing countries doubly exposed.

The first shock of the oil price rise had been absorbed. During this period the world monetary system recycled the petro-dollar surplus and the oil producers stepped up their imports, though not always for economic development. But then new dangers threatened which were partly due to the weakness of the whole international economic system and partly to the fact that the remedies for the first crisis were applied in a merely piecemeal fashion. The concentration of the oil surplus in a few countries; the uneven pace of recovery in the West and the fact that the recovery was less than expected; the strain on the American dollar and the lack of another reserve currency; the dependence of each of the non-oil producing countries on one or more commodities; the vulnerability of these commodities to a fickle world market system which favoured the rich countries—all of these factors had an impact.

By mid-1982 the picture was one of bright areas with increasingly dark patches appearing. Developing countries as a whole did reasonably well in 1981 in terms of growth, recording an average of 4 per cent. However, whereas the current account of the industrialized countries improved from a combined deficit of $44,000 million in 1980 to one of only $15,000 million in 1981, the non-oil developing countries fared badly. Low demand for exports and falling terms of trade more than offset any benefit of stable oil prices. The combined current account deficits of all non-oil developing countries rose by

Table 1

DIETARY ENERGY SUPPLY
(per person per day)

	Calories				Protein (grammes)
	Supply		Supply as percentage of requirement		
	1961–63	1972–74	1961–63	1972–74	1972–74
Developed Countries					
Australia	3,245	3,339	122	126	99·4
New Zealand	3,514	3,501	133	133	107·3
U.S.S.R.	3,272	3,483	128	136	105·5
U.S.A.	3,340	3,542	127	134	104·7
Developing Countries					
Afghanistan	2,107	2,000	86	82	61·5
Bangladesh	1,953	1,949	85	84	43·9
Burma	1,920	2,131	89	99	56·0
Fiji	2,487	2,647	109	116	57·1
India	2,046	1,970	93	89	48·6
Indonesia	1,945	2,033	90	94	42·3
Kampuchea (Cambodia)	2,198	2,095	99	94	48·9
Korea, Dem. People's Repub.	2,429	2,641	104	113	77·6
Korea, Republic	2,081	2,749	89	117	73·7
Laos	1,845	2,076	83	94	57·6
Malaysia (Peninsular)	2,445	2,534	110	114	45·0
Nepal	2,023	2,015	92	92	49·2
Pakistan	1,830	2,132	79	92	54·0
Philippines	1,880	1,953	83	86	46·6
Singapore	2,412	2,825	105	123	75·4
Solomon Islands	2,115	2,056	93	90	40·2
Sri Lanka	2,140	2,078	96	94	41·5
Thailand	2,105	2,315	95	104	49·9
Viet-Nam	2,101	2,288	97	106	56·9

Source: The Fourth World Food Survey, 1977, Food and Agriculture Organization.

$15,000 million in a single year to $97,000 million (double what it was in 1977).

Within Asia and the Pacific, the immediate figures looked good, much higher than the average for developing countries. The Asian Development Bank's *Annual Report* for 1982 provides a good chronicle of the times: "During 1981, the bank's developing member countries (DMCs), as a group, continued to have an overall economic growth rate higher than the average for other groups of developing countries. Many DMCs had rates of growth of over 5 per cent in 1981. Some DMCs in east and southeast Asia continued to be among the fastest growing economies in the world. The rate of increase in output in most of the south Asian DMCs was above the average for all developing countries. Many DMCs were also able to reduce inflation. However, the rates of economic growth in a majority of DMCs were lower than those achieved by them in 1980. The trade deficits of most DMCs widened, causing them to have larger recourse to high-cost external finance."

The prospects right across Asia and the Pacific looked increasingly gloomy. The very fast-growing countries faced sharp falls in their growth rates. Recession was already forcing revisions in Hong Kong and Singapore. Restrictive and protective measures by the industrialized countries would further curb rates by making it difficult to sell goods. Commodity producers continued to suffer.

When rich Malaysia, with a string of commodity exports including oil, had to cut its growth rate expectations, it augured badly for less well-endowed countries. Australia, too, was facing a halt to its resources boom and the likelihood of only modest growth. At the other end of the scale, the very poor countries could see cutbacks in aid which would force them to the commercial money markets for borrowings. In Asia, if not in the vulnerable tiny Pacific island countries, growth rates may still be positive, but they will be so small in 1982 and 1983 that social objectives will be impossible.

Stemming from these points, there are two sets of implications to be examined. One is the prospect for overall economic growth of the countries of the region. The other is the extent to which economic growth has meant real development.

ECONOMIC GROWTH

In trying to assess the first question there is no easy nor single answer. Growth rates in fact show enormous differences. In Japan, as has been pointed out, growth rates were soaring into double figures during the 1960s and early 1970s, and although they have since slowed down, rapid growth has taken Japan to prosperity. Likewise, Singapore, by following a process of guided capitalism plus heavy dependence on foreign investment, has managed to increase its per caput income to more than U.S. $5,000 per year while retaining high tax rates. Hong Kong has also achieved relative prosperity on the strength of low rates of taxation which attracted foreign investment. If it is protested that Hong Kong and Singapore should be disregarded because they are small and island states, which enjoy advantages which larger states cannot have, then Taiwan (admittedly a larger island) and South Korea have enjoyed a great deal of success by pursuing vigorous capitalist policies. Malaysia has built a rich economy using the base of its rich commodity resources.

On the other hand, India and the rest of South Asia, including the island republic of Sri Lanka, have lagged behind, with growth rates which have hardly covered their population increases. The Philippines and Thailand have done reasonably well—and grown—without performing startlingly. On the communist side, China has done well, and shown great strides and previously unparalleled growth but with major flaws exposed when it began to try to modernize. The other communist states have not done so well.

In a stimulating essay in *The Economist* in May 1977*, Norman Macrae studied all of the factors involved in the economic growth of those countries in Asia which had gone beyond the "take-off point" and concluded with various points, which he called the steps to take-off:

"1. Go for total employment in the countryside, at just the moment when unsuccessful poor countries are usually industrialising.

2. Put a lot of money into the hands of rural landlords, at just the moment when "progressive" poor countries are usually expropriating them. If it is politically necessary to expropriate or murder landlords before G.N.P. reaches an annual $300 a head, then find some alternative high-investing and above all wide-investing new squires (like the chairmen of revolutionary committees of Chinese rural communes).

3. Then go through a period of exploiting urban workers (i.e. paying them wages below their marginal productivity), in order to increase industrial profits. Unfortunately, the economically right moment at which to exploit the urban workers will usually come at just the moment when they are most liable to launch revolutions.

4. Then, but generally at this late stage only, with annual G.N.P. over about $300 a head, tactfully overthrow the rural squires, by a land reform that transfers agricultural production to entrepreneurial small farmers, but without causing class bitterness.

There are two other essential steps to development, which are (5) introduce cost-conscious technology, and (6) make big business beloved and get government out of its way."

Looking at the evidence, some of Mr. Macrae's arguments may be valid, particularly that which argues for total employment. One of India's major mistakes has been to neglect employment and thus fail to bring the masses into the economy. In consequence there has not been enough purchasing power to sustain economic take-off. Industries have been running at well below capacity, encouraged to be inefficient.

* *The Economist*, May 7th–13th.

Certainly the experience of Japan also suggests that with full employment and incentives to big business, it is possible to make enormous progress. But the Japanese system is entirely different from those of the western countries—or of their former colonies—in that a man joins a company for life. The tightly-knit Japanese society means that the country can move together without being split into "them and us" or having to cope with the demands of individualism. In these circumstances, and with Japan's particular situation of being humiliated in defeat after the war, it was not unnatural that it was able to grow quickly. An added advantage was that the country had been shattered by the war and could start with a clean slate, as did the Federal Republic of Germany in the West.

In the case of other countries, for example India, some of Mr. Macrae's suggestions, if implemented, would contradict one another. In India money is already in the hands of rural landlords and in the experience of a number of agronomists this is one of the reasons why food production in India has been slow.

A more valid prescription would be that the Government should be able to pursue efficiently a coherent, cohesive and lasting course, and should be able to do it efficiently. China and Japan have been able to do this, and so have Singapore, Taiwan, South Korea and all the other countries with high growth rates. On the other hand, those with slow growth rates have not. Indian policies have fallen foul of the self-contradictory tendencies in the Indian ruling élite. Precisely because the large landowners were rich providers for the ruling Congress Party, land reforms were fulfilled only on paper. Precisely because industrialists back the ruling élite, the Government's "socialist" promises have remained as mere promises. Mass education is clearly a key factor in stimulating development, though not of the Western style so openly aped in developing countries. Another qualification for growth would be a certain degree of some sort of democracy to make sure that there is access to the élite and that policies are regularly tested. Some of the fast-growing countries have not passed this test and may face problems.

The case of Pakistan is worth considering. During the 1960s, under Ayub Khan, Pakistan grew by rates of more than 7 per cent a year. Big business was encouraged. Large landlords were encouraged too, and the Green Revolution flourished. It was the only period when Pakistan's economic policy has pursued a smoothly consistent path for several years without being altered for political expediency. But interest-

Table 2

BALANCE OF TRADE OF SELECTED DEVELOPING COUNTRIES, 1978–81

(U.S. $ million)

	1978	1979	1980	1981*
Afghanistan	−74	49	118	201
Bangladesh	−646	−723	−1,639	−1,823
Burma	−92	−229	−194	−354
Cook Islands	−16	−16	−19	−16
Fiji	−157	−213	−187	−265
Hong Kong	−1,952	−1,979	−2,695	−2,899
India	−1,199	−2,015	−6,088	−6,040
Indonesia	4,953	8,388	11,075	9,435
Kiribati	8	7	−16	−18
Korea, Republic	−2,261	−5,283	−4,787	−4,877
Laos	−64	−59	−100	n.a.
Malaysia	1,470	3,225	2,142	95
Maldives	−8	−15	−16	−18
Nepal	−124	−186	−231	−239
Pakistan	−1,499	−1,966	−2,375	−2,450
Papua New Guinea	11	61	93	44
Philippines	−1,718	−2,012	−2,507	−2,538
Singapore	−2,909	−3,400	−4,620	−6,606
Solomon Islands	—	11	−1	−15
Sri Lanka	−121	−470	−990	−718
Taiwan	1,660	1,329	78	1,413
Thailand	−1,271	−2,304	−2,710	−2,771
Tonga	−19	−21	−25	−31
Vanuatu	−22	−25	−31	−26
Viet-Nam	−677	−690	−606	n.a.
Western Samoa	−41	−56	−45	−48
TOTAL	−6,768	−8,592	−16,376	−21,359

* Preliminary estimates.

Sources: IMF, *International Financial Statistics*, February 1982, and country sources.

ingly enough, the lopsidedness which Ayub's era created in Pakistan, with a handful of men from selected families controlling large slices of business, banking and insurance, caused much of the outcry that led to the inconsistency in the 1970s.

Another country which has grown quite quickly but not quickly enough to avoid the tremendous problems of poverty is Indonesia, where the low level of income and inefficient bureaucracy have led to corruption and an inability to improve the economic situation—which perhaps suggests that another prerequisite of strong and sustained economic growth is a sufficiently high level of per capita income to approach the "take-off" point. Indonesia and Malaysia are the only countries in the region with net exports of petroleum, though China has tremendous potential, but when the Indonesian Pertamina oil company ran into difficulties and debts, the whole foundation of the country's drive for growth was frustrated.

The serious question faced by developing Asian and Pacific nations is whether the Japanese experience of rapid growth can be repeated, and particularly whether it can be repeated by a large country such as India, Indonesia, Bangladesh, Pakistan or, for that matter, China. Together these countries make up almost 80 per cent of the total population of the region.

Various factors militate against any state today seeking fast growth. There is growing protectionism in the rich countries and a tendency to try to shut markets as soon as there is danger of a domestic crisis in an old, even if decaying, industry. This happened in the 1970s with European restrictions on Hong Kong textiles, with unwillingness to grant concessions to Bangladesh jute goods by the countries of Western Europe which had a small jute sector, and with Britain imposing restrictions on Pakistan knitted textiles. The exaggerated reaction against Hong Kong is an interesting case. If India were to hope to achieve the sort of export-led growth of Hong Kong, Taiwan, and even Korea, it would have to export on a massive scale and starting with such basic products that it would cause an outcry in the rich countries where vulnerable older industries would be affected.

In recent years the world has become a more uncertain place and this has led to a more protectionist attitude within the rich industrialized world. The countries which have been most severely affected have been the non-oil developing countries, which means all of Asia and the Pacific except Malaysia and Indonesia, which have been saddled with huge oil bills. It was always difficult to break into the rich world; it has now become more so.

[*continued on page 20*

Table 3

OIL PRODUCTION AND IMPORTS OF SELECTED DEVELOPING COUNTRIES, 1979–81

	Production of Crude Petroleum ('000 metric tons)				Imports of Petroleum and Petroleum Products (U.S. $ million)			
	1979	1980	1981*	% Increase 1980/81	1979	1980	1981*	% Increase 1980/81
Afghanistan	16	11	n.a.	n.a.	65	124	n.a.	n.a.
Bangladesh	—	—	—	—	140	162	185	14.2
Burma	1,499	1,521	1,905	25.2	n.a.	8	22	175.0
Fiji	—	—	—	—	87	127	158	24.4
Hong Kong	—	—	—	—	951	1,536	2,988	94.5
India	12,839	9,397	15,229	62.1	3,095	6,127	n.a.	n.a.
Indonesia	78,132	77,874	79,790	2.6	793	1,774	1,648	−7.1
Korea, Republic	—	—	—	—	3,416	6,164	7,210	17.0
Malaysia	13,754	13,365	12,150	−9.1	943	1,626	4,600	182.9
Nepal	—	—	—	—	19	42	45	7.1
Pakistan	471	491	484	−1.4	530	1,079	1,535	42.3
Philippines	1,048	517	993	92.1	1,371	2,226	2,700	21.3
Singapore	—	—	—	—	4,446	6,949	9,381	35.0
Solomon Islands	—	—	—	—	7	11	16	45.4
Sri Lanka	1,311	1,303	n.a.	n.a.	251	487	506	3.9
Taiwan	198	181	160	−11.6	2,176	4,741	4,428	−6.6
Thailand	11	14	15	7.1	1,599	2,867	3,330	16.1
Tonga	—	—	—	—	3	4	4	—
Vanuatu	—	—	—	—	4	12	10	−16.7
Western Samoa	—	—	—	—	7	10	12	20.0
Total (Reporting)	109,279	104,584	112,135	7.2	19,903	36,076	46,905	30.0

* Preliminary estimates.

Sources: UN, *Monthly Bulletin of Statistics*, December 1981, and country sources.

Table 4

BASIC ECONOMIC INDICATORS OF SELECTED COUNTRIES*

	Estimated Population (millions)	Area ('000 sq. km.)	Per Caput G.N.P. Amount (U.S. $)	Per Caput G.N.P. Average Annual Growth (%)	Index of Per Caput Food Production (1969–71=100)	Energy: Average P.A. Growth of Production (%)	Energy: Per Caput Consumption (kg. of coal equivalent)	Average Annual Rate of Inflation (%)	
	mid-1978	1978	1978	1960–78	Av. 1976–78	1974–78	1978	1960–70	1970–78
Low Income Countries†			200	1.6	97	8.2	161	3.0	10.6
1 Kampuchea (Cambodia)	8.4	181	n.a.	n.a.	57	n.a.	4	3.8	n.a.
2 Bangladesh	84.7	144	90	−0.4	90	12.8	43	3.7	17.9
3 Laos	3.3	237	90	n.a.	96	−0.6	60	n.a.	n.a.
4 Bhutan	1.2	47	100	−0.3	100	n.a.	n.a.	n.a.	n.a.
7 Nepal	13.6	141	120	0.8	92	4.6	11	7.7	9.1
12 Burma	32.2	677	150	1.0	96	11.2	64	2.7	13.7
14 Viet-Nam	51.7	330	170	n.a.	102	12.3	125	n.a.	n.a.
15 India	643.9	3,288	180	1.4	100	5.5	176	7.1	8.2
18 Sri Lanka	14.3	66	190	2.0	114	3.5	109	1.8	11.8
24 Pakistan	77.3	804	230	2.8	101	2.4	172	3.3	14.6
26 Afghanistan	14.6	647	240	0.4	100	−4.2	47	11.9	4.4
38 Indonesia (excl. East Timor)	136.0	2,027	360	4.1	100	11.3	278	n.a.	20.0
Middle Income Countries†			1,250	3.7	106	1.7	903	3.1	13.1
47 Thailand	44.5	514	490	4.6	122	11.4	327	1.9	9.1
49 Philippines	45.6	300	510	2.6	115	12.4	339	5.8	13.4
53 Papua New Guinea	2.9	462	560	3.6	106	16.2	292	3.6	8.8
67 Malaysia	13.3	330	1,090	3.9	110	27.1	716	−0.3	7.2
70 Korea, Republic	36.6	99	1,160	6.9	116	3.2	1,359	17.5	19.3
75 Taiwan	17.1	36	1,400	6.6	105	1.4	2,202	4.1	10.3
86 Hong Kong	4.5	1	3,040	6.5	30	n.a.	1,657	2.3	7.7
88 Singapore	2.3	1	3,290	7.4	112	n.a.	2,461	1.1	6.1
Industrialized Countries†			8,070	3.7	108	0.8	7,060	4.2	9.4
93 New Zealand	3.2	269	4,790	1.7	107	11.4	3,790	3.3	11.0
94 United Kingdom	55.8	244	5,030	2.1	111	13.5	5,212	4.1	14.1
97 Japan	114.9	372	7,280	7.6	97	−0.8	3,825	4.8	9.6
98 Australia	14.2	7,687	7,990	2.9	121	5.3	6,622	3.1	12.8
105 U.S.A.	221.9	9,363	9,590	2.4	114	−0.5	11,374	2.8	6.8
Centrally Planned Economies†			1,190	4.0	112	6.5	2,117	n.a.	n.a.
114 China, People's Repub.	952.2	9,561	230	3.7	111	9.1	805	n.a.	n.a.
115 Korea, Dem. People's Repub.	17.1	121	730	4.5	130	4.3	2,702	n.a.	n.a.
118 Mongolia	1.6	1,565	940	1.5	94	9.3	1,240	n.a.	n.a.
123 U.S.S.R.	261.0	22,402	3,700	4.3	111	5.5	5,500	n.a.	n.a.

* The countries are listed within their group in ascending order of income per caput. The reference numbers indicate that order in terms of all countries in the world with over 1 million inhabitants. Capital-surplus oil exporters (five countries) and countries with centrally planned economies are not listed in terms of the rest of the countries in the world.

† The figures shown in this band are the median values of indicators for each group of countries.

Sources: World Bank, *World Development Report*, 1980.

continued from page 18].

Much more important, the former colonies have been impeded by their colonial past and by the fact that they were largely suppliers of goods to the metropolitan markets. If there has been a shift in the metropolis, the terms of relationships have not changed much. This applies even to a country as rich as Malaysia, which has managed to diversify to produce four rather than one or two world-ranking commodities—rubber, tin, tropical hardwood and palm oil.

All the developing countries of the Asian-Pacific region have to depend upon a small number of primary commodities, and have had to struggle to build up and diversify their exports into industrial fields. Afghanistan exports dried fruit and a certain amount of natural gas, which is tied to the Soviet Union as recompense for help in building a pipeline (it should be pointed out that the Soviet Union is at least as bad if not worse than the other rich industrial countries in the terms it extracts from poor nations). Pakistan depends on rice and cotton exports. India

Table 5

CHANGES IN SHARES OF WORLD TRADE IN SELECTED AGRICULTURAL COMMODITIES

	Value Share in Total World Trade		Percentage Change
	1963–67	1970–74	
Raw Cotton	%	%	
Pakistan*	3.53	2.60	−26
Afghanistan	0.51	0.32	−37
Bangladesh	0.02	0.02	0
	4.06	2.94	−28
Jute/Similar Fibres			
Bangladesh	73.00	66.89	−8
Burma	0.15	2.43	1,500
Nepal	0.94	1.13	20
	74.09	70.45	−5
Tea			
India	34.82	27.02	−22
Sri Lanka	32.71	25.96	−21
Bangladesh	6.20	5.10	−18
Viet-Nam†	0.38	0.31	−18
	74.11	58.39	−21
Tobacco			
India	3.56	3.98	12
Indonesia	1.65	2.14	30
Korea, Republic	0.24	1.28	433
Pakistan	0.97	0.92	−5
Bangladesh	0.05	0.05	0
	6.47	8.37	30
Rice			
Thailand	17.78	12.40	−30
Japan	—	5.21	n.a.
Pakistan	4.23	5.10	21
Nepal	5.87	2.56	−56
Burma	11.45	2.35	−79
Kampuchea	37.77	0.23	−94
Viet-Nam	0.08	0.22	175
	43.18	28.07	−35
Natural Rubber			
Malaysia	45.29	51.55	14
Indonesia	21.52	21.31	−1
Thailand	8.84	10.52	19
Sri Lanka	5.90	5.14	−13
Viet-Nam	2.45	0.57	−77
Kampuchea	2.30	0.52	−77
Burma	0.36	0.28	−22
	86.66	89.89	4
Sugar	%	%	
Philippines	7.23	7.38	2
Thailand	0.20	1.73	765
India	1.55	1.57	1
Korea, Republic	0.04	0.16	300
	9.02	10.84	20
Coffee			
Indonesia	1.35	2.12	57
Viet-Nam	0.28	0.07	−75
Laos	0.01	0.00	−90
	1.64	2.19	33
Palm Oil			
Malaysia	25.09	48.51	93
Indonesia	20.41	17.25	−15
	45.50	65.76	45
Coconut Oil			
Philippines	49.58	56.17	13
Malaysia	5.02	6.27	25
Sri Lanka	18.62	6.17	−67
	73.22	68.61	−6
Copra			
Philippines	63.58	61.71	−3
Coconuts (desiccated)			
Philippines	56.58	57.40	1
Sri Lanka	40.47	36.42	−10
	97.05	93.82	−3

Countries for which data is given are those Developing Countries which had the particular commodity among its four leading agricultural exports (in value terms) in 1970–74.

* Countries are ranked under each commodity heading according to their share of world trade in 1970–74.

† Includes all of what is now the Socialist Republic of Viet-Nam.

Source: FAO, *Trade Yearbook.*

used to depend on jute and tea. Bangladesh still does depend on jute and jute goods, Burma on rice, Sri Lanka on tea and a little rubber, Thailand on rice, tin and rubber, Malaysia on rubber, tin, timber and palm oil, Indonesia on rubber and spices and other natural resources, the Philippines on sugar and coconuts, Fiji on sugar and New Caledonia on nickel.

In most cases, industrialization, offering the chance of providing more jobs and diversifying development, has meant treading a well-beaten path starting with textiles, then going on to electronic and semi-skilled assembly jobs which rely on low labour costs. In each of these, the developing countries have been competing with one another and have had to keep their labour under control so as not to price themselves out of the market. That has made the job easier for small, compact areas like Singapore and Hong Kong, but impossibly difficult for those with rambling rural hinterlands and large-scale infrastructural problems. Attempts by the bigger countries to break into industrial markets have been held back by a vicious circle of underdevelopment. The developing countries have never had enough spare capital to start their own industries to compete with the already rich as this would require a big enough market to support industry and a sufficiently skilled labour force. They also have inadequate infrastructures and a low level of education. Thus, most poor countries have been unable to find an area to provide extra thrust for economic development. Interestingly India, which has been most criticized, especially for its educational developments, stands far above the rest of Asia in terms of the sophistication of its industry. Unfortunately, India's other policies have not helped in releasing the energies of its trained people to beneficial purposes.

STANDARDS OF LIVING

Beyond this is perhaps the most important question of all, which applies to both the fast and slow growing countries of the Asian-Pacific region—will they see that their citizens have a say in their own lives as well as a decent standard of living? What Gunnar Myrdal wrote in *Asian Drama* is still true: "The plight of the masses of people in the underdeveloped economies of South Asia would be serious enough if income were evenly distributed . . . the high degree of inequality means that the vast majority in each nation are forced to eke out an existence on annual incomes well below the quite inadequate national average. Regardless of the crudity of the empirical evidence . . . it cannot and in fact does not conceal the reality of massive poverty." Such a judgement would apply to practically all the countries of the region apart from the rich ones of Australia, Japan and New Zealand, and perhaps Taiwan.

The greatest failure of the leaders of the Third World countries is that they have tended to be a self-perpetuating élite who have lived lifestyles very little different from that of the élites in the rich countries. In most countries of this region, large and growing numbers of poor have been marooned right at the bottom of the ladder, with little hope of any stake in their country. According to the Asian Development Bank *Asian Agricultural Survey*, published in 1978: "There is a remarkable consistency in the patterns of rural consumption expenditure. About 60 per cent of household budgets are spent on food, 20–25 per cent on non-food items, and the rest on services. This shows the relatively low buying power of the rural population and the lack of demand for both agricultural and non-agricultural outputs which it implies. There has been no appreciable change in these patterns since the mid-1960s. It is the failure of the rural consumption link to develop (this being a function of poverty) which mainly constrained the development of stronger linkages between agriculture and non-agriculture."

In country after country, poverty and underdevelopment have reinforced one another, and led to further underdevelopment and renewed poverty. In a recently published book,* Michael Lipton of Sussex University analyses the question why the poor stay poor, and concludes that it is largely because of the urban bias in the developing countries. There is much to be said for this thesis. A demonstration of it can be seen in India, Thailand, Indonesia and in practically every country of Asia and the Pacific. The politicians and the bureaucrats sit in their often air-conditioned capitals enjoying modern comforts while the peasants toil in the fields. Much of the grain that they produce may be taken away to the cities where it is sold at low prices which tend to depress the incentive of farmers to produce more. The politicians and bureaucratic planners cannot afford to pay more because they are afraid that higher prices would cause the urban masses to feel tempted to show off their hostility in a way that might threaten the government. The discomfiture of the rural masses can be more safely ignored as they are a long way away from the centres of power and too busy cultivating their crops and eking out a living to start thinking of marching in any demonstration of protest.

It is a thesis which carries much conviction, but in India and in much of the rest of Asia there is another factor which is that many of the rural landlords are allies of the middle class élite which simply creates another barrier to progress.

Again as the Asian Development Bank *Agricultural Survey* eloquently puts it:

> "The broad objectives for Asian agricultural and rural development during the next decade are clear:
>
> (i) the rate of growth in agricultural output must be accelerated considerably;
>
> (ii) this has to be done in a manner which allows the small and currently marginal farmers to contribute to, and benefit from, this growth:
>
> (iii) wage paid employment or supplementary occupations in both farm and non-farm activity have to be provided for the substantial and growing number of rural workers who do not have a viable production base, i.e. the landless laborers and farmers with tiny

* Lipton, Michael. *Why Poor People Stay Poor: Urban Bias in World Development* (Temple Smith, London, 1977).

holdings, the unemployed and underemployed, and many of the new labor force entrants during the next decade;

(iv) links between agricultural and non-agricultural sectors have to be strengthened so that growth in these sectors become mutually reinforcing; and

(v) the production and trade in agricultural commodities must be so organized that the DMCs' economies can share in global increases in productivity and income, and at the same time be more adequately safeguarded from the vulnerability characteristic of involvement in international trade.

Many of the factors which will determine the success with which these goals can be achieved lie beyond the control of the DMCs, even as a group, yet there clearly are also crucial areas of policy and action which lie within their competence."

The lack of these prerequisites combines to produce more misery and to take countries further away from a solution. In the villages, the educational system tends to tap the most promising children (though often only of the rich classes) and to lure them to the cities, thus sapping the strength they may give to their home areas. The poor peasants continue to have more children than the State can afford, although there may be a short-term advantage for their parents, or at least those who are lucky enough to be able to think of the short-term. The pressures on the land increase, so that they are intolerable even for peasants and landless who have managed to eke out an existence from tiny strips. So on the one hand peasants move to the cities in a hopeless search for work, while on the other, the hard-pressed try to use land which is not economically nor agriculturally suitable. At a certain stage, which is happening now in some countries, the pressure on the land begins to threaten the delicate balance of nature. There are too many examples to mention of forests which have been torn down for agriculture, only to leave the soil exposed for the rains to wash away its nutrient value. Sometimes too, it is the same large landowners who greedily tear down the forest for short-term profits. This has been done to a large extent in Malaysia, where it has been sanctioned at high levels. Tun Mustapha in timber-rich Sabah kept himself in power by putting people under an obligation to him by granting them timber concessions.

There is another ugly dimension of underdevelopment. Mr. Lipton's thesis about urban bias rings true in the villages and in the salons of the middle class élite, but walking round the slums of Calcutta, Jakarta or Bangkok, one is hard-pressed to think of the advantages to millions of urban dwellers exposed without a roof over their heads and possibly too poor even to afford the Government's ration-price rice or wheat.

At this point all the reinforcing factors begin to come into play. The Government's room for manoeuvre is limited. It probably has a population where the literacy rate is low, it cannot add to its budget spending without expanding the deficit, increasing inflation and harming most of all the poorest section of the community. On top of this, it has all its other worries of how to set up a decent infrastructure, how to keep its defence forces in readiness against an attack from a neighbour that it does not trust or from guerrillas supported by aid from a foreign power. Its own imagination is probably limited even if it has the inclination to look to the countryside. And in any case, its immediate political friends are probably located within the cities and the middle class bourgeoisie, and it dare not desert them and their interests without provoking a revolt or revolution.

Internationally, few countries have much room for manoeuvre. Too many of them are dependent on one or two commodities, in which prices are determined partly by nature, partly by demand from the rich countries, and partly by the way in which they indulge in cut-throat competition with other developing countries. To industrialize would be one solution, but industrialization is not easy without infrastructure, etc. Aid has been promised from the rich countries, but aid meets only 10 per cent of investment spending by poor countries and has so often been filtered to projects which are either completely wasteful or which do not take cognizance of the real needs to create employment. So the poor countries are stuck. In 1977, there were flickers of hope with the new Carter Administration and a less self-contained American policy. But as time went on Carter became preoccupied with other problems and the world slipped towards recession, promoting a spurt in self-interest but not in moves towards imaginative solutions. At the industrialized summit in Venice former British Prime Minister Edward Heath fought to interest the heads of government in the proposals of the North-South Commission under Willy Brandt. This had called for a "New Deal" for the developing world, with higher aid, better commercial lending and assured prices for commodities from developing countries. The best the big seven leaders could do was to utter polite noises.

The coming of the new Reagan Administration in the U.S.A. posed new challenges and issued new threats to the developing world. High interest rates (in 1981 and 1982 people were asking "when would American interest rates come down and give a lead to expansion and world recovery?"; although the worst predictions of rates of more than 20 per cent were not fulfilled, by mid-1982 rates were still stubbornly high at 15 per cent and were considerably higher than inflation), the struggle to control inflation, the demands from industrial workers in the West that their jobs should be protected, the political pressures of a complex international world, the general lack of confidence among the leaders of the West were all difficult enough. Then the conservative policies of President Reagan added extra squeezes. The U.S.A. has, for several years, been the biggest delinquent in its laggardliness in supplying funds to the World Bank and its "soft loan" arm, the International Development Agency (IDA). Because of congressional delays, the IDA ran out of funds in 1981. The problem was that the American funds were needed as the trigger to release other countries' contributions, but then Reagan came in, keener on bilateral rather than multilateral aid, and pledged to look again at aid. Mr. Robert McNamara retired as President of the World Bank in June 1981 and was succeeded by A. W. (Tom) Clausen, former chairman of the Bank of America. McNamara admitted that his speeches over 13 years as President of the World Bank had been better reported abroad than in the U.S.A. "I don't believe we have been successful in raising the consciousness of the American public in terms of where their own interests lie", said McNamara in his valedictory interviews.

In Asia's case, finding finance was likely to be an increasingly tough proposition. By 1982 the cutback in IDA funds had particularly hurt India. Of all IDA recipients, only Bangladesh survived without a cutback, although, in real terms (taking account of inflation), the value of assistance to Bangladesh was also trimmed. The new World Bank President, A. W. Clausen, made a powerful plea for the IDA. Speaking in Washington at the end of 1981, he said: "The same professional staff in the World Bank negotiates and administers IDA projects; the same high rates of economic return are insisted upon; the same supervision and international competitive bidding for procurement are rigorously applied; and the same full government guarantees of repayment are required.

"For an IDA project to be approved at all, it must have an estimated rate of economic return of at least 10 per cent in real terms. So IDA is not a give-away program, or a welfare agency, or a philanthropic society, or a soft-hearted and soft-headed 'soft-loan window'. There is nothing soft about IDA at all. It is a hard, tough, realistic development agency doing a hard, tough, realistic job. And doing it well.

"I say that as a former commercial banker, with 31 years of experience in a tough, competitive banking market-place—and with no personal reputation, I think it's fair to say, for banking softness.

"IDA is having difficulties in the U.S. Congress, as we all know—but, in my view, it is having difficulties for the wrong reason. If IDA were just a kind of international entitlement program—just a relic of a more prosperous economic period in the past when the United States felt more generous—then I could understand that in a time of budgetary pressures it might make good economic sense to cut it back, and pare it down, and string it out in a severely reduced form.

"But IDA is not an international entitlement program. And the basic issue is not generosity. On the contrary, IDA is a hard-headed investment in international trade, and economic growth, and greater global stability and cohesion, and the U.S. ought to live up to the international agreements it has made with respect to IDA because it is in its own best self-interest to do so."

The pressures will get even tougher because in 1981 China, for the first time, was approved as a World Bank borrower. Although entitled to IDA terms, it will not receive IDA money. Even so, its borrowing presence will squeeze the funds available. India decided, for the first time, to seek funds from the Asian Development Bank (ADB) and Delhi officials were hoping to obtain $400 million per year, a large sum compared with the ADB's total lending of $1,678 million in 1981. That sort of money would further squeeze other smaller countries. Like the World Bank, the ADB is experiencing a shortage of funds and talking of co-financing projects and other schemes to eke out the money.

Middle-income countries, those too rich to be given the very soft loans from IDA, faced other difficulties. Some of them, South Korea and the Philippines among them in Asia, had borrowed heavily from commercial banks. By the 1980s the interest rates were high, and higher than inflation in many countries: the end of cheap money imposed heavy debt burdens. Middle-income countries also faced the sharp end of the renewed protectionist squeeze as they tried to diversify their exports. Bitter battles were fought over the renewal of the Multi-Fibre Arrangement concerning textiles. It was renewed, but the struggle continued even more fiercely into 1982 as individual agreements were sought within the agreement. The European Economic Community was fighting especially hard and protectively. Questions of a so-called dialogue between the north (industrialized countries) and the south (developing countries) were taken up at the North-South summit in Mexico in October 1981. When the leaders of the "big seven" industrial countries met at Versailles in mid-1982, however, the problems of the developing world received little attention. There was reference in the communiqué to the launching of "global negotiations" and maintaining aid flows. For the most part, the rich countries had other things to distract them, such as their own plight.

And over it all hangs the shadow of the growth of population. The Asian and Pacific region contains 60 per cent of the world's teenagers and children. Populations are growing at between 2 and 3 per cent a year. By the year 2000 the region may contain as many people as the whole world does now. Already large numbers are without jobs. An estimated 40 to 68 per cent (the latter figure was given by the Janata Party, later the Government, in its election manifesto) of the population of India lives below the officially designated poverty line. Other poor countries in the region cannot be much better off. The cities are hard-pressed to provide minimum facilities. The land supply in the villages is sufficiently low to drive peasants to the cities. With effort and foresight, great things can be done and agricultural and industrial revolutions begun. But without something being done quickly, a grim future awaits the poor countries of the developing Asian and the Pacific region.

A clear warning about the size of the problem and the time for action was given in the first *World Development Report* published by the World Bank in the autumn of 1978. The report estimated that there were 800 million people throughout the world living

Table 6

POPULATION CHANGES AND PROJECTIONS FOR SELECTED DEVELOPING COUNTRIES

	Mid-Year Population (in millions)			Percentage Increase	
	1950	1975	2000	1950 to 1975	1975 to 2000
India	368.5	618.8	960.6	68.0	55.2
Indonesia (excl. E. Timor) .	80.0	135.7	198.7	69.6	46.4
Bangladesh . . .	40.6	76.6	148.4	88.7	93.7
Pakistan	38.5	75.5	140.0	96.2	85.4
Philippines	20.9	43.1	77.0	106.4	78.9

Source: World Population Prospects as Assessed in 1980 (UN Department of International Economic and Social Affairs, New York, 1981).

in absolute poverty, of whom 600 million were in developing Asia. Economists from the World Bank contrived to paint a picture of some optimism which was in part a public relations exercise designed to spur on the faint-hearted to new efforts, but even if the optimism were fulfilled there would still be 600 million absolutely poor people in the world by the year 2000. To get prospects off to a good start the Bank expected greater aid flows, a continuing flow of commercial capital to the developing countries, growth rates averaging 4.2 per cent a year in the industrialized countries between 1975 and 1985, and open trade policies. By the start of the 1980s these seemed like heroic projections of optimism.

BIBLIOGRAPHY

GENERAL

Asia and Pacific 1980 & 1981 (Annual Review). Editor K. Rafferty (World of Information, Saffron Walden).

Asia 1981 Yearbook (Far Eastern Economic Review, Hong Kong, 1980).

Avramovic, Dragoslav. Stabilization, adjustment and diversification: a study of the weakest commodities produced by the poorest regions (World Bank Paper No. 245, November 1976).

Balassa, Bela. Export incentives and export performance in developing countries: a comparative analysis (World Bank Paper No. 248, January 1977).

Barnet, R. J., and Muller, R. E. Global Reach: The Power of the Multinational Corporations (New York, 1974).

Bhagwati, J. N. (ed.). The New International Economic Order: The North-South Debate (Massachusetts Institute of Technology, Cambridge, Mass. and London, England, 1977).

Bhattacharya, A. K. Foreign Trade—International Development (Lexington Books, Massachusetts, Toronto and London, 1976).

Chenery, Hollis B., and Syrquin, M. with Elkington, H. Patterns of Development, 1950–70 (Oxford University Press, London, 1975).

Critchfield, Richard. The Golden Bowl Be Broken: Peasant Life in Four Cultures (Bloomington and London, 1973).

George, Susan. How the Other Half Dies—The Real Reasons for World Hunger (Penguin Books, Harmondsworth, 1976).

Griffin, Keith. The Green Revolution: An Economic Analysis (UNRISD, Geneva, 1972).

Hadler, Sandra C. Developing Country Foodgrain Projections for 1985 (World Bank Paper No. 247, November 1976).

Haq, M. The Poverty Curtain (World Bank, New York).

Haq, M., and Burki, S. J. Meeting Basic Needs: an Overview (Poverty and Basic Needs series, World Bank, September 1980).

Hayami, Yujiro. Anatomy of a Peasant Economy (International Rice Research Institute, Manila, 1978).

Hicks, Norman L. "A model of trade and growth for the developing world" reprinted from *European Economy*, Review 7, 1976, Reprint 28.

Hughes, Helen et al. Capital Utilization in Manufacturing in Developing Countries (World Bank Paper No. 242, September 1976).

Jolly, Richard (ed.). Disarmament and World Development (Institute of Development Studies, University of Sussex and Pergamon Press, London, 1978).

Jolly, Richard et al. (ed.). Third World Employment (Harmondsworth, 1973).

Leontief, Wassily et al. The Future of the World Economy: a United Nations Study (Oxford University Press, New York, 1977).

Lowe, Peter. Great Britain and the Origins of the Pacific War: A Study of British Policy. East Asia 1937–1941 (Oxford University Press, London, 1977).

MAZUMDAR, DIPAK. The Urban Informal Sector (World Bank Paper No. 211, July 1975).

MELLOR, JOHN W. Agricultural price policy and income distribution in low income nations (World Bank Paper No. 214, September 1975).

"The Land and the Landless" in *Ceres*, 61, Jan.–Feb. 1978.

MORAWETZ, DAVID. Employment implications of industrialization in developing countries: a survey (World Bank Paper No. 170, January 1974).

MORRISON, RALPH H., and GRILLI, ENZO R. Jute and Synthetics (World Bank Paper No. 171, January 1974).

PAYER, CHERYL. The Debt Trap: The IMF and the Third World (Harmondsworth, 1974).

REUTLINGER, SCHLOMO et al. Should Developing Nations Carry Grain Reserves? (World Bank Paper No. 171, January 1974).

SCHUMACHER, E. F. Small is Beautiful (London, 1973).

SINGH, SHAMSHER. Commodity trade and price trends (World Bank, 1976).

STOCKHOLM INTERNATIONAL PEACE RESEARCH INSTITUTE. SIPRI Yearbook 1978 (World Armaments and Disarmaments) (London, 1978).

Arms Control: A Survey and Appraisal of Multilateral Agreements (London, 1978).

Outer Space—Battlefield of the Future? (London, 1978).

Strategic Disarmament, Verification and National Security (London, August 1977).

Weapons of Mass Destruction and the Environment (London, October 1977).

TRIDENTE, ALBERTO. "Eliminating the divisions and competition among countries exporting manpower is the only way to order the international labour market" in *Ceres*, 59, Sept.–Oct. 1977.

WARD, BARBARA. The Home of Man (Penguin Books, Harmondsworth, and André Deutsche, London, 1976).

WARD, BARBARA, and DUBOS, RENÉ. Only One Earth (Penguin Books, Harmondsworth, 1972).

WEBB, RICHARD C. On the Statistical Mapping of Urban Poverty and Employment (World Bank Paper No. 227, January 1976).

WORLD BANK. World Debt Tables (regular intervals). World Development Report, 1978, 1979, 1980, 1981.

ASIA

ANGELOPOULOS, ANGELOS. "Up to its neck in debt, the Third World, whose strength grows constantly, demands the lightening of its burden" in *Ceres*, 59, Sept.–Oct. 1977.

ASIAN DEVELOPMENT BANK. Asian Agricultural Survey 1976 (Manila, 1977).

Annual Reports 1977–80 (published Manila, in following year).

South Pacific Agriculture—Choices and Constraints (Manila, 1979).

BHAGAVAN, M. R. et al. The Death of the Green Revolution (Haslemere Group, London, 1973).

BRECHER, M. The New States of Asia: political analysis (1964).

BROWN, JUDITH M. Gandhi and Civil Disobedience: The Mahatma in Indian Politics, 1928–34 (Cambridge University Press, 1977).

BROWN, W. N. The United States and India, Pakistan and Bangladesh (3rd. edn., 1972).

CARTIER-BRESSON, H. The Face of Asia (1972).

COLBERT, EVELYN. South-east Asia in International Politics 1941–56 (Cornell University Press, Ithaca, New York and London, 1977).

CRAMPTON, E., and JACKSON, J. The Asian Highway. Handbook for the traveller between Turkey and India (1977).

FRIEDMAN, EDWARD, and SELDEN, MARK (eds.). America's Asia: Dissenting essays on Asian-American Relations (New York, 1971).

GALE, ROGER. "Security Micronesia . . . for the Pentagon" in AMPO (Tokyo) July–Sept. 1975, pp. 62–67.

HALLIDAY, JON. A Political History of Japanese Capitalism (New York, 1975).

HALLIDAY, JON, and MCCORMACK, GAVAN. Japanese Imperialism Today (Harmondsworth, 1973).

HANNEH, LESLIE. The Rise of the Corporate Economy (Methuen & Co. Ltd., London, 1976).

HAWKES, J. The First Great Civilisations: life in Mesopotamia, the Indus Valley and Egypt (Pelican, 1973).

HORNE, DONALD. The Lucky Country (Harmondsworth, 1964).

HOWELL, LEON, and MORROW, MICHAEL. Asia, Oil Politics and the Energy Crisis (IDOC/North America, New York, 1974).

INTERNATIONAL LABOUR OFFICE. Poverty and Landlessness in Rural Asia (Geneva, 1977).

JOHNSON, SHEILA K. American Attitudes to Japan, 1941–75 (AEI-Hoover Policy Study, November 1975).

KARCHER, MARTIN. "Unemployment and Underemployment in the People's Republic of China" reprinted from *China Report* 11, Sept.–Dec. 1975, Reprint 25.

KAYSER, BERNARD. "The bloodletting exchanges and mobility are necessary to progress. But to what extent do migrations favour development?" in *Ceres* 59, Sept.–Oct. 1977.

KERSHAW, ROGER. "Thailand after Vietnam; after Vietnam, Thailand?—The direction of Thai diplomacy in 1975" in *Asian Affairs*, Vol. 63, February 1976.

MACFARQUHAR, R. (ed.). Sino-American Relations, 1949–71 (1972).

MCHENRY, DONALD F. Micronesia—Trust Betrayed (Carnegie Endowment).

MARTIN, EDWIN W. South-east Asia and China; The End of Containment (Westview Press for Centre for Strategic and International Studies, Georgetown University, Washington, D.C., 1977).

MISRA, B. B. The Indian Political Parties—An Historical Analysis of Political Behaviour up to 1947 (Oxford University Press, London, 1977).

MOULDER, FRANCES V. Japan, China and the Modern World Economy. Towards a reinterpretation of East Asian Development 1600–1918 (Cambridge University Press, London, New York and Melbourne).

MYRDAL, GUNNAR. Asian Drama: An Inquiry into the Poverty of Nations (Pantheon Books, New York and London, 1968).

The Challenge of World Poverty: a summary and continuation of Asian Drama (1970).

PANIKKAR, K. M. Asia and Western Dominance (London, 1953).

RAWSON, PHILIP. Indian Asia (Elsevier-Phaidon Press, 1977).

REISCHAUER, E. O., and FAIRBANK, J. K. East Asia: Tradition and Transformation (1973).

SIGUARDSON, JON. Rural Industrialization in China (Harvard University Press, Cambridge, Mass., 1977).

TAKEUCHI, KENJI. Tropical hardwood trade in Asia-Pacific region (Johns Hopkins University Press for the World Bank, Baltimore and London, 1974).

TINKER, H. Ballot Box and Bayonet; People and Government in Emergent Countries (1964).

The Banyan: Overseas Emigrants, India, Pakistan and Bangladesh (1977).

VELLI, F. A. Politics of the Indian Ocean Region (Free Press, 1976).

WALL, P. The Indian Ocean and the Threat to the West. Four Studies in Global Strategy (1975).

WENKHAM, ROBERT. The Great Pacific Rip-Off: Corporate Rape in the Far East (Chicago, 1974).

WILCOX, W. A. Asia and the United States Policy (1967).

WILCOX, W. A. et al. Asia and the International System (1972).

WILSON, DICK. (ed.) Mao Tse-tung in the Scales of History (Cambridge University Press for the Contemporary Chinese Institute of Publications, 1977).

Population in Asia and the Pacific

Michael Williams

THE IMPORTANCE OF ASIA'S POPULATION

The overwhelming features of the population of Asia are its total size and its density. Outside Soviet Asia, there were an estimated 2,601 million people,* or 58.7 per cent of the world's total population, living in this region (including Oceania) at mid-1980, occupying a mere 26.6 per cent of the earth's surface, or only 20.7 per cent if the large but sparsely populated areas of Australia and New Zealand are excluded. This total includes 38 million people living in Iran (considered to be part of Middle South Asia) and a further 98 million in Western South Asia (i.e. the Middle East), areas not covered in this essay. It is possible to relate the total population of the countries of the region to their total area in order to give some indication of the density of people per square kilometre, but, as will be shown later, while such figures do give a very general indication of "crowding" they can be very misleading, if interpreted to mean an absolute level of well-being.

Between mid-1975 and mid-1980 the average annual rate of population increase in the major areas of the Asian and Pacific region (excluding the Middle East) varied from 0.9 per cent for Japan to 2.2 per cent for Middle South Asia. While high, these rates of increase must be seen in perspective against the trends in other continents. When compared with the average annual growth rate of 3.1 per cent for Western Africa, or 3.0 per cent for mainland Middle America, they are not so spectacular; on the other hand, when compared with the rate of 0.4 per cent for Europe (excluding the U.S.S.R.), they are enormous. The implications of these figures are made clearer if we think of the time it takes to double a population at a constant growth rate. At 0.5 per cent it takes 139 years; at 1 per cent it takes 70 years; at 2 per cent it takes 35 years; and at 3 per cent it takes 23 years.

Nevertheless, it is the large base population from which this annual growth emanates which is the crucial factor, for, in the case of Asia, this produced a large annual increment of people of, in round figures, 47 million persons annually over the period 1970–80.

* Unless otherwise stated, the population figures refer to mid-1980 and are based on *World Population Prospects as Assessed in 1980* (UN, Population Studies, No. 78, 1981).

Table 1

POPULATION IN THE ASIAN-PACIFIC REGION

	Mid-Year Population (millions)*			Average Annual Rate of Growth (%) 1975–80*	Average Annual Birth Rate (per 1,000) 1975–80*	Average Annual Death Rate (per 1,000) 1975–80*	Area ('000 sq. km.)	Population Density (per sq. km.) 1980
	1960	1970	1980					
Asia (excl. U.S.S.R.)†	1,692	2,111	2,579	1.85	n.a.	n.a.	27,576	94
East Asia	816	994	1,175	1.38	21.0	7.3	11,756	100
China (incl. Taiwan)	682	838	995	1.40	21.3	7.4	9,597	104
Japan	94	104	117	0.88	15.1	6.3	372	313
Others	40	51	63	2.05	27.1	7.9	1,786	36
South Asia†	877	1,117	1,404	2.22	37.1	14.8	15,820	89
Middle	592	752	944	2.21	37.6	15.5	6,785	139
Eastern	229	291	361	2.08	35.2	13.7	4,493	80
Western†	56	74	98	2.84	39.6	11.7	4,542	22
Oceania (excl. Hawaii)	15.8	19.3	22.8	1.47	21.8	9.0	8,510	3
Australia and New Zealand	12.7	15.4	17.8	1.21	16.8	7.9	7,956	2
Melanesia	2.2	2.8	3.6	2.70	42.3	15.1	524	7
Polynesia and Micronesia	0.9	1.2	1.4	1.73	34.0	7.0	30	47
Africa	275	355	470	2.90	46.0	17.2	30,330	15
Northern America (incl. Hawaii)	199	226	248	0.95	16.3	9.1	21,515	12
Latin America	216	283	364	2.44	33.6	8.9	20,566	18
Europe (excl. U.S.S.R.)†	425	459	484	0.40	14.4	10.5	4,937	98
U.S.S.R.	214	242	265	0.93	18.3	9.0	22,402	12
World (excl. Antarctica)	3,037	3,696	4,432	1.72	28.5	11.4	135,837	33

* UN estimates and projections from *World Population Prospects as Assessed in 1980.*

† The European portion of Turkey is included in Asia.

Because of this, Asia's share of the world population increased from 55.0 per cent in 1950 to 58.2 per cent in 1980. However, it is predicted that, largely because of the recent sharp decline in the growth rate of China's population, this proportion will remain roughly constant until the end of the century and then decline. Even so, Asia will retain the preponderant share of the world's population for the foreseeable future. Put crudely, Asia's population in 1980 was greater than that of the world in 1950; by 2000 it will nearly equal that of the world in 1970.

These facts and figures are very familiar and tend to lose their impact through constant repetition; nevertheless, this annual increment of people makes Asia one of the most critical areas of the world, not only demographically but also economically, socially and, of course, politically. All these aspects of life are linked inextricably with the discussion on population. Demographically, as mentioned already, the region is characterized by high rates of population growth (despite high death rates), high crude densities, and high dependency levels. Economically there are serious problems of unemployment and under-employment leading to low productivity and low per caput incomes. Socially there are serious problems of malnutrition, illiteracy, sub-standard housing, inadequate medical care, and poverty. The International Labour Office calculates that some 40 per cent of the population is destitute. The reduction of the annual increment of people through a decrease in births, encouraged by a variety of family planning programmes, is seen as a key factor in the planning policies of nearly all of the less developed countries of the region, for it is commonly felt that many of the social and economic problems stem from (or, at least, are linked to) the demographic situation. However, the linkages of what is cause and what is effect are by no means clear.

Some of the economic and social problems, and the attempts to limit population growth, are elaborated below, but the understanding of population growth is more complex than appears at first. Fertility and mortality, and the efforts made to control them are but the dynamic aspects of Asia's population which spring from the present base population and its composition. It is important, therefore, to examine the total numbers in each country, the relationship of the population to land resources, and the sex structure and the age structure of the population, for within these lies the potential for future growth. In addition, the degree of urban and rural living is important.

CHARACTERISTCS OF THE PRESENT POPULATION

Total Numbers

The population of Asia contains the two largest population units in the world, the People's Republic of China (estimated to have 996,220,000 inhabitants at December 31st, 1981) and India (where the census of March 1st, 1981, recorded a population of 683,998,000). These both tower above the next two largest entities, the U.S.S.R. (population 267,700,000 at July 1st, 1981) and the U.S.A. (229,810,000 at mid-1981). Recent census results confirm that Indonesia (population 147,490,000 at October 1st, 1980), Japan (117,057,000 at October 31st, 1980), Bangladesh (89,940,000 at March 6th, 1981), and Pakistan (83,782,000 at March 15th, 1981) exceed all other nations of the world except Brazil (119,099,000 at September 1st, 1980). In addition, there were at mid-1980 five other countries in Asia (excluding the Middle East) with populations exceeding 25 million, namely Viet-Nam (53.7 million), the Philippines (48.4 million), Thailand (47.2 million), South Korea (38.1 million) and Burma (33.6 million). The remaining countries of the region are substantially smaller. In many ways the size of the population of a country is not of great significance but in one respect it is. Administrative efficiency, the co-ordination of economic and social development, and the diffusion of innovations are more difficult within larger population entities than within smaller ones.

Population Density

A warning has already been sounded on interpreting overall population density as an indicator of "crowding". The crudeness of the measure is refined somewhat by relating population to the amount of agricultural land, but even then the density does not reflect wholly the true position because the quality of the land, the level of technology, the productivity per person, and the patterns of settlement all alter the significance of any given ratio. Having said that, however, if we do relate population to arable land, then densities such as 1,822 persons per square kilometre were recorded for Japan in 1970, 1,384 per square kilometre for South Korea, while those for Afghanistan were 216, Sri Lanka 637, China 695, Papua New Guinea 1,614, Indonesia 1,138, India 347, New Zealand 367, and a mere 172 for Burma (ECAFE, 1972). The atypical figures of 21,050 per square kilometre for Singapore and 41,680 for Hong Kong show the difficulties of assessing the significance of these ratios. On 1979 estimates these two territories had among the highest per caput G.N.P. of any countries in the Asian and Pacific region, which shows the importance of trade, commerce and industry in mitigating the problems inherent in high population densities.

However, in more rural countries the ratio has some validity for unless there is the development of more industry and commerce to absorb the ever-increasing number of people, then the pressure on land resources will become greater. The availability of new land, taking a 10- to 20-year viewpoint, is practically nil. Some land will be engulfed in the expansion of cities (which are usually sited on the best land), while the depletion of arable land through soil erosion, exhaustion and other forms of degradation must also be taken into account. It is probable that land being taken out of production will counteract the amount of land gained through the extension of cultivation, so that not only will the population of Asia increase in the future but the supply of productive land will barely increase.

[*continued on page* 30

Table 2

POPULATION AND INCOME OF SELECTED COUNTRIES OF THE ASIAN-PACIFIC REGION

Country	Estimated Mid-1980 Population (million)	Average Annual Birth Rate (per 1,000) 1975–80	Average Annual Death Rate (per 1,000) 1975–80	Infant Mortality Rate (per 1,000 live births)*	Annual Population Increase (%) 1975–80	Doubling Rate (years)	Life Expectancy at Birth (years) 1975–80		Per Caput G.N.P. (U.S. $) 1979
							Males	Females	
Asia:									
Afghanistan	15.9	48.5	23.2	237	2.54	27.6	40.0	41.0	n.a.
Bangladesh	88.7	46.8	18.7	153	2.82	24.9	46.0	45.5	110
Bhutan	1.3	42.7	20.6	c. 150	2.21	31.7	44.0	42.5	80
Burma	33.6	38.6	14.3	195	2.44	28.8	51.0	54.1	150
China (incl. Taiwan)	994.9	21.3	7.4	56	1.40	49.9	66.0	68.6	260†
Hong Kong	5.0	18.6	4.4	14	3.00	23.4	73.5	78.6	3,640
India	663.6	35.3	15.1	125	2.02	34.7	50.0	48.7	210
Indonesia (excl. East Timor)	148.0	33.6	16.2	90	1.74	40.2	46.4	48.7	370
Japan	116.8	15.1	6.3	8.9	0.88	79.1	73.1	78.3	8,730
Kampuchea	6.7	30.9	29.4	150	−1.01	—	29.0	31.4	n.a.
Korea, Dem. People's Republic	17.9	32.5	8.3	c. 70	2.42	29.0	60.5	64.6	n.a.
Korea, Republic	38.1	25.3	8.1	38	1.72	40.6	60.5	64.6	1,510
Laos	3.7	44.1	20.3	170	2.39	29.3	42.1	45.0	n.a.
Malaysia	13.4	33.1	7.9	32	2.53	27.7	61.5	65.1	1,450
Mongolia	1.7	37.1	8.3	c. 70	2.89	24.3	60.5	64.6	n.a.
Nepal	14.0	43.7	20.7	182	2.30	30.5	44.0	42.5	130
Pakistan	82.1	43.1	15.0	124	2.81	25.0	51.9	49.7	270
Philippines	48.4	36.2	8.6	48	2.67	26.3	59.1	62.4	640
Singapore	2.4	17.2	5.1	13	1.21	57.6	68.6	73.1	3,770
Sri Lanka	14.7	27.6	7.6	32	1.71	40.9	63.5	66.5	230
Thailand	47.2	32.3	8.9	25	2.34	30.0	57.6	63.0	600
Viet-Nam	53.7	40.1	14.3	c. 60	2.30	30.5	51.1	54.3	n.a.
Oceania:									
Australia	14.6	16.6	7.9	12.5	1.23	56.7	70.1	76.3	8,870
Fiji	0.6	28.6	4.2	17.1	1.78	39.3	69.5	73.1	1,650
New Zealand	3.1	17.8	7.9	13.8	1.14	61.1	69.8	75.9	6,400
Papua New Guinea	3.0	42.5	15.7	c. 50	2.69	26.1	50.5	50.0	760

* Latest available year. † Excluding Taiwan.

Sources: mainly UN, *Monthly Bulletin of Statistics, World Population Prospects as Assessed in 1980* and *Demographic Yearbook 1979; World Bank Atlas 1981; Quarterly Bulletin of Statistics, Asia and Pacific, 1980.*

continued from page 28].

In so many ways we are talking here of food availability and an indication of the increasing density is given by the ever-increasing food imports within the region. The whole topic of food availability is looked at below, but the ever-increasing scale of grain imports into the region does pinpoint the deficiencies of local production. In 1950 the continent was largely self-sufficient, although at the cost of great malnutrition and periodic famine. By about 1960, 25–30 million tons of grain were being imported annually, half of which was in the form of food aid. By the 1970s imports had reached about 50 million tons a year; in 1980 imports were 94.0 million tons throughout all Asia.

Sex Composition

Sex, together with age, is one of the two most important controls of future growth, and also, incidentally, of social ranking. In countries which are aiming towards economic and social development the position and proportion of women and youth in society are important because of their influence on the composition of the workforce, their ability to contribute to national prosperity, and their ability to reproduce and so contribute to future population growth.

Asian society has nearly always had a predominance of males, which has a lot to do with the lower social status of women, their higher mortality rate as a consequence of frequent pregnancies, poor health care, and the tendency to favour the care of male babies and children. Also, in census taking there would appear to be a frequent under-enumeration of females. Usually, and particularly in developed economies, the life expectancy of women is greater than that of men by 6 or 7 years, but in some of the countries of Asia it is equal to or below that of men, e.g. Bangladesh, India, Nepal, Pakistan and Papua New Guinea (*see* Table 2).

The sex ratio, where it can be calculated, can be expressed as the number of males per 1,000 females, and it is high in Pakistan (1,129 in 1974), the People's Republic of China (1,076 in 1953), India (1,075 in 1971) and Bangladesh (1,077 in 1974). Female predominance is usually a feature of developed economies (e.g. Australia was at unity in 1976), but sub-parity ratios of males per 1,000 females have been recorded for Kampuchea (999 in 1962), Indonesia (973 in 1971) and Thailand (991 in 1970). The changes in female survival are occurring as a result of the spectacular decline in female mortality.

The literacy rate for women is uniformly below that for males, the enrolment rate into primary education is markedly less and the drop-out rate in secondary and tertiary education is greater. This inequality of access to education and continuation of education results in a great wastage of human resources, both in the labour market and in the performance of domestic duties. Attitudes to education and society are therefore handed down to children and the lack of exposure of women to "modernization" may well be crucial in the acceptance of birth control, and hence future population growth, although it is by no means the only consideration (ESCAP, 1976, pp. 54–57).

Age Composition

High fertility and rapidly declining mortality have resulted in a changing age composition for most of the countries of Asia. The younger age groups are expanding at a faster rate than the older age groups. For most countries the proportion of the population under 15 is over 40 per cent (*see* Table 3), reaching as high as 44.0 per cent in the case of Indonesia. This can be

Table 3

DISTRIBUTION OF TOTAL POPULATION BY BROAD AGE GROUPS AND BY URBAN AND RURAL RESIDENCE FOR SELECTED COUNTRIES

(latest available data)

	Percentage of Total Population in the Age Group			Percentage of Total Population Living in Urban or Rural Areas	
	0–14	15–64	65 and over	Rural	Urban
Asia:					
Hong Kong	29.1	65.2	5.7	2.0	98.0
India	40.8	55.9	3.3	78.8	21.2
Indonesia (excl. East Timor)	44.0	53.5	2.5	81.8	18.2
Japan	24.3	67.6	8.1	24.1	75.9
Korea, Republic	38.1	58.4	3.5	51.6	48.4
Malaysia, Peninsular	41.5	55.0	3.5	71.2	28.8
Nepal	40.4	56.5	3.1	96.0	4.0
Philippines	42.9	54.2	2.9	68.2	31.8
Sri Lanka	39.0	56.8	4.2	77.6	22.4
Thailand	42.8	54.0	3.2	86.8	13.2
Oceania:					
Australia	27.2	63.9	8.9	14.4	85.6
Fiji	41.1	56.4	2.5	62.8	37.2

Source: UN, ***Demographic Yearbook 1977.***

compared with about 24 per cent for Europe, 26 per cent for the U.S.S.R., and 25 per cent for North America.

The situation is more complex than that, however, because within the 15-64 age group in Asia, about 20 per cent is made up of 'youths' of 15-24, again a larger percentage than in many other parts of the world. The implication for the developing countries of this heavy preponderance of young people (0-14 years) and of youth (15-24) are manifold. First, the very youngest contingent requires expanded health services; a large proportion of this age group in Asia already suffer from malnutrition, and a further increase in their number is a cause for special concern. Clearly those who survive will constitute the future labour force, and malnutrition suffered during early years may have undesirable effects on their physical and mental development, and thus on their subsequent well-being and productivity when they enter the work force. Despite the great wastage of human lives, however, it is estimated that the region's pre-school population alone grew by about another 50 million between 1970 and 1975, from 306 million to about 356 million, and an ever greater investment will have to be made in primary schools and similar facilities, thus diverting scarce funds away from more conventional "resource producing" activities such as agriculture and manufacturing (ECAFE 1973, pp. 61–72).

By and large the youth group (15-24) are more vocal and critical of their elders than any others and they will apply pressure for more radical solutions to social inequalities, such as inadequate health care, scarce food supplies, sub-standard housing, and particularly unemployment, especially as the concentration of this particular age group is far greater in urban than in rural areas. Expanding secondary and tertiary education has, in a sense, mobilized this feeling in student protest, a potent factor for purposeful change.

The burden of youth can be expressed as a dependency ratio, i.e. the number of dependants, conventionally considered to be those of 0-14 and the old of 65 and over, in relation to the economically productive 15-64 year olds. These ratios are higher for Asia than elsewhere and have obvious economic ramifications. However, when the unemployed dependent component of the youth group (15-24) is considered, then the burden is worsened considerably. In a sense all these considerations are, hopefully, short-term, but the long-term implications are far greater. The people have already been born who will increase Asia's population by about 50 per cent by the end of the century. No birth control programme will change that.

The emphasis on the "burden" of dependants under 15 should not obscure the existence of a burden at the other end of the age range—those over 65. Up till now the numbers and proportions have been small, but increasing life-expectancy is going to cause a great swelling of numbers in the foreseeable future. Will the traditional family units be able to cope with this increase? Will Asian governments, already poor, be able to institute and finance workers' pension schemes? Will the old become the new poor?

Urban-rural Population

In nearly every country of the region about four-fifths of the population is located in rural areas (*see* Table 3) and between two-thirds and three-quarters of the total population is engaged in agriculture (*see* Table 5). Among developing countries it is only in Peninsular Malaysia and the Philippines that the proportion of rural dwellers falls to about 70 per cent of the population. Of all the countries in the region, only in Japan, Australia and New Zealand are all the proportions completely reversed so that three-quarters to four-fifths of the population live in urban centres, the degree of urbanization in Australia (86 per cent in 1976) being one of the highest in the world.

This is not to say, however, that the characteristically rural, less-developed countries have no urban problems. The continued and alarming high rate of rural to urban migration is upsetting the delicately balanced distribution of population. Urbanization is proceeding at a faster rate than the growth of employment (certainly of manufacturing), and it is straining the economic and social facilities and infrastructures that are available. In this respect the less well-developed world is reversing the historical experiences of the developed countries where urbanization was a response to a rapid increase in industrialization which provided ample employment opportunities for the rapidly growing labour force.

The causes of migration are varied but it seems that the expected higher wage in the urban areas, rather than the actual wage earned, is what attracts the migrants, particularly the young with some education. Most migrants are prepared to move in the probability of finding new employment, and once a job is found the differential in earnings is sufficient to compensate for the unemployment (ESCAP, 1977, pp. 72–73). But this cannot be accomplished without a period of extended (and even permanent) unemployment, and hence the presence of dire poverty in housing conditions; dwellings (if they can be called such) bereft of nearly all amenities, with the barest minima of conveniences such as furniture, kitchen utensils, and bedding, rudimentary sanitation, and no tap water or electricity. While rural households are, on the whole, of inferior quality to urban households throughout Asia it is in the urban areas that the situation is reaching a critical level. It results in the growth of spontaneous slums and shanty towns on the fringes of the large cities which are squalid, congested and socially disorganized.

Estimates have been made that one-third of the population of Calcutta (total population 7 million, including suburbs, in 1971), Manila (1.4 million in 1975) and Seoul (6.9 million in 1975), and two-fifths of Colombo (0.6 million in 1974), live in squatter settlements. The situation in Bangkok (population 4.2 million in 1975), Jakarta (4.6 million in 1971) and Karachi (3.5 million in 1972) is little better, with squatter settlements accounting for one-fifth to one-quarter of the population. The need for massive urban redevelopment programmes on the scale of those completed in Singapore (total population 2.3 million in 1977) and Hong Kong and, from what can be made out, in Beijing (Peking) (7.6 million in 1970), Shanghai (10.8 million in 1970) and other large Chinese cities, is clear. Such programmes may be one of the ways of reducing unemployment by the intensive use of labour (ECAFE, 1973, pp. 67-79, and 94-95).

Although this is not the place to discuss future trends in any detail, it is appropriate to note that the urban problem will not diminish as the years progress. According to UN projections, the total Asian urban population (including the Middle East) will more than double by the end of the century from 595 million in 1975 to nearly 1,400 million, while the number of cities with a population over one million will increase from 68 to 164, up to 50 of them growing to over five million, and Bombay, Calcutta, Karachi and Jakarta reaching over 15 million each. The already serious problems of slums, traffic congestion, environmental pollution and the general accentuation of inequalities in standards of living will become worse. In the rural areas the expected addition of 590 million to the population between 1975 and 2000 is much less than the predicted rise in town-dwellers but the problem of housing will still be there, although not so starkly obvious as it will be in the concentrated masses of the cities.

THE DYNAMIC ASPECTS OF POPULATION

The sheer bulk of Asia's population tends to hide underlying dynamics of the demographic structure of the various societies that make up the region. Increase in numbers is made up from migration movements and the excess of births over deaths. The first, migration, can be discarded as of negligible significance except in the cases of Australia and New Zealand where European migration makes up a significant element of population growth. Therefore the following discussion focuses upon fertility and mortality, and the observable trends in these.

Fertility

Between 1965 and 1980 the population of Asia (including the Middle East) increased at an average annual rate of 2.1 per cent. It is the past decline in the mortality rate which has caused such a surge in population numbers, which continues despite recent reductions in the fertility rate. Taking 1970 as a datum point we can see that fertility has fallen, not only in those countries that had been experiencing substantial declines in fertility in the 1960s (e.g. Japan) but also in many other countries where fertility levels had remained virtually unchanged during the 1960s.

Examples of the decline in the 1970s include Sri Lanka, where the crude birth rate (CBR) fell from 29 per 1,000 in 1970 to 26 per 1,000 in 1979; Hong Kong, from 20.0 per 1,000 to 16.8; and Singapore, from 23.0 to 17.3. Other significant examples are Peninsular Malaysia, where the CBR declined from 33.9 per 1,000 in 1970 to 30.7 per 1,000 in 1979; India, where

Table 4

FERTILITY AND INFANT MORTALITY LEVELS IN COUNTRIES OF THE ASIAN-PACIFIC REGION CLASSIFIED BY ACHIEVEMENTS IN FERTILITY REGULATION

	Birth Rate (per 1,000)	Infant Mortality Rate (per 1,000 live births)	Mid-1980 Population	
			Millions	Percentage of Region's Total
I *Low level of fertility achieved* Australia, Hong Kong, Japan, Macau, New Zealand, Singapore .	15–19	8–15	142.1	5.76
II *Noticeable lowering of fertility being experienced* China, Fiji, Repub. of Korea, Malaysia, Sri Lanka . . .	21–33	14–60	1,062.9	43.12
III *Programmes established but effect on fertility not clearly measurable* India, Pakistan	35–43	121–125	771.4	31.29
IV *Programme in early stages* Bangladesh, Indonesia, Nepal, Philippines, Thailand . . .	32–47	25–185	346.8	14.07
V *No announced policy and programme, or no information* All other countries . . .	30–50	40–184	141.9	5.76
Total	—	—	2,465.0	100.00

Source: Based on ECAFE, 1972, p. 93; UN, *Demographic Yearbook 1979* and *World Population Prospects as Assessed in 1980*; and Berelson, 1970.

the estimated CBR fell from 36.6 per 1,000 in 1972 to 34.4 per 1,000 in 1979; and, most significant of all because of its immense population base, China, where (according to UN estimates) the average annual CBR was 29.5 per 1,000 in 1970–75, yet claims for 1979 put the rate as low as a startling 20 per 1,000. These declines are confirmed by other statistics. According to a survey carried out in 1973, the average number of children per woman in Indonesia declined from 6.4 in 1969/70 to 5.2 in 1971/72, while in Thailand another survey showed that completed family size for women aged 14 to 44 had fallen from 9.6 children in 1969/70 to 8.6 children in 1972/73. The extent of the change indicated by these claims may be exaggerated but there is little doubt that fertility has fallen significantly. Again, in the Philippines the decline in marital fertility has been in the order of 11.2 to 10.0 children in urban areas, and 11.6 to 9.0 in rural areas, which is reflected marginally in a decline in the overall growth rate from 3.0 per cent to 2.9 per cent (ESCAP, 1977, pp. 5–6).

The aim in the majority of countries is to reduce the number of births, either by actually conducting a family planning programme or at least by permitting one to operate. Between 1970 and 1979 approximately U.S. $2,500 million was budgeted for national family planning programmes, or roughly 70 cents per caput over the ten-year period. These programmes will cover about 90 per cent of Asia's population. For example, India wishes to halve its CBR by the year 2000, Pakistan to reduce its CBR to 25 per 1,000 in 1985, the Philippines from 43.8 per 1,000 in 1970 to 35.9 in 1977, and Singapore from 17.8 per 1,000 in 1975 to bare replacement level in 1980.

The contents of parts of Table 2 can now be regrouped as in Table 4 above, according to the achievements in lowering fertility and the scope of the programme put forward so far. The "Group I" countries contain less than 6 per cent of the region's population and they have managed to achieve and sustain a low level of fertility. Undoubtedly the success of regulating fertility has been the result of almost total literacy in the adult population and the availability of a wide range of contraceptive techniques, strategies and inducements. For example, cheap, efficient and safe abortion in Japan since 1948 and in Singapore since 1969 have been very effective. In addition, in Singapore a wide range of sophisticated monetary disincentives apply to people having large families. Income tax relief is limited to the first three children, maternity leave is restricted to the first two pregnancies, childbirth costs are increased after the first two deliveries, and priority is given to small families for public housing—in fact a reversal of all the normally accepted democratic welfare principles (ESCAP, 1977, pp. 6–7).

Health services in "Group I" countries are good, and infant mortality rates (IMR) amongst some of the lowest in the world, varying from 8 to 15 infant deaths per 1,000 live births. Parents know that the probability is high that a calculated number of pregnancies will achieve a calculated desirable family size, therefore people are not reproducing to beat infant mortality. Per caput incomes in these countries are the highest in the Asian and Pacific region and there are moderate to good social services for the aged, which again takes away one of the incentives for having large families. These are the most urbanized and most industrialized countries of the region.

"Group II" countries have all experienced a noticeable lowering of fertility and have CBRs ranging from 21 to 33, and IMRs ranging from 14 to 60. Again, a wide range of contraceptive techniques have become available. For example, both South Korea and the People's Republic of China have legalized abortion. The greatest achievement in this group has undoubtedly been that of China, where, according to official sources, the CBR has fallen to about 20 per 1,000. After an initial period of regarding population control as anathema under conventional Marxist doctrine, the country began a birth control programme during the early 1960s which moved forward with great impact following the period of political instability and unrest which resulted from the Cultural Revolution and the death of Chairman Mao Zedong (Mao Tse-tung). Through a rigorous control of marriage age at 22 for men and 20 for women, families are being limited. Only one child is normally permitted, and a second only in special circumstances. Some local authorities provide special treatment for families with one child, including priority in entry to kindergarten and schools, health care, jobs, housing and rations. In some places, fines are levied against three-child families. China is now accepting funds and technical assistance from the UN Fund for Population Activities, and a Population Research Institute has been established at Beijing University. A major census was to be undertaken in July 1982 that will at last, it is hoped, settle the question of the exact magnitude of China's massive population. South Korea has similarly experienced a major drop in fertility, with the average annual CBR falling from 45.9 per 1,000 in 1955–60 to 25.3 per 1,000 in 1975–80. This decline reflects spectacular rises in the standard of living, the availability of legalized abortion and the introduction of anti-natal fiscal measures, such as the granting of income tax deductions up to the third child only.

The "Group III" countries constitute 31 per cent of the region's population and include India and Pakistan. CBRs are believed to have fallen in both countries since 1970, from 38 per 1,000 to 34.4 per 1,000 (1979) in India and from 43 to a claimed 34.4 per 1,000 (1979) in Pakistan. In India the government's emphasis on birth control programmes, particularly on the socially sensitive method of sterilization by vasectomy, was heavy-handed and inept. The mismanagement of the programme is thought by many observers to have been partly responsible for the defeat of Mrs. Gandhi's Congress Party in the general elections of March 1977. A backlash developed to the dictatorial and over-zealous attitudes of local officials in the contraception programme and this has many lessons for those countries wishing to speed up their birth control programmes (Bird, 1976). Experience suggests that at least five years are needed merely to arrange and organize any programme, to recruit and train staff, and to obtain funds and facilities, and an even longer period is needed for a programme to get under way and disseminate through the population; a total of anything from 5 to 12 years. Another mistake is to place too much emphasis on the use of one contraceptive technique; a multi-faceted approach, through fiscal as well as medical methods and economic motivation, is the most successful. To that end both India and Pakistan introduced oral contraceptives into their national family planning programmes. All monetary incentives and duress have been scrapped in favour of purely voluntary schemes, an approach continued by Mrs. Gandhi after her re-election. The policy has been changed, however, at the cost of a reduced acceptance rate, particularly in the rural areas. Consequently the CBR was reduced from 39 per 1,000 in 1968 to 34.4 per 1,000 in 1979, rather than the 33 per 1,000 that was anticipated. Pakistan's population programme has been obscured by political events during the last few years. The declared aim of reducing the CBR from 43 per 1,000 in 1970 to 33.2 per 1,000 in 1975 was not achieved; the rate was 36 per 1,000 in 1979 and some estimates put it even higher, so that the hope of reducing it to 25 per 1,000 by 1985 seems remote under present conditions.

"Group IV" countries include Bangladesh, Indonesia, Nepal, the Philippines and Thailand, all of which have high CBRs in the 32 to 42 per 1,000 range and even higher IMRs of 25 to 185 per 1,000 live births. Their planning programmes are still in their infancy and we have no way of estimating overall success because of the lack of accurate and complete information. Bangladesh now considers population control to be an integral part of economic planning and up to 20,000 trained family planning personnel have been sent into rural areas to advise and to motivate people to accept and act upon the ideal of smaller families, but there is little money available to tackle the problem. Indonesian progress seems varied, with marked successes in Bali, where the average number of children per family fell from 5.8 in 1971 to 3.8 in 1980, and similar falls in parts of Java.

The fifth Group consists of those countries for which there is either no precise information or no announced policy. They constitute only 5.8 per cent of the population of the region but, because of their high-level CBRs and IMRs, they are in dire need of some regulation.

Mortality and Life Expectancy

Mortality is the other part of population increase. Crude death rates (CDRs) have fallen steadily since 1945, but are unlikely to fall much lower for some time (*see* Table 2). Indeed, in a few countries, CDRs have risen slightly as the age structure has changed and as health and nutritional standards have deteriorated. Rates of less than 12 per 1,000 are experienced by 15 of the independent countries of the region, and are usually associated with a high life expectancy of more than 60 years for both sexes, often being well into the 70s. Countries such as Thailand, with an average annual CDR of 8.9 per 1,000 in 1975–80 (UN estimate), or the Philippines with one of 8.6 per 1,000 (but with average CBRs of 32.3 and 36.2 per 1,000, respectively, in the same period) have achieved death control long before they have achieved birth control, and their average annual growth rates in 1975–80 were between 2.3 and 2.7 per cent, some of the highest in the region, leading to a doubling of their population in 25 to 30 years if maintained.

Birth Control, Ideology and Social Well-being

The previous discussion of fertility and mortality has made only passing reference to the controversy concerning the relationship between birth control programmes and the efforts made to eliminate inequalities and to raise the standard of social well-being for the bulk of the population. Most observers would agree that many of the economic and social problems of the Asian and Pacific region stem from, or at least are linked to, the demographic situation, but what causes that situation and what can be done to lessen its impact are open to different interpretations. The arguments in this dispute on approaches to the socio-economic and population problems of the region are important because upon them hinges the social and economic welfare of a large portion of mankind, and in them are hints of the possible causal mechanisms of population regulation.

The undoubted growth of population in absolute numbers and the undoubted lag in economic production have led to a restatement of the Malthusian hypothesis that population numbers are outstripping the resources of the region, and that a balance between the two might be resolved in the future only through the occurrence of great hardship, poverty and outright death. The growth rates in Asia are high not only because people are having a great number of children, but also because fewer people are dying; death control has been easier to achieve than birth control largely because it is not fraught with the moral, sociological and cultural implications of birth control. In short, stopping people from dying is unquestionably "good" but stopping people from being born is not so clearly desirable. Dramatic changes in the CDR have been achieved through the widespread use of antibiotics, improved public health facilities, better drinking water and the elimination of endemic and epidemic diseases. The task now, many would argue, is to encourage Asians to reduce their number of births and to bring their CBRs into a new equilibrium with the new CDRs. In this way a "breathing space" will be achieved and the production of resources will catch up with the increase in population. The result will be a greater material well-being and hence a voluntary lowering of births as couples perceive the financial benefits to be gained from having fewer children.

A somewhat different point of view is put forward by others and may be summarized thus. Social and economic progress are a prerequisite for improving the standard of living and reducing the birth rate, not a consequence of the reduction. Others would take the argument further and say that birth control is a move on the part of the more affluent countries of the world to attempt to solve the problem of over-population without upsetting the established social and political order of the countries involved, thereby ensuring the continued reservation of the world's resources for their own profit and profligate use. There is no population problem in Asia, such people would argue, only an unequal distribution of the means of dominating and using the world's resources by the "White Centre" at the expense of the "coloured periphery", thus leading, incidentally, to global pollution (Buchanan, 1977; Jalée, 1964).

The examples of the two most populous countries of the world are used to typify these arguments. On the one hand there is India, largely democratic with a mixed laissez-faire/socialist economy, a very traditional society and a poor record of increasing production and limiting population growth. On the other hand there is the People's Republic of China with its rigid centralized control of society and economy, an elimination of traditional society, and a clear record of success in raising average economic standards and in reducing population growth. A perusal of the 1970s issues of *Ceres*, a magazine produced by the Food and Agriculture Organization (FAO), would soon reveal the extremes and variations of these points of view which often have strong ideological overtones. The argument is a healthy one, however, because it does question past assumptions and it does draw attention to some of the important causal mechanisms in reducing births and increasing the provision of resources and standards, which both sides, at least, would agree was a desirable and common aim.

One example of the questioning of past assumptions is that of the priority of funding to reduce deaths or to reduce births. If greater resources were invested in death control rather than in birth control, couples would respond by having less children because they would perceive that those who have been born will survive into adulthood. In support of this it is known that the reverse is true, and those couples who lose children at a young age quickly have more children (Brown and Way, 1974).

Another example of questioning past assumptions is that of the desirability of small families. In Asia this fails if patterned on the western developed countries' ideal of two or three children. Such small families are not related to the cultural and economic milieux of many of the developing countries of Asia, where male children are the only security and insurance for old age, and are a source of wealth because they provide labour in the fields at critical times, producing a wealth that far exceeds the cost of rearing children, and also eliminating the cost of wages that would be payable if such labour was provided by an outsider. In short, there is no motivation for a rural working family to accept the proposal to limit births as large families are an economic and social security if they use manpower intensively (Mamdani, 1974). Thus the concept of the "desirable" family size is determined by the balance between human labour and the means of production open to the family, and this has not been understood readily by many western "advisers".

Birth control by itself is unlikely to achieve any solution to economic problems unless it is accompanied by other measures to stimulate the economy, including aid, land reform, social reform, women's education and emancipation, and in general the ironing out of the extremes of gross inequalities. In other words, couples are unlikely to plan their families unless they can plan their whole lives in terms of income, employment, security, adequate health, shelter and education. Family planning is the desired aim, however achieved, while birth control is merely the technological means of achieving it. Finally, birth control can have little effect on the problems of immediate starvation, malnutrition, unemployment and poor housing; it is essentially a long-term process taking from one or two decades to produce a result.

Certainly the heavy-handedness and ineptness of India's birth control programme and the reaction against it in the 1977 elections was a manifestation of the failure of experts and officials to perceive the cultural psychology of the population which they were administering. However, in pointing out the lack of sensitivity in applying birth control measures in India and the success of such measures in China it is often conveniently forgotten that the result in China was, and is being, achieved only through a great deal of coercion and deliberate lack of sensitivity to the country's cultural traditions in the first instance. So in the end the argument resolves itself very much into the degree of revolutionary restructuring of society necessary to achieve the desired result, which basically depends upon one's ideological stance.

The task of finding the right approach to achieving the threshold of self-motivation in family limitation can be achieved by other means. To assert that there is no relationship between low rates of population growth and high rates of economic growth is to shut one's eyes to the facts of the situation. Japan, South Korea and Taiwan have achieved these successfully, albeit with massive American aid, just as North Korea has achieved it with aid from the U.S.S.R. Aid, after all, is what the critics of the existing order would like to see applied in even greater amounts than now in order to achieve a more equitable distribution of resources and development. This is not to say that there are not different paths to the goals of lowering birth rates and raising standards of well-being.

The major positive argument that the pro-Chinese (or "restructuring of society prior to reducing the birth rate") lobby can point to is that, given the level of technology, the mobilization of the massive unemployed and under-employed labour of that country for general public works programme has been beneficial. In this sense Marxists and Catholics have much in common in the belief that every new mouth has a pair of hands, and it is remarkable that this has not been a stronger point in the approach of western nations, for their development in the past has been dependent on the adequate and full utilization of all labour resources. Unfortunately, technological advances have blinded some to the virtues and efficiency of hard physical work. However, coercion in forcing people to work, either for profit or for the public good, is difficult to condone anywhere.

In the final analysis, all the evidence points to the fact that family planning is essential for Asia's future, but that the incubus of massive population numbers cannot be solved by tacking a programme of birth control on to an unchanged rural society. Much aid gets dissipated and diverted away from those very people whom it is intended to help, and there is much evidence to suggest that the poor are getting poorer in some societies. In other words, internal inequalities widen and, as long as this occurs, there can be little true hope of reducing the number of births.

POPULATION, FOOD AND NUTRITION

At the core of the discussion on population has been the question of the availability of food and nourishment for the 2,600 million people living in the whole of Asia (excluding the U.S.S.R.) and Oceania. Levels of nutrition are still appallingly low in some countries, people are still dying from the sheer lack of food, while millions of children are growing up seriously debilitated physically and mentally by malnutrition. The limitation of births, to allow food production to catch up with or to overtake population growth, is a long-term solution; more important in the short-term and during the coming years is the ability of the nations of the region to produce the food they need, or at least to be able to purchase it from elsewhere. Since 1970 the record has been bad, especially after the widespread publicity given to the "green revolution" as a means of meeting the food needs of the growing population. Again, Asia has been beset by a number of natural disasters, such as floods and drought, all of which have reduced crop yields, while at the same time the cost of imports has risen sharply in the wake of the enormous increases in the price of petroleum. A particular casualty in this rise in costs has been the reluctance or inability of countries to import artificial fertilizer which is the means of raising productivity in so many cases.

Food Production

Asian food production cannot be viewed except in a global context because food surpluses elsewhere (the U.S.A., Canada, Australia, Argentina and the EEC) are the source of the imports, so that poor harvests in

Table 5

ASPECTS OF AGRICULTURE AND FOOD PRODUCTION AND NUTRITION FOR SELECTED COUNTRIES IN THE ASIAN-PACIFIC REGION

	Index of Production per Person, 1980 (1969–71 = 100)		Daily Calorific Intake per Person, 1977–79	Percentage of Labour Force Employed in Agriculture, etc., 1980
	Agriculture	Food (net)		
Asia:				
Afghanistan	91	92	1,974*	77·8
Bangladesh	94	97	1,787*	83·8
Bhutan	100	99	2,058*	93·4
Burma	106	106	2,223*	51·8
China (incl. Taiwan)	119	119	2,439	59·8
Hong Kong	76	76	2,745	2·5
India	101	101	1,996*	63·2
Indonesia (excl. East Timor)	109	112	2,203*	58·9
Japan	88	88	2,847	11·0
Kampuchea	39	39	1,767*	74·9
Korea, Democratic People's Republic	133	135	2,833	45·9
Korea, Republic	120	121	2,837	38·6
Laos	105	103	1,842*	73·8
Malaysia	114	124	2,562	47·8
Mongolia	93	95	2,764	48·9
Nepal	89	90	1,941*	92·6
Pakistan	99	101	2,270	53·5
Philippines	115	114	2,211*	46·0
Singapore	163	166	3,003	2·2
Sri Lanka	107	128	2,200*	53·2
Thailand	121	125	2,175*	75·4
Viet-Nam	108	107	2,033*	70·6
Oceania:				
Australia	100	108	3,413	5·8
Fiji	110	109	2,577	40·1
New Zealand	103	104	3,443	9·3
Papua New Guinea	105	102	2,250	82·3

* Below minimum nutritional levels.

Source: FAO, *Production Yearbook 1980*, Tables 7, 6, 97 and 3 respectively.

these producing countries in 1972–73 caused more hardship in Asia than elsewhere in the world. Output trends, carry-over stocks and hence prices are vitally important to Asia and are quickly reflected in nutritional levels.

A summary of the performance of some of the countries in the region with regard to food production and nutrition is given in Table 5. Two-thirds of the countries show an increase in production, the cases of Burma, the People's Republic of China, Indonesia, Laos, Malaysia, Singapore, Viet-Nam and Fiji being of great significance. While the indices went up for many countries in total output terms, they experienced an actual decline in rice and wheat output, compared with several years before, or at least a rise so slight as to constitute a decline in real terms, considering the population increase during the interval. The indices for Afghanistan, Hong Kong, India, Japan, Kampuchea, Nepal, Australia and Papua New Guinea actually fell. Deficiencies in Hong Kong and Japan were more than made up for from outside sources; Australian export surpluses were reduced. In war-torn South-East Asia, Viet-Nam and Laos reversed previous trends and showed increases, but Kampuchea showed a drastic decline yet again.

Food grain production during 1981 appears to have reached record levels, both in Asia and in the world as a whole. For example, world output of paddy rice (almost all grown in Asia) passed 400 million metric tons for the first time. However, if FAO forecasts are correct, by 1985 domestic grain production will fall short of needs in Bangladesh, India, Pakistan, Sri Lanka, Peninsular Malaysia, the Philippines and South Korea. Only Burma and Thailand will achieve surpluses.

Asian agriculture still needs massive and radical reorganization. There is a crying need for land reform and the elimination of landlords and middlemen who hamper production; there is need of water regulation and availability, and for the introduction of higher-yielding varieties (HYV) and multiple cropping, all of which need to be attempted singly or together by small farmers. India seems suddenly to have become successful by pursuing a variety of small-scale improvements and by intensively using existing labour rather than by importing tractors and machinery. With good reason, past deficits have been transformed into surpluses and the country is now a modest exporter of grain. China, on the other hand, has suffered from climatic extremes and violent political reorganization, and the recent tough controls on family size are a recognition and response to food deficiencies.

The much vaunted success of the HYV has given a breathing space in the fight to match food increase to population increase. The penetration of the new varieties into the traditional crop programme has been very uneven. With wheat it has been as much as 62 per cent of plantings in Pakistan in 1974/75, compared with 23.4 per cent in Bangladesh at the same time. With rice it has been as high as 64 per cent in the Philippines, but as low as 6.4 per cent in Burma. Clearly much more can be done to increase yields by adopting new varieties, and it is possible that even better varieties will come onto the market in due course. For example, it was recently reported that a new strain of rice had been developed in the Philippines that will mature in 65 days, compared with the present 100 days or more. The new rice can therefore be harvested four times each year on irrigated fields, or twice a year on unirrigated fields, but the amount of fertilizer needed to sustain these continuous periods of growth is enormous (ESCAP, 1977, pp. 11–12).

One major innovation in the region during 1981 was the introduction of private plots and profit motives in the communist nations of Asia in an effort to boost production. In the People's Republic of China, communes are to be reorganized, with the family as the basic production unit. Each family will be assigned quotas by the commune, but private plots will be enlarged. Viet-Nam has similarly allowed peasants to keep or sell food over and above targets, and output has increased significantly in both countries. In Mongolia, privately raised livestock is to be allowed in order to stop imports from the U.S.S.R.

Local shortfalls in production can be made up for by imports and the implications of this on the world grain market need to be looked at more closely. Estimated carry-over stocks of cereals throughout the world reached a record 273.7 million metric tons in 1979, compared with 179.7 million tons in 1975. Stocks fell to 253 million tons in 1980 and to 228 million tons in 1981. World production of cereals in 1981 rose to 1,664 million tons (provisional estimate), an increase of more than 100 million tons over the 1980 harvest. However, rising production is often accompanied by falling prices which, while excellent for the food importing countries of Asia, does affect those few countries which are net exporters of grains or other primary produce. The ramifications of falling prices are more far-reaching because North American farmers are reducing their wheat acreages as a consequence of the low returns. If the reduction in planting coincides with another set of harvest failures elsewhere in the world, then a new food shortage will appear. Continuing poor harvests in the U.S.S.R. and China have meant massive food imports; grain imports by the U.S.S.R. roughly tripled between 1977 and 1981 from 11.8 million tons to 33 million tons. However, it seems clear that, unless indigenous food production can be raised significantly and enormous food stocks built up, the spectre of another famine, recalling that of 1973, looms large. The achievement of large carry-over stocks and their storage costs money which the developing countries do not have, and which the developed countries may not be willing to part with at this stage, with their own domestic problems of inflation in the wake of the rise in energy costs since 1973/74 and the world recession. In fact, there has been a definite downturn in food aid. With food grain imports throughout Asia totalling 94 million tons in 1981, even slight fluctuations of production and price anywhere in the world can have dire effects on Asia's population.

Nutritional Levels

The delicate balance between domestic production, imports and population growth is hinted at in Table 5, showing the daily calorific intake per person. Only a few of the developing countries have an average nutritional level that comfortably exceeds the minimum health requirements of around 2,250 calories per day. Affluent countries such as Japan, North Korea, South Korea, Singapore, Australia and New Zealand have an intake either just above or comfortably well above the minimum intake required to maintain good health. Notable newcomers in this category are China and Pakistan. In many countries (such as Afghanistan, Bangladesh and India) the figures shown in Table 5 are actually lower than they were during the early 1960s.

The other point to note is that the average intake is spread across the whole of the population, but we know that food supplies are not distributed equally, and that probably about half (some would say more than half) of the population receives amounts considerably less than the national average. There are many examples of this, but one for Indonesia (*see* Table 6) must suffice. The various levels of income for 1969/70 are broken down into urban and rural in order to pinpoint the regional inequalities as well as the inequalities of nutrition that accompany affluence. The situation is, in fact, worse than it looks because the poorest income classes are involved in more continuous labour than others, and usually need a greater nutritional intake in order to maintain their effort. How many people fall below absolutely critical intake levels in the poorer income groups is unknown (ESCAP, 1977, pp. 63–65).

What we do know is that, if food prices continue to rise, more poor peasants and urban slum dwellers will not be able to afford the food, either home-produced or imported.

Active Engagement in Agriculture

Finally, one other aspect of agriculture and food production is worth looking at. A clear hallmark of an economically advanced economy is the low proportion of the working population engaged in agriculture, forestry and fishing. In Asia and Oceania there are the examples of Australia (5.8 per cent in 1980), Hong Kong (2.5 per cent), Japan (11.0 per cent), New Zealand (9.3 per cent) and Singapore (2.2 per cent), or even, at a somewhat higher level but still low by the standards of the region, Fiji (40.1 per cent), North Korea (45.9 per cent), South Korea (38.6 per cent) and the Philippines (46.0 per cent). All other countries have well over half of their labour force engaged in agriculture, the proportion reaching as high as 93.4 per cent in Bhutan, 92.6 per cent in Nepal and 83.8 per cent in Bangladesh.

The percentage figures for all countries have dropped markedly during the last decade as more and more of the population increase has been syphoned off into secondary and tertiary activities, but the percentage decline hides the fact that the absolute numbers on the land are increasing rapidly. For example, although 86.4 per cent of the population in Bangladesh was engaged in agriculture in 1965, decreasing to 83.8 per cent in 1980, the actual number of people in agriculture increased by 7.5 million from 17.8 to 25.3 million. Similarly, in India the proportion fell from 71.7 per cent in 1965 to 63.2 per cent in 1980 but the actual number rose from 142.9 million to 168.1 million; in Pakistan the percentage drop was from 59.8 per cent to 53.5 per cent but the absolute number rose from 9.4 to 11.9 million. Even China's massive drop from 72.3 per cent to 59.8 per cent was in fact an increase in absolute numbers from 240.7 to 265.9 million. The pressure on the productive land is not diminishing but increasing, and more is needed out of the land to feed the growing urban populations as well.

Table 6

AVERAGE DAILY INTAKE OF CALORIES PER PERSON BY HOUSEHOLD INCOME GROUP, INDONESIA, 1969/70

Average Monthly Income (Rupiahs)	Urban Areas		Rural Areas	
	% of Total Population	Average Calorie Intake	% of Total Population	Average Calorie Intake
Under 500	3	790	10	1,117
501–750	9	1,060	18	1,420
751–1,000	12	1,232	19	1,629
1,001–1,250	14	1,417	14	1,812
1,251–1,500	12	1,449	11	2,027
1,501–2,000	19	1,728	13	2,267
2,001–2,500	12	1,874	7	2,519
2,501–3,000	8	1,951	3	2,804
Over 3,000	13	2,408	5	3,344
All Groups	100	1,633	100	1,855

Source: Republic of Indonesia, *Survey social ekonomi nasional* (Biro Pusat, Statistik, Jakarta, 1973) (Mimeo).

The implication of this discussion on food and nutrition is that the countries of the region need to grow more food and/or pay for more food. There is a need to diversify crops, and to grow, for example, tubers and "green leaf" vegetables such as those found in Papua New Guinea, as well as to adopt HYV, and to undertake all the other reforms and re-organizations noted before. The question is not merely one of food but one of job expansion throughout the economy. There is clearly scope for improvement, and it should be possible for the region to feed its increasing population during the next few decades if all solutions and remedies are applied, but the outlook is not one which promotes a great deal of enthusiasm beyond the year 2000, on the present state of knowledge. W. H. Pawley predicts that Asia could support 50 times its present population provided enough water can be desalinated for irrigation and the problem of cultivating tropical soils can be solved (Pawley, 1974), but, as these two provisos seem a long way off (particularly when the energy costs of desalinization are really calculated), this and similar predictions are so over-optimistic as to enter the realms of science fiction. Hopefully Asia's population growth will have tapered off significantly in another two decades.

POPULATION, DEVELOPMENT AND INTERNAL INEQUALITIES

The preoccupation with the narrowing gap postulated by Malthus between the means of production (particularly food) and population numbers has led to an obvious emphasis on the need for rapid economic growth or "development", and the deceleration of population growth. Unfortunately the analysis has usually been carried out at the national, gross level, and usually purely in monetary (per caput income) terms. Only recently have attempts been made to extend the concept of development beyond that of economic performance and to see social needs and aspirations as being intimately intertwined in the process of development. Similarly, only recently have attempts been made to analyse the scope and nature of the internal inequalities within nations (Drewnowski, 1974).

The problem arises because the chances are that the growth that has been achieved in the mixed economies of the region has accentuated internal patterns of inequality; a process which, if continued, must ultimately work against further advances. If this occurs fewer people will identify the benefits of economic growth with their own personal lives, and the obvious result will be their failure to respond to family planning. As pointed out before, couples are unlikely to plan their families unless they can plan their whole lives (in terms of income, employment, shelter and security) with some degree of assurance.

There are many examples of inequalities, that of food supply being perhaps the most obvious and basic, and which has already been singled out for special consideration. But there are others. For example, the per caput income figures in Table 2 do give a reasonably correct view of the relative levels of affluence between countries, but they do not identify the enormous inequalities of income that occur in the least developed of the countries of the region. Estimates of the amount of the population living at poverty level vary enormously but, whichever measure is taken, the result is disturbing. Shail Jain suggests that in 1969 32.5 per cent of India's population had an income below U.S. $50, while one-twentieth of households had 25 per cent of the income. In Sri Lanka in 1973, 35 per cent were below the same poverty level and 19 per cent of the country's wealth was in the hands of one-twentieth of the households. On the whole, the tendency is for urban areas to have slightly less inequality than rural areas. Nevertheless, even in the urban areas inequality is increasing rapidly. If poverty is measured not in income but in terms of access to facilities, then urban areas have a clear advantage. For example, there were approximately 24,200 persons per doctor in rural Pakistan in 1970, compared with 3,700 in urban areas. Reasonable access to supplies of drinking water also vary regionally between town and country, with anything from 50 to 90 per cent of the urban populations of the region having adequate supplies, with the reverse proportions (but usually in the 10–15 per cent range) having adequate supplies in the rural areas (ESCAP, 1977, p. 61). Urban/rural inequalities are typified by literacy rates and infant mortality rates in a variety of locations in India (*see* Table 7).

Table 7

REGIONAL INEQUALITIES IN INDIA

PERCENTAGE LITERATE IN TOTAL POPULATION

	Rural Areas		Urban Areas	
	Male	Female	Male	Female
1961 . .	29.1	8.5	57.5	34.5
1971 . .	33.1	12.9	61.0	41.5

INFANT MORTALITY RATE, 1969

(per 1,000 live births)

State	Rural Areas	Urban Areas
Assam . .	130	101
Mysore (now Karnataka) .	110	57
Punjab . .	98	78
Rajasthan . .	169	92
Uttar Pradesh . .	179	110

Source: Indian Censuses, 1961 and 1971, reproduced from ESCAP, 1976, p. 61.

Within rural areas, land ownership is a crucial measure and criterion of poverty and social well-being, for from it stem status, employment and leisure (Myrdal, 1968, vol. 1, p. 569). The statistics on the distribution of holdings by size groups are endless, but typically, the poorest 25 per cent of the rural households hold hardly any land, while the bulk of the land is held by the top 25 per cent of the households. The landless labourers who are products of this inequality of ownership create problems of precisely unknown but undoubtedly great magnitude, and their ranks are swelled continuously by the small owner-occupiers, tenants, share-croppers and artisans displaced by population growth, and also by the centralization of the means of production. They may constitute up to 50 per cent of all households, as was the estimate for Java in 1973, a proportion in that island which had grown from about 20 per cent of households in 1963.

Next to starvation, unemployment is the ultimate measure of poverty in societies without the welfare and social support mechanisms of developed countries. Traditional concepts of what is employed and unemployed have rarely had much meaning in rural or urban Asia, where kinship bonds, much under-employment and the seasonal nature of agriculture are common in rural areas, and concepts of the duration of the working day or week are poorly defined in urban areas. Official surveys totally underplay the extent of unemployment. For example, in India the 1971 census revealed an unemployment rate of 1.8 per cent of the workforce, a figure that any country of the developed world would be delighted to record. However, small-scale surveys show that unemployment could be as high as 20 per cent of the workforce and in the Philippines it could be even 25 per cent (ECAFE, 1973; ESCAP, 1977, pp. 46–51).

Whatever the correct percentage, the fact is clear that a large proportion of the population is not able to contribute to national growth. Their numbers are probably higher in the urban areas than in rural areas, higher for the young than for the old, and they tend to increase with educational level, and for men as compared with women. Only South Korea, Singapore, Japan, Hong Kong, Australia and New Zealand have experienced labour shortages, but everywhere else there are high labour surpluses. These high rates of unemployment are a result of rapid population growth, an increase in the number of women in the labour force, and a high rate of migration to urban areas where it is difficult to provide new jobs (e.g. 15 per cent of Greater Calcutta's 8-9 million people are unemployed).

The numbers of unemployed are also being swelled by technological change. The rate of industrial growth is too slow to absorb the population, the excessive introduction of capital-intensive labour-saving techniques in factory and farm do not absorb but actually replace people, and there is difficulty in finding markets in the developed world for the labour-intensive exports of developing countries. To all this must be added the ever-rising aspirations brought about by the expansion of the educational system, and of the type of education given. Young people feel unfitted for the jobs that are available. The number of unemployed is increasing rapidly and will reach a crisis point by the 1990s when well over another 100 million will be looking for jobs.

The inter-relationship between economic inequality and social inequality with family size is important. There is an observable inverse relationship between per caput income (and consumption) and family size. Thus, in India, Dandekar and Rath (1971) have shown that the average number of children per family in the poorest 10 per cent of the rural population was 5.87. As one moved through each successive 10 per cent band of the population with more income, so family size fell, until in the richest 5 per cent of households it was 3.78 children. Similar results have been recorded for Thailand and elsewhere, and this relationship is a well attested fact in the developed countries of the world. One point about this sort of analysis, however, is that it is worth considering whether smaller family sizes produce higher incomes or higher incomes produce smaller families—an argument of cause and effect that has far-reaching ramifications. There is also a clear association between the level of education received and the level of personal earnings, and hence family size.

THE ROLE OF AID

One way of redressing the imbalance between the affluence of the countries of the developed world and the poverty of the developing world is by the donation of aid. A target of 1 per cent of the Gross National Product (G.N.P.) to be set aside for aid is the objective of the countries of the OECD, but on 1974 returns this was attained by only a few member countries—Belgium, Canada, France, the Netherlands and the United Kingdom. However, the average for all the OECD countries in 1974 was 0.75 per cent of the G.N.P., which compared favourably with the effort of the centrally planned economies (0.16 per cent), but was below that of the OPEC countries (1.4 per cent). The total of all recorded non-military transfers in 1974 was U.S. $40,000 million, or one-fifth of the resources of all the developing countries, the other four-fifths being made up of export earnings (FAO *Ceres*, 52; ESCAP 1977, pp. 28–41).

The flow of the transfers is shown in diagrammatic form in Figure 1 (*see* below) and needs little elaboration, except in one regard. The bulk of the aid is given on a bilateral basis, often through technical assistance and credits in order to promote goodwill and trade between the donor nation and the recipient nation. However, the feeling is growing that aid should not be narrowly focused on purely economic goals, and that the main aim of the aid should be the eradication of the complex nexus of socio-economic poverty. The perfect way to do this is by giving money, which can be used on the projects the recipient country needs most. Increasingly more money is being channelled into multilateral organizations (such as the World Bank, the regional development banks and UN agencies) and the untied money in loans of a liberal nature and outright gifts is now the main concern. The United Nations would like 70 per cent of all aid donated to be in this form, called Official Development Assistance (ODA), which only Sweden and about half of the OPEC countries achieve. The swing away from package loans to the exploration of the normal commercial credit facilities in order to raise cash explains the very great increase of Eurocurrency loans, but the servicing of debts is now assuming massive proportions.

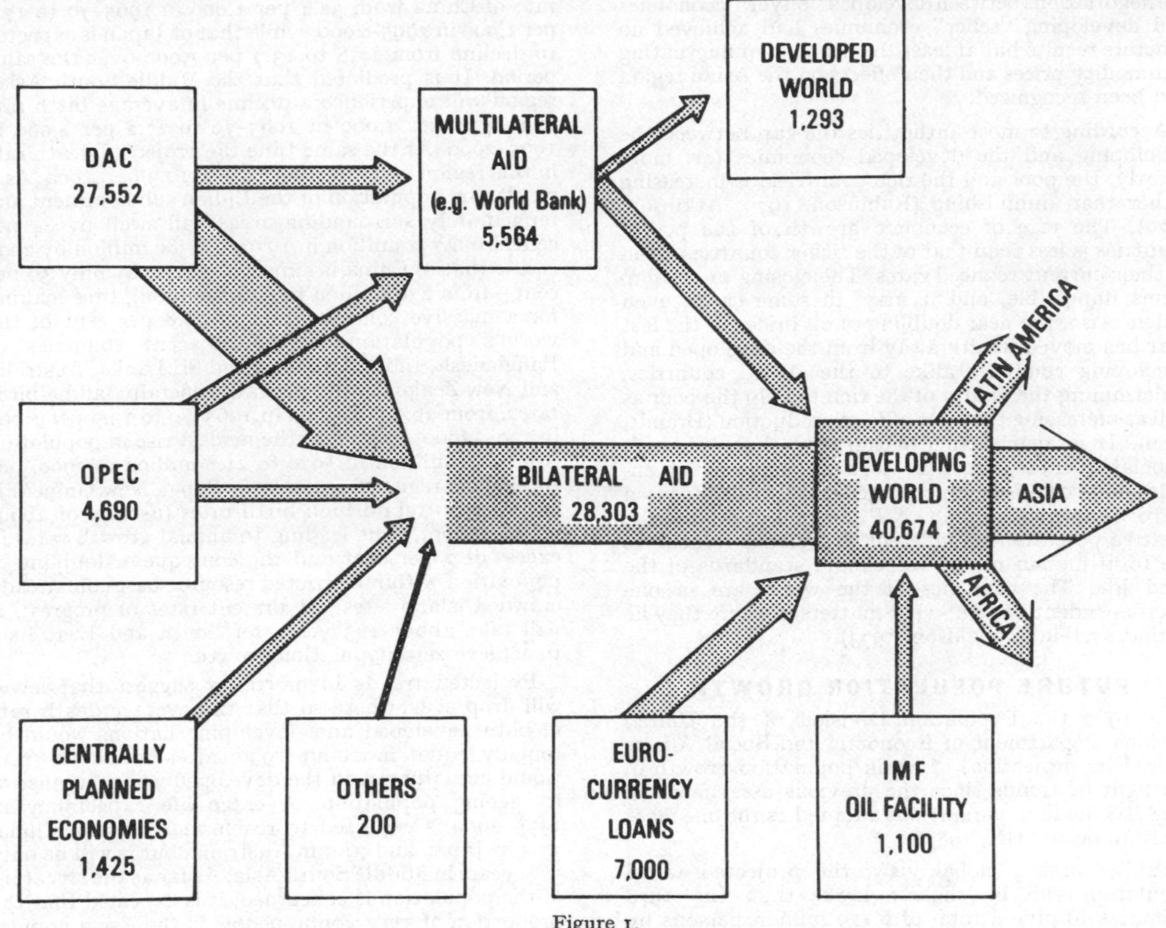

Figure 1.
AID FLOWS (U.S. $ million).
Based on FAO, *Ceres* 52 (1976), pp. 20–21.
(*Note:* DAC = members of the Development Assistance Committee of the OECD.)

Aid is by no means the universal panacea that some would think. A central problem of all aid is the prevention of the "leakage" of benefits from the poverty-ridden section of the population, at which the aid is aimed, to the more affluent section which is often far more capable of taking advantage of it. A second and important problem is that aid does not necessarily promote productive employment. Indeed, it may have the opposite effect because capital-intensive and labour-saving projects may be given priority. What is needed is the creation of efficient labour-intensive technology to absorb the under-employed and unemployed (Stewart, 1972). Thus, the expansion of small family farms (given that all back-up facilities are provided), the most efficient sector of the economy and the most deserving of aid, may be the way of striking in one blow at the problems of food supply, social well-being, employment and ultimately, at family size. Therefore it would be desirable to abandon aims of maximizing efficiency through aid, and to concentrate on employment creation which would mop up the un- and under-employed, and would lead to the growth of the G.N.P., rather than to its retardation, as is commonly supposed.

The countries of the developing world still need the investment of private money, but the pursuit by lenders of increased productivity must be seen as secondary to that of increasing employment. Too often investment by large companies is not helpful because they tend to import their own technology and to promote the goods which have been most successful in their own home markets and which, incidentally, will probably appeal to the most affluent section of the community in the recipient country (Singer, 1976).

During 1978 the United Nations Conference on Trade and Development (UNCTAD) pressed ahead with establishing a Common Fund in order to achieve the stabilization of commodity prices. By July 1979 the negotiations between developed "buyer" economies and developing "seller" economies had achieved no concrete results but at least the problem of fluctuating commodity prices and their effects on the Asian region had been recognized.

According to most authorities the gap between the developing and the developed economies (or, more bluntly, the poor and the rich countries) is increasing rather than diminishing (Robinson, 1970; Atkinson, 1970). The rate of economic growth of the poorer countries is less than that of the richer countries, even at their current reduced rates. The closing of the gap seems impossible, and it may, in some cases, even widen. Also, the near doubling of oil prices in the last year has moved wealth away from the developed and developing countries alike to the OPEC countries, undermining the ability of the rich to help the poor as well as increasing the costs of food production (Brandt, 1980). It is against this background that aid, with associated trade, must be seen as a means of encouraging socio-economic progress, not being focused narrowly on raising the G.N.P., but on unfolding the creative potentialities inherent in societies to achieve the total human needs, values and standards of the good life. The countries of the world are in one interdependent system; what matters is where they lie in that system (Donaldson, 1973).

FUTURE POPULATION GROWTH

In 1980 the Population Division of the United Nations Department of Economic and Social Affairs revised its projections of world population growth in the light of trends since the previous assessment in 1978. Its medium variant was adopted as the one most likely to occur (UN, 1981).

Taking first a global view, the projected world population will be slightly lower than the 1978 estimates to give a total of 6,119 million persons by 2000, largely because of the decline in annual population growth rates since 1975. Nevertheless, it is expected that the population of the less developed countries of the world will continue to expand at a far greater rate than that of developed countries (up from 2,648 million in 1970 to 4,847 million, compared with a rise of 1,047 million to 1,272 million), because of the net decline in population in many of the most highly developed economies. The share of the world population of the developed countries would then shrink from 28.3 per cent in 1970 to 20.8 per cent in 2000, while that of the developing nations would expand from 71.7 to 79.2 per cent.

As far as Asia (excluding the U.S.S.R.) and Oceania are concerned, the projected increase in population will be 68.4 per cent, a rise from 2,126 million in 1970 to 3,579 million in 2000. Patterns of fertility will change, and the most striking feature of this will be the estimated reduction in the average annual birth rate of China from 32.4 per 1,000 in 1965–70 to 17.3 per 1,000 in 1995–2000, while that of Japan is expected to decline from 17.8 to 13.7 per 1,000 over the same period. It is predicted that the Middle South Asian region will experience a decline in average birth rate from 43.2 per 1,000 in 1965–70 to 27.2 per 1,000 in 1995–2000. At the same time the projected death rate in this region will fall from 18.9 to 10.3 per 1,000. As a result, the population of the Indian sub-continent and immediately surrounding areas will swell by 84 per cent, from 752 million in 1970 to 1,386 million by 2000 (while that of China is expected to rise by only 50 per cent—from 838 million to 1,257 million), thus making for a massive concentration of 20.8 per cent of the world's population in the adjacent countries of Bangladesh, India, Pakistan and Sri Lanka. Australia and New Zealand will also have generally falling birth rates, from 20.3 per 1,000 in 1965–70 to 15.3 per 1,000 in 1995–2000, leading to the modest rise in population from 15.4 million in 1970 to 21.8 million in 2000, but the Pacific region (particularly Papua New Guinea) is expected to retain high birth rates (usually of about 30 per 1,000), thus leading to annual growth rates in excess of 2 per cent and the consequent doubling of population within restricted resource bases on already crowded island sites. At present rates of progress, it will take about 125 years for South and East Asia to achieve zero population growth.

Projected trends in mortality suggest that levels will drop everywhere so that the average death rate in both developed and developing nations would be roughly equal in about 1990, after which the rate would actually rise in the developed world because of its ageing population. Average life expectancy in 1995–2000 is expected to reach 72.6 years in China, 77.3 in Japan and 74.7 in Australia, but it will be only 57.9 years in Middle South Asia. As far as the structure of the population is concerned, it is expected that the proportion of very young people in the Asian population will decline because of lowering birth rates and that the proportion of old persons will increase by a few per cent, but those of working age (15–64) will increase much more, by anything from 3 to 7 per cent, with obvious implication for employment. The drift from rural areas to urban areas will continue at an increasing and alarming rate.

The total projected increase in population is not quite as great as was formerly expected, but it is still large, and the challenges implicit in the present demographic situation will be multiplied enormously. It will take all the ingenuity and hard work of the countries concerned to provide adequate social justice and food supplies for their populations, and it will require all the generosity and sympathy of the more affluent world to assist in this task; a task currently all the more complex and difficult in a world in the throes of spectacular rises in energy prices, high rates of inflation and potential recession.

BIBLIOGRAPHY

ATKINSON, A. B. "On the measurement of inequality" in *Journal of Economic Theory*, Vol. 2, pp. 244–263 (1970).

BERELSON, B. "The present state of family planning programmes" in *Studies in Family Planning*, No. 57 (New York, 1970).

BIRD, KAI. "Sterilization in India. Indira Gandhi uses force" in *The Nation*, June 19th (New York, 1976).

BRANDT, WILLY. North-South: a Programme for Survival. Report of the Independent Commission on International Development Issues; under the Chairmanship of Willy Brandt (London, 1980).

BROWN, ROY E., and WAY, JOE D. "The starving roots of population growth" in *Natural History*, Vol. 83, No. 1 (1974).

BUCHANAN, KEITH. "Population in Asia" in *The Far East and Australasia 1976–77*, pp. 29–40 (London, 1976).

CLARKE, JOHN I. Population Geography and the Developing Countries (Pergamon, Oxford, 1971).

DANDEKAR, V. M., and RATH, N. "Poverty in India: dimensions and trends" in *Economic and Political Weekly*, Vol. 6, pp. 32–33 (1971).

DONALDSON, P. Worlds Apart: The Economic Gulf between Nations (Penguin, Harmondsworth, 1973).

DREWNOWSKI, J. On Measuring and Planning the Quality of Life (Menton, The Hague, 1974).

ECONOMIC COMMISSION FOR ASIA AND THE FAR EAST (ECAFE). Economic Survey of Asia and the Far East 1972 (Bangkok, 1973) (*see* also the *Survey* for 1973).

"Growth and distribution of the rural and the urban population of the ECAFE Region'," pp. 47–67 of Report and Selected Papers of the Regional Seminar on Ecological Implications of Rural and Urban Population Growth, Asian Population Series No. 10 (Bangkok, 1972).

ECONOMIC AND SOCIAL COMMISSION FOR ASIA AND THE PACIFIC (ESCAP). Economic and Social Survey of Asia and the Pacific 1976 (Bangkok, 1977).

FOOD AND AGRICULTURE ORGANIZATION (FAO) *Ceres, see* "The quality of life" in No. 61 (1971); "Rural poverty" in No. 58 (1977), "Aid transfers" in No. 52 (1976), "Dynamics of Poverty" in No. 45 (1975), and Special Population issue (1974) to commemorate World Population Year.

FAO, Production Yearbook 1978 and Trade Yearbook 1979.

JALÉE, P. The Pillage of the Third World (New York, 1969).

MAMDANI, M. The Myth of Population Control: Family, Caste and Class in an Indian Village (New York, 1972).

MYRDAL, GUNNAR. Asian Drama: Inquiry into the Poverty of Nations, 3 vols. (Pantheon Books, New York, 1968).

PAWLEY, W. H. "In the Year 2070" in *Ceres*, Special Population Issue, 1974.

ROBINSON, E. A. G. (ed.). The Gap between the Rich and the Poor Countries (Macmillan, Canada, 1970).

SHAIL, JAIN. Size, Distribution of Income: A Compilation of Data (International Bank for Rural Development, Washington, D.C., 1975).

SINGER, H. "An elusive concept" in *Ceres*, No. 52, pp. 22–26.

STEWART, F. "Choices of techniques in developing countries" in *Journal of Development Studies* (October 1972).

UNITED NATIONS. Demographic Yearbook (1977, 1978 and 1979).

Proceedings of World Population Conference (Bucharest Report, 1974).

Quarterly Bulletin of Statistics, Asia and the Pacific, Vol. ix, No. 2.

"World Population prospects as Assessed in 1980" in *Population Studies* No. 78 (1981).

"World Population Trends and Prospects by Country, 1950–2000: Summary report of the 1978 assessment" (1979).

VISARIA, P. "The inter-relationship between economic development and population growth during the second and third development decades" in *Economic Bulletin for Asia and the Far East*, Vol. 24, pp. 1–9 (1973).

The Religions of Asia

Geoffrey Parrinder

Islam

Islam means "submission" or surrender to God, and a Muslim, from the same root, is a surrendered man. This faith was taught by Muhammad but Muslims object to being called Muhammadan or Mahometan, because they do not worship the founder of their religion. Although a late starter among the world's great religions, Islam is a universal faith with some 600 or 700 million followers in Asia and Africa.

HISTORY

Muhammad lived from A.D. 570–632 in Arabia, which was largely pagan and polytheistic with small communities of Jews and Christians. The town of Mecca was already a sacred place and it was part of the religious genius of Muhammad to purge some of its holy sites of idolatrous associations and incorporate them into the new religion, particularly the Ka'ba shrine, a cube-like sanctuary in the middle of Mecca. Jewish and Christian figures were also honoured by Muhammad, especially Abraham, Moses and Jesus, and many of their stories occur in the sacred book, the Koran. But the central themes of Muhammad's teaching came in his own experience: the unity of God, His word to man, the judgement of unbelievers and paradise for the righteous. From 610 onwards Muhammad received divine visions and messages and preached a monotheistic faith, but most of the leaders of Mecca rejected it and in 622 Muhammad migrated to Medina 200 miles to the north. This "migration" (*Hijra* or *Hegira*) was later taken as the beginning of the Muslim era from which its calendar is dated. In Medina, Muhammad became leader of a community and after successful battles against the Meccans he eventually ruled over most of Arabia, and returned to Mecca in triumph in 630, cleansing the Ka'ba of idols but going back to Medina where he died two years later.

Muhammad was followed by Caliphs (*Khalifas*, "successors") who greatly extended the rule of Islam. Under Abu Bakr the Arab armies conquered Babylon, and under 'Umar (Omar) Syria, Palestine and Egypt fell to their rule. Jerusalem and Alexandria surrendered, led by their Christian patriarchs who were glad to be rid of Byzantine Greek overlords. Arab rule was not unduly oppressive, allowing the survival of Christian communities to this day in Syrian, Coptic, Greek and other churches. Arab armies slowly pressed on into North Africa, crossed into Spain in 711, and were only repelled from central France by Charles Martel in 732 at the Battle of Poitiers. To the east the second Persian empire fell to the Arabs, who entered northern India in 705 and sent embassies as far as China. As the Arab empire settled down it absorbed eastern and western cultures and produced its own contributions; Greek philosophy, mathematics and medicine were preserved by the Arabs during the Dark Ages of Europe.

The Arab empire dominated the Near and Middle East, from Spain to central Asia, and the caliphate came to be located in Baghdad till its fall to the Mongols in 1258. After the capture of Constantinople (Istanbul) the caliph lived there till his office was abolished by the Turkish Government in 1924. In modern times the Turkish empire broke up into independent nation states and Turkey itself became westernized and secularized, a tendency which has operated in varying degrees in many Islamic countries.

BELIEF AND PRACTICE

There are Five Pillars of practical religion in Islam:

The first is the Witness that "there is no god but God" (*Allah*) and that "Muhammad is the Apostle of God". This confession is called from the minaret or a mosque by a *muezzin* ("crier") at the times of daily prayer. It stresses the unity and omnipotence of God, but it does not necessarily make Muslims into fatalists, an attitude which may derive as much from social as from theological reasons;

The second Pillar is Prayer which is to be said five times a day, turning towards the Ka'ba shrine in Mecca. Muslims unroll prayer mats and pray in a *mosque* (a "place of prostration"), at home, or wherever they are, bowing and prostrating to God and reciting set verses from the Koran in Arabic. On Fridays there is congregational worship in central mosques attended by men but not normally by women, in which worship includes the formal prayers and usually a short sermon;

No collection of money is made in the mosque but the third Pillar is Almsgiving which provides for the sick and poor in lands where there are few social services;

The fourth Pillar is Fasting from food and drink, which is obligatory on all healthy adults during the hours of daylight for the whole of the ninth month, Ramadan. The sick, pregnant women, travellers and children are exempt, but adults should fast when restored to normal life. Some modern states extend exemption to students, soldiers and factory workers, and it is said that the true fast is from sin. Since the Islamic year is lunar, the date of Ramadan gets a little earlier each year compared with the solar calendar and in northern countries in summer fasting is a considerable trial. The fast ends with one of the two great Muslim festivals, *Id al Fitr* or *Little Bairam*.

The fifth Pillar is Pilgrimage (*hajj*) to Mecca which is incumbent at least once in a lifetime on every Muslim, who may then take the title *Hajji*. About a million pilgrims go every year to Mecca, which is the holy city forbidden to all but Muslims, and some take months or years to perform the ambition of a lifetime, travelling by air, sea, lorry or on foot. The pilgrimage is in the twelfth month and must be performed in simple dress donned at ten miles distance from Mecca, women's heads covered, faces usually unveiled. The central ritual entails going round the Ka'ba seven times, kissing a Black Stone in its walls, and visiting hills outside Mecca where sheep and other animals are sacrificed. At the same time Muslims all over the world sacrifice sheep and this makes the chief festival, *Id al Kabir, Qurban* or *Bairam*. This ceremony unites all Muslims and is popularly linked with Abraham's sacrifice of a sheep in place of his son Isaac (Ishaq). The birthday of the Prophet is another popular modern anniversary.

The Holy War (*Jihad*) was the means of the unparalleled spread of Islam in the first centuries, but despite pressures it has not been elevated into a Pillar of religion and today theologians interpret the Jihad as war against sin in the soul.

The Koran (*Qur'an*, "recitation" or "reading") is regarded as the very Word of God and not to be subjected to criticism. The Koran is about as long as the New Testament, in 114 chapters (*suras*) of uneven length, the longest ones coming first after the opening chapter. The Opening (*Fatiha*) is repeated twice at least at all times of daily prayer, preceded by the ascription "in the name of God, the Merciful, the Compassionate". Two short chapters at the end are also used in prayers, and instructed and pious Muslims may repeat other chapters, always in Arabic. Modern translations of the Koran are now allowed for private use and there have always been many commentaries. The chief message of the Koran is the majesty of God, His oneness, demand for human obedience and coming judgement. The later and longer chapters include much family and social legislation, for marriage, divorce, personal and communal behaviour.

The Koran is not the only authority for Muslims, but it is supplemented by masses of Traditions (*Hadith*) which include sayings attributed to the Prophet and his companions, and doctrine and morals are further interpreted by Comparison and Consent. Four law schools arose which apply Islamic law (*shari'a*) to all activities of life. In Asia the two principal law schools are the *Hanafi* in central Asia and the Indian sub-continent, and the *Shafi'i* in the East Indies. In modern times interpretation of law ranges between conservative rigorism and modernism; many of the Traditions are questioned but the Koran remains sacrosanct.

The Islamic community (*umma*) is the basis of the brotherhood of Islam, which from the early centuries aimed at making this religion international and above tribal rivalries. This is still the ideal, though the rise of nationalism has brought divisive interests into the Muslim world.

SECTS AND MYSTICS

The great majority, probably over 80 per cent, of Muslims are *Sunni*, followers of "the path", custom or tradition. They accept the first four caliphs (Abu Bakr, 'Umar, 'Uthman, 'Ali) as "rightly guided", receive six authentic books of Traditions, and belong to one of the four schools of law. Other Muslims claim to follow true tradition but differ on its interpretation.

Shi'a Muslims

The major division came early. The Shi'a or "followers" of 'Ali believed that as cousin and son-in-law of Muhammad, 'Ali should have been his first successor. When at last his turn came there was a division and another caliph was set up in Damascus. The Shi'a became linked with patriotism in Iraq which objected to rule from Syria, and Husain, a son of 'Ali, went to found a kingdom in Iraq but was intercepted by rival troops and slain at Karbala. Husain became the great Shi'a martyr, the anniversary of whose death in Muharram, the first month of the year, is the occasion for days of mourning and long Passion Plays in Shi'a towns. At the climax of the play Husain receives the key of intercession from Gabriel and promises paradise to all who call upon him.

The basic Shi'a beliefs are the same as those of the Sunni but 'Ali is added after Muhammad in the confession of faith. Their most distinctive doctrine is that of the *Imam*, spiritual "leader", which was used in preference to caliph for the head of state. Most Shi'a are Twelvers, recognizing twelve Imams, of whom the last disappeared in A.D. 878, but it is believed that he will return again as the *Mahdi* ("guided one") to put down evil and restore righteousness on earth. In 1502, Shi'ism became the established religion of Iran and it is strongest there and in Iraq and north India. *Ayatollahs* ("signs of God") are conservative religious leaders in Iran.

Isma'ilis

Some of the Shi'a are Isma'ilis, believing that it was the seventh Imam, Isma'il, who was the last when he disappeared in 765, hence they are also called Seveners. There were political as well as religious reasons for the schism. There are mystical beliefs in the "light" of the Imam, eternal and ever-present, and various grades of initiation into mysteries. There are small groups of Isma'ilis in Afghanistan and Turkestan, and larger ones in Pakistan, Bangladesh and India. Offshoots are most of the Khojas whose leader is the Aga Khan. These Isma'ili Khojas are found in Bombay, Gujarat, Sind, East Africa, and other Indian and neighbouring towns. They number over 200,000, in active and educated communities, noted for social works.

Ahmadiyya Movement

At Qadian in India and Lahore in Pakistan are centres of a modern movement called Ahmadiyya, after Ghulam Ahmad of the Punjab who, from 1890, was set forth as the expected Mahdi, Messiah and Avatar. After struggles and divisions the Ahmadiyya have published many books in English, sent missionaries to Africa, and propounded teachings most of which are orthodox Islam but with some modern polemics.

Sufis

Sufi mystics have been found in all branches of Islam from the early days, so called from the woollen (*suf*) robes which they wore, like Christian monks. In face of orthodox formalism and deism, the Sufis taught the love of God and sometimes this became almost pantheism or identity with God. The Sufis came to be accepted, partly through the efforts of the Persian philosopher Ghazali, himself a mystic. Many popular shrines are tombs of holy men or shaikhs, where relics are revered and votive gifts are placed.

DISTRIBUTION

Most of the population are Sunni Muslims in Afghanistan, while in Pakistan Islam is the state religion and the 1961 census found that 97.1 percent of the population were Muslims. In Bangladesh at the 1974 census over 85 per cent, 60.6 million, were Muslims and according to the 1971 census in India there were 61.4 million Indian Muslims. Indonesia is predominantly Muslim with 94 per cent of the population, over 112 million, adherents at the 1971 census. Islam is the state religion in Malaysia, followed by most Malays. There are Muslim minorities in Sri Lanka, Burma, Thailand and the Philippines and in Soviet Central Asia and China there are some large Muslim communities.

Hinduism

Hinduism is the name given by Europeans to the major religion of India, estimated to have 453 million adherents in the 1971 Census.

HISTORY

The name is derived from India and the river Indus in the north-west. Here flourished an extensive city culture from about 2,500 to 1,500 B.C., contemporary with ancient Mesopotamia and Egypt. These cities were destroyed by invading Aryans but remains indicate that Indus Valley religion included worship of a Mother Goddess, and a Lord of Yogis and animals, like Shiva, a great god today. A caste system arose from conquest and colour at the head of which were the Brahmin priests who imposed their religion.

The Brahmins compiled the most ancient religious texts, the *Vedas* ("knowledge"), in four collections, though these were not written down for many centuries but passed on orally. The history of Hinduism is scanty, with no historical founder and no organized church, but development can be traced in religious texts. The Vedas are hymns to many gods of heaven and earth, and they portray a relatively simple religion in some ways like that of the Homeric Greeks who were also Aryans. The Vedic hymns were probably compiled between 1500 and 800 B.C. but their use was restricted to the upper castes, and today they are used only by priests and at marriage and funeral ceremonies. They were followed by the *Upanishads* ("sitting-down-near", teaching sessions), dialogues of which the chief were compiled between 800 and 300 B.C. The Upanishads are called *Vedanta* ("end of the Vedas") though this term is also used for some later philosophies. They discuss philosophical questions, like those which Greek thinkers considered a little later: the origins of the world and man, the nature of divinity and the human soul, death and immortality, self-discipline and devotion.

From this time onwards arose masses of religious works which became the chief inspiration of most Hindus. Two great epic poems, the *Mahabharata*, "great India" story, and the *Ramayana*, "the story of Rama", include myth, history, theology and ethics. The personal gods of the Vedas reappear but with many others, no doubt from the Indus Valley and indigenous sources. A creating deity Brahma plays a small part, but Shiva, Vishnu and the Goddess come from now on to be the major deities of Hinduism. Vishnu, a minor Vedic god, became important through his *Avatars* ("descents"), visible embodiments on earth in animal and human form. The two chief human Avatars were Rama and Krishna, the latter a dark god of herdsmen, a warrior king, and a lover of the soul. A small section of the Great Epic is the *Bhagavad-Gita*, "the Song of the Lord" Krishna, the best known of all Indian scriptures, which gives the teaching of the god Krishna on reincarnation, salvation, deity and devotion. Stories of Krishna and other gods continued in the *Puranas*, "ancient tales", composed down to the Middle Ages. Many medieval Indian poets also produced popular songs in praise of Krishna, Rama, Shiva and the Goddess, and devotional groups flourished especially in Bengal and southern India.

In modern times external influences and internal pressures brought reforms of Hinduism. Muslim invasions began in the eighth century but became most potent under the rule of the Mughals from the sixteenth to the nineteenth centuries. Christian missions and European trade developed especially in the nineteenth and twentieth centuries. Both Islam and Christianity criticized Hinduism for polytheism and idolatry, and practices such as *suttee* (*satī*, widow-burning). Modern Hinduism is presented as "eternal truth", including all that is best from other faiths but with its special emphasis either in pantheism or devotion.

BELIEFS

Belief in the indestructibility of the soul is basic to Hinduism, it is both pre-existence and post-existence. Transmigration from one life to another, or reincarnation, is universally held, but the endless births and deaths are a harsh cycle from which ways of salvation are offered, through knowledge, works or devotion. The next life is conditioned by *Karma*, "works" or the entail of works. This explains the inequalities and sufferings of life, to those who accept it in faith, but it does not necessarily lead to fatalism. Karma can be improved by good actions and the next rebirth be to a higher level. But those who do wrong may descend to the animal level or even lower, hence there is a great respect for animal life and many Hindus are vegetarians.

From early times Indians have practised self-discipline and there are many holy men, sadhus, swamis, and the like. *Yoga* is a general name for both discipline and union, related to the English "yoke". It may consist in forms of physical exercise and control, in Hatha ("force") Yoga. Some adepts claim supernatural powers, like levitation. Most practitioners engage in breath-control and sit in cross-legged postures. Raja ("royal") Yoga proceeds to mastery of mind, concentration or emptying of thought, and attainment of supreme knowledge or bliss.

The Caste System

The caste system greatly developed over the centuries. There are four basic castes: Brahmin priests, Raja or Kshatriya rulers and warriors, Vaishya artisan merchants, and Shudra servants. The first three are "twice born" through initiation with sacred threads at adolescence. But the castes have been expanded with many local and occupational castes, said to number over 3,000, with further sub-castes, and below these are millions of outcastes who perform the most menial tasks. Caste distinctions are rigid in theory, and Brahmins in particular are offended by any contact with low castes; eating between castes is prohibited. Many occupational and guild distinctions remain but modern conditions, liberal laws and closer communications, are breaking down exclusiveness. Communal quarrels arise between castes and religions, particularly in anything that touches the sacredness of the cow.

TEMPLES AND WORSHIP

India is a land of magnificent architectural monuments, most of them religious. The temples have small inner sanctuaries surrounded by large open paved courtyards, tanks for ritual washing, and walls with stone gates and towers. Temple worship is performed by priests without much lay assistance, but people visit the courtyards for quiet prayer and meditation.

Modern temples are less impressive but there are countless little shrines by the wayside or in the middle of streets, at which people stop to place gifts and pray. Hindu homes have rooms or corners for images and devotion, where flowers are placed and incense burns. Worship is performed at home and there is no sabbath or regular obligation to visit temples, though for festivals and annual events great crowds assemble there, when images are carried in procession in chariots or on elephants.

There are countless holy places, from the Himalayas in the north to the extreme southern capes, and pilgrimages are made to seven chief sites. The holiest place of all is Varanasi (Banaras) on the middle Ganges, where steps (*ghats*) lead down from temples into the sacred river in which people wash and pray. "Burning ghats" are reserved for cremation, the normal lot of the Hindu dead. Varanasi is full of holy men, dressed in yellow robes or smeared with ashes, begging and awaiting death in the sacred city. Great assemblies are held here and at other places every few years, at which millions of people gather to bathe in the river.

There are many Hindu festivals and all deities have sacred days. *Holi* in the spring is an ancient fertility feast when coloured water is squirted on participants and the praises of Krishna and his loves are chanted. *Dashara* or *Dassehra* in the autumn is marked by carnival figures of the hero Rama and his demon enemy Ravana, the latter being packed with crackers which are set alight at the end. *Divali* in November is a feast of lights for the gracious goddess Lakshmi, consort of Vishnu, when lamps welcome the patroness of wealth, business and learning. In other popular feasts the god of fortune, Ganesha, son of Shiva, is carried in the form of images of pink elephants, or Shiva the lord both of Yoga and the dance is depicted as the dancing god within a flaming circle, often represented in bronze images.

ORGANIZATION AND DISTRIBUTION

There is little widespread organization in Hindu religion. The followers of Shiva, Vishnu and the Mother are joined in their own cult sympathy, and sometimes divided between cults in antagonism. There are centres of learning and worship, but many local differences of practice. Monasteries and retreat houses (*ashrams*) cater for cults and societies, but no large-scale monastic organization compares with those of Buddhism and Christianity. Many Hindu holy men are solitaries and may be seen sitting alone or living in secluded places with a few disciples.

In modern times the Brahmo and Arya Samaj have organized themselves, and also significant is the Ramakrishna Mission. Taking its name from a nineteenth-century holy man of Bengal, Shri Ramakrishna, and directed by his disciple Swami Vivekananda, the Mission initiated religious, educational and social works and undertakes much literary propaganda. From its centre in Calcutta the Ramakrishna Mission has established branches throughout India and in Europe and America, and by using English as well as Indian languages it is one of the most effective propagandists of Vedantic pantheism. From Pondicherry, south of Madras, the Aurobindo Ashram also engages in meditation, education, industrial work, and literary propaganda, and there are many smaller similar agencies.

Hinduism is virtually confined to the peoples of the Indian sub-continent, though it is practised also in Bali and by peoples of Indian origin in Sri Lanka. It has commonly been said that a Hindu is one born into a caste and who accepts the Vedic scriptures, and therefore it is an ethnic and not a missionary religion. But in past centuries Hinduism spread as far away as Bali and Kampuchea (Cambodia), and today some of its missionaries choose Europe and America as their fields.

Other Indian Religions

PARSIS

An ancient religion which in origins was akin to that of the Aryan Indians was practised by related peoples in Iran, but it survives today mainly in small communities in India. The Parsis (Persians) migrated to India from the ninth century onwards under pressure from Muslim invaders and settled chiefly in the region of Bombay, though there are groups elsewhere in India and East Africa, numbering in all about 120,000. The prophetic reformer of the religion was Zoroaster (Zarathushtra), generally dated 630–553 B.C. He taught faith in one God, *Ahura Mazda* ("Lord Wisdom"), who was goodness opposed to the spirit of evil, *Ahriman*. In hymns, *Gathas*, attributed to him, Zoroaster told of visions of the heavenly court to which he was summoned and received the doctrines and duties which would reform his country's religion. He was not successful at first but after some ten years he did better in Bactria to the east of Persia, and after years of preaching Zoroaster was killed in a struggle with opposing priests. His religion slowly developed, led by priests called *Magi*, and in the early Christian centuries it became the state religion of Iran until the Muslim invasion.

Belief and Practice

The basic Parsi scriptures are the *Avesta*, which include hymns and ritual and practical regulations and are still recited in ancient Persian. Belief in the opposition of the good and evil spirits has caused this religion to be called dualistic, but Parsis claim that the dualism is temporary since at the end Ahura Mazda will triumph. There is a strong moral emphasis and its followers call it the Religion of the Good Life; by virtuous conduct and moderation men help God to overcome evil. Ahura Mazda is the supreme God but there are other angelic and demonic spirits; especially important is Mithra or Meher, a god of the old Iranian religion who now becomes the judge of death. Belief in life after death is strong in Zoroastrianism and probably influenced Judaism and Christianity with its ideas of angels and demons, the end of the world, judgement and eternal life. It is believed that departed souls have their deeds weighed in scales and then cross a narrow bridge to paradise; the evil fall into a purgatory but eventually all are saved.

Parsi temples contain no images but sacred fire always burns there, fed by sandalwood, and so they are called "fire temples" by other Indians. The dead are disposed of in "towers of silence" where vultures destroy the flesh, which must not defile the earth or fire. Some of these towers are outside Bombay, though closed to the public, but elsewhere Parsi dead are buried in lead coffins. There have been reforms in modern times and religious instruction is given in new expositions of the faith. Parsi priests wear white robes and old Parsis have traditional dress with hard hats and robes, but many Parsis wear modern European or Indian dress. As a small ingrown community the Parsis are highly educated and in trade and public service they play a role out of all proportion to their size. Women are emancipated, enter temples equally with men, and take part in educational and public affairs.

JAINS

The Jains are an Indian religious community numbering 2.6 million at the 1971 census. It is possible that the religion existed in India before the arrival of the Aryan invaders about 1,500 B.C., since its beliefs in reincarnation and types of asceticism seem to have been non-Aryan. The Jains say that their religion is eternal and is renewed in successive ages by *Jinas* ("conquerors"), of whom there have been twenty-four at long intervals in the present world eon. The last Jina was given the title of Mahavira ("great man") and lived in the sixth century B.C., a little before Gautama Buddha whose life was similar in some ways. After the death of his parents Mahavira left his wife and family (though one sect says he was celibate) and went about naked begging alms and seeking enlightenment. He achieved this after thirteen years and became a Jina and omniscient. He is said to have had great success, with a community of 50,000 monks and nuns and many lay followers. Mahavira died in the lower Ganges valley, entering *Nirvana*, the "blowing out" of desire and life.

Belief and Practice

Jains do not believe in a creator God, since the world is eternal, and they have been called atheistic. But the twenty-four Jinas are objects of worship and some Hindu gods also figure in their temple imagery. Jains believe in the eternity of countless souls, which are immersed in matter and evil, but by renunciation of desire they can rise to Nirvana at the ceiling of the universe. Monksare the nearest to salvation and sectarian differences divide the "white-clad" monks in robes from the "sky-clad" who are naked. The best known Jain doctrine is "non-violence" or harmlessness (*ahimsa*). All life is sacred; this involves vegetarianism and abstention from taking any life by hunting, farming or fishing. Monks sweep the ground in their path to avoid treading on insects, filter their drink, and wear cloths before their mouths to keep out insects. In modern times Jain stress on non-violence has inspired reformers, like the Hindu Gandhi.

Despite ascetic practices and absence of deity, the Jains have built some of the most splendid temples in India through the patronage of rich followers. The main anniversary is at the end of August when wrongs are confessed, fasting practised, and the birthday of Mahavira is celebrated. The Hindu feast of Divali is also popular and the goddess Lakshmi is invoked for success. Being excluded from many occupations that involve taking or endangering life, the Jains have prospered in commerce and are influential in public affairs. Some modern Jains try to adapt asceticism to current conditions, but monks continue on the hard way to Nirvana.

SIKHS

The Sikhs are one of the largest Indian religious minorities with 10.3 million followers at the 1971 census, the men easily recognizable by turbans and beards. The Sikh religion is relatively modern and developed like Hindu devotional movements with some influence from Islam.

Medieval Hindu poets sang the praises of Krishna and Rama, the Avatars of Vishnu, and in the fifteenth century Kabir concentrated on Rama as the sole deity. Kabir was a Muslim weaver of Varanasi but trained by a Hindu teacher, and he taught that there is one God behind the many names of Allah, Rama and Krishna. Kabir composed and sang poems denouncing priests and scriptures and he suffered persecution, though at his death both Hindus and Muslims claimed him for their own and rival shrines commemorate him. The followers of the path of Kabir, *Kabir-panthis*, number about a million, chiefly in north-central India.

A little later in the Punjab lived Nanak (1469–1538) who founded the Sikhs. He was a Hindu who also sought the unity of God and had a vision in which he was told to teach faith in God as the True Name. He travelled widely but was most successful in the Punjab where groups of *Sikhs* ("disciples") followed him. Nanak was the great *Guru* ("teacher") and though he was followed by nine other Gurus they were regarded as essentially identical with Guru Nanak. The Sikhs suffered persecution from the Muslims and the tenth Guru, Govind Singh, founded an inner militant society, Khalsa, with initiation by a sword and adding the name Singh ("lion") to all initiates. Members of the Khalsa have five marks: beard and hair uncut (hence the turban), wearing shorts, steel comb in hair, steel bangle on the right wrist, and steel dagger at the side. With this militant force the Sikhs won independence in the Punjab till British rule came. But at the partition of India in 1947 the line between India and Pakistan ran right through the Punjab and the Sikhs rose to assert their independence. They were expelled from Pakistan and had to accept a place in the Indian state, though constant moves have been made towards fuller autonomy, with leaders fasting to gain their end.

Belief and Practice

Sikhs believe in one God, with Guru Nanak his perfect teacher, and their temples have no images. Their scriptures, the *Adi Granth* ("first book"), contain poems by Kabir and Hindu and Muslim composers, as well as by Guru Nanak and other Gurus. It is an anthology of lofty religious verse which is chanted daily, in the Punjabi language, by Sikhs in public and private devotion.

Sikh temples are usually white buildings with golden domes, and alongside is a tank or small lake for ritual washing. The Adi Granth scriptures are carried into the temple at dawn and chanted by relays of readers till night, when the book is returned to a treasury. The principal shrine is the Golden Temple at Amritsar, the most sacred Sikh town and centre of administration. Beside the temple are free hostels and kitchens for the community and for visitors of any race or religion. Sikhs are found in many Indian cities, as well as in Africa and Europe, but their strength remains in the Punjab.

Buddhism

Buddhism arose in India though it has almost disappeared there, and its great successes as a missionary religion have been in South-East and East Asia, to which it took Indian thought and culture.

HISTORY

The founder was named Siddhartha but is more generally known by the family name of Gautama (the Sanskrit form; Gotama in Pali), or from his clan Shakyamuni, "the sage of the Shakyas". The dates commonly accepted for Gautama by Western scholars are 563–483 B.C., though Chinese Buddhists put them hundreds of years earlier. Primary evidence is scanty and begins with inscriptions made by the emperor Asoka from about 260 B.C., some of which still remain.

Gautama was born in Kapilavastu in north-central India, or Nepal, of a local king and into the warrior caste rather than the priestly Brahmin. From many legends it is clear that his parents were married, the birth was not virginal, and the boy grew up in relative seclusion but was married and had a son. Riding outside the palace at the age of twenty-nine Gautama saw four signs: an old man, a sick man, a corpse and an ascetic. These showed him the suffering of the world, and the calm of leaving it, and led to his great renunciation. He left his wife and child by night, and for years tried various teachers and ways towards enlightenment but without success. Finally, near Gaya on a tributary of the Ganges, Gautama sat under a tree called the Bo or Bodhi-tree, the "tree of enlightenment", and waited for light to come. After a day and a night knowledge came; he understood the rising and passing away of beings, the cause of suffering, the end of rebirth and the way to Nirvana. Now he was a Buddha, an "enlightened one", and went to preach his doctrine in a park to the north of the holy city of Varanasi.

The Buddha was followed at first by small groups of monks and laymen but soon became successful, especially in middle India where the town of Rajagriha (modern Rajgir) was a centre for the religion. For some 40 years the Buddha went about teaching, retiring to monastic buildings during the rains. The monastic order (*Sangha*) was the centre of activity, and after some hesitation orders of nuns were formed as well. Finally, the Buddha died after eating tainted pork and was cremated, tradition saying that his relics were divided between eight regions.

At the Buddha's death 500 monks met in a cave and the chief disciple, Ananda, recited the *Vinaya*, the monkish rules that form the first part of the Buddhist scriptures. The Buddha himself and his followers came into conflict with Brahmin priests, Jains, Yoga teachers and others, and taught that the way of the Buddha was best. They rejected the Hindu scriptures and were regarded as heretics. There was also some caste rivalry and possibly Buddhism inherited both some of the communal differences and the religious beliefs of the ancient Indus Valley cultures.

A great impulse to the spread of Buddhism was given by Asoka in the third century B.C., who turned from martial conquests to the peaceful way of Buddhism, inscribing decrees ordering faith and morality, restoring Buddhist sacred sites, and sending missionaries to Sri Lanka and elsewhere. Buddhism became the dominant religion of South-East Asia, despite some remains of ancient animism. In the first Christian century Buddhist monks took scriptures, images and relics to China, and in the sixth century to Japan, in both countries mingling with local religions which retained much of their appeal. In the land of its origin Buddhism flourished for over a thousand years, but finally almost died out in India under pressure from reviving Hindu devotional cults and destruction of temples and monasteries by invading Muslims. Recently there has been some Buddhist success among the Indian outcastes, claiming three million converts.

BELIEFS

The Buddha taught *Dharma* (or *Dhamma*) which is law, virtue, right, religion or truth, and this is expounded as the Middle Way between the extremes of sensuality and asceticism. At his enlightenment Gautama saw the solution of the suffering that had troubled him and enunciated it in the Four Noble Truths. These are: the universal fact of suffering, the cause of suffering which is craving or desire, the cessation of suffering by ending craving, and the method of cessation by the Noble Eightfold Path. This Path is a way of discipline in eight steps, each of which is called Right. They fall into three groups, the first beginning the path in Right View and Resolve. Then come practical activity in Right Speech, Action and Livelihood. Finally, there are higher spiritual states: Right Effort, Concentration and Contemplation.

This is a scheme of moral and spiritual improvement without reference to the Hindu gods. Some of them appear in Buddhist legend but always subservient to the Buddha. The Hindu teaching of the impersonal divine Brahman seems to have been unknown to the Buddha and his system has been called atheistic or agnostic. But in fact the Buddha himself is the supreme and omniscient teacher and object of adoration. A Buddhist does not save himself, but he relies on the teaching of experts and the celestial Buddha.

The Buddha also criticized the Hindu doctrine of the soul, which he declared could not be identified with any of the bodily elements. At death the five constituents of the body dissolved and were not passed on to another life. Yet Buddhism held firmly to the Indian belief in rebirth, and the cycle of existence was caused by desire from which one could escape only by following the path of the Buddha. The link between one life and another was *Karma*, the entail of deeds which determined a higher or lower destiny in the next life. To become free from this round of existence was the supreme goal, the indescribable *Nirvana* (*Nibbana*), the "blowing out" of desire and life.

Northern Buddhism

These are the basic beliefs of southern Buddhists, but in the north further doctrines developed in which multitudes of celestial beings offered gracious help to mankind. Southern Buddhists believe that there have been several Buddhas in the past and there will be some in the future, the next one, Maitreya, being a fat jolly figure bringing fortune. But in the present long world eon there is only one Buddha, the supreme Gautama. In northern Buddhism not only are thousands of Buddhas accepted now but there are countless *Bodhisattvas* ("beings of enlightenment"), who have deferred their own salvation until all beings are saved. This led to a universalism and a religion of faith and grace which was able to absorb many Chinese and other deities in the guise of Bodhisattvas. The Chinese Kwanyin (Japanese Kwannon) is the "lady of compassion", not a goddess but a Bodhisattva, a kindly giver of children and a saviour who immediately hears the cries of all suppliants. In Tibet the Dalai Lama is the incarnation of this Bodhisattva, not of Gautama.

More abstruse philosophical doctrines were also taught in northern Buddhism: the three bodies of the Buddha, and an idealistic doctrine of the Void in which Buddhas and believers are merged in a neutral monism somewhat like the Hindu Brahman. There were links with Chinese Daoism in this pantheism, and later Zen Buddhism emerged from the fusion of ideas. On the popular level, *Pure Land* Buddhism offered the hope of a Western paradise where another Buddha, Amida, called men to himself.

SCHOOLS AND ORGANIZATION

The southern Buddhists call themselves *Theravada*, followers of the "tradition of the elders". They are found in Sri Lanka, Burma and other parts of South-East Asia, where their graceful buildings, dagobas, pagodas or wats, decorate towns and countryside. Here relics are enshrined, innumerable Buddha images sit in various postures, and worshippers go to meditate. Traditional education was in the monasteries which are still strong. Yellow-robed monks go on begging-rounds every morning, and scholars study the scriptures, the *Tripitaka* ("three baskets"). There are minor sects but general uniformity of belief and practice.

The northern Buddhists are *Mahayana*, followers of the "great Vehicle" to salvation, as against the others whom they call *Hinayana*, of the "small Vehicle". In Tibet Mahayana Buddhism has traditionally been the state religion, incorporating some beliefs of a primitive Bon religion whose gods are taken as guardians of Buddhism. There are two chief schools of monks, the Yellow Hats being reformed and dominant, and the Red Hats of an earlier tradition. The chief monks are Lamas, of whom the chief is the Dalai Lama who lived in the Potala palace in Lhasa. In 1959 he fled from the Chinese to India and lives there in exile. Despite oppression, Buddhism remains the religion of the Tibetan people.

Buddhism in China and Japan

Buddhism was at first opposed in China, since it withdrew young men from active life into monasteries and its teaching seemed to be contrary to the popular cults of the ancestors. But despite some fierce persecutions Buddhism became part of Chinese life and exercised a great influence not only on religion but on culture and the arts. Confucian scholars criticized the use of relics but popular devotion cherished them, and Buddhist monks became particularly active in reciting texts at funerals and memorial services. Chinese Buddhism evolved the popular *Pure Land* sects, the meditative *Chan*, and the scholarly and tolerant *Dian-Dai* (*Tien-Tai*). Under Communism Buddhist activity has been severely restricted and many monasteries have been closed or converted into schools and barracks. But there has also been extensive restoration of Buddhist centres in the interests of antiquarian study and the preservation of monuments of national culture, in famous cave-temples and grottoes in Shanxi (Shansi), Henan (Honan) and Xinjiang (Sinkiang). A strictly controlled Chinese Buddhist Association was founded in 1953, and with the suppression of the monastic order the future of Buddhism in China depends upon the ability of its lay followers to adapt themselves to modern conditions.

In Japan Buddhism appealed to both leaders and people. In the sixth century A.D. it came first from Korea and then from China, and brought with it writing and Chinese culture. Buddhism soon gained a firm footing in Japan under the regent Prince Shotoku, who was regarded as an incarnation of the Bodhisattva Kwannon. Buddhism came to terms with the ancient Japanese Shinto religion by declaring that the Shinto gods were manifestations of Buddha originals. When the colossal bronze Buddha at Nara was begun the emperor received the blessing of the chief Shinto deity. A synthesis called Dual (*Ryobu*) Shinto was formed in which Buddhists controlled all but the most important Shinto shrines. This lasted over a thousand years, till the Shinto revival in 1868 when Ryobu Shinto was abolished. Buddhism came under attack for a time, but it had entered too deeply into Japanese life and its contribution to thought and the arts could not be hidden.

Japanese Buddhism adopted Chinese schools: *Pure Land* as *Jodo*, and *Dian-Dai* as *Tendai*. The school of Nichiren opposed the emotional cults by claiming to return to the original teaching of the Buddha, but he was still the glorified Shakyamuni sitting on a Vulture Peak in the Himalayas. Chinese Chan became known to a wider world through Japanese *Zen* (both based on an Indian word for "meditation"). It stressed the search for enlightenment in daily work and so encouraged many arts. It also became popular with the military, the Samurai warriors, in Zen teaching of judo, archery and swordsmanship. Zen teachers are critical of some traditional texts, but they use basic ones in meditation techniques and they have monasteries where Zen is taught. Zen monks are the only ones in Japan who continue the daily begging round.

Japanese Buddhism has developed congregational worship more than other parts of the Buddhist world, and there are great temples with lavish ritual services. There are modern sectarian movements which show the influence of Shinto naturalism and sometimes of Christianity. From Japan Buddhist missions have gone to the Pacific islands, especially Hawaii, and the western parts of the U.S.A.

Organization

The different Buddhist schools have loose organization. Traditionally monasteries have been the centres of doctrine and discipline, and their chief abbots are the religious authorities; in centralized systems such as Tibet the Dalai Lama and the Panchen Lama disputed the supremacy. Monks and nuns are, of course, celibate, but where there are large numbers of priests, as in Japan, they are usually married. Since the days of Asoka, laymen have been encouraged to attend the monasteries at weekly or fortnightly special days, and many go there also for meditation during the rainy season.

Other East Asian Religions

CONFUCIANISM

It has been debated whether Confucianism was a religion, but what has been known in the West under this title was a compound of ancient Chinese popular cults, ancestral worship, state ritual and moral precepts. Alongside and often mingling with this Confucianism were also indigenous Daoism and imported Buddhism, which together have been called the Three Religions or rather Three Ways of China, since none of them was an exclusive system.

Kongfuzi (K'ung Fu-tzu) or Master Kong, latinized as Confucius, lived in the state of Lu in north China, 551–478 B.C. Of humble rank and largely self-educated, he became a teacher asking questions and giving maxims, like a Chinese Socrates, rather than a systematic philosopher. Some of his pupils came to occupy high office, but although in later life Confucius toured the country looking for a state which would put his ideas into practice, he was unsuccessful. It is said, on dubious grounds, that he then compiled the Chinese Classics, the *Book of History*, the *Book of Odes* and the *Book of Changes*, and also the *Annals of Lu*. Confucius was not a founder of a religion, though he criticized some forms of ritual. His thoughts are found in a small book called *Analects* (*Lun Yu*) and they emphasize the importance of propriety (*li*) in personal and social conduct. Filial piety and correct observance of ancestral cults are commended, and the duties of rulers to subjects as well as servants to masters. His personal religious attitude appears in the sense of Heaven (*Tian*) inspiring him, judging his acts and hearing prayer.

About a hundred years later his most famous follower, Mencius, praised Confucius as the greatest of all sages and he was more successful in advising rulers to follow just and peaceful ways. The cult of Confucius grew slowly: by the second century B.C. Chinese emperors adapted his teachings to their purposes, and in A.D. 59 sacrifice was ordered to Confucius in every school. He was called "the Teacher of ten thousand generations", but he was not deified and Confucian halls were different from the temples of other religions, with memorial tablets instead of images. The scholars (mandarins) were concerned with the preservation of the teachings of Confucius and until this century examinations for public service were in the Confucian classics.

The popular religion of China was a worship of nature and hero gods, similar to those of India or ancient Greece. In the villages the gods of earth were the most important for work, and the god of the hearth dominated homes. "Wall and moat" gods protected towns, and storm and disease spirits were propitiated at need. The local cults were idealized in great state functions when the emperor sacrificed to heaven on the marble terraces of the Temple of Heaven in Beijing (Peking), or paid homage to the agricultural gods at a great altar of Land and Grain. The emperor ploughed the first furrow in spring and cut the first corn in summer, as a model for the country.

Cults of the ancestors were highly developed in China, though it has been claimed that they were filial piety and not religious worship. Great expense was made at funerals and incense burnt daily before the tablets of the recently dead. Later the tablets were removed to ancestral halls, with the tablet of the family founder on the highest shelf. At the winter solstice sacrifices were offered and food eaten communally, while in the Festival of Hungry Souls lighted paper boats are sent sailing down rivers to help the dead in their journey to the afterworld.

In modern times many of the old temples and images of village and town gods have been destroyed, but ancestral ceremonies are still widely observed. Confucius has been attacked as a feudalist but also honoured as the greatest national teacher. In 1961 his tomb was redecorated but Red Guards ransacked it in 1967. Yet Confucianism has not been classified as a religion and remains as an invisible force in which some of the old attitudes continue in new guise.

DAOISM (TAOISM)

Daoism is China's indigenous nature and personal religion and inspires much of its culture and philosophy. The word Dao (Tao) is a path or way, regarded as the true principle of life and the universe. There is a Dao of heaven, a Dao of earth and a Dao of man which is harmony with these. In Confucian writings Dao is moral and practical, but in Daoism it is mystical and universal.

Lao Zi (Lao Tzu) is a legendary figure who is said to have lived just before Confucius and rebuked him, but this reflects later controversy. Lao Zi is said to have written the *Dao De Jing* (*Tao Te Ching*), the classic of "the Way and its Power", in 81 chapters. This is a charming and profound work, perhaps written in the third century B.C. by an anonymous quietist. Dao is here called indefinable and eternal, it cannot be grasped, but by quietness its influence extends over the 10,000 material things. This is a nature mysticism, in which a favourite symbol is water which passively overcomes everything. Formal morality is opposed by "actionless activity", and militarism is strongly repudiated.

Two centuries later this quietism was taken further by Zhuang Zi (Chuang Tzu) who taught that men should live according to nature, and practise a kind of Yoga or "sitting in forgetfulness". The *Yang* and *Yin*, positive and negative principles of nature, are seen in heaven and earth, light and dark, male and female, and are symbolized in the circle with two pear-shaped halves that appears in much oriental decoration. Daoists began the search for supernatural powers which would come by living naturally, controlling breathing, eating uncooked food and walking through fire. Anchorites lived in the country drinking dew, and expeditions set out for the Isles of the Blest whose inhabitants were supposed to be immortal. The unfortunate associations with magic led Daoism into superstition, and the close link of its priests with the people brought many temples of earth and city gods under their care.

When Buddhism arrived in China it was both opposed and imitated by the indigenous religions. Daoist temples and images multiplied, and rituals for helping the living and the dead developed from Buddhist examples. Lao Zi received the title of "Emperor of Mysterious Origin" and other gods were added to form a pantheon which had huge and often frightening images, while heavens and hells dazzled the pious. More philosophical was the mingling of Daoism and Buddhism in the Chan (Zen) sect which sought enlightenment by the way of nature. In the arts Daoism had great influence by applying the principle of "seeing without looking" to painting and writing.

Nowadays attack on superstitions has led to the outward decline of Daoism, except in Hong Kong, Taiwan and Malaysia. In China the association of Daoism with secret societies made it the potent force in revolts like the Boxer Rising in 1900, and the Pervading-Unity Dao society which was crushed only in the 1950s. A governmental Chinese Daoist Association was established in 1957, later than societies controlling other religions. But the spirit of Daoism remains as a pervading influence in Chinese life, appealing to the traditional love of nature, reflecting scepticism towards doctrinaire programmes and military excesses, and cultivating physical and spiritual health.

SHINTO

When Buddhist monks arrived in Japan in the sixth century A.D. they called the religion of the country *Shen-Tao*, the "Way of the Gods", contrasted with the Way of the Buddha. There was no writing, and the monks wrote down the Chronicles of Japan (*Nihongi*) which give Shinto mythology and traditional stories of the country.

It is said that in the beginning heaven and earth were not yet separated into *Yo* and *In*, like the Chinese Yang and Yin. Then appeared the chief deity, the sun goddess Amaterasu. Her brother the storm god, Susanowo, made Amaterasu hide in the cave of heaven till she was induced to emerge by other deities, a myth explaining light and dark, summer and winter, and eclipses. Later Amaterasu sent her grandson

Ninigi to rule the earth and marry the goddess of Mount Fuji, and they were the ancestors of the first emperor of Japan, Jimmu Tenno. Thus, the royal family claimed descent from the supreme deity, while other notables took various gods as their ancestors.

There are countless Shinto deities, associated with mountains and earth, rain and wind, sea and harbours, food and fertility. One of the most popular is Inari the rice god who is represented by the fox and has many images in this form. Japanese love of nature appears in pilgrimages which are made to sacred mountains, and in the location of their temples. Traditionally Shinto temples were small wooden buildings, based on ancient patterns which are constantly renewed, situated in large parks with fountains and decorative rocks, but many smaller shrines are by the wayside or in towns.

When Buddhism came, Dual Shinto was formed and many temples came under Buddhist control, being embellished with images and ritual. After the first contact with Europeans Japan was closed to the West from the seventeenth century to 1854 and the country was ruled by feudal dictators (Shoguns). But Shinto revival gathered strength and was associated with the emperor as the descendant of Amaterasu. In 1868 the emperor Meiji was restored to effective power and State Shinto was established. Adoration of the emperor grew and reverence to the imperial portrait was imposed in all public life and in schools, even those of Buddhists and Christians. For a time it was said that Shinto was a world religion, since the emperor was child of the sun. This emperor-centred Shinto was not traditional though it inspired fanatical patriotism, and in 1946 the emperor repudiated "the fictitious idea that the emperor is manifest god".

The State Shinto shrines were disestablished in 1947 and had to rely on public support. But many great national shrines, like that of Amaterasu at Ise, have remained important and are attended on occasions of national significance. The ordinary Shinto shrines are directed by bodies of priests who perform the rituals, and lay people attend to offer prayers and recite texts. The quietness and beauty of the surroundings add to their attraction and they are visited by parents and children. In Japanese homes there are shelves for Shinto or Buddhist symbols, at which incense, leaves and water are regularly offered.

Sect Shinto

After the establishment of State Shinto it was seen that distinction would have to be made for popular modern movements which were called Sect Shinto. Some of the new sects are Buddhist, and others centre on mountain pilgrimages, but the most notable are communities in which healing by faith is important. They are like societies or churches, with known founders, and relatively monotheistic. "The Teaching of Golden Light" (*Konko-kyo*) was founded in the last century by Kawade Bunjiro who said that the god of golden metal possessed him and was the sole deity. Though a Shinto priest Bunjiro denounced narrow patriotism and taught the need for sincere rather than ritual prayer. About the same time a woman, Miki Nakayama, founded "the Teaching of Heavenly Wisdom" (*Tenri-kyo*). She practised healing by faith and encouraged her followers to work communally at building temples, schools and houses. A new city of Tenri has been built round a sanctuary where it is believed that a new age will soon begin. This is one of the richest and largest religious organizations, with more than 2 million followers and thousands of missionary teachers.

In 1930 the "Creative-Value Study Society" (*Soka Gakkai*) arose from the militant Nichiren sect of Japanese Buddhism. Suppressed during the war, it has strong support among the working classes and has been linked with a political party (*Komeito*) which has members in the Japanese Diet.

Christianity in Asia and the Pacific

Christianity began as an Asian religion, and although its chief expansion was to the West yet it has remained in minorities in the Near East and has spread in missions to most Asian countries. The Syrian Orthodox Church in India claims to have been founded by the Apostle Thomas and there is evidence of its existence at least from the fifth century. The rites and traditions are derived from the Jacobite Church of Syria, which separated from other Orthodox churches after the Council of Chalcedon in 451. These Indian churches are divided into Orthodox Syrian and Mar Thoma Syrian, and a further section has been in communion with Rome since the seventeenth century as one of its Uniate churches. These Syrian Christians are found almost exclusively in Malabar, Travancore and Cochin, and number over a million. Other Christian communities all over India are the result of modern Western missions and have 12 million adherents, of whom more than half are Roman Catholics. In Pakistan there are a million Christians.

Burma and Sri Lanka have each about a million Christians, the latter being largely Roman Catholic and strong among the mixed Ceylonese peoples. In Indonesia there are over 6 million Christians, mostly Protestant, and about 3 million in Viet-Nam and over 5 million in Korea. Japan has a profusion of Christian sects, with over a million members. Christianity has had a long and chequered history in China. Nestorian missionaries were active there from the seventh century to the ninth, Jesuits and others from the sixteenth, and there were many missions in modern times. The last censuses gave over 3 million Chinese Christians, but all foreign missionaries have been expelled. There are Patriotic Catholic and Protestant Associations, and two Roman Catholic cardinals visited Beijing in 1980.

The Philippines is the one Christian nation in Asia, with over 30 million Roman Catholics and 4 million Protestants. The first missionaries arrived in the sixteenth century and mass movements led to the formal Christianization of the whole population within a century, with the non-Christian culture largely replaced by that of the Spanish missionaries.

In Oceania both missions to indigenous populations and the influx of many Europeans, especially in Australia and New Zealand, led to the dominance of Christianity. Most of the Maoris, Fijians, Samoans and Tongans were converted from the nineteenth century onwards, but there are smaller numbers of Christians in Papua New Guinea. There are an estimated 10 million Protestants and 4 million Roman Catholics in Oceania, including Australia and New Zealand.

BIBLIOGRAPHY

GENERAL

LING, T. O. A History of Religion East and West (London and New York, 1968).

MOORE, A. C. Iconography of Religions (London, 1977).

PARRINDER, E. G. (ed.) Man and his Gods (London, 1971).

A Dictionary of Non-Christian Religions (London and Philadelphia, 2nd edn., 1981).

ISLAM

CRAGG, K. Counsels in Contemporary Islam (Edinburgh and Chicago, 1965).

The Wisdom of the Sufis (London, 1976).

DAWOOD, N. The Koran (Harmondsworth, 4th edn., 1974).

FISHER, H. J. Ahmadiyya (Oxford, 1963).

GUILLAUME, A. Islam (Harmondsworth and Baltimore, 1954).

KHAN, M. Z. Muhammad, Seal of the Prophets (London, 1980).

NASR, S. H. Living Sufism (London, 1972).

PARRINDER, E. G. Jesus in the Qur'ān (London, 2nd edn., 1976).

RAHMAN, F. Islam (London, 1966).

SMITH, M. The Way of the Mystics (London, 1976).

TRIMINGHAM, J. S. The Sufi Orders in Islam (Oxford, 1971).

WATT, W. M. Muhammad, Prophet and Statesman (Oxford and New York, 1961).

Bell's Introduction to the Qur'ān (Edinburgh and Chicago, 1970).

HINDUISM

BASHAM, A. L. (ed.) A Cultural History of India (Oxford, 1975).

CHAUDHURI, NIRAD C. Hinduism: A Religion to Live By (Chatto and Windus, London, 1979).

DE BARY, W. T. (ed.) Sources of Indian Tradition (New York and London, 1958).

DESHPANDE, P. Y. The Authentic Yoga (London, 1978).

EMBREE, A. T. The Hindu Tradition: Readings in Oriental Thought (New York, 1966).

MICHELL, G. The Hindu Temple (London, 1977).

O'FLAHERTY, W. D. Hindu Myths (Harmondsworth, 1975).

The Rig Veda, An Anthology (Harmondsworth, 1981).

PARRINDER, E. G. The Wisdom of the Forest: Sages of the Indian Upanishads (London, 1975).

SINGH, K. Gurus, Godmen and Good People (Delhi, 1975).

STUTLEY, MARGARET and JAMES. A Dictionary of Hinduism (Routledge and Kegan Paul, London, 1977).

ZAEHNER, R. C. Hinduism (Oxford and New York, 1962).

Hindu Scriptures (London and New York, 1965).

PARSIS

BARUCHA, E. S. D. Zoroastrian Religion and Customs (Bombay, 3rd edn., 1979).

BOYCE, M. Zoroastrians (London, 1979).

DUCHESNE-GUILLEMIN, J. The Hymns of Zarathustra (London, 1952).

HINNELLS, J. Persian Mythology (London, 1973).

ZAEHNER, R. C. The Teachings of the Magi (London and New York, 1975).

JAINS

JAINI, P. S. The Jaina Path of Perfection (Berkeley, 1979).

MOOKERJEE, S. The Jaina Philosophy of Non-absolutism (Delhi, 2nd edn., 1978).

SCHUBRING, W. The Doctrine of the Jains (Varanasi, 1962).

SIKHS

COLE, W. O., and SAMBHI, P. S. The Sikhs (London, 1978).

MCLEOD, W. H. Gurū Nānak and the Sikh Religion (Oxford, 1968).

SINGH, D. Indian Bhakti Tradition and the Sikh Gurus (Chandigarh, 1968).

SINGH, T. (ed.) Selections from the Sacred Writings of the Sikhs (London, 1960).

VAUDEVILLE, C. Kabīr (Oxford, 1974).

BUDDHISM

BRANNEN, N. S. Sōka Gakkai (Richmond, Virginia, 1968).

CONZE, E. A Short History of Buddhism (London, 1980).

DALE, K. T. Circle of Harmony (Kawata Press, Tokyo, 1975).

DUMOULIN, H. Zen Enlightenment (New York and Tokyo, 1979).

HOFFMAN, H. The Religions of Tibet (London and Münich, 1956).

LING, T. O. The Buddha: Buddhist Civiliziation in India and Ceylon (London, 1973). Buddhist Revival in India (1975).

The Buddha's Philosophy of Man; Early Indian Buddhist Dialogues (London, 1981).

PARRINDER, E. G. The Wisdom of the Early Buddhists (London, 1977).

PYE, M. The Buddha (London, 1979).

ROBINSON, R. H. The Buddhist Religion (London, 1970).

SCHLOEGEL, I. The Wisdom of the Zen Masters (London, 1975).

TUCCI, E. The Religions of Tibet (London, 1980).

WELCH, H. The Buddhist Revival in China (Harvard, 1968).

ZWOLF, W. Heritage of Tibet (London, 1981).

CONFUCIANISM AND DAOISM

BLOFELD, J. The Secret and Sublime: Taoist Mysteries and Magic (London, 1973).

CHRISTIE, A. Chinese Mythology (London, 1968).

DAWSON, R. Confucius (Oxford, 1981).

DE BARY, W. T. (ed.) Sources of Chinese Tradition (New York and London, 1960).

NEEDHAM, J., and RONAN, C. A. The Shorter Science and Civilisation in China, Vol. I (Cambridge, 1978).

SMITH, D. H. Chinese Religions (London, 1968).

Confucius (London, 1973).

The Wisdom of the Taoist Mystics (London, 1980).

WALEY, A. (Translator). The Analects of Confucius (London, 4th edn., 1956).

WALEY, A. The Way and its Power (London, 3rd edn., 1949).

WELCH, H. The Parting of the Way (London, 1957).

SHINTO

BLACKER, C. The Catalpa Bow (London, 1975).

BUNCE, W. K. Religions in Japan (Tuttle, Tokyo, 2nd edn., 1973).

HAMMER, R. Japan's Religious Ferment (London and New York, 1961).

HERBERT, J. Shinto (London, 1967).

KIDDER, E. Ancient Japan (Oxford, 1977).

MORRIS, I. The World of the Shining Prince: Court Life in Ancient Japan (Oxford, 1964).

PHILIPPI, D. L. (Translator). Kojiki (Univ. of Tokyo Press, 1968).

TSUNODA, R. (ed.) Sources of Japanese Tradition (New York and London, 1958).

VAN STRAELEN, H. The Religion of Divine Wisdom (Tokyo, 1954).

CHRISTIANITY

BARRACLOUGH, G. (ed.) The Christian World (London, 1981).

BROWN, L. W. The Indian Christians of St. Thomas (Cambridge, 1956).

COXHILL, H. W. (ed.) World Christian Handbook (London, 1972).

CROSS, F. L. (ed.) The Oxford Dictionary of the Christian Church (Oxford, 2nd edn., 1958).

DRUMMOND, R. H. A History of Christianity in Japan (Michigan, 1971).

DUMOULIN, H. Christianity meets Buddhism (La Salle, Illinois, 1974).

NEILL, S. A. History of Christian Missions (Harmondsworth, 1964).

SCHIMMEL, A., and FALATURI, A. We Believe in One God: The Experience of God in Christianity and Islam (London, 1979).

Development Problems of Asia

Dick Wilson

When Gunnar Myrdal, the renowned Swedish economist, published in 1968 his long-awaited book on Asian economic development problems, he called it *Asian Drama: An Inquiry Into the Poverty of Nations*. The drama, he explained, lay in the "inner conflicts operating on peoples' minds; between their high-pitched aspirations and the bitter experience of a harsh reality; between the desire for change and improvement and mental reservations and inhibitions about accepting the consequences and paying the price." Such conflicts are part of human history all over the world, but never have they raged with such intensity as in the Asia of our day.

Asia is, of course, increasingly difficult to view as a whole. On the one hand it embraces the world's most successful industrialized state, Japan. On the other it includes two countries of enormous size—India and China—which stand almost at the bottom of the ladder of economic development, and because of their huge populations they dwarf the better achievements of some of the smaller states of South-East Asia, and Korea, when it comes to continental generalizations.

But if one leaves Japan aside and takes what has until now been loosely called "developing Asia", then one can begin by saying that, like the countries of Africa, Latin America and the Arab world, Asia is part of the developing, under-developed or Third World. Like theirs, its economic life is for the most part old-fashioned and inefficient, characterized by subsistence farming and the minor role played by modern manufacturing industry. Many of its people are not yet touched by the money system, living by barter and exchange.

Indeed, Asia is the Cinderella of the developing world, or of what in contemporary United Nations parlance is called the "South", as distinct from the economically advanced and industrialized countries of the "North" (Europe, the U.S.A. and Japan). The dead hand of the past lies heavier on Asia than on either Africa or Latin America: the pattern of society is for the most part near-feudal. The typical peasant, who accounts for more than 70 per cent of the total population, is untutored, superstitious and sceptical about the possibility of re-ordering his environment.

Only in the 1930s and 1940s did concerted efforts begin to be made to overcome these handicaps and set in train a process of purposive economic change. Thus Myrdal, concerned to examine why the gap between North and South was widening rather than narrowing, chose to examine Asia (and especially India) because Asia represented the worst case in the development tragedy. The developing countries of Asia (excluding the Middle East), with more than one-half of the world's population, enjoy only about one-tenth of the world's wealth and production, and this share is dwindling, albeit slightly, rather than expanding. Their average Gross National Product per head in 1979 was a derisory U.S. $310, compared with $700 in Africa, $1,700 in Latin America, $4,310 in the Middle East, $6,760 in Europe and $10,500 in North America.

Yet within this overall sad picture there are enormous differences. Japan's G.N.P. per head in 1979 was $8,730, whereas India's was only $210. The best estimate for China is $260, and that is not far off the level of the South-East Asian countries. Yet the two "city-states", Hong Kong and Singapore, both enjoyed a G.N.P. per head in excess of $3,600, and these two states, together with South Korea and Taiwan, are now so successful in manufacturing industry that the West is no longer willing to accord automatic preference for their products in its own markets, and they are beginning to be termed the "threshold", "super-competitive" or "Newly Industrializing" countries.

These G.N.P. figures must be used with caution as their comparability is increasingly disputed. It is very hard to find accurate indicators of the differences in wealth between societies living in quite different climates and also in such different political systems as the communism of China or the free-enterprise democracy of India. But whatever the figures, Myrdal was right: Asia has the worst poverty in the world, with eight out of the 29 "least developed" states in the world according to the UN (Afghanistan, Bangladesh, Bhutan, Laos, Maldives, Nepal, Sikkim and Western Samoa), and almost half their population.

The Example of Japan

One country in Asia, however, stands out as a symbol of hope. In 1868 the Meiji reformers inaugurated their country's first deliberate attempt to modernize itself along Western lines. The ground which Japan has traversed since then has enabled its economy to rank third in the world after the American and the Russian in the late 1970s, after having overtaken the British and West German in terms of Gross National Product. Japan is, of course, about twice as populous as Britain or the Federal Republic of Germany, and ranks only about fifteenth in the world league for income per head or living standards, but it disposes of more current wealth and goods than any single West European country.

Since Japan is an Asian nation, and one which stubbornly refused to deal with Europeans for two decisive centuries prior to 1868, this achievement gives some vicarious pleasure, and ground for hope to other Asian countries. Recent research, however, suggests that conditions in early nineteenth-century Japan were such as to render the development of a modern form of capitalism probable, even without the Meiji revolution, and scholars are less willing now simplistically to equate the economic situation of Japan a hundred years ago with that of India or China today.

Nevertheless, Japan's success in economic modernization gives encouragement to those who yearn for a similar breakthrough in other Asian countries, just as the Japanese military defeat of Tsarist Russia in 1905 stirred the political ambitions of other Asians impatient with the European imperialist yoke. It also means that the development problems of contemporary Asia have to be discussed to the exclusion of Japan, and most of the remarks that follow are concerned with Asia minus Japan.

AGRICULTURE

The central issue in the Asian development drama is agriculture, the traditional source of livelihood for the population and still for most countries the largest single source of wealth. The methods by which rice, wheat and other crops are grown by peasants in many parts of Asia are extraordinarily old-fashioned. Pandit Nehru, the late Prime Minister of India, often used to express his astonishment that so many Indian peasants still used the plough that had been developed in Vedic times more than 3,000 years ago. Irrigation systems had been developed in many Asian civilizations (an outstanding example is to be found near the ruins of Angkor Wat in Kampuchea (Cambodia)), but chemical fertilizer, modern machinery and the development of better strains of seeds were only introduced in many Asian villages in the past decade or so.

During the first half of this century India's production of food grains increased by an annual average of about 0.5 per cent, and this was probably typical of other countries as well. Since the 1950s the tempo of improvement has quickened, and yet the average annual increase over the past two decades has been in the region of only 3 per cent. During the 1950s, harvests more or less regained their pre-war levels, but from then on it became apparent that costly inputs would be needed to maintain the momentum. As late as 1967 it was possible for the President of the Asian Development Bank (ADB) to argue that food production was still below the 1930s level. The United Nations Economic and Social Commission for Asia and the Pacific (ESCAP) calculates the average annual rate of increase in food production over developing Asia in 1970–77 at only 2.9 per cent. With the population growing at about 2 per cent a year, the per caput food increase remains marginal. Food-grain production as a whole rose by 4.9 per cent in 1981, according to the ADB.

In the 1960s the technological advances of the so-called "green revolution" quickened the tempo slightly. In conditions where weather can cause the loss of tens of millions of tons of rice or wheat in a single country, trends are difficult to establish over a short period. These crops require the application of water, neither too much nor too little, at certain stages of their growth. If the rains come too early or too late, continue too long or are unusually heavy, then crops can either shrivel into the ground or be washed out of the fields. Drought and flood are the twin terrors of the Asian farmer, and only a well-planned, sustained and expensive programme of water conservancy (strengthening river banks, reafforestation to prevent soil erosion, measures against silting, systems of irrigation and drainage canals) can provide some protection.

China suffered three consecutive years of bad weather from 1959–61, during which many people died of malnutrition and others survived on bark, grass and insects. A similar disaster, enough to impel the Communist Government to seek food aid from the UN, occurred in limited areas in the early 1980s. The Huanghe (Yellow River) flood in Northern China at the end of the Second World War took almost a million lives, and the Bengal famine of the early 1940s cost about 3 million deaths. There have been cases of actual starvation in recent years in such poor regions as Bihar in India and Java in Indonesia.

Land Reform

The reform of land tenure is one improvement which almost every Asian government has tried to make. It has both political and economic implications. Much of the success of Japan's post-war "miracle" and of Taiwan's and South Korea's rapid development in the past twenty years is owed to land reform—American-imposed during the occupation period in Japan's case. In China, Viet-Nam and North Korea, land reform was followed swiftly by co-operativization and collectivization of agriculture. China introduced the so-called People's Commune in 1958 as a model for socialist agriculture and rural life in an Asian context, but it has not so far been followed elsewhere and its future in China itself seems now in doubt. In the non-communist countries the progress of land redistribution has been slow and this has held back modernization, especially in the Indian sub-continent and the Philippines.

The consequences of collectivization are disputed by scholars: it allows public works (notably irrigation) to be carried out on a scale impossible for owners of small-holdings, yet it would appear also to diminish the incentive for enterprising peasants to produce more. The question how far collective ownership should be carried in China's villages was a central issue in the Cultural Revolution of 1966–69, and today a certain latitude is being given to the "private sector", which accounts for at least one-tenth of farm output, as well as to incentives for production. In India politicians and planners, in private at least, seem resigned to a situation where improvements in agriculture are bound initially to benefit the already better-off peasants rather than the worse-off, although this ultimately will pose a political problem. This is a matter which was given the highest priority in the sixth Five-Year Plan drafted in 1978.

Improvements in Agricultural Yield

Crop yields vary enormously in Asia. To quote from the most recent ADB report, rice production is given at 1.6 to 1.7 metric tons per hectare in India, Burma, Bangladesh, Nepal and the Philippines, but as high as 4 in Taiwan and 4.9 in South Korea. Technical reforms are now being carried out throughout the continent to level up these performances and to improve them. Only a third of Asia's land area is arable, but in most countries it has been found possible to extend the acreage sown to crops by a small proportion, and also to increase the extent of double-cropping (even, treble-cropping in some areas) on the same piece of soil. But the most important contribution to bigger harvests has been to increase yields. This is done by providing four new inputs: chemical fertilizer, artificial water supply, new and better strains of seeds and improved machinery with electrification.

The Japanese farmer applies as much chemical fertilizer to his land as the European, but his Indian or Chinese counterpart uses at best one-eighth of that amount, acre for acre. Irrigation is gradually spreading, but still fewer than one-third of Asia's farmlands are irrigated. Mechanization is not popular with the planners because it is costly and because labour is plentiful. But after years of laboratory work new hybrid strains of rice and wheat have been developed which combine the qualities of the highest yielding types in the world with the essential characteristics of the local types. To take one example, there is increased use of dwarf varieties of wheat which make the crops less vulnerable to wind and rain. But the benefits of the "green revolution" seemed to stabilize by the mid-1970s, and it is not clear how the momentum of improving yields per acre can be maintained.

Trade in Agricultural Produce

Asia continues to be a significant importer of foods from other continents. In the early 1970s Asia was importing as much as 20 million metric tons of wheat annually, and had become a net importer of rice in spite of producing almost two-thirds of the world crop. Most of this wheat and rice was shipped from North and South America and Australia, and a large proportion of it was supplied free or with liberal repayment terms under American aid. But, in a bad weather year, India has had to import up to 9 million metric tons, and China even more. In a favourable year these imports can be greatly reduced, but in a normal or average year India probably has to pay the equivalent of almost half of its total export earnings, and China and Pakistan a quarter of theirs, merely to acquire food for consumption. This is obviously unsatisfactory when the long-term need is for machinery and industrial materials to speed Asian modernization. Average calorie intake in Asia is thought to be around 2,050 per day, which is less than the minimum requirement suggested by the United Nations.

Agricultural problems extend beyond food grains to the various cash crops, ranging from tea and sugar to oilseeds and rubber, which are also economically important. Like minerals, these were an original cause of Europe's attraction to the Orient, and their commercial development (even, in some cases, introduction from other continents) was often the work of Europeans over the past century or so. Most Asian countries are still dependent on these primary commodities for their export earnings. Sri Lanka relies on tea, rubber and coconuts for 90 per cent of its export earnings and Malaysia on tin and rubber for 60 per cent. But the modern international trading system ensures that the price for such commodities (which are often perishable, with little margin for improvement and can increasingly easily be substituted by synthetic materials) tends to decline, relative to the price of the machinery and manufactured goods which Asia buys from the West.

The stabilization of commodity prices has proved an elusive goal of Asian and other under-developed countries. Asian agriculture is so old-fashioned that European and American farmers can compete, in spite of their higher labour costs, in a number of products formerly the preserve of tropical farmers and planters—soy beans and rice, for instance.

The success of the oil producers in the mid-1970s in achieving a quadrupling of the world oil price led to hopes in Asia that a similar strategy could be followed for other commodities. Commodity price trends since the early 1970s have indeed been more favourable to Asia than usual, but there is little hope of applying to other commodities the same strategies which the OPEC countries were able to use so successfully with oil.

In Malaysia the fall in the world rubber price can cause a loss of as much as £50 million in export earnings—and every time this kind of thing happens, the Government has to make painful cuts in the country's development programmes. Small wonder that the Asian governments have been vocal supporters of the UN programme for a New International Economic Order, and of UNCTAD's Integrated Commodity Programme with its Common Fund. Malaysia has, in fact, taken the lead in organizing natural rubber producers to co-ordinate their efforts to stabilize the price of natural rubber and South-East Asian producers have taken a new initiative regarding tin.

INDUSTRY

It is in this context that the urgency of industrialization in Asia should be seen. Only by developing modern industry can Asia hope to become truly independent of the West, psychologically self-confident and able to meet its own capital development needs. In fact, the roots of modern industry go back a long way, in both India and China. Jamsetji Tata launched his pioneer cotton mill in Nagpur in 1877, while Dwarkanath Tagore, the poet's grandfather, bought India's largest coal mine in 1836. Steel has been made in Manzhou (Manchuria), in north-eastern China, and in Bihar, in eastern India, since the beginning of this century. These early enterprises were small and isolated, however, and it was only in the 1950s that comprehensive industrialization schemes were pursued.

In the 1950s and 1960s industrial output in Asia expanded about tenfold, and if only heavy industry is considered, the rise was even larger. Industry was thus expanding about twice as fast as other sectors of the economy. During the 1970s expansion has been approximately 12 per cent in East and South-East Asia and a more disappointing 4 per cent in South Asia. By 1978 steel output had reached the level of about 45 million tons (Japan's production was around 120 million tons a year, more than either

Britain or West Germany, but this is not included in the calculation). Asia and Australasia (including Japan) were responsible for about one-fifth of the world's steel production.

The construction of machinery has grown tremendously. By the late 1970s both India and China were self-sufficient not only in consumer goods but also in most of the capital goods needed to make them, as well as advanced automated metallurgical and chemical equipment. Both countries are thus able to export complete industrial plant. Both also have a well developed nuclear industry, which in China's case has seen the explosion of an H-bomb several years after political disagreements which caused the departure of the Soviet scientists advising her. India too has conducted an independent peaceful nuclear explosion, but it has also utilized U.S. and European atomic technology.

China's industry was based on Soviet tutelage in the 1950s, but has since moved to a largely self-reliant basis. The "Four Modernizations" programme extending to the end of the century will, however, rely on a few key inputs of Western industrial technology as well as a more general mid-level inflow from Hong Kong. India has leant more unequivocally on foreign expertise and help. The first giant steel works to be put up under public ownership were designed by Britain, West Germany and the Soviet Union respectively—but subsequent ones were to be fully Indian-designed and Indian-built. Both countries aim at self-reliance, but India has opted more consistently for the short cuts which foreign help can provide. No country in Asia has yet been able to produce jet aircraft or large ships, except Japan, which is not only the world's biggest ship-builder, but is also responsible for more than half of current world production.

The most remarkable development of the 1970s was the growth of light industry in the smaller countries of East and South-East Asia, especially South Korea, Taiwan, Hong Kong, Singapore and the Philippines. Based fully on private enterprise, and mixing indigenous enterprise with overseas Chinese skills and the input of Western multinationals, these countries have led the Third World in the export of manufactured goods.

Industrial Priorities

In the 1950s developing Asia tended to lay stress on heavy industry, following the Soviet model in the case of China and India. By the 1960s, however, the planners in both Beijing and New Delhi had been forced to recognize the significance of light industry and the need to take into account the interests of agriculture. It was light industry which provided the household consumer goods which farmers needed, and which constituted an important incentive for their work, while agriculture and light industry also brought in the greater part of export earnings so essential for the purchase of foreign food, fertilizer and capital equipment.

But controversy continued about the role of the state and private enterprise in industry. In China and the other communist states private enterprise was eliminated or suffocated by the mid-1950s. But in the rest of Asia industrial ownership and management has been shared between the government and the private sector. In the 1940s Asian nationalist politicians were sometimes suspicious of native capitalists and their almost "unpatriotic" collaboration with foreign interests. Thus Pandit Nehru was a notable advocate of the public sector, and his daughter Indira Gandhi, during her premiership of India, reduced yet further the role of the private sector. But the trend of the 1970s seemed to go on the whole in favour of incentives and private enterprise, even in the China of Vice-Chairman Deng Xiaoping. It is those few countries which have firmly turned their back on private enterprise, such as Burma, which have been the least successful in development.

FINANCE

The speed of development of Asian agriculture and industry depends heavily on the amount of funds available. This in turn is primarily dictated by the domestic savings and taxes of each country itself, but, given the low standard of living, the margin for capital accumulation is naturally small. Assistance is therefore sought from outside, in four principal forms: aid, export earnings, remittances and foreign investment.

Domestic Savings

Most Asian governments derive only about a fifth of their revenues from direct taxation such as income tax. Unlike the typical Western government, they depend more on customs duties and other indirect taxes. The tendency is for them to find it increasingly hard to obtain compulsory savings from their people through taxation.

Improvement of agricultural yields has primarily benefited the farmer, on whom the state finds it difficult to impose taxation. Some of the Indian states are actually abolishing land revenue at a time when the planners in the centre are desperately calling for more funds to be raised from the land. It is politically impossible, within India's democratic structure, for the Government to impose an agricultural income tax. And even in China, where more authoritarian methods are accepted, the central government is not always able to get what it wants from the localities. As the political balance of power shifts from the urban to the rural population throughout developing Asia, the prospect for centrally organized savings diminishes.

Domestic savings are not encouraged by the severe inflation which has periodically plagued most of the Asian countries, rising to some 600 per cent a year in Indonesia during the mid-1960s, for example.

Aid

Asia is an important beneficiary of the West's economic aid programme, currently receiving about half of the total which is annually disbursed to the Third World. A similar proportion of the communist states' aid (including China's, China being until recently a donor rather than a beneficiary) goes to the developing countries of Asia. In the early 1970s the total net flow of aid from the West to developing Asia was between $4,000 million and $5,000 million a year, having maintained an average of about $3,000 million a year during the 1960s. But there was something of a standstill after 1973, with the recession and the oil crisis. Communist aid to developing Asia has been calculated at $7,250 million in the 23 years ending December 1976—of which about $5,000 million came from the Soviet Union, $1,250 million from Eastern Europe and $1,000 million from China. But the climate for aid worsened appreciably in the 1970s with the diminution of the Cold War rivalry between the U.S.A. and the Soviet Union; the political disenchantment of the "North" with the politics, extravagance and corruption of the "South"; and the resentment in the North of the South's success in raising the world oil price through cartel action. Graft tarnishes the image of Asian development, a spectacular case being that of Thai dictator Field Marshal Sarit, who amassed at least £12 million during his five years as Prime Minister.

Aid has to be paid for, and the burden of debt service has now become a major issue in the North-South dialogue. Western donors have only just begun to consider writing off past debts, and yet a country like India or Pakistan might have to earmark between a fifth and a quarter of its entire export earnings for debt service. The capacity of such countries to borrow further is questioned, and this alone would seem enough to ensure the de-emphasis of aid as an agent of development. Willy Brandt, the former West German Chancellor, has said that the traditional concept of foreign aid has now become obsolete, and certainly the greater part of the diplomatic energy expended by Asia goes into the quest to restructure the world economy rather than to seek more financial handouts. It is in any event recognized that foreign aid contributes only a small fraction of the total funds which are devoted to Asian development, the vastly greater part coming from the people's own savings and taxes.

Investments, Remittances and Exports

Foreign private investment is also a relatively small item in the total picture. Many Asian governments, notably that of India, regulate private investment too closely for Western businessmen's comfort. In China, it was ruled out until 1978–79. But an influential place is nevertheless occupied in India, and in the smaller developing countries in Asia, by Western firms usually operating in association with local capital. Their role in the transmission of techniques, both managerial and technological, is particularly appreciated. Pioneer industries in many newly industrializing countries are favoured by tax holidays, tariff protection and other privileges; the South-East Asian countries are especially noted for this. At the same time, there is a certain suspicion on the part of local businessmen and politicians, as well as civil servants and economists, about the trans-national corporations which are felt to be skilled at minimizing their financial contribution to the host country.

A relatively underestimated factor in external finance is remittances from nationals living overseas. China and India have always had a regular income in foreign exchange from this source, mainly from those living in South-East Asia, East Africa and the Persian Gulf, and the Indian Government has from time to time sought to encourage the flow of such funds back into India. But recently the flow of Indian immigration into Britain has resulted in a much larger source of foreign exchange, and China too is planning to encourage its overseas Chinese to send more funds home to development, as well as "exporting" labour for big overseas construction projects.

But the basic way for a country to earn its own foreign exchange is by exporting, and increasing attention is now being paid to this. Unfortunately, as we have seen, the traditional crops and other primary commodities in which Asia is so rich are tending to fall behind in prices. High hopes are therefore placed on the export potential of Asia's new light industry, especially textiles, plastic goods, electronics and other light machinery. The trouble is that the rich industrialized markets have now become reluctant to allow an unlimited increase in the entry of cheap manufactures. With the economic recession of the past few years and rising unemployment in most Western countries, protectionism has become more common.

Nevertheless, the most enterprising of the Asian developers have gained substantial shares of North American and European markets in these manufactures in spite of attempts to regulate them, notably under the international long-term textile export arrangements which have been negotiated in Geneva since 1962. The extension of the so-called Multi-Fibre Agreement at the end of 1981 was made conditional on a much more restrictive regime demanded in particular by the EEC. So far the experiment of internationally regulating the import of low-cost manufactures from Asia has been confined to textiles, although the industrialized countries have unilateral quotas on some household goods, toys, radios and television sets when they come from low-wage countries in Asia and elsewhere. This has become a matter of very great concern to GATT, particularly when the EEC tried to make the so-called Tokyo Round of multilateral tariff cuts dependent on a new mechanism by which it could more readily restrict low-cost imports.

POPULATION

All of Asia's problems are compounded by population growth. The various national censuses taken in 1960–61 showed, for the first time beyond doubt, that population growth in the continent was running at about 2.5 per cent a year—half as much again as what had been supposed earlier. The reasons for the faster increase are clear. In many parts of Asia the death rate was halved during the 1950s as a result of improvements in public health, medicine and hygiene. But there was no corresponding fall in the birth rate, since that is a product not only of medical progress but more importantly of changing social attitudes and economic environment. Asians are probably less troubled than Westerners by religious objections to birth control, but their traditions attach supreme importance to the family as a social unit and channel of social forces. The Indian or Chinese peasant feels that there is a premium in having a large family, especially of sons, since they alone can ensure their parents' comfortable old age and provide the hands necessary to swell the family's fortunes. Neither the authoritarian Chinese Marxists nor the Nehruvian gradualists of India have been able to make much general impact on these sentiments except among the intellectuals and urban populations.

Family planning requires a big investment in terms of propaganda, instruction and materials, and only recently has it been recognized that the allocation of funds is sufficiently worthwhile. Abortion was the principal factor in Japan's success in reducing its population growth to 1 per cent a year, but it is both costly and distasteful. India is now emphasizing sterilization as a partial answer. A Minister of Family Planning recently submitted himself for voluntary sterilization after his third child, but when Mrs. Gandhi's government tried to go too fast for public opinion on sterilization it lost popularity and a general election. The consensus is that it will take another decade or more for the results of the present family planning campaigns to be seen in a lower birth rate, and that the population growth will go on for another generation or so.

Implications of Population Growth

The latest annual survey by ESCAP shows that the 1975–80 population growth for all the developing countries of Asia was just below 1.8 per cent. China's rate was 1.3 per cent, India's 2.0, Indonesia's 2.2, Bangladesh's 2.8 and that of Pakistan 3 per cent. These figures mean that, unless there is some exceptional disaster, Asia is expected to increase its numbers by nearly 1,000 million in the last 20 years of the century—from 2,579 million at mid-1980 to 3,549 million in the year 2000. In historical perspective, one could perhaps argue that what we are seeing is the restoration of the pre-Industrial Revolution balance between the continents or civilizations. Asia probably accounted for two-thirds of mankind at the time of Napoleon, but the population expansion in nineteenth century Europe and its offshoots in other continents reduced that proportion to 55 per cent by 1950. Asia's share of world population reached 58 per cent in 1980 and this is expected to remain roughly constant until the end of the century.

In the 1950s Asian intellectuals often disbelieved Western warnings about population pressure, thinking that the West was frightened of the prospect of larger numbers of Asians, but today there is agreement in Asia about the need, for domestic reasons, for limiting population growth. The Asian Conference on Children and Youth in National Planning and Development in 1967 concluded that, "Population growth is endangering the quality of mankind, as a large part of national resources must be devoted to simply maintaining existing levels of living, leaving few resources available for improving those levels." In a year of reasonable weather a typical Asian economy will expand by perhaps 4 per cent, but half of that painfully gained advance must be written off from the start because of the 2 per cent growth in population. To put it another way, if the Indian population had remained stable since 1947, the gain in per caput annual income since then would be four times bigger than it actually is. Economics, as one commentator has put it, "just does not have a chance against reproduction." Even the anti-Malthusian Chinese communists now concede that birth control promotes economic development.

It will also help to alleviate what is going to be Asia's most distressing problem in the decades to come, namely how to provide gainful employment for the vast numbers of school leavers now entering the adult labour market. The age structure is such that every other Asian is under 21. The workforce in Asia was expected to expand by more than half during the 1960s and 1970s, according to the 1965 Asian Conference on Industrialization report, creating a need for 336 million new jobs. Even in authoritarian China the communists find it difficult to get school leavers to work on the land. Education in the past has been a passport to white-collar work, and manual labour is still despised. Hence the Chinese communists' insistence on everybody, no matter how important they may be, doing some manual work every year, and the Chinese preference for part-time schools which pay their own way from their own part-time production. The most recent ADB agricultural survey predicted that unemployment could rise to a level of 15 per cent or even 20 per cent in developing Asia unless governments act quickly to create new job opportunities.

EDUCATION

If anything has been learned in Asia in the past two or three decades it is that modernization means more than juggling with economic structure and putting in new investments. The burden of Myrdal's *Asian Drama* was the necessity to change the social structure —people's social and traditional values—if a modern type of economic development were to succeed. What is the use of creating an ultra-modern steel mill in India if you can see in its shadow peasants continuing to use pre-historic methods of cultivation, refusing to limit their families and faithfully observing such traditional Hindu taboos as that against slaughtering useless cows. Educational reform—what the economist calls the human factor—is fundamental to everything else.

Probably about 6 out of 10 of Asia's school-age children actually attend school between the ages of five and fourteen. Another one goes out to work, while the remaining three stay at home to help in the house. The Asian governments agreed at a 1960 UNESCO Conference in Karachi that they would try to achieve seven years of compulsory free primary education by 1980. But even that modest goal is held up by lack of funds and a shortage of trained teachers.

The strain which the population growth places on educational services can be enormous: in the Indian state of Orissa the number of school children has quadrupled in the past decade. Teachers are badly paid in most Asian countries, and whereas Asian Ministers of Education agreed at a conference in Tokyo in 1962 that they would spend between 4 and 5 per cent of their G.N.P. on education, their actual subsequent performance was only about two-thirds of that. The average annual spending on education is about $2 per head, compared with about $75 in Britain.

Illiteracy thus remains a damaging problem in Asia, where only one in three people can read and write. In Nepal the ratio is only one in twenty. Illiteracy tends to be self-perpetuating in a society like India where the education system discriminates against women. It is estimated that more than three-quarters of Indian mothers are illiterate, and thus unable to teach their children.

Asia is not lacking in brilliant intellects, and has produced many Nobel Prize winners in scientific subjects. The Chinese and Indian nuclear programmes are evidence of what can be done when the political authorities consider it important enough, but the diffusion of knowledge and science down to the schools, especially in the rural areas, leaves much to be desired.

PLANNING

These are the principal problems facing the drive for modernization in Asia. How has economic strategy itself developed over recent years? It goes without saying that the concept of central planning is now broadly accepted. When India, China and Pakistan launched their first Five-Year Plans in the first half of the 1950s, Asia demonstrated its preference for planning. Only colonial Hong Kong maintains an unfashionable laissez-faire policy towards its economy, and with considerable success. But then, its challenge is a small one by comparison with India or China.

Not that the plans have kept out of trouble. China's Second Plan was thrown out almost before it began in favour of the ill-fated Great Leap Forward, while the Third Plan had to be delayed for three years because of the economic setbacks that followed. The Chinese Government was unable to publish comprehensive targets or details of its current Plan because of the uncertainties surrounding the economy. India's Fourth Plan was also delayed by three years because of the stagnation caused by crop failures and war with Pakistan. Today, China seems in practice to be working on annual rather than quinquennial plans, while India has now decided to proceed by "rolling" five-year plans, although the Sixth Plan draft was made ready in early 1978.

CHINESE AND INDIAN PERFORMANCE

The idea of planning, however, remains a fixed part of the Asian scene. Its content has altered as experience gradually reveals the deficiency of the so-called Mahalanobis model in India or the Soviet pattern in China, both of which placed great stress on heavy industry which needed either a high rate of savings or a large inflow of aid. Most countries have now learnt that there is a political limit to the forcing upwards of savings in a poor economy, as well as a limit to aid handouts in a growingly sceptical world, and that a balance between agriculture, heavy industry and light industry is a condition of steady growth.

It is surprising, perhaps, that China has shown itself to be the more temperamental developer. In 1958 China plunged with little preparation into an entirely new and imaginative policy, the Great Leap Forward. By mobilizing manpower on an unprecedented scale, decentralizing planning and stimulating the whole nation into a frenzy of hard work, the Chinese leaders managed to double the growth rate from about 6 to 12 per cent. But this tempo could not be maintained, and the economy then entered a recession which lasted for several years, compounded by bad weather. Tremendous resources were wasted, for example, in the campaign to construct backyard steel furnaces in every village. Yet the Leap contained some features that made sense for Chinese conditions, notably the emphasis on the development of rural industries as a means of preventing open-ended urbanization: there was no question of China going back again to the Russian model.

The Indian Plans have gained universal fame as models of a distinctively Indian reconciliation between three goals—a high rate of economic growth, greater social justice and democratic freedom. But the emphasis has changed over the past 30 years and, after pressure from the growing Indian business community and external advisers (notably the Americans, the source of most of India's foreign aid, and the World Bank), the Government after Nehru's death began to liberalize the controls by which it had enforced planning. From the mid-1960s onwards, entrepreneurs and industrialists had more freedom, while the rural sector was given more attention. The Indian case is not only the largest, but it is perhaps the most difficult development challenge in Asia. India hoped to double the per caput income of its people over a generation. This would have meant an annual per caput income growth of about 3 per cent, which (because of the population growth rate) in turn meant an overall economic growth rate of over 5 per cent. If this could have been maintained after five Plans by the mid-1970s, the average Indian could have hoped to enjoy the far from princely annual income of £50.

But this modest goal proved over-ambitious. After three Plans costing £16,000 million in new investment, per caput income at constant prices rose by only 2 per cent a year. India began to do better in the late 1970s, and the Fifth Plan covering 1974 to 1979 aimed at a growth rate of 4.5 per cent.

Most of the other developing countries in Asia have done little better than India, and ESCAP reported average annual growth of about 5 per cent in developing Asia as a whole in the three years 1975–77, to bring up the Gross Domestic Product per head to about $165 in 1977. China's growth has been estimated in the period 1952–75 at 5.8 per cent, a surprisingly high figure, but one fixed on a base year when the effect of decades of civil war and fighting against Japan were still evident in the economy. The 1981 growth rate was officially calculated at 4.5 per cent.

In the so-called economic development race between India and China, the two contenders for big-power status on the Asian mainland, conclusive comparisons are impossible because of the different methods by which the figures are calculated. The best conclusion is that the Indian tortoise has not, so far, compared unfavourably with the Chinese hare, but that the revolutionary base for future modernization is better secured in China than in India. Development in China has been better spread, but also more fluctuating. Critics used to deplore the excesses of the Chinese communists, but it is now being realized that rapid modernization requires changes in social attitudes which only a forceful overthrow of vested interests can decisively accelerate.

INTERNATIONAL ORGANIZATIONS

The international forums and frameworks within which Asian economic development issues are discussed are now legion. The earliest in the field were the Colombo Plan, a largely British initiative which pioneered the concept of long-term planning, and ESCAP which has a permanent secretariat in Bangkok dealing with all problems of development affecting the area. Its annual conference provides a sounding board for the region's economic preoccupations, and its research studies are invaluable. It has helped to set up the Asian Institute for Economic Development and Planning, the Asian Development Bank and the Asian-Pacific Telecommunity. It is justifiably proud of its achievement in gaining the co-operation for most of the time of the four riparian countries sharing the Mekong River (Kampuchea, Laos, Thailand and Viet-Nam, a quartet which is far from harmonious politically and from which Kampuchea is currently dissociating itself) in an ambitious multinational project to harness the river's energy for the common good.

But ESCAP is a creature of its governments and a prisoner of the UN bureaucratic style, inhibited by the attendance of non-Asian states (including the United Kingdom, France, the Netherlands and the U.S.A.). It has failed to achieve the authority of its sister organizations in Africa and Latin America, if only because of the extraordinary heterogeneity of the area it has to cover.

Asia is of course a prominent voice in many of the international organizations dealing with development, of which the United Nations Conference on Trade and Development (UNCTAD) is perhaps the most important. The Asian governments have shared with others the disappointment over the UN's failure to carry through the goals of the First Development Decade of the 1960s and the Second Development Decade of the 1970s, which had as its target an annual growth of 6 per cent in all developing countries. Similarly, Asian delegates took a leading role in the formulation of the demands at the UN for a "new international economic order", and for UNCTAD's programme for commodity price stabilization. It has been generally noted, however, that the radical drive for these campaigns tends to come more from the African and Latin American delegations, and it is fairly common comment in the UN that the Asians are too busy with their own development to lend themselves to international extremism.

After a number of false starts, five South-East Asian nations have organized a grouping of their own called ASEAN (Association of South East Asian Nations) which has now taken the first steps towards regional economic co-operation, especially in communications and transport, and even, in a very limited way, in tariff reductions. A preferential trade scheme started in 1978 for 70 items whose trade between the five countries was estimated at $500 million, but intra-ASEAN trade remains at only about 12 per cent of the five countries' global trade. ASEAN, with an economic growth rate of 6.5 per cent in 1977 was recently hailed by *The Economist* as the next big capitalist bloc to join the U.S.A., Western Europe and Japan among the developed regions of the world.

From time to time there are proposals for a larger grouping centred on the Indian sub-continent. In 1977 the Government of Iran proposed a common market comprising Afghanistan, Bangladesh, India, Iran and Pakistan. ESCAP has also pioneered efforts to get the Asian developing countries to collaborate and to promote their trade with each other, with such institutions as a Clearing Union and, most recently, a food bank. But political trust between these countries is still fragile and the atmosphere can be guessed from the fact that none of them is willing to merge its national airline into a regional enterprise.

JAPAN AND AUSTRALIA

Japan was the first country whose Prime Minister was invited to meet the five ASEAN heads of government after their summit in 1977, and Australia and New Zealand were the second and third. No other countries were accorded this honour. Japan, Australia and New Zealand are also full regional members of ESCAP, a particular compliment for the two Anglo-Saxon powers which enjoy considerable goodwill in the continent, especially among the other Commonwealth countries. There was even in 1978 the first Asian and Pacific heads of government Regional Commonwealth Meeting, held in Sydney.

Japan is not only the biggest donor of aid to the Asian region after the U.S.A., but is also the only big industrial power to have an unreservedly vital stake in the stability and progress of the area. While the European states have withdrawn militarily from Asia, and the U.S.A. has left the mainland and could always retreat further in an excess of isolationism, Japan, as one of its foreign ministers used to remark, cannot move to the other side of the Pacific. Until very recently, Japan left the initiative in Asian affairs to the Americans, but is now taking a more active role. Regular conferences are held at a ministerial level with many of the Asian developing countries, under Japanese sponsorship, to promote co-operation in various economic matters. Indonesia in particular, whose economic waywardness was the despair of most Western governments, is now widely seen as a "Japanese responsibility" in the sense that Japan is expected to take the most active interest in its progress. Asians remember with indignation the Greater East Asia Co-Prosperity Sphere of an earlier generation, and the Japanese are still regarded with some reserve. But they are bound to play an increasingly helpful part in the region and have pledged a considerable increase in aid. The plan endorsed in 1977 by the Trilateral Commission to double Asian rice output over fifteen years by doubling investment in agriculture to $3,500 million was the invention of Japan's great development economist and subsequent Foreign Minister, Saburo Okita.

Australia's and New Zealand's position is ambivalent. On the one hand their standard of living exceeds that even of many European countries, let alone Asia, and they have fairly strict barriers against Asian immigration. On the other hand, like the Asian developing countries, they are still largely dependent on primary commodities rather than manufacturing, and are fully in favour of international commodity price stabilization programmes. The relationship between Australia and Japan is an awkward one, and some Australians still criticize the process by which Australia is apparently condemning herself to a role of providing raw materials (iron in particular) to feed Japan's industries. But as Britain gradually recedes from South-East Asia, and as American support becomes more questionable, the Australians and New Zealanders become aware that their self-interest lies in forging closer links with their Asian neighbours.

BIBLIOGRAPHY

ASIAN DEVELOPMENT BANK. Asian Agricultural Survey (Tokyo, 1969).

Rural Asia: Challenge and Opportunity (New York, 1978).

BRANDT REPORT: NORTH–SOUTH. A Programme for Survival (London, 1980).

THE COLOMBO PLAN. 29th Annual Report (Colombo, 1981).

EAST-WEST CENTER. Asia and the Future (Honolulu, Hawaii, 1970).

FAR EASTERN ECONOMIC REVIEW. Asia 1982 Yearbook (Hong Kong, 1981).

INTERNATIONAL DEVELOPMENT CENTRE OF JAPAN. A Study of Industrialization of Five Countries in Southeast Asia (Tokyo, 1974).

JOURNAL OF DEVELOPMENT PLANNING NO. 1. Economic Cooperation among the Member Countries of the Association of South East Asian Nations (New York, 1974).

KOJIMA, KYOSHI. (ed.) Structural Adjustments in Asia-Pacific Trade (Tokyo, 1973).

LEHMANN, DAVID. (ed.) Agrarian Reform and Agrarian Reformism (London, 1974).

MYRDAL, GUNNAR. Asian Drama: An Inquiry into the Poverty of Nations (Pantheon Books, New York and London, 1968).

OHKAWA, KAZUSHI, and KEY, BERNARD. Asian Socio-economic Development (Tokyo, 1980).

OKITA, SABURO. The Developing Economies and Japan (Tokyo, 1980).

SHINOHARA, MIYOHEI. Emerging Industrial Adjustment in Asian-Pacific Area (in Asian Pacific Community, Tokyo, 1981).

TURNER, LOUIS (et al.). Living with The Newly Industrializing Countries (Royal Institute of International Affairs, London, 1980).

UN. Economic Survey of Asia and the Pacific, 1978 (Bangkok and New York, 1979).

Industrial Developments in Asia and the Far East, Vols. I-IV (New York, 1966).

WILSON, DICK. Asia Awakes (London and New York, 1970).

WONG, JOHN. ASEAN Economies in Perspective (London, 1979).

Major Commodities of Asia and the Pacific

Aluminium

Aluminium is the most abundant metallic element in the earth's crust, comprising about 8 per cent of the total. It has important applications as a metal because of its lightness, ease of fabrication and other desirable properties. Other products of alumina (aluminium oxide) are also important industrial minerals for use as refractories, abrasives, glass manufacture, other ceramic products, catalysts and absorbers. Alumina hydrates are used for the production of aluminium chemicals, fire retardant in carpet backing, industrial fillers in plastics and related products. The major markets for aluminium are in building and construction, transportation, consumer durables, electrical machinery and equipment, and the packaging industry. About one-third of aluminium output is consumed in the manufacture of transport equipment, especially road motor vehicles, where the metal is increasingly being used as a substitute for steel. Also, the development of an aluminium/air energy cell for electric car propulsion, producing recyclable aluminium tri-hydroxide, promises a substantial extension of the use of the metal in the transportation industry. Another 15 per cent is used on packaging and cans. Aluminium cans may be recycled more easily than glass or plastic containers.

Bauxite is the principal aluminium ore, although experimental plants have used nepheline syenite. The developing countries, with 70 per cent of known bauxite reserves, supply 50 per cent of the ore required. The industry is structured in three stages: bauxite mining, alumina refining and smelting. The aluminium is separated from the ore by modifications of the Bayer-Hall processes. After mining, bauxite is fed to process directly if mine material is adequate (as is the case in Jamaica and the U.S.A.) or it is crushed and beneficiated. Where the ore presents handling problems, or weight reduction is desirable, it may be dried.

At the alumina plant the ore is slurried with spent-liquor directly, if the soft Caribbean type is used, or, in the case of other types, it is ball-milled to reduce it to a size which will facilitate the extraction of the alumina. The bauxite slurry is then digested with caustic soda to extract the alumina from the ore while leaving the impurities as an insoluble residue. The liquor, with the dissolved alumina, is then separated from the insoluble impurities by combinations of sedimentation, decantation and filtration and the residue washed to minimize the soda losses. The clarified liquor is concentrated and the alumina precipitated by seeding with hydrate. The precipitated alumina is filtered, washed and calcined to produce alumina. The smelting of the aluminium is generally by electrolysis in molten cryolite, but one producer has recently introduced a smelting process where a molten mixture of lithium and sodium chlorides is used. Because of the high consumption of electricity by the smelting process (it takes 16,000–17,000 kWh. of electricity to produce one metric ton of aluminium), alumina is usually smelted in areas where low-cost electricity is available. In 1982, however, Mitsui Alumina of Japan announced that it had developed a method of smelting and refining aluminium which does not require electricity (the Kuwahara process).

Australia is the world's largest producer of bauxite ore (about 35 per cent and nearly 30 per cent of world alumina), with huge deposits in Western Australia, the Northern Territory and Queensland. The availability of bauxite and alumina and of cheap power (the country's huge coal resources) also means that Australia is a desirable location for aluminium smelters; there are three operating, with an annual capacity of about 350,000 metric tons of aluminium. The largest of the smelters is at Bell Bay in Tasmania and at least eight new smelters were planned or under construction (although three projects have been either cancelled or deferred in Queensland and New South Wales and increased electricity charges in Victoria threatened the cancellation of another at Portland for a time), which will boost Australia's production of aluminium to about 1.5 million tons by the end of the 1980s.

India and Indonesia are both relatively important producers in Asia. Indeed, experts say that India, with reserves estimated at 2,270 million tons (only Australia and Guinea have more), could become one of the world's leading aluminium producers in the next ten years. However, despite plans to increase production capacity, India is struggling to keep pace with demand. The Japanese Government has given a loan to Indonesia of U.S. $87.5 million towards a project for an aluminium smelter and hydro-power plant due to begin operations in 1982. During the 1960s Malaysia was exporting about 200,000 tons of bauxite a year, but production declined considerably from over 1 million tons in 1972 to less than 400,000 tons in 1979. Malaysia is now increasing in importance as a site for aluminium smelters and an investment of $49 million for the expansion of aluminium production facilities was announced in November 1980. Meanwhile, in early 1980 an agreement was reached for a U.S. $450 million aluminium industry in the Philippines, producing 140,000 tons per year. New Zealand should have its second smelter in production by mid-1984, providing that the consortium involved finds a replacement for Alusuisse, which withdrew from the project in 1981.

In 1980 the estimated world output of primary aluminium was 15.8 million metric tons, of which about 29 per cent was produced in the U.S.A., mostly from imported ores. Prices of aluminium have recently been more stable than those of other metals. In the U.S.A. the domestic price of ingots per lb. remained steady at 25 cents during 1973, but, partly because of increased energy costs, it rose in gradual stages to 58 cents by February 1979 and to 66 cents per lb. in October. During 1980 the price increased to more than 70 cents per lb., but then fell. In May 1981, however, the price was increased from 66 to 76 cents per lb.

Despite opposition from aluminium producers, the London Metal Exchange (LME) began trading in aluminium in October 1978. Most aluminium is sold at prices fixed by producers but there is also a small "free market" and it is in this area that the LME operates. When dealing began in the new metal, in the form of primary aluminium ingots (minimum purity 99.5 per cent), it was confined to "futures" trading, i.e. buying and selling three months in advance. However, a "spot" market, for immediate delivery, was also launched the following December and opened at a price of around £620 per metric ton. The London aluminium price increased steadily, rising to £799 per ton in June 1979, although slipping in July to less than £650, before a recovery to £800 per ton in October and £900 in November.

After another fall, the London aluminium price climbed to £956 per ton in February 1980. Following a brief decline, it quickly rose to a record £962.5 per ton on April 1st but by June had declined to £681.5 per ton. The price rose to £776.5 per ton in August, fell to £662.5 in September but recovered to £702 in October. Thereafter it showed a steady downward trend, falling to £576 per ton in January 1981. It climbed to nearly £700 per ton in August, but in November fell to £539, before recovering to £628.5 in December. In June 1982 the price fell to £506.5 per ton, the lowest level since trading began, but in July it recovered to £567.5.

In March 1974 seven major bauxite-producing countries, including Australia, agreed to set up the International Bauxite Association (IBA) to promote the orderly development of the industry and to "secure fair and reasonable returns for member countries". After ratification by the seven states, representing over 60 per cent of world bauxite production, the IBA's Ministerial Council held its inaugural meeting in Georgetown, Guyana, in November 1974. The Council approved the establishment of a permanent secretariat in Kingston, Jamaica.

At the second ministerial meeting in November 1975, Indonesia joined the IBA while the Council, unable to agree a long-term price formula, made non-binding recommendations that members adopt a minimum pricing policy for all bauxite ore exported in 1976. Australia, however, had reservations about the long-term proposals. In September 1976 the IBA's executive board agreed on further recommendations to govern bauxite prices, but again, at the third Council meeting, no agreement was reached on a long-term pricing policy. The earlier recommendations on (undisclosed) minimum price levels were renewed for 1977. In December 1977 the IBA Council decided on a fixed minimum price for base grade bauxite in the North American market, but left member countries free to negotiate prices for other markets and grades.

In December 1978 the IBA abandoned its fixed minimum price and instead agreed to index bauxite prices from 1979, initially at 2 per cent of the average U.S. list price for aluminium ingots. At the same time the IBA broadened its pricing policy to include alumina, with a recommendation that members should sell the material at 16 to 19 per cent of aluminium ingot prices. Australia again expressed reservations about IBA pricing policy, preferring to set prices after consultation with consumers. For 1982 the IBA recommended an increase of 2 per cent in the price of base-grade bauxite and of 2.5 to 3 per cent for metallurgical grade ore. These changes took into account the anticipated poor demand for aluminium in 1982.

In December 1980, at the first meeting of its type to discuss bauxite, the IBA had talks in Jamaica with the world's major aluminium-producing firms. Broad agreement was reached on the future course of the industry. The members of the IBA indicated that they would continue to seek "fair and equitable" revenues for their exports but that they did not intend to operate as a price-fixing cartel such as OPEC. In dealing with prices, the IBA did no more than make several recommendations to its members. An increase in the "floor" price of bauxite to be sold in 1981 from $26 to $30 per metric ton was suggested and it was proposed that alumina should be sold at between 16 and 19 per cent of the U.S. price for ingot.

In 1976 the OECD estimated that known world bauxite reserves were adequate to meet demand for the next 50 years. IBA member states have about 70 per cent of these reserves, produce 75 per cent of world output, but account for only 4 per cent of aluminium production. The Association's share will be increased by the participation of Brazil, whose eventual accession to membership is considered a formality. Since about 1970, however, aluminium supplies have been tight because of a surge in demand from the motor vehicle and aerospace industries. Demand continues to grow as aluminium, being lighter than steel, is important to the various transport manufacturing industries as a conserver of valuable energy. Yet in most cases new capacity has not been added to cope with this growth. The latest prediction, in the light of this, is that demand for aluminium will probably outstrip supply

PRODUCTION OF BAUXITE

(crude ore. '000 metric tons)

	1978	1979
WORLD TOTAL	82,552	85,135
Far East	4,687	4,896
Oceania*	24,642	25,541
Leading Regional Producers:		
Australia*	24,642	25,541
China, People's Republic†	1,400	1,500
India	1,663	1,949
Indonesia‡	1,008	1,058
Malaysia, Peninsular	615	387
Other Leading Producers:		
Guinea§	11,648	12,199
Jamaica‡	11,732	11,574
Suriname	5,025	4,769
U.S.S.R.†	4,600	4,600

* Twelve months ending June 30th of year stated.
† U.S. Bureau of Mines estimates.
‡ Figures refer to the dried equivalent of crude ore.
§ *Source: World Metal Statistics.*

in the 1980s, rising by 4 per cent annually. World smelting capacity, meanwhile, is likely to rise to 18 million metric tons per year by the mid-1980s.

The world economic recession and high power costs have recently caused a slump in international demand for aluminium. According to an International Primary Aluminium Institute (IPAI) report in January 1981, the aluminium ingot stocks of western aluminium producing countries had risen by 50 per cent in six months to 2 million metric tons. Further rises took stocks to over 3 million tons by the end of 1981.

Cassava (Manioc, Tapioca, Yuca) (*Manihot esculenta*)

Cassava is a perennial woody shrub, 1 to 5 metres in height, cultivated for its high starch yielding roots, principally as a food source. A native of South and Central America, it is now the most important source of non-cereal starchy food in the developing countries (except at the highest altitudes) in spite of its extreme perishability. A hardy plant with a wide range of adaption, it can withstand drought (but not frost) after early development and yields well in acidic, infertile soils—hence its exploitation as a cheap food source.

Cassava is a staple source of carbohydrates for 300 million people in the tropics. The form in which cassava is consumed is partly determined by its content of hydrocyanic (prussic) acid which, according to the level, can produce a range of tastes from bitter to sweet. Cassava is rarely eaten raw. Usually, if it is sweet, it is boiled and then eaten, or it may be soaked, pounded and fermented to make a paste (though not in Asia). After harvest, cassava is highly perishable and, if not consumed immediately, it must be processed into other forms (flour, starch, pellets, etc.). With rising wheat imports by developing countries, cassava flour can be substituted up to 20 per cent in producing composite flour. It is a cheap energy source and, when combined with a protein source, makes an ideal substitute for cereals such as barley and maize. As cereal prices have risen in the EEC, the search for cheaper alternatives to grains and the fact that cassava is not subject to the variable levy has led to an increase in cassava imports in Europe.

In the last few years there has been a marked interest in the utilization of cassava as an industrial crop rather than a food crop. Indeed, cassava has the potential to become a basic energy source for animal feed or a feedstock for ethyl alcohol (ethanol), a substitute for petroleum. In a time of high-cost energy the attraction of this is obvious. It has been estimated that from 11 U.S. cents' worth of cassava 40 per cent more "alcogas" (a blend of cassava alcohol and petrol) can be produced than from an equivalent amount of crude petroleum, with one ton of cassava yielding up to 180 litres of alcohol. It can be mixed with petrol to provide motor fuel, while the high-protein residue from its production can be used for animal feed, so there is little wastage. In the early 1980s Brazil was hoping to produce up to 400,000 automobiles per year that utilized pure alcohol. The Brazilian programme, however, relies on substantial subsidies to make its alcohol competitive.

Production of Cassava
('000 metric tons)

	1979	1980
World Total	117,505*	122,134*
Far East	40,852*	43,559*
Oceania	219*	222*
Leading Regional Producers:		
China, People's Republic	2,500*	3,000*
India	6,053	6,500*
Indonesia	13,751	13,300†
Malaysia	409*	410*
Philippines	2,249	1,900*
Sri Lanka	535	530*
Taiwan	226	174*
Thailand	11,100†	13,500†
Viet-Nam	3,800*	4,000*
Other Leading Producers:		
Brazil	24,935	24,554
Nigeria	10,500*	11,000*
Tanzania	4,500*	4,600*
Zaire	12,000†	12,500*

* FAO estimate. † Unofficial figure.

In 1981 fears of a shortage of domestically produced alcohol sent the price of hybrid fuel up and sales of alcohol-fuelled cars plummeted. Programmes designed to exploit this cheap energy source are now being formulated, notably in Thailand (largely sugar cane-based), the Philippines and Papua New Guinea.

In 1980 Asia accounted for 36 per cent of world cassava production, an increase of 12 per cent since 1970. The leading producer of cassava in the region is Indonesia but the principal exporter is Thailand. Together they produce over 60 per cent of all Asia's cassava. In 1978 Thailand sold 6.3 million metric tons of processed cassava products (pellets, starch and flour), valued at 10,892 million baht (U.S. $536 million), though exports in 1979 fell to about 4.0 million tons, valued at 9,891 million baht, due to drought and the decreased production of cassava roots to only 10.7 million tons. Thailand's export earnings from tapioca products rose to 14,866 million baht in 1980 and to 16,857 million baht (U.S. $732.9 million) in 1981, when 6.67 million tons were shipped. The main importers of these products, mostly in the form of pellets, are the Netherlands, the Federal Republic of Germany, France and Belgium. Total imports by the EEC rose from 1.35 million metric tons in 1971 to 5.9 million tons (more than 90 per cent of Thailand's exports) in 1978. However, from January 1981 the EEC and Thailand agreed to limit the export of tapioca products to between 5.0 and 5.5 million tons for the next two years. This arrangement was subsequently extended to cover 1983 and 1984 as well. Import reductions will not now begin until 1985. Also in 1981, Thai exports, formerly free, were placed under the control of a government quota system.

The area under cassava has increased considerably in recent years and the number of people for whom it is a principal component of the diet could double by the year 2000. Indonesia has about 1.4 million hectares under cultivation. However, there is growing concern over evidence that the rapid expansion of cassava root planting may threaten the fertility of the soil and subsequently other crops. Under cropping systems where no fertilizer is used, cassava is the last crop in the succession because of its particular adaptability to infertile soils. Cassava itself, however, does not threaten soil fertility but rather the cultivation systems which employ it without fertilizer use.

Production figures in the table refer to fresh cassava, but may not be accurate since it is a subsistence crop.

Coal

Coal is a mineral of organic origin, formed from the remains of vegetation over millions of years. There are several grades: anthracite, the hardest coal with the highest proportion of carbon, which burns smoke-free; bituminous and sub-bituminous coal, used for industrial power, some is made into coke when the volatile matter is driven off by heating; lignite or brown coal, the lowest grade and nearest to the peat stage. Anthracite and bituminous coal are classed as "hard" coal. Coal gas is made from brown coal, but is not widely used for energy except in the U.S.S.R.

World trade in hard coal rose steadily between 1970 and 1975, reaching an estimated 194.6 million metric tons. Exports fell in 1976 to 191.0 million tons (7.9 per cent of world production), partly because of cutbacks in steel production, but recovered in 1977 to reach 198.6 million tons. In 1981 a small percentage increase took trade to 200 million tons (excluding eastern bloc trade). The main exporters are the U.S.A., Australia, South Africa, Poland (whose exports have been disrupted by recent political events), Canada and the U.S.S.R. The leading coal importer is Japan, which wants to reduce its dependence on petroleum for energy and whose own coal seams are mainly deep and therefore too expensive to mine. Production of hard coal throughout the world rose to record levels in 1980, with estimated output of 2,740 million tons, and remained at the same level in 1981.

The People's Republic of China is the world's second largest coal producer, behind the U.S.A., and has possible reserves of 600,000 million metric tons, mostly located in the North and Central regions. Recent discoveries in Anhui (Anhwei) province in eastern China have led to the development of a major new field. Official figures show that China's coal production reached 620 million metric tons in 1980, 15 million tons down on 1979's output, and stayed at this level in 1981. Only 50 per cent of China's mines are fully mechanized, however, and many of these employ out-dated Soviet technology from the 1950s. Nevertheless, with improvements, outside technical and financial assistance and the expansion of mining operations, coal production is targeted to reach 725 million tons by 1985. Coal provides about 80 per cent of China's total energy requirements and a comparatively small amount is exported. Japan reached a succession of agreements to import increasing amounts of steam coal from China (2.5 million to 2.7 million tons in 1981) and there are also nominal exports to the

PRODUCTION OF HARD COAL
('000 metric tons, excluding brown coal and lignite)

	1978	1979
WORLD TOTAL‡	2,568,873	2,695,985
Far East‡	799,606	817,728
Oceania	74,732	76,600
Leading Regional Producers:		
Australia	72,700*	74,800*
China, People's Repub.‡	618,000	635,000
India	101,290	103,445*
Japan‡	18,992*	17,644*
Korea, Democratic People's Republic†	35,000*	35,000*
Korea, Republic	18,054	18,209
Viet-Nam†	6,000*	6,000*
Other Leading Producers		
U.S.S.R.	501,536*	495,000*
U.S.A.	566,646	665,748

* Provisional or estimated figure.

† *Source:* U.S. Bureau of Mines.

‡ Figures for Japan include brown coal production (about 7 per cent of total production). Figures for China include lignite and brown coal production.

Democratic People's Republic of Korea, Pakistan, Romania and the U.S.A.

India has the fourth largest coal reserves in the world, but still needs to import some coal to meet domestic requirements. Production stagnated at about 100 million metric tons per year from 1975/76, although 1979/80 and 1980/81 saw output rise by about one-fifth. Coal mining was nationalized in 1973 but, despite enormous investment in the industry since then, it is still largely unmechanized and inefficient. Nevertheless, with foreign technology and a programme of modernization, India aims to become a coal exporter by the mid-1980s and increase production to 220 million tons per year by 1990; the Government has estimated output for 1980/81 at 133 million tons as against an expected domestic demand of just over 131 million tons. Australia is also an important coal producer in the region, mining an estimated record of 111.7 million metric tons in 1981. Coal is now one of Australia's largest export income earners, bringing in $A1,700 million in 1979/80. About one-half of Australia's production is exported, the majority of this to Japan, in particular for its steel industry. Although Australia has only 5 per cent of the world's coal reserves, it is likely to become the worlds' leading exporter because of comparatively low domestic demand for coal and its situation in unpopulated areas, inexpensive to mine. Australia is also involved with Japan in a joint project to two coal liquefaction plants. A big future is foreseen for this process, with petroleum prices rising and conventional reserves rapidly being depleted.

A report presented to the World Energy Conference in 1977 predicted that world demand for coal would rise rapidly after the mid-1980s and would reach four to six times the current level by 2020. In December 1978 the International Energy Agency of the OECD issued a report advocating "massive substitution" of coal for petroleum as a fuel source since it was expected that after 1985 the world demand for energy would outstrip supply because of oil shortages. Experts predict that coal will have to supply between one-half and two-thirds of the additional energy required by the world between 1980 and the end of the century. To do this, world coal production will have to increase by between two and three times and international trade by three to five times.

Coconut (*Cocos nucifera*)

The coconut palm is a tropical tree, up to 25 metres tall, with a slender trunk surmounted by a feathery crown of leaves. Its fruits first appear after about six years, though the palm may not reach full bearing until it is about 20 years old. It may go on fruiting for another 60 years. The fruits, green at first but turning yellow as they ripen, are often left to fall naturally but many are then over-ripe so harvesting by hand is widely practised.

Coconut, the most important of all cultivated palms, is essentially a smallholder's crop, found mainly in small plots around houses and in gardens. Its fruit, fronds and wood provide many thousands of families with a cash income as well as basic necessities such as food, drink, fuel and shelter. The palms grow with little or no attention where conditions are favourable. Over 80 varieties are known, divided broadly into tall palms produced by cross-pollination and dwarf palms which are self-pollinating. The sap of the coconut palm can be evaporated to produce sugar or fermented to make an alcoholic drink called "toddy". This may be distilled to produce a spirit called "arrack".

All parts of the fruit have their uses. Beneath the outer skin is a thick layer of fibrous husk. The fibres can be combed out to produce coir, a material used for making ropes, coconut matting, brushes, mattresses and upholstery. Inside the husk is the nut—what people in temperate areas think of as a "coconut" since the whole fruit is not usually imported. The nut has a hard shell, inside which is a thin white fleshy layer of edible "meat". The nut's hollow interior is partially filled with a watery liquid called "coconut milk" which is gradually absorbed as the fruit ripens. This "milk" is a refreshing and nutritious drink. The shells are mainly consumed locally as fuel but small quantities are used to make containers, ornaments, ladles and buttons.

After harvesting, the fruits are split open, the husk removed and the nuts usually broken open. The "meat" is sometimes eaten directly or used to prepare desiccated coconut, widely used in the bakery and confectionery trades. However, by far the most important economic product of the plant is obtained by drying the "meat" into copra, either in the sun or in a kiln which may be heated by burning the coconut shells. The dried copra is the source of coconut oil, used mainly in the manufacture of soap, detergent and cosmetics, but also as a cooking oil and in margarine production. World coconut oil production rose to more than 3 million tons in 1976, but it ranked only fifth among vegetable oils, compared with second in the early 1950s. By 1978 it was in sixth place, with production below 3 million tons. As technology advances, more uses for coconut oil are being developed. Recent experiments have shown that it can be converted into diesel fuel and the high price of petroleum suggests that a programme of conversion may be economically viable. Good copra has an oil content of about 60 per cent. Some extraction is done in the coconut-growing countries but there is a large trade in copra to countries which extract the oil themselves. The residue left after the extraction of oil from copra is a valuable oilcake for livestock feed.

The Philippines is by far the world's most important coconut producer and exporter, with coconut products accounting for 27 per cent of the country's export earnings in 1979. The country accounts for nearly 85 per cent of world coconut oil exports and over 30 per cent of world copra exports. However, copra and coconut oil represent less than one-tenth of the world's fats and oil trade. About a third of the

PRODUCTION OF COCONUTS
('000 metric tons)

	1979	1980
WORLD TOTAL	34,386*	35,422*
Far East	28,504*	29,476*
Oceania	2,498*	2,488*
Leading Regional Producers:		
India	4,300*	4,500*
Indonesia	10,700†	10,900†
Malaysia	1,364†	1,567†
Papua New Guinea	870*	780*
Philippines	9,154*	9,575*
Sri Lanka	1,819	1,550†
Thailand	688†	900†
Vanuatu	340*	346*
Other Leading Producers:		
Ghana	300*	300*
Mexico	700†	710†
Mozambique	400*	420*
Tanzania	300*	310*

* FAO estimate. † Unofficial figure.

PRODUCTION OF COPRA
('000 metric tons)

	1979	1980
WORLD TOTAL	4,491*	4,710*
Far East	3,769*	3,952*
Oceania	352*	330*
Leading Regional Producers:		
India	370*	375†
Indonesia	1,169	1,301
Malaysia	218*	219*
Papua New Guinea	160	148
Philippines	1,752	1,855
Sri Lanka	166	98
Thailand	42*	51*
Vanuatu	49†	34†
Other Leading Producers:		
Mexico	130	173†
Mozambique	65*	68*

* FAO estimate. † Unofficial figure.

population is directly or indirectly dependent on coconut for a livelihood. As a result of growing world demand, the Philippines Government is undertaking a coconut replanting programme which aims to double production by 1987. In recent years the Philippines has been crushing more of its copra production into crude coconut oil for export and gradually phasing out exports of copra. In 1981 exports of coconut oil totalled 1.05 million metric tons, compared with 914,008 metric tons in 1980. However, coconut oil exports declined in value from $564.6 million in 1980 to $533 million in 1981. Although coconut oil exports grew, due to weak demand and abortive efforts by Philippines exporters to stockpile huge amounts of the oil, the price of coconut oil fell in 1980 to 50 per cent of its 1979 high of $1,011 per metric ton and the slump continued in 1981. Output of coconut products in 1981 rose by an estimated 10 per cent from the 1980 figure of 2.1 million tons (measured in copra equivalent). Exports were also up but, due to the slump in prices, earnings actually fell to $768.8 million, compared with $833.9 million in 1980.

Production figures for copra relate only to quantities traded, no allowance being made for copra treated for oil by primitive methods. World output in 1976 reached a record level of 5.1 million metric tons, but fell to 4.6 million in 1978. Because of reduced Philippine production and increased export duties aimed at discouraging export sales, copra prices more than doubled in two years. The average import price at European ports rose from $320 per metric ton in August 1977 to $736 in July 1979, but fell steadily to $365 in October 1980. The price rose to $405 per ton in January 1981 but had fallen to $330 by May 1982. Provisional figures for 1981 indicate an increase in world output to approaching the record figures of 1976, mainly because of the continued recovery of the Philippines coconut crop, which had fallen 10 per cent below the 1978 level in 1979, due to poor weather.

A meeting of the Intergovernmental Group on Hard Fibres in March 1977 approved a proposal for the establishment of Coir International, an association of about 25 countries to promote the sale of coir and coir goods. The proposal was accepted in October by the UN Conference on Trade and Development. At present about 90 per cent of coir fibre is thrown away as waste.

Cotton (*Gossypium*)

The seed of the commercial cotton plant bears a lint or growth of hair on its epidermis. This collapses on drying and forms a ribbon which can be detached and spun. Cotton is classified by length; staple length being the length of fibre of a sample of raw cotton. Generally speaking, this length determines the texture of the resulting yarn, the longer the staple, the finer and stronger the textile. Staple lengths are between ⅝ in. and 2 in. (1.6 to 5.1 cm.) and are classified as short, medium, long and extra long. After the lint has been removed from the seed, there remains a short fuzz of fibres, known as cotton linters, which is used to make paper, cotton wool, surgical lint, rayon and other cellulose products. Cotton textiles are made into clothes, household articles and industrial products.

Cotton is the world's leading textile fibre. However, between 1960 and 1973, as the use of synthetics grew, its share in the world's total consumption of fibre declined from 68 per cent to about 50 per cent, despite an overall increase in cotton consumption of about 2 per cent each year. The rate of growth in consumption of other fibres began to decrease after 1967 and cotton prices became more competitive, partly because of the rise in costs of man-made fibres manufactured from petrochemicals but also because of the introduction of cotton market development programmes. At the same time, cotton denims and corduroy grew in popularity. However, by 1976 cotton's share of total fibre consumption had fallen below 50 per cent. Compared with cotton, man-made fibres have the advantage of producing fabrics with better "easy care" qualities, such as non-shrinking and non-creasing, but, again, cotton research and development is producing cotton textiles with improved "easy care" properties. Cotton is just managing to hold its share of the fibre market in the major consuming areas of Western Europe and Japan, although consumption of all fibres has been affected by the world economic recession.

In spite of competition from man-made fibres such as polyesters, world production of cotton lint has generally been increasing in recent years, rising from 10.7 million metric tons in 1967 to 13.9 million tons in 1974. Output fell sharply in 1975 and was even lower in 1976, partly due to a recession in the world textile industry, but recovered in 1977, mainly as a result of an expansion in the area planted because of higher prices. Cotton production exceeded 14 million tons for the first time in 1979 and remained above that figure in 1980 and 1981.

Between 1974 and 1980 world trade in cotton lint averaged about 19.3 million bales per year. The leading exporters in 1980/81 were the U.S.A. (about 30 per cent of the world total) and the U.S.S.R.

PRODUCTION OF COTTON LINT
('000 metric tons, excluding linters)

	1980/81	1981/82*
WORLD TOTAL	14,197	15,410
Far East	4,827	5,208
Oceania	104	121
Leading Regional Producers:		
China, People's Republic	2,710	2,884
India	1,301	1,409
Pakistan	695	781
Other Leading Producers:		
Brazil	613	564
Egypt	529	517
Mexico	352	305
Turkey	499	488
U.S.S.R.	3,079	2,992
U.S.A.	2,422	3,426

* Provisional.

Source: International Cotton Advisory Committee.

(about 23 per cent). The major cotton exporters are the People's Republic of China, Japan and the Republic of Korea.

Cotton is the second most important agricultural export for both Afghanistan and Pakistan. Thailand and the Philippines are increasing the area under cotton. In the Philippines a cotton development programme aims to make the country self-sufficient in cotton.

As with other commodities, cotton prices have varied considerably in recent years. However, taking a three-year moving average, prices over the period 1967–81 show a strong upward trend rising from around 30 U.S. cents per lb. at the beginning of the period to about 80 cents per lb. at the end. Various factors have contributed to these price increases, not least the improved demand for cotton in the major textile markets of Western Europe and Japan. During the first three months of 1981 the price of strict middling 1 $\frac{1}{16}$ in. cotton averaged about 96 cents per lb.

Cotton is not controlled by any international agreement but co-operation in cotton affairs has a long history. Ten producing countries held a conference in 1939, when world cotton stocks had reached about 5 million tons, to take concerted international action to maintain a sound world cotton economy. They agreed to establish the International Cotton Advisory Committee (ICAC), an intergovernmental body with its headquarters in Washington, D.C. At first, membership was limited to producing countries but after 1945 it was extended to importers. By 1980 the ICAC had 49 members, eight of them Asian countries (including Australia). It aims to promote co-operation in the solution of cotton problems and to provide a forum for international consultation and discussion.

Because of the problems faced by cotton from competition with man-made fibres in the 1960s, the ICAC recognized the need for a programme of research and promotion. To this end it was instrumental in the formation of the International Institute for Cotton (IIC), incorporated in January 1966. By 1980 the IIC, with its headquarters in Brussels, had 11 cotton-producing countries, including India, as members. The IIC is financed by contributions from its members, assessed on the basis of their exports of raw cotton and cotton textiles. It also receives voluntary financial support from a number of cotton-consuming developed countries. The IIC aims to increase consumption of raw cotton and cotton products, concentrating its efforts on Western Europe and Japan—which together account for some 60 per cent of world imports of raw cotton.

The official cotton "season" runs from August 1st to July 31st of the following year and quantities are measured in bales. In the U.S.A. one bale of cotton is conventionally 500 lb. (226.8 kg.) gross or 480 lb. (217.7 kg.) net, but international data are recorded in terms of net bales of 478 lb. (216.8 kg.) each. In 1980/81, according to the ICAC, world production was 65.5 million bales (14.2 million metric tons) while estimated consumption reached a record 66.6 million bales (14.4 million tons). World cotton stocks in August 1981 stood at 21.6 million bales (4.7 million tons), low by historical standards.

In 1979/80 world output was 66.04 million bales (14.3 million metric tons). In February 1982 the 1981/82 crop was projected to reach 71.1 million bales, mainly because of increased production in the U.S.A., China, India and Pakistan. However, consumption was not expected to be equal to this figure, so stocks were forecast to increase. Cotton consumption prospects in India, which earlier had appeared less favourable, have now improved as a result of an amelioration in power availability, labour problems and cotton's competitive position *vis-à-vis* man-made fibres derived from petroleum. As a consequence, consumption in 1981/81 is now estimated at 6.3 million bales, considerably above previous levels. Consumption in Pakistan is expected to remain around 2 million bales but production has increased substantially to over 4 million bales per year and exports of new cotton from Pakistan soared from 256,000 bales in 1978/79 to 1.2 million bales in 1979/80, with an estimate of 1.5 million bales in 1980/81. Cotton is Pakistan's biggest foreign exchange earner. Projections of consumption in the People's Republic of China are now estimated at 16.0 million bales in 1981/82, against 15.3 million bales in 1980/81. Expansion of the cotton industry is being encouraged because of the contribution it can make to economic development.

In June 1977 the secretariat of the UN Conference on Trade and Development (UNCTAD) proposed an international agreement on cotton, with the operation of a buffer stock to stabilize prices as the central feature. The UNCTAD proposals envisage that the stockpile would be financed from a common commodity fund, part of its "integrated programme" aimed at stabilizing market conditions for major primary products. Cotton is one of ten "core" commodities chosen by UNCTAD for special attention but little progress has been made on establishing a cotton agreement.

There have now been six "preparatory meetings" convened by UNCTAD to discuss the possibility of an international cotton agreement which would include price stabilization and "other measures" such as cotton research, marketing and promotion. The UNCTAD secretariat favours the establishment of a buffer stock, calculating that a reserve stock of 3 million bales (about 10 per cent of the total stocks held by cotton traders) could stabilize prices of raw cotton within an acceptable range. This proposal, supported by some developing countries which depend on cotton for foreign exchange, was opposed by the U.S.A., Japan and the EEC as an unnecessary interference with market forces.

An UNCTAD report of March 1981 found that a group of 15 multi-national companies controls nearly 90 per cent of the world's cotton trade, while developing countries, responsible for 80 per cent of production, have minimal control over prices. In 1982 the Third World's 21 main cotton-growing nations set up their own promoting body, The International Cotton Producers' Association (ICPA).

Cottonseed (*Gossypium*)

After the lint and linters have been removed from the "seed cotton", the seed itself can be processed into valuable subsidiary products. The oil extracted from cottonseed is mainly used to make margarine and cooking fat, and the residual oilcake is used as fodder and fertilizer. The husk may be used for fertilizer or fuel. Cottonseed is a significant source of protein in addition to oil. As processing methods improve, the seed element is becoming increasingly important in the cotton economy. Cottonseed is not suitable for human consumption because it contains a toxic substance known as gossypol. However, new technology is being developed to remove this toxin and so open up a new market for cottonseed flour.

PRODUCTION OF COTTONSEED
('000 metric tons)

	1979	1980
WORLD TOTAL	26,810*	26,830*
Far East	8,670*	9,632*
Oceania	87	136
Leading Regional Producers:		
China, People's Republic	4,414*	5,414*
India	2,618	2,600*
Pakistan	1,436	1,400†
Other Leading Producers:		
Brazil	1,145†	1,110†
Egypt	792	844
Mexico	605	534
Turkey	769	783
U.S.S.R.	5,954†	6,500†
U.S.A.	5,242	4,056

* FAO estimate. † Unofficial figure.

World production of cottonseed rose steadily between 1969 and 1974 (when it exceeded 26 million metric tons) but fell by 3 million tons in 1975. In 1977 world output rose to 25.7 million tons, but production fell to 24.7 million tons in 1978. World output reached record levels in 1979, 1980 and, provisionally, in 1981, a major portion of the increase coming from the U.S.A. and the People's Republic of China, with the remainder from Pakistan and the U.S.S.R.

Production of cottonseed oil reached an estimated 3,050,000 metric tons (protein equivalent) in 1975, making it the fourth most important soft vegetable oil, accounting for 12.5 per cent of the total output of such oils. In the same year exports of cottonseed oil totalled 410,000 tons, about 6.5 per cent of the world trade in soft edible oils. In the 1977/78 season cottonseed yielded 3.4 million tons of edible oil, so retaining its fourth position.

Groundnut (Peanut, Monkey Nut, Earth Nut) (*Arachis hypogaea*)

This is not a true nut, though the underground pod, which contains the kernels, forms a more or less dry shell at maturity. The plant is a low-growing annual herb introduced from South America.

Each groundnut pod contains between one and four kernels enclosed in a reddish skin. The kernels are very nutritious because of their high content of both protein (about 30 per cent) and oil (40 to 50 per cent). In tropical countries the crop is grown partly for domestic consumption and partly for export. Whole nuts of selected large dessert types, with the skin removed, are eaten raw or roasted. Peanut butter is made by removing the skin and germ and grinding the roasted nuts. The most important commercial use of groundnuts is the extraction of oil. Groundnut oil is used as a cooking and salad oil, as an ingredient in margarine and, in the case of lower quality oil, in soap manufacture. The oil faces strong competition from soya, cottonseed and sunflower oils—all produced in the U.S.A. The residue left after oil extraction is an oilcake used in animal feeding. However, trade in this groundnut meal is limited by health laws in some countries.

Production of groundnuts, having doubled since the 1920s, has fluctuated considerably in recent years, with the annual world output generally ranging from 17 to 19 million metric tons. A record crop of 19.7 million tons was produced in 1975 and provisional figures indicate that a similar level may have been achieved in 1981. About 80 per cent of the world's groundnut output comes from developing countries. India, the world's largest producer of groundnuts, is taking steps to increase production of groundnut oil for domestic consumption and aims to reach self-sufficiency in edible oils by 1983. It is therefore expected to restrict groundnut exports.

In continental Europe the average import price of groundnuts per metric ton was U.S. $500 in February 1980. It fell to $440 in May but climbed to $535 in November. The sharp reduction in the U.S. groundnut crop, due to drought, fuelled prices in late 1980 after a stable period. The second half of 1981 saw a sharp drop in the price of groundnuts. It recovered to over $700 per ton in early 1982 but fell back to $660 in May. The average Rotterdam price of groundnut oil

PRODUCTION OF GROUNDNUTS
(in shell, '000 metric tons)

	1979	1980
WORLD TOTAL	18,488*	18,286*
Far East	10,245*	11,200*
Oceania	72*	51*
Leading Regional Producers:		
Burma	384	337
China, People's Republic	2,822	3,500*
India	5,772	6,000†
Indonesia	709	793
Thailand	132	130†
Other Leading Producers:		
Argentina	671	293
Brazil	462	514†
Nigeria	540†	570†
Senegal	600†	489†
Sudan	880†	810†
U.S.A.	1,800	1,047

* FAO estimate. † Unofficial figure.

stood at $1,245 per metric ton in November 1978. It fell to $719 per ton in January 1980, but rose to $1,179 in December. A prolonged decline began in mid-1981 and by April 1982 the price had fallen to under $700 per ton.

In 1975 groundnut oil was the third most important of soft edible oils, both in terms of production and export. The estimated output was 3,310,000 metric tons (protein equivalent) or 13.5 per cent of all soft edible oils, while exports totalled 720,000 tons. Groundnut oil is one of several oils currently being investigated as possible sources of energy to provide an alternative to petroleum.

Production of groundnut cake in 1975 was estimated at 2,100,000 tons, with exports of 750,000 tons. By 1978 world production of groundnut oil had risen to 3.5 million tons but its position had dropped to fifth.

Jute

Jute fibres are obtained from *Corchorus capsularis* and *C. olitorius*. Jute-like fibres include a number of jute substitutes, the main ones being kenaf or mesta and roselle (*Hibiscus* spp.) and Congo jute or paka (*Urena lobata*). The genus *Corchorus* includes about 40 species distributed throughout the tropics, with the largest number of species being found in Africa.

Jute flourishes in the hot damp regions of Asia. Commercial fibre varies from yellow to brown in colour and consists of tow (bunches of strands), which is pressed into bales of 400 lb. (181.4 kg.) after it has been retted (softened).

Jute has a number of uses. The relatively cheap fibre is used to manufacture sacks, bags and wrapping, twine and carpet backing, for which, despite a fall of about 35 per cent in consumption in the early 1970s, jute still provides 40 per cent of the material. The finest jute standards are spun into carpet yarn and woven into curtains and wall coverings. Jute is mixed with wool, after treatment with caustic soda, and processed into cheap clothing fabrics or blankets in developing Asian countries.

In 1978/79 the world jute and kenaf harvest was a record 4.4 million tons, an increase of about 20 per cent compared with the previous season. In 1979/80 and 1980/81, however, annual world production dropped to about 4 million tons.

India and Bangladesh are the principal producers of raw jute and fabrics. In both countries most of the growers of jute are small farmers whose livelihood depends entirely on their annual crop of the fibre. Jute is the major cash crop in Bangladesh and provides about 75 per cent of the country's export earnings. About one-half of the annual output is exported as raw fibre and the rest is processed in the local mills for export as jute goods. Bangladesh's production of raw jute reached 1,168,930 tons in 1978/79 (compared with 972,378 tons in 1977/78), 1,095,000 tons in 1979/80 but only 904,000 tons in 1980/81. The Government is engaged in an effort to support producers' prices. While Bangladesh would like to diversify from its high dependence on sales of jute and jute products for foreign currencies, there are few options available. Bangladesh is trying, so far without success, to strengthen its share of the carpet market by reducing the gap between the country's capacity of 140,000 sq. metres and the global demand for 3.5 million sq. metres per year. As the world's leading exporter of jute and jute goods, its sales in general seem to be holding up better than those of India in the current world recession. However, declining prices and competition on the international market and from synthetics are likely to hurt Bangladesh more than the next largest jute producer, India. Bangladesh exports over 90 per cent of its jute and jute goods while India consumes over 70 per cent of its jute manufactures domestically.

In terms of its market position, jute is one of the world's weakest commodities, with demand declining by an average of 5 per cent a year since the mid-1960s. The fall in consumption by the industrialized states has been most severe, almost 10 per cent a year since 1969 so that by 1977 the "rich" world consumed only 280,000 tons of jute, compared with nearly 700,000 tons in the late 1960s. By the late 1970s jute had a slight edge in price over the synthetic fibres which had been adversely affected by successive oil price rises. However, this advantage was not sufficient to halt falling demand, and the long-term prospects for the industry are gloomy. Almost everywhere there is a need for rationalization, modernization and greater organization in jute production.

Prospects for the Indian jute industry have deteriorated since the start of the 1980s, with the recession in the U.S.A. hitting demand. Bangladesh overtook India as the world's largest exporter of jute goods in the mid-1970s. However, domestic consumption is increasing and already absorbs nearly two-thirds of the total output. Raw jute production is becoming cheaper but mill costs have risen sharply. A major problem is, in fact, the abundance of supply in recent years, which has necessitated a number of price support operations to protect the country's 4 million growers. In 1981/82 the crop is put at about 7 million bales (of 180 kg.) and raw jute production at an estimated 1,440,000 tons, compared with a record 1,493,000 tons in 1978/79. India is faced with large surplus stocks (2.2 million bales in March 1982), even after exports and domestic sales, and the value of exports fell by an estimated 33 per cent in 1981/82, much mores harply than by quantity. In the meantime workers' strikes, power shortages and the high cost of production, compared with steadily falling market prices, have disrupted the production of jute goods and caused the closure of 14 of India's 72 jute mills, although government purchases of surplus jute may enable some of them to resume operations. According to the Indian Government, 50 of the operating jute mills needed to be modernized. In September 1980, in an effort to revive exports of jute goods, the Government abolished the Rs. 1,000 per metric ton export duty on hessian (introduced in February), which had discouraged foreign buyers from buying more than their miniumum requirements.

In early 1980 Thailand (with 13 mills in operation)

placed a ban on jute imports as they were depressing local prices of kenaf and jute.

There are two international forums for discussion of world jute developments: the UN Food and Agriculture Organization (FAO) and UNCTAD. The FAO International Group on Jute held its 15th Session in October 1979. Jute is one of the 18 commodities being discussed within the framework of UNCTAD's proposed integrated commodity programme (under discussion since 1976) which aims to establish a series of agreements designed to stabilize commodity prices. However, little has been achieved and, due to the opposition of the major consumer-nations to any external control of free market prices, jute-producing countries are now moving towards an agreement aimed at promoting production and consumption rather than stabilizing prices. This is the purpose of Jute International, conceived by the UN Industrial Development Organization (UNIDO) as long ago as 1971 but whose formation has been dogged by political difficulties. However, talks resumed in late 1978 and four major producers—Bangladesh, India, Thailand and Nepal—have agreed to be members. These four countries took a major step towards an international agreement for jute fibre in 1979, when they agreed on a draft version of a pact.

Since then a series of talks has taken place involving the other principal jute-producing nations (China's part was usually that of observer). In April 1981, in Calcutta, India, Bangladesh, Thailand and Nepal agreed on the need for co-ordinated international action to fight the inroads of synthetic fibres into the natural fibres market. Subsequent talks between producers and consumers in Geneva in May 1981 failed to produce an agreement for jute. The proposed International Jute Organization was brought one step nearer, however, when agreement on equal producer voting rights in any such body was reached at talks in Bangkok in May 1982.

PRODUCTION OF JUTE, KENAF AND ALLIED FIBRES
('000 metric tons)

	1979	1980
WORLD TOTAL	4,269*	4,078*
Far East	4,105*	3,907*
Leading Regional Producers:		
Bangladesh	1,095	904
Burma	95*	90
China, People's Republic	1,089	1,098
India	1,433	1,475
Nepal	68	59
Thailand	278	228
Viet-Nam	26	31
Other Leading Producers:		
Brazil	80	76
U.S.S.R.	44†	44*

* FAO estimate. † Unofficial figure.

Millet and Sorghum

Millet and sorghum are cereals grown chiefly as feed for livestock and poultry in Europe and North America, but are used to a large extent as food in Asia, Africa and the U.S.S.R. Provisional figures for 1981 indicated a rise in world output of millet and sorghum to a record 101 million metric tons, although Asia's 1981 crop rose only slightly to 37 million tons.

Data on millet relate mainly to the following: cattail millet (*Pennisetum glaucum* or *typhoides*), also known as bulrush millet, pearl millet or, in India and Pakistan, as "bajra"; finger millet (*Eleusine coracana*), known in India as "ragi"; common or bread millet (*Panicum miliaceum*), also called proso; foxtail millet (*Setaria italica*), or Italian millet; and barnyard millet (*Echinochloa crusgalli*), also often called Japanese millet.

PRODUCTION OF MILLET AND SORGHUM
('000 metric tons)
M = Millet; S = Sorghum; U = Unspecified (only combined figures reported)

	1979	1980
WORLD TOTAL: M and U	27,417*	28,521*
S	65,169*	56,151*
Far East: M and U	15,203*	15,363*
S	19,984*	18,971*
Oceania: M	36	14
S	1,131*	929*
Leading Regional Producers:		
Australia: M	36	14
S	1,125	922
China, People's Repub. M	6,150*	6,000*
S	7,650*	7,700*
India: M	8,094	9,461
S	11,648	10,504
Korea, Dem. People's Repub.: M	440*	440*
S	130*	130*
Pakistan: M	277	214
S	249	234
Thailand: S	260†	350†
Other Leading Producers:		
Argentina: M	310	188
S	6,200	2,960
Mexico: S	3,917	4,812
Nigeria: M	3,130†	3,130†
S	3,785†	3,800†
Sudan: M	550	450*
S	2,408	2,200*
U.S.S.R.: M	1,553	1,873
S	89	119
U.S.A.: S	20,546	14,712

* FAO estimate. †Unofficial figure.

In Asian countries millet is an important cereal crop, the largest producers being the People's Republic of China and India. In India millet accounts for about one-sixth of total foodgrain production and is a cheap supplement for wheat and rice. It is grown in areas of low soil fertility and minimal rainfall and thrives in conditions unsuitable for most other crops. Millet has a higher mineral and vitamin content than wheat or rice and a similar protein content, although it is an inferior form of protein. There is still very little mechanical extraction; millet flour is ground in mortars and is frequently used combined with wheat flour to make types of pasta and dough. As such it provides a highly nutritious foodstuff.

Sorghum statistics refer mainly to the several varieties of *Sorghum vulgare* known by various names, such as great millet, Guinea corn, kafir or kafircorn, milo, feterita, durra, jowar, sorgo, maicillo, etc. Other species included in the table are Sudan grass (*S. sudanense*) and Columbus grass or sorgo negro (*S. almum*). The use of grain sorghum hybrids has resulted in a considerable increase in yields in recent years. Sorghum is less important in Asia than in Africa.

Wherever possible, statistics are given separately for millet and sorghum, but many countries do not make any distinction between the two grains in their reports; in such cases, combined figures are given.

Nickel

Nickel is a white, malleable metal which occurs in various types of ores, the most important being sulphide ores, arsenides and antimonides. It is mined both underground and open-cast, depending on the type of ore. Nickel is often found in conjunction with copper and similar extraction processes are used. The ore is subjected to crushing and grinding, with final treatment by the flotation method. The resulting concentrate is roasted and smelted in furnaces to remove the sulphur. Nickel production is an energy-intensive operation and the cost of energy to the industry has risen steeply in recent years. Mining companies are faced with falling world demand and prices. World nickel ore reserves are put at 68 million metric tons, divided into 26 million tons of sulphide and 42 million tons of laterite ores. The distinction is significant as sulphide ores are cheaper to process.

Nickel is used in a wide range of alloys where it contributes to resistance to corrosion, strength and high levels of heat and electrical conductivity. Its most important use is in steel production, and the majority of high tensile steels contain nickel. Nickel still has a very significant consumer role in military equipment. High-nickel alloys are used in power and chemical plants and it is also used in high-temperature applications, such as gas turbines.

During the 1960s world consumption of nickel generally exceeded production and a reduction in stocks was necessary to meet demand. The end of the Viet-Nam war, combined with the world recession of the early 1970s, led to a fall in consumption from 710,700 metric tons in 1974 to 577,400 tons in 1975. This led to huge surpluses and a build-up of world stocks which by 1977 totalled an estimated 227,000 tons. In the second half of 1977 severe cutbacks in production were implemented, with the result that in 1978 demand exceeded supply for the first time in four years. With increased world production of stainless steel in 1978, nickel production in 1979 was again short of demand, which was a record 620,000 tons. Nickel stocks, having fallen in 1979 to about 130,000 tons (their lowest level for five years), were expected to rise to about 180,000 tons in 1980. Consumption for 1980 was estimated at 521,000 tons, 15 per cent down from the previous year, while supplies of nickel were put at 535,000 tons.

The major nickel-producing countries in the region are Australia and New Caledonia. Australia increased production of refined nickel from an estimated 1,000 metric tons in 1970 to 32,900 metric tons in 1975. Output dropped slightly for the first time in 1977, due to the general cutback in production. Large deposits have recently been discovered in Western Australia. New Caledonia possesses the world's largest known nickel deposit and the economy relies almost entirely on nickel. Production of refined nickel reached a peak of 52,800 metric tons in 1975, but has dropped considerably since then. In 1979 International Nickel (Inco) began new operations in Indonesia. However, owing to the depressed world market for nickel, production was cut by 50 per cent in 1982. The Philippines, meanwhile, opened another nickel mine, the country's fourth, at the end of 1980 following the commencement of the Isabela nickel project. The latter should produce 15 million lb. of ferro-nickel alloy annually as part of a projected 21 per cent growth in national nickel production from 1979 to 1982.

The U.S.A. is the world's largest nickel consumer, accounting for about one-third of total consumption. The U.S.S.R. and the EEC, especially the Federal Republic of Germany, are also important consumers. Japan is a major producer of refined nickel, all from imported raw materials.

World nickel prices have traditionally been governed by the four largest producing companies—Inco, Falconbridge, Western Mining and Société Le Nickel—who together account for about 60 per cent of world production. In July 1977 Inco stopped officially quoting prices because of the very competitive conditions in the market and did not resume until February 1979, during which time the price slumped from U.S. $2.10 to $1.59 per lb. The price quoted by Inco in February 1979 was $2.10 per lb. for plating nickel and $2.05 for melting nickel, lower than the last official quotation of $2.41 for plating nickel in October 1976. In March Falconbridge raised the price to $2.30 per lb. for plating and $2.25 for melting, and in May 1979 Inco quoted prices of $2.90 and $2.85 respectively. In 1979 Inco received for its nickel products an average of $2.43 per lb., compared with $1.98 in 1978, while in February 1980 nickel prices were at $3.25 per lb. The price subsequently rose, but in November 1981 Inco cut the price of plating nickel from $3.50 to $3.29 per lb. and melting nickel from $3.20 to $3.15 per lb.

There has been a growing free market in nickel and in April 1979 dealing in nickel began on the London Metal Exchange, despite opposition from the major producers who feared that speculative buying would increase volatility in prices. However, the amount of nickel traded in this way is still relatively small. The free market price for nickel is currently firmly below the producer price.

Recent research has revealed the existence of extensive deposits of ferromanganese nodules—also containing nickel, copper and cobalt—on the floor of the world's oceans. A conservative estimate puts world nodule reserves at 290 million metric tons of nickel, 240 million tons of cobalt and 6,000 million tons of manganese. It is considered unlikely, however, quite apart from the question of rights of recovery tortuously negotiated at the UN conference on the law of the sea, that it will be practicable to extract metals from the nodules until the 1990s.

PRODUCTION OF NICKEL ORE
(nickel content, metric tons)

	1978	1979
WORLD TOTAL	642,589	783,483
Far East	58,506	58,736
Oceania	153,087	158,248
Leading Regional Producers:		
Australia[1]	86,991	80,385
Indonesia	28,960	37,240
New Caledonia	66,096	77,863
Philippines	29,528	21,478
Other Leading Producers:		
Canada[2]	128,310	131,579
Cuba	34,787	32,324
Dominican Republic	14,302	25,112
South Africa[3,4]	21,999	21,999
U.S.S.R.[4]	148,000	152,000

[1] Nickel content of concentrates in 12 months ending June 30th of year stated.

[2] Refined nickel, nickel in oxides and salts sold, nickel in matte exported and recoverable nickel in concentrates shipped to smelters.

[3] Nickel content of matte and refined nickel.

[4] *Source:* U.S. Bureau of Mines (figures for the U.S.S.R. are estimates).

Oil Palm (*Elaeis guineensis*)

This plant, native to West Africa, is now grown in the Far East. The entire fruit is of use commercially; palm oil is made from its pulp, and palm kernel oil from the seed. Palm oil is a versatile product, used in margarine and other edible fats; as a "shortener" for pastry and biscuits; as an ingredient in ice cream; and in the manufacture of soaps and detergents. Palm kernel oil, which is similar to coconut oil, is also used for making soaps and fats. The sap from the stems of the tree produces palm wine, an intoxicating beverage which ferments by itself.

Palm oil can be produced virtually all the year round once the palms have reached oil-bearing age, which takes about five years. The palms continue to bear oil for 30 years or more and the yield far exceeds that of any other oil plant. However, it is an intensive crop, needing considerable investment and skilled labour.

The leading world producer of palm oil is Malaysia, which accounts for over 60 per cent of world exports. It is the fastest growing industry in the country, with production of crude palm oil rising from 92,000 metric tons in 1960 to 1.75 million tons in 1978, half of which was exported. Palm oil production in 1981 reached a record 2.8 million tons, making Malaysia's share of the world market 56 per cent. In 1972 Malaysia overtook Nigeria as the world's leading supplier of palm oil. The most important markets for Malaysian palm oil are, India, the EEC, the U.S.A., Japan and Pakistan. During the Second Malaysian Plan (1971–75) palm oil exports rose by more than 25 per cent and projections indicated that they would rise by an annual rate of 19 per cent during the Third Malaysian Plan (1976–80). Exports were 1.8 million tons in 1979 and are expected to rise to 2.08 million tons in 1980. By 1985 palm oil production in Malaysia is expected to be over 4 million tons and will probably replace rubber as Malaysia's leading export. Because of continued growing world demand the Government is actively encouraging the industry; in 1978 a Palm Oil Registration and Licensing Authority was set up to supervise all aspects of production—research, replanting and marketing. In 1980 a palm oil exchange offering contracts was established in Kuala Lumpur—a logical development from Malaysia's status as the world's leading palm oil producer.

Indonesia's production is growing and the aim is to increase output to just under 1 million tons by the end of 1983 and to over 12 million tons by 1988. However, earnings from exports of palm oil fell by 65 per cent in value in 1981, compared with 1980, largely as a result of the government's policy of substituting palm oil for coconut oil in cooking. Export volume in 1981 was the lowest for more than a decade. The area under palm oil more than doubled in the 1970s to about 260,000 hectares and a further programme of planting is under way. Oil palm projects are also being undertaken in Burma and Papua New Guinea.

In the United Kingdom the import price of palm oil per long ton averaged U.S. $217 in 1972, rising to $376 in 1973 and reaching more than $800 per ton in October 1974. Following a sharp decline in 1975, the price remained fairly stable in 1976, averaging $403 per ton, but during 1977 it rose above $650. After falling below $500 per ton, another surge took the price of palm oil to more than $700 in February 1979. In 1980 palm oil oscillated between

PRODUCTION OF PALM KERNELS
('000 metric tons)

	1979	1980
WORLD TOTAL	1,706*	1,825*
Far East	636*	728*
Oceania	16*	17*
Leading Regional Producers:		
China, People's Republic	44*	46*
Indonesia	113	121
Malaysia	475	557
Other Leading Producers:		
Benin	70*	73*
Brazil‡	262†	266†
Nigeria	335†	345†
Zaire	70*	65*

* FAO estimate. † Unofficial figure.
‡ Babassu kernels.

a high of $725 per ton and a low of $475 per ton. The price was $635 per ton in February 1981 but fell through most of the year and in May 1982 was $507 per ton.

Provisional figures for 1981 indicated record production levels: 1.9 million tons of kernels and 5.4 million tons of palm oil.

Despite competition from soyabean oil, palm oil increased its share of the oils and fats market (from just over 4 per cent) throughout the 1970s. By 1985 palm oil is expected to have captured 23 per cent of the vegetable oils market, against 14 per cent in 1977, whereas soyabean's share is expected to remain in the region of 30 per cent. In 1981 palm oil accounted for 15 per cent of the market. The increase in palm oil output has posed a threat to the soyabean industry, particularly in the U.S.A., which has attempted to reduce palm oil imports and is opposed to the use of international aid in the expansion of palm oil production. U.S. imports of palm oil fell from 480,000 metric tons in 1975 to 160,000 tons in 1978.

Production of Palm Oil
('000 metric tons)

	1979	1980
World Total	4,556*	5,105*
Far East	2,999*	3,461*
Oceania	103*	112*
Leading Regional Producers:		
China, People's Republic	184*	190*
Indonesia	606	677†
Malaysia	2,188	2,573†
Other Leading Producers:		
Ivory Coast	132†	170†
Nigeria	650*	675*
Zaire	170*	160*

* FAO estimate. † Unofficial figure.

Petroleum (by Iain Buchanan and the Editor)

In total terms, the hydrocarbon potential of Asia and the Pacific is considerable. In the three million square kilometres of off-shore concessions alone, extending from the Gulf of Cambay, through the continental shelves of Australia and Indonesia, to offshore Korea, there are an estimated 300,000 million barrels of oil (15 per cent of the world's recoverable reserves) and over 200,000,000 million cubic feet of recoverable gas reserves.

Six major characteristics define the position of oil and gas in Asia. Firstly, there is the imbalance between export surpluses and dependence on imports, in their relation to national development needs. Here, Brunei contrasts with Bangladesh, 70 per cent of whose import expenditure goes to OPEC. For the developing member countries of the Asian Development Bank the cost of oil imports rose from $13,500 million in 1978 to $32,100 million in 1980, increasing current account deficits and foreign debts.

Secondly, import dependence has encouraged the development of domestic energy sources. For example, the Philippines and India are each spending over $10,000 million on oil exploration for the period 1980–85.

Thirdly, Japan is an increasingly significant importer of regional oil and liquefied natural gas (LNG). It takes half of Indonesia's oil and it is expected that by 1984 it will take 14 million metric tons of Indonesian LNG (compared with 8 million tons in 1980) in addition to all of Brunei's LNG output and half of Australia's North West Shelf LNG output (6 million tons per year).

Fourthly, recent years have seen the growth of a "downstream" petro-chemical/LNG industry, which has major implications for industrialization. Indonesia, Thailand, Singapore and Malaysia are all developing major ethane and ethylene projects for an ASEAN market which can absorb 600–700,000 tons of ethylene equivalent every year.

Fifthly, with a policy of "depletion" like Malaysia's and new discoveries, oil producers can regulate production to enable it to last for up to 20 years. However, increasing rates of domestic consumption and costs of oil development and imports place all Asian countries, apart from Brunei and China, in a weak long-term position.

Finally, what characterizes Asian oil activities is the dominance of Western capital. Most exploration, especially offshore, from Australia's North West Shelf to China's offshore concessions, has strong Western financial and technical support. This is a function of the size and organization of necessary investments, of an established and comprehensive pattern of ownership and control and of advanced Western oil and gas technology. Western control of the oil industry contrasts with the uneven performance of Asian governments (including those of Indonesia and Japan) in the energy field.

On the basis of oil production and consumption patterns, the Asian–Pacific countries can be divided into five categories.

(i) Producers which, because of smallness and/or lack of economic development, export most of their output. For example, Brunei exported virtually all its 250,000 barrels per day (b.p.d.) average 1980 production and is exporting 5.14 million tons of LNG per year to Japan in the period 1973–95; Indonesia, with recoverable oil reserves of about 16,000 million barrels, "ultimate recoverable" oil reserves of up to 50,000 million barrels and gas reserves of some 34,000,000 million cubic feet, exported 80 per cent of its 1980 average output of 1.54 million b.p.d. (set to rise to 1.83 million b.p.d. by 1984), as well as 8 million tons of LNG (making it the world's largest LNG exporter); Malaysia exported 86 per cent of its 280,000 b.p.d. output in 1980, importing light Middle Eastern crudes for domestic refining. Malaysia's reserves are estimated at 1,800 million barrels of oil and over 33,000,000 million cubic feet of gas. Indonesia, however, spent $4,300 million (42.5 per cent of its 1979–80 gross oil revenue) on oil imports and associated services.

(ii) Producers with marginal exports. Non-Soviet Asia's largest producer, China, exported about 11 per cent of an average 1980 production of 2.1 million b.p.d., but this export is hard to maintain given declining production at the inland Daqing field (about half of total output), accelerated industrialization and agricultural modernization. As offshore fields are developed, with heavy use of foreign technology, China, holding oil reserves of 100,000–500,000 million barrels, should be a major exporter by 1990. Burma, with a 1980 production of 30,000 b.p.d., exports 10 per cent of crude output and imports refined oil.

(iii) Producers with a significant degree of self-sufficiency. Australia's production, largely from the Bass Strait, approaches two-thirds self-sufficiency at about 450,000 b.p.d. (1979). When the $6,000 million Northwest Shelf gas project (with total reserves of 20,000,000 million cubic ft.) and Central Queensland shale oil development (of at least 9,000 million barrels) come on stream in 1984, Australia could become a net exporter. India has an estimated 95,000 million barrels equivalent of hydro-carbon reserves but scarcely 2,500 million barrels are proven. In 1980 India's average consumption was over 600,000 b.p.d. and its production about 200,000 b.p.d. (down nearly 15 per cent from 1979 because of troubles in Assam); thus, imports in 1980 absorbed almost 80 per cent of export earnings. Oil needs by 1984 should exceed 950,000 b.p.d., with production about 440,000 b.p.d. from doubled output in the Western Continental Shelf fields of Bombay High and North Bassein, the coming on stream of the associated Ratnagiri field and offshore production in the Bay of Bengal.

(iv) Countries largely, or totally, dependent upon imports. Japan, with a consumption of 5.3 million b.p.d., imports all but a tiny proportion, mainly from the Middle East. A little over 2 million b.p.d. are refined in Japan. Although not a major user of LNG, Japan accounts for 50 per cent of world imports. Japan's total indigenous reserves, as yet little developed, are estimated at 8,200 million barrels of off-shore oil and gas. However, Japan planned to lower its crude oil imports for the financial year 1981/82 by 12.3 per cent to five million b.p.d. and to revise downwards other energy-related targets for the 1980s. Singapore, with no production but a refinery of one million b.p.d. (giving it the third largest oil refinery complex in the world) and another one planned, supplies part of the balance with refined crude from the Middle East and South-East Asia. Some countries, like Bangladesh, Sri Lanka, the Philippines and New Zealand (although the Maui gas field has estimated reserves of 11,800,000 million cubic ft.) are likely to remain very heavy importers, while others, such as Thailand (with up to 18,000,000 million cubic ft. of natural gas off-shore) and Viet-Nam, could, with sufficient investment, achieve a far higher degree of self-sufficiency than at present.

(v) Soviet Asia. Most of the U.S.S.R.'s oil and gas is produced in Soviet Asia, especially Western Siberia which has estimated oil reserves of 48,000 million barrels and the world's largest natural gas deposits. Most of the increase in Soviet gas production to 15,400,000 million cubic ft. in 1980, was due to the Western Siberian output reaching 4,600,000 million cubic ft. Oil production in Western Siberia reached 5.9 million b.p.d. in February 1980, or half the U.S.S.R.'s average 1980 production of just under 12 million b.p.d. The Yakutia gas field in the Yakut A.S.S.R., with confirmed deposits of 30,000,000 million cubic feet, is the basis of a joint U.S.S.R.–U.S.A.–Japan pipeline scheme. Similarly, a U.S.S.R.–Japan team is working off Sakhalin Island in an area with estimated oil reserves of 35,000 million barrels.

Late 1975 was the peak of South-East Asian off-shore oil activities: Indonesia had 66 off-shore rigs at work (fewer only than the U.S.A., Canada and Mexico) and Singapore had become the world's leading builder of jack-up rigs, with over a third of world orders for such rigs under construction. After 1975 the focus of

PETROLEUM PRODUCTION
('000 metric tons, including natural gas liquids)

	1978†	1978 '000 Barrels Per Day	1979*	1979 '000 Barrels Per Day
Australia	20,690	433	21,390	448
Brunei/Sarawak	21,640	457	25,260	533
Burma	1,350	28	1,470	30
China, People's Republic	104,000	2,080	106,100	2,122
India	11,500	235	12,140	247
Indonesia	80,820	1,643	78,750	1,601
Japan	540	11	490	10
Pakistan	470	9	530	11
TOTAL (including New Zealand, Taiwan and Philippines)	241,880	4,914	247,840	5,036

* Preliminary. † Revised.

Source: Institute of Petroleum, London.

attention shifted from Indonesia towards Australia, partly because of the Indonesian Government's decision to scrap the original production-sharing system in 1976. With Malaysia's Petronas and Indonesia's Pertamina offering better terms, with oil prices tripling since late-1976 (the price of Malaysian oil, for example, rose from $12 to nearly $36 per barrel in June 1980) the opening of China's vast off-shore potential to foreign exploration teams, and the growing instability of the Gulf region, the situation has improved. By 1981 there were 71 off-shore rigs in Asia, compared with 48 in late-1978. It would be unwise to predict a decline in South-East Asia's and the China Sea's significance much before 1990, given the fact, for example, that most of Indonesia has not been properly surveyed, and that investment of at least $50,000 million is planned down the length of the Western Pacific between 1980 and 1985. Likewise, hydrocarbon development around Australia will absorb considerable foreign investment during the 1980s. China, too, though unable to increase exports over the next few years, will absorb large foreign funds. Finally, it is worth noting that in 1972 American sources estimated that there were only 34 gas fields with reserves of over 10,000,000 million cubic ft.: 20 in the U.S.S.R., none in Southern Asia. In 1981, estimated gas reserves in Southern Asia/Australasia totalled over 160,000,000 million cubic ft. Natural gas liquefaction, transport and gasification are among the most costly energy activities, but also the most important for the region during the 1980s.

REFINERY CAPACITY

('000 metric tons)

	1975	1976	1977	1978‡	1979*
Australia	33,650	34,500	34,500	35,100	36,350
Bangladesh	1,500	1,500	1,500	1,500	1,500
Burma	1,300	1,300	1,300	1,300	1,300
China, People's Republic*†	62,000	70,000	73,500	78,900	80,000
India	26,220	26,220	30,920	30,920	31,120
Indonesia	21,020	21,020	26,020	26,270	26,270
Japan	270,950	276,200	274,500	284,650	284,650
Korea, Republic	19,000	19,000	21,000	23,850	27,325
Malaysia	6,200	6,200	6,200	6,200	6,200
New Zealand	2,700	2,700	2,700	3,700	3,700
Pakistan	3,500	3,500	5,100	5,350	5,350
Philippines	13,350	13,400	13,400	13,400	11,900
Sarawak	1,000	2,250	850	2,250	2,250
Singapore	45,750	45,750	45,750	45,750	45,750
Sri Lanka	2,000	2,000	2,000	2,000	2,000
Taiwan	15,000	15,000	20,000	23,500	23,500
Thailand	7,810	7,810	7,810	8,060	9,360

* Preliminary. † Includes oil from shale and coal. ‡ Revised.

Source: Institute of Petroleum, London.

Rice (*Oryza sativa*)

Rice is the staple food of all the countries of Monsoon Asia and 90 per cent of the total world area under rice lies within the region. The predominance of rice as a food crop is based on its ability to give yields very high in nutritional value and frequently to produce satisfactory yields where no other crop will grow, e.g. in coastal marshes. Wet rice cultivation is typically associated with the alluvial lowlands of Monsoon Asia, since the best natural conditions for this type of agriculture are obtained there, but rice tolerates a wide range of geographic, climatic and ecological conditions and can be adapted to various locations including non-submerged land, where upland rice is grown. All varieties of rice can be classified into two main groups: *indica* and *japonica*. (There is also an intermediate or *java* type, cultivated in parts of Indonesia.) The *indica* group, prevalent in tropical Asia, and covering a very high proportion of the total rice area of Asia, has been associated with a very low yield and primitive production techniques. The *japonica* type, which predominates in China, Taiwan, Korea and Japan, is very responsive to natural and artificial fertilizers and gives a high average yield.

The main reasons for the low rice yields in South and South-East Asia (including India, Bangladesh, Sri Lanka, Laos, Kampuchea, Viet-Nam and Thailand), compared with those in East Asia (China, the Koreas, Japan and Taiwan), are the scarcity of inputs, appropriate water supplies and fertilizers, and the lack of modern varieties. Conventional rice varieties are unresponsive to increased fertilizer usage and tend to lodge (fall over), affecting grain yields. During the 1960s, in the Philippines, the International Rice Research Institute (IRRI) developed a series of stiff-stemmed, semi-dwarf varieties with upright leaves that respond positively to high rates of fertilizers and other improved cultural practices. Similar varieties have also been developed in several other tropical and subtropical countries. Improved varieties may yield as much as 8 to 9 metric tons of paddy rice per hectare, while old varieties may not even yield 1 ton per hectare. Most of the newly-developed varieties are also resistant to common pests, diseases and some soil problems. Agronomists at the IRRI, as well as in various countries, are in the process of developing varieties that will also have tolerance to drought, flood, deep water and sub-optimum temperatures. Farmers growing these varieties face less risk of crop-failures and are therefore more prone to invest in other production inputs. Both improved varieties and improved agronomic practices are essential for a sustained increase in production.

The People's Republic of China developed its own high yielding semi-dwarf varieties in the late-1950s and these were widely disseminated in China by the mid-1960s, prior to the release of the first IRRI varieties. Of recent interest has been the development in Hunan Province of a true hybrid rice which increases yields by as much as 20 per cent and was planted on more than 5 million hectares (about 10 per cent of rice area) throughout South China by 1979. A major limitation of the hybrids (apart from the high cost of seed production) is their rather long maturation period which limits their suitability for intensive cropping patterns.

If estimates are proved accurate, the world rice million harvest in 1981 set a new record, exceeding 400 tons for the first time. About 90 per cent of world production comes from Asian countries, including more than a third of the total from the People's Republic of China, the world's leading rice-growing nation. Many countries, including India, faced for the first time the problems associated with abundant harvests

PRODUCTION OF PADDY RICE
('000 metric tons)

	1979	1980
WORLD TOTAL	377,390*	397,494*
Far East	341,495*	359,084*
Oceania	723*	637*
Leading Regional Producers:		
Bangladesh	19,599	20,822
Burma	10,448	13,107
China, People's Republic	143,750	139,255
India	63,476	79,930
Indonesia	26,283	29,774
Japan	14,948	12,189
Korea, Dem. People's Rep.	4,800*	4,800*
Korea, Republic	7,881	5,311
Malaysia	2,095	2,171
Nepal	2,060	2,464
Pakistan	4,824	4,679
Philippines	7,504	7,840
Sri Lanka	1,917	2,133
Taiwan	3,209	3,083
Thailand	15,758	17,366†
Viet-Nam	10,758	11,679
Other Leading Producers:		
Brazil	7,595	9,748
Egypt	2,517	2,350
Madagascar	2,045	2,109
U.S.S.R.	2,394	2,791
U.S.A.	5,985	6,629

* FAO estimate. † Unofficial figure.

—accumulating stocks due to lack of demand among the poor, losses as a result of inadequate storage facilities, and declining export prices. Such conditions were very different from those of the 1979/80 season, when world and Asian production was estimated to be at least 5 per cent below the 1978 level and production in India fell by over 20 per cent, due to the worst drought this century.

Due to strong increases in demand for rice in Indonesia (the world's biggest rice importer, accounting for about 17 per cent of total imports) and several Middle Eastern countries, world rice exports in 1978 and 1979 reached record levels in excess of 11.5 million metric tons. However, in spite of Asia's leading role as a rice producer, only about 4 per cent of the total rice crop is exported. Thailand, the leading Asian exporter, exported 3 million tons of rice in 1981. Rice is now Thailand's principal export earner. The next largest exporters are Pakistan (1.1 million tons in 1981), Burma (0.8 million tons) and China (0.6 million tons).

The export price of Thai white rice (5 per cent broken), a good barometer of world rice prices, increased from $300 to over $400 per ton between 1979 and 1980. In 1980 Thai white rice averaged $433 per ton. The price rose to $535 per ton in June 1981 but fell to $420 in November.

Rubber (Para Rubber) (*Hevea brasiliensis*)

Rubber cultivation is suited to both estate and smallholder methods of farming but productivity on rubber estates is greater as it is the estates which have pioneered both the development of cultivation techniques and the improvement of the clones, or selected high-yield strains. These may either be planted as seedlings or propagated by grafting on to seedlings of ordinary trees (root stock) and planted out subsequently.

Of a total 1980 world production of 3.8 million metric tons of natural rubber, Asian countries produced all but 240,000 tons. The principal producers are Malaysia, Indonesia, Thailand, Sri Lanka and India. In value terms, rubber is Malaysia's most important export commodity, the second most important for Sri Lanka and the third for Indonesia. Malaysia's rubber output has shown little variation in recent years at about 1.6 million tons, roughly 40 per cent of world production. Estate production has declined due to the switch in emphasis from rubber to palm oil. In 1980 petroleum overtook natural rubber as Malaysia's leading export earner. However, with Government encouragement, in the form of tax incentives and higher replanting grants, average smallholder yields have risen to 700–800 kg. per hectare and smallholders now account for 59 per cent of Malaysian rubber production (about 38 per cent of the area planted with rubber is the property of smallholders). Nevertheless, output remained at the level of recent years in 1981, growth being hampered by a decline in the rate of replanting, particularly among smallholders who, without assistance, cannot afford the money to replant, or the time it takes (six years) for a new rubber tree to mature.

In 1965 technical specifications for the grading of rubber were introduced in Malaysia (Standard Malaysian Rubber, SMR) and other countries later followed with their own standard forms. By 1976 exports of these standard (block) natural rubbers exceeded one million tons a year.

Petroleum-based synthetic rubber outrivals natural rubber, with production reaching 9.3 million tons in 1979, of which 1,107,250 tons were produced in Japan, 42,800 tons in Australia, 32,100 tons in India, 60,300 tons in the Republic of Korea and an estimated 80,000 tons in Taiwan. It is thought that a further 80,000 tons is produced in the People's Republic of China. Competition from synthetic rubber was affected by the sharp price increases during 1973/74 for petroleum, but in the following years natural rubber failed to capture any significant part of the market from the synthetic products as output cannot be raised rapidly. Also, producers of natural rubber are themselves faced with rising costs such as increased prices for fertilizers.

Natural rubber increased its share of total new rubber consumption from 31 per cent in 1973 to 32.4 per cent in 1975 but the proportion fell in 1978 to 29.8 per cent, the lowest for more than 10 years. It recovered to 30.1 per cent in 1979 and climbed to 30.9 per cent in 1980. It is estimated that total world consumption of natural rubber will reach 5.6 million tons by 1985. However, according to a joint World Bank/FAO report, production is unlikely to keep pace with demand and a shortage of up to 1 million tons may occur.

In April 1978 it was forecast that natural rubber's market share would fall to 28 per cent by 1985. However, some leading rubber producing countries have announced plans to increase substantially the area planted with rubber in order to meet future requirements. Although rising petroleum costs pushed up the price of synthetic rubber, thus increasing the competitiveness of the natural product, the recent massive rises in the cost of oil and the general world economic recession have reduced the demand for natural rubber in proportion to the fall in demand for road vehicles. The stabilizing of petroleum prices in 1981 is possibly, therefore, something of a mixed blessing. Nearly four-fifths of world annual natural rubber production is used in making tyres. Notwithstanding current difficulties it is generally agreed that world demand for natural rubber will rise by some 50 per cent between 1980 and 1990.

The Association of Natural Rubber Producing Countries (ANRPC) was set up in 1970 and in December 1975 its eight members (Malaysia, Indonesia, Thailand, Singapore, Viet-Nam, Sri Lanka, India and Papua New Guinea) adopted a draft agreement to establish an international buffer stock and to "rationalize" national rubber supplies by keeping surplus stocks off the market.

Following a period of relative inactivity, the ANRPC was reactivated in May 1982 in response to producer disenchantment over the International Rubber Agreement (*see* below), in particular the consumer-inspired 1 per cent downward revision of the buffer stock price range. In a bid to improve rubber prices, members of the ANPRC proposed a reduction of 350,000 metric tons (8 per cent) in their output for the second half of 1982.

In January 1977 a meeting of producers and consumers was held under the auspices of the UN Conference on Trade and Development (UNCTAD) and considered proposals for stabilizing rubber prices, including the establishment of an international buffer stock of possibly 450,000 metric tons. The proposals were intended to form part of UNCTAD's "integrated programme" of commodity agreements covering major primary products, based on a Common Fund to provide financial support. A full negotiating conference for an international rubber agreement was held in Geneva, under UNCTAD auspices, in November and December 1978. The conference was adjourned without producing an agreement but talks were renewed in March 1979, when the main elements of a revised pact, including a buffer stock of 550,000 tons, were settled. However, further UNCTAD discussions in June and July failed to resolve key issues. In particular, producing countries objected to the U.S.A.'s insistence that the proposed pact should commit them to disclose their production and supply plans to consumers.

Eventually, at a fourth session in September and October 1979, the 55-nation talks reached accord on the terms of a new International Natural Rubber Agreement (INRA). It is the first commodity pact to be completed under UNCTAD auspices. The Agreement, to run until October 1985, was opened for signature in January 1980. INRA remained open for nine months and came into force provisionally on October 24th, the necessary 65 per cent of producers and 65 per cent of consumers having ratified it (votes are weighted according to the proportion of rubber trading by the countries participating in the negotiations). The U.S.A. agreed to apply the terms of the accord, if only on a provisional basis. The agreement became fully operational in April 1982, the requisite participation of 80 per cent of both producer and consumer nations having been achieved (the actual percentage ratification was 91 per cent of producers and 84 per cent of consumers).

INRA provides for an adjustable price range, quoted in Malaysian currency, to be maintained by means of a buffer stock. The "floor" price is M$1.50 per kg. and the "ceiling" price M$2.70 per kg. The buffer stock will normally be 400,000 metric tons, with an additional contingency stock of 150,000 tons. It was agreed that the stock management (buying in times of surplus and selling in times of shortage) should attempt to maintain market prices within a range initially set at M$1.68 to M$2.52 per kg., i.e. 20 per cent above or below a central reference level of M$2.10 per kg. The INRA price range would be subject to review by the INRC every 18 months.

At its first meeting, in Geneva, in November 1980, the INRC decided that the headquarters of the International Natural Rubber Organization should be in Kuala Lumpur, capital city of Malaysia, the world's largest rubber producer and exporter.

Although world output of natural rubber rose to a record level in 1979, production was still about 80,000 metric tons below expected consumption and rubber stocks fell to their lowest level since 1968. World output of synthetic rubber also reached an all-time peak in 1979, when production totalled 9.3 million tons. A joint study by the FAO and the World Bank published in September 1978, forecast an increase in annual production of natural rubber to 6.1 million metric tons by 1990, about 500,000 tons less than the projected annual demand. Rubber growers were advised to increase plantings in order to be able to meet the expected increase in demand.

The International Rubber Study Group's estimate for world consumption in 1981 was 12.50 million tons (natural and synthetic rubber), compared with 12.92 million tons in 1979. World natural rubber production in 1981 was put at 3.86 million tons.

As with other commodities, rubber prices have varied considerably in recent years. In London the import price of ribbed smoked sheets per metric ton rose from less than £150 in September 1972 to £635 in November 1976. It fell below £500 per ton in December 1976 and then fluctuated between £455 and £640 until November 1978. Rubber rose to more than £670 per ton in June 1979 but fell to below £560 in July.

From September 1979 the London rubber price steadily increased and in January 1980 it passed £700 per ton, exceeding the previous all-time peak set in 1950, when the Korean war caused prices to soar. In February 1980 the London price climbed to a record £900 per ton (with "futures" trading at over £1,000 per ton for the first time) but it then fell sharply, reaching £555 in May. The price recovered to £610 per ton in June, fell to £555 again in July but climbed to £650 in August. The sudden price increase in 1979–80 was partly due to speculative buying, caused by nervousness about the international situation. In April 1981, however, rubber fell to £515 per ton. Although the price recovered to £625.5 per ton in August, further falls later in 1981 led to the intervention of INRA (not then fully in force) in the market. Support buying failed to prevent prices from falling in February 1982 to £430 per ton, the lowest level since April 1976. However, rumoured producer buying pushed the price up to £587.5 per ton in April 1982. Rubber fell to £460 per ton in June.

PRODUCTION OF NATURAL RUBBER
('000 metric tons)

	1979	1980
WORLD TOTAL	3,867*	3,796*
Far East	3,625*	3,558*
Oceania	4*	4*
Leading Regional Producers:		
China, People's Republic	98*	102*
India	147	155
Indonesia	947	919
Malaysia	1,617	1,600
Philippines	55*	68
Sri Lanka	153	133
Thailand	540	510*
Viet-Nam	43	45
Other Leading Producers:		
Liberia	75	77
Nigeria	56†	45†

* FAO estimate. † Unofficial figure.

Sugar

This is principally the product either of sugar beet (*Beta vulgaris*) or sugar cane, a giant perennial grass of the genus *Saccharum*, although it may be derived, in uncommercial quantities, from the juices of various plants. Until seedling canes were introduced about 1920, all cultivated canes were ascribed to one species, *S. officinarum*. Sugar cane, found in tropical areas, grows to between 4 and 5 metres tall. The plant is native to Asia but its distribution is now widespread. It is not necessary to plant cane every season as, if the root of the plant is left in the ground, it will grow again in the following year. This practice, known as "ratooning", may be continued for five or six years, sometimes longer, and gives the plant an advantage over annual crops. Cane is ready for cutting between 12 and 24 months after planting, depending on local conditions. Much of the world's sugar cane is still cut by hand, but rising costs are forcing producers to introduce mechanical harvesting methods.

Sugar cane deteriorates quickly after it has been cut and should be processed as quickly as possible. At the sugar factory, after passing through shredding, crushing, squeezing and heating processes, the cane is separated into sugar crystals (raw cane sugar) and sugar syrup (cane molasses) by means of a succession of centrifuges.

The greater part of the raw cane sugar produced in the world is sent to refineries unless the sugar is for local consumption. Most countries where cane is grown export sugar in the raw state, though some (including Cuba, Thailand, Brazil and India) also export part of their output as refined sugar. Beet sugar is generally refined in the country of origin and, in most producing countries, is consumed domestically. The major exceptions are, usually, the EEC, Czechoslovakia and Poland, which (in that order) are substantial exporters of white refined sugar. The refining process further purifies the sugar crystals and eventually results in finished products of various grades, such as granulated, icing or castor sugar. The ratio of refined to raw sugar is usually about 0.9 : 1.

As well as providing sugar, quantities of cane are grown in some countries for seed, feed, fresh consumption, the manufacture of alcohol and other uses. Molasses may be used as cattle feed or fermented to produce alcoholic beverages for human consumption, such as rum. Sugar cane juice may be used to produce ethyl alcohol (ethanol). This chemical can be mixed with petroleum derivatives to produce fuel for motor vehicles. The steep rise in the price of petroleum since 1973 has made the large-scale conversion of sugar cane into alcohol economically attractive, especially as sugar, unlike petroleum, is a renewable source of energy. The blended fuel derived from sugar is known as "gasohol", "alcogas" or "green petrol". The pioneer in this field was Brazil, which has the largest "gasohol" programme in the world. A technical problem, and one that has slowed down the Brazilian programme, is that of an increase in the rate of engine rusting caused by the use of "gasohol". More seriously, a shortage of domestically produced alcohol sent the price of "gasohol" up and sales of alcohol fuelled cars have plummeted.

The Philippines Government plans to build two distilleries for the production of this hybrid fuel and hopes to produce 159 million litres per year by 1985. In following Brazil's example, the Philippines has been joined by countries such as Australia, Kenya, Tanzania, Malawi, Fiji, Taiwan, Thailand and others who have initiated commercial gasohol projects.

After the milling of sugar, the cane has dry fibrous remnants known as bagasse, which is usually burned as fuel in sugar mills but can be pulped and used for making fireboard, particle board and most grades of paper. As the costs of imported wood pulp have risen, cane-growing regions have turned increasingly to the manufacture of paper from bagasse. In view of rising energy costs, some countries, Cuba for example, are once again reverting to using bagasse as fuel to save on foreign exchange for imports of oil.

The production of raw sugar has shown a steadily rising trend in recent years. World output first passed 70 million metric tons in 1970 and reached 79.5 million tons in 1974. The total passed 90 million tons for the first time in 1978. It remained at about this level in 1979 but fell back slightly in 1980. World sugar production for 1981 was estimated at 92 million tons. Meanwhile, consumption is not expected to have kept pace with production, leading to an increase in stocks which had been declining in the previous two or three years.

The major sugar producers in Asia are India, the Philippines, China, Thailand and Indonesia. Of these, only China and Indonesia are net importers rather than net exporters. The main exporters in the Far East and Australasia are Australia, the Philippines and Thailand; the main importers are Indonesia and Japan. Total Asian sugar exports were 2.5 million metric tons in 1980. India is usually the largest producer of cane sugar in the world, but is not a major exporter. Due to a severe drought in India and other countries in the region during 1978 and 1979, a shortfall in overall production was recorded in many countries and India and Thailand had to import sugar in 1980. In India production was expected to exceed consumption by 2 million tons in the 1981/82 season reaching a record 7 million tons. Indonesia, meanwhile, has announced a plan for building 200 mini-sugar mills over the next five years, with a view to achieving self-sufficiency by 1985. Thailand, having moved, in recent years, for a reduction in its sugar production, encouraging a switch to other crops, has now introduced a programme for the controlled expansion of sugar production. Sugar is Australia's most important export crop after wheat. Sales were up 30 per cent to a record U.S. $777 million in 1981/82, compared with 1980/81. Production in 1981/82 is estimated at 3.43 million tons.

Most of the world's sugar output is traded at fixed prices under long-term agreements. On the free market, however, sugar prices have often fluctuated with extreme volatility. An International Sugar Agreement negotiated in 1958 lapsed as a result of the disruption in the market caused by the cessation of trade between Cuba and the U.S.A. in 1961. In London the import price of raw cane sugar per long ton rose to £105 in November 1963 but fell to only £12 (about 1.4 U.S. cents per lb. and considerably below production costs) in January 1967. As a result, there was a desire for new arrangements to cover the portion of sugar production traded on the open market, which grew to 19.6 million tons in 1977, fell back to about 17.5 million tons in 1978 and 1979 and rose again to 19.5 million tons in 1980.

Negotiations in 1968 produced another International Sugar Agreement (ISA), which included provisions for regulating prices and set up the International Sugar Organization (ISO) to administer it. However, the U.S.A. and the six original members of the EEC did not participate. The ISA was in force from January 1st, 1969, to December 31st, 1973, but, as a result of shortages the price of sugar rose above the stipulated "ceiling" in 1971 and the ISA export quotas were suspended in January 1972. After a failure to reach accord at two international conferences, held in 1973, the ISA expired and was replaced by a purely administrative interim Agreement from January 1st, 1974. This arrangement was subsequently extended in 1975 and 1976. At the end of 1976 the ISA had 56 member countries.

Sugar is one of the 18 primary products in the proposed "integrated programme" for commodity agreements, based on a common fund to stabilize prices, which is a main objective of the UN Conference

PRODUCTION OF SUGAR CANE
('000 metric tons)

	1979	1980
WORLD TOTAL	754,536*	719,800*
Far East	282,487*	253,792*
Oceania	25,222*	27,321*
Leading Regional Producers:		
Australia	21,151	23,948
China, People's Republic	21,508	22,807
India	151,655	128,833
Indonesia	15,995*	17,085*
Pakistan	27,326	27,498
Philippines	20,007*	19,846*
Thailand	20,244	12,460
Other Leading Producers:		
Brazil	138,899	146,065
Colombia	24,700*	26,100*
Cuba	77,311	62,374
Mexico	34,587	36,480
U.S.A.	24,069	24,460

* FAO estimate.

PRODUCTION OF SUGAR BEET
('000 metric tons)

	1979	1980
WORLD TOTAL	263,618*	262,892*
Far East	6,887*	10,298*
Leading Regional Producers:		
China, People's Republic	3,106	6,305
Japan	3,344	3,550
Other Leading Producers:		
France	26,060	26,347
U.S.S.R.	76,214	79,559
U.S.A.	19,954	21,321

* FAO estimate.

on Trade and Development (UNCTAD). Because of this, the UN took a prominent part in moves to produce an effective new ISA.

A full negotiating conference for a new ISA was held, under UN auspices, at Geneva in April and May 1977, but it failed to reach agreement. The 72-nation UN Sugar Conference resumed in September and, after four weeks of talks, a text was agreed for a new five-year ISA to enter into force on January 1st, 1978, with a provision for renegotiation of the basic export tonnages for the third, fourth and fifth quota years. It was also agreed to establish an International Sugar Council (ISC) to supervise implementation of the Agreement. The new ISA aimed to raise the level of international trade in sugar, particularly to increase the export earnings of developing sugar-producing countries, and to achieve stable conditions in this trade, including the avoidance of excessive price fluctuations.

To this end, the new Agreement established a price range of 11 to 21 U.S. cents per lb. for imports on the free market, to be maintained by the use of export quotas and the creation of an internationally controlled special stock of 2.5 million metric tons, to be financed by a levy on exports of 0.28 cent per lb. The storage costs of stock-holding members were to be partly assisted at the annual rate of 1.5 cents per lb. as an interest-free loan from the ISO's Stock Financing Fund. Money for this was to be raised by a contribution on all trade between members of the ISO and on exports by members to non-members. The scheme was due to be brought into effect on July 1st, 1978, but in June the ISC recommended that it should be postponed until October 1st. Further postponements were announced in September and December 1978, in March, June and November 1979 and in March 1980, as U.S. ratification of the ISA was delayed by a legislative deadlock over a domestic sugar programme. With the ratification of the ISA by the U.S.A. in early 1980, the Council agreed that contributions to the Fund should begin from July 1st, 1980, but at a greatly reduced rate of 50 cents per metric ton. In December 1977 the IMF announced that member states would be entitled to use its buffer stock financing facility to help with the cost of maintaining the necessary sugar stocks.

For the first two quota years of the new ISA, basic export quotas were set at 17.4 million metric tons a year for 51 countries. To achieve the price range envisaged in the Agreement, the 29 principal exporting countries (whose quotas totalled 15.9 million tons) agreed to reduce shipments by an initial 15 per cent below their allocated quotas during 1978 and by a further 2.5 per cent if the price was below 11 cents per lb., as was the case in both 1978 and 1979.

In October 1977, when the Sugar Conference reached agreement, the sugar price on the free market was only about 8 U.S. cents per lb. and subsequently fell even further, the decline being attributed partly to sales by exporters from surplus stocks in advance of the ISA's entry into force.

After acceptance by 32 countries (24 exporters and eight importers), the Agreement took effect provisionally on January 1st, 1978. A further 20 countries had signed, but not ratified, the Agreement. The EEC, which had 12 per cent of the exporters' votes, did not sign because of its opposition to export quotas but was expected to resume negotiations later. The main barrier to EEC acceptance is its "structural" surplus of subsidized beet sugar, boosted by imports of cane sugar under the Lomé Convention (*see* below). The EEC is seeking a form of association with the ISA, short of full membership, and exploratory talks on this began in June 1978, but little progress had been made by early 1982. Meanwhile the EEC disposes of its surplus of heavily subsidized sugar on the free market, selling about 3.5 to 4 million tons per year, though it was agreed that the EEC would withold 1.7 million tons of sugar for sale in the 1982/83 season with the possibility of further voluntary restraint in the future.

The ISC held its first session in January 1978 and set a time limit for ratification of June 30th that year. However, in June several members had still to ratify and the time limit was extended. Three further extensions subsequently took the time limit for ratification to June 1980. Meanwhile, by March 1980, 58 countries (42 exporters and 16 importers) had agreed to be bound by the Agreement. From April 1st, 1980, the ISA price range was revised slightly, becoming 12 to 22 cents per lb. It was revised again from November 19th, 1980, to between 13 and 23 cents. However, the ISC failed to reach agreement on the renegotiation of basic tonnages for export quotas and, as a result, the "fall-back" formula for the calculation of basic export tonnages for 1980/82 came into force.

During 1978 and the first half of 1979 prices remained depressed (*see* below), so the new ISA did not become effectively established. In early 1978 it was reported, though, that several larger sugar producers had abandoned expansion plans or had begun to reduce production. In April 1978, with the market price continuing below the ISA's "floor" price, export quotas were reduced by a further 2.5 per cent, the maximum cut permitted. Despite restricting exporters to 82.5 per cent of their export quotas, the ISA failed to have any significant effect until late in 1979, owing to the existence of huge stocks accumulated by over-production. Also hampering the Agreement was the failure of the U.S.A. (the leading sugar importer) to ratify and the refusal of the EEC to join.

The U.S.A. ratified the Agreement in December 1979 and the implementing legislation was passed by Congress in April 1980. Meanwhile, in January 1980, with world prices rising dramatically, the ISO first increased export quotas by 10 per cent and then suspended them altogether. For 1980 there was no limit on the volume of sugar which exporters could sell (the U.S.A., for example, having exported only 14,000 metric tons in 1979, sold 587,000 tons abroad in 1980) and the ISO lost most of its power to regulate the sugar market. Later, when average prices had passed 19, 20 and 21 cents per lb. respectively, the ISO had to authorize the release of one-third of its special stock (837,000 metric tons) of sugar at each stage. The market, however, continued to rise to over 40 cents in November, from which point it declined rapidly. In April 1981 the sugar price fell below 21 cents per lb. and the ISA had to support the market. When, in May, the 15-day average price stayed below 16 cents per lb. for five market days, export quotas totalling 14.3 million tons of sugar per year were automatically imposed on ISO members in proportion to their 1980 basic export tonnages.

In November 1981 the ISC agreed in principle to extend the ISA for two years (i.e. up to December 31st, 1984), subject to settlement of the question of basic export tonnages, for which no solution covering 1983 and 1984 had been found by June 1982.

In London the import price of raw cane sugar reached a record £650 per long ton in November 1974 but quickly fell. During 1975 and 1976 the price was generally between £110 and £235 per ton. From the beginning of 1977 London sugar prices were quoted per metric ton (2,204.6 lb.) instead of per long ton (2,240 lb.). In 1977 the price oscillated between a high of £151 per ton in April and a low of £85 in November.

Following the entry into force of the new ISA, the sugar price climbed to £114 per ton in January 1978 but fell to £94 in March. It rose above £105 per ton in June but in July dropped to £81, the lowest level since December 1972 and well below even the most efficient producers' costs. The price recovered to £112 per ton in October 1978 but declined to £93 in January 1979. Sugar then hovered at around £100 per ton.

However, from September 1979, following reports of hurricane damage to sugar plantations in the Caribbean, the London sugar price began to rise steadily and by the end of the year had reached £182 per ton. In January 1980 the price passed £200 per ton and in February, with news of reduced sugar crops in Cuba, the U.S.S.R. and elsewhere, it rose to £287. In March 1980 sugar fell to £190 per ton but in May it

Production of Centrifugal Sugar

(raw value, '000 metric tons)

	1979	1980
World Total	88,984*	84,212*
Far East	17,317*	14,454*
Oceania	3,436	3,725
Leading Regional Producers:		
Australia	2,963	3,329
China (incl. Taiwan)	3,587*	3,615*
India‡	6,367	4,191
Indonesia	1,307	1,403†
Philippines	2,342	2,343
Thailand	1,862	1,098
Other Leading Producers:		
Brazil	7,027†	8,547†
Cuba	8,048	6,787
France	4,332	4,253
U.S.S.R.	7,700†	7,150†
U.S.A.	5,061	5,331

* FAO estimate. † Unofficial figure.

‡ Includes sugar (raw value) refined from gur.

moved up to £362. In June the price slipped to £285 per ton but recovered to £334. In July it fell to £235 per ton. The dramatic upsurge in prices was partly due to speculative activity but it was also assisted by earlier ISA export restrictions and by the prospect of the first production deficit since 1972/73, which in fact occurred in both 1979 and 1980. However, after so many years of surplus, world sugar stocks, which were near peak levels, have been sharply reduced. In November 1980 the London sugar price reached £410 per ton, its highest level for almost six years, with March 1981 "futures" touching £423 at one stage. From this point, however, sugar fell dramatically, high prices having hit demand. In December the London price slumped to £245 per ton, although it soon climbed to £310. After another fall, the price reached £315 per ton in January 1981. In February it fell to £235 per ton but rose again to £285. Further sharp falls took the sugar price to £168 per ton in May. The price fluctuated between £148 and £235 for the rest of the year but the overall trend was downwards and in June 1982 sugar fell to £95 per ton, the lowest level since August 1979.

During the period of depressed prices, sugar producers were faced by rising production costs, particularly of fuel based on petroleum, and generally inflationary trends in consumer prices for other goods. The low sugar prices prevailing between mid-1977 and mid-1979 were due to the existence of large surplus sugar stocks, standing at 31 million tons in August 1979, resulting from a steep rise in output. This rise was a reflection of the expansionary policies pursued by sugar producers, especially in cane-growing countries, following the record prices of 1974. Estimated world sugar consumption, which averaged about 20 kg. (raw value) per head in 1973 and 1974, fell in 1975 to 18.9 kg. per head as a reaction to the same high prices. With lower prices, average sugar consumption rose to a record 21.1 kg. per head in 1979. With some decline in total consumption in 1980, especially in the industrialized countries, per caput consumption was also expected to fall.

In October 1978 a market for white sugar was established in London, where previously trading had been confined to raw sugar. Prior to this the world's only white sugar market was in Paris.

Two of the more important special trading arrangements—the U.S. Sugar Act (laying down a system of domestic and foreign import quotas) and the Commonwealth Sugar Agreement (CSA), covering the United Kingdom's imports from Commonwealth sugar producers—both expired at the end of 1974. The former arrangement has ceased completely while the latter was replaced to a great extent by the first Lomé Convention, adopted in February 1975, between the enlarged EEC and a group of African, Caribbean and Pacific (ACP) countries. A special Protocol on sugar, forming part of the Convention, required the EEC to import not less than 1.4 million metric tons of raw sugar per year from ACP countries. The price to be paid to the supplying countries was linked to the minimum EEC intervention price each year, but, as the agreement was made when world prices were high, it was agreed that a supplementary payment would be made for 1975. This had the effect of raising the price per long ton from about £160 to £260. The first Lomé Convention became fully effective on April 1st, 1976. In June 1976, when the world price was below £180 per long ton, the EEC and ACP countries agreed on a price of 267 units of account (then about £194) per metric ton for the 12 months ending June 30th, 1977.

In May 1977 agreement was reached on a guaranteed price of 272.5 Units of Account (UA), then about £215, per metric ton to be paid by the EEC for 1,250,000 tons of raw sugar between May 1st, 1977, and June 30th, 1978. Representatives of the ACP countries met the EEC Commission in May 1978 to discuss terms for sugar supplies in 1978/79. The ACP countries asked for a 9 per cent rise in the guaranteed price of cane sugar, back-dated to May 1st, but in June they accepted the EEC offer of a 2 per cent increase, to UA 278.1, equal to 336.2 European Currency Units (ECU), per ton, for 12 months from July 1st. The agreed price for sales of raw sugar was 127 per cent above the current free market price. The price per metric ton of sugar was equivalent to 341.3 ECU in 1979/80, 358.9 ECU in 1980/81 and 389.4 ECU in 1981/82. In June 1979 the ACP countries agreed to accept an increase of 1.5 per cent in the EEC's guaranteed price for 1.3 million tons of raw sugar to be exported to the Community in the 12 months from July 1st. The second Lomé Convention, also incorporating a Sugar Protocol and running until February 28th, 1985, took effect on January 1st, 1981.

Production data for sugar cane and sugar beet cover generally all crops harvested, except crops grown explicity for feed. Provisional figures for 1981 indicate a world cane crop of 775.3 million metric tons (including 288.7 million tons from the Far East) and a beet crop of 281.5 million tons. The third table covers the production of raw sugar by the centrifugal process. In some countries sugar cane is used to produce sugar by much simpler methods than the centrifugal process. The resulting sugar is usually unrefined and brown in colour and is called gur or jaggery in India. The largest producer of non-centrifugal sugar is India, which produces between 5 and 6 million tons out of a total annual world production of 12 to 13 million tons.

In September 1976, when New York sugar prices stood at only 8 cents per lb., the U.S.A. trebled import tariffs to protect the country's sugar producers. The import duty on raw sugar was reduced in December 1977 and removed altogether from January 1st, 1980. However, in December 1981 the U.S. introduced new and increased import duties, with a further rise in April 1982 adding almost 1 cent per lb. to duty. A quota was also announced for sugar imports, which was a particular setback for developing nations which rely heavily on the U.S. market for their sugar sales. Moreover, the lowering of world oil prices was expected to reduce the demand for sugar by major petroleum exporters such as Indonesia, Mexico and Venezuela, all net sugar importers on a fairly large scale. The continued world economic recession, combined with high interest rates and a stronger U.S. dollar, have depressed demand for sugar in industrialized countries generally, despite a lowering of sugar prices since November 1980.

As sugar prices rose, the competition faced from other sweeteners, including maize-based products (e.g. isoglucose, a high-fructose syrup) and chemical additives (such as saccharine, aspartame and zylitol), increased. Natural substitutes expanded their share of the market for sweeteners from 18 to 30 per cent between 1973 and 1977. In March 1977 the Canadian and U.S. Governments announced plans to ban, on health grounds, the use of saccharine as a food sweetener. In November, however, this proposal was postponed for 18 months, although the moratorium was not renewed when it ended in May 1979. Approval of five new sweeteners has been recommended in the United Kingdom, and aspartame is now approved by several countries. The growth of high-fructose corn syrup has decreased, but it has made sizeable inroads in the sweetener markets of many industrialized nations, and several developing countries are establishing plants for its production.

In 1979 Malaysia announced plans to cultivate stevia, a plant containing stevioside, which is a non-calorific substance about 300 times as sweet as sugar. Stevioside will be exported initally to Japan.

Sweet Potatoes (*Ipomoea*)

Sweet potatoes are an important root crop in many tropical and sub-tropical countries. Like cassava, much of the crop is grown on small plots and consumed locally.

The People's Republic of China is by far the largest producer of sweet potatoes.

PRODUCTION OF SWEET POTATOES
('000 metric tons)

	1979	1980
WORLD TOTAL . . .	109,036*	107,254*
Far East . . .	100,450*	98,595*
Oceania . . .	595*	600*
Leading Regional Producers:		
Bangladesh . . .	795	795*
China, People's Republic .	87,500*	86,000*
India . . .	1,545	1,600*
Indonesia . . .	2,194	2,025†
Japan . . .	1,360	1,400*
Korea, Republic . .	1,387	1,103
Philippines . . .	1,120	1,050*
Taiwan . . .	1,225	1,080
Viet-Nam . . .	2,200*	2,400*
Other Leading Producers:		
Brazil . . .	900*	1,000*
Burundi‡ . . .	870*	920*
Rwanda . . .	865*	888*
Uganda‡ . . .	670*	670*
U.S.A. . . .	607	497

* FAO estimate. † Unofficial figure.
‡ Including yams.

Tea (*Camellia sinensis*)

Tea is a beverage made by infusing in boiling water the dried young leaves and unopened leaf-buds of the tea plant, an evergreen shrub or small tree. Black and green tea are the most common finished products. The former counts for the bulk of the world's supply and is associated with machine manufacture and generally the plantation system, which guarantees an adequate supply of leaf to the factory. The latter, mainly produced in China and Japan, is to a great extent the product of peasants, and much of it is consumed locally. There are two main varieties of tea, the China and the Assam, although hybrids may be obtained, such as Darjeeling.

Total recorded tea exports by producing countries were less than 600,000 metric tons in 1969 but thereafter rose steadily, passing 700,000 tons for the first time in 1974 and 800,000 tons in 1977. Exports declined slightly in 1978, but rose during the following two tears, reaching 873,000 tons in 1980. The principal exporting countries are India and Sri Lanka, with roughly equal sales, but the quantity which they jointly supply has remained fairly stable (between 360,000 and 440,000 tons per year), so their share of trade has been declining. During the 1960s they were responsible for over two-thirds of all the tea sold by producing countries, whereas in 1978 Sri Lanka overtook India as the world's largest tea exporter, with total sales of 193,000 metric tons, despite lower production than in 1977, but lost that position in 1979, when India exported 199,700 tons. Sri Lanka's production has been gradually declining since its peak of 228,000 metric tons in 1965, but, with World Bank assistance, the Government is undertaking a massive replanting and improvement programme (almost 90 per cent of the country's tea acreage is over 100 years old). In an effort to correct the deficiencies of management since nationalization in 1975, foreigners are being invited back to run the country's tea plantations.

PRODUCTION OF MADE TEA
('000 metric tons)

	1979	1980
WORLD TOTAL . . .	1,821*	1,857*
Far East . . .	1,313*	1,359*
Oceania . . .	8*	8*
Leading Regional Producers:		
Bangladesh . . .	37	40
China, People's Republic .	277	304
India . . .	552	577
Indonesia . . .	89	95
Japan . . .	98	102
Sri Lanka . . .	208	191
Taiwan . . .	27	24
Other Leading Producers:		
Kenya . . .	99	90
Turkey . . .	102	96
U.S.S.R. . . .	118	130

* FAO estimate. † Unofficial figure.

Indian tea production in 1981 was expected to be slightly down on the record 577,000 metric tons of 1980. In early 1979 the Government lifted all export duties on tea, when India held nearly 30 per cent of the world market. Exports were 224,000 tons in 1980 and rose to a record 245,000 tons in 1981. Meanwhile, new tax concessions on exports are being instituted. In 1979 the area planted with tea was estimated at 350, 000 hectares and it was planned to increase this by a further 100,000 hectares over a five-year period. Following recent record crops, India plans to raise its exports by 10,000 metric tons per year and two packaging centres were established in Singapore and Egypt during 1981. Nevertheless, India's share of the market declined from 45 per cent in 1951 to 28 per cent in 1980 and, unless exports rise to keep pace with planned increases in production, the country would be faced with large tea surpluses in the future. On the other hand, India is the largest consumer of tea, as well as the largest producer, and the domestic market continues to expand by about 6 per cent every year.

World production of tea grew at an average annual rate of 3.3 per cent between 1955 and 1973 but a continuing surplus, as well as the difficulty of storing tea for long periods, led to a steady decline in prices. However, world output has continued to rise steadily and provisional figures for 1981 indicate a crop of about the same size as that of 1980. China's output rose to 343,000 tons in 1981.

Quantitative restrictions on tea imports have been removed by nearly all developed countries. In the United Kingdom, the largest single importer (taking about 30 per cent of world trade), consumption of tea per person fell from 10 lb. (4.5 kg.) in 1958 to 7.58 lb. (3.44 kg.) in 1975, but increased in 1976 to 8.13 lb. (3.69 kg.), partly because of the sharp rise in the price of coffee, its main competitor. As tea prices also rose in late 1976 and early 1977, British consumption fell. It averaged 7.1 lb. (3.2 kg.) per head in 1977 and only 6.4 lb. (2.9 kg.) in 1978, the lowest level since 1945. Average tea consumption was back up to 7.1 lb. per head in 1977 and 7.23 lb. (3.28 kg.) in 1980. The United Kingdom's tea imports of 177,694 metric tons in 1978 were the lowest since 1950, but the figure rose to 197,732 tons in 1979 and to 211,035 tons in 1980. Average tea demand has been falling recently in other developed countries but consumption and imports in developing countries have expanded significantly.

Much of the tea traded internationally is sold by auction, first in the exporting country and then again in the importing country. In 1976 and 1977, despite steadily rising production, tea prices increased considerably as a result of growing demand, partly due to the sharp rise in coffee prices.

From 1956 to 1967 the average import price of Northern India tea at London auctions varied between £450 and £530 per metric ton. The average price fell to £405 per ton in 1969 and remained below £500 until 1973. Thereafter the price began to rise, reaching more than £1,000 per ton in September 1976. A more dramatic price surge began in January 1977 and the peak prices, reached in March, were £2,500 per ton for plain tea, £2,700 for medium and £2,890 for quality, although, because of inflation, even these record tea prices were more than 15 per cent lower in real terms than the prices prevailing at the beginning of the 1960s. By September 1977 London tea prices had fallen, with medium tea at £1,050 per ton. In 1978 prices for medium tea oscillated between £1,060 and £1,250 per ton. During 1979 the average London auction price for all teas was generally between £930 and £1,130 per ton. In July the average price of plain tea was only £580 per ton, its lowest level since February 1976. By July 1980 plain tea was £700 per ton, but fell to £540 in September, only slowly recovering to £670 per ton in April 1981. Quality tea reached a low of £1,220 per ton in 1980, having begun the year at £1,370. In 1981 the price fluctuated between £1,170 and £1,400 per ton. In April 1982 the price was £1,170 per ton.

The first official International Tea Agreement, signed in 1933, established the International Tea Committee, based in London, as an administrative body. The Agreement's provisions were enforced by the governments of India, Ceylon (now Sri Lanka) and the Netherlands East Indies (now Indonesia). It was renewed for five years in 1938 and again in 1943. A two-year Agreement was made for 1948–50 and another five-year Agreement signed in 1950. This was not renewed after 1955 but the Committee remained in existence to provide a link between producing countries. Until 1979 it was financed by subscription from producers, in proportion to their share of world exports. In June 1979 the Committee adopted a new constitution, under which it is financed equally by producers/exporters and consumers. In 1980 there were seven producer/exporter members (Bangladesh, India, Indonesia, Sri Lanka and three African countries), four consumer members and one associate member.

In 1969, when tea prices fell to a low point, the FAO Consultative Committee on Tea was formed and an exporters' group, meeting under this Committee's auspices, set export quotas in order to maintain tea prices. These quotas have applied since 1970 but are generally regarded as too liberal to have more than a minimal effect on prices. The perishability of tea makes the effective operation of a buffer stock very difficult.

In September 1976 representatives of leading tea producers met in Geneva to discuss the establishment of an International Tea Promotion Association (ITPA). The meeting, sponsored by the International Trade Centre of UNCTAD and GATT, was attended by 17 countries but China and Kenya did not take part. Fourteen of the participating countries, representing 81 per cent of the world's tea exports, agreed terms for the proposed Association, to be submitted to their governments. The ITPA is intended to develop and intensify the co-ordination of policy and action by tea exporters to increase demand for the beverage. Members will contribute to promotional budgets in proportion to their share of the relevant market. The agreement to establish the ITPA was ratified by India and Sri Lanka, the two leading exporters, in November 1977 and by Indonesia and five African countries in September 1978. The agreement came into force in February 1979 and the ITPA became operational in April, when the first session of its governing body was held in Geneva. In November 1979, when the ITPA had nine members (including Bangladesh), it was announced that the Association's headquarters would be established at Rotterdam in the Netherlands.

Tea is one of the 18 commodities in the "integrated programme" proposed by UNCTAD for stabilizing the prices of major primary products through a common fund. In February 1977 the FAO intergovernmental group on tea met in London for talks aimed at preparing the way for an UNCTAD conference to establish a new International Tea Agreement. It was decided that a new agreement should be based on export controls. Since then a series of talks has taken place in which various proposals have been discussed. However, the fact remains that no new agreement acceptable to both importers and exporters has been arrived at to regulate prices, which have fallen by 25 per cent since 1972, owing to over-supply. At a 40-nation meeting in December 1979 the tea exporters proposed a price stabilization plan with the aim of keeping 1980 auction prices within a range of £940 to £1,160 per metric ton.

In May 1980 a Conference in Indonesia of the world's ten leading tea exporters, accounting for about 95 per cent of total world exports, could agree only in principle to set a global net export quota for 1981 and no accord of any kind was reached on fixing country-specific export quotas as a preliminary to an international tea agreement. A further meeting was held in Salisbury, Zimbabwe, in November 1980. This, too, was unsuccessful, with producing countries, particularly those such as Kenya (where tea production is expanding), loath to accept voluntarily any kind of restraint on exports. The objective was to achieve an average price of £1,050 per metric ton. According to the International Tea Committee, world tea exports in 1979 traded at an average price of £940 per ton.

Talks continue on a regular basis and a conference of producing and consuming countries which sat in Geneva in May 1982 outlined broad terms for a quota and price-control mechanism. The main European tea-importing countries agreed to make price stabilization the principal aim of any agreement.

Tin

The world's main tin deposits occur in the equatorial zones of Asia and Africa, in central South America and in Australia. Cassiterite is the only economically important tin-bearing mineral, and it is generally associated with tungsten, silver and tantalum minerals. There is a clear association of cassiterite with igneous rocks of granitic composition, and "primary" cassiterite deposits occur as disseminations, or in veins and fissures in or around granites. If the primary deposits are eroded, by rivers for instance, cassiterite may be concentrated and deposited in "secondary", sedimentary deposits. These secondary deposits comprise the bulk of the world's tin reserves. The ore is treated, generally by gravity method or flotation, to produce concentrates prior to smelting.

Tin owes its special place in industry to its unique combination of properties; low melting point, the ability to form alloys with most other metals, resistance to corrosion, non-toxicity and good appearance. Its main uses are in tinplate (about 40 per cent of world tin consumption), in alloys (tin-lead solder, bronze, brass, pewter, bearing and type metal), and in chemical compounds (in paints, plastics, medicines, coatings and as fungicides and insecticides).

In 1980 world* production of tin-in-concentrates was 199,500 metric tons. In recent years the production of tin-in-concentrates from Australia, Indonesia and Thailand has reached relatively high levels while that of Malaysia, the world's largest producer (accounting for about 30 per cent of total ouput) and exporter, fell in 1977 to its lowest level since 1962, but recovered in 1978. South-East Asian production comes mainly from gravel pump mines and dredges, working alluvial deposits, although there are underground and open-cast mines working hard-rock deposits. In Australia underground and open-cast mines and alluvial dredges are of equal importance.

World smelter production of primary tin metal reached 198,500 metric tons in 1980, slightly less than in the previous year, but 6,000 tons more than in 1978 and almost 19,000 tons more than in 1977. Indonesia and Thailand now smelt virtually the whole of their mine production, as do Malaysia and Japan which also import concentrates. Australia smelts about half of its mine production, most of the remainder being sent to Penang in Malaysia. Concentrates from Burma, Laos, the Republic of Korea, and those of unspecified origin are mainly exported to Malaysia, Europe and the U.S.S.R.

Until comparatively recently, despite a recession in the steel industry, consumption of primary tin has generally exceeded production, leading to a reduction in surplus stocks. However, since the mid-1970s the trend appears to have been reversed, with production exceeding consumption in each of the last three years for which complete figures are available. In 1980, consumption of primary tin was 23,100 metric tons below the production figure of 198,500 tons. A similar surplus was expected in 1981.

The total mine production of tin fell steadily between 1972 and 1976. While mining generally recovered in 1977, the output from Malaysia, the world's leading tin producer, fell to its lowest level since 1961. However, world mine production passed the previous peak in 1978, rose even higher in 1979 and held at that level in 1980.

Since 1956 much of the world's tin production and trade has been covered by successive international agreements, administered by the International Tin Council (ITC), based in London. The main object of each International Tin Agreement (ITA) has been to stabilize prices within an agreed range by using a buffer stock to regulate the supply of tin. The buffer stock has been financed by producing countries, with voluntary contributions by some consuming countries. "Floor" and "ceiling" prices are fixed, and the range between the two prices is divided into lower, middle and upper sectors. If the price is above the "ceiling", the Buffer Stock Manager sells, at the market price, such tin as is at his disposal until the price falls below the "ceiling" or his stock is exhausted. In the upper sector he may operate at his discretion, provided he is a net seller, and in the lower sector provided he is a net buyer. If the price is below the "floor", he buys tin at the "floor" price until the price rises above the "floor" or his funds are exhausted. The ITA also includes provisions for the IMF to assist producing countries in funding the buffer stock. For added protection, the ITC can introduce export controls as a last resort if the "floor" price is being threatened. It took such action in April 1975, when an export cut of about 18 per cent was imposed. Again, in April 1982, in an attempt to support falling prices, an export cut of 15 per cent (4,500 metric tons) was made.

At a UN conference on tin, held at Geneva in May and June 1975, delegates from 36 countries negotiated the Fifth ITA, covering 1976–81. The new Agreement entered into force provisionally on July 1st, 1976. An important change from the previous ITA was the inclusion of a target buffer stock of 40,000 metric tons, double the limit in the 1971–76 Agreement. The increase was to be achieved by supplementing the producers' compulsory contribution of 20,000 metric tons by voluntary "additional contributions" of 20,000 tons of tin or its cash equivalent from consuming countries. By April 1977 the ITA had been ratified by 26 of the participating countries, including the U.S.A. (the world's leading tin consumer) for the

* World totals of production and consumption exclude Albania, the People's Republic of China, the German Democratic Republic, the Democratic People's Republic of Korea, Mongolia, the U.S.S.R. and Viet-Nam.

first time. The provisional operation of the new ITA was extended to June 30th, 1977, after a decision had been reached on incorporating a permanent price review mechanism into the Agreement. This was to meet the reservations expressed by representatives of Bolivia, a high-cost tin producer, who felt that the ITA's price range was too low and had initially declined to ratify it. Bolivia finally ratified on June 14th, 1977 and the Agreement came into force definitively on the same date. By 1979 the ITA had been ratified by 30 countries (seven producers and 23 consumers).

In January 1977 the free market price broke through the ITC's "ceiling" and the Council exhausted the tin available in its buffer stock, thus effectively losing its ability to intervene in the tin market. An ITC meeting in July raised the intervention prices by more than 10 per cent but the "ceiling" price still remained below the free market price. Despite pressure from producing countries for intervention prices to be brought into line with the world market, another ITC meeting in January 1978 left them unchanged. In April 1978 the free market price of tin fell below the ITA's "ceiling" for the first time in almost 15 months. In July the ITC fixed a higher price range, with the "floor" price increased by 12.5 per cent, and it was informally agreed to leave the range unaltered for twelve months. Free market prices, however, remained above the ITA "ceiling".

In July 1979 a ministerial meeting of seven leading tin producers, together accounting for 83 per cent of world production, took place in Indonesia. This gathering, the first of its kind, was held to discuss a common position for producers at the ITC meeting later in the month. When the ITC met, it was agreed to raise the ITA "floor" price by 11.1 per cent and the "ceiling" price by 14.7 per cent. As a result, the "ceiling" price was briefly above the current market price again. After another ministerial meeting of producers in February 1980, the ITC raised both intervention prices a further 10 per cent in March, although the new "ceiling" price was still below current free market levels. By November 1980, however, the market price of tin had fallen below the "ceiling" and the buffer stock manager accepted 1,500 metric tons of tin from the U.S.A., his stocks having run out as he sold them in a vain attempt to put a brake on soaring prices.

In February 1981 the ITA "floor" price was set at £5,900 per ton. If the market price fell to that level, the ITA's international price-support mechanism would come into operation.

The first session of a UN conference to negotiate the Sixth ITA, to operate from 1981, was held in Geneva in April and May 1980. Producers sought further changes in the price range and also proposed revision of ITC voting procedures. By contrast, the U.S.A. proposed a larger buffer stock and the abolition of the provision for export controls which, it claimed, discouraged investment in new production. The talks ended with key issues still unresolved.

In December 1980 further negotiations were held in Geneva for a Sixth ITA. They broke down, however, mainly because the U.S.A. insisted that export quotas should be scrapped and a bigger buffer stock than the 50,000 metric tons agreed by the producers created to protect consumers in times of shortage and high prices. The producer nations, for their part, believed that too large a buffer stock would act as a permanent depressant on tin prices.

As a consequence of the failure of these talks, in January 1981 the Fifth ITA was extended until June 1982 to allow for further negotiations towards a new agreement. In March 1981 a third session of talks was held in Geneva and again members were unable to reach any firm agreement. Consumers, led by the U.S.A., could not agree to a rise in the ITA price range demanded by the producing nations, and a compromise formula presented by the conference chairman, Peter Lai, was rejected. Another round of talks in April produced deadlock and, to allow more time for negotiations, the Fifth ITA was extended a further year to its limit of June 1983.

Talks in Geneva in June 1981, which were seen as the last chance to formulate a new ITA, seemed destined to the same fate as all those before them. The producing nations were critical of the U.S.A. for selling tin from its stockpile (*see* below), and, although most of them were prepared to compromise on the size of the buffer stock and the extent of price range alterations, Bolivia was not. The U.S.A. reduced its figure for the buffer stock by 5,000 metric tons to 50,000 tons, but major differences remained. However, 50 countries (excluding the U.S.A. and Bolivia) finally accepted a compromise package put forward by Peter Lai. Under the terms of this proposal, the buffer stock would compromise a permanent supply of 30,000 metric tons and a back-up stock of 20,000 tons, to be financed equally by producers and consumers; the "ceiling" price would be 130 per cent of the "floor price" and export controls would be triggered by buffer levels of 35,000 and 40,000 metric tons.

The Sixth ITA was opened for a period of ratification running from August 3rd, 1981, to April 30th, 1982, and was due to come into force (provisional or definitive) depending on the extent of membership of tin-producing and -consuming countries.

By April 30th, 1982, the U.S.A. and Bolivia had still not signed the agreement and, although 70 of the producers had done so, it appeared unlikely that the balancing 65 per cent level of consumer support required for the ITA even to be adopted provisionally would be forthcoming. Malaysia agreed to remain a member of the new ITA in June, but at the same time joined with Indonesia and Thailand, the other major producing nations, in setting up an independent group, on the pattern of OPEC, to protect their interests.

Meanwhile, it was expected that the U.S.A.'s contribution to the buffer stock would be in the form of metal released from its strategic stockpile of about 200,000 tons. In 1977 and 1978 several attempts were made to obtain legislative approval for a proposal to transfer 5,000 long tons of tin to the ITC buffer stock and to sell a further 30,000 tons from the stockpile.

However, the necessary legislation was repeatedly delayed and did not come into effect until January 1980. The prospect of the proposed sale was a source of concern to producing countries, which feared that the disposal of such a large amount would lower prices. However, the U.S. Government has announced that the tin sales will be made gradually (10,000 long tons per year for three years) so as not to depress prices too severely. Disposals began in July 1980.

On the free market, tin prices increased considerably in recent years. On the London Metal Exchange the price of standard grade tin per metric ton rose from less than £1,700 in February 1973 to reach £4,245 in September 1974, then fell to below £3,000 in the following month. The price hovered between £3,000 and £3,500 per ton in 1975.

During 1976 tin recorded a low price of about £3,000 per ton and a high of £5,000. The average price for the year was £4,255 per ton.

In 1977 the rising trend of the London tin price was maintained. The price per ton rose as high as £7,355 in December and did not fall below £5,000 all year, the annual average being £6,181 per ton.

Tin was thus a remarkable exception to the general 1977 pattern of over-supply and low prices for metals. Despite falls early in the year, 1978 saw the London tin price climb still higher, passing the previous peak in October and reaching £8,090 per ton in November. Although the price subsequently fell rather abruptly to below £7,000, the 1978 average was £6,706 per ton.

PRODUCTION OF TIN CONCENTRATES
(tin content, metric tons)

	1979	1980
WORLD TOTAL†	200,700	199,500
Far East	136,300	136,870
Oceania	12,571	10,391
Leading Regional Producers:		
Australia	12,571	10,391
Burma	1,000*	1,100*
Indonesia	29,440	32,527
Japan	658	549
Korea, Republic	40	9
Laos	600*	600*
Malaysia	62,995	61,404
Thailand‡	33,962	33,685
Unspecified origin	7,600*	7,000*
Other Leading Producers:		
Bolivia	27,781	27,271
Brazil	6,645	6,930
Zaire‡	3,300*	3,159

* Estimate.

† As defined on p. 89. Tin is also produced in the People's Republic of China, the German Democratic Republic and the U.S.S.R. For 1979 *World Metal Statistics* has estimated production (in metric tons) as: G.D.R. 1,600; U.S.S.R. 18,000; People's Republic of China 17,000.

‡ Including tin in tin-tungsten concentrates.

Note: Total figures for the Far East are rounded off to the nearest 10 tons. World figures are rounded off to the nearest 100 tons.

Source: International Tin Council, London.

Amid general fluctuations, the London tin price reached a new high of £8,150 per ton in June 1979 but fell back to £6,325 in July before climbing steadily towards the end of the year to nearly £8,000 per ton. The average price in 1979 was £7,276 per ton.

In January 1980 the London tin price dropped to £7,235 per ton but moved up quickly to £7,935. Tin fell to £7,225 per ton in February but rose to £8,350 in March. Thereafter, however, tin prices went into a steady decline. The effect of the world recession on tin consumption (which fell while production continued to rise gradually, adding to existing stocks) and the intention of the U.S.A. to sell from its strategic tin stockpile combined to depress prices. After falling throughout most of 1980, the London

PRODUCTION OF PRIMARY TIN METAL
(metric tons)

	1979	1980
WORLD TOTAL*	201,300	198,500
Far East	139,620	142,160
Oceania	5,423	4,819
Leading Regional Producers:		
Australia	5,423	4,819
Indonesia	27,790	30,465
Japan	1,252	1,319
Malaysia	73,068	71,318
Thailand	33,058	34,689

* As defined on p. 89.

Note: Total figures for the Far East are rounded off to the nearest 10 tons. World figures are rounded off to the nearest 100 tons.

Source: International Tin Council, *Monthly Statistical Bulletin.*

tin price slumped to £5,700 per ton in January 1981. Tin recovered to £6,425 per ton in April but fell to £5,875 in May.

Under the influence of a mystery buyer, believed to be acting for Malaysia and other producer interests, the tin price was pushed to a succession of new peaks in the second half of 1981 and early 1982. In February 1982 the London tin price was a record £8,985 per ton. In March the price fell dramatically to £6,845 per ton but recovered to more than £7,200. In June tin slumped to £5,460 per ton, its lowest level for five years, but quickly rose to more than £7,000 after Malaysia agreed to join the new International Tin Agreement (*see* above).

Tobacco

Two tobaccos are grown in Asia, *Nicotiana tabacum* and *Nicotiana rustica*. The former is used in commercially manufactured products while the latter is consumed in "cottage industry" products such as snuff, simple cigars and cigarettes. Commercially grown tobacco can be subdivided into four major types according to how the leaf is cured or dried: flue-cured, air-cured (including Burley, cigar, light and dark), fire-cured and sun-cured (including oriental). Each has specific chemical and smoking characteristics and each is used in specific products (e.g. flue-cured in Virginia cigarettes). All types are grown in Asia.

As in other major producing areas, new cultivars have been developed by local research organizations with specific, desirable chemical characteristics, disease resistance characteristics and improved yields. Almost all tobacco production comes from small farmer production; there is no estate production of tobacco such as is common in tea. Emphasis has been placed on improving yields by the selection of cultivars, by the increased use of fertilizers and by the elimination or reduction of crop loss (through use of crop chemicals) and on reducing hand labour requirements through the mechanization of land preparation and the use of crop chemicals. Harvesting is still entirely a manual operation as the size of farmers' holdings and the cost of harvesting devices (now commonly used in the U.S.A. and Canada) preclude such development in Asia. The flue-curing process demands energy in the form of oil, gas, coal or wood. To ensure that supplies of wood are continuously renewed, the tobacco industry in, for example, Pakistan and Sri Lanka, encourages the planting of trees. Research is also being done into the possibility of converting waste materials, such as rice husks, into energy.

The principal type of tobacco grown is flue-cured. Of the countries producing this tobacco the most important are China, India, Japan and Korea. While most of China's production is locally consumed, there are exports to Europe. Production in China decreased significantly in the period 1978 to 1980. This decline was considered to be the result of a failure to increase tobacco prices to farmers in line with other farm and rural products; it was exacerbated by the increased domestic competition for tobacco (some 140 small cigarette factories had been set up in rural China). Farm prices have now been increased and many of the small cigarette factories in the rural areas closed. Consequently, between 1979 and 1981, China purchased large quantities of flue-cured tobacco from Bangladesh, Brazil, Canada, India, Thailand and Zimbabwe.

Japan is unable to produce sufficient flue-cured tobacco for domestic consumption, mainly due to land pressure, and thus has to rely on substantial imports, though these have been reduced over the past few years. India, an important supplier of flue-cured tobacco, has increased production since 1965 and Korean flue-cured is now accepted on the world markets. In both Korea and Thailand domestic requirements are likely to maintain pressure on production; exports, however, have shown signs of levelling off since 1977 but this situation is unlikely to be reversed despite the increased supplies of flue-cured tobacco now available on the world market as a result of the settlement in Zimbabwe.

Of the other tobacco producing countries in the Far East, production in Bangladesh has been increased to meet the need to replace tobaccos once produced in West Pakistan and exported to East Pakistan (now Bangladesh). Indonesia is a significant producer and exporter of cigar tobaccos, yet still requires to import flue-cured tobacco to sustain its domestic market; increasing quantities of domestic flue-cured are now available ofrm Sulawesi, Bali and Lombok through the efforts of a large domestic manufacturer. Domestic tobacco production is increasing in Malaysia under the aegis of the National Tobacco Board. The Philippines produces both flue-cured and air-cured tobacco acceptable to world markets. Sri Lanka, once solely a producer of tobacco for domestic consumption, now exports quantities of both flue-cured and air-cured tobacco.

The only significant producers of Burley tobacco are Japan (for domestic consumption) and Korea (for domestic consumption and for export), although Thailand is increasing production. Dark air-cured tobacco production is monopolized by India, China, Pakistan and Indonesia. India's production is almost entirely for domestic consumption. Insignificant quantities of fire-cured and oriental tobaccos are produced in Asia.

Growing conditions in New Zealand and Australia are totally dissimilar from those in other countries in the Far East. Tobacco holdings are large, mechanization is significant and cultural problems, such as the occurrence of blue mould in Australia, are unique. Domestic production, mainly flue-cured, is encouraged through government legislation stipulating a minimum quantity of such tobacco to be incorporated into tobacco products marketed in Australia and, currently, New Zealand. The main sources of imported tobacco are the U.S.A. and Korea.

PRODUCTION OF TOBACCO—ALL TYPES
(farm sales weight, '000 metric tons)

	1980	1981*
WORLD TOTAL	5,575	5,823
Far East	2,414	2,651
Oceania	18	17
Leading Regional Producers:		
Burma	75	75
China, People's Republic	1,148	1,400
India	447	450
Indonesia	137	125
Japan	141	143
Korea, Republic	93	87
Pakistan	71	61
Philippines	75	81
Thailand	87	87
Other Leading Producers:		
Brazil	350	315
Turkey	250	200
U.S.S.R.	289	295
U.S.A.	810	919

* Preliminary figures.

Source: United States Department of Agriculture.

Tungsten

Tungsten, one of the world's rarer and more valuable metals, derives its name from the Swedish words *tung*, meaning heavy, and *sten*, meaning stone. It occurs in both vein-type and disseminated deposits and is mined both underground and open-cast, depending on the type of deposit. There are two basic types of ores: wolframites (black ores where the tungsten is mixed in oxide form with iron and manganese) and scheelites (white ores where calcium has replaced the iron and manganese). Tungsten minerals are normally concentrated by gravity methods, with final removal of deleterious elements being achieved with magnetic and electrostatic separators and sometimes by flotation.

As a metal, tungsten has many exceptional properties including a high density, equal to that of gold and surpassed only by the platinum group of metals, a melting point of 3,410°C and a boiling point of 5,900°C, which are the highest of all metals and of all elements except carbon. These properties make tungsten invaluable in the manufacture of carbides used in armaments, cutting tools, drilling machines and wear parts. A wide use of pure tungsten is filaments for light bulbs. Tungsten is also an important constituent of alloy high-speed and tool steels.

The People's Republic of China is the world's leading producer and exporter of tungsten, with an estimated annual production of 9,000 metric tons. Other important producers in the region are North and South Korea, Thailand and Australia. The world's most important consumers are the U.S.A. and the U.S.S.R. (both of which are also important producers), the EEC and Japan.

As with many metals, tungsten prices have been somewhat volatile. In the early 1970s prices were depressed, reaching a nadir of U.S. $3,000 per metric ton in 1972, principally as a result of excessive releases of U.S. strategic stockpile surpluses in 1969 and 1970. After 1975 prices recovered and from mid-1979 until mid-1981 the price for concentrates was relatively stable at between $13,000 and $15,000 per metric ton. However, with world consumption having fallen by about 3 per cent per year since 1980, the price of tungsten had declined to $9,700 per ton by May 1982.

In 1976 leading producers from Bolivia, Australia, Portugal and some other countries formed a trade association known as the Primary Tungsten Association (PTA) to protect and further the interests of the tungsten industry. Two tungsten mining companies in Australia are prominent members and the People's Republic of China attends meetings as an observer. Thailand, formerly an observer, is now a full member of the Association. The PTA gives technical support to producer governments and, through the auspices of the UN Conference on Trade and Development (UNCTAD), is seeking an international commodity agreement for tungsten whereby excessive fluctuations in prices can be regulated by a system of nationally-held stocks. Despite years of deliberations under a Committee on Tungsten, little progress has been made owing to consumer opposition.

Negotiations on tungsten have been in progress in a sporadic manner since 1965. China, strongly supported by the other producer nations and especially Australia, wants to have tungsten prices stabilized "at levels to be agreed as remunerative and just to producers and equitable to consumers, and to provide long-term equilibrium between production and consumption". An agreement based on these proposals would be used to set up a reserve stock system to maintain the world price of a representative grade of tungsten between approved maximum and minimum limits.

The main consumers, however, led by the U.S.A., Britain, West Germany, Japan and Sweden, want to go no further than establishing an informal forum for consultations among consumers and producers.

PRODUCTION OF TUNGSTEN ORE AND CONCENTRATES
(tungsten content, metric tons)

	1978	1979
WORLD TOTAL . . .	44,691*	43,895*
Far East	19,228*	23,308
Oceania	2,680	3,168
Leading Regional Producers:		
Australia . . .	2,680	3,168
Burma	471	703
China, People's Republic .	9,980*	12,000*
Japan	754	751
Korea, Democratic People's Republic .	2,150*	2,150*
Korea, Republic . .	2,589	2,617
Thailand . . .	3,186	1,826
Other Leading Producers:		
Bolivia	3,170	2,647
U.S.S.R. . . .	8,500*	8,620*
U.S.A.	3,128	3,013

* Estimate.

Source: UNCTAD Statistics, January 1981.

Together with some consumers, the PTA was instrumental in creating an industry price index known as the International Tungsten Indicator (ITI). This came into operation in July 1978 and is made up of the weighted average of the prices of all the transactions of subscribers, both "spot" and long-term, occurring in the preceding two-week period and confidentially collated by an independent collator. After almost a year in operation the indicator was based on more than 50 per cent of the world's trade in tungsten.

The First International Tungsten Symposium was held in September 1979, indicating the growing importance of tungsten as a metal. Speakers from China and Australia took part. A second Symposium took place in San Francisco in June 1982.

Wheat (*Triticum*)

The most common species of wheat, *T. vulgare*, includes hard, semi-hard and soft varieties which have different milling characteristics but which, in general, are suitable for bread-making. Another species, *T. durum*, is grown mainly in semi-arid areas. This wheat is very hard and is suitable for the manufacture of semolina. A third species, spelt (*T. spelta*), is also included in production figures for wheat.

In the long term, world wheat production has been increasing at over 3 per cent a year, but there are wide year-to-year fluctuations due to variations in weather conditions in main producing areas, especially the occurrence of drought. The 1978 world wheat crop reached 450 million metric tons but production declined to 427 million tons in 1979, mainly because of a reduced U.S.S.R. crop. In 1980 production increased again to 444 million tons, and in 1981 a new record of 457 million tons was reached, mainly as a result of bumper crops in North America. World wheat consumption, which has been growing at a similar rate to production, fluctuates much less. About 75 per cent of total consumption is directly used as human food, while about 15 per cent is used for animal feed, mainly in developed countries and the U.S.S.R. Wheat is thought to be the principal food of about 42 per cent of the world's population.

Asia accounts for about 30 per cent of total world wheat production (including 5 per cent in Near East Asia and 25 per cent in Far East Asia) and Australasia for a further 4 per cent. In Far East Asia, the largest producer is the People's Republic of China, with a 1981 crop of 58.5 million tons. Although production has increased in recent years, large imports are still required. In India the introduction of high-yielding and high-response varieties, more extensive irrigation and greater use of fertilizers have boosted production. The 1979 wheat harvest of 35 million tons was the fourth record in successive years. In 1980, however, due to drought, output fell by about 3 million tons, but in 1981 production recovered to exceed 36 million tons. The other major producer in the region is Pakistan, whose output was over 11 million tons in 1980. Australia is one of the world's major wheat-exporting nations. Its production varies from year to year, largely according to the rainfall received in the major producing areas. Areas sown have been increasing steadily since the early 1970s. Drought affected production in 1980 and it reached only 11 million tons, down 5 million tons from the previous year, but in 1981 production recovered to over 16 million tons.

Far East Asian imports averaged about 25 million tons in the second half of the 1970s, accounting for 30 per cent of world trade. The largest importing country in the region, and sometimes in the world, is the People's Republic of China. In 1980/81 it imported 13.7 million tons and is expected to import 13 million tons in 1981/82. Japan usually imports between 5 and 6 million tons a year. India, which was a major importing country in the mid-1970s, has become self-sufficient because of increased production. It needed to import about 2.5 million tons in 1981/82, however, to replenish depleted stocks. Other countries in the region which regularly import 1 million tons or more in most seasons are Bangladesh, Indonesia, the Republic of Korea and Viet-Nam.

World trade in wheat has been growing rapidly in recent years. In the 1980/81 (July-June) crop year it was 93 million tons, compared with about 54 million tons ten years earlier. Total trade is expected to reach a record of about 99 million tons in 1981/82. Principal exporters are the U.S.A., Canada, Australia, the EEC and Argentina. About half of world wheat imports are by developing countries, of which over 85 per cent (i.e. about 42 million tons in 1980/81) are on commercial terms. The remaining 6 million tons per year are provided on concessional terms, including food aid.

As with other commodities, the price of wheat has fluctuated considerably in recent years. For example, the export price of one widely traded variety, U.S. No. 2 Hard Winter (Ordinary), reached a peak of over U.S. $220 per ton (f.o.b., Gulf ports) in February 1974. It fell to less than $100 per ton in mid-1977 but then rose to more than $180 in late 1979. A declining trend set in again in early 1980 but prices subsequently recovered, exceeding $200 in November 1980. After a renewed decline, prices stood at around $170 per ton in early 1982.

Since 1949 nearly all world trade in wheat has been conducted under the auspices of successive international agreements, administered by the International Wheat Council (IWC) in London. The last agreement to contain provisions which attempted directly to restrain price movements was that negotiated in 1967, which expired in 1971. The current International Wheat Agreement took effect in 1971 and was originally due to expire on June 30th, 1974, although it was later extended. The Agreement includes a Wheat Trade Convention, with a membership of 60 countries, and the Food Aid Convention, 1980 (administered by a Food Aid Committee), with twelve donor members. Asian countries currently parties to the Wheat Trade Convention include India, Japan, Pakistan and the Republic of Korea—all of which are importing members. Australia is an exporting member of the Convention. Under the Food Aid Convention, developing countries in Far East Asia (such as Bangladesh, Indonesia, Pakistan and Sri Lanka) usually receive considerable quantities of grain (in excess of 2.5 million tons in recent seasons) as outright gifts. Now that the needs of India have been reduced, the principal Asian recipient of food aid under the Convention is usually Bangladesh. Australia and Japan are donor members of the Food Aid Convention.

Much of the IWC's activity in recent years has been devoted to a detailed exploration of the possible bases for a new international arrangement to replace the 1971 International Wheat Agreement. In early 1978 the Council requested the Secretary-General of the UN Conference on Trade and Development (UNCTAD) to convene a negotiating Conference, but this was adjourned in February 1979 without the completion of an agreed text. As there seemed little prospect in the foreseeable future of successfully negotiating a new convention on the bases evolved during the UN Conference, it was decided that alternative solutions would have to be found to fulfil the twin objectives of market stability and world food security.

By the middle of the 1980/81 crop year discussions had progressed to the point where the Council could declare that the proposal under consideration (a flexible scheme based on the international co-ordination of the accumulation or release of nationally-held reserve stocks) appeared to be technically feasible. However, some delegations refused to accept the proposed scheme. At its 95th session, in November 1981, the Council decided to continue the search for a new agreement and the 1971 Convention was extended once again until June 30th, 1983.

Despite its inability so far to develop a new Wheat Trade Convention, the IWC continues to function as an instrument of international co-operation in wheat matters, within the limitations of the 1971 Convention, which does not contain substantive economic provisions. For example, the Advisory Sub-Committee on Market Conditions is useful to wheat producers and consumers alike in providing a comprehensive assessment of market conditions and prospects.

The 1980 Food Aid Convention was brought into force on July 1st 1980 as one of the constituent instruments of the extended 1971 International Wheat Agreement. The Food Aid Committee, whose membership consists of all parties to the Convention, continues to be a focus for international co-operation in food aid matters which began with the 1967 Food Aid Convention. Since the latter came into force, some 55 million metric tons of aid have been distributed to over 80 developing countries in the form of wheat and other grains suitable for human consumption. As before, the obligations are basically quantitative, ensuring that the volume of aid is not reduced in times of very short supplies and rising grain prices.

The minimum annual contributions of the present members of the Convention towards the overall target total about 7.6 million metric tons (compared with 4.2 million tons under the 1971 Convention). Efforts are continuing to encourage new potential donors, especially oil-exporting countries, to join the traditional donor countries in order to reach the target of 10 million metric tons.

PRODUCTION OF WHEAT
('000 metric tons, including spelt)

	1980	1981†
WORLD TOTAL	444,528	457,100
Far East	102,000	110,000
Oceania	11,242	16,800
Leading Regional Producers:		
Afghanistan	2,750	2,600
Australia	10,870	16,400
China, People's Republic	54,155	57,000‡
India	31,564	36,500
Pakistan	10,805	11,400
Other Leading Producers:		
Canada	19,158	24,500
France	23,632	22,800
Turkey	17,400	17,000
U.S.S.R.*	98,182	88,000
U.S.A.	64,492	76,000

* Excluding spelt. † Provisional.

‡ The official Chinese estimate is 58,490,000 metric tons.

Source: IWC.

We acknowledge with many thanks the assistance of the following bodies in the preparation of certain articles: the International Bauxite Association, the Thai Tapioca Trade Association, the Asian and Pacific Coconut Community, the International Cotton Advisory Committee, the International Institute for Cotton, the Malaysian Palm Oil Producers' Association, the Institute of Petroleum, the International Rice Research Institute, the Natural Rubber Producers' Research Association, the International Rubber Study Group, New York State College of Agriculture and Life Sciences, the International Sugar Organization, the International Tea Committee, the International Tin Council, British-American Tobacco Ltd., the Primary Tungsten Association and the International Wheat Council.

Sources for Tables (unless otherwise indicated): FAO, *Production Yearbook 1980* (Rome, 1981); FAO, *Monthly Bulletin of Statistics*, issues to April 1982; UN, *Statistical Yearbook 1979/80*.

PART TWO
Regional Organizations

REGIONAL ORGANIZATIONS

Page

The United Nations in the Far East and Australasia 99

Member States, with Contributions and Year of Admission 99

Permanent Missions 99

The Trusteeship Council 100

Economic and Social Commission for Asia and the Pacific—ESCAP 101

Committee for Co-ordination of Investigations of the Lower Mekong Basin 104

Food and Agriculture Organization—FAO 105

International Bank for Reconstruction and Development—IBRD (World Bank) 106

International Development Association—IDA 107

International Finance Corporation—IFC 108

United Nations Development Programme—UNDP 108

United Nations Educational, Scientific and Cultural Organization—UNESCO 110

United Nations High Commissioner for Refugees—UNHCR 111

World Health Organization—WHO 112

Other Regional Offices of the UN System 113

UN Information Centres 114

ANZUS 115

Asian Development Bank—ADB 116

Asian Productivity Organization—APO 120

Association of South East Asian Nations—ASEAN 121

The Colombo Plan for Co-operative Economic and Social Development in Asia and the Pacific 125

The Commonwealth 128

European Community 130

South Pacific Commission—SPC 131

South Pacific Forum 134

South Pacific Bureau for Economic Co-operation—SPEC 134

Directory of Other Regional Organizations 136

INDEX OF REGIONAL ORGANIZATIONS 142

The United Nations in the Far East and Australasia

MEMBER STATES, WITH CONTRIBUTIONS AND YEAR OF ADMISSION

(assessments for percentage contributions to UN Budget for 1981/82)

Country	Contribution	Year	Country	Contribution	Year
Afghanistan	0.01	1946	Maldives	0.01	1965
Australia	1.83	1945	Mongolia	0.01	1961
Bangladesh	0.04	1974	Nepal	0.01	1955
Bhutan	0.01	1971	New Zealand	0.27	1945
Burma	0.01	1948	Pakistan	0.07	1947
China, People's Republic*	1.62	1945	Papua New Guinea	0.01	1975
Fiji	0.01	1970	Philippines	0.10	1945
India	0.60	1945	Singapore	0.08	1965
Indonesia	0.16	1950	Solomon Islands	0.01	1978
Japan	9.58	1956	Sri Lanka	0.02	1955
Kampuchea	0.01	1955	Thailand	0.10	1946
Laos	0.01	1955	Viet-Nam	0.03	1977
Malaysia	0.09	1957	Western Samoa	0.01	1976

* From 1945 to 1971 the Chinese seat was occupied by the Republic of China (confined to Taiwan since 1949).

SOVEREIGN COUNTRIES NOT IN THE UNITED NATIONS

China (Taiwan)
Kiribati
Democratic People's Republic of Korea
Republic of Korea
Nauru
Tonga
Tuvalu
Vanuatu

PERMANENT MISSIONS TO THE UNITED NATIONS

(with Permanent Representatives)

(June 1982)

Afghanistan: 866 United Nations Plaza, Suite 520, New York, N.Y. 10017; MOHAMMAD FARID ZARIF.

Australia: One Dag Hammarskjöld Plaza, 885 Second Ave., 16th Floor, New York, N.Y. 10017; H. D. ANDERSON, O.B.E.

Bangladesh: 821 United Nations Plaza, 8th Floor, New York, N.Y. 10017; KHWAJA MOHAMMED KAISER.

Bhutan: 866 Second Ave., New York, N.Y. 10017; OM PRADHAN.

Burma: 10 East 77th St., New York, N.Y. 10021; SAW HLAING.

China, People's Republic: 155 West 66th St., New York, N.Y. 10023; LING QING.

Fiji: One United Nations Plaza, 26th Floor, New York, N.Y. 10017; FILIPE NAGERA BOLE.

India: 750 Third Ave., 21st Floor, New York, N.Y. 10017; NATARAJAN KRISHNAN.

Indonesia: 666 Third Ave., 12th Floor, New York, N.Y. 10017; ABDULLAH KAMIL.

Japan: 866 United Nations Plaza, 2nd Floor, New York, N.Y. 10017; MASAHIRO NISIBORI.

Kampuchea: 212 East 47th St., Suite 24G, New York, N.Y. 10017; PRASITH THIOUNN.*

Laos: 321 East 45th St., Apartment 7G, New York, N.Y. 10017; Dr. VITHAYA SOURINHO.

Malaysia: 666 Third Ave., 30th Floor, New York, N.Y. 10017; Datuk ZAINAL ABIDIN BIN SULONG.

Maldives: 212 East 47th St., 15B, New York, N.Y. 10017; AHMED ZAKI.

Mongolia: 6 East 77th St., New York, N.Y. 10021; BUYANTYN DASHTSEREN.

Nepal: 711 Third Ave., Room 1806, New York, N.Y. 10017; UDDHAV DEO BHATT.

New Zealand: One United Nations Plaza, 25th Floor, New York, N.Y. 10017; HAROLD H. FRANCIS.

Pakistan: Pakistan House, 8 East 65th St., New York, N.Y. 10021; NIAZ A. NAIK.

Papua New Guinea: 100 East 42nd St., Room 1005, New York, N.Y. 10071; KUBLAN LOS.

Philippines: 556 Fifth Ave., 5th Floor, New York, N.Y. 10036; ALEJANDRO D. YANGO.

Singapore: One United Nations Plaza, 26th Floor, New York, N.Y. 10017; T. T. B. KOH.

Solomon Islands: FRANCIS BUGOTU.

Sri Lanka: 630 Third Ave., 20th Floor, New York, N.Y. 10017; IGNATIUS BENEDICT FONSEKA.

Thailand: 628 Second Ave., New York, N.Y. 10016; BIRABHONGSE KASEMSRI.

Viet-Nam: 20 Waterside Plaza (Lobby), New York, N.Y. 10010.

Western Samoa: 211 East 43rd St., Suite 1400, New York, N.Y. 10017; MAIAVA IULAI TOMA.

OBSERVERS

Asian-African Legal Consultative Committee: 24 Manning Pelham Circle, New York, N.Y. 10803; Dr. SOELEIMAN H. TAJIBNAPIS.

Korea, Democratic People's Republic: 40 East 80th St., 25th Floor, New York, N.Y. 10021; HAN SI HAE.

Korea, Republic: 866 United Nations Plaza, Suite 300, New York, N.Y. 10017.

* Representing the government of Democratic Kampuchea, overthrown in January 1979. The People's Republic of Kampuchea, which succeeded the deposed regime, has not been recognized by the UN.

THE TRUSTEESHIP COUNCIL

The Trusteeship Council has supervised United Nations' Trust Territories through the administering authorities to promote the political, economic, social and educational advancement of the inhabitants towards self-government or independence.

MEMBERS

The Council consists of member states administering Trust Territories, permanent members of the Security Council which do not administer Trust Territories, and other non-administering countries elected by the Assembly for three-year terms.

Administering Country:	*Other Countries:*
United States	China, People's Republic*
	France
	U.S.S.R.
	United Kingdom

*China does not participate in the work of the Council.

ORGANIZATION

The Council meets once a year, generally in May–June. Each member has one vote, and decisions are made by a simple majority of the members present and voting. A new President is elected at the beginning of the Council's regular session each year.

The only territory remaining under United Nations trusteeship is the Trust Territory of the Pacific Islands which consists of the Caroline Islands and the Marshall Islands, island groups in Micronesia. The Northern Mariana Islands, formerly the Marianas District of the Trust Territory, became a Commonwealth territory of the U.S.A. in January 1978, although it remains legally part of the area covered by the Trusteeship Agreement. The Trust Territory of the Pacific Islands has been designated a strategic area, and the supervisory functions of the United Nations are, in its case, exercised by the Trusteeship Council under the authority of the Security Council.

The Constitution of the Marshall Islands entered into force on May 1st, 1979. The Constitution of the Federated States of Micronesia, four districts of the Caroline Islands, entered into force on May 10th, 1979. A referendum held in July 1979 in the Palau district approved a proposed local constitution, and in January 1981 it became the Republic of Palau. With the entries into force of the Constitutions, the High Commissioner, the chief executive of the Trust Territory, retained only the authority necessary to carry out the obligations of the U.S.A. under the Trusteeship and other agreements. In October and November 1980 agreements were initialled providing for the future self-government of the islands under a compact of "free association" with the U.S.A., subject to approval by the U.S. Congress and by plebiscite in the islands, after which the agreements would be submitted to the UN for formal termination of the trusteeship agreements (*see* chapter on the Trust Territory of the Pacific Islands).

High Commissioner: JANET MCCOY.

ECONOMIC AND SOCIAL COMMISSION FOR ASIA AND THE PACIFIC—ESCAP

United Nations Building, Rajadamnern Avenue, Bangkok 2, Thailand
Telephone: 2829181.

Founded in 1947 to encourage the economic and social development of Asia and the Far East; originally known as the Economic Commission for Asia and the Far East (ECAFE). The title ESCAP, which replaced ECAFE, was adopted after a reorganization in 1974.

MEMBERS

Afghanistan	India	Mongolia	Solomon Islands
Australia	Indonesia	Nauru	Sri Lanka
Bangladesh	Iran	Nepal	Thailand
Bhutan	Japan	Netherlands	Tonga
Burma	Kampuchea	New Zealand	U.S.S.R.
China, People's Republic	Korea, Republic	Pakistan	United Kingdom
Fiji	Laos	Papua New Guinea	U.S.A.
France	Malaysia	Philippines	Viet-Nam
	Maldives	Singapore	Western Samoa

ASSOCIATE MEMBERS

Brunei, Cook Islands, Guam, Hong Kong, Kiribati, Niue, Trust Territory of the Pacific Islands, Tuvalu, Vanuatu

ORGANIZATION

(June 1982)

COMMISSION

The work of the Commission is conducted through its annual sessions and conference structure, through the meetings of its main committee, *ad hoc* conferences and *ad hoc* working groups of government officials or experts. Other activity includes field missions, training courses and seminars. Technical assistance is provided for governments, while the secretariat continually provides its services at headquarters in Bangkok.

The nine main legislative committees cover:

Agricultural development;
Development planning;
Industry, technology, human settlements and the environment;
Natural resources;
Population;
Shipping, transport and communications;
Social development;
Statistics;
Trade.

Executive Secretary: Shah A. M. S. KIBRIA (Bangladesh).

Deputy Executive Secretary: KOJI NAKAGAWA.

Pacific Liaison Office: Nauru; Liaison Officer PAULA E. SOTUTU.

FUNCTIONS

ESCAP's fields of activity are as follows: promoting regional co-operation on social and economic problems, with increasing attention to sub-regional approaches as well as assistance to individual governments in planning and carrying out balanced development programmes. Since 1974, following the guidance of its members, ESCAP has gradually concentrated its efforts in six priority areas: food and agriculture; energy; raw materials and commodities; transfer of technology; international trade, transnational corporations and external financial resources transfers; and integrated rural development.

Efforts have also been made to encourage technical and economic co-operation among the developing countries (TCDC and ECDC) in ESCAP's activities and to increase the direct involvement of all social groups, especially women, in the development process. Greater attention has also been given to the least developed of the developing countries including the land-locked and island countries.

The post of a Liaison Officer to be based in the South Pacific, was approved by the UN General Assembly at its 34th session in 1979. The Liaison Office was opened in Nauru in October 1980.

Although ESCAP does not itself distribute capital aid, it has helped to set up and attract funds for regional and sub-regional projects that, in turn, provide development assistance. It is also increasingly becoming the executing agency for regional projects.

ANNUAL SESSIONS

At its yearly sessions the Commission examines the region's problems, reviews progress, sets new goals and priorities and may launch new projects.

37th Session, Bangkok, March 1981: priorities for the continued work of the organization were as follows:

1. promotion of the integration of women in the development process;

2. review and appraisal of the implementation of the new International Development Strategy;
3. unified approach to economic and social development and planning;
4. United Nations Conference on the Least Developed Countries;
5. Charter of the Asian and Pacific Development Centre;
6. role of the co-operative movement in the social and economic development of the developing countries of Asia and the Pacific;
7. role of qualified national personnel in the social and economic development of developing countries;
8. expanding and strengthening the functions of the Commission in the context of the restructuring of the economic and social sectors of the United Nations system.

BUDGET

For 1980/81, ESCAP's regular budget, an appropriation from the UN Budget, was U.S. $26 million. The regular budget is supplemented each year by funds from various technical assistance sources which amounted to about U.S. $22.4 million in 1980/81.

Regional advisers and supporting personnel are paid from technical assistance funds. In addition, a UN Development Advisory Team (UNDAT), for which ESCAP is the executing agency, is stationed in Fiji to serve the South Pacific area.

REGIONAL PROJECTS

Set up by ESCAP or with its aid.

ECONOMICS AND FINANCE

Asian Clearing Union (ACU): c/o Bank Markazi, Teheran, Iran; f. 1974 to provide clearing arrangements to save foreign exchange and promote the use of domestic currencies in trade transactions among developing countries; part of ESCAP's Asian trade expansion programme; the Bank Markazi, Teheran, is the Union's agent; mems.: Bangladesh, Burma, India, Iran, Nepal, Pakistan, Sri Lanka; Chair. W. Rasaputram, Governor, Central Bank of Ceylon.

Asian Reinsurance Corporation: Ocean Insurance Bldg., 175 Sukhumvit Soi 21, Bangkok 11, Thailand; f. 1979 to provide backing for local insurance companies who, during 1979, paid an estimated U.S. $200 million in reinsurance premiums to foreign countries; the inaugural meeting of the Council of Members was held in Bangkok in May 1979; mems.: Afghanistan, Bangladesh, Bhutan, the People's Republic of China, India, the Republic of Korea, the Philippines, Sri Lanka, Thailand.

NATURAL RESOURCES

Committee for Co-ordination of Joint Prospecting for Mineral Resources in Asian Offshore Areas (CCOP/East Asia): The White Inn, No. 41, Sukhumvit Soi 4, Bangkok, Thailand; f. 1966 to reduce the cost of advanced mineral surveying and prospecting to member nations by a co-ordinated regional approach involving the pooling of expertise and resources such as ships, aircraft and expensive scientific equipment; works in partnership with developed nations which have provided geologists and geophysicists as technical advisers; has received aid from the UNDP and other sources since 1972; mems.: People's Republic of China, Indonesia, Japan, Kampuchea, the Republic of Korea, Malaysia, Papua New Guinea, the Philippines, Singapore, Thailand, the Trust Territory of the Pacific Islands, Viet-Nam; Project Manager/Co-ordinator A. Johannes.

Committee for Co-ordination of Joint Prospecting for Mineral Resources in the South Pacific Area (CCOP/SOPAC): c/o Mineral Resources Department, Private Mailbag, G.P.O., Suva, Fiji; has received support from the UNDP since 1974; mems.: Cook Islands, Fiji, Kiribati, New Zealand, Papua New Guinea, Solomon Islands, Tonga, the Trust Territory of the Pacific Islands, Vanuatu, Western Samoa; Project Manager Cruz A. Matos.

Regional Mineral Resources Development Centre: Jalan Jenderal Sudirman 623, Bandung, Indonesia; f. 1973 to achieve rapid discovery and use of the region's deposits of minerals, and to make use of research capacity; Governing Council mems.: Bangladesh, India, Indonesia, Japan, the Republic of Korea, Malaysia, the Philippines, Sri Lanka, Thailand; Co-ordinator P. H. Ljunggren.

South-East Asia Tin Research and Development Centre: 14 Tiger Lane, Ipoh, Malaysia; established in April 1977 by Indonesia, Malaysia and Thailand, who produce about two-thirds of the world's output of tin. The Centre aims at developing methods of locating new primary ore deposits, efficient mining, ore beneficiation and smelting; Dir. Dr. Abdullah Hasbi bin Hassan.

RESEARCH AND TRAINING

Asian and Pacific Development Centre: P.O.B. 2224, Kuala Lumpur, Malaysia; f. 1980 as the integration of four former regional training and research institutions (Asian and Pacific Development Institute, Asian and Pacific Development Administration Centre, Asian and Pacific Centre for Women and Development, Social Welfare and Development Centre); acts as a "think-tank" for accelerating the development of the region; Dir. Aftab Ahmad Khan.

Regional Co-ordinating Centre for Research and Development of Coarse Grains, Pulses, Roots and Tuber Crops: c/o ESCAP Agricultural Division; f. 1981; Co-ordinator Shiro Okabe.

Statistical Institute for Asia and the Pacific: Akasaka, P.O.B. 13, Tokyo 107, Japan; f. 1970; trains professional statisticians; prepares teaching materials, provides facilities for special studies and research of a statistical nature, assists in the development of statistical education and training at all levels in national and sub-regional centres; Dir. J. G. Miller.

TECHNOLOGY

Regional Centre for Technology Transfer: P.O.B. 115, Bangalore 560052, India; f. 1977 to assist countries of the ESCAP region in all their problems concerning technology development and transfer; Dir. B. R. Devarajan.

Regional Network for Agricultural Machinery: c/o UNDP, P.O. Box 7285 ADC, Manila, Philippines; f. 1978 to supplement and co-ordinate the efforts of national institutes designated by participating governments to design, develop and manufacture simple farm machinery to meet the needs of small farmers; provides prototypes of selected machinery; organizes training facilities, study tours and international symposia; Officer-in-Charge: C. S. SRIDHARAN.

TRADE

Asian and Pacific Coconut Community: 4th Floor, Jaya Bldg., Jalan Thamrin 12, Jakarta, Indonesia; f. 1969 to promote, co-ordinate, and harmonize all activities of the coconut industry towards better production, processing, marketing and research; mems.: India, Indonesia, Malaysia, Papua New Guinea, the Philippines, Solomon Islands, Sri Lanka, Thailand, the Trust Territory of the Pacific Islands, Western Samoa, Vanuatu; Dir. GODOFREDO P. REYES, Jr.

Asian Free Trade Zone: f. 1975; provides for the reduction and eventual elimination of tariff and non-tariff barriers in trade; co-operation in commodities, industrial and other goods; and preferences for the least developed countries; mems.: Bangladesh, India, the Republic of Korea, Laos, Sri Lanka; the agreement on which it is based is known as the Bangkok Agreement which entered into force in 1976.

International Pepper Community: 4th Floor, Jaya Bldg., 12 Jalan M.H. Thamrin, Jakarta, Indonesia; f. 1972 for joint action among world producing countries on the standards, supplies, marketing and promotion of pepper; mems.: Brazil, India, Indonesia, Madagascar, Malaysia; Dir. LAKSHMI NARAIN SALKANI.

TRANSPORT AND COMMUNICATIONS

Asia-Pacific Telecommunity: Office Compound of the Communications Authority of Thailand, Bangkok 5, Thailand; f. 1979 to create telecommunications networks linking the countries of the region, and to serve as a forum for technical questions. Mems.: Afghanistan, Australia, Bangladesh, Burma, the People's Republic of China, India, Iran, Japan, the Republic of Korea, Malaysia, Maldives, Nauru, Nepal, Pakistan, Papua New Guinea, the Philippines, Singapore, Sri Lanka, Thailand, Viet-Nam; assoc. mems. Hong Kong, Brunei; two affiliated mems. in Hong Kong, two in Japan, and five in the Philippines; Exec. Dir. BOONCHOO PHIENPANIJ.

Asian Highway Network Project: comprises a network of 65,000 kilometres in 15 Asian countries from the Iranian-Turkish border to Viet-Nam in East Asia and to Bali, Indonesia in South-East Asia, with a linking route to Sri Lanka.

MISCELLANEOUS

ESCAP/WMO Typhoon Committee: c/o UNDP, P.O.B. 7285 ADC, Manila, the Philippines; f. 1968, an intergovernmental body sponsored by ESCAP and WMO for mitigation of typhoon damage. It aims at establishing efficient typhoon and flood warning systems through improved meteorological and telecommunication facilities. Other activities include promotion of disaster preparedness, training of personnel and co-ordination of research. The committee's programme is supported from national resources and also through international and bilateral assistance. Mems.: People's Republic of China, Hong Kong, Japan, Kampuchea, Republic of Korea, Laos, Malaysia, the Philippines, Thailand, Viet-Nam; Co-ordinator of Secretariat: Dr. ROMAN L. KINTANAR.

WMO/ESCAP Panel on Tropical Cyclones: Technical Support Unit, c/o Meteorological Dept., Colombo, Sri Lanka; f. 1973 to mitigate damage caused by tropical cyclones in the Bay of Bengal and the Arabian Sea; mems.: Bangladesh, Burma, India, Pakistan, Sri Lanka, Thailand; Chief Technical Adviser R. L. SOUTHERN.

ESCAP PUBLICATIONS

Annual Report.
Agricultural Development Information Bulletin.
Agro-chemicals, fertilizers and agro-pesticides news-in-brief.
Economic and Social Survey of Asia and the Pacific.
Economic Bulletin for Asia and the Pacific.
Small Industry Bulletin for Asia and the Pacific.
Electric Power in Asia and the Pacific.
Water Resources Series.
Oil and Natural Gas Map of Asia.
Mineral Resources Development Series.
Asian Population Programme News.
Energy Resources Development Series.
Asia Population Studies Series.
Statistical Yearbook for Asia and the Pacific.
Quarterly Bulletin of Statistics for Asia and the Pacific.
Statistical Indicators in ESCAP Countries.
Foreign Trade Statistics of Asia and the Pacific.
Transport and Communication Bulletin for Asia and the Pacific.
TCDC: Training Courses Available in Developing ESCAP Countries, 1979.
TCDC: Experts of Developing ESCAP Countries (Supplement).
Inter-Country Institutional Arrangements for ECDC TCDC.

COMMITTEE FOR CO-ORDINATION OF INVESTIGATIONS OF THE LOWER MEKONG BASIN

c/o ESCAP, United Nations Building, Rajadamnern Avenue, Bangkok 2, Thailand

To develop the water resources of the lower Mekong basin, including mainstream and tributaries, for hydro-electric power, irrigation, navigation, fisheries, flood control and other purposes.

MEMBERS

Laos Thailand Viet-Nam

CO-OPERATING COUNTRIES

Australia
Austria
Belgium
Canada
Denmark
Egypt
Finland
France
Federal Republic of Germany
Hong Kong
India
Indonesia
Iran
Israel
Italy
Japan
Netherlands
New Zealand
Norway
Pakistan
Philippines
Sweden
Switzerland
United Kingdom
U.S.A.

INTERIM COMMITTEE

The functioning of the Co-ordination Committee was interrupted by upheavals in Indochina in 1975 but the work of the Secretariat in Bangkok continued. In January 1978 Laos, Thailand and Viet-Nam agreed to establish the Interim Committee for Co-ordination of Investigations of the Lower Mekong Basin to promote the development of water resources of the lower Mekong basin and to increase agricultural and power production in order to meet the needs for reconstruction and development of Laos and Viet-Nam and the economic needs of Thailand. The Interim Committee is intended to function only until Kampuchea (formerly a member) resumes participation in the Co-ordination Committee. At its twelfth session in Vientiane, Laos, in September 1981 the Committee considered the work programme for 1982. About U.S. $400 million of foreign assistance was required to implement the main projects to increase food and energy production. Other projects include agricultural development, irrigation, fishing and navigation.

EXECUTIVE AGENT

Responsible for day-to-day management and co-ordination between sessions of the Committee. Assisted by a staff provided by the member countries, the co-operating countries and the United Nations (UNDP).

Executive Agent: B. A. BERNANDER.

ACTIVITIES

Contributions pledged at the end of 1980 amounted to U.S. $427,715,586, of which some $159.3 million was provided by member states, $193.5 million by co-operating countries, $44.2 million by UN agencies (chiefly UNDP) and $30.7 million by other international agencies (chiefly the Asian Development Bank, the European Community and the OPEC Special Fund).

Data collection is carried out in such fields as hydrology, meteorology, mapping and levelling, agriculture and industry. An indicative development plan for the water resources of the Basin was published in 1972.

Feasibility reports have been completed for the Pa Mong project in northern Laos. The cost of the Pa Mong project (installed capacity of 4,800 MW.) is estimated at U.S. $2,000 million (at 1975 prices).

Thirteen dams have been built on tributaries of the Mekong, mostly with bilateral help from the donor countries. Six more are under construction.

The Committee has undertaken the Nam Ngum project in Laos, the first phase of which was completed in 1971. The second phase, to provide an additional 80 MW. of hydro-electric power, was completed in October 1978.

Pre-investment preparation for 12 pioneer agricultural projects has been completed for the Committee by the World Bank, the FAO and the Asian Development Bank, with multilateral financial support. Four pioneer projects and part of another have been started; the total current financial commitment for these is U.S. $36 million.

Included in the construction programme of the Interim Committee are agricultural production projects in Laos, Thailand and Viet-Nam for which studies have been completed. The implementation of these would require about U.S. $150 million in assistance.

The Committee also sponsors experimental and demonstration farms in the basin.

The Committee conducts hydrographic surveys, rock-blasting, channel marking and dredging, improvement in cargo-handling facilities and craft construction.

Other projects include mineral surveys, fisheries and forestry, power market surveys, socio-economic and environmental studies and professional training.

FOOD AND AGRICULTURE ORGANIZATION—FAO

Via delle Terme di Caracalla, 00100 Rome, Italy

Telephone: 57971.

The FAO, the first specialized agency of the UN to be founded, was established in Quebec, Canada, in October 1945. The Organization fights malnutrition and hunger and serves as an organizing and co-ordinating agency which brings together representatives of national governments, scientific bodies, non-governmental organizations, industry and banking to plan and carry out development programmes in the whole range of food and agriculture, including forestry and fisheries. It helps developing member countries to promote educational and training facilities and institution-building.

ORGANIZATION

(June 1982)

SECRETARIAT

Director-General (1982–88): EDOUARD SAOUMA (Lebanon).

Deputy Director-General: EDWARD WEST (United Kingdom).

REGIONAL OFFICE FOR ASIA AND THE PACIFIC

Maliwan Mansion, Phra Atit Rd., Bangkok 2, Thailand; Regional Rep. SURJIT SINGH PURI (India).

REGIONAL COUNCILS AND COMMISSIONS

(at FAO Regional Office unless otherwise stated)

Animal Production and Health Commission for Asia, the Far East and the South-West Pacific (APHCA): f. 1973 to promote livestock development in general and national and international research and action with respect to animal health and husbandry problems in the region. Mems. 13 states.

Asia and Far East Commission on Agricultural Statistics: f. 1962; to review the state of food and agricultural statistics in the region and to advise member countries on the development and standardization of agricultural statistics. Mems. 19 states.

Asia-Pacific Forestry Commission: f. 1949. Aims: to co-ordinate national forest policies; to exchange information and to make recomendations. Mems. 22 states.

Indo-Pacific Fishery Commission: f. 1948 to develop fisheries, encourage and co-ordinate research, disseminate information, recommend projects to governments, propose standards in technique and nomenclature. Mems. 19 states.

International Rice Commission: c/o FAO, Via delle Terme di Caracalla, 00100 Rome, Italy; f. 1948 to promote national and international action on production, conservation, distribution and consumption of rice, except matters relating to international trade. Mems. 47 states.

Regional Commission on Farm Management for Asia and the Far East: f. 1966 to stimulate and co-ordinate farm management research and extension activities and to serve as a clearing house for the exchange of information and experience among the member countries in the region.

ACTIVITIES IN ASIA AND THE PACIFIC

Examples of recent activities in the region to which FAO has given financial or technical assistance include the following: a forestry project in the Philippines, launched by FAO and UNDP in 1979, to develop a forest land management scheme based on permanent cultivation instead of "slash and burn" techniques; a programme to form a reserve of rice for planting in Kampuchea in 1982; a 20-year forestry development scheme in Nepal, begun in 1980 by FAO, UNDP and the Nepalese Government, to halt deforestation; support for a rural dairy co-operatives scheme in India; operation of a service known as INFOFISH to promote regional trade in fish products; and a project to improve rice storage facilities in Burma.

WORLD FOOD PROGRAMME—WFP

WFP is a joint UN-FAO effort to stimulate economic and social development through food and to provide emergency relief, using contributions of commodities, cash and services made by member governments of the UN and FAO. It became operational in 1963.

WFP development projects in Asia and the Pacific approved in 1981 included food-for-work supplies for irrigation and forestry schemes in Bhutan; provision of food as part-payment for workers on farm development and flood control projects in the People's Republic of China; rations for women participating in development training schemes in Indonesia; and food-for-work on afforestation in Sri Lanka.

Emergency supplies of food were given to the following countries (value indicated in U.S. $ million): People's Republic of China (2.5), Kampuchea (3.9), Pakistan (for refugees from Afghanistan) (80.1), Philippines (0.2), Sri Lanka (1.7) and Viet-Nam (2.9).

Executive Director: JAMES CHARLES INGRAM (Australia).

INTERNATIONAL BANK FOR RECONSTRUCTION AND DEVELOPMENT—IBRD (WORLD BANK)

1818 H Street, N.W., Washington, D.C. 20433, U.S.A.

Telephone: (202) 477-1234.

The World Bank was established in 1945. It aims to assist the economic development of member nations by making loans, in cases where private capital is not available on reasonable terms, to finance productive investments. Loans are made either direct to member governments, or to private enterprises with the guarantee of their governments.

ORGANIZATION

(June 1982)

President and Chairman of Executive Directors: ALDEN W. CLAUSEN (U.S.A.).

Regional Vice-President, East Asia and the Pacific: S. SHAHID HUSAIN (Pakistan).

Regional Vice-President, South Asia: W. DAVID HOPPER (Canada).

OFFICES

There are offices in New York, London, Paris, Geneva and Tokyo.

Tokyo Office: Kokusai Bldg., 1-1 Marunouchi 3-chome, Chiyoda-ku, Tokyo 100, Japan; Dir. SEIGO NOZAKI.

Regional Mission in Thailand: Udom Vidhya Bldg., 956 Rama IV Road, Sala Daeng, Bangkok 5; Chief HENDRIK VAN DER HEIJDEN.

LOANS TO COUNTRIES IN ASIA AND THE PACIFIC

TOTAL LOANS
(cumulative to June 30th, 1981)

	NUMBER	AMOUNT (U.S. $ million)
Australia	7	417.7
Bangladesh	1	46.1
Burma	3	33.4
Fiji	8	83.7
India	61	3,200.6
Indonesia	57	3,729.0
Japan	31	862.9
Korea, Republic	56	3,338.5
Malaysia	52	1,314.6
New Zealand	6	126.8
Pakistan	38	884.0
Papua New Guinea	9	94.0
Philippines	75	2,922.9
Singapore	14	181.3
Sri Lanka	8	93.9
Taiwan*	14	329.4
Thailand	66	2,286.3

* In May 1980 the People's Republic of China became a member of the Bank. The Bank's board voted to exclude Taiwan, whose shareholding was allocated to the People's Republic.

APPROVED BANK LOANS July 1980–June 1981.

	PURPOSE	AMOUNT (U.S. $ million)
Fiji	Non-project (Cyclone reconstruction)	18.0
India	Agriculture and rural development	30.0
	Energy	400.0
Indonesia	Agriculture and rural development	229.0
	Education	45.0
	Energy	250.0
	Urbanization	43.0
	Small-scale enterprises	106.0
Korea, Republic	Agriculture and rural development	50.0
	Urbanization	90.0
Korea, Republic (Guarantor)	Development finance companies	250.0
Malaysia	Agriculture and rural development	182.0
Papua New Guinea	Education	6.0
Philippines	Agriculture and rural development	83.0
	Non-project (structural adjustment)	200.0
	Education	100.0
Philippines (Guarantor)	Development finance companies	150.0
Thailand	Transportation	100.0
	Agriculture and rural development	87.0
	Industry	8.9
Thailand (Guarantor)	Development finance companies	30.0
	Energy	100.0

Source: World Bank, *Annual Report* 1981.

INTERNATIONAL DEVELOPMENT ASSOCIATION—IDA

1818 H Street, N.W., Washington, D.C. 20433, U.S.A.

Telephone: (202) 477-1234.

The International Development Association began operations in November 1960. Affiliated to the World Bank, the IDA advances capital on more flexible terms to developing countries. The officers of the World Bank direct the International Development Association.

DEVELOPMENT CREDITS TO COUNTRIES IN ASIA AND THE PACIFIC

TOTAL CREDITS (cumulative to June 30th, 1981)

	Number	Amount (U.S. $ million)
Afghanistan	20	230.1
Bangladesh	72	1,788.2
Burma	17	418.0
India	137	9,566.2
Indonesia	46	931.8
Korea, Republic	6	110.8
Laos	3	32.0
Maldives	1	3.2
Nepal	26	297.9
Pakistan	52	1,446.9
Papua New Guinea	8	108.2
Philippines	3	122.2
Solomon Islands	1	1.5
Sri Lanka	27	536.6
Taiwan*	4	15.3
Thailand	6	125.1
Viet-Nam	1	60.0
Western Samoa	3	14.4

*In May 1980 the People's Republic of China became a member of the Association, thereby excluding Taiwan.

APPROVED IDA CREDITS July 1980–June 1981.

	Purpose	Amount (U.S. $ million)
Bangladesh	Small-scale enterprises	35.0
	Non-project (imports programme)	65.0
	Energy	85.0
	Transportation	25.0
	Development finance companies	50.0
	Technical assistance	16.0
	Agriculture and rural development	58.0
Burma	Agriculture and rural development	55.0
China, People's Republic	Education	100.0
India	Transportation	35.0
	Agriculture and rural development	490.0
	Urbanization	42.0
	Telecommunications	314.0
	Industry	400.0
Nepal	Water supply and sewerage	27.0
	Agriculture and rural development	35.2
Pakistan	Non-project (fertilizer imports)	50.0
	Education	25.0
	Small-scale enterprises	30.0
	Agriculture and rural development	97.0
Papua New Guinea	Education	12.0
	Agriculture and rural development	15.0
Solomon Islands	Development finance companies	1.5
Sri Lanka	Agriculture and rural development	153.5
	Transportation	13.5
Western Samoa	Agriculture and rural development	2.0

Source: World Bank, *Annual Report* 1981.

INTERNATIONAL FINANCE CORPORATION—IFC

1818 H Street, N.W., Washington, D.C. 20433, U.S.A.

Telephone: (202) 477-1234.

Founded in 1956 as an affiliate of the World Bank to encourage the growth of productive private enterprise in its member countries, particularly in the less-developed areas.

Special Representative, Far East: Naokado Nishihara.
Director, Department of Investments, Asia: Torstein Stephansen.
Chief, Regional Mission in East Asia: Sakdiyiam Kupasrimonkol.

IFC INVESTMENTS IN THE FAR EAST AND AUSTRALASIA

TOTAL CUMULATIVE INVESTMENT TO JUNE 1981
(U.S. $ '000)

Country	Number of Enterprises	Cumulative Gross Commitments (Including Syndications)
Afghanistan	1	322
Bangladesh	2	2,614
India	18	148,620
Indonesia	12	132,484
Korea, Republic	12	133,662
Malaysia	4	8,691
Nepal	1	3,128
Pakistan	14	73,595
Philippines	24	143,816
Sri Lanka	7	33,332
Taiwan*	2	9,844
Thailand	9	110,591

APPROVED INVESTMENTS, JULY 1980–JUNE 1981
(U.S. $ '000)

Country	Purpose	Amount (Including Syndications)
Bangladesh	Leather industry	2,272
India	Cement and construction material	15,875
	Motor vehicles	15,000
	Iron and steel	45,274
Korea, Republic	Grain bulk terminal	9,500
Pakistan	Food processing	3,352
Philippines	Cement and construction material	16,000
	Mining	5,000
	Money and capital market	19,235
Sri Lanka	Money and capital market	5,000
	Textiles and fibres	79
	Tourism	18,000
Thailand	Mining	604
	Cement and construction	27,000

* In May 1980 the People's Republic of China became a member of the Corporation, thereby excluding the Republic of China (Taiwan).

Source: IFC 1981 Annual Report.

UNITED NATIONS DEVELOPMENT PROGRAMME—UNDP

One United Nations Plaza, New York, N.Y. 10017, U.S.A.

Telephone: (212) 745-1234.

Established in 1965 by the General Assembly to help the developing countries increase the wealth-producing capabilities of their natural and human resources by supporting economic growth and social progress through projects of technical co-operation. The UNDP came into effect in January 1966, bringing together the previous activities of the expanded Programme of Technical Assistance and the UN Special Fund.

ORGANIZATION

(June 1982)

AGENCIES PARTICIPATING

The following act as executing agencies or otherwise participate in the work of the UNDP; the UN Department of Technical Co-operation for Development and 24 of the UN agencies and organizations, three regional development banks, five regional economic commissions, the International Fund for Agricultural Development and the Arab Fund for Economic and Social Development.

The UNDP is responsible to the General Assembly, to which it reports through ECOSOC.

Governing Council: representatives of 48 countries; 27 seats filled by developing countries and 21 by economically more advanced countries; the policy-making body of the UNDP. Meets annually. One-third of the membership changes each year. President (1982): DOUGLAS LINDORES (Canada).

Administrator: F. BRADFORD MORSE (U.S.A.).

Inter-Agency Consultative Board (IACB): composed of the UN Secretary-General and the Executive Heads of the UNDP's participating and executing Agencies; provides guidance and advice.

Secretariat: composed of an international staff from over 100 countries.

REGIONAL BUREAUX

Headed by assistant administrators, the regional bureaux share the responsibility for implementing the programme with the Administrator's office. Within certain limitations, large-scale projects may be approved and funding allocated by the Administrator, and smaller-scale projects by the Resident Representatives, based in 114 countries.

The four regional bureaux, all at the Secretariat in New York, cover: Africa; Asia and the Pacific; the Arab states; and Latin America; there is also a Unit for Europe.

FIELD OFFICES

In almost every country receiving UNDP assistance there is a Country Office, headed by the UNDP Resident Representative, who co-ordinates all UN technical assistance. He advises the Government on formulating the country programme, sees that the field activities are carried out, and acts as the leader of the UN team of experts working in the country. Resident Representatives are normally designated as co-ordinators for all UN operational development activities; the field offices function as the primary presence of the UN in most developing countries.

UNDP REPRESENTATIVES IN THE FAR EAST AND AUSTRALASIA

Afghanistan: P.O.B. 5, Kabul; EVLOGUI BONEV.

Bangladesh: P.O.B. 224, Ramna, Dacca; JEHAN RAHEEM.

Bhutan: G.P.O. Box 162, Thimphu; TILAK MALHOTRA.

Burma: P.O.B. 650, Rangoon; ERLING DESSAU.

China, People's Republic: c/o United Nations, Beijing; NESSIM SHALLON.

Fiji: Private Mail Bag, Suva; ARTHUR HOLCOMBE.

India: P.O.B. 3059, New Delhi 110003; MICHAEL PRIESTLEY.

Bombay Sub-Office: Ravindra Mansion, Dinsha Vachha Rd., Bombay 40020.

Calcutta Sub-Office: P.O.B. 9011, Calcutta 700016.

Indonesia: P.O.B. 2338, Jakarta; GAMIL HAMDY.

Korea, Democratic People's Republic: P.O. Box 27, Pyongyang; FILIP MARUSIC.

Korea, Republic: Central P.O.B. 143, Seoul; B. VUNIBOBO.

Laos: rue Phone Keng, B.P. 345, Vientiane; CASPAR KAMP.

Malaysia: P.O.B. 2544, Kuala Lumpur; K. SATRAP.

Maldives: Alivaage 6, Lainoofaru Magu, Malé.

Mongolia: P.O.B. 49/207, Ulan Bator.

Nepal: P.O.B. 107, Kathmandu; JOHN MELFORD.

Pakistan: P.O.B. 1051, Islamabad; HIMALAYA RANA.

Papua New Guinea: P.O.B. 3041, Port Moresby; N. SUBBARAMAN.

Philippines: P.O.B. 1864/P.O.B. 7285 ADC, Manila; EUAN E. SMITH.

Sri Lanka: P.O.B. 1505, Colombo 7; Y. Y. KIM.

Thailand: G.P.O. Box 618, Bangkok; WINSTON PRATTLEY.

Viet-Nam: P.O.B. 59, Hanoi; KARL ENGLUND.

Western Samoa: Private Mail Bag, Apia; ROY MOREY.

ACTIVITIES IN THE FAR EAST AND AUSTRALASIA

In 1980 31.5 per cent (U.S. $207.1 million) of UNDP expenditure was allocated to Asia and the Pacific (1,521 projects).

Agriculture remains the largest component of UNDP's activities, accounting for 25.5 per cent of total programme outlays in 1980. Some 15.5 per cent went to trade, transportation and communication; 12 per cent to development policies; 10 per cent to industry; 11 per cent to natural resources development; 7 per cent to education, 6 per cent to employment schemes, 4 per cent to health, and the rest to other related sectors. The majority of this work was carried out in the field by the United Nations and 35 of its related international agencies.

Project work covers five main areas: locating, assessing and activating latent natural resources and other development assets; stimulating capital investment to help realize these possibilities; support for professional and vocational training; expansion of scientific research and applied technology; and strengthening of national and regional development planning.

Assistance under the UNDP is planned with reference to the Indicative Planning Figure (IPF) for the country concerned. This is a projection of the total financial resources the UNDP can expect to have at its disposal for the country over a five-year period.

Individual countries submit to the Governing Council of the UNDP a programme outlining areas needing assistance. The programme sets out the various national priorities and takes into account aid from other sources. The IPF gives an indication of future assistance so that overall national development plans can be formulated with more certainty.

UNDP INDICATIVE PLANNING FIGURES FOR PROJECTS IN THE FAR EAST AND AUSTRALASIA
(U.S. $ million)

COUNTRY	IPF 1977–81	IPF (illustrative) 1982–86*	COUNTRY	IPF 1977–81	IPF (illustrative) 1982–86*
Afghanistan	38.00	71.50	Nauru	—	0.06
Bangladesh	65.50	201.00	Nepal	32.50	98.00
Bhutan	12.25	36.50	Niue	1.00	1.00
Brunei	—	0.20	Pakistan	52.50	118.00
Burma	41.50	102.00	Papua New Guinea	8.75	13.50
China, People's Republic	—	142.00	Philippines	30.50	46.00
Cook Islands	—	1.40	Singapore	7.50	7.50
Fiji	5.00	5.00	Solomon Islands	2.30	4.00
Hong Kong	0.50	0.50	Sri Lanka	31.50	76.00
India	97.00	252.00	Thailand	29.50	43.00
Indonesia	69.50	106.00	Tokelau	—	0.95
Kampuchea	25.50	n.a.	Tonga	2.00	2.50
Kiribati	1.10†	1.30	Trust Territory of the Pacific Islands	1.00	1.00
Korea, Democratic People's Republic	—	24.75	Tuvalu	1.10†	1.14
Korea, Republic	18.00	18.00	Vanuatu	—	2.00
Laos	17.75	52.50	Viet-Nam	—	118.00
Malaysia	15.00	15.00	Western Samoa	5.25	5.25
Maldives	2.50	7.00	Regional	95.70	296.10
Mongolia	10.00	10.00			

* Owing to the insufficient level of contributions by member governments, illustrative figures for 1982–86 are likely to exceed actual figures.

† The IPF for 1977–81 is for the Gilbert Islands (now Kiribati) and Tuvalu combined.

UNITED NATIONS EDUCATIONAL, SCIENTIFIC AND CULTURAL ORGANIZATION—UNESCO

7 place de Fontenoy, 75700 Paris, France

Telephone: 577-16-10.

UNESCO was established in 1945 "for the purpose of advancing, through the educational, scientific and cultural relations of the peoples of the world, the objectives of international peace and the common welfare of mankind".

ORGANIZATION

(June 1982)

SECRETARIAT

Director-General: AMADOU MAHTAR M'BOW (Senegal).

Deputy Director-General: FEDERICO MAYOR (Spain).

Head, Executive Office of the Director-General: CHIKH BEKRI (Algeria).

REGIONAL OFFICES

Regional Office for Culture and Book Development in Asia: P.O. Box 8950, 44/J/6 Razi Road P.E.C.H.S., Karachi 2904, Pakistan.

Regional Office for Education in Asia and Oceania: Darakarn Bldg., 920 Sukhumvit Rd., P.O.B. 1425, Bangkok 11, Thailand.

Regional Office for Science and Technology in South and Central Asia: UNESCO House, 17 Jor Bagh (Lodi Road), New Delhi 11 0 003, India.

Regional Office for Science and Technology in South-East Asia: UN Bldg., Jalan Thamrin 14, Tromol Pos 273/JKT, Jakarta, Indonesia.

ACTIVITIES IN THE FAR EAST AND AUSTRALASIA

Directed by its constitution to advance "the mutual knowledge and understanding of peoples" and to "give fresh impulse to popular education and to the spread of culture" the Organization promotes the exchange of information and the defining of policies by convening intergovernmental and other conferences and seminars.

Education

UNESCO prepared an Asian model of education development that was adopted by a ministerial conference at Bangkok in 1965 and which also served as a guide for each country. Work in educational projects is co-ordinated by UNESCO's regional education office in Bangkok.

Science

Apart from the establishment of regional science offices in New Delhi and Jakarta, UNESCO was drawn into large-scale scientific programmes whose success depended on international co-operation.

In 1951, UNESCO co-ordinated the international effort to improve the productivity of Asia's arid and humid lands. This developed into a major project, lasting eleven years; the region is still served by the Central Arid Zone Research Institute at Jodhpur, India.

The Intergovernmental Oceanographic Commission (IOC) was created in 1958 and co-ordinated two major expeditions in Asia, with a total of 31 participating countries and 76 research vessels.

With UNESCO assistance, the International Institute of Seismology and Earthquake Engineering in Japan has been expanded.

Following the Conference on the Application of Science and Technology to the Development of Asia, UNESCO became the executive agency for over 25 UNDP-financed projects. UNESCO's own projects included science teaching equipment, standards and testing, and zoology.

Culture

Another UNESCO project is the expansion of the mutual appreciation of cultural values. Institutes have been established in Tokyo, New Delhi and Teheran to study Asian civilizations. Representative works have been published, and over 360 Asian classics have been translated into English and French while western works have been published in Asian languages. UNESCO has also initiated several international campaigns for the conservation and renovation of monuments and historical sites. In June-July 1980 the Organization collaborated in the South Pacific Arts Festival in New Guinea.

UNESCO has participated in schemes to preserve the ancient buildings of Borobdur, Indonesia, and Moenjodaro, Pakistan, and in 1981 it launched an international campaign for the restoration of historic monuments in Viet-Nam.

Communications

UNESCO has a Centre for Book Development in Karachi, which trains specialists in book production and assists national and regional promotions.

UNESCO assists Asian states to train their own media specialists. It helped to set up a regional Mass Communications Institute at the University of the Philippines and collaborated on the establishment of an Asian Institute for Broadcasting Development at Kuala Lumpur.

In February 1979 UNESCO convened an Intergovernmental Conference on Communication Policies in Asia which was attended by representatives of 22 countries.

Under the International Programme for the Development of Communications, launched in 1981, an information exchange network and a film bank were planned for the region.

UNITED NATIONS HIGH COMMISSIONER FOR REFUGEES—UNHCR

Palais des Nations, 1211 Geneva 10, Switzerland

Telephone: 31 02 61.

The Office of the High Commissioner was established in 1951 to provide international protection for refugees and to seek permanent solutions to their problems. In 1977 the mandate of UNHCR was extended until the end of 1983.

ORGANIZATION

(June 1982)

HIGH COMMISSIONER

High Commissioner (1978–82): POUL HARTLING (Denmark).

Deputy High Commissioner: WILLIAM R. SMYSER (U.S.A.).

The High Commissioner is elected by the United Nations General Assembly on the nomination of the Secretary-General, and is responsible to the General Assembly and to ECOSOC.

EXECUTIVE COMMITTEE

The Executive Committee of the High Commissioner's Programme, established by ECOSOC, gives the High Commissioner directives in respect of material assistance programmes and advice at his request in the field of international protection. It meets once a year at Geneva. It includes representatives of 40 states, both members and non-members of the UN.

Chairman: OMAR BIRIDO (Sudan).

Vice-Chairman: P. H. R. MARSHALL (U.K.).

ADMINISTRATION

Headquarters includes the High Commissioner's Office, and the following divisions: External Affairs, Protection, Assistance, and Administration and Management. As at May 1981 there were 10 Regional Offices, 34 Branch Offices and 17 Sub-Offices, 8 Chargés de Mission and 7 Honorary Representatives located in 61 countries.

Offices in the Far East and Australasia: G.P.O. Box 4045, Sydney 2001, Australia; Shin Aoyama Building Nishikan, 22nd Floor, 1-1 Minami Aoyama, Minato-ku, Tokyo 107, Japan.

ACTIVITIES IN THE FAR EAST AND AUSTRALASIA

The two main functions of UNHCR are the legal protection of refugees and the provision of material assistance. In the field of protection, the UNHCR continues to encourage national practices and procedures benefiting refugees and, as elsewhere, seeks to promote accessions to the basic international instruments concerning refugees, the 1951 Convention and the 1967 Protocol relating to the Status of Refugees, to which Australia, Japan, New Zealand and the Philippines are currently parties in the region covered by this volume. Without such accessions, the countries of an area such as South-East Asia have no common policy on the granting of asylum, the prevention of *refoulement* (enforced repatriation) and expulsion, or the legal status of refugees.

Since 1975 the UNHCR'S assistance activities in the Far East and Australasia have been dominated by the problems of refugees and displaced persons in and from the Indo-Chinese peninsula: Laotians, Kampucheans and Vietnamese, needing both immediate assistance in the countries of temporary asylum to which they had fled, and help in finding a place of permanent resettlement. Between 1975 and 1981 UNHCR provided assistance to over 570,000 refugees in Thailand, at a cost of U.S. $184 million; in 1981, however, departures began to outnumber arrivals. The total number of refugee arrivals in South-East Asian countries of temporary asylum fell from 119,402 in 1980 to 99,168 in 1981. By August 1980 over half a million Indo-Chinese refugees had been resettled, chiefly in the U.S.A. (about 283,600), the People's Republic of China (265,000), France (67,000), Canada (63,400) and Australia (40,500): over 200,000, however, still remained in camps, mostly in Thailand, awaiting resettlement. A programme of aid was launched in 1980 for some 300,000 Kampucheans who had returned to their homeland from Thailand, Viet-Nam and Laos.

In May 1979 UNHCR and Viet-Nam signed a "memorandum of understanding" on the orderly departure of persons wishing to leave: under the Orderly Departure Programme which resulted, 6,598 people left the country in 1980, and 11,212 in 1981.

Refugees from Afghanistan began to enter Pakistan early in 1979; by October they numbered 200,000. UNHCR established a programme to help the Pakistan Government transfer the refugees from the north-western frontier to resettlement areas in the interior; the cost was originally estimated at U.S. $10 million, but numbers increased so rapidly, reaching 2.34 million by September 1981, that successive appeals had to be made to the international community, for $26.4 million in January 1980, for $99.8 million in June, and for a further $56.6 million in June 1981. The total amount needed to cover the assistance programme in 1981 was estimated at $98 million.

UNHCR's 1982 budget allocated $180 million to Asia, of which $71 million was for Afghan refugees in Pakistan.

WORLD HEALTH ORGANIZATION—WHO

Avenue Appia, 1211 Geneva 27, Switzerland

Telephone: 34 60 61.

Established in 1948 as the central agency directing international health work. Of its many activities, the most important single aspect is technical co-operation with national health administrations, particularly in the developing countries.

ORGANIZATION

(June 1982)

SECRETARIAT

Director-General: Dr. HALFDAN MAHLER (Denmark).

Deputy Director-General: Dr. ADEOYE T. LAMBO (Nigeria).

Assistant Directors-General: Dr. CHEN WENJIE (People's Republic of China), Dr. JACQUES HAMON (France), WARREN W. FURTH (U.S.A.), Dr. I. D. LADNYI (U.S.S.R.), Dr. DAVID TEJADA-DE-RIVERO (Peru).

REGIONAL OFFICES

South-East Asia: Indraprastha Estate, Ring Rd., New Delhi 110002, India; Regional Dir. Dr. U Ko Ko (Burma).

Western Pacific: P.O.B. 2932, 12115 Manila, the Philippines; covers 32 countries and areas; staff of 300; regular budget (1982–83) U.S. $39 million; Regional Dir. Dr. HIROSHI NAKAJIMA (Japan).

ACTIVITIES IN THE FAR EAST AND AUSTRALASIA

In February 1980 the Asian Charter for Health Development was signed by Bangladesh, India, Sri Lanka and Thailand; Indonesia signed in April and other countries of the region were due to sign later in the year. The Charter serves to declare health priorities, to enable the mobilization of funds and resources, to promote inter-country co-operation, and to provide a common basis for formulating health plans. The Charter lists the following priority areas: primary health care; appropriate manpower development; provision of safe water and sanitation; promotion of maternal and child health; control of communicable diseases (especially malaria and the diseases against which effective immunization agents are available); and the improvement of nutrition.

During 1980–81 WHO promoted national, regional and global strategies for the attainment of the main target of member states for the next two decades: "Health for all by the year 2000", or the attainment by all citizens of the world of a level of health that will permit them to lead a socially and economically productive life. In May 1981 the World Health Assembly adopted a Global Strategy in support of this aim. Primary health care was seen as the key to "Health for all", with the following as minimum requirements:

Safe water in the home or within 15 minutes' walking distance, and adequate sanitary facilities in the home or immediate vicinity;

Immunization against diphtheria, pertussis, tetanus, poliomyelitis, measles and tuberculosis;

Local health care, including availability of at least 20 essential drugs, within one hour's travel;

Trained personnel to attend childbirth, and to care for pregnant mothers and children up to at least one year old.

In many countries of Asia and the Pacific, WHO staff work with national health leaders to assess health needs and resources, and to formulate realistic health plans. These plans form an integral part of the overall national development programmes, since health and socio-economic development are viewed as closely interlinked. Support was given to Burma in drawing up the "People's Health Plan" for 1982–86, and to other member states in developing managerial training for national health development. Assessment of health resource needs was being carried out in Burma, Indonesia, Nepal and Sri Lanka in 1982.

The Organization supports its members' efforts to create broadly-based community-centred health services. Much importance is attached to bringing the education and training of health professionals into accord with specific local health problems, making judicious use of the available manpower and resources, and preparing community health workers and other categories of personnel to function in a health care system best suited to answer the community's health needs. An important aspect of manpower development is the award of fellowships: for example, about 400 are granted annually to workers in the Western Pacific region.

The International Drinking Water Supply and Sanitation Decade (1981–1990) aims to eradicate a major cause of ill-health by providing hygienic water supply and sewage facilties: WHO assists the national water supply agencies in drawing up realistic programmes, and recommends the programmes to international and bilateral agencies for funding. The Maldives, the hills of Nepal and the arid areas of India have received particular attention.

An outstanding success that Asian governments have achieved with WHO's co-operation is the eradication of smallpox. The last case in Asia occurred in Bangladesh in 1975. In 1980 the disease was declared to have been eradicated throughout the world. The Expanded Programme on Immunization against six childhood diseases—diphtheria, pertussis (whooping cough), tetanus, poliomyelitis, measles and tuberculosis—is active in many countries of the region. In 1976 WHO set up a Special Programme for Research and Training in Tropical Diseases, namely malaria, schistosomiasis, filariasis (including onchocerciasis or river blindness), trypanosomiasis or sleeping sickness, leishmaniasis and leprosy. Programmes are under way to eradicate the vectors of diseases, such as the mosquito vector of malaria, the blackfly vector of onchocerciasis and the water-snail vector of schistosomiasis.

In May 1981 the International Code of Marketing of Breastmilk Substitutes was adopted by the World Health Assembly, aiming to provide safe and adequate nutrition for infants by promoting breast-feeding and by ensuring the proper use of breastmilk substitutes, when necessary, with controls on production, storage and advertising.

OTHER REGIONAL OFFICES OF THE UN SYSTEM

INTERNATIONAL CIVIL AVIATION ORGANIZATION—ICAO

100 Sherbrooke St. West, Montreal, P.Q. H3A 2R2, Canada

Regional Office for Asia and the Pacific: Sala Santitham, Rajadamnern Ave., P.O.B. 614, Bangkok, Thailand.

INTERNATIONAL LABOUR ORGANISATION—ILO

1211 Geneva 22, Switzerland

Regional Office for Asia and the Pacific: United Nations Bldg., Rajadamnern Ave., Bangkok 2; P.O.B. 1759, Bangkok, Thailand.

UNITED NATIONS CHILDREN'S FUND—UNICEF

866 United Nations Plaza, New York, N.Y. 10017, U.S.A.

Regional Office for Australia: G.P.O. Box 4045, Sydney, N.S.W. 2001.

Regional Office for East Asia and Pakistan: P.O.B. 2-154, Bangkok, Thailand.

Regional Office for Japan: c/o UN Information Centre, 22nd Floor, Shin Aoyama Bldg., Nishikan, 1-1, Minami-Aoyama 1-chome, Minato-ku, Tokyo 107.

Regional Office for South and Central Asia: 73 Lodi Estate, New Delhi 110003, India.

UNITED NATIONS ENVIRONMENT PROGRAMME—UNEP

P.O.B. 30552, Nairobi, Kenya

Regional Office for Asia and the Pacific: United Nations Bldg., Rajadamnern Ave., Bangkok 2, Thailand; Dir. C. SURIYAKUMARAN.

UNITED NATIONS UNIVERSITY

University Centre and Headquarters: 29th Floor, Toho Seimei Building, 15-1 Shibuya 2-chome, Shibuya-ku, Tokyo 150, Japan.

UNITED NATIONS INFORMATION CENTRES

Afghanistan: Shah Mahmoud Ghazi Watt, P.O.B. 5, Kabul.

Australia: 77 King St., Sydney, N.S.W. 2000; P.O.B. 4045, G.P.O., Sydney, N.S.W. 2001 (also covers Fiji and New Zealand).

Burma: 28A Manawhari Rd., P.O.B. 230, Rangoon.

India: 55 Lodi Estate, New Delhi 110003 (also covers Bhutan).

Japan: Shin Aoyama Bldg., Nishikan, 22nd Floor, 1-1, Minami Aoyama 1-chome, Minato-ku, Tokyo.

Nepal: Lainchaur, Lazimpat, P.O.B. 107, Kathmandu.

Pakistan: House No. 26, Ramna 6/3, 88th Street, P.O.B. 1107, Islamabad.

Papua New Guinea: Musgrave St., Ela Beach, P.O.B. 472, Port Moresby (also covers Solomon Islands).

Philippines: Ground Floor, NEDA Bldg., 106 Amorsolo St., Legaspi Village, Makati, Metro Manila; P.O.B. 7285 (ADC).

Sri Lanka: 202-204 Bauddhaloka Mawatha, P.O.B. 1505, Colombo 7.

Thailand: Information Service, ESCAP, United Nations Bldg., Rajadamnern Ave., Bangkok 2 (also covers Hong Kong, Kampuchea, Laos, Malaysia, Singapore and Viet-Nam).

ANZUS

c/o Department of Foreign Affairs, Canberra, A.C.T. 2600, Australia

The ANZUS Security Treaty was signed in San Francisco in September 1951 and ratified in April 1952 to co-ordinate defence as the first step to a more comprehensive system of regional security in the Pacific. This system was developed further in 1954 by the South-East Asia Collective Defence Treaty (the Manila Treaty).

MEMBERS

Australia New Zealand U.S.A.

ORGANIZATION

ANZUS COUNCIL

The ANZUS Council is the main consultative organ of the ANZUS Treaty, consisting of the Foreign Ministers, or their deputies, of the three signatory powers. Meetings are held annually, rotating between the three capitals. The 30th meeting was held in Wellington in June 1981. Talks between officials, and other forms of practical co-operation, are held more frequently.

At the 30th meeting of the Council, members agreed that the Soviet invasion and continuing occupation of Afghanistan was a direct violation of the fundamental principles governing international relations, that it remained totally unacceptable to the international community and constituted a serious threat to global and regional stability and to the independence of all states. The Council members also reaffirmed their belief that Poland should be left to settle its own affairs without outside intervention; stressed their continued firm commitment to the goal of arms limitation through negotiations which could lead to effective, balanced and verifiable agreements (while noting that this could not be a substitute for the necessary efforts which the West had to undertake to redress the adverse trend in the military balance); emphasized the need to sustain efforts to prevent the further spread of nuclear weapons, reaffirmed their commitment to strengthen the international non-proliferation regime; and reaffirmed their support for the United Nations General Assembly Resolution 35/6 on Kampuchea.

The organization has no permanent staff or secretariat, and costs are borne by the Government in whose territory the meeting is held.

The instruments of ratification are deposited with the Government of Australia in Canberra.

MILITARY REPRESENTATIVES

The Council meetings are attended also by a military officer representing each country. These officers also meet separately, and it is their function to advise the Council on military co-operation.

SECURITY TREATY

The treaty itself is brief, containing only 11 articles. Like the NATO treaty upon which it was based, the ANZUS Treaty is largely a declaratory, constitutional document which is not drafted in precise and detailed legal terms.

In the words of the preamble to the treaty, the purposes of the signatory powers are: "to strengthen the fabric of peace in the Pacific Area"; "to declare publicly and formally their sense of unity, so that no potential aggressor could be under the illusion that any of them stand alone in the Pacific Area"; "to co-ordinate further their efforts for collective defence for the preservation of peace and security pending the development of a more comprehensive system of regional security in the Pacific Area".

The Parties to the treaty undertake to "consult together whenever in the opinion of any of them, the territorial integrity, political independence or security of any of the parties is threatened in the Pacific" (Article 3). Each Party is bound to act to meet the common danger according to its constitutional processes, since each Party recognizes that an armed attack on any of the Parties would be dangerous to its own peace and safety (Article 4).

An armed attack in the terms of the treaty includes an armed attack on the metropolitan territory of any of the Parties, or on the island territories under its jurisdiction in the Pacific, or on its armed forces, public vessels or aircraft in the Pacific.

Any armed attack and all measures taken as a result thereof shall be immediately reported to the Security Council of the UN. These measures are to be terminated when the Security Council has taken the measures necessary to restore and maintain international peace and security (Article 4).

Asian Development Bank—ADB

2330 Roxas Boulevard, Metro Manila, Philippines
P.O.B. 789, Manila, Philippines 2800
Telephone: 831-7211; 831-7251.

The Bank commenced operations in December 1966; its aims are to raise funds from private and public sources for development purposes in the region, to assist member states in co-ordinating economic policies, and to give technical assistance in development projects.

MEMBERS

There are 30 member countries within the ESCAP region and 14 others (*see* list of subscriptions below).

ORGANIZATION

(June 1982)

BOARD OF GOVERNORS

All powers of the Bank are vested in the Board which may delegate its powers to the Board of Directors except in such matters as admission of new members, changes in the Bank's authorized capital stock, election of Directors and President, amendment of the Charter. One Governor and one Alternate Governor are appointed by each member country. The Board meets at least once a year. Fifteenth Annual Meeting: Manila, Philippines, April 1982.

BOARD OF DIRECTORS

Responsible for general direction of operations and exercises all powers delegated by the Board of Governors. Composed of twelve Directors elected by the Board of Governors, of whom eight represent member countries within the ESCAP region and four represent the rest of the member countries. Each Director serves for two years and may be re-elected. The President of the Bank, though not a Director, is Chairman of the Board.

Chairman of Board of Directors and President: MASAO FUJIOKA (Japan).

Vice-Presidents: A. T. BAMBAWALE (India); S. STANLEY KATZ (U.S.A.).

ADMINISTRATION

Departments: Country, Development Policy, Agriculture and Rural Development, Infrastructure, Industry and Development Banks, Central Projects Services, Budget, Personnel and Management Systems, Controller's, Treasurer's.

Offices: President, Secretary, General Counsel, Development Policy, Central Projects Services, Administrative Services, Economic, Information, Computer Services, Internal Auditor and Post-Evaluation.

Secretary: WILFRED A. VAWDREY.

General Counsel: CHUN PYO JHONG (Republic of Korea).

BUDGET

Internal administrative expenses for 1981 amounted to $51.9 million: the 1982 budget was $68.6 million. Services to member countries financed from the Bank's own resources (e.g. project preparation and advisory services) accounted for $6 million in actual disbursements in 1981, and the 1982 budget allowed for $10.5 million in disbursements.

FINANCIAL STRUCTURE

CAPITAL

(as of December 31st, 1981)

(U.S. $ million, valued at SDR 1= U.S. $1.16396)

Authorized	8,404.5
Subscribed	8,296.8
Paid-in	1,609.1

The Bank has also borrowed funds from the world capital markets. Total borrowings up to the end of December 1981 were equivalent to $3,123 million (gross contracted borrowings converted to U.S. dollars at exchange rates prevailing at the end of the year of each borrowing).

ORDINARY CAPITAL RESOURCES

Composed of subscribed capital and borrowings. Subscriptions and voting power at the end of December 1981 were:

	Subscriptions (U.S. $ '000)*	Voting Power (% of Total)
Regional:		
Afghanistan	13,909	0.589
Australia	581,246	6.059
Bangladesh	102,568	1.444
Burma	54,706	0.982
Cook Islands	268	0.457
Fiji	6,833	0.520

[*continued on next page*

continued from previous page]

Hong Kong	54,706	0.982
India	635,953	6.587
Indonesia	547,061	5.730
Japan	1,367,653	13.642
Kampuchea	10,185	0.553
Kiribati	407	0.458
Korea, Republic	506,032	5.334
Laos	2,863	0.482
Malaysia	273,531	3.092
Maldives	407	0.458
Nepal	14,771	0.597
New Zealand	154,271	1.942
Pakistan	218,825	2.565
Papua New Guinea	9,428	0.545
Philippines	239,334	2.762
Singapore	34,186	0.784
Solomon Islands	675	0.461
Sri Lanka	58,256	1.016
Taiwan	109,412	1.510
Thailand	136,765	1.773
Tonga	407	0.458
Vanuatu	675	0.461
Viet-Nam	82,059	1.246
Western Samoa	675	0.461
	5,218,067	63.950
Non-regional:		
Austria	34,186	0.784
Belgium	34,186	0.784
Canada	525,446	5.521
Denmark	34,186	0.784
Finland	13,676	0.587
France	170,951	2.103
Germany, Fed. Repub.	434,553	4.645
Italy	136,765	1.773
Netherlands	75,215	1.180
Norway	34,186	0.784
Sweden	13,676	0.587
Switzerland	46,989	0.907
United Kingdom	205,148	2.433
U.S.A.	1,319,558	13.178
	3,078,721	36.050
TOTAL	8,296,788	100.000

* Valued in terms of SDR at the rate of U.S. $1.16396 per SDR.

SPECIAL FUNDS

The Asian Development Fund (ADF) was established in June 1974 in order to provide a systematic mechanism for mobilizing and administering resources for the Bank to lend on concessional terms. Administration of the earlier Special Funds—the Multi-Purpose Special Fund (MPSF) and the Agricultural Special Fund (ASF)—had been complicated by the fact that contributions of individual donors had been made voluntarily at the initiative of the countries concerned and were frequently tied to procurement in those countries. Under the restructuring proposals, the ASF was wound up in the first half of 1973 and its resources consolidated with those of the MPSF. By the end of 1980 all the resources of the MPSF had been transferred to the ASF.

The initial mobilization of ADF resources (ADF I) was intended to finance the Bank's concessional lending programme for the three-year period ending December 31st, 1975. Contributions to ADF I totalling $486.1 million were received from 14 countries. At the end of 1975 the Board of Governors authorized a replenishment of the resources of the ADF (ADF II), intended to finance the Bank's concessional lending programme over the period 1976–78. The amount initially authorized was $830 million,

[*continued on page* 118

RESOURCES OF ASIAN DEVELOPMENT FUND

(U.S. $'000 equivalent, December 31st, 1981)

CONTRIBUTED RESOURCES	
Australia	146,850
Austria	19,870
Belgium	25,100
Canada	218,280
Denmark	19,590
Finland	13,240
France	63,610[1]
Germany, Federal Republic	216,650
Italy	67,620[1]
Japan	1,402,960
Netherlands	64,390
New Zealand	9,870[1]
Norway	19,250
Sweden	23,850[1]
Switzerland	42,830
United Kingdom	154,120
U.S.A.	496,040[2]
TOTAL CONTRIBUTED RESOURCES	3,004,130
Set-aside resources	55,420
Other resources[3]	4,680
Accumulated translation adjustments	(3,890)
Accumulated net income	124,400
TOTAL ADDITIONAL RESOURCES	180,610
Total resources	3,184,740
Less amounts disbursed and outstanding	872,240
Less amounts committed but undisbursed	2,055,370
TOTAL UNCOMMITTED RESOURCES	257,130
Less provision for exchange rate fluctuations[4]	166,700
NET AMOUNT AVAILABLE FOR LOAN COMMITMENTS	90,430

[1] Not including advance payments by the Federal Republic of Germany ($31,810,000), Japan ($30,659,000), Norway ($49,000), and Switzerland ($228,000) on account of their respective contributions to ADF III, since these were not available for loan commitment purposes.

[2] Excluding the third instalment ($56,465,000) of the U.S.A.'s contribution to ADF II, and the two final instalments ($222,500,000) of its contribution to ADF III.

[3] Net income of MPSF of prior years transferred to ADF.

[4] Equivalent to the sum of accumulated net income, accumulated translation adjustments, other resources and loan principal repayments.

continued from page 117]

but this was subsequently reduced to $809 million. By the end of 1978, 15 of the Bank's developed member countries had participated in ADF II with total contributions of $701 million; in January 1982 $56.5 million of the United States contribution was still to be paid. In 1978 the ADF was replenished a second time (ADF III) to finance the Bank's concessional lending programme until 1982. The amount authorized was $2,150 million. By the end of 1980 17 countries had agreed to contribute. Total contributed resources of the ADF stood at $3,004.1 million in December 1981.

Discussions of a proposed third replenishment (ADF IV) of $4,100 million were held in 1981, but owing to restrictions on American aid policy, this figure was cut to $3,200 million.

The Bank provides technical assistance grants from its Technical Assistance Special Fund. By the end of 1981, contributions to this fund amounted to $52 million, of which $39 million had been utilized.

ACTIVITIES

The Bank gives priority to three sectors: agriculture and agro-industry (which accounted for 32.3 per cent of lending in 1981), energy (28.6 per cent) and social infrastructure, including water supply, sewerage, housing, education and health (21.7 per cent). Loans from ordinary capital resources amounted to $1,147 million in 1981, and loans from Special Funds to $531 million, a total of $1,678 million, compared with $1,436 million in 1980. Disbursements in 1981 came to $667 million ($579 million in 1980). Fifty-seven loans were made for 54 projects in 15 developing member countries: 23 projects involved co-financing, mainly with bilateral and multilateral official sources.

Technical assistance worth $14.8 million was provided for 49 projects in 1981: over half was for agriculture and agro-industrial projects.

The Bank also carries out regional studies, for example a regional energy survey completed in 1981; other activities undertaken in that year included a fish market study and a study of agricultural research facilities and requirements in the South Pacific, and an industrial survey of the South Pacific. The Bank's Post-Evaluation Office reviewed 35 completed projects in order to assess achievements and problems.

BANK ACTIVITIES BY SECTOR
(to December 1981)

	Loan Approvals (U.S. $ million)		Technical Assistance Approvals[1] (U.S. $ '000)	
	1967–81	1981	1967–81	1981
Agriculture and agro-industry	2,806.01	541.60	49,785.84	8,175.30
Energy	2,443.44	480.10	11,633.84[2]	2,754.00
Industry and non-fuel minerals	375.24	13.00	3,297.90	190.00
Development banks	1,310.10	204.00	3,017.60	—
Transport and communications	1,353.75	72.40	9,954.30	1,726.00
Water supply	829.52	123.70	4,999.50	350.00
Urban development	239.25	99.30	1,579.00	680.00
Education	296.30	82.50	3,278.92	927.72
Health	113.40	59.30	1,074.00	—
Multiproject	3.88	1.68	140.00	—
Others	—	—	1,451.70	—
Total	9,770.89	1,677.58	90,242.60	14,803.02

[1] Excluding regional projects and technical assistance loans.

[2] Adjusted to include additional UNDP financing of $200,000 for Energy Master Plan (Thailand) which was approved in 1979.

LENDING ACTIVITIES BY COUNTRY
(U.S. $ million)

	Cumulative to End of 1981			Loans Approved in 1981		
	Ordinary Capital	Special Funds	Total	Ordinary Capital	Special Funds	Total
Afghanistan	—	95.10	95.10	—	—	—
Bangladesh	11.40	810.93	822.33	—	191.00	191.00
Burma	6.60	343.46	350.06	—	59.50	59.50
Cook Islands	—	1.00	1.00	—	—	—
Fiji	45.90	—	45.90	16.00	—	16.00
Hong Kong	101.50	—	101.50	—	—	—
Indonesia	1,406.78	162.28	1,569.06	337.80	—	337.80
Kampuchea (Cambodia)	—	1.67	1.67	—	—	—
Kiribati	—	1.75	1.75	—	—	—
Korea, Republic	1,373.53	3.70	1,377.23	205.20	—	205,20
Laos	—	36.84	36.84	—	—	—
Malaysia	706.75	3.30	710.05	116.80	—	116.80
Maldives	—	1.00	1.00	—	1.00	1.00
Nepal	2.00	262.92	264.92	—	45.20	45.20
Pakistan	534.37	680.95	1,215.32	55.00	155.00	210.00
Papua New Guinea	43.95	69.94	113.89	8.00	8.00	16.00
Philippines	1,267.55	79.30	1,346.85	200.50	15.00	215.50
Singapore	178.08	3.00	181.08	—	—	—
Solomon Islands	—	14.85	14.85	—	—	—
Sri Lanka	14.13	245.61	259.74	—	35.50	35.50
Taiwan	100.39	—	100.39	—	—	—
Thailand	1,002.58	72.10	1,074.68	207.40	15.00	222.40
Tonga	—	6.05	6.05	—	1.68	1.68
Viet-Nam	3.93	40.67	44.60	—	—	—
Western Samoa	—	35.03	35.03	—	4.00	4.00
Total	6,799.44	2,971.45	9,770.89	1,146.70	530.88	1,677.58

Source: ADB Annual Report 1981.

PUBLICATIONS

Annual Report.

ADB Quarterly Review.

Annual Review of Post-Evaluation Reports.

Studies and papers.

Asian Productivity Organization—APO

4-14, Akasaka, 8-chome, Minato-ku, Tokyo 107, Japan.
Telephone: (03) 408-7221/9.

Established by Convention in 1961 by eight governments in Asia to hasten their respective economic development.

MEMBERS

Open to all Asian Governments that are members of the Economic and Social Commission for Asia and the Pacific (ESCAP). Governments outside the ESCAP region may become Associate Members. The founding members were the Republic of China (Taiwan), India, Japan, the Republic of Korea, Nepal, Pakistan, the Philippines, and Thailand, subsequently joined by Hong Kong (1963), Iran and the Republic of (South) Viet-Nam (1965), Sri Lanka (1967), Indonesia (1968) and Singapore (1970).

ORGANIZATION

(June 1982)

The Governing Body is the supreme organ of the APO and is composed of Directors designated by member Governments. It meets once a year to decide on policy matters concerning programmes, budget, finance, and membership. At each annual session it elects from among Directors a Chairman and two Vice-Chairmen, who, assisted by the Secretary-General, act on important matters when the Governing Body is not in session.

National Productivity Organizations (NPOs) in member countries, or similar institutes dealing with productivity activities at the national level, act as implementing agencies for APO projects and participants in APO programmes. The Heads of NPOs meet once a year to exchange experiences and to review and work out projects and implementation details of APO's programme of activities.

The Secretariat, headed by a Secretary-General, is the executive arm of the Governing Body. It has four divisions: Industry, Agriculture, Research and Planning, and Administration and Public Relations. Staff members are recruited from among member countries.

Chairman: Surya Prasad Shrestha (Nepal).

Vice-Chairmen: Danang Joedonagoro (Indonesia), Dr. Gerardo P. Sicat (Philippines).

Secretary-General: Hiroshi Yokota (Japan).

AIMS AND ACTIVITIES

The APO aims to increase productivity, and consequently accelerate economic development, in the Asian region, by mutual co-operation. It seeks to realize its objectives by propagating productivity consciousness and disseminating productivity knowledge, techniques, and experiences in agriculture, industry, and service sectors. APO activities are grouped under three broad categories:

Productivity improvement in general, through the study of productivity issues relevant to the development of the region: the APO organizes conferences, symposia, and undertakes researches and surveys to identify common needs of the member countries and to plan and design programmes based on the findings.

Institution building and meeting needs of member countries: the APO organizes multi-country training projects in management and technology for the development of trainers and consultants; technical expert services; observational study missions to observe latest techniques in a particular sector. Fellowships are also awarded.

Propagation of productivity concepts through dissemination of knowledge and promotion of mutual co-operation among member countries and with other countries and organizations: the APO issues publications, develops training material and audio-visual aids, encourages the exchange of information among its member countries, and co-operates with various international organizations and governments on matters of mutual interest. Non-member countries within the ESCAP region are also encouraged to participate in selected APO programmes by special arrangements.

PUBLICATIONS

APO NEWS (monthly), *Annual Report*, reports of surveys and symposia, monographs, etc.

Association of South East Asian Nations—ASEAN

ASEAN Secretariat, Jalan Sisingamangaraja, P.O.B. 2072, Jakarta, Indonesia
Telephone: 348838.

Established August 1967 at Bangkok, Thailand, to accelerate economic progress and to increase the stability of the South-East Asian region.

MEMBERS

Indonesia	Philippines	Thailand
Malaysia	Singapore	

Observer: Papua New Guinea.

ORGANIZATION

(June 1982)

SUMMIT MEETING

The highest authority of ASEAN, bringing together the Heads of Government of member countries. The first meeting was held in Bali in February 1976; the second in Kuala Lumpur in August 1977.

MINISTERIAL CONFERENCES

Composed of the Foreign Ministry of member states; meets annually in each member country in turn. Economic and other Ministers also meet frequently.

STANDING COMMITTEE

Meets when necessary between Ministerial meetings for consultations in one of the five countries in annual rotation: Philippines in 1980–81. Consists of the Foreign Minister of the host country and Ambassadors of the other four.

SECRETARIAT

A permanent secretariat was established in Jakarta, Indonesia, in 1976. A "Headquarters Agreement" was signed in September 1978. The Secretary-General serves for a two-year term.

Secretary-General: Narciso G. Reyes (Philippines).

COMMITTEES

The seats of the Committees are distributed among the ASEAN capitals, and move in rotation at 2–3 year intervals. There are nine Committees:

Trade and Tourism; Industry, Minerals and Energy; Food, Agriculture and Forestry; Transportation and Communications; Finance and Banking; Science and Technology; Social Development; Culture and Information; Budget.

These committees are serviced by a network of subsidiary technical bodies comprising sub-committees, expert groups, ad-hoc working groups, working parties, etc.

To support the conduct of relations with other countries and international organizations, ASEAN committees (composed of heads of diplomatic missions) have been established in ten foreign capitals: those of Australia, Belgium, Canada, France, the Federal Republic of Germany, Japan, New Zealand, Switzerland, the United Kingdom and the U.S.A.

A study group was set up in February 1982 to consider the establishment of an ASEAN parliament.

AIMS

ASEAN was established in 1967 with the signing of the ASEAN Declaration, otherwise known as the Bangkok Declaration. This set out the objectives of the organization as follows:

To accelerate economic growth, social progress and cultural development in the region through joint endeavours in the spirit of equality and partnership in order to strengthen the foundation for a prosperous and peaceful community of South East Asian nations.

To promote regional peace and stability through abiding respect for justice and the rule of law in the relationship among countries of the region and adherence to the principles of the United Nations Charter.

To promote active collaboration and mutual assistance on matters of common interest in the economic, social, cultural, technical, scientific and administrative fields.

To provide assistance to each other in the form of training and research facilities in the educational, professional, technical and administrative spheres.

To collaborate more effectively for the greater utilization of their agriculture and industries, the expansion of their trade, including the study of the problems of international commodity trade, the improvement of their transportation and communication facilities and the raising of the living standards of their people.

To promote South East Asian studies.

To maintain close and beneficial co-operation with existing international and regional organizations with similar aims and purposes, and explore all avenues for even closer co-operation among themselves.

ASEAN's first summit meeting was held at Denpasar, Bali, Indonesia, in February 1976. Two major documents were signed:

Treaty of Amity and Co-operation, laying down principles

of mutual respect for the independence and sovereignty of all nations; non-interference in the internal affairs of one another; settlement of disputes by peaceful means; and effective co-operation among the five countries.

Declaration of Concord, giving guidelines for action in economic, social and cultural relations. This included co-operation in the pursuit of political stability in the region; the members would give priority to the supply of one another's needs for commodities, particularly food and energy, in any emergency. This last aim would be approached by forming industrial projects in common.

The long-term objective of a preferential trade arrangement was acknowledged; the first priority in trade, however, was to develop joint action in the international markets.

The declaration called for assistance between member states in the event of a natural disaster.

ACTIVITIES

EXTERNAL RELATIONS

GATT: The ASEAN-Geneva Committee was formed in 1973 to assist member countries in their participation in the Multilateral Trade Negotiations at the GATT Secretariat. GATT has endorsed the ASEAN Preferential Trade Agreements and this will contribute to the expansion of intra-ASEAN trade.

EEC: A Joint Study Group was set up by ASEAN and the EEC Commission in 1975 to discuss the possibilities for economic co-operation between the two regions, and to act as a forum for contacts with European officials and companies. The principal achievement in the ASEAN countries' negotiations with the EEC Commission was a reduction of duties under the EEC's Generalized System of Preferences in favour of ASEAN countries. In March 1980 a five-year co-operation agreement was signed between ASEAN and the EEC, following a joint ministerial conference. The agreement, which entered into force on October 1st, provides for the strengthening of existing trade links and increased co-operation in the scientific and agricultural spheres. A joint co-operation committee met in Manila in November; it drew up a programme of scientific and technological co-operation, approved measures to promote contracts between industrialists from the two regions, and agreed on the financing of ASEAN regional projects by the Community.

Japan: In September 1978 the Japan-ASEAN Economic Council was founded by business organizations from Japan and ASEAN as a machinery for regular consultation on mutual economic co-operation and Japan promised U.S. $1,000 million for implementing joint industrial projects, but during 1978 and 1979 Japan's attention was focused on the People's Republic of China and ASEAN increasingly turned to the EEC for trading links. In January 1981 the Japanese Prime Minister made a tour of ASEAN countries, declaring support for their opposition to the Vietnamese over Kampuchea, and announcing the approval of yen-based credits worth $870,000,000 for Indonesia, Malaysia, the Philippines and Thailand.

China and Indochina: The question of relations with the new communist governments in Indochina was prominent at the Bali summit in February 1976. The documents signed at the summit made clear that ASEAN countries wished to form a zone of peace, freedom and neutrality, a concept adopted by ASEAN in 1971, and would respect the independence and sovereignty of all nations. ASEAN was to be an economic and diplomatic forum, with no question of a military alliance. Diplomatic relations with the communist governments were established in 1976. In 1978 the hostilities between Viet-Nam, Kampuchea and the People's Republic of China caused both Viet-Nam and China to seek closer ties with ASEAN and to negotiate with ASEAN as a group, not in bilateral terms. Fears of Viet-Nam's military ambitions stirred by the invasion of Kampuchea in December 1978 and the severe strain placed on the ASEAN countries by the exodus of refugees from Viet-Nam, however, caused ASEAN to reassess its relations with Viet-Nam, which it accused of trying to destabilize South-East Asia, and to seek new ways of establishing peace. At the 12th meeting of Foreign Ministers in June 1979 grave concern was expressed over the thousands of displaced persons from Indochina, and the delegates deplored the fact that Viet-Nam had not taken effective measures to stop the exodus. The ASEAN Foreign Ministers also reiterated their support for the right of the Kampuchean people to self-determination. In July 1981 the United Nations held a conference on Kampuchea, sponsored by ASEAN: the ASEAN countries proposed a coalition of the three main factions in Kampuchea, the withdrawal of Vietnamese troops, and elections supervised by the UN. ASEAN made it clear that it would not, as a group, supply arms to any faction.

The Chinese Prime Minister, Zhao Ziyang, made a tour of ASEAN countries in August 1981 and assured them that, in spite of its backing for the *Khmer Rouge* in Kampuchea and its "political and moral" support for communist parties in the region, the People's Republic had no ambition to create a sphere of influence in South-East Asia.

Other countries: There have been increased contacts with Australia, New Zealand and Canada. Discussions with the U.S.A. began in September 1977, with a meeting of officials in Manila, and a second meeting was held at ministerial level in Washington, D.C., in August 1978. It was agreed in September 1980 to establish an Economic Co-ordination Committee to promote trade, investment and improved economic relations between ASEAN and the U.S.A.

INTERNAL RELATIONS

Internal Security: Whilst the policy of peace and neutrality was a major feature of the Treaty of Amity and Co-operation, the ASEAN countries recognized a common problem in combating communist insurgency. It had been necessary during 1976 and 1977 for Thailand and Malaysia to co-ordinate their military activity against the communists in the area of their mutual border, and this was reflected in the section of the Declaration of Concord (*see* above) concerning the pursuit of political stability in the region. In 1978–80 the large numbers of refugees from Viet-Nam revived fears of destabilization in the area and placed severe strains on the internal security of the recipient countries, particularly Malaysia, Thailand and Indonesia.

Industry: The Bali summit and the joint industrial projects launched in 1976 were the first actions which gave expression to the new solidarity. A meeting of Economic Ministers in Kuala Lumpur in March 1976 agreed to set up five medium-sized industries by forming joint projects; a 60 per cent share of each was to be owned by the host country, and the remaining 40 per cent by the other four members. The projects originally comprised the manufacture of diesel engines in Singapore, urea in Indonesia and Malaysia, superphosphates in the Philippines, and soda ash in Thailand. At the sixth meeting of ASEAN Economic Ministers in Jakarta in June 1978, the text of the Basic Agreement on ASEAN Industrial Projects was agreed. By 1982, however, only the urea projects in Indonesia and Malaysia were ready to be implemented. The Indonesian project had its ASEAN company incorporated in March 1979 and was expected to be completed by 1982 to produce 500,000 tons of urea annually. The Malaysian project will have an annual production capacity of 530,000 tons of urea and 360,000 tons of ammonia, to come on stream in 1984. In April 1980 an Integrated Pulp and Paper Project in the Philippines was accepted as the fourth ASEAN industrial project, but at the end of the year it was announced that a copper fabrication plant was to take its place. The Singapore diesel engine project was also abandoned and alternative schemes were being considered in 1982. The Thai soda ash project was due to become operational in 1985, but a rival Indonesian project, announced in 1981, appeared likely to delay the Thai scheme and create further obstacles to co-operation.

In July 1980 ASEAN representatives agreed to set up their first joint private banking institution, the ASEAN Finance Corporation, to provide financing for industrial projects of benefit to the region. The Corporation was to have an initial capital of $50 million.

Trade: Meeting in Manila in January 1977 the Economic Ministers concluded a Basic Agreement on the Establishment of ASEAN Preferential Trade Arrangements. This was not intended to lead directly to the formation of a free trade zone. The Philippines, Thailand and Singapore have been in favour of trade liberalization, and early in 1977 they concluded bilateral agreements for 10 per cent tariff cuts on a wide range of items traded between themselves. Indonesia, on the other hand, has been opposed to trade liberalization, taking the view that its own economy is of a type that would be bound to suffer under free trade. The ASEAN agreement therefore provides for negotiations to lead to the introduction of preferences product by product.

Under the agreement, the five countries were to accord priority to buying and selling their products to each other at preferential rates during gluts or shortages, as from January 1978. At their sixth meeting in Jakarta in June, the Economic Ministers agreed that in each future round of negotiations on trade preferences, to take place every three months, each country will make offers of at least 100 items. By July 1980 4,325 items were covered by a tariff reduction of 10 per cent, and in that month it was decided that all imports with trade values of less than U.S. $50,000 (as recorded in the trade statistics for 1978) should have the existing tariff reduced by 20 per cent, bringing the number of items under the preferential trading arrangements to over 6,000. By April 1981 5,825 items were included.

In 1980 the Committee on Finance and Banking agreed in principle to the establishment of an ASEAN Bankers' Acceptance Market, as a tool to promote intra-ASEAN trade.

At the first ASEAN Agriculture Ministers' meeting in Manila an emergency grain reserve agreement was signed on August 29th, 1979. During the year an emergency reserve of 50,000 tons of rice was established, available to any member country at three days' notice. Proposals towards the creation of a common agricultural policy were also adopted.

Communications: The Malaysian and Thai national airlines have pooled some of their services. During 1979 disagreements arose between ASEAN and Australia over the volume of passenger traffic carried by ASEAN airlines between Europe and Australia. In May an agreement was reached limiting such traffic. Telecommunications networks in the region have been improved. The first section of the ASEAN Submarine Cable Network went into operation in August 1978. It runs between the Philippines and Singapore. The second section, between Indonesia and Singapore, was inaugurated in August 1980. An ASEAN Regional Satellite system was proposed in June 1978 and some member countries use the Indonesian communications satellite, purchased from the U.S.A. in 1979.

Joint research and technology: The ASEAN Committee on Science and Technology has co-ordinated projects such as the Protein Project, investigating low-cost alternative sources of protein; research in food technology and the management of food waste materials; preparation of a Climatic Atlas and Regional Compendium of Climatic Statistics; a nature conservation scheme; and non-conventional energy research. An energy exploration programme was planned for 1981–85 at a cost of U.S. $33,100 million.

Education: Under the ASEAN Development Education Programme five projects (financed by Australia) have been set up: Special Education; Education Management Information System; Teacher Education Reform; Work-oriented Education; Test Development. A National Agency of Development Education has been set up in each country.

Social development: Programmes include a Population Programme to promote family planning; co-operation against drug abuse; mutual assistance in natural disasters; collaboration in health and nutrition programmes; and co-operation in labour administration and vocational training.

Tourism: Visits of up to 14 days may be made to other member countries without a visa; tourists may also obtain ASEAN Common Collective Travel Documents for package tours and may use these in lieu of a passport within the member countries.

Culture: Tours by theatrical and dance groups, holding of art exhibitions and exchange of radio and television programmes, films and visual aids. A film festival and a Youth Music Workshop are held annually, and a directory of museums in the ASEAN region was being compiled in 1981. Cultural exchanges are also arranged. At the 11th ministerial meeting it was agreed to establish an ASEAN Cultural Fund to promote regional cultural development. In December 1978 Japan pledged 5,000 million yen towards the fund, the initial disbursement taking place in mid-1979.

PUBLICATIONS

Annual Report; *ASEAN Newsletter* (monthly), *ASEAN Journal* (quarterly).

The Colombo Plan for Co-operative Economic and Social Development in Asia and the Pacific

12 Melbourne Avenue, P.O.B. 596, Colombo 4, Sri Lanka
Telephone: 81813.

Founded by seven Commonwealth countries in 1950, the Colombo Plan was subsequently joined by more countries in Asia and the Pacific as well as the U.S.A. and Japan.

MEMBERS

Afghanistan
Australia
Bangladesh
Bhutan
Burma
Canada
Fiji
India
Indonesia
Iran
Japan
Kampuchea
Korea, Republic
Laos
Malaysia
Maldives
Nepal
New Zealand
Pakistan
Papua New Guinea
Philippines
Singapore
Sri Lanka
Thailand
United Kingdom
U.S.A.

ORGANIZATION

(June 1982)

CONSULTATIVE COMMITTEE

The highest deliberative body of the Colombo Plan, consisting of Ministers representing member governments. It meets every two years in a member country. The ministers' meeting is preceded by a meeting of senior officials who are directly concerned with the operation of the Plan in their respective countries, to identify issues for discussion by the ministers.

COLOMBO PLAN COUNCIL

The Council meets twice a year in Colombo to review the economic and social development of the region and promote co-operation among member countries. Its executive arm is the Colombo Plan Bureau.

President: U MYAUNG MYAUNG GYI (Burma).

COLOMBO PLAN BUREAU

The only permanent institution of the Plan, with its headquarters in Colombo, participates in Consultative Committee meetings, serves the Council, records the flow of bilateral assistance and disseminates information on the Colombo Plan as a whole. It also provides assistance to the host government for the holding of Consultative Committee Meetings. The Bureau represents the Colombo Plan at meetings where such representation is necessary.

The operating costs of the Bureau are met by equal contributions from member states.

Director: ERIK INGEVICS (Australia).

Chief Economic Adviser: Dr. MAHFUZUL HUQ (Bangladesh).

Information Officer: MANIK LAL MANANDHAR (Nepal).

ACTIVITIES

CAPITAL AID

Capital aid takes the form of grants and loans for national projects mainly from six developed countries to the developing member countries of the Plan. The capital aid covers almost all aspects of social and economic development.

From 1950 to 1980 total amounts of assistance from the major donors were as follows:

	U.S. $ million
Australia	3,666.03
Canada	3,197.67
India	727.38
Japan	10,062.68
New Zealand	205.91
United Kingdom	4,689.74
U.S.A.	38,745.80
TOTAL	61,295.21

TECHNICAL CO-OPERATION

Under the Technical Co-operation programme experts are supplied, fellowships are awarded and equipment for training and research is supplied.

From 1950 to December 1980, 153,457 trainees and students had received technical training and 44,425 experts and 1,892 volunteers and equipment to the value of U.S. $832.3 million had been provided.

During 1980, 15,677 trainees and students received training; 6,335 experts and 834 volunteers were engaged; value of equipment supplied was $35.2 million; total value of co-operation activities from the inception of the Plan to December 1980 was nearly $3,938 million, disbursements in 1980 totalling $397.6 million.

Japan provided 35 per cent of the 15,677 training and student places available in 1980; the United Kingdom was the second largest donor, followed by Australia and the U.S.A.

Indonesia was the largest recipient of training and student awards during 1980 with 2,240 awards, followed by Thailand (1,694), India (1,389) and Bangladesh (1,372).

Of the 3,911 experts provided in 1980, Japan was the major donor country, providing 2,209 or nearly 57 per cent of the total. The U.S.A. was the second largest donor with 21 per cent. If experts whose assignments continued into 1980 from a previous year are also taken into account, Japan, Australia, the U.S.A., and the United Kingdom provided respectively 56.9 per cent (3,607), 15.5 per cent (981), 12.9 per cent (820) and 8.5 per cent (537) of a total of 6,335 experts financed in 1980.

Indonesia was the largest recipient of experts (1,554) during 1980 followed by Thailand (1,217) and the Philippines (770).

DISBURSEMENTS FOR BILATERAL TECHNICAL ASSISTANCE

(U.S. $ '000)

BY SECTOR, 1950–80

	1978	1979	1980	1950–80
Students and trainees	64,933	80,239	84,928	795,467
Experts and volunteers	119,018	114,169	149,913	1,894,239
Equipment and commodities	26,222	20,515	35,251	832,285
Other	56,541	83,571	109,488	415,533
TOTAL	226,714	298,494	379,580	3,937,524

BY DONOR AND SECTOR, 1980*

(U.S. $'000)

	Students and Trainees	Experts and Volunteers	Equipment	Other	Total
Australia	14,507.0	20,173.0	411.0	3,964.0	39,055.0
Canada	n.a.	n.a.	n.a.	n.a.	3,060.0
India	1,038.3	150.1	—	3,398.8	4,587.2
Japan	36,130.5	59,892.1	20,954.2	11,885.4	128,952.3
Korea, Republic	139.2	24.3	—	—	163.5
Malaysia	45.1	—	—	—	45.1
New Zealand	1,801.2	3,279.6	3,955.6	3,944.9	12,981.3
Pakistan	240.5	40.0	—	7.5	288.0
Singapore	261.2	—	—	—	261.2
Thailand	0.7	—	—	—	0.7
United Kingdom	283.3	14.0	—	—	297.3
U.S.A.	23,343.0	21,268.0	9,930.0	27,498.0	82,039.0
	7,138.1	44,981.9	—	55,729.4	107,849.4
TOTAL	84,928.1	149,913.0	35,250.8	109,448.1	379,580.0

* Difference in vertical and horizontal totals due to rounding.

DRUG ADVISORY PROGRAMME

The programme was launched in 1973 to help develop co-operative schemes to eliminate the cause and ameliorate the effects of drug abuse in member states. The programme is supplementary in nature and does not duplicate the efforts of international and other agencies involved. Its activities are directed towards the promotion of effective national, regional and sub-regional efforts in tackling problems and identifying areas in which bilateral and multilateral assistance and international co-operation under the Colombo Plan would be useful.

Seminars are held in member countries to inform governments and the public and to help organize remedial measures. Assistance is given in training narcotics officials in all aspects of drug abuse prevention by means of exchanges, fellowships, study, training and observation. Bilateral and multilateral talks among member countries are held.

Member countries are helped in establishing narcotics control offices or boards, revising legislation on narcotics, improving law enforcement, treatment, rehabilitation and prevention education, and in improving public understanding of these matters by the use of mass media, workshops and seminars.

Drug Adviser: Pio A. Abarro (Philippines).

STAFF COLLEGE FOR TECHNICIAN EDUCATION

Paterson Road, P.O.B. 187, Singapore 10.

Established in Singapore in 1974 as the first multilateral project of the Colombo Plan. All 26 member governments contribute to its operating costs.

The College is administered by a Governing Board consisting of a representative from each member government, the Director of the College and the Director of the Colombo Plan Bureau.

The main functions of the College are:

(i) to undertake programmes in the development of staff and in the training of staff for technician education;

(ii) to conduct study conferences and courses in technician education for senior administrators;

(iii) to undertake research in any special problems in the training of technicians in the region;

(iv) to give advice and other facilities for training of technicians within and outside the region.

Chairman of the Governing Board: Harry E. Thayer (U.S.A.).

Director: Prof. Y. Saran (India).

PUBLICATIONS

Bureau Publications:

The Colombo Plan Newsletter (monthly).

Proceedings and Conclusions of the Consultative Committee.

Annual Report of the Colombo Plan Council.

The Colombo Plan: What It Does, How It Works.

Development Perspectives: Country Issues, Papers by Member Governments to the Consultative Committee.

Staff College for Technician Education *Newsletter* (quarterly).

The Commonwealth

Commonwealth Secretariat: Marlborough House, Pall Mall, London, SW1Y 5HX, England

Telephone: 01-839 3411.

The Commonwealth is a voluntary association of 44 independent states comprising nearly a quarter of the world's population. It comprises the United Kingdom and most of its former dependencies, plus former dependencies of Australia and New Zealand (themselves Commonwealth countries).

MEMBERS IN THE FAR EAST AND AUSTRALASIA

Australia	Malaysia	Solomon Islands
Bangladesh	Nauru*	Sri Lanka
Fiji	New Zealand	Tonga
India	Papua New Guinea	Tuvalu*
Kiribati	Singapore	Vanuatu
		Western Samoa

* Nauru and Tuvalu are special members of the Commonwealth; they have the right to participate in functional activities but are not represented at Meetings of Commonwealth Heads of Government.

DEPENDENCIES

Australia:	*New Zealand:*	*United Kingdom:*
Christmas Island	Cook Islands	Brunei
Cocos (Keeling) Islands	Niue	Hong Kong
Coral Sea Islands Territory	Tokelau	Pitcairn Islands
Norfolk Island		

ORGANIZATION

(June 1982)

The Commonwealth is not a federation, there is no central government nor are there any rigid contractual obligations such as bind the members of the United Nations.

The Commonwealth has no written constitution but its members subscribe to the ideals of the Declaration of Commonwealth Principles unanimously approved by a meeting of Heads of Government in Singapore in 1971.

MEETINGS OF HEADS OF GOVERNMENT

Meetings are private and informal and operate not by voting but by consensus. The emphasis is on consultation and exchange of views for co-operation. Meetings are held every two years in different capitals in the Commonwealth. Last meeting: Melbourne, Australia, September-October 1981.

Heads of Government within regions of the Commonwealth hold occasional meetings to discuss matters of particular interest to them. First meeting of Asian and Pacific Regional Heads of Government: Sydney, Australia, February 1978. Second meeting: New Delhi, India, September 1980. Third meeting: Fiji, October 1982.

COMMONWEALTH SECRETARIAT

The Secretariat, established by Commonwealth Heads of Government at their meeting in London in 1965, operates as an international organization at the service of all Commonwealth countries, responsible to Commonwealth governments collectively and is the main agency for multilateral communication between them. It promotes consultation and disseminates information on matters of common concern to member governments, services the meetings of Commonwealth Heads of Government, Ministers and officials and assists appropriate agencies in fostering Commonwealth links.

Secretary-General (1975–85): Sir SHRIDATH RAMPHAL, C.M.G., Q.C. (Guyana).

Deputy Secretaries-General: E. C. ANYAOKU (Nigeria), C. J. SMALL (Canada).

COMMONWEALTH FUND FOR TECHNICAL CO-OPERATION (CFTC)

All member countries contribute to the Commonwealth Fund For Technical Co-operation, a mutual assistance agency which forms part of the Commonwealth Secretariat. The Fund provides Commonwealth experts and advisers, arranges training for nationals in other member countries, and offers assistance in improving export performance. In 1978 there were 280 long-term and 30 short-term expert advisers in the field, but, owing to a drop in income, activities were curtailed over the next two years, and the number of CFTC experts in 1981 was only 130. A working party established by Commonwealth finance ministers in 1980 recommended that CFTC's activities should be restored to their higher level, and an operational reserve set up to ensure stability of income. Examples of CFTC's activities in the region in 1981 include help in the establishment of an administrative planning unit in Vanuatu; providing advisers for regional working groups on agriculture, energy, trade and industry; marketing assistance for the South Pacific Forum Fisheries Agency; and training in telecommunications, technical education planning and agriculture at various regional centres.

ACTIVITIES

The countries of the Asian and Pacific Region, together with their dependencies, that are represented at the Commonwealth Heads of Government Regional Meeting form three distinct regions of the Commonwealth (South Asia, South-East Asia and the Pacific), and comprise nearly 80 per cent of its population. Despite the physical, geographical and social disparities of a region that stretches from India to Nauru, the tendency of Indian and Australian foreign policies to take an increasingly active part in regional co-operation has encouraged the formation of the group, while the small islands have supported an international meeting of a size that is more responsive to their views than the majority of such conferences.

The idea for an Asian and Pacific meeting was put forward by Malcolm Fraser, Prime Minister of Australia, at the Commonwealth Meeting of Heads of Government in London in June 1977. The original proposal called for the establishment of a regional office of the Commonwealth Secretariat in Canberra but was not accepted. The first meeting of the Commonwealth Asian and Pacific Heads of Government was held in Sydney in February 1978; working groups were established to discuss co-operation on energy resources, the problems of small states, combatting terrorism and stopping the traffic of narcotics.

On the question of regional trade, however, the possibility of co-operation was smaller and the problems of development greater. Though all the countries agreed that the development of trade in Asia and the Pacific was necessary to increase the region's prosperity and to protect it from the effects of recession and protectionism in the industrialized world, both the variety of the countries' economies and the small volume of trade between them, made it difficult to agree on a common trade policy. A regional consultative group on trade was established, however, to attempt to improve regional communications, simplify procedures for trade, reduce non-tariff barriers, examine ways to persuade the U.S.A., Japan and the EEC to reduce non-tariff barriers and consider long-term preferential purchases of goods from countries in the region. The meeting also called upon the industrialized world to liberalize the international trading system within the current Multilateral Trade Negotiations (MTN) and asked the EEC to address itself to the effects of Britain's entry into the EEC upon its former trading partners in Asia and the Pacific.

The second meeting of regional Heads of Government was held in New Delhi in September 1980. The participants condemned foreign intervention in Afghanistan and Kampuchea and the increased military presence of the major powers in the Indian Ocean. A Working Group on Industry was set up to examine proposals for industrial co-operation in the region, and the Secretary-General was asked to appoint a study group of experts from the region to draw up a programme of action for co-operation in agricultural research and development (including fisheries development). The study group held its third meeting in February 1982 and was to report to the meeting of Heads of Government later in the year.

In 1980 a Commonwealth Regional Renewable Energy Resources Information System (CRRERIS) was set up with headquarters in Melbourne and liaison centres in each country of the Asian and Pacific region.

In July 1981 a regional rural technology workshop, organized by the Food Production and Rural Development Division of the Commonwealth Secretariat, was held in Fiji, to encourage the use of new low-cost equipment in fishing and farming.

The second meeting of a regional Working Group on Industrial Co-operation, established in 1980, was held in November 1981 and drew up a programme for identifying members' needs and, with the help of the Industrial Development Unit of the CFTC, examining the feasibility of projects, such as industry based on coconut products in the Pacific islands.

During 1978–80 four new states in the Asian and Pacific Region acceded to membership of the Commonwealth on attaining independence: Solomon Islands on July 7th, 1978; Tuvalu on October 1st, 1978; and Kiribati (formerly the Gilbert Islands) on July 12th, 1979. Tuvalu became a special member, Kiribati and Solomon Islands full members. The former Anglo-French Condominium of New Hebrides became independent as Vanuatu on July 31st, 1980, and became a full member of the Commonwealth.

In April 1981 Pakistan, which left the Commonwealth in 1972, expressed its willingness to re-join if invited to do so. Opposition from India was expected to be the chief obstacle to Pakistan's re-admission.

PUBLICATIONS

Report of the Commonwealth Secretary-General (every two years).

Commonwealth Currents (every two months).

Commonwealth Youth Programme Annual Report.

Numerous papers, reports and handbooks.

European Community

MEMBERS

Belgium	Federal Republic of Germany	Ireland	Netherlands
Denmark	Greece	Italy	United Kingdom
France		Luxembourg	

The Community's relations with the developed countries of the Far East and Australasia have been dominated by problems of competition in trade. The traditional agricultural exports to the United Kingdom by Australia and New Zealand clash with Community preferences, although the Community has made some concessions on meat and butter.

Discussions on the Community's trade deficit with Japan were held in 1981: the Community requested in particular a reduction of some Japanese exports and the opening of the Japanese market to European imports.

Non-preferential trading agreements were signed with Bangladesh, India, Pakistan and Sri Lanka between 1974 and 1976. A further agreement with India, extended to include co-operation in trade, industry, energy, science and finance, came into force in December 1981. A trade agreement with the People's Republic of China was also signed in 1978, and co-operation with China in energy research was begun in 1982.

A five-year EEC-ASEAN co-operation agreement came into force in October 1980. It provided for the strengthening of existing trade links and a programme of co-operation in science and technology.

Eight Pacific states (Fiji, Kiribati, Papua New Guinea, Solomon Islands, Tonga, Tuvalu, Vanuatu and Western Samoa) adhere to the Second Lomé Convention concluded in 1979 with 58 African, Caribbean and Pacific (ACP) states.

The First Lomé Convention (Lomé I), which came into force on April 1st, 1976, replaced the Yaoundé Conventions and the Arusha Agreement and was designed to provide a new framework of co-operation, taking into account the varying needs of developing countries. Under Lomé I, provision was made for the bulk of ACP agricultural exports to enter the EEC market duty free. The STABEX (Stabilization of Export Earnings) scheme was designed to help developing countries to withstand fluctuations in the price of their products. In 1981, for example, compensation was paid to Fiji, Kiribati, Tonga and Tuvalu for a fall in export earnings derived from coconut products (oil and copra). The Convention also provided for Community funds to help finance projects in ACP countries. The Second Lomé Convention came into force on January 1st, 1981, to run until the end of February 1985. One of the most important innovations is a scheme (SYSMIN), similar to STABEX, to safeguard mineral production. Other chapters concern new rules on investment protection, migrant labour, fishing, sea transport, co-operation in energy policy and agricultural development, and procedures to speed the administration of aid.

The Centre for Industrial Development and the Technical Centre for Agricultural and Rural Co-operation are intended to promote development by co-ordinating information and advisory services.

ACP Secretariat: Africa House, Brussels, Belgium; Sec.-Gen. T. Okelo-Odongo (Kenya).

South Pacific Commission—SPC

Post Box D5, Nouméa, New Caledonia

Telephone: 26.20.00.

The Commission was established by an agreement signed in Canberra, Australia in February 1947, effective from July 1948. Its purpose is to promote the economic and social welfare and advancement of the peoples of the South Pacific region. The region contains approximately 5 million people, scattered over some 30 million square kilometres.

MEMBERS

PARTICIPATING GOVERNMENTS

Australia
Cook Islands
Fiji
France
Nauru
New Zealand
Niue
Papua New Guinea
Solomon Islands
Tuvalu
United Kingdom
U.S.A.
Western Samoa

COUNTRIES AND TERRITORIES ALSO ENTITLED TO BE REPRESENTED AT THE SOUTH PACIFIC CONFERENCE

American Samoa
Federated States of Micronesia
French Polynesia
Guam
Kiribati
Marshall Islands
New Caledonia
Northern Mariana Islands
Palau
Pitcairn Islands
Tokelau
Tonga
Vanuatu
Wallis and Futuna Islands

ORGANIZATION

(July 1982)

SOUTH PACIFIC CONFERENCE

The Conference is held annually and since 1974 has combined the former South Pacific Conference, attended by delegates from the countries and territories within the Commission's area of action, and the former Commission Session, attended by representatives of the participating governments. Each government and territorial administration has the right to send a representative and alternates to the Conference and each representative (or in his absence an alternate) has the right to cast one vote on behalf of the government or territorial administration which he represents. The 21st Conference was held at Port Vila, Vanuatu, in October 1981. The 22nd Conference was to be held in Pago Pago, American Samoa, in 1982.

The Conference examines and adopts the Commission's work programme and budget for the coming year, and discusses any other matters within the competence of the Commission.

Planning and Evaluation Committee: meets each year to evaluate the preceding year's work programme and to draft the programme and budget for the coming year; it decides on two themes of regional interest to be discussed by the Conference.

Committee of Representatives of Participating Governments: approves the Commission's administrative budget and nominates the Commission's principal officers.

SECRETARIAT

Since November 1976 the Secretariat has had a Management Committee which has a supervisory and advisory role over all Commission activities. Committee members are the Principal Officers of the Commission.

COMMITTEE MEMBERS

Secretary-General: FRANCIS BUGOTU (Solomon Islands).

Director of Programmes: W. T. BROWN (Australia).

Deputy Director of Programmes: T. PIERRE (Cook Islands).

AIMS

Each territory has its own programme of development activities. The Commission assists these programmes by bringing people together for discussion and study, by research into some of the problems common to the region, by providing expert advice and assistance and by disseminating technical information.

ACTIVITIES

The 16th South Pacific Conference adopted a recommendation by the 1976 Review Committee that the Commission should carry out the following specific activities:

(*a*) rural development
(*b*) youth and community development
(*c*) *ad hoc* expert consultancies
(*d*) cultural exchanges (in arts, sports and education)
(*e*) training facilitation
(*f*) assessment and development of marine resources and research;

and that special consideration should be given to projects and grants-in-aid which do not necessarily fall within these specific activities, but which respond to pressing regional or sub-regional needs or to the expressed needs of the smaller Pacific countries. The work programme adopted by the 21st South Pacific Conference was developed in response to these guidelines. It gave priority to projects in the following areas for 1982:

Food and Materials: Agriculture; Plant protection.

Marine Resources: Artisanal fisheries; Oceanic fisheries.

Rural Management and Technology: Conservation and environmental management; Rural health, sanitation and water supply; Rural employment; Rural technology.

Community Services: Community education training; Youth and adult education; Women's programmes and activities; Family and community health services; Public health.

Socio-economic Statistical Services.

Education Services: English language programme: media unit.

Cultural Conservation and Exchange.

Awards and Grants: Short-term experts and specialist services; Assistance to applied research, experiments and field work; Inter-territorial study visits and travel grants.

Some highlights of the 1981 Work Programme and follow-up activities in the 1982 Work Programme include:

Marine resources

The Skipjack Survey and Assessment Programme was completed in September 1981, and in October 1981 the Tuna and Billfish Assessment Programme began, both programmes being externally funded. The estimates of the skipjack and baitfish resources were discussed at the Thirteenth Regional Meeting on Fisheries in Nouméa in August 1981. The meeting concluded that the total resource of skipjack in the region, estimated at approximately 3 million metric tons, is under-exploited, but that the strategy for harvesting these resources must be carefully studied.

The activities of the Deep Sea Fisheries Project, which operated in 13 countries from 1978–81 and trained over 500 government officers and fishermen, was to be diversified in 1982 to include development and evaluation of other practical fishing equipment and techniques.

Rural management and technology

The South Pacific Regional Environment Programme (SPREP), involving the participation of the South Pacific Bureau for Economic Co-operation (SPEC), South Pacific Commission (SPC), Economic and Social Commission for Asia and the Pacific (ESCAP) and United Nations Environment Programme (UNEP), organized a Technical Meeting in June 1981 to draft an Action Plan for activities. This was submitted for adoption at the Conference on the Human Environment in the South Pacific, held in March 1982 in Rarotonga, Cook Islands. At this conference, the South Pacific Declaration on Natural Resources and the Environment (the Rarotonga Declaration) was adopted. This declaration gives guidance to the South Pacific Region for the sustainable management of land, sea and air resources. It provides a statement of regional policy on the environment, and can serve as a model for the development of national policies.

The Project to Increase Self-sufficiency on Atolls, which has been approved for United Nations Development Programme funding, was considered during the Regional Technical Meeting on Atolls, held in Majuro, Marshall Islands, in April 1982. The meeting recommended quick action in five priority areas: fresh water resources, energy, food production, coconut utilization, and health and nutrition.

Community services

One of the activities for 1981 in the Public Health programme was the UNDP-funded project on the effects of urbanization and western diet on health of Pacific Island populations, for which three workshops and a Regional Meeting were held. Recommendations of the Regional Meeting included the establishment of national food and nutrition committees/councils to formulate national food and nutrition policies and that the South Pacific Commission employ a Regional Adviser in nutrition. One of the follow-up activities in this programme was to be the meeting in Nouméa in June 1982 of a Working Group on Pacific Food (Composition) Tables.

The 21st South Pacific Conference approved the establishment of a Women's Resource Bureau at the South Pacific Commission, following a recommendation from the Seminar of South Pacific Women, held in Papeete in July 1981. Two Women's Programmes Development Officers, an Anglophone and a Francophone, will be the professional staff for this programme.

Socio-economic statistical services

One of the highlights in this area was the beginning in early 1981 of Phase 1 of the International Labour Organization/SPC project on Migration, Employment and Development in the South Pacific, to collect and analyse data on migration and employment in the region. A conference, funded by UNFPA (United Nations Fund for Population Activities), was held in Nouméa in 1982 to discuss the data and to identify problems and trends. Subject to funding, Phase 2 of the project was to commence in the second half of 1982.

BUDGET

(1982)

ESTIMATED REVENUE	'000 francs CFP
Contributions of Participating Governments	351,048
Grants from Territories	3,200
Other Sources	35,772
TOTAL	390,020

ESTIMATED EXPENDITURE	'000 francs CFP
Administration	129,250
Work Programme and Services .	260,770
TOTAL	390,020

PUBLICATIONS

South Pacific Commission Publications Bureau, P.O.B. A245, Sydney South, N.S.W. 2000, Australia.

Technical Publications (published as the need arises), *South Pacific Conference Proceedings, Annual Report.*

South Pacific Forum

c/o SPEC (*see* below)

MEMBERS

Australia	Federated States of Micronesia (observer)	New Zealand	Tonga
Cook Islands		Niue	Tuvalu
Fiji		Papua New Guinea	Vanuatu
Kiribati	Nauru	Solomon Islands	Western Samoa

The South Pacific Forum is the gathering of Heads of Government of the independent and self-governing states of the South Pacific. Its first meeting was held on August 5th, 1971, in Wellington, New Zealand. It provides an opportunity for informal discussions to be held on a wide range of common issues and problems and meets annually or when issues require urgent attention. The Forum has no written constitution or international agreement governing its activities nor any formal rules relating to its purpose, membership or conduct of meeting. Decisions are always reached by consensus, it never having been found necessary or desirable to vote formally on issues.

The 12th meeting of the Forum was held in August 1981 in Port Vila, Vanuatu. The 13th meeting was to be held in August 1982 in Rotorua, New Zealand.

SOUTH PACIFIC BUREAU FOR ECONOMIC CO-OPERATION—SPEC

G.P.O. Box 856, Suva, Fiji

Telephone: 312600.

Established by an agreement signed on April 17th, 1973, at the third meeting of the South Pacific Forum in Apia, Western Samoa.

ORGANIZATION

(July 1982)

COMMITTEE

The Committee is the Bureau's executive board. It comprises representatives and senior officials from all member countries. It meets twice a year, immediately before the meetings of the South Pacific Forum and at the end of the year, to discuss in detail the Bureau's work programme and annual budget.

SECRETARIAT

The Secretariat carries out the day-to-day activities of the Bureau. It is headed by a Director, with an executive staff of 11 drawn from the member countries. In 1975 the Bureau became the official secretariat of the South Pacific Forum and its secretariat is responsible for the administration of the Forum.

Director: (acting, until August 1982) JONATHAN P. SHEPPARD.

Deputy Director: Dr. PETER ADAMS.

AIMS AND ACTIVITIES

The Bureau was set up as a result of proposals for establishing a "Trade Bureau" which were put forward at the second meeting of the South Pacific Forum in 1972. It is to facilitate continuing co-operation and consultation between members on trade, economic development, transport, tourism and other related matters. In 1974 the Bureau absorbed the functions of the Pacific Islands Producers' Association (PIPA).

The current work programme includes regional activities in the following areas: trade; trade promotion; transport (shipping and civil aviation); telecommunications; tourism; agriculture; industrial development; aid and air co-ordination; Law of the Sea; fisheries and seabed resources; the environment; energy; secretariat duties.

Since its establishment, the Bureau has established the Pacific Forum Line (a regional shipping line), the South Pacific Forum Fisheries Agency, a South Pacific Trade Commission in Australia, the Association of South Pacific Airlines, a SPEC Fellowship scheme and a South Pacific Regional National Disaster Fund and has co-ordinated the establishment of the South Pacific Regional Environment Programme.

The South Pacific Regional Trade and Economic Co-operation Agreement (SPARTECA) came into force in January 1981, aiming to redress the trade deficit of the South Pacific countries with Australia and New Zealand.

BUDGET

The Governments of Australia and New Zealand each contribute one-third of the annual budget and the remaining third is equally shared by the other member Governments.

BUDGET ESTIMATES, 1981
($F)

Revenue		Expenditure	
Contributions from members	735,540	Administration and services	286,055
Revote and other income	22,500	Work Programme	463,285
		Capital expenditure	8,700
Total	758,040	Total	758,040

AFFILIATED ORGANIZATIONS

Association of South Pacific Airlines (ASPA): c/o Air Pacific, Private Bag, Suva, Fiji; f. 1979 at a meeting of airlines in the South Pacific convened by the SPEC to promote co-operation among the member airlines for the development of regular, safe and economical commercial aviation within, to and from the South Pacific; mems.: Air Calédonie, Air Mélanésie, Air Nauru, Air Niugini, Air Pacific, Fiji Air, Norfolk Island Airlines Ltd., Polynesian Airlines, Solair, South Pacific Island Airways, Talair Pty.

Chair. T. Betham; Sec. and Treas. N. Menon.

Pacific Forum Line: P.O.B. 655, Apia, Western Samoa. Chair. H. Julian; Gen. Man. G. W. Fulcher.

South Pacific Forum Fisheries Agency (FFA): P.O.B. 627, Honiara, Solomon Islands; f. 1978 by the South Pacific Forum to facilitate, promote and co-ordinate co-operation and mutual assistance among coastal states in the region in the matter of fisheries; polices an Exclusive Economic Zone within 200 nautical miles (370 km.) of the coastlines of member states; mems.: South Pacific Forum members.

Dir. D. A. P. Muller.

South Pacific Trade Commission: 225 Clarence House, Sydney, N.S.W. 2000, Australia.

Trade Commissioner: R. Hegerhorst.

PUBLICATIONS

Annual Report.

SPEC Activities (monthly).

Directory of Aid Agencies.

Reports of Forum and Bureau meetings.

Other Regional Organizations

(*see* also under ESCAP, p. 101–103)

These organizations are arranged under the following sub-headings:

Agricultural Research
Aid and Development
Economics and Finance
Education
Government and Politics
Labour
Law
Medicine and Health
Planning and Housing
Press, Radio and Telecommunications
Religion
Science
Students
Tourism
Trade and Industry
Transport
Women's Associations

AGRICULTURAL RESEARCH

Asian Vegetable Research and Development Center: P.O.B. 42, Shanhua, Tainan 741, Taiwan; f. 1971 to improve diet and standard of living of rural populations in the Asian tropics by increased production of vegetable crops through the breeding of better varieties and the development of improved cultural methods; research programme includes plant breeding, plant pathology, plant physiology, soil science, entomology and chemistry; the Centre has an experimental farm, laboratories and weather station and provides training for research and production specialists in tropical vegetables. Mems.: Federal Republic of Germany, Japan, the Republic of Korea, the Philippines, Taiwan, Thailand and the U.S.A.

Dir. Dr. G. W. SELLECK; Assoc. Dir. PAUL M.H. SUN. Publs. *Annual Report, Technical Bulletin, CENTERPOINT*, crop research reports, scientific papers.

International Crops Research Institute for the Semi-Arid Tropics (ICRISAT): ICRISAT Patancheru Post Office, Andhra Pradesh 502 324, India; f. 1972 as world centre for genetic improvement of sorghum, pearl millet, pigeonpea, chickpea and groundnut and for development of improved farming systems for the world's semi-arid tropics; research covers all physical and socio-economic aspects of improving the entire system of agriculture on unirrigated land.

Dir. LESLIE D. SWINDALE (New Zealand).

International Rice Research Institute: P.O.B. 933, Manila, Philippines; f. 1960; conducts basic research on the rice plant and its cultural management with the objective of increasing the quantity and quality of rice available for human consumption; disseminates results of research and plant materials; operates a training programme for rice scientists, maintains a library and information centre on rice research, holds periodic conferences and symposia.

Dir.-Gen. M. R. VEGA (acting). Publs. *Annual Report, Technical Bulletins, Technical Papers, The IRRI Reporter, Research Highlights, International Rice Research Newsletter, IRRI Research Paper Series, International Bibliography on Cropping Systems, International Bibliography of Rice Research.*

AID AND DEVELOPMENT

Afro-Asian Rural Reconstruction Organization (AARRO): C-117/118 Defence Colony, New Delhi 110024, India; f. 1962 to restructure the economy of the rural population of Africa and Asia, and to explore collectively opportunities for co-ordination of efforts for promoting welfare and eradicating hunger, thirst, disease, illiteracy and poverty amongst the rural people; activities include launching of Integrated Rural Development Pilot Projects, organizing international seminars at AARRO's own training centres in Japan and Egypt, and awarding individual fellowships; mems.: 12 African, 15 Asian countries and the Central Union of Agricultural Co-operatives, Japan.

Pres. Republic of Korea; Sec.-Gen. Dr. B. S. MINHAS; Dir. M. R. KAUSHAL (India). Publ. *Rural Reconstruction* (half-yearly).

Foundation for the Peoples of the South Pacific (FSP): 200 West 57th Street, New York, N.Y. 10019, U.S.A.; f. 1965 to research and implement a programme of development related to basic needs as perceived by the indigenous people, encouraging self-help. Regional Secretaries at Sydney, Australia; Nandi, Fiji; Suva, Fiji; Port Moresby, Papua New Guinea; Geneva, Switzerland; Honiara, Solomon Islands; Nuku'alofa, Tonga; Port Vila, Vanuatu; Apia, Western Samoa. Affiliates: South Pacific People's Foundation of Canada (Vancouver); U.K. Foundation for the Peoples of the South Pacific (Lincoln).

Pres. ELIZABETH SILVERSTEIN; Exec. Dir. Rev. STANLEY W. HOSIE (U.S.A.). Publ. *Annual Report*, technical reports (e.g. on intermediate technology, nutrition, teaching aids).

ECONOMICS AND FINANCE

Asian Confederation of Credit Unions: P.O.B. 155, Suhdaemoon, Seoul, Republic of Korea; links and promotes credit unions in Asia, provides research facilities and training programmes. Mems. in Hong Kong, Japan, Republic of Korea, Papua New Guinea, Taiwan, Thailand; assoc. mems. in Indonesia and Malaysia.

Gen. Man. A. J. R. KANG. Publ. *Asia-Con News* (quarterly).

Association of Development Financing Institutions in Asia and the Pacific: c/o Private Development Corporation of the Philippines, Ayala Ave., Makati, Manila, Philippines; f. 1977 to promote the interest and economic development of the respective countries of its member institutions through development financing; membership comprises institutions engaged in the financing of development, whether industrial or agricultural, as their main activity; 44 ordinary, four special and seven associate mems.

Chair. Management Cttee. VICENTE R. JAYME (Philippines).

Council for Mutual Economic Assistance—CMEA (COMECON): Prospekt Kalinina 56, Moscow 121205, U.S.S.R.; f. 1949 to assist the economic development of its member states through joint utilization and co-ordination of efforts. Annual Council. Mems.: Bulgaria, Cuba, Czechoslovakia, German Democratic Republic, Hungary, Mongolia, Poland, Romania, U.S.S.R., Viet-Nam. The CMEA has co-operation agreements with Finland,

Iraq and Mexico. Afghanistan, Angola, Ethiopia, Laos, Mozambique and the People's Democratic Republic of Yemen send observers to certain CMEA bodies. Yugoslavia has participated in certain CMEA activities.

Sec. NIKOLAI V. FADDEYEV (U.S.S.R.).

Institute of Economic Growth, Asian Research Centre: University Enclave, Delhi 7, India; f. 1967 to bring the resources of social science to bear upon the solution of problems connected with social and economic development in South and South East Asia; specialized library and documentation services; biennial regional training programmes in sociology of development.

Dir. of Institute Prof. P. C. JOSHI; Head of Centre Prof. T. N. MADAN. Publs. *Asian Social Science Bibliography* (annual), *Contributions to Indian Sociology: New Series* (annual), *Studies in Asian Social Development* (occasional).

Pacific Basin Economic Council: Confederation of Australian Industry, Industry House, Barton, A.C.T. 2600, Australia; f. 1967 as Pacific Basin Economic Co-operation Council, present name adopted 1971; the Council is a businessmen's organization composed of the representatives of business circles of Australia, Canada, Japan, New Zealand and the U.S.A., and special participants from developing countries; the Council aims to co-operate with governments and international institutions in the economic development of the Pacific Area. The Council's activities are the promotion of economic collaboration among the member countries and co-operation with the developing countries in their effort to achieve self-sustaining economic growth. Fourteenth General Meeting, Hong Kong, May 1981.

Chair. J. B. CLARKSON, C.B.E.; Exec. Dir.-Gen. W. J. HENDERSON.

EDUCATION

Asia Foundation: 550 Kearny St., San Francisco, Calif. 94108, U.S.A.; f. 1954 to strengthen Asian educational, cultural and voluntary activities with private American assistance; provides small-size grants in the fields of law, public administration, women's activities, business and management, community development, communications, population and health, food and nutrition, and Asian-American exchange; representatives in 13 Asian countries.

Chair. RUDOLPH A. PETERSON; Pres. HAYDN WILLIAMS; Sec. TURNER H. MCBAINE. Publs. *President's Review* (annual), *The Asia Foundation News* (every two months).

Asian and South Pacific Bureau of Adult Education: P.O.B. 1225, Canberra 2601, Australia; f. 1964 to assist non-formal education and adult literacy. Mems. in 28 countries and territories.

Sec.-Gen. Dr. C. DUKE. Publ. *Courier* (quarterly).

Asian Institute of Technology: P.O.B. 2754, Bangkok, Thailand; f. 1959 by SEATO; became independent 1967; Master's, Doctor's and Diploma programmes are offered in the Divisions of Agriculture and Food Engineering, Computer Applications, Environmental Engineering, Geotechnical and Transportation Engineering, Human Settlements Development, Industrial Engineering and Management, Structural Engineering and Construction, Water Resources Engineering and Energy Technology. Student enrolment in 1979/80 was 516 from 26 nations; there are 70 faculty mems. from Asia, Australia, Europe, Canada and the U.S.A.

Pres. Dr. ROBERT B. BANKS.

Association of Southeast Asian Institutions of Higher Learning (ASAIHL): Secretariat, Ratasastra Building, Chulalongkorn University, Henri Dunant Street, Bangkok 5, Thailand; f. 1956 to promote the economic, cultural and social welfare of the people of South-East Asia by means of educational co-operation and research programmes. Mems.: 70 university institutions in 9 countries.

Pres. Dr. RAYSON L. HUANG (Hong Kong); Exec. Sec. Dr. NINNAT OLANVORAVUTH. Publs. *Newsletter*, *Handbook of Southeast Asian Institutions of Higher Learning* (annual), Reports.

International Union for Oriental and Asian Studies: Institut d'Etudes Turques, 13 rue de Santeuil, 75005 Paris, France; f. 1951 by the 22nd International Congress of Orientalists under the auspices of UNESCO. Object: to promote contacts between orientalists throughout the world, and to organize congresses, research and publications. Twenty-six member countries.

Pres. H. C. L. BERG (Netherlands); Sec.-Gen. LOUIS BAZIN (France). Publs. Four oriental bibliographies, *Philologiae Turcicae Fundamenta*, *Materialien zum Sumerischen Lexikon*, *Sanskrit Dictionary*, *Corpus Inscriptionum Iranicarum*, *Linguistic Atlas of Iran*, *Matériels des parlers iraniens*, *Turcica*.

Southeast Asian Ministers of Education Organization (SEAMEO): c/o SEAMES, Darakarn Bldg., 920 Sukhumvit Rd., Bangkok 10110, Thailand; f. 1965. Objects: to promote co-operation among the South-East Asian nations through co-operative projects and programmes in education, science and culture. SEAMEO has a permanent secretariat (SEAMES) in Bangkok; seven regional centres: BIOTROP for tropical biology in Bogor, Indonesia; INNOTECH for educational innovation and technology at the University of the Philippines, Quezon City; RECSAM for education in science and mathematics in Penang, Malaysia; RELC for language in Singapore; SEARCA for graduate study and research in agriculture in Los Baños, the Philippines; SPAFA for archaeology and fine arts with sub-centres in Indonesia, the Philippines and Thailand and a co-ordinating unit in Bangkok, Thailand, and TROPMED for tropical medicine and public health with national centres in Indonesia, Malaysia, the Philippines and Thailand and a central office in Bangkok, Thailand. SEAMES implements the activities of SNEP, the SEAMEO Non-Formal Education Programme. Mems.: Indonesia, Kampuchea, Laos, Malaysia, the Philippines, Singapore and Thailand. Assoc. mems.: Australia, France, New Zealand.

Council Pres. Dr. DAOED JOESOEF (Indonesia); SEAMES Dir. Dr. ADUL WICHIENCHAROEN. Publs. The Centres and Projects publish academic journals, reports of conferences and seminars, brochures, monthly or quarterly newsletters and occasional publications. SEAMES publishes annual reports, reports of conferences and meetings, brochures, a quarterly, and technical publications.

GOVERNMENT AND POLITICS

Afro-Asian People's Solidarity Organization (AAPSO): 89 Abdel Aziz Al-Saoud St., Manial El-Roda, Cairo, Egypt; f. 1957 as the Organization for Afro-Asian Peoples' Solidarity; acts as a permanent liaison body between the peoples of Africa and Asia and aims to ensure their economic, social and cultural development. Board of Secretaries is composed of members from Algeria, Angola, Congo, Egypt, Ethiopia, German Democratic Republic, Guinea, India, Japan, Madagascar, Palestine Liberation Organization, Somalia, African National Congress of South Africa, Sri Lanka, Sudan, SWAPO of Namibia, U.S.S.R., Viet-Nam, People's Democratic Republic of Yemen, Zambia. Mems.: national committees and affiliated organizations in 88 countries.

Sec.-Gen. NOURI ABDEL RAZZAK (Iraq). Publ. *Socio-Economic Development and Progress* (quarterly), *Afro-Asian Publications* (series).

Eastern Regional Organization for Public Administration (EROPA): Rizal Hall, Padre Faura St., Manila, Philippines; f. 1960 to promote regional co-operation in improving knowledge, systems and practices of governmental administration, to help accelerate economic and social development; organizes regional conferences, seminars, special studies, surveys and training programmes. There are three technical centres covering Training (New Delhi), Local Government (Tokyo) and Organization and Management (Seoul). Mems.: 11 countries, 57 organizations, 159 individuals.

Chair. Dr. SONDANG P. SIAGIAN (Indonesia); Sec.-Gen. RAUL P. DE GUZMAN (Philippines). Publs. *EROPA Review* (bi-annual), *EROPA Bulletin* (quarterly), occasional books.

World Anti-Communist League (WACL): Freedom Center, C.P.O. Box 7173, Seoul, Republic of Korea; f. 1966 by the Asian People's Anti-Communist League to strive to remove all forms of totalitarianism, including Communism, and to uphold human rights of liberty, freedom of religious belief, social justice, self-determination, etc. Annual General Conference elects Council, which elects Executive Board of 19 for a three-year term. Mems.: 8 regional organizations, 91 countries and territories, 13 international orgs.; 10 orgs. are assoc. mems.

Hon. Chair. Dr. KU CHENG-KANG (Taiwan); Sec.-Gen. Prof. WOO JAE-SUNG (Republic of Korea). Publs. *WACL Bulletin* (quarterly), *WACL Newsletter* (monthly).

LABOUR

Brotherhood of Asian Trade Unionists (BATU): Suite F, Vermont Towers, Julio Nakpil St., Malate, P.O.B. 163, Manila, the Philippines; f. 1963 as the regional body in Asia of the World Confederation of Labour, to develop mutual co-operation among Asian Trade Unionists through exchanges of information, conferences, and educational activities; 5 million mems. and 34 delegates from 9 countries.

Pres. JUAN C. TAN (Pres. Federation of Free Workers, the Philippines). Publs. *The Asian Worker* (quarterly), and workers' education pamphlets and training manuals.

International Confederation of Free Trade Unions—Asian Regional Organization (ICFTU—ARO): P-20 Green Park Extension, New Delhi 110016, India; f. 1951; runs the Asian Trade Union College in New Delhi and a Programme and Education Bureau in Singapore; there is a Liaison Office in Indonesia and a Field Representative in Thailand. Mems.: 23 million in 31 organizations in 20 countries.

Pres. C. V. DEVAN NAIR; Asian Regional Sec. V. S. MATHUR. Publs. *Asian Labour* (monthly), *Asian Trade Union Information Service* (fortnightly).

LAW

Asian-African Legal Consultative Committee: 27 Ring Rd., Lajpat Nagar IV, New Delhi 110024, India; f. 1956 to consider legal problems referred to it by member countries and to serve as a forum for Asian-African co-operation in international law and economic relations; provides background material for conferences, prepares standard/model contract forms suited to the needs of the region; promotes arbitration as a means of settling international commercial disputes; trains officers of member states; has permanent UN observer status. Mems.: 40 states.

Pres. N. D. M. SAMARAKOON (Sri Lanka); Vice-Pres. YUSUF ELMI ROBLEH (Somalia); Sec.-Gen. B. SEN (India).

Law Association for Asia and the Western Pacific (Lawasia): 8th Floor, 170 Phillip St., Sydney, N.S.W. 2000, Australia; f. 1966 to promote the administration of justice, the protection of human rights and the maintenance of the rule of law within the region, to advance the standard of legal education, to promote uniformity within the region in appropriate fields of law and to advance the interests of the legal profession. Mems.: 55 asscns. in 21 countries; 2,500 individual mems.

Pres. KHUN MARUT BUNNAG (Thailand); Sec.-Gen. Dr. D. H. GEDDES. Publs. *Lawasia* (annual journal), proceedings of conference, research reports.

MEDICINE AND HEALTH

Asia Pacific Academy of Ophthalmology: 1013 Bishop St., Honolulu, Hawaii, U.S.A.

Pres. Dr. W. J. HOLMES; Sec. Dr. AKIRA NAKAJIMA (Japan).

Asian Pacific League of Physical Medicine and Rehabilitation: c/o Dr. P. L. Colville, 28 Collins St., Melbourne, Victoria 3000, Australia; f. 1968, Montreal, Canada; assembly held every four years.

Pres. Dr. KOADLOW (Australia); Sec. Dr. P. L. COLVILLE (Australia).

Asian-Pacific Dental Federation: 165A Jalan SS 2/24, Petaling Jaya, Malaysia; f. 1955 to establish closer relationship among dental associations in Asian and Pacific countries and to encourage research, with particular emphasis on dental health in rural areas. Mems.: 13 national associations. Eleventh congress: Hong Kong, November 1984.

Pres. Dr. OLIVER HENNEDIGE (Singapore); Sec.-Gen. Dr. LOW TEONG (Malaysia). Publ. *APDF APRO Newsletter* (3 a year).

Asian Parasite Control Organization: c/o Hoken Kaikan Bekkan, 1-2 Sadohara-cho, Ichigaya Shinjuku-ku, Tokyo, Japan; f. 1974; holds annual conferences. Mems.: six national committees.

Sec. CHOJIRO KUNII (Japan).

Federation of Asian Nutrition Societies: c/o Dr. F. G. Winarno, Food Technology Development Centre, Bogor Agricultural University, Kampus IPB, Darmaga, Bogor, Indonesia; f. 1973; encourages regional links in nutrition research and training. Mems.: 15 national societies.

Sec.-Gen. Dr. F. G. WINARNO.

Federation of Asian Pharmaceutical Associations (FAPA) 5th Floor, Cardinal Bldg., Pedro Gil cnr. F. Agoncillo, Ermita, Manila, the Philippines; f. 1964; aims to develop pharmacy as a profession and as an applied science; membership comprises national pharmaceutical associations in the following countries: Australia, India, Indonesia, Israel, Hong Kong, Japan, Republic of Korea, Malaysia, Pakistan, the Philippines, Singapore, Taiwan, Thailand.

Pres. Mrs. LOURDES T. ECHUAZ (Philippines); Sec.-Gen. Dr. JESUSA A. CONCHA (Philippines). Publ. *Journal* (yearly).

International Congress on Tropical Medicine and Malaria: c/o Dr. E. C. Garcia, Institute of Public Health, P.O.B. EA-460, Manila, Philippines; congresses are held every five years.

Pres. of 10th Congress Prof. B. D. CABRERA; Sec.-Gen. Dr. E. C. GARCIA.

Pan-Pacific Surgical Association: P.O. Box 553, Honolulu, Hawaii 96809, U.S.A.; f. 1929 to bring together surgeons to exchange scientific knowledge relating to surgery and medicine. Mems.: 3,200 regular associate, and senior mems. from over 50 countries. Sixteenth congress: Honolulu, Jan. 1982. Seventeenth congress: Sydney, Australia, March 1984.

Chair. of the Board JOHN S. SMITH, M.D. (Hawaii).

PLANNING AND HOUSING

Afro-Asian Housing Organization (AAHO): 28 Ramses St., P.O.B. 523, Cairo, Egypt; f. 1965 to promote co-operation between African and Asian countries in housing, reconstruction, physical planning and related matters.

Sec.-Gen. HASSAN M. HASSAN (Egypt).

Eastern Regional Organization for Planning and Housing: 4A Ring Rd., Indraprastha Estate, New Delhi 110001, India; f. 1958 to promote and co-ordinate the study and practice of housing and regional town and country planning. Mems.: 72 organizations and 145 individuals in 13 countries; regional offices in Tokyo, Bandung and Kuala Lumpur.

Pres. Prof. CESAR H. CONCIO (Philippines); Sec.-Gen. C. S. CHANDRASEKHARA (India). Publs. *EAROPH News and Notes* (monthly), *Town and Country Planning* (bibliography), conference reports.

International Planned Parenthood Federation: 18-20 Lower Regent St., London, SW1Y 4PW; f. 1952. Supports and co-ordinates the work of national family planning associations in 108 countries; provides technical assistance for family planning and population programmes; collaborates with other international bodies including the United Nations; provides information on all aspects of family planning and produces medical handbooks and educational literature. Regional Office in New York; sub-regional office in Lomé, Togo. Mems.: 95 associations.

Pres. Mrs. AZIZA HUSSEIN; Sec.-Gen. Dr. CARL WAHREN. Publs. *People* (quarterly in English, French and Spanish), *Medical Bulletin* (every two months, in English, French and Spanish), *Research in Reproduction* (quarterly).

PRESS, RADIO AND TELECOMMUNICATIONS

Asia-Pacific Broadcasting Union: Headquarters: NHK Broadcasting Centre, 2-2-1 Jinnan, Shibuya-ku, Tokyo 150, Japan; f. 1964 to assist in the development of radio and television in the Asian/Pacific area, particularly in its use for educational purposes. Annual General Assembly. Mems.: 67 mems. in 46 countries.

Pres. Dr. SUMADI (Indonesia); Vice-Pres. Dato ABDULLAH MOHAMAD (Malaysia), TOMOKAZU SAKAMOTO (Japan); Sec.-Gen. ROKU ITO (Japan) (P.O.Box 1164, Jalan Pantai Bharu, Kuala Lumpur 22-07, Malaysia). Publs. *ABU Newsletter* (monthly in English), *ABU Technical Review* (bi-monthly in English).

Asian Pacific Postal Union: Post Office Bldg., Manila 2801, the Philippines; f. 1962 to extend, facilitate and improve the postal relations between the member countries and to promote co-operation in the field of postal services. 16 mem. countries.

Dir Gen. FELIZARDO R. TANABE; Exec. Officer RUBEN O. RUIZ. Publs. *APPU Annual Report, Exchange Program of Postal Officials, APPTS Newsletter.*

Confederation of ASEAN Journalists: Jalan Veteran 7-C, Jakarta, Indonesia; f. 1975.

Exec. Sec. DJA'FAR H. ASSEGAFF. Publs. *CAJ Newsletter* (quarterly), *CAJ Year Book* (annual).

Organization of Asia-Pacific News Agencies (OANA): c/o BERNAMA News Agency, P.O.B. 24, Kuala Lumpur 01-02, Malaysia; f. 1961 to promote co-operation in professional matters and mutual exchange of news, features, etc. among the news agencies of Asia and the Pacific via the Asia-Pacific News Network (ANN). Mems.: Antara (Indonesia), APP (Pakistan), Bakhtar News Agency (Afghanistan), BERNAMA (Malaysia), BSS (Bangladesh), Hindusthan Samachar (India), IRNA (Iran), KCNA (Korea, Democratic People's Republic), KPL (Laos), Kyodo (Japan), Lankapuvath (Sri Lanka), Montsame (Mongolia), PNA (Philippines), PPI (Pakistan), PTI (India), RSS (Nepal), Samachar Barati (India), Tass (U.S.S.R.), TNA (Thailand), UNI (India), Viet-Nam News Agency, Yonhap (Republic of Korea), Xinhua (People's Republic of China).

Pres. AHMAD MUSTAPHA HASSAN (Malaysia); Sec.-Gen. YUSOF BADOR (Malaysia).

Press Foundation of Asia: P.O.B. 1843, Manila, the Philippines; f. 1967; an independent, non-profit-making organization governed by its newspaper members; acts as a professional forum for about 300 newspapers in Asia; aims to reduce cost of newspapers to potential readers, to improve editorial and management techniques through research and training programmes and to encourage the growth of the Asian press. Mems.: 300 newspapers; regional offices in Bangkok, Hong Kong, Kuala Lumpur, New Delhi, Tokyo and Seoul. The Foundation owns and operates *DEPTH-news*, a feature service for newspapers in the region.

Chair. KIM SANG MAN (Repub. of Korea); Dir.-Gen. MOCHTAR LUBIS (Indonesia). Publ. *Data Asia* (weekly).

RELIGION

Christian Conference in Asia: 480 Lorong 2, Toa Payoh. Singapore 1 231; f. 1959 under title East Asia Christian Conference; structure rearranged and title changed to CCA at 5th Assembly, Singapore, 1973. Aims: to promote co-operation and joint study into matters of common concern among the Churches of the region and to encourage interaction with other regional Conferences and the World Council of Churches. Mems.: 15 national Christian Councils and 92 churches in 17 countries: Australia, Bangladesh, Burma, Hong Kong, India, Indonesia, Japan, Republic of Korea, Laos, Malaysia, New Zealand, Pakistan, the Philippines, Singapore, Sri Lanka, Taiwan and Thailand.

Presidium: VICTOR OORJITHAM (Malaysia), JAN COMACK (New Zealand), Canon ALAN CHAN CHOR CHOI (Hong Kong), PRASANNAKUMARI THOTTATHIL; Gen. Sec. Dr. YAP KIM HAO. Publs. *Directory, CCA News* (monthly) and various others.

World Fellowship of Buddhists: 33 Sukhumvit Rd., between Soi 1 and 3, Bangkok 10110, Thailand; f. 1950 to promote among members strict observance and practice of the teachings of the Buddha; to secure unity, solidarity and brotherhood among Buddhists; to promote the sublime doctrine of the Buddha; to organize and carry out activities in the field of social, educational, cultural and other humanitarian services; to work for securing peace, harmony among men and happiness for all beings and to collaborate with other organizations working to the same ends. Thirteenth General Congress, November 1980. Regional centres in 35 countries.

Pres. H.S.H. Princess POON PISMAI DISKUL; Hon. Gen. Sec. PRASERT RUANGSKUL; Hon. Treas. PRASONG BUNCHOEM. Publ. *WFB Review* (bi-monthly).

SCIENCE

Pacific Science Association: P.O.B. 17801, Honolulu, Hawaii 96817, U.S.A.; f. 1920 to promote co-operation in the study of scientific problems relating to the Pacific region, more particularly those affecting the prosperity and well-being of Pacific peoples; sponsors Pacific Science Congresses and Inter-Congresses. Fifteenth Congress, Dunedin, New Zealand, 1983; fifth Inter-Congress, Baguio, Philippines, 1985. Mems.: institutional representatives from 35 areas, scientific societies, individual and corporate mems.

Pres. J. A. R. MILES (New Zealand); Sec. BRENDA BISHOP. Publs. *Congress and Inter-Congress Record of Proceedings, Information Bulletin* (six issues a year).

STUDENTS

Asian Students' Association: 511 Nathan Rd., 1/F, Kowloon, Hong Kong; f. 1969 to help in the solution of local and regional problems; to assist in promotion of an Asian identity; to promote programmes of common benefit to member organizations; since 1972 the organization has opposed all forms of colonialism or foreign intervention in Asia; activities: defence of students' rights, self-determination, social development; standing commissions on education, women, economics, travel. Mems.: 14 national or regional student unions, one assoc. mem.

Sec.-Gen. LO CHI KIN. Publ. *Asian Student News.*

TOURISM

East Asia Travel Association: c/o Japan National Tourist Organization, 2-10-1 Yurakucho, Chiyoda-ku, Tokyo, Japan; f. 1966 to promote tourism in the East Asian region, encourage and facilitate the flow of tourists to that region from other parts of the world, and to develop regional tourist industries by close collaboration among members. Twenty-second General Meeting, Nov. 1982, Japan. Mems.: 8 national tourist organizations, 7 airlines, 3 travel agent associations and 1 hotels association.

Pres. YOSHINARI TEZUKA (Japan); Sec.-Gen. KENJI SAKUMA (Japan).

Pacific Area Travel Association (PATA): 228 Grant Ave., San Francisco, Calif. 94108, U.S.A.; f. 1951 for the promotion of travel to and between the countries and islands of the Pacific. Annual Conference and Workshops between January and April each year (Bangkok 1982, Acapulco 1983, Sri Lanka 1984). Mems.: over 2,100 in 67 countries.

Exec. Vice-Pres. KENNETH L. CHAMBERLAIN. Publs. *Pacific Travel News, Pacific Area Destinations Handbook, Pacific Hotel Directory and Travel Guide, Events in the Pacific.*

TRADE AND INDUSTRY

Association of Natural Rubber Producing Countries (ANRPC): 1st Floor, Bangunan Getah Asli, 150 Jalan Ampang, Kuala Lumpur, Malaysia; f. 1970; the association aims to bring about co-ordination in the production and marketing of natural rubber, to promote technical co-operation amongst members and to bring about fair and stable prices for natural rubber. Structure: Assembly, Executive Committee, Committee of Experts, Secretariat. An International Natural Rubber Agreement on Price Stabilization has been signed by all the members except India and Papua New Guinea. The first international council on the agreement met in January 1978. Seminars and meetings on technical and statistical subjects are held. Mems.: India, Indonesia, Malaysia, Papua New Guinea, Singapore, Sri Lanka, Thailand and Viet-Nam.

Sec.-Gen. B. K. ABEYARATNA (Sri Lanka). Publs. reports of meetings, technical papers, *Quarterly Statistical Bulletin, Development of Rubber Smallholders Proceedings.*

Commission on Asian and Pacific Affairs of the International Chamber of Commerce: c/o The Board of Trade, 150 Rajbopit Rd., Bangkok 2, Thailand; f. 1952 to act as spokesman of businessmen of Asia and the Pacific region. Mems.: ICC National Committees in 12 countries.

Exec. Sec. ARCOT C. POULIER.

Confederation of Asian Chambers of Commerce and Industry: Philippines Chamber of Commerce and Industry, CCPF Bldg., Magallanes Drive, Intramuros, Manila 2801, Philippines; f. 1966; composed of the national chambers of commerce and industry of Australia, India, Japan, Republic of Korea, Nepal, New Zealand, the Philippines and Taiwan.

Pres. FRED J. ELIZALDE (Philippines); Sec.-Gen. R. J. DELA CUESTA (Philippines).

International Co-operative Alliance: Regional Office and Educational Centre for South-East Asia: Bonow House, 43 Friends' Colony, P.O.B. 3312, New Delhi 110014, India; f. 1960; promotes economic relations and encourages technical assistance among the national co-operative movements; represents the ICA in other regional forums; holds courses, seminars and conferences. Mems.: 14 countries.

Regional Dir. R. B. RAJAGURU; Dir. (Education) J. M. RANA. Publs. *ICA Regional Bulletin* (quarterly), *Documentation Bulletin for S.E. Asia* (quarterly), *Annotated Bibl. of Lit. on Co-operative Mvt. in S.E. Asia* (half-yearly supplement).

International Cotton Advisory Committee: 1225 19th St., N.W., Suite 320, Washington, D.C. 20036, U.S.A.; f. 1939 to keep in close touch with developments affecting the world cotton situation; to collect and disseminate statistics; to suggest to the governments represented any measures for the furtherance of international collaboration in maintaining and developing a sound world cotton economy. Mems.: 49 countries.

Exec. Dir. J. C. SANTLEY. Publs. *Cotton-Monthly Review* (English, French and Spanish editions), *Quarterly Statistical Bulletin.*

International Federation of Asian and Western Pacific Contractors' Associations: Makati Commercial Centre, P.O.B. 1664, Manila, Philippines; f. 1956. Mems. in 13 countries.

Sec.-Gen. Dr. R. BAH NEO.

International Natural Rubber Organization (INRO): 12th Floor, MUI Plaza, Jalan Parry, P.O.B. 374, Kuala

Lumpur 01-02, Malaysia; f. 1980 under the International Rubber Agreement (1979) to stabilize natural rubber prices and maintain buffer stock; seven exporting and 25 importing members (March 1982).

Exec. Dir. K. ALGAMAR; Deputy Exec. Dir. D. STIEPEL; Buffer Stock Man. J. J. RIEDL.

International Rubber Study Group: Brettenham House, 5–6 Lancaster Place, London, WC2E 7ET, England; f. 1945 to provide a forum for the discussion of problems affecting rubber and to provide statistical and other general information on rubber. Mems.: 27 countries.

Sec.-Gen. Dr. L. BATEMAN. Publs. *Rubber Statistical Bulletin, International Rubber Digest* (monthly), *Statistical Commentaries, Proceedings of Annual Meetings* and special reports.

International Sugar Organization: 28 Haymarket, London, SW1Y 4SP, England; set up to administer the International Sugar Agreement negotiated in 1977 by the United Nations Sugar Conference. Mems.: 44 exporting countries and 15 importing countries.

Exec. Dir. WILLIAM K. MILLER; Sec. C. POLITOFF. Publs. *Pocket Sugar Year Book, Monthly Statistical Bulletin, Annual Report, World Sugar Economy, Structure and Policies* 1976.

International Tea Committee: Sir John Lyon House, 5 High Timber St., London, EC4V 3NII, England; f. 1933 to administer the International Tea Agreement. Now serves as a statistical and information centre. New Constitution adopted June 1979 extended membership to consuming countries. Mems. under new Constitution are—Producers: Tea Board of India, Sri Lanka Tea Board, Tea Board of Kenya, Government of Indonesia, Tea Association (Central Africa) Ltd., Bangladesh Tea Board, ENACOMO (Mozambique), Zimbabwe Tea Growers' Association; Consumers: Tea Trade Committee (U.K.), Comité Européen du Thé, Australian Tea & Coffee Traders' Association, the Tea Council of Canada; Contributor: Tea Association of the U.S.A., Inc.

Chair. A. C. DAVIES; Sec. Mrs. N. C. CARNEGIE-BROWN. Publs. Annual Bulletin of Statistics and Supplement. Monthly Statistical Summary.

International Tea Promotion Association: P.O.B. 30007, Coolsingel 58, 3011 AE Rotterdam, Netherlands; f. 1979; by July 1980 nine countries (Bangladesh, India, Indonesia, Kenya, Malawi, Mauritius, Sri Lanka, Tanzania, and Uganda), accounting for about 90 per cent of world exports of black tea, had acceded to the international agreement establishing the Association; governing board meets twice a year.

Exec. Dir. T. S. BROCA; Admin. and Finance Officer T. G. PEIRIS. Publ. *International Tea Journal* (2 a year).

International Tin Council: Haymarket House, 1 Oxendon St., London, SW1Y 4EQ, England; f. July 1956; now operates the Fifth International Tin Agreement (1976–1982), which is intended to achieve a long-term balance between world production and consumption of tin and to prevent excessive fluctuations in the price of tin; the Council sets floor and ceiling prices, operates a buffer stock and may regulate tin exports from producing members. The council meets at least four times a year. Mems.: governments of 30 countries, and the EEC.

Exec. Chair. PETER LAI (Malaysia); Sec. N. L. PHELPS; Buffer Stock Man. P. A. A. DE KONING. Publs. *Monthly Statistical Bulletin, Tin Statistics* (annual), *Annual Reports, Notes on Tin* (monthly), *Proceedings: Conference on Tin Consumption London* 1972 (1 vol.), *Fourth World Conference on Tin Kuala Lumpur* 1974 (4 vols.), *Tin Production and Investment*, tinplate consumption surveys.

International Wheat Council: Haymarket House, Haymarket, London, SW1Y 4SS, England; f. 1949; responsible for the administration of the Wheat Trade Convention, 1971 (as extended). Mems.: 8 exporting countries and 40 importing countries, and the EEC which is both an importing and exporting member. Provides administrative services for the Food Aid Committee, established by the Food Aid Convention, 1980 (as extended) (mems.: 12 donor countries).

Exec. Sec. J. H. PAROTTE. Publs. *World Wheat Statistics* (annually), *Review of the World Wheat Situation* (annually), *Market Report* (monthly), Annual Report, Secretariat Papers (occasional).

South-East Asia Iron and Steel Institute: P.O.B. 7759, Airmail Distribution Center, Manila International Airport (MIA), Pasay City, Philippines; f. 1971 to further the development of the iron and steel industry in the region, encourage regional co-operation, provide advisory services and a forum for the exchange of knowledge, establish training programmes, promote standardization, collate statistics and issue publications. Mems.: Indonesia, Malaysia, Philippines, Singapore, Taiwan, Thailand; supporting mems.: Australia, Japan.

Exec. Consultant TAKASHI ITAOKA. Publs. *SEAISI Quarterly, SEAISI Directory, Iron and Steel Statistics, Newsletter* (monthly), technical papers.

TRANSPORT

Orient Airlines Association: 5th Floor, Standard Bldg., 151 Paseo de Roxas Ave. cnr. Pasay Rd., Makati, Metro Manila, Philippines; f. 1967; enables members to exchange information and plan the development of the industry within the region by means of research, technical, security, data processing and marketing committees. Mems.: Air Niugini, Air Viet-Nam (inactive), Cathay Pacific Airways Ltd., China Air Lines, Japan Air Lines, Korean Air Lines, Malaysian Airline System, Philippine Airlines, Qantas Airways Ltd., Singapore Airlines, Royal Brunei Airlines and Thai Airways International.

Sec.-Gen. HIDEO MITSUHASHI. Publs. *Cost Study Group Report* (annual). *Statistical Research Report* (annual).

WOMEN'S ASSOCIATION

Pan-Pacific and South East Asia Women's Association (PPSEAWA): 78 Esplanade, Kaikoura, New Zealand; f. 1928 (Hawaii) to strengthen the bonds of peace by fostering better understanding and friendship among women of all Pacific and South-East Asian areas, and to promote co-operation among women of these regions for the study and improvement of social conditions.

INDEX OF REGIONAL ORGANIZATIONS

(main reference only)

A

ACP States, 130
Afro-Asian Housing Organization, 139
— People's Solidarity Organization, 137
— Rural Reconstruction Organization, 136
Animal Production and Health Commission for Asia, the Far East and the South-West Pacific (FAO), 105
ANZUS, 115
ASEAN, 121
Asia and Far East Commission on Agricultural Statistics (FAO), 105
— Foundation, 137
— Pacific Academy of Ophthalmology, 138
Asia-Pacific Broadcasting Union, 139
— Forestry Commission (FAO), 105
— Telecommunity, 103
Asian and Pacific Coconut Community, 103
— — — Development Centre, 102
— — South Pacific Bureau of Adult Education, 137
— Charter for Health Development (WHO), 112
— Clearing Union, 102
— Confederation of Credit Unions, 136
— Development Bank—ADB, 116
— Free Trade Zone, 103
— Highway Network Project, 103
— Institute for Broadcasting Development, 111
— — of Technology, 137
— Pacific League of Physical Medicine and Rehabilitation, 138
— — Postal Union, 139
— Parasite Control Organization, 138
— Productivity Organization, 120
— Reinsurance Corporation, 102
— Students' Association, 140
— Vegetable Research and Development Center, 136
Asian-African Legal Consultative Committee, 138
Asian-Pacific Dental Federation, 138
Association of Development Financing Institutions in Asia and the Pacific, 136
— — Natural Rubber Producing Countries, 140
— — South East Asian Nations—ASEAN, 121
— — South Pacific Airlines, 135
— — Southeast Asian Institutions of Higher Learning, 137

B

Brotherhood of Asian Trade Unionists, 138

C

Central Arid Zone Research Institute, 111
Christian Conference in Asia, 139
Colombo Plan for Co-operative Economic and Social Development in Asia and the Pacific, 125
COMECON, 136
Commission on Asian and Pacific Affairs of the International Chamber of Commerce, 140
Committee for Co-ordination of Investigations of the Lower Mekong Basin, 104
— — — — Joint Prospecting for Mineral Resources, 102
Commonwealth, 128
— Fund for Technical Co-operation, 128
Commonwealth Regional Renewable Energy Resources Information System, 129
Confederation of ASEAN Journalists, 139
— — Asian Chambers of Commerce and Industry, 140
Council for Mutual Economic Assistance—CMEA, 136

E

East Asia Travel Association, 140
Eastern Regional Organization for Planning and Housing, 139
— — — — Public Administration, 138
Economic and Social Commission for Asia and the Pacific—ESCAP, 101
— Commission for Asia and the Far East, 101
European Community, 130

F

Federation of Asian Nutrition Societies, 138
— — — Pharmaceutical Associations, 138
Food and Agriculture Organization—FAO, 105
Foundation for the Peoples of the South Pacific, 136

I

Indo-Pacific Fishery Commission (FAO), 105
INFOFISH, 105
Institute of Economic Growth, Asian Research Centre, 137
Intergovernmental Oceanographic Commission, 111
International Bank for Reconstruction and Development—IBRD, 106
— Chamber of Commerce, 140
— Civil Aviation Organization—ICAO, 113
— Confederation of Free Trade Unions, Asian Regional Organization, 138
— Congress on Tropical Medicine and Malaria, 139
— Co-operative Alliance Regional Office and Education Centre, 140
— Cotton Advisory Committee, 140
— Crops Research Institute for the Semi-Arid Tropics, 136
— Development Association—IDA, 107
— Federation of Asian and Western Pacific Contractors' Associations, 140
— Finance Corporation—IFC, 108
— Institute of Seismology and Earthquake Engineering, 111
— Labour Organisation—ILO, 113
— Natural Rubber Organization, 140
— Pepper Community, 103
— Planned Parenthood Federation, 139
— Programme for the Development of Communications, 111
— Rice Commission (FAO), 105
— — Research Institute, 136
— Rubber Study Group, 141
— Sugar Organization, 141
— Tea Committee, 141
— Tea Promotion Association, 141
— Tin Council, 141
— Union for Oriental and Asian Studies, 137
— Wheat Council, 141

L

Law Association for Asia and the Western Pacific, 138
Lomé Convention, 130

O

Organization of Asia-Pacific News Agencies, 139
Orient Airlines Association, 141

P

Pacific Area Travel Association, 140
— Basin Economic Council, 137
— Forum Line, 135
— Science Association, 140
Pan-Pacific and South East Asia Women's Association, 141
— Surgical Association, 139
Panel on Tropical Cyclones (WMO/ESCAP), 103
Press Foundation of Asia, 139

R

Regional Centre for Technology Transfer, 102
— Commission on Farm Management for Asia and the Far East (FAO), 105
— Mineral Resources Development Centre, 102
— Network for Agricultural Machinery, 102

S

South Pacific Arts Festival, 111
— — Bureau for Economic Co-operation—SPEC, 134
— — Commission—SPC, 131
— — Forum, 134
— — — Fisheries Agency, 135
— — Regional Trade and Economic Co-operation Agreement, 134
South-East Asia Iron and Steel Institute, 141
— — Tin Research and Development Centre, 102
Southeast Asian Ministers of Education Organization, 137
Statistical Institute for Asia and the Pacific, 102
STABEX Scheme, 130
Staff College for Technician Education, 127
SYSMIN scheme, 130

T

Typhoon Committee (ESCAP/WMO), 103

U

United Nations, 99
— — Children's Fund, 113
— — Development Programme—UNDP, 108
— — Economic and Social Commission for Asia and the Pacific—ESCAP, 101
— — Educational, Scientific and Cultural Organization—UNESCO, 110
— — Environment Programme—UNEP, 113
— — High Commissioner for Refugees—UNHCR, 111
— — Trusteeship Council, 100
— — University, 113

W

World Anti-Communist League, 138
— Bank, 106
— Fellowship of Buddhists, 139
— Food Programme, 105
— Health Organization—WHO, 112

PART THREE

Country Surveys

Afghanistan

PHYSICAL AND SOCIAL GEOGRAPHY

W. B. Fisher

Occupying an area of approximately 650,000 square kilometres (estimates range between 620,000 and 700,000 square kilometres), Afghanistan has the shape of a very irregular oval with its major axis running N.E.-S.W. and extending over roughly 1,125 kilometres, and the minor axis at right angles to this, covering about 560 kilometres. The country is in the main a highland mass lying mostly at an altitude of 1,200 metres (4,000 ft.) or more, but it presents a highly variable pattern of extremely high and irregular mountain ridges, some of which exceed 6,000 metres (20,000 ft.), ravines and broader valleys, parts of which are very fertile, and an outer expanse of undulating plateau, wide river basins, and lake sumps.

Politically, Afghanistan has two frontiers of major length: one on the north with the Turkmen, Uzbek and Tadzhik Republics of the U.S.S.R., the other on the south and east with Pakistan.

This frontier follows what was once termed the Durand Line (after the representative of British India, Sir Mortimer Durand, who negotiated it in 1893 with the Ruler of Afghanistan). So long as the British occupied India, it was generally accepted as forming the Indo-Afghan frontier, but in 1947 with the recognition of Pakistan as a successor to the British, the Afghan government recalled that for much of the eighteenth century, Peshawar and other parts of the Indus Valley had formed part of a larger Afghan state, and were moreover occupied largely by Pashtuns, who are of closely similar ethnic character to many Afghans. Accordingly, the Durand Line frontier was denounced by Afghanistan, and claims were made that the territories as far as the line of the Indus, including Chitral, Swat, and Peshawar, and continuing as far as the Pashtun areas of the North-west Frontier Province and Baluchistan, ought to be recognized as an autonomous state, "Pashtunistan". This remains a topic of dispute between Afghanistan and Pakistan.

There are shorter but no less significant frontiers on the west with Iran and on the north-east with Kashmir and with China. This last was fully agreed only in 1963, and the precise location of others in the south and west has not been fully delimited: an indication of the extreme difficulties of terrain, and an explanation of the uncertainty regarding the actual area of Afghanistan. It is noteworthy that, in order to erect a "buffer" between the then competing empires of Russia and India, under the Durand treaty of 1893 the Wakhan district, a narrow strip of land 200 miles long and under 10 miles wide in its narrowest part, was attached to Afghanistan. This strip controls the Baroghil pass over the Pamir and avoids having a Soviet-Indian frontier.

PHYSICAL FEATURES

The main topographical feature of Afghanistan is a complex of irregular highlands that is relatively broad and low in the west, and very much higher and also narrower towards the east. In this eastern part the mountains form a group of well-defined chains that are known by the general name of the Hindu Kush (Hindu destroyer), and are linked further eastward first to the Pamirs and then to the main Himalaya system. The Eastern Hindu Kush ranges form the southern defining limit of the Wakhan strip whilst a short distance to the north and east, a small but high ridge, the Little Pamir, forms the topographic link between the Hindu Kush and the main Pamir. From maximum heights of 6,000–7,000 metres (20,000–24,000 ft.) the peaks decline in altitude westwards, attaining 4,500–6,000 metres (15,000–20,000 ft.) in the zone close to Kabul. Further west still, the ridges are no more than 3,500–4,500 metres (12,000–15,000 ft.) and in the extreme west they open out rather like the digits of a hand, with the much lower Parapamisus ridges (proto-Pamir) forming the last member of the mountain complex. The various ridges are distinguished by separate names. The Hindu Kush, which has a general altitude of about 4,500 metres, with peaks 2,000–3,000 metres (7,000–10,000 ft.) higher still, is, however, narrow and crossable by quite a number of passes, some of which are indirect and snow-bound for much of the year.

In geological structure, Afghanistan has close affinities both to Iran further west, and, as has just been stated, to the massive Himalayan system further east. Development of present-day land-forms has been greatly influenced by the existence of several large, stable masses of ancient rocks, which, by drifting northwards, have acted as cores or plates around which rock series of younger age first developed and were then closely wrapped as fold structures. Most important of these ancient massifs, or "plate" areas so far as Afghanistan is concerned, is the plateau of the Deccan, the effect of which was to "bunch" a series of tight folds in a double loop or garland on its northern side. In this way can be explained the existence of the "knot" or "bunch" of fold structures lying partly in Afghanistan, and comprising the Pamir which forms the eastern limb and the Hindu Kush that makes up the western segment of the "garland". The abrupt change of direction and swinging of the fold structures from an east-west to, in some places, a north-south direction are a direct result of the presence of the resistant mass of the Deccan. The fold ranges themselves are composed in part of sediments mainly laid down under water, and include limestones with some sandstones and are of Cretaceous and later age, Eocene especially. Extensive heat and pressure in some regions have metamorphosed original series into schists and gneiss, and there has been much shattering and cracking of the rock generally, with the consequent development of fault-lines and overthrust zones. A further feature in much of Afghanistan has been a good deal of differential earth movement, uptilting, downwarping and local adjustment, making the region particularly susceptible to earth tremors, which occur frequently, usually on a small scale. Occasionally, however, a major disaster occurs, such as that in the Uzbek Republic of the U.S.S.R., just north of Afghanistan, in 1976.

As a consequence of frequent crustal disturbance, the rise of magma from the earth's interior has produced lava-flows and minor volcanos. Most of these are in a stage of old age—being merely fissures from which emanate gas, steam and mud flows, and the presence of soft volcanic debris adds considerably in places to soil fertility.

As far as river drainage is concerned, Afghanistan forms a major watershed, from which rivers flow outward. The Amu-Dar'ya (Oxus) rises on the north side of the Hindu Kush and flows northwestwards into the U.S.S.R. Here, away from the mountains, the presence of loess (a yellowish soil of high fertility) in small pockets offers scope for agriculture. The Hari Rud rises a short distance only from the Amu-Dar'ya but flows westward through Herat to terminate in a salt, closed basin on the Iranian frontier. From the south and west of the Hindu Kush flow a number of streams that become tributaries of the Indus; and in the extreme south-west the Helmand river flows through to end like the Hari Rud in a closed basin that is partly within Iranian territory. The Helmand basin is of interest in that because of a curious balance in water-level at its lowest part, the river here reverses its flow seasonally, and remains for much of its length non-brackish instead of becoming progressively more saline, as is normal when there is no outlet to the sea. The Helmand basin thus offers distinct potential for agricultural improvement, and in fact schemes for irrigation are in process of development. But political difficulties (part of the lower basin is Iranian territory) and remoteness have been inhibiting factors.

The lower-lying areas, which are in the main more densely peopled, occur either as a series of peripheral zones to north and south, or as a series of interior valleys and basins between the main mountain ridges of the centre. Largest of these areas is the piedmont lying on the northern flanks of the mountains, and dropping northwards in altitude to merge into the steppelands of Soviet Central Asia. This is Bactria (Balkh), a region of, in places, light yellowish loessic soils. An interior situation, shut off from the sea by mountains, means that rainfall is deficient and falls mainly over the mountains. Streams fed partly by mountain snow-melt straggle across the plain, to lose themselves in the sand, feed salt swamps, or in a few cases, join others to form larger rivers such as the Hari Rud. Much of Bactria thus consists of semi or full desert with sheets of sand and gravel in many places, with, nearer the mountains, outwash of larger, coarser scree. Given stable political conditions this area with its areas of highly fertile loess soils and moderate water supplies offers much scope for economic development. For long inhabited by pastoral nomads, and disputed politically between various claimants (Afghan, Iranian and Soviet), this northern zone is now developing rapidly with irrigated cotton growing as a main element. Links with the U.S.S.R. are considerable, and the two chief towns of Herat in the west and Mazar-i-Sharif in the north have grown considerably in size over the past few years.

On the south, towards the east, is the Kabul basin, which is a relatively flat zone hemmed in closely by steep mountain ridges. Some distance away to the north-west, and reachable through two major passes is the narrower Vale of Bamian; whilst south-east of Kabul occurs another fertile lowland zone around Jalalabad. Here lower elevation and southerly situation produce warmer conditions, especially in winter, as compared with most of the rest of Afghanistan.

In the south-west, extending through Ghazni as far as Qandahar, there is another series of cultivated zones; but the extent of this piedmont area is much smaller than the corresponding one we have just described as Bactria. To the west aridity, the price of declining altitude, increases, so the lowland passes into the desert areas of Registan and the Dasht-i-Mayo. Registan has seasonal flushes of grass, which support relatively large numbers of pastoral nomads, who, however, are becoming increasingly settled following irrigation development on the Helmand and Arghandab rivers.

Two other regional units may be mentioned. South of the Parapamisus and Kuh-i-Baba mountain ranges are a number of parallel but lower massifs, with narrow valleys between. Here because of altitude there is relatively abundant rainfall, but owing to topography, the region is one of remoteness and difficulty. This is the Hazarat, so called from the name of the Hazara inhabitants, and it still remains, despite a central position, one of the least known and visited parts of the country. Another equally remote highland, this time located north-east of Kabul, is Nuristan, again high and mountainous, but well-wooded in places, and supporting a small population of cultivators and pastoralists who use the summer pastures of the high hills and move to lower levels in winter.

CLIMATE

Climatically, Afghanistan demonstrates a very clear relationship with Iran and the Middle East, rather than with Monsoon Asia, in that it has an almost arid summer, a small amount of rainfall which is largely confined to the winter season, and considerable seasonal variation in temperature. The monsoonal condition of heavy summer rainfall does not occur, despite Afghanistan's nearness to India. Annual rainfall ranges from 100–150 mm. (4–6 in.) in the drier, lower areas of the west and north, to 250–400 mm. (10–15 in.) in the east; on the highest mountains there is more still. Kabul, with an average of 330 mm. (13 in.) per annum, is typical of conditions in the east, and Herat with 125 mm. typical of the west. Almost all this falls in the period December to April, though there can be a very occasional downpour at other times, even in summer, when a rare damp monsoonal current penetrates from the Indian lowlands. Temperatures are best described as extreme. In July, the lowlands experience temperatures of 43°C. (110°F.) with 49°C. not uncommon—this is true of Jalalabad on the edge of the Indus lowlands. But the effects of altitude are important, and Kabul, at an elevation of 1,800 m., does not often experience temperatures of over 38°C. (100°F.). Winter cold can be bitter, with minima of −22° to −26°C. (−10° to −15°F.) on the higher plateau areas, and as a result there are heavy blizzards in many mountain areas. The January mean at Kabul is −4°C. (25°F.). Generally speaking, a seasonal temperature range of 45–55°C. is characteristic of many areas (cf. 14°C. for London). A further difficulty is the prevalence of strong winds, especially in the west, where a persistent and regular wind blows almost daily from June to September and affects especially the Sistan area of the lower Helmand basin, where it is known as the *Wind of 120 Days*.

With highly varied topography and climate, Afghanistan has a wide range of plant life—a good real of which is not yet fully recorded. Conditions dange from Arctic and Alpine type flora on the highest parts to salt-tolerant arid zone species in the deserts. Woodland occurs in a few areas, but much has been used for fuel in a country that has cold winters.

PEOPLE AND ACTIVITIES

The considerable variation in the types of terrain, and the considerable obstacles imposed by high mountains and deserts, have given rise to marked ethnic and cultural differences, so that heterogeneity in human populations is most characteristic. The Pashtuns live mainly in the centre, south and east of the country, and are probably numerically the largest group. The Ghilzays, also of the areas adjacent to Pakistan, are thought to be of Turkish origin, like the Uzbeks who live in the north, mainly in the Amu-Dar'ya lowlands. Another important element are the Tadzhiks or Parziwans who are of Persian origin, and in the opinion of some represent the earliest inhabitants of the country. Other groups, such as the Hazara (who are reputed to have come in as followers of Genghis Khan) and the Chahar Aimak, may have Mongol ancestry, but they now speak Persian and the Hazara are Shi'a Muslims. In the north-east, the presence of fair-haired groups has suggested connection with Europe. Another possibly indigenous group of long-standing, is the Nuristani or Kafirs, now small in number. Most Afghans (the Hazara and Qizilbash of Kabul excepted) are Sunni. Pashtu, one of the Eastern group of Iranian languages, is spoken by about 30 per cent of the total population (another 1½–2 million Pashtu-speakers live across the frontier in Pakistan). Since 1936 Pashtu and Farsi (Iranian) have been the official languages of the country, using an augmented Arabic script.

For long a difficult topography, extreme climate with a generally deficient rainfall, and political instability inhibited economic progress. Small communities lived by cultivation where water and soil were available, and there were relatively numerous pastoralists, mostly nomads, who formed an important section of the community. Even today, it is estimated that about 15 per cent of the population is nomadic, and tribal organization is strong. In fact, only 12 per cent of the land area is cultivated.

Two major handicaps, arising directly from its geography, have long been the fragmented nature of the settlement pattern and the difficulties of physical communications between the various communities. Scale of production and size of markets have consequently been very limited: local standards often prevail and the central Government does not find it easy to develop full control. So inherently strong is this fact of regional subdivision and diversity that the improvement of infrastructure (roads, airfields, radio and telephonic communication), undertaken with vigour over the past few years, has largely resulted in the intensification of regionalism.

In common with other countries of south-west Asia, Afghanistan experienced severe drought between 1968–72. This is thought to have been due to a major cyclical climatic shift that is traceable over a very wide area of the Northern Hemisphere. The economic consequences of this drought have been considerable, though varied regionally within Afghanistan, not only for the 75 per cent or so of the population who still live directly by agriculture, but also through restriction on water supplies for developing manufacturing and other activities.

Because of Afghanistan's former location as a buffer between Russia and British India, railways approached from various sides, but none actually penetrated the country, and so Afghanistan is one of the few parts of the world still to be without railways. In the 1970s a programme of road development was undertaken, resulting in considerable improvements. Since Soviet occupation in 1979, vigorous attempts have been made to link Afghanistan with the Soviet economy. A national development plan, financed from Soviet and COMECON (CMEA) sources, has been undertaken, which has had the effect of diverting trade (already moving that way) strongly towards the Soviet bloc, and hence reducing traditional commercial links with India and Pakistan to 10 per cent or less of former levels. Prospecting for various minerals known to exist in some quantity—chrome, coal, iron, uranium, petroleum and especially gas—has increased and, where production has occurred, all are exported to the U.S.S.R. Opponents of the new regime declare that prices paid to Afghanistan for these are little more than half of current world prices; and these are offset against charges levied by the U.S.S.R. for military costs in Afghanistan, again stated by opponents of the regime as having reached $3–4,000 million by early 1982. In 1981 an attempt was made to popularize the regime by largely abandoning an earlier scheme of land reform aimed at reducing holdings by individuals. This hasty, badly planned agrarian reform, undertaken without necessary supporting measures (such as technical and financial assistance), together with military action against insurrection (including destruction of food stocks in villages), has greatly reduced overall living standards. Shortages of basic food have thus been a feature of the last few years.

HISTORY

Malcolm E. Yapp

The history of Afghanistan has been largely determined by its geography. It stands at the meeting place of three geographical and cultural regions: the Iranian plateau to the west, Turkestan to the north, and the Indian sub-continent to the south. Throughout its history Afghanistan has been subject to influences and invasions from these neighbouring regions and until the eighteenth century was commonly divided, politically, between regimes based on the more fertile and populous regions which surrounded it. At the same time the mountainous terrain and poor communications have enabled large parts of Afghanistan to enjoy local independence of any government and permitted widely differing ethnic and religious groups to retain their identities. The great variety of Afghan historical experience consequent upon this situation makes it difficult to construct an intelligible narrative of Afghan history prior to the emergence of something which may be termed an Afghan state during the second half of the eighteenth century.

PREHISTORY

Significant archaeological investigation in Afghanistan developed only after 1949. Flints and bones discovered indicate human occupation in northern Afghanistan as early as *c.* 30,000 B.C. and the northern slopes of the Hindu Kush may have been one of the earliest centres of the domestication of plants and animals during the Neolithic period (*c.* 10,000 B.C.). Further south, at Mundigak, north-west of Qandahar, excavations have revealed the development of a small village into an urban centre during the period 3000 to 1500 B.C. Archaeological evidence of nomadic occupation is less easy to find but there is some indication of the presence of pastoral peoples in northern Afghanistan during the Iron Age.

EARLY HISTORY

The Achaemenids

Although scholars have argued that references to Afghanistan exist in the early religious works of India (the *Rig Veda*) and Iran (the *Avesta*), this is uncertain and the existence of various tribal kingdoms during this early period can only be postulated. Afghanistan's first appearance in recorded history dates from the sixth century B.C., when parts of western Afghanistan were conquered by the Achaemenid ruler of Iran, Cyrus the Great (reigned 559–530 B.C.), and much of the remainder was incorporated as provinces in the empire of Darius the Great (522–486 B.C.).

The Greeks

In 330 B.C. Afghanistan was invaded by the Macedonian, Alexander the Great, following his defeat of the Achaemenids. Alexander fought several campaigns in Afghanistan and founded cities near Herat, on an unknown site between Qandahar and Ghazni, near Begram, and at Bactria (Balkh), before moving on to India in 327 B.C.

Alexander's empire disintegrated after his death in 323 B.C. Afghanistan fell to the share of his general Seleucus, but revolts led to the establishment of several independent "Greek" kingdoms (that is kingdoms in which the names of the rulers, the language of the inscriptions and the style of the architecture were Greek). The most notable of these kingdoms were those of Bactria (north of the Hindu Kush) and the so-called Indo-Greek kingdom south of the mountains. In 1963 the important remains of one Greek city were discovered at Ai Khanoum in northern Afghanistan. From the third century B.C. these kingdoms were subjected to attacks from the Parthians from the west and the Mauryas from the south; and from the second century they were assaulted by nomads from the north.

The Kushans

During the first century A.D. Afghanistan (with Turkestan) became part of the empire of the Kushans, a Central Asian people who employed an Indo-European language. Under the remarkable ruler, Kanishka I (probably early second century A.D.), the Kushans also took control of much of northern India. The capital was moved from the vicinity of Bactria to that of Peshawar, while Begram (near Kabul) was used as a summer capital. The Kushan period saw two important developments in Afghanistan: a major increase in the trade of the region, which became an entrepôt for commerce between Rome, China and India; and the spread of Buddhism, which had been introduced to Afghanistan by the Mauryas and whose presence is witnessed by several remarkable monuments including the great stone statues of the Buddha at Bamian.

During the third century A.D. the Kushan empire broke up under attack from the Sasanian rulers of Iran and for the next two centuries Afghanistan appears to have been divided among semi-independent Sasanian or Kushan rulers. In the mid-fifth century these petty states crumbled before the invasion of the so-called White Huns, or Hephthalites, from Central Asia. The regime of the White Huns endured for approximately 100 years before submitting to the attacks of a Turkish people from the north and the Sasanians from the west.

THE EARLY ISLAMIC PERIOD

The final Arab defeat of the Sasanians in A.D. 642 left the fragmented Afghan kingdoms independent. Although the Arabs raided into Afghanistan, they did not establish a permanent government in the area, preferring to work through local rulers. With the decline of the power of the Abbasid Caliphs in Baghdad during the ninth century, new local Iranian Muslim dynasties established themselves in the east and at various times parts of Afghanistan were included in the dominions of the Tahirids, Samanids and Saffarids. At the end of the tenth century new dynasties of Turkish origin emerged, notably that of the Ghaznavids.

The Ghaznavids

The Ghaznavid dynasty was founded by a Turkish mercenary soldier named Alptegin who settled in Ghazni. His son-in-law, Subuktigin (reigned 977–997), developed the new state which reached its climax under Subuktigin's son, Mahmud of Ghazni (998–1030), who defeated the rival Ghurid dynasty in central Afghanistan, raided extensively into surrounding areas, especially northern India, and made his court a centre of scholarship and the arts. Mahmud's tomb and his two great towers of victory may still be seen in the vicinity of Ghazni. During the twelfth century the Ghaznavid state was eaten away by regimes based upon Iran (the Seljuks), Turkestan (the Qarakhanids) and India. The final blow was administered by the resurgent Ghurids in 1186, although the Ghurids were quickly replaced by another Turkestan-based dynasty, that of the Khwarazmshahs.

The Mongols, Timur and the Timurids

In 1220 the Mongol conqueror, Genghis Khan, smashed his way through Turkestan and invaded Afghanistan. Political authority was fragmented and a confused period followed in which predominance belonged to the descendants of Genghis in Central Asia (the Chaghatay Khans). At the end of the fourteenth century a new great eastern empire was created by Timur (Tamerlane; 1370–1405), which included Afghanistan. Timur's empire broke up after his death but his descendants continued to rule in various parts of the region and, under Shah Rukh (1405–47) and Husayn Bayqara (1470–1506), Herat became one of the most notable cultural centres in the eastern Muslim world. Evidence of its architectural splendour still survives. In Turkestan power passed to the Uzbek Turks who invaded from the north. One of Timur's descendants, Babur, fled to Kabul, from where he launched a campaign into India which resulted in the establishment of the great Mughal Empire in the sub-continent.

Mughals and Safavids

In the early fifteenth century Afghanistan was once more surrounded by three powerful states. In Turkestan the Uzbeks quickly became divided into a number of small states, although they retained influence in northern Afghanistan. In India and in Iran the powerful Mughal and Safavid states became established and laid claim to Afghanistan, for the possession of which they contended for much of the following two centuries. Broadly speaking, western Afghanistan, including Qandahar, usually fell into the Safavid orbit while eastern Afghanistan, including Kabul, was often under Mughal control, although when Mughal power declined during the seventeenth century the area enjoyed greater independence.

Although imposing in appearance, the Safavid state was in reality weak and unstable and in the early eighteenth century it was overthrown by a revolt of the western Ghilzay Afghans. Under their leader, Mir Wais (died 1715), the Ghilzays defeated the Safavids at Qandahar in 1711. In 1721–22 Mir Wais's son, Mahmud, led a raid into Iran which ended in the siege and capture of Isfahan and the effective destruction of the Safavid state. The Afghans lacked the resources to create a new empire and were eventually defeated and expelled from Iran in 1730 by another great Asian conqueror, Nadir Shah, who went on to create a vast eastern empire in which Afghanistan was included. Many Afghans served in his victorious armies.

THE DURRANI EMPIRE (1747–1818)

In 1747 Nadir Shah was assassinated and his empire dissolved in anarchy. In Qandahar power was seized by one of his Afghan officers, Ahmad Shah (1722–72) of the Abdali Afghans. Ahmad renamed his tribe the Durranis. He constructed a new empire based upon Afghanistan and resting primarily upon the military power of the Afghan tribes. For these achievements Ahmad Shah is usually acknowledged as the founder of the Afghan state. After winning the support of the Abdalis and gaining acceptance by the Ghilzay Afghans, Ahmad went on to consolidate his hold on Afghanistan by seizing Kabul in 1748, Herat in 1749 and the area of northern Afghanistan between the Hindu Kush and the Amu-Dar'ya (Oxus) in 1751. He also made Khurasan into a dependency. His main efforts, however, were directed towards northern India, whither he led a total of eight campaigns. At its peak in 1757 his authority extended over the Punjab, Kashmir and Sind, but in his later years Ahmad met increasing competition from the Marathas (whom he defeated in 1761 at Panipat) and from the Sikhs, who gradually loosened the Afghan hold on the Punjab. The Durrani Empire was essentially a military empire and Ahmad relied upon a constant series of victorious campaigns to provide the booty which purchased the allegiance of the Afghan tribal chiefs. His military skills, his piety and his normally good relations with the Afghan chiefs maintained Ahmad's authority until his death. He also patronized the arts and built the new city of Qandahar.

Ahmad Shah was succeeded by his second son, Timur (reigned 1772–93), who adopted a less belligerent policy and allowed some outlying dependencies to gain substantial independence. Nevertheless Timur held the core of the Durrani empire intact and it was only during the civil war which followed his death that Afghan power crumbled. Between 1793 and 1818 the sons of Timur, notably Zaman Shah (1793–1800), Mahmud Shah (1800–03; 1809–18) and Shah Shuja (1803–09), contended for power, enlisting the support of tribal groups. This resulted in Afghanistan's becoming divided into several states. Mahmud retained possession of Herat but the remainder of Afghanistan proper was divided among chiefs from the Barakzay section of the Durrani confederation. Of the dependencies, Bactria, Sind, Baluchistan and the Punjab all became independent and the ruler of the Sikh state of Lahore, Ranjit Singh, went on to take control of Kashmir, Peshawar and other Afghan districts west of the river Indus.

EVENTS LEADING TO INDEPENDENCE

Gradually the situation in Afghanistan crystallized and three states emerged based upon the principal towns. In the west, in Herat, Mahmud extended his power into Sistan and amongst the petty states on the north slope of the Paropamisus mountains. The area between the Helmand river and Kalat-i Ghilzay fell under the control of the Barakzay Sirdars of Qandahar. In the east Dost Muhammad of Kabul took control of Ghazni and Jalalabad and enforced his authority in the region of the Hindu Kush. The dissensions of these three states, however, aided their external foes: the Qajar state of Iran in the west and the state of Lahore in the east. In 1837 Afghans and Sikhs fought in the Khaibar Pass and the Iranians beseiged Herat. In consequence two new actors were introduced to the scene: Russia and Britain.

The First Anglo-Afghan War, 1839–42

British interest in Afghanistan derived from the establishment of British power in India through the agency of the East India Company. In 1809, as part of a series of diplomatic arrangements designed to protect India from a possible French invasion, a treaty was negotiated with Shah Shuja in Afghanistan, but, because of the disappearance of the alleged French threat and the fall of Shah Shuja, the treaty remained a dead letter. British interest in Afghanistan languished, to be revived from 1830 onwards as a result of fears of the spread of Russian influence towards India. An attempt was made to develop commercial relations with the Barakzay states but the deteriorating Sikh-Afghan and Iranian-Afghan relations caused difficulties. In the event, in 1838, the Governor-General, Lord Auckland, abandoned hope of reaching agreement with the Barakzays and decided to replace them in Qandahar and Kabul with Shah Shuja and, through him, to establish a powerful British influence in Afghanistan as a counterpoise to Russian influence in Iran. In 1839 Shah Shuja was re-established on the throne with the aid of British and Company troops and a Sikh diversionary action. For various reasons it proved impossible to withdraw the British and Company troops. Hostility to British influence multiplied and in November 1841 a rising took place in Kabul which led to the withdrawal of the British garrison from Kabul and its massacre during its retreat to Jalalabad. At Jalalabad and Qandahar the British garrisons held out and were reinforced in 1842 when Kabul was recaptured. It was then decided to abandon Afghanistan. Shah Shuja had been murdered and the Barakzay rulers returned from exile in 1843 to resume their rule in Kabul and Qandahar.

The Unification of Afghanistan, 1843–63

Following his return to power, Dost Muhammad resumed his previous policy of extending his authority over the other Afghan states. In northern Afghanistan he established his power in Bactria and Khulm (1850), Shibarghan (1854), Maymana and Andkhuy (1855) and Kunduz (1859). In the west he took Qandahar (1855) and Herat (1863). At the same time he increased his power over the tribal chiefs, reduced the power of the Ghilzays, and developed a regular army to replace the feudal militia. By the time of his death in 1863 he had established the outlines of modern Afghanistan. He also restored good relations with Britain and signed agreements with her in 1855 and 1857.

The Civil War and the Reign of Shir Ali, 1863–78

After Dost Muhammad's death his sons, whom he had employed as provincial governors, contended for supreme power. After five years and many vicissitudes Shir Ali Khan emerged triumphant and resumed the policy of consolidating Afghanistan and developing a reliable regular army. Britain had abstained from intervention until the issue was settled but when Shir Ali emerged as the victor good relations were established with him in 1869. However, these good relations did not last.

The Second Anglo-Afghan War, 1878–80

British interest in Afghanistan, which had waned after 1842, was revived first by a new Iranian threat to Herat and then, during the 1860s and 1870s, by the Russian conquest of Turkestan and its apparent threat to the security of British India. One school of thought held that Britain should seek friendly but distant relations with Afghanistan and negotiate an agreement with Russia; another, represented by Lord Lytton (Viceroy 1876–80), believed that British influence should be firmly planted in Afghanistan through a British Resident in Kabul. Shir Ali's unwilling acceptance of a Russian mission during the Eastern Crisis of 1878 provided an excuse for insisting on the reception of a British mission and when this demand was refused Afghanistan was invaded, Shir Ali fled and died, and his son, Yaqub, was obliged to surrender certain lands to Britain and accept a British Resident under the Treaty of Gandamak of 1879. The murder of the British Resident in September 1879 led to a further expedition to Afghanistan and a decision by Lytton to break up Afghanistan, giving Herat to Iran, dominating Qandahar, and leaving Kabul largely to its own devices. However, before this policy could be implemented the British forces in western Afghanistan suffered a severe defeat in 1880 at Maiwand at the hands of Ayyub Khan, the second son of Shir Ali, and were beseiged in Qandahar. Although the troops were rescued by the famous march of a British column under Gen. Sir Frederick Roberts from Kabul to Qandahar, the new Liberal Government in London decided to withdraw from Afghanistan. Of the gains made by Britain at Gandamak, the Khaibar Pass and the districts of Kurram, Pishin and Sibi were retained, and Britain retained control of Afghanistan's foreign relations.

The Amir Abd al-Rahman, 1880–1901

The British installed, as ruler of Kabul, a grandson of Dost Muhammad named Abd al-Rahman and in 1881 Abd al-Rahman took possession of Qandahar and Herat and so reunited Afghanistan. It was during his reign that the boundaries of Afghanistan assumed their present form. The western frontier with Iran had been delimited in 1872; the northern frontier with Russian-controlled Turkestan was demarcated in two stages, in 1885–87 and 1895; and the southern and eastern frontiers with British India and its dependencies were outlined in the Durand Agreement of 1893 and demarcated in 1894–96. Within these limits Abd al-Rahman established a strong autocratic government. He pacified eastern Afghanistan, defeating tribal opposition and extending his power over outlying areas, including Kafiristan (renamed Nuristan); suppressed a major Ghilzay rising (1886–88); crushed a major uprising in northern Afghanistan (1888); and brought the Hazaras of central Afghanistan under control in a long and bitter war (1891–93). He also made major reforms in local government, law and taxation, and established new industries and constructed roads and bridges. His principal instrument was his new, regular, disciplined, conscript army, a great development from the models of Dost Muhammad and Shir Ali. He was also aided by a British subsidy. Although obliged to accept British control of his foreign relations, Abd al-Rahman preserved Afghanistan's internal independence and established some of the main features of the modern state.

MODERN AFGHANISTAN, 1901–73

Abd al-Rahman was succeeded as Amir by his son, Habibullah, who maintained the absolutist system of his father, while making more concessions to tribal and religious leaders. Habibullah introduced educational reforms: the first secondary school was founded in 1904 and the curriculum of the traditional religious schools was broadened. During his reign a modernizing, nationalist movement of Afghan intellectuals developed around the newspaper *Siraj al-Akhbar* (1911–19), edited by Mahmud Tarzi (1866–1935). During the First World War Habibullah successfully resisted pressure to join the Central Powers; Afghanistan remained neutral.

On February 20th, 1919, Habibullah was assassinated and was succeeded by his youngest son, Amanullah, who immediately proclaimed the independence of Afghanistan. War with Britain broke out when Afghan forces entered British Indian territory. Afghan forces in the Khaibar Pass were quickly repulsed but those in Waziristan achieved some successes before an armistice was signed. By the treaty of Rawalpindi in August 1919, peace was established, the British subsidy ended and the Durand frontier confirmed. A separate letter effectively recognized Afghanistan's independence. In November 1921 a treaty between Britain and Afghanistan was signed.

Amanullah, 1919–29

Amanullah confirmed Afghanistan's independence by agreements with other countries. In September 1920 he signed an agreement with Soviet Russia, in March 1921 with Kemalist Turkey, and in June 1921 with Iran. Diplomatic relations were opened with other countries. His hopes of territorial expansion were ended when neighbouring regimes consolidated their power. Amanullah began an extensive programme of modernization. First he concentrated on improving the legal, judicial and administrative framework of government. The first Afghan constitution was promulgated in 1923 and the whole administrative system was reorganized; a system of legislative councils was established; a new system of courts was set up with secular codes of law; major reforms were made in taxation and budgeting (the first government budget was introduced in 1922); and efforts at economic modernization were made. After his visit to Europe in 1927–28 Amanullah became more ambitious and announced a further series of reforms especially directed against traditional social customs, including the wearing of the veil. Without doubt Amanullah saw himself as a modernizer in the mould of Atatürk in Turkey and Reza Shah in Iran; his mistake was to allow his army to become weak. In the autumn of 1928 tribal risings began in eastern Afghanistan, culminating in the occupation of Kabul in January 1929 by a Tajik bandit, known as the Baccha-i Saqqaw, who proclaimed himself Habibullah II of Afghanistan. After vain efforts to recover his power Amanullah fled to India and thence to Europe.

Nadir Shah, 1929–33

Leadership of the opposition to Habibullah II fell to a group of able brothers, Nadir, Hashim, Aziz, Shah Wali and Shah Muhammad Khan, who were members of the Musahiban family and were descended from a brother of Dost Muhammad Khan. Political disagreements with Amanullah had driven them into self-imposed exile. In 1929 they returned to rally the Pathan tribes against the Tajik, Habibullah, and in October captured Kabul. Habibullah and some of his followers were executed. Nadir Khan was elected ruler and began a programme of pacification, conciliation and cautious reform, beginning with the reconstitution of the army. In 1931 he introduced a new constitution. In foreign policy he followed the traditional neutralist policy, seeking good relations with the U.S.S.R. and Britain, while attempting to win the support of other European countries and the U.S.A.

The replacement of Amanullah by the Musahiban deeply divided the Afghan élite. In 1933 first Aziz and then Nadir were assassinated. Nadir was succeeded by his only son, Zahir Shah, but real power resided with the family as a whole and especially with Hashim, who became Prime Minister.

Afghanistan, 1933–53

The policy of the Musahibans was to preserve national independence, foster nationalist feeling and pursue modernization with circumspection. In foreign affairs they sought correct relations with Britain and the U.S.S.R. and close connections with other Muslim countries, especially Turkey, Iran and Iraq, with whom Afghanistan had signed the Sa'adabad Pact in 1937. Attempts to form close links with the U.S.A. had little success but important economic and technical connections were made with Germany. Nevertheless, during the Second World War Afghanistan resisted invitations to identify with the Axis cause, preserved its neutrality, and expelled Axis subjects when the Allies demanded this. The growth of nationalism was encouraged by the adoption of Pashtu as the official language in 1937; by the development of education at all levels, leading up to various institutions of higher education which were eventually grouped together in the University of Kabul in 1946; by the improvement of communications; and by the spread of newspapers. Economic modernization concentrated on improving the infrastructure. A bank was founded in 1932 and roads were developed, including a major new route to northern Afghanistan, which became the scene of important developments in the cotton and textile industries. However, as in previous periods, all modernization projects were hampered by lack of money and during the Second World War the prevailing economic dislocation set back programmes still further and led to discontent and tribal risings in 1944 and 1945.

Hashim was succeeded as Prime Minister by his brother, Shah Mahmud Khan. Economic difficulties (which obliged Afghanistan to import grain in 1946) continued, but an improvement in 1947 enabled Afghanistan to contemplate major economic development centring on the massive Helmand Valley scheme designed to irrigate a large area of western Afghanistan. It was badly planned and failed to yield any results commensurate with the cost. Between 1951 and 1953 Afghanistan once again found itself in severe economic trouble. The post-war period also saw Afghanistan's first experiment with parliamentary democracy. In 1947 the "Awakened Youth" movement began to agitate for social reform and to criticize government policy. In 1949 relatively free elections were permitted and the seventh Afghan Parliament (1949–51) gave voice to criticisms of the Government and traditional institutions, and enacted some liberal reforms including laws providing for a free press. Outside Parliament, radical groups became stronger, especially among students. The critics belonged to a tiny middle-class group, without real support in the country, and were easily silenced when the Government abandoned conciliation and returned to a policy of strict control in the elections for the eighth Parliament in 1952. Several of the liberal leaders were imprisoned. The seeds of a new type of opposition, however, had been planted in Afghanistan.

In foreign affairs the most notable event was the end of British rule in India and the creation in 1947 of the new states of Pakistan and India. Afghanistan's former balancing role was no longer possible and the country inevitably inclined more towards the U.S.S.R. This new direction was increased by the re-opening of the question of the tribal lands on Pakistan's north-western frontier. The Afghans contended that the Pathan tribesmen should be given the choice of joining Pakistan or forming an independent Pashtunistan. The issue led to bad relations between Afghanistan and Pakistan and handicapped Afghanistan's transit trade through Pakistan.

Daud Khan, 1953–63

In September 1953 Shah Mahmud was replaced as Prime Minister by his nephew, Lt.-Gen. Muhammad Daud, son of Aziz. Under Daud, Afghanistan returned to the path of autocratic modernization, now pursued with greater determination and ruthlessness. Daud favoured state-directed economic development aimed at improving communications. Large-scale economic aid was obtained from the U.S.S.R. from 1955 onwards and also considerable help from the U.S.A. Afghanistan's first five-year plan began in 1956. Daud also obtained military assistance, arms and training facilities from the U.S.S.R. and greatly strengthened the army. Daud introduced important social reforms, especially improving the status of women. In 1959 a campaign against the wearing of the veil was launched and opposition by tribal and religious leaders was crushed.

In foreign affairs Daud pressed more strongly the case for Pashtunistan, especially after West Pakistan's "one unit" scheme of 1955 threatened the considerable autonomy which the tribal areas had enjoyed since 1947. Daud denounced the 1921 Anglo-Afghan treaty, which had endorsed the frontier line, and summoned a national assembly to pass a resolution supporting Pashtunistan. Eventually Afghan-Pakistan relations deterioriated to the point where Afghan troops entered Pakistan tribal territory, and in 1961 diplomatic relations were broken off and the border closed. Afghanistan was obliged to make new arrangements with the U.S.S.R. for transit facilities for its exports. Grapes were airlifted to both the U.S.S.R. and India, while greater use was made of road links to Iran. Nevertheless, Afghanistan's economic development was disrupted. In December 1955 the Soviet leaders, Nikolay Bulganin and Nikita Khrushchev, visited Kabul and voiced limited support for Afghanistan's stand on the Pashtunistan issue.

The Constitutional Period, 1963–73

In March 1963 Daud resigned because of the failure of his foreign policy and the desire for a more liberal regime. A new Government was formed by Dr. Muhammad Yusuf, the first Prime Minister not of royal birth. With Iranian help, relations between Afghanistan and Pakistan were quickly restored and the border re-opened. Relations with the U.S.S.R. remained good and close economic and other links continued. Nevertheless, Afghanistan recovered greater freedom in its dealings with the outside world. The new Government's main concern was with a programme of liberal domestic reform, of which the centre-piece was a new constitution promulgated in October 1964. The constitution provided for an elected lower house and partially elected upper house of Parliament. Elections were held in September 1965, with women voting for the first time. The new constitutional system did not work easily. Factions within the lower house bitterly attacked the Government while students demonstrated. In October 1965 riots led to three deaths and the Government of Dr. Yusuf resigned. Further disturbances took place under the Government of Muhammad Hashim Maiwandwal, who resigned in November 1967. There were continued student riots and even fighting in Parliament. Apart from a reorganization of provincial administration, by which 27 provinces were created to replace the old system, and a new liberal Press Law which led to a mushrooming growth of unofficial newspapers, there was little legislative reform. Government and Parliament were usually deadlocked in opposition, with the result that political parties were not legalized and democracy was not extended downwards to provincial and municipal councils. Although numerically insignificant, the radical left was especially vocal and grouped itself around a succession of newspapers (*Khalq*, *Parcham* and *Shu'la-yi Jawed*). There was no improvement in the situation under the new Prime Minister, Nur Ahmad Etemadi (November 1967–June 1971). In the thirteenth Parliament, elected in

August 1969, there was a marked change as compared with the twelfth. The 1965 Parliament had been elected on a very small turn-out which had led to the vocal predominance of Kabuli radicals; the thirteenth Parliament attracted much greater attention from the traditional Afghan élite, the turn-out in the election was much higher, and the radicals were almost extinguished. Nevertheless, although the basis of their opposition was different, the traditional élite were just as loud in their denunciations of the Government as the radicals were. In June 1971 Etemadi's Government resigned, over a dispute concerning the manner in which Ministers should answer parliamentary questions, and a new Government was formed under Abd al-Zahir (June 1971–December 1972). The new Government did establish better relations with Parliament and managed to get some long-delayed bills passed.

In the early 1970s Afghanistan was severely afflicted by three successive seasons of drought in central and north-western regions, including, in 1971, the worst ever recorded. A very large proportion of the sheep stock was lost, there was starvation (with considerable loss of life in some provinces, especially Ghor) and a substantial emigration to Pakistan and Iran. International aid alleviated, but did not eliminate, the problems and there was serious criticism of the Government's handling of the problem. Abd al-Zahir attempted to resign in September 1972 but was persuaded to stay until December, when a massive vote of "no confidence" in Parliament led to the formation of a new Government under Muhammad Musa Shafiq.

THE REPUBLIC OF AFGHANISTAN, 1973–78

On July 17th, 1973, a virtually bloodless military coup resulted in the deposition of King Zahir Shah and the creation of a republic headed by the former Prime Minister, Lt.-Gen. Muhammad Daud. Daud created a dictatorship dominated by himself, his relations and intimates. The 1977 constitution provided for a single political party. Elections for a new parliament were scheduled for November 1979. Daud was elected President for a six year term.

Daud's main objective was rapid economic development, centred on the improvement of communications, including the construction of a railway to develop the extensive mineral resources of central Afghanistan. To finance this work he increased tax yields three-fold and sought foreign aid from traditional suppliers, including the Western and Eastern blocs, and, increasingly, from Iran and the oil-rich Arab states. Daud tightened state control over the economy; in 1975 the principal private bank, the Banke Milli Afghan, was nationalized; in 1976 a major seven-year plan was unveiled; and a modest measure of land reform was announced but not implemented. In foreign affairs Daud followed a traditional policy of neutrality, maintaining good relations with the U.S.A. and the U.S.S.R. In 1975 the Soviet-Afghan Treaty of Neutrality and Non-Aggression was renewed for a further ten years. Relations with Pakistan, which deteriorated when Daud revived the Pashtunistan dispute, improved after 1976 following Soviet and Iranian mediation.

THE REVOLUTION OF APRIL 1978

During the latter part of 1977 and in 1978 Daud increased his attacks on his political opponents of the right and left. Following leftist anti-government demonstrations in Kabul in April 1978, Daud arrested seven leaders of the People's Democratic Party of Afghanistan (PDPA, founded 1965, divided into Khalq and Parcham factions in 1967, reunited in 1976) and began a purge of army officers and civil servants. On April 27th the commanders of military and air force units in the Kabul area staged a coup, which became known as the Great Saur (April) Revolution and on the following day, after heavy fighting against troops loyal to Daud, the rebels gained the victory. Daud, nearly all his family, the leading ministers and the principal military commanders were killed. The military rebels released the imprisoned PDPA leaders and brought them to power. There is no good evidence of outside intervention; the revolution appears to have been a purely internal struggle. As a result of the revolution the 1977 constitution was abolished, the Republic of Afghanistan was renamed the Democratic Republic of Afghanistan (DRA), power was vested in a Revolutionary Council, and the PDPA became the only political party. The PDPA leader, Nur Muhammad Taraki, became President of the Revolutionary Council and Prime Minister.

AFGHANISTAN UNDER TARAKI AND AMIN 1978–79

The PDPA came to power without any previously-agreed programme of reform and their long-term strategy was not fully unveiled until the publication of the draft Five-Year Plan in August 1979. This plan envisaged a state socialist system: economic growth at 5 per cent per annum, universal primary education by 1984 and a major adult literacy programme. But the central element in the PDPA policy, land reform, had already been put into practice. This was contained in three edicts issued between July and November 1978. These edicts provided for the gradual reduction of rural indebtedness, the abolition of dowries, and a major distribution of land holdings in favour of landless peasants. The land redistribution programme began on January 1st, 1979, and after six months it was announced that it had been successfully completed. The object was political: to destroy the basis of the political power of the former landlord-backed regimes and to win for the PDPA the allegiance of the peasant masses. In the absence of an industrial proletariat in Afghanistan, PDPA support was drawn from a tiny urban intelligentsia and professional group. The programme failed in its aim and the land reform and adult literacy campaigns caused widespread opposition to the DRA Government which led to armed insurrection in almost all provinces, the flight of thousands of refugees to Pakistan and Iran, and great economic dislocation.

From the start the PDPA Government was torn by factional disputes. In July 1978 some leading Parchamis were dismissed and took refuge in eastern Europe; in August 1978 two of the coup leaders, Abdul Qader and Mohammad Rafie, were arrested. Purges of party and army and arrests of opponents of the regime became regular features. In March 1979 more Parchamis were arrested and the Government again reorganized. The Foreign Minister, Hafizullah Amin, already Secretary of the PDPA since July 1978, now replaced Taraki as Prime Minister. Amin's power continued to increase in subsequent months. In July 1979 he added the Ministry of Defence to his responsibilities and in September attempted to remove rivals from the Cabinet. This became the occasion for an armed showdown with Taraki. Amin won and on September 16th became President of the Revolutionary Council. Taraki was put under house arrest and apparently strangled on October 8th. The dispute between Taraki and Amin was partly one of personality and partly of policy; whether the DRA should proceed with its radical politics, as Amin wished, or whether it should pursue more moderate, conciliatory policies, as Taraki and his Soviet backers desired.

Amin now pursued a radical, uncompromising policy. Opponents were imprisoned and executed, a counter-coup was defeated in October, and, after the failure of an amnesty appeal, a new campaign against the rebels in the provinces was launched. To legalize his own position, in October 1979 he appointed a committee to draft a new constitution and he tried to set up a new broad front organization—the National Organization for the Defence of the Revolution in the DRA.

Amin failed either to win over the rebels or to suppress them, and the flight of refugees from Afghanistan increased rapidly. Guerrilla organizations were formed among the refugees in Pakistan. The greater part of rebel military activity was the work of local groups within Afghanistan. The DRA Government accused China, Pakistan, Iran, the U.S.A., Egypt and other countries of aiding the rebels. Relations between the DRA and the U.S.A. steadily deteriorated; in February 1979 U.S.Ambassador Dubbs was killed in a kidnap attempt and the U.S.A. cut aid to Afghanistan. The DRA leaned more heavily on the U.S.S.R. (with which a Treaty of Friendship and Co-operation was signed on November 7th, 1978) for civil and military advice and equipment and for financial aid.

THE SOVIET INVASION OF AFGHANISTAN

From the early summer of 1979 the U.S.S.R. pressed for the adoption of moderate policies and the formation of a broad-based government in Afghanistan. These demands led to increasing friction with the radical elements in the PDPA, which culminated in December 1979 in a Soviet invasion of Afghanistan and the overthrow and execution of Amin on December 27th. A new Government, under the leader of the Parcham faction, Babrak Karmal, was formed, an event described as the inauguration of the second, new developmental stage of the revolution. The Karmal regime announced a policy of conciliation, respect for Islam and for Afghan traditions, particularly tribal customs, and the formation of a broad-based national government. These policies were embodied in the new Provisional Basic Principles, forming an interim constitution, approved by the Revolutionary Council on April 14th, 1980. In subsequent months a number of organizations of religious leaders, young people, women, private businessmen and workers were set up or reinvigorated. In June 1981 a Supreme Council of Afghan Tribes was established. Finally, and after much delay, the promised National Fatherland Front, bringing all these organizations under PDPA leadership, was organized on June 15th, 1981, with Saleh Mohammad Zirai as chairman. This event was accompanied by the introduction of a new political structure: the Revolutionary Council was enlarged and its Presidium separated from the Council of Ministers. This involved ministerial changes, including the replacement of Karmal by Sultan Ali Kishtmand as Prime Minister, although Karmal retained power through the offices of Chairman of the Revolutionary Council and Secretary-General of the PDPA. Land reform remained a key element in the policies of the regime but mistakes in its implementation during the first stage were admitted. Under the revised plan, the system of land redistribution was maintained, although major exemptions were allowed for supporters of the regime. Its implementation, however, was now made subject to surveys, the solution of the water problem and the formation of agricultural co-operatives. The campaign against illiteracy was also maintained but concessions were announced in respect of the education of women. Continued efforts were made to check bureaucratic corruption by the creation of a General Inspectorate under the Prime Minister's Office. In an effort to involve the people in government, a major scheme of decentralized local government, with elected councils, was unveiled at the end of September 1981.

The Karmal regime failed to achieve its objectives. The first essential was the achievement of party unity but disputes between Khalq and Parcham factions continued and there were accusations of corruption, nepotism and tribalism. Efforts to heal the divisions culminated in the PDPA National Conference of March 14th–15th, 1982, at which the Party Charter was amended and a new programme of action adopted. These efforts were evidently unsuccessful. The regime also failed to rebuild the army. Weakened by purges, desertions and mutinies, the Afghan army shrank from about 90,000 in 1978 to about 30,000 in 1981. In attempts to increase its strength, the age of conscription was reduced from 22 to 20 in January 1981 and to 19 in April 1982. On August 30th, 1981, it was decided to recall all reservists under the age of 35 who were released prior to October 22nd, 1978. The regime also made use of other forces: police, security forces, revolutionary guards and social order brigades, formed from those too young for military service. The formation of local defence groups was also publicized. Changes in the command structure were announced in August 1981, when a DRA Defence Council was formed to control all state and military power and to work through a new system in which provinces were grouped into eight zones under party officials. The Minister of Defence, Mohammad Rafie, and other senior officers disappeared at this time to reappear much later in the U.S.S.R. After some delay, Maj.-Gen. Abdul Qader became acting Minister of Defence.

The major problem for the Soviet-backed Karmal regime was the continuing civil war in Afghanistan. This war, mounted by local resistance groups in most areas of Afghanistan and supported by guerrilla organizations operating from the Afghan refugee communities in Pakistan and Iran, caused widespread destruction of roads, bridges, schools and other public buildings, interrupted communications, deprived the Government of authority over large areas of countryside, caused disturbances in towns, dislocated production, and killed many supporters of the regime. Although the regime often proclaimed that it had broken the back of the resistance and frequently announced victories over groups of rebels, it is clear that opposition to its authority was not overcome and in the summers of 1980 and 1981 the Government was in very grave difficulties. In June 1982 a major campaign was mounted against the rebels in their stronghold of the Panjsher Valley, north of Kabul; the Government claimed complete success. Meanwhile the efflux of refugees from Afghanistan continued, the number rising to a reported 2.6 million in Pakistan in February 1982. Including those in Iran, about one in five Afghan citizens had left the country in three years.

INTERNATIONAL RELATIONS

The Soviet invasion was defended on the basis of the November 1978 treaty and Article 51 of the UN Charter. It was claimed that Afghanistan had been attacked by forces from outside, that Amin had requested Soviet aid, and the Karmal Government (after achieving power by its own efforts) had renewed that request. It was alleged that Amin had plotted with the U.S.A., China, Egypt, Pakistan, etc., to partition Afghanistan and that the U.S.S.R. had been obliged to protect its own southern frontier.

World opinion was sceptical and hostile to the Soviet and DRA arguments, and the presence of Soviet forces was opposed by the UN General Assembly, the Organization of the Islamic Conference, ASEAN and the non-aligned movement as well as the Western powers. The U.S.A. took a number of measures against the U.S.S.R., including postponing ratification of SALT II and banning grain exports to the U.S.S.R. (ban lifted April 1981). A partial boycott of the Moscow Olympic Games was arranged. New defensive agreements were negotiated by the U.S.A. with Oman, Kenya and Somalia. In February 1980 attempts were made to persuade the U.S.S.R. to withdraw by neutralizing Afghanistan, but this was denounced by the U.S.S.R. and the DRA as interference in the internal affairs of Afghanistan. The Afghan revolution, it was asserted, was irreversible and on April 17th the DRA put forward its own peace plan, elaborated on May 14th and repeated in the joint DRA/U.S.S.R. announcement on October 16th, 1980. The plan involved bilateral talks with Iran and Pakistan, a regional conference and a U.S. promise not to interfere in Afghanistan *before* discussion of a Soviet withdrawal. Pakistan rejected the plan and offered talks *after* the withdrawal of Soviet troops. In May 1980 the Islamic Foreign Ministers set up a committee to hold talks but this initiative made little progress. Relations between Pakistan and the DRA Government continued to deteriorate, with mutual accusations of frontier violations. In January 1981 it was agreed to hold talks between Pakistan and the DRA through a special representative of the UN Secretary-General. In April and August 1981 Dr. Javier Pérez de Cuellar held talks with Pakistan and the DRA independently. On June 30th, 1981, the EEC also launched a plan for a two-stage international conference which was rejected by the DRA. On August 26th, in the light of these discussions, the DRA refurbished its proposals, agreeing to trilateral talks with Iran and Pakistan in the presence of the Secretary-General and offering some apparent concessions on the timing of the withdrawal of Soviet troops. In September talks were held between Pakistan and Soviet representatives. The talks under UN auspices were resumed in New York in November 1981, and in April 1982 the new special representative of the Secretary-General, Diego Cordovez, visited Afghanistan and Pakistan. As a result of these meetings, there appeared to be some lessening of the differences between Pakistan and the DRA although considerable problems remained: those relating to the withdrawal of Soviet troops, recognition of the DRA Government by Pakistan and the question of the representation of Afghan opposition groups at any talks. Judging by a plan unveiled on November 10th, 1981, the Iranian position, based on the establishment of a purely Islamic regime in Afghanistan, remained very far apart. Indirect discussions between Iran, Pakistan and the DRA were held in Geneva in June 1982 and further discussions were promised for the autumn. Some progress on procedural matters was reported.

ECONOMIC SURVEY

Kevin Rafferty

The greatest problem in trying to present an accurate economic profile of Afghanistan used to be that it was a backward, underdeveloped country where information was hard to come by. That difficulty has now been compounded by the Soviet invasion and the cruel war of attrition that has gone on since 1980. There was always a gulf between the small number of educated urban élite and the majority of traditional tribal Afghans living in close community with a harsh and testing environment. The Soviet invasion and occupying force have widened these divisions. About 20 per cent of the population (over 3 million Afghans by mid-1982) has been driven out of the country into wretched refugee exile in Pakistan; others have fled their homes because of bombing or strafing. There is frequently more than one way of looking at the economies of developing countries. There is the view of the government planners, accustomed to nicely rounded numbers and the assumption that the capital can pull the strings; on the other hand there are the harsher facts of life. In Afghanistan, perhaps more than anywhere else in the world, the lines of communication never ran straight between the capital and the countryside; the effectiveness of the Kabul government was always tested by the rugged terrain of steep mountains, high desert plateaux and narrow valleys and by tribal and feudal laws. The Soviet invasion and the unrest and turmoil which it brought in its wake have merely added to these problems. Even in calmer days, Afghanistan's official statistics gave grounds for scepticism.

That is only the start of the problems of dealing with Afghanistan's statistics. There is the difficulty that no one really knows the size of the population, except that it is somewhere between 12 and 18 million (late 1970s). The Government's own figures would have surpassed 20 million by 1976 were it not for the fact that a substantial downward revision was made in mid-1976 to bring the estimated population to 16,665,000 at mid-1975, of whom 2.4 million were estimated to be nomads. Afghanistan's first national census, conducted in June 1979, gave a population figure of 15,551,358. This includes a nomadic population of 2,500,000. In figures supplied to the Asian Development Bank, the Kabul regime ignored any exodus of refugees and put the mid-1981 population at 16,370,000, a steady 2.6 per cent increase each year, as if the refugees were still solid Afghan citizens. It did acknowledge a large decline in G.N.P. in 1979 but said that the economy picked up in the following year so that total G.N.P. was Afs. 159,700 million ($3,400 million or $220 per caput at the official exchange rates then prevailing). The 1981 *World Bank Atlas* was more cautious and gave no figures for 1979 or 1980 G.N.P. In the previous edition it estimated G.N.P. (in average 1977–79 prices) as $2,290 million in 1978 and $2,590 million ($170 per caput) in 1979.

For much of the period since 1960 Afghanistan's economy has been stagnant. During the 1960s and early 1970s the rate of growth in real terms was below the rate of population increase. The years 1970 and 1971 marked the nadir as the serious droughts caused a 20 per cent drop in wheat production and killed livestock in large numbers. Since then economic performance has picked up. Better rains pushed the annual wheat crop to about 3 million tons so that in a normal year Afghanistan should be self-sufficient in food production. Industrial performance improved. Capital inflows pushed the foreign exchange reserves from U.S. $22 million at the end of 1974 to $411 million at the end of 1979 and led to an appreciation in the value of the afghani to 43 per U.S. dollar by late 1979, compared with 80.50 in 1972/73. By the late 1970s the time had come for a serious attempt to be made at planning Afghanistan's future economic development, taking into account all the disadvantages imaginable in a poor, land-locked country. However, then came the foreign invasion to make a mockery of all these projects.

THE START OF ECONOMIC PLANNING

Prior to the 1930s Afghanistan was still in the Middle Ages as far as economic development was concerned. The great armies and trade caravans of ancient times had struggled over it, but modern development had ignored it because, with the coming of sea power from the fifteenth century onwards, there were less arduous ways to India and China. Even the railway age bypassed Afghanistan. Only in 1932 when the Banke Milli Afghan (National Bank) was established did modern economic development begin. Before that the only modern features were the Government's workshops in Kabul chiefly providing for the needs of the army, and one small hydroelectric station. The formation of the bank gave an impetus to the foundation of private companies. These were mainly dealing in trade for karakul and lamb skins and wool, but textile and sugar companies were also set up. However, progress was slow and even at the end of the Second World War, internal trade was carried by caravan and inter-city roads were not paved. Only about 20,000 kilowatts of power was produced and few consumer goods were made locally.

In 1946 the new Prime Minister, Shah Mahmud Khan, began what he wanted to develop as an ambitious economic development programme using Afghanistan's agricultural exports as its base. But he failed for lack of finance. The next attempt to start economic planning came when Muhammad Daud took over as Prime Minister in 1953. Again, he ran into problems in finding foreign finance, and Washington refused to lend general support to the first five-year plan which got under way in 1957. It was ready only to provide money for individual projects. However, the Prime Minister, Daud, neatly sidestepped that problem by improving relations with the Soviet Union and delicately playing off the U.S.S.R. and the U.S.A. so that the U.S.A. closely followed and almost matched Soviet aid to Afghanistan. Moscow was prepared to underwrite a general five-year exercise. In all, between 1957 and 1972 the Soviet Union offered more than $900 million to support these plans, that is nearly 60 per cent of foreign aid, although some Western experts say that the sums promised were larger than the money handed over. The U.S.A. provided the second largest amount of aid but it usually offered better terms.

The first three plans (from 1957 to 1961 for the first; 1962 to 1967 for the second; 1968 to 1972 for the third) cannot really be described as an attempt to control the whole economy, though the Government described the economy as its "guided economy" and later "mixed guided economy". The plans offered a series of projects basically to improve the infrastructure and bring Afghanistan at least closer to the twentieth century.

The first plan set the pattern by putting great emphasis on communications, particularly road building and the establishment of air links, both national and international. In addition, 32 industrial projects were due to begin, though not all were started. The achievements of the first plan were patchy. Its great merits were the attempt to establish planned economy development, to tap external sources of finance, and at the same time to realize the need for internal finance. The great drawback was that this daring in planning was not matched by daring or so much success in implementation.

By the time of the second plan, the difficulties of the planning were beginning to be apparent, at least to outsiders. Proper cost-benefit studies were neglected, and the impact of projects on income and job opportunities was virtually ignored. The second plan also attempted to expand the role of the public sector because private industry was not big enough to undertake developments in power, gas, supply and making of cement, chemicals, and other important capital intensive industry. One problem which was not properly examined beforehand was where to find competent operators and managers to run the plants. At the start of the third plan, the Government reviewed the achievements and the lessons of the first two plans and emphasized the need to turn to more quickly yielding projects. However, in practice this proved more difficult.

For all this, 16 years of planning and public investment of Afs. 53,000 million produced an impressive list of achievements. Before planning started there were no paved roads in Afghanistan, few permanent bridges and air transport was almost non-existent. By the end of the third plan, in 1972, the country had 2,780 kilometres of paved roads and two international and 29 local airports. Dams and bridges were constructed. Registration of motor vehicles in Kabul went up from 16,000 in 1962 to 52,000 in 1971. In industry, production of cotton cloth quadrupled to 62 million metres, cement making and shoe manufacturing began, and output of the soap, sugar and coal industries increased by between 100 and 300 per cent. Electricity production rose almost nine-fold to 422.6 million kilowatt hours. Natural gas production was started and reached 2,635 million cubic metres annually, much of which is exported to the Soviet Union. There were big achievements in education where the number of schools rose from 804 to nearly 4,000, teachers from 4,000 to 20,000, and students from 125,000 to 700,000. Industrial employment rose from 18,000 in 1962 to nearly 27,000 in 1971. More than 60 private enterprise industries were set up employing nearly 5,000 people.

The fourth plan was published in 1973 and looked again to Soviet help as its mainstay but the planning procedure was disrupted by the coup and actual planning was on an annual basis. By 1976 an ambitious seven-year plan was announced, but before it had time to take effect President Daud was overthrown in the April 1978 coup and the future of the plan became uncertain.

THE ECONOMY IN THE LATE 1970s

Agriculture

Agriculture is in normal times the most important contributor to Afghanistan's economy, providing half the national income and four-fifths of the country's exports. Of the total land area of about 65 million hectares, 8 million hectares are considered to be arable, only half of which are cultivated every year. Experts estimate that a mere 2.6 million hectares of irrigated land provide 85 per cent of the crops. Irrigation is often primitive but ingenious. The impact of lack of water was shown sharply in 1971 when there was severe drought as a result of which the production of wheat, the main crop, dropped from nearly 2.5 million tons to below 2 million tons and millions of important livestock were slaughtered. It took two years for the crops to recover. Because of the large migrations of people, it is foolish to try to give specific annual production figures, but Afghanistan is capable of producing over 3 million tons of wheat a year, 160,000 tons of cotton, 400,000 tons of rice, 800,000 tons of maize, up to 400,000 tons of barley, about 1 million tons of fruit, 100,000 tons of sugar beet and 65,000 tons of sugar cane.

The severe drought of 1970 and 1971 is estimated to have cost between 30 per cent and 50 per cent of Afghanistan's livestock which in 1970 were estimated at 6.5 million karakul sheep, 15 million ordinary sheep, 3.7 million cattle, 3.2 million goats and 500,000 horses. By 1975 they were estimated to have increased to the 1970 levels. There was a 9 per cent shortfall in the agricultural production plan for 1979/80. In particular, the number of livestock declined considerably and it has been estimated that it will take four or five years to restore the cattle herds to an adequate level.

Industry

Although its series of economic plans set up modern industry and took Afghanistan out of the handicraft age, the contribution of industry to the G.D.P. is small, less than 10 per cent. Handicrafts, especially carpet making and weaving, still contribute more to the G.D.P. than modern industry. Industrial employment has hardly changed since 1971 when it was estimated that 27,000 people had paid jobs out of the total working population of about 4 million. Even the oldest established and largest industry, cotton textiles, is not able yet to produce enough cloth—output was 43.3 million metres in 1980/81—to satisfy domestic demand. Cement production fell to 87,200 metric tons in 1980/81 which was higher than the 1971 trough of 73,000 tons, but well below the 1966 peak of 174,000 tons. Changes in construction activity are responsible for these fluctuations. In 1972, owing to government concern to expand new industries, an Industrial Development Bank was established. The Daud Government said that it was anxious to encourage private enterprise, but subject to government surveillance.

Mining

Afghanistan has extensive mining resources of coal, salt, chrome, iron ore, silver, gold, fluorite, talc, mica, copper and lapis lazuli, but the country's problems of access and transport have posed questions about whether it is worth mining them. The most successful find has been of natural gas, most of which is piped to the Soviet Union in payment for imports and debts. The annual volume of these exports was projected to double when operations at the new Jarquduq field commence. Production may soon rise to 4,000 million cubic metres per year, compared with 2,790.3 million in 1980/81 but even gas prodution has had problems due to rebel activity. However, unless new gas finds are made the existing fields may be exhausted some time before the turn of the century.

Iron ore reserves at Hajigak in Bamian province, with 1,700 million tons of high-grade ore (62 per cent), are the most promising of recent discoveries. However, although the ore would fetch a good price, much of it is located at heights of 3,500 metres or more. Moreover, there would be high costs involved in exporting it from remote Afghanistan, which has no sea-port of its own, nor even rail lines. There were hopes that the iron and natural gas could be used to make steel, but this has not been realized. Another potentially important mineral is copper, with estimated reserves of 4.7 million tons of ore. Provision to open up these deposits has been made in the 1979–84 Five-Year Plan. Two small oil-fields with total estimated reserves of 12 million tons have also been discovered in the north of the country.

Trade

Afghanistan's trade is small and it has become increasingly dependent on the Soviet Union, its northern neighbour. This is because of the mounting difficulties of using land routes to Pakistan and India, Afghanistan's principal trade outlets, both for fresh fruit going to the sub-continent and for other goods going beyond. In addition, turmoil in Iran made trade via the west difficult, and, of course, any organized road traffic would have to run the risks of rebel attack.

Through the 1970s, the balance of payments showed a surplus, thanks to tourism and remittances from Afghans working abroad. The main export items are fresh fruit and vegetables to Pakistan and India, natural gas to the Soviet Union, karakul to the fur markets of Europe, and carpets and rugs, raw cotton and dried fruits and nuts, which are just beginning to make inroads into the developed country markets. Imports include machinery, petroleum, pharmaceuticals, textiles and other consumer goods. Afghanistan is in the happy position, practically unique to the poor non-oil-producing countries, in that its oil-producing neighbours, Iran and the Soviet Union, have provided it with oil at low prices. Exports of natural gas meant that Afghanistan used to have a surplus on its energy account, yet figures supplied to the ADB show petroleum imports worth $124 million but no figures for gas exports.

Before the Soviet involvement, Afghanistan's main trading partner was the Soviet Union, which in 1977/78 provided 26 per cent of imports and took 37 per cent of the country's exports. Trade turnover between the two countries increased by 44 per cent in 1979, compared with the previous year, and further huge increases were planned. According to Kabul Radio, trade with the U.S.S.R. was $670 million in 1980 and this was expected to increase to $2,000 million in 1981. Thus dependence on the Soviet Union increased as other countries were either unable or unwilling to export their products, and as foreign aid from the West began to decrease and then to disappear.

Since 1978 the Afghan Chamber of Commerce and Industry had acted as the sole agent for the twenty-two importers' associations and had controlled all import business. However, in order to encourage the private sector, the Government returned these exclusive export rights to the private merchants in 1980.

Money and Finance

The slow growth of the economy has created difficulties in raising the Government's internal revenues and the budget deficit has risen steadily. Half of the ordinary revenues come from indirect taxes. The next largest contributor is revenue from natural gas (21 per cent in 1979 and expected to reach 34 per cent in 1980). Only 10 per cent of the revenues comes from direct taxes. In 1978/79 domestic revenues were estimated at Afs. 15,684 million, leaving a huge deficit of Afs. 9,196 million, a rise of Afs. 2,400 million. Highest expenditure was on defence, accounting for almost 40 per cent. Social services were allocated 34 per cent of the budget.

In 1975 the Government decreed that all banks in Afghanistan had been nationalized in an attempt to bring about a more organized banking system. The move was directed at the Banke Milli Afghan, as the other banks were already under Government control. The chief bank is the Da Afghanistan Bank, the central bank which also does commercial business.

Tourism

In the 1970s tourism was an important contributor to Afghanistan's earnings, raising up to $10 million a year from visitors who numbered between 90,000 and 100,000 a year. The peak was 117,000 in 1977. Afghanistan's location off the main air routes of the world and its poor hotel facilities (apart from two international hotels in Kabul) meant that it was not able to tap the lucrative Western package holiday market. Its main tourist visitors were travellers going overland to or from Pakistan and India. The development of tourism suffered from the change of regime and internal unrest, which caused the number of tourists almost to disappear, as overland travel was too dangerous and even Kabul became unsafe for visitors.

The Seven-year Plan and After

In 1976 President Daud inaugurated an ambitious Seven-Year Economic and Social Development Plan intended to make major strides towards solving the problems of poverty and underdevelopment. The Plan is academic now because of the change of governments. Given the political setbacks to the economy, its targets—to increase the G.N.P. by more than 50 per cent by 1983, with annual growth rates of 6.3 per cent or double those of the past—also seem hopelessly optimistic.

Two things about the Plan are still worth noting. It aimed to bring Afghanistan into the railway age, through a U.S. $2,000 million project to build a 1,800-kilometres system linking with Iran in the west and with Pakistan, at Spin Boldak, in the east. Economically, it was a doubtful venture; politically, it is now dead because of the distrust of Afghanistan's neighbours. The other factor was that Daud saw the main thrust of development effort coming from the public sector and the main assistance coming from the U.S.S.R.

Over the past half-century, governments in Kabul had tried hard to lay the foundation of a modern state. The now much-abused Daud had introduced the notion of planning and been instrumental in securing Moscow's help. Some 3,000 kilometres of properly metalled roads were built and air links were established. Of course, plenty of questions can be asked about the efficiency of the plan expenditure. For example, more than 30 per cent of the money from the first three plans went on building the giant highways which opened up the country—some of them truly magnificent works of engineering like the Salang tunnel—but what use were they in helping local people living in scattered villages to get their crops to market? Although 85 per cent of the Afghans live in rural areas, although agriculture contributes 50 per cent of G.N.P. and although 90 per cent of export earnings have traditionally come from agricultural products, a much smaller proportion of the plan expenditure went to help agriculture or livestock, and little of the money went to the smaller farmers. Of the Afs. 12,500 million spent on the agricultural sector, half went on two huge irrigation projects. More attention to feeder roads to get crops to market, to small irrigation schemes and to agricultural extension work might have been better to increase agricultural production and to bring the ordinary Afghans into the market economy.

In addition, a lot of money was poured into grandiose schemes which were out of place in a poor and sparsely populated country. Qandahar airport, an American-aided project, never had enough traffic even when tourists and others could move about freely. Other schemes, such as the French-assisted Balkh textile mill, exceeded their original budget. Sometimes this was because the Kabul planners were always working in an ideal world and tended to forget their own and the country's slow pace. Yet other ventures were based on out-of-date technology, including the Soviet built Mazar-i-Sharif fertilizer factory.

Nevertheless, by the end of the Daud era, economists who looked at Afghanistan made two points. Firstly, there was hope of building a twentieth-century country with the prospect of prosperity ahead of it. There was scope for greatly increased agricultural yields and export earnings. Tree and field crops and livestock all have potential that has not been realized. Cottön has proved competitive in world markets, fresh fruit from the orchards of Afghanistan was in demand around the Gulf, while dried fruits, such as raisins, could be marketed worldwide. Mineral reserves are yet to be opened up. Industry, especially that devoted to the processing of agricultural products, offered increased value-added as well as jobs in the modern sector.

Secondly, though, all these projects would take time. In spite of progress, Afghanistan has a long way to go. Simple statistics tell one side of the story. According to comparative figures published in 1982 by the Asian Development Bank, 77.8 per cent of Afghans in 1980 were employed in agriculture, the fourth highest figure of all Asian countries. In terms of adult literacy, Afghanistan was well behind with a literacy rate of 11 per cent. (The next most illiterate country in the Asian-Pacific region is Solomon Islands with literacy of 19 per cent.) School enrolment does not offer any early hope of a dramatic improvement. Only 28 per cent of Afghan children enrolled for primary school and only 5 per cent for secondary school. Other social indicators also present a grim picture. Average life at birth in 1975–80 was only 40.5 years, the lowest in Asia and the Pacific (except for the special case of Kampuchea), infant mortality is 185 per 1,000 live births, the highest in the region (having actually increased from 182 per 1,000 in 1970). Only 20 per cent of the Afghans in urban areas and only 3 per cent in rural areas have access to safe water.

The statistics do not tell the whole story of the struggle that will be necessary. Socially, in tribal and nomadic Afghanistan, the barriers to progress are as high as the Hindu Kush mountains which Babur the Mogul called "the theatre of Heaven".

THE ECONOMY AND SOCIAL BENEFITS

The pattern of society in Afghanistan is remarkably static. Though there is some marginal movement, the tendency is for a son, if he survives (since the child mortality rate up to the age of 5 is 50 per cent), to follow in his father's footsteps. Outside the cities, the chances are that he will not have any schooling and that he will not have any adolescence and hardly any childhood. As soon as he is big enough to walk and talk, a son can be usefully employed looking after sheep or other animals.

To make any breakthrough the authorities would have somehow to penetrate the traditional hostility to government. Officials are usually met by a "mud curtain" of the village because of the suspicion—justifiable in the past—that the officials have come to extract something from the village.

There is also the problem of the role of women. In 1959, Prime Minister Daud passed a law saying that women no longer had to veil themselves. Yet the status of women has hardly changed. When a boy is born, he is greeted with bonfires and pistol shots signifying rejoicing that another man, a warrior, has entered the world. Yet when a girl comes into the world, the reaction is more likely to be one of shame. Educational opportunities for girls have increased, although of the roll of 720,000 pupils in all educational institutions in 1970, only 96,000 were girls. In village schools, there were only 13,000 girls. Of an estimated 100,000 Afghan women who have finished some kind of schooling only about 5,000 are employed, mainly in the professions and the majority of these in teaching. There are hardly any women in industry—because of the high unemployment rate.

In many ways, the Afghanistan that entered the 1980s was ripe for a reform or revolution that would tip the balance towards the less privileged members of society, especially the poor, the landless and women. This was the stage onto which the Soviet Union and its soldiers stepped. Although Afghanistan in many ways seemed ripe for revolution, the established system had its strengths and posed difficulties. The Kabul Government and its Soviet masters made the most of them. The Soviet operation came in two stages: firstly, after the Saur Revolution in which Daud was overthrown, when the new ruler, Nur Mohammed Taraki, invited hosts of advisers from Moscow as he tried to remodel the economy and then, when Moscow invaded, to get rid of Hafizullah Amin and put in 85,000 soldiers to support Babrak Karmal.

The Taraki Government quickly formulated plans to tackle the problems of those people so far unaffected by economic change. A Five-Year Plan started in 1979. This proposed a total investment of Afs. 105,000 million, 25 per cent of which would be allocated to agriculture in order to triple output. Investment in industry (in 1979 employing only 12 per cent of the working population) and mining was to amount to Afs. 43,654 million and should increase the contribution of industry to G.N.P. from 23 per cent to 41 per cent. The Plan envisaged the comprehensive development of both heavy and light industry based on the effective utilization of natural resources. Towards the end of 1978 it decreed important new measures: a major land reform limiting families to 15 irrigated acres each; a decree remitting debts of peasants; and dowry rules outlawing payment of more than Afs. 300 (about U.S. $8) in dowries and raising the minimum age for marriage to 16 years for women and 18 years for men. These measures caused head-on conflict with the powers of the old village and tribal order. The wisdom of such a direct attack could clearly be doubted. Given the distrust of officialdom it was not surprising that the reforms were ignored or circumvented. However, the Government claimed at the beginning of 1980 that there were already almost 1,200 agricultural co-operatives in the country. The Five-Year Plan aims for a total of 4,500, uniting over one million people.

The room for manoeuvre economically is likely to be reduced with the return of large numbers of Afghan workers from Iran. The remittances from these workers had allowed the country to run a growing trade deficit. Without this cushion of about U.S. $100 million each year Afghanistan will have to rely even more on foreign help to pursue its economic plans. Western protests over the presence of Soviet troops in the country have affected the amount of aid coming into Afghanistan. The 1979/80 budget called for a 15 per cent decrease in development spending, which seemed to indicate that previously pledged aid would not necessarily be forthcoming. In January 1980 the World Bank stopped disbursing funds for development projects in Afghanistan as Bank representatives had been unable to supervise the projects. This decision affected the payment of U.S. $115 million out of a total $227 million which had been approved. Socialist countries are expected to contribute 66 per cent of the foreign aid needed for basic projects in the 1979–84 Plan.

The unreality of all the plans of the new regime and their Soviet advisers became apparent by the middle of 1981. Links with the West were almost completely cut. Bright Afghan students, who would in the past have gone to universities in the West, now went to Soviet universities. The whole education system had been remoulded to fit an Eastern European system, with much emphasis on the virtues of Communism. The judicial system was also reformed. Even Western planners and technical advisers, attached to the United Nations, were weeded out and replaced by East Europeans or Indians. Daily, reports appeared in 1980 and 1981 of new co-operation agreements signed between Kabul and Moscow.

For all that, however, the life and the economy actually controlled from the capital was limited. The rebels opposed to the Kabul–Moscow axis had a free run of the countryside, and even towns like Qandahar, the second largest city, had their "no go" areas as far as the Kabul regime was concerned. The traditional economy, however, did suffer, a fact which was marked by the outflow of refugees. Much of the money sent from abroad never reached the Afghan people. In addition, by early 1981 it was clear that the Soviet leaders were trying to use food as a weapon against the rebellion. Food shortages became acute as the tribal groups preferred fighting to farming and as the regime destroyed grain stores, cattle and crops to try to bring dissidents to heel. By the middle of 1981 this began to cause a drift from the countryside to the towns, bringing new upheaval and the deterioration of what little remained of the traditional ways.

In Manila in April 1982 Kabul pleaded for a resumption of aid. Fazl Haque Khaliqyar, First Deputy Minister of Finance, said: "We find it regrettable and unfair that the flow of aid to our country should remain suspended even by international financial institutions because of political considerations and pressures". He spoke of Democratic Afghanistan's righteous cause". However, the President of the Asian Development Bank, Masao Fujioka, said that aid to Afghanistan would have to wait until the situation was "more conducive".

Total aid fell from more than $100 million per year in the late 1970s to only $34 million in 1980, with the prospect of further falls. Flows of funds from the industrialized countries, from multilateral agencies such as the World Bank and from the oil producers also dropped. In 1977, before Daud was killed,

Afghanistan received more than $20 million from OPEC; by 1980, such aid was only $1.5 million.

The various pressures on the economy were beginning to tell. Khaliqyar put a brave face on things and claimed that there had been a 1.6 per cent increase in G.N.P. in the Afghan year 1359 (1980/81). He said, however, that in that year agriculture had declined by about 1 per cent and industry had been "relatively stagnant", so his optimism may not have been justified. In 1360 (1981/82) he promised greater growth, with a rise of 9.5 per cent in industry and 3.5 per cent in agriculture. He mentioned the support which the Government had given, including provision of inputs, setting of remunerative prices and ensuring of bank credit. Yet he conceded that it was an uphill struggle because of recession and what he termed "the destructive activities of counter-revolutionaries supported by international imperialism and regional reactionaries".

The impact of these pressures showed in both the statistics and the policies. Figures supplied by the Asian Development Bank showed a trade deficit which reached $300 million in 1979 and was $200 million in the following year. In spite of increased sales to the Soviet Union, which took 95 per cent of Afghanistan's natural gas (though at lower prices than Moscow received for sales of its own gas to Western Europe), and in spite of increased Soviet aid—$240 million in 1980—the budget and balance of-payments positions were strained. In addition, the interlock between Afghanistan and the Soviet Union meant that most of the new project aid was for schemes, such as in coal and natural gas development-which would benefit the Soviet Union.

The Prime Minister, Sultan Ali Kishtmand, admitted to the Kabul press that the financial position was "rather tough", with revenues down and expenditures up. Some sources said that revenue collection had come to a virtual standstill in some provinces because of rebel activity. If taxes were levied in such areas, they were levied by the rebels. Khaliqyar said that Afghanistan's convertible foreign exchange reserves had declined by 16 per cent in the first 10 months of the 1981/82 financial year. He also said that "in the 1361 (1982/83) Development Plan several concessions are also being provided for promoting greater investment in the private sector". It was a good sign that the attempts to foist Marxism on a traditional people were acknowledged to be failing. The Government had to abandon its efforts at rural reform. In August 1981 it reversed its programme of land reform, and in February 1982 it dropped other rural measures and promised local tribal leaders control over internal affairs. This they had had anyway, so the Government's move was an attempt to woo the tribes back within Kabul's framework.

STATISTICAL SURVEY

AREA AND POPULATION

Area	Estimated Mid-Year Population			Density (per sq. km.)
	1977	1978	1979	1979
652,090 sq. km.*	14,795,733	15,158,632	15,551,358†	23.8

* 251,773 sq. miles.

† Result of Afghanistan's first national census, conducted on June 23rd, 1979. It includes an estimated nomadic population of 2,500,000.

Population (official mid-year estimates): 15,950,000 in 1980; 16,360,000 in 1981.

Note: In February 1982 it was estimated that over 2,600,000 Afghan refugees were living in Pakistan.

PROVINCES*

(Census of June 23rd, 1979)

	AREA (sq. km.)	POPULATION	DENSITY (per sq. km.)	CAPITAL (with population)
Kabul	17,548	1,864,000	106.2	Kabul (913,164)
Parwan	11,269	755,285	67.0	Charikar (22,424)
Bamian	17,411	268,517	15.4	Bamian (7,355)
Ghazni	23,373	646,623	27.7	Ghazni (30,425)
Paktika	19,333	245,229	12.7	Sharan (1,398)
Paktia	10,286	497,503	48.4	Gardiz (9,550)
Nangarhar	7,614	745,986	98.0	Jalalabad (53,915)
Laghman	7,209	310,751	43.1	Meterlam (3,987)
Kunar	10,477	250,132	23.9	Hasan Abad (2,089)
Badakhshan	47,393	497,758	10.5	Faizabad (9,098)
Takhar	12,373	519,752	42.0	Taluqan (19,925)
Baghlan	17,106	493,882	28.9	Baghlan (39,228)
Kunduz	7,825	555,437	71.0	Kunduz (53,251)
Samangan	16,220	272,584	16.8	Uiback (4,938)
Balkh	11,833	569,255	48.1	Mazar-i-Sharif (103,372)
Jawzjan	25,548	588,609	23.0	Shibarghan (18,995)
Fariab	22,274	582,705	26.2	Maymana (38,251)
Badghis	21,854	233,613	10.7	Qala-i-nau (5,340)
Herat	61,301	769,111	12.5	Herat (140,323)
Farah	47,778	234,621	4.9	Farah (18,797)
Neemroze	41,347	103,634	2.5	Zarunj (6,477)
Helmand	61,816	517,645	8.4	Bost (21,600)
Qandahar	47,666	567,204	11.9	Qandahar (178,409)
Zabul	17,289	179,362	10.4	Qalat (5,946)
Uruzgan	29,289	444,168	15.2	Tareenkoot (3,362)
Ghor	38,658	337,992	8.7	Cheghcheran (2,974)
TOTAL	652,090	13,051,358	20.0	

* Population figures refer to settled inhabitants only, excluding kuchies (nomads), estimated at 2,500,000 for the whole country.

PRINCIPAL CITIES

(population at June 23rd, 1979)

Kabul (capital)	913,164	Kunduz	53,251
Qandahar	178,409	Baghlan	39,228
Herat	140,323	Maymana	38,251
Mazar-i-Sharif	103,372	Pul-i-Khomri	31,101
Jalalabad	53,915	Ghazni	30,425

Births and Deaths (1979): Birth rate 48.1 per 1,000; death rate 23.3 per 1,000.

ECONOMICALLY ACTIVE POPULATION*

(ISIC Major Divisions, persons aged 8 years and over)

	1979 Census
Agriculture, forestry, hunting and fishing	2,369,481
Mining and quarrying	59,339
Manufacturing	423,373
Electricity, gas and water	11,354
Construction	51,086
Trade, restaurants and hotels	137,860
Transport, storage and communications	66,243
Other services	749,345
Total	3,868,081

* Figures refer to settled population only and exclude persons seeking work for the first time.

AGRICULTURE

LAND USE

('000 hectares)

	1973	1976	1979
Arable land	7,910*	7,910	7,910*
Land under permanent crops	138*	138*	140*
Permanent meadows and pastures	50,000*	50,000*	50,000*
Forest and woodland	1,900	1,900	1,900*
Other land and inland water	4,802	4,802	4,800
Total	64,750	64,750	64,750

* FAO estimate.

Source: FAO, *Production Yearbook*.

PRINCIPAL CROPS

(year ending March 20th)

	Area ('000 hectares)			Production ('000 metric tons)		
	1978/79	1979/80	1980/81	1978/79	1979/80	1980/81
Wheat	2,348	2,162	2,192	2,813	2,663	2,750
Maize	482	472.3	477	780	759.8	797
Rice (paddy)	210	205.8	212	428	439	461
Barley	310	303.8	306	325	318.4	321
Seed cotton	112	84.1	45	132	105	65
Sugar beet	4.9	3.2	2	73	70	35
Sugar cane	3.8	3.7	4	64	63.7	70
Vegetables	94.0	130.3	95	766	1,069.2	828
Fruits	140.2	139.2	142.6	824	836	891
Oil seeds	50	59	59	35	42	43

LIVESTOCK
('000)

	1976/77*	1977/78	1978/79	1979/80	1980/81
Cattle	3,835	3,650	3,730	3,710	3,710
Sheep†	22,000	20,244	19,075	18,400	18,700
Goats	3,000	3,000	3,000	2,885	2,850
Horses	370	392*	400	1,730 (Horses, Asses and Mules)	1,730
Asses	1,250	1,300	1,300		
Mules	26	48	40		
Buffaloes	35	n.a.	n.a.	n.a.	n.a.
Camels	290	300	300	270	265
Poultry	19,690	6,000	6,200	6,400	6,400

* FAO estimate.

† Including Karakul sheep, numbering 4.4 million in 1979/80, and 4.5 million in 1980/81.

Sources: FAO, *Production Yearbook*, and Central Statistics Office, Kabul.

LIVESTOCK PRODUCTS
('000 metric tons)

	1978	1979*	1980*
Beef and veal	67	67	67
Mutton and lamb	103	99	100
Goats' meat	25*	25	25
Poultry meat	11*	11	11
Cows' milk	533	640	640
Sheep's milk	225*	230	230
Goats' milk	48*	48	48
Butter	5.6*	5.8	5.8
Cheese	9.8*	9.9	9.9
Hen eggs	16.8*	16.9	16.9
Honey	3.6†	3.6†	3.6
Wool: greasy	26.5*	27.0	27.5
Wool: clean	14.3*	14.5	14.8
Cattle and buffalo hides	11.1*	11.2	11.4
Sheep skins	16.1*	16.8	17.1
Goat skins	3.8*	3.8	3.8

* FAO estimate. † Unofficial figure.

Source: FAO, *Production Yearbook*.

FORESTRY

ROUNDWOOD REMOVALS
(FAO estimates, '000 cubic metres, excluding bark)

	Coniferous (soft wood)			Broadleaved (hard wood)			Total		
	1977	1978	1979	1977	1978	1979	1977	1978	1979
Sawlogs, veneer logs and logs for sleepers*	820	820	820	36	36	36	856	856	856
Other industrial wood	122	125	129	488	501	515	610	626	644
Fuel wood	1,830	1,879	1,931	4,381	4,500	4,622	6,211	6,379	6,553
Total	2,772	2,824	2,880	4,905	5,037	5,173	7,677	7,861	8,053

* Assumed to be unchanged from 1977.

Source: FAO, *Yearbook of Forest Products*.

SAWNWOOD PRODUCTION
('000 cubic metres, including boxboards)

	1971	1972	1973	1974*	1975*	1976*
Coniferous	345	305	360*	360	310	380
Broadleaved	60	55	50	50	20	20
TOTAL	405	360	410	410	330	400

* FAO estimate.

1977-79: Annual production as in 1976 (FAO estimates).

Source: FAO, *Yearbook of Forest Products.*

Inland Fishing (1964–80): Total catch 1,500 metric tons each year (FAO estimate).

MINING

(Twelve months ending March 20th)

		1977/78	1978/79	1979/80	1980/81
Hard coal	'000 metric tons	170.3	218.2	131.9	118.7
Salt (unrefined)	,, ,, ,,	77.7	81.1	67.6	37.1
Natural gas	million cu. metres	2,548	2,461	2,327	2,790.3

INDUSTRY

SELECTED PRODUCTS
(Twelve months ending March 20th)

		1977/78	1978/79	1979/80	1980/81
Ginned cotton	'000 metric tons	41.5	45.3	29.4	22.9
Cotton fabrics	million metres	76.8	76.6	63.3	43.3
Woollen fabrics*	'000 metres	400.0	405.2	401.0	405.3
Rayon fabrics	,, ,,	29,700.6	23,100.0	21,300.0	14,800.0
Cement	'000 metric tons	149.7	126.5	99.3	87.2
Electricity†	million kWh.	776.1	845.4	907.8	958.8
Wheat flour	'000 metric tons	80.9	97.0	122.6	113.1
Refined sugar	,, ,, ,,	11.2	10.8	8.6	2.7
Vegetable oil	,, ,, ,,	9.9	10.4	9.6	6.5
Nitrogenous fertilizers‡	,, ,, ,,	99.7	105.7	106.2	106.3

* Including blankets.
† Production for public use, excluding industrial establishments generating electricity for their own use.
‡ Production in terms of nitrogen.

FINANCE

100 puls (puli) = 2 krans = 1 afghani (Af.).
Coins: 25 and 50 puls; 1, 2 and 5 afghanis.
Notes: 10, 20, 50, 100, 500 and 1,000 afghanis.

Exchange rates (June 1982): £1 sterling = 118.21 afghanis; U.S. $1 = 68.25 afghanis.
1,000 afghanis = £8.46 = $14.65.

Note: Multiple exchange rates were in operation before March 1963. Between 1956 and 1963 the official base rate was U.S. $1 = 20.00 afghanis. In March 1963 a single official rate of $1 = 45.00 afghanis was introduced. This remained in force until May 1979. The year-end exchange rate (afghanis per U.S. dollar) was: 42.25 in 1979; 45.85 in 1980; 50.60 in 1981. In terms of sterling, the official rate was £1 = 108.00 afghanis from November 1967 to August 1971; and £1 = 117.26 afghanis from December 1971 to June 1972.

BUDGET

(million afghanis, twelve months ending September 21st)

Revenue	1976/77	1977/78	1978/79
Direct taxes	1,713	2,428	2,535
Indirect taxes	6,159	6,830	6,913
Revenue from monopolies and other enterprises	887	1,316	1,192
Natural gas revenue	2,336	1,510	2,637
Revenue from other property and services	2,179	2,357	1,954
Other revenue	676	480	1,224
Total Revenue	13,950	14,921	16,455

Expenditure	1976/77	1977/78	1978/79
Administration	1,223	1,255	1,690
Defence, Security	2,381	2,656	3,007
Social services	2,254	2,538	3,186
Economic services	1,219	870	985
Total Ministries	7,077	7,319	8,868
Foreign debt service	1,320	2,087	2,493
Subsidies (exchange, etc.)	2,771	2,532	1,024
Total Ordinary	11,168	11,938	12,385
Development Budget	5,060	5,200	6,845

1980/81 (estimates in million afghanis): Revenue: internal sources 23,478, grants-in-aid from U.S.S.R. 1,735, loans and project assistance 8,546, total revenue 33,759; Expenditure: ministries' allocation 19,213, development budget 14,546, total expenditure 33,759.

BANK OF AFGHANISTAN RESERVES

(U.S. $ million at December)

	1975	1976	1977	1978	1979	1980
Gold*	39.35	39.35	39.69	40.02	42.97	270.32
IMF Special Drawing Rights	6.23	5.95	6.90	7.01	17.68	15.46
Reserve Position in IMF	—	—	10.02	11.69	12.42	19.22
Foreign Exchange	80.32	124.97	258.90	371.86	411.11	336.49
Total	125.90	170.27	315.51	430.58	484.18	641.49

* National valuation. In March 1980 gold was revalued at U.S. $300 per troy ounce (31.1 grammes).

Source: IMF, *International Financial Statistics.*

MONEY SUPPLY

(million afghanis at March 21st)

	1977	1978	1979	1980	1981
Currency outside banks	15,232	17,968	22,046	28,624	33,545
Private sector deposits at Bank of Afghanistan	3,412	5,179	5,596	5,993	5,512
Demand deposits at commercial banks	1,339	1,427	1,304	1,814	1,877
Total Money	19,983	24,574	28,946	36,431	40,934

Source: IMF, *International Financial Statistics.*

COST OF LIVING

(twelve months ending March 20th. Base: 1961/62=100)

	1975/76	1976/77	1977/78	1978/79	1979/80*	1980/81
Cereals	308.6	303.5	351.2	366.2	113.2	105.1
Meat	368.6	389.3	399.4	385.7	100.8	123.3
Fruits	305.9	361.7	358.9	390.3	118.2	109.1
Vegetables	335.3	349.6	349.3	350.7	122.5	99.3
TOTAL (incl. others)	298.2	300.8	335.6	346.1	112.2	109.6

* Base: 1978/79=100.

NATIONAL ACCOUNTS

('000 million afghanis at 1978 prices, twelve months ending March 20th)

GROSS NATIONAL PRODUCT BY ECONOMIC ACTIVITY

	1976/77	1977/78	1978/79	1979/80
Agriculture, hunting, forestry and fishing	86.6	77.3	82.1	84.3
Mining Manufacturing Electricity, gas and water	29.3	30.4	33.2	30.7
Construction	5.7	6.9	8.6	7.6
Trade, restaurants and hotels	11.8	11.1	11.5	10.3
Transport, storage and communications	5.3	6.0	6.1	5.2
Other services	2.1	2.0	18.2	19.5
Foreign transactions	6.7	14.2		
G.N.P. IN MARKET PRICES	147.5	147.9	159.7	157.6

BALANCE OF PAYMENTS

(U.S. $ million, year ending March 20th)

	1976/77	1977/78	1978/79	1979/80
Merchandise exports f.o.b.	282.5	326.7	336.7	481.2
Merchandise imports c.i.f.	−349.8	−521.3	−638.6	−681.1
TRADE BALANCE	−67.3	−194.6	−301.9	−199.9
Travel (net)	30.2	38.0	28.0	7.0
Service component of project aid	−20.1	−18.9	−17.1	—
Official loans and grants: project	120.8	198.1	204.3	264.5
other	39.5	20.3	31.5	52.6
External public debt service	−28.2	−50.8	−58.0	−18.0
Other transactions (net)*	−10.0	163.4	212.0	17.5
CHANGES IN RESERVES, etc.	64.7	155.5	98.8	60.7

*Including errors and omissions.

EXTERNAL TRADE

(million afghanis, year ending March 20th)

	1975/76	1976/77	1977/78	1978/79	1979/80	1980/81
Imports c.i.f.*	20,442	18,313	24,214	32,021	29,860	23,482
Exports f.o.b.	13,085	16,320	15,296	15,120	21,476	32,362

* Including imports under commodity loans and grants from foreign countries and international organizations.

PRINCIPAL COMMODITIES

(distribution by SITC, U.S. $'000, year ending March 20th)

Imports c.i.f.*	1973/74	1974/75	1975/76	1976/77
Food and live animals	25,687	44,891	74,817	38,885
Sugar, sugar preparations and honey	13,139	26,285	39,494	12,790
Refined sugar	13,071	26,097	33,811	12,768
Coffee, tea, cocoa and spices	10,849	15,648	31,436	22,976
Tea	10,143	15,066	30,492	21,940
Crude materials (inedible) except fuels	4,540	7,552	5,412	5,896
Mineral fuels, lubricants, etc.	8,521	22,617	27,072	35,676
Petroleum and petroleum products	8,507	22,582	27,060	35,624
Petroleum products	8,386	22,510	27,000	35,597
Motor spirit (petrol), etc.	2,900	4,998	9,265	12,073
Lamp oil and white spirit (kerosene)	533	9,504	1,693	5,022
Distillate fuels	3,598	6,400	13,391	15,280
Animal and vegetable oils and fats	3,725	6,676	8,618	13,746
Chemicals	10,819	23,268	23,941	30,447
Medicinal and pharmaceutical products	4,998	6,353	6,704	9,062
Medicaments	n.a.	6,324	6,700	9,035
Manufactured fertilizers	n.a.	8,754	7,850	8,533
Nitrogenous fertilizers	n.a.	7,811	—	—
Phosphatic fertilizers	n.a.	943	7,850	8,533
Basic manufactures	49,022	85,448	92,024	93,888
Rubber manufactures	11,677	11,323	21,699	18,917
Tyres and tubes	11,612	11,298	21,631	18,761
Textile yarn, fabrics, etc.	27,520	60,040	49,983	55,159
Textile yarn and thread	14,730	13,276	10,661	10,422
Yarn of flax, ramie and true hemp	13,428	10,947	7,868	7,068
Woven cotton fabrics†	2,032	7,881	2,968	3,145
Other woven fabrics†	11,209	38,883	36,353	40,070
Fabrics of linen, ramie and true hemp†	4,940	11,927	8,998	6,353
Fabrics of synthetic fibres†	3,278	20,657	18,839	21,809
Machinery and transport equipment	16,208	19,229	34,482	29,025
Electrical machinery, apparatus, etc.	3,294	5,384	6,459	12,682
Transport equipment	9,750	10,499	24,351	10,912
Road motor vehicles and parts‡	9,403	9,812	n.a.	10,025
Buses	876	1,236	13,228	924
Miscellaneous manufactured articles	9,136	9,033	12,535	14,479
Total (incl. others)	127,560	223,794	268,313	264,183

* Excluding imports under commodity loans and grants for which the distribution by commodity is not known (U.S. $'000): 26 in 1973/74; 19,169 in 1974/75; 67,815 in 1975/76; 71,346 in 1976/77.

† Excluding narrow or special fabrics.

‡ Excluding tyres, engines and electrical parts.

1977/78 (U.S. $'000): Sugar 16,569; Tea 27,935; Edible oil 9,790; Medicaments 11,384; Tyres and tubes 19,308; Textile yarn and thread 18,199; Textile fabrics etc. 51,469; Road vehicles 10,760; Petroleum products 34,426; Total (incl. others) 321,347 (excl. project imports 143,789; other loans and grants 26,141).

[*continued on following page*

PRINCIPAL COMMODITIES—*continued*]

EXPORTS f.o.b.	1973/74	1974/75	1975/76	1976/77
Food and live animals	72,633	95,612	n.a.	94,326
Fruit and vegetables	69,779	n.a.	77,007	92,328
Fresh fruit and nuts (excl. oil nuts)*	29,310	44,423	29,746	46,684
Fresh grapes	8,808	18,488	13,235	15,108
Edible nuts	5,965	12,913	n.a.	23,480
Dried fruit*	47,134	n.a.	47,261	43,604
Dried grapes (raisins)	n.a.	37,238	n.a.	41,844
Crude materials (inedible) except fuels	n.a.	80,476	89,123	130,688
Hides, skins and fur skins	29,902	19,326	22,099	33,402
Hides and skins (undressed)	5,668	7,053	11,748	11,524
Hides of cattle, etc.	1,566	2,777	6,647	8,866
Fur skins (undressed)	18,239	12,273	10,351	21,878
Oil-seeds, oil nuts and oil kernels	3,597	4,133	8,251	12,912
Textile fibres and waste	13,640	40,876	39,538	68,728
Wool and other animal hair	n.a.	6,193	7,980	7,212
Cotton	7,221	34,883	31,558	60,758
Raw cotton (excl. linters)	7,221	34,883	31,558	60,706
Plants mainly for medicines, perfumes, etc.	2,395	8,980	10,436	5,814
Mineral fuels, lubricants, etc.	17,985	32,095	45,342	39,540
Natural gas	17,985	32,095	45,342	39,540
Basic manufactures	n.a.	n.a.	n.a.	30,654
Textile yarn, fabrics, etc.	15,898	20,077	18,469	30,084
Floor coverings, tapestries, etc.	14,474	19,900	16,785	24,024
Knotted carpets, carpeting and rugs	14,474	19,900	16,738	23,528
TOTAL (incl. others)	159,102	230,550	223,363	298,997

* Dried citrus fruit are included with "fresh fruit and nuts".

1977/78 (U.S. $'000): Fresh fruit and nuts 22,874; Dried fruit 83,840; Hides and skins 11,448; Fur skins 18,443; Raw cotton 55,040; Natural gas 39,349; Carpets and rugs 38,408; Total (incl. others) 313,374.

PRINCIPAL TRADING PARTNERS

(U.S. $ million)

IMPORTS	1977/78	1978/79
France	7.1	10.6
Germany, Federal Republic	31.9	46.6
India	24.5	39.1
Japan	101.5	123.5
Pakistan	12.5	16.9
United Kingdom	15.6	21.9
U.S.A.	16.8	30.9
TOTAL (incl. others)	497.7	681.7

EXPORTS	1977/78	1978/79
Germany, Federal Republic	17.4	22.5
India	24.0	37.5
Iran	2.4	2.1
Pakistan	36.7	41.1
Switzerland	7.8	8.9
United Kingdom	37.1	30.2
U.S.A.	15.0	11.3
TOTAL (incl. others)	314.4	321.8

1977/78 (U.S. $ million): Imports from U.S.S.R. 108.1, Iran 62.2; Exports to U.S.S.R. 117.4.

TOURISM

INTERNATIONAL TOURIST ARRIVALS BY COUNTRY

	1975	1976	1977	1978	1979
Australia	1,094	1,055	4,397	3,070	967
France	9,431	7,794	6,779	4,781	1,153
Germany, Federal Republic	8,649	8,907	9,085	7,496	1,817
India	8,717	8,521	11,158	9,744	4,350
Pakistan	13,648	20,213	35,105	23,663	10,126
United Kingdom	9,777	10,108	11,526	9,102	1,850
U.S.A.	9,501	8,950	9,011	6,389	1,039
Others	27,662	23,406	31,299	27,744	8,902
TOTAL	85,479	88,954	118,360	91,989	30,204

Receipts from tourism: U.S. $11 million in 1973; $12 million in 1974; $12 million in 1975.

TRANSPORT

CIVIL AVIATION

(twelve months ending March 20th)

	1977/78	1978/79	1979/80	1980/81
Kilometres flown ('000)	4,514	3,931	3,765	3,012
Passengers carried	97,100	69,800	104,000	86,199
Passenger-km. ('000)	298,200	206,200	238,068	173,855
Freight ton-km. ('000)	40,300	32,600	19,084	21,366
Cargo	13,300	14,000	7,070	n.a.
Mail	174	153	n.a.	n.a.

ROAD TRAFFIC

(motor vehicles in use)

	1976/77	1977/78	1978/79	1979/80	1980/81
Passenger cars	28,098	31,471	34,772	34,192	34,080
Commercial vehicles	19,298	29,737	34,435	27,555	28,714

COMMUNICATIONS MEDIA

Telephones in use: 20,831 in 1977/78.

Radio sets in use: *c.* 1,000,000 in 1977.

Television sets in use: 120,000 in January 1980.

EDUCATION

(1977/78)

	INSTITUTIONS	PUPILS
Primary schools	1,778	751,252
Village schools	1,593	121,070
Secondary schools (to Grade nine)	134	10,177
General high schools	199	99,563
Vocational high schools	27	10,816
Universities and Polytechnics	3	9,352

Note: Teachers in all institutions totalled 12,399 in 1975/76.

Source (unless otherwise stated): Central Statistics Office, Kabul.

THE CONSTITUTION

Immediately after the coup of April 27th, 1978 (the Saur Revolution), the 1977 Constitution was abolished. Both Taraki and Amin promised new constitutions but were removed from power before special commissions appointed by them had prepared any drafts. On April 21st, 1980, the Revolutionary Council ratified the Basic Principles of the Democratic Republic of Afghanistan. These are to remain valid until the ratification of the Constitution by a Loya Jirgah (National Assembly). The following is a summary of the Basic Principles.

General Provisions. The role of the State is to serve the well-being and prosperity of the people, to safeguard their peaceful life and to protect their rights.

The People's Democratic Party of Afghanistan, the party of the workers and the working class, is the country's guiding force. It aims to realize the ideals of the Great Saur Revolution for the creation of a new, just society.

Muslims are free to practise religious rites, as are members of other religions provided they pose no threat to Afghan society.

All nationalities, tribes and ethnic groups are equal.

Foreign policy is based on the principle of peaceful co-existence and active and positive non-alignment. Friendship and co-operation is to be strengthened with the U.S.S.R. as it will be with all countries of the socialist community. Afghanistan abides by the UN Charter, professes its desire for peace between neighbouring countries of the region and supports the struggle against colonialism, imperialism, Zionism, racism and fascism. Afghanistan favours disarmament and the prevention of proliferation of nuclear weapons. War propaganda is prohibited.

The State protects private ownership and guarantees the law of inheritance of private ownership. Banks, mines, institutes, insurance, heavy industries, radio and television are state-owned. The establishment of agricultural and industrial co-operatives is encouraged.

One of the State's major duties is to provide adequate housing for the workers. Family, mother and child are given special protection by the State.

The capital is Kabul.

Rights and duties of the people. All subjects of Afghanistan are equal before the law. The following rights are guaranteed: the right to life and security, to observe the religious rites of Islam and of other religions, to work, to protection of health and social welfare, to education, to scientific, technical, cultural and artistic activities, to freedom of speech and thought, to security of residence and privacy of correspondence and to complain to the appropriate government organs.

In crime, the accused is considered innocent until guilt is recognized by the court. Nobody may be arrested, detained or punished except in accordance with the law.

The defence of the homeland and of the achievements of the Saur Revolution, loyalty to its aims and ideals and services to the people are the responsibilities of every subject.

Loya Jirgah. This is the highest organ of State power. Its composition and the election of its representatives will be regulated by law. Elections to the Loya Jirgah will be based on a general, secret, free, direct and equal vote. The Loya Jirgah will ratify the Constitution at its first session.

The Revolutionary Council is the highest organ of State power until the necessary conditions for elections to the Loya Jirgah are met.

The number and election or selection of new members is proposed by the Presidium of the Revolutionary Council and ratified by the Revolutionary Council. It is empowered to ratify laws, decrees, state economic and social development plans and to form the Presidium and the Council of Ministers. It also has the authority to call elections for the Loya Jirgah and to declare war. Laws and decrees are ratified by a majority vote of the members and are enforced after their publication in the official gazette. Sessions of the Revolutionary Council are held twice a year and they require a minimum attendance of two-thirds of the members.

The permanent organ of the Revolutionary Council is the Presidium. The Revolutionary Council elects the Presidium from amongst its members. The President of the Revolutionary Council is the Chairman of the Presidium. The Presidium's responsibilities include the interpretation and enforcement of laws, the granting of amnesty and the commuting of punishment. Between sessions all responsibilities of the Revolutionary Council are transferred to the Presidium.

Until the appointment or election of a Prime Minister, the President of the Revolutionary Council is the Prime Minister.

The Council of Ministers is the supreme executive organ of State power and is responsible to the Revolutionary Council and to the Presidium when the Revolutionary Council is in recess. It is vested with the authority to implement domestic and foreign policy and to submit draft laws to the Revolutionary Council (or Presidium) for consideration and ratification. It comprises the President of the Council of Ministers (also known as the Prime Minister), his deputy or deputies and ministers.

Local administrative organs. Local committees and councils are to be formed in the provinces, cities, sub-districts and villages for the solution of all questions relating to the locality. All matters of election and representation will be regulated by law. Local executive committees of State power are to be established too. Besides taking decisions within the limits of their authority, these local organs are authorized to implement the decisions of higher organs.

The Judiciary. (*see* Judicial System section).

The Public Prosecution Department. The Attorney-General guides the activities of the country's prosecution organs. The Department consists of the Prosecutor General and the prosecution department of the provinces, cities, districts and sub-districts. These organs are independent of local organs, answerable only to the Prosecutor General. The Attorney-General, who is responsible to the Revolutionary Council, and the prosecutors supervise the implementation and observance of all laws. Until the appointment of the Prosecutor General his authority and duties are vested in the Minister of Justice.

Final Orders. Any alteration of these Basic Principles may be implemented on the proposal of the Presidium and the ratification by two-thirds of the members of the Revolutionary Council. The Basic Principles will remain valid until the ratification of the Constitution of the Democratic Republic of Afghanistan. Decrees, laws and other documents issued prior to the enforcement of the Basic Principles remain valid provided they are not contradictory to the Basic Principles.

THE GOVERNMENT

HEAD OF STATE

President of the Revolutionary Council and General Secretary of the People's Democratic Party Central Committee: BABRAK KARMAL (took office December 27th, 1979).

PRESIDIUM OF THE REVOLUTIONARY COUNCIL

President: BABRAK KARMAL.

Vice-Presidents: Maj.-Gen. ABDUL QADER, Lt.-Col. GUL AQA.

Secretary: MOHAMMAD ANWAR FARZAN.

Members: NOOR AHMAD NOOR, ABDURRASHID ARYAN, ANAHITA RATEBZAD, NEJMUDDIN KAWYANI, Lt.-Col. NASER MOHAMMAD, ABDUL GHAFFAR LAKANWAL, Dr. SALEH MOHAMMAD ZEARAI.

COUNCIL OF MINISTERS

(May 1982)

President of the Revolutionary Council: BABRAK KARMAL.

President of the Council of Ministers: SULTAN ALI KISHTMAND.

Vice-President of the Council of Ministers and Minister of Information and Culture: ABDUL MAJID SARBULAND.

Vice-President of the Council of Ministers and Minister of Higher Education: GUL DAD.

Vice-President of the Council of Ministers and President of the State Planning Committee: Dr. KHALIL AHMAD ABAWI.

Minister of Justice: ABDUL WAHAB SAFI.

Minister of Defence: Maj.-Gen. MOHAMMAD RAFIE.

Minister of Foreign Affairs: SHAH MOHAMMAD DOST.

Minister of the Interior: SAYED MOHAMMAD GULABZOI.

Minister of Communications: Lt.-Col. MOHAMMAD ASLAM WATANJAR.

Minister of Education: FAQIR MOHAMMAD YAQUBI.

Minister of Nationalities and Tribes: SULIEMAN ALI LAIQ.

Minister of Agriculture and Land Reform: FAZUL RAHIM MOHMAND.

Minister of Finance: ABDUL WAKIL.

Minister of Commerce: MOHAMMAD KHAN JALALAR.

Minister of Mines and Industries: Eng. MOHAMMAD ESMA'IL DANESH.

Minister of Transport: Lt.-Col. SHERJAN MAZDOORYAR.

Minister of Public Works: Eng. NAZAR MOHAMMAD.

Minister of Power: Prof. RAS MOHAMMAD PAKTIN.

Minister of Irrigation: Eng. AHMAD SHAH SORKHABI.

Minister of Public Health: Dr. MOHAMMAD NABI KAMYAR.

POLITBURO OF THE CENTRAL COMMITTEE OF THE PEOPLE'S DEMOCRATIC PARTY OF AFGHANISTAN

General Secretary: BABRAK KARMAL.

Full Members: ANAHITA RATEBZAD, SULTAN ALI KISHTMAND, Dr. SALEH MOHAMMAD ZEARAI, GHULAM DASTAGIR PANJSHERI, NOOR AHMAD NOOR, Maj.-Gen. MOHAMMAD RAFIE, Lt.-Col. MOHAMMAD ASLAM WATANJAR, MOHAMMAD NAJIBULLAH.

Alternate Members: MOHAMMAD ISMAIL DANESH, MAHMOUD BARYALAI.

POLITICAL PARTY

People's Democratic Party of Afghanistan (PDPA): Kabul; f. 1965, split 1967; re-founded 1976, when the Khalq (Masses) Party and its splinter Parcham (Flag) Party re-united and annexed the Musawat Party; Communist; Secretariat of the Central Cttee. BABRAK KARMAL, Dr. SALEH MOHAMMAD ZEARAI, NOOR AHMAD NOOR, MAHMOUD BARIALAI, NEYAZ MOHD. MOHMAND; publ. *Haqiqat Enqelab Saur*.

National Fatherland Front: f. 1981 as union of PDPA representatives, national and tribal groups; aims to promote national unity under the leadership of the PDPA; Exec. Bd. of 23 mems.; Chair. National Committee Dr. SALEH MOHAMMAD ZEARAI; Vice-Chair. SULIEMAN ALI LAIQ, SAYED AFGHANI, NEJMUDDIN KAWYANI, SAYED EKRAM PAYGIR.

No other political parties are allowed to function. There are many insurgent groups (*Mujaheddin*) fighting against the Government in Afghanistan. The principal ones are the two factions of Hizb-i Islami (leaders: GULBUDDIN HIKMATYAR and YUNUS KHALIS), Jamiat-i Islami (leader: BURHANEDDIN RABBANI), Harakat-i Inqilab-i Islami (leader: MOHAMMAD NABI MOHAMMADI), the National Islamic Front (leader: SAYED AHMAD GAILANI) and the National Liberation Front (leader: SEBQATULLAH MOJADDEDI). The different groups co-operate to varying degrees; the last three groups joined forces in June 1981 to form the Islamic Unity of Mujaheddin of Afghanistan, but the alliance has been strained by rivalry and feuding. Efforts were being made in March 1982 to form a grand alliance of the six major groups.

DIPLOMATIC REPRESENTATION

EMBASSIES ACCREDITED TO AFGHANISTAN*

(In Kabul unless otherwise stated)

(E) Embassy.

Algeria: New Delhi, India (E).

Argentina: Teheran, Iran (E).

Australia: Islamabad, Pakistan (E).

Austria: P.O.B. 24, Zarghouna Wat (E); *Chargé d'affaires a.i.:* MAXIMILIAN FREISCHLAGER (Ambassador resident in Teheran, Iran).

Bahrain: Teheran, Iran (E).

Bangladesh: House no. 19, Sarak "H", Wazir Akbar Khan Mena, P.O.B. 510 (E); *Chargé d'affaires a.i.:* MD. MIZANUR RAHMAN.

Belgium: Teheran, Iran (E).

Brazil: Teheran, Iran (E).

Bulgaria: Wazir Akbar Khan Mena (E); *Ambassador:* MLADEN NIKOLOV MLADENOV.

Burma: New Delhi, India (E).

Canada: Islamabad, Pakistan (E).

China, People's Republic: Shah Mahmoud Ghazi Wat (E); *Chargé d'affaires a.i.:* JIN CHANGRU.

Cuba: Char Rahi Haji Yaqub, opp. Shar-e-Nau Park (E); *Ambassador:* MANUEL PENADO CASANOVA.

Czechoslovakia: Taimani Wat, Kala-i-Fatullah (E); *Ambassador:* Dr. VACLAV KOUBA.

Denmark: Teheran, Iran (E).

Egypt: c/o Yugoslav Embassy.

Finland: Moscow, U.S.S.R. (E).

France: Avenue Enqelab Saur (E); *Chargé d'affaires a.i.:* ROLAND BARRAUX.

German Democratic Republic: Ghazi Ayub Wat, Shar-e-Nau (E); *Ambassador:* KRAFT BUMBEL.

Germany, Federal Republic: P.O.B. 83, Wazir Akbar Khan Mena (E); *Chargé d'affaires a.i.:* JOHANNES BAUCH.

Ghana: New Delhi, India (E).

Greece: Baghdad, Iraq (E).

Hungary: sin 306–308, Wazir Akbar Khan Mena, P.O.B. 830 (E); *Ambassador:* DEZSŐ KISS.

India: Malalai Wat, Shar-e-Nau (E); *Ambassador:* J. N. DIXIT.

Indonesia: Wazir Akbar Khan Mena (E); *Chargé d'affaires a.i.:* HADI MARTOYO.

Iran: Malekyar Wat (E); *Chargé d'affaires a.i.:* SEYYED ALIREZA NIKUNIA.

Iraq: P.O.B. 523, Wazir Akbar Khan Mena (E); *Chargé d'affaires a.i.:* HASSAN IBRAHIM D. AL-ADHAMI.

Italy: Khoja Abdullah Ansari Wat (E); *Chargé d'affaires a.i.:* CESARE CAPITANI.

Japan: No. 240–241, Wazir Akbar Khan Mena (E); *Chargé d'affaires a.i.:* AKIHISA TANAKA.

Jordan: Teheran, Iran (E).

Korea, Democratic People's Republic: Wazir Akbar Khan Mena (E); *Ambassador:* LI CHONG-RIM.

Korea, Republic: New Delhi, India (E).

Kuwait: Teheran, Iran (E).

Lebanon: Teheran, Iran (E).

Libya: 103 Wazir Akbar Khan Mena (People's Bureau); *Secretary:* MOHD HASAN AL-BURKI.

Malaysia: Teheran, Iran (E).

Mexico: New Delhi, India (E).

Mongolia: Wazir Akbar Khan Mena (E); *Ambassador:* (vacant).

Morocco: Teheran, Iran (E).

Nepal: New Delhi, India (E).

Netherlands: Teheran, Iran (E).

Norway: Teheran, Iran (E).

Pakistan: Zarghouna Wat (E); *Chargé d'affaires a.i.:* FEDA YUNIS.

Philippines: New Delhi, India (E).

Poland: Gozargah St. (E); *Ambassador:* Dr. EDWARD BARADZIEJ.

Portugal: New Delhi, India (E).

Qatar: Teheran, Iran (E).

Romania: Teheran, Iran (E).

Saudi Arabia: c/o French Embassy.

Senegal: Teheran, Iran (E).

Spain: Teheran, Iran (E).

Sri Lanka: New Delhi, India (E).

Sudan: Teheran, Iran (E).

Sweden: Teheran, Iran (E).

Switzerland: Teheran, Iran (E).

Syria: New Delhi, India (E).

Thailand: New Delhi, India (E).

Turkey: Shah Mahmoud Ghazi Wat (E); *Chargé d'affaires a.i.:* ALTAN GÜVEN.

U.S.S.R.: Dar-ul-Aman Wat (E); *Ambassador:* FIKRYAT A. TABEYEV.

United Arab Emirates: Teheran, Iran (E).

United Kingdom: Karte Parwan (E); *Chargé d'affaires a.i.:* JOHN D. GARNER.

U.S.A.: Khwaja Abdullah Ansari Wat (E); *Chargé d'affaires a.i.:* CHARLES F. DUNBAR.

Viet-Nam: No. 3 Nijat St., Wazir Akbar Khan Mena (E); *Ambassador:* NGUYEN SI HOAT.

Yugoslavia: No. 923 Main Rd., Wazir Akbar Khan Mena (E); *Ambassador:* BOGDAN MALBASIĆ.

* Not all of the above mentioned countries recognize the administration of Babrak Karmal as the legitimate government of Afghanistan.

Afghanistan also has diplomatic relations with Chile, Laos, Tunisia and the People's Democratic Republic of Yemen.

JUDICIAL SYSTEM

The functions and structure of the judiciary are established in Articles 54–58 of the Basic Principles ratified by the Revolutionary Council in April 1980.

Judgment is made by the courts on the basis of democratic principles. The courts implement the laws of the Democratic Republic of Afghanistan and, in cases of ambivalence, will judge in accordance with the rules of *Shari'ah* (Islamic religious law). Trials are held in open session except when circumstances defined by law deem the trial to be held in closed session. Trials are conducted in Pashtu and Dari or in the language of the majority of the inhabitants of the locality. The right to speak in court in one's mother tongue is guaranteed to the two sides of the lawsuit.

The judiciary comprises the Supreme Court, provincial, city and district courts, the courts of the armed forces and other such special courts as are formed in accordance with the directives of the law.

The supreme judicial organ is the Supreme Court, which consists of a President, Vice-President and other members. It supervises the judicial activities of the courts and ensures the uniformity of law enforcement and interpretation by those courts.

The Presidium of the Revolutionary Council appoints all judges. Death sentences are carried out after ratification by the Presidium.

RELIGION

The official religion of Afghanistan is Islam. Ninety-nine per cent of Afghans are Muslims, approximately 80 per cent of them of the Sunni and the remainder of the Shi'ite sect. There are small minority groups of Hindus, Sikhs and Jews.

THE PRESS

PRINCIPAL DAILIES

The newspapers and periodicals marked * were reported to be the only ones appearing regularly in May 1982.

***Anis** (*Friendship*): Kabul; f. 1927; evening; independent; Dari and Pashtu; news and literary articles; Chief Editor ZAMON MOMAND; circ. 1,717.

Badakhshan: Faizabad; f. 1944; Dari and Pashtu; Chief Editor HADI ROSTAQI; circ. 1,000.

Bedar: Mazar-i-Sharif; f. 1922; Dari and Pashtu; Chief Editor ROZEQ FANI; circ. 2,500.

Ettehadi-Baghlan: Baghlan; f. 1930; Dari and Pashtu; Chief Editor SHAFIQULLAH MOSHFEQ; circ. 1,200.

***Haqiqat Enqelab Saur** (*Truth of the April Revolution*): Kabul; f. 1980; Dari and Pashtu; organ of the Government; Editor-in-Chief MAHMUD BARIALAY; circ. 50,000.

***Hewad:** Kabul; f. 1959; Dari and Pashtu; Editor-in-Chief ABDULLAH BAKHTIANAE; circ. 12,200.

Jawzjan: Jawzjan; f. 1942; Dari and Pashtu; Chief Editor A. RAHEM HAMRO; circ. 1,500.

***Kabul New Times:** Ansari Wat, Kabul; f. 1962 as Kabul Times, renamed 1980; State-owned; English; Editor-in-Chief DANESHYOR; circ. 2,200.

Nangarhor: Jalalabad; f. 1919; Pashtu; Chief Editor MORAD SANGARMAL; circ. 1,500.

Sanae: Parwan; f. 1953; Dari and Pashtu; Chief Editor G. SAKHI ESHANZADA; circ. 1,700.

Tulu-i-Afghan: Qandahar; f. 1922; Pashtu; Chief Editor TAHER SHAFEQ; circ. 1,200.

Wolanga: Paktia; f. 1943; Pashtu; Chief Editor M. ANWAR; circ. 1,500.

PERIODICALS

Afghan Journal of Public Health: Institute of Public Health, Ansari Wat, Kabul; quarterly; Pashtu and Dari; Editor-in-Chief A. W. LATIFI; circ. 500.

Afghan Standard: Kabul; f. 1979; quarterly; Dari and Pashtu; Editor-in-Chief TAJMOHAMAD YORMAND; circ. 1,000.

***Afghanistan:** Historical Society of Afghanistan, Kabul; f. 1948; quarterly; English; historical and cultural; Editor MALIHA ZAFAR.

***Aryana:** Historical Society of Afghanistan, Kabul; f. 1943; quarterly; Pashtu and Dari; cultural and historical; Editor FAQIR MUHAMMAD KHAIRKHAH.

Awaz: Kabul; f. 1940; radio and television programmes; Pashtu and Dari; twice a month; Editor NASIR TOHORI; circ. 20,000.

De Kano Aw Sanayo (*Mines and Industry*): Kabul; f. 1955; quarterly; Dari and Pashtu; Editor-in-Chief MESBA SABA; circ. 1,500.

Eqtesad (*Economist*): Afghan Chambers of Commerce and Industry, Darulaman Watt, Kabul; f. 1922; weekly; Dari and Pashtu; Editor MUHAMMAD TAHIR PAYAM.

Erfan: Ministry of Education, Mohd. Jan Khan Wat, Kabul; f. 1923; monthly; Dari and Pashtu; Chief Editor KUBRA MAZHARI MALORAW; circ. 2,500.

Foreign Affairs Bulletin: Directorate of Information and Publicity, Ministry of Foreign Affairs, Shar-e-Nau, Kabul; f. 1982; fortnightly; official documents on government foreign policy and international issues.

Geography: Kabul; f. 1965; monthly; Pashtu and Dari; Editor-in-Chief STANAMIR ZAHER; circ. 2,500.

Gorash: Ministry of Information and Culture, Mohd. Jan Khan Wat, Kabul; f. 1979; weekly; Turkmani; Chief Editor S. MISEDIQ AMINI; circ. 1,000.

***Haqiqat-e-Sarbaz:** Ministry of Defence, Kabul; f. 1980; Dari and Pashtu; three times a week; Chief Editor MER JAMALUDIN FAKHR; circ. 18,370.

Helmand: Bost; f. 1954; weekly; Pashtu; Editor-in-Chief M. OMER FARHAT BALEGH; circ. 1,700.

Herat: Ministry of Information and Culture, Mohd. Jan Khan Wat, Kabul; f. 1923; monthly; Dari and Pashtu; Chief Editor JALIL SHABGER FOLADYON.

Kabul: Academy of Sciences, Scientific Research Centre for Languages and Literature, Kabul; f. 1931; monthly; Pashtu; literature and language research; Editor N. M. SAHEEM.

Kamkyono Anis: Ministry of Information and Culture, Mohd. Jan Khan Wat, Kabul; f. 1969; weekly; Dari and Pashtu; Chief Editor NADIA; circ. 1,500.

Karhana: Ministry of Agriculture, Jamal Mena, Kabul; f. 1953; monthly; Dari and Pashtu; Editor Dr. BABRAK ARGHAND; circ. 1,500.

Mairmun: Kabul; f. 1955; Dari and Pashtu; produced by the Women's Welfare Association.

Mojalae Rana (*Light*): Kabul; f. 1978; monthly; Dari and Pashtu; Editor-in-Chief RASHID ASHTI; circ. 1,000.

Nengarhar: Kabul; f. 1919; weekly; Pashtu; Editor-in-Chief KARIM HASHIMI; circ. 1,500.

Paim Haq: Kabul; f. 1953; monthly; Dari and Pashtu; Editor-in-Chief FARAH SHAH MOHIBI; circ. 1,000.

Pamir: Kabul; f. 1952; organ of the Municipality; weekly; Dari and Pashtu; Chief Editor ZIA ROSHAN; circ. 2,000.

Samangon: Aybak; f. 1978; weekly; Dari; Editor-in-Chief M. MOHSEN HASSAN; circ. 1,500.

Seistan: Fareh; f. 1944; weekly; Dari and Pashtu; Editor-in-Chief M. ANWAR MAHAL; circ. 2,500.

Seramiasht: Afghan Red Crescent Society, Afshar, Kabul; f. 1958; Dari and Pashtu; quarterly; Editor H. R. JADIR; circ, 1,500.

Sewad (*Literacy*): Kabul; f. 1954; monthly; Dari and Pashtu; Editor-in-Chief MALEM GOL ZADRON; circ. 1,000.

Sob: Kabul; f. 1979; weekly; Balochi; Editor-in-Chief WALIMOHAMAD ROKHSHONI; circ. 1,000.

Talim Wa Tarbia: Kabul; f. 1954; monthly; published by Institute of Education.

Tanzimi Khanawada (*Family Management*): Kabul; f. 1981; Dari and Pashtu; monthly; Editor-in-Chief Ms. SORAYA KOHISTANI; circ. 1,500.

Urdu (*Military*): Kabul; f. 1922; quarterly; military journal; issued by the Ministry of National Defence; Dari and Pashtu; Chief Editor KHALILULAH AKBARI; circ. 500.

Yoduz (*Star*): Ministry of Information and Culture, Mohd. Jan Khan Wat, Kabul; f. 1979; weekly; Uzbeki; Chief Editor EKHAN BAYONI; circ. 2,000.

Zeray: Academy of Sciences, Scientific Research Centre for Languages and Literature, Kabul; f. 1938; weekly; Pashtu; Pashtu folklore, literature and language; Editor A. W. WAJID; circ. 1,000.

Zhwandoon (*Life*): Kabul; f. 1944; weekly; Pashtu and Dari; illustrated; Editor ROHELA ROSEKH KHORAMI; circ. 1,400.

NEWS AGENCIES

Bakhtar News Agency: Ministry of Information and Culture, Mohd. Jan Khan Wat, Kabul; f. 1939; Pres. ABDOLQADER MAL; Dir. ABDOLQODDUS TANDER.

FOREIGN BUREAUX

The following foreign agencies are represented in Kabul: APN (U.S.S.R.), TASS (U.S.S.R.), Tanjug (Yugoslavia) and Xinhua (People's Republic of China).

PRESS ASSOCIATION

Union of Journalists of Afghanistan: Wazir Akbar Khan Mena, St. No. 13, Kabul.

PUBLISHERS

Afghan Book: P.O.B. 206, Kabul; f. 1969 by Kabir A. Ahang; books on various subjects, translations of foreign works on Afghanistan, books in English on Afghanistan and Dari language textbooks for foreigners; Man. Dir. JAMILA AHANG.

Afghanistan Publicity Department: c/o Kabul New Times, Ansari Wat, Kabul; publicity materials; answers enquiries about Afghanistan.

Baihaqi Book Publishing and Importing Institute: P.O.B. 2025, Kabul; f. 1971 by co-operation of the Government Printing House, Bakhtar News Agency and leading newspapers; publishers and importers of books; Pres. MOHAMMAD ANWAR NUMYALAI.

Book Publishing Institute: Herat; f. 1970 by co-operation of Government Printing House and citizens of Herat; books on literature, history and religion.

Book Publishing Institute: Qandahar; f. 1970 by citizens of Qandahar, supervised by Government Printing House; mainly books in Pashtu language.

Educational Publications: Ministry of Education, Char Rahi Malek Asghar, Kabul; textbooks for primary and secondary schools in the Pashtu and Dari languages; also three monthly magazines in Pashtu and in Dari.

Government Printing House: Kabul; f. 1870 under supervision of the Ministry of Information and Culture; four daily newspapers in Kabul, one in English; weekly, fortnightly and monthly magazines, one of them in English; books on Afghan history and literature, as well as textbooks for the Ministry of Education; thirteen daily newspapers in thirteen provincial centres and one journal and also magazines in three provincial centres; Dir. MUHAMMAD AYAN AYAN.

Historical Society of Afghanistan: Kabul; f. 1931; mainly historical and cultural works and two quarterly magazines: *Afghanistan* (English and French), *Aryana* (Dari and Pashtu); Pres. AHMAD ALI MOTAMEDI.

Institute of Geography: Kabul University, Kabul; geographical and related works.

Kabul University Press: Kabul; publishes textbooks for Kabul and Nangarhar Universities, College Journals, etc.

Pashtu Tolana (*Pashtu Academy*): Sher Alikhan St., Kabul; f. 1937 by the Department of Press and Information; research works on Pashtu language and literature; Pres. POHAND RSHTEENE; publs. *Zeray* (weekly), *Kabul* (monthly).

RADIO AND TELEVISION

National Radio-TV of Afghanistan: P.O.B. 544, Ansari Wat, Kabul; Pres. (Radio) ABDUL LATIF NAZEMI; Pres. (Television) ABDULLAH SHADAN; the Afghan Broadcasting station is under the supervision of the Ministry of Communications and Culture; Home service in Dari, Pashtu, Pashai, Nuristani, Uzbeki, Turkmani and Balochi; Foreign service in Urdu, Arabic, English, Russian, German, Dari and Pashtu.

Number of radio receivers: over 1m. (approx.) in 1981.

Television broadcasting began in August 1978 with a transmission range of 50 kilometres.

Number of television sets: 120,000 in January 1980.

FINANCE

BANKING

(cap. = capital; auth. = authorized; p.u. = paid up; res. = reserves; m. = million; brs. = branches; Afs. = Afghanis).

In June 1975 all banks were nationalized.

Da Afghanistan Bank (*Central Bank of Afghanistan*): Ibne Sina Wat, Kabul; f. 1939; main functions: banknote issue, foreign exchange regulation, credit extensions to banks and leading enterprises and companies, government and private depository, government fiscal agency; 67 local brs.; cap. Afs. 2,000m.; dep. Afs. 20,839m.; res. Afs. 1,210m. (March 1981); Gov. MEHRABUDDIN PAKTIAWAL; 65 brs.

Agricultural Development Bank of Afghanistan: P.O.B. 414, Kabul; f. 1955; makes available credits for farmers, co-operatives and agro-business; aid provided by IBRD and UNDP; auth. share cap. Afs. 1,000m.; Pres. Eng. ABDUL WAHAD ASSEFI.

Banke Milli Afghan (*Afghan National Bank*): Jada Ibn Sina, Kabul; f. 1932; brs. throughout Afghanistan; cap. Afs. 500m.; total resources Afs. 3,807m. (March 1980); Pres. MOHAMMAD AKRAM KHALIL.

Export Promotion Bank of Afghanistan: 24 Mohammed Jan Khan Wat, Kabul; provides financing for exports and export-oriented investments; cap. Afs. 100m.; Pres. Prof. Dr. ZABIOULLAH A. ELTEZAM.

Industrial Development Bank of Afghanistan: P.O.B. 14, Kabul; f. 1973; provides financing for industrial development; total financial resources including cap. Afs. 842m.; Pres. T. SURKHABI; Gen. Man. SUNIT GUPTA.

Mortgage and Construction Bank: 2 Jade' Maiwand, Kabul; f. 1955 to provide short and long term building loans; cap. Afs. 100m.; Pres. (vacant).

Pashtany Tejaraty Bank (*Afghan Commercial Bank*): Mohd. Jan Khan Wat, Kabul; f. 1954 to provide long- and short-term credits, forwarding facilities, opening letters of credit, purchase and sale of foreign exchange, transfer of capital; cap. p.u. Afs. 500m.; total assets Afs. 6,997m. (March 1981); Pres. and Chief Exec. MOHD. NAIM ASKARYAR; 20 brs. in Afghanistan and abroad.

There are no foreign banks operating in Afghanistan.

INSURANCE

There is one national insurance company:

Afghan National Insurance Co.: P.O.B. 329, Timore Shahi Park, Kabul; f. 1964; mem. of Asian Reinsurance Corp.; marine, aviation, fire, motor and accident insurance; cap. Afs. 75m.; Pres. M. Y. DEEN; Vice-Pres. SANAULLAH DARWISH.

No foreign insurance companies are permitted to operate in Afghanistan.

TRADE AND INDUSTRY

CHAMBER OF COMMERCE

Federation of Afghan Chambers of Commerce and Industry: Mohd. Jan Khan Wat, Kabul; includes chambers of commerce and industry at Ghazni, Qandahar, Herat, Mazar-i-Sharif, Fariab, Jawzjan, Kunduz, Jalalabad and Andkhoy; Pres. MEHR CHAND VERMA.

TRADING CORPORATIONS

Afghan Carpet Exporters' Guild: P.O.B. 3159, Darul Aman Rd., Kabul; f. 1968; a non-profit making association for carpet exporters; Pres. A RATEB; publs. catalogues and pamphlets in English, Dari and Pashtu.

Afghan Raisins Export Promotion Institute: P.O.B. 3034, Kabul; exporters of dried fruit.

Afghanistan Karakul Institute: P.O.B. 506, Mohammed Jan Khan Wat, Kabul; exporters of furs.

TRADE UNIONS

Central Council of Afghan Trade Unions: P.O.B. 756, Kabul; f. 1978 to establish and develop the trade union movement, including the setting up of provincial councils and organizational committees in the provinces; 41 mems. and 7 alt. mems.; Pres. ABDUL SATAR PORDELY; Vice-Pres. ABDUL GHANY KARGAR; publ. *Kar* (Labour). The provincial councils are as follows:

Kabul Province: 6,500 mems.; Pres. MAIRAM JAN.

Kabul City: 72,000 mems.; Pres. ABDUL RAZAQ.

Balkh Province: 17,000 mems.; Pres. SALIM KARGAR.

Jawzjan Province: 8,500 mems.; Pres. JANATH GOUL.

Baghlan Province: 10,000 mems.; Pres. SIDIQ.

Kunduz Province: 2,000 mems.; Pres. JABAR.

Parwan Province: 10,000 mems.; Pres. NAPEES.

Kapisa Province: 3,000 mems.

Nangarhar Province: 13,000 mems.; Vice-Pres. NAZEER KARGAR.

Kandahar Province: 6,000 mems.; Pres. HAJI SHARAPUDIN.

Helmand Province: 8,000 mems.; Pres. MOHAMMAD SAPY.

Herat Province: 7,000 mems.; Pres. AZIZ KARGAR.

Badakhshan Province: 1,000 mems.; Pres. A. AHMAD ROWSHAN.

Bamian Province: 700 mems.; Pres. S. TAHER.

Samangan Province: 1,200 mems.; Pres. ZAHER.

Takhar Province: 700 mems.; Pres. HAFIZ.

Fariab Province: 1,000 mems.; Pres. MURTAZA.

Farah Province: 300 mems.; Pres. KARIM.

Neemroze Province: 700 mems.; Pres. FAKIRI.

Kunar Province: 300 mems.; Pres. SAIDAN GUL.

Laghman Province: 600 mems.; Pres. MASOOM.

Paktia Province: 1,200 mems.; Pres. SHAH JEHAN.

TRANSPORT

RAILWAYS

In 1977 the Government approved plans for a railway system. The proposed railway (1,815 km. long) was to connect Kabul to Qandahar and Herat, and to run through Islamqala and Mashed to join the Iranian railway network. Another branch was to run from Qandahar to link with Pakistan Railways at Quetta. By 1982 work had not yet begun on the proposed railway..

ROADS

Ministry of Communications and Ministry of Public Works: Kabul; in 1978 there were 2,812 kilometres of paved roads out of a total distance of 18,752 kilometres. All-weather highways now link Kabul with Qandahar and Herat in the south and west, Jalalabad in the east and Mazar-i-Sharif and the Amu-Dar'ya river in the north.

Land Transport Company: Khoshal Mena, Kabul; f. 1943; commercial transportation within Afghanistan.

Afghan International Transport Company: Wazir Akbar Khan Mena, behind American Embassy, P.O.B. 768, Kabul.

The Millie Bus Enterprise: Ministry of Transport and Tourism, Kabul; government-owned and run; Pres. Dip. Eng. AZIZ NAGHABAN.

INLAND WATERWAYS

River ports on the Amu-Dar'ya are linked by road to Kabul.

CIVIL AVIATION

Civil Aviation and Tourism Authority: Ansari Wat, P.O.B. 165, Kabul; Pres. NOOR MOHAMMAD DALILI; Dir.-Gen. of Air Operations ABDUL WASEH HAIDARI.

There are international airports at Kabul and Qandahar and there are plans to rebuild Kabul airport and construct six airports in the northeast, with Soviet help.

NATIONAL AIRLINES

Ariana Afghan Airlines Co. Ltd.: P.O.B. 76, Ansari Wat, Kabul; f. 1955; services to India, U.S.S.R. and Europe; services to Iran, Turkey and Pakistan temporarily suspended; Pres. Capt. SAYED BABA; 1 DC 10-30, 2 Boeing 727-100C.

Bakhtar Afghan Airlines: Ansari Wat, P.O.B. 3058, Kabul; f. 1968; internal services between Kabul and 12 regional locations; 3 DHC-6 Twin Otter projects, 2 YAK-40 jets, 2 Antonov-24 aircraft; Pres. NIAZ MUHAMMAD; Dir. of Operations Capt. R. NAWROZ; Gen. Dir. Lt.-Col. ABDOL LATIF.

FOREIGN AIRLINES

The following airlines also operate services to Afghanistan: Aeroflot (U.S.S.R.), Indian Airlines and PIA (Pakistan) (suspended Sept. 1981).

TOURISM

Afghan Tourist Organization: Shar-e-Nau, Kabul; f. 1958; Pres. H. KYANWAR; Vice-Pres. S. J. BARAKZAI; publ. *Statistical Bulletin* (quarterly).

Afghan Tour: Salang Wat, Kabul; official travel agency supervised by A.T.O.

ATOMIC ENERGY

Atomic Energy Commission: Faculty of Science, Kabul University, Kabul; Pres. of Commission and Dean of Faculty Dr. MOHAMMAD RASUL.

DEFENCE

Commander-in-Chief of the Army: Gen. BABAJAN.

Commander-in-Chief of the Air Force and Air Defence Force: Maj.-Gen. NAZAR MOHAMMAD.

Supreme Defence Council: Kabul; founded March 1979 to improve defence, supervise the armed forces, approve the Defence Budget and safeguard internal security.

Armed Forces (July 1981 estimates): Army 35,000; air force 8,000 and para-military forces comprise 30,000 gendarmes; military service lasting two years is compulsory for every able-bodied man, but conscription is difficult to enforce and desertions are frequent.

Equipment: The army's equipment and training are very largely provided by the Soviet Union. The air force is equipped with Soviet built combat aircraft.

Defence Expenditure: Estimated defence expenditure in 1978/79 was 2,870 million afghanis (U.S. $63.8 million).

EDUCATION

The traditional system of education in Afghanistan was religious instruction in Madrasas, or Mosque schools. These centres are still active, but a modern educational system has been built up since 1904.

Since 1933 primary, middle and secondary schools have been opened all over the country. In March 1980 it was announced that the education system would comprise primary schools (four classes), basic middle schools (eight classes), full middle schools (ten classes) and religious schools. Those children aged 10 to 14 with no previous opportunity to attend school can study in specially accelerated training classes covering the elementary school curriculum in two years. The development of education since 1961 has been rapid especially at the primary level. It is estimated that the proportion of children aged 6 to 11 years receiving primary education increased from 9 per cent in 1960 to 23 per cent in 1975. Only 7 per cent of girls in this age-group were enrolled and only 8 per cent of all children aged 12 to 16 attended secondary schools. In 1979 the Government announced the introduction of free and compulsory primary education for children over seven years of age. Competitive examinations for high-school entrance were abolished in 1978 and in 1980 the Government claimed that the total number of schools (excepting religious and vocational schools) had increased by 13 per cent compared with 1979 and that the number of students at these schools had increased by 21 per cent in the same period.

Under the Five-year Social and Economic Development Plan (1979–84), a massive programme to combat adult illiteracy has been launched. (It has been estimated that only 10 per cent of males and 2 per cent of females are literate.) The programme aims to reach over 8 million people by the end of the Plan.

Teacher training began on an organized scale in the early 1950s. The University of Kabul was founded in 1932 when the Faculty of Medicine was established. It now has 10 Faculties. In 1962 a second university was founded in Jalalabad, Nangarhar province; again the nucleus was provided by the Medical Faculty of Kabul University.

Progress is also being made in women's education, and girls' schools are now found in all major cities.

In 1980 it was reported that up to 80 per cent of university staff had fled their posts.

BIBLIOGRAPHY

GENERAL

AFGHAN TRANSPORT & TRAVEL SERVICE. Afghanistan—Ancient Land with Modern Ways (London, 1961).

CAROE, OLAF. The Pathans.

DUPREE, LOUIS. Afghanistan (Princeton University Press, Princeton, N.J., 1973).

GRASSMUCK, GEORGE, and ADAMEC, LUDWIG. (eds.) Afghanistan: Some new approaches (Center for Near Eastern and North African Studies, University of Michigan, Ann Arbor, Mich., 1969).

GRIFFITHS, JOHN C. Afghanistan (Pall Mall Press, London, 1967).

KESSEL, FLINKER and KLIMBURG. Afghanistan (photographs, 1959).

KING, PETER. Afghanistan, Cockpit in Asia (Bles, London, 1966, Taplinger, N.Y., 1967).

KLIMBURG, M. Afghanistan (Austrian UNESCO Commission, Vienna, 1966).

SHALISI, PRITA K. Here and There in Afghanistan.

WILBER, DONALD N. Afghanistan (New Haven, Conn., 1956).

Annotated Bibliography of Afghanistan (New Haven, Conn., 1962).

GEOGRAPHY AND TRAVELS

BURNES, Sir ALEXANDER. Cabool (John Murray, London, 1842, reprinted Lahore 1961).

BYRON, ROBERT. Road to Oxiana (Jonathan Cape, London, 1937).

ELPHINSTONE, M. An Account of the Kingdom of Caubul and its Dependencies in Persia, Tartary and India (John Murray, London, 1815, reprinted Oxford University Press, London, 1972).

FERRIER, J. P. Caravan Journeys (1857, reprinted Oxford University Press, London).

HAHN, H. Die Stadt Kabul und ihr Umland (2 vols., Bonn, 1964–65).

HAMILTON, ANGUS. Afghanistan (Heinemann, London, 1906).

HUMLUM, J. La Géographie de l'Afghanistan (Gyldendal, Copenhagen, 1959).

MASSON, CHARLES. Narrative of various journeys in Baluchistan, Afghanistan and the Punjab (Bentley, London, 1842, reprinted Oxford University Press, London).

WOLFE, N. H. Herat (Afghan Tourist Organization, Kabul, 1966).

WOOD, JOHN. A Personal Narrative of a Journey to the Source of the River Oxus by the Route of Indus, Kabul and Badakshan (John Murray, London, 1841, reprinted Oxford University Press, London, 1976).

HISTORY

ADAMEC, LUDWIG W. Afghanistan 1900–1923 (University of California, Berkeley, 1967).

Afghanistan's Foreign Affairs to the Mid-Twentieth Century (University of Arizona Press, Tucson, 1974).

AKHRAMOVICH, R. T. Outline History of Afghanistan after the Second World War (Moscow, 1966).

ALDER, G. J. British India's Northern Frontier, 1865–1895 (Longmans, London, 1963).

BOSWORTH, C. E. The Ghaznavids (Edinburgh University Press, 1963).

CAMBRIDGE HISTORY OF INDIA, Vols. I, III, IV, V, VI.

DOLLOT, RENÉ. Afghanistan (Payot, Paris, 1937).

DUPREE, LOUIS and LINNET, ALBERT (eds.). Afghanistan in the 1970s (Praeger, New York, 1974 and Pall Mall Press, London).

FLETCHER, ARNOLD. Afghanistan, Highway of Conquest (Cornell and Oxford University Presses, 1965).

FRASER-TYTLER, Sir W. KERR. Afghanistan (Oxford University Press, 1950, 3rd edn., 1967).

GREGORIAN, VARTAN. The Emergence of Modern Afghanistan (Stanford University Press, Stanford, Calif., 1969).

KAKAR, HASAN, Afghanistan, 1880–1896 (Karachi, 1971). Government and Society in Afghanistan (University of Arizona Press, Tucson, Ariz., 1979).

KHAN, M. M. S. M. (ed.) The Life of Abdur Rahman, Amir of Afghanistan (John Murray, London, 1900).

KOHZAD, A. A. Men and Events (Government Printing House, Kabul).

MACRORY, PATRICK. Signal Catastrophe (Hodder & Stoughton, London, 1966).

MASSON, V. M., and ROMODIN, V. A. Istoriya Afghanistana (Akad. Nauk, Moscow, 1964–65).

MOHUN LAL. Life of the Amir Dost Mohammed Khan of Kabul (Longmans, London, 1846, reprinted Oxford University Press, London, 1978).

NEWELL, RICHARD S. The Politics of Afghanistan (Cornell University Press, Ithaca, N.Y., 1972).

NORRIS, J. A. The First Afghan War, 1838–42 (Cambridge University Press, 1967).

POULLADA, LEON B. Reform and Rebellion in Afghanistan, 1919-1929 (Cornell University Press, Ithaca, N.Y., 1972).

SYKES, Sir PERCY. A History of Afghanistan (Macmillan, London, 1940).

ECONOMY

FRY, MAXWELL J. The Afghan Economy (Leiden, 1974).

MALEKYAR, ABDUL WAHED. Die Verkehrsentwicklung in Afghanistan (Cologne, 1966).

RHEIN, E. and GHAUSSY. A. GHANIE. Die wirtschaftliche Entwicklung Afghanistans, 1880–1965 (C. W. Leske Verlag, Hamburg, 1966).

Australia

PHYSICAL AND SOCIAL GEOGRAPHY

A. E. McQueen

Australia covers 7,682,300 square kilometres (2,966,150 square miles). Nearly 39 per cent of its land mass lies within the tropics; Cape York, the northernmost point, is only 10° S. of the equator. At the other extreme, the southern limit of the mainland lies at 39° S. or, if Tasmania is included, at 44° S., a distance on the mainland alone of 3,134 km. (1,959 miles) from north to south. From east to west Australia is 3,782 km. (2,489 miles) broad.

CLIMATE AND VEGETATION

The wide latitudinal range as well as the size and compact shape of Australia produce a climate with widely varying effects in different parts ofthe country. The climatic differences can be assigned generally to latitude, and therefore to its liability to influence rainfall either from tropical rain-bearing air masses or from the westerly wind belt which affects the southern areas of Australia. It is important to note, too, that the average elevation of the land surface is only about 275 metres (900 ft.); nearly three-quarters of Australia is a great central plain, almost all of it between 185 m. (600 ft.) and 460 m. (1,500 ft.) above sea level, with few high mountains. The Dividing Range, running parallel to most of the east coast, is the most notable—the highest peak, Kosciusko, reaches 2,249 m. (7,313 ft.). This general lack of mountains, coupled with the moderating effects of the surrounding oceans, means that there are fewer abrupt regional climatic changes than would be found on land masses in comparable latitudes in other parts of the world.

The northern part of the continent except the Queensland coast comes under the influence of summer tropical monsoons. This produces a wet summer as the moist air flows in from the north-west; but winter is dry, with the prevailing wind coming from the south-east across the dry interior. Both the north-east and north-west coasts are liable to experience tropical cyclones between December and April, and these storms, with accompanying heavy rain, will occasionally continue some distance inland.

On the other hand, the southern half of Australia lies in the mid-latitude westerly wind belt for the winter half of the year; consequently winter is the wet season. Winter rainfall in the south-east and south-west corners of Australia and Tasmania is particularly high—at least by Australian levels—with maximum falls occurring on the windward sides of the mountains in each area. Rainfall decreases rapidly inland with distance from the coast, with the result that parts of central Australia record some very low annual average rainfall figures; the area of lowest average annual rainfall is the 460,000 sq. km. (180,000 sq. miles) around Lake Eyre in South Australia which receives an average of some 10–15 cm. (4–6 in.) a year. At the other extreme lies Tully (17° 55′ S.), on the east coast of Queensland, with an annual average of 449 cm. (177 in.). Overall, few parts of Australia enjoy abundant rainfall; and even where occasional heavy falls are recorded the unreliability of its seasonal distribution may well count against its value in terms of pasture growth. Only south-west Western Australia, western Tasmania and Victoria south of the divide can be counted as areas of reliable precipitation; elsewhere reliability decreases away from the coast, with wide variations being recorded at stations such as Whim Creek (20° 52′ S., 117° 51′ E.) where 74.5 cm. (29.41 in.) once fell in a single day, but only 0.43 cm. (0.17 in.) was recorded in all of 1924.

Very high temperatures are experienced during the summer months over the central parts of the country and for some distance to the south, as well as during the pre-monsoon months in the north. Australia's insular nature and other features tend to hold temperatures at a rather lower general level than other southern hemisphere land areas in the same latitudes but temperatures are high enough to produce an evaporation rate, especially in inland areas, which in turn is high enough to exert a marked influence on soil and vegetation patterns. In much of the interior xerophytic plant species adapted to very dry and variable conditions, such as spinifex, salt bush, blue bush and dwarf eucalyptus, are capable of supporting a limited cattle population. Between these arid areas and the zones of higher rainfall lie the semi-arid plains on which the main vegetation is mulga (*Acacia*) and mallee scrub (*Eucalyptus spp*) in which several stems rise from a common woody base. It is this type of land that carries most of the sheep in New South Wales and Western Australia; it is also here, as well as in the still drier interior, that the major effects of drought are felt—and drought occurs with sufficient regularity to have a limiting effect upon the long-term stock population. In the last hundred years Australia has suffered from at least seven major droughts affecting most of the country, as well as several others causing severe losses in particular areas. The effects of these climatic vagaries are felt throughout the economy.

In the colder southeastern areas the length of the growing season is mainly dependent upon temperatures, but elsewhere the availability of soil moisture is the major variable. The growing season lasts for 9 months or more along the east coast and in south-western Australia; elsewhere, and especially in the interior, there are wide variations according to both the intensity and seasonal distribution of rainfall.

Underground water supplies are fairly widespread in the semi-arid parts of Australia, including the resources of the Great Artesian Basin, fed from inland slopes of the mountain to make one of the largest such catchments in the world. In some areas, notably the Barkly Tableland, stock-raising is largely dependent upon bore water.

SOILS AND LAND USE

Soils do little to ease the problems of the Australian pastoralist. They are very diverse in both type and origin, and are of low natural fertility over large areas due to the great geological age of Australia and the subsequent poor qualities of the parent materials. Climate has a marked effect on soil type with seasonal desiccation and surface erosion coinciding with the extreme dry and wet seasons which affect much of the continent. Salinity and alkalinity are also problems, especially in arid southern Australia; investigations into these factors, as well as into more complex aspects of maintaining and building up soil fertility, form a continuing part of the Commonwealth Scientific and Industrial Research Organization's soil research programme, a programme conducted as part of the broad government assistance schemes to improve the overall productivity of Australia's farmlands.

These various physical influences combine to give a generalized pattern of land use which falls into three broad zones. The first comprises some 70 per cent of the land area, and covers all central Australia, reaching the coast along the shores of the Bight and in north-west Australia. About one-third of the area is desert, useless for farming; the rest is of only marginal value for pastoral activities, and then only in the areas close to the rather more favourable conditions of the second zone. This second zone covers only some 17 per cent of Australia, and contains a wide variety of climate and soil types; it is included within a broad belt over 300 kilometres wide extending from the Eyre peninsula paralleling the east coast, and across the northern part of Australia to the Kimberleys. In this zone most farming is practised in the temperate part of the area, including more than 90 per cent of all wheat sown; the zone also supports some 40 per cent of the nation's sheep, 30 per cent of the beef cattle and 20 per cent of the dairy cattle.

The third general zone comprises a belt of land along the east coast from Cairns southward and then westward to south-east South Australia, all of Tasmania, south-west Western Australia and a small part of the Northern Territory around Darwin. Much of this zone (which covers some 13 per cent of the continent) is of broken relief; in the remaining areas the pattern of land use is quite complex. In the northern parts beef grazing dominates, but in the remainder most forms of cropping and livestock production are found. Nearly all Australia's forests are within this zone, as are almost all of the dairying, sugar, fat-lamb, horticulture and high-producing beef cattle areas. The potential for pasture improvement, especially in the southern areas, is considerable.

POPULATION

Australia's population at the end of 1981 was 15,053,555: a density of less than 2 persons per square kilometre, one of the lowest national figures in the world. The reasons for the sparse average population density can be found, first, in the physical geography of the continent, and, second, in its history of settlement—itself a function in time of the physical geography.

As with land use, so with population, Australia can be divided into three broad zones corresponding in many respects to those outlined in the last section; one part almost unpopulated, another sparsely populated, and the final part containing the great majority of the people. This distribution pattern means that any discussion of "averages" in terms of population densities is of only limited value; this is specially so when the proportion of each State's population living in the respective State capitals is revealed (*see* Statistical Survey). The concentration of population within each state is matched by a concentration, on a national scale, in the south-east of Australia. New South Wales and Victoria contain 62 per cent of the nation's population; if Tasmania is added, the proportion rises to 65 per cent. Over the country as a whole settlement is closely related to the areas of moderate rainfall and less extreme temperatures, a pattern initiated by the early growth of towns and cities based on a predominantly pastoral farming community dependent upon farm exports for a livelihood. The result has been the rapid growth of settlement around major ports on which State railway systems were centred, and a subsequent development of manufacturing industry at these port centres where imported raw materials were available, where a skilled labour force could be found, and where distribution facilities to all parts of the respective States were readily available. Only in Queensland and Tasmania did this basic pattern vary to any extent; in Queensland because of the widespread distribution of intensive farming (especially sugar) along a coast well serviced with ports, and in Tasmania because the more dispersed distribution of agricultural and other resources called into being a number of moderate-sized towns and commercial centres.

The majority of the population is from European stock; more than 50,000 full-blood and 50,000 half-caste aborigines are concentrated mainly in rural areas.

HISTORY

E. J. Tapp

COLONIZATION

The continent of Australia was first discovered by the Dutch in the early half of the seventeenth century, but was left in the undisturbed possession of its few widely scattered palaeolithic aborigines until 1770 when the English navigator, Captain James Cook, charted some of its shores and took possession of its eastern half. The annexation was timely, for a few years later the British Government was confronted by a penal problem consequent upon the forced cessation of transportation to the North American colonies which in 1776 had broken away. To relieve the subsequent congestion of convicts in gaols and hulks the Government adopted the suggestion that felons be sent to the newly acquired territory of New South Wales. Accordingly, in 1787, Captain Arthur Phillip sailed in command of the "First Fleet" to establish a penal settlement at Port Jackson (Sydney).

For several years this lonely "gaol" struggled desperately against a harsh, niggardly environment, the constant threat of starvation and internal factions. To ease the pressure on the scanty resources of Port Jackson a branch settlement was established on Norfolk Island, and in 1803, to forestall French designs, a further extension of the penal settlement was made on Van Diemen's Land (Tasmania). Fortunately, Australia was spared from being no more than a penal settlement by the introduction of fine-wool sheep in 1796 and by the penetration in 1813 of the forbidding Blue Mountains to the inviting and endless plains beyond. Such developments led to a broadening of English policy to admit land settlement by emancipists, discharged prison guards and a trickle of free migrants. Even under the sterner conditions of Van Diemen's Land settlement developed and extended to spill over in the 1830s into Port Phillip district of the mainland.

Meanwhile, in 1829 in far Western Australia an entirely free English colony was attempted by private entrepreneurs on the Swan River. Lack of good leadership and planning led to failure and to intervention by the British Government to rescue the misguided settlers from their wretched predicament. For years what remained of the colony languished in the doldrums for want of labour.

From the lessons learnt from the failure of the Swan River settlement South Australia was founded in 1837 on the principles of systematic colonization put forward by Edward Gibbon Wakefield. Here too insufficient preparation caused several years of financial stringency and ultimately necessitated official intervention: but under the vigorous governorship of Captain George Grey and with the opening up of fertile country for wheat growing, South Australia, aided by a locally invented harvester, entered an era of steady prosperity.

Political and Economic Developments 1840–1901

So too did New South Wales which by this time was developing rapidly and supporting scattered settlements of pastoralists. Shortly after the establishment of a penal colony in Moreton Bay (Brisbane) squatters opened up the rich and extensive Darling Downs. By 1840 the free settlers of the colony forced the British Government to end the convict transportation system to New South Wales. Ten years later when the Australian colonies were given power to make their own constitutions, they lost little time in doing so. During the 1850s the five colonies of New South Wales, Tasmania (after 1853), South Australia, Victoria and Queensland, the latter two having been separated from New South Wales in 1850 and 1859 respectively, all gained a wide measure of representative and responsible government, including vote by ballot and manhood suffrage. The demand for self-government was largely stimulated by the discovery of gold and by the great flood of immigrants which came to swell the population. Many of them, inflamed by reform and revolutionary movements in Europe, not only quickened and diversified the purely pastoral economy but introduced radically new social and economic forces which were to have lasting effect. As the gold miners' resistance at Eureka (Victoria) in 1854 against overbearing authority tragically showed, their demands for greater democratic freedom could not be brooked. In education the new spirit worked to break down a dual system of national and denominational schools, and by the 1870s the principle of free, secular and compulsory education through government schools had been adopted. Church schools were allowed to keep open but without government subsidies. From the sharpening and clash of conflicting interests there emerged a colonial democracy, militant in tone, placing a premium upon egalitarianism.

After the first flush of the gold-rush period the increased demand for land led in the 1860s to a series of Selection Acts in New South Wales and Victoria which unlocked vast areas for settlement. Unfortunately, the intractable nature of much of the country, drought and the malpractices of squatters partly defeated the purpose of these Acts and intensified sectional bitterness. The eastern colonies were rescued from years of frustration and social conflict by railway construction, by improved yields from the use of superphosphates, by the invention of refrigeration in the 1880s and at the end of the century by the discovery of drought-resistant varieties of wheat. The prosperity of the Australian colonies in the 1870s and 1880s was general, for by this time Western Australia had, partly through a belated recourse to transportation to solve its labour shortage, achieved some measure of economic stability and independence. Prosperity, however, intensified the forces making for colonial separatism. Different railway gauges and conflicting fiscal policies, especially between free trade New South Wales and protectionist Victoria, were symptomatic of an intense and narrow parochialism. Yet, cutting across colonial borders and differences were social divisions which in the hands of trade unions hardened into a lasting pattern of employer-employee antagonism and led to much industrial strife in eastern Australia. A series of bitterly fought strikes, the failure of banks and a prolonged drought, which halved the flocks of sheep, brought to an end an era of carefree expansion and prodigal expenditure of men and money. Only Western Australia, through a timely discovery of gold deposits at Kalgoorlie and Coolgardie, escaped the depression of the 1880s.

Notwithstanding their primary absorption in internal and domestic matters the eastern colonies towards the end of the century began to show concern for their external relationships. Since their inception all the Australian colonies had subscribed to two basic assumptions: that the continent must be preserved for British settlement only and that the purity of the white race must be safeguarded. Queensland and New South Wales had long been apprehensive of the activities of the French in the south-west Pacific; but they were roused to a sense of danger and dismay when, following the occupation by Germany of the northern half of New Guinea, Queensland's annexation of the southern half was disavowed by the Colonial Office. Of a more general social and economic nature was the Chinese problem which had begun in the 1840s with the importation of cheap coolie labour to replace the convict assignees. With the gold rushes tens of thousands of Asiatics, mainly Chinese, poured into the country to create explosive racial situations on the gold fields. The fiercely competitive practices of the Chinese intensified racial antipathy, and the Colonial Governments' attempts to restrict their entry provoked the intervention of the British Government. Perturbed at such exclusionist policies against a nascent power it wished to placate, Great Britain forced the repeal of the restrictions. But popular feeling in Australia against Asiatic immigration continued to grow and to give rise to alarmist talk of a "Yellow Peril". To labour unions in particular the Chinese were a threat to wages and conditions of employment, so that by the end of the century a white Australia policy had emerged with sufficient support to insist on restriction of Chinese immigration.

The Commonwealth of Australia

The common dangers from without served to strengthen arguments for closer political integration among the colonies. Federation had often been discussed and an abortive attempt at colonial union had been made with the Federal Council of Australasia in 1884. But subsequent events were to give federation a sense of urgency. Alarmed at the defenceless position of Australia and acutely aware during times of depression of the folly of tariff barriers against each other's goods, colonial statesmen rose above their parochial loyalties and gave expression to mounting public opinion in a series of federation conventions. Common characteristics and interests triumphed over their differences; and in 1901 five Australian colonies federated to form the Commonwealth of Australia, leaving Western Australia to join a few years later. Adopting a system of parliamentary executive, the constitution provided for specific powers for the Federal Government and left the residual powers with the States. It gave what the colonies wanted, union but not unity.

The first Commonwealth Parliament lost no time in dealing with matters of common concern. One of its first actions was to give legislative sanction to the White Australia policy in the Immigration Restrictions Bill of 1901. This caused the repatriation of Pacific islanders (Kanakas) employed in the Queensland sugar cane fields. Federation brought for the first time a uniform fiscal policy of protection for the whole of Australia. In 1906 a Commonwealth Court of Conciliation and Arbitration was established to deal with labour disputes extending beyond the borders of any State. An early decision of that Court laid down the basic wage as "the normal needs of the average employee regarded as a human being living in a civilized community". With the Labor Party in power after 1909, the Commonwealth Bank was established and a Federal land tax was imposed. At the same time Australia's growing sense of nationhood was reflected in its insistence upon a separate Australian navy and in the introduction of compulsory military training.

In spite of such defence measures and the Prime Minister's pledge that Australia would support the United Kingdom "to the last man and the last shilling", the country was ill-prepared in 1914 for the consequences of its almost automatic committal to the war. Twice did its mercurial wartime leader, W. M. (Billy) Hughes, try to carry referenda to conscript manpower for war service; but in two bitterly fought campaigns, in which a powerful Irish element with strong *Sinn Fein* sympathies took a leading part, conscription was rejected; and the Labor Party, seriously divided on the issue, fell from office. For all that, the part Australia played in the war was vigorous and substantial, both in men and material. Not only did the war toughen the national fibre but it also strengthened the forces making for national unity and gave Australia an enhanced status among the nations of the world. Recognition of this status was made when, along with the other Dominions, it secured the right of separate representation at the Versailles peace conference and of independent membership of the League of Nations. As a member it was entrusted with the mandate over the ex-German territory in New Guinea and with a share in the mandate over the phosphate island of Nauru.

THE INTER-WAR YEARS

Throughout Australia the war had so disturbed and changed the structure of the economy as to create lasting problems. In the struggle fought on the home front for concerted action, liberalism had been the chief casualty. Never strongly entrenched among vigorously intolerant communities, it fell victim to the clash between capital and labour, which even before the war had ended had resulted in open conflict. The exigencies of war had strengthened and developed heavy and secondary industries in the eastern States. From the consequent development of large industrial monopolies on the one hand and the trade unions on the other came class bitterness and hostility, leading to an era of lock-outs and strikes which continued well after the war. But the fillip given to the Australian economy was such as to cause the Federal Government to set up a tariff board to protect secondary industries and to secure a well-balanced commercial and industrial development of the country. Yet too often tariff protection gave shelter to obsolete or obsolescent plants.

In general the 1920s were years of prosperity and economic expansion. High prices for its primary products of wool and meat enabled Australia to spend freely on public works. During this period over 300,000 immigrants were absorbed into the labour force. At the same time, the opening up of some of the back-country and the attempted development of the Northern Territory by the Federal Government led to a revised appraisal of Australia's resources. The popular conception of Australia Unlimited was replaced by more cautious estimates of its economic and demographic potentialities. This too was a period in which the States, freed from the unifying bonds of war, tended to assume a more parochial outlook. In Western Australia this even went to the length of a short-lived movement for secession. In Queensland, and New South Wales in particular, a newly formed Country Party gave support to fissiparous political trends manifest in New State movements.

By 1928 a hardening of trade and financial conditions had strengthened the position of the Federal Government. After eight years of endless wrangling and before that twenty years of uncertainty the States entered into a financial agreement with the Commonwealth by which the Federal Government took over all State debts. But so dependent was Australia's economy on the United Kingdom's in particular that it could not escape the world depression which developed in the early 1930s. A slump in export prices and a sudden cessation of overseas borrowing gave rise to widespread unemployment and distress. Unfortunately for Australia the crisis had developed at a time when it was facing serious problems arising out of a shortage of overseas funds. To meet the emergency the Commonwealth and State Governments imposed drastic deflationary policies involving a 20 per cent reduction in wages and a 25 per cent depreciation of the Australian pound. Feverish attempts were made to balance budgets in all States except New South Wales where the problems were tackled by the Labor Government by such unorthodox methods as repudiation of interest on overseas loans that they led to a constitutional crisis and the dismissal in 1932 of the State Premier. To honour the State's obligations the Commonwealth paid the interest in default and furnished the amount from the State Treasury. With nearly 30 per cent of union labour unemployed, Australia sought desperately to find markets and economic security. The Ottawa Trade Agreement of 1932 gave it preferential treatment for dried fruits, dairy produce and sugar in return for reduced duties on English goods. But at best the Agreement afforded only a breathing space in which to find new markets outside the British Commonwealth and Empire. Such efforts led to a trade diversion policy in which reciprocal trade treaties were made with Japan, China, the United States and Egypt in addition to some European countries.

Meanwhile, Australia struggled out of the depression. It was no longer able to shelter inefficient secondary industries, but import restrictions stimulated the growth of some industries. To offset the prevailing low returns the Federal Government gave bounties to wheat farmers, but failed to secure increased powers for marketing and aviation. Yet trade gradually expanded and, when in 1937 an end was put to a tariff war with Japan, temporary advantages were gained for Australian wool and textiles. Greater internal investment replacing public borrowing abroad contributed to expansion and stability in secondary production.

Foreign Affairs

The depression and efforts at recovery quickened Australia to a keener awareness of its position in world affairs. Not unnaturally in the absence of international tension isolationist tendencies had re-emerged, but never to the point of making Australia complacently indifferent to its foreign commitments and defence. Not only did it honour the Washington disarmament agreement of 1922 by reducing its naval armaments, but it administered New Guinea in the spirit of the mandate and continued to support the League of Nations. This did not prevent it, especially under a non-Labor Federal Government, from still placing its faith in the United Kingdom and from contributing towards the British naval base being built at Singapore. With traditional loyalties to the United Kingdom unimpaired, Australian statesmen saw little need at the 1926 Imperial Conference to try and define the Dominion Status enjoyed by members of the British Commonwealth. Hence, Australia was in no hurry to adopt the Statute of Westminster of 1931 which granted complete autonomy to the various self-governing Dominions.

Yet world events in the late 1930s were for Australia charged with a new sense of urgency. It was apprehensive at the rapid industrial rise of Japan and its military conquests in Manzhou (Manchuria). Although reluctant to support the imposition of sanctions upon Italy for unprovoked aggression in Abyssinia, it became increasingly concerned with defence problems, especially in view of the deterioration of the international situation and the impotence of the League of Nations to deal with it. Even the Labor Party, which when in power had suspended compulsory military training, urged stronger air defence. The government under Joseph Lyons placed its trust in full co-operation with the United Kingdom and in a balanced development of all armed services. Though remote from the scene of European events Australia watched the gathering storm with fatalistic calm and generally supported every move made by the British Government to prevent it breaking. When it did in 1939, Australia never hesitated to throw in its lot with that of the Mother Country and to place its navy at the disposal of the British Admiralty.

THE SECOND WORLD WAR

Australia entered the Second World War with more maturity and greater realism than it had the First. Although it still harboured old illusions as to its defence and did not yet fully appreciate the nature of the new forces to its north, it was aware that it could no longer escape the consequences of its geographical position in the Pacific. Without delay it began to mobilize all its resources. The United Australia Party, which was in power, invited the Labor Party to form a coalition for the duration of the war, but with its traditional opposition to conscription the Labor Party rejected the offer on the grounds that the interests of democracy could best be safeguarded even in war by a vigilant opposition. With the assistance of State governments the Commonwealth enforced vigorous measures for the prosecution of the war effort. Controls were imposed on exchange, imports, prices and investments, while its wheat and wool were bought by the United Kingdom. In 1941 the State governments agreed to surrender their taxing powers for the duration of the war and to accept in return single uniform taxation by the Commonwealth Government.

But the United Australia Party sat uneasily in government. Apart from appointing Australian ministers to Washington and Tokyo, its record was undistinguished, and after losing strength at the 1940 Federal elections it surrendered its precarious tenure of office to the Labor Party under John Curtin in the following year. With the sudden entry in 1942 of the Japanese on the side of the Axis Powers the Australian Government was charged with unprecedented responsibility. For the first time in its history Australia was faced with the threat of imminent invasion. The fall of Singapore shattered the somewhat pathetic faith it had placed in that bastion of defence and in the British navy. The immediate public reaction was a stiffening of support for the Federal Government's demand for a more direct voice in the determination of Allied war policy. This not being forthcoming, the Prime Minister insisted upon the return from the Middle East of Australian forces to defend Australia. At the same time he turned to the United States for aid. Response was immediate; and U.S. General Douglas MacArthur was ordered to escape from the beleaguered Philippines and to make of Australia a base from which to conduct combined service operations to drive back the Japanese. To implement this plan hundreds of thousands of American troops poured into eastern Australia together with much lend-lease assistance. The Commonwealth accelerated its war effort by enforcing manpower direction and tightening control over wages and profits. This policy of austerity was wholeheartedly endorsed in 1943 at the Federal elections.

With Allied victory nearer in Europe and the Japanese invasion turned back in the south-west Pacific, the Federal Government in 1943 began to plan for post-war reconstruction. Although its successful war policy carried it some distance towards planning for peace, the Federal Government met with opposition from the States which, while weakened by the centralizing wartime trends, still clung to their not inconsiderable powers. In this they were supported by the general public which refused the Commonwealth the special powers that it sought to give effect to its post-war planning. For all that, the State governments supported the Federal Government's attempt to avoid another post-war depression by a policy of full employment, and co-operated in settling ex-servicemen on the land, in housing, in the continuation of price control and in reconstruction training.

THE POST-WAR PERIOD

All this post-war development had the full support of the Labor Party which was in power in most of the States as well as in the Commonwealth. But in regarding the post-war era as the critical period in which they should consolidate their gains, trade unions were often at odds with Federal and State governments. Communist-inspired strikes seriously embarrassed an unsympathetic Federal Labor Government which was at the same time being pressed on all sides for the relaxation of wartime controls. The first concessions were made in 1946 when building controls were handed back to the States. But to prevent inflation resulting from the removal of restrictions and to preserve a favourable trade balance drastic cuts were made in dollar imports. In 1947, the new Labor Prime Minister, Joseph Chifley, sought to control the machinery of credit by nationalizing through the forced purchase of their shares the trading banks of Australia. In this he was thwarted by the opposition of the private banks which successfully appealed against the Banking Act to the Judicial Committee of the Privy Council in the United Kingdom, the final court of appeal in civil cases. Further setbacks to increased Federal control were met when the Australian people rejected a request by referendum for special powers to control rents and prices. Bowing to the public will, the Federal Government in 1948 abandoned all economic controls, but instead sought to set up a social welfare state. Social security measures, such as increased child endowments (first introduced during the war), old age, widow and invalid pensions and hospital benefits were introduced.

Notwithstanding such concessions, return to peace and an era of rising prices hastened the fall of the Federal Labor Government. Not even his own personal popularity and successful handling of a paralyzing coal strike were sufficient to save Chifley and his party at the 1950 elections. Addressing itself mainly to the business sections of the community and playing on public fears of socialization and regimentation, the newly formed Liberal Party was returned to office to form a coalition government with the Country Party. Wartime rationing was abolished and, with the help of a U.S. $100 million loan from the International Bank for Reconstruction and Development, irrigation, land clearance and increased power schemes were undertaken. But the Senate or upper house, which has never operated as it was intended as a safeguard for the member States but has tended to follow the party lines of the lower house, remained predominantly Labor and therefore opposed to the legislation of the new government. At a double dissolution of the Federal Parliament Robert Menzies, the new Prime Minister, secured at the following elections clear majorities in both houses and an endorsement of his policies. Yet in spite of the mandate it had given the Government, the public in its dislike of the politics of proscription rejected Menzies' proposals to deal more effectively with Communism. But the Korean war provided support for firmer anti-communist policies, including secret ballot in trade union elections. Meanwhile, spiralling inflation consequent upon a spectacular rise in wool income intensified industrial unrest which did not abate until lower wool prices stabilized the economy.

Among the chief sufferers from inflation were the State governments which had to bargain fiercely for the annual Commonwealth "hand-outs". Yet when in 1953 they were offered the return of their taxing powers they preferred to leave the unpopular task of raising money to Canberra. More and more was being expected of the Federal Government, and in 1953 it introduced a health scheme to include anti-T.B. treatment and hospital, medical and pharmaceutical benefits. But in 1970 the Government introduced a national health scheme to reduce the cost of medical and hospital services to the public. Increased public and State demands forced the Federal Government to press its constitutional powers to their limit. In the bold and imaginative Snowy Mountains water conservation and hydroelectric scheme, begun in the 1950s, involving the three States of New South Wales, Victoria and South Australia, it undertook the administration and paid the cost of about £500 million.

Although by the mid-1950s Labor had gained popular support in all State governments, except in South Australia where the electoral system until 1970 was weighted in favour of rural constituencies, the Liberal-Country Coalition rode comfortably into Federal office again in 1955 on a buoyant economy. Again, in 1958, Menzies was returned not only with slightly increased gains but with a badly needed Senate majority which he had lost. This enabled him to reform the banking system and make the Reserve Bank of Australia the central bank for the Commonwealth.

Meanwhile, torn by internal dissension, its public image marred in 1954 by a spy case and split by an anti-communist, Catholic-led group which formed itself into the Democratic Labor Party, the Australian Labor Party retired into the political wilderness to lick its wounds. Economic prosperity, full employment and rising wages had blunted the force of much of Labor's original appeal. Even the resignation of its controversial leader, Dr. Herbert Evatt, and his succession by Arthur Calwell, a Roman Catholic, made little difference to the fortunes of the party. The political tide had also turned against Labor by the early 1960s in all States including even New South Wales, a hitherto Labor stronghold, but in 1970 the party was returned to power in South Australia.

It was undoubtedly the serious division in the Labor Party and fear of its extremists, especially in Victoria, which allowed Menzies in 1966 to retire gracefully after sixteen consecutive years of office as Prime Minister. His successor, Harold Holt, although his Liberal Party was returned to office, was unable to secure referendum support to break the constitutional numerical nexus between the Senate and the House of Representatives. After Holt's tragic drowning at the end of 1967, the Federal Government was led by John Gorton, a former prominent Liberal senator, while the leadership of the Labor Opposition was in the strengthening hands of Gough Whitlam. A move to increase the membership of the House of Representatives was defeated in a national referendum. Growing disillusionment with existing political parties led in 1969 to the formation of a short-lived and ineffectual Australia Party. At that year's Federal elections the Liberal-Country Party under John Gorton lost heavily and was returned to office with a bare working majority. Bitter internal party strife led to the replacement of John Gorton by William McMahon in March 1971. Yet it was high time for wider change, for neither the Government nor its leader was popular. Their uncertain and timid handling of inflation, together with growing industrial unrest arising out of penal clauses of the Arbitration Act, proved their downfall. At the Federal elections in December 1972 the Labor Party under Gough Whitlam decisively gained the Treasury benches after 23 years of Liberal-Country Party control.

With the moral support of Labor Governments in the States of South Australia, Western Australia and Tasmania, and more importantly the trade union movement under its new (1969) and dynamic president, Robert Hawke, the Labor Government began life in a general euphoria of great expectations. But Labor's attempts to promote socialistic legislation were frustrated by a hostile Senate, so that after the rejection of a Supply Bill the Prime Minister in 1973 ordered a dissolution of both the House of Representatives and the Senate. The results were disappointing for the Government. Not only was its majority in the House of Representatives reduced, but a stalemate resulted in the Senate and four referenda seeking constitutional reform were rejected by the electorate. In addition the Democratic Labor Party accelerated its long slide to virtual eclipse. Nor could the Liberal Party take much comfort from the result; discredited and weakened by internal dissension, it replaced its leader, Billy Snedden, by Malcolm Fraser in March 1975.

However, the Federal Labor Government's attempt to do too much too quickly led to political disaster. In July 1975 the Deputy Prime Minister, Dr. James Cairns, was removed from office for an irregular move to raise loans of up to $A4,000 million, mainly from Arab sources, to develop the country's mineral resources. Following this, the Government was trenchantly attacked for its lavish spending and borrowing policies. To add to the Government's embarrassment, both the Queensland and New South Wales Governments failed to observe the normal convention of filling vacant Senate seats with nominees of a like political persuasion to those being replaced, thus giving the Federal Opposition a slight but critical Senate majority. With supply repeatedly blocked by a hostile Senate, which constitutionally has the power to pass or reject money bills, Parliament was deadlocked in an intolerable crisis. In a surprise intervention on November 11th the Governor-General, Sir John Kerr, dismissed Prime Minister Whitlam and dissolved both Houses of Parliament. This unprecedented, hotly debated and criticized use of his powers incurred for the Governor-General and his office much public odium and kindled incipient republicanism in Australia. In December 1977 he resigned and was replaced by Sir Zelman Cowen, an eminent constitutionalist and university vice-chancellor.

Meanwhile, the bitterly fought general election in December 1975 resulted in a landslide victory for the Liberal-Country Party and a humiliating defeat for Whitlam and the Labor Party. With an overwhelming majority of 55 (91 seats compared with Labor's 36) in the House of Representatives and a majority of 6 in the Senate, the new Prime Minister, Malcolm Fraser, had a clear mandate to embark on a policy of retrenchment and economy to reduce the rate of inflation and Australia's overseas indebtedness. In December 1977 Gough Whitlam resigned from the leadership of the Labor Party and was replaced by William Hayden, a former Federal Treasurer. Although torn by internal dissension resulting in a breakaway party, the Australian Democrats under Donald Chipp, the Fraser Government was returned to power in December 1977 with a majority in both Houses and has since been seriously challenged only by differences which threatened the coalition of the Liberal and National Country Parties.

In spite of internal dissension and growing public unpopularity, the Government retained office at the general elections in October 1980, but with a much reduced majority (54 seats in the House of Representatives to Labor's 51 and the Country Party's 20). In 1982 Andrew Peacock, who had resigned as Minister for Industrial Relations, unsuccessfully challenged Malcolm Fraser for the leadership of the Government. The Prime Minister, however, continued to be troubled by ministerial scandals and resignations. His position was further weakened by changes in the Senate, where the Government lost its majority and the Australian Democrats held the balance of power. The Federal opposition, meanwhile, was strengthened by the election to the House of Representatives of Bob Hawke, the former outstanding president of the Australian Council of Trade Unions.

In spite of a growing homogeneous political culture, State politics still play a very important part in the life of the nation. In Queensland and Western Australia, owing largely to gerrymandered constituencies, the Country Party was easily returned to power in the former State in 1980 while the Liberal-Country Party alliance retained office in the latter, although with a slim majority. In Victoria, however, a major upset occurred when, after 27 years, the Labor Party returned to the Treasury benches. In New South Wales in 1976, after 13 years in the political wilderness, Labor regained power, managing to retain it with increased majorities in two succeeding elections in 1979 and 1982. So strengthened, it has been able to change the nominated Legislative Council into an elected body. After nearly 10 years in office under a very able Premier, Donald Dunstan, Labor was forced to surrender the government of South Australia in 1979 to the Liberals, who gained a very slender majority. The Liberal Party was also narrowly returned to office in the Tasmanian elections of May 1982. However, it is in the Northern Territory that the major political changes have taken place. Since gaining self-government from Canberra in 1978, the Territory has elected a Country-Liberal Party coalition but there is a strong Labor opposition, thanks largely to the voting of the aborigines.

Australia and the World

After the Second World War Australia became alive not only to the strategic importance of, but also to its obligations to Papua and New Guinea over which it exercised control and a United Nations Trusteeship mandate respectively. In the face of earlier Indonesian expansionist designs in West Irian (then Dutch West New Guinea) and of United Nations' criticism of its treatment of the dependent peoples in the Trust Territory of New Guinea, Australia initiated a policy for both territories of gradual preparation for eventual independence. In 1963 a House of Assembly was set up, providing for an elective native majority. With the gradual transfer of power from Canberra, Papua New Guinea (as it became known) secured self-government in December 1973 and became independent in September 1975, with the blessing of Australia and a bilateral aid commitment of $A930 million over five years. In addition, Australia provided for the construction of the Port Moresby airport and for education and training schemes.

The assumption of such responsibilities towards its dependent peoples has partly quickened the greater maturity Australia has shown since the Second World War in international affairs. Under the vigorous and independent direction of Dr. Herbert Evatt, the Federal Labor Government, while maintaining co-operation with the United Kingdom and with the British Commonwealth of Nations, laid greater store by the United Nations. If somewhat stridently assertive, Australia has in its keen awareness of its vulnerability insisted on a greater measure of control over policy in the Pacific. As a preliminary measure in 1944 it entered into a regional agreement with New Zealand. At the same time the Federal Government emphasized the need to raise living standards in the under-privileged countries of South-East Asia with whose radical nationalist movements it has shown open sympathy.

But with the fall of the Labor Party from Federal power in 1949 the shift of political emphasis under Robert Menzies returned to the British Commonwealth. With a pragmatic rather than a doctrinaire approach to world affairs and with less confidence in untried Asian nationalism, Liberal-Country Party Governments failed to accord diplomatic recognition to the People's Republic of China and sought mainly to contain communism in South-East Asia. Hence, Australia was a prime mover in the Colombo Plan of 1950 designed to give economic and technical aid to non-communist Asian peoples. To this end it gave large sums for rehabilitation in South Viet-Nam and technical assistance in South Korea.

Recognizing that its own security lay largely with the U.S.A., Australia concluded in 1952 (along with New Zealand, with which it had made a defence treaty in 1951) the Australia, New Zealand and United States (ANZUS) Pact. This collective defence treaty, the first which Australia had entered into without Britain, was supplemented in 1954 with its subscription to SEATO (the South East Asia Treaty Organization). Further moves to strengthen defence ties with the U.S.A. led to the establishment in 1963 of a U.S. radio communication station at North Cape in Western Australia, and in 1967 to the construction of a secret defence research station at Pine Gap, in the centre of the continent. Meanwhile, under the terms of ANZUS, Australia sent about 8,000 troops in the late 1960s to aid the Americans in South Viet-Nam but widespread opposition to their involvement in the war led to their withdrawal at the end of 1972.

At the same time, with the advent of a Labor Government, Australia began to assert a more independent foreign policy. As the richest and most powerful country in the south-west Pacific, fully conscious of the importance of its geographical position and international responsibilities, it lost no time in establishing wider diplomatic contacts, first with the People's Republic of China and later with the German Democratic Republic. To Indonesia, with which Australia has had close association, the Federal Government gave large quantities of rice to alleviate a severe local shortage, and also military aid, and in 1974 it provided a loan of $A25 million for economic development. In 1976 it promised a further $A56 million in bilateral aid over three years and, although it protested at Indonesia's annexation of former Portuguese Timor, it has since recognized the *fait accompli* and given assistance for the rehabilitation of its inhabitants. Unfortunately, a rocket range established in 1960 at Woomera in South Australia, with the assistance of Britain and France, has had disappointing results, leading to a decline in its launching activities. Together with New Zealand, with which it has strengthened its alliance, Australia has protested against French nuclear testing in the South Pacific and has successfully brought a case against France before the International Court of Justice. In 1979 it settled its maritime boundaries with Papua New Guinea, sent a peace service corps to Fiji and troops to Namibia as part of a United Nations peace-keeping force.

The intensification of the "cold war", on the other hand, led Australia to strengthen further its ties with the U.S.A. In 1975 it allowed the establishment of an American navigational station and the use of the naval base at Cockburn Sound, Western Australia. It has supported the construction of an American defence base on the island of Diego Garcia in the British Indian Ocean Territory. To strengthen its own defences and to expand its military role in the Indian Ocean, Australia has purchased American anti-submarine aircraft and was to purchase a British aircraft-carrier in 1982. It has also signed a United Nations arms convention.

It has, however, been in the affairs of south-east Asia that Australia has begun to play a leading role. With lessening emphasis upon military pacts, it has supported the Association of South East Asian Nations (ASEAN) in its call for the neutralization of the region. While protesting at the Vietnamese occupation of Kampuchea (formerly Cambodia), Australia has, for political reasons only, recognized the Vietnamese-backed regime in Laos. More significantly, it concluded in 1976 a new co-operation and friendship treaty with Japan and established an Australian-Japanese Foundation to expand cultural relations. To safeguard its northern approaches, especially in view of Britain's withdrawal of armed forces east of Suez, the Federal Government, in agreement with their owner, assumed sovereignty over the strategically placed Cocos Islands in 1978. In Africa, with which Australia has had little contact, it assisted the native independence movement in Rhodesia and sent a monitoring force during the elections for an independent Zimbabwe. To meet Australia's total defence commitments, the Federal Government budgeted for $A3,649 million in 1981/82.

In its international relations, Australia has actively pursued humanitarian policies. Since 1950 more than 400,000 refugees and displaced people from some 40 countries, mainly European, have been settled as "New Australians". Refugee settlement accommodated some 40,000 Indo-Chinese during the 1970s; and for the triennium 1981-83 a target of 250,000 new immigrants has been set. East Timorese have also been allowed to settle in Australia. In addition, much aid has been given, including a yearly grant of $A244 million to Papua New Guinea, while a grant of $A102 million for three years in forward aid commitment has made Australia the principal source of development funds in the South Pacific region. To alleviate distress in Kampuchea, the Federal Government sent over 4,000 metric tons of rice and much medical aid, and in 1982 sent food to the typhoon-battered Solomon Islands. Altogether, in 1981/82 Australia distributed 403,000 tons of food-grain in aid throughout the world. In south-west China it has established a large demonstration farm. To assist fishing within 200 nautical miles (370 km.) of the Australian coastline, it has established a South Pacific fisheries agency, but it has opposed whaling everywhere. Of a cultural nature has been the training of nearly 2,000 Asian students in Australian tertiary institutions.

Diplomatically the Federal Government has also pursued an increasingly important foreign policy. It has established bilateral relations with the People's Republic of China and, in spite of Labor opposition, has strengthened ANZUS ties with the U.S.A. by allowing the construction of an American communication base at North West Cape (Western Australia), bringing the number of such Australian bases to four. On the other hand, it has applied sanctions against the U.S.S.R. for the occupation of Afghanistan and against Iran for its hostility to the West. However, attempts to boycott the Moscow Olympic Games were only partly successful but, to honour the Gleneagles Agreement, Australia has banned participation in South African sporting events. Nearer home, it assisted in quelling rebellion in the New Hebrides (now Vanuatu). More recently, in the face of public opposition, Australia contributed towards an international peace-keeping force in the Sinai region of Egypt and has boycotted trade with Argentina for that country's illegal occupation of the Falkland Islands. In October 1981 Australia mounted the Commonwealth Heads of Government meeting in Melbourne to consider ways and means of combating world poverty. Meanwhile, popular anti-nuclear rallies continue to be held in the major cities.

Social Development

Among the most difficult and pressing of Australia's social problems is that of the aborigines. In recent years, the public conscience has been quickened by the realization of the white man's inhumanity to Australia's earliest inhabitants. After nearly two centuries of indifference and neglect, the Liberal-Country Party Government (1955–72) gave to those of aboriginal descent (numbering 161,000 in 1982), who live primarily in the Northern Territory, Queensland and Western Australia, the franchise and social benefits hitherto denied them. In 1971, the Federal Senate admitted its first aboriginal senator. But aborigines are beginning seriously to question the wisdom of Federal paternalism and assimilation into the white community. In consequence, the Federal Labor Government placed a better deal for the aborigines high on its list of domestic priorities. As the Prime Minister fairly observed, "Australia's treatment of her aboriginal people will judge Australia and the Australians". Accordingly, a Cabinet Minister with exclusive responsibility for aboriginal affairs embarked upon a vigorous new dual policy designed to end discriminatory State practices and to give those who do not wish to integrate into white society educational opportunities, including the provision of teaching in their own language and the preservation of the aboriginal cultural heritage. In 1976 a Federal Act was passed giving aborigines rights to land but reserving mineral rights for the Federal Government. Unfortunately, in the inevitable clash of mining interests with native rights, it has been the latter which have generally suffered, especially in northern Queensland and in Western Australia. Although safeguards against the desecration of sacred sites and pollution from uranium mining have been partly secured, together with some compensation, aborigines, even with the help of the Australian Council of Trade Unions, have not been very successful in resisting the erosion of their land rights by mining companies, or (in 1981) in opposing oil drilling at Noonkanbah in Western Australia. To redress the balance, the Federal Government in 1978 granted $A176 million for assistance to the aborigines but, in so doing, clashed with the Queensland Government over aborigine mission sites, to the disadvantage of the aborigines. A 1981/82 Federal grant of $A147 million is to be spent on aboriginal development, including health, education, training and employment. In 1982 a High Court decision upheld the constitutional validity of the Commonwealth Racial Discrimination Act to give the Federal Government the right to apply national standards in civil liberties to aborigines as well as to all other peoples. Yet thousands of Australian native peoples still live in squalor on their reserves and on the fringe of many country towns. Afflicted with numerous diseases, including glaucoma, they are deprived of most civilized amenities, except alcohol. For all that, they were able in 1976 to supply South Australia with the continent's first aboriginal State governor.

In striking contrast to his treatment of the aborigine, the white man has surrounded himself with all the cultural and civilized amenities of a thoroughly materialistic society. Since the Second World War, largely through the policy of the Federal Government, the number of universities has been increased from 12 to 19, and some 78 Colleges of Advanced Education have been established in the various States. Since 1974 private schools have enjoyed Federal aid, subject to the right of inspection, and about 1,000 ethnic schools have been opened for over 100,000 migrants. In spite of a falling school population, apprentice and student assistance schemes have been initiated, to bring the total Federal expenditure on education for 1981/82 to $A3,255 million, an increase of 16 per cent on the previous budget. For primary and secondary education generally, this is more than equalled by the State governments.

Not surprisingly, the post-war period has seen significant changes to social welfare and health policies. In keeping with its egalitarian philosophy, the Federal Labor Government established a universal contributory system of social security and a voluntary health insurance scheme (Medibank). However, in 1978 the Liberal-Country Party Government, in a major move to cut Federal expenditure by $A2,500 million, abolished Medibank and replaced it with a comprehensive Commonwealth medical and health benefit insurance for all the country's inhabitants, including aborigines. To assist in the implementation of social assistance, an Administrative Appeal Tribunal and an ombudsman have been appointed in every State. None the less the physical health of the nation is giving increasing concern. Heart disease is the biggest killer and is largely exacerbated by tobacco smoking, which in 1981 cost over $A1,000 million in lost wages, medical and other expenses. It is also estimated that there are 1 million handicapped people in the community.

Even more disturbing are the man-made problems, many of which are consequent upon the high urban concentration of population, with 10 million people living in the major cities. Unemployment has steadily risen over the last few years, there being 351,400 registered as unemployed in 1982. Partly in consequence, crime, especially "white collar" crime, has increased and is often associated with drug trafficking and alcohol addiction. To help protect women from abuses, hundreds of refuges have been established throughout the States.

Like most large continents, Australia is subject to the vagaries of extreme climatic conditions. Every year some parts are swept with bush-fires or floods. The town of Darwin was destroyed in December 1974 by a devastating cyclone: it has since been rebuilt and its population increased. In 1978 a cyclone brought death and destruction to the south-west of Western Australia, while periodically locust plagues lay waste large areas of crops and pasture in the southern States. Drought is almost endemic in Western Australia, western New South Wales and western Queensland. Most recent (1981) of such disasters have been widespread bush-fires in Tasmania. Ironically, heavy rain in normally arid central Australia has turned desert areas temporarily into swampland. To cover such contingencies, the Federal Government has instituted a comprehensive insurance scheme. Meanwhile, conservationists have become alarmed at the depredations being made by people upon the native fauna and flora. For some time now, parakeets and other birds have been smuggled out of the country, the kangaroo has been indiscriminately hunted and killed while the koala faces extinction. Even the ubiquitous eucalypt has been afflicted by the so-called "die-back" disease which appears to be consequent upon the decline of bird life, due in part to large-scale mining operations.

Largely indifferent to the plight of its natural heritage, the great majority of Australians continue to indulge in a hedonistic and materialistic way of life. Blessed with a moderate to warm climate, almost all enjoy outdoor recreation. Moreover, it is estimated that more than 5 million people are actively engaged in sport. The Commonwealth Games, due to be held in Brisbane in October 1982, were expected to boost the tourist industry, which in 1981 brought about 1 million visitors (including 115,000 from the U.S.A.) to spend $A1,000 million. To promote tourism further, casinos have been established in Hobart and Darwin, and others are planned for Townsville and Adelaide. While 150 television stations, numerous radio stations and about 600 newspapers continue to provide amusement, news and information to an increasingly passive public, the culturally inclined are also well served with opera, theatre and ballet, which flourish in such venues as the Sydney Opera House, the Melbourne Cultural Centre and the Adelaide Festival Complex. A flourishing film industry benefits from Federal financial support for cultural and recreational activities, which in 1982 amounted to $A461 million.

ECONOMIC SURVEY

C. G. F. Simkin

(Revised for this edition by W. J. Merrilees)

Australia has a comparatively high level of real income per head, although it is about 25 per cent below that of the U.S.A. and further below recent levels in the richer countries of Western Europe. The average annual growth rate of its real income, moreover, slowed down from 4.6 per cent between 1965/66 and 1975/76 to 2.5 per cent in the following five years to 1980/81. The annual rate of population growth slowed to 1.0 per cent in 1975/76, but reached 1.6 per cent in 1980/81.

Most of this income is generated by service industries, whose contribution to G.D.P. rose from 47 per cent in 1955/56 to 60 per cent in 1978/79. There has also been a relative expansion, over this period, of the mining sector because of important discoveries, and exploitation, of iron ore, petroleum, natural gas, coal and other minerals. Despite this growth, mining accounted for only 3.6 per cent of G.D.P. in 1978/79. The construction sector's contribution did not alter from about 8 per cent, but there was a relative decline for manufacturing from 29 to 22 per cent and a bigger drop for agriculture from 14 to 7 per cent. The share of manufacturing has been declining from 1965/66 while that of farming has fallen steadily since about 1960.

Farming industries are still the most important source of export income, although their share of total exports fell from 65 per cent in 1965/66 to 46 per cent in 1979/80. Over the same period, the share of manufacturing in Australia's exports rose from 15 to 22 per cent and that of mining from 18 to 32 per cent. Unprocessed minerals were three-quarters of mining exports.

Australia has continued to recover from the effects of a severe recession, but the relatively slow rate of economic growth, a high level of unemployment (averaging 6 per cent in 1981/82), and a fall in employment in manufacturing have led to official awareness of the need for structural adjustment in the economy, particularly in the manufacturing sector. However, there has been little concrete action in this direction. Concern about an increasing current account external deficit led to heavy government borrowing overseas in 1977/78. Subsequently this was suspended due to a heavy inflow of private capital. The Australian dollar, in terms of a trade-weighted index of the currencies of Australia's principal trading partners, progressively depreciated in value (by 34 per cent between 1974 and 1979) and, after a slight recovery, has continued to fall since mid-1981.

PRIMARY INDUSTRIES

Farming

Much of Australia is low-rainfall, barren desert. Little more than two-fifths of the total area is used for farming. Of the total area (7.8 million square kilometres), only 1 per cent is under crops and only a twelfth of that crop area is irrigated. Droughts and other harsh climatic factors cause large seasonal variations in farm output. Many agricultural commodities also show considerable fluctuations in value from year to year through variations in world prices for wool, wheat, meat, sugar and other farm products. It is better, therefore, to make comparisons on a quinquennial rather than on an annual basis. Between 1974/75 and 1978/79 pastoral activities contributed 43 per cent to gross farm output, crops contributed 48 per cent and most of the remainder came from poultry and pigs.

The most important pastoral activities are sheep farming and beef cattle raising. Meat has become rather more important than wool as a contributor to gross farm output. Over the period 1974/75 to 1978/79 sheep farming accounted for half the gross value of pastoral production. The value of wool sold was four times the gross value of lamb and mutton and beef was three times their value.

Dairy products accounted for 8 per cent of gross farm output, two-thirds of which came from the production of butter and cheese. Butter production has been fairly static since the mid-1950s while cheese production has been rising. Pig and cattle numbers doubled between 1951 and 1979, while poultry farming developed into a separate, highly mechanized and rapidly growing industry. In the 1974–79 period it produced more than 5 per cent of gross farm output.

Wheat, the most important crop, is grown on a large scale in all states, contributing 21 per cent of gross farm output in 1979/80. It is especially vulnerable to climatic changes and rainfall variation. Output has more than doubled since 1955, due to growing world demand for cereals. In 1972/73, a bad year, it contributed only 7 per cent of gross farm output. In 1974/75 and 1978/79, both good years, its share rose to 21 per cent. Barley, the next most important cereal, contributed 2 per cent in 1972/73 and 5 per cent in its best year, 1975/76. Other cereals, including sorghum, rice, maize, rye and millet, made a combined contribution of 3 per cent to gross farm output in 1978/79.

The most important industrial crop is sugar cane, grown in the coastal regions of Queensland and northern New South Wales. Its output has trebled since the late 1950s but it is subject to wide fluctuations in price, which raised the gross value of its output from $A219 million in 1973/74 to $A548 million in 1979/80, when it was 4.6 per cent of gross farm output. Other industrial crops, principally tobacco and cotton, contributed 2 per cent in 1979/80, while fruit and vegetables provided 15 per cent. There is a great variety of fruit and vegetables grown, mostly for the domestic market, due to the wide climatic range of the continent.

Forestry

Australia is not well endowed with forests. Little more than 5 per cent of its area is actually or potentially productive forests. Conservation movements are active, trying to limit logging, especially of rain forests and wilderness areas. There is a surplus of hardwoods for domestic requirements but a considerable deficiency of softwoods, made up by imports. The gross value of forest products in 1979/80 was only 3 per cent of that of agriculture. Most of the forest area is natural forest, four-fifths of which consists of eucalypts or related species. Of a total forest area of 42.5 million hectares, only about 500,000 hectares are plantations of exotic species, principally the Monterey pine (*Pinus radiata*) from California, but these plantations produce about one-fifth of the total volume of forest production.

Fishing

The industry is small-scale and its output is insufficient for local requirements. Australia imports three-fifths of its domestic consumption of seafoods. Lobsters and prawns account for more than three-fifths of the gross value of fishing products. Oysters (commercially cultured in New South Wales and Queensland) and mussels produce 10 per cent of the gross value of fishing products.

Mining

Australia is self-sufficient in most important minerals and has exportable surpluses of aluminium, steaming and coking coal, copper, iron ore, lead, manganese, natural gas, silver, tin, titanium, tungsten, uranium, zinc and zircon. Its main deficiencies, in terms of known deposits, are in crude petroleum, asbestos, cobalt, graphite, fluorite, magnesite, mercury, molybdenum, nitrates, platinum, potassium salts and sulphur.

The added value of mineral products in 1977/78 was nearly $4,400 million. Metallic minerals contributed 40 per cent of this and coal and petroleum 53 per cent. The most important minerals were black coal (34.5 per cent), iron ore (16 per cent), petroleum (18 per cent), silver, lead and zinc (8 per cent),

Australia has long been an important producer of lead, zinc and copper and has had more than enough iron ore for local requirements. In the 1960s there was modest growth of lead, zinc and iron ore production while that of copper trebled during the decade. During the 1960s huge reserves of iron ore in Western Australia were discovered and developed. As a result, the output of iron ore (64 per cent iron) grew from less than 5 million metric tons in 1962 to 96.4 million tons in 1978/79. Large, highly-mechanized mines have been developed in remote, inhospitable areas, accompanied by the construction of ports, railways and habitable towns. Most of the construction and infrastructure cost has been financed by a massive inflow of foreign capital. These mines are almost entirely export-oriented, the principal customer being Japan. Sales have been on a long-time contractual basis to provide the required cash flow to service this large-scale investment.

On the energy side, one of the most important developments was the proving-up to commercial production of a major oilfield in Bass Strait. In addition, a number of small fields have come into production, becoming economic as the result of the continued rise in the world price of oil. The output of crude petroleum increased from 2.5 million cubic metres in 1968/69 to 23.6 million in 1979/80, by which time the country had become two-thirds self-sufficient in petroleum. By then, too, 9 million cubic metres of natural gas were also being produced from Bass Strait, and new fields in South and Western Australia. The potential of the Western Australian fields, in particular, is still in the early stages of assessment.

The other important energy source is coal. Australia's output of black coal rose from 25 million tons in 1962 to 81 million tons in 1979/80. This expansion resulted from development of both new and old fields in Queensland and New South Wales, in response to sharp rises in demand by energy-importing developed countries which sought substitutes for oil. Most of the brown coal deposits are in Victoria and Queensland, and substantial efforts are being made to establish an efficient coal-to-oil liquefaction operation. In 1979/80 production of brown coal, entirely for electricity generation purposes, was 33 million tons.

Major discoveries of nickel and bauxite have been made in Western Australia, while large deposits of bauxite have also been found in Queensland and the Northern Territory. Output of nickel concentrates increased from 36,000 tons in 1972/73 to 75,000 tons in 1979/80. To process the ore, a smelter and a refinery have been built in Western Australia. Output of bauxite increased from 14.7 million tons in 1972/73 to 28 million tons in 1979/80. Australia provided over 60 per cent of Japan's imports of bauxite in 1980.

Tin output has also increased through new discoveries and more efficient exploitation of old ones. It rose from 2,758 metric tons in 1962 to 11,367 tons in 1979/80. The main deposits are in Queensland, New South Wales and Western Australia. Queensland and New South Wales also produce most of Australia's output of rutile (a titanium ore), which increased from 119,000 tons in 1962 to 287,000 tons in 1979/80. Other notable mineral discoveries in recent years include manganese, phosphates, tungsten and a range of mineral sands.

Australia has only one uranium mine operating fully. A number of other deposits have been proven up. Four in the Northern Territory have estimated reserves of 310,000 tons and one in Western Australia has 13,500 tons. There is considerable controversy about uranium mining and aboriginal land rights, which has impeded development of these deposits. Two new mines have been authorized and should make a substantial contribution to exports in the 1980s if the world market demand recovers.

MANUFACTURING

In 1977/78 manufacturing contributed 22.9 per cent of Australia's gross national product, and absorbed about 20 per cent of the civilian labour force. Of the manufacturing sectors, food, beverages and tobacco was easily the most important, yielding 23.1 per cent of manufacturing's contribution to G.N.P. Textiles yielded only 2.5 per cent and clothing and footwear only 3.9 per cent. Wood and its products, including paper and printing, yielded 12.8 per cent, and chemicals, petroleum and coal products 11.8 per cent. Comparable figures for other sectors were: non-metallic mineral products 4.6 per cent, basic metal products 8.8 per cent, fabricated metal products 7.1 per cent, transport equipment 9.6 per cent, other machinery and equipment 10.5 per cent, and miscellaneous manufacturing 4.6 per cent. This supports the claim that Australia has become an industrialized country.

Within the food, beverages and tobacco sector, the processing of meat, milk, cereals and vegetables account for over half the gross value added. Processing of sugar is estimated to account for 12 per cent.

Clothing is the biggest category in the textiles and clothing sector, contributing 51 per cent of its added value. Women's garments are statistically more important than men's. The value of knitwear is about a third that of clothing and the value of footwear is 28 per cent. Fabric production is 63 per cent of the value of clothing and is fairly evenly divided between cottons, woollens, synthetic fabrics and other products such as carpets, felt products, canvas, rope and cordage. The spinning part of this sector is about as important as the fabric part. Synthetic fibres are nearly four times as important as wool in spinning, while cotton spinning is a quite minor activity. A notable feature of the clothing and footwear industries is the high proportion of female labour employed (78 per cent). Textile industries have a much smaller proportion of female labour (42 per cent) and the food, beverage and tobacco group is even less dependent on female labour (26 per cent). Concentration ratios, as measured by the share of the five largest firms in industry sales, were 24 per cent for clothing in 1977/78, 70 per cent for footwear and from 34 per cent to 100 per cent in the various sections of the food, tobacco and beverage sector.

Wood products and furniture contribute 5.4 per cent of the total value added in manufacturing; furniture, joinery and sawmilling are the most important activities in this sector. The female labour ratio is only 15 per cent and the concentration ratios range from 24 per cent to 34 per cent.

The chemical sector (excluding petroleum products) contributes 7.4 per cent to the total value added in manufacturing. Basic chemicals, mainly fertilizers and plastics, account for 40 per cent of this contribution, and pharmaceuticals and agricultural chemicals for another 20 per cent. Paints, soaps and cosmetics account for most of the remainder. Women comprise one-third of the industry's work force and concentration ratios range from 31 per cent for pharmaceuticals to 74 per cent for paints.

Petroleum refining contributes only 1 per cent to total value added in manufacturing. It is highly capital-intensive, and is highly concentrated because of the dominance of the industry by transnational corporations. Local refineries supply over 90 per cent of Australian consumption of motor spirit (petrol), aviation turbine fuel, power kerosene, industrial diesel fuel, automotive distillate and liquefied natural gas. The only petroleum product for which they fail to supply two-thirds of the local market is aviation gasoline. After the oil strikes in 1969, Australia's imports of crude petroleum halved in volume and now domestic crude accounts for 68 per cent of the total input. Since 1969 the combined exports of crude and refined products have quintupled to reach a value of $A414 million in 1979/80.

Non-metallic mineral products account for 5 per cent of manufacturing's value added. Nine-tenths of this sector's contribution comes from the production of bricks, cement, concrete and glass, and half of it from cement and concrete together. Women are an insignificant proportion of the work force, and concentration ratios range from 40 per cent for clay products to 70 per cent for glass.

Basic metal products, which contribute 10.6 per cent to net manufacturing output, are dominated by iron and steel, which account for more than two-thirds of the sector's total value added. The dominant producer of iron and steel is the Broken Hill Proprietary Company. This company also has important interests in petroleum and a range of other basic metals. Activities here include smelting, refining and processing of copper, aluminium, lead, zinc and silver. All these industries are highly concentrated and capital-intensive. The whole sector supplies about nine-tenths of the local market's demand for such products and, in addition, exports three-fifths of its production.

Fabricated metal products had an added value of $A1,845 million in 1978/79, compared with $A2,356 million for basic metal products themselves. By far the biggest contribution came from structural steel, followed by architectural metal products and then by boiler and plate work.

The transport equipment sector contributes 10 per cent of net manufacturing output and two-thirds of this comes from the motor industry. Helped by various protective measures, it supplied about three-quarters of the local market for motor vehicles and parts in 1973/74 but has since had its market share reduced by strong competition from Japanese producers. It is not regarded as an efficient industry, partly owing to the undue proliferation of models for a relatively small domestic market. Only a small proportion of its output is exported.

The "other machinery and equipment" category contributes 12.5 per cent of the value of net manufacturing output. A wide range of activities is included in this group. In order of importance the leading sectors are industrial machinery, electrical machinery, television and radio receivers, refrigerators and other household appliances. Local production supplies about three-quarters of the domestic demand for such products and only 9 per cent of output is exported.

On the whole, Australian manufactures are highly protected. Nominal rates of tariff range from 4 per cent for mineral manufactures to 66 per cent for clothing, which is also protected by quotas. This is also true of footwear, on which the nominal tariff rate is 27.5 per cent. On average the nominal rate of protection is 15 per cent, compared with 5.8 per cent for the U.S.A., 7.5 per cent for the EEC and 11 per cent for Japan. Effective rates of protection (in 1978/79) were 151 per cent for clothing and footwear together, 59 per cent for transport equipment and 61 per cent for textiles. The average for all items was 26 per cent.

Such high rates grew out of an earlier policy of fostering import-substitution industries. While more than one-tenth of manufacturing output is exported, three-quarters of such exports come from industries processing basic metals and foodstuffs. The international competitiveness of Australian manufacturing industry has declined since 1970. The index of competitiveness for import-competing industries declined from a base of 100 in 1970/71 to 78 in 1973/74. Subsequently the index recovered to 89. Many of the reasons for the decline in competitiveness are still present. They include the severe wage explosion in the 1970s (now being repeated in the early 1980s), the move to equal pay for women and an intensification of industrial disputes.

Using the indicator "operating profits as a percentage of funds employed", the least profitable industries in 1978/79 were motor vehicles, leather, rubber, clay products, fruit and vegetable products and basic metal products.

EXTERNAL TRANSACTIONS

Australia is markedly dependent on trade with the rest of the world. Since 1960 the ratio of exports of goods and services to gross domestic product has varied from 14 to 19 per cent, while the ratio of imports to G.D.P. has ranged from 13 to 18 per cent.

Food, beverages and tobacco (mainly wheat, meat and sugar) have provided a fairly steady proportion of merchandise exports, usually somewhat over a third. Wool's proportion fell dramatically from 36 per cent in 1962/63 to 8.5 per cent in 1979/80. The share of iron ore and other basic metal ores has risen dramatically, from less than 3 per cent in 1962/63 to 17 per cent in 1979/80. Coal also rose from 1 to 9 per cent of exports over this period. Manufactures have risen from 14 to 23 per cent of merchandise exports. Basic manufactures have been most important, with metal products contributing 12.5 per cent of total merchandise exports. Chemicals rose from 1 per cent in 1962/63 to 7.5 per cent in 1979/80. Machinery and transport equipment rose from 2 per cent in 1962/63 to 4.5 per cent in 1979/80.

Australia's most important customers in recent years have been Japan, the U.S.A. and the United Kingdom, but there have been marked changes in their relative shares of exports. Between 1962/63 and 1979/80 Japan's share rose from 16 to 27 per cent, touching a peak of 34 per cent in 1976/77. That of the U.S.A. was fairly steady at about 11 per cent and that of the United Kingdom fell sharply from 19 to 5 per cent. New Zealand is now a more important export market for Australia than the United Kingdom and is the largest single market for Australia's manufactured exports. Exports to Europe were 38 per cent of the total in 1962/63, falling to 14 per cent in 1979/80. After the United Kingdom, the main European markets are the Federal Republic of Germany, Italy and France, with shares of between 2 and 3 per cent. The most striking feature of changes in the direction of Australia's trade is its large and growing involvement with the Pacific Basin. This area took three-fifths of Australia's exports in 1962/63 and three-quarters in 1979/80. Exports to China have fluctuated greatly with its need for imported wheat, of which Australia is a major supplier.

On the import side, the largest category has been industrial supplies (mainly processed) 30 per cent, capital goods (excluding transport equipment) 22.4 per cent, consumer goods 15 per cent, transport equipment (including parts) 13 per cent and fuels 12.8 per cent. Owing to high protective duties, imports of clothing were relatively small, at 2 to 3 per cent of the total. The 25 per cent cut in tariff rates in 1973 was so damaging, in terms of profitability and employment, to some import-affected industries that quantitative restrictions became a progressively more important form of assistance to some industries—especially textiles, clothing and footwear, motor vehicles and "white goods". With the exception of the "white goods" industry, this assistance has been maintained or increased. It has been estimated that in 1977/78 quotas increased the average level of assistance to the manufacturing sector by 40 per cent. The textile quotas have been particularly detrimental to the developing countries in East Asia.

For some years Australia has had a substantial deficit on current external account. It has ranged from an average of $A409 million per annum in 1960–64 to $A880 million in 1965–69, falling back to $A416 million for the period 1970–74. As a proportion of total export receipts, the current account deficit has varied from 7 per cent in 1970–74 to 18 per cent in 1960–64 and 28 per cent in 1965–69. There were heavy capital inflows in the 1960s, due to the attraction of mining investment, and this effect has been substantial again since 1979.

INFLATION, EMPLOYMENT AND GOVERNMENT POLICY

Australia has been strongly affected by the world inflation which began in 1973. The buffer of increasing self-sufficiency in oil supplies has been offset by the government's adoption of an import parity pricing policy. The annual increase of consumer prices rose from 3 per cent between 1965 and 1969 to 9 per cent in 1973 and 15 per cent in 1974, falling to 8 per cent in 1978/79. In early 1982 it was about 11 per cent on an annual basis. External influences played a part as import prices rose by 40 per cent in 1974 and by 26 per cent in 1975. Export prices, after rising by 29 per cent in 1973, rose by 17 per cent in both 1974 and 1975. Import prices have since settled down to an average annual increase of 11 per cent while the annual increase of export prices has ranged from 5 per cent in 1977/78 to 21 per cent in 1979/80. Wages (as measured by average adult male weekly earnings) rose by 12 per cent in 1973, 22 per cent in 1974 and 19 per cent in 1975. Subsequent annual increases have ranged between 8 and 11 per cent, with the latter figure holding since 1978.

In the period 1969–71, money (defined in the widest sense) increased by 7 per cent per year, but in 1971–73 the rate of growth rose to 19 per cent. Thereafter it fell to a low of 9 per cent and in 1981 was growing at 11 per cent. Banking sector loans to the Government contributed to monetary expansion between 1969 and 1976, reaching a high of $10,500 million in 1976, but have since slackened off.

The Liberal/National Country Party's re-election as a Government in October 1980 brought no significant shift in policy. A leading research institute has characterized current policy as dominated by a myopic monetarist view. Primary emphasis is placed on restraining the rate of growth of the money supply, currently running at 13 per cent per annum. In addition, there have been attempts, mostly unsuccessful, to hold down wage demands. More successful have been the efforts to reduce the budget deficit, which dropped from 12 per cent of total expenditure in 1977/78 and 1978/79 to just over 6 per cent in 1979/80 and 4 per cent in 1980/81.

The most dramatic reduction has been in the size of the domestic deficit, the aim being to eliminate it in 1981/82. However, it is unlikely that this target will be achieved, partly because of unexpectedly high wage increases in the government sector. The share of the domestic deficit in the total deficit (domestic plus overseas) fell from 71 per cent in 1977/78 to 65 per cent in 1978/79 and 28 per cent 1979/80. In recent years there have been considerable shifts in the relative significance of different sources of revenue for the Federal Government. "Pay as you earn" taxes, which yielded an average of 25.6 per cent of total budget receipts over the period 1964/65 to 1968/69, rose to 41 per cent in 1977/78, a level which has been maintained subsequently. There have been variations in the contribution of indirect taxes, ranging from an average of 26.6 per cent for 1964/65 to 1968/69, to 24.4 per cent in 1974/75, then rising to a peak of 28.5 per cent in 1979/80. The fastest growing source of revenue is the oil levy, which is associated with the Government's world parity oil pricing policy. From a modest 2 per cent of total Government revenue in 1977/78, it rose to 9 per cent in 1980/81. The severely contractionary thrust of fiscal policy is one of the main reasons for the modest growth of consumer demand, especially for consumer durables, in recent years. At the same time, measures to reduce inflation have been largely ineffective due to continued high levels of private capital inflow and the rigidities and imbalances in the structure of interest rates.

Unemployment has become a very serious problem with (at mid-1982) 6 per cent of the civilian workforce registered as seeking jobs. The Government's official view remains that only by reducing inflation, and thus expected inflation, will the preconditions be established for recovery in demand and employment.

STATISTICAL SURVEY

AREA AND POPULATION

Area	Population†						
	Census Results‡						Estimate (December 31st, 1981)§
	June 30th, 1976			June 30th, 1981			
	Males	Females	Total	Males	Females	Total	Total
7,682,300 sq. km.*	6,774,948	6,773,501	13,548,448	7,276,603	7,297,885	14,574,488	15,053,555

* 2,966,150 square miles.

† Excluding diplomatic personnel and armed forces stationed outside the country. Also excluded are alien armed forces within Australia.

‡ Excluding adjustment for under-enumeration, estimated to have been 1.92 per cent in 1981.

§ Provisional.

ETHNIC GROUPS
(census results)

	June 30th, 1971			June 30th, 1976		
	Males	Females	Total	Males	Females	Total
European	6,298,511	6,243,456	12,541,967	6,022,786	6,014,365	12,037,152
Aboriginal	53,917	52,371	106,288	72,824	71,557	144,381
Chinese	15,173	11,025	26,198	19,418	17,220	36,638
Torres Strait Islanders	4,815	4,848	9,663	8,330	8,201	16,531
Pacific Islanders } Others }	40,295	31,227	71,522	5,394	5,179	10,573
				83,524	78,750	162,274
Not stated*	—	—	—	562,672	578,228	1,140,900
Total	6,412,711	6,342,927	12,755,638	6,774,948	6,773,501	13,548,448

* A "Not stated" category for the 1971 census did not exist because in the processing a racial origin was imputed from the respondents' other answers.

STATES AND TERRITORIES

	Area (sq. km.)	Population (December 31st, 1981)*
New South Wales	801,600	5,269,803
Victoria	227,600	3,970,965
Queensland	1,727,200	2,386,229
South Australia	984,000	1,325,874
Western Australia	2,525,500	1,317,602
Tasmania	67,800	428,573
Northern Territory	1,346,200	126,310
Australian Capital Territory	2,400	228,199
Total	7,682,300	15,053,555

* Provisional.

PRINCIPAL CITIES*

Population (June 30th, 1980)

Canberra (national capital)†	245,500	Perth (capital W. Australia)	902,000
Sydney (capital N.S.W.)	3,231,700	Newcastle	385,000
Melbourne (capital Victoria)	2,759,700	Wollongong	226,300
Brisbane (capital Queensland)	1,028,900	Hobart (capital Tasmania)	170,200
Adelaide (capital S. Australia)	934,200	Geelong	142,300

* Statistical divisions or districts. † Includes the municipality of Queanbeyan in New South Wales.

BIRTHS, MARRIAGES AND DEATHS

(Year ending December 1980)

	Births	Marriages	Deaths
New South Wales	79,455	38,965	40,282
Victoria	58,206	27,724	29,374
Queensland	34,972	17,157	16,497
S. Australia	18,499	10,064	9,580
W. Australia	20,607	9,594	8,166
Tasmania	6,735	3,433	3,392
Northern Territory	2,587	661	512
Australian Capital Territory	4,466	1,642	892
Total	225,527	109,240	108,695

PERMANENT AND LONG-TERM MIGRATION*

(Year ending December)

	Arrivals			Departures			Net Increase
	Males	Females	Total	Males	Females	Total	
1977	82,773	78,039	160,812	55,541	50,493	106,034	54,778
1978	81,288	73,457	154,745	54,946	48,176	103,122	51,623
1979	87,887	79,240	167,128	52,704	45,404	98,107	69,020
1980	97,420	86,868	184,288	48,235	42,627	90,862	93,426
1981	113,035	99,650	212,685	45,616	39,996	85,612	127,073

* i.e. intending to stay for more than one year.

EMPLOYMENT*

('000 persons at August)

	1979	1980	1981
Agriculture and services to agriculture	375.7	378.3	384.7
Forestry, logging, fishing and hunting	23.6	28.9	29.5
Mining	82.3	84.3	98.3
Manufacturing	1,220.8	1,233.6	1,230.9
Construction	465.9	483.3	472.2
Transport and storage	344.4	341.8	349.3
Wholesale and retail trade	1,224.2	1,265.4	1,265.5
Finance, property and business services	483.1	510.5	554.9
Community services	940.4	1,007.8	1,022.0
Recreational, personal and other services	366.5	386.4	396.2
Other industries	514.5	526.3	552.7
TOTAL	6,041.5	6,246.6	6,356.3

* Estimates refer to all employed persons and are derived from a monthly population survey.

AGRICULTURE

AREA CULTIVATED

('000 hectares, year ending March 31st)

	1977/78	1978/79	1979/80	1980/81
Cereals for grain:				
Wheat	9,955	10,249	11,153	11,283
Oats	1,076	1,359	1,123	1,093
Barley	2,803	2,785	2,482	2,451
Maize	45	50	54	56
Sugar cane (for crushing)	295	252	267	288
Potatoes	36	35	37	36
Grapevines	71	71	70	70
Fruit	94	97	98	101

CROP PRODUCTION

('000 metric tons, year ending March 31st)

	1976/77	1977/78	1978/79	1979/80	1980/81
Wheat for grain	11,800	9,370	18,090	16,188	10,856
Oats for grain	1,072	990	1,763	1,411	1,128
Barley for grain	2,847	2,383	4,006	3,703	2,682
Maize for grain	144	130	169	151	173
Sugar cane for crushing	23,344	23,493	21,457	21,151	23,976

FRUIT PRODUCTION

(metric tons, year ending March 31st)

	1977/78	1978/79	1979/80	1980/81
Apples	258,360	344,948	298,812	306,921
Apricots	24,834	31,049	26,353	30,621
Bananas	97,808	113,132	125,123	124,341
Oranges	356,538	368,554	392,092	424,494
Peaches	62,168	64,777	71,523	79,194
Pears	108,019	127,590	124,268	145,643
Plums and prunes	18,597	28,899	14,971*	20,827

* Incomplete due to rotational item.

LIVESTOCK

('000 head at March 31st)

	1979	1980	1981*
Cattle and calves	27,112	26,203	25,168
Sheep and lambs	134,222	135,985	134,407
Pigs	2,301	2,518	2,430
Horses	476	494	489

* Provisional.

DAIRY PRODUCE

(Year ending June 30th)

		1978/79	1979/80	1980/81
Whole milk	million litres	5,671	5,398	5,181
Factory butter	'000 metric tons	105	84	79
Factory cheese	,, ,, ,,	142	154	137
Market milk sales by factories	million litres	1,453	1,485	1,514

OTHER LIVESTOCK PRODUCTS

('000 metric tons, year ending June 30th)

	1978/79	1979/80	1980/81
Beef and veal	2,018	1,564	1,466
Mutton	239	275	299
Lamb	253	273	280
Pig meat	199	220	234
Poultry meat	271	313	303
Hen eggs	196	195	202
Wool: greasy	704	709	700
clean	425	430	424

FORESTRY

ROUNDWOOD REMOVALS

('000 cubic metres, excluding fuel wood)

	Coniferous (soft wood)			Broadleaved (hard wood)			Total		
	1977/78	1978/79	1979/80	1977/78	1978/79	1979/80	1977/78	1978/79	1979/80
Sawlogs, veneer logs and logs for sleepers	2,216	2,324	2,713	5,852	5,362	5,621	8,068	7,686	8,334
Pitprops (mine timber)	—	—	—	222	213	180	222	213	180
Pulpwood	937	930	982	4,382	4,332	5,270	5,319	5,262	6,252
Other industrial wood	114	124	176	346	359	397	460	483	573
Total	3,267	3,378	3,871	10,802	10,266	11,468	14,069	13,644	15,339

Source: Forestry Branch, Department of Primary Industry, Canberra, A.C.T.

SAWNWOOD PRODUCTION

('000 cubic metres)

	1975/76	1976/77	1977/78	1978/79	1979/80
Coniferous sawnwood*	716	768	774	797	943
Broadleaved sawnwood*	2,569	2,528	2,201	2,122	2,217
	3,285	3,296	2,975	2,919	3,160
Railway sleepers	205	192	216	249	229
Total	3,490	3,488	3,191	3,168	3,389

* Including boxboards.

Source: Forestry Branch, Department of Primary Industry, Canberra, A.C.T.

FISHING

('000 metric tons, live weight)

	1975	1976	1977	1978	1979	1980
Inland waters	1.5	1.5	1.5	1.3	0.9	1.4
Indian Ocean	57.5	61.1	73.4	66.2	65.1	75.3
Pacific Ocean	49.7	48.8	53.0	55.5	61.7	59.6
Total Catch	108.7	111.4	127.8	122.9	127.7	136.2

MINING*

(year ending June 30th)

		1978/79	1979/80	1980/81
Coal (black)	'000 metric tons	81,197	81,249	96,074
Coal, brown (lignite)[1]	,, ,, ,,	29,095	32,895	29,212
Coal, brown (briquettes)	,, ,, ,,	1,131	1,253	1,081
Bauxite	,, ,, ,,	25,541	27,629	25,450
Zircon[2]	metric tons	347,474	331,190	342,480
Iron	'000 metric tons	53,248	61,319	59,064
Lead	,, ,, ,,	423	n.a.	381
Zinc	,, ,, ,,	498	518	582
Copper	,, ,, ,,	239	235	246
Titanium[3]	,, ,, ,,	958	1,029	1,008
Tin	metric tons	12,011	12,379	12,690
Crude petroleum	'000 cubic metres	24,839	23,647	22,095
Natural gas	million cubic metres	7,686	8,876	9,161
Gold	kilogrammes	19,584	18,273	16,672
Silver	,,	874,075	791,760	758,800
Nickel	metric tons	80,385	64,393	73,367

* Figures for metallic minerals represent metal contents based on chemical assay, except figures for bauxite, which are in terms of gross quantities produced.

[1] Excludes coal used in making briquettes.

[2] In terms of zircon (ZrO_2) contained in zircon and rutile concentrates.

[3] In terms of TiO_2 contained in bauxite and mineral sands.

INDUSTRY

SELECTED PRODUCTS

(year ending June 30th)

		1978/79	1979/80	1980/81
Steel (ingots)	'000 metric tons	7,541	7,895	7,954
Electric motors (under 720 watts)	'000	2,841	3,352	3,648
Clay bricks	million	1,936	2,200	2,251
Sulphuric acid	'000 metric tons	1,922	2,175	1,963
Nitric acid	metric tons	168,596	179,654	182,219
Television receivers	'000	284	325	375
Motor vehicles	,,	435	416	373
Cotton yarn	'000 metric tons	21	22	22
Cotton cloth	'000 sq. metres	41,557	42,144	43,519
Tinplate	'000 metric tons	337	379	333
Electricity	million kWh.	90,857	95,910	100,782
Cement	'000 metric tons	5,117	5,354	5,734

FINANCE

100 cents = 1 Australian dollar ($A).
Coins: 1, 2, 5, 10, 20 and 50 cents.
Notes: 1, 2, 5, 10, 20 and 50 dollars.
Exchange rates (June 1982): £1 sterling = $A1.6925; U.S. $1 = 97.9 Australian cents.
$A100 = £59.08 = U.S. $102.17.

Note: The Australian dollar was introduced in February 1966, replacing the Australian pound (exchange rate: £A1 = U.S. $2.24 from September 1949) at the rate of $A2 = £A1. From February 1966 to August 1971 the exchange rate remained at $A1 = U.S. $1.12 (U.S. $1 = 89.29 Australian cents). Between December 1971 and December 1972 the par value of the Australian dollar was U.S. $1.216 (U.S. $1 = 82.24 Australian cents), though the effective mid-point exchange rate was $A1 = U.S. $1.191. Revaluations were made in December 1972 ($A1 = U.S. $1.275), in February 1973 ($A1 = U.S. $1.4167) and in September 1973 ($A1 = U.S. $1.4875). This last valuation remained in effect until September 1974, when the direct relationship with the U.S. dollar was ended and the Australian dollar was linked to a weighted "basket" of the currencies of Australia's main trading partners. The Australian dollar's value immediately fell to U.S. $1.31, representing an effective devaluation by 11.9 per cent. The currency maintained its weighted value until November 1976, when it was devalued by 17.5 per cent. The average value of the Australian dollar in U.S. dollars was: 1.4227 in 1973; 1.4408 in 1974; 1.3102 in 1975; 1.2252 in 1976; 1.1090 in 1977; 1.1447 in 1978; 1.1179 in 1979; 1.1395 in 1980; 1.1493 in 1981. In terms of sterling, the average exchange rate was £1 = $A1.469 in 1976; $A1.573 in 1977; $A1.676 in 1978; $A1.895 in 1979; $A2.042 in 1980.

GENERAL GOVERNMENT BUDGET*
($A million, years ending June 30th)

Revenue	1978/79	1979/80	1980/81	Expenditure	1978/79	1979/80	1980/81
Income from public enterprises	1,645	1,857	1,952	Final consumption	16,815	18,762	22,055
Interest, etc.	1,028	1,304	1,482	Subsidies	584	807	1,053
Indirect taxes	12,672	14,908	17,270	Interest, etc.	3,028	3,487	4,193
Direct taxes (paid) on income	15,913	18,542	22,343	Personal benefits to residents	9,350	10,160	11,476
Other direct taxes, fees, fines, etc.	850	816	836	Unfunded employee retirement benefits	162	181	207
				Transfers overseas	515	565	633
Total	32,108	37,426	43,884	Total	30,454	33,941	39,618

* Consolidated accounts of Commonwealth, State and local authorities.

STATE GOVERNMENT FINANCES*
($A million, year ending June 30th)

	Receipts		Expenditure	
	1978/79	1979/80	1978/79	1979/80
New South Wales	5,146	5,895	6,116	6,823
Victoria	4,079	4,632	5,160	5,626
Queensland	2,381	2,670	2,778	3,157
South Australia	1,520	1,666	1,787	1,865
Western Australia	1,563	1,748	1,874	2,049
Tasmania	598	665	731	804
Northern Territory	301	378	300	499

* Includes all State Government Authorities.

OFFICIAL RESERVE ASSETS
(June 30th—$A million)

	1979	1980	1981
Gold . . .	1,939	4,117	3,184
SDRs . . .	195	30	46
IMF reserve position	186	179	256
Foreign exchange	1,565	1,355	2,223
TOTAL . .	3,885	5,681	5,709

NOTES IN CIRCULATION
(June 30th—$A million)

	1979	1980	1981
Notes . . .	4,107.4	4,586.1	5,187.3

COST OF LIVING
CONSUMER PRICE INDEX*
(base: 1970=100)

	1978	1979	1980	1981
Food	211.4	240.9	271.3	296.4
Fuel and light	192.0	217.5	249.8	283.5
Clothing	244.6	261.5	279.2	300.0
Rent	237.6	253.4	275.7	304.5
ALL ITEMS . . .	224.0	244.3	269.2	295.3

* Weighted average of six State capitals.

NATIONAL ACCOUNTS
($A million at current prices, year ending June 30th)

	1978/79	1979/80	1980/81
GROSS DOMESTIC PRODUCT . . .	102,070	114,464	131,055
Indirect taxes *less* subsidies . .	12,088	14,069	16,175
GROSS DOMESTIC PRODUCT AT FACTOR COST .	89,982	100,395	114,880
Consumption of fixed capital . . .	6,928	7,725	8,663
DOMESTIC FACTOR INCOMES . . .	83,054	92,670	106,217
Indirect taxes *less* subsidies . . .	12,088	14,069	16,175
Net income paid overseas	1,390	1,760	1,939
NATIONAL INCOME (AT MARKET PRICES) .	93,752	104,977	120,453
EXPENDITURE ON GROSS DOMESTIC PRODUCT .	102,070	114,464	131,055
of which:			
Private final consumption expenditure .	62,097	69,678	78,609
Government final consumption expenditure	16,835	18,804	22,204
Gross fixed capital formation . . .	23,275	25,482	31,581
Increase in stocks	1,271	576	287
Statistical discrepancy	−28	−779	875
Export of goods and services . . .	16,513	21,617	22,267
Less import of goods and services . .	17,892	20,914	24,768

BALANCE OF PAYMENTS

($A million, year ending June 30th)

	1979/80			1980/81		
	Credit	Debit	Balance	Credit	Debit	Balance
Goods and Services:						
Merchandise	18,579	15,828	2,751	18,816	19,186	−371
Transportation	1,891	3,021	−1,130	2,026	3,344	−1,318
Travel	801	1,479	−678	999	1,561	−562
Investment income	581	2,945	−2,364	592	2,840	−2,248
Government n.e.s.	123	264	−141	126	287	−161
Other services	232	417	−185	279	501	−222
Total	22,207	23,954	−1,747	22,838	27,719	−4,881
Transfer Payments:						
Private	588	347	241	715	435	280
Central Government	—	565	−565	—	625	−625
Total	588	912	−324	715	1,060	−345
CURRENT BALANCE	—	—	−2,071	—	—	−5,225
Capital and Monetary Gold:						
Non-Monetary:						
Government transactions (net)	—	80	−80	—	69	−69
Private investment	3,091	533	2,558	5,569	429	5,140
Trade credit n.e.s.	—	758	−758	93	134	−41
Total	3,091	1,371	1,720	5,662	632	5,030
Monetary:						
Changes in official reserve assets	348	—	348	—	1,101	−1,101
Allocation of Special Drawing Rights	98	—	98	86	—	86
Other official monetary institutions transactions	—	145	−145	—	134	−134
Other	143	—	143	—	34	−34
Total	589	145	444	86	1,269	−1,183
Balancing item	—	94	−94	1,378	—	1,378
CAPITAL BALANCE	—	—	2,071	—	—	5,225

Note: Any discrepancies between totals and sums of components in the above table are due to rounding.

FOREIGN INVESTMENT

($A million, year ending June 30th)

INFLOW	1975/76	1976/77	1977/78	1978/79	1979/80	1980/81*
EEC—United Kingdom	310	369	374	807	1,038	1,870
—Other	33	528	1,168	433	551	445
U.S.A.	477	737	994	765	725	1,151
Canada	14	68	−13	−11	55	100
Japan	97	138	380	871	654	841
Other countries	−18	88	76	555	245	1,096
IBRD	−6	−4	−4	−4	−5	−8
TOTAL	905	1,923	2,975	3,415	3,263	5,495

[*continued on next page*

FOREIGN INVESTMENT—*continued*]

OUTFLOW	1975/76	1976/77	1977/78	1978/79	1979/80	1980/81*
EEC—United Kingdom	25	28	71	30	189	−9
—Other	8	9	−1	13	27	19
New Zealand	10	71	47	18	36	108
U.S.A. and Canada	47	60	4	75	105	182
Papua New Guinea†	51	26	26	16	54	−32
ASEAN‡	9	17	23	43	38	92
Other countries	35	42	30	77	83	68
TOTAL	184	252	199	272	532	429

* Provisional.

†From January 1976, includes portfolio investment in Papua New Guinea. Prior to April 1975 excludes such investment; between April and December 1975, includes transactions with Papua New Guinea only where amounts involved were denominated in kina.

‡ Indonesia, Malaysia, the Philippines, Singapore and Thailand.

FOREIGN AID EXTENDED BY AUSTRALIA*

($A million, year ending June 30th)

	1977/78	1978/79	1979/80†	1980/81‡	1981/82‡§
Aid Payments:					
Bilateral:					
Papua New Guinea	219	237	236	245	253
Other	120	154	175	212	267
Multilateral	79	69	89	101	142
TOTAL	418	460	500	558	662

* Official only; excludes transfers by private persons and organizations to overseas recipients.

† *Source:* Statistical summary, Australian Official Development Assistance to Developing Countries 1979–80.

‡ *Source:* Budget Paper No. 8: Australia's Overseas Development Assistance Program 1981-82.

§ Provisional.

EXTERNAL TRADE

($A million, year ending June 30th)

	1975/76	1976/77	1977/78	1978/79	1979/80	1980/81
Imports	8,241	10,411	11,167	13,752	16,218	18,964
Exports	9,640	11,646	12,270	14,243	18,870	19,169

PRINCIPAL COMMODITIES

($A million)

Imports	1978/79	1979/80	1980/81
Food and live animals	532.9	655.2	654.8
Beverages and tobacco	131.1	141.8	169.1
Crude materials (inedible) except fuels	562.3	699.6	763.4
Mineral fuels, lubricants, etc.	1,140.2	2,098.2	2,725.9
Animal and vegetable oils, fats and waxes	65.9	81.2	63.4
Chemicals and related products	1,200.8	1,578.8	1,587.8
Basic manufactures	2,407.5	2,900.2	3,268.9
Paper, paperboard and manufactures	345.6	420.0	458.0
Textile yarns, fabrics, etc.	831.3	953.3	981.2
Machinery and transport equipment	5,731.1	5,655.7	7,033.1
Machinery	3,645.2	3,932.3	4,995.3
Transport equipment	2,086.0	1,723.4	2,037.7
Miscellaneous manufactured articles	1,741.8	2,004.9	2,263.5
Other commodities and transactions	125.1	225.7	258.1
Total merchandise	13,638.7	16,041.4	18,788.0
Non-merchandise trade	113.1	176.1	176.3
Total	13,751.8	16,217.5	18,964.3

Exports	1978/79	1979/80	1980/81
Food and live animals	4,124.1	6,310.4	6,121.7
Meat and meat preparations	1,712.6	1,729.5	1,587.0
Dairy products and birds' eggs	219.1	264.0	270.5
Cereals and cereal preparations	1,174.2	2,891.4	2,325.8
Sugar, sugar preparations and honey	463.7	700.4	1,168.9
Beverages and tobacco	29.6	41.4	47.1
Crude materials (inedible) except fuels	4,597.9	5,568.8	5,761.8
Wool and other animal hair*	1,433.6	1,532.6	1,774.6
Hides, skins and furskins (raw)	374.2	377.4	210.4
Metalliferous ores and metal scrap	2,478.4	3,244.7	3,306.3
Mineral fuels, lubricants, etc.†	n.a.	2,114.4	2,497.3
Animal and vegetable oils, fats and waxes	133.9	99.7	91.8
Chemicals and related products	308.2	379.7	396.8
Basic manufactures	1,798.2	2,360.9	2,036.9
Machinery and transport equipment	673.0	856.7	1,077.7
Machinery	404.4	500.8	606.2
Transport equipment	268.7	355.9	471.6
Miscellaneous manufactured articles	228.3	308.1	342.9
Other commodities and transactions‡	331.1	565.0	567.8
Total merchandise	14,072.6	18,605.0	18,941.5
Non-merchandise trade	170.2	265.1	227.8
Total	14,242.7	18,870.1	19,169.2

* Excluding wool tops.

† Excluding natural and manufactured gas.

‡ Including natural and manufactured gas.

PRINCIPAL TRADING PARTNERS

($A '000)

	Exports		Imports	
	1979/80	1980/81	1979/80	1980/81
Bahrain	59,606	56,176	135,481	109,848
Belgium-Luxembourg	200,532	171,516	120,975	119,300
Canada	338,673	434,120	446,079	500,192
China, People's Republic	845,456	671,201	199,653	269,789
Egypt*	326,913	393,514	79	172
France	351,481	366,305	306,332	305,229
Germany, Federal Republic	495,327	473,677	1,021,207	1,079,380
Hong Kong	281,069	309,252	380,386	394,947
India	173,444	176,859	119,220	108,682
Indonesia	293,151	358,575	241,779	416,875
Iran	251,815	196,471	83,688	33,418
Iraq	226,042	59,265	150,612	95,738
Italy	427,008	393,976	420,498	427,656
Japan	5,070,548	5,227,105	2,526,973	3,628,927
Korea, Republic	406,038	531,849	138,484	203,601
Kuwait	97,165	182,539	311,065	350,768
Malaysia	427,843	442,431	185,820	186,741
Netherlands	234,596	208,048	190,449	198,988
New Zealand	864,480	915,543	546,589	636,193
Norway*	51,341	25,983	41,153	36,415
Papua New Guinea	369,034	433,430	86,412	73,641
Philippines	160,813	169,999	82,565	91,827
Saudi Arabia	218,476	276,305	625,607	1,032,210
Singapore	393,685	513,025	442,631	507,289
South Africa	93,395	132,758	105,835	110,643
Spain	56,717	66,379	54,034	63,666
Sweden	71,994	56,775	307,899	294,618
Switzerland	14,035	17,146	160,648	177,538
Taiwan	323,251	395,093	440,559	508,607
U.S.S.R.	978,283	831,758	66,406	8,974
United Kingdom	951,578	715,329	1,647,850	1,584,605
U.S.A.	2,044,105	2,147,012	3,577,306	4,168,673
Other countries	1,772,185	1,813,829	1,053,231	1,239,107
Total	18,870,079	19,169,243	16,217,505	18,964,266

* From January 1st, 1981, exports of alumina to Egypt and Norway are included only in the figure for other countries.

TRANSPORT

		1976/77	1977/78	1978/79	1979/80§
Railways:					
Route kilometres*	number	40,133	39,710	39,388	40,565
Passengers	'000	331,568	322,895	374,785‡	401,293
Goods and livestock	'000 metric tons	109,943	107,329	111,125	125,671
Road traffic:					
Motor vehicles registered*	'000	6,818	7,115	7,358	7,573
Overseas shipping:					
Vessels entered†	'000 tons	79,666	80,154	82,755	244,433
Vessels cleared†	,, ,,	79,485	80,443	82,509	244,891
Air transport, internal services:					
Kilometres flown	'000	122,933	134,702	135,409	138,185
Passengers carried		9,348,697	10,289,477	10,724,181	11,504,957
Freight	metric tons	108,108	120,887	127,528	129,775
Mail	,, ,,	9,636	11,307	13,126	15,053
Air transport, overseas services:					
Kilometres flown	'000	61,586	58,962	59,040	59,109
Passengers carried		1,551,679	1,569,374	1,782,673	1,933,580
Freight	metric tons	34,380	40,972	51,373	52,326
Mail	,, ,,	3,205	2,981	3,238	3,878

* Figures as at end of period.

† Figures to June 30th, 1979, are for total registered net tonnage of vessels; from July 1st, 1979, figures are for deadweight tonnage of vessels.

‡ Figure includes details of tram and bus operations for the State of South Australia. § Provisional.

1980/81: Road traffic: motor vehicles registered 7,917,000; Overseas shipping ('000 tons): vessels entered 237,223, vessels cleared 234,618.

TOURISM

	1977	1978	1979	1980
Number of Visitors (Arrivals)*	563,281	630,594	793,345	904,558

* i.e. intending to stay less than one year.

COMMUNICATIONS MEDIA

(At June 30th)

	1975	1976	1977	1978	1979	1980
Telephones in use ('000)	5,267	5,502	5,835	6,181	6,677	7,153

Radio receivers (1981): 15,000,000 in use (estimate).

Television receivers (1981): 5,525,000 in use (estimate). **Books** (1979): 8,392 titles (including 2,642 pamphlets) produced.

Newspapers (1979): 63 dailies (combined circulation 4,851,000); 470 non-dailies (circulation 8,930,000).

EDUCATION

(1981)

	Institutions	Teaching Staff*	Students
Government schools	7,472	140,525	2,299,403§
Non-government schools	2,261	37,225	687,996§
Universities	19	11,962	166,611
Colleges of advanced education	68	9,995	165,067
Technical education†	1,248‡	10,600	983,262

* Full-time staff plus full-time equivalents of part-time staff. Technical education staff are shown in units of 1,000 hours.

† The figures are for 1980 and relate to technical and further education (T.A.F.E.) activities of agricultural and college of advanced education authorities as well as the activities in major government departments/divisions of T.A.F.E. The T.A.F.E. enrolments are total enrolments registered during the year up to October 31st, no adjustment being made for students enrolled in more than one course. *Source:* Commonwealth Tertiary Education Commission, *Selected T.A.F.E. Statistics*, 1980.

‡ Includes parent institutions and affiliated branches or annexes as separate institutions.

§ Excludes all pre-primary education undertaken on a sessional basis or in a recognized pre-school class.

Source (unless otherwise stated): Australian Bureau of Statistics, Belconnen, A.C.T. 2616.

THE CONSTITUTION

PARLIAMENT

The legislative power of the Commonwealth of Australia is vested in a Federal Parliament, consisting of H.M. the Queen, represented by the Governor-General, a Senate, and a House of Representatives. The Governor-General may appoint such times for holding the sessions of the Parliament as he thinks fit, and may also from time to time, by proclamation or otherwise, prorogue the Parliament, and may in like manner dissolve the House of Representatives. This power is limited by strict, although unwritten, constitutional convention, and it is rare for such decisions to be made at the sole discretion of the Governor-General. After any general election Parliament must be summoned to meet not later than thirty days after the day appointed for the return of the writs.

THE SENATE

The Senate is composed of ten Senators from each State, two Senators representing the Australian Capital Territory and two representing the Northern Territory. The Senators are directly chosen for a period of six years by the people of the State or Territory, voting in each case as one electorate, and are elected by proportional representation. They retire by rotation, half from each State or Territory, on June 30th of each third year. In the case of a State, if a Senator vacates his seat before the expiration of his term of service, the Houses of Parliament of the State for which he was chosen shall, in joint session, choose a person to hold the place until the expiration of the term or until the election of a successor. If the State Parliament is not in session, the Governor of the State, acting on the advice of the State's Executive Council, may appoint a Senator to hold office until Parliament reassembles, or until a new Senator is elected.

The Senate may proceed to the dispatch of business notwithstanding the failure of any State to provide for its representation in the Senate.

THE HOUSE OF REPRESENTATIVES

In accordance with the Australian Constitution, the total number of members of the House of Representatives must be as nearly as practicable double that of the Senate. The number in each State is in proportion to population, but under the Constitution must be at least five. The House of Representatives is composed of 124 members, which includes two members for the Australian Capital Territory and one member for the Northern Territory.

Members are elected by universal adult suffrage and voting is compulsory. Qualifications for Commonwealth franchise are possessed by any British subject, not under 18 years of age, subject to certain disqualifications (e.g. if of unsound mind), who has lived in Australia for six months continuously.

Members are chosen by the electors of their respective electorates by the preferential voting system.

The duration of the Parliament is limited to three years.

Qualification for membership of the House of Representatives is possessed by any British subject 18 years of age or over who has resided in the Commonwealth for at least three years and who is, or is qualified to become, an elector of the Commonwealth.

THE EXECUTIVE GOVERNMENT

The executive power of the Federal Government is vested in the Queen, and is exercised by the Governor-General, assisted by an Executive Council of Ministers of State, known as the Federal Executive Council. These Ministers are, or must become within three months, members of the Federal Parliament.

The Australian Constitution is construed as subject to the principles of responsible government and the Governor-General acts on the advice of his Ministers in relation to most matters.

THE JUDICIAL POWER

See Judicial System, p. 213.

THE STATES

The Australian Constitution safeguards the Constitution of each State by providing that it shall continue as at the establishment of the Commonwealth, except as altered in accordance with its own provisions. The legislative power of the Federal Parliament is limited in the main to those matters which are listed in section 51 of the Constitution, while the States possess, as well as concurrent powers in those matters, residual legislative powers enabling them to legislate in any way for "the peace, order and good Government" of their respective territories. When a State law is inconsistent with a law of the Commonwealth, the latter prevails, and the former is invalid to the extent of the inconsistency.

The States may not, without the consent of the Commonwealth, raise or maintain naval or military forces, or impose taxes on any property belonging to the Commonwealth of Australia, nor may the Commonwealth tax State property. The States may not coin money.

The Federal Parliament may not enact any law for establishing any religion or for prohibiting the exercise of any religion, and no religious test may be imposed as a qualification for any office under the Commonwealth.

The Commonwealth of Australia is charged with protecting every State against invasion, and, on the application of a State Executive Government, against domestic violence.

Provision is made under the Constitution for the admission of new States and for the establishment of new States within the Commonwealth of Australia.

ALTERATION OF THE CONSTITUTION

Proposed laws for the amendment of the Constitution must be passed by an absolute majority in both Houses of the Federal Parliament, and not less than two or more than six months after its passage through both Houses the proposed law must be submitted in each State to the qualified electors.

In the event of one House twice refusing to pass a proposed amendment which has already received an absolute majority in the other House, the Governor-General may, notwithstanding such refusal, submit the proposed amendment to the electors. If in a majority of the States a majority of the electors voting approve the proposed law and if a majority of all the electors voting also approve, it shall be presented to the Governor-General for Royal Assent.

No alteration diminishing the proportionate representation of any State in either House of the Federal Parliament, or the minimum number of representatives of a State in the House of Representatives, or increasing, diminishing or altering the limits of the State, or in any way affecting the provisions of the Constitution in relation thereto, shall become law unless the majority of the electors voting in that State approve the proposed law.

NEW SOUTH WALES

The State's executive power is vested in the Governor, appointed by the Crown, who is assisted by a Cabinet.

The State's legislative power is vested in a bicameral Parliament, the Legislative Council and the Legislative Assembly. The Legislative Council, formerly consisting of 60 members, began, in late 1978, a process of reconstitution at the end of which it will consist of 45 members directly elected for a term of nine years, fifteen members retiring every three years. The Legislative Assembly consists of ninety-nine members and sits for three years.

VICTORIA

The State's legislative power is vested in a bicameral Parliament: the Upper House, or Legislative Council, of forty-four members, elected for six years, and the Lower House, or Legislative Assembly, of eighty-one members, elected for three years. One-half of the members of the Council retire every three years.

In the exercise of the executive power the Governor is assisted by a Cabinet of responsible Ministers. Not more than five members of the Council and not more than thirteen members of the Assembly may occupy salaried office at any one time.

The State has eighty-one electoral districts, each returning one member, and twenty-two electoral provinces, each returning two Council members.

QUEENSLAND

The State's legislative power is vested in a unicameral Parliament composed of eighty-two members who are elected from eighty-two districts for a term of three years.

SOUTH AUSTRALIA

The State's Constitution vests the legislative power in a Parliament elected by the people and consisting of a Legislative Council and a House of Assembly. The Council is composed of twenty-two members, half of whom retire every three years. Their places are filled by new members elected under a system of optional proportional representation, with the whole State as a single electorate. The executive has no authority to dissolve this body.

The forty-seven members of the House of Assembly are elected for three years from forty-seven electoral districts.

The executive power is vested in a Governor, appointed by the Crown, and an Executive Council consisting of thirteen responsible Ministers.

WESTERN AUSTRALIA

The State's administration is vested in the Governor, a Legislative Council and a Legislative Assembly.

The Legislative Council consists of thirty-two members, each of the sixteen provinces returning two members. Election is for a term of six years, one-half of the members retiring every three years.

The Legislative Assembly consists of fifty-five members, elected for three years, each representing one electorate.

TASMANIA

The State's executive authority is vested in a Governor, appointed by the Crown, who acts upon the advice of a Legislative Council and House of Assembly. The Council consists of nineteen members who sit for six years, retiring in rotation. There is no power to dissolve the Council. The House of Assembly has 35 members elected for four years.

NORTHERN TERRITORY

On July 1st, 1978, the Northern Territory was established as a body politic with executive authority for specified functions of government. Most functions of the Government were transferred to the Territory Government in 1978, and all other functions except Aboriginal Affairs and uranium mining were transferred in 1979.

The Territory Parliament consists of a single house, the Legislative Assembly, with 19 members. The first Parliament stayed in office for three years, but as from the election held in August 1980 members are elected for a term of four years.

The Office of Administrator continues. The Northern Territory (Self-Government) Act provides for the appointment of an Administrator by the Governor-General charged with the duty of administering the Territory. In respect of matters transferred to the Territory Government, the Administrator acts with the advice of the Territory Executive Council; in respect of matters retained by the Commonwealth, he acts on Commonwealth advice.

AUSTRALIAN CAPITAL TERRITORY

The Australian Capital Territory, within which the Federal Seat of Government is situated, is administered by the Federal Government. Under legislation passed by the Parliament the Governor-General is given power to make ordinances for the peace, order and good government of the Territory. There is established in the Territory an elected Legislative Assembly, consisting of 18 elected members, which may advise the Government on matters affecting the Territory.

THE GOVERNMENT

(July 1982)

Head of State: H.M. Queen ELIZABETH II.

Governor-General: Rt. Hon. Sir NINIAN STEPHEN, K.B.E. (took office July 29th, 1982).

FEDERAL EXECUTIVE COUNCIL

(Coalition of the Liberal Party and the National Country Party (NCP)).

INNER CABINET

Prime Minister: Rt. Hon. J. MALCOLM FRASER, C.H.

Deputy Prime Minister and Minister for Trade and Resources: Rt. Hon. JOHN DOUGLAS ANTHONY, C.H. (NCP).

Treasurer: Hon. JOHN HOWARD.

Minister of Defence: Rt. Hon. IAN SINCLAIR (NCP).

Minister for National Development and Energy: Senator the Hon. Sir JOHN CARRICK, K.C.M.G.

Minister for Industry and Commerce: Rt. Hon. Sir PHILIP REGINALD LYNCH, K.C.M.G.

Minister for Foreign Affairs: Hon. ANTHONY AUSTIN STREET.

Minister for Primary Industry: Hon. PETER JAMES NIXON (NCP).

Vice-President of the Executive Council: Hon. Sir JAMES KILLEN, K.C.M.G.

Minister for Finance: Senator the Hon. Dame MARGARET GUILFOYLE, D.B.E.

Attorney-General: Senator the Hon. PETER DURACK, Q.C.

Minister for Social Security: Senator Hon. FRED CHANEY.

Minister for Aviation and Minister Assisting the Prime Minister in Federal Affairs and Public Service Matters: Hon. WALLACE FIFE.

Minister for Employment and Industrial Relations: Hon. IAN MACPHEE.

Minister of Education: Hon. PETER BAUME.

OTHER MINISTERS

Minister of Transport and Construction: Hon. RALPH HUNT (NCP).

Minister for Defence Support and Minister Assisting the Minister for Defence: Hon. ROBERT IAN VINER.

Minister for Science and Technology: Hon. DAVID THOMPSON, M.C. (NCP).

Minister for Administrative Services: Hon. KEVIN NEWMAN.

Minister for Communications and Minister Assisting the Attorney-General: Hon. NEIL ANTHONY BROWN, Q.C.

Minister for the Capital Territory and Minister Assisting the Minister for Industry and Commerce: Hon. WILLIAM MICHAEL HODGMAN.

Minister for Veterans' Affairs and Minister Assisting the Treasurer: Senator the Hon. JOHN MESSNER.

Minister for Home Affairs and Environment and Minister Assisting the Minister for Trade and Resources: Hon. D. T. MCVEIGH (NCP).

Minister for Aboriginal Affairs and Minister Assisting the Minister for Social Security: Hon. IAN WILSON.

Minister for Health and Minister Assisting the Minister for National Development and Energy: Hon. J. J. CARLTON.

Minister for Immigration and Ethnic Affairs: Hon. JOHN HODGES.

ADMINISTRATORS OF TERRITORIES

Northern Territory: Commodore E. E. JOHNSTON, A.M., O.B.E., C. ST. J.

Norfolk Island: DESMOND O'LEARY.

Cocos (Keeling) Islands: ERIC H. HANFIELD.

Christmas Island: W. YATES.

LEGISLATURE

FEDERAL PARLIAMENT

Elections to the House of Representatives and for 34 of the 64 Senate seats were held on October 18th, 1980.

SENATE

(1982)

President: Senator the Hon. HAROLD WILLIAM YOUNG (Lib.).

Chairman of Committees: Senator DOUGLAS MCCLELLAND (NCP).

Leader of the Government: Senator the Hon. Sir JOHN CARRICK (Lib.).

Leader of the Opposition: Senator the Hon. J. N. BUTTON (Lab.).

	SEATS
Liberal	28
National Country Party	3
Labor Party	27
Australian Democrats	5
Independents	1
TOTAL	64

HOUSE OF REPRESENTATIVES
(July 1982)

Speaker: Rt. Hon. Sir BILLY MACKIE SNEDDEN, K.C.M.G., Q.C.

Chairman of Committees: PERCIVAL CLARENCE MILLAR (NCP).

Leader of the House: Rt. Hon. IAN SINCLAIR (NCP).

Leader of the Opposition: Hon. WILLIAM HAYDEN (Lab.).

	SEATS
Liberal Party . .	53
National Country Party .	20
Labor Party . . .	52
TOTAL	125

STATE GOVERNMENTS

NEW SOUTH WALES

Governor: Air Marshal Sir JAMES ROWLAND, K.B.E., D.F.C., A.F.C.

LABOR MINISTRY
(July 1982)

Premier: Hon. NEVILLE K. WRAN, Q.C., M.P.

LEGISLATURE

Legislative Council: Pres. Hon. JOHN RICHARD JOHNSON, M.L.C.; Chair. of Committees Hon. CLIVE HEALEY, M.L.C.

Legislative Assembly: Speaker Hon. LAWRENCE BORTHWICK KELLY; Chair. of Committees Hon. THOMAS JAMES CAHILL.

VICTORIA

Governor: Rear-Admiral Sir BRIAN MURRAY, K.C.M.G., A.O.

LABOR MINISTRY
(July 1982)

Premier: Hon. JOHN CAIN.

LEGISLATURE

Legislative Council: Pres. F. S. GRIMWADE, M.L.C.; Chair. of Committees WILLIAM M. CAMPBELL, M.L.C.; Clerk of the Council ALFRED R. B. MCDONNELL, J.P.

Legislative Assembly: Speaker CYRIL THOMAS EDMUNDS, M.P.; Chair. of Committees JOHN THOMAS WILTON, M.P.; Clerk of the Assembly JOHN H. CAMPBELL, J.P.

QUEENSLAND

Governor: Commodore Sir JAMES MAXWELL RAMSAY, K.C.M.G., C.B.E., D.S.C.

NATIONAL PARTY (NP)-LIBERAL (L)
COALITION MINISTRY
(July 1982)

Premier: JOHANNES BJELKE-PETERSEN, M.L.A. (NP).

LEGISLATURE

Legislative Assembly: Speaker SELWYN JOHN MULLER; Chair. of Committees C. J. MILLER, M.L.A.; Clerk A. R. WOODWARD.

SOUTH AUSTRALIA

Governor: Lt.-Gen. Sir DONALD BEAUMONT DUNSTAN, K.B.E., C.B.

LIBERAL MINISTRY
(July 1982)

Premier: DAVID OLIVER TONKIN.

LEGISLATURE

Legislative Council: Pres. and Chair. of Committees ARTHUR MORNINGTON WHYTE; Clerk of the Legislative Council C. H. MERTIN.

House of Assembly: Speaker BRUCE CHARLES EASTICK; Chair. of Committees GRAHAM MCDONALD GUNN; Clerk of the Parliaments and of the House of Assembly G. D. MITCHELL.

WESTERN AUSTRALIA

Governor: Rear-Admiral Sir RICHARD TROWBRIDGE, K.C.V.O., K.ST.J.

LIBERAL (L)-NATIONAL COUNTRY PARTY (NCP)
COALITION MINISTRY
(July 1982)

Premier: Hon. RAYMOND JAMES O'CONNOR (L).

LEGISLATURE

Legislative Council: Pres. CLIVE EDWARD GRIFFITHS; Chair. of Committees VICTOR J. FERRY, D.F.C.

Legislative Assembly: Speaker IAN DAVID THOMPSON; Chair. of Committees BARRY ROY BLAIKIE.

TASMANIA

Governor: Sir JAMES PLIMSOLL, A.C., C.B.E., K.ST.J.

LIBERAL MINISTRY
(July 1982)

Premier: ROBIN GRAY.

LEGISLATURE

Legislative Council: Pres. Hon. C. B. M. FENTON; Chair. of Committees K. F. LOWRIE; Clerk of the Council A. J. SHAW, J.P.

House of Assembly: Speaker MAX BUSHBY; Chair. of Committees JOHN BEATTIE; Clerk of the House PAUL TREVOR MCKAY.

NORTHERN TERRITORY

Administrator: Commodore E. E. JOHNSTON, A.M., O.B.E., C.ST.J.

LEGISLATIVE ASSEMBLY

Chief Minister: Hon. PAUL ANTHONY EDWARD EVERINGHAM.

Speaker: Hon. J. L. S. MACFARLANE, C.M.G.

POLITICAL PARTIES

Liberal Party of Australia: Federal Secretariat, cnr. Blackall and Macquarie Sts., Barton, A.C.T. 2600; f. 1944; the Party supports private enterprise, individual liberty and initiative, and social justice. It is committed to Australia's development, prosperity and security; Federal Pres. Sir JOHN ATWILL; Parliamentary Leader Rt. Hon. J. MALCOLM FRASER, C.H., M.P.

National Country Party of Australia: John McEwen House, National Circuit, Barton, A.C.T. 2600; f. 1916; formerly called the Country Party; principal objectives are balanced national development based on free enterprise, with special emphasis on the needs of people outside the major metropolitan areas; known as the National Party in Queensland and Victoria as it seeks support equally in the towns and the country; Federal Parliamentary Leader Rt. Hon. JOHN DOUGLAS ANTHONY; Federal Dir. (vacant).

Australian Labor Party: John Curtin House, 22 Brisbane Ave., Barton, A.C.T. 2600; f. 1891; supports the democratic socialization of industry, production, distribution and exchange; Leader of the Federal Parliamentary Labor Party the Hon. WILLIAM HAYDEN; National Pres. NEVILLE K. WRAN, Q.C., M.L.A.; National Sec. BOB MCMULLAN.

Australian Democratic Labor Party: 155-159 Castlereagh St., Sydney, N.S.W.; f. 1956 following a split in the Australian Labor Party; Pres. P. J. KEOGH; Gen. Sec. JOHN KANE.

Australian Democrats Party: 400 Flinders St., Melbourne, Vic. 3000; f. 1977; comprises the former Liberal Movement and the Australia Party; Party Leader Senator The Hon. DONALD L. CHIPP.

Communist Party of Australia: 4 Dixon St., Sydney, N.S.W. 2000; f. 1920; independent of both Soviet and Chinese influence; Pres. JUDY MUNDEY; Nat. Secs. E. AARONS, B. TAFT, R. DURBRIDGE, M. TAFT; publ. *Tribune* (weekly).

Communist Party of Australia (Marxist-Leninist): f. 1967 after split in Communist Party of Australia; supports Maoist principles; Chair. E. F. HILL.

Socialist Party of Australia: 237 Sussex St., Sydney, N.S.W.; f. 1971; aims to bring about a socialist society in Australia through public ownership of the means of production and working-class political power, and to build a united front of workers allied to other progressive forces; fosters international co-operation; Pres. P. CLANCY; Gen. Sec. P. SYMON; publs. *The Socialist, Australian Marxist Review.*

Other political parties include the Farm and Town Party

DIPLOMATIC REPRESENTATION

EMBASSIES AND HIGH COMMISSIONS ACCREDITED TO AUSTRALIA

(In Canberra unless otherwise stated)

Argentina: Room 102, 1st Floor, MLC Tower, Woden, A.C.T. 2606; *Ambassador:* J. ORLANDO CAPPELLINI.

Austria: 107 Endeavour St., Red Hill, A.C.T. 2603; *Ambassador:* Dr. HEINRICH BLECHNER.

Bangladesh: 2 Somers Crescent, Forrest, A.C.T. 2603; *High Commissioner:* (vacant).

Belgium: 19 Arkana St., Yarralumla, A.C.T. 2600; *Ambassador:* ANDRÉ DOMUS.

Brazil: 11th Floor, Canberra House, 40 Marcus Clarke St., A.C.T. 2601; *Ambassador:* MARCOS HENRIQUE CAMILLO CÔRTES.

Bulgaria: Jakarta, Indonesia.

Burma: 85 Mugga Way, Red Hill, A.C.T. 2603; *Ambassador:* U KYEE MYINT.

Canada: Commonwealth Ave., A.C.T. 2600; *High Commissioner:* R. C. ANDERSON.

Chile: 93 Endeavour St., Red Hill, A.C.T. 2603; *Ambassador:* JORGE VALDOVINOS.

China, People's Republic: 247 Federal Highway, Watson, A.C.T. 2602; *Ambassador:* LIN PING.

Colombia: Beijing, People's Republic of China.

Cyprus: 37 Endeavour St., Red Hill, A.C.T. 2603; *High Commissioner:* Dr. PROKOPIS VANEZIS.

Czechoslovakia: Jakarta, Indonesia.

Denmark: 24 Beagle St., Red Hill, A.C.T. 2603; *Ambassador:* HENNING HALCK.

Egypt: 125 Monaro Crescent, Red Hill, A.C.T. 2603; *Ambassador:* ABDEL-HAKEIM MAMDOUGH GOBBAH.

Fiji: 9 Beagle St., Red Hill, A.C.T. 2603; *High Commissioner:* F. M. K. SHERANI.

Finland: 10 Darwin Ave., Yarralumla, A.C.T. 2600; *Ambassador:* VEIKKO O. HUTTUNEN.

France: 6 Perth Ave., Yarralumla, A.C.T. 2600; *Ambassador:* JEAN-BERNARD MÉRIMÉE.

German Democratic Republic: 12 Beagle St., Red Hill, A.C.T. 2603; *Ambassador:* JOACHIM ELM.

Germany, Federal Republic: 119 Empire Circuit, Yarralumla, A.C.T. 2600; *Ambassador:* WILHELM FABRICIUS.

Ghana: 44 Endeavour St., Red Hill, A.C.T. 2603; *High Commissioner:* Rear-Admiral CHEMOGOH K. DZANG.

Greece: 22 Arthur Circle, Forrest, A.C.T. 2603; *Ambassador:* ALEXANDER VAYENAS.

Guatemala: Tokyo, Japan.

Hungary: 79 Hopetoun Circuit, Yarralumla, A.C.T. 2600; *Ambassador:* ISTVÁN MOLNAR.

India: 3-5 Moonah Place, Yarralumla, A.C.T. 2600; *High Commissioner:* KRISHNA D. SHARMA.

Indonesia: 8 Darwin Ave., Yarralumla, A.C.T. 2600; *Ambassador:* ERMAN HARIRUSTAMAN.

Iran: 14 Torres St., Red Hill, P.O.B. 219, Manuka, A.C.T. 2603; *Chargé d'affaires a.i.:* A. A. JEDDI.

Iraq: 48 Culgoa Circuit, O'Malley, A.C.T. 2606; *Ambassador:* FARIS A. K. AL-ANI.

Ireland: 20 Arkana St., Yarralumla, A.C.T. 2600; *Ambassador:* JOSEPH SMALL.

Israel: 6 Turrana St., Yarralumla, A.C.T. 2600; *Ambassador:* ABRAHAM KIDRON.

Italy: 12 Grey St., Deakin, A.C.T. 2600; *Ambassador:* SERGIO ANGELETTI.

Japan: 112 Empire Circuit, Yarralumla, A.C.T. 2600; *Ambassador:* MIZUO KURODA.

Jordan: 20 Roebuck St., Red Hill, A.C.T. 2603; *Chargé d'affaires a.i.:* SAMIR NAOURI.

Korea, Republic: 113 Empire Circuit, Yarralumla, A.C.T. 2602; *Ambassador:* HA JONG YOON.

Kuwait: Tokyo, Japan.

Laos: 113 Kitchener St., Garran, A.C.T. 2605; *Chargé d'affaires a.i.:* AXANAY VILAIHONGS.

Lebanon: 73 Endeavour St., Red Hill, A.C.T. 2603; *Ambassador:* RAYMOND HENEINE.

Libya: 50 Culgoa Circuit, O'Malley, A.C.T. 2606; *Secretary of the People's Committee:* SULEIMAN A. OREIBI.

Malaysia: 71 State Circle, Yarralumla, A.C.T. 2600; *High Commissioner:* Tan Sri Datuk LIM TAIK CHOON.

Malta: 261 La Perouse St., Red Hill, A.C.T. 2603; *Acting High Commissioner:* JOSEPH A. CARUANA.

Mauritius: 43 Hampton Circuit, Yarralumla, A.C.T. 2600; *High Commissioner:* L. R. DEVIENNE.

Mexico: 1 Beagle St., Red Hill, A.C.T. 2603; *Ambassador:* JESÚS CABRERA MUÑOZ LEDO.

Mongolia: Tokyo, Japan.

Nepal: Tokyo, Japan.

Netherlands: 120 Empire Circuit, Yarralumla, A.C.T. 2600; *Ambassador:* EMILE L. C. SCHIFF.

New Zealand: Commonwealth Ave., A.C.T. 2600; *High Commissioner:* Sir LAURIE FRANCIS.

Nigeria: 27 State Circle, Deakin, A.C.T. 2600; *High Commissioner:* EDWARD O. SANU.

Norway: 3 Zeehan St., Red Hill, A.C.T. 2603; *Ambassador:* TORLEIV ANDA.

Pakistan: 59 Franklin St., Forrest, A.C.T. 2603; *Ambassador:* S. W. HUSAIN.

Panama: Tokyo, Japan.

Papua New Guinea: Forster Crescent, Yarralumla, A.C.T. 2600; *High Commissioner:* AUSTIN SAPIAS.

Peru: 94 Captain Cook Crescent, Griffith, A.C.T. 2603; *Ambassador:* JOSÉ F. TORRES-MUGA.

Philippines: 1 Moonah Place, Yarralumla, A.C.T. 2600; *Chargé d'affaires a.i.:* ROSARIO CARINO.

Poland: 7 Turrana St., Yarralumla, A.C.T. 2600; *Ambassador:* RYSZARD FRACKIEWICZ.

Portugal: 8 Astrolabe St., Red Hill, A.C.T. 2603; *Ambassador:* Dr. I. J. REBELLO DE ANDRADE.

Romania: 3 Tyagarah St., O'Malley, A.C.T. 2606; *Chargé d'affaires:* GHEORGHE ZAMFIR.

Singapore: 81 Mugga Way, Red Hill, A.C.T. 2603; *High Commissioner:* LOW CHOON MING.

Somalia: Beijing, People's Republic of China.

South Africa: cnr. State Circle and Rhodes Place, Yarralumla, A.C.T. 2600; *Ambassador:* A. J. OXLEY.

Spain: 15 Arkana St., Yarralumla, A.C.T. 2600; *Ambassador:* CARLOS M. FERNANDEZ-SHAW.

Sri Lanka: 35 Empire Circuit, Forrest, A.C.T. 2603; *High Commissioner:* Lt.-Gen. J. E. D. PERERA.

Sweden: 5 Turrana St., Yarralumla, A.C.T. 2600; *Ambassador:* LARS-ERIK HEDSTRÖM.

Switzerland: 7 Melbourne Ave., Forrest, A.C.T. 2603; *Ambassador:* Dr. HENRI ROSSI.

Thailand: 111 Empire Circuit, Yarralumla, A.C.T. 2600; *Ambassador:* PADANG PADAMASANKH.

Turkey: 60 Mugga Way, Red Hill, A.C.T. 2603; *Ambassador:* FARUK SAHINBAS.

Uganda: Mezzanine Floor, MLC Tower, Woden, A.C.T. 2606; *High Commissioner:* Prof. J. W. KIBUKAMUSOKE.

U.S.S.R.: 78 Canberra Ave., Griffith, A.C.T. 2603; *Ambassador:* Dr. NIKOLAY SUDARIKOV.

United Kingdom: Commonwealth Ave., A.C.T. 2600; *High Commissioner:* Sir JOHN MASON, K.C.M.G.

U.S.A.: Chancery, Yarralumla, A.C.T. 2600; *Ambassador:* ROBERT D. NESEN.

Uruguay: Suite 5, Bonner House, P.O.B. 318, Woden, A.C.T. 2606; *Chargé d'affaires a.i.:* LUIS A. CARRESSE.

Vatican: 2 Vancouver St., Red Hill, A.C.T. 2603; *Apostolic Pro-Nuncio:* The Most Rev. Dr. LUIGI BARBARITO.

Venezuela: Suite 106, M. L. C. Tower, Woden, A.C.T. 2606; *Ambassador:* Dr. I. ARCAYA.

Viet-Nam: 31 Endeavour St., Red Hill, A.C.T. 2603; *Chargé d'affaires a.i.:* NGUYEN THAI HUNG.

Yugoslavia: 11 Nuyts St., Red Hill, A.C.T. 2603; *Ambassador:* SIME KARAMAN.

Australia also has diplomatic relations with Afghanistan, Algeria, the Bahamas, Bahrain, Barbados, Botswana, Costa Rica, Cuba, Dominica, the Dominican Republic, Ecuador, Ethiopia, Gabon, Grenada, Guyana, Haiti, Honduras, Iceland, the Ivory Coast, Jamaica, Kenya, Kiribati, the Democratic People's Republic of Korea, Lesotho, Liberia, Liechtenstein, Luxembourg, Madagascar, Maldives, Monaco, Morocco, Nauru, Oman, Paraguay, Qatar, Saint Lucia, Saint Vincent and the Grenadines, Saudi Arabia, Seychellés, Sierra Leone, Solomon Islands, Sudan, Swaziland, Syria, Tanzania, Tonga, Trinidad and Tobago, Tunisia, Tuvalu, the United Arab Emirates, Vanuatu, Western Samoa, the Yemen Arab Republic, Zaire, Zambia and Zimbabwe.

JUDICIAL SYSTEM

The judicial power of the Commonwealth of Australia is vested in the High Court of Australia, in such other Federal Courts as the Federal Parliament creates, and in such other courts as it invests with Federal jurisdiction.

The High Court consists of a Chief Justice and six other Justices, each of whom is appointed by the Governor-General in Council, and has both original and appellate jurisdiction.

The High Court's original jurisdiction extends to all matters arising under any treaty, affecting representatives of other countries, in which the Commonwealth of Australia or its representative is a party, between States or between residents of different States or between a State and a resident of another State, and in which a writ of *mandamus*, or prohibition, or an injunction is sought against an officer of the Commonwealth of Australia. It also extends to matters arising under the Constitution or involving its interpretation, and to any other matters empowered by the Federal Parliament.

The High Court's appellate jurisdiction extends to appeals from all judgments, decrees, orders and sentences of its own Justices exercising original jurisdiction, and, in a limited way, to appeals from any other Federal Court or court exercising Federal jurisdiction, and from the Supreme Court of any State or any other State court from which an appeal lies to the Queen in Council.

Legislation enacted by the Federal Parliament in 1976 substantially changed the exercise of Federal and Territory judicial power, and, by creating the Federal Court of Australia in February 1977, enabled the High Court of Australia to give greater attention to its primary function as interpreter of the Australian Constitution. The Federal Court of Australia has assumed, in two divisions, the jurisdiction previously exercised by the Australian Industrial Court and the Federal Court of Bankruptcy and has additionally been given jurisdiction in trade practices and in the developing field of administrative law. It also hears appeals from the Court constituted by a single Judge, from the Supreme Courts of the Territories, and in certain specific matters from State Courts, other than a Full Court of the Supreme Court of a State, exercising Federal jurisdiction. The Federal Court is composed of a Chief Judge and twenty-five other Judges.

FEDERAL COURTS

HIGH COURT OF AUSTRALIA

Chief Justice: Rt. Hon. Sir HARRY TALBOT GIBBS, G.C.M.G.

Justices:

Hon. Sir ANTHONY FRANK MASON, K.B.E.
Hon. LIONEL KEITH MURPHY.
Hon. Sir RONALD DARLING WILSON, K.B.E.
Hon. Sir GERARD BRENNAN, K.B.E.

Registrar: F. W. D. JONES.

FEDERAL COURT OF AUSTRALIA

Chief Judge: Sir NIGEL HUBERT BOWEN, K.B.E.

25 other Judges.

FAMILY COURT OF AUSTRALIA

Chief Judge: Hon. ELIZABETH ANDREAS EVATT.

40 other Judges.

NEW SOUTH WALES

SUPREME COURT

Chief Justice: Hon. Sir LAURENCE WHISTLER STREET, K.C.M.G., K.ST.J.

President of the Court of Appeal: Hon. ATHOL RANDOLPH MOFFIT, C.M.G.

Chief Judge in Equity: Hon. MICHAEL M. HELSHAM, O.A., D.F.C.

Chief Judge at Common Law: Hon. JOHN FLOOD NAGLE, O.A.

Masters: B. J. K. COHEN, Q.C., C. R. ALLEN, G. S. SHARPE. J. HOGAN (acting).

Principal Registrar: L. JAMES (acting).

Prothonotary: J. LESLIE (acting).

VICTORIA

SUPREME COURT

Chief Justice: Hon. Sir. JOHN MCINTOSH YOUNG, K.C.M.G.

Masters: C. P. JACOBS, M.B.E., P. A. BARKER, E. N. BERGERE, G. S. BRETT, T. P. BRUCE, V. M. GAWNE.

Prothonotary: P. S. MALBON.

QUEENSLAND

SUPREME COURT

Southern District (Brisbane)

Chief Justice: Hon. Sir WALTER BENJAMIN CAMPBELL.

Senior Puisne Judge: Hon. D. G. ANDREWS.

Registrar and Prothonotary: M. J. CAMPBELL.

Central District (Rockhampton)

Puisne Judge: Hon. A. G. DEMACK.

Registrar: G. D. ROBERTS.

Northern District (Townsville)

Puisne Judge: Hon. Sir JOSEPH KNEIPP.

Registrar: R. J. KEANE.

SOUTH AUSTRALIA

SUPREME COURT

Chief Justice: Hon. LEONARD JAMES KING.

Registrar: J. B. GARSDEN.

WESTERN AUSTRALIA

SUPREME COURT

Chief Justice: Hon. Sir FRANCIS BURT, K.C.M.G.

Master: G. T. STAPLES.

Principal Registrar: M. S. NG.

TASMANIA

SUPREME COURT

Chief Justice: Hon. Sir GUY STEPHEN MONTAGUE GREEN, K.B.E.

Master: C. G. BRETTINGHAM-MOORE, M.C.

Registrar: J. DALE.

AUSTRALIAN CAPITAL TERRITORY

SUPREME COURT

Chief Judge: Hon. RICHARD A. BLACKBURN, O.B.E.

Registrar: B. J. PROCTOR.

NORTHERN TERRITORY

SUPREME COURT

Chief Justice: Hon. Sir WILLIAM EDWARD STANLEY FORSTER.

Master: NARENDRA PATEL.

RELIGION

ANGLICAN CHURCH OF AUSTRALIA

In 1979 there were over 3.75 million members of the Anglican Church of Australia. The national office is: General Synod Office, P.O.B. Q190, Queen Victoria P.O., Sydney, N.S.W. 2000; Gen. Sec. J. G. DENTON.

Primate of Australia, Archbishop of Brisbane and Metropolitan of Queensland: Most Rev. JOHN B. R. GRINDROD.

Archbishop of Sydney and Metropolitan of New South Wales: Most Rev. DONALD W. B. ROBINSON.

Archbishop of Melbourne and Metropolitan of Victoria: Most Rev. ROBERT W. DANN.

Archbishop of Perth and Metropolitan of Western Australia: Most Rev. PETER F. CARNLEY.

Archbishop of Adelaide and Metropolitan of South Australia: Most Rev. KEITH RAYNER.

ROMAN CATHOLIC CHURCH

In 1981 there were about 3.5 million Roman Catholics in the 29 dioceses of Australia.

Archbishops

Adelaide	Most Rev. JAMES W. GLEESON.
Brisbane	Most Rev. FRANCIS R. RUSH.
Canberra and Goulburn	Most Rev. EDWARD B. CLANCY.
Hobart	Most Rev. GUILFORD C. YOUNG, K.B.E.
Melbourne	Most Rev. THOMAS F. LITTLE, K.B.E.
Perth	Most Rev. LAUNCELOT JOHN GOODY, K.B.E.
Sydney	His Eminence Cardinal JAMES DARCY FREEMAN, K.B.E., Most Rev. JAMES P. CARROLL, Most Rev. ABDO KHALIFE.

OTHER CHURCHES

Baptist Union of Australia: P.O.B. 136, Glen Waverley, Vic. 3150; f. 1926; Pres.-Gen. Rev. J. D. WILLIAMS; Sec. Rev. G. G. ASHWORTH; 53,116 mems.; 702 churches; publs. *Australian Baptist* (fortnightly) and *State Papers* (monthly).

Lutheran Church of Australia: Lutheran Church House, 58 O'Connell St., North Adelaide, S.A. 5006; f. 1966; 157,000 mems.; Pres. Rev. L. B. GROPE; Sec. Rev. H. F. W. PROEVE; publs. *The Lutheran* (official organ; every 3 weeks), *Lutheran Women, Lutheran Men, Children's Friend, Prism* (all monthly), *Lutheran Theological Journal* (quarterly), *Lutheran Year Book.*

Greek Orthodox Church: Greek Orthodox Archdiocese, 242 Cleveland St., Redfern, Sydney, N.S.W. 2016; leader in Australia, Archbishop STYLIANOS; 380,500 mems.; Archdiocesan offices in Melbourne and Adelaide; Greek Orthodox Communities throughout Australia.

Uniting Church in Australia: Box C103, Clarence St. Post Office, Sydney, N.S.W. 2000; f. 1977 when the Methodist, Presbyterian and Congregational Churches united; Pres. Rev. Prof. R. A. BUSCH, O.B.E.; Sec. Rev. DAVID GILL; 2,000,000 mems.

JUDAISM

Great Synagogue: Elizabeth St., Sydney, N.S.W.; f. 1828; Senior Minister Rabbi RAYMOND APPLE, A.M.; Sec. RAPHAEL A. SEIDMAN, 166 Castlereagh St., Sydney, N.S.W.

THE PRESS

Australia's legislation relating to the Press varies in different States.

Under the law concerning contempt of court, to publish names or photographs before proceedings begin may draw heavy penalties. Though accurate reporting of a case while it is being tried is privileged, a judge is empowered to ban all reports until the conclusion of the case.

Each state has its legislation against obscene publications, which is particularly severe in the State of Queensland, whose broadly defined Objectionable Literature Act of 1954 covers a wide range of offences.

The libel law ranges from seditious libel for matter liable to cause a breach of the peace, or for excessive abuse of government officials, to defamatory libel. Certain government agencies have privilege. A journalist, if prosecuted, is obliged to justify every material part of an allegedly defamatory statement, and this has led to a marked tendency not to publish outspoken comment where there is a risk of prosecution. In all States the author, editor, owner, publisher, printer and, to some extent, the distributor of a publication are liable for damages to the person defamed.

The total circulation of Australia's daily newspapers is very high but in the remoter parts of the country weekly papers are even more popular. Most of Australia's newspapers are published in sparsely populated rural areas where the demand for local news is strong. The only newspapers which may fairly claim a national circulation are the dailies *The Australian* and *Australian Financial Review,* and the weeklies *The Bulletin,* the *National Times* and the *Nation Review,* the circulation of most newspapers being almost entirely confined to the State in which each is produced.

All newspapers in the state capitals are owned by limited companies. The trend towards concentration of ownership has led to the development of three principal groups of newspapers. Economic conditions have necessitated the extension of the activities of newspaper companies into related spheres, magazine and book publishing, radio and television, etc. The main groups are as follows:

The John Fairfax Group: 235 Jones St., Broadway, P.O.B. 506, Sydney, N.S.W. 2001; f. 1841; Chair. J. O. FAIRFAX; with its subsidiary Associated Newspapers Ltd., controls *The Sydney Morning Herald, The Sun, National Times, Australian Financial Review* and the *Sun-Herald* (Sydney), *The Age* (Melbourne), *The Canberra Times* (Canberra), *Illawarra Mercury* (Wollongong), and *The Newcastle Herald* (Newcastle); also has radio and television interests.

The Herald and Weekly Times Ltd. Group: 44 Flinders St., Melbourne, Vic. 3000; Chair. Sir KEITH MACPHERSON; controls, among other publications, *The Herald, The Sun News-Pictorial, The Bendigo Advertiser* and *The Geelong Advertiser* (Melbourne), *The West Australian, Daily News* (Perth), *Kalgoorlie Miner, Papua New Guinea Post-*

Courier, *Fiji Times*, and also has holdings in several magazines and radio and television companies.

News Ltd.: 2 Holt St., Surry Hills, Sydney, N.S.W. 2010; Chair. R. H. SEARBY; Chief Exec. RUPERT MURDOCH; controls *Adelaide News* (Adelaide), *The Australian*, *Daily Mirror* (Sydney), *The News* (Darwin), *Sunday Times* (Perth), *Sunday Sun* (Brisbane), *Daily Telegraph* and *Sunday Telegraph* (Sydney), *Northern Daily Leader* (Tamworth), Progress Press (Melbourne). Assoc. publs.: *New Idea* and *TV Week* (Melbourne), *The Sun*, *News of the World*, *The Times* and *The Sunday Times* (London), *New York Post* and *New York Magazine* (New York), *New West* (Los Angeles), *Express-News* (Texas). Owns television channels TEN-10 (Sydney), ATV-10 (Melbourne).

Also of some importance are the following:

Consolidated Press Group: 54 Park St., Sydney, N.S.W.; publishes *The Australian Women's Weekly*, *The Bulletin* and *Cleo* magazines; holds a controlling interest in the Murray Leisure Group and several country newspapers including *The Maitland Mercury*; controls various television and radio stations.

David Syme & Co. Ltd.: Melbourne, Vic.; of which John Fairfax Ltd. owns 57 per cent; publishes *The Age* and other newspapers and magazines in Victoria and Hong Kong.

NEWSPAPERS

AUSTRALIAN CAPITAL TERRITORY

The Canberra Times: 18 Mort St., Braddon, Canberra 2601; f. 1926; daily and Sun.; morning; Editor I. R. MATHEWS; circ. 45,846.

NEW SOUTH WALES

DAILIES

The Australian: News Ltd., 2 Holt St., Surry Hills, N.S.W. 2010, P.O.B. 4245; f. 1964; edited in Sydney, published simultaneously in Sydney, Melbourne, Perth and Brisbane; Propr. RUPERT MURDOCH; Editor WARREN BEEBY; circ. 126,000.

Australian Financial Review: 235 Jones St., Broadway, P.O.B. 506, Sydney 2001; f. 1951; Mon. to Fri.; distributed nationally; Editor-in-Chief P. P. MCGUINNESS; circ. 63,000.

Daily Commercial News: P.O.B. 1552, Sydney 2001; f. 1891; Gen. Man. C. S. WYNDHAM.

Daily Mirror: 2 Holt St., Surry Hills 2010; f. 1941; evening; Chief Exec. RUPERT MURDOCH; Editor KEITH HARRIS; circ. 390,500.

Daily Telegraph: 2 Holt St., Surry Hills 2010; f. 1879; morning; Editor G. HUSSEY; circ. 326,000.

The Manly Daily: 26 Sydney Rd., Manly 2095; f. 1906; Tues. to Sat.; Gen. Man. M. C. G. UTTING; circ. 73,930.

The Newcastle Herald: 28–30 Bolton St., Newcastle 2300; f. 1858; morning; Editor J. A. ALLAN; circ. 64,000.

The Sun: 235 Jones St., Broadway, P.O.B. 506, Sydney 2001; f. 1910; evening; Editor-in-Chief G. R. FORD; circ. 350,000.

The Sydney Morning Herald: 235 Jones St., Broadway, P.O.B. 506, Sydney 2001; f. 1831; morning; Editor V. J. CARROLL; circ. 266,000.

WEEKLY NEWSPAPERS

The Advertiser: 142 Macquarie St., Parramatta 2150; Wed. and Sat.; Man. Editor S. JACKSON; circ. 102,000.

Bankstown Canterbury Torch: 47 Allingham St., Bankstown 2200; f. 1920; Wed.; Editor P. C. L. ENGLISCH; circ. 75,000.

National Times: 235 Jones St., Broadway, Sydney 2007; f. 1971; weekly; published in all capital cities; Editor BRIAN TOOHEY; circ. 96,000.

Northern District Times: 116 Rowe St., Eastwood 2122; f. 1921; Wed.; Man. M. PACEY; Editor J. MITCHELL; circ. 67,162.

Parramatta and District Mercury: 1st Floor, 38 George St., Parramatta 2150; f. 1977; Tues.; circ. 101,500.

St. George and Sutherland Shire Leader: 172 Forest Rd., Hurstville 2220; f. 1960; Wed.; Exec. Dir. J. D. CHICKEN; Editor K. HARGRAVE; circ. 118,000.

Sun-Herald: 235 Jones St., Broadway, P.O.B. 506, Sydney 2001; f. 1953; Sunday; Editor P. R. ALLEN; circ. 692,088.

Sunday Telegraph: 2 Holt St., Surry Hills 2010; f. 1938; Editor ALAN FARRELLY; circ. 665,000.

VICTORIA

DAILIES

The Age: 250 Spencer St. (cnr. Lonsdale St.), Melbourne 3001; f. 1854; independent; morning; Man. Dir. C. R. MACDONALD; Editor CREIGHTON BURNS; circ. 251,178.

The Herald: 44–74 Flinders St., Melbourne 3000; f. 1840; evening; Editor P. V. HINTON; circ. 390,000.

Sun News-Pictorial: 44–74 Flinders St., Melbourne 3000; f. 1922; morning; Editor LEIGH STEVENS; circ. 640,000.

WEEKLY NEWSPAPERS

Chadstone Progress: 2 Keys Rd., P.O.B. 301, Moorabbin 3189; f. 1960; Wed.; Editor O. A. HAYES; circ. 98,600.

Melbourne Sunday Press: 250 Spencer St., Melbourne 3000; f. 1973; Editor JACK CANNON; circ. 137,000.

Sporting Globe: 44 Flinders St., Melbourne 3000; f. 1922; Tues.; Editor G. HOBBS.

Sunday Observer: 45–49 Porter St., Prahran 3181; f. 1971; Editor ANTONY CHEESEWRIGHT; circ. 129,000.

Truth: 32 Walsh St., Melbourne 3000; f. 1902; Mon. and Thurs.; Editor B. KAPLAN; circ. 303,700.

QUEENSLAND

DAILIES

Courier-Mail: Campbell St., Bowen Hills, Brisbane 4006; f. 1933; morning; Editor K. J. KAVANAGH; circ. 270,500.

Telegraph: Campbell St., Bowen Hills, Brisbane 4006; f. 1872; evening; Editor D. C. SMITH; circ. 154,000.

WEEKLY NEWSPAPERS

The Suburban: 10 Aspinall St., Nundah; P.O.B. 10, Nundah; 2 editions, for north-western and north-eastern suburbs respectively; publr. Mrs. HEATHER JEFFERY; combined circ. 90,000.

Sunday Mail: Campbell St., Bowen Hills, Brisbane 4006; f. 1933; Editor D. FLAHERTY; circ. 366,000.

Sunday Sun: cnr. Brunswick and McLachlan Sts., Fortitude Valley, Brisbane 4000; f. 1971; Man. Editor R. RICHARDS; circ. 311,000.

SOUTH AUSTRALIA

DAILIES

Advertiser: 121 King William St., Adelaide 5001; f. 1858; morning; Editor D. V. RIDDELL; circ. 230,261.

News: 112 North Terrace, Adelaide 5000, Box 1771 G.P.O., Adelaide 5001; f. 1923; evening; Mon. to Fri.; Editor-in-Chief KERRY SULLIVAN; circ. 188,000.

SUNDAY NEWSPAPER

Sunday Mail: 116–120 North Terrace, Adelaide 5000; f. 1912; Editor KERRY SULLIVAN; circ. 258,590.

WESTERN AUSTRALIA

DAILIES

Daily News: Newspaper House, St. George's Terrace, Box D162 G.P.O., Perth 6001; f. 1882; evening, Mon.-Fri.; Editor I. L. HUMMERSTON; circ. 125,000.

West Australian: Newspaper House, St. George's Terrace, Box D 162 G.P.O., Perth 6001; f. 1833; morning; Editor M. C. UREN; circ. 254,672.

WEEKLY NEWSPAPERS

The Countryman: Newspaper House, St. George's Terrace, Perth; f. 1885; Thurs.; a farmers' magazine; Editor G. A. BOYLEN; circ. 16,000.

Sunday Independent: East Victoria Park 6101, Box 40 P.O., Bentley 6102; f. 1969; Sunday; Editor NEVILLE CATCHPOLE.

Sunday Times: 34-36 Stirling St., Perth 6000; f. 1897; Man. Dir. D. M. WEBB; Editor F. DUNN; circ. 265,000.

Weekend News: 125 St. George's Terrace, Perth 6001; f. 1960; Saturday; Editor J. R. DAVIES; circ. 80,000.

TASMANIA

DAILIES

Advocate: P.O.B. 63, Burnie 7320; f. 1890; morning; Editor D. J. CHERRY; circ. 26,300.

Examiner: 71–75 Paterson St., Launceston 7250; f. 1842; morning; independent; Gen. Man. B. J. MCKENDRICK; Editor M. C. P. COURTNEY; circ. 38,480.

Mercury: 91–93 Macquarie St., Hobart 7000; f. 1854; morning; Editor D. N. HAWKER; circ. 57,693.

WEEKLY NEWSPAPERS

Advocate Weekender: P.O.B. 63, Burnie 7320; f. 1968; Saturday afternoon; Editor D. J. CHERRY; circ. 16,600.

Saturday Evening Mercury: 91–93 Macquarie St., Hobart 7000; f. 1954; Editor D. N. HAWKER; circ. 39,296.

Sunday Examiner-Express: 71–75 Paterson St., Launceston 7250; f. 1924; Editor M. C. P. COURTNEY; circ. 38,700.

The Tasmanian Mail: 130 Collins St., Hobart 7000; f. 1978; weekly; Man. Editor W. A. J. HASWELL; circ. 132,000.

NORTHERN TERRITORY

DAILY

Northern Territory News: 28 Mitchell St., P.O.B. 1300, Darwin 5794; f. 1952; Mon. to Sat.; Man. Editor J. HOGAN; circ. 15,000.

TWICE-WEEKLY

The Darwin Star: 31 Bishop St., P.O.B. 39330 Winnellie, Darwin, N.T. 5789; f. 1976; Wed. and Sat.; Man. Editor ALEC MARTIN; circ. 13,000.

SELECTED PERIODICALS

WEEKLIES AND FORTNIGHTLIES

The Advocate: 143 a'Beckett St., Melbourne, Vic.; f. 1868; Thurs.; Catholic; Editor NEVILLE WEERERATNE; circ. 19,000.

Australasian Post: 61 Flinders Lane, Melbourne, Vic. 3000; f. 1946; factual, general interest, particularly Australiana; Fri.; Editor G. R. ECCLES; circ. 316,000.

Australian Cricket: Murray Publishing Pty. Ltd., 152-156 Clarence St., Sydney, N.S.W. 2000; f. 1968; fortnightly October-March; Man. Editor IAN HEADS.

Australian Women's Weekly: 54 Park St., Sydney, N.S.W. 2000; f. 1933; Wed.; Editor-in-Chief TREVOR KENNEDY; circ. 900,000.

The Bulletin: 54 Park St., Sydney, N.S.W.; f. 1880; Wed.; Editor-in-Chief TREVOR SYKES.

The Medical Journal of Australia: 71–79 Arundel St., Glebe, N.S.W. 2037; f. 1914; fortnightly; Editor DR. ALAN BLUM; circ. 21,500.

New Idea: 32 Walsh St., Melbourne, Vic.; weekly; women's magazine; Editor D. BOLING.

News Weekly: G.P.O. Box 66A, Melbourne, Vic. 3001; f. 1943; Wed.; political and trade union affairs in Australia; int. affairs, particularly Indian Ocean and South-East Asian area; National Civic Council organ; Man. Dir. P. ANDERSON; circ. 16,500.

People Magazine: P.O.B. 156, Chippendale 2008; weekly; Publr. J. ZANETTI; News Editor DAVID NAYLOR; circ. 180,000.

Queensland Country Life: 432 Queen St., Brisbane, Qld.; f. 1935; Thurs.; Editor MALCOLM MCCOSKER; circ. 35,305.

Scene: 61 Flinders Lane, Melbourne, Vic. 3000; f. 1925; Wed.; Editor G. J. MANSFIELD; circ. 98,275.

Stock and Land: Stock and Land Publishing Co. Pty. Ltd., Box 82, North Melbourne, Vic. 3051; f. 1914; weekly; livestock, land and wool market journal; Man. Editor C. T. DEB. GRIFFITH; circ. 25,000.

TV Week: 32 Walsh St., Melbourne, Vic.; f. 1957; Mon.; colour national; Editor TONY FAWCETT; circ. 673,000.

Weekly Times: Box 751F, G.P.O. Melbourne, Vic. 3001; f. 1869; farming, gardening, country life and sport; Weds.; Editor J. BALFOUR BROWN; circ. 120,000.

Woman's Day: 57-59 Regent St., P.O.B. 148, Chippendale, N.S.W. 2008; circulates throughout Australia and New Zealand; Editor VICKI GREEN; circ. 500,000.

MONTHLIES AND OTHERS

Archaeology in Oceania: University of Sydney, N.S.W. 2006; f. 1966; archaeology and physical anthropology; 3 issues a year; Editor J. PETER WHITE.

Architecture Australia: Strand Publishing, P.O.B. 1185, Brisbane 4001.

Australian Architecture and Design: 26–29 Beatty Ave., Armadale, Vic. 3143; f. 1980; independent architectural journal posted to architects and designers throughout Australia; 6 issues a year; circ. 7,000.

Australian Forest Research: C.S.I.R.O., 314 Albert St., East Melbourne, Vic. 3002; quarterly; Editor J. J. LENAGHAN.

Australian Home Beautiful: 44–74 Flinders St., Melbourne, Vic. 3000; f. 1925; monthly; Editor A. J. HITCHIN.

Australian House and Garden: 152 Clarence St., Sydney, N.S.W. 2000; monthly; building, furnishing, decorating, handicrafts, gardening, etc.; Editor BERYL CLARKE.

Australian Journal of Agricultural Research: C.S.I.R.O., 314 Albert St., East Melbourne, Vic. 3002; f. 1950; alternate months; Editor G. A. FORSTER.

Australian Journal of Biological Sciences: C.S.I.R.O., 314 Albert St. East Melbourne, Vic. 3002; f. 1953; alternate months; Editor L. A. BENNETT.

Australian Journal of Botany: C.S.I.R.O., 314 Albert St., East Melbourne, Vic. 3002; f. 1953; alternate months; Editor L. W. MARTINELLI.

Australian Journal of Chemistry: C.S.I.R.O., 314 Albert St., East Melbourne, Vic. 3002; f. 1953; monthly; Editor R. SCHOENFELD.

Australian Journal of Marine and Freshwater Research: C.S.I.R.O., 314 Albert St., East Melbourne, Vic. 3002; f. 1950; alternate months; Editor L. A. BENNETT.

Australian Journal of Pharmacy: 35 Walsh St., West Melbourne, Vic. 3003; f. 1886; monthly; official journal of the associated pharmaceutical organizations of Australia; Editor S. L. DICKSON; Man. I. G. LLOYD; circ. 8,500.

Australian Journal of Physics: C.S.I.R.O., 314 Albert St., East Melbourne, Vic. 3002; f. 1953; alternate months; Editor D. E. BOYD.

Australian Journal of Plant Physiology: C.S.I.R.O., 314 Albert St., East Melbourne, Vic. 3002; f. 1974; alternate months; Editor L. W. MARTINELLI.

Australian Journal of Politics and History: University of Queensland, St. Lucia, Qld. 4067; f. 1955; 3 times a year; Editor G. GREENWOOD; circ. 1,000.

Australian Journal of Soil Research: C.S.I.R.O., 314, Albert St., East Melbourne, Vic. 3002; f. 1963; quarterly; Editor G. A. FORSTER.

Australian Journal of Zoology: C.S.I.R.O., 314 Albert St., East Melbourne, Vic. 3002; f. 1953; alternate months; Editor SUSAN E. INGHAM.

Australian Law Journal: 19th Floor, St. Martins Tower, 31 Market St., Sydney, N.S.W.; f. 1927; monthly; General Editor J. G. STARKE, Q.C.; Asst. Editor C. A. SWEENEY.

Australian Left Review: Box A247, Sydney South P.O. 200, N.S.W.; f. 1966; five issues a year.

Australian Outdoors: 154 Clarence St., Sydney, N.S.W. 2000; monthly; Editor PETER SCOTT.

Australian Photography: 381 Pitt St., P.O.B. 4689, Sydney, N.S.W. 2001; monthly; an official organ of the Australian Photographic Society; Editor MARTIN COLOMAN.

Australian Quarterly: Australian Institute of Political Science, Archway House, 32 Market St., Sydney, N.S.W. 2000; f. 1929; quarterly; Editors HUGH PRITCHARD, ELAINE THOMPSON.

Australian Video and Communications: P.O.B. 451, Hawthorn, Vic. 3122; f. 1981; monthly; Editor GEOFFREY M. GOLD; circ. 28,300.

Australian Wildlife Research: C.S.I.R.O., 314 Albert St., East Melbourne, Vic. 3002; f. 1974; three issues per year; Editor-in-Chief B. J. WALBY.

The Australian Worker incorporating The Worker: 321 Pitt St., Sydney, N.S.W. 2000; f. 1891; monthly; official organ of the Australian Workers' Union; published by D. F. Austin Publishing Pty. Ltd.; circ. 105,000.

Brunonia: C.S.I.R.O., 314 Albert St., East Melbourne, Vic. 3002; f. 1978; two issues per year; Editor-in-Chief B. J. WALBY.

Cleo: 168 Castlereagh St., Sydney, N.S.W. 2000; P.O.B. 4088, Sydney, N.S.W. 2001; monthly; women's; Editor PATSY HOLLIS.

Commerce, Industrial and Mining Review: Invicta Publications, Box 142, Bentley, W.A. 6102; quarterly.

Current Affairs Bulletin: University of Sydney, Sydney, N.S.W. 2006; f. 1947; monthly; Exec. Editor G. WILSON; circ. 12,500.

Economic Record: School of Agriculture, La Trobe University, Bundoora, Vic. 3083; f. 1925; 4 a year; journal of Economic Society of Australia and New Zealand; Joint Editors Prof. J. W. FREEBAIRN, Dr. R. G. GREGORY.

Ecos: C.S.I.R.O., P.O.B. 225, Dickson, A.C.T. 2602; f. 1974; quarterly; reports of C.S.I.R.O. environmental research findings for the non-specialist reader; Editor ROBERT LEHANE; circ. 14,000.

Electronics Australia: P.O.B. 163, Chippendale, N.S.W. 2008; f. 1939; technical, radio, television, microcomputers, hi-fi and electronics; monthly; Editor LEO SIMPSON.

Historical Studies: Department of History, University of Melbourne, Parkville, Vic. 3052; f. 1940; 2 a year, April and October; Editor J. B. HIRST.

Industrial and Commercial Photography: 381 Pitt St., P.O.B. 4689, Sydney, N.S.W. 2001; 2 a month; official journal of the Professional Photographers Association of Australia, Australian Cinematographers Society and Photographic Industrial Marketing Association of Australia; Editor TERRY SWAN.

Journal of Pacific History: Australian National University, P.O.B. 4, Canberra, A.C.T. 2600; f. 1966; 2 a year; Editors W. N. GUNSON, D. A. SCARR.

Manufacturers' Monthly: 72 Clarence St., Sydney, N.S.W. 2000; f. 1961; circ. 11,440.

The Mathematical Scientist: C.S.I.R.O., DMS, P.O.B. 1965, Canberra City, A.C.T. 2601; 2 a year; Editor C. C. HEYDE.

Modern Boating: Murray Publishers, 154 Clarence St., Sydney, N.S.W. 2000; monthly; Man. Editor CHRIS NIXON.

Modern Motor: 154 Clarence St., Sydney, N.S.W. 2000; f. 1954; monthly; Man. Editor BRIAN WOODWARD; Editor BARRY LAKE; circ. 50,000.

Nation Review: P.O.B. 339, P.O Camberwell, Melbourne 3124; f. 1958; independent, progressive monthly; Editor-in-Chief GEOFFREY M. GOLD; circ. 45,490.

New Horizons in Education: c/o Dept. of Education, University of Sydney, Sydney, N.S.W. 2006; f. 1938; published twice a year by the World Education Fellowship; Editor Dr. YVONNE LARSSON.

Oceania: The University of Sydney, Sydney, N.S.W. 2006; f. 1930; social anthropology; quarterly; Editor PETER LAWRENCE.

Open Road: 151 Clarence St., Sydney, N.S.W.; f. 1927; official journal of National Roads and Motorists' Asscn. (N.R.M.A.); every two months; Editor B. GIULIANO; circ. 1,188,653.

Overland: G.P.O. Box 98A, Melbourne, Vic. 3001; f. 1954; literary, social, political; Editor S. MURRAY-SMITH.

Pacific Islands Monthly: 76 Clarence St., Sydney, N.S.W. 2000; f. 1930; specialist journal dealing with political, economic and cultural affairs in the Pacific Islands; Editor ANGUS SMALES; Man. JOHN BERRY.

POL: ADC House, 77 Pacific Highway, North Sydney, N.S.W. 2060; monthly; women's; Editor ROBIN INGRAM.

Progress: 31 Hardware St., Melbourne, Vic. 3000; economics, land reform; monthly; Editors A. R. HUTCHINSON, H. B. EVERY, G. A. FORSTER.

Queensland Countrywoman: 89–95 Gregory Terrace, Brisbane, Qld.; f. 1929; monthly journal of the Queensland Country Women's Association; Editor Mrs. RAE PENNYCUICK.

Rural Research: C.S.I.R.O., P.O.B. 225, Dickson, A.C.T. 2602; f. 1952; reports of C.S.I.R.O. agricultural and biological research findings for the non-specialist reader; quarterly; Editor ROBERT LEHANE; circ. 24,000.

Search-Science Technology and Society: Box 873, G.P.O. Sydney, N.S.W. 2001; f. 1970; journal of Australian and N.Z. Association for the Advancement of Science;

monthly; Hon. Editor R. STRAHAN; Exec. Editor E. F. F. WHEELER; circ. 3,700.

Theatre Australia: 8th Floor, 36 Clarence St., Sydney, N.S.W. 2000; f. 1976; monthly; Editor ROBERT PAGE; Exec. Editor LUCY WAGNER; circ. 10,000.

VideoMag: P.O.B. 163, Chippendale, N.S.W. 2008; f. 1982; 2 a month; Editor NEVILLE WILLIAMS.

Wildlife in Australia: 8 Clifton St., Petrie Terrace, Brisbane, Qld. 4000; quarterly; official publication of the Wildlife Preservation Society of Queensland; Editor VINCENT SERVENTY.

World Review: P.O.B. 279, Indooroopilly, Qld. 4068; f. 1962; four times a year; published by the Australian Institute of International Affairs, Queensland Branch; Editor NANCY VIVIANI.

Your Garden: 61 Flinders Lane, Melbourne, Vic. 3000; monthly; Editor A. BALHORN; circ. 85,000.

PRESS AGENCIES

Australian Associated Press: 364 Sussex St., Sydney, N.S.W.; f. 1935; owned by principal daily newspapers of Australia; Chair. G. J. TAYLOR; Joint Man. Dirs. A. H. MCLACHLAN and E. J. L. TURNBULL; Gen. Man. C. L. CASEY.

FOREIGN BUREAUX

Agence France-Presse (AFP): P.O.B. 48, Canberra, A.C.T. 2600; Chief of Bureau FRANK S. CHAMBERLAIN.

Agenzia EFE (Spain): 6 Crossles Close, Melba, Canberra, A.C.T. 2615; Stringer Corresp. ANTONIO-JOSE ARJONILLA.

Agenzia Nazionale Stampa Associata (ANSA) (*Italy*): Wynyard House, 291 George St., Sydney, N.S.W. 2000; Chief of Bureau EVASIO COSTANZO.

Associated Press (AP) (*U.S.A.*): P.O.B. K35, Haymarket, Sydney, N.S.W. 2000; Chief of Bureau PETER O'LOUGHLIN.

Deutsche Presse-Agentur (dpa) (*Federal Republic of Germany*): 67 Kipling Ave., Mooroolbark, Melbourne, Vic. 3138.

Jiji Tsushin-Sha (Japan): Suite 1, 1st Floor, Wynyard House, 291 George St., Sydney, N.S.W. 2000; postal: P.O.B. 2584, Sydney, N.S.W. 2001; Chief of Bureau HIROSHI YAMAYA.

Kyodo Tsushin (*Japan*): 364 Sussex St., Sydney, N.S.W. 2000; Bureau Chief YOICHI YOKOBORI.

Reuters Ltd. (*U.K.*): Macquarie Building, 364 Sussex St., Sydney, N.S.W. 2000; G.P.O. Box 3888, Sydney 2001.

United Press International (UPI) (*U.S.A.*): First Floor, News House, 2 Holt St., Sydney, N.S.W. 2010; Man. BRIAN DEWHURST.

The following foreign bureaux are represented in Sydney: New Zealand Press Association and TASS (U.S.S.R.), Antara (Indonesia) is represented in Canberra.

PRESS ASSOCIATIONS

Australian Newspapers Council: 44–74 Flinders St., Melbourne, Vic. 3000; f. 1958; membership 6, confined to metropolitan daily or Sunday papers; Pres. J. J. D'ARCY; Sec. K. H. MARSH.

Australian Provincial Press Association: Underwood House, 37 Pitt St., Sydney, N.S.W. 2000; f. 1906; 280 mems.; Exec. Dir. I. D. DAVIDSON.

Country Press Association of South Australia Incorporated: 130 Franklin St., Adelaide, S.A.; f. 1912; represents South Australian country newspapers; Pres. T. ELLIS; Sec. M. R. TOWNSEND.

New South Wales Country Press Association: Underwood House, 37 Pitt St., Sydney, N.S.W. 2000; f. 1900; 103 mems.; Exec. Dir. I. D. DAVIDSON.

Queensland Country Press Association: P.O.B. 103, Paddington, Qld. 4064; Pres. IAN JEFFERS; Sec. G. P. W. WILLCOCKS.

Regional Dailies of Australia Ltd.: 247 Collins St., Melbourne, Vic. 3000; f. 1936; Chair. K. J. FLECKNOE; Chief Exec. Officer R. W. SINCLAIR; 34 mems.

Tasmanian Press Association Pty. Ltd.: 71–75 Paterson St., Launceston; Sec. B. J. MCKENDRICK.

Victorian Country Press Association Ltd.: 33 Rathdowne St., Carlton, Vic. 3053; f. 1910; Pres. D. F. MORRIS; Exec. Dir. K. B. LAURIE; 110 mems.

PUBLISHERS

Addison-Wesley Publishing Co.: Unit 1A, 6-8 Byfield St., North Ryde, N.S.W. 2113; educational, scientific, technical, juvenile; Gen. Man. S. DANE.

George Allen and Unwin: 11th Floor, NCR House, 8 Napier St., P.O.B. 764, North Sydney, N.S.W. 2060; educational, general, non-fiction; Chair. R. S. UNWIN; Man. Dir. P. A. GALLAGHER.

Angus and Robertson Publishers: Unit 4, 31 Waterloo Rd., North Ryde, P.O.B. 290, North Ryde, N.S.W. 2113; f. 1886; fiction, general and children's; Dir. RICHARD WALSH.

Edward Arnold (Australia) Pty. Ltd.: 373 Bay St., P.O.B. 146, Port Melbourne, Vic. 3207; all categories; Chair. E. A. HAMILTON; Man. Dir. R. BLACKMORE.

Ashton Scholastic: Railway Crescent, Lisarow, Gosford, N.S.W. 2250; educational, children's paperbacks; Chair. M. SINCLAIR; Man. Dir. KEN JOLLY.

Associated Book Publishers (Australia) Ltd.: 21st Floor, St. Martins Tower, 31 Market St., Sydney, N.S.W. 2000; legal, educational, general non-fiction; Chair. K. T. FELLOW; Man. Dir. W. J. MACKARELL.

Australasian Medical Publishing Co. Ltd.: 71–79 Arundel St., Glebe, N.S.W. 2037; f. 1913; scientific, medical and educational; Man. JAMES G. ASTLES.

The Australasian Publishing Co. Pty. Ltd.: Cnr. Bridge Rd. and Jersey St., Hornsby, N.S.W. 2077; f. 1937; fiction, educational, children's books, general; Man. A. S. M. HARRAP.

Australia and New Zealand Book Co. Pty. Ltd.: 10 Aquatic Drive, Frenchs Forest, N.S.W. 2086; P.O.B. 459, Brookvale, N.S.W. 2100; f. 1964; general non-fiction, technical, scientific; Chair. GEOFFREY M. KING; Man. Dir. G. ROSS KING.

Australian Government Publishing Service: P.O.B. 84, Canberra, A.C.T. 2600; f. 1970; Publishing Dir. B. P. SHURMAN.

Australian National University Press: P.O.B. 4, Canberra, A.C.T. 2600; f. 1966; scholarly; publishes 60–70 new books annually; Man. C. MAKEPEACE.

S. John Bacon Pty. Ltd.: 13 Windsor Ave., Mount Waverley, Melbourne, Vic. 3149; f. 1938; theology and Christian education, educational; Dirs. Mrs. M. BACON, Mrs. J. DIEMAR; Gen. Man. H. EADON.

Butterworths Pty. Ltd.: 271–273 Lane Cove Rd., North Ryde, N.S.W. 2113; f. 1912; law, medical, scientific and accountancy publications; Chair. W. G. GRAHAM; Man. Dir. D. J. JACKSON.

Cambridge University Press (Australia) Pty. Ltd.: 296 Beaconsfield Parade, Middle Park, Vic. 3206; scholarly and educational; Dir. Brian W. Harris.

Collins, Wm. Pty. Ltd.: 55 Clarence St., Sydney, N.S.W. 2000; fiction, non-fiction, religious, Bibles, children's, reference, natural history, paperbacks; Man. Dir. K. W. Wilder.

Commonwealth Scientific and Industrial Research Organization (C.S.I.R.O.): 314 Albert St., East Melbourne, Vic. 3002; f. 1948; 15 journals of original scientific research and two scientific indexes; Editor-in-Chief B. J. Walby.

Doubleday Australia Pty. Ltd.: 14 Mars Rd., Lane Cove, N.S.W. 2066; general; Man. Dir. P. Madgwick.

Encyclopaedia Britannica (Australia) Inc.: 44 Miller St., North Sydney, N.S.W. 2060; reference, education, art, science and commerce; Pres. R. F. Grott.

Georgian House Pty. Ltd.: 296 Beaconsfield Parade, Middle Park, Vic. 3206; f. 1943; general, including educational; Man. Dir. B. W. Harris.

Golden Press Pty. Ltd.: 2–12 Tennyson Rd., Gladesville, Sydney, N.S.W. 2111; children's, general non-fiction, education; Man. Dir. Ron Bunt.

Gordon and Gotch Ltd.: 114 William St., P.O.B. 767G, Melbourne, Vic. 3001; Gen. Man. F. P. Dwyer.

Granada Publishing Australia Pty. Ltd.: Toga House, 117 York St., Sydney, N.S.W. 2000; general; Man. Dir. E. G. Grigor.

Harcourt Brace Jovanovich Group (Australia) Pty. Ltd.: Centrecourt, 25–27 Paul St., North Ryde, N.S.W. 2113; incl. Academic Press Australia and Grune & Stratton Australia; educational, technical, scientific, medical; Man. Dir. Barry Dingley.

Harper and Row (Australasia) Pty. Ltd.: Cnr. Reserve Rd. and Campbell St., P.O.B. 226, Artarmon, N.S.W. 2064; reference, educational, medical, paperbacks; Man. Dir. B. D. Wilder.

Heinemann Publishers Australia Pty. Ltd.: 81-85 Abinger St., Richmond, Melbourne, Vic. 3121; educational and general; Man. Dir. Nicholas Hudson.

Hodder and Stoughton (Australia) Pty. Ltd.: 2 Apollo Place, Lane Cove, N.S.W. 2066; offices in Melbourne, Brisbane, Adelaide and Perth; fiction, general, educational, technical, children's; Man. Dir. E. Coffey.

Holt-Saunders Pty. Ltd.: 9 Waltham St., Artarmon, N.S.W. 2064; all categories; Man. Dir. A. Taylor.

Horwitz Grahame Books Pty. Ltd.: 506 Miller St., Cammeray, N.S.W. 2062; fiction, reference, educational, Australiana, general; imprints: *Horwitz Publications*, *Carrolls*, *Martin Educational*; Man. Dir. L. J. Moore; Deputy Man. Dir. and Financial Dir. M. C. Phillips.

Hutchinson Group (Australia) Pty. Ltd.: 30–32 Cremorne St., Richmond, Vic. 3121; 330–370 Wattle St., Ultimo, N.S.W. 2007; Man. Dir. Otto Hofner.

Hyland House Publishing Pty. Ltd.: 23 Bray St., South Yarra, Vic. 3141; trade, general; Official Rep. Al Knight.

Jacaranda Wiley Ltd.: 65 Park Rd., Milton, Qld. 4064; P.O.B. 859, Brisbane, Q4001; f. 1954; general, educational, technical and cartographic; Man. Dir. John Collins.

L. & S. Publishing Co.: 99–101 Argus St., Cheltenham, Vic. 3192; educational, children's and Australiana; Gen. Man. L. R. Flight; Publr. B. Barratt.

Lansdowne Press: 176 South Creek Rd., P.O.B. 60, Dee Why, N.S.W. 2099; history, lifestyle; practical and leisure subjects; natural history and art; Official Rep. Laurie Muller.

Longman Cheshire Pty. Ltd.: 346 St. Kilda Rd., Melbourne, Vic. 3004; f. 1947; mainly educational, some general; Man. Dir. N. J. Ryan.

Thomas C. Lothian Pty. Ltd.: 4–12 Tattersalls Lane, Melbourne, Vic. 3000; f. 1905; Dirs. Louis A. Lothian, K. A. Lothian, Peter H. T. Lothian, L. N. Jupp; general, practical, educational.

McGraw-Hill Book Co. Australia Pty. Ltd.: 4 Barcoo St., East Roseville, Sydney, N.S.W. 2069; educational and technical books, training and development films and materials; Man. Dir. D. J. Pegrem.

Macmillan Company of Australia Pty. Ltd.: 107 Moray St., South Melbourne, Vic. 3205; f. 1967; general and educational; Man. Dir. Brian Stonier.

McPhee Gribble Publishers Pty. Ltd.: 203 Drummond St., Carlton, Vic. 3053; general; Man. Dirs. Hilary McPhee, Diana Gribble.

Melbourne University Press: 932 Swanston St., Carlton, Vic. 3053; f. 1923; academic, educational, Australiana, general (all fields except fiction and children's); Chair. Prof. J. R. Poynter; Dir. P. A. Ryan.

National Library of Australia: Canberra, A.C.T. 2600; national bibliographical publs.; books and reproductions based on materials in the library's collections; Dir. A. T. Bolton.

Thomas Nelson Australia: 480 La Trobe St., Melbourne, Vic. 3000; all categories; Man. Dir. B. J. Rivers.

New South Wales University Press Ltd.: P.O.B. 1, Kensington, N.S.W. 2033; f. 1961; general, especially educational; Gen. Man. Douglas Howie.

Oxford University Press: P.O.B. 2784Y, Melbourne, Vic. 3001; f. 1908; general, excluding fiction; Dir. D. C. Cunningham.

Penguin Books Australia Ltd.: 487/493 Maroondah Highway, Ringwood, Vic. 3134; general paperbacks; Man. Dir. T. D. Glover; Publishing Dir. Brian Johns.

Pergamon Press (Australia) Pty. Ltd.: 19A Boundary St., Rushcutters Bay, N.S.W. 2011; educational, general, scientific; Chair. I. R. Maxwell, M.C.; Deputy Chair. R. McLeod; Man. Dir. J. Mayer.

Pitman Publishing Pty. Ltd.: 158 Bouverie St., Carlton, Vic. 3053; f. 1968; secretarial and management sciences, art, craft, medical, educational, technical, general, B.B.C. Publs.; Chair. Nicolas Thompson; Man. Dir. Philip J. Harris.

Prentice-Hall of Australia Pty. Ltd.: 7 Grosvenor Place, P.O.B. 151, Brookvale, N.S.W. 2100; educational textbooks, popular trade books, reference, audiovisual material; Man. Dir. P. F. Gleeson.

Reader's Digest Services Pty. Ltd.: 26–32 Waterloo St., Surry Hills, N.S.W. 2010; P.O.B. 4353, Sydney, N.S.W.; general; Chair. A. W. Glassford; Man. Dir. M. Maton.

Reed (A. H., and A. W.) Pty. Ltd.: 2 Aquatic Drive, Frenchs Forest, Sydney, N.S.W. 2086; f. 1964; books on Australia and all general non-fiction; Man. Dir. J. M. Reed.

Rigby Publishers Ltd.: 30 North Terrace, Kent Town, S.A. 5067; f. 1859; general and educational; Man. Dir. R. A. Davis.

Science Research Associates Pty. Ltd.: 82-84 Waterloo Rd., North Ryde, N.S.W. 2113; educational; Chair. and Man. Dir. R. J. Barton.

Schwartz Publishing Group Pty. Ltd.: Suite 602, Wellesley House, 126 Wellington Parade, East Melbourne, Vic. 3002; fiction, non-fiction; Dir. Morry Schwartz.

Sydney University Press: Press Building, University of Sydney, Sydney, N.S.W. 2006; f. 1964; scholarly, academic and educational books and journals; Dir. DAVID NEW.

Thames and Hudson (Australia) Pty. Ltd.: 86 Stanley St., West Melbourne, Vic. 3003; art and general; Man. Dir. RICHARD M. GILMOUR.

D. W. Thorpe Pty. Ltd.: 384 Spencer St., Melbourne, Vic. 3003; biographies, trade, paperbacks; Chair. J. NICHOLSON; Man. Dir. M. WEBSTER.

Time Life International (Australia) Pty. Ltd.: 15th Floor, AMP Centre, 50 Bridge St., Sydney, N.S.W. 2000; general; Man. Dir. ED BARNUM.

Transworld Publishers (Aust.) Pty. Ltd.: 26 Harley Cres., Condell Park, N.S.W. 2200; general, fiction, juvenile, education; Man. Dir. G. S. RUMPF.

University of Queensland Press: P.O.B. 42, St. Lucia, Qld. 4067; f. 1948; scholarly and general cultural interest; microfilm; Man. FRANK W. THOMPSON; Chief Editor MERRIL E. YULE.

University of Western Australia Press: Nedlands, W.A. 6009; f. 1954; educational, secondary and university, technical and scientific, scholarly, humanities; second imprint *Cygnet Books*; Man. V. S. GREAVES.

PUBLISHERS' ASSOCIATION

Australian Book Publishers' Association: 161 Clarence St., Sydney, N.S.W. 2000; f. 1949; about 150 mems.; Pres. WILLIAM J. MACKARELL; Dir. SANDRA FORBES.

RADIO AND TELEVISION

Australian Broadcasting Commission: 145–153 Elizabeth St., P.O.B. 487, Sydney, N.S.W. 2001; f. 1932; Chair. J. D. NORGARD; Gen. Man. Sir TALBOT DUCKMANTON, C.B.E.

The programmes for the National Broadcasting Service and National Television are provided by the non-commercial statutory corporation, the Australian Broadcasting Commission. All studio technical services are manned by the A.B.C.; transmitting stations in both broadcasting and television are manned by the staff of Telecom Australia. Radio: 92 medium-wave stations, 13 F.M., 6 domestic and 12 overseas (Radio Australia) short-wave stations broadcasting in English, French, Indonesian, Japanese, Standard Chinese, Cantonese, Neo-Melanesian, Thai and Vietnamese. Television: one national network of 6 metropolitan channels with 85 transmitters and 132 translator stations.

RADIO

Federation of Australian Radio Broadcasters: P.O.B. 294, Milson's Point, N.S.W. 2061; association of privately-owned stations; Federal Dir. D. L. FOSTER; Deputy Federal Dir. J. M. RUSHTON; Federal Sec. J. H. FINLAYSON.

Commercial services are provided by stations operated by companies under licences granted and renewed by the Australian Broadcasting Tribunal. They rely for their income on the broadcasting of advertisements. On January 1st, 1982, there were 134 commercial broadcasting stations in operation.

MAJOR COMMERCIAL BROADCASTING STATION LICENSEES

Advertiser Broadcasting Network Pty. Ltd.: 121 King William St., Adelaide, S.A. 5000; operates station 5AD in Adelaide and regional stations 5PI and 5SE in other parts of the State; Gen. Man. L. J. SUTTON; Man. BOB FRANCIS.

Amalgamated Wireless (Australasia) Ltd.: 47 York St., Sydney, N.S.W.; operates stations at Sydney, Grafton, Goulburn, Albury, Bendigo, Townsville and Cairns; Chair. and Chief Exec. J. A. L. HOOKE.

Associated Broadcasting Services Ltd.: 290 La Trobe St., Melbourne, Vic. 3000; f. 1957; operates stations at Shepparton, Warragul and Warrnambool; Chair. Sir JOHN KNOTT; Gen. Man. R. W. ELLENBY.

Commonwealth Broadcasting Network: 11 Rangers Rd., Neutral Bay, N.S.W. 2089; operates station 2UW Sydney; Stations at Brisbane, Toowoomba, Rockhampton and Maryborough; Chief Exec. B. E. BYRNE.

Consolidated Broadcasting System (W.A.) Pty. Ltd.: 283 Rokeby Rd., Subiaco, W.A.; operates stations 6GE Geraldton, 6KG Kalgoorlie, 6AM Northam and 6PM Perth; Chief Execs. K. A. GANNAWAY and R. BIGUM.

Macquarie Broadcasting Service Pty. Ltd.: Cnr. Liverpool and Sussex Sts., G.P.O. Box 4290, Sydney, N.S.W. 2001; represents stations in Sydney, Canberra, Adelaide, Wollongong, Melbourne, Brisbane and more than 20 other stations; Chair. and Gen. Man. R. A. JOHNSON.

South Australia Broadcasting Network: 43 Franklin St., Adelaide, S.A.; operates stations in Adelaide, Port Augusta and Renmark.

Tamworth Radio Development Company Pty. Ltd.: P.O.B. 497, Tamworth, N.S.W. 2340; controls stations 2TM Tamworth, 2MO Gunnedah, 4 WK Warwick and 2RE Taree and operates 2AD Armidale through the New England network; Man. E. C. WILKINSON.

Victorian Broadcasting Network Ltd.: Lily St., Bendigo, Vic.; operates stations at Sale and Mackay.

6IX Radio Network Pty. Ltd.: P.O.B. 77, Tuart Hill, W.A. 6060; operates stations 61X Perth; Station Man. R. L. LUCAS.

TELEVISION

Federation of Australian Commercial Television Stations: 447 Kent St., Sydney, N.S.W. 2000; f. 1960; represents 49 of 50 commercial television stations; Chair. W. BARKER; Federal Dir. and Chief Exec. JAMES MALONE; Deputy Federal Dir. and Gen. Man. DAVID MORGAN.

The commercial television service is provided by stations operated by companies under licences granted and renewed by the Australian Broadcasting Tribunal. In December 1981 there were 50 commercial television stations in operation. Colour services came into operation in March 1975.

COMMERCIAL TELEVISION STATION LICENSEES

Amalgamated Television Services Pty. Ltd.: TV Centre, Epping, N.S.W. 2121; f. 1956; operates one station at Sydney, ATN7; Gen. Man. E. F. THOMAS.

Austarama Television Pty. Ltd.: P.O.B. 42, Hawthorn Rd., Nunawading, Vic. 3131; operates station ATV-10 at Melbourne; Station Man. R. B. CAMPBELL.

Australian Capital Television Pty. Ltd.: P.O.B. 21, Watson, A.C.T. 2602; f. 1962; station CTC-7; Chief Exec. W. G. RAYNER.

Ballarat and Western Victoria Television Ltd.: Box 464, Ballarat, Vic. 3350; f. 1962; operates BTV-6, and translators Channel 9 (Warrnambool), Channel 11 (Portland) and Channel 7 (Nhill); Chair. W. H. HEINZ; Gen. Man. G. W. RICE.

Brisbane TV Ltd.: Sir Samuel Griffith Drive, Mt. Coot-tha, Box 604J, G.P.O., Brisbane, Qld. 4001; operates station BTQ-7; Man. G. M. MOLLER.

Broadcast Operations Pty. Ltd.: Remembrance Driveway, Griffith, N.S.W. 2680; f. 1965; operates station MTN-9; Man. Dir. W. R. GAMBLE; Gen. Man. B. W. MERCHANT.

Broken Hill Television Ltd.: P.O.B. 472, Broken Hill, N.S.W. 2880; station BKN-7; Chair. P. MARTIN; Man. Dir. J. M. STURROCK; Administrator THELMA WATTS.

Country Television Services Ltd.: P.O.B. 465, Orange, N.S.W. 2800; f. 1962; operates country stations CBN-8, CWN-6, 2GZ Orange and 2NZ Inverell; Man. Dir. E. YELF; Gen. Man. I. RIDLEY.

Darling Downs TV Ltd.: P.O.B. 670, Toowoomba, Qld. 4350; f. 1962; operates country stations DDQ-10, SDQ-4 and Channel 5, Toowoomba; Gen. Man. L. R. BURROWS.

Far Northern Television Ltd.: 101 Aumuller St., Cairns, Qld. 4870; f. 1966; operates station FNQ-10 on relay from Telecasters North Queensland Ltd.; Station Man. COLIN S. LINDSAY.

General Television Corporation Pty. Ltd.: 22–46 Bendigo St., P.O.B. 100, Richmond, Vic. 3121; f. 1957; operates station GTV-9 at Melbourne; Pres. D. J. EVANS.

Geraldton Telecasters Pty. Ltd.: Fifth St., Wonthella, P.O.B. 46, Geraldton, W.A. 6530; operates station GTW-11; Gen. Man. BRUCE E. CARTY.

Golden West Network Ltd.: P.O.B. 112, Bunbury, W.A. 6230; f. 1967; operates channels BTW-3 (Bunbury), GSW-9 (Mt. Barker), BTW-10 (Katanning), BTW-6 (Narrogin), BTW-10 (Quairading), BTW-11 (Wagin), GSW-10 (Albany) and BTW-UHF-55 (Northam); Gen. Man. B. F. HOPWOOD; T.V. Man. R. J. COX.

Goulburn-Murray Television Ltd.: P.O.B. 666, Shepparton, Vic. 3630; f. 1961; operates country station GMV-6, Shepparton; Chair. Sir JOHN KNOTT; Gen. Man. RONALD EULING.

Herald-Sun TV Pty. Ltd.: G.P.O. Box 215D, Melbourne, Vic. 3001; f. 1956; operates station HSV-7 in Melbourne; parent company, The Herald and Weekly Times Ltd.; Chair. R. H. SAMPSON; Gen. Man. R. P. CASEY.

Mackay Television Ltd.: Box 496, P.O. Mackay, Qld.; f. 1965; operates MVQ6; Gen. Man. M. R. WILLIAMS.

Mid Western Television Pty. Ltd.: 2 Killarney St., Kargoolie, W.A. 6430; operates station VEW-8; Man. Dir. H. LILBURN.

Mt. Isa Television Pty. Ltd.: 110 Camooweal St., Mt. Isa, Qld. 4825; operates station ITQ-8; Man. Dir. Sir A. JOEL; Gen. Man. P. DOOLEY.

NBN Ltd.: Mosbri Crescent, Newcastle, N.S.W. 2300; f. 1962; operates regional station NBN-3; Man. Dir. GEORGE BROWN.

Northern Rivers Television Ltd.: Pacific Highway, Coff's Harbour, P.O.B. 920, N.S.W. 2450; operates stations NRN-11 and RTN-8; Gen. Man. J. W. MCKENZIE.

Northern Television (TNT9) Pty. Ltd.: Watchorn St., Launceston, Tas. 7250; f. 1962; operates Tasmanian country station TNT-9; Gen. Man. D. M. MCQUESTIN.

Queensland Television Ltd.: G.P.O. Box 72, Brisbane, Qld. 4001; f. 1958; operates QTQ-9; Gen. Man. H. K. CORNISH.

Regional Television Australia Pty. Ltd.: 82-84 Sydenham Rd., Marrickville, N.S.W. 2204; P.O.B. 285, Sydney, N.S.W. 2001.

Riverina and North East Victoria TV Ltd.: P.O.B. 2, Kooringal via Wagga, N.S.W. 2650; f. 1964; operates country stations RVN-2 and AMV-4; Gen. Man. W. MARSDEN.

Riverland Television Pty. Ltd.: Murray Bridge Rd., P.O.B. 471, Loxton, S.A. 5333; operates station RTS-5A; Exec. Chair. E. H. URLWIN.

Rockhampton Television Ltd.: Dean St., P.O.B. 568 Rockhampton, Qld. 4700; f. 1963; operates CSEQ and RTQ-7 Television; Man. Dir. B. SAUNDERS.

South Australian Telecasters Ltd.: 45–49 Park Terrace, Gilberton, S.A. 5081; f. 1965; operates station SAS-10; Gen. Man. K. CAMPBELL.

South East Telecasters Ltd.: P.O.B. 821, Mount Gambier, S.A. 5290; f. 1962; operates regional station SES-8; Chair. G. T. BARNFIELD; Station Man. A. D. PHILLIPS.

Southern Television Corporation Ltd.: 202 Tynte St., North Adelaide, S.A.; f. 1958; station NWS-9 at Adelaide; Man. Dir. TYRRELL TALBOT.

Spencer Gulf Telecasters Ltd.: P.O.B. 305, 4 Port Pirie, S. A. 5540; f. 1968; stations GTS-4, 5 and 8; Studio Man. R.M. DAVIS.

Swan Television and Radio Broadcasters Ltd.: P.O.B. 99, Tuart Hill, W.A. 6060; f. 1965; operates station STW-9; Man. Dir. L. J. KIERNAN; Gen. Man. D. R. ASPINALL.

Tasmanian Television Limited: 52 New Town Rd., Hobart, Tas.; f. 1959; started operating TVT-6 at Hobart in 1960; Man. Dir. D. L. CARTER.

TCN Channel Nine Pty. Ltd.: 54-58 Park St., Sydney, N.S.W.; f. 1956; operates station TCN-9 at Sydney; Chair. K. F. B. PACKER; Man. Dir. S. H. CHISHOLM.

Telecasters North Queensland Ltd.: 12 The Strand, P.O.B. 1016, Townsville, Qld. 4810; f. 1962; operates TNQ-7; Chair. J. F. GLEESON; Man. Dir. K. R. CHRISTENSEN.

Television New England Ltd.: P.O.B. 317, Tamworth, N.S.W. 2340; f. 1965; operates stations NEN-9 and ECN-8; Chair. H. JOSEPH; Gen. Man. M. M. MORONEY.

Territory Television Pty. Ltd.: Gardens Hill, P.O.B. 1764, Darwin, N.T. 5794; f. 1971; operates station NTD-8; Man. D. R. ASTLEY.

TV Broadcasters Ltd.: 125 Strangways Terrace, North Adelaide, S.A. 5006; f. 1958; station ADS-7 at Adelaide; Gen. Man. J. S. DOHERTY.

TVW Enterprises Ltd.: P.O.B. 77, Tuart Hill, W.A. 6060; f. 1959; commercial stations TVW-7 in Perth, SAS-10 in Adelaide and 6IX, 6BY, 6VA and 6WB in W.A.; Chair. and Chief Exec. M. R. H. HOLMES A'COURT.

United Telecasters Sydney Ltd.: Epping and Pittwater Rds., North Ryde, N.S.W. 2113; operates station TEN-10, Sydney; Man. Dir. B. P. MORRIS.

Universal Telecasters Qld. Ltd.: Box 751, G.P.O., Brisbane, Qld. 4001; f. 1965; operating TVQ-0; Gen. Man. R. G. ARCHER.

Victorian Broadcasting Network Ltd.: P.O.B. 240, Lily St., Bendigo, Vic. 3350; f. 1961; operates regional stations BCV-8 Bendigo, BCV-11 Swan Hill, GLV-8 Gippsland, GLV-6 Foster, GLV-11 Lakes Entrance and GLV-7 Orbost; relays programmes to STV-8 Mildura; Gen. Man. I. R. MÜLLER.

FINANCE

BANKING

(cap.=capital; p.u.=paid up; res.=reserves; dep.=deposits; m.=million; $A=$ Australian; brs.=branches)

Central Bank

Reserve Bank of Australia: 65 Martin Place, Sydney, N.S.W. 2001; f. 1911; sole bank of issue for Australia and Territories; has separate dept. for commodity marketing finance; cap. $A49.4m.; res. funds $A3,111.3m.; dep. and other accounts $A3,236.8m. (June 30th, 1981); Gov. Sir Harold Knight, K.B.E., D.S.C.; Deputy Gov. D. N. Sanders.

Commonwealth Banks

Commonwealth Banking Corporation: G.P.O. Box 2719, Pitt St. and Martin Place, Sydney, N.S.W. 2001; f. 1960; controlling body for three member banks; Chair. Prof. L. F. Crisp; Man. Dir. V. T. Christie.

Commonwealth Development Bank of Australia: Prudential Bldg., 39 Martin Place, Sydney, N.S.W. 2000; f. 1960; loans, advances and bills discounted $A541.8m. (June 1981); Gen. Man. Alwyn Richards.

Commonwealth Savings Bank of Australia: Pitt St. and Martin Place, Sydney, N.S.W. 2000; f. 1912; dep. $A8,099.5m. (June 1981); Gen. Man. E. J. Brighton.

Commonwealth Trading Bank of Australia: Pitt St. and Martin Place, Sydney, N.S.W. 2000; est. 1953 to take over business of General Banking Division of Commonwealth Bank of Australia; cap. $A14.9m; dep. $A6,670.4m. (June 1981); Gen. Man. W. H. Clark.

Development Bank

Australian Resources Development Bank Ltd.: 379 Collins St., Melbourne, Vic. 3000; f. 1967 by major Australian trading banks with support of Reserve Bank of Australia, the Rural Bank of New South Wales and the Rural and Industries Bank of Western Australia to marshal funds from local and overseas sources for the financing of Australian participation in projects of national importance; took over Australian Banks' Export Re-Finance Corporation Ltd. in 1980; cap. p.u. $A11m.; dep. $A708.3m. (Sept. 1981); Chair. D. Dobbie; Gen. Man. M. K. R. Wills.

Trading Banks

Australia and New Zealand Banking Group Ltd.: Collins Place, 55 Collins St., Melbourne, Vic. 3000; f. 1970; cap. $A126.7m.; res. $A300.3m.; dep. $A7,979.3m. (Sept. 1978); over 1,250 brs. in Australia, New Zealand, U.K., U.S.A. and Pacific Islands; took over the Bank of Adelaide in 1979; Chair. Sir William Vines, C.M.G.; Man. Dir. John D. Milne.

Australian Bank Ltd.: 17 O'Connell Street, Sydney, N.S.W. 2000; f. 1981; cap. p.u. $A30m.; Chief Exec. Mark Johnson.

Bank of Queensland Ltd.: 115 Queen St., Brisbane, Qld.; f. 1874; cap. p.u. $A5.67m.; dep. $A71.9m. (1981); Chair. Sir Ernest Savage; Gen. Man. A. N. Murrell.

Commercial Banking Co. of Sydney Ltd.: 343 George St., Sydney, N.S.W. 2000; f. 1834; cap. p.u. $A43.0m.; dep. $A3,528.1m. (1979); 529 brs.; merger proceeding with National Bank of Australasia, 1981; Chair. Sir Robert Crichton-Brown, C.B.E.; Man. Dir. V. E. Martin.

National Bank of Australasia Ltd.: 500 Bourke St., Melbourne, Vic.; f. 1858; group cap. p.u. $A149m.; dep. $A6,527.8m. (Sept. 1981); merger proceeding with Commercial Banking Co. of Sydney, 1981; Chair. Sir Robert Law-Smith; Group Gen. Man. J. D. Booth.

Rural and Industries Bank of Western Australia: 54–58 Barrack St., P.O.B. E237, Perth, W.A. 6001; f. 1945; State Government Bank; cap. $A22m.; dep. $A906m. (1981); Chair. David P. Fischer; Gen. Man. Andrew J. Gordon.

State Bank of New South Wales: 52–56 Martin Place, Sydney, N.S.W. 2000; 242 offices in N.S.W.; cap. $A25.80m.; res. $A151.09m.; dep. $A2,137.25m.; Man. Dir. N. Whitlam; Sec. P. P. Turner.

State Bank of South Australia: 51 Pirie St., Adelaide, S.A.; f. 1896; cap. $A434.1m.; dep. $A240.5m. (June 1981); Chair. G. F. Seaman, C.M.G., B.EC., A.U.E., F.A.S.A.; Gen. Man. P. E. Byrnes.

Westpac Banking Corporation: 60 Martin Place, Sydney, N.S.W.; postal: P.O.B. 1, Sydney, N.S.W. 2001; f. 1982 following merger of the Bank of New South Wales and The Commercial Bank of Australia.

Savings Banks

Bank of New South Wales Savings Bank Ltd.: 60 Martin Place, Sydney, N.S.W.; f. 1956; cap. p.u. $A40m.; group dep. $A3,128m. (1980); Chair. Sir Noel Foley, C.B.E.; Chief Gen. Man. R. J. White.

The Savings Bank of South Australia: King William St., Adelaide, S.A.; f. 1848; assets $A1,315.2m. (1981); 158 brs.; Chair. L. Barrett; Gen. Man. P. J. Simmons.

The Savings Bank of Tasmania (The Hobart Savings Bank): 39 Murray St., Hobart, Tasmania; f. 1845; Pres. H. A. Cuthbertson; Gen. Man. H. A. Parker.

State Bank of Victoria: 385 Bourke St., Melbourne, Vic. 3000; f. 1842; dep. $A4,260m.: total resources $A4,995 m. (June 1981); 541 brs.; Chair. Prof. Donald Cochrane, C.B.E.; Gen. Man. H. E. Torrens.

Foreign Banks

Most of the major foreign banks have representative offices in Australia but only the Banque Nationale de Paris has full branches.

Banque Nationale de Paris (*France*): 12 Castlereagh St., Sydney, N.S.W.; 6 brs.

STOCK EXCHANGES

Australian Associated Stock Exchanges: King George Tower, 388 George St., Sydney, N.S.W. 2000; f. 1937; mems. stock exchanges in the six capital cities; Exec. Dir. Ronald L. Coppel.

The Brisbane Stock Exchange Ltd.: 344 Queen St., Brisbane, Qld. 4000; f. 1885; 39 mems.; Chair. W. J. B. Earnshaw; Man. G. P. Chapman.

Hobart Stock Exchange: 86 Collins St., Hobart, Tasmania; f. 1891.

Stock Exchange of Adelaide Ltd.: 55 Exchange Place, Adelaide, S.A.; f. 1887; 64 mems.; Chair. H. E. Bowman; Gen. Man. I. G. Bogle.

Stock Exchange of Melbourne Ltd.: 351 Collins St., Melbourne, Vic.; f. 1859 (inc. 1970); 232 mems.; Chair. L. Ian Roach; Gen. Man. R. B. Lee.

Stock Exchange of Perth Ltd.: Exchange House, 68 St. George's Terrace, Perth, W.A.; f. 1889; 34 mems.; Chair. R. S. Punch; Gen. Man. Mark Heelan.

Sydney Stock Exchange: 20 Bond St., P.O.B. H224, Australia Sq., Sydney, N.S.W. 2000; f. 1871; 144 mems.; Chair. F. H. MULLENS; Gen. Man. P. W. MARSHMAN; publs. *Australian Stock Exchange Journal* (monthly), *Stock Exchange Research Handbook* (annually).

PRINCIPAL INSURANCE COMPANIES

A.G.C. (Insurances) Ltd.: A.G.C. House, Philip and Hunter Sts., Sydney, N.S.W.; f. 1938; Chair. E. C. TAIT; Gen. Man. H. E. WOOD.

A.M.P. Fire & General Insurance Co. Ltd.: A.M.P. Bldg., Sydney Cove, N.S.W. 2000; f. 1958; Chair. J. W. UTZ; Man. Dir. J. K. STAVELEY.

Australian Natives' Association Insurance Co. Ltd.: 28–32 Elizabeth St., Melbourne, Vic. 3000; f. 1948; Chair. L. D. BROOKS; Man. F. R. ARCHER.

Australian Reinsurance Co. Ltd.: 325 Collins St., Melbourne, Vic. 3000; f. 1962; reinsurance; Chair. R. S. TURNER, C.B.E.; Man. Dir. J. H. WINTER; Gen. Mans. O. HOFSTETTER, P. C. HEFFERNAN.

Catholic Church Insurances Ltd.: 387 St. Kilda Rd., Melbourne, Vic. 3004; f. 1911; Chair. Rev. Mgr. P. H. JONES; Gen. Man. C. R. O'MALLEY.

The Chamber of Manufactures Insurance Ltd.: 368-374 St. Kilda Rd., Melbourne, Vic. 3004; f. 1914; Chair. W. D. MCPHERSON; Man. Dir. G. P. SUTHERLAND.

City Mutual General Insurance Ltd.: 60 Hunter St., P.O.B. 505, Sydney, N.S.W. 2000; f. 1889; Chair. GERALD WELLS; Gen. Man. R. J. LAWSON.

City Mutual Life Assurance Society Ltd.: 60 Hunter St., Sydney, N.S.W. 2001; f. 1878; Chair GERALD WELLS; Gen. Man. R. W. GUEST, F.A.I.I.

Colonial Mutual General Insurance Co. Ltd.: 330 Collins St., Melbourne, Vic. 3000; f. 1958; Chair. H. MCE. SCAMBLER; Chief Man. G. D. C. SWANTON.

The Colonial Mutual Life Assurance Society Ltd.: 330 Collins St., Melbourne, Vic. 3000; f. 1873; Chair. H. MCE. SCAMBLER; Gen. Man. M. S. MAINPRIZE.

Commercial Union Assurance Co. of Australia Ltd.: Temple Court, 428 Collins St., Melbourne, Vic.; f. 1960; fire, accident, marine; Chair. Sir EDWARD COHEN; Gen. Man. A. L. BREND.

Copenhagen Reinsurance Company (Aust.) Ltd.: 60 Margaret St., Sydney, N.S.W. 2000; f. 1961; reinsurance; Chair. J. G. DUFF; Gen. Man. A. FALKANGER.

Farmers Grazcos Co-operative Ltd.: 3 Spring St., Sydney, N.S.W. 2000; f. 1980 by merger of The Farmers & Graziers' Co-operative Co. Ltd. and Grazcos Co-operative Ltd.; Chief Gen. Man. H. T. HALSTED.

Federation Insurance Ltd.: Level 34, 360 Collins St., Melbourne, Vic. 3000; f. 1926; Chair. R. L. M. SUMMERBELL; Gen. Man. E. MILLER.

GRE Insurance Ltd.: 604 St. Kilda Rd., Melbourne, Vic.; fire, marine, accident; Man. Dir. K. GILBERT.

Manufacturers' Mutual Insurance Ltd.: 60–62 York St., Sydney, N.S.W. 2000; f. 1914; workers' compensation; fire, general accident, motor and marine; Chair. C. W. LOVE; Gen. Man. A. T. C. VENNING.

Mercantile & General Life Reassurance Co. of Australia Ltd.: Royal Exchange Bldg., 56 Pitt St., Sydney, N.S.W. 2000; f. 1956; reinsurance; Chair. J. H. G. GUEST, O.B.E.; Gen. Man. S. R. B. FRANCE.

Mercantile Mutual Insurance Ltd.: 117 Pitt St., Sydney, N.S.W.; f. 1878; Chair. M. C. DAVIS; Man. Dirs. A. E. M. GEDDES, J. N. TAVERNE.

M.L.C. Fire & General Insurance Company Pty. Ltd.: Victoria Cross, North Sydney, N.S.W. 2060; f. 1958; Chair. G. W. E. BARRACLOUGH, O.B.E.; Gen. Man. D. A. WHIPP.

Mutual Life and Citizens' Assurance Co. Ltd.: P.O.B. 200, North Sydney, N.S.W. 2060; f. 1886; Chair. B. J. D. PAGE, C.B.E.; Gen. Man. G. W. WEIGHTMAN.

National & General Insurance Co. Ltd.: 10 Bond St., Sydney, N.S.W.; f. 1954; fire, marine, general; Chair. SIR PETER FINLEY, O.B.E., D.F.C.; Gen. Man. J. WOODCOCK.

The National Mutual Life Association of Australasia Ltd.: 447 Collins St., Melbourne, Vic.; f. 1869; Chair. G. M. NIALL; Man. Dir. R. L. BIENVENU.

New Zealand Life Ltd.: 20 Bond St., Sydney, N.S.W.; Chair. F. R. A. HELLABY; Gen. Man. J. R. MARKLEY.

N.R.M.A. Insurance Ltd.: 151 Clarence St., Sydney, N.S.W. 2000; f. 1926; associated with National Roads and Motorists' Association; Gen. Man. R. J. LAMBLE.

QBE Insurance Limited: 82 Pitt St., Sydney, N.S.W. 2000; f. 1886; Chair. J. D. O. BURNS; Man. Dir. E. J. CLONEY.

Reinsurance Co. of Australasia Ltd.: 1 York St., Sydney, N.S.W.; f. 1961; reinsurance, fire, accident, marine; Chair. Sir JOHN MARKS, C.B.E.; Gen. Man. P. J. MILLER.

South British United Life Assurance Co. Ltd.: 55 Lavender St., Milsons Point, N.S.W.; f. 1921; Gen. Man. JOHN T. CORBETT.

Southern Pacific Insurance Co. Ltd.: 80 Alfred St., Milson's Point, N.S.W. 2061; f. 1935; fire, accident, marine; Chair. C. H. V. CARPENTER; Chief Gen. Man. B. A. SELF.

Sun Alliance Insurance Ltd.: Sun Alliance Bldg., 22 Bridge St., Sydney, N.S.W. 2000; fire, accident and marine insurance; Man. Dir. N. GREENWOOD.

T & G Fire and General Insurance Co. Ltd.: Collins and Russell Sts., Melbourne, Vic.; f. 1958; Chair. L. J. YEO; Gen. Man. M. A. KEMP.

T and G Mutual Life Society Ltd.: Collins and Russell Sts., Melbourne, Vic.; f. 1876; Gen. Man. K. D. J. COVENTRY.

Traders Prudent Insurance Co. Ltd.: 23 Leigh St., Adelaide, S.A. 5000; f. 1956; Chair. N. E. MUTTON; Gen. Man. Dr. G. WEIPPERT.

Westralian Farmers Co-operative Ltd.: 172 St. George's Terrace, Perth, W.A. 6000; Chair. M. CLAYTON; Insurance Man. T. I. CORNFORD.

INSURANCE ASSOCIATIONS

Australian Insurance Association: 11th Floor, 82 Pitt St., Sydney, N.S.W. 2000; f. 1968; Pres. R. J. LAWSON; Exec. Dir. I. J. FREW, B.E.C., A.A.S.A.

Australian Insurance Institute: 257 Collins St., Melbourne, Vic. 3000; f. 1919; Pres. S. I. MCDONALD; Chief Exec. Officer A. V. SMYTHE; 4,430 mems.

Insurance Council of Australia Ltd.: Head Office: 31 Queen St., Melbourne, Vic. 3000; Chief Exec. R. G. A. SMITH.

Life Insurance Federation of Australia: 303 Collins St., Melbourne, Vic. 3000; f. 1979; Chair. A. W. COATES; Exec. Dir. N. E. RENTON; 41 mems.

TRADE AND INDUSTRY

CHAMBERS OF COMMERCE

International Chamber of Commerce: Australian Council, Commerce House, Brisbane Ave., Barton, P.O.B. E118, Canberra, A.C.T. 2600; f. 1927; 70 mems.; many publs. on international trade, Court of Arbitration, banking, documentation and trade procedures; Chair. P. J. DUNSTAN.

Australian Chamber of Commerce: Brisbane Ave., Barton, A.C.T. 2600; f. 1901; membership includes Chambers of Commerce in Sydney, Melbourne, Canberra, Brisbane, Adelaide, Perth, Hobart, Newcastle, Darwin, Gove, Tamworth, Cairns, Norfolk Island, and State Federations of Chambers of Commerce in Victoria, Queensland, Western Australia and Tasmania; Pres. W. J. WILLS; Exec. Dir. R. PELHAM THORMAN; Sec. A. O. DAWSON.

Brisbane Chamber of Commerce Inc.: 243 Edward St. (cnr. Adelaide St.), Brisbane, Qld. 4000; f. 1868; Dir. C. ROBERTSON, O.B.E., F.C.I.S., F.A.S.A.; publ. *The Voice of Business*.

Chamber of Commerce and Industry, South Australia, Inc.: 12–18 Pirie St., Adelaide, S.A. 5000; 3,500 mems.; Gen. Man. A. C. SCHRAPE, F.A.I.M., J.P.; publ. *Journal of Industry* (fortnightly).

Hobart Chamber of Commerce: 65 Murray St., Hobart, Tasmania; f. 1851; Dir. B. A. JENNINGS; publs. *Members' classified directory*, *Tasmanian Business Reporter* (monthly; circ. 10,000), tourist brochures.

Launceston Chamber of Commerce: 57 George St., Launceston, Tasmania; f. 1849; Pres. B. J. MCKENDRICK.

Melbourne Chamber of Commerce: 60 Market St., Melbourne, Vic. 3000; f. 1851.

Perth Chamber of Commerce (Inc.): 14 Parliament Place, West Perth, W.A.; f. 1890; 1,200 mems.; Dir. B. KUSEL.

Sydney Chamber of Commerce Inc.: 95–99 York St., G.P.O. Box 4280, Sydney, N.S.W. 2001; f. 1826; Dir. DAVID ABBA; publ. *The Business Bulletin*.

AGRICULTURAL AND INDUSTRIAL ORGANIZATIONS

The Australian Agricultural Council: Dept. of Primary Industry, Barton, Canberra, A.C.T. 2605; f. 1934 to provide means for consultation between individual States and Commonwealth on agricultural production and marketing (excluding forestry and fisheries), to promote the welfare and standards of Australian agricultural industries and to foster the adoption of national policies in regard to these industries; 8 mems. comprising the agricultural Ministers of the six States and the Northern Territory and the Commonwealth Minister for Primary Industry; Sec. W. D. SALTER.

Standing Committee on Agriculture: f. 1927; associated as an advisory body with the Australian Agricultural Council; additional functions are the coordination of agricultural research and of quarantine measures relating to pests and diseases of plants and animals; comprises the State and Northern Territory Directors of Agriculture and heads of Commonwealth Departments with a direct or indirect interest in agriculture; Sec. W. D. SALTER.

There is also a Standing Committee on Soil Conservation associated with the Council.

Australian Dairy Corporation: Dairy Industry House, 576 St. Kilda Rd., Melbourne, Vic. 3004; promotes local consumption and controls the export of dairy produce; Chair. M. L. VAWSER; Gen. Man. B. A. NORWOOD.

Australian Industry Development Corporation: 212 Northbourne Ave., Canberra, A.C.T. 2601; f. 1970; a Commonwealth Statutory Authority providing a wide range of financial facilities including loan and equity financing to promote the development of Australian manufacturing and mining industries, and supporting local participation in the ownership and control of industries and resources; brs. in Sydney, Melbourne, Perth and Brisbane; cap. p.u. $A62.5m. (1980); Chair. Sir ALAN WESTERMAN, C.B.E.; Chief Exec. J. ROBERT THOMAS.

Australian Meat and Livestock Corporation: P.O.B. 4129, Sydney, N.S.W. 2001; Chair. R. G. JONES.

Australian Trade Development Council: c/o Department of Trade and Resources, Canberra, A.C.T. 2600; f. 1958; advises the Minister for Trade and Resources on all aspects of the development of overseas trade; Chair. J. B. GOUGH, O.B.E.

Australian Wheat Board: 179 Queen St., Melbourne, Vic.; f. 1939; sole marketing authority of wheat and flour on both domestic and export markets; 14 mems.; Chair. Sir LESLIE PRICE; Gen. Man. M. W. MOORE-WILTON; publs. *Wheat Australia* (monthly), *Annual Report*.

Australian Wool Corporation: Wool House, 369 Royal Parade, Parkville, Vic. 3052; f. 1973; responsible for wool marketing, research and testing; board of 10 mems. (chairman, 4 wool growers, 4 from commerce, 1 Govt. mem.); Chair. DAVID ASIMUS; publ. *Perspective* (monthly).

Department of National Development and Energy: South Tower, CAGA Centre, Akuna St., P.O.B. 5, Canberra, A.C.T. 2600; deals mainly with: national energy policy, including planning and research into coal, oil and gas, uranium, solar energy and other forms of energy; radioactive waste management; minerals exploration and resource assessment; water resources and electricity; geodesy and mapping; local government; Minister for National Development and Energy Senator the Hon. Sir JOHN CARRICK; Sec. A. J. WOODS.

Wool Council of Australia: P.O.B. 10, Canberra, A.C.T. 2600; composed of 20 Councillors from seven State member organizations; participates in selection and nomination of Australian Wool Corporation members and advises the Minister for Primary Industry on Australian wool industry policy; replaces the Australian Wool Industry Conference; Chair. I. M. MCLACHLAN.

EMPLOYERS' ORGANIZATIONS

Confederation of Australian Industry: P.O.B. 14, Canberra, A.C.T. 2600; f. 1977 following a merger of Assoc. Chambers of Manufacturers of Australia and the Australian Council of Employers' Federations; mems.: over 30 national asscns. representing over 50,000 firms; Pres. H. G. ASTON, C.B.E.; Sec. M. J. OVERLAND.

Confederation of Australian Industry Industrial Council: 128 Exhibition St., Melbourne, Vic. 3000; Dir.Gen. G. POLITES, C.M.G., M.B.E.

National Trade and Industry Council: Industry House, Canberra, A.C.T. 2600; f. 1977; Chair. W. D. ADCOCK, O.B.E.; Dir.-Gen. W. J. HENDERSON; 30,000 mems.

Dairy Farmers Co-operative Ltd.: 700 Harris St., Ultimo, N.S.W. 2007; f. 1900; Gen. Man. MEAD; Sec. E. L. YORK.

Film and Television Production Association of Australia: Suite 306, 26 College St., Sydney, N.S.W. 2000; Pres. JOHN CHAMBERS; Nat. Dir. JAMES MITCHELL.

The Livestock and Grain Producers' Association of New South Wales: Box 1068, G.P.O., Sydney, N.S.W. 2001; 56 Young St., Sydney, N.S.W. 2000; f. 1980.

The Master Builders' Association of New South Wales: Private Bag 9, P.O., Broadway, N.S.W. 2007; f. 1873; 3,500 mems.; Exec. Dir. R. L. ROCHER; publs. *Builder N.S.W.* (monthly); *M.B.A. Handbook*.

Meat and Allied Trades Federation of Australia: 5th Floor, 210 George St., Sydney; postal address: P.O.B. R199, Royal Exchange, Sydney, N.S.W. 2000; f. 1928; Pres. J. H. MEDWAY; National Dir. R. H. J. NOBLE; publ. *Australian Meat Industry Bulletin* (monthly).

Metal Trades Industry Association of Australia: 105 Walker St., North Sydney, N.S.W.; National Pres. J. E. DIXON, O.B.E.; Nat. Dir. and Chief Exec. A. C. EVANS.

New South Wales Flour Millers' Council: B.N.Z. House, 333 George St., P.O.B. 2125, Sydney, N.S.W. 2001; Sec. K. G. WILLIAMS.

Timber Trade Industrial Association: 155 Castlereagh St., Sydney, N.S.W. 2000; f. 1940; 530 mems.; Man. H. J. MCCARTHY.

MANUFACTURERS' ORGANIZATIONS

Australian British Trade Association: P.O.B. 141, Manuka, A.C.T. 2603; Dir. D. C. DOUGLAS, O.B.E., A.A.S.A.

Australian Industries Development Association: Head Office and Research Centre, 10 Queen's Rd., Melbourne, Vic. 3004; P.O.B. 387D, Melbourne, Vic. 3001; an industry-sponsored research and advocacy organization; studies business–Government relations; Dir. G. D. ALLEN; publs. *A.I.D.A. Bulletin* and research monographs.

Australian Manufacturers' Export Council: Industry House, P.O.B. 14, Canberra, A.C.T. 2600; f. 1955; Exec. Officer G. M. CARR.

Chamber of Manufactures of New South Wales: Box 3968, G.P.O., Sydney, N.S.W. 2001; f. 1885; Dir. NOEL J. MASON.

Confederation of Western Australian Industry, Inc.: P.O.B. 6209, Hay St. East, Perth, W.A. 6000; Exec. Dir. B. G. ATKINSON; Dirs. W. J. BROWN, G. A. BLACK.

Queensland Confederation of Industry: Industry House, 375 Wickham Terrace, Brisbane, Qld. 4000; f. 1976; 2,400 mems.; Gen. Man. G. B. SIEBENHAUSEN.

Tasmanian Chamber of Industries: 191 Liverpool St., Hobart, Tasmania 7000; f. 1898; Exec. Dir. E. C. ILES.

The Victorian Chamber of Manufactures: Industry House, 370 St. Kilda Rd., G.P.O. Box 1469N, Melbourne, Vic. 3001; f. 1877; 5,500 mems.; Dir. B. H. B. POWELL.

PRINCIPAL TRADE UNIONS

Australian Council of Trade Unions (A.C.T.U.): 254 La Trobe St., Melbourne, Vic.; f. 1927; the organization includes a branch in each State generally known as a Trades and Labour Council; 149 Trade Unions are affiliated to the A.C.T.U.; Pres. C. O. DOLAN; Sec. P. I. NOLAN.

Administrative and Clerical Officers' Association: 75 King St., Sydney, N.S.W. 2000; 38,978 mems.; Nat. Sec. P. R. MUNRO.

Amalgamated Metal Workers' & Shipwrights' Union: 136 Chalmers St., Surry Hills, N.S.W. 2010; 131,029 mems.

Australasian Meat Industry Employees' Union: 377 Sussex St., Sydney, N.S.W. 2000; 50,753 mems.

Australian Building Construction Employees' and Builders' Labourers' Federation: 4 Goulburn St., Sydney, N.S.W. 2000; 28,598 mems.

Australian Insurance Employees' Union: 21st Floor, 114 William St., Melbourne, Vic. 3000; Federal Pres. KEVIN DAVERN; Federal Sec. KEN H. MCLEOD; 22,470 mems.

Australian Postal and Telecommunications Union: 400 Sussex St., Sydney, N.S.W.; 46,423 mems.

Australian Public Service Association: 4th Floor, Wingello House, Angel Place, Sydney, N.S.W. 2000; f. 1912; Pres. BRUCE MARTIN; Sec. FRANK O'DONNELL; 8,000 mems.

Australian Railways Union: 7th Floor, 377 Sussex St., Sydney, N.S.W. 2000; 42,054 mems.; National Sec. R. C. TAYLOR.

Australian Teachers' Federation: P.O.B. 1891, Canberra City, A.C.T. 2601; f. 1920; 138,771 mems.; Pres. W. G. TICKELL; Gen. Sec. R. V. BLUER.

Australian Telecommunications Employees Association: P.O.B. A129, Sydney South; 4th Floor, 245 Castlereagh St., Sydney, N.S.W. 2000; 25,200 mems.; Pres. J. HALL; Sec. and Treas. C. P. COOPER; publ. *A.T.E.A. Technical Worker*.

Australian Textile Workers' Union: Box 68, Trades Hall, Lygon St., Carlton South, Vic. 3053; f. 1919; 28,500 mems.; Gen. Pres. R. B. MOSS; Gen. Sec. W. A. C. HUGHES; publ. *Textile Topics*.

Australian Workers' Union: 219/227 Elizabeth St., Sydney, N.S.W.; f. 1886; Pres. E. WILLIAMS; Gen. Sec. F. V. MITCHELL; 111,851 mems.

Building Workers' Industrial Union of Australia: 535 George St., Sydney, N.S.W. 2000; f. 1945; Pres. N. A. CURRIE; Gen. Sec. P. M. CLANCY; 41,260 mems.

Electrical Trades Union of Australia: National Council, 302-306 Elizabeth St., Sydney, N.S.W. 2010; f. 1919; Pres. R. M. GLASTONBURY; Nat. Sec. R. J. PERRIAM; 70,000 mems.

Federated Clerks' Union of Australia: 26 King St., Melbourne, Vic. 3000; 83,624 mems.

Federated Ironworkers' Association of Australia: 188 George St., Sydney, N.S.W. 2000; 65,432 mems.

The Federated Miscellaneous Workers' Union of Australia: Federal Council, First Floor, 365 Sussex St., Sydney, N.S.W. 2000; f. 1916; Gen. Sec. R. GIETZELT; 125,000 mems.; publ. *Federation News*.

Federated Municipal and Shire Council Employees' Union of Australia: P.O.B 3511, Sydney, N.S.W. 2001; 49,158 mems.

Hospital Employees' Federation: 240 Macquarie Rd., Greystanes, N.S.W. 2145; 30,579 mems.

Printing and Kindred Industries Union: Third Floor, 377-383 Sussex St., Sydney, N.S.W. 2000; f. 1916; Sec. C. L. N. HARVEY; 51,307 mems.; publ. *Printing Trades Journal* (monthly).

Transport Workers' Union of Australia: Transport House, 388-390 Sussex St., Sydney, N.S.W. 2000; 94,499 mems.

Vehicle Builders' Employees' Federation of Australia: 8th Floor, 377 Sussex St., Sydney, N.S.W. 2000; Sec. J. S. THOMPSON; 33,671 mems.

Waterside Workers' Federation of Australia: 365-375 Sussex St., Sydney, N.S.W. 2000.

MAJOR INDUSTRIAL COMPANIES

The following are some of the major industrial and trading companies in Australia, arranged by sector.

MINING AND METALS

Alcoa of Australia Ltd.: 535 Bourke St., Melbourne; Vic.; cap. $A350m.

Bauxite miner and producer of alumina; producer of aluminium ingot and fabricator of aluminium extrusions, tube, rod, bar, sheet and foil.

Chair. Sir ARVI PARBO; Man. Dir. J. L. DEIDERICH; employees: 6,180.

BH South Ltd.: 360 Collins St., Melbourne, Vic. 3000; f. 1918; cap. $A27.8m.

Mining of phosphate; mineral exploration.

Chair. Sir ARVI PARBO.

Boral Ltd.: 11th Floor, Boral House, 221 Miller St., North Sydney, N.S.W. 2060.

Sand and gravel extraction; asphalt and bitumen surfacing; pre-mixed concrete; clay and concrete products; pre-cast wall and floor panels; steel reinforcing; aluminium windows and doors; plaster wallboards and ceiling panels; insulation; insect screening; fencing; hand and garden tools; electronic timers, control relays and switchgear; wire conveyors, screens and sieves; furnaces and refractory installations; steel-framed buildings and storage silos; scaffolding and builders' plant hire; distribution of town gas, natural gas and l.p.g.

Chair. Sir PETER FINLEY, O.B.E., D.F.C.; Chief Exec. Sir ERIC NEAL; employees: 8,000.

British Phosphate Commissioners: 515 Collins St., Melbourne, Vic. 3001.

Managing agents for Christmas Island Phosphate Commission for mining at Christmas Island and for distribution from there and from other sources, to Australia and New Zealand.

Commissioners: M. C. TIMBS (Australia); W. D. M. BREMNER, C.M.G. (New Zealand); C. M. CARRUTHERS, C.M.G. (U.K.); Gen. Man. A. E. GAZE.

The Broken Hill Proprietary Co. Ltd.: 140 William St., Melbourne, Vic. 3000; f. 1885; cap p.u. $A589m.

Mining of iron ore, bauxite, manganese, copper, gold, nickel and coal; iron and steelmaking, oil and natural gas exploration and development, ironstone, manganese and coal mining. Operates in every state of Australia, the Northern Territory, Papua New Guinea, Indonesia, Taiwan, Malaysia, Fiji and the Philippines.

Twenty-four subsidiary companies; twelve major associated companies; Chair. and Dir. of Admin. Sir JAMES MCNEILL; Man. Dir. B. T. LOTON; employees: 72,000.

Consolidated Gold Fields Australia Ltd.: Gold Fields House, 1 Alfred St., Sydney Cove, N.S.W. 2000; cap. $A27.1m.

Numerous mining interests throughout Australia.

Chair. S. L. SEGAL; Man. Dir. B. C RYAN.

Conzinc Riotinto of Australia (CRA) Limited: 55 Collins St., Melbourne, Vic. 3001; f. 1981; cap. issued $A217.4m.

CRA is a mining, development and investment company and, through its subsidiary and associate companies, has wide and various interests in most metals and minerals of economic importance, principally copper, iron ore, lead, zinc, aluminium, uranium, tin, coal, salt, gold, silver and diamonds. The CRA group operates mining and processing ventures which extend into fabrication, distribution and marketing. Active exploration and research programmes are maintained. CRA's principal interests are in: Bougainville Copper Ltd. (copper), Australian Mining Smelting Ltd. (lead/zinc), Hamersely Holdings Ltd. (iron ore), Comalco Ltd. (bauxite) and Mary Kathleen Uranium Ltd.

Chair. and Chief Exec. Sir RODERICK CARNEGIE; Deputy Chair. Sir RUSSEL MADIGAN, O.B.E.; Group employees: 38,000.

EZ Industries Ltd.: 390 Lonsdale St., P.O.B. 856K, Melbourne, Vic.3001; f. 1956; cap. $A75.6m.

Operates as a holding company for the wholly-owned operating subsidiaries, Electrolytic Zinc Company of Australasia Ltd., The Emu Bay Railway Company Ltd., EZ Europe Ltd, EZ America Ltd. and North-West Acid Pty. Ltd. Lead and zinc mining and concentrating; transport of concentrates; production of zinc and zinc alloys; fertilizer; marketing in Europe and U.S.A. of zinc metal and cadmium.

Four subsidiaries; Chair. Sir EDWARD COHEN; employees of subsidiaries: 3,394.

John Lysaght (Australia) Ltd.: 50 Young St., Sydney, N.S.W.; P.O.B. 196, G.P.O., Sydney, N.S.W. 2001; f. 1921; issued cap. $A100m.; p.u. cap. $A50m.

Manufacture of coated and uncoated steel sheets and coils; roofing, walling and floor decking, electrical laminations; other building and industrial products.

Twenty-four subsidiary companies inc. abroad; Chair. Sir JAMES MCNEILL; Man. Dir. S. W. H. FAIRBAIRN; employees: 7,200.

Metal Manufactures Ltd.: 168 Kent Street, P.O.B. 7047, Sydney, N.S.W. 2000; f. 1916; cap. $A37.9m.

Manufacturers of copper and other non-ferrous wire, strand and tubes, covered wire and strip, cables, and steel cored aluminium conductors.

Eleven wholly-owned subsidiary companies and three partly-owned subsidiaries; Man. Dir. Dr. D. R. STEWART; employees: about 5,000.

M.I.M. Holdings Ltd.: 160 Ann St., Brisbane, Qld. 4000, f. 1970; authorized cap. $A300m.

Mining and milling of silver-lead, zinc and copper; smelting and refining of copper and silver-lead; mining of coal and participation in iron ore and nickel mining.

Chair. Sir JAMES FOOTS; Man. Dir. B. D. WATSON; employees: 7,400.

North Broken Hill Holdings Ltd.: 360 Collins St., Melbourne, Vic. 3000; f. 1912; cap. $A150m.

Mines and treats lead, silver and zinc ore to produce lead and zinc concentrates; mineral exploration.

Chair. L. M. JARMAN; Exec. Dir. R. L. BAILLIEU; employees: 1,116.

Pancontinental Mining Ltd.: 1 York St., Sydney, N.S.W. 2000.

Mineral exploration and mining company.

Chair. A. J. GREY; Dir. R. R. MILES.

Peko-Wallsend Ltd.: 1–33 Macquarie St., Sydney, N.S.W. 2000.

Holding company for miners of gold, bismuth, copper, tungsten, coal, mineral sands; refiner, assayer and marketer of precious metals; manufacturer of industrial pumps, agricultural equipment, lead acid storage batteries; mini steel mill operator; processor of scrap metal; transport and warehousing.

Chair. KEITH W. HALKERSTON; Chief Exec. A. C. COPEMAN; Sec. ALLAN EDWARDS; employees: 7,982.

Tubemakers of Australia Ltd.: 1 York St., Sydney, N.S.W. 2000; f. 1946; cap. $A192m.

Manufacturer of steel and cast iron pipes, tubes and fittings; merchandiser of steel products.

Several subsidiary companies; Chair. Sir JAMES MCNEILL; Man. Dir. J. M. GRIGGS; employees: 7,000.

Western Mining Corporation Ltd.: 360 Collins St., Melbourne, Vic. 3001; f. 1933; cap. $A103.6m.

Mining and processing of nickel, gold and talc; interests in aluminium, phosphate, copper and uranium.

Chair. and Man. Dir. Sir ARVI PARBO; employees: 4,700.

MOTOR VEHICLES

Ford Motor Company of Australia Ltd.: 1735 Sydney Rd., Campbellfield, Vic.; f. 1925; cap. $A50m.

Manufactures for sale in domestic and export markets passenger and commercial motor vehicles, tractors, construction equipment, implements and parts and accessories.

Chair. Sir BRIAN INGLIS; Man. Dir. W. L. DIX; employees: 12,600.

General Motors-Holden's Ltd.: 241 Salmon Street, Port Melbourne, Vic. 3207; f. 1926; cap. $A140m.

GMH is a wholly-owned subsidiary of General Motors Corporation. Manufactures Commodore, Holden, Torana, Gemini, Sunbird and Statesman passenger vehicles, Holden commercial vehicles, and Holden engines for marine and industrial use. Assembles Chevrolet and Bedford commercial vehicles. Manufacture and distribution of spare parts and accessories. Assembles Terex earth-moving equipment.

One subsidiary company; Man. Dir. C. S. CHAPMAN; employees: 21,495.

International Harvester Australia Ltd.: 211 Sturt St., South Melbourne, Vic. 3205; f. 1912; cap. $A20m.

Manufacturers and marketers of trucks, tractors, farm, industrial and construction equipment, etc.,

One subsidiary company; Chair. and Man. Dir. A. ROBERT ABERCROMBIE; employees: 3,000.

Leyland Motor Corporation of Australia Ltd.: P.O.B. 59, Liverpool, N.S.W. 2170.

Assemblers and distributors of cars, light and heavy commercial motor vehicles and marine engines; importers and distributors of selected high class motor cars made by the parent company, B.L. Limited of England. Branches in N.S.W., Victoria, Queensland, S. Australia and Western Australia.

Chair. J. M. SNOWDON; Man. Dir. PHILIP HOVELL; employees: 2,000.

Mitsubishi Motors Australia Ltd.: 1284 South Rd., Clovelly Park, S.A.; issued cap. $A59.4m.

Manufacturers of cars, service parts, accessories, automotive components, engines.

Chair. Y. SHIMAMURA; Man. Dir. G. G. SPURLING; employees: 4,400.

Repco Ltd.: 630 St. Kilda St., Melbourne, Vic. 3004.

Manufacturer of automotive components and service equipment, accessories, hand and machine tools, industrial products and services. Largest suppliers of original equipment to vehicle manufacturers in Australia; has overseas manufacturing and/or merchandising operations in: the U.K., New Zealand, Canada, India, South Africa, Singapore, Hong Kong, Thailand, Malaysia and the U.S.A.

There are also associated companies in Australia, South Africa, Singapore, Hong Kong and India; Man. Dir. ANTHONY B. AVERY; Sec. NEIL K. ANGUS; employees: 11,595.

PETROLEUM

Ampol Petroleum Ltd.: 84 Pacific Highway, North Sydney, N.S.W. 2060; f. 1936; cap. $A114.5m.

Group's activities: oil, gas, coal, uranium and mineral exploration and exploitation; refining, shipping, distribution and marketing of petroleum products; property development; finance and leasing; computer services; television and leisure services.

Fifteen subsidiary companies, all in Australia; Chair. Sir TRISTAN ANTICO; Man. Dir. and Chief Exec. ALFRED E. HARRIS; Chief Gen. Man. RICHARD C. H. MASON; employees: 1,949.

The British Petroleum Company of Australia Ltd.: BP House, 1 Albert Rd., Melbourne, Vic. 3004; f. 1962; cap. $A110m.

The Holding Company for the BP Group Companies in Australia; wholly-owned by The British Petroleum Company Ltd., U.K. Activities in Australia: refining, marketing, exploration, transportation of petroleum products, fertilizer production, coal production and mineral exploration.

Twelve subsidiary companies; Chair. J. DARLING; Man. Dir. A. W. GORRIE; employees: 4,000.

Esso Australia Ltd.: Esso House, 127 Kent St., Sydney, N.S.W. 2000; cap. $A30m.

All spheres of the petroleum business. The parent company is the Exxon Corporation through Esso Eastern Inc.

Five subsidiary companies; six associated companies; Chair. and Man. Dir. JAMES F. KIRK; employees: 2,300.

Mobil Oil Australia Ltd.: 2 City Rd., South Melbourne, Vic. 3205; f. 1904; cap. $A50m.

Marketers in Australia and the Pacific Islands of a full range of petroleum products.

Subsidiary companies: 6 at home, 1 in Papua New Guinea; Chief Exec. GEORGE W. PUSACK.

Petroleum Refineries (Australia) Pty. Ltd.: 2 City Rd., South Melbourne, Vic. 3205; cap. $A10m.

Petroleum refiners.

Chair. G. W. PUSACK; Man. Dir. W. R. YEO; employees: 560.

Shell Australia Limited: Shell Corner, 155 William St., Melbourne, Vic. 3001, P.O.B. 872K; inc. 1958; cap. $A450m.

Manufactures and markets petroleum and petroleum products and chemicals; exploration and production of oil, gas, coal and minerals.

Sixteen subsidiary companies; Chair. and Man. Dir. R. K. GOSPER; Sec. D. W. JAFFER.

H. C. Sleigh Ltd.: 160 Queen St., Melbourne, Vic. 3000; f. 1895, inc. 1947; cap. $A55.1m.

Forest resources, earthmoving equipment, exporting and international trading, coal mining, food processing, shipping and travel, aviation.

Thirty-one subsidiary companies; Chair. R. N. MILLAR; Man. Dir. A. F. WARBURTON; employees: 2,000.

West Australian Petroleum Pty. Ltd.: 12 St. George's Terrace, P.O.B. C1580, Perth, W.A. 6001.

Exploration and production of petroleum and natural gas.

Man. Dir. ROBERT B. MITCHELL.

RUBBER AND TEXTILES

Dunlop Olympic Ltd.: 23rd Floor, 500 Bourke St., Melbourne, Vic. 3000; cap. $A96.5m.

Marketing and manufacturing. Batteries, tyres and rubber products; aircraft braking systems; building supplies; automative and engineering products; textiles and clothing; footwear; mattresses; latex and polyurethane foam; polystyrene and cold storage; sporting goods and under-water equipment; electrical and telecommunications cables; timber products.

Chair. Sir BRIAN MASSY-GREENE; Man. Dir. J. B. GOUGH; employees: 22,000.

The Goodyear Tyre and Rubber Co. (Australia) Ltd.: 4 Yurong Street, Sydney, N.S.W.; cap. $A26.6m.

Manufacturers of tyres and tubes, industrial rubber products, general rubber products, fan belts, adhesives. Goodyear aviation products, film packaging.

Chair. P. B. BLACKFORD; employees: 2,800.

PAPER AND PULP

Australian Paper Manufacturers Ltd.: South Gate, South Melbourne, Vic. 3205; f. 1926; cap. $A161m.

Australia's principal producer of woodpulp, paper and paperboard.

Subsidiary companies: 33 at home, 2 in New Zealand; Chair. J. G. WILSON; Man. Dir. S. D. M. WALLIS; employees: 5,590.

Associated Pulp and Paper Mills Ltd.: 360 Collins St., Melbourne, Vic.; G.P.O. Box 509H, Melbourne, Vic. 3001; f. 1936; cap. $A60.63m.

Manufacture of various papers and boards as well as paper merchandising and converting, forestry, farming and mining and production of filler and superfine coating clays.

Thirteen subsidiary companies in Australia; Chair. Sir WILLIAM VINES, C.M.G.; Man. Dir. W. H. THORNTON; employees: 5,183.

FOOD AND DRINK, ETC.

AMATIL Ltd.: Box 145, G.P.O., Sydney, N.S.W. 2001; f. 1904; cap. $A97.7m.

Manufacturing and distribution of tobacco products; foods and beverages and meat products; printing and packaging. investment in poultry and fishing.

About 55 subsidiary companies, of which 11 are overseas; Chair. H. WIDDUP; employees: over 13,000.

Cadbury Schweppes Australia Ltd.: 636 St. Kilda Rd., Melbourne, Vic. 3004; f. 1971; cap. $A31.16m.

Manufacture and distribution of chocolate and sugar confectionery, jams, soft fruit drinks, post mix syrups, fruit juices.

Chief Exec. D. J. HUGHES; Man. Dir. (Drinks) F. J. SWAN; Man. Dir. (Confectionery) K. A. HAYES; Sec. A. E. PETHERBRIDGE; 3,350 employees.

Carlton and United Breweries Ltd.: 16 Bouverie St., Carlton, Vic.; cap. $A191m.

Sixty-two subsidiary companies; Chair. Sir EDWARD COHEN; Man. Dir. L. J. MANGAN; employees: 4,500.

Henry Jones (IXL) Ltd.: 20 Garden St., South Yarra, Vic. 3141; f. 1909; shareholders funds $A38m.

Farming, processing and marketing food products including jam, fruit and fruit juices, pineapples, fresh and frozen vegetables and meat. Interests include timber milling, hop growing and marketing, television and radio. Major interests are in Australia, South Africa, the United Kingdom and Hong Kong.

Subsidiary companies: 16 at home, 6 in South Africa, 2 in Hong Kong, 2 in the U.K.; Chair. T. MARCUS CLARK; Man. Dir. J. D. ELLIOTT; Sec. S. J. KELSO.

Petersville Australia Ltd.: 258–294 Wellington Rd., Mulgrave, Vic. 3170; f. 1929.

Processor of vegetables, ice cream, dairy products, meat and pastries. Manufacturer of sheet metal and refrigeration products. Importers of gourmet foods.

Chair. and Man. Dir. J. S. SHAW; employees: 5,500 (approx.).

Philip Morris Ltd.: 252 Chesterville Rd., P.O.B. 93, Moorabbin, Vic. 3189.

Manufacturer of tobacco products.

Chair. WILLIAM R. IRVINE; Man. Dir. G. D. W. CURLEWIS; employees: 1,550.

Tooth & Co. Ltd.: 26 Broadway, N.S.W. 2007; f. 1835; issued cap. $A73.0m.

Brewer; wine and spirit merchants; hotel and property owners.

Chair. W. L. FESQ; Vice-Chair. R. H. MINTER; Man. Dir. G. A. HAINES; Sec. C. J. HENSON.

Unilever Australia Export Pty. Ltd.: 1-33 Macquarie St., Sydney, N.S.W. 2000; Box No. 1590 G.P.O., Sydney, N.S.W. 2001.

Marketing ice cream, food, edible oils, toiletries, soap and detergents.

Fourteen subsidiary companies; employees: 5,000.

MISCELLANEOUS

Acmil Ltd.: 168 Walker St., North Sydney, N.S.W. 2060.

Manufacturers of all kinds of specialized building materials and bricks, quarry tiles, clay pipes, corrosion control systems, adhesives, marina systems, building chemicals, non-woven vinyl floor coverings, PVC furnishing fabrics, plastic houseware, containers, toys and components, moulded boats, rubber carpet underlays, aluminium and timber windows and doors, multi-nail connector plates, locks; glass merchants, timber millers and shop fitters.

Subsidiary companies in Australia, New Zealand, S.E. Asia, U.S.A.; Chair. L. W. R. CAVE; Man. Dir. K. B. GODSON; employees: 7,000.

Ansett Transport Industries Ltd.: 489 Swanston St., Melbourne, Vic. 3000.

Airline and road passenger and freight services, general trading, manufacturing, hotels and tourist resorts, television station operation, general insurance.

Chairmen and Jt. Man. Dirs. Sir PETER ABELES, K. RUPERT MURDOCH; Exec. Dirs. FRANK PASCOE, C.B.E., B. RITZMANN, A. NOTLEY; Sec. J. K. SIMPSON; employees: 14,700.

Australian Consolidated Industries Ltd.: 550 Bourke St., Melbourne, Vic.; f. 1872; auth. cap. $A150m.

Manufacturers and distributors of glass containers, float, decorative rolled and wire reinforced glass, pressed and blown glassware and pyrex ovenware, fibreglass insulants and textiles, plastic piping, corrugated fibre containers—Australia, New Zealand, South-East Asia, Papua New Guinea and Fiji.

One hundred and twenty-two subsidiary companies, 50 in Australia, 72 abroad (N.Z., Fiji, Papua New Guinea, Indonesia, Singapore, Malaysia and Hong Kong); Chair. Andrew Grimwade; Man. Dir. R. W. Brack; employees: 23,000.

BMI Limited: 6 O'Connell St., Sydney, N.S.W. 2000; f. 1952; cap. $A54.7m.

Quarrying; supply of all types of aggregates, road base and sand materials; manufacturing and laying of premixed asphaltic materials; building stone and terrazzo; ready-mixed concrete; timber milling and merchandising; furniture manufacture and retail; bricks; concrete roofing tiles; pre-cast and pre-stressed concrete; fly-ash; road transport; tyre retread manufacture and processing; general engineering; mining; dairy farming; cattle breeding.

Man. Dir. R. A. Robson, C.B.E.

Brambles Industries Ltd.: Gold Fields House, 1 Alfred St., Sydney Cove, N.S.W. 2000; f. 1875; cap. $A24.8m.

Materials movement and distribution, including industrial plant hire, equipment pools, scheduled freight forwarding by road, rail, sea and air, heavy haulage, logistical support programmes for major projects, marine towage and transportation, pollution control services, etc.

Chief Exec. Officer Warwick J. Holcroft; employees: 5,000.

CSR Ltd.: 1 O'Connell St., P.O.B. 483, Sydney, N.S.W. 2001; f. 1855; issued cap. $A259m.

Sugar milling, refining and marketing, distilling, sheep, cattle, shipping, macadamia nuts, manufacture of building and construction materials, mining and mineral exploration, industrial chemicals.

One hundred and thirty-eight subsids.; Chair. Sir Noel Foley; Gen. Man. R. G. Jackson; employees: 14,100.

Commonwealth Industrial Gases Ltd., CIG: 46 Kippax St., Surry Hills, N.S.W. 2010.

Manufacturers and suppliers of industrial and medical gases, electric and gas welding equipment and consumables, safety equipment, medical equipment, ground engaging tools, food freezing equipment, paint sprays and safety equipment. Industrial and medical gas plants throughout Australia; equipment and welding consumables factories in Melbourne. Overseas subsidiaries in Papua New Guinea, Fiji, Indonesia and Thailand, each with its own gas manufacturing facilities.

Chair. J. A. Davidson, A.O.; Man. Dir. G. A. Scott; employees: 4,309.

Containers Ltd.: 265–275 Franklin St., Melbourne, Vic. 3000; f. 1950.

Manufacture of metal food and beverage cans, aerosols, plastic containers, paper labels and cartons, flexible laminates, shipping containers and Regency greeting cards and wrapping.

Man. Dir. L. N. Price; Group Gen. Man. R. Cameron; employees: 4,200.

James Hardie & Co. Pty. Ltd.: 65 York St., Sydney, N.S.W. 2000; f. 1937.

Manufacturers of fibre cement building products and asbestos-cement pipes.

Chair. D. K. Macfarlane; Sec. B. K. Sugg; employees: 3,300.

The Herald and Weekly Times Limited: 44–74 Flinders St., Melbourne, Vic. 3000; f. 1902; cap. $A48.3m.

Newspaper proprietors, publishers, printers, radio and television broadcasters.

Thirty-one subsidiary companies; Chair. Sir Keith Macpherson; employees: 3,500.

ICI Australia Ltd.: ICI House, 1 Nicholson St., Melbourne, Vic. 3000.

Manufacturers of industrial explosives, industrial and agricultural chemicals, dyes, polythene, polypropylene, plastic, fibres, paint, etc.; 62 per cent owned by Imperial Chemical Industries, United Kingdom.

Chair. and Man. Dir. M. D. Bridgland; Sec. A. E. Paine; employees: 12,000.

Kodak (Australasia) Pty. Ltd.: 173 Elizabeth St., Coburg, Vic. 3058.

Manufacturers of sensitized photographic materials, photographic chemicals and equipment; distributors and retailers.

One subsidiary company in New Zealand; Chair. D. Hogarth; Man. Dir. and Chief Exec. Officer E. G. Woods; employees: 2,500.

McPherson's Ltd.: 500 Collins St., Melbourne, Vic.; issued cap. $A27.3m.

Distributors of industrial products and machine tools. Also manufacturers of pumps for industrial and agricultural purposes, mechanical fasteners, and cold formed parts, cutting tools, fence and gate fittings.

Chair. W. D. McPherson; Man. Dir. C. R. Ward-Ambler; employees: 5,500.

Thiess Holdings Ltd.: 20th Floor, National Mutual Centre, 144 Edward St., Brisbane, Qld. 4000.

Coal mining, coal exploration; civil engineering and building, land development; pastoral activities.

Pres. Sir Leslie Thiess, C.B.E.; Chair. R. G. Jackson, A.C.; Gen. Man. A. S. Honey; employees: 1,500.

Thomas Nationwide Transport Limited (TNT): TNT Plaza, Tower 1, Lawson Square, Redfern, N.S.W. 2016; f. 1946; cap. and res. $A93m. (1976/77).

Local, bulk, refrigerated and long-haul trucking, rail, sea, air freight forwarding, bond and free stores, warehousing, customs agents, courier services, computer services, armed security, pallet hiring, forklift distribution, waste disposal, ship owners and operators. Operates in Australia, Canada, the U.S.A., Brazil, the U.K., Europe, Malaysia, Singapore, Taiwan, Hong Kong, the Philippines, Mexico and New Zealand.

One hundred and seventy Australian overseas subsidiaries; Chair. F. W. Millar; Man. Dir. and Chief Exec. Sir Peter Abeles; Chief Gen. Man. J. R. Cribb, O.B.E.; employees: 11,000.

RETAIL AND WHOLESALE TRADE

Burns Philp & Co. Ltd.: 7 Bridge St., Sydney, N.S.W. 2000.

General merchandise wholesalers; general and shipping agents; branches throughout the Pacific.

Chair. and Man. Dir. James D. O. Burns; Sec. B. C. Porter.

G. J. Coles & Co. Ltd.: 236 Bourke St., Melbourne, Vic. 3000; cap. $A100.4m.

Variety chain stores, supermarkets and food stores.

Three grocery subsidiary companies; Chair. T. L. North; Man. Dir. and Chief Exec. Bevan P. Bradbury; employees: 63,500.

Dalgety Australia Ltd.: 38 Bridge St., Sydney, N.S.W. 2000; cap. $A30m.

Wool selling brokers, stud stock specialists, livestock exporters, finance, produce salesmen, suppliers of graziers' and farmers' merchandise and agricultural seeds requirements, wholesale merchandisers, shipping agents, stevedores, insurance agents, pastoralists, exporters, mining and industrial equipment manufacturers, domestic and commercial air-conditioning manufacturer.

Twenty-two subsidiary trading companies in Australia. Chair. and Man. Dir. R. B. Vaughan; Sec. J. S. Burgess; employees: 2,600.

Elder Smith Goldsbrough Mort Ltd.: Elder House, 27–39 Currie St., Adelaide, South Australia; cap. $A43.57m.

Importers and exporters, wool brokers, buyers and scourers, general merchants, land and livestock insurance, shipping and travel agents, ship chartering brokers, fruit exporters, station owners, trustees and executors, merchant bankers, rural and real estate financiers, steel and metal distributors, coastal marine service, stevedoring and general transport operators.

Nine main subsidiary companies; Chair. Sir Ian McLennan; Deputy Chair. J. I. N. Winter; Man. Dir. and Chief Exec. J. D. Elliott; employees: 7,500.

David Jones Ltd.: 86–108 Castlereagh St., Sydney, N.S.W. 2000; f. 1838; cap. $A25.6m.

Department store chain retailers; 23 stores in Australia; trades under name of Buffums in California, U.S.A.

Chair. K. Russell; employees: 11,000.

The Myer Emporium Ltd.: 250 Elizabeth St., Melbourne, Vic. 3000; f. 1925.

Holding company of the largest group of department and discount stores in the Southern Hemisphere. Major department stores in all States.

Chair. S. B. Myer; Man. Dir. K. A. Rosenhain; employees: 29,995.

Waltons Ltd.: George, Park and Pitt Sts., Sydney, N.S.W. 2000; f. 1926; cap. $A29.1m.

Department store chain retailers.

Chair. John S. Walton; employees: 6,000.

Woolworths Ltd.: 534 George St., Sydney, N.S.W. 2000; cap. $A82.9m.

Retail chain stores.

Chair. E. McClintock; Man. Dir. A. J. Harding; employees: 45,500.

TRANSPORT

Australian Transport Advisory Council: Lombard House, Allara St., Canberra, A.C.T. 2600; f. 1946; Members: Commonwealth Minister for Transport, State and Territory Ministers of Transport and Roads; Observer: the New Zealand Minister for Transport, Civil Aviation and Railways; advises the Commonwealth and State Governments on transport policies and seeks to secure uniformity in transport regulations, promote co-ordination of development and maintain research.

Urban Transit Authority of New South Wales: 11-31 York St., Sydney, N.S.W. 2000; ensures co-ordination of bus, rail and ferry services in Sydney, Newcastle and Wollongong; operates publicly owned buses and ferries; exercises broad policy control over privately operated public vehicles in the above areas. Buses operate on routes totalling 1,090 km.

RAILWAYS

Before July 1975 there were seven government-owned railway systems in Australia. In July 1975 Australian National was formed to incorporate the Commonwealth Railways, non-metropolitan South Australian Railways and the Tasmanian Government Railways.

Australian National: 55 King William Rd., North Adelaide, S.A. 5006; a federally owned, statutory authority operating 7,649 km. of railways in 1982; Chair. L. E. Marks; Gen. Man. Dr. D. G. Williams.

Queensland Government Railways: Railway Centre, 305 Edward St., Brisbane, Qld. 4000; operates 9,967 km. of track; Commissioner P. J. Goldston; Deputy Commissioner and Sec. A. J. Neeson.

State Rail Authority of New South Wales: 11–31 York St., Sydney, N.S.W. 2000; administers passenger and freight rail service in N.S.W. over a network of 9,773 km.; Chief Exec. David Hill.

State Transport Authority—(South Australia): G.P.O. Box 2351, Adelaide, S.A. 5001; Railway Bldg., North Terrace, Adelaide, S.A.; f. 1856; operates 136 km. of metropolitan track; Gen. Man. F. R. Harris.

Victorian Railways (VicRail): 67 Spencer St., Melbourne. Vic. 3000; f. 1856; operates 5,870 km. of track; Chair, A. S. Reiher; Dep. Chair. I. G. Hodges; Gen. Man. R. J. Gallacher.

Western Australian Government Railways (Westrail): Perth, W.A.; operates passenger and freight transport services mainly in the south of Western Australia; 7,415 main line route km. of track, 7,006 bus route km. and 3,542 truck route km. of road services; Commissioner W. I. McCullough; Sec. W. T. Tobin.

ROADS

At June 30th, 1978 there were 816,832 km. of roads, including 108,982 km. of main roads.

SHIPPING

Commonwealth of Australia, Australian National Line: (Australian Shipping Commission), 65–79 Riverside Ave., South Melbourne, Vic. 3205; postal: P.O.B. 2238T, Melbourne, Vic. 3001; f. 1956; services: Australian coastal trade and passenger and car services between mainland and Tasmania; overseas container services to Europe, the U.S.A., Hong Kong, Taiwan, the Philippines, Korea, Singapore, Malaysia, Thailand, Indonesia and Japan; Chair. V. G. Jenner; Gen. Man. J. L. Morgan.

The Adelaide Steamship Co. Ltd.: 123 Greenhill Rd., Unley, S.A. 5061; f. 1875; Man. Dir. J. G. Spalvins.

Ampol Petroleum Ltd.: 84 Pacific Highway, North Sydney, N.S.W.; Chair. Sir TRISTAN ANTICO; Man. Dir. A. E. HARRIS; bulk carriage of crude oil from Westernport, Victoria, to Brisbane, and carriage of refined products from the Brisbane refinery to Queensland ports; 2 vessels.

TNT Bulkships Ltd.: Tower 1, TNT Plaza, Lawson Sq., Redfern, N.S.W. 2016; f. 1958; wholly-owned subsidiary company of Thomas Nationwide Transport Ltd.; shipowner and operator; charters vessels; Man. Dir. Sir PETER ABELES; Exec. Dir. ROLAND J. HOY; Sec. J. REUBEN RATTRAY.

John Burke Shipping: Macquarie St., New Farm, P.O.B. 509, Fortitude Valley, Qld. 4006; f. 1887; Chair. D. J. DALY; 5 vessels; coastal services.

Burns, Philp and Co. Ltd.: 7 Bridge St., P.O.B. 543, Sydney, N.S.W.; f. 1883; Chair. and Man. Dir. J. D. O. BURNS; Chief Exec. Officer P. C. BEST.

Holyman and Sons Pty. Ltd.: 54 Brisbane St., P.O.B. 70, Launceston, Tas.; Chair. and Man. Dir. K. C. HOLYMAN; coastal services.

Howard Smith Industries Pty. Ltd.: 1 York St., Sydney, N.S.W.; Chair. W. HOWARD-SMITH; Chief Gen. Man. J. G. EVANS; ownership or interest in 8 vessels and 46 tugs.

McIlwraith McEacharn Ltd.: Scottish House, 90 William St., Melbourne, Vic.; Chair. Sir IAN POTTER; Man. Dir. F. M. MURPHY; tug, launch and shipowners, agents; ship management, repair and cleaning.

Mason Shipping Co. Pty. Ltd.: Smith's Creek, P.O.B. 840, Cairns, Qld. 4870; 4 vessels; Man. R. A. MASON; coastal services and stevedoring.

Western Australian Coastal Shipping Commission (Stateships): 6 Short St., P.O.B. 394, Fremantle, W.A.; Chair. R. M. ROWELL, O.B.E.; Gen. Man. D. F. WILSON.

CIVIL AVIATION

Airlines of South Australia (*Division of Ansett Transport Industries (Operations) Pty. Ltd.*): 150 North Terrace, Adelaide, S.A. 5000; services in South Australia between Adelaide and Kangaroo Island, Port Lincoln, Whyalla, Ceduna, Mount Gambier and Broken Hill; fleet of 3 Fokker F.27; Gen. Man. L. CONNELLY.

Airlines of Western Australia (*Division of Ansett Transport Industries (Operations) Pty. Ltd.*): International House, 26 St. George's Terrace, Perth, W.A. 6000; f. 1934 (formerly Mac. Robertson Miller Airline Services); F-28 and DC-9 jet services Perth–Darwin via north-west ports and throughout Western Australia; fleet: 7 Fokker F-28, 1 DC-9; Gen. Man. J. E. KARASEK.

Air New South Wales (*Divison of Ansett Transport Industries (Operations) Pty. Ltd.*): Kingsford Smith Airport, Mascot, Sydney, N.S.W. 2020; f. 1934; operates extensive services from Sydney throughout N.S.W.; fleet includes 6 Fokker F.27-500; Gen. Man. J. BUCHANAN.

Air Queensland: P.O.B. 1381, Cairns, Qld.; f. 1951; operates an extensive network of scheduled services throughout the State to 83 centres; fleet of 3 F-27, 6 DC-3, 4 Trislander BN-3, 4 Cessna 402, 2 Cessna 310R, 1 Fokker F-27, 2 Cessna 404, 6 Swearingen Metro II, 5 de Havilland Twin Otters, 1 Nomad; Chair. H. S. WILLIAMS; Gen. Man. R. H. ENTSCH.

Ansett Airlines of Australia (*Division of Ansett Transport Industries (Operations) Pty. Ltd.*): 501 Swanston St., Melbourne, Vic. 3000; f. 1936; commercial airline operators; passenger and cargo air services throughout Australia and to New Zealand; fleet includes 16 Boeing 727-200, 8 Boeing 737-200, 4 DC-9-30, 5 Fokker F.27, 3 Electra Freighters and 2 Sikorsky S-61N; Chairmen and Jt. Man. Dirs. K. R. MURDOCH, Sir PETER ABELES; Exec. Dir. F. PASCOE, C.B.E.

East-West Airlines Ltd.: P.O.B. 249, Tamworth, N.S.W. 2340; f. 1947; routes total 10,200 km.; services to N.S.W., Queensland, Tasmania and Norfolk Island; 10 F-27; Chair. and Man. Dir. J. G. RILEY.

Northern Airlines: 30 Daly St., P.O.B. 1490, Darwin, N.T. 5790; f. 1980; Chair. G. HARRISON; Exec. Dir. B. TEAGUE; Gen. Man. M. CATHCART.

Qantas Airways Ltd.: Qantas House, 70 Hunter St., Sydney, N.S.W. 2000 (P.O.B. 489); f. 1920; wholly-owned by the Commonwealth of Australia; routes totalling 200,266 unduplicated km. at March 1981; services to 33 cities in 24 countries including from Australia to the U.K. via South-East Asia and the Middle East or India and Europe, U.S.A. and Canada, Japan, Hong Kong via Manila, Papua New Guinea, various routes across the Tasman Sea to New Zealand and Nouméa; fleet: 21 Boeing 747-238B, 2 Boeing 747 SP-38, 1 HS-125; Chair. J. B. LESLIE, M.C.; Dir. and Chief Exec. K. R. HAMILTON.

Trans-Australia Airlines (TAA): 50 Franklin St. (P.O.B. 2806AA), Melbourne, Vic. 3001; f. 1946; operated by Australian National Airlines Commission (Chair. Sir ROBERT LAW-SMITH); routes totalling 65,492 unduplicated km. to 46 points covering every Australian State and Christchurch, New Zealand; fleet includes 3 Airbus A300, 12 Boeing 727-276, 12 Douglas DC-9 and 10 Fokker F-27; Gen. Man. F. J. BALL.

FOREIGN AIRLINES

The following foreign airlines serve Australia: Air Canada, Air France, Air India, Air Nauru, Air New Zealand, Air Niugini (Papua New Guinea), Air Pacific International (Guam), Alitalia, British Airways, Canadian Pacific, Cathay Pacific (Hong Kong), JAL (Japan), JAT (Yugoslavia), KLM (Netherlands), Lan-Chile, Lufthansa (Federal Republic of Germany), MAS (Malaysia), Pan American (U.S.A.), PAL (Philippines), Garuda (Indonesia), PT Merpati Nusantara Airlines (Indonesia), SAA (South Africa), SIA (Singapore), Thai International and UTA (France).

TOURISM AND CULTURE

Australian Tourist Commission: 324 St. Kilda Rd., Melbourne, Vic. 3001; f. 1967; Government organization for encouraging overseas tourists; Chair. Sir PETER DERHAM; Gen. Man. K. A. MCDONALD; offices in Sydney, London, Auckland, Los Angeles, New York, Tokyo, Frankfurt-am-Main and Singapore.

CULTURAL ORGANIZATIONS

Australia Council: 168 Walker St., P.O.B. 302, North Sydney, N.S.W. 2060; f. 1975; statutory authority providing support for the arts in Australia. Seven boards: Aboriginal Arts, Crafts, Literature, Music, Theatre, Visual and Community Arts; administers grants, provides public information services, acts in an advisory capacity to the Federal Government and is involved in policy development, research and international activities; Chair. Dr. TIMOTHY PASCOE; publs. include information booklets, the newsletter *Artforce*, *Annual Report*.

The Australian Ballet: 11 Mount Alexander Rd., Flemington, Vic. 3031; f. 1962 by The Australian Ballet Foundation; 60 full-time dancers; Artistic Dir. MARILYN JONES, O.B.E.; Administrator PETER F. BAHEN, M.B.E.

Australian Elizabethan Theatre Trust: 153 Dowling St., Potts Point, N.S.W.; f. 1954; controls and administers Elizabethan Sydney Orchestra and Elizabethan Melbourne Orchestra, The N.S.W. Theatre of the Deaf and Theatrical Services Division, the Entrepreneurial Division of which is the official national entrepreneur for overseas and Australian companies and artists, including drama, dance, jazz and puppetry; financed by subsidies from Commonwealth and State Governments and city councils of approximately $A3,000,000 a year, and private donations and subscriptions; Pres. Sir JAMES DARLING, C.M.G., O.B.E.; Chair. Sir IAN POTTER; Gen. Man. JEFFRY JOYTON-SMITH.

The Australian Opera: A.M.P. Centre, 50 Bridge St., Sydney, N.S.W. 2000; f. 1955; full-time professional opera company, tours Melbourne, Canberra, Adelaide, Brisbane; 230 singers and staff mems.; Chair. CHARLES J. BERG, O.B.E.; Gen. Man. PATRICK L. VEITCH.

Sydney Opera House Trust: Box 4274 G.P.O., Sydney, N.S.W. 2001; f. 1961 to manage Sydney Opera House as a performing arts complex and convention centre; 8 mems.; Gen. Man. LLOYD MARTIN.

ORCHESTRAS

Australian Broadcasting Commission: 145–49 Elizabeth St., Sydney, N.S.W.; f. 1932; organizes more than 750 concerts and recitals each year throughout Australia; has established a major symphony orchestra in each of the six State capitals, as well as a national training orchestra based in Sydney. All orchestras are maintained and administered by the A.B.C. with, in addition, subsidies from State and municipal authorities.

FESTIVALS

There are many festivals in each of the States, the Northern Territory and Tasmania which are listed in a directory of festivals published by the Australian Council (*see above*, Cultural Organizations). The following is Australia's major festival of the arts.

Adelaide Festival: Adelaide Festival Centre, King William Rd., Adelaide, S.A. 5000; f. 1960; biennial; international; performing, visual and creative arts; Gen. Man. KEVIN EARLE.

ATOMIC ENERGY

Australian Atomic Energy Commission: Lucas Heights Research Laboratories, New Illawarra Road, Lucas Heights, N.S.W.; Private Mail Bag, Sutherland, N.S.W. 2232; Chair. Prof. D. W. GEORGE, PH.D.; Sec. L. H. KEHER (acting); Dir. of Research Establishment Prof. S. T. BUTLER; publs. Annual Report, *Atomic Energy in Australia* (quarterly journal), *A.A.E.C. Nuclear News*.

The Commission is concerned with scientific research, development of practical uses of atomic energy, the training of scientists and engineers, the discovery and production of uranium, the production of radioisotopes and radiopharmaceuticals. The Commission's Research Establishment is situated at Lucas Heights, near Sydney.

HIFAR: 10 MW. research reactor; critical 1958; for production of radioisotopes, studies of effects of high intensity radiation and as a source of neutrons.

MOATA: 100 kW. research reactor; critical 1962; provides neutron radiography, uranium analysis and general activation services and beams and irradiation space for physical chemistry and materials research.

Australian Institute of Nuclear Science and Engineering: Lucas Heights, N.S.W.; the Institute supports university research and training projects in all branches of nuclear science and engineering. Its membership comprises seventeen Universities, A.A.E.C. and CSIRO; Pres. (1981-82) Prof. S. C. HAYDON; Exec. Officer E. A. PALMER.

Australian School of Nuclear Technology: Private Mail Bag, PO, Sutherland, N.S.W. 2232; provides courses for Australian and overseas students in nuclear medicine, radioisotope techniques and applications and radiation protection; Principal B. TONER.

The following universities have facilities for nuclear research and training: Universities of Adelaide, New South Wales, Newcastle, Queensland, Sydney and Tasmania, The Australian National University, Flinders University of South Australia and La Trobe University.

DEFENCE

Armed Forces (Feb. 1982): Total strength 73,261; army 33,126, navy 17,515, air force 22,620; military service is voluntary.

Equipment: The Army has Leopard medium tanks, armoured personnel carriers, fire support vehicles and light observation helicopters. Other materiel includes Pilatus Porter and Nomad light aircraft, field artillery and the Rapier surface to air guided weapon system. The Navy has an aircraft carrier, guided missile destroyers and frigates, destroyer escorts, Oberon class submarines, patrol boats and a wide range of support and training vessels. The Air Force is equipped with American F111 C strike aircraft and French designed Mirage fighters. Other aircraft include Caribou and Hercules transports, Iroquois and Chinook helicopters and Orion maritime aircraft.

Defence Expenditure: Defence expenditure for 1980/81 was $A3,645.6m.

Chief of the Defence Force Staff: Air Chief Marshal Sir Neville McNamara, K.B.E., A.O., A.F.C., A.E.

Chief of Naval Staff: Vice-Admiral D. W. Leach, A.O., C.B.E., M.V.O., R.A.N.

Chief of the General Staff: Lt.-Gen. P. H. Bennett, A.O., D.S.O.

Chief of the Air Staff: Air Marshal S. D. Evans, A.O., D.S.O., A.F.C.

EDUCATION

Compulsory education was first established in Victoria by the 1872 Education Act, which was followed by similar acts in Queensland in 1875, in New South Wales and South Australia in 1880 and in Tasmania and Western Australia in 1893. After the federation of the 6 states was established in 1901 each State retained responsibility for education. The responsibility for framing educational policy and putting it into effect rests with the Minister of Education, and an Education Department headed by a director-general deals with all aspects of education within each State. Although the State systems are not identical they have many similar features. The education of people in isolated areas is an important problem, although only a small proportion of Australia's school-age children live in remote districts. The Australian government gives high priority to equality of educational opportunity. School attendance in Australia is compulsory and free between the ages of 6-15 (16 in Tasmania) for all children except those exempted on account of distance, for whom a special form of education is provided. The academic year, which is divided into 4 terms in Queensland and into 3 terms in the other States, begins at the end of January or the beginning of February in schools and at the end of February or March in universities and ends in December for the long vacation. The Federal Government has full responsibility for education in the Australian Capital Territory and makes very substantial contributions to the States for recurrent and capital expenditure in both governmental and non-governmental schools. Since 1974 the Federal Government, by agreement with the States, has become responsible for the full financing of higher education throughout Australia. In the financial year 1979/80 the Federal Government provided $A2,607 million for education and the State Governments $A4,174 million.

Government Schools

In 1981 there were 7,472 government primary and secondary schools with an enrolment of 2,299,403 children and 140,525 teachers, of whom about half are women.

Pre-school. Only a small proportion of Australian children attend pre-school centres or kindergartens. Such centres are sometimes run by church bodies and private groups, more frequently by Government-subsidized Kindergarten Unions.

Most children start school at the age of five, attending infants' school or classes attached to the primary school. Primary schools are generally mixed and cater for children up to the age of twelve to thirteen with 4½–5 hours of daily instruction. Syllabuses are prescribed by the Educational departments, although teachers are to a certain extent free to modify courses to suit local circumstances.

Secondary education is largely co-educational, although in the larger cities segregated schools are not uncommon. Children are grouped in classes according to the subjects that they intend to pursue. Curricula vary in each State but usually include English language and literature, foreign languages, mathematics, chemistry and physics and other natural and social sciences. However, while a purely academic course is still available it is becoming increasingly common for high schools to be of the comprehensive type. In more sparsely populated areas junior secondary classes are sometimes attached to a primary school, but the increasing tendency is to bring children in by bus from outlying areas to high schools in the nearest town.

In some States junior technical, agricutural area and rural schools offer up to four years of the secondary courses and a curriculum combining general education with subjects related to their special emphasis.

Public examinations are being phased out in Australian schools. A variety of forms of assessment, including periodic tests and examinations in class are used to help teachers assess students' abilities and performance. Alternative methods are being developed for the selection of students for tertiary study, which use objective tests in conjunction with teacher assessment in the final year of a student's secondary schooling.

In 1974 the Federal Government replaced its former scheme of secondary scholarships awarded on merit with a secondary allowance scheme under which grants, subject to a means test, may be given to parents to encourage all children to complete the final two years of secondary schooling.

Private Schools or Independent Schools

In 1981 there were 687,996 pupils attending 2,200 private schools with 37,225 teachers. Approximately one child in five attends private schools which are fee-paying. The majority of non-government schools are conducted by various religious denominations, and many of the larger ones make provision for boarders; courses in private schools are similar to those in state schools. About 80 per cent of the total number of private schools are Roman Catholic schools, which form a highly developed system, usually run on a diocesan basis under the general direction of the Bishop. In 1979 there were an estimated 1,694

Roman Catholic schools, with 512,345 pupils, of whom more than a third were at secondary level.

Special Education for Children in Isolated Areas

Education in isolated areas has been provided for in a variety of ways. In areas where there are sufficient children of school age, a school may be formed with all primary grades in one room, under the control of one teacher. Children who complete their primary education in such a school and cannot obtain a secondary school education may take secondary correspondence lessons under the teacher's supervision. At one time over a third of Government schools were of this type, but now all state education departments are closing schools with small enrolments. Instead, pupils are transported each day by bus to a consolidated school in the nearest large centre of population. These schools provide primary instruction and from two to four years of post-primary instruction. The curriculum usually has a bias towards practical activities of the locality. All States have systems of subsidies, whereby transport is made available free or at a concessionary rate for children who have to travel daily to school. For children whose homes are too far from a secondary school to allow daily travel some States run hostels or give financial assistance to privately owned hostels, while others pay boarding allowances to the holders of scholarships. In 1973 the Federal Government introduced the Isolated Children Allowance Scheme, under which allowances are payable to the parents of all children of school age who live some distance from the nearest school of appropriate standard

Correspondence Schools have been established in each capital city to meet the needs of children whose daily attendance at school is prevented by distance or illness. These schools originally began with primary grades only but were soon expanded to secondary level and it is now possible to do a complete matriculation course. As many as 20,000 children including Australian children overseas receive instruction each year through correspondence courses.

Schools of the Air, first established in 1950, are an attempt to give the outback children of school age some of the benefits of school life and at the same time to supplement correspondence education. Two-way wireless equipment is used.

Higher Education

Since January 1st, 1974, all Australian students gaining entry to an approved tertiary institution may receive maintenance grants, subject to a means test, under the Tertiary Education Assistance Scheme. At the same date all tuition fees for approved tertiary courses were abolished. Various other forms of financial assistance to students are available from the Australian Government and the State Governments.

Universities: Australian universities are autonomous institutions, though members of their respective State governments are among the members of their governing bodies. There are 19 universities and 68 colleges of advanced education. In 1981 the enrolment was 166,611 in the former and 165,067 in the latter. Most of the courses last from three to six years. Some of the universities have limited systems of external tuition, whereby students in country areas may do certain courses by correspondence. Postgraduate research facilities are available at all Australian universities and assistance is available either in the form of research grants from the universities themselves, or from the scheme of Commonwealth postgraduate awards.

Colleges of Advanced Education: This term covers a wide variety of institutions, other than universities, which provide higher education and teacher training courses, including Institutes of Technology and Agricultural Colleges.

Adult Education is used mainly to refer to non-vocational education in which adults participate voluntarily. There are also full-time and part-time classes for teaching English to immigrants and refugees under a programme conducted jointly by the State Education Departments and the Commonwealth Government. In 1979/80 about 111,500 adult immigrants attended courses in English language and in aspects of Australian life, services and institutions. In 1977/78 57,972 adult immigrants were enrolled in continuation classes and over 16,168 were participating in the various radio and correspondence courses.

BIBLIOGRAPHY

GENERAL

Aitken, J. Land of Fortune, a study of the New Australia (Secker and Warburg, London, 1976).

Australia: Yearbook of the Commonwealth of Australia (Commonwealth Bureau of Census and Statistics).

Australian Encyclopedia. 6 vols. (Grolier Society, Sydney, latest edn. 1977).

Berndt, R. M. and C. H. The world of the First Australian (Ure Smith, Sydney, 1964).

Davies, A. F. (ed.). Australian Society; a sociological introduction (Cheshire, Melbourne, 2nd edn. 1970).

Encel, S. Equality and Authority, a study of class, status and power (Cheshire, Melbourne, 1970).

Horne, D. The Australian People, biography of a nation (Angus and Robertson, Sydney, 1976).

Jeans, D. N. (ed.). Australia, a Geography (Sydney University Press, Sydney, 1977).

Kewley, T. Social Security in Australia (Sydney University Press, Sydney, 1972).

Maddock, K. J. The Australian Aborigines (Penguin, London, 1973).

Simpson, C. The New Australia (Angus and Robertson Sydney, 1971).

Spate, O. H. K. Australia (Nations of the Modern World Series, Benn, London, 1968).

Stone, Sharman. Aborigines in White Australia (Heinemann Educational Books, Adelaide, 1974).

Venturini, V. G. (ed.). Australia: a survey (Otto Harrassowitz, Wiesbaden, 1970).

HISTORY

Australian Dictionary of Biography (Melbourne University Press, 1966).

Blainey, G. The Tyranny of Distance (Sun Books, Melbourne, 2nd edn. 1976).

Clark, M. A History of Australia (to 1888, 4 vols.) (Melbourne University Press, 1972).

Crowley, F. K. (ed.). A New History of Australia (Heinemann, Melbourne, 1974).

GRIFFITHS, J. Contemporary Australia (St. Martin's Press, New York, 1977).

LACOUR-GAYET, R. A Concise History of Australia (Penguin, London, 1976).

LA NAUZE, J. The Making of the Australian Constitution (Melbourne University Press, Melbourne, 1972).

MCINTYRE, K. G. The Secret Discovery of Australia (Souvenir Press, London, 1977).

SHARP, C. A. The discovery of Australia (Oxford University Press, London, 1963).

SHAW, A. G. L., and NICOLSON, H. D. Australia in the Twentieth Century (Angus and Robertson, Sydney, 1967).

POLITICS

ALEXANDER, F. From Curtin to Menzies and After (Nelson, Melbourne, 1973).

ATKINS, B. Governing Australia (Wiley, Sydney, 1972).

BENNETT, S. C. The Making of the Commonwealth (Cassell, Melbourne, 1971).

CRISP, L. F. Australian National Government (Longman, Melbourne, latest edn. 1975).

DAVIES, S. R. (ed.). The Government of the Australian States (Longman, London, 1960).

HUGHES, C. A. A Handbook of Australian Government and Politics, 1965–74.

MEYER, H. Australian Politics (Cheshire, Melbourne, 1971).

MILLER, J. D. B. Australian Government and Politics (Duckworth, London, 1971).

SAWER, G. The Australian Constitution (Government Publications, Canberra, 1975).

THEOPHANOUS, ANDREW. Australian Democracy in Crisis: A New Theoretical Introduction to Australian Politics (Oxford University Press, 1980).

WATT, A. The Evolution of Australian Foreign Policy (Cambridge University Press, 1967).

WHITINGTON, B. L. The Menzies Era and After (Cheshire, Melbourne, 1972).

ECONOMY

ANDREWS, J. A. Australia's Resources and their Utilisation (University Press, Sydney, rev. edn., 1970).

COGHILL, I. G. Australia's Mineral Wealth (Sorrett Publishing, Melbourne, 1971).

CORDEN, W. M. Australian Economic Policy Discussion: a survey (Melbourne University Press, Melbourne, 1968).

CRAWFORD, J. G., and others. Study Group on Structural Adjustment, March 1979 (Australian Government Publishing Service, Canberra, 1979).

CRAWFORD, J. G., and OKITA, S. (eds.). Raw Materials and Pacific Economic Integration (Croom Helm Ltd., London, 1978).

DOWNING, R. I. National Income and Social Accounts; an Australian Study (Melbourne University Press, 12th edn., reprinted with supplement, 1971).

FITZPATRICK, B. C. British Imperialism and Australia 1783–1833: an economic history of Australasia (Sydney University Press, Sydney, 1971).

The British Empire in Australia: an economic history, 1834–1939 (Macmillan, Melbourne, 1969).

GROENEWEGEN, P. D. Public Finance in Australia, Theory and Practice (Prentice-Hall of Australia Pty. Ltd., Sydney, 1979).

ISAAC, J. E., and FORD, G. Australian Labour Relations: readings (Sun Books, Melbourne, 2nd edn. 1971).

ISAAC, J. E., and NILAND, J. R. (eds.). Australian Labor Economics Readings (Melbourne, 1975).

KARMEL, P. H. The Structure of the Australian Economy (Cheshire, Melbourne, rev. edn., 1966).

NANKERVIS, F. T. Descriptive Economics; Australian Economic Institutions and Problems (Longmans, Melbourne, 7th edn., 1966).

PALMER, G. R. A Guide to Australian Economic Statistics (Macmillan, Melbourne, 2nd edn., 1966).

SINCLAIR, W. A. The Process of Economic Development in Australia (Cheshire, Melbourne, 1976).

SINDEN, J. A. (ed.). The Natural Resources of Australia: Prospects and Problems for Development (Angus and Robertson, Sydney, 1972).

Australian Dependencies in the Indian Ocean

CHRISTMAS ISLAND

Christmas Island covers an area of about 135 square kilometres and lies 360 kilometres south of Java Head in the Indian Ocean. The nearest point on the Australian coast is North West Cape, 1,408 kilometres to the south-east.

Administration was transferred from Singapore to Britain on January 1st, 1958, pending final transfer to Australia. It became an Australian territory on October 1st, 1958. An Administrator, appointed by the Governor-General of Australia and responsible to the Minister for Home Affairs and the Environment, is the senior government representative on the island. Christmas Island has no indigenous population. At March 31st, 1981, the estimated population was 3,214 (1,854 Chinese, 859 Malays, 369 Europeans and 132 others). Residents consist of employees of the Phosphate Mining Company of Christmas Island and the Administration and their families. The recovery of phosphates is the sole economic activity, and exports were 1,321,000 metric tons of phosphate rock, 96,393 tons of phosphate dust and 8,800 tons of citraphos dust for the year ending June 30th, 1981. In 1980 it was estimated that there were sufficient recoverable reserves to ensure the continuation of mining for eight years.

Administrator: W. YATES.

Supreme Court: Judge: The Hon. Mr. Justice W. E. S. FORSTER; Additional Judges The Hon. Mr. Justice E. A. DUNPHY, The Hon. Mr. Justice J. F. GALLOP.

Christmas Island Broadcasting Service: Christmas Island 6798; f. 1967; owned and operated by Australian Administration; daily broadcasting service by Radio VLU-2 on 1422 KHz. in English, Malay, Mandarin and Cantonese; on air Monday to Saturday 23.00–15.00 G.M.T., Sunday 01.00–14.00 G.M.T.; Broadcasting Officer RICHARD ANDREWARTHA.

There were about 3,800 radio sets in 1981.

Christmas Island Phosphate Commission: 515 Collins St., Melbourne, Vic. 3000, Australia; f. 1948. The Commission is responsible to the Australian and New Zealand Governments for the mining and distribution of phosphate from Christmas Island and the purchase of phosphate for Australia and New Zealand from other world sources. The Commission's operations are performed by the Phosphate Mining Company of Christmas Island.

Transport: Australian Government charter aircraft operate a fortnightly service from Perth via the Cocos (Keeling) Islands. The Phosphate Mining Company of Christmas Island conducts a cargo-shipping service to Singapore and to New Zealand, Malaysian and Australian ports. They also operate flights from Singapore to Christmas Island.

COCOS (KEELING) ISLANDS

The Cocos (Keeling) Islands are 27 in number and lie 2,768 kilometres north-west of Perth, in the Indian Ocean. The islands, which have an area of 14 square kilometres, form two low-lying coral atolls, densely covered with coconut palms. The population on June 30th, 1981, was 569, comprising 242 residents on West Island and 312 Cocos Malays and 15 Europeans on Home Island, the only inhabited islands in the group. The Cocos Malays are descendants of the people brought to the islands in 1826 by Alexander Hare and of labourers subsequently introduced by John Clunies-Ross.

The islands were declared a British possession in 1857 and came successively under the authority of the Governor of Ceylon (1878) and the Governor of the Straits Settlements (1886); they were annexed to the Straits Settlements and incorporated with the Settlement (later Colony) of Singapore in 1903. Administration of the islands was transferred to the Commonwealth of Australia in November 1955.

An Administrator, appointed by the Governor-General of Australia and responsible to the Minister for Home Affairs and Environment, is the senior government representative in the islands.

The Government announced new policies concerning the islands in June 1977 which resulted in the Commonwealth's purchase from Mr. John Clunies-Ross of the whole of his interests in the Cocos (Keeling) Islands with the exception of his residence and associated buildings. The purchase took effect on September 1st, 1978.

In July 1979 the Cocos (Keeling) Islands Council was established, with a wide range of functions in the Home Island village area, which the Government has transferred to the Council on trust for the benefit of the Cocos Malay community. The Council may advise the Administrator on any matter affecting the Territory.

Although local fishing is good and domestic gardens provide vegetables, bananas and pawpaws, the islands are not self-sufficient and other foodstuffs, fuels and consumer items are imported from mainland Australia. A Cocos Postal Service (including a philatelic bureau) came into operation in September 1979 and revenue from the Service is to be used for the benefit of the community.

The sole cash crop is the coconut, which is grown throughout the islands. Total exports in 1980/81 were 187 metric tons.

Primary education is provided at the schools on Home and West Islands. Secondary education is provided to year 10 on West Island.

Administrator: ERIC H. HANFIELD.

Supreme Court, Cocos (Keeling) Islands: Judge: The Hon. Mr. Justice WILLIAM E. D. FORSTER; Additional Judges: The Hon. Mr. Justice EDWARD A. DUNPHY, The Hon. Mr. Justice JAMES H. MUIRHEAD.

Radio Cocos: daily broadcasting service from 0.630 to 00.30 by Radio VKW, West Island; Man. LEONARD WATSON.

Australian Government charter aircraft from Perth carry passengers, supplies and mail to and from the Cocos every fortnight. Cargo vessels from Perth deliver supplies, at intervals of six to eight weeks.

Bangladesh

PHYSICAL AND SOCIAL GEOGRAPHY

B. H. Farmer

Bangladesh covers 143,998 square kilometres (55,598 square miles). It straddles the Tropic of Cancer, extending between 21° 5′ and 26° 40′ North latitude, and between 88° 5′ and 92° 50′ East longitude. It is almost surrounded by India, except for a short southeastern frontier with Burma and a southern, deltaic coast fronting the Bay of Bengal.

From the granting of independence to India and Pakistan on August 15th, 1947, until the end of the Indo-Pakistan war of December 1971, what was to become Bangladesh was the eastern wing of Pakistan: that is, East Pakistan or East Bengal. At the conclusion of the war, Bangladesh became an independent country.

PHYSICAL FEATURES

Almost all of Bangladesh is a plain, largely made up of the still-growing, annually-flooded Ganges-Brahmaputra delta, together with a tongue of similar wet plain running up the Surma River between the Assam Plateau and the Lushai Hills (both in India; though Bangladesh includes a very small portion of lower foothills country, on the Assam boundary, which contains some tea plantations). As in West Bengal (India), belts of older and less fertile deposits lend some little diversity to the plains: notably in the regions known as Barind and the Madhupur Jungle Tract. To the east of the delta lie the Chittagong Hill Tracts, an area of steep, roughly parallel ranges largely covered with jungle, much of it bamboo.

For the most part, however, Bangladesh is deltaic, and its rural people have evolved a remarkable semi-aquatic life style adapted to deep flooding in the monsoon: for instance, by constructing earthen plinths four metres (15 ft.) or more high to raise their houses above flood-level (or so they hope) and by sowing varieties of rice which will grow in deep water.

CLIMATE

The climate of Bangladesh is dominated by the seasonally-reversing monsoons. There is no real cool season. In the capital, Dacca, for example, the average January temperature is 19°C. (67°F.), and the average July temperature 29°C. (84°F.). The "summer", if it can be called such, is remarkably equable: the average monthly temperature is 29°C. from May right through to September. The "winter" is dry, and crops (in the absence of irrigation or of water-holding depressions, where winter rice can be grown) have to depend on moisture remaining in the soil from the monsoon. There are pre-monsoon rains in April and May, but it is the south-west monsoon that brings heavy rain in earnest: 75 per cent of Dacca's annual average total of 188 cm. (74 in.) falls between June and September. Bangladesh has, in fact, a typical humid tropical monsoon climate. But it is a climate subject to violence from time to time, for example when a tropical cyclone sweeps in, charged with energy and with water vapour and accompanied by high winds, and devastates low-lying areas in the coastal parts of the delta. Such "extreme natural events" tend to bring high seas and flooding with salt water, so that there is damage to the soil as well as terrible loss of life and of crops.

SOILS

Much of Bangladesh has relatively good alluvial soils, many of them benefiting from renewal by flooding. There is considerable local variation: for example, areas of sandy soils on the one hand, and of swamp soils on the other (alluvium varying with the rivers that brought it), to say nothing of Barind and the Madhupur Jungle Tract. The Chittagong Hills have, as might be expected, poor skeletal soils.

POPULATION

Bangladesh had a population of 89,940,000 in March 1981, according to preliminary census figures, an average density of 625 per square kilometre. Apart from territories less than 1,200 square kilometres in area, Bangladesh is the most densely populated country in the world, despite its overwhelmingly rural and agricultural nature.

Even then, average densities are misleading: the density of population is lower than the average in such areas as Barind and the Madhupur Jungle Tract, and higher than the very high average in other areas, notably those along the lower Padma and Meghna Rivers.

Bangladesh has one rapidly-growing conurbation, that around the capital, Dacca, with a population of 1.7 million, including suburbs, in 1974.

ETHNIC GROUPS

Most of the inhabitants of Bangladesh are short, dark people with subdued Mongolian features; but there are rather different tribal groups in the Chittagong Hill Tracts. Bengali is the principal language (as it is in Indian West Bengal); some tribal peoples retain their own languages.

HISTORY

Peter Robb

The existence of Bangladesh is the result of a number of historical accidents. There has not been, from time immemorial, a Bangla nation. The concept of the nation, in its modern exclusive sense, is new to the subcontinent. Yet Bangladesh does have roots in the past: in the distinctions between the Bengali region and the rest of South Asia, and in the divisions between Bengali Muslims and Hindus, between East and West Bengal. The distinct character of Bengal has truly ancient origins; the separate identity of the Muslims is a more recent phenomenon.

During the period of British rule about two-thirds of the population of the eastern divisions (Rajshahi, Dacca and Chittagong) were Muslim. The number of Muslims in Bengal was probably due to the activities of Muslim saints in the thirteenth century, before the thorough establishment there of Brahminical Hinduism; and this helped determine the character of Islam in this region. The Mughal administration and even more that of the Nawab of Bengal after the Mughal decline in the eighteenth century, was carried on except at the highest levels largely by Hindu intermediaries. Although a Muslim élite was drawn to Bengal from North India and further afield, and though it was estimated in 1901 that as many as one-sixth of Bengali Muslims may have had foreign blood, the bulk of the Muslim population remained what it had been in the thirteenth century: poor, almost wholly rural, strongly influenced by Hindu custom. The use of *sunni* law was notable in Bengal under British rule, and knowledge of Persian and the influence of Islam had spread even to the Hindu élite; but the poor agriculturists, though notionally Muslim, were as distant from Islamic culture as from their rulers, and continued in some cases even the worship of local Hindu gods.

BRITISH RULE

The establishment of British rule quickened the decline of the Muslim ruling classes. Muslim *faujdars* (district officials) were replaced by Europeans, and, though the progressive centralization of revenue administration deprived mainly Hindu officials, it also diverted income from Muslims. Only in the judicial service did Muslims continue to thrive, until the 1830s and the abolition of the use of Persian; elsewhere, with the frank Europeanization adopted after the 1790s, Muslims found only minor administrative careers open to them. The Muslim rulers had not engaged in trade, and thus were denied the benefits which some Indians were able to find under the British; nor had they been much involved as revenue farmers or *zamindars*, and thus did not become English-style landlords with the permanent settlement of the revenue in 1793.

The bulk of the Muslim population was not immediately affected by the coming of the British. But gradually, during the early nineteenth century, their position declined. The tendency of the permanent settlement and of the initially high level of taxation was to depress the status of the peasantry until increasing numbers became landless labourers. The competition of British manufactures and the demand for raw materials transformed the economy into one subservient to that of Britain; the Muslim weavers of Dacca were particularly badly affected. Dacca's population is estimated to have dropped dramatically in the thirty years after 1801, probably by more than half. In the later nineteenth century, with the growth of Calcutta and of road and rail networks which ignored the old centres up-river, and under an administration that was overstretched and ill-informed about local conditions, East Bengal became increasingly a backwater.

There was some reaction to these changes. The Fara'idi movement led by Hajji Shariat-Allah (1781–1840) and his son, Didu Miyan, embodied both religious and economic responses: it preached the strict adherence to Quranic duties and abandonment of Hindu practices, but also opposition to Hindu landlords. Thus among possible reactions to the West, for Muslims as for Hindus, were attempts to purify and standardize religion. Though the Fara'idi movement went underground and dwindled in importance, the impulse it represented was taken up elsewhere during the nineteenth century. By the end of the nineteenth century, Muslims were under-represented in the administration and hardly represented at all in the boards and committees of local self-government. (In 1886 Muslims held less than 13 per cent of executive and just over 3 per cent of judicial posts, with over 31 per cent of the population.) There was a competitive system of appointment; thus Muslim failure was blamed on their reluctance to take up Western education: certainly in 1871/72 they made up only a little more than 14 per cent of school and college-goers in Bengal. The proportion was to increase (23 per cent in 1881/82) and, thanks largely to the formation of Dacca University, numbers were to go on rising even after the proportion began to drop again in the 1920s; but it is clear that there were fewer among Bengali Muslims ready to groom themselves as minor officials for the British than there were among Hindus, where some had traditional callings as writers and administrators.

In the early twentieth century the mass of the Muslim population had interests which could be seen as distinct from those of the Hindus; and, though the Western-educated Muslim élite had more in common with their Hindu colleagues than with their co-religionists, it was easy for them to feel at a disadvantage. The next step was for them to begin to consider the Muslim masses as their community. The British helped by treating Muslims as a separate political interest at least from the late nineteenth century; the Muslim élite could use the size of the

Muslim population as an argument for a greater share of offices and privileges.

The Muslim élite began obviously to diverge from the Hindu early in the twentieth century. The partition of Bengal (allegedly for administrative reasons) in 1905 created a controversy in which some Muslims were to be found on both sides; but the anti-partition agitation proved rather aggressively Hindu, and, even more important, the experience between 1905 and 1911 (when the partition was annulled) revealed to East Bengalis the advantages of a separate administration centred on Dacca. The concession of separate electorates for Muslims in 1909, 1919 and 1935 encouraged the development of separate political organizations, while a long series of communal riots hardened attitudes between the rank and file of the communities. The more conscious each became of the unique features of his religion, the more likely friction became; and the more local administration passed into Indian hands, the more this friction could be expressed in political terms by such measures as, for example, regulations by municipal authorities for or against cow-killing. During this century, moreover, changes in the constitution, including after 1920 limited (but, in relative terms, enormous) expansions of the elective principle, sent the Muslim elite politicians in search of a constituency; thus they began to bridge the gap between them and the depressed mass of their co-religionists, reaching at least to the higher sections of the Muslim peasantry, often in the context of an appeal to their religion.

Even so, for a long time, the political élites of both communities continued to meet at several points, and in Bengal it seemed that regional feeling was on the whole more potent than communal passions. Bengal Muslims as well as Hindus reacted to the fact that Bengal, which in the nineteenth century, for the first time, had been central to a great empire, had become once more peripheral to the development of the initially Bombay-dominated Indian National Congress and the moving of the imperial capital from Calcutta to Delhi.

The strategies of those Muslims who feared Hindu dominance shifted during the twentieth century from reliance on the British, to reliance on Islamic power outside India and then to reliance on the strength of the Muslim-majority provinces in India. But the fears were naturally most powerful in minority provinces. In the late 1930s the growth area of the Muslim League was the United Provinces. Thus in the 1937 elections in Bengal, Fazlul Huq's Krishak Proja Samiti was overwhelmingly successful and the Muslim League won only 39 of 119 Muslim seats. Fazlul Huq defied the central organization under Jinnah, and the local League as well, until he was eventually forced to resign in 1943 and a League ministry was formed under Khwaja Nazim al-din. The experience of power in the 1940s repeated for many middle-class Muslims the lesson learnt by an earlier generation after 1905, and persuaded them of the possible advantages of Pakistan. Fazlul Huq did not campaign against this in 1945–46. The conversion to Pakistan in Bengal was, therefore, sudden and late. Even then it is probably true that Bengali Muslims endorsed the separation of the whole of Bengal from India and not the "moth-eaten" Pakistan they received in 1947.

ESTABLISHMENT AND DIVISION OF PAKISTAN

The new country comprised peoples who were predominantly Muslim but otherwise radically different in race and language. Several factors exacerbated the divisions. First, East Pakistan had been a sub-region subordinate to Calcutta and one that was not flourishing: thus, after independence, it experienced an influx of mainly Punjabi officials and merchants. Second, East Pakistanis were less well versed than Punjabis or Sindhis in Urdu, which was declared a national language in March 1948. Third, because of British policies, the East was scarcely represented in the army, which was to become the most important organ of the Pakistani state. Finally, independence encouraged the growth and ambitions of younger, middle-class Bengali-speakers, who came to supplant the few land-owning families which had been socially dominant in the East before 1947.

A belief arose that West Pakistan was treating the East as a colony, exploiting its resources to the detriment of the local population. Such concessions as the West made proved to be too few and too late. The language issue led to demonstrations and riots, notably a "Martyrs' day" in February 1952, and to the routing of the Muslim League in the provincial elections of March 1954. Bengali was then admitted to equal status with Urdu, but Fazlul Huq's ministry was dismissed on a charge of separatism. Again, in October 1955, the country was divided into supposedly equal halves, but no elections were held: General Ayub Khan dismissed his popular military governor, Azam Khan, and instituted his own "Basic Democracy" system which made the local assembly into a puppet. In 1965, too, a vote was held to re-elect Ayub Khan as President, but the defeat of Fatima Jinnah in the East was held to be engineered.

The malcontents came to be led by Sheikh Mujibur Rahman and his Awami League, which stood for the limitation of the central authority to defence and foreign affairs and the retention by each wing of its own resources. Mujib was imprisoned in 1966, but released in 1969 with the fall of Ayub. Elections were held in December 1970. The Awami League was assisted in its campaign by the devastation of the East in recent floods, the West being blamed for negligence in sending relief; the League won all but two of the East's seats in both Provincial and National Assemblies. President Yahya Khan refused to accept Mujib as Prime Minister; Mujib in turn demanded the implementation of his party's radical form of autonomy. The impasse was broken by a general strike, the Awami League's seizure of power (March 10th, 1971), and its declaration of Bangladeshi independence (March 26th). The West retaliated with severe repression by the army. Refugees flooded into India, which, on December 4th, invaded in support of the *Mukhti Bahini* (freedom fighters) and other irregular

Bengali groups operating inside East Pakistan. The campaign was brief and successful, and Pakistan's forces surrendered on December 16th. Bangladesh's independence became a reality.

The new country gained prompt international recognition, but was beset by enormous difficulties. There were delicate diplomatic issues to be resolved, and a pressing need for international aid. The loss of professionals through the murder of Bengalis and the removal of Punjabis and Sindhis led to serious manning problems in commerce and the public services. A problem of order was exacerbated by the failure of armed cadres to disband completely, and by campaigns against Biharis: as Urdu-speakers, the Biharis' loyalty was held to be suspect. The change of regime made no contribution to the region's economic problems, and the participation of India raised the spectre of another colonialism to replace those of the past.

POLITICAL CHANGES IN BANGLADESH

Sheikh Mujib, released from prison in Pakistan, became the first Prime Minister, confirmed with a sweeping majority in 1973. Bangladesh was given a secular and parliamentary constitution. On February 22nd, 1974, it was finally recognized by Pakistan. Political stability was not easily maintained, however. Opposition groups of both extremes resorted to terrorism, including Muslim fundamentalists opposed to secession and secularism, and Maoist groups co-operating with Indian Naxalites. In October 1973 the Awami League formed an alliance with the Communist party and the pro-Soviet wing of the National Awami party with a joint policy of suppressing terrorism. A militia, the *Rakkhi Bahini*, was formed to assist the police. Economic problems also mounted. In July and August 1974 disastrous floods led to widespread famine. In some areas prices rose by 400 per cent, and there was talk of official corruption, even close to the still-popular Mujib. At the end of December the Government declared a state of emergency and all fundamental rights guaranteed by the constitution were suspended. Four weeks later, the Bangladesh Parliament adopted a constitution Bill which replaced the parliamentary by a presidential form of government and provided for the introduction of a one-party system. Mujib became President for a second time, assuming absolute powers, and created the Bangladesh *Krishak-Sramik* (Peasants and Workers) Awami League, excluding all other parties from government.

If nothing else, however, Bangladesh's war and independence created a local military power-base, which was bound to play a political role. It began to do so on August 15th, 1975, when a group of discontented young army majors assassinated Mujib and his family and put Mushtaq Ahmed, the former Minister of Commerce, in power. The army majors themselves went into residence in the President's palace, remaining involved to the extent of promoting their supporters in the armed services. This was to prove dangerous; but for the moment the accession of Mushtaq continued the dominance of the Awami League, of which he had long been an important leader. Soon further signs of strain appeared, and on November 2nd, 1975, the expected counter-coup took place. In a period of confusion a former Prime Minister and several other prominent figures were murdered in jail, and General Khalid Musharaf, a pro-Mujib figure, came briefly to power. Major Dalim and the other authors of the August coup were exiled. Musharaf's control was incomplete, however, and after a day's serious fighting in the Dacca cantonment he and many of his supporters were killed. Mushtaq resigned as President in favour of the Chief Justice of the Supreme Court, Abusadat Mohammad Sayem, who was sworn in as President on November 6th. Power was assumed by the three service chiefs jointly, as Deputy Martial Law Administrators; but Major-Gen. Ziaur Rahman, Chief of Army Staff, who had led the overthrow of Khalid Musharaf after being at one stage his prisoner, took precedence over his colleagues, Mosharraf Hossain Khan, Chief of Naval Staff, and M. G. Tawab, then Chief of Air Staff. Gen. Zia promised an early return to representative government. From August 1976 political parties were permitted to operate, providing their manifesto had been approved by the Government. Parishad council elections were held in February 1977, but the general election foreseen for that date was postponed indefinitely in November 1976. The major political change was the supremacy of the army and the end of Awami League rule. This change was consolidated by the arrest of Mushtaq Ahmed and other possible opponents in November 1976, and by Ziaur Rahman's assumption first of the powers of Chief Martial Law Administrator in November 1976, and then of the Presidency in April 1977, following the resignation of President Sayem.

In May 1977 a national referendum resulted in a 99 per cent vote in favour of the President and his martial rule policies. A presidential election in June 1978 confirmed this position and in July the Council of Advisers was replaced by a 28-member Council of Ministers. In September the President formed a new party, the Bangladesh Jatiyatabadi Dal (Bangladesh Nationalist Party or BNP), after a failed attempt to create a "grand coalition". In December the President's "undemocratic" powers were abolished and in January 1979 a number of political prisoners were released. In February the delayed elections to the Jatiya Sangsad (Parliament) were finally held. Major opposition parties had agreed to take part, after prolonged manoeuvring. A 40 per cent poll produced a two-thirds majority for the President's allies. In March 1979 Azizur Rahman took over as Prime Minister. A new Cabinet was formed and at the beginning of April martial law was lifted.

Foreign policy after independence was characterized by growing animosity towards India whose role in the liberation war is apparently being written out of history. Several contentious issues were raised on both sides, and there were border incidents in mid-1976. The central issue, alleged disruption of water supply in Bangladesh by India's Farakka barrage, was raised at the UN towards the end of 1976. After several unsuccessful meetings with India it was announced in April 1977 that an understanding had been reached over sharing the waters of the River Ganges, and an interim agreement was signed in December. Since then, however, in spite of hopeful talk of a permanent solution, there have been repeated failures on the Joint Rivers Commission, and in 1981 continuing boundary disagreements, including those over a new island in the Bay of Bengal. Nonetheless, co-operation has continued in other fields, from a tripartate jute agreement with India and Nepal, to a three-year agreement with India in October 1980, designed to reduce the imbalance of trade.

The four years after Mujib could thus be seen as a period of continual upheaval, but also one of consolidation, in which Gen. Zia sought legitimacy and allowed a slow liberalization. Civil unrest (including attempted coups in 1976 and 1977) continued with rumours of conspiracy against the regime in 1980, a year which was notable for repeated strikes, especially among public employees. Mutinies had to be suppressed on at least six occasions, in the army, the navy or air force; but the military position was strengthened, especially after 1979, by the expansion of the Bangladesh Rifles, a reduction in the *Rakkhi Bahini* and the exclusion of supporters of the left.

A continuing theme in Bangladesh has been corruption in government, sometimes real and serious but always indicative of the failure either to promote efficiency at all levels or to alter the fundamental realities of poverty and a concentration of wealth and influence. Zia himself was not accused of corruption but did not succeed in reforming the top-heavy administration, creating the necessary intermediate linkages or reducing the dependence on foreign aid. His personal interventions and helicopter tours, which characterized his rule, did not provide any institutional means whereby the existing "colonial" system could be ended in the rural areas.

Bangladesh politics, too, have been élite, even parochial, in character, beset with what are little more than personal or family rivalries. This may seem an advantage to the rulers in that it prevents the growth of effective opposition: only the Awami League, with its history of mass following, could be a real political threat to Zia, and it was repeatedly split into factions. In February 1980 parties tried to boycott the Jatiya Sangsad but were unable to preserve a united front; Zia was able to strain the alliance by releasing Mushtaq Ahmed, whose claims to leadership were disputed; by April opposition groups were engaging in public brawls in Dacca. However, the political weakness divided Zia's own supporters as well. His government had sought to capitalize on the growth of cultural militancy, after initially maintaining a secular stance, by adopting an Islamic amendment to the constitution in April 1977 and thus benefiting from a decline in the popularity of leftist parties. However, internal quarrels still divided Zia's own party, the BNP. In January 1980 he was obliged to reshuffle his Cabinet and to replace his deputy, to counter restlessness among his supporters, and in April 1980 a further Cabinet reshuffle, for similar reasons, brought in a team largely made up of political unknowns.

The major problem perhaps was that Zia's rule was essentially personal, as shown in his dislike of political ideology, his long reluctance to work through legislative means and the polyglot nature of the party he formed. In the end it was a reversion to the instability of personal politics, to old rivalries, which killed him: he was murdered in Chittagong on May 30th, 1981. The details are uncertain: if a coup was planned, it was poorly done, and its leader, Maj.-Gen. Mohammad Abdul Manzur (an army divisional commander only recently sent to Chittagong), was soon captured and then killed in confused circumstances. The country drew back from civil war and waited 180 days for a new President. Once again, a President had been removed by a disappointed former ally, who would fail to succeed to power.

Zia's Vice-President, Abdus Sattar, became acting Head of State pending a presidential election, which he won in November 1981. Sattar was elected because he had important backers who sought continuity at a time of potential upheaval, because he had few (if any) sworn enemies, and because the reputation of the assassinated Zia was strong enough to hold public support to his party. However, President Sattar was elderly and in poor health. Accusations of corruption and ineffectiveness soon came to be heard again, implying, among other things, a dissatisfaction with the way in which the system was working on the part of the powerful, especially in the armed forces. The Army Chief of Staff, Lt.-Gen. Hossain Mohammad Ershad, originally a supporter of Sattar and a man who denied personal ambition ("I am a soldier"), none the less sought successfully to extend the army's political involvement, against the President's wishes. In January 1982 Sattar was persuaded to set up a National Security Council, formally bringing the military chiefs into government. In February he dismissed the Cabinet and formed a smaller group with executive powers. The two moves made clear that he was losing the battle for civilian control, partly because of yet another struggle between sections of the ruling party. A coup was widely expected and took place on March 24th, 1982, forestalling a political rumpus which it had been thought would follow Sattar's appointment of a new Vice-President. General Ershad succeeded to supreme power, his takeover eased by Sattar's own announcement which blamed the deterioration of law and order. The new leader has promised to work for his own replacement by a civilian government, and, immediately after the coup, he nominated a retired judge (Abul Fazal Mohammad Ashanuddin Chowdhury) as President. The result, however, has been to confirm the formal involvement of the military in government, with Gen. Ershad as Chief Martial Law Administrator, at the expense of civillian opponents such as the former Prime Minister, Azizur Rahman, leader of the rightist faction of the BNP. The last factor explains the support which the military have supposedly received from the Awami League and leftist politicians.

ECONOMIC SURVEY

Kevin Rafferty

Bangladesh gained its independence in 1971, as almost the poorest country in the world. By 1981 the population, now swollen to more than 90 million, had not achieved even the modest levels of "prosperity" of 1969/70, the last full year in which the territory was part of Pakistan. At independence the new rulers took over a land which had been devastated by the bitter struggle for freedom and which was then hit by drought and floods and by the inexperience of the politicians. In 1975 Sheikh Mujibur Rahman, the "father of the nation", was assassinated and Major-Gen. (later Lt.-Gen.) Ziaur Rahman became the dominant figure. For a time, things seemed to improve. Aided by better weather and military discipline, respectable economic growth rates were achieved. However, by 1980 corruption had begun to eat its way into the society and to cut the very poorest Bangladeshis off from even the slightest hope of getting a square meal a day and a secure roof over their heads. In May 1981 President Zia was himself assassinated, leaving doubts about economic stability and many problems to be solved, even if an economic mastermind took over. Any ruler of Bangladesh must first fight through a number of political problems before tackling the economic difficulties.

In March 1982 a new regime came into power under Lt.-Gen. Hossain Mohammad Ershad, who became Chief Martial Law Administrator after seizing control from the crumbling civilian government of President Abdus Sattar. In June Ershad's government announced vigorous measures to restore much of industry to the private sector.

Bangladesh will remain for years to come among the poorest countries in the world. Its land area is small but its population in March 1981 was 89,940,000, making it the eighth most populous country in the world. Bangladesh has more people per square kilometre (625 in 1981) than any other country, apart from city states such as Hong Kong and Singapore. If account is taken of all river areas, population density would be 1,000 per square km. of land. That alone would be bad enough, but Bangladesh is also poor. With its degree of poverty, figures become academic because their translation in hard currency turns on unreliable or unrealistic exchange rate valuations. The World Bank gives per caput income in 1980 at only U.S. $120. Half the population has a deficiency in calorie intake, and more than 80 per cent a deficiency in vitamins. Cloth consumption allows for a single simple loin cloth per person per year. About 20 per cent of the people are literate. Bangladesh has fewer than 6,000 buses, only 12,000 private cars, 50,000 telephones, 300,000 radios and 10,000 televisions. Such statistics also illustrate that a few Bengalis do enjoy a privileged life and that the lot of the ordinary man is worse than even the humble average quoted. Yet, more than that, Bangladesh has few resources with which it can begin to build prosperity. The population is increasing at about 2.8 per cent annually, so that by the turn of the century it is expected to be about 150 million. Moreover, Bangladesh has been traditionally dependent on jute for between 80 and 90 per cent of its export earnings, and jute is in constant decline on the world markets.

ECONOMIC HISTORY BEFORE INDEPENDENCE

The area which is today Bangladesh used to be the rural hinterland of Calcutta in the days of British India. Long before that, the land had been renowned for its spices, for soil fertility, and the fine quality Dacca muslin. With the coming of the British and the creation of Calcutta as the great port and industrial centre of India, Eastern Bengal began to suffer as the most able people drifted towards the opportunities of the metropolis, and the new industries sprang up in and around it. By the time of partition in 1947, East Bengal was the richest jute-growing area in the world, but had very little industry of its own. All but a few jute-processing mills were in and around Calcutta. At partition, it was decided that Calcutta should go to India, leaving East Pakistan without a large town of its own.

The new Pakistan was split into two and separated by 1,500 km. of India. East Pakistan contained 55 per cent of the population, but the capital was in the West. West Pakistanis dominated Pakistan: they composed the majority of the senior civil servants and, more important, from 1958 (when General Ayub Khan became President) only a few of the army generals were Bengalis and then none of the senior ones. The war and struggle with India for Kashmir only concentrated more attention by the West Pakistani rulers on the needs of West Pakistan.

East Pakistan was neglected. The Government of Pakistan did encourage the building of jute mills but few other industries were established. However, for the first 20 years, Pakistan relied on jute earnings which were the most important supplier of foreign exchange for all Pakistan, on which industry, chiefly in the west, could be built up. The West received the major share of Plan development spending and, comparatively, grew more affluent. In the 1950s the West was 20 per cent richer; by 1960 it was 30 per cent; by 1970 per caput income in West Pakistan was probably 50 per cent or more higher than that of the East.

By the time of the independence war in 1971, economists from the East pointed bitterly to the disparities of resources between the two wings of Pakistan. They claimed that, allowing for the overvalue of the Pakistan rupee, actions of successive Governments based in the West had resulted in the transfer of resources from West to East Pakistan of 30,000 million rupees. This would be $3,000 million given a rate of 10 rupees to one U.S. dollar. The official rate was 4.76 rupees to the dollar, but the complaint of the Bengalis was that the true rate was 10 rupees per dollar and East Pakistan's jute exports were contributing enormously to Pakistan but the province was not getting a fair share of either internal resources or foreign assistance.

THE ECONOMY, 1971-1975

When independence came late in 1971, Bangladesh, desperately poor, was ill-suited to face the difficult economic climate of the 1970s. It had to recover from the devastation of the liberation struggle when millions of refugees had fled to India: homes had been destroyed, livestock killed and much of the (albeit poor) infrastructure destroyed. It had a lack of experience in bureaucratic and economic management and administration which had been run for so long from the West. For the first year, it received massive funds from the United Nations relief operation and from friendly countries, such as India, and generous ones, such as the United States. In subsequent years, Bangladesh was hit first by drought and then by floods which reduced harvests and meant that the country was having to import nearly 2 million tons of food per year, a sixth of its needs. Given the soaring world prices of food grains, this was a heavy drain on Bangladesh's funds and the cost of food imports alone was more than Bangladesh was earning for all its exports.

Then there were the political ramifications. Sheikh Mujibur Rahman, the new leader of the country, had little experience in administration. The new rulers dedicated the country to socialism and quickly nationalized the jute mills, textile factories and most of the other major industries. The Biharis, Urdu-speaking Muslims who migrated from Bihar and Uttar Pradesh to East Pakistan after Partition, were excluded from the economy because many of them had sided with the Pakistan forces during the liberation struggle. Yet they had industrial skills and experience and their exclusion put a greater strain on the economy.

The inexperience of labour was matched by the inexperience of management and exacerbated by the extravagant and unrealistic promises of socialism. Industry's contribution to gross domestic product was small, about 8 per cent, but one of the industries was jute manufacturing, providing a major part of foreign exchange reserves.

Then there was political manipulation. Large-scale smuggling, backed by prominent people, increased prices and caused uncertainty over food supplies. Prices of essential commodities rose by up to 300 per cent. The long-maintained refusal to devalue the taka, the Bangladesh currency fixed at independence at par with the Indian rupee, meant that jute prices were kept far too high on world markets to be competitive while the benefit was not felt in lower import prices which were kept high by scarcities and bureaucracy.

Sheikh Mujib had gathered into his planning commission the most talented economists of Bangladesh, probably a team unparallelled in the world. They produced an eminently sensible five-year plan, hoping to produce real growth of 5.5 per cent a year until 1977/78. The plan concentrated on the simple but essential things, like rural development and food production, and was surprisingly honest about Bangladesh's shortcomings; but its targets were hopelessly optimistic and the "bench-mark" output was well above the actual economic performance in 1972/73, the opening year of the plan. But even if the plan had been fulfilled in all its details, the state of Bangladesh can be seen from some of the plan's per capita targets. Rice consumption per day in 1977/78 was to be 15.61 ounces compared with 15.41 in 1969/70 and 12.91 in 1972/73; sugar consumption per year in 1977/78 was to be 4.48 lb. compared with 4.22 in 1969/70 and 3.0 in 1972/73; textiles consumption in 1977/78 was to be 8.14 yards per year compared with 7.5 in 1969/70 and 4.96 in 1972/73; tea consumption in 1977/78 was to be 0.22 lb. per year compared with 0.14 in 1969/70 and 0.16 in 1972/73; consumption of electricity in 1977/78 was to be 3.56 kWh. per year compared with 1.63 in 1969/70 and 1.64 in 1972/73; consumption of gas in 1977/78 was to be 21.37 cubic feet per year compared with 5.27 in 1969/70 and 4.93 in 1972/73.

Given all the natural calamities and the poor political performance, Bangladesh got nowhere near its aims. When Sheikh Mujib was killed in 1975, the country was still poorer than it had been in 1969/70, its last "normal" year as part of Pakistan, yet the population had increased by 10 million since then.

That is not wholly to condemn the economic performance of Sheikh Mujibur Rahman's Bangladesh. In many ways, his was an inexperienced regime feeling its way. Its failures were magnified by the political squabbling and by a distinct shift in the world economic climate against Bangladesh. In fact, towards the end of his rule, stimulated by the International Monetary Fund (IMF), a more disciplined economy began to emerge. Sheikh Mujib finally devalued the taka and curbed the growth of money supply. Credit for such successes has fallen to his successors.

THE ECONOMY FROM 1975

From 1975 to 1981 the commanding figure in Bangladesh was Ziaur Rahman (popularly known as Zia), who became President in April 1977. Zia lost the services of the brilliant economists and planners whom Sheikh Mujib had at his disposal. Instead, he relied on a team of economists and professional experts under Dr. M. N. Huda. The mark of the new economic team was soundness and efficiency rather than brilliance.

The army began to tidy up law and order, to help lay new foundation stones. Zia himself had a reputation as "Mr. Clean". He himself tried hard to chart a new path for Bangladesh. This included a more open approach to the rest of the world, involving a search for foreign aid and investment and a dedication to basic domestic order. The President repeatedly emphasized the need to double food production, to improve irrigation facilities and to reduce population growth. Throughout 1979 and 1980 he made numerous journeys by helicopter to try to get the message across to thousands of villages.

At least on the surface, the policy seemed to be paying off. More and more foreign businessmen began to visit Bangladesh and to look at potential investment projects. It helped that Bangladesh had "come of age" internationally by winning the second Asian seat on the UN Security Council in 1978 against stiff competition from Japan. The official news agencies paid more and more attention to the need to set the basic house in order. By 1980, however, some things were turning sour. There was a noticeable gap between official pronouncements and what was actually achieved. Aid agencies began to complain that corruption was on the increase and the new political ministers were corruptly enriching themselves on a large scale. Bangladeshis even commented that, in spite of Zia's personal reputation, his ministers were much more professional in the game of corruption than Sheikh Mujib's ministers had ever been. In addition, the dispute with India over the sharing of the waters of the River Ganga (Ganges) also flared up again, putting new pressures on Zia.

Economic growth throughout the Zia years was higher than during the rule of Sheikh Mujibur Rahman. In only one year, 1976/77, did it drop below the rate of population increase. Overall, G.D.P. rose by an average of 4 per cent a year in the First Five-Year Plan period and by 3.9 per cent in 1978/79 and 1979/80, though in each case the rate was much diluted by the increase in population so that the per caput rise was only just over 1 per cent. In the final year of Zia's rule growth rose sharply to more than 7 per cent, owing to better weather and the benefits of improved irrigation facilities. Nevertheless, enormous problems remained. In spite of more than $1,000 million in aid each year, Bangladesh's trade gap became wider than ever. It was difficult to stimulate exports, while the need for imports continued to grow.

Zia's main achievements, according to his supporters, were that he realized the necessity to raise food production and to curb the population. He also tried to vitalize the people to see that their salvation lay literally in their own hands. However, each of these objectives is, of necessity, a long-term project and Zia is no longer alive to urge and direct operations. In his last year in office Zia had also failed to break through the effective dominance of landed and other vested interest groups. If now there is a protracted struggle or a weak coalition of successors to Zia, it will be harder still to make the economic breakthroughs.

AGRICULTURE

Agriculture is the most important sector of the Bangladesh economy. It accounts for nearly 60 per cent of the G.D.P. and employs 80 per cent of the working population. Rice is the main food crop and production of milled rice in 1980/81 reached a record of just over 13.6 million tons. The main crop is harvested from October onwards after the monsoon and usually yields about 7 million tons (milled). Two other rice crops are grown: one dependent on irrigation and harvested in spring, which produces up to 3 million tons, and the summer crop which provides a similar amount. Ten per cent of production goes to waste or to provide seed. Traditionally, a small amount of wheat is also grown, but in the last few years a strong effort has been made to grow more and more wheat, a grain which is more nutritious than rice and cheaper to produce. Wheat can also be turned into chappaties, which are easier to carry for lunch than rice. Production of wheat rose sharply to nearly a million tons in 1979/80 and the harvest was so successful that the Government planned to increase it ambitiously. With so many people to feed, the need to import grain has been a heavy drain on foreign reserves. Annual food imports were reduced to 1.5 million tons in 1977/78 and stocks were built up, but in 1979, as the crop fell short, the country had to import almost 3 million tons of grain.

By 1982 there were hopes that Bangladesh was within sight of reaching food self-sufficiency. This hope came, perversely, as total food-grain production dropped to 14.1 million tons in 1981/82 from almost 15 million tons the year before. The argument of the agriculture ministry was that the 1981/82 total was the second highest ever and was achieved in spite of bad weather. "If we can achieve this in a bad year, then we can do much better in a normal or good year." said A. Z. M. Obaidullah Khan, the adviser on agriculture. He said that improvements were due to better irrigation facilities, especially the use of small irrigation systems such as shallow tube-wells and low-lift pumps.

Allowing for all grains, per caput food grain consumption is only 16 ounces (450 grammes) per day and, unlike in many other countries, grain is practically the only source of food. Fish consumption, for example, is only 4 lb. (1.8 kg.) per person each year. (The proviso has to be made that all production figures must be treated with scepticism. What can be said with certainty is that the ordinary Bengali gets little enough to eat.)

Yields of food grain have traditionally been low, averaging about 12.5 maunds per acre (1 maund = 82.27 lb.). The highest yields have been obtained from the spring crop, in which new seeds have been used most successfully, and yields of up to 24 maunds per acre have been realized there. Bangladesh varieties of new seed stock have done extremely well in international rice trials, but the problem has always been how to transplant the experiments successfully to the farms. Bangladesh's combined rice crops occupy 24.2 million acres, which is more than the total cultivated land of 21 million acres.

In 1980 the Zia Government devised a plan to achieve food-grain self-sufficiency by 1985. This involved revision of the programme of the Second Five-Year Plan and aimed at boosting production to 20 million tons of food grains by 1984/85. Of this total, just under 18 million tons would be rice and just over 2 million tons wheat. In addition, fish and livestock products were to increase substantially. Foreign experts thought that the aim of self-sufficiency in food grains was feasible, given the improvements in irrigation facilities which have allowed Bangladesh more freedom from the weather, the traditional destroyer of agricultural hopes.

There were still considerable doubts about whether Bangladesh would go from a feasible target to an actual one. Although the country had tried to insure against the weather, it was rather more difficult to do anything about the deteriorating world aid climate: Bangladesh is still heavily dependent on aid to achieve its targets. In addition, the local bureaucracy would have to increase its efficiency greatly to see that fertilizers, seeds, pesticides and other essential inputs arrived on time and were distributed effectively. Above all, there were questions of whether "self-sufficiency" would mean that the ordinary Bangladeshi received enough food. One aid worker commented gloomily that there was no certainty that the landless Bangladeshi would find the work and the money to buy food. National "self-sufficiency" could still mean increasing numbers of hungry people.

There is evidence lately of a drift of people from the countryside to the towns. One problem typical of the sub-continent is that farms are small and landholdings liable to be fragmented. This creates inefficiencies in production and means that economies of scale often cannot be realized. In time of hardship it means that a farmer may sell his land to stay alive, and there is evidence that this happened in 1973 and 1974, increasing the number of landless to possibly 40 per cent of the population. According to the 1977 Land Occupancy Survey, almost 50 per cent of the rural population was effectively landless (i.e. those with holdings of less than 0.5 of an acre) and the number of landless was growing two to three times as fast as the overall rural population.

JUTE

Jute is the main non-food crop and the cash crop of Bangladesh. It was traditionally sown on 2.5 million acres yielding up to 7 million bales (1 bale is 400 lb.). About half the crop is exported as raw jute and the rest processed in Bangladesh for export as jute goods. Since independence, jute has gone from one crisis to another. In the early years, production fluctuated as the Government struggled to get its rice and rice pricing policies right; jute competes for land with one of the three rice crops. Not until the late 1970s did production begin to approach the level of 6.5 million bales. When it did, it was affected by poor quality, mainly because of weather, and by the problem of a high backlog of stocks due to declining world demand and difficulties in the Bangladesh mills. Farmgate prices for jute fell to 45–50 taka per maund. By 1980/81, production was estimated to have slumped to just over 4 million bales. Even so, total availability was almost 8 million bales because of carry-over stocks.

For some years the Government has been trying to encourage use of new seeds and regular inputs of fertilizers and pesticides which can increase yields from 3 to 4.5 or 5 bales per acre. The idea is that land can then be freed for other crops while production remains the same. Bangladesh had high hopes that its jute might be able to benefit from the higher oil prices which would make synthetic substitutes for jute bags and sacks more costly. However, as the jute industry ran into difficulties, it did not look as if the planners would be able to ensure the necessary market stability to seize the opportunities that higher oil prices offered. Economists pointed out that synthetics did not have the problems of availability or regular shipments that Bangladesh jute experienced.

INDUSTRY

Industry is small in Bangladesh and contributes less than 10 per cent to G.D.P. It is dominated by jute processing, which contributes a third of the value added by all manufacturing. Cotton textiles and cigarettes come next. The performance of industry since independence has been disappointing and up to 1974/75 only cotton and sugar had surpassed the 1969/70 performance in terms of output. Industries have had problems with inefficient production, poor quality management and distorted pricing policies, with goods sometimes sold at prices below their cost of production. The capacity utilization rate has been poor. The nationalized Jute Industries Corporation, in particular, has made big losses which have been a considerable drain on the Government budget. Since President Zia took over there has been greater emphasis on private enterprise, with attempts made to stimulate both local and foreign investment. In 1979 there was renewed speculation that the jute mills might be handed back to private entrepreneurs, but the political storms it would raise stayed Zia's hand. Getting the public sector corporations into better shape was a major task in the 1980s, as the public sector accounts for 75 per cent of total industry.

After the March 1982 coup, the new leader, Lt.-Gen. Ershad, did not waste time; early in June the government announced that about one-half of the jute and textile industries taken over by the government in Sheikh Mujibur Rahman's time would be returned to the private sector.

MINING

Mining so far has not been very important in Bangladesh because the country has few proven mineral resources apart from natural gas. Reserves of gas are estimated at several million million cubic feet and the country is hoping to use them for setting up fertilizer plants and eventually for a petrochemical complex. The 500,000-ton Ashuganj fertilizer complex built with World Bank help, came belatedly "on stream" in 1981. In 1975 Bangladesh made contracts with six foreign companies for off-shore oil exploration in the Bay of Bengal. Although expectations were high, several oil companies pulled out as commercial finds proved elusive. The only other mineral resources are coal, of which large reserves of 700 million tons have been discovered, though the quality of the coal is low grade. In 1980 there were renewed hopes of oil finds on land.

TRADE AND PLANNING

Exports of jute and jute goods used to dominate Bangladesh's export to the tune of 85 per cent, but in the late 1970s there was a slight shift in emphasis and its contribution was reduced to about 66 per cent. This was partly due to problems in the jute industry, but partly also because other commodities improved. Tea production increased and other exports, such as leather goods, newsprint, fish and naphtha, began to figure in the export account. By international standards, however, the sums were small, e.g. 1,200 million taka ($80 million) for leather and leather goods.

Jute goods have also suffered since independence because of both internal and external factors. Internally, the labour unions whose leaders were close to the Awami League caused endless problems; moreover management was inexperienced and unequal to the difficulties after nationalization. Externally, the world recession led to a sharp drop in demand for prime products such as carpet backing. And, all the time, jute is under serious threat from synthetic substitutes.

By the late 1970s Bangladesh jute had a slight edge in price over the synthetics affected by successive oil price rises. But, according to all international studies, prospects for jute are gloomy except in the poorer and developing countries where the market is smaller and growth likely to be slower. If jute is to survive it needs a more vigorous marketing policy and more reliable production and delivery in which costs will be kept down to make jute goods competitive in price with rival products.

Other plans for improving exports include the setting up of an export zone south of the main port of Chittagong. The country would hope to use its plentiful source of cheap labour and some local products for processing, and industries such as leather goods and electronic products could be established. It was not until mid-1980 that the Bangladesh Parliament passed the necessary bill for not one, but three export processing zones. The first zone, at Chittagong, was in place in 1982 but was not fully operational.

When Ziaur Rahman was assassinated, Bangladesh stood on the verge of its most serious trade and payment crisis. The trade gap continued to widen as Bangladesh found it difficult to promote exports or to reduce imports. The best year for exports was 1979/80, when they rose to $727 million, compared with $490 million in 1978/79. Imports also rose to $1,645 million, almost a doubling on the previous year. Subsequently, exports actually fell and were estimated to be $640 million in 1981/82. The rise in imports was limited—to around $2,400 million—principally because Bangladesh had virtually no foreign exchange to pay for other than essential imports. However, World Bank economists foresaw a possible rise in imports to $2,670 million in 1982/83 (which would mean a trade gap of almost $2,000 million) if petroleum prices went up again.

In the wider area of the balance of payments, Bangladesh was receiving a welcome boost from remittances sent home by Bangladeshis working abroad. These sums rose to an unexpectedly high $400 million in 1981. Even so, the current account deficit was expected to stay close to $1,800 million in 1982/81 and possibly ro rise to $2,000 million in the following year. Bangladesh was counting on large injections of foreign aid, just to keep the economy ticking over. However, it was by no means certain that it would get the aid it wanted, or even whether it would receive the commodity aid essential to ensure food self-sufficiency. The ramifications of failure cast gloom over the whole economy: failure to get commodity aid would also mean inability to generate the counterpart taka funds and thus undermine the Government's budget planning. The country had almost exhausted opportunities for remedying the situation. By 1981 foreign exchange reserves had fallen to about $100 million, or sufficient for about two weeks' imports. Normally a cushion of three or four months' import requirement is considered advisable. Dacca finance officials confessed that, were it not for special sums on deposit with Bangladesh from friendly Middle Eastern countries, their reserves would be negative.

A three-year loan of 800 million Special Drawing Rights (SDRs), equal to more than $900 million, was negotiated with the International Monetary Fund under the "extended Fund facility" in late 1980, but was suspended in August 1981 when Bangladesh failed to keep agreed credit ceilings. The IMF said that the agreement could not be resumed as the targets could not be kept. Bangladesh officials pointed out that, since the suspension, the country had put its house in order and credit creation was under control. Unfortunately, the other targets could not be met because world conditions and the terms of trade had moved against Bangladesh.

With the help of 60 million SDRs from the IMF's "compensatory Fund facility", Bangladesh was able to survive 1981/82 and wait for fresh negotiations with the Fund. It had to borrow commercially about $180 million in small "packets" of about $25 million at a time on a 180-day basis in order to pay for oil imports. The one bright spot was that Bangladesh, almost alone, escaped a cut-back in funds from the World Bank's "soft" loan agency, the International Development Association. However, the Bank said that expansion of its loans would be slower than originally planned.

Even if it can find a way out of the present crisis, Bangladesh faces a long haul before it can even hope to bring either trade or payments into balance. There is no quick way of raising exports while there is a long queue of demands for imports. Prices rise of oil and food grains helped to push up the import bill to its high levels. Some aid donors suggested that Bangladesh should encourage exports of handicrafts and fish products, but such items are likely to raise only negligible sums. The Export Processing Zone might offer hopes of attracting new investment, new jobs, and new exports, but the politicallv sensitive

Bangladeshis may not be prepared to allow foreigners sufficient freedom to attract them to Bangladesh. To foreigners, the very name of Bangladesh suggests exhausting time, money and patience working through bureaucratic procedures and political objections. Finally, even assuming that the Zone went into full production there are large questions about whether some industrial countries would be prepared to allow Bangladesh concessions in their markets. Even exports of jute goods faced quotas in Europe because of European countries' wishes to protect a few thousand jobs. On a more practical level, there is little industrial tradition in Bangladesh, levels of education and skills are low, and the very topography of the country makes communications difficult.

GOVERNMENT FINANCIAL AND ECONOMIC POLICY

In 1975 and 1976 the Bangladesh Government tightened its economic policy. The measures started in April 1975, under Sheikh Mujibur Rahman, when the money supply was reduced by 22 per cent. In May 1975 the Government devalued the taka, changing the exchange rate against the pound sterling from 18.97 to 30.00, allowing more flexibility for rewarding jute farmers while keeping the international price competitive (in 1976 the currency was revalued against the falling pound, to 28.10 on April 30th and to 26.70 on June 7th). Along with these measures, the Government undertook to abstain from deficit financing, to fix a ceiling on credit and to improve its tax efforts. The price of rationed rice was increased by 50 per cent and that of wheat by 40 per cent.

As a result of all these policies, an annual increase in the money supply of 30 per cent and an inflation rate of 50 per cent were checked: in 1975/76 retail prices fell by about 10 per cent. A reform programme was started, thanks largely to the good harvest. Hoarding and smuggling were cut.

By the late 1970s and early 1980 many problems began to occur again. The fall in food grain crops imposed strains. The annual rate of inflation soared well into double figures. Potentially more serious were the contradictions in the administration, the gaps between what Zia was aiming at and what was happening and the tensions between politicians, military and bureaucrats, with much mutual antagonism between the major power groups as each strove both for power and the profits associated with power. All this threatened to wreck the Second Five-Year Plan before it was started.

The plan was unveiled in the middle of 1980 and involves a total proposed development outlay of $16,500 million. Of this, 9,000 million is expected to be provided from foreign sources. The plan aims at an average annual growth rate of 7.2 per cent, much higher than the 4.3 per cent actually achieved over the previous seven years. The private sector has been given 22 per cent, compared with 11 per cent in the first plan. Targets are ambitious and include a 7 per cent annual increase in food grain production, 8.6 per cent in manufacturing, an increase in the area sown with high-yielding varieties from 3 million to 8 million acres and a doubling of the acreage given to improved varieties, more than tripling of irrigated land to 10.2 million acres of the 22.5 million acres of cultivated land.

Critics of the plan are not lacking. Dr. Rahman Sobhan, a member of the Planning Commission under Sheikh Mujib, called the plan "a series of papers just glued together". He pointed to internal inconsistencies. Most notably, President Zia had called for the doubling of food production during the plan, whereas ministry experts believe that the best that can happen is self-sufficiency in food production; the plan accepts both targets in its anxiety to conceal any disagreement.

The new regime of Lt.-Gen. Ershad intended to tighten controls, eradicate corruption and yet bring all of Bangladesh's resources into the economy. Several ministers of the former Zia and Sattar governments were arrested, tried and sentenced by special courts to prison terms involving hard labour. At the same time, the new rulers urged businessmen to come forward with their "black" (illegal) money and put it into productive projects. No questions would be asked, the regime promised. However, businessmen were uncertain and found that promise difficult to reconcile with the imprisonment of ministers and the arrest of prominent businessmen.

As part of his economic team, Ershad brought in officials or retired officials as advisers with the status of ministers. Among them was A. M. A. Muhith, who became, in effect, Minister of Finance, having retired from the Civil Service at the end of 1981 and given up lucrative consultancies to serve his country again.

DEVELOPMENT

In per caput terms, Bangladesh has not yet returned to the levels of "prosperity" of Pakistan days. Tackling the development problem is a longer way off. It is difficult to describe Bangladesh's real poverty to people used to Western comforts. Dacca, the capital, is a city which has few of the graces of a capital. Its population expanded from about 100,000 in 1947 to about 2 million in 1976. Unemployment is a problem and the pressure on the land in the villages has led to a constant influx of people from the countryside.

If progress is to be made, the Government has to tackle the immense poverty, underemployment and unemployment of the rural areas. Food is always a problem, nutrition is even more so. Proper irrigation is a key, ensuring better crop yields and therefore economic development; although Bangladesh has so much water, only 2 million acres have ensured irrigation supplies. Work is not always available to the young. Although more than 50 per cent of children enrol for school, regular schooling is foreign to perhaps the majority of children. Health care is rudimentary.

One international expert wrote graphically: "Per capita income is only a proxy for many different kinds of deprivation. More than half of all families are below the acceptable calorific intake, while more than two-thirds are deficient in proteins and vitamins. Houses are single rooms ... and have no water or

electricity. Less than 20 per cent of the population are literate. Estimates of unemployment and under-employment range from one-quarter to one-third of the labour force. About one in every four live-born children dies before their fifth birthday. The expectation of life of 48 years contrasts with 70 years in developed countries. In addition to all these indicators, the special disabilities faced by women in Bangladesh substantially reduce the quality of life."

Ziaur Rahman did at least realize that the uplift of the people of Bangladesh had to come from the village roots upwards. His many journeys, even to the remotest parts of the country, spoke of his commitment to the ordinary people. His campaign of canal digging was intended to show that improvements could be made to the infrastructure and to ordinary lives without massive doses of foreign aid. However, in the end, Zia's radical words fell down on his failure to do anything to change the power structure, and indeed he came to depend on the old groups. Looking at village power groupings, political analysts found that the people who dominated were often the very people who had been the leading lights of Ayub Khan's "basic democracies". Village politics are frequently vicious and leaders often come to the fore literally over the dead bodies of numbers of their opponents. Once in power, they can make alliances with the local bureaucracy and the forces of law and order to carve out for themselves what little Bangladesh has to offer, depriving the really poor of even below-average starvation levels. Given that half of the people effectively have no land, and thus not even the slenderest hold on vital resources, the future of Bangladesh is bleak unless someone can hold the polity and the economy together and begin to think of new solutions to the country's massive difficulties.

STATISTICAL SURVEY

AREA AND POPULATION

Area	Population (census results)†		
	Feb. 1st, 1961	March 1st, 1974	March 6th, 1981
143,998 sq. km.*	50,853,721	71,479,071	87,052,024

* 55,598 sq. miles.

† Excluding adjustment for underenumeration. According to the Pakistan Planning Commission, the 1961 census result understated the total population (in both wings of pre-1971 Pakistan) by about 8.3 per cent. The estimated underenumeration was 6.88 per cent in 1974 and 3.32 per cent in 1981. The adjusted total for 1981 is 89,940,000.

DIVISIONS

	1974 Census	1981 Census
Chittagong	18,636,177	22,565,000
Dacca	21,316,067	26,249,000
Khulna	14,195,274	17,150,000
Rajshahi	17,331,553	21,087,000
Total	71,479,071	87,052,000

CHIEF TOWNS

	1961 Census	1974 Census
Dacca (capital)	556,712	1,679,572
Chittagong	364,205	889,760
Khulna	127,970	437,304
Narayanganj	162,054	270,680

Births and Deaths: Average annual birth rate 47.4 per 1,000 in 1970–75 (UN estimate), 44 per 1,000 in 1978; death rate 20.5 per 1,000 in 1970–75 (UN estimate), 19 per 1,000 in 1978.

ECONOMICALLY ACTIVE POPULATION
(1974 census, provisional results)

	Males	Females	Total
Agriculture, hunting, forestry and fishing	15,212,622	610,256	15,822,878
Mining and quarrying	1,900	22	1,922
Manufacturing	909,829	36,297	946,126
Electricity, gas and water	7,401	142	7,543
Construction	32,417	469	32,886
Trade, restaurants and hotels	762,168	8,739	770,907
Transport, storage and communications	318,448	1,567	320,015
Financing, insurance, real estate and business services	55,000	567	55,567
Community, social and personal services	1,877,663	182,355	2,060,018
Activities not adequately described	1,895	129	2,024
Total Employed	19,179,343	840,543	20,019,886
Unemployed	471,254	31,452	502,706
Total Labour Force	19,650,597	871,995	20,522,592

Source: ILO, *Year Book of Labour Statistics.*

AGRICULTURE

LAND USE, 1979/80
(million acres)

Total area	35·3
Forests	5·4
Not available for cultivation	6.7
Other uncultivated land	0.6
Total non-agricultural area	12.7
Fallow land	1.7
Net sown area	20.9
Total cultivated area	22.6
Sown more than once	9.5
Total cropped area	32.0

PRINCIPAL CROPS
(Twelve months ending June 30th)

	Area (million acres)		Production (million long tons)	
	1979/80	1980/81	1979/80	1980/81
Rice (milled)	25.11	25.47	12.54	13.66
Wheat	1.07	1.46	0.81	1.07
Sugar cane	0.36	0.37	6.34	0.65
Potatoes	0.24	0.25	1.03	0.98
Sweet potatoes	0.18	0.17	0.78	0.69
Pulses	0.82	0.81	0.21	0.21
Oilseeds	0.77	0.69	0.25	0.17
Jute	1.87	1.57	1.06	0.88

Tobacco (production in '000 metric tons): 44 in 1979; 40 in 1980; 47 in 1981.

LIVESTOCK

('000 head)

	1979	1980	1981
Cattle	21,024	21,288	21,590
Buffaloes	492	504	512
Sheep	512	514	516
Goats	8,842	9,051	9,266
Chickens	45,153	47,119	49,170
Ducks	14,692	16,173	17,803

LIVESTOCK PRODUCTS

		1978	1979	1980	1981
Beef and veal	metric tons	116,312	117,693	119,224	120,903
Buffalo meat	,, ,,	1,792	1,866	1,866	1,941
Mutton and lamb	,, ,,	896	896	896	896
Goats' meat	,, ,,	30,235	30,944	31,619	32,437
Poultry meat	,, ,,	41,209	43,524	46,062	48,750
Edible offals	,, ,,	44,000	48,000*	47,000	47,000
Cows' and buffalo milk	,, ,,	672,639	681,150	690,108	705,039
Sheep's milk*	,, ,,	15,000	15,000	15,000	16,000
Goats' milk*	,, ,,	462,000	495,000	501,000	507,000
Butter*	,, ,,	16,463	16,973	17,255	n.a.
Cheese	,, ,,	858	859	859	933
Hen eggs	'000	623,008	650,196	678,528	708,048
Other poultry eggs	,,	500,550	550,950	606,450	667,650
Wool: greasy*	metric tons	1,200	1,270	1,270	n.a.
clean*	,, ,,	720	760	760	n.a.
Cattle and buffalo hides	'000	2,637	2,670	2,703	2,743
Sheep skins	,,	159	159	159	160
Goat skins	,,	4,836	4,951	5,069	5,185

* FAO estimates.

FORESTRY

ROUNDWOOD REMOVALS

('000 cubic metres, all non-coniferous)

	1974	1975	1976	1977	1978	1979	1980*
Sawlogs, veneer logs and logs for sleepers	778	614	760	730	436	555	555
Pulpwood	74	63	63*	63*	63*	63*	63
Other industrial wood	230*	236*	242*	248*	256*	263*	271
Fuel wood	8,149*	8,421*	8,653*	8,907*	9,180*	9,464*	9,754
TOTAL	9,231	9,334	9,718	9,948	9,935	10,345	10,643

* FAO estimate.

Source: FAO, *Yearbook of Forest Products*.

SAWNWOOD PRODUCTION

('000 cubic metres, all non-coniferous)

	1972	1973	1974	1975	1976	1977	1978
TOTAL (incl. boxboards)	116	210	280	236	142	159	170*

* FAO estimate.

1979-80: Annual production as in 1978 (FAO estimates).

Source: FAO, *Yearbook o j Forest Products.*

FISHING

('000 long tons, year ending June 30th)

	1975/76	1976/77	1977/78	1978/79	1979/80	1980/81
Inland	536	532	525	519	516	517
Marine	94	98	108	116	120	123
TOTAL CATCH	630	630	633	635	636	640

Source: Directorate of Fisheries.

INDUSTRY

SELECTED PRODUCTS

(Public sector only, July 1st to June 30th)

		1976/77	1977/78	1978/79	1979/80	1980/81
Jute textiles	'000 tons	490	546	500	523	581
Hessian	,, ,,	166	177	175	190	202
Sacking	,, ,,	227	265	232	247	305
Carpet backing	,, ,,	70	76	75	77	70
Others	,, ,,	26	28	18	8	4
Cotton cloth	million yards	67	83	85	89	86
Cotton yarn	million lb.	83	90	97	95	102
Newsprint	'000 tons	15	28	34	38	30
Other paper	,, ,,	26	32	31	31	33
Cement	,, ,,	303	334	317	331	340
Steel ingots	,, ,,	106	115	124	135	137
Re-rolled steel products	,, ,,	97	146	207	178	194
Petroleum products	,, ,,	1,058	1,001	1,016	1,162	1,189
Urea fertilizer	,, ,,	282	209	290	355	336
Ammonium sulphate	,, ,,	9.2	9.3	5	9	9
Chemicals	,, ,,	13	15	23	15	16
Refined sugar	,, ,,	139	175	131	93	143
Wine and spirits	'000 liquid proof galls.	896	1,129	1,173	1,225	1,033
Tea*	million lb.	75	77	75	82	90
Edible oil and vegetable ghee	'000 tons	25	27	23	31	25
Cigarettes	'000 million	12	12	14	14	15

* Including production in the private sector.

FINANCE

100 paisa=1 taka.
Coins: 1, 2, 5, 10, 25 and 50 paisa.
Notes: 1, 5, 10, 50, 100 and 500 taka.
Exchange rates (June 1982): £1 sterling=38.25 taka; U.S. $1=22.145 taka.
1,000 taka=£26.14=$45.16.

Note: The taka was introduced in January 1972, replacing the Pakistan rupee. At the same time the currency was devalued by 34.6 per cent, so that the taka would be at par with the Indian rupee. Until May 1975 the link with India was retained and Bangladesh maintained an official exchange rate against sterling at a mid-point of £1=18.9677 taka. Before the "floating" of the pound in June 1972 this was equivalent to a rate of U.S. $1=7.279 taka. In May 1975 the currency was devalued by 36.8 per cent against sterling, the new exchange rate being £1=30.00 taka. This remained in effect until April 1976, when a new rate of £1=28.10 taka was introduced. This was adjusted to £1=26.70 taka in June 1976 and to £1=25.45 taka in November 1976. In January 1977 the rate reverted to £1=26.70 taka but since November 1977 it has been adjusted frequently. The average market rate of the taka per U.S. dollar was 7.595 in 1972; 7.742 in 1973; 8.113 in 1974; 12.019 in 1975; 15.347 in 1976; 15.375 in 1977; 15.016 in 1978; 15.552 in 1979; 15.454 in 1980; 17.987 in 1981.

BUDGET

(estimates, million taka, July 1st to June 30th)

Revenue	1978/79	1979/80	1980/81	1981/82
Customs duties	4,931	6,548	7,927	9,500
Excise duties	2,417	2,936	3,798	4,630
Sales tax	1,898	2,606	3,015	4,050
Stamps	220	290	375	645
Motor vehicle taxes	28	30	38	39
Entertainment taxes	83	95	105	n.a.
Income taxes	1,417	1,756	2,368	2,599
Land revenue	280	257	288	312
Other taxes and duties	9	10	16	112
Interest receipts	708	1,097	1,396	1,945
Railways	768	846	1,043	1,165
Other revenue	1,300	1,650	2,382	3,623
Total	14,059	18,121	22,951	28,620

Expenditure	1978/79	1979/80	1980/81	1981/82
General administration	2,016	1,917	2,111	2,665
Justice and police	1,150	1,222	1,568	2,017
Defence	1,756	2,200	2,524	3,065
Scientific departments	64	72	81	93
Education	1,389	1,651	1,957	2,209
Health	469	628	798	909
Social welfare	102	120	130	144
Agriculture	143	191	291	323
Manufacturing and construction	260	293	317	371
Transport and communication	299	359	406	542
Debt service	858	986	1,172	1,321
Food subsidy	729	886	1,145	978
Railways	795	864	1,030	1,337
Contingency	500	550	550	650
Total	10,530	11,939	14,080	16,624

Revised totals for 1980/81 (in million taka) are: Revenue 23,430; Expenditure 14,816.

Source: **Ministry of Finance.**

PUBLIC SECTOR DEVELOPMENT EXPENDITURES

(estimates, million taka)

	1979/80	1980/81*	1981/82
Agriculture	2,623	3,580	4,181
Rural development	858	924	950
Water and flood control	2,123	3,940	4,508
Industry	3,420	3,890	3,965
Power, scientific research and natural resources	3,033	4,898	4,705
Transport	3,467	3,697	4,212
Communication	845	815	1,013
Physical planning and housing	1,376	1,460	1,975
Education and training	614	1,189	1,347
Health	672	750	841
Population planning	670	830	944
Social welfare	184	316	354
Manpower and employment	113	185	201
Cyclone reconstruction	—	—	—
Miscellaneous	702	526	963
Total Development Expenditure	20,700	27,000	30,150

* Revised total 23,690 million taka.

Source: Ministry of Finance.

FOREIGN AID

(U.S. $ million, July 1st to June 30th)

Donor	1979/80	1980/81	1981/82*
Canada	60	70	69
India	1	3	2
Japan	224	161	184
Netherlands/Belgium	29	56	70
Sweden	23	27	23
U.S.S.R.	9	4	6
United Kingdom	65	52	70
U.S.A.	184	133	166
Total	595	506	590

* Estimate.

Source: Ministry of Finance.

COST OF LIVING

(Middle class families in Dacca, 1969/70=100)

	1976/77	1977/78	1978/79	1979/80	1980/81
Food	367	431	466	550	604
Fuel and lighting	391	401	437	500	658
Housing and household requisites	476	564	656	775	880
Clothing and footwear	387	466	514	560	654
Miscellaneous	365	395	440	486	531
All items	382	441	486	561	628

NATIONAL ACCOUNTS

(million taka at current prices, year ending June 30th)

Expenditure on the Gross Domestic Product

	1976/77	1977/78	1978/79	1979/80	1980/81*
Government final consumption expenditure	5,726	6,827	9,715	11,509	14,577
Private final consumption expenditure	97,148	121,160	130,252	156,043	169,666
Increase in stocks } Gross fixed capital formation	9,810	13,341	16,901	21,534	30,861
Total Domestic Expenditure	112,684	141,328	156,868	189,086	215,104
Exports of goods and services	6,670	7,178	9,632	10,415	11,748
Less Imports of goods and services	13,993	18,216	21,726	27,254	28,348
G.D.P. in Purchasers' Values	105,361	130,290	144,774	172,247	198,504

* Provisional.

Gross Domestic Product by Economic Activity

	1975/76	1976/77	1977/78	1978/79	1979/80	1980/81*
Agriculture and hunting	49,446	44,666	61,268	67,105	81,238	95,000
Forestry and logging	2,094	2,112	4,064	4,754	4,860	5,407
Fishing	5,799	6,893	6,916	6,886	6,998	7,111
Mining and quarrying	2	2	2	2	2	2
Manufacturing	8,173	8,660	9,403	10,315	12,511	15,050
Electricity, gas and water	189	231	245	260	369	470
Construction	5,514	5,807	6,155	7,232	9,289	11,930
Wholesale and retail trade	10,747	10,384	12,832	15,634	19,048	21,575
Transport, storage and communications	6,633	7,334	8,819	9,547	11,521	11,902
Owner-occupied dwellings	8,945	8,024	8,249	9,338	11,464	12,953
Finance, insurance, real estate and business services	974	1,002	1,034	1,454	1,833	2,192
Public administration and defence	2,820	3,350	3,457	3,567	4,231	5,019
Other services	6,122	6,896	7,846	8,680	8,883	9,893
Total	107,458	105,361	130,290	144,774	172,247	198,504

* Provisional.

BALANCE OF PAYMENTS

(U.S. $ million)

	1975	1976	1977	1978	1979	1980
Merchandise exports f.o.b.	322.9	400.5	476.3	549.1	655.5	793.4
Merchandise imports f.o.b.	−1,170.2	−819.9	−1,019.1	−1,339.7	−1,738.0	−2,322.6
Trade Balance	−847.3	−419.4	−542.8	−790.6	−1,082.5	−1,529.2
Exports of services	74.4	84.7	90.7	135.6	197.0	286.8
Imports of services	−221.3	−172.5	−243.4	−314.4	−457.2	−550.0
Balance on Goods and Services	−994.2	−507.2	−695.5	−969.4	−1,342.7	−1,792.4
Private unrequited transfers (net)	31.2	33.3	95.3	126.1	161.7	301.0
Government unrequited transfers (net)	356.9	195.0	316.9	456.3	741.1	727.3
Balance on Current Account	−606.1	−278.9	−283.3	−387.0	−439.9	−764.1
Long-term capital (net)	610.7	324.6	290.1	400.0	498.8	439.4
Short-term capital (net)	1.9	−8.7	−30.4	6.7	−66.5	16.7
Net errors and omissions	−38.6	14.2	−14.5	21.8	36.2	−10.6
Total (net monetary movements)	−32.1	51.2	−38.1	41.5	28.6	−318.6
Allocation of IMF Special Drawing Rights	—	—	—	—	20.4	20.9
Valuation changes (net)	18.8	−2.5	−5.6	5.8	15.0	11.2
IMF Subsidy Account grants	—	0.7	2.3	2.4	2.5	2.2
IMF Trust Fund loans	—	—	15.7	47.8	49.3	41.5
Official financing (net)	−20.6	20.1	4.8	—	21.5	114.8
Changes in Reserves	−33.9	69.5	−20.9	97.5	137.3	−128.0

Source: IMF, *International Financial Statistics.*

EXTERNAL TRADE

(million taka, July 1st to June 30th)

	1976/77	1977/78	1978/79	1979/80*	1980/81*
Imports	13,992.9	18,216.3	21,726.6	27,254.4	31,265.9
Exports	6,670.1	7,178.2	9,631.8	10,415.0	11,207.7

* Provisional.

PRINCIPAL COMMODITIES

(million taka, July 1st to June 30th)

IMPORTS	1979/80*	1980/81*
Food and live animals	6,206.3	4,666.6
Wheat	3,209.1	3,188.6
Rice	1,902.8	232.5
Beverages and tobacco	51.9	87.2
Crude materials (inedible) except fuels	1,977.8	2,426.9
Mineral fuels, lubricants, etc.	2,575.5	3,126.2
Animal and vegetable oils and fats	1,486.1	1,835.1
Chemicals, drugs and medicines	3,364.7	3,665.0
Basic manufactures	4,939.4	7,259.8
Machinery and transport equipment	5,855.6	7,136.2
Miscellaneous manufactured articles	442.3	546.2
Other commodities and transactions	269.9	374.4
TOTAL	27,254.4	31,265.9

EXPORTS	1979/80*	1980/81*
Raw jute and jute cuttings	2,134.7	1,892.0
Jute goods	5,738.6	6,771.8
Tea	571.8	729.9
Hides, skins and leather goods	927.9	862.2
Fish and fish preparations	558.8	510.9
Newsprint and other paper	108.5	58.2
Spices	5.1	2.6
All other items	354.2	380.1
TOTAL	10,415.0	11,207.7

* Provisional.

TRANSPORT

RAILWAYS

(July 1st to June 30th)

	1976/77	1977/78	1978/79	1979/80	1980/81
Passenger-miles (million)	2,879.3	3,110.4	3,003.3	3,180.7	3,229.6
Freight-miles (million)	435.7	480.7	512.8	522.7	481.1

Source: Bangladesh Railway.

ROAD TRAFFIC

(motor vehicles in use)

	1974	1975	1976	1977	1978	1979
Private motor cars	11,160	11,882	12,409	14,869	16,692	17,344
Taxis	904	815	837	836	881	904
Buses and coaches	6,207	5,223	5,264	5,494	5,773	5,794
Trucks	9,380	9,457	9,369	9,757	10,871	11,155
Jeeps	4,100	4,112	4,370	5,828	6,354	6,556
Station wagons	1,360	1,583	1,686	2,015	2,385	2,671
Auto-rickshaws	8,424	7,398	7,486	7,953	8,762	8,723
Motor-cycles	17,026	20,194	22,605	26,739	31,705	33,046
Others	1,358	1,403	1,753	3,263	3,561	2,995
TOTAL	59,919	62,067	65,979	76,754	86,984	89,188

Source: Ministry of Communications, Government of Bangladesh.

INTERNATIONAL SEA-BORNE SHIPPING
(freight traffic in '000 long tons, July 1st to June 30th)

	GOODS LOADED				GOODS UNLOADED			
	1976/77	1977/78	1978/79	1979/80	1976/77	1977/78	1978/79	1979/80
Chalna . . .	681	654	677	643	407	1,122	1,026	1,593
Chittagong . . .	511	455	345	329	2,936	4,689	4,190	5,905
TOTAL . .	1,192	1,109	1,022	972	3,343	5,811	5,216	7,498

EDUCATION
(1977/78)

	NUMBER	STUDENTS
Primary schools . .	39,914	8,531,000
Secondary schools . .	8,327	1,943,000
Technical colleges and institutes (government)* .	588	393,000
Universities . . .	6	32,000

* In addition to government-owned and managed nstitutes, there are many privately-run vocational training centres.

Source: Ministry of Education.

Source (unless otherwise stated): Bangladesh Bureau of Statistics.

THE CONSTITUTION

(Promulgated November 1972; amended 1973, 1974, 1975, 1977, 1979, 1981.)

SUMMARY

Fundamental Principles of State Policy

The 1977 amendment to the Constitution, which was initially based on the fundamental principles of nationalism, socialism, democracy and secularism, replaced secularism with Islam. The amendment states that the country shall be guided by "the principles of absolute trust and faith in the Almighty Allah, nationalism, democracy and socialism". The Constitution aims to establish a society free from exploitation in which the rule of law, fundamental human rights and freedoms, justice and equality are to be secured for all citizens. A socialist economic system is to be established to ensure the attainment of a just and egalitarian society through state and co-operative ownership as well as private ownership within limits prescribed by law. A universal, free and compulsory system of education shall be established. In foreign policy the State shall endeavour to consolidate, preserve, and strengthen fraternal relations among Muslim countries based on Islamic solidarity.

Fundamental Rights

All citizens are equal before the law and have a right to its protection. Arbitrary arrest or detention, discrimination based on race, age, sex, birth, caste or religion, and forced labour are prohibited. Subject to law, public order and morality, every citizen has freedom of movement, of assembly and of association. Freedom of conscience, of speech, of the press and of religious worship are guaranteed.

GOVERNMENT

The President

The President is the constitutional Head of State and is elected for a term of five years. He is eligible for re-election. The supreme control of the armed forces is vested in the President. He appoints the Vice-President, the Prime Minister and other Ministers as well as the Chief Justice and other judges. The President is elected by universal adult suffrage.

The Executive

Executive authority shall rest in the President and shall be exercised by him either directly or through officers subordinate to him in accordance with the Constitution.

There shall be a Council of Ministers to aid and advise the President. All ministers shall hold office during the pleasure of the President.

The Legislature

Parliament (*Jatiya Sangsad*) is a unicameral legislature. It comprises 300 members and an additional 30 women members elected by the other members. Members of

Parliament, other than the 30 women members, are directly elected on the basis of universal adult franchise from single territorial constituencies. Persons aged 18 and over are entitled to vote. The parliamentary term lasts for five years unless Parliament is dissolved sooner by the President. War can be declared only with the assent of Parliament. In the case of actual or imminent invasion, the President may take whatever action he may consider appropriate.

THE JUDICIARY

The Judiciary comprises a Supreme Court with High Court and an Appelate Division. The Supreme Court consists of a Chief Justice and such other judges as may be appointed by the President. The High Court division has such original appelate and other jurisdiction and powers as are conferred on it by the Constitution and by other law. The Appelate Division has jurisdiction to determine appeals from decisions of the High Court division. Subordinate courts, in addition to the Supreme Court, have been established by law. The new military regime has retained the structure of the Supreme Court, but the High Court division has been split into five, one being located in each of the administrative divisions of the country.

ELECTIONS

An Election Commission supervises elections for the Presidency and for Parliament, delimits constituencies and prepares electoral rolls. It consists of a Chief Election Commissioner and other Commissioners as may be appointed by the President. The Election Commission is independent in the exercise of its functions. Subject to the Constitution, Parliament may make provision as to elections where necessary.

THE GOVERNMENT

HEAD OF STATE

President, in charge of President's Secretariat, Cabinet Division and Ministries of Defence and Planning: Justice ABUL FAZAL MOHAMMAD ASHANUDDIN CHOWDHURY (took office March 27th, 1982).

Chief Martial Law Administrator: Lt.-Gen. HOSSAIN MOHAMMAD ERSHAD.

COUNCIL OF ADVISERS

(June 1982)

Ministry of Industry: S. M. SHAFIUL AZAM.

Minister of Energy: Air Vice-Marshal SULTAN MAHMUD.

Ministry of Finance and Planning: A. M. A. MUHITH.

Ministry of Food and Relief: Air Vice-Marshal (Retd.) ABDUL GAFUR MAHMOOD.

Ministry of Local Government, Rural Development and Cooperatives: MAHBUBUR RAHMAN.

Ministry of Agriculture, Forest and Flood Control: A. Z. M. OBAIDULLAH KHAN.

Ministry of Education and Religious Affairs: A. MAJEED KHAN.

Ministry of Social Welfare and Women's Affairs: Dr. SHAFIA KHATUN.

Ministry of Transport and Communications: Rear-Admiral MAHBUB ALI KHAN.

Ministry of Information and Broadcasting: A. R. SHAMS-UD DOHA.

Ministry of Health and Population Control: Maj.-Gen. M SHAMSUL HAQ.

Ministry of Law, Land Administration and Reforms: K. A. BAKR.

Ministry of Public Works and Urban Development: Maj.-Gen. ABDUL MANNAN SIDDIQUI.

Ministry of Labour and Manpower: Air Vice-Marshal (Retd.) AMINUL ISLAM.

Six ministries, including Foreign and Home Affairs, are held by the Chief Martial Law Administrator.

PRESIDENT AND LEGISLATURE

The elected President was deposed and the Jatiya Sangsad (Parliament) dissolved following promulgation of martial law and the take-over of power by Lt.-Gen. H. M. Ershad on March 24th, 1982. Three days later, Gen. Ershad appointed a retired judge to be President.

POLITICAL PARTIES*

In August 1975 the then President, Mushtaq Ahmed, banned all political parties and disbanded the Bangladesh Awami League. In August 1976 the Government permitted political activities to be resumed, and final restrictions were lifted at the end of 1978. There are 29 political parties, of which the following are the most influential:

Awami League (Hasina): 23 Bangabandhu Ave., Dacca; f. 1949; Chair. Sheikh HASINA WAZED; Gen. Sec. ABDUR RASSAQ; *c.* 1,025,000 mems.

Awami League (Mizan): 271/4 Elephant Rd., Dacca; f. 1978; Leader MIZANUR RAHMAN CHOUDHURY.

Bangladesh Communist Party: Dacca; Leader MONI SINGH; Gen.-Sec. MOHAMMAD FARHAD.

Bangladesh Jatiya League: 500A Dhanmandi R/A, Road No. 7, Dacca; f. 1970 as Pakistan National League; renamed in 1972; Leader ATAUR RAHMAN KHAN.

Bangladesh Democratic Movement: Dacca; f. 1978; Convenor RASHED KHAN MENON.

Bangladesh Jatiyatabadi Dal (*Bangladesh Nationalist Party*): House No. 19A, Road No. 27 (Old) and 16 (New), Dhanmandi R/A, Dacca; f. 1978 by merger of groups supporting Ziaur Rahman, including Jatiyatabadi Ganatantrik Dal (Jagodal-Nationalist Democratic Party); stands for presidential system of government; Chair. Justice ABDUS SATTAR; Sec.-Gen. BADRUDDOZA CHOWDHURY.

Bangladesh Muslim League: 281 Road No. 25, Dhanmandi R/A, Dacca; f. 1947; conservative, pro-Islam; Leader (vacant).

Democratic League: 68 Jigatola, Dacca 9; f. 1976; conservative; Leader KHANDAKAR MUSHTAQ AHMED.

Gonoazadi League: 30 Banagran Lane, Dacca; Leader MOULANA A. R. TARKABAGISH.

Jatiya Janata Party: Dacca; f. 1976; socio-democratic; Convenor Gen. MUHAMMAD ATAUL GHANI OSMANY.

Jatiya Samajtantrik Dal (*National Socialist Party*): 23 D.I.T. Ave., Malibagh (Choudhury para), Dacca; f. 1972; socialist; Leader SHAJAHAN SIRAJ.

National Awami Party-Bhashani NAP: 226 Outer Circular Rd., Dacca; f. 1957; left-wing, pro-Beijing; Pres. ABU NASSER KHAN BHASHANI; Gen.-Sec. ABDUS SUBHANI.

National Awami Party-NAP(M): 21 Dhanmandi Hawkers' Market (1st Floor), Dacca 5; pro-Moscow; Leader MUZAFFAR AHMED.

People's League: House No. 72, Dhanmandi R/A, Road No. 7/A, Dacca; f. 1976; Leader Dr. ALIM AL-RAZEE.

Samyabadi Dal: Dacca; secular, pro-Beijing; Leader MOHAMMAD TOAHA.

United People's Party: 42/43 Purana Paltan, Dacca; f. 1974; pro-Beijing; left-wing; Leader KAZI JAFAR AHMED.

* All political activities are suspended under Martial Law Regulations.

DIPLOMATIC REPRESENTATION

EMBASSIES AND HIGH COMMISSIONS ACCREDITED TO BANGLADESH

(In Dacca unless otherwise stated)

HC=High Commission

Afghanistan: House CES(A)49, 96 Gulshan Ave., Gulshan Model Town; *Chargé d'affaires:* GOLAM GAUS WAZIRI.

Algeria: Hanoi, Viet-Nam.

Argentina: New Delhi, India.

Australia: Hotel Purbani, 9th Floor, Dilkusha Commercial Area; *High Commissioner:* M. H. G. WILLIAMS.

Austria: New Delhi, India.

Belgium: House 40, Rd. 21, Block B, Banani; *Ambassador:* RAYMOND VAN ROY.

Bhutan: House 58, Rd. 3A, Dhanmondi R/A, P.O.B. 3141; *Ambassador:* DAGO TSHERING.

Brazil: 10-A, Circuit House Rd.; *Ambassador:* ALDO DE FREITAS.

Bulgaria: House 12, Rd. 127, Gulshan Model Town; *Ambassador:* ASPARUH TODOROV PAPALEZOV.

Burma: No. 89(B), Rd. 4, Banani; *Ambassador:* U THEIN WIN.

Canada: House 16A, Rd. 48, Gulshan Model Town; *High Commissioner:* ARTHUR ROBERT WRIGHT.

China, People's Republic: Plot NE(L)6, Rd. 83, Gulshan Model Town; *Ambassador:* LIU SHUQING.

Cuba: New Delhi, India.

Czechoslovakia: House 71, Gulshan Ave., Gulshan Model Town; *Ambassador:* ALEXANDER VENGLAR.

Denmark: House No. 1, Rd. 51, Gulshan Model Town; *Ambassador:* BJØRN OLSEN.

Egypt: House NE(N)-9, Rd. 90, Gulshan Model Town; *Ambassador:* EZZ ELDIN EL SAYED ISSA.

Ethiopia: New Delhi, India.

Finland: New Delhi, India.

France: P.O.B. 22, House 18, Rd. 108, Gulshan; *Ambassador:* LOUIS MOREAU.

Gabon: Paris, France.

German Democratic Republic: 32/34, Rd. 74, Gulshan Model Town; *Chargé d'affaires:* GERHARD MUELLER.

Germany, Federal Republic: House Kalpana, 7, Green Rd., P.O.B. 108, Dhanmandi R/A; *Ambassador:* Baron WALTER VON MARSCHALL.

Ghana: New Delhi, India (HC).

Greece: New Delhi, India.

Hungary: House 10, Rd. 9, Gulshan Model Town; *Ambassador:* ENDRE GALAMBOS.

India: House 120 and 129, Rd. 2, Dhanmondi R/A; *Ambassador:* MUCHKUND DUBEY.

Indonesia: CWS(A) 10, 75 Gulshan Ave., Rd. 30; *Ambassador:* SAJID BASUKI SASTROHARTOJO.

Iran: 171 Gulshan Ave., Gulshan Model Town; *Ambassador:* MAHMOUD SADAK MADARSHAHI.

Iraq: 112 Gulshan Ave.; *Ambassador:* ARIF MOHAMMAD ALI KARIM.

Italy: House No. 4, Rd. No. 58/6, Gulshan; *Ambassador:* Dr. FAUSTO MARIA PENNACCHIO.

Japan: Gulshan Model Towm; *Ambassador:* HIROHIKO OTSUKA.

Korea, Democratic People's Republic: Plot No. 157, Rd. No. 12, Block E, Banani Model Town; *Ambassador:* JONG TAE GUN.

Korea, Republic: House NW(E)17, Rd. 55, Gulshan Model Town; *Ambassador:* KIE YUL MOON.

Kuwait: House 53, Gulshan Ave.; *Ambassador:* SALEH MOHAMMAD SALEH AL-MOHAMMAD.

Libya: House 4 CWN(C), Gulshan Ave.; *Secretary of People's Bureau:* ABUBAKAR AHMED ABUSHAMA.

Malaysia: Plot 18, Gulshan South Ave., Gulshan; *High Commissioner:* MOHAMMAD HARON.

Mauritius: New Delhi, India (HC).

Mongolia: New Delhi, India.

Morocco: New Delhi, India.

Nepal: 248 (Old), 82 (New), Dhanmandi R/A, Rd. 21 (Old), 11A (New); *Ambassador:* GEHENDRA BAHADUR RAJ BHANDARY.

Netherlands: House 19, Rd. 99, Gulshan Model Town; *Ambassador:* WILLIAM SINNINGHE DAMSTE.

New Zealand: New Delhi, India (HC).

Nigeria: New Delhi, India (HC).

Norway: New Delhi, India.

Oman: New Delhi, India.

Pakistan: 22 Gulshan Ave., House No. SE(D)-9, Rd. No. 140, Gulshan Model Town; *Ambassador:* TANVIR AHMAD KHAN.

Philippines: Hotel Sonargaon; *Chargé d'affaires:* RODRIGO S. A. ARAGON.

Poland: Rd. 71, NE/A/5, Gulshan; *Ambassador:* WŁADYSŁAW DOMAGALA.

Portugal: New Delhi, India.

Romania: 126 Gulshan Ave., Rd. 111; *Ambassador:* IOSIF CHIVU.

Saudi Arabia: SW(A)25, Rd. 10, Gulshan Ave.; *Ambassador:* Sheikh FOUAD ABDUL HAMMED AL-KHATEEB.

Senegal: New Delhi, India.

Sierra Leone: Beijing, People's Republic of China (HC).

Singapore: New Delhi, India (HC).

Somalia: Islamabad, Pakistan.

Spain: New Delhi, India.

Sri Lanka: House No. 4, Rd. No. 72, Gulshan; *High Commissioner:* CHARITA RANASINHA.

Sweden: P.O.B. 304, 73 Gulshan Ave.; *Ambassador:* PEDER HAMMARSKJÖLD.

Switzerland: House 15, Rd. 81, Gulshan Model Town; *Chargé d'affaires a.i.:* PAUL ERB (Ambassador resident in New Delhi, India).

Syria: New Delhi, India.

Thailand: 21, Block B, Rd. No. 16, Banani Residential Area; *Ambassador:* THAWEE MANASCHUANG.

Turkey: House 7, Rd. 62, Gulshan Model Town; *Ambassador:* METIN SIRMAN.

Uganda: New Delhi, India (HC).

U.S.S.R.: NR(J) 9, Rd. 79, Gulshan; *Ambassador:* V. P. STEPANOV.

United Arab Emirates: SWB(I), Rd. 7, Gulshan Model Town; *Chargé d'affaires:* ABDULLAH MOHAMMAD AL-TAKAWI.

United Kingdom: P.O.B. 90, Abu Bakr House, Plot 7, Rd. No. 84, Gulshan; *High Commissioner:* FRANK MILLS, C.M.G.

U.S.A.: Adamjee Court, Motijheel; *Ambassador:* Mrs. JEANE A. COON.

Vatican City: House NW(K) 9, Rd. 50, Gulshan; *Apostolic Pro-Nuncio:* Most Rev. LUIGI ACCOGLI.

Viet-Nam: Plot NW(A) 4, Rd. 69, Gulshan; *Chargé d'affaires:* DO NGOE AN.

Yugoslavia: House 10, Rd. 62, Gulshan Model Town; *Ambassador:* GUSTAB ZADNIK.

Zambia: New Delhi, India (HC).

Bangladesh also has diplomatic relations with Albania, Bahrain, Barbados, Guyana, Iceland, Jamaica, Jordan, Lebanon, Luxembourg, Maldives, Mali, Malta, Mauritania, Mexico, Sudan, Tuvalu, Upper Volta and the People's Democratic Republic of Yemen.

JUDICIAL SYSTEM

Chief Justice: Justice F. K. M. A. MUNIM.

Attorney-General: K. A. BAKR.

Note: See also under the Constitution.

RELIGION

According to preliminary results of the 1974 census, over 85 per cent of the population are Muslims, the rest are caste Hindus, scheduled castes, Buddhists, Christians and tribals.

Complete freedom of religious worship is guaranteed under the Constitution (suspended by Martial Law Proclamation of March 24th, 1982) but, under the 1977 amendment to the Constitution, secularism was replaced with Islam as one of the guiding principles.

CHURCH OF BANGLADESH

The Bishop of Dacca: Rt. Rev. B. D. MONDAL, St. Thomas' Church, 54 Johnson Rd., Dacca 1.

ROMAN CATHOLIC CHURCH

Archbishop of Dacca: Most Rev. MICHAEL ROZARIO, Archbishop's House, 1 Kakrail, Dacca 2.

There were 150,000 Catholics in Bangladesh in 1981.

THE PRESS

PRINCIPAL DAILIES

BENGALI

Azad: 27A Dhakeswari Rd., Ramna, Dacca 5; f. 1936; Editor MOHAMMAD ZAINUL ABEDIN KHAN; circ. 7,000.

Azadi: Andarkilla, Chittagong; f. 1960; Editor Prof. MOHAMMAD KHALED; circ. 11,000.

Daily Abarta: 141 Arambagh, Motijeel, Dacca 2, P.O.B. 628; Editor S. M. TAUFIQUL ISLAM; circ. 3701.

Banglar Bani: 81 Motijheel CA, Dacca 2; f. 1971, re-published 1981; Editor SHEIKH FAZLUL KARIM SELIM.

Banglar Mukh: 31A Rankin Street, Dacca; Editor SIDDIQUR RAHMAN ASHRAFI.

Dainik Bangla: 1 D.I.T. Ave., Dacca 2; f. 1964; Editor SHAMSUR RAHMAN; circ. 30,000.

Dainik Burta: Natore Rd., Rajshahi; f. 1976; Editor MIR MAHBUB ALI; circ. 5,000.

Dainik Desh: 27 Purana Paltan, Dacca; f. 1979; Editor SANAULLAH NOORI; circ. 10,000.

Dainik Kishan: 369 Outer Circular Rd., Dacca; f. 1976; Editor KAZI ABDUL QADER; circ. 8,000.

Dainik Purbanchal: 36 Shamsur Rahman Rd., Khulna; f. 1974; Editor LIAQUAT ALI; circ. 4,500.

Dainik Rupashi Bangla: Natun Chowdhury Para, Bagichagaon, Comilla; f. 1979; Editor ABDUL WAHAB.

Dainik Samachar: 31/32 P. K. Roy Road, Banglabazar, Dacca 1; f. 1964; evening; Editor SEKANDAR HAYAT MAJUMDER; circ. 25,000.

Dainik Uttara: Dinajpur Town, Dinajpur; f. 1974; Editor Prof. MUHAMMAD MOHSIN; circ. 7,500.

Deshbangla: 6 Folder St., Wari, Dacca 3; f. 1977; Editor FERDOUS AHMAD QURESHI; circ. 4,000.

Gonokantha: 24 Tipusultan Rd., Dacca; f. 1972; Editor-in-Chief MIRZA SULTAN RAZA; circ. 5,000.

Ittefaq: 1 Ramkrishna Mission Rd., Dacca 3; f. 1953; Editor ANWAR HOSSAIN MANJU; circ. 125,000.

Janabarta: Khanjahan Ali Rd., Khulna; f. 1974; Editor SYED SOHRAB ALI; circ. 4,000.

Karatoa: Thana Rd., Bogra; f. 1976; Editor MOHAMMAD ABOUL MATIN; circ. 4,000.

Naya Bangla: 22 Miranda Lane, Patharghata, Chittagong; f. 1978; Editor ABDULLAH AL SAGIR; circ. 4,000.

Prabaha: Roypara Cross Rd., Khulna; f. 1977; Editor ASHRAFUL HUQ; circ. 3,000.

Protidin: Ganashtola, Dinajpur; f. 1980; Editor KHAIROL ALAM.

Runner: Pyari Mohan Das Rd., Jessore; f. 1980; Editor GULAM MAJED.

Sangbad: 263 Bangshal Rd., Dacca 1; f. 1951; Editor AHMEDUL KABIR; circ. 13,000.

Sangram: 423 Elephant Rd., Bara Maghbazar, Dacca; f. 1970; Editor ABUL ASAD; circ. 15,000.

Sphulinga: P.O.B. 12, Jessore; f. 1971; Editor MIA ABDUS SATTAR; circ. 3,000.

Swadhinata: 99A Zamal Khan Lane, Chittagong; f. 1972; Editor ABDULLAH-AL-HARUN; circ. 4,000.

Zamana: Qazir Dewry, Chittagong; f. 1955; Editor MOYEENUL ALAM.

ENGLISH

Bangladesh Observer: Observer House, 33 Toynbee Circular Rd., Dacca 2; f. 1948; Editor OBAIDUL HUQ; circ. 41,000.

Bangladesh Times: 1 D. I. T. Ave., Dacca 2; f. 1974; Editor A. M. MUFAZZAL; circ. 25,000.

Daily Life: 27 Sadarghat Rd., Chittagong; f. 1977; Editor ANWARUL ISLAM BOBBY; circ. 9,000.

The Daily Tribune: 38 Iqbalnagar Mosque Lane, Khulna; f. 1978; Editor Mrs. FERDOUSI ALI; circ. 14,560.

Millat: 27 Purana Paltan, Dacca; f. 1977; Editor A. T. M. ABDUL MATEEN; circ. 6,000.

Morning Post: 33 Topjhana Rd., Dacca 2; f. 1969; Editor HABIBUL BASHAR; circ. 5,000.

New Nation: 1 R.K. Mission Rd., Dacca; f. 1977; Editor MOTHAR HOSSAIN SIDDIQUI; circ. 10,200.

People's View: 129 Panchlaish R/A, Chittagong; f. 1969; Editor NURUL ISLAM; circ. 5,000.

PERIODICALS

BENGALI

Adab Sangbad: House No. 79, Rd. No. 11/A, Dhanmandi R/A, Dacca; f. 1974; 2 a month; Editor Dr. KHAWJA SHAMSUL HUDA; circ. 9,000.

Ad-Dawat: Rajshahi Town; f. 1976; monthly; Editor MOHAMMAD ABUL QASEM.

Ahmadi: 4 Bakshi Bazar, Dacca; f. 1925; fortnightly; Editor A. H. M. ALI ANWAR.

Ajker Samabaya: 114 Motijheel C/A, Dacca; f. 1974; fortnightly; Editor KH. REASUL KARIM; circ. 10,000.

Amod: Comilla Town; f. 1953; weekly; Editor MOHAMMAD FAZLE RABBI; circ. 2,000.

Begum: 66 Lyall St., Dacca 1; f. 1947; women's illustrated weekly; Editor NURJAHAN BEGUM; circ. 23,000.

Bichitra: 1 D.I.T. Ave., Dacca; f. 1972; weekly; Editor SHAMSUR RAHMAN; circ. 45,000.

Chitrali: Observer House, 33 Toynbee Circular Rd., Dacca 2; f. 1963; film weekly; Editor AHMED ZAMAN CHOWDHURY; circ. 48,000.

Dacca Digest: 34 Topkhana Rd., Dacca; f. 1974; monthly; Editor RASHID CHOWDHURY; circ. 7,000.

Fashal: 114 Fakirapool, Dacca; f. 1965; agricultural weekly; Editor ERSHAD MAJUMDAR; circ. 6,500.

Ispat: Kushtia Town, Kushtia; f. 1976; weekly; Editor WALIUR BARI CHOUDHURY; circ. 2,000.

Ittehad: 42/3 Purana Paltan, Dacca; f. 1969; weekly; Editor OLI AHAD; circ. 12,000.

Jahan-e-Nau: 13 Karkun Bari Lane, Dacca; f. 1960; weekly; Editor Md. HABIBIUR RAHMAN; circ. 15,000.

Jugabheri: Lipika Printers, Sylhet; f. 1971; weekly; Editor AMINUR RASHID CHOWDHURY; circ. 6,000.

Kalantar: 87 Khanjahan Ali Rd., Khulna; f. 1971; weekly; Editor NOOR MOHAMMAD; circ. 2,200.

Kaukon: Nawab Bari Rd., Bogra; f. 1974; weekly; Editor SUFIA KHATUN; circ. 6,000.

Khabar: 137 Shanti Nagar, Dacca; f. 1977; weekly; Editor MIZANUR RAHMAN MIZAN; circ. 15,000.

Kishore Bangla: Observer House, Motijheel C/A, Dacca; juvenile weekly; f. 1976; Editor RAFIQUL HAQUE; circ. 5,000.

Krira Jagat: National Sports Control Bd., Dacca; f. 1977; fortnightly; Editor UMMESALMA RAFIQ; circ. 10,000.

Krishi Katha: 3 R.K. Mission Rd., Dacca; f. 1964; monthly; Editor A. H. M. A. HALIM; circ. 6,000.

Muktibani: 70 R. K. Mission Rd., Dacca; f. 1972; weekly; Editor NIZAMUDDIN AHMED; circ. 15,000.

Nayajug: 32 Purana Paltan, Dacca; f. 1976; weekly; Editor KAZI ZAFAR AHMED; circ. 9,000.

Patuakhali Samachar: Patuakhali Town; f. 1970; fortnightly; Editor SHAMSUL HAQ KHAN.

Protirodh: Ministry of Home Affairs, Bangladesh Secretariat, Dacca; f. 1977; fortnightly; Editor AREFIN BADAL; circ. 20,000.

Purbani: 1 Ramkrishna Mission Rd., Dacca; f. 1951; film weekly; Editor SHAHADAT HOSSAIN; circ. 58,000.

Reporter: 114 Fakirapool, Dacca; f. 1977; weekly; Editor ERSHAD MAJUMDAR; circ. 6,000.

Robbar: 1 R. K. Mission Rd., Dacca; f. 1978; weekly; Editor ABDUL HAFIZ; circ. 20,000.

Sachitra Bangladesh: Film and Publications Dept., Ministry of Information and Broadcasting, Dacca; f. 1979; fortnightly; Editor M. A. WAHAB; circ. 8,000.

Sachitra Sandhani: 41 Naya Paltan, Dacca; f. 1978; weekly; Editor GAZI SAHABUDDIN AHMED; circ. 10,000.

Shishu: Shishu Academy, Old High Court Area, Dacca; f. 1977; children's monthly; Editor JOBEDA KHANAM; circ. 5,000.

ENGLISH

Adab News: House No. 79, Rd. No. 11/A, Dhanmandi R/A, Dacca; f. 1976; 2 a month; Editor Dr. KHAWJA SHAMSUL HUDA; circ. 4,000.

Bangladesh Gazette: Bangladesh Government Press, Tejgaon, Dacca; f. 1947, title changed 1972; weekly; government publication.

Bangladesh Illustrated Weekly: 31/A Rankin St., Wari, Dacca; Editor ATIQUZZAMAN KHAN; circ. 3,000.

Detective: Naya Paltan, Dacca; f. 1960; weekly; also published in Bengali; Editor KAZI ZAHURUL HAQ; circ. 3,000.

Eastern Tribune: 62/1 Purana Paltan, Dacca; f. 1969; weekly; Editor ABUL HOSSAIN MALLICK; circ. 3,500.

Economic Times: 42-43 Purana Paltan, Dacca; f. 1973; weekly; Editor A. K. M. SHAMSUL HUDA.

Financial Times: 7/G Motijheel C/A, Dacca; f. 1974; Editor OSMAN HAIDER CHOWDHURY.

Herald: 79 Motijheel C/A, Dacca; f. 1981; weekly; Editor A. AHMED YUSUF.

Holiday: 40/1 Naya Paltan, Dacca; f. 1965; weekly; independent; Editor FAZAL M. KAMAL; circ. 16,000.

Karnaphuli Shipping News: 88 Ghatforhadbeg, Kazem Ali Rd., Chittagong; f. 1977; twice a week; Editor F. KARIM; circ. 10,000.

Motherland: Khanjahan Ali Rd., Khulna; f. 1974; weekly; Editor MUKTADIR HOSSAIN.

Saturday Post: 33 Topkhana Rd., Dacca 2; f. 1975; weekly; Editor HABIBUL BASHAR; circ. 15,000.

Sunday Star: 149/A D.I.T. Extension Ave., Dacca; f. 1981; weekly; Editor MOHIUDDIN AHMED.

Voice From the North: Dinajpur Town, Dinajpur; f. 1981; weekly; Editor Prof. MUHAMMAD MOHSIN; circ. 5,000.

NEWS AGENCIES

Bangladesh Sangbad Sangstha (*Bangladesh News Agency*): 68/2 Purana Paltan, Dacca 2; Gen. Man. and Chief Editor ABUL HASHEM.

Eastern News Agency (E.N.A.): 3/3C Purana Paltan, Dacca 2; Man. Dir. and Chief Editor GOLAM RASUL MALLICK.

PRESS ASSOCIATIONS

Bangladesh Council of Newspapers and News Agencies: Dacca; Gen. Sec. HABIBUL BASHAR.

Bangladesh Federal Union of Journalists: National Press Club Bldg., 18 Topkhana Rd., Dacca 2; f. 1973; Pres. A. HUMAYUN; Sec.-Gen. REAZUDDIN AHMED.

Bangladesh Sangbadpatra Karmachari Federation (*Newspaper Employees Federation*): 47/3 Toynbee Circular Rd., Bikrampur House, Dacca 2; f. 1972; Pres. JAHANGIR KABIR; Sec.-Gen. MIR MOZAMMEL HOSSAIN.

Bangladesh Sangbadpatra Press Sramik Federation (*Newspaper Press Workers' Federation*): 1 R.K. Mission Rd., Dacca; f. 1960; Pres. ABDUL KARIM; Sec. FAZLE IMAM.

Overseas Correspondents' Association Bangladesh (OCAB): 18 Topkhana Road, Dacca 2; f. 1979; 38 members; Pres. S. KAMALUDDIN.

PUBLISHERS

Adyle Brothers: 60 Patuatuly, Dacca 1.

Ahmed Publishing House: 7 Zindabahar 1st Lane, Dacca 1; publ. books on literature, history, science, religion, children's books, maps and charts.

Ashrafia Library: 4 Hakim Habibur Rahman Rd., Chawk Bazar, Dacca 2; publ. Islamic religious books, texts, and reference books of Islamic institutions.

Asiatic Society of Bangladesh: 2 Old Secretariat Rd., Ramna, Dacca; f. 1951; publ. periodicals on science and humanities; Pres. KHAN BAHADUR ABDUL HAKIM.

Bangla Academy: Burdwan House, Dacca 2; f. 1957; higher ecduation text books in Bengali, research works, drama, children's books, translations of world classics, various dictionaries; Dir. (publ. and sales) AL-KAMAL ABDUL WAHHAB.

Bangladesh Book Corporation: Patuatuly, Dacca.

Bangladesh Bureau of Statistics: Bangladesh Secretariat Bldg., Dacca; publ. statistical yearbooks and monthly bulletins; Publication Officer MENHAJUDDIN AHMAD.

Bangladesh Publishers: 45 Patuatuly, Dacca.

Bangladesh Books International Ltd.: P.O.B. 337, Ittefaq Bhavan, 1 R.K. Mission Rd., Dacca 3; f. 1975; reference, academic, research, literary and books for children in Bengali and English; Chair. MOINUL HOSSEIN; Man. Dir. ANOWER HOSSAIN.

Barnamala Prakashani: 30 Banglabazar, Dacca.

Bidar Publications: 48 Johnson Rd., Dacca.

Boi Prakashani: 38A Banglabazar, Dacca.

Boighar: 286 Bipani Bitan, Chittagong.

Book Society: 38 Banglabazar, Dacca.

Co-operative Book Society Ltd.: Motijheel, Dacca.

Emdadia Library: Chawk Bazar, Dacca.

Ferdaus Publications: 41 North Brook Hall Rd., Dacca.

Great Bengal Library: Islampur, Dacca.

Green Book House: Motijheel, Dacca.

Habibia Library: Chawk Bazar, Dacca.

Islamia Library: Patuatuly, Dacca.

Islamic Foundation: Baitul Mukarram, Dacca.

Jatiya Sahitya Prakashani: P.O.B. 3416, 51 Purana Paltan, Dacca 2; f. 1970; Principal Officer MOFIDUL HOQUE.

Khan Brothers & Co.: 67 Pyari Das Rd., Dacca.

Knowledge Home: Pyari Das Rd., Dacca.

Liaquat Publications: 34 North Brook Hall Rd., Dacca.

Model Publishing: 34 Banglabazzar, Dacca.

Modina Publications: Pyari Das Rd., Dacca.

Mofiz Book House: 37 Banglabazar, Dacca.

Mowla Brothers: Banglabazar, Dacca.

Muktadhara: 74 Farashganj, Dacca; f. 1971; publ. educational, literary and general books in Bengali and English; Man. Dir. C. R. SAHA; Chief Editor S. P. LAHIRY.

National Book Centre of Bangladesh: 67A Purana Paltan, Dacca; f. 1963, an autonomous organization to promote the cause of "more, better and cheaper books"; Dir. FAZLE RABBI.

Osmania Book Depot: 71–72 Islampur, Dacca 1.

Provincial Library: Banglabazar, Dacca.

Puthighar: 74 Farashganj, Dacca; f. 1951; educational books in Bengali and English; Man. Dir. C. R. SAHA; Chief Editor S. P. LAHIRY.

Puthipatra: 1/6 Shirish Das Lane, Banglabazar, Dacca 1; f. 1952.

Rangpur Publications: 13/3 Haramohan St., Amligola, Dacca.

Royal Library: Islampur, Dacca.

Sahitya Kutir: Bogra.

Sahityika: 6 Banglabazar, Dacca.

Samakal Prakashani: 36A, Toynbee Circular Rd., Dacca 2.

Standard Publishers Ltd.: 3-10 Liaquat Ave., Dacca 1.

Student Ways: Banglabazar, Dacca.

University Press Ltd.: 114 Motijheel, Dacca.

PUBLISHERS' ASSOCIATION

The Bangladesh Publishers' and Booksellers' Association: 3rd Floor, 3 Liaquat Ave., Dacca 1; Pres. JAHANGIR MOHAMMED ADEL.

RADIO AND TELEVISION

RADIO

Radio Bangladesh 36 (New) Rd. No. 3, Dhanmandi Residential Area, Dacca 5; f. 1971; regional stations at Dacca, Rajshahi, Chittagong, Sylhet, Rangpur and Khulna broadcast a total of 80 hours on week-days and 84 hours on Sundays; external service broadcasts 6 programmes daily in Arabic, Bengali, English, Hindi, Nepali and Urdu; Dir.-Gen. AMIR-UZ-ZAMAN KHAN.

TELEVISION

Bangladesh Television (BTV): Television Bhavan, P.O.B. 456, Rampura, Dacca; f. 1964, under state control since 1972; colour transmission from 1981; morning transmission on weekdays ceased in April 1982; daily broadcasts on two channels from Dacca station of 10 hours on weekdays and 13 hours on Sundays; transmissions also from station at Chittagong, Khulna, Mymensingh, Natore, Rangpur, Sylhet and Noakhali; stations planned at Cox's Bazar and Rangamati by 1982; Dir. Gen. SYED AHMED; Dir. of Programmes KHALIDA FAHMI.

FINANCE

(cap. = capital; p.u. = paid up; dep. = deposits; res. = reserves; m. = million; brs. = branches)

BANKING

CENTRAL BANK

Bangladesh Bank: Head Office, Motijheel C/A, P.O.B. 325, Dacca 2; f. 1971; 6 brs.; cap. p.u. 30m. taka, total assets 19,623m. taka (June 1981); Gov. M. NURUL ISLAM.

COMMERCIAL BANKS

In 1972 all 12 commercial banks were nationalized and six incorporated banks established:

Agrani Bank: Agrani Bank Bhavan, Motijheel C/A, Dacca; f. 1972; 776 brs.; cap. 30m. taka, res. 36m. taka, dep. 3,801.5m. taka (1979); Chair. Prof. M. SHAFIULLAH; Man. Dir. M. FAZLUR RAHMAN.

Janata Bank: P.O.B. 468, 1 Dilkusha C/A, Dacca 2; f. 1972; 830 brs.; cap. p.u. 30m. taka, res. 7,240m. taka, dep. 8,110m. taka (June 1981); Chair. Dr. ABDULLAH FAROOQ; Man. Dir. KAMALUDDIN AHMED; Gen. Mans. MD. AFZALUR RAHMAN, A. K. M. GHAFFAR.

Pubali Bank: P.O.B. 853, 24–25 Dilkusha C/A, Dacca 2; f. 1972; 433 brs.; cap. p.u. 20m. taka, dep. 2,890.1m. taka (1981); res. 32.5m. taka (1979); Chair. Dr. K. T. HUSSAIN; Man. Dir. ASHRAFUL HUQ.

Rupali Bank: 34 Dilkusha C/A, P.O.B. 719, Dacca 2; f. 1972; 538 brs.; cap. 20m. taka, dep. 2,887m. taka (1979); Chair. and Man. Dir. ABDUL WAHID.

Sonali Bank: P.O.B. 147, Motijheel C/A, Dacca 2; f. 1972; over 890 brs.; cap. 30m. taka, dep. 10,233.8m. taka (Dec. 1979); Chair. S. A. KHAIR; Man. Dir. EZAZUR RAHMAN.

Uttara Bank: 42 Dilkusha C/A, P.O.B. 818, Dacca 2; f. 1965; 201 brs.; cap. 20m. taka, res. 27.5m. taka, dep. 1,878,4m. taka (1981); Chair. Dr. HABIBULLAH; Man. Dir. AZIZ AHMED.

PRIVATE BANKS

Arab Bangladesh Bank Ltd.: Bangladesh Steel House, Kawran Bazar, Dacca; f. 1982 as first joint-venture Bangladeshi Bank in private sector; Chief Exec. HAFIZUL ISLAM.

FOREIGN BANKS

American Express International Banking Corpn. (*U.S.A.*): ALICO Bldg., 18–20 Motijheel C/A, Dacca 2; f. 1966; 3 brs. in Dacca, Chittagong and Khulna; Vice-Pres. and Head (Bangladesh) GARY JOHNS.

Bank of Credit and Commerce International (Overseas) Ltd. (*Cayman Islands*): 10 Dilkusha C/A, Box 896, Dacca 2; f. 1976; 3 brs.; Chief Exec. ANWARUL AMIN.

Banque de L'Indo-Chine et de Suez (*France*): Motijheel C/A, Dacca 2; f. 1981.

Chartered Bank (*U.K.*): Box 536, 18–20 Motijheel C/A, Dacca 2; also in Chittagong; Gen. Man. M. INMAN.

Grindlays Bank (*U.K.*): 2 Dilkusha C/A, P.O.B. 502, Dacca; 9 brs.; Gen. Man. A. R. DICKSON.

Habib Bank Ltd. (*Pakistan*): 53 Motijheel C/A, Dacca 2; f. 1979; Man. HABIB H. MIRZA.

State Bank of India: 24–25 Dilkusha C/A, Dacca 2; f. 1975; Chief Exec. N. K. SEN GUPTA.

DEVELOPMENT FINANCE ORGANIZATIONS

Bangladesh House Building Finance Corporation: HBFC Bldg., 22 Purana Paltan, Dacca 2; f. 1952; provides credit facilities at low interest for house-building; cap. authorized 100m. taka (subscribed by the Bangladesh Government); credit facilities exist in all urban areas; 5 zonal offices and 12 regional offices; Chair. A. K. M. MUSA; Man. Dir. KAMALUDDIN AHMED.

Bangladesh Krishi Bank (*Agricultural Development Bank*): 84 Motijheel C/A, Dacca 2; f. 1971; 632 brs.; cap. p.u. 200m. taka, total assets 2,959m. taka, dep. 258m. (Dec. 1977), res. 751m. taka (June 1980); Chair. A. K. M. ASHAN; Man. Dir. KHAIRUL KABIR.

Bangladesh Shilpa Bank (*Industrial Development Bank*): 4–6 Floor, Agrani Bank Bldg., Motijheel C/A, P.O.B. 975, Dacca 2; f. 1972; cap. p.u. 100m. taka, total assets 2,805m. taka, dep. 273m. take (Dec. 1977), res. 259m. taka (1980); Chair. Prof. MUZAFFAR AHMED; Man. Dir. AMINUL ISLAM KHAN.

Bangladesh Shilpa Rin Sangstha (*Industrial Loan Agency*): 1–2 Floor, Agrani Bhavan, Motijheel C/A, P.O.B. 473, Dacca 2; f. 1972; cap. p.u. 150m. taka, total assets 2,310m. taka (June 1981); Chair. Dr. IQBAL MAHMOOD; Man. Dir. A. H. M. KAMALUDDIN.

Investment Corporation of Bangladesh: 64 Motijheel C/A, Dacca 2; f. 1976; cap. p.u. 87.5m. taka (1981); Chair. MANSURUL KARIM; Man. Dir. BAZAL AHMED.

INSURANCE

Department of Insurance (attached to Ministry of Commerce): 74 Motijheel C/A, Dacca 2; government-owned; Controller of Insurance M. HARUNUR RASHID; controls activities of all insurers, local and foreign, incl. Bima Corporations, as per provisions of the Insurance Act, 1938.

The Bangladesh Government in August 1972 set up a National Insurance Corporation to regulate and supervise all nationalized Life and general insurance companies. This was abolished in May 1973 and the two corporations listed below were set up, one to handle life insurance and the other general insurance.

Jiban Bima Corporation: 24 Motijheel C/A, Dacca 2; government-owned; amalgamation of 36 national life insurance companies formerly operating in East Pakistan; life insurance; publ. *Jiban Bima* (quarterly, Bengali and English).

Shadharan Bima Corporation: 33 Dilkusha C/A, Dacca 2; government-owned; general insurance; Man. Dir. SHAMSUL ALAM.

TRADE AND INDUSTRY

In 1972 the Government took over all cotton, jute and other major industrial enterprises and the tea estates. Management Boards were appointed by the Government. During 1976 and 1977 many tea plantations and the smaller industrial units were returned to the private sector.

GOVERNMENT SPONSORED ORGANIZATIONS

Bangladesh Chemical Industries Corporation: Shilpa Bhaban, 2nd Floor, Motijheel C/A, Dacca 2; Chair. A. K. M. MOSHARRAF HOSSAIN.

Bangladesh Export Processing Zones Authority: C.D. Bldg., Court Rd., Chittagong; Shilpa Bhaban, Motijheel C/A, Dacca 2; f. 1981 to operate and control export processing zones in Bangladesh.

Bangladesh Fisheries Development Corporation: 24/25 Dilkusha C/A, Dacca 2; f. 1964; Chair. Dr. M. B. RAHMAN.

Bangladesh Forest Industries Development Corporation: 186 Circular Rd., Motijheel C/A, Dacca 2; Chair. M. ATIKULLAH.

Bangladesh Jute Mills Corporation: Adamjee Court, 4th Floor, Motijheel C/A, Dacca 2; operates 71 jute mills with over 15,000 looms; Chair. M. A. SYED.

Bangladesh Mineral Exploration and Development Corporation: H.B.F.C. Bldg., 22 Purana Paltan, Dacca 2; Chair. Air Commodore (retd.) M. WAJIULLAH.

Bangladesh Oil and Gas Corporation (Petro Bangla): 122/124 Motijheel C/A, Chamber Bldg., Dacca 2; Chair. Dr. HABIBUR RAHMAN.

Bangladesh Small and Cottage Industries Corporation (BSCIC): 137/138 Motijheel C/A, Dacca 2; f. 1957; Chair. SERAJUDDIN AHMED.

Bangladesh Steel and Engineering Corporation: Shilpa Bhaban, 4th Floor, Motijheel C/A, Dacca 2; Chair. Dr. NAZRUL ISLAM.

Bangladesh Sugar and Food Industries Corporation: Shilpa Bhaban, Motijheel C/A, Dacca 2; f. 1972; Chair. DELWAR HOSSAIN.

Bangladesh Textile Mills Corporation: Shadharan Bima Bhaban, 33 Dilkusha C/A, Dacca 2; f. 1972; Chair. MOHAMMAD NEFAUR RAHMAN.

Trading Corporation of Bangladesh: H.B.F.C. Bldg., 22 Purana Paltan, Dacca 2; f. 1972; Chair. KAZI AZUAR ALI.

Export Promotion Bureau: 122-124 Motijheel C/A, Dacca 2; f. 1972; under the Ministry of Commerce; regional offices in Chittagong, Khulna and Rajshahi; brs. in Comilla, Sylhet, Bogra and Barisal; foreign offices in Milan and Rotterdam; Vice-Chair. RUHUL AMIN MAJUMDER.

Planning Commission: Planning Commission Secretariat, G. O. Hostel, Sher-e-Bangla Nagar, Dacca; f. 1972; government agency responsible for all aspects of economic planning and development including the preparation of the Five-Year Plans and annual development programmes (in conjunction with appropriate government ministries), promotion of savings and investment, compilation of statistics and evaluation of development schemes and projects.

CHAMBERS OF COMMERCE

Federation of Bangladesh Chambers of Commerce and Industry: 60 Motijheel C/A, Dacca 2; Pres. NURUDDIN AHMED.

Agrabad Chamber of Commerce and Industry: P.O.B. 70, Chamber Bldg., Bangabandhu Rd., Chittagong; Pres. L. D. B. BRYCESON.

Barisal Chamber of Commerce and Industry: Asad Mansion (1st Floor), Sadar Rd., Barisal; Pres. KAZI ISRAIL HOSSAIN.

Bogra Chamber of Commerce and Industry: Rajabazar. Bogra; Pres NIZAMUDDIN HAYDER.

Chittagong Chamber of Commerce and Industry: Chamber House, Agrabad C/A, P.O.B. Chittagong; f. 1963; 2,319 mems.; Pres. SIJANDAR HUSAIN MEAH.

Comilla Chamber of Commerce and Industry: Ranibazar, Comilla; Pres. AFZAL KHAN.

Dacca Chamber of Commerce and Industry: Dacca Chamber Bldg., 65–66 Motijheel C/A, P.O.B. 2641, Dacca 2; f. 1960; 4,000 mems.; Pres. M. A. SATTAR; Vice-Pres. (Sr.) M. REZA, Vice-Pres. (Jr.) MUJIBUR RAHMAN; publ. *Review* (fortnightly).

Dinajpur Chamber of Commerce and Industry; Jail Rd., Dinajpur; Pres. M. E. MOJUMBER.

Faridpur Chamber of Commerce and Industry: Chamber House, Niltuly, Faridpur; Pres. KHANDOKER MOHSIN ALI.

Khulna Chamber of Commerce and Industry: P.O.B. 26, Shams House (3rd Floor), Sir Iqbal Rd., Khulna; f. 1934; Pres. S. K. ZAHOIUL ISLAM.

Khustia Chamber of Commerce and Industry: 15, N.S. Rd., Kustia; Pres. DIN MOHAMMAD.

Metropolitan Chamber of Commerce and Industry: Chamber Bldg. (4th Floor), 122–124 Motijheel C/A, Dacca 2; Narayanganj Office: 137 Bangabandhu Sharak; f. 1904; 184 mems.; Pres. M. MORSHED KHAN; Sec. C. K. HYDER; publs. *Chamber News* (monthly), *Summary of Taxation Rules, Economic Profile, Annual Report.*

Noakhali Chamber of Commerce and Industry: Pourashavha Bldg., Maizdi Court, Noakhali; Pres. MOHAMMAD NAZIBUR RAHMAN.

Rajshahi Chamber of Commerce and Industry: Kabil Mansion, Rajshahi; f. 1960; 48 mems.; Pres. MESBAHUDDIN AHMED.

Sylhet Chamber of Commerce and Industry: Chamber Bldg., P.O.B. 97, Jail Rd., Sylhet; Administrator ABDUL KHALEQUE KHAN.

TRADE ASSOCIATIONS

Bangladesh Cha Sangsad (*Bangladesh Tea Association*): No. 6, Jahan Bldg., P.O.B. 287, Chamber Bldg., Bangabandhu Ave., Chittagong; f. 1972; Chair. WILLIAM MURDOCH.

Bangladesh Jute Association: B.J.A.Bldg., 137 Bangabandhu Rd., P.O.B. 59, Narayanganj, Dacca; Chair. (vacant).

Bangladesh Jute Export Corporation: 14 Topkhana Road, Dacca 2; f. 1972; Chair. S. M. MATIUR RAHMAN.

Bangladesh Jute Goods Association: Nahar Mansion, 56 Motijheel C/A, Dacca; f. 1979; 17 mems.; Chair. M. A. KASHEM; Chair. HAJI MOHAMMAD ALI.

Bangladesh Jute Spinners Association: Chamber Bldg., (4th Floor), 122–124 Motijheel C/A, Dacca 22.

Bangladesh Tea Board: 111/113 Motijheel C/A, Dacca 2; Acting Chair. Dr. K. A. HASSAN.

Jute Marketing Corporation: Goadnail, Narayanganj, Dacca.

CO-OPERATIVES

Bangladesh Co-operative Marketing Society: 9D Motijheel C/A, Dacca 2.

Chattagram Bahini Kalyan Shamabaya Samity Ltd.: 70 Agrabad C/A, Osman Court, Chittagong; f. 1972.

MAJOR INDUSTRIAL COMPANIES

AUTOMOBILE INDUSTRY

Navana Ltd.: 125/A Motijheel Commercial Area, Dacca 2.

Progoti Industries Ltd.: 18–20 Motijheel Commercial Area, Dacca 2; automobiles and machinery.

CHEMICALS

Ashuganj Fertilizer and Chemical Co. Ltd.: Ellal Chamber, 11 Motijheel Commercial Area, Dacca 2; urea and ammonia fertilizer producers; Man. Dir. MOHAMMAD YUSUF.

Chemical Industries of Bangladesh: Facy Bldg., 87 Agrabad, Chittagong.

Karnaphuli Rayon and Chemicals Ltd.: 92 Sadarghat Rd., Chittagong.

Pharmapak Laboratories Ltd.: 26 Tejgaon Industrial Area, Dacca; pharmaceuticals; Man. Dir. ABDUS SATTAR.

COTTON TEXTILES, JUTE, MAN-MADE FIBRES

Adamjee Jute Mills Ltd.: Adamjee Nagar, Dacca; Gen. Man. NURUL HAQUE.

Bangladesh Jute Mills Corporation: Adamjee Court, Motijheel Commercial Area, Dacca 2.

Dacca Dyeing and Manufacturing Co. Ltd.: 22 Purana Paltan, Dacca 2; bed sheets and covers.

Jute Trading Corporation Ltd.: Agrani Bank Bldg., Motijheel Commercial Area, Dacca 2; f. 1967; raw jute; Chair. and Man. Dir. BADRUDDIN AHMAD.

Karim Jute Mills Ltd.: Karim Chambers, 99 Motijheel Commercial Area, Dacca 2; jute products; Dir. ABDUL GHANI AHMED; 3,200 employees.

Paris Garments: 12 Nanda Kumar Datta Rd., Dacca 1; ready-made garments.

Reaz Garments: 37 Urdu Rd., Dacca 1; ready-made garments.

PAPER

Bangladesh Paper Products Ltd.: 7D Sholashahar I, Chittagong.

Eagle Box and Carton Group: Postagola, Dacca 4.

Khulna Newsprint Mills Ltd.: Kalishpur, Khulna.

Sylhet Pulp & Paper Mills: Chatak, Sylhet.

MISCELLANEOUS

Bangladesh Cutleries Ltd.: 67 Bangabandhu Ave., Dacca 2.

Eastern Refinery Ltd.: 338 Segun Bagicha, Dacca 2; Dir. Dr. M. AZIZUR RAHMAN.

Meher Industries (Bangladesh) Ltd.: Airport Rd., Dacca 2; electronics.

People's Ceramic Industries Ltd.: 64 Motijheel Commercial Area, Dacca 2.

Poly Tube Industries: 46 Chawk Circular Rd., Dacca.

Other industries presently in operation include the Bangladesh metal tools and machinery complex and match and battery factories at Dacca, an oil refinery and sheet glass factory at Chittagong, natural gas plants at Sylhet and Titas, Chattack, Rashidpur, Kailash Tila, Haluganj and Ashuganj, a cement factory at Chattack, the Khulna shipyard, as well as petrochemical and pharmaceutical plants at Fenchuganj and Ghorasal.

TRANSPORT

RAILWAYS

Railway Wing, Ministry of Railways, Roads, Highways and Road Transport: Bangladesh Secretariat, Dacca; responsible for deciding policy and exercising government control over the railway system. A five-member Railway Board was set up in 1976 to supervise the 2,858 km. of track; Chair. Railway Bd. MAQBOOL AHMED.

ROADS

Of the 6,240 km. of road, 3,840 km. are metalled.

Bangladesh Road Transport Corporation: Paribhaban, D.I.T. Ave., Dacca; f. 1961; land transportation services including a Truck Division, transporting government food grain; 700 vehicles (March 1980).

INLAND WATERWAYS

In Bangladesh there are some 8,430 km. of navigable waterways on which are located the main river ports of Dacca, Narayanganj, Chandpur, Barisal and Khulna. A river steamer service connects these ports several times a week. Vessels of up to 175 metres in overall length can be manoeuvred on the Karnaphuli river.

Bangladesh Inland Water Transport Corporation: 5 Dilkusha C/A, Dacca 2; f. 1972; water transportation services; 600 vessels (March 1980).

SHIPPING

The chief ports are Chittagong, where the construction of a second dry-dock is planned, and Chalna. A modern seaport is being developed at Mangla.

Bangladesh Shipping Corporation: 28/1 Toynbee Circular Rd., Motijheel C/A, P.O.B. 53, Dacca 2; f. 1972; maritime shipping line; 25 vessels, over 392,488 tons capacity; Chair. and Man. Dir. Commodore M. RAHMAN; Financial Dir. MAHBUB KABIR.

Bangladesh Steam Navigation Co. Ltd.: Red Cross Bldg., 87 Motijheel C/A, Dacca 2; coastal services; Chair. A. K. KHAN; Man. Dir. A. M. Z. KHAN.

Chittagong Port Authority: P.O.B. 2013, Chittagong; provides bunkering and lighterage facilities as well as provisions and drinking water supplies.

CIVIL AVIATION

Dacca and Chittagong are international airports. (Dacca International Airport was renamed Zia International Airport in June 1981). A third international airport at Kurmitola was opened in September 1980 and is expected to handle 5 million passengers annually, ten times the capacity of Dacca airport. There are also airports at all major towns.

Biman (*Bangladesh Airlines*): Biman Bhaban, Motijheel C/A, Dacca 2; f. 1972; fleet of 5 Fokker Friendship, 4 Boeing 707 320-C and two F-28 on services to Abu Dhabi, Burma, Dubai, Greece, India, Indonesia, Italy, Japan, Libya, Malaysia, Nepal, the Netherlands, Oman, Pakistan, Qatar, Saudi Arabia, Singapore, Thailand and the United Kingdom, and proposed services to Kuwait, Iraq and the Philippines; Chief Exec. ABDUL MANNAN.

Foreign airlines serving Bangladesh include Aeroflot (U.S.S.R.), British Airways, Burma Airways Corporation, Indian Airlines, Kuwait Airways Corporation, PIA (Pakistan), Royal Nepal Airlines Corporation, Saudi (Saudi Arabia) and Thai International.

TOURISM

Bangladesh Parjatan Corporation (*National Tourist Organization*): Old Airport Bldg., Tegazon, Dacca 15; there are two Tourist Information Centres in Dacca, and one each in Chittagong, Cox's Bazar, Rajshahi, Rangamati, Moulvi Bazar, Khulna and Bogra; Chair. SYED AHMED REZA-HUSSAIN; Man. GAZI SADEQ.

ATOMIC ENERGY

Bangladesh Atomic Energy Commission (BAEC): P.O.B. 158, 7 Mymensingh Rd., Ramna, Dacca 2; inaugurated as Atomic Energy Centre of fmr. Pakistan Atomic Energy Commission in East Pakistan (now Bangladesh) in 1965, reorganized under present name in 1973; Chair. Dr. ANWAR HOSSAIN; publs. *Nuclear Science & Applications* (Series A and B), *BAEC Annual Report*, *BAEC News Letter* (quarterly, Bengali).

DEFENCE

Armed Forces (July 1981): Total strength 77,000: army 70,000; navy 4,000; air force 3,000; military service is voluntary.

Equipment: The army has 5 infantry divisions, 12 infantry brigades, 2 armoured regiments, 12 artillery regiments, and 6 engineer battalions. The navy has 3 ex-British frigates, 4 ex-Chinese Shanghai TI fast attack craft, 5 large patrol craft, 5 river patrol boats and 1 training ship; 2 more ex-Chinese patrol boats commissioned in Dacca on May 28th, 1982. The air force has 19 combat aircraft. Spares are in short supply and some equipment unserviceable. Paramilitary forces include Bangladesh Rifles (30,000) and armed police reserve (36,000).

Defence Expenditure: The estimated defence budget for 1981/82 was 3,065 million taka.

Army Chief of Staff: Lt.-Gen. HOSSAIN MOHAMMAD.

Chief of Naval Staff: Rear-Admiral MAHBUB ALI.

Chief of Air Staff: Air Vice-Marshal SULTAN MAHMUD.

EDUCATION

In 1972 the Government set up an Education Commission with the aim of effecting radical reforms in the system of education. Reforms are designed to help meet the manpower needs of the country and emphasis is given to primary, technical and vocational education. Some pilot schemes for compulsory attendance in primary schools are in progress and there are plans to introduce universal primary education by 1985. In 1980 the Government launched a programme for the eradication of illiteracy over a five-year period. The National Committee on Curriculum and Syllabus is engaged in reviewing and revising the curriculum for the grades 1–12.

The administration and organization of the educational system in Bangladesh, run by both public and private enterprise, is the responsibility of the Ministry of Education. Education is not compulsory but the Government provides free primary education for five years. Secondary schools and colleges in the private sector (recognized and aided by the Government) vastly outnumber government institutions. In 1976 government secondary schools comprised about 2 per cent of the country's total, whilst only 48 colleges, out of a total of 626, were government-owned. In 1980 there were 40,300 primary schools, 9,000 secondary schools and 717 institutions for further education.

BIBLIOGRAPHY

HISTORY

AHMAD, AZIZ. Studies in Islamic Culture in the Indian Environment (Oxford University Press, 1964).

Islamic Modernism in India and Pakistan 1857–1964 (Oxford University Press, London and New York, 1967).

AHMED, SUFIA. Muslim Community in Bengal 1884–1912 (Dacca, 1974).

ALI, S. M. After the Dark Night. Problems of Sheikh Mujibur Rahman (Delhi, 1973).

AMIMUL ISLAM, A. K. M. A Bangladesh Village (Cambridge, Mass., 1974).

AYOOB, MOHAMMAD, et al. Bangla Desh. A Struggle for Nationhood (Vikas Publications, Delhi, 1971).

BALL, NICOLE. Regional Conflicts and the International System (Brighton, ISOI monographs, 1978).

BHATTACHARJEE, ARUN. Dateline Mujibnagar (Delhi, 1973).

BHATTACHARJEE, G. P. Renaissance and Freedom Movement in Bangladesh (Calcutta, 1973).

BROOMFIELD, J. H. Elite Conflict in a Plural Society (University of California Press, Berkeley, Calif., 1968).

CHOWDHARY, S. R. The Genesis of Bangladesh (Bombay, 1972).

GOPAL, RAM. The Indian Muslims (Calcutta, 1959).

GORDON, LEONARD A. Bengal: the Nationalist Movement (Delhi, 1974).

HABIBULLAH, A. B. M. The Foundation of Muslim Rule in India (Allahabad, 2nd edn., 1961).

HARDY, PETER. The Muslims of British India (Cambridge University Press, 1972).

HUNTER, W. W. The Indian Musalmans (Lahore, reprinted 1964).

KABIR, HUMAYUN. Muslim Politics 1906–42 (Calcutta, 1944).

KARIM, ABDUL. Social History of the Muslims in Bengal (Dacca, 1959).

KHAN, ABDUL MAJED. The Transition in Bengal 1765–1775 (Cambridge University Press, 1969).

KHAN, MUIN-UD-DIN AHMAD. History of the Fara'idi Movement in Bengal 1818–1906 (Karachi, 1965).

MAJUMDAR, R. C., and SARKAR, Sir JADUNATH. (eds.) The History of Bengal (University of Dacca, 2 vols., 1942 and 1948).

MARSHALL, P.J. East Indian Fortunes (Oxford University Press, 1976).

MUHITH, A. M. A. Bangladesh: Emergence of a Nation (Bangladesh Books International, Dacca, 1978).

MUJEEB, M. The Indian Muslims (Allen and Unwin, London, 1967).

MUKHERJEE, RAMKRISHNA. Six Villages of Bengal (Bombay, 1971).

RAHMAN, MUJIBUR. Bangladesh, My Bangladesh (New Delhi and Dacca, 1972).

SARKAR, SUMIT. The Swadeshi Movement in Bengal 1903–1908 (New Delhi, 1973).

SEN GUPTA, JYOTI. History of the Freedom Movement in Bangladesh, 1943–47 (Calcutta, 1974).

SIDDIQUI, KALIM. Conflict, Crisis and War in Pakistan (Macmillan, London, 1972)

SINGH, MALA. (ed.) Khushwant Singh on War and Peace in India, Pakistan and Bangladesh (Delhi, 1976).

ECONOMY

AHMAD, K. U. Breakup of Pakistan: Background and Prospects of Bangladesh (London, 1972).

AHMAD, MOUDUD. Bangladesh: Constitutional Quest for Autonomy (Germany, 1976, later Dacca).

AHMAD, N. A. New Economic Geography of Bangladesh (New Delhi, 1976).

ALAMGIR, MOHIUDDIN. Bangladesh: A Case of Below Poverty Level Equilibrium Trap (Bangladesh Institute of Development Studies, Dacca, 1978).

ARENS, J. and BEWDEN, J. V. Jhagrapur: Poor Peasants and Women in a Village in Bangladesh (Third World Publications, Birmingham, 1977).

CHEN, L. C. Disaster in Bangladesh (Oxford University Press, London, 1973).

CHOWDHURY, ANWARULLAH. A Bangladesh Village (Centre for Social Studies, Dacca, 1978).

FAALAND, J. and PARKINSON, J. R. Bangladesh, The Test Case for Development (C. Hurst and Co., London, 1976).

GREENHIL, B. Boats and Boatmen of Pakistan (David & Charles (Publishers) Ltd., Newton Abbot, 1971).

HAFEEZ, ZAIDI S. M. The Village Culture in Transition: a Study of East Pakistan Rural Society (East-West Center, Honolulu, 1971).

ISLAM, N. Development Planning in Bangladesh; Study in Political Economy (London, 1977).

Development Strategy of Bangladesh (Oxford, Pergamon Press, 1978).

JAHAN, ROUNAQ. Bangladesh Politics: Problems and Issues (Dacca, 1980).

JOHNSON, B. L. C. Bangladesh (London, Heinemann, 1975).

KHAN, AZIZUR RAHMAN. The Economy of Bangladesh (London, 1972).

LOSHAK, DAVID. Pakistan Crisis (Heinemann, London, 1972).

RAHIM, A. M. A. (ed.) Bangladesh Economy Problems and Issues (Dacca, 1976).

Bangladesh Economy: Problems and Policies (Dacca, 1980).

ROBINSON, AUSTIN. Economic Prospects of Bangladesh (Overseas Development Institute, London, 1973).

ROBINSON, E. A. and GRIFFIN, K. The Economic Development of Bangladesh within a Socialist Framework: Proceedings of a Conference held by the I.E.A. at Dacca (1974).

STEPANER, J. F. Bangladesh: Equitable Growth (Oxford, Pergamon Press, 1979).

WILCOX, W. The Emergence of Bangladesh: Problems and Opportunities for a redefined American Policy in South Asia (A Foreign Affairs Study, 1973).

[*See also India and Pakistan.*]

Bhutan

PHYSICAL AND SOCIAL GEOGRAPHY

B. H. Farmer

Bhutan is situated between the high Himalayas and the Ganges Plains, between India and the Xizang A.R. (Tibet) in China. It extends approximately from 26° 45′ to 28° 20′ north latitude, and from 88° 50′ to 92° 05′ east longitude, covering 47,000 square kilometres (18,000 square miles).

PHYSICAL FEATURES

Bhutan's physiography is similar to that of Nepal, the Terai belt being known here, as in nearby Bengal and Assam, as the Duars. From them the outermost ranges rise abruptly; then range piles upon range till, as in Nepal, the snow-capped ranges are reached. Bhutan's highest peak is 7,554 metres (24,784 feet) above sea-level. There are a series of striking transverse gorges, useful as gateways.

CLIMATE

It is difficult to be precise in the absence of reliable data. Darjeeling, at 2,250 metres (7,376 ft.) between Nepal and Bhutan, moves from 4.4°C. (40°F.) (mean January) to 17°C. (62°F.) (mean July); and receives 305 cm. (123 inches) of rainfall in an average year, over 255 cm. (100 inches) between June and September.

SOILS AND NATURAL RESOURCES

There is little reliable scientific information on soils. In the Himalayas natural soils are likely to be thin, skeletal and poor (though improved by terracing), better soils being confined to valley bottoms and the Duars.

Vegetation (and the widespread clearing thereof) shows similarities with eastern Nepal.

Bhutan has not revealed mineral deposits of any importance, though there is a proposal to mine coal in the south-east of the kingdom.

POPULATION AND ETHNIC GROUPS

Bhutan's first census was conducted in 1969 and revealed a total population of 931,514. The population was estimated to have risen to 1,101,053 in mid-1977. Population density was 23 per square kilometre in 1977 but the population is unevenly distributed, being densest along valleys in the Duars.

In Bhutan the Bhutias seem to be the indigenous people, with Tibetans constituting the second major ethnic group. There are also numerous Nepalese settlers in the Duars.

HISTORY

the late Dorothy Woodman

(Revised by the Editor)

Bhutan's high valleys lying between the foothills of Assam and West Bengal to the south and the Tibetan plateau to the north have made this the most isolated of all Himalayan countries and its history the least recorded. The larger monasteries and forts were built in the sixteenth century and there is evidence, mainly in manuscripts found in Tibetan monasteries, of an earlier period. The first King, known as the Dharma Raja, was a lama, Sheptoon La-Pha, and he gave the country some political entity in the seventeenth century. His successor, Doopgein Sheptoon, appointed governors of territories (penlops) and governors of forts (jungpens) to administer the country. The third Dharma Raja, probably influenced by Tibet, conceived the idea of separating temporal and spiritual authority. Henceforth, until the present century, the Dharma Raja fulfilled only a spiritual role and appointed a dewan, later to be known as the Deb Raja, to exercise temporal rule.

The country, divided among a number of warring chieftains, acquired importance in 1771 when the Court of Directors of the East India Company suggested that the exploration of Assam and Bhutan might disclose fresh channels for British trade. The Collectors of Rangpur and Cooch Behar were instructed to ascertain the prospects of Bhutan as a market for British goods and, later, as a through route to Lhasa. A number of missions followed, the most famous of which was led by Bogle. They were rebuffed by the Bhutanese who had their own less organized methods of barter in the Duars. In 1775 the Bengal Government ordered Mr. Purling to secure the possession of all cultivated tracts extending to the foothills and to consider the hills as the frontier. When Assam was occupied in 1826, after the first Anglo-Burmese war, the frontier with Bhutan became a more serious affair. More missions were sent to Bhutan, but they became increasingly unwelcome. The Eden Mission of 1864 was a complete failure which led to the annexation of the Bengal Duars and the Anglo-Bhutanese war. The British had vastly superior military organization and forces and it was only the extremely difficult mountainous terrain which made them decide not to annex Bhutan. By the 1865 Treaty Bhutan agreed to the formal cession of the Duars to British India in return for an annual subsidy to be paid from the revenues of the ceded territory. This comprised an area of rich lands 346 km. in length averaging about 35 km. in width. In 1910 a new Anglo-Bhutanese Treaty was signed which placed all Bhutan's foreign relations under the supervision of the Government of British India. Following the independence of India, that treaty was replaced by the Indo-Bhutan Treaty of Friendship, signed in 1949. Under Article 2 the Government of Bhutan agrees to seek the advice of the Government of India with regard to its foreign relations, but remains free to decide whether or not to accept such advice.

Bhutan maintains close and friendly relations with India, and recognizes the help which India has contributed, particularly towards communications in Bhutan, without which little progress could be made. However, Bhutan has asserted itself as a fully sovereign, independent state. In the 1960s the Bhutanese gained Indian agreement to have their country marked as a separate entity on Indian maps, and in the 1970s Bhutan became a member of the United Nations, the Non-Aligned Movement and other international organizations. In 1981 it joined the IMF.

Bhutan is an absolute monarchy. However, in 1968 the King, Jigme Dorji Wangchuk, initiated an amendment to the Constitution, by which he would voluntarily surrender the absolute powers of the monarchy, in order to establish a new political system described as "Democratic Monarchy". The amendment, making the continuity of any monarch's rule dependent on popular assent, was promulgated in 1969. A vote of confidence in the king was to be taken every three years. However, in 1973 this amendment was abrogated following the death of King Jigme Dorji Wangchuk.

A national assembly, the Tsogdu, was established in 1953. A number of seats are reserved for ecclesiastical bodies. Lamas still play an important role in every part of life, and are as influential as they were in the lives of the Tibetan people in pre-communist days. The system of government is unusual since power is in effect shared between the monarch, the executive and legislative branches and the *Jey Khempo* or monastic head of Bhutan's 6,000 Lamas.

King Jigme Dorji Wangchuk died on July 21st, 1972, at the age of 43, and was succeeded by the 16-year-old Crown Prince Jigme Singye Wangchuk. The new King had been educated in Bhutan and England and when proclaimed Crown Prince had been made Chairman of the Planning Commission. At a press conference in August 1972 King Singye stated that he wished to strengthen friendship with India further, that the Indo-Bhutan Treaty did not need any review and acknowledged the contribution that Indian technical assistance was playing. In 1978 Article 2 of the Treaty was heavily criticized in the Tsogdu, but the King reiterated his belief that the Treaty was not in need of revision. Relations with India remained very strong and in 1978 the respective diplomatic missions were designated embassies. However, during the non-aligned conference and later at the UN General Assembly session, Bhutan decided to vote in opposition to India, in favour of Chinese policy. King Singye stated that the Indo-Bhutan Treaty needed up-dating and that there was no need to consult India on all foreign policies.

In the 1970s Bhutan faced problems with Tibetan refugees in the country. When Chinese authority was established in Tibet in 1959, about 4,000 Tibetans were granted asylum by the Bhutanese, with whom they had close ethnic, cultural and religious links. Bhutan carried out a programme of rehabilitating about 500 refugees at a time in land settlement areas. However, in 1974 it was discovered that many refugees were engaged in spying and subversive activities, and the Bhutan Government decided to disperse the refugees in small groups and to introduce a number of Bhutanese families into each settlement to lessen the security risk. The Dalai Lama of Tibet tried to impose certain conditions on this, but the Government, anxious also not to spoil its relations with China, rejected the conditions and went ahead with the dispersal of refugees. To facilitate their integration into the community, the refugees were offered Bhutanese citizenship, more land and tax and other concessions, and in June 1979 the National Assembly passed a directive giving the refugees until the end of the year to decide whether to take out Bhutanese citizenship or accept repatriation to Tibet. Despite India's announcement that it would not be able to accept any more refugees, by July 1980 most of the Tibetans had chosen Bhutanese citizenship and the rest were to be accepted by India.

ECONOMIC SURVEY

In Bhutan, as in the other Himalayan kingdoms, real or suspected needs of strategy provided a catalyst for economic development, social services and education. The first Five-Year Plan was started in 1961. The aim of this plan and of the second Five-Year Plan (1966–71) was to create an infrastructure for Bhutan's social and economic development. The aim of the third and fourth Five-Year Plans (1971–76 and 1976–81) was to achieve economic self-reliance by developing revenue-gathering projects.

DEVELOPMENT

More than 1,700 km. of roads connect different parts of Bhutan and in addition surfaced roads link important border towns in southern Bhutan with towns in India. However, the shortage of proper all-weather roads is still a major impediment to development. There are two airports: Paro, the chief one, is served by a weekly flight to and from Hashimara, in West Bengal, while an airport at Yangphulla serves the east. A telephone system operates between the main towns and from the capital, Thimphu, to the outside world. Internal administration has extended with the development of communications between high, isolated valleys.

The economy is mainly agrarian, with well over

90 per cent of the population engaged in agriculture and livestock raising. Timber and fruit are exported. Apples have become a major crop and an important export item. Improved irrigation has been the main aim of agricultural development; between the end of the first Plan and 1978 about 34,000 acres of land were brought under irrigation. Under the second and third Five-Year Plans the emphasis was on the development of modern scientific methods of cultivation and livestock rearing, regional specialization, and research and development of new cropping patterns. Under the fourth Five-Year Plan (1976–81), which envisaged a total outlay of Nu 778 million (to be provided mainly by India), priority was to be given to the development of agriculture and animal husbandry. The fifth Five-Year Plan (1981–86), with a proposed total outlay of Nu 2,646 million, envisages a real growth rate of between 8 and 8.5 per cent annually. Bhutan hopes to achieve self-sufficiency in food-grain production and in animal products, and emphasis is being given to the improvement of internal communications.

Recent developments in industry include the establishing of wood-work, bamboo-work and weaving centres. Timber, food preservation and liquor industries have also been set up. Other manufactures include matches, soap, candles, carpets and textiles. The Penden Cement Factory, with a production capacity of 1,000 tons a day, is being installed at Pugli in southern Bhutan and was expected to go into production by 1979. Several minerals of economic importance have been discovered, including beryl, calc-tufa, copper, dolomite, graphite, gypsum, lead, zinc, limestone, marble, mica, pyrite slate and talc. Small mineral-based units have been set up, such as the graphite beneficiation plant at Paro. The Government is encouraging private entrepreneurs to set up small units. Small industrial estates have been established in Phuntsholing, Gaylegphug and Semdrup Jongkhar in southern Bhutan, producing a variety of consumer and industrial raw materials. Their development is aided by the ready availability of power and labour from India. Being under-populated, Bhutan is dependent on foreign labour. To lessen this dependence, many construction activities are to be mechanized.

There is, however, an inadequate development of domestic power resources, although six hydro-electricity stations have been set up and Bhutan expects to export a surplus of energy in the future. The 360 MW. Chukha hydro-electric project, on which construction work began in 1975, is expected to start operation in 1984. The total availability of hydro-electric power in the country is about 4,000 kW., purchased from India. The principal towns in Bhutan have electricity, and the total generating capacity of all stations exceeds 4,000 kW. The Indian Government is financing the establishment of an East-West link and the Indo-Bhutanese microwave link which, when completed, would provide Bhutan with instant communication internally and abroad.

Financial developments since 1961 include the creation of Bhutan's first bank in Phuntsholing in 1968. From 1974 the bank has issued Bhutan's own paper currency, whereas previously Indian rupees were used.

AID

The principal source of aid is India, which provides financial assistance in the form of grants, loans and subsidies, while further aid is provided by UN agencies and the Colombo Plan. Between 1961 and 1975 India granted 620 million rupees to Bhutan, financing 100 per cent of the first and second Five-Year Plans and 90 per cent of the third. India provided Nu 410 million of the Nu 500 million development expenditure in 1978/79 and Nu 170 million to finance the plan for 1979/80. The UN Development Programme gave assistance of U.S. $3.3 million during the third Plan and committed $12.25 million for the plan period 1976–81. During this period the UN Children's Fund was to provide $965,000, together with an additional $2.4 million for education, health and nutrition projects, and the World Food programme made a food commitment of $1,015,000 for school children. In addition, the UN Fund for Population Activities agreed to provide $5 million for the period 1978–82. Out of the proposed outlay of Nu 2,646 million for the fifth Five-Year Plan, Bhutan expects to provide Nu 446 million, with the rest being made up by India and several UN organizations.

Attempts to raise internal resources for development projects are being made. A health contribution and an agricultural tax have been introduced.

TRADE

Nearly all Bhutan's trade is with India and the main exports are timber, minerals and agricultural products. Other exports include liquor from three Bhutanese distilleries and canned fruit products. Timber, liquor and cardamom are also exported to the Middle East and Western Europe. Bhutan also has surpluses of oranges, apples and ginger and, following an agreement with India in 1978, has been exporting these to other countries, notably Bangladesh and Nepal.

After the inauguration of the postal system in 1972 Bhutan's postage stamps became the main source of foreign exchange earnings. Since 1976, however, tourism has become the main source of foreign exchange, bringing in an estimated U.S. $1 million in 1979.

HEALTH SERVICES

Smallpox has been totally eradicated, but tuberculosis and malaria are still widespread. In 1981 Bhutan had 19 hospitals, with a total of 570 beds. There were also 36 dispensaries, 46 basic health units and one hospital based on the indigenous school of medicine. The basic health units provide basic medical services, ante-natal and midwifery services and post-natal care. In 1979 a national immunization programme was launched and has been extended to cover the whole country, with the help of the World Health Organization.

STATISTICAL SURVEY

AREA AND POPULATION

Area	Census Population Nov.-Dec. 1969	Estimated Population mid-1977
47,000 sq. km.* (18,000 sq. miles)	931,514	1,101,053

* 30,000 sq. km. are forested.

Capital: Thimphu (population 8,922 at July 1st, 1977).

Births and Deaths: Average annual birth rate 43.2 per 1,000 in 1970–75, 42.7 per 1,000 in 1975–80; death rate 22.3 per 1,000 in 1970–75, 20.6 per 1,000 in 1975–80 (UN estimates).

Life expectancy: 46.1 years (1977).

ECONOMICALLY ACTIVE POPULATION

(ILO estimates, '000 persons at mid-year)

	1960			1970		
	Males	Females	Total	Males	Females	Total
Agriculture, etc.	249	168	417	294	197	491
Industry	7	1	8	8	2	10
Services	11	2	13	16	3	19
Total	267	171	438	318	202	520

Source: ILO, *Labour Force Estimates and Projections, 1950–2000.*

Mid-1978 (estimates in '000): Agriculture, etc. 564; Total 603.
Mid-1979 (estimates in '000): Agriculture, etc. 575; Total 615.
Mid-1980 (estimates in '000): Agriculture, etc. 586; Total 627.

Source: FAO, *Production Yearbook.*

AGRICULTURE

PRINCIPAL CROPS

(FAO estimates, '000 metric tons)

	1978	1979	1980
Rice (paddy)	290	295	300
Wheat	63	64	65
Maize	58	59	60
Barley	8	9	10
Buckwheat	5	n.a.	n.a.
Millet	5	5	5
Potatoes	40	42	43
Other roots and tubers	5	5	5
Pulses	2	2	2
Tobacco	1	1	1
Jute	6	6	6

Source: FAO, *Production Yearbook.*

LIVESTOCK

(FAO estimates, '000 head)

	1978	1979	1980
Cattle	205	207	210
Pigs	58	59	60
Sheep	41	41	42
Goats	21	21	22
Buffaloes	4	5	5
Horses	20	20	20
Asses	17	17	17
Mules	8	8	8
Poultry	105	107	109

Source: FAO, *Production Yearbook.*

Cows' Milk: 13,000 metric tons per year in 1979–80 (FAO estimate).

FINANCE

Bhutanese and Indian currency are both legal tender.
Bhutanese currency: 100 chetrums (Ch) = 1 ngultrum (Nu).
Coins: 5, 10, 25, 50 chetrums, 1 ngultrum.
Notes: 1, 5, 10 and 100 ngultrums.
Indian currency: 100 paisa = 1 rupee.
Coins: 1, 2, 3, 5, 10, 20, 25 and 50 paisa; 1 rupee.
Notes: 1, 2, 5, 10, 20, 50, 100, 1,000, 5,000 and 10,000 rupees.
Exchange rates (June 1982): £1 sterling = 16.55 ngultrums or rupees; U.S. $1 = 9.555 ngultrums or rupees;
100 ngultrums or Indian rupees = £6.042 = $10.465.

Note: Since April 1974 Bhutan has issued its own currency, the ngultrum, which is at par with the Indian rupee and circulates with it inside the country. From December 1971 to September 1975 India maintained an exchange rate against sterling at a mid-point of £1 = 18.9677 rupees. Since September 1975 the rupee has been pegged to a "basket" of currencies of India's principal trading partners. The average exchange rates (rupees per U.S. dollar) were: 8.102 in 1974; 8.376 in 1975; 8.960 in 1976; 8.739 in 1977; 8.193 in 1978; 8.126 in 1979; 7.863 in 1980; 8.659 in 1981.

BUDGET
(million ngultrums)

Revenue	1977/78
Indirect taxes:	
Customs duties	0.07
Excise duties	8.24
Sales tax	3.31
Direct taxes:	
Income tax	1.03
Registration and licence fees	1.61
Land revenue	1.16
Other taxes	4.40
Other:	
Forestry	7.76
Miscellaneous	54.87
Total	82.45
Source of finance for excess of expenditure over revenue	139.95
Grand Total	222.40

Expenditure	1977/78
Non-development expenditure:	
Defence	n.a.
General	6.20
General administration	21.42
Others	50.96
Total	78.58
Development expenditure:	
Agriculture	35.30
Industries, forests and mining	17.36
Transport, communications	7.23
Education	25.62
Planning secretariat	5.93
Health	9.94
Power	4.01
Public works	31.38
Others	7.05
Total	143.82
Grand Total	222.40

FOURTH FIVE-YEAR PLAN
(1976–81)
Estimated expenditure
(million ngultrums)

Agriculture	184.24
Animal husbandry	43.06
Education (incl. technical education)	130.08
Power	40.50
Health	48.37
Development Headquarters	34.30
Information and Press	9.71
Public Works Department	118.21
Industries	30.00
Forests	81.98
Food Corporation of Bhutan	10.00
Broadcasting, wireless, telephone and post and telegraphs	54.25
Tourism	12.50
Total	797.20

Source: The Colombo Plan, Twenty-second annual report.

ROAD TRAFFIC

In 1979 there were 2,179 vehicles, of which 1,432 were private cars and 747 were heavy vehicles.

Source: Directorate of Motor Vehicles.

EDUCATION
(1979)

Primary schools	108
Junior high schools	19
Central schools	6
Teachers' training institutes	2
Schools for Buddhist studies	2
Junior college	1
Technical schools	2
Total pupils	28,548
Total teachers	1,210

Source (unless otherwise stated): Royal Government of Bhutan.

THE GOVERNMENT

Head of State: His Majesty Druk Gyalpo JIGME SINGYE WANGCHUK, succeeded to the Throne in July 1972.

Royal Advisory Council: Established 1965 and composed of nine members, one representing H.M. the King, two representing religious bodies and six regional representatives of the people.

COUNCIL OF MINISTERS

(June 1982)

Representative of His Majesty in the Ministry of Finance: H.R.H. Princess SONAM CHHODEN WANGCHUK.

Representative of His Majesty in the Ministry of Development: H.R.H. Princess DECHEN WANGMO WANGCHUK.

Minister of Trade, Industry and Forests: H.R.H. NAMGYEL WANGCHUK.

Home Minister: LYONPO TAMJI JAGAR.

Minister of Foreign Affairs: LYONPO DAWA TSERING.

Minister of Communications and Tourism: LYNPO SANGYE PENJOR.

LEGISLATURE

TSOGDU

A National Assembly (*Tsogdu*) was established in 1953. The Assembly has a three-year term and meets twice yearly in spring and autumn. There are 150 members, of whom 101 are directly elected by the public. Ten seats are reserved for religious bodies and the remainder are occupied by officials, the ministers and members of the Royal Advisory Council. The Assembly enacts laws, advises on constitutional and political matters and debates all important issues. Both the Royal Advisory Council and the Council of Ministers are responsible to it. In 1979 the Assembly accepted its first woman member.

LOCAL ADMINISTRATION

There are 18 districts, each headed by a Dzongda (in charge of administration and law and order) and a Thrimpon (in charge of judicial matters). Land revenue is collected by the village headmen and remitted to the Dzongda. Under the proposed Fifth Five-Year Plan (1982–86), with the introduction of decentralization, there will be 17 districts, as Punakha and Thimphu will be merged as one district.

POLITICAL PARTIES

There are no political parties in Bhutan.

DIPLOMATIC REPRESENTATION

EMBASSIES ACCREDITED TO BHUTAN

Bangladesh: Thorilam, Thimphu; *Ambassador:* MOHIUDDIN AHMED JAIGIRDAR.

India: Lungtenzampa, Thimphu; *Ambassador:* SALMAN HAIDAR.

JUDICIAL SYSTEM

Bhutan has a Civil and a Criminal Code.

High Court: Established 1968 to review appeals from Lower Courts; 6 Judges.

Appeal Court: The Supreme Court of Appeal is H.M. the King.

Magistrates Courts: All cases are heard by the Thrimpon (District Magistrates). Appeals are made to the High Court.

RELIGION

The State religion is Mahayana Buddhism. Buddhism was introduced into Bhutan in the eighth century A.D. by the Indian saint Padma Sambhava, known in Bhutan as Guru Rimpoche. In the thirteenth century Phajo Dugom Shigpo made the Drukpa school of Kagyupa Buddhism dominant in Bhutan and this sect is still supported by the dominant race in Bhutan, the Bhutias. Monasteries are numerous. The chief monastery is situated at Tashichhodzong and contains 2,000 Lamas. There are 6,000 state-supported Lamas in the kingdom, with the *Jey Khempo* as their head.

THE PRESS

Druk Losel: Department of Information, Thimphu; f. 1979; quarterly; in English, Dzongkha and Nepali; Editor RIGZIN DORJI; combined circ. 3,000.

Kuensel: Department of Information, Thimphu; f. 1965; weekly government bulletin; in English, Dzongkha and Nepali; Editor-in-Chief RIGZIN DORJI; Sub-editors G. S. UPADHYA (Nepali), Miss NIMA OM (English, GOEMPO DORJI (Dzongkha); combined circ. 5,000.

RADIO

Radio National Youth Association of Bhutan (NYAB): P.O.B. 1, Thimpu; short-wave radio station broadcasting in Dzongkha, Nepali, Sharchop and English; Sec. LOUISE DORJI.

There are 27 radio stations in Bhutan. Eight of them are for transmitting flood warning data.

In 1978 there were estimated to be about 6,500 radio receivers.

FINANCE

(cap.=capital; auth.=authorized; p.u.=paid up; dep.=deposits; m.=million; brs.=branches)

BANKING

Bank of Bhutan: Phuntsholing; f. 1968; 25 per cent shares held by State Bank of India; auth. cap. Nu 5m. and cap. p.u. Nu 2.5m. (in Indian rupees and Bhutanese currency in fully paid shares of Nu 1,000 each), dep. Nu 154.6m. (Dec. 1980); Dirs. nominated by the Bhutan Govt.: Dasho (Dr.) DORJI TSHERING (Chair.), Dasho LAM PENJOR, Dasho PEMA WANGCHUK, Dasho CHENKYAP DORJI, YESHEY ZIMBA, DORJI WANGDI; Dirs. nominated by the State Bank of India: B. K. BOSE, K. S. NANJAPPAN; Man. Dir. M. S. VERMA; 14 brs.

INSURANCE

Royal Insurance Corporation of Bhutan: P.O.B. 77, Phuntsholing; f. 1975; cap. Nu 12m.; Chair. H.R.H. ASHI SONAM CHHODEN WANGCHUK; Man. Dir. Dasho U. DORJI; Tech. Dir. D. DAS GUPTA; Dir. D. WANGDI.

TRADE AND INDUSTRY

Food Corporation of Bhutan (FCB): f. 1974; activities include retailing, marketing, storage, import and export of agricultural products; operates a rural finance scheme, receiving loans from the Bank of Bhutan and the Royal Insurance Corporation, to assist farmers.

National Commission for Trade and Industry: regulates the type, quality and quantity of industrial projects to be set up in Bhutan; Chair. H.M. Druk Gyalpo JIGME SINGYE WANGCHUK.

TRANSPORT

ROADS AND TRACKS

In 1978 there were 1,775 km. of roads (most of which are surfaced). In addition, surfaced roads link the important border towns of Phuntsholing, Gaylephug, Sarbhang and Samdrup Jongkhar in southern Bhutan to towns in West Bengal and Assam in India. Yaks, ponies and mules are still the chief means of transport on the rough mountain tracks.

State Transport Department (*Bhutan Government Transport Corporation*): Phuntsholing; f. 1962; operates a fleet of 90 buses (1977).

Lorries for transporting goods are operated by the private sector.

CIVIL AVIATION

The main airport is at Paro; an airport at Yangphulla serves the east of the country. There are numerous helicopter landing pads. Druk Airways is expected to become operational with the help of Indian Airlines by 1982 and will link Paro with Calcutta.

TOURISM

Bhutan Travel Agency: P.O. Thimphu; government-run.

The Kingdom was opened to tourism in the autumn of 1974 and the tourist seasons are from March to June and September to December. Tourists travel in organized package or trekking tours, or individually, accompanied by guides. Hotels have been constructed by the Department of Tourism at Phuntsholing, Paro and Thimphu. There are also many small privately run hotels.

DEFENCE

The strength of The Royal Bhutan Army, which is under the direct command of the King, is classified information. As well as the regular standing army Bhutan has a large militia. Army training facilities are provided by an Indian Military Training Team. No reference is made in the Indo-Bhutan Treaty to any aid by India for the defence of Bhutan, but when the Prime Minister of India visited Bhutan in November 1958 he declared that any act of aggression against Bhutan would be regarded as an act of aggression against India.

Military Chief-of-Staff: Maj.-Gen. LAM DORJI.

EDUCATION

Free education is provided by the Government, including degree courses. Some of the schools are co-educational and run along the lines of an American private school but using a British syllabus. In 1981 there were over 150 schools, including six central schools, one junior college (to be upgraded to a three- year degree college), two technical schools, one Buddhist grammar school, one painting and one sculpture school, two teacher-training schools and a number of monastic schools. There are no mission or private schools, all schools in Bhutan being subsidized by the Government. In addition to the schools and training institutes in Bhutan, regular courses are organized by different Government departments in agriculture, health, secretarial work, etc. A number of students are receiving higher education and training in various technical fields in India, Australia, Japan, New Zealand, Singapore, the U.K., Switzerland, Austria and the U.S.A. There are five main linguistic groups in Bhutan but Dzongkha, spoken in western Bhutan, has been designated the official language. The Dzongkha textbook section of the Department of Education has produced a complete set of textbooks for students up to school-leaving age. The Government encourages students from one part of the country to seek admission in schools and educational institutions in other regions, as part of its policy to increase integration of people throughout the country. Schools have been instructed to take senior students on educational tours to the various regions.

INDO-BHUTAN TREATY

The Treaty of Friendship with India was signed on August 8th, 1949.

Treaty of Friendship between the Government of India and the Government of Bhutan.

***Article* 1 There shall be perpetual peace and friendship between the Government of India and the Government of Bhutan.**

***Article* 2 The Government of India undertakes to exercise no interference in the internal administration of Bhutan. On its part the Government of Bhutan agrees to be guided by the advice of the Government of India in regard to its external relations.**

***Article* 3 In place of the compensation granted to the Government of Bhutan under Article 4 of the Treaty of Sinchula and enhanced by the treaty of the eighth day of January 1910 and the temporary subsidy of Rupees one lakh per annum granted in 1942, the Government of India agrees to make an annual payment of Rupees five lakhs to the Government of Bhutan. And it is further hereby agreed that the said annual payment shall be made on the tenth day of January every year, the first payment being made on the tenth day of January 1950. This payment shall continue so long as this treaty remains a force and its terms are duly observed.**

***Article* 4 Further to make the friendship existing and continuing between the said governments, the Government of India shall, within one year from the date of signature of this treaty, return to the Government of Bhutan about thirty-two square miles of territory in the area known as Dewangiri. The Government of India shall appoint a**

competent officer or officers to mark out the area so returned to the Government of Bhutan.

Article 5 There shall, as heretofore, be free trade and commerce between the Government of India and the Government of Bhutan; and the Government of India agrees to grant to the Government of Bhutan every facility for the carriage, by land and water, of its produce throughout the territory of the Government of India, including the right to use such forest roads as may be specified by mutual agreement from time to time.

Article 6 The Government of India agrees that the Government of Bhutan shall be free to import with the assistance and approval of the Government of India, from or through India into Bhutan, whatever arms, ammunition, machinery, warlike materials or stores may be required or desired for the strength and welfare of Bhutan and that this arrangement shall hold good for all time as long as the Government of India is satisfied that the intentions of the Government of Bhutan are friendly and that there is no danger to the Government of India from such importations. The Government of Bhutan, on the other hand, agrees that there shall be no export of such arms, ammunition, etc., across the frontier of Bhutan either by the Government of Bhutan or by private individuals.

Article 7 The Government of India and the Government of Bhutan agree that Bhutanese subjects residing in Indian territories shall have equal justice with Indian subjects and that Indian subjects residing in Bhutan shall have equal justice with the subjects of the Government of Bhutan.

Article 8 (1) The Government of India shall, on demand being duly made by the Government of Bhutan, take proceedings in accordance with the provisions of Indian Extradition Act, 1903 (of which a copy shall be furnished to the Government of Bhutan), for the surrender of all Bhutanese subjects accused of any of the crimes specified in the first schedule of the said Act who may take refuge in Indian territory.

(2) The Government of Bhutan shall, on requisition being duly made by the Government of India, or by any officer authorized by the Government of India in this behalf, surrender any Indian subjects, or subjects of a foreign power, whose extradition may be required in pursuance of any agreement or arrangements made by the Government of India with the said power, accused of any of the crimes specified in the first schedule of Act XV of 1903, who may take refuge in the territory under the jurisdiction of the Government of Bhutan and also any Bhutanese subjects who, after committing any of the crimes referred to in Indian territory shall flee into Bhutan, on such evidence of their guilt being produced as that satisfy the local court of the district in which the offence may have been committed.

Article 9 Any differences and disputes arising in the application or interpretation of this treaty shall in the first instance be settled by negotiation. If within three months of the start of negotiations no settlement is arrived at, then the matter shall be referred to the Arbitration of three arbitrators, who shall be nationals of either India or Bhutan, chosen in the following manner:

(i) one person nominated by the Government of India;
(ii) one person nominated by the Government of Bhutan;
(iii) a Judge of the Federal court or of a High Court of India, to be chosen by the Government of Bhutan, who shall be Chairman.

The judgment of this tribunal shall be final and executed without delay by either party.

Article 10 This treaty shall continue in force in perpetuity unless terminated or modified by mutual consent.

BIBLIOGRAPHY

CHAKRAVARTI, P. C. India's China Policy (Indiana University Press, Bloomington, 1962).

GORDON, EUGENE. Nepal, Sikkim and Bhutan (Oak Tree Press, London, 1972).

HAAB, ARMIN, and VELLIS, NINON. Bhutan-Fürstenstaat am Götterthron (Mohn. Gütersloh, 1961).

HERMANNS, Father MATTHIAS. The Indo-Tibetans (Fernandes, Bombay, 1954).

KARAN, P. P. Bhutan: A Physical and Cultural Geography (University of Kentucky Press, Lexington, 1967).

KARAN, P. P., and JENKINS, W. M. The Himalayan Kingdoms: Bhutan, Sikkim and Nepal (Van Nostrand, Princeton, 1963).

KUHN, DELIA, and KUHN, FERDINAND. Borderlands (Knopf, New York, 1962).

LAMB, ALISTAIR. The China-India Border: The Origins of the Disputed Boundaries (Chatham House Essays, Oxford University Press, London, 1946).

Asian Frontiers: Studies in a Continuing Problem (Pall Mall Press, London, 1968).

LEIFER, M. Himalaya: Mountains of Destiny (Galley Press, London, 1962).

MEHRA, PARSHOTAM. The Younghusband Expedition. An Interpretation (Asia Publishing House, 1968).

NEBESKY-WOJKOWITZ, RENE VON. Where the Mountains are Gods (Weidenfeld and Nicolson, London, 1956).

PALLIS, MARCO. The Way and the Mountains (Owen, London, 1961).

ROSE, LEO E. The Politics of Bhutan (Cornell University Press, Ithaca, N.Y., 1977).

RUSTOMJI, N. K. Enchanted Frontiers: Sikkim, Bhutan and India's North-Eastern borderlands (Oxford University Press, London, 1970).

The Dragon Kingdom in Crisis (Oxford University Press, New Delhi, 1978).

SINGH, NAGENDRA. Bhutan, a Kingdom in the Himalayas (Thomson Press, New Delhi, 1980).

SNELLGROVE, DAVID L. Himalayan Pilgrimage (Bruno Cassirer, Oxford, 1961).

The Sino-Indian Boundary Question (Foreign Language Press, Beijing, 1962).

WHITE, CLAUDE. Sikkim and Bhutan: Twenty-One Years on the North-East Frontier, 1887–1908 (Arnold, London, 1909).

WOODMAN, DOROTHY. Himalayan Frontiers: a political review of British, Chinese, Indian and Russian rivalries (Barrie and Jenkins, London, 1969).

Brunei

PHYSICAL AND SOCIAL GEOGRAPHY

C. A. Fisher

(Revised for this edition by HARVEY DEMAINE)

Brunei covers 5,765 square kilometres (2,226 square miles) facing the South China Sea along the coast of northern Kalimantan (Borneo). On its landward side it is both surrounded and split into two separate units by Sarawak, part of Malaysia.

PHYSICAL FEATURES AND CLIMATE

The greater part of Brunei's small territory consists of a low coastal plain, and only on its southern margins does it attain heights of over 300 metres (1,000 feet). Situated as it is, only 4°–5° N. of the equator, Brunei has a consistently hot and humid climate, with mean monthly temperatures around 27°C. (80°F.) and a heavy rainfall of over 250 cm. (100 inches), well distributed throughout the year. Except for those areas which have been cleared for permanent cultivation in the coastal zone, the country is covered by dense equatorial forest, though this has deteriorated in places as a result of shifting cultivation.

MINERALS

Apart from agricultural land adequate to feed its population and to produce a minute export of rubber, Brunei's natural resources consist exclusively of petroleum and natural gas. Production from the old Seria oilfield, close to the Sarawak border, is now of minor significance but the off-shore fields of Fairley, South-West Ampa and, in particular, Champion (all discovered since 1964), offer significant reserves. Petroleum reserves are expected to last some 20 years at present rates of production (about 125,000 barrels per day), but the real future lies in natural gas, of which reserves are put at 218,000 million cubic metres. These are currently being exploited at the rate of almost 9,000 million cubic metres per year under long-term contracts with Japan.

POPULATION

The estimated population at mid-1982 was 228,500, of whom about 55 per cent were Brunei Malays and 25 per cent Chinese, mainly in Bandar Seri Begawan (formerly Brunei Town) and Seria. Bandar Seri Begawan, the capital, which occupies an impressive site overlooking the large natural inlet of Brunei Bay, had an estimated population of 75,000 in 1976.

HISTORY

John Bastin

(Revised by T. M. BURLEY since 1975)

Brunei has long been a centre of human settlement although little is known about its early history. Chinese coins of the eighth century A.D. have been found at Kota Batu, 3 km. from Bandar Seri Begawan, but these may have been introduced at a later period when Chinese trade with western Borneo was more extensively developed. Brunei is listed among the tributary states of the Hindu-Javanese empire of Majapahit in the second half of the fourteenth century but it soon afterwards became an independent sultanate. As the Brunei royal chronicles give only the names of rulers and not specific dates (the present ruler, Sultan Hassanal Bolkiah, is the twenty-ninth in the list), the date of the origin of the sultanate is uncertain. However, the Malay-Arabic inscription of the oldest tombstone at Brunei carries the equivalent Hijra date of A.D. 1432 so that by then, at least, Islam was already well established.

The first rulers of Brunei may not have been Malays, but Bisayas or Muruts, the designation *Malay* being applied to the peoples of western Borneo as they became Muslims. Islam only marginally affected the Kayans and Ibans but it made considerable progress among such peoples as the Melanaus whose chiefs were frequently replaced by Brunei princelings who married Melanau women. Together with the spread of Islam went a corresponding increase in Brunei's political power. By the sixteenth century the sultanate embraced most of the coastal regions of present-day Sarawak and Sabah. Tribute from the imperial domains was collected by Malays (and Arabs) settled at the mouths of the rivers.

The prosperity of the sultanate depended upon trade, a large part of which was carried on with Chinese merchants from the southern ports of China. In exchange for hornbill-ivory, bezoar stones, woods and edible birds' nests, the Chinese brought silks, metals, stoneware and fine porcelains. The fact that large quantities of Tang, Song and Ming porcelain have been found attests to the extent and importance of the trade with China which continued until the late eighteenth century. Early European commercial contacts with Brunei, on the other hand, were minimal, and it was not until the arrival of James Brooke, an English adventurer, in Sarawak that Brunei was forced to adjust to the Western presence in South-East Asia.

The adjustment was often painful. In 1842, Sultan Omar Ali Saifuddin was obliged to appoint Brooke as Rajah of Sarawak, and four years later to cede the island of Labuan to the United Kingdom. Thereafter the sultanate was under growing pressure from the Brooke regime in the south and from American and European speculators in Sabah to cede more territory.

The coast beyond Bintulu was in Brooke's hands by the 1860s, and during the following twenty-odd years the Sarawak frontier was advanced to include the Baram, Trusan and Limbang Rivers. During the same period (1877–78) the Brunei and Sulu rulers ceded 72,500 sq. km. of Sabah, from Gaya Bay to the Sibuco River, to agents of the embryo British North Borneo Company, formed in 1881. Sandwiched between the Company in the north and the Brooke state in the south, the formerly powerful sultanate of Brunei was reduced in size to a little more than 5,500 sq. km., its Belait and Tutong districts being divided from Temburong by the lands of Sarawak. In 1888, the U.K. formally extended its protection over the sultanate, and in 1906 a British Resident (later High Commissioner) was appointed to the court of the ruler to advise on all matters of government except those relating to Islam and Malay custom.

Administrative and Political Structure

Brunei was occupied by Japan from 1941 to 1945. In 1948 the Governor of Sarawak was appointed High Commissioner for Brunei. An agreement was concluded between the British Government and the Sultan in September 1959, by which the U.K. retained responsibility for Brunei's defence and foreign relations. The agreement also provided for the appointment of a resident High Commissioner in Brunei.

Five councils were established to govern the state: the Privy Council, presided over by the Sultan and concerned with amendments to the constitution and appointments to Malay customary posts; the executive Council of Ministers, also presided over by the Sultan and composed of the British High Commissioner, four unofficial members appointed by the Legislative Council, and six *ex officio* members; the Legislative Council, possessing general legislative powers, including finance, and comprised of six *ex officio* members, ten official and five unofficial members; the Religious Council, advising the Sultan on all matters relating to Islam; and a Council of Succession. At local government level four District Councils, having a majority of members elected by universal suffrage, were established.

Moves towards introducing more popular government were halted by a revolt in December 1962, led by A. M. Azahari and the Brunei People's Party, which was sparked off by the prospect of Brunei joining the new federation of Malaysia. A state of emergency was declared, the disorders were suppressed and the Brunei People's Party was banned. Azahari went into exile in Malaya. In 1963 the Sultan decided against joining the proposed Malaysian federation, but the state of emergency remained in force and he continued to rule by decree.

The Brunei People's Independence Front has been vocal in demanding constitutional reform by the implementation of a full ministerial system and an elective Legislative Council as proposed in the White Paper of 1964; but the failure of the Front to win a majority of seats in the District Council elections in May 1968 suggested that there was no general dissatisfaction with the existing arrangements. In these elections the Independence Front, the only party to participate, lost in 15 of the 25 wards in which it was opposed by "royalist" independents, and finished with only 24 of the total of 55 District Council seats. The independents refused to exert any pressure on Sultan Hassanal Bolkiah preparatory to his talks with the British Government in London late in 1968 over the future of Brunei. In view of the partial withdrawal of British forces "East of Suez" the United Kingdom's commitments under the 1959 agreement were reduced.

Under a new treaty signed on November 23rd, 1971, and presented to Parliament in April 1972, the United Kingdom, though continuing to assume responsibility for external affairs, was to advise only on defence while leaving the Sultan in control of all internal matters. A separate agreement provided for the stationing of a battalion of British Gurkhas in Brunei.

Recent Trends

During the early 1970s Brunei's energies were focused upon developing its natural gas resources and spending its oil revenues. Despite the general lack of political discontent and the wide-ranging welfare state benefits made possible by oil and gas revenues, there is some resentment of the continuing large numbers of expatriates employed in key government positions and of the slow progress of "localization" of the Royal Brunei Regiment. The presence of the battalion of British Gurkhas was another irritant.

Political activity was muted until November 1975, when a mass demonstration by government supporters took place at Seria to protest at "outside interference" (i.e. Malaysian) and at attempts to revive the Brunei People's Party. However, Malaysia did not withdraw its sponsorship of a 1976 UN resolution calling on Brunei to hold elections in the near future, and this was adopted by the UN in November 1977. The resolution, which also called for the abolition of restrictions on political parties and the return of political exiles, received 117 votes in favour and none against. The United Kingdom was one of 15 nations that abstained.

The Brunei Government remained reluctant to review the terms of its agreement with the United Kingdom and negotiations proceeded only when assurances were received from Malaysia and Indonesia that they would respect the independence of Brunei. The agreement that resulted was signed in 1979. It envisaged that the state would become fully independent from the United Kingdom in 1983. A visit to Brunei, the first since 1968, by the Malaysian Prime Minister, Datuk Hussein bin Onn, in 1979 symbolized the changed attitude of Malaysia towards Brunei that now manifests itself in increasingly close social and cultural links. In financial and economic matters, however, Brunei's closest ties in the region remain with Singapore. It is expected that Brunei will become a member of ASEAN after independence. Then, Brunei's Chinese population—which numbers some 60,000 and has become the backbone of the economy—may become stateless and leave for Singapore as a result.

ECONOMIC SURVEY

T. M. Burley

Brunei possesses an urban and industrial economy based on the exploitation of rich petroleum and gas resources. According to World Bank estimates, Brunei's Gross National Product in 1979 was U.S. $2,240 million, equal to U.S. $10,680 per person. Between 1970 and 1976, estimated G.N.P. per head increased at an average annual rate of 16 per cent, mainly owing to the sharp increases in petroleum prices; in the following three years it jumped a further 60 per cent. Of Brunei's population (estimated to be 228,500 at mid-1982), about 30 per cent are foreign nationals, mostly Malaysians. About 30 per cent of the population is in employment, half being government and public service workers.

The small size of the indigenous work force and its preference for tertiary employment are major constraints to development. Infrastructural and industrial projects have to rely on foreign workers and incentives have to be chosen with care to avoid an excess of foreign nationals. It is hoped that industry will be attracted to Brunei by the 1975 Investment Incentives Act. This exempts new investments from the 30 per cent tax charged on companies for periods of two to eight years depending on the size of the investment. Exemption from import duties on plans and machinery may also be given. A scheme for financing small and medium-sized businesses was started in 1977.

The 1980–84 Development Plan projects expenditure at B$1,700 million, to be compared with the B$760 million spent on the previous (1975–79) Plan. The objectives of the 1980–84 Plan are similar to those of the 1975–79 Plan. This, it is claimed, achieved considerable improvements in health, education, communications and agriculture. Among new projects will be improvements to road, sea and air communications, more schools, hospitals and mosques, and an extension of public utilities, including water and electricity supplies, radio, television, telecommunications and the postal service. The primary sector will be the subject of research to find new sources of income when, as expected, oil and gas production declines in the 1990s.

Agriculture

Brunei is dependent on imports for about 80 per cent of its food requirements, including the staple cereal, rice. Only 10 per cent of the land area is cultivated but much potential agricultural land lies undeveloped and is currently under evaluation by ULG Consultants of the United Kingdom. Concern has been expressed over indiscriminate logging in the coastal forests. Rice production meets only 25 per cent of requirements. Rice, along with other cereals, livestock and livestock feeds, is a priority area for development. Attention is also being given to the production of coffee, coconuts, cocoa, sugar and tobacco and to increasing local production of fruits, spices and vegetables. Rubber, once the main source of Brunei's foreign earnings, is now of minor importance.

The main protein ingredient in the Brunei diet is fish. With the aid of the United Kingdom's White Fish Authority, surveys are being undertaken of off-shore waters with a view to developing deep-sea fishing. In 1978 two companies were operating poultry farms; these supplement a previously established pig farm. The Mitsubishi Corporation is investing B$4 million in the first phase of a cattle-breeding project. Its aim is to make Brunei self-sufficient in livestock by 1984 through a 350-strong herd of bulls and breeding heifers.

Petroleum and natural gas

Brunei is one of the most important petroleum and gas producers in the Commonwealth: government revenues from oil and gas in 1981 are estimated at B$7,560 million. Early in 1975 the Government took a controlling interest in the Brunei Shell Petroleum Company, the only oil company operating in the country. Production in 1978 averaged 240,210 barrels per day (b.p.d.), mainly from off-shore fields. In 1979 output averaged 254,154 b.p.d., of which 214,721 b.p.d. came from off-shore fields; in 1980 output stayed in the region of 230,000 to 240,000 b.p.d. Since then, with the current world oil glut and a desire to ration known reserves, output has been cut to 176,000 b.p.d. in 1981 and to around 160,000 b.p.d. in 1982. Some of the oil is refined locally but the bulk of it is pumped to Lutong and Miri in Sarawak. Following completion of Shell's blending plant (designed ultimately to blend all local requirements of premium petrol), a five-fold increase in capacity (to 10,000 b.p.d.) is planned for the Seria refinery.

Gross production of natural gas rose from 4,500 million cubic metres in 1972 to 10,511 million cubic metres in 1977, when exports of natural gas earned B$1,121.3 million. In 1978 and 1979 output was slightly lower, but the value of gas exports rose to B$1,320.8 million in 1978 and to B$1,480.4 million in 1979. In 1979, 12.6 million cubic metres of liquefied natural gas (LNG) was exported, comprising 168 cargoes of 75,000 cubic metres each. The natural gas liquefaction plant at Lumut, the largest in the world, cost U.S. $120 million and is designed to produce at its full capacity about 6 million tons of liquid gas a year. In 1981 it operated at over 80 per cent of capacity. A contract has been signed to supply Japan with LNG to the value of B$6,000 million over a 20-year period.

Infrastructure

Links with the outside world were greatly improved in 1974 with the establishment of the Royal Brunei Airlines. From an international standard airport at Bandar Seri Begawan, it operates to Bangkok, Hong

Kong, Singapore, Manila, Kuching and Kota Kinabalu. The opening of the $32 million port at Muara, able to handle 150,000 d.w.t. vessels, has prompted plans for a national shipping line. The volume of imports through Muara exceeded 400,000 tons for the first time in 1979. Royal Brunei Airlines is now carrying over 100,000 passengers per year. In 1979 there were 52,113 registered motor vehicles. The number of telephones has been more than doubled under a telecommunications scheme which included the construction of the first of two earth satellite stations and a U.S. $23 million central telephone exchange. Current projects under construction or recently completed include a shopping centre incorporating Brunei's first department store, a 500-bed hospital and a coastal road 60 km. (37 miles) long between Tutong and Muara. Brunei's first international standard hotel, the Sheraton Utama, was opened in 1981, and at least two more hotels should be ready in time for independence. There are plans for a second shopping centre, a major bridge over the Brunei River and a road link to Sarawak, to be achieved by bridging the Lawas river in Sarawak and extending the road to Temburong in Brunei. There is also to be a new palace for the Sultan.

Foreign trade

Brunei has a healthy balance of trade due to the rising value of oil and gas exports since 1972. The trade surplus in the first half of 1980 was a record B$4,290 million, exactly double the 1979 surplus. Exports totalled B$4,840 million, up by 87.4 per cent; imports rose by 25 per cent to B$550 million. For 1980 as a whole, the trade surplus was B$8,620 million, with exports of B$9,853 million and imports of B$1,231 million. Brunei's major export markets are Japan (which accounted for 84 per cent of Brunei's total export earnings in 1979), the U.S.A., Singapore, Taiwan and Sarawak. Imports come chiefly from Japan, Singapore, the U.S.A. and the United Kingdom. Data for the first half of 1980 indicates that 24.4 per cent of imports came from Japan, which also took 72.5 per cent of exports.

Food and manufactured goods account for one half of Brunei's imports, machinery and transport equipment make up a further third. Rice is the main food import, with Thailand the main source, supplying between 20,000 and 25,000 tons a year.

Finance

Government revenues are managed by local commercial banks. In 1980, however, the Legislative Council called for the training of local staff with a view to establishing a central bank. The largest banking network is operated by the National Bank of Brunei, whose nine branches represent 30 per cent of all banking outlets. Its total assets in 1979 were B$632.7 million. Government revenue in 1978 totalled B$1,923 million, compared with $975 million in 1974, and in 1979 was provisionally estimated at $1,882 million.

There is no personal income tax in Brunei and companies pay a flat 30 per cent tax on profits. The bulk of government revenue is derived from taxes paid by the four Shell companies: Brunei Shell Petroleum, which produces and sells oil, and produces gas which it transports by pipeline to sell to Brunei LNG; Brunei LNG, which produces liquefied natural gas and sells it to Brunei Coldgas; Brunei Coldgas, a two-man trading company which transports the LNG and sells it to Japan. The fourth company is Brunei Shell Marketing, which distributes and sells Shell products in Brunei. The effect of the rise in oil prices helped Brunei's oil revenue to jump to $1,970 million in 1974 and $762 million in 1973. Similarly, oil royalties and mining rents earned the state $216.9 million in 1974, compared with $62.9 million in 1973. Oil royalties and mining rents for 1979 were $282 million. Revenue sources have been expanded since 1977, when the Government took a one-third interest in Brunei LNG Ltd., the holding company for the LNG plant. This places it on an equal footing with the two other shareholders, Shell and Mitsubishi. The Government has also taken an undisclosed share in Brunei Coldgas, the company set up by Shell and Mitsubishi to ship liquid natural gas to Japan.

Consumer prices rise along similar lines to those of Malaysia. Although the rate of increase appears to be accelerating, the underlying annual rate had been about 5–6 per cent, but more recently imported inflation has pushed the rate to over 10 per cent.

The consolidated revenue account at the end of 1978 stood at B$6,640 million. It had risen to about B$10,500 million at the end of 1980 and jumped to B$19,880 million by the end of 1981. It is expected to total B$25,070 million by the end of 1982. The budget for 1980 anticipated revenues of B$4,490 million and expenditure of just under B$1,000 million. G.D.P. grew more slowly in 1981 than in 1980, increasing by about 12.5 per cent at constant prices, or by 6.5 per cent if oil and gas are not included. The 1982 budget sets recurrent expenditure at B$1,590 million and development expenditure at B$399 million, increases of 19 and 38 per cent respectively from 1981. Defence continues to take the largest share of expenditure, followed by education. Concern has been expressed that not enough of the development budget is spent on public utilities and that more effort should be made to encourage non-government economic activity. Most excess revenue is banked, rather than invested in development, and, as such, is held overseas. These reserves totalled B$19,800 million at the end of 1981.

STATISTICAL SURVEY

AREA AND POPULATION

Area	Population†							
	Census Results						Estimates (mid-year)	
	August 10th, 1960			August 10th, 1971				
	Males	Females	Total	Males	Females	Total	1978	1979
5,765 sq. km.*	43,676	40,201	83,877	72,772	63,484	136,256	201,260	212,840

* 2,226 square miles. † Excluding transients afloat.

Capital: Bandar Seri Begawan (formerly Brunei Town), population 75,000 (1976 estimate).

ETHNIC GROUPS (mid-1979)

Malay	118,190
Chinese	54,150
Other indigenous	25,800
Others	14,700

DISTRICTS

District	Population (mid-1979 estimate)
Brunei/Muara	114,410
Belait	70,520
Tutong	20,350
Temburong	7,560

BIRTHS, MARRIAGES AND DEATHS

	Live Births		Marriages		Deaths	
	Number	Rate (per 1,000)	Number	Rate (per 1,000)	Number	Rate (per 1,000)
1973	5,034	34·7	658*	4·5	708	4·9
1974	5,013	33·4	664*	4·4	640	4·3
1975	5,141	31·7	1,052	6·5	728	4·5
1976	5,300	29·9	1,135	6·4	667	3·8
1977	5,397	28·4	1,103	5·8	748	3·9
1978	5,598	27·8	1,164	5·8	731	3·6
1979	5,752	27·0	n.a.	n.a.	728	3·4

* Muslim marriages only.

ECONOMICALLY ACTIVE POPULATION
(census of August 10th, 1971)

	Males	Females	Total
Agriculture, hunting, forestry and fishing	3,296	1,480	4,776
Mining and quarrying	2,720	195	2,915
Manufacturing	1,466	285	1,751
Electricity, gas and water	1,061	25	1,086
Construction	7,929	161	8,090
Trade, restaurants and hotels	3,332	857	4,189
Transport, storage and communications	2,034	93	2,127
Finance, insurance, property and business services	527	118	645
Community, social and personal services	11,146	3,217	14,363
Other activities (not adequately described)	51	19	70
Total in Employment	33,562	6,450	40,012
Unemployed	649	438	1,087
Total Labour Force	34,211	6,888	41,099

Source: International Labour Office, *Year Book of Labour Statistics.*

AGRICULTURE

LAND USE, 1979
('000 hectares)

Arable land	4*
Land under permanent crops	9*
Permanent meadows and pastures	6*
Forests and woodland	415†
Other land	93
Inland water	50
Total	577

* Unofficial figures. † FAO estimate.

PRINCIPAL CROPS
('000 metric tons)

	1978	1979*	1980*
Rice (paddy)	7	7	7
Sweet potatoes	1*	1	1
Cassava (manioc)	3*	3	3
Bananas	3*	3	3
Pineapples	2*	3	3
Vegetables (incl. melons)	4*	4	4

* FAO estimates.

Source: FAO, *Production Yearbook.*

LIVESTOCK
(FAO estimates—'000 head)

	1978	1979	1980
Cattle	3	3	4
Buffaloes	13	14	14
Pigs	13	13	14
Goats	1	1	1
Chickens	995	1,040	1,090
Ducks	45	46	46

LIVESTOCK PRODUCTS
(FAO estimates—metric tons)

	1978	1979	1980
Poultry meat	3,000	3,000	3,000
Hen eggs	1,800	1,850	1,900
Cattle and buffalo hides (fresh)	109	111	117

Source: FAO, *Production Yearbook.*

FORESTRY

ROUNDWOOD REMOVALS

('000 cubic metres, all non-coniferous)

	1975	1976	1977	1978	1979	1980
Sawlogs, veneer logs and logs for sleepers	115	148	144	124	135	128
Other industrial wood	5	7*	8*	8*	8*	8*
Fuel wood	74*	75*	76*	78*	79*	79*
TOTAL	194	230	228	210	222	215

* FAO estimate.

Source: FAO, *Yearbook of Forest Products.*

SAWNWOOD PRODUCTION

('000 cubic metres, all non-coniferous)

	1975	1976	1977	1978	1979	1980
Total (incl. boxboards)	51	65	72	63	85	77

Source: FAO, *Yearbook of Forest Products.*

FISHING

(metric tons)

	1975	1976	1977	1978	1979
Marine fishing	1,500	1,561	2,110	2,621	2,709
Inland waters	70	83	83	83	83

1980: Catch as in 1979 (FAO estimates).

Source: FAO, *Yearbook of Fishery Statistics.*

MINING

('000 metric tons)

	1974	1975	1976	1977	1978	1979
Crude petroleum	9,433	8,777	10,004	10,540	11,146	12,000
Natural gasolene	45	41	59	83	90	96
Natural gas*	7,409	8,156	9,666	10,511	10,043	10,277
Sand, silica and quartz	78	45	25	n.a.	n.a.	n.a.
Gravel and crushed stone	22	35	21	n.a.	n.a.	n.a.

* Million cubic metres, gross production.

INDUSTRY

SELECTED PRODUCTS

('000 metric tons)

	1974	1975	1976	1977	1978	1979
Motor spirit (petrol)	14	19	18	17	19	19
Naphthas	6	5	4	4	5	5
Distillate fuel oils	32	30	29	30	52	55
Liquefied petroleum gas from natural gas plants*	186	143	144	166	182	205
Electric energy†	212	230	264	312	361	415

* '000 barrels. † Million kWh. generated during twelve months ending June 30th of year stated.

FINANCE

100 sen (cents) = 1 Brunei dollar (B$).

Coins: 5, 10, 20 and 50 cents.

Notes: 1, 5, 10, 50, 100, 500 and 1,000 dollars.

Exchange rates (June 1982): B$1 = 1 Singapore dollar; £1 sterling = B$3.753; U.S. $1 = 2.1665.
B$100 = £26.65 = $46.16.

Note: The Brunei dollar (B$) was introduced in June 1967, replacing (at par) the Malayan dollar (M$). From September 1949 the Malayan dollar was valued at 2s. 4d. sterling (£1 = M$8.5714) or 32.667 U.S. cents (U.S. $1 = M$3.0612). This valuation in terms of U.S. currency remained in effect until August 1971. Between December 1971 and February 1973 the Brunei dollar was valued at 35.467 U.S. cents (U.S. $1 = B$2.8195). From February to June 1973 the Brunei dollar's value was 39.407 U.S. cents (U.S. $1 = B$2.5376). In terms of sterling, the exchange rate was £1 = B$7.347 from November 1967 to June 1972. The formal link with the Malaysian dollar, begun in June 1967, ended in May 1973 but the Brunei dollar remained tied to the Singapore dollar. Since June 1973 the Singapore dollar has been allowed to "float". The average market exchange rate (B$ per U.S. $) was: 2.809 in 1972; 2.444 in 1973; 2.437 in 1974; 2.371 in 1975; 2.471 in 1976; 2.439 in 1977; 2.274 in 1978; 2.175 in 1979; 2.141 in 1980; 2.113 in 1981.

BUDGET ESTIMATES

(B$ million)

Revenue	1978*	1979
Taxes	1,200	1,350
Royalties	273	282
Interest on investments	150	250
Total	1,623	1,882

Expenditure	1980	1981
Royal Brunei Malay Regiment	288	416
Education	115	161
Public works	101	110
Medical services	49	67
Police	46	n.a.
Religious affairs	27	40
Other current expenditure	360	346
Transfer to Development Fund	250	215
Total	1,236	1,355

* Revised estimates.

Revenue (forecasts in B$ million): 4,490 in 1980; 7,560 in 1981.

DEVELOPMENT EXPENDITURE

(Revised estimates, B$ million)

	1980
Agriculture	6
Education	36
Roads	59
Civil aviation	17
Electricity	40
Telecommunications	17
Government housing	51
Water supplies	13
Medical and Health	31
Marine	17
TOTAL	287

GROSS DOMESTIC PRODUCT

(B$ million, estimates at market prices)

1975	1976	1977	1978	1979	1980
2,770	3,516	4,227	4,416	6,117	10,413

EXTERNAL TRADE

(B$ million)

	1972	1973	1974	1975	1976	1977	1978	1979	1980
Imports c.i.f.	300.2	323.2	450.9	648.9	642.5	680.4	639.2	862.1	1,230.6
Exports f.o.b.	497.4	852.1	2,388.3	2,494.8	3,293.2	4,000.0	4,195.2	5,796.5	9,852.9

PRINCIPAL COMMODITIES

(B$ million)

IMPORTS	1977	1978	1979
Food and live animals	90.7	95.7	110.4
Beverages and tobacco	18.5	22.6	25.5
Crude materials (inedible) except fuels	7.3	7.4	10.2
Mineral fuels, lubricants, etc.	13.2	14.4	15.9
Animal and vegetable oils and fats	3.4	3.9	4.9
Chemicals	52.1	42.5	58.5
Basic manufactures	210.1	192.7	193.2
Machinery and transport equipment	228.7	193.9	349.1
Miscellaneous manufactured articles	38.7	47.9	67.9
TOTAL (incl. others)	680.4	639.2	862.1

EXPORTS	1977	1978	1979
Crude petroleum	2,704.7	2,618.7	3,936.4
Petroleum products	126.8	165.2	285.6
Natural gas	1,121.3	1,320.8	1,480.4
TOTAL (incl. others)	4,000.0	4,195.2	5,796.5

PRINCIPAL TRADING PARTNERS
(B$'000)

Imports	1977	1978	1979
Australia	12,335	11,353	19,117
China, People's Republic	17,093	19,171	23,822
Germany, Fed. Republic	28,000	14,953	18,148
Japan	145,652	154,622	221,331
Malaysia (Peninsular)	29,951	28,104	31,960
Singapore	117,650	140,484	183,284
United Kingdom	82,091	68,250	85,770
U.S.A.	143,320	97,085	144,902

Exports	1977	1978	1979
Japan	3,061,006	3,107,530	4,109,360
Malaysia (Sarawak)	107,937	78,946*	52,955
Singapore	159,763	203,378	348,077
South Africa	n.a.	197,400	n.a.
Taiwan	117,771	168,249	240,946
U.S.A.	366,379	383,322	485,305

* Includes exports to Sabah.

TRANSPORT

ROAD TRAFFIC
(number of registered vehicles)

	1978	1979
Private cars	34,335	36,042
Taxis	104	104
Motor-cycles and scooters	2,234	2,077
Goods vehicles	5,815	3,733
Buses	214	159
Jeeps	n.a.	8,977
Other vehicles	1,142	1,021
Total	43,844	52,113

INTERNATIONAL SEA-BORNE SHIPPING

	1974	1975	1976	1977	1978
Vessels ('000 net registered tons):					
Entered	14,838	12,121	14,610	18,152	18,341
Cleared	9,756	7,294	7,951	10,594	11,544
Goods ('000 metric tons):					
Loaded	11,253	13,171	21,091	23,101	22,456
Unloaded	405	445	415	608	746

CIVIL AVIATION

	1974	1975	1976	1977	1978
Passengers embarked	73,292	78,258	82,404	92,244	103,808

TOURISM

	1975	1976	1977	1978	1979
Tourist arrivals	3,200	3,441	3,345	3,336	3,561

EDUCATION
(1978)

	Schools	Pupils
Kindergarten	25	2,661
Primary	157	33,053
Secondary*	27	15,571
Teacher Training	2	533
Vocational	3	306

* Including Sixth-Form Centres.

In 1978, 494 Brunei students were studying abroad.

Source (unless otherwise stated): Economic Planning Unit, State Secretariat, Bandar Seri Begawan.

THE CONSTITUTION

Note: Parts of the constitution have been in abeyance since 1962.

A new constitution was promulgated on September 29th, 1959. Under it sovereign authority is vested in the Sultan, who is assisted and advised by five Councils:

The Religious Council: In his capacity as head of the Islamic Faith, the Sultan is advised in all Islamic matters by the Religious Council, whose members are appointed by the Sultan.

The Privy Council: This Council, presided over by the Sultan, is to advise the Sultan on matters concerning the Royal prerogative of mercy, the amendment of the constitution and the conferment of ranks, titles and honours.

The Council of Ministers: Presided over by the Sultan, the Council of Ministers considers all executive matters as well as those raised by the Legislative Council. It is composed of 11 members.

The Legislative Council: This council is presided over by a Speaker appointed by the Sultan. The Council introduces Bills, passes laws, exercises financial controls and scrutinizes government policies.

The Council of Succession: Subject to the Constitution this Council is to determine the succession to the throne should the need arise.

A Mentri Besar (Chief Minister) is responsible to the Sultan for the exercise of all executive authority. He is assisted by a State Secretary, an Attorney-General and a State Financial Officer.

The State is divided into four administrative districts, in each of which is a District Officer (Malay) responsible to the State Secretary.

THE GOVERNMENT

(June 1982)

The Sultan: H.H. Sir MUDA HASSANAL BOLKIAH MU'IZZADDIN WADDAULAH (succeeded October 5th, 1967; crowned August 1st, 1968).

General Adviser to H.H. The Sultan: Pehin Dato Haji ISA.

Mentri Besar: Pehin Dato Haji ABDUL AZIZ.

State Secretary (acting): Pehin Dato ABDUL RAHMAN TAIB.

State Financial Officer: Pehin Datuk JOHN LEE, C.B.E.

Attorney-General: Pengiran LAILA KANUN DI-RAJA Pengiran BAHRIN.

Head of Religious Affairs: Pehin Dato Haji MOHAMMAD ZAIN bin Haji SERUDDIN.

POLITICAL PARTIES

Barisan Kemerdeka'an Rakyat—BAKER (*People's Independence Front*): Bandar Seri Begawan; f. 1966.

There are two other political organizations, Parti Ra'ayat Brunei (Brunei People's Party), which is banned and whose members are all in exile, and Parti Perdapuan Kebangsaan Ra'ayat Perkara (Brunei People's National United Party), founded in 1968 but no longer active.

DIPLOMATIC REPRESENTATION

Brunei's external relations are conducted by the United Kingdom.

The British High Commission: Jalan Residency, Bandar Seri Begawan; *High Commissioner:* ARTHUR C. WATSON, C.M.G.

JUDICIAL SYSTEM

The Supreme Court consists of the High Court and the Court of Appeal. There are also Magistrates' Courts of First, Second and Third Class.

The Supreme Court: Consists of the Chief Justice and Commissioners of the Supreme Court appointed by the Sultan. The High Court has unlimited original jurisdiction in most civil matters and unlimited criminal jurisdiction.

Courts of Magistrates: There are Courts of Magistrates of the First, Second and Third Class. They have original jurisdiction in minor civil and criminal cases.

Courts of Kathis: Deal solely with questions concerning Muslim religion, marriage and divorce. Appeals lie from these Courts to the Sultan in the Religious Council.

Chief Justice: Sir DENYS ROBERTS.

President, Court of Appeal: Dato Sir GEOFFREY BRIGGS.

Chief Kathi: Pehin Datu IMAM Dato PADUKA Seri SETIA Awang Haji ABDUL HAMID BIN BAKAL.

RELIGION

The official religion of Brunei is Islam, and the Sultan is head of the Islamic population. Muslims number about 60,000, most of them Malays. The Chinese population is either Buddhist, Confucianist, Daoist or Christian. Large numbers of the indigenous races are animists of various types. The remainder of the population are Roman Catholics, Anglicans or members of the American Methodist Church of Southern Asia.

ANGLICAN CHURCH

Bishop of Kuching: The Rt. Rev. Datuk BASIL TEMENGONG, Bishop's House, P.O.B. 347, Kuching, Sarawak, Malaysia.

ROMAN CATHOLIC CHURCH

Archbishop of Kuala Lumpur: Rt. Rev. Tan Sri DOMINIC VENDARGON, 528 Jalan Bukit Nanas, Kuala Lumpur 04-01, Malaysia.

THE PRESS

NEWSPAPERS

Borneo Bulletin: 74 Jalan Sungei, P.O.B. 69, Kuala Belait; f. 1953; independent; English; weekly; Saturday; Man. I. M. MACGREGOR; Editor L. J. BRINSDON; circ. 32,000.

Pelita Brunei: Information Section of the State Secretariat, Bandar Seri Begawan; f. 1956; free newspaper in Malay and Chinese; weekly; circ. 33,000.

Petroleum di-Brunei: c/o Brunei Shell Petroleum Co. Ltd., Seria; magazine published by Brunei Shell Petroleum Co. Ltd.; English and Malay; quarterly; circ. 6,000.

Salam: c/o Brunei Shell Petroleum Co. Ltd., Seria; f. 1953; free employee newspaper published by the Brunei Shell Petroleum Co. Ltd.; Malay, English and Chinese in one edition; fortnightly on Tuesdays; circ. 6,000.

PUBLISHERS

The Brunei Press: P.O.B. 69, Kuala Belait; f. 1959; Gen. Man. I. M. MACGREGOR.

Eastern Printers and Trading Co. Ltd.: Bandar Seri Begawan; Man. Haji UMAR MUHAMMED.

Leong Bros.: 52 Jalan Bunga Kuning, P.O.B. 164, Seria.

The Star Press: Bandar Seri Begawan; f. 1963; Man. F. W. ZIMMERMAN.

RADIO AND TELEVISION

Radio and Television Brunei: Bandar Seri Begawan; f. 1957; two networks, one broadcasting in Malay and local dialects, the other in English, Chinese and Gurkha; an all-colour television service was opened in July 1975 and is on VHF CCIR-PAL 'B' system of 625 lines with sound/vision separation 5.5MHz; Dir. ABDUL RAZAK Haji MUHAMMAD; Deputy Dir. MOHD. ALIMIN BIN Haji ABDUL WAHAB.

In 1981 there were 37,500 radio receivers and 29,000 television sets.

FINANCE

BANKING

(cap. = capital; dep. = deposits; m. = million; brs. = branches)

In December 1981 there were 9 banks with a total of 27 branches operating in Brunei.

National Bank of Brunei Ltd.: P.O.B. 321, Bandar Seri Begawan; f. 1965; cap. B$90m., dep. B$839m. (Dec. 1981); Pres. Prince MOHAMMED BOLKIAH; Deputy Pres. Prince Hj. SUFRI BOLKIAH; Chair. Dato KHOO BAN HOCK; brs. in Seria, Kuala Belait, Tutong, Muara Port, Airport, Jalan Tutong, Bangar, Gadong and Princess Amal Rakiah Building.

FOREIGN BANKS

Bank of America National Trust and Savings Association (*U.S.A.*): Suri Bldg., Jalan Tutong, P.O.B. 2280, Bandar Seri Begawan; Man. ROGER H. YOUEL.

The Chartered Bank (*U.K.*): 145 Jalan Chevalier, P.O.B. 186, Bandar Seri Begawan; Man. D. W. G. HEWETT.

Citibank N.A. (*U.S.A.*): 147 Jalan Chevalier, P.O.B. 2209, Bandar Seri Begawan; Vice-Pres. DOUGLAS L. HARDY.

The Hongkong and Shanghai Banking Corporation (*Hong Kong*): Jalan Sultan, P.O.B. 59, Bandar Seri Begawan; 4 brs.; Man. J. H. MASON.

The Island Development Bank Ltd.: 22–23 Jalan Sultan, Bandar Seri Begawan.

Malayan Banking Berhad (*Malaysia*): 148 Jalan Chevalier, P.O.B. 167, Bandar Seri Begawan; Man. Haji ZAINAL LAMDIN.

Overseas Union Bank Ltd. (*Singapore*): 72 Jalan Roberts, P.O.B. 2218, Bandar Seri Begawan; Man. EDMOND Y. L. LEE.

United Malayan Banking Corporation Berhad (*Malaysia*): 141 Jalan Chevalier, P.O.B. 435, Bandar Seri Begawan; Man. LIOW CHEE HWA.

INSURANCE

A number of British insurance companies have agencies in Brunei.

TRADE AND INDUSTRY

Trade in Brunei is largely conducted by the agency houses, European and Chinese, and by Chinese merchants.

Brunei Coldgas Ltd.: formed by Shell and Mitsubishi as a trading company to buy, transport and sell LNG from Brunei LNG Ltd. to customers in Japan.

Brunei LNG Ltd.: Seria; f. 1969; natural gas liquefaction; owned jointly by Shell, Mitsubishi and the Brunei Government; 1981 intake 680 million cubic feet per day; operates LNG plant at Lumut which has a capacity of 6 million tons per year.

Brunei Shell Marketing Co. Ltd.: 36/37 Jalan Sultan, Bandar Seri Begawan; f. 1978 from the Shell Marketing Company of Brunei Ltd. when the Government became equal partners with Shell; markets petroleum products throughout Brunei; Gen. Man. B. LIVINGSTONE.

Brunei Shell Petroleum Co. Ltd.: Seria; the largest industrial concern in the State and the only oil company at present in production in Brunei; 50 per cent state holding; output (1981) 175,000 barrels per day; Man. Dir. PETER EVERETT.

CHAMBER OF COMMERCE

Brunei State Chamber of Commerce: P.O.B. 2246, Bandar Seri Begawan; 48 mems.; Chair. T. K. LOW.

TRADE UNIONS

Brunei Government Junior Officers' Union: P.O.B. 2290, Bandar Seri Begawan; 378 mems.; Pres. Haji ALI BIN Haji NASAR; Gen. Sec. Haji OMARALI BIN Haji MOHIDDIN; Treas. Haji PUTEH BIN JUKIN.

Brunei Government Medical and Health Workers' Union: P.O.B. 459, Bandar Seri Begawan; 300 mems.; Pres. Pengiran Haji MOHIDDIN BIN Pengiran TAJUDDIN; Gen. Sec. HANAFI BIN ANAI; Treas. Haji SABTU BIN ALI.

Brunei Oilfield Workers' Union: P.O.B. 175, Seria; f. 1961; *c.* 505 mems.; Pres. SEMITH BIN SABLI; Vice-Pres. IBRAHIM BIN METUSSIN; Sec.-Gen. MOHD. ALI BIN Haji YUSOF; Treas. MOHD. BIN ABDULLAH.

Royal Brunei Custom Department Staff Union: Custom Department, Kuala Belait; f. 1972; 51 mems.; Pres. HASSAN BIN BAKAR; Gen. Sec. ABDUL ADIS BIN TARIP; Treas. Pengiran DANI BIN Pengiran Haji IDRIS.

TRANSPORT

RAILWAYS

There are no public railways in Brunei. The Brunei Shell Petroleum Co. Ltd. maintains a 19.3-km. section of light railway between Seria and Badas.

ROADS

There are some 576 kilometres of roads in Brunei and these are supplemented by 132 kilometres of district tracks. The main highway connects Bandar Seri Begawan, Tutong and Kuala Belait. A new 59-km. coastal road is currently under construction between Muara and Tutong.

SHIPPING

Most sea traffic is handled by a deep-water port at Muara, 27 km. from the capital. The original, smaller port at Bandar Seri Begawan itself is mainly used for river-going vessels. There is a port at Kuala Belait which takes shallow-draught vessels. At Seria crude oil from the oil terminal is shipped through SBMs. At Lumut there is a two-mile jetty for liquefied natural gas (LNG) carriers.

Rivers are the principal means of communication in the interior.

SHIPPING COMPANY

Bee Seng Shipping Company: 1½ Miles Jalan Tutong, P.O.B. 92, Bandar Seri Begawan.

CIVIL AVIATION

There is an international airport at Bandar Seri Begawan. The Brunei Shell Petroleum Co. Ltd. operates a private airfield at Anduki.

Director of Civil Aviation: H. C. BLACK, O.B.E.; Brunei International Airport.

Royal Brunei Airlines Ltd.: P.O.B. 737, Bandar Seri Begawan; f. 1974; operates services to Bangkok, Hong Kong, Singapore, Manila, Kuching, Kuala Lumpur and Kota Kinabalu; Chair. Pehin Dato ISA; Gen. Man. DAVID LOWE; 3 Boeing 737-200.

The following airlines also serve Brunei: British Airways, Cathay Pacific Airways (Hong Kong), MAS (Malaysia) and SIA (Singapore).

TOURISM

Tourist Information Centre: The Chief Information Officer, Information Section, State Secretariat Office, Bandar Seri Begawan.

DEFENCE

The Royal Brunei Malay Regiment numbered 2,850 men in 1981. The allocation made in the 1981 budget to the Regiment was B$416 million. Since 1971 the first line of defence is the responsibility of the Brunei Government, although the British Government is represented on the Brunei Defence Council and a Gurkha battalion of the British Army is stationed in Brunei. In mid-1978 it was agreed that the Gurkhas would remain until Brunei becomes fully independent from the United Kingdom in 1983.

Commander of the Royal Brunei Regiment: Brigadier JOHN FRIEDBERGER.

EDUCATION

In Brunei education is carried out in three different languages, Malay, English and Chinese, and schools are divided accordingly. There are also religious schools.

All Malay schools are government-administered and are in general co-educational. Primary education in the Malay schools lasts six years. Examinations at the end of the fourth year determine whether the pupils go on to prepare for entry to a government English medium or Malay medium secondary school, or to a religious school.

Secondary schooling lasts for seven years. After the third year promotion to the higher forms depends on examination performance. In 1975 there were 111 Malay schools with 19,850 pupils.

English medium schools are either government-administered or independent. Government English schools offer a three-year preparatory course for entry to English medium secondary schools. These prepare pupils for both Malay and English medium examinations. There were 13,681 pupils studying at 25 government English schools in 1975.

Chinese schools are not assisted by the government and cater for pupils at both primary and secondary levels. Religious schools are administered by the Religious Affairs Department. They take in pupils after the fourth year in Malay primary schools.

The only form of higher education offered in Brunei is teacher training. Students wishing to pursue other forms of higher education may go abroad to continue their studies at government expense. The state runs two teacher training institutions, one for religious teachers and one which caters for Malay and English schools. (*See* also *Statistical Survey p.* 287).

BIBLIOGRAPHY

Brunei Annual Report, H.M.S.O., London.

See Malaysia.

Burma

PHYSICAL AND SOCIAL GEOGRAPHY

C. A. Fisher

(Revised for this edition by HARVEY DEMAINE)

Burma, which covers a total area of 261,218 square miles (676,552 square kilometres), lies to the east of India and Bangladesh and to the south-west of China, and has a long coastline facing the Bay of Bengal and the Andaman Sea. Much the greater part of its territory, between latitudes 28½° and 16° N., forms a compact unit surrounded on three sides by a great horseshoe of mountains and focusing on the triple river system of the Irrawaddy, Chindwin and Sittang. But in addition, Tenasserim, consisting of a narrow coastal zone backed by steep mountains, extends south from the Gulf of Martaban to Victoria Point only 10° N. of the equator.

PHYSICAL FEATURES

Structurally, Burma falls into three well-marked divisions, of which the first comprises the mid-Tertiary fold mountains of the west. These ranges, swinging in a great arc from the Hukwang valley to Cape Negrais, appear to represent a southward continuation of the eastern Himalayan series, though only after the latter has made a right-angled bend in the vicinity of the Tibeto-Burman border. From north to south these western ranges are known successively as the Patkai, Naga, and Chin Hills, and the Arakan Yoma, though the name hills is a singularly misleading designation for ranges whose summits exceed 12,000 ft. (3,650 metres) in the Patkai and 6,000 ft. to 8,000 ft. (1,800 to 2,400 metres) in the Chin and Naga sectors. Further south, in the Arakan Yoma, the summit levels gradually decrease to between 3,000 ft. (900 metres) and 5,000 ft. (1,500 metres), but even there the mountains, consisting of a series of parallel serrated ridges, densely forested and fever-ridden, continue to provide a tremendous natural barrier between Burma and the Indian sub-continent, and even in British colonial times, when Burma formed part of the Indian Empire, the links between the two were almost exclusively by sea.

The second major structural unit consists of the eastern mountain systems, of Mesozoic or earlier origin, which, beginning as a continuation of the Yunnan plateau of China across the Burma border into the northeastern corner of Kachin State, extend thence through the Shan and Karenni plateaux into the more subdued but still rugged upland which forms the divide between Tenasserim and peninsular Thailand. In the far north, where this system adjoins the western mountain system, the general plateau level is of the order of 6,000 ft. (1,800 metres) with higher ridges frequently attaining 10,000 ft. (3,050 metres). The corresponding altitudes in the Shan area, however, are only about half as great, though here also the surface is severely dissected, with the main rivers, notably the great Salween, rushing southwards in deeply incised gorges.

In between the two main mountain systems described above lies the third major structural unit, namely the vast longitudinal trough of central Burma, formerly occupied by an arm of the early Tertiary sea, and now containing the great alluvial lowlands which form the cultural and economic heart of the country. Throughout the entire length of these lowlands the Irrawaddy provides the central artery, both of drainage and of communication. To the north it is paralleled by its largest tributary, the Chindwin, which joins it near the centre of the Dry Zone (*see below*) and farther south by the Sittang, which flows separately to the sea on the opposite side of the recent volcanic uplands of the Pegu Yoma. Central Burma is a zone of crustal instability; a severe earthquake in July 1975 caused extensive damage. Altogether, the Irrawaddy drains a total area of some 158,000 square miles (409,000 square kilometres), and its huge delta, originally covered with dense forest and swamp vegetation, has been cleared during the past hundred years to provide one of the greatest rice bowls of the world.

CLIMATE

Apart from the highest uplands in the far north of the country, the climate of practically the whole of Burma may be classified as tropical monsoonal, though important regional variations nevertheless occur within that overall category. In all parts of the country the main rains come during the period of the S.W. monsoon, i.e. between May and October inclusive, and those areas, notably Arakan and Tenasserim, which face the prevailing winds and are backed by steep and high ranges, receive some of the heaviest rainfall in the world, as, for example, Akyab, with an annual total of 204 in. (518 cm.), of which 196 in. (498 cm.) falls during the six months in question, and Amherst with 190 in. (483 cm.) of its 196 in. (498 cm.) also falling during the same period. Moreover, even the flat and low-lying Irrawaddy delta receives an annual rainfall of about 100 in. (250 cm.), again with some 95 per cent of it during the same half-year, and in all of these three areas mean annual temperatures are around 80°F. (27°C.), though the seasonal range varies from 12°F. (6.5°C.) in Akyab to 6°F. (3.5°C.) in Amherst.

However, over a considerable area in the interior of the central lowland, which constitutes a rain-shadow area relative to the S.W. monsoon, the total annual precipitation is less than 40 in. (100 cm.), and in some places even below 25 in. (64 cm.). And even though in this Dry Zone the seasonal incidence is essentially similar to that in the other areas already considered, the spectacular difference in total amount is reflected in a major change of vegetation from the prevailing heavy tropical monsoon forest elsewhere to a much more open cover and in places a mere thorny scrub. Moreover, the relative aridity is also responsible for a wider range of temperature, as is shown by Mandalay's 70°F. (21°C.) in January and 90°F. (32°C.) in April, immediately before the onset of the rains. Finally, in the eastern plateaux rainfall, though well above that of the Dry Zone, is nevertheless much less than along the western coastal margins, and this fact, combined with temperatures some 10° to 15°F. (6° to 8°C.) below those of the torrid plains gives the Shan plateau the pleasantest climate of any part of the country.

NATURAL RESOURCES

Natural resources in Burma are closely related to the salient features of the country's physical geography. Thus, the greatest wealth of the humid mountain slopes lies in their timber, particularly teak, and while the young folded mountains of the west are not noted for mineral wealth, the older plateaux of the east have long been noted for a variety of metallic minerals, including the silver, lead and zinc of Bawdwin and the tungsten of Mawchi. The current reserve position of such minerals is somewhat uncertain, because of their location in areas of insecurity, and only recently have attempts been made to rehabilitate former production facilities. Output remains significantly below pre-war levels. Further south Tenasserim forms a minor part of the South-East Asian tin zone, though its resources in this respect are very small compared with those of Malaysia and Thailand. More important than any of these metals, or the sub-bituminous coal deposits at Kalewa, near the Chindwin/Myittha confluence, are the petroleum and natural gas deposits which occur in the Tertiary structures underlying the middle Irrawaddy lowlands. As the original fields at Chauk and Yenangyaung have become exhausted, further discoveries have been made, notably at Man (petroleum) and Myanaung (natural gas). Production of petroleum, while small by world standards, recently surpassed pre-war levels, with an output of 11.5 million tons in 1980, but the country has yet to discover expected commercial fields off-shore and the present self-sufficient position seems likely to disappear in the near future as consumption continues to rise.

It is in agricultural resources that Burma is potentially most richly endowed and the Irrawaddy delta seems capable of both meeting local needs and providing an even greater surplus for export than at present when long-neglected water control facilities are completed in the mid-1980s. The Dry Zone is also well-suited for the production of oil-seeds and cotton, especially under irrigation, and in Tenasserim conditions are appropriate, though not ideal, for the cultivation of rubber and fruit crops.

POPULATION AND ETHNIC GROUPS

By March 1981 Burma's population was estimated at 34,083,000, a density of only 50.4 per square km., which is not merely far below that of India and China, but also well below the South-East Asian average of approximately 77. The greatest concentrations occur in the delta, and it is likewise in the lowlands, including also those of Arakan and Tenasserim, that the Burmese form the majority element in the population, while the uplands are more sparsely inhabited by a series of minority groups at varying levels of advancement. The Burmese, whose ancestors came from the Sino-Tibetan borders and eventually in early historical times supplanted all but a minor remnant of the earlier Mon population of lowland Burma, now form some 65 per cent of the total Burman population. A further 7–8 per cent consists of Shans, who are ethnic kinsfolk of the Thai and Lao, and, like the Burmese and the half-million Mons, follow the Theravada form of Buddhism.

Of the non-Buddhist indigenous groups, often referred to collectively as hill peoples, the Karens are the most numerous and indeed slightly outnumber the Shans. Their homeland occupies the uplands between the Shan plateau and Tenasserim, but many have migrated into the lowlands around Moulmein and to the Irrawaddy delta, and considerable numbers have discarded animism and adopted Christianity. Other upland peoples include the Kachins, Chins, Wa-Palaung, Lolo-Muhso and Nagas, who are still mostly animists and respectively form from 2.5 to 0.5 per cent of the total population.

Until recently Burma had a large Indian community, which before 1941 numbered over a million, but has since been successively reduced by repatriation so that today it is probably exceeded by the Chinese. Largely because of its arrested economic development since around 1960, Burma remains below the South-East Asian average in respect of urbanization, with Rangoon, its capital, totalling 2.3 million inhabitants in March 1980 and only three other towns exceeding 100,000 in the 1973 census.

HISTORY

Josef Silverstein

History and geography have much in common in Burma. The pattern of predominantly north-south rivers and valleys, enveloped by a crown of sharp and sometimes inhospitable hills and mountains, proved to be a strong barrier to those seeking easy access to the fertile land on the banks of its major rivers; one result of this was that the permanent population of Burma lived in relative isolation from its neighbours, India and China. Barriers, however, did not prevent contact with the outside; through wars, some trading and other means of contact, some migration and cultural exchange took place. The coastline also is deceiving. For lying back and away from the main sea routes of the monsoon traders, commerce never developed and flourished.

Among the people who settled in Burma, a pattern of separation predominated. Despite the above-mentioned natural barriers, migration to the country via land is believed to be the main avenue of population movement. The earliest known races who left traces of significant civilizations were the Pyus and Mons. Both lived in lower Burma along the banks or in the delta of the Irrawaddy River. Their successors were the Tibeto-Burman peoples, the ancestors of the contemporary Burmans. The Shan-Thai, who entered Burma somewhat later from Nanchao—an area which today is located in southern China—settled to the north and east of the Burmans in the hill areas of the country. Others, such as the Karens, Chins and Kachins entered at various times from the pre-Christian era to the late eighteenth century and also made their homes in the same area. Only the Karens moved gradually in large numbers to the plains area and settled among the Burmans and remnants of the ancient Mons. As a result of this migration pattern, together with the geographical features of Burma, most of the racial groups in Burma lived separated from each other. Each retained its own culture and identity. Only local warfare, intermarriage and intermingling among the racial groups living in close proximity provided for significant social and cultural exchange. No thoroughgoing assimilation took place.

BURMA BEFORE BRITISH RULE

The Burmans, from the tenth century on, were the most numerous and, in terms of cultural, historical and political contribution to the varied heritage of Burma, were the most important group. Between their founding of the Pagan Dynasty in the eleventh century and the conquest of Burma in the nineteenth, the Burmans succeeded in unifying Burma under a single political authority on three separate and relatively short occasions.

The Pagan Dynasty lasted from the eleventh to the end of the thirteenth century. The Burman king Anahwrahta, the founder of the empire, succeeded in bringing the Mons under Burman rule and, more important, adopting Buddhism from them and propagating it throughout the developing empire. The Pagan Dynasty proved to be Burma's Golden Age, in which Indian-influenced culture—from written language to architectural development—flourished. The Mongol invaders in 1287 brought the period to an end when they sacked Pagan, drove the last kings from the city and destroyed the political and military power of the empire.

For the next two centuries, the Shans seemed on the verge of creating their own empire out of the remnants of the Pagan Dynasty. However, internal rivalries among the Shan princes prevented them from uniting and it was not until a new line of Burman kings arose (the Toungoo Dynasty) in the sixteenth century that Burma once again came under a single ruler. The Toungoo kings brought the Shans under permanent Burman rule and sought to increase the size of the empire at the expense of the neighbouring Thais. But continuous warfare weakened the power of the new line of kings and by the seventeenth century, the Toungoo Dynasty came to an end; Burma once again became the centre of quarrelling races, none strong enough to subdue and hold the rest.

Toward the end of the eighteenth century, Alaungpaya became the third Burman king to unite the country. Within a few years he not only conquered his indigenous rivals but in addition expanded the influence of his empire to the neighbouring areas of Assam, Manipur and Siam. During the era of this dynasty (the Konbaung) the Burmans repelled four invasion attempts by the Chinese. Early in the nineteenth century, rivalry with the British East India Company over border areas adjoining Burma and India—Arakan—and over influence in Assam and Manipur, brought the two powers into open warfare. Beginning in 1824, the Burmese and the British engaged in three wars, each ending in defeat for the former and the loss of territory and power. The third and final war in 1885–86 brought an end to Burman rule when the last king was captured and exiled.

Although the bare outline of history, suggested above, stresses the disunity among the peoples of Burma and the rise and fall of short-lived dynasties, there are other aspects of this history which suggest stability and continuity throughout this long period. The mass conversion of the Burmans and many of the minorities to Buddhism provided the basis for Burmese thought and values from the past to the present. The tradition of self-reliance among the peasantry, from the production of food and clothing to the education of the young, provides a picture of relative stability in the countryside, which stands in marked contrast to the rivalry and occasional chaos at the royal level. The self-contained racial groups husbanded their cultures and identities in the face of conquest and competition and emerged in the modern period as separate and distinct groups, which gave allegiance to rivals stronger than themselves, but little else. Finally, the general isolation of Burma from the outside world cut the country and its people off from the changes in other countries and left them unprepared for modifications in their social, economic and political institutions, which the British imposed on them.

BRITISH RULE

The development of colonial institutions and programmes was slow and pragmatic. Until the second Anglo-Burmese War in 1852, little was done in the two ceded territories—Arakan and Tenasserim—beyond the maintenance, as cheaply as possible, of law and order. Following that war and the acquisition of the rest of lower Burma, the British gave greater attention to making the area economically viable. Law and order in the countryside together with a policy of encouraging both indigenous and foreign peasants to clear and cultivate the land laid the foundation for Burma's development into the world's largest rice exporter. Economic transformation to a food-exporting nation brought with it the problems of foreign landowners, money lending, tenancy and land alienation. During this period, the British sought to use the existing system of local rule.

International rivalry in 1885 between France and Britain over the strategic area of upper Burma, together with problems encountered by a British firm over its timber leases in upper Burma provided the basis for launching a third war against the Burmans. The British forces met with little or no opposition and all of Burma came under British rule in 1886. The Shan princes generally accepted the changes and in turn were confirmed in their local authority. In time, the other minorities in the hill areas followed the Shans.

Between 1897 and 1942, British rule flowered and Burma underwent vast changes. Administratively, the first change occurred when the traditional system of local government was altered to make authority territorial, instead of personal, and the village headman replaced the local chieftain; the headmen became directly responsible to the district officer and a part of the central administrative hierarchy. Also about this time, the Chief Commissioner was raised to the office of Lieutenant-Governor and assisted by a council; Burma became a province of India. Reforms leading to self-government did not get under way until 1923, when a system of dyarchy was introduced and a partially elected legislative council was formed. In 1937 Burma was separated from India, received its own constitution, a fully elected legislature and a responsible cabinet. Four popular governments served until Burma was occupied by the Japanese in 1942. Although political instability and personal rivalries dominated Burma's political life during this period, the political élite learned the mechanics of parliamentary government. Through the period of reforms the hill areas were kept administratively separate from Burma proper with the result that uneven political development occurred in the two areas.

The administrative changes in Burma proper together with the development of Christian mission and Anglo-vernacular schools rendered invalid the traditional forms of education carried on by the Buddhist monks. The new indigenous élite and the recruits for the Western business firms were drawn from those who spoke English and had experienced Western-type education. The emergence of a commercial export economy, together with the development of an expansion of mineral and timber extractions complemented the administrative and educational changes and all contributed to undermining the traditions and customs of the people; social dislocation, instability, increased crime and the impoverishment of the peasantry resulted. Rangoon grew to importance as a major port and commercial centre for foreign commercial interests, while among the hill peoples little or no change occurred.

The Burman response to all these changes was to react politically. The first popular movement, the Young Men's Buddhist Association (YMBA), appeared before the First World War. Its main concern was religion not politics; however, following Britain's promise to India (given during the First World War) of eventual self-government, the YMBA was transformed to the General Council of Burmese Associations (GCBA) and the new organization headed the nascent nationalist movement. In 1920 university students called a strike which won popular backing and thrust them into national politics. Following the introduction of dyarchy, the GCBA split as its leaders contested with each other for seats in the legislative council and for followers. The key issue was whether to accept the reforms or fight for new ones.

In 1930, a new phase in Burmese politics developed. The impact of the world economic depression provoked a minority of rural Burmans to revert to superstition and challenge British rule in a hopeless gesture of revolt. The Saya San Revolt marked the first effort in the twentieth century to expel the British by force and violence. More important was the second movement. Drawn in the main from among the young intelligentsia and university students, who called themselves *Thakins* (masters), the movement sought to revive popular interest in the national language, traditions, identity and culture. It rejected the course of political development in progress and worked instead directly with peasant organizations, labour unions and youth. When Burma became involved in the Second World War, thirty of its leaders were in secret training for military activity, under the Japanese. From its ranks sprang the new generation of leaders who guided the nation through the war and to independence.

Burma in Transition (1942-48)

The invading Japanese Army scored rapid successes against the British defenders of Burma and within six months forced the Allied Forces out of Burma proper and parts of the hill areas. Accompanying the victorious Japanese were the new recruits and leaders of the Burmese Independence Army (BIA)—secretly created and trained by the Japanese before the war. Administration broke down inside Burma when the government and thousands of civil servants and

Indians evacuated in the train of the defeated army. The BIA leaders expected to fill the administrative void and establish an independent Burma under their leadership; however, they found that the Japanese had other plans. Dr. Ba Maw, Burma's first Prime Minister in 1937, was called to head the administration and in 1943 was chosen to head the nominally independent Burma Government. Neither the Japanese nor the Burma Government under its control ever became popular with the people. Loss of the rice export market, shortages of consumer goods, brutal treatment by the Japanese and the hardships of war combined to prevent all efforts of the invaders to win local support.

The youthful leaders of the new Burma Army, together with their colleagues in government and outside, organized a resistance movement. Under the leadership of Aung San and in secret communication with the British in India, the Anti-Fascist People's Freedom League (AFPFL) rose in revolt in March 1945, and participated in the final stages of the Allied victory in Burma. When the Burma Government-in-exile returned in October 1945, it found a well-organized nationalist movement under strong leadership and equipped with goals and programmes confronting it. Until mid-1946, the Governor could make no headway with economic reconstruction due to his unwillingness to work with and through the AFPFL. A change in governors, a general strike and a change in policy in London broke the deadlock; in January 1947, Aung San travelled to London to discuss Burma's political future with the British Prime Minister. Agreement was reached and the Burmese returned home to carry out the necessary steps to realize their goal of independence. Crucial to the success of their plans was the support of the hill peoples. This was secured and delegations from all the major ethnic groups participated in drafting the constitution.

Tragedy befell the nation on July 19th, 1947, when Aung San and six members of the Executive Council were assassinated. Quick work by the Governor, the success of Thakin Nu in stepping into Aung San's office, and support from the AFPFL permitted Burma to complete all necessary steps in time to declare its independence outside the Commonwealth on January 4th, 1948.

THE CONSTITUTIONAL PERIOD: 1948-62

The Union of Burma began its independent political life as a constitutional democracy. The fundamental law provided for an elected two-house legislature, a responsible Prime Minister and Cabinet, and an independent judiciary. More important, however, was the manner in which it attempted to answer the ethnic question. In theory, a federal form of government was created with each of the states enjoying certain common powers, such as authority in local matters, education and taxation. Each state had an elected council and head. In practice, however, the federal structure was overlaid by strong central control. The Prime Minister had the final say in the selection of state heads, the allocation of central revenues for state use, and, through a variety of Burmanization policies, the central government tended to supersede the states and thereby nullify the constitutional guarantees of unity in diversity. Although certain states had the right of secession, none in fact ever attempted to employ it.

When Burma became independent in 1948, the governing party was the AFPFL. Although it held an overwhelming majority of seats in Parliament, it was faced with serious rivals, both in and out of Burma. The major threat came from the communists who went into open revolt three months after independence. The People's Volunteer Organization (PVO), a mainstay in the AFPFL, split and a majority followed the communists. In 1949 the Karen National Defence Organization (KNDO) revolted over the failure of their people to receive the area and cultural protection they thought they deserved. Other ethnic groups also revolted. Despite the preponderance of opposition, the government did not collapse, mainly because the rebels fought each other as well as the Government. The leadership of Nu united the people in support of the Government and by 1951 the armed forces had reorganized and won back control of the major portion of the countryside.

During the 1950s, two elections were held. In both cases the AFPFL won overwhelmingly. However, all was not right in the party, and in 1958 it split into two rival factions. To avoid open revolt, the Prime Minister invited the head of the army, General Ne Win, to form a caretaker government and prepare the country for new elections. Elections were held in 1960 and Nu's faction of the AFPFL was returned to power. Nu once again became Prime Minister and he pledged his government to restore public confidence in democratic processes and bring racial harmony to the people. Internal troubles in his party together with increased demands by the Shans and Kachins for greater autonomy or even secession prevented the Government from attaining its goals. On March 2nd, 1962, the military, under the leadership of Ne Win, engineered a coup. All the members of the Government were arrested along with the key leaders of the minorities. The constitution was set aside and the self-chosen Revolutionary Council began to rule by decree.

During the Constitutional period Burma's major social problem was how to bring unity to the diverse peoples living in the hills and on the plains. While some measure of success was achieved in securing the loyalty of the hill peoples, especially the Shans, Kachins and Chins, other minority groups, primarily the Karens and Mons, remained in opposition. Under the caretaker regime, dissidents among the Shans and Kachins went into open revolt and joined forces, in some areas, with the KNDO and the Communists. When elected government was restored in 1960, the divisions between the Burmans and the various minorities continued to widen. Finally, in 1962, the Prime Minister called a conference of all ethnic leaders to seek a solution to the problem of unity. No answer was found and when the coup took place, nearly all the participants were arrested.

From 1948 to 1962, the Burmese made several and varied attempts to cope with the economic problems of the nation. Little or no reconstruction was carried out after the Second World War mainly because the AFPFL leaders did not agree with the plans and priorities. Therefore, with independence, the people inherited an economy badly in need of capital and technical assistance, both to restore it to its pre-war status and then transform it to meet the needs of a nation desirous of transforming itself from a primary producing economy to one that was mixed. Under the original leaders of the AFPFL, socialism was seen as the best means of achieving this end. As a result of the failure of successive economic plans, in 1957 the Burmese chose a new road to economic health. The socialist goals were postponed and following the restoration of elected government in 1960, a new policy came into effect. Private enterprise was encouraged to enter into partnership with the government, and once its know-how had been passed along, to drop out. This policy never got very far in view of the coup and the different outlook of the military in economic matters.

Throughout the period of 1948–62, the economy languished while the population grew and popular expectation of improved conditions increased. Rice and extraction remained the basic means of earning foreign exchange. As a result, the economy was subject to the instability of world demand for its products. Little or no headway was made in developing an industrial sector or training personnel for manning it. By the time of the coup, Burma had experimented with several approaches to development—capitalism, socialism or mixed economy—but had not resolved the question of which was best for its needs.

MILITARY RULE, 1962–74

During the greater part of the first decade of military rule (1962–72), the new leaders devoted themselves to demolishing and sweeping away the liberal constitutional system of their predecessors and replacing it with an arbitrary dictatorial system which sought to organize and maintain the support of the people. The "new order" was based on the rule of a few military senior officers, under the leadership of General Ne Win, and organized as the Revolutionary Council (RC). The ideas underlying the "new order" were incorporated in an ideological statement entitled the *Burmese Way to Socialism*, published in April 1962; it remained unchanged throughout the ten-year period, providing the basis for much of the RC's programme. In form and theory, Burma was still a federal state; in fact, the new leaders created a centralized bureaucracy which, for all practical purposes, treats the nation as a unitary state. A new hierarchy of Security and Administration Councils (SAC), composed of representatives of the army, the police and the civil service, formed a network of administrative units which were linked together in a hierarchy with its apex in Rangoon and extending through the nation. To mobilize the people under its leadership, the RC created a new political party, the Burma Socialist Programme Party (BSPP) or *Lanzin* in July 1962. Building slowly, with emphasis upon loyalty, training and testing, the party finally emerged as a major organization of the military regime in 1971, when it called its first congress. With only 73,369 full members of which 41,921 were drawn from the armed forces, the party was an élite group largely isolated from the civilian mass. At the Congress, General Ne Win was formally elected as its leader and a committee of 150 was chosen to assist the leader. The party identified its mission as twofold: to transform itself from a cadre to a mass party and replace centralism with democratic centralism; to aid in the transformation of the nation to a socialist democratic state under a new constitution. Its ideological basis remained the same as that of the Government, the *Burmese Way to Socialism.* The third new set of institutions created by the military to mobilize and involve the people was the establishment of a dual hierarchy of peasant and worker councils. Ultimately, it was planned that a single Peasants' and Workers' Council would bind the two hierarchies and together serve as a popular backdrop to the military government.

In July 1971 the military leaders announced plans to draw up a new constitution and to transfer power to civilian hands. To match the move toward constitutionalism, in April 1972 General Ne Win and twenty of his senior commanders retired from the Army and became civilian members of government. At the same time, the RC proclaimed the end of the Revolutionary Government and its replacement by the Government of the Union of Burma. U (formerly General) Ne Win became Prime Minister, nine of his retired officers, three active military senior officers and two civilians made up the first cabinet under this new order. Brigadier San Yu was promoted to General and took over command of the Army, became Deputy Prime Minister and Minister of Defence; he became the most powerful figure in the nation after U Ne Win. The intent of these changes was to restore the image of civilian rule and constitutional government. Also, to make the Government more responsive to the people, the central administrative structure was overhauled, reducing the number of Ministries from 25 to 20 and abolishing the Secretariat and the post of District Officer.

Throughout the period of military rule, there was a remarkable stability in the nation's leadership. The Revolutionary Council came into existence in 1962 with a membership of 17 and was reorganized only once. The Council of Ministers—the Government of Burma—was also stable. During the 12 years of military rule, it was reorganized only twice. The military in Burma monopolized all power and in 12 years only three genuine civilians were given cabinet rank and only three in the final phase were admitted to membership in the highest level of government, the Revolutionary Council. This marked a significant difference between the caretaker government of Ne Win in 1958–60 and military rule from 1962 to 1974. In the earlier period, Ne Win drew upon highly qualified civilians to share power with members of the military both in making and implementing policy. The results then, unlike those achieved in the later period, were highly beneficial to the nation.

Over the years of military rule, despite Ne Win's pleas to the contrary, the ruling group began to further their own wealth and power. Their reputation was tarnished due to the sharp contrast between their wealth and the poverty of the people. Despite more than a decade of military rule, memories of popular government did not disappear. In an obvious bid for support and co-operation of the pre-coup political leaders, the RC in November 1968 established a committee of 33 former political leaders—called the Internal Unity Advisory Body—to advise it on ways and means of establishing national unity. The work of the committee received wide publicity inside Burma; General Ne Win took no official note of it however, until November 1969, when at a *Lanzin* national meeting, he dismissed or denounced most of the recommendations and called for national support of the programmes and policies of his government.

The awakening of the former political leaders did not end with the committee. U Nu, abroad in Europe and the U.S.A., denounced the Ne Win Government and called for its overthrow, either by persuasion or revolt. Following his trip, Nu and his supporters settled in Bangkok, Thailand, from where they launched their revolt. In the autumn of 1970 Nu reported agreement between himself and factions of dissidents from amongst the Shans, Karens and other indigenous minorities. During the two years which followed, the movement was unable to penetrate deeply into Burma and its numbers remained small and it was unsuccessful in winning the support of any of the government forces or their commanders. Despite the backing of foreign oil interests, eager to support Nu in exchange for the right to explore Burma's coastline for oil deposits, the movement proved to be no real match for the army of General Ne Win. In January 1972 U Nu resigned as President of the National United Liberation Front over the issue of the future of the federal state in Burma, and retired from politics.

A second source of opposition was the remnant of the Burma Communist Party which, in spite of internal dissension, remained a serious challenge to the military inside Burma. Despite the constant pressure the military sought to keep upon the Communists, they remained strong because of their ability to operate in the remote sections of the country and because they established strong links with the dissident minorities as well as with individual Burmese who sought political change. In order to weaken their foreign support, the Burmese Government, in October 1970, re-established diplomatic relations with the People's Republic of China after three years of intensive propaganda warfare and occasional military clashes. Despite the willingness of the People's Republic to restore normal relations with the Burmese, it continued to give military aid and training to the Burma Communist Party.

Political opposition emanated also from a third source, the indigenous minorities. The military rulers tried to bring about an end to their opposition in 1963, when they sought to negotiate directly with all factions. However, these negotiations broke down and rebellion was resumed. Until U Nu entered into agreement in 1970 with several minority groups, they had only the Burma Communist Party as their link with dissident Burmans. The resignation of Nu from the Liberation Front weakened the effort to weld together a solid opposition and at the end of military rule in 1974 the minorities were still in revolt, but their threat to Ne Win's government was no stronger than it had been at the beginning of military rule.

The reformation of values and attitudes among the people was a major concern of the RC. It sought to alter the character of the Burmese through educational reform. With all means of communications in government hands, the military rulers enjoyed a monopoly in this area. By concentrating on the school children, the leaders hoped to develop new attitudes and loyalties, which in time would come to replace the traditional ones.

Since becoming an independent nation in 1948, Burma has pursued a policy of non-alignment in world affairs. It supported the United Nations and contributed the third Secretary-General, U Thant, to that organization. It sought to maintain friendly relations with its neighbours, India, Pakistan, Bangladesh, the People's Republic of China, Laos and Thailand. In 1960 Burma signed a boundary agreement and a treaty of friendship with the People's Republic of China. However, in June 1967 a dispute arose with China over local Chinese demonstrations supporting the Cultural Revolution. Violence flared in Rangoon and Sino-Burmese relations deteriorated. China went so far as to give support to the Burmese communist insurgents, thus worsening an already difficult internal problem. The restoration of full diplomatic relations with China in 1970 permitted Burma to resume using the unexpended loans given to it a decade earlier. However, the resumption of diplomatic relations did not lead, as the Burmese Government had hoped, to a lessening of aid to the Burma Communist Party or to a reduction in tension between Burma and China. Throughout the period, Burma continued to have good relations with neighbours who had joined local regional organizations, but it did not alter its non-aligned policy and join any, despite an invitation from the Association of South East Asian Nations (ASEAN) to do so.

Following the coup in 1962 the military began to bring the whole economy under its control and drive out all private interests. Only agriculture and peasant land ownership remained in private hands, but the produce had to be sold to the government for distribution internally and for marketing abroad. All this was done in the name of the people by soldiers and state employees without business or trade experience. It succeeded in driving thousands of Indian merchants out of the country and caused the economy to stagnate, production to decline, distribution to break down and black markets and shortages to develop. From 1966 onward, the military oscillated between strict economic control and partial relaxation in the hope of encouraging the peasants to produce and deliver greater quantities of their product. But given the natural population increase and the state of the economy, the military never achieved the levels of production, distribution and exports in effect at the time they seized power.

CONSTITUTIONAL DICTATORSHIP

Military rule ended formally in March 1974. The new constitution of Burma, promulgated in January 1974, differed widely from its predecessor. Although the state is nominally federal, in practice it is unitary. The five states and Burma proper were replaced by seven states and seven divisions, all united in an administrative and political hierarchy. Real power is vested in the Burma Socialist Programme Party (BSPP). It is proclaimed as the only party in the nation and it is commanded to lead. As the author of the constitution, the only recognized party in the country, and as the chief agent for selecting candidates for elected office, it stands both inside and outside the formal structure of the state. Neither its constitution and rules nor its leaders and members are limited by the constitution. As the creation of the men who made the coup in 1962 and continue to lead in this period, it does not effect a real change in leadership between the past and present period; despite the elaborate wording of the basic law, there are no real limits on the party and its leaders.

Following a rigid timetable, elections for all four tiers of government were held and the new constitution and the institutions it created came into existence on March 2nd, 1974. General Ne Win, now U Ne Win, was elected as Chairman of the Council of State and therefore became the first president under the new basic law. Brigadier Sein Win, now U Sein Win, became Prime Minister. General San Yu was chosen as Secretary of the Council of Ministers and was therefore, under the constitution, the legal successor to Ne Win. The other seats in the two Councils were filled with familiar military leaders from the immediate past. In all, 11 of the 29 members of the Council of Ministers were carried over from the previous Revolutionary Council. Following its organization, the People's Assembly adjourned, leaving the running of the state to the members of the two Councils and the hierarchies they commanded at all three subordinate levels of government.

Despite the institutional changes, the people were still plagued with the economic problems of the past. In June 1974 riots broke out over food shortages and maldistribution. During the rainy season excessive flooding caused severe damage to the new crop and heralded another possible poor crop and further problems for the people. In December there were riots following the return of U Thant's body to Burma for burial and martial law was proclaimed. While the immediate cause of this unrest was the question of proper burial of U Thant, in fact it was clearly associated with popular discontent over the continuing declining economic conditions in the country, growing corruption and ostentatious living among those in power and the inability to provide good government and social stability.

A government campaign against corruption and inefficiency in administration and state enterprises began. The Government also launched a campaign against criminals and blackmarketeers, smugglers and heroin dealers. Against this background, the Government made two important ministerial changes and added 17 deputy ministers. It sought to placate the people through larger expenditures for education and health, and the importation of consumer goods.

Unrest in Burma was not limited to students and workers; ethnic and political rebellion continued as it has since 1949.

In 1976 social problems increased and forced the nation's leaders to rethink their approach both to politics and ideology. In March another student demonstration erupted on the university campus in Rangoon. The students seized buildings and demonstrated both for the release of their fellow student leaders, imprisoned earlier, and against conditions in the country. The student demonstration came shortly after U Ne Win had surprised the nation by dismissing General Tin U, the Armed Forces Chief of Staff and thought to be a rival of San Yu as successor to Ne Win, reportedly because of corruption.

In July the nation was shaken further by the announcement that an attempted coup by young officers of the armed forces had failed. General Tin U was accused of failing to inform the authorities of the impending coup attempt. The trial was given wide publicity in the press. The revelations of young officers, who had been educated under the Revolutionary Council regime and who had enjoyed the special privileges available to members of the military, that they were dissatisfied with the nation's economic failings and mismanagement raised serious doubts about the efforts made since 1962 to create a new socialist man, devoted to the ideology of the *Burmese Way to Socialism*. It also indicated how deeply the social discontent had penetrated the new élite. All the accused who had not turned state's evidence were convicted with the leaders, receiving sentences of death, and General Tin U receiving a sentence of seven years' hard labour.

In the face of the continuing political unrest and the economic shortcomings of the regime, the BSPP called a special meeting in October to review the past and plan for the future. It decided to expel more than 50,000 party members and candidates who had failed to live up to the ideals and directives of the party and to hold a third congress in February 1977. The Congress was attended by 1,311 delegates representing a membership of 885,460. The report of the Secretary-General, San Yu, stated that 17,894 full members and 131,490 candidate members had been dropped because they were "out of contact with the party".

The Congress focused upon several problems both within the structure of the party and the governance of the nation. Clearly, one major problem was in the party itself. As an institution it had grown rapidly and had failed fully to indoctrinate its members. More important, it had admitted persons whose values and interests were inconsistent with the party ideology, even within the defence services, the mainstay of the

Government since the coup. The party leaders were not free of criticism either. The Central Committee was accused of lacking dynamism and failing to give leadership or follow the resolution adopted at the previous congress. Through the process of self-criticism, 55 per cent of the members of the Central Committee were expected to resign and make way for new leaders. Although it was anticipated that the Central Committee would be enlarged to 240 members, only 180 were elected.

The Congress abolished the existing five-year plan for economic development and adopted a new programme. In doing this, the party seemingly moved to the right by approving the idea of foreign aid and controlled investment by private firms from capitalist countries. These and other changes were stated to be consistent with the nation's ideology in that the constitution argued that everything was impermanent and subject to change. Thus, while continuing to approve the socialist goals laid down by the Revolutionary Council and embodied in the constitution, it was argued that the modifications being adopted were in line with the changes facing Burma.

Following the adjournment of the Congress, the People's Assembly met. In addition to taking note of the work of the Congress, several members of the Council of Ministers, including U Sein Win, the Prime Minister, resigned. The People's Assembly elected new members to the Council of Ministers upon the recommendation of the Council of State. Among those elevated to leadership were U Maung Maung Kha as Prime Minister, U Than Sein as Minister of Finance, U Kyaw Zaw as Minister of Labour and Mines, U Kyi Maung as Minister of Health and Information and Colonel Sein Lwin as Minister of Home and Religious Affairs.

The changes in leadership and policy were followed in September 1977 by the removal from office and arrest of two leading members of the BSPP who were recently chosen as Ministers (U Than Sein and U Tin Lin), on the orders of Ne Win, as "threats" to presidential authority. Two members of the Central Committee and three members of the Secretariat were also dismissed and placed under detention. Earlier, other plots to assassinate the President had been uncovered. In order to offset these defections and the dissent within the party leadership, a special congress was held to elect a new Central Committee in February 1978, when 113 of those elected only the year before were dropped and in their place the party elected at least 80 active or recently retired military officers, thus almost eliminating civilian participation at top party levels. The remilitarization of Burma's constitutional dictatorship was also reflected a few weeks later in the naming of the new Council of Ministers. The party instituted new regulations which called upon leaders at all levels to disclose their assets and property holdings so that corruption among those in power could be more readily detected. The purges, arrests, trials and leadership changes suggest that the unity which once characterized the military dictatorship was faltering. Yet, despite this, Ne Win continued to take frequent trips abroad without apparent fear of being overthrown during his absence.

If the decisions taken at the Third Congress of the BSPP were intended to give a clear signal both to the Burmese and foreigners alike, laws passed by the People's Assembly during 1977 confused its message. The Private Enterprises Law reinforced the socialist objectives embodied in the constitution by declaring that there would be no private foreign investment, although local private enterprise could continue in areas not yet taken over by the State or co-operatives. The second law declared that Burma's territorial waters extended 200 nautical miles (370 km.) off-shore and that this would become an exclusive economic zone for Burma. Taken together, the two laws seemed to reverse the liberal trends toward foreign investment and aid which were advocated by some of the leaders at the Third Congress of the BSPP a few months earlier.

In January 1978 the second national election was held. Approximately 16 million voters participated. With only one party authorized to field candidates, the results brought new persons to the legislature, but no real changes either in the nation's leadership or its policies. In March 1978 the new Pyithu Hluttaw (People's Assembly) met and replaced several members of the Council of Ministers and Council of State with active or recently retired military officers.

The Fourth Party Congress and the third national election were held in 1981. At the party congress, Ne Win announced his intention to give up the office of President of the Socialist Republic of the Union of Burma while continuing as head of the party. His stated reasons for resigning were old age and the desire to see a peaceful transition of the nation's leadership. His successor is San Yu. The other important change was the elevation of Aye Ko to be General Secretary of the party and Secretary of the Supreme Council, making him the second-ranking member of the party and the Government. In his report to the party, the outgoing Secretary-General announced that membership rose to 1,500,902, of whom 143,747 were members of the armed forces. Although they represented only 9 per cent of the total party membership, they constituted more than 82 per cent of the total number of men under arms. It must also be noted that 60 of the 260 members of the party's Central Committee and four of the 15 members of the Executive Committee were uniformed officers. If these numbers are added to those officers, such as San Yu, who are retired from service, it is clear that the military's tight hold on the party which it created and the Government which it runs is as firm as ever. The report also suggested that the continuing problems of national unity were being solved. However, the Government's failure to end the insurgency of the Burma Communist Party (BCP) and the Kachin Independence Organization after extended negotiations during 1980–81, and their continuing military action against these and other insurgent groups, suggests that the new leaders have inherited old problems with little prospect for solution.

The national election took place in October 1981 and was expected to attract 90 per cent of the 17.4 million registered voters. The voting merely confirmed the party's choice of candidates for each of the seats in the four levels of councils because the constitution makes no provision for voters' choice, since the BSPP is the only legal party in the nation. The newly-elected members took their seats in November and the new President and other elected and appointed officials took up their duties.

As before, opposition remained outlawed. The BCP, located on the China border in the northern part of the Shan State, posed the most serious military challenge to the Burma Armed Forces. A pitched battle was fought in February 1978 and both sides sustained heavy casualties. The Communists were unable to gain their objective, the capture of Kunlong and Tang Yan in the northern Salween region; but the military also failed in its aim—the defeat and destruction of the BCP militarily. In November 1979 the Government quietly launched another major campaign, which lasted into mid-1980. Although the government forces scored some early successes, the tide turned against them and independent foreign sources suggested that it sustained very heavy casualties. The Communists were well armed and supported by anti-government, pro-BCP broadcasts from its China-based secret radio transmitter, the Voice of the People of Burma. In addition, the several ethnic insurgents—Kachins, Shans and Karens—continued their low-level warfare. The Burma Army challenged the Karens, located on both sides of the Thai border, but here, too, after initial success, the Karens fought back and continue to hold their enclaves on the Burma-Thai border.

Within Burmese society there remained one group which eluded control by the Government. The Buddhist *sangha* (order of monks) resisted government efforts to register its members and force them to carry identity cards when the effort was first made in 1965. Over the years, the Government has moved quietly to bring a majority of the orders under its control. Having established a Ministry of Religion and acknowledged the importance of the Buddhist tradition to the history and culture of the nation, it was able in May 1980 to sponsor a nationwide Congregation for the Purification, Perpetuation and Propagation of Buddhism. At this convention the representatives of the monks created a centralized authority to control the *sangha* throughout the nation and approved the idea that monks and nuns would carry identification cards. In response to its success in bringing the Buddhist clergy under its control, the Government proclaimed an amnesty which made it possible for U Nu and other political dissidents to return to Burma, and released thousands of prisoners including General Tin U. In 1981 the religious courts, which for years had been inactive, were revived. Two sects were brought before them, charged with teaching heretical doctrines. After an extended trial, both sects were found guilty and ordered to be dissolved. The monks belonging to the two orders were to recant publicly or cease to be monks. The trials were followed closely by the press and the results suggest that the Government was making headway in bringing the religious orders under its control.

Burma's renewed interest in Western culture was demonstrated in two important ways. In 1979 Ne Win called for the re-establishment of a strong English-language programme to allow the Burmese to keep up with scientific and technical information which was being generated in the West. This confirmed a trend toward interest in Western popular literature which remained strong despite government policies against it. Of equal importance was the government decision to introduce colour television to the nation. With the help of the Japanese, transmission facilities were installed and receivers were imported and distributed so that broadcasting began on June 3rd, 1980. This marked a significant advance in communications as Burma has not had any television facilities before.

In the latter half of the 1970s, talks between representatives of Burma and of the World Bank took place and in September 1976 the Burmese announced that the World Bank would form a consortium of Western nations to assist Burma. Later in the year, representatives of Burma, the World Bank and Western states met in Tokyo to discuss Burma's financial and economic requirements. In February 1978 the Burma Aid Group (comprising 10 members: Australia, Canada, France, the Federal Republic of Germany, the United Kingdom, Japan, the U.S.A., the Asian Development Bank, the International Monetary Fund and the United Nations Development Programme) met in Paris under the co-ordinating leadership of the World Bank to discuss further Burma's needs. No pledges were made but several nations began to discuss particular bilateral aid projects. In April 1979 the Group met again, this time in Tokyo, where Burma's Deputy Prime Minister, Tun Tin, outlined his nation's development goals and how aid would be used to realize them. It was reported that members of the Group tentatively pledged U.S. $400 million to support various projects on a bilateral basis. In December 1980 the Burma Aid Group, pleased with Burma's progress and use of previous grants, offered a further $500 million in aid. During 1979 the U.S.A. completed talks, initiated by the Burmese, and agreed to resume economic assistance, allotting $5 million for improving rural public health. This was the second time that the U.S.A. had formed links with Burma through assistance. The U.S.A. gave a further $30 million in 1981 to support corn and oil-seed production in order to achieve self-sufficiency within five years. In 1976 the Burmese authorities had realized that the opium which was grown in the "Golden Triangle" area of north-eastern Burma was being marketed illegally in the country and causing sizeable portion of the nation's youth to become addicted. In order to halt this growing problem, Burma began co-operating with the drug enforcement programmes of the United Nations and the U.S.A., and purchased 18 helicopters from the U.S.A. to give its Armed Forces more mobility in pursuing smugglers and raiding usually inaccessible areas. In January 1980 a U.S. delegation visited Burma to help its drug suppression programme.

The present Government continues the foreign policy of its predecessors. With a continued emphasis upon independence, non-alignment and friendship with all, especially its neighbours, the Government has sought to adapt to the political changes in the area while broadening its contacts with the states beyond. Despite this, the Burmese Government faces a persistent threat from the BCP, whose support from the fraternal Chinese Communist Party allows it to engage in nearly continuous warfare against the Government. Although there have been several visits to China by Ne Win and by Chinese leaders to Burma, Chinese support for the BCP continues. Towards other states in the region, Burma continues to pursue its policy of being a good neighbour. During 1978 Thailand's leader, Gen. Kriangsak Chomanan, visited Burma in order to reduce tension between the two states which stemmed from long-standing issues such as smuggling and the provision of sanctuary for Burmese rebels in Thai territory. The Thais ordered Burmese rebels out of their hiding places inside Thailand and took other steps calculated to please the Burmese. In July and August 1978 the two nations exchanged trade and economic missions. All this, however, must be balanced against the Burmese declaration of an off-shore exploration zone, extending 200 nautical miles (370 km.) from the coast, which drew an immediate rejection from Thai authorities, who saw the move as having a potentially adverse effects upon Thailand's fishing industry. In the summer of 1980, the Thai Foreign Minister and Prime Minister visited Burma and accomplished, among other things, the formulation of a treaty concerning their disputed maritime boundaries and Burma's newly declared economic zone. The Burmese Government continues to approve of ASEAN, but it shows no desire to join. Burma startled the world at the Havana Non-Aligned Summit Conference in September 1979, when its delegation, under the leadership of the Minister for Foreign Affairs, Brig. Myint Maung, denounced the movement's drift towards partisanship as exemplified by its support for the Heng Samrin government of Kampuchea; he called upon the members to return to the principles which it established at the movement's creation in Belgrade in 1971. When his suggestion was ignored, he informed the world at the UN General Assembly meeting that same month that Burma was withdrawing from the Non-Aligned movement which it had helped to create.

Towards the nations beyond South-East Asia, Burma elevated its relations with the two Koreas to ambassadorial level. It continued its good relations with Japan during 1977 by accepting two large loans, one for commodity purchases and the second for use in the building of a new medical research centre. Diplomatic visits and delegations have been exchanged with the three great powers, the U.S.S.R., the U.S.A. and the People's Republic of China. Relations with neighbouring Bangladesh deteriorated sharply in May 1978 over the problem of the flight of an estimated 200,000 Burmese Muslims across the border during April and May from Arakan State. The refugees complained of persecution by the Burmese authorities, while the Government claimed that it had only been attempting to stamp out illegal immigration from Bangladesh into the region. Talks between Burma and Bangladesh, begun in June in an attempt to resolve the problem, resulted in an agreement, signed in July, to return the refugees to Burma and to co-operate in future to prevent illegal border-crossing between the countries. In February 1982 an agreement was reached on the demarcation line along the boundary of 88 miles (142 km.) between Burma and Bangladesh.

ECONOMIC SURVEY

David I. Steinberg*

Closely following the military coup of March 2nd, 1962, Gen. Ne Win initiated the dual economic policies of the new revolutionary government, policies that were to characterize the first decade of military rule. These were: to create an industrialized socialist state devoid of foreign exploitation while concurrently improving income and access to social services throughout Burmese society. The theoretical formulation of these policies were explicitly stated shortly after the coup in two seminal documents, *The Burmese Way to Socialism* and *The System of Correlation of Man and His Environment*, the latter an eclectic mixture of Buddhist and socialist philosophy.

These policies were based on a joint effort to exclude foreigners (primarily Europeans, Indians, Pakistanis and Chinese) from the major modes of production and trade while at the same time fostering the harmonious relationships between all indigenous ethnic groups. Because of ethnic separatism and insurgency, the Revolutionary Government determined that centralized control, including the economy, should be in the hands of the Burmans, who had politically dominated all previous governments and who comprise over two-thirds of the population.

The decade following the coup could be characterized as one of nationalist economic involution. It was marked by efforts to strengthen the nascent industrial sector of the economy while improving access to social

* The views presented in this paper are solely those of the author and do not necessarily represent either those of the Agency for International Development or the Department of State.

services throughout Burma proper and those areas of the periphery controlled by the central government. Investment in industry was stressed. Banking and businesses, over 15,000 private enterprises including those involved in internal and external trade, were nationalized. The State, which had previously assumed legal ownership of all agricultural land, reinforced this claim and eliminated both landlords and private agricultural debt through the 1963 Law to Protect Peasant Rights and the Land Tenancy Law of the same year, guaranteeing to the tillers its use during their lifetime. Access to primary and secondary education as well as health services were improved in rural areas. In effect, however, the peasants paid for such benefits through the very low purchase price for paddy rice paid by the Government to farmers. In 1980/81† farmers received 438 kyats per ton for ordinary paddy, which the Government sold on the international market for 2.64 times that amount, while the Burmese consumer had to pay 39 per cent more for the same rice on the free market.

More equitable distribution of income did result as rural debt was eliminated, at least that officially recognized. However, the stress on industry and social services resulted in inattention to and stagnation of the agriculture and forestry sectors which were essential both to improved overall economic growth and a higher standard of living for the bulk of the population. During this decade, the acreage under rice production remained relatively constant, still not reaching levels achieved in 1940/41. Yields also stabilized at 1,400–1,500 lb. of paddy harvested per acre. Ominously, as production stabilized, population grew at about 2.2 per cent a year according to official figures, but the increase may well have been higher. These factors resulted in a major drop in rice exports in spite of a minimal 15 per cent increase in the government-controlled purchase price for paddy from 1962–72. Exports, which had risen to well over 3 million tons a year prior to the Second World War, dropped to 1,309,000 tons in 1964/65, and by 1972/73 had fallen to 262,000 tons, earning only U.S. $23.3 million in foreign exchange. Capacity utilization of major industries averaged about 50 per cent. Although 44.9 per cent of public capital expenditures in 1970 were allocated to processing and manufacturing, these sectors provided only 12.1 per cent of G.D.P. Yet agriculture, which was allocated only 6.2 per cent of capital expenditures in the same year, provided 27.2 per cent of G.D.P. Rice alone accounted for 49.5 per cent of all export earnings in 1970 while all agricultural products, including forestry, accounted for 84 per cent of total earnings. At the same time, the large military budget necessitated by the various insurgencies continued to drain meagre government resources. G.D.P. grew by 2.7 per cent a year, with agricultural growth for the decade beginning in 1963/64 estimated at 2.4 per cent. Unemployment emerged as an important social problem. The "black" (or "parallel") market became, and remains, ubiquitous, and smuggling increased.

In September 1972 a profound policy shift was approved at the fourth meeting of the Central Committee of the Burma Socialist Programme Party (BSPP), culminating with the publication of the "Long-Term and Short-Term Economic Policies of the Burma Socialist Programme Party." The Party leadership recognized that its economic programme was failing. It was determined to "establish the economic system on a commercial basis", while still retaining the long-range goal of an industrialized socialist state.

A series of economic reforms, initiated over a period of five years, began to reverse the patterns of stagnation of the previous decade. The Burmese Government determined that the basis for growth lay in those sectors of the economy where Burma was naturally well-endowed. Agriculture, forestry, fishing and mining were to be given priority. At the same time, the Government determined that financial incentives, personal and institutional, were an appropriate response to the previous malaise, even in a socialist state. These incentives included reforms which, over several years, hesitatingly raised the paddy purchase price paid to farmers by the Government, and authorized the State Economic Enterprises to be run along commercial lines, rewarding economic units with bonuses for meeting production targets. Interest rates were raised to encourage domestic savings. The tax system was reformed and a law passed encouraging private investment in sectors where State-run corporation activities were weak. Consumer industries were given emphasis.

As a result of, or concurrently with, these changes, the Government began to modify its policy of intense economic isolation. Burma re-established relationships with the IBRD in 1973, and in 1974 joined the Asian Development Bank. Bilateral assistance was promoted. Foreign assistance commitments which averaged $50–$60 million at the close of the military government's first decade rose to $320 million in 1976/77, with over $400 million expected for 1979/80. At the donor group meeting held in Paris in December 1980, under IBRD auspices, it was indicated that Burma could expect $500 million in aid in 1981/82. Bilateral loans in 1980/81 totalled $288.3 million, and multilateral loans $216.2 million. Grants of $44 million are expected for 1982. Visas for tourist travel were also liberalized.

These slow but, as a whole, momentous changes were related to the increased political confidence of the regime internally, and the control which it exercised over the heartland of the nation. Although the ethnic and communist insurgencies did not disappear, they at least offered no immediate threat to national survival. The BSPP was transformed from a "cadre" party to a mass party and, following this shift, a new Constitution was promulgated in 1974 after much public fanfare and a census the previous year. The Constitution stipulated that the BSPP was to be the only legal political party. Politically the Government felt more secure but, economically,

† Dates indicated with an oblique stroke represent fiscal years. Until 1973 the Burmese fiscal year was October 1st to September 30th. After 1973 it became April 1st to March 31st. All data for 1980/81 are provisional.

changes had to be made, although it took several years for these reforms to be implemented.

In 1972 the Twenty-Year Plan was inaugurated. It was hoped that by the end of the Plan period in 1993/94 Burma would have achieved an annual growth rate of 5.9 per cent, that the public sector contribution to G.D.P. would have increased from 36 per cent to 48 per cent, that the co-operative sector's share would rise from approximately 3 per cent to 26 per cent and that the private sector's contribution to G.D.P. would decline from 61 per cent to 26 per cent.

The Twenty-Year Plan was divided into five four-year plans. The First Four-Year Plan, inaugurated in October 1971, was a truncated effort which ended in March 1974, as the new policies enunciated in 1972 began to take effect. The Second Four-Year Plan (1974/75–1977/78) resulted in marked improvement in overall economic performance, especially in its last two years. G.D.P. grew by 4.8 per cent a year, compared with 2.7 per cent during the first decade of military rule. Agricultural production increased by 3.6 per cent a year and that of fisheries and livestock by 3.2 per cent. However, a much more marked improvement was noted in the forestry (7.7 per cent a year), mining (10.5 per cent), construction (6.3 per cent), and trade (4.2 per cent) sectors.

The Third Four-Year Plan (1978/79–1981/82) produced excellent growth. G.D.P. was planned to rise by 6.5 per cent annually, but in the third year of the Plan (1980/81) the growth rate reached 8.3 per cent, including growth of 14.6 per cent in agriculture, 8.2 per cent in livestock and fisheries, 5.9 per cent in forestry, 17.2 per cent in mining, and 13.8 per cent in industry. The aim for the last year of the Plan was a more modest 5.7 per cent growth, and, overall, the growth targets have been achieved, with the highest growth by the public works sector at 20.1 per cent.

On March 18th, 1981, the Constitution was amended to allow the convening of the Pyithu Hluttaw in November 1981 instead of March 1982, to facilitate the planning and approval of the Fourth Four-Year Plan.

AGRICULTURE

Three-quarters of Burma's population is rural and agriculture supports two-thirds of Burma's 34 million inhabitants. Much of Burmese agriculture is still traditional: only 1.6 million acres are ploughed by tractors and the use of chemical fertilizers is still limited; pesticides are in short supply relative to needs. In the hill areas of Burma traditional "slash and burn" techniques remain, untouched by new and improved policies. Burma is fortunate in Asian terms to have an area of cultivable and virgin land approximately equal to that of land under production. Although much of it is difficult to reach, it provides a potential for development that could both improve Burma's export position and provide a livelihood for Burma's expanding population. Because of seasonal rural labour shortages, such expansion, at least at present, is regarded by the Government as necessary for increased agricultural production in spite of relatively high urban unemployment. Burma therefore continues to have a pro-natalist policy, and family planning is officially proscribed.

The Burmese Government had early in its rule eliminated the absentee and foreign landlord. Village People's Councils allocate plots of land to farmers for their lifetime, and then determine who shall farm the land after their death. Burma has been transformed into a state of small land-holders. At the last survey, 62.5 per cent of all farm families held under five acres of land, and this accounted for 26.2 per cent of all cultivated land in Burma. A further 24.1 per cent of farm families tilled between 5 and 10 acres, or 32.1 per cent of the total cultivated area. Thus, 86.6 per cent of all farm families have holdings under 10 acres, and their land represents 58.3 per cent of all agricultural land. Few large landowners exist; only 0.05 per cent till more than 50 acres, and most of these comprise rubber plantations which were not nationalized in 1963. In 1978, by Burmese estimates, the average farm family holding was 4.76 acres, larger in lower Burma and smaller in upper Burma. Population pressure on cultivated land is increasing. There were approximately 1.39 cultivated acres per person in 1940/41, but by 1977/78 that figure had fallen to 0.77 of an acre per person. To rise above the rural poverty line requires holdings of about 10 acres, unless high-yielding varieties of rice are grown. Therefore over five-sixths of the rural population are considered poor.

Increases in Burmese agricultural yield are largely dependent upon the availability of fertilizer, new varieties of seed, and a controlled water supply. While urea is produced locally, and a third urea plant is being financed by the Federal Republic of Germany, potash and phosphates must be imported. There is a 50–70 per cent subsidy on fertilizer distributed to farmers and the bulk of fertilizer is used for paddy production. Population pressure on farmland is growing, both among the tribes who practice "slash and burn" agriculture in the hills, and among those engaged in stabilized farming in both the Divisions and the States.

In 1980/81, 98.3 per cent of the value of agricultural output was in private hands, 1.4 per cent in the co-operative sector and only 0.3 per cent in the State sector.

Rice

Paddy is Burma's principal crop and the major source of employment, foreign exchange and, in its edible form (rice), of caloric and protein intake for the population. Rice provides 77 per cent of calories for the lower-income urban groups and 66 per cent for the rural population. The acreage under paddy production has remained relatively constant since 1964, when it attained the levels achieved just prior to the Second World War. The area under paddy in 1980/81 was 12,668,000 acres, representing 52 per cent of all land under cultivation. Total paddy production was a record 9,313,000 long tons in 1977/78, an average yield of 1,736 lb. per acre. Output rose once again in

1978/79 to an estimated 10.3 million tons. Production in 1979/80 reached 10,283,000 tons, with an average yield of 2,099 lb. per acre. Provisionally, the 1980/81 harvest was 13,107,000 tons, or an average of 2,475 lb. per acre. There has been a slow but steady rise in production per acre, primarily due to the recent introduction of new rice strains, although it still remains one of the lower rates of production in Asia. Availability of fertilizer is critical to increased yields. Figures for 1980/81 indicate that production of urea will be about 130,000 tons, about half the required amount, and imports of all fertilizers are expected to reach 108,000 tons. In 1980/81, the Government spent 300 million kyats on fertilizer subsidies. Domestic use of fertilizer has increased by 60 per cent since 1977/78, but imports are expected to increase five fold by 1983/84.

The Government procures about 32–35 per cent of the total yield (provisional figures for 1980/81 indicated that the proportion was 32 per cent, a procurement of 4,145,000 tons). This must be distributed to the rice-deficit areas in the dry zone of central Burma, to urban areas, and to the constituent states, as well as be used for export. Approximately 20 per cent of Government-procured paddy is exported as milled rice, and provisional figures for 1977/78 give total rice exports of approximately 636,000 tons, 189,000 tons in 1978/79, and 759,000 tons in 1979/80. The major buyers of Burmese rice are Sri Lanka and Indonesia. In the early 1950s Burma controlled 28 per cent of the world rice trade. By 1970 it was 2 per cent.

The Government has made efforts to improve yields and to expand both the acreage under cultivation and irrigation, but much more needs to be done. Only 5 per cent of paddy land in lower Burma, the rice-surplus area, is irrigated, and only 3.6 million acres of all land is double-cropped. High-yielding varieties of paddy have been introduced into lower Burma in 72 township-level campaigns (the "Whole Township Programme") which, because of their intensive nature, have been reasonably successful. Yet only about 46 per cent of paddy acreage is sown with high-yielding varieties, including areas under less efficacious locally-produced improved strains. Priority fertilizer distribution is concentrated in such areas, and increased extension services are provided, as is short-term agricultural credit of 140 kyats per acre, increasing in some areas to 200 kyats. Water control remains a problem, as does the lack of pesticides, used by perhaps 2 per cent of farmers. In April 1981 three dams were under construction: the Chuang Magyi dam, the Nawin dam in Prome township and the Sedawgyi dam, funded by the ADB. They were planned to irrigate an additional 20,000 acres of land in 1980/81. Burma's milling factor (the percentage of rice derived from a given weight of paddy) was only 58–62 per cent, owing to aged milling capability, but in 1980/81 apparently dropped to 46 per cent. By comparison, Thailand's milling factor is 67 per cent. Losses also occur because of inadequate storage facilities and a decayed transportation network. The lower imputed conversion rate may also be due to overestimation of production, underestimation of consumption, unreported free market trading or even smuggling.

Perhaps the single greatest deterrent to increased production is the improved, but still low, paddy purchase price. Theoretically the State has a monopoly of all major commercial sales of rice, inter-township paddy shipments, and exports. Farmers in 171 of the 314 townships are obliged to sell their surplus to the government. Although the Burmese Government has raised the paddy purchase price three times since 1971, it still remains perhaps 40–50 per cent below the internal "parallel" market price, depending on the area. The Burmese farmer receives one of the lowest prices for paddy within the region. In Sri Lanka, the farmer gets 12.2 U.S. cents per kilogramme, in the Philippines between 11.6 and 17.8 cents, and in Thailand 22 cents. In Burma the figure is 6.42 cents. Quotas are set for procurement from individual farms. The farmer retains fixed amounts for home consumption, together with a small additional amount for ceremonial activities and seed. He is required to sell most of the surplus up to his quota to the Government. He may sell the remainder to any individual consumer within his township, except in specified rice surplus townships, which comprise over half of the total number of 314. However, internal and external smuggling of rice is extensive, and probably led to the Government purchase shortfall in 1977/78. This accounted for more stringent Government supervision of procurement of quotas in 1978/79, and increased involvement of the military in the process.

Other Crops

Although paddy dwarfs all other forms of agriculture, important local crops include groundnuts, sesame seed, jute, pulses and sugar cane. Except for pulses, which are exported (earning an estimated $9.9 million in 1977/78), these crops are consumed locally. Exports of pulses and beans in 1979/80 reached an estimated 63,200 tons, worth $19.3 million.

Groundnut production amounted to 431,000 long tons in 1980/81, cultivated on 1,271,000 acres. In 1980/81 155,000 tons of sesame seed was produced on 3,231,000 acres. Yields increased 70 per cent in a decade but acreage fluctuated in response to local conditions. Production of pulses in 1980/81 was 402,000 tons on 1,995,000 acres. Sugar cane production has increased both in acreage sown and in production (248,000 acres and 2,003,000 tons in 1980/81). A major sugar refining improvement project has been funded by the ADB. Rubber and jute are the two other crops which are exported. Provisional estimates placed the value of jute exports in 1979/80 at $6.2 million and that of rubber at $11.3 million. Rubber production has remained constant at 16,000 tons on 200,000 acres. The IBRD is to assist in rehabilitation of the rubber sector, while the ADB provided $25.3 million for a jute mill in 1975. Cotton production in 1980/81 was 73,000 tons.

In addition to paddy, the Government officially controls the price of certain pulses, cotton, jute, sugar cane and tobacco and has extended its "Whole Township Programme" for paddy to include a wide variety of other crops.

Forestry

The Burmese Government estimates that forests cover approximately 57 per cent of the total land area, and about half of the forests comprise teak and other hardwoods. This figure may be questioned, as it has remained constant since 1952 while Burma's population has steadily increased and much of the area said to be forested is outside the control of the Government. Teak has been extensively smuggled into Thailand. The management of forests is the responsibility of the Forest Department but the Timber Corporation handles engineering, extraction, transport, milling and marketing. Reserved forest areas totalled 38,315 square miles in 1978/79.

Burma has about 75–85 per cent of the world's teak reserves. Due to insurgent activity, a paucity of extraction equipment and spare parts, occasional localized shortages of fuel, and transport problems, Burma has, until recently, neglected this sector which, with careful management, can and now does yield considerable revenue. As rice exports began to decline, the Burmese Government recognized that expansion of the forestry sector, which is dominated by teak, could provide the additional foreign exchange necessary to expand imports. Teak exports, which had averaged 227,283 cubic tons (i.e. tons of 63.66 cubic feet) a year between 1936 and 1940, declined to 145,889 cubic tons in 1962 and fell further to 120,000 cubic tons in 1972/73 and only 76,000 cubic tons in 1976/77. However, increased international prices in 1977 and 1978 provided greater revenue although exports were low. In 1977/78 Burma earned $54.2 million and in 1978/79 $117.5 million from teak alone. In 1979/80 Burma exported 103,000 tons, earning $73.6 million.

During the decade 1963/64–1973/74 the forestry sector received 2.0 per cent of public capital expenditures but, in recognition of its new importance, it was allocated 6.7 per cent of such expenditures during the Second Four-Year Plan and a target of 5.0 per cent during the Third Four-Year Plan (1978/79–1981/82). In 1978 forestry contributed 7.0 per cent to G.D.P. although it employed only 1.2 per cent of the labour force. Annual growth in the forestry field between 1964/65–1974/75 averaged 1.2 per cent. This increased to 5.7 per cent in 1976/77, 6.6 per cent in 1977/78, 10.5 per cent (provisional) in 1978/79, and is projected to fall to 6.6 per cent in 1979/80. The growth target for 1981/82 is 7.7 per cent. Teak production in 1978/79 was 380,000 cubic tons, exceeding Plan estimates, and was expected to reach 390,000 tons in 1980/81.

Timber extraction is receiving assistance from the IBRD and the ADB and promises to be an important continuing source of foreign exchange. Sawmills, which had been operating at only 56.2 per cent capacity in 1973/74, had reached 79.5 per cent by 1977/78. While the Government has set targets for reforestation, these do not seem an adequate response to what may be the rapid deterioration of the major river watersheds.

Livestock and Fishing

Livestock and fishing employed only 1.3 per cent of the labour force in 1978 but accounted for 7 per cent of G.D.P. while receiving 2.6 per cent of public capital allocations in the same year. The budget for this sector in 1978 was 627 million kyats. This sector expanded at an average annual rate of 3.3 per cent during 1963/64–1973/74, and grew by 3.2 per cent a year during the succeeding Four-Year Plan. It is expected to grow by 5.0 per cent annually during the Third Fourth-Year Plan (1978/79–1981/82). Production increases were 5.3 per cent in 1978/79, 1.3 per cent in 1979/80 and 1.4 per cent in 1980/81. Much of the growth predicted under the Third Plan will come from the offshore fisheries production which is now beginning to be exploited by the People's Pearl and Fishery Corporation (PPFC). The 1976/77 receipts of that organization were 72 million kyats, compared with 6 million kyats for the Livestock Development and Marketing Corporation. The importance of livestock is not for food production, although this is a goal, but for ploughing. Meat production in 1979/80 was 78.8 million viss (1 viss= 3.6 lb. or 1.63 kg.).

There is no doubt that the new guidelines offering incentives for the operation of State Economic Enterprises have greatly assisted the PPFC by reducing smuggling. Foreign assistance to develop off-shore fishing has been received from the ADB, the United Kingdom, Norway and Denmark. The FAO believes that such fisheries could provide a maximum sustainable yield of 600,000 metric tons a year, compared with the 1972 output of 367,000 metric tons. Fresh-water fisheries are also within the scope of the PPFC. Catches for 1979/80 were 95.3 million viss for fresh water, 262.85 million viss for marine fisheries and 12.85 million viss for shrimp and prawns (1978/79). Public investment in livestock and fisheries reached 9.7 per cent of total expenditure in 1979/80.

About 95 per cent of the output of the fisheries sector is in private hands. In 1977/78 fishing accounted for 1.6 per cent of all exports, but it is planned that this will rise to 4.8 per cent at the end of the Third Four-Year Plan in 1981/82. Although fishery export earnings have grown by almost 40 per cent annually, only about 2 per cent of catches are exported.

MINING AND PETROLEUM

The mining sector is under the control of the Ministry of Mines, which includes, under a reorganization in July 1979, four corporations within its structure. These are No. 1 Mining Corporation, responsible for non-ferrous metals; No. 2 Mining Corporation, concerned with tin, tungsten and antimony; No. 3 Mining Corporation, with responsibility for coal, various clays, bentonite and feldspar; and the Myanma Gems Corporation. Responsibility for petroleum exploitation is vested in three corporations under the authority of Ministry of Industries II: the Petrochemical Industries Corporation; the Petroleum Products Supply Corporation; and the Myanma Oil Corporation.

Mining, including petroleum, is one of the sectors stressed under the Twenty-Year Plan. Although Burma is regarded as well-endowed with minerals, much of the mining activity takes place in areas periodically subject to insurgent activity. This, coupled with an antiquated internal transport system and relatively high costs for the movement of commodities, has prevented Burma from attaining many pre-war production levels. The rates of growth for mining were disappointing during the decade 1963/64–1973/74, when mining averaged only 1.9 per cent of G.D.P. During the Second Four-Year Plan (1974/75–1977/78), its contribution to G.D.P. increased to 10.5 per cent and under the Third Four-Year Plan it is expected to reach 12.2 per cent.

The rapid growth of the mining sector has been attributed largely to increased production of petroleum, and the targets for the Third Four-Year Plan were predicated on the optimistic assumption of producing 17 million barrels a year by 1981/82. Production of oil increased from 3.81 million barrels in 1965 to 11.7 million barrels in 1979/80 but has since stagnated. Until a few years ago Burma imported a modest amount (1.70 million barrels in 1976). In 1977 Burma exported petroleum for the first time in many years (140,000 barrels), but at present output is barely sufficient to meet the country's needs, which are kept artificially low under stringent controls, resulting in localized shortages sometimes affecting development projects. Since 1979 Burma has been exporting 1 million barrels of crude oil annually to Japan. In order to improve Burma's position, a day pipeline, capable of transporting 20,000 barrels a day from the Mann Oilfield, and financed by the Chase Manhattan Bank, was completed in April 1979. In October 1978 off-shore drilling sites were opened to bids by foreign oil companies but as of mid-1979 the results were not encouraging. There were 462 on-shore wells in 1977/78. An increase to 527 wells was planned for 1978/79 and the discovery of three new fields was announced in 1981. Natural gas production in 1977/78 was 8.7 million cubic feet, and was expected to reach 12.8 million cubic feet in 1979/80.

The mining sector as a whole received 5.4 per cent of public capital expenditure between 1964 and 1974, and 13.3 per cent under the Second Four-Year Plan. It was anticipated that it would receive 6.6 per cent under the Third Four-Year Plan, but estimates have been revised upwards to 11.0 per cent.

Figures for 1977/78 showed exports of 10,000 long tons of base metals and ores, providing $11.5 million in foreign exchange. Estimates for 1979/80 indicate that exports reached 11,300 tons, valued at $29 million, excluding precious metals. Production during 1980/81 was estimated at 1,000 tons of tin concentrates, 888 tons of tungsten concentrates, 6,992 tons of zinc concentrates, 6,488 tons of refined lead, 11,036 tons of coal and 28,395 viss of jade, as well as copper matte, nickel speiss, refined silver and antimonial lead.

INDUSTRY

Although the political and economic focus of the Burmese Government between 1962 and 1972 was on industry, this sector expanded by only 2.8 per cent a year during that period. During the Second Four-Year Plan the sector grew by 7.0 per cent a year and this growth rate is expected to increase to 12.2 per cent a year during the Third Four-Year Plan. Processing and manufacturing grew by 9.2 per cent in 1979/80. This may seem to be an unusually high rate of change, especially in the light of Government stress on agriculture. In fact much of the investment in industry is in areas which will support the growth of agriculture, such as fertilizer plants and food-processing. During the Second Four-Year Plan, capacity utilization, especially in light industries, improved by about 10–15 per cent. Heavy industries did not fare so well; they accounted for only 10 per cent of value added, compared with 40 per cent for light industries. Public capital expenditure on industry was 25.5 per cent of the total and this was expected to rise to 36.1 per cent during the Third Plan. Capacity utilization in 1979/80 was 70 per cent, and was increasing.

In 1979/80 there were 1,699 state-owned factories and establishments, and an additional 330 under construction. This contrasts with 35,345 private factories and manufacturing concerns, and only 1,183 in co-operative hands. In 1978/79 the total production of the state section was valued at 2,951 million kyats, of which 57 per cent was in the food and beverage field. Total production of the private sector that year was 3,617 million kyats, and only 393 million kyats in the co-operatives. In 1978/79 processing and manufacturing contributed 10.8 per cent of G.D.P., of which 55.5 per cent was in the state sector and 4.9 per cent in the co-operative movement.

The gross output of the State Economic Enterprises under the auspices of Ministry of Industry I was valued at 996 million kyats and that of Ministry of Industry II at 806 million kyats in 1977/78 (in 1969/70 constant value kyats). Almost half of the latter was devoted to the Petrochemical Industries Corporation. Ministry of Industry I, which essentially handles consumer goods, had a per capita production of only $4.65 in 1977/78. Under this Ministry the Textile Industry Corporation dominated the light industrial field with current receipts in 1976/77 of 1,020 million kyats, compared with the next largest light industry, the Foodstuff Industry Corporation, which received 643 million kyats during the same year. Manufacturing employed 7.35 per cent of the labour force in 1978. In 1980/81 public sector investment in processing and manufacturing was 32.6 per cent, of which 9.9 per cent was in "agriculture support industries" and 4.1 per cent in "processing of agricultural commodities".

The economic reforms of 1972 have had their most positive effect in the processing and manufacturing sector. Yet, in many of the traditional industries, production has not reached pre-military coup levels while the population has increased by 50 per cent. The consumer is still disadvantaged in Burma.

TRANSPORT

Transport bottlenecks remain one of the more enduring constraints to Burmese growth and, indeed, to Burmese control of some of the peripheral regions on its northern and eastern frontiers. Equipment for river, rail, road and air transport is largely outmoded and is subject to constant breakdown, a lack of spare parts and occasional shortages of fuel.

The Union-estimated requirements for transport were calculated to be 55.9 million tons in 1978/79 for all types of transportation and from both the public and private sectors. Of this amount, only 4.04 million tons could be carried by the state, the remainder being in the hands of the private sector and the co-operative movement (capacity provisionally estimated at 44.5 million tons in 1978/79).

In 1975, the Burma Railways Corporation operated 279 miles of double-track railway from Rangoon to Mandalay, and 1,670 miles of single-track railway. In 1978 these figures were reported to be 179 and 1,770 respectively. The number of passengers carried reached 57.9 million in 1980/81. However, freight tonnage had declined to 1.88 million long tons in 1978/79, and only in 1980/81 reached the 2.3 million tons carried in the period before the coup.

The Burmese Government lists one international-class airport (Rangoon) and 45 domestic civilian airfields within the country. Provisional figures for 1980/81 indicated that 261,386 passengers were flown, internally and externally, some 3.6 million passenger-miles.

In 1980/81 there were 17,388 miles of all-weather roads in Burma, including 2,452 miles regarded as national highways, 11,676 miles of main roads, and 3,260 miles of locally maintained roads. There are an additional 10,000 miles of farm roads passable only in the dry season. Between 1971/72 and 1979/80 the number of passengers on state-operated buses declined to 174,600,000 (provisional) from 297,618,000 while the number of passenger-miles reached 787,050,000 in 1979/80. Freight tonnage hauled by road reached 967,000 long tons in 1979/80, a decrease from 1,844,000 in 1971/72. The bulk of freight transport remains in private hands, including the co-operative movements. In 1977/78 1,059,000 tons were transported by the Road Transport Corporation whereas 16,653,000 tons were transported by privately-owned lorries.

River transport has always played an important role in the Burmese economy, especially with regard to north-south communications along the Irrawaddy and its tributary, the Chindwin, and, to a lesser degree, along the Sittang and the Lower Salween. Burma has 5,000 miles of navigable rivers at high water, and 3,700 miles at low water. The number of passengers carried by state-owned inland water transport increased to 13.6 million in 1979/80, but there has been a marked decline since 1974–75 in the freight tonnage carried, to 1,108,000 long tons in 1977/78. The vast majority of river transport is controlled by the private sector and the co-operatives, which in 1977/78 shipped 29 million tons of freight along the rivers and coasts of Burma.

Investment allocations in the public sector during the Third Four-Year Plan call for the Burmese Railway Corporation to receive 29.5 per cent of the allocation to the transport sector, the Inland Water Transport Corporation 16.2 per cent and the Road Transport Corporation 8.9 per cent. 1979/80 witnessed an 8.6 per cent growth in the transport sector, although this sector continues to be one which will have to be improved if Burma is to increase its exports and avoid internal food and commodity shortages at various points throughout the country.

DOMESTIC COMMERCE AND PRICES

The Government has succeeded in its efforts to "Burmanize" the domestic economy through the nationalization of most major forms of industry and commerce. Since 1962 more than 15,000 firms have been nationalized but, even with the reorganization of the state trading corporations in 1976, a great deal of trade is still officially in the hands of the private sector. A "parallel" market is tolerated but, although it is clearly extensive, its volume of trade is unknown. Some unofficial estimates calculate that it may equal the known volume of internal commerce. Improvements in the State Economic Enterprises have become apparent with the promulgation of the "Guidelines for Operating State Economic Enterprises along Commercial Lines", introduced in 1976/77. In August 1977 the "Bill on the Rights of Private Enterprises" was passed. Approximately 10,000 applications have been received for the establishment of private enterprises, of which about 1,000 have been approved. There has been no foreign investment in Burma since 1962, although official documents indicate that the Government is prepared to consider mutually beneficial investments, but only with the Burmese public sector. In April 1976 a major tax reform was enacted which has improved the capacity of the government to manage its internal fiscal affairs.

For long periods Burma avoided the inflationary spiral, as it has been the only less-developed country that exports both oil and food. Earlier calculations in the 1960s may have been based on controlled prices that did not reflect consumer realities. However, in the 1970s the consumer price index may have been more responsive to actuality. In any case, inflation did strike Burma. The Rangoon consumer price index (base: 1972=100) rose to 123.5 in 1973, stood at 206.4 in 1975 and reached a high of 249.7 in 1977. By 1978, however, it had dropped to 234.1. It rose once again to 252.6 in 1979, and to 258.9 in June 1980, and was 248.3 in 1981. Burma's concern about raising official procurement prices, especially for paddy, is related to their efforts to hold down the consumer price index. Investment has grown during the Second Four-Year Plan. As a proportion of G.D.P., it was 6.5 per cent in 1974/75, 10.5 per cent in 1975/76, 19.6 per cent in 1978/79 and 20.4 per cent in 1979/80. Of this last figure, 5.4 per cent is from foreign sources and 14.9 per cent domestically financed. Investment for 1980/81 is scheduled to reach 5,375 million kyats, of which 33 per cent will be from foreign loans and grants.

FOREIGN TRADE

The change in policy by the Burmese Government in 1972 was designed to return Burma to its traditional export strengths—agriculture, forestry and mining.

With the development of the Irrawaddy delta following the opening of the Suez Canal in 1869, Burma became the world's leading rice exporter. In 1940/41 it exported 3,123,000 long tons. Following independence and the early insurrections that threatened the political and economic structure of the state, exports declined to 1,309,000 tons in 1964/65, and then further to 262,000 tons in 1972/73. With policy changes and stringent procurement regulations, they had risen to 646,000 tons in 1976/77, earning $110.3 million in foreign exchange. Exports were 636,000 tons in 1977/78, dropped to 189,900 tons in 1978/79, but rose again to 759,400 tons in 1979/80, with stricter enforcement of Government paddy procurement.

Teak exports between 1936 and 1940 averaged 120,000 cubic tons a year and were the same in 1972/73. Provisional figures for 1980 indicated that, with paddy, these two traditional exports continued to dominate the export market. In that year Burmese exports totalled $407.6 million, of which $182.4 million came from rice and rice products. Teak exports were valued at $59.4 million in 1977/78, $121.4 million in 1978/79 and $73.6 million in 1979/80. Trade with other Asian countries, Burma's traditional markets for rice, accounted for 73.9 per cent of exports, with most rice exports destined for Sri Lanka and Indonesia. The EEC received 14.8 per cent of exports in 1978, and exports to Japan were 18.4 per cent the same year.

Imports continue to be dominated by capital goods and raw materials. Figures for 1979/80 showed that capital goods constituted 58.0 per cent (of which machinery represented 35.9 per cent, transport equipment 8.5 per cent and building materials 11.7 per cent). Consumer goods comprised 5.7 per cent of total imports. Since 1974/75 imports have increased from 1,106 million kyats to 2,220 million kyats in 1977/78. Of total imports, 44.7 per cent came from Japan, 22.2 per cent from the EEC, 5.1 per cent from Singapore and 3.6 per cent from the People's Republic of China. These official figures do not account for the high volume of illegal foreign trade. Because of controlled prices, unauthorized supplies of rice, teak, fish, tin, rubber, precious stones and jade, fertilizers and minerals find their way into foreign markets, as do antiques. A wide range of foreign consumer goods imported illegally may be seen in all major markets in Burma. They operate openly and with the tacit knowledge of the government. The volume of this illicit trade is unknown but it probably greatly exceeds official imports in all categories. This informal trade provides the means by which the centrally-controlled economy can respond to increased public demand for consumer goods when local production is limited, imports restricted and population growing.

FOREIGN EXCHANGE RESERVES AND FOREIGN ASSISTANCE

In 1980/81 Burma's gross foreign exchange reserves stood at $274.8 million, or 3.6 months of imports. Total external debt was $2,740.2 million on March 31st, 1981, of which slightly less than half was undisbursed, while debt servicing was $90.3 million in 1979/80 and is expected to rise to $127.7 million in 1980/81. In 1981/82 the debt service ratio was 28.4 per cent of foreign exchange receipts. It has grown rapidly since 1965, when it was 4.5 per cent of exports. Continued good weather, a strong demand for rice on the world market, especially in the Asia region, and vigorous implementation of the economic reforms already begun should mean that Burma will be able to meet these demands, as they are still less than 3 per cent of G.N.P.

During 1979 the money supply increased by 14 per cent, but during 1980/81 this expansion is expected to slow to 10 per cent. For 1979/80 the overall government deficit is put at 3,500 million kyats, or 10.7 per cent of G.D.P., caused by the expansion of capital expenditures by the State. This rose from 3 per cent of G.D.P. in 1975/76 to 18 per cent in 1979/80. Foreign exchange reserves in 1977/78 were 869.6 million kyats, and provisionally in September 1979 stood at 1,425.7 million kyats.

Burma has been a frequent user of IMF resources over the past several years. Since 1974, SDR 39 million have been purchased under the compensatory financing facility and SDR 24 million and SDR 35 million under stand-by arrangements concluded in 1974 and May 1977 respectively. In July 1978 Burma and the IMF concluded a stand-by arrangement for SDR 30 million. In addition, Burma has 20.8 million from the Special Drawing Rights accounts and a loan of about SDR 32 million from the Trust Fund.

Burma's foreign assistance, both multilateral and bilateral, reached a low of $21.7 million in 1971, before major planning reforms took place, and before Burma turned increasingly to the outside world. Foreign assistance thereafter expanded rapidly. In 1977 loans of $320.6 million were contracted and by 1979/80, the level of assistance increased to $511.8 million. The largest donors continue to be Japan and West Germany, who allotted $164.6 million to Burma in 1979/80, while Japan provided $122.3 million (these figures exclude grants). The IBRD and the ADB have provided the bulk of multilateral lending. In July 1979 the People's Republic of China and Burma agreed to support from China of $64 million for as yet unspecified projects. In April 1979 the third meeting of the Burma Aid Group took place in Tokyo under IBRD auspices. The Burmese Government estimated that $350 million would be required annually in foreign loans and grants, beginning in 1979.

Burmese development planning is dependent on foreign assistance. The delicacy with which such assistance is negotiated with the Burmese, and Burma's sovereignty perceived to be respected, may well determine the amount and path of Burmese growth as much as her absorptive capacity.

OBJECTIVES OF THE FOURTH FOUR-YEAR PLAN

The targets of the Fourth Four-Year Plan (1982/83–1985/86) are calculated on the basis of the results of the final year of the Third Four-Year Plan (1981/82).

During the new Plan, the Government hopes to continue the successes attributed to the previous one.

These goals include an average annual growth rate of 6.2 per cent, compared with an average of 6.6 per cent during the previous Plan, and an increase in the G.N.P. (at constant prices) to 21,280 million kyats at the end of the plan in 1985/86. This is in contrast to a G.N.P. of 16,760 million kyats at the close of the Third Four-Year Plan. If Plan targets are met, there is to be a 54.9 per cent increase in commodity production, a 24.0 per cent increase in services, and a 21.1 per cent increase in trade. This is to be accompanied by a 40.5 per cent increase in the value of services in the state sector, 4.8 per cent among the co-operatives, and 54.7 per cent in the private sector. 37,110 million kyats will be invested in the state sector over the life of the Plan, and by the final year exports are to reach 6,070 million kyats. Also anticipated are increases in per capita production and services of 3.8 per cent per year, a 3.3 per cent improvement in real annual income, a 3.1 per cent increase in consumption, and a 4.9 per cent improvement in investment. Co-operative ownership is planned to grow at an annual rate of 13.2 per cent, so that by the end of the Twenty-Year Plan, in 1993/94, 50 per cent of ownership in the agricultural sector will be in the hand of the co-operatives.

For the first year of the Plan (1982/83), the G.N.P. goal is 17,680 million kyats, an increase of 5.9 per cent. It is anticipated that the G.N.P. will be composed of 54.0 per cent in production, 24.8 per cent in services, and 21.2 per cent in trade. These figures in turn represent a state sector of 39.2 per cent, 3.9 per cent in co-operatives, and 56.9 per cent in the private sector. The private sector figure remains more than double the 26 per cent of the economy that is calculated to be still in that sector at the end of the Twenty-Year Plan. Exports are expected to reach 4,250 million kyats, with 8,700 million kyats invested in the state sector that year.

The Government anticipates an average annual growth in employment of 2.8 per cent, compared with the annual estimated increase in the labour force of 2.3 per cent, which may, however, be underestimated for the nation as a whole.

The success of the Plan is, in large part, predicated on the continued growth in real terms of the agricultural sector at about 4 per cent per year, and careful selection of development projects with improvement in capacity utilization and continuous foreign assistance. These conditions may be difficult to accomplish. Agricultural production may continue to increase, but it may do so at a slower rate, for the spectacular increases in paddy production over the past several years have made future increases more difficult, given the paucity of irrigation and the need for enhanced fertilizer production and distribution. The weather has been generally favourable in recent years but, of course, there is no guarantee that it will continue to be so. Oil production, which has been disappointing, may require additional scrutiny and its consumption may have to be further curtailed. It has been carefully controlled in the past, even though consumer prices have been abnormally low.

The outlook, therefore, for the Fourth Four-Year Plan is cautiously optimistic, although structural changes in the contribution of the private sector are recommended for enhanced growth and productivity. Such developments, however, are at odds with the stated objectives of the Twenty-Year Plan and thus seem to remain inimical to the political leadership.

CONSTRAINTS TO BURMESE GROWTH

Burmese policy shifts since 1972 have provided the basis for much improved economic progress. To reach the goals which the Government has set for the termination of its Twenty-Year Plan in 1993/94, considerable attention will have to be paid by the State to factors which continue to impede economic growth. The highly centralized economic planning structure does not allow the various Government corporations or the co-operative or private sector sufficient latitude to plan and respond quickly to changing circumstances. Although the higher levels of Burmese bureaucracy are staffed with qualified technicians, they are spread very thinly. Whether the revamped technical education system which Burma has implemented will provide mid-level management and skills, especially at the local level, is as yet unclear and unlikely. Project planning occurs at the departmental level, and is co-ordinated through the Ministry of Planning and Finance. There are few, if any, ways to relate projects to each other, although they are expected to conform with government overall priorities. Thus the plans are a mosaic of individual projects without coherent interrelationships. Planning co-ordination needs to be improved.

Since agriculture is the backbone of the economy, the development of incentives for farmers is especially important. Responsive pricing policies, particularly for paddy but for other crops as well, are required for increased production and thus foreign exchange earnings. Security of tenure for farmers, now lacking, might encourage spontaneous investment in land improvement—investment that the government cannot now provide. Long-term productive agricultural credit is almost totally lacking, and needs more emphasis. More flexible methods for anticipating and ordering spare parts are essential if present equipment is to function with the greatest possible efficiency. Decentralization of some economic planning is desirable. The multi-ethnic insurgencies, as well as that of the Burma Communist Party, show no sign of abatement in spite of a 90-day amnesty declared in May 1980, and are likely to continue indefinitely, denying the Government access to a large part of its hinterland and its natural resources and population, and causing defence expenditure to remain high, thus draining the capacity of the government to expand social services.

The latent mistrust of the private sector is still evident even though "Burmanization" has eliminated foreign activity in this field. Increased participation by the private sector could expand Burma's growth rate if assurances were given that productive enterprises would not be nationalized. The private sector still controls about 50 per cent of manufacturing, all of its small-scale, 90 per cent of trade and virtually all of agricultural production. There are encouraging signs that Burma is interested in foreign investment in partnership with state corporations.

In spite of ethnic fragmentation and lack of an effective system of political succession, Burma's two major problems, the nation has many advantages. The Government has achieved its goal of indigenous control of the Burmese economy. It has progressed markedly in its efforts to improve income distribution in Burmese society, a society traditionally lacking in caste or rigid class structure and providing exceptional social mobility. The status of women is high, and has traditionally been so. There are no conservative religious groups that could stifle progress.

Burma has proceeded, perhaps too rapidly considering the lack of trained staff and adequate planning mechanisms, to nationalize and control the economy. However, the pragmatism which the State has shown since 1972 has begun to have effect. If this pragmatism continues and expands, Burma could increase both its overall growth rate and improve the well-being of its populace commensurate with its potential.

STATISTICAL SURVEY

AREA AND POPULATION

Area	Census Population† (March 31st, 1973)			Estimated Population (mid-year)		
	Males	Females	Total	1979	1980‡	1981‡
261,218 sq. miles*	14,356,754	14,529,113	28,885,867	32,913,000	33,313,000	34,083,000

* 676,552 square kilometres.

† Including an estimate of 800,000 persons for six townships not covered by the census. The figures also include 1,600 residents who were absent at the time of the census. ‡ At March.

PRINCIPAL TOWNS

(population at 1973 census)

Rangoon	2,056,118*	Bassein	126,152
Mandalay	417,266	Akyab	82,544
Moulmein	171,767	Taunggyi	80,678

* Population at March 1980 was 2.3 million.

Births and Deaths: Birth rate 26.8 per 1,000 in 1979; death rate 10.2 per 1,000 in 1979 (estimates).

ECONOMICALLY ACTIVE POPULATION*

(official estimates, '000 persons, year ending March 31st)

	1977/78	1978/79	1979/80
Agriculture, hunting, forestry and fishing	8,531	8,697	8,864
Mining and quarrying	67	68	68
Manufacturing	929	968	1,009
Electricity, gas and water	15	15	16
Construction	184	189	195
Trade, restaurants and hotels	1,206	1,239	1,262
Transport, storage and communications	420	430	443
Financing, insurance, real estate and business services; Community, social and personal services	729	760	772
Activities not adequately described	559	569	579
Total	12,640	12,935	13,208

* Excluding unemployed persons, numbering 512,000 in 1979/80.

AGRICULTURE

LAND USE, 1979
('000 hectares)

Arable land	9,579
Land under permanent crops	449
Permanent meadows and pastures	361
Forests and woodland	32,169
Other land	23,216
Inland water	1,881
TOTAL	67,655

Source: FAO, *Production Yearbook.*

PRINCIPAL CROPS

	AREA HARVESTED ('000 hectares)			PRODUCTION ('000 metric tons)		
	1978	1979	1980	1978	1979	1980
Wheat	91	83	82	92	41	74
Rice (paddy)	5,011	4,442	5,040	10,500	10,448	13,317
Maize	87	83	80	77	102	100
Sugar cane	50	50	42*	1,763	1,812	1,472
Pulses	474	567	573*	329	326	330*
Groundnuts (in shell)	563	523	525	457	384	494
Cottonseed	130	165	165*	27†	34†	34*
Cotton (lint)				14†	17†	17*
Sesame seed	606	958	763	109	206	165
Tobacco	65	61	62*	58	51	55*
Jute and substitutes	51	54*	58*	82	85*	88*
Natural rubber	n.a.	n.a.	n.a.	15	15	15*
Millet	186	183	180*	59	56	60*
Vegetables (incl. melons)	n.a.	n.a.	n.a.	1,826	1,823	1,855*
Fruit (excl. melons)	n.a.	n.a.	n.a.	1,065	1,055*	1,064*

* FAO estimate. † Unofficial estimate.

Source: FAO, *Production Yearbook.*

LIVESTOCK
(FAO estimates—'000 head)

	1978	1979	1980
Cattle	7,550	7,560	7,702
Buffaloes	1,750	1,750	1,803
Pigs	2,100	2,200	2,279
Sheep	210	215	217
Goats	570	575	577
Chickens	17,000	17,100	17,420
Ducks	3,500	3,600	3,839

LIVESTOCK PRODUCTS
(FAO estimates—'000 metric tons)

	1978	1979	1980
Beef and veal	74	75	76
Buffalo meat	16	17	17
Mutton and lamb	1	1	1
Goats' meat	3	3	3
Pig meat	74	78	81
Poultry meat	20	20	21
Cows' milk	221	225	227
Buffaloes' milk	51	52	53
Goats' milk	5	5	5
Butter and ghee	4·9	4·9	5·0
Cheese	13·9	14·1	14·3
Hen eggs	24·7	25·6	25·9
Other poultry eggs	4·3	4·4	4·4
Cattle and buffalo hides	23·5	23·9	24·4

Source: FAO, *Production Yearbook.*

FORESTRY

ROUNDWOOD REMOVALS

('000 cubic metres, all non-coniferous)

	1974	1975	1976	1977	1978	1979	1980
Sawlogs, veneer logs and logs for sleepers	1,404	1,119	1,155	1,152	1,227	1,531	1,909
Other industrial wood*	915	937	960	983	1,007	1,030	1,055
Fuel wood*	20,286	20,909	21,421	21,947	22,489	23,046	23,618
TOTAL	22,605	22,965	23,536	24,082	24,723	25,607	26,582

* FAO estimate.

Source: FAO, *Yearbook of Forest Products.*

SAWNWOOD PRODUCTION

('000 cubic metres, all non-coniferous)

	1971	1972	1973	1974	1975	1976	1977
Sawnwood (incl. boxboards)	615	653	595	455	396	324	404
Railway sleepers	14	17	11	11*	11*	11*	11*
TOTAL	629	670	606	466	407	335	415

* FAO estimate.

1978-80: Annual production as in 1977 (FAO estimates).

Source: FAO, *Yearbook of Forest Products.*

FISHING

('000 metric tons, live weight)

	1973	1974	1975	1976	1977	1978	1979	1980
Inland waters	125.3	126.2	130.0	134.4	138.9	144.4	152.5	155.8
Indian Ocean	338.1	307.6	355.1	367.2	379.8	396.1	412.8	429.3
TOTAL CATCH	463.4	433.8	485.1	501.6	518.7	540.5	565.3	585.1

Source: FAO, *Yearbook of Fishery Statistics.*

MINING

(year ending March 31st)

		1976/77	1977/78*	1978/79	1979/80*
Coal	long tons	19,166	28,361	11,992	38,000
Crude petroleum	'000 U.S. barrels	8,586	9,556	9,999	11,676
Natural gas	million cu. ft.	8,481	8,784	9,892	12,846
Refined lead	long tons	2,721	5,242	5,460	5,198
Antimonal lead	,, ,,	116	169	200	125
Zinc concentrates	,, ,,	3,860	4,170	5,255	6,000
Tin concentrates	,, ,,	360	276	726	1,372
Tungsten concentrates	,, ,,	332	402	702	568
Refined silver	'000 troy oz.	187	400	422	410

* Provisional.

1980-81: 11,180,000 barrels of crude petroleum were produced.

Note: Figures for metallic minerals refer to the metal content of ores mined.

INDUSTRY

SELECTED PRODUCTS

(year ending March 31st)

		1976/77	1977/78*	1978/79	1979/80*
Salt	'000 tons	196	198	239	263
Sugar	,, ,,	29	34	39	36
Cigarettes	million	2,458	2,440	2,545	2,591
Cotton yarn	'000 tons	13.2	14.2	14.5	12.7
Soap	,, ,,	50.0	43.8	37.1	36.6
Cement	,, ,,	255	273	274	370
Motor spirit (petrol)	'000 gallons	61,000	65,100	66,000	71,100
Kerosene	,, ,,	357	307	23,400	34,700

* Provisional.

FINANCE

100 pyas=1 kyat.

Coins: 1, 5, 10, 25 and 50 pyas; 1 kyat.

Notes: 1, 5, 10, 20, 25, 50 and 100 kyats.

Exchange rates (June 1982): £1 sterling=11.17 kyats; U.S. $1=6.45 kyats.

100 kyats=£8.95=$15.50.

Note: Between September 1949 and August 1971 the kyat (known as the Burmese rupee before 1952) had a par value of 21 U.S. cents (U.S. $1=4.7619 kyats). From December 1971 to February 1973 the central exchange rate was $1=5.3487 kyats (1 kyat=18.696 U.S. cents). Between February 1973 and August 1974 the rate was $1=4.8138 kyats (1 kyat=20.773 U.S. cents). From August 1974 to January 1975 the currency was subject to "controlled floating". In January 1975 the kyat was linked to the IMF Special Drawing Right, initially at a mid-point of 1 SDR=7.7429 kyats. In May 1977 a new rate of 1 SDR=8.5085 kyats was established. The exchange rate against the U.S. dollar is adjusted from month to month. The average market rate (kyats per $) was: 5.454 in 1972; 4.907 in 1973; 4.858 in 1974; 6.454 in 1975; 6.770 in 1976; 7.136 in 1977; 6.865 in 1978; 6.651 in 1979; 6.609 in 1980; 7.308 in 1981. In terms of sterling, the value of the kyat between November 1967 and August 1971 was 1s. 9d. (8.75p), the exchange rate being £1=11.4286 kyats; from December 1971 to June 1972 the rate was £1=13.937 kyats.

BUDGET

(million kyats, April 1st to March 31st)

Receipts	1976/77	1977/78*	Expenditure	1976/77	1977/78*
Current revenue	2,414.8	2,912.9	Current expenditure	13,151.7	16,526.1
Current account	12,493.3	15,549.2	*of which:*		
Current capital	278.1	547.2	Economic enterprises	5,854.0	7,580.9
Debts	55.9	120.1	Trade	3,480.7	4,354.9
Loans and advances	25.3	42.3	Social welfare	948.2	1,052.1
Savings	—	—	National defence	935.5	1,060.6
			Transport and communications	723.2	819.7
			Construction	450.6	617.9
			Administration	759.5	1,040.0
			Capital account	2,172.7	4,360.3
			of which:		
			Mines	29.3	86.4
			Industry	474.0	1,491.8
			Transport and communications	197.5	647.5
			Agriculture	283.4	770.0
			Administration	370.8	645.2
			Investments	288.3	16.3
			Debts	448.6	555.5
			Contributions	—	—
			Loans and advances	59.0	121.5
			Savings	21.8	26.1
Total	15,267.4	19,171.7	**Total**	15,324.4	20,886.4

* Revised estimates.

INTERNATIONAL RESERVES

(U.S. $ million at December 31st)

	1975	1976	1977	1978	1979	1980	1981
Gold	8.2	8.1	9.6	10.9	11.6	11.2	10.2
IMF Special Drawing Rights	9.4	8.8	9.1	3.8	6.2	6.9	2.8
Reserve position in IMF	—	—	—	—	—	—	10.5
Foreign exchange	123.4	109.5	94.2	92.6	197.1	253.7	198.8
TOTAL	141.0	126.4	112.9	107.2	214.9	271.8	222.2

Source: IMF, *International Financial Statistics.*

COST OF LIVING

(Consumer Price Index for Rangoon. Base: 1970=100)

	1972	1973	1974	1975	1976	1977	1978	1979	1980
Food	114.8	150.0	187.4	254.4	299.7	290.7	269.3	284.4	289.5
Fuel and light	102.2	108.9	175.5	196.5	292.1	304.1	298.5	336.3	334.8
Clothing	100.0	108.1	132.7	157.4	226.8	237.8	203.1	190.3	178.8
Rent and repairs	90.1	102.1	124.8	155.7	188.7	194.5	179.6	174.4	181.1
ALL ITEMS	109.9	135.8	172.4	226.9	285.4	274.5	257.9	272.5	274.2

Source: ILO, *Year Book of Labour Statistics.*

NATIONAL ACCOUNTS

(million kyats at current prices, 12 months ending March 31st)

EXPENDITURE ON THE GROSS DOMESTIC PRODUCT

	1973/74	1974/75	1975/76	1976/77	1977/78	1978/79
Final consumption expenditure	12,824	17,710	21,393	24,984	26,469	26,674
Increase in stocks	352	475	659	515	87	44
Gross fixed capital formation	1,146	1,267	1,677	2,142	3,447	6,006
TOTAL DOMESTIC EXPENDITURE	14,322	19,452	23,729	27,641	30,003	32,724
Exports of goods and services	953	912	1,191	1,414	1,728	2,120
Less Imports of goods and services	575	1,016	1,443	1,628	2,220	3,994
G.D.P. IN PURCHASERS' VALUES	14,700	19,348	23,477	27,427	29,511	30,850

COST STRUCTURE OF THE GROSS DOMESTIC PRODUCT

	1972/73	1973/74	1974/75	1975/76	1976/77	1977/78
Compensation of employees	5,165	6,385	8,153	9,494	10,509	11,320
Operating surplus	4,642	5,924	7,684	9,810	12,214	13,212
DOMESTIC FACTOR INCOMES	9,807	12,309	15,837	19,304	22,723	24,532
Consumption of fixed capital	830	982	1,669	1,903	2,004	2,108
G.D.P. AT FACTOR COST	10,637	13,291	17,506	21,207	24,727	26,640
Indirect taxes, *less* subsidies	1,098	1,409	1,842	2,270	2,700	2,871
G.D.P. IN PURCHASERS' VALUES	11,735	14,700	19,348	23,477	27,427	29,511

Gross Domestic Product by Economic Activity

	1972/73	1973/74	1974/75	1975/76	1976/77	1977/78
Agriculture (excl. livestock) and hunting	3,414	5,009	7,320	9,307	10,639	11,000
Forestry and logging	313	282	306	324	358	422
Livestock and fishing	804	868	1,204	1,420	1,791	2,168
Mining and quarrying	196	154	164	136	193	248
Manufacturing	1,049	1,276	1,568	2,106	2,656	2,899
Electricity	72	76	59	66	70	88
Construction	208	195	198	221	237	310
Wholesale and retail trade	2,972	4,070	5,530	6,846	8,115	8,594
Transport, storage and communications	621	629	691	740	797	889
Other services	2,086	2,141	2,312	2,311	2,571	2,893
	11,735	14,700	19,348	23,477	27,427	29,511

BALANCE OF PAYMENTS

(U.S. $ million)

	1975	1976	1977	1978	1979	1980
Merchandise exports f.o.b.	162.3	172.6	205.6	273.1	362.9	427.7
Merchandise imports f.o.b.	−249.3	−212.6	−307.1	−496.8	−732.2	−763.8
Trade Balance	−87.0	−40.0	−101.5	−223.7	−369.3	−336.1
Exports of services	29.5	30.7	39.4	30.8	49.3	66.2
Imports of services	−38.9	−40.8	−49.7	−50.5	−95.6	−134.1
Balance of Goods and Services	−96.4	−50.1	−111.8	−243.4	−415.6	−404.0
Unrequited transfers (net)	16.8	16.3	10.9	27.8	58.0	80.6
Balance on Current Account	−79.6	−33.8	100.8	−215.7	−357.6	−323.3
Long-term capital (net)	40.2	20.5	67.1	193.6	422.7	351.6
Short-term capital (net)	−7.5	−4.7	−11.8	−9.6	6.1	−0.3
Net errors and omissions	1.7	−4.1	−3.5	−9.7	9.0	35.8
Total (net monetary movements)	−45.2	−22.1	−48.9	−41.5	80.2	63.5
Allocation of IMF Special Drawing Rights	—	—	—	—	9.8	10.0
Valuation changes (net)	−7.1	15.0	4.7	−3.7	1.5	−2.4
IMF Trust Fund loans	—	—	7.5	22.9	23.6	19.9
Change in Reserves	−52.3	−7.1	−36.7	−22.3	115.1	91.0

Source: IMF, *International Financial Statistics.*

EXTERNAL TRADE

(million kyats)

	1975	1976	1977	1978	1979	1980
Imports c.i.f.	1,612.6	1,311.1	2,200.3	2,114.0	2,116.1	2,337.3
Exports f.o.b.	1,104.6	1,629.4	1,648.9	1,665.9	2,412.3	3,122.6

1981: Exports 3,305.4 million kyats.

PRINCIPAL COMMODITIES

(million kyats, year ending March 31st)

IMPORTS	1977/78	1978/79*	1979/80*
Milk and milk products	35.2	41.6	81.4
Pharmaceuticals	44.0	53.2	26.8
Chemicals	74.7	91.3	112.9
Fertilizers	2.9	115.9	166.6
Cotton yarn	102.9	70.4	40.8
Cotton fabrics	64.9	14.4	2.5
Fabrics of mixed fibres	1.2	—	—
Coke and coal	2.0	0.1	—
Refined mineral oil	14.2	26.3	7.0
Base metals and base metal manufactures	312.6	210.1	258.0
Machinery (non-electric) Transport equipment	747.6	1,465.2	1,181.3
Electric machinery	138.2	213.2	114.9
Paper and paper products	76.6	68.8	59.3
Rubber manufactures	57.6	62.9	22.6

EXPORTS	1977/78	1978/79	1979/80*
Rice and rice products	867.7	288.2	1,217.9
Teak and hardwood	396.7	904.5	717.2
Metals and ores	85.2	165.3	189.1
Oilcakes	55.8	65.6	51.7
Pulses	73.4	59.1	125.0
Jute	21.9	56.9	40.3
Rubber	41.6	61.5	68.6

* Provisional.

PRINCIPAL TRADING PARTNERS

('000 kyats)

IMPORTS	1975	1976	1977
Australia	25,949	23,637	32,914
China, People's Repub.	117,834	65,173	132,412
France	17,166	16,407	70,158
Germany, Fed. Repub.	89,545	97,126	142,490
Japan	398,313	488,194	546,038
Singapore	72,749	155,681	261,116

EXPORTS	1975	1976	1977
China, People's Repub.	105,506	1,894	1,305
Denmark	18,653	31,280	33,288
Germany, Fed. Repub.	28,922	53,303	76,572
Hong Kong	50,802	83,908	91,692
Indonesia	80,047	266,099	220,587
Japan	138,586	142,477	139,701
Pakistan	38,956	15,786	15,053
Singapore	152,906	391,059	239,964
United Kingdom	157,820	43,546	31,419

TRANSPORT

RAILWAYS (Burma Railways Corporation)

(million)

	1975/76	1976/77	1977/78	1978/79	1979/80*
Freight ton-miles	237.3	242.5	276.6	287.7	367.4
Passenger-miles	2,155.4	1,728.2	1,779.3	1,903.1	2,339.1

* Provisional.

ROAD TRAFFIC (Road Transport Corporation)

(vehicles in use)

	1974/75	1975/76	1976/77	1977/78	1978/79	1979/80
Passenger buses	1,791	1,860	1,506	1,490	1,400	1,550
Taxis	993	1,008	1,008	1,008	840	819
Haulage trucks	2,593	2,638	2,693	2,696	2,638	2,762

INLAND WATER TRANSPORT CORPORATION

(million)

	1977/78*	1978/79*	1979/80
Passengers	11.7	13.2	13.7
Freight tons	1.0	1.0	1.2

* Provisional.

INTERNATIONAL SEA-BORNE SHIPPING*

('000 metric tons)

	1977/78	1978/79	1979/80
Freight loaded	862	723	1,290
Freight unloaded	371	454	466

* Twelve months beginning April 1st.

CIVIL AVIATION

(Burma Airways Corporation)

	1976/77	1977/78	1978/79	1979/80
Passenger miles	115,834	132,789	126,502	161,273
Freight tons ('000)	4.9	5.4	5.1	8.2

TOURISM

	1976	1977	1978	1979*
Number of visitors	18,581	22,076	21,908	22,164
Tourist revenue (million kyats)	16.7	23.1	30.4	37.2

* Provisional.

EDUCATION

(1978/79)

	INSTITUTIONS	TEACHERS	STUDENTS
Primary Schools	23,099	84,593	3,731,160
Middle Schools	1,302	19,964	754,079
High Schools	596	11,469	170,660
Teacher Training Colleges	16	367	5,163
Agricultural and Technical Institutes	52	786	9,576
Universities and Colleges	35	3,922	112,671

Source (unless otherwise stated): Central Statistical Organization, Rangoon, and Ministry of Planning and Finance, Rangoon.

THE CONSTITUTION

The constitution came into force on January 3rd, 1974, following a national referendum held in December 1973. It is the basic law of the State. A summary of the main provisions follows:

GENERAL PRINCIPLES

The Socialist Republic of the Union of Burma is a sovereign, independent, social state. There shall be only one political party, the Burma Socialist Programme Party. Sovereign power rests with the people as represented by the People's Assembly. The State is the ultimate owner of all natural resources and shall exploit them in the interests of the people. The means of production shall be nationalized. National groups shall have the right to practise their religion and culture freely within the law and the national interest. The State shall follow an independent and peaceful foreign policy.

STATE ORGANS

The structure of the State is based on a system of local autonomy under central leadership. Government operates at four levels of administration: wards or village tracts, townships, states or divisions and at national level.

People's Assembly (Pyithu Hluttaw)

A unicameral legislature, the highest organ of State power, it exercises sovereign power on behalf of the people. It is elected directly by secret ballot for a term of four years. Regular sessions take place twice a year, the intervening period being no more than eight months. The People's Assembly may be dissolved if three-quarters of its members agree to it. It may delegate executive and judicial power to central and local state organs. It has the power to enact economic legislation, declare war and peace and the right to call referenda. It may constitute committees and commissions and invest them with powers and duties. Under certain circumstances the People's Assembly may dissolve the People's Councils.

State Council

The State Council is composed of 29 members including one representative from each of the 14 states and divisions, and the Prime Minister, elected by the People's Assembly from its members. The State Council elects a Chairman from its members who becomes President of the Union and represents the State. The term of office of the Council and the President is the same as that of the People's Assembly. The State Council is vested with executive power to carry out the provisions of the Constitution. It has the power to convene the People's Assembly in consultation with the panel of Chairmen of the Assembly. It interprets and promulgates legislation, makes decisions concerning diplomatic relations, international treaties and agreements. It is responsible for the appointment of the heads of the bodies of the public services. The State Council has the power to grant pardons and amnesties. It may make orders with the force of law between sessions of the People's Assembly, and may order military action in defence of the State, declare a state of emergency and martial law subject to the subsequent approval of the People's Assembly.

Council of Ministers

The highest organ of public administration, elected by the People's Assembly from a list of candidates submitted by the State Council. Its term of office is the same as that of the People's Assembly. The Prime Minister is elected by the Council of Ministers from among its members. It is responsible for the management of public administration and drafting economic measures and submitting them to the People's Assembly for enactment.

Council of People's Justices

The highest judicial organ. Elected by the People's Assembly from a list of its members submitted by the State Council. Its term of office is the same as that of the People's Assembly. The People's Councils form judges' committees at local levels.

Council of People's Attorneys

Elected by the People's Assembly from a list of members submitted by the State Council. Its term of office is the same as that of the People's Assembly. It is responsible to the People's Assembly for directing state, divisional and township law officers, protecting the rights of the people and supervising the central and local organs of state power.

Council of People's Inspectors

Elected by the People's Assembly from a list of candidates submitted by the State Council. Its term of office is the same as that of the People's Assembly. It is responsible to the People's Assembly for the inspection of the activities of the local organs of state power, ministries and public bodies. There are also local inspectorates at each administrative level, responsible to the People's Council concerned.

People's Councils

The term of office of the People's Councils is the same as that of the People's Assembly. They are elected at different levels according to law. They are responsible for local economic and social affairs and public administration, the administration of local justice, local security, defence and the maintenance of law and order. Each of the People's Councils elects an executive committee to implement its decisions. The Executive Committees each elect a Chairman and a Secretary from among themselves who are also the Chairman and Secretary of the People's Council concerned.

FUNDAMENTAL RIGHTS AND DUTIES OF CITIZENS

All citizens are equal before the law irrespective of race, religion, sex or other distinction. Every citizen has the right to enjoy the benefits derived from labour, to inherit, to settle anywhere in the State according to law, to medical treatment, education and rest and recreation. Freedom of thought, conscience and expression are upheld subject to the law and the interests of state security. All citizens are bound to abstain from undermining the sovereignty and security of the State and the socialist system.

ELECTORAL SYSTEM

All citizens over 18 years are entitled to vote. Those whose parents are both citizens may stand for election to office having attained the age of 20 years (Village and Township Councils), 24 years (State and Divisional Councils), 28 years (People's Assembly). Members of religious orders and others disqualified by law are prohibited from voting or standing for election.

THE GOVERNMENT

(June 1982)

HEAD OF STATE

President, Chairman of the State Council: U SAN YU (elected by the Third People's Assembly, November 9th, 1981).

STATE COUNCIL

Chairman: U SAN YU.

Secretary: U AYE KO.

Members:

U KYAW SEIN
U KHIN MAUNG
U SAW OHN
THAKIN KHIN ZAW
U SOE HLAING
U SEIN WIN
U SEIN LWIN
Brig.-Gen. TIN OO
U KHIN AYE
U ZAW WIN
U VAN KULH
Dr. MAUNG MAUNG
Dr. MAUNG LWIN
Thura U MIN THEIN
U HPAU YU KHA
U BA THAW
U SAN KYI
U HLA MAUNG
Dr. HLA HAN
U THA KYAW
U MAHN SAN MYAT SHWE
THAUNG TIN
U THAING THAN TIN
Thura U AUNG PE
THAKIN AUNG MIN
U MAUNG MAUNG KHA
U THAN SEIN

COUNCIL OF MINISTERS

Prime Minister: U MAUNG MAUNG KHA.

Deputy Prime Minister, Minister for Planning and Finance: Thura U TUN TIN.

Deputy Prime Minister, Minister for Defence: Gen. Thura KYAW HTIN.

Minister for Home and Religious Affairs: U BO NI.

Ministers for Industry: U TINT SWE (I), U MAUNG CHO (II).

Minister for Mines: U THAN TIN.

Minister for Construction: U HLA TUN.

Minister for Transport and Communications: Thura U SAW PRU.

Minister of Information and Culture: U AUNG KYAW MYINT.

Minister for Education: U KYAW NYEIN.

Minister for Agriculture and Forests: U YE GOUNG.

Minister for Social Welfare and Labour: U OHN KYAW.

Minister for Foreign Affairs: U CHIT HLAING.

Minister for Co-operatives: U SEIN TUN.

Minister for Trade: U KHIN MAUNG GYI.

Minister for Health: U TUN WAY.

LEGISLATURE

PYITHU HLUTTAW (*People's Assembly*)

Following national elections early in 1974, the inaugural session of the Pyithu Hluttaw was convened on March 2nd, 1974. New elections were held in October 1981. All the candidates were members of the BSPP. There are 475 seats and sessions are presided over by the members of a panel of chairmen in rotation.

POLITICAL PARTY

Burma Socialist Programme Party (BSPP) (*Lanzin Party*): Rangoon; f. 1962; the only recognized political party; set up by the Revolutionary Council to implement its policies; 1,500,902 full mems. (1981); publs. *Lanzin Thadin* (*Party News*) (twice a month), *Party Affairs Journal* (monthly), *International Affairs Journal* (monthly); Chair. U NE WIN; Gen. Sec. U AYE KO; Jt. Secs. Brig.-Gen. TIN OO and U THAN SEIN.

DIPLOMATIC REPRESENTATION

EMBASSIES ACCREDITED TO BURMA

(In Rangoon unless otherwise stated)

Afghanistan: New Delhi, India.

Albania: Beijing, People's Republic of China.

Argentina: Bangkok, Thailand.

Australia: 88 Strand Rd.; *Ambassador:* RICHARD K. GATE.

Austria: Bangkok, Thailand.

Bangladesh: 340 Prome Rd.; *Ambassador;* SYED NAJMUDDIN HASHIM.

Belgium: Dacca, Bangladesh.

Bulgaria: Dacca, Bangladesh.

Canada: Dacca, Bangladesh.

China, People's Republic: 1 Pyidaungsu Yeiktha Rd.; *Ambassador:* MO YANZHONG.

Czechoslovakia: 326 Prome Rd.; *Ambassador:* JOSEF BOZEK.

Denmark: Bangkok, Thailand.

Egypt: 81 Pyidaungsu Yeiktha Rd.; *Ambassador:* AZIZ NOUR EL DIN.

Finland: Manila, Philippines.

France: 102 Pyidaungsu Yeiktha Rd., P.O.B. 858; *Ambassador:* MICHEL CADOL.

German Democratic Republic: 60C Golden Valley, P.O.B. 1305; *Ambassador:* KLAUS MÄSER.

Germany, Federal Republic: 32 Natmauk Rd., P.O.B. 12; *Ambassador:* Dr. HELMUT TUERK.

Greece: New Delhi, India.

Hungary: Bangkok, Thailand.

India: 545–547 Merchant St.; *Ambassador:* G. G. SWELL.

Indonesia: 100 Halpin, P.O.B. 1401; *Ambassador:* ASNAWI MANGKUALAM.

Iran: New Delhi, India.

Iraq: New Delhi, India.

Israel: 49 Prome Rd.; *Ambassador:* KALMAN ANNER.

Italy: 3 Lowis Rd., Golden Valley; *Ambassador:* JOLANDA BRUNETTI.

Japan: 100 Natmauk Rd.; *Ambassador:* M. TACHIBANA.

Korea, Democratic People's Republic: 30 Tank Rd., *Ambassador:* LI SONG HO.

Korea, Republic: 591 Prome Rd.; *Ambassador:* KAE CHUL LEE.

Laos: Bangkok, Thailand.

Malaysia: 65 Windsor Rd.; *Ambassador:* Encik LOOI CHEOK HUN.

Mongolia: Beijing, People's Republic of China.

Nepal: 16 Nat. Mauk Yeiktha Rd.; *Ambassador:* K. BARAL.

Netherlands: Bangkok, Thailand.

New Zealand: Kuala Lumpur, Malaysia.

Nigeria: New Delhi, India.

Norway: Singapore.

Pakistan: 18 Windsor Rd.; *Ambassador:* AFZAL MAHMOOD.

Philippines: 56 Prome Rd.; *Ambassador:* CONSTANTE MA. CRUZ.

Poland: 31 Aung Mingaung Ave.; *Ambassador:* WŁADYSŁAW DOMAGALA (resident in Bangladesh).

Romania: 71 Mission Rd.; *Ambassador:* NICOLAE GAVRILESCU (resident in Beijing, People's Republic of China).

Singapore: Bangkok, Thailand.

Spain: Bangkok, Thailand.

Sri Lanka: 34 Fraser Rd.; *Ambassador:* (vacant).

Sweden: Kuala Lumpur, Malaysia.

Switzerland: Bangkok, Thailand.

Syria: New Delhi, India.

Thailand: 91 Prome Rd.; *Ambassador:* B. ISRASENA.

Turkey: New Delhi, India.

U.S.S.R.: 52 Prome Rd.; *Ambassador:* V. N. KOUZNETSOV.

United Kingdom: 80 Strand Rd., P.O.B. 638; *Ambassador:* C. L. BOOTH, C.M.G., M.V.O.

U.S.A.: 581 Merchant St.; *Ambassador:* PATRICIA M. BYRNE.

Viet-Nam: 40 Komin Kochin Rd.; *Ambassador:* PHAM MANH DIEM.

Yugoslavia: 39 Windsor Rd.; *Ambassador:* RANKO RADULOVIĆ.

Burma also has diplomatic relations with Algeria, Costa Rica, Cuba, Maldives, Mauritania, Mauritius, Mexico, Morocco, Portugal and Zaire.

JUDICIAL SYSTEM

A new judicial structure was established in March 1974. Its highest organ, composed of members of the People's Assembly, is the Council of People's Justices. This Council, with three members of it selected for each occasion, serves as the central Court of Justice.

Chairman of the Council of People's Justices: U MOUN MOUN KYAW WINN.

Below this Council are the state, divisional, township, ward and village tract courts formed with members of local People's Councils.

RELIGION

Freedom of religious belief and practice is guaranteed for every citizen. About 80 per cent of the population are Buddhists.

Roman Catholic Bishop of Rangoon: Mgr. GABRIEL THOHEY, Mahn Gaby, Archbishop's House, 289 Theinbyu St., Rangoon.

Episcopalian Bishop of Rangoon and Archbishop of Burma (Anglican): The Most Rev. GREGORY HLA GYAW, Bishopscourt, 140 Pyidaungsu Yeiktha Rd., Dagon P.O., Rangoon.

THE PRESS

DAILIES

Daily newspaper readership in 1977 was estimated at 820,000.

Botahtaung (*Vanguard Daily*): 22/30 Strand Rd., P.O.B. 539, Rangoon; f. 1958; Burmese; nationalized; Chief Editor U THEIN; circ. 100,000.

Guardian: 392 Merchant St., P.O.B. 1522, Rangoon; f. 1956; nationalized 1964; English; Chief Editor U SOE MYINT; circ. 14,000.

Kyemon (*Mirror*): 77 52nd St., Pazundaung P.O., P.O.B. 819, Rangoon; f. 1951; Burmese; nationalized; Chief Editor U SOE NYUNT; circ. 77,000.

Loketha Phithu Nayzin (*Working People's Daily*): 212 Theinbyu Rd., P.O.B. 48, Rangoon; f. 1963; Burmese and English; official newspaper; Chief Editor U HLA MYAING; circ. 101,500.

Myanma Alin (*New Light of Burma*): 58 Komin Kochin Rd., P.O.B. 21, Rangoon; f. 1914; Burmese; nationalized 1969; Chief Editor U KYAW MYINT; circ. 45,000.

Working People's Daily: 212 Theinbyu Rd., Rangoon; f. 1963; English; Chief Editor U KO KO LAY; circ. 21,000.

PERIODICALS

Aurora (*Moethaukpan*): 184 32nd St., Rangoon; Publr. Myawaddy Press; Burmese and English; monthly; circ. 32,000.

Do Kyaung Tha: 184 32nd St., Rangoon; Publr. Myawaddy Press; monthly; circ. 20,000.

Gita Padetha: Rangoon; journal of Burma Music Council; circ. 10,000.

Guardian Magazine: 392 Merchant St., P.O.B. 1522, Rangoon; f. 1953; nationalized 1964; English; literary magazine; monthly.

Myawaddy Magazine: 184 32nd St., Rangoon; f. 1952; Burmese; literary magazine; monthly.

Pyinnya Lawka Journal: 529 Merchant St., Rangoon; Publr. Sarpay Beikman Management Board; quarterly; circ. 18,000.

Shetho (*Forward*): 22/24 Pansodan St., Rangoon; Burmese and English editions; published by the Information and Broadcasting Department; monthly; circ. 36,000.

Shu Ma Wa Magazine: 146 Western Wing, Bogyoke Market, Rangoon; Burmese; literary; monthly.

Shwe Thwe: 529 Merchant St., Rangoon; bilingual children's journal; Publr. Sarpay Beikman Management Board; weekly; circ. 100,000.

Teza: 184 32nd St., Rangoon; Publr. Myawaddy Press; English and Burmese; monthly; circ. 60,100.

Thwe/Thauk Magazine: 185 48th St., Rangoon; f. 1946; Burmese; literary; monthly.

NEWS AGENCIES

News Agency of Burma (NAB): 212 Theinbyu Rd., Rangoon; f. 1963; Government sponsored; Chief Editors U YE TINT (domestic section), U KYAW MIN (external section).

FOREIGN BUREAUX

Agence France-Presse (AFP) (*France*): 58A Golden Valley, Rangoon.

Agenzia Nazionale Stampa Associata (ANSA) (*Italy*): Building 215, Room 28, Yankin, Rangoon; Representative U TIN AYE.

Associated Press (AP) (*U.S.A.*): 283 U Wisara Rd., Sanchaung P.O., Rangoon; Representative U SEIN WIN.

Deutsche Presse-Agentur (dpa) (*Federal Republic of Germany*): U Chit Tun, 55 Kalagar St., Kemmendine P.O., Rangoon.

Reuters (*United Kingdom*): 162 Phayre St., Rangoon.

Telegrafnoye Agentstvo Sovietskogo Soyuza (TASS) (*U.S.S.R.*): 54-A Lowis Rd., Rangoon; Representative N. ANDREYEV.

Xinhua (*People's Republic of China*): 67 Prome Rd., Rangoon; Representative LI JIASHENG.

PUBLISHERS

Hanthawaddy Press: 157 Bo Aung Gyaw St., Rangoon; f. 1889; general publisher of books and journals; Man. Editor U ZAW WIN.

Knowledge Publishing House: 130 Bogyoke St., Rangoon; travel, fiction, religious and political books and directories.

Kyipwaye Press: 84th St., Letsaigan, Mandalay; arts, travel, religion, fiction and children's books.

Myawaddy Press: 184 32nd St., Rangoon; journals and magazines; Chief Editor Major MYA THEIN.

Sarpay Beikman Management Board: 529 Merchant St., Rangoon; f. 1947; Burmese encyclopaedia, literature, fine arts and general; also magazines and translations; Chair. Col. AUNG HTAY (Deputy Information Minister); Vice-Chair. Col. MAUNG MAUNG KHIN.

Shumawa Press: 146 West Wing, Bogyoke Market, Rangoon; non-fiction of all kinds.

Thu Dhama Wadi Press: 55–56 Maung Khine St., P.O.B. 419, Rangoon; f. 1903; religious books; Propr. U TIN HTOO; Man. U PAN MAUNG.

RADIO AND TELEVISION

Burma Broadcasting Service (BBS): Prome Rd., Kamayut P.O., Rangoon; f. 1946; broadcasts are made in Burmese, Arakanese, Mon, Shan, Karen, Chin, Kachin, Kayah and English; a colour television service began functioning in 1980, broadcasting two hours daily from a modern Japanese studio and transmitter in Rangoon; Dir.-Gen. U TIN AUNG TUN; Dir. of Broadcasting U KYAW MINN.

There were an estimated 670,000 radio receivers in 1979,

FINANCE

All banks in Burma were nationalized in 1963 and amalgamated to form the People's Bank of the Union of Burma from November 1969. In April 1972 this was renamed the Union of Burma Bank and was reconstituted as the Central Bank in April 1976.

Under a law of November 1975 there are four separate state-owned banks: the Union of Burma Bank, the Myanma Economic Bank, the Myanma Foreign Trade Bank and the Myanma Agricultural Bank each with its own management board. The Myanma Insurance Corporation was also established separately.

BANKING

(cap. = capital; p.u. = paid up; dep. = deposits; m. = million; Ks. = kyats.)

CENTRAL BANK

Union of Burma Bank: 24/26 Sule Pagoda Rd., Rangoon; f. 1976; cap. p.u. Ks. 200m., dep. Ks. 948m.; Chair. U AUNG SINT; Adviser Dr. AYE HLAING.

Myanma Economic Bank: 1/7 Latha St., Rangoon; cap. Ks. 80m. (1976); provides savings and credit facilities; Man. Dir. U MAUNG MAUNG HAN.

Myanma Foreign Trade Bank: P.O.B. 203, Theingyizay C Block, Shwedagon Pagoda Rd., Rangoon; f. 1976; cap. Ks. 30m. (1979); handles all foreign exchange and all international banking transactions; Man. Dir. U KO KO LAY; Gen. Man. U AUNG NYUNT PE.

Myanma Agricultural Bank: 1/7 Latha St., Rangoon; cap. Ks. 40m.; Man. Dir. U HLA THAN.

INSURANCE

Myanma Insurance Corporation: 163/167 Phayre St., Rangoon; Man. Dir. U WAN TUN.

TRADE AND INDUSTRY

Socialist Economic Planning Committee: Rangoon; f. 1967; 10 mems.; Chair. U NE WIN; Vice-Chair. U SAN YU.

GOVERNMENT CORPORATIONS

Agricultural and Farm Produce Trade Corporation: Rangoon; Man. Dir. U KYI THEIN.

Agriculture Corporation: 72–74 Shwedagon Pagoda Rd., Rangoon; Man. Dir. U KHIN WIN.

Construction Corporation: Rangoon; Man. Dir. U Kyin Hlaing.

Electric Power Corporation: 197–199 Lower Kemmendine Rd., Rangoon; Man. Dir. U Khin Maung Thein.

Foodstuff Industries Corporation: Rangoon; Man. Dir. U Maung Maung Than Tun.

Heavy Industries Corporation: Rangoon; Man. Dir. Lt.-Col. Htay Tint.

Hotel and Tourist Corporation: 77–91 Sule Pagoda Rd., Rangoon; Man. Dir. Maj. Maung Maung Aye.

Industrial Planning Department: 192 Kaba-Aye Pagoda Rd., Bahan P.O., P.O.B. 11201, Rangoon; f. 1952; Dir.-Gen. Lt.-Col. Aye Kyin.

Livestock Development and Marketing Corporation: Rangoon; Man. Dir. U Pyi Soe.

Myanma Export-Import Corporation: 622–624 Merchant St., Rangoon; Man. Dir. U Soe Nyunt.

Myanma Gems Corporation: 66 Kaba-Aye Pagoda Rd., P.O.B. 1397, Rangoon; under Ministry of Mines; Man. Dir. Lt.-Col. Myint Htun.

Myanma Oil Corporation: 604 Merchant St., P.O.B. 1049, Rangoon; under Ministry of Industries II; formerly Burmah Oil Company: nationalized 1963; Man. Dir. U Than Nyunt.

No. 1 Mining Corporation: 226 Mahabandoola St., Rangoon; under Ministry of Mines; formerly Myanma Bawdwin Corporation; development and mining of non-ferrous metals; Man. Dir. U Ko Ko Than.

No. 2 Mining Corporation: Rangoon; under Ministry of Mines; formerly Myanma Tin Tungsten Development Corporation; development and mining of tin, tungsten and antimony; Man. Dir. Lt.-Col. Maung Thaung.

No. 3 Mining Corporation: 80 Rangoon-Insein Rd., Thamine P.O., Rangoon; under Ministry of Mines; production of various clays, coal, byrite, gypsum, limestone, etc.; Man. Dir. Col. San Maung.

People's Pearl and Fishery Corporation (PPFC): 654 Merchant St., Rangoon; Man. Dir. Capt. Sein Tun.

Petrochemicals Industries Corporation: Rangoon; under Ministry of Industries II; Man. Dir. U Kyan Khin.

Petroleum Products Supply Corporation: Rangoon; under Ministry of Industries II; Man. Dir. Col. Myint Soe.

Textiles Industries Corporation: 53 Pyidaungsu Yeiktha Rd., Rangoon; Man. Dir. U Khin Nyo.

Timber Corporation: Rangoon; f. 1948; extraction, processing, and main exporter of Burma teak and other timber, veneers, plywood and other forest products; Man. Dir. U Kyaw Shein.

CO-OPERATIVES

By the end of February 1980 a total of 21,095 co-operative societies had been formed.

Central Co-operative Society (CCS) Council: Rangoon; Chair. U San Tint; Sec. U Hla Tin.

WORKERS' AND PEASANTS' COUNCILS

Central People's Workers' Council: Rangoon; f. 1968 to provide organization for self-government of workers; Chair. U Ohn Kyaw; Sec. U Thura Tin Myat.

Central People's Peasants' Council: Rangoon; f. 1969; Chair. U Ye Goung; Sec. U Than Yu.

TRANSPORT

RAILWAYS

Burma Railways Corporation: Head Office: Bogyoke Aung San St., Rangoon, P.O.B. 118; f. 1972; government organization which manages State railways; railway mileage (1979/80) was 2,705 track miles (4,354 km.); Man. Dir. U Tin Tun; Gen. Man. U Saw Clyde.

ROADS

The total length of motorable roads in Burma was 34,776 km. in 1980.

Road Transport Corporation: Rangoon; f. 1963 to nationalize gradually all passenger and freight road transport; by 1979/80 operated 2,762 haulage trucks and 1,550 passenger buses in Burma; Man. Dir. U Myo Aung.

INLAND WATERWAYS

Inland Water Transport Corporation: 50 Pansodan St., Rangoon; state-owned; operates cargo and passenger launch services throughout Burma. During 1979/80 13.7 million passengers and 1.2 million tons of freight were carried. Man. Dir. U Hla Win; Gen. Man. U Maung Maung.

SHIPPING

Rangoon is the chief port. Vessels up to 15,000 tons can be accommodated.

Burma Ports Corporation: P.O.B. 1, 10 Pansodan St., Rangoon; Man. Dir. Commdr. Tin Maung Soe; services: general port and harbour duties; fleet: 9 vessels totalling 4,700 tons gross and 20 smaller craft.

Burma Five Star Shipping Corporation: 132–136 Theinbyu Rd., Rangoon; f. 1959; 24 coastal and ocean-going vessels; cargo services to Europe and Japan; Man. Dir. U Shwe Than.

CIVIL AVIATION

Mingaladon Airport, near Rangoon, is equipped to international standards.

Burma Airways Corporation (BAC): 104 Strand Rd., Rangoon; f. 1948; internal network operates services to 33 stations; external services to Bangladesh, India, Nepal, Singapore and Thailand; services to Kampuchea and Hong Kong are currently suspended; operated by the Government; Man. Dir. U Thaung Nyunt; Operations Man. U Tin Tun; fleet of 3 F-28, 8 F-27, 7 Twin Otter, 2 SA-Puma.

Burma is also served by CAAC (People's Republic of China), KLM (Netherlands) and Thai Airways International.

ATOMIC ENERGY

Atomic Energy Committee: The establishment of the Atomic Energy Committee was announced in October 1978; Chair. U Win Maung.

Union of Burma Atomic Energy Centre: Central Research Organization, Yankin Post Office, Rangoon; f. 1955; departments of nuclear mineralogical research; nuclear research; radiation protection research; nucleonic instrumentation; Chair. Col. Oo Saw Hla.

DEFENCE

Armed Forces (1981): Total strength 179,000: army 163,000, navy 7,000, air force 9,000; para-military forces number 73,000.

Equipment: The army is mainly infantry, with American, British and Yugoslav light arms. There are also some British tanks and armoured cars. The navy is equipped with small craft (mainly gunboats). The air force has 17 combat aircraft and various transport planes and helicopters.

Defence Expenditure: Expenditure allocated for 1980/81 was 1,114.7 million kyats.

Chief of Staff of the Armed Forces: Gen. Thura KYAW HTIN.

EDUCATION

The organization and administration of education in the Union of Burma is the responsibility of the Ministry of Education. Three Directorates are in turn responsible to the Ministry for: (*a*) Basic education (primary, upper and lower secondary); (*b*) Technical and Vocational education; and (*c*) University Administration (including Higher Institutes). The main emphasis continues to be on primary education so that, for example, in 1969/70 86 per cent of all those receiving education were enrolled in State primary schools. Moreover, in the same period 65 per cent of State expenditure on education was allocated to this sector. Since 1962 considerable improvements in education have taken place. A Five-Year Education Plan (1965–70) was introduced which aimed to establish a network of primary schools throughout the country. Attendance, which lasts from the age of 5 to 9, is to be made compulsory by 1985/86. The study of science is being given priority in the school curriculum. Expansion of technical and vocational education at secondary (middle and high school) level and of education for the professions will, it is envisaged, be integrated with the requirements in the National Development Plans for skilled manpower. In 1981, as a result of the Government's desire to raise educational standards, the English language was restored to a prominent position in the curriculum, and is now taught from kindergarten. In 1979/80 the budget allocation for education was 560 million kyats, compared with an expenditure of 416 million kyats in 1977/78.

Primary Schools

In 1978/79 the total enrolment in the State primary schools was 3.7 million in 23,009 schools, in which there were 84,593 teachers.

Lower Secondary (Middle) Schools

Education in lower secondary schools lasts four years from the age of 10 to 13 when pupils take the external government examination. In 1978/79 total enrolment at this level was 754,079 pupils in 1,302 schools, in which there were 19,964 teachers.

Upper Secondary (High) Schools

These schools cater for those in the age range 14 to 19. In 1978/79 there were 170,660 pupils enrolled in 596 schools with 11,469 teachers.

Technical and Vocational

The total number of students attending agricultural and technical institutes in 1978/79 was 9,576, in 52 institutions with 786 teachers.

Universities and Colleges

The total number of students attending universities and colleges in 1978/79 was 112,671.

BIBLIOGRAPHY

GENERAL

CHHIBBER, H. L. The Physiography of Burma (Calcutta and London, 1933).

CHRISTIAN, J. LE ROY. Modern Burma (University of California Press, Berkeley, Calif., 1942).

DONNISON, F. S. V. Burma (Benn, London, 1970).

HALL, D. G. E. Burma (Hutchinson, London, 2nd edn., 1956).

KHAING, MI MI. Burmese Family (Longman, Green & Co., London, 1946).

NASH, MANNING. The Golden Road to Modernity: Village Life in Contemporary Burma (John Wiley & Sons, Inc., New York, 1965).

SHWE YOE (Sir George Scott). The Burman: His Life and Notions (London, 1982).

SPIRO, MELFORD E. Kinship and Marriage in Burma (University of California Press, Berkeley, Calif., 1977).

STEINBERG, DAVID I. Burma: A Socialist Nation of South-east Asia (Westview Press, Boulder, Colorado, 1982).

TINKER, H. The Union of Burma (Oxford University Press, London, 4th edn., 1967).

HISTORY

ADAS, MICHAEL. The Burma Delta: Economic Development and Social Change on an Asian Rice Frontier, 1852–1941 (University of Wisconsin Press, Madison, Wis., 1974).

AUNG, MAUNG HTIN. A History of Burma (Columbia University Press, New York, 1968).

CADY, J. F. A. History of Modern Burma (Cornell University Press, Ithaca, N.Y. 1958).

The United States and Burma (Harvard University Press, Cambridge, Mass., 1976).

HALL, D. G. E. Early English Intercourse with Burma 1587–1743 (Frank Cass & Co., London, 1968).

HARVEY, G. E. History of Burma from the earliest times to the beginning of the English conquest (London, 1925).

British Rule in Burma (London, 1946).

LEHMAN, F. K. (ed.) Military Rule in Burma Since 1962 (Maruzan Asia (Institute of Southeast Asian Studies), Singapore, 1981).

MAW, BA. Breakthrough in Burma (Yale University Press, New Haven, Conn., 1968).

NU, THAKIN. Burma under the Japanese (Macmillan, London, 1954).

POLLAK, OLIVER B. Empires in Collision: Anglo-Burmese Relations in the Mid-Nineteenth Century (Greenwood Press, Westport, Conn., 1979).

STEINBERG, DAVID I. Burma's Road toward Development: Growth and Ideology under Military Rule (Westview Press, Boulder, Colorado, 1981).

STEWART, A. T. Q. The Pagoda War: Lord Dufferin and the Fall of the Kingdom of Ava, 1885–86 (Faber and Faber, London, 1972).

WOODMAN, D. The Making of Burma (Cresset Press, London, 1962).

ECONOMICS AND POLITICS

ANDRUS, J. R. Burmese Economic Life (Stanford University Press, Stanford, Calif., 1948).

CHAKRAVARTI, N. The Indian Minority in Burma: The Rise and Decline of an Immigrant Community (Oxford University Press, London, 1971).

DONNISON, F. S. V. Public Administration in Burma (London, 1953).

FURNIVALL, J. S. Colonial Policy and Practice: A Co-operative Study of Burma and Netherlands India (Cambridge University Press, London, 1957).

The Governance of Modern Burma (Institute of Pacific Relations, New York, 1960).

HAGEN, E. E. The Economic Development of Burma (Washington, 1956).

JOHNSTONE, W. C. Burma's Foreign Policy: a Study in Neutralism (Harvard University Press, Cambridge, Mass., 1963).

LEACH, E. R. Political Systems of Highland Burma (Harvard University Press, Cambridge, Mass., 1954).

LEHMAN, F. K. The Structure of Chin Society (University of Illinois, Urbana, Ill., 1963).

LISSAK, MOSHE. Military Roles in Modernization: Civil-Military Relations in Thailand and Burma (Sage Publications, Beverly Hills, 1976).

MAUNG, MAUNG. Burma's Constitution (Nijhoff, The Hague, 2nd edn., 1961).

Burma and General Ne Win (Asia Publishing House, London, 1969).

MENDELSON, E. MICHAEL, and FERGUSON, JOHN (ed.). Sangha and State in Burma (Cornell University Press, Ithaca, N.Y., 1975).

MOSCOTTI, ALBERT D. Burma's Constitution and the Elections of 1974 (Institute of Southeast Asian Studies, Singapore, 1977).

NU, U. U Nu—Saturday's Son (Yale University Press, New Haven, Conn., 1975).

PYE, L. W. Politics, Personality, and Nation Building (Yale University Press, New Haven, Conn., 1962).

SARKISYANZ, E. Buddhist Backgrounds of the Burmese Revolution (Martinus Nijhoff, The Hague, 1965).

SILVERSTEIN, JOSEF. Burma: Military Rule and the Politics of Stagnation (Cornell University Press, Ithaca, N.Y., 1977).

Burmese Politics: The Dilemma of National Unity (Rutgers University Press, New Brunswick, N.J., 1980).

SIOK-HWA, CHENG. The Rice Industry of Burma, 1852–1940 (University of Malaya Press, Kuala Lumpur, and Oxford University Press, London, 1969).

SMITH, D. E. Religion and Politics in Burma (Princeton University Press, Princeton, N.J., 1965).

SPIRO, MELFORD E. Buddhism and Society: A Great Tradition and its Burmese Vicissitudes (Allen & Unwin, Ltd., London, 1971).

WALINSKY, LOUIS. Economic Development in Burma 1951–1960 (Twentieth Century Fund, New York, 1962).

The People's Republic of China

China

Note: The Pinyin system of transliteration has been adopted for this edition. Where necessary, the traditional Wade-Giles spelling is given in brackets. For a full list of provinces *see* p. 355.

PHYSICAL AND SOCIAL GEOGRAPHY

Michael Freeberne

(Revised by the Editor, 1977-82)

The third largest country in the world (after the U.S.S.R. and Canada), China's territory covers 9.6 million square kilometres (over three and a half million square miles) and measures about 4,000 km. north to south and 4,800 km. from east to west. China and the United States are approximately the same size, but because of China's relief and the comparatively backward state of transport, distance creates major economic and political problems. For example, not only is it difficult to build a dense communications network but also the current policies of industrial re-location are seriously hindered, due to such factors as the long haul for minerals or the distance from the market. Similarly, the vastness of China has made it very hard to provide strong central government from Beijing (Peking). This is illustrated by the widespread tendency toward localism which became apparent after the onset of the Cultural Revolution in mid-1966. Offsetting these disadvantages is the inestimable psychological pressure which China's bulk exerts over its Asian neighbours.

China's land frontiers extend for a total of 20,000 km. (official), in an arc of actual and potential conflict. The eleven countries which share frontiers with China are North Korea, the Soviet Union, Mongolia, Afghanistan, Pakistan, India, Nepal, Bhutan, Burma, Laos and Viet-Nam. Although frontier agreements have been concluded with countries such as Mongolia, Pakistan and Burma since 1949, these have not prevented frontier tensions. The dispute over the boundary between China and India resulted in the border war of 1962. Meanwhile, the most recent Chinese maps show large stretches of the north-eastern boundary with the Soviet Union and the Sino-Soviet boundary in the Pamir area as "un-delimited", whilst border incidents have increased dramatically both in the north-east and north-west since 1960, as in the clashes along Heilongjiang's borders in 1969.

The eastern seaboard is 14,000 km. in length. China's territorial waters are dotted with over 5,000 islands, ranging from provincial sized Hainan and Taiwan down to minute atolls. Rich in fish, these waters make an important contribution to the output of aquatic products (marine and fresh water combined), estimated at between five and seven million tons a year. China lacks an important sea-faring tradition, however, partly because the relatively smooth coastline is largely without good natural harbours.

Administratively, China is divided into twenty-two provinces (including Taiwan); five autonomous regions (Nei Monggol (Inner Mongolia) A.R., Ningxia Hui A.R., Xinjiang Uygur A.R., Guangxi Zhuang A.R. and Xizang (Tibet) A.R.), and three cities (Beijing, Tianjin (Tientsin) and Shanghai), all of which are directly under the central government. In addition there are over two thousand counties and cities, which are subdivided into 74,000 people's communes. As the communes have undergone striking changes since their introduction in 1958, much of the effective economic and political organization in China is at production brigade and production team level, which probably frequently coincides with the natural village. Other organizational structures such as macro-economic and military regions may embrace several provinces, whilst tiny urban street organizations complete the administration network.

PHYSICAL FEATURES

Physical size on its own cannot automatically raise China to the rank of a first-class world power. The West regarded China as a land of fabulous wealth at the height of the Qing (Ch'ing) empire, but in fact the geographical environment presents considerable obstacles to modern development, which if not insurmountable put a brake on progress. For example, a Chinese source published in 1964 reveals that approximately 10 per cent of China's surface is in agricultural use, 10 per cent is forest, 28 per cent is pasture, whilst a further 12 per cent is classified as reclaimable wasteland; this leaves roughly 40 per cent unclassified wasteland.

Relief, configuration and climate are critical in suggesting possible settlement areas and zones suitable for economic development. For the most part high in the west and relatively low in the east, comparison has been made with a three section staircase. The Qinghai-Xizang Plateau at over 4,000 metres is the highest flight; next is an arc of plateaux and basins between 1,000 and 2,000 metres extending eastwards from the Tarim Basin, across Nei Monggol and the loess lands, then turning south to include the immensely fertile Sichuan Basin, and the Yunnan-Guizhou Plateau; much of the land which constitutes the lowest flight lies below 500 metres and includes the most densely settled areas, such as the middle and lower Changjiang (Yangtze) Basin, the North China Plain and the northeastern plain. About a third of China's total area is highland; 26 per cent is plateau land; 10 per cent is hill country; 20 per cent is occupied by basins; but only 12 per cent of the surface is composed of plains.

Watering these plains are rivers which in some years bring rich harvests, whilst in other years they may cause flooding, or dry up altogether with resulting drought famines, which were frequent before 1949. In the north, the Huanghe (Yellow River) is 4,845 km. in length and has a drainage basin of 745,000 sq. km. In central China the Changjiang is 5,800 km. long with a massive drainage basin of 1,800,000 sq. km., covering one-fifth of the country. The shorter Xijiang (Sikiang) is the most important river in south China. The long history of flood control and water conservation continues into the contemporary period, as in the case of the taming of the Huai River, a project encouraged by Mao Zedong (Mao Tse-tung). Flood control, irrigation, navigation and power generation are all stressed in this and similar multi-purpose projects. The Chinese claim that China is high in world ranking in hydro-electric power potential and that the Hengduan Mountains in the south-west have an "unlimited" potential; what they fail to point out is that this area is difficult of access and economically backward. Indeed China has been characterized as a land which suffers from having either too much water or not enough water, both in terms of regional and seasonal distribution. Since 1969 there has been a national campaign to build small and medium-sized hydro-electric power stations which was said to have doubled the total capacity of rural hydro-electricity stations constructed over the previous twenty years during the winter and spring of 1969–70 alone.

CLIMATE

Climatically, China is dominated by a monsoonal regime. Cold air masses build up over the Asian land mass in winter, and the prevailing winds are offshore and dry. In summer there is a reversal of this pattern, and the rainy season is concentrated in the summer months over the most densely settled parts of the country in the east and the south. Running from south to north there are six broad temperature zones; tropical and sub-tropical, warm-temperate and temperate, cold-temperate and the Qinghai-Xizang plateau area, which has its own characteristic regime. January is generally the coldest month and July the hottest. There is a great range in winter temperatures—as much as 15°C. between the average for Guangzhou (Canton) in the south and Harbin in the north. South of the Nanling Mountains January temperatures average around 8°C., but they drop to between −8°C. and −15°C. over much of the north-east, Nei Monggol and the north-west. In summer the temperature difference between Guangzhou and Harbin is only 12°C. and summer temperatures over much of the country average above 20°C.

The summer monsoon brings abundant rain to coastal China, especially in the south and east, but amounts decrease drastically to the north and west. A humid zone covers much of southeastern China and the average annual rainfall is above 75 cm. In the semi-humid zone, extending across the north-east, the North China Plain and the southeastern region of the Qinghai-Xizang Plateau, the average falls to less than 50 cm. The remainder of the Qinghai-Xizang, the Loess, and the Nei Monggol Plateaux receive only about 30 cm., whilst western Nei Monggol and Xinjiang receive less than 25 cm. and include extensive deserts.

Eighty per cent of the precipitation falls between May and October, with July and August the wettest months. Not infrequently the rain turns the rivers into raging torrents and disastrous floods occur, or alternatively not enough rain falls. In the late 1870s, for instance, four northern provinces were devastated by a drought famine which cost between nine and thirteen million lives. To flood and drought can be added other calamities: typhoons, earthquakes, frosts, hailstorms, plant and animal pests and diseases. The grave economic difficulties of the early 1960s may be attributed to three main factors, namely the withdrawal of Soviet aid, internal mistakes, and bad weather. The Chinese refer to the years 1959, 1960 and 1961 as the "three bitter years" and they claim that in 1960 and again in 1961 half the agricultural land was affected by natural disasters.

VEGETATION AND NATURAL RESOURCES

During many hundreds of years a great deal of China's natural vegetation has been stripped. The basic contrast is between the forests and woodlands of the eastern half of the country and the grassland-desert complex of the western half. Tree types vary from the tropical rain forests in the south, through evergreen broad-leaved forests, mixed mesophytic forests, temperate deciduous broad-leaved forests, and mixed northern hardwood and boreal coniferous forests in the north. Sixty per cent of China's forest reserves are found in the area of the eastern Mongolian Plateau, the Xiao Hingan Ling and Da Hingdao Ling (the Lesser and Greater Khingan Mountains), and the Changbaishan massif. Other natural forests are located in Yunnan, Jiangxi, Fujian, Guizhou, Sichuan, on Hainan Island, in the Qinling Mountains and along the eastern edge of the Qinghai-Xizang Plateau. Most of China's forests are largely inaccessible, however, and there is a serious shortage of workable timber.

Due to the widespread destruction of natural vegetation, soil erosion is a major problem. Sheet and gulley erosion are common; water and wind erosion do great damage in the north, whilst water erosion is the chief enemy in the south; also, farming malpractices, such as deep ploughing, have aggravated the situation both historically and since 1949. A recent Chinese source states that about 40 per cent of the total cultivated area comprises "poor" soils: red loams, saline-alkaline soil and some of the rice paddy soils. Thus the legendary fertility of China's soils cannot be taken for granted.

Information concerning mineral wealth is incomplete, but the best available estimates suggest that China is extremely rich in coal and iron ore. Between 1966 and 1973 many thousands of small coal mines and pits were opened, especially in areas south of the Changjiang river. Following a major petroleum discovery at Daqing (Taching) and explorations elsewhere, China increased its annual production of crude oil from about 3 million tons in 1960 to an estimated 106 million tons in 1979. China has abundant reserves of manganese, tungsten and molybdenum, but is relatively poor in copper, lead and zinc, and nickel supplies are meagre. There are rich resources of salt, moderate reserves of sulphur, whilst phosphates require development; supplies of tin, fluorite-graphite, magnesite, talc, asbestos and barytes are also comparatively good.

HUMAN GEOGRAPHY

In June 1979 the State Statistical Bureau gave a population figure for China (including Taiwan) of 975,230,000 at the end of 1978. According to a Bureau communiqué in April 1980, China's population (excluding Taiwan) was 970,920,000 at the end of 1979, compared with 958,090,000 a year earlier. The Bureau estimated the total as 982,550,000 at December 31st, 1980, rising to 996,220,000 at the end of 1981. These figures, which represent 22 per cent of the world's population, are formidable in view of the pressures which Chinese numbers have exerted on the Chinese realm in the past, and in view of the continuing problems in the physical environment already outlined. There is, for instance, a striking imbalance in the distribution of population, which is heavily concentrated in the plain and riverine lands of the southeastern half of the country, whilst most of the northwestern half is, by comparison, virtually uninhabited. This results in very high densities of population in the richest areas for settlement, such as the Changjiang delta or the Red Basin of Sichuan. Indeed, 90 per cent of the population inhabit little more than 15 per cent of the country's surface area.

Some 94 per cent of the population are Han Chinese. The remaining 6 per cent belong to one of the national minority groups. Altogether there are over fifty million non-Chinese living within China, chiefly in the peripheral areas beyond the Great Wall, in the north, the north-west and the south-west. There are over fifty different minorities scattered throughout 60 per cent of the country. Ten minorities number more than one million each: the Zhuangs (Chuangs), Wei Wu Er (Uighurs), Huis, Yis, Xizangzu (Tibetans), Miaos, Manzus (Manchus), Menggus (Mongolians), Buyis (Puyis), and Chaoxian (Koreans). There are over seven million Zhuangs in Guangxi, whilst the smallest of all the minorities, the Hezhe (Hochih), from the banks of the Wusuli Jiang (Ussuri River), number only about 600.

Although so-called autonomous regions (and also districts and counties) have been established, the larger minority groups have presented the central government with serious administrative difficulties. Racial, religious and linguistic problems, as in Muslim Xinjiang and Buddhist Xizang, have resulted in several anti-Chinese uprisings since 1949; these have been forcibly suppressed.

Linguistic differences between the seven main Chinese dialects, as well as between Chinese and minority languages, have proved an intractable issue, despite the adoption of Mandarin as the national language, despite attempts at the simplification of the written language by reducing the number of strokes in individual characters and by romanization, and despite literacy drives. In 1957 Mao Zedong forecast that illiteracy would be wiped out by 1963; by the early 1980s the Chinese had not achieved this goal.

Well over 100 million people in China live in cities or towns, but this is still predominantly a rural country with possibly 85 per cent of the population living in the countryside. The inequalities in living standards which exist between the "parasitic" cities and the rural areas confront the Chinese with some of their most urgent ideological and practical problems. One answer is to advertise life in the countryside by applauding the progress of model villages like Dazhai (Tachai), a tiny community in the northern province of Shanxi.

About 20 million Chinese live beyond the frontiers of China. These Overseas Chinese are found mostly in South-East Asia. Because of its proximity to the People's Republic and because this part of Asia is rich in items such as rice, oil, timber and rubber, which China lacks in sufficient quantities, some authorities see in the presence of these communities a threat to the security of the area.

The population of China is expanding at a rate of approximately 1.4 per cent a year. Birth control programmes since the early 1960s failed to make any noticeable inroads in the increase in Chinese numbers and in 1979 further directives were issued favouring couples with only one child and penalizing those who practise "anarchism in parenthood". Internal migration offers no solution to the population problem.

Despite high grain harvests in the 1970s (an estimated 279 million tons in 1978), and because the agricultural sector has to provide not only food for a rapidly growing population but also investment for individual growth, population pressure must remain central to all domestic and external issues within the foreseeable future.

TAIWAN

The province of Taiwan is one of a mountainous arc of islands offshore from the Asian land mass. Separated from the mainland by the Taiwan Strait (about 145 km. wide at the narrowest point), Taiwan is 36,002 square km. in area and measures 390 km. from north to south and 142 km. from east to west, and straddles the Tropic of Capricorn.

Due to the mountainous character of the relief only about one quarter of the island is cultivated, while forests cover about two-thirds of the total land area.

The climate is sub-tropical in the north and tropical in the south, being strongly modified by oceanic and relief factors. Apart from the mountainous core, winter temperatures average 15°C. and summer temperatures about 26°C. Monsoon rains visit the north-east in winter (October to March) but come to the south in summer, and are abundant, the mean annual average rainfall being 256 cm. Typhoons are often serious, particularly between July and September.

The population numbered 18,145,810 at January 31st, 1982, giving Taiwan a population density of more than 500 per square kilometre, one of the highest in the world.

In 1964 the rate of natural increase fell below 3 per cent for the first time; it was 3.7 per cent in 1952 and 1.8 per cent in 1981. The crude birth rate in 1981 was 23.0 per 1,000 (compared with 46.6 per 1,000 in 1952), and the crude death rate in 1981 was 4.8 per 1,000 (compared with 9.9 per 1,000 in 1952). The death rate is one of the lowest in Asia, and the infant mortality rate (deaths under 1 year of age per 1,000 live births) of 10.1 in 1980 was among the lowest in Asia. At the end of 1980, 32.1 per cent of Taiwan's population were under 15 years of age; 61.1 per cent were aged between 15 and 59; and 6.8 per cent of the population were 60 and over. This is a youthful population, with 43.3 per cent under 20 years of age (at the end of 1980), and therefore a high potential for growth.

With the expansion of industry, Taiwan's population is becoming increasingly urbanized. Between 1960 and 1980 the proportion living in towns of 100,000 or more increased from 28.9 per cent to 47.2 per cent.

HISTORY

C. P. FitzGerald

China has a long history, but it does not reach quite so far back as is often claimed. The earliest written Chinese records date from the period round 1500 B.C., and recorded history is uncertain and partly legendary until after 1000 B.C. These dates are late for Egypt, Iraq, or Asia Minor. On the other hand, the civilization first appearing in the second millennium B.C. is the direct ancestor of the culture of modern China, the written language is an early form of the present script, and the connection between spoken Chinese of today and that of a remote age can be traced. There is good archaeological evidence that the present-day Chinese, especially in north China, are the descendants of the people of Shang, the first certainly known kingdom of that region. It would not, of course, be historical to speak of "China" and the "Chinese" in this early period. Next to nothing is known of the culture of what is now more than half of China, the south, until centuries later. The north China kingdom of Shang was probably confined to the valley of the Huanghe (Yellow River).

In the next age, the first millennium B.C., a new kingdom was established over a much wider area of north China, but was divided into feudal fiefs, some of which were very large. This kingdom, or dynasty, the Zhou (Chou), endured nominally from *c.* 1100 to 221 B.C., but in the later centuries the kings had lost all power and retained only the old capital city. The country was divided among warring feudal lords, the most powerful of whom finally set up as independent kings and virtually abolished the nominal overlordship of the King of Zhou. Other, originally ethnically different, peoples in the Changjiang (Yangtze) valley, acquired Chinese civilization in this age and also established strong states in the south and centre of China. In the same age as the early Chinese philosophers taught and wrote, of whom the first was Confucius (died 479 B.C.), the Chinese Feudal System broke down, and a period of intense strife known as the "Age of the Warring States" (481–221 B.C.) ravaged the country both north and south. This was in reality a contest to unite the whole of the Chinese civilized world under one rule, and was ultimately won by a powerful ruthless monarch, king of the western state of Qin (Ch'in).

IMPERIAL CHINA

Qin had been a state dedicated to war and conquest: its official ideology despised the arts, literature and philosophy, but exalted law, by which was meant a harsh criminal code to which all, rich and poor, noble and serf, were alike subject. When the king of Qin had conquered all his rivals (221 B.C.) he proclaimed himself First Emperor, choosing a new and lofty title which we have translated as "emperor" although the Chinese words *Huang Di* do not have the military connotations of the Latin *imperator*. Once in power the Qin applied their own harsh system of government to the whole country, and thereby provoked a violent and fatal reaction. On the death of the First Emperor after a reign of eleven years his incompetent successor was soon engulfed in a national revolt, from which emerged, after several years of civil war, the Han dynasty, which restored the central unified empire but ruled it with more moderate policies and thus established the new form of the state. Before the Qin-Han empire there had been no political unity in China; the rule of even the earliest Zhou kings had been limited, and the later fiction of an original unified empire, from which the feudal system was a degeneration, is an imaginative reconstruction of largely unknown periods in the light of the reality of the first century B.C.

One of the acts of Qin which was most condemned at the time and has subsequently been bitterly denounced by Chinese historians was the "burning of the books"—a decree by which all the works of the philosophers and much other literature were collected and destroyed, in order to crush the intellectual opposition to Qin rule. In the Han period scholars laboured, with some success, to restore the lost works, but our knowledge of earlier China has undoubtedly suffered greatly from this proscription. The ancient Chinese did not inscribe on clay tablets, nor carve long inscriptions on stone: they wrote on slips of bamboo, a perishable material which rarely survives long periods of interment. The Han empire, which expanded the frontiers to limits close to those of the present People's Republic, and also extended its conquests far into central Asia, has left very full historical records, which became the model for all later dynastic histories.

Ruling all China for over four hundred years (206 B.C.–A.D. 221) it was contemporary with the great age of the Roman Republic and the first centuries of the Roman Empire. The imperial state as constructed by the Han remained the model for the subsequent regimes, right down to modern times, although innovations and advances in the art of government were made at later times. The Emperor was the supreme and absolute monarch, in theory, and when a vigorous personality occupied the throne, in practice also. He was advised, and often controlled, by a council of ministers chosen from the heads of the civil service, who were thus not politicians but bureaucrats. In Han times the civil service was recruited by recommendation, not yet by public examinations. High officials recommended their followers or clients, but these had to be men of education, usually of some means, and also capable. An incompetent or corrupt official would bring his patron into trouble and disgrace. The hereditary aristocracy of pre-imperial days had been abolished. Only the imperial family and a small number of their eminent supporters held such titles, and after the middle of the Han period these ranks no longer gave any effective jurisdiction over territory, which was divided into units governed by imperial officials. As both the imperial family of the Han dynasty and their early chief supporters were all men of poor origin and low social class, the advent to power of this group made a social revolution almost inevitable. Feudal land tenure vanished, to be replaced by the free ownership of land, and as a consequence the rise of the landlord class and a mixed farming class of free peasants and tenants.

Division and Reunification under the Tang and Song

On this basis the Han dynasty retained power for a long period, which was one of rapid and varied development both in the economy and in the art and literature of China. In the early third century A.D. the Han empire collapsed due to a variety of internal tensions and the increasing weakness of the ruling family. Civil wars at first divided the empire into three kingdoms (221–265), then, after a very brief reunion, the empire was invaded in the north by Tartar tribes, who seized the northern provinces. Chinese dynasties ruling from Nanjing (Nanking), held the south, and developed it. This period of division between north and south lasted for more than 250 years (316–589). It was a period of political weakness, but not a "Dark Age". Literature flourished, and in these centuries Buddhism was introduced from India and established a major place in the Chinese civilization, from whence it spread to Japan. In both north and south military power tended to overshadow the civil service, but that institution did not wholly disappear.

Reunion of the empire was accomplished by the short-lived Sui dynasty (589-618) and then consolidated by the great Tang dynasty (618–907). This period of three hundred years marks what many would call the apogee of the old Chinese civilization (contemporary with the European Dark Ages). The Tang empire was as extensive as the Han, and at one time also included all of Korea. It was governed on the same principles but with significant improvements on Han practice. Public examinations for the choice of civil service candidates came steadily into prominence, displacing the recommendation system This was partly the Tang emperors' response to the dangerous power of the highly placed military aristocracy who had dominated the court in the period of the division between north and south. It had the consequence of bringing to power a much larger class of literates who had neither territorial nor military power bases. The Tang bureaucracy could thus draw on a wide field of talent, and the extent to which it mastered the practice of government is evidenced by the elaborate and detailed census taking in 754, which enumerated the population of China as 52,880,488, a figure which archaeological discovery has proved to be founded on exact and detailed returns of families, in which men, women and children were counted. The second half of the Tang dynasty was disturbed by a major rebellion, which weakened central government control in the provinces. Art and literature, especially poetry, early forms of the drama and the novel, all flourished during this great age, in which China was also in closer contact with western Asia and Byzantium, as with India and Japan, than ever before.

When Tang fell in 907 a short interval of fifty years of confused struggle and separation divided it from the rise of the next great unifying dynasty, the Song (Sung) (960–1280). This period is again divided at 1127 when the Song lost north China to the invading Kin Tartars. The Song regime differed in some respects from its predecessor. The civil service now reigned supreme, recruited by public examination. Song rule was rather gentle; disgraced statesmen were sent to govern small provincial towns, not imprisoned or executed, and even rival kings at the foundation of the dynasty were spared if they surrendered. Art excelled, and the Song is also the age of the reshaping and modernization of Confucianism (finally perfected by the philosopher Zhu Xi (Chu Hsi), which was the main intellectual interest of the age. The Song were in fact too civilized for their age; beyond their northern frontier powerful and violent nomadic peoples were emerging and were to break into the empire first in 1127 when they conquered north China, and later, from 1212 to 1280, when the Mongol ruler Genghis Khan and his successors maintained continuous attacks upon China, both north and south, till they had conquered the whole country and extinguished the Song dynasty. During that dynasty the economy had made great advances. It has been suggested that the Song economy was approaching the point of "take-off" to an industrial revolution. Shipping and overseas commerce were for the first time more important sources of revenue, in the southern Song, than the land tax.

Mongol and Ming Rule

All this was checked, indeed largely destroyed, by the Mongol conquest which was particularly destructive in north China. Large areas were reduced to uninhabited wilderness, and made into imperial Mongol hunting grounds. A very great number of people perished, either by slaughter or starvation. Europe was soon to learn of the glory of Kubilai Khan, the first Mongol to rule all China, but Marco Polo was in large part describing the surviving prosperity of parts of the Song empire which had escaped the worst devastation. The Mongols ruled China with foreigners, such as Polo, who took service under the Khans. They came from all over Asia as well as some from Europe, and they did not speak or read Chinese. Consequently, Mongol rule was alien and hated. Chinese in their service were often employed in non-Chinese parts of their empire. The successors of Kubilai Khan were weak and incompetent; in 1368, after less than a century of full control, they were driven out by a large-scale Chinese rebellion, which was finally led and organized by the founder of the following Ming dynasty. The main contribution of the Mongol period to Chinese culture was the rise of the drama, possibly under some foreign inspiration, but essentially the work of Chinese scholars. The widespread Mongol empire of the early Khans, which included Persia, Asia Minor and much of Russia, made communication better for a time than ever before. It was in this age that, thanks to Marco Polo and other travellers, Europeans for the first time obtained some accurate information about China. Chinese scholars, in the Song period, using Arab informants, had also gained more knowledge of western Asia and Europe.

The Ming dynasty not only restored Chinese rule, but expanded the limits of the empire. South Manzhou (Manchuria) was settled and incorporated, as was Yunnan, at the opposite extremity of the empire. But the land route to the west decayed in importance after the Mongol period, and the sea route round India to the Red Sea and Persian Gulf became more important. Early in the fifteenth century, from 1405 to 1433, the Ming court sent out several large-scale maritime expeditions carrying up to 70,000 men in specially built large ships. These expeditions roamed over the seas south of China, established Ming suzerainty over the kingdoms of Malaya and parts of what is now Indonesia, visited Ceylon, India, Burma, the Philippines, the Persian Gulf, Arabia, the Red Sea, and the east coast of Africa down to Zanzibar, from which region they brought back a live giraffe as a gift to the Emperor. Ming sea power, had it been maintained in the southern seas, would have barred the Portuguese when they arrived seventy years later. But there was a change of policy in Beijing (Peking): the maritime effort was discontinued and never resumed. Unwittingly, the Ming court thus exposed China to many calamities.

From the middle of the fifteenth century China was also to an increasing extent menaced by the growth of a new power in what is called Manzhou, or the Three Eastern Provinces. The Manzu (Manchu) tribes, kindred of the Kin Tartars who had ruled north China in the late Song period, were at first tributary to the Ming. From China, through this contact, they acquired a knowledge of governing techniques, literacy, and organization. Late in the sixteenth century they coalesced into a new kingdom which threw off allegiance to the Ming, and before long began to encroach on the Ming territory of south Manzhou, or modern Liaoning province. By the middle of the seventeenth century they had seized this region and were raiding the Great Wall frontier of China proper. In 1644 an internal rebellion overthrew the Ming government in Beijing, and the general commanding the frontier army, Wu Sangui, decided to admit the Manzus rather than acknowledge the rebel chief as a new emperor. Aided by his powerful Chinese army (which could probably have denied them entry to China indefinitely), the Manzus occupied north China, while Wu destroyed the rebels. Later he broke with the Manzus and tried to establish his own dynasty in south China. His death during this campaign enabled the Manzus to conquer south China also. But Manzhou (Manchu) rule was not firmly established in the south of China until 1682, nearly forty years after their unopposed entry into Beijing. This difference between the history of north and south had great importance for later times. The north had accepted the Manzus, and remained loyal to them; the south had resisted them, and remained hostile and unreconciled. In the first century of Manzhou rule the difference was unimportant, although even then moulding Manzhou policy. In later times, when the dynasty was losing power, the hostile traditions of the south became the main source of trouble and rebellion from which the failing regime was never delivered.

Manzhou (Qing)

The Qing (Ch'ing) or Manzhou dynasty (1644–1912) was the last age of imperial China. In many ways, although a dynasty of alien origin, the Qing were more conservative and traditional than any of their Chinese predecessors. Being of foreign origin, and a small minority in a vast sea of Chinese subjects, they sought to conciliate the Chinese intellectual class, the scholar-officials, by adopting all their opinions and endorsing their outlook. They became more Confucian than the Chinese Confucianists. Had the Qing had no more to contribute than an extreme conservative standpoint and a reverence for Chinese culture which distrusted all change and advance, it is probable that they would not have lasted very long. They had the fortune to produce, within a generation of their accession to the throne, three successive very capable rulers, the Emperors Kang Xi (K'ang Hsi) (1662–1723), Yong Zheng (Yung Cheng) (1723–1736), and Qian Long (Ch'ien Lung) (1736–1796). The first and last of these also reigned for sixty years each. Long reigns are conducive to stability in an authoritarian government. The gains acquired through a period of such stability lasting nearly 150 years were great. Peace was maintained throughout China; only frontier wars, to pacify the nomads of Mongolia, kept the army in good training. The population rose very rapidly; for a time prosperity grew proportionately. New grains and plants, such as maize, the potato and sweet potato introduced through the Philippines from the Americas, added to the productivity of the soil.

But these successes were themselves productive of trouble and danger. The pacification of the Mongolian tribes ended the nomad menace for ever, for at the same time the advance of Russia in Siberia cut off and destroyed the reservoir of nomad power. Consequently, the Manzhou army, originally a highly trained and very efficient force, had now no wars to fight, and degenerated. No one at court considered the activity of European shipping on the coasts to be a latent menace; no one heeded the fate of India. The long internal peace is believed to have doubled the population from 100 million to over 200 million. Land became hard to find and prices rose; tenants were rack-rented and free peasants bought or squeezed out. Industry was not developed to meet the rising population and provide new employment. Industry and mining were held to be occupations which, needing some foreign technology, could only prove subversive and anti-Confucian in their operation. The ruling scholar-officials were not trained to engage in this sort of enterprise and the court endorsed their attitude.

Foreign Relations under the Manzhous

The Manzhous needed trade, which was at first very profitable to China, but they distrusted the foreign traders, confined them to one port, Guangzhou (Canton), forced them to deal only with a selected group of Chinese merchants and hedged them about with innumerable vexatious restrictions, as if they were dangerous pirates. Chinese were forbidden on pain of death to travel overseas.

All these restrictions were imposed without relaxation throughout the eighteenth century, and the otherwise able and enlightened Emperor Qian Long upheld them. He would not accept any permanent foreign diplomatic representation in Beijing; it had never been customary. Foreigners came to pay tribute, were given magnificent gifts, and sent back home. The same treatment was given to the British, Dutch and other embassies who tried to open up relations. The Manzhous did not wish to learn about a new world which would upset their basic assumptions and challenge their traditional claims. Tension built up at Guangzhou, and the discovery that opium, produced in India, could have a ready and spreading sale in China, turned the favourable trade balance from China to Britain. Opium was an illegal import; British traders, and their officials, connived at an extensive smuggling trade; Chinese officials were easily corrupted to turn a blind eye and win a share in the profits. Early in the nineteenth century the opium trade was an open scandal and doing great harm to China's economy and to social life. The court was finally induced by earnest and patriotic officials to decree the total suppression of the trade. The resulting action, and high-handed methods employed, touched off the powder keg and brought about the Opium War of 1842.

China was defeated; its navy was wholly inadequate to face the British fleets; its old-style army could not overcome the more modern arms of small British landing forces. China was compelled to sue for peace, and this was consummated by the Treaty of Nanjing, the first of the "Unequal Treaties" as they came to be called, which established the system of Treaty Ports, concession areas and the right of extraterritorial jurisdiction. This system was to endure for just one century until, in 1942, it was swept away by the Japanese invasion of China.

Reform Movement

It was not, at first, the terms of the Treaty of Nanjing which did harm to the Chinese Government of the Qing dynasty; it was the loss of prestige following defeat in war, and defeat in the south, where the population was hostile. Within a few years the great unrest of the south, aggravated by economic pressures, burst out in the Taiping rebellion (1851–1864). This rebellion swept the south and centre of China, and narrowly failed to capture Beijing and dethrone the dynasty. Its leader was a man with some imperfect knowledge of the Christian Protestant religion, who claimed to be a prophet inspired directly by God. Established in Nanjing, he ruled the Taiping Heavenly Kingdom and for a time tried to enforce many advanced reforms, especially in the condition of women and land tenure. But the pressure of the imperial armies was too constant to make these efforts fruitful. At the end Nanjing was recaptured, the Heavenly King dying of disease, for which he refused all attention, shortly before the city fell. The salient fact about this campaign was that the Manzhou army had been proved useless, and the imperial cause was won by Chinese armies commanded by Chinese loyalists. They could not thereafter be disbanded and their commanders became the highest officials of the dynasty, and dominated political life for the next fifty years. The Manzhou government now survived on Chinese arms and loyalty; so long as it could command both, it could endure; when these were lost the dynasty had no further resource.

Preserved against all likelihood in the 1860s, the Manzus were compelled to permit some few modernizing reforms, mainly concerned with the armed forces. These were to be equipped with modern weapons, and arsenals were built. A modern navy was constructed, and its future officers sent to England to serve with the British Fleet and learn their art. This was, in fact, the flaw in the new movement. "Chinese learning as a base, foreign skills for use" was the new slogan. But foreign skills require foreign learning; the young men had to study English, or French; they did not confine their reading to technology, they read about democracy and other strange notions. They became at first reformers and when reform was denied, they became revolutionaries. The patrons of the young students now beginning to be sent abroad were the great officials who had commanded and raised armies to fight the Taipings, and now exercised unquestioned power. Change and reform were thus built into the power structure, but this could still be obstructed by the supreme authority of the Emperor. For nearly half a century since the death of the Emperor Xian Feng in 1862 until her own death in 1908 this power was exercised by the Regent, the Empress Dowager Cu Xi (Tz'u Hsi), first in the name of her infant son and when he died in youth in that of her infant nephew Emperor Guang Xu (Kuang Hsu). She was an able but basically ignorant woman who hated foreign innovations. She did her best to obstruct reform, and she was very successful.

If the great reforming officials of the early 1870s had had the leadership of the sovereign to back them, as their contemporaries in Japan had, it is at least possible that they might have achieved in China some reformed system not unlike the Meiji system in Japan. China is a larger country and the task harder; but there were plenty of able men willing to undertake it. Instead they had to hold on to power by conciliating the prejudices of an obscurantist court arbitrarily ruled by a strong-minded but conservative woman. When Emperor Guang Xu came of age he tried, in a brief three months in 1898, to implement a programme of sweeping reforms, inspired by young and progressive officials who had gained his confidence. He was never fully free to act, and when it seemed that he might become so, the Empress Dowager emerged from a very partial retirement to carry out a *coup d'état*, imprison the Emperor for the rest of his life, and execute all reformers she could catch. Thus tragically ended the last real hope of reform under the monarchy.

Meanwhile, since the 1870s, China had been steadily suffering the encroachment of the European Powers. Russia had taken the opportunity of the Taiping war to obtain what is now the Maritime Province of Siberia and land north of the Heilong Jiang (Amur River). These territories had been Manzu, but never Chinese. France had in the 1880s seized Indochina and forced Beijing to renounce its suzerainty. The United Kingdom and France together had been at war with China (1858) and had actually occupied Beijing, exacting a further "Unequal Treaty". Towards the end of the century Japan entered the lists, and in the war of 1894–95 drove the Chinese out of Korea, and destroyed the new fleet. China had to yield suzerainty over Korea, and also the ports of Dalianwan (Talienwan) or Dalian (Dairen) and Lushun (Port Arthur) to Japan. Russia, aided by France and Germany, then put pressure on Japan to give up these two ports to Russia. A government which is laggard in reform at home, and unable to defend itself abroad, is not likely to retain loyalty and support. When the younger generation, towards the turn of the century, realized that reform would be frustrated, and that the country was running the real risk of partition by foreign powers—already "spheres of influence" were openly marked out—there was a sharp turn to revolutionary ideas and action. This movement will for ever be associated with the name of Dr. Sun Yat-sen.

REPUBLICAN CHINA

Sun Yat-sen was a Cantonese, who had been educated from childhood in Hawaii and then took a medical degree at the medical school of Hong Kong, which later became Hong Kong University. His formation was thus largely foreign and Western. Finding that radical reform was unacceptable to the official world of China, he turned revolutionary and republican, and for more than ten years maintained an unceasing effort to stir up rebellion in China. He was for long unsuccessful; but his influence grew steadily among the young Chinese studying abroad, particularly in Japan, where the majority of them went. He built up a party and a secret organization, obtained funds from the overseas Chinese of South-East Asia, always anti-Manzu, and finally his followers were able to infiltrate the army—the new model army whose officers had also studied abroad. Army officers, who must necessarily learn modern techniques, have in many countries of Asia proved to be the most effective revolutionaries. They at least can command armed support.

Thus, when in 1911 the revolution broke out it was from the first dominated by the army men, a servitude from which it was not to escape for many years. The court had lost further prestige in 1900 by backing the peasant anti-foreign movement known as the Boxer Rebellion, which for a time threatened to massacre the diplomatic corps in Beijing, and was finally crushed by an international expedition, which took Beijing and drove the court to retreat to the west of China. The southern provinces under their great viceroys refused to follow court policy over the Boxers, and virtually concluded a separate peace with the Foreign Powers. This was a sign of coming disruption which proved a portent. After signing a further humiliating peace the court returned to Beijing, and in its last years attempted to put through reforms which might have saved it fifty years earlier. It was too late. When the Empress Dowager died in 1908 no strong character remained to carry on the Regency in the name of the next infant Emperor, Xuan Tong or Pu Yi. Within three years the revolution had broken out and the dynasty was doomed.

In its last extremity it called upon the former commander-in-chief Yuan Shikai, who was out of favour with the new Regent, to save it. The northern troops would only obey their old commander; the southern army had gone over to the revolution. Yuan took command, but he did not intend to save the dynasty; he hoped to set up his own. First he showed by a brief campaign that he was a serious contender, then began to negotiate with the republicans. A deal was soon arranged. Yuan would bring about the peaceful abdication of the dynasty, which would in return be granted very favourable terms, and the republic would elect Yuan to be president. When the first Parliament was called (under conditions of flagrant corruption) Yuan had some of the more able members assassinated, and soon, having obtained a loan from the Foreign Powers without the assent of Parliament, dissolved that body and ruled by decree. Futile and ineffective resistance in the south was speedily crushed. Yuan now moved to obtain support for a new dynasty with himself as Emperor (1914).

The outbreak of the First World War was a factor which worked against this programme. It divided the Foreign Powers, and left Japan a comparatively free hand in Asia. Japan bribed and armed Yuan's secret opponents, his own generals, who were jealous of his pretensions to the throne. On December 25th, 1915, a revolt broke out, and within a few months it was evident that the generals had turned against him, and the projected monarchy was impossible. He renounced his plans, tried to cling to the Presidency, and died in June 1916. His death was soon followed by the contests among his former generals who controlled the provinces. The "warlord era" from 1917 to 1927 was marked by a series of short civil wars fought entirely between rival militarists to gain control of revenues, and above all of the impotent government in Beijing, which could dispense the custom revenue collected under foreign supervision to service the foreign loans, but which still left a valuable revenue for whichever general could dominate Beijing. The international position of China fell to its lowest point, and within the country there was an increasing breakdown of law and order, banditry, and rural distress. The seeds of revolution in a real sense were rapidly maturing.

Nationalism and Communism

If to foreign observers China had never seemed so chaotic and purposeless, there were, in fact, beneath the surface, forces stirring which were very little understood abroad. In May 1919 the students of Beijing had rioted against the Beijing Government's acceptance of the secret deal by which Japan was to acquire the former German leased port of Qingdao (Tsingtao) in Shandong. It was generally known that the corrupt politicians and their militarist master had received large sums from Japan for this virtually treasonable decision. The "May Fourth Movement", as it has become known, spread widely in all parts of China; it was the first sign of a new phase of the revolution, a revolt against Western dictation of China's affairs and fate, the first overt reaction of the generation who had grown up since the empire fell. Today the Communist government commemorates it as the opening of a new era.

In May 1925, six years later, another violent outbreak followed upon the shooting by International Settlement police of student demonstrators in Shanghai. This time the wave of anger, directed against the United Kingdom and Japan, was nation-wide. There was a total boycott of British and Japanese trade and enterprise. Hong Kong's labour was withdrawn and its life all but paralysed. Further riots and shootings occurred at Guangzhou, and missionaries were compelled to leave the interior of China. Boycott pickets were established in the Treaty Ports and became an extra-legal militia.

Dr. Sun Yat-sen, having failed to obtain any help from the Western Powers to reinstate his government—which he and his followers regarded as the only legal one—had turned to the Soviet Union, who gave him the necessary support in arms, advisers and possibly money. He regained control of Guangzhou in 1923 and swiftly set about the organization of an efficient government and a new model army. In 1921 the Chinese Communist Party had been formally set up at a meeting attended by eleven members, one of whom was Mao Zedong (Mao Tse-tung). At almost the same time a Chinese Communist Party had been formed in France by students living in Paris. One of the founders was Zhou Enlai (Chou En-lai). The two parties, the Communists still very small, the Nationalists already gaining wide support, co-operated on the basis that Communists might join the Nationalists (Kuomintang) as individuals, but there was no affiliation of the two parties. Aided by the repercussions of May 1925, revolutionary agitation increased rapidly.

After Dr. Sun's death in 1925, all hope of peaceful reunion was ended, and the Nationalist government in Guangzhou prepared for war, which was launched in 1926 against the southern warlords. Success was rapid, and early in 1927 the whole of the middle Changjiang region had fallen into Nationalist hands, and their armies, commanded by Jiang Gaishek (Chiang Kai-shek), were approaching Shanghai. Alarmed, the Treaty Powers landed troops to defend the International Settlement. The Shanghai workers and boycott pickets, organized by the Communists, rose and seized the Chinese-governed part of Shanghai, expelling the warlord army. When Jiang's forces arrived they found Chinese Shanghai already in the hands of the revolutionaries, and a critical situation pregnant with acute danger of war with the Foreign Powers. Jiang had close connections with Chinese big business and finance in Shanghai. These people, good Nationalists, and no friends of the plundering warlords, were equally very frightened of social revolution and the Communist-controlled workers. Jiang, knowing he had their support, carried out a sudden coup and massacre of the Communists (from which Zhou Enlai narrowly escaped) and broke with the Communist Party. A confused situation followed for several months. Jiang set up his right-wing Nationalist government at Nanjing; the former Guangzhou government was now established at Wuhan, further up the Changjiang, and did not at first break with the Communist Party. In much of south China, particularly Hunan province, social revolution, inspired by rural agitators led by Mao Zedong, was sweeping the country.

Before long the two Nationalist governments coalesced at Nanjing, and Jiang could turn his attention to combating the Communists. From 1929 to 1935 Jiang launched successive extermination campaigns against the Communists, who had now under the leadership of Mao Zedong and Zhu De (Chu Teh), established a Soviet area in the hill country on the Hunan-Jiangxi border. Jiang's campaigns failed until he devised, on the advice of his German staff officers, the plan of blockading the Jiangxi Soviet and thus forcing the Communists to break out or be starved into surrender.

The Communists set out on the Long March in 1935 with about 100,000 men and many of their dependants. A year later they reached Yanan, in north Shaanxi, after marching and counter-marching for more than 6,000 miles, with 30,000 fighting men. But they had not been defeated; and during that epic march Mao Zedong had emerged as the unquestioned leader of the Party, a position he retained until his death. The Party, also, was fully emancipated from long-distance control by Moscow, which had proved uniformly disastrous for several years. The Communists reached Yanan, in the far north-west, difficult to attack, almost impossible to blockade, and close to the areas soon to be threatened by the impending Japanese invasion.

Japanese Invasion

Everyone in China knew that the Japanese were bent on an all-out effort to conquer China; Japan feared that if it waited China would grow strong and it also feared the rise of Communist influence. But the Nanjing government was still bent on destroying the Communists before resisting the Japanese. It was not until December 1936, when his own army, facing the Communists at Xian in Shaanxi, mutinied and held him prisoner until he agreed to cease the civil war, that Chiang was forced to agree to the slogans "Chinese do not fight Chinese" and "unite to resist Japanese aggression". The Japanese did not wait; in July 1937 they struck near Beijing, and the fighting soon escalated into a large-scale, but still undeclared, war.

In the early stages, Nationalist resistance, as at Shanghai and the battle of Taierzhuang in Shandong had been at times effective; but the weight of Japanese armament was far superior. They had almost unchallenged air power and complete control of the sea. The Nationalist forces were forced back from the coast to the mountainous interior of western China, losing nearly two-thirds of the provinces. The difficulties of forcing the Changjiang gorges halted the Japanese at that point, and the added difficulty of holding vast conquered territories prevented any further advance. In those conquered territories, particularly north China, the Communists were organizing the guerrilla resistance which was soon to shake Japanese authority. The hope of a quick Chinese surrender had faded; Japan was now involved in the Second World War in the Pacific, and here, too, early victory was turning into stalemate and presaged defeat. The Chinese Communists steadily expanded their guerrilla war until large areas were liberated and in these they set up their own administration. Japanese retaliation was brutal and ruthless, forcing the Chinese peasantry to rely on guerrilla groups for their protection. It roused the national consciousness of an indifferent apolitical peasantry, and was the main factor in building the power of the Communist Party to a national level.

COMMUNIST CHINA

The war was ended neither by the still passive resistance of the Nationalists in western China, nor by the activity of the guerrillas, but by the Japanese surrender in the Pacific War. It left China deeply divided. The Nationalists took over from the Japanese in the south and eastern provinces. The Communists controlled the rural north, and cut the communications when the Nationalists flew in men to take over the Japanese-held cities. Civil war loomed close. The U.S.A. sent General Marshal to mediate and build, if possible, a coalition government. He failed; neither side trusted the other, and the demands made by the Nationalist side would have been a death warrant for the Communists. Early in 1946 the dreaded civil war began, but was neither as long nor as destructive as most Chinese feared it would be. From the first it became evident that the Communists were going to win. Their troops fought well under firm discipline; the Nationalist forces had no will to war, and plundered wherever they went. Gross inflation was wrecking the economy, corruption was notorious and fantastic in the Nationalist Government and army, business was almost paralysed, there was nothing that the Nationalists could offer to enlist the support of any social class, not even the capitalists of Shanghai, where government-protected racketeers preyed on business.

Therefore, despite massive American arms supply, full control of the air, and vastly superior numbers, the Nationalist armies were wholly destroyed and defeated in less than three years. Vast numbers surrendered; relatively few were killed in battle. By the end of 1948 the Communists already held all north China and Manzhou; they were on the banks of the Changjiang opposite Nanjing. The Nationalist side was no longer united. A large group favoured peace and negotiation. They compelled Jiang to renounce his Presidency, but were not able to shake his under-cover control over many units of the army. The Nanjing government tried to secure peace, and nearly did so, but this effort was sabotaged by the agents of Jiang at the last moment, and the acting President Li Zongren (Li Tsung-jen) was forced into exile. The war resumed, the Communists crossed the Changjiang, took Nanjing, then Shanghai, and swept on into the south and west. By the middle of 1949, when the People's Republic was proclaimed on October 1st in Beijing, the Communists were the masters of China, and Jiang and his remnant forces were retreating to Taiwan (Formosa), where they have since then remained (*see* section on Taiwan on p. 340).

Yet the failure to end the war by negotiation did China, and the Communists, one serious piece of harm. It destroyed the continuity of the legitimate internationally recognized government. If the Nanjing regime had made peace—any sort of peace—it would have remained the legal government, even if it was now run by the Communists. By failing to win this diplomatic victory the Communists found their new regime subject to recognition, or non-recognition, at the will of foreign states, and their claim to China's seat at the UN disputed by the Nationalist protégés of the U.S.A. This situation continued to be one of the main causes of friction between China and the Western Powers, who in their attitudes to the new China have also been deeply divided. To many of the Western and in particular the European Powers the fate of China was settled; the Nationalists on Taiwan were no longer significant. To the U.S.A., on the other hand, they were the "real China" and the Communists considered to be Soviet puppets. Thus, the Communist regime started its career with the open ill-will of the U.S.A., the doubtful and wary acceptance of the United Kingdom and other smaller Western Powers, and the half-hearted and cautious approval of the U.S.S.R. Only two years earlier Stalin had assured the U.S.A. that he recognized only Jiang as the legitimate ruler of China.

Economic and Social Reform

The early policy of the new regime in Beijing was necessarily one of national salvage. The economy was at a standstill, communications almost wholly interrupted, inflation rampant, public utilities run down by years of neglect. Even foreign trade was deflected into the supply of quick-selling consumer goods, largely useless to the economy, while valuable exports could not be moved and needed imports could not be paid for. To the general surprise of both Chinese and foreign observers, the new regime, headed by men who had had no urban life nor experience for more than 25 years, tackled these tasks with great skill and expedition. Within weeks the railways were running, and supplying coal to Shanghai in place of the normal seaborne supplies which the Nationalist navy blocked. Inflation was brought under steady control and ended, with a new currency, in the next year. Since then the Chinese currency, subjected to violent fluctuations for longer than living memory, has remained stable. Foreign trade began to revive, cautiously, and limited to imports which the country really required, and to exports which would earn foreign exchange. The restoration of the cities, some of which were still in partial ruins from wartime bombing, and all neglected, insanitary and decaying, was made a high priority. In one year the transformation was profound.

All these things should have been done by any competent government of any political complexion; they were not specifically Communist. But it was, in fact, the Communist government which first undertook them. This gained them widespread popular support, and served to offset other policies less immediately appealing to many people. Land reform was the first major socialist, or Communist, policy implemented. It was at first a simple redistribution of land in equal lots to all cultivators, including the families of former landlords, if still willing to remain and work. With it went the trial and frequent condemnation of those landlords who were accused of maltreating their tenants, oppressing the peasants and dominating the villages with their armed retainers. Not all those found guilty were put to death; probably a larger number were sentenced to terms of imprisonment. It is at least probable that the institution of such courts, rough and ready as their justice often was, prevented a much more widespread and savage vengeance from the peasants, which could have attained the proportions of wholesale massacre.

The Communist Party did not intend to leave the matter at the level of peasant proprietorship of tiny plots. From the first, co-operative work teams were organized to co-ordinate crop sowing and harvesting. Later these were developed into the two stages of co-operative farming, and still later the co-operative farms were grouped together into communes. By these stages private ownership of agricultural land was abolished and replaced by the communal system under which each former owner has a share of the commune's revenue allotted by "work points", based on hours worked. State-owned collective farms were confined to newly opened lands or reclaimed land not previously privately owned. Whatever other defects and difficulties the new land system has encountered, due to bad weather or administrative over-centralization, it can be said with certainty to have achieved two major gains. No peasant family now starves to death in bad times; irrigation and water conservancy with flood control was made possible on a large and beneficial scale by the abolition of smallholdings. These factors enabled the commune system to withstand the great drought years 1960–62 without wholesale famine and thousands of deaths, although not without stern rationing and some malnutrition. In earlier less severe droughts the victims were often numbered by the million.

The Korean War and Relations with the U.S.S.R.

The Korean War has given rise to a large literature, and its origin and the responsibility for its outbreak are still in dispute. Chinese intervention, after the United Nations forces began to move northwards into North Korea, was forewarned, but the warnings were not heeded. To the Chinese this movement was a direct threat to their vital industrial area of south Manzhou (Liaoning province) adjoining Korea. It was also widely feared in China to be the preliminary move to an invasion of China itself. How far the Chinese intervention was intended to reassert Chinese authority, rather than Soviet influence, in Manzhou and in Korea, remains conjectural. Later developments seem to indicate that this consideration was important. It was certainly a consequence of the war, for after the cease-fire the Soviet Union soon renounced the special position which the Chinese had conceded to her in the port of Dalianwan (Dalian) and over the railways across Manzhou. In China the effect of the war was to strengthen the prestige of the government which had, for the first time for more than a century, if ever, shown itself able to meet and match a large-scale Western army. In the years since the truce signed at Panmunjom, Chinese relations with North Korea have not always been smooth. The pretensions of President Kim Il-sung to be a major ideological leader cannot have been much appreciated in Beijing. North Korea's attitude of neutrality in the Sino-Soviet dispute, although undoubtedly very wise, cooled relations with China. On the other hand foreign observers have drawn the conclusion that China has exercised a restraining influence on the bellicose ambitions of President Kim in respect of South Korea. But North Korea is certainly not a Chinese satellite.

In 1957 the Government permitted, in the "Hundred Flowers" movement, open criticism of its methods, if not of its basic policies. The extent of the resulting criticisms was probably disconcerting to the authorities, yet much of what was said made its mark and led to some change of style in the Party. The "Hundred Flowers" movement, it is now known, was almost contemporary with the first phase of the Sino-Soviet dispute which has grown over the years until the two countries have become completely estranged. The original quarrel over ideology developed into a dispute more concerned with national interests, especially after the U.S.S.R. withdrew its technical aid and experts from China in 1960. This was a hard blow to the developing Chinese industrialization but has been overcome. After a series of border clashes in 1969, negotiations for a settlement of Sino-Soviet differences concerning the border regions opened in Beijing in October 1969. However, subsequent relations between the two countries have shown no signs of improvement, and they have continued to confront each other with a barrage of invective and propaganda. The fear of a possible Soviet attack, either using conventional or nuclear weapons, has a strong influence on China's military and diplomatic planning. The expectation entertained by the Soviet leaders that, after the death of Mao Zedong, China would prove willing to renew the former friendship, or at least to modify its criticisms of the U.S.S.R., has not been realized. Under Chairman Hua Guofeng (Hua Kuo-feng), policy remains unchanged, and the U.S.S.R. continues to be described as a "Socialist-Imperialist" state and the major threat to world peace.

All Chinese governments since the fall of the Manzhou Dynasty have continued to assert sovereignty over Xizang (Tibet), although the western two-thirds of the country had been in practice independent since 1912. In 1951 the Communist regime reoccupied the country and placed it under an autonomous region status. In 1961 a rebellion originating in the eastern part of Xizang spread to the reoccupied western part and was followed by the flight of the Dalai Lama, temporal ruler of Xizang, to India. Chinese occupation was consolidated and social changes and reforms imposed. In 1962 the establishment of Chinese forces on the Indian border with Xizang led to disputes upon the position of the undefined and unmarked boundary. China proposed negotiations, but the Indian side rejected them, asserting that the frontier had been established by the United Kingdom before Indian independence. The tension escalated into a border war when Indian forces attempted to expel Chinese troops from some disputed positions. The clash resulted in a Chinese victory, which could have led to an invasion of Indian Assam. China unilaterally called off the operations and withdrew to the positions already established before the clash. Soviet verbal support for the Indian claim considerably embittered relations between China and Russia. The frontier dispute remains unsettled, the Chinese holding what they claim is the correct frontier line. However, in 1978 there were signs that better relations between India and China were in prospect. Diplomatic approaches, preparing the way for negotiations on the frontier dispute, began. This may have been due to a more accommodating attitude assumed by the Janata Party government in India.

The Cultural Revolution

The programme called the Great Leap Forward, contemporary with the establishment of the commune system in 1958–59, was intended to push Chinese industrialization forward by a great effort to the level of the United Kingdom. It did not achieve this result, partly because of the great drought of 1960–62, partly because of the Soviet withdrawal of technical assistance. It is known that disagreements in the higher leadership following this set-back lie at the bottom of the open political struggle associated with the Cultural Revolution. Peng Dehuai, then Defence Minister, did not believe in the Great Leap programme. At a session of the Politburo held at Lushan in August 1959 he was dismissed from his post and rusticated. Although this decision appears to have been accepted by Liu Shaoqi (Liu Shao-ch'i) and the majority of the Politburo, there was subsequent criticism of Mao with regard to the Great Leap, and possibly the Commune programme also. In December 1958 Mao had yielded the post of President of the Government to Liu Shaoqi before the dismissal of Peng and this resignation was later, in the Cultural Revolution, attributed to pressure from influential critics in the higher Party hierarchy. Mao retained the all-important post of Chairman of the Communist Party. These problems must be seen in proportion; it is certain that Chinese industrial progress has not attained the level of the Western advanced nations; it is equally evident that enormous transformations of the virtually pre-industrial economy of China have been achieved, and that the essential change to a modern economy has been made.

In 1966 Mao Zedong, emerging from a partial seclusion, which has been variously interpreted, launched the "Great Proletarian Cultural Revolution" and raised, to carry it out, the Red Guards, composed for the most part of middle-school children from fourteen to eighteen years old. Contrary to a widespread belief, university students did not form a large proportion of the Red Guards. The movement, at first directed against "old ways of thinking, acting, and working", and leading to attacks on "bourgeois" people of professional and academic standing, was soon directed to an attack upon the leadership of the Communist Party itself, and in particular upon Liu Shaoqi, Head of the State and long-time organizer of the Party machine. Mao's aim was to create a new form of Communist society, free from the rigidity and hierarchy of the Communist Party of earlier times. He claimed that unless this were done the whole of Chinese society would slide back, as he saw the Soviet Union sliding, to a bourgeois way of life, with privilege hardening into new class divisions and revolutionary enthusiasm disappearing.

It is admitted that this movement encountered a considerable opposition, but it could not easily be identified. It would not appear that any group openly repudiated the "Thoughts of Mao Zedong". Rather many, claiming to be his true followers, still continued practices which others condemned as "revisionist". There was faction brawling, and at times more serious clashes. The army was called upon to maintain order and guard essential installations. The picture remains obscure, due largely to lack of objective news. Certain large and important fields of national life were hardly affected at all. Agriculture, the nuclear fission programme, the revenue collection, and also foreign trade remained outside the battle. Political life was galvanized into violent struggle centred round the "Top Party persons taking the capitalist road", by which were meant Liu Shaoqi, Head of the State, and Deng Xiaoping (Teng Hsiao-p'ing), Secretary-General of the Communist Party. Liu and Deng, with some others, were dismissed from all posts including that of Head of State, at the Ninth Party Congress of the Chinese Communist Party in April 1969.

The Ninth Congress of the Chinese Communist Party, the first to meet for some years, was convened in Beijing in April 1969. It ratified changes in the Constitution including the new power structure of three-part committees which govern provinces and cities. They are composed of Army, Revolutionary Cadres and Workers. The Army component seems in most cases to hold the predominant positions. Although the Ninth Congress seems to have formally ended the active phase of the Cultural Revolution, and was accompanied by measures disbanding the large Red Guard groups, conflicting factions still existed in the Chinese leadership. One indication was the dramatic fall and death of Marshal Lin Biao, Minister of Defence and proclaimed heir to Mao Zedong. In July 1972 the Chinese Government disclosed that Lin Biao had conspired to assassinate Mao Zedong and seize power, that his plot was detected, and that he and some companions had died in an aircraft crash in September 1971 while fleeing from China. His companions have not been officially identified. The other senior officers who disappeared from public view were brought to trial in Beijing in 1980. The official account of the military plot and death of Lin Biao has been doubted by foreign observers and is, at best, incomplete. Conjectures upon the possible role of the "gang of four", headed by Jiang Qing (Chiang Ching), Mao's wife, suggesting that they feared a too powerful successor to Mao, who would block their road to power, cannot be verified from the few facts available.

These events have been variously interpreted, but in the years that followed the Chinese government waged a propaganda campaign seeking to prove that Lin Biao was an arch-reactionary, comparable to Confucius in antiquity. The situation after his fall was clarified and settled by the decisions of the Fourth National People's Congress, the supreme organ of the Chinese state, in January 1975. The Congress promulgated a new Constitution, superseding that of 1954. One major change was that the Chairman of the Central Committee of the Communist Party became commander-in-chief of the armed forces. The post of Head of State, whether President or Chairman of the Government, was abolished, leaving the Chairman of the Central Committee of the Communist Party as the supreme power. Another important outcome of this Congress was the apparent rehabilitation of Deng Xiaoping, who re-emerged as first Vice-Premier and Chief of the General Staff.

China and the World

After the quarrel with the U.S.S.R., Mao Zedong postulated a new formula for foreign policy. The world is divided into three categories of states, replacing the simple dichotomy of Communist and Capitalist-Imperialist states of the old formulation. In the first category are the super-powers, the U.S.A. and the Soviet Union, whose conflict is the greatest danger to peace; the U.S.S.R. is judged to be the more aggressive of the two. Secondly, there are the middle powers which are virtually identical with the other advanced economies and industrialized nations, with some borderline cases such as Australia. Thirdly, the developing and under-developed nations (the Third World), of which China is the leader. This guideline remains in force for Chinese foreign policy and is frequently reasserted under Hua Guofeng in diplomatic contacts with foreign ambassadors and visiting Prime Ministers. It is notable that it takes little account of the divergent ideologies of the nations assigned to the three categories.

China sees itself as the leader of the Third World against the domination of the two super-powers. The Cultural Revolution was marked by xenophobia but a policy of détente has since been pursued. Diplomatic relations with many countries have been achieved since 1971. In 1972 Japan broke off diplomatic relations with the Taiwan government, recognized the People's Republic of China and opened negotiations for a treaty of friendship with China designed to end the long antagonism between the two nations. The question of Chinese representation at the United Nations was resolved in October 1971 with the adoption in the UN General Assembly of an Albanian resolution proposing the People's Republic as one of the five permanent members of the Security Council and the representatives of its Government as the only legitimate representatives of China to the United Nations, and also proposing the expulsion of the representatives of Taiwan from the United Nations.

The Viet-Nam cease-fire agreement in January 1973 opened the way for a further improvement in relations with the U.S.A. A visit by the then U.S. Secretary of State, Dr. Henry Kissinger, in February led to the establishment of liaison offices in the respective capitals, and a further visit in November confirmed the progress made.

The year 1976 was one of great upheaval for China. Zhou Enlai died in January and it was assumed that Deng Xiaoping would succeed him. However, after an apparent split in the Party leadership, Hua Guofeng, the Minister of Public Security, was appointed acting Premier in February. A campaign denouncing Deng and others as "capitalist roaders" then developed. Demonstrations in memory of Zhou Enlai took place in early April, and were regarded as a display of popular support for Deng. This culminated in serious rioting in Beijing, followed by widespread disturbances throughout the country. On April 7th Hua Guofeng's appointment as Premier was confirmed, and Deng Xiaoping was dismissed from all his official posts. Mass demonstrations in favour of the Politburo's decisions were then organized. The death of Marshal Zhu De, Chairman of the Standing Committee of the National People's Congress, in July was a serious loss to the Party, and placed a further strain on the leadership. In the same month, a massive earthquake killed over 650,000 people, and devastated the city of Tangshan and other important industrial centres.

On September 9th, 1976, against this background of turmoil, Mao Zedong died at the age of 82. His widow, Jiang Qing, who had begun to exert an increasing influence, then tried to seize control with the help of three radical members of the Politburo, Zhang Chunqiao, Wang Hongwen and Yao Wenyuan. Their attempt was foiled, and in October they were arrested, along with a number of other radicals. A vigorous campaign against the "gang of four" was subsequently mounted. They were accused of various crimes, including the forgery of Mao's will and a plot to assassinate Hua Guofeng, who was to succeed Mao.

In early 1977 there were a number of disturbances but these had been brought under control by late in the year when Deng Xiaoping was reinstated as a senior member of the Politburo. In 1978, and with increasing emphasis in 1979, the new policy of the "Four Modernizations" (industry, technology, defence and agriculture) has been implemented. The campaign against the "gang of four" was continued vehemently until early 1979 when, presumably having achieved its objective of totally discrediting the recent policies (including the Cultural Revolution), it was replaced by announcements that they would be brought to trial. This took place in 1980. Jiang Qing and Zhang Chunqiao were given suspended death sentences which are not expected to be carried out. The other two received long terms of imprisonment. Concurrently, eminent people who had been imprisoned or under house arrest for the past ten years or more, have been rehabilitated, even posthumously, like Peng Dehuai and Liu Shaoqi. Lin Biao has remained under condemnation although no longer mentioned. He was perhaps not only the enemy of the "gang of four" but of others also.

By October 1978 the Cultural Revolution was being violently condemned by university academics and other intellectuals, although as yet not by the media. However, in rural areas slogans in praise of the Cultural Revolution were still displayed. This new liberty of expression of personal opinions is an outstanding change in the social order and had expanded into public demands for more "democracy" in politics and social life expressed in wall posters (*dazibao*) in Beijing and other cities. These social and political pressures continue and their final outcome cannot yet be discerned.

In December 1978 the Chinese launched a "punitive" expedition against Viet-Nam; the Chinese army advanced against strong opposition until it had captured the city of Lang Son which opened the direct route across the plains to Hanoi. Then, declaring its objective achieved, the Chinese army withdrew behind its own frontier. Withdrawal was completed by mid-March 1979. Deng Xiaoping, during his state visit to the U.S.A. immediately prior to the Chinese action, had publicly, and no doubt privately, announced that "Viet-Nam must be taught a lesson", the reason being the anti-China policy of the Vietnamese government, expressed in the mass expulsion of ethnic Chinese residents, established there for centuries, and continued border provocations and frontier violations. A further more important reason was the Vietnamese invasion of Kampuchea earlier in December 1978 and the overthrow by Vietnamese forces of the Pol Pot regime which China, along with India and the West, had recognized. It has been replaced by a regime obviously created by Viet-Nam and totally dependent on that country. Viet-Nam has also openly adhered to the U.S.S.R. in its foreign policy and had signed a treaty of alliance with the Soviet Union in 1978.

These developments were seen in China as a direct threat. China's reaction shocked Western and Asian countries alike; it was held to be a reckless act and, even if a response to provocation, dangerously likely to invite Soviet retaliation or even intervention to protect its new ally, Viet-Nam. In the event, the U.S.S.R. has waged a vehement propaganda campaign against China and has certainly shipped arms to Viet-Nam, even though it has taken no direct military action. The world has felt profound relief at the U.S.S.R.'s restraint. The Chinese believe, and clearly calculated, that their firm action against Viet-Nam demonstrated to the world that the U.S.S.R. is a "paper tiger", and that this was the real lesson which Viet-Nam had to be taught.

During the years 1979 and 1980 the internal policy of China continued to be the development of the industrial plan for modernization of the economy, making much wider use of foreign technology. Some of the more ambitious programmes have been modified to conform with the realities which experiment had revealed. China is still short of highly-skilled technicians and much of the existing stock of machinery in the factories is outmoded. Progress is none the less steady and comprehensive. The emphasis on modernization and industry has inevitably been accompanied by some problems in the social sphere. The younger generation who were brought up in the period of the Cultural Revolution—now condemned openly—have demanded greater freedom, and for a time were freely expressing these expectations by putting up *dazibao* on Beijing's "Freedom Wall", although this was eventually closed down. At the same time, changes in the Politburo, the supreme organ of government in practice, also reflected this more liberal policy. The remaining members who had been at least tolerant, it not active, supporters of the "gang of four" were removed from their positions and were replaced by men known to be strong supporters of Deng Xiaoping, Vice-Premier and the real power in the Government. Hua Guofeng, the only remaining powerful figure from the Maoist past, continued in office but began to assume a role more formal than executive.

In June 1981 Hua Guofeng resigned from his post as Chairman of the Chinese Communist Party and was replaced by Hu Yaobang, former Secretary-General of the Politburo. Hua, now a vice-chairman, also relinquished his post as Chairman of the Military Affairs Commission to Deng Xiaoping, who is said to have refused the chairmanship of the party in order to make way for younger leaders. This reshuffle is thought to be the result of a campaign over a long period by Deng to oust Hua because of his left-leaning policies.

The demotion of Mao's appointed successor marks the completion of a purge of top-level leftist elements in the Politburo. It is also a further indication of the gradual change in attitude towards the historical role of Mao who, while still praised for his early revolutionary activities, is now publicly criticized for the "grave errors" which he is said to have committed in his later years.

In 1982 Deng Xiaoping continued to dominate the Government, although eschewing the highest-ranking post. Two of his close followers, Zhao Ziyang and Hu Yaobang, were placed in the most influential posts of Premier and Chairman of the Chinese Communist Party respectively. A reconstruction of the Government, with the elimination of several ministries and a reduction in the number of Vice-Premiers, was undertaken for the declared purpose of "streamlining" the administration and reducing the excessive number of public servants. It is conjectured abroad that this operation also had the purpose of removing from office, and influence, people who were not whole-hearted supporters of the current policy. That there has remained an element of leftist tendency, still hankering for the methods of Mao, has been apparent. Many hundreds of officials who joined the Party in the years of the Cultural Revolution and its aftermath had not been reconciled to the major reversals which followed Mao's death.

The policy of the Government in economic matters has continued to stress modernization and, in particular, the necessity to involve foreign firms in the process. It is in the new and very important sphere of petroleum production that this development is most conspicuous. It has now been proved that the offshore oilfields on the south-east China coast, and also in the Bohai gulf in the North China Sea, are possibly the largest undeveloped oilfields now known in the world. The fields are indisputably on the continental shelf of China, and thus Chinese. The water, by comparison with the North Sea, is shallow, and the seas less stormy. In May 1982 China offered the leases for development of these fields to a number of foreign oil companies, which have expressed great interest, but are somewhat uncertain about the very strict terms, the degree of Chinese Government participation, political control and disposal of the oil, matters all still under negotiation. Whatever the outcome, the development of these oilfields will profoundly change the Chinese economy, enrich the country, and enhance its power and status in international affairs.

In foreign affairs, 1982 was marked by three developments, the outcome of which is not yet clear. The U.S.S.R., by means of a speech delivered by Brezhnev himself at Tashkent, re-opened the possibility of renewed approaches to China to settle the quarrel, now mainly concerned with frontier territories, which has estranged the two powers for many years. The U.S.S.R. appears ready to drop all preconditions, thus meeting a former Chinese proposal. China has neither rejected nor fully accepted this approach. It would seem at least probable that China is waiting to see whether the U.S.A. can be induced to change its attitude on the Taiwan problem, and also whether Japan will agree to much closer co-operation with China.

These two questions constitute the second and third developments in Chinese foreign affairs. The Reagan Administration, which (even before it won power) was foreseen to be likely to take a different line on Taiwan than that of the Carter Administration, proved, in fact, to be strongly influenced by Republicans who held to the old enmity towards Communist China, and the old support for the Nationalist regime in Taiwan. Unable to make a major change in U.S. policy, this influence within the Administration has secured the continued sale of modern arms and aircraft to the Nationalist regime in Taiwan, which, for its part, continues to reject apparently favourable terms of reunion with China. American policy on this matter has seriously offended the Chinese Government and sown manifest distrust of the Reagan Government, which sent Vice-President Bush to Beijing to try to restore good relations. He was received with some aloofness by the Chinese, and it is clear that no real agreement was reached. Deng Xiaoping and other Chinese leaders subsequently emphasized their real concern at what they regard as the unfriendly policy of the U.S.A.

In May 1982 Zhao Ziyang visited Japan, the avowed purpose being to conclude agreements for closer co-operation between Japanese industry and the economic development of China. In this sphere it seems that progress was made, acceptable to both sides. There was, however, a wider aim: a project amounting to an alliance between the two Far Eastern powers was hinted at. It was, of course, publicly stated that no idea of military alliance was under consideration; but, as has been noted by observers of Japan, the very idea of even having to deny such a possibility would have been very recently unthinkable. The denial publicly admits that such an idea is "thinkable": a seed has been sown.

Taken together, the Soviet approach to China, the American policy on arms sales to Taiwan and the Chinese approach to Japan can be suspected of being linked. The U.S.S.R. would naturally seek to exploit a difference or disagreement between China and the U.S.A. China, equally, can seek closer ties with Japan, now an industrial giant, to offset any coolness which may develop between China and the U.S.A. over Taiwan arms sales. Clearly not unconnected with these moves is the fact that those immensely valuable Chinese oilfields lie off the south-east coast, close to Taiwan. It is in China's interest to make offers to Japan which Taiwan cannot match. It is unlikely that any Chinese response to Soviet advances would assume the proportions of a real change of alignment. The quarrel is deep, ideological as well as territorial, but both sides might welcome a relaxation of tension, and reduction of the very large forces which watch each other along a lengthy frontier. It is also possible that an appreciation of the risks and disadvantages of alienating China for the sake of some sales of arms to Taiwan may bring about a change in U.S. policy, which would probably be swiftly acknowledged in Beijing.

TAIWAN

The location of the island has determined its history. Situated between the Malayan Archipelago, China and Japan, the island has had a chequered past. The original inhabitants were tribes of Malayan origin. China's relations with the island date from A.D. 607, but the first small Chinese settlements were not established there until the fourteenth century. During the seventeenth century, Portuguese, Spanish, and Dutch traders visited the island from time to time. In 1624 the Dutch settled the southern part. Two years later came the Spanish, who occupied the northern part. In 1642 the Dutch drove out the Spanish and in 1661 the Dutch were driven out by the Chinese Ming loyalist Zheng Zheng Gong (Coxinga) who ruled, with his sons, for 22 years. In 1663 the Manzhou Emperor Kang Xi invaded and conquered the island which became a part of his empire until ceded to the Japanese at the end of the Sino-Japanese war of 1895. During the period of independence and Manzhou rule, massive immigration from the mainland established the ethnic Chinese character of the island.

As a result of Japan's defeat in the Second World War, Taiwan was returned to China in 1945. The island became one of the thirty-five provinces of the Republic of China. Practically all the exportable surpluses went to China, and Chinese government control replaced that of the Japanese. In 1947 misgovernment by the mainland officials led to a large-scale, but peaceful, political uprising which was repressed with great brutality by the Nationalist government.

Early in 1949 the Nationalist government authorities, driven from the mainland by the Communists, moved to Taiwan's capital, Taipei, along with approximately 2 million soldiers, officials and their dependants. Thus the island's population increased from 6.8 million to 7.5 million in 1950, excluding military personnel numbering 600,000.

Taiwan under the Chinese Nationalist Government

Communist control of the mainland meant the loss of the island's chief market. Taiwan was thus forced to seek a world market, and the economy of the island changed from that of a colony to that of an independent state. The Nationalist government in Taiwan has tried to achieve three major engineering feats: the cross-island highway, the Shihmen Reservoir project, and the port of Kaohsiung on the west coast. These three efforts parallel the three great Japanese achievements: the hydro-electric power plant at Sun-Moon Lake, the irrigation system at Chianan, and the mountain railway. The Nationalist government in Taiwan has achieved a remarkable record and regeneration in the period since 1949 with massive American aid. The years 1951 and 1952 were years of government reorganization. Then followed a four-year period (1953–56) of adjustment and planning. In 1957 and 1958 the cumulative effect of domestic reform and United States aid brought a great improvement in economic and other fields. The prominent developments include the following: the land reform programme, which was internationally acclaimed as a model; the rapid development of industry, with new types of export products, such as bicycles, plate glass, electric fans, plastics, aviation gasoline, and even jeeps and cars, which previously had been unknown in Taiwan; the establishment of a system of nine-year free public education. No longer receiving American economic aid, the economy of the island is prosperous.

In October 1971 the People's Republic of China was admitted to the United Nations in place of Taiwan. Consequently a number of countries broke off diplomatic relations with Taiwan and recognized the People's Republic of China. On establishing full diplomatic relations with Beijing in March 1972, the British Government issued a communiqué acknowledging " . . . the position of the Chinese Government that Taiwan is a province of China . . . ".

When Japan sought rapprochement with Beijing in September 1972 Taiwan angrily broke off diplomatic relations with Japan. In February 1973 the U.S. Government announced that they would continue to maintain diplomatic relations with Taiwan, but at the same time would set up an "American mission" in Beijing and allow a "Chinese liaison office" to open in Washington. By 1981 only 22 countries still recognized the Government of Taiwan.

President Chiang Kai-shek died in April 1975. He was succeeded as President by the former vice-president, Dr. Yen Chia-kan, and by his son, General Chiang Ching-kuo, the Prime Minister, as Chairman of Kuomintang, the ruling Nationalist Party of China. Chiang Ching-kuo succeeded Yen Chia-kan as President in May 1978. Although no dramatic changes were expected, Chiang Kai-shek's death cannot fail to have profound implications for the future status of Taiwan, which the People's Republic of China continues to claim to be that of a province of China. Although no immediate prospect of hostilities with the People's Republic of China is apparent, mutually conflicting claims to the sea-bed off the China coast, and to potential under-sea oilfields in the region, must be recognized as a latent danger.

In December 1978, prior to Deng Xiaoping's visit to Washington, there had been a dramatic change in U.S. policy towards Taiwan. Diplomatic recognition was withdrawn from Taiwan as constituting the Republic of China, and the U.S. embassy was closed. However, Taiwan as an unrecognized but existing state is assured of continuing U.S. protection and trade until some form of reconciliation between China and Taiwan can be brought about. China has stopped denouncing the Taiwan leadership and has been offering suggestions for forms of autonomy within the People's Republic of China. These approaches have so far been rejected by Taiwan, where public indignation has been manifested against the American policy. Elections to the National Assembly and the Legislative Yuan, which were postponed when this policy was announced, were held in December 1980. In the Legislative Yuan, 70 new members were elected and

26 appointed by the President. In November 1981 there occurred the first major government reshuffle since Premier Sun Yun-suan's appointment in 1978.

In October 1981 Taiwan rejected the latest of China's proposals for reunification, under which Taiwan would become a "special administrative region" and would have a high degree of autonomy, including the retention of its own armed forces and its relatively high standard of living.

U.S. policy towards Taiwan is ambiguous. While assuring Taiwan of its continuing support, the U.S.A. is at the same time trying to maintain good relations with the People's Republic of China. Relations with both countries have become strained as a result.

ECONOMIC SURVEY OF THE PEOPLE'S REPUBLIC OF CHINA (1949-1982)

Christopher Howe

PRIORITIES AND POLICIES: THE CHANGING ECONOMIC STRATEGY

The Chinese economy has been growing in size and complexity for several hundred years. Population increased approximately eightfold between the 15th and 20th centuries, and agricultural development broadly kept pace with this expansion. At the same time, tertiary activities and urban growth increased in extent and sophistication, and after 1914 significant industrialization occurred. The starting point for the Communist phase of industrialization was, therefore, not a primitive or stagnant economy. In some senses the economy was mature, but at the same time it was suffering from the consequences of war, of over-population, of foreign economic aggrandizement, and of failures of national leadership.

The economy in 1949 was still largely agrarian. Over 80 per cent of the labour force worked in agriculture, where incomes were generally both low and unstable. Modern techniques were rare and the degree of commercialization very variable. Landlordism in some regions was oppressive and extractive, although this was not universal and appears to have been less of a problem in north China.

Most of China's modern industry was located in Tianjin, Shanghai, and Manchurian cities. Foreign ownership accounted for about one-half of the assets, and managerial and technical positions in foreign companies were usually held by foreigners.

As a result of war finance, hyper-inflation became rife in the late 1940s and political and military uncertainties led to falling output and uncontrollable mass movements of population.

It was against this background that Communist China's experiments in economic planning began. From the start, the gaps between what was feasible in China, what had worked in the U.S.S.R., and what Chairman Mao Zedong believed should happen in China, were large. The twisting pattern of development since 1949 can be understood only in terms of these contradictions and the interplay between them.

The First Five-Year Plan (1953–57)

The Chinese adopted from the U.S.S.R. the practice of one-year, five-year and longer-term perspective planning. The First Plan began in 1953 and, in principle, the Sixth Plan started in 1981. In practice, however, Chinese economic developments do not fit sensibly into these planning periods, and, apart from the First Plan and the period since 1978, details of Plans and their results have not been published in a systematic and reliable way.

The First Plan was drawn up with Soviet assistance on the basis of agreements for the importation into China of 156 major industrial plants. The Plan envisaged rapid industrial and agricultural developments, with rising living standards. These goals were to be achieved by a state investment programme that concentrated on state-owned heavy industry, and were to be effected by a new, centralized economic administration. Private rural and urban economic activities were to continue, but were to be brought gradually into the public sector over a 15-year period.

In broad terms, the industrial targets set in the Plan were achieved (although many of the projects started in the Plan came "on stream" only in 1958 and 1959). Agriculture performed less well. Year-to-year fluctuations in performance were large and there were serious shortfalls in non-grain crops. Grain output performed tolerably well, but control and distribution were difficult. These problems were a major factor behind the decision to collectivize agriculture (1955) which later led to the parallel collectivization of small-scale urban activity (1956).

The differing performance of industry and agriculture was reflected in incomes. Urban incomes increased by over 30 per cent, while agricultural incomes increased far more slowly and unevenly. This stimulated mass inward urban migration which compounded agricultural problems. Thus the overall situation at the end of the plan period was unstable and reflected the failure of the Chinese planners to appreciate the complexities of the agricultural problem, the implications of rapid population growth, and the full implications of the long-term agreements with the U.S.S.R.

The "Great Leap Forward" and its aftermath (1958–65)

One school of thought wished to react to these difficulties by reducing growth rates and by placing more emphasis on agriculture and light industry, and less on socialist organization. Mao on the other hand, refused to retreat in this way. Instead, he advocated even higher growth rates, an enlarged investment programme, abandonment of central planning and the creation of new, large-scale People's Communes.

Behind these policies lay a variety of thoughts and theories—some sensible, some catastrophically mistaken. On the positive side was the appreciation that China's economy could not be planned on lines mechanically transposed from other "socialist" economies. Mao saw that China's abundance of labour, shortage of land and lack of transportation and infrastructure called for new policies and institutions. At the same time he was obsessed with the theory that the way to increase the dynamism of the economy was deliberately to destabilize it.

The acute setbacks that followed the "Great Leap" produced a set of new priorities and policies. Grain output fell by about one-third and new agricultural policies were therefore imperative. These included new investment in electrification, chemical fertilizers and machinery. The People's Communes were reorganized so that the scale of planning and the operation of revived incentive systems were improved. Throughout the economy, planning was moderately re-centralized and the acute imbalances of the earlier period corrected. By 1965 the economy was functioning tolerably well and the overall output of major sectors had recovered or exceeded their previous best levels (although continued population growth implied that per capita outputs were still below the best levels of the 1950s).

The "Cultural Revolution" (1966–70)

The "Cultural Revolution" was not primarily motivated by economic objectives. It was a struggle in the political and cultural spheres which had economic effects—most of them harmful. In the short run, industrial output in late 1966 and early 1967 was interrupted and the volume of production fell in 1967. These setbacks affected export deliveries which, combined with the general xenophobia of the period, severely prejudiced the resumption of foreign trade that had begun in the mid-1960s. In agriculture the impact of the "Cultural Revolution" was more insidious and long-term in character. Although direct intervention was not important, the "Cultural Revolution" did undermine incentives. Prices for farm goods were not increased and, at the level of the Production Team, incentive systems failed to encourage individual effort. Private plots were attacked in spite of the crucial role that they had played in the recovery of agriculture after the "Great Leap".

There were two other ways in which the "Cultural Revolution" affected the economy: through educational policies and the declining effectiveness of the planning system. The former severely disrupted advanced education and training, while planning was disrupted by waves of political factionalism which reverberated for years.

After 1970 Mao allowed Zhou Enlai to return economic objectives to the forefront. This was certainly necessary. The trends in agriculture were deteriorating while population growth was increasing as a result of a loosening of discipline in the "Cultural Revolution". In industry it was becoming apparent that, in spite of the remarkable progress in the 1950s, China was 10 to 15 years behind the best technological practice in advanced economies. Statistical evidence, available internally (but not externally), also revealed that the efficiency of new investment in the economy was well below the level of the 1950s and falling.

Zhou's programme for the economy included a sharp attack on the population problem (*see* over), renewed large-scale plant imports from abroad and the re-establishment of the objectives of the Four Modernizations—a programme actually announced as early as 1964—the modernization of industry, agriculture, defence and science and technology. Between 1970 and 1976 there were continuing conflicts within the leadership about the economic programme, and lack of consistent leadership at the centre was undoubtedly reflected in confusion at lower levels. Thus, although Zhou had re-established certain policy principles, the actual implementation of priorities was only partial and the inefficiency of the economy continued to increase. It was only after the death of Mao that the full extent of China's economic problems became apparent.

The strategies of Hua Guofeng and Deng Xiaoping (1976–82)

The leadership that took power immediately after Mao's death in 1976 embarked on a three-part strategy for China's economic growth. Industrial growth was to accelerate and to focus on 120 major projects—mainly in the sectors of metallurgy, energy and heavy industry. This industrial plan was to be supported by large-scale imports of plant from overseas and a general expansion of China's international relations (*see* over). In agriculture the expansion of output was to be promoted by a continuation of the programme of mechanization. The organizational plans that accompanied these sectoral plans were complex. In agriculture Hua pressed for more centralization and large units of organization; in industry some recentralization of power over large enterprises was combined with less specific talk of the benefits of decentralization. The latter was reinforced by publication of Mao's 1956 speech on the "Ten Great Relations", which had emphasized the need for local initiative.

In 1977 the economy began to recover from the paralysis caused by Mao's death, and in 1978 output and construction expenditures began to grow rapidly. At the same time very large commitments for imports of capital goods were undertaken. During this period criticism of several aspects of Hua's policies began to surface in China, and from Sichuan province came reports of the successes of very different approaches. These were published, both locally and nationally, and were signals that China's economic strategy had become the subject of intense inner-Party struggle. This struggle was resolved in 1978 at the Third Plenum of the Eleventh Central Committee.

This Plenum was described at the time as "the great turning point". It certainly marked the beginning of the end for Hua and many of his policies, and the emergence at the top of Deng Xiaoping and Zhao Ziyang—the latter the author of the new Sichuan policies and later to become Premier.

The basic economic strategy of this group was, first, to reduce both the rate of growth of the economy and the level of investment. The pursuit of excessively ambitious targets was seen to have been a major cause of long-run inefficiencies in the economy. The reduction in investment was to be accompanied by a rise in consumption. This implied that both agriculture and light industry were to be promoted at the expense of heavy industry. Foreign trade policy remained positive in the sense that the new leadership saw contact with the world economy as a major source of economic advantage. However, whereas previous thinking had emphasized large-scale plants and visible trade, the new policy emphasized selectivity (*see* below).

Changes in priority were only part of the new package. Accompanying them were proposals for radical changes in organization and incentives. Agriculture, industry and foreign trade were all to be decentralized in different ways, and incentive systems were to be revived to encourage both individuals and organizations to perform more effectively.

These policies were incorporated in a detailed annual plan for 1979. During 1979 and 1980, however, disorder and confusion in the economy continued. The total volume of investment, the domestic budgetary balance, the external trade balance and the level of domestic prices all began to move out of control. As a result, the Chairman of the State Planning Commission (who favoured heavy industry) and the Minister of Finance were both demoted. In the winter of 1980 new plans were prepared to reduce the level of activity and to restructure the economy. The policies of "readjustment" initiated after the Central Work Conference in December 1980 remain the core of present policy and are intended to last until 1986.

During 1981 and 1982 considerable progress in meeting readjustment targets was made. The situation and outlook were summed up by Premier Zhao Ziyang in his "Report on Government Work" (December 1981) and in his address to the Conference on Industry and Communication (March 1982). The message of these speeches was conservative. Planning was to be strengthened, reforms to be "reviewed and summarized" and economic abuses to be stopped. The proposed policies for the future were summed up in Premier Zhao's "Ten Principles for Future Economic Construction". These principles include continued sectoral emphasis on agriculture, consumer goods and energy, gradual economic reforms and the maintenance of an "open door" policy towards foreign economic relations.

These statements (and arguments) at the political level have been underpinned by debates among Chinese economists. Differences of opinion on priorities and economic reform are clearly considerable. During late 1981 it appears that critics of retrenchment and anti-heavy industry policies were very active. The orthodox line has probably best been summed up by Liu Guoguang (November 1981) in an article in which he analysed the characteristics of what he called "benignant" economic cycles, and addressed the question of whether re-adjustment would not lead to a "malignant" cycle. Liu argued that "benignant" cycles occurred when policies ensured (*a*) balance, (*b*) productivity growth, and (*c*) rising living standards in the economy. He noted that, while (*a*) and (*c*) were moving in the right direction, (*b*) was proving difficult to maintain. Liu emphasized that, to avoid putting the economy into a malignant phase, it was essential to keep output, investment and fiscal revenue rising at reasonable rates. In stating this, Liu was probably attacking extreme supporters of readjustment and providing a rationale for the cautious, but more balanced, approach now adopted.

POPULATION, EMPLOYMENT AND INCOMES

Population

According to official estimates, China's population at the end of 1981 was 996,220,000. This represented an absolute increase of about 450 million since 1949—an average annual growth rate of 1.9 per cent. This rate of population increase is only marginally slower than that of the food supply and has posed immense problems for the maintenance of employment, economic growth and stability generally. The course of population growth seems to have been uneven, as is illustrated below:

Population increase rates (annual averages)

1949–57	1957–66	1966–72	1972–80
2.2%	1.6%	2.6%	1.6%

The initial spurt of growth reflected the relative calm and economic progress of this period, which led to falling death rates and perhaps slightly rising birth rates. During 1960–61 death rates rose sharply and birth rates fell in response to the collapse of the food supply. Subsequently population growth spurted again, only to be slowed in the early 1970s. Between 1972 and 1980 the annual rate of natural increase fell from 2.2 per cent to 1.2 per cent. The latter rate was reported to be the product of a birth rate of 17.9 per 1,000 and a death rate of 6.2 per 1,000. Clearly the fall in the birth rate in the 1970s was remarkably rapid, although non-Chinese observers believe that both birth and death rates are understated. Life expectancy at birth is now about 70 years.

Population policy has oscillated considerably since the early 1950s. After an initial enthusiasm for population growth, numerous Party officials and specialists began to call in 1954 and later for measures of fertility control. In 1957 these reformers were crushed by Mao in an "Anti-Rightist" campaign. Subsequently, although there were developments in policy, serious demographic study was suspended for 20 years.

The important turning-point in policy came in 1971, when a new policy of fertility control was initiated. Under this, detailed plans for marriage and births are formulated at each major level of the administrative hierarchy and, finally, at the level of the workplace. These plans are supported by moral, economic and coercive sanctions of many kinds. The evidence suggests that, after initial success, there is now increasinging difficulty in securing compliance with these plans. The aim for the future is to stabilize population growth by the year 2000 and, in the longer term, to reduce it to an "optimal level" of 650 to 700 million.

In July 1982 China began to carry out the largest census operation in world history. Supported by UN technical assistance, the census involves a form containing 19 questions and the results will be published over a period of years. It is anticipated that this census could provide answers to many problems about the Chinese population that existing data leave obscure.

Labour

China's labour force in 1979 was estimated to be 406 million. (42 per cent of the population). Of this total 306 million were employed in agriculture (including 29 million in commune and brigade enterprises). Outside agriculture, state employment of various kinds accounted for 77 million, while the remainder were employed in collective or private enterprises. Since 1979 the proportion employed in the latter has grown.

The level of skill within the labour force is low. Only 0.5 per cent have had post-secondary education of any kind and only an estimated 8 per cent have had education above the lower middle school (i.e. nine years' total education). Up to about one-third have probably not had the equivalent of full primary education.

Control of employment has been fairly comprehensive. The hiring and transfer of workers in the cities has had to go through local Bureaus and, in the state sector, dismissal was generally impermissible. Skilled workers have always been in very short supply. In principle, new graduates are assigned to their work-places and, because of shortages, enterprises and organizations tend to hoard graduates irrespective of their immediate usefulness.

Unemployment is a major problem in China and was particularly acute in the 1970s, when people born in the population expansion of the 1950s came onto the labour market. Since 1977 the problem has been admitted and measures taken to alleviate it. These include expanded state sector employment, pressure on older workers to retire, and a major liberalization of private and collective activities in the cities. Between 1979 and 1981, 8,660,000 per annum were reported to have found employment, leaving a backlog of only 3 million at the end of 1981. One other source of employment in recent years has been the Manpower Services Companies. These companies are available to foreigners for civil construction and other works around the world. In 1979 an estimate of the employment potential in these companies was 1 million, although the numbers employed are thought to be well below this level.

In the countryside the reorganization of agriculture has not helped the employment problem created by the pressure of population on land. In the short term, reorganization has forced all able-bodied members of the labour force to seek work without ensuring a comparable expansion of work. In the longer term it is hoped that the liberalization of private activity and the policy of diversification will relieve the difficulties to some extent.

Non-agricultural incomes in China are mainly fixed by reference to tables of basic rates.These relate wages and salaries to occupations, sectors, skills, levels of responsibility and geographical locations. Around these basic rates are bonus systems which have grown in importance as a result of recent reforms. There is little doubt that both wage and bonus systems are in a state of confusion. At some stage a major reform of the system seems inevitable.

In agriculture the commune system has, in the past, included a variety of payment systems, most of which assign a notional credit to each member of the labour force, reflecting the worker's contribution to output. These notional credits are turned into real annual rewards on the basis of the net real income of the team to which each commune member and his household is attached. Recent agricultural reforms have strengthened the links between individual reward and payment, and have encouraged the further development of private agriculture.

The long-term trend of real incomes is not known in great detail. In terms of the major components of expenditure, one may deduce from output and population figures that, up to 1978, neither food nor housing had increased in per capita supply to any significant extent since 1957. This is confirmed by a Chinese report that between 1957 and 1979 the real wages of non-agricultural workers in the state and collective sectors declined by 1.4 per cent. Since 1978, however, consumption standards for many have improved as output of consumer goods and housing construction have been increased very rapidly. In 1980 and 1981 wages of workers and staff rose 22 per cent, during which time the official retail price index increased 14 per cent, although a more comprehensive index would have shown a higher rise in prices. The price rises have undoubtedly been a serious problem. Some groups of urban workers will not have had rises equal to the average, while official sources have reported that, in the countryside, up to 100 million peasants are living in serious poverty. The problem of acute poverty in the countryside has been intensified in the short term by the reorganization of the People's Communes, since this has led to some undermining of the "Five Guarantees" (food, shelter, clothing, health and burial expenses). In the short run, dismantling the planned economy is bound to lead to some welfare problems, although, in the longer run, it is to be hoped that rising productivity will bring higher and reasonably distributed incomes.

ORGANIZATION AND PLANNING

At the Centre of the Chinese planning system are a group of key administrative and political organizations. These include the National People's Congress, which meets periodically to approve major plans and the State Budget; the Central Committee and Politburo of the Chinese Communist Party, which have over-arching political functions; and the State Council, the body to which are subordinate a large number of Commissions, Ministries and agencies, including all those with significant economic functions. Among these, the most important, with economic co-ordination functions, are the State Planning Commission and the State Economic Commission (long and short-term planning respectively). The economic Ministries correspond either to a sector or industry (e.g. agriculture or textiles), or to a function (e.g. finance or prices). State Council responsibilities also include the whole of the financial system and the organization of foreign trade.

Although Five-Year Plans are often given great prominence in the press and in literature about China, the plan of pre-eminent importance is the annual one. The details of the annual plan and of the results of the plan for the previous year are, together with the annual budget, the most important documents produced by the planning system.

The Chinese adopted a great deal of the Soviet planning technique, although, from the outset, they included new variations of their own. The essence of this system in the non-agricultural sector is that enterprises are provided with detailed physical and related plans which it is their legal duty to fulfil. Necessary inputs are provided and, while losses are offset through subsidies, surpluses of all kinds are automatically appropriated by the centre.

The Chinese system has differed from the Soviet model in two particularly important respects: lack of provision of large managerial incentives to encourage plan fulfilment and a much larger role for local planners, who have total responsibility for many enterprises in light industry and other smaller-scale activities.

In agriculture the People's Communes, with their three-tier organization (commune, brigade and team), have played a central planning role since 1958. The working of the system has varied, but the system, as it survived nutil the late 1970s, provided for agreed plans for the area to be sown with major crops (especially grain and cotton) while leaving day-to-day management to be conducted at the team level. Output flowed out of the commune in the forms of tax, compulsory purchase and voluntary, above-norm offerings to the State. The balance is then allocated for various local needs and individual income.

The economic reforms

Since 1978 the whole planning organization has been subject to a series of reforms. In industry the reform began in Sichuan Province, where 100 enterprises were allowed to operate under new rules. This experiment was later extended to 1,200 enterprises nationwide and subsequently became generalized throughout the economy. The reformed regulations have developed the following characteristics: (i) enterprises are allowed to keep a small proportion of planned and a larger proportion of above-plan profits; (ii) output produced above the planned level may be disposed of either through the state system or by alternative distribution channels; (iii) some raw materials can be obtained by routes other than the state monopoly organizations; (iv) loans can be obtained from banks for development purposes; (v) enterprises are allowed limited breaches of the state monopoly of foreign trade.

The intention behind these reforms was to provide direct links between individual effort, the performance of enterprises and individual and collective rewards. The allocation of retained profits for bonuses and investment was a key link in this chain.

Early evidence from the reformed enterprises suggested that the reforms were having positive effects. More recent evidence is less promising and a number of problems have emerged. First, the mixture of planning and market allocation causes great confusion and bureaucratic backlash. Secondly, the scale and use of retained funds have been unsatisfactory. Enterprises have twisted the rules to retain large sums and have spent these on large bonuses and uncontrolled investment projects. Further, the allocation of profits (the source of benefits in the system) has been irrational because these are largely determined by the prices of goods produced and these are arbitrary. Thus, inland and extractive enterprises have done particularly badly. For example, 33,000 workers at a Peking petrochemical enterprise earned more profits than China's 2 million coal miners. These problems were a major reason for the emergence of China's large domestic fiscal deficit and consequent inflation, As a result, in December 1981 it was announced that, while reforms were to be continued, they were to be subject to careful review. Serious abuses were to be halted immediately by use of courts of law and by a more general attack on corrupting bourgeois ideology.

In agriculture, output was stimulated by three measures: a large increase in purchase prices for agricultural goods, a reorganization of the commune system, and an expansion of the land allocated to private plots and increased freedom to market privately. These measures had some sharp initial impact, as can be seen from data on output and peasant incomes. By 1981 the planners were, however, concerned about the loss of control over the production of grain and vegetables and about difficulties in controlling market prices. As a result, important directives on price practices were implemented and, in the Spring of 1982, steps were taken to try to ensure that the land sown with grain and vegetables was adequate.

The banking system

The most important domestic bank is the People's Bank of China. This bank is directly under the State Council and has a key role as the location of settlement and supplier of money to the economic system. Until very recently the main functions of the People's Bank have been twofold. First, it oversees the activities of units and enterprises in the economy, all of whom have accounts at the Bank. The main purpose of this is to ensure that enterprises comply with the economic plans laid down for them. Secondly, the Bank controls the money supply through credit policies. Funds supplied to enterprises have been predominantly short-term working capital (long-term finance coming directly, interest-free, from the Budget). An important part of monetary control has also been the Bank's function as the medium for encouraging private savings. The scale of the Bank's activities is indicated by the fact that it has 29 major branches, about 2,500 "central sub-branches" and 37,000 "offices". Also linked to the system are 60,000 rural credit co-operatives. Total employment in all these units is probably close to 500,000.

Economic reforms have begun to change the nature of the banking system quite significantly. First, the Agricultural Bank of China was re-established and has begun to make loans to support the new agricultural policies. Secondly, a revitalized People's Construction Bank of China is now allowed to make longer-term investment loans to industry. These latter developments were paralleled by allowing the People's Bank to make short- and medium-term loans for capital and capital renovation purposes. These loans have been particularly important in light industry, which for many years was kept short of directly budgeted state funds. Two other aspects of banking reform have been a greater use of interest rates and the reform in the management of the People's Bank itself. The effect of the latter is to make individual parts of the system more independent and operationally flexible. This loss of central control is partially offset by the use of interest rate policy. In this way, the Bank of China is beginning to look more like a central bank in a country with a market economy.

The experiments in banking reform have caused many problems, of which the greatest was the system's role in the loss of control over investment expenditures. Even so, unless there is a sharp reversal in the policy of reforming the rest of the economic system, the function of the banking system as a controlling agency is likely to grow.

INDUSTRY

According to official (State Statistical Bureau) statistics, China's industry grew at 11.1 per cent per annum between 1953 and 1979. In 1980 and 1981 the rate fell sharply as a result of "readjustment". Nonetheless, this growth has put China quite high in the world rankings for absolute output of some industrial products. For example, China ranks third in the output of coal, natural gas and petroleum; fourth in cement; fifth in steel, and first in cotton yarn. In spite of these achievements, the Chinese are concerned about the backwardness of their industrial technology, the low levels of operating efficiency, and inter-industry imbalances. Current policy is to reduce the trend rate of growth and to improve quality and efficiency. Most emphasis is being placed at present on energy, transport and consumer goods.

Energy

China's estimated level of energy consumption per head in 1980 was 602 kg. of coal equivalent. In 1979 industrial consumption accounted for 69 per cent of total consumption, and private household consumption for only 17 per cent. China's per capita consumption is about 6 per cent of the level for market economies and slightly higher, for example, than that for Africa among developing areas. Growth of energy output in China has been high. Between 1961 and 1976 it averaged 8.8 per cent per annum, compared to a world average of 5.5 per cent. Within that total, crude petroleum (21 per cent), natural gas (16.6 per cent), and hydro-electric power (12.3 per cent) have been the mainstays of growth. In 1978 coal still accounted for 67 per cent of total primary energy output.

Coal

China's coal reserves have been estimated at 600,000 million metric tons and coal remains central to China's energy strategy. Annual output rose from 550 million tons in 1977 to 635 million tons in 1979 but production fell to 620 million tons in 1980 and remained at this level in 1981. As a result the Chinese have been rethinking the details of their plan for coal. The main problems in recent years have been lack of transportation, regional imbalances between production and consumption, very low recovery rates, poor utilization of output, and ineffective planning. The lack of regional balance arises from the presence of major deposits in north-west China, a long way from the major consumers in east, south and north China. The problem in the south is particularly serious, since eight southern provinces, producing nearly 40 per cent of China's industrial output, have only 2 per cent of known coal reserves.

In 1978 the Minister for Coal proposed that coal production be doubled within a decade. This would imply a 1988 output of more than 1,000 million tons. The unrealistic nature of this plan is shown by the fact that annual production has since levelled out. A major explanation for this has been the closure of many of the 1 `,000 small rural pits. Many of these make a loss financially and the loss of central deficiency payments has led to closure.

Future policies now look to improvements in coal utilization as a key to alleviating shortages for consumption. An immediate target of a 15 per cent improvement has been established. In the spring of 1981 a new Minister for coal announced major plans for the introduction of new techniques in extraction, washing, gasification and liquefaction. Coal mining is still very labour-intensive and it is possible that labour-intensive deep mining will begin to give way to more mechanized open-cast methods.

Petroleum

The poor long-run performance of coal between 1957 and 1981 was, until recently, compensated for by extraordinarily high growth rates of petroleum output. Soviet assistance in the 1950s in prospecting and development laid the foundations for petroleum self-sufficiency in the 1960s. Since 1978, however, output has fluctuated around 100 million tons per year and, while some observers believe that official data are still not wholly accurate, the growth of output has undoubtedly eased. This reflects growing difficulties with the large oilfield at Daqing (Taching), in Heilongjiang province, which has held back the overall level of output in spite of the coming on stream of major new fields such as Renqui, in Hobei province.

Foreign assistance has always played an important part in China's oil development. The need for more sophisticated techniques of surveying, secondary recovery and off-shore exploration and development offer major opportunities for foreign technology. Economically recoverable on-shore reserves are estimated to be about 6,000 million tons, and off-shore reserves may add a further 4,000 million tons. Although the off-shore figures are particularly problematic, the Chinese have now codified the rules relating to foreign participation in off-shore oil and a first round of bids was announced in February 1982. This development is overseen by the China Offshore Oil Corporation and bids have been received for an area of 150,000 sq. km.

If off-shore exploration and development is successful, the situation regarding energy and the balance of payments in the late 1980s will be markedly improved. The imponderables, however, remain large, so that policies for conservation and improved utilization will remain critical.

Metals and machine-building

China's raw materials for the metallurgical and related industries are extensive. Iron ore, coking coal, molybdenum, nickel, titanium and other metals are all exploited in China. In the past, however, there has been inadequate investment in extraction and processing. In the crucial case of iron ore, China seems to lack concentrated high-quality deposits. This has hampered the development of the iron and steel industry, and has led to a policy of importing ore.

In the 1950s the Chinese, with Soviet technical help, attained steady growth in the iron and steel industry. This progress was cut short by the drive during the "Great Leap Forward" for an expansion of small-scale steel-making. Between 1949 and 1979 steel output grew at 12 per cent per annum, and in 1981 the industry employed 3.8 million workers and staff. Since 1979 output has plateaued in the "readjustment". A good deal of the readjustment consisted of the elimination or merging of small-scale plants. Steel was central to Hua Guofeng's strategy, which included a target annual output of 60 million metric tons by 1985. This was to be achieved largely with the aid of imported plant, including the huge Baoshan project at Shanghai. These new projects ran into severe difficulties due to supply problems with energy and raw materials, and the Hua target has now been dropped. Current policies emphasize improvements in quality, in raw materials, in energy use, in plant reorganization and in relating the structure of output to the needs of customers.

The machinery industry is closely related to the metal-processing industries and progress in these has been impressive. From a very small base, machinery output has grown remarkably, so that domestic production now accounts for nearly all of domestic consumption (although the foreign share of consumption has great value). Machinery output is organized in a wide variety of enterprises, including some very large, integrated organizations in Wuhan, Shanghai and north-east China. A feature of development in recent years has been the appearance of machinery among China's exports, and its medium technology products clearly have a market in developing countries.

Since 1978 the industry has undergone its own process of readjustment. The main problems have been gross duplication and under-utilization of capacity, lack of standardization and weakness at the design stage. In general the industry has failed to relate sufficiently to customer needs and is bedevilled by the division between the defence and civilian departments with it.

Consumer goods

By far the largest sectors in this group are the various branches of the textile industry. Textiles were a major industry in pre-war China. Shanghai and Tianjin remain large textile centres, although official policy has been to disperse the industry much more widely and there are now large textile plants in the interior. Since the early 1960s, traditional textiles have been supplemented by synthetic goods. Given the problems in the agricultural sector, synthetic products seem certain to grow in importance.

In 1981 the total output of cotton yarn (including mixed yarn) was 3,170,000 metric tons while the output of cotton cloth was 14,270 million linear metres. Woollen and silk goods are also important and their output is growing rapidly. Although textiles are crucial to Chinese domestic living standards, the sector is also very important for international trade. Textiles, clothing and related products have regularly contributed up to one-quarter of China's visible foreign exchange earnings.

Since policies to improve living standards began in 1978, output of other consumer goods has increased rapidly. Watches, bicycles and radios had been produced in substantial quantities since the 1960s, but recently the output of television receivers, washing machines, cameras and sewing machines has also increased considerably.

Transport

China has major facilities in rail, road, water and air transport. Of rail, road and water facilities, increases in operational distances between 1949 and 1980 were 2.36 times, 10.85 times and 1.46 times respectively. At the end of 1981 the rail network totalled 50,000 km., of which 8,000 km. were double-tracked.

The transport sector remains one of the weakest links in the Chinese economy. Railway utilization, for example, is exceptionally intensive and yet facilities for grain, coal and other industrial goods remain inadequate. Road building, too, has not kept pace with demand. If there were an effective programme for the building of metalled roads, the effects would be very great, particularly in the countryside. Internal water transport remains very important, with navigable waterways estimated to total 109,000 km. in 1981. The mechanization of water transport is proceeding.

Transport has a high priority in China's economic strategy. The main lines of policy are: to invest in new facilities (especially railway locomotives and rolling stock) in order to reduce the strains of overuse; to promote energy-saving forms of water transport where feasible; and to make dramatic improvements in the management and pricing of transport services in order to achieve better value from existing resources.

New industries

China has begun the development of industries employing new technologies. These include electronics and chemicals. Computer production (controlled by the Fourth Ministry of Machine Building) is advancing rapidly. The Chinese have been producing a number of main-frame computers for several years now, but recent developments have included production of micros, ancillary equipment and software. Much of this has been supported by licensing and other agreements with foreign companies. Western experts believe that prospects for parts of the industry may be very good, including, in the long run, the software end, which is very labour-intensive and hence expensive in the West and Japan.

AGRICULTURE

China's cultivated land totals about 100 million hectares—11 per cent of the total land area. With total and rural populations of about 1,000 and 800 million respectively, this represents about 0.4 of an acre per head or 0.5 of an acre per head of the rural population. The potential for increasing the cultivated acreage is not large and the costs of doing so are high and rising. The high man-to-land ratio and China's natural conditions have produced an agrarian economy in which instability and inequalities are major problems. The growth of population puts continuous pressure on the system to grow, which, given the land shortage, means that an improvement in productivity is essential.

Grain is the most important output of agriculture since it supplies four-fifths of the population's calorie intake. The rural economy is divided into a northern grain-producing and a southern rice-producing region. (Grain in China is defined to include coarse grains, soyabeans, pulses and tubers "in grain equivalent"). In general, the "fine grain" of wheat and rice is much preferred by consumers to the coarser cereals which tend to be consumed in the countryside.

Total grain output grew by an annual average of 2.6 per cent from 1952 to 1980. This is slightly in excess of the rate of growth of population. In the same period the gross value of all agricultural output grew at 3.4 per cent annually. The pattern of this growth through time has been: (*a*) above-average growth up to 1958, followed by (*b*) decline and sharp recovery in the first half of the 1960s, (*c*) steady progress up to the early 1970s, followed by some very variable years thereafter. From the early 1960s, Mao emphasized the primacy of grain production at the expense of industrial crops, forestry, fishing and livestock. As a result, output of non-grain crops has been very variable, with particular difficulties in production of cotton and soyabeans in the years before Mao's death.

During the 1950s, state investment in agriculture was small. After 1961, however, the provision of modern inputs, notably electricity, irrigation and chemical fertilizers increased rapidly. These investments had good short-term effects, but these began to decline in the early 1970s. The difficulties in securing steady growth in the 1970s were partly technical, but were reinforced by the lack of effective incentive systems in agriculture and the failure to provide an adequate overall level of farm purchase prices.

Since 1978 there have been major attempts to rectify these problems. For example, the index of procurement prices, which increased from 185 in 1965 to 201 in 1975, jumped to 243 in 1979. Within the index, increases in cotton and sugar prices were particularly marked. Organizational change, enlargement of private farming possibilities and the provision of large quantities of consumer goods to the countryside also increased incentives. More generally, the Government reversed the policy of giving priority to grain and encouraged widespread diversification into other food, non-food and forestry development.

Output in agriculture responded to these changes. Some crops have increased markedly but there is growing concern about the decline in the area sown with grain, which fell by 6 million hectares between 1979 and 1981. It is also clear that the pricing and distribution of agricultural commodities are having unforeseen effects on both living standards and the procurement policies of industrial users of agricultural output.

The net effect of China's agricultural policies and performance since the 1950s has been to make the economy dependent on imports. Grain is a large item but other products, including cotton, have also had to be imported. Current policies tend to reinforce the need for grain imports, although diversified production should also help to pay for these by increasing exports.

FOREIGN INTERNATIONAL RELATIONS

Visible trade

China's visible trade turnover (imports plus exports) totalled an estimated U.S. $42,000 million in 1981. Since 1970 the average nominal growth rate has been 23 per cent, although the volatility of China's trade is particularly great. In spite of the rapid growth of the 1970s, total trade is equal to only about 14 per cent of national income and, on a per capita basis, is, for example, only 1/84th of the Japanese level.

During the 1950s trade was essentially an exchange of agricultural output for industrial machinery and inputs. After 1960 food imports became essential and the structure and year-to-year level of trade became more variable. In 1979 the commodity structure of trade was as follows:

Imports (% of total)		*Exports* (% of total)	
Capital goods	27	Agricultural goods	29
(of which machinery	18)	Extractive products	15
		Manufactures	56
Consumer goods	2	(of which textiles	25)
Food	13		
Industrial materials	58		
TOTAL	100	TOTAL	100

It will be seen that manufactured goods are more than one-half of total exports, although the high level of textile exports implies that the dependence of export performance on agriculture remains considerable. Within imports, the proportions accounted for by capital goods and machinery have become quite high, although these shares have not regained the peaks of the late 1950s.

China's major trading partners in recent years have been Japan, Hong Kong, the U.S.A. and Western Europe. With the exception of Hong-Kong, China runs a deficit with the richer, more industrialized partners which has to be covered by surpluses with poorer countries and by credits. Trade with other Communist countries has recovered somewhat in recent years but this tends to be fairly balanced trade.

Balance of payments, reserves and financing

For most years since 1950, China has achieved a visible trade surplus. Altogether there have been 10 deficit years. These include the four years 1977 to 1981, during which the scale of the deficits was unprecedentedly large. In 1981 the deficit is estimated to have been U.S. $2,440 million. To offset this, China is estimated to have had an invisibles surplus of up to $2,000 million. Even after the trade deficit, China had foreign exchange reserves of $4,773 million at the end of 1981.

China's policy towards credit has fluctuated. In the 1950s China had short-term loans from the U.S.S.R., but later, after the collapse of the Sino-Soviet link, the Chinese rejected credit as likely to lead to a loss of national independence. Large-scale imports of plant in the 1970s brought with them access to suppliers' credits and, since 1977, the Chinese attitude has changed considerably. China has sought lines of buyers' credit and inter-governmental help of various kinds. In total, credits estimated to amount to $28,000 million are known to have been offered to China but, since this was nearly all at commercial rates, the Chinese have taken up only a small fraction of it.

In May 1980 China joined the World Bank and the IMF. The link with the World Bank was undoubtedly made in the hope of access to money at highly concessional rates. Some has been offered but China has not yet been offered very large-scale support.

Trade organization

Until 1977, China's trade organization was modelled on the Soviet system in which the state has a monopoly of imports, exports and foreign exchange payments. This system is an effective means of keeping control over foreign trade and of ensuring that it serves priority needs. It does, however, lead to inefficiencies of all kinds. Since 1977 a number of innovations have been made in this system. Provinces, municipalities and enterprises have all been given some limited roles in the processes of foreign trade. Also, four special economic zones have been set up in Guangdong and Fujian provinces. In these zones, local governments have special powers to encourage foreign investment under the terms of regulations promulgated in 1979 and 1981.

To handle the growing complexity of China's foreign economic links, numerous new organizations have been established for export, import, foreign investment and foreign exchange control. Relations between these, at both central and local levels, clearly became very tangled. To remedy this, a new coordinating agency was established in the Spring of 1982. This is the Ministry of Foreign Trade and Economic Relations, which is headed by Miss Chen Muhua.

The foreign exchange side of China's international relations will continue to be handled on a day-to-day basis by the Bank of China. This is the overseas counterpart of the People's Bank, and it has branches in London, Singapore, Hong Kong and Luxembourg. Internally, the Bank has to work under the State Council and in conjunction with the State General Administration of Exchange Control. Since 1979, problems in the foreign exchange control field have been very acute and new regulations of March 1981 were designed to re-tighten central direction of foreign exchange responsibilities.

ECONOMIC SURVEY OF TAIWAN

Ramon H. Myers

Taiwan's post-war economic growth, one of the fastest on record, originated from three developments. First, 50 years of Japanese colonial rule modernized the island's transport, public health and farming. Second, U.S. economic aid in the 1950s enabled the Government to divert more domestic resources to capital formation. Finally, the Government reversed its strategy of import-substitution industrialization of the early 1950s and in 1958 initiated reforms that oriented Taiwan toward the world economy.

On December 15th, 1978, President Jimmy Carter announced that on January 1st, 1979, the U.S.A. would recognize the People's Republic of China as the sole legal government of China and terminate diplomatic relations and the Mutual Defense Treaty with the Republic of China on Taiwan. On March 16th, 1979, the U.S. Congress passed the Taiwan Relations Act which made it possible for the U.S.A. and Taiwan to continue their economic and cultural ties of the past. Throughout 1979 and into 1980 Taiwan's economy continued to grow and become more productive in spite of its acute diplomatic isolation in the world.

Post-War Economic Development

Under Japan's colonial rule, Taiwan's economic structure gradually began to shift from a dependency on agriculture to manufacturing. This trend accelerated after the war so that by 1980 only 9.1 per cent of the goods and services produced originated from agriculture compared with 35 per cent in 1952, whereas manufacturing produced 45.7 per cent compared with 18 per cent in 1952. The share of the service sector declined to 45.2 per cent. This transformation in economic structure is unusual because it was associated with a rapid population growth of 3.5 per cent in the 1950s and a very rapid annual growth of per capita income of 3 and 7 per cent respectively during the 1950s and 1960s.

In 1981 the Taiwan economy grew by 5.5 per cent, compared with 6.6 per cent in 1980. Per capita income for the year averaged U.S. $2,362, compared with $2,280 in 1980. The population of 18.1 million enjoyed living standards comparable to the developed countries in the west.

Between 1960 and 1973 the island economy enjoyed an unprecedented economic boom; the value of exports rose 20-fold and real G.N.P. (in 1978 prices) increased 3.3 times. A study of the sources for this growth concluded that between 1963 and 1972 half of the output expansion originated from technical progress and 36 per cent from capital accumulation. The remaining 14 per cent of output growth came from labour.

Prior to 1967 foreign sources played a large role in financing net capital formation expansion, but after 1967 domestic savings financed the entire growth of net capital formation. The structure of capital also changed in the late 1960s shifting from mainly construction items toward a larger share comprised of transport equipment, machinery, and equipment. The expansion of foreign trade is the major reason for Taiwan's rapid capital growth. Eighty per cent of the growth in exports can be attributed to the competitiveness of Taiwan's exports in price and quality in world markets for food, crude materials, machinery, transport equipment, and other manufactured goods. The sources for this competitiveness are to be found in low cost, high skilled labour, efficient management, the strong profit incentive of businessmen, and social and political stability within the country.

This rapid economic boom naturally created new problems. After 1965 farm labour became scarce, and the sudden rise in rural wages began to adversely influence farm costs and product prices. In the early 1970s overcrowding of public transportation and shipping congestion in major ports revealed for the first time that demand had outstripped the capacity of Taiwan's infrastructure to provide the same services as in the recent past. In the 1970s the Government launched 10 projects to expand and improve roads, harbours, airfields and rail transport, as well as to establish new industries producing petrochemical and steel products.

The economy's capacity to save has risen enormously. In the late 1960s the rate of savings to national income exceeded 20 per cent, and in the 1970s it was around 30 per cent. High government savings since 1975 have accounted for about one-third of domestic savings and have been a major financial source for public investment. Also, income distribution became more equal. In 1950 the richest 20 per cent of all households had 15 times as much income as the poorest 20 per cent. In 1979 this disparity had dropped to 4.4 times, compared with 4.1 times for Japan in 1977, 7.9 times for the Republic of Korea in 1976 and 9.3 times for the U.S.A. in 1972.

Current Economic Development

Since 1978 the rate of economic growth of Taiwan has declined, like that of all developed economies afflicted by inflation and declining productivity. Even so, Taiwan's 1981 increase in G.N.P. of 5.5 per cent (at 1981 prices) was much higher than that of the developed countries. In 1979 and 1980 wholesale prices jumped by 13 and 21 per cent respectively but in 1981 inflation fell to 7.6 per cent. Taiwan's economic performance has been adversely influenced by the world recession. Its rate of export growth has declined since 1978, and exports increased by only 14 per cent in 1981, compared with a 23 per cent rise in 1980. Tough restrictions on money supply expansion kept the growth rate to only 11 per cent in 1981, compared with nearly 20 per cent in 1980.

RESOURCES

Forests covered 2,319,000 hectares, about two-thirds of Taiwan's land area, in 1969. These forests include broad-leaved evergreens, coniferous trees, shrub and bamboo. Only 24 per cent of the land surface is under cultivation. Rapid population growth has increased the cultivated area from 1,665,000 acres in 1910 to 2,124,000 acres in 1940 and a near maximum limit of 2,197,220 acres in 1965. Cultivated soil in Taiwan is mainly of the alluvial type. The fertility of this alluvial soil is rather high, and its physical properties are well-suited for crop-growing.

Mineral resources are poor and it is unlikely that important mineral reserves still remain to be discovered. The chief minerals produced are coal, gold, and sulphur; other resources of importance include copper, petroleum, and salt. Bituminous coal is found in shales and sandstone in the north. At the present rate of coal exploitation, about 3 million tons annually in the late 1970s, current coal reserves can be expected to last somewhat less than 50 years.

Manpower

Taiwan's population was officially estimated to be 18,135,508 at December 31st, 1981, compared with only 7,869,247 at the end of 1951. The population will probably increase much more slowly over the next 30 years. In 1981 the annual population growth was 1.9 per cent, compared with 3.0 per cent in the 1960s. Rapid urbanization, high literacy and high per capita income are the factors now encouraging young couples to have fewer children.

Between October 1965 and October 1976 the non-agricultural workforce doubled to reach 4,181,000 workers, but the agricultural workforce began to decline from a peak of 1.7 million in 1969 to 1.6 million in 1979. A 1978 study found that the main reason for the decline was the reduced number of workers entering the rural workforce each year. These young people have moved to towns and cities for employment and education. Therefore, the average age of the rural workforce has risen from 34 years in 1967 to 39 in 1977 and was expected to rise further to 42 in 1982.

The workforce increased most rapidly in manufacturing, construction, commerce, and in services such as administration, clerical and sales. Until 1970 the population between 0 and 15 years of age had slowly increased. This trend meant that the economy had to expand rapidly in order to absorb persons entering the economically active age group over 15 years of age. As the economy develops, more college-educated men and women will be demanding professional and "white collar" jobs. Taiwan might soon face a serious problem of under-employment amongst its educated élite, a problem that confronts nearly all advanced economies.

AGRICULTURE

Until 1965 agriculture produced the largest share of national income, but thereafter its share steadily declined as industrial production expanded rapidly and the growth rate of agricultural production slowed. Land used for food-grain production had been diverted to producing more vegetables, mushrooms and fruit. More farm capital and labour were also shifted to increase the supply of poultry and pigs. But, due to a decline in the agricultural labour force since the mid-1960s, the multiple cropping index also declined slightly. While some farm mechanization had increased, the trend of more costly farm specialization can only mean that food-grain production might not meet future demand, necessitating some importing of food or food price rises. Over 85 per cent of the farms have less than 3 hectares, and 45 per cent of this number are smaller than 1 hectare. In 1977 the average farm family contained 6.4 persons. A total of 872,509 households farmed 922,778 hectares.

Crops

The main crops ranked by area of cultivation are rice, sugar, sweet potatoes and groundnuts. Rice accounted for more than half of total farm production and nearly half of the cultivated farm land. However, the acreage used for these main crops has been declining since 1969 as farmers have switched land use to maize and soya beans which are used as feed for hogs and poultry. Farming areas around metropolitan areas are being converted into vegetable and fruit lands. Pigmeat production was 652,104 metric tons in 1981, compared with 224,000 tons in 1964. The production of hen eggs more than quadrupled between 1964 and 1978.

Improvements in Yield

Until 1910 farm production increased due to the expansion of farming inputs such as land, labour and farm capital produced by farmers themselves. Between 1910 and 1970 it expanded three times more rapidly than the historical growth trend and new farm capital and technology began to account for roughly half of this output expansion. This rise in productivity must be attributed to the activities of an efficient farm extension service which was established in 1898.

There was notable progress achieved in expanding irrigation facilities and using chemical fertilizers, pesticides, and new farm machinery. Irrigated land increased greatly in the 1930s because of the completion of several large reservoirs and numerous networks of canals and ponds started in the 1920s. By 1955 three-fifths of the farm land was irrigated. Before 1940 farmers used night soil and soya bean cake but few chemical fertilizers on their fields. By 1965 farmers had already shifted from using nitrogenous compounds to phosphate and sulphate fertilizer compounds. Taiwan's fertilizer industry now supplies farmers with all the nitrogenous fertilizer required. Pesticides are widely used, and rice de-huskers, rotary tiller ploughs, power-driven sprayers and dusters, pumps, and spacing gauges can be found on many farms. However, less than one-quarter of the farming population possess these implements, and the potential is great for increasing yield still further when the majority of farmers own and use these implements.

Land Tenure

One of the most striking post-war changes in the countryside was the creation of a freehold farming class and the elimination of powerful absentee landlords. This was accomplished by a land reform programme carried out between 1949 and 1953. By paying landlords a fair price for their land and encouraging them to invest in urban enterprises, the Government induced this class to shift its wealth and energies from farming to finance and industry. By establishing a land bank and providing easy credit terms to tenant farmers, the Government made it possible for eight out of every ten households to own their farms compared with three out of ten households before the war. Although the farming population rose from 4,488,763 to 5,996,889 between 1956 and 1970, this number began to decline thereafter and in 1977 stood at 5,572,130. In 1976 the percentage of tenant and part-owner households was 9 per cent each, compared with 19 and 58 per cent in 1956.

INDUSTRY

The shortage of fuel and minerals has not prevented the development of new industries. Between 1946 and 1952 the nucleus of industry constructed by the Japanese during the war slowly recovered. Government import controls and foreign exchange licensing gave importers of intermediate products a premium to be earned. Exports declined, and as imports rose, the productive capacity of the pre-war industries rapidly expanded. Two new industries, textiles and chemicals, also grew rapidly as a result of this programme of protecting infant industries.

By 1954, however, industrial production began to falter. As manufacturers found their inventories rising, idle capacity in plants increased; textile and chemical factories were especially hard hit. In 1958 the Government reversed its former policy and liberalized trade. Import controls on numerous products were removed, and many industries were encouraged to produce for world markets as the Government reduced the costs of products they imported from abroad. The growth rate of manufacturing began to accelerate once again, and between 1961 and 1973 overall manufacturing output expanded at a growth rate of 17 per cent a year. Between 1974 and 1975 manufacturing output expansion slowed down considerably because of government steps to curb inflation. In 1975 the Government gave tax rebates to certain industries to encourage businessmen to reduce their unit costs and remain competitive in world markets. These measures paid off when industrial production rose by 11.2 per cent in 1977. However, renewed inflation in 1980 slowed the growth rate to 7.2 per cent.

Taiwan's industrial structure has altered considerably since 1960. In that year light industry made up 60 per cent of industry's contribution to the net national product and the remainder (comprising chemicals, machine tools, metals, construction, etc.) accounted for 40 per cent. By 1977 light industry's share had fallen to 48 per cent. Most basic industries are located in Kaohsiung city. Light industries are situated around Taipei which uses the facilities of Keelung harbour to import raw materials such as cotton for nearby textile mills. Industries depending on local agricultural products such as sugar cane, are concentrated in the south. Food processing industries, such as rice hulling, grain milling, manufacturing of edible oil, bean curd, and of condiments, are located in larger cities of the rural areas.

In 1965 the Government designated Kaohsiung as the site for an industrial zone to stimulate investors and businessmen to develop new export industries on the model of Hong Kong's free entrepôt economy. A site of 165 acres was set aside for establishing factories which would produce optical equipment, plastics, electrical appliances, chemicals, garments, furniture and packaging materials for export. By late 1973 two additional zones in Nantze and Taichung were in operation, with a fourth being planned. At the end of 1977, 267 factories were in operation in these zones. Their combined investment totalled U.S. $300 million; they employed 80,000 workers and exported goods valued at U.S. $1,000 million in 1979.

Steel production from the integrated and expanding mill at Kaohsiung now produces 3 million tons annually. A fourth naphtha cracker plant in the petrochemical industry was expected to be operating in 1980. The island has six vehicle manufacturers and the motor industry is turning out nearly 200,000 units annually, mostly for export. The output of passenger cars exceeds 100,000 per year. In February 1982 the state-owned China Steel Corporation signed an agreement with Nissan and Toyota of Japan for the construction of a 200,000 vehicle-per-year car manufacturing plant. Electrical machinery was expected to overtake textiles in dollar volume by 1982.

In 1980 new industries emerged. The United Microelectronics Corporation started to construct an electronics manufacturing plant, which was expected to speed up the transfer of electronics technology to Taiwan by late 1981. The first Science Industry Park was completed at Hsinchu in late 1980, and 14 high-technology manufacturers, including Wang Laboratories Ltd., received approval to set up plants there, Under the new Statute for Encouragement of Investment, the Government has offered incentives to high-technology industries if they earmark a certain percentage of their revenues for research and development.

FOREIGN AID AND INVESTMENTS

Without U.S. economic and military assistance Taiwan's economic recovery would have been protracted and the economy could have floundered in inflation and stagnated. The Nationalist Government has used economic aid for both agriculture and industry. Between 1951 and 1965 Taiwan received U.S. $1,465.4 million worth of economic aid. The importance of this aid for economic development can be seen in the financing of capital formation between 1952 and 1960: U.S. aid financed 26 per cent of the total value of capital formed during this period.

It was also responsible for reducing the annual trade deficit of approximately U.S. $100 million. U.S. aid was also used for building the fertilizer industry, financing the Shihmen dam, launching many agricultural programmes, establishing schools and distributing teaching guides. In 1965 the aid programme was terminated, and by 1970 all grants had been used.

In 1977 overseas Chinese and foreign investments in Taiwan totalled U.S. $163.9 million, an increase of 5.8 per cent over the amount invested during the previous year. Foreign investments by 50 firms accounted for 60 per cent of this total. The electronics and electrical appliance industries led with U.S. $52.8 million or 32.2 per cent of the total. This was followed by service industries, with 31.3 per cent, and the chemical products industry with 8.6 per cent. Among foreign investments, those from Japan and the United States ranked first. Twenty Japanese firms had invested a total of U.S. $24.1 million, while 17 U.S. firms had invested U.S. $24.2 million.

OVERSEAS TRADE

Taiwan depends greatly on trade to obtain raw materials and capital for industrial expansion and consumer goods which it is still unable to produce. Before the war sugar and rice accounted for three-fifths of the island's exports. Food and fibres made up two-fifths of the imports and the remainder consisted of textiles and assorted goods. Industrial development in the post-war period greatly increased the demand for raw materials, semi-finished goods and machinery. Food and fibres now account for less than one-quarter of total imports. Exports have also undergone changes. During the 1950s industrial products in exports averaged less than 21 per cent, but by 1965 they made up over half of the export trade. Agricultural raw materials and processed goods accounted for only 12.5 per cent of exports in 1977, whereas industrial products made up 87.5 per cent of exports.

In 1964 an export surplus of U.S. $16 million was achieved for the first time, but this was followed by six years of moderate trade deficit. Then, between 1971 and 1973, large export surpluses accumulated, to be followed by a huge deficit of U.S. $1,327 million in 1974 because of the sudden rise in petroleum prices. This deficit fell to U.S. $620 million in 1975, when the Government initiated various policies to stem domestic inflation.

In 1981 exports to the U.S.A. accounted for 36.1 per cent of Taiwan's exports, followed by Japan (11.0 per cent) and Hong Kong (8.4 per cent). Japan supplied 28.0 per cent of Taiwan's imports, followed by the U.S.A. (52.2 per cent) and Kuwait (10.6 per cent). Taiwan exports great quantities of cement, fertilizers and textiles to South-East Asia.

Due to rapidly rising prices of imports around the end of 1972, the Government reduced the tariffs on 10 categories of imports. In March 1973 the Government removed 2,360 additional items of import from the control list, which means that except for military items, heroin, and precious metals such as gold, trade restrictions on general commodities have been completely removed. In February of the same year the Government revalued the currency, the New Taiwan dollar (NT$). The official exchange rate, U.S. $1=NT $40 since 1961, was adjusted to U.S. $=NT $38. This rate remained in effect until July 1978, when the currency was revalued and a new rate of U.S. $1= NT $36 was introduced.

As the NT$ has been pegged to the U.S. $, the depreciation of the U.S. $ in 1978–80 weakened the NT $, especially with respect to the Japanese yen. In December 1978 the Legislative Yuan authorized the Central Bank to "float" the NT dollar against the U.S. dollar. Under the new system, foreign exchange earners may hold foreign exchange in the form of special deposit accounts, either passbook or time deposits. The Central Bank will no longer buy and sell foreign exchange, and market supply and demand fluctuations will freely determine the NT $/U.S. $ exchange rate. The Central Bank will intervene only if violent swings in demand and supply occur.

FINANCE

The Bank of Taiwan serves as the country's central bank and issues notes, controls foreign exchange and makes loans to other banks. In 1961 the Central Bank of China resumed its operations in Taipei after 11 years of suspension. It also makes loans to other banks, handles U.S. aid funds, and assists the Government in its transactions.

The Bank of Taiwan and the national banks have maintained tight control over the money supply whenever prices began to rise unexpectedly. During the 1960s these institutions allowed the money supply to rise steadily in order to satisfy transactions and speculative demands. But in 1974 restrictions were vigorously applied, with the money supply rising by only 7 per cent, compared with 47 per cent the previous year.

Although wholesale prices increased by 22 and 40 per cent respectively in 1973 and 1974 because of the oil crisis, prudent monetary and fiscal action cooled the temporary inflation. As a result the wholesale price index fell by 5.1 per cent in 1975, but rose by 2.8 per cent in 1976 and 1977. Again in 1980 the sharp rise in world oil prices contributed to a huge rise in wholesale prices of 21 per cent. Banks reacted by slowing down the growth of money supply and by raising interest rates, and inflation fell to 7.6 per cent in 1981.

Taiwan operates with a national, provincial and district budget. Government receipts of income tax, estate tax and commodity taxes accounted for roughly 64 per cent of total revenue in the 1970s. The remainder comes from profits of public enterprises, sale of foreign exchange certificates, monopoly revenue, indemnities and fees. Expenditures on national defence and administration as a share of the budget gradually declined during the 1970s to 38.6 per cent in 1976. Expenditures for education, science, and culture accounted for 17.5 per cent of the total. Net budget expenditures average around 20 per cent of national income. However, following the withdrawal of U.S. support, the 1979/80 budget envisaged an increase of 25.2 per cent over the previous year, national defence and foreign affairs expenditure accounting for 41.5 per cent of the total.

INFRASTRUCTURE

Crowded roads and railways and congested harbours have plagued Taiwan since the late 1960s, and by 1974 the Government had realized that a serious imbalance, between the available infrastructure and the demands on resources originating from Taiwan's rapid economic growth, had arisen. To correct this it launched the "Ten Major Construction Projects" including the building of two new ports and an airport, constructing one railway and electrifying another, building an island-long freeway, establishing nuclear power as a source of energy, constructing an integrated steel plant and shipbuilding facilities, and creating a petrochemical industry. Originally the estimated cost of these projects was U.S. $6,500 million but the probable cost is $10,000 million or more. This is to be followed by a scheme of "Twelve Construction Projects", five of which are related to the further improvement of the transport system.

The Kaohsiung shipyard and Taichung harbour have been constructed. Taipei's new international airport at Taoyuan was opened in February 1979. The North Bend Railway, linking Suao and Taitung on the west coast, is still under construction and electrification of the railway system was completed in 1979. The North-South Freeway was completed in 1978. Taiwan's first nuclear power station was completed in 1978. Further plants are under construction, and total capacity is scheduled to exceed 5,000 MW. by 1985. Petrochemical development involves three naphtha cracking plants at Kaohsiung and 12 downstream projects with a planned annual capacity of 1.4 million tons of various petrochemical products. Taiwan continues to search for off-shore and on-shore petroleum. Prospects for new industrial growth from shipbuilding and steel production are not as promising as they were several years ago but it is hoped that the projected shipbuilding facilities and steel plant will improve the situation.

Transport

The Taiwan Railway Administration (TRA) is a government enterprise operating 1,091.1 km. of railway track in 1981; there are also 1,957.1 km. of private lines operated by the Taiwan Sugar Corporation, the Taiwan Forestry Administration and the Taiwan Metal Mining Corporation. The main line, located in the west, links the port of Keelung in the north with Kaohsiung in the south. Most of the major cities and their industries are served by this line. On the eastern side a 175-km. line connects Hualien with Taitung. TRA passenger traffic increased from 121 million persons in 1966 to 145 million in 1974, but was down to 131.7 million in 1981; in that year 32 million tons of freight were transported by rail, compared with 14 million tons in 1966. Electrification of Taiwan's west coast railways, completed in 1979, was expected to increase its carrying capacity by one-third and reduce travel time.

Highways in 1981 totalled 17,522 km. Roads are more developed on the western side of the island, and a four-carriage expressway connects Taipei with Kaohsiung. A cross-island highway links Taichung in the west with Hualien in the east. The bus service throughout the island is excellent.

Taiwan's four major harbours of Keelung, Kaohsiung, Taichung and Hualien handle marine traffic and service ocean vessels of all sizes. The tonnage handled by these harbours nearly trebled between 1968 and 1975. To relieve the problem of congested harbours, Keelung harbour has operated at night since 1973 and all existing harbour facilities are being expanded.

There are two domestic airlines that provide all major cities of over 100,000 people with air service. Taipei International Airport is a major stop-off for all flights from Japan to South-East Asia and beyond. Air traffic has increased greatly since the mid-1960s, and a new international airport at Taoyuan was completed in 1979.

Power

Energy has always been a serious problem for this island economy. Taiwan now derives 80 per cent of its total energy supply from imported oil. Its industries alone consume 70 per cent of the total energy supply. In 1946 the Taiwan Power Company, a government enterprise, was set up to supply electricity and administer electricity rates. Electric power output totalled 34,432 million kWh. in 1978, compared with 9,802 million kWh. in 1968. Industry consumed 21,436 million kWh. in 1978.

Eighty per cent of Taiwan's electrical power is produced by thermal stations, using mainly petroleum. In consequence the 1973–74 increase in energy prices created a new source for domestic inflation. The Government introduced a new energy conservation programme in November 1973 with government agencies taking the lead by reducing their power and oil consumption by one-quarter. Rising energy costs are likely to reduce the growth of industrial production, adversely influence exports, and worsen the balance of payments unless cheap, alternative energy is found in the near future. The Government has tried to diversify the island's sources of energy by developing nuclear power. So far, two plants are in operation. The third will be completed by the end of 1985, at which time the three nuclear plants are expected to have an installed capacity of more than 5 million kilowatts and account for one-third of Taiwan's electrical power supply.

STATISTICAL SURVEY

Note: Wherever possible, figures in this Survey exclude Taiwan province. In the case of unofficial estimates for China, it is not always clear if Taiwan is included or excluded. Where a Taiwan component is known, either it has been deducted from the all-China figure or its inclusion is noted.

AREA AND POPULATION

Area	Population				Density (per sq. km.)
	Census	Official Estimates (at December 31st)			
	June 30th, 1953	1979	1980	1981	1981
9,561,000 sq. km.*	582,603,417	970,920,000	982,550,000	996,220,000	104

* 3,691,500 sq. miles.

PROVINCES AND AUTONOMOUS REGIONS

(Previous spelling given in brackets)

	Area ('000 sq. km.)	Population (million) 1953 (census)	1968 (est.)*	1978 (est.)†	Capital of Province or Region	Estimated Population of Capital ('000), 1958
Provinces						
Sichuan (Szechwan)	569.0	66	70	97	Chengdu (Chengtu)	1,130
Shandong (Shantung)	153.3	49	56	71	Jinan (Tsinan)	880
Henan (Honan)	167.0	44	50	71	Zhengzhou (Chengchow)	780
Jiangsu (Kiangsu)	102.6	41	47	58	Nanjing (Nanking)	1,450
Hebei (Hopei)	202.7	39	47	58	Tianjin (Tientsin)	3,280
Guangdong (Kwangtung)	231.4	35	40	56	Guangzhou (Canton)	2,200
Hunan (Hunan)	210.5	33	38	52	Changsha (Changsha)	710
Anhui (Anhwei)	139.9	30	35	47	Hefei (Hofei)	360
Hubei (Hupeh)	187.5	28	32	46	Wuhan (Wuhan)	2,230
Zhejiang (Chekiang)	101.8	23	31	37	Hangzhou (Hangchow)	790
Liaoning (Liaoning)	151.0	24	28	37	Shenyang (Shenyang)	2,420
Yunnan (Yunnan)	436.2	17	23	31	Kunming (Kunming)	900
Jiangxi (Kiangsi)	164.8	17	22	32	Nanchang (Nanchang)	520
Shaanxi (Shensi)	195.8	16	21	28	Xian (Sian)	1,370
Heilongjiang (Heilungkiang)	463.6	12	21	34	Harbin (Harbin)	1,590
Shanxi (Shansi)	157.1	14	18	24	Taiyuan (Taiyuan)	1,050
Guizhou (Kweichow)	174.0	15	17	27	Guiyang (Kweiyang)	530
Fujian (Fukien)	123.1	13	17	24	Fuzhou (Foochow)	620
Jilin (Kirin)	187.0	11	17	25	Changchun (Changchun)	990
Gansu (Kansu)	366.5	11	13	19	Lanzhou (Lanchow)	730
Qinghai (Tsinghai)	721.0	2	2	4	Xining (Hsining)	150
Autonomous Regions						
Guangxi Zhuang (Kwangsi Chuang)	220.4	20	24	34	Nanning (Nanning)	260
Nei Monggol (Inner Mongolia)	1,177.5	6	13	9	Hohhot (Huhehot)	320
Xinjiang Uygur (Sinkiang Uighur)	1,646.9	5	8	12	Urumqi (Urumchi)	320
Ningxia Hui (Ninghsia Hui)	66.4	2	2	4	Yinchuan (Yinchuen)	90
Xizang (Tibet)	1,221.6	1	1	2	Lhasa (Lhasa)	50
Special Municipalities						
Beijing (Peking)	7.1	3	7	8	—	4,150
Shanghai (Shanghai)	5.8	6	11	11	—	6,980
Total	9,561.0	583	711	958		

* As announced during the "Great Proletarian Cultural Revolution" (1967–68).

† *Source:* Cartographical Publishing House, Beijing (as quoted by A. John Jowett in *China Quarterly* No. 81, 1980).

PRINCIPAL TOWNS

(Wade-Giles or other spellings in brackets)

POPULATION AT MID-1975
(UN estimates in '000)

Town	Population	Town	Population
Shanghai (Shang-hai)	12,382	Changsha (Chang-sha)	939
Beijing (Pei-ching or Peking, the capital)	9,335	Zhangjiakou (Chang-chia-k'ou or Kalgan)	938
Tianjin (T'ien-chin or Tientsin)	4,657	Zibo (Tzu-po or Tzepo)	927
Shenyang (Shen-yang or Mukden)	3,174	Hefei (Ho-fei)	899
Guangzhou (Kuang-chou or Canton)	3,016	Luoyang (Lo-yang)	887
Wuhan (Wu-han or Hankow)	2,932	Jinzhou (Chin-chou or Chinchow)	854
Chongqing (Ch'ung-ch'ing or Chungking)	2,692	Qiqihar (Ch'i-ch'i-ha-erh or Tsitsihar)	854
Lanzhou (Lan-chou or Lanchow)	2,072	Jilin (Chi-lin or Kirin)	845
Nanjing (Nan-ching or Nanking)	2,032	Suzhou (Su-chou or Soochow)	825
Xian (Hsi-an or Sian)	1,850	Nanchang (Nan-ch'ang)	808
Harbin (Ha-erh-pin)	1,836	Nanning (Nan-ning)	788
Luda (Lü-ta)	1,826	Guiyang (Kuei-yang or Kweiyang)	784
Taiyuan (T'ai-yüan)	1,612	Huainan (Huai-nan or Hwainan)	776
Qingdao (Ch'ing-tao or Tsingtao)	1,473	Xuzhou (Hsü-chou or Süchow)	758
Chengdu (Ch'eng-tu)	1,401	Fuzhou (Fu-chou or Foochow)	755
Changchun (Ch'ang-ch'un)	1,392	Wuxi (Wu-hsi or Wusih)	710
Jinan (Chi-nan or Tsinan)	1,294	Benxi (Pen-ch'i or Penki)	697
Kunming (K'un-ming)	1,284	Hohhot (Huhehot)	697
Zhengzhou (Cheng-chou or Chengchow)	1,271	Urumqi (Urumchi)	677
Anshan (An-shan)	1,247	Xining (Hsi-ning or Sining)	654
Fushun (F'u-shun)	1,196	Changzhou (Ch'ang-chou or Changchow)	631
Baotau (Pao-t'ou or Paotow)	1,135	Hantan (Han-tan)	615
Hangzhou (Hang-chou or Hangchow)	1,112	Kaifeng (K'ai-feng)	600
Tangshan (T'ang-shan)	1,086	Zigong (Tzu-kung or Tzekung)	600
Shijiazhuang (Shih-chia-chuang or Shihkiachwang)	960		

Source: UN Population Division, *Urban, Rural and City Population, 1950–2000, as Assessed in 1978* (Working Paper 66, June 1980).

Births and Deaths (1979): Birth rate 17.9 per 1,000; Death rate 6.2 per 1,000.

Life expectancy (years at birth): Males 61.8 in 1970–75, 66.0 in 1975–80; Females 64.6 in 1970–75, 68.6 in 1975–80 (UN estimates, including Taiwan).

AGRICULTURE

LAND USE

(FAO estimates, '000 hectares, including Taiwan)

	1973	1976	1979
Arable land	100,500	99,570	98,550
Land under permanent crops	700	730	760
Permanent meadows and pastures	220,000	220,000	220,000
Forests and woodland	111,400	113,600	115,700
Other land	497,896	496,596	495,486
Inland waters	29,200	29,200	29,200
TOTAL AREA*	959,696	959,696	959,696

* Comprising (in '000 hectares): Mainland China 956,100; Taiwan 3,596.

Source: FAO, *Production Yearbook.*

PRINCIPAL CROPS

(FAO estimates, unless otherwise indicated)

	Area Harvested ('000 hectares)			Production ('000 metric tons)		
	1978	1979	1980	1978	1979	1980
Wheat	26,500	29,360†	28,000	52,000	62,800†	54,155†
Rice (paddy)	33,000	33,870†	33,400	135,000	143,750†	139,255†
Barley	5,000	4,500	4,400	5,500	5,000	4,800
Maize	19,000	20,130†	20,000	53,000	60,000†	59,600
Rye	1,400	1,450	1,500	1,800	2,000	2,000
Oats	900	900	900	1,000	1,000	1,000
Millet	4,100	4,170†	4,100	5,900	6,000†	5,800
Sorghum	3,100	3,170†	3,200	7,500	8,000†	7,700
Other cereals	6,200	6,200	6,300	5,300	5,600	5,800
Potatoes	1,450	1,450	1,460	12,500	12,500	12,500
Sweet potatoes	10,800	10,600	10,500	87,500	87,500	86,000
Cassava (Manioc)	195	195	220	2,300	2,500	3,000
Other roots and tubers	96	98	100	1,270	1,260	1,250
Dry beans	4,000	4,100	4,100	3,500	3,600	3,300
Dry broad beans	5,300	5,400	5,500	5,400	5,500	5,200
Dry peas	4,300	4,500	4,400	4,500	4,700	4,300
Soybeans (Soyabeans)	8,500	9,300	9,600	9,000	10,000	10,000
Groundnuts (in shell)	2,300	2,400	2,900	2,400	2,822†	3,600†
Castor beans	190	190	200	98	115	120
Sunflower seed	320	356	600	279	375	625
Rapeseed	2,900	3,600	3,750	1,870	2,402†	2,384†
Sesame seed	950	1,000	800	320	417†	259†
Linseed	90	93	95	50	70	70
Flax fibre				65	70	75
Cottonseed	4,650	4,500	5,000	4,335	4,414	5,414
Cotton (lint)				2,167	2,207	2,707†
Vegetables and melons*	n.a.	n.a.	n.a.	75,269	77,687	79,596
Fruit (excl. melons)*	n.a.	n.a.	n.a.	7,408	8,103	8,335
Tree nuts*	n.a.	n.a.	n.a.	304	306	324
Sugar cane	300	310	320	21,117†	21,508†	22,807†
Sugar beet	110	130	230	2,702†	3,106†	6,305†
Tea (made)	665	670	700	268†	277†	304†
Tobacco (leaves)	725	730	700	1,000	970	900
Jute and jute substitutes	270	270	270	1,088†	1,089†	1,098†
Natural rubber	n.a.	n.a.	n.a.	95	108†	113†

* Including Taiwan. † Official estimate.

Source: mainly FAO, *Production Yearbook.*

1981 (official estimates, production in '000 metric tons): Wheat 58,490; Rice 143,205; Soybeans 9,245; Groundnuts 3,826; Rapeseed 4,065; Sesame seed 510; Cotton (lint) 2,968; Sugar cane 29,668; Sugar beet 6,360; Tea 343; Jute etc. 1,260; Natural rubber 128.

LIVESTOCK

(FAO estimates, '000 head, year ending September)

	1977/78	1978/79	1979/80
Horses	6,700	6,600	6,500
Mules*	1,520	1,510	1,500
Asses*	11,500	11,450	11,400
Cattle	63,750	63,890	64,600
Buffaloes	30,000	30,000	30,000
Camels	1,150	1,150	1,150
Pigs†	291,780	301,290	319,705
Sheep‡	90,360	94,940	102,880
Goats‡	71,000	75,000	80,262
Poultry	720,000	760,000	800,000

* Including Taiwan.

† Official estimate for December 31st within the 12-month period.

‡ Derived from official data for sheep and goats combined.

Other official estimates ('000 head at December 31st): Large animals (horses, mules, asses, cattle, camels) 93,750 in 1977, 93,890 in 1978, 94,591 (incl. cattle 71,346) in 1979, 95,246 in 1980, 97,641 in 1981; Pigs 305,431 in 1980, 293,702 in 1981; Sheep and goats 187,311 in 1980, 187,730 in 1981.

LIVESTOCK PRODUCTS

(FAO estimates, '000 metric tons)

	1978	1979	1980
Beef and veal*	1,623	1,668	1,683
Buffalo meat*	614	631	648
Mutton and lamb*	392	395	398
Goats' meat*	323	331	349
Pig meat*	14,566	15,580	16,486
Horse meat*	65	64	62
Poultry meat*	2,421	2,678	2,981
Other meat*	226	274	325
Edible offals*	1,042	1,073	1,091
Lard*	705	722	738
Tallow*	58	59	61
Cows' milk	4,750	5,200	5,350
Buffaloes' milk	1,290	1,340	1,390
Sheep's milk	477	483	489
Goats' milk	65	90	110
Butter*	94.3	99.2	102.2
Cheese*	156.8	163.0	167.2
Hen eggs	4,000	4,300	4,500
Other poultry eggs*	31.1	32.0	32.6
Honey*	247.3	256.5	264.5
Raw silk (incl. waste)	24.8	29.7†	35.4†
Wool: greasy	144.5	153.0	176.0†
clean	86.7	91.8	105.6
Cattle and buffalo hides*	379.4	390.0	395.2
Sheep skins*	73.1	73.6	74.2
Goat skins*	49.5	50.7	53.5

* Including Taiwan. † Official estimate.

Source: FAO, mainly *Production Yearbook*.

Other official estimates ('000 metric tons): Beef, mutton and pig meat 10,624 in 1979, 12,055 (beef 269, mutton 445, pig meat 11,341) in 1980, 12,609 (beef 249, mutton 476, pig meat 11,884) in 1981; Milk 1,141 in 1980, 1,291 in 1981; Raw silk 37.4 in 1981; Wool (greasy) 189 in 1981.

FORESTRY

ROUNDWOOD REMOVALS

(FAO estimates, '000 cubic metres, excluding bark)

	Coniferous (soft wood)			Broadleaved (hard wood)			Total		
	1978	1979	1980	1978	1979	1980	1978	1979	1980
Industrial wood	38,670	40,583	42,637	22,598	23,705	24,840	61,268	64,288	67,477
Fuel wood	60,170	61,370	62,600	90,304	92,073	93,882	150,474	153,443	156,482
Total	98,840	101,953	105,237	112,902	115,778	118,722	211,742	217,731	223,959

Source: FAO, *Yearbook of Forest Products.*

Timber production (official estimates, '000 cubic metres): 51,620 in 1978; 54,390 in 1979; 53,590 in 1980; 49,420 in 1981.

SAWNWOOD PRODUCTION

(FAO estimates, '000 cubic metres, including Taiwan)

	1975	1976	1977	1978	1979	1980
Coniferous sawnwood	10,442	10,973	11,532	12,090	12,676	13,292
Broadleaved sawnwood	6,150	6,450	6,765	7,096	7,443	7,807
	16,592	17,423	18,297	19,186	20,119	21,099
Railway sleepers	60	62	64	66	66	66
Total	16,652	17,485	18,361	19,252	20,185	21,165

Source: FAO, *Yearbook of Forest Products.*

FISHING

('000 metric tons, live weight)

	1975	1976	1977	1978	1979	1980
Fishes	3,482.9	3,509.7	3,518.2	3,396.0	3,120.9	3,281.6*
Crustaceans	442.7	433.8	477.8	544.0	484.8	499.0*
Molluscs	304.7	371.7	455.6	450.1	435.5	446.2*
Jellyfishes	17.1	5.1	11.7	3.5	13.0	13.2*
Total Catch	4,247.4	4,320.3	4,463.3	4,393.6	4,054.3	4,240.0
of which:						
Inland waters	1,065.0	1,056.5	1,076.1	1,058.7	1,115.9	1,240.0
Pacific Ocean	3,182.3	3,263.8	3,387.2	3,334.9	2,938.4	3,000.0

* FAO estimate.

Aquatic plants ('000 metric tons): 986.4 in 1975; 934.9 in 1976; 1,388.4 in 1977; 1,559.0 in 1978; 1,543.2 in 1979; 1,575.7 in 1980.

Source: FAO, *Yearbook of Fishery Statistics.*

Aquatic products ('000 metric tons): 4,660 in 1978; 4,305 in 1979; 4,497 in 1980; 4,605 in 1981.

MINING

(Unofficial estimates)

		1976	1977	1978	1979
Coal[1]	'000 metric tons	480,000	490,000*	n.a.*	n.a.*
Crude petroleum	" " "	85,000	100,000*	n.a.*	n.a.*
Iron ore[2]	" " "	22,500	25,000	31,500	33,700
Bauxite	" " "	1,000	1,200	1,400	1,500
Copper ore[2]	" " "	100	100	150	150
Lead ore[2]	" " "	100	100	120	120
Magnesite	" " "	1,000	1,000	1,000	n.a.
Manganese ore[2]	" " "	200	200	250	300
Zinc ore[2]	" " "	100	100	120	120
Salt (unrefined)	" " "	30,000	30,000	n.a.*	n.a.*
Phosphate rock	" " "	4,000	4,000	4,500	5,000
Potash[3]	" " "	150	150	150	150
Sulphur (native)	" " "	150	170	200	200
Asbestos	" " "	176	n.a.*	n.a.*	n.a.*
Iron pyrites (unroasted)	" " "	2,000	2,000	2,200	2,400
Natural graphite	" " "	50	60	80	100
Antimony ore[2]	metric tons	12,000	12,000	13,000	15,000
Mercury	" "	900	700	700	700
Molybdenum ore[2]	" "	1,500	1,500	2,000	2,000
Silver[2]	" "	31	31	47	62
Tin concentrates[2]	" "	20,000	18,000	18,000	17,000
Tungsten concentrates[2]	" "	12,300	12,300	13,700	13,700
Gold[2]	kilogrammes	2,488	3,110	4,666	6,221
Natural gas	million cu. metres	10,225	12,480	13,731	14,500

* Revised data are available in official estimates (*see* below).

[1] Including brown coal and lignite.

[2] Figures refer to the metal content of ores and concentrates.

[3] Potassium oxide (K_2O) content of potash salts mined in the 12 months ending June 30th of the year stated.

Sources: For tin, Metallgesellschaft Aktiengesellschaft (Frankfurt am Main, Federal Republic of Germany); for all other minerals, U.S. Bureau of Mines.

Official estimates ('000 metric tons): Coal 550,000 in 1977, 618,000 in 1978, 635,000 in 1979, 620,000 in 1980, 620,000 in 1981; Crude petroleum 93,640 in 1977, 104,050 in 1978, 106,150 in 1979, 105,590 in 1980, 101,220 in 1981; Salt 17,100 in 1977, 19,530 in 1978, 14,770 in 1979, 17,280 in 1980, 18,320 in 1981; Asbestos 139 in 1977, 143 in 1978, 141 in 1979; Natural gas (million cubic metres) 14,510 in 1979, 14,270 in 1980, 12,740 in 1981.

INDUSTRY

SELECTED PRODUCTS

UNOFFICIAL ESTIMATES

		1976	1977	1978	1979
Soyabean oil (crude)[1]	'000 metric tons	800	720	n.a.	n.a.
Cottonseed oil (crude)[1]	,, ,, ,,	520	n.a.	n.a.	n.a.
Groundnut oil (crude)[1]	,, ,, ,,	450	390	n.a.	n.a.
Palm oil (crude)[2]	,, ,, ,,	160	168	176	184
Tung oil[2]	,, ,, ,,	76	63	70	74
Raw sugar[3]	,, ,, ,,	1,750	1,950	2,250*	2,750*
Beer[4]	'000 hectolitres	1,750	n.a.	n.a.	n.a.
Rayon continuous filaments[5]	'000 metric tons	55.0	61.0	65.0	68.0
Rayon discontinuous fibres[5]	,, ,, ,,	70.0	77.0	80.0	85.0
Non-cellulosic continuous filaments[5]	,, ,, ,,	15.0	18.0	30.0	45.0
Non-cellulosic discontinuous fibres[5]	,, ,, ,,	37.0	42.0	106.6	128.0
Plywood[2, 6]	'000 cubic metres	1,170	1,167	1,527	1,539
Mechanical wood pulp[2, 6]	'000 metric tons	723	757	796	862
Chemical wood pulp[2, 6]	,, ,, ,,	1,054	1,151	1,233	1,319
Other fibre pulp[2, 6]	,, ,, ,,	3,440	3,695	3,919	4,214
Newsprint[2]	,, ,, ,,	1,140	1,187	1,252	1,348
Other paper and paperboard[2]	,, ,, ,,	4,862	5,023	5,250	5,563
Synthetic rubber[7]	,, ,, ,,	50	60	70	80
Sulphur[8, 9] (a)	,, ,, ,,	300	300	350	400
(b)	,, ,, ,,	1,000	1,000	1,100	1,200
Nitrogenous fertilizers (a)[2, 6, 10]	,, ,, ,,	3,172	3,842	4,600*	n.a.*
Phosphate fertilizers (b)[2, 6, 10]	,, ,, ,,	1,349	1,387	1,775*	n.a.*
Potash fertilizers (c)[2, 6, 10]	,, ,, ,,	240	270	310*	n.a.*
Motor spirit (petrol)[8]	,, ,, ,,	9,340	10,300	10,800	11,000
Kerosene[8]	,, ,, ,,	13,340	14,680	16,440	17,000
Distillate fuel oils[8]	,, ,, ,,	19,340	21,820	23,120	24,000
Residual fuel oil[8]	,, ,, ,,	24,700	28,700	30,250	31,000
Coke-oven coke[8, 11]	,, ,, ,,	28,000	29,000	34,000	35,000
Cement[8]	,, ,, ,,	35,000	40,000	n.a.*	n.a.*
Pig-iron[8]	,, ,, ,,	30,000	30,000	n.a.*	n.a.*
Crude steel[8]	,, ,, ,,	27,000	27,000	n.a.*	n.a.*
Aluminium (unwrought)[8]	,, ,, ,,	200	250	300	330
Refined copper (unwrought)[8]	,, ,, ,,	100	100	150	150
Lead (unwrought)[8]	,, ,, ,,	100	110	150	150
Tin (unwrought)[12]	,, ,, ,,	19	18	18	17
Zinc (unwrought)[8]	,, ,, ,,	100	100	120	120
Electric energy[4]	million kWh.	203,500	n.a.	n.a.*	n.a.*

* Revised data are available in official estimates (*see* next table).

[1] *Source:* U.S. Department of Agriculture.

[2] *Source:* FAO.

[3] *Source:* International Sugar Organization.

[4] *Source:* UN, *Yearbook of Industrial Statistics.*

[5] *Source:* Textile Economics Bureau Inc., New York, U.S.A.

[6] Including Taiwan.

[7] *Source:* International Rubber Study Group.

[8] *Source:* U.S. Bureau of Mines.

[9] Figures refer to (a) sulphur recovered as a by-product in the purification of coal-gas, in petroleum refineries, gas plants and from copper, lead and zinc sulphide ores; and (b) the sulphur content of iron and copper pyrites, including pyrite concentrates obtained from copper, lead and zinc ores.

[10] Twelve months ending June 30th of the year stated. Figures refer to (a) nitrogen; (b) phosphoric acid (P_2O_5); and (c) potassium oxide (K_2O).

[11] Excluding breeze.

[12] *Source:* Metallgesellschaft Aktiengesellschaft, Frankfurt am Main, Federal Republic of Germany.

1980 ('000 metric tons): Palm oil 190; Tung oil 77; Plywood ('000 cubic metres) 1,563; Mechanical wood pulp 934; Chemical wood pulp 1,412; Other fibre pulp 4,534; Newsprint 1,435; Other paper and paperboard 5,929; Synthetic rubber 90.

1981 ('000 metric tons): Palm oil 190; Tung oil 80.

OFFICIAL ESTIMATES

		1978	1979	1980	1981
Raw sugar	'000 metric tons	2,267	2,500	2,570	3,166
Cotton yarn	,, ,, ,,	2,382	2,630	2,930	3,170
Woven cotton fabrics	million metres	11,029	12,150	13,470	14,270
Woollen fabrics	'000 metres	88,850	90,170	101,000	113,000
Silk fabrics	,, ,,	610,350	663,450	759,000	835,000
Chemical fibres	'000 metric tons	284.6	326.0	450	527
Paper and paperboard	,, ,, ,,	4,390	4,930	5,350	5,400
Rubber tyres	'000	9,360	11,690	11,460	7,290
Ethylene (Ethene)	'000 metric tons	380.3	435.0	490.0	500.0
Sulphuric acid	,, ,, ,,	6,610	7,000	7,640	7,810
Caustic soda (Sodium hydroxide)	,, ,, ,,	1,640	1,826	1,923	1,923
Soda ash (Sodium carbonate)	,, ,, ,,	1,329	1,486	1,613	1,652
Insecticides	,, ,, ,,	533	537	537	484
Nitrogenous fertilizers (a)*	,, ,, ,,	7,639	8,821	9,990	9,860
Phosphate fertilizers (b)*	,, ,, ,,	1,033	1,817	2,310	2,510
Potash fertilizers (c)*	,, ,, ,,	21	16	20	20
Plastics	,, ,, ,,	679	793	898	916
Coke (machine-made)	,, ,, ,,	n.a.	33,540	34,050	31,720
Cement	,, ,, ,,	65,240	73,900	79,860	84,000
Pig-iron	,, ,, ,,	34,790	36,730	38,020	34,170
Crude steel	,, ,, ,,	31,780	34,480	37,120	35,600
Internal combustion engines†	'000 horse-power	28,180	29,080	25,290	20,040
Tractors (over 10 horse-power)	'000	113.5	125.6	98.0	53.0
Sewing machines	,,	4,865	5,870	7,680	10,390
Railway locomotives (diesel)	number	521	573	512	398
Railway freight wagons	,,	16,950	16,042	10,571	8,779
Road motor vehicles	'000	149.1	186.0	222.0	176.0
Bicycles	,,	8,540	10,090	13,020	17,540
Wrist watches	,,	13,510	17,070	22,160	28,720
Radio receivers‡	,,	11,677	13,807	30,040	40,570
Television receivers	,,	517	1,329	2,492	5,394
Cameras	,,	179	238	373	623
Electric energy	million kWh.	256,550	281,950	300,600	309,300

* Production in terms of (a) nitrogen; (b) phosphoric acid; or (c) potassium oxide.

† Sales.

‡ Portable battery sets only.

FINANCE

Renminbi (RMB or "People's Currency"):
100 fen (cents) = 10 jiao (chiao) = 1 Renminbiao (People's Bank Dollar), usually called a yuan.

Coins: 1, 2 and 5 fen.
Notes: 10, 20 and 50 fen; 1, 2, 5 and 10 yuan.

Exchange rates (June 1982): £1 sterling = 3.365 yuan; U.S. $1 = 1.943 yuan.
100 yuan = £29.72 = $51.47.

Note: The new yuan, equal to 10,000 old yuan, was introduced in March 1955. The initial exchange rate was U.S. $1 = 2.4618 new yuan (1 yuan = 40.62 U.S. cents) and this remained in effect until August 1971. The market rate was $1 = 2.2673 yuan from January to June 1972; $1 = 2.2174 yuan from July to October 1972; and $1 = 2.2401 yuan from November 1972 to January 1973. Since February 1973 the rate against the dollar has been frequently adjusted. The average exchange rate (yuan per dollar) was: 1.9612 in 1974; 1.8598 in 1975; 1.9414 in 1976; 1.8578 in 1977; 1.6836 in 1978; 1.5550 in 1979; 1.4984 in 1980; 1.7050 in 1981. In terms of sterling, the exchange rate between November 1967 and June 1972 was £1 = 5.908 yuan.

BUDGET ESTIMATES*

(million yuan)

Revenue	1980	1981	1982	Expenditure	1980	1981	1982
Industrial and commercial taxes	106,290	115,460	64,600	Capital construction	37,350	37,580	29,730
Income from state-owned industrial enterprises			34,410	Agriculture	7,740	8,800	7,610
Other receipts			11,440	Culture, education, health and science	14,830	16,950	18,000
				Defence	19,330	20,170	17,870
Total	106,290	115,460	110,450	Total (incl. others)	114,290	120,460	113,450

* Figures represent a consolidation of the budgets of the central government, provinces, counties and municipal governments. Actual results (in million yuan) were: Revenue 108,520 in 1980, 106,430 in 1981; Expenditure 121,270 in 1980, 108,970 in 1981.

INTERNATIONAL RESERVES

(U.S. $ million at December 31st)

	1978	1979	1980	1981
Gold*	584	590	571	516
IMF Special Drawing Rights		—	92	275
Reserve position in IMF	—	—	191	—
Foreign exchange	1,557	2,154	2,262	4,773
Total	2,141	2,744	3,116	5,564

* Valued at 35 SDRs per troy ounce.

Source: IMF, *International Financial Statistics.*

MONEY SUPPLY

(million yuan at December 31st)

	1978	1979	1980	1981
Total money	58,040	73,660	91,930	109,780
of which: Currency in circulation	21,200	26,770	34,620	39,630

Source: IMF, *International Financial Statistics.*

COST OF LIVING INDEX

(base: 1975 = 100)

	1976	1977	1978	1979	1980
All items	100.3	103.0	103.7	105.7	113.6

NATIONAL ACCOUNTS

(million yuan at current prices)

	1978	1979	1980	1981
Net material product*	301,000	335,000	366,000	388,000

* Defined as the total net value of goods and "productive" services, including turnover taxes, produced by the economy. This excludes economic activities not contributing directly to material production, such as public administration, defence and personal and professional services.

EXTERNAL TRADE

(million yuan)

	1977	1978	1979	1980	1981
Imports f.o.b.	13,280	18,740	24,390	29,880	36,770
Exports f.o.b.*	13,970	16,760	21,170	27,120	36,760

* Excluding exports of complete plant in the form of foreign aid.

COMMODITIES

(per cent)

Imports	1978
Food	17
Fuels	0
Other primary commodities	43
Machinery and transport equipment	18
Other manufactures	22
Total	100

Exports	1978
Fuels, minerals and metals	13
Other primary commodities	38
Textiles and clothing	24
Machinery and transport equipment	3
Other manufactures	22
Total	100

Source: World Bank, *World Development Report* 1981.

PRINCIPAL TRADING PARTNERS

(U.S. $ million—based on partner-country statistics)

Imports	1975	1976	1977	1978*	1979*
Australia	359	291	507	531	750
Canada	407	220	381	486	858
France	410	390	105	219	373
Germany, Federal Republic	575	685	552	1,095	1,642
Hong Kong	37	33	49	69	385
Italy	159	140	98	207	285
Japan	2,484	1,832	2,150	3,381	4,048
Malaysia and Singapore	102	92	197	185	365
Pakistan	15	19	16	68	100
Romania	242	274	263	289	530
Sri Lanka	72	63	52	34	70
U.S.S.R.	130	240	160	241	255
United Kingdom	196	138	120	193	510
U.S.A.	334	149	188	906	1,896

Exports	1975	1976	1977	1978*	1979*
Australia	86	100	124	140	166
Canada	55	90	78	53	143
France	158	177	176	205	297
Germany, Federal Republic	204	246	261	333	485
Hong Kong	1,247	1,448	1,578	2,045	2,985
Italy	117	141	148	182	310
Japan	1,390	1,248	1,418	1,859	2,664
Malaysia and Singapore	396	365	377	511	580
Pakistan	49	58	58	64	90
Romania	215	202	273	400	560
Sri Lanka	85	6	28	16	60
U.S.S.R.	150	180	177	257	229
United Kingdom	120	142	166	194	294
U.S.A.	158	200	203	324	594

* Preliminary.

Sources: IMF, *Direction of Trade*, and Soviet trade statistics.

TRANSPORT

	1978	1979	1980	1981
Freight (million ton-km.). .				
Railways . . .	533,300	558,800	571,700	571,200
Roads	n.a.	74,500	76,400	78,000
Inland waterways . .	377,900	456,400	505,300	515,000
Air	97	123	141	170
Passenger-km. (million):				
Railways . . .	109,100	121,400	138,300	147,300
Roads	52,100	60,300	72,900	83,900
Inland waterways . .	10,100	11,400	12,900	13,800
Air	2,800	3,500	4,000	5,000

SEA-BORNE SHIPPING

(freight traffic in '000 metric tons)

	1978	1979	1980	1981
Goods loaded and unloaded .	200,000	212,570	217,310	219,310

COMMUNICATIONS MEDIA

		1980	1981
Newspapers . .	million copies	14,040	14,070
Magazines	,, ,,	1,120	1,460
Books . . .	,, ,,	4,590	5,580

Television receivers: 500,000 in 1973.

EDUCATION

('000 pupils)

	1979	1980	1981
Pre-primary . . .	8,790	11,508	10,562
Primary	146,630	146,270	143,330
Middle	59,050	55,535	48,596
Secondary technical .	1,199	1,243	1,069
Higher	1,020	1,144	1,280

Source: (unless otherwise indicated): State Statistical Bureau, Beijing.

DRAFT OF THE REVISED CONSTITUTION

(April 21st, 1982)

The Preamble, which is not included here, states that "Taiwan is part of the sacred territory of the People's Republic of China"

Chapter 1
General Principles

Article 1: The People's Republic of China is a socialist state of the people's democratic dictatorship led by the working class and based on the alliance of workers and peasants.

The socialist system is the basic system of the People's Republic of China. Disruption of the socialist system by any individual and in any form is prohibited.

Article 2: All power in the People's Republic of China belongs to the people.

The organs through which the people exercise state power are the National People's Congress and the local people's congresses at various levels.

The people have the right to administer the affairs of the country and its economic, cultural and social affairs, according to provisions of the law, through various channels and in various forms.

Article 3: The state institutions of the People's Republic of China apply the principle of democratic centralism.

The National People's Congress and the local people's congresses at various levels are elected democratically, responsible to the people and subject to their supervision.

All organs of state administration and all judicial and procuratorial organs are originated by the organs of state power to which they are responsible and to whose supervision they are subject.

The division of functions and powers between the central and local state institutions shall conform to the principle of giving full play to the initiative and enthusiasm of the local authorities under the unified leadership of the central authorities.

Article 4: All nationalities in the People's Republic of China are equal. The state protects the lawful rights and interests of the various minority nationalities and upholds and develops the relationship of equality, unity and mutual assistance among all the nationalities of China. Discrimination or oppression with regard to any of the nationalities, and acts which undermine the unity between them are prohibited; big-nationality chauvinism and local-nationality chauvinism must be opposed.

Regional autonomy applies to any area where a minority nationality lives in a compact community; in each such area an organ of self-government shall be established for the exercise of national autonomy. All the national autonomous areas are inalienable parts of the People's Republic of China.

All nationalities have the freedom to use and develop their own spoken and written languages and to preserve or reform their own customs and ways.

Article 5: The state upholds the uniformity and dignity of the socialist legal system.

No laws, decrees or statutes shall contradict the Constitution.

All organs of state and people's armed forces, all political parties and public organizations and all enterprises and institutions must abide by the Constitution and the law. No organization or individual shall enjoy privileges that transcend the Constitution and the law.

Article 6: The basis of the socialist economic system of the People's Republic of China is socialist public ownership of the means of production, that is, ownership by the whole people, and collective ownership by working people. The socialist economic system has abolished the system of exploitation of man by man; it applies the principle "from each according to his ability, to each according to his work".

Article 7: The state sector of the economy, that is, the socialist sector owned by the whole people, is the dominant force in the national economy. The state ensures the consolidation and development of the state sector of the economy.

Article 8: Mineral resources, waters, forests, mountainous lands, grasslands, undeveloped lands, beaches and other natural resources, sea and land, are owned by the state, that is, by the whole people, with the exception of forests, mountainous lands, grasslands, undeveloped lands and beaches which are owned by the collectives according to provisions of the law.

Article 9: Rural people's communes, agricultural producers' co-operatives and other forms of the co-operative economy constitute a socialist sector of the economy collectively owned by the working people. Working people who are members of organizations of the rural collective economy have the right, within limits prescribed by law, to farm plots of agricultural and hilly land, engage in household sideline production and keep livestock for their own needs.

The various forms of the co-operative economy in the cities and towns, such as those in the handicraft, industrial, building, transport, commercial and service trades, also constitute a socialist sector of the economy collectively owned by the working people.

The state protects the lawful rights and interests of collective economic units both urban and rural; the state encourages, guides and helps the development of the collective economy.

Article 10: Land in the cities is the property of the state. Land in villages, towns and the suburban areas is the property of the collective except for the portion which belongs to the state according to provisions of the law; land used for building houses and the plots of agricultural and hilly land farmed for personal needs are also the property of the collectives.

The state may take over land for its use, as required by the public interest, according to provisions of the law.

No organization or individual shall seize, buy, sell or lease land.

Article 11: The individual economy of the urban and rural working people, within limits prescribed by law, is a complement to the socialist sector of the economy owned by the public. The state protects the lawful rights and interests of the individual economy.

The state guides, helps and supervises the individual economy by means of administrative measures and through the economic links of the state and collective economy with the individual economy.

Article 12: The People's Republic of China permits foreign enterprises, other foreign economic organizations or foreign individuals to invest in China or to undertake various forms of economic co-operation with Chinese enterprises or other Chinese economic organizations; all such investments or joint undertakings in China must accord with provisions of the laws of the People's Republic of China.

All foreign enterprises and other foreign economic organizations in China, as well as joint ventures with Chinese and foreign investment located in China, must abide by the laws of the People's Republic of China. Their lawful rights and interests are protected by laws of the People's Republic of China.

Article 13: Socialist public property shall be sacred and inviolable.

The state protects socialist public property, ensures the rational use of the land, forests, waters and other natural resources and protects rare animals and plants.

All organizations and individuals are prohibited from seizing or damaging, by any means, any state and collective property or any mineral resources, waters, forests, grasslands and other natural resources, sea and land.

Article 14: The state protects the right of citizens to own lawfully earned income, savings, houses and other lawful property.

Article 15: The state protects, according to provisions of the law, the right of citizens to inherit private property.

Article 16: The state continually raises labour productivity, increases economic effectiveness and develops the social productive forces by enhancing the political consciousness of the working people, increasing their cultural, scientific and technical knowledge, perfecting systems of economic management and enterprise management, applying various forms of socialist responsibility system for production and other work, practising strict economy and checking waste.

The state makes appropriate arrangements with regard to accumulation and consumption, takes into account the interests of the state, the collective and the individual and, on the basis of the development of production, gradually improves the material and cultural life of the people and enhances national defence capabilities.

Article 17: The state plans the national economy on the basis of socialist public ownership. It ensures the proportionate and co-ordinated development of the national economy through the comprehensive balancing of economic plans, with market regulation as a subsidiary.

All organizations and individuals are prohibited from disrupting, by any means whatsoever, the orderly functioning of the social economy or of the economic plans of the state.

Article 18: The state enterprises enjoy powers of decision in management, within the limits specified by law, on condition that they submit to the unified leadership of the state and comprehensively fulfil their obligations under the state plans.

Workers and staff members of the state enterprise participate in the management of their respective enterprises through the congresses of workers and staff members and other channels, in accordance with provisions of the law.

Article 19: Units of the collective economy have powers of decision in conducting independent economic activities, on condition that they accept the guidance of the state plans and abide by the relevant laws.

Units of the collective economy practise democratic management according to provisions of the law; their managerial personnel shall be elected and removed and decisions on major issues concerning enterprise management shall be taken by the entire body of their workers and staff members.

Article 20: The state promotes the planned, socialist development of education, science, public health and sports, culture and art, publishing and distribution of publications, and of the press, television and broadcasting, libraries, museums and cultural centres and other cultural undertakings.

The state operates, and encourages non-governmental bodies to operate, various types of schools in order to wipe out illiteracy, universalize primary education and develop secondary, vocational and higher education.

The state increases various types of cultural and educational facilities and promotes political, cultural, scientific, technical and professional education among the workers, peasants and other working people.

The state promotes the spoken Han language in wide use throughout the country to facilitate the development of the cultural and educational work.

Article 21: The state, in a planned way, trains intellectuals who serve socialism, increases their number and gives full scope to their role in socialist modernization.

Article 22: The state promotes the virtues of love for the motherland, the people, labour, science and socialism; it educates the people in the ideas and ethics of patriotism, collectivism, internationalism and communism; and it opposes the influence of capitalist ideas, the remaining feudal ideas and other decadent ideology.

Article 23: The state advocates and encourages family planning so that population growth can conform to the plans of economic and social development in various fields.

Article 24: The state protects the environment and the ecological balance; and it organizes and encourages afforestation, and prevents and eliminates pollution and other hazards to public health.

Article 25: The state protects places of scenic or historical interest, valuable cultural relics and other important items of the historical and cultural legacies.

Article 26: All organs of state must strictly carry out the system of responsibility for work, constantly improve their functioning, raise efficiency and combat bureaucratism.

All state organs and personnel must rely on the support of the people, constantly keep in close touch with them, heed their opinions and suggestions, accept their supervision and strive to serve them.

Article 27: The state safeguards public order and suppresses treasonable and counter-revolutionary activities; the state penalizes actions that endanger public security, actions that wreck the socialist economy and other criminal activities; and the state punishes and reforms criminal offenders.

Article 28: The armed forces of the People's Republic of China belong to the people. Their tasks are to consolidate the national defence, resist aggression, defend the motherland, safeguard the people's peaceful labour, participate in national construction, and work in the interests of the people at all times and in all places.

The state steps up the revolutionization, modernization and regularization of the armed forces.

Article 29: The administrative divisions of the People's Republic of China are as follows:

1. The country is divided into provinces, autonomous regions, and municipalities directly under the Central Government;

2. Provinces and autonomous regions are divided into autonomous prefectures, counties, autonomous counties, and cities;

3. Counties and autonomous counties are divided into townships, nationality townships, and towns.

Municipalities directly under the Central Government, and other large cities are divided into districts and counties. Autonomous prefectures are divided into counties, autonomous counties, and cities.

Autonomous regions, autonomous prefectures and autonomous counties are all national autonomous areas.

Article 30: The state may, where necessary, establish special administrative regions. The rules and regulations in force in special administrative regions shall be stipulated by law according to specific conditons.

Article 31: The People's Republic of China grants the right of residence to any foreign national persecuted for striving for human progress, for defending the cause of peace or for engaging in scientific work.

Chapter 2
The Fundamental Rights and Duties of Citizens

Article 32: All citizens of the People's Republic of China are equal before the law.

The rights of citizens are inseparable from their duties. Every citizen enjoys the rights prescribed by the Constitution and the law and at the same time has the duty to abide by the Constitution and the law.

Article 33: Citizens of the People's Republic of China who have reached the age of 18, with the exception of persons deprived of political rights by law, have the right to vote and stand for election irrespective of their nationality, race, sex, occupation, family origin, religious belief, education, property status, or length of residence.

Article 34: Citizens of the People's Republic of China enjoy freedom of speech, the press, assembly, association, procession and demonstration.

Article 35: Citizens of the People's Republic of China enjoy freedom of religious belief.

No organs of state, public organizations or individuals shall compel citizens to believe in religion or disbelieve in religion, nor shall they discriminate against citizens who believe, or do not believe, in religion.

The state protects legitimate religious activities. No one may use religion to carry out counter-revolutionary activities or activities that disrupt public order, harm the health of citizens or obstruct the educational system of the state.

No religious affairs may be dominated by any foreign country.

Article 36: The freedom of person of citizens of the People's Republic of China is inviolable.

No citizen may be arrested except with the sanction of a people's procuratorate or by decision of a people's court, and arrests must be made by a public security organ.

Extra-legal detention of citizens, or extra-legal deprivation or restriction of citizens' freedom of person by other means, is prohibited; and extra-legal search of the person of citizens is prohibited.

Article 37: The personal dignity of citizens of the People's Republic of China is inviolable. Insult or slander against citizens in any form is prohibited.

Article 38: The homes of citizens of the People's Republic of China are inviolable. Searches of, or intrusions into, citizens' domiciles, in contravention of law, are prohibited.

Article 39: The freedom and privacy of correspondence of citizens of the People's Republic of China are protected by law. No organization or individual shall, for any reason, infringe upon citizens' freedom and privacy of correspondence other than in cases where, to meet the needs of state security or of investigation into criminal offences, public security or procuratorial organs are permitted to censor correspondence in accordance with procedures prescribed by law.

Article 40: Citizens of the People's Republic of China have the right to make criticisms of and proposals to any organ of state or any functionary therein; citizens have the right to appeal, complain or report to relevant organs of state against transgression of law or neglect of duty by any organ of state or any functionary therein; but no one is permitted to make deliberately false charges through fabrication or distortion of fact.

The organs of state concerned must handle appeals, complaints or reports submitted to them, by investigating the facts. No one shall suppress such appeals, complaints or reports or retaliate against citizens making them.

People suffering loss through infringement of their rights as citizens by organs of state or functionaries therein have the right to compensation according to provisions of the law.

Article 41: Citizens of the People's Republic of China have the right and obligation to work.

The state creates conditions for employment through various channels and, on the basis of increased production, gradually improves working conditions, strengthens labour protection and raises remuneration for work.

Work is a glorious duty of every able-bodied citizen. Workers in the state enterprises and in units of the collective economy, urban or rural, should preform their tasks with the attitude of masters of the country. The state promotes socialist labour emulation, commends model and advanced workers, and protects and rewards inventions. The state encourages citizens to take part in voluntary labour.

The state provides necessary vocational training to citizens who have not yet been assigned work.

Article 42: Working people in the People's Republic of China have the right to rest.

The state expands facilities for rest and recuperation by the working people, and prescribes working hours and regulations concerning vacations for workers and staff members.

Article 43: Citizens of the People's Republic of China have the right to material assistance from the state and society in old age, illness or disability. To ensure that citizens can enjoy this right, the state expands social insurance, social assistance and public health services.

The state applies the system of retirement for workers and staff members.

The state ensures the livelihood of disabled members of the armed forces, provides allowances to the families of revolutionary martyrs and gives preferential treatment to the families of military personnel.

The state helps arrange for the livelihood of the blind, deaf-mutes and other handicapped persons and provides them with special education.

Article 44: Citizens of the People's Republic of China have the right and obligation to receive education.

The state promotes the all-round development—moral, intellectual and physical—of young people and children.

Article 45: Citizens of the People's Republic of China have the freedom to engage in scientific research, literary and artistic creation and other cultural pursuits. The state encourages and assists creative endeavours, conducive to the interests of the people and human progress, by citizens engaged in education, science, technology, literature, art and other cultural work.

Article 46: Women in the People's Republic of China enjoy equal rights with men in all spheres of political, economic, cultural, social and family life. Men and women shall receive equal pay for equal work.

The state protects marriage, the family and the mother and child. Children have the duty to support their parents. Violations of the freedom of marriage are prohibited. Maltreatment of old people, women and children is prohibited.

Article 47: The People's Republic of China protects the legitimate rights and interests of Chinese residents abroad and protects the lawful rights and interests of returned overseas Chinese and the relatives of Chinese residents abroad living in China.

Article 48: When exercising their freedoms and rights, citizens of the People's Republic of China must not infringe upon the interests of the state, of society and of the collective, or upon the lawful freedoms and rights of other citizens.

Article 49: Citizens of the People's Republic of China are duty-bound to safeguard the unity of the country and the unity of all its nationalities.

Article 50: Citizens of the People's Republic of China must safeguard state secrets, take care of public property, observe labour discipline, observe public order and respect social ethics and beneficial customs and habits.

Article 51: Citizens of the People's Republic of China are duty-bound to safeguard the security, honour and interests of the motherland; acts damaging to the security, honour and interests of the motherland are prohibited.

Article 52: It is the sacred duty of every citizen of the People's Republic of China to defend the motherland and resist aggression.

It is the honourable obligation of citizens of the People's Republic of China to perform military service and to join the militia according to the law.

Article 53: Citizens of the People's Republic of China are duty-bound to pay taxes according to the law.

Chapter 3

The Structure of the State

SECTION I

THE NATIONAL PEOPLE'S CONGRESS

Article 54: The National People's Congress of the People's Republic of China is the highest organ of state power. Its permanent organ is the Standing Committee of the National People's Congress.

Article 55: The National People's Congress and its Standing Committee exercise legislative authority in the country and enact laws and decrees.

Except for laws, all the decisions and resolutions adopted by the National People's Congress and its Standing Committee are called decrees, with the same binding force as laws.

Article 56: The National People's Congress is composed of deputies elected by the provinces, autonomous regions and municipalities directly under the Central Government, and by the armed forces. All the minority nationalities are entitled to appropriate representation.

Elections of deputies to the National People's Congress are conducted by its Standing Committee.

The number of deputies to the National People's Congress and the manner of their election are prescribed by electoral law.

Article 57: The National People's Congress is elected for a term of five years.

Two months before the term of office of a National People's Congress expires, its Standing Committee must ensure that the election of deputies to the succeeding National People's Congress is completed. Should exceptional circumstances prevent such an election, the term of office of the sitting National People's Congress may be prolonged until the first session of the succeeding National People's Congress; such prolongation must be approved by a majority vote of more than two-thirds of all the members of its Standing Committee.

Article 58: Sessions of the National People's Congress meet once a year and are convened by its Standing Committee. Extraordinary sessions may be convened when the Standing Committee deems this necessary or when more than one-fifth of the deputies so propose.

Article 59: When the National People's Congress meets, it elects a presidium to conduct its session.

Article 60: The National People's Congress exercises the following functions and powers:

1. to amend the Constitution;
2. to make and amend basic laws concerning criminal offences, civil affairs, the structure of the state and other matters;
3. to elect the Chairman and the Vice-Chairman of the People's Republic of China;
4. to decide on the choice of the Premier of the State Council upon the recommendation of the Chairman of the People's Republic of China, and to decide on the choice of the Vice-Premiers, Commissioners of State, Ministers, Chairmen of Commissions, Chief Auditor and Secretary-General of the State Council upon the recommendation of the Premier;
5. to elect the Chairman of the Central Military Commission and, upon his recommendation, to decide on the choice of other members of the Central Military Commission;
6. to elect the President of the Supreme People's Court;
7. to elect the Chief Procurator of the Supreme People's Procuratorate;
8. to examine and approve plans of national economic and social development and the reports on their implementation;
9. to examine and approve the state budget and the report on its implementation;
10. to approve the establishment of provinces, autonomous regions, and municipalities directly under the Central Government;
11. to decide on the establishment of special administrative regions and their rules and regulations;
12. to decide on questions of war and peace; and
13. to exercise other functions and powers that shall be exercised by the highest organ of state power.

Article 61: The National People's Congress has the power to recall or remove from office the following persons:

1. the Chairman and the Vice-Chairman of the People's Republic of China;
2. the Premier, Vice-Premiers, Commissioners of State, Ministers, Chairmen of Commissions, Chief Auditor and Secretary-General of the State Council;

3. the Chairman and other members of the Central Military Commission;

4. the President of the Supreme People's Court; and

5. the Chief Procurator of the Supreme People's Procuratorate.

Article 62: Amendments to the Constitution should be proposed by the Standing Committee of the National People's Congress or by more than one-fifth of the deputies to the National People's Congress; such amendments require, for their adoption, a majority vote of more than two-thirds of all the deputies to the National People's Congress.

Laws, decrees and other bills require, for their adoption, a simple majority vote of all the deputies to the National People's Congress.

Article 63: The Standing Committee of the National People's Congress is composed of the following members: the Chairman; the Vice-Chairmen; the Secretary-General; and other members.

Minority nationalities are entitled to appropriate representation on the Standing Committee of the National People's Congress.

The National People's Congress elects, and has the power to recall, members of its Standing Committee.

Members of the Standing Committee of the National People's Congress shall not hold posts in organs of state administration and the judicial and procuratorial organs.

Article 64: The Standing Committee of the National People's Congress is elected for the same term as the National People's Congress; it exercises its functions and powers until a new Standing Committee is elected by the succeeding National People's Congress.

The Chairman and Vice-Chairmen of the Standing Committee may be re-elected but shall not serve more than two consecutive terms.

Article 65: The Standing Committee of the National People's Congress exercise the following functions and powers:

1. to interpret the Constitution and supervise its enforcement;

2. to enact and amend laws with the exception of those to be enacted by the National People's Congress;

3. to partially amend and supplement the basic laws enacted by the National People's Congress when the latter is not in session;

4. to interpret laws and decrees;

5. to examine and approve, when the National People's Congress is not in session, partial adjustments that are deemed necessary to plans of national economic and social development and to the state budget, in the course of their implementation;

6. to supervise the work of the State Council, the Central Military Commission, the Supreme People's Court and the Supreme People's Procuratorate;

7. to annul administrative statutes, decisions and orders of the State Council which contravene the Constitution, laws or decrees;

8. to annul local statutes and decisions of the organs of state power of provinces, autonomous regions and municipalities directly under the Central Government which contravene the Constitution, laws, decrees or general administrative statutes;

9. to decide on the appointment and removal of Ministers, Chairmen of Commissions, the Chief Auditor and the Secretary-General of the State Council upon the recommendation of the Premier of the State Council when the National People's Congress is not in session;

10. to decide on the appointment and removal of members of the Central Military Commission other than its Chairman, upon the recommendation of the latter, at times when the National People's Congress is not in session;

11. to appoint and remove the Vice-Presidents, judges and members of the Judicial Committee of the Supreme People's Court upon the request of the President of the Supreme People's Court;

12. to appoint and remove the Deputy Chief Procurators, procurators and members of the Procuratorial Committee of the Supreme People's Procuratorate upon the request of the Chief Procurator of the Supreme People's Procuratorate, and to approve the appointment and removal of the chief procurators of the people's procuratorates of provinces, autonomous regions and municipalities directly under the Central Government;

13. to appoint and remove Deputy Chief Auditors and auditors upon the request of the Chief Auditor, and to approve the appointment and removal of the chief auditors of provinces, autonomous regions and municipalities directly under the Central Government;

14. to decide on the appointment and recall of plenipotentiary representatives stationed abroad;

15. to decide on the ratification or abrogation of treaties and important agreements concluded with foreign states;

16. to institute military, diplomatic and other special titles and ranks;

17. to institute state orders, medals and titles of honour and decide on their conferment;

18. to decide on the granting of special pardons;

19. to decide, when the National People's Congress is not in session, on the proclamation of a state of war in the event of armed attack on the country or in fulfilment of international treaty obligations concerning common defence against aggression;

20. to decide on general mobilization throughout the country, or partial mobilization;

21. to decide on the enforcement of martial law throughout the country or in particular provinces, autonomous regions or municipalities directly under the Central Government; and

22. to exercise such other functions and powers as are vested in it by the National People's Congress.

Article 66: The Chairman of the Standing Committee of the National People's Congress presides over the work of the Standing Committee and convenes its sessions. The Vice-Chairmen and the Secretary-General assist the Chairman in his work.

The Chairman, Vice-Chairmen and Secretary-General of the Standing Committee of the National People's Congress are the participants in the Chairmanship Conference to attend to its important routine work.

Article 67: The chairman or a vice-chairman of the standing committee of the people's congress of each province, autonomous region and municipality directly under the Central Government attends the sessions of the Standing Committee of the National People's Congress.

Article 68: The Standing Committee of the National People's Congress is responsible and accountable to the National People's Congress.

Article 69: The National People's Congress has a Nationalities Committee, a Law Committee, a Financial and Economic Affairs Committee, an Education and Science Committee, a Foreign Affairs Committee and other necessary special committees. These special committees work under the direction of the Standing Committee of the National People's Congress when the National People's Congress is not in session.

The special committees examine, discuss and draw up relevant bills under the direction of the National People's Congress and its Standing Committee.

Article 70: The National People's Congress and its Standing Committee may, when deemed necessary, appoint commissions of inquiry for the investigation of specific questions and make relevant decisions in the light of the reports of these commissions.

All organs of state, public organizations and citizens concerned are obliged to supply the necessary information to these commissions when they conduct investigations.

Article 71: Deputies to the National People's Congress and Members of its Standing Committee have the right to submit, according to procedures prescribed by law, legislative bills within the scope of the functions and powers of the National People's Congress and its Standing Committee.

Article 72: Deputies to the National People's Congress, during its sessions, and Members of its Standing Committee, during sessions of the latter, have the right to put forward bills of inquiry, according to procedures prescribed by law, to the State Council, the Supreme People's Court, the Supreme People's Procuratorate and the ministries and commissions under the State Council, which are all under obligation to answer.

Article 73: No deputy to the National People's Congress may be arrested or placed on trial without the consent of the Presidium of the current session of the National People's Congress or, when the National People's Congress is not in session, the consent of its Standing Committee.

Article 74: Deputies to the National People's Congress shall not be subjected to legal investigation for speeches or votes at its meetings.

Article 75: Deputies to the National People's Congress should maintain close contact with the units which elect them and with the people, listen to and report the opinions and demands of the people and, in their own production and other work and public activities, assist in the enforcement of the Constitution and the law.

Article 76: Deputies to the National People's Congress are subject to the supervision of the units which elect them. These electoral units have the power to replace the deputies they elect at any time, through procedures prescribed by law.

Article 77: The organization and working procedures of the National People's Congress and its Standing Committee are specified by law.

SECTION II
THE CHAIRMAN OF THE PEOPLE'S REPUBLIC OF CHINA

Article 78: The Chairman of the People's Republic of China represents the state in its domestic affairs and its relations with foreign states.

The Vice-Chairman of the People's Republic of China assists the Chairman in his work.

Article 79: Citizens of the People's Republic of China who have the right to vote and to stand for election and who have reached the age of 45 are eligible to stand for election as Chairman or Vice-Chairman of the People's Republic of China.

The term of office of the Chairman and Vice-Chairman of the People's Republic of China is five years. They may be re-elected but shall not serve more than two consecutive terms.

Article 80: The Chairman of the People's Republic of China, in pursuance of the decisions of the National People's Congress and its Standing Committee, promulgates laws; appoints and removes the Premier, Vice-Premiers, Commissioners of State, Ministers, Chairmen of Commissions, Chief Auditor and Secretary-General of the State Council; confers state orders, medals and titles of honour; grants special pardons; proclaims martial law; proclaims a state of war; and orders mobilization.

Article 81: The Chairman of the People's Republic of China receives foreign diplomatic representatives and, in pursuance of the decisions of the Standing Committee of the National People's Congress, appoints and recalls plenipotentiary representatives stationed abroad, ratifies and abrogates treaties and important agreements concluded with foreign states.

Article 82: The Vice-Chairman of the People's Republic of China may exercise such part of the functions and powers of the Chairman as the Chairman may entrust to the Vice-Chairman.

Article 83: The Chairman and Vice-Chairman of the People's Republic of China exercise their functions and powers until the new Chairman and Vice-Chairman elected by the succeeding National People's Congress take office.

Article 84: Should the office of the Chairman of the People's Republic of China fall vacant, the Vice-Chairman succeeds to the office of the Chairman.

Should the office of the Vice-Chairman of the People's Republic of China fall vacant, the National People's Congress holds a by-election to elect a new Vice-Chairman.

Should the offices of both the Chairman and the Vice-Chairman fall vacant, the National People's Congress holds by-elections to elect a new Chairman and a new Vice-Chairman. Prior to the by-elections, the Chairman of the Standing Committee of the National People's Congress functions as the Acting Chairman of the People's Republic of China.

SECTION III
THE STATE COUNCIL

Article 85: The State Council, that is, the Central People's Government, of the People's Republic of China, is the executive organ of the highest organ of state power; it is the highest organ of state administration.

Article 86: The State Council is composed of the following members: the Premier; two to four Vice-Premiers; the Commissioners of State; the Ministers; the Chairmen of Commissions; the Chief Auditor; and the Secretary-General.

The State Council applies the system of decision by the Premier. The ministries and commissions apply the system of decision by their respective ministers or chairmen.

The organization of the State Council is specified by law.

Article 87: The term of office of the State Council is the same as that of the National People's Congress.

The Premier, Vice-Premiers and Commissioners of State shall not serve more than two consecutive terms.

Article 88: The Premier directs the work of the State Council. The Vice-Premiers and Commissioners of State assist the Premier in his work.

The Premier, Vice-Premiers, Commissioners of State and Secretary-General of the State Council are the participants in its regular meetings.

The Premier convenes and presides over the regular meetings and plenary meetings of the State Council.

Article 89: The State Council exercises the following functions and powers:

1. to formulate administrative measures, draw up and approve administrative statutes and issue decisions and orders in accordance with the Constitution, laws and decrees;

2. to specify the tasks and responsibilities of the ministries and commissions of the State Council, and to exercise unified leadership over the work of the ministries and commissions and all other administrative work for the whole country which does not fall within the functions and powers of the ministries and commissions;

3. to exercise unified leadership over the work of local organs of state administration at various levels throughout the country, and to specify the division of the functions and powers of the organs of state administration of the Central Government, provinces, autonomous regions and municipalities directly under the Central Government;

4. to draw up and implement the plans of national economic and social development and the state budget;

5. to direct and administer economic work and urban and rural construction;

6. to direct and administer the work of education, science, culture, public health, physical culture and family planning;

7. to direct and administer affairs concerning the nationalities, to safeguard the equal rights of minority nationalities and the right of autonomy of the national autonomous areas;

8. to protect the legitimate rights and interests of Chinese residents abroad;

9. to direct and administer civil affairs, public security work, legal administration and supervisory work;

10. to administer external affairs and conclude treaties and agreements with foreign states;

11. to direct the building of the armed forces;

12. to revise or annul inappropriate administrative statutes, orders and directives issued by Ministers or by Chairmen of Commissions;

13. to revise or annul inappropriate decisions and orders issued by local organs of state administration at various levels;

14. to approve the administrative divisions of provinces, autonomous regions and municipalities directly under the Central Government and to approve the establishment and administrative divisions of autonomous prefectures, counties, autonomous counties and cities;

15. to decide on the enforcement of martial law in parts of provinces, of autonomous regions, and of municipalities directly under the Central Government;

16. to examine and decide on the size of administrative organs and appoint, remove, train, check up on the work of, reward and punish administrative personnel according to provisions of the law; and

17. to exercise such other functions and powers as are vested in it by the National People's Congress or its Standing Committee.

Article 90: The State Council may submit to the National People's Congress or its Standing Committee bills concerning the following:

1. plans of national economic and social development and their implementation;

2. the state budget and its implementation;

3. those treaties and important agreements concluded with foreign states, subject to ratification and annulment by the Standing Committee of the National People's Congress;

4. appointment and removal of personnel which shall be decided on by the National People's Congress or its Standing Committee; and

5. other matters which shall be decided on by the National People's Congress or its Standing Committee through laws or decrees.

Article 91: The Ministers and Chairmen of Commissions under the State Council direct the work of their respective departments, convene and preside over meetings of ministries or commissions and issue orders, directives and departmental administrative statutes within the jurisdiction of their respective departments and in accordance with laws and decrees and the administrative statutes, decisions and orders issued by the State Council.

Article 92: The State Council has an auditing body to audit and supervise the financial work, the revenues and expenditures of the governments at various levels and of the financial and monetary departments and enterprises and institutions under them.

The auditing body exercises its auditing and supervisory powers independently, according to provisions of the law and subject to no interference by any other administrative organs or any organizations and individuals.

Article 93; The State Council is responsible and accountable to the National People's Congress or, when the National People's Congress is not in session, to its Standing Committee.

Section IV

THE CENTRAL MILITARY COMMISSION

Article 94: The People's Republic of China has a Central Military Commission to lead the armed forces of the country.

Article 95: The Central Military Commission applies the system of decision by its Chairman.

Article 96: The term of office of the Chairman of the Central Military Commission is five years. He may be re-elected but shall not serve more than two consecutive terms.

Article 97: The Chairman of the Central Military Commission is responsible to the National People's Congress or to its Standing Committee when the former is not in session.

Sections V and VI, which are not included here, deal with the Local People's Congresses and Governments and with the Organs of Self-Government of National Autonomous Areas respectively.

Section VII

THE PEOPLE'S COURTS AND THE PEOPLE'S PROCURATORATES

Article 125: The people's courts in the People's Republic of China are the judicial organs of the state.

Article 126: The People's Republic of China has its Supreme People's Court, local people's courts at various levels and special people's courts.

The term of office of the President of the Supreme People's Court is five years; he may be re-elected but shall not serve more than two consecutive terms.

The organization of people's courts is specified by law.

Article 127: All cases in the people's courts are heard in public except those involving special circumstances as prescribed by law. The accused has the right to defence.

Article 128: People's courts shall exercise judicial authority independently according to provisions of the law and are not subject to interference by administrative organs, organizations or individuals.

Article 129: The Supreme People's Court is the highest judicial organ.

The Supreme People's Court supervises the administration of justice by local people's courts at various levels and by the special people's courts; people's courts at the higher levels supervise the administration of justice by those at lower levels.

Article 130: The Supreme People's Court is responsible to the National People's Congress and to the latter's Standing Committee. Local people's courts at various levels are responsible to the organs of state power which elect them.

Article 131: The people's procuratorates of the People's Republic of China are state organs of legal supervision.

Article 132: The People's Republic of China has its Supreme People's Procuratorate, local people's procuratorates at various levels and special people's procuratorates.

The term of office of the Chief Procurator of the Supreme People's Procuratorate is five years; the incumbent may be re-elected but shall not serve more than two consecutive terms.

The organization of people's procuratorates is specified by law.

Article 133: People's procuratorates exercise procuratorial authority independently according to provisions of the law and are not subject to interference by administrative organs, organizations and individuals.

Article 134: The Supreme People's Procuratorate is the highest procuratorial organ.

The Supreme People's Procuratorate directs the work of the local people's procuratorates at various levels and of the special people's procuratorates; people's procuratorates at the higher levels direct the work of those at the lower levels.

Article 135: The Supreme People's Procuratorate is responsible to the National People's Congress and to the latter's Standing Committee. Local people's procuratorates at various levels are responsible to the organs of state power at the corresponding levels and to the people's procuratorates at the higher levels.

Article 136: Citizens of all nationalities have the right to use their own spoken and written languages in court proceedings. The people's courts and people's procuratorates are required to provide interpretation in the court proceedings for any party not well acquainted with the spoken or written languages commonly used in the locality.

In an area where people of a minority nationality live in a compact community or where a number of nationalities live together, hearings should be conducted in the language commonly used in the locality; indictments, judgments, notices and other documents should be written in that language.

Article 137: People's courts, people's procuratorates and public security organs shall, in handling criminal cases, divide their functions, each taking responsibility for their own work, and they shall co-ordinate with each other and restrict each other to ensure accurate and effective application of the law.

Chapter 4

The National Flag, the National Emblem and the Capital

Article 138: The national flag of the People's Republic of China has five stars on a field of red.

Article 139: The national emblem of the People's Republic of China is: Tian An Men in the centre, illuminated by five stars and encircled by ears of grain and a cogwheel.

Article 140: The capital of the People's Republic of China is Beijing.

THE GOVERNMENT

HEAD OF STATE

The functions of Head of State are at present exercised by the Standing Committee of the National People's Congress (*see* below). The new Constitution proposes to restore the office of Head of State and elections are likely to be held in 1983.

STATE COUNCIL

(May 1982)

Premier: Zhao Ziyang.

Vice-Premiers:

Wan Li
Yao Yilin

State Councillors

Yu Qiuli
Geng Biao
Fang Yi
Gu Mu
Kang Shien
Chen Muhua
Bo Yibo
Ji Pengfei
Huang Hua
Zhang Jingfu

Secretary-General: Du Xingyuan.

Minister of Foreign Affairs: Huang Hua.

Minister of National Defence: Geng Biao.

Minister in Charge of the State Planning Commission: Yao Yilin.

Minister in Charge of the State Economic Commission: Zhang Jingfu.

Minister in Charge of the State Commission for Restructuring the Economic System: Zhao Ziyang.

Minister in Charge of the State Scientific and Technological Commission: FANG YI.
Minister in Charge of the State Nationalities Affairs Commission: YANG JINGREN.
Minister of Public Security: ZHAO CANGBI.
Minister of Civil Affairs: CUI NAIFU.
Minister of Justice: LIU FUZHI.
Minister of Finance: WANG BINGQIAN.
President of the People's Bank of China: LU PEIJIAN.
Minister of Commerce: LIU YI.
Minister of Foreign Economic Relations and Trade: CHEN MUHUA.
Minister of Agriculture, Animal Husbandry and Fishery: LIN HUJIA.
Minister of Forestry: YANG ZHONG.
Minister of Water Conservancy and Power: QIAN ZHENGYING.
Minister of Urban and Rural Construction and Environmental Protection: LI XIMING.
Minister of Geology and Minerals: SUN DAGUANG.
Minister of Metallurgical Industry: LI DONGYE.
Minister of Machine-Building Industry: ZHOU JIANNAN.
Minister of Nuclear Industry: ZHANG CHEN.
Minister of Aviation Industry: MO WENZIANG.
Minister of Electronics Industry: ZHANG TING.
Minister of Ordnance Industry: YU YI.
Minister of Space Industry: ZHANG JUN.
Minister of Coal Industry: GAO YANGWEN.
Minister of Petroleum Industry: TANG KE.
Minister of Chemical Industry: QIN ZHONGDA.
Minister of Textile Industry: HAO JIANXIU.
Minister of Light Industry: YANG BO.
Minister of Railways: CHEN PURU.
Minister of Communications: LI QING.
Minister of Posts and Telecommunications: WEN MINSHENG.
Minister of Labour and Personnel: ZHAO SHOUYI.
Minister of Culture: ZHU MUZHI.
Minister of Radio and Television: WU LENGXI.
Minister of Education: HE DONGCHANG.
Minister of Public Health: CUI YUELI.
Minister in Charge of the State Physical Culture and Sports Commission: LI MENGHUA.
Minister in Charge of the State Family Planning Commission: QIAN XINZHONG.

LEGISLATURE

QUANGUO RENMIN DIABIAO DAHUI

(*National People's Congress*)

The National People's Congress (NPC) is the highest organ of state power. The Fourth Session of the Fifth NPC was convened in Beijing in December 1981, and was attended by 3,154 deputies. The Fourth Session of the Fifth National Committee of the Chinese People's Political Consultative Conference (CPPCC), a revolutionary united front organization led by the Communist Party, took place simultaneously and was attended by 2,054 members. The CPPCC holds democratic discussions and consultations on the important affairs in the nation's political life. Members of the CPPCC National Committee or of its Standing Committee may be invited to attend the NPC or its Standing Committee as observers.

STANDING COMMITTEE

Chairman: Marshal YE JIANYING.

Vice-Chairmen:

PENG ZHEN
DENG YINGCHAO
Gen. ULANHU
Gen. WEI GUOQING
TAN ZHENLIN
LI JINGQUAN
PENG CHONG
Gen. SEYPIDIN
LIAO CHENGZHI
NGAPOI NGAWANG JIGME
XU DEHENG
HU JUEWEN
XIAO JINGGUANG
SHI LIANG
XI ZHONGXUN
SU YU
YANG SHANGKUN
BAINQEN ERDINI QOIGYI GYAINCAIN (Panchen Lama)
ZHU XUEFAN

Secretary-General: YANG SHANGKUN.

In March 1978, 175 members were elected to the Standing Committee.

LOCAL PEOPLE'S CONGRESSES

Province	*Chairman of People's Congress*
Anhui	Gu Zhuoxin
Fujian	Liao Zhigao
Gansu	Wang Shitai
Guangdong	Li Jianzhen
Guizhou	Xu Jiansheng
Hebei	Jiang Yizhen
Heilongjiang	Zhao Dezun
Henan	Liu Jie
Hubei	Chen Pixian
Hunan	Wan Da
Jiangsu	Xu Jiatun
Jiangxi	Yang Shangkui
Jilin	Li Youwen
Liaoning	HuangOudong
Qinghai	Zhaxi Wangqug
Shaanxi	Ma Wenrui
Shandong	Zhao Lin
Shanxi	Ruan Bosheng
Sichuan	Du Xinyuan
Yunnan	An Pingsheng
Zhejiang	Tie Ying

Special Municipalities	
Beijing	Jia Tingsan
Shanghai	Hu Lijiao
Tianjin	Yan Dakai

Autonomous Regions	
Guangxi Zhuang	Huang Rong
Nei Monggol	Ting Mao
Ningxia Hui	Ma Qingnian
Xinjiang Uygur	Tomur Dawamat
Xizang	Yang Dongsheng

PEOPLE'S GOVERNMENTS

Revolutionary Committees were established to administer each of the 29 provinces, special municipalities and autonomous regions in 1967 and 1968 during the "Great Proletarian Cultural Revolution" and received official recognition in the 1975 constitution. This was reaffirmed in the March 1978 constitution but in July 1979 the Second Session of the Fifth NPC resolved to abolish the Revolutionary Committees and replace them by People's Governments with effect from January 1980.

Province	*Governor*
Anhui	Zhou Zijian
Fujian	Ma Xingyuan
Gansu	Li Dengying
Guangdong	Liu Tianfu
Guizhou	Su Gang
Hebei	Li Erzhong
Heilongjiang	Chen Lei
Henan	Dai Suli (acting)
Hubei	Han Ningfu
Hunan	Sun Guozhi
Jiangsu	Hui Yuyu
Jiangxi	Bai Dongcai
Jilin	Zhang Gensheng (acting)
Liaoning	Chen Puru
Qinghai	Zhang Guosheng
Shaanxi	Yu Mingtao
Shandong	Su Yirian
Shanxi	Luo Guibo
Sichuan	Lu Dadong
Yunnan	Liu Minghui
Zhejiang	Li Fengping

Special Municipalities	*Mayor*
Beijing	Jiao Ruoyu
Shanghai	Wang Daohan
Tianjin	Li Ruihuan (acting)

Autonomous Regions	*Governor*
Guangxi Zhuang	Qin Yingji
Nei Monggol	Kong Fei
Ningxia Hui	Ma Xin
Xinjiang Uygur	Ismail Amat
Xizang	Ngapoi Ngawang Jigme

POLITICAL PARTIES

COMMUNIST PARTY

Zhongguo Gongchan Dang (*Chinese Communist Party*): Beijing; f. 1921; publ. *People's Daily* (*Renmin Ribao*).

The Chinese Communist Party is defined in the Constitution as "the core of leadership of the whole Chinese people". There were over 35 million members in 1977. The Sixth Plenary Session of the Eleventh Central Committee was held in June 1981.

ELEVENTH CENTRAL COMMITTEE

Chairman: Hu Yaobang.

Vice-Chairmen:

Marshal Ye Jianying
Deng Xiaoping
Zhao Ziyang
Li Xiannian
Chen Yun
Hua Guofeng

In August 1977, 201 Members and 132 Alternate Members were elected to the Eleventh Central Committee. Nine additional Members were elected in December 1978 and a further 12 Members in September 1979.

POLITBURO

Members of the Standing Committee:

Hu Yaobang
Marshal Ye Jianying
Deng Xiaoping
Zhao Ziyang
Li Xiannian
Chen Yun
Hua Guofeng

Other Full Members:

Gen. Wei Guoqing
Gen. Ulanhu
Gen. Xu Shiyou
Gen. Li Desheng
Yu Qiuli
Gen. Zhang Tingfa

Geng Biao
Fang Yi
Marshal Liu Bocheng
Marshal Nie Rongzhen
Ni Zhifu
Marshal Xu Xiangqian
Peng Chong
Deng Yingchao
Wang Zhen
Peng Zhen

Alternate Members: Chen Muhua, Gen. Seypidin.

General Secretary: Hu Yaobang.

Secretariat:

Wan Li
Wang Renzhong
Fang Yi
Gu Mu
Song Renqiong
Yu Qiuli
Gen. Yang Dezhi
Hu Qiaomu
Yao Yilin
Peng Chong.
Xi Zhongxun
Hu Yaobang

OTHER POLITICAL BODIES

China Association for Promoting Democracy: f. Shanghai 1945; membership mainly drawn from cultural and educational circles, especially teachers of middle and primary schools, editors and publishers; Chair. Zhou Jianren.

China Democratic League: f. 1941; formed from reorganization of League of Democratic Parties and Organizations of China; membership mainly intellectuals working in education and culture; Chair. Shi Liang; Vice-Chair. Hu Yuzhi.

China Democratic National Construction Association: f. 1945; membership mainly former industrialists and businessmen; Chair. Hu Juewen; Sec. Gen. Huang Liangchen.

China Zhi Gong Dang: f. 1925; re-organized 1947; membership mainly drawn from returned expatriate Chinese; Chair. Huang Dingchen.

Chinese Peasants' and Workers' Democratic Party: f. 1947; Chair. Ji Fang; Vice-Chair. Zhou Gucheng.

Communist Youth League: f. 1922; 48 million members; First Sec. of Central Committee Han Ying.

Guomindang (Kuomintang) Revolutionary Committee: f. 1948; Chair. Wang Kunlun (acting); Vice-Chair. Zhu Xuefan.

Jiu San Society: Chair. Xu Deheng; Vice-Chair. Mao Yisheng.

Taiwan Democratic Self-Government League: f. 1947; recruits Taiwanese living on the Mainland; Chair. Cai Xiao.

THE PEOPLE'S LIBERATION ARMY

Apart from its strategic role as a defensive force, the People's Liberation Army is closely tied to the political leadership of the country. The People's Republic of China is divided into eleven Military Units.

Chairman of Military Affairs Commission: Deng Xiaoping.

Secretary-General of Military Affairs Commission: Yang Shangkun.

Chief of General Staff: Gen. Yang Dezhi.

Chief of the General Political Department (Chief Political Commissar): Gen. Wei Guoqing.

Commander, PLA Navy: Ye Fei.

Commander, PLA Air Force: Gen. Zhang Tingfa.

Head, General Logistics Department: Hong Xuezhi.

Military Units	*Commander*
Beijing	Qin Jiwei
Chengdu	You Taizhong
Fuzhou	Yang Chengwu
Guangzhou	Wu Kehua
Jinan	Rao Shoukun
Kunming	Zhang Zhixiu
Lanzhou	Du Yide
Nanjing	Nie Fengzhi
Shenyang	Gen. Li Desheng
Urumqi (Xinjiang)	Xiao Quanfu
Wuhan	Zhang Caiqian

DIPLOMATIC REPRESENTATION

EMBASSIES ACCREDITED TO THE PEOPLE'S REPUBLIC OF CHINA

(In Beijing unless otherwise stated)

Afghanistan: 8 Dong Zhi Men Wai, Da Jie Chao Yang Qu; *Ambassador:* (vacant).

Albania: 28 Guang Hua Lu; *Ambassador:* Jonuz Mersini.

Algeria: Dong Zhi Men Wai Da Jie, 7 San Li Tun; *Ambassador:* Ali Abdallaoui.

Argentina: 11 Dong Wu Jie, San Li Tun; *Ambassador:* Héctor Alberto Subiza.

Australia: 15 Dong Zhi Men Wai Da Jie; *Ambassador:* Hugh Alexander Dunn.

Austria: Jian Guo Men Wai, Xiu Shui Nan Jie 5; *Ambassador:* Wolfgang Wolte.

Bangladesh: 42 Guang Hua Lu; *Ambassador:* Rezaul Karim.

Belgium: San Li Tun Lu, 6; *Ambassador:* Roger Denorme.

Benin: 38 Guang Hua Lu; *Ambassador:* Cosme Deguenon.

Brazil: 27 Guang Hua Lu; *Ambassador:* Aluizio Napoleão.

Bulgaria: 4 Xiu Shui Bei Jie, Jian Guo Men Wai; *Ambassador:* Nayden Beltchev.

Burma: 6 Dong Zhi Men Wai Da Jie Chao Yang Qu; *Ambassador:* U Aung Win.

Burundi: 25 Guang Hua Lu; *Ambassador:* Sylvere Gahungu.

Cameroon: 7 San Li Tun, Dong Wu Jie; *Ambassador:* Jacob Achidi Kisob.

Canada: 10 San Li Tun Lu; *Ambassador:* MICHEL GAUVIN.

Central African Republic: 1 Dong San Jie, San Li Tun; *Ambassador:* AUGUSTE MBOE.

Chad: *Ambassador:* (vacant).

Chile: Dong Si Jie, San Li Tun; *Ambassador:* BENJAMÍN AGUSTÍN OPAZO BRULL.

Colombia: 34 Guang Hua Lu; *Ambassador:* JULIO MARIO SANTODOMINGO.

Congo: 7 San Li Tun, Dong Si Jie; *Ambassador:* ALBERT MATOKO.

Cuba: 1 Xiu Shui Nan Jie, Jian Guo Men Wai; *Ambassador:* LADISLAO GONZÁLEZ CARBAJAL.

Cyprus: *Ambassador:* DINOS MOUSHOUTAS.

Czechoslovakia: Ri Tan Lu, Jian Guo Men, Wai; *Ambassador:* ZDENĚK TRHLÍK.

Denmark: 1 Dong Wu Jie, San Li Tun; *Ambassador:* RUDOLPH ANTON THORNING-PETERSEN.

Ecuador: 2-41 San Li Tun; *Ambassador:* GONZALO PAREDES.

Egypt: 2 Ri Tan Dong Lu; *Ambassador:* EZZ-ELARAB AMIN IBRAHIM.

Equatorial Guinea: 2 Dong Si Jie, San Li Tun; *Ambassador:* SALVADOR ELA NSENG ABEGUE.

Ethiopia: 3 Xiu Shui Nan Jie, Jian Guo Men Wai; *Ambassador:* (vacant).

Finland: 30 Guang Hua Lu; *Ambassador:* PENTTI SUOMELA.

France: 3 Dong San Jie, San Li Tun; CHARLES MALO.

Gabon: 36 Guang Hua Lu; *Ambassador:* ALAIN MAURICE MAYOMBO.

German Democratic Republic: 3 Dong Si Jie, San Li Tun; *Ambassador:* HELMUT LIEBERMANN.

Germany, Federal Republic: 5 Dong Zhi Men Wai, Da Jie; *Ambassador:* GUENTHER SCHOEDEL.

Ghana: 8 San Li Tun, Lu; *Ambassador:* G. H. ARTHUR.

Greece: 19 Guang Hua Lu; *Ambassador:* PANAYOTIS RELLAS.

Guinea: 7 Dong San Jie, San Li Tun; *Ambassador:* THIERNO HABIB DIALLO.

Guyana: 1 Xiu Shui Doug Jie, Jian Guo Men Wai; *Ambassador:* A. MOHAMMED.

Hungary: 10 Dong Zhi Men Wai Da Jie; *Ambassador:* RÓBERT RIBÁNSZKY.

Iceland: *Ambassador:* PETUR THORSTEINSSON.

India: 1 Ri Tan Dong Lu; *Ambassador:* KAYATYANI SHANKAR BAJPAI.

Iran: *Ambassador:* ALI KHORRAM.

Iraq: 25 Xiu Shui Bei Jie, Jian Guo Men Wai; *Ambassador:* BADRI KARIM KADHIM.

Ireland: 3 Ri Tan Dong Lu; *Ambassador:* JOHN CAMPBELL.

Italy: 2 Dong Er Jie, San Li Tun; *Ambassador:* GIULIO TAMAGNINI.

Japan: 7 Ri Tan Lu, Jian Guo Men Wai; *Ambassador:* YASUE KATORI.

Jordan: 54 Dong Liu Jie, San Li Tun; *Ambassador:* KEMAL AI HOMOUD.

Kenya: 1-81 San Li Tun; *Ambassador:* JOSHUA S. ODANGA.

Korea, Democratic People's Republic: Ri Tan Bei Lu, Jian Guo Men Wai; *Ambassador:* JON MYONG SU.

Kuwait: 23 Guang Hua Lu; *Ambassador:* MOHAMMAD ZAID AL-HERBISH.

Lebanon: 51 Dong Liu Jie, San Li Tun; *Ambassador:* ELIE J. BOUSTANY.

Liberia: 2-62 San Li Tun; *Ambassador:* GEORGE TOE WASHINGTON.,

Libya: 55 Dong Liu Jie, San Li Tun; *Secretary of the People's Committee:* ABDALLA A. ALHARARI.

Luxembourg: *Ambassador:* CARLO KETTER.

Madagascar: 3 Dong Jie, San Li Tun; *Ambassador:* SOLOHERY CRESCENT RAKOTOFIRINGA.

Malaysia: 13 Dong Zhi Men Wai Da Jie; *Ambassador:* ALBERT S. TALALLA.

Mali: 8 Dong Si Jie, San Li Tun; *Ambassador:* SEKOU ALMAMY KOREISI.

Malta: *Ambassador:* ALFRED J. FALZON.

Mauritania: 9 Dong San Jie, San Li Tun; *Ambassador:* BA MOHAMED ABDALLAHI.

Mexico: San Li Tun, Dong Wu Jie 5; *Ambassador:* EUGENIO ANGUIANO ROCH.

Mongolia: 2 Xiu Shui Bei Jie, Jian Guo Men Wai; *Ambassador:* PUNTSAGYN SHAGDARSUREN.

Morocco: 16 San Li Tun Lu; *Ambassador:* ABDERRAHIM HARKETT.

Nepal: 12 San Li Tun Lu; *Ambassador:* GUNA SHUMSHER JUNG BAHADUR RANA.

Netherlands: 10 San Li Tun, Dong Si Jie; *Chargé d'affaires:* A. G. O. SMITSENDONK.

New Zealand: Ritan Dongerjie 1, Chaoyang District; *Ambassador:* FRANCIS ANTHONY SMALL.

Niger: 50 Dong Liu Jie, San Li Tun; *Ambassador:* IDRISSA AROUNA.

Nigeria: 2 Dong Wu Jie, San Li Tun; *Ambassador:* SULE SAMUEL SALIFU.

Norway: 1 San Li Tun, Dong Yi Jie; *Ambassador:* TANRCED IBSEN.

Oman: *Ambassador:* (vacant).

Pakistan: 1 Dong Zhi Men Wai Da Jie; *Ambassador:* DR. MAQBOOL AHMAD BHATTY.

Peru: 2-82 San Li Tun; *Ambassador:* JUAN ALAYZA ROSPIGLIOSI.

Philippines: *Ambassador:* FORTUNATO U. ABAT.

Poland: 1 Ri Tan Lu, Jian Guo Men Wai; *Ambassador:* WTADYSTAW WOJTASIK.

Portugal: 2-72 San Li Tun; *Ambassador:* ANTÓNIO RESSANO GARCIA.

Romania: Dong Er Jie, Ri Tan Lu; *Ambassador:* FLOREA DUMITRESCU.

Rwanda: 30 Xiu Shui Bei Jie; *Ambassador:* SYLVESTRE KAMALI.

Senegal: 1 Ri Tan Dong Yi Jie, Jian Guo Men Wai; *Ambassador:* MAMADOU SEYNI MBENGUE.

Sierra Leone: 7 Dong Zhi Men Wai, Da Jie; *Ambassador:* CALEB BABATUNDA AUBEE.

Somalia: *Ambassador:* SALAH MOHAMED ALI.

Spain: 9 San Li Tun Lu; *Ambassador;* FELIPE DE LA MORENA.

Sri Lanka: 3 Jian Hua Lu, Jian Guo Men Wai; *Ambassador:* C. MAHENDRAN.

Sudan: 1 Dong Er Jie, San Li Tun; *Ambassador:* MUHAMMAD HAMAD MUHAMMAD MATTAR.

Sweden: 3 Dong Zhi Men Wai Da Jie; *Ambassador:* STEN SUNDFELDT.

Switzerland: 3 Dong Wu Jie, San Li Tun; *Ambassador:* WERNER SIGG.

Syria: 6 Dong Si Jie, San Li Tun; *Ambassador:* ZAKARIA SHURAIKI.

Tanzania: 53 Dong Liu Jie, San Li Tun; *Ambassador:* JOB M. LUSINDE.

Thailand: 40 Guang Hua Lu; *Ambassador:* KOSON SINTHUWANON.

Togo: 11 Dong Zhi Men Wai Da Jie; *Ambassador:* BLOUA YAO AGBO.

Tunisia: 1 Dong Jie, San Li Tun; *Ambassador:* RIDHA BACH BAOUAB.

Turkey: 9 Dong Wu Jie, San Li Tun; *Ambassador:* NECDET TEZEL.

Uganda: 5 Dong Jie, San Li Tun; *Ambassador:* GEORGE PALIEL OFOYURU.

U.S.S.R.: 4 Dong Zhi Men Wai Zhong Jie; *Ambassador:* I. S. SHCHERBAKOV.

United Kingdom: 11 Guang Hua Lu, Jian Guo Men Wai; *Ambassador:* Sir PERCY CRADOCK, K.C.M.G.

U.S.A.: 17 Guang Hua Lu; *Ambassador:* ARTHUR W. HUMMEL, Jr.

Upper Volta: 52 Dong Liu Jie, San Li Tun; *Ambassador:* MONVEL MICHEL DAH.

Vanuatu: *Ambassador:* BARAK SOPE.

Venezuela: 14 San Li Tun Lu; *Ambassador:* REGULO BURELLI RIVAS.

Viet-Nam: 32 Guang Hua Lu, Jian Guo Men Wai; *Ambassador:* NGUYEN TRONG VINH.

Yemen Arab Republic: *Ambassador:* AHMED MUHAMMAD AL-WADIDI.

Yemen, People's Democratic Republic: 5 Dong San Jie, San Li Tun; *Ambassador:* YASSIN AHMED SALEH.

Yugoslavia: 56 Dong Liu Jie, San Li Tun; *Ambassador:* (vacant).

Zaire: 6 Dong Wu Jie, San Li Tun; *Ambassador:* TUMA WAKU DIA BAZIKA.

Zambia: 5 Dong Si Jie, San Li Tun; *Ambassador:* WILLIE R. MWONDELA.

Zimbabwe: *Ambassador:* GABRIEL PHINEAS CHISESE.

China also has diplomatic relations with Barbados, Botswana, Cape Verde, the Comoros, Djibouti, Fiji, The Gambia, Guinea-Bissau, Jamaica, Kiribati, Laos, Maldives, Mauritius, Mozambique, Papua New Guinea, Qatar, São Tomé and Príncipe, Seychelles, Suriname, Trinidad and Tobago, and Western Samoa. Consular relations have been established with San Marino.

JUDICIAL SYSTEM

The general principles of the Chinese judicial system are laid down in Articles 41–43 of the January 1980 constitution (*see* page 126).

PEOPLE'S COURTS

Supreme People's Court: Beijing; f. 1949; the highest judicial organ of the State; directs and supervises work of lower courts; Pres. JIANG HUA (term of office four years); Vice-Pres. WANG HUA'AN.

Special People's Courts.

Local People's Courts.

PEOPLE'S PROCURATORATES

Supreme People's Procuratorate: Beijing; acts for the National People's Congress in examining government departments, civil servants and citizens, to ensure observance of the law; prosecutes in criminal cases Chief Procurator HUANG HUOQING (elected by the National People's Congress for four years).

Local People's Procuratorates: undertake the same duties at the local level. Ensure that the judicial activities of the people's courts, the execution of sentences in criminal cases, and the activities of departments in charge of reform through labour, conform to the law; institute or intervene in, important civil cases which affect the interest of the State and the people.

RELIGION

During the Cultural Revolution places of worship were closed. Since 1977 the Government has adopted a policy of religious tolerance, and many churches and mosques are reopening.

ANCESTOR WORSHIP

Ancestor worship is believed to have originated with the deification and worship of all important natural phenomena. The divine and human were not clearly defined; all the dead became gods and were worshipped by their descendants. The practice has no code or dogma and the ritual is limited to sacrifices made during festivals and on birth and death anniversaries.

CONFUCIANISM

Confucianism is a philosophy and a system of ethics, without ritual or priesthood. The respects accorded Confucius are not paid to a prophet or god, but to a great sage whose teachings promote peace and good order in society and whose philosophy encourages moral living.

DAOISM

Daoism originated as a philosophy expounded by Lao Zi, born 604 B.C. The establishment of a religion was contrary to his doctrines, but seven centuries after his death his teachings were embodied into a ritual.

China Daoist Association: Beijing; Pres. CHEN YINGNING Chair. LI YUHANG.

BUDDHISM

Buddhism was introduced into China from India in A.D. 61, and flourished during the Sui and Tang dynasties (6th-8th century). It now bears little resemblance to the religion in its original form, a number of native Chinese legends, traditions, rites and deities having been added. The Ch'an and Pure Land sects are the most popular.

Buddhist Association of China: f. 1953; Chair. ZHAO PUCHU; Vice-Chair. LI RONGXI; publ. *Dharma-ghosa* (2 a month).

ISLAM

According to Muslim history, Islam was introduced into China in A.D. 651. It has over 11 million adherents in China, chiefly among the Wei Wuer and Hui people.

Beijing Islamic Association: Dongsi Mosque, Beijing; f. 1979; Chair. Imam Al-Hadji SALAH AN SHIWEI.

China Islamic Association: Beijing; f. 1953; Hon. Chair. BURHAN SHAHIDI; Chair. Al-Hadji MOHAMMED ALI ZHANG JIE.

CHRISTIANITY

During the 19th century and the first half of the 20th large numbers of foreign Christian missionaries worked in China.

Protestant Church: Chair. of Council Bishop DING GUANGXUN; 1 million adherents.

Roman Catholic Church: Catholic Mission, Si-She-Ku, Beijing; Bishop of Beijing MICHAEL FU TIESHAN.

Chinese Catholic Patriotic Association: Chair. Mgr. ZONG HUAIDE; Vice-Chair. Bishop YANG 3,000 mems.

THE PRESS

There are 43 daily newspapers with a combined circulation of 34 million per issue. Each province publishes its own daily. There are approximately 1,882 periodicals published for national distribution, of which 900 deal with science and technology, 170 with politics and social sciences and 130 with art and literature. A further 610 periodicals are published in regional centres. Only the major newspapers and periodicals are listed below, and only a restricted number are allowed abroad.

NEWSPAPERS

Beijing Daily (*Beijing Ribao*): Beijing; f. 1952; Editor-in-Chief HUANG SEN.

Beijing Evening News (*Beijing Wanbao*): Beijing; f. 1980; Editor GU XING; circ. 500,000.

China Daily: 2 Jintai Xilu, Beijing; f. 1981; in English; coverage: China's political, economic and cultural developments; world, financial and sports news; Man. Ed. FENG XILIANG.

China Peasant News (*Zhongguo Nongmin Bao*): Beijing; f. 1980; 2 a week.

China Youth News (*Zhongguo Qingmian Bao*): Beijing; f. 1951; aimed at 14–25 age-group; Dir. and Chief Editor SHE SHIGUANG; 4 a week; circ. 3,100,000.

Dazhong Daily: Jinan, Shandong Province; f. 1939.

Fu Xiao Bao: Suxian County, Anhui Province; f. 1981; 3 a week.

Guangming Daily (*Guangming Ribao*): Beijing; f. 1949; literature, art, science, history, economics, philosophy; Editor-in-Chief FAN KE; circ. 1,500,000 (mainly among intellectuals).

Guizhou Daily: Guiying, Guizhou Province.

Hebei Daily: Shijiazhuang, Hebei Province; f. 1949.

Hunan Daily: Changsha, Hunan.

Jiangxi Daily: Nanchang, Jiangxi Province; f. 1949.

Liberation Army Daily (*Jiefangjun Bao*): Beijing; f. 1955; official organ of the PLA.

Liberation Daily (*Jiefang Ribao*): Shanghai; f. 1949; circ. 900,000.

Nanfang Daily: Guangzhou, Guangdong Province.

People's Daily (*Renmin Ribao*): 2 Jin Tai Xi Lu, Beijing; f. 1948; organ of the Communist Party of China; Pres. HU JIWEI; Editor-in-Chief QIN CHUAN; circ. 5,000,000.

Qinghai Tibetan Language Newspaper: Xining, Qinghai Province; 3 a week.

Reference News (*Can Kao Xiao Xi*): Beijing; reprints from foreign newspapers; published by Xinhua (New China News Agency); circ. 8,000,000.

Shanxi Daily: Taiyuan, Shanxi Province.

Sichuan Daily: Chengdu, Sichuan; f. 1952.

Southern Daily (*Nan Fang*): Guangdong; circ. 1,000,000.

Tianjin Daily: 66 Am Shan Rd., Tianjin; f. 1949; Editor-in-Chief SHI JIAN; circ. 600,000.

Wen Hui Bao: Shanghai; f. 1938; circ. 1,200,000.

Wenxue Qingnian (*Youth Literature Journal*): Wenzhou, Zhejiang Province; f. 1981; 2 a week.

Workers' Daily (Gongren Ribao): Beijing; f. 1949; trade union activities and workers' lives; also major home and overseas news items; circ. 1,800.000.

Xinmin Evening News: Shanghai.

Xin Hua Daily: Nanjing, Jiangsu.

Xizang Daily: Lhasa, Xizang; f. 1956.

Zhongguo cai mao bao (*Finance-Trade Journal*): Beijing; f. 1978; 3 a week.

Zhongguo Nongmin Bao: Beijing; f. 1980; national paper directed at peasants in rural areas; Principal Officer ZHOU TEXIN; 2 a week; circ. 700,000.

PERIODICALS

Ban Yue Tan (*Fortnightly Conversations*): Beijing; f. 1980.

Beijing Review: Beijing 37; weekly; in English, French, Spanish, Japanese and German; monthly editions; Chief Editor WANG XI.

China Radio and Television (*Zhongguo Guangbo Dianshi*): Newspaper and Periodical Distribution Bureau, Beijing; f. 1982; sponsored by Ministry of Radio and Television; reports and comments on radio and television; monthly.

China Reconstructs: China Welfare Institute, Wai Wen Bldg., Beijing 37; monthly; economic, social and cultural affairs; illustrated; in English, Spanish, French, Arabic, Portuguese, Chinese and German.

China's Foreign Trade: Fu Xing Men Wai St., Beijing; f. 1956; every 2 months; in Chinese, English, French and Spanish.

China Sports: Beijing; f. 1957; monthly; illustrated; in English.

Chinese Acupuncture and Moxibustion: f. 1981; 2 a month; produced by Chinese Society of Acupuncture and Institute of Acupuncture under Academy of Traditional Chinese Medicine; partly in English; available abroad.

Chinese Literature: Bai Wan Zhuang, Beijing 37; f. 1951; literary; includes reproductions of art works; monthly in English and quarterly in French.

Feitian (*Fly Skywards*): Lanzhou, Qinghai Province; f. 1961; monthly.

Friends of the Fine Arts: Art review journal, providing professional and amateur artists with information on fine arts publications in China and abroad; f. 1982; quarterly.

Hai Xia: Fuzhou, Fujian Province; f. 1981; literary journal; quarterly.

Liaowang (*Observation Post*): Beijing; f. 1981; monthly.

Market (*Shichang*): Beijing; f. 1979; 3 a month in Chinese; commercial and economic affairs; published by Renmin Ribao; circ. 1,000,000.

New Film Era: Xian, Shanxi Province; f. 1981; film magazine; 6 a year.

New Sports: 8 Tiyuguan Road, Beijing; f. 1950; sponsored by the All-China Sports Federation; monthly; in Chinese; circ. 1,000,000.

People's Pictorial: Beijing; f. 1950; monthly; published in 16 languages, including English.

Red Flag (*Hong Qi*): Beijing; f. 1958; 2 a month; official organ of the Chinese Communist Party; Chief Editor Xiong Fu.

Rensheng (Family Planning): Beijing; f. 1981; quarterly.

Tibet Science and Technology Journal: 2 a month.

Tourist: China Youth Publishing House, Beijing; f. 1955; monthly; Chinese beauty spots, customs, cultural relics.

Urban Construction: Beijing; monthly.

Wen Zhai Bao (*Newspaper Digest*): Beijing; f. 1981; weekly.

Women of China: 50 Deng Shi Kou, Beijing; f. 1956; monthly; illustrated; in English.

Xinghuo Liaoyuan: Beijing; f. 1980; revolutionary educational journal; quarterly.

Zhongguo Shaonian Bao: Beijing; f. 1951; weekly illustrated; wide readership among children; circ. 7,260,000.

NEWS AGENCIES

Xinhua (*New China News Agency*): 57 Xuanwumen St., Beijing; f. 1937; offices in all large Chinese towns and some foreign capitals; Dir. Zeng Tao.

China News Service: P.O.B. 1114, Beijing; f. 1952; office in Hong Kong; supplies news features, special articles and photographs for newspapers and magazines in Chinese printed overseas; services in Chinese.

Foreign Bureaux

Agence France-Presse (AFP) (*France*): Qi jiayuan 10–83, Beijing; Bureau Chief Charles-Antoine de Nerciat; Correspondents Gilles Campion, Elisabeth Chang.

Agencia EFE (*Spain*): Jian Gou Men Wai 2-2-132, Beijing; Representative Manuel Dompablo Bernaldo de Quiros.

Agenzia Nazionale Stampa Associata (ANSA) (*Italy*): Ban Gong Lou 2-81 San Li Tun, Beijing; agent Mino Brunetti.

Allgemeiner Deutscher Nachrichtendienst (ADN) (*German Democratic Republic*): Jian Guo Men Wai, Qi Jia Yuan Gong Yu 3-62, Beijing; Correspondent Jurgen Siemund.

Associated Press (AP) (*U.S.A.*): Beijing; Correspondents Phil Brown, Victoria Graham, Liu Heung Shing.

Bulgarian Telegraph Agency (BTA): 1-4-13 Jian Guo Men Wai, Beijing; Bureau Chief Dimitre Ivanov Maslarov.

Deutsche Presse-Agentur (dpa) (*Federal Republic of Germany*): San Li Tun, Ban Gong Lou, Apt. 1-31, Beijing; Correspondent Dietmar Schulz.

Jiji Tsushin-Sha (*Japan*): Correspondent Motoo Hoshino.

Kyodo News Service (*Japan*): 8-41 Jijiayuan Apt.,Beijing; Correspondent Hiroshi Nakajima.

Prensa Latina (*Cuba*): 6 Wai Jiao Da Lou; Correspondent Francisco Robaina.

Reuters (*U.K.*): 1-11 Ban Gong Lou, San Li Tun, Beijing.

United Press International (UPI) (*U.S.A.*): Qi Jia Yuan, 7-1-11, Beijing; Correspondents William J. Holstein, Paul Loong.

The following are also represented: Agerpres (Romania), ČTK (Czechoslovakia), Korean Central News Agency (Democratic People's Republic of Korea), Magyar Távirati Iroda (Hungary), Tanjug (Yugoslavia), TASS (U.S.S.R.), and VNA (Viet-Nam).

PUBLISHERS

There are 203 publishing houses in China, of which 108 are in Beijing.

National Publishing Administration of China (NPA): Beijing; administers publishing, printing and distribution under the State Council; Acting Dir. Chen Hanbo.

China Printing Corporation: administers printing of books and periodicals.

Xinhua (New China) Book Store: Beijing; in charge of distribution; over 5,200 brs.; Gen. Man. Wang Jing.

China Social Science Publishing House: 29 Wusi Dajie, Beijing; f. 1978; Dir. Guo Jing.

China Youth Publishing House: Beijing; f. 1949; books and periodicals; Dir. and Chief Editor Zhu Yujin.

Chinese Cultural Relics Publishing House: Beijing; f. 1956; publishes books and materials on Chinese relics in museums and on those recently discovered; Dir. Wang Fangzi.

Commercial Press: 36 Wang Fu Jing Street, Beijing; f. 1897; state publishers; specializes in translation of foreign books on social sciences and publication of dictionaries and reference books of Chinese and foreign languages; Principal Officer Chen Yuan.

Encyclopaedia of China Publishing House: A-1 Wai Guan Dong Jie, Beijing; f. 1978; specializes in publication of encyclopaedias; Dir. and Chief Editor Jiang Chunfang.

Fighters' Publishing House: Beijing; f. 1966; Dir. Ma Faran.

Foreign Languages Press: Beijing 37; f. 1951; state publishing house; publishes books in foreign languages reflecting political, economic and cultural progress in People's Republic of China; Dir. and Chief Editor Fan Yuan.

Fujian People's Publishing House: Fuzhou, Fujian Province; f. 1951.

Guangdong People's Publishing House: Guangzhou; Dir. Ma Bingshan.

Guangdong Scientific and Technological Publishing House: Guangzhou; f. 1928; Dir. and Chief Editor Wu Jian.

Guoji Shudian (*China Publications Centre*): P.O.B. 399; Chegongzhuang Xilu 21, Beijing; foreign trade organization, specializing in publications, including books, periodicals, stationery items etc.; import and export distribution; Gen. Man. CAO JIANFEI.

Hunan People's Publishing House: Changsha, Hunan Province, Dir. LI WEIXIN.

Lingnan Art Publishing House: Guangzhou, Guangdong Province; f. 1980.

National Minorities Publishing House: Beijing; f. 1953; publishes books in minority languages, e.g. Wei Wuer, Mongolian, Tibetan, Kazakh, S.E. language group, etc.

People's Educational Publishing House: Beijing; f. 1950; educational, scientific, engineering.

People's Medical Publishing House: Beijing; f. 1953; Dir. LIU XUEWEN.

People's Fine Arts Publishing House: 32 Beizongbu Hutong, Beijing; f. 1951; publishes works by Chinese and foreign painters, books on ancient Chinese art; Dir. SHAO YU.

People's Literature Publishing House: Beijing; f. 1951; largest state publisher of literary works and translations into Chinese; Dir. YAN WENJING.

People's Sports Publishing House: 8 Tiyuguan Rd., Beijing; f. 1954; sports books, pictures and pictorial magazines.

People's Publishing House: Beijing; f. 1950; political, economic and other books; Dir. CHEN MAOYI; Chief Editor ZENG YANXIU.

Qinghai Nationalities Publishing House: Xining, Qinghai Province; f. 1976.

San Lian Publishers: Beijing; f. 1950; a state publishing house; philosophy and social science; Gen. Man. FAN YONG.

Shanxi People's Publishing House: Taiyuan, Shanxi Province; f. 1951; Chief Editor LI PING.

Scholar Books Publishing House: Shanghai; f. 1982; specializes in publication of academic works, including personal academic works at author's own expense.

Workers' Press: Beijing; f. 1949; publishing house of All-China Federation of Trade Unions; Dir. and Chief Editor XING FANGQUN.

The Workers' Publishing House: Beijing; f. 1949; Dir. XING FANGQUN.

Yangtze Art and Literature Publishing House: Wuhan, Hubei Province.

Zhong Hua Book Co.: 36 Wangfujing St., Beijing; f. 1912; specializes in Chinese classics; Gen. Man. CHEN ZHIXIANG.

PUBLISHERS' ASSOCIATION

Publishers' Association of China: Beijing; f. 1979; arranges academic exchanges with foreign publishing houses; Chair. CHEN HANBO; Vice-Chair. WANG ZIYE.

RADIO AND TELEVISION

RADIO

Central Broadcasting Administration: Outside Fu Xing Men Street 2, Beijing; controls the Central People's Broadcasting Station, the Central TV Station, Radio Beijing, China Record Company and the Central Broadcasting Art Troupe; Dir. ZHANG XIANGSHAN.

Central People's Broadcasting Station: Outside Fu Xing Men Street 2, Beijing; domestic service in Chinese, Guanghua (Cantonese), Zang Wen (Tibetan), Chaozhou, Min Nan Hua (Amoy), Ke Jia (Hakka), Fuzhou Hua (Foochow dialect), Hasaka (Kazakh), Wei Wuer (Uygur), Menggu Hua (Mongolian) and Chaoxian (Korean).

Radio Beijing: Outside Fu Xing Men Street 2, Beijing; foreign service in 38 languages including Arabic, Burmese, Czech, English, Esperanto, French, German, Indonesian, Italian, Japanese, Lao, Polish, Portuguese, Russian, Spanish, Turkish and Vietnamese.

There are 106 broadcasting stations and 502 transmitting and relay stations.

In 1978, 63 per cent of households in the countryside had loudspeakers connected to the radio rediffusion system.

TELEVISION

Central People's Television Broadcasting Section: Bureau of Broadcasting Affairs of the State Council, Beijing; f. 1958.

There are 38 television stations and 246 transmitting and relay stations equipped with transmitters of 1,000 W. or more. A Beijing station transmits experimental colour broadcasts daily.

In 1979 there were an estimated 2 million television receivers.

FINANCE

BANKING

(cap.=capital; p.u.=paid up; res.=reserves; m.=million; brs.=branches; amounts in yuan)

Agricultural Bank of China: Beijing; f. 1963; functions directly under the State Council and handles State agricultural investments; total deposits 6,200m. (Aug. 1979); Pres. HU JINGYUN.

Bank of China: 17 Xi Jiao Min Xiang, Beijing; f. 1912; handles foreign exchange and international settlements; cap. p.u. 1,000m., res. 968m. (1979); Pres. BU MING; Vice-Pres. LI FAKUI; 78 brs., 22 abroad.

Bank of Communications: 17 Xi Jiao Min Xiang, Beijing; f. 1908; operates for the People's Bank of China; handles state investments in the joint state-private enterprises; cap. p.u. 400m., res. 188m.; Gen. Man. CHANG YANQING.

China and South Sea Bank Ltd.: 17 Xi Jiao Min Xiang, Beijing; f. 1920; cap. p.u. 250m., res. 95m.; Gen. Man. CUI PING.

China International Trust and Investment Corporation: 2 Qianmen Dongdajie, Beijing; f. 1979; functions under the State Council; raises funds abroad for investment in China and engages in joint investment ventures in China and abroad; auth. cap. 600m.; Chair. and Pres. RONG YIREN; Vice-Chair. LEI RENMIN.

China Investment Bank: Beijing; f. 1981; specializes in raising foreign funds for domestic investment and credit; Chair. WU BOSHAN.

China State Bank Ltd.: 17 Xi Jiao Min Xiang, Beijing; cap. p.u. 250m., res. 103m.; Gen. Man. LI PINZHOU.

Guangdong Provincial Bank: 17 Xi Jiao Min Xiang, Beijing; cap. p.u. 300m., res. 104m.; Gen. Man. CHENG KEDONG.

Jincheng Banking Corporation: 17 Xi Jiao Min Xiang, Beijing; f. 1917; cap. p.u. 300m., res. 123m.; Gen. Man. XIANG KEFANG.

National Commercial Bank Ltd.: 17 Xi Jiao Min Xiang, Beijing; f. 1907; cap. p.u. 250m., res. 95m.; Gen. Man. WANG WEICAI.

People's Bank of China: San Li Ho, West City, Beijing; f. 1948; the state bank of the People's Republic of China; more than 34,000 brs.; Pres. LU PEIJIAN; Vice-Pres. ZHU TIANSHUN.

People's Construction Bank of China: Ministry of Finance, Beijing; f. 1954 to make payments for capital construction according to plan and budget approval by the State; issues long- and medium-term loans to enterprises and short-term loans to contractors.

Xin Hua Trust, Savings and Commercial Bank Ltd.: 17 Xi Jiao Min Xiang, Beijing; cap. p.u. 300m., res. 133m.; Gen. Man. CUI YANXU.

Yian Yie Commercial Bank Ltd.: 17 Xi Jiao Min Xiang, Beijing; cap. p.u. 250m., res. 114m.; Gen. Man. JIANG WENGUI.

FOREIGN BANKS

Chartered Bank (*U.K.*): P.O.B. 2135, 185 Yuan Ming Yuan Lu, Shanghai; f. 1853.

First National Bank of Chicago (*U.S.A.*): Peking Hotel 7022, Beijing; Man. FONG CHI.

Hongkong and Shanghai Banking Corporation (*Hong Kong*): 185 Yuan Ming Yuan Lu, P.O.B. 151, Shanghai; f. 1865; Man. R. T. M. COTTON.

Midland Bank Ltd. (*U.K.*): Room 4088, West Wing, Beijing Hotel, Beijing; Group Rep. DAVID MARKHAM.

Oversea-Chinese Banking Corporation Ltd. (*Singapore*): f. 1932; brs. in Xiamen (Amoy) and Shanghai; Chair. Tan Sri TAN CHIN TUAN.

The following foreign banks also have branches in Beijing: Banca Commerciale Italiana, Banque Nationale de Paris, Banque de Paris et des Pays-Bas, Bank of America, Bank of Tokyo, Barclays Bank International, Chase Manhattan, Crédit Lyonnais, Deutsche Bank, Dresdner Bank, Export-Import Bank of Japan, Industrial Bank of Japan, National Bank of Pakistan, Royal Bank of Canada.

INSURANCE

China Insurance Company Ltd.: P.O.B. 20, Beijing; f. 1931; cargo, hull, freight, fire, life, personal accident, industrial injury, motor insurance, etc.

The People's Insurance Company of China (P.I.C.C.): 22 Xi Jiao Min Xiang, P.O.B. 2149, Beijing; f. 1949; hull, marine cargo, aviation, motor, fire and reinsurance, etc.

Tai Ping Insurance Co. Ltd.: 22 Xi Jiao Min Xiang, Beijing; marine freight, hull, cargo, fire, life, personal accident, industrial injury, motor insurance, reinsurance, etc.

TRADE AND INDUSTRY

EXTERNAL TRADE

Ministry of Foreign Economic Relations and Trade: Beijing; f. 1972; Minister CHEN MUHUA.

China Council for the Promotion of International Trade: 4 Taipingqiao Street, Beijing; f. 1952; encourages; foreign trade; arranges Chinese exhibitions at home and abroad; Chair. WANG YAODING; Vice-Chair. XIAO FANGZHOU.

EXPORT AND IMPORT CORPORATIONS

China Coal Industry Technology and Equipment Corporation: 16 Heping Rd., N. outside An Ding Men, Beijing; imports and exports technology and equipment for coal industry.

China National Aerotechnology Import-Export Corporation: P.O.B. 1671, Beijing; exports signal flares, electric detonators, tachometers, parachutes, general-purpose aircraft, etc.

China National Arts and Crafts Import and Export Corporation: 82 Donganmen, Beijing; deals in jewellery, ceramics, handicrafts, etc.

China National Breeding Stock Import and Export Corporation: Hepingli, Beijing; sole agency for import and export of stud animals including cattle, sheep, goats, swine, horses, donkeys, camels, rabbits, etc.

China National Cereals, Oils and Foodstuffs Import and Export Corporation: 82 Donganmen, Beijing; imports and exports cereals, vegetable oils, meat, eggs, fruit, dairy produce, vegetables, wines and spirits etc.

China National Chartering Corporation (SINOCHART): Import Building, Erlikou, Xijiao, Beijing; run by Ministry of Foreign Trade; agents for SINOTRANS (*see below*); arranges chartering of ships, booking space, etc.

China National Chemicals Import and Export Corporation: Erlikou, Xijiao, Beijing; deals in rubber, petroleum, paints, chemicals and drugs.

China National Foreign Trade Transportation Corporation (SINOTRANS): Import Building, Erlikou, Xijiao, Beijing; run by Ministry of Foreign Trade; agents for Ministry's import and export corporations; arranges customs clearance, deliveries, forwarding and insurance for sea, land and air transportation.

China National Hydraulic Engineering Corporation: Baiguang Rd., Beijing; contracts survey, design and construction of projects using water resources; drainage planning, hydraulic and hydro-power engineering.

China National Import and Export Commodities Inspection Corporation: 2 Changan St. E., Beijing; inspects, tests and surveys import and export commodities for overseas trade, transport, insurance and manufacturing firms.

China National Instruments Import and Export Corporation: Erlikou, Xijiao, Beijing; imports telecommunications, electronic and laboratory equipment etc.

China National Light Industrial Products Import and Export Corporation: 82 Donganmen, Beijing; imports and exports electrical appliances, radio and TV sets, photographic equipment, paper goods etc.

China National Machine Tools Corporation: San Li He, Beijing; single and multipurpose machines, indexing-table and indexing-drum machines, multispindal vertical drilling and boring machines and transfer lines.

China National Machinery and Equipment Import and Export Corporation: 12 Fuxing Menwai, Beijing; f. 1978; imports and exports machine tools, all kinds of machinery, automobiles, hoisting and transport equipment, electric motors, photographic equipment, etc.; Gen. Dir. JIA QINGLIN.

China National Machinery Import and Export Corporation: Erlikou, Xijiao, Beijing; imports and exports machine tools, diesel engines and boilers and all kinds of machinery.

China Metallurgical Import and Export Corporation: 46 Dongsi Xidajie, Beijing; imports spare parts, automation and control systems, exports metallurgical products, technology and equipment; establishes joint ventures and trade with foreign companies.

China National Metals and Minerals Import and Export Corporation: Erlikou, Xijiao, Beijing; f. 1961; principal imports and exports include steel, antimony, tungsten concentrates and trioxide, ferrotungsten, zinc ingots, tin, mercury, pig iron, cement, coal, etc.; Man. Dir. CAO ZHONGSU.

China National Native Produce and Animal By-products Import and Export Corporation: 82 Donganmen, Beijing; imports and exports tea, coffee, cocoa, tobacco, fibres, etc.

China National Packaging Import and Export Corporation: 2 Changan St. E., Beijing; handles import and export of packaging materials, containers, machines and tools; contracts for the processing and converting of packaging machines and materials using raw materials supplied by foreign clients.

China National Publications Import and Export Corporation: P.O.B. 88, Beijing; imports principally foreign books, newspapers, records, etc.; Man. DING BO.

China National Publishing Industry Trading Corporation: P.O.B. 614, Beijing; exports books, magazines, paintings, woodcuts, watercolour prints and rubbings; holds book fairs abroad; undertakes joint publication.

China National Seed Corporation: 16 North Donghuan Rd., Beijing; imports and exports crop seeds, including cereals, cotton, oil-bearing crops, vegetables, etc.

China National Technical Import Corporation: Erlikou, Xijiao, Beijing; imports all kinds of complete plant and equipment.

China National Textiles Import and Export Corporation: 82 Donganmen, Beijing; imports synthetic fibres, raw cotton, etc.; exports cotton yarn, knitwear, silk garments, etc.; Man. Dir. ZHEN ZHENGZHONG.

China Nuclear Energy Industry Corporation: P.O.B. 2139, Beijing; exports air filters, vacuum valves, dosimeters, radioactive detection elements and optical instruments.

China Road and Bridge Engineering Co.: 10 Fuxing Rd., Beijing; overseas building of highways, urban roads, bridges, airport runways and parking areas; contracts to do all surveying, designing, building, etc., and/or to provide technical or labour services.

Guoji Shudian: *See* under Publishers.

North China Industrial Corporation: P.O.B. 2137, Beijing; exports measuring tools, bearings, calipers, optical instruments, hydraulic presses, dynamite, etc.

Peking Foreign Trade Corporation: 190 Chaonie St., Beijing; controls import-export trade, foreign trade transportation, export commodity packaging and advertising for Beijing.

Shanghai Foreign Trade Corporation: 27 Zhongshan Rd., E.1, Shanghai; controls import-export trade, foreign trade transportation, chartering, export commodity packaging, storage and advertising for Shanghai municipality.

Shanghai International Trust Service Corporation: P.O.B. 3066, Shanghai; f. 1979; provides purchasing and mail order facilities for overseas buyers of art works and certain consumer goods, etc.

Waiwen Shudian: P.O.B. 88, Beijing; f. 1964; importers of newspapers, books and periodicals.

INTERNAL TRADE

General Administration for Industry and Commerce: Beijing; under the direct supervision of the State Council; Dir. WEI JINFEI.

All-China Federation of Industry and Commerce: 93 Donganmen Bei Jie, Beijing; f. 1953; promotes overseas trade relations; Pres. HU ZIANG; Sec.-Gen. HUANG JIARAN.

TRADE UNIONS

All-China Federation of Trade Unions: 10 Fuxingmenwai St., Beijing; f. 1925; comprises 376,000 trade union organizations; affiliated to WFTU; organized on an industrial basis; 17 affiliated national industrial unions, 29 affiliated local trade unions councils; membership is voluntary; trade unionists enjoy extensive benefits; in 1981 there were 411,000 primary trade union organizations and about 68.4 million members; Pres. NI ZHIFU; publ. *The Workers' Daily*.

TRADE FAIR

Chinese Export Commodities Fair (CECF): Guangzhou Foreign Trade Centre, Guangzhou; f. 1957; 2 a year; April 15th-May 5th; October 15th-November 5th.

TRANSPORT

RAILWAYS

Ministry of Communications: Beijing; controls all railways through regional divisions. The railway network has been extended to all provinces and regions except Xizang, where construction is in progress. Total length exceeded 50,000 km. in 1981, of which about 1,170 km. was electrified. In addition, special railways serve factories and mines. Some of the major routes are Beijing–Guangzhou, Tianjin–Shanghai, Manzhouli–Vladivostok, Jiaozuo–Zhicheng and Lanzhou–Badou.

Note: An underground system serves Beijing. Its total length is 23 km. and further lines are under construction.

ROADS

In 1978 there were 890,200 km. of paved and unsurfaced roads of which 200,000 km. were national and provincial highways. Four major highways link Lhasa with Sichuan, Xinjiang, Qinghai Hu and Kathmandu (Nepal). Further construction of mountain roads is under way.

WATER TRANSPORT

Bureau of Water Transportation: Controls rivers and coast traffic. In 1981 there were 108,000 km. of inland waterways in China, 57,000 of which were open to motor ships. The main rivers are the Huanghe, Changjiang and Zhu. The Changjiang is navigable by vessels of 10,000 tons as far as Wuhan, over 1,000 km. from the coast. Vessels of 1,000 tons can continue to Chongqing upstream. Over one-third of internal freight traffic is carried by water. In 1981 the 1,782 km.-long, 1,400-year old-Grand Canal was opened to foreign tourists for the first time since 1949.

SHIPPING

The greater part of China's shipping is handled in nine major ports: Dalian, Qinhuangdao, Xingang, Qingdao, Lianyungang, Shanghai, Huangpu (Whampoa), Guangzhou and Zhanjiang. Three quarters of the handling facilities are mechanical, and harbour improvement schemes are constantly in progress. In 1980 China's merchant fleet totalled over 400 ships with a deadweight capacity of 7 million tons.

China Ocean Shipping Company (COSCO): 6 Dongchangan St., Beijing; br. offices: Shanghai, Guangzhou, Tianjin, Qingdao, Dalian; merchant fleet of 431 vessels of various types with a d.w.t. of 7.92 million tons; also operates chartered foreign ships amounting to 1.7 million d.w.t.; serves China/Japan, China/S. E. Asia, China/Australia, China/Gulf, China/Europe and China/ N. America.

China Ocean Shipping Agency: 6 Dongchangan St., Beijing; br. offices at Chinese foreign trade ports; the sole agency which undertakes business for ocean-going vessels calling at Chinese ports; arranges sea passage, booking space, transhipment of cargoes; attends to chartering, purchase or sale of ships etc.

Foreign Lines Serving China

Blue Funnel Line: Liverpool; services to Shanghai.

Glen Line: London; services to Chinese ports.

Rickmers-Linie: Hamburg; serves Europe/China.

Toho Line: Tokyo; serves Europe/China.

Lloydiano: Trieste; serves Mediterranean/China.

CIVIL AVIATION

General Administration of Civil Aviation of China (CAAC): 115 Dong-si (West) Street, Beijing; established in 1949, superseded the Civil Aviation Administration of China. CAAC controls all civil aviation activities in China, including the current domestic network of more than 166 routes, with a total length of 190,000 km. and with services to all 29 provinces and autonomous regions except Taiwan. External services operate from Beijing to Addis Ababa, Baghdad, Bangkok, Belgrade, Frankfurt, Hanoi, Karachi, London, Moscow, Nagasaki, New York, Osaka, Paris, Pyongyang, Rangoon, San Francisco, Sharjah, Teheran, Tokyo and Zurich; there is a weekly charter service between Chengdu and Hong Kong; Dir.-Gen. Shen Tu; fleet of 3 Boeing 747, 4 707-320B, 6 707-320C, 5 Ilyushin Il-62, Il-18, Trident, Viscount 800, Antonov An-24, Il-14/ Li-2 plus a number of smaller aircraft.

Foreign Airlines

The following foreign airlines also serve the People's Republic of China: Aeroflot (U.S.S.R.), Air France, British Airways, Cathay Pacific (Hong Kong), Civil Aviation Administration of the Democratic People's Republic of Korea, Ethiopian Airlines, Iran Air, JAL (Japan), JAT (Yugoslavia), Lufthansa (Federal Republic of Germany), PAL (Philippines), Pan Am (U.S.A.), PIA (Pakistan), SIA (Singapore), Swissair, TAROM (Romania), and Thai International.

There are plans for the following airlines to operate flights into China: Alitalia, Canadian Pacific Airlines and KLM (Netherlands).

A new international airport at Beijing was opened in 1980. The construction of international airports at other major centres is planned.

TOURISM

China International Travel Service (Lüxingshe): 6 Dongchangan, Beijing; makes travel arrangements for foreign parties; Gen. Dir. and Man. Zhang Lian Hua; offices in London, Paris, New York, Tokyo and Hong Kong.

Chinese People's Association for Friendship with Foreign Countries: Beijing; Pres. Wang Bingnan.

General Administration for Travel and Tourism of China: Beijing; Dir. Han Ke Hua.

7.8 million tourists visited China in 1981, including many from Hong Kong and Macau. China's expanding tourist industry brought in $780 million in foreign exchange.

ATOMIC ENERGY

China was believed to have a total of about 40 nuclear reactors in operation at the end of 1966.

Atomic Energy Institute: Chinese Academy of Sciences, Beijing; contains an enriched uranium heavy water reactor and a cyclotron; Dir. Jian Sanjiang.

Atomic Research Centre: Tarim Pendi, Xinjiang; f. 1953; Dir. Wang Ganzhang.

Military Scientific Council: Beijing; Dir. Dr. Jian Xuesan.

DEFENCE

Armed Forces and Equipment (July 1981): Total regular forces estimated at 4,750,000: army 3,900,000, navy 360,000 (including 38,000 naval air force and 38,000 coast defence forces), air force 490,000. The army is equipped with some early Soviet-made tanks and artillery but mostly with its own manufactured weapons. The navy has 97 submarines, one of which is nuclear-powered, and a variety of other vessels mainly deployed in three fleets, the North Sea (500 vessels), the East Sea, i.e. around the Chinese coast (750 vessels), and the South Sea mainly around North Viet-Nam and the Gulf of Tonkin (600 vessels). The air force has 5,200 combat planes including some Soviet aircraft. China also has 65–85 IRBM and 40–50 MRBM. In addition to these forces there are several million paramilitary troops.

Defence Expenditure: Between 1960 and 1979 China issued no budget figures. Western estimates put annual defence spending at about U.S. $35,000 million. In July 1979 the Minister of Finance stated that expenditure on national defence and preparations against war totalled 16,784 million yuan in 1978, an increase of 12.6 per cent over the previous year. Defence expenditure for 1981 was planned at U.S. $12,500 million, but was subsequently cut to $10,800 million.

Military Service: Army 3–4 years; air force 4 years; navy 5 years.

For further information on the People's Liberation Army, *see* p. 376.

EDUCATION

The aim of education in the People's Republic of China is the transformation of society by the development of new patterns of thought and the discarding of traditions which hamper the growth of the communist state, together with the aim of training people in those disciplines which are dictated by the needs of the State. Experiment and changes of plan have characterized the period since 1949. Education policy has veered between the conflicting aims of the pursuit of scientific knowledge seen as an end in itself, and the abandonment of book learning in favour of practical experience. Ideology and indoctrination play a prominent part in educational curricula. The Great Proletarian Cultural Revolution of 1966 sparked off a further reorganization and reorientation of the system, with still greater emphasis on student and worker participation, communist ideology and physical labour. However, since 1977 this policy has been reversed.

The overall level of literacy in China is difficult to assess; probably it is over 60 per cent; it was claimed in 1960 that by 1957 67 per cent of the counties and municipalities had eliminated illiteracy. But in a largely rural population the provision of any kind of schooling to outlying districts is still a difficulty, and the relapse from partial literacy to inability to read for lack of practice is clearly a continuing problem.

Educational System

Education in China today is based on the two principles of fulfilling the need for trained manpower and developing the student into the communist ideal of the all-round man: worker, intellectual and soldier. The two principles have not always been given equal weight. During the "Hundred Flowers" campaign of 1956–57 education in an atmosphere of free discussion was actively encouraged; after 1966, in the wake of the Cultural Revolution, politics came to take precedence over content, and knowledge suffered at the expense of proletarian socialism. Since 1977 there has been a return to more conventional standards in education, including the reintroduction of the examination system.

Alongside book learning, physical work is promoted; this is to break down the traditional contempt for manual labour among the educated classes. This trend has the added advantage of releasing school buildings for double-shift teaching, and encouraging modern attitudes in agriculture and industry.

Administrative Reorganization, 1949–54

One of the most immediate consequences of the Communist victory in 1949 was the reorganization of education, particularly at higher levels, to eliminate content deemed superfluous, replacing it with constructive courses oriented to the new concept of society. The majority of private schools were closed down or taken over by the State. Higher education, following the Soviet model, became specialized along those channels which served the needs of Chinese society, and very few of the universities retained the broad spectrum of courses in all subjects typical of western institutions.

Outside the State educational system, factories, communes and similar organizations are encouraged to develop their own teaching institutions, the "people's schools". Most are work-schools in which labour pays for tuition.

Only higher education in China is free. Both State and people's schools charge some form of fees.

Pre-School Education

Kindergartens are regarded as important in introducing the child to ideas which will shape his thought in later life, and they have economic significance in releasing women for productive work. In 1979, 8,792,000 children attended kindergarten.

Primary Education

In the ten years following the proclamation of the People's Republic of China in 1949, primary education grew fourfold. In 1965 it was claimed that between 35 and 50 per cent of rural youths had completed a primary course. The curriculum for the four- or five-year course includes Chinese language, arithmetic, geography, history and music. Songs and slogans, parades and demonstrations provide the main ideological content of the curriculum, although politics is not taught until the fourth or fifth year. Pupils are also required to spend some time engaged in manual labour. In 1978 it was reported that children would be allowed to start school at the age of six instead of seven. In 1981 more than 143 million children were enrolled in primary schools.

Secondary Education

The middle school course of general education lasts four to five years and it is divided into two separate phases. Entry and departure are controlled by examination. The curriculum includes compulsory courses in mathematics, Chinese and foreign languages, physics, chemistry, biology and history. As with primary education, much of the expansion of secondary facilities in the 1960s was in the field of people's schools giving technical instruction through work-study. Within the State system there is also a division between general and vocational schools, the latter being almost all part-time work-study institutions. A few full-time vocational schools give a two- to three-year course, but most work-study schools give part-time courses lasting up to four years. The curriculum includes politics, Chinese language and mathematics. In addition to specialized practical instruction, senior pupils may spend several months of the year working in factories or on farms. In 1979 there were 59,050,000 middle school students.

Higher Education

Prior to 1966, entrance to university education was by examination, with family and political background playing a necessary but subordinate role in selection. But after the Cultural Revolution, students of proletarian origin showing close familiarity with the writings of Mao Zedong were given preference. Entrance examinations were abandoned in favour of admitting students selected from the workers, peasants and soldiers themselves, but in 1977 they were reintroduced, and academic merit again takes precedence over political background. University courses last four to five years. There are also two- to three-year courses in specialized institutes and basic colleges. Institutions of higher education totalled 598 in 1978, and they enrolled 1,020 students in 1979. In 1981 10,000 graduate students were enrolled to study for a master's degree within the country and 1,500 graduate students were enrolled for overseas preparatory courses.

Courses in higher institutions are determined largely by national requirements for various specialized skills. All students must in addition to their normal courses study politics, economics, Marxist philosophy, Communist Party history and one foreign language, normally Russian or English. No degrees are awarded on graduation. College graduates may be required to spend some time engaged in factory or farm work.

It was announced in June 1981 that China is to receive its first World Bank loan ($100 million) to aid the development of higher education in the fields of science and engineering.

Teacher Training

The special position of the teacher in Chinese society has been eroded and attacked by the Communist regime. Teachers are expected to ensure political conformity in their classes as well as educational progress. In 1961 official figures indicated a total of three million teachers for a total of 100 million pupils in full-time schools. Many of the teachers are recent graduates of secondary and even of primary schools. Teacher training is mostly undertaken in specialist secondary schools. Special schools and short courses are among many methods employed to increase the available resources of teaching manpower and to raise standards among existing teachers. In 1982 there were 123 training colleges for junior-high school teachers.

Special Schools

Much of China's educational effort is devoted to part-time and spare-time systems, both for professional training and ideological dissemination. Almost all the special schools are people's schools set up by factories, government agencies, street committees, communes and similar organs. Many of the Government schools also provide extension classes, and a few special institutes provide correspondence courses. Content and standards are closely adapted to local conditions. In addition, television has been adopted in urban areas to provide a "TV University" offering specialized lectures to classes assembled at convenient reception points.

CHINA (TAIWAN)

STATISTICAL SURVEY

AREA AND POPULATION

Area (sq. km.)	Population (at December 31st)				
	1977	1978	1979	1980	1981
36,002.08	16,813,127	17,135,714	17,479,314	17,805,067	18,135,508

February 28th, 1982: Population 18,175,645.

PRINCIPAL TOWNS
(December 31st, 1981)

Town	Population	Town	Population
Taipei (capital)	2,270,983	Hsinchu	243,218
Kaohsiung	1,227,454	Fengshan	227,310
Taichung	607,238	Chungli	215,414
Tainan	594,739	Yungho	213,787
Panchiau	422,260	Pingtun	189,347
Keelung	347,828	Changhwa	185,816
Shanchung	334,726	Taoyuan	185,257
Chiayi	251,840	Hsintien	171,315

BIRTHS, MARRIAGES AND DEATHS

	Live Births		Marriages		Deaths	
	Number	Rate (per 1,000)	Number	Rate (per 1,000)	Number	Rate (per 1,000)
1971	380,424	25.64	106,812	7.20	70,954	4.78
1972	365,749	24.15	112,331	7.42	71,486	4.72
1973	366,942	23.79	122,135	7.92	73,476	4.76
1974	367,823	23.42	127,684	8.13	74,760	4.76
1975	367,647	22.98	151,437	9.47	75,061	4.69
1976	423,356	25.93	152,090	9.31	76,596	4.69
1977	395,796	23.76	154,483	9.27	79,366	4.76
1978	409,203	24.11	163,313	9.62	79,359	4.68
1979	422,518	24.41	152,685	8.82	81,860	4.73
1980	412,558	23.38	174,743	9.91	83,965	4.76
1981	412,772	22.97	167,165	9.30	86,848	4.83

ECONOMICALLY ACTIVE POPULATION

(annual average in '000)

	1978	1979	1980	1981
Agriculture, forestry and fishing	1,553	1,380	1,277	1,257
Mining and quarrying	51	60	45	42
Manufacturing	1,901	2,081	2,149	2,158
Construction	469	514	554	587
Electricity, gas and water	26	29	26	27
Commerce	918	986	1,046	1,059
Transport, storage and communications	343	378	387	373
Finance and insurance	111	120	139	139
Other services	855	875	925	927
TOTAL IN EMPLOYMENT	6,228	6,424	6,547	6,672
Unemployed	106	83	82	95
TOTAL LABOUR FORCE	6,333	6,507	6,629	6,764

AGRICULTURE

PRINCIPAL CROPS

('000 metric tons)

	1977	1978	1979	1980	1981*
Rice†	2,648.9	2,444.5	2,449.8	2,353.6	2,356.8
Sweet potatoes	1,694.9	1,463.0	1,224.8	1,055.1	860.3
Asparagus	102.1	97.4	102.8	112.9	81.0
Soybeans	51.7	40.8	31.8	25.9	15.9
Maize	95.0	107.2	98.5	115.1	100.5
Tea	26.3	25.9	27.1	24.5	24.5
Tobacco	24.7	22.1	21.5	19.7	21.5
Groundnuts	77.1	92.2	85.9	86.1	84.7
Cassava (manioc)	274.8	250.0	225.6	184.9	155.8
Sugar cane	11,036.9	7,941.1	9,363.1	8,851.3	7,570.7
Bananas	252.3	182.1	226.8	214.3	180.0
Pineapples	282.2	249.6	244.8	228.8	140.0
Citrus fruit	368.6	373.7	398.8	374.4	391.8
Vegetables	2,587.2	2,814.5	3,029.7	3,260.9	2,725.1
Mushrooms	88.3	119.5	103.4	76.2	67.0

* Preliminary.

† Figures are in terms of brown rice. The paddy equivalent (in '000 metric tons) was 3,351 in 1977; 3,093 in 1978; 3,096 in 1979.

LIVESTOCK

('000 head at December 31st)

	1977	1978	1979	1980
Cattle	103.6	87.9	80.2	80.1
Buffaloes	84.0	71.3	62.6	53.7
Pigs	3,760.4	4,322.2	5,417.7	4,870.2
Sheep and goats	200.8	198.4	187.9	183.9
Chickens	35,488.6	38,360.4	38,940.5	41,393.4
Ducks	9,585.5	10,122.8	9,994.9	9,927.7
Geese	1,422.7	1,498.0	1,456.2	1,499.2
Turkeys	695.4	702.6	706.1	675.3

LIVESTOCK PRODUCTS

		1978	1979	1980	1981†
Beef	metric tons	9,710	8,518	5,499	5,276
Pigmeat	,, ,,	579,327	694,822	658,416	652,104
Goatmeat	,, ,,	977	639	633	632
Chickens*	'ooo head	91,463	94,253	104,684	114,785
Ducks*	,, ,,	26,406	27,381	27,585	32,340
Geese*	,, ,,	2,920	2,954	2,855	2,754
Turkeys*	,, ,,	1,398	1,409	1,381	1,312
Milk	metric tons	44,615	44,418	47,740	51,710
Duck eggs	'ooo	517,664	524,489	475,522	479,180
Hen eggs	,,	1,743,175	1,875,003	2,023,649	2,046,291

* Figures refer to numbers slaughtered.

† Preliminary.

FORESTRY

ROUNDWOOD REMOVALS
('ooo cubic metres)

	Coniferous (soft wood)			Broadleaved (hard wood)			Total		
	1978	1979	1980	1978	1979	1980	1978	1979	1980
Industrial wood	422.1	411.9	355.6	253.1	242.3	227.1	675.2	654.2	582.7
Fuel wood	—	—	—	94.0	92.0	86.1	94.0	92.0	86.1
Total	422.1	411.9	355.6	347.1	334.3	313.2	769.2	746.2	668.8

FISHING
('ooo metric tons, live weight)

	1975	1976	1977	1978	1979	1980	1981*
Total catch	780.0	810.6	854.9	885.0	929.3	936.3	911.5

* Preliminary.

MINING*

	1978	1979	1980	1981
Coal	2,883,904	2,719,751	2,573,530	2,445,782
Gold (kilogrammes)	417.0	443.0	413.0	17,634
Silver (kilogrammes)	2,342.6	2,655.7	2,957.1	6,683.5
Electrolytic copper	14,353	15,305	19,495	52,230
Pyrite	767	536	150	20
Crude petroleum ('ooo litres)	246,765	230,625	211,426	182,812
Natural gas ('ooo cu. metres)	1,840,582	1,720,516	1,708,327	1,501,959
Salt	340,552	366,355	722,425	351,330
Gypsum	1,526	2,535	3,364	1,985
Sulphur	9,506	8,946	8,099	9,849
Marble (cu. metres)	1,641,223	1,976,347	2,838,726	3,269,094
Talc	9,946	11,194	9,911	24,774
Asbestos	2,031	2,957	683	2,317
Dolomite	417,397	530,183	488,725	359,405

* Amounts in metric tons unless otherwise specified.

INDUSTRY

SELECTED PRODUCTS

		1979	1980	1981
Wheat flour	'000 metric tons	515.5	512.1	500.3
Refined sugar	,, ,, ,,	871.8	726.2	796.7
Alcoholic beverages (excl. beer)	'000 hectolitres	1,716.9	1,933.8	1,911.5
Cigarettes	million	24,835	25,933	27,361
Cotton yarn	'000 metric tons	158.9	171.0	156.4
Paper	,, ,, ,,	450.8	490.3	471.4
Sulphuric acid	,, ,, ,,	776.7	769.2	818.6
Spun synthetic yarn	,, ,, ,,	104.9	128.3	126.7
Motor spirit (petrol)	,, ,, ,,	1,996.8	2,080.5	2,068.1
Diesel oil	(million litres)	3,282.0	3,564.3	3,301.9
Cement	'000 metric tons	11,897.3	14,062.2	14,342.0
Pig iron	,, ,, ,,	324.9	271.6	184.9
Steel ingots	,, ,, ,,	1,570.2	1,764.9	1,600.2
Transistor radios	'000 units	8,720.5	9,489.9	9,657.3
Television receivers	,, ,,	6,080.0	6,090.9	6,239.5
Ships	'000 gross tons	382.1	572.2	776.2
Electric energy	million kWh.	37,897	40,814	40,149
Liquefied petroleum gas	'000 metric tons	429.2	458.4	434.6

FINANCE

100 cents = 1 New Taiwan dollar (NT$).

Coins: 10, 20 and 50 cents; 1, 5 and 10 dollars.

Notes: 1, 5, 10, 50, 100, 500 and 1,000 dollars.

Exchange rates (June 1982): £1 sterling = NT$67.46; U.S. $1 = NT$38.95.
NT$1,000 = £14.82 = U.S. $25.67.

Note: Multiple exchange rate systems were in operation from 1951 to August 1959. From March 1956 the certificate rate (used for foreign trade transactions) was U.S. $1 = NT$24.78 (NT$1 = 4.04 U.S. cents). In 1958 the rate became U.S. $1 = NT$36.38 (NT$1 = 2.75 U.S. cents). In August 1959 the currency was devalued and the exchange rate fluctuated close to U.S. $1 = NT$40.00 (NT$1 = 2.50 U.S. cents), which became the par value in September 1970. Foreign trade was valued at this rate from January 1961 and it became the official basic rate in June 1961, though from October 1963 a selling rate of U.S. $1 = NT$40.10 came into force. These rates remained in effect until February 1973. From February 1973 to July 1978 the exchange rate (par value) was U.S. $1 = NT$38.00 (NT$1 = 2.63 U.S. cents). A new rate of U.S. $1 = NT$36.00 was introduced in July 1978. The market rate was adjusted to U.S. $1 = NT$36.10 in June 1979 but this was revised in 1980. The average rate (NT $ per U.S. $) was: 37.054 in 1978; 36.048 in 1979; 36.015 in 1980. In terms of sterling, the exchange rate was £1 = NT$96.00 from November 1967 to August 1971; and £1 = NT$104.23 from December 1971 to June 1972.

BUDGET

(NT$ million, year ending June 30th)

Revenue	1981/82
Taxes	197,595
Monopoly profits	24,434
Non-tax revenue from other sources	96,063
Total	318,092

Expenditure	1981/82
General administration and defence	141,416
Education, science and culture	28,904
Reconstruction and communications	12,816
Enterprise fund	48,789
Social affairs, relief and health	43,552
Cbligations	6,007
Others	36,608
Total	318,092

1982/83 (NT$ million): Budget 338,841.

NATIONAL ACCOUNTS

(NT$ million at current prices)

	1978	1979	1980	1981*
Gross Domestic Product (at market price)	970,269	1,164,073	1,442,870	1,706,389
Net Domestic Product (at factor cost)	749,782	892,326	1,124,973	1,346,297
of which:				
Agriculture and fisheries	84,800	92,758	104,697	116,761
Mining	8,588	9,646	12,617	14,297
Manufacturing	258,577	311,871	382,811	440,414
Electricity	20,841	21,391	29,830	45,052
Construction	53,098	64,669	84,066	99,321
Transport and communications	45,116	53,712	71,162	83,770
Commerce	101,423	123,454	165,862	199,052
Net National Product (National Income)	747,451	892,726	1,122,881	1,343,621
Gross National Product	967,938	1,164,473	1,440,778	1,703,713
Balance of exports and imports of goods and services	65,088	10,477	19,643	21,512
Available External Resources (end of year)	203,020	202,498	195,184	245,718

* Preliminary.

EXTERNAL TRADE

(NT$ million)

	1977	1978	1979	1980	1981
Imports	323,839.3	408,378.0	532,928.0	711,432.7	778,633.3
Exports	355,238.9	468,509.3	579,298.6	712,195.2	829,756.0

PRINCIPAL COMMODITIES

(NT$ million)

Imports	1978	1979	1980	1981
Wheat (unmilled)	3,418.0	4,271.3	5,271.5	4,890.7
Maize (unmilled)	9,850.9	13,120.0	15,752.9	18,340.3
Soybeans	8,947.7	11,424.1	10,523.7	14,073.7
Logs	24,499.8	38,123.3	22,216.6	17,917.0
Natural rubber	1,830.5	2,328.4	2,835.1	2,319.6
Crude petroleum	58,783.4	78,480.1	147,969.6	163,599.2
Raw cotton	11,918.0	10,377.2	14,453.1	11,782.0
Yarn from synthetic fibres	583.0	917.0	1,082.9	1,230.7
Distillate fuels	6,169.6	5,773.9	16,296.0	16,956.2
Polyacids and derivatives	5,995.5	8,264.4	6,070.7	6,288.3
Thin iron and steel sheets	8,237.2	10,375.4	12,297.5	13,218.8
Thermoplastic resins	4,335.0	5,734.3	5,740.9	6,021.0
Iron and steel scrap	2,187.2	3,511.5	6,609.4	4,436.2
Spinning, extruding machines	2,511.7	3,061.8	4,280.1	5,106.5
Electrical switchgear	4,688.4	6,166.4	6,727.7	7,949.6
Television receivers	169.3	229.9	302.2	347.8
Internal combustion engines other than for aircraft	2,808.4	3,797.7	3,981.6	4,335.6
Ships for breaking	10,454.9	12,102.7	14,906.1	9,636.6
Total (incl. others)	407,565.0	532,393.5	711,432.7	788,633.3

[*continued on next page*

PRINCIPAL COMMODITIES—*continued*]

EXPORTS	1978	1979	1980	1981
Fresh bananas	647.8	892.4	919.8	919.6
Canned mushrooms	3,721.7	3,007.8	3,426.3	1,928.7
Canned asparagus	4,206.4	3,966.4	4,841.9	3,984.6
Raw sugar	2,342.2	2,704.6	7,635.3	4,310.5
Cotton fabrics	3,937.6	5,363.3	4,838.6	5,765.3
Yarn from synthetic fibres	7,392.4	7,463.8	6,460.1	9,366.6
Synthetic fabrics	11,161.2	14,244.2	16,844.4	17,180.2
Plywood	12,016.6	15,139.2	13,394.9	14,658.7
Clothing (incl. knitted and crocheted fabrics)	61,383.5	68,719.3	85,632.2	96,358.1
Thermionic articles, valves, tubes, photo-cells, transistors etc.	9,154.4	12,369.8	17,505.6	21,619.8
Calculating machines	3,161.9	4,217.9	4,657.4	8,138.0
Television receivers	17,416.9	17,218.4	19,602.0	20,431.8
Radio receivers	12,459.2	13,464.6	15,019.1	12,689.7
Plastic articles	30,498.3	38,362.4	52,469.7	59,325.0
Dolls and toys	7,823.6	10,525.7	13,378.4	19,377.2
TOTAL (incl. others)	468,509.3	579,298.5	712,195.2	829,756.0

PRINCIPAL TRADING PARTNERS

(NT$ million)

	IMPORTS			EXPORTS		
	1979	1980	1981	1979	1980	1981
Australia	16,399.2	18,466.7	21,802.3	15,082.6	19,388.4	24,886.9
Canada	4,746.8	8,975.0	9,848.7	14,908.2	16,526.4	20,834.5
Germany, Federal Republic	22,947.0	26,041.2	23,760.4	26,714.0	38,680.9	33,196.4
Hong Kong	7,414.8	9,010.1	11,356.4	41,022.7	55,738.7	69,560.7
Indonesia	16,312.4	19,454.5	17,127.9	14,347.9	17,191.9	15,556.9
Italy	5,331.1	6,603.7	7,176.8	7,010.6	10,347.6	7,869.7
Japan	164,655.4	193,002.0	217,842.6	80,884.9	78,136.8	91,032.5
Korea, Republic	6,402.3	7,517.5	11,056.1	6,156.7	9,581.2	10,288.3
Kuwait	41,669.5	80,791.9	82,571.6	4,820.2	7,071.1	6,134.8
Malaysia	11,867.2	15,315.8	16,621.8	4,686.8	6,109.0	6,881.2
Philippines	2,649.5	4,227.3	4,436.2	7,227.1	7,010.0	16,283.4
Saudi Arabia	31,182.5	51,159.8	65,909.0	17,126.8	19,578.3	22,227.6
Singapore	4,484.3	7,994.3	7,289.2	15,195.3	19,598.7	22,154.1
Thailand	2,434.4	3,241.7	4,297.1	6,678.4	6,337.9	7,170.6
United Kingdom	10,691.0	10,409.5	11,154.6	14,605.9	16,954.7	20,755.2
U.S.A.	122,046.0	168,496.1	174,869.3	203,336.6	243,041.2	299,799.9
TOTAL (incl. others)	471,211.4	630,707.1	778,659.5	479,804.7	570,932.8	829,830.9

TRANSPORT

RAILWAYS
(1981)

Passengers	'000	131,666
Passenger/km.	,,	7,981,907
Freight	'000 metric tons	31,723
Freight ton/km.	'000	2,527,152

ROADS
(1981)

Passengers	'000	2,037,249
Passenger/km.	,,	29,511,090
Freight	'000 metric tons	182,713
Freight ton/km.	'000	8,720,987

INTERNATIONAL SEA-BORNE SHIPPING
(freight traffic in '000 metric tons)

	1977	1978	1979	1980	1981
Goods loaded	7,877	10,065	9,681	9,095	11,289
Goods unloaded	35,879	44,129	46,317	51,168	46,609

CIVIL AVIATION

	1978	1979	1980	1981
Passengers	10,918,563	11,246,890	9,933,619	9,701,436
Freight (metric tons)	183,113	220,813	234,985	250,400

COMMUNICATIONS MEDIA

	1978	1979	1980	1981
Television receivers	2,505,360	3,247,896	3,992,675	n.a.
Telephones	2,099,310	2,566,078	3,166,169	3,774,821

EDUCATION
(1980/81)

	Schools	Full-time Teachers	Pupils/ Students
Pre-school	1,186	6,690	178,216
Primary	2,428	69,141	2,233,706
Secondary (incl. Vocational)	1,023	69,698	1,605,567
Higher	104	16,495	342,528
Special	8	465	2,645
Supplementary	347	4,238	235,059
Total (incl. others)	5,096	166,727	4,597,721

Source (unless otherwise stated): Directorate-General of Budget, Accounting and Statistics, Executive Yuan, Taipei.

THE CONSTITUTION

The form of government incorporated in the Constitution, adopted in December 1946, follows the five-power system envisaged by Dr. Sun Yat-sen, which has the major features of both cabinet and presidential government. The following are the chief organs of government:

National Assembly: Composed of elected delegates; meets to elect or recall the President and Vice-President, to amend the Constitution, or to vote on proposed Constitutional amendments submitted by the Legislative Yuan.

President: Elected by the National Assembly for a term of 6 years, and may be re-elected for a second term (the two-term restriction is at present suspended). Represents country at all state functions, including foreign relations; commands land, sea, and air forces, promulgates laws, issues mandates, concludes treaties, declares war, makes peace, declares martial law, grants amnesties, appoints and removes civil and military officers, and confers honours and decorations. He also convenes the National Assembly, and subject to certain limitations, may issue emergency orders to deal with national calamities and ensure national security.

Executive Yuan: Is the highest administrative organ of the nation and is responsible to the Legislative Yuan; has five categories of subordinate organization:

Executive Yuan Council
Ministries and Commissions
Secretariat
Government Information Office and Personnel Administration Bureau
Directorate-General of Budget, Accounting and Statistics.

Legislative Yuan: Is the highest legislative organ of the state, composed of elected members; holds two sessions a year; is empowered to hear administrative reports of the Executive Yuan, and to change Government policy.

Judicial Yuan: Is the highest judicial organ of state and has charge of civil, criminal, and administrative cases, and of cases concerning disciplinary measures against public functionaries (*see* Judicial System).

Examination Yuan: Supervises examinations for entry into public offices, and deals with personal questions of the civil service.

Control Yuan: Is a body elected by local councils to impeach or investigate the work of the Executive Yuan and the Ministries and Executives; meets once a month, and has a subordinate body, the Ministry of Audit.

THE GOVERNMENT

HEAD OF STATE

President: CHIANG CHING-KUO (took office May 20th, 1978).

Vice-President: SHIEH TUNG-MIN.

Secretary-General: MA CHI-CHUANG.

THE EXECUTIVE YUAN

(July 1982)

Prime Minister: SUN YUN-SUAN.
Deputy Prime Minister: CHIU CHUANG-HUAN.
Secretary-General: CHU SHAO-HWA.
Minister of the Interior: LIN YANG-KANG.
Minister of Foreign Affairs: CHU FU-SUNG.
Minister of National Defence: SOONG CHANG-CHIH.
Minister of Finance: HSU LI-TEH.
Minister of Education: CHU HWEI-SEN.
Minister of Justice: LI YUAN-ZU.
Minister of Economic Affairs: CHAO YAO-TUNG.
Minister of Communications: LIEN CHAN.
Minister of State: YU KUO-HWA, LI KWOH-TING, KAO YU-SHU, CHEN CHI-LU, CHANG FENG-SHU, WALTER H. FEI, CHOW HONG-TAO, LIN CHIN-SHENG.

Chairman of the Overseas Chinese Affairs Commission: MO SUNG-NIEN.

Chairman of the Mongolian and Tibetan Affairs Commission: HSUEH JEN-YANG.

Director-General of the Government Information Office: JAMES SOONG.

Director-General of Directorate-General of Budget, Accounting and Statistics: CHUNG SHIH-YI.

Director-General of Central Personnel Administration: CHEN KWEI-HWA.

Director-General of National Health Administration: HSU TZU-CHIU.

LEGISLATURE

KUO-MIN TA-HUI

(*National Assembly*)

The last general election was held on December 7th, 1980. In May 1982 the National Assembly had 1,145 members. In the 1980 elections 76 new members were elected. Delegates meet to elect or recall the President and Vice-President, to amend the Constitution or to vote on Constitutional amendments submitted by the Legislative Yuan.

LI-FA YUAN

(*Legislative Yuan*)

The Legislative Yuan is the highest legislative organ of state. In the elections held throughout China in 1948 members elected to the Legislative Yuan totalled 760. Membership after the elections in April 1982 comprised 392 members, 70 new members having been elected and 27 appointd by the President.

President: NIEH WEN-YAH.

POLITICAL PARTIES

Kuomintang (KMT) (*Nationalist Party of China*): 11 Chung Shan S. Rd., Taipei; f. 1894; aims to overthrow Communist rule in China and promote constitutional government; mems. 2,000,000; Chair. CHIANG CHING-KUO; Sec.-Gen. TSIANG YIEN-SI; Deputy Secs.-Gen. WU CHEN-TSAI, CHEN LI-AN, CHEN SHUI-FONG.

Young China Party: Taipei; f. 1923; aims: to recover and maintain territorial sovereignty; to safeguard the Constitution, and democracy; to better international understanding between free China and the free world.

China Democratic Socialist Party: Taipei; f. 1932; aims: to promote democracy; to protect fundamental freedoms; to promote public welfare and social security.

DIPLOMATIC REPRESENTATION

EMBASSIES ACCREDITED TO THE REPUBLIC OF CHINA

(In Taipei unless otherwise stated)

Bolivia: 576 Tun Hua S. Rd.; *Chargé d'affaires a.i.:* RENÉ SORIA GALVARRO.

Costa Rica: 2nd Floor, 164 Chung Shan N. Rd., Sec. 6; *Ambassador:* (vacant).

Dominican Republic: 54 Nanking E. Rd., Sec. 3; *Ambassador:* FRANCISCO ANSELMO GUZMÁN.

El Salvador: 2nd Floor, Room A, 12 Min Chu E. Rd.; *Ambassador:* JOSÉ DOLORES GERARDO HERRERA.

Guatemala: 6 Lane 44, Chien Kuo N. Rd.; *Ambassador:* EDGAR ARTURO LÓPEZ CALVO.

Haiti: 4th Floor, 432 Kuang Fu South Rd.; *Ambassador:* RAYMOND PERODIN.

Honduras: Tokyo, Japan.

Ivory Coast: Tokyo, Japan.

Korea, Republic: 345 Chunghsiao E. Rd., Sec. 4; *Ambassador:* CHONG KON KIM.

Nicaragua: 3rd Floor, 270 Chung Shan N. Rd., Sec. 6; *Ambassador:* (vacant).

Panama: 4th Floor, 614 Linsen N. Rd.; *Ambassador:* RAMÓN SIEIRO MURGAS.

Paraguay: 2nd Floor, Room B-5, 98 Fu Kuo Rd., Shih Lin; *Ambassador:* TIMOTEO ALVARENGA.

Saudi Arabia: 321 Shih Pai Rd., Sec. 2, Pei Tou; *Ambassador:* Gen. ASSAD ABDUL AZIZ AL-ZUHAIR.

South Africa: 13th Floor, Bank Tower, 205 Tun Hua N. Rd.; *Ambassador:* LOUIS VORSTER.

Uruguay: 7th Floor, 16 Mintsu E. Rd.; *Ambassador:* (vacant).

Vatican: 6, Lane 63, Chin Shan St.; *Chargé d'affaires:* Mgr. PAUL GIGLIO.

Taiwan also has diplomatic relations with Lesotho, Malawi, Nauru, Saint Vincent and the Grenadines, Swaziland, Ronga and Tuvalu.

JUDICIAL SYSTEM

Judicial Yuan: Pres. HUANG SHAO-KU; Vice-Pres. HUNG SHOU-NAN; Sec.-Gen. FAN KUEI-SHU; highest judicial organ, and the interpreter of the Constitution and national laws and ordinances. Its judicial powers are exercised by:

Supreme Court: Chief Justice CHIEN KUO-CHEN; court of appeal for civil and criminal cases.

Administrative Court: Chief Justice WANG CHIA-YI; aims at the redress of administrative wrongs.

Committee on the Discipline of Public Functionaries: Chair. KU RU-SHING; metes out disciplinary measures to persons impeached by the Control Yuan.

The interpretive powers of the Judicial Yuan are exercised by the Council of Grand Justices nominated and appointed for nine years by the President of the Republic of China with the consent of the Control Yuan. The President of the Judicial Yuan also presides over the Council of Grand Justices.

The Judicial Yuan has jurisdiction over the high court and district courts. The Ministry of Justice is under the jurisdiction of the Executive Yuan.

Control Yuan: Exercises powers of impeachment and censure, and powers of consent in the appointment of the President, Vice-President and the grand justices of the Judicial Yuan, and the president, vice-president and the members of the Examination Yuan (*see* the Constitution).

President: YU CHUN-HSIEN.

Vice-President: HWYNG TZUN-CHIOU.

RELIGION

BUDDHISM

Buddhists belong to the Mahayana and Theravada schools. Leader CHIEN LI. The Buddhist Association of Taiwan has about 1,900 group members and more than 705,303 devotees.

DAOISM (TAOISM)

Leader CHAO CHIA-CHO. There are about 721,140 devotees.

ISLAM

Leaders HSIAO YUNG-TAI, DAWUD FS HSU. About 54,000 adherents.

CHRISTIANITY

Roman Catholic: Archbishop of Taipei MATTHEW KIA YEN-WEN; Archbishop's House, 94 Loli Rd., Taipei; about 286,088 adherents for entire Taiwan Province.

Episcopal: There are about 2,250 adherents; Bishop of Taiwan (Episcopal Church of America) Rt. Rev. PUI-YEUNG CHEUNG, 7, Lane 105, Hangchow S. Rd. Sec. 1, Taipei.

Tai-oan Ki-tok Tiu-Lo Kau-Hoe (Presbyterian Church in Taiwan): 89-5 Chang-Chun Rd., Taipei 104; f. 1865; Gen. Sec. Dr. C. M. KAO; 161,800 mems. (1979).

THE PRESS

DAILIES

TAIPEI

Central Daily News: 83 Chung Hsiao West Rd., Sec. 1; f. 1928; morning; official Kuomintang paper; Publr. YAO PENG.

China Daily News (*Northern Edition*): 131 Sungkiang Rd.; morning; Chinese; f. 1946; Publr. CHIEN CHEN; Pres. YEN HAI-CHIU; Editor-in-Chief CHEN HUAI-CHIEH.

China News: 277 Hsinyi Rd., Sec. 2; f. 1949; afternoon; English; Publishers SHELLY LO; Dir. TING WEI-TUNG.

China Post: 8 Fu Shun St.; f. 1952; morning; English; Publisher NANCY YU-HUANG; Editor HUANG CHIH-HSIANG.

China Times: 132 Da Li St.; f. 1950; morning; Chinese; general and financial; Chair. YU CHI-CHUNG; Publr. CHU CHING-CHIH; Editor CHANG PING-FENG.

Chung Cheng Pao: 70 Li-hsing Rd., Shing-den, Taipei; f. 1948; morning; armed forces; Publr. HUANG WEI; Editor LIANG CHI-TUNG.

Commercial Times: 132 Tali St.; f. 1978; Publr. YU CHI-CHUNG; Editor-in-Chief JUAN TENG-FA.

Economic Daily News: 555 Chung Hsiao E. Rd., Sec. 4; f. 1967; morning; Publr. WANG PI-LY; Editor YIN CHENG-KUO.

Independent Evening Post: 15 Chinan Rd., Sec. 2; f. 1947; afternoon; Chinese; Publisher WU SAN-LIEN; Editor-in-Chief YEN WEN-SHUAN.

Mandarin Daily News: 10 Fuchow St.; f. 1948; morning; Publr. HSIA CHENG-YING; Editor YANG RU DER.

Min Sheng Pao: 555 Chung Hsiao E. Rd., Sec. 4; f. 1978; Publr. WANG HSIAO-LAN; Editor SHIH MIN.

Min Tsu Evening News: 235 Kunming St.; f. 1950; afternoon; Chinese; Publisher WANG CHENG-YUNG; Editor YANG SHANG-CHIANG.

Ta Hua (Great China) Evening News: 61 Chiu Chuen St.; f. 1950; afternoon; Publr. KENG HSIU-YEH; Editor TUAN SHOU-YU.

Taiwan Shin Sheng Pao: 127 Yenping S. Rd.; f. 1945; morning; Chinese; Publr. SHEN YUEH; Editor HSU HSÜ.

United Daily News: 555 Chung Hsiao East Rd., Sec. 4; f. 1951; morning; Publr. WANG PI-CHENG; Editor CHANG TSO-CHIN.

Youth Warrior Daily: 3 Hsin Yi Rd., Sec. 1; f. 1952; morning; Chinese; armed forces; Publr. LIU YEN-SHENG; Editor LO CHO-CHUN.

PROVINCIAL DAILIES

Cheng Kung Evening News: 233 Chung Chen Rd., Hsiao Kang Li, Kaohsiung; f. 1956; afternoon; Publr. YEN HAI-CHIU; Dir. SUN WU-NAN.

Chien Kuo Daily News: 36 Min Sheng Rd., Makung, Chen, Penghu; f. 1949; morning; Publr. CHAO CHUAN-FANG; Editor HUANG CHAO-JUNG.

China Daily News (*South Edition*): 57, Hsi Hwa St., Tainan; f. 1946; morning; Publr. CHIEN CHEN; Editor HSIUNG CHAU.

China Kuo Evening News: 38 Chung Cheng 4th Rd., Kaohsiung; f. 1955; afternoon;Publr. LIU HEN-HSIU; Editor CHANG TZU-CHIANG.

Chung Kuo Daily News: 147-10 Chung Ching Rd., Sec. 2, Taichung; f. 1956; morning; Publr. CHENG SHEN-CHI; Editor CHANG YU-CHI.

Daily Free Press: 409-12 Peitun Rd., Taichung; f. 1978; morning; Publr. CHIEN WEN-FA; Editor TSAI HSIN-CHANG.

Keng Sheng Daily News: 36 Wuchuan St., Hualien; f. 1947; morning; Publr. HSIEH YING YI; Editor CHEN HSING.

Kinmen Daily News: Wu Chiang Village, Kinmen; f. 1965; morning; Publr. WU SHIH-SUNG; Editor LEE YEN-PO.

Matsu Daily News: Matsu; f. 1957; morning; Publr. LEE CHIEN-SHENG; Editor CHIN I-PING.

Min Chung Daily News: 410 Chung Shan 2 Rd., Kaohsiung; f. 1950; morning; Publr. LEE SHUI-PIAO; Editor YAO CHIH-HAI.

Min Sheng Daily News: 406 Fu-Shing Rd., Sec. 1, Taichung; f. 1946; morning; Publr. HSU KENG-NAN; Editor HSU SHIH-YÜ.

Shang Kung Daily News: 218 Kuo Hua St., Chiayi; f. 1953; morning; Publr. LIN FU-TI; Editor LIU KUEI-NAN.

Taiwan Daily News: 24 Chung Shan Rd., Taichung; morning; f. 1964; Publr. CHEN MAO-PANG; Pres. and Man. Editor HSICH TIEN-CHYU.

Taiwan Shin Wen Pao Daily News: 249 Chung Cheng 4 Rd., Kaohsiung; f. 1949; morning; Publr. YEN CHUNG-TSE; Editor YEH YEN-I.

Taiwan Times: 167 Chung Cheng 4 Rd., Fengshan, Kaohsiung; f. 1971; Publr. WU CHI-FU; Editor SU TENG-CHI.

SELECTED PERIODICALS

Agri-week: 14 Wenchow St., Taipei; f. 1975; weekly; Editor NED LIANG; Publr. H. T. CHANG.

The Artist: 129–1 Wenchow St., Taipei; Publr. HO CHENG KWANG.

Biographical Literature: 4th Floor, 230 Hsinyi Rd., Sec. 2, Taipei; Publr. LIU TSUNG-HSIANG.

The Chinese Literary Monthly: Hua Hsin Publications, 2nd Floor, 51 Po Ai Rd., Taipei; Editor-in-Chief CHAO YÜ-MIN.

Chung Hua Magazine: 3-2 31 St., Tienmou 1 Rd., Taipei; f. 1963; Publr. HU CHIU YUAN.

Continent Magazine: 11-6 Fu Chou Rd., Taipei; f. 1950; archaeology, history and literature; fortnightly; Publr. HSU KOU-PIAO.

Crown: 52 Lane 120, Tun Hua N. Rd., Taipei; Publr. PING SIN TAO.

Free China Review: 3 Chung Hsiao E. Rd., Sec. 1, Taipei; illustrated; English; monthly; Publr. C. Y. SOONG; Editor-in-Chief S. C. CHEN.

Free China Weekly: 3 Chung Hsiao E. Rd., Sec. 1, Taipei; news review; English; Publr. SUNG TZU-LI; Editor YIN LAI.

The Gleaner: Kaohsiung Refinery, P.O.B. 25–12, Tsoying, Kaohsiung; Publr. CHIN KAI-YIN.

Harvest Farm Magazine: 14 Wenchow St., Taipei; f. 1951; fortnightly; Editor NED N. LIANG; Publr. H. T. CHANG.

The Kaleidoscope Monthly: 7–2 Hsin Sheng S. Rd., Sec. 3, Taipei; Publr. WANG CHENG SHENG.

Music & Audiophile: 3rd Floor, 3 Hangchow S. Rd., Sec. 2, Taipei; f. 1973; Publr. ADAM CHANG.

National Palace Museum Quarterly: Wai Shuang Hsi, Shih Lin, Taipei; f. 1966; art history research in Chinese with summaries in English; Dir. CHIANG FU-TSUNG.

Reader's Digest (Chinese Edn.): Taipei; monthly; Editor-in-Chief LIEN HO PAO.

Sinorama: 3 Chung Hsiao E. Rd., Sec. 1, Taipei; cultural; English; monthly; Publr. SUNG TZU-LI.

Taiwan Pictorial: 150 Tzyou Rd., Sec. 1, Taichung; f. 1951; general illustrated; fortnightly; Chinese; Publr. CHUNG CHEN-HUNG; Editor-in-Chief WANG HSIAO.

NEWS AGENCIES

Central News Agency Inc. (CNA): 209 Sungkiang Rd., Taipei; f. 1924; Pres. HUAN-KUN PAN; Editor-in-Chief WILLIE K. CHU.

Chiao Kwang News Photo Service: 6th Floor, 3 Lane 1, Ta-an St., Taipei; Dir. YEH FENG-CHUN.

China Youth News Agency: 131 Teng Hua N. Rd., Taipei 105; Dir. CHI CHIH-PING.

FOREIGN BUREAUX

Agence France-Presse (AFP): 48 Lane 369, Tunhua S. Rd., Taipei; Correspondent CALIX CHU.

Associated Press (AP) (*U.S.A.*): 6th Floor 209 Sungkiang Rd., Taipei; Correspondents WILLY MA, TINA CHOU, PAN YUEH-KAN.

United Press International (UPI) (*U.S.A.*): 3rd Floor, 137 Nanking E. Rd., Taipei; Bureau Chief SHULLEN SHAW.

PRESS ASSOCIATION

Taipei Journalists Association: 100 Kuang Fu S. Rd., Taipei; 2,798 mems. representing editorial and business executives of newspapers and broadcasting stations; publ. *Chinese Journalism Yearbook*.

PUBLISHERS

Art Book Company: 4th Floor, 18 Lane 283, Roosevelt Rd., Sec. 3, Taipei; Publr. HO KUNG SHANG.

Buffalo Publishing Co.: 48 Lane 143, Hang Chou S. Rd., Sec. 1, Taipei; Publr. PENG CHUNG HANG.

Cheng Chung Book Co.: 20 Hengyang Rd., Taipei; humanities, social sciences, medicine, fine arts; Gen. Man. CHIANG LIEN-JU.

Cheng Wen Publishing Co.: 9, Lane 6, Hang Chou South Rd., Taipei; Publr. HUANG CHENG CHU.

Chung Hwa Book Co. Ltd.: 94, Chungking S. Rd., Sec. 1, Taipei; humanities, social sciences, medicine, fine arts, school books; Gen. Man. HSIUNG DUN SENG.

Far East Book Co.: 66–1 Chungking S. Rd., Sec. 1, 10th Floor, Taipei; art, education, history, physics, mathematics, literature, dictionaries; Chair. GEORGE C. L. PU.

Globe International Corporation: 2nd Floor, 271 Roosevelt Rd., Sec. 3, Taipei; Publr. TSAI HUNG-TA.

Ho Chi Book Co.: 249 Wuhsing St., Taipei; Publr. WU FU CHANG.

Hua Hsin Culture and Publications Center: 4th Floor, 86 Ning-Po St. W., Taipei; f. 1971; Dir. Dr. JAMES K. CHENG; Editor-in-Chief Miss FEI-FEI YU.

Hua Kuo Publishing Co.: 218 Chin San St., Taipei; f. 1950; Publr. YEH YO-MO.

International Cultural Enterprises: 6th Floor, 25 Po Ai Rd., Taipei; Publr. HU TZE-DAN.

Li-Ming Cultural Enterprise Co.: 11th Floor, 213 Hsin Yi Rd., Sec. 2, Taipei; Gen. Man. LIU YEN-SHENG.

Mei Ya Publications Inc.: 6th Floor, 192 Hoping East Rd., Sec. 1, Taipei; f. 1965; copyrighted Taiwan reprints; Chair. SUELING LI.

San Min Book Co.: 61 Chungking S. Rd., Sec. 1, Taipei; f. 1953; literature, history, philosophy, social sciences; Gen. Man. LIU CHEN-CHIANG.

Taiwan Kaiming Book Co.: 77 Chung Shan N. Rd., Sec. 1, Taipei; Publr. FAN SHOU-K'ANG; Gen. Man. LIU FU-CH'IN.

The World Book Co.: 99 Chungking S. Rd., Sec. 1, Taipei; f. 1921; Chair. CHEN SHEH WOO; Gen. Man. SHAW TSUNG MOU.

Youth Cultural Enterprise Co. Ltd.: 3rd. Floor, 66-1 Chungking S. Rd., Sec. 1, Taipei; Gen. Man. CHI-CHUN TSEN.

RADIO AND TELEVISION

RADIO

Broadcasting stations are mostly privately owned, but the Ministry of Communications determines power and frequencies and supervises the operation of all stations, whether private or governmental. Principal networks:

Broadcasting Corporation of China: 53 Jen Ai Rd., Sec. 3, Taipei 106; f. 1928; Domestic (6 networks) and Overseas services (all AM); FM and Stereo production; 44 stations, 97 transmitters; 18 languages and dialects; total power output 2,405.85 kW.; Pres. CHIANG HSIAO-WU; Chair. MAH SOO-LAY.

Cheng Sheng Broadcasting Corporation: 7–8th Floors, 66-1 Chungking S. Rd., Sec. 1, Taipei; f. 1959; 7 stations; Chair. LEE LIEN; Gen. Man. WANG HSING-CHUNG.

Fu Hsing Broadcasting Corporation: P.O.B. 799, Taipei; 27 stations; Dir. HO MUH-CHAO.

In 1981 there were 13,000,000 licensed radio receivers.

TELEVISION

Taiwan Television Enterprise Ltd.: 10 Pa Te Rd., Sec. 3, Taipei; f. 1962; Chair. HSU CHING-TEH; Pres. STONE K. SHIH; publs. *TTV* (weekly), *Families* (monthly).

China Television Company Ltd.: 53 Jen-Ai Rd., Sec. 3, Taipei; f. 1969; Chair. TSU SUNG-CHIU; Pres. MEI CHANG-LING; publ. *TV Scan* (monthly).

Chinese Television Service Ltd.: 100 Kuang Fu S. Rd., Taipei; f. 1971; cultural and educational; Chair. YEE CHIEN-CHIU; Pres. WU PAO-HWA; publ. *CTS* (weekly).

In 1981 there were 4,200,000 licensed television sets.

FINANCE

BANKING

(cap.=capital; p.u.=paid up; dep.=deposits; m.=million)

Central Bank

Central Bank of China: 2 Roosevelt Rd., Sec. 1, Taipei; f. 1928; issuing bank; cap. NT$12,000m.; dep. NT$ 295,250m. (Dec. 1981); Gov. Kuo-hwa Yu; Deputy Govs. Robert C. Chien, Shirley W. Y. Kuo.

National Banks

Bank of Communications: 91 Heng Yang Rd., Taipei; f. 1907; cap. NT$7,500m.; dep. NT$21,834m. (Dec. 1981); Chair. M. S. Chen; Pres. H. P. Chia.

Bank of Taiwan: 120 Chungking S. Rd., Sec. 1, Taipei 100; f. 1946; cap. NT$4,000m.; dep. NT$224,571m. (Dec. 1981); Chair. Liu Shih-cheng; Pres. C. D. Wang.

Co-operative Bank of Taiwan: 77 Kuan Chien Rd., Taipei; f. 1946; acts as central bank for co-operatives, and as major agricultural credit institution; 66 brs.; cap; NT$1,000m.; dep. NT$125,380m. (Dec. 1981); Chair. C. H. Yang; Pres. H. M. H. Hsu.

Farmers Bank of China: 53 Huai Ning St., Taipei; f. 1933; cap. NT$2,389m.; dep. NT$28,025m. (Dec. 1981); Chair. K. H. King; Pres. L. S. Lin.

International Commercial Bank of China: 100 Chi Lin Rd., Taipei 104; f. 1912; cap. NT$2,400m.; dep. NT$ 43,312m. (Dec. 1981); Chair. T. T. Way; Pres. Ronald H. C. Ho.

Land Bank of Taiwan: 46 Kuan Chien Rd., Taipei; f. 1946; cap. NT$2,000m.; dep. NT$77,865m. (Dec. 1981); Chair. C. C. Yang; Pres. C. C. Lee.

Commercial Banks

Central Trust of China: 49 Wu Chang St., Sec. 1, Taipei; f. 1935; government institution; cap. NT$2,300m.; dep. NT$5,686m. (Dec. 1981); Chair. C. C. Chang; Pres. W. S. King.

Chang Hwa Commercial Bank Ltd.: 38 Sec. 2, Tsuyu Rd., Taichung; f. 1905; cap. NT$2,000m.; dep. NT$85,920m. (Dec. 1981); Chair. Chen Pao-chuan; Pres. Kenneth K. H. Lo; 101 brs.

First Commercial Bank: 30, Sec. 1, Chungking S. Rd., Taipei; f. 1899; cap. NT$2,176m.; dep. NT$86,756m. (Dec. 1981); Chair. Dr. Liang Kuo-shu; Pres. H. A. Lee; 104 brs.

Hua Nan Commercial Bank Ltd.: 33 Kaifeng St., Sec. 1, Taipei; f. 1919; cap. NT$1,680m.; dep. NT$81,331m. (Dec. 1981); Chair. F. H. Chang; Pres. H. A. Chen.

Overseas Chinese Commercial Banking Corporation: 8 Hsiang Yang Rd., Taipei; f. 1961; general and foreign exchange banking business; cap. p.u. NT$720m.; dep. NT$7,715m. (Dec. 1981); Chair. H. K. Thua; Gen. Man. C. H. Lin.

Shanghai Commercial and Savings Bank: 16 Jen Ai Rd., Sec. 2, Taipei; f. 1915; cap. p.u. NT$450m.; dep. NT$3,136m. (Dec. 1981); Chair. J. T. Chu; Man. Dir. Z. B. Yue.

Taipei City Bank: 7 Chingtao W. Rd., Taipei 100; f. 1969; cap. NT$2,000m.; dep. NT$44,688m. (Dec. 1981); Chair. Y. C. Chu; Pres. C. Y. Lee.

United World Chinese Commercial Bank: 65 Kuan Chien Rd., Taipei 100; f. 1975; cap. NT$500m.; dep. NT$12,866m. (Dec. 1981); Chair. Snit Viravan; Pres. T. M. Yee.

There are also a number of Medium Business Banks throughout the country.

Foreign Banks

American Express International Banking Corpn. (*U.S.A.*): 137 Nanking E. Rd., Sec. 2., Taipei; Vice-Pres. James M. Kaul.

Bangkok Bank Ltd. (*Thailand*): No. 125, Sec. 2., Nanking East Rd., P.O.B. 22419, Taipei; Vice-Pres. and Man. Prasong Uthaisangchai.

Bank of America NT and SA (*U.S.A.*): 205 Tung Hwa N. Rd., Taipei; Vice-Pres. and Man. Stephen B. Hunt.

Chase Manhattan Bank N.A. (*U.S.A.*): 72 Nanking E. Rd., Sec. 2, P.O.B. 3996, Taipei; Vice-Pres. and Gen. Man. Carter Booth.

Chemical Bank (*U.S.A.*): 261 Nanking E. Rd., Sec. 3, P.O.B. 48-11, Taipei; Vice-Pres. and Gen. Man. George Cooper.

Citibank N.A. (*U.S.A.*): 742 Min Sheng E. Rd., P.O.B. 3343, Taipei; Vice-Pres. Michael J. Cannon-Brookes.

Continental Bank (*U.S.A.*): 62 Nanking E. Rd., Sec. 2, Taipei; Gen. Man. Steven R. Champion.

Dai-Ichi Kangyo Bank Ltd. (*Japan*): 23 Chang An E. Rd., Sec. 1, Taipei; Pres. Kyozo Yumoto.

First Interstate Bank of California (*U.S.A.*): 221 Nanking E. Rd., Sec. 3, Taipei; Vice-Pres. and Gen. Man. Donald D. Snyder.

Irving Trust Company (*U.S.A.*): 10-12 Chungking S. Rd., Sec. 1, Taipei; Vice-Pres. William P. van Vooren.

Metropolitan Bank and Trust Co. (*Philippines*): 52 Nanking E. Rd., Sec. 1, Taipei; Gen. Man. Godofredo Aranza-mendez.

Toronto Dominion Bank (*Canada*): 20 Pa Teh Rd., Sec. 3, Taipei; Man. William H. Mack.

The following foreign banks also have branches in Taipei; International Bank of Singapore, Rainier National Bank (U.S.A.), First National Bank of Boston (U.S.A.), Seattle First National Bank (U.S.A.), Grindlays Bank (U.K.), European Asian Bank (F.R.G.), Société Générale (France), Banque de Paris et des Pays-Bas (France), Hollandsche Bank-Unie N.V. (Netherlands), Lloyds Bank International (U.K.), Morgan Guaranty Trust Co. of New York (U.S.A.), Bankers Trust Co. (U.S.A.), Manufacturers Hanover Trust Co. (U.S.A.).

DEVELOPMENT CORPORATION

China Development Corporation: 131 Nanking East Rd., Sec. 5, Taipei 105; f. 1959 as privately owned development finance company to assist in creation, modernization and expansion of private industrial enterprises in Taiwan, to encourage participation of private capital in such enterprises, and to help to promote and develop a capital market; cap. NT$850m. (1982); Chair. Yung-Liang Lin; Pres. Yen Shen.

STOCK EXCHANGE

Taiwan Stock Exchange Corporation: 9th Floor, City Bldg., 85 Yen-ping South Rd., Taipei; f. 1962; 45 mems.; Chair. T. Y. Tsai.

INSURANCE

Cathay Life Insurance Co. Ltd.: 1 Hsiang Yang Rd., Taipei; f. 1962; Chair. Tsai Wan-Lin; Exec. Man. Dir. Hong-tu Tsai.

Central Trust of China, Life Insurance Dept.: 5-7th Floor, 76 Poai Rd., Taipei; life insurance; Chair. Jen-kong; Gen. Man. Li Chia-chuan.

China Mariners' Assurance Corporation Ltd.: 62 Hsinsheng S. Rd., Sec. 1, Taipei; Chair. S. S. CHANG; Gen. Man. K. T. FAN.

Chung Kuo Insurance Co. Ltd.: 10th–12th Floor, ICBC Building, 100 Chilin Rd., Taipei; fmrly. China Insurance Co. Ltd.; Chair. J. W. HSIEH; Gen. Man. C. C. LIN.

Tai Ping Insurance Co. Ltd.: 42 Hsu Chang St., Taipei; f. 1929; Chair. GEORGE Y. L. WU; Man. Dir. CHANG HOO-CHUNG.

Taiwan Life Insurance Co. Ltd.: 45 Kuan Chien Rd., Taipei; Chair. W. K. WU; Gen. Man. M. H. TSAI.

There are 16 other insurance companies in Taipei.

TRADE AND INDUSTRY

CHAMBER OF COMMERCE

General Chamber of Commerce of the Republic of China: Rose Mansion, 7th Floor, 162 Shin Yee Rd., Sec. 3, Taipei; Chair. LIN CHI-CHUN; Sec.-Gen. YUAN HSIAO-CHIEH.

TRADE AND INDUSTRIAL ORGANIZATIONS

China External Trade Development Council: 201 Tun Hua N. Rd., Taipei; trade promotion body.

China Productivity Centre: 11th Floor, 201/26 Tunhua N. Rd., Taipei; f. 1955; industrial management and technical consultative organization; Gen. Man. WANG SZE-CHEH.

Chinese National Association of Industry and Commerce: 4th Floor, 7 Roosevelt Rd., Sec. 1, Taipei; Chair. KOO CHEN-FU; Sec.-Gen. RICHARD C. Y. WANG.

Chinese National Federation of Industries: 17th Floor, 30 Chungking S. Rd., Sec. 1, Taipei; f. 1948; 124 mems.; Chair. KOO CHEN-FU; Sec.-Gen. HO CHUN-YIH.

Industrial Development and Investment Centre: 10th Floor, 7 Roosevelt Rd., Taipei 104; f. 1959 to assist investment and planning; 6 overseas brs.; Dir. LAWRENCE LU.

Taiwan Handicraft Promotion Centre: 1 Hsu Chow Rd., Taipei; f. 1956; Chair. K. C. WANG; Man. Dir. PHILLIP P. C. LIU.

Trading Department of Central Trust of China: 49 Wuchang St., Sec. 1, Taipei; export and import agent for private and government-owned enterprises.

CO-OPERATIVES

In December 1981 there were 4,208 co-operatives with a total membership of 2,822,024 people and total capital of NT$3,569.9m. Of the specialized co-operatives the most important was the consumers' co-operative (3,413 co-ops; 1,735,131 mems.; cap. NT$151.3).

The centre of co-operative financing is the Co-operative Bank of Taiwan, owned jointly by the Taiwan Provincial Government and 495 co-operative units (*see* Finance section). The Co-operative Institute (f. 1918) and the Co-operative League (f. 1940), which has 420 institutional and 14,503 individual members, exist to further the co-operative movement's national and international interests; and departments of co-operative business have been set up at the National Chung Hsing University and other colleges.

RURAL RECONSTRUCTION

Council for Agricultural Planning and Development (CAPD): 37 Nanhai Rd., Taipei 107; f. 1979 to replace the Sino-American Joint Commission on Rural Reconstruction (JCRR); government agency directly under the Executive Yuan; assists in planning agricultural policies, co-ordinating programmes, promoting technology and providing external assistance; Chair. Dr. H. T. CHANG; Sec.-Gen. C. C. KOH.

TRADE UNIONS

Chinese Federation of Labour: 11th Floor, 201–18 Tunhua N. Rd., Taipei; f. 1948; mems.: 1,802 industrial unions representing 1,172,954 workers; Pres. CHEN HSI-CHI; Gen. Sec. LU KUO-HUA.

NATIONAL FEDERATIONS

Chinese Federation of Postal Workers: 4th Floor, 99 Kweilin Rd., Taipei; f. 1930; 15,485 mems.; Pres. CHEN SHEE-SHING.

Chinese National Federation of Railway Workers: 107 Chin Chou Rd., Taipei; f. 1947; 23,259 mems.; Chair. LIU CHIA-YÜ.

National Chinese Seamen's Union: 2nd Floor, 115 Chang-chou S. Rd., Sec. 1, Taipei; f. 1913; 64,639 mems.; Pres. LI CHING-CHIH; publ. *Chinese Seamen's Monthly News* (in Chinese).

REGIONAL FEDERATIONS

Taiwan Federation of Textile and Dyeing Industry Workers' Union (TFTDWU): 2 Lane 64, Chung Hsiao E. Rd., Section 2, Taipei; f. 1957; 41,848 mems.; Chair. J. H. LIU.

Taiwan Provincial Federation of Labour: 11th Floor, 44 Roosevelt Rd., Sec. 2, Taipei; f. 1948; 43 mem. unions and 655,052 mems.; Pres. H. C. CHEN; Sec.-Gen. S. W. KUO.

MAJOR INDUSTRIAL COMPANIES

STATE ENTERPRISES

The following are the major state enterprises operating in Taiwan under the Ministry of Economic Affairs:

China Fisheries Corporation: 25 Tung Shan St., Taipei; f. 1955; Pres. P. K. LIU; Gen. Man. Y. C. LEE; employees: 700.

China Shipbuilding Corporation: 6th Floor, Tai Tze Bldg., 20 Pa-Teh Rd. Sec. 3, Taipei; f. 1973; shipbuilding and repairing up to 1 million d.w.t.; machinery manufacture; Chair. WILLIAM Y. N. WEI; Pres. T. W. WU; employees: 9,244.

China Steel Corporation: Lin Hai Industrial District, Hsiao Kang, Kaohsiung; plates, wire, rods, bars, billets, pig irons; Chair. T. K. LIN; Pres. FU TZU-HAN.

Chinese Petroleum Corporation: 83 Chung Hwa Rd., P.O.B. 135, Taipei; f. 1946; natural gas, petroleum products, petrochemical feedstocks; refineries at Kaohsiung and Taoyuan; Chair. T. H. LEE; Pres. Y. S. CHEN; employees: 19,965.

Taiwan Aluminium Corporation: 15 Chengkung 2nd Rd., P.O.B. 19, Kaohsiung; f. 1946; aluminium sheets, ingots and plates, foils, cans, shipping containers and other finished products, etc.; Pres. W. L. LEE; employees 3,850.

Taiwan Fertilizer Co. Ltd.: 101 Yenping South Rd., Taipei; manufacturers of compound fertilizers, urea, ammonium sulphate, calcium super-phosphate, melamine; Pres. T. H. HUANG; employees: 4,800.

Taiwan Machinery Manufacturing Corporation: 3 Tai chi Rd., Hsiaokang, Kaohsiung; f. 1946; machine manufacturing, shipbuilding and repairing, pre-fabricated steel frameworks, steel and iron casting, various steel products, and marine diesel engines; Pres. P. S. Yu; Gen. Man. Lay Ying; employees: 4,500.

Taiwan Power Co.: 39 Hoping E. Rd., Sec. 1, P.O.B. 171, Taipei; f. 1946; electricity generating company; Chair. L. K. Chen; Pres. David S. L. Chu; employees: 17,248.

Taiwan Sugar Corporation: 25 Paoching Rd., Taipei; f. 1946; sugar, yeast powder, alcohol, soya bean oil, pulp and hogs; Chair. Y. T. Wong; Pres. H. S. Tan; employees: 14,000.

PRIVATE COMPANIES

The following is a selected list of some of Taiwan's major industrial enterprises in the private sector:

Canned Food

Weichuan Foods Corporation: 125 Sung Chiang Rd., Taipei; f. 1953; milk products, monosodium glutamate, canned foods and soy sauce; Pres. L. H. Huang; employees: 3,000.

Cement

Taiwan Cement Corporation: 113 Chung Shan N. Rd., Sec. 2, Taipei; f. 1946; cement manufacturers and exporters; Chair. and Pres. C. F. Koo; employees: 2,396.

Chemicals

Formosa Chemicals and Fibre Corporation: 359 Chung Shan Rd., Sec. 3, Changhwa; f. 1956; manufacturers of chemicals, pulp, rayon staple, yarns, cloth and nylon filament; Pres. Yung-ching Wang; employees: 8,369.

Kaohsiung Ammonium-Sulphate Corporation Ltd.: 100-2 Chung Shan 3rd Rd., P.O.B. 52, Kaohsiung; manufacturers of ammonium sulphate, ammonium nitrate, anhydrous ammonia, nitric acid, sulphuric acid and oleum; employees: 957; Chair. Ling Shih-Cheng; Gen. Man. Lee Wu-Ting.

Engineering and Motorworks

Tatung Co.: 22 Chung Shan N. Rd., Sec. 3, Taipei; f. 1918; household electric appliances, audio equipment, computers, telecommunications, wires and cables, heavy electrical apparatus, steel and machinery, material industry, construction and transport equipment; Chair. T. S. Lin; Pres. W. S. Lin; employees: 25,000.

Yue Loong Motor Co. Ltd.: 150 Nanking E. Rd., Sec. 2, Taipei; f. 1953; cars and pick-up trucks; Pres. Vivian W. Yen; employees: 3,537.

Iron and Steel

Tang Eng Iron Works Co. Ltd.: 109 San To 4th Rd., Kaohsiung; f. 1947; ingots, bars, sections, wire rods, castings, machining and repairing, concrete products, construction engineering, bricks, refractory bricks, oxygen gas, vehicle manufacturing and mechanical engineering, transport equipment; Chair. Yung Kuo; Pres. T. D. Zah; employees; 4,392.

Taiwan Iron Manufacturing Corporation: 208-5 Nanking E. Rd., Sec. 3, Taipei Hsien; f. 1945; steel plate, steel and iron casting, ferro-silicon and pig iron; Pres. F. Y. Chen; Gen. Man. Y. L. Fang; employees: 985.

Mining

Taiwan Metal Mining Corporation: 4th Floor, 83 Chunghua Rd., Taipei; f. 1948; gold, silver, copper, coal, copper alloy strips, gold and aluminium bonding wire, sulphuric acid and copper powder; Chair. Yao Chen; Pres. Y. Y. Wang; employees: 1,900.

Tai Yang Co.: 3rd Floor, 208 Hsinyi Rd., Taipei; f. 1948; gold, silver copper, coal; Pres. C. H. Yen; employees: 2,800.

Plywood and Timber

Lin Shan Hao Plywood Corporation: 150 Hoping W. Rd., Sec. 2, Taipei; f. 1938; factories at Kaohsiung and Chiayi; Pres. and Gen. Man. T. S. Lin; employees: 2,000.

Fu Shing Manufacturing & Lumber Co. Ltd.: 9th Floor, 53 Nanking E. Rd., Sec. 2, Taipei; f. 1948; Chair. P. L. Cheng; Gen. Man. David Y. W. Cheng; employees: 1,100.

Textiles and Synthetic Fibres

China Wool Textiles Inc.: 162-37 Hsinyi Rd., Sec. 3, Taipei; f. 1953; yarns, worsted fabrics, knitted garments; Gen. Man. N. T. Cheng.

Far Eastern Textile Ltd.: 128 Yen Ping S. Rd., Taipei; f. 1951; cotton yarn, blended yarn, piece goods, shirts, underwear, pyjamas, polyester pants/suits, etc.; Chair. Y. Z. Hsu; Pres. D. T. Hsu; employees: 15,000.

Lio Ho Cotton Weaving Mill Co. Ltd.: 8th Floor, 201-1 Tung Hwa N. Rd., Taipei; f. 1948; cotton yarn and cloth and ready-made garments; Pres. K. C. Tsung; employees: 1,982.

Tai Yuen Textile Co. Ltd.: 8th Floor, 150 Nanking E. Rd., Sec. 2, Taipei; f. 1951; yarn, cloth, garments and sewing thread; Pres. Vivian Wu; Gen. Man. T. L. Yen; employees: 5,500.

Tainan Spinning Co. Ltd.: 511 Yu-Nung Rd., Tainan; f. 1955; cotton, blended and synthetic yarns, etc.; Pres. San Lien Wu; Gen. Man. Cheng Kuo-hui; employees: 3000.

Miscellaneous

Chinaimex Industry Development Inc.: P.O.B. 3584, Taipei; f. 1976; exporters of footwear, garments, machinery, industrial products, foodstuffs, frozen foods, electrical products, etc.; Gen. Man. Willi Chen.

Nan Ya Plastics Corporation: 201 Tung Hwa N. Rd., Taipei; f. 1958; P.V.C. products, footwear, polyester fibre, etc.; 4 divisions; Chair. Y. C. Wang; employees: 7,500.

Taiwan Salt Works: 191 Chien Kang Rd., Tainan; Pres. C. Pei; employees: 1,337.

TRANSPORT

RAILWAYS

Taiwan Railway Administration (TRA): 2 Yen Ping N. Rd., Sec. 1, Taipei; a public utility under the provincial government of Taiwan, it operates both the west line and east line systems with a route length of 1,091.1 km.; the west line is the main trunk line from Keelung in the north to Kaohsiung in the south, with several branches; electrification of the main trunk line was completed in 1979; the east line runs down the east coast linking Hualien with Taitung; the north link line, with a length of 81 km. from New Suao to Tienpu, connecting

Suao and Hualien, was inaugurated in February 1980; Man. Dir. TONG PING.

There are also 1,957.1 km. of private narrow-gauge railroads operated by the Taiwan Sugar Corporation, the Forestry Administration and other organizations. These railroads are mostly used for freight but they also provide public passenger and freight services which connect with those of TRA.

ROADS

Taiwan Highway Bureau: 70 Chung Hsiao West Rd., Sec. 1, Taipei; Dir.-Gen. MEI-HUANG HU.

Taiwan Motor Transport Company: f. 1980; operates national bus service.

There were 17,521.8 km. of highways in 1981, most of them asphalt-paved, representing about 50 km. of road per 100 sq. km. of land. The North-South Freeway was completed in 1978.

SHIPPING

Taiwan has four international ports: Kaohsiung, Keelung, Taichung and Hualien.

China Merchants' Steam Navigation Co. Ltd.: 4th Floor, 2 Han Kou St., Sec. 2, Taipei; 1 refrigerator vessel; Chair. CHIH MENG-BING.

China Union Lines Ltd.: 3rd Floor, 46 Kwan Chien Rd., Taipei; f. 1948; 3 cargo vessels, 6 bulk carriers, 1 banana carrier; liner and tramp services; Chair. Y. S. KUNG; Pres. C. H. CHEN.

Evergreen Marine Corp.: 63 Sung-chiang Rd., Taipei; f. 1968; 24 container vessels, 1 multi-purpose ship, 1 training ship; container liner services from the Far East to the U.S.A., Central and South America, the Red Sea, the Mediterranean, Europe and South-East Asia; Chair. CHANG YUNG-FA; Pres. YEH FU-SING.

Far Eastern Navigation Corp. Ltd.: 7th Floor, 10 Chung King S. Rd., Sec. 1, Taipei; 1 bulk carrier; Chair. W. H. E. HSU.

First Steamship Co. Ltd.: 42 Hsu Chang St., 7th Floor, Taipei; 4 cargo vessels; worldwide service; Chair. H. C. TUNG; Pres. S. C. CHU.

Great Pacific Navigation Co. Ltd.: 2nd Floor, 79 Chung Shan N. Rd., Sec. 2, Taipei; 5 reefer vessels; fruit and refrigeration cargo services worldwide; Chair. CHEN CHA-MOU.

Taiwan Navigation Co. Ltd.: 6 Chungking S. Rd., Sec. 1, Taipei; f. 1947; 6 bulk carriers, 2 tankers, 4 general cargo, 1 refrigerator, 1 passenger vessel; Chair. H. L. HUANG; Pres. T. H. CHEN.

Yangming Marine Transport Corp.: Hwai Ning Bldg., 4th Floor, 53 Hwai Ning St., Taipei; 17 cargo vessels, 5 bulk carriers, 5 tankers; Chair. CHIH MENG-BING; Pres. KUO HUNG-WEI.

CIVIL AVIATION

There are two international airports, C.K.S. (Taoyuan) near Taipei, which opened in 1979, Kaohsiung. The former Taipei international airport at Sungshan is now used for domestic flights.

China Air Lines Ltd. (CAL): 131 Nanking East Rd., Sec. 3, Taipei; f. 1959; domestic services and international services to Hong Kong, Indonesia, Japan, Malaysia, the Philippines, Saudi Arabia, Singapore, Thailand, Korea and the U.S.A.; fleet comprises 4 Boeing 707, 4 727, 3 737, 7 747; Chair. SZETO FU; Pres. Gen. CHANG LIN-TEH.

Far Eastern Air Transport Corporation: 4th Floor, 9 Nanking E. Rd., Sec. 3, Taipei; f. 1957; domestic services and chartered flights to Indonesia; fleet: 6 Boeing 737, 3 Caravelle, 11 Viscount, 2 Herald, 3 Bell 212, 2 DC-3; Chair. K. T. SIAO; Pres. T. C. HWOO.

FOREIGN AIRLINES

Taiwan is also served by the following foreign airlines: Air Nauru, Cathay Pacific (Hong Kong), Flying Tiger Lines (U.S.A.), Japan Asia Airways, Korean Airlines, MAS (Malaysia), Northwest Orient (U.S.A.), PAL (Philippines), SIA (Singapore), Thai Airways International, TMA (Lebanon), Cargo LUX, South Africa Airlines.

TOURISM AND CULTURE

Tourism Bureau, Ministry of Communications: 9th Floor, 280 Chung Hsiao E. Rd., Sec. 4, Taipei; f. 1960; Dir.-Gen. YU WEI.

Taiwan Visitors Association: 5th Floor, Minchuan E. Rd., Taipei; f. 1956; Chair. A. C. SAMMY YUAN.

In 1981 there were 1,409,465 foreign visitors to Taiwan.

CULTURAL ORGANIZATIONS

PRINCIPAL OPERA COMPANIES

National Foo Hsing Opera Experimental Academy: 177 2nd Ne-hou Rd., Ne-hou, Taipei; f. 1957; Dir. LIU PO-CHI.

Ta Peng Chinese Opera: 11 Alley 9, Lane 5, Chiu-Chuan St., Taipei; f. 1965.

PRINCIPAL ORCHESTRA

Taiwan Symphony Orchestra: P.O.B. 8-7, Taichung; f. 1945; Government body under Taiwan Provincial Dept. of Education; Music Dir. Prof. DENG HAN-CHING.

ATOMIC ENERGY

Atomic Energy Council: 67, Lane 144, Keelung Rd., Sec. 4, Taipei; Chair. CHEN-HSING YEN; Sec. G. CHEN-HWA CHENG; publs. *Nuclear Science Journal* (quarterly), *Chinese AEC Bulletin* (every 2 months).

Institute of Nuclear Energy Research (INER): P.O.B. 3, Lung Tan, Taiwan 325; f. 1968; national nuclear research centre; Dir. Dr. CHIEN JI-PENG; publ. INER series reports.

Two nuclear power stations were operational in 1980. Further plants are under construction, and total capacity is scheduled to exceed 5,000 MW by 1985.

DEFENCE

Armed Forces (July 1981): Total strength 451,000; army 310,000, navy 35,000, and a marine corps of 39,000, air force 67,000. Military service is for 2 years.

Equipment: The army is equipped with U.S. manufactured weapons including medium and heavy tanks, armoured personnel carriers, heavy guns and surface-to-air missiles. The navy largely comprises destroyers, escort vessels, minesweepers and landing craft, and also has 2 submarines. The air force has 386 combat planes including tactical aircraft, interceptors, transports, trainers and 12 armed helicopters.

Defence Expenditure: Defence spending for 1977/78 was estimated at NT$63,470 million.

Chief of the General Staff: Gen. SOONG CHANG-CHIH.

EDUCATION

Taiwan's educational policy, as set out in the Constitution, places the stress on national morality, the Chinese cultural tradition, scientific knowledge and the ability to work and to contribute to the community. Hence the Government efforts in education have been mainly directed towards (*a*) promoting advanced study in higher instituf tions of learning, (*b*) stepping up the in-service training o, teaching staff to enable them to keep abreast of the times- (*c*) to co-ordinate education to the economic and social needs of the country.

Elementary Education

Pre-school kindergarten education is optional, though in 1981/82, 191,693 children attended kindergartens and kindergartens attached to primary schools. In 1968 an educational development programme was begun; this extended compulsory and free education for children of school-age to 9 years. Children above school-age and adults who have had no education whatsoever receive supplementary education in the form of supplementary courses of four to six months' and six months' to one year's duration, which are held in the central elementary schools. Primary education has expanded in recent years; in 1981/82 there were 2,444 schools with 69,613 teachers and 2,213,179 pupils. With the extension of compulsory education to junior high school, the junior high school entrance examinations have been abolished.

Secondary Education

Secondary, including vocational, education has shown substantial growth in past years with 1,034 schools and 1,627,652 pupils enrolled in the 1981/82 academic year with 71,099 teachers.

Secondary education involves three types of school: junior high, senior high and vocational. Senior high schools admit junior high school graduates and prepare them for higher education. They offer a three-year programme. Vocational schools also offer a three-year programme and provide training in agriculture, fisheries, commerce and industry, etc.

Higher Education

In 1981/82 there were 104 universities, junior colleges and independent colleges. Most of them offer postgraduate facilities. Students are selected by entrance examination under the joint sponsorship of private and public universities. The great majority of courses are of four years' duration. Junior colleges run two-, three- and five-year courses. The 1981/82 enrolment was 358,437 students with 17,452 teachers. In order to utilize the existing educational facilities to the full, colleges and universities have to set up night departments and conduct summer courses.

Under a 1963 plan the university curriculum was revised in order to adapt Taiwan's higher education to modern academic research at the higher level. As part of the Government policy to promote advanced education and academic standards, it has been encouraging existing universities to set up graduate schools with special budgets made available for the purpose. In 1981/82 there were 262 graduate schools, of which 110 were in science and engineering, 91 in the humanities and social sciences, 24 in agriculture, 19 in medicine, and 18 in the fields of education, law and fine arts.

The Government also encourages the establishment of overseas Chinese institutes of higher learning for the study of Chinese as a means of promoting international understanding. Recently rules have been considerably relaxed to allow more students to go abroad for further education, mostly to the U.S.A., Latin America and Europe.

Government lectureships and research professorships have been established to encourage Chinese scholars abroad to return to Taiwan. In 1981 a total of 937 graduates returned to teach or undertake research.

Teacher Training

The Government attaches great importance to the improvement of teacher training in schools and universities and in-service courses have been running since 1959. In 1979 there were nine teachers' junior colleges. They provide a five-year course which is open to junior high school leavers. High school teachers are trained at the National Taiwan Normal University and a teachers' college.

Adult Education

The main aim has been to raise the literacy rate and standard of general knowledge. In 1981/82 there were 365 supplementary schools with an enrolment of 248,438. Chinese language, general knowledge, arithmetic, music and vocational skills are taught.

Radio and television also play an important part in the expansion of education. The Chinese Television Service and the Educational Broadcasting Station are both run by the Ministry of Education to broadcast cultural and educational programmes, the former for 2¾ hours daily and the latter 9 hours daily.

BIBLIOGRAPHY*

BOOKS

BAARK, ERICK. Dissemination of Technology Information in China (Research Policy Institute, Washington).

BARTKE, WOLFGANG. Who's Who in the People's Republic of China (M. E. Sharpe, Armonk, N.Y., 1981).

BAUM, RICHARD (Editor). China's Four Modernisations: The New Technological Revolution (Distributed by Ernest Benn, Tonbridge, 1980).

BONAVIA, DAVID. The Chinese: A Portrait (Allen Lane, London, 1980).

BROYELLE, CLAUDIE and JACQUES. Apocalypse Mao (Grasset, Paris, 1980).

BUTTERFIELD, FOX. China: Alive in the Bitter Sea (Times Books, New York , 1982).

CHANG, PARRIS H. Power and Policy in China (Pennsylvania State University Press, 1978).

CHENG, CHESTER. Documents of Dissent: Chinese Political Thought since Mao (Hoover Institution Press, Stanford, 1980).

CHINA DIRECTORY (Radio Press Inc., Tokyo, 1978).

DE KEIJZER, ARNE J. and KAPLAN, FREDERIC. The China Guidebook (Eurasia Press, 1979).

DERNBERGER, ROBERT F. (Editor). China's Development Experience in Comparative Perspective (Harvard University Press, 1980).

FITZGERALD, C. P. Revolution in China (Cresset Press, London, 1952).

China: A Short Cultural History (Cresset Press, London, revised edition, 1964, 1976).

Birth of Communist China (Penguin Books, London, 1964).

The Southern Expansion of the Chinese People (Barrie and Jenkins, London, 1972).

Mao Tse-Tung and China (Hodder and Stoughton, London, 1976).

GARSIDE, ROGER. Coming Alive: China after Mao (André Deutsch, London, 1981).

GEELAN, P. J. M. and TWITCHETT, D. C. The Times Atlas of China (Times Newspapers Ltd., London, 1974).

A GREAT TRIAL IN CHINESE HISTORY (New World Press, distributed in U.K., U.S.A. and Canada by Pergamon Press, Oxford, 1981).

HARRIS, PETER. Political China Observed (Croom Helm, London, 1981).

HONGKONG AND SHANGHAI BANKING CORPORATION. The People's Republic of China (Business Profiles Series, Hong Kong, 1980).

HOWE, CHRISTOPHER. China's Economy: A Basic Guide (Paul Elek Ltd., London, 1978).

JOINT ECONOMIC COMMITTEE (U.S.). Chinese Economy Post-Mao (U.S. Government Printing Office, Washington, 1978).

KAPLAN, FREDERIC M., SOBIN, JULIAN M., and ANDORS, STEPHEN. Encyclopaedia of China Today (Eurasia Press/Harper & Row, New York, 1979).

LEE, HONG YUNG. The Politics of the Chinese Cultural Revolution (University of California Press, 1980).

MACDOUGALL, COLINA. Trading with China: A Practical Guide (McGraw Hill, New York, 1980).

MCKAY, DAVID. Fodor's People's Republic of China (David McKay Co. Inc., New York, 1979).

POPULATION AND OTHER PROBLEMS: first volume of *China Today* (*Beijing Review* Special Feature Series): distrib. Guoji Shudian, China Publications Centre, Chegongzhuang Xiln 21, P.O.B. 399, Beijing.

PYE, LUCIAN W. The Dynamics of Faction and Consensus in Chinese Politics: A Model and some Propositions (The Rand Corporation, 1980).

QI WEN. China—A General Survey (Foreign Languages Press, Beijing, 1979).

RAWSKI, THOMAS G. China's Transition to Industrialization: Producer Goods and Economic Development in the Twentieth Century (Univ. of Michigan Press, Ann Arbor, 1980).

Economic Growth and Development in China (Oxford University Press, New York, for World Bank, 1980).

RESOLUTION ON CPC HISTORY (1949–81) (Guoji Shudian—China Publications Centre, Beijing, 1981).

SCHERER, JOHN L. China Facts and Figures Annual, Vol. 1, 1978, Vol. 2, 1979 (Academic International Press, Florida).

SHABAD, THEODORE. China's Changing Map (Praeger, New York, 1972).

SUTTMEIER, RICHARD P. Science, Technology and China's Drive for Modernization (Hoover Institution Press, Stanford, 1980).

SZUPROWICZ, B. O. and M. R. Doing Business with the People's Republic of China—Industries and Markets (John Wiley and Sons, New York, 1978).

TREGEAR, T. R. A Geography of China (University of London Press, 1965).

WILSON, DICK. When Tigers Fight: The Story of the Sino-Japanese War 1937–1945 (Hutchinson, 1982).

XUE MUQIAO. China's Socialist Economy (Guoji Shudian—China Publications Centre, Beijing, 1981).

YAHUDA, MICHAEL B. China's Role in World Affairs (Croom Helm, London, 1979).

YUAN LI WU (Editor). China—A Handbook (David and Charles, Newton Abbot, 1973).

ZHU LI. Tibet: No longer mediaeval (English edition); ed. JIN ZHOU (Foreign Languages Press, Beijing 1981, distrib. Guoji Shudian, P.O.B. 399, Beijing).

* We are most grateful to the Hongkong and Shanghai Banking Corporation for allowing us to draw extensively from the Bibliography published in *China*, in their Business Profile Series, July 1980.

PERIODICALS

AUJOURD'HUI LA CHINE. Association des Amitiés Franco-Chinoises, Paris; quarterly.

BEIJING REVIEW. Guoji Shudian (China Publications Centre), Peking; weekly.

BRITAIN-CHINA. Newsletter of the Great Britain-China Centre, London; quarterly.

BULLETIN DE L'ASSOCIATION FRANÇAISE D'ETUDES CHINOISES. Paris.

BUSINESS CHINA. Business International, Hong Kong; every two months.

CHINA BUSINESS REPORT. Institute for International Research, London; monthly.

CHINA BUSINESS REVIEW. National Council for U.S.-China Trade, Washington, D.C.; every two months.

CHINA ECONOMIC NEWS. Economic Information and Consultancy Co., Hong Kong; weekly.

CHINA ECONOMIC AND TRADE NEWSLETTER. Monitor Consultants, London; monthly.

CHINA ECONOMIC TIMES. Far East Publications, Hong Kong; monthly.

CHINA: INTERNATIONAL TRADE. National Foreign Assessment Centre, Washington, D.C.; quarterly.

CHINA LETTER, THE. The Asia Letter Ltd., Hong Kong; monthly.

CHINA NEWSLETTER. Japan External Trade Organization, Tokyo; every two months.

CHINA NOW. Society for Anglo-Chinese Understanding, London; every two months.

CHINA QUARTERLY. Contemporary China Institute, School of Oriental and African Studies, London; quarterly.

CHINA RECONSTRUCTS. Guoji Shudian (China Publications Centre), Beijing; monthly.

CHINA REPORT. Centre for the Study of Developing Societies, Delhi, India; six times a year.

CHINA TRADE AND ECONOMIC NEWSLETTER. The Forty-eight Group of British Traders with China.

CHINA TRADE REPORT. Far Eastern Economic Review, Hong Kong; monthly.

CHINA'S FOREIGN TRADE. Guoji Shudian (China Publications Centre), Beijing; every two months.

CHINESE ECONOMIC STUDIES. M. E. Sharpe Inc., Armonk, New York; four times yearly.

CONTEMPORARY CHINA. Westview Press, Boulder, Colorado, for East Asian Institute, Columbia University, N.Y.; quarterly.

CURRENT BIBLIOGRAPHY OF AGRICULTURE IN CHINA. Centre for Agricultural Publishing and Documentation, Wageningen, Netherlands; monthly.

EASTERN HORIZON. Eastern Horizon Press, Hong Kong; monthly.

ECONOMIC REPORTER. Economic Information and Agency, Hong Kong; monthly.

MODERN CHINA. Sage Publications, Beverly Hills, U.S.A., and London; quarterly.

FAR EASTERN ECONOMIC REVIEW. Hong Kong; weekly.

PEKING INFORMERS, THE. Continental Research Institute, Hong Kong; fortnightly.

TA KUNG PAO (English Edition). Ta Kung Pao, Hong Kong; weekly.

XINHUA WEEKLY (English Edition). Xinhua News Agency, Hong Kong; weekly.

TAIWAN

GENERAL

CHINA YEARBOOK. Annual (China Publishing Co., Taipei).

CROZIER, BRIAN. The Man Who Lost China: The First Full Biography of Chiang Kai-Shek (Angus and Robertson, London, 1977).

GODDARD, W. G. Formosa: A Study in Chinese History (Macmillan, London, 1966).

HSU, LONG-HSUEN, and CHANG, MING-KAI. History of the Sino-Japanese War (Chung Wu Publishing Co., 1971).

ECONOMY

CHANG, HAN-YU, and MYERS, R. H. Japanese Colonial Development Policy in Taiwan 1895–1906: A Case of Bureaucratic Entrepreneurship (*The Journal of Asian Studies*, Vol. XXII, No. 4, 1963).

CHANG, KOWEI. Economic Development in Taiwan (Cheng Chung Co., Taipei, 1968).

CLOUGH, RALPH N. Island China (Harvard University Press, Cambridge, Mass., 1978).

HO, C. S., and others. Economic Minerals of Taiwan Geological Survey of Taiwan, 1963.

HO, SAMUEL P. S. Economic Development of Taiwan, 1860–1970 (Yale University Press, 1978).

HO, YHI-MIN. Agricultural Development of Taiwan: 1903–1960 (Vanderbilt University Press, Tennessee, 1966).

JACOBY, N. H. An Evaluation of U.S. Economic Aid to Free China 1951–1965 (Praeger, New York, 1967).

MINISTRY OF INTERIOR AND COUNCIL FOR INTERNATIONAL ECONOMIC CO-OPERATION AND DEVELOPMENT. Labor Laws and Regulations of the Republic of China (Taipei, 1965).

SHEN, TSUNG-HAN. Agricultural Development on Taiwan since World War II (Mei Ya Publications Inc., Taipei, 1971).

STATISTICAL YEARBOOK OF THE REPUBLIC OF CHINA. Directorate-General of Budget, Accounting and Statistics, Executive Yuan.

TANG, H. S., and HSIEH, S. C. Land Reform and Agricultural Development in Taiwan (*The Malayan Economic Review*, Vol. VI, No. 1, 1961).

Hong Kong

PHYSICAL AND SOCIAL GEOGRAPHY

Michael Freeberne
(Revised by the Editor, 1976-1982)

Hong Kong's population occupies a total area of only 1,063.4 sq. km. (410.6 square miles). The Crown Colony is situated off the south-east coast of China, to the east of the mouth of the Zhujiang (Pearl River), between latitudes 22° 9′ and 22° 37′ N. and longitudes 113° 52′ and 114° 30′ E. Hong Kong includes the island of Hong Kong, ceded to Britain by China in 1842, the Kowloon peninsula, ceded in 1860, and the New Territories, which are part of the mainland leased to Britain in 1898 for a period of 99 years, together with Deep Bay and Mirs Bay and various outlying islands. The fine anchorages between the capital of Victoria on the northern shore of Hong Kong island and Kowloon, provided an ideal situation for the growth of one of the world's leading entrepôt ports.

Physical Features

Hong Kong Island is roughly 17 km. (11 miles) long and between 3 and 8 km. (2 and 5 miles) wide. An irregular range of hills rises abruptly from the sea; several peaks are over 300 metres (1,000 ft.) in height, and Victoria Peak reaches 551 metres (1,809 ft.). Granites, basalt and other volcanic rocks account for the main geological formations. These rocks are most common, too, on Lantau and Lamma islands and in the Kowloon peninsula and New Territories, which are mostly hilly, rising to 958 metres (3,144 ft.) in Tai Mo Shan, and have rugged deeply indented coastlines. The Colony is poor in minerals and largely stripped of natural vegetation. Flat land and agricultural land is scarce everywhere. Reclamation of land from the sea for building purposes is very important, and the new land is used for housing and factories, as well as projects like the extension of the runway of Kai Tak international airport.

Climate

The climate of Hong Kong is tropical monsoon. Winter lasts from October to April, when the winds are from the north or north-east, while during the summer months from May to September south or southwesterly winds predominate. Average daily temperatures are highest in July with 28°C. and lowest in January with 15°C. The wet summer is very humid. Annual rainfall averages 2,225 mm., over two-thirds of which falls between June and September. Devastating typhoons occasionally strike in summer, taking an especially heavy toll amongst the squatter colonies which crowd some of the hill-sides.

Notwithstanding the high rainfall it has proved difficult to supply sufficient domestic and industrial water, and water is piped from neighbouring Guangdong Province in the People's Republic of China. The Plover Cove reservoir, inaugurated in 1969, and holding 37,000 million gallons, trebled Hong Kong's reservoir capacity and further reservoirs came into operation in the 1970s including the world's first seabed reservoir with a capacity of 50,000 million gallons. A further hazard which frequently threatens the sub-standard housing of the large refugee population is the danger of fire and disease, despite the brave housing and health schemes of the Government.

POPULATION

The population of Hong Kong in June 1981 was estimated at 5,154,100, an average densisty of 4,847 per square kilometre. However, average density in the New Territories in March 1981 was only 1,338 per square kilometre, whereas for Hong Kong Island it was 15,103, and in the Mong Kok district over 200,000. These higher figures represent some of the highest population densities in the world. In 1979 the population was greatly swelled by the entry of many thousands of illegal immigrants from China and "boat people" from Viet-Nam.

Hong Kong has experienced an extraordinary growth in population. About 59 per cent of the population in 1978 was born in Hong Kong. Between 1841, when only about 2,500 people lived on the island, and 1941, the colony received wave after wave of migrants; then the population was estimated at about 1.5 million. There was a drastic reduction during the Japanese occupation in the early 1940s, but by 1949 the population had grown to 1,857,000. After the establishment of the People's Republic of China in 1949 large numbers of refugees arrived in Hong Kong, where the rate of natural increase was already high. Over 98 per cent of the population are Chinese, on the basis of language and place of origin. The Cantonese are the largest community.

Land Use

About three-quarters of Hong Kong's land area is marginal land; 15.7 per cent comprises built-up areas; and 7.7 per cent is in agricultural use. Only the alluvial soils around Yuen Long in the Deep Bay area have any depth. Hong Kong belongs to the frost-free double-cropping rice zone of East Asia. Increasingly, however, more profitable forms of land utilization are replacing rice: market gardens, including vegetables, fruit and cut flowers for the dense urban populations; poultry farms and fish ponds.

HISTORY

N. J. Miners

The area of the present colony was acquired in three stages. The First Opium War of 1840–42 began after the Chinese Commissioner in Guangzhou (Canton) had seized and destroyed large stocks of opium held by the British traders there, who then left the city. The British Government demanded compensation and a commercial treaty, and an expedition was dispatched to enforce these demands. During the hostilities a naval force occupied the island of Hong Kong, which was ceded to Britain "in perpetuity" by the Treaty of Nanjing (Nanking) of 1842. As soon as this was ratified the colony was formally proclaimed in June 1843.

Continuing disputes between Britain and China over trade and shipping led to renewed warfare in 1856. This was ended by the Convention of Beijing (Peking) of 1860, by which the peninsula of Kowloon on the mainland opposite the island was annexed.

In 1895 China was defeated by Japan, and the Western powers seized the opportunity to exact further concessions. Britain obtained a 99-year lease of the mainland north of Kowloon together with the adjoining islands, on the grounds that this was needed for the colony's defence. These New Territories increased the area of the colony from 43 to 400 square miles. The terms of the 1898 Convention of Beijing allowed the existing Chinese magistrates to remain in the Old Walled City of Kowloon, but in 1899 they were unilaterally expelled by the British on the pretext that they had encouraged resistance to the British occupation. The Chinese Government protested at the time and reasserted a claim to jurisdiction over this small area in 1933, 1948 and 1962, though this interpretation of the 1898 Convention has been rejected by the Hong Kong courts.

Since 1949 spokesmen for the People's Republic of China have asserted that all the unequal treaties forced upon China in the days of its weakness are no longer recognized as binding; but the treaties of 1842, 1860 and 1898 have not yet been formally abrogated. After admission to the United Nations in 1971, Beijing's permanent representative informed the Special Committee on Colonialism that "Hong Kong and Macau are part of Chinese territory occupied by the British and Portuguese authorities. The settlement of the questions of Hong Kong and Macau is entirely within China's sovereign right and does not at all fall under the ordinary category of colonial territories. . . . The Chinese Government has consistently held that they should be settled in an appropriate way when conditions are ripe".

In deference to China's wishes, Hong Kong and Macau were deleted from the list of colonial territories. However, the United Kingdom still considers the treaties to be valid. All leases of Crown land in the New Territories terminate on June 27th, 1997, three days before the expiry of the British lease. What may happen in 1997 is uncertain. The New Territories are now fully integrated into the rest of the colony and it is inconceivable that Britain could or would wish to retain Hong Kong island and Kowloon if the New Territories should revert to Chinese administration. In March 1981 Deng Xiaoping told the British Foreign Secretary: "If in sixteen years' time or after there is a change in the status of Hong Kong, the interests of investors will not be harmed". This repeated previous assurances by other Chinese leaders. He also indicated, however, that China was not yet ready to make a definitive statement on Hong Kong's future.

Early Development to 1945

The main reason for the British occupation of Hong Kong in 1841 was its magnificent harbour. Attracted by its free port status, the entrepôt trade between the West and China grew steadily for the next 100 years. The great trading companies set up their headquarters under the British flag; banks, insurance companies and other commercial enterprises were established to serve the China traders as well as shipbuilding, ship-repairing and other industries dependent on the port. At the same time the population grew from about 5,000 in 1841 to more than 500,000 in 1916 and over a million by 1939, of which fewer than 20,000 were non-Chinese. Chinese were allowed free access and the flow of migrants increased whenever China was disturbed by wars or rebellions, reversing itself when peaceful conditions had been restored on the mainland. Apart from the settled farming population of the New Territories, relatively few Chinese regarded Hong Kong as their permanent home until after the Second World War. Most came to trade or seek employment and then returned to their home-towns. Europeans were similarly transient, whether they were government officials or in private employment. Few, apart from some Portuguese from Macau and Eurasians, considered Hong Kong their permanent home.

The colony's administration followed the usual Crown Colony pattern, with power concentrated in the hands of a Governor advised by nominated Executive and Legislative Councils on which government officials had an overall majority over the unofficial members. The first unofficial members were appointed to the Legislative Council in 1850, and the first Chinese in 1880; the first unofficials in the Executive Council were appointed in 1896, and the first Chinese in 1926. In 1894, 1916 and 1922 the British residents pressed for an unofficial majority in the Legislative Council and the election of some or all of the unofficials on a franchise confined to British subjects, citing the constitutional progress made in other colonies; but on all occasions the British Government was unwilling to allow the Chinese majority to be politically subjected to a small European minority. A Sanitary Board was set up in 1883 and this was made partly elective in 1887. In 1936 it was renamed the Urban Council, though its powers were not significantly increased.

Little of note happened in Hong Kong throughout this period, apart from commercial expansion, land reclamation, the building of reservoirs and minor squabbles between British officialdom and the trading community. There were a number of large-scale strikes in the early 1920s, notably that of 1925/26 which closed the port for several months, but, other than these incidents, anti-foreigner agitation in China had little effect on Hong Kong's prosperity.

The increasing threat of war in the late 1930s led to an increase in defence expenditure, which forced the institution of income and profits tax for the first time; this wartime expedient was made permanent in 1947. Japanese forces occupied most of the Chinese province of Guangdong, north of the colony, in 1938, and in December 1941 invaded Hong Kong, which was forced to surrender. The Japanese occupation lasted three years eight months until August 1945, when the Japanese authorities handed power back to the surviving colonial officials who had been interned with the rest of the British community throughout the occupation. A British naval force arrived in late August to set up an interim military administration, thus forestalling pressures from the United States Government for Hong Kong to be handed back to China.

The Post-War Period

After the loss of Hong Kong in 1941 a planning unit was set up in London to prepare for the post-war rehabilitation of the colony. Its members staffed the interim military administration, which restored public services on a minimum basis. During the war the colony's population had dropped to about 600,000 as a result of privation and mass deportations by the Japanese. The population quickly regained pre-war levels and then rose to about 2,000,000 in 1950 as a result of a massive influx of refugees from the civil war in China. The pressures caused by this inflow forced the colony to abandon its policy of free access and the frontier was closed in 1950. Since then, movement over the border has been tightly controlled by the Chinese authorities, with the exception of 1962, when the frontier was unexpectedly opened and 120,000 refugees were allowed to leave. Individual escapers also attempt to enter clandestinely. From 1974 to 1980 any illegal immigrants caught in the frontier region were handed over to the Chinese authorities, but those who succeeded in reaching the urban areas were allowed to remain. This concession continued to encourage escape attempts and after a massive surge in illegal immigration in 1979/80, when it is estimated over 200,000 succeeded in settling in the colony in spite of the fact that 170,000 were captured and repatriated, it was announced in October 1980 that in future all illegals found anywhere in the colony would be repatriated. This caused a sharp decline in illegal attempts to enter, but China continues to allow 150 legal migrants to cross the frontier daily, in spite of Hong Kong's representations.

The United Kingdom recognized the new Communist Government of China in 1950, having heavily reinforced the garrison in Hong Kong in 1949 to deter any possible Chinese attack. The only serious violation of the frontier occurred in 1967. The garrison was run down at successive defence reviews in the 1970s, but was then increased in 1979 to provide greater security along the frontier against illegal immigrants. From 1982 the garrison will consist of five infantry battalions (four of them Gurkha) and supporting services, together with the locally raised Hong Kong Regiment.

The problem of feeding the refugees and providing employment was made worse by the outbreak of the Korean war in 1950 which led to the imposition of an embargo on the export of strategic goods to China and gravely damaged Hong Kong's entrepôt trade. However, the refugees provided a pool of docile, hard-working labour. Local businessmen and industrialists who had fled from Shanghai took advantage of this and, by making use of the colony's existing financial infrastructure and worldwide trading connections, they reoriented the economy to manufacturing for export. The value of domestic exports fluctuated during the 1950s but there have been continued rapid increases since 1960.

The refugees put an immense strain on all public services and the newcomers were left to build themselves shanty towns which spread over the hillsides. A devastating fire at one of these shanty towns in 1953 spurred the Government into a resettlement programme; huge estates were built with rooms allocated on the scale of 25 square feet (2.3 square metres) for each adult. The early designs provided few amenities, as the main consideration was speed of erection. The housing programme has continued steadily since then with an added boost in 1972 when a ten-year programme to house a further 1,500,000 people, mainly in new towns in the New Territories, was announced. At the same time various government housing agencies were amalgamated in a new Housing Authority to take over the planning, construction and management of all public housing in Hong Kong. The latest estates are being built to improved standards, with separate washrooms and kitchens for each family and a space allocation of 50 square feet per adult. The target set in 1972 was not attained, largely because of the economic recession of the mid-1970s caused by the oil crisis; but the Government is now building 35,000 public housing units per year and this rate of construction is to be continued.

Since 1945 the people of Hong Kong have shown a marked apathy towards any form of political activity or agitation for democratic self-government. This political calm has been disturbed only three times: in 1956 there were faction fights between communist and nationalist supporters; in 1966 there were three nights of rioting sparked off by a fare increase on the cross-harbour ferry; and for several months in 1967 there were disturbances and bomb attacks, led by communist sympathizers inspired by the example of the Cultural Revolution in China. Since then, relations with China have greatly improved, particularly since the death of Mao Zedong (Mao Tse-tung) and the launching of China's new drive for modernization. In April 1979 the

Governor paid an official visit to Beijing at China's invitation. The main benefit to China of the present position is the huge surplus which it earns on trade and commercial transactions with the colony. Estimates of China's total foreign exchange receipts range up to U.S. $6,000 million, which is about 40 per cent of China's total foreign income. Agencies of the Chinese government have recently made large commercial investments in the colony, and Hong Kong businessmen have set up joint enterprises inside China. This has encouraged speculation that China may agree to extend the lease of the New Territories. Officially the Government's long term plans take no account of 1997 and large public investments are being made in the New Territories, including five new towns, a new underground railway and a projected new airport. (*Editorial Note:* In July 1982 there was speculation that China's intention was now to integrate the whole of Hong Kong into the People's Republic.)

Administrative and Political Developments

Civil government was restored after the Japanese occupation in May 1946. The returning governor promised a greater measure of self-government and, after inviting suggestions from the public, proposed that an elected municipal council with wide powers over local affairs in the urban area should be set up. The detailed bills to implement this proposal were not published until June 1949, but then the unofficial members of the Legislative Council objected that reforms of their council to provide for elected members and an unofficial majority should have priority, and voted unanimously against the plan. Consultations were recommenced but, in the absence of widespread agitation for changes and amid the continuing uncertainty over the colony's future caused by the communist victory in China in 1949, reform was abandoned in 1952 and has not been revived, largely because China has made plain her dislike of any such moves.

Instead, the number of appointed unofficial members on the Legislative Council has been steadily increased, to 8 in 1951, 13 in 1964, 15 in 1973, 22 in 1976, 24 in 1977 and 27 in 1981. In 1982 twenty-one of the unofficials were Chinese. Until 1976 the number of officials was always equal to the unofficials, enabling the Governor, as President, to use his casting vote in the event of a tie. Since 1976 the unofficials have had a clear majority over the officials (27–23 in 1982) though a further four official members could be added to the Council if needed. In practice the official majority has not been used to overrule the unanimous view of the unofficials since 1953. The unofficials also form a Finance Committee which meets in private to scrutinize in detail all government expenditure proposals. Since 1945, if the unofficials have rejected any item, the administration has always taken this as final.

The number of unofficial members on the Executive Council was increased to eight in 1966 and nine in 1978, thus outnumbering the six official members. In 1982 five members of the Council were Chinese (all unofficials). The Governor is empowered to reject the advice given to him by the majority of the Council, but in fact is most unlikely to do so.

The British Government and Parliament retain the power to legislate for the colony, to veto ordinances passed by the Legislative Council, and to issue mandatory instructions to the Governor. The veto has not been invoked since 1913 and the power to legislate is confined almost entirely to matters which concern the United Kingdom's international or Commonwealth obligations. Hong Kong is normally allowed to run its internal affairs without reference to Britain.

The Urban Council was reorganized in 1973 with 12 appointed and 12 elected members, and responsibility for public health and sanitation, recreation, amenities and cultural services in the urban area. From 1983 there will be 15 appointed and 15 elected members, and the right to vote has been extended to all those over 21 years old who have been resident in Hong Kong for seven years. Previously the franchise was more restricted and such was popular apathy that only about 2 per cent of those eligible to vote cast their ballots (6,195 in 1981). The Reform Club and Civic Association run candidates but voting is largely on the basis of personalities.

The New Territories are divided into eight districts and the urban area into 10. In each of these there is a management committee of officials from various government departments working in the area, presided over by a senior administrative officer. This committee is assisted by an advisory District Board composed partly of officials, partly of nominated unofficials, and partly of unofficials elected on the same wide franchise as the Urban Council. District Board elections were held for the first time in 1982 and attracted greater interest than previous Urban Council elections. The interests of the rural indigenous inhabitants of the New Territories are served by an elected advisory body, the *Heung Yee Kuk*. Although it has no executive powers, it is heard with the greatest respect by the administration, particularly on the question of compensation when land is recovered for development. There are also advisory committees attached to most government departments.

In 1973 revelations of widespread corruption in the police force led to the establishment of the Independent Commission Against Corruption (I.C.A.C.). As a result, a number of police officers and businessmen were convicted and imprisoned, but its methods of investigation gave rise to increasing dissatisfaction among the police, culminating in a near mutiny in November 1977. The situation was calmed only when the Governor instructed the I.C.A.C. to confine its enquiries to offences committed since January 1977. Later, in April 1978, 118 policemen who had been under suspicion were compulsorily retired from the force without prosecution.

ECONOMIC SURVEY

Frank H. H. King

(Revised for this edition by Carla Rapoport)

In 1981, Hong Kong's economy experienced yet another year of rapid growth. The growth rate of the Gross Domestic Product (G.D.P.) in real terms was as high as 10 per cent, easily matching the growth rates in the earlier post-recession years. Given that world economic prospects remained uncertain and economic conditions in Hong Kong's major markets were unimpressive, such a performance continued to be remarkable.

Unlike the previous two years, however, the impetus to Hong Kong's impressive economic growth lay with domestic demand, rather than with domestic exports, in 1981. The growth rate in real terms of domestic demand was 11 per cent, significantly higher than that of domestic exports (at 7 per cent). Given that the export sector is still the backbone of the Hong Kong economy, the situation in which economic growth is led by domestic demand is one that inevitably causes uneasiness. The situation in 1981 developed against a background of historically high interest and inflation rates, relatively low growth rates in domestic exports and a relatively weak Hong Kong dollar. With the recession still squeezing its major Western markets, Hong Kong's export-based economy faces strong challenges ahead and still cannot afford to ignore its exposed international position despite high priority social needs.

With a population of 5.2 million at the end of 1981 and a land area of only 1,063 sq. kilometres, Hong Kong is one of the mostly densely populated areas of the world. While the rate of natural increase in population dropped from 14.9 to 11.5 per 1,000 in the 1970s, illegal and legal immigration from China during the same period presented a threat to the orderly development of the territory. This threat was exacerbated in 1978 and 1979 by the influx of refugees from Viet-Nam. In October 1980 Hong Kong abolished legislation which had allowed illegal immigrants from China who reached the urban centre of Hong Kong to remain. This substantially reduced the flow of illegal immigration during 1981, but the challenge of Hong Kong's dense population remains awesome.

Some 36 per cent of this large population is below the age of 20 and the percentage of those over the age of 65 is increasing. All these factors require a high-performance economy and, as Hong Kong has few natural resources, the territory's very survival depends on its ability to sustain a reasonable level of economic growth supporting an ever-increasing level of exports.

While overall growth rates may support the territory's strong arguments for free enterprise, sectoral economic problems and social questions involve the Government in activities which challenge the popular concept of laissez-faire by which its policy has been usually characterized. The under-staffed colonial government of the early 1950s faced problems which, in the Hong Kong context, were virtually indeterminable, given a potentially unlimited influx of refugees, an uncertain political future, and an almost total lack of control of the resources necessary for planning. However, when the Hong Kong Government left decisions to market forces it did so knowing that there were both skilled workers and entrepreneurs with adequate capital among the refugees, that the former entrepôt trade provided the territory with shipping facilities and financial institutions, and that the private sector was in communication with world markets. Equally important for Hong Kong's economic growth was insistence on a relatively independent internal policy. Thus Hong Kong escaped many of the restraints implied in Britain's sterling area policies and delayed implementation of social measures which the home country considered essential.

The troubles of 1966 and 1967, a spill-over of China's Cultural Revolution, revealed on the one hand the basic loyalty of the population to an open society but on the other hand served as a warning to the Government that it must take a more active role in ordering the use of economic resources. The realistic approach of Hong Kong workers was revealed in the 1974 recession when real wages were allowed to fall without significant labour disturbance, but by then a basic change in government attitude had been declared and since then steps have been taken on many fronts to achieve a redistribution of resources.

Since 1953 the Government has been involved in extensive housing schemes. In 1981 about 44 per cent of the population were living in government-subsidized accommodation. Some 35,400 flats, for rent or sale, were built in 1981 and this construction rate is scheduled to be maintained for five years. However, there are about 163,000 families on the waiting list and the typical waiting time is about seven years. At the same time standards are improving, and non-housing amenities are being integrated into the estates. The Government is also implementing an extensive house-ownership scheme which reflects recognition of the permanence of the territory.

Land is the scarce commodity and the Government's long-standing policy (since 1844) of allocation by auction, modified by private treaty for educational and charitable purposes, has been further modified under the pressures of an increasingly crowded environment. The Government has been actively attracting high-technology industry as part of its diversification policy and, consistent with this, has since 1974 made sites available on arranged terms. Intensive land development for industrial purposes has made 445 hectares available over the last few years, and a second industrial estate has been planned. These developments coincide with the construction of new towns at Tsuen Wan, Tuen Mun and Sha Tin.

If housing and land appear to be the most spectacular departures from the image of passive government, there are others of considerable significance. The growth of leisure has dictated the need to preserve the countryside and beaches, and five country parks have been established. Government expenditure on education reached HK $3,700 million in 1981/82, although its share of the total budget dropped from 16 to 13 per cent. The social welfare programme has developed more cautiously, with expenditure limited to $885 million in 1981/82.

Despite its attempts at diversification and its developed financial services, Hong Kong's prosperity depends on exports, of which textiles (including clothing) comprised 42 per cent by value in 1981. These goods and others, such as footwear, are subject to increasingly restrictive quotas and controls, and diversification has been pursued in the face not only of quotas, but also of the increasing competitiveness of countries like South Korea and Taiwan. Hong Kong also remains primarily dependent on the U.S. market, where 36.1 per cent of its exports were sold in 1981. Thus the territory, without political authority in international affairs, is doubly vulnerable at a time when domestic demands in its major markets are still under recessionary pressure.

Against this several factors must be noted. Firstly, with the new stress on economic development within the People's Republic of China, the demands on Hong Kong are increasing and the territory's economy is becoming more integrated with that of the neighbouring Guangdong Province in the People's Republic of China. This change is difficult to assess statistically, but mainland banks, trading enterprises, retail stores, real estate ventures, and other direct activities complement China's use of Hong Kong's port facilities, including the connecting railroad from Guangzhou (Canton). Secondly, foreign investment, nearly 45 per cent of which comes from the U.S.A., totalled over HK $2,500 million by February 1981. Gross domestic fixed capital formation is nearly 25 per cent of the G.D.P., a percentage which, while not exceptional in the region, is considered adequate.

Hong Kong may not be master of its economic destiny, but the Government has now joined the private sector in attempting to set a course which will avoid the still random barriers to overseas trade not only by planning the general infrastructure but also by positive attraction of new industries whose exports are likely to be acceptable on world markets, judged both by their relative competitiveness and their impact on the domestic economic policies of the importing country.

AGRICULTURE AND FISHING

The New Territories, i.e. the land leased from China for 99 years in 1898, comprise 90 per cent of Hong Kong's total land area and include 234 islands, including the largely undeveloped island of Lantau. Once largely rural with a few market towns, the area is rapidly becoming more urban. As a result there has been a fall in the area of land given over to rice production from 9,450 hectares in 1954 to 30 hectares in 1980, although the yield on two-crop rice land has reached five metric tons per half-hectare due to the increased use of fertilizer. Rice production continues to give way to intensive vegetable production which gives a far higher return where there is adequate water.

Recent figures show that less than 2 per cent of the economically active population is engaged in farming on 9.2 per cent of the total land area. However, with modern techniques and constant experimentation, the value of crop production increased by 524 per cent between 1963 and 1981, with vegetable production contributing 86 per cent of the total value, at HK $555 million, in 1981. Consequently, Hong Kong's farmers can produce 38 per cent of the vegetables consumed, 66 per cent of the total live chicken requirements and 18 per cent of all pigs slaughtered. Total food imports in 1981 were valued at HK $13,993 million, with China as the main supplier.

Although only 1.19 per cent of the economically active population are engaged in fishing, the total marine catch in 1981 was 182,000 metric tons. This represented 90 per cent of local consumer demand.

Facilities in the existing wholesale markets are inadequate for handling the ever-increasing quantities of imported fresh vegetables, fruit, poultry and eggs. There is widespread obstruction, traffic congestion and low marketing efficiency at high costs. Plans are going ahead to establish new wholesale markets in Kowloon and on Hong Kong Island. In the interim, the government has brought a number of temporary wholesale markets into operation.

These rapid developments have been aided not only by extensive research but also by a highly developed government marketing system which both protected the income of primary producers and gave them a credit standing which they use to finance mechanization and modernization. However, this has also contributed towards the urbanization of the population in that small farmers and fishermen are not in a position to take advantage of these schemes.

INDUSTRY AND TRADE

The Hong Kong Government is playing an increasing role in directing the course of industry. This is being followed up by an involvement in international commercial relations at a level which approximates to that of an active foreign policy. Hong Kong, for example, must negotiate its own bilateral agreement with the European Economic Community; the 1978 agreement on textile and clothing exports was signed, according to Acting Governor Sir Denys Roberts, "reluctantly and with many misgivings". Little support came from the United Kingdom.

While the total value of domestic exports rose by 18 per cent in 1981 to a total of HK $80,423 million, the textile and clothing industry continued to dominate, employing some 40 per cent of the total industrial workforce and producing 42 per cent of total domestic exports. This does not, of course, suggest a static situation; since the early Shanghai-financed textile operations of the early 1950s, the industry has grown, modernized and diversified. The boom in 1976 was due not only to a building of stocks overseas but also to exploitation of the new demand for denim, and the slowdown in 1977 partly reflected a reaction to both these factors. The export performance of this sector improved over 1979, despite the restrictive terms of its current bilateral textile agreements with the EEC and the U.S. Total domestic exports of textiles and clothing in 1981 were valued at HK $33,590 million, against HK $27,793 million in 1980. Other light industries include electronics, plastic products, toys, watches, clocks and accessories industries. In 1981 the electronics industry maintained its position as the second largest export-earner among Hong Kong's manufacturing industries, with domestic exports of electronic products valued at HK $9,174 million. Toys constitute the bulk of the items produced in the plastics sector and Hong Kong continues to be the world's largest supplier of toys.

The impact of new industrial policies, including the developments planned by the Hong Kong Industrial Estates Corporation, established in March 1977, has not as yet shown itself in aggregate statistics. However, by the end of 1981 some 45 hectares of the Tai Po Industrial Estate had been developed and the third stage of the Industrial Estate had begun. It is expected to take three years to complete and will add another 20 hectares to the Estate. A second industrial estate, under construction in Yuen Long, will provide another 65 hectares when completed in 1983. The number of industrial sites made available outside these estates increased in 1981 to a total of 53 sites with an area of over 150,037 sq. metres.

Gross domestic fixed capital formation is estimated at about 25 per cent of G.D.P. in real terms. There was considerable investment in textile plant and equipment in 1976 and in electronics in 1977 and the growth rate of investment in plant and machinery in 1980 was expected to be more than 10 per cent. In order to encourage overseas industrialists to invest in Hong Kong's manufacturing industry, a series of industrial investment promotion missions were sent in 1980 to the United Kingdom, the Federal Republic of Germany, Japan, Australia, Sweden and the U.S.A. Although the great majority of industrial enterprises are locally financed and managed, the number of factories either fully or partly-owned by foreign interests in 1981 was nearly 430. The main target industries are electronics and textiles and the total direct investment involved was over HK $900 million as of February 1980. The main sources of these funds were the U.S.A. Japan, the United Kingdom, the Netherlands and Switzerland. The development of joint enterprises with China is, on the other hand, evidence both of Hong Kong's capital export role and of the continuing integration of its economy with that of neighbouring Guangdong Province.

The Hong Kong Government claims that it neither protects nor subsidizes manufacturers. Some policies come very close to indirect subsidy but, true to its free port tradition and consistent with the needs of a territory without natural resources, Hong Kong does not protect industry. Import tariffs and revenue duties are levied only on tobacco, alcoholic liquors and some hydrocarbon oils. In contrast, Hong Kong's exports suffer from various agreed and ad hoc restrictions which are the subject of continual negotiation. Although the market share of Hong Kong's domestic exports in its major foreign markets is nowhere in excess of 2.5 per cent (Australia) and for its principal target, the U.S.A., the share is only 1.8 per cent, the impact of textiles and footwear, to mention two problem categories, has led to restraints which in turn have forced the Government into a more active role in industrial development.

Hong Kong's external economic relations are constrained by the United Kingdom's membership of the International Monetary Fund and by the rules of the General Agreement on Tariffs and Trade. But of major concern are the restraints on textiles imposed by adherence to the Multi-Fibre Agreement and membership of the Textiles Surveillance Body. These latter arangements, first made in 1974, were recently renewed for four years from January 1982. A bilateral textile agreement with the U.S.A. also came into force in January 1978. Hong Kong does, however, benefit from various generalized preference schemes designed by developed countries to benefit the exports of developing territories, but Hong Kong is excluded from the Finland scheme and certain of its products are specifically excluded from the schemes of the EEC, Japan, Australia, Norway and Austria.

Total merchandise trade in 1981 was up 24 per cent to HK $260,537 million. Imports amounted to HK $138,375 million, an increase of 24 per cent over 1980. Consumer goods represented 27 per cent of Hong Kong's imports, with foodstuffs alone accounting for 11 per cent. Japan, with 23 per cent, remained the principal supplier, China was second with 21 per cent, providing 49 per cent of all foodstuffs and live animals, and the United States third with 10 per cent. Finally, Hong Kong's entrepôt trade improved, with re-exports accounting for 34 per cent of total exports. Re-exports, totalling HK $41,739 million, came mainly from China, Japan and the U.S.A. and were destined primarily for China but also for the U.S.A., Indonesia, Singapore and Taiwan. With imports increasing faster than exports, the territory's visible trade deficit in 1981 reached HK $16,213 million, more than four times the 1977 figure. This trade gap has led to a depreciation in the Hong Kong dollar which, in turn, has been helpful in maintaining Hong Kong's export competitiveness.

In March 1981 Hong Kong had a total working population of 2,404,067, with 990,365 working in manufacturing establishments (which numbered 46,729 in September 1981). At the same time, trade union membership was about 400,000 and there were 366 registered unions. Political affiliations are of primary consideration, and there is evidence that labour relations are handled at levels other than that of the union, including direct influence from the People's Republic of China. Daily wages in manufacturing industries in September 1980 averaged HK $54.18. Despite the lack of strong union intervention, the average rates had increased by 142 per cent (32 per cent in real terms) over the base period of July 1973–June 1974. On no other subject is Hong Kong under greater pressure from the United Kingdom, and a complex body of labour legislation is developing. A Labour Tribunal has been instituted, and the Labour Relations Service dealt with 15,288 labour problems during 1981. In the same year there were 49 work stoppages, with 15,319 working days lost, compared with 21,069 days lost in 37 work stoppages in 1980.

FINANCE

With its still relatively sound currency, stock markets, commodity exchange, gold and silver exchange, banking, deposit-taking and other financial institutions, its absence of exchange controls, low tax rates, non-discriminatory economic policies, communications facilities and ease of international movement (except for Eastern bloc nationals), Hong Kong has become a world financial centre. A tax on interest prevents the territory from reaching its full potential in this direction and Singapore is a determined rival. Hong Kong has therefore become the base of multinationals' regional headquarters, the channel through which funds from overseas Chinese reach the People's Republic, the base of much of China's overseas financial operations, and the source of funds for Hong Kong dollar-denominated bond issues. Yet, despite the interlocking aspects of all these activities, the absence of full statistical information—a product of the absence of controls—leaves local economists unable to agree on, for example, the sources or even the size of capital inflows, or the meaning of a rapid growth in money supply at any given time.

Given the dependence on external economic factors, Hong Kong's fiscal policy might be expected to show a conservative trend, and indeed, surpluses have been achieved in all but three problem years since the Second World War. On the other hand, a surplus in an economy requiring considerable social expenditure may prove surprising, and the explanation is not to be found in terms of economic philosophy alone. Dependence on external factors makes prediction difficult. Thus in 1977/78 revenue from earnings and profits tax was underestimated when the economic recovery was sharper than expected. In both 1979/80 and 1980/81 large surpluses were recorded, largely as a result of unexpectedly high revenues from land sales. As the Hong Kong property market experienced a boom in the late 1970s and early 80s, the Government's income from land sales soared to HK $10,784 million in 1980/81, more than three times the previous year's figures and some HK $4,000 million more than the Government's estimates. Not surprisingly, the Government's overall surplus for 1980/81 was a huge HK $6,696 million. A surplus of HK $5,417 million is estimated for 1981/82.

Yet in another way the Government's fiscal policy appears somewhat more progressive. Estimated expenditure of HK $25,061 million for 1981/82 is more than five times the level for 1972/73, despite three low growth years between 1974 and 1977. Social services accounted for 38 per cent of 1981/82 expenditure forecasts. Education received HK $3,300 million in 1981/82. With defence expenditure limited by the Defence Costs Agreement with the United Kingdom at an estimated HK $1,787 million in 1981/82, the Government can afford to spend 21 per cent of its budget on community services.

Nevertheless the uncertainties place a strain on the capacity of the Government to plan effectively, to recruit and train, to obtain supplies, and to overcome the obstacles which a crowded environment and conflicting priorities present. These factors, together with uncertainty, provide Hong Kong with its justifiable reputation for economic sanity.

For its revenue, Hong Kong depends first on earnings and profits taxes which were forecast to account for 45 per cent of the HK $20,605.5 million recurrent revenue for 1981/82. General rates and excise duties are also important, while capital account receipts comprise approximately 31 per cent of total revenue, with land sales of prime importance.

Although capital expenditures now exceed the surplus on recurrent account, they are almost entirely financed in any one year by the revenue of that year, and public borrowing is minimal. Indeed on March 31st, 1981, while net available public financial assets totalled HK $11,674 million, the public debt was only HK 277 million. Hong Kong is a member in its own right of the Asian Development Bank and has borrowed for a desalinization plant, for the Sha Tin new town Sewage Treatment Works, and for housing facilities in the same area. There are also Government guaranteed debts and contingent liabilities.

Hong Kong has no central bank and the bulk of its currency is issued by two commercial banks, the Hongkong and Shanghai Banking Corporation and the Chartered Bank. However, apart from a small authorized note issue against which approved securities have to be deposited, the Banks can issue bank notes only against the purchase on a one-for-one basis of non-interest bearing certificates of indebtedness which are liabilities of the Government's Exchange Fund. Originally established to permit management of the foreign exchange value of the Hong Kong dollar when China and Hong Kong went "off silver" in 1935, the Exchange Fund operated *de facto* in a neutral way, much as a colonial currency board. But since the Basel Agreement, Hong Kong has been diversifying its foreign exchange reserves, and only 15 per cent are now in sterling. The decision to float the dollar in November 1974 provided the Exchange Fund with the resources and the need to act positively in support of a foreign exchange policy. The transfer of other government foreign exchange assets to the Fund has given it considerable flexibility and since 1977 it has been actively involved in the market to implement foreign exchange policies.

Some would argue that a dependent economy cannot afford a monetary policy and that there is no need for a central bank. However, as stated, the Exchange Fund operates one aspect of monetary policy; other authority is in the hands of the Government's Monetary Affairs Branch, and banks are regulated by the appropriate ordinance. It is nevertheless true that the Hongkong and Shanghai Banking Corporation acts as the Government's banker and that it has shown itself a lender of last resort by intervening positively in the 1964 banking crisis, in the affair of the Hang Seng Bank, and in recent business reorganizations.

Since the 1973 share market speculative boom, when the share price index reached 1,775 (1964=100), more attention has been paid to controlling the potential excesses of the financial sector. In August 1980, the Stock Exchange Unification Ordinance was enacted, which provides for the establishment of one exchange in place of the existing four. Under the ordinance, the Stock Exchange of Hong Kong Ltd. will have the exclusive right to operate a market by not later than early 1984. All members of the existing exchanges have been invited to apply for shares in the new exchange. This unification is expected to result in a broader market, to increase the attractiveness of Hong Kong securities to overseas investors and assist the better management of the market and more effective regulation of the stockbrokers. In June 1982 the Hang Seng index stood at around 1,300, compared with the peak of 1,780 a year earlier. In 1981 total turnover was HK $105,985 million, an increase of 10.8 per cent on 1980's figure. There is now a commodities exchange and in 1978 the traditional gold and silver exchange began dealing in silver for the first time since the Second World War.

The 123 licenced banks in Hong Kong are subject to the Banking Ordinance. There are 1,301 bank branches, reflecting the need for even the largest banks with worldwide operations to seek funds at the grass-roots; otherwise Hong Kong would surely be considered "over-banked" at the retail level. This growth since 1978 reflected in part the Government's lifting of its ten-year moratorium on new banks in Hong Kong (there was one exception). Also, some of the existing foreign banks with representative offices established full branches. At the same time the territory's banks are supplemented by the 350 so-called "deposit-taking" companies and finance companies, for which special legislation exists. A second moratorium on new banking licenses, in place since August 1979, was lifted in May 1980 by the outgoing Financial Secretary, Sir Philip Haddon-Cave. He raised the asset requirement for a foreign bank seeking a Hong Kong licence, but said that there was little prospect of further moratoriums.

Monetary analysis is difficult in the absence of reliable international balance of payments data to supplement the money supply statistics. Hong Kong's money supply, defined to include savings and time deposits, rose by 22 per cent in 1981, or twice the growth rate of the G.D.P. Domestic bank lending played a key role, and there was significant growth in the entire financial sector. However, the bank's liquidity ratio remained significantly above the legal minimum of 25 per cent. Statistics from the deposit-taking companies became available for the first time in December 1978. During 1981 public deposits with these companies grew from HK $42,716 million to HK $60,479 million at the end of the year. Interest rates follow overseas trends and are used as a tool of policy. By the mid-1970s worldwide inflation had caught up with Hong Kong, and was running at some 15 per cent during 1981. High interest rates, however, had cooled down the property market by mid-1981 and cut down on the high level of speculation that had been prevailing in 1979–80.

INFRASTRUCTURE, TOURISM, etc.

There are two historical explanations for Hong Kong's industrial success. Firstly, Chinese entrepreneurs and skilled workers made Hong Kong their first stop to exile and remained by choice or from necessity. Secondly, the territory, although it had no natural resources other than an excellent harbour, did have a sufficiently advanced infrastructure to permit immediate development.

Hong Kong ranks among the three largest container terminals in the world. The Kwai Chung Container Terminal handled the equivalent of 1.55 million 20-foot containers in 1981. There are six berths, fronting 85 hectares of cargo-handling space. The importance of the associated feeder-trade is reflected in the re-export statistics. Consideration is being given to a branch rail line to the container port to facilitate trade with China, and a search is being made for a suitable site for a new container terminal. For the harbour as a whole there were some 10,600 calls by ocean-going vessels in 1981, importing and exporting 39 million metric tons of cargo. There are facilities for shipping repairs for vessels up to 100,000 d.w.t., including the five new floating dry docks located off Tsing Yi Island and some 130 minor shipyards.

Hong Kong's busy Kai Tak airport will soon reach capacity despite HK $600 million of improvements carried out over the last few years. It handles more than 1,000 scheduled flights per week by 31 international airlines. In July 1981 the government decided to proceed with an airport master planning study for a replacement airport at Chek Lap Kok, off Lantau Island. The estimated cost of the project, if undertaken, is HK $5,000 million at 1977 prices. Should construction be approved it would help to justify a planned bridge from the New Territories, on the mainland, to Lantau and would speed industrial development at the island's northern end, with the rest remaining for resort, recreational and other low-density activity.

Work started in mid-1981 on the third and most ambitious stage of Hong Kong's underground railway. The new link is a 12.5-km. stretch on Hong Kong island, extending along the northern shoreline from Western Market to Chai Wan. The extension is expected to cost HK $7,000 million and, when it is completed in 1986, Hong Kong will have an underground system of almost 40 km. The first stage of the railway was opened in February 1980 and runs 16 km. along the spine of Kowloon and under the harbour to Central District. The Tsuen Wan extension, 10.5 km., opened early in 1982 and runs from Tsuen Wan to join the existing system at the north end of Nathan Road.

In 1981 the system was used by about 223 million passengers, with daily passenger volume running at around 700,000. The cost of the initial stage linking Central District on Hong Kong Island with Kwun Tong in Kowloon was HK $5,000 million, excluding government equity payments, and has been financed by Hong Kong dollar government-guaranteed bonds, suppliers' credits and short and medium-term loans from banking syndicates. The extension to Tsuen Wan will cost another HK $4,100 million.

Complementing the Mass Transit System are the modernized Kowloon-Canton Railway and the second Beacon Hill tunnel, which was opened in April 1981. China began exporting petroleum to Hong Kong in 1974 and necessary provisions for this and other freight requirements have been made. A high-speed suburban service was opened in February 1981, linking the new town of Sha Tin in the New Territories with Kowloon. Additionally, Hong Kong has a complex privately-operated system of buses, trams, mini-buses, ferries, the Peak Tram and, at Ocean Park, the world's largest capacity passenger-carrying aerial ropeway.

By agreement with the People's Council of Guangdong Province, China supplies Hong Kong with about one-third of its total water consumption. The actual amount is negotiated every year but reached 168 million cubic metres in 1980. Hong Kong's own supply comes from 18 storage reservoirs with a total capacity of 363 million gallons and from the world's first seabed reservoir which has a capacity of 50,000 million gallons.

Electricity is supplied almost entirely by two private companies. Consumption of electricity in 1981 was 42,427 million megajoules, giving Hong Kong the second highest per capita consumption rate in Asia. Of the total, 75 per cent is almost evenly divided between industrial and commercial usage.

Tourism remains a major source of Hong Kong's foreign exchange earnings, amounting to HK $7,547 million from 2,501,473 visitors in 1981. In the same year 22 per cent of visitors came from South-East Asia, 20.1 per cent from Japan, 18.3 per cent from the U.S.A., 16.3 per cent from Western Europe and 9.1 per cent from Australasia. Hotel capacity, which expanded by 62 per cent between 1970 and 1977, totalled 16,666 by December 1981. By the end of 1983 more than 20,000 rooms should be available. Considerable effort is being made to change Hong Kong's image from that of a short-stay shopping stop to a territory with scenery, beaches, temples, customs, fine food and an entire culture on view. The Asian Arts Festival and the Hong Kong Arts Festival provide two concentrated periods of cultural activity, typical of those available around the year. Hong Kong is also a base for visiting Macau, the Portuguese territory only 75 minutes by hydrofoil to the west. Tourism to China continues to grow, bringing with it a bonus for Hong Kong in the form of visitors who stay there on their way to or from China. These visitors in 1980 accounted for 10.5 per cent of the total number of arrivals. A through train service from Kowloon to Guangzhou (Canton) was re-established in April 1979, eliminating the walk across the frontier bridge and symbolizing the changed approach of the Chinese Government. Daily charter flights to Guangzhou are now available, and there is also a frequent hoverferry service on the Zhujiang (Pearl River) via Whampoa to Guangzhou.

ECONOMIC OUTLOOK

In his 1982 budget speech, the Financial Secretary forecast a real G.D.P. growth rate of 8 per cent for the year, compared with 10 per cent in 1981. Domestic exports in 1982 are officially estimated to grow by 7 per cent in real terms. By April 1982 the Financial Secretary was suggesting that the target would be difficult to reach and the Government's first-quarter economic report suggests that he was correct. While growth in money terms was 9 per cent over the first quarter of 1981, real growth was nil. This seems to indicate that the government's estimate on G.D.P. growth may be somewhat over-ambitious. While the expanding financial sector will cushion overall G.D.P. against a manufacturing slow-down, an estimate of perhaps 5 to 6 per cent for export growth would be more accurate for 1982.

There has been no sign of any significant shift in the distribution of labour resources away from the manufacturing sector, nor any sign of a significant widening in the visible trade gap. As a result, revenue and expenditure are estimated to grow more slowly in 1982. Revenue is forecast to go up by 8.3 per cent to HK $32,888 million, while gross expenditure is expected to increase by 6.2 per cent to HK $25,062 million, with an estimated surplus of HK $7,826 million for the year.

Restrictive textile agreements, reflecting what is seen in Hong Kong as a shift towards protectionism, make the territory's short-range ability to sustain necessary economic growth dependent on its ability to increase trade, find new markets and, more realistically, diversify industry. Hong Kong enjoyed a 6 per cent per caput growth rate between 1977 and 1980; whether it can sustain this rate into the mid-1980s is open to question.

The government is nevertheless committed to a programme of increased participation in the economy. As Hong Kong's public expenditure policies are highly redistributive, this is equivalent to stressing the commitment to improve educational and social services. The basis for a successful conclusion to the housing problem has been realized, technical and secondary educational opportunities are improving, social services are being broadened, and the infrastructure is subject to overall planning despite the nature of its ownership. With regard to this, land production, although limited, is seen as a key to the provision of adequate space for the new industries which will provide the necessary product diversification.

The constraints on improved welfare programmes are real in terms of financial capacity, staff and planning capabilities, and the nature of the society itself. Yet pressure from the United Kingdom is expected to continue, especially in the field of labour organization. There is a growing feeling that, unless certain British schemes are adopted, whatever their relevance, it may be the United Kingdom rather than the People's Republic of China which will question the status of Hong Kong; reform may be seen as the price which supposedly wealthy residents must pay to "rent" the British flag. Although this is an extreme view and is not reflected in official British Government statements, the point is made with sufficient frequency for Hong Kong to take note.

Despite the stress on economic development now current in China, it would be wrong to assess the future of Hong Kong solely in terms of economic benefit to China. If, however, economics is considered in combination with political factors, there would seem to be no reason why China should press for a change of status. Nevertheless, and regardless of whether China recognizes the "unequal treaties" of the nineteenth century, by British law the right of the Crown to administer the New Territories ends in 1997. Politically it is possible to assume that the crucial day could come and go without incident or that a last-minute ad hoc arrangement might be made. Economically this is impossible since investment decisions, the key to Hong Kong's survival, require a more definite arrangement in the not too distant future. Already the 1997 date affects decisions by overseas firms considering investment in the new industrial estates. The matter is not one of urgency, but it is one which is being discussed in board rooms as well as at academic seminars.

STATISTICAL SURVEY

AREA AND POPULATION

Area (sq. km.)				Population (June 1981 estimate)	
Total	Hong Kong Island	Kowloon and Stonecutters Island	New Territories (leased)	Total	Chinese (approx.)
1,063.43*	78.37	11.29	973.77	5,154,100	98 per cent

* 410.6 square miles.

DISTRIBUTION OF POPULATION

(Census of March 9th, 1981)

Hong Kong Island	Kowloon	New Kowloon	Marine	New Territories
1,183,621	799,123	1,681,064	49,747	1,303,005

* Unadjusted for non-contacted population.

REGISTERED BIRTHS AND DEATHS

(1981)

Births		Deaths	
Number	Rate per '000	Number	Rate per '000
87,104	16.9	24,978	4.8

Capital: Victoria (population 501,680 at August 1976).

ECONOMICALLY ACTIVE POPULATION

(Census of March 1981)

	Employed			Unemployed*		
	Males	Females	Total	Males	Females	Total
Agriculture and fishing	31,057	15,947	47,004	979	290	1,269
Mining and quarrying	1,412	144	1,556	63	25	8
Manufacturing	537,755	452,610	990,365	20,333	14,311	34,644
Electricity, gas and water	13,223	1,446	14,669	218	45	263
Construction	173,874	12,125	185,999	10,274	1,217	11,491
Trade, restaurants and hotels	320,778	140,711	461,489	9,980	4,629	14,609
Transport, storage and communications	159,737	21,631	181,368	6,787	1,050	7,837
Financing, insurance, real estate and business services	69,159	46,711	115,870	799	619	1,418
Services	223,938	151,765	375,703	4,183	2,464	6,647
Unclassifiable	20,510	9,534	30,044	2,784	1,619	4,403
Total	1,551,443	852,624	2,404,067	56,400	26,269	82,669

* Excluding unemployed persons without previous job and first-time job-seekers, numbering 17,068 (10,546 males, 6,522 females).

AGRICULTURE

LAND USE

(1981)

	Area (sq. km.)
Built-up (urban areas incl. roads and railways)	170
Woodlands	125
Grass and scrub lands	624
Badlands	46
Swamp and mangrove lands	1
Fish ponds	18
Arable (incl. orchards and market gardens)	80

PRINCIPAL CROPS

		1978	1979	1980	1981
Rice (unhusked)	metric tons	400	100	70	30
Other field crops*	,, ,,	2,700	2,800	2,400	2,500
Vegetables†	,, ,,	175,000	192,000	195,000	176,000
Fresh fruit and nuts	,, ,,	2,600	1,070	3,090	4,980
Flowers	HK $'000	39,414	42,440	42,450	55,550

* Includes yam, millet, groundnut, soybean, sugar cane, sweet potato and water chestnut.
† Fresh, frozen or preserved.

LIVESTOCK

(Estimates—head)

	1978/79	1979/80	1980/81
Cattle	11,450	6,930	5,199
Water Buffaloes	500	140	154
Pigs	532,530	554,950	471,800
Chickens	5,882,800	6,755,800	6,287,800
Ducks	881,250	867,600	760,140
Geese	4,930	4,100	1,920
Quail	408,000	690,500	598,200
Pigeons (pairs)	167,000	174,300	189,900

FISHING*

('000 metric tons, live weight)

	1976	1977	1978	1979	1980	1981
Inland waters:						
Freshwater fish	5.2	4.2	5.8	6.5	7.0	6.8
Pacific Ocean:						
Marine fish	124.9	129.4	133.5	151.4	161.0	147.8
Crustaceans	15.7	15.5	13.5	20.0	15.8	14.1
Molluscs	10.1	8.4	8.8	11.0	9.9	12.7
TOTAL CATCH	155.9	157.5	161.6	188.9	193.7	181.4

* Including estimated quantities landed directly from Hong Kong vessels in Chinese ports.

MINING

(metric tons)

	1977	1978	1979	1980	1981
Kaolin	2,466	89,460*	2,841	748	8,216
Quartz	2,063	665	2	12	—
Feldspar	3,378	3,157	742	2,974	194

* Including 64,414 tons of crude clay.

INDUSTRY

(September 15th, 1981)

INDUSTRY GROUPS	ESTABLISHMENTS	EMPLOYED
Food, beverages and tobacco	1,143	22,292
Textiles, wearing apparel, leather and leather products, footwear	15,061	393,483
Wood and cork products, furniture and fixtures	2,750	18,125
Paper and paper products, printing, publishing and allied industries	4,042	40,281
Chemicals and chemical products, products of petroleum and coal, rubber and plastic products	6,118	101,814
Non-metallic mineral products	378	4,886
Basic metal industries	301	4,684
Fabricated metal products	7,622	82,114
Machinery, apparatus, appliances and supplies	4,352	138,969
Transport equipment	438	15,805
Professional and scientific, measuring and controlling equipment not elsewhere classified, and photographic and optical goods	1,479	48,287
Other manufacturing industries	3,047	33,906
TOTAL	46,729	904,646

FINANCE

100 cents=1 Hong Kong dollar (HK $).
Coins: 5, 10, 20 and 50 cents; 1, 2, 5 and 1,000 dollars.
Notes: 1 cent; 5, 10, 50, 100, 500 and 1,000 dollars.
Exchange rates (June 1982): £1 sterling=HK $10.27; U.S. $1=HK 5.93.
HK $100=£9.74=U.S. $16.87.

Note: From September 1949 to November 1967 the Hong Kong dollar was officially valued at 1s. 3d. sterling (£1=HK $16.00) or 17.5 U.S. cents (U.S. $1=HK $5.714). On November 20th, 1967, the Hong Kong dollar was devalued, in line with sterling, to 15 U.S. cents (U.S. $1=HK $6.667) but, three days later, it was revalued at 1s. 4½d. or 6.875p (£1=HK $14.545), worth 16.5 U.S. cents (U.S. $1=HK $6.061). In August 1971 the U.S. dollar was "floated" but the Hong Kong dollar's relationship to sterling remained unchanged and a rate of U.S. $1=HK $5.582 (HK $1=17.91 U.S. cents) came into operation in December 1971. After sterling was allowed to "float" in June 1972, the Hong Kong dollar was devalued in July 1972, when the central exchange rate became U.S. $1=HK $5.65 (HK $1=17.70 U.S. cents). This was retained until February 1973, after which the central rate was U.S. $1=HK $5.085 (HK $1=19.666 U.S. cents) until November 1974, since when the Hong Kong dollar has been "floating". For calculating the value of foreign trade transactions, the average value of the Hong Kong dollar in U.S. cents was: 19.50 in 1973; 19.84 in 1974; 20.18 in 1975; 20.52 in 1976; 21.47 in 1977; 21.33 in 1978; 19.96 in 1979; 20.07 in 1980; 17.88 in 1981.

BUDGET ESTIMATES*
(HK $ million, year ending March 31st)

Revenue	1980/81	1981/82†
Direct taxes	8,216.0	9,160.0
Indirect taxes	5,843.1	5,086.6
Other Revenue	15,875.1	18,165.9
Reimbursements, contributions and loan repayments	356.1	475.2
Total	30,290.3	32,887.7

Expenditure	1980/81	1981/82†
General services	4,079.7	4,775.8
Economic services	1,467.0	1,992.1
Community services	7,754.8	5,499.7
Social services	8,367.1	9,441.7
Common supporting services	660.6	862.3
Others	1,264.3	2,490.2
Total	23,593.5	25,061.8

* Excluding income and expenditure of the Housing Authority, the Urban Council and various funds established by resolution of the Legislative Council.

† Estimate.

CURRENCY IN CIRCULATION
(HK $ million at December 31st)

1976	1977	1978	1979	1980	1981
5,177.1	6,355.2	7,775.6	8,784.7	10,464.3	12,306.42

COST OF LIVING
Consumer Price Index*
(July 1973–June 1974=100)

	1978	1979	1980	1981
All items	124.7	139.2	160.8	185.5
Foodstuffs	121.3	134.3	154.1	178.5
Housing	130.3	142.6	152.6	171.9
Fuel and light	134.7	172.7	264.4	328.1
Alcoholic drinks and tobacco	141.7	160.0	181.8	200.0
Clothing and footwear	103.3	110.0	121.1	134.4
Durable goods	114.4	126.0	134.4	145.2
Miscellaneous goods	133.2	146.2	168.9	182.8
Transport and vehicles	121.7	152.3	196.7	239.3
Services	137.1	148.0	169.5	196.5

* Households with monthly expenditure between HK $400 and $1,499 in 1973–74.

EXTERNAL TRADE

(HK $ million)

	1976	1977	1978	1979	1980	1981
Imports	43,293	48,701	63,056	85,837	111,651	138,375
Exports	32,629	35,004	40,711	55,912	68,171	80,423
Re-exports	8,928	9,829	13,197	20,022	30,072	41,739

PRINCIPAL COMMODITIES

(HK $ million)

IMPORTS	1979	1980	1981
Food and live animals	9,646	11,558	13,993
Live animals	1,332	1,635	1,897
Meat and meat preparations	1,186	1,475	1,631
Dairy products and eggs	636	698	926
Fish, crustaceans, molluscs and fish preparations	1,533	1,776	2,007
Cereals and cereal preparations	1,304	1,556	1,893
Fruit and vegetables	2,397	2,843	3,705
Beverages and tobacco	1,353	1,583	2,060
Crude materials (inedible) except fuels	4,312	5,267	5,616
Textile fibres and waste	1,929	2,371	2,319
Other animal and vegetable crude materials	1,378	1,671	1,680
Mineral fuels, lubricants, etc.	4,906	7,882	10,966
Petroleum and petroleum products	4,759	7,642	10,646
Chemicals	6,819	7,934	9,059
Dyeing, tanning and colouring materials	903	960	1,154
Medicinal and pharmaceutical products	967	1,064	1,267
Plastic materials	2,294	2,605	2,705
Basic manufactures	26,931	33,720	40,149
Textile yarn, fabrics, made-up articles, etc.	11,863	14,895	19,335
Non-metallic mineral manufactures	5,739	6,963	7,009
Iron and steel	2,884	3,426	3,843
Paper, paperboard, and articles thereof	1,767	2,262	2,582
Machinery and transport equipment	18,609	25,133	32,298
Telecommunications and sound recording and reproducing apparatus and equipment	3,257	4,471	6,122
Electrical machinery, apparatus and appliances n.e.s., and electrical parts thereof	5,821	7,526	9,931
Road vehicles	1,982	3,311	4,398
Miscellaneous manufactured articles	12,525	17,628	23,179
Photographic apparatus, optical goods, watches and clocks, etc.	5,765	7,647	9,503

[*continued on next page*

PRINCIPAL COMMODITIES—*continued*]

EXPORTS	1979	1980	1981
Food and live animals	844	813	3,145
Fish, crustaceans, molluscs and fish preparations	461	346	998
Cereals and cereal preparations	48	54	142
Fruit and vegetables	133	164	1,141
Sugar, sugar preparations and honey	17	22	72
Beverages and tobacco	73	114	657
Tobacco and tobacco manufactures	65	103	518
Crude materials (inedible) except fuels	650	1,108	4,234
Metalliferous ores and metal scrap	371	762	1,224
Chemicals	432	542	4,336
Essential oils, perfume materials, toilet, polishing and cleansing preparations	138	182	17
Artificial resins, plastic materials, cellulose esters and ethers	106	123	765
Basic manufactures	6,509	7,733	20,839
Textile yarn, fabrics, made-up articles, etc.	4,065	4,535	12,283
Non-metallic mineral manufactures	394	472	3,215
Paper, paperboard, and their articles	166	209	486
Manufactures of metals (others)	1,537	2,037	2,988
Machinery and transport equipment	9,314	12,375	25,458
Office machines and automatic data processing equipment	1,457	2,079	3,408
Telecommunications and sound recording and reproducing apparatus and equipment	4,063	5,030	7,741
Electrical machinery, apparatus and appliances n.e.s., and electrical parts thereof	3,235	4,490	8,881
Miscellaneous manufactured articles	37,525	44,814	62,168
Clothing	20,131	23,258	30,485
Photographic apparatus, optical goods, watches and clocks, etc.	5,126	7,119	11,494

RE-EXPORTS	1979	1980	1981
Food and live animals	1,220	1,418	2,128
Fruit and vegetables	407	442	931
Coffee, tea, cocoa and spices	148	157	241
Fish, crustaceans, molluscs and fish preparations	490	472	556
Cereals and cereal preparations	40	62	82
Crude materials (inedible) except fuels	1,580	2,373	3,249
Textile fibres and waste	288	463	694
Chemicals	2,201	2,817	3,581
Dyeing, tanning and colouring materials	422	462	658
Medicinal and pharmaceutical products	535	594	758
Basic manufactures	6,440	8,762	12,233
Textile yarn, fabrics, made-up articles, etc.	2,772	4,311	6,981
Non-metallic mineral manufactures	2,379	2,388	2,708
Machinery and transport equipment	3,916	6,762	10,415
Machinery specialized for particular industries	514	727	1,088
Telecommunications and sound recording and reproducing apparatus and equipment	641	1,283	2,123
Electric machinery, apparatus and appliances n.e.s., and electrical parts thereof	1,195	1,963	3,069
Miscellaneous manufactured articles	4,091	6,565	8,788
Clothing	935	1,554	2,197
Photographic apparatus, optical goods, watches and clocks, etc.	1,802	2,810	3,393

PRINCIPAL TRADING PARTNERS

(HK $ million)

Imports	1979	1980	1981
Australia	1,579	1,698	2,005
China, People's Republic	15,130	21,948	29,510
France	1,472	1,404	1,828
Germany, Federal Republic	2,775	2,883	3,383
Israel	996	1,138	1,081
Japan	19,320	25,644	32,130
Korea, Republic	2,529	3,869	5,495
Singapore	4,821	7,384	10,627
Switzerland	2,592	2,897	2,848
Taiwan	6,035	7,961	10,762
Thailand	1,321	1,578	1,834
United Kingdom	4,350	5,456	6,283
U.S.A.	10,365	13,210	14,442

Exports	1979	1980	1981
Australia	1,789	1,941	2,910
Canada	1,637	1,782	2,355
France	1,004	1,407	1,483
Germany, Federal Republic	6,344	7,384	7,048
Japan	2,656	2,329	2,940
Netherlands	1,406	1,575	1,598
Nigeria	443	1,025	1,282
Saudi Arabia	711	962	1,226
Singapore	1,413	1,791	1,732
Sweden	908	974	1,013
Switzerland	949	1,280	1,332
United Kingdom	5,974	6,791	7,710
U.S.A.	18,797	22,591	29,200

Re-Exports	1979	1980	1981
Belgium	411	348	276
China, People's Republic	1,315	4,642	8,044
Indonesia	1,684	2,761	4,272
Japan	2,477	2,201	2,792
Korea, Republic	818	899	1,401
Macau	605	923	1,407
Nigeria	377	843	1,073
Philippines	777	904	1,294
Singapore	1,804	2,510	3,243
Switzerland	487	622	437
Taiwan	1,730	2,229	2,420
Thailand	542	661	847
U.S.A.	1,995	3,085	4,785

TRANSPORT

RAILWAYS

(Kowloon–Canton railway, British section)

	1980	1981
Passengers	18,452,048	16,138,857
Freight (metric tons)	1,949,706	1,779,707

ROAD TRAFFIC

(Motor vehicle registrations)

	1981
Private cars	211,556
Goods vehicles	64,214
Motor cycles (incl. scooters)	27,438
Taxis	11,061
Crown vehicles (excl. H.M. Forces)	5,041
Buses	5,496
Public light buses	4,350
Private light buses	924
Motor tricycles	5
Total (incl. others)	330,309

SHIPPING
(1981)

		Ocean-going	River Steamers	Junks	Launches	Hover-Ferries*	Hydrofoil Vessels
Vessels entered .	number	10,667	1,991	15,308	12,192	1,189	21,044
Tonnage entered .	'000 n.r.t.	60,206,772	2,393,203	2,972,905	1,830,630	54,308	2,877,537
Passengers landed .	number	53,351	1,015,748	—	—	60,949	2,714,375
Passengers embarked	,,	78,774	988,654	—	—	76,691	2,853,892
Cargo tons landed .	metric tons	23,374,531	592	1,462,752	1,610,443	—	—
Cargo tons loaded .	,,	8,594,279	2,363	420,811	153,172	—	—

* A new route between Hong Kong and Guangzhou (Canton) opened in November 1978.

CIVIL AVIATION

	1979	1980	1981
Passengers:			
Arrivals	2,836,120	3,036,939	3,509,028
Departures	2,909,541	3,164,026	3,619,688
Freight (in metric tons):			
Arrivals	107,019	105,200	121,405
Departures	150,389	152,666	168,900

TOURISM
VISITORS BY COUNTRY OF RESIDENCE

	1977	1978	1979	1980	1981
Australia	154,849	160,004	139,236	166,170	201,793
Germany, Federal Republic	41,356	51,851	58,426	61,869	62,926
Indonesia	56,664	68,040	64,008	79,400	96,731
Japan	485,495	487,250	508,011	472,182	507,960
Korea, Republic . .	45,672	70,139	61,563	45,187	44,943
Malaysia	73,316	80,491	86,307	99,867	111,230
Philippines	52,844	86,381	89,549	98,628	104,690
Singapore	62,946	66,920	77,191	89,661	101,373
Taiwan	87,488	128,924	206,344	123,644	135,621
Thailand	80,775	99,764	132,551	148,671	137,715
United Kingdom . . .	71,097	84,324	95,344	121,054	167,117
U.S.A.	254,186	284,642	303,583	346,910	372,133
Total (incl. others) .	1,755,669	2,054,739	2,213,209	2,301,473	2,535,203

COMMUNICATIONS MEDIA

	1980	1981
Telephones	1,676,000*	1,829,000*
Periodicals	388	413
Newspapers	97	72

* Estimate.

Over 90 per cent of all homes in Hong Kong have at least one television set.

EDUCATION
(1981)

	Pupils
Kindergarten	200,426
Primary	548,759
Secondary	521,581
Post-Secondary	15,382
Adult education	105,954
Special education	12,117

Source: Hong Kong Government, *Official Statistics.*

THE CONSTITUTION

The Government of Hong Kong, which consists of the Governor, the Executive Council and the Legislative Council, is constituted under the authority of Letters Patent and Standing Instructions.

The Executive Council is consulted by the Governor on all important administrative questions. In addition to five *ex officio* members, there are nine unofficial members and one nominated official member.

The Legislative Council, which advises on and approves the enactment of the Colony's laws and approves all expenditure from public funds, presently consists of the five *ex officio* members, 18 other official members and 27 unofficial members meets in private to scrutinize all government expenditure proposals; two subcommittees deal with public works capital expenditure, and with government staff increases.

THE GOVERNMENT

Governor: Sir EDWARD YOUDE, K.C.M.G.

EXECUTIVE COUNCIL

(July 1982)

President: The Governor.

Ex Officio Members:

The Chief Secretary Sir PHILIP HADDON-CAVE, K.B.E., C.M.G., J.P.

The Commander British Forces Maj.-Gen. JOHN LYON CHAPPLE, C.B.E.

The Financial Secretary JOHN H. BREMRIDGE, O.B.E.

The Attorney General JOHN CALVERT GRIFFITHS, Q.C.

The Secretary for Home Affairs DENIS CAMPBELL BRAY, C.M.G., C.V.O., J.P.

Nominated Official Member: DAVID AKERS-JONES, C.M.G. J.P. (Secretary for City and New Territories Administration).

Unofficial Members:

Sir SZE-YUEN CHUNG, C.B.E., J.P.

OSWALD VICTOR CHEUNG, C.B.E., J.P.

Dr. HARRY FANG SIN-YANG, O.B.E., J.P.

LI FOOK-WO, C.B.E., J.P.

ROGERIO HYNDMAN LOBO, O.B.E., J.P.

MICHAEL GRAHAM RUDDOCK SANDBERG, O.B.E., J.P.

The Rev. PATRICK TERENCE MCGOVERN, O.B.E., S.J., J.P.

DAVID KENNEDY NEWBIGGING, J.P.

LO TAK-SHING, O.B.E., J.P.

LEGISLATIVE COUNCIL

President: The Governor.

Ex Officio Members: The Chief Secretary, the Attorney General, the Secretary for Home Affairs, the Financial Secretary.

There are also 18 nominated official members and 27 unofficial members. Provision exists for a maximum membership of 54, comprising 27 official and 27 unofficial members.

POLITICAL ORGANIZATIONS

The **Reform Club** and **Civic Association**, which worked in alliance between 1961 and 1964, stand for moderate constitutional changes in Hong Kong's Government.

The **Communists** and **Kuomintang** (Nationalist of Party China, based in Taiwan) also maintain organizations.

JUDICIAL SYSTEM

The Supreme Court consists of a Court of Appeal and of a High Court.

The High Court of Justice has unlimited jurisdiction in civil and criminal cases, the District Court having limited jurisdiction. Appeals from these courts lie to the Court of Appeal, presided over by the Chief Justice or a Vice-President of the Court of Appeal with one or two Justices of Appeal. Appeals from Magistrates' Courts are heard by a High Court judge.

SUPREME COURT

Chief Justice: Sir DENYS ROBERTS, K.B.E., Q.C., J.P.

Justices of Appeal: Sir ALAN HUGGINS, A. M. MCMULLIN, P. F. X. LEONARD, SIMON F. S. LI, D. CONS, T. L. YANG, A. ZIMMERN, W. J. SILKE, D. A. BARKER.

High Court Judges:

E. G. BABER
R. O'CONNOR
F. ADDISON
A. GARCIA
N. P. POWER
R. G. PENLINGTON
B. T. M. LIU
E. DE B. BEWLEY
J. J. RHIND
N. MACDOUGALL
K. T. FUAD
S. H. MAYO
N. B. HOOPER
B. L. JONES
Lieut.-Commdr. M. H. JACKSON-LIPKIN
E. C. BARNES
M. E. I. KEMPSTER
D. S. HUNTER
G. A. DE BASTO.

District Courts: There are 31 District Judges with Courts in Victoria, Kowloon, Tsuen Wan and Fanling.

Magistrates' Courts: There are 43 Magistrates, sitting in 8 Magistracies.

RELIGION

The Chinese population is predominantly Buddhist, although Confucianism and Daoism are also practised, The three religions are frequently found in the same temple. There are more than 440,000 Chinese Christians, approximately 30,000 Muslims, 8,000 Hindus and 500 Jews.

ANGLICAN CHURCH

Bishop of Hong Kong and Macau: Rt. Rev. PETER K. K. KWONG, Bishop's House, 1 Loer Albert Rd.

ROMAN CATHOLIC CHURCH

Bishop of Hong Kong and Macau: JOHN BAPTIST WU, Catholic Diocese Centre, 16 Caine Rd., Hong Kong.

THE PRESS

Hong Kong has a thriving press, with, after Japan, the highest newspaper readership in Asia. In early 1981 these newspapers included 6 English dailies and 63 Chinese language dailies. In 1979 there were 284 periodicals, of which 196 were Chinese language, 61 English language and 27 bi-lingual.

PRINCIPAL DAILY NEWSPAPERS

English Language

Asian Wall Street Journal: P.O.B. 9825; f. 1976; daily business newspaper; Editor ROBERT KEATLEY; Publr. JOHN C. ORR; circ. 25,500.

Hongkong Standard: News Building, 635 King's Rd., North Point; f. 1949; Editor-in-Chief ALAN CASTRO; circ. 100,000.

International Herald Tribune: Cheney and Associates Ltd., 703 Car Po Commercial Bldg., 18 Lyndhurst Terrace Central.

South China Morning Post: Tong Chong St., P.O.B. 47; f. 1903; Editor ROBIN HUTCHEON; circ. 60,000.

The Star: News Bldg., 6th Floor, 635 King's Rd., North Point; f. 1965; morning and evening; Editor EDWARD HUNG; circ. 35,000.

English and Chinese

Daily Commodity Quotations: 12 Moon St., Ground Floor, Wanchai; f. 1948; morning; quotations and commercial news; Editor EDWARD IP.

Chinese Language

Ching Pao: 141 Queen's Rd. East, 3rd Floor; f. 1956; Editor MOK GON; circ. 120,000.

Chiu Yin Pao: 458 Lockhart Rd., 11th Floor; f. 1950; morning; Editor KWONG LAI; circ. 30,000.

Chun Pao (*Truth Daily*): 29–33 Gage St.; evening; Editor LUK KOON-CHEUNG; circ. 45,000.

Fai Pao (*Express*): News Bldg., 633 King's Rd., 5th Floor, North Point; f. 1963; morning; Editor KWONG YAN-CHUN; circ. 100,000.

Hong Kong Daily News: 7–9 New St., P.O.B. 1586; f. 1958; morning; Editor JOSEPH LAW; circ. 119,078.

Hong Kong Evening Post: 5–13A New St., Western District; f. 1969; Editor JOSEPH LAW; circ. 50,000.

Hong Kong Sheung Po (*Hong Kong Commercial Daily*): 499 King's Rd., North Pt.; f. 1952; morning; Editor-in-Chief H. CHEUNG; circ. 110,000.

Hong Kong Shih Pao (*Hong Kong Times*): Hua Hsia Bldg., 64 Gloucester Rd.; f. 1949; morning; right-wing; Editor BENITO T. SHU; circ. 60,000.

Hsin Wan Pao (*New Evening Post*): 342 Hennessy Rd.; f. 1950; left-wing; Editor LO FU; circ. 90,000.

Hung Look Yat Po (*Hung Look Daily News*): 37 Gough St.; f. 1939; morning; Prop. YAM TAT-NIN; circ. 50,000.

Kung Sheung Man Po (*Industrial and Commercial Evening News*): 18 Fenwick St., Wanchai; f. 1930; evening; Editor MICHAEL K. W. LI; circ. 65,100.

Kung Sheung Yat Po (*Industrial and Commercial Daily News*): 18 Fenwick St, Wanchai; f. 1925; morning, independent; Editor LAM YAU-PUI; circ. 110,100.

Ming Pao: 651 King's Rd., 9th Floor; f. 1959; morning; Editor DAVID Y. S. POON; circ. 110,000.

Ming Pao Evening News: 651 King's Rd., 9th Floor; f. 1969; Exec. Editor LEE MAN-KAI; circ. 22,685.

Ming Tang Yat Pao: 196-198 Tsat Tse Mui Rd.; morning; Editor L. FONG; circ. 45,000.

Nah Wah Man Po: 4th Floor, 241-243 Nathan Rd., Kowloon; f. 1963; evening; Editor LAM YAU-PUI; circ; 40,000.

Seng Weng Evening News: 3 Wing Lok Lane; f. 1957; Editor YAM PING-YAN; circ. 60,000.

Sing Pao: Sing Pao Building, 101 King's Rd.; f. 1939; morning; Editor HO MAN FAT; circ. 300,000.

Sing Tao Jih Pao: 635 King's Rd., North Point; f. 1938; morning; Editor CHOW TING; circ. 76,737.

Sing Tao Man Pao: 635 King's Rd.; f. 1938; evening; Editor TONG BIK-CHUEN; circ. 121,700.

The Star: News Bldg., 6th Floor, 635 King's Rd., North Point; f. 1969; morning; Editor EDWARD HUNG; circ. 45,000.

Ta Kung Pao: 342 Hennessy Rd.; f. 1902; morning; Editor LI HSIA WEN; circ. 82,000.

Tin Tin Yat Pao: 3rd Floor, Block A, Aik San Factory Bldg., Westlands Rd., Quarry Bay; f. 1960; Editor CHEUNG CHOK LEUNG; circ. 140,000.

Wah Kiu Man Po: 106-116 Hollywood Rd.; f. 1945; evening; independent; Editor CHAN SIU CHIU; circ. 58,860.

Wah Kiu Yat Po (*Overseas Chinese Daily News Ltd.*): 106-116 Hollywood Rd.; f. 1925; morning; independent; Chief Editor HO KIN CHEUNG; circ. 125,000.

Wen Wei Po: 197–199 Wanchai Rd.; f. 1948; morning; left-wing; Editor KIM YIU YU; circ. 100,000.

SELECTED PERIODICALS

English Language

Asia Magazine: Morning Post Bldg., Tong Chong St., Quarry Bay; f. 1961; general interest; Sunday supplement distributed to English language newspapers; Editor JOHN HARDIE; circ. 350,000.

Asia Travel Trade: Interasia Publications, 200 Lockhart Rd., 13th Floor; f. 1969; monthly; travel trade; Editor MURRAY BAILEY; circ. 20,000.

Asian Business: c/o Far East Trade Press Ltd., 1913 Hanglung Centre, 2-20 Paterson St., Causeway Bay; monthly; Publr. SIMON HALLEY; Editor JOHN C. MAISANO; circ. 37,000.

Asian Finance: Suite 9-D, Hyde Centre, 223 Gloucester Rd.; f. 1975; monthly; Editor T. K. SESHADRI; circ. 15,000.

Asiaweek: 7F Toppan Bldg., 22 Westlands Rd.; f. 1975; Asian news weekly; Editor-in-Chief MICHAEL O'NEILL; Man. Editor SALMAN W. MORRISON; circ. 35,000.

Business Traveller Asia/Pacific: Interasia Publications, 200 Lockhart Rd., 13th Floor; f. 1982; consumer travel; 10 per year; Editor KEN MCKENZIE.

Far Eastern Economic Review: 6th Floor, Centre Point, 181–185 Gloucester Rd., G.P.O. Box 160; f. 1946; weekly; Editor DEREK DAVIES; circ. 57,000.

Hong Kong Enterprise: Connaught Centre, 1 Connaught Place, Hong Kong; f. 1967; published by the Hong Kong Trade Development Council; shows the range of products available in Hong Kong; monthly; Editor ANDREW SIMPSON; circ. 65,000.

Hong Kong Government Gazette: Govt. Printing Dept., Java Rd., North Point; weekly.

Hong Kong Trader: Connaught Centre, 1 Connaught Place, Hong Kong; f. 1976; published by the Hong Kong Trade Development Council; trade, investment, financial and general news on Hong Kong; every 2 months; Editor CHARLES CHAPMAN; circ. 27,000.

Insight: Pacific Magazines Ltd., 13th Floor, 200 Lockhart Rd.; f. 1972; monthly; business; Editor MURRAY BAILEY; circ. 20,000.

Modern Asia: P.O.B. 9765; f. 1967; business government and industry; 11 issues a year; Editor DAVID CREFFIELD; circ. 24,000.

Orientations: 13th Floor, 200 Lockhart Rd.; monthly; arts of the Far East, the Indian sub-continent, South-East Asia and the Near East; Editor HINCHEUNG LOVELL.

The Reader's Digest (Asia Edn.:) Reader's Digest Association Far East Ltd., Tung Sun Bldg., 9th Floor, 194–200 Lockhart Rd.; f. 1963; general topics; monthly; Editor-in-Chief VICTOR LANIAUSKAS; circ. 338,000.

Sunday Examiner: Catholic Centre, Catholic Diocese Centre, 16 Caine Road; f. 1946; weekly; religious; Editor Fr. A. BIRMINGHAM.

Textile Asia: c/o Business Press Ltd., Tak Yan Commercial Bldg., 11th Floor, 30-32 D'Aguilar St.; f. 1970; monthly; Editor-in-Chief KAYSER SUNG; circ. 15,000.

Travel Business Analyst: Interasia Publications, 200 Lockhart Rd., 13th Floor; f. 1981; travel trade; 10 per year; Editor MURRAY BAILEY.

Travelling Magazine: Room 903, Yat Fat Bldg., 44 Des Voeux Rd. Central; f. 1965; monthly; Publr. SHAU-FU POK; circ. 50,500.

Chinese Language

Hong Fook (*Pictorial Happiness*): monthly.

Hsin Kar Ting (*New Home*): monthly.

Kar Ting Sang Wood (*Home Life Journal*): 326 Jaffe Rd.; f. 1950; every ten days; Editor TONG BIG CHUEN; circ. 30,000.

Kung Kao Po: Catholic Diocese Centre, 11th Floor, 16 Caine Rd.; weekly; f. 1928; religious; Editor Fr. LOUIS HA.

The Reader's Digest (Chinese Edn.): Reader's Digest Association Far East Ltd., Tung Sun Commercial Centre, 8th Floor, 194–200 Lockhart Rd.; f. 1965; general topics; monthly; Chief Editor Miss LIN TAI-YI; circ. 300,000.

Sin Chung Hwa Pictorial: monthly.

Sing Tao Weekly: 179 Wanchai Rd.

Sinwen Tienti (*Newsdom Weekly*): Room 903, Yat Fat Bldg., 44 Des Voeux Rd. Central; f. 1945; weekly; Publr. SHAU-FU POK; circ. 60,550.

Tien Wen Tai (*Observatory Review*): 6th Floor, 60 Leighton Rd.; f. 1936; weekly; Editor LAI CHUN WAI; circ. 20,000.

Tse Yau Chun Hsin (*Freedom Front*): weekly.

Tsing Nin Wen Yu (*Literary Youth*): monthly.

Tung Sai (*East and West*): fortnightly.

Zheng Ming: Pro-Communist magazine.

NEWS AGENCIES

International News Service: 217 Queen's Rd. Central; Rep. AU KIT MING.

Rapid News Agency: 7th Floor, On Cheung Bldg., 454-A Nathan Rd., Kowloon; Chair. CHAN CHI BUN.

FOREIGN BUREAUX

Agence France-Presse (AFP): New Mercury House, 11th Floor, 22 Fenwick St., P.O.B. 15613, Wanchai; Correspondent EDOUARD DILLON.

Agencia EFE (*Spain*): 10/A Emerald Garden, 86 Pokfulam Rd.; Correspondent JOSÉ M. SOTO RAMÍREZ.

Agenzia Nazionale Stampa Associata (ANSA) (*Italy*): c/o Hong Kong Hotel, Kowloon; Correspondent GIROLAMA BRUNETTI.

Associated Press (AP) (*U.S.A.*): 1282 New Mercury House, 22 Fenwick St.; Bureau Chief ROBERT LIU.

Central News Agency Inc. (*Taiwan*): Hua Hsia Bldg., 20th Floor, 64–66 Gloucester Rd.; Bureau Chief EDDIE P. TSENG.

Jiji Tsushin-Sha (*Japan*): Room B 3/F, On Hing Bldg., 1–4 On Hing Terrace, Wyndham St.; Correspondent YUICHIRO NISHIDA.

Kyodo Tsushin (*Japan*): 9th Floor, Block B, Seaview Mansion, 34B Kennedy Rd.; Correspondent MIKIO KOBAYASHI.

New Zealand Press Association: 3D/22 Baguio Villa, 555 Victoria Rd.; Correspondent ROBERT HORROCKS.

Reuters (*U.K.*): 5th Floor, Gloucester Tower, 11 Pedder St. Central.

United Press International (UPI) (*U.S.A.*): 1260 New Mercury House, 22 Fenwick St., P.O.B. 5692; Gen. Man. ALBERT E. KAFF; Editor (Asia) MICHAEL KEATS.

Xinhua (New China News Agency) (*People's Republic of China*): 5 Sharp St., West; Dir. WANG GUANG.

PRESS ASSOCIATIONS

Newspaper Society of Hong Kong: P.O.B. 47; f. 1954; 24 mems. and 4 assoc. mems.; Chair. G. A. PILGRIM.

Hong Kong Journalist Association: P.O.B. 11726, Hong Kong; f. 1968; 300 mems.; Chair. DAVID WONG.

PUBLISHERS

Asia Press Ltd.: 88 Yee Wo St., Causeway Bay; f. 1952; books and magazines; Pres. CHANG KUO-SIN; Gen. Man. CHEN LIU-TO.

Business Press Ltd.: Tak Yan Commercial Bldg., 11th Floor, 30-32 D'Aguilar St.; f. 1970; publr. of *Textile Asia*; Man. Dir. KAYSER SUNG.

Excerpta Medica Asia Ltd.: 67 Wyndham St., 9th Fl.; f. 1980; medical books, newspapers and magazines; Man. ROSEMARY IRELAND.

Far East Trade Press Ltd.: 1913 Hanglung Centre, 2–20 Paterson St., Causeway Bay; trade magazines and directories; Publr. and Man. Dir. MICHAEL BRIERLEY.

Hong Kong University Press: 139 Pokfulam Rd., University of Hong Kong; f. 1955; academic, scholarly, educational, general; Publr. C. W. TOOGOOD; Editor Y. K. FUNG.

Ling Kee Publishing Co.: Zung Fu Industrial Bldg., 1067 King's Rd.; f. 1949; educational and reference books; Man. Dir. B. L. AU.

PUBLISHERS' ASSOCIATION

Hong Kong Publishers' and Distributors' Association: National Bldg., 4th Floor, 240–246 Nathan Rd., Kowloon

RADIO AND TELEVISION

RADIO

Radio Television Hong Kong: Broadcasting House, Broadcast Drive, P.O.B. 200, Kowloon Central Post Office; f. 1928; public service broadcasting department of the Government; 24-hour services in English and Chinese transmitted on five radio channels; Dir. JOHN TISDALL.

Hong Kong Commercial Broadcasting Co. Ltd.: P.O.B. 3000, Hong Kong; f. 1959; broadcasts in English and Chinese on three radio channels; Man. Dir. GEORGE HO.

British Forces Broadcasting Service: BFPO 1, Hong Kong; f. 1971; broadcasts in English and Nepali; Station Controller J. W. NATION; Nepali Programme Organizer Major (QGO) KISHORKUMAR GURUNG; English Programme Organizer NICK BAILEY.

In 1981 there were an estimated 2,550,000 radio receivers in use.

Radio Television Hong Kong: Broadcasting House, Broadcast Drive, P.O.B. 200, Kowloon Central Post Office; government-owned; news, drama, documentaries and public affairs; broadcasts in English and Chinese; also operates an educational service (ETV) transmitted by the commercial stations; Dir. JOHN TISDALL.

TELEVISION

Rediffusion Television Ltd.: Television House, 81 Broadcast Drive, Kowloon; f. 1973; operates two commercial television services (English and Chinese); Man. Dir. BERNARD T. HOOLEY.

Television Broadcasts Ltd.: 77 Broadcast Drive, Kowloon; f. 1967; 2 colour networks; operates Chinese and English language services; Exec. Dir. KEVIN LO.

In 1981 there were an estimated 1,114,000 television receivers in use.

FINANCE

BANKING

There were 115 licensed banks operating in June 1981 including the Bank of China and other banks based in the People's Republic of China. All banks are free to conduct foreign exchange business. The distinction between authorized and non-authorized banks no longer applies.

(cap.=capital; p.u.=paid up; res.=reserves; dep.=deposits; m.=million; brs.=branches; HK $=Hong Kong dollars)

Banking Commission: 1604 Hang Chong Bldg., 5 Queen's Rd. Central; f. 1964; Commr. C. D. W. MARTIN; Asst. Commrs. C. S. LEUNG, W. K. KWOK; publs. monthly statistics on banking and on deposit-taking companies and other information connected with the monetary system.

ISSUING BANKS

The Chartered Bank (Standard Chartered Banking Group): 4–4A Des Voeux Rd. Central; f. 1853; Area Gen. Man. Hon. W. C. L. BROWN, J.P.; 105 brs.

Hongkong and Shanghai Banking Corporation: G.P.O. Box 64, 1 Queen's Rd. Central; f. 1865; cap. issued and p.u. HK $3,899m.; dep. HK $269,707m. (1981); Chair. M. G. R. SANDBERG, O.B.E.; Sec. F. R. FRAME.

HONG KONG BANKS

The Bank of Canton Ltd.: 6 Des Voeux Rd. Central; incorp. in Hong Kong in 1912; cap. p.u. HK $115m.; total resources (1981) HK $3,811m.; Chief Man. F. G. MARTIN; Chair. RESSEL FOK.

Bank of East Asia Ltd.: 10 Des Voeux Rd. Central; inc. in Hong Kong in 1918; cap. p.u. HK $144.1m.; dep. HK $6,492.4m. (1981); Chair. Hon. Sir Y. K. KAN.

The British Bank of the Middle East: G.P.O. Box 64, 1 Queen's Rd. Central; f. 1889; cap. p.u. £52.5m.; dep. £1,079m. (Dec. 1981); Chair. M. G. R. SANDBERG, O.B.E.

Chekiang First Bank Ltd.: Prince's Bldg., 3 Statue Square; f. 1950; cap. p.u HK $75m.; dep. and other accounts HK $1,423.5m. (1981); Chair. HU SZU-CHI.

Chiyu Banking Corporation Ltd.: 80 Des Voeux Rd. Central; f. 1947; cap. p.u. HK $30m.; dep. HK $498m. (1979); Man. GEORGE TAN.

Commercial Bank of Hong Kong Ltd.: 120 Des Voeux Rd. Central; f. 1934; cap. HK $40m.; dep HK $798m. (1979); Chair. ROBIN S. K. LOH; Vice-Chair. and Man. Dir. ROBIN Y. H. CHAN; Exec. Dir. and Gen. Man. JOHN C. C. CHEUNG.

Grindlays Dao Heng Bank Ltd.: 7–19 Bonham Strand, Hong Kong; f. 1921; cap. HK $20m.; resources HK $5,620m. (1980); Chair. Sir S. Y. CHUNG; Chief Man. GEORGE CUNNINGHAM; 17 brs.

Hang Seng Bank Ltd.: 77 Des Voeux Rd. Central; f. 1933; cap. and res. HK $1,831.2m. (Dec. 1981); dep. HK $30,134.9m. (Dec. 1981); Chair. S. H. HO, O.B.E.; Gen. Man. Q. W. LEE, C.B.E.

The Hong Kong Chinese Bank Ltd.: The Hong Kong Chinese Bank Bldg., 61–65 Des Voeux Rd. Central; f. 1954; cap. HK $90m.; dep. HK $526m. (1981); 8 brs.; Chair. MING THIEN-CHANG; Man. Dir. and Chief Exec. JOHN K. L. CHAN.

Hong Kong Industrial and Commercial Bank: 99–105 Des Voeux Rd. Central; f. 1964; cap. and res. HK $168.1m.; dep. HK $1,398.9m. (1981); Man. Dir. SUN SE CHUN; Gen. Man. WAI-BUN CHEUNG; 19 brs.

Hong Kong Metropolitan Bank Ltd.: Admiralty Centre, 5/F., Tower I, 18 Harcourt Rd., P.O.B. 4612; f. 1961; cap. p.u. HK $50m.; dep. HK $796m. (Dec. 1980); Chief Gen. Man. HENRY W. K. WAT.

Kwong On Bank Ltd.: 137–141 Queen's Rd. Central, Hong Kong; f. 1938; inc. 1954, cap. HK $100m.; dep. HK $1,546m. (1981); Chair. RONALD LEUNG DING-BONG; Senior Man. Dir. SHIGETAKA KONDO; 21 brs.

Liu Chong Hing Bank Ltd.: 24 Des Voeux Rd. Central; f. 1955; cap. HK $150m.; Chair. NGAN SHING-KWAN, C.B.E., J.P.; 26 brs.

Mercantile Bank Ltd.: 1 Queen's Rd. Central, Hong Kong; cap. p.u. £2.94m.; dep. £225.2m.; Chair. M. G. R. SANDBERG, O.B.E.

Nanyang Commercial Bank Ltd.: 151 Des Voeux Rd. Central; f. 1949; cap. p.u. HK $200m.; dep. HK $4,053.3m. (1980); Chair. and Gen. Man. CHUANG SHIH PING; 25 brs.

Overseas Trust Bank Ltd.: O.T.B. Bldg., cnr. Gloucester and Tonnochy Rds.; cap. p.u. HK $69m.; dep. HK $1,229.2m. (1977); Man. Dir. HUANG TIONG CHAN.

Shanghai Commercial Bank Ltd.: 12 Queen's Rd. Central; f. 1950; cap. p.u. HK $200m.; dep. HK $5,903m. (1981); Chair. J. T. CHU; Man. Dir. and Gen. Man. K. K. CHEN.

Wing Lung Bank Ltd.: 45 Des Voeux Rd. Central; f. 1933; cap. HK $100m.; dep. HK $3,581m. (Dec. 1981); Chair. WU JIEH-YEE; Gen. Man. PATRICK P. K. WU; 20 brs.

Wing On Bank Ltd.: 22 Des Voeux Rd. Central; f. 1931; cap. p.u. HK $25m.; dep. HK $578m. (Dec. 1977); Chair. LAMSON KWOK; Chief Man. ALBERT KWOK; 11 brs.

PRINCIPAL FOREIGN BANKS

Algemene Bank Nederland N.V. (*Netherlands*): Holland House, 9 Ice House St.; Chief Man. J. D. ALTINK.

American Express International Banking Corpn. (*U.S.A.*): Connaught Centre, 28th Floor; Vice-Pres. LANCY I. ALMEIDA.

Bangkok Bank Ltd. (*Thailand*): 28 Queen's Rd. Central West; Pres. CHATRI SOPHONPANICH.

Bank of America N.T. and S.A. (*U.S.A.*): Gloucester Tower 12F, 11 Pedder St.; Senior Vice-Pres. HEINZ A. WASCHECK.

Bank of China (*People's Repub. of China*): 2A Des Voeux Rd. Central; Man. CHANG CHI.

Bank of Communications (*People's Repub. of China*): 3A Des Voeux Rd. Central; Gen. Man. S. M. WANG.

Bank of India: Dina House, 3–5 Duddell St., P.O.B. 13763; Man. K. L. SAMANT.

Bank Negara Indonesia 1946: 25 Des Voeux Rd. Central; Man. H. W. TEHUBIJULUW.

Bank of Scotland: Connaught Centre; Asst. Gen. Man. I. M. ROBERTSON.

Bank of Tokyo Ltd. (*Japan*): Sutherland House, 3 Chater Rd., Hong Kong; Dir. and Gen. Man. R. ARAI.

Banque Belge pour l'Etranger S.A. (*Belgium*): New World Centre, 10/F, P.O.B. 98453 Tsim Sha Tsui, Kowloon; 13 brs.

Banque de l'Indochine et de Suez (*France*): Alexandra House, 11 Des Voeux Rd. Central, G.P.O. Box 16; Man. R. PH. MARTIN; 9 brs.

Banque Nationale de Paris (*France*): Central Bldg., 23 Queen's Rd., Central f. 1966; Chief Exec. Man. F. DE LAJUGIE; Group Man. O. LACOIN.

Banque Worms et Cie (*France*): Admiralty Centre II, 18 Harcourt Rd., Hong Kong; Man. MICHEL CURE.

Barclays Bank International Ltd. (*U.K.*): 5th Floor, Connaught Centre, Connaught Rd. Central (P.O.B. 9716); f. 1973; Gen. Man. C. STEVENS.

Bayerische Vereinsbank (*Federal Republic of Germany*): 1208-09, 12th Floor, Alexandra House, Chater Rd.

Chase Manhattan Bank, N.A. (*U.S.A.*): World Trade Centre, P.O.B. 104; 720 Nathan Rd., Kowloon; Gen. Man. CARL F. GUSTAVSON.

China and South Sea Bank Ltd. (*People's Repub. of China*): 77–83 Queen's Rd. Central; Gen. Man. Y. H. SUN.

China State Bank Ltd. (*People's Repub. of China*): 39 & 41 Des Voeux Rd. Central; Man. LIU HUNG JU.

Chung Khiaw Bank Ltd. (*Singapore*): 15–18 Connaught Rd. Central; Gen. Man. LO POON KEU.

Citibank (*U.S.A.*): Citibank Tower, 8 Queen's Rd. Central; Vice-Pres. KENT DEM. PRICE.

Commerzbank (*Federal Repub. of Germany*): 1 Connaught Centre, 42nd Floor.

Crédit Lyonnais (*France*): 32/F Gloucester Tower, 11 Pedder St., P.O.B. 9757.

Equitable Banking Corporation (*Philippines*): 4 Duddell St.; Senior Vice-Pres. CHARLES GO.

European Asian Bank (*Federal Repub. of Germany*): New World Tower, 16–18 Queen's Rd. Central (P.O.B. 3193); Chief Mans. HORST KAISER, JÜRGEN-LEWIN VON SCHLABRENDORFF.

Four Seas Communications Bank Ltd. (*Singapore*): 49–51 Bonham Strand West; Man. LOW CHUCK TIEW.

Indian Overseas Bank: 9th Floor, Pacific House, 20 Queen's Rd. Central; Regional Man. S. K. BALAKRISHNAN; 7 brs.

Kincheng Banking Corporation (*People's Repub. of China*): 51–57 Des Voeux Rd. Central; Man. P. L. CHEN.

Korea Exchange Bank (*Repub. of Korea*): 5th Floor, China Bldg., 29 Queen's Rd. Central; Dir. and Gen. Man. I. K. CHOO; 2 brs.

Kwangtung Provincial Bank (*People's Repub. of China*): 21–22 Connaught Rd. Central; Gen. Man. WU WEI-LEUNG.

Lloyds Bank International (*U.K.*): 2901–4 Admiralty Centre Tower 1; 18 Harcourt Rd., Principal Man. V. FOLCH VERNET.

Malayan Banking Berhad (*Malaysia*): 1st Floor, Pacific House, 20 Queen's Rd. Central; Man. WONG KIM LING; 1 br.

Manufacturers Hanover Asia (*U.S.A.*): 27th Floor, Alexandra House, 16–20 Chater Rd. Central; f. 1977; Man. MILTON D. BAUGHMAN.

Midland Bank Ltd. (*U.K.*): 3802 Gloucester Tower, 11 Pedder St; Man. R. A. N. HENLEY.

Morgan Guaranty Trust Co. of New York (*U.S.A.*): Alexandra House, 16–20 Chater Rd. Central; Vice-Pres. and Gen. Man. TIMOTHY L. BOYD WILSON.

National Bank of Pakistan: 129 Central Bldg., Queen's Rd. Central: Gen. Man. MUSHTAQUE AHMED; 4 brs.

National Commercial Bank Ltd. (*People's Repub. of China*) 1–3 Wyndham St.; Gen. Man. C. T. DONG.

National Westminster Bank Plc. (*U.K.*): 6/F St. George's Bldg., 2 Ice House St.; Chief Man. COLIN J. HOOD.

Nippon Credit Bank (*Japan*): 1701 Gloucester Tower, Pedder St.; Chief Rep. TAKASHI KISHINAMI.

Oversea-Chinese Banking Corpn. Ltd. (*Singapore*): American International Tower, 16–18 Queen's Rd. Central.

Overseas Union Bank (*Singapore*): 14–16 Pedder St.; Area Man. JOHN AU YEUNG.

Rainier International Bank (*U.S.A.*): 32nd Floor, United Centre, 95 Queensway; Sr. Vice-Pres. and Gen. Man. CHEUNG SUT-LOI.

Royal Bank of Canada: 12th Floor, 10 Ice House St. Central; Man. N. BAILEY.

Sanwa Bank Ltd. (*Japan*): 30–32 Connaught Rd. Central; Gen. Man. A. KATO.

Security Pacific National Bank (*U.S.A.*): 2101 Bank of Canton Bldg., 6 Des Voeux Rd.; f. 1971; Senior Vice-Pres. ROBERT P. WILLIAMSON.

Sumitomo Bank Ltd. (*Japan*): 5 Queen's Rd. Central; Gen. Man. TOSIO MORIKAWA.

Toyo Trust and Banking Co. Ltd. (*Japan*): 1504–6 Gloucester Tower, 11 Pedder St., The Landmark.

United Commercial Bank (*India*): Prince's Bldg., 5 Statue Square; Asst. Gen. Man. M. L. DHAWAN.

United Overseas Bank Ltd. (*Singapore*): 34–38 Des Voeux Rd. Central; Chair. and Man. Dir. WEE CHO YAW; 2 brs.

Xin Hua Trust, Savings and Commercial Bank Ltd. (*People's Repub. of China*): 1A Des Voeux Rd. Central; f. 1914; Man. SU TRAN SING.

Yien Yieh Commercial Bank Ltd. (*People's Repub. of China*): 242 Des Voeux Rd. Central; Gen. Man. LEE CHAO KUANG.

BANKING ASSOCIATION

The Hong Kong Association of Banks: P.O.B. 11391, General Post Office; f. 1981 to succeed The Exchange Banks' Asscn. of Hong Kong; f. 1897; all licensed banks in Hong Kong are by law members of this statutory body whose main purpose is to represent and further the interests of the banking sector in Hong Kong; Chair. The Hongkong and Shanghai Banking Corporation represented by T. WELSH; from January 1983 the Chartered Bank is to take over as Chair.

STOCK EXCHANGES

Far East Exchange Ltd.: 8th Floor, New World Tower, 16–18 Queen's Rd. Central; f. 1969; 352 mems.; Chair. RONALD FOOK-SHIU LI.

Hong Kong Stock Exchange Ltd.: 21st Floor, Hutchison House; f. 1891; 145 mems.; Chair. MOK YING KIE; Sec. B. J. N. OGDEN; publs. *Daily Quotations, Weekly Report, Monthly Gazette, Year Book, Profile*.

Kan Ngan Stock Exchange: 7th Floor, Connaught Centre, Connaught Rd. Central; f. 1970; 350 mems.; Chair. WOO HON FAI; publs. *Daily Quotation, Monthly Bulletin*.

Kowloon Stock Exchange Ltd.: f. 1972; 175 mems.; Chair. PETER P. F. CHAN.

The four exchanges are due to merge in 1983 to form **The Stock Exchange of Hong Kong.**

INSURANCE ASSOCIATION

Insurance Institute of Hong Kong: G.P.O. Box 6747, Hong Kong; f. 1967; Pres. STAN T. K. WU; Hon. Sec. ANDREW C. S. LO.

TRADE AND INDUSTRY

CHAMBERS OF COMMERCE

Hong Kong General Chamber of Commerce: Swire House, 9th Floor, P.O.B. 852; f. 1861; 2,700 mems.; Chair. Hon. D. K. NEWBIGGING, J.P.; Dir. JAMES MCGREGOR, O.B.E.; publs. *The Bulletin—Business Magazine* (monthly), *Hong Kong Progress* (basic figures, quarterly), *Hong Kong Overall Merchandise Trade* (statistics, annually), *Annual Report* and others.

Chinese General Chamber of Commerce: 24 Connaught Rd. Central; f. 1900; 7,000 mems.; Chair. WONG KWAN-CHENG.

Hong Kong Junior Chamber: 272 Queen's Rd. Central, 15th Floor, Flat C; f. 1950; 950 mems.; Pres. EDMOND PANG; Sec.-Gen. JUNIA HO; publ. *Harbour Lights*.

Kowloon Chamber of Commerce: 2 Liberty Ave., Kowloon; Chair. ROBERT DER; Sec. PETER C. S. LEE.

EXTERNAL TRADE ORGANIZATIONS

Hong Kong Trade Development Council: Connaught Centre, 1 Connaught Place, Hong Kong; f. 1966; Chair. Sir Y. K. KAN; Exec. Dir. L. DUNNING; publs. *Hong Kong Enterprise* (monthly), *Hong Kong Trader* (every 2 months), *Hong Kong Apparel* (bi-annual), *Hong Kong Toys* (annual).

Hong Kong Exporters' Association: K.C.P.O.B. K1864; Office: 1625 Star House, Kowloon; f. 1955; 200 mems. consisting of the leading merchants and manufacturing exporters of Hong Kong; Chair. L. KNEER; Exec. Sec. GEORGINA WHYATT.

INDUSTRIAL ORGANIZATIONS

Hong Kong Productivity Council: 20th and 21st Floors, Sincere Bldg., 173 Des Voeux Rd. Central; f. 1967 to promote increased productivity of industry and to encourage more efficient utilization of resources; Council of Chairman and 20 members, all appointed by the Governor, of whom 14 represent management, labour, academic and professional interests, the other 6 representing government departments closely associated with productivity matters; Chair. of Council and Exec. Cttee. ALLEN LEE PENG-FEI; Exec. Dir. S. K. CHAN; publs. *Hong Kong Productivity News* (monthly, bilingual), *Bulletins* on Plastics, Electronics, Metals, Environmental Control, Technology, Transfer (quarterly, bilingual), *Industry Data Sheets* (annually, bilingual), *Directory of Hong Kong Industries* (annually, bilingual), *Report on Salary Trends and Fringe Benefits* (annually).

Chinese Manufacturers' Association of Hong Kong: 9F Wing Hang Bank Bldg., 161 Queen's Rd. Central; f. 1934; seeks to promote and protect industrial and trading interests, operates CMA Testing and Certification Laboratories; over 2,300 mems.; Pres. NGAI SHIU KIT; Sec.-Gen. J. P. LEE; publs. *Monthly Bulletin, Annual Report, Directory of Members*.

Employers' Federation of Hong Kong: 2005 Asian House; 1 Hennessy Rd., P.O.B. 2067; f. 1947; 162 mems.; Chair. F. L. WALKER; Sec. and Treas. J. A. CHEETHAM.

Federation of Hong Kong Cotton Weavers: 14/F, Flat B, Ashley Rd., Kowloon; f. 1955; 48 mems.; Chair. J. H. YU; Exec. Officer P. K. WAN.

Federation of Hong Kong Industries: Eldex Industrial Bldg., 12th Floor, Unit A, 21 Ma Tau Wei Rd., Hung Hom, Kowloon; f. 1960; about 1,300 member firms, divided into 21 groups according to type of industry; Chair. H. C. TANG; Deputy Chair. ALLEN LEE; publ. *Hong Kong Industrial News* (monthly).

Hong Kong Cotton Spinners' Association: 1041 Swire House; f. 1955; 32 mems.; Chair. C. S. LOH.

Hong Kong Jade and Stone Manufacturers' Association: Hang Lung House, 16th Floor, 184–192 Queen's Rd. Central; f. 1965; Pres. R. Y. C. LEE.

Hong Kong Printers' Association: 48–50 Johnston Rd. 1/F, Wanchai; f. 1939; 335 mems.; Chair. HO WAI CHUEN; Vice-Chair. WONG SHIU KEUNG.

TRADE UNIONS

In January 1981 there were 357 trade unions in Hong Kong with an estimated membership of 401,300. Of these unions, 220 were independent and the others affiliated to the following organizations:

Hong Kong and Kowloon Trades Union Council (TUC): Labour Bldg., 11 Chang Sha St., Kowloon; f. 1949; 71 affiliated unions, mostly covering the catering and building trades; 36,770 mems.; supports the Republic of China; affiliated to ICFTU; Gen. Sec. WONG YIU KAM.

Hong Kong Federation of Trade Unions (FTU): 142 Lockhart Rd., 3rd Floor; f. 1948; 66 affiliated unions, mostly concentrated in the shipyards, public transport, textile mills and public utilities, and 29 nominally independent unions which subscribe to the policy and participate in the activities of the FTU; left-wing; supports the People's Republic of China; estimated membership: 203,020.

CO-OPERATIVES

Registrar of Co-operatives: The Director of Agriculture and Fisheries, 393 Canton Rd., Kowloon; as at March 31st, 1982 there were 407 Co-operatives with a membership of 22,520 and paid-up capital of HK $1,911,768.

CO-OPERATIVE SOCIETIES

(socs. = societies; mems. = membership; cap. = paid-up share capital in HK $; feds. = federations)

Agricultural Credit: socs. 8, mems. 250, cap. $51,740.

Apartment Owners': socs. 2, mems. 156, cap. $10,800.

Better Living: socs. 23, mems. 1,950, cap. $36,415.

Consumers': socs. 10, mems. 2,575, cap. $16,985.

Farmers' Irrigation: socs. 1, mems. 68, cap. $340.

Federation of Fishermen's Societies: feds. 4, member-socs. 50, cap. $5,175.

Federation of Pig Raising Societies: fed. 1, member-socs. 25, cap. $10,975.

Federation of Vegetable Marketing Societies: fed. 1, member-socs. 28, cap. $5,600.

Fishermen's Credit: socs. 56, mems. 1,027, cap. $17,245.

Fishermen's Credit and Housing: socs. 2, mems. 70, cap. $380.

Housing: socs. 238, mems. 5,702, cap. $1,391,600.

Pig Raising: socs. 24, mems. 1,329, cap. $146,490.

Salaried Workers' Thrift and Loan: socs. 4, mems. 666, cap. $12,889.

Vegetable Marketing: socs. 31, mems. 8,842, cap. $107,297.

There are also 61 Credit Unions (1982).

MARKETING ORGANIZATIONS

Fish Marketing Organization: f. 1945; statutory organization to control wholesale fish marketing; in 1979 landings marketed through wholesale fish markets totalled 88,308 metric tons valued at HK $400m.

Vegetable Marketing Organization: f. 1946; Government agency for collection, transportation and sale of vegetables; loan fund to farmers; in 1980, 56,567 metric tons of vegetables, valued at HK $132.4m. were sold through the organization.

DEVELOPMENT CORPORATIONS

Hong Kong Housing Authority: 101 Princess Margaret Rd., Kowloon; Chair. DONALD P. H. LIAO; Vice-Chair. and Dir. of Housing BERNARD V. WILLIAMS.

Kadoorie Agricultural Aid Association: f. 1951; assists farmers in capital construction by technical direction and by donations of livestock, trees, plants, seeds, fertilizers, cement, road and building materials, farming equipment, etc.

Kadoorie Agricultural Aid Loan Fund: f. 1954; in conjunction with the Hong Kong Government, provides interest-free loans to assist farmers in the development of projects. During the year 1980/81 an amount of HK $7,022,000 was issued.

J. E. Joseph Trust Fund: c/o Director of Agriculture and Fisheries, Canton Rd. Govt. Offices: 12th-14th Floor, 393 Canton Rd., Kowloon, Hong Kong; f. 1954; grants credit facilities to farmers; up to March 31st, 1981, the accumulated total of loans amounted to HK $47,544,820.

TRADE FAIR

Hong Kong Trade Fair Ltd.: 805 Wing On Plaza, Tsimshatsui East, Kowloon; fair scheduled every autumn; even years consumer goods, odd years industrial goods; *Expoship* Far East International Shipping Exhibition scheduled for alternate even-numbered years.

MAJOR INDUSTRIAL COMPANIES

The following are some of Hong Kong's leading industrial organizations, arranged in alphabetical order:

China Light & Power Co. Ltd.: 147 Argyle St., Kowloon; electricity suppliers; Chair. Lord KADOORIE.

Gilman & Co. Ltd.: G.P.O.B. 56, Hong Kong; subsid. of Inchcape & Co. Ltd., London; importers, exporters, engineers, shipping and insurance agents; Man. Dir. J. F. HOLMES; 1,500 employees.

Hong Kong Electric Holdings Ltd.: Electric House, 44 Kennedy Rd., G.P.O. Box 915, Hong Kong; holding company; activities of subsidiaries include electricity generation, property holding and development, trading, hire purchase, insurance; Chair. D. K. NEWBIGGING, J.P.; Group Man. Dir. J. PEACOCK.

Hong Kong Spinners Ltd.: 1501 Prince's Bldg., Chater Rd., Hong Kong; cotton yarn; Man. Dir. T. Y. WONG; Asst. Man. Dir. JAMES ST. WONG.

Hutchison Whampoa Ltd.: Hutchison House, 22nd Floor, 10 Harcourt Rd., Hong Kong; investment holding and management company; Chair. K. S. LI; Chief Exec. J. A. RICHARDSON.

Jardine, Matheson & Co. Ltd.: Connaught Centre; f. 1832; general merchants; Chair. and Sr. Man. Dir. D. K. NEWBIGGING, J.P.

Kader Industrial Co. Ltd.: 24 Tanner Rd., North Point, Hong Kong; plastic goods including dolls, toys, model trains, household articles, table-wares and unbreakable chairs; Joint Man. Dirs. H. S. TING, J.P., KENNETH W. S. TING.

Soco Textiles (HK) Ltd.: 10th Floor, Yu To Sang Bldg., 37 Queen's Rd. Central, Hong Kong; spinners of cotton and synthetic/cotton blended yarns; importers of raw cotton and exporters of cotton and synthetic/cotton blended yarns and finished piece-goods; Man. Dirs. W. H. CHOU, T. K. ANN, H. C. TANG.

Sonca Industries Ltd.: 34 Tai Yau St., San Po Kong, Kowloon; manufacturers of consumer goods including aluminium, brass, steel and plastic flashlights, battery lanterns, precision machinery, battery chargers, electronic devices; Man. Dir. T. S. CHAN.

Swire Group: John Swire and Sons (HK) Ltd.: Swire House, 9 Connaught Rd. Central, Hong Kong; shipping managers and agents, airline operators, marine and aviation engineering, trading, insurance, China trade development, property development, operators of offshore drilling rigs and associated offshore oil drilling support equipment, and manufacturers of soft drinks and paints, packagers and distributors of sugar, chemical manufacturer; Chair. D. R. Y. BLUCK.

W. Haking Marketing Ltd.: 981 King's Rd., North Point, Hong Kong; binoculars, cameras and film projectors.

Wheelock Marden & Co. Ltd.: 22nd Floor, Lane Crawford House, Hong Kong; investment holding company; Chair. J. L. MARDEN; Deputy Chair. P. J. GRIFFITHS; Man. Dirs. W. J. LEES, H. W. LEUNG.

Yangtzekiang Garment Manufacturing Co. Ltd.: 22 Tai Yau St., San Po Kong, Kowloon; clothing manufacturers; Man. Dir. S. K. CHAN.

TRANSPORT

Transport Department: Guardian House, 32 Oi Kwan Rd., 6th Floor, Hong Kong; Transport Commr. A. T. ARMSTRONG-WRIGHT.

RAILWAYS

Mass Transit Railway Corporation (MTRC): the first section of the underground railway system opened in October 1979; a 15.6-km. line from Kwun Tong to Chater opened in February 1980; a 10.5-km. Tsuen Wan extension opened in May 1982; the 12.5-km. Island Line is under construction, the first section of which is to open in July 1985, the second section in 1986; Chair. NORMAN THOMPSON.

Kowloon-Canton (Guangzhou) Railway: the line is 35 km. long and runs from the terminus at Kowloon to the Chinese frontier at Lo Wu. Through passenger services to China, in abeyance since 1949, were reinstated in April 1979. The railway is undergoing an extensive modernization programme, including complete electrification which is due to be completed by late 1982. The entire length is to be double-tracked, and the first section, from Kowloon to Sha Tin, began operating in 1981. All existing stations are to be reconstructed or improved, and three new stations are planned for Kowloon Tong, Tai Wai and Fo Tan. Gen. Man. U. L. WONG.

ROADS

In 1981 there were 1,161.3 km. of officially maintained roads, 347.8 on Hong Kong Island, 346.2 in Kowloon and 467.3 in the New Territories. Almost all of them are concrete or asphalt surfaced. Construction of the Sha Tin-Tai Po Coastal Highway in the New Territories began in 1981, to be completed by 1984; it consists of a 7-km. dual three-lane highway.

FERRIES

Steamers, hydrofoils and jetfoils operate between Hong Kong and Macau. There is also an extensive network of private ferry services to outlying districts.

Hong Kong and Yaumati Ferry Co. Ltd.: Hong Kong; 16 passenger and three car ferry services within harbour limits and 16 services to outlying districts (including recreational and excursion services); also operates hoverferry services between Hong Kong and Guangzhou (Canton), Hong Kong and Shekou (Deep Bay); fleet of 96 vessels.

"Star" Ferry Company Ltd.: Kowloon; operates passenger ferries between the Kowloon Peninsula and the main business district of Hong Kong and between Central and Hung Hom; fleet of 10 vessels; Gen. Man. W. D. McCluskie.

SHIPPING

Hong Kong is the world's seventh largest port in terms of tonnages of shipping using its facilities, cargo handled and number of passengers, and the world's third largest in terms of container handling. In 1981 some 10,600 ocean-going vessels calling at Hong Kong loaded and discharged more than 32 million metric tons of cargo. This included 25 million metric tons of general goods, of which 55 per cent was container cargo.

Marine Department: 102 Connaught Rd., Central, G.P.O. Box 4155; Dir. of Marine P. E. J. Davy.

Shipping Agents

Ben Line Steamers Ltd.: The Chartered Bank Building, 7th Floor, 4–4a Des Voeux Rd. Central; Man. Keith Welsh.

East Asiatic Co. Ltd.: The Connaught Centre, 19th Floor, 1 Connaught Place, Central; Dir. Mr. Lockenwitz.

Ednasa Shipping Co. Ltd.: 19th Floor, New World Tower, 16–18 Queen's Rd. Central; Pres. R. S. K. Loh.

Everett Steamship Corpn. S.A: 24/f Sincere Bldg., 84–86 Connaught Rd. Central; Gen. Man. J. G. Davison.

Jardine, Matheson & Co. Ltd.: 48th Floor, Connaught Centre, P.O.B. 70, G.P.O.; f. 1832; Chair. and Senior Man. Dir. Hon. D. K. Newbigging.

Kin Wah Maritime Co.: 1603a Tai Sang Commercial Bldg. 24–34 Hennessy Rd., Wanchai; f. 1968; Man. S. H. Lo

Maersk Line (Hong Kong) Ltd.: Sunning Plaza, 17–19/f, 10 Hysan Ave., Causeway Bay; Man. Dir. Per Jorgensen.

John Manners & Co. Ltd.: 17th Floor, Swire House, Chater Rd.; Man. Dir. E. F. de Lasala.

Nedlloyd (Hong Kong) Ltd.: Sincere Building, 22nd Floor, 173 Des Voeux Rd. Central; Dir. J. A. W. Weddepohl.

Sime Darby Shipping (Hong Kong) Ltd.: 35th Floor, Windsor House, 311 Gloucester Rd., Causeway Bay.

Sun Hing Shipping Co. Ltd.: South China Bldg., 7th/9th Floor, 1 Wyndham St.; Man. Dir. Simon K. Y. Lee.

John Swire & Sons (Hong Kong) Ltd.: Shipping Dept., Swire House, 3rd Floor, Chair. D. R. Y. Bluck.

Teh-Hu Cargocean Management Co. Ltd.: Asian House 17f, 1 Hennessy Rd.; f. 1974; Man. Dir. K. W. Lo.

Unique Shipping Agencies Ltd.: 604 Hang Chong Bldg., 5 Queen's Rd. Central; Exec. Dir. Edward S. C. Cheng.

Wah Kwong & Co. (Hong Kong) Ltd.: Wah Kwong Building, 26th Floor, 48 Hennessy Rd.; d.w.t. 3.2m.; Chair. Tsong-yen Chao.

Wallem & Co. Ltd.: Hopewell Centre, 48th Floor, 183 Queen's Rd. East; Chair. A. J. Hardy.

World-Wide Shipping Agency Ltd.: 15–17 Floor, World Shipping Centre, Harbour City, 7 Canton Rd., Kowloon; Chair. Sir Yue-kong Pao.

CIVIL AVIATION

Hong Kong's international airport is Kai Tak. Its runway can accommodate all types of conventional wide-bodied aircraft and supersonic aircraft.

Civil Aviation Department: United Centre, 10th Floor, 95 Queensway, New Rodney Block; Dir. B. D. Keep.

Cathay Pacific Airways Ltd.: Swire House, 9 Connaught Rd.; f. 1946; services to 24 major cities in the Far East, Middle East, the U.K. and Australia, using a fleet of 9 Lockheed TriStar L-1011S, 6 Boeing 747-200B, 4 Boeing 707-320C; Chair. D. R. Y. Bluck; Man. Dir. H. M. P. Miles.

In addition, British Airways, British Caledonian, CAAC (People's Republic of China) and about 30 other foreign airlines serve Hong Kong.

TOURISM AND CULTURE

Hong Kong Tourist Association: 35th Floor, Connaught Centre, Connaught Rd. Central, Hong Kong; f. 1957; co-ordinates and promotes the tourist industry; has government support and financial assistance; 11 mems. of the Board representing government, the private sector and the tourist industry; Chair. D. R. Y. Bluck; Exec. Dir. J. Pain, o.b.e.; Sec. H. B. Cheung; publ. *Hong Kong Travel Bulletin*.

In 1981 there were over 2.5 million visitors to Hong Kong.

CULTURAL ORGANIZATIONS

Hong Kong Arts Centre: 2 Harbour Rd., Hong Kong; opened 1977; 19-storey building contains three auditoria, two floors of galleries, restaurants, libraries, and practice and rehearsal facilities; Chair. Sir Run Run Shaw; Gen. Man. Andrew Welch.

Hong Kong Arts Festival: G.P.O. Box 2547; takes place annually in February; Gen. Man. Keith Statham.

The Hong Kong Philharmonic Society Ltd.: Harbour View Commercial Bldg. 20f, 2 Percival St., Causeway Bay; Chair. Dr. Philip Kwok; Gen. Man. John Duffus; orchestra of 82 mems.

Society for the Advancement of Chinese Folklore Ltd.: 35th Floor, Connaught Centre, Connaught Rd. Central, Hong Kong; f. 1976; promotes, fosters, improves and advances public appreciation of and interest in Chinese folklore and culture; Hon. Sec. H. B. Cheung.

DEFENCE

The British Army, Navy and Air Force are all represented in Hong Kong under the overall command of the Commander British Forces who advises the Governor on matters affecting the security of Hong Kong.

Defence forces include five Royal Navy patrol craft, one U.K. and three Gurkha Infantry battalions, one Gurkha engineer squadron and one army helicopter squadron. In 1979 and 1980 additional troops were sent to help halt the flow of illegal immigrants. There are also two auxiliary service units; the Royal Hong Kong Regiment, consisting of 700 volunteers, and the Royal Hong Kong Auxiliary Air Force which has 54 permanent staff and 111 volunteers. Defence expenditure for 1980/81 was estimated at HK $867 million.

EDUCATION

Schools in Hong Kong fall into three main categories: those wholly maintained by the government; those run by private non-profit-making bodies with government financial aid; and those run independently by private organizations. There are also specialized schools for handicapped children run by government and voluntary organizations. In 1981 they provided education for 12,117 children.

Pre-primary and Primary Schools

Kindergartens are run by private bodies without government assistance for children between the ages of four and six. In 1981 there were 729 such schools with an enrolment of 200,426. The age of entry into primary school is six and the schools provide a six-year course of basic primary education. Compulsory primary education was first introduced in 1971 when fees were abolished in all government and aided primary schools. There are eight government-subsidized primary schools catering for the education of English-speaking children. At the end of six years, every primary school-leaver is allocated a free place in a secondary school for three years. The method of allocation is based on schools' internal assessments, monitored by an Academic Aptitude Test under the Secondary School Places Allocation scheme.

Secondary Schools

In 1981 there were 521,581 pupils in secondary schools. There are four main types of secondary school in Hong Kong: Anglo-Chinese grammar schools, prevocational schools, the Chinese middle schools and the secondary technical schools. The Hong Kong Certificate of Education Examination may be taken after a five-year course; a furher course of one or two years leads to the Hong Kong Higher Level Examination and the Hong Kong Advanced Level Examination respectively. The prevocational schools provide shorter courses with a higher vocational content. From September 1980, the government has begun to provide three years of free and compulsory secondary education for children aged under 15.

Higher Education

Higher education is provided at the University of Hong Kong, the Chinese University of Hong Kong and the Hong Kong Polytechnic. They are autonomous institutions and receive government subventions through the University and Polytechnic Grants Committee. In 1981 the two universities had 11,485 students while the Hong Kong Polytechnic, running a large number of full- and part-time courses up to higher diploma levels, registered an enrolment of 24,796 students. Technological training is also provided, with effect from April 1st, 1982, by the newly established Technical Education and Industrial Training Department, which has five technical institutes under its technical education division. Post-secondary education is also provided for 7,543 students in the three approved post-secondary colleges.

Teachers' Training

There are four government-run colleges of education which provide training for teachers of primary schools and secondary schools. The total number of students in 1981 was 3,176 and the government provides interest-free loans and grants for needy students. All four colleges offer full-time courses of two and three years' duration. Both universities also provide a postgraduate part-time preservice or postservice course in education of two years' duration. The Chinese University of Hong Kong also provides a full-time one-year course in education.

BIBLIOGRAPHY

GENERAL

HARRIS, PETER. Hong Kong: A Study in Bureaucratic Politics (Heinemann Asia, 1978).

HONG KONG GOVERNMENT, Annual Reports (H.M.S.O., London, and Government Publications Centre, Hong Kong).

Hong Kong 1981 (Government Publications Centre, Hong Kong).

HOPKINS, KEITH (ed.). Hong Kong: The Industrial Colony (Oxford University Press, Hong Kong, 1971).

HUGHES, R. Hong Kong: Borrowed Place, Borrowed Time (Andre Deutsch, London, 1976).

JARVIE, IAN C. (ed.). Hong Kong: A Society in Transition (Routledge and Kegan Paul, 1969).

JONES, JOHN F. (ed.). The Common Welfare, Hong Kong's Social Services (Chinese University Press, Hong Kong, 1981).

KING, AMBROSE Y. C. (ed.). Social Life and Development in Hong Kong (Chinese University Press, Hong Kong, 1981).

LEE, RANCE P. L. (ed.). Corruption and its control in Hong Kong (Chinese University Press, Hong Kong, 1981).

LEEMING, F. Street Stuaies in Hong Kong (Oxford University Press, 1977).

MINERS, N. J. The Government and Politics of Hong Kong (Oxford University Press, 3rd edn. 1981).

OSGOOD, CORNELIUS. The Chinese: A Study of a Hong Kong Community (3 vols.) (University of Arizona Press, Tucson, Arizona, 1975).

VAID, K. N. The Overseas Indian Community in Hong Kong (Centre of Asian Studies, University of Hong Kong, 1972).

WATSON, JAMES L. Emigration and the Chinese Lineage. The Mans in Hong Kong and London (University of California Press, Berkeley, Los Angeles and London, 1975).

HISTORY

ENDACOTT, G. B. A History of Hong Kong (Oxford University Press, London, 1958).

Government and People in Hong Kong, 1841–1962: A Constitutional History (Hong Kong University Press, 1964).

ENDACOTT, G. B., and BIRCH, A. H. Hong Kong Eclipse (Oxford University Press, 1978).

GLEASON, G. Hong Kong (Robert Hale, London, 1964).

HAYES, JAMES W. The Hong Kong Region 1850–1911, Institutions and Leadership in Town and Countryside (William Dawson Ltd., New Haven, Conn. and London, 1977).

LETHBRIDGE, HENRY J. Hong Kong: Stability and Change (Oxford University Press, London, 1979).

LINDSAY, OLIVER. The Lasting Honour: The Fall of Hong Kong (Hamish Hamilton, London, 1978).

LUARD, E. Britain and China (Chatto and Windus London, 1962).

MILLS, A. British Rule in Eastern Asia (Oxford University Press, London, 1942).

SAYER, G. R. Hong Kong: Birth, Adolescence and Coming of Age (Oxford University Press, London, 1937).
Hong Kong, 1862–1919 (Hong Kong University Press, 1975).

WESLEY-SMITH, P. Unequal Treaty 1898–1997 (Oxford University Press, 1980).

ECONOMY

BEAZER, WILLIAM F. The Commercial Future of Hong Kong (Praeger, New York and London, 1978).

CHENG, T. Y. The Economy of Hong Kong (Far East Publs., Hong Kong, 1977).

COLLIS, MAURICE. Wayfoong, the History of the Hongkong and Shanghai Banking Corporation (Faber and Faber, London, 1965).

ENGLAND, J., and REAR, J. Industrial Relations and Law in Hong Kong (Oxford University Press, 1981).

GEIGER, T. and F. M. Tales of Two City States: the Development Progress of Hong Kong and Singapore (Washington, 1973 and MacMillan, London, 1975).

HSIA, RONALD, and CHAU, L. Industrialisation, Employment and Income Distribution (Croon Helm, London, 1978).

JAO, Y. C. Banking and Currency in Hong Kong, a Study of Post-War Financial Development (MacMillan, London, 1974).

LETHBRIDGE, DAVID (ed.). The Business Environment in Hong Kong (Oxford University Press, 1980).

LIN, T. B. Das monetäre System und Monetäre Verhalten in Hong Kong (Eberhard Albert Verlag, Freiburg, 1970).

RABUSHKA, ALVIN. Value for Money, the Hong Kong Budgetary Process (Hoover Institution, Stanford, 1976).
Hong Kong. A Study in Economic Freedom (University of Chicago Press, Ill., 1979).

RIBEIRO, R. A. The Hong Kong Labour Tribunal (Centre of Asian Studies, University of Hong Kong, 1978).

TURNER, H. A. The Last Colony: But Whose? A Study of the Labour Movement (Cambridge University Press, 1980).

India

PHYSICAL AND SOCIAL GEOGRAPHY

B. H. Farmer

India is one of the largest countries in the world, with an area of 3,287,782 square kilometres (1,269,420 square miles), including the Indian portion of Jammu and Kashmir, which is disputed between India and Pakistan. India stretches from 8° to 33° 15′ North latitude, and from 68° 5′ to 97° 25′ East longitude. Its northern frontiers are with Xizang (Tibet), in the People's Republic of China, Nepal and Bhutan. Its great southern peninsula stretches far down into the tropical waters of the Indian Ocean. On the north-west it bounds Pakistan; on the north-east, it borders on Burma; in the east, Bangladesh.

PHYSICAL FEATURES

India has three well-marked and, indeed, obvious relief regions: the Himalayan system in the north, the plateaux of the peninsula and, in between, the great plains of the Indus and Ganga (Ganges) basins.

The Himalayan system, between the Xizang Plateau and the Indo-Gangetic Plains, is made up of complex ranges arranged more or less in parallel, but in places combining and then dividing again, in others (particularly in the highest places) taking on the apparent form of a series of peaks divided by deep gorges rather than that of a range. The Great Himalaya is, in general, just such an array of giant peaks, mostly over 6,100 metres (20,000 ft.) in height, covered by perpetual snows, and nurturing great glaciers which in turn feed the rivers flowing to the Indus, Ganga and Brahmaputra. The southernmost range of the system, the Siwaliks, presents a wall-like margin to the plains; while in the extreme north-east the whole system bends very sharply on crossing the Brahmaputra and forms the wild, forest-clad country of the Naga and other hills on the marches of Burma.

Peninsular India, the Deccan or South Country, begins at another but more broken wall that fringes the plains to the south, and stretches away to Kanyakumari, the southernmost extremity of India. The whole peninsula is built, fundamentally, of ancient and largely (though not entirely) crystalline rocks which have been worn down through long geological ages and now form a series of plateaux, mostly sloping eastward and drained by great rivers, like the Mahanadi, Krishna and Godavari, flowing to the Bay of Bengal. Where plateaux end abruptly their edges present, from the lower plains or plateaux below, the appearance of mountain ranges. This feature is most evident in the Western Ghats, the great scarp overlooking the narrow western coastal plain. Two rivers, the Narmada and Tapti, flow east. Between them, and on east into the jungle country of Chota Nagpur, lies wild hilly territory that has done much to isolate the southern Deccan from the plains through long periods of Indian history. The Garo and Khasi Hills of Meghalaya form a detached piece of plateau country.

In places there are variants on the ancient crystalline-rock plateau theme. Thus in the northeastern Deccan narrow, down-faulted basins preserve the most important of India's coal measures; while inland of Bombay, and covering most of the State of Maharashtra, great basalt flows have given rise to distinctive countryside with broad open valleys floored by fertile (though difficult) "black cotton soils" separated by flat-topped hills.

The west coast is fringed by a narrow alluvial plain. That on the east coast is generally wider, especially where it broadens out into the highly productive deltas of the great east-flowing rivers.

The Indo-Gangetic Plain, between the Siwaliks and the northernmost plateau-edges of the Deccan, is one of the really great plains of the world. Consisting entirely of alluvium, it presents an appearance of monotonous flatness from the air or, indeed, to the uninitiate traveller on land. In fact, however, its general flatness conceals a great deal of variety. The fine muds and clays of the Ganga-Brahmaputra delta contrast, for instance, with the sands of the Rajasthan Desert at the western extremity of the Indian portion of the plains. Almost everywhere, too, there is a contrast of floodplains (along the rivers) and naturally dry belts, often of older alluvium, well above the reach of even the highest floods.

CLIMATE

"As is well known, the climate of India is dominated by the monsoon; that is, by the seasonal reversal of wind which brings a seasonal change from dry weather to wet." Simple statements like this, though true in a very broad sense, take no account of a great deal of local variation and complexity—not surprising features of a country like India with a vast size and extremely varied relief. Thus, in north India at any rate, there are not two seasons, but three. A "cool season" lasts from December to February, and brings average temperatures of 10–15°C. (50–60°F.) to Delhi and the Punjab, but with a high diurnal range (from as high as 26°C. (80°F.) by day to freezing point or below at night) and, although this is the season of the "dry" north-east monsoon, depressions from the north-west may bring rain to the Punjab and, indeed, farther down the plains to the east. In the "hot season" of the north temperatures rise till, in May, the average is 32–35°C. (90–95°F.) (as high as 48°C. (120°F.) by day), and rain is very rare. With the "burst" of the monsoon in June and July, temperatures fall and the rains begin, to last till September or October.

In the Ganga delta, to take another regional example, the "cool season" is less cool than in Delhi (19°C. average for January in Calcutta), the hot season less hot (30°C. May average), and the rains much heavier—there is hardly a year in which Calcutta's streets do not suffer serious flooding at least once. The "hot season" is, moreover, punctuated by "mango showers", which are even more significant in Assam.

In the peninsula, the coolness of the "cool season" tends to be diminished as one goes south, as does the striking heat of the "hot season", partly because in places like Bombay temperatures are never as high as in, say, Delhi, and partly because in the far south it is always hot, except where temperatures are mitigated by altitude. In Tamil Nadu, for example, average monthly temperatures vary only from 24°C. in January to 32°C. in May and June. In the peninsula, too, the south-west monsoon brings particularly heavy rains to the westward-facing scarps of the Western Ghats, which receive 200 to 250 cm. (80 to 100 in.) in four months. The dry season also decreases southward till in Kerala, in the far south-west, it lasts for only a month or two. In Tamil Nadu, there is an almost complete reversal of the normal monsoonal rainfall regime: the heaviest rains fall in what, in the north, is the dry season (October to January, inclusive) and the south-west monsoon period is relatively dry (principally because the state lies in the lee of the Western Ghats).

The theme of contrast in Indian climate is best expressed by drawing attention to the tremendous difference between, on the one hand, the deserts of Rajasthan and the rather less dry sands of Ramanathapuram, in southeastern Tamil Nadu, and, on the other, the verdant landscapes of the north-eastern Deccan and of Kerala. Sometimes these contrasts are to be seen during a very short journey, such as that from Trivandrum, the capital of Kerala, to Kanyakumari and on into Tamil Nadu.

There is another dominant theme in Indian climate —violence: violent rains and floods when the monsoon bursts, violent rain almost whenever rain falls (so that rapid run-off and soil erosion are almost omnipresent hazards), violent heat and violent wind at least seasonally; and violent fluctuations between wet years and dry years, and between good years and bad years (for extreme climatic variability also characterizes much of India, especially the semi-arid regions). Agriculture in many parts of India is indeed a perpetual gamble with the weather.

SOILS

India unfortunately lacks a good modern soil map compiled on a uniform and scientific basis. Certain general statements, however, may be made. Thus the soils of the Himalayan mountains and plateaux are generally thin, skeletal and infertile, except in intermont basins or in areas of artificial terracing, and therefore artificial depth and fertility. The soils of the peninsula are also generally poor, though for a different reason—that in general they have been derived from long years of weathering from unpromising crystalline rocks. There are, however, noteworthy exceptions—particularly the rich alluvia, with a generally high potential for improvement by means of fertilizers, to be found in the east coast deltas of the Mahanadi, Godavari, Krishna and Kaveri, and the *regur* (black cotton soils) of the basalt areas of Maharashtra. The latter are naturally of quite high fertility and retain moisture (an important property in a monsoon climate especially in the axis of semi-aridity that runs east of the Ghats through Pune) but are sticky, erodible and hard to cultivate when wet, and also difficult to irrigate satisfactorily.

The soils of the plains are, by nature, generally much more fertile than those of the Himalayas or of the Deccan, though this does not apply to the sandier soils that are to be found (for example) in the Rajasthan Desert, or to the leached soils of old alluvial terraces like those on the western margins of the Bengal delta. But infertility has tended to creep in as a result of human occupancy. This is partly, and very widely, a matter of long continued cultivation without adequate manuring, partly a matter of salinity and alkalinity induced by a causal chain that stretches from canal irrigation through rising water-tables to the capillary ascent of salts to the surface. The problem of salinity particularly afflicts the fields of Uttar Pradesh.

VEGETATION

The tremendous variations in rainfall, not to say temperature and relief to be met in India mean that there must have been, far back in time, very wide variations in natural vegetation. These probably ranged from near-desert or even complete desert (in Rajasthan); through thorn scrub (in semi-arid regions like the western Maharashtran Deccan) and tropical dry deciduous forest (in slightly wetter areas lying along a broad crescentic belt from the middle Ganga plains to Hyderabad and Madras) and tropical moist deciduous forest (in the north-east Deccan); to tropical wet evergreen forest, approaching rain forest (along the Western Ghats and in Kerala). There must also have been a complete altitudinal gradation from plains vegetation through deciduous and coniferous forests to montane vegetation in the Himalayas.

But over much of India the hand of man has lain heavily on the vegetation. Little natural vegetation of any sort survives in the plains or in the east and west coast deltas and coastal strips, except in rare groves; or, for that matter, over much of Tamil Nadu or the plateau areas of Maharashtra (apart from the still-forested eastern districts of the latter state). In all these regions, and many more, the landscape is dominated not by natural vegetation but by arable cultivation. Even in apparently uncultivated areas the natural vegetation has been modified out of all recognition. It may well be that part of the Rajasthan Desert is man-made or, at any rate, degraded by man. The savanna-like jungles of parts of central India have developed from denser forest formations, by the action of man and his animals. Even the pleasant forests of the north-east Deccan, dominated by *sal* (*Shorea robusta*, a useful timber tree), are often, if not generally, derived from more heterogeneous forests by the action of fire. Not surprisingly, India's forest resources, though not by any means inconsiderable, do not match its needs.

MINERALS

India possesses some of the largest and richest reserves of iron ore in the world. These occur particularly in the north-east Deccan, in the states of Bihar, Orissa and in the western part of West Bengal. Other deposits occur farther afield—for example, round Salem, in Tamil Nadu; in Karnataka; and in Goa. Altogether it has been estimated that India has reserves of no less than 22,000 million tons of iron ore. This is ample to supply the country's present industrial needs and to allow for exports to such countries as Japan.

Unfortunately, resources of coal, particularly of coking coal, are much more meagre, though by no means negligible (perhaps 80,000 million tons of poor and medium coals but only 2,500 million tons of coking coals). Some 95 per cent of Indian production, and nearly all of the coking coal, comes from seams in the down-faulted basins in the north-east Deccan to which reference has already been made. It will be appreciated that the bulk of the iron ore reserves are in the same region: this is India's good fortune so long as reserves of coking coal last. Elsewhere, there is a little coal in Assam and lignite in Rajasthan and Tamil Nadu.

India is rich in the non-ferrous minerals used in alloys, notably in manganese (of which India in most years is the second or third largest producer in the world; ores are found widely distributed in the Deccan). About 75 per cent of the world's mica comes from India, notably from Bihar, Tamil Nadu and Rajasthan. The known reserves of various minerals are: haematite 9,000 million metric tons; magnetite 2,800 million tons; lignite 2,000 million tons; limestone 50,000 million tons; dolomite 1,800 million tons; china clay 365 million tons; fireclay 300 million tons; copper 333 million tons; kyanite 143 million tons; lead 120 million tons; zinc 101 million tons; manganese 98 million tons; nickel 78 million tons and phosphorite 78 million tons (December 1976).

In-shore deposits of petroleum have been found in Assam, Gujarat and Nagaland, and off-shore oilfields have been discovered in the Western continental shelf off the Maharashtra coast, notably in the Bombay High. India expects to become self-sufficient in oil by 1986.

There is no shortage of building-stone or of the raw materials for the cement industry.

POPULATION

India's population at the March 1981 census was 683,997,512 (including the Indian-held part of the disputed territory of Jammu and Kashmir). The average annual population increase rate was about 2.3 per cent in 1961–71 and in 1971–81. By any standards, large areas of India are now over-populated; economic development is a constant race against population increase; and the control of future growth has become a burning issue.

There are great variations in population density in the Indian countryside. There are very high densities of rural population in the rice-growing areas of the lower Ganga plain and in the Bengal delta; in parts of Assam; in parts of the eastern peninsular deltas and around Madras; in Kerala; and in the coastal plains stretching from south of Bombay north into Gujarat. Less spectacular, but still high densities are to be found in the upper Ganga plains and in the Punjab, in Assam, and in Tamil Nadu generally. At the other extreme, low densities occur in the Himalayas and Rajasthan Desert (not surprisingly), in the jungle-covered hills and plateaux of the northeastern Deccan (though these have been invaded by mining, by the iron and steel industry, and by agricultural colonists, refugees from Bangladesh); in inland Gujarat and Saurashtra; and in the marchland-hills that stretch from west to east in the region of the Narmada and Tapti.

India also has its great and growing urban concentrations, especially in and around Bombay, Calcutta and Madras.

ETHNIC GROUPS

The peoples of India are extremely varied in composition. It is not particularly profitable to attempt to divide them into "racial" groups distinguished by physical characteristics (though it may be of interest that representatives of what are often held to be primitive stocks may be met, especially among jungle tribes). It is more profitable to consider the linguistic divisions of the Indian people, particularly since these in large measure form the basis for the current division of the federal Union into states. The languages of north India are of the Indo-Aryan family, the most important member of which is Hindi, the language particularly of Uttar Pradesh and Haryana (now separated by an inter-state boundary from the Punjabi-speaking area to the west). Other members of the family (whose corresponding linguistic states will be readily identified) are Rajasthani, Bihari, Bengali, Oriya and Marathi. In south India the languages are of a quite different family, the Dravidian; and include Tamil (in Tamil Nadu), Malayalam (in Kerala), Telugu (in Andhra Pradesh), and Kannada (in Karnataka). There are also many tribal languages in the jungle areas and Tibetan languages in the Himalayas.

As is well known, Indian society is also divided into castes, each of which is endogamous and into one of which a man or woman enters irrevocably at birth. Status and, to some extent, occupation are still largely determined by caste, and caste considerations enter greatly into politics; though the scene is a complex and rapidly shifting one in many regions.

Religion is in India both a divisive and a cohesive force. Communal friction and disharmony are often largely a matter of religion, especially as between Hindus and Muslims in north India. But most of India's peoples, apart from certain tribal groups, are united to a greater or lesser extent by cultural traits and the consciousness of a common heritage, and these derive in very large measure from age-old Hinduism.

HISTORY

Peter Robb*

HINDU INDIA

A mature Indian civilization began, so far as our present knowledge goes, about the middle of the third millenium B.C. About that time, amidst the cultures of the Baluch hills, based on villages of mud brick houses, apparently stable communities occupying sites of not more than two acres, a radically different culture arose in the Indus valley. The sophisticated trading cities which developed are known as the Indus valley or Harappa culture. This civilization extended from Indian Punjab to the Arabian Sea, Gujarat and the Gulf of Cambay. The cities were laid out in grid patterns with efficient drainage systems, writing was practised in a script as yet undeciphered, and trade was carried on by sea with the Sumerians of ancient Iraq. Little is known of their religion, but it may be that this culture provided some of the groundwork of later Hindu civilization. The culture lasted about a thousand years, showing remarkable physical and apparently administrative continuity, until it was suddenly overthrown, probably by the non-urban illiterate Aryan tribes of the Vedic period.

A pastoral people with aristocratic organization, the Aryans spread in migratory waves over Sind and the Punjab, tending their cattle. They also composed hymns to the nature deities, later written down as the *Rg Veda*. These include the beginnings of philosophic reflection and rituals. The people were evidently vigorous and they, or those who followed them, moved on into the Ganga valley. Eventually there arose agriculture and cities, and there was a gradual mixing with the original inhabitants. The Aryans are the first of many invaders from the northwest who (until modern times) have partly been absorbed and partly added to the polyglot nature of Indian society. The special and lasting contribution of the Aryans, however, was that out of a gradual coalescing of tribes into kingdoms, and a diversification of pastoral into specialist occupations, there came eventually a hardening of social divisions into the four classes of priest, warrior, farmer and serf. Racial integration deepened as the tribes continued their move east as far as Bengal. The pastoralists of the Punjab had now become agriculturists, centred on cities with palaces and temples of wood. Even in the early period, before they began to build in brick or stone, the tribes seem to have had skilled bronze smiths. They drove chariots to battle (and must have had the supply of artisans which this required); they had begun to include in their pantheon gods connected with earlier tradition; and they were developing the caste system. The Indo-Aryans had become Hindus. Their heartland remained in the Doab.

India enters the historical period about 600 B.C. There were two major movements at this time. The clash of cults produced a series of universal religions and organized kingdoms began to develop into empires. In reaction to the ritualism and spell-making of the Brahmins there appeared many protesting sects, from which Jainism and the religion of Gautama the Buddha have survived. Hinduism in response itself underwent radical changes which produced a higher religion.

At the time of the Buddha, Bimbisara had begun to consolidate his kingdom, Magadha, an area formerly on the periphery of Aryan influence, to the east of Kasi (Varanasi). After about 494 B.C., Magadha emerged as the first major power of India; it lasted about 150 years, and its territories, in the 4th century B.C., included the Ganga basin and much of the rest of North India. The brief invasion of the northwest by Alexander between about 327 and 325 B.C., provided an opportunity for Candragupta Maurya to overthrow the last of the Magadhan Nandas, and to establish the greatest of the ancient Indian empires, the Mauryan. This empire developed a sophisticated administrative structure and provided a degree of unity to much of North India. Candragupta's grandson, Asoka (273–232 B.C.), the greatest of the Mauryans, left the earliest significant contemporary records, showing his rule as humane internally and non-aggressive externally, clearly influenced by Buddhism. Some of the features of a certain strand of Hinduism: non-violence, vegetarianism, pilgrimages, were evident in this period.

Within fifty years of Asoka's death the empire collapsed. For a time the Sungas of Malwa ruled not a centralized state but, setting the pattern of the future, a loose confederacy of semi-autonomous peoples. The northwest experienced a series of invasions. Meanwhile other kingdoms rose and fell in Orissa, Gujarat and Malwa and in the south.

Out of this confusion, in 320 A.D., arose the second of the great empires: that of the Guptas. In the time of Candra Gupta II the Guptas became the paramount power of India, their realm stretching from the Bay of Bengal to the Gulf of Cambay and far into the north-west. It is generally agreed that ancient India attained its apogee under the Guptas and their efficient bureaucracy. Indian literature reached its peak with the poet Kalidas; art, science, philosophy and law all flourished. It was an age of achievement and consolidation.

Towards the end of the fifth century the White Huns and associated tribes descended on north India, destroying the Gupta empire and all political unity. From this period come many of the customs of Hindus which, in a later age, reformers sought to eradicate, such as *sati* (widow-burning) and tantric practices. Power became localized again.

MUSLIM INDIA

In the late twelfth century armies of Turkish slaves and Afghan chieftains spilled over into the Ganga valley. Subsequently cut off from Central

* This article is in part a revision of an earlier version by Percival Spear.

Asia by the Mongols, these people were reinforced by some Muslim refugees and mixed with local populations; they set up a military empire, the Delhi sultanate, which, for a brief period in the fourteenth century, controlled a vast area extending to the Hindu empire of Vijayanagar in the far south. It was succeeded by regional sultanates after the sack of Delhi by Timur (Tamerlane) at the end of the century, until, in the fifteenth, the Lodi Afghans restored Delhi's authority over most of north India. They fell in turn in 1526 to the Mughal ruler of Kabul, Babur, whose successors, in particular Akbar, extended enormously the territory over which they had control. Through a complex system of indirect rule, utilizing existing administrations and officials as much as possible, Mughal authority was maintained with a minimum of imperial officials. Thus, too, the influence of Mughal culture came to be supreme in the Hindu as well as the Muslim élite.

The empire collapsed during the eighteenth century as cohesive forces were weakened. Aurangzib became embroiled in a major war in the Deccan. The situation worsened after his death in 1707, with the sack of Delhi by the Persian ruler, Nadir Shah, in 1739, and with the subsequent establishment of Afghan power in the northwest under Ahmad Shah Abdali. Aurangzib's successors eventually became pensioners of first the Marathas (strong again under Brahmin leadership) and then the British; former Mughal governors, or non-Mughals such as Europeans, Marathas, and the Sikhs under Ranjit Singh, established independent centres of power. Thus the third great Indian empire went the way of its predecessors; like them it left a cultural and political legacy which was obscured but not lost.

BRITISH RULE

The British East India Company came to India in Mughal times to trade. In the eighteenth century, however, from insignificant and peripheral trading posts, the Company began to accumulate territory and then, in Bengal after 1765, to administer one of the Mughal provinces. Later the British expanded their territories to protect those they had already, and then to reach "natural" frontiers taking on the Marathas and later the Sikhs. By the mid-nineteenth century they ruled most of India directly, and all of it was under their ultimate control: theirs was the first empire to achieve this completeness.

British rule may be usefully divided into three periods. In the first, lasting until the 1840s, they were preoccupied with establishing hegemony or refining the administration. In the second, lasting until the First World War, they were able to put their system to work. In the third, their attention shifted to the gradual transfer of power to the Indians.

At first, ignorant of Indian conditions, the British had to follow Mughal precedent and administer indirectly; except at the highest levels, government always remained in Indian hands. Inevitably, however, British rule tended to strengthen those institutions for which the British found a use: they introduced Western notions of property and sovereignty, and later on the rule of law, legal equality, progress, social justice, nationalism, and representative democracy. Moreover, the early revenue settlements and the development of commercial agriculture subtly distorted the shape of rural society.

Although some of the British had thought it their mission to 'bring light' to India, by the time such interference was practical it had been discredited by the North Indian revolt of 1857–58; and, in the second period of their rule, laissez-faire became the justification for policies, just as utilitarianism had been earlier. This did not wholly prevent government involvement in economic development, famine relief, tenancy relations, and even social reform. After the 1860s the increasingly centralized administration, the long continuation of peace, and the building of telegraphs, railways and canals, left their mark on India. It became a market and a source of raw materials rather than a producer of finished goods, and many former centres found themselves without a role in the new economic system. The cultivated area and agricultural production increased, and, with the growth of coastal and railway cities, offset the pressure of population until the beginning of the twentieth century, but rising prices strained the relationships of rural society, and the right to partition and transfer property rights disturbed the operation of rural credit. In the balance sheet of benefit and loss from British rule, some areas and classes fared much worse than others.

From the first there were reactions to the changes and the most important in the long term were on the periphery of Indian society. The need for the cooperation of Indians, not only in the traditional roles of prince and *zamindar*, but also in a modern-style bureaucracy, encouraged deliberate attempts to educate Indians in English, so that they could provide the minor officials without whom government as the British conceived it could not function. In the towns the British impact created new classes: those engaged in Western-style commerce, those in government service, and those in professions such as law and medicine and teaching. These people had a number of shared interests which superseded, at least on occasions, caste, communal and regional differences. If the British did not create Indian unity, then certainly, for these people, they made it necessary. After 1885, with the consolidation of administration at Calcutta, and the development of the press and communications, members of the Western-educated élites began to come together in an annual alliance called the Indian National Congress.

There were social and religious reactions as well. British rule, being non-Islamic, posed a special problem for orthodox Muslims, and, while most adapted themselves, a few took the logical step of regarding India as *dar-al harb* (land of war). Among Hindus, Rammohan Roy's *Brahmo Samaj* (1830) was followed by various movements for social reform, or to achieve the benefits of Western ethics and education without the risks of religious contamination. After 1875 some Muslims followed suit in Sayyid Ahmad Khan's Aligarh movement. Late nineteenth century traditional society and religion turned increasingly back on itself. Lower classes of Muslims were trained or influenced by newly-founded seminaries; a Hindu revival was marked by renewed interest in popular festivals.

In the nineteenth century the spokesmen to whom the central government listened most easily, for all the careful rapport in the districts between officials and traditional power networks, were naturally those who spoke their language both literally (in English) and metaphorically (in the appeal to a British liberal rhetoric). It was enough for such Indians in their annual Congress debates, that they should stand for India because of their class and education. With successive constitutional changes, however, they began to need wider support, and to justify their role through their popularity, not their talents. Inevitably they came into contact with the popular religious movements. These were new men, even though in many ways they did closely resemble the stalwarts of the Congress (Gokhale, Mehta, Naoroji) in their background and hopes for India, because of their standing with the mainstream of Indian society and the methods of permanent concerted agitation which they were thus able to employ. Such men were succeeded in the twentieth century by Mohandas Gandhi, whose rise marked a rethinking of the organization and approach of the Congress, and the advent of new regions and levels of politics on the national scene to replace the long dominance of Bombay. The change was assisted by the Amritsar massacre of 1919 and Muslim objections to the Turkish peace terms after 1918.

After 1857 the British had shown their determination to hold on to power by recruiting for the Indian army only from "loyal" classes, by reserving the higher reaches of administration for Europeans, and by demonstrating in a number of other ways that India was a subject empire. But, if only to help overcome financial difficulties, they had to listen to educated opinion. After 1885 they introduced local self-government (with powers to raise local revenue); in 1892, indirectly, and again in 1909, they conceded the elective principle in choosing who were to advise, though not control, the executive through the legislative councils. Finally between 1915 and 1919, an even more important breakthrough, they admitted publicly that they would have to transfer power (not sovereignty) to Indian hands. In the 1920s and 1930s this promise, by affecting a wide range of policies and because of the radical transformation in Indian politics, was translated into an expectation that the British would relinquish sovereignty as well. The problem then was how to resolve India's regional, communal and constitutional disunity.

The Indian princes, semi-autonomous rulers of areas vast and small, made difficulties that were not so much solved as shelved. The unrepresentative character of the Indian political élite was an argument canvassed by conservatives but not something that could be much diminished while the British continued to fashion a Western-style constitution which emphasized the politician's talents. It was the Muslim problem which had to be answered. Muslims were not one community; but their élites had begun to unite, for reasons of linguistic, social and religious competition, and because of separate Muslim electorates (1909) and Muslim issues in political agitations. During the last thirty years of British rule, the Congress under Gandhi conducted campaigns (1919–22, 1929–32, 1942) of non-co-operation or civil disobedience (*satyagraha*), often using local issues and less peaceful methods. In between, the Congress participated in dyarchy (the partial transfer of responsibility to Indians, 1919) and provincial self-government (1935). Both activities required mobilization of support, and, especially at local levels, tended to use religious appeals and organization. Thus, though it rested on fundamental differences between the two religions, the Muslim sense of danger from the Hindu majority grew as the prospect of majority rule came closer, and this sense was transmitted from the political classes, who hoped to inherit British power, through the *ulama* to the population at large. It was not helped by the Congress insistence that it was an alternative government to the British, and thus superior in status to other political associations; the fact that the dangers were real, at least at the street level, was shown in many savage communal riots, which though due to faults on both sides were obviously more alarming for the community in a minority. In the 1940s, Muslim demands hardened, after the resignation of Congress ministries and its subsequent outlawing because of Gandhi's "Quit India" campaign. The British began to treat the Muslim League, which had at last consolidated its all-India status, as an equal with the Congress. After the war the British believed they could hold India only by force, and they had lost the will for this. Thus, after 1945, the British wanted to go, and when the Muslim League under Muhammad Ali Jinnah stood in their way, the British Prime Minister, Clement Attlee, and the last Viceroy, the Earl Mountbatten of Burma, cut the knot and partitioned the country. The majority Muslim areas, never wholeheartedly behind the League, found themselves yoked, for a time, as a new country: Pakistan.

INDEPENDENT INDIA AND THE RULE OF NEHRU

India became an independent Dominion on August 15th, 1947. The new Prime Minister, Jawaharlal Nehru, promised that it now would "awake to life and freedom". His administration, however, was marked by continuity as well as change.

The immediate task was to restore the authority of the government following a rising tide of panic and massacre as refugees fled from one part to the other of divided Punjab. Millions were uprooted and hundreds of thousands killed as the Boundary Force set up by Mountbatten proved wholly inadequate to its task. Both the migration and the enormous death toll have left permanent marks on India and Pakistan, but in the short term order was restored quite quickly. To do so, however, took the life of Gandhi who had rushed to Delhi to try to stop the communal violence, and was assassinated in January 1948 by a Hindu extremist who seems to have considered him too conciliatory to the Muslims. Nehru told the nation "the light has gone out"; but the shock of Gandhi's death restored it, at least for a time, by discrediting communalists.

It was necessary also to unify the country. When the British left there were 362 princely states, varying enormously in size and population. The British had absolved them from their allegiance to the Crown, but apparently left uncertain their future and even the basis on which a decision about their future would be taken, whether, for example, it should be by the rulers or the governments or the people. But, although in theory a state could opt for independence or for union with either India or Pakistan, in practice the withdrawal of British suzerainty made the first option difficult (if not impossible), while the second was a real choice only for those states adjacent to the borders between the two new countries. By independence day all but four had acceded to one or the other; and during 1948 the Home Minister, Vallabhbhai Patel, aided by V. P. Menon, bullied and cajoled those which had joined India into being absorbed into the new states of the Indian federation.

Of the princely states which were still aloof, two had Muslim rulers but largely Hindu populations. The ruler of the first, Junagadh (on the Kathiawar coast), finally opted for Pakistan. There were disturbances, Indian troops marched in, and, the prince having fled to Pakistan, the state was united with India after a plebiscite. The Nizam of Hyderabad, the second of these mainly Hindu states and the largest princely domain of British India, had hoped for independence, but this depended (as the state was landlocked) on Indian goodwill, which was not forthcoming. Eventually, after an extremist group had taken power in the state, it was invaded by Indian forces and taken into the Indian union. (At the same time Kalat was absorbed by Pakistan.)

Kashmir, with its predominantly Muslim population and Hindu ruler, also had remained undecided, until October 1947 when Pathan tribesmen from Pakistan invaded in support of an internal rising. The Maharaja was promptly persuaded to opt for India, whose troops retained for him Jammu (with its Hindu-Sikh majority) and the Vale. A "popular" government was installed under Sheikh Abdullah, with a promise of a plebescite to follow. Later, when the Sheikh quarrelled with the raja, and began to speak of independence, the idea of a plebiscite was dropped, and the Sheikh was removed and imprisoned without trial. India has regarded the state as part of India since 1954 (when the Kashmir assembly proclaimed that it had joined the union) and, although the dispute with Pakistan continues, the border now seems bound to harden more or less along the truce lines arranged by the United Nations after the brief war of 1948, thus leaving most of the territory with India, but with Pakistan the areas overrun in 1947.

Unity was maintained within India firstly through the Constitution, which established the union as a secular parliamentary democracy on the Western model, with a federal structure but a strong centre. Jawaharlal Nehru's own wishes were closely reflected in the shape of the administration, though he recognized that, as a whole, the document might cause difficulties in future. In January 1950 India became a republic with a President as its constitutional head, but recognizing the British sovereign as Head of the Commonwealth. There are two Houses of Parliament, the Lok Sabha (House of the People) and the Rajya Sabha (Council of States), the former elected by adult suffrage, the latter representing states' interest. The executive, a Cabinet under a Prime Minister, is responsible to the Lok Sabha; and thus India followed the British model. In other respects, however, the example of the U.S.A. was followed: the Supreme Court is empowered to decide constitutional questions, including those relating to the declaration of fundamental rights which the Constitution contains. The diversity of India and a fear of "Balkanization" were reflected, however, in the distribution of functions. The centre controls defence, foreign affairs, railways, ports and currency, and is vested with residuary powers; also, in listed subjects, it can override the states, while the President's emergency powers allow, for example, the suspension of a state government and the imposition of President's rule.

Indian unity was threatened further by reorganization of the former British provinces along linguistic lines. What was conceded to Andhra in 1952–53 was refused to Bombay until 1960 (when Gujarat and Maharashtra were separated) and to Punjab until 1966 (when Haryana was formed out of "Hindu" Punjab). Nehru had opposed linguistic states but it seems that the limited and gradual responses by the centre to some extent defused separatist tendencies, and that secession can be avoided in spite of the linguistic divisions as long as local interests are served by the union.

The role of English as an official language (scheduled to end in 1965) has been championed by non-Hindi speakers, especially in Tamil Nadu, as a means of preventing Hindi dominance of the civil service and central institutions. Nehru again proved accommodating and promised vernacular examinations for the services and the continuing use of English, thus ensuring that any move to Hindi would be gradual and that Hindi enthusiasts would have to be restrained in the interests of non-Hindi speakers.

The supremacy of the Congress was ensured by the resolution of internal struggles in favour of Nehru, and by campaigns outside it against communalist and communist parties. Through the election of P. N. Tandon as Congress President against the Prime Minister's wishes, Vallabhbhai Patel sought, it seems, to limit his old rival's power and the accretion of influence by the office of Prime Minister, though probably not actually to displace Nehru himself. With Patel's death, and by gathering support in Tandon's Working Committee, Nehru was able to outflank this movement and became undisputed dictator of his party. He had to pay the price, if such he saw it, of working with rightists in his Cabinet and the Congress.

From 1951 until the Chinese invasion in 1962 Nehru reigned supreme. Parallel to the assertion of his personal will came the securing of Congress dominance. The assassination of Gandhi provided the occasion for an outright attack on communalist parties (as well as communalists with Congress) who had been encouraged by the war with Pakistan and the influx of Hindi refugees. The issue was further defused by the Nehru-Liaquat pact in 1950, temporarily settling the relations between the two countries. At the first general election in 1951–52 communist parties fared badly and Congress scored an overwhelming victory.

Against communists, too, Nehru waged a constant campaign, especially in Andhra and Kerala. He was successful largely through tireless electioneering, though once, under the influence of his daughter, Indira Gandhi (as Congress President), he intervened in Kerala to remove a communist government.

The very success of Nehru's Congress posed a problem, however. In British times Congress repeatedly had been faced with the incompatibility of its twin roles, as disciplined political movement committed to a definite programme, and as alternative government containing a variety of points of view. In so far as Congress became the inevitable party of government after independence, it was bound to attract the ambitious and thus to find it difficult to evolve a consistent ideology: a compendium of more or less diverse interests could not also be a unified force for, say, socialism. For there did not evolve after independence, any more than before, a fully democratic structure with a credible alternative party or parties of government. This lack resulted partly from deliberate Congress policy, partly from the wide slice of the political sphere encompassed by the Congress as a result of its history as the central nationalist movement, and partly from the divisions among opposition groups. Potential or long-standing opposition leaders were ready to take office at times under the Congress while permanent opposition groupings of any size have proved elusive. Socialists, for example, originating in the Congress Socialist Party (1934), formed the Socialist Party in 1948, which evolved into the PSP in 1952. But in 1955 Rammanohar Lohia and others split from their colleagues over the police firing under a PSP government in Kerala, and over possible co-operation with the Congress. Thereafter only short-term periods of unity were possible. The leaders, Lohia, Jayaprakash Narayan, Asok Mehta, J. B. Kripalani and so on, tended to be individualists rather than organization-men. Thus, under Nehru, the pre-eminence of Congress during the independence struggle was modified and preserved.

There was broad continuity too, under Nehru, in the personnel of government. In spite of a certain shift in legislative and party membership towards agricultural classes and peasant castes, the beneficiaries tended to be those already dominant socially or economically; individuals whose ability and resources brought them to the top proved mostly to be members of dominant landholding castes. Even the communist government in Kerala seems to have been largely upper class (though supported in factories and villages) and by no means immune from opportunists or free from self-seeking and corruption. The monopoly of politics by an English-speaking professional élite, whose talents fitted them to negotiate with the British, may have continued slowly to be weakened as it began to be with the advent of popular agitation in the 1920s; but independence and democracy have also further emphasized the resilience of customary power structures which had operated all along beside the British-inspired politicians. In this way, caste has accommodated itself to democracy, though the meaning of both has been subtly changed in the process.

Neither did change spread to the bureaucracy, widely regarded as being inefficient and corrupt. Nehru opted for continuity among the administrators, partly through necessity, for the Congress cadres could not replace the bureaucracy the British had built. At the highest levels, it is true, political leaders displaced the administrator-rulers, often not receiving the advice of civil servants except on the bare question of legality, and combined bureaucratic and political functions. At lower levels, however, the executive functions of the higher civil servant remained, as for example in the district officer as the fount of authority in the locality. The advent of *panchayati raj* and the involvement of local elected agencies in development programmes after 1959 represented a contrary trend, but the bureaucrats have mostly reasserted their role. *Panchayati raj* has become, rather, a means of extending state and national political allegiances and networks to lower levels.

Independence did change the priorities of government, even when policies continued existing trends. Thus Nehru continued the social reforming tendencies which resulted from Western influence in British days, but with a determination impossible for alien rulers. He insisted on the secular nature of India's government, on equality before the law (untouchability was formally abolished under the Constitution), and on the passage of Acts providing, among other things, for divorce, monogamy, and equal rights of inheritance for women. Though he had to draw on his personal prestige to secure this major achievement, it is safe to say that he would not have insisted if there had not been a sufficient body of opinion in favour of the changes, and if it had not been politically safe. (In 1951 he agreed to drop the Hindu Code Bill.) On the other hand it is also true that this favourable opinion is largely limited to sections of the middle classes, and that change, for example in the position of women, has not been rapid. Under Nehru too, education was greatly expanded, but (repeating the mistake of the British) most notably at university and higher technical levels, and in towns; in the countryside the literacy rate is still very low, about one in four.

The diversion of resources to development was the other major example of change within continuity. The creation of the National Planning Commission in 1950 was followed by three Five-Year Plans during the rule of Nehru. His main remedy was industrialization. The Plans were largely successful and industrial production expanded by 50 per cent between 1951 and 1959. What was new and remarkable in these programmes was the conscious attempt to plan a mixed economy as a weapon against poverty. What was unfortunate perhaps was the perpetuation of the British emphasis on large-scale projects and imported remedies, and the neglect of agriculture in favour of heavy industry. In spite of the "green revolution" in wheat, food production lagged behind industrial growth.

Nor has growth resulted in a fundamental redistribution of wealth. There was an attack on the great estate-holders of northern India, but, though the estates were divided, the great volume of landless labourers was little diminished. The abolition of landlordism, and more recently princely purses, has affected the families at the very highest levels; but the undoubted benefits of economic development since independence have been absorbed almost exclusively by middle groups or minorities of rich peasants, while the inhabitants of India's innumerable villages have become, if anything, poorer than before. This, more than corruption or bureaucracy, seems to be the stumbling block in such programmes as the one for family planning.

During the 1950s Nehru conducted foreign affairs with little interference. He began with the support of nationalist forces in Indonesia, mainland S.E. Asia and elsewhere. Acutely aware of East-West tension, and of the dangers of an atomic war in the post-war years he declared the policy of non-involvement, and strove to build up a third force of uncommitted nations. This led him to welcome the Communist rise to power in China in 1949 and brought him to the Bandung conference of Afro-Asian states in 1955.

This was the zenith of Nehru's international influence and from this moment his star seemed to decline. He was forthright in condemning Britain and France over Suez in 1956, but offended Indian right-wing opinion by being less clear on the U.S.S.R. in Hungary. In 1959 the Chinese decision to rule, instead of control, Xizang, followed by the Dalai Lama's flight to India, put him under further pressure from right-wing opinion and embroiled him with China itself. It gradually became clear that China did not regard its border with India as settled, and, partly under pressure from public opinion and the army, Nehru agreed to a policy of asserting Indian presence up to the border it claimed. The dispute became serious with the discovery of a Chinese road across the desolate Aksi Chin plateau in northeast Kashmir. Nehru made some war-like speeches, and the Indians engaged in minor skirmishes. Suddenly, in 1962, the Chinese advanced in full force against apparently unprepared Indian positions, overran them, continued rapidly on into India, and then withdrew to their earlier positions. Thus Nehru's plan for an unaligned bloc headed by India in close friendship with China was finally destroyed, and the way was open for even closer ties with the Soviet Union. India's remaining credit as a peace-maker was undermined with the occupation of Goa, Nehru having finally abandoned, under heavy internal pressure, the unpromising negotiations with Portugal to have the territory accede to India without force.

THE PERIOD SINCE NEHRU

Although in the last 18 months of his life Nehru was much criticized, there were serious doubts about what would happen after his death. In the event, in May 1964, the transition was smooth and the succession passed to Lal Bahadur Shastri, not the most able nor the closest to Nehru among the outgoing Cabinet, but something of a consensus figure. Before he had fully found his feet he was faced with a national crisis over the proclamation of Hindi as the national language in January 1965. There followed the Rann of Kutch incident with Pakistan in April and the three-weeks war with Pakistan in September. His stature grew with this last event. He died, however, in January 1966, after going to Tashkent to meet President Ayub Khan and the Soviet Premier, Aleksei Kosygin. His successor was Nehru's daughter, Mrs. Indira Gandhi, with the kingmaker Kamaraj in the background and the existing Congress team except for Morarji Desai, who left because he would be Prime Minister or nothing.

In 1967 the general election ended the nearly general domination of the Congress in the states, and returned it to power at Delhi with a much reduced majority. Indira Gandhi continued as Prime Minister but was now strengthened by a deal with Morarji Desai who became Deputy Premier and Finance Minister. In Madras (subsequently re-named Tamil Nadu) the separatist Dravida Munnetra Kazhagam (DMK) took power and in Kerala Communist rule was restored. Anti-Congress ministries were set up in several other states, but proved so unstable that mid-term elections were held from Haryana to West Bengal. The chief beneficiaries of the Congress losses were the left-wing pro-Communist groups and the Hindu nationalist party, the Jana Sangh.

In Bengal political anarchy reigned. Leaders and supporters on all sides became embroiled in campaigns of violence; revolutionary terrorists, the Naxalites, murdered landowners and political leaders in the countryside and also in Calcutta itself. To cope with this menace, Indira Gandhi's government armed itself in 1971 with special powers.

The Congress managers had supported Indira Gandhi as another consensus figure, and had no intention of reducing their influence in her favour, or condoning any substantial change in the Congress programme. The events of 1967, however, had shaken their credibility, and shown to many, including Mrs. Gandhi, that the Congress needed a new image and revitalized organization if it was to remain in power. It was not in Mrs. Gandhi's personal style, either, to leave the initiative in the hands of others. The crisis was precipitated by the death of the respected President Zakir Husain in May 1969. The Presidency possessed considerable reserve powers which would place it in a key position in the event, as then seemed quite possible, of the next general election failing to give the Congress an overall majority. The right-wing adopted K. C. Reddy as the Congress candidate. Mrs. Gandhi retorted by implementing the long-standing Congress promise to nationalize the banks, by dismissing Mr. Desai from the Finance Ministry and by supporting the Vice-President, V. V. Giri, a left-wing Congressman, for the Presidency. His success greatly strengthened her hand. In November the Congress openly split, the Syndicate retaining the party organization and Mrs. Gandhi the popular support, depending for a majority in the Lok Sabha on the left-wing group outside Congress. In 1970 Congress success with Communist allies in the Kerala elections encouraged her to dissolve the Lok Sabha. The elections of February-March 1971 proved a notable success, both for Mrs. Gandhi herself and her wing of the Congress. Once again an effective opposition had failed to emerge, largely because Mrs. Gandhi's Congress occupied the middle ground ideologically and, by being in power, attracted recruits as the party of government. Congress (O) was left with little positive policy; and the degree to which Mrs. Gandhi had commandeered the territory of the socialists was marked by their evident confusion about how to react to her.

Hard on the election results came a fresh crisis with Pakistan: its army's intervention in East Pakistan (now Bangladesh). India was faced with an immense refugee problem: about 7 million in August and nearly all in West Bengal. First, India publicized the problem and asked for help. Next she concluded in August 1971 a treaty with the Soviet Union: "non alignment" was safeguarded, but the two countries promised mutual support, short of actual military involvement, in the event of either being attacked by a third. Finally, thus assured of non-interference, India first sheltered then trained and armed, and finally gave support to Bangladeshi guerilla forces along and across the border. The Pakistan Government commenced hostilities on December 6th with raids on Indian airfields in the west. The war lasted twelve days. India maintained its position in the west, but gained an unexpectedly rapid victory in the east.

In July 1972 Pakistan and India renounced the use of force and agreed to respect the 1971 ceasefire line in Kashmir and international borders elsewhere.

However the explosion of India's first nuclear device in May 1974 set back the improvement in relations with Pakistan, and resulted in much criticism throughout the world. India, apparently supreme in the subcontinent in 1971, once again found its position threatened. The fall of Mujib in Bangladesh (August 1975) brought into the open several disputes and fears of Indian dominance. The inclusion of Sikkim in the Indian Union (April 1975) soured relations with Nepal. Indian foreign policy became more pragmatic. In mid-1976 agreement was reached with Pakistan on exchange of ambassadors and restoration of air links, and relations have improved with China to the point of an exchange of ambassadors.

Indira Gandhi's personal position had been further strengthened by state elections in 1972. With Congress ministries in almost all states, she was able to secure Chief Ministers who would carry out her policies. Nevertheless a number of her measures were thwarted by the Supreme Court and, in the long term, economic disasters made it impossible for her to make much improvement in conditions, let alone carry out her promise to abolish poverty. During 1973 and 1974 unprecedented drought brought appalling famine to west and central India. Inflation, intensified by the worldwide oil crisis, seriously reduced the standard of living of the middle classes, and further reduced the circumstances of the urban poor. Riots broke out in a number of states, and in Gujarat street fighting forced the resignation of the state government and the imposition of President's rule. A strike of railway staff was suppressed by the army. In Bihar, the veteran socialist, Jayaprakash Narayan, headed a popular campaign against the local Congress government, alleging corruption, and during 1974 he sought allies outside Bihar and began also to attack the central government. His coalition lacked ideological conviction, including parties both to the right and left of Congress, but in May 1975, as the Janata Front, it contested and won the election in Gujarat which followed the ending of President's rule.

In June 1975 the Allahabad High Court found Mrs. Gandhi guilty of election malpractices (largely, though perhaps not entirely, of a technical nature). Mrs. Gandhi then proclaimed a state of emergency and arrested large numbers of her opponents. The Houses of Parliament were recalled and, in the absence of non-government members (other than the CPI), rapidly approved constitutional amendments to strengthen the executive and legislature and protect the Prime Minister.

Mrs. Gandhi's motives were obscure. The opposition campaign was real enough, but accusations of foreign involvement were never substantiated, and the most recent examples of disorder to be cited were riots in Gujarat and Bihar in 1973 and 1974, and the assassination in 1975 of L. N. Mishra, Central Minister for Railways, which was not blamed on the opposition. The need to improve administration and revitalize development programmes was a justification rather than a cause. Obviously the Allahabad judgment was crucial, but the real question is why Mrs. Gandhi chose to seek immunity through retrospective legislation rather than fight in the courts, and the answer may well be that she needed to counter-attack opponents within her own party. Rumour at the time suggested that Jagjivan Ram had favoured her resignation.

The emergency saw some gains in administrative efficiency, an apparently successful attack on the black market and some reduction in the expected rate of inflation. Opponents were silenced where they were not imprisoned. Newspapers were muzzled. Non-Congress state governments in Tamil Nadu and Gujarat were removed. It ended unexpectedly when Mrs. Gandhi announced that the general election, hitherto postponed, would be held in March 1977. Three explanations for this seem more likely than others: that Mrs. Gandhi was misinformed about her popularity or, being informed, saw this as her last chance to gain a popular mandate; that she wished to allow the political advance of her second son, Sanjay and members of his Youth Congress; and that once again she needed to outflank opponents within her own party, an idea supported by the resignation of Jagjivan Ram after the elections were announced.

The Congress faced a large number of straight contests, as the opposition groups had either come together formally in the Janata Party, under Morarji Desai, or had entered into electoral agreements, as was the case with Jagjivan Ram's new Congress for Democracy. The results must rank among the most extraordinary in recent times. Mrs. Gandhi lost her own seat in the Lok Sabha and the Congress was defeated throughout North India, winning no seats at all in areas where they had always seemed invincible. Mrs. Gandhi had alienated local political machines through her assertions of central power and her encouragement of Sanjay, the middle classes through the attacks on the courts, the press, and freedom of expression, the farmers through the development tax, the workers through the freezing of wages and the ban on strike action, and the poor through excesses in (or rumours about) slum clearance and sterilization. However, in the south the Congress and its allies improved their position: there emergency measures were less effective and fewer leaders were imprisoned, Jagjivan Ram was less well-known and the Jana Sangh unimportant, the government-controlled radio was still the main source of outside information, and the major opposition party, Tamil Nadu's DMK, had been discredited by charges of corruption.

The first tasks for the Janata Government were to dismantle the machinery of the emergency and to repair the Constitution. It had its successes. It turned an electoral alliance into a ruling party, helped by the reluctant agreement of Jagjivan Ram and his supporters to merge with the majority. It secured its candidate, Neelam Sanjiva Reddy, as President in July 1977. As late as November 1978 it had some representation in southern state assemblies, had toppled the ruling Congress alliance in the Bombay municipality and remained powerful in the north.

However, serious rifts soon appeared: they widened or narrowed in tandem with Mrs. Gandhi's fortunes. In 1977 she had been unsuccessful in a tour of the south and in seeking control of the defeated Congress. She was strongly criticized by the Shah Commission, set up to investigate the emergency, and criminal charges were finally lodged against her in July 1978. By this time, Charan Singh and Raj Narain (Home and Health Ministers) had provoked their dismissals; dissent was reported between Prime Minister, Morarji Desai, and his External Affairs Minister, A. B. Vajpayee; President Reddy had threatened to resign; Industry Minister George Fernandes had had his plan for nationalizing key industries turned down by the Cabinet (and later he would propose a realignment to outflank the Jana Sangh). In November 1978 Desai called for criticism of himself in preference to destruction of the party. In 1978, however, Mrs. Gandhi's supporters won overall majorities in state elections in Karnataka and Andhra Pradesh, formed a short-lived coalition in Maharashtra, and became the major opposition group in the Lok Sabha. In November Mrs. Gandhi herself won a by-election for a Karnataka seat in the Lok Sabha. The Janata leadership rallied. When Mrs. Gandhi tried to take her seat she was expelled for contempt and imprisoned for a week. Charan Singh returned to the government as Finance Minister and Deputy Prime Minister in January 1979. By July, however, Mrs. Gandhi's Congress had lost its position as official opposition, a split having resulted from her quarrels with Devaraj Urs, the dominant figure in Karnataka. Coincidentally, Raj Narain was suspended from the Janata party, and many other defections followed, including the resignation of Charan Singh.

Janata's decline was marked by public disorder, including police riots over pay, the restoration of preventive detention, and by economic problems. However, the damage was chiefly due to internal faction-fighting. Morarji Desai's huge majority melted away and eventually the withdrawal of Communist and Socialist support forced him to resign in July 1979. President Reddy, in an unprecedented situation, first called on Y. B. Chavan, leader of the then official opposition; and later asked Charan Singh, now head of the Lok Dal, to form a government. He was dependent on the tacit support of Mrs. Gandhi, which was withdrawn as soon as he took office. Finally, ignoring the claims of Jagjivan Ram, who eventually succeeded Desai as Janata leader, the President dissolved Parliament in August. Elections to the Lok Sabha were held in January 1980. Two trends could be discerned: disarray and fragmentation of the former Janata coalition, and opportunist support for Mrs. Gandhi. Although personalities were foremost, the issue was also clear: Janata's manifesto harked back to the emergency, while Mrs. Gandhi's emphasized the need for order and stability.

Mrs. Gandhi won an overwhelming victory, though with only 42 per cent of the total vote. Sanjay Gandhi entered the Lok Sabha for the first time. On the whole, elderly politicians, in the past, retained power and advanced their protégés: energies were devoted to dynastic ambitions or to suspicions of them. Sanjay, however, had come to have the backing of men of his own generation and, because of his influence on the selection of candidates, many were elected with him. He was, of course, himself influential by virtue of being the heir apparent, and, when he met his death in an air crash in June 1980, this need continued to be felt. By 1981 some people spoke of the inevitable succession of his elder brother Rajiv and in June 1981 Rajiv won, by a large majority, Sanjay's former seat of Amethi in Uttar Pradesh.

Mrs. Gandhi's return to power saw some shifts in foreign policy but, while consolidating her country's relations with the Soviet Union (entering into a large arms deal in mid-1980), she continued to seek normal relations with both the U.S.A. and China. In East Asian affairs she projected herself as an honest broker, deploring American intervention in Iran while regretting any foreign involvement in Afghanistan. In February 1980, following earlier examples,

Mrs. Gandhi precipitated new elections in most states, partly to secure a majority in the Rajya Sabha. Very substantial Congress (I) majorities were returned in seven of the assemblies, and by-elections in November 1980 confirmed this success. With other states, notably Sheikh Abdullah's Kashmir and Bengal under the CPI (M), relations have been poor and, in the latter case, productive of local disorder. In 1982 there was some diminution of Congress(I) support, and some attempts by opposition parties to form a common front. A serious test was provided by a series of by-elections for the Lok Sabha and assembly elections in four states, held on May 19th. In Kerala the United Democratic Front under K. Karunakaran, for Congress(I), was confirmed in government, which it had formed as a coalition since January. In West Bengal there was an overwhelming victory for the Left Front and, particularly, Jyoti Basu's CPI(M). In Himachal Pradesh the ruling Congress(I) suffered reverses at the hands of the BJP and was able to maintain a majority only by welcoming back and rewarding with ministerial posts rebels whom it had expelled in a show of party discipline on the eve of the poll. In Haryana a confused result, also representing marked reverses for the ruling Congress(I), was resolved only by the wooing of independents and defectors, with a mixture of violence, intrigue and farce, and by the refusal of the Governor to call the Lok Dal leader to form a government. The verdict of the electorate was clearly against Mrs. Gandhi and her party, especially in the north, but not overwhelmingly so. The outcome was almost everywhere the maintenance of the *status quo*. In the process, the nature of the political system was once again exposed: parties on all sides were shown to be uneasy coalitions of factions, and politicians to be attracted more by the lure of office than by the discipline of party allegiance. The Left Front success in West Bengal was thus marred and almost shattered by rows between the parties over the allocation of ministries. In Kerala the multi-party government ensured its support partly by sharing out the largest-ever number of ministerial posts. In Himachal Pradesh and Haryana, office had to be offered to politicians who had been rejected by the ruling party or who had defeated party candidates at the polls. The centripetal force represented by the consensus party of government, now the Congress(I), continues to be powerful, but in the states, despite some polarization of voting, the existence of splinter groups and uneasy co-operation between them is still the main feature of politics, one which makes majorities difficult to secure and preserve, voting difficult to interpret, and the popular will unlikely to be accurately reflected in the formation of ministries.

The Indian economy has shown some encouraging signs, especially in the fight against inflation, and this, with some good harvests, has been to the advantage of the central government. Another Five-Year Plan has been announced: there have been some budgetary liberalizations and some relaxation towards foreign investment. There are, however, two phenomena which suggest an underlying economic and social malaise. One is a resurgence of caste and communal feeling, which has led in recent years to uncommonly violent rioting, most notably between low castes, with some higher caste backing, and Harijans (or "outcastes"), with their statutory and constitutional privileges. The backward, non-Harijan sector had supported, but become disillusioned with, the Janata party; Mrs. Gandhi's victory was, to some extent, their defeat, and their alienation remains a time-bomb.

The second development is the violent regional feeling being expressed in Assam and north-east India against Bengali residents and immigrants, feelings expressed in murders, bomb outrages, strikes and a non-co-operation campaign. Mrs. Gandhi criticized this "distressing trend" without being able to reverse it. Matters have improved since June 1981, after talks held by the Central Minister of Home Affairs; and in February 1982 President's rule in Assam was at last replaced by a Congress(I) government under K. C. Gogoi. However, continuing minor disorder suggests that the fundamental problems, of which the troubles are symptoms, have not disappeared. It remains to be seen whether such crises, or the undoubted technological and economic progress which India has made, will be the trend for the future.

ECONOMIC SURVEY

Kevin Rafferty

It is difficult to talk of the Indian e conomy because there are in fact several different ec onomies working in the country at the same time. For example, although India manufactures highly developed heavy industrial goods (some of them as sophisticated as any in the world), it is also one of the world's poorest countries, where the bottom 50 per cent of the people earn hardly enough to stay alive. Some statistics illustrate well this incongruity within the economy, In terms of population, India, with about 684 million people at the 1981 census, is the second largest country, after China, in the world. In terms of area, it is the fifth largest. In terms of aggregate Gross Domestic Product (G.D.P.), India comes about 13th in the world, after countries such as Brazil, Canada, Poland and Spain, as well as behind all the obviously rich countries. In per capita terms, it is much further behind and has slipped to about the 15th poorest country in the non-communist world, according to World Bank figures. Putting a reliable dollar figure either on G.D.P. or on per capita income has become surprisingly difficult. The Asian Development Bank (ADB), in its annual report issued in 1982, assesses India's per capita income at $240 in 1980. Such a figure is higher than the direct dollar conversion of India's rupee figures. The official Economic Survey for 1981/82 gives total net national product in 1980/81 of Rs. 1,042,010 million and per capita national product of Rs. 1,536.9. At the average 1980 exchange rate of Rs. 7.863 to the U.S. dollar, that would work out at $195 per head; at the 1981 rate of Rs. 8.659 per dollar, it would work out at only $177. An additional difficulty is that such direct convesions do not take account of the real purchasing value of the rupee, which would take you further in India than its dollar equivalent, for example, would in the U.S.A.

At the time of the British industrial revolution, India was split by wars and warring factions and was easy prey for the European mercantile powers. As British rule increased so India became united. Many British made great sums of money out of India; and although many district officers cared deeply for the Indians under their charge, British Government policy was rather more concerned about the fact that India was the jewel in the British crown which had to be kept secure and well-polished. In a talk with the author in 1977, the then Indian Prime Minister, Morarji Desai, showed a real feeling of anger only when discussing the link between the old India and the new. "You British," he said. "It was you who destroyed our flourishing textile industry by loading taxes on us so that your cotton industry could grow. But you had to cripple us because we were so much more efficient."

At the time of Independence in 1947 India had a narrow industrial base, with jute and cotton textile mills based in Bengal and Bombay, coal mining in Bihar and Bengal and the steel mill which had been set up by the Tata family in the first decade of the century. Under the Government of Jawaharlal Nehru, a vigorous industrial expansion programme was undertaken and India quickly developed a modern industrial sector, capable of turning out goods on a par with those from the rich industrialized countries. By 1966 agriculture accounted for less than 50 per cent of India's national income. But the way in which the industrialization programme was carried out and the way in which agriculture developed, have led to important unsolved questions with regard to India's development.

RESOURCES

India's resources are considerable, though generally not as fabled as the travellers of old assumed. Two of the most important are the land, (3,287,782 square kilometres) and the people (684.0 million according to the 1981 census or about 11 million higher than forecast and increasing at 13.5 million a year). But these have yet to have their full potential unlocked. The land needs better irrigation and management; and too many people lie below the poverty line and outside the market economy to give their energy and intelligence to the country. Recent studies suggest that much of India's agricultural land can be rich when properly irrigated and tended. The country is wealthy in certain minerals, notably iron ore, coal, mica and bauxite. India also has oil reserves in Assam, Gujarat and Nagaland and off the Maharashtra coast.

In terms of infrastructure in its widest sense, India is reasonably well off, and certainly rich compared with other developing countries in Asia and Africa. When the British departed, they left behind a civil service which, in its top ranks, contained men as intelligent and efficient as those anywhere in the world. Since Independence, the standard of the Indian civil service has been maintained and the top ranks have always been well populated with men highly sought after by international agencies. However, the system does become too easily entangled in red tape. Other criticisms of the civil service are that, in its lower rungs, it is weaker and prone to corrupting influences and that the officials are encouraged to look to their promotions and to what is happening in the towns rather than to the wider development interest of the rural people.

The British also left behind the Indian railway network which is the biggest in the world after that of the U.S.A. The network has more than 60,000 route kilometres and annually carries more than 200 million metric tons of goods and about 3,000 million passengers over 140,000 million passenger-kilometres. India's railways, however, have been hit by various problems. Road transport is increasing at the expense of the railways and railway freight traffic has stagnated at around 200 million metric tons a year since about 1965. The railways were particularly bedevilled by labour unrest in the years before Mrs. Gandhi declared a state of emergency and in 1979 when there was renewed discontent over pay and bonuses. With regard to efficiency, wagon use on India railways is higher than on British, Canadian, French, German and American first class railways. However, the late 1960s and early 1970s saw a deterioration in services, measured by the turn-round time for wagons. The average speed of trains is also incredibly slow at about 25 kilometres an hour. Further difficulties were caused by the quadrupling of oil prices after 1973. In 1960/61 steam trains hauled 90 per cent of the freight traffic. By 1972/73, shortly before oil prices increased, diesel and electric-powered engines pulled 75 per cent of freight traffic. Since then, there have been plans to switch some traffic back to steam but this may be difficult.

India's road network is more extensive and increased from 400,000 km. in 1961 to 1,604,110 km. in 1979, of which 623,402 km. were surfaced. In terms of maintenance, Indian roads are less impressive than the railways, but road traffic has grown whereas the railways have stagnated. The number of lorries has grown steadily by 7 per cent a year. More than 33 per cent of India's goods were transported by road in 1976/77, compared with 17 per cent in 1960/61. The weight of goods carried rose four-fold in the same period. In terms of passenger-kilometres, roads had the advantage, carrying 61 per cent of passenger traffic by 1976/77.

India's shipping and ports are also impressive but are facing many problems. India's merchant navy is the second largest in Asia, and India has considerable facilities for shipbuilding, including those for constructing military vessels. Indian registered vessels totalled over 5.6 million gross registered tons at the end of 1980, compared with a mere 857,000 g.r.t. in 1961. However, India's ports require considerable improvement. Calcutta port has suffered from congestion and silting for many years but it is hoped that the construction of new ports such as Haldia, Mormugao (Goa) and Vishakhapatnam will relieve such problems. The biggest port in terms of annual volume of traffic is Bombay, with about 17 million metric tons, followed by Mormugao with between 13 and 14 million tons and Calcutta and Madras with about 7.5 million tons each.

In air transport India has entered the Jumbo jet age. Air India, the international carrier, flies Boeing 747s to all corners of the world except South America, and Indian Airlines, the domestic and regional carrier, uses A-300B European airbuses on its trunk routes. However, Indian Airlines has been criticized for poor booking and service standards.

AGRICULTURE

India's agriculture is dominated by food production although large amounts of non-food crops are also grown. Food grain crops account for 70 per cent of India's crop area which itself covers about 40 per cent of the country's total land area. Of the cash crops grown, oil-seeds, cotton, jute and tea are the most important. India is the biggest producer in the world of sugar cane, groundnuts, rapeseed, sesame seed and tea. It vies with Bangladesh as the biggest world producer of jute, with annual production averaging between 6 and 7 million bales (one bale is 180 kg.) in the 1970s. Both jute and tea, important traditional crops and exports, faced difficulties in the early 1980s because of international competition and poor world prices. Tea exports reached a record 245,000 metric tons in 1981 but higher costs were damaging the industry. India is also the world's second largest producer of rice and castor beans. Production of raw sugar steadily increased from about 12 million tons annually at the beginning of the 1970s to 18 million tons in 1977/78, although the size of the crop fell subsequently and was still only 15.4 million tons in 1980/81.

One of the most critical questions facing the Indian economy is still food production. Since independence, much precious foreign exchange has been spent on importing food grains to feed the Indian people. For much of the 1960s and 1970s the prophets of doom seemed justified as the gap grew between plan targets and actual performance. However, in the late 1970s things began to go exceptionally well and India's harvest of food grains (cereals and pulses) climbed to a record 131.4 million metric tons (including rice on a milled basis) in 1978/79, with stocks at more than 18 million tons: enough to see India through two bad monsoons. Of course, a bad monsoon followed and in 1979/80 production of food grains slumped to about 109 million tons, according to figures given in 1981, which were revised downwards considerably. Stocks were drawn down, but still amounted to 14 million tons at the end of the year. The inevitable outcome was that many hungry Indians went even hungrier in the bad year. Production of food grains recovered in the two following years, but there were still difficulties in reaching the previous record. Production for 1980/81 was finally assessed at just under 130 million tons and the best hopes were for 134 million tons in 1981/82, but there was argument about whether these expectations would be fulfilled.

In spite of the successful year and the apparent achievement of self-sufficiency in food grain production, India still faces two problems with regard to food production: finding ways to raise production from what are low levels in comparison with its potential, and enabling poor people to have the means of obtaining at least one square meal a day (even in a "good" year millions of Indians go hungry).

Given India's resources, there is no reason why food grain production should be low. India, according to most experts, could feed a population three times its present size if full use were made of the land and the potential it offers. In trials, rice yields have been up to seven times the actual performance of the 1960s, and yields of wheat and pulses four times higher. Dr. M. S. Swaminathan, at that time the member of the Planning Commission responsible for agriculture, said in 1981 that India could reach 240 million tons of food-grain production by the end of the century. In 1982 Dr. Swaminathan moved to the Philippines to become director of the International Rice Research Institute.

The ways forward are clear enough. In 1969/70 only 30.3 million hectares, or 22 per cent of the net area sown, received assured irrigation. The irrigated area had increased to 51 million hectares by the end of the 1970s. In 1982, the Minister of Agriculture, Rao Birendra Singh, said that India's irrigated area had risen to 60 million hectares and that fertilizer use had risen eightfold to 6 million tons in 20 pears. Only about one-fifth of the net area sown yielded more than one crop. Yet the potentially irrigable area is more than double that which is irrigated today, so that, with double cropping and the introduction of new seeds and more fertilizer, the tripling, quadrupling or even quintupling of India's food grain crops should not be too difficult. However, achieving this is quite another matter, and putting together the essential inputs for it has so far proved elusive. The short-term step of increasing the use of fertilizer is the easiest one, and recent governments have done their best to increase fertilizer use. The medium- and long-term steps are much more difficult. These include better attention to irrigation and soil management and an effort to get the best and most efficient use made of the land.

It has been said before, and it is still true, that the performance of high-yielding varieties of wheat has been successful, but that of rice has not. This is all the more important as rice is India's main crop, accounting for 40 per cent of total food-grain production. The annual output of milled rice was proving static at about 55 million tons, but wheat production continued to improve and a record 38 million tons was forceast for 1981/82. Wheat is more able to benefit from improved irrigation because it is grown in the spring or *rabi* season, whereas rice is produced mainly during the monsoon or *kharif* season. Cereals account for 90 per cent of India's food-grain production, with pulses, notably chick-peas (gram), forming the rest.

In studying the factors which lead to the shortfall of rice production compared with both hopes and official targets, one realizes that it is not just agricultural practice which is involved but the whole of India's socio-economic life. If India is to be confident of self-sufficiency in food, it will have to incorporate many factors. Moreover, it should be pointed out that many of the existing irrigation facilities were intended merely to supplement the monsoon and not to be the main providers of water.

In these and other aspects there is a lesson for India's wheat-growing farmers, but not one that can be learnt easily to increase rice production. As wheat is a second crop, the farmers have money from the first crop to pay for inputs. The wheat-growing area also has a great degree of ecological and agro-climatic uniformity, unlike India's rice areas. Moreover, the Punjab, where the wheat revolution flourished, is dominated by owner-occupiers and by larger farm holdings. Also the Punjabis have been prominent both in the army and in migration abroad; two factors which may have helped to increase family incomes and expand horizons, both of which are important to the progress of new crops.

Rice farmers are a more mixed group. At one extreme there are the landowners who have close ties with India's political élite. They have large holdings and many have managed to evade the land reform provisions. At the other extreme there are owners of tiny strips of land which may often be repeatedly subdivided so that one man possesses many unconsolidated strips. Outside this system are a number of landless labourers. The big farmer is not sufficiently involved to take up new farming methods, and the small farmer does not have enough money to do so; if he grows more rice, he simply eats more that year. An additional problem is that Government officials and extension workers are either unconcerned or so badly trained they do not know enough to help the poor farmer. More important still, agricultural credit is difficult to obtain.

INDUSTRY

Industry has also changed considerably since Independence, but has slowed markedly since 1965. Before Independence India had the rudimentary foundations for industrial development, dominated by textiles and jute, and the Tata steel mill established in the early years of the century. There were also some consumer goods industries based on raw materials, including tea, sugar, cigarettes and vegetable oils. India was also producing more than 30 million metric tons of coal a year, 2 million tons of cement and one million tons of steel. It took Independence to accelerate growth in both the size and type of industrial capacity. Through the series of Five-Year Plans, with the first plan covering the period 1951/52 to 1955/56 submitted to Parliament in December 1952, India's industrial potential began to improve and to take India towards the league of the big industrialized countries.

That certainly was the intention of the planners. They argued that India was a big country with a variety of natural resources as well as a potentially large domestic market. Therefore, the best strategy was to use what foreign exchange there was to import "machines to make machines". With a heavy capital base firmly established, it would be possible to develop downwards, and to set up a consumer goods industry. The stated planning objective was to "raise living standards and open out to the people new opportunities for a richer and more varied life." In addition, planning was "an integral part of a wider process aiming not merely at the development of resources in a narrow technical sense, but at the development of human faculties in the building up of an institutional framework adequate to the needs and aspirations of the people". The first Prime Minister, Jawaharlal Nehru, took a personal interest in planning; he was Chairman of the Planning Commission. His admiration for Soviet planning was recognizable in the new approach, and at times his own prose, the blend of concern for India and for Indians, shone through plan documents.

In the early stages, the new planning paid off handsomely. Many new industries were established, including heavy electrical and heavy machine tool industries, machine building and heavy engineering. Chemicals and chemical products, penicillin, explosives, fertilizer, synthetic fibres, bicycles, sewing machines, textile machinery, power-driven pumps, diesel engines, electrical motors, power transformers and typewriters were all produced. Annual rates of growth of industrial production reached almost 7 per cent for the period 1951–61 and 9.2 per cent for the period between 1958 and 1965. Between 1951 and 1965 annual steel production quadrupled to 4.5 million metric tons and volume of electricity generated rose by six times to 32,000 million kWh. However, between 1965 and 1975 the growth rate slowed. The annual increase in manufacturing output averaged 2.7 per cent to 3.3 per cent, depending on whether the index used was one of gross production or value added. This performance was far below the average of other countries, whether developed or developing. The annual average of developing countries in the late 1960s and early 1970s was 7.3 per cent, while the developed economies' industry grew at a rate of 4.7 per cent.

All the major industrial sectors (mining and quarrying, manufacturing and utilities) were affected by this slow-down. The capital goods industry showed the sharpest deceleration, followed by the intermediate goods and consumer goods sectors. Between 1965 and 1975 production of textiles (which alone account for more than a quarter of the production index) and transport equipment was below the level reached in the growth years before 1965. Between 1951 and 1965, because of the industrial strategy of import substitution and encouraging production of capital and intermediate goods at the expense of consumer goods, there was a change in the contributions of these three types of goods to the manufacturing industry as a whole. Consumer goods, which had accounted for 68 per cent of manufacturing value added in 1951, had dropped to 38 per cent in 1965, whilst capital goods increased their share from 17 per cent in 1951 to 34 per cent in 1965. Between 1966 and 1975, the capital goods industries were the worst hit and grew by only 1.5 per cent a year. Durable consumer goods did best with an annual growth rate of almost 6 per cent against 2.2 per cent for non-durable consumer goods. But this in turn reflected the uneven pattern of income distribution and has been criticized itself as a major factor leading to stagnation of economic growth. A slow-down in investment also added to the decline in India's growth. Investment in real terms had increased rapidly between 1952 and 1965. Gross investment increased at a rate of 10 per cent a year during the First Plan (1951–56), 14.4 per cent in the second (1956–61) and 17.8 per cent in the third (1961–66). The average annual increase of gross fixed investment rose from 9.2 per cent during the First Plan to 16.1 per cent in the third. There was no further improvement until 1974. In the Fourth Plan (1969–74) the annual rate of increase of gross investment was 18 per cent and of gross fixed investment only 15.8 per cent.

Some economists held that the slow-down was caused by factors external to the Government and its economic policies, but the view of economists in the World Bank is that the slow-down in industry and in the Indian economy would have asserted itself even without external setbacks to growth. There is a better explanation: that an imbalance arose between capacity created and demand, and that this became accentuated and acute without a dynamic export market to absorb some of the goods. In addition, inefficiencies in investment allocation and production within industry eroded the self-perpetuating dynamism which should have developed. As well as all this, the growth in the non-industrial sectors of the economy was slow and failed to give necessary impetus to the industrial sectors. Some proof of this thesis comes from the fact that Indian industry has been suffering from under-capacity for some time. According to studies made by the Reserve Bank of India, capacity utilization in the capital goods sector was only 76.8 per cent in the 1960s, rising to 84.9 per cent by 1965 before falling to 61.6 per cent in 1975. These figures are based on "potential production" as an indicator of capacity. Consumer goods industries capacity utilization was more than 90 per cent in 1960 but had fallen to almost 80 per cent by 1975. Figures produced by the Central Statistical Office (CSO), using installed capacity as a basis, give even lower percentages.

The slower growth of agriculture during the 1960s and early 1970s hardly helped the situation. Expenditure statistics illustrate the vicious circle into which the economy has fallen. The ratio of food expenditure to total income has remained the same in constant prices, at about 50 per cent, and has even increased in current prices from 61 per cent in 1965/66 to 65 per cent in 1973/74, thus indicating a squeeze on non-food expenditure. Two other components of demand—capital accumulation and import substitution—were progressively weakened, as by 1965/66 domestic production took care of more than 90 per cent of the total supply of most consumer goods. Only in the capital goods industry was there much scope left for import substitution, which was perhaps reflected in the growing capital/output and capital/labour ratios. The capital/output ratio rose from 2.06 in 1950, to 2.15 in 1961 and 2.58 in 1971. Industry has picked up since 1975 but still shows major structural weaknesses.

In the early years of the 1980s the second Government of Mrs. Indira Gandhi began to put new stress on performance and on a more open regime. It remains to be seen, however, how easy it is to make the changes effective.

TRADE

In its *World Development Report, 1979*, the World Bank had some comments which were very appropriate to India, and indeed India was specially mentioned as a country which could do with more competition through trade. "Once early import substitution opportunities have been fully exploited, a continued reliance on protection imposes increasingly higher costs on the economy, because the production of goods associated with later stages—intermediate goods, capital goods and durable consumer goods—has relatively advanced technological requirements, is more demanding of skilled labour, and needs to be organized on a relatively large scale if it is to use resources efficiently. Limited domestic markets and a structure of incentives that discourages exports have condemned capital-intensive industries to efficient levels of production in countries that have pursued import-substitution strategies for too long. Even in larger economies such as Brazil (at least until 1965), India, Mexico and Turkey, the prolonged use of protective measures has contributed to the development of high-cost, inefficient domestic industries. Moreover, an important corollary of the protection afforded to manufacturing is its disincentive effect on agricultural production. Import-substitution policies have tended to limit agricultural growth, and hence domestic demand for manufactured goods, while simultaneously keeping industrial production dependent on internal purchasing power."

Lack of attention to foreign trade has made India vulnerable to higher petroleum prices and in 1979/80 the country had a massive trade deficit of Rs. 22,000 million (more than $2,800 million), with every prospect that it would grow worse, subsequently fulfilled as the deficit doubled. For years India's dependence on trade was low, at between 10 and 11 per cent of the G.N.P. Throughout the 1960s and early 1970s, India and a substantial trade deficit which was covered by aid inflows. Then, in late 1973 the oil-producing countries quadrupled their prices and India faced a huge extra burden. By 1974/75 and 1975/76 the trade gap had widened alarmingly to more than U.S. $1,500 million, as the average annual cost of oil and oil products increased from $180 million in the period between 1960 and 1965 to $322 million between 1970 and 1974, and then to $1,450 million in 1974 and 1975. Besides oil prices, those of fertilizers and food grains also shot up, leaving India in a very desperate state in the eyes of most economists.

However, exports suddenly began to rise rapidly, so rapidly that some experts said that India had discovered an "export culture". The trade balance was also helped by the good harvest and the fall in imports of food grains and fertilizers. Also the petroleum from the Bombay High off-shore field meant that oil imports could be reduced slightly. In 1976/77 exports rose by 27 per cent, much higher than the world growth of exports of 13.6 per cent and that of the industrialized countries of 11 per cent. Such growth helped India to show a small trade surplus by the late 1970s. But then export growth began to slow down and the liberalized imports began to rise in 1977/78. The fall of food imports kept India's trade balance reasonably healthy and remittances from Indians working abroad added to the large growth of foreign exchange reserves. However, by 1979 a trade gap had opened up once more and in the following years it widened alarmingly.

The composition of Indian exports has remained more or less the same from the 1960s, with food and live animals accounting for 31 per cent of total exports, manufactures 35 per cent and crude materials 13 per cent. One of the factors which probably contributed to the slow growth of exports was the close association in the 1960s between India and the Eastern European bloc. More than half the growth of exports in the 1960s was the result of exports to Eastern Europe. Then the 1973 oil price rise threatened disaster. However, it also forced India to review its policies and offered trade opportunities in the growing Middle East market. Policies began to change and exports began to rise, reaching more than $5,600 million and almost touching 7 per cent of the G.N.P. in 1976/77. Exporters were given greater freedom and urged to send their goods abroad. In addition, some goods were exported because of sluggish domestic demand; for example, steel, where exports rose to U.S. $350 million in 1976/77, a rise of 200 per cent over the previous year. Various other goods also began to reach their take-off point, including oil products, leisure goods, chemicals, engineering products and cotton textiles. India also developed a reputation as a supplier of "turnkey" projects, especially in the Middle East.

Another important question is whether the export performance can be sustained. Some economists would like India to use exports as the motor for its whole economic growth, as countries such as the Republic of Korea, Taiwan and Hong Kong have done. However, critics can point out that India had entered the export game too late and that competitors had taken most of the richest market opportunities. In terms of the G.N.P., exports are still small when India is compared with countries like the Republic of Korea or Hong Kong. Yet India is so large that even a small increase in exports could lead to protectionist responses abroad. There is also the question of whether India could ever hope to attain export-led growth. Given the problem of the large subsistance rural sector outside the market economy, it is doubtful whether anything other than massive export growth could shift the whole of India to new economic prosperity, if exports are to be the vehicle of growth.

By 1979 there was renewed doubt as to whether India had really developed an export culture. In 1977/78 there was a trade deficit of 6,525 million rupees as exports rose by only 4.3 per cent whilst imports increased by 15.8 per cent. This deficit widened during the latter part of the calendar year 1978, with marginally lower exports and imports rising by about 20 per cent. One factor which certainly prevented the growth of exports was that, as India's growth rate increased, the domestic market became more attractive and manufacturers showed preference for the home rather than the cut-throat foreign market. This protected domestic market had long bedevilled India's balances of trade and payments but the payments position has become more secure thanks to workers' remittances and tourist receipts. An additional problem affecting exports was growing protectionism abroad. The largest item on the import side was petroleum and petroleum products, which accounted for 15,564 million rupees in 1977/78, in spite of the impressive growth of India's own Bombay High petroleum supplies. This item accounted for a quarter of all imports by value although the volume was maintained at a steady rate as domestic oil production has risen.

By 1980 the deficit had widened disastrously as imports rose by 24.6 per cent while exports could increase by only 8.2 per cent. As far as imports were concerned, the near doubling of petroleum prices was a body blow, but India also imported large quantities of oilseeds and other products because of poor planning of the domestic economy. Exports were hit by many factors also bedevilling the overall economy, such as power shortages, labour unrest and transport and shipping delays. The official *Economic Survey* for 1979/80 warned that "the shadow on the economy of the continuously rising oil prices seems to be growing longer day by day". It feared that import prices would rise faster than export prices, and to go back to a strict import regime could add to delays and impose extra costs through bureaucratic formalities and corruption.

Petroleum prices did rise and formed about 55 per cent of the total import bill in 1980/81. In spite of a substantial increase in domestic oil production and a stabilization of prices of imported oil in 1981, India continued to have substantial problems with a growing trade deficit. The revised figure for the 1980/81 deficit was Rs. 58,000 million (probably close to $6,500 million), double even the heavily revised and increased figure of Rs. 25,000 million for 1979/80. Ministers said, however, that the 1981/82 trade deficit was likely to be yet another new record. Besides petroleum, fertilizers, vegetable products, capital goods and chemicals were imported in greater quantities. On the export side, India managed to increase its sales by about 14 per cent, although mainly in traditional areas such as tobacco, marine products, leather, gems and garments. In spite of an increase in invisible earnings (thanks to remittances sent home by Indians working abroad), the current account of the balance of payments also went into deficit, reaching Rs. 27,000 million in 1980/81. In his 1982 budget, the new Finance Minister, Pranab Kumar Mukherjee, also warned that workers' remittances were likely to show a decline and that the unsettled conditions in the Middle East could disrupt the potential of the area. In 1981 and 1982 India also tried to open up its economy—which was part of the price of taking the International Monetary Fund's largest-ever loan of 5,000 million SDRs (about $5,700 million).

RECENT ECONOMIC DEVELOPMENT

In 1975 changes began to take place in India's economic policy. Although Mrs. Gandhi declared the State of Emergency only at the end of June 1975, tightening of the Government's policy was noticeable from the end of the previous year. Early indications were the crack-down on smugglers and the attempt to bring "black money" into the economy proper; some economists said that the "black money" economy was at least as large as the official economy. Another sign was the firm line taken with the striking railwaymen; yet another was the impounding by the Government of half of the "dearness allowance" automatically given to public sector workers when the cost of living rose beyond certain points. These measures, together with the assistance of the record food grain harvest of 121 million metric tons in 1975/76, produced dramatic results. Between June 1975 and March 1976 consumer prices fell by 12.8 per cent. Deficiencies in crucial areas like electricity supply and transport were remedied. Basic commodities such as cement, coal and steel showed production increases of more than 10 per cent each. Time lost through strikes was drastically reduced. This had reached a peak of 40 million man-days in 1974, but fell to 21 million in 1975 and further still to 11 million in 1976. All in all, there was a startling change in an economy which, in 1973, had been suffering and had been almost written off by international commentators because of the drought, higher oil prices and alarming trade and payments deficits.

By 1979 the strengths and weaknesses of the modern Indian economy had become apparent. The trade balance and the balance of payments had begun to improve, but this was only temporary and the figures for 1980 demonstrated the need for more vigorous planning. India also received a substantial boost of U.S. $1,000 million a year in remittances from Indians working abroad, mainly in the Middle East. (Some international economists have shown concern regarding the impact of the drain of skilled workers on India itself.) Foreign exchange reserves increased to $6,300 million, or the equivalent of almost eleven months' imports.

The Janata Government's first Minister of Finance, Hirubhai Patel, had followed a cautious policy, in some ways too cautious to take sufficient advantage of the extra room for manoeuvre. He indicated his fear of a widening trade gap, renewed inflation or further bad harvests, which seemed unnecessary to other countries. Indeed, the rich countries, which have traditionally given aid to India ($2,000 million a year in gross terms by the mid-1970s) questioned whether this aid was in fact needed in the face of such large reserves and Patel's cautious policies. However, although the annual net contribution of aid amounted to only 1.8 per cent of India's G.D.P. or $2.50 per capita, too sharp a cutback in aid could lead to problems in repaying past loans.

The 5 per cent growth of G.N.P. in 1977/78 was almost entirely the result of an improved agricultural performance due mainly to good weather conditions. Industrial production rose by 5 per cent, although important industries like power generation, coal, steel, cement and commercial vehicles showed decelerating rates of growth. The output of the cotton textile industry, of vital importance, actually declined. Some industries, including steel and textiles, were supported largely by exports. Investment was sluggish; no higher than the level reached in the mid-1960s.

With high food grain production and large foreign exchange reserves, there were none of the traditional constraints on growth. But there was evidence to suggest that there was not a sufficient increase in demand to provide the necessary impetus for further investment. This seemed to be particularly the case in both the rural and urban sectors of the textile industry. Employment in the whole of the manufacturing sector had risen by a mere 75,000 a year since 1974/75, only a fraction of the annual addition to the labour force. It was apparent that only small sections of society, mainly those who were better-off, had benefited from the growth of the economy. So, in spite of the superficially improved economic performance, there were signs that, without a change in government policy to improve the conditions of the poorer sections of society, India could face an ever-growing number of people below the poverty line.

Morarji Desai's Government gave notice that it was dissatisfied with the pattern of India's growth and sought to change the approach to put more emphasis on rural development. In an interview with the author, Mr. Desai said that India had had 1,000 years of village civilization, yet, since Independence, it had neglected the villages and created a society which had taken away Indians' self-reliance. He commented that the universities were producing large numbers of graduates who could not find work even though education was supposed to make a person self-reliant. What room he had for manoeuvre in making his plans to foster village level development was another matter.

By 1979 further strains had begun to appear in the economy. Apart from the widening trade deficit, real G.N.P. growth was estimated at about 3.5 per cent. Nevertheless, the official *Economic Survey* emphasized the good aspects: it pointed to the 8 per cent growth in industrial production and added that "the satisfactory agricultural performance coming on top of a record achievement in 1977/78 gives cause for hope that Indian agriculture is entering an era of steady and reasonable growth." Other favourable factors were a growth of almost 13 per cent in power generation, low inflation, increasing investment and the use of foreign exchange reserves for development. However, by mid-1979 price rises had begun to cause concern and threatened to spark off disputes amongst the restless labour unions. The power supply deteriorated sharply both in Maharashtra state and Calcutta, where cuts of six or eight hours a day became common in the pre-monsoon heat, with temperatures reaching 40°C. Political uncertainty aggravated the economic situation; the introduction of measures to curb inflation and keep prices down was halted abruptly by the resignation of the Janata Government in July 1979.

By 1980 the gloom was complete. Gross National Product actually fell by 4.8 per cent, according to revised figures. Both agriculture and industry fell. Foreign exchange reserves dropped by Rs. 2,740 million to Rs. 48,900 million, still a high level, however. Prices, steady for 23 months, rose by about 20 per cent on a point-to-point basis and were particularly high in a handful of key commodities like gur, sugar, oilseeds, edible oils, coal and petroleum. Strikes, go-slows and other forms of industrial action were also a problem. There were widespread power cuts, and political agitation in Assam reduced the flow of petroleum.

Production of important industrial goods, such as coal, fell. Saleable steel production declined by 8.4 per cent; cement fell by 9.1 per cent, cotton cloth by 5.7 per cent, sugar by 26.2 per cent and vanaspaties by 7.7 per cent; petroleum production rose by a mere 0.9 per cent.

The *Economic Survey* commented in 1980: "What is surprising is that this turnround has been so fast: for the *Economic Survey 1978/79* was confidently looking forward to a period of steady growth on the basis of the economy's performance in that year. The situation arose from a combination of a number of adverse factors affecting the economy in 1979/80. Firstly, the economy faced a severe drought. Secondly, it ran into constraints imposed by poor performance in infrastructure sectors such as power, coal and transport where shortages cannot be overcome by imports. Thirdly, political instability for a major part of the year produced a lack of effective direction from government. This made firm and consistent action to tackle problems of infrastructure and other economic problems very difficult. Finally, the substantial rise in petroleum prices and disruption of supply caused damage to the economy directly and indirectly."

Better agricultural performance gave an optimistic gloss to the results for 1980/81. In fact the national accounts showed that India's G.D.P. had actually grown by 7.5 per cent in real terms, compared with the fall of 4.8 per cent the previous year, according to revised figures. Most of the improvement was due to agriculture. Industrial production, although the *Economic Survey* showed a slight rise of just over 1 per cent, was bedevilled by the old problems in the basic power, coal and railway infrastructure. Inflation was reduced, though still running at a high rate of 15 per cent. The biggest constraint, however, was the ever-looming payments deficit. India took steps in 1981 to increase its domestic oil production, which was expected to grow to 16.9 million tons in 1981/82, provided disruptions in Assam could be kept under control. Increasing oil production is not, however, as easy as turning on a tap: it requires money and time, so India's oil imports bill is expected to grow in spite of higher domestic production.

Early in 1981 the Government released the revamped Sixth Five-Year Plan (1980–85). It was already a year late. The Plan was by far the biggest and most ambitious ever, calling for total resources of Rs 1,722,100 million (equivalent to about $215,000 million) and for annual real growth rates of 5.2 per cent, compared with the annual average of 3.5 per cent in the previous three decades. The aims of the Plan were to achieve modernization, economic growth and self-reliance, along with social justice.

The *Economic Survey* produced a neat summary of the Plan objectives which, by its very length, indicated that it would be a long haul to reach the targets: "It emphasizes a significant step up in the rate of growth together with more efficient use of existing resources through improved productivity; strengthening the impulses of modernization for the achievement of economic and technological self-reliance; progressive reduction in poverty, unemployment and regional inequalities; speedy development of indigenous energy sources and efficiency in energy use; conservation of natural resources; a minimum programme for the economically and socially handicapped section of the population; and promotion of policies for controlling population. Another important objective of the Plan is to strengthen the redistributive bias of public policies and services in favour of the poor."

The Plan implementers faced the difficult task of bridging the gap between the two Indias. Much of the investment was earmarked for projects to combat the big constraints on production: poor infrastructure and heavy dependence on imported energy. Yet these thrust the responsibility back towards the big public sector corporations and the bureaucracy, both of which had shown themselves in the past to be ponderously slow in movement. In 1981 the then Finance Minister, Mr. R. Venkataraman, commented that the public enterprises had yet "to deliver results commensurate with the massive investments which have gone into them at great public sacrifice". The financial constraints were tight. Many economists thought that India had reached the limits of taxation yield, and in his 1981 Budget the Finance Minister did lift some taxes while raising those facing foreign tourists using hotels. The Minister, in effect, had to do a juggling act: somehow to encourage effort and initiative without increasing the budget deficit which had increased substantially in 1980/81. More difficult was the task of raising exports to keep the external account deficit within bounds. An additional constraint here was the Plan ambition, backed by many politicians, for "self-reliance". This would invite "tit-for-tat" restrictions if India did manage to get its exports moving and then tried to restrict the entry of goods from abroad into its own ports.

The 1981/82 financial year showed continuing improvement in economic growth, which was again positive by about 4.5 per cent, according to the first estimates. Industrial production rose by about 8 per cent, double the rate achieved in the previous year. The increase in agricultural production was more modest, at about 3 per cent, but followed a large rise of 15 per cent in 1980/81. Nevertheless, the external account was still poor and the Government needed to try new policies.

Without assistance from the IMF, the country's foreign exchange reserves might have been eaten up in as little as three years. India negotiated for a record loan of 5,000 million SDRs and, in return, the IMF tried to push the Indian economy to a more open position. In his 1982 budget, Finance Minister Mukherjee also added his own incentives by opening the door to investment in India's stock exchanges by Indians residing abroad.

The country was also squeezed by cut-backs in funds from the World Bank's "soft-loan window," the International Development Association (IDA). India was the most heavily hit. In 1981 it had received 40 per cent of all IDA loans, or $1,300 million. The Government had hoped to see IDA assistance increasing to $1,600 million but, with the revised amounts of aid available, India seemed likely to receive only $800 to $900 million from IDA. So India began to tap commercial markets and gave notice to the Asian Development Bank that it hoped to receive ADB funds for the first time in 1983.

In 1980 Indian borrowings from the Euromarket were about $60 million. In 1981 a huge 10-year loan of $680 million was signed for international funds to build a new aluminium plant in Orissa. This was followed by negotiations for a new steel plant, also in Orissa. The international component of the $2,500 million deal might be as much as $1,000 million. India originally signed a letter of intent with the Davy McKee company of Britain but in May 1982, India having changed the actual site and some of the details for the plant, talks with Davy McKee broke down.

It seemed likely that India would put together its own revised deal for the plant. This was what a number of economists, both Indian and foreign, had urged all along, saying that international companies were charging too much.

In Mrs. Gandhi's new Government there seems to be more commitment to get the economy moving and, if necessary, to import technology and know-how from abroad. Another sign was a deal with the Japanese Suzuki company to build India's first small car factory. However, there were still problems, notably the poor performance in the power industry, where Indian rates of capacity utilization were among the lowest in the world and transmission losses among the highest.

Yet above all there was the question of whether India in the 1980s was open enough or flexible enough to make the quick changes and the implications of efficiency that the Sixth Plan indicated. That would require big changes in the minds of the rulers, both political and bureaucratic, as well as imaginative policies.

THE DEVELOPMENT PERSPECTIVE

In spite of India's achievements, it still remains a fact that the 40 to 50 per cent of the people at the bottom of India's economy have been neglected and have fallen further into poverty, even assessed according to the Government's austerely defined official poverty line. The country which, in the early 1970s, had joined the exclusive nuclear club when it exploded an atomic device, only half a step away from making atomic bombs, cannot provide for the minimum needs of its people. The actual number of those below the poverty line is disputed, but official surveys in the early 1970s stated that at least 40 per cent of the population fell below the line. The Janata Party manifesto in 1977 claimed that 68 per cent of the population was below the poverty line. This figure means that more than 400 million Indians were living in poverty. Tarlok Singh, one of those intimately involved in the early planning of India's economy, noted: "Despite notable advances in several directions, India's economy has been open to criticism on at least three grounds: inadequate performance in terms of economic growth, continued dependence on external support, and inability thus far to provide for the minimum needs of its citizens."* It is possible to look at the problem in two ways. One is to examine the national economy and to see how policies have led to contradictions in the mechanism which might have brought about sustained economic growth, and at the same time to see how little attention was given to eliminating the basic causes of poverty. The other is to look at the problem from the grass roots upwards.

From the time of the first Five-Year Plan, India's politicians tried to attain a modern economy through industrialization, concentrating on import substitution with a bias towards capital goods. The belief was that the benefits of this programme would somehow automatically filter down and assure jobs and prosperity throughout the whole economy and population. What in fact happened was that pressure on scarce resources encouraged protection for the infant Indian industry. The distortions thus induced were accentuated by bureaucratic controls which encouraged slowness and inefficiency, so that Indian prices were often higher than those of its competitors. This led to pressure for further controls to prevent imports of non-capital goods which might eat up scarce foreign resources. However, as Indian manufacturers were on the whole less efficient than their competitors, there was no export culture and capacity utilization was also low. For a time, as has been shown in the review of industry, things appeared to go well and new factories, new products and new jobs were created. In some of them India's performance was impressive and rivalled that of any country in the

* Singh, Tarlok. *India's development experience* (Macmillan, 1974).

world. But then, as the history of the last decade has shown, problems arose and the economy settled down to slow growth so that there could be no hope of solving underlying problems of poverty.

International economic studies have tended to show that total economic growth of over 5.5 per cent a year is necessary before a country can begin to eliminate poverty. Also, deliberate policies are needed to distribute the growth evenly and to prevent the benefits from accruing only to the already rich. India by no means achieved the necessary growth rate. Since Independence the growth rate has been of the order of 3.5 per cent, admittedly much higher than during the British colonial era, but not high enough to enable the Government to tackle the basic problem of ingrained poverty, especially when it is taken into account that the population is growing by about 2 per cent a year. To compound this, the planners did little to redistribute whatever small increase in wealth there was. There were land reforms, but those with useful political connections found a way around them. There was a big upsurge in education. Far more Indian children go to school today than ever before, although the very poor still cannot afford to send their children to school. The largest banks were nationalized in 1970 and more were taken into the public sector when Mrs. Gandhi returned to power in 1980, but credit remained largely in the cities or townships or went to the larger landowners. Hopes that industry would provide extra jobs have proved false. The contribution of agriculture to the G.N.P. fell below 50 per cent for the first time in 1966, but it still comprises the largest sector, accounting for 40 per cent of the G.N.P. In addition, 75 per cent of the people still depend on the countryside for their jobs. And, as Tarlok Singh writes: "Basically, the agrarian structure has remained unchanged, and the rural social system has lacked both the goal and the capacity of harnessing the available human resources for productive use."

In industry, too, the machines and their organization have been put before the encouragement of human resources. Again to quote Tarlok Singh: "Economic organization and the deployment of human resources have been subservient to the approach of capital investment, development of modern industry and the infrastructure associated with it, and the mobilization of resources for financing public outlays. Thus, too limited an approach came to be adopted to industrial priorities, expansion of employment opportunities, raising of productivity for the mass of the people, and the role of the modern sector of the economy as an instrument for transforming the character of agriculture and the unorganized sector. It has become increasingly clear that the two principal drawbacks mentioned above have restricted the total effort of which the country was and is capable, having regard to its human resources, natural endowments and available economic capacities. In turn, this has diminished the scope and magnitude of the capital formation which could be undertaken as well as the ability of the economy to withstand strains, mishaps and adversities arising from internal and external causes." It is also clear that Mrs. Gandhi's promises of "socialism", which were usually a reaction to political pressures and given to avoid difficult problems, were frustrated by the organization of the ruling groups which had too much at stake to allow even the limited reforms. Thus, at the industrial and urban level, the Congress Party constantly protested about the large industrial establishments, but depended upon funds from big business to keep the party machine going and to win the elections. In the rural areas, too, attempted or paper reforms failed because the pillars of rural society, even down to quite small villages, were usually the people responsible for ensuring that the masses voted Congress.

Another indication of the unevenness of India's growth is shown in a study carried out for the Ford Foundation by Tata Economic Consultancy Services. This pointed out that India differed from China in that it lagged far behind in the production of wage goods—goods produced for mass consumption. An economic approach which had paid more attention to the masses might have created a market which fully used India's huge population, as well as providing more jobs and bringing more people into the market economy. The study also pointed out that if India wished to have a per capita G.D.P. (in 1970/71 prices) of U.S. $300 a year by the turn of the century, assuming a population of 945 million by then, the country would have to achieve a growth rate of between 5 and 7 per cent a year. Production of many ordinary items would have to grow by between three and 30 times. Food grain production would have to grow by only 2.3 times.

A brief visit to any Indian village, with the object of judging India's economic performance from the bottom upwards, will bring to light some of the constraints. In one village in Uttar Pradesh for example the author found that one family had a stranglehold over all the main sources of power. The family was by far the largest land-holder and an important source of loans to villagers in a position to borrow. It controlled the village panchayat (council) which had power to levy fines for non-repayment of loans. And even this village had to take its place in India's oppressive power structure. Progress was inhibited because the bureaucrats had not thought to supply a power line, although power cables were laid only a kilometre away. Mrs. Gandhi's 20-point programme to defeat poverty also made matters worse for the villagers. They were afraid to go into the town because of the sterilization campaign. Local bureaucrats were also told by their masters to show that there had been development in the villages, so they increased taxes by imposing a development tax as if development had in fact taken place.

Some economists have spoken or written as if there were a dualistic economy in India: one for the rich and the ruling classes in towns and another for the poor in the villages. In reality there are interlocking factors between the towns and the villages and there are seepages from the market economy. There are links between the rich in the towns and in the countryside, and the poor in both towns and villages are, in a sense, the victims of this interlocking system. Nor is there an easy dichotomy between the market economy and the subsistence economy. Some of the poor, though only a few, filter from the villages to the towns and the education system encourages the development of urban values.

Also, there is always the pressure of population to take into consideration. India's population growth has slowed to about 2 per cent a year, or perhaps less, but that is still sufficient to offset the benefits of economic growth and to create additional problems in the years ahead. Of course, another dimension of the development problem is that it may not be in the interest of the villager to have fewer children, for an extra child may prove useful, if only for minding the cattle for a few paisa (pennies) a day. When the child grows up he must look after himself and may support his parents. World Bank economists have pointed out that as yet there is little evidence of any massive drifts from the countryside to the towns in search of work. However, between harvests the villagers who do not own enough land drift to the towns for work and then return to the village for the next harvest. In the Uttar Pradesh village already mentioned, 75 per cent of the men went into the town at some time to look for jobs. Official studies suggest that 32 per cent of the rural labour force and about 20 per cent of the urban labour force does not have stable or adequate employment. Moreover, there is always pressure on the land. At present slightly less than 10 per cent of India's rural households own no land, and another 68 per cent own less than two hectares of agricultural land.

In 1978 the Planning Commission announced the draft sixth Five-Year Plan. It attempts to rectify some of the deficiencies under which India's poor have been by-passed by economic progress. It suggests that village committees should be formed to help superintend a large-scale transfer of resources to the rural poor. It hopes that organized pressure by potential beneficiaries would "counteract the weaknesses of the administration and the opposition with vested interests". The Plan stated that 20 per cent of households with assets of less than 1,000 rupees each accounted for less than 1 per cent of total rural assets, while 4 per cent of households with 50,000 rupees or more each owned 30 per cent of total rural assets.

In his 1979 budget the then Minister of Finance, Charan Singh, gave expression to his ideas of village development by favouring the middle-level farmers, the "five-acre kulaks" as they became known. The urban dwellers, who had to put up with a broad range of tax increases on common household goods, were infuriated. There were doubts about how the new approach would help the really poor, which justified complaints that the measures would make it more difficult for the landless to become integrated into the economy. In the large, backward states such as Bihar and parts of Uttar Pradesh there were riots and deaths as rural interest groups pitted their strength against one another. At the same time large industrial concerns were threatened with nationalization and reminders that emphasis was on small-scale and cottage industry. However, these large concerns did not object too strongly to industrial licensing and other constrictions which, to a certain extent, protected their markets and safeguarded them against competition. One of the owners of an up-and-coming industrial concern admitted that his enterprise had reached a stage and size where he preferred it to be protected against competition from other newcomers. He kept bureaucrats at bay with donations to the right political party. He kept the union leaders happy by paying them only to shout in favour of socialism, but not to disrupt production more than it suited him.

The new Gandhi Government again spoke eloquently of the need to look to the poor, and large chunks of the Sixth Plan were devoted to the demands of "social justice". Yet by the 1980s the Indian economy was becoming more complicated. One of the most powerful developments was the rise of the middle farmers. Several times in 1980 they staged marches on the streets of Delhi or in the state capitals to protest that they were suffering from the effects of inflation, fuel shortages or poor prices for their produce. Yet the protesters are much better off than the really poor people of India: they have land and they have work and income, unlike many of the more than 300 million Indians below the poverty line.

With savings rates of more than 20 per cent a year, which India now has, Japan was able to grow at more than 9 per cent a year. Yet India remains marooned at 3.5 per cent. The answer, according to a growing number of economists, is that millions of Indians are trapped below the poverty line and excluded from the economy; a smaller, but more influential and more powerful group actually benefits from the misery of the poor. If nothing is done about this, the prospects are bleak for real economic take-off, let alone economic or social justice.

STATISTICAL SURVEY

AREA AND POPULATION*

Area	Population (Census Results)					Density (per sq. km.)
	March 1st, 1961	April 1st, 1971	March 1st, 1981‖			
			Males	Females	Total	1981
3,287,782 sq. km.†	439,234,771‡	548,159,652§	353,502,987	330,494,525	683,997,512	208

* Including Sikkim (incorporated into India on April 26th, 1975) and the Indian-held part of Jammu and Kashmir.
† 1,269,420 sq. miles.
‡ Including an estimate of 626,667 for the former Portuguese territories of Goa, Daman and Diu, incorporated into India in December 1961.
§ Excluding adjustment for underenumeration, estimated at 1.67 per cent.
‖ Including estimates for Assam.

STATES AND TERRITORIES

		Area (sq. km.)	Population April 1971	Population March 1981
States	**Capitals**			
Andhra Pradesh	Hyderabad	276,814	43,502,708	53,592,605
Assam	Dispur	78,523	14,625,152	19,902,826‡
Bihar	Patna	173,876	56,353,369	69,823,154
Gujarat	Gandhinagar	195,984	26,697,475	33,960,905
Haryana	Chandigarh†	44,222	10,036,808	12,850,902
Himachal Pradesh	Simla	55,673	3,460,434	4,237,569
Jammu and Kashmir*	Srinagar	222,236	4,616,632	5,954,010
Karnataka	Bangalore	191,773	29,299,014	37,043,451
Kerala	Trivandrum	38,864	21,347,375	25,403,217
Madhya Pradesh	Bhopal	442,841	41,654,119	52,138,467
Maharashtra	Bombay	307,762	50,412,235	62,715,300
Manipur	Imphal	22,356	1,072,753	1,411,375
Meghalaya	Shillong	22,489	1,011,699	1,328,343
Nagaland	Kohima	16,527	516,449	773,281
Orissa	Bhubaneswar	155,782	21,944,615	26,272,054
Punjab	Chandigarh†	50,362	13,551,060	16,669,755
Rajasthan	Jaipur	342,214	25,765,806	34,108,292
Sikkim	Gangtok	7,299	209,843	314,999
Tamil Nadu	Madras	130,069	41,199,168	48,297,456
Tripura	Agartala	10,477	1,556,342	2,047,351
Uttar Pradesh	Lucknow	294,413	88,341,144	110,885,874
West Bengal	Calcutta	87,853	44,312,011	54,485,560
Territories	**Capitals**			
Andaman and Nicobar Islands	Port Blair	8,293	115,133	188,254
Arunachal Pradesh	Itanagar	83,578	467,511	628,050
Chandigarh	Chandigarh	114	257,251	450,061
Dadra and Nagar Haveli	Silvassa	491	74,170	103,677
Delhi	Delhi	1,485	4,065,698	6,196,414
Goa, Daman and Diu	Panaji	3,813	857,771	1,082,117
Lakshadweep	Kavaratti	32	31,810	40,237
Mizoram	Aizawl	21,087	332,390	487,774
Pondicherry	Pondicherry	480	471,707	604,182

* The area figure refers to the whole of Jammu and Kashmir State, of which 84,112 sq. km. is occupied by Pakistan. The population figure refers only to the Indian-held part of the territory.
† Chandigarh forms a separate Union Territory, not within Haryana or Punjab.
‡ Estimate.

Sources: Census of India, 1971 and 1981, *Data Asia/Pacific* 1979, and the Registrar General, India.

PRINCIPAL TOWNS

(population at 1981 census*)

Town	Population	Town	Population	Town	Population
Greater Bombay	8,227,332	Varanasi (Banaras)	704,772	Meerut	417,288
Delhi	4,865,077	Coimbatore	700,923	Jalandhar	405,709
Calcutta	3,291,655	Bhopal	672,329	Kozhikode (Calicut)	394,440
Madras	3,266,034	Jabalpur (Jubbulpore)	614,879	Bareilly	375,124
Bangalore	2,482,507	Allahabad	609,232	Ajmer	374,350
Hyderabad	2,142,087	Ludhiana	606,250	Chandigarh	371,992
Ahmedabad	2,024,917	Visakhapatnam	558,117	Guntur	367,219
Kanpur (Cawnpore)	1,531,345	Gwalior	542,924	Salem	361,177
Nagpur	1,215,425	Hubli-Dharwar	526,493	Tiruchirapalli	360,919
Pune (Poona)	1,202,848	Cochin	513,081	Kota	346,928
Jaipur (Jeypore)	966,677	Sholapur	510,707	Kolhapur	340,306
Lucknow	895,947	Trivandrum	499,168	Raipur	338,973
Indore	827,071	Jodhpur	493,609	Warangal	336,018
Madurai	817,562	Ranchi	487,485	Moradabad	332,663
Surat	776,004	Jamshedpur	457,440	Aligarh	319,981
Patna	773,720	Vijaywada (Vijayavada)	453,414	Bhilai Nagar	319,428
Howrah	742,298	Rajkot	444,156	Thane	309,271
Vadodara (Baroda)	733,656	Mysore	439,185	Durgapur	305,838
Agra	723,676				

* Figures refer to the city proper in each case. For urban agglomerations, the following populations were recorded: Calcutta 9,165,650; Greater Bombay 8,227,332; Delhi 5,713,581; Madras 4,276,635; Bangalore 2,913,537; Hyderabad 2,528,198; Ahmedabad 2,515,195; Kanpur 1,688,242; Pune 1,685,300; Nagpur 1,297,977; Lucknow 1,006,538; Jaipur 1,004,669; Coimbatore 917,155; Patna 916,102; Surat 912,568; Madurai 904,362; Indore 827,071; Varanasi 793,542; Agra 770,352; Jabalpur 757,726; Vadodara 744,043; Cochin 685,686; Dhanbad 676,736; Bhopal 672,329; Jamshedpur 669,984; Ulhasnagar 648,149; Allahabad 642,420; Tiruchirapalli 607,815; Ludhiana 606,250; Visakhapatnam 594,259; Amritsar 589,229; Gwalior 559,776; Kozhikode 546,060; Vijaywada 544,958; Meerut 538,461; Hubli-Dharwar 526,493; Trivandrum 519,766; Salem 515,021; Solapur 514,461; Ranchi 500,593.

BIRTH AND DEATH RATES

	Birth Rate (per 1,000)	Death Rate (per 1,000)	Life Expectancy at Birth (years)
1975	35·2	15·9	49·5
1977	33·0	14·7	n.a.
1978	33·3	14·2	n.a.
1979	33·2	12·8	n.a.

Source: Registrar General, India.

ECONOMICALLY ACTIVE POPULATION*

(1971 census)

	Males	Females	Total
Agriculture, hunting, forestry and fishing	104,175,289	25,882,808	130,058,097
Mining and quarrying	798,755	124,066	922,821
Manufacturing (incl. repair services)	14,872,986	2,195,972	17,068,958
Electricity, gas and water supply	525,193	9,511	534,704
Construction	2,015,272	203,829	2,219,101
Trade, restaurants and hotels	8,310,820	520,629	8,831,449
Transport, storage and communications	4,256,865	146,114	4,402,979
Finance, insurance, property and business services	1,173,417	35,765	1,209,182
Community, social and personal services (excl. repair services)	13,017,472	2,220,243	15,237,715
Total	149,146,069	31,338,937	180,485,006

* Figures exclude persons who were unemployed or seeking work for the first time.

AGRICULTURE

LAND USE

(FAO estimates, '000 hectares)

	1978/79
Arable land	164,928
Land under permanent crops	3,910
Permanent meadows and pastures	12,155
Forests and woodland	67,441
Other land	48,904
Inland waters	31,440
Total	328,778

Source: Directorate of Economics and Statistics, Ministry of Agriculture.

PRINCIPAL CROPS

(July 1st to June 30th)

	Area ('000 hectares)			Production ('000 metric tons)		
	1978/79	1979/80	1980/81	1978/79	1979/80	1980/81
Rice (milled)	40,482	39,414	39,773	53,774	42,330	53,231
Sorghum (Jowar)	16,146	16,674	15,610	11,436	11,648	10,504
Cat-tail millet (Bajra)	11,393	10,579	11,630	5,566	3,948	5,418
Maize	5,760	5,720	5,983	6,199	5,603	6,804
Finger millet (Ragi)	2,705	2,615	2,341	3,200	2,721	2,465
Small millets	4,397	4,002	3,895	1,894	1,425	1,578
Wheat	22,641	22,172	22,104	35,508	31,830	36,460
Barley	1,828	1,771	1,821	2,142	1,624	2,242
Total cereals	105,352	102,947	103,157	119,719	101,129	118,702
Chick-peas (Gram)	7,708	6,985	6,720	5,739	3,356	4,652
Pigeon peas (Tur)	2,635	2,731	2,811	1,887	1,757	2,015
Dry beans, dry peas, lentils and other pulses	13,314	12,543	13,103	4,557	3,458	4,498
Total food grains	129,009	125,206	125,791	131,902	109,701	129,867
Groundnuts	7,433	7,165	6,905	6,208	5,768	5,020
Sesame seed	2,389	2,377	2,443	514	348	437
Rapeseed and mustard	3,544	3,471	4,063	1,860	1,428	2,247
Linseed	2,092	1,614	1,710	535	269	428
Castor beans	447	441	501	229	227	210
Total oil seeds	15,905	15,068	15,622	9,346	8,040	8,342
Cotton (lint)	8,119	8,078	7,870	7,958*	7,698*	7,600
Jute	884	834	942	6,470†	6,072†	6,515†
Kenaf (Mesta)	380	383	358	1,863†	1,890†	1,680†
Tea (made)	369	374	378	564	552	575
Sugar cane: production gur	3,088	2,610	2,648	15,734	13,091	15,402
Sugar cane: production cane				151,655	128,833	150,522
Tobacco (leaves)	409	425	428	454	439	456
Potatoes	807	685	685	10,133	8,327	9,599
Chillies (dry)	826	854	854	566	508	485

* Production in '000 bales of 170 kg. each. † Production in '000 bales of 180 kg. each.

Source: Directorate of Economics and Statistics, Ministry of Agriculture.

LIVESTOCK
(FAO estimates, '000 head)

	1978	1979	1980
Cattle	181,992	181,849	182,500
Sheep	40,700	41,000	41,300
Goats	70,580	71,000	71,650
Pigs	9,410	9,900	10,000
Horses	771	760	760
Asses	1,000	1,000	1,000
Mules	125	125	128
Buffaloes	60,698	60,651	61,300
Camels	1,150	1,150	1,150
Poultry	144,000	145,000	146,000

Source: FAO, *Production Yearbook.*

LIVESTOCK PRODUCTS
(FAO estimates, '000 metric tons)

	1977	1978	1979	1980
Beef and veal	70	71	72	74
Buffalo meat	119	120	120	123
Mutton and lamb	118	119	120	122
Goats' meat	275	277	278	280
Pig meat	63	66	67	70
Poultry meat	104	106	107	109
Cows' milk	n.a.	12,180*	12,600*	13,000
Buffaloes' milk	14,500	15,950*	16,500*	17,000
Goats' milk	n.a.	870*	900*	930
Butter and ghee	570	570	581	588
Hen eggs	85	86	87	88
Wool: greasy	34.0*	34.5*	35.0*	36
clean	22.0	22.4	22.7	23.4
Cattle and buffalo hides (fresh)	766.0	771.0	771.0	790.0
Sheep skins (fresh)	35.6	35.8	36.4	36.7
Goat skins (fresh)	70.2	70.9	71.3	72.0

* Unofficial estimate.
Source: FAO, *Production Yearbook.*

FORESTRY

ROUNDWOOD REMOVALS
('000 cubic metres, excluding bark)

	Coniferous (soft wood)			Broadleaved (hard wood)			Total		
	1978	1979	1980*	1978	1979	1980*	1978	1979	1980*
Sawlogs, veneer logs and logs for sleepers	790	968	968	2,517	2,419	2,419	3,307	3,387	3,387
Pitprops (mine timber)*	—	—	—	1,250	1,250	1,250	1,250	1,250	1,250
Pulpwood*	145	145	145	1,063	1,063	1,063	1,208	1,208	1,208
Other industrial wood*	66	68	69	2,577	2,642	2,702	2,643	2,710	2,771
Total Industrial Wood	1,001	1,181	1,182	7,407	7,374	7,434	8,408	8,555	8,616
Fuel wood	6,000†	6,500†	6,649	181,509*	185,712*	189,992	187,509*	192,212*	196,641
Total	7,001	7,681	7,831	188,916	193,086	197,426	195,917	200,767	205,257

* FAO estimates. † Unofficial estimate.
Source: FAO, *Yearbook of Forest Products.*

SAWNWOOD PRODUCTION

('000 cubic metres)

	1974	1975	1976	1977*	1978	1979
Coniferous sawnwood (incl. boxboards)	800*	850*	900*	950	790	968
Broadleaved sawnwood (incl. boxboards)	2,200*	2,400*	2,500*	2,600	2,517	2,419
	3,000*	3,250*	3,400*	3,550	3,307	3,387
Railway sleepers	132	120	161	124*	124	252
TOTAL	3,132	3,370	3,561	3,674	3,431	3,639

* FAO estimate.

1980: Production as in 1979 (FAO estimates).

Source: FAO, *Yearbook of Forest Products.*

FISHING

('000 metric tons, live weight)

	1975	1976	1977	1978	1979	1980
Indian Ocean:						
Bombay-duck	110.2	134.1	140.5	118.4	121.6	116.2
Marine catfishes	73.5	45.3	38.4	46.0	47.1	61.1
Croakers and drums	110.6	91.9	119.5	109.2	127.9	125.1
Indian oil-sardine (sardinella)	245.7	261.3	232.4	237.8	274.4	212.4
Anchovies	58.7	63.6	70.1	70.7	50.1	64.7
Hairtails and cutlass fishes	47.6	74.2	43.0	77.0	72.2	75.6
Indian mackerel	40.7	46.9	76.4	102.0	86.2	58.4
Other marine fishes (incl. unspecified)	535.1	447.5	473.6	519.2	499.5	558.4
TOTAL SEA FISH	1,222.2	1,164.8	1,194.0	1,280.4	1,279.9	1,271.8
Shrimps and prawns	246.2	197.8	232.7	186.7	183.2	244.5
Other marine animals	13.7	12.1	21.7	22.6	28.9	31.9
TOTAL SEA CATCH	1,482.1	1,374.7	1,448.4	1,489.7	1,492.0	1,548.2
Inland waters:						
Freshwater fishes	783.8	799.2	863.4	816.5	847.6	875.3
TOTAL CATCH	2,265.9	2,173.9	2,311.9	2,306.1	2,339.5	2,423.5

* Provisional.

Source: Ministry of Agriculture, Government of India.

MINING

		1977	1978	1979	1980*
Coal	'000 metric tons	100,358	101,340	103,364	109,102
Lignite	,, ,, ,,	3,632	3,613	3,264	4,549
Iron ore†	,, ,, ,,	26,759	24,776	25,066	25,742
Manganese ore†	,, ,, ,,	677	598	659	619
Bauxite	,, ,, ,,	1,519	1,663	1,952	1,775
Chalk (Fireclay)	,, ,, ,,	720	733	789	737
Kaolin (China clay)	,, ,, ,,	399	418	495	452
Dolomite	,, ,, ,,	2,193	2,003	2,157	2,018
Gypsum	,, ,, ,,	778	888	877	868
Limestone	,, ,, ,,	30,380	30,915	31,317	29,211
Crude petroleum	,, ,, ,,	10,185	11,271	12,841	9,397
Salt‡	,, ,, ,,	5,328	6,696	7,032	8,004
Chromium	,, ,, ,,	253	266	310	321
Phosphorite	,, ,, ,,	706	760	661	523
Kyanite	,, ,, ,,	42	31	41	49
Magnesite	,, ,, ,,	402	414	396	385
Steatite	,, ,, ,,	247	315	352	332
Copper ore†	metric tons	29,011	26,640	27,717	26,819
Lead concentrates†	,, ,,	10,914	10,553	12,805	10,794
Zinc concentrates†	,, ,,	24,375	24,396	37,028	24,406
Mica (crude)	,, ,,	9,352	9,593	9,073	7,930
Gold†	kilogrammes	3,014	3,774	2,637	2,452
Diamonds	Carats	18,297	15,953	15,229	14,432
Natural gas§	million cubic metres	1,631	1,731	1,925	1,462

* Provisional.

† Figures refer to the metal content of ores and concentrates.

‡ Figures refer to sea salt.

§ Figures refer to gas utilized.

Source: Indian Bureau of Mines.

INDUSTRY

SELECTED PRODUCTS

		1977	1978	1979	1980
Refined Sugar*	'000 metric tons	4,804	6,501	5,791	3,849
Cotton Cloth	million metres	6,895	7,327	7,531	8,314
Jute Manufactures	'000 metric tons	1,159	1,173	1,150	1,385
Paper and Paper Board	,, ,, ,,	937	1,006	1,010	1,066
Sulphuric Acid	,, ,, ,,	2,017	2,087	2,228	989†
Soda Ash	,, ,, ,,	568	581	544	603
Fertilizers	,, ,, ,,	2,642	2,826	3,064	2,888
Petroleum Products	,, ,, ,,	22,795	24,200	26,347	23,601
Cement	,, ,, ,,	19,171	19,626	18,270	17,803
Pig Iron	,, ,, ,,	9,784	9,431	8,687	8,480
Finished Steel	,, ,, ,,	6,738	6,492	6,156	5,537
Aluminium	metric tons	183,854	205,386	211,637	184,509
Diesel Engines (stationary)	number	136,031	136,934	143,290	154,527
Sewing Machines	,,	381,600	244,900	355,073	345,393
Radio Receivers	,,	1,814,370	1,937,150	2,030,483	1,918,000
Electric Fans	,,	3,393,200	3,011,400	3,721,000	4,102,000
Passenger Cars and Jeeps	,,	47,900	45,634	42,774	47,533
Passenger Buses and Trucks	,,	36,485	48,462	58,367	66,016
Motor Cycles and Scooters	,,	221,165	254,735	240,501	301,671
Bicycles	,,	3,057,900	3,479,900	3,994,145	3,892,700

* Figures relate to crop year (beginning November) and are in respect of cane sugar only.

† January–June.

Source: Ministry of Industry, Government of India.

FINANCE

100 paisa (singular, paise) = 1 Indian rupee.
Coins: 1, 2, 3, 5, 10, 20, 25 and 50 paisa; 1, 10 and 50 rupees.
Notes: 1, 2, 5, 10, 20, 50 and 100 rupees.
Exchange rates (June 1982): £1 sterling = 16.55 rupees; U.S. $1 = 9.555 rupees;
100 Indian rupees = £6.042 = $10.465.

Note: Between September 1949 and June 1966 the Indian rupee had a par value of 21 U.S. cents (U.S. $1 = 4.7619 rupees). From June 1966 to December 1971 the exchange rate was $1 = 7.50 rupees (1 rupee = 13.33 U.S. cents). In terms of sterling the rate between November 1967 and August 1971 was £1 = 18.00 rupees. In December 1971 a new central exchange rate of £1 = 18.9677 rupees was established. Until the "floating" of the pound in June 1972 this was equivalent to a rate of U.S. $1 = 7.279 rupees. Until September 1975 the Indian authorities maintained the exchange rate against sterling, thus allowing the rupee to "float" in relation to other currencies. Since September 1975 the rupee has been pegged to a "basket" of currencies of India's principal trading partners. The average market rates (rupees per U.S. dollar) were: 7.594 in 1972; 7.742 in 1973; 8.102 in 1974; 8.376 in 1975; 8.960 in 1976; 8.739 in 1977; 8.193 in 1978; 8.126 in 1979; 7.863 in 1980; 8.659 in 1981.

BUDGET

(million rupees, year ending March 31st)

Revenue	1981/82*	1982/83
Tax revenue:		
Customs	41,400.0	49,973.5
Union excise duties	75,031.4	85,249.3
Corporation tax	19,620.0	23,820.0
Income tax	15,200.0	15,740.0
Estate duty	170.0	170.0
Wealth taxes	750.0	800.0
Interest tax	2,000.0	2,200.0
Gift tax	67.5	67.5
Others	3,322.3	3,460.9
Gross tax revenue	157,543.2	181,481.2
Less states' share	42,744.8	47,796.7
Net tax revenue	114,798.4	133,684.5
Non-tax revenue:		
Interest receipts	21,652.0	23,642.8
Dividends and profits	3,605.5	3,235.7
Others	13,674.5	15,445.5
Total non-tax revenue	38,932.0	42,324.0
Total current receipts	153,730.4	176,008.5
Total capital receipts	94,806.1	102,533.8
Grand Total	248,536.5	278,542.3

Expenditure	1980/81	1981/82
General services:		
Organs of states	1,099.3	1,212.9
Fiscal services	3,498.7	3,531.8
Interest payments	32,000.0	38,000.0
Administrative services	6,531.2	10,128.0
Pensions and miscellaneous services	2,750.7	3,183.8
Defence (net)	41,356.8	45,987.0
Total general services	87,236.7	102,043.5
Social and community services	10,909.7	12,531.5
Economic services:		
General economic services	7,111.9	6,948.2
Agriculture and allied services	10,695.0	11,748.2
Industry and minerals	8,726.5	9,608.5
Water and power development	2,015.4	2,606.4
Transport and communications	2,985.6	3,141.9
Total economic services	31,534.4	34,053.2
Aid and contributions	29,795.6	33,644.7
Total current expenditure	159,476.4	182,272.9
Total capital expenditure	106,057.2	109,919.6
Grand Total	265,533.6	292,192.5

* Revised budget.

Source: Government of India, Annual Budget Papers, 1982/83.

INTERNATIONAL RESERVES

(U.S. $ million at December 31st)

	1975	1976	1977	1978	1979	1980	1981
Gold	204	205	235	262	284	284	248
IMF Special Drawing Rights	248	220	181	294	489	480	545
Reserve position in IMF	—	—	—	90	213	420	384
Foreign exchange	841	2,572	4,691	6,042	6,731	6,043	3,764
TOTAL	1,293	2,997	5,107	6,688	7,717	7,227	4,941

Source: IMF, *International Financial Statistics.*

MONEY SUPPLY

(million rupees, last Friday of the year)

	1974	1975	1976	1977	1978	1979	1980	1981*
Currency with the public	61,380	64,430	73,170	84,100	94,540	107,960	126,290	138,760
Demand deposits with banks	53,760	61,490	77,970	92,710	113,030	74,410	86,660	105,320
Other deposits with Reserve Bank	490	600	910	700	1,900	3,050	2,180	2,040
TOTAL MONEY	115,630	126,520	152,050	177,510	209,470	185,420	215,130	246,120

* Provisional.

Source: Reserve Bank of India.

COST OF LIVING

(Consumer price index for industrial workers. Base: 1970=100)

	1974	1975	1976	1977	1978	1979	1980
Food	171.0	178.5	156.0	171.5	173.0	181.0	203.0
Fuel and light	170.1	187.4	195.2	201.2	215.0	253.3	282.6
Clothing	189.3	198.7	198.7	217.0	234.0	248.4	271.1
Rent	113.6	122.7	129.5	137.1	143.9	150.0	158.3
ALL ITEMS (incl. others)	165.2	174.5	160.9	174.5	178.8	190.2	212.0

1981: Food 232.9; All items 233.1.

NATIONAL ACCOUNTS

('000 million rupees at current prices, year ending March 31st)

National Income and Product

	1974/75	1975/76	1976/77	1977/78	1978/79	1979/80
Compensation of employees	213.50	243.54	265.18	294.69	318.27	349.88
Operating surplus*	383.87	380.40	410.79	466.99	493.21	531.96
Domestic Factor Incomes	597.37	623.94	675.97	761.68	811.48	871.84
Consumption of fixed capital	35.26	40.54	44.64	50.11	57.62	67.99
Gross Domestic Product at Factor Cost	632.63	664.48	720.61	811.79	869.10	939.83
Indirect taxes	75.15	88.34	99.26	106.89	127.35	145.94
Less Subsidies	11.83	11.20	13.93	17.72	22.01	84.26
G.D.P. in Purchasers' Values	695.95	741.62	805.94	900.96	974.44	1,061.51
Factor income from abroad	0.96	1.18	1.92	} −2.33	−1.56	0.69
Less Factor income paid abroad	3.87	3.73	4.27			
Gross National Product	693.04	739.07	803.59	898.63	972.88	1,062.20
Less Consumption of fixed capital	35.26	40.54	44.64	50.11	57.62	67.99
National Income in Market Prices	657.78	698.53	758.95	848.52	915.26	994.21
Other current transfers from abroad	2.80	5.41	7.46	10.29	} 10.42	12.13
Less Other current transfers paid abroad	0.06	0.13	0.07	0.07		
National Disposable Income	660.52	703.81	766.34	858.74	925.68	1,006.34

* Including mixed income of self-employed ('000 million rupees): 297.95 in 1974/75; 284.03 in 1975/76; 290.61 in 1976/77; 341.90 in 1977/78; 350.58 in 1978/79; 366.21 in 1979/80.

Expenditure on the Gross Domestic Product

	1974/75	1975/76	1976/77	1977/78	1978/79	1979/80
Government final consumption expenditure	61.43	73.51	82.06	86.67	96.24	109.24
Private final consumption expenditure	519.05	525.58	542.62	626.89	669.44	729.67
Increase in stocks	35.79	31.50	23.82	12.58	37.44	41.63
Gross fixed capital formation	109.30	132.65	153.58	170.83	192.05	205.20
Total Domestic Expenditure	725.57	763.24	802.08	896.97	995.17	1,085.74
Exports of goods and services	38.35	48.12	61.39	66.36	71.15	77.65
Less Imports of goods and services	47.79	56.64	56.14	65.22	74.26	95.55
Sub-Total	716.13	754.72	807.33	898.11	992.06	1,067.84
Statistical discrepancy	−20.18	−13.10	−1.39	2.85	−17.62	−6.33
G.D.P. in Purchasers' Values	696.95	741.62	805.94	900.96	974.44	1,061.51

GROSS DOMESTIC PRODUCT BY ECONOMIC ACTIVITY
('000 million rupees at current factor cost)

	1973/74	1974/75	1975/76	1976/77	1977/78*	1978/79*	1979/80*
Agriculture and hunting	258.79	280.29	267.70	277.77	318.36	316.18	320.10
Forestry and logging	5.16	5.62	6.40	7.35	8.26	10.00	12.65
Fishing	3.93	4.54	5.67	6.50	6.71	8.01	8.13
Mining and quarrying	4.87	6.95	8.84	10.11	11.17	12.32	14.77
Manufacturing	75.72	98.58	103.52	115.55	128.78	152.45	175.40
Electricity, gas and water	5.25	6.75	8.35	10.75	12.21	15.02	16.64
Construction	24.05	26.37	32.94	39.35	45.34	48.94	49.19
Trade, restaurants and hotels	60.25	81.05	91.65	95.42	109.74	118.31	160.06
Transport, storage and communications	24.90	31.34	35.24	41.43	45.27	49.70	57.22
Banking and insurance	11.01	13.79	17.77	21.04	23.25	25.73	28.36
Real estate and business services	19.09	21.44	23.41	26.20	28.76	31.78	35.09
Public administration and defence	22.21	28.56	32.37	34.53	36.94	40.66	46.11
Other services	22.49	27.35	30.62	34.61	38.47	42.18	46.79
TOTAL	537.72	632.63	664.48	720.61	813.26	871.28	970.51

* Provisional.

Revised totals (in '000 million rupees) are: 811.79 in 1977/78; 869.10 in 1978/79; 939.83 in 1979/80.

BALANCE OF PAYMENTS
(U.S. $ million)

	1975	1976	1977	1978	1979
Merchandise exports f.o.b.	4,666	5,410	6,249	6,518	7,603
Merchandise imports f.o.b.	−4,952	−4,623	−5,317	−7,402	−9,819
TRADE BALANCE	−286	787	932	−884	−2,216
Exports of services	971	1,251	1,592	1,997	2,831
Imports of services	−1,442	−1,495	−1,711	−2,047	−2,605
BALANCE ON GOODS AND SERVICES	−757	543	813	−934	−1,990
Private unrequited transfers (net)	414	634	926	1,147	1,424
Government unrequited transfers (net)	196	394	368	447	618
CURRENT BALANCE	−147	1,571	2,107	660	53
Long-term capital (net)	933	1,034	652	683	353
Short-term capital (net)	12	−102	−220	129	135
Net errors and omissions	−450	−293	−132	450	308
TOTAL (net monetary movements)	357	2,210	2,408	1,921	850
Allocation of IMF Special Drawing Rights	—	—	—	—	154
Valuation changes (net)	−68	−28	131	425	180
IMF Subsidy Account grants	—	8	12	9	3
CHANGES IN RESERVES	289	2,190	2,551	2,355	1,187

Source: IMF, *International Financial Statistics.*

EXTERNAL TRADE
(million rupees, year ending March 31st)

	1977/78	1978/79	1979/80	1980/81	1981/82*
Imports c.i.f.	60,202	68,106	90,217	124,346	132,713
Exports f.o.b.	53,975	57,080	64,588	67,088	75,575

* Provisional.

PRINCIPAL COMMODITIES

(million rupees)

Exports	1979/80	1980/81
Fish, crustaceans, molluscs and preparations	2,494.3	2,236.6
Meat and meat preparations	413.4	546.6
Rice	1,238.1	1,559.8
Wheat	565.5	184.4
Cashew kernels	1,181.0	1,232.1
Other vegetables and fruit	635.4	844.6
Crude vegetable materials	865.3	660.1
Sugar and sugar preparations	1,289.4	359.6
Coffee and coffee substitutes	1,633.1	2,250.1
Tea and maté	3,678.4	3,851.6
Spices	1,493.7	1,061.8
Oil cakes	1,275.3	1,092.4
Unmanufactured tobacco, tobacco refuse	1,022.5	1,225.5
Cotton (raw)	751.0	1,296.4
Cotton fabrics	2,874.0	2,938.4
Ready-made garments	4,596.7	4,809.7
Jute manufactures	3,361.3	2,432.6
Carpets (hand-made)	1,397.6	1,403.1
Leather and leather manufactures	4,855.6	3,412.4
Pearls, precious and semi-precious stones	5,189.5	5,424.6
Works of art	1,055.0	1,090.4
Iron ore	2,852.4	2,894.1
Other ores and minerals	877.9	913.8
Iron and steel	1,052.2	823.3
Metal manufactures (excl. iron and steel)	2,165.8	2,088.1
Machinery and transport equipment	4,473.3	4,940.6
Chemicals and allied products	1,978.1	2,098.4
Total (incl. others)	64,587.7	67,088.4

Imports	1979/80	1980/81
Wheat	843.1	580.5
Milk and cream	527.9	254.8
Fruit and nuts (excl. cashew nuts)	301.5	425.9
Textile yarn, fabrics, etc.	523.0	542.3
Synthetic and regenerated fibres	81.7	903.7
Crude rubber (incl. synthetic and reclaimed)	514.0	267.8
Crude fertilizers	596.9	633.0
Manufactured fertilizers	3,712.2	5,900.8
Sulphur and unroasted iron pyrites	845.1	747.5
Other crude minerals	376.9	310.6
Metalliferous ores and metal scrap	908.3	1,044.2
Iron and steel	8,342.0	7,792.0
Non-ferrous metals	3,363.0	4,242.3
Edible vegetable oil	4,298.3	5,677.8
Mineral fuels, lubricants, etc.	32,670.8	55,868.7
Organic chemicals	1,974.6	1,914.0
Inorganic chemicals	1,173.2	1,333.1
Chemical materials and products	617.5	677.9
Artificial resins, plastic materials	950.9	1,166.0
Medicinal and pharmaceutical products	739.7	812.1
Paper, paperboard and manufactures	1,552.6	1,758.6
Pulp and waste paper	302.5	148.3
Pearls, precious and semi-precious stones	3,473.6	3,882.3
Non-electric machinery	8,596.0	9,781.8
Electrical machinery, apparatus, etc.	1,716.9	2,012.1
Transport equipment	3,365.2	3,933.5
Professional, scientific and controlling instruments, photographic and optical goods, watches and clocks	1,552.8	1,553.4
Wool (raw)	287.5	381.2
Total (incl. others)	90,217.5	124,345.8

Source: Ministry of Commerce, Government of India, *Annual Report 1981/82.*

PRINCIPAL TRADING PARTNERS

(million rupees)

IMPORTS c.i.f.	1979/80	1980/81
Australia	1,628.4	1,819.7
Belgium	2,636.9	3,060.4
Brazil	647.6	2,179.0
Canada	2,264.8	2,759.1
France	2,077.5	2,675.0
Germany, Federal Republic	6,445.5	7,584.5
Iran	6,206.9	13,489.4
Iraq	9,172.7	8,041.1
Italy	1,788.9	2,949.7
Japan	6,094.0	6,432.8
Korea, Republic	884.5	1,283.3
Kuwait	1,655.1	3,313.4
Malaysia	2,073.3	2,534.8
Netherlands	1,451.9	2,541.6
Saudi Arabia	3,631.2	4,343.6
Singapore	1,508.4	4,519.2
Switzerland	1,005.8	1,411.4
U.S.S.R.	8,243.3	9,552.5
United Arab Emirates	2,088.0	3,190.7
United Kingdom	7,088.1	8,254.3
U.S.A.	9,260.7	15,108.8

EXPORTS f.o.b.	1979/80	1980/81
Australia	1,020.0	914.4
Bangladesh	982.2	580.0
Belgium	1,668.5	1,482.5
Egypt	697.7	828.8
France	1,973.2	1,551.4
Germany, Federal Republic	3,801.0	3,558.0
Hong Kong	1,184.9	1,200.9
Iran	961.1	1,219.7
Italy	2,131.9	1,627.8
Japan	6,462.6	6,115.9
Kuwait	1,238.1	966.9
Nepal	634.2	877.6
Netherlands	2,204.6	1,645.6
Saudi Arabia	1,556.4	1,713.7
Singapore	830.6	999.3
Sri Lanka	1,019.5	891.4
Switzerland	1,037.3	1,041.7
U.S.S.R.	6,382.3	11,573.0
United Arab Emirates	1,328.3	1,512.8
United Kingdom	5,160.5	4,277.6
U.S.A.	8,169.9	8,522.3

Source: Ministry of Commerce, Government of India, *Annual Report 1981/82*.

TRANSPORT

RAILWAYS

(million, year ending March 31st)

	1976/77	1977/78	1978/79	1979/80	1979/80	1980/81
Passengers	3,300.5	3,503.8	3,719.0	3,505	3,505	3,612
Passenger-kilometres	163,836.2	176,635.0	192,946.0	198,642	198,657	208,558
Freight (metric tons)	239.1	237.3	223.4	217.8	217.1	220
Freight (metric ton-kilometres)	156,755.8	162,687.1	154,824.0	155,955.0	155,955	158,474

Source: Ministry of Railways.

ROAD TRAFFIC

(Motor vehicles in use at March 31st)

	1977	1978	1979
Private cars	630,925	676,888	722,511
Jeeps	98,364	105,053	119,414
Taxis	79,519	76,891	82,999
Buses and coaches	114,656	119,479	126,671
Goods vehicles	361,396	375,303	411,610
Motor cycles and scooters	1,235,137	1,431,602	1,678,142
Others	448,200	618,977	555,021
TOTAL	2,968,197	3,304,283	3,696,368

Source: Transport Wing, Ministry of Shipping and Transport.

INTERNATIONAL SEA-BORNE SHIPPING
(Twelve months ending March 31st)

	1975/76	1976/77	1977/78	1978/79
Vessels* ('000 net reg. tons):				
Entered	20,261	21,222	20,766	n.a.
Cleared	18,505	21,343	19,195	n.a.
Freight† ('000 metric tons):				
Loaded	32,120	36,153	31,263	31,041
Unloaded	30,932	28,989	26,798	29,264

* Excluding minor and intermediate ports. † Including bunkers.

Sources: United Nations, *Statistical Yearbook*.

CIVIL AVIATION
('000)

	1977	1978	1979	1980
Kilometres flown	80,100	82,284	82,248	84,120
Passenger kilometres	8,278,932	8,995,344	9,720,156	10,689,372
Freight ton-kilometres	284,184	294,744	304,464	374,532
Mail ton-kilometres	27,648	28,944	31,260	35,412

Sources: United Nations, *Statistical Yearbook* and *Monthly Bulletin of Statistics*, and Directorate General of Civil Aviation, New Delhi.

TOURISM
FOREIGN VISITORS

	1979	1980	1981
Australia	23,172	22,294	20,612
Canada	23,737	23,783	25,358
France	53,129	58,682	57,272
Germany, Federal Republic	51,084	54,736	54,311
Italy	27,413	29,002	28,503
Japan	29,954	30,575	29,032
Malaysia	23,877	26,405	26,458
Switzerland	11,903	13,287	14,411
United Kingdom	101,193	102,483	116,684
U.S.A.	82,420	78,608	82,052
Total (incl. others)	747,552	800,150	853,148

Source: Ministry of Tourism and Civil Aviation.

COMMUNICATIONS MEDIA

	1977	1978	1979
Radios	20,096,453	19,611,444	20,723,040
Television sets	676,615	899,123	1,150,000†
Telephones*	n.a.	1,613,000	2,016,000
Newspapers	14,531	15,814	17,168

* Figures refer to year ending March 31st.

† Figures refer to year ending December 31st.

Sources: Ministry of Communications and Registrar of Newspapers for India, Ministry of Information and Broadcasting.

EDUCATION
(1979/80)

	Institutions	Students	Teachers
Primary: lower	478,249	70,940,386	1,311,931
middle	114,720	18,701,230	835,292
Secondary (High school)	37,419	7,515,640	633,642
Higher secondary (Old course)	3,127	961,515	65,283
Higher secondary (New pattern)	5,044	1,193,954	160,434

Source: Ministry of Education and Social Welfare.

Source (unless otherwise stated): Central Statistical Organization, Ministry of Planning, Government of India.

THE CONSTITUTION

The Constitution of India, adopted by the Constituent Assembly on November 26th, 1949, was inaugurated on January 26th, 1950. The Preamble declares that the People of India solemnly resolve to constitute a Sovereign Democratic Republic and to secure to all its citizens justice, liberty, equality and fraternity. There are 397 articles and 9 schedules, which form a comprehensive document.

Union of States. The Union of India comprises 22 states and 9 Union Territories. There are provisions for the formation and admission of new states.

The Constitution confers citizenship on a threefold basis of birth, descent, and residence. Provisions are made for refugees who have migrated from Pakistan and for persons of Indian origin residing abroad.

Fundamental Rights and Directive Principles. The rights of the citizen contained in Part III of the Constitution are declared fundamental and enforceable in law. "Untouchability" is abolished and its practice in any form is a punishable offence. The Directive Principles of State Policy provide a code intended to ensure promotion of the economic, social and educational welfare of the State in future legislation.

The President is the head of the Union, exercising all executive powers on the advice of the Council of Ministers responsible to Parliament. He is elected by an electoral college consisting of elected members of both Houses of Parliament and the Legislatures of the States. The President holds office for a term of five years and is eligible for re-election. He may be impeached for violation of the Constitution. The Vice-President is the *ex officio* Chairman of the Rajya Sabha and is elected by a joint sitting of both Houses of Parliament.

The Parliament of the Union consists of the President and two Houses: the Rajya Sabha (Council of States) and the Lok Sabha (House of the People). The Rajya Sabha consists of 244 members, of whom 8 are nominated by the President. One-third of its members retire every two years. Elections are indirect, each state's legislative quota being elected by the members of the state's legislative assembly. The Lok Sahba consists of 544 members elected by adult franchise; not more than 17 represent the Union Territories. It may also include a number of members nominated by the President.

Government of the States. The governmental machinery of states closely resembles that of the Union. Each of these states has a governor at its head appointed by the President for a term of five years to exercise executive power on the advice of a Council of Ministers. The state's legislatures consist of the Governor and either one house (legislative assembly) or two houses (legislative assembly and legislative council). The term of the assembly is five years, but the council is not subject to dissolution.

Language. The Constitution provides that the official language of the Union shall be Hindi. (The English language will continue to be an associate language for many official purposes.)

Legislation—Federal System. The Constitution provides that bills, other than money bills, can be introduced in either House. To become law, they must be passed by both Houses and receive the assent of the President. In financial affairs, the authority of the Lower House is final. The various subjects of legislation are enumerated on three lists in the seventh schedule of the Constitution: the Union List, containing nearly 100 entries, including external affairs, defence, communications, and atomic energy; the State List, containing 65 entries, including local government, police, public health, education; and the Concurrent List, with over 40 entries, including criminal law, marriage and divorce, labour welfare. The Constitution vests residuary authority in the Centre. All matters not enumerated in the Concurrent or State Lists will be deemed to be included in the Union List, and in the event of conflict between Union and State Law on any subject enumerated in the Concurrent List the Union Law will prevail. In time of emergency Parliament may even exercise powers otherwise exclusively vested in the states. Under Article 356, "If the President on receipt of a report from the Government of a state or otherwise is satisfied that a situation has arisen in which the Government of the state cannot be carried on in accordance with the provisions of this Constitution, the President may by Proclamation: (a) assume to himself all or any of the functions of the Government of the state and all or any of the powers of the Governor or any body or authority in the state other than the Legislature of the state; (b) declare that the powers of the Legislature of the state shall be exercisable by or under the authority of Parliament; (c) make such incidental provisions as appear to the President to be necessary": provided that none of the powers of a High Court be assumed by the President or suspended in any way. Unless such a Proclamation is approved by both Houses of Parliament, it ceases to operate after two months. A Proclamation so approved ceases to operate after six months, unless renewed by Parliament. Its renewal cannot be extended beyond a total period of three years. An independent judiciary exists to define and interpret the Constitution and to resolve constitutional disputes arising between states, or between a state and the Government of India.

Other Provisions of the Constitution deal with the administration of tribal areas, relations between the Union and states, inter-state trade and finance.

Amendments. The Constitution is flexible in character, and a simple process of amendment has been adopted. For amendment of provisions concerning the Supreme Courts and the High Courts, the distribution of legislative powers between the Union and the states, the representation of the states in Parliament, etc., the amendment must be passed by both Houses of Parliament and must further be ratified by the legislatures of not less than half the states. In other cases no reference to the state legislatures is necessary.

Numerous amendments were adopted in August 1975, following the declaration of a state of emergency in June. The Constitution (39th Amendment) Bill laid down that the President's reasons for proclaiming an emergency may not be challenged in any court. Under the Constitution (40th Amendment) Bill, 38 existing laws may not be challenged before any court on the ground of violation of fundamental rights. Thus detainees under the Maintenance of Internal Security Act could not be told the grounds of their detention and were forbidden bail and any claim to liberty through natural or common law. The Constitution (41st Amendment) Bill provided that the President, Prime Minister and state Governors should be immune from criminal prosecution for life and from civil prosecution during their term of office.

In November 1976 a 59-clause Constitution (42nd Amendment) Bill was approved by Parliament and came into force in January 1977. Some of the provisions of the Bill are that the Indian Democratic Republic shall be named a "Democratic Secular and Socialist Republic";

that the President "shall act in accordance with" the advice given to him by the Prime Minister and Cabinet, and, acting at the Prime Minister's direction, shall be empowered for two years to amend the Constitution by executive order, in any way beneficial to the enforcement of the whole; that the term of the Lok Sabha and of the State Assemblies shall be extended from five to six years; that there shall be no limitation on the constituent power of Parliament to amend the Constitution, and that India's Supreme Court shall be barred from hearing petitions challenging Constitutional amendments; that strikes shall be forbidden in the public services and the Union Government have the power to deploy police or other forces under its own superintendence and control in any state. Directive Principles are given precedence over Fundamental Rights: ten basic duties of citizens are listed, including the duty to "defend the country and render national service when called upon to do so".

The Janata Party Government, which came into power in March 1977, promised to amend the Constitution during the year, so as to "restore the balance between the people and Parliament, Parliament and the judiciary, the judiciary and the executive, the states and the centre, and the citizen and the Government that the founding fathers of the Constitution had worked out". The Constitution (43rd Amendment) Bill, passed by Parliament in December 1977, the Constitution (44th Amendment) Bill, passed by Parliament in December 1977 and later redesignated the 43rd Amendment, and the Constitution (45th Amendment) Bill, passed by Parliament in December 1978 and later redesignated the 44th Amendment, reversed most of the changes enacted by the Constitution (42nd Amendment) Bill. The 44th Amendment is particularly detailed on emergency provisions: An emergency may not be proclaimed unless "the security of India or any part of its territory was threatened by war or external aggression or by armed rebellion." Its introduction must be approved by a two-thirds majority of Parliament within a month, and after six months the emergency may be continued only with the approval of Parliament. Among the provisions left unchanged after these Bills were a section subordinating Fundamental Rights to Directive Principles and a clause empowering the central Government to deploy armed forces under its control in any state without the state government's consent. In May 1980 the Indian Supreme Court repealed sections 4 and 55 of the 42nd Amendment Act, thus curtailing Parliament's power to enforce directive principles and to amend the Constitution. The death penalty was declared constitutionally valid.

The Panchayat Raj scheme is designed to decentralize the powers of the Union and state Governments. This scheme is based on the Panchayat (Village Council) and the Gram Sabha (Village Parliament) and envisages the gradual transference of local government from state to local authority. Revenue and internal security will remain state responsibilities at present. By 1978 the scheme had been introduced in all the states except Meghalaya, Nagaland and 23 out of 31 districts in Bihar. The Panchayat existed in all the Union Territories except Lakshadweep, Mizoram and Pondicherry.

THE GOVERNMENT

President: Giani Zail Singh (sworn in July 25th, 1982).

Vice-President: Mohammad Hidayatullah.

THE COUNCIL OF MINISTERS

(July 1982)

Prime Minister and Minister of Atomic Energy, Science and Technology and Space: Indira Gandhi.

Minister of Defence: Ramaswami Venkataraman.

Minister of Home Affairs: (vacant; temporarily under Ministry of Defence).

Minister of Finance: Pranab Kumar Mukherjee.

Minister of External Affairs: P. V. Narsimha Rao.

Minister of Railways: P. C. Sethi.

Minister of Planning: S. Rao B. Chavan.

Minister of Energy: A. B. A. Ghani Khan Chaudhuri.

Minister of Health and Family Welfare: B. Shankaranand.

Minister of Information and Broadcasting: Vasanth Sathe.

Minister of Communications: C. M. Stephen.

Minister of Law, Justice and Company Affairs: Jagannath Kaushal.

Minister of Shipping and Transport: Virendra Patil.

Minister of Agriculture and Rural Reconstruction: Rao Birendra Singh.

Minister of Tourism and Civil Aviation: A. P. Sharma.

Minister of Industry, Steel and Mines: Narain Dutt Tiwari.

Minister of Parliamentary Affairs, Works and Housing: Bhisham Narain Singh.

Minister of Petroleum, Chemicals and Fertilizers: P. Shiv Shankar.

Minister of Irrigation: Kedar Pandey.

There are also twenty-one State Ministers and fifteen Deputy Ministers.

LEGISLATURE

PARLIAMENT

RAJYA SABHA
(Council of States)

Chairman: MOHAMMAD HIDAYATULLAH.

(April 1982)

PARTY	SEATS
Congress (I)	120
Congress (S)	5
Janata	15
Bharatiya Janata Party	14
Communist (CPM-Marxist)	15
Lok Dal	14
All-India Anna Dravida Munnetra Kazhagam (ADMK)	9
Communist (CPI)	5
Dravida Munnetra Kazhagam (DMK)	4
Akali Dal	3
Independents	8
Nominated	8
Others	14
Vacant	10
TOTAL	244

LOK SABHA
(House of the People)

Speaker: BAL RAM JAKHAR.

(June 1982)

PARTY	SEATS
Congress (I)	356
Communist (CPM-Marxist)	36
Lok Dal	32
Dravida Munnetra Kazhagam (DMK)	16
Bharatiya Janata Party	17
Janata	12
Communist (CPI)	12
Democratic Socialist Party	12
Congress (S)	4
Revolutionary Socialist Party	4
Forward Bloc	3
Muslim League	3
Independents and others	24
Vacant	12
Speaker	1
TOTAL	544

STATE GOVERNMENTS

(June 1982)

ANDHRA PRADESH
(Capital—Hyderabad)

Governor: K. C. ABRAHAM.
Chief Minister: B. VENKATARAMA REDDY (Congress—I).
Legislative Assembly: 294 seats (Congress—I 248, Lok Dal 9, Communist-CPM 8, Janata 7, Communist-CPI 6, Bharatiya Janata Party 3, Congress—S 3, independents and others 10).
Legislative Council: 90 seats.

ASSAM
(Capital—Dispur)

Governor: PRAKASH CHANDRA MEHROTRA.
Chief Minister: KESHAV CHANDRA GOGOI (Congress—I).
Legislative Assembly: dissolved; under President's rule since March 17th, 1982.

BIHAR
(Capital—Patna)

Governor: A. R. KIDWAI.
Chief Minister: Dr. JAGANNATH MISHRA (Congress—I).
Legislative Assembly: 324 seats (Congress—I 191, Lok Dal 42, Communist-CPI 23, Bharatiya Janata Party 19, Congress—S 12, Janata 11, Communist-CPM 6, independents and others 20).
Legislative Council: 90 seats.

GUJARAT
(Capital—Gandhinagar)

Governor: Mrs. SHARDA MUKHERJEE.
Chief Minister: Justice M. P. THAKKAR (Congress—I).
Legislative Assembly: 182 seats (Congress—I 140, Janata 21, Bharatiya Janata Party 11, Lok Dal 1, independents 9).

HARYANA
(Capital—Chandigarh)

Governor: G. D. TAPASE.
Chief Minister: BHAJAN LAL (Congress—I).
Legislative Assembly: 90 seats (Congress—I 36, Haryana Janata Secular (Lok Dal) 31, Bharatiya Janata Party 6, others and independents 16, vacant 1).

HIMACHAL PRADESH
(Capital—Simla)

Governor: A. N. BANERJEE.
Chief Minister: RAM LAL (Congress—I).
Legislative Assembly: 68 seats (Congress—I 32, Bharatiya Janata Party 29, Lok Dal 1, Janata 2, Communist-CPM 1, independents 5, vacant 2).

JAMMU AND KASHMIR
(Capitals—Srinagar (Summer), Jammu (Winter))

Governor: B. K. NEHRU.
Chief Minister: Sheikh MOHAMMED ABDULLAH (Jammu and Kashmir National Conference Party).
Legislative Assembly: 76 seats (National Conference Party 50, Congress—I 7, Janata 11, Congress—S 1, Janata (S) 2, independents and others 5).
Legislative Council: 36 seats.

KARNATAKA
(Capital—Bangalore)

Governor: GOVIND NARAIN.
Chief Minister: R. GUNDU RAO (Congress—I).

Legislative Assembly: 224 seats (Congress—I 154, Congress—S 35, Janata 28, independents and others 7).
Legislative Council: 63 seats.

KERALA
(Capital—Trivandrum)

Governor: Mrs. JYOTI VENKATACHALAM.
Chief Minister: K. KARUNAKARAN (Congress—I).
Legislative Assembly: 140 seats (Communist-CPM) 26, Communist-CPI 12, Congress—I 19, Congress-S (Antony Group) 15, Indian Union Muslim League 14, Kerala Congress (Mani Group) 9, Kerala Congress (Joseph Group) 8, Congress—S 7, All-India Muslim League 5, Janata 5, Revolutionary Socialist Party 5, Independents and others 12).

MADHYA PRADESH
(Capital—Bhopal)

Governor: BHAGWAT DAYAL SHARMA.
Chief Minister: ARJUN SINGH (Congress—I).
Legislative Assembly: 320 seats (Congress—I 246, Bharatiya Janata Party 61, Janata 2, Communist-CPI 2, independents and others 9).
Legislative Council: 90 seats.

MAHARASHTRA
(Capital—Bombay)

Governor: IDRIS HASAN LATIF.
Chief Minister: BABA SAHEB ANANTRAO BHONSLE (Congress—I).
Legislative Assembly: 288 seats (Congress—I 229, Congress—S 17, Janata 17, Bharatiya Janata Party 14, independents and others 11).
Legislative Council: 78 seats.

MANIPUR
(Capital—Imphal)

Governor: S. M. H. BURNEY.
Chief Minister: RISHANG KEISHING (Congress—I).
Legislative Assembly: 60 seats (Congress—I 42, People's Democratic Front and Peoples Legislative Party 18).

MEGHALAYA
(Capital—Shillong)

Governor: PRAKASH CHANDRA MEHROTRA.
Chief Minister: Capt. WILLIAMSON SANGMA (All Party Hill Leaders Conference).
Legislative Assembly: 60 seats (All Party Hill Leaders Conference (Lyngdoh Group) 14, State Hill People's Democratic Party 14, All Party Hill Leaders Conference (Pugh Group) 9, Congress—I 18, others 3, vacant 2).

NAGALAND
(Capital—Kohima)

Governor: S. M. H. BURNEY.
Chief Minister: J. B. JASOKIE (Naga National Democratic Party).
Legislative Assembly: 60 seats (Naga National Democratic Party 32, Congress—I 27, others 1).

ORISSA
(Capital—Bhubaneswar)

Governor: C. M. POONACHA.
Chief Minister: JANAKI BALLABH PATNAIK (Congress—I).
Legislative Assembly: 147 seats (Congress—I 121, Lok Dal 12, Communist-CPI 4, Janata 3, Congress—S 2, independents and others 5).

PUNJAB
(Capital—Chandigarh)

Governor: Dr. M. CHENNA REDDY.
Chief Minister: DARBARA SINGH (Congress—I).
Legislative Assembly: 117 seats (Congress—I 64, Akali 38, Communist-CPI 9, Communist-CPM 5, independents 2, Bharatiya Janata Party 1).

RAJASTHAN
(Capital—Jaipur)

Governor: O. P. MEHRA.
Chief Minister: SHIV CHARAN MATHUR (Congress—I).
Legislative Assembly: 200 seats (Congress—I 137, Bharatiya Janata Party 32, Janata 8, Lok Dal 7, Congress—S 3, Communist-CPI 1, Communist-CPM 1, independents and others 11).

SIKKIM
(Capital—Gangtok)

Governor: HOMI J. H. TALYARKHAN.
Chief Minister: N. S. BHANDARI (Congress—I).
Legislative Assembly: 32 seats (Congress—I 21, Revolutionary Congress 8, others 3).

TAMIL NADU
(Capital—Madras)

Governor: SADIQ ALI.
Chief Minister: M. G. RAMACHANDRAN (ADMK).
Legislative Assembly: 234 seats (ADMK 131, DMK 35, Congress—I 30, Communist-CPM 11, Communist-CPI 10, Gandhi-Kamaraj National Congress 6, Forward Bloc 3, Janata, independents and others 8).
Legislative Council: 63 seats.

TRIPURA
(Capital—Agartala)

Governor: S. M. H. BURNEY.
Chief Minister: NRIPEN CHAKRABARTY (Communist-CPM).
Legislative Assembly: 60 seats (Communist—CPM 52, independent 1, others 7).

UTTAR PRADESH
(Capital—Lucknow)

Governor: (vacant).
Chief Minister: SHRIPATI SINGH (Congress—I).
Legislative Assembly: 425 seats (Congress—I 316, Lok Dal 53, Congress—S 13, Bharatiya Janata Party 11, Janata 5, Communist-CPI 7, independents and others 20).
Legislative Council: 108 seats.

WEST BENGAL
(Capital—Calcutta)

Governor: BHAIRAB DUTT PANDEY.
Chief Minister: JYOTI BASU (Communist-CPM).
Legislative Assembly: 294 seats (Communist-CPM 174, Congress—I 49, Forward Bloc 28, Revolutionary Socialist 19, Communist CPI 7, others 17).

UNION TERRITORIES

Andaman and Nicobar Islands (Headquarters—Port Blair): *Chief Commissioner:* S. M. KRISHNATRY.
Arunachal Pradesh—(Capital Itanagar): *Lieut.-Governor:* H. S. DUBEY.
Chief Minister: GAGONG APANG (Congress—I).
Assembly: 30 seats (Congress—I 13, People's Party of Arunachal 13, independent 4).
Chandigarh (Headquarters—Chandigarh): *Chief Commissioner:* KRISHNA BANARJY.
Dadra and Nagar Haveli (Headquarters—Silvassa): *Administrator:* Col. PARTAP SINGH GILL.
Delhi (Headquarters—Delhi): *Lieut.-Governor:* S. L. KHURANA.
etropolitan Council: 56 seats.

Goa, Daman and Diu (Capital—Panaji): *Lieut.-Governor:* JAGMOHAN.
Chief Minister: PRATAP SINGH RANE (Congress—S).
Assembly: 30 seats (Congress 27, Maharashtrawadi Gomantak Party 2, independents 1).

Lakshadweep (Headquarters—Kavaratti): *Administrator:* P M. NAIR.

Mizoram (Headquarters—Aizawl): *Lieut.-Governor:* S. N. KOHLI.
Chief Minister: THENPHUNGA SAILO (People's Conference Party).
Assembly: 30 seats (People's Conference 21, Mizoram Congress Group 7, others 2.)

Pondicherry (Capital—Pondicherry): *Lieut.-Governor:* KIZHEKETHIL MATHEW CHANDY.
Chief Minister: D. RAMACHANDRAN (DMK).
Assembly: 30 seats (DMK 15, Congress—I 10, Janata 3, others 2).

POLITICAL PARTIES

In 1907 Congress was split in two—the Extremists and the Moderates. In 1969 Congress again split into two distinct organizations, with Indira Gandhi's Government continuing in office while the Indian National Congress (Organization) became India's first recognized opposition party. A further split occurred in January 1978, when Mrs. Gandhi formed a breakaway group. In July 1981 a Supreme Court ruling confirmed Congress (I) as the official Congress party.

Indian National Congress (I): 24 Akbar Rd., New Delhi 110011; f. 1978 when Mrs. Gandhi formed a breakaway group; Pres. INDIRA GANDHI; Gen. Secs. G. KARUPPIAH MOORPANAR, CHANDULAL CHANDRAKAR, Dr. RAJENDRA KUMARI BAJPAL, M. SATYANARAYANA RAO, VASANTDADA PATIL.

Indian National Congress (S): 3 Raisina Rd., New Delhi 110001; f. 1885. Aims: the well-being and advancement of the people and the establishment by peaceful means of a socialist, co-operative Commonwealth based on equality of opportunity and rights, aiming at world peace; the provision of basic needs and opportunities for culture; full employment; Government control of large-scale industries and services; co-operative industry and agriculture; a neutral foreign policy; Pres. SHARAD PAWAR.

The five other principal parties are:

Janata Party: 7 Jantar Mantar Rd., New Delhi 110001; f. May 1st, 1977, by the official merger of the Indian National Congress (Organization), the Bharatiya Lok Dal (BLD), the Bharatiya Jana Sangh (People's Party of India) and the Socialist Party, who had combined as the Janata Party to fight the general election of March 1977; Congress for Democracy, a party formed in February 1977 by Jagjivan Ram, merged into the Janata Party in May 1977; aims to achieve by democratic and peaceful means a socialist society, free from social, political and economic exploitation of individual by individual and nation by nation; Leaders MADHU DANDAVATE (Parliament), PILOO MODY (Rajya Sabha); Pres. CHANDRA SHEKHAR; Gen. Secs. RAVINDRA VARMA, RAMAKRISHNA HEGDE, SYED SHAHABUDDIN, Dr. BAPU KALDATE, Dr. SAROJINI MAHISHI; 3 million mems.; publ. *Janata Bulletin* (English and Hindi).

Lok Dal: 15 Windsor Place, New Delhi 110001; f. 1979 by merger of a splinter group from the Janata Party with a socialist group and others; advocates secularism, the primacy of agriculture and small industry; Pres. CHARAN SINGH; Gen. Sec. RABI RAY (Acting); 5 million mems.; publ. *Lok Dal Bulletin* (fortnightly, English and Hindi).

The Communist Party of India (CPI): Ajoy Bhavan, Kotla Marg, New Delhi 110002; f. 1925; aims: the establishment of a socialist society led by the working class, and ultimately of a communist society; Leaders INDRAJIT GUPTA, YOGENDRA SHARMA; Sec.-Gen. C. RAJENSWARA RAO; mems.: 466,483 (1981); publs. *New Age* (weekly) and 82 Jourals.

Communist Party of India (CPM-Marxist) 14 Ashoka Rd., New Delhi 110001; f. 1964 as pro-Beijing breakaway group of CPI; the Party declared its independence of Beijing in 1968 and is managed by a politbureau of ten members; Leaders SAMAR MUKHERJEE, P. RAMAMURTI; Gen. Sec. E. M. SANKARAN NAMBOODIRIPAD; 267,200 mems.; publs. *People's Democracy* (weekly), *Lok Lahar* (weekly, Hindi and Urdu) and several language publs.

Bharatiya Janata Party: 11 Ashok Rd., New Delhi 110001; f. 1979; breakaway group from main Janata Party after the Janata executive agreed to ban dual membership of Janata and the Rashtriya Swayam Sewak Sangh, an extremist body; based on right-wing Hindu Jana Sangh party; Pres. ATAL BEHARI VAJPAYEE; Gen. Secs. LALKRISHNA ADVANI, SIKANDER BAKHT, YAGYA DUTT SHARMA, JANA KRISHNA MOORTHY.

Akhil Bharat Hindu Mahasabha: Hindu Mahasabha Bhavan, Mandir Marg, New Delhi 110001; aims: to establish a democratic Hindu state; Pres. VIKRAM SAVARKAR; Gen. Sec. GOPAL GODSE; mems.: 100,000; publ. *Hindu Sabha Varta* (weekly).

All-India Anna Dravida Munnetra Kazhagam (ADMK): 160 Lloyds Rd., Madras 600004; f. 1972; splinter group of the DMK; Leader M. G. RAMACHANDRAN.

All India Forward Bloc: 128 North Ave., New Delhi 110001; f. 1940 by Netaji Subhash Chandra Bose; socialistic principles, including nationalization of key industries, land reform and redistribution; advocates right to work and full employment, education for all, fixation of prices, rapid development of villages, etc.; Chair. P. D. PALIWAL; Gen. Sec. CHITTA BASU.

Communist Bolshevik Party: f. 1978; Leaders K. P. R. GOPALAN, A. V. ERIAN, VARU VISHWAN.

Congress (J): 6 Krishna Menon Marg, New Delhi 110011; f. 1981 as a breakaway group from the main Congress party; Pres. JAGJIVAN RAM.

Dravida Munnetra Kazhagam (DMK): Arivagam, Royapuram, Madras 600013; f. 1949; aims at full state autonomy for Tamil Nadu within the Union, to establish regional languages as State languages and English as the official language; Pres. Dr. M. KARUNANDHI; Gen. Sec. K. ANBUZHAN; mems.: over 1,600,000.

Peasants' and Workers' Party of India: Mahatma Phule Rd., Naigaum, Bombay 400014; aims to establish a People's Democracy, to nationalize all basic industries, to promote industrialization, and establish a unitary state with provincial boundaries drawn on linguistic basis; Marxist; Gen. Sec. DAJIBA DESAI; mems.: about 10,000.

Republican Party of India: Azad Maidan, Fort, Bombay 400001, Maharashtra; main aim is to realize the aims and objects set out in the preamble to the Indian Constitution; Pres. R. S. GAVAI; Gen. Sec. N. H. KUMBHARE.

Shiromani Akali dal: Amristar; Sikh party; campaigns against Government interference in Sikh affairs and for greater power to individual states and allocation of heavy industry to Amristar; Pres. HARCHAND SINGH LONGOWAL; Gen. Secs. PARKASH SINGH MAJITHIA, SUKHJINDER SINGH, RAJINDER SINFH.

DIPLOMATIC REPRESENTATION

EMBASSIES AND HIGH COMMISSIONS ACCREDITED TO INDIA

(E) Embassy.

Afghanistan: B-54, Greater Kailash, Part I, New Delhi 110048 (E); *Ambassador:* Dr. MOHAMMAD HASSAN SHARQ.

Algeria: 13 Sunder Nagar, New Delhi 110003 (E); *Chargé d'affaires:* BENGHEZAL ALI.

Argentina: B-8/9 Vasant Vihar, Paschimi Marg, New Delhi 110057 (E); *Ambassador:* FERNANDO MARÍA FERNANDEZ ESCALANTE.

Australia: No. 1/50-G Shantipath, Chanakyapuri, New Delhi 110021; *High Commissioner:* G. N. UPTON.

Austria: EP/13 Chandragupta Marg, New Delhi 110021 (E); *Ambassador:* Dr. GEORG HENNIG.

Bangladesh: 56 Ring Rd., Lajpatnagar, New Delhi 110024; *High Commissioner:* A. K. KHANDAKAR.

Belgium: 7 Golf Links, New Delhi 110003 (E); *Ambassador:* J. HOLLANDS VAN LOOCKE.

Bhutan: Chandragupta Marg, Chanakyapuri, New Delhi 110021 (E); *Ambassador:* TASHI TOBGYAL.

Brazil: 8 Aurangzeb Rd., New Delhi 110011 (E); *Ambassador:* ROBERTO LUIZ ASSUMPÇÃO DE ARAÚJO.

Bulgaria: 16/17 Chandragupta Marg, Chanakyapuri, New Delhi 110021 (E); *Ambassador:* TOCHO KIRYAKOV TOCHEV.

Burma: Burma House, 3/50-F Nyaya Marg, Chanakyapuri, New Delhi 110021 (E); *Ambassador:* U KO KO LAY.

Canada: 7/8 Shanti Path, Chanakyapuri, New Delhi 110021; *High Commissioner:* JOHN G. HADWEN.

Chile: 1/13 Shantiniketan, New Delhi 110021 (E); *Ambassador:* TOMÁS VÁSQUEZ-FLORES.

China, People's Republic: 50-D Shanti Path, Chanakyapuri, New Delhi 110021 (E); *Ambassador:* SHEN JIANG.

Colombia: 82D Malcha Marg, Chanakyapuri, New Delhi 110021 (E); *Ambassador:* Dr. NELLY TURBAY DE MUÑOZ.

Cuba: D-5 South Extension, Part II, New Delhi 110049 (E); *Ambassador:* JOSÉ PÉREZ NOVOA.

Cyprus: 52 Jor Bagh, New Delhi, 110003; *High Commissioner:* ANDROS A. NICOLAIDES.

Czechoslovakia: 50-M Niti Marg, Chanakyapuri, New Delhi 110021 (E); *Ambassador:* PAVEL KANKA.

Denmark: 2 Golf Links, New Delhi 110003 (E); *Ambassador:* BJØRN HARRY OLSEN.

Egypt: 55–57 Sunder Nagar, New Delhi 110003 (E); *Ambassador:* NABIL E. ELARABY.

Ethiopia: 7/50-G, Satya Marg, Chanakyapuri, New Delhi 110021 (E); *Ambassador:* Brig.-Gen. AMDEMIKAEL BELACHEW.

Finland: 25 Golf Links, New Delhi 110003 (E); *Ambassador:* RISTO HYVÄRINEN.

France: 2 Aurangzeb Rd., New Delhi 110011 (E); *Ambassador:* ANDRÉ ROSS.

Gabon: Paris, France (E).

German Democratic Republic: 2 Nyaya Marg, Chanakyapuri, New Delhi 110021 (E); *Ambassador:* HEINZ BIRCH.

Germany, Federal Republic: 6 Block 50G, Shanti Path, Chanakyapuri, New Delhi 110021 (E); *Ambassador:* ROLF RAMISCH.

Ghana: A-42 Vasant Marg, Vasant Vihar, New Delhi 110057; *High Commissioner:* SILVESTER KWADA ANKAMA.

Greece: 16 Sundar Nagar, New Delhi 110003 (E); *Ambassador:* JOHN N. SOSSIDIS.

Guyana: 85 Poorvi Marg, Vasant Vihar, New Delhi 110057; *High Commissioner:* E. V. LUCKHOO.

Hungary: Plot 2, Block No. 50-M, Niti Marg, Chanakyapuri, New Delhi 110021 (E); *Ambassador:* Dr. FERENC TURI.

Indonesia: 50A Chanakyapuri, New Delhi 110021 (E); *Ambassador:* R. S. SASRAPRAWIRA.

Iran: 5 Bapakhamba Road, New Delhi 110001 (E); *Ambassador:* HASSAN ASSADI LASI.

Iraq: 169–171 Jor Bagh, New Delhi 110003 (E); *Ambassador:* ADNAN JAMIL MOHAMMAD AL-OBAIDI.

Ireland: 13 Jor Bagh, New Delhi 110003 (E); *Ambassador:* BERNARD MCHUGH.

Italy: 13 Golf Links, New Delhi 110003 (E); *Ambassador:* Dr. EMILIO PAOLO BASSI.

Japan: Plot Nos. 4 and 5, Block 50G, Shanti Path, Chanakyapuri, New Delhi 110021 (E); *Ambassador:* EIKICHI HARA.

Jordan: 35 Malcha Marg, Chanakyapuri, New Delhi 110021 (E); *Ambassador:* W. AL-DUAHRRA.

Kampuchea: C4/4, Paschimi Marg, Vasant Vihar, New Delhi 110057 (E); *Ambassador:* DITH MUNTY.

Kenya: 66 Vasant Marg, Vasant Vihar, New Delhi 110057; *High Commissioner:* P. G. GITONGA.

Korea, Democratic People's Republic: 42/44 Sundar Nagar, New Delhi 110003 (E); *Ambassador:* RYU TAE-SOP.

Korea, Republic: 9 Chandragupta Marg, Chanakyapuri, New Delhi 110021 (E); *Ambassador:* CHUNG-TAI KIM.

Kuwait: 5A Shanti Path, Chanakyapuri, New Delhi 110021 (E); *Ambassador:* ESSA A. REHMAN AL-ESSA.

Laos: 20 Jor Bagh, New Delhi 110003 (E); *Ambassador:* Dr. KITHONG VONGSAY.

Lebanon: 10 Sardar Patel Marg, Chanakyapuri, New Delhi 110021 (E); *Ambassador:* RABIA HAIDAR.

Liberia: Tokyo, Japan (E).

Libya: 22 Golf Links, New Delhi 110003; *Secretary of People's Bureau:* MUKHTAR AL-MESHIRI (acting).

Malaysia: 50-M Satya Marg, Chanakyapuri, New Delhi 110021; *High Commissioner:* RAZALI BIN ISMAIL.

Maldives: New Delhi (E); *Ambassador:* MOHAMED MUSTHAFA HUSSAIN.

Mauritius: 5 Kautilya Marg, Chanakyapuri, New Delhi 110021; *High Commissioner:* RAJMOHUNSING JODAMAR.

Mexico: N-88 Panchshila Park, New Delhi 110017 (E); *Ambassador:* GRACIELA DE LA LAMA.

Mongolia: 34 Golf Links, New Delhi 110003 (E); *Ambassador:* BAYARYN JARGALSAIKHAN.

Morocco: 33 Golf Links, New Delhi 110003 (E); *Chargé d'affaires a.i.:* ABDEL KHALEK IBN IBRAHIM.

Nepal: Barakhamba Rd., New Delhi 110001 (E); *Ambassador:* VEDANAND JHA.

Netherlands: 6/50 F, Shanti Path, Chanakyapuri, New Delhi 110021 (E); *Ambassador:* HENDRICUS LEOPOLD.

New Zealand: 39 Golf Links, New Delhi 110003; *High Commissioner:* B. H. BROOKS.

Nigeria: 21 Palam Marg, Vasant Vihar, New Delhi 110057; *High Commissioner:* THEOPHILUS OLADEGA ASIWAJU DAOA.

Norway: Kautilya Marg, Chanakyapuri, New Delhi 110021 (E); *Ambassador:* TANCRED IBSEN.

Oman: 16 Palam Marg, New Delhi 110057 (E); *Ambassador:* AHMED HAMOUD AL-MAAMIRY.

Pakistan: 2/50 G, Shanti Path, Chanakyapuri, New Delhi 110021 (E); *Ambassador:* RYAZ PIRACHA.

Panama: S-260, Greater Kailash, Part II, New Delhi 110048 (E); *Ambassador:* IRMA RILTER.

Paraguay: Tokyo, Japan (E).

Peru: 3/5 Shanti Niketan, New Delhi 110021 (E); *Ambassador:* JUAN VARGAS QUINTANILLABONDY.

Philippines: 50-N Nyaya Marg, Chanakyapuri, New Delhi 110021 (E); *Ambassador:* ROMEO S. BUSUEGO.

Poland: Shanti Path, Chanakyapuri, New Delhi 110021 (E); *Ambassador:* RYSZARD FIJALKOWSKI.

Portugal: A-24 West End Colony, New Delhi 110021 (E); *Ambassador:* ANTÓNIO MANUEL DA VIEGO EMENEZES CORDEIRO.

Qatar: A-3 West End Colony, New Delhi 110021 (E); *Ambassador:* (vacant).

Romania: 9 Tees January Marg, New Delhi 110011 (E); *Ambassador:* Dr. DUMITRU NICULESCU.

Saudi Arabia: 1 Ring Road, Kilokri, New Delhi 110014 (E); *Chargé d'affaires:* MOHAMED A. AL-GHAMDI.

Singapore: B-70, Greater Kailash, Part I, New Delhi 110048; *High Commissioner:* Haji YA'ACOB BIN MOHAMED.

Somalia: B-23, Greater Kailash, Part I, New Delhi 110048 (E); *Ambassador:* ABDULLAHI EGAL NOOR.

Spain: 12 Prithviraj Rd., New Delhi 110011 (E); *Ambassador:* ENRIQUE MAHOU STAUFFER.

Sri Lanka: 27 Kautilya Marg, Chanakyapuri, New Delhi 110021; *High Commissioner:* (vacant).

Sudan: 6 Jor Bagh, New Delhi 110003 (E); *Ambassador:* IBRAHIM TAHA AYOUB.

Sweden: Nyaya Marg, Chanakyapuri, New Delhi 110021 (E); *Ambassador:* LENNART FINNMARK.

Switzerland: Nyaya Marg, Chanakyapuri, New Delhi 110021 (E); *Ambassador:* PETER S. ERNI.

Syria: 28 Vasant Marg, Vasant Vihar, New Delhi 110057 (E); *Ambassador:* MOHAMMAD KHODAR.

Tanzania: 27 Golf Links, New Delhi 110003; *High Commissioner:* MUHAMMAD ALI FOUM.

Thailand: 56-N Nyaya Marg, Chanakyapuri, New Delhi 110021 (E); *Ambassador:* SUMESR SIRIMONGKOL.

Trinidad and Tobago: 131 Jor Bagh, New Delhi 110003; *High Commissioner:* NATHAN HAZEL.

Tunisia: B 9/22, Vasant Vihar, New Delhi 110057 (E); *Ambassador:* ABDERRAOUF OUNAIES.

Turkey: N-50, Chanakyapuri, New Delhi 110021 (E); *Ambassador:* ALI HIKMET ALP.

Uganda: 19A Rajdoot Marg, New Delhi 110021; *High Commissioner:* GURDIAL SINGH.

U.S.S.R.: Shanti Path, Chanakyapuri, New Delhi 110021 (E); *Ambassador:* YULI MIKHAYLOVICH VORONTSOV.

United Arab Emirates: A-7 West End, New Delhi 110021 (E); *Ambassador:* ABDUL AZIZ BIN NASSER AL-OWEIS.

United Kingdom: Shanti Path, Chanakyapuri, New Delhi 110021; *High Commissioner:* ROBERT WADE-GERY, C.M.G.

U.S.A.: Shanti Path, Chanakyapuri, New Delhi 110021 (E); *Ambassador:* HARRY C. BARNES.

Uruguay: Tokyo, Japan (E).

Vatican: 50-C Niti Marg, Chanakyapuri (Apostolic Nunciature), New Delhi 110021; *Pro-Nuncio:* Most Rev. AGOSTINO CACCIAVILLAN.

Venezuela: N-114 Panchshila Park, New Delhi 110017 (E); *Ambassador:* Dr. EDUARDO SOTO ALVAREZ.

Viet-Nam: 35 Prithviraj Rd., New Delhi 110011 (E); *Ambassador:* NGUYEN QUANG TAO.

Yemen Arab Republic: B-55, Paschimi Marg, Vasant Vihar, New Delhi 110057 (E); *Ambassador:* AHMED MOHAMMAD HAIDER.

Yemen, People's Democratic Republic: 29 Mahatma Gandhi Marg (Ring Rd.), Lajpat Nagar IV, New Delhi 110024 (E); *Ambassador:* TAHA AHMED GHANIM.

Yugoslavia: 3/50G, Niti Marg, Chanakyapuri, New Delhi 110021 (E); *Ambassador:* DANILO BILANCOVIĆ.

Zaire: 160 Jor Bagh, New Delhi 110003 (E); *Ambassador:* BOKINGI EMBEYOLO.

Zambia: 14 Jor Bagh, New Delhi 110003; *High Commissioner:* A. C. CHALIKULIMA.

Bolivia, Costa Rica, the Dominican Republic, Ecuador, El Salvador, Haiti, Honduras, Iceland, Israel, Monaco, Nauru, Nicaragua, San Marino and Upper Volta are represented by Consuls-General.

India also has diplomatic relations with Albania, Angola, the Bahamas, Barbados, Benin, Burundi, Cameroon, Cape Verde, Chad, the Comoros, the Congo, Djibouti, Fiji, The Gambia, Grenada, Guatemala, Guinea, Guinea-Bissau, the Ivory Coast, Jamaica, Lesotho, Luxembourg, Madagascar, Malawi, Mali, Malta, Mauritania, Mozambique, Niger, Papua New Guinea, Rwanda, Saint Lucia, Senegal, Seychelles, Sierra Leone, Suriname, Swaziland, Togo, Tonga, Vanuatu, Western Samoa and Zimbabwe.

JUDICIAL SYSTEM

THE SUPREME COURT

The Supreme Court, consisting of a Chief Justice and not more than 17 judges appointed by the President, exercises exclusive jurisdiction in any dispute between the Union and the states (although there are certain restrictions where an acceding state is involved). It has appellate jurisdiction over any judgment, decree or order of the High Court where that Court certifies that either a substantial question of law or the interpretation of the Constitution is involved.

Provision is made for the appointment by the Chief Justice of India of judges of High Courts as ad hoc judges at sittings of the Supreme Court for specified periods, and for the attendance of retired judges at sittings of the Supreme Court. The Supreme Court has advisory jurisdiction in respect of questions which may be referred to it by the President for opinion. The Supreme Court is also empowered to hear appeals against a sentence of death passed by a State High Court in reversal of an order of acquittal by a lower court, and in a case in which a High Court has granted a certificate of fitness.

The Supreme Court also hears appeals which are certified

by High Courts to be fit for appeal, subject to rules made by the Court. Parliament may, by law, confer on the Supreme Court any further powers of appeal.

Chief Justice of India: The Hon. YESHWANT VISHNU CHANDRACHUD.

Judges of the Supreme Court: Hons. P. N. BHAGWATI, S. MURTAZA FAZAL ALI, V. D. TULZAPURKAR, D. A. DESAI, R. S. PATHAK, O. CHINNAPPA REDDY, A. P. SEN, E. S. VENKATARAMIAH, APPAJEE VARDARAJAN, BAHARUL ISLAM, AMARENDRA NATH SEN, V. BALAKRISHNA ERADI, RAMBRIKSH MISRA.

Attorney-General: L. N. SINHA.

Solicitor-General: K. PARASARN.

HIGH COURTS

The High Courts are the Courts of Appeal from the lower courts, and their decisions are final except in cases where appeal lies to the Supreme Court.

LOWER COURTS

Provision is made in the Code of Criminal Procedure for the constitution of lower criminal courts called Courts of Session and Courts of Magistrates. The Courts of Session are competent to try all persons duly committed for trial, and inflict any punishment authorized by the law. The President and the local government concerned exercise the prerogative of mercy.

The constitution of inferior civil courts is determined by regulations within each state.

RELIGION

INDIAN FAITHS

Buddhism: The Buddhists in Ladakh (Jammu and Kashmir) owe allegiance to the Dalai Lama. Head Lama of Ladakh: KAUSHAK SAKULA, Dalgate, Srinagar, Kashmir. In 1971 there were 3.81 million Buddhists in India (0.70 per cent of the population).

Hinduism: According to the 1971 census, Hindus form 82.72 per cent of the population (453.3 million).

Islam: Muslims are divided into two main sects, Shi'as and Sunnis. Most of the Indian Muslims are Sunnis. In 1979 the Muslim population numbered 80 million.

Jainism: 2.6 million adherents (1971 census), 0.48 per cent of the population.

Sikhism: According to the 1971 census, there were 10.3 million Sikhs in India (1.89 per cent of the population), the majority living in the Punjab.

Zoorastrians: More than 120,000 Parsis practise the Zoroastrian religion.

CHRISTIAN CHURCHES

In 1971 there were 14.2 million Christians in India, of whom more than half were Roman Catholics, the others being members of the ancient Syrian and the Protestant churches.

THE ROMAN CATHOLIC CHURCH

Apostolic Pro-Nuncio to India: *See* Diplomatic Representation.

The Church has 16 archdioceses, 70 suffragan dioceses (including 7 eparchies of Syro-Malabar Rite) and 2 apostolic prefectures for Catholics of the Latin Rite. There are 3 archdioceses, 11 suffragan bishoprics and 7 eparchies for the Oriental Rite. Total number of Roman Catholics: 9,704,000.

PROTESTANT

Church of North India: Moderator Rt. Rev. Dr. R. S. BHANDARA, Cathedral House, Nagpur 440001.

The Church has 22 dioceses with 22 Bishops and Diocesan Councils, elected by the diocese and synod. Total membership of CNI: 700,500. Office of General Secretary: "Wesley Lodge", 16 Pandit Pant Marg, New Delhi 110001; publs. *Communicate* (fortnightly), *North India Churchman* (monthly).

Church of South India: Moderator Most Rev. Dr. SOLOMON DORAISAWMY, B.A., L.T., B.D.; 8 Racquet Court Lane, P.O.B. 31, Tiruchirapalli 620001.

There is a total congregation of about 1,530,000; publ. *The South India Churchman.*

National Council of Churches in India: Christian Council Lodge, Nagpur, M. S. 440001; mems.: 20 reformed and 3 orthodox churches, 14 regional Christian Councils, 12 All India Ecumenical organizations and 5 related agencies; Pres. DAISY L. GOPAL RATNAM; Gen. Sec. Rev. M. A. Z. ROLSTON; publ. *National Christian Council Review.*

Federation of Evangelical Lutheran Churches in India: Ranchi, Bihar; Pres. Rt. Rev. R. B. MANIKAM; Sec. Dr. M. BAGE.

Malankara Orthodox Syrian Church: Catholicate Palace, Kottayam-4, Kerala; f. A.D. 52 by St. Thomas; Catholicos of the East and Malankara Metropolitan: His Holiness BASELIUS MAR THOMA MATHEWS I; Sec. Metropolitan DANIEL MAR PHILOXENOS; 1,500,000 mems.

Mar Thoma Syrian Church of Malabar: Mar Thoma Sabha Office, Tiruvalla 689101, Kerala; f. A.D. 52 by St. Thomas; Metropolitan: Most Rev. Dr. ALEXANDER MAR THOMA; Sec. Rev. C. G. ALEXANDER; 500,000 mems.; publs. *Malankara Sabha Tharaka, Yuva Deepam, Vanitha Bhodhini, Gospel Messenger.*

United Church of North India and Pakistan: Church House, Mhow, Madhya Pradesh; Sec. (vacant).

Other groups include Baptist and Methodist Churches.

THE PRESS

Freedom of the Press was guaranteed under articles 13 and 19 of the Constitution. A measure giving the Press the right to publish proceedings of Parliament without being subjected to censorship or the fear of civil or criminal action was popularly known as the "Feroz Gandhi Act". This privilege was withdrawn when Mrs. Indira Gandhi's Government declared a state of emergency in June 1975 and article 19 of the Constitution, which guaranteed the right to freedom of speech and expression, was suspended. In order to facilitate censorship of all news, a merger of the existing news agencies was enforced in January 1975, and *Samachar*, the state news agency, was established. However, pre-censorship was declared illegal by the courts in September 1975, and censorship of foreign correspondents ended in September 1976, but the Prevention of Publication of Objectionable Matter Act, passed by Parliament in early 1976, still greatly restricted press freedom. In April 1977 the new Government introduced bills to repeal the Prevention of Publication of Objectionable Matter Act and to restore the rights of the "Feroz Gandhi Act", which were both subsequently approved by Parliament. The right to report Parliamentary proceedings was further guaranteed under the Constitution (45th Amendment) Bill of December 1978, later redesignated the 44th Amendment. In April 1978 *Samachar* was disbanded and the original agencies were re-established.

In March 1979 a Press Council was set up (the previous one was abolished in 1975). It function is to uphold the freedom of the Press and maintain and improve journalistic standards. In 1980 a second Press Commission was appointed to inquire into the growth and status of the press since the first commission gave its report, and suggest how best it should develop in the future.

The growth of a thriving Press has been made difficult by cultural barriers caused by religious, caste and language differences. Consequently the English Press, with its appeal to the educated middle-class urban readership throughout the States, has retained its dominance. The English metropolitan dailies, such as the *Times of India* (published in three cities), *Indian Express* (published in ten cities), the *Hindu* (published in five cities) and the *Statesman* (published in two cities), are some of the widest circulating and most influential newspapers. In 1979 there were 17,168 newspapers and magazines: 1,087 were dailies, 5,023 weeklies and 11,058 other periodicals. More were published in Hindi than in English, and the total circulation for Hindi papers was 11,408,000, while the English language press had a total circulation of 10,224,000. The readership of daily newspapers is just over 21 per thousand. There were 559 government publications in 1979.

The main Indian language dailies, such as the *Navbharat Times* (Hindi), *Malayala Manorama* (Malayalam), the *Jugantar* (Bengali), and *Ananda Bazar Patrika* (Bengali), by paying attention to rural affairs, cater for the increasingly literate provincial population who know no English. Most Indian language papers have a relatively small circulation.

The more popular weekly and fortnightly periodicals include the cultural Tamil publications *Kumudam*, *Kalki*, *Rani* and *Ananda Vikatan*, the English *Illustrated Weekly of India*, *India Today*, *Sunday*, and *Indian Express* (Sunday edition) and the sensationalist *Blitz*, published in English, Hindi and Urdu. The main monthly periodicals are the *Reader's Digest* and the Hindi *Manohar Kahaniyan*.

The majority of publications in India are under individual ownership (64.5 per cent in 1977), whilst newspapers owned by joint stock companies claim the largest part of the total circulation (38.5 per cent in 1979). The most powerful groups own most of the large English dailies and frequently have considerable private commercial and industrial holdings. Four of the major groups are as follows:

Times of India Group (controlled by ASHOK JAIN and family): dailies: the *Times of India*, *Economic Times*, the *Evening News of India* (Bombay), the Hindi *Navbharat Times*, the *Maharashtra Times* (Bombay); periodicals: the *Illustrated Weekly of India*, the Hindi weeklies *Dharmayug* and *Dinaman*, the English fortnightlies *Femina* and *Filmfare* and the Hindi publications *Parag* and *Sarita*, etc.

Indian Express Group (controlled by the GOENKA family): dailies: the *Indian Express*, the Marathi *Loksatta*, the Tamil *Dinamani*, the Telugu *Andhra Prabha*, the Kannada *Kannada Prabha* and the English *Financial Express*; periodicals: the English weeklies the *Indian Express* (Sunday edition), *Screen*, *Cinema Express* (fortnightly) and the Telugu *Andhra Prabha Illustrated Weekly*.

Hindustan Times Group (controlled by the BIRLA family): dailies: the *Hindustan Times* (Delhi), the *Searchlight* (Patna), *Pradeep* (Patna), the Hindi *Hindustan* (Delhi) and *Bharat* (Allahabad); periodicals: the weeklies the *Overseas Hindustan Times*, the *Eastern Economist*, the Hindi *Saptahik Hindustan* (Delhi) and the Hindi monthly *Nandan* (New Delhi).

Ananda Bazar Patrika Group (controlled by ASOKE SARKAR and family): dailies: the *Ananda Bazar Patrika* (Calcutta), the English *Business Standard* and *Hindustan Standard*; periodicals: the English weeklies *Sunday* and *Sports World*, the English fortnightly *Business World*, Bengali weekly *Desh*, Hindi weekly *Ravivar*, Bengali monthly *Anandamela*, Bengali fortnightly *Anandlok*, etc.

PRINCIPAL DAILIES

DELHI (incl. NEW DELHI)

The Economic Times: Bahadur Shah Zafar Marg; published in Delhi from 1974 and in Calcutta from 1976; *see* under Bombay; circ. (Delhi) 18,267.

The Financial Express: Bahadur Shah Zafar Marg; *see* under Bombay.

Hindustan: 18/20 Kasturba Gandhi Marg; f. 1936; morning; Hindi; Editor C. L. CHANDRAKAR; circ. 172,740.

Hindustan Times: 18/20 Kasturba Gandhi Marg; f. 1923; morning; English; Editor KHUSWANT SINGH; circ. 255,188.

Indian Express: Bahadur Shah Zafar Marg, 110002; also published from Bombay, Chandigarh, Cochin, Bangladore, Ahmedabad, Madras, Madaurai, Hyderabad and Vijayawada; Editor-in-Chief B. G. VERGHESE; circ. (Delhi and Chandigarh) 146,464.

Milap: 8A Bahadurshah Zafar Marg; f. 1923; Urdu; Nationalist; also published from Jullundur and Hyderabad; Managing Partner PUNAM SURI; circ. 49,000.

National Herald: Herald House, Bahadur Shah Zafar Marg, New Delhi 110002; nationalist; also published from Lucknow; Editor HARI JAISINGH.

Navbharat Times: 7 Bahadurshah Zafar Marg; f. 1947; also published from Bombay; Hindi; Editor S. VATSYAYAN; circ. (national) 378,645, (Delhi) 292,993.

Patriot: P.B. 727, Link House, Bahadur Shah Zafar Marg; f. 1963; English; Chair. of Editorial Board ARUNA ASAF ALI; circ. 31,877.

Pratap: Pratap Bhawan, Bahadur Shah Zafar Marg; f. 1919; Urdu; Editor K. NARENDRA; circ. 20,689.

Statesman: Connaught Circus; Delhi Editor S. SAHAY; *see* under Calcutta.

Times of India: 7 Bahadur Shah Zafar Marg; *see* under Bombay; circ. (Delhi) 172,873.

ANDHRA PRADESH

Hyderabad

Deccan Chronicle: 36 Sarojini Devi Rd., Secunderabad; f. 1938; English; Editor T. CHANDRASEKHAR REDDY; circ. 48,441.

Eenadu: Somajiguda, Hyderabad 500004; f. 1974; Telugu; also published from Visakhapatnam and Vijayawada; Editor RAMOJI RAO; circ. 197,605.

Rahnuma-e-Deccan: Afzalgunj, Hyderabad 12; f. 1949; morning; Urdu; independent; Editor SYED VICARUDDIN; circ. 22,328.

Siasat Daily: Jawaharlal Nehru Rd., Hyderabad 500001; f. 1949; morning; Urdu; Editor ABID ALI KHAN; circ. 27,040.

Vijayawada

Andhra Jyoti: P.O.B. 712, Bunder Rd., 10; f. 1960; Telugu; Editor NANDURI RAMAMOHANA RAO; circ. 48,111.

Andhra Patrika: P.O.B. 534, Vijayawada 520003; f. 1914; Telugu; also published from Hyderabad; Editor S. RADHAKRISHNA; circ. 36,282.

Andhra Prabha: f. 1959; Telugu; also published from Bangalore and Hyderabad; Editor K. S. SUBRAHMANYAM; circ. (national) 100,474.

Indian Express: George Oakes Building, Besant Rd., Gandhinagar 3; circ. (Vijayawada, Bangalore, Madras, Cochin, Hyderabad and Madurai) 263,370.

ASSAM

Gauhati

Assam Tribune: Tribune Bldgs., Gauhati 3; f. 1938; English; Editor R. N. BOROOAH; circ. 37,241.

Dainik Assam: Tribune Bldgs., Gauhati; f. 1965; Assamese; Editor K. N. HAZARIKA; circ. 59,924.

BIHAR

Patna

Aryavarta: Mazharul Haque Path; f. 1940; Hindi; morning: Editor H. JHA SHASHTRI; circ. 98,140.

The Indian Nation: Mazharul Haque Path; f. 1930; morning; Editor DEENA NATH JHA; circ. 53,741.

Pradeep: Buddha Marg; f. 1947; Hindi; morning; Editor HARI OM PANDE; circ. 32,654.

Searchlight: Buddha Marg; f. 1918; English; morning; Editor R. K. MUKKER; circ. 20,859.

GOA

Panaji

Gomantak: Gomantak Bhavan, St. Inez, Panaji-Goa; f. 1962; Marathi; morning; Editor NARAYAN G. ATHAWALAY; circ. 15,000.

Navhind Times: Rua Ismael Gracias; f. 1963; English; morning; Editor K. S. K. MENON; circ. 19,800.

GUJARAT

Ahmedabad

Gujarat Samachar: Gujarat Samachar Bhavan; f. 1932; Gujarati; morning; also published from Surat; Editor SHANTILAL A. SHAH; circ. 193,824.

Indian Express: Janasatta Bldg., Mirzapur Rd.; English; circ. (Ahmedabad) 18,154.

Janasatta: Post Bag No. 191, Mirzapur Rd.; f. 1953; Gujarati; morning; also published from Rajkot; Editor ISHWAR J. PANCHOLI; circ. (national) 82,943.

Sandesh: Sandesh Bldg., Cheekanta Rd.; f. 1923; Gujarati; Editor C. S. PATEL; circ. 141,962.

Times of India: P.O.B. 4046, 139 Ashram Rd., 380009; *see* under Bombay; circ. (Ahmedabad) 52,003.

Western Times: Gujarat Samachar Bhavan, Khanpur; f. 1967; English; Editor RAMU PATEL; circ. 16,100.

Rajkot

Jai Hind: P.O.B. 59, Sharda Baug; f. 1948; also published from Ahmedabad; Gujarati; Editor N. L. SHAH; circ. 40,000 (Rajkot), 20,000 (Ahmedabad).

Phulchhab: Opp. Parsi Agiary; f. 1950; Gujarati; morning; Editor HARSUKH M. SANGHANI; circ. 89,428.

Surat

Gujaratmitra and Gujaratdarpan: Gujaratmitra Bhavan, near Old Civil Hospital, Sonifalia, 395003; f. 1863; Gujarati; morning; Editor P. U. RESHAMWALA; Man. Editor B. P. RESHAMWALA; circ. 65,180.

Pratap: Pratap Sadan, Nanavat, P.O.B. 242, 395003; f. 1926; Gujarati; morning and evening; Editor RAVINDRA P. BHATT; circ. 17,785.

JAMMU AND KASHMIR

Jammu

Kashmir Times: Residency Rd.; f. 1955; English; morning; Editor V. BHASIN; circ. 16,000.

Shrinagar

Shrinagar Times: Badshah Bridge; f. 1969; Urdu; circ. 14,000.

KARNATAKA

Bangalore

Deccan Herald: 16 Mahatma Gandhi Rd., 560001; f. 1948; morning; English; Editor M. P. YASHWANTH KUMAR; circ. 115,800.

Indian Express: 1 Queen's Rd.; circ. (Bangalore, Cochin, Hyderabad, Madras, Madurai and Vijayawada) 263,730.

Kannada Prabha: 1 Queen's Rd.; Kannada; circ. 77,071.

Prajavani: 16 Mahatma Gandhi Rd., 560001; f. 1948; Kannada; morning; Editor Y. N. KRISHNA MURTHY; circ. 171,783.

KERALA

Kottayam

Deepika: P.B. 7, Kottayam 1; f. 1887; Malayalam; independent; also published from Trichur; Editor VICTOR Z. NARIVELY; circ. 62,307.

Malayala Manorama: Kottayam 1; f. 1888; also published from Kozhikode and Cochin; Malayalam; morning; Chief Editor K. M. MATHEW; circ. 539,607.

Kozhikode

Deshabhimani: 157 Convent Rd.; f. 1942; Malayalam; morning; also published from Cochin; Editor P. GOVINDA PILLAI; circ. 45,286.

Mathrubhumi: P.B. No. 46, Robinson Rd., Calicut 673001; f. 1923; Malayalam; Editor V. P. RAMACHANDRAN; also published from Trivandrum and Cochin; circ. 344,030.

Trichur

Express: P.B. 15, Trichur 680001; f. 1944; Malayalam; Editor K. BALAKRISHNAN; circ. 48,003.

Trivandrum

Kerala Kaumudi: P.B. 77, Pettah, Trivandrum 695024; f. 1911; Malayalam; Editor M. S. MADHUSOODANAN; circ. 126,535.

MADHYA PRADESH

Bhopal

Dainik Bhaskar: Agrawal Bhawan, Sultania Rd.; f. 1958; Hindi; morning; also published from Gwalior; Editor R. C. AGRAWAL; circ. 41,762.

Hitavada: Central T.T. Nagar; f. 1911; English; morning; also published from Nagpur and Raipur; Editor N. RAJAN; circ. 20,000.

Indore

Nai Duniya: Kesharbagh Rd.; f. 1947; Hindi; morning; Editor RAJENDRA MATHUR; circ. 130,000.

MAHARASHTRA

Bombay

Bombay Samachar: Red House, Sayed Abdulla Brelvi Rd., Fort; f. 1822; morning and Sunday weekly; Gujarati; political and commercial; Editor JEHAN D. DARUWALA; circ. 141,597 (daily).

The Economic Times: Head Office, P.O.B. 213, Bombay 400001; f. 1961; published daily from Bombay, New Delhi and Calcutta; English; Editor Dr. HANNAN EZEKIEL; circ. (national) 65,085.

Evening News of India: Dr. Dadabhai Naoroji Rd.; f. 1923; evening; English; Editor GIRILAL JAIN; circ. 24,101.

The Financial Express: Express Towers, Nariman Point, Bombay 400021; f. 1961; morning; English; also published from New Delhi and Madras; Editor N. S. JAGANNATHAN; circ. (Bombay, Madras and New Delhi) 31,258.

Free Press Journal: Journal Bldgs., 21 Dalal St.; f. 1930; English; Editor S. KRISHNAMURTHY; circ. 33,802.

Indian Express: Express Towers, Nariman Point, Bombay 400021; English; Editor-in-Chief B. G. VERGHESE; circ. 124,582.

Inquilab: 156D J. Dasajee Rd., Tardeo, 400034; f. 1938; Urdu; Man. Editor KHALID ANSARI; circ. 22,928.

Jam-e-Jamshed: Ballard House, Mangalore St.; f. 1832; English and Gujarati; Chair. NANABHOY JEEJEEBHOY; Editor ADI MARZBAN; circ. 7,900 (daily), 11,800 (Sunday).

Janmabhoomi: Janmabhoomi Bhavan, Ghoga St., Fort, Bombay 400001; f. 1934; Gujarati; Propr. Saurashtra Trust; Editor HARINDRA J. DAVE; circ. 40,104.

Loksatta: Express Towers, Nariman Point, Bombay 400021; f. 1948; Marathi; morning (except Sunday); Editor V. S. GOKHALE; circ. 204,065.

Maharashtra Times: The Times of India Press, P.O.B. 213, Dr. Dadabhai Naoroji Rd.; f. 1962; Marathi; Editor G. S. TALWALKAR; circ. 194,121.

Mid-Day: 156D J. Dadajee Rd., Tardeo, 400034; f. 1979; English; daily and Sunday; Man. Editor KHALID ANSARI; circ. 76,000.

Mumbai Sakal: N. B. Parulekar Rd., Prabhadevi, 40025; f. 1970; daily and Sunday; Marathi; *see* under Pune.

Navbharat Times: Dr. Dadabhai Naoroji Rd.; f. 1950; *see* under New Delhi; circ. (Bombay) 85,652.

Navshakti: 21 Dalal St., Fort, Bombay 400001; f. 1932; Marathi; Editor P. R. BEHERE; circ. 27,720.

Times of India: Dr. Dadabhai Naoroji Rd.; f. 1838; morning; English; published from Bombay, Delhi and Ahmedabad; Editor GIRILAL JAIN; circ. (Bombay) 291,705.

Nagpur

Maharashtra: House No. 510, Ogale Rd., Mahal; f. 1941; Marathi; Nationalist; Editor M. R. DANGRE; circ. 17,300.

Nagpur Times: 37 Farmland, Ramdaspeth; f. 1933; English; Editor S. B. BEDARKAR; circ. 22,999.

Nava Bharat: Cotton Market; f. 1938; Hindi; morning; also published from Bhopal, Indore, Jabalpur and Raipur; Editor R. G. MAHESWARI; circ. 135,300.

Tarun Bharat: Ramdaspeth Nagpur; f. 1944; Marathi; independent; also published from Pune; Editor M. G. VAIDYA; circ. 62,909.

Pune

Kesari: 568 Narayan Peth, 30; f. 1881; Marathi; Editor CHANDRAKANT GHORPADE; circ. 85,000.

Sakal: 595 Budhwar Peth, Pune 411002; f. 1932; daily and Sunday; Marathi; Editor S. G. MUNAGEKAR; Gen. Man. S. V. NAGARKAR; circ. daily (Bombay and Pune) 122,460.

ORISSA

Cuttack

Samaj: Buxibazar; . 1919; Oriya; Editor R. N. RATH; circ. 81,325.

PUNJAB

Jullundur

Ajit: Nehru Garden Rd., Jullundur City; f. 1955; Punjabi: Editor S. S. HAMDARD; circ. 65,285.

Hind Samachar: Pacca Bagh, Jullundur City; f. 1948; Urdu; morning; Editor ROMESH CHANDER; circ. 68,773.

Jagbani: Pacca Bagh, Jullundur; f. 1978; Punjabi; published by Hind Samachar Ltd.; Editor ROMESH CHANDER; circ. 24,034.

Punjab Kesari: Jullundur City; f. 1965; Hindi; morning; Editor ROMESH CHANDER; circ. 194,209.

Chandigarh

The Tribune: 29-C Chandigarh 160020; f. 1881; English, Hindi and Punjabi; Editor-in-Chief PREM BHATIA; circ. 176,000 (English), 32,680 (Hindi), 42,011 (Punjabi).

RAJASTHAN

Jaipur

Rajasthan Chronicle: A-31, Bassi Sitarampur, Jaipur 302006; f. 1951; English; Editor K. S. NARANG.

Rajasthan Patrika: Kesargarh, Jawahar Lal Nehru Marg, Jaipur 302004; f. 1956; Hindi; also published from Jodphur; Editor K. C. KULISH; circ. 109,273.

Rashtradoot: H.O., P.O.B. 30, M.I. Rd., Jaipur 302001; f. 1951; Hindi; also published from Kota and Bikaner; Editor RAJESH SHARMA; circ. (Jaipur) 62,000, (Kota) 21,000, (Bikaner) 20,000.

TAMIL NADU

Madras

Daily Thanti: 46 E.V.K. Sampath Rd., 600007; f. 1942; Tamil; also published from Bangalore, Coimbatore, Cuddalore, Madurai, Salem, Tiruchi, Tirunelveli and Vellore; Editor R. S. RATHNAM; circ. 255,522.

Dinakaran: 106–107 Kutchery Rd., Mylapore; f. 1977; Tamil; also published from Madurai and Coimbatore; Editor S. JAYAPANDIAN; circ. 139,140.

The Hindu: 859/860 Mount Rd.; f. 1878; morning; English; independent; also published from Bangalore, Coimbatore, Hyderabad and Madurai; Editor G. KASTURI; circ. 330,722.

Indian Express: Express Estates, Mount Rd., 600002; *see* under Delhi; Editor-in-Chief B. G. VERGHESE; circ. (Madras, Madurai, Bangalore, Cochin, Hyderabad and Vijayawada) 263,370.

Murasoli: 93 Kodambakkam High Road, Madras 34; f. 1960; Tamil; also published from Madurai; Editor MURASOL MARAN; circ. 39,233.

Madurai

Dinamani: 137 Ramnad Rd., 9; f. 1951; morning; Tamil; Editor A. N. SIVRARAMAN; circ. (Madurai and Madras) 169,401.

UTTAR PRADESH

Agra

Amar Ujala: Guru-Ka-Tal, Udyog Nagar, Agra 282007; also 19 Civil Lines, Bareilly; f. 1948 and 1969 respectively; Hindi; Editors ANIL K. AGARWAL (Agra), ASHOK K. AGARWAL (Bareilly); circ. (Agra) 67,515, (Bareilly) 40,447.

Sainik: Sainik Bhavan, Moti Katra, Agra 3; f. 1925; Hindi; Editor R. S. SHARMA; circ. 16,000.

Allahabad

Amrita Prabhat: 10 Edmonstone Rd.; f. 1977; Hindi; also published from Lucknow; Chief Editor TUSHAR KANTI GHOSH; Gen. Man. SISIR MISRA; Editor S. N. JAISWAL; circ. 40,824.

Bharat: Leader Bldg., 3 Leader Rd.; f. 1928; Hindi; Chief Editor Dr. M. D. SHARMA; circ. 12,000.

Northern India Patrika: 10 Edmonstone Rd., Allahabad 211001; f. 1959; English; also published from Lucknow; Chief Editor TUSHAR KANTI GHOSH; Gen. Man. SISIR MISRA; Editor S. K. BOSE; circ. 61,400.

Kanpur

Daily Veer Bharat: 48/15 Lathi Mohal, Kanpur 208001; f. 1926; Hindi; Editor A. K. PANDEY; circ. 15,000.

Pratap: 22/120 Shri Ganesh Shankar Vidyarathi Rd.; f. 1932; Hindi; Editor SURESH CHANDRA BHATTACHARYA; circ. 16,300.

Vyapar Sandesh: 48/12 Lathi Mohal Lane, Kanpur; f. 1958; Hindi; commercial news and economic trends; Editor HARI SHANKAR SHARMA; circ. 13,225.

Lucknow

National Herald: published by Associated Journals Ltd., P.O.B. 122; f. 1938 Lucknow, 1968 Delhi; English; Editor HARI JAISINGH.

The Pioneer: 20 Vidhan Sabha Marg; f. 1865; English; Man. Editor Dr. K. P. AGARWAL; circ. 44,711.

Swatantra Bharat: Pioneer House, 20 Vidhan Sabha Marg; f. 1947; Hindi; Chief Editor Dr. K. P. AGARWAL; circ. 63,971.

Varanasi

Aj: Sant Kabir Rd., Kabirchaura, P.O.B. 7 & 52, 221001; f. 1920; Hindi; also published from Patna and Kanpur; Exec. Dir. S. V. GUPTA; circ. 77,599 (Varanasi), 32,754 (Kanpur), 35,255 (Patna).

WEST BENGAL

Calcutta

Aaj Kaal: 96 Raja Rammohan Sarani, 700009; f. 1981; morning; Bengali; Editor GOUR KISHORE GHOSH; circ. 80,000.

Amrita Bazar Patrika: 14 Ananda Chatterji Lane, 700003; f. 1868; morning; English; Nationalist; Editor T. K. GHOSH; circ. 138,299.

Ananda Bazar Patrika: 6 Prafulla Sarkar St., 700001; f. 1922; morning; Bengali; Editor A. K. SARKAR; circ. 406,269.

Business Standard: 6 Prafulla Sarkar St., 700001; f. 1975; morning; English; Editor Dr. D. K. RANGNEKAR; circ. 18,988.

Dainik Basumati: 166 Bepin Behari Ganguly St.; f. 1914; Bengali; independent Nationalist; Editor PRASANTA SARKAR; circ. 32,926.

The Economic Times: 105/7A, S. N. Banerjee Rd.; *see* under Bombay; circ. (Calcutta) 13,918.

Hindustan Standard: 6 Prafulla Sarkar St.; f. 1937; evening; English; Editor AVEEK SARKAR (acting).

Jugantar: 72/1 Baghbazar St., Calcutta 3; f. 1937; Bengali; Editor T. K. GHOSH; circ. 307,172.

Paigam: 26/1 Market St.; f. 1948; Bengali; morning; Editor ABDUL JALIL TARAFDAR; circ. 16,000.

Sanmarg: 160C Chittaranjan Ave.; f. 1948; Hindi; Nationalist; Editor B. S. GUPTA; circ. 51,686.

Satyajug: 13 Prafulla Sarkar St.; f. 1972; Bengali; morning; Editor JIBANLAL BANERJEE; circ. 15,000.

Statesman: Statesman House, 4 Chowringhee Square, 700001; f. 1875; morning; English; independent; also published from New Delhi; Editor AMALENDU DASGUPTA; circ. 223,331.

Vishwamitra: 74 Lenin Sarani; f. 1916; morning; Hindi; commercial; also published from Bombay and Kanpur; Editor KRISHNA CHANDRA AGRAWALLA; circ. 70,000.

SELECTED PERIODICALS

DELHI (incl. NEW DELHI)

Akashvani: Samachar Bhavan, 2nd Floor, New Delhi 110001, Post Bag 12; f. 1936; All-India Radio programmes; Urdu, English and Hindi editions; Chief Editor GYAN SINGH; circ. 1,800 (Urdu), 11,500 (English), 4,000 (Hindi).

Bal Bharati: Patiala House, Publication Division, Ministry of Information and Broadcasting, Govt. of India; f. 1948; Hindi; monthly; for children; Editor P. K. BHARGAVA; circ. 45,000.

Biswin Sadi: Daryaganj; f. 1937; monthly; Urdu; Editor REHMAN NAYYAR; circ. 20,387.

Caravan: Jhandewalan Estate, Rani Jhansi Rd.; f. 1940; fortnightly; English; political and cultural; Editor VISHWA NATH; circ. 28,000.

Careers and Courses: 94 Baird Rd.; f. 1949; monthly; English; Editor A. C. GOYLE; circ. 44,300.

Careers Digest: 21 Shankar Market; f. 1963; English; monthly; Editor O. P. VARMA; circ. 35,000.

Champak: Rani Jhansi Rd., 110055; f. 1968; Hindi; fortnightly; Editor VISHWA NATH; circ. 110,000.

Children's World: Nehru House, 4 Bahadur Shah Zafar Marg, 110002; f. 1968; English; monthly; Editor K. RAMAKRISHNAN.

Competition Success Review: 604 Prabhat Kiran, Rajendra Place; monthly; English; f. 1963; Editor T. N. SACHDEVA; circ. 185,435.

Dinaman: 10 Daryaganj; f. 1965; Hindi news weekly; Editor KANHAIYA LAL NANDAN; circ. 34,790.

Eastern Economist: United Commercial Bank Bldg; Parliament St., P.O.B. 34; f. 1943; weekly; English; Editor SWAMINATHAN S. AIYAR; circ. 7,000.

Ekta Sandesh: 8/818 Ajmeri Gate, Delhi 110006; f. 1963; weekly; Hindi; Editor PREM CHAND VERMA; circ. 12,355.

Employment News: Publications Division, Ministry of Information and Broadcasting, Govt. of India; f. 1976; weekly; Hindi, Urdu and English editions; Editor (English edition) N. N. CHATTERJEE; circ. 280,000.

Film Mirror: 26F Connaught Place; f. 1964; monthly; English; Editor HARBHAJAN SINGH; circ. 21,021.

Filmi Duniya: 16 Darya Ganj, Delhi 6; f. 1958; monthly; Hindi; Editor NARENDRA KUMAR; circ. 119,551.

Filmi Kaliyan: 16/39 Subhash Nagar, New Delhi 110027; f. 1969; monthly; English; films; Editor-in-Chief V. S. DEWAN; circ. 86,488.

Grih Shobha: Delhi Press Bldg., E-3 Jhandelwala Estate, Rani Jhansi Rd., New Delhi 110055; f. 1979; monthly; Hindi; Editor VISHWA NATH; circ. 163,738.

India Today: 40-F, Connaught Place, 2nd Floor, 110001; f. 1975; fortnightly; English; Editor AROON PURIE; circ. 174,883.

Indian and Foreign Review: Shastri Bhavan; f. 1963; fortnightly; review of political, socio-economic and cultural aspects of India and India in relation to the world; Chief Editor H. B. MATHUR.

Indian Horizons: Azad Bhavan, Indraprastha Estate; f. 1951; quarterly; English; published by the Indian Council for Cultural Relations; Editor Dr. J. MANGAMMA; circ. 5,200.

Indian Railways: P.O.B. 467, New Delhi 110001; f. 1956; English; monthly; published by the Ministry of Railways; Editor P. U. C. CHOWDARY; circ. 12,000.

Intensive Agriculture: Ministry of Agriculture and Irrigation; f. 1955; monthly; English; Editor SHUKLA HAZRA; circ. 20,000 (1979).

Jagat (Hindi) Monthly: 8/818 Ajmeri Gate, Delhi 110006; f. 1958; Hindi; popular and family magazine; Editor PREM CHAND VERMA; circ. 17,738.

Jagat Weekly: 8/818 Ajmeri Gate, Delhi 110006; f. 1956; progressive Urdu paper of the people; Editor PREM CHAND VERMA; circ. 10,838.

Journal of Industry and Trade: Ministry of Commerce; f. 1952; English; monthly; Man. Dir. A. C. BANERJEE; circ. 2,000–2,500.

Kadambini: Hindustan Times House, Kasturba Gandhi Marg, New Delhi; f. 1960; Hindi; monthly; Editor RAJENDRA AWASTHY; circ. 81,259.

Krishak Samachar: A-1 Nizamuddin West; f. 1957; monthly; English, Hindi, Marathi; agriculture; Editor Dr. D. A. BHOLAY; circ. (English) 6,500, (Hindi) 6,500, (Marathi) 7,000.

Kurukshetra: Krishi Bhavan; fortnightly (English), monthly (Hindi); rural development; Editor R. THUKRAL; circ. 13,000.

Lalita: 92 Daryaganj; f. 1959; monthly; Hindi; Editor L. RANIGUPTA; circ. 20,000.

Link Indian News Magazine: Link House, Mathura Rd.; f. 1958; independent; weekly; Editor M. V. RAO; circ. 11,730.

Mayapuri Weekly: A-5, Mayapuri, 110064; f. 1974; weekly; Hindi; Editor P. K. BAJAJ; circ. 144,058.

Nandan: Hindustan Times House, New Delhi 110001; f. 1963; monthly; Hindi; Editor JAI PRAKASH BHARTI; circ. 204,051.

Nav Chitrapat: 92 Daryaganj; f. 1932; monthly; Hindi; Editor SATYENDRA SHYAM; circ. 35,980.

New Age: 15 Kotla Rd., 1; f. 1953; central organ of the Communist Party of India; weekly; English; Editor BHUPESH GUPTA; circ. 205,000.

Organiser: 29 Rani Jhansi Rd., New Delhi 110055; f. 1947; weekly; English; Editor K. R. MALKANI; circ. 65,625.

Overseas Hindustan Times: Hindustan Times House, Kasturba Gandhi Marg; English; weekly.

Panchajanya: 29 Rani Jhansi Marg, New Delhi 110055; f. 1947; weekly; Hindi; Man. N. N. KAUL; Chief Editor BHANU PRATAP SHUKLA; circ. 69,312.

Parag: 10 Daryaganj, New Delhi 110002; f. 1958; monthly; Hindi; Editor K. L. NANDAN; circ. 106,585.

Priya: 92 Daryaganj; f. 1960; monthly; Hindi; Editor SATYENDRA SMYAM; circ. 27,800.

Punjabi Digest: 9 Hemkunt House, Rajindera Place, P.O.B. 2549, New Delhi 110005; f. 1971; literary monthly; Gurmukhi; Chair. S. KAPUR SINGH; Gen. Man. Sardar PARVESH BAHADUR SINGH; Chief Editor Sardar JANG BAHADUR SINGH; circ. 27,319.

Rang Bhumi: 5A/15 Ansari Rd., Darya Ganj; f. 1941; Hindi; films; Editor S. K. GUPTA; circ. 30,000.

Ruby Magazine: Daryaganj, 110002; f. 1966; monthly; Urdu; Editor REHMAN NAYYAR; circ. 40,000.

Sainik Samachar: Block L-1, Church Rd., New Delhi 110001; f. 1909; pictorial weekly for Indian Defence Services; English, Hindi, Urdu, Tamil, Punjabi, Telugu, Marathi, Gorkhali, Malayalam and Bengali edns.; Editor-in-Chief Col. R. K. MATHUR; circ. (Hindi and English) 30,000.

Saptahik Hindustan: Kasturba Gandhi Marg; f. 1950; weekly; Hindi; Editor M. S. JOSHI; circ. 110,969.

Sarita: Jhandewalan Estate, Rani Jhansi Rd.; f. 1945; fortnightly; Hindi; Editor VISHWA NATH; circ. 260,000.

Shama: 13/14 Asaf Ali Rd., Ajmeri Gate; f. 1939; monthly; Urdu; Editor M. YUSUF DEHLVI; circ. 95,637.

Sher-i-Punjab: Hemkunt House, 6 Rajindera Place, P.O.B. 2549, New Delhi 110005; f. 1911; weekly news magazine; only Urdu paper for Sikhs in India and abroad; Chief Editor Sardar JANG BAHADUR SINGH; Editor S. B. SINGH; circ. over 15,000.

Sun Weekly: 88 Bahadur Shah Zafar Marg; f. 1977; English; Editor V. B. GUPTA; circ. 70,211.

Surya India: Kanchenjunga, 18 Barakhamba Rd.; f. 1977; monthly; English; Editor ANURAG MATHUR.

Sushama: 13/14 Asaf Ali Rd.; f. 1959; monthly; Hindi, Editor M. YUNUS DEHLVI; circ. 66,873.

Vigyan Pragati: Hillside Rd., 110012; f. 1952; monthly; Hindi; popular science; Editor O. P. SHARMA; circ. 50,000.

Women's Era: Jhandewalan Estate, Rani Jhansi Rd.; f. 1963; fortnightly; English; Editor VISHWA NATH; circ. 25,000.

Yojana: Planning Commission, Yojana Bhavan, Parliament St.; f. 1957; fortnightly; English, Tamil, Bengali, Marathi, Gujarati, Assamese, Malayalam, Telugu, Urdu and Hindi; Chief Editor P. SRINIVASAN; circ. 42,000.

ANDHRA PRADESH

Hyderabad

Islamic Culture: P.O.B. 171; f. 1927; quarterly; English; Editor Dr. M. A. MUID KHAN; circ. 11,300.

Vijayawada

Andhra Jyoti Sachitra Vara Patrika: Labbipet 520010; f. 1967; weekly; Telugu; Editor P. S. SARMA; circ. 77,817.

BIHAR

Patna

Anand Digest: P.O.B. 5, Govind Mitra Rd.; f. 1981; monthly; Hindi; family magazine; Editors M. S. SINGH, Dr. S. S. SINGH, S. R. SARAN, J. B. SARAN; circ. 50,000.

Balak: P.O.B. 5, Govind Mitra Rd.; f. 1926; monthly; Hindi; for children; Editors M. S. SINGH, Dr. S. S. SINGH, S. R. SARAN and J. B. SARAN; circ. 49,000.

Bihar Information: P.R. D. Govt. of Bihar; f. 1952; weekly; English, Hindi and Urdu editions; Chief Editor G. S. VERMA; circ. 14,000.

Jyotsana: Rejendranagar; f. 1947; monthly; Hindi; Editor S. NARAYAN; circ. 10,550.

Nar Nari: Nari Prakashan, 800004; f. 1949; monthly; Hindi; Editor V. VATSYAYAN; circ. 10,000.

GUJARAT

Ahmedabad

Aaspas: Nr. Khanpur Gate, Khanpur, 380001; f. 1976; weekly; Gujarati; Editor SHALIBHADRA S. SHAH; circ. 95,131.

Akhand Anand: P.O.B. 50, Bhadra; f. 1947; monthly; Gujarati; Editor T. K. THAKKAR; circ. 49,075.

Chitralok: Gujarat Samachar Bhavan, Khanpur, P.O.B. 254; f. 1952; weekly; Gujarati; films; Editor SHREYANS SHAH; circ. 17,986.

Stree: Sandesh Bhavan, Gheekanta; f. 1962; weekly; Gujarati; Editor Mrs. LEELABEN C. PATEL; circ. 54,979.

Zagmag: Gujarat Samachar Bhavan, Khanpur; f. 1952; weekly; Gujarati; for children; Editor SHREYANS S. SHAH; circ. 17,007.

Rajkot

Amruta: opp. Sharda Baug; f. 1967; weekly; Gujarati; films; Editor Y. N. SHAH; circ. 32,484.

Parmarth: opp. Sharda Baug; monthly; Gujarati; religion; Editor N. L. SHAH; circ. 25,000.

Phulwadi: opp. Sharda Baug; weekly; for children; Editor Y. N. SHAH; circ. 55,394.

KARNATAKA

Bangalore

Mysindia: 38A Mahatma Gandhi Rd.; f. 1939; weekly; English; news and current affairs; Editor D. N. HOSALI; circ. 14,000.

New Leader: 93 North Rd., St. Mary's Town, Bangalore 560005; f. 1887; weekly; English; Editor Rt. Rev. Mgr. HERMAN D'SOUZA; circ. 10,000.

Prajamata: North Anjaneya Temple Rd., Basavangudi; f. 1931; weekly; Kannada; news and current affairs; Chief Editor H. V. NAGARAJA RAO; circ. 105,856.

KERALA

Kottayam

Balarama: B.O.P. 226, Kottayam, 686001; f. 1972; children's monthly; Malayalam; Editor MAMMEN MATHEW; circ. 113,927.

Malayala Manorama: P.O.B. 26; f. 1956; weekly; Malayalam; Editor MAMMEN VERGHESE; circ. 584,973.

Vanitha: P.B. No. 226, Kottayam 686001; f. 1975; women's monthly; Malayalam; Editor Mrs. K. M. MATHEW; circ. 234,288.

MADHYA PRADESH

Krishak Jagat: P.O.B. 3, Bhopal 462001; f. 1946; weekly; Hindi; agriculture; Editor S. C. GANGRADE; Chief Editor M. C. BONDRIYA; circ. 11,438.

MAHARASHTRA

Bombay

Beautiful: 34 Mittal Chambers, Nariman Point, 400021; f. 1974; monthly; English; Editor LYNN DEAS; circ. 53,000.

Bhavan's Journal: Bharatiya Vidya Bhavan, Bombay 400007; f. 1954; fortnightly; English; Man. Editor J. H. DAVE; Editor S. RAMAKRISHNAN; circ. 25,000.

Blitz News Magazine: 17/17-H Cowasji Patel St., Bombay 400001; f. 1941; weekly; English, Hindi and Urdu editions; also publishes film monthly *Cine Blitz*; Editor-in-Chief R. K. KARANJIA; combined circ. 353,766.

Bombay: 28 A&B Jolly Maker Chambers-II, Nariman Point, 400021; f. 1979; fortnightly; English; Editor AROON PURIE.

Business India: Wadia Bldg., 17/19 Dalal St., 400023; f. 1978; fortnightly; English; Publr. ASHOK ADVANI; circ. 16,883.

Business World: 145 Atlanta, 209 Ceremonial Blvd., Nariman Point, 400021; f. 1980; fortnightly; English; Editor DILIP THAKORE.

Chitralekha: 62 Vaju Kotak Marg, Fort; f. 1950; weekly; Gujarati; Editors Mrs. M. V. KOTAK, H. L. MEHTA; circ. 168,064.

Cine Blitz: 17/17-H Cowsaji Patel St., 400001; f. 1974; monthly; English; films; Editor Mrs. RITA MEHTA; circ. 67,714.

Commerce: Manek Mahal, 90 Veer Nariman Rd., Churchgate, 20; f. 1910; weekly; English; Editor VADILAL DAGLI; circ. 6,645.

Current: 15th Floor, Nariman Bhavan, Nariman Point; f. 1949; weekly; English; Editor AYUB SYED; circ. 80,000.

Dharmayug: Dadabhai Naoroji Rd.; f. 1950; weekly; Hindi; Editor D. V. BHARATI; circ. 218,861.

Eve's Weekly: Bombay Samachar Marg; f. 1947; English; Editor G. EWING; circ. 41,460.

Femina: Times of India Bldg., Dr. D. N. Rd.; f. 1959 fortnightly; English; Editor VIMLA PATIL; circ. 103,058.

Filmfare: Dr. D. N. Road; f. 1952; fortnightly; English; Editor VIKRAM SINGH; circ. 145,235.

Illustrated Weekly of India: Dr. Dadabhai Naoroji Rd.; f. 1929; weekly; English; Editor K. C. KANNA; circ. 203,909.

Imprint: Surya Mahal, 5 Burjorji Bharucha Marg, Bombay 400023; f. 1961; monthly, English; Editor ARUN GANDHI; circ. 16,528.

Indian and Eastern Engineer: Piramal Mansion, 235 Dadabhai Naoroji Rd., Bombay 400001; f. 1858; monthly; English; Editors MICK DE SOUZA, S. K. GHASWALA; circ. 7,000.

Indian PEN: Theosophy Hall, 40 New Marine Lines, Bombay 400020; f. 1934; 6 issues a year; organ of Indian Centre of the International PEN; Editor SOPHIA WADIA.

Janmabhoomi Pravasi: Janmabhoomi Bhavan, Ghoga St., Fort, Bombay 400001; f. 1939; weekly; Gujarati; Editor HARINDRA J. DAVE; circ. 100,700.

Mirror: Apollo St., Fort; f. 1961; monthly; English; Editor SHEKHAR HATTANGADI; circ. 57,825.

Mother India: Sumati Publications Ltd., 15 Sir. P. M. Rd., Fort, Bombay 400001; f. 1935; 2 a month; English; Editor BABURAO PATEL; circ. 12,500.

Navaneet: Tardeo 341; f. 1951; monthly; published in Hindi, Marathi and Gujarati editions; Editors N. DUTT (Hindi), U. THOMRAY (Marathi), K. KAPADIA (Gujarati); circ. respectively 23,900, 4,200, 12,600.

Onlooker: 21 Dalal St., Bombay 400023; f. 1939; fortnightly; news magazine; English; Editor YOGESH SHARMA; circ. 50,744.

People's Raj (*Lokrajya*): Directorate-General of Information and Public Relations, Sachivalaya, Bombay 400032; f. 1947; government activities and publicity; fortnightly; editions in Marathi, Urdu and English; circ. (all editions) 121,600.

Reader's Digest: Orient House, Mangalore St., Ballard Estate, Bombay 400038; f. 1954; monthly; English; Man. Dir. and Publisher T. PARAMESHWAR; Editor RAHUL SINGH; circ. 203,812.

Screen: Express Towers, Nariman Point, Bombay 400021; f. 1951; film weekly; English; Editor B. K. KARANJIA; circ. 139,733.

Shree: 40 Cawasji Patel St., Bombay 400023; f. 1967; weekly; Marathi; Editor LALITA BHUTTA; circ. 92,160.

Shreewarsha: 40 Cawasji Patel St., 400023; f. 1980; weekly; Hindi; Editor and Man. Dir. R. M. BHUTTA; circ. 50,000.

Sportsweek: 156D J. Dadajee Rd., Tardeo, 400034; f. 1968; weekly; English; Man. Editor KHALID ANSARI; circ. 42,952.

Star and Style: Bombay Samachar Marg; f. 1965; film and fashion; fortnightly; English; Editor GULSHAN EWING; circ. 105,911.

Stardust: Lana Publishing Company, 14 Advent, 1st Floor; 12A Gen. J. Bhonsale Marg, 400021; f. 1971; monthly, English; Editor VANITA GHOSH; circ. 119,634.

Sudha: Janmabhoomi Bhavan, Ghoga St., Fort; f. 1965; women's weekly; Gujarati; Propr. Saurashtra Trust; Editor D. G. PATEL; circ. 113,300.

Sunday Loksatta: Express Towers, Nariman Point, Bombay 400021; f. 1948; Marathi; Editor V. S. GOKHALE; Gen. Man. N. M. DUGAR; circ. 339,727.

Sunday Mid-Day: 156D J. Dadajee Rd., Tardeo, 400034; f. 1980; Man. Editor KHALID ANSARI; circ. 140,000.

Vyapar: Janmabhoomi Bhavan, Ghoga St., Fort, Bombay 400001; f. 1949; financial journal; weekly; Gujarati; Editor S. J. VASANI; circ. 35,746.

Yuvdarhsan: c/o Warsha Publications Pvt. Ltd., Warsha House, 6 Zakaria Bunder House, Sewri, 400015; f. 1975; weekly; Gujarati; Editor and Man. Dir. R. M. BHUTTA; circ. 44,448.

Nagpur

All India Reporter: A.I.R. Ltd., P.O.B. 209, Congress Nagar, Nagpur 440012; f. 1914; law journal; monthly; English; Editor V. R. MANOHAR; circ. 32,000.

Pune (Poona)

Swaraj: Bombay Papers Ltd., 595 Budhwar Peth, Pune 411002; f. 1936; weekly; Marathi; Gen. Man. S. V. NAGARKAR; circ. 57,750.

Trivandrum

Mathrubhumi Illustrated Weekly: Perunthanni, Trivandrum 695008; f. 1932; weekly; Malayalam; Editor V. P. RAMACHANDRAN; circ. 89,198.

TAMIL NADU

Madras

Ambulimama: 188 Arcot Rd., Vadapalani; f. 1947; monthly; Tamil; Editor NAGI REDDI; circ. 78,000.

Amgili Ammavan: 188 Arcot Rd., Vadapalani, 600026; f. 1970; children's monthly; Malayalam; Editor NAGI REDDI; circ. 43,000.

Ananda Vikatan: 757 Mount Rd.; f. 1924; weekly; Tamil; Editor S. BALASUBRAMANIAN; circ. 267,915.

Andhra Prabha Illustrated Weekly: Express Estates, Mount Rd., 600002; f. 1952; weekly; Telugu; Editor VIDWAN VISWAM; circ. 80,167.

Chandamama: 188 Arcot Rd., Vadapalani, 600026; f. 1947; children's monthly; Hindi, Gujarati, Telugu, Kannada, English, Bengali, Punjabi, Assamese; Editor NAGI REDDI; combined circ. 484,000.

Chandoba: 188 Arcot Rd., Vadapalani, 60026; f. 1952; monthly; Marathi; Editor NAGI REDDI; circ. 107,000.

Dinamani Kadir: 137 Ramnad Rd., 9; Tamil; weekly; Editor K. R. VASUDEVAN (acting); circ. 66,818.

Jahnamamrt (Oriya): 188 Arcot Rd., Vadapalani, 600026; f. 1972; childrens' monthly; Editor NAGI REDDI; circ. 56,000.

Kalai Magal: P.O.B. 604, Madras 4; f. 1932; literary and cultural; monthly; Tamil; Editor K. V. JAGANNATHAN; circ. 49,060.

Kalkandu: 151 Purasawalkam High Rd.; f. 1948; weekly; Tamil; Editor TAMIL VANAN; circ. 167,610.

Kalki: 84/1C Race Course Rd., Guindy, Madras 600032; f. 1941; literary and cultural; weekly; Tamil; Editor K. RAJENDRAN; circ. 64,316.

Kumudam: 83 Purasawalkam High Rd.; f. 1947; weekly; Tamil; Editor S. A. P. ANNAMALAI; circ 556,953.

Malai Mathi: 50 Edward Elliots Rd.; f. 1958; monthly; Tamil; Editor P. S. ELANGO; circ. 81,052.

Pesum Padam: 325 Arcot Rd.; f. 1942; monthly; Tamil; films; Editor R. V. RAMANI; circ. 29,897.

Picturpost: 325 Arcot Rd., 24; f. 1943; monthly; English; films; Editor CHITRA V. RAMANI; circ. 24,176.

Puthumai: 101 Purusawalkam High Rd.; f. 1957; monthly; Tamil; Editor K. T. KOSALRAM; circ. 27,100.

Rani: 1091 Poonamallee High Rd., Madras 600007; f. 1962; Tamil; weekly; Managing Partner B. S. ADITYAN; circ. 378,458.

Sunday Times: 69 Peters Rd.; f. 1956; weekly; English; Editor S. V. S. VINOD; circ. 50,000 .

Thayaga Kural: 2-16 Mount Rd.; f. 1961; weekly; Tamil; Editor A. MA. SAMY; circ. 50,000.

Vani: f. 1949; fortnightly; Telugu; All India Radio journal; circ. 18,000.

Vanoli: f. 1939; fortnightly; Tamil; All India Radio journal; circ. 51,300.

Other Towns

Mathajothidam: 3 Arasamaram, Vellore; f. 1949; monthly; astrology; Tamil; Editor V. K. V. SUBRAMANYAM; circ. 27,700.

UTTAR PRADESH

Allahabad

Jasoosi Duniya: 5 Kolhan Tola St.; f. 1953; monthly; Urdu and Hindi editions; Editor S. ABBAS HUSAINY; circ. (both) 70,000.

Manohar Kahaniyan: Mitra Prakashan (Pvt.) Ltd., 281 Muthiganj 211003; f. 1940; monthly; Hindi; Editor A. MITRA; circ. 344,977.

Manorama: Mitra Parkashan (Pvt.) Ltd., 281 Muthiganj 211003; f. 1924; fortnightly; Hindi; Editor A. MITRA; circ. 181,311.

Maya: Mitra Prakashan (Pvt.) Ltd. 281 Muthiganj 211003; f. 1929; monthly; Hindi; Editor A. MITRA; circ. 121,015.

Probe India: Mitra Prakashan (Pvt.) Ltd., 281 Muthiganj 211003; f. 1979; monthly; English; Editor A. MITRA; circ. 70,498.

Satyakatha: Mitra Prakashan (Pvt.) Ltd., 281 Muthiganj 211003; f. 1972; monthly; Hindi; Editor A. MITRA; circ. 145,000.

Kanpur

Kanchan Prabha: 2 Sarvodaya Nagar, P.O.B. 214; f. 1974; Hindi; monthly; Man. Editor P. C. GUPTA; Editor Y. M. GUPTA; circ. 25,948.

Lucknow

Rashtra Dharma: P.O.B. 207, Dr. Raghubir Nagar; f. 1964; monthly; Hindi; Editor VACHNESH TRIPATHI; Man. V. C. MAHESHWARI; circ. 15,000.

Other Towns

Current Events: 15 Rajpur Rd., Dehra Dun; f. 1955; monthly review of national and international affairs; English; Editor DEV DUTT; circ. 5,000.

Jeevan Shiksha: Sarvodaya Sahitya Prakashan, Chowk, Varanasi; f. 1957; monthly; Hindi; Editor TARUN BHAI; circ. 13,400.

WEST BENGAL

Calcutta

All India Appointment Gazette: 7 Old Court House St.; f. 1973; weekly; English; Editor S. C. TALUKDAR; circ. 81,098.

Anandalok: 6 Prafulla Sarkar St.; f. 1975; fortnightly; Bengali; film; Editor SEVABRATA GUPTA; circ. 57,016.

Anandamela: 6 Prafulla Sarkar St.; f. 1975; monthly; Bengali; juvenile; Editor NIRENDRANATH CHAKRAVARTI; circ. 95,023.

Betar Jagat: All India Radio, Akashvani Bhavan, Eden Gardens, 700001; f. 1929; twice a month; Bengali; radio journal; Editor S. C. BASU; circ. about 16,150.

Capital: 19 R. N. Mookerjee Rd., 700001; f. 1888; weekly; English; financial; Editor JOLLY M. KAUL; circ. 7,900.

Desh: 6 Prafulla Sarkar St.; f. 1933; arts; weekly; Bengali; Editor S. GHOSH; circ. 100,038.

Economic Age: P-36 India Exchange Place, 2nd Floor, 700001; f. 1968; monthly; English; economic and business; Editor SIB BANERJEE; circ. 7,500.

Engineering Times: Wachel Molla Mansion, 8 Lenin Sarani; f. 1955; weekly; English; Editor E. H. TIPPOO; circ. 19,030.

Naba Kallol: 11 Jhamapooker Lane; f. 1960; monthly; Bengali; Editor S. C. MAZUMDAR; circ. 80,088.

Neetee: 4 Sukhlal Johari Lane; f. 1955; weekly; English; Editor M. P. PODDAR.

Ravivar: 6 Prafulla Sarkar Street; f. 1977; weekly; Hindi; Editor S. P. SINGH; circ. 59,458.

Screen: P-5, Kalakar St., Calcutta 700070; f. 1960; weekly; Hindi; Editor M. P. PODDAR; circ. 58,150.

Sportsworld: 6 Prafulla Sarkar St.; weekly; English; Editor MANSUR ALI KHAN PATAUDI; circ. 59,833.

Statesman: 4 Chowringhee Square, 700001; f. 1875; overseas weekly; English; Editor AMALENDU DAS GUPTA.

Suktara: 11 Jhamapooker Lane, 700009; f. 1948; monthly; juvenile; Bengali; Editor M. MAJUMDAR; circ. 150,000.

Sunday: 6 Prafulla Sarkar St.; f. 1973; weekly; English; Editor M. J. AKBAR; circ. 204,528.

NEWS AGENCIES

Hindustan Samachar: 2 Connaught Lane, New Delhi 110001; Gen. Man. BALESHWAR AGARWAL.

Press Trust of India Ltd.: 357 Dr. Dadabhai Naoroji Rd., Bombay 400001; f. 1949, re-established 1978; Gen. Man. NARAYAN RAMA CHANDRAN; Deputy Gen. Man. P. UNNIKRISHNAN.

Samachar Bharati: 12 Fire Brigade Lane, New Delhi 110001; f. 1966, re-established 1978; Gen. Man. B. B. MATHUR.

United News of India (UNI): 9 Rafi Marg, New Delhi 110001; operates special services devoted to banking, business, economic affairs, agriculture, overseas news and features; news service to Gulf countries by satellite; operates in over 90 centres in India; over 15 foreign correspondents; Gen. Man. and Chief Editor G. G. MIRCHANDANI.

FOREIGN BUREAUX

Agence France-Presse (AFP): Room 20, P.T.I. Bldg., 4 Parliament St., New Delhi 110001; Chief Rep. HENRI JOEL CHARLES.

Agencia EFE (*Spain*): Ambassador Hotel, Sujan Singh Park, New Delhi, 110003; Correspondent MARÍA PALOMA MARTÍNEZ AVILÉS.

Agentstvo Pechati Novosti (*U.S.S.R.*). C-3 West End Colony, New Delhi 110021; Correspondent E. K. CHOUBITCHEV.

Agenzia Nazionale Stampa Associata (ANSA) (*Italy*): A-293, New Friends Colony, New Delhi; Chief Rep. RICCARDO EHRMAN.

Allgemeiner Deutscher Nachrichtendienst (ADN) (*German Democratic Republic*): C-64, Anand Niketan, New Delhi 110021; Correspondent (vacant).

Associated Press (AP) (*U.S.A.*): 19 Narendra Place, Parliament St., New Delhi 110001; Chief EUGENE KRAMER.

Československá tisková kancelář (ČTK) (*Czechoslovakia*): C-59, Ananda Niketan, New Delhi 110021; Correspondent P. JANDOUREK.

Deutsche Presse-Agentur (dpa) (*Federal Republic of Germany*): E 14/3 Vasant Vihar, New Delhi 110067; Chief Rep. MARTIN E. PENDL.

Kyodo Tsushin (*Japan*): 1st Floor, PTI Bldg., 4 Parliament St., New Delhi 110001; Chief TAKAO MAYAMA.

Novinska Agencija Tanjug (*Yugoslavia*): D-1/11 Vasant Vihar, New Delhi 110067; Correspondent PREDRAG STAMENKOVIC.

Prensa Latina (*Cuba*): C-105 Anad Niketand, New Delhi; Corresp. TOMÁS ANAEL GRANADOS.

Reuters (*U.K.*): Hansalaya, Barakhamba Road, New Delhi 110001; Chief BERNARD MELUNSKY.

Telegrafnoye Agentstvo Sovietskogo Soyuza (TASS) (*U.S.S.R.*): A-32 West End Colony, New Delhi 110021; Chief BORIS I. CHEKHONIN.

United Press International (UPI) (*U.S.A.*): Ambassador Hotel, Suite 204, Sujan Singh Park, New Delhi 110003; Bureau Chief (vacant).

Xinhua News Agency (*People's Republic of China*): Nyaya Margi, Chanakyapuri, New Delhi 110021; Chief LI NAN.

The following agencies are also represented: Associated Press of Pakistan, Bangladesh Sangbad Sangsta, BTA (Bulgaria), PAP (Poland) and Viet-Nam News Agency.

CO-ORDINATING BODIES

Press Information Bureau: Shastri Bhavan, Dr. Rajendra Prasad Rd., New Delhi 110001; f. 1975 to co-ordinate press affairs with the Government; represents newspaper management, journalistic profession, news agencies, Parliament; has power to examine journalists under oath and may censor objectionable material; Principal Information Officer U. C. TIWARI.

Registrar of Newspapers for India: Ministry of Information and Broadcasting, Vandhana Building, 11 Tolstoy Marg, New Delhi 110001; f. 1956; a statutory body set up to collect statistics regarding the Press in India. It maintains a register of newspapers containing particulars about every newspaper published in India; Registrar G. VENKATARAMAN.

PRESS ASSOCIATIONS

All-India Newspaper Editors' Conference: 36–37 Northend Complex, Rama Krishna Ashram Marg, New Delhi 110001; f. 1940; 330 mems.; Pres. VISHWA BANDHU GUPTA; Sec.-Gen. M. S. MADHUSOODANAN.

Indian and Eastern Newspaper Society: IENS Bldgs., Rafi Marg, New Delhi 110001; f. 1939; 390 mems.; Pres. MAMMEN VARGHESE; Sec. S. C. RAO; publ. *IENS Annual Press Handbook*.

Indian Federation of Working Journalists: Flat No. 29, New Central Mkt., Connaught Circus, New Delhi 110001; f. 1950; Pres. A. RAGHAVAN; Sec.-Gen. SANTOSH KUMAR; publ. *The Working Journalist* (monthly).

Indian Language Newspapers' Association: Janmabhoomi Bhavan, Ghoga St., Fort, Bombay 400001; f. 1941; 326 mems.; Pres. RATILAL SHETH; Gen. Secs. L. M. D'COSTA, A. D. POTNIS; publ. *Language Press Bulletin* (non-political monthly).

Press Institute of India: Sapru House Annexe, Barakhamba Rd., New Delhi 110001; f. 1963; 42 mem. newspapers and other organizations; Chair. G. KASTURI; Dir. K. BHUPAL; publs. *Vidura* (every 2 months), *Data India* (weekly), *DEPTHnews India* (a feature service), and special surveys; training courses.

PUBLISHERS

BOMBAY

Allied Publishers Private Ltd.: 15 J. N. Heredia Marg, Ballard Estate, 400038; f. 1934; economics, politics, history, philosophy; brs. at New Delhi, Calcutta, Madras, Bangalore, Hyderabad; Man. Dir. R. N. SACHDEV.

Asia Publishing House (Private) Ltd.: 14/18 Calicut St., Ballard Estate, Bombay 400038; f. 1961; humanities, social sciences, science and general; English and Indian languages; Man. Dir. ANANDA JAISINGH.

Bharatiya Vidya Bhavan: Munshi Sadan, Kulapati, K. M. Munshi Marg, Bombay 400007; f. 1938; art, literature, culture, philosophy, religion, history of India in English, Hindi, Sanskrit and Gujarati; various periodicals; brs. all over India and in the U.K. and U.S.A.; Pres. DHARAMSEY M. KHATAU; Vice-Pres. JAISHUKLAL HATHI, GIRDHARILAL MEHTA.

Blackie and Son (Private) Ltd.: Blackie House, 103–105 Walchand Hirachand Marg, P.B. 21, Bombay 400001; f. 1901; educational, scientific and technical, general and juvenile; br. at Madras; Man. Dir. D. R. BHAGI.

Chetana Private Ltd.: 34 Rampart Row, Bombay 400023; religion, philosophy; Dir. S. K. DIKSHIT.

Himalaya Publishing House: 'Ramdoot', Dr. Balerao Marg (Kelevadi), opp. Sharni Rd., Station (east), Girgaon, Bombay 400004; text books; Dir. D. P. PANDEY.

Hind Kitab Ltd.: 32–34 Veer Nariman Rd., 400001.

IBH Publishing Co.: 412 Tulsiani Chambers, 4th Floor, Nariman Point, Bombay 400021; Managing Editor P. C. MANAKTALA.

International Book House Private Ltd.: Indian Mercantile Mansions (extn.), Madame Cama Rd., Bombay 400049; f. 1941; general, educational, scientific and law books; Man. Dir. S. K. GUPTA.

Jaico Publishing House: 121 Mahatma Gandhi Rd.; f. 1947; general paperbacks; imports scientific, technical and educational books; Man. Dir. JAMAN SHAH.

Mid-Day Publications Pvt. Ltd.: 156D J. Dadajee Rd., Tardeo, 400034; publr. of *Mid-Day* (daily), *Inquilab Daily*, *Sportsweek*, *Sportsweek's World of Cricket*, *Sportsweek Annual*, *Sunday Mid-Day;* Man. Editor KHALID ANSARI.

Popular Prakashan Private Ltd.: 35-C Madan Mohan Malaviya Rd., Tardeo, Bombay 400034; f. 1968; sociology, biographies, current affairs, medicine, history, economics and literature in English and Marathi; Man. Dir. R. G. BHATKAL; Jnt. Dir. S. G. BHATKAL.

Somaiya Publications Private Ltd.: 172 Mumbai Marathi Grantha Sangrahalaya Marg, Dadar; f. 1967; economics, sociology, history, politics, mathematics, sciences; Chief Editor W. H. PATWARDHAN.

Taraporevala, Sons and Co. (Private) Ltd.: 210 Dr. D. Naroji Rd., Fort, Bombay 400001; f. 1864; Indian art, culture, history, sociology, scientific, technical and general in English; Dirs. M. J. TARAPOREVALA, S. J. TARAPOREVALA.

N. M. Tripathi (Private) Ltd.: 164 Samaldas Gandhi Marg, 400002; f. 1888; law and general books in English and Gujarati; Chair. D. M. TRIVEDI; Dir. and Gen. Man. A. S. PANDYA.

CALCUTTA

Academic Publishers: 5A Bhawani Dutta Lane, P.O.B. 12341, Calcutta 700073; text books; br. in New Delhi; Managing Partner B. K. DHUR.

Allied Book Agency: 18/A Shyama Charan De St., Calcutta 700073; medical text books; Dir. B. SARKAR.

Assam Review Publishing Co.: 29 Waterloo St., 700001; f. 1926; tea, tea plantations, directory; Partners G. L. BANERJEE, S. BANERJEE.

Book Land Private Ltd.: 1 Shankar Ghosh Lane, 700007; economics, politics, history and general; Man. Dir. J. N. BASU.

Chuckerverty, Chatterjee and Co. Ltd.: 15 College Square, 700012; Dir. BINODELAL CHAKRAVARTI.

Eastern Law House Private Ltd.: 54 Ganesh Chunder Ave., Calcutta 700013; f. 1918; legal, commercial and accountancy; br. in New Delhi; Man. Dir. ARUP DE; Dir. ASOK DE.

Firma KLM Private Ltd.: 257B B. B. Ganguly St., 700012; f. 1950; Indology, scholarly books in English, Bengali, Sanskrit and Hindi; Man. Dir. K. L. MUKHOPADHYAY.

Intertrade Publications (India) Private Ltd.: 55 Gariahat Rd., P.O.B. 10210; f. 1954; economics, medicine, law, history and trade directories; Man. Dir. Dr. K. K. ROY.

A. Mukherjee & Co. Pvt. Ltd.: 2 Bankim Chatterjee St., 700012; f. 1940; educational and general in Bengali and English; Man. Dir. J. CHATTERJEE.

New Era Publishing Co.: 31 Gauri Bari Lane, 700004; f. 1944; Propr. Dr. P. N. MITRA; Man. S. K. MITRA.

W. Newman and Co. Ltd.: 3 Old Court House St., 700001; f. 1851; general; Man. Dir. L. P. N. BHARGAVAL.

Oriental Publishing Co.: f. 1910; Propr. D. N. BOSE; Man. D. P. BOSE.

Renaissance Publishers Private Ltd.: 15 Bankim Chatterjee St., 700012; f. 1949; politics; Man. Dir. J. C. GOSWAMI.

M. C. Sarkar and Sons (Private) Ltd.: 14 Bankim Chatterjee St., 700012; f. 1910; publr. of *Hindustan Year Book* and *Who's Who*; Dirs. SUPRIYA SARKAR, SAMIT SARKAR.

Thacker's Press and Directories: M.P. Works Private Ltd., 6-B, Bentinck St., P.O.B. 2512, 700001; industrial publications and directories; Chair. JUTHIKA ROY; Dirs. B. B. ROY, A. BOSE.

DELHI and NEW DELHI

Affiliated East West Press (Pvt.) Ltd.: 104 Nirmal Tower, 26 Barakhamba Rd., New Delhi 110001; text books; Man. Dir. KAMAL MALIK.

Amerind Publishing Co. (Pvt.) Ltd.: 66 Janpath, New Delhi 110001; f. 1970; offices at Calcutta, Bombay and New York; scientific and technical; Dirs. G. PRIMLANI, M. PRIMLANI.

Arnold Heinemann Publishers India (Pvt.) Ltd.: AB/9 Safdarjung Enclave, New Delhi 110016; Literature and general; Dir. G. A. VAZIRANI.

Atma Ram and Sons: Kashmere Gate, Delhi 110006; f. 1909; br. in Lucknow; scientific, technical, humanities, medical; Man. Dir. ISH K. PURI.

B.R. Publishing Corporation: 461 Vivekanand Nagar, Delhi 110052; Partner PARMIL MITTAL.

Cambridge Publishing House: D-36 South Extn., Part 1, New Delhi 110049; children's books; Dir. RAM AVTAR GUPTA.

S. Chand and Co. Ltd.: P.O.B. 5733, Ram Nagar, New Delhi 110055; f. 1917; educational and general books in Hindi and English, exporters and importers of books; Man. Dir. SHYAM LAL GUPTA.

Concept Publishing Co.: H-13 Bali Nagar, New Delhi 110015; sociology, economics, commerce, anthropology, psychology, political science, etc.; Dir. NAURANG RAI.

Eurasia Publishing House (Private) Ltd.: Ram Nagar, New Delhi 110055; f. 1964; educational books in English and Hindi; Man. Dir. S. L. GUPTA.

Heritage Publishers: 4348 Madan Mohan St., 4C Ansari Rd., Darya Ganj, New Delhi 110002; economics, commerce, literature; Dir. B. R. CHAWLA.

Hind Pocket Books Private Ltd.: G. T. Rd., Shahdara, Delhi 110032; f. 1958; fiction and non-fiction paperbacks in English, Hindi, Punjabi and Urdu; Man. Dir. DINANATH MALHOTRA.

Hindustan Publishing Corporation: 6 U.B. Jawahar Nagar, Delhi 110007; archaeology, sciences, chemistry and chemical engineering, economics, geology, maths, physics, sociology, anthropology, etc.; Dir. S. K. JAIN.

Inter-India Publications: 105 Anand Nagar, Old Rohtak Rd., Delhi 110035; economics, commerce, sociology; Dir. MOOLCHAND MITTAL.

Lancers Publishers: P.O.B. 4235, New Delhi 110048; f. 1977; politics with special emphasis on north-east India; Prop. S. KUMAR.

Macmillan India Ltd.: 4 Community Centre, Naraina Industrial Area, Phase I, New Delhi 110028; text books; Marketing Man. SUBHASH WAGHRAY.

Motilal Banarsidass: Bungalow Rd., Jawahar Nagar, 110007; f. 1903; Indological publishers, in English and Sanskrit; Dirs. S. L. JAIN, N. P. JAIN, J. P. JAIN, R. P. JAIN, RAVI JAIN, RAVIJ JAIN.

Neel Kamal Prakashan: Raj Bhawan, 4/C Daryaganj; educational; Propr. S. K. AGGARWAL.

Orient Longman Ltd.: 3/5 Asaf Ali Rd., 110002; f. 1948; educational, technical, general and children's books in almost all Indian languages; Publisher Dr. SUJIT MUKHERJEE; Chair. J. RAMESHWAR RAO.

Oxford and IBH Publishing Co.: 66 Janpath, New Delhi 110001; f. 1964; science, technology and reference books in English; offices at Calcutta and Bombay; Gen. Mans. GULAB PRIMLANI, MOHAN PRIMLANI.

Oxford University Press: 2/11 Ansari Rd., Daryaganj. New Delhi 110002; brs. in Bombay, Calcutta and Madras; Gen. Man. R. DAYAL.

People's Publishing House (Private) Ltd.: 5E Rani Jhansi Rd. 110055; f. 1943; paperbacks, history, biographies, economics, politics, philosophy, sociology, literature, textbooks; Chair. H. K. VYAS.

Publications Division: Ministry of Information and Broadcasting, Government of India, Patiala House, New Delhi 110001; f. 1941; culture, art, literature, planning and development, general publications; publishes 21 magazines in English and several Indian languages; Dir. D. S. MEHTA.

Rajkamal Prakashan (Private) Ltd.: 8 Netaji Subhas Marg, 110002; f. 1946; Hindi; literary books, quarterly journal of literary criticism, monthly trade journal.

Rajpal and Sons: Madrasa Rd., Kashmere Gate, 110006; f. 1891; humanities, social sciences, art, juvenile; Hindi; Man. Partner VISHWANATH MALHOTRA.

Sahgal, N. D., and Sons: Dariba Kalan; f. 1917; politics, history, general knowledge, sport, fiction and children's books in Hindi; Man. G. SAHGAL.

Shiksha Bharati: Madrasa Rd., Kashmere Gate, Delhi 110006; f. 1955; textbooks, popular science books and children's books in Hindi and English; Man. Partner VEENA MALHOTRA.

Sterling Publishers (Private) Ltd.: AB/9 Safdarjang Enclave, New Delhi 110029; f. 1965; academic books on the humanities and social sciences, paperbacks; Indian Book Industry (monthly journal); Man. Dirs. O. P. GHAI, S. K. GHAI.

Technical and Commercial Book Co.: 75 Gokhale Market, Tis Hazari, Delhi 110054; f. 1913; technical books; Propr. B. R. MALHOTRA; Man. D. N. MEHRA.

Thomson Press (India) Ltd.: 9K Connaught Circus, New Delhi 110001; children's books; Dir. AROON PURIE.

MADRAS

Higginbothams Ltd.: 814 Anna Salai, 600002; f. 1844; general; Dir. and Man. V. BALARAMAN.

B. G. Paul and Co.: 4 Francis Joseph St.; f. 1923; general, educational and oriental; Man. K. NILAKANTAN.

Srinivasa Varadachari and Co.: 2–16 Mount Rd.; f. 1879; educational; Propr. G. VENKATACHARI.

Thompson and Co. (Private) Ltd.: 33 Broadway, 600001; f. 1890; directories in English, Tamil, Telugu and Malayalam; Man. Dir. K. M. CHERIAN.

OTHER TOWNS

Bharat Bharti Prakashan: Western Kutchery Rd., Meerut; text books; Dir. RAJENDRA AGARWAL.

Bharati Bhawan: (publishers and distributors); Govind Mitra Rd., Patna 800004; f. 1942; educational and juvenile; Partners M. M. BOSE, T. K. BOSE and SANJIB BOSE.

Bishen Singh Mahendra Pal Singh: P.O.B. 137, Dehradun 248001; botany; Dir. GAJENDRA SINGH.

Catholic Press: Ranchi 834001 (Bihar); f. 1928; books and periodicals; Dir. WILLIAM TIGGA, S.J.

Chugh Publications: P.O.B. 101, 2 Strachey Rd., Allahabad; sociology, economics, history and general; Prop. RAMESH KUMAR.

Geetha Book House: New Statue Circle, Mysore 570001; general; Dir. M. SATHYA NARAYANA RAO.

Goel Publishing House: Subhash Bazar, Meerut 250002; text books; Dir. KAMAL K. RASTOGI.

Kalyani Publishers: 1/1 Rajinder Nagar, Ludhiana (Punjab); text books; Dir. RAJ KUMAR.

Kitabistan: 30 Chak, Allahabad 211003; f. 1932; general, agriculture and fine arts; Partners A. U. KHAN, SULTAN ZAMAN, NASEEM FAROOQI.

Law Book Co.: Sardar Patel Marg, Allahabad 211001; f. 1970; legal books in English; Partners J. N. BAGGA, L. R. BAGGA, R. R. BAGGA, RAKESH BAGGA, RITU BAGGA.

Macmillan India Ltd.: 248 Upper Palace Orchards, Bangalore 560080; brs. in Delhi, Bombay, Calcutta and Madras; English scholarly monographs, text books and general, Hindi university monographs and text books, export typesetting and printing; Pres. and Man. Dir. S. G. WASANI.

Navajivan Publishing House: P.O. Navajivan, Ahmedabad 380014; f. 1919; Gandhian literature in English, Hindi and Gujarati; run by the Navajivan Trust; Man. Trustee JITENDRA DESAI.

Nem Chand & Bros.: Civil Lines, Roorkee 247667; f. 1951; engineering text books and journals.

Pioneer Publishing Co.: Sardar Patel Marg, Allahabad 211001; f. 1972; law books; Partners A. BAGGA, R. BAGGA, Mrs. R. BAGGA, Mrs. S. BAGGA.

Publication Bureau: Punjab University, Chandigarh 160014; text books and general; Head of Bureau and Sec. R. K. MALHOTRA.

Ram Prasad and Sons: Hospital Rd., Agra 282003; f. 1905; agricultural, arts, commerce, education, general, science, technical, economics, mathematics, sociology; Dirs. H. N., R. N., B. N. and Y. N. AGARWAL; Mans. S. N. AGARWAL and R. S. TANDON.

Upper India Publishing House Private Ltd.: Aminabad, Lucknow 226001; f. 1921; publishers of books in English and Hindi special subjects—Indian history, religion, art and science; Man. Dir. S. BHARGAVA.

Vikas Publishing House Private Ltd.: 20/4 Industrial Area, Sahibabad, Ghaziabad, Uttar Pradesh; medicine, sciences, engineering, children's books, textbooks, academic journals, etc.; Man. Dir. NARENDRA KUMAR.

RADIO AND TELEVISION

Radio broadcasting in India began in 1927 and was taken over by the Government in 1930. Commercial television began in 1976 and by 1981 covered 18 per cent of the population spread over 6.5 per cent of the country. In 1978 it was decided that All India Radio and Doordarshan India should become autonomous corporations. To enable broadcasting to reach as many people as possible the Government installs and maintains radio and television sets in community centres. Both radio and television carry advertising.

RADIO

All India Radio (AIR): Akashvani Bhavan, Parliament St., New Delhi 110001; broadcasting in India is controlled by the Ministry of Information and Broadcasting by a network of 85 broadcasting centres, covering about 89 per cent of the population and about 78 per cent of the total area of the country. The service is financed from the grants voted by Parliament annually. Dir.-Gen. K. C. SHARMA.

Radio broadcasting stations are grouped into five zones:

East: Agartala, Aizawl, Bhagalpur, Calcutta, Cuttack, Darbhanga, Dibrugarh, Gauhati, Imphal, Jeypore, Kohima, Kurseong, Pasighat, Patna, Ranchi, Sambalpur, Shillong, Silchar, Siliguri, Tawang and Tezu.

North: Ajmer, Allahabad, Bikaner, Chandigarh, Delhi, Gorakhpur, Jaipur, Jodhpur, Jullundur, Kanpur, Lucknow, Mathura, Najibabad, Rampur, Rohtak, Simla, Udaipur and Varanasi.

South: Alleppey, Bangalore, Bhadravati, Coimbatore, Cuddapah, Dharwar, Gulbarga, Hyderabad, Kozhikode (Calicut), Madras, Mangalore, Mysore, Pondicherry, Port Blair, Tiruchirapalli, Tirunelveli, Trichur, Trivandrum, Vijayawada and Vishakhapatnam.

West: Ahmedabad, Ambikapur, Aurangabad, Bhopal, Bhuj, Bombay, Chhatarpur, Gwalior, Indore, Jabalpur, Jagdalpur, Jalgaon, Nagpur, Panaji, Parbhani, Pune, Raipur, Rajkot, Ratnagiri, Rewa, Sangli, Suratgarh and Vahdodara (Baroda).

Kashmir: Jammu, Leh and Srinagar.

The News Services Division of **AIR**, centralized in New Delhi, is one of the largest news organizations in the world. It has 40 regional news units, which broadcast 116 bulletins daily in 23 languages and 33 dialects. Sixty-eight bulletins in 19 languages are broadcast in the Home Services and 65 bulletins in 25 languages in the External Services.

In 1980 there were an estimated 17,868,506 radio licences issued.

TELEVISION

Doordarshan India (*Television India*): Mandi House, Copernicus Marg, New Delhi 110001; f. 1976, when television broadcasting became independent of All India Radio; 7 centres, 3 base production centres, 7 Satellite Instructional Television Experiment (SITE) on-going transmitters and 5 relay centres; programmes: 266.35 hours weekly; colour transmission began on an experimental basis in 1981 and is to be generally introduced on August 15th, 1982. While only 0.2 per cent of India's 684 million people (1981) own a television receiver, 15 per cent—102 million—have access to one through community centres; Dir.-Gen. SHAILENDRA SHANKAR.

Television stations are located at:

Amritsar: began transmissions in 1973.
Bangalore: began transmissions in 1981.
Bombay: began transmissions in 1972; comprises TV studio at Worli and relay transmitter at Sinhagarh, near Pune.
Calcutta: began transmissions in 1975.
Delhi: began transmissions in 1959.
Gulbarga: began transmissions in 1977.
Hyderabad: began transmissions in 1977.
Jaipur: began transmissions in 1977.
Jullundur: began transmissions in 1977.
Kanpur: began transmissions in 1979.

Lucknow: began broadcasting in 1975; a relay transmitter at Kanpur has extended the range of Lucknow's transmissions.

Madras: began transmissions in 1975.

Mussoorie: began transmissions in 1977.

Muzaffarpur: began transmissions in 1978.

Pij (Ahmedabad): began transmissions in 1976.

Pune: began transmissions in 1973.

Raipur: began transmissions in 1977.

Sambalpur: commissioned in 1978.

Srinagar: commenced broadcasting in 1973 in Urdu and Kashmiri.

In 1981 an estimated 1,548,000 television sets were in operation.

FINANCE

BANKING

(cap. = capital; p.u. = paid up; auth. = authorized; dep. = deposits; m. = million; res. = reserves; Rs. = rupees; brs. = branches.)

State Banks

Reserve Bank of India: Central Office, P.O.B. 406, Mint Rd., Bombay 400001; f. 1935; nationalized 1949; sole right to issue notes; cap. Rs. 50m., dep. Rs. 61,634.9m. (Dec. 1979); Gov. I. G. Patel; 11 brs.

State Bank of India: New Administration Bldg., Madame Cama Rd., Bombay 400021; f. 1955; cap. p.u. Rs. 56.2m., res. Rs. 2,407.3m., dep. Rs. 111,335.9m. (Dec. 1981); Chair. P. C. D. Nambiar; Man. Dir. V. S. Natarajan; 6,000 brs.

The State Bank of India has subsidiaries in Bikaner and Jaipur, Hyderabad, Indore, Mysore, Patiala, Saurashtra and Travancore. There are 26 state co-operative banks and 341 district co-operative banks. It has offices worldwide and off-shore branches in Nassau (Bahamas) and Bahrain.

Commercial Banks

Fourteen of India's major commercial banks were nationalized in July 1969 and a further six in April 1980 (listed below). They are managed by fifteen-member Boards of Directors (2 directors to be appointed by the Central Government, 1 employee director, 1 representing employees who are not workmen, 1 representing depositors, 3 representing farmers, workers, artisans, etc., 5 representing persons with special knowledge or experience, 1 Reserve Bank of India Official and 1 Government of India Official). The day-to-day administration of the bank is one of the chief functions of the Government Custodian or Bank Chairman. The Department of Banking of the Ministry of Finance controls all banking operations.

There were 35,707 branches of public sector and other commercial banks on June 30th, 1982.

Allahabad Bank: 2 Netaji Subhas Rd., Calcutta 700001; f. 1865; cap. p.u. Rs. 10.5m., dep. Rs. 10,428.2m. (Dec. 1981); Chair. and Man. Dir. P. K. Sengupta; 999 brs.

Andhra Bank: Andhra Bank Bldg., P.O.B. 161, Sultan Bazar, Hyderabad 500001; f. 1923; nationalized April 1980; cap. p.u. Rs. 10m., dep. 7,652.1m. (Dec. 1981); Chair. and Man. Dir. K. Gopalkrishna Muthy; 775 brs.

Bank of Baroda: Post Bag 10046, 3 Walchand Hirachand Marg, Ballard Pier, Bombay 400038; f. 1908; cap. p.u. Rs. 100m., dep. Rs. 37,114m. (Dec. 1981); Chair. and Man. Dir. Y. V. Sivaramakrishnayya; Exec. Dir. A. C. Sheth; 1,669 brs.

Bank of India: Express Towers, Nariman Point, Bombay 400021; f. 1906; cap. p.u. Rs. 100m., dep. Rs. 29,595.7m. (Dec. 1980); Chair. and Man. Dir. N. Vaghul; Exec. Dir. D. N. Shukla; 1,440 brs. (incl. overseas).

Bank of Madura Ltd.: 33 North Chitrai St., Madurai 625001; cap. p.u. Rs. 7.5m., dep. Rs. 1,173m.; Chair. R. M. Muthiah.

Bank of Maharashtra: 1501 Shivajinagar, Lokmangal, Pune 411005; f. 1935; cap. Rs. 23m. (1981), dep. Rs. 9,600m. (Dec. 1981); Chair. and Man. Dir. Dr. M. V. Patwardhan; Exec. Dir. P. S. Deshpande; 792 brs.

Canara Bank: P.O.B. 6648, 112 Jayachamarajendra Rd., Bangalore 560002; f. 1906; cap. p.u. Rs. 50m., dep. Rs. 25,460m. (Dec. 1981); Exec. Dir. B. Ratnakar; Gen. Man. K. S. Kamath; 1,095 brs.; publ. *Shreyas* (twice a month).

Central Bank of India: Chandermukhi, Nariman Point, Bombay 400021; f. 1911; cap. p.u. Rs. 72.5m., dep. Rs. 32,680m. (Dec. 1981); Chair. and Man. Dir. B. V. Sonalker; Exec. Dir. R. M. Pradhan; 2,057 brs. (incl. overseas).

Corporation Bank: Mangaladevi Temple Rd., P.O.B. 88; Mangalore 575001; f. 1906; nationalized April 1980, cap. and res. Rs. 26m., dep. Rs. 3,569m. (Dec. 1981); Chair. and Man. Dir. J. B. Kamath; Exec. Dir. Y. S. Hegde; 323 brs.

Dena Bank: P.O.B. 6058, Maker Towers 'E', Cuffe Parade, Bombay 400005; f. 1938; cap. Rs. 12.5m., dep. Rs. 9,727m. (Dec. 1981); Chair. and Man. Dir. M. N. Goiporia; Exec. Dir. C. R. Trivedi; Gen. Man. L. S. Mehta; 870 brs.

Indian Bank: P.O.B. 1384, 31 Rajaji Rd., Madras 600001; f. 1907; cap. p.u. Rs. 40m., dep. Rs. 9,123.9m. (Dec. 1980); Chair. and Man. Dir. M. V. Subba Rao; Exec. Dir. M. G. K. Nair; 832 brs.

Indian Overseas Bank: P.O.B. 3765, 762 Anna Salai, Madras 600002; f. 1937; cap. p.u. Rs. 100m., dep. Rs. 19,500m. (Dec. 1981); Chair. and Man. Dir. K. V. Murthy Yerkadithaya; Exec. Dir. P. B. Sreenivasan; 819 brs.

The New Bank of India: 1 Tolstoy Marg, New Delhi 110001; f. 1936; nationalized April 1980; cap. p.u. Rs. 25m., dep. Rs. 5,852.1m. (Dec. 1981); Chair. and Man. Dir. R. Srinivasan; Exec. Dir. B. L. Khurana; 455 brs.

The Oriental Bank of Commerce: P.O.B. 329, E Block, Connaught Place, New Delhi 110001; f. 1943; nationalized April 1980; cap. p.u. Rs. 2.2m., dep. Rs. 2,583.2m. (Dec. 1980); Chair. and Man. Dir. M. K. Vig; Gen. Man. R. C. Suneja; 327 brs.

Punjab and Sind Bank: B-45/47, Connaught Place, New Delhi 110001; f. 1908; nationalized April 1980; cap. Rs. 8.9m., dep. Rs. 7,020.3m. (Dec. 1981); Chair. and Man. Dir. Mohinder Singh; Gen. Man. S. Autar Singh Bagga; 558 brs.

Punjab National Bank: P.O.B. 274, 5 Sansad Marg., New Delhi 110001; f. 1895; cap. p.u. Rs. 50m., dep. Rs.

33,760m. (Dec. 1981); Chair. and Man. Dir. SUNDERLAL BALUJA; Gen. Mans. K. C. BERRY, S. P. MEHRA, A. K. MAHAJAN, HARISH C. NAKRA; 1,812 brs. (incl. overseas).

Syndicate Bank: Manipal, Karnataka State 576119; f. 1925; cap. Rs. 75m., dep. Rs. 18,433m. (Dec. 1981); Chair. R. RAGHUPATHY; Exec. Dir. H. N. RAO; 1,207 brs.

Union Bank of India: 239 Backbay Reclamation, Nariman Point, Bombay 400021; f. 1919; cap. p.u. Rs. 12.5m., res. Rs. 68.2m., dep. Rs. 17,228m. (Dec. 1981); Chair. and Man. Dir. R. R. KUMAR; Gen. Mans. L. C. MISTRY, R. L. WADHWA; 1,309 brs.

United Bank of India: 16 Old Court House St., Calcutta 700001; f. 1950; cap. p.u. Rs. 26.9m., dep. Rs. 15,591.9 m. (Dec. 1981); Chair. and Man. Dir. K. L. ROY; Exec. Dir. K. B. DAMPLE; 875 brs.

United Commercial Bank: 10 Biplabi Trailokya Maharaj Sarani (Brabourne Rd.), Calcutta 700001; f. 1943; cap. p.u. Rs. 50m., dep. Rs. 19,050m. (Dec. 1980); Chair. and Man. Dir. B. K. CHATTERJI; Exec. Dir. J. N. PATHAK; Gen. Mans. H. N. VOHRA, C. T. THAKUR. 1,436 brs.

Vijaya Bank: 2 Residency Rd., Bangalore 560025; f. 1931; nationalized April 1980; cap. p.u. Rs. 11.8m., dep. Rs. 4,363.1m. (Dec. 1980); Chair. and Man. Dir. R. VIJAYARAGHAVAN; Gen. Man. K. SADANANDA; 578 brs.

MAJOR PRIVATE BANKS

Bank of Cochin Ltd.: Ernakulam North, P.O.B. 1938, Cochin 682018; f. 1928; cap. p.u. Rs. 3.9m., dep. Rs. 622m. (Dec. 1980); Chair. E. K. ANDREW; Gen. Man. C. D. ANTHONY; 103 brs.

The Bombay Mercantile Co-operative Bank Ltd.: 78 Mohamedali Rd., Bombay 400003; f. 1939; cap. p.u. Rs. 11.9m., dep. Rs. 682.1m. (Dec. 1980); Chair. HOOSEINI S. DOCTOR; Man. Dir. Z. G. RANGOONWALA; 26 brs.

Karnataka Bank Ltd.: Dongerkery, Mangalore 3; f. 1924; cap. Rs. 2m., dep. Rs. 60m. (Dec. 1977); Chair. P. RAGHURAM; 210 brs.

The Sangli Bank Ltd.: Rajwada Chowk, P.O.B. 158, Sangli 416416; f. 1916; cap. p.u. Rs. 3.9m., dep. Rs. 1,105.9m. (Dec. 1980); Chair. M. S. APTE; Gen. Man. M. S. GUJARATH; 144 brs.

United Western Bank Ltd.: P.O.B. 2, 172-4 Raviwar Peth, Shivaji Circle, Satara 415001; f. 1936; cap. Rs. 3.0m., dep. Rs. 1,240m. (Nov. 1981); Chair. V. S. DAMLE; Gen. Man. R. P. MIRAJKAR; 149 brs.

FOREIGN BANKS

Algemene Bank Nederland, N.V. (*Netherlands*): 14 Veer Nariman Rd., Bombay 400023; Gen. Man. (India) A. OORTMAN GERLINGS; 3 brs.

American Express International Banking Corpn. (*U.S.A.*): Dalamal Towers, First Floor 211, Nariman Point, Bombay 400021; Vice-Pres. (India) H. R. QUIRING; 3 brs.

Bank of America National Trust and Savings Association (*U.S.A.*): Express Towers, Nariman Point, Bombay 400021; Regional Vice-Pres. JOHN O. SIMS; 4 brs.

Bank of Credit and Commerce International (Overseas) Ltd. (*Cayman Islands*): Atlanta Building, 209 Nariman Point, Bombay 400021; Man. M. JURUDUTT.

Bank of Oman Ltd.: 4–6 Maker Arcade, Cuffe Parade, Bombay 400005.

Bank of Tokyo Ltd. (*Japan*): Jeevan Prakash, Sir P. Mehta Rd., Bombay 400001; Gen. Man. H. KOISI; 3 brs.

Banque Nationale de Paris (*France*): French Bank Bldg., P.O.B. 45, 62 Homji St., Fort, Bombay 400001; Man. G. HOYAMI; 5 brs.

British Bank of the Middle East (*Hong Kong*): 16 Veer Nariman Rd., Fort, Bombay 400023; Man. J. R. HARGREAVES.

Chartered Bank (*U.K.*): P.O.B. 1806, 4th Floor, New Excelsior Bldg., A. K. Naik Marg, Bombay 400001; Chief Man. H. J. WATSON; 24 brs.

Citibank (*U.S.A.*): 293 Dr. D.N. Rd., Bombay 400001; Vice-Pres. N. G. PAMNANI; 5 brs.

Emirates Commercial Bank Ltd.: Rehmat Manzil, 75 Veer Nariman Rd., Bombay 400020.

European Asian Bank (*Federal Republic of Germany*) Tulsiani Chambers, Post Bag 9995, Nariman Point Bombay 400021.

Grindlays Bank Ltd. (*U.K.*): P.O.B. 725, 90 Mahatma Gandhi Rd., Bombay 400023; Regional Dir. ASHOK DAYAL; 54 brs.

Mercantile Bank Ltd. (*U.K.*): 52/60 Mahatma Gandhi Rd., Bombay 400023; Chief Exec. Officer R. W. CAMPBELL; 20 brs.

Mitsui Bank Ltd. (*Japan*): 6 Wallace St., Bombay 400001; Gen. Man. N. SUZUKI; 1 br.

Sonali Bank (*Bangladesh*): 15 Park St., Calcutta 700016; Asst. Gen. Man. ANWARUL AZIM; 1 br.

BANKING ORGANIZATIONS

Indian Banks' Association: Stadium House, 81–83 Veer Nariman Rd., Bombay 400020; 84 mems.; Chair. M. V. SUBBA RAO; Sec. N. S. PRADHAN; publs. include *IBA Bulletin* (monthly).

Indian Institute of Bankers: 'The Arcade', World Trade Centre, Second Floor, East Wing, Cuffe Parade, Bombay 400005; f. 1928; 157,315 mems.; Pres. I. G. PATEL; Chief Sec. R. D. PANDYA.

National Institute of Bank Management: 85 Nepean Sea Rd., Bombay 400006; f. 1968; Dir. Shri P. D. KASBEKAR; publs. incl. *Prajnan* (quarterly).

DEVELOPMENT FINANCE ORGANIZATIONS

Agricultural Finance Corpn. Ltd.: Dhanraj Mahal, Chatrapati Shivaji Maharaj Marg, Bombay 400039; f. 1968; a consortium of commercial banks, set up for financing agricultural and rural development projects directly, or jointly in collaboration with its member banks; provides project consultancy services to commercial banks, Union and State Governments, public sector corporations, the World Bank, the Asian Development Bank, the Food and Agricultural Organization of the United Nations, the International Fund for Agricultural Development and other institutions and to individuals; undertakes techno-economic and investment surveys in agriculture and agro-industries, projects on dairy and livestock; also provides consultancy services for the formulation of projects in backward areas, including Integrated Tribal Development Projects, Drought-prone Area Projects, etc.; regional offices at Calcutta, Lucknow and Madras; br. offices at Patna, Kota, Shillong, Surat, Chandigarh and Trivendrum; cap. p.u. Rs. 50m.; auth. cap. Rs. 1,000m.; Chair. V. M. BHIDE; Man. Dir. GHULAM GHOUSE.

Agricultural Refinance and Development Corporation: P.O.B. 6552, Shrineketan, Shivsagar Estate, Dr. A.B. Rd., Worli, Bombay 400018; f. 1963 to provide medium-term or long-term finance to schemes of agricultural development which cannot be satisfactorily financed by existing credit agencies; 14 regional offices; cap. p.u. Rs. 575m.; res. Rs. 355.1m.; Chair. M. Ramakrishnayya; Man. Dir. M. A. Chidambaram; publ. *ARDC News* (quarterly).

Credit Guarantee Corporation of India Ltd.: Vidyut Bhavan, 3rd Floor, BEST Bldg., Pathakwadi, Bombay 400002; f. 1971; promoted by the Reserve Bank of India; guarantees loans and other credit facilities extended by (i) scheduled and non-scheduled commercial banks to small traders, farmers and self-employed persons and small borrowers under the Differential Interest Rates Scheme, (ii) scheduled and non-scheduled commercial banks and state financial corporations to small transport and business enterprises, (iii) scheduled commercial banks and certain state and central co-operative banks to service co-operative societies assisting their members who are engaged in industrial activity; Chair. Dr. R. K. Hazari; Man. C. S. Subramaniam; Sec. N. D. Mirani.

Industrial Credit and Investment Corporation of India Ltd.: 163 Backbay Reclamation, Bombay 400020; f. 1955 to assist industrial enterprises by providing finance in both rupee and foreign currencies in the form of long- or medium-term loans or equity participation, sponsoring and underwriting new issues of shares and securities, guaranteeing loans from other private investment sources, furnishing managerial, technical and administrative advice to Indian industry; regional offices at Calcutta, Madras and New Delhi; share cap. Rs. 247.5m.; res. Rs. 343.8m.; Chair. S. S. Mehta; Man. Dir. S. S. Nadkarni.

Industrial Development Bank of India (IDBI): Nariman Bhavan, 227 Vinay K. Shah Marg, Nariman Point, Bombay 400021; f. 1964 as wholly owned subsidiary of the Reserve Bank to co-ordinate and supplement other financial organizations and to finance and promote industrial development; became independent 1976, following amendments to the Public Financial Institutions Laws; 5 regional offices and 11 branch offices; cap. p.u. Rs. 1,050m.; res. Rs. 798.2m.; Chair. Nileshwar Narayan Pai; Gen. Man. O. P. Berry Rao.

Industrial Finance Corporation of India: Bank of Baroda Bldg., 16 Sansad Marg, P.O.B. 363, New Delhi 110001; 17 brs.; f. 1948 to provide medium- and long-term finance to companies and co-operative societies in India, engaged in manufacture, preservation or processing of goods, shipping, mining, hotels and power generation and distribution. The Corporation promotes industrialization of less developed areas, and sponsors training in management techniques and development banking; cap. p.u. Rs. 150m.; res. Rs. 401.2m.; Chair. B. B. Singh; Gen. Man. D. N. Davar.

STOCK EXCHANGES

Ahmedabad Share and Stock Brokers' Association: Manekchowk, Ahmedabad 1; f. 1894; 228 mems., 111 active brokers; Pres. Hasmukhlal Mulchand; Exec. Dir. Chhotalal Pandya; Sec. D. M. Panchal.

Bangalore Stock Exchange: Indian Bank Bldg., Kempegowda Rd., Bangalore 560009; 31 mems.; Pres. M. N. Venkata Subban; Sec. M. Raghavendra; publ. *Investment Focus* (quarterly).

Bombay Stock Exchange: Dalal St., Bombay 400001; f. 1875; 504 mems.; Pres. Laldas Jamnadas; Exec. Dir. V. B. Sonde; Sec. A. J. Shah; publ. *The Stock Exchange Official Directory*.

Calcutta Stock Exchange Association Ltd.: 7 Lyons Range, Calcutta 700001; f. 1908; 643 mems.; Pres. B. N. Khandelwal; Exec. Dir. S. R. Basu; Sec. B. Majumdar; publ. *The Calcutta Stock Exchange Official Year Book*.

Delhi Stock Exchange Association Ltd.: 3 & 4/4B Asaf Ali Rd., New Delhi 110002; f. 1947; 110 active mems.; Pres. Harish C. Bhasin; Exec. Dir. R. K. Pandey; publ. Year Book of listed companies.

Madras Stock Exchange Ltd.: P.O.B. 183, Exchange Bldg., 11 Second Line Beach, Madras 600001; f. 1937; 51 mems.; Pres. R. M. Ramanathan; Exec. Dir. E. R. Krishnamurti; publ. *Official Yearbook*.

INSURANCE

In January 1973 all Indian and foreign insurance companies were nationalized. The general insurance business in India is now transacted by only four companies, subsidiaries of the General Insurance Corporation of India.

Deposit Insurance Corporation: Vidyut Bhavan, Pathakwadi, Bombay 400002; provides insurance of up to Rs. 10,000 to a depositor with funds in any of the 956 banks insured by the corporation; cap. Rs. 20m.; Chair. K. R. Puri; Man. V. S. Moharir.

General Insurance Corporation of India: Industrial Assurance Bldg., 4th floor, Churchgate, Bombay 400020; Chair. Ashok Goenka; Man. Dirs. S. R. V. Madhavarao, K. S. Shenoy; subsidiaries:

National Insurance Co. Ltd.: 3 Middleton St., Calcutta 700071; cap. p.u. Rs. 80m.; res. Rs. 348m.; Chair. and Man. Dir. N. N. Lahiri.

New India Assurance Co. Ltd.: New India Assurance Bldg., 87 Mahatma Gandhi Rd., Bombay 400023; Chair. and Man. Dir. A. C. Mukherji.

Oriental Fire & General Insurance Co. Ltd.: Oriental House, A-25/27 Asaf Ali Rd., New Delhi 110002; Chair. and Man. Dir. K. N. Malhotra.

United India Insurance Co. Ltd.: 24 Whites Rd., Madras 600014; cap. p.u. Rs. 116m.; res. Rs. 442m.; Chair. and Man. Dir. M. R. Rayaker; Gen. Mans. C. P. Varghese, R. Radakrhishnan, M. N. Seshagiri.

Life Insurance Corporation of India: Jeevan Bima Marg, Bombay 400021; f. 1956; cap. 50m.; controls all life insurance business; Chair. J. R. Joshi; Man. Dirs. A. S. Gupta, V. Dixit.

Insurance Association

Indian Insurance Companies' Association: Co-operative Insurance Bldg., Sir P. Mehta Rd., Fort, Bombay; f. 1928 to protect the interests of the insurance industry in India; 43 mems.

TRADE AND INDUSTRY

TRADE ORGANIZATIONS

CHAMBERS OF COMMERCE

Chambers of Commerce have been established in almost all commercial and industrial centres. The following are among the most important.

Associated Chambers of Commerce and Industry of India: 2nd Floor, Allahabad Bank Bldg., 17 Parliament St., New Delhi 110001; f. 1921; a central organization of Chambers of Commerce and Industry representing over 6,000 companies throughout India; 4 industrial associations, 170 associate mems. and 16 constituent chambers; Pres. RAUNAQ SINGH; Sec. C. BALAKRISHNAN; publs. *Assocham Bulletin* (monthly), *Foreign Trade and Investment Digest* (weekly).

Federation of Indian Chambers of Commerce and Industry: Federation House, Tansen Marg, New Delhi 110001; 500 asscns. affiliated as ordinary mems. and 1,200 concerns as associate mems.; Pres. G. K. DEVARAJULU; Sec.-Gen. D. H. PAI PANANDIKAR; publ. *Economic Trends*.

Indian National Committee of International Chamber of Commerce: Federation House, Tansen Marg, New Delhi 110001; f. 1929; 50 organization mems., 226 associate mems., 74 committee mems.; Pres. J. N. GUZDER; Sec.-Gen. D. H. PAI PANANDIKER.

Bengal Chamber of Commerce and Industry: 6 Netaji Subhas Rd., Calcutta 700001; f. 1853; 205 mems.; Pres. S. P. ACHARYA; Sec. M. GHOSE; publ. *Monthly Bulletin*.

Bengal National Chamber of Commerce and Industry: 23 R. N. Mukherjee Rd., Calcutta 700001; f. 1887; 315 mems. and 30 industrial and trading associations are affiliated, some having common working arrangements; Pres. H. N. DUTTA GUPTA; Sec. A. R. DUTTA GUPTA; publ. *Economic Bulletin* (monthly).

Bharat Chamber of Commerce: 8 Old Court House St., Calcutta 700001; f. 1900; 616 mems., 39 association mems.; Pres. C. I. GANDHI; Sec. K. C. MUKHERJEE.

Bihar Chamber of Commerce: Judges' Court Rd., P.O.B. No. 71, Patna 800001; f. 1926; 800 mems., 100 association mems.; Pres. S. R. RUNGTA; Sec.-Gen. K. P. JHUNJHUNWALA.

Bombay Chamber of Commerce and Industry: Mackinnon Mackenzie Bldg., Ballard Estate, P.O.B. 473, Bombay 400038; f. 1836; 1,024 mems.; Pres. N. C. CHAUDHURI; Sec. B. P. GUNAJI; publs. *Information Bi-Weekly*, *Monthly Bulletin*, *Annual Report*, *Directory of Members*.

Cocanada Chamber of Commerce: Commercial Rd., Kakinada 533007, Andhra Pradesh; f. 1868; 34 mem. firms; Chair. H. SITARAM; Sec. D. RADHA KRISHNA MURTY.

Gujarat Chamber of Commerce and Industry: Gujarat Chamber Bldg., Ranchhodlal Rd., P.O.B. 4045, Ahmedabad 380009; f. 1949; 5,504 mems.; Pres. B. DOSABHAI PATEL; Hon. Sec. RAMESHCHANDRA NANDLAL PARIKH; publ. *Monthly Bulletin*.

Indian Chamber of Commerce: India Exchange, India Exchange Place, Calcutta 700001; f. 1926; 22 association mems., 58 associate mems., 378 ordinary mems.; Pres. B. D. BANGUR; Sec.-Gen. C. S. PANDE.

Indian Merchants' Chamber: 76 Veer Nariman Rd., Bombay 400020; f. 1907; 160 association mems., 2,053 mem. firms, 38 associate mems.; Pres. KANTIKUMAR PODDAR; Sec. RAMU PANDIT; publs. *Trade, Commerce and Industry Bulletin* (weekly), *Journal* (monthly).

Madras Chamber of Commerce and Industry: Dare House Annexe, 44 Moore St., Madras 600001; f. 1836; 160 mem. firms, 15 associated, 6 affiliated and 8 honorary; Chair. M. K. KUMAR; Sec. C. S. KRISHNASWAMI; publs. *Annual Report*, *Quarterly Review*.

Maharashtra Chamber of Commerce: 12 Rampart Row, Bombay 400023; f. 1927; over 2,300 mems.; Pres. DILIP S. DAHANUKAR; Sec. R. G. MOHADIKAR; publs. *Trade, Commerce and Industry Bulletin* (English), *Vaibhav* (Marathi; monthly).

Merchants' Chamber of Uttar Pradesh: 14/76 Civil Lines, Kanpur; f. 1932; 200 mems, 15 association mems., 56 mem. firms; Pres. M. P. JHUNJHUNWALA; Sec. J. V. KRISHNAN.

North India Chamber of Commerce and Industry: 9 Gandhi Rd., Dehra Dun, Uttar Pradesh; f. 1967; 99 mems, 29 association mems., 12 mem. firms, 76 associate mems.; Pres. P. R. NARANG; Hon. Sec. S. S. ARORA; Gen. Sec. B. L. JAIN.

Oriental Chamber of Commerce: 6 Clive Row, Calcutta 700001; f. 1932; 160 mems.; Pres. K. G. DOSSANI; Asst. Sec. K. A. ZOBER.

PHD Chamber of Commerce and Industry: PHD House, 4/2 Siri Institutional Area, behind Hauz Khas, P.B. 130, New Delhi 110016; f. 1905; 650 mems.; Pres. V. P. PUNJ; Sec.-Gen. M. L. NANDRAJOG.

Southern India Chamber of Commerce and Industry: Indian Chamber Bldgs., Esplanade, Madras 600001; f. 1909; 1,000 mems.; Pres. A. C. MUTHIA; Sec. J. PRASAD DAVIDS.

United Chamber of Trade Associations: Amirchand Marg, Katra Rathi, Delhi 110006; 35 mem. firms; Pres. MAHESHAWR DAYAL; Gen. Sec. P. R. MITTAL.

Upper India Chamber of Commerce: 14/69 Civil Lines; Kanpur; f. 1888; 105 mems.; Pres. DEOKI NANDAN DIKSHIT; Vice-Pres. DEVENDRA SWARUP, A. P. GUPTA.

Uttar Pradesh Chamber of Commerce: 15/197 Civil Lines, Kanpur 268001; f. 1914; 200 mems.; Pres. V. K. SRIVASTAVA.

FOREIGN TRADE CORPORATIONS

Export Credit and Guarantee Corporation Ltd.: Express Towers, 10th Floor, Nariman Point, Bombay 400021; f. 1964; to assist exporters by insuring risks involved in exports on credit terms and to supplement credit facilities by issuing guarantees, etc.; Chair. and Man. Dir. D. D. SATHE; Gen. Man. K. GOPALAKRISHNAN.

Minerals and Metals Trading Corporation of India Ltd.: Express Bldg., 9 and 10, Bahadur Shah Zafar Marg, New Delhi 110002; f. 1963; export of iron and manganese ore, ferro-manganese, mica, coal and other minor minerals; import of steel, non-ferrous metals, rough diamonds, fertilizers, etc. for supply to industrial units in the country; auth. cap. Rs. 120m.; six regional offices in India; foreign offices in Japan and Poland; Chair. P. K. DASGUPTA; Sec. O. P. GARG.

State Trading Corporation of India Ltd.: Chandralok, 36 Janpath, New Delhi 110001; f. 1956; Government undertaking dealing in exports and imports; brs. in Bombay, Calcutta, Madras, and 21 offices overseas; Chair. P. K. KAUL; Exec. Dir. P. K. SHUNGLU.

SUBSIDIARIES

Cashew Corporation of India Ltd.: P.B. 1261, Mahatma Gandhi Rd., Cochin 682011; imports raw cashew nuts for distribution to the export orientated sector of the cashew processing industry; also undertakes exports of cashew kernels; Chair. B. S. THACKER.

Handicrafts and Handloom Export Corporation of India Ltd.: Lok Kalyan Bhavan, 11A Rouse Ave. Lane, New Delhi 110001; f. 1958; undertakes export of handicrafts, handloom goods and ready-to-wear clothes while promoting exports and trade development; auth. cap. Rs. 40m.; Chair. Dr. N. C. B. NATH; Man. Dir. R. S. PAL.

Projects and Equipment Corporation of India Ltd.: Hansalaya, 15 Barakhamba Rd., New Delhi 110001; f. 1971; export of engineering, industrial and railway equipment; undertakes turnkey and other projects and management consultancy abroad; Chair. VIKRAM PRAKASH; Exec. Dirs. SURESH CHANDRA, ANAND KRISHNA.

Trade Development Authority: P.O.B. 767, Bank of Baroda Bldg., 16 Parliament St., New Delhi 110001; f. 1970 to promote selective development of exports of non-traditional products; arranges investment in export-oriented ventures undertaken by India with foreign collaboration; brs. in Frankfurt, New York, Tokyo, Monrovia; Man. Dir. ZAFAR SAIFULLAH.

INDUSTRIAL AND AGRICULTURAL ORGANIZATIONS

The following are among the more important industrial and agricultural organizations.

GENERAL

Banana and Fruit Development Corporation: 49/2-B Mowbrays' Rd., Alwarpet, Madras 600018; f. 1964 with Govt. of India as the major shareholder; responsible for the promotion, cultivation and marketing of bananas; Chair. K. C. SANKARANARAYANAN.

Coal India Ltd.: 10 N. Subhas Rd., Calcutta 700001; Govt. of India holding co., responsible for planning and production of coal mines throughout India; Chair. R. N. SHARMA.

Cotton Corporation of India Ltd.: Air India Bldg., 12th Floor, Nariman Point, Bombay 400021; f. 1970 to act as an agency in the public sector for the purchase, sale and distribution of home-produced cotton and cotton staple fibre imported from abroad; exports long staple cotton; Chair. and Man. Dir. N. S. KULKARNI.

Fertilizer Corporation of India Ltd.: Madhuban, 55 Nehru Place, New Delhi 110024; f. 1961; two operating fertilizer factories at Sindri and Gorakhpur; two at Talcher and Ramagundam, producing nitrogenous, phosphatic and complex fertilizers and some industrial products; Chair. and Man. Dir. P. L. KUKREJA.

Food Corporation of India: 16-20 Barakhamba Lane, New Delhi 110001; f. 1965 to undertake trading in foodgrains on a commercial scale but within the framework of an overall government policy; to provide the farmer an assured price for his produce, supply food grains to the consumer at reasonable prices. The Corporation purchases, stores, distributes and sells foodgrains and other foodstuffs and arranges imports and handling of foodgrains and fertilizers at the ports. It also distributes sugar in a number of states and has set up rice mills; Chair. P. RAMACHANDRAN; Man. Dir. S. K. S. CHIB.

Forest Development Corporation of Maharashtra Ltd.: 6A Nawab Layout, Tilak Nagar, Nagpur 440010; f. 1974 to undertake large-scale forest redevelopment, by felling areas of uneconomic forest and planting them with teak to increase the income from timber and provide employment; Man. Dir. M. Y. SOWANI.

Housing and Urban Development Corporation Ltd.: HUDCO House, Lodhi Rd., New Delhi 110013; f. 1970; to finance and undertake housing and urban development programmes including the setting-up of new or satellite towns and building material industries; auth. cap. Rs. 420m. (March 1982); Chair. and Man. Dir. H. U. BILJANI.

Indian Dairy Corporation: Darpan Bldg., R. C. Dutt Rd., Baroda 390005; objects: to promote dairying in India; to execute the IDA/EEC/Govt. of India dairy development programme "Operation Flood" which aims at covering 155 districts for dairy development to link them to major urban centres for milk marketing to enable the organized dairy sector to obtain a commanding share of these markets, to set up a national milk herd and a national milk grid; Chair. Dr. V. KURIEN; Man. Dir. G. M. JHALA.

Jute Corporation of India Ltd.: 1 Shakespeare Sarani, Calcutta 700071; f. 1971; objects: (i) to undertake price support operations in respect of raw jute; (ii) to ensure remunerative prices to producers through efficient marketing; (iii) to operate a buffer stock to stabilize raw jute prices; (iv) to handle the import and export of raw jute; (v) to promote the export of jute goods; Chair. and Man. Dir. A. K. MOITRA.

National Co-operative Development Corporation: 4 Siri Institutional Area, behind Hauz Khas, New Delhi 110016; f. 1962 to plan and promote country-wide programmes through co-operative societies for the production, processing, marketing, storage, export and import of agricultural produce, foodstuffs and notified commodities; also programmes for the development of poultry, dairy, fish products, coir, handlooms, distribution of consumer articles in rural areas and minor forest produce in the co-operative sector; Pres. RAO BIRENDRA SINGH; Man. Dir. V. B. L. MATHUR.

National Industrial Development Corporation Ltd.: Chanakya Bhavan, N.D.M.C. Complex, Vinay Marg, P.O.B. 5212, New Delhi 110021; f. 1954; auth. cap. Rs. 10m.; consultative engineering services to Central and State Governments, public and private sector enterprises, the UN and overseas investors; Chair. and Man. Dir. (vacant); Sec. K. C. BHALLA.

National Mineral Development Corporation Ltd.: Pioneer House, P.O.B. 52, Somajiguda, Hyderabad 500004; f. 1958; Government of India undertaking under the Ministry of Steel and Mines; to exploit minerals (excluding coal, atomic minerals, lignite, petroleum and natural gas) in public sector; may buy, take on lease or otherwise acquire mines for prospecting, development and exploitation; iron ore mines at Bailadila-14 and Bailadila-5 in Madhya Pradesh, and at Donimalai in Karnataka State, and diamond mines at Panna in Madhya Pradesh; research and development laboratories at Hyderabad; consultancy wing and research and development laboratories at Hyderabad; investigates a number of mineral projects; iron ore production in 1981/82 was an estimated 7.5 million metric tons, diamond production 14,544 carats; Chair. and Man. Dir. C. S. VENUGOPALA RAO.

National Productivity Council: Productivity House, Lodi Rd., New Delhi 110003; f. 1958 to increase productivity and to improve quality by improved techniques which aim at efficient and proper utilization of available resources; autonomous body representing national organizations of employers and labour, government ministries, professional organizations, Local Productivity Councils, small-scale industries and other interests; total mems.: 75.

National Research Development Corporation of India: 20–22, Zamroodpur Community Centre, Kailash Colony Extension, New Delhi 110048; f. 1953 to stimulate development and commercial exploitation of new inventions with financial and technical aid; finances development projects to set up demonstration units in collaboration with industry; exports technology; Chair. GURBACHAN SINGH SIDHU; Man. Dir. H. S. RAO.

National Seeds Corporation Ltd.: Beej Bhavan, Pusa, New Delhi 110012; f. 1963 to improve and develop the seed industry in India; Chair. ANNA MALHOLTRA; Man. Dir. T. BALARAMAN.

National Small Industries Corporation Ltd.: Near Industrial Estate, Okhla, New Delhi 110020; f. 1955 to aid, counsel, finance, protect and promote the interests of small industries; cap. auth. Rs. 100m., issued Rs. 75m., all shares held by the Government; Chair. J. S. JUNEJA.

Rehabilitation Industries Corporation Ltd.: 25 Free School St., Calcutta 700016; f. 1959 to create employment opportunities through industries for refugees from Bangladesh and migrants from West Pakistan, repatriates from Burma and Sri Lanka, and other persons of Indian extraction who have immigrated to India; Chair. B. K. DASCHOWDHURY; Man. Dir. A. R. KOHLI.

State Farms Corporation of India Ltd.: Beej Bhavan, C.T.O. Bldg., Pusa Complex, New Delhi 110012; f. 1969 to administer the Central State Farms; activities include the production of quality seeds of high-yielding varieties of wheat, paddy, maize, bajra and jowar; advises on soil conservation, reclamation and development of waste and forest land; consultancy services on farm mechanization; auth. cap. Rs. 150m.; Chair. (vacant); Man. Dir. K. RAJAN.

Steel Authority of India Ltd.: Ispat Bhawan, Lodhi Rd., New Delhi 110003; f. 1973 to provide co-ordinated development of the steel industry in both the public and private sectors; steel plants at Bhilai, Bokaro, Durgapur, Rourkela; Salem alloy steel projects at Durgapur; Vijaynagar Steel; subsidiary Indian Iron and Steel Corpn. Ltd., Burnpur and Kulti; combined ingot steel capacity is 9.4m. tonnes annually; Chair. SUBRAHMANYAM SAMARPUNGAVAN.

Tea Board of India: 14 Brabourne Rd., Calcutta 700001; f. to provide financial assistance to tea research stations; also sponsors and finances independent research projects in universities and technical institutions to supplement the work of tea research establishments; Chair. B. K. GOSWAMI.

There are also industrial development corporations in the separate states. Organizations engaged in the financing of agricultural and industrial development are listed under *Finance*.

PRINCIPAL INDUSTRIAL ASSOCIATIONS

Ahmedabad Textile Mills Association: Ranchhodlal Marg, Navarangpura, Ahmedabad 380009; f. 1891; Pres. PRIYAKANT T. MUNSHAW; Exec. Dir. M. D. RAJPAL.

Association of the Indian Engineering Industry: 172 Jor Bagh, New Delhi 110003; f. 1974 by merger of Engineering Association of India and Indian Engineering Association; *c.* 1,500 mem. companies, 41 affiliated asscns.; Pres. VINOD L. DOSHI; Sec. T. DAS; publs. *Engineering Metals Review* (monthly), *Overseas Opportunities* (weekly), *Information on Projects* (fortnightly).

Bharat Krishak Samaj (*Farmers' Forum, India*): A-1 Nizamuddin West, New Delhi 110013; f. 1954; 21,000 mems.; national organization of farmers; Pres. Ex-Officio Union Minister for Agriculture; Chair. Dr. BALRAM JAKHAR; Sec.-Gen. Dr. D. A. BHOLAY; publ. *Krishak Samachar* (monthly; English, Hindi and Marathi).

Bombay Millowners' Association: P.O.B. 95, Elphinstone Bldg., 10 Veer Nariman Rd., Fort, Bombay 400023; f. 1875; 86 mem. companies; Chair. HARESH CHANDRA MAGANLAL; Sec.-Gen. R. L. N. VIJAYANAGAR.

Bombay Motor Merchants' Association Ltd.: Sukh Sagar, 3rd Floor, Sandhurst Bridge, Bombay 400007; 601 mems.; Pres. JASBIR SINGH CHANDHOK; Gen. Sec. NARINDER SINGH SETHI.

Bombay Piece-Goods Merchants' Mahajan: Shaikh Memon St., Bombay 400002; f. 1881; 1,757 mems.; Pres. N. L. SHAH; Sec. N. M. BORADIA.

Bombay Presidency Association: 107 M. Gandhi Rd., Bombay 400023; f. 1886; Pres. NAUSHIR BHARUCHA.

Bombay Textile and Engineering Association: 343 Sattar Bldg., Grant Rd., Bombay 400007; f. 1900; Pres. N. F. BHARUCHA.

Calcutta Baled Jute Association: 6 Netaji Subhas Rd., Calcutta 700001; f. 1892; 58 mems.; Chair. SHANTI CHAND BOTHRA; Sec. M. GHOSH.

Calcutta Flour Mills Association: 6 Netaji Subhas Rd., Calcutta 700001; f. 1932; 25 mems.; Sec. M. GHOSE.

Calcutta Trades Association: 18H Park St., Stephen Court, Calcutta 700071; f. 1830; Master N. K. JALAN.

East India Cotton Association Ltd.: Cotton Exchange, Marwari Bazar, Bombay 400002; f. 1921; 354 mems.; Pres. PURSHOTTAMDAS JHUNJHUNWALA; Sec. D. G. DAMLE; publs. *Indian Cotton Annual, Cotton Statistics* (weekly).

Federation of Gujarat Mills and Industries: Federation Bldg., R. C. Dutt Rd., Vadodara 390005; f. 1918; 300 mems.; Pres. VISHWAJIT M. MEHTA; Sec. DINESH P. AMIN; publ. *FGMI Members' Monthly*.

Grain, Rice and Oilseeds Merchants' Association: Grainseeds House, 72/80 Yusef Meheralli Rd., Bombay 400003; f. 1899; 903 mems.; Pres. PREMJI VELJI LAKHAMSI; Hon. Secs. VASANJI LAKHAMSHI, VASANT KUMAR DEVJI; publ. *Vanijya* (monthly).

Indian Chemical Manufacturers Association: India Exchange, Calcutta; f. 1938; 210 mems.; Pres. M. B. MEHTA; Sec.-Gen. C. S. PANDE; publs. *Chemical Industry News* (monthly), and others.

Industries and Commerce Association: I.C.O. Association Rd., P.O.B. 70, Dhanbad 826001 (Bihar); f. 1933; 89 mems.; Pres. P. K. AGARWALLA.

Indian Jute Mills Association: Royal Exchange, 6 Netaji Subhas Rd., Calcutta 700001; sponsors and operates export promotion, research and product development; regulates labour relations; Chair. G. SIVARAMAN.

Indian Mining Association: 6 Netaji Subhas Rd., Calcutta 700001; f. 1892; 50 mems.; Sec. K. MUKERJEE.

Indian Mining Federation: 135 Biplabi Rashbehari Basu Rd., Calcutta 700001; est. 1913 to aid and stimulate mining, particularly coal, and to protect the commercial interests; 70 mems.; Chair. H. S. CHOPRA; Sec. M. DAS.

Indian National Shipowners' Association: Scindia House. Ballard Estate, Bombay; f. 1930; 34 mems.; Pres, Vice-Admiral R. K. S. GHANDHI; Sec. B. V. NILKUND; publ. *Indian Shipping*.

Indian Paper Mills Association: India Exchange, 8th Floor, India Exchange Place, Calcutta 700001; f. 1939; 36 mems.; Pres. S. BISWAS; Asst. Sec. B. GHOSH

Indian Sugar Mills Association: Sugar House, 39 Nehru Place, New Delhi 110019; f. 1932; 162 mems.; Pres. H. C. Kothari; Sec.-Gen. J. S. Mehta; publs. *Sugar Industry* (weekly), *Indian Sugar* (monthly).

Indian Tea Association: Royal Exchange, 6 Netaji Subhas Rd., Calcutta 700001; f. 1881; 249 mems. (incl. brs.); 499 tea states; Chair. S. K. Mehera; Sec. J. D'Souza.

Jute Balers' Association: 12 India Exchange Place, Calcutta 700001; f. 1909; over 500 ordinary and exchange mems.; represents all Indian Jute Balers; Chair. N. C. Toshniwal; Sec. R. N. Mohnot; publ. *The Jute Trade* (English, fortnightly).

Master Stevedores' Association: Royal Exchange, Calcutta; f. 1934; 11 mems.; Pres. D. S. Bose; Sec. M. Ghose.

Silk and Art Silk Mills' Association Ltd.: Resham Bhavan, 78 Veer Nariman Rd., Bombay 400020; f. 1939; 891 mems.; Chair. M. H. Doshi; Sec. D. A. Joshi.

Southern India Mills' Association: Racecourse, Coimbatore 641018, Tamil Nadu; f. 1933; 200 mems.; Chair. S. Devaraj; Sec. T. Rangaswamy.

EMPLOYERS' FEDERATIONS

Council of Indian Employers: Federation House, Tansen Marg, New Delhi 110001; f. 1956; Sec. B. M. Sethi; comprises:

All-India Organization of Employers: Federation House, Tansen Marg, New Delhi 110001; f. 1932; mems. 47 industrial associations and 130 large industrial concerns; Pres. Sudhir Jalan; Sec.-Gen. D. H. Pai Panandikar; Sec. B. M. Sethi; publ. *AIOE Labour News* (fortnightly).

Employers' Federation of India: Army and Navy Building, 148 Mahatma Gandhi Rd., Bombay 400023; f. 1933; 221 mems.; Pres. Naval H. Tata; Sec. N. M. Vakil.

Standing Conference of Public Enterprises (SCOPE): Chandralok Bldg., 36 Janpath, New Delhi 110001; f. 1973; representative body of all central public enterprises in India; advises the Government and public enterprises on matters of major policy and co-ordination; 159 mems.; Chair. B. L. Wadhera; Sec. Waris Rasheed Kidwai.

Employers' Association of Northern India: 14/69 Civil Lines, P.O.B. 344, Kanpur 208001; f. 1937; 142 mems.; Chair. R. C. Agarwal; Sec. D. Massey (acting).

Employers' Federation of Southern India: Dare House Annexe, 44 Moore St., P.O.B. 35, Madras 600001; f. 1920; 170 mem. firms; Chair. N. Venkataramani; Sec. C. S. Krishnaswami.

TRADE UNIONS

Indian National Trade Union Congress—INTUC: 1B Maulana Azad Rd., New Delhi 110011; f. 1947; the largest and most representative trade union organization in India; 3,731 affiliated unions with a total membership of 3,604,157; affiliated to ICFTU; 25 state brs. and 25 national industrial federations; Pres. Nand Kishore Bhatt; Gen. Sec. G. Ramanujam; Treas. V. R. Hoshing; publs. *The Indian Worker* (weekly, English), *Labour Information Service* (monthly, English).

Centre of Indian Trade Unions: 6 Talkatora Rd., New Delhi 110001; f. 1970; 1.7 million mems.; 3,641 affiliated unions; Pres. B. T. Ranadive; Gen. Sec. P. Ramamurti; publs. monthly journals *The Working Class* (English), *CITU Mazdoor* (Hindi).

National Industrial Federations

All India Council of Atomic Energy Employees: Tel Rasayan Bhavan, Tilak Rd., Dadar, Bombay 400014; f. 1981; 3,000 mems.; Pres. Raja Kulkarni.

Indian National Cement and Allied Workers' Federation: Mazdoor Karyalaya, Congress House, Bombay 400004; 87,000 mems.; Pres. H. N. Trivedi; Gen. Sec. I. M. Moinuddin.

Indian National Chemical Workers' Federation: Tel Rasayan Bhavan, Tilak Rd., Dadar, Bombay 400014; Pres. Raja Kulkarni; Gen. Sec. K. H. Dastoor.

Indian National Defence Workers' Federation: 25/19 Karachi Khana, Kanpur; Pres. Kali Mukherjee.

Indian National Electricity Workers' Federation: 19 Mazdoor Maidan, Power House, Jaipur 302006; Pres. J. C. Dikshit.

Indian National Metal Workers' Federation: 26K Rd., Jamshedpur 831001; Pres. V. G. Gopal; Gen. Sec. S. Gopeshwar.

Indian National Mineworkers' Federation: Rajendra Path, Dhanbad, Bihar; f. 1949; 300,835 mems. in 139 affiliated unions; Pres. Kanti Mehta; Gen. Sec. S. Das Gupta; publs. *Khan Mazdoor* (Hindi, weekly), *Mine and Metalworker* (English, fortnightly).

Indian National Paper Mill Workers' Federation: Ballarpur, Chanda; Pres. G. Sanjeeva Reddy; Gen. Sec. P. J. Nair.

Indian National Plantation Workers' Federation: P.O.B. 13, Rehabari, Dibrugarh; 261,000 mems. (est.) in 24 affiliated unions; Pres. K. P. Tripathi; Gen. Sec. G. Sarmah.

Indian National Port and Dock Workers' Federation: P.B. 87, Vasco-da-Gama 403802, Goa; f. 1954; 15 affiliated unions; 75,000 mems.; Pres. Mohan Nair; Gen. Sec. Janaki Mukherjee.

Indian National Press Workers' Federation: 162 South Ave., New Delhi 110011; Pres. S. W. Dhabe.

Indian National Sugar Mills Workers' Federation: 19 Lajpatrai Marg, Lucknow; 181 affiliated unions; 200,000 mems.; Pres. C. Singh; Gen. Sec. Ramnath Bharti.

Indian National Textile Workers' Federation: Mazdoor Manzil, G. D. Ambekar Marg Parel, Bombay 400012; f. 1948; 368 affiliated unions; 535,251 mems.; Pres. M. S. Ramchandran; Gen. Sec. A. T. Bhosale.

Indian National Transport Workers' Federation: Sham Shivir, Tansen Marg, Gwalior 474002; Pres. T. S. Viyogi; Gen. Sec. K. S. Verma.

National Federation of Petroleum Workers: Tel Rasayan Bhavan, Tilak Rd., Dadar, Bombay 400014; f. 1959; 22,340 mems.; Pres. Raja Kulkarni.

All-India Trade Union Congress: 24 K. M. Munshi Lane, New Delhi 110001; f. 1920; affiliated to WFTU; 2.74 million mems., 3,004 affiliated unions; 18 regional brs.; Pres. S. A. Dange; Gen. Sec. Indrajit Gupta; publ. *Trade Union Record* (English).

Major Affiliated Unions

Annamalai Plantation Workers' Union: Valparai, Via Pollachi, Tamil Nadu; over 21,000 mems.

Zilla Cha Bagan Workers' Union: Malabar, Jalpaiguri, West Bengal; 21,000 mems.

United Trades Union Congress—UTUC: 249 Bepin Behari Ganguly St., Calcutta 700012; f. 1949; 608,052 mems. from 607 affiliated unions; 10 state brs.; Pres. N. Srikantan Nair; Gen. Sec. Jatin Chakravorty.

MAJOR AFFILIATED UNIONS

All-India Farm Labour Union: c/o U.T.U.C. Jakkanpur New Area, Patna 800001, Bihar; over 35,000 mems. (est.).

Bengal Provincial Chatkal Mazdoor Union: 64 Chittarajan Ave., Calcutta 700012; textile workers; 28,330 mems.

Hind Mazdoor Sabha—HMS: Nagindas Chambers, 167 P. D'Mello Rd., Bombay 400038; f. 1948; affiliated to ICFTU; 1,849,990 mems. from 1,100 affiliated unions; 16 regional brs.; Pres. P. S. CHINNADURAI; Chief Exec. and Gen. Sec. D. D. VASISHT; publ. *Hind Mazdoor* (monthly).

MAJOR AFFILIATED UNIONS

Bombay Port Trust Employees Union: Pres. Dr. SHANTI PATEL; Gen. Sec. S. K. SHETYE.

Colliery Mazdoor Congress (*Coalminers' Union*) **& Koyala Ispat Mazdoor Panchayat Jharia-Asansol:** coal and steel workers; Working Pres. P. TIWARI; Gen. Sec. JAYANTA PODDER.

Oil & Natural Gas Commission Employees Mazdoor Sabha: Vadodara; 4,000 mems.; Pres. R. DULARE; Gen. Sec. G. G. PARADKAR.

South Central Railway Mazdoor Union: 7-C, Railway Bldg., Accounts Office Compound, Secunderabad 25, A.P.; 67,550 mems.; Gen. Sec. A. U. K. CHAITANYA.

West Bengal Chah Sramik Union: Jalpaiguri, West Bengal; 43,350 mems.; Pres. B. D. RAI; Gen. Sec. DEVEN SARKAR.

Confederation of Central Government Employees' Unions: New Delhi; 700,000 mems. (est.); Pres. M. BHAKAT; Sec.-Gen. S. K. VYAS.

AFFILIATED UNION

National Federation of Post, Telephone and Telegraph Employees—NFPTTE: 9 Pusa Rd., New Delhi; f. 1954; 175,000 mems. (est.); Gen. Sec. O. P. GUPTA.

All-India Bank Employees' Association—AIBEA: 10/9 East Patel Nagar, New Delhi; Gen. Sec. TARAKESWAR CHAKRAVARTY; publ. *Bank Karmchari*.

All-India Defence Employees' Federation—AIDEF: 70 Market Rd., Kirkee, Pune; 264 affiliated unions; over 400,000 mems.; Pres. S. M. BANERJEE; Gen. Sec. K. M. MATHEW.

All-India Port and Dock Workers' Federation: No. 9 Second Line Beach, Madras, 600001; f. 1948; 177,000 mems. in 30 affiliated unions; Pres. S. R. KULKARMI; Gen. Sec. S. C. C. ANTHONY PILLAI.

All-India Railwaymen's Federation—AIRF: 4 State Entry Road, New Delhi 110055; f. 1924; 753,727 mems.; Pres. U. M. PUROHIT; Gen. Sec. J. P. CHAUBEY; publs. *Indian Railwaymen, Bhartiya Railwaymen* (monthly).

National Federation of Indian Railwaymen—NFIR: 3 Chelmsford Rd., New Delhi 110055; f. 1952; 15 affiliated unions; 600,162 mems.; Pres. T. V. ANANDAN; Gen. Sec. KESHAV H. KULKARNI; publ. *Indian Rail Worker* (monthly).

MAJOR INDUSTRIAL COMPANIES

GOVERNMENT INDUSTRIAL UNDERTAKINGS

The following are some of the more important industrial and commercial undertakings in which the Government holds the majority of shares.

Bharat Aluminium Co. Ltd.: Punj House, 18 Nehru Place, New Delhi 110019; f. 1965; cap. Rs. 1,598.7m., total assets Rs. 3,453.4m. (1980/81).

Runs integrated aluminium project at Korba (Madhya Pradesh); plans to set up alumina plants in Andhra Pradesh (with Soviet aid).

Chair. and Man. Dir. I. M. AGA.

Bharat Coking Coal Ltd.: Bhuggatdih Bldgs., Jharia 828111, Dhanbad, Bihar; f. 1972; auth. cap. Rs. 1,500m.

A subsidiary of Coal India Ltd.; manages coking coal mines nationalized in 1972; coal production in 1978/79: 19.72m. tonnes.

Chair. and Man. Dir. B. R. PRASHAD (acting).

Bharat Electronics Ltd.: Jalahalli P.O., Bangalore 560013; f. 1954; cap. Rs. 130m., total assets Rs. 1,399m. (1977/78).

Manufacture of electronic and radar equipment and electronic components; units at Ghaziabad and Pune.

Chair. M. G. K. MENON; Man. Dir. N. L. KRISHNAN; employees: 16,000.

Bharat Heavy Electricals Ltd.: Hindustan Times House, 18–20 Kasturba Gandhi Marg, New Delhi 110001; f. 1964; Share cap. Rs. 1,500m.; res. and surplus Rs. 1,264 m.

Integrated world-wide service in power generation, transmission and utilization equipment; plants at Bhopal, Jhansi, Hardwar, Hyderabad, Bangalore and Tiruchirapau; overseas offices in London and Moscow.

Chair. and Man. Dir. K. L. PURI.

Bharat Petroleum Corporation Ltd.: P.O.B. 688, Bharat Bhavan, Ballard Estate, Bombay 400038; f. 1952 as Burmah-Shell Refineries Ltd., nationalized 1976; cap. res. 145.4m.; res. 497.9m.

Refinery at Trombay with crude processing capacity of 6m. metric tons a year. Manufactures motor spirit, kerosene, aviation turbine fuel, high speed diesel oil, light diesel oil, jute batching oil, fuel oil, bitumen, liquefied petroleum gas, solvents, refinery gas, aviation gasoline, naphthas, mineral turpentines, carbon black feedstock, hot heavy stock and cutbacks. Owns five port installations, two lubricating oil blending plants, 69 depots and 3,315 retail outlets throughout the country.

Chair. and Man. Dir. U. K. KINI; employees: about 5,000.

Bokaro Steel Ltd.: Main Administrative Bldg., Bokaro Steel City 827011, Dhanbad District, Bihar; f. 1964; part of Steel Authority of India Ltd. (SAIL); cap. Rs. 5,000m., total assets Rs. 13,823m. (1977/78).

To manage the fourth steel plant in the public sector, under construction at Bokaro. The first stage of construction is complete. Bokaro markets hot rolled sheets. plates and coils and cold rolled sheets and coils.

Man. Dir. D. R. AHUJA; Sec. L. A. K. PRASAD.

Cement Corporation of India Ltd.: Shakuntla Apts., 59 Nehru Place, New Delhi 110019; f. 1965; cap. Rs. 300m.

To set up cement factories in various parts of the country, survey and prospect for limestone deposits; also offers consultancy services.

Man. Dir. A. P. MAHESWARI.

Central Coalfields Ltd.: Darbhanga House, Ranchi 834001, Bihar; f. 1973; auth. cap. Rs. 1,500m.

Wholly-owned subsidiary of Coal India Ltd.; the Company had 64 collieries, 4 washeries, 2 workshops and 2 coke oven plants in 1978/79; coal production in 1978/79: 23.43m. tonnes.

Chair. and Man. Dir. B. L. WADHERA.

Damodar Valley Corporation: Bhabani Bhavan, Alipore, Calcutta 700027; f. 1948; cap. p.u. Rs. 2,147.2m.

Set up to administer the Damodar Valley Project, which aims at unified development of irrigation, flood control and power generation in West Bengal and Bihar; runs 3 hydel and 3 thermal power stations; power generating capacity 1,361.5 MW (March 1982).

Chair. P. C. LUTHAR.

Eastern Coalfields Ltd.: Sanctoria, P.O. Dishergarh 713333, Burdwan, West Bengal; f. 1975; auth. cap. Rs. 1,500m.

Subsidiary of Coal India Ltd.; coal production in 1978/79: 22.06m. tonnes.

Chair. and Man. Dir. N. MITRA (acting).

Fertilizers and Chemicals (Travancore) Ltd.: P.O.B. 14, Udyogamandal 683501, Via Cochin, Kerala; f. 1943; auth. cap. Rs. 1,500m.

Major share-holdings were passed onto the Government in 1963; engaged in the manufacture of fertilizers and chemicals of different qualities.

Chair. and Man. Dir. V. SUBRAMANIAM.

Fertilizer Corporation of India: Madhuban, 55 Nehru Place, New Delhi 110024; f. 1961; cap. Rs. 7,000 m., total assets Rs. 11,497m. (1977/78); in 1978 the Corporation was reorganized into four units:

Fertilizer Corporation of India:

Runs Sindri, Gorakhpur, Talcher, Ramagundam and Korba fertilizer plants.

Chair. and Man. Dir. P. L. KUKREJA.

Rashtriya Chemicals and Fertilizers Ltd.: Administrative Bldg., Marvali, Chembur, Bombay 400074.

Runs Trombay fertilizer plant; expansion projects and proposed new projects.

Chair. and Man. Dir. DULEEP SINGH.

Hindustan Fertilizer Corporation Ltd.: 55 Nehru Place, New Delhi 110019.

Runs Barauni, Durgapur, Haldia and Namrup fertilizer plants.

Chair. P. K. GHOSH.

Projects and Development India Ltd.: CIFT Bldg., Sindri 828122, Dhanbad, Bihar.

Chair. and Man. Dir. K. S. SARMA.

Heavy Engineering Corporation Ltd.: Plant Plaza Rd., Ranchi 834004; f. 1956; cap. Rs. 1,618m., total assets Rs. 3,315m. (1977/78).

Runs a heavy machine building plant, a foundry forge plant and heavy machine tools plant; employees: 21,000.

Chair. and Man. Dir. S. R. JAIN.

Hindustan Aeronautics Ltd.: Indian Express Bldg., P.B. 5150, Vidhana Veedhi, Bangalore 560001, Karnataka; f. 1964; total cap. Rs. 2,004.9m.

Manufactures aircraft, helicopters, aero-engines, airborne electronic equipment and accessories; undertakes overhaul of aircraft, etc.; mainly manufactures for the Indian Air Force; 11 divisions; factories at Bangalore, Hyderabad, Koraput, Nasik, Kanpur and Lucknow.

Chair. Capt. B. K. KAPUR; Man. Dir. (Bangalore) P. D. CHOPRA; employees: 41,195.

Hindustan Copper Ltd.: Industry House, 10 Camac St., Calcutta 700017; f. 1967; auth. cap. Rs. 1,000m.

Responsible for the development of Indian Copper Complex, Ghatsila, Bihar, Khetri Copper Complex, Dariba Copper Deposit and Chamdmari Copper Deposit in Rajasthan, Rakha Copper Project, Bihar and Malanjkhand Copper Project, Madhya Pradesh; produced 21,888 tonnes of blister copper in 1978/79.

Chair. and Man. Dir. O. P. VASUDEVA.

Hindustan Machine Tools Ltd. (HMT): 36 Cunningham Rd., Bangalore 560052; f. 1953; cap. Rs. 373m., total assets Rs. 1,625m.

India's largest machine tools manufacturer with units at Bangalore, Pinjore (Haryana), Kalamassery (Kerala), Hyderabad, Ajmer, Tumkur and Srinagar.

Chair. and Man. Dir. T. B. MANSUKHANI; employees: 24,722.

Hindustan Petroleum Corporation Ltd.: 17 J. Tata Rd., Bombay 400020; f. 1952 as Esso Standard Refining Co. of India Ltd.; fully nationalized 1976; total assets Rs. 1,224m. (1977/78).

Petroleum refining, manufacture of lubricating oil base stocks and marketing of petroleum products. Refinery at Trombay (capacity 3.5m. metric tons a year), producing petrol, kerosene, diesel oils, fuel oils, solvents, LPG, asphalts, etc., and at Visakhapatnam (AP) (capacity 1.6m. metric tons a year), producing liquid petroleum gas, naphtha, motor gasoline, aviation turbine fuel, mineral turpentine, kerosene, etc. Lube refinery uses crude from fuel refinery; production exceeds designed capacity of 164,000 metric tons a year. Has about 17 per cent share in the Indian oil market.

Chair. and Man. Dir. R. M. BHANDARI.

Hindustan Zinc Ltd.: 6 New Fatehpura, Udaipur 313001 Rajasthan; f. 1966; share cap. Rs. 902m., res. and surplus Rs. 295.1m.

Established to develop mining and smelting capacities for metal, particularly zinc and lead; units: zinc smelter, Dibari, Rajasthan, lead smelter, Tundoo, Bihar and lead smelter, Vishakhapatnam, Andhra Pradesh; produces zinc ingots, cadmium, refined lead, refined silver, sulphuric acid, etc.

Chair. and Man. Dir. RAM PRAKASH KAPUR.

Indian Iron and Steel Co. Ltd.: 50 Chowringhee Rd., Calcutta 700071; f. 1918; cap. p.u. Rs. 877.7m.; res. 44m.

A subsidiary of Steel Authority of India Ltd. (SAIL); major establishments; iron and steel works at Burnpur and foundry at Kulti and the township of Burnpur and Kulti, West Bengal; ore mines (iron ore and manganese deposits) in Singhbhum district of Bihar; mining rights for phosphate rock and phosphate of lime near Ghatsila; collieries and coal lands at Ramnagore, Noonodih Jitpur and Chasnalla.

Man. Dir. K. R. SANGANESWARAN.

Indian Oil Corporation Ltd.: 254-C, Dr. Annie Besant Rd., Prabhadevi, Bombay 400025; f. 1964; share cap. Rs. 821.8m.; res. and surplus Rs. 4,236.7m.

The Refineries and Pipelines Division in New Delhi manages five refineries. The division lays pipelines and manages the Gauhati–Siliguri, Haldia–Barauni–Kanpur, Haldia–Mourigram–Rajbandh, Salaya–Koyali–Mathura and Koyali–Ahmedabad oil pipelines. The Marketing Division in Bombay distributes petroleum products and has about 60 per cent share in the Indian oil market. Lube blending plant at Madras; Research and Development Centre at Faridabad, New Delhi; Indian Oil Blending Ltd., a fully-owned subsidiary, has blending plants at Calcutta and Bombay; Assam Oil Division manages Digboi Refinery (Assam) and markets petroleum products in the north-east.

Chair. A. J. A. TAURO.

Indian Petrochemicals Corporation Ltd.: P.O. Petrochemicals, Gujarat 391346; f. 1969; cap. Rs. 1,860m., total assets Rs. 3,657m. (1977/78).

Established to aid and initiate the development of petrochemical complexes in the public sector.

Chair. and Man. Dir. Dr. S. VARADARAJAN.

Indian Telephone Industries Ltd.: Dooravani Nagar, Bangalore 560016, Karnataka; total assets Rs. 1,264m. (1977/78).

Manufacturers of all types of telecommunication equipment: telephones, automatic exchanges, long-distance transmission equipment, microwave equipment; will manufacture all ground communication equipment for the 22 earth stations of the Indian National Satellite; in conjunction with the Post and Telegraph Department, a newly designed 2,000 line exchange has been completed.

Chair. and Man. Dir. C. S. S. RAO; Gen. Man. K. THOMAS KORA.

Instrumentation Ltd.: Kota 324005, Rajasthan; f. 1964.

The largest manufacturers of industrial process control instruments in India; designs, builds, erects and commissions instrumentation systems; manufactures control valves and allied items with the technical collaboration of Japan, gas analysers used in pollution control with the Federal Republic of Germany and modernized process control instruments with the U.K.

Chair. and Man. Dir. Brig. Y. NIRULA.

National Mineral Development Corporation Ltd.: Pioneer House, P.B. 52, Somajiguda, Hyderabad 500004; f. 1958.

The exploitation and evaluation of minerals in the public sector, excluding coal, lignite, oil and natural gas; the acquisition of mines for prospecting and development for optimum utilization of the country's mineral resources. Projects include iron ore at Kiriburu (Bihar), Bailadila (Madhya Pradesh), Dominalai (Karnataka), Meghahatuburu (Bihar) and diamonds at Panna (Madhya Pradesh); carries out a consultancy service for several major organizations in India and abroad; produced 7.13 million tons of iron ore and 14,210 carats of diamonds in 1978/79, now diversifying into iron ore pelletization.

Chair. and Man. Dir. C. S. VENUGOPALA RAO.

Neyveli Lignite Corporation Ltd.: Neyveli, South Arcot Dist., Tamil Nadu 607801; f. 1956; auth. cap. Rs. 2,550m.

Activities include power generation and production of urea and carbonized briquettes.

Chair. and Man. Dir. G. L. TANDON.

Oil India Ltd.: Allahabad Bank Bldg., 17 Parliament St., New Delhi 110001; f. 1959.

Formed as a result of an agreement between the Government of India, the Burmah Oil Company Ltd. and the Assam Oil Company Ltd., for the development of new oilfields in Assam. The company has mining leases for the exploration and production of crude oil and natural gas in Nahorkatiya, Hugrijan, Moran and Dum Duma and a petroleum exploration licence in Arunachal Pradesh. It has begun off-shore exploration in the Bay of Bengal (Mahanadi). It supplies crude oil to the refineries at Barauni, Gauhati, Bongaigaon and Digboi. It is also engaged in the transport of oil and the sale of gas. For this purpose the company has constructed and is operating a network of pipelines. In 1982, Oil India Ltd. plans to commission a plant for the manufacture of liquefied petroleum gas.

Man. Dir. C. R. JAGANNATHAN; employees: 5,311; publ. *O.I.L. News*, monthly; circ. 6,100.

Oil and Natural Gas Commission: Tel Bhavan, Dehradun 248001; f. 1956; cap. Rs. 3,429m., total assets Rs. 12,594m. (1980/81).

Engaged in exploration and exploitation of oil in India and abroad.

Chair. S. P. WAHI.

Tea Trading Corpn. of India Ltd.: 7 Wood St., (2nd Floor), Calcutta 700016; f. 1973.

Promotes the export and local sale of tea; owns and manages tea estates; processes and manufactures tea in blended and packaged form; is expanding into export of sea foods and processed fruit and food products.

Gen. Man. V. ANAND.

Tungabhadra Steel Products Ltd.: P.O. Tungabhadra Dam, Bellary District, Karnataka; f. 1960, acquired by Govt. of India 1967.

Designs, manufactures and erects steel structures including hoists, gantries, cranes, pressure vessels, heavy structurals and galvanized high transmission line towers; operates a galvanizing plant with a capacity of 3,000 metric tons a year. Solar water heating system for domestic, industrial and commercial purposes.

Man. Dir. Y. ADINARAYANA SASTRI; Gen. Man. M. KALAPPA.

Western Coalfields Ltd.: Bisesar House, Temple Rd., Nagpur 440001, Maharashtra; f. 1975; auth. cap. Rs. 1,500m.

Wholly-owned subsidiary of Coal India Ltd.; coal production in 1978/79: 24.23m. tonnes.

Chair. and Man. Dir. D. P. GUPTA.

PRIVATE COMPANIES

The following are India's major industrial firms in the private sector, arranged by industry.

AUTOMOBILE INDUSTRY

Ashok Leyland Ltd.: Ennore, Madras; f. 1948; cap. Rs. 165m., res. 446.9m.

Manufactures Leyland Comet trucks and buses, Beaver, Hipo and Jumbo trucks in range of 5 to over 16 metric tons.

Chair. and Man. Dir. R. J. SHAHANEY.

Hindustan Motors Ltd.: Birla Bldg., 9–1 R. N. Mukherjee Rd., Calcutta 1; f. 1942; cap. Rs. 300m.

Manufactures cars, truck chassis, cranes, presses, excavators, steel structurals, steel castings and forgings at factory at Hindmotor (Hooghly District) and dumpers, crawler tractors, front end loaders at factory in Trivellore.

Chair. B. M. BIRLA.

Mahindra & Mahindra Ltd.: Gateway Bldg., Apollo Bunder, Bombay 400039; f. 1945; cap. Rs. 131.9m.; res. 244.6m.

Manufactures "Mahindra" range of vehicles, tractors and agricultural implements, industrial engines, industrial process and control instruments. Trades in steel and machine tools, exports and imports chemicals, engineering goods, diesel engines etc. Four subsidiaries in India.

Chair. KESHUB MAHINDRA; Man. Dir. B. R. SULE.

Premier Automobiles Ltd.: Construction House, Ballard Estate, Bombay 400038; f. 1944; cap. Rs. 74.8m.

Manufactures cars and commercial vehicles, industrial

and marine diesel engines, MS Tubes and air conditioners.

Chair. LALCHAND HIRACHAND; Man. Dir. P. N. VENCATESAN; employees: 9,143.

Tata Engineering & Locomotive Co. Ltd.: Bombay House, 24 Homi Mody St., Bombay 400023; Export Dept.: Shiv Sagar Estate, Worli, Bombay 400018; f. 1945; cap. p.u. Rs. 315.1m.; res. 809.5m.

Manufactures and sells Tata Diesel truck and bus chassis, Tata P & H earth moving equipment, press tools and dies, special purpose machines. Factories at Jamshedpur and Pune.

Chair. S. MOOLGAOKAR; Vice-Chair. N. A. PALKHIWALA; employees: 39,090.

CEMENT INDUSTRY

Associated Cement Companies Ltd.: Cement House, 121 Maharshi Karve Rd., Bombay 400020; f. 1936; cap. Rs. 332.3m.; res. Rs. 190.1m.

Manufacture and sale of cement (17 cement works in 9 states), refractories (Katni), coal (Kotma and Nowrozabad), special products (Porbandar), engineering (Shahabad). Subsidiaries: ACC-Vickers-Babcock Ltd., and Associated Tyre Machinery Co. Ltd.

Chair N. A. PALKHIVALA; Man. Dir. S. KRISHNASWAMI; employees: 28,300.

India Cements Ltd.: 4th Floor, Dhun Bldg., 175/1 Mount Rd., Madras 600002; f. 1946; cap. Rs. 52m.

Manufactures cement, cement clinker, grinding media, malleable cast' iron material, etc. Factories at Sankarnagar (Tirunelveli District), Sankaridrug (Salem District).

Chair. R. RAMJEEDASS IYER; Man. Dir. K. S. NARAYANAN.

CHEMICALS

The Alkali & Chemical Corporation of India Ltd.: 34 Chowringhee, Calcutta 700071; f. 1937; cap. Rs. 51.2m.

Manufacturers of liquid chlorine, caustic soda, hydrochloric acid, BHC (tech.), "Alfloc" water treatment chemicals, paints, polythene, agricultural chemicals, rubber chemicals, phenothiazine and various pharmaceuticals.

Chair. A. L. MUDALIAR; Man. Dir. Dr. S. GANGULY; employees: 3,469.

Atul Products Ltd. (Gujarat): Atul 396020 (Bulsar District); f. 1947; cap. Rs. 49m.

Manufacture dyes, chemicals, pesticides and pharmaceuticals.

Chair. and Man. Dir. SIDDHARTH K. LALBHAI; Man-Dirs. CHINUBHAI CHIMANBHAI, MANAN NIRANJAN LALBHAI.

See also some of the companies listed under Cotton Textiles, etc.

CONSTRUCTION

The Hindustan Construction Co. Ltd.: Construction House, Walchand Hirachand Marg, Ballard Estate, Bombay 400038; f. 1926; cap. Rs. 27m.

Constructs concrete dams, railways and hydro tunnels, power houses, docks, jetties, barrages, industrial structures, environmental engineering projects, etc. Major projects: Maneri Bhali, Salal, Idamalayar and Kadamparai Hydro-electric works, Teesta, Mahananda Barrages, tunnelling by shield method for Calcutta Metro, Narora Atomic Power project, Barauni, Titagarh, Farakka and Ramagundam Thermal Power projects, Cochin Tanker Terminal and fertilizer berths at Cochin port, construction at Upper Kolab Dam. Brs. in New Delhi, Calcutta, Madras; civil works in Iraq and Tanzania.

Chief Exec. A. NAGABHUSHANA RAU; employees: 30,000.

COTTON TEXTILES, JUTE, MAN-MADE FIBRES

Birla Jute Manufacturing Co. Ltd.: Birlapur, 24 Parganas, West Bengal; f. 1919; cap. Rs. 60m.

Manufacture and sale of jute goods, calcium carbide, staple fibre yarn and cement, jute carpets and webbing. Three subsidiary companies.

Chief officials: R. K. CHHAOCHHARIA, R. L. THIRANI, J. R. BIRLA, S. N. PRASAD, B. L. SHAH, C. B. NEVATIA, G. D. DADOO, C. L. GOSWAMI, M. D. PODDAR, U. S. SETHIA; employees: 16,000.

The Bombay Dyeing & Manufacturing Co. Ltd.: Neville House, Ballard Estate, Bombay 400038; f. 1879; cap. Rs. 104.1m.

Manufacturers and exporters of cotton yarn and textiles, and blends of cotton and synthetic fibres. Two mills and a processing works in Bombay and Roha (Maharashtra).

Chair. and Man. Dir. NUSLI N. WADIA; employees: 14,400.

Century Spinning and Manufacturing Company Ltd.: Century Bhavan, Dr. Annie Besant Rd., Bombay 400025; f. 1897; cap. Rs. 270m.

Manufactures cotton fabrics, grey, bleached, dyed and printed sheetings, cotton yarn, poplin, organdie, mulls, voiles, shirtings, etc.; mill at Worli (Bombay), viscose rayon yarn, tyre yarn and caustic soda plants at Kalyan, portland cement plants at Baikunth and Sarlanagar (Madhya Pradesh).

Chair. B. K. BIRLA.

Delhi Cloth & General Mills Co. Ltd.: P.O.B. 1039, Bara Hindu Rao, Delhi 110006; f. 1889; cap. Rs. 196m.

Manufactures cotton and synthetic textiles, sulphuric acid, urea, PVC, caustic soda, alums, superphosphate, sugar, confectionery, alcohol, edible vegetable oils, calcium carbide, rayon type cord, electronic desk calculators, etc. One subsidiary company.

Man. Dirs. Dr. BHARAT RAM, Dr. CHARAT RAM; employees: 35,000.

The Gwalior Rayon Silk Mfg. (Wvg.) Co. Ltd.: Birlagram, Nagda; f. 1947; cap. Rs. 963m.

Viscose staple fibre; dissolving pulp and paper; man-made fabrics; cotton textiles; also manufactures rayon and allied chemical plant and machinery.

Chair. A. BIRLA; Pres. INDU H. PAREKH; employees: 15,000.

Jiyajeerao Cotton Mills Ltd.: Birlanagar, Gwalior; f. 1921; cap. Rs. 72m.

Manufactures variety of cloths and runs own power house. Chemical plant at Porbandar producing soda ash and caustic soda.

Chair. M. P. BIRLA.

Kesoram Industries and Cotton Mills Ltd.: 9/1 R. N. Mukherjee Rd., Calcutta 1; f. 1919; cap. Rs. 75m.

Manufactures cotton textiles and piece goods, rayon yarn, transparent paper, cellulose film, sulphuric acid, carbon disulphide, cast iron spun pipes and fittings, cement, refractories, etc.

Dirs. B. K. BIRLA, B. P. RAY, B. S. BHATT, P. D. HIMAT SINGKA, K. G. MAHESWARI, A. S. GUPTA, PROMAD KHAITAN.

The National Rayon Corporation Ltd.: Ewart House, Homi Mody St., Fort, Bombay 400023; f. 1946; cap. Rs. 60.75m.

Manufactures textile rayon yarn, rayon tyre yarn, nylon tyre yarn, caustic soda, liquid chlorine, hydrochloric acid, hydrogen, sulphuric acid, carbon disulphide, carbon tetrachloride and anhydrous sodium sulphate. Factory at Mohone, Kalyan; six other branches.

Chair. B. R. PATEL; employees: 8,000.

ELECTRICAL GOODS

Peico Electronics and Electricals Ltd.: Philips House, 7 Justice Chandra Madhab Rd., Calcutta 700020; f. 1930; total cap. Rs. 306m.

Manufactures lighting equipment and other radio and electronic goods; factories at Calcutta, Bombay and Pune.

Chair. and Man. Dir. C. J. SEELEN.

Union Carbide India Ltd.: 1 Middleton St., Calcutta 700071; f. 1934; cap. p.u. Rs. 326m.; res. 202m.

Manufactures all types of dry cells and batteries for radio and telecommunication purposes, zinc alloys, various organic chemicals, polyethelene and allied products, pesticides, etc.; engaged in commercial fishing and processing of marine products for export. One subsidiary company, Nepal Battery Co. Ltd.

Chair. KESHUB MAHINDRA; Man. Dir. W. R. CORREA.

Voltas Ltd.: Volkart Bldg., 19 Graham Rd., Ballard Estate, Bombay 400038; P.O.B. 900; f. 1954; cap. Rs. 62.3m.

An integrated marketing, engineering and manufacturing company with country-wide selling and service organization. Manufactures air-conditioning and refrigeration equipment, water coolers, core drills, diamond bits, water well drills, fork-lift trucks, power capacitators and air and water pollution control equipment.

Chair. AKBAR HYDARI; Vice-Chair. and Man. Dir. A. H. TOBACCOWALA.

INDUSTRIAL AND BUILDING SUPPLIES

ACC-Vickers Babcock Ltd.: 18th Floor, Express Towers, Nariman Point, Bombay 400021; f. 1959; cap. Rs. 100m.

Manufactures cement making machinery, mining equipment, boilers and pressure vessels. Factories at Durgapur and Shahabad (Karnataka).

Chair. S. MOOLGAOKAR.

Indian Oxygen Ltd.: Oxygen House, P34 Taratala Rd., Calcutta 700053; f. 1935; cap. p.u. Rs. 82.1m.; res. 239.6m.

Manufacturers and suppliers of industrial and medical gases, including special gases and gas mixtures of ultra high purity; electrodes and other welding equipment including fluxes; cutting apparatus, medical and surgical equipment; oxygen and other gas plants and high-pressure industrial and medical pipelines; liquid oxygen explosives. Factories and depots all over India; subsidiaries of BOC Ltd., London.

Chair. RUSSI MODY; Man. Dir. SAT DEV SINGH; employees: 6,000.

Larsen & Toubro Ltd.: L&T House, Narottam Morarji Marg, Ballard Estate, Bombay 400038; f. 1938; cap. Rs. 480m.

Manufacturers and suppliers of equipment to atomic energy, power, steel, cement, minerals and oil, chemical, food and pulp and paper industries, construction, earth moving, instruments and valves, and other industrial appliances and accessories; six subsidiary companies.

Chair. and Pres. N. M. DESAI; employees: 10,000.

Textile Machinery Corporation Ltd.: P.O. Belgharia, 24 Parganas, Calcutta 700056; f. 1939; cap. Rs. 50m.

Manufactures textile machinery, rolling stock, boilers of all types, sugar mill machinery, steel and cast iron castings, machine tools, heavy, medium and light structurals and other engineering goods.

Dirs. K. K. BIRLA, D. P. GOENKA, D. N. KAPUR, Dr. S. C. LAW, SUROTTAM P. HUTHEESING, G. R. PODAR, A. L. GOENKA.

METALS

Guest Keen Williams Ltd.: 97 Andul Rd., Howrah 711103, West Bengal; f. 1931; cap. Rs. 100m.

Manufacture metal pressings, alloys and special steels, industrial fasteners, automative forgings, electrical stamping and laminations, strip wound cores, railway track fasteners and accessories.

Chair. K. B. LALL; Man. Dir. S. RAY.

Hindustan Aluminium Corporation Ltd.: 45 Race Course Rd., Bangalore 560001; f. 1958; cap. Rs. 200m.

Produces alumina, aluminium and aluminium products and by-products.

Chair. G. D. BIRLA.

Indian Aluminium Co. Ltd.: 1 Middleton St., Calcutta 700071, P.O.B. 361; f. 1938; cap. p.u. Rs. 304.7m.

Owns and operates bauxite mines (Lohardaga, Bihar: 210,767 metric tons a year) (Chandgad, Maharashtra: 406,013 metric tons); alumina plants (Muri, Bihar: 75,000 metric tons) (Belgaum, Karnataka: 160,000 metric tons); smelters (Alupuram, Kerala: 15,850 metric tons) (Hirakud, Orissa: 20,320 metric tons) (Belgaum: 60,000 metric tons); sheet mills (Belur, West Bengal: 18,000 metric tons) (Taloja, Maharashtra: 15,175 metric tons); Properzi plant (Alupuram, Kerala: 8,000 metric tons); foil plant (Kalwa, Maharashtra: 4,000 metric tons); powder and paste plant (Kalwa, Maharashtra: 1,600 metric tons); extrusion plant (Alupuram, Kerala: 3,760 metric tons).

Chair. KESHUB MAHINDRA; Man. Dir. T. D. SINHA; employees: 7,917.

Indian Tube Company Ltd.: 43 Chowringhee Rd., Calcutta 700071; P.O.B. 270; f. 1954; cap. Rs. 250m. (authorized).

Manufactures steel tubes, rectangular and square hollow sections and cold rolled steel strips at Jamshedpur and Bihar.

Chair. R. H. MODY; Man. Dir. R. K. BHASIN.

The Tata Iron and Steel Co. Ltd.: Bombay House, 24 Homi Mody St., Fort, Bombay 400023; f. 1907; cap. Rs. 628.5m.

Integrated iron and steel plant at Jamshedpur (Bihar) with annual saleable steel capacity of 1.5m. metric tons. Main steel products comprise sheets, narrow strips, plates, structurals, bars, billets, high silicon sheets, rolled rings, rails, wheels, axles and agricultural implements such as hoes, picks, beaters; by-products such as benzol, ammonium sulphate.

Chair. J. R. D. TATA; Vice-Chair. R. H. MODY; employees: 65,000.

PAPER

Orient Paper and Industries Ltd.: Brajrajnagar, near Jharsuguda, District Sambalpur, Orissa; f. 1936; cap. Rs. 11m.

There are mills at Brajrajnagar, with a capacity of

76,000 metric tons per year, and at Amlai (Madhya Pradesh), with a capacity of 85,000 metric tons per year. A cement plant with a capacity of 900,000 tons has been commissioned at Devapur (Andhra Pradesh).

Chair. G. P. BIRLA.

Rohtas Industries Ltd.: Dalmiangar, Shahabad District (Bihar), Railway Station, Dehri-on-Sone; f. 1933; cap. Rs. 150m.

Manufactures cement, paper, chemicals, asbestos cement sheets, vanaspati, vulcanized fibre, etc. Also has an electricity generating plant and workshop.

Chair. ASHOK JAIN; Sec. P. R. KRISHNAMOORTHY.

RUBBER

Dunlop India Ltd.: 57B Mirza Ghalib St., Calcutta 700016; f. 1926; cap. Rs. 157m.

Manufactures tyres and tubes for bicycles, automobiles, aircraft, earth-moving equipment, tractors, conveyor and transmission belting, hoses, bicycle rims and Metalastik products.

Chair. and Man. Dir. L. J. TOMPSETT; employees: 10,200.

Synthetics and Chemicals Ltd.: 7 Jamshedji Tata Rd., Churchgate Reclamation, Bombay 400020; f. 1960; cap. Rs. 150m.

Manufactures synthetic rubbers, including styrene-butadiene rubbers (SBR), acrylonitrile-butadiene rubbers (NBR) and synthetic latices; also ABS plastics.

Chair. S. L. KIRLOSKAR.

MISCELLANEOUS

Hindustan Lever Ltd.: Hindustan Lever House, 165/166 Backbay Reclamation, Bombay 400020; P.O.B. 409; f. 1933; cap. p.u. Rs. 291.6m., res. and surplus Rs. 551.7m.

Manufacture and sale of washing products, toilet preparations, edible fats, food products, animal and poultry feeds, ossein, di-calcium phosphate and chemicals. One subsidiary company and three trust companies for administering pensions, etc.

Chair. A. S. GANGULY; employees: 7,300.

ITC Ltd.: Virginia House, 37 Chowringhee, Calcutta 700071; P.O.B. 89; f. 1910; cap. Rs. 272.9m.; res. 238m.

Manufacture and sale of cigarettes, smoking tobaccos, printed and packaging material; development of tobacco and tobacco cultivation; purchase, processing and sale of tobacco for industrial use in the export and domestic markets; hoteliering; export of foods, including marine foods and general merchandise.

Chair. A. N. HAKSAR.

Tata Oil Mills Co. Ltd.: Bombay House, 24 Homi Mody St., Fort, Bombay 400023; f. 1917.

Manufactures edible oils, soaps, detergents, toiletries, glycerine, processed marine products, animal feed and food products.

Employees: 5,343.

TRANSPORT

RAILWAYS

Indian Government Administration (Ministry of Railways, Railway Board): Rail Bhawan, Raisina Rd., New Delhi; Chair. M. S. GUJRAL.

The Indian Government exercises direct or indirect control over all railways in the Republic of India through the medium of the Railway Board.

ZONAL RAILWAYS

The railways are grouped into nine zones:

Northern: Delhi; Gen. Man. R. SRINIVASAN.

Western: Bombay; Gen. Man. S. SARATH.

Central: Bombay-VT; Gen. Man. T. N. RAMACHANDRAN.

Southern: Madras; Gen. Man. VERGHESE ANVER.

Eastern: Calcutta; Gen. Man. C. K. SWAMINATHAN.

South Eastern: Calcutta; Gen. Man. R. P. SINGH.

South Central: Secunderabad; Gen. Man. S. M. KAUL.

North Eastern: Gorakhpur; Gen. Man. A. K. BHADURI.

Northeast Frontier: Maligaon and Gauhati; Gen. Man. K. T. V. RAGHAVAN.

India's railway system is the largest in Asia and the fourth largest in the world. The total length of Indian railways in March 1981 was 61,240 route km.

Note: An underground railway for Calcutta is scheduled for completion by 1986. It is expected to serve more than one million people daily and to total 17 km. in length.

ROADS

In December 1979 there were 1,604,110 km. of roads in India, 29,340 km. of which were main roads and 485,997 km. secondary roads. Estimated expenditure on roads in 1978/79 was Rs. 1,000m.

Ministry of Shipping and Transport (Roads Wing): Transport Bhawan No. 1, Parliament St., New Delhi 110001; responsible for the maintenance of India's system of National Highways, with an aggregate length of about 29,340 km. in 1980, connecting the State capitals and major ports and linking with the highway systems of its neighbours. This system includes 57 highways and they constitute the main trunk roads of the country. There are also four express highways and work on a fifth was in progress in 1979.

Border Roads Development Board: f. 1960 to accelerate the economic development of the north and north-eastern border areas; it has constructed 7,470 km. of new roads, improved 4,904 km. of existing roads and surfaced 8,913 km. (1976).

Central Road Transport Corporation Ltd.: 4 Fairlie Place, Calcutta 700001; f. 1964 to supplement the transport capacity in the eastern sector of the country; fleet of over 200 trucks; Chair. Commdr. K. CHELLIAH; Man. Dir. M. YUSUF KHAN.

INLAND WATERWAYS

About 16,180 km. of rivers are navigable by mechanically propelled country vessels and 3,631 km. by large country boats. Services are mainly on the Ganga and Brahmaputra and their tributaries, the Godavari and Krishna.

Central Inland Water Transport Corpn. Ltd.: 4 Fairlie Place, Calcutta 1; f. 1967; inland water transport services in Bangladesh and the north-east Indian states; also shipbuilding and repairing, general engineering, dredging, lightening of ships and barge services; Chair. and Man. Dir. S. K. GHOSAL; Gen. Man. (River Services) T. K. SENGUPTA.

East Bengal River Steam Service Ltd.: 87 Sovabazar St., Calcutta 700005; f. 1906; Man. Dirs. K. D. ROY, B. K. ROY.

SHIPPING

India is sixteenth on the list of principal merchant fleets of the world. In 1980 the fleet had 384 vessels totalling 9.35 million d.w.t. There are some 60 shipping companies in India. The major ports are Bombay, Calcutta, Cochin, Kandla, Madras, Mangalore, Mormugao, Pradip (Paradeep), Tuticorin and Vishakhapatnam (Visakhapatnam). An auxiliary port to Calcutta at Haldia was opened to international shipping in 1977 and in 1979 a five-year plan was launched to modernize the port. Its coal berth is complete and will eventually have an annual throughput capacity of 5 million metric tons. An auxiliary port to Bombay is also proposed, at Nhava-sheva. The cost is estimated at Rs. 6,000 million and it is to be finished by 1985. Provision of Rs. 3,900m. has been made in the Sixth Plan for development of the ten major ports.

Among the largest shipping companies are:

BOMBAY

Bharat Line Ltd.: Bharat House, 104 Apollo St., Fort, 400001; coastal services; Chair. and Man. Dir. GUNVANTRAI T. KAMDAR; brs. in Calcutta, Bhavnagar and Madras.

Great Eastern Shipping Co. Ltd.: Mercantile Bank Bldg., 60 Mahatma Gandhi Rd., Bombay 400023; f. 1948; cargo services; 19 vessels; Chair. VASANT J. SHETH; Deputy Chair. and Man. Dir. K. M. SHETH; offices in New Delhi and London.

Malabar Steamship Co. Ltd., The: 4th Floor, Express Towers, Nariman Point, 400021, P.O. Box 34; f. 1935; cargo and transport services; 3 vessels; Gen. Man. R. H. NARECHANIA; brs. in Calcutta and Cochin.

Mogul Line Ltd.: 16 Bank St., Fort, 400023; f. 1877; state-owned; world-wide passenger and cargo services; 17 vessels; Chair. and Man. Dir. J. G. SAGGI.

Scindia Steam Navigation Co. Ltd.: Scindia House, Narottam Morarjee Marg, Ballard Estate, 400038; f. 1919; cargo services; 40 vessels; Chair. and Man. Dir. Mrs. SUMATI MORARJEE; brs. at Calcutta, Jamnagar, Bhavnagar, Porbandar, Gandhidham, Mangalore and London.

Shipping Corporation of India Ltd.: Shipping House, 245 Madame Cama Rd., Bombay 400021; f. 1961 as a government undertaking and took over Jayanti Shipping Co. Ltd. in 1973; fleet of 147 vessels of 5.02m. d.w.t., consisting of tankers, freighters, VLCCs, combination carriers, product carriers, passenger-cum-cargo ships, bulk carriers; operates 24 services; br. offices in Calcutta, New Delhi, Mombasa, Port Blair, Rameshwaram and London; Chair. N. S. MAHIDA; Vice-Chair. and Man. Dir. Vice-Admiral R. K. S. GHANDHI.

South-East Asia Shipping Co. Ltd.: Himalaya House, Dr. Dadabhoy Naoroji Rd., Bombay 400001; f. 1948; world-wide cargo services; 5 vessels of 61,259 d.w.t.; Chair. N. H. DHUNJIBHOY; Chief Exec. D. P. ADENWALLA; Dirs. J. P. BRAGG, K. N .DHUNJIBHOY.

CALCUTTA

India Steamship Co. Ltd.: 21 Old Court House St., P.O.B. 2090, Calcutta 700001; cargo services; 20 vessels; Chair. K. K. BIRLA; Chief Exec. Capt. J. C. ANAND; brs. in Bombay, Kakinada, Vishakhapatnam, Delhi and London.

Ratnakar Shipping Co. Ltd.: 16 Strand Rd., Calcutta 700001; worldwide tramping services; 6 vessels (5 cargo vessels and one tanker); Chair. K. K. BIRLA; Gen. Man. K. C. MATHUR.

Surrendra Overseas Ltd.: 15 Park St., Calcutta 700016; cargo services; 4 vessels (2 bulk carriers and 2 cargo vessels); Chair. JIT PAUL; Chief Exec. Capt. B. S. KUMAR.

GOA

Chowgule Steamships Ltd.: Chowgule House, Mormugao Harbour, Goa 403803; f. 1963; 5 bulk carriers, of 269,654 d.w.t., two trawlers; Chair. VISHWASRAO DATTAJI CHOWGULE; Man. Dir. SHIVAJIRAO DATTAJI CHOWGULE.

MADRAS

South India Shipping Corpn. Ltd.: Chennai House, 7 Esplanade, Madras 600001; 6 bulk carriers; Chair. J. H. TARAPORE; Man. Dir. F. G. DASTUR.

CIVIL AVIATION

There are 6 international airports in India, at Bombay Airport, Calcutta Airport, Delhi Airport, Trivandrum Airport, Amritsar Airport and Madras Airport. There were over 85 other airports in 1978.

Air India: 218 Backbay Reclamation, Nariman Point, Bombay 400021; f. 1932 (as Tata Airlines; renamed Air India 1946), in 1953 became a state corporation responsible for international flights; extensive services to 44 countries covering five continents; fleet of ten Boeing 747-237B, three Boeing 707-337B, two 707-337C and one 707-437; Chair. and Man. Dir. RAGHU RAJ.

Indian Airlines: Airlines House, 113 Gurudwara Rakab Ganj Rd., New Delhi 110001; f. 1953; state corporation responsible for regional and domestic flights; services throughout India and to Afghanistan, Bangladesh, Maldives, Nepal, Pakistan, Sri Lanka; unduplicated route length: 51,000 km.; fleet of twenty-two Boeing, fourteen HS-748, eight F-27 and eight Airbus; Chair. and Man. Dir. K. CHADHA.

Vayudoot Private Ltd.: f. 1981 to operate fleet of Fokker Friendship aircraft to link the smaller towns of north-eastern India; jointly owned by Indian Airlines and Air India; Chair. K. N. KATHJU.

FOREIGN AIRLINES

The following airlines also serve India: Aeroflot (U.S.S.R.), Air France, Air Lanka, Alitalia, Ariana Afghan, Bangladesh Biman, British Airways, BAC (Burma), CAAC (People's Republic of China), Cathay Pacific Ltd. (Hong Kong), ČSA (Czechoslovakia), Egypt-Air, Ethiopian Airlines, Garuda (Indonesia), Gulf Air, Iran Air, Iraqi Airways, JAL (Japan), Kenya Air, KLM (Netherlands), Kuwait Airways, LOT (Poland), Lufthansa (Federal Republic of Germany), Maldive International Airlines, Nigeria Airways, Pan Am (U.S.A.), PIA (Pakistan), Qantas (Australia), Royal Nepal, Sabena (Belgium), Saudia, SAS (Sweden), SIA (Singapore), Swissair, Thai International, Uganda Airlines Corporation and Yemen Airways (Yemen Arab Republic).

TOURISM AND CULTURE

Department of Tourism of the Government of India: Ministry of Tourism and Civil Aviation, No. 1 Parliament St., Transport Bhavan, New Delhi; responsible for the formulation and administration of government policy for active promotion of tourist traffic to India, and for planning the organization and development of tourist facilities; has a network of tourist information offices in India and Overseas; Dir.-Gen. K. K. SRIVASTAVA.

India Tourism Development Corporation Ltd.: Jeevan Vihar, 3 Parliament St., New Delhi 110001; f. 1966 to promote tourism in India; runs hotels (largest hotel chain owner), beach resorts, forest and travellers lodges, tourist transport services, duty free shops; owns Ashok Travels & Tours; production of tourist literature, tourism and hotel consultancy services; Chair. and Man. Dir. S. K. MISRA.

CULTURAL ORGANIZATIONS

Lalit Kala Akademi (*National Academy of Art*): Rabindra Bhavan, New Delhi 110001; f. 1954; autonomous, government financed; sponsors national and international exhibitions; arranges seminars, lectures, films, etc.; runs a studio complex with workshop and facilities for sculpture, ceramics and graphics; Chair. Dr. K. K. HEBBAR; publs. on ancient and modern Indian art, two journals *Lalit Kala* (ancient Indian art, annually), *Lalit Kala Contemporary* (modern art, half-yearly).

Sangeet Natak Akademi (*National Academy of Dance, Drama and Music*): Rabindra Bhavan, 35 Feroze Shah Rd., New Delhi 110001; f. 1953; autonomous body responsible for promotion and organization of the performing arts; maintains Asavari, a gallery of musical instruments, Yavanika, a gallery of theatre arts, a listening room for research scholars, a library, a collection of photographs, films, tape-recordings and slides; Chair. KAMALADEVI CHATTOPADHYAYA; Sec. A. N. DHAWAN; publ. *Sangeet Natak* (quarterly).

Indian Council for Cultural Relations: Azad Bhavan, Indraprastha Estate, New Delhi 110002; f. 1950 to strengthen cultural relations between India and other countries and to promote cultural exchanges; Pres. Minister of External Affairs; Sec. Mrs. MANORAMA BHALLA; publs. *Indian Horizons* (English, quarterly), *Thaqafatul-Hind* (Arabic, quarterly), *Papels de la India* (Spanish, quarterly), *Rencontre avec L'Inde* (French, quarterly), *ICCR Newsletter* (English, quarterly), *Africa* (English, quarterly), *Gagananchal* (Hindi, quarterly).

THEATRE GROUPS

Bharatiya Natya Sangh: 34 New Central Market, New Delhi 110001; Pres. IQBAL MOHD. KHAN.

Bohurupee: 7 Lower Range, Calcutta 700017; f. 1948; Pres. KUMAR ROY.

Children's Little Theatre: Abanmahal, Gariahat Rd., Calcutta 700029; f. 1951; Pres. Dr. BHABATOSH DUTTA; Hon. Gen. Sec. SAMAR CHATTERJEE; publ. *Rhythms & Rhymes* (quarterly).

There are fourteen state Academies of Music, Dance and Drama, ten Colleges of Music, sixteen of Dance and Ballet and fourteen other Theatre Institutes, some of which have semi-professional companies.

ATOMIC ENERGY

There are two nuclear power stations, at Tarapur near Bombay and at Kota (Rajasthan). Two more are being built at Narora (Uttar Pradesh) and Kalpakkam (Tamil Nadu) and there are plans to set up a fifth at Kakrapar (Surat). India has five heavy water plants in operation or nearing completion and three more have been sanctioned.

Atomic Energy Commission: Chhatrapati Shivaji Maharaj Marg, Bombay 400039; organizes research on the release of atomic energy for peaceful purposes; Chair. and Principal Sec. Dept. of Atomic Energy Dr. H. N. SETHNA; Sec. Dept. of Atomic Energy Dr. RAJA RAMANNA.

Bhabha Atomic Research Centre (BARC): Trombay, Bombay 400085; f. 1957; national centre for research in and development of atomic energy for peaceful uses; 4 reactors: APSARA (1 MW, research and isotope production), CIRUS (40 MW, research, isotope production and materials testing), ZERLINA (Zero Energy Reactor for Lattice Investigations and New Assemblies), PURNIMA (Zero Energy Plutonium Oxide Fast Reactor); a fifth nuclear reactor R-5 (100 MW) is under construction; the centre successfully exploded India's first underground nuclear device in May 1974 at Pokaran, Rajasthan; Dir. Dr. RAJA RAMANNA; publ. *Nuclear India* (monthly).

DEFENCE

Armed Forces (July 1981): Total strength 1,104,000: army 944,000, navy 47,000 (incl. naval air force), air force 113,000; there is also a Border Security Force of 200,000 and other para-military forces number 100,000.

Defence Budget: The defence budget for 1981/82 was estimated at Rs. 51,000 million.

CHIEFS OF STAFF

Chief of the Army: Gen. K. V. KRISHNA RAO.

Chief of the Navy: Admiral OSCAR STANLEY DAWSON.

Chief of the Air Force: Air Marshal DILBAGH SINGH.

EDUCATION

Under the Constitution, education in India is primarily the responsibility of the individual state governments, although the Government of India has several direct responsibilities, some specified in the Constitution, as for example, responsibility for the Central Universities, all higher institutions, promotion and propagation of Hindi, co-ordination and maintenance of higher education standards, scientific and technological research and welfare of Indian students abroad.

Education in India is administered at the centre by the Ministry of Education which is headed by a Union Minister of Education who is assisted by two Deputy Ministers. At state level, there is an Education Minister assisted by an Education Secretariat or in certain instances, by a Minister of State/Deputy Minister. Priority has been given to an expansion in elementary and community education as well as in education for girls. Improvements are to be effected in teacher training and science education; standards are to be raised in postgraduate education and research; a reorganization of Polytechnic education and the development of Hindi and of textbook production are to take place. There are facilities for free lower primary education in the age-group 6–11 in all the states. Education in the upper primary stage is also free in twelve states. The Sixth Plan aims for free universal and compulsory education to the age of 14 years by 1983. Expenditure on education in 1976 was Rs. 19,633 million.

Elementary Education: In lower primary classes (6–11 age-group) the total number of pupils increased from 48 million in 1965 to 71 million in 1979/80. Enrolment in higher primary classes (age-group 11–14) in 1979/80 was 18.7 million. Similarly the number of primary schools has risen from about 387,963 in 1965 to 478,249 in 1979/80.

Basic Education: The notable characteristic of elementary education in India is the use of what is known as basic education. There is an activity-centred curriculum which correlates teaching with the physical and social environment of the child. Education is imparted through socially useful, productive activities such as spinning, weaving, gardening, leather work, book craft, domestic crafts, pottery, elementary engineering, etc. The emphasis is on introducing important features of basic education in non-basic schools. Basic education is the national pattern of all elementary education and all elementary schools will ultimately be brought over to the basic system. Twenty per cent already have, and the rest are gradually being converted under the "orientation" system which consists of programmes for teachers to reduce the differences between basic and non-basic education.

Secondary Education: Education at this level is provided for those at between the ages of 14 and 17. Many state governments have taken steps to reorganize secondary schools, resulting in great expansion since 1965. In 1979/80 there were 45,590 such schools with 9.7 million pupils and 859,359 teachers.

Most schools follow what is known as the "three language formula" which comprises teaching of: (1) the regional dialect, (2) Hindi, (3) English. Much emphasis is now also being laid on physical training, which has become a compulsory subject, particularly at secondary school level in conjunction with the programme of the National Fitness Corps.

Higher Education: The Universities are for the most part autonomous as regards administration. The Inter-University Board was founded in 1925 for the discussion of university problems. The University Grants Commission is responsible for the promotion and co-ordination of University Education and has the authority to make appropriate grants and to implement development schemes.

India had a total of 108 universities at the end of 1979, including 11 institutions with university status, and some 4,558 university and affiliated colleges. University enrolment was 2.65 million in 1979/80.

Higher Technical Education: In 1976 there were 142 engineering and technology degree colleges with about 68,000 students.

Rural Higher Education: On the recommendation of the Rural Higher Education Committee, a National Council for higher education in rural areas was established in 1953 to advise the Government on all matters relating to the development of rural higher education. In 1977 there were 10 rural institutes functioning in 7 states, most of them affiliated to the state university.

Social Education: provides an educational base for community development programmes in the country, and includes eradication of illiteracy, education in citizenship, cultural and recreational activities and organization of youth and women's groups for community development.

Adult Education: A National Board for Adult Education has been set up, but the state governments are largely responsible for adult education programmes. The main emphasis is on improving literacy rates, especially in rural areas; there are also Urban Adult Education Programmes and in 1976 a major programme of non-formal education was launched for the 15–25 age group.

BIBLIOGRAPHY

GENERAL

BASHAM, A. L. The Wonder that was India (Revised edn., Hawthorn, New York, 1963).
A Cultural History of India (Clarendon Press, Oxford).

DE BARY, W. THEODORE. (ed.) Sources of Indian Tradition, 2 vols. (Columbia University Press, New York and London, 1958).

HIRO, DILIP. Inside India Today (Routledge and Kegan Paul, London, 1976).

JOHNSON, B. L. C. India: Resources and Development (Heinemann, London, 1978).

MEHTA, VED. A New India (Penguin, London, 1978).

MOON, PENDEREL. Strangers in India (Faber and Faber, London, 1944).

NAIPAUL, V. S. An Area of Darkness: An Experience of India (1964).
India: A Wounded Civilization (André Deutsch, London, 1977).

SINGH, R. L. (ed.) India: Regional Studies (for 21st Int. Geog. Congress by Indian Nat. Cttee. for Geog., Calcutta, 1968).

SPATE, O. H. K. and LEARMONTH, A. T. A. India and Pakistan (3rd edn., Methuen, London, 1967).

WESTWOOD, J. N. Railways of India (1974).

HISTORY AND POLITICS

AHMAD, AZIZ. Islamic Modernization in India and Pakistan 1857–1964 (Oxford University Press, London and New York, 1966).

APPADORAI, A. (ed.) Documents on Political Thought in Modern India (Oxford University Press, 1977).

AYOOB, MOHAMMED. India, Pakistan and Bangladesh: Search for a New Relationship (Indian Council of World Affairs, New Delhi, 1975).

BAKER, C. J. and WASHBROOK, D. A. South India, Political Institutions and Political Change 1880–1920 (Macmillan, Delhi, 1975).

BATTACHARJEA, AJIT. Jayaprakash Narayan: A Political Biography (New Delhi).

BAYLY, C. A. The Local Roots of Indian Politics, Allahabad 1880–1920 (Clarendon Press, Oxford, 1975).

BRASS, PAUL R. Language, Religion and Politics in North India (Cambridge University Press, London, 1975).

BRECHER, MICHAEL. Nehru: A Political Biography (Oxford University Press, London, 1959).

BROWN, JUDITH M. Gandhi and Civil Disobedience: The Mahatma in Indian Politics, 1928–1934 (Cambridge University Press, 1977).

HISTORY

COLLINS, L., and LAPIERRE, D. Freedom at Midnight (Collins, London, 1975).

CROOKE, W. W. The North-West Provinces of India 1897–1972 (Oxford in Asia Historical Reprints).

CURRAN, J. A., Jr. Militant Hinduism in Indian Politics; A Story of the R.S.S. (Institute of Pacific Relations, New York, 1951).

DERRETT, J. DUNCAN M. Religion, Law and the State in India (Faber and Faber, London).

DEWEY, CLIVE, and HOPKINS, A. G. (ed.) The Imperial Impact (Athlone Press, London, 1977).

DONALDSON, R. H. Soviet Policy towards India: Ideology and Strategy (1974).

DURAND, A. The making of a Frontier—1899 (1975).

EDWARDES, MICHAEL. British India 1772–1947 (Sidgwick and Jackson, London, 1967).

EPSTEIN, T. S. South India: Yesterday, Today and Tomorrow (1973).

FAIRSERVIS, WALKER A., Jr. The Roots of Ancient India (University of Chicago, Chicago and London, 2nd edn., 1975).

FRANKEL, FRANCINE R. India's Green Revolution: Political Costs of Economic Growth (1971).
India's Political Economy, 1947–77: The Gradual Revolution (Princeton University Press, Princeton, N.J., 1979).

FUCHS, STEPHEN. The Aboriginal Tribes of India (Macmillan, 1973).

GUPTA, K. The Hidden History of the Sino-Indian Frontier (Minerva Associates, Calcutta, 1974).

HABIBULLAH, A. B. M. The Foundation of Muslim Rule in India (Allahabad, 2nd edn., 1961).

HARDY, PETER. The Muslims of British Empire (Cambridge University Press, 1972).

JACKSON, R. South Asian Crisis: India, Pakistan and Bangladesh (1975).

JEFFREY, ROBIN. (ed.) People, Princes and Paramount Power: Society and Politics in the Indian Princely States (Oxford University Press, 1979).

JOHNSON, G. Provincial Politics and Indian Nationalism. Bombay and the Indian National Congress 1880–1915 (Cambridge University Press, 1974).

JOSHI, G. N. Constitution of India (6 edns., 1975).

JOSHI, NIRMALA. Foundations of Indo-Soviet Relations: 1917–1947 (Radiant Publishers, New Delhi, 1975).

KAPUR, ASHOK. India's Nuclear Option: Atomic Diplomacy and Decision Making (Praeger, New York, 1976).

KARUNAKARAN, K. P. Continuity and Change in Indian Politics: a study of the Indian National Congress (People's Publishing House, New Delhi, 1964).

KOPF, D. A. British Orientalism and the Bengal Renaissance (University of California, Berkeley and Los Angeles, 1969).

LIPTON, M., and FIRN, J. The Erosion of a Relationship: India and Britain since 1960 (Oxford University Press for the Institute of International Affairs, 1975).

LUMBY, E. W. R. The Transfer of Power in India (Allen and Unwin, London, 1954).

MANSERGH, NICHOLAS, LUMBY, E. W. and MOON, PENDEREL. (eds.) India: The Transfer of Power, 1942–47, 7 vols. (H.M.S.O., London, 1970–77).

MARSHALL, P. J. (ed.) Problems of Empire, Britain and India 1757–1813 (Allen and Unwin, London, 1968).

MASANI, Z. Indira Gandhi: A Biography (London, 1974).

MASON, PHILIP. (ed.) India and Ceylon: Unity and Diversity (Oxford University Press, London, 1967).

MEHROTRA, S. R. India and the Commonwealth 1885–1929 (Allen and Unwin, London, 1965).

MEHTA, VED. Mahatma Gandhi and his Apostles (André Deutsch, London, 1977).

MENON, V. P. The Integration of the Indian States (Orient Longmans, Bombay, 1956).
The Transfer of Power in India (Orient Longmans, Bombay, 1957).

MOORE, R. J. Liberalism and Indian Politics 1872–1922 (Edward Arnold, London, 1966).
The Crisis of Indian Unity (Clarendon Press, Oxford, 1975).

NANDA, B. R. (ed.) Indian Foreign Policy: The Nehru Years (Vikas Publishing House, Delhi and Bombay, 1976).
Socialism in India (Delhi, 1972).

NANDA, B. R., and JOSHI, V. C. (ed.) Studies in Modern Indian History (Delhi, 1972).

NOSSITER, T. J. Communism in Kerala: a Study in Political Adaptation (Hurst, for Royal Institute of International Affairs, London, 1980).

PANDEY, B. N. Nehru (Macmillan, London, 1976).

PHILIPS, C. H., and WAINRIGHT, MARY. (ed.) Indian Society and the Beginnings of Modernization (SOAS, London, 1976).

PRASAD, BIMLA. The Origins of Indian Foreign Policy (Bookland, Calcutta, 1960).

ROBB, P. G. The Government of India and Reform (Oxford University Press, 1976).

ROBINSON, F. C. R. Separatism among Indian Muslims. The Politics of the United Provinces' Muslims 1860–1923 (Cambridge University Press, 1974).

RUDOLPH, L. I., and S. H. The Modernity of Tradition (Chicago, 1967).

SAHGAL, NAYANTARA. Indira Gandhi: Emergence and Style (Vikas Publications, 1978).

SCHWARTZBERG, J. E. (ed.) A Historical Atlas of South Asia (University of Chicago Press, London and Chicago, 1978).

SEAL, ANIL. The Emergence of Indian Nationalism (Cambridge University Press, 1967).

SEN GUPTA, B. Soviet-Asian Relations in the 1970s and Beyond: Interpretational Study (1976).

SHUKLA, SATYENDRA R. Sikkim. The Story of Integration (S. Chand & Co. (Pvt.) Ltd., New Delhi, 1976).

SINGH, KUSHWANT. A History of the Sikhs, 2 vols. (1964–1966).

SMITH, D. E. India as a Secular State (Princeton University Press, New Jersey, 1963).

SPEAR, PERCIVAL. A History of India (Penguin Books, Harmondsworth).

STOKES, ERIC. The Peasant and the Raj (Cambridge University Press, 1978).

TANDON, PRAKASH. Punjabi Century 1857–1957 (University of California, 1968).

THAPAR, R. A. History of India Vol. I (Penguin, Harmondsworth, 1966).
Asoka and the Decline of the Mauryas.

TINKER, HUGH. Experiment with Freedom: India and Pakistan, 1947 (Oxford University Press, London, 1967).
India and Pakistan: A Political Analysis (Pall Mall Press, London, 2nd edn., 1967).
South Asia: A Short History (Pall Mall Press, London, 1966).

TOMLINSON, B. R. The Indian National Congress and the Raj 1929–1942 (Macmillan, London, 1976).

WAVELL, Lord. (ed. MOON, P.) The Viceroy's Journal (1973).

WEINER, MYRON. (ed.) State Politics in India (Oxford University Press, London).
Party Politics in India: The Development of a Multi-Party System (Princeton University Press, New Jersey, 1957).

WOLPERT, STANLEY. A New History of India (Oxford University Press, New York, 1976).

SOCIAL LIFE

BÉTEILLE, A. Studies in Agrarian Social Structure (Oxford University Press, 1974).

CHAKRAVARTI, ANAND. Contradiction and Change: Emerging Patterns of Authority in a Rajasthan Village (Oxford University Press, Delhi, Bombay, Calcutta, Madras, 1975; London, 1976).

COHN, B. S. India: the Social Anthropology of a Civilisation (Chicago University Press, Chicago, 1971).

DOIG, D. Mother Teresa: Her People and Her Work (1976).

FREEMAN, J. M. Scarcity and Opportunity in an Indian Village (1977).

GUPTA, G. I. Marriage, Religion and Society, Tradition and Change in an Indian Village (1974).

HUSAIN, ABID. National Culture of India (Asia Publishing House, New York, 2nd edn., 1961).

HUTTON, J. H. Caste in India (Oxford University Press, London, 3rd edn., 1961).

KESSINGER, T. Vilayatpur 1848–1968: Social and Economic Change in a North Indian Village (1974).

MANDELBAUM, D. G. Society in India, 2 vols. (University of California, Berkeley and Los Angeles, 1970).

MITRA, ASHOK. Calcutta Diary (1977).

MOHANTI, P. My Village, My Life, Nanpur: A Portrait of an Indian Village (1973).
Indian Village Tales (1975).

NARASIMHAN, V. A., et al. (ed.) The Languages of India (Varadachari, Madras, 1958).

RENOU, LOUIS. The Nature of Hinduism (Walker, New York, 1951).

SANKHDHER, L. M. Caste Interaction in a Village Tribe (1974).

ART AND CULTURE

AMBROSE, KAY. Classical Dances and Costumes of India (Black, London, 1950).

ARCHER, M. British Drawings in the India Office Library: Vol. I: Amateur Artists; Vol. II: Official and Professional Artists (1969).
Company Drawings in the Indian Office Library (1972).
Indian Popular Paintings in the Indian Office Library (1977).

ARCHER, W. G. Indian Paintings from Punjab Hills (1973).
Visions of Courtly India (1976).
Pahari Miniatures: Concise History (1976).

BROOM, P. Indian Architecture: Vol. I: Hindu and Buddhist Period (1968); Vol. II: Islamic Period (1971).

BROWN, PERCY. Indian Architecture (Taraporevala, Bombay, 2 Vols., 1942).

COOMARASWAMY, ANANDA K. The Arts and Crafts of India and Ceylon (Foulis, London, 1913).

DUBOIS, JEAN ANTOINE. Hindu Manners, Customs and Ceremonies (Clarendon Press, Oxford, 3rd edn., 1906).

GOPAL, RAM and SEROZH, DADACHANJI. Indian Dancing (Phoenix House, London, 1951).

GUPTA, CHANDRA BHAN. Indian Theatre (Motilal Banarsidass, Benares, 1953).

KRAMRISCH, STELLA. The Art of India (Phaidon, New York, 1954).

MARSHALL, Sir J. Mohenjo-Daro and the Indus Civilisation (1973).
Taxila: Illustrated Account of Archaeological Excavations at Taxila 1933–34 (1975).

MICHELL, G. The Hindu Temple: Introduction to its Meanings and Forms (1977).

NATH, R. Some Aspects of Mughal Architecture (1976).

OMAN, JOHN CAMPBELL. The Brahmans, Theists and Muslims of India (Unwin, London, 2nd edn., 1907).
Cults, Customs and Superstitions of India (Unwin, London, 1908).

POPLEY, HERBERT A. The Music of India (Y.M.C.A., Calcutta, 2nd edn., 1950).

RAO, RAMACHANDRA. Modern Indian Painting (Rachana, Madras, 1953).

WHEELER, Sir MORTIMER. Early India and Pakistan (1959).
The Indus Civilization (1968).
My Archaeological Mission to India and Pakistan (1976).

ECONOMY

BASU, S. K. Studies in Economic Problems (Asia Publishing House, Bombay, 1965)

BAUER, P. T. Indian Economic Policy and Development (Allen and Unwin, London; Praeger, New York, 1961).

BHATT, V. V. Aspects of Economic Change and Policy in India, 1800–1960 (Allied Publishers, Bombay, 1962). A Decade of Performance of Industrial Development Bank of India (World Bank Paper).

CASSEN, R. H. India: Population, Economy and Society (Macmillan, London, 1977).

CHANDHURI, P. The Indian Economy: Poverty and Development (Crosby Lockwood Staples, London, 1978).

DASGUPTA, B. The Oil Industry in India: Some Economic Aspects (1971).
Agrarian Changes and the New Technology in India (UNRCSP, Geneva, 1977).

DUTT, R. C. Economic History of India (Publications Division, Delhi, 1960).

EPSTEIN, T. A. Economic Development and Social Change in South India (Oxford University Press, Bombay, 1962).

ETIENNE, GILBERT (translation by MOTHERSOLE, MEGAN). Studies in Indian Agriculture: the Art of the Possible (University of California Press, Berkeley, Calif., 1968).

FARMER, B. H. Agricultural Colonization in India since Independence (Oxford University Press, 1974).

FARMER, B. H. (ed.) Green Revolution? Technology and Changes in Rice Growing Areas of Tamil Nadu and Sri Lanka (Macmillan, London, 1977).

FONSECA, A. J. Wage Issues in a Developing Economy: The Indian Experience (Oxford University Press, Bombay, 1975; Delhi, Calcutta, Madras, 1976).

GYAN, CHAND. The Socialist Transformation of the Indian Economy (Allen and Unwin, London, 1965).

HANSON, A. H. The Process of Planning: A Study of India's Five-Year Plans 1950–1964 (Oxford University Press, London, 1966).

HENDERSON, P. D. India: The Energy Sector (Published for the World Bank by Oxford University Press, Delhi, 1975; London, 1976).

JAIN, J. P. Nuclear India (Radiant Publishers, New Delhi, 1974).

JAYARAMAN, Dr. T. K. Economic Cooperation in the Indian Subcontinent (Orient Longman, 1978).

JHA, PREM SHANKAR The Economy of India (Oxford University Press. 1979).

KREUGER, A. O. The Benefit and Costs of Substitution in India: A Microeconomic Study (1975).

MADDISON, A. Class Structure and Economic Growth: India and Pakistan since the Moguls (1971).

MANDEL, G. C., and GHOSH, M. G. Economics of the Green Revolution: A Study in East India (1976).

MEHTA, B. India and the World Oil Crisis (1974).

MELLOR, JOHN W. The New Economics of Growth: A Strategy for India and the Developing World (Cornell University Press, Ithaca and London, 1976).

MONGIA, J. N. (ed.) Readings in Indian Labour and Social Welfare (Atmar Ram, Delhi, 1976).

MUKHERJEE, SADHAN. India's Economic Relations with the U.S.A. and the U.S.S.R. (Sterling Publishers Pvt. Ltd., New Delhi, 1978).

NAIR, K. Three Bowls of Rice: India & Japan, a century of effort (1973).

OJNE, P. D. Pattern of Income Distribution in India: 1933–1955 to 1963–1965 (World Bank Paper).

PACHAURI, R. K. Energy and Economic Development in India (Praeger Special Studies, New York, 1977).

SINGH, CHARAN. India's Economic Policy: The Gandhian Blueprint (Vikas Publishing, 1978).

RAO, V. K. R. V., and NARAIN, DHARM. Foreign Aid and India's Economic Development (Asia Publishing House, London, 1964).

ROSEN, G. Democracy and Economic Change in India (Cambridge University Press for University of California Press, 2nd. edn., 1967).

STREETEN, P., and LIPTON, M. (eds.) The Crisis of Indian Planning (Oxford University Press, London, 1968).

SWAMY, S. Economic Growth in China and India 1952–1970 (1973).

TURNER, R. (ed.) India's Urban Future (University of California Press, Berkeley and Los Angeles, Calif.; Cambridge University Press, London, 1962).

VEDAVALLI, R. Private Foreign Investment and Economic Development: A Case Study of Petroleum in India (Cambridge University Press, London, 1976).

WADHVA, C. D. Some Problems of India's Economic Policy (1973).

ZINKIN, MAURICE, and WARD, BARBARA. Why Help India? (Pergamon Press, London, 1963).

Indonesia

PHYSICAL AND SOCIAL GEOGRAPHY

C. A. Fisher

(Revised for this edition by Harvey Demaine)

Indonesia, which today comprises the same area as the former Netherlands East Indies (the former Portuguese colony of East Timor was incorporated into Indonesia in 1976), lies along the equator between the south-eastern tip of the Asian mainland and Australia. Along its western and southern coasts it abuts upon the Indian Ocean (which the former President Sukarno renamed the Indonesian Ocean); to the north it looks towards the Straits of Malacca and the South China Sea, and on the remote northern shore of Irian Jaya (West New Guinea) it has a direct frontage on to the Pacific Ocean.

With an overall distance of over 4,800 km. (3,000 miles) from east to west and 2,000 km. (1,250 miles) from north to south, Indonesia stretches over an area almost as big as Europe west of the U.S.S.R. However, since nearly four-fifths of the area between these outer extremities consists of sea, the total land surface of Indonesia covers 1,904,569 square kilometres (excluding East Timor), which makes it the fourteenth largest territorial unit in the world.

PHYSICAL FEATURES

This territory is divided between some 13,000 islands of very varied size and character. The largest exclusively Indonesian island is Sumatra covering 473,606 square kilometres, though this is exceeded by the Indonesian two-thirds (539,460 square kilometres) of Kalimantan (Borneo). These are followed by the 412,781 square kilometres of Irian Jaya, then Sulawesi (Celebes) with 189,216 square kilometres and Java which, with the neighbouring island of Madura, totals 132,187 square kilometres and the remainder is made up by a series of much smaller islands comprising Bali and the Nusatenggara group, and the small scattered islands of the Moluccas (Maluku) group lying between Sulawesi and Irian Jaya.

These differences in size reflect fundamental differences in geological structure. All the large islands except Sulawesi stand on one of two great continental shelves, namely the Sunda Shelf, representing a prolongation of the Asian mainland though now largely covered by the shallow waters of the Malacca Straits, the Java Sea and the southernmost part of the South China Sea, and the Sahul Shelf which, beneath the similarly shallow Arafura Sea, links Irian (New Guinea) with Australia. Geologically speaking, these two shelves represent ancient stable surfaces on the edges of which, as in Sumatra, Java and northeastern Kalimantan to the west, and Irian Jaya to the east, extensive folding has taken place in Tertiary and/or more recent times, as a result of compressional movements between the two. In all the above-mentioned islands, therefore, there are pronounced mountain ranges facing the deep seas along the outer edges of the shelves, and extensive lowland tracts, facing the shallow inner seas whose coastlines show all the characteristics of recent submergence. In contrast to these larger islands of western and eastern Indonesia, most of those lying between the two shelves, including Sulawesi as well as those of the Nusatenggara and Maluku groups, rise steeply from deep seas on all sides, and have only extremely narrow coastal plains.

Related to the recency of mountain building in most parts of the archipelago is the widespread vulcanity, much of it still in the active stage. Except in Kalimantan and Irian Jaya, the culminating relief normally consists of volcanic cones, many of which exceed 3,000 metres in altitude, though the loftiest peaks of all are in fact the non-volcanic Punjak Jaya (5,000 metres) and Idenburg-top (4,800 metres) in the Snow Mountains of Irian Jaya.

However, although the most extensive lowlands occur along the eastern coast of Sumatra and the southern coasts of Kalimantan and Irian Jaya, the larger part of all three lowland areas consists of tidal swamp which, until very recently, has been virtually ignored for cultivation purposes, and still constitutes a major obstacle to the opening up of the better-drained areas further inland. Reclamation is now being undertaken in some of these lands, under the transmigration programme, but it still cannot match that of the narrower coastal lowlands of the smaller central island of Java.

SOILS AND NATURAL RESOURCES

The much greater fertility of the soils of the eastern two-thirds of Java and nearby Bali, by comparison with nearly all the rest of Indonesia, apart from a small part of interior and coastal northeastern Sumatra, arises from the neutral-basic character (as opposed to the prevailingly acidic composition elsewhere) of the volcanic ejecta from which they are derived. In the remaining nine-tenths or more of Indonesia, the soils—whether volcanically derived or not—are altogether poorer in quality than they are popularly assumed to be, and indeed are not noticeably better than in most other parts of the humid tropics.

As regards mineral wealth, there remains controversy about the scale of Indonesia's resources. It must be stressed that exploration is still continuing in many parts of the archipelago and, while mineral wealth may not justify the boasts of former President Sukarno, there are certainly substantial deposits.

Pride of place must go to hydrocarbons. Although proven reserves of petroleum remain at an estimated 15,000 million barrels, geological reports of several of Indonesia's Tertiary basin structures have suggested that there could be as much as 223,000 million barrels available when all are fully explored. Even a minimum 10 per cent confirmation of such estimates would double the estimated production life at current levels of extraction (1.6 million barrels per day in 1981). The largest producing field is still at Minas in Sumatra.

Similarly, reserves of natural gas may also be substantially greater than previously thought, with some estimates now put at 73,000,000 million cubic metres, compared with the proven 1,100,000 million. In 1980, production of gas rose to 28,750,000 million cubic metres, the bulk coming from two fields at Badak, off East Kalimantan, and Arun, off-shore of Aceh's north coast, whence the gas is sent, in liquefied form, chiefly to Japan. It is reported, moreover, that a recent discovery near the Natuna Islands, in the South China Sea, may be one of the largest gas fields in the world.

Other minerals are naturally overshadowed by the hydrocarbon sector, which makes such an important contribution to the Indonesian economy. Nevertheless, it was estimated in 1975 that the tin deposits in the Sunda Shelf islands of Bangka, Belitung and Singkep accounted for about 23 per cent of the remaining world reserves; the Ertsberg copper ore body in Irian Jaya may have up to 45 million metric tons of ore and other low-grade deposits have been reported from Sumatra, while at least 824 million tons of nickel-bearing laterites have been estimated in southern Sulawesi.

CLIMATE AND VEGETATION

Climatically the greater part of Indonesia may be described as maritime equatorial, with consistently high temperatures (except at higher altitudes) and heavy rainfall at all seasons, though in many parts of western Indonesia there are distinct peak periods of exceptionally heavy rain when either the north-east or the south-west monsoon winds are blowing onshore. However, the eastern half of Java, Bali, southern Sulawesi and Nusatenggara, which lie further to the south and nearer to the Australian desert, experience a clearly marked dry season during the period of the south-east monsoon (which changes direction to become the south-west monsoon over western Indonesia) between June–July and September–October. Thus, whereas in Pontianak, situated almost exactly on the equator on the west coast of Kalimantan, the monthly mean temperature varies only from 25.6°C. (78°F.) in December to 26.7°C. (80°F.) in July, and average monthly rainfall varies from 16 cm. (6.3 inches) in July to 40 cm. (15.7 inches) in December, out of a total annual rainfall of 320 cm. (126 inches), Surabaya in eastern Java, while showing even less variation in mean monthly temperature, which fluctuates between 26.1°C. (79°F.) and 26.7°C. (80°F.) throughout the year, has four months (December-March) each with over 24 cm. (9.4 inches) of rain, and four others (July-October) with less than 5 cm. (2 inches) each, out of an annual total of 173.5 cm. (68.3 inches).

While nearly all of Indonesia in its natural state supports a very dense vegetation, though with significant variations in type as between tidal swamps, normal lowlands and lower slopes, and higher altitudes, the natural forest cover becomes progressively thinner as one goes eastwards from central Java to Timor, and over much of Nusatenggara the vegetation is better described as savanna.

POPULATION AND CULTURE

With an estimated population of over 151 million at mid-1982 and suggestions that even this (based on the October 1980 census total of 147,490,298) may be an underestimate, Indonesia ranks as the fifth most populous country in the world, after the People's Republic of China, India, the U.S.S.R. and the U.S.A. Despite a growing family planning programme, this huge total continues to increase at about 2 per cent per annum. So large a population spread over so vast and fragmented a territory presents a wide range of variation, notably in ethnic type, religion and language.

As a result of the combination of distinctly richer soils, less dense vegetation, a high proportion of lowland, an absence of extensive and unhealthy tidal swamp and, not least, a central position within Indonesia as a whole, Java, together with the neighbouring islands of Madura and Bali, has in historic times proved to be by far the most favourable area to man. This situation is reflected, in exaggerated form, in the astonishing fact that these three islands, which all told comprise less than one-thirteenth of the total area of Indonesia, contain almost two-thirds of its population. This situation has persisted despite extensive efforts to shift population out of Java and Bali since as early as 1905 under colonization schemes, latterly known as "transmigration". Altogether it is estimated that some three-quarters of a million people had moved under such schemes by 1977, but even so, whereas the population density for Java and Madura had reached 678 per sq. km. by 1981, for the rest of Indonesia it was still only 29.

Over the western two-thirds of Indonesia the predominant ethnic type is the so-called Deutero-Malay, basically southern Mongoloid in origin, to which belong virtually the entire indigenous populations of Java, Madura and Bali; the coastal peoples, together with many of the uplanders, of Sumatra; and most of the coastal inhabitants of Kalimantan, though the majority of the inland peoples of Kalimantan and of some parts of Sumatra are descendants of the earlier Proto-Malays. In the eastern third of the country the pattern is more complicated, with a preponderance of Proto-Malay, or mixed Proto-Malay, Melanesoid and in some cases also Australoid elements, in all but the coastal fringe, except in Irian Jaya whose indigenous population is predominantly Papuan. In the coastal areas of Sulawesi, Nusatenggara and Maluku the Deutero-Malay type is again evident, though in relation to the total population of these islands it forms a much smaller percentage than further west.

To a significant extent the main cultural divisions run parallel to the ethnic divisions already described. Thus the indigenous coastal peoples throughout western Indonesia are all Muslim with the solitary exception of the Balinese, who remain faithful to the Hinduism which formerly predominated over all the more advanced parts of western Indonesia. Nevertheless, although over 90 per cent of the total Indonesian population profess Islam, there are considerable variations in the degree of attachment to that religion as, for example, between the extremely staunch Acenese and Sundanese, of northern Sumatra and western Java respectively, the much laxer Sasaks of Lombok, the more typically orthodox coast Malays of eastern Sumatra and coastal Kalimantan, and the Javanese whose Islam is much modified by earlier Hindu survivals.

By contrast, most of the Proto-Malay peoples in the interiors of all these islands (except Java) are animists, though some have in recent times adopted Christianity. In the eastern third of the country the operative distinction lies between a much narrower Muslim coastal fringe and a predominantly animist interior, though in some of the islands the Muslim element is almost completely absent, and in several Christianity has made deep inroads.

Altogether some 25 different languages and 250 dialects have been recognized in Indonesia, and again the divisions tend to follow the basic ethnic divide between coastal and interior peoples in the several parts of the archipelago. However, since the achievement of independence great progress has been made in modernizing the old traders' *lingua franca*, often referred to as "market Malay", and propagating it as the national language, Bahasa Indonesia, in all parts of the country.

Besides the indigenous population, with whom the foregoing paragraphs are concerned, Indonesia contains one of the largest Chinese communities in South-East Asia. This community may number over 2 million and (although a substantial proportion have been born and brought up in Indonesia, have already accepted citizenship and have become "Indonesianized") up to one-half may remain stateless and a source of friction in the society.

As elsewhere in South-East Asia, the Chinese and smaller non-indigenous groups such as Arabs and Eurasians, are largely concentrated in the towns. These have grown rapidly in recent years, with Jakarta increasing its population from 4,564,000 in 1971 to an estimated 6,500,000 in 1980 and some nine other cities now claiming a population of over 1 million. These include Surabaya and Bandung in Java, Medan and Palembang in Sumatra and Ujungpandang (formerly Makasar) in Sulawesi. Rapid growth has brought with it severe social problems and well over one-third of Jakarta's population is estimated to live in slums and squatter settlements containing few basic facilities.

HISTORY

Jan M. Pluvier

EARLY HISTORY

Situated in an area through which important trade routes ran, the Indonesian island world could not fail to be affected by influences from outside. Around the beginning of the Christian era these influences came from India. During the so-called Hindu period two great Indonesian empires emerged: Srivijaya, with its centre in Sumatra and controlling the Malacca Straits (roughly A.D. 700–1200); and Majapahit, a Javanese state which from about A.D. 1300 held the greater part of the archipelago for a century and a half. A few remarks about the nature of these empires should be made. First, their control over large territories, especially over those far away from the capital city, was very much indirect rule, with the real power in the hands of local princes—a situation which accounted for the strength of centrifugal forces whenever the power of the central government was on the wane. Secondly, the Indonesian states of the Hindu period were neither Indian colonies nor in any other way politically linked with India. India's expansion was exclusively cultural and its influence was confined to the higher strata of a society which continued to be essentially Indonesian in character. The "Hindu kingdoms" were Indonesian states in which the upper classes had, for several reasons, adopted elements of Indian civilization.

Somewhere between 1100 and 1300 another culture made its appearance in Indonesia. It came from India, too, but it was not indigenous there: Islam. Like Indian civilization it was adopted by the ruling classes in the Indonesian states, but unlike the Indian cultural elements of the previous millennium it also descended to the mass of the population. From the first Islamic centres in Malacca, Northern Sumatra (Achin) and East Java it spread over the entire archipelago, a process which lasted from roughly 1400 to 1900. In the structure of Indonesian society, however, this process of Islamization did not bring about any more essential changes than the process of Indianization had done. The village community, a social organization, living on *sawah* agriculture, based on communal labour and responsibility and economically self-sufficient, continued to be the fundamental unit of Indonesian society. Some industry and cattle breeding did exist and there were some signs of a monetary economy, but these were exceptions; in general there was neither production for a market nor profit-making. Socially and economically the villages had hardly any contacts with the outside world, the only link with which was provided by the authority of the princes or the local aristocratic classes. Towns were administrative and, seen from an economic point of view, almost entirely consumptive units.

European Influence

The third of the external influences which affected Indonesia—Europe—did not in any sense transform this basic structure of society, at least not until well into the nineteenth century. The Dutch traders, who in 1602 joined forces in the United East Indian Company, the armed commercial organization with sovereign rights which represented Holland in the archipelago for nearly two centuries, were a more powerful challenge to Indonesian society than Indian civilization and Islam had been in previous periods. However, they too had to adapt themselves to the existing social structure. In the seventeenth century the Dutch establishments (Malacca, Batavia, Ambon) were mere enclaves in a huge territory where the power of the greater Indonesian kingdoms (Achin, Mataram, Banjarmasin) was still predominant, and their trade and shipping constituted just one element, albeit an aggressive one, of the commercial intercourse in the area in which Chinese, Japanese, Siamese, Javanese, Indians and Arabs took part. A century later the situation had changed in that the Dutch company had monopolized the trade in the Moluccas, had guaranteed for itself a sort of unstable preponderance over Java and had conquered places like Padang and Makassar, but it was not yet an inter-insular power in the archipelago. Direct Dutch influence, in the territories which they controlled, did not, in general, go beyond the upper classes of native society; in fact, this society, not at all affected by the presence of the Europeans and hardly influenced by their power, went its natural course until the end of the eighteenth century.

DUTCH COLONIAL POLICY

At the time the Dutch state took over the possessions and assets of the company (1799), a change was taking place in the approach of the Dutch towards their overseas territories. The policy of passive adaptation to the feudal structure of society was abandoned. Stimulated by the industrial revolution and a sudden consciousness of European technical superiority, an urge to organize and regulate led to an active policy of penetrating deeper into the interior of Java. The main concern of the colonial politicians was to continue and to intensify the exploitation of the archipelago's material resources. That the first decades of the nineteenth century in Dutch colonial history became known as the "period of doubt" was the result not of any difference of opinion on this primary goal but of conflicting theories about the method which was most likely to guarantee the highest profits. During the British period, under (Sir) Stamford Raffles' responsibility (1811–16), more liberal ideas had been introduced in Java, and after the Dutch had returned it seemed for a while that these new theories would prevail. They did not, however, for the leading colonial circles feared foreign competition and they were not convinced that private enterprise would be successful in speeding up production. The financial difficulties caused by the Java war (1825–30), in which the Dutch reduced the entire island to submission, and the insufficient proceeds of the land-rent, led to a restoration of a system of forced labour and exploitation by the state.

During the period that the Culture System, introduced in 1830, was in force, the Dutch focused their attention primarily on Java. After their return to Indonesia (1816) they controlled outside Java only the Moluccas and some points in Sumatra and the Celebes. By the Anglo-Dutch Treaty of 1824, in which they exchanged Malacca for Bencoolen, the archipelago, with the exception of Achin, was recognized as their sphere of influence, but they did not embark upon any comprehensive policy to impose their rule. They were definitely less aloof than the British were *vis-à-vis* Malaya during the same decades and they made their presence felt in large areas of Sumatra (particularly West Sumatra) and in Borneo. However, their attitude towards the "Outer Islands", as the territories outside Java were referred to, was, on the whole, one of indifference.

This situation continued until the 1870s. By this time the industrial revolution had transformed the Netherlands into a more industrialized state and this economic change affected the Dutch approach to their overseas territories. Criticism of the Culture System on humanitarian grounds (*Multatuli*) coincided with criticism of the economic aspects of the system of state exploitation; and as the economically interested circles, which represented industrial capitalism, had become quite a powerful force in the Netherlands, their liberal tenets of free trade and private enterprise could not fail to prevail. Indonesia had to supply the raw materials for industries in the Netherlands, it had to become a market for Dutch industrial products and the opportunities it offered for capital investment had to be explored. In 1870 private enterprise was allowed to operate in the colony, where it found a rich field for its activities. The new liberal policy brought about a change of attitude towards the Outer Islands with their large natural resources. Between 1870 and 1910 the whole of Indonesia was brought under effective Dutch rule and, either by conquest (e.g. Achin War) or by treaty, incorporated into the Netherlands East Indies, which was now given definite shape.

Social Policy

It was also during this period that the Indonesian social structure was most affected by influences from outside. Western penetration, which led to a direct confrontation between a capitalist economy with its dynamic and active elements on the one hand and the traditional pre-capitalist system on the other, in fact undermined the very foundations of the Indonesian native economy. The result was that while the Netherlands East Indies, judged by its production capacity and its import and export figures, developed into one of the most prosperous European colonies in the world, the standard of living of the mass of the population steadily declined. An attempt to remedy this situation was undertaken during the first decades of the twentieth century. This so-called "Ethical Course", introduced in 1901, was a combination of free enterprise and a state-managed native welfare policy, which could boast of some substantial achievements. The magnitude of the problem, however, aggravated by the rapid growth of the population, seriously jeopardized the efforts to make amends for the neglect that in the past had characterized the official attitude in this field. Moreover, the ambiguous nature of Ethical colonial policy, which often forced the administration to choose between the conflicting interests of either Western enterprise or the Indonesian population, resulted in a failure to bring about any essential improvement. During the trade depression of the 1930s the Government increased its regulatory and managerial powers in the economic sphere, but its primary goal in this was to prevent the success of Japanese competition and to carry European business safely through the economic disaster which hit Indonesia with unprecedented savagery, rather than to protect the Indonesian population. Ethical policy was never officially repealed, but in practice it ceased.

THE NATIONALIST MOVEMENT

In the political, as in the economic, sphere the 1930s showed a similar retrogression of Ethical principles. At the turn of the century Dutch colonial policy towards Indonesia was not unlike that of the British *vis-à-vis* India and in 1918 the People's Council was introduced as a representative body. In the same year the so-called "November Promises" referred to a future transfer of authority from the Netherlands to the Indies and to constitutional reforms which would give the native population a greater share in administrative matters. From 1922, however, after the rise of the nationalist movement had caused fear in a great many Dutch hearts and the revolutionary high tide which had accompanied the end of the First World War had ebbed away, hardly anything was done in this respect: during the trade depression interference from The Hague was increasing instead of diminishing, while constitutional stagnation set in. In 1938 the Government rejected an Indonesian proposal, the Soetardjo Petition, put forward in the People's Council in 1936, to convene a conference of representatives of the Netherlands and the Indies in order to discuss gradual reforms which, over a period of ten years or more if the conference should decide so, would lead to self-rule for Indonesia within the realm of the Kingdom of the Netherlands.

The nationalist movement, with its main centres in Java and West Sumatra, was originally moderate in nature, but during the First World War and under the influence of Marxist ideas, it took on a more radical appearance; the great Muslim association *Sarekat Islam*, founded in 1912, changed its policy from one of "collaboration with the administration for the well-being of the Indies" to one of opposition to the government and to "sinful" (i.e. non-native) capitalism. For some years some kind of co-operation between the Sarekat Islam and the Communist Party existed, but after the break of 1921 the Muslim party lost a good deal of its mass following, while the Communists had manoeuvred themselves into a rebellion (Java, 1926; Sumatra, 1927) which was suppressed and followed by a ban on Communism. The next stage of the development brought the genuine nationalists to the fore, genuine in the sense that they did not base their actions on any international ideal, such as Islam or Communism, but on pure Indonesian nationalism. The years between 1926 and 1934 were the years of Sukarno, Hatta and Sjahrir, characterized on the nationalist side by a policy of non-co-operation with the colonial authorities, and on the Dutch side by an intensification of political repression. Realizing that it was primarily the non-co-operative nationalist parties which were persecuted by the Government, the nationalists changed tactics and dropped non-co-operation as a means of political struggle. Thus a process of reorientation began around 1934–35, giving the impression that the nationalist movement had returned to moderation—a false impression as the ultimate end of the struggle continued to be independence. The more moderate behaviour of nationalism induced the administration to relax its oppressive policy, though not, however, to change its course of withholding constitutional or political reforms. After the Netherlands itself had become involved in the Second World War such reforms were not even taken into consideration, in spite of the nationalists' insistence on this as a pre-requisite for a closer co-operation between the Dutch and the Indonesians against a common enemy.

The Effect of Japanese Occupation

During the Japanese occupation (1942–45) the nationalist movement gained considerable strength. From its early beginnings Japanese policy, in Java at least, was directed to winning over the population with the help of those leaders who, because of their links with the masses, might be useful to this end. Some of the nationalist leaders were given official advisory posts in the Japanese-sponsored mass movements, but as they did not command a sufficiently large following among the population and as the Japanese fully realized that they collaborated only in order to prepare themselves for post-war contingencies it was not until late 1944 that the occupying authorities allowed them to obtain a more substantial share in political life. In the intervening years the Japanese accorded their favours to the aristocratic classes and, to a far greater extent, to Muslim religious leaders, the only group which held considerable influence over the population at grass-roots level.

The most important result of the Japanese occupation was the psychological effect of the sudden disappearance of the colonial regime, which, combined with the practical effect of Indonesians holding the administrative and technical positions formerly reserved for Europeans, gave fresh impetus to Indonesian self-confidence. The nationalist movement which arose after the war was, for the first time, a real mass movement, partly led by Islamic leaders whose influence had been greatly strengthened in comparison with the pre-war situation, partly by the nationalist politicians who had managed to win control over the quasi-political organizations as soon as the Japanese, in the last phase of the war, had committed themselves to the idea of granting independence to Indonesia.

The Revolutionary Years: 1945–49

The leadership of the nationalist movement was still essentially middle class, but during the revolution of August 1945, its hand was often forced by the younger generation which had developed new and radical ideals. Between the older nationalists and the young revolutionaries Sjahrir emerged as Prime Minister in November 1945, at the same time that Surabaya was the scene of stubborn Indonesian resistance against the British occupying forces. The conflict between the middle-class leaders and the revolutionary young generation lasted until the attempted coup in July 1946, after which the country's leadership slid back into the hands of the old guard.

In the social field the Indonesian revolution was clearly characterized by the bourgeois nature of the leading élite; it was essentially a middle-class and primarily a nationalist, not in any sense a proletarian, revolution. The political leadership of this élite group was never endangered during the revolutionary years (1945–49), either by the small group around Sjahrir and Sjarifuddin (Prime Ministers 1945–47 and 1947–48 respectively) who advocated a parliamentary democracy along bourgeois lines, or by the Communists. Neither were the Dutch, after their return and their take-over of responsibility from the British occupying power in 1946, successful in creating a counterweight. Their so-called Malino-policy (1946–49) of setting up separate states as constituent parts of a projected United States of Indonesia was an attempt at isolating the revolutionary government of the Indonesian Republic as much as it was an attempt at a counter-revolution. It was based on the traditionally loyal aristocracy and the aristocracy's fear of the emerging middle-class nationalist leaders. In the end, however, it was not strong enough to counterbalance the influence of the latter.

INDEPENDENT INDONESIA

Negotiations between the Dutch and the government of the Indonesian Republic led to an initial agreement in November 1946, the Linggadjati Treaty, but misunderstandings over its interpretation and especially the Dutch insistence that the Republic give up its sovereign rights and incorporate itself in the United States of Indonesia during a transitional period under Dutch sovereignty, resulted in a break. In July 1947 full-scale fighting broke out, but under the auspices of the United Nations a truce was arranged in January 1948. New negotiations were unsuccessful; in a new military campaign the Dutch captured the entire republican government in December 1948, but facing hostile world opinion, intensifying guerrilla operations and distrust among the loyal politicians of the Malino states, they had to give in: on December 27th, 1949, Indonesia became independent. It was a federal state—thus far the Dutch had been successful—but the United States of Indonesia did not survive the withdrawal of Dutch power for long. A strong unitarian movement, supported by republican leaders, swept the constituent states and the Malino authorities aside and in August 1950 Indonesia was proclaimed a unitary republic.

Parliamentary Democracy: 1949–57

After independence Indonesia faced many problems and, as these were emerging in a society which was politically far more articulate than in pre-war years, it also experienced greater difficulties in solving them than the colonial regime had done. No Indonesian government could afford to disregard public opinion and incur public discontent from which the opposition might make political capital. Any governmental system based on principles which for the most part are derived from abroad needs some time to mature. This is valid in almost any country; it was the more so in a nation which obtained its freedom after eight years of war and revolutionary turbulence. The coming of independence was accompanied by an upsurge of enthusiasm and a desire to build up a new state and society. At the same time, however, various dissonant forces were released once the only factor that had cemented them together had been eliminated. There was disappointment among the younger generation which had played a leading part in conducting the revolutionary struggle from the more dangerous outposts, and which now discovered that the country's leadership had reverted to the old-guard nationalists who were claiming superiority on the grounds of their experience and their better education.

Such a situation created problems which required a strong governmental structure and a sound party system. Neither of these conditions was met. Owing to a lack of experts and competent civil servants after the dismissal of many Dutch and Eurasian officials, the administration functioned inefficiently and clumsily in the executive sphere as well as in the legislature. This last factor also accounted for the defects in the party system; capable and authoritative leaders were usually drawn into the higher ranks of the government and the civil service, leaving the parties under the command of second-rate people. Another factor was that most parties had come into being, and their leaders had begun their political careers, during the colonial period: their activities had been directed against the administration and after a national government had supplanted the foreign regime many parties still persisted in displaying an element of opposition and enmity towards all authority. As no party commanded an absolute majority in the legislature, all governments during the period of parliamentary democracy (1949–57) were coalition cabinets, none of them stable and none capable of finding either a common platform or a solution to any of the more pressing problems. Only in combating illiteracy did independent Indonesia achieve a great and most admirable success.

There were many fundamental problems with which the Indonesian governments had to cope. First the religious issue: whether or not Indonesia should be an Islamic state. The second problem concerned the integration of the army into the state and its position *vis-à-vis* the civilian government. On several occasions the downfall of a cabinet was caused by army interference and in many more cases the authority of the Government and its appointees in the armed forces was openly defied by insubordinate actions—

a factor which greatly contributed to political instability. Thirdly there was the problem of regionalism which outwardly seemed to have been overcome in 1950, but which was definitely not extinct. The mood of dissatisfaction which crept into the regions outside Java was based not only on ethnological and cultural differences, but also, and primarily so, on economic considerations: income earned for Indonesia in Sumatra flowed to Java, a situation which confronted the government in Jakarta with an ugly and almost insoluble dilemma.

Guided Democracy: 1957–65

In 1957 parliamentary democracy gave way to a type of authoritarianism which was dubbed "guided democracy". In the course of a few years Sukarno, the leading architect of the new system, strengthened the executive power of the government, replaced the elected parliament by an appointed legislature and reintroduced the constitution of 1945.

During this period of "guided democracy", which lasted from 1957 until 1965, Sukarno was the central figure. He was able to demonstrate a mysterious mastery over the population, while at the same time he successfully played the two great contending power factions off against each other: on the one side the army, on the other the Communist Party which in the previous years had been capable both of emerging as the best organized political party and of capturing a large mass following.

Great emphasis was put on the unity of Indonesia, not only in a geographical sense—and directed against regional tendencies—but also in a national and social sense: hence Sukarno's insistence on close co-operation between all classes and sections of Indonesian society (*Nasakom*). In its foreign policy Indonesia, since independence a staunch advocate of "neutralism", followed an anti-Western course, as became evident in its actions against the Netherlands, which could be regarded as a completion of the nationalist revolution (the incorporation of Irian Jaya—West New Guinea—in 1963), as well as by its opposition to "neo-colonialism": confrontation with Malaysia (1963–66).

This anti-Western course, the take-over of Dutch business firms, the inclusion of communism in the *Nasakom*-ideal and of some individual communists in the cabinet, contributed to give Indonesian policy a leftist image. In its essence it was not leftist, however. The opposition to imperialism and neo-colonialism served to arouse feelings of nationalist self-consciousness and to create a national consensus of opinion. Taking over foreign business was not the outcome of any socialist ideal, but part of a nationalist campaign. The Communist Party was not banned—in this Sukarno's government differed from traditional authoritarian systems—but it did not come any closer to the take-over which many observers seemed to fear. In the constitutional framework of guided democracy there was no opportunity for the Communist Party, which in 1955 had polled 16.4 per cent of the votes, to show its strength in national elections; its growing influence among the masses, caused by the deteriorating economic situation, was most effectively counter-balanced by the increasing power of the army and by the government's policies which diverted the communists' activities from social to nationalist issues. In fact, guided democracy contributed to maintaining the social status quo in which Indonesia continued to be ruled by the middle-class élite which had captured the direction of political and economic affairs from the Japanese in 1945.

The New Order

The abortive coup by some army sections in October 1965 totally changed the situation. The military establishment used the event as an excuse to crack down on the communists, who were murdered by the thousands in one of the worst single massacres in South-East Asian history: in fact the entire left wing was eliminated. At the same time President Sukarno was deprived of his prerogatives. In March 1966 military commanders, led by General Suharto, assumed emergency powers. General Suharto used his new executive authority gradually to establish his "New Order". In February 1967 Sukarno handed over all power to Suharto. In March the People's Consultative Assembly removed the President from office and named Suharto acting President and, after being elected by the Assembly, he was inaugurated as President in March 1968.

The delicate balance of power on which Sukarno's authority had been based was completely destroyed. The armed forces became the most important power-factor, while the political parties were relegated to an even more inferior position than during "Guided Democracy". Even the Muslims, the staunchest allies of the army in the drive against the Communist Party and Sukarno, were not allowed to regain the political influence they commanded before the 1958 revolt. Yet, in spite of the changes, the coming to power of Suharto did not essentially alter the situation in which the middle class élite continued to rule the country. There was a change from a moderately right-wing authoritarian type of government to a harsh military dictatorship, but there was not, in fact, a switch from a really left-wing to a right-wing regime. The New Order represented a counter-revolution only in the sense that the social forces working towards improving the living conditions of the mass of the population were effectively blocked: the land-reform programme of 1960 was discontinued, peasants' associations and trade unions were banned.

Under the New Order the problems besetting the Government were the same as before, and even more acute. There was no real solution to the economic difficulties although, with the help of Western countries and Japan, a programme of economic stabilization and rehabilitation was introduced in October 1966. The new regime offered better opportunities for foreign investment than the previous one and its general political orientation fitted in better with Western policy and strategy in South-East Asia. Up to mid-1980 Indonesia received nearly $10,000 million in loans from the so-called donor-countries (officially the Inter-Governmental Group for Indonesia, IGGI).

In spite of these huge financial injections, the Five-Year Plan introduced in April 1969 failed. By resorting to a tight-money policy as well as by allowing the importation of foreign goods, the Government's policy led to the ruin of Indonesian business firms. In 1968 a crash programme to improve rice production also failed: undue pressure was put on Javanese peasants to sell their crops at low prices and to buy expensive imported fertilizers. If anyone benefited from whatever economic improvements were made, it was certainly not the rural mass of the population, but a few categories of urban consumers: in order to satisfy their needs, to keep the towns quiet and to create the impression in the outside world that Indonesia was developing as a welfare state, the prices of rice and other necessities were artificially kept at a low level.

On the other hand the increasing dependence of Indonesia's economy on the West and Japan, endangered its freedom of economic and political action. Western and Japanese capital are heavily involved in exploiting Indonesia's natural resources, particularly oil, timber and fishing. By mid-1981 its foreign debt amounted to over $20,000 million; the following year the balance of payments showed a deficit of $2,500 million. However, record harvests meant that by 1982 Indonesia was no longer dependent on rice imports, and in a report by the World Bank it was stated that, with a G.N.P. of $520 per caput, it was no longer one of the "poor nations".

Indonesia's dependence on the Western world also resulted in a new foreign policy. In 1966/67 the good relations with China were ended, and diplomatic relations with Malaysia re-established. The Suharto government still adhered formally to the principle of non-alignment and did not participate in any Western military alliance. However, it was a member of ASEAN which, although referring to Asian neutralism, fitted in with United States policy towards South-East Asia.

In the early 1970s Indonesia had moved towards the West and this the more so when, in view of the débâcle of U.S. policy in Indochina, insular South-East Asia was more and more regarded as the last American line of defence in the region.

In July 1971 general elections were held. The Government strongly supported the so-called *Sekber Golkar* (Secretariat of Functional Groups) which consequently won a handsome victory. In addition to the seats allotted to the armed forces the members of *Sekber Golkar* guaranteed the regime a comfortable parliamentary majority, and early in 1972 Suharto was re-elected. In January 1973 the political parties were forced to merge into two large organizations, one for the Islamic groups, and one for the non-Muslim parties. In fact the regime often declared itself against "politics" and *Sekber Golkar* was described as a non-political body. In spite of the manoeuvres to increase the number of civilian cabinet ministers the regime remains predominantly military: the majority of local officials at all levels are military officers.

During the early 1970s, in spite of the extent of popular support for the New Order indicated by election results, there was significant opposition to Suharto's regime. Small guerrilla bands were operating in Kalimantan and Irian Jaya and among Islamic leaders there was dissatisfaction over their minimal role in the political process. In August 1973 there were riots when the Government introduced a new marriage law. Students frequently demonstrated over corruption and rising prices. In January 1974 the outward stability of the regime was badly shaken by serious disturbances in Jakarta. Students played a major role in these, but they were probably manipulated by some elements within the military establishment who were displeased with their own position and with the government's policies.

In 1974 the increasing revenues from the oil industry caused a temporary improvement in Indonesia's balance of payments. Yet this did not produce any rise in the standard of living of the majority of the population. Discontent was expressed towards the widespread corruption within government departments which was heightened by the near-collapse of Pertamina, the state oil concern, and the revelation of the dubious financial activities of its former President, Lt.-Gen. Ibnu Sutowo. The repressive nature of the regime, which, according to estimates by Amnesty International, held 100,000 political prisoners, has also provoked severe criticism both at home and abroad. The Government responded to this pressure by releasing 10,000 political prisoners in December 1977 and the remainder in 1978 and 1979. However, it became clear that in many cases the freed prisoners were being either forcibly moved to outlying islands as part of the Government's transmigration policy or detained under house arrest.

In September 1976 there was an alleged attempt to overthrow Suharto and replace him with Muhammad Hatta, who had signed a document criticizing the regime as had several other leading figures from military and religious circles. While it became clear that the signatories of the document did not intend to engineer a coup, it was significant that their discontent with the Government should have led them to make such a protest.

General elections were held in May 1977. There were only three parties contesting the 350 seats up for election: *Sekber Golkar*, the Development Unity Party (PPP), an amalgamation of all the Islamic parties that had participated in the 1971 elections, and the Indonesian Democratic Party (PDI), comprising all the former secular opposition parties. As anticipated, *Sekber Golkar* won an overwhelming majority.

Towards the end of 1977 criticism of the Suharto regime increased. Several prominent and respected personalities, including the former Commander of the Armed Forces, Gen. Nasution, as well as students, voiced their dissatisfaction with the Government and the level of corruption within it. There was also discontent among the Islamic leadership and the PPP who felt that they were not being given sufficient influence over government policies.

Between November 1977 and January 1978 there was a series of student riots which resulted in a ban on newspapers and the repression of student political activity. However, Suharto remained firmly in control and was re-elected unopposed by the People's Consultative Assembly for a third five-year term as President in March 1978. Elections in May 1982 gave *Sekber Golkar* an increased majority, with 64 per cent of the vote. The campaign leading up to the elections was often violent and resulted in about 50 deaths, many injuries and several hundred arrests. Several newspapers were temporarily banned as a consequence of reporting these events. There were also allegations from the other political parties of corruption during the voting by the ruling majority.

Opposition to the Suharto Government was also manifested in the continuing separatist rebellions in East Timor and Irian Jaya. Following the withdrawal of Portugal from the former in 1975, the Indonesian Government intervened to prevent Fretilin, the independence movement, from taking control, and in July 1976 formally integrated East Timor as the 27th province of Indonesia. Resistance by Fretilin continues in spite of a brutal campaign of suppression by the Indonesian army, and leaders of the movement maintain that their forces still control a large part of East Timor. During 1978 both Australia and New Zealand formally recognized the integration of East Timor, which resulted in an improvement in their relations, but the UN has passed several resolutions calling for the withdrawal of Indonesian troops from the territory. Reports from various sources recorded a severe famine raging in the territory but by 1981 conditions had improved. The Government allocated $100 million for development in East Timor in 1981. In the 1982 election, East Timor was allocated four seats for the first time.

In Irian Jaya, rebellion against Indonesian control by the Free Papua Movement (OPM), which aims for unification with Papua New Guinea, presented a further threat to the stability of Suharto's regime, following a major uprising in May 1977. In mid-1978 Indonesian troops led a concerted campaign against the OPM rebels, thus renewing suspicions in Papua New Guinea of Indonesian expansionism. In December 1979, however, a new border agreement was finalized between the two countries.

ECONOMIC SURVEY

Iain Buchanan

(Revised for this edition by CHRISTOPHER DIXON)

In terms of population, Indonesia is the fifth largest country in the world, with an estimated 151 million people in 1982. In terms of resources, it is one of the richest in the Third World, with sizeable petroleum, natural gas and other mineral deposits and some of the richest timber stands in the world. Its position is economically and politically strategic, curving from the Indian Ocean, adjacent to the Malacca Straits and the South China Sea (Japan's main link with Europe and the Middle East), through to the Pacific Ocean and Micronesia. Yet Indonesia is among the poorer countries in the world. According to the World Bank, it had an estimated per caput G.N.P. of U.S. $520 in 1981, with 58 per cent of the population living officially in "absolute poverty", in a poor and overpopulated agricultural economy. The bulk of the population (66 per cent) is concentrated in the islands of Java and Madura (7 per cent of total area), and in Java, too, there is concentrated most of Indonesia's urban population, manufacturing and modern transport facilities, as well as some of the most productive agriculture and the majority of the country's poorest peasantry.

ECONOMIC TRENDS, 1950-65

During the Sukarno years Indonesia was inherently unstable economically, reflecting a combination of political obstacles to effective development. While Sukarno tried to develop a badly disrupted economy his policies were often counter-productive, overcompromising and sabotaged by the complex of powerful vested interests. A radical restructuring of the economic and political system was essential but impossible, given the chronic antagonism between the nationalists, the Muslim establishment, communists and regional interests.

With an overwhelmingly agrarian economy, Indonesia's first priority was rural development. Agriculture was marked by high rates of tenancy, indebtedness, landlessness, under-employment and a majority of landholdings of unviable size (in 1955 the average holding in Java was officially 0.6 of a hectare, with over 50 per cent of the farming population in holdings of less than one hectare or half the size necessary for adequate family subsistence).

However, the two main reform laws, the 1960 Basic Agrarian Law and the Sharecroppers Act were too late, too moderate, and were sabotaged by a combination of landlord, orthodox Muslim and military interests. When the Indonesian Communist Party encouraged the peasantry to make unilateral land transfers, to enact legislation already on the books, those interests were threatened. When Sukarno nationalized Dutch, British, American and local Chinese interests, he was asserting a double-edged anti-imperialism: first, the short-term advantages of using foreign investment to gain foreign exchange for development were lost, for Indonesia had neither the capital nor the expertise to develop effectively its own resources, and the institutional framework of a corrupt military, in-

Table 1

Production of selected items, 1955–64
('000 metric tons)

	1955	1959	1964
Food crops:			
Rice (milled)	7,125	7,950	8,096
Maize	1,882	2,101	3,769
Cassava	9,380	11,923	12,223
Sweet potatoes	1,866	2,719	3,931
Groundnuts	216	255	261
Soybeans	345	431	392
	1954	1958	1964
Export products:			
Rubber	759.6	695.7	732
Copra (smallholder)	973.5	1,050.0	1,193
Palm oil (estate)	169.0	147.6	195
Tin concentrates	32.8	22.8	16.6
Crude petroleum	10,775	16,295	23,172

competent bureaucracy, and strongly capitalist entrepreneurial élite negated any possible benefits of economic independence; second, anti-Western moves alienated the Western-subsidized military establishment, the trader class and the large class of commercial croppers in Sumatra.

One result of this was deepening antagonism between Sumatra and other outer islands (which accounted for 85 per cent of all export income) on the one hand, and Java (whose imports were subsidized by the outer islands' earnings) on the other. Sumatra, in particular, began direct trading with Malaysia and Singapore, thus depriving the central government of vital revenue. In this situation, corruption became endemic, and smuggling mushroomed and continued despite confrontation with Malaysia and Singapore (1963–66). Hence trade figures are unreliable (since 1962 Singapore, through which most of Indonesia's exports go, has refused to publish figures on trade with Indonesia).

Export production is poorly reflected in trade figures, partly because of world price changes and partly because of cash crop smuggling. In 1959 rubber, petroleum and tin accounted for, respectively, 48 per cent, 27 per cent and 4 per cent of the value of reported trade. Allowing for smuggling, more than 80 per cent of the value of Indonesia's exports came from these three commodities. Indonesia's visible trade balance deteriorated between 1959 and 1964 from a surplus of 47 per cent to one of 14 per cent. As for financial stability, the cost of living rose by 19 per cent in 1959 and 594 per cent in 1965.

As Table 1 shows, production during the decade 1954-1964 showed a sluggishness or decline for the most part: of the major export commodities only petroleum showed a notable increase in production (115 per cent). More significant, however, are the figures for food crop production. Rice production increased by 1.3 per cent per annum and per capita annual consumption of rice declined from 91 kilogrammes in 1958 to 86 kilogrammes in 1964. However, aggregating rice and maize production (given the major boost to maize production which was part of Sukarno's policy), gross production per capita increased from 107 kilogrammes per annum in 1955 to 111 kilogrammes in 1964 (with net consumption some 5 per cent less). By the mid-1960s, net food supplies available per capita (average 1964–66) were the second lowest in the world, and so too was average daily protein intake.

Thus, by 1965 the Indonesian economy was virtually stagnant. The population remained amongst the poorest in the world (the average annual income per caput fell from $73 in 1960 to $65 in 1963). Wide disparities remained between a densely populated Java and the less densely populated outer islands. Infrastructural development had not brought transport facilities back to pre-war efficiency, despite considerable investment, and production suffered as a result of this and wider neglect. By 1966, Indonesia had incurred a foreign debt of $1,630 million and the trading economy was bordering on chaos. Besides, little attempt had been made to exploit effectively large known reserves of timber and many basic minerals—commodities vital to the industrialized West and Japan.

CONSOLIDATION OF THE "NEW ORDER"

After the 1965–66 crisis, the new Suharto administration began a change from a bureaucratic, badly-managed, centrally-controlled economy to a liberal market economy underpinned by State planning and foreign investment. The "New Order" openly reflected Western development concepts and strategies: Indonesia accepted the International Monetary Fund (IMF) stabilization programme; the new economic leaders were trained in the U.S.A.; Western aid resumed, channelled largely through the Inter-Governmental Group for Indonesia (IGGI); food imports resumed from the West; and foreign investors were encouraged.

The IMF stabilization model was followed closely. First, the Government instituted anti-inflation measures. The 1967–72 period was marked by the achievement of a balanced budget by 1969, cuts in social expenditure (for example, free schooling was abolished), emphasis in government spending upon infrastructure, and tight credit control through high interest rates. Inflation dropped from 650 per cent in 1966 to 10 per cent in 1969.

Secondly, the rupiah was devalued. The exchange rate moved from U.S. \$1=Rs. 156 (1967) to \$1=Rs. 415 (1971). At the same time, the complicated foreign exchange control was ended in 1970 after 30 years, by the merging of multiple exchange rates.

Thirdly, foreign investment was encouraged by the 1967 Foreign Investment Law. This encouraged investment outside transport, power, and telecommunications; but, even here, joint ventures were allowed, with the foreign investor having full powers to appoint managers and foreign personnel. Priority sectors for foreign capital included export-oriented industries, those using local raw materials, and manufacturing of basic consumer goods. Major incentives, including tax exemptions, were given to foreign investors. There was a guarantee of free profit repatriation and against expropriation (a vague rider provided for eventual local participation).

Thus by 1970 a complete reversal of economic policy was accomplished within three years of the overthrow of Sukarno. The implications of this, and subsequent developments, are examined below.

Economic Planning: REPELITA I to REPELITA III

Since 1967 planning has been closely guided by Western and Japanese interests working bilaterally or through multilateral agencies, especially the IGGI, the aid consortium which approves Indonesia's annual aid requests, and through which planning policy is influenced. Thus, of the three plans, REPELITA I (1969-74) was 66 per cent aid-financed, REPELITA II (1974-79) 35 per cent, and REPELITA III (1979-84) a projected 42 per cent. Plan emphases reflect the interests of the patrons as much as of the client-élite.

In 1969 the First Five-Year Plan (REPELITA I) began (*see* also *The Far East and Australasia* 1977–78 and 1978–79). Formulated by the National Planning Board (BAPPENAS) with American guidance, it aimed to build an infrastructure to serve both foreign investment and agriculture and to modernize agriculture by irrigation rehabilitation and the introduction of a "Green Revolution" strategy, using high-yielding varieties (HYV) of rice, and increased use of fertilizers, pesticides, and mechanical equipment to achieve food self-sufficiency. Agriculture, producing 55 per cent of the 1968 G.N.P. and 60 per cent of exports, and involving 72 per cent of the population was clearly a priority for planning.

There was to be an increase in rice area from 8.5 million hectares to 9.3 million, and the introduction of HYV rice into four million hectares, by 1974, to reach a production of 15.4 million tons of milled rice. Of the allocation to agriculture, 82.5 per cent was for irrigation development and rice intensification.

Infrastructural development, excluding irrigation, absorbed 33 per cent of planned expenditure. Poor communications had long been a major obstacle to development: infrastructural development had been very uneven, being concentrated in Java and eastern Sumatra, and 70 per cent of the roads were virtually unfit for use.

As for industry, the high profitability of manufacturing (because of low labour costs, generous fiscal incentives, and ample local raw materials) meant greater appeal to private capital; thus, the Government's allocation was to be matched by private (largely foreign) investment of 140,500 million rupiahs. Five categories of industry were to be emphasized: agriculture-supporting industries, import-substituting industries, industries processing local raw materials, labour-intensive industries and industries that induced regional development through spread effect.

Overall, productive capacity was to be raised by 90 per cent over the Plan period. Near self-sufficiency was hoped for by 1974 in fertilizers (90 per cent imported), cement (50 per cent imported), and textiles (95 per cent imported). Petroleum and timber based industries were expected to increase output dramatically, reducing import-dependence on chemicals, plastics, synthetic fibres, processed timber, and paper.

Except for provision of infrastructure, metal mining was left largely to foreign investors. The greatest potential for mineral development was in petroleum and natural gas, especially off-shore. Apart from that from the Caltex Sumatran fields, there was little petroleum production (on-shore or off-shore) in 1968. By 1970, however, over 30 oil companies had production-sharing agreements with the state oil company Pertamina.

Pertamina was virtually autonomous from BAPPENAS, and was overseer of potentially the most profitable sector of the economy. In considering the evolution of the Indonesian economy after 1968, the role of petroleum as a source of revenue, and of Pertamina as an entrepreneur, is of critical importance. By contracting with foreign oil companies, by controlling Indonesia's increasing oil revenues (U.S. \$388 million in 1969 and \$10,000 million in 1979), and by mortgaging this revenue to heavy foreign loans, Pertamina developed a "parallel economy" with major influence in every sector of the national economy. Its management differed from that of BAPPENAS, its budget was separate (and at least half the value of the total national budget), and its priorities often clashed with those of the technocrats managing REPELITA I. Thus a clear distinction must be made, in terms of the structure of the "modern" economy and development policy followed, between the economy of Lt.-Gen. Ibnu Sutowo, the President of Pertamina, and the economy of Dr. Widjojo Nitisastro, the architect of REPELITA I.

By the end of REPELITA I, however, Pertamina was on the verge of collapse. REPELITA II (1974–79) was to build upon the quantitative achievements of

REPELITA I, aiming for greater job creation, a more equitable distribution of income and improved material living standards (better housing, food, and clothing), expansion and improvement of economic and social infrastructure, and investment policies better aimed at protecting domestic and small industries. There was an explicit admission that REPELITA I had neglected many important areas of development.

Agriculture received first priority. Emphasis was on achieving self-sufficiency in rice, and increasing secondary food crop production. Only 7.6 per cent of Plan spending was allocated to increasing production of paddy, *palawija* (secondary food) crops, fruit and vegetables, with an expected increase in the production of milled rice to 18.2 million metric tons in 1978/79. BIMAS programmes (*see* under Agriculture) would be greatly expanded, farm incentives increased, and an attempt made to lessen reliance on rice as a staple by encouraging BIMAS *palawija* production (e.g. maize and soybeans). A further 9.5 per cent of expenditure was allocated to rehabilitation of the irrigation network and to build new irrigation works for 820,000 hectares. This was linked with opening new land for transmigration and flood control as well as increasing productivity.

To prevent the continuing abuse of forest resources, it was planned to increase control over forestry operations, to reafforest and "green" 3.8 million hectares, and to complete a major national survey of forest resources.

Industrial growth was projected at 11–13 per cent during the period, providing more consumer goods, about 1.2 million new jobs, and greater export earnings. It was planned that textile production would rise by about 39 per cent, for example, and that cement, paper and fertilizer production would more than double. Some increases in production would be large as major projects (such as most of the PUSRI fertilizer complex at Palembang) begun during REPELITA I, often by Pertamina, would come on stream during REPELITA II. As during the first Plan, mining was left largely to foreign investment, although its importance to the economy was recognized, with petroleum providing a projected 51 per cent of foreign exchange, and petroleum and gas providing raw materials for fertilizer, liquid natural gas and petrochemical production.

As for infrastructure excluding irrigation, under REPELITA II, electricity development (7.5 per cent of Plan spending) would increase generating capacity from less than 3 million MWh. in 1973 to about 7 million in 1978. Transport and communications development (15.6 per cent of Plan spending) would emphasize road improvements, bringing the percentage of roads classified as "in good condition" from 23 to 50 per cent, and shipping and port development, expanding both inter-island and ocean-going shipping by 50 per cent.

The need for employment expansion was obvious, with open unemployment around 20 per cent. This was to be achieved by trying to prevent bias (in any sector) towards either capital intensity or urban concentration, by expanding the *kabupaten* and provincial level programmes of local development, transmigration, and such projects as the *Padat Karya* (Labour Intensive Works Programme). Such schemes are also important in relation to another basic aim of

Table 2

REPELITA II (1974–79)

	'000 million rupiahs	%
Economic sector:		
Agriculture and irrigation	1,001.6	19.1
Industry and mining	185.8	3.5
Electricity and power	387.8	7.4
Communications and tourism	831.7	15.8
Trade and co-operatives	37.9	0.7
Manpower and transmigration	69.7	1.3
Regional and local development	930.6	17.7
Social sector:		
Health, family planning and social welfare	192.1	3.7
Education, culture and religion	540.8	10.3
Housing and water supply	101.6	1.9
General sector:		
Defence and security	156.0	3.0
Scientific and technical research	101.3	1.9
State apparatus	123.0	2.3
Government capital participation	562.9	10.7
Information and communications	26.7	0.5
TOTAL	5,249.2*	100.0

* U.S. $12,650 million at 1973 exchange rate ($1=415 rupiahs).

REPELITA III (1979–84)

	'000 million rupiahs	%
Economic sector:		
Agriculture and irrigation	3,048.9	14.0
Industry and mining	1,589.3	7.3
Electricity and power	2,528.6	11.6
Communications and tourism	3,384.3	15.5
Trade and co-operatives	191.9	0.9
Manpower and transmigration	1,240.7	5.7
Regional and local development	2,142.9	9.8
Social sector:		
Health, family planning and social welfare	829.1	3.8
Education, culture and religion	2,429.3	11.0
Housing and water supply	532.0	2.4
General sector:		
Defence and security	1,676.6	7.7
Scientific and technical research	1,154.8	5.3
State apparatus	730.7	3.3
Business development	370.3	1.7
TOTAL	21,849.4†	100.0

† U.S. $34,960 million at 1979 exchange rate ($1=625 pruiahs).

REPELITA II, that of ensuring balanced local and regional development. Transmigration, for example, was planned to move 250,000 families from over-populated Java, Bali and Lombok to such islands as Kalimantan and Sumatra, at an estimated cost of U.S. $2,400 per family. Whether such "transfer of poverty", modestly funded rural health plans, or subsidies for such local works programmes as the *kabupaten* programme, will provoke a more equitable distribution of development, especially for rural areas, remains to be seen.

Another inequality, that of income and living standards, is being tackled, according to the Plan, simply by accelerating economic development. Such matters as housing and water supply have low priority in the Plan (1.9 per cent of expenditure), and consist mainly of stimulating middle-class housing and providing 225,000 serviced "sites" for low-income homes.

In assessing developments since 1969, it must be remembered that REPELITA I and II were not plans for thorough-going state-controlled economic change, setting imperative targets to be met. They were indicative sets of guidelines for government investment, with public sector activities detailed in annual budgets (in effect, annual plans) and annual reviews. Thus, it is instructive to compare planned REPELITA II expenditure with annual total and development budget estimates. Some anomalies exist. On average, as a proportion of the annual development budget, agriculture and irrigation receive 17.8 per cent of funds, industry 8 per cent, transport and tourism 18 per cent, and regional development 11 per cent. Priorities in total public spending (including routine and administrative spending) are very different, averaging annual budgets: state apparatus 19.6 per cent, regional development 15.9 per cent, defence 15.4 per cent, agriculture and irrigation 10.3 per cent, and health and welfare 1.5 per cent. Clearly, too, Plan spending as an indication of development priorities must be qualified by private investment. Taking this into account, total expenditure on agriculture and irrigation would be relatively much smaller for instance, while that on industry and mining would be far higher.

REPELITA III is a logical successor to REPELITA I, which rehabilitated infrastructure and began agricultural improvement; REPELITA II, which approached self-sufficiency in most agro-chemicals and petrochemicals and which expanded production of agricultural equipment; and the Pertamina era, during which Indonesian minerals were heavily exploited to achieve an industrial "take-off" in large-scale, capital-intensive projects. REPELITA III aims to help create an agriculture-based economy and society strong enough to initiate and support the development of a dual-programme industrialization by 1985. The two programmes are, firstly, the extension of the already developing large-scale projects and secondly, the smaller, often more traditional activities such as subcontracting, crafts, local production of consumer goods and export-oriented processing industries (e.g. garments, shoes, plastics, electronics and tinned food).

To support this development, the following will be emphasized:

(i) Greater effort to achieve food self-sufficiency and a more stable and diversified rural economy and society. This involves enlarged credit programmes and administrative reform, co-operative development and moderate land reform, greater emphasis on estate production, encouragement of village industries, the transmigration of 500,000 families from Java and Bali and expansion of the planted area by one million hectares.

(ii) Expansion of non-oil exports, in the hope that they will surpass oil exports as revenue earners by 1982. Four main elements are involved: agriculture (e.g. palm oil); forestry (up to 30 million cubic metres of timber cut annually); minerals (e.g. bauxite and coal); and manufactures (e.g. plastics and electronics).

(iii) Particular effort in mobilizing domestic funds for small-scale industrialization with a high degree of export-orientation, preferably outside Jakarta; for example, tax concessions are given to small companies if they submit to external auditing.

(iv) Encouragement of foreign investment in manufacturing, including the development of numerous Free Trade Zones hosting multinational companies using cheap local labour for export production.

(v) Expansion of infrastructure, especially transport and energy. An estimated $25,000 million is to be spent on oil and natural gas ($17,500 million), electricity and urban gas, and coal—40 per cent from foreign sources.

(vi) Encouragement of Malay Indonesian (*pribumi*) enterprise, in such fields as forestry and government construction and servicing contracts.

The general aim of attaining the "eight development equalities" specifically for the poor (e.g. more equal income distribution) is announced; and the broad aim of creating 6.4 million jobs (less than the projected addition to the work force) is stated.

AGRICULTURE

Food crops

To assess progress in the agricultural sector since 1967, it is essential we recognize a number of key points.

Firstly, most of the 70 per cent of Indonesians living in rural areas work within an agrarian structure characterized by small, non-viable holdings; a marked disparity in land-ownership (60–70 per cent of land is owned by 10 to 20 per cent of rural families); a high degree of landlessness (over 50 per cent); a high degree of under- and unemployment, respectively about 18 per cent and 35 per cent; heavy indebtedness of over 60 per cent of Javanese peasants; a combination of high rents and high interest charges to local moneylenders, meaning that the renting small-holder retains little more than 30 per cent of his harvest. These features combine with inefficient marketing, credit and infrastructural facilities, and considerable administrative corruption. The result is a generally low-yielding agriculture marked by extensive poverty, malnutrition and inefficiency.

Secondly, there are regional disparities within Java, and between Java and the outer islands.

Thirdly, non-agricultural activities are insufficiently developed to absorb much excess rural labour. The decline of village industries because of urban industrialization, increasing capital-intensity in agriculture, and a high rate of population growth have increased under- and unemployment.

Fourthly, higher average production or productivity do not necessarily mean increasing returns to most farmers, and increasing and more widespread rural prosperity. A country may achieve self-sufficiency at a certain level of average production per capita without most of the population (especially rural) being individually self-sufficient.

Finally, while parts of Java are overpopulated (about 2,000 per square kilometre) the problem of Java's overpopulation is more correctly one of under-employment. This has major relevance to policies of economic planning and population control.

Between 1969 and 1981, the gross production of milled rice rose erratically (*see* Table 3) from 12.3 million metric tons to a provisional 21.9 million tons. The REPELITA II target for rice production was almost reached by 1978/79, but the key point is that the increase was achieved by intensification of farming, benefiting relatively few, and not by any major extension of cultivated land. Over the decade, planted rice area—including transmigration schemes—increased by about 400,000 hectares, compared with a planned 800,000 hectares during REPELITA I alone. Irrigation improvement had affected 45–50 per cent of all wet rice lands by 1980.

To extend the area under intensified cropping, the Government used the two key programmes of BIMAS (*Bimbingan Massa,* or Mass Guidance) and INMAS (*Intensifikasi Massa,* Mass Intensification). The first grew out of Sukarno's 1965 Mass Guidance for Self-sufficiency in Food Programme (*Bimbingan Masal Swasembada Bahan Makanan*). In its revised form it is basically a programme to provide cheap credit from Bank Rakyat Indonesia (the State People's Bank) for essential inputs like fertilizers, pesticides and seeds. INMAS (also inspired in 1965) is geared to areas where farmers are financially more secure, and provides for the distribution of essential agricultural equipment. The two programmes are serviced within an organizational structure comprising the *Badan Usaha Unit Desa* (BUUD, or Hamlet Unit Enterprise Body) and the *Koperasi Usaha Unit Desa* (KUUD, or Hamlet Unit Enterprise Co-operative), and covering a BIMAS area of 600 to 1,000 hectares. The hamlet unit is the focal point for agricultural development, and the BUUD/KUUDs were designed to co-ordinate economic activities at this level, as well as to service the BIMAS/INMAS programmes. They have four functions: to provide credit from the State Bank, extension services, production needs such as fertilizers and seeds at fixed prices, and processing equipment (e.g., huskers and driers) to allow farmers to process their own grain and earn higher prices. The State Procurement Agency (BULOG) is responsible for collecting surplus grain through the BUUD/KUUDs, and stockpiling rice.

After a disastrous resumption of BIMAS intensification schemes, during 1967–70, in conjunction with multinational companies such as CIBA and Hoechst, the Government introduced a new BIMAS in 1970. Loans were granted directly to farmers by new village banks of the State Bank; supplies of subsidized fertilizer and pesticide went through the usual marketing channels instead of by direct government distribution, and farmers were given more freedom to choose the mix of inputs.

BIMAS went hand in hand with the INMAS scheme, and both worked at the hamlet level through the BUUD/KUUD scheme of co-operative development. By late 1977 there were 3,800 BUUDS, involving mostly better-off farmers. Since 1973 BUUDS and KUUDS have combined in many areas, and the BIMAS and INMAS programmes they service covered some 5 million hectares by 1980, with about 3 million hectares (36 per cent of rice-land) planted with HYV rice—especially the *wereng*-resistant IR36. Administrative re-organization was needed, largely because of mismanagement and corruption in the distribution of BIMAS credit, especially for fertilizers. Half of all BUUDs are believed to be insolvent, and making them sole distributors of fertilizer and pesticides almost certainly led to the decline in fertilizer consumption in 1976. In mid-1977, the Government began to tighten the reins on dubious BUUD operations. Another problem was the conflict between assuring a low rice price for the urban population and giving farmers a fair return. Over the past decade, the rice price has been subsidized, but the farm price has also been kept down. To counter this, fertilizer was subsidized. Now the farm price of urea, relative to the rice support price is low by Asian standards, but most farmers still have no access to fertilizers, and face price rises in other commodities.

By suppressing on-farm prices, the Government dampened rural development and penalized the indebted farmer who had to sell or buy rice on the open market at low selling prices and high buying prices. The tenant's or sharecropper's burden was aggravated by landowners and creditors passing down losses in heavier exactions. Equally, the small peasant benefits little from increased rice prices. In October 1979, BULOG increased the floor price of locally purchased rice for the fourth time in 18 months (a total increase of 50 per cent). However, since the November 1978 devaluation, most commodities have risen in price: the price of kerosene—the "poor man's fuel"—rose by over 100 per cent between May 1979 and May 1980, for example.

In such a situation, BIMAS schemes have had a detrimental effect on the small farmer: loans, and other facilities for increasing yields, were monopolized by larger farmers, and the smaller peasant's only incentive to grow more rice was the need to pay higher exactions, not to boost his real income.

Little rice is purchased at or above the floor price through the KUUD. BULOG normally buys only 5 per cent of the domestic crop; the main buyers are private, often buying below the floor price at harvest time in payment of debt. On balance, because of inefficiency, corruption, limited coverage and convergence of interest between KUUD managers and landowners, only slight significance should be placed on the co-operative scheme. Changes in rice and fertilizer prices, and BIMAS credit per hectare have merely aggravated the peasant's indebtedness. On BIMAS account alone, this rose as a proportion of total lending from 5 per cent in 1972 to 90 per cent in 1977; partly reflecting this, the number of individual farmers under BIMAS and INMAS schemes fell between 1975 and 1980. After a slump in fertilizer demand and indifferent harvests during 1976 and 1977, an increase in fertilizer consumption during the following two years accompanied significantly improved harvests. Grain imports dropped to 2 million tons in 1980 and to an estimated 500,000 tons in 1981. Major programmes to plant the *wereng*-resistant IR36, and fertilizer subsidies maintained at a high level, helped to increase paddy production. It is, however, doubtful if much of this increase resulted from the indifferent progress made in irrigation since 1975; besides, serious institutional problems remain. The record harvests of 1980 and 1981 are primarily a result of a favourably long wet season in Java.

Subsidies, official loans and extension of technology usually by-pass the smallholder and accumulate among the wealthy—smallholders and the landless have been poorly represented in BIMAS, let alone INMAS, programmes. Even in villages where ecological conditions were optimal for the success of HYV rice, and where class divisions were not as sharp as elsewhere, fewer than 30 per cent of farm households were using loans in the late 1970s, and to do so often carried the threat of dispossession.

The reason lay in the tenure system. With most farms well below viable size, and a high degree of landlessness, there is extreme concentration of landownership and debt-bondage—meaning that a few large landowners (owning over 10 hectares) use BIMAS credit, intensify production with low-wage labour under the *ijon kereja* system (work through debt bondage) over extensive areas, and thus control the bulk of the harvest at the same time as they increase it.

Table 3

Milled rice production

('000 metric tons)

	Gross	Net*
1969	12,349	10,000
1976	15,850	14,899
1977	15,900	14,946
1978	17,600	16,544
1979	17,900	16,826
1980	19,600	18,400
1981†	21,900	20,586

* Allowing 6 per cent for seed and losses.

† Provisional.

While the *ijon kereja* system is common, with many farmers preferring to use labour rather than capital-intensive measures the relationship between rich and poor in rural Java has gone beyond increasing debt-bondage: wealthy households use increased productivity to buy land from poorer peasants or to buy Japanese rice-field tractors and home-milling equipment, and labour-saving harvesting equipment. In both cases, consolidation of the wealthy farmer's position leads to increasing rural-urban migration in an effort to escape deepening poverty: 130,000 migrants enter Jakarta annually, for example, despite a 1971 edict declaring it a "closed city".

Certainly, in terms of overall increased productivity, BIMAS has had notable results. Average productivity in areas affected by BIMAS/INMAS schemes is about twice that of ordinary fields.

But overall production figures are misleading. While gross rice production increased between 1968 and 1979 at an average annual rate of 3.6 per cent (about 1.6 per cent per caput), supplies are still low: average annual net rice availability per caput (including imports) rose from 87 kilogrammes per caput in 1968 to an estimated 141 kilogrammes per caput in 1981. Further, this average conceals wide disparities between urban and rural dwellers and between social classes. Most rural dwellers exist on well below the average. The record harvests of 1980 and 1981 have highlighted the long-term problems of storage. BULOG has expanded its storage capacity to 2.75 million tons, but by the end of 1981 this was proving to be inadequate and causing serious loss.

Another necessary qualification is that the increase in rice production was achieved partly by concentrating effort, irrigation facilities, and fertilizers to produce a second crop on land previously used for other crops. As a result, acreage and production of other food crops declined by 3.5 per cent and 3.4 per cent respectively. During 1974–77, there was a decline of 232,000 hectares in harvested area of *palawija* crops, despite an emphasis on them in REPELITA II. This was associated with an estimated decline of 760,000 metric tons in the harvest of maize, cassava, sweet potatoes, groundnuts and soybeans over the same period. This qualitative change in farming had two main effects: first, with lower increases in production of higher protein staples like groundnuts and soybeans, and declines in production of sweet potatoes, cassava, and maize together with poor production of fish, animal meat, and milk, the average rural diet is more starchy and less nutritious than it was in 1968; secondly, total non-rice staple food production per caput fell, according to government figures, from 151.9 kilogrammes to 143.3 kilogrammes between 1968 and 1978. Since 1979 with the exception of maize, the production of these non-rice staple crops has stagnated.

It would therefore seem that, although priority was given (at least theoretically) to agriculture in the two Plans, there has been little qualitative improvement in rural conditions. Gross rice production increased, infrastructure such as irrigation works improved, and the area under HYV rice increased but the effects of these achievements were concentrated in a relatively small proportion of cropland and within a relatively small group of the population.

Cash crops

Available evidence suggests that progress in cash crop production has been variable especially in terms of the relative positions of estate and smallholder agriculture.

In 1969 estate and smallholder cash-cropping occupied about 35 per cent of arable area (over 6 million hectares) and provided 70 per cent of Indonesia's exports by value contributing such products as rubber, palm oil, tea, coffee, pepper, hard fibre, and copra. Coffee, tea and tobacco production went mainly to domestic consumption.

Of the 1969 rubber output of 778,000 metric tons, over 70 per cent came from smallholdings (rubber then contributed over a quarter of all exports by value); smallholdings also accounted for 45 per cent of tea output, 80 per cent of tobacco, and almost all pepper, kapok, copra, coffee and spices (especially clove and nutmeg). Oil palm and sugar are predominantly estate crops.

Up to 1979, the most marked production increases were in these two crops: sugar production, for example, rose 70 per cent between 1969 and 1979 to 1.5 million tons, (but this was still 500,000 tons below consumption) while production of palm oil increased from 188,000 tons to over 500,000 tons.

Oil palm was produced mainly for export until 1980, when the Government enforced regulations that required the bulk of production to be sold on the domestic market. The intention is to substitute palm oil for the more valuable coconut oil as the country's main cooking oil. As a result, an estimated 150,000 tons of coconut oil, out of a crop in 1981 of 750,000 tons, will become available for export.

Sugar production declined in 1980, largely because of the introduction of TRI (conversion of estates to smallholder production), which reduced yields. Domestic sugar consumption has been increasingly met by imports, averaging 500,000 tons in 1980 and 1981. The sugar processing sector has suffered from inadequate supplies of cane as a result of the low prices paid to growers. A change in the pricing policy in 1981 offered growers more than double the 1979 price. It is hoped that high prices will bring an expansion of the area planted and an increase in the yields, which are very low by international standards. The Government's current plans are ambitious: a production target of 3 million tons per annum by 1988. This will involve the renovation of 27 Javanese mills and the construction of 18 new mills. Production expansion is also planned in Sumatra and Sulawesi, where the building of new mills is already under way. Some concern has been expressed that sugar may replace rice on some irrigated land.

From 1970–79, rubber production increased by 1.1 per cent a year to reach 900,000 tons. Despite good prices in recent years, the planted area has remained about 2.3 million hectares. Under both REPELITA I and II, rubber small-holders were neglected, and most of the increase in production was from estates. Under REPELITA III, barely 10 per cent of rubber land was to be replanted. In 1981 the Government proposed a 10-year programme of expansion, with an investment in rubber of $4.500 million. Replanting and rehabilitation will take place on 1.8 million of the 1981 total of 4.5 million hectares. In addition, 500,000 hectares of new land for rubber will be developed, mainly in association with transmigration projects in Riau, Jambi, Aceh and Kalimantan. In 1981 export earnings from rubber fell by 20 per cent to an estimated $889 million.

Overall, "plantation" crops occupy about 6.7 million hectares, mostly in small-holdings. The export value of these crops rose from $421 million in 1969 to $1,950 million in 1979, and the government had hoped that such crops, together, will constitute the second main export earner after oil by 1984. However, in view of the fall in commodity prices during the latter part of 1981, this target is unlikely to be realized. Other planned developments include upgrading 68,000 hectares (17 per cent) of coffee area and 185,000 hectares (8 per cent) of coconut land, and increasing coconut and coffee area by 101,000 and 26,000 hectares respectively. Such diversification may be desirable, but the problems of the "plantation" crop sector are so great that many of these programmes seem inadequate. More than one-half of all rubber trees are well past peak maturity, and some 60 per cent of coconut trees over 50 years old. The smallholder is sector getting little finance from public sources to aid recovery: the 1980–81 Development Budget allocates it a mere five per cent of agriculture and irrigation's share of funds. Government policy points generally towards an encouragement of larger-scale private estate companies, rather than more diversified small-holding agriculture.

Animal husbandry and fishing

The main sources of animal protein in rural Indonesia are fish, poultry and eggs. Beef products are more for urban consumption, and almost all high-grade meat is imported. Rural consumption of beef is limited by the need to maintain buffaloes as draught animals and cows as milk producers. Pork is produced and consumed by the Hindu Balinese, the mainly urban Chinese and the non-Malay population of eastern Indonesia.

In 1978, the fishing industry contributed about 1 per cent of G.N.P. and employed about 1.2 million people. Of an estimated total 1979 catch of 1.7 million tons, only 2 per cent was gained by modern methods, and a good proportion of the inland catch comes from irrigation canals, as a secondary activity to wet-rice farming; marine fishing is poorly developed and subject to increasing Japanese competition. Fishing has a considerable potential for development: the potential sea catch alone is over 4.5 million tons.

MINING

Petroleum and natural gas

Petroleum deserves special attention for its decisive role in shaping the pattern and progress of Indonesian economic development, under the management of Pertamina, since 1968. Indonesia has 16,000 million barrels of estimated recoverable reserves of oil, and 34,700,000 million cubic feet of recoverable gas reserves. With a prospective area of 809,600 square kilometres on land, and 1,500,000 square kilometres off-shore (to the 300-metre isobath), designated oil areas in Indonesia are ten times the size of the European North Sea area, with dozens of sedimentary basins not yet tested. With the most promising land and off-shore area in South-East Asia, Indonesia has seen the most comprehensive oil search in the region. In 1974 231 wells were drilled: 28 were oil producers, 18 gas producers, and 25 both oil and gas producers; in 1981, 317 wells were drilled. Exploration and development expenditure rose from U.S. $78 million in 1969, to and estimated $690 million in 1975, declined to $145 million in 1977, rose to $700 million in 1980 and reached an estimated $3,400 million in 1981. Most of this activity involves United States investment: U.S. companies have over $5,000 million invested in Indonesian oil, and pump 90 per cent of all crude petroleum. Production is particularly sensitive to current investments levels because of the small size of the oil-fields and consequent short productive life.

Crude oil production rose, erratically, from 189 million barrels in 1967 to 584 million in 1981, when domestic consumption was 20 per cent of production (Japan took 50 per cent and the United States about 25 per cent). On a per caput basis, Indonesia's oil consumption is 2 per cent that of the United States but, if the country accelerates industrialization, fuel demand and depletion of reserves will increase. The continuation of subsidies for domestic fuel oil is contributing to the annual rate of increase of 12 to 14 per cent. At the 1980 rate of extraction, the country has about 26 years supply of oil and over 50 years' supply of natural gas. However, the rate of new discoveries is high, and in 1980 it exceeded production. The most important exploratory developments in 1981 were gas-fields in the South China Sea near the Natuna Islands. Gas could be the most important hydrocarbon resource for export and feed stock: in 1980 Indonesia exported 8 million tons of liquefied natural gas (LNG), all to Japan, making Indonesia the world's largest LNG exporter. Tied to the price of oil, Indonesia's gas exports rose in value from $540 million in 1978 to $2,300 million in 1980. Production of LNG is concentrated at the Arun plant (Aceh, Sumatra) and the Badak plant (Kalimantan). Both plants are working at capacity and, after planned expansion, should double production by 1984. Of major significance to offshore—and therefore most oil—exploration, was the formal declaration, in April 1979, of an exclusive 200-mile economic zone for exploration and exploitation of the sea and seabed around Indonesian territorial waters. Boundary problems exist, especially with Australia, Viet-Nam and Malaysia, as the economic zone is defined by the archipelagic principle—the baseline from which territorial and economic boundaries are drawn being an imaginary line connecting all outer-most points of outlying islands.

Except for Caltex, which gives the Government a 60:40 profit split, most oil companies in Indonesia operate under the production-sharing formula which leaves resource ownership with the Government, while the company acts as contractor and puts up necessary capital. Of petroleum and gas produced, until August 1976, 40 per cent was retained by the company as production costs, and the remainder split 35:65 between company and Government. In August an 85:15 split in the Government's favour was proposed. In early 1977, this was modified with exceptions increasing the company's share allowance for accelerated depreciation write-off of up to 100 per cent of costs, investment credits for all new exploration, and more favourable government oil purchase terms. With falling reserves and exploration, the Government had to temper its "oil nationalism".

Between 1978 and 1980, net oil and LNG earnings rose from $4,000 million to $9,400 million (aided by a doubling of prices in 1979); the crude oil and product import bill rose from $4,700 million in 1979 to $9,400 million. Oil company taxes provided 71 per cent of Government revenue in 1980–a level of contribution unlikely to be affected by the agreement in May 1981 to cut production 7 per cent from an average 1.64 million b.p.d. to 1.53 million b.p.d., and to freeze prices (based on a $36 per barrel marker price) in line with OPEC policy. The stagnation of oil prices, coupled with a reduction in export volume following a growth in domestic consumption which exceeded production expansion, resulted in a decline in oil and gas earnings to $7,700 million from the projected level of $8,600 million in 1981/82.

A balance needs to be established between a hasty recovery of oil production for immediate gain and slower recovery for long-term benefit. In so far as oil revenues are not fundamentally affecting Indonesia's major development problems but, because of the institutional framework within which they are collected and used, actually exacerbating most of these problems, a proper utilization of oil revenue must wait on a thorough reappraisal of development priorities and structures. However, the change in management at Pertamina in April 1981, with the return of some Sutowo aides, has been seen as an alignment of policy closer to President Suharto's view of oil's importance: that it should be used as fast as possible to finance modernization.

Other minerals

Mineral production outside the oil sector has developed considerably since 1967, with the exception of coal, which has shown a marked drop from its pre-war level of 2 million tons: while tin has yet to regain its 1954 peak output of 36,500 metric tons. The revival of bauxite production was already underway in the early 1960s, and the high post-1967 levels indicate a levelling off of production. The most

Table 4

Mineral production, selected years 1959–81
(metric tons)

	1959	1964	1967	1973	1977	1979	1981
Tin . .	21,960	16,607	13,819	22,297	25,926	29,436	34,500
Bauxite . .	387,300	647,805	912,266	1,229,375	1,301,400	1,057,900	1,200,000
Nickel* . .	n.a.	47,950	170,601	867,046	1,302,512	1,551,872	1,461,000
Coal . .	637,600	445,862	208,313	148,855	230,627	278,589	402,680
Copper† . .	—	—	—	125,600	189,103	188,769	189,240

* Gross weight. The nickel content (in metric tons) was: 1,678 in 1964; 5,118 in 1967; 20,816 in 1973; 31,260 in 1977; 37,240 in 1979.

† Copper content (in '000 metric tons): 37.9 in 1973; 56.4 in 1977; 56.6 in 1979.

‡ Provisional.

dramatic increases have been in nickel and copper production. However, due to high production costs and low world prices, numerous mining projects have been shelved since 1977.

All minerals are highly localized in production. Nickel is mined in Sulawesi, although major reserves in Maluku will soon be exploited. Indonesia has reserves of over 40 million tons of nickel ore, sufficient, at 1974 extraction rates, for 47 years' production.

Copper is almost entirely produced in the Ertsberg Mountains area of Irian Jaya by Freeport Minerals, the first investor to take advantage of the 1967 Foreign Investment Law. Two ore bodies, one mined since 1973, have total reserves of about 63 million tons, with a copper content of 2.7 per cent and associated gold and silver. At present extraction rates, Freeport has sufficient for 23 years' mining.

Bauxite is mined entirely on Bintan island, in the Riau archipelago, by ALCOA. However, ALCOA have confirmed a further major reserve of bauxite in West Kalimantan. At present 90 per cent of bauxite is exported to Japan.

Tin production (an estimated 34,500 metric tons in 1981) comes from three state-owned mines on the islands of Banka, Belitung and Singkep. Annually, 3,000–5,000 metric tons (valued at $4.5–7.5 million) are smuggled through Singapore.

Coal production is undergoing major rehabilitation at its main producing region in South Sumatra, and a major increase in the use of coal as a domestic energy source will result—from 260,000 metric tons in 1980 to 4 million in 1985. Lack of infrastructure is hindering the expansion of existing mines and the opening of new fields. It is considered by some observers that the rate of construction of coal-powered cement and electricity generating plants will outrun the growth in coal output. Latest estimates of reserves are about 20,000 million metric tons (of largely low-grade coal, in Sumatra and Kalimantan).

FORESTRY

Forests cover 120 million hectares, or two-thirds of Indonesia's land area. While this is 35 per cent of all tropical forest reserves (comprising 70 per cent hardwood stands), only 24 million hectares are exploitable. However, Indonesian forests contain the most extensive concentrations of tropical hardwoods in the world.

The timber industry has grown rapidly. Between 1963 and 1977, output of industrial logs rose from 4 million cubic metres to 26.6 million, with a serious slump during 1974/75. Timber is Indonesia's second largest export earner, accounting for 11.6 per cent of exports in 1979—the export of logs and sawnwood rose from 3.4 million cubic metres in 1966 to 18 million in 1979, but fell to an estimated 12 million cubic metres in 1980 (due partly to falling demand, and partly to new export restrictions). In 1981 the Government banned raw log exports in an attempt to stimulate domestic wood processing. This policy, in conjunction with the continued fall in demand, resulted in a decline in the volume of timber exports in the first and second quarters of 1981, by 37 per cent and 59.9 per cent respectively, compared with the same periods in 1980.

An ambitious programme has been drawn up for plywood production. It calls for an investment of $1,000 million by 1985 and will involve the construction of 60 mills. Output will be raised to between 7 and 8 million cubic metres. Most observers consider that a lack of investment, shortages of skilled labour and inadequate infrastructure make this target unrealistic. 1981 saw the output of plywood rise sharply, but the aim of 1.6 million cubic metres by the end of 1982 seems unlikely to be met.

A number of problems face Indonesian forestry. The first is robber-cutting; with over 220 million cubic metres of saleable timber extracted since 1966 over 5 million hectares of forest have been felled including most of the best stands with little replanting. This exploitation reflects a lack of political control over private (and foreign) firms. The second problem is the high degree of speculation and therefore corruption involved in the industry. Thirdly, investors' excessive mechanization and employment of Filipino and Malaysian workers led to a relatively low creation of jobs for Indonesians and a banning of further foreign workers. Fourthly, there has been very little timber processing: although foreign concessionaires are expected to set up processing plants within three years of starting operations (leading to 60 per cent of log output being processed domestically within 10 years), few have done so: in 1979, 23 per cent of total output was processed domestically. The reasons are the high profitability of logging; the lack of infrastructure; the desire to keep processing in home countries; the difficulty of meeting international quality standards, due to shortage of skilled manpower; excessive bureaucracy, and the absence of price incentives to process logs—in 1979, the domestic price for meranti was $30–45 per cubic metre, while the export price was $135.

Government concern over the decline of productive area, the neglect of replanting, and company reluctance to "Indonesianize" led to a ban in 1974 on further concessions to foreigners (although domestic investment and sub-contracting to foreigners were still allowed). In 1975 the Government decreed that within 10 years of starting a logging project, indigenous Indonesian participation should be 51 per cent, while in 1980 it was ruled that all concessions operating for over 7 years must sell 60 per cent of logs on the domestic market, and 40 per cent of log production must be processed domestically. However, with skilled Indonesian labour and capital scarce, together with a run-down of the best stands and ending of the five-year tax exemption for most companies, the industry is facing a difficult future: increased exploitative cutting, inefficiency and run-down are becoming characteristic.

MANUFACTURING

As a result of expansion in other sectors of the economy, notably mining and forestry, the proportion of G.N.P. from manufacturing fell from 13.2 per cent in 1958 to 12.6 per cent in 1979. However, for most main products, the increase in output between 1968 and 1979 was respectable. From 1977 to 1979 the manufacturing sector grew at an average annual rate of 11.3 per cent while G.D.P. grew by an average of only 6.9 per cent. The sharp upswing in the rate of manufacturing growth, up to 21.1 per cent in 1980, reflects the "boom" conditions of 1980–81, increased foreign investment and an element of "catching up" from the 1978 devaluation and subsequent monetary restraints. Self-sufficiency in manufacturing is still remote (with some exceptions, such as rubber tyres and electronic components, the bulk of which are exported). Between 1977 and 1979, a contrast can be seen between production in the car assembly industry (a 22 per cent drop) and production of textiles (a 36 per cent increase). Imports in 1979 included nearly 2 million tons of steel and steel products, 62 per cent of paper needs, and about 15 per cent of textile requirements.

After 1969 a number of major manufacturing projects were initiated or completed by Pertamina. By 1978, the expanded PUSRI urea complex at Palembang had an annual capacity of 1.6 million tons (reputedly the largest in the world). A major petrochemical complex in South Sumatra (PLAJU) began producing polypropylene in early 1974, and the Krakatau Steel Company plant at Cilegon was expanded—at a cost of $2,500 million by 1979.

The Government's industrialization policy has come under criticism on a number of points: through the generous incentive scheme for foreign investors, capital-intensive industries and foreign control have been encouraged, while labour-intensive industries have gone bankrupt and domestic capital has been pushed into smaller and less profitable industries; a sharp regional imbalance has developed with most approved foreign investment in manufacturing concentrating in Java (80 per cent of the total in Jakarta and West Java) and most domestic manufacturing investment following suit; there has been excessive dependence on Pertamina, allowing it to channel oil earnings and foreign loans into whatever project its director, Gen. Ibnu Sutowo, agreed upon with President Suharto, thus (through its pattern of investment) aggravating the localized, capital-intensive nature of development; finally, there has been a related over-emphasis upon industrializing on the narrow base of oil resources.

Table 5

Approved foreign and domestic investments in manufacturing (1967–1978)

Total foreign (million $)	7,123.6
Number of foreign projects	805
Textiles (million $)	1,124
(projects)	70
Total domestic (million $)	8,100
Number of domestic projects	3,080
Textiles (million $)	1,664
(projects)	522
Capital-intensity (million $ per project)	
Foreign (total)	8.8
Domestic (total)	2.6
Foreign (textiles)	16.1
Domestic (textiles)	3.2

Source: Investment Co-ordinating Board, Jakarta.

Labour displacement has certainly occurred as a result of modernization in the rubber processing, tobacco, and textile industries, and small-scale industries based on handicrafts, fisheries, food and drink, plastics, and chemicals have also suffered. An example of both labour displacement and the centripetal tendency in industrial development is the situation in southern Sulawesi where, between 1968 and 1972, the number of small industries decreased from 3,855 to 2,432 (a 37 per cent decrease in four years): the number of textile factories (based mainly on handloom production) declined from 974 to 111 and handicraft industries from 1,243 to 537.

The problem of job creation is highlighted by the estimate that, during the REPELITA II period, about 2.2 million jobs were created outside manufacturing, leaving four million new entrants to the labour force to be absorbed by manufacturing. At a conservative $5,000 per worker for capital-intensity, there would have needed to be a total investment in manufacturing of $20,000 million to absorb new entrants alone.

Finally, during 1980/81, plans were expedited for at least six major oil-related projects—including the $1,000 million Dumai hydrocracker, a $1,600 million olefins complex at Arun, and a $1,000 million plant at Plaju, making polyester. With "wind-fall" oil revenue, the Government re-emphasized the central place of large petrochemical projects in the REPELITA III industrialization programme, hoping to "increase linkages", reduce imports, and provide industrial raw materials.

The structure of the Indonesian economy encourages this official obsession with the narrow, capital-intensive sector—it also makes such an emphasis contrary to sound overall development.

INFRASTRUCTURE

Transport

During REPELITAs I and II, about 16 per cent of state spending ($2,600 million) was allocated to improvement of communications. Most of this went to improvements in Java, where, for example, all highways have been asphalted and 90 per cent of provincial roads improved. In Sumatra, road repair and building between 1968 and 1978 cost $500 million. This includes the 1,800 km. Trans-Sumatran Highway, due for completion in 1982.

In 1974, of 85,000 km. of roads, 21,000 km. were asphalted. Officially, 23 per cent of all roads were described as in "good condition", 26 per cent "fair", and 41 per cent "very bad". By the end of REPELITA II (1979), it was hoped that the proportions would be, respectively, 50 per cent, 41 per cent and 9 per cent. Of the 7,250 km. of railway track, all is in Java and Sumatra: track and bridges are in poor condition and 50 per cent of railway motive power is over 40 years old.

Indonesia's merchant fleet comprises 540 vessels, with a gross tonnage of 640,000 tons, and nine local shipping companies. There are eight ocean ports with a loading capacity of 40,000 metric tons per day. The two major ports, Tanjung Priok near Jakarta (8.7 million tons handled in 1975, accounting for 70 per cent of Indonesia's imports and a high proportion of exports) and Tanjung Perak near Surabaya (3.9 million tons), have been modernized with the aid of foreign loans, with Indonesia's first container terminal opened in 1979 at Tanjung Priok, and container facilities being built at four other ports. Inter-island communication is poorly developed, a serious deficiency for an archipelago nation the size of Indonesia.

In 1980, Garuda was Asia's second largest airline (after Japan Airlines), with an all-jet fleet of 71 aircraft operating domestically and increasingly internationally—at marginal profit and 40 per cent capacity. Merpati, a Garuda subsidiary, operates domestically and regionally. There are also about 45 private or semi-private airlines operating, some foreign-controlled and some involved primarily with mineral development, including Pelita, the Pertamina airline.

Airports are small and geared to domestic use, with the exception of Jakarta's Halim airport, Medan in Sumatra, and Denpasar in Bali.

Power

Indonesia is almost totally dependent on oil for power. In 1980, only 3.8 per cent of energy requirements were derived from coal and hydroelectric generation. In 1978 electricity generating capacity was 3,737 MW. (30 per cent privately owned and 1,310 MW. in Java). This compares with 653 MW. in 1966. Per caput consumption of electricity, in 1978, was little over 20 kWh.—a low figure compared with other poor Asian countries—and only 10 per cent of the total population have access to electricity. While Indonesia produced 267,000 tons of coal in 1979, coal imports are needed for gas production. Similarly, despite its position as an oil exporter, Indonesia must import certain grades of oil; refinery capacity is 400,000 barrels per day, from nine refineries, with domestic consumption absorbing 20 per cent of production. In April 1980, all domestic oil fuel prices were increased by 50 per cent; the previous year, in April, all fuel prices save that of kerosene were increased by 40 per cent.

A major development of energy resources will result from the ($2,000 million) Bukit Assam power project—converting coal to electricity at a planned 3,000 MW. power station at Suralaya for the electrification of Java. This will be the first of 18 coal-fired plants, providing 12,000 MW., to be built by 2006.

TRADE

Indonesia's exports are dominated by petroleum, which has been the largest export earner since the early 1960s: in 1964, petroleum and its derivatives accounted for 36.4 per cent of export earnings, compared with rubber's 32 per cent; by 1979 oil and LNG's share of export value was 65 per cent. Because of oil price increases and the growth of LNG exports, export trade almost quintupled in value between 1974 and 1979 from $3,210 million to $15,578 million. Over 95 per cent of Indonesia's exports are raw or semi-processed materials.

Imports for 1979 were valued officially at $7,225 million, and consisted of 32 per cent machinery and transport equipment, 36 per cent "other manufactured goods", 14 per cent food and livestock, 14 per cent chemical goods, and four per cent "others". Official figures fail to account for the $4,700 million paid for oil imports during 1979–80.

Indonesia's main trading partner is Japan (with 46 per cent of exports and 29 per cent of imports in 1979), followed by the U.S.A. (20 per cent of exports and 14 per cent of imports) and Singapore (12.5 per cent of exports and 7 per cent of imports). Accurate figures for Indonesia-Singapore trade are lacking; official data greatly underestimate the value of this trade. Besides official reticence over Singapore trade, there is considerable "unofficial" trade with Malaysia and Philippines (including barter and smuggling). In September 1975 international reserves stood at only $437 million because of the repayment of Pertamina debts. However, by April 1981, they stood at $12,000 million.

Table 6

Exports of petroleum, timber and rubber, by value (%).

	Rubber	Timber	Petroleum
1970/71 . . .	24.6	9.8	37.3
1971/72 . . .	17.9	13.5	44.0
1972/73 . . .	10.6	12.8	51.4
1973/74 . . .	12.1	17.9	50.0
1974/75 . . .	5.9	8.8	71.0
1978/79 . . .	6.2	8.6	68.6
1979/80 . . .	6.0	11.6	65.2

PLANNING, FOREIGN AID AND FOREIGN INVESTMENT

The five-year Plans are heavily aid-financed, with the 12-member Inter-Governmental Group for Indonesia (IGGI), together with the International Monetary Fund (IMF), the World Bank and the Asian Development Bank (ADB), providing about half of all funds. During REPELITA II Indonesia obtained loans amounting to $10,570 million from the IGGI (compared with a total outlay in the Plan of $12,650 million). There is criticism by many, including influential generals, of over-reliance on foreign aid: the main complaint was that the IGGI consortium had appropriated the State's budgetary powers and had imposed a model of development which did not suit most Indonesians, and that aid was, in fact, a restraint on development. The development model Indonesia was following was undoubtedly Western-inspired and supported; through aid, control over planning was considerable. This was clear in 1979, when World Bank pressure led to cuts in import-substitution policies and budgetary subsidies. Whatever the letter of REPELITA II, the Bank saw little export potential in either agriculture or non-oil minerals. Emphasis was on export-oriented industrialization and a great increase in private (both domestic and foreign) investment. However, the relationship between Indonesia and its patrons is unstable. In particular, the country has moved only recently from a position of heavy dependence upon aid to one of sharp friction with the World Bank.

By 1981, Indonesia's outstanding public debt had reached $23,000 million, $15,000 million of which was disbursed. Circumstances began to change dramatically after the 1974 IGGI allocation of $900 million. The 1975 official aid support amounted to $1,800 million (half from IGGI sources); by 1979, aid stood at $2,575 million ($1,971 million on concessional terms and $604 million commercial borrowing). Pertamina's debt, confirmed at $11,700 million in 1976 and reduced to a total $3,800 million by 1978, was still a major charge on the aid account in 1979—when over 60 per cent of Indonesia's "aid" was promptly returned as principal and interest.

Further, debt repayment as a proportion of export earning rose from 13.6 per cent in 1976 to 18.6 per cent in 1978. This was both a drain on foreign exchange reserves, and affected the funding of REPELITA II. For example, it was planned to reduce the foreign aid component of plan spending from 35 per cent in 1974 to 18 per cent in 1978: in 1980, the development budget was still 30 per cent aid-funded. The debt-service ratio was 12 per cent in 1981/82 but this is expected to rise to 17.5 per cent in 1982/83.

Since 1978, however, there has been a marked improvement in Indonesia's solvency. Oil earnings and foreign exchange reserves have rocketed, the debt service ratio dropped to less than 10 per cent by 1981, and the IGGI's 1981 commitment of $2,100 million was made largely because of World Bank insistence that Indonesia remain within the Western aid system.

It has been noted that REPELITAs I and II were, to a large extent, vehicles for creating a favourable infrastructural framework for foreign investment by freeing funds going to rice imports (through rural development) for other uses, and by investment in infrastructure needed to effectively develop manufacturing, forestry and mining.

An indication of this can be seen by combining foreign investment during the plan period with official spending: this shows that the spread of total investment bears no relation to that of government investment. By the end of the Second Plan, commited foreign investment in industry, mining (including oil) and forestry amounted to over $15,000 million; less $1,000 million as pre-plan investment, this, combined with government investment, shows a total investment divided in terms of 50 per cent for industry, mining (including oil) and forestry, and only 16 per cent for all agricultural development. Since the end of the Second Plan, the proportion of new approved foreign investment in the non-oil sector has declined: from 40 per cent in 1976–78 to 25 per cent in 1979–81. The level of realization also fell, by the same percentages, in the same period. There is a considerable distortion in overall investment priorities towards the three sectors of forestry, metal-mining and oil in the extractive export industries, and manufacturing. There are a number of significant implications of this pattern of investment. First it is, by definition, largely for foreign benefit. Given the generous provisions of the 1967 Foreign Investment Law, and the high profitability of mining, forestry, and the oil industry the most lucrative parts of the economy have been subject to high repatriation of capital and an accelerated rundown of resources which would be needed for any major domestic industrialization. Secondly, it is for the most part capital-intensive. For example, modern mining has a capital-intensity of between $60,000 and $90,000 per worker.

Investment in the extractive sector (66 per cent of all foreign investment), then, contributes little to job creation. However, manufacturing is more labour-intensive—but this raises a third problem. Virtually all manufacturing investment is in West Java, particularly around Jakarta, and thus the sectoral spread of investment is linked with a high concentration of manufacturing development (and

Table 7

Foreign Investment Approvals, Implementation, and Employment Creation (1967–March 1979)

Sector	No. of Projects	Investment (U.S. $ million)		% Implementation	Employment*	
		Approved	Realized		Planned	Actual
Agriculture	58	171	64.8	38	94,620	36,901
Forestry	78	607	299.4	49	87,586	44,842
Fishing	23	127	85.1	67	n.a.	n.a.
Mining and quarrying	11	1,453	385.6	27	11,392	2,962
Manufacturing	466	4,730	2,216.8	47	143,915	68,917
Construction	63	77	38.9	51	26,173	11,246
Trade and hotels	14	183	106.2	58	9,995†	3,498
Transport and communications	20	97	37.0	38	n.a.	n.a.
Real estate and business services	51	307	108.3	35	15,819‡	6,855 (Real estate and business services and Other combined)
Other			117.6	—	5,602	
Total	784	7,752	3,459.7	44	395,102	175,221

* To August 1976. † Hotels only. ‡ Real estate/housing.

Source: Far Eastern Economic Review and BIES.

proportionately high employment creation) within a small and well-serviced area of the archipelago. This metropolitan concentration of manufacturing reflects both gravitation of investment to the already most developed area in terms of infrastructure, business and administrative facilities, and readily available cheap labour, as well as a reluctance to decentralize to areas less well serviced and marked by lower standards of living. The process is circular: government policy is Java-centric, and so is investment not tied to a raw material; 60 per cent of jobs created by foreign investment are in Java, while development of the outer islands depends on capital-intensive "enclave" activities in the extractive sector.

Given Java's high rate of underemployment and unemployment, this might be a logical process. However, three factors limit local job creation: the high degree of capital-intensity; the concomitant decline of traditional occupations and local business with foreign investment in competitive modern industry; and the preference for foreign skilled workers such as Filipinos and non-Indonesian Malays in forestry and managerial staff in expatriate industries. With about 600,000 jobs created by foreign and domestic private investment (two-thirds by local investment), the annual rate of job creation between 1967 and 1979 was about 55,000, at most, in a job market increasing by over 1.5 million annually.

A final consideration relating to foreign investment is its concentration within a few non-traditional sectors: there is already the danger that the Indonesian economy may rely too heavily upon oil and timber, and localized industrialization, for development. Of increasing importance to the country's industrial growth will be the installation of Free Trade Zones, virtual foreign "enclaves" of multinational subsidiaries operating large-scale and often capital-intensive plants (as in vehicle assembly) or large labour-intensive plants (as in electronics), geared almost wholly to the export market. These export "platforms" make good use of cheap and non-unionized local labour, and Indonesia has one of the cheapest unskilled labour forces in the world. Little linkage exists with the rest of the manufacturing economy, and there is relatively little emphasis on import-substitution (the market for consumer goods is smaller than that of South Korea, which has a population one-quarter the size of Indonesia's). Yet these "enclaves" of foreign "putting out" industries, seen by the World Bank as the key to Indonesia's manufacturing role, are expected to increase manufacturing's share of exports to 25 per cent in a decade.

Between 1974 and 1980 foreign investment slumped—from $1,392 million to $489 million approved non-oil investment—reflecting partly the world recession, but also more regulations and greater bureaucracy. In this context, the World Bank produced a confidential report for submission to the 1981 IGGI meeting (it was never submitted), warning that Indonesia was neglecting to prepare a proper industrial infrastructure and industrial export facilities with its expanding oil revenues. The Bank was concerned at growing state intervention, in an economic climate far more favourable to economic nationalism. Since 1975, the Government had moved to control equity and technology transfers, foreign workers, and the distribution and influence of foreign investment, and to promote a *pribumi* (indigenous Indonesian) capitalist élite. For example, it is stipulated that a foreign company must have 51 per cent Indonesian equity after 10 years—though this usually involves passing equity, not management or control, to an Indonesian "sleeping partner". This applies in the non-oil sector (with $8,700 million foreign and $11,600 million local, mainly Indonesian Chinese, investment approved by 1981) but not in the oil sector (with about $8,500 million foreign investment). In April 1980, two presidential decrees strengthened *pribumi* participation: KEPPRES 14A defined the priority given to "economically weak" *pribumi* companies in government contracts—especially those up to 100 million rupiahs ($160,000); KEPPRES 10 ruled that every contract or subcontract using government funds above 500 million rupiahs must be cleared for *pribumi* preference (including within the oil sector). One implication of such decrees is to boost the economic role of politically favoured Indonesians, another is to delay projects.

In addition, the Government has pursued money control through state-defined credit ceilings (as opposed to free-market-defined interest rates), and protection of local markets and inefficient local businesses through quotas, subsidies and tariffs.

The World Bank saw such policies dampening investment. They were concerned at preference given to state enterprises, but only partly because of the distorting effect of political-military patronage in the public sector: the Bank wanted a more open capitalist economy, with freedom of investment within an ASEAN framework of co-ordinated investment incentives for Western capital, and greater encouragement of export-oriented manufacturing.

FINANCE

Apart from the introduction of mandatory balanced budgets, Indonesian finance during the 1970s was marked by the use of high interest rates and low credit ceilings to control inflation and direct funds, especially into state and *pribumi* private enterprise. Currency was devalued, exchange controls lifted, and inflation controlled. By 1974 the financial system had been completely redefined. In 1980, however, the credit structure remained inadequate both in the limited number of institutions able to extend credit and in the types of loan available. The five State Banks control 80 per cent of banking assets, and are responsible for funding the creation of a *pribumi* entrepreneurial class. Like public and private local banks, they suffer from corruption: over the decade 1969–79, they were involved in fraud involving a possible write-off of $1,700 million (33 per cent of outstanding bank credit). The 28 Development Banks—including 26 regional banks owned, or partly owned, by provincial governments—channel official credit (in five to 15 year loans) to industries with priority under the Five Year Plan. In 1979, there were 74 private commercial banks, with about 11 per cent of banking assets.

The State Bank's tight credit policy was seen by the World Bank as one element of an administrative impediment to free investment, especially by foreigners and local investors lacking political patronage. In the World Bank's critique of Indonesian policy, three inter-related measures were proposed: first, changing budgetary priorities from balance to surplus in overall budget, and from deficit to balance in domestic budget—thus controlling liquidity in an economy marked by heavy spending of large oil surpluses, and freeing these surpluses for spending on capital imports (presupposing a less protective trade policy); second, as credit ceilings are relaxed in favour of budgetary control of liquidity, freeing interest rates from central bank control and allowing them to reflect market conditions; third, using the rediscount rate for state bank lending as a control on credit—by redefining it to reflect cost of capital. Through this redefinition of the financial system, capital would move more freely into the hands of those whom the World Bank saw as the key entrepreneurs.

Again, contrary to World Bank demands, subsidies on fertilizer, rice and oil were not reduced in 1980/81; for the budget year 1981/82, these were set at, respectively, $500 million, $500 million and $2,400 million (the last an increase from $1,300 million). The World Bank argues against subsidies partly in terms of the revenue thus removed from circulation; ironically, however, it is also true that subsidies usually accrue to those best able to afford them.

International reserves reached $12,000 million by 1981—$7,000 million in central banks and $5,000 million in commercial banks. As oil and LNG earnings moved through the country's financial system, time and demand rupiah deposits increased in dollar value from $4,300 million in early 1979 to $8,100 million in September 1980— while Government deposits in commercial banks rose from $400 million to $1,200 million. Yet bank credit rose from $6,000 million to $8,500 million. The balance of $2,100 million went overseas, mainly into Eurodollar accounts. Commercial banks exchanged rupiah funds for foreign assets, increasing these assets over 18 months from $400 million to $3,300 million. This transfer of funds overseas is partly due to restrictions on credit for non-*pribumi* borrowers—the few credit-worthy *pribumi* borrowers often borrow only to relend, perhaps to a foreigner or a Chinese, while many needy borrowers must go overseas for credit.

The large surpluses on the current balance of payments in 1979/80 and 1980/81 were associated with increases in budget expenditure of 20 per cent in real terms. During these two years the economy grew rapidly: G.N.P. increased by 9.6 per cent in 1980/81. A cautious financial policy during this period resulted in less expansionary budgets than would have otherwise been possible. The central banking institutions absorbed funds and greatly expanded Indonesian foreign reserves.

After the latter half of 1981, the economic outlook changed drastically. The deepening international recession brought a stagnation in oil prices and a sharp fall in the prices of other commodities. During 1981 the price of rubber, for example, fell by over 50 per cent, and coffee prices by nearly 30 per cent. The 1982/83 budget reflects these changed circumstances. Increases in expenditure are to be restricted to 10 per cent. Export earnings from oil and gas are expected to fall by 5 per cent in real terms and non-oil earnings by 30 per cent.

The balance of payments has deteriorated sharply.

The expected surplus on the current account of $930 million for 1981/82 has given way to a deficit of $2,500 million, a striking change from the previous year's surplus of $2,700 million. The reserves accumulated in 1980 and early 1981 are being used to finance this deficit.

This sudden reversal in the fortunes of the Indonesian economy reveals its basic weakness: "development" is mortgaged to world prices for a narrow range of primary products, and there has yet to emerge a sound, stable and diversified base for (especially) rural, social and economic progress.

STATISTICAL SURVEY

Note: **Unless otherwise stated, figures for East Timor (incorporated by Indonesia in July 1976) are not included in the tables.**

AREA
(sq. km.)

Total	Java and Madura	Sumatra	Kalimantan (Borneo)	Sulawesi (Celebes)	Other Islands*
1,904,569	132,187	473,606	539,460	189,216	570,100

* Comprises Bali, Nusatenggara, Maluku and Irian Jaya.

East Timor: 14,874 sq. km.

POPULATION
('000)

	1972	1973	1974	1980*
Java and Madura	77,137	77,882	79,004	91,270
Sumatra	21,425	21,870	22,658	28,016
Kalimantan	5,229	5,448	5,574	6,723
Sulawesi	8,729	8,896	8,964	10,410
Bali	2,159	2,174	2,217	2,470
Nusatenggara	4,602	4,657	4,718	5,462
Maluku	1,159	1,179	1,187	1,411
Irian Jaya	926	982	1,007	1,174
Total	121,366	123,088	125,329	146,936

* Census of October 31st, 1980.

East Timor: 636,553 (1972 mid-year estimate); 720,000 (mid-1978 UN estimate); 555,350 (1980 census).

CHIEF TOWNS
Population ('000)

	1971 Census	1980 Census		1971 Census	1980 Census
Jakarta (capital)	4,546	6,480	Malang	422	510
Surabaya	1,552	2,017	Padang	196	480
Bandung	1,200	1,461	Yogyakarta	341	398
Medan	636	1,373	Banjarmasin	282	381
Semarang	642	1,024	Pontianak	218	304
Palembang	583	786	Bogor	195	246
Ujungpandang (Makassar)	434	709	Tjirebon	179	223

Births and Deaths: Average annual birth rate 39.5 per 1,000 in 1970–75, 33.6 per 1,000 in 1975-80; death rate 18.6 per 1,000 in 1970–75, 16.2 per 1,000 in 1975–80 (UN estimates). Estimates for 1981: Birth rate 35 per 1,000; Death rate 15 per 1,000.

ECONOMICALLY ACTIVE POPULATION

(1978 National Labour Force Survey)

	Males	Females	Total
Agriculture, hunting, forestry and fishing	20,647,361	10,898,038	31,545,399
Mining and quarrying	105,418	17,301	122,719
Manufacturing	1,935,531	1,920,029	3,855,560
Electricity, gas and water	13,106	242	13,348
Construction	786,157	19,761	805,918
Trade, restaurants and hotels	3,688,318	4,020,213	7,708,531
Transport, storage and communications	1,273,531	15,053	1,288,584
Financing, insurance, real estate and business services	36,359	6,336	42,695
Community, social and personal services	4,416,853	1,977,905	6,394,758
Activities not adequately described	2,424	423	2,847
Total	32,905,058	18,875,301	51,780,359

AGRICULTURE

LAND USE, 1979

('000 hectares)

Arable land	14,168
Land under permanent crops	5,250*
Permanent meadows and pastures	12,000*
Forests and woodland	121,800†
Other land	27,917
Total Land Area	181,135
Inland water	9,300
Total Area	190,435

* FAO estimate. † Unofficial figure.

Source: FAO, *Production Yearbook.*

PRINCIPAL CROPS

	Area Harvested ('000 hectares)			Production ('000 metric tons)		
	1978	1979	1980†	1978	1979	1980†
Rice (milled)	8,929	8,850	9,018	17,525	17,918	20,246
Maize	3,025	2,575	2,711	4,029	3,305	4,012
Sweet potatoes	301	273	287	2,083	2,043	2,193
Cassava (Manioc)	1,383	1,418	1,414	12,902	13,330	13,532
Soybeans	733	764	726	617	674	642
Groundnuts (in shell)	506	490	507	446	418	476
Copra (incl. coconuts)	n.a.	n.a.	2,386	1,467	1,559	1,593
Palm kernels	n.a.	n.a.	212 (Palm kernels and Palm oil)	102	115	113
Palm oil	n.a.	n.a.		519	622.8	670
Vegetables and melons	692	884	710	2,031	3,477	1,994
Other fruit (excl. melons)	436	500	477	2,709	3,559	4,102
Sugar cane	77.6	91.7	229	1,616	1,686	1,639
Coffee (green)	n.a.	n.a.	520	222	223	234
Tea (made)	n.a.	n.a.	42	88	91	102
Tobacco (leaves)	n.a.	n.a.	172	81	82	88
Natural rubber	n.a.	n.a.	2,302	844	892.8	923

† *Source: Attachment* to 1981 President's National Day Speech.

LIVESTOCK
('000 head)

	1978	1979	1980
Cattle	6,305	6,276	6,534
Sheep	4,101	4,361	4,197
Goats	7,419	7,402	7,906
Pigs	2,890	2,855	3,296
Horses	689	719	616
Buffaloes	2,275	2,269	2,506
Chickens	115,617	121,357	127,705
Ducks	17,541	18,689	19,810

LIVESTOCK PRODUCTS
('000 metric tons)

	1978	1979	1980*
Beef and veal	129.21	130.96	133
Buffalo meat	33.81	34.72	35
Mutton and lamb	20.40	19.30	22
Goats' meat	36.80	34.25	38
Pig meat	83.52	83.84	86
Poultry meat*	96	102	105
Cows' milk	62.30	60.70	69
Hen and other poultry eggs	151	131.40	175
Cattle and buffalo hides	26	25.40	27.19

Note: Figures for meat refer to inspected production only, i.e. from animals slaughtered under government supervision.

* FAO estimates.

FORESTRY

ROUNDWOOD REMOVALS
('000 cubic metres, excluding bark)

	1974	1975	1976	1977	1978	1979	1980
Sawlogs, veneer logs and logs for sleepers:							
Coniferous	90	400	500*	550*	550*	600*	600*
Non-coniferous	23,190	16,296	23,300	26,080	25,000	21,200	21,200*
Pitprops (mine timber)	20	20	20*	20*	20*	20*	20*
Pulpwood	30	20	20*	20*	20*	20*	20*
Other industrial wood	1,988†	2,041†	2,095†	2,150†	2,206†	2,264†	2,316*
TOTAL INDUSTRIAL WOOD	25,318	18,777	25,935	28,820	27,796	24,104	24,156
Fuel wood*	115,059	117,873	120,714	123,580	126,476	129,414	132,398
TOTAL	140,377	136,650	146,649	152,400	154,272	153,518	156,554

* FAO estimate.

† Unofficial estimate.

Source: FAO, *Yearbook of Forest Products*.

SAWNWOOD PRODUCTION

('000 cubic metres)

	1973	1974	1975	1976	1977	1978	1979	1980
Coniferous sawnwood†	20	—	5*	10*	—	—	—	—
Non-coniferous sawnwood†	1,380	1,819	2,400	3,000	3,500	3,500	3,400	3,400*
Railway sleepers	11	10	10	12	10	—	7	7*
TOTAL	1,411	1,829	2,415	3,022	3,510	3,500	3,407	3,407*

* FAO estimate. † Including boxboards.

Source: FAO, *Yearbook of Forest Products*.

FISHING

('000 metric tons)

	1974	1975	1976	1977	1978	1979	1980
Inland waters	387.7	393.2	401.4	414.2	420.3	430.5	439.1
Indian Ocean	71.8	72.8	109.2	131.8	116.3	113.8	137.7
Pacific Ocean	873.8	915.6	968.6	1,021.8	1,105.5	1,221.9	1,276.4
TOTAL CATCH	1,333.3	1,381.6	1,479.2	1,567.8	1,642.0	1,766.2	1,853.2

Aquatic plants ('000 metric tons): 3.0 in 1974; 8.4 in 1975; 3.8 in 1976; 4.1 in 1977; 5.6 in 1978; 5.9 in 1979; 5.9 in 1980.

Source: FAO, *Yearbook of Fishery Statistics*.

MINING

		1977	1978	1979	1980	1981‡
Crude petroleum	'000 barrels	615,123	596,700	580,446.6	577,015	580,660
Natural gas	'000 million cu. ft.	542,784	820,130	998,446	1,045,000	1,118,000
Bauxite	'000 metric tons	1,301.4	1,007.7	1,057.9	1,249	1,200
Coal	metric tons	230,627	264,184	278,589	304,000	402,680
Nickel ore (gross weight)*	,, ,,	1,302,512	1,256,450	1,551,872	1,537,000	1,461,000
Copper (gross weight)†	,, ,,	189,103	180,933	188,769	186,000	189,240
Tin	,, ,,	25,926	27,409	29,436	30,460	34,500
Gold	kilogrammes	255.9	254.0	170.0	248	179
Silver	,,	2,832.0	2,506.4	1,644.6	2,196	1,932

* The nickel content (in metric tons) was: 31,260 in 1977; 28,960 in 1978; 37,240 in 1979.
† The copper content (in '000 metric tons) was: 56.4 in 1977; 54.3 in 1978; 56.6 in 1979.
‡ Provisional.

Source: Ministry of Mines and Energy.

INDUSTRY

PETROLEUM PRODUCTS

('000 metric tons)

	1976	1977	1978	1979	1980
Motor spirit (petrol)	1,546	2,154.9	2,409.2	2,291.6	2,039.0
Kerosene	2,650	4,149.5	4,096.1	4,503.0	3,347.3
Jet fuel	108	115.3	34.7	317.4	22.4
Distillate fuel oils	2,703	3,740.9	4,102.2	4,680.9	2,653.1
Residual fuel oils	7,662	9,469	11,363	11,610	11,337

Source: UN, ***Statistical Yearbook***, and Central Bureau of Statistics, Jakarta.

OTHER PRODUCTS

		1976/77	1977/78	1978/79	1979/80	1980/81
Wheat flour	'000 metric tons	650	690	774	1,291	1,331
Sugar	" " "	1,200	1,150	1,200	1,290	1,309
Cotton yarn	" " "	623	678	900	206	230
Nitrogenous fertilizers	" " "	406	990	1,430	1,827	1,985
Cement	" " "	1,980	2,878	3,640	4,705	5,851
Cigarettes	million	60,537	64,000	69,400	70,100	83,900
Tyres	'000	1,883	2,340	2,641	2,898	3,320
Radio receivers	"	1,100	1,000	1,128	1,018	1,110
Television receivers	"	212.8	482	611	659	729
Motor vehicles (assembly)	"	343	356	419	323	580

Tin (primary metal, metric tons): 23,322 in 1976; 24,005 in 1977; 25,830 in 1978; 27,790 in 1979; 30,465 in 1980.

Source: Ministry of Industry.

FINANCE

100 sen = 1 rupiah (Rp.).

Coins: 5, 10, 25, 50 and 100 rupiahs.

Notes: 100, 500, 1,000, 5,000 and 10,000 rupiahs.

Exchange rates (June 1982): £1 sterling = 1,137.5 rupiahs; U.S. $1 = 656.75 rupiahs;
10,000 rupiahs = £8.79 = $15.23.

Note: The new rupiah, equal to 1,000 old rupiahs, was introduced in December 1965. For converting the value of foreign trade transactions the average import rates (rupiahs) per U.S. dollar) were: 365.0 in 1970; 394.4 in 1971. In August 1971 new rates of U.S. $1 = 374 rupiahs (exports) and U.S. $1 = 415 rupiahs (imports) were introduced. The import rate remained in force as the market rate until November 1978. In terms of sterling the exchange rates from December 1971 to June 1972 were £1 = 974.54 rupiahs (exports) and £1 = 1,081.37 rupiahs (imports). In November 1978 it was announced that the rupiah would be subjected to a "managed float", with an initial exchange rate of $1 = 625 rupiahs. The average rate (rupiahs per dollar) was: 442.05 in 1978; 623.06 in 1979; 626.99 in 1980; 631.76 in 1981.

BUDGET ESTIMATES

('000 million rupiahs—year ending March 31st)

Revenue	1981/82	1982/83
Direct Taxes	10,038.2	11,112.8
Income tax	207.1	256.1
Company tax	558.4	822.5
Oil companies tax	8,575.2	9,121.7
MPO*	512.6	680.4
Ipeda†	87.6	108.9
Miscellaneous	97.3	123.2
Indirect Taxes	2,016.9	2,251.3
Sales tax (products)	293.7	442.1
Import duties	538.9	298.6
Excise	553.0	618.4
Sales tax (imports)	222.4	677.9
Export duties	381.1	170.0
Miscellaneous	27.8	44.3
Non-tax Receipts	219.3	392.4
Total Domestic Revenue	12,274.4	13,756.5
Foreign Aid Receipts	1,625.9	1,850.8
Programme aid	64.8	25.0
Project aid and export credits	1,561.1	1,825.8
Total	13,900.3	15,607.3

Expenditure	1981/82	1982/83
Personnel Emoluments	2,412.3	2,491.8
Rice allowances	n.a.	294.4
Salaries and pensions	n.a.	1,782.0
Food allowances	n.a.	267.7
Other remunerations	n.a.	94.3
Missions abroad	n.a.	54.3
Purchases of Goods	994.3	1,067.7
Domestic products	n.a.	1,021.1
Foreign products	n.a.	46.6
Regional Subsidies	1,209.4	1,315.4
Irian Jaya	n.a.	43.0
Other regions	n.a.	1,272.4
Debt Servicing	963.7	976.2
Domestic debts	n.a.	30.0
Foreign debts	n.a.	946.2
Others	1,921.4	1,150.4
Food subsidy	309.7	188.4
Fuel oil subsidy	1,511.1	924.0
General elections	81.0	14.5
Miscellaneous	19.6	23.5
Total Ordinary Budget	7,501.1	7,001.5
Total Development Budget	6,399.2	8,605.8
Total	13,900.3	15,607.3

* Pre-payments on income or corporate taxes.

† Revenues from regional development contributions.

Source: Ministry of Finance.

DEVELOPMENT EXPENDITURE*

('000 million rupiahs)

	1980/81	1981/82	1982/83
Agriculture	739	531	1,252.5
Irrigation		411	
Industry	275	330	366.1
Mining	484	191	938.2
Energy		492	
Tourism and communications	708	810	1,098.4
Manpower and transmigration	299	436	605.9
Regional and town development	482	613	740.6
Education	575	787	1,301.7
Health, social welfare, women's affairs and family planning	197	258	322.1
National defence and security	387	481	568.7
TOTAL (incl. others)	5,028	5,340	8,605.8

* Planned.

Source: Ministry of Finance.

INTERNATIONAL RESERVES

(U.S. $ million at December 31st)

	1974	1975	1976	1977	1978	1979	1980	1981
Gold	2	2	2	7	37	105	1,108	1,062
IMF Special Drawing Rights	68	7	5	26	75	170	175	264
Reserve position in IMF	35	—	—	83	90	97	205	229
Foreign exchange	1,386	577	1,492	2,400	2,461	3,795	5,012	4,521
TOTAL	1,492	586	1,499	2,516	2,663	4,167	6,500	6,076

Source: IMF, *International Financial Statistics.*

MONEY SUPPLY

('000 million rupiahs at December 31st)

	1974	1975	1976	1977	1978	1979	1980	1981
Currency outside banks	496.9	649.6	779.0	979.1	1,239.9	1,545.5	2,169.5	2,545.5

Source: IMF, *International Financial Statistics.*

COST OF LIVING

Consumer Price Index

(average of monthly figures. Base: April 1977—March 1978 = 100)

	1979*	1980
Food	133.2	152.9
Fuel and light	133.2	147.9
Clothing	152.4	181.6
Rent	138.4	160.8
ALL ITEMS	132.3	156.3

* April to December only.

1981: Food 175.7; All items 175.4.

Source: International Labour Office, mainly *Year Book of Labour Statistics.*

NATIONAL ACCOUNTS

National Income and Product

('000 million rupiahs at current prices)

	1976	1977	1978	1979	1980
Domestic factor incomes*	13,769.9	16,929	19,970	27,702	39,311
Consumption of fixed capital	1,006.3	1,235	1,460	2,017	2,848
Gross Domestic Product at Factor Cost	14,776.2	18,165	21,430	29,719	42,159
Indirect taxes, *less* subsidies	690.5	846	1,029	1,305	1,607
G.D.P. in Purchasers' Values	15,466.7	19,011	22,458	31,023	43,765
Net factor income from abroad	−432.2	−679	−852	−1,489	−2,169
Gross National Product	15,034.5	18,332	21,606	29,534	41,596
Less Consumption of fixed capital	1,006.3	1,235	1,460	2,017	2,845
National Income in Market Prices	14,028.2	17,097	20,146	27,517	38,751

* Compensation of employees and the operating surplus of enterprises.

Expenditure on the Gross Domestic Product

('000 million rupiahs at current prices)

	1976	1977	1978	1979	1980
Government final consumption expenditure	1,590.5	2,077.3	2,659	3,733	5,565
Private final consumption expenditure	10,463.8	12,458.4	14,900	18,505	25,045
Increase in stocks	3,204.9	3,826.4	4,671	6,704	9,485
Gross fixed capital formation					
Total Domestic Expenditure	15,259.2	18,362.1	22,229	28,942	40,095
Exports of goods and services	3,429.6	4,465.8	4,788	9,461	13,353
Less Imports of goods and services	3,222.1	3,817.2	4,559	7,381	9,683
G.D.P. in Purchasers' Values	15,466.7	19,010.7	22,458	31,023	43,765

Gross Domestic Product by Economic Activity

('000 million rupiahs at current prices)

	1976	1977	1978	1979	1980
Agriculture and livestock production	4,084.0	5,905.7	6,706	8,984	11,253
Forestry and logging	512.8				
Fishing	215.2				
Mining and quarrying	2,930.0	3,599.7	4,358	6,980	11,673
Manufacturing	1,453.3	1,816.9	2,185	2,614	3,846
Electricity, gas and water	98.1	105.6	118	149	225
Construction	812.6	1,023.3	1,242	1,790	2,524
Transport and communications	662.6	820.6	980	1,300	1,706
Wholesale and retail trade	4,698.1	5,738.9	3,450	4,603	6,168
Finance and other services			3,420	4,604	6,372
Total	15,466.7	19,010.7	22,458	31,023	43,765

BALANCE OF PAYMENTS
(U.S. $ million)

	1976	1977	1978	1979	1980	1981
Merchandise exports f.o.b.	8,613	10,763	11,035	15,154	21,757	23,120
Merchandise imports f.o.b.	−6,815	−7,478	−8,386	−9,245	−12,603	−16,923
TRADE BALANCE	1,798	3,285	2,649	5,909	9,154	6,197
Exports of services	160	166	291	398	446	608
Imports of services	−2,881	−3,525	−4,368	−5,357	−6,804	−8,017
BALANCE OF GOODS AND SERVICES	−923	−74	−1,428	950	2,796	−1,212
Unrequited transfers (net)	15	24	14	30	54	44
CURRENT BALANCE	−907	−50	−1,414	980	2,850	−1,168
Direct capital investment (net)	344	235	279	226	184	152
Other long-term capital (net)	1,638	1,256	1,317	1,094	1,970	2,197
Short-term capital (net)	−268	−391	121	−454	−821	192
Net errors and omissions	−186	−54	−133	−402	−1,931	−1,671
TOTAL (net monetary movements)	622	996	171	1,444	2,253	−298
Allocation of IMF Special Drawing Rights	—	—	—	65	66	62
Valuation changes (net)	10	21	−54	−73	−989	−142
Loans to Government and Central Bank	280	—	—	—	—	—
CHANGES IN RESERVES	912	1,017	117	1,436	1,330	−378

Source: IMF, *International Financial Statistics.*

FOREIGN AID*
(U.S. $ million)

	1979/80	1980/81
Soft loans from IGGI	1,954.2	1,969.5
Bilateral	916.2	797.1
Australia	38.6	41.8
Austria	—	—
Belgium	10.6	12.2
Canada	129.6	15.2
Denmark	—	—
France	119.8	73.5
Germany, Fed. Republic	63.8	67.3
Italy	0.9	3.0
Japan	307.8	335.8
Netherlands	59.6	65.5
New Zealand	—	—
Switzerland	—	—
United Kingdom	14.5	22.4
U.S.A.	171.0	160.4
Multilateral (*international agencies*)	1,038.0	1,172.4
IBRD	800.0	850.0
ADB	238.0	281.0
UNDP	—	31.4
EEC	—	10.0
Semi-concessionary loans and commercial loans, including export credit for projects	1,274.6	884.7
Cash loans	450.1	445.9
TOTAL	3,678.9	3,300.1

* As agreed by the 20th and 21st Inter-Governmental Group for Indonesia (IGGI) meetings, April 1977 and May 1978.

†*Source: Attachment* to 1981 President's National Day Speech.

EXTERNAL TRADE

(U.S. $ million)

	1976	1977	1978	1979	1980	1981
Imports c.i.f.	5,673.1	6,230.3	6,690.4	7,202.3	10,834.4	13,270.0
Exports f.o.b.	8,546.5	10,852.6	11,643.2	15,590.1	21,908.9	22,260.0

PRINCIPAL COMMODITIES

(U.S. $ million)

IMPORTS c.i.f.	1977	1978	1979	1980
Food and live animals	958.8	1,042.5	1,037.6	1,285.0
Cereals and cereal preparations	736.3	692.7	714.8	872.3
Rice	678.0	591.5	596.3	690.4
Crude materials (inedible) except fuels	227.1	295.1	367.5	491.2
Mineral fuels, lubricants, etc.	734.7	582.5	797.1	1,753.8
Petroleum and petroleum products	732.0	579.7	793.3	1,744.0
Crude and partly refined petroleum	353.9	276.9	443.4	1,051.8
Crude petroleum	291.3	229.3	355.6	963.0
Petroleum products	378.1	302.9	349.9	692.2
Chemicals	619.0	756.2	1,011.6	1,255.0
Chemical elements and compounds	211.8	272.5	421.7	516.0
Basic manufactures	1,224.8	1,262.7	1,402.9	2,053.3
Iron and steel	401.7	505.4	599.5	966.7
Universals, plates and sheets	180.3	221.0	299.8	450.6
Machinery and transport equipment	2,270.3	2,434.4	2,291.4	3,633.8
Non-electric machinery	956.0	1,071.5	1,172.8	1,855.0
Electrical machinery, apparatus, etc.	765.3	577.7	550.7	748.6
Transport equipment	549.1	785.2	567.9	1,030.2
Road motor vehicle and parts*	465.4	654.5	477.0	891.0
Lorries and trucks (incl. ambulances)	226.0	376.9	233.2	506.3
TOTAL (incl. others)	6,230.3	6,690.4	7,202.3	10,834.4

* Excluding tyres, engines and electrical parts.

EXPORTS f.o.b.	1977	1978	1979	1980
Food and live animals	1,066.2	989.1	1,208.2	1,290.8
Coffee, tea, cocoa and spices	807.5	688.4	785.9	875.8
Coffee (incl. extracts, etc.)	599.3	491.3	614.5	658.3
Crude materials (inedible) except fuels	1,760.9	1,891.2	3,064.2	3,569.3
Crude rubber, etc.	589.5	717.7	940.3	1,173.8
Wood, lumber and cork	952.8	996.5	1,798.7	1,816.3
Rough or roughly squared wood	901.0	909.3	1,551.3	1,559.3
Coniferous logs	816.0	814.9	1,355.3	1,311.6
Metalliferous ores and metal scrap	167.3	117.9	195.6	428.3
Non-ferrous ores and concentrates	142.9	117.7	188.5	407.5
Mineral fuels, lubricants, etc.	7,378.6	7,986.2	10,165.5	15,743.1
Petroleum and petroleum products	7,297.8	7,438.5	8,870.9	12,858.8
Crude petroleum	6,826.5	7,014.6	8,124.2	11,671.3
Petroleum products	471.4	423.9	746.6	1,187.5
Lamp oil and white spirit	426.9	3.8	1.1	0.1
Residual fuel oils	18.4	393.1	726.7	1,178.3
Gas (natural and manufactured)	80.3	546.9	1,292.9	2,881.2
Basic manufactures	235.9	331.6	571.4	614.7
Non-ferrous metals	206.8	281.4	384.0	427.1
Tin	206.4	281.2	382.0	423.3
TOTAL (incl. others)	10,852.6	11,643.2	15,590.1	21,908.9

Source: Central Bureau of Statistics, Jakarta, and Department of Trade.

PRINCIPAL TRADING PARTNERS

(U.S. $ million)

IMPORTS	1979	1980	1981
Australia	222.5	377.6	362.0
China, People's Republic	131.8	197.3	n.a.
France	143.4	235.6	n.a.
Germany, Fed. Republic	462.2	685.3	904.0
Hong Kong	101.6	139.4	n.a.
India	125.6	43.2	n.a.
Japan	2,103.4	3,413.0	3,990.0
Korea, Republic	117.3	234.1	488.0
Netherlands	119.1	115.5	n.a.
Saudi Arabia	355.8	964.7	671.0
Singapore	536.4	936.3	1,240.0
Taiwan	407.1	432.5	400.0
Thailand	218.6	288.0	n.a.
United Kingdom	198.0	261.2	546.0
U.S.A.	1,027.8	1,409.2	1,800.0
TOTAL (incl. others)	7,202.3	10,834.4	13,270.0

EXPORTS	1979	1980	1981
Australia	190.0	339.1	447.3
Bahamas	—	33.4	825.2
Brazil	0.6	138.3	n.a.
Germany, Fed. Republic	337.6	389.0	n.a.
Hong Kong	99.1	151.9	n.a.
Italy	209.9	254.4	n.a.
Japan	7,191.9	10,792.4	10,540.0
Korea, Republic	387.5	293.6	n.a.
Netherlands	399.1	414.9	n.a.
Philippines	165.0	181.2	410.8
Singapore	1,963.8	2,483.5	2,170.0
Taiwan	287.4	n.a.	n.a.
Trinidad and Tobago	420.0	734.8	896.6
United Kingdom	88.9	141.7	n.a.
U.S.A.	3,170.7	4,303.3	4,080.0
TOTAL (incl. others)	15,590.1	21,908.9	22,260.0

Source: Central Bureau of Statistics, Jakarta, and Department of Trade.

TRANSPORT

RAILWAYS

	1977	1978	1979	1980
Passenger-kilometres (million)	3,809	4,063	5,981	6,229
Freight ton-kilometres (million)	853	762	1,016	980

ROAD TRAFFIC

(motor vehicles in use at December 31st)

	1975	1976	1977	1978	1979	1980
Cars	383,061	420,945	479,335	532,299	1,013,744	1,482,801
Trucks	196,416	222,062	278,979	331,658	632,991	925,750
Buses	35,103	40,001	48,089	58,365	121,082	177,083
Motor cycles	1,191,771	1,419,375	1,704,964	1,960,237	3,735,749	5,463,533

INTERNATIONAL SEA-BORNE SHIPPING

		1976	1977	1978	1979
Goods loaded	'000 metric tons	83,717.0	95,298	101,262	99,972
Goods unloaded	,, ,, ,,	12,038.6	13,908	13,334	14,880
Merchant shipping fleet*	'000 g.r.t.	1,046	1,163	1,272	1,310

* At June 30th.

CIVIL AVIATION
(scheduled services)

	1977	1978	1979	1980
Kilometres flown (million)	72·3	85·3	91·4	96·4
Passengers carried ('000)	3,781	4,706	4,535	4,936
Passenger-kilometres (million)	3,917	4,246	n.a.	n.a.
Freight ton-kilometres (million)	52·1	45·7	48·3	60·6
Mail ton-kilometres (million)	4·8	n.a.	n.a.	n.a.

Source: UN, *Statistical Yearbook*, and *Attachment* to 1980 President's National Day Speech.

TOURISM

	1979	1980	1981
Visitors ('000)	501.4	561.2	600.2
Receipts (U.S. $ million)	200.0	210.4	310.0

Source: Directorate General of Tourism.

COMMUNICATIONS MEDIA

	1977	1978	1979
Radio sets*	1,741,069	1,579,652	1,430,917
Television sets	863,227	1,156,747	1,539,198
Telephones*	347,030	447,034	460,100

*Number of licences issued.

EDUCATION
(1979)

	Schools	Teachers	Pupils and Students
Primary	98,026	676,236	21,123,482
General secondary*	24,424	188,406	3,321,383
Technological	928	25,228	304,496
Teacher training	630	14,858	227,965

* 1978 figures, including secondary vocational schools.

1981: Pupils and Students; 25,500,000 (primary), 5,100,000 (secondary), 454,000 (tertiary).

Source: Far Eastern Economic Review.

Source (unless otherwise stated): Central Bureau of Statistics, Jakarta.

THE CONSTITUTION

(A Summary)

Indonesia has had three provisional Constitutions: August 1945, February 1950 and August 1950. In July 1959 the Constitution of 1945 was re-enacted by Presidential decree. The General Elections Law of 1969 supplemented the 1945 Constitution, which has been adopted permanently by the People's Consultative Assembly.

GENERAL PRINCIPLES

The 1945 Constitution consists of 37 articles, 4 transitional clauses and 2 additional provisions, and is preceded by a preamble. The preamble contains an indictment of all forms of colonialism, an account of Indonesia's struggle for independence, the declaration of that independence and a statement of fundamental aims and principles. Indonesia's National Independence, according to the text of the preamble, has the state form of a Republic, with sovereignty residing in the People, and is based upon the *Pancasila:*

1. Belief in the One Supreme God.
2. Just and Civilized Humanity.
3. The Unity of Indonesia.
4. Democracy led by the wisdom of deliberations (*musyawarah*) among representatives.
5. Social Justice for all the people of Indonesia.

THE STATE ORGANS

Majelis Permusyawaratan Rakyat—MPR (*People's Consultative Assembly*)

Sovereignty is in the hands of the People and is exercised in full by the People's Consultative Assembly as the embodiment of the whole Indonesian People. The Consultative Assembly is the highest authority of the State, and is to be distinguished from the legislative body proper (Dewan Perwakilan Rakyat, *see below*) which is incorporated within the Consultative Assembly. The Consultative Assembly, with a total of 920 members, is composed of all members of the Dewan, augmented by delegates from the regions and representatives of the functional groups in society (farmers, workers, businessmen, the clergy, intelligentsia, armed forces, students, etc.). The Assembly sits at least once every five years, and its primary competence is to determine the Constitution and the broad lines of the policy of the State and the Government. It also elects the President and Vice-President, who are responsible for implementing that policy. All decisions are taken unanimously in keeping with the traditions of *musyawarah*.

The President

The highest executive of the Government, the President, holds office for a term of five years and may be re-elected. As Mandatory of the MPR he must execute the policy of the State according to the Decrees determined by the MPR during its Fourth General and Special Sessions. In conducting the administration of the State, authority and responsibility are concentrated in the President. The Ministers of the State are his assistants and are responsible only to him.

Dewan Perwakilan Rakyat—DPR (*House of Representatives*)

The legislative branch of the State, the House of Representatives, sits at least once a year. It has 460 members: 364 elected, 96 appointed from Functional Groups. Every statute requires the approval of the DPR. Members of the House of Representatives have the right to submit draft bills which require ratification by the President, who has the right of veto. In times of emergency the President may enact ordinances which have the force of law, but such Ordinances must be ratified by the House of Representatives during the following session or be revoked.

Dewan Pertimbangan Agung—DPA (*Supreme Advisory Council*)

The DPA is an advisory body assisting the President who chooses its members from political parties, functional groups and groups of prominent persons.

Mahkamah Agung (*Supreme Court*)

The judicial branch of the State, the Supreme Court and the other courts of law are independent of the Executive in exercising their judicial powers.

Badan Pemeriksa Keuangan (*Supreme Audit Board*)

Controls the accountability of public finance, enjoys investigatory powers and is independent of the Executive. Its findings are presented to the DPR.

THE GOVERNMENT

HEAD OF STATE

President: SUHARTO (inaugurated March 27th, 1968; re-elected March 1973 and March 1978).

Vice-President: ADAM MALIK.

CABINET

(July 1982)

Minister-Co-ordinator for Political Affairs and Defence: MARADEN PANGGABEAN.

Minister-Co-ordinator for Economic, Financial and Industrial Affairs, concurrently Chairman of the National Planning Board: Prof. Dr. WIDJOJO NITISASTRO.

Minister-Co-ordinator for Social Welfare: SURONO REKSODIMEJO.

Minister of State for Administrative Reform, concurrently Deputy Chairman of the National Planning Board: Dr. JOHANNES B. SUMARLIN.

Minister of State for Supervision of Development and the Environment: Prof. Dr. EMIL SALIM.

Minister of State for Research and Technology: Prof. Dr. BUCHARUDDIN JUSUF HABIBIE.

Minister of State and State Secretary: Lieut.-Gen. SUDHARMONO, S.H.

Minister of Home Affairs: AMIR MACHMUD.

Minister of Foreign Affairs: Prof. Dr. MOCHTAR KUSUMAATMADJA, S.H.

Minister of Defence and Security, concurrently Commander-in-Chief of the Armed Forces: Gen. ANDI MOHAMMAD JUSUF.

Minister of Justice: Lieut.-Gen. ALI SAID, S.H.

Minister of Information: ALI MURTOPO.

Minister of Finance: Prof. Dr. ALI WARDHANA.

Minister of Trade and Co-operatives: Drs. RADIUS PRAWIRO.

Minister of Agriculture: Prof. Ir. SOEDARSONO HADISAPUTRO.

Minister of Industry: Ir. ABDOEL RAOEF SOEHOED.

Minister of Mining and Energy: Prof. Dr. SOEBROTO.

Minister of Public Works: Dr. Ir. PURNOMOSIDI HADJISAROSO.

Minister of Communications: RUSMIN NURJADIN.

Minister of Manpower and Transmigration: Prof. Drs. HARUN ALRASYID ZAIN.

Minister of Education and Culture: Dr. DAOED JUSUF.

Minister of Health: Dr. SOEWARDJONO SURJONINGRAT.

Minister of Religious Affairs: H. ALAMSJAH RATU PRAWIRANEGARA.

Minister of Social Affairs: SAPARDJO.

Junior Minister for Increasing Food Production: Ir. ACHMAD AFFANDI.

Junior Minister for Co-operatives: BUSTANIL ARIFIN.

Junior Minister for Transmigration: MARTONO.

Junior Minister for Public Housing: Drs. COSMAS BATUBARA.

Junior Minister for Youth Affairs: Dr. ABDUL GAFUR.

Junior Minister for Women's Affairs: Mrs. L. SUTNATO.

LEGISLATURE

MAJELIS PERMUSYAWARATAN RAKYAT—MPR

(*People's Consultative Assembly*)

The Assembly consists of the members of the House of Representatives, regional delegates, members of Golkar and the Armed Forces, and of the two parties appointed in proportion to their share of DPR seats. Total membership is 920. The table below shows the distribution of seats in the People's Consultative Assembly.

Chairman: DARYATMO.

	SEATS
Golkar	461
Armed forces	230
Partai Persatuan Pembangunan	148
Partai Demokrasi Indonesia	43
Non-affiliated regional representatives	34
Members from East Timor	4
TOTAL	920

HOUSE OF REPRESENTATIVES
(Dewan Perwakilan Rakyat—DPR)

In March 1960, a Presidential decree prorogued the elected Council of Representatives and replaced it by a nominated House of 283 members (increased to 460 in 1968). Subsequently, the number of appointed members was reduced to 96. The remaining 364 are directly elected.

Speaker: DARYATMO.

(General Election, May 4th, 1982)

	SEATS
Golkar	244
Partai Persatuan Pembangunan	96
Partai Demokrasi Indonesia	24
Appointed members*	96
TOTAL	460

* Members of the political wing of the Armed Forces (ABRI).

POLITICAL PARTIES

A Presidential decree of January 1960 enables the President to dissolve any party whose membership does not cover a quarter of Indonesia, or whose policies are at variance with the aims of the State.

The following parties and groups participated in the general elections held in May 1982:

Sekber Golongan Karya (Golkar) (*Joint Secretariat of Functional Groups*): Jakarta; f. 1964, reorganized 1971; a Government alliance of groups representing farmers, fishermen and the professions; Pres. and Chair. of Advisory Board SUHARTO; Gen. Chair. AMIR MOERTONO, S.H. (1978–83); Sec.-Gen. SUGIANTO.

Partai Demokrasi Indonesia (PDI) (*Indonesian Democratic Party*): Jakarta; f. 1973 as a result of the merger of five nationalist and Christian parties; Gen. Chair. Maj.-Gen. SUNAWAR SUKO-WATI (acting).

Partai Persatuan Pembangunan (PPP) (*United Development Party*): Jakarta; f. 1973 as a result of the merger of four Islamic parties; Pres. IDHAM CHALID; Chair. JONY NARO; Sec.-Gen. JAHJA UBEID, S.H.

DIPLOMATIC REPRESENTATION

EMBASSIES ACCREDITED TO INDONESIA
(In Jakarta unless otherwise stated)

Afghanistan: Jalan Dr. Kusuma Atmaja 15; *Ambassador:* Prof. Dr. MOHAMMAD EHSSAN ROUSTAMAL.

Algeria: Jalan Diponegoro 8; *Ambassador:* MOHAMMED AISSA MESSAOUDI.

Argentina: Jalan Panarukan 17; *Ambassador:* MARIO ALFONSE PEPE.

Australia: Jalan Thamrin 15; *Ambassador:* FREDERICK R. DALRYMPLE.

Austria: Jalan Diponegoro 44; *Ambassador:* Dr. EDGAR SELZER.

Bangladesh: Jalan Mendut 3; *Ambassador:* M. SHAMSUL ISLAM.

Belgium: Jalan Cicurug 4; *Ambassador:* JACQUES IVAN D'HONDT.

Bolivia: Kuala Lumpur, Malaysia.

Brazil: Jalan Cik Ditiro 39, Menteng; *Ambassador:* JORGE DE SÁ ALMEIDA.

Bulgaria: Jalan Imam Bonjol 34; *Ambassador:* Dr. MATEY KARASIMEONOV.

Burma: Jalan Haji Agus Salim 109; *Ambassador:* Dr. BO LAY.

Canada: 5th Floor, Wisma Metropolitan, Jalan Jendral Sudirman, P.O.B. 52/JKT; *Ambassador:* WILLIAM HARP MONTGOMERY.

Chile: 14th Floor, Arthaloka Bldg., Jalan Jendral Sudirman 2; *Ambassador:* ENRIQUE CARVALLO.

Cuba: Manila, Philippines.

Czechoslovakia: Jalan Prof. Mohd. Yamin 29, P.O.B. 319; *Ambassador:* MILAN MACHA.

Denmark: Jalan Abdul Muis 34, Jakarta Pusat; *Ambassador:* ERIK SKOV.

Egypt: Jalan Teuku Umar 68; *Ambassador:* WAGEEH MOHD. ROUSHDI.

Finland: Jalan Dr. Kusuma Atmaja 15A; *Ambassador:* TUURE MENTULA.

France: Jalan Thamrin 20; *Ambassador:* Count DIMITRI DE FAVITSKI.

German Democratic Republic: Jalan Raden Saleh 56, P.O.B. 2252; *Ambassador:* WERNER PETERS.

Germany, Federal Republic: Jalan M. H. Thamrin 1; *Ambassador:* Dr. HANS-JOACHIM HALLIER.

Ghana: Canberra, A.C.T., Australia.

Greece: New Delhi, India.

Guinea: Tokyo, Japan.

Hungary: Jalan Rasuna Said, Kav. 13; *Ambassador:* ISTVÁN DEBRECENI.

India: Jalan Kebonsirih 44; *Ambassador:* S. K. BHUTAN.

Iran: Jalan Cokroaminoto 110; *Chargé d'affaires:* MAHMUD KAMIABI-PUR.

Iraq: Jalan Teuku Umar 38; *Ambassador:* HISHAM TABAQCHALI.

Italy: Jalan Diponegoro 45; *Ambassador:* GERARDO ZAMPAGLIONE.

Japan: Jalan Mohammad Hoesni Thamrin 24; *Chargé d'affaires:* TAIZO NAKAMURA.

Jordan: Islamabad, Pakistan.

Korea, Democratic People's Republic: Jalan Teuku Umar 72/74; *Ambassador:* PAK MIN SOP.

Korea, Republic: Jalan Jenderal Gatot Subroto 57; *Ambassador:* WOO SUK HAN.

Kuwait: Tokyo, Japan.

Laos: Bangkok, Thailand.

Lebanon: New Delhi, India.

Liberia: Tokyo, Japan.

Malaysia: Jalan Imam Bonjol 17; *Ambassador:* Datuk MOHAMED RAHMAT.

Mexico: Jalan Thamrin 59; *Ambassador:* JUAN MANUEL RAMÍREZ GÓMEZ.

Mongolia: Tokyo, Japan.

Nepal: Rangoon, Burma.

Netherlands: Jalan H. R. Rasuna Said: *Ambassador:* L. H. J. B. VAN GORKOM.

New Zealand: Jalan Diponegoro 41; *Ambassador:* MICHAEL POWLES.

Nigeria: Arthaloka Bldg., 7th Floor, Jalan Jenderal Sudiman No. 2; *Ambassador:* O. O. ADESOLA.

Norway: Jalan Padalarang 4; *Ambassador:* CARL ODDVAR JORGENSEN.

Pakistan: Jalan Teuku Umar 50; *Ambassador:* MATAHAR HUSEIN.

Papua New Guinea: Wisma Metropolitan, 4th Floor, Jalan Jendral Sudirman; *Ambassador:* BENSON GEGEYO (recalled May 1982).

Philippines: Jalan Imam Bonjol 6–8; *Ambassador:* MANUEL T. YAN.

Poland: Jalan Diponegoro 65; *Ambassador:* LUCJAN LIK.

Qatar: Islamabad, Pakistan.

Romania: Jalan Cik Ditiro 42A; *Ambassador:* ION COTOȚ.

Saudi Arabia: Jalan Imam Bonjol 3; *Ambassador:* Shaikh BAKR ABBAS KHOMAIS.

Singapore: Jalan Proklamasi 23; *Ambassador:* JOSEPH FRANCIS CONCEICAO.

Somalia: Islamabad, Pakistan.

Spain: Wisma Kosgoro 14th Floor, Jalan Thamrin 53; *Ambassador:* ALBERTO PASCUAL VILLAR.

Sri Lanka: Jalan Diponegoro 70; *Chargé d'affaires:* D. SERASINGHE.

Sudan: New Delhi, India.

Sweden: Jalan Taman Cut Mutiah 12, P.O.B. 2824; *Ambassador:* ARNE LELLKI.

Switzerland: Jalan J. Latuharhary, S.H. 23; *Ambassador:* JEAN BOURGEOIS.

Syria: Jalan Gondangdia Lama 38; *Ambassador:* NADIM DOUAY.

Thailand: Jalan Imam Bonjol 74; *Ambassador:* CHUAY KANNAWAT.

Trinidad and Tobago: New Delhi, India.

Turkey: Jalan Bonjol 43; *Ambassador:* PULAT Y. TACAR.

U.S.S.R.: Jalan Thamrin 13; *Ambassador:* I. F. SHPEDKO.

United Kingdom: Jalan M. H. Thamrin 75; *Ambassador:* ROBERT BRASH, C.M.G.

U.S.A.: Jalan Merdeka Selatan 5; *Chargé d'affaires:* JOHN C. MONJO.

Vatican City: Jalan Merdeka Timur 18 (Apostolic Nunciature); *Apostolic Pro-Nuncio:* PABLO PUENTE.

Venezuela: Hotel Hilton; *Ambassador:* JOSÉ DE JESÚS OSIO.

Viet-Nam: Jalan Teuku Umar 25; *Ambassador:* TRINH XUAN LANG.

Yugoslavia: Jalan Cokroaminoto 109; *Ambassador:* ZLATAN SAŽUNIĆ.

Indonesia also has diplomatic relations with the Bahamas, Bahrain, Djibouti, Ethiopia, Fiji, Gabon, Iceland, the Ivory Coast, Kenya, Luxembourg, Madagascar, Maldives, Mali, Malta, Morocco, Oman, Suriname, Tanzania, Tunisia, the United Arab Emirates, Western Samoa and Zambia.

JUDICIAL SYSTEM

There is one codified criminal law for the whole of Indonesia. Europeans are subject to the Code of Civil Law published in the State Gazette in 1847. For Indonesians the civil law is the uncodified customary law (*Hukum Adat*) which varies from region to region. Alien orientals (i.e. Arabs, Indians, etc.) and Chinese are subject to certain parts of the Code of Civil Law and the Code of Commerce. The work of codifying this law has started but in view of the great complexity and diversity of customary law it may be expected to take a considerable time to achieve.

Supreme Court. The final court of appeal (cassation).

High Courts in Jakarta, Surabaya, Medan, Ujungpandang (Makassar), Banda Aceh, Padang, Palembang, Bandung, Semarang, Banjarmasin, Menado, Denpasar, Ambon and Jayapura deal with appeals from the District Courts.

District Courts deal with marriage, divorce and reconciliation.

Chief Justice of the Supreme Court: Maj.-Gen. MOEDJONO, S.H.

Attorney-General: ISMAIL SALEH, S.H.

RELIGION

In 1978 percentage estimates were as follows:

	Per cent
Muslim	90
Christian	9
Hindu	} 1
Others	

ISLAM

Leader: Prof. Dr. Haji ABDUL MALIK KARIM AMRULLAH (HAMKA).

Indonesian Ulama Council (MUI): Central Muslim organization; Chair. KHM SYVKRIGHOZALI.

CHRISTIANITY

In 1977 there were an estimated 2.9 million Roman Catholics in Indonesia.

Archbishop of Jakarta: Mgr. LEO SOEKOTO, S.J.; Jalan Kathedral 7, Jakarta Pusat.

THE PRESS

PRINCIPAL DAILIES

Java

Berita Buana: Jalan Tanah Abang 11/35, Jakarta; f. 1970; Indonesian; Editor SUKARNO WIBOWO; circ. 150,000.

Berita Yudha: Jalan Bangka II/2, 2nd Floor Kebayoran Baru, Jakarta; f. 1970; general newspaper; Editor SUNARDI, D.M.; circ. 75,000.

Harian Umum AB: CTC Building 2nd Floor, Kramat Raya 94, Jakarta Pusat; official armed forces paper; Dir. GOENARSO, S.F.; Editor-in-Chief M. H. NASUTION; circ. 100,000.

Indonesia (*Indonesia Rze Pao*): Jalan Toko Tiga Seberang 21, Jakarta Barat; f. 1966; Chinese; Editors Drs. T. W. SLAMET, Sk. HADI WIBOWO; circ. 80,000.

The Indonesia Times: Jalan Letjen S. Parman Kav. 72, P.O.B. 224, Jakarta; f. 1974; English language; Chief Editor R. P. HENDRO; circ. 35,000.

Indonesian Daily News: Jalan Jend. Basuki Rachmat 52, Surabaya; f. 1957; English; Editor Hos. NURYAHYA; circ. 6,500.

Indonesian Observer: Jalan A. M. Sangaji 11, Jakarta; f. 1950; English; independent; Chief Editor Mrs. HERAWATI DIAH; circ. 18,000.

Jawa Pos: Jalan Kembang Jepun 166, Tromolpos 5149, Surabaya; f. 1949; Indonesia; Editor SETYONO; circ. 20,000.

Jurnal Ekuin: Jalan Kenari 11/12, P.O.B. 3065, Jakarta; Indonesian; economic; Editor N. DIAH; circ. 15,000.

Kedaulatan Rakyat: Jalan P. Mangkubumi 40–42, Yogyakarta; f. 1945; Indonesian; independent; Editor IMAN SUTRISNO; circ. 50,000.

Kompas: Jalan Palmerah Selatan 26-28, P.O.B. 615/DAK, Jakarta; f. 1965; Editor Drs. JAKOB OETAMA; circ. 300,000.

Masa Kini: Jalan Mayor Suryotomo 23, Yogyakarta; f. 1966; Chief Editor H. ACHMAD BASUNI; circ. 25,000.

Merdeka: Jalan A. M. Sangaji 11, Jakarta; f. 1945; Indonesian; independent; Dir. B. M. DIAH; Editor B. M. DIAH; circ. 130,000.

Pelita: Jalan Diponegoro 60, Jakarta; f. 1974; Indonesian; Muslim; Editor BARLIANTA HARAHAP; circ. 80,000.

Pewarta Surabaya: Jalan Karet 23, P.O.B. 85, Surabaya; f. 1905; Indonesian; Editor RADEN DJAROT SOEBIANTORO; circ. 10,000.

Pikiran Rakyat: Jalan Asia-Afrika 77, Bandung; f. 1950; independent; Editor ATANG ROSWITA; circ. 80,000.

Pos Kota: Jalan Gajah Mada 63, Jakarta; f. 1970; Indonesian; Chief Editor HARMOKO; circ. 215,000.

Pos Sore: Jalan Asemka 29/30, Jakarta; f. 1971; Indonesian; Editor S. ABIJASA; circ. 40,000.

Sinar Harapan (*Ray of Hope*): Jalan Dewi Sartika 136-D, Cawang, Jakarta Timur; f. 1961; independent; Publr. H. G. RORIMPANDEY; Editor SUBAGYO PR.; circ. 200,000.

Sinar Pagi: Jalan Letjen Haryono MT 22, Jakarta Selatan; f. 1971; Indonesian; Editor C. T. SIAHAAN; circ. 25,000.

Suara Karya: Jalan Bangka 11/2, Kebayoran Baru, Jakarta; f. 1971; Indonesian; Editor Drs. D. H. ASSEGAF; circ. 91,400.

Suara Merdeka: Jalan Merak 11A, Semarang; f. 1950; Indonesian; Publr. and Editor Ir. BUDI SANTOSO; circ. 105,000.

Surabaya Post: Jalan AIS Nasution 1, Surayaba; independent; Publr. Mrs. TUTY AZIS; Editor A. AZIS; circ. 85,000.

Kalimantan

Banjarmasin Post: Jalan Pasar Baru 222, Banjarmasin; f. 1971; Indonesian; Chief Editor H. J. DJOK MENTAYA; circ. 50,000.

Gawi Manuntung: Jalan Pangeran Samudra 97B, Banjarmasin; f. 1972; Indonesian; Editor M. ALI SRI INDRADJAYA; circ. 5,000.

Sumatra

Analisa: Jalan A. Yani 43, Medan; f. 1972; Indonesian; Editor SOFFYAN; circ. 50,000.

Haluan: Jalan Damar 57 C/F, Padang; f. 1948; Editor-in-Chief RIVAI MARLAUT; circ. 40,000.

Mimbar Umum: Jalan Riau 79, Medan; f. 1947; Indonesian; independent; Editor SAMSUDDIN MANAN; circ. 30,000.

Sinar Indonesia Baru: Jalan Katamso 50C, ABCD Medan; f. 1970; Indonesian; Chief Editor G. M. PANGGABEAN; circ. 60,000.

Suara Rakyat Semesta: Jalan K. H. Ashari 52, Palembang; Indonesian; Editor DJADIL ABDULLAH; circ. 10,000.

Waspada: Jalan Suprapto/Katamso 1, Medan; f. 1947; Indonesian; Editors PRABUDI SAID, AMMARY IRABI; circ. 55,000 (daily), 50,000 (Sundays).

Sulawesi

Pedoman Rakyat: Jalan H. A. Mappanyukki 28, Ujungpandang; f. 1947; independent; Editor M. BASIR; circ. 30,000.

Bali

Harian Pagi Umum (*Bali Post*): Jalan Kepudang 67A, Denpasar; f. 1948; weekly (Indonesian edition), monthly (English edition); Editor RAKA WIRATMA; circ. 5,000.

PRINCIPAL PERIODICALS

Bahasa dan Sastra: Jalan Diponegoro 82, P.O.B. 2625, Jakarta Pusat; f. 1975; linguistics and literature; every 2 months; Dir. Prof. Dr. AMRAN HALIM; circ. 5,000.

Basis: P.O.B. 20, Yogyakarta; f. 1951; general Indonesian culture; monthly; Editor DICK HARTOKO; circ. 3,000.

Berita Negara: Jalan Pertjetakan Negara 21, Kotakpos 2111, Jakarta; f. 1960; official gazette; 3 times a week.

Bobo: Jalan Palmerah Selatan 22, Jakarta; f. 1973; children's magazine; weekly; Editor TINEKE LATUMETEN; circ. 160,000.

Budaja Djaja: Jalan Gajah Mada 104–110A, Jakarta Barat; f. 1968; cultural; independent; Editor AJIP ROSIDI; circ. 4,000.

Business News: Jalan H. Abdul Muis 70, Jakarta; f. 1956; Indonesian and English; 3 a week (Indonesian edition), 2 a week (English edition); Chief Editor SANJOTO SASTROMIHARDJO; circ. 15,000.

Depthnews Indonesia: Jalan Jatinegara Barat III/6, Jakarta Timur; f. 1972; Publr. Press Foundation of Indonesia; weekly; Editor SUMONO MUSTOFFA.

Dunia Wanita: Jalan Brigjen. Katamso 1, Medan; f. 1949; Indonesian; women; fortnightly; Chief Editor Mrs. PRAPUDI SAID; circ. 10,000.

Economic Review: Jalan Lada 1, Jakarta; f. 1947; English; quarterly.

Economics and Finance in Indonesia: Institute for Economic and Social Research, University of Indonesia, Jalan Raya Salemba 4, P.O.B. 295/JKT, Jakarta; quarterly; circ. 4,000.

Ekonomi Indonesia: Piola Bldg., 5th Floor, Jalan Kramat Raya; English; fortnightly; Editor Z. ACHMAD; circ. 20,000.

Femina: Jalan H. R. Rasuna Said, Blok B, Kav. 31–32–33, Kuningan, Jakarta Selatan; women's magazine; weekly; Editor WIDARTI GUNAWAN; circ. 120,000.

Gema Jusani: Jalan Salemba Tengah 47, Jakarta Pusat; f. 1981; Indonesian; monthly; organ of Corps of Invalids; Editor H. ANWAN BEY; circ. 20,000.

Hai: Jalan Gajah Mada 104, Jakarta; f. 1973; youth magazine; weekly; Editor Drs. ANTON SUMANGOONO.

Horison: Jalan Gajah Mada 104–110A, Jakarta Barat; f. 1966; literary and cultural; independent; monthly; Editors MOCHTAR LUBIS, H. B. JASSIN, TAUFIC ISMAEL; circ. 4,000.

Hukum & Keadilan: Jalan Gajah Mada 110A, Jakarta Barat; f. 1974; independent law journal; 2 a month; Editors SUARDI TASRIF, S.H., SOENARDI, ADNAN BUYUNG NASUTION, S.H.; circ. 3,000.

Indonesia Magazine: Merdeka Barat 20, Jakarta; f. 1969; English; monthly; Dir. G. DWIPAJANA; circ. 10,000.

Intisari: P.O.B. 615/DAK, Jakarta; f. 1963; monthly digest; Editors IRAWATI, Drs. J. OETAMA; circ. 134,000.

Keluarga: Jalan Sangaji 9–11, Jakarta; women's and family magazine; monthly; Editor D. S. MULYANTO.

Majalah Ekonomis: P.O.B. 4195, Jakarta; business journal; English; monthly; Chief Editor S. ARIFIN HUTABARAT; circ. 15,000.

Majalah Kedokteran Indonesia (*Journal of the Indonesian Medical Association*): Jalan Kesehatan 111/29, Jakarta 11/16; f. 1951; monthly; Indonesian, English.

Mangle: Jalan Lodaya 19–21, Bandung; f. 1957; Sundanese; weekly; Chief Editor R. H. UTON MUCHTAR; circ. 74,000.

Mimbar Kabinet Pembangunan: Jalan Merdeka-Barat 7, Jakarta; f. 1966; monthly; Indonesian; published by Dept. of Information.

Mimbar Pembangunan: Jalan Merdeka-Barat 7, Jakarta; f. 1968; Indonesian; quarterly; published by Dept. of Information.

Mimbar Penerangan: Jalan Merdeka-Barat 7, Jakarta; f. 1950; Indonesian; quarterly; published by Dept. of Information.

Mutiara: Jalan Petak Asem 1/40, Jakarta; family; Dir. TIOLINA ADRIANA LAUPASE.

Peraba: Bintaran Kidul 5, Yogyakarta; Indonesian and Javanese; Catholic; weekly; Editor W. KARTOSOEHARSONO.

Pertani P.T.: Jalan Pasar Minggu, Jakarta; f. 1974; Indonesian; agricultural; monthly; Pres./Dir. Ir. RUSLI YAHYA.

Rajawali: Jalan Ir. H. Juanda 15, Jakarta; Indonesian; monthly; civil air transport and tourism; Dir. R. A. J. LUMENTA; Man. Editor KARYONO ADHY.

Selecta: Kebon Kacang 29/4, Jakarta; illustrated; fortnightly; Editor SAMSUDIN LUBIS; circ. 80,000.

Sinar Jaya: Jalan Sultan Agung 67A, Jakarta Selatan; agricultural newspaper; bi-weekly; Chief Editor Ir. SURYONO PROJOPRANOTO.

Tempo: Pusat Perdagangan Senen, Blok II, Lantai III, Jakarta; current affairs; weekly; Editor GOENAWAN MOHAMMAD; circ. 80,000.

NEWS AGENCIES

Antara (*Indonesian National News Agency*): Wisma Antara 19th and 20th Floors, Merdeka Selatan 17, P.O.B. 257 Jakarta; f. 1937; State Radio, TV and 50 newspapers suscribe to the Agency (1982); 27 brs. in Indonesia, 3 abroad; connected with 27 foreign agencies and members of ASEAN New Agencies Association, Organization of Asia–Pacific News Agencies, International Islamic News Agencies and Non-Aligned Press Agencies Pool; 10 bulletins in Indonesian and 11 in English and one European edition and one Asian edition; Gen. Man. AUGUST MARPAUNG, S.H.

Kantorberita Nasional Indonesia (*KNI News Service*): Jalan Jatinegara Barat III/6, Jakarta Timur; f. 1966; independent national news agency; foreign and domestic news in Indonesian and English; Dir. Drs. T. S. S. SUTANTO; Editor-in-Chief SUDJARWO.

FOREIGN BUREAUX

Agence France-Presse (AFP): Jalan Indramayu 18, Jakarta; Chief Correspondent PIERRE COMPARET.

Associated Press (AP) (*U.S.A.*): Jalan Kebon Sirih 40 (flat 30), P.O.B. 2056, Jakarta; Corresp. GHAFUR FADYL.

Deutsche Presse-Agentur (dpa) (*Federal Republic of Germany*): P.O.B. 2021, Jakarta; Corresp. AMIR DAUD.

Jiji Tsushin-sha (*Japan*): Jalan Pasuruan No. 15, Jakarta; Bureau Chief IWAO AMANO.

Kyodo Tsushin (*Japan*): c/o Reuters, Jalan Medan Merdeka Selatan 17, Jakarta; Correspondent MICHITAKA YAMADA.

Reuters (*United Kingdom*): Jalan Medan Merdeka Selatan 17, P.O.B. 2318, Jakarta.

TASS (*U.S.S.R.*): Hotel Indonesia Sheraton, Jakarta.

United Press International (UPI) (*U.S.A.*): Hotel Borobudur, Jakarta Pusat, Corresp. ISABEL ISMAIL.

Agencia EFE (Spain) also has an office in Jakarta.

PRESS ASSOCIATION

Persatuan Wartawan Indonesia (*Indonesian Journalists' Association*): Jalan Veteran 7-C, Jakarta; f. 1946; 2,858 mems. (Feb. 1981); Exec. Chair. HARMOKO; Gen. Sec. D. H. ASSEGAFF.

Serikat Penerbit Suratkabar (SPS) (*Indonesian Newspaper Publishers Association*): Jalan Taman Tanah Abang III/23, Jakarta Pusat; f. 1946; Chair. SUNARDI D. M.; Sec.-Gen. ZULHARMANS.

Yayasan Pembina Pers Indonesia (*The Press Foundation of Indonesia*): Jalan Jatinegara Barat III/6, Jakarta Timur; f. 1967; Chairs. SUGIARSO SUROYO, MOCHTAR LUBIS.

PUBLISHERS

Jakarta

Aries Lima: Jalan Rawa Gelam II/4, Industrial Estate, Pulogadung; f. 1974; general and children's books; Pres. Drs. AZMI SJAHBUDDIN.

Balai Pustaka: Jalan Dr. Wahidin 1, P.O.B. 29; f. 1908; children's books, literary, scientific publications and periodicals; Pres. Drs. SOETOJO GONDO.

P.T. Bhratara Karya Aksara: Jalan Rawabali II/5, Kawasan Industri Pulogadong, Jakarta Timur; f. 1958; university/educational textbooks; Pres. AHMAD JAYUSMAN.

Bulan Bintang: Jalan Kramat Kwitang 1/8; f. 1956; religious, social science, natural and applied sciences, art; Man. AMELZ.

Djambatan: Jalan Kramat Raya 152, Tromolpos 116; f. 1954; children's books, textbooks, social sciences, fiction; Dir. ROSWITHA PAMOENTJAK.

Dunia Pustaka Jaya: Jalan Kramat 11/31A; f. 1971; fiction, religion, essays, poetry, drama, criticism, art, philosophy and children's books; Man. RACHMAT M. A. S.

Erlangga: Kramat IV/11; f. 1952; secondary school and university textbooks; Dir. M. HUTAURUK, S.H.

Gaya Favorit Press: Jalan Proklamasi 71; f. 1971; fiction, popular science and children's books; Dir. SOFJAN ALISJAHBANA.

Gramedia: Jalan Palmerah Selatan 22, Lantai IV; f. 1970; university textbooks, general non-fiction, magazines and children's books; Gen. Man. Y. ADISUBRATA.

Gunung Aung: Jalan Kwitang 8, P.O.B. 145, Jakarta Pusat; f. 1953; general books, textbooks, scientific publications; Chair. and Man. Dir. MASAGUNG.

BPK Gunung Mulia: Jalan Kwitang 22; f. 1951; general books, children's books, religious books, home economics; Man. A. SIMANDJUNTAK.

Harapan Masa: Jalan Karet Tengsin 20; f. 1952; textbooks, children's books, general books; Man. AMIN KROMOMIHARDJO.

Ikhtiar: Jalan Majapahit 6; f. 1957; textbooks, law, social sciences, economics; Mans. J. and R. SEMERU.

Kinta: Jalan Cik Ditiro 54A; f. 1950; textbooks, social science, general books; Man. Drs. MOHAMAD SALEH.

Mutiara: Jalan Pulo Kambing 9, Industrial Estate P. Gandung; f. 1966; textbooks, religious books, social sciences, general books, children's books; Man. H. OEMAR BARKY DT. TAN-BESAR.

Pembangunan: Jalan Grinting, Kebayoran Baru 1/15; brs. in Bandung, Yogyakarta, Madiun and Surabaya; f. 1953; textbooks, children's books and scientific publications; Mans. SUMANTRI, SOEWEDO.

Penerbit Universitas Indonesia: Jalan Raya Salemba 4; f. 1969; scientific publications; Man. Dr. EDI SWASONO.

Pradnya Paramita P.T.: Jalan Kebon Sirih 46, P.O.B. 146/JKT; f. 1963; children's, general, educational, technical and social science books; Man. SADONO DIBYOWIROYO, S.H.

Pustaka Antara: Jalan Majapahit 28; f. 1952; textbooks, political and religious books, children's books and general books; Man. H. M. JOESOEF AHMAD.

Sastra Hudaya: Jalan Proklamasi 61; f. 1967; religious books, textbooks, children's books and general books: Man. ADAM SALEH.

Soeroengan: Jalan Pecenongan 58; f. 1950; textbooks and agriculture; Man. G. SILITONGA, S.H.

Tintamas Indonesia: Jalan Kramat Raya 60, Jakarta Pusat; f. 1947; biography, history, modern science and culture, especially Islamic works; Man. MARHAMAH DJAMBEK.

Wijaya: Jalan Pecenongan 48C; f. 1950; textbooks, children's books, religious and general books; Man. NAZAR YAHYA.

Yasaguna: Jalan Dr. Saharjo 50, Jakarta Selatan; f. 1964; agricultural books; Dir. HILMAN MADEWA.

Bandung

Alumni: Jalan Geusanulun 17, P.O.B. 272; f. 1969; university textbooks; Man. EDDY DAMIAN.

Binacipta: Jalan Ganesya 4; f. 1967; textbooks, scientific publications, general books; Man. O. BARDIN.

Diponegoro: Jalan Mohamad Toha 44-46; f. 1963; religious, textbooks, fiction and non-fiction; Man. A. DAHLAN.

Eresco: Jalan Hasanudin 9; f. 1957; scientific publications and general books; Man. Mrs. P. ROCHMAT SOEMITRO.

Ganaco/Masa Baru/Sanggabuwana: Jalan Gereja 3; primary and secondary school textbooks, information and children's books; Man. MOH. ISA DARNAKUSUMA.

Al Ma'arif: Jalan Tamblong 48-50; f. 1949; textbooks, religious books and general books; Man. H. M. BAHARTHAH.

Pelita Masa: Jalan Lodaya 25, Bandung; f. 1973; information and children's books; Man. ROCHDI PARTAATMADJA.

Remaja Kanya: Jalan Ciateul 34-36, P.O.B. 284; textbooks and children's fiction; Man. ROZALI USMAN, S.H.

Rosda: Jalan Ciateul 33; f. 1969; primary and secondary school textbooks, children's books; Man. H. MURSJIDAH.

Sumur Bandung: Jalan Asia-Afrika 82; f. 1972; textbooks; Man. H. MOH. RISAN.

Flores

Nusa Indah: Jalan Katedral 5, Ende-Flores; f. 1973; religious and general books and periodicals; Man. ALEXANDER BEDING SVD.

Kudus

Menara: Jalan Menara 2; f. 1958; religious books; Man. HILMAN NAJIB.

Medan

Hasmar: Jalan Letjen Haryono M.T. 1, P.O.B. 446; primary school textbooks; Man. HASBULLAH LUBIS.

Islamiyah: Jalan Sutomo 328–329; f. 1954; Man. H. ABD DJALIL SIREGAR.

Maju: Jalan Singamangaraja 25; f. 1950; textbooks, children's books and general books; Pres. Dir. H. MOHAMED ARBIE.

Surabaya

Assegaff: Jalan Panggung 136; f. 1951; religious books, language books, lower school textbooks; Man. HASAN ASSEGAFF.

Bina Ilmu: Jalan Tunjungan 53E; f. 1973; primary and secondary school textbooks; Pres. ARIFIN NOOR.

Grip: Jalan Kawung 2, P.O.B. 129; f. 1958; textbooks and general books; Man. Mrs. SURIPTO.

Institut Dagang Moechtar: Jalan Embong Wungu 8; textbooks for business colleges; Pres. Z. A. MOECHTAR.

Jaya Baya: Jalan Penghela 2 (atas), P.O.B. 250; f. 1945; religion, philosophy and ethics; Man. TADJIB ERMADI.

Karunia C.V.: Jalan Peneleh 18; f. 1971; textbooks and general books; Man. HASAN ABDAN.

Marfiah: Jalan Kalibutuh 131; information books and primary school textbooks; Man. ACHMAD NOTOATMODJO.

Ujungpandang

Bhakti Baru: Jalan A. Yani 15; f. 1972; textbooks and general books; Man. ALWI HAMU.

Yogyakarta

Yayasan Kanisius: Jalan P. Senopati 24; f. 1922; textbooks, religious books and general books; Man. R. P. S. PADMOBUSONO.

PUBLISHERS' ASSOCIATION

IKAPI (*Association of Indonesian Book-Publishers*): Jalan Pengarengan (Kalipasir) 32, Jakarta III/4; f. 1950; 154 mems.; Pres. RACHMAT M. A. S.; Sec. ROZALI USMAN.

RADIO AND TELEVISION

Directorate-General of Posts and Telecommunications: Jalan Kebon Sirih 37, Jakarta; Dir.-Gen. SURYADI.

RADIO

Radio Republik Indonesia (RRI): Jalan Merdeka Barat 4–5, P.O.B. 157, Jakarta; f. 1945; 49 stations; Dir. H. M. SANI; Deputy Dirs. PURBOYO (Overseas Service), I. M. P. TANTRAWAN (Domestic Service), MOH. RAMLI (News), S. BROTODIREDJO (Engineering Planning and Development), MUNAYIK SALAM (Engineering Operation), FADJAR MADRADJI (Administration), Drs. SUWARDI HASSAN (Head of Training Centre); publ. *Radio Bulletin* (daily).

Voice of Indonesia: P.O.B. 157, Jakarta; foreign service; daily broadcasts in Arabic, English, French, German, Indonesian, Japanese, Malay, Mandarin and Thai; publ. *RRI Radio dan Televisi* (weekly).

In 1980 there were an estimated 20 million radio receivers.

TELEVISION

Yayasan Televisi Republik Indonesia (TVRI): Senayan, Jakarta; f. 1962; government controlled; Dir. Drs. H. SOEBRATA; publ. *Monitor TVRI*.

In 1980 there were an estimated 1,600,000 televisions registered.

FINANCE

BANKING

(cap. = capital; dep. = deposits; p.u. = paid up; auth. = authorized; m. = million; amounts in rupiahs; brs. = branches.)

Central Bank

Bank Indonesia: Jalan M.H. Thamrin 2, Jakarta; f. 1828; nationalized 1951; promulgated the Central Bank in 1953; cap. 1,000m.; dep. (banks) 496,043m. (March 1979); Gov. Rachmat Saleh; publs. *Weekly Report, Indonesian Financial Statistics* (monthly), *Annual Report.*

State Banks

Bank Bumi Daya: Jalan Imam Bonjol 61, P.O.B. 106; Jakarta; f. 1959; commercial and foreign exchange bank, specializes in credits to the plantation and forestry sector; cap. p.u. 300m.; dep. 1,608,579m. (Sept. 1981); Pres. Omar Abdalla; 70 brs.

Bank Dagang Negara: Jalan M. H. Thamrin 5, P.O.B. 338/JKT, Jakarta; f. 1960; authorized state foreign exchange bank; specializes in credits to the mining sector; cap. p.u. 250m.; dep. 273,239m. (Dec. 1978); Pres. H. M. Widarsadipradja; 66 brs.

Bank Ekspor Impor Indonesia: Jalan Lapangan Setasiun 1, P.O.B. 32, Jakarta Kota; f. 1968; commercial foreign exchange bank; specializes in credits for manufacture and export; cap. 200m.; dep. 507,961m. (Dec. 1979); Pres. Moeljoto Djojomartono; 45 brs.

Bank Negara Indonesia 1946: Jalan Lada 1, P.O.B. 1946/KB/JAK, Jakarta Kota; f. 1946; cap. 500m.; dep. 2,434,827m. (Dec. 1981); commercial foreign exchange bank; specializes in credits to the industrial sector as well as commercial transactions; Pres. H. Somala Wiria; 229 brs.; publ. *Economic Review.*

Bank Rakyat Indonesia: Jalan Veteran 8, P.O.B. 94, Jakarta; f. 1946; cap. 300m., dep. 256,600m. (Dec. 1976); commercial foreign exchange bank; specializes in credits to co-operatives in agriculture and fisheries, in rural credit generally and international business; Pres. Permadi, s.e.; 272 brs.

Bank Tabungan Negara (*State Savings Bank*): Jalan Gajah Mada 1, Jakarta; f. 1964; cap. p.u. 100m.; dep. 7,713m. (Dec. 1976); specializes in promotion of savings among the general public; Dir. Prayogo Mirhad; 6 brs.

Development Bank

Bank Pembangunan Indonesia (BAPINDO) (*Development Bank of Indonesia*): Gondangdia Lama 2–4, Jakarta; f. 1960; state bank; financial assistance to Government enterprises and privately-owned industrial and other productive enterprises; helps in development or establishment of new industries and other productive ventures, or expansion and modernization of existing enterprises; conducts feasibility studies of Government projects; auth. cap. 50,000m.; cap. p.u. 49,981m.; total financial resources 134,746m. (June 1977); Pres. Kuntoadji.

Finance Corporations

P.T. Bahana Pembinaan Usaha Indonesia: Jalan Cik Ditiro 23, Jakarta; f. 1973; cap. p.u. 2,500m.; Pres. Trasno Kaliprogo.

P.T. Inter-Pacific Financial Corporation: 4th Floor-Nusantara Bldg., Jalan M.H. Thamrin 59, Jakarta Pusat; f. 1973; cap. p.u. 449m.; Pres. Dir. Frank Jan Dictus.

P.T. Multinational Finance Corporation: Wisma Kosgoro, 20th Floor, Jalan M. H. Thamrin 53, Jakarta; f. 1974; Pres. Dir. K. R. Wynn.

P.T. Mutual International Finance Corporation: Nusantara Bldg., 17th Floor, Jalan M. H. Thamrin 12, Jakarta; f. 1973; cap. p.u. 300m.; Pres. Dir. E. Hiratsuka.

P.T. Private Development Finance Company of Indonesia: Jalan Abdul Muis 60, Jakarta; f. 1973; cap. p.u. 3,700m.; Pres. Sulaksana Supart.

P.T. Usaha Pembiayaan Pembangunan Indonesia (*Indonesian Development Finance Company*): UPPINDO Bldg., Jalan Abdul Muis 28, P.O.B. 24, Jakarta; f. 1972; cap. p.u. 6,592m.; Chair. T. M. Zahirsjah, s.h.; Pres. Dir. Drs. Moerdyono Soemadyono; Man. Dir. G. L. S. Kapitan, s.h.

National Private Banks

In 1978 there were 80 private commercial banks in Indonesia.

P.T. Bank Amerta: Jalan Palatehan 1/30, Jakarta; f. 1951; cap. p.u. 3,000m.; dep. 6,978m. (Dec. 1980); Pres. Idham; Chair. Soedarpo Sastrosatomo.

P.T. Bank Bali: Jalan Pasar Pagi 24, Jakarta; f. 1954; foreign exchange bank; cap. p.u. 1,181m.; dep. 19,487m. (Dec. 1980); Pres. D. Ramli; Chair. L. Sandjaja; Man. Dirs. G. Karjadi, W. Kidarsa and P. H. Sugiri; 4 brs., 1 sub-br.

P.T. Bank Buana Indonesia: Jalan Asemka 33–35, Jakarta; f. 1956; foreign exchange bank; cap. p.u. 3,000m.; dep. 41,073m. (Dec. 1980); Pres. Hendra Suryadi (acting); 8 brs.

P.T. Bank Central Asia: Jalan Asemka 25–26, Jakarta; f. 1957; cap. p.u. 10,000m.; dep. 126,000m. (Dec. 1981); Pres. A. Ali; Chief Exec. Dir. Mochtar Riady; 26 brs.

P.T. Bank Duta Ekonomi: Jalan Sultan Hasanuddin 47–48, Kebayoran Baru, Jakarta; f. 1966; foreign exchange bank; cap. p.u. 2,400m.; dep. 22,084m. (Dec. 1980); Pres. Abdulgani; 4 brs.

P.T. Bank Niaga: Jalan Gajah Mada 18, Jakarta; f. 1955; foreign exchange bank; cap. p.u. 1,271m.; dep. 30,185m. (Oct. 1980); Pres. Idham; Man. Dir. Jonosewojo; 5 brs.

P.T. Bank N.I.S.P.: Jalan Taman Cibeunying Selatan 31, Bandung; f. 1941; cap. p.u. 1,052m.; dep. 20,912m. (Sept. 1981); Pres. Karmaka Surjaudaja; Man. Dir. Peter Eko Sutioso, s.h.; 2 brs.

P.T. Overseas Express Bank: Jalan Pecenongan 84, Jakarta; f. 1974; cap. p.u. 6,000m.; dep. 18,881m.; Pres. I. Nyoman Moena; Chair. Soetianto Soemali; 9 brs.

P.T. Bank Pacific: Jalan K. H. Samanhudi 17–19, Jakarta; f. 1958; cap. p.u. 8,000m.; dep. 14,225m. (Dec. 1981); Pres. Iman Sukotjo; Man. Dirs. R. Oemar Said, Abdul Firman, H. A. Toar; 6 brs.

P.T. Pan Indonesia (Panin) Bank: Panin Bldg., Jalan Jen. Sudirman, Senayan, Jakarta; f. 1971; foreign exchange bank; cap. p.u. 6,047m.; dep. 94,456m. (Dec. 1981); Pres. H. Andi Gappa; Exec. Vice-Pres. Mu'min Ali G. and Tidjan Ananto; 20 brs.

P.T. Bank Perdania: Jalan Raya Mangga Besar 7–11, Jakarta; Pres. Jusuf Wibisono, s.h.

P.T. Sejahtera Bank Umum: Jalan Tiang Bendera 15, Jakarta Barat; f. 1952; cap. p.u. 1,500m.; total assets 17,547m. (Dec. 1980); Pres. Dr. J. PANGLAYKIM; 4 brs.

P.T. South East Asia Bank Ltd.: Jalan Asemka 17, Jakarta; f. 1957; cap. p.u. 6,000m.; dep. 1 ,000m. (M r h 1981); Pres. MOERTOLO, S.H.; Man. Dirs. Drs. H. ABUCHAERI, TRISNO HARIANTO, HARIONO; 3 brs.

P.T. Bank Umum Nasional: Jalan Cikini Raya 78, Jakarta; f. 1952; foreign exchange bank; cap. p.u. 7,000m.; dep. 58,323m. (Dec. 1981); Pres. Dir. KAHARUDIN ONGKO; Deputy Pres. H. CHANDRA; Exec. Dir. M. DJAILANI.

P.T. United City Bank: Jalan Hayam Wuruk 121, Jakarta; f. 1967; cap. p.u. 1,600m.; dep. 7,155m. (March 1977); Pres. AGUS ANANDATIO; 3 brs.

FOREIGN BANKS

Algemene Bank Nederland N.V. (*Netherlands*): Jalan Ir. H. Juanda 23–24, P.O.B. 2950, Jakarta; Man. J. A. BRANDT.

Bangkok Bank Ltd. (*Thailand*): Jalan Thamrin 3, Jakarta; Man. and Vice-Pres. ADISORN TANTIMEDH.

Bank of America N.T. & S.A. (*U.S.A.*): P.O.B. 195, Jakarta; Vice-Pres. and Man. PETER K. STERNAD.

Bank of Tokyo Ltd. (*Japan*): Nusantara Bldg., Jalan Thamrin 59, Jakarta; Gen. Man. KENJI YOSHIZAWA.

The Chartered Bank (*U.K.*): Wisma Kosgoro, Jalan Thamrin 53, Jakarta; Man. K. N. RADFORD.

The Chase Manhattan Bank, N.A. (*U.S.A.*): Jalan Medan Merdeka Barat 6, P.O.B. 311/JKT, Jakarta; Country Man. NORMAN J. BUCHAN.

Citibank, N.A. (*U.S.A.*): Jalan M.H. Thamrin 55; f. 1912; Vice-Pres. A. R. BATUBARA, M. M. MISTRI.

European Asian Bank (*Federal Republic of Germany*): Eurasbank Bldg., Jalan Imam Bonjol 80, P.O.B. 135, Jakarta; Man. Dr. KLAUS ZEIDLER.

Hongkong and Shanghai Banking Corpn. (*Hong Kong*): Jalan Hayam Wuruk 8, P.O.B. 2307, Jakarta; br. at Jalan Pintu Besar Seletan 109B; Man. K. R. WHITSON.

Westpac Banking Corpn. (Australia): 5th Floor, Bangkok Bank Bldg., Jalan Thamrin 3, Jakarta.

BANKING ASSOCIATION

Indonesian National Private Banks Association (*Perbankan Nasional Swasta—PERBANAS*): Jalan Sindanglaja 1, Jakarta; f. 1952; 127 mems.; Chair. SARONO; Sec.-Gen. O. P. SIMORANGKIR.

STOCK EXCHANGE

Badan Pelaksana Pasar Modal (BAPEPAM) (*Capital Market Executive Agency*): Jalan Medan Merdeka Selatan 13, Jakarta; Chair. Drs. J. A. TURANGAN.

INSURANCE

Regulations have been introduced to limit the number of foreign companies licensed to operate to 12. In February 1974 a statement was issued by the Ministry of Finance emphasizing the need to form bigger units among the domestic companies, advising foreign companies to co-operate with domestic companies in joint ventures, and forbidding foreign investment in the life insurance sector. By 1980, all twelve foreign companies licensed to operate had merged with one or more domestic companies. In July 1976 the Government ruled that foreign non-life insurance companies should conduct business through local companies.

In 1980 there were 75 insurance companies, including 55 non-life companies, 12 life companies and 3 reinsurance companies.

Insurance Supervising Authority of Indonesia: Directorate of Financial Institutions, Ministry of Finance, Jalan Lapangan Banteng Timur 2, Jakarta; Dir. MARZUKI USMAN.

SELECTED LIFE INSURANCE COMPANIES

Bumiputera 1912 Mutual Life Insurance Co.: Jalan Hos. Cokroaminoto 85-89, Jakarta Pusat; Pres. I. K. SUPRAKTO.

P.T. Asuransi Jiwa Bumi Asih Jaya: Jalan Jatinegara Barat 144, Jakarta; f. 1967; Pres. K. M. SINAGA.

P.T. Asuransi Jiwa Central Asia Raya: Jalan Pintu Besar Selatan 101, Jakarta; f. 1968; Man. WARDOJO.

P.T. Asuransi Jiwa Ikrar Abadi: Jalan Let. Jen. S. Parman 108, Slipi, Jakarta Barat; Man. HARRY HARMAIN DIAH.

P.T. Asuransi Jiwa Iman Adi: Jalan Haryono, Kar. 16, Jakarta; Man. MAMAN SUWARMAN KOWARA.

P.T. Asuransi Jiwa Mahkota Jaya Abadi: Jalan Sisingamangaraja 11, Kebayoran Baru, Jakarta; Man. WIDODO SUKARNO.

P.T. Asuransi Jiwa "Panin Putra": 1–2 Jalan Pejagalan Raya 182, Jakarta-Barat; f. 1974; Pres. ACHMAD DANUNINGRAT; Chair. NORMAN BATUBARA; Man. Dir. SLAMET SUDIRGA.

P.T. Asuransi Jiwasraya: Jalan Ir. H. Juanda 34, P.O.B. 240, Jakarta; f. 1859; Pres. ALIBASYAH SATARI.

P.T. Asuransi Pensiun Bumiputera 1974: Jalan Hos. Cokroaminoto 85, Jakarta; f. 1974; Gen. Man. HUGO W. SMID.

SELECTED NON-LIFE INSURANCE COMPANIES

P.T. Asuransi Bintang: Jalan Hayam Wuruk 4CX, Jakarta; Dir. Z. A. ACHIR.

P.T. Asuransi Jasa Indonesia: Jalan M. T. Haryono, Kav. 61, Jakarta; Pres. Dir. Z. NASUTION.

P.T. Maskapai Asuransi Indonesia: Jalan Sultan Hasannuddin 53/54, Jakarta; Pres. Dir. R. ABDULRAHMAN SURIOKUSOMO; Man. Dir. Z. U. SALAWATI.

P.T. Maskapai Asuransi Indrapura: Gedung Jaya, Jalan Thamrin, Jakarta; f. 1954; Chair. HENRI GUNANTO, S.H.

P.T. Maskapai Asuransi Murni: Jalan Tiang Bendera 90, Jakarta; f. 1953; Pres. Dir. M. J. P. PATTY; Dir. BACHZAD M.A.

P.T. Maskapai Asuransi Ramayana: Jalan Cengkeh 19H, Jakarta; f. 1956; Pres. Dir. R. G. DOERIAT; Dirs. SADIJONO HARJOKUSUMO S.H., F. X. WIDIASTANTO.

P.T. Maskapai Asuransi Timur Jauh: 13th Floor, Sarinah Bldg., Jakarta; f. 1954; Pres. Dir. H. A. AZIS HASSAN; Financial Dir. OSMAN SUNARTO; Underwriting Dir. MUSTAFA KAMAL.

Periscope Insurance Co. Ltd.: Jalan Pintu Besar Selatan 97, Jakarta; Pres. Dir. Drs. SJARIFUDDIN HARAHAP.

INSURANCE ASSOCIATION

Dewan Asuransi Indonesia (*Insurance Association of Indonesia*): Jalan Majapahit 34, Blok V, 29, Jakarta; Chair. I. K. SUPRAKTO; Exec. Sec. B. HADIKUSUMO.

TRADE AND INDUSTRY

Badan Koordinasi Penamanaman Modal (BKPM) (*Capital Investment Co-ordinating Board*): Jalan Gatot Subroto 6, Jakarta; f. 1976; Chair. R. SUHARTOYO.

National Development Planning Agency (BAPPENAS): Taman Suropati 2, Jakarta; Chair. Prof. WIDJOJO NITISASTRO; Vice-Chair. J. B. SUMARLIN.

Perusahaan Pertambangan Minyak dan Gas Bumi Negara (PERTAMINA): Jalan Merdeka Timur 1, Jakarta; f. 1957; state oil and gas corporation; Pres./Dir. Brig.-Gen. JUDO SUMBONO.

CHAMBER OF COMMERCE

Kamar Dagang dan Industri Indonesia (KADIN) (*Indonesian Chamber of Commerce and Industry*): Jalan Merdeka Timur 11, Jakarta Pusat; f. 1968; 27 regional offices throughout Indonesia; Pres. Dr. H. M. N. M. HASJIM NING; Sec.-Gen. ALI NOOR LUDDIN.

TRADE ORGANIZATIONS

Association of State-Owned Companies: C.T.C. Bldg., Jalan Kramat Raya 4, Jakarta; Pres. ODANG, S.H.

CAFI (*Commercial Advisory Foundation in Indonesia*): Jalan Probolinggo 5, P.O.B. 249, Jakarta; f. 1958; information, consultancy and translation services; Chair. Dr. R. Ng. S. SOSROHADIKOESOEMO; Man. Dir. D. HAGE; publ. daily economic bulletin.

Export Arbitration Board: Jalan Kramat Raya 4-6, Jakarta; Chair. Ir. R. M. SOSROHADIKUSUMO; Vice-Chair. SANUSI.

Gabungan Perusahaan Ekspor Indonesia (*Indonesian Exporters' Federation*): Jalan Kramat Raya 4-6, Jakarta; Pres. NAAFII; Sec. SOFYAN MUNAF.

GINSI (*Importers' Association of Indonesia*): Wisma Nusantara, Jalan Majapahit 1, P.O.B. 2744/JKT, Jakarta Pusat; f. 1956; 2,360 mems.; Chair. ZAHRI ACHMAD; Sec. (acting) Gen. H. ARIF RANI KONO.

Indonesian Timber Association (INDOTA): Gedung Arthaloka, 2nd Floor, Jalan Jenderal Sudirman 2, Jakarta Pusat.

Indonesian Tobacco Association: Jalan Kramat Raya 4-6, Jakarta; Pres. H. A. ISMAIL.

Shippers' Council of Indonesia: Jalan Kramat Raya 4-6, Jakarta; Pres. R. S. PARTOKUSUMO.

STATE TRADING ORGANIZATIONS

General Management Board of the State Trading Corporations (BPU-PNN): Jakarta; f. 1961; Pres. Col. SUHARDIMAN; publ. *Majalah Perekonomian Nasional.*

Anekatambang: Jakarta; government minerals corporation.

P.N. Dharma Niaga Ltd.: Jalan Abdul Muis 6/8/10, P.O.B. 2028, Jakarta; f. 1964; import of technical articles, equipment and plant; factory representatives, repair and after sales service; export.

Perum Perhutani (*State Forestry Corporation*): Jalan Jenderal Gatot Subroto 17-18, P.O.B. 232/KBJ, Jakarta; f. 1972; Pres. Dir. Ir. HARTONG WIRJODARMODJO.

P.T. Tjipta Niaga: Jalan Kalibesar Timur IV/1, P.O.B. 1213/DAK, Jakarta Kota; f. 1964; import and distribution of basic goods, bulk articles, sundries, provisions and drinks, and export of Indonesian produce.

TRADE UNION FEDERATION

Federasi Buruh Seleruh Indonesia (FBSI) (*All Indonesia Labour Federation*): Jalan Tanah Abang III/21, Jakarta; f. 1973; consists of 20 national industrial unions; Chair. AGUS SUDONO; Vice-Chair. SUTANTO MARTOPRASONO.

MAJOR INDUSTRIAL COMPANIES

The following is a selected list of some of the prominent companies in the more important industries currently operating in Indonesia. With a few exceptions, such as oil, rubber and tin, the industrial sector remains in its infancy and at present is composed of a very large number of small enterprises producing mainly consumer goods.

(All addresses in Jakarta except where otherwise stated.)

BICYCLE ASSEMBLY

Bunda Safia: Comador Sudarso 347, Medan.

Firam I.N.I.: Jembatan Lima 48.

CEMENT

P.T. Perkasa Agung: Cibinong, Jakarta.

ELECTRICAL GOODS

Central Electric Wire and Cable: Budiharto Angawijaya 57, Jalan Sukarjo Wiryopranoto.

ENAMEL WARE

Pabriek Emaile Takari: Jalan Prof. Latumeten.

P.T. Sedjati: Jalan Pinangsia 14.

P.T. Sedjati Ltd.: Jalan Pinangsia 14.

Sri Kentjana: Bandengan Utara 93.

FOOD CANNING

Canning Indonesian Products: Pelabuhan, Bali.

Jakti Products: Batu, Malang.

Ong Tjay Bo: Muka Kampanan, Malang.

P.T. PIDO Manufacturing and Trading Company: Jalan Garuda 36; f. 1981; Pres. Dir. J. MAWEIKERE; Chair. Dr. B. P. PAULUS.

FOUNDRIES

P.N. Kerata Api: Perusahaan Jawatan Kereta Api, Jalan Perintis Kermerdekaan 1, Bandung.

P.N. Tambang Timah Banka: Sungeiliat, Banka Island; tin corporation.

P.T. Barata Metalworks and Engineering: Jalan Ngagel 109, Surabaya; f. 1971; foundries, road-building equipment, steel fabrications, machinery and equipment manufacturing and general contracting; Pres. I. SOESENO.

P.T. Dok Dan Perkapalan Surabaya (*Indonesian Navy Dockyard*): Jalan Tanjung Perak Barat 433-435, Surabaya; f. 1910; shipbuilders, ship repairs and offshore platform builders; Pres. Dir. O. M. MARKABAN.

P.T. Krakatau Steel: Cilegon, West Java.

GLASS FACTORIES

The First National Glassware Ltd. P.T.: Jalan Raya Bekasi Km. 21 Pulogadung, Jakarta Timur.

IMPORTERS

P.T. Empat Tunggal Chakrawarti: Jalan K. H. Hasyim Ashari No. 3; f. 1954.

STATE OIL CONCERN

Perusahaan Pertambangan Minyak dan Gas Bumi Negara (PERTAMINA): Jalan Merdeka Timur 1; f. 1957; Pres. Dir. Brig.-Gen. JUDO SUMBONO.

Paint

P.T. Warna Agung (Patna Paint Factory): Gunung Sahar Ancol 3.

Paper Mill

P.N. Letjes: Letjes, Probolinggo, East Java.

Pharmaceuticals

Indonesian Drug House: Jalan Cikini Raya 88, P.O.B. 3339.

Nellco Indophama P.T.: Jalan Kebon Jeruk 18/6, P.O.B. 2805.

P.T. Bintang Tuju: Jalan Jenderal A-Yani.

P.T. Bison: Jalan Kemenangan 1A; f. 1948; Man. Dir. Widjojo Lusli.

P.T. Darya Varia Laboratoria: Cicadas-Gunung Putri, Bogor; Pres. Dr. Wim Kalona.

P.T. Dupa: Jalan H.O.S. Tjokroaminoto 83; f. 1959; Dirs. Drs. E. Looho, Drs. J. Mokoginta.

P.T. Japhar Pharmaceutical Laboratories: Jati Petamburan 11c/30.

P.T. Kemboja: Jalan Kemboja 6.

P.T. Kimia Farma: Jalan Budi Utomo 1, P.O.B. 204/JKT; production units in Jakarta, Bandung, Simongan and Tjg. Morawa.

P.T. Medi Pharma: Jen. Sudirman 276.

P.T. Merck Indonesia: Pasar Rebo, Jakarta; f. 1974.

Raja Pharma: Mojopahit 18.

P.T. Tempo: Jalan Kebon Sirih 45.

Plastics

Golden Star Plastics Company: Jalan Bandangan Utara 2c.

Kantjing Kimia Indonesian Industries: Jalan Jembatan Tiga 2; Pres. Lie Ing Fen.

Pabriek Plastik Mega: Raya Jembatan Lima 84.

Pabriek Plastik Naga Sakhti: Bandangan Utara 52A.

Pioneer Plastics Limited: Jalan Bandangan Utara 43.

Plastik Factory Dewi Mulia: Jalan Raya Barat 524, Bandung.

P.T. Cimone Jaya Chemical Industry: Cimone Km. 2, Tangerang.

P.T. Industri Dinar Makmur: Jalan Palmerah Utara 69-71; Dir. Ichwan Hartono.

P.T. Sinar Panah: Jalan Prof. Dr. Latumeten, Gg. Karung 39; f. 1963; Man. Hendra Widjaja.

Wellex Plastics Limited: Bandangan Utara 91.

Rubber

Hevea Latex Rubber Works: Pekalangan, Tjeribon.

Java Rubber Industrie: Jalan Jakarta 12, Bandung.

Perushaan Sepatu "Bata": Tromol Pos 69, Jakarta Pusat; f. 1931; Pres. Dir. P. Z. Baldik.

P.T. Goodyear Indonesia: Jalan Pedjagalan, Bogor.

P.T. Intirub (*Indonesian Tyre & Rubber Works*): Jalan Cililitan Besar 454, Jakarta Timur.

Textiles

Hoa An Weaving Mill: Kampung Malebar 215, Bandung.

Ling Ling Weaving Mill: Raya Timur 268, Bandung.

P.T. Badan Tekstil Nasional: Jalan Oto Iskandardinata 89, Bandung; textile and garment manufacturers.

P.T. Industrial Sandang I. Senayan: Gedung Baru, Jakarta Selantan.

Tooth Paste

Wisma Usaha: Tjigarelang, Bandung.

Yo Kang Tek: Raya Barat 415, Bandung.

Unilever Indonesia: Jalan Medan Merdeka Barat 1, P.O.B. 162; Chair. Yamani Hasan.

TRANSPORT

RAILWAYS

Perusahaan Jawatan Kereta Api (*State Railways*): Jalan Gereja 1, Bandung; six regional offices; controls 6,877 km. (1978) of track on Java, Madura and Sumatra, of which 55 km. are electrified; Chief Dir. Ir. Pantiarso.

ROADS

Directorate General of Highways: Ministry of Public Works, Jalan Pattimura 20, Kebayoran Baru, P.O.B. 181/KBY, Jakarta; Dir. Gen. Ir. Suryatin.

Total length of roads in 1982 was about 105,000 km., of which 21,095 km. were asphalted. A road development programme was due to start in April 1982 to construct roads and bridges totalling 5,400 km. and to repair 2,500 km. of damaged roads. The project will cost $300 million and is due to be completed in 1986.

SHIPPING

Indonesia has 15 ocean ports, the two major ports being Tanjung Priok, near Jakarta, and Tanjung Perak, near Surabaya. A major development programme for Tanjung Perak port to make it Indonesia's first container terminal was completed in 1979. Container facilities have also been improved at Tanjung Perak and several other ports.

Indonesian National Ship Owners' Association (INSA): Jalan Bungur Besar 54, Jakarta; Pres. S. Boedihardjo.

Jakarta Lloyd P.T. Indonesian National Shipping Line: Jalan Haji Agus Salim 28, Jakarta; f. 1950; services to U.S.A., Europe, Japan, Australia and the Middle East; 14 cargo vessels, 2 semi containers, 3 full containers; Pres. Drs. H. Norman Razak.

Ocean Transport and Trading Ltd.: Speed Building, Jalan Gajah Mada 18, P.O.B. 74/JKWK, Jakarta; owners' representatives for regular worldwide shipping services; Snr. Owners' Rep. R. J. Valk.

P.T. Pelayaran Nasional Indonesia—Pelni Lines: Jalan Angkasa-Kemayoran, Jakarta; State-owned national shipping company; 67 ships.

P.T. Pelayaran Nusantara SRIWIJAYA RAYA: Jalan Tiang Bendera 52, Jakarta Barat; inter-island cargo and passenger services; fleet of 4 cargo and 5 passenger-cargo vessels; Dir. Sjahrul Ghozi Bajumi.

P.T. Perusahaan Pelayaran Samudera—SAMUDERA INDONESIA: Jalan Kali Besar Barat 43, Jakarta Kota; private company.

P.T. Trikora Lloyd: Jalan Malaka 1, P.O.B. 1076/DAK, Jakarta Kota; f. 1964; Pres. and Dir. S. Boedihardjo.

CIVIL AVIATION

The main airports are Halim Airport, Jakarta, Medan Airport, Sumatra and Denpasar Airport, Bali. A new international airport under construction at Cengkareng, near Jakarta, is expected to be completed by 1984.

P.T. Garuda Indonesian Airways: Jalan Ir. H. Juanda 15, Jakarta; f. 1950; government-controlled; operates domestic, regional and international services to Australia, Austria, Hong Kong, India, Japan, Malaysia, Pakistan, The Philippines, Saudi Arabia, Singapore, Sri Lanka, Thailand, France, Federal Republic of Germany, Greece, Italy, Netherlands, the United Kingdom and Switzerland; fleet (1981): 4 Boeing 747, 37 F-28, 24 DC-9, 6 DC-10, 6 Airbus A-300; Pres. Drs. WIWEKO SOEPONO.

P.T. AOA Zamrud Aviation Corporation: Jalan Dr. Wahidin, P.O.B. 56, Denpasar; f. 1969; domestic services and charter flights; 4 DC-3; Pres. UTOJO UTOMO; Dir. DJOEBER AFFANDI.

P.T. Bouraq Indonesia Airlines (BIA): Jalan Angkasa 1, Jakarta; f. 1970; private company; domestic services linking Jakarta with points in Kalimantan, Sulawesi, Maluku and Tawau (Malaysia); 11 HS 748, 3 DC-3, 3 Casa C-212; Pres. J. A. SUMENDAP; Exec. Vice-Pres. G. B. RUNGKAT.

P.T. Bali International Air Service: subsidiary of BIA; charter services; 5 Trislander, 4 BN Islander 2 Cessna 404; Pres. J. A. SUMENDAP; Gen. Man. Capt. SOEJONO.

P.T. Merpati Nusantara Airlines: Jalan Angkasa 2, Jakarta; f. 1962; subsidiary of P.T. Garuda Indonesian Airways; domestic and regional service to Australia, Malaysia and Singapore; 4 Vanguard 953, 5 Viscount 800, 16 F-27, 2 HS 748, 19 Twin Otter, 4 C-212; Pres. R. A. J. LUMENTA; Sec. H. M. IDRUS.

P.T. Sempati Air Transport: Jalan Medan Merdeka, Timur 7, P.O.B. 2068, Jakarta Pusat; f. 1968; subsidiary of P.T. Tri Usaha Bhakti; passenger and cargo services throughout ASEAN countries; 6 Fokker F-27, 1 DC-3; Pres. Capt. DOLF LATUMAHINA.

FOREIGN AIRLINES

The following foreign airlines also serve Indonesia: Aeroflot (U.S.S.R.), Air France, Air India, Air Niugini (Papua New Guinea), Alitalia, British Airways, Cathay Pacific (Hong Kong), ČSA (Czechoslovakia), China Airlines (Taiwan), EgyptAir, JAL (Japan), KLM (Netherlands), Lufthansa (Fed. Repub. of Germany), MAS (Malaysia), Pan Am (U.S.A.), PAL (Philippines), PIA (Pakistan), Qantas (Australia), SAS (Sweden), SIA (Singapore), Swissair, Thai Airways International and UTA (France).

TOURISM

Dewan Pariwisata Indonesia (*Indonesian Council for Tourism*): Jalan Diponegoro 25, Jakarta; f. 1957; private body to promote national and international tourism; Chair. HAMENGKU BUWONO; Vice-Chair. Sri BUDOYO.

ATOMIC ENERGY

National Atomic Energy Agency (*Badan Tenaga Atom Nasional*): Jalan KH. Abdul Rokhim, Kuningan Barat, Mampang Prapatan, P.O.B. 85 KBY, Jakarta Selatan; f. 1958; Dir.-Gen. Prof. Dr. A. BAIQUINI; publs. *Majalah Batan, Atom Indonesia, Bulletin Batan.*

DEFENCE

Armed Forces (1981): Total strength 273,000: army 195,000, navy 52,000, air force 26,000; military service is selective.

Equipment: The army has some British and Soviet equipment, while the navy and air force have Soviet and U.S. equipment.

Defence Expenditure: U.S. $2,390 million (1981).

Commander-in-Chief of the Armed Forces: Gen. ANDI MOHAMMAD JUSUF.

CHIEFS OF STAFF

Army: Gen. PONIMAN.

Navy: Admiral WALUYO SUGITO.

Air Force: Air Marshal ASHADI TJAHJADI.

EDUCATION

Education is mainly controlled by the Ministry of Education and Culture but the Ministry of Religious Affairs also runs *Madrasahs* (Islamic religious schools) at the primary level. General administration of the Ministry, including co-ordination and activities relating to staff assistance, is carried out by the Secretariat-General. Under the Minister four Directorates-General perform executive technical functions in the fields of elementary and secondary education, higher education, out of school education and youth affairs, and cultural development. An Inspectorate-General assists the Minister and supervises other ministerial organs while the Office of Educational and Cultural Research and Development assists similarly in the field of research and development.

The general pattern of education is as follows: elementary education starts from the age of 6 or 7 and lasts for six years. This is followed by three years of junior secondary school education and another three years of senior secondary school education. A further three years of academic level or five years of higher education may follow. Government education expenditure in 1980/81 was 574,637 million rupiahs (10.1 per cent of the national budget).

Primary Education

In the 1960s and 1970s primary education grew considerably: by 1980, 25,500,000 pupils were enrolled, compared with 7,970,000 in 1960. This marked a considerable achievement, though some 10 per cent of pupils drop out of their last year of primary schooling. However, it was expected that free universal education to grade six will be introduced by 1980.

Secondary Education

In the junior high schools 2,721,712 pupils were enrolled in 1977 which represented 27.2 per cent of the school age population of 9,997,378. At the senior high school level 13.8 per cent or 1,246,937 pupils out of a school age population of 9,020,896 were enrolled in 1977. By 1979, there was a total of 3,321,383 pupils at 24,424 general secondary education institutions (including secondary vocational schools).

Technical and Vocational Education

This is the least developed aspect of the educational system but plans have been introduced to establish vocational subjects in the secondary schools. In 1979, there were 304,496 pupils at 928 technological schools.

University Education

The total number of students attending courses in academies and universities in 1980 was 454,000. In 1978, there were 29 state universities and technical institutes and 21 private universities and instutites.

Further Developments

Since 1970 the State examinations have been gradually replaced by schools examinations. The Five-Year Educational Development Plan (1969/70-73/74) aimed to improve the curricula and teaching methods in both primary and secondary schools. New mathematics projects have been introduced and eight comprehensive schools were established on an experimental basis in 1972. By the end of Repelita II, 31,000 new elementary school buildings had been completed and many other school facilities greatly improved. The universities have been allocated increased funds to enable them to develop more rapidly.

BIBLIOGRAPHY

GENERAL

CALDWELL, M. Indonesia (Oxford University Press, 1968).

GRANT, B. Indonesia (Penguin Books, Harmondsworth, 1967).

MCVEY, R. T. (ed.). Indonesia (Human Relations Area Files Inc., New Haven, 1967).

MINTZ, J. Indonesia—A Profile (Princeton University Press, 1961).

HISTORY AND POLITICS

ALLEN, G. C., and DONNITHORNE, A. C. Western Enterprise in Indonesia and Malaya (London, 1957).

ANAK AGUNG GDE AGUNG, I. Twenty Years of Indonesian Foreign Policy 1945–1965 (The Hague, 1973).

ANDERSON, B. R. Java in a Time of Revolution; Occupation and Resistance 1944–1946 (Cornell University Press, Ithaca, N.Y., 1972).

ANDERSON, B. R., and MCVEY, R. T. A Preliminary Analysis of the October 1, 1965 Coup in Indonesia (Cornell University Press, Ithaca, N.Y., 1971).

BRACKMAN, ARNOLD. Indonesian Communism (Praeger, New York, 1963).
The Communist Collapse in Indonesia (New York, 1969).

CALDWELL, MALCOLM. (ed.) Ten Years' Military Terror in Indonesia (Spokesman Books, Nottingham, 1975).

CALDWELL, MALCOLM, and UTRECHT, ERNST. Indonesia: an alternative history (Alternative Publishing Coop., Sydney, 1979).

CROUCH, HAROLD. The Army and Politics in Indonesia (Cornell University Press, Ithaca, N.Y., 1978).

DAHM, BERNARD. History of Indonesia in the Twentieth Century (London, 1970).

DAY, C. The Policy and Administration of the Dutch in Java (Oxford University Press, London, 1967).

EMMERSON, DONALD K. Indonesia's Elite: Political Culture and Cultural Politics (Cornell University Press, Ithaca and London, 1976).

FEITH, H. The Decline of Constitutional Democracy in Indonesia (Cornell University Press, Ithaca, N.Y., 1962).

HOLT, CLAIRE (ed.). Culture and Politics in Indonesia (Cornell University Press, 1972).

HUGHES, J. The End of Sukarno (Angus and Robertson, London, 1968).

JACKSON, KARL D., and PYE, LUCIAN W. (eds.) Political Power and Communication in Indonesia (University of California Press, Berkeley and London, 1978).

LEGGE, J. D. Sukarno—A Political Biography (London 1972).

LEV, DANIEL S. The Transition to Guided Democracy: Indonesian Politics 1957–1958 (Cornell University Press, Ithaca, N.Y., 1966).

MACKIE, J. A. C. Konfrontasi: The Indonesia-Malay Dispute 1963–66 (Oxford University Press, London, 1975).

MAY, BRIAN. The Indonesian Tragedy (Routledge and Kegan Paul, London, 1978).

NICOL, BILL. Timor: The Stillborn Nation (Visa Books, 1979).

OEY HONG LEE. (ed.) Indonesia after the 1971 Elections (Oxford University Press, 1974).

PALMIER, L. H. Indonesia and the Dutch (Oxford University Press, London, 1962).

POLOMKA, P. Indonesia since Sukarno (Penguin Books, Harmondsworth, 1971).

ROEDER, O. G. The Smiling President: President Soeharto of Indonesia (Gunung Agung Ltd., Jakarta, 1969).

SCHILLER, A. A. The Formation of Federal Indonesia (The Hague, 1955).

VLEKKE, B. M. H. Nusantara, A History of Indonesia (W. Van Hoeve Ltd., The Hague and Bandung, 1959).

WEINSTEIN, FRANKLIN B. Indonesian Foreign Policy and the Dilemma of Dependence: From Sukarno to Soeharto (Cornell University Press, Ithaca, N.Y., 1977).

WERTHEIM, W. F. Indonesian Society in Transition (Van Hoeve, The Hague, 1959).

ECONOMICS

AMPO (Japan Asia Quarterly Review). Free Trade Zones and Industrialization of Asia (Pacific-Asia Resources Centre, Tokyo, 1977).

BARTLETT, A. G. et al. PERTAMINA: Indonesian National Oil (Amerasia, Jakarta, Singapore and Tulsa, 1972).

BIRO PUSAT STATISTIK. Statistical Pocketbook of Indonesia (Jakarta, annually).

BULLETIN OF INDONESIAN ECONOMIC STUDIES (Australian National University, three annually).

GEERTZ, C. Agricultural Involution: The Process of Ecological Change in Indonesia (University of California, 1971).

HICKS, G. L., and MCNICOLL, G. The Indonesian Economy, 1950–67—A Bibliography (Yale University Press, New Haven, Conn., 1968).

HIGGINS, B. Indonesia's Economic Stabilization and Development (New York, 1957).

HO KWON PING. "Back to the Drawing Board" in the *Far Eastern Economic Review*, April 27th, 1979).

MORTIMER, R. (ed.) Showcase State: The Illusion of Indonesia's "Accelerated Modernization" (Angus and Robertson, Sydney, 1973).

PALMER, INGRID. The Indonesian Economy since 1965. A Case Study of Political Economy (Frank Cass, London, 1977).

PENNY, D. H. and SINGARIMBUN. Population and Poverty in Rural Java: Some Economic Arithmetic from Sriharjo (Cornell University, 1973).

SACERDOTI, G. "Technocrats in Indonesian balancing act", (*Far Eastern Economic Review*, May 16th, 1980).
"Overdraft of Inefficiency" (*Far Eastern Economic Review*, May 29th, 1981).

SIE KWAT SOEN. Prospects for Agricultural Development in Indonesia (Wageningen, 1968).

Japan

PHYSICAL AND SOCIAL GEOGRAPHY

John Sargent

(Revised by the Editor for this edition)

The Japanese islands lie off the Asian continent in an arc stretching from latitude 45° N. to latitude 35° N., covering a land area of 377,708 square kilometres. The Tsushima Strait, which separates Japan from Korea, is about 190 km. wide, while 800 km. of open sea lie between Japan and the nearest point on the coast of the Chinese mainland.

Four large and closely grouped islands—Hokkaido, Honshu, Shikoku, and Kyushu—constitute 98 per cent of the territory of Japan, the remainder being made up by a large number of smaller islands.

PHYSICAL FEATURES

The Japanese archipelago belongs to a belt of recent mountain building which extends around the rim of the Pacific Ocean, and which is characterized by frequent volcanic activity and crustal movement. Around the fringes of the western Pacific, this belt takes the form of a complex series of island arcs, stretching southwards from the Aleutians and including Japan. In the Japanese islands, the Kurile, Kamchatka, Bonin, Ryukyu, and Korean arcs converge. Where two or more of these major arcs meet, as in Hokkaido and in central Honshu, conspicuous knots of highland occur. In the latter area, the Japan Alps, which rise to over 3,000 metres, form the highest terrain in the country, although the highest single peak, Mount Fuji (3,776 metres), is an extinct volcano unrelated to the fold mountains of the Alps.

Three major zones of active volcanoes and hot springs occur: in Hokkaido, in northern and central Honshu, and in southern Kyushu. Further evidence of crustal instability is provided by the occurrence, each year, of over a thousand earth tremors. Earthquakes strong enough to cause damage to buildings are, however, less frequent, and occur, on average, once every five years.

While the major arcs determine the basic alignment of the main mountain ranges, complex folding and faulting has resulted in an intricate mosaic of landform types, in which rugged, forested mountains alternate with small pockets of intensively cultivated lowland.

In the mountains, short, fast flowing torrents, fed by meltwater in the spring and by heavy rains in the summer, have carved a landscape which is everywhere characterized by steep and sharply angled slopes. Narrow, severely eroded ridges predominate and rounded surfaces are rare. Although the mountain torrents provide many opportunities for the generation of hydroelectric power, marked seasonal changes in precipitation cause wide fluctuations in the rate of flow, and consequently hinder the efficient operation of hydroelectric plant throughout the year.

The extreme scarcity of level land is one of the salient features of the geography of Japan. In a country where the population was the seventh largest in the world in 1980, only 15 per cent of the total land area is cultivable. Thus, the small areas of lowland, which contain not only most of the cultivated land but also all the major concentrations of population and industry, are of vital importance.

Most Japanese lowlands consist of small coastal plains which have been formed through the regular deposition of river-borne alluvium. On encountering the low-lying land of the coastal plain, the typical torrent becomes a sluggish river which meanders across the gently sloping surface of the plain, to terminate in a shallow estuary. The river bed is usually raised above the surface of the surrounding plain, and the braided channel is contained by levees, both man-made and natural. Most alluvial plains are bounded inland by rugged upland, and many are flanked by discontinuous benches of old and poorly consolidated alluvial material. None of the alluvial plains of Japan is extensive: the Kanto, which is the largest, has an area of only 12,800 sq. km. Many plains are merely small pockets of nearly level land, closely hemmed in by the sea and the steeply sloping mountains.

The coastline of Japan is long and intricate. On the Pacific coast, where major faults cut across the prevailing grain of the land, large bays, flanked by relatively extensive alluvial plains, are conspicuous features. Three of these bay-head plains—the Kanto, the Nobi, and the Kansai—contain over a third of the population of the country, and over half of its industrial output. Farther west along the Pacific coast, two narrow channels lead into the sheltered waters of the Inland Sea, which occupies a zone of subsidence between Shikoku and western Honshu. By contrast with the Pacific coasts, the Japan Sea coastline is fairly smooth. The overall insularity of Japan may be indicated by reference to the fact that very few parts of the country are more than 100 km. from the sea.

CLIMATE

While relief conditions in Japan often impose severe limits upon economic activity, climatic conditions are, on the whole, more favourable. Japanese summers are of sufficient warmth and humidity to allow the widespread cultivation of paddy rice; yet cold, dry winters clearly differentiate Japan from those countries of sub-tropical and tropical Asia, where constant heat prohibits prolonged human effort.

The climate of Japan, like the climates of the rest of Monsoon Asia, is characterized by a marked seasonal alternation in the direction of the prevailing winds. In winter, in association with the establishment of a centre of high atmospheric pressure over Siberia, cold dry air masses flow outwards from the continent. During their passage over the Japan Sea, these air masses are warmed in their lower layers, and pick up moisture, which, when the air masses rise on contact with the Japanese coast, is precipitated in the form of snow. Thus, winter weather along the Japan Sea coastlands is dull, cloudy, and characterized by heavy falls of snow. By contrast, the Pacific side of the country experiences cold dry weather, with low amounts of cloud. Near the Pacific coast, winter temperatures are ameliorated by the influence of the warm Kuro Shio sea current.

Besides this contrast between the two sides of the country, a latitudinal variation in temperature, similar to that of the Atlantic seaboard of the United States, is also apparent. Thus, north of latitude 38° N., average January temperatures fall below 0°C. (32°F.), and reach −10°C. (20°F.) in Hokkaido. In this northern zone, winter weather conditions prohibit the double cropping which is elsewhere characteristic of Japanese agriculture. South of latitude 38°N., January temperatures gradually rise, reaching 4°C. (40°F.) at Tokyo, and 6°C. (44°F.) at Kagoshima in southern Kyushu.

After mid-March, the winter pattern of atmospheric circulation begins to change, with high pressure developing over the Aleutians, and low pressure over Siberia. In association with these unstable conditions, the first of the two annual rainfall maxima occurs, with the onset of the Bai-u rains in June. By July, however, the high pressure centre to the east of Japan has fully developed, and, with low pressure prevailing over the continent, a southeasterly flow of warm moist air covers the entire country. On the Pacific coast, August temperatures rise to over 26°C. (80°F.), and the weather becomes unpleasantly hot and humid. To the north, however, August temperatures are lower, reaching only 18°C. (66°F.) in Hokkaido.

In late August and early September, the Pacific high pressure centre begins to weaken, and the second rainfall maximum occurs, with the arrival of typhoons, or tropical cyclones, which travel northwards to Japan from the equatorial regions of the Pacific Ocean. These severe storms, which frequently coincide with the rice harvest, cause widespread damage.

By October, high pressure has again developed over Siberia, and the northwesterly winter monsoon is consequently re-established.

Annual precipitation in Japan varies from 84 cm. (33 in.) in eastern Hokkaido to over 305 cm. (120 in.) in the mountains of central Honshu, and in those parts of the Pacific coast which are fully exposed to the force of the late summer typhoons.

RESOURCES

Although 67 per cent of the total area of Japan is forested, not all of the forest cover is commercially valuable, and large areas of woodland must be preserved to prevent soil erosion. Because many houses are still built of wood, the domestic demand for timber is high, and the home output is supplemented by imports.

In terms of value, and, since 1972, also of volume, the Japanese fish catch is the world's largest. In Japan, fish still supplies a large proportion of the protein content of the average diet, and demand is therefore high. Rich fishing grounds occur in both the Japan Sea and the Pacific to the east of Japan.

Japan is poorly endowed with mineral resources, and industry is heavily dependent upon imported raw materials and fuels. Japan's coal is of poor to medium quality, and seams are thin and badly faulted. The two main coalfields are located towards the extremities of the country, in Hokkaido and in northern Kyushu. In 1979 coal output amounted to only 17.6 million tons. Japanese coal deposits are particularly weak in coking coal, much of which is imported, mainly from the U.S.A. and Australia.

The small Japanese oilfields, which are located in north-east Honshu, supply only 0.3 per cent of the domestic demand. The remaining 99.7 per cent, which now constitutes Japan's biggest import category in terms of value, is shipped mainly from the Middle East.

In 1980 Japanese domestic iron ore production was only 477,000 metric tons. Japan is thus heavily dependent on foreign ores, imported mainly from Australia, Brazil and India.

A wide variety of other minerals is mined, but none exists in large quantities. Japan is self-sufficient only in limestone and sulphur.

POPULATION

The population of Japan in October 1981 was 117,884,000, giving it an average density of over 312 per square kilometre. However, only 15 per cent of the land area is cultivable lowland and the population density in these areas is among the highest in the world.

Three conspicuous urban-industrial concentrations, centred upon Tokyo, Osaka and Nagoya, contain more than a third of the population of Japan. With ten cities containing populations of 1 million and over in 1981, and a further 64 with populations of between 250,000 and 1 million, Japan is by far the most urbanized country in Asia. Tokyo, the capital of Japan and one of the four largest cities in the world, had a population of 8,334,866, Yokohama, with 2,806,523, was the second largest city, followed by Osaka, with 2,635,189, and Nagoya, with 2,089,163. Kyoto, Sapporo, Kobe, Fukuoka, Kitakyushu and Kawasaki also have populations of over 1 million.

In 1867, on the eve of modernization, the population of Japan was already approximately 30 million, a level at which it had stood for the preceding 150 years. With industrialization, population increased rapidly and by 1930 had reached 65 million. After the Second World War, the population policy initiated by the Japanese government succeeded in drastically lowering the rate of population increase, and, since 1954, the growth rate has closely corresponded to the rates prevailing in Western Europe.

Apart from the very small number of Ainu, a people who exhibit certain Caucasian characteristics, the Japanese population has been, since early times, ethnically and linguistically uniform. The racial origins of the Japanese are still obscure, but both Mongolian and southern Pacific strains can be seen in the present-day population.

HISTORY

Richard Storry

(Subsequently revised by Jean-Pierre Lehmann and the Editor)

ANTIQUITY AND THE MIDDLE AGES

It is generally agreed that the ancestors of the Japanese must have been immigrants from the mainland of Asia. It is also claimed that there was probably some migration to Japan from the islands of South-East Asia. But the whole subject is still one of pure conjecture. What does seem undeniable is that the forbears of the dwindling little Ainu communities of Hokkaido once occupied the whole country and were in fact the original inhabitants. Be that as it may, an elaborate mythology surrounds the origins of Japan and the Japanese. This declares, for example, that the country itself was created by the gods, and that the first emperor was a direct descendant, in the fifth generation, of the sun goddess.

Yamato Period

At all events, what seems to have happened is that the invading immigrants from Asia, who no doubt crossed over from Korea, gradually forced their way eastward from Kyushu along the shores of the Inland Sea; until, around the beginning of the Christian era, they found themselves in the fertile Kansai plain (the modern Kyoto-Osaka region). Here, in the Yamato district, they established an ordered society under chieftains who became priest-kings, dedicated to the cult of the Sun.

This early Japanese society was profoundly influenced by the civilizations of Korea and China. The Chinese ideographic script is only one important and very striking example of many cultural importations from or through Korea. Of even greater significance was the introduction of Buddhism in the sixth century A.D. It was at this stage that the existing body of religious practices, associated with sun worship and animism, became known as Shinto, or "The Way of the Gods". Neither the theology of Buddhism nor the ethics of Confucianism (another import from the continent) made Shinto superfluous. Old beliefs existed side by side with the new. And in course of time, as one would expect, Chinese ideas of religion, of morality, of artistic excellence, of good government, of sound agriculture, were adapted to Japanese conditions and thus suffered a degree of change in the process.

Nara and Heian Periods

At the beginning of the eighth century Nara became the capital, being built on the contemporary Chinese model. This was the heyday of the early Buddhist sects in Japan; and the splendid temples surviving at Nara have a particular interest today, since they are the best remaining examples anywhere of Chinese architecture of the Tang period. Nara was meant to be a permanent capital. But this was in fact Heian-kyo, later to be known as Kyoto, founded in 794 and constructed, like Nara, on the model of the Chinese capital. It was to be the home of the Japanese imperial family until 1868. The establishment of this city marks the opening of the Heian age (794–1185), a period remarkable for the artistic sophistication of the court and metropolitan aristocracy.

By the middle of the twelfth century effective power in Kyoto was in the hands of a warrior household, the Taira. Their great rivals were another family, the Minamoto. The strife between the two gave rise to many later epics; and the story of Taira-Minamoto rivalry has never ceased to appeal to the imagination of the Japanese. At first the Taira carried all before them; and Kiyomori, the head of the family, ruled Japan in the emperor's name for a generation. But after his death in 1181 the tables were turned; and in a final battle, in 1185, the Minamoto annihilated their enemies. Thereafter the leader of the Minamoto, Yoritomo, set up a new system of government, known as the *Bakufu* (literally, "camp office"), at Kamakura in the east of the country, far from the imperial capital. The emperor gave Yoritomo the title, *Sei-i Tai Shogun*, or "Barbarian-subduing generalissimo"—usually abbreviated, in Western publications on Japan, as "shogun".

Kamakura Period

The original purpose of Yoritomo's *Bakufu* was the control and administration of the Japanese warrior class, which was now a distinctive entity, and one that was rapidly becoming all-powerful in society. Here was a striking contrast with the situation in China, where the fighting man as such tended to be despised, or at least was held in relatively low esteem by comparison with those who had risen by competitive examination to the peaks of the government service. The Japanese fighting man was already a member of an élite class by the twelfth century. The true rulers of the country from that time forward, to a period well within living memory, would tend nearly always to belong to the warrior class. Not for a moment did this class seek to overthrow the imperial dynasty. The idea was indeed unthinkable, since the emperor's line was descended from the sun goddess. So ceremonious respect was always paid to the Kyoto court; but it was exceptional, and usually a sign of uncharacteristic weakness, for any warrior administration to allow the reality of power to slip back into the hands of the imperial household. Every shogun governed in the emperor's name and received his appointment from the emperor.

The Kamakura *Bakufu* lasted until well into the fourteenth century. Yoritomo was a man of exceptional energy, organizing ability, and ruthlessness, who did not hesitate to pursue a vendetta against his own younger half-brother Yoshitsune, who as a military commander had been chiefly responsible for the ultimate defeat of the Taira. Yoritomo died in 1199. His successors in the office of shogun were leaders of inferior calibre, and the *Bakufu* was run by the house of Hojo, related to the Minamoto by marriage. It was the Hojo who rallied the country in resistance to the Mongol invasions of 1274 and 1281. Japanese martial courage was a vital element in the discomfiture of the invaders; but the decisive factor, both in 1274 and 1281, seems to have been the storms which wrecked the Mongol ships lying off the coast. With some justice the Japanese described the great typhoon of 1281 as a *Kami-kaze*, or "Divine Wind".

Some fifty years later both the Hojo family and the Kamakura *Bakufu* were overthrown in the course of a civil war. The climax occurred in 1331 when, with their enemies overrunning Kamakura, the Hojo and their supporters—more than 800 in all—committed *seppuku*, the formal term for the act of hara-kiri, the warrior's suicide by self-disembowelling.

Muromachi Period

Over the succeeding 250 years and more there was great disorder, including much bitter fighting in and near Kyoto. A new *Bakufu* was established, this time in the Muromachi district of the capital, with members of the Ashikaga house (of the Minamoto line) holding office as shogun. From the fall of Kamakura to the latter half of the sixteenth century political events, so often shaped by domestic warfare, are extremely complicated. They require, however, no elaboration here. It should be noted only that Ashikaga power was on the whole limited, and that this was a period in which, thanks to the troubled times, established families were ruined and new men, leading new warrior households, rose to eminence, often from nothing. However, this period was by no means an unrelieved Dark Age. It was marked not only by civil war but also by economic growth and artistic achievement. For the breakdown of central government gave at least some provincial lords the freedom and incentive to embark on foreign trade on their own account, especially with China. One consequence of this commerce was a substantial importation in the fifteenth century of copper cash from China, which promoted the growth of money instead of rice as a medium for exchange. At the same time painting, classical drama, architecture, landscape gardening, ceramics, the tea ceremony, flower arrangement—a great deal of what is recognized today as Japan's magnificent cultural heritage—blossomed in these stormy years. Here Zen Buddhism, in all its manifestations, played a central part. Japan presented a paradoxical scene of savagery and civilization, of barbarism and beauty, intertwined.

TOKUGAWA RULE

Effective central government and internal peace were not finally secured until the early years of the seventeenth century, after Ieyasu founded the Tokugawa *Bakufu* in Yedo (the modern Tokyo), giving the whole country a domestic order that would endure until the coming of American and European men-of-war in the 1850s. Tokugawa Ieyasu built on the work already performed by two notable captains, Oda Nobunaga (1534–82) and Toyotomi Hideyoshi (1536–98). The former contrived, before his death, to unify about half the provinces of Japan. Hideyoshi, the son of a foot-soldier, was one of Nobunaga's commanders. Within ten years of Nobunaga's death he made himself master of the whole country, with the help of a wise and cautious ally in the shape of Tokugawa Ieyasu. Once Japan was under his control (in the emperor's name, of course) Hideyoshi dispatched a host of warriors against Korea, his ambition being to threaten China itself. This venture was a failure. Korea was devastated but could not be permanently conquered and held.

"The Closed Country"

After Hideyoshi's death Ieyasu lost little time in making his own position supreme. He defeated his most formidable rivals in battle in 1600, and three years later he was appointed shogun by the emperor. The history of Japan in Ashikaga days taught him, no doubt, the lesson that the shogun's government was best conducted, like Yoritomo's regime, well away from Kyoto. At any rate he made Yedo castle the headquarters of his administration.

Ieyasu and his immediate descendants adopted a number of important measures to buttress the dominant position of the Tokugawa house (a branch of the seemingly indestructible Minamoto line). Their basic concern was to make sure that no provincial lord or coalition of lords should ever be able to challenge the *Bakufu*. Careful watch at all times was kept on those lords considered to be unreliable. But a more effective way of controlling all feudatories was the rule, strictly enforced, that they spend part of every year in the shogun's capital at Yedo. It was also decreed that when a lord returned to his own province he must leave his wife and family behind him, in Yedo.

Moreover, the Tokugawa *Bakufu* adopted a policy of severe national isolation. From 1628 only the Chinese and Dutch were allowed in, as traders; and their commerce was confined to the port of Nagasaki, where the handful of Dutch merchants was restricted to the tiny island of Deshima. No other foreigners were granted access. No Japanese was permitted to go abroad. Vessels above a certain tonnage could not be built. The modest foreign trade at Nagasaki was a Tokugawa monopoly, controlled by officials appointed by Yedo.

This situation, of what was called *sakoku* or "the closed country", was in sharp contrast with the state of affairs in the previous century. For when, from 1543 onwards, Portuguese traders and missionaries had begun to appear in Japanese waters they had been received with goodwill. More than this, the Christian missionaries had made considerable headway in south-west Japan, especially in Kyushu. They were nearly all of them Jesuits, picked men, who impressed the Japanese by their high standards of personal conduct, by their sincerity, and by their intellectual capacity. Over the years they made thousands of converts. But both Hideyoshi and Ieyasu came to be suspicious of the new faith, which seemed scarcely compatible with many of Japan's own religious practices. Furthermore, it was perceived that in the Philippines, Spanish missionary endeavour had gone hand-in-hand with Spanish invasion and conquest. Erratic and capricious at first, persecution of Christianity came to be conducted with brutal efficiency as the seventeenth century advanced. Christians refusing to recant faced painful torments and death.

National isolation was not broken until 1853 and 1854, when Commodore Perry's squadron of American warships paid visits to Yedo (now Tokyo) Bay. On his second visit Perry secured *Bakufu* consent to the opening of two ports and the acceptance at a future date of a resident American consul. The door having been forced ajar it was soon widened. Other powers lost no time in following the example of the United States; and a decade after Perry's expedition a community of foreign diplomats and traders had settled on Japanese soil.

While none of Japan's leaders really welcomed this intrusion by the West, some were implacable in their hostility, insisting that the "barbarians" be expelled. Others perceived the weakness of their country and argued that it must come to terms with the situation, learning the techniques of modern Western civilization. Only then would Japan attain the necessary power to hold its own. At the cost of much humiliation—a great deal of pride had to be swallowed—the second, more realistic, course was adopted as the national policy.

THE RISE OF IMPERIAL JAPAN

Modernization followed the domestic transformation known as the Meiji Restoration. The Tokugawa shogunate had lost face from the moment the first concessions were made to Perry and other intruders. Eventually, in 1868, the much weakened *Bakufu* was overthrown by provincial lords from the south-west, acting in concert and impelled by a coalition of their own most vigorous, far-sighted, warrior retainers. The emperor, still in his teens, was persuaded to leave Kyoto for Yedo, which was renamed Tokyo and became the new capital. Nominally, full governing powers were "restored" to the ancient monarchy; but the young emperor, Meiji, reigned rather than governed. Real power was exercised by an oligarchy composed almost entirely of the provincial warriors (all of them young or still in the prime of life) who had engineered the downfall of the shogunate. These men, the Meiji modernizers, dominated Japanese politics, actively or from their retirement, for the best part of fifty years. They pushed their country out of feudalism into the late nineteenth century world of battleships, telegraphs, steam technology, and Great Power politics. The pace of modernization, the abolition of so many cherished customs and privileges inevitably gave acute offence to many conservatives. There was more than one unsuccessful armed rising against the government in the decade following the Restoration of 1868.

On the other hand, the Meiji leaders were equally unsympathetic with those who called for guarantees of human rights and individual liberty, together with popular participation in central and local government. It was a question of priorities. Even when such demands were not considered to be actually subversive they were held to be premature. "A rich country and strong military forces"—this was the slogan of the modernizers in the early years. Factories and blast furnaces must come before freedom and the ballot box.

The heritage of Confucian ethics, with their strong emphasis on loyalty to seniors and superiors, fortified the traditions of Shinto, with its veneration of the imperial house, in sustaining a spirit of harmony and hard work, deeply influencing the great majority of the people. Educational indoctrination played a great part here. The Meiji government founded an impressive structure of schools, colleges, and universities. Primary education was compulsory. All came under the aegis of the state, in one way or another. State schoolmasters were civil servants, and therefore loyal vassals of the emperor. In 1890 the emperor issued his famous *Rescript on Education*, an exhortation commending the nation's fundamental ethical code to all young people. The Rescript, stressing the patriotic virtues of obedience and self-sacrifice, was read aloud in all schools on days of national festival and commemoration.

A Constitution promulgated in 1889, setting up a bicameral parliament, represented a concession by the oligarchy to the growing demand for some kind of national legislative assembly. But the powers of the Diet (as the new parliament was known) were modest. Nevertheless, the party leaders in the Diet soon became a serious irritant to the government.

Wars with China and Russia

Domestic political squabbles, however, were put aside in the face of a crisis with China over Korea, in 1894, which led to a war in which Japan won spectacular victories on land and sea. By the Treaty of Shimonoseki (1895) China surrendered to Japan the island of Formosa and the Liaodong peninsula in South Manzhou (Manchuria), including Lushun (Port Arthur). Within a few days Japan was forced by Russia, Germany and France to waive its claim to the Manzhou prize. A few years later Russia established itself in control of Lushun and its hinterland. Revenge came in 1904, when Japan took the gamble of waging war on Russia. But the Anglo-Japanese Alliance (concluded in 1902) meant that Russia's ally, France, could not intervene unless it was prepared to fight England also. The Russo-Japanese War of 1904–05 was a much more costly affair for Japan in men and material resources than the Sino-Japanese

War ten years earlier. But Japan's victories, including the destruction of the Tzar's Baltic Fleet off Tsushima in May, 1905, were dramatic. Asia in particular was deeply moved by what happened. The hegemony of the white race seemed to be shaken by Russia's defeat in the East.

THE TAISHO ERA

The death of Emperor Meiji in 1912 was decidedly a landmark, the end of a not inglorious chapter. For the Meiji era is Japan's Victorian age, when despite set-backs and disappointments everything seemed to move forward. The new emperor proved to be mentally unstable, and in 1921 his eldest son, Crown Prince Hirohito, became Regent, succeeding to the throne at the end of 1926.

The period 1912–26 is known as the Taisho era, after the title chosen for the reign of Meiji's successor. It is noteworthy for three important developments and one shocking disaster. In the first place, thanks to the World War of 1914–18, the nation's economic power began to swell in dynamic fashion, as the Japanese shipyards, factories, and foundries were overwhelmed with orders from the Allied countries. There were demands, too, from markets in Asia and Africa which could no longer be supplied by British and German exporters. Secondly, as Britain's ally, Japan invaded and occupied Germany's leased territory in Shandong, China. This brought Japan firmly into China's affairs. The temptation to dictate to China could not be resisted, with the result that Chinese dislike and distrust of Japan increased dramatically, souring the relations between the two countries for years to come. Thirdly, Lenin's triumph in Russia gave some impetus to movements of protest created by the contrast in the standards of living between those who had done well out of the war and the poorer sections of the urban working class. Left-wing groups began to obtain a measure of representation in the Diet. But those who called themselves Communists faced continual harassment by the police and were not allowed to form a legal party. Marxism, however, became fashionable in the academic world. In parts of Tokyo, at any rate, the old-fashioned virtues of patriotism and loyalty seemed faintly outmoded; democracy appeared to be coming into vogue.

And then there occurred the disaster. In September 1923 more than half the city of Tokyo and the whole of Yokohama were destroyed in a series of earth tremors and subsequent fires. In recorded history there have been few comparable natural disasters so calamitous in loss of life and destruction of property.

THE PRE-WAR SHOWA PERIOD

After Emperor Taisho's death in 1926 his successor chose as the title for the new reign two Chinese characters, Sho Wa, which can be translated as "Bright Harmony". But the years that followed belied the promise implicit in these words. A prime minister, Hamaguchi, was shot and wounded by a nationalist fanatic in 1930, and died some months later from his injuries. In 1932 another prime minister, Inukai, was assassinated; and in 1936 two former premiers, Saito Makoto and Takahashi Korekiyo, were shot down in their homes by parties of mutinous troops. These and other instances of domestic bloodshed and violence were among the more lurid symptoms of a wave of irrational nationalist hysteria prompted partly by events on the continent of Asia and in part by the economic consequences for Japan of the world depression, which hit the country hard at the beginning of the 1930s. Unrest and dissatisfaction exploded in anger against Diet politicians, wealthy capitalists, and liberal-minded men at the palace and in other influential positions. Public opinion came to regard such figures as weak-kneed, corrupt, and incompetent. The man in uniform, on the other hand, was back in favour, and in power. For in the early autumn of 1931 Japanese forces in South Manzhou carried out a coup against the Chinese in Shenyang (Mukden), and this soon developed into the forcible seizure of all Manzhou.

The army and navy had long enjoyed a key position at the apex of government. For the minister of war and the navy minister were invariably active officers of their respective services. If the army disliked the policy of a cabinet it could usually make its opposition felt by requiring the minister of war to resign. Again, no general on the active list would defy his own service by taking office in a cabinet of which the army disapproved. The same considerations applied to the navy minister. But the army was the more powerful service. During the 1930s indeed it was the single most powerful force shaping the destinies of the country; although the Constitution was never overtly modified, much less overruled.

Expansion in Asia

Condemned by the League of Nations for aggression in Manzhou, Japan left that body in 1933. Manzhou became a puppet state (Manchukuo), an appanage of the empire, only in name more independent than Formosa, or Korea, which had been annexed in 1910. Domination of Manzhou led to involvement in North China; and out of this came undeclared war in the summer of 1937. By the end of that year Japan and China were locked in a combat that would not end until 1945. Chiang Kai-shek resisted with determination, retreating from Nanjing to Wuhan, and then, further up the Changjiang (Yangtze), to Chongqing (Chungking) in the far west. As the war continued, Japan's relations with other powers underwent a change. It drew closer to Nazi Germany and Fascist Italy, eventually joining them in full alliance in September 1940. Increasingly, both the United Kingdom and the U.S.A., powers which supported the Chinese government in Chongqing, were seen as potential enemies. The Soviet Union, with whom Japan always expected to be at war sooner or later, dealt some hard blows when Soviet forces clashed with the Japanese on the Manzhou-Outer Mongolia frontier region in 1939.

In July 1941 Vichy France agreed to the Japanese occupation of bases in the Saigon area—bases in northern French Indochina had been occupied by Japan in the previous year. The move southward seemed a clear threat to both Malaya and the Dutch East Indies. It indicated, too, that for the time being at least Japan was not going to join its ally Germany in the assault on the Soviet Union. There was a quick response by the British Commonwealth, the U.S.A., and the Netherlands, in the form of a virtual embargo on all trade with Japan. This was serious for it meant that oil imports into that country must cease. Japanese-American talks in Washington led nowhere. Inexorably Japan drifted towards armed confrontation with the western imperial powers.

The Sino-Japanese War of 1894–95 and the Russo-Japanese War of 1904–05 had started with surprise attacks by the Japanese navy. In December 1941, Japan followed the same strategy, attacking not only Pearl Harbor in Hawaii but also Hong Kong, Malaya and Singapore.

THE PACIFIC WAR

For the first six months it was victory all the way. Hong Kong, Malaya, Singapore, Java and the Indies, the Philippines, Burma and the Andamans, New Britain and the Solomons—all these fell to Japanese arms.

But there had been a grave miscalculation of the spirit and resources of the nation's principal enemies. Allied submarines, American island-hopping strategy, and superior fire-power turned the tables in Japan. From early summer in 1944 it was defeat all the way—in the Pacific, on the eastern frontier of India, in Burma, in the Philippines, in Okinawa. By mid-summer 1945 the position was desperate. American air raids had inflicted fearful punishment. The merchant fleet, like the battle fleet, had practically ceased to exist. Germany was out of the war. The Soviet Union was an unknown but menacing factor, returning no answer to pleas that Moscow should act as a mediator. The civilian population, exhausted and undernourished, drilled with bamboo spears against the day of invasion, hoping to match the heroism of the *kamikaze* suicide pilots.

The Potsdam Proclamation at the end of July 1945 seemed to leave the government unmoved, although in reality the premier, the aged Admiral Suzuki, was seeking ways and means of ending the war short of abject capitulation. On August 6th the first atomic bomb laid waste Hiroshima. On August 9th the second descended on the suburbs of Nagasaki. Between those dates the Soviet army invaded Manchukuo at several points in great strength.

In this supreme crisis the nation's leaders were divided between those who favoured surrender (with the proviso that the monarchy be maintained) and those who were ready to fight on in spite of everything. It was the emperor, invited to give an unprecedented decision of his own, who tipped the balance by declaring that the Potsdam terms must be accepted.

THE OCCUPATION

U.S. General Douglas MacArthur represented all the Allies in Japan, but the Occupation was nevertheless an almost exclusively American undertaking and to a very great extent MacArthur went his own way, took his own decisions, with or without the agreement of Washington. He rejected the view that the Japanese would be better off without the age-old institution of the monarchy. He felt that the emperor was a stabilizing factor in a society shaken to its roots by the capitulation. Popular regard for the emperor, however, no longer rested on the belief that he partook of divinity because of his descent from the sun goddess. The capitulation—something hardly imagined, even as a nightmare, by most of the people up to August 1945—had shattered the old concept of the state, so intimately bound up with Shinto mythology. When the emperor formally renounced his "divinity" at the beginning of 1946 it created little interest among most Japanese.

In ruling Japan MacArthur acted through the Japanese Government, a procedure that worked smoothly in nearly every instance. Between conquerors and conquered there was indeed a harmony that nobody could have foreseen during the years of warfare. The Japanese, however, can be intensely pragmatic. The events of 1945 seemed to demonstrate that their own way of conducting affairs was inefficient and harmful to themselves. So when the Americans arrived, and once it was clear that their general behaviour was by no means vengeful and oppressive, the Japanese were ready to be their pupils in all manner of activities. During what can be described as the honeymoon period of the Occupation—let us say the first two years—the Americans, exemplifying Democracy triumphant, could do little wrong in the eyes of at least the younger generation in Japan.

Political, Economic and Social Reforms

The watchwords of the Occupation, in the early days especially, were disarmament and democratization. A new Constitution, promulgated in 1946, reflected both these aims. One clause (Article 9) stated that the Japanese people renounced war; and it went on to say that "land, sea, and air forces, as well as other war potential, will never be maintained". A further clause (Article 66) laid down that the prime minister and his cabinet colleagues must be civilians. The other Articles of the Constitution reflected the authentic spirit of North American democracy, with full emphasis on the rights of the individual. Sovereignty of the people was declared. The emperor was made "the symbol of the State and of the unity of the people", and it was affirmed that he derived his position "from the will of the people".

Although undeniably the concoction of American brains, the post-war Constitution captured the imagination of the Japanese. To this day its defenders are sufficiently numerous to make it unlikely that the Constitution will be so radically amended as to change its basic character. Amendment requires the assent of two-thirds of the members of both houses of the Diet, confirmed by a referendum of the people as a whole. So far, conservative governments, wishing to undertake some revision, have been unable to secure the necessary two-thirds majority in the houses of the Diet.

Another measure of profound social and political importance, instigated by MacArthur's headquarters, was the Land Reform. Scores of thousands of tenant farmers were able to obtain ownership of the land they cultivated. Up to the war a depressed class, the farmers of Japan, thanks to the Land Reform, became firm, if not always satisfied, upholders of the political status quo. Left-wing parties found the farming vote difficult to entice. The average farmer, freed from the burden of rent and assured of sales for his crop at guaranteed prices, was not impressed by advocates of collectivization and other projects of agrarian socialism.

The educational system was reformed from top to bottom. In terms alike of organization and syllabus it was reworked to a pattern resembling that of the U.S.A. The famous Rescript, needless to say, was discarded; and there was a thorough revision of school-books concerned with history, political science, and ethics.

These manifold and generally liberating changes were not far short of revolutionary in character. The tentacles of reform also reached out to rectify the position of women, who had so far been deprived of political and many civil rights. The 1920s had witnessed a number of nascent feminist movements which were suppressed in the 1930s. The occupation authorities granted women the right to vote, to divorce, to obtain property rights and equal access to education and the professions. Article 14 of the new Constitution proclaimed that "All the people are equal under the law and there shall be no discrimination in political, economic or social relations because of race, creed, sex, social status or family origin". However, the degree to which constitutional theory has been put into practice with regard to the equality of the sexes is another matter.

Political freedom gave the parties of the Left an opportunity to exploit the changes that had occurred, and to make them even more far-reaching. But except for the period between May 1947 and March 1948, when a coalition cabinet under the socialist Katayama was in office, electoral success always attended the conservative parties. Until the end of 1954 the political scene was dominated by Yoshida Shigeru; and even after his retirement the old man was influential, as adviser to successive cabinets, up to his death in 1967.

Consolidation of Relations with the West

As the international situation hardened into the Cold War the attitude of MacArthur's headquarters underwent a subtle but definite change. The emphasis shifted from reform to rehabilitation; and whereas at first the Japanese Left were looked upon as a progressive, liberating force this point of view was no longer fashionable among MacArthur's entourage after about 1947. In particular, as the armies of Mao began to gain ground in China, and as it became clear that American influence on the Chinese mainland might soon be eliminated, the importance of Japan as part of the free world was perceived with growing clarity. After the Korean War broke out in the summer of 1950 it seemed all the more desirable, and in fact urgent, to nourish the revival of Japan. In other words Japan was now regarded not as a recent enemy but rather as a new friend and junior ally. In these circumstances the disarmament clause of the Constitution appeared as an embarrassment. In practice, however, it was to be blandly ignored. The first steps in rearmament were taken in 1950, after war had started in Korea, when MacArthur authorized the Yoshida cabinet to recruit gendarmerie (the National Police Reserve) of 75,000 men.

The Occupation lasted up to the end of April 1952. This was much longer than had been planned. For soon after his basic reforms had been introduced, MacArthur had decided that the situation called for a treaty of peace. When he was dismissed by President Truman in 1951 the Japanese feared that progress towards a peace treaty would be checked. However, in September 1951 the treaty was concluded between Japan and 48 nations (but not the Soviet Union) at San Francisco. It was a magnanimous settlement, free from punitive clauses, although Japan's territorial losses were confirmed. On the same day a bilateral security pact was signed by Japan and the United States. In this Japan asked the U.S.A. to retain their forces in and around the Japanese islands as a defence against outside attack. When all the signatories of the San Francisco Treaty had ratified the document, it came into force; and in the spring of 1952 Japan became once again formally an independent state.

DEMOCRATIC JAPAN—"ECONOMICS BEFORE POLITICS"

The story since 1952 has been one of astonishing material success, bringing solid practical benefits to the Japanese people in terms of the comfort and enjoyment of their daily lives. The speed and extent of this economic leap forward was something that few had predicted, even after it was clear that the Korean War was going to put industry on its feet again. The problems facing the country in the early 1950s seemed too great to encourage much optimism about the future. The population, after all, was approaching the figure of 100 million. The China market was lost and so was the market in Korea. The Soviet Union had put a stop to nearly all Japanese fishing in the seas between Hokkaido and Kamchatka—where the richest harvest of salmon and crab was garnered before the war, for both home consumption and the export trade. Above all, the nation was very poorly endowed with natural resources. It seemed logical to expect that recovery, although real, would be fairly modest.

But a number of factors worked in Japan's favour. During the post-war years, for example, the importance of primary products, of raw materials, declined—thanks to the development of synthetic products. New discoveries, in various parts of the world, of oil and iron ore helped to create a buyer's market. Thus, the loss of access to the high-grade coal and ore of Manzhou and North China was less vexatious than had been feared.

Nevertheless, these and other factors would have been of minor significance had they not been intelligently utilized. The real secret of the country's success lay elsewhere. It may be summed up in the words of Yoshida Shigeru, written shortly before his death.

> It was the diligence, initiative, and creative ability of the Japanese people that enabled them to exploit the advantages offered. The precept "God helps those who help themselves" was certainly valid for post-war Japan. The economic rehabilitation and advance of Japan was due less to political factors than to hard toil and good fortune.
>
> *Japan's Decisive Century:* 1867–1967 (Praeger, New York, 1967).

Fundamentally, it was "hard toil" by a literate and, indeed, technologically well-educated population which made Japan a world leader in shipbuilding, the world's third greatest producer of steel (with a production exceeding that of the United Kingdom, France and Western Germany combined), and a striking example of *speed* in economic growth which other industrial societies have so far failed to emulate.

Since independence it has been government policy (in Tokyo's own words) "to give priority to economics over politics". For instance, in foreign affairs the close association with the U.S.A. has been sustained; and a revised security pact was concluded and ratified in 1960 against shrill and determined popular criticism expressed in repeated street demonstrations on a massive scale. Yet there has been a refusal, quite firm and consistent, to adopt more positive measures. Japan has rejected the idea that it should join any regional defence organization. Although a conscientious member of the United Nations, it has declined to participate in any active peace-keeping role by contributing a detachment—or even observers—to a UN military force. No doubt to the disappointment of Washington, the Japanese never considered for a moment that they might follow South Korea's example and send a contingent to Viet-Nam. The fact is that such a display of national power would be political suicide. The conservative cabinets—of the *Jiyu-Minshuto* (Liberal-Democratic) party—maintained their political ascendancy through the 1950s, 1960s and 1970s on the strength of their remarkable success in running the economy. The recollection of what total war meant to them has not faded from the consciousness of the Japanese, although a new generation has reached maturity since 1945. Although Japan is now a well-armed state, at least in conventional non-nuclear weapons, the distaste for militarism is still deep enough, and the pacifism symbolized by Article 9 still strong enough, to turn the voters against a government which became involved in any commitment beyond the country's own shores.

If Japan had a definable, short-term, foreign policy goal it was to regain possession of the southern Kuriles, captured by the Soviet Union in 1945. The Ryukyu Islands, including Okinawa, were returned to Japanese sovereignty by the U.S.A. in May 1972.

The same emphasis in internal political affairs, namely priority of economics over politics, was given expression in foreign policy. Japan sought to ensure secure access to sources of much needed raw materials, especially petroleum, and to develop markets for its manufactured products. Japan's international trade grew phenominally and, especially in South-East Asia, its economic presence was felt. Not all relations, however, could be maintained at a purely economic level. The problem of relations with Korea was a highly sensitive one; this was due partly to the existence of two mutually antagonistic Korean states, partly to Japan's colonial legacy in that country and partly to what can only be described as popular reciprocal suspicion and hostility. By the late 1960s a normalization of relations between Japan and South Korea was achieved; economic ties between the two are considerable, but political tensions remain.

Another complex issue was that of China. The Chinese people suffered most under the excesses of Japanese expansionism during the Second World War. Under strong pressure from the Americans, however, the Yoshida cabinet in 1951 had agreed to recognize Chiang Kai-shek's Government in Taiwan. Certainly Japan's economic ties with Taiwan became very strong. The China question, however, was both economic and political. It was economic in that, as China's industrialization gathered speed, Japanese businessmen realized the potential of the Chinese market and the possible complementarity of the two economies. It was also, however, an emotional issue for many Japanese: these sentiments combined guilt for the past and fascination for the present developments. Especially after China's first atom bomb explosion in 1964—not a welcome event for the Japanese—it was also recognized that China was becoming a world power. For Japan to be at loggerheads with its huge neighbour was both dangerous and stupid. Some formula had to be found to get Japan out of this diplomatic impasse.

In 1964 Japan was host-country for the Olympic Games and in 1970 the first world exhibition held in Asia opened at Osaka; both successes seemed to epitomize Japan's remarkable economic miracle. Yet at the same time pollution of the environment, by industry and its products (especially the motor-car), became the main topic of public interest. The people of Japan showed signs of dissatisfaction with the frustrations and dangers that technology had produced.

The Sato government's victory at the polls in 1969 was due in great part, no doubt, to satisfaction at the agreement reached with the U.S.A. on Okinawa. But the conservatives' success also reflected the growing public revulsion against the extreme left-wing student violence that disturbed universities and colleges in all parts of Japan during 1968 and 1969. The traditional relationship between teachers and students, deriving ultimately from Confucian ethics, incurred much damage.

In the summer of 1972 Eisaku Sato resigned, having held the office of Prime Minister for a longer period than any of his predecessors. To succeed him the ruling Liberal-Democratic Party (L.D.P.) voted into office Kakuei Tanaka, Minister of Trade and Industry, a largely self-made man, noted for his dynamic political style. This was soon confirmed by his visit to Beijing in September 1972, an event of great historic importance; it involved not only the recognition of the People's Government of China as the only legitimate government of China, but also the termination of Japan's diplomatic links with the Chinese Nationalist Government in Taiwan. Moreover, both sides at Beijing declared their intention to negotiate a Sino-Japanese Treaty of Friendship.

Japan's new China policy was hailed with enthusiasm by nearly all political groups in Japan. Great interest was also aroused by a plan, *The Remodelling of the Japanese Archipelago*, which, it was widely believed, would form the basis of the Government's domestic policies. One of the major proposals was the movement of industry to less developed parts of the country.

The success of his visit to China and the interest in his domestic plans were among the factors believed to have influenced Mr. Tanaka to decide on an early dissolution of the House of Representatives. The House was dissolved in November 1972 and elections held in the following month. The L.D.P. was returned to power, though with a reduced majority. Important gains were made by left-wing parties, including Communist victories in all six districts of Osaka.

Early in 1973 Mr. Tanaka attempted to introduce a reform of the electoral system but an Opposition boycott forced him to abandon the proposal. By the autumn the Government's popularity had greatly diminished. Mr. Tanaka had been unable to check Japan's rampant inflation (consumer prices rose 12 per cent in the year to August 1973) and he was blamed for the rush of speculative activities which followed publication of his plans for relocating industry. Following the death of the Finance Minister, Kiichi Aichi, in November, Mr. Tanaka carried out an extensive Cabinet reshuffle to tide Japan over "the most difficult time in our post-war economic history".

This was a reference to a series of events late in 1973, when Japan's rapid economic growth, sustained over more than 20 years, became seriously threatened. Following the Middle East war in October, the governments of Arab oil-producing countries agreed to reduce the output of crude petroleum as a means of putting pressure on countries supporting Israel. The oil cutback exposed Japan's vulnerability to outside pressures, due to the country's dependence on imported raw materials. In December the Deputy Prime Minister made a three-week tour of eight Middle East countries, with the hope of developing closer ties. Nevertheless, more stringent legislation was introduced to control energy consumption.

Following the 10 per cent devaluation of the U.S. dollar in February 1973, the Japanese yen (valued at 308 per dollar since December 1971) was allowed to "float" and immediately showed an appreciation of about 14 per cent against U.S. currency. A rate of around 265 yen per dollar was maintained until November 1973, when the oil crisis threatened the Japanese economy. The yen was effectively devalued three times in November and again in January 1974. However, from 1975 the Japanese economy strongly recovered and by July 1977 the exchange rate was again 265 yen per U.S. dollar, rising further to 176 yen per U.S. dollar in October 1978. The yen subsequently weakened and by early 1980 the exchange rate was about 250 yen per dollar. In early 1981 the currency recovered to about 200 yen per dollar but by July 1982 the rate had fallen to 259 yen, the lowest level since September 1977.

Meanwhile, Japan continued to pursue its aim of gaining greater recognition as a world power. In September 1972 it was reported that the Japanese Government was to make a bid for a permanent seat on the United Nations Security Council.

In 1973 the Prime Minister and other officials visited France, the United Kingdom, the Federal Republic of Germany and the Soviet Union. The Soviet visit produced a joint communiqué which included agreement to resume in 1974 the deadlocked negotiations for the conclusion of a peace treaty. The main stumbling block to the signing of this treaty has been the Soviet occupation of the northern Kurile Islands. Relations with Moscow thus remain lukewarm, despite provisional agreements on joint efforts to develop Soviet oil and gas fields. Japan's relations with China were further strengthened in December 1973, when a three-year trade agreement was initialled. The Prime Minister then visited South-East Asia in January 1974. This tour was marked by hostile demonstrations, notably in Thailand and Indonesia, directed against Japan's economic penetration of the region.

What some commentators interpreted as a turning-point in Japan's post-war politics took place in July 1974, when the House of Councillors' election occurred. This Upper House election is held every three years, for half the seats in the House. The July election reduced the overall majority of the Liberal-Democratic Party in the House from 26 to 7. This blow to the government party's position harmed Premier Tanaka's standing in the country, and this was undermined further when the Prime Minister came under strong criticism as a result of allegations that he had used irregular means to amass his personal fortune. A political storm blew up, and late in November Mr. Tanaka announced his intention to resign. His successor, appointed early in December, was Takeo Miki, the former Deputy Prime Minister.

Miki seemed to be a popular choice. He had the reputation of being rather to the left of his party, and he was not associated in the public eye with "money power". The standing of the L.D.P. was severely damaged in February 1976 by allegations of leading politicians' and businessmen's involvement in a financial scandal concerning massive bribes accepted from the Lockheed Aircraft Corporation, a leading U.S. aerospace company. In July Kakuei Tanaka was arrested on charges concerning the "Lockheed scandal".

A split developed within the L.D.P., and by September Miki was under considerable pressure from within the Party to resign. In November 1976 Takeo Fukuda resigned from the post of Deputy Prime

Minister, in order to launch his campaign against Miki. In December 1976 the political trend against the Liberal-Democratic Party was confirmed by the results of the general election, when L.D.P. seats in the Lower House were reduced from 265 to 249. Miki resigned, and was replaced as Prime Minister by Takeo Fukuda.

In the Upper House election of July 1977 the L.D.P. lost its majority, emerging with only 124 of the 252 seats. The Japan Socialist Party and the Communist Party also lost ground, while the Komeito Party made significant gains.

In the mid-1970s Japan maintained a position of virtual balance, if not immobility, *vis-à-vis* its powerful neighbours, China and the Soviet Union. No progress was made towards an agreement with the latter on the northern islands' question (Southern Kuriles, Shikotan and Habomai) and, with the build-up of Soviet forces on the Southern Kurile islands of Etorufu and Kunashiri in 1979, a solution seemed even more remote. In early 1981 Soviet anger was incurred by several demonstrations in Japan to campaign for the return of the Southern Kurile Islands and by the proclamation of February 4th as "Day of the Northern Territories". However, in August 1978, after six years of talks and in the face of strong criticism from the U.S.S.R., Japan signed a treaty of peace and friendship with the People's Republic of China.

The Liberal-Democratic Party presidential election of November 1978 was contested by four candidates. Voting was no longer restricted to members of the Diet and party officials, but for the first time was extended to the 1.5 million members of the Party. Takeo Fukuda was unexpectedly defeated in the primary election by the L.D.P. Secretary-General, Masayoshi Ohira, who polled 42 per cent of the votes, compared with Fukuda's 36 per cent. Fukuda was obliged to step down in favour of Ohira, whose success was widely attributed to support received from Kakuei Tanaka's faction. Ohira was subsequently appointed Prime Minister, and a new Cabinet was formed.

In the local elections held in April 1979, the L.D.P. won all 15 governorships at stake, including that of Tokyo which had been held by Dr. Ryokichi Minobe, jointly sponsored by the Socialist and Communist parties, for 12 years. This resounding victory led Ohira to call an early general election in October. The over-confident ruling party, however, was in for a rude shock. For the first time since 1955 the L.D.P. failed to achieve an overall majority. Ohira's rivals blamed him for this severe setback and called upon him to resign.

Ohira, however, remained in office and, with the scholarly and dynamic Dr. Saburo Okita (appointed Minister of Foreign Affairs in November), sought to enhance Japan's influence in world affairs. In the summer of 1979 Tokyo was the venue for the Seven World Powers' summit conference. Most popular Japanese attention was focused on Margaret Thatcher, it still being inconceivable in Japan for a lady to become head of government. Japan has been severely affected by the more traumatic recent political events, namely the "Islamic revolution" in Iran and the Soviet invasion of Afghanistan. The U.S. administration of Jimmy Carter sought to put great pressure on Japan to increase markedly its defence expenditure (at present 0.9 per cent of G.N.P., which the U.S.A. would like to see rise to 1.5 per cent) and to join the U.S.A. in economic sanctions against Iran and to boycott the Moscow Olympics. Japan has acceded to both latter requests, though without much enthusiasm, especially in regard to Iran, a country of great economic significance for Japan and in January 1981, Japan announced the lifting of the economic sanctions, although normal trade relations were not expected until the ending of the Iran-Iraq war.

There were renewed demands by the U.S.A. in 1981 for Japan to increase its defence spending and the Government also came under pressure from the Socialists, who accused it of building up Japan's military defence machine at the expense of social welfare. The 9.7 per cent increase in defence spending, originally agreed with the U.S.A., was subsequently reduced to 7.6 per cent. In April Japan announced its intention to achieve the goals of its 1977 defence build-up programme by 1987 at the latest.

In economic terms, Japan reacted far more positively to the 1978 oil crisis than had been the case following the 1973 crisis. Economic growth remains in the area of 6 per cent per annum and the forecasts are, on the whole, reasonably optimistic. The country's dependence on imported petroleum, the deficit which this has incurred in its balance of payments and the consequent low value of the yen, however, have created tensions with the U.S.A. and Western Europe; Japanese manufactured goods continue to penetrate the Western economies, with certain areas—the automobile industry in the U.S.A. and the United Kingdom, for example—seemingly threatened. The government is seeking to attenuate the trade imbalance by more direct overseas investments. In April 1981 the Prime Minister visited Western Europe on the first official tour by a Japanese Premier since 1973. The talks centred largely on proposals for limiting Japanese car sales to Europe, as Japan had voluntarily done with the U.S.A. However, no definite agreement was reached.

If in the pre-war era Japan's politics were characterized by constant turmoil, the post-war scene has been a generally placid one. Suddenly, however, on May 17th, 1980, events took a fairly dramatic turn. The Japan Socialist Party called for a motion of no-confidence in the Ohira Government. This was earlier perceived as mere ritual; to general astonishment, including that of the Prime Minister, the motion was carried. This was due to the fact that 69 L.D.P. members of the Diet, but belonging to anti-Ohira factions, had abstained. The Prime Minister, according to the Constitution, had the choice either to offer the resignation of his government or to dissolve the House; he chose the latter course. Elections were set for June 22nd and the Upper House, which in any case was due for the election of half its members on

June 29th, now also had to face the polls on the same day.

Pundits predicted heavy losses for the L.D.P. There was talk of a possible coalition government, the L.D.P. joining forces with the more moderate opposition parties, namely the Komeito and the Japan Democratic Socialist Party. In the meantime, the opposition parties were also looking for the possibility of an anti-L.D.P. alliance. In any case, the L.D.P.'s epitaph was being written, prematurely, as it happened. Ohira had suffered what was described as a mild heart attack, as a result of which it was announced that he would not participate directly in the campaigns, nor would he attend the Venice summit conference. On June 12th, however, Ohira died. He was the first Japanese prime minister to die in office since the assassination of Tsunayoshi Inukai by young army officers on May 15th, 1932.

The elections of June 22nd provided a resounding victory for the L.D.P. The party increased the number of its seats in the Lower House from 248 to 284, giving it the largest majority since 1969. The New Liberal Club, a splinter group from the L.D.P. but in basic alliance with it, gained eight seats, an increase from four to 12. If one adds the seats won by the L.D.P. with those of the New Liberal Club and the pro-L.D.P. Independents, the Government enjoys a most comfortable majority, with 305 seats out of 511. The Japan Socialist Party remained static at 107 seats, while heavy losses were incurred by the Communist Party (39 to 29 seats) and the Komeito (57 to 33), and a small decline by the Democratic Socialist Party (35 to 32).

The L.D.P. victory can be attributed to a number of factors: a sympathy vote for the late Prime Minister, the continued disarray of the opposition parties, the Japanese population's conservative instincts, justified by the government's able management of the economy, the uncertainty of the world political situation encouraging caution at home. On July 15th Zenko Suzuki, a relatively unknown middle-of-the-road conservative, was elected President of the L.D.P. He succeeded Ohira as Prime Minister when Parliament was convened a week later. Suzuki emerged as a compromise choice to avoid open confrontation between the ambitious leaders of warring factions within the Party. In terms of both internal and external affairs, assuming the absence of any cataclysmic world event, no major departure from current trends was expected.

In 1981 a number of developments put severe strains on relations with Washington. The main factor involved a joint communiqué issued after the Prime Minister's summit meeting in Washington with President Reagan. The main contention was the wording of a phrase calling for the strengthening of the "alliance" between the two countries. This was widely interpreted in Japan as a commitment to greater military co-operation. The Foreign Minister, Masayoshi Ito, resigned to take responsibility for the row, but Mr. Suzuki's personal credibility appeared to suffer because, as was pointed out, it was unprecedented for a Prime Minister to find fault with a joint communiqué after signing it.

In the wake of this, a former U.S. Ambassador to Japan claimed that, in 1960, the Japanese Government had verbally agreed that American warships could call at Japanese ports and pass through Japanese territorial waters with nuclear weapons, without unloading them. This caused great uproar as the Government had always assured the public that, under Japan's post-war anti-nuclear policy, U.S. ships were prohibited from carrying nuclear weapons in Japanese waters.

Economic tensions with the U.S.A. and the EEC also became heightened, owing to the continued growth of Japanese exports and restrictive tariffs covering imports. Japan voluntarily agreed to limit car sales to the U.S.A. and was seeking ways to ease the trade gap with the EEC. In November Suzuki carried out a major reshuffle of the Cabinet, distributing major posts among the five feuding L.D.P. factions.

ECONOMIC SURVEY

Hisao Kanamori

Japan has a total area of 377,708 square kilometres and had a population of 117,884,000 in October 1981. The population density is high, at 312 persons per square kilometre. Much of the land is mountainous; 67 per cent of the total area is forested, 15 per cent is cultivated and 1 per cent is wilderness. The proportion of cultivated land to total area is very low compared with many European countries. As Japan has few natural resources it must rely for its growth on importing fuel, raw materials and food and on exporting manufactured goods.

The Meiji Restoration in 1868 began Japan's transformation from a feudal society into a modern industrialized state. The changes experienced in Japan in the succeeding century were enormous. The Japanese economy grew by approximately 3.3 per cent a year over the period from the Meiji Restoration to the start of the Second World War and was one of the fastest growing economies in the world. By the 1930s Japan had become a major world exporter of industrial goods and a major importer of raw materials.

The economy suffered drastically from the effects of the Second World War. Immediately following Japan's surrender in 1945, mining and manufacturing output fell to only 31 per cent of its pre-war level. The subsequent recovery, however, was rapid. Between 1960 and 1970 the economy grew at an average annual rate of 10 per cent. The growth rate fell in 1974, due to the effects of the oil crisis, but by 1981 the Gross National Product (G.N.P.) had increased to about

U.S. $1,127,000 million, with per caput G.N.P. at $9,577 (cf. $12,730 in the U.S.A.).

The principal reasons for Japan's high growth rates are as follows:

1. during the U.S. military occupation after the Japanese surrender, agricultural land reform, the dissolution of the *zaibatsu* (large financial combines) and the organization of a modern trade union system were carried out;

2. the high investment: capital spending accounted for as much as 20 per cent of the G.N.P. in the 1960s;

3. the high rate of savings: personal savings exceeded 20 per cent of net incomes in the 1960s and 1970s;

4. Japan adopted new industrial techniques from the U.S.A.;

5. Japan had the highest level of education in the world after the U.S.A. with 38 per cent of the population in the pertinent age group enrolled in universities and 93 per cent of children enrolled in high schools in 1977;

6. stable industrial relations, due to the common interest existing between management and workers caused partly by Japan's unique system of life-long employment within one firm;

7. the positive lending policy of financial institutions: the ratio of net worth to total capital in manufacturing was only 17.3 per cent in 1975, compared with 53 per cent in the U.S.A. and 33 per cent in the Federal Republic of Germany;

8. the low rate of defence expenditure: 0.9 per cent of the G.N.P. in 1980;

9. world peace: so that Japan was able to import raw materials and fuels at low prices and to expand its exports;

10. the stable political situation: with conservative political parties in power for most of the time since the Second World War there has been little disruptive social unrest or political confrontation.

GROSS NATIONAL PRODUCT

Japan's G.N.P. reached an estimated $1,127,000 million in 1981 and is the second largest in the non-communist world, after the U.S.A. The most important sector of the economy is manufacturing, which contributed about 30 per cent of Japan's total output in 1980. However, its share in the G.N.P. has fallen since reaching its peak of 36 per cent in 1970. The share of banking, insurance and services has been increasing and reached 59 per cent; thus, Japan may be said to be entering a post-industrial society. The share of agriculture in the total national product has been falling rapidly but is still higher, at 3.8 per cent, than in the U.S.A., the United Kingdom and the Federal Republic of Germany.

A striking feature of Gross National Expenditure (*see* Table 1) is the high percentage of investment in plant and equipment during the 1960s. The percentage of capital investment, however, fell in the 1970s to only 14 per cent in 1981. Low consumption and high capital expenditure are major reasons for the rapid growth of the Japanese economy and there is an opinion in some quarters that the recently declining rate of capital investment indicates the end of Japan's impressive record of growth. However, this decline in capital investment could be attributable to a period of recession within the general economic cycle.

Prior to 1979 government fixed capital formation was tending to increase. This was the result of government policies designed to raise such capital formation in order to recover from the delay in the formation of social overhead capital caused by the rapid industrial development of the 1960s. The percentage, however, has declined since 1979 due to the government's difficulty in raising the necessary funds. The percentage of investment in housing, which was lower than in many other countries, is now rising. Exports rose due to the stagnation of domestic demand after the oil crisis and imports also increased due to rising crude petroleum prices.

Table 1

GROSS NATIONAL EXPENDITURE
(percentage distribution)

	1965	1975	1981
Private consumption expenditure	58	58	58
General government consumption expenditure	9	10	10
Private equipment investment	16	16	15
Private housing investment	6	7	6
Government fixed capital formation	9	9	10
Increase in stocks	2	0	0
Exports, etc.	11	14	17
Less Imports, etc.	10	14	16

The distribution of national income can be seen below:

Table 2

NATIONAL INCOME
(percentage distribution)

	1965	1970	1980
Employees' income	55	54	68
Income from property	9	9	14
Income from enterprises	36	38	23
Less Income from property due to non-commercial activity	0	1	4

The rise in the income of employees from 56 per cent of the national income in 1965 to 68 per cent in 1980 reflects a decrease in the number of farmers and unincorporated enterprises and an increase in the number of employees. On the other hand, the income of enterprises fell sharply due to the recession. The income from property increased thanks to a rise in interest income.

AGRICULTURE, FORESTRY AND FISHING

Agriculture

Until the end of the Second World War approximately half of Japan's cultivated land was owned by landlords to whom the tenants paid rent in kind. In the post-war land reform absentee landlords were forbidden to own land and the holding of resident landlords was limited to one hectare. As a result, 95 per cent of the total cultivated land area came into the possession of owner-farmers. This wide-ranging land reform contributed greatly to increased agricultural production after the war but the resulting fragmentation of holdings is a deterrent to extensive modernization. In 1981 Japan's agricultural labour force totalled 5.6 million. There were 4.5 million farms, of which 70 per cent were less than one hectare. Twenty-two per cent were between one and two hectares and only 8 per cent were more than two hectares (with the exception of Hokkaido).

Japanese agriculture is characterized by labour-intensive farming. The number of people employed in agriculture is 142 per 100 hectares (compared to 19 in the Federal Republic of Germany, 9 in the U.K. and 1 in the U.S.A.). Nevertheless, only 13 per cent of farmers are exclusively engaged in farming; the rest combine farming with employment in other industries.

The most important crop is rice, which contributed 34 per cent to total agricultural output in 1979. A large variety of other crops such as wheat, sweet potatoes, potatoes, soybeans, radishes, cabbages, mandarin oranges, apples, persimmons, pears etc. are also grown. Japan produces 72 per cent of its food requirements. Under the Staple Food Management Law the producer price of rice is set by the Government every year; this is an issue of great political significance. Since the price is usually advantageous to growers, rice is usually overproduced and the Government is trying to decrease production in favour of other products.

Forestry

Sixty-seven per cent of Japan's total land area is forested. Nevertheless, 56 per cent of domestic timber requirements had to be imported in 1980 and timber was the largest import item after petroleum and coal. There is a large variety of trees including cedar, Japanese cypress, pine, Japanese oak and beech.

Fishing

Japan's 1980 catch was 11.1 million metric tons (including aquatic plants), accounting for 14.7 per cent of the world total. The establishment by most nations after 1976 of fishing zones extending 200 nautical miles (370 km.) offshore had a profound effect on the Japanese fishing industry as about 40 per cent of its catch came from within the 200-mile limits of these countries. Japan's catch in the 200-mile fishing zones of other countries fell to 27 per cent in 1977.

INDUSTRY

Mining

Japan's mineral resources are rich in variety but meagre in quantity. While the domestic output of limestone, sulphur etc. is sufficient to meet domestic demand, all of Japan's requirements of bauxite, crude petroleum and iron ore, 94 per cent of its requirements of copper ore and 98 per cent of coking coal had to be met by imports in 1980.

Manufacturing

In 1981 there were 13.9 million, that is approximately 25 per cent of the total labour force, employed in manufacturing. Industrial production is concentrated in four regions, Tokyo-Yokohama, Osaka-Kobe, Nagoya and northern Kyushu, which together produce 47 per cent of Japan's total manufacturing output. In 1981 Japan was the world's major producer of ships, the largest producer of passenger cars and the second largest producer of synthetic fibres, paper, cement, synthetic resins and steel. As a whole Japan ranks second in the world, after the U.S.A., in industrial production.

It can be seen from Table 3 that Japanese industry is undergoing a structural change. Textiles have become markedly less important whereas the machine-building industry is gaining in importance.

Table 3

COMPOSITION OF MANUFACTURING

(percentage distribution of value-added)

	1965	1980
Foodstuffs	10.0	9.3
Textiles	8.0	4.2
Timber and timber products	3.3	2.3
Paper and pulp	3.5	2.7
Printing and publishing	4.9	5.1
Chemicals	10.6	8.5
Ceramics	4.7	5.0
Steel	6.5	7.4
Non-ferrous metals	2.5	2.8
Metal products	5.9	6.3
General machinery	9.2	10.5
Electrical machinery	9.1	12.2
Transport equipment	9.7	9.4
Precision instruments	1.7	2.0
Others	10.4	12.3

Transport Equipment. This is the most important industry in Japan, accounting for 9.4 per cent of total industrial output in 1980. The industry consists of two sectors: car manufacturing, which is a growing industry, and shipbuilding, which is a declining industry.

Japan ranks first in the world in the production of passenger cars, with an output of 7 million in 1981, and first in its production of buses and lorries. There are nine major passenger car manufacturers in Japan continuously competing for larger shares in the world market. Fifty-four per cent of the 1981 output was exported and the U.S.A. is the largest customer for Japanese cars, taking 38 per cent in 1981. Exports to Saudi Arabia, South-East Asia and Africa are growing. Domestic demand is growing rapidly, with 59 per cent of Japanese families owning cars. Japan's automotive industry is the most competitive of its industries, and continued to earn high profits through expanding exports even after the outbreak of the oil crisis. The increase in exports of Japanese motor vehicles is attributed to their superior quality, good after-service and a larger world demand for small cars which have a low fuel consumption. This sharp increase in the volume of Japanese car exports, however, has given rise to trade frictions with EEC countries and with the U.S.A. and in 1981 Japan voluntarily reduced its automobile exports to the U.S.A.

Traditionally Japan's shipbuilding industry has had an outstanding competitive strength in the international market. In 1975 it produced 18 million gross tons of ships and accounted for about 50 per cent of the total world output. Eighty per cent of Japan's output was exported. However, since the oil crisis in 1973 orders from abroad have been decreasing due to a sharp fall in the world demand for oil tankers, and several Japanese shipyards have been forced to close. In addition the shipbuilding industries of South Korea and Taiwan have become more competitive and are now rivalling Japan's low production costs as Japan was earlier able to do against its European counterparts. In 1978 the Japanese shipbuilding industry attempted to cut production costs by scrapping 35 per cent of its equipment and by laying off large numbers of its work force. Consequently its production dropped to 4.3 million tons in 1979. However, the industry has passed through the worst of the crisis and production recovered to 7.3 million tons in 1980.

General and Electrical Machinery. Machinery production has grown rapidly because of an expanding domestic demand resulting from the country's rapid economic growth. Until 1973 only a small percentage of output was exported but with the stagnation of domestic demand, manufacturers began to place emphasis on exports, which had risen to more than 40 per cent of the total output by 1977. Japan also produces heavy electrical machines, domestic electrical appliances and electronics apparatus. All are growing industries but the electronics industry is growing at a much faster pace and is strongly competitive on the world market for goods such as video recorders, television sets, radios, tape recorders, stereo sets, calculators and computers.

Precision instruments. The camera industry has played a central role in this sector but recently the growth of the watch-making industry has been spectacular, with the output of watches in Japan surpassing that of Switzerland in and after 1977.

Iron and Steel. Although Japan has only small deposits of iron ore and coal, it is the second largest producer of iron and steel in the world and the biggest exporter, accounting for 30 per cent of total world exports. This was achieved because of the advanced nature of the industry but, as demand for iron and steel dwindled after the oil crisis, the industry has been suffering from an excessive production capacity. Production of crude steel dropped from 120 million tons in 1973 to 102 million in 1981 although production capacity is about 160 million tons. Approximately one-third of output is exported, the largest proportion to the U.S.A. However, now that the U.S.A. is moving towards restricting imports of iron and steel from Japan, hopes are being placed on the Chinese market. Exports to the People's Republic of China are expected to exceed shipments to the U.S.A. in the future. Iron ore is imported from Australia, Brazil and India and coal from Australia, the U.S.A. and Canada.

Chemicals. Traditionally the principal products within the chemical industry have been chemical fertilizers such as ammonium sulphate but recently, petrochemical products have grown in importance. The petrochemical industry is now in a difficult position due to rising petroleum prices and a declining demand for petrochemical products, and Japanese firms are attempting to build plants in Iran, Singapore and Saudi Arabia.

Textiles. The textile industry was the first industry to develop in Japan. Until the 1920s raw silk was Japan's principal export but exports have decreased rapidly even though Japan's production of raw silk in 1980 comprised 24 per cent of total world output. Since 1966 Japan has been importing raw silk. The cotton industry was also a major industry in pre-war Japan but, with the development of synthetic fibres and the growth of the cotton industry in China, India, Hong Kong and South Korea, Japan's production and exports have become stagnant. On the other hand, the synthetic fibres industry, producing nylon and polyester, has grown. Output in 1980 was 1.4 million tons and Japan contributes 13 per cent to total world production, ranking second after the U.S.A. But even this industry is stagnating due to low demand and competition from South Korea.

Ceramics. The principal products are tableware, tiles and porcelain insulators. Thirty per cent of output is exported, chiefly to the U.S.A.

BALANCE OF PAYMENTS

The structure of Japan's balance of payments is characterized by a trade account surplus and an invisible trade account deficit; also since 1965 the long-term capital account has registered excessive outflows. Japan's overall balance of payments has been in surplus since 1969 due to the export competitiveness of its products, which has been aided by the fact that the value of the yen was maintained at 360 to the U.S. dollar from 1949 until 1971 in spite of the rapid growth of the economy. The yen was revalued in December 1971 and then allowed to float in February 1973. While the balance of payments registered a deficit in 1974 and 1975, growing surpluses were recorded in 1976, 1977 and 1978, thus bringing about a sharp rise in the yen's exchange value. In 1979 and 1980 the current-account balance of international payments registered a deficit, owing to a sharp rise in petroleum prices. In 1981, however, it swung back to a surplus of $4,700 million.

Foreign Trade

Japan's rate of dependence on foreign trade (the ratio of foreign trade to G.N.P.) is low, at 17.2 per cent for exports and 16.5 per cent for imports in 1981, compared with those of major European countries, which are around 20 per cent. This may be ascribed to the facts that Japan is geographically remote from other countries and that there is a large domestic market. Even though the rate is low, foreign trade is very important in the Japanese economy because it depends on imports for the supply of the greater part of its major raw material and fuel requirements.

Japan's exports in 1981 totalled U.S. $152,030 million. Before the Second World War the principal export items were raw silk, green tea, cotton fabrics, ceramics, toys etc., but the development of heavy industry in Japan has brought about a vast change in the composition of its exports. Exports of passenger cars, iron and steel and ships are by far the largest by value. Until 1977 iron and steel was the principal export but in that year it was overtaken by passenger car exports. Other important exports include radios, cameras, synthetic fibre fabrics, television sets, motorcycles, engines, office appliances, machine tools, plastics, video recorders, tape recorders, watches, etc.

In 1981 Japan's imports totalled U.S. $143,290 million, the principal item being petroleum, which accounted for 37 per cent of the total by value. About 80 per cent of Japan's petroleum imports come from the Middle East, a fact which has prompted the Government to develop nuclear energy and to diversify the source of its petroleum imports in order to obtain more security. Other major imports are coal, timber, iron ore, non-ferrous ores, wheat, soybeans (soya beans), sugar, cotton, meat, maize and wool.

The U.S.A. is Japan's principal trading partner although its importance is declining. In 1981 Japanese exports to the U.S.A. totalled $38,609 million, 25 per cent of the total, and imports from the U.S.A. totalled $25,297 million or 18 per cent of the total. In 1981 exports to the Federal Republic of Germany, Saudi Arabia, South Korea, Taiwan, Hong Kong and the People's Republic of China were also considerable. In recent years more of Japan's imports have come from the Middle East due to the rising cost of petroleum; the second largest exporter to Japan in 1981 was Saudi Arabia with a total of $21,482 million. Others included Indonesia, the United Arab Emirates, Australia, the People's Republic of China and Canada. In recent years there has been concern in the U.S.A. and Europe over the low ratio of Japanese manufactured imports and its high ratio of manufactured exports. In spite of the appreciation of the yen's exchange value, exports continued to rise sharply through the first half of 1978, thus adding to trade frictions with Western countries. The Japanese government therefore requested business enterprises to exercise self-restraint in their exports of motor cars, motor cycles, duplicating machines, watches, cameras, iron and steel, television sets, ships, etc. In the second half of 1978, the growth of exports levelled off as the appreciation of the yen's exchange value began to take effect. As regards imports, the U.S.A. strongly requested Japan to expand its import quota of agricultural products, to reduce tariffs on electronic computers and to expand the limit on government-procured goods. In 1981 Japan registered a $13,300 million trade surplus with regard to the U.S.A. and one of about $10,300 million with regard to the EEC.

Invisible Trade

The deficit of $13,700 million in Japan's invisible trade balance in 1981 can be attributed to large deficits in freightage, patent fees, tourism, and to the expenses of overseas branch offices. The long-term capital balance showed an excess of payments over receipts reaching $6,500 million in 1981. Direct investment abroad can be categorized into those aimed at obtaining natural resources such as iron ore and coal, those designed to locate industries in South Korea, Taiwan and Hong Kong, and those connected with establishing branch offices of banks, trading firms or hotels abroad. Of total Japanese long-term investment, direct investment accounted for $4,900 million and securities investment for $8,800 million.

LABOUR AND LIVING STANDARDS

Labour

Post-war Japan was faced with considerable unemployment due to the economic depression resulting from its military defeat and to the increase in labour supply following the evacuation of its former colonies and demobilization. But with the upsurge in economic growth the demand for labour increased, resulting in a serious shortage in the 1960s. As a result the average wage rose by 10 per cent a year in the early 1960s and by the even higher rate of 15 per cent in the late 1960s and labour began to move from the rural villages to the cities. A number of small businesses, which had relied on cheap labour, became bankrupt due to rising wage costs. However, after 1974 the problem of unemployment re-emerged as the rate of economic growth slowed. Nevertheless, compared with Western countries the unemployment rate is low (2.2 per cent in 1981) due to the Japanese practice of retaining employees even in times of depression.

In 1981 Japan's labour force totalled 57.1 million or 48 per cent of the population. Of the working population 10 per cent are engaged in agriculture, forestry and fishing, 35 per cent in mining, construction and manufacturing and 55 per cent in the service industries. Sixty-one per cent of the labour force are male and thirty-nine per cent are female. Some 73 per cent of the working population are employees, a figure which is rising rapidly. Trade unions are usually organized enterprise by enterprise and these form federations by industries. The federations, in turn, are organized into larger groupings; typical of which are *Sohyo*, which had a membership of 4.6 million and *Domei*, with a membership of 2.2 million in 1981. Thirty-one per cent of employed workers are members of trade unions. Important characteristics of the Japanese employment system are the enterprise trade union system and the importance attached to length of service within one firm.

Standard of Living

The standard of living in Japan is quite high. In 1981 the average monthly income before tax of a worker's household (3.8 persons per household) was $1,665. The rate of savings (the percentage of savings in the disposable income) is high at 21 per cent so that the average monthly expenditure per household is only $1,366. According to a 1976 OECD survey, incomes are the most evenly distributed in the world after Sweden, Norway and Australia.

Life expectancy in Japan is the highest in the world at 73 years for men and 79 years for women in 1980. Educational attainment is also high with the proportion of those enrolled in universities at 38 per cent. Durable consumer goods are remarkably widespread; in 1981, 99 per cent of households possessed colour television sets, refrigerators and washing machines. One of the less developed aspects of Japanese society is housing. Because of the concentration of population into urban areas, land prices have risen markedly, thus slowing down house building. Another major cause for concern is pollution of the environment. As pollution became more widespread in the late 1960s various legislative measures were taken, which have resulted in an improvement in the situation.

Another serious problem has been the rise in consumer prices. Between 1965 and 1972 they rose by an annual average rate of 5.5 per cent due to increases in service charges resulting from rising wages and increases in prices for agricultural products. The rate of increase accelerated between 1973 and 1975, due to the impact of the oil crisis, reaching a peak of 24 per cent in 1974. The rise subsequently slowed to 3.8 per cent in 1978 and 3.6 per cent in 1979. In 1980, however, prices rose again by 8 per cent, due to increased petroleum prices, but in 1981 they became stable, rising by only 4.9 per cent.

FINANCIAL, MONETARY AND ECONOMIC POLICIES

Government expenditure accounts for about 20 per cent of the Gross National Product, a figure which is not high in comparison with that of other countries as there is little government expenditure on defence and social security. Taxes are also low, amounting to only 24 per cent of the national income. Of the total, direct taxes such as personal income tax and corporation tax account for 67 per cent and indirect tax 31 per cent in 1981. The budget was more or less balanced until 1964 but then government expenditure increased, exceeding revenue. Public bonds were therefore issued. After the oil crisis, while government revenue decreased due to the recession, expenditure was increased in order to stimulate the economy. This brought about a sharp issuance of public bonds; the share of public bonds in the general account therefore rose sharply to reach 32 per cent in 1978 and 40 per cent in 1979. It is a major policy goal for the Government to reduce the percentage of public bonds and this was lowered to 21 per cent in the 1981 budget.

A conspicuous feature of the present Japanese economy is that, while private enterprise has extremely modern equipment, public utilities such as roads, hospitals, schools and sewerage are undeveloped. Also, insufficient measures have been taken to combat pollution. In future more government funds are to be applied to public works and social programmes. The Government, however, is having difficulty in putting this into practice, due to its budget deficit.

Monetary Policies

The central bank, the Bank of Japan, is responsible for basic monetary policies such as changes in the official discount rate and the reserve rate. It also issues bank notes, makes loans to other banks, discounts bills and purchases and sells bonds. Other banks wholly financed by the Government include the Japan Development Bank, the Export-Import Bank of Japan, the Small Business Finance Corporation, the People's Finance Corporation and the Agriculture, Forestry and Fisheries Finance Corporation. There are 76 private commercial banks and numerous banking facilities for small businesses.

One characteristic of Japan's monetary policy is that the commercial banks receive large loans from the Bank of Japan, while private enterprise, in its turn, borrows heavily from the commercial banks. In 1980 the percentage of owned capital in private enterprise was only 17 per cent compared with a figure of 83 per cent for borrowed capital. The reasons for the low percentage of owned capital are that businesses expanded so rapidly that they could not procure enough funds through internal capital accumulation alone; that sufficient capital could not be raised through shares because the capital market was undeveloped and that the tax system was such that it is more profitable for firms to borrow from banks than to try to raise funds by issuing stocks. This heavy dependence on borrowed capital is one of the reasons why private enterprise is so liable to instability during any period of flux. On the other hand, this increases the efficacy of monetary policies established by the Bank of Japan. Such policies are chiefly effected through changes in the official discount rate. The Bank of Japan also purchases or sells bonds and changes the reserve rate or limits the level of loans to be made by commercial banks as part of is monetary policy.

Implementation of Economic Policies

In Japan economic affairs are conducted on the principle of a free economy. Adjustments of business trends and economic growth rates are made mainly through financial and monetary policies. There is the view that the State interferes with private enterprise to so great an extent that the two are incorporated into one body: "Japan, Inc.", but this is incorrect. It cannot be denied, however, that the Government has an unusual way of intervening in the national economy. One example is that, since the Second World War, the State has formulated medium-term economic plans, ranging from five to ten years in length, and has used these plans as the basis for managing the national economy. The plans have never been compulsory as far as the private sector is concerned, but a great many entrepreneurs, trade union officials, consumer representatives, economists etc., as well as civil servants, have been involved in formulating them so that a common view has emerged on the management of the economy as a whole. Another example is administrative guidance. When the Government judges that an industry is investing too heavily in capital equipment, or over-producing, exporting too much, or overpricing, it can often persuade firms to follow its intentions without having recourse to law. An example of this is the Bank of Japan's ability to limit the level of loans given by commercial banks.

THE ECONOMY AFTER THE OIL CRISIS

As mentioned previously, Japan depends on imports for almost all of its petroleum requirements, and as there are few domestic sources of energy the nation relies on imports for 88 per cent of its total energy needs. As a result, the economy was seriously affected by the crisis which was triggered by the oil embargo imposed by OPEC countries in October 1973. There were fears that the oil crisis might affect the Japanese economy in the following three ways: (1) it might become impossible to accomplish further growth due to a shortage of oil supplies; (2) rising oil prices might increase domestic prices for goods and services; (3) an increase in the import bill might put the balance of payments into deficit. In fact, as can be seen from the table below, in 1974 the G.N.P. was reduced, prices rose sharply and the balance of payments registered a huge deficit. However, by 1976 the shock had been absorbed to a considerable degree; the rate of inflation has slowed and the balance of payments is in surplus. These may be attributed to the fact that demand for petroleum decreased due to its higher price and the worldwide recession on the one hand, while the supply of petroleum increased on the other; that an inflationary spiral of wage-price increases was avoided as demand declined due to the recession and trade unions became more moderate in their demands; and that exports of passenger cars, colour television sets and industrial machinery increased to offset the increase in petroleum imports.

In 1978 the economic growth rate was 5.5 per cent, the highest rate of any OECD country. Consumer prices increased by only 3.4 per cent, the lowest rate in the world after the Federal Republic of Germany and the U.S.A. The current balance of payments registered a huge surplus of $16,534 million, the biggest surplus of any OECD country and the largest in the world after that of Saudi Arabia. In 1980 consumer prices rose sharply and the current balance of payments swung into deficit due to the second oil crisis. In 1981, however, prices stabilized and the current balance is recovering. It is therefore safe to say that the Japanese economy has overcome the effects of the oil crisis fairly well.

However, two problems remain. First, even though after 1976 the economy had a growth rate of more than 5 per cent a year, this is still considered low when compared with the growth potential of the Japanese economy. With the continued recession private enterprise is still suffering from low profits and low capacity utilization (80 per cent) and unemployment is increasing. Many industries, including the aluminium, petrochemical, shipbuilding, textile and plywood industries, have been particularly badly affected by the rising oil prices, sharply decreased demand and the rapid development of the developing countries. Secondly, Japan is being criticized by the rest of the world, especially the U.S.A., on the ground that it has aggravated the unfavourable balance of payments of other countries by registering excessively large balance of payments surpluses. In addition the Japanese yen appreciated sharply in the foreign exchange markets from 293 to the U.S. dollar in early 1977 to 176 to the U.S. dollar in October 1978 This abrupt rise decreased the profitability of the nation's export industry.

As a result, the Government adopted policies to expand public capital expenditure substantially in fiscal 1978 in order to stimulate the economy and to reduce the balance of payments surplus. The Government set the rate of increase in government fixed capital formation at 16 per cent in real terms and increased bond issues to finance its capital expenditure programme. At the same time the official discount rate was reduced from 9 per cent in late 1973 to 3.5 per cent in March 1978. Thanks to these measures, the economy began to improve in the latter half of 1978, and in early 1979 there was a recovery of corporate profits, a decline in the unemployment rate and a reduction in the balance of payments surplus. This shows the capacity of the Japanese economy to adapt to different circumstances. However, the growth rate of the economy dropped to 2–3 per cent in 1980 and 1981, owing to the oil crisis of 1979.

THE FUTURE OF THE JAPANESE ECONOMY

It is considered that the future economy of Japan will differ from the present one in the following ways: the rate of increase in the labour force will fall from 1.2 per cent to less than 1 per cent; the percentage of people over the age of 65 years will increase; private capital expenditure will decline; there will be increasing uncertainty over energy supplies and resistance against an increase in Japanese exports will become stronger throughout the world.

Taking all these points into consideration the Government adopted, in 1979, a new Seven-Year Economic Plan which was designed to serve as a guide for public and private economic activity by setting forth the future outlook of the economy. The Plan gave priority to an increase in the rate of self-sufficiency in energy through the development of nuclear power, aimed at an expansion of the social security system and, lastly, envisaged increases in taxes and social security contributions. It set the average annual growth rate of the economy at 5.5 per cent for the period 1980–85. This target was revised in January 1982 to 5.1 per cent annually for fiscal years 1981–85. This is low when compared with past growth rates but does indicate that the Government aims to achieve the highest growth rate among the advanced nations of the world. The Government also made public in 1982 a long-term economic outlook which forecast the nation's real economic growth rate up to the year 2000 at about 4 per cent annually.

Table 4

(fiscal years, i.e. 12 months beginning April 1st of the year stated)

	1974	1975	1976	1977	1978	1979	1980
Rate of economic growth (real, %)	0.0	3.2	5.9	5.8	5.7	6.1	5.1
Rate of increase in consumer prices (%)	21.8	10.4	9.4	8.1	3.4	4.8	7.8
Current balance of payments (U.S. $ '000 million)	−2.3	0.1	4.7	14.0	12.0	−13.9	−7.3

Table 5

JAPANESE ECONOMIC OUTLINE IN FISCAL YEAR 1985

Items	Fiscal 1980	Fiscal 1985 (Projected)	Average Annual Growth, 1980–85
G.N.P. ('000 million yen at 1978 prices)	210,700 (1981)	282,900	5.1%
National income ('000 million yen)	166,000	300,000	about 9%
Mining and industrial production (annual increase)	4.6%	n.a.	about 5.2%
Public investment ('000 million yen at 1978 prices, incl. land compensation costs)	about 190,000 in FY1979–85		
Social security transfers (as percentages of national income)	12.8%	about 14½ %	—
Social security contributions (,,)	9.3%	about 11%	—
Tax burden (,,)	23.4%	about 26½%	—
Government balance ('000 million yen)	−14,100	−10,000	—
Increase in consumer prices	7.8%	n.a.	about 5%
Increase in wholesale prices	13.3%	n.a.	about 4%
Unemployment rate	2.1%	about 1.7%	—
Propensity to consume	80.5%	about 80%	—

STATISTICAL SURVEY

AREA AND POPULATION

Area		Population ('000) at October 1st*		
		Total	Male	Female
377,708.09 square kilometres	1975†	111,940	55,091	56,849
	1977	114,154	56,199	57,956
	1978	115,174	56,704	58,470
	1979	116,133	57,180	58,953
	1980‡	117,060	57,594	59,467
	1981	117,884	58,002	59,882

* Excluding foreign military and diplomatic personnel and their dependants.
† Final result of 1975 census.
‡ Final result of 1980 census.

PRINCIPAL CITIES*
(population at October 1st, 1981)

City	Population	City	Population	City	Population
Tokyo (capital)†	8,334,866	Himeji	448,111	Takamatsu	318,815
Yokohama	2,806,523	Yokosuka	424,077	Toyohashi	308,776
Osaka	2,635,189	Kanazawa	419,971	Fujisawa	306,982
Nagoya	2,089,163	Nishinomiya	410,413	Toyama	306,866
Kyoto	1,476,956	Gifu	410,399	Nara	305,210
Sapporo	1,433,355	Matsudo	408,226	Kochi	302,524
Kobe	1,375,006	Matsuyama	407,969	Machida	300,060
Fukuoka (Hukuoka)	1,104,483	Kurashiki	406,633	Naha	296,982
Kitakyushu	1,065,038	Wakayama	405,329	Koriyama	289,770
Kawasaki	1,045,244	Toyonaka	403,969	Aomori	289,329
Hiroshima	910,768	Hachioji	394,232	Akita	287,791
Sakai	815,291	Kawaguchi	386,633	Toyota	285,160
Chiba	755,729	Utsunomiya	383,246	Yao	273,106
Sendai	645,331	Ichikawa	372,498	Miyazaki	268,786
Okayama	550,767	Oita	368,079	Shimonoseki	268,630
Kumamoto	532,590	Urawa	363,041	Maebashi	267,845
Higashiosaka	522,359	Hirakata	360,830	Okazaki	267,540
Amagasaki	519,141	Omiya	357,687	Fukushima	264,213
Kagoshima	510,882	Asahikawa	353,255	Kawagoe	263,380
Hamamatsu	496,073	Fukuyama	349,160	Akashi	258,640
Funabashi	487,808	Iwaki	343,677	Yokkaichi	257,131
Niigata	462,445	Takatsuki	340,508	Neyagawa	256,453
Shizuoka	459,392	Suita	338,389	Ichinomiya	254,611
Sagamihara	449,815	Nagano	326,472	Sasebo	251,717
Nagasaki	449,321	Hakodate	319,244	Tokushima	251,032

* Except for Tokyo, the data for each city refer to an urban county (*shi*), an administrative division which may include some scattered or rural population as well as an urban centre.
† The figure refers to the 23 wards (*ku*) of Tokyo. The population of Tokyo-to (Tokyo Prefecture) was 11,634,927.

BIRTHS, MARRIAGES AND DEATHS

	Births	Birth Rate (per 1,000)	Marriages	Marriage Rate (per 1,000)	Deaths	Death Rate (per 1,000)
1975	1,901,440	17.1	941,628	8.5	702,275	6.3
1976	1,832,617	16.3	871,543	7.8	703,270	6.3
1977	1,755,100	15.5	821,029	7.2	690,074	6.1
1978	1,708,643	14.9	793,257	6.9	695,821	6.1
1979	1,642,580	14.2	788,505	6.8	689,664	6.0
1980	1,576,889	13.6	774,702	6.7	722,801	6.2

EMPLOYMENT

(annual averages, '000 persons aged 15 and over)

	1978	1979	1980	1981
Agriculture and forestry	5,890	5,680	5,320	5,100
Fishery and aquatic culture	440	450	450	470
Mining	150	120	110	100
Construction	5,200	5,360	5,480	5,440
Manufacturing	13,260	13,330	13,670	13,850
Wholesaling, retailing, finance, insurance and real estate	13,900	14,130	14,390	14,740
Transport, communications and public utility	3,740	3,820	3,800	4,070
Services	9,430	9,800	10,010	10,300
Government service	1,970	2,010	1,990	1,940
TOTAL IN EMPLOYMENT (incl. others)	54,080	54,790	55,360	55,810
Unemployed	1,240	1,170	1,140	1,260
TOTAL LABOUR FORCE	55,320	55,960	56,500	57,070

AGRICULTURE

LAND USE

('000 hectares)

	1973	1976	1979
Arable land	4,584	4,415	4,315
Land under permanent crops	632	615	592
Permanent meadows and pastures	431	506	567
Forests and woodland	25,043	25,011	25,011
Other land	6,413	6,556	6,618
Inland water	128	128	128
TOTAL AREA	37,231	37,231	37,231

Source: FAO, *Production Yearbook.*

PRINCIPAL CROPS†

('000 metric tons)

	1976	1977	1978	1979	1980
Rice (brown)*	11,772	13,095	12,589	11,958	9,751
Barley	170	167	276	347	332
Wheat	222	236	367	541	583
Potatoes	3,742	3,520	3,316	3,381	3,345
Sweet potatoes	1,279	1,431	1,371	1,360	1,317
Silk cocoons	88	79	78	81	73
Soybeans (Soya beans)	110	111	190	192	174
Tobacco	176	173	172	153	141

* To obtain the equivalent in paddy rice, the conversion factor is 150 kg. of brown rice equals 186.6 kg. of paddy.

† Data at harvest time.

1981 ('000 metric tons): Barley 330; Wheat 587.

LIVESTOCK

('000 head)

	1977	1978	1979	1980	1981
Cattle	3,875	4,009	4,150	4,248	4,385
Sheep	11	11	12	12	16
Goats	82	79	71	67	62
Horses	31	25	22	n.a.	24
Pigs	8,132	8,780	9,491	9,998	10,065
Chickens	263,882	281,448	291,845	n.a.	295,968

LIVESTOCK PRODUCTS

(metric tons)

	1977	1978	1979	1980	1981
Beef and veal	361,175	403,340	401,685	418,062	470,734
Pig meat	1,169,465	1,284,473	1,475,005	1 429 927	1,395,614
Poultry meat	1,092,838	1,239,339	1,419,032	1,365,433	1,395,114
Cows' milk	5,734,988	6,116,615	6,462,822	6,504,457	6,619,749
Butter*	54,091	62,188	69,421	64,052	63,621
Cheese*	60,654	66,375	67,420	65,949	71,078
Hen eggs	1,882,774	1,965,416	1,990,924	1,999,143	1,999,091
Raw silk	16,083	15,957	15,949	16,156	14,820

***Industrial production only (i.e. butter and cheese manufactured at milk plants), excluding farm production.**

FORESTRY

INDUSTRIAL ROUNDWOOD

('000 cubic metres)

	1976	1977	1978	1979	1980
Sawn timber	21,378	20,526	20,482	21,461	20,953
Pulp	2,856	2,504	1,986	1,852	2,144
Pit props	340	369	373	335	329
Veneer sheets and plywood	659	658	597	603	514
Others	10,038	9,736	8,707	9,019	10,111
TOTAL	35,271	33,793	32,145	33,270	34,051

Source: Ministry of Agriculture, Forestry and Fisheries, *Report on Demand and Supply of Lumber.*

FISHING

('000 metric tons, live weight)

	1976	1977	1978	1979	1980
Freshwater fishes	95.7	99.0	106.6	105.8	105.2
Chum salmon (Keta or Dog salmon)	78.4	71.9	74.1	101.5	96.9
Flounders, halibuts, soles, etc.	352.2	286.9	313.8	288.9	288.9
Alaska pollack	2,445.4	1,927.6	1,546.2	1,551.1	1,552.4
Pacific sandlance	224.3	137.2	99.1	110.5	201.2
Atka mackerel	229.2	235.0	135.7	118.9	117.4
Pacific saury (Skipper)	105.4	253.5	360.2	278.0	187.2
Japanese jack mackerel	128.4	88.2	58.8	84.2	56.2
Japanese scad	79.0	98.3	95.1	101.2	91.3
Japanese amberjack	101.6	114.9	121.6	154.9	149.3
Japanese pilchard (sardine)	1,065.7	1,420.5	1,637.4	1,740.2	2,197.7
Japanese anchovy	216.7	244.9	152.4	134.6	150.6
Skipjack tuna (Oceanic skipjack)	331.1	309.4	369.5	329.9	354.1
Albacore	108.7	53.2	84.1	67.3	69.6
Yellowfin tuna	85.1	86.0	106.1	100.3	109.1
Bigeye tuna	114.3	134.5	126.4	125.1	128.1
Chub mackerel	978.8	1,354.5	1,625.9	1,491.0	1,301.0
Other fish (incl. unspecified)	1,829.5	1,755.9	1,680.7	1,608.2	1,640.2
TOTAL FISH	8,569.5	8,671.6	8,693.6	8,491.4	8,796.5
Crustaceans	136.0	142.8	171.0	179.0	165.9
Pacific cupped oyster	226.3	212.8	232.1	205.5	261.3
Japanese scallop	95.2	126.7	127.4	123.4	123.5
Japanese (Manila) clam	135.6	155.5	154.3	132.6	127.4
Other marine clams	165.6	132.6	116.2	131.5	114.2
Japanese flying squid	280.5	207.8	215.9	212.8	311.9
Other squids	185.6	251.8	278.4	291.6	357.8
Other molluscs	166.5	185.2	158.7	141.1	118.8
Other sea creatures*	33.7	36.7	36.1	35.9	33.2
TOTAL CATCH*	9,994.4	10,123.4	10,183.7	9,945.0	10,410.4
of which:					
Inland waters	200.1	207.5	227.6	230.3	220.8
Atlantic Ocean	231.8	215.2	180.3	185.8	151.8
Indian Ocean	48.8	59.0	66.9	73.7	68.2
Pacific Ocean	9,513.7	9,641.7	9,708.9	9,455.1	9,969.7

* Excluding aquatic mammals (including whales, *see* below).

Source: FAO, *Yearbook of Fishery Statistics.*

WHALING*

	1974	1975	1976	1977	1978	1979
Number of whales caught	14,277	13,427	9,632	9,299	5,924	4,918

* Figures include whales caught during the Antarctic summer season beginning in the year prior to the year stated.

Aquatic plants ('000 metric tons): 666.0 in 1976; 638.5 in 1977; 638.6 in 1978; 643.1 in 1979; 695.0 in 1980.

Source: FAO, *Yearbook of Fishery Statistics.*

MINING

		1976	1977	1978	1979	1980
Coal	'000 metric tons	18,396	18,246	18,992	17,643	18,029
Zinc	,, ,, ,,	260	276	275	243	238
Iron	,, ,, ,,	563	559	528	458	477
Iron pyrites	,, ,, ,,	1,474	1,284	1,117	863	823
Manganese	,, ,, ,,	142	126	104	88	80
Quartzite	,, ,, ,,	8,929	9,815	11,979	13,745	14,470
Limestone	,, ,, ,,	147,530	154,121	172,543	182,781	184,780
Chromite	metric tons	22,150	17,881	8,696	11,905	13,610
Copper	,, ,,	81,606	81,395	71,951	59,100	52,553
Lead	,, ,,	51,666	54,764	56,489	46,929	44,746
Gold ore	kg.	4,281	4,635	4,517	3,970	3,183
Crude petroleum	million litres	674	689	630	561	503
Natural gas	'000 cu. metres	2,493,197	2,804,064	2,640,670	2,414,005	2,197,189

Source: Ministry of International Trade and Industry.

INDUSTRY

SELECTED PRODUCTS

		1978	1979	1980	1981
Wheat flour[1]	'000 metric tons	4,013	4,150	4,184	n.a.
Sugar*	,, ,, ,,	2,730	2,561	n.a.	n.a.
Distilled alcoholic beverages[1]	'000 hectolitres	6,333	6,634	n.a.	n.a.
Beer[1]	,, ,,	44,230.9	46,833.8	n.a.	n.a.
Cigarettes[1]	million	302,573	308,259	303,177	n.a.
Cotton yarn (pure)	metric tons	412,602	475,417	472,735	423,463
Cotton yarn (mixed)	,, ,,	35,270	32,317	31,037	32,066
Woven cotton fabrics (pure and mixed)	million sq. metres	2,315.3	2,338.8	2,202.0	2,066.5
Flax, ramie and hemp yarn	metric tons	2,090	1,991	2,119	2,362
Jute yarn	,, ,,	25,063	22,464	21,933	14,773
Linen fabrics	'000 sq. metres	17,059	18,464	16,101	15,115
Jute fabrics	,, ,, ,,	12,919	12,857	10,984	4,988
Woven silk fabrics (pure and mixed)	,, ,, ,,	159,234	157,975	151,889	137,111
Wool yarn (pure and mixed)	metric tons	109,436	124,196	119,119	114,366
Woven woollen fabrics (pure and mixed)[2]	'000 sq. metres	335,996	325,651	294,192	290,654
Rayon continuous filaments	metric tons	81,868	83,445	87,488	86,432
Acetate continuous filaments	,, ,,	27,943	30,865	31,819	32,286
Rayon discontinuous fibres	,, ,,	279,362	290,416	277,954	273,546
Acetate discontinuous fibres[3]	,, ,,	34,881	35,606	35,124	36,516
Woven rayon fabrics (pure and mixed)[2]	million sq. metres	780.9	830.7	800.3	702.7
Woven acetate fabrics (pure and mixed)[2]	,, ,, ,,	69.9	71.2	81.6	72.2
Non-cellulosic continuous filaments	metric tons	644,492	649,138	641,641	620,824
Non-cellulosic discontinuous fibres	,, ,,	774,169	760,731	757,810	747,888
Woven fabrics of non-cellulosic fibres[2,4]	million sq. metres	2,916.0	2,980.6	3,158.6	3,121.0
Leather footwear[5]	'000 pairs	51,442	53,426	50,195	51,227
Mechanical wood pulp	'000 metric tons	9,391.6	9,992.8	9,788.4	8,611.7
Chemical wood pulp[6]	,, ,, ,,				
Newsprint	,, ,, ,,	2,482.3	2,566.3	2,674.0	2,575.2
Other printing and writing paper	,, ,, ,,	3,416.2	3,770.6	4,137.7	3,814.0
Other paper	,, ,, ,,	3,465.1	3,644.1	3,724.6	3,554.3
Paperboard	,, ,, ,,	7,136.2	7,879.8	7,551.5	7,036.7
Synthetic rubber	,, ,, ,,	1,028.9	1,107.3	1,094.1	1,010.3
Motor vehicle tyres	'000	106,143	115,612	131,459	127,782
Rubber shoes	'000 pairs	63,443	63,849	65,877	65,653
Ethylene (Ethene)	'000 metric tons	4,387.4	4,783.7	4,175.3	3,654.6
Propylene (Propene)	,, ,, ,,	2,963.7	3,112.5	2,636.9	2,537.7
Benzene (Benzol)	,, ,, ,,	2,014.6	2,179.0	2,059.7	1,887.9

[*continued on next page*

SELECTED PRODUCTS—*continued*]

		1978	1979	1980	1981
Toluene (Toluol)	'000 metric tons	884.1	961.9	907.6	843.2
Xylenes (Xylol)	" " "	1,248.9	1,318.2	1,195.1	1,201.8
Methyl alcohol (Methanol)	" " "	907.3	940.2	835.7	734.3
Ethyl alcohol (95 per cent)	kilolitres	138,984	153,506	154,744	n.a.
Sulphuric acid (100 per cent)	'000 metric tons	6,437.3	6,581.8	6,777.3	6,571.8
Caustic soda (Sodium hydroxide)	" " "	2,776.2	3,020.9	3,157.4	2,871.8
Soda ash (Sodium carbonate)	" " "	1,161.6	1,354.4	1,355.4	1,177.7
Ammonium sulphate	" " "	1,929.1	1,883.3	1,878.3	1,816.9
Nitrogenous fertilizers (a)[7]	" " "	1,446	1,457	1,458	1,202
Phosphate fertilizers (b)[7]	" " "	696	707	744	648
Plastics and synthetic resins	" " "	9,471	11,346	10,377	n.a.
Liquefied petroleum gas	" " "	8,671	9,089	7,996	7,781
Naphtha	million litres	25,689	25,083	22,308	18,259
Motor spirit (Gasoline)[8]	" "	33,493	34,517	34,230	35,102
Kerosene	" "	25,613	26,546	23,839	23,254
Jet fuel	" "	4,147	4,239	4,592	4,496
Gas oil	" "	19,571	21,571	21,571	21,387
Heavy fuel oil	" "	124,270	124,047	111,023	95,746
Lubricating oil	" "	2,200	2,303	2,338	2,185
Petroleum bitumen (Asphalt)	'000 metric tons	5,212	5,132	4,777	n.a.
Coke-oven coke	" " "	38,459	} 46,414†	50,958†	50,690†
Gas coke	" " "	3,342			
Cement	" " "	84,882	87,804	87,957	n.a.
Pig-iron	" " "	78,589	83,825	87,041	80,049
Ferro-alloys[9]	" " "	1,513	1,901	1,866	1,639
Crude steel	'000 metric tons	102,105	111,748	111,395	101,676
Aluminium (unwrought): primary	" " "	1,057.7	1,010.4	1,091.5	n.a.
secondary[10]	" " "	660.0	788.3	800.4	n.a.
Electrolytic copper	metric tons	959,070	983,700	1,014,292	n.a.
Refined lead (unwrought)	" "	228,442	221,247	220,934	n.a.
Electrolytic, distilled and rectified zinc (unwrought)	" "	767,949	789,352	735,187	n.a.
Calculating machines	'000	42,319	45,996	60,356	52,433
Radio receivers	"	18,781	15,421	16,623	n.a.
Television receivers	"	13,927	14,236	16,327	11,630‡
Merchant vessels launched	'000 gross reg. tons	4,801	4,249	7,308	9,140
Passenger motor cars	'000	5,976.0	6,175.8	7,038.1	6,976.8
Lorries and trucks[11]	"	3,237.1	3,397.2	3,913.2	4,103.0
Motorcycles, scooters and mopeds	"	5,999.9	4,476.0	6,434.7	7,412.6
Cameras: photographic	"	10,932	12,266	13,987	n.a.
cinematographic	"	1,014.9	960.6	897.7	621.4
Watches and clocks	"	88,807	95,631	132,749	n.a.
Construction: new dwellings started[12]	"	1,549.4	1,493.0	1,268.6	1,151.7
Electric energy[1]	million kWh.	563,990	589,644	612,040	n.a.
Town gas	teracalories	87,662	89,746	99,123	105,173

* Twelve months ending September.
† Coke of all grades (43,888,000 metric tons in 1978).
‡ Colour sets only (10,909,000 in 1980).
1 Twelve months beginning April 1st of the year stated.
2 Including finished fabrics.
3 Including cigarette filtration tow.
4 Including blankets made of synthetic fibres.
5 Sales.
6 Including pulp prepared by semi-chemical processes.
7 Figures refer to the 12 months ending June 30th of the year stated and are in terms of (a) nitrogen, 100 per cent, and (b) phosphoric acid, 100 per cent.
8 Including aviation gasoline.
9 Including silico-chromium.
10 Including alloys.
11 Including three-wheeled vehicles.
12 Including buildings and dwelling units created by conversion.

Sources: Ministry of Agriculture, Forestry and Fisheries, Ministry of International Trade and Industry, Ministry of Finance and Ministry of Construction.

FINANCE

1,000 rin = 100 sen = 1 yen.

Coins: 1, 5, 10, 50 and 100 yen.

Notes: 500, 1,000, 5,000 and 10,000 yen.

Exchange rates (June 1982): £1 sterling = 443.0 yen; U.S. $1 = 255.6 yen.

1,000 yen = £2.26 = $3.91.

Note: From April 1949 to August 1971 the official exchange rate was U.S. $1 = 360 yen. Between December 1971 and February 1973 the rate was 308 yen per $. Since February 1973 the yen has been allowed to "float", though the exchange rate was maintained at around 265 yen to the $ until November 1973. The average market rates (yen per U.S. $) were: 271.70 in 1973; 292.08 in 1974; 296.79 in 1975; 296.55 in 1976; 268.51 in 1977; 210.44 in 1978; 219.14 in 1979; 226.75 in 1980; 220.53 in 1981. In terms of sterling, the exchange rate was £1 = 864 yen from November 1967 to August 1971; and £1 = 802.56 yen from December 1971 to June 1972.

GENERAL BUDGET ESTIMATES

Twelve months ending March 31st

(million yen)

Revenue	1979/80	1980/81	1981/82
Taxes and Stamps	21,487,000	26,411,000	32,284,000
Public Bonds	15,270,000	14,270,000	12,270,000
Others	1,843,143	1,907,843	2,234,131
Total	38,600,143	42,588,843	46,788,131

Expenditure	1979/80	1980/81	1981/82
Social Security	7,626,569	8,212,441	8,836,914
Education and Science	4,299,692	4,524,955	4,741,998
Defence	2,094,489	2,230,202	2,400,019
Public Works	6,540,132	6,655,448	6,655,448
Local Finance	5,993,161	7,387,698	8,766,595
Pensions	1,499,848	1,639,888	1,802,972
Total (incl. others)	38,600,143	42,588,843	46,788,131

INTERNATIONAL RESERVES
(U.S. $ million at December 31st)

	1975	1976	1977	1978	1979	1980	1981
Gold	865	859	920	1,093	1,117	1,082	987
IMF Special Drawing Rights	520	535	600	1,372	1,688	1,738	1,934
Reserve position in IMF	804	1,329	1,615	2,139	1,477	1,331	1,558
Foreign exchange	10,627	13,883	20,126	28,896	16,357	21,567	24,716
TOTAL	12,816	16,606	23,261	33,500	20,639	25,718	29,195

Source: IMF, *International Financial Statistics.*

MONEY SUPPLY
('000 million yen at December 31st)

	1975	1976	1977	1978	1979	1980	1981
Currency outside banks	11,578.6	12,858.1	14,122.4	16,259.0	17,051.9	17,475.3	18,584
Demand deposits	38,370.1	43,321.0	46,664.3	52,669.9	53,968.2	52,097.4	57,923
TOTAL MONEY	49,948.7	56,179.1	60,786.7	68,928.9	71,020.1	69,572.7	76,507

COST OF LIVING
Consumer Price Index*
(Average of monthly figures. Base: 1980=100)

	1972	1973	1974	1975	1976	1977	1978	1979	1981
Food (incl. beverages)	47.0	53.1	67.8	76.6	83.6	89.2	92.3	94.3	105.3
Housing	44.8	50.9	62.9	68.8	75.2	82.0	87.3	92.4	104.0
Rent	54.2	58.8	63.2	69.3	76.3	84.1	91.0	95.8	104.8
Fuel and light	39.9	41.9	52.6	59.8	65.8	72.0	71.6	74.9	107.7
Clothing	47.6	58.4	71.7	76.0	82.3	87.3	90.4	94.8	104.0
Miscellaneous	46.5	49.8	58.8	65.7	79.5	84.3	86.7	89.2	104.5
ALL ITEMS	46.9	52.4	65.2	72.9	79.7	86.1	89.4	92.6	104.9

NATIONAL ACCOUNTS

('000 million yen at current prices)

	1976	1977	1978	1979	1980
Government final consumption expenditure	16,417.2	18,243.2	19,752.5	21,486.2	23,531.9
Private final consumption expenditure	95,148.8	105,789.0	115,909.6	127,066.3	136,779.2
Increase in stocks	1,072.8	1,210.6	1,037.3	1,816.6	1,595.1
Gross fixed capital formation	51,877.2	56,177.0	62,383.6	70,248.4	75,192.7
TOTAL DOMESTIC EXPENDITURE	164,516.0	181,419.8	199,083.0	220,617.5	237,098.9
Exports of goods and services	22,582.0	24,307.6	22,728.5	25,627.3	32,886.5
Less Imports of goods and services	21,246.9	21,267.3	19,173.9	27,628.6	35,036.2
GROSS DOMESTIC PRODUCT	165,851.1	184,460.0	202,637.6	218,616.3	234,949.2
Factor income received from abroad	1,257.1	1,253.7	1,376.3	2,276.3	2,820.1
Less Factor income paid abroad	1,413.5	1,345.6	1,306.0	1,998.4	2,897.6
GROSS NATIONAL PRODUCT	165,694.7	184,368.2	202,707.9	218,894.1	234,871.7
Less Consumption of fixed capital	21,288.4	24,033.5	26,379.1	28,939.4	31,515.9
	144,406.3	160,334.7	176,328.8	189,954.7	203,355.8
Statistical discrepancy	52.5	−1,415.3	−1,571.2	−1,011.9	−190.3
NATIONAL INCOME IN MARKET PRICES	144,458.7	158,919.4	174,757.7	188,942.8	203,165.5

GROSS DOMESTIC PRODUCT BY ECONOMIC ACTIVITY

('000 million yen at current prices)

	1976	1977	1978	1979	1980
Agriculture, forestry and fishing	8,821.9	9,310.2	9,337.7	9,508.4	8,934.5
Mining and quarrying	840.1	962.5	1,129.2	1,267.1	1,379.2
Manufacturing	50,731.5	55,286.4	60,772.5	65,846.8	71,079.2
Electricity, gas and water	3,585.4	4,330.9	4,857.8	4,796.2	6,825.4
Construction	15,016.2	15,806.2	18,069.0	20,148.0	21,480.2
Wholesale and retail trade	24,291.5	25,735.4	26,858.2	28,143.7	29,195.4
Transport, storage and communications	11,113.1	13,151.9	14,185.4	15,018.1	16,187.5
Finance and insurance	8,645.0	9,338.7	10,263.5	11,114.4	12,621.6
Real estate	14,476.1	16,977.1	19,464.5	21,880.2	24,345.2
Public administration	7,979.0	8,854.8	9,591.8	10,388.3	11,268.4
Other services	27,464.9	30,751.8	34,444.8	38,251.8	41,536.9
SUB-TOTAL	172,964.9	190,505.9	208,974.5	226,363.2	244,853.6
Import duties	711.4	776.6	758.8	946.1	923.9
Less Imputed bank service charge	7,772.7	8,237.7	8,666.9	9,704.9	11,018.6
TOTAL	165,903.6	183,044.7	201,066.3	217,604.3	234,758.9
Statistical discrepancy	−52.4	1,415.3	1,571.2	1,011.9	190.3
GROSS DOMESTIC PRODUCT	165,851.1	184,460.0	202,637.6	218,616.3	234,949.2

BALANCE OF PAYMENTS
(U.S. $ million)

	1980			1981		
	Credit	Debit	Balance	Credit	Debit	Balance
Goods and Services:						
Merchandise f.o.b.	126,736	124,611	2,125	149,379	129,350	20,029
Freight	7,155	3,770	3,385	8,253	3,433	4,820
Insurance on merchandise	255	446	−191	266	442	−176
Non-merchandise insurance	57	309	−252	43	292	−249
Other transportation	5,581	13,118	−7,537	6,888	14,702	−7,814
Tourists	415	2,653	−2,238	465	2,553	−2,088
Other travel	229	1,940	−1,711	270	2,065	−1,795
Investment income	11,115	10,261	854	15,678	16,535	−857
Military transactions	1,032	—	1,032	1,124	—	1,134
Other government services	443	264	179	834	305	529
Other private services	5,217	10,081	−4,864	5,690	12,862	−7,172
TOTAL	158,235	167,453	−9,218	188,900	182,539	6,361
Unrequited Transfers:						
Private transfer payments	322	562	−240	354	574	−220
Reparations	—	—	—	—	—	—
Other government transfers	65	1,353	−1,288	78	1,490	−1,412
TOTAL	387	1,915	−1,528	432	2,064	−1,632
TOTAL CURRENT ACCOUNT	158,622	169,368	−10,746	189,332	184,603	4,729
Capital Flows:						
Long-term Capital:						
Direct investments	278	2,385	−2,107	189	4,894	−4,705
Trade credits (net)	−16	717	−733	−19	2,696	−2,715
Loans (net)	−231	2,553	−2,784	−186	5,083	−5,269
Securities (net)	11,947	3,753	8,194	15,034	8,777	6,257
External bonds	3,452	2,216	1,236	4,659	3,291	1,368
Others (net)	−3	1,409	−1,412	−71	1,322	−1,393
BALANCE	15,427	13,033	2,394	19,606	26,063	−6,457
Short-term Capital:						
Trade credits (net)	2,067	—	2,067	—	1,279	−1,279
Others (net)	1,004	—	1,004	457	—	457
BALANCE ON CAPITAL ACCOUNT	18,498	13,033	5,465	20,063	27,342	−7,279
NET ERRORS AND OMISSIONS	—	3,115	−3,115	406	—	406
OVERALL BALANCE (NET MONETARY MOVEMENTS)			−8,396			−2,144
of which:						
Gold and foreign exchange reserves			4,905			3,171
Others			−13,301			−5,315
of which: commercial banks			−13,144			−6,386

Source: Bank of Japan, *Balance of Payments, Monthly.*

JAPANESE DEVELOPMENT ASSISTANCE

(U.S. $'000)

	1977	1978	1979	1980
Official:				
Bilateral Grants:				
Donations	236,700	383,400	560,200	652,600
Reparations	88,800	162,200	318,300	374,800
Technical Assistance	147,800	221,200	241,900	277,800
Direct Loans	662,600	1,147,600	1,361,000	1,308,200
TOTAL	899,300	1,531,000	1,921,200	1,960,800
Capital Subscriptions or Grants to International Agencies	525,200	684,400	716,300	1,342,900
TOTAL	1,424,400	2,215,400	2,637,500	3,303,700
Other Government Capital:				
Export Credits	1,081,600	1,286,500	−235,100	822,900
Direct Investment Capital	417,400	703,800	675,400	767,000
Loans to International Agencies	123,600	162,400	−230,200	−111,900
TOTAL	1,622,600	2,152,600	210,100	1,478,000
TOTAL OFFICIAL	3,047,000	4,368,000	2,847,600	4,781,700
Private:				
Export Credits	913,800	412,100	642,500	73,700
Direct Investments	1,223,600	5,014,500	3,405,800	1,566,300
Loans to International Agencies	332,200	890,100	640,700	317,800
Donations to non-profit Organizations	18,300	18,900	19,000	26,400
TOTAL	2,487,900	6,335,600	4,708,000	1,984,200
GRAND TOTAL	5,534,900	10,703,500	7,555,600	6,765,900

EXTERNAL TRADE*

(U.S. $ million)

	1974	1975	1976	1977	1978	1979	1980	1981
Imports c.i.f.	62,110	57,863	64,799	70,809	79,343	110,672	140,528	143,290
Exports f.o.b.	55,536	55,753	67,225	80,495	97,543	103,032	129,807	152,030

* Excluding the payment of reparations and all trade in gold, silver and goods valued at less than $100. Also excluded are fish and other marine products landed directly from the high seas.

Source: Ministry of Finance, *The Summary Report, Trade of Japan.*

PRINCIPAL COMMODITIES

(U.S. $ million)

IMPORTS C.I.F.	1978	1979	1980	1981
Food and live animals	10,786.3	13,682.7	13,954.1	15,121.6
Meat and meat preparations	1,296.0	1,712.5	1,523.2	1,927.0
Fresh, chilled or frozen meat	1,241.8	1,625.0	1,457.5	n.a.
Fish and fish preparations*	3,016.6	3,957.4	3,025.7	3,653.1
Fresh and simply preserved fish*	2,883.1	3,781.2	2,842.6	n.a.
Crustacea and molluscs	1,643.9	2,265.3	1,785.1	n.a.
Cereals and cereal preparations	3,063.6	3,719.3	4,426.3	4,989.6
Wheat and meslin (unmilled)	827.8	1,090.0	1,229.3	1,273.2
Maize (unmilled)	1,230.5	1,486.5	2,008.6	1,866.9
Fruit and vegetables	1,150.9	1,356.0	1,386.6	1,678.0
Sugar, sugar preparations and honey	753.4	894.0	1,423.9	918.1
Sugar and honey	714.9	867.1	1,403.8	n.a.
Raw sugar	592.0	707.5	1,224.4	732.0
Coffee, tea, cocoa and spices	727.1	1,072.4	1,074.8	870.2
Beverages and tobacco	616.6	732.7	712.0	791.8
Crude materials (inedible) except fuels	15,105.4	21,842.0	23,457.7	19,720.3
Oil-seeds, oil nuts and oil kernels	1,571.8	1,841.9	1,880.4	2,018.4
Soya beans (excl. flour)	1,130.9	1,271.8	1,310.2	1,395.8
Wood, lumber and cork	4,154.1	7,378.2	6,940.1	4,483.4
Rough or roughly squared wood	3,557.0	6,270.0	5,679.6	3,674.2
Coniferous sawlogs and veneer logs	1,814.6	2,851.6	2,677.8	n.a.
Non-coniferous sawlogs and veneer logs	1,710.2	3,351.7	2,913.0	n.a.
Textile fibres and waste	2,102.5	2,448.6	2,393.4	2,403.7
Cotton	1,068.1	1,263.7	1,359.2	1,415.6
Raw cotton (excl. linters)	1,045.9	1,239.5	1,328.9	1,383.1
Metalliferous ores and metal scrap	4,836.5	6,850.1	8,429.6	7,284.4
Iron ore and concentrates	2,453.2	2,999.3	3,448.7	3,504.1
Non-ferrous ores and concentrates	1,754.2	2,879.4	3,730.8	3,011.2
Copper ores and concentrates (excl. matte)	939.3	1,511.9	2,040.0	1,676.3
Mineral fuels, lubricants, etc.	31,336.3	45,286.1	69,991.2	72,562.7
Coal, coke and briquettes	3,084.1	3,555.0	4,469.1	5,532.3
Coal (excl. briquettes)	3,076.9	3,548.8	4,458.3	5,520.9
Petroleum and petroleum products	25,705.9	37,970.8	57,850.9	58,673.9
Crude and partly refined petroleum	23,432.6	33,471.0	52,762.9	53,343.1
Crude petroleum	22,661.5	32,512.2	51,032.7	n.a.
Petroleum products	2,273.2	4,499.8	5,088.0	5,330.7
Residual fuel oils	1,021.2	2,052.7	2,215.3	1,847.8
Gas (natural and manufactured)	2,546.3	3,760.4	7,671.2	8,356.6
Animal and vegetable oils and fats	274.5	353.6	302.6	314.8
Chemicals	3,763.3	5,178.2	6,202.4	6,486.7
Chemical elements and compounds	1,514.2	2,255.2	2,834.4	3,027.8
Organic chemicals	883.7	1,463.8	1,678.8	1,847.0
Basic manufactures	6,639.5	9,410.6	10,578.4	10,157.6
Textile yarn, fabrics, etc.	1,495.7	2,030.7	1,650.0	1,627.9
Non-metallic mineral manufactures	983.8	1,146.2	1,136.2	1,117.9
Non-ferrous metals	2,354.3	3,416.4	4,479.7	4,189.0
Machinery and transport equipment	5,715.5	7,330.5	8,756.2	9,239.7
Non-electric machinery	2,489.2	3,195.5	3,789.0	3,597.4
Electrical machinery, apparatus, etc.	1,732.7	2,364.2	2,721.5	2,938.8
Transport equipment	1,493.6	1,770.9	2,245.7	2,703.5
Miscellaneous manufactured articles	3,874.2	5,213.5	5,030.5	5,385.7
Clothing (excl. footwear)	1,235.1	1,801.2	1,529.9	1,801.8
Other commodities and transactions	1,231.4	1,642.3	1,542.5	3,508.8
Re-imports	575.2	1,009.1	829.3	965.8
TOTAL	79,343.0	110,672.2	140,527.7	143,289.7

* Including crustacea and molluscs.

[*continued on next page*

PRINCIPAL COMMODITIES—*continued*]

(U.S. $ million)

EXPORTS F.O.B.	1978	1979	1980	1981
Food and live animals	950.4	1,069.0	1,446.0	1,582.8
Beverages and tobacco	96.5	137.8	142.4	156.2
Crude materials (inedible) except fuels	1,051.1	1,152.9	1,354.8	1,380.9
Mineral fuels, lubricants, etc.	260.8	356.2	503.7	553.7
Animal and vegetable oils and fats	119.1	114.9	114.0	96.2
Chemicals	5,102.2	6,100.2	6,766.7	6,840.7
Chemical elements and compounds	2,315.8	2,822.0	3,050.1	2,960.8
Organic chemicals	1,812.3	2,209.1	2,275.5	2,184.0
Plastic materials, etc.	1,416.9	1,674.7	1,866.6	1,915.3
Basic manufactures	23,141.0	26,140.1	31,170.9	33,686.6
Textile yarn, fabrics, etc.	3,827.2	3,996.6	5,094.0	5,833.2
Woven textile fabrics (excl. narrow or special fabrics)	2,582.1	2,741.6	3,331.0	3,937.2
Fabrics of synthetic (excl. regenerated) fibres	1,751.3	1,922.1	2,242.4	2,650.1
Non-metallic mineral manufactures	1,378.7	1,547.1	1,862.7	2,122.5
Iron and steel	11,854.8	14,113.4	15,454.2	16,668.9
Ingots and other primary forms	1,134.5	1,489.7	1,392.8	n.a.
Coils for re-rolling	1,105.3	1,444.7	1,333.6	1,402.3
Bars, rods, angles, shapes, etc.	1,901.1	2,678.1	2,221.7	2,014.9
Universals, plates and sheets	4,608.5	5,167.6	5,388.2	4,989.4
Thin plates and sheets (uncoated)	2,219.5	2,609.8	2,810.5	2,471.3
Tubes, pipes and fittings	3,412.2	3,914.9	4,747.1	7,217.7
Seamless tubes and pipes	1,638.7*	2,004.0*	2,593.6*	n.a.
Welded (excl. cast iron) tubes and pipes	1,455.0*	1,586.5*	1,760.8*	n.a.
Non-ferrous metals	1,035.3	1,138.5	1,917.4	1,467.2
Other metal manufactures	3,151.9	3,127.0	3,947.0	4,319.6
Machinery and transport equipment	55,526.2	55,284.2	71,155.7	86,362.1
Non-electric machinery	14,187.4	14,872.4	18,088.5	22,628.1
Power generating machinery	2,375.0	2,103.4	2,548.1	3,173.5
Internal combustion engines (non-aircraft)	1,344.3	1,429.7	1,782.8	2,294.4
Office machines	1,654.3	1,830.5	2,279.7	2,636.9
Metalworking machinery	1,264.6	1,534.2	1,743.2	2,071.0
Heating and cooling equipment	1,260.7	1,132.8	1,523.8	2,554.3
Electrical machinery, apparatus, etc.	13,899.2	14,690.4	18,694.7	22,466.5
Electric power machinery and switchgear	2,520.0*	n.a.	1,629.4*	n.a.
Electric power machinery	1,323.4	1,243.4	1,503.4	2,038.6
Switchgear, etc.	1,196.6*	1,272.4*	1,629.4*	n.a.
Telecommunications apparatus	6,603.5	6,590.0	8,157.5	9,801.0
Television receivers	1,318.4	1,282.7	1,660.4	1,928.7
Radio receivers	2,635.9	2,497.2	3,008.9	3,223.2
Thermionic valves, tubes, etc.	1,268.9	1,679.2	2,306.9	2,661.9
Transport equipment	27,439.6	25,721.4	34,372.5	41,267.5
Road motor vehicles and parts†	19,297.2	20,954.6	28,467.8	32,899.0
Passenger cars (excl. buses)	10,616.8	11,964.3	16,114.6	18,445.4
Lorries and trucks (incl. ambulances)	4,218.2	3,118.5	4,681.1	6,069.4
Parts for cars, buses, etc.†	1,622.9	1,743.4	2,015.3	2,564.6
Motorcycles and parts	2,143.6	2,189.9	3,179.1	3,812.9
Motorcycles	1,886.5	1,925.2	2,802.3	3,338.9
Ships and boats	7,172.5	3,868.8	4,681.9	7,273.6
Miscellaneous manufactured articles	10,460.1	11,562.5	15,556.8	19,984.9
Scientific instruments, watches, etc.	5,168.1	5,684.4	7,134.9	8,536.3
Scientific instruments and photographic equipment	3,448.3	3,860.7	4,526.3	5,512.5
Watches, clocks and parts	1,276.7	1,286.4	1,733.5	2,014.3
Musical instruments, sound recorders, etc.	2,904.0	3,527.7	5,138.2	7,849.3
Sound recorders, phonographs and parts	2,258.8	2,751.2	4,065.6	6,273.8
Sound recorders and phonographs	2,003.5	2,442.7	3,718.0	n.a.
Other commodities and transactions	835.8	1,113.9	1,596.0	1,386.2
Re-exports	793.3	1,045.3	1,329.9	1,264.7
TOTAL	97,543.1	103,031.6	129,807.0	152,030.2

* Provisional. † Excluding tyres, engines and electrical parts.

PRINCIPAL TRADING PARTNERS*
(U.S. $ million)

IMPORTS C.I.F.	1977	1978	1979	1980	1981
Australia	5,287.6	5,300.4	6,297.6	6,981.6	7,419.3
Brazil	946.8	787.0	1,240.4	1,560.9	1,578.5
Brunei	1,419.7	1,393.5	1,891.3	3,244.8	2,907.5
Canada	2,880.8	3,190.6	4,104.7	4,724.2	4,463.9
China, People's Republic	1,546.9	2,030.3	2,954.8	4,323.4	5 291.9
France	560.7	754.4	1,078.1	1,295.6	1 171.4
Germany, Federal Republic	1,496.2	1,997.4	2,584.1	2,500.8	2,429.4
India	800.0	793.1	1,053.0	1,014.3	1,056.7
Indonesia	4,996.6	5,246.6	8,794.0	13,167.0	13,305.3
Iran	4,242.9	4,243.6	4,271.3	4,101.0	1,920.1
Iraq	735.2	776.9	1,815.7	4,339.1	n.a.
Italy	466.3	656.0	992.7	938.5	n.a.
Korea, Republic	2,113.8	2,591.0	3,359.4	2,996.3	3,388.9
Kuwait	2,487.6	2,481.9	4,413.8	3,457.6	3,608.6
Malaysia	1,560.5	1,899.7	3,257.1	3,470.9	2,927.0
Oman	883.0	904.1	1,339.8	1,732.8	2,327.8
Philippines	897.4	1,057.8	1,582.8	1,951.4	1,731.2
Qatar	197.3	560.5	971.4	1,803.1	2,234.6
Saudi Arabia	8,505.5	8,459.7	12,133.9	19,538.1	21,482.1
Singapore	687.4	869.1	1,473.4	1,507.2	1,943.8
South Africa	895.9	1,041.6	1,299.4	1,740.9	1,728.3
Switzerland	648.3	986.1	1,032.6	1,076.5	1,542.4
Taiwan	1,288.7	1,750.2	2,475.9	2,293.4	2,522.6
Thailand	748.2	842.7	1,169.4	1,119.5	1,061.6
U.S.S.R.	1,421.9	1,441.7	1,910.7	1,859.9	2,020.7
United Arab Emirates	2,748.2	2,621.9	3,633.4	8,190.4	8,836.0
United Kingdom	959.3	1,378.8	1,681.1	1,954.4	2,694.5
U.S.A.	12,396.1	14,790.4	20,430.8	24,408.0	25,297.1
TOTAL (incl. others)	70,808.7	79,343.0	110,672.2	140,527.7	143,289.7

EXPORTS F.O.B.	1977	1978	1979	1980	1981
Australia	2,329.6	2,692.2	2,606.6	3,388.9	4,779.2
Belgium and Luxembourg	817.9	965.1	1,091.8	1,425.5	1,441.7
Brazil	839.7	1,252.5	1,125.0	1,114.8	1,367.5
Canada	1,707.8	1,871.1	1,738.3	2,436.6	3,399.0
China, People's Republic	1,938.6	3,048.7	3,698.7	5,078.3	5,095.5
France	1,005.9	1,102.7	1,395.2	2,021.2	2,221.8
Germany, Federal Republic	2,781.7	3,654.4	4,266.1	5,756.4	5,967.5
Greece	1,095.1	891.4	758.6	545.0	n.a.
Hong Kong	2,320.2	3,087.8	3,678.8	4,760.7	5,310.5
Indonesia	1,797.5	2,094.9	2,223.8	3,457.6	4,122.8
Iran	1,926.4	2,691.1	925.4	1,529.5	1,485.5
Iraq	872.2	951.5	1,608.8	2,169.5	3,026.0
Korea, Republic	4,079.6	6,003.0	6,246.9	5,368.3	5,657.9
Kuwait	935.5	774.1	885.5	1,272.9	1,647.9
Liberia	2,486.8	1,645.7	930.7	1,415.5	1,690.1
Malaysia	863.4	1,157.1	1,507.0	2,060.9	2,424.4
Netherlands	1,305.3	1,598.8	1,671.4	2,060.6	1,902.3
Nigeria	1,009.5	953.4	806.9	1,493.6	2,158.9
Panama	1,328.5	1,445.5	894.6	1,415.8	2,209.7
Philippines	1,099.9	1,545.7	1,622.0	1,683.3	1,928.3
Saudi Arabia	2,342.3	3,254.3	3,828.8	4,855.7	5,876.4
Singapore	1,719.2	2,324.8	2,679.1	3,910.9	4,467.9
South Africa	757.2	979.2	993.4	1,800.3	2,222.0
Taiwan	2,552.7	3,584.7	4,366.9	5,145.8	5,404.6
Thailand	1,359.8	1,527.8	1,713.7	1,916.5	2,250.6
U.S.S.R.	1,933.9	2,502.2	2,461.5	2,778.2	3,259.4
United Arab Emirates	845.9	1.015.3	1,045.0	1,355.9	1,493.8
United Kingdom	1,950.0	2,341.2	3,096.8	3,781.9	4,789.2
U.S.A.	19,716.9	24,914.7	26,402.5	31,367.3	38,608.8
TOTAL (incl. others)	80,494.8	97,543.1	103,031.6	129,807.0	152,030.2

* Imports by country of production; exports by country of last consignment.

Source: Ministry of Finance, *The Summary Report, Trade of Japan.*

TOURISM

	1977	1978	1979	1980	1981
Foreign Visitors . . .	1,028,140	1,038,875	1,112,606	1,316,632	n.a.
Money Received (U.S. $ million)	425	470	644	644	735

TRANSPORT

RAILWAYS
(million)

	1976/77	1977/78	1978/79	1979/80	1980/81
National Railways					
Passengers . . .	7,180	7,068	6,997	6,931	6,825
Freight ton-km. . .	45,526	40,587	40,413	42,284	36,961
Private Railways					
Passengers . . .	10,402	10,699	10,763	10,907	11,180
Freight ton-km. . .	779	746	791	803	740

ROAD TRAFFIC
(licensed vehicles—'000)

	1976/77	1977/78	1978/79	1979/80	1980/81
Cars	18,618.2	19,942.5	21,409.3	22,751.1	23,646.1
Buses	222.3	224.1	226.7	228.4	229.4
Lorries	10,829.2	11,369.6	12,020.0	12,697.8	13,303.2
Special Purpose Vehicles .	631.0	670.8	720.1	765.8	794.0
Total	30,300.8	32,207.0	34,376.1	36,443.0	37,972.8

Source: Ministry of Transport.

SHIPPING

MERCHANT FLEET
(registered at June 30th)

	VESSELS	DISPLACEMENT ('000 g.t.)
1977 . .	9,642	40,036
1978 . .	9,321	39,182
1979 . .	9,981	39,993
1980 . .	10,568	40,960
1981 . .	10,422	40,836

Source: Lloyd's Register of Shipping.

INTERNATIONAL SEA-BORNE TRAFFIC ENTERED

	NUMBER OF SHIPS	'000 NET TONS
1975 . .	37,909	280,196
1976 . .	39,465	299,983
1977 . .	40,202	315,125
1978 . .	40,761	318,371
1979 . .	40,699	341,252
1980 . .	39,848	353,314
1981 . .	38,464	337,657

Source: Ministry of Finance.

CIVIL AVIATION
(Domestic and International Services)

		1976	1977	1978	1979	1980
Passengers carried .	'000	29,799	36,014	40,011	45,415	45,739
Passenger-km. . .	million	34,372	40,729	45,441	52,505	53,169
Freight ton-km.* .	'000	1,095,037	1,147,920	1,307,921	1,514,315	1,723,130

* Including excess baggage.

Original Source: Ministry of Transport.

COMMUNICATIONS MEDIA

('000)

	1978	1979	1980	1981
Radio Receivers	89,000	90,000	n.a.	n.a.
Television Subscribers*	28,394	28,932	29,263	n.a.
Daily Newspaper Circulation†	44,277	45,852	46,391	47,260

* At March 31st. † In October.

EDUCATION

(1981)

	Institutions	Teachers	Students
Primary Schools	25,004	473,957	11,924,706
Secondary Schools	10,810	258,479	5,299,281
High Schools	5,219	247,719	4,682,829
Technological Colleges	62	5,765	46,468
Junior Colleges	523	40,897	372,406
Graduate Schools and Universities	451	174,429	1,822,117

Source (unless otherwise stated): Statistics Bureau, Prime Minister's Office, Tokyo, *Monthly Statistics of Japan, Japan Statistical Yearbook*.

THE CONSTITUTION

(Summary of the Constitution promulgated November 3rd, 1946, in force May 3rd, 1947).

The Emperor: Articles 1–8. The Emperor derives his position from the will of the people. In the performance of any State act as defined in the Constitution, he must seek the advice and approval of the Cabinet though he may delegate the exercise of his functions, which include: (i) the appointment of the Prime Minister and the Chief Justice of the Supreme Court; (ii) promulgation of laws, cabinet orders, treaties and constitutional amendments; (iii) the convocation of the Diet, dissolution of the House of Representatives and proclamation of elections to the Diet; (iv) the appointment and dismissal of Ministers of State and as well as the granting of amnesties, reprieves and pardons and the ratification of treaties, conventions or protocols; (v) the awarding of honours and performance of ceremonial functions.

Renunciation of War: Article 9. Japan renounces for ever the use of war as a means of settling international disputes.

Articles 10–40 refer to the legal and human rights of individuals guaranteed by the constitution.

The Diet: Articles 41–64. The Diet is convened once a year, is the highest organ of State power and has exclusive legislative authority. It comprises the House of Representatives (511 seats) and the House of Councillors (252 seats). The members of the former are elected for four years whilst those of the latter are elected for six years and election for half the members takes place every three years. If the House of Representatives is dissolved, a general election must take place within 40 days and the Diet must be convoked within 30 days of the date of the election. Extraordinary sessions of the Diet may be convened by the Cabinet when one quarter or more of the members of either House request it. Emergency sessions of the House of Councillors may also be held. A quorum of at least one third of the Diet members is needed to carry on Parliamentary business. Any decision arising therefrom must be passed by a majority vote of those present. A bill becomes law having passed both Houses except as provided by the constitution. If the House of Councillors either vetoes or fails to take action within 60 days upon a bill already passed by the House of Representatives, the bill becomes law when passed a second time by the House of Representatives, by at least a two-thirds majority of those members present.

The Budget must first be submitted to the House of Representatives. If, when it is approved by the House of Representatives, the House of Councillors votes against it or fails to take action on it within 30 days, or failing agreement being reached by a joint committee of both Houses, a decision of the House of Representatives shall be the decision of the Diet. The above procedure also applies in respect of the conclusion of treaties.

The Executive: Articles 65–75. Executive power is vested in the cabinet consisting of a Prime Minister and such other Ministers as may be appointed. The Cabinet is collectively responsible to the Diet. The Prime Minister is designated from among members of the Diet by a resolution thereof.

If the House of Representatives and the House of Councillors disagree on the designation of the Prime Minister, and if no agreement can be reached even through a joint committee of both Houses, provided for by law, or if the House of Councillors fails to make designation within 10 days, exclusive of the period of recess, after the House of Representatives has made designation, the decision of the House of Representatives shall be the decision of the Diet.

The Prime Minister appoints and may remove other Ministers, a majority of whom must be from the Diet. If the House of Representatives passes a no-confidence motion or rejects a confidence motion, the whole Cabinet resigns unless the House of Representatives is dissolved within 10 days. When there is a vacancy in the post of Prime Minister, or upon the first convocation of the Diet after a general election of members of the House of Representatives, the whole Cabinet resigns.

The Prime Minister submits bills, reports on national affairs and foreign relations to the Diet. He exercises control and supervision over various administrative branches of the Government. The Cabinet's primary functions (in addition to administrative ones) are to: (a) administer the law faithfully; (b) conduct State affairs; (c) conclude treaties subject to prior (or subsequent) Diet approval; (d) administer the civil service in accordance with law; (e) prepare and present the budget to the Diet; (f) enact Cabinet orders in order to make effective legal and constitutional provisions; (g) decide on amnesties, reprieves or pardons. All laws and Cabinet orders are signed by the competent Minister of State and countersigned by the Prime Minister. The Ministers of State, during their tenure of office, are not subject to legal action without the consent of the Prime Minister. However, the right to take that action is not impaired.

Articles 76–95. Relate to the Judiciary, Finance and Local Government.

Amendments: Article 96. Amendments to the Constitution are initiated by the Diet, through a concurring vote of two-thirds or more of all the members of each House and are submitted to the people for ratification, which requires the affirmative vote of a majority of all votes cast at a special referendum or at such election as the Diet may specify.

Amendments when so ratified must immediately be promulgated by the Emperor in the name of the people, as an integral part of the Constitution.

Articles 97–99 outline the Supreme Law, while Articles 100–103 consist of Supplementary Provisions.

THE GOVERNMENT

HEAD OF STATE

His Imperial Majesty HIROHITO, Emperor of Japan; succeeded to the throne December 25th, 1926.

THE CABINET

(July 1982)

Prime Minister: ZENKO SUZUKI.

Minister of Justice: MICHITA SAKATA.

Minister of Foreign Affairs: YOSHIO SAKURAUCHI.

Minister of Finance: MICHIO WATANABE.

Minister of Education: HEIJI OGAWA.

Minister of Health and Welfare: MOTOHARU MORISHITA.

Minister of Agriculture, Forestry and Fisheries: KICHIRO TAZAWA.

Minister of International Trade and Industry: SHINTARO ABE.

Minister of Transport: TOKUSABURO KOSAKA.

Minister of Posts and Telecommunications: NOBORU MINOWA.

Minister of Labour: TAKIICHIRO HATSUMURA.

Minister of Construction: IHEI SHISEKI.

Minister of Home Affairs and Chairman of National Public Safety Commission: MASATAKO SEKO.

Minister of State and Chief Cabinet Secretary: KIICH MIYAZAWA.

Minister of State, Director-General of the Prime Minister's Office and Director-General of Okinawa Development Agency: KUNIO TANABE.

Minister of State and Director-General of the Administrative Management Agency: YASUHIRO NAKASONE.

Minister of State and Director-General of the Defence Agency: SOICHIRO ITO.

Minister of State and Director-General of the Economic Planning Agency: TOSHIO KOMOTO.

Minister of State, Director-General of the Science and Technology Agency and Chairman of the Atomic Energy Commission: ICHIRO NAKAGAWA.

Minister of State and Director-General of the Environment Agency: BUNBEI HARA.

Minister of State, Director-General of the National Land Agency and of Hokkaido Development Agency: YUKIYASU MATSUNO.

Director of the Cabinet Legislature Bureau: REIJIRO TSUNODA.

LEGISLATURE

KOKKAI

(The Diet)

The Diet consists of two Chambers: the House of Councillors (Upper House), which replaced the House of Peers, and the House of Representatives. The 511 members of the House of Representatives are elected for a period of four years (subject to dissolution). For the House of Councillors, which has 252 members, the term of office is six years, half the members being elected every three years.

HOUSE OF COUNCILLORS

Speaker: MASOTOSHI TOKUNAGA.

PARTY	SEATS	
	Election, July 10th, 1977	Election, June 22nd, 1980
Liberal-Democratic	124	135
Socialist	56	47
Komeito	28	26
Communist	16	12
Democratic Socialist	11	12
New Liberal Club	4	2
Independent	12	15
Social Democratic Alliance	—	2
Vacant	1	1

HOUSE OF REPRESENTATIVES

Speaker: HAJIME FUKUDA.

PARTY	SEATS	
	Election Oct. 7th, 1979	Election, June 22nd, 1980
Liberal-Democratic	248	284
Socialist	107	107
Komeito	57	33
Democratic Socialist	35	32
Communist	39	29
New Liberal Club	4	12
Independent	19	11
Social Democratic Alliance	2	3

POLITICAL PARTIES

The Political Funds Regulation Law provides that any organization which wishes to support a candidate for an elective public office must be registered as a political party. There are over 10,000 registered parties in the country, mostly of local or regional significance. The conservative Liberal-Democratic Party has the support of big business and the rural population and is also by far the richest of the political parties. The proportion of votes for the two socialist parties increased slowly at each election after 1952. The split between the two parties reflects a long-standing division between supporters of a mass popular party (now represented by the DSP) and those seeking a class party on Socialist lines. The Communist Party of Japan split in 1964, the official party being independent and supporting neither the U.S.S.R. nor the People's Republic of China.

Liberal-Democratic Party (LDP) (Jiyu-Minshuto): 7, 2-chome, Hirakawacho, Chiyoda-ku, Tokyo; f. 1955; programme includes the establishment of a welfare state, the build-up of industrial development, the levelling up of educational and cultural systems and the revision of the Constitution where necessary; follows a foreign policy of alignment with the U.S.A.; 1.5 million mems. (1978); Pres. ZENKO SUZUKI; Sec.-Gen. YOSHIO SAKURAUCHI; publ. *Jiyu Shimpo* (weekly).

Japan Socialist Party (JSP) (Nippon Shakaito): 1-8-1 Nagata-cho, Chiyoda-ku, Tokyo; f. 1945; aims at the establishment of collective non-aggression and mutual security system, including Japan, the U.S.A., the U.S.S.R. and the People's Republic of China; 50,000 mems. (1979); Chair. ICHIO ASUKATA; Sec.-Gen. NOBORU BABA; publ. *Shakai Shimpo* (twice a week).

Komeito (*Clean Government Party*): 17 Minamimoto-machi, Shinjuku-ku, Tokyo; f. 1964; based on middle-of-the-road principle and humanitarian socialism, promotes policies in best regard of "dignity of human life"; 167,000 mems. (1980); Founder DAISAKU IKEDA; Chair. YOSHIKATSU TAKEIRI; Sec.-Gen. JUNYA YANO; publs. *Komei Shimbun* (daily), *The Komei* (monthly), *Komei Graphic* (monthly).

Democratic Socialist Party (DSP) (Minshato): Shiba Sakuragawa-cho, Minato-ku, Tokyo; f. 1961 by Right-Wing Socialists of the Socialist Party of Japan; aims at the pursuit of an independent foreign policy; 35,000 mems. (1975); Chair. RYOSAKU SASAKI; Sec.-Gen. SABURO TSUKAMOTO; publs. *Shukan Minsha* (daily), *Gekkan Kakushin* (monthly).

Japanese Communist Party (JCP): Sendagaya 4-26-7, Shibuya-ku, Tokyo; f. 1922; 440,000 mems. (1980); Chair. (Central Cttee.) SANZO NOSAKA; Chair. (Presidium) KENJI MIYAMOTO; Chief Sec. TETSUZO FUWA; publs. *Akahata* (Red Flag) (daily and weekly), *Zen'ei* (Vanguard) (monthly), *Josei no Hiroba* (Women's Forum) (monthly).

New Liberal and Democratic Alliance: f. 1981 by merger of the new Liberal Party and the United Social Democratic Party; Leader TOSHIO YAMAGUCHI.

Second Chamber Club (Ni-In Club): c/o House of Councillors, Nagata-cho 1-7-1, Chiyoda-ku, Tokyo; remnant of the Green Wind Club (Ryokufukai), which originated in the House of Councillors in 1946-47; Sec. ISAMU YAMADA.

DIPLOMATIC REPRESENTATION

EMBASSIES ACCREDITED TO JAPAN

(In Tokyo unless otherwise stated)

(E) Embassy.

Afghanistan: Rm. 503, Olympia Annexe Apartments, 31-21, Jingumae 6-chome, Shibuya-ku (E); *Ambassador:* ABDOLHAMID MOHTAT.

Algeria: 12-23, Higashi 4-chome, Shibuya-ku (E); *Ambassador:* MOURAD BENCHEIKH.

Argentina: Chiyoda House, 17-8, Nagata-cho 2-chome, Chiyoda-ku (E); *Ambassador:* CARLOS JAIME FRAGUIO.

Australia: 1-14, Mita 2-chome, Minato-ku (E); *Ambassador:* Sir JAMES PLIMSOLL.

Austria: 1-20, Moto Azabu 1-chome, Minato-ku (E); *Ambassador:* Dr. CLEMENS WEICHS AN DER GLON.

Bangladesh: 7–45, Shirogane 2-chome, Minato-ku (E); *Ambassador:* MANZOOR AHMED CHOUDHURY.

Belgium: 5, Niban-cho, Chiyoda-ku (E); *Ambassador:* HERMAN DEHENNIN.

Bolivia: Edinburgh House 101, 13-6, Higashi Gotanda 3-chome, Shinagawa-ku (E); *Ambassador:* ROBERTO PACHECO HERTZOG.

Brazil: 2nd, 3rd and 4th Floor, Aoyama Daiichi Mansion, 4-14, Akasaka 8-chome, Minato-ku (E); *Ambassador:* RONALDO COSTA.

Bulgaria: 36-3, Yoyogi 5-chome, Shibuya-ku (E); *Ambassador:* TODOR DICHEV.

Burma: 8-26, Kita-Shinagawa 4-chome, Shinagawa-ku (E); *Ambassador:* U SAW TUN.

Canada: 3-38, Akasaka 7-chome, Minato-ku (E); *Ambassador:* BRUCE I. RANKIN.

Central African Republic: Azabu Koyo Heights 1-13, Moto-Azabu 2-chome, Minato-ku (E); *Ambassador:* VINCENT NBANDA.

Chad: Beijing, People's Republic of China (E).

Chile: 14-12, Nishi Azabu 4-chome, Minato-ku, She Azaub (E); *Ambassador:* CÉSAR RUIZ DANYAU.

China, People's Republic: 4-5-30, Minami Azabu, Minato-ku (E); *Ambassador:* SONG ZHIGUANG.

Colombia: 8-15, Minami-Azabu 3-chome, Minato-ku (E); *Ambassador:* GUSTAVO MEDINA O.

Costa Rica: 1-1, Higashi-Ikebukuro 3-chome, Toshima-ku (E); *Ambassador:* Dr. JAIME BOTEY BRENES.

Cuba: 2-51 Minami-Azabu 4-chome, Minato-ku (E); *Ambassador:* JOSÉ ARMANDO GUERRA MENCHERO.

Czechoslovakia: 16-14, Hiroo 2-chome, Shibuya-ku; *Ambassador:* KAREL HOUŠKA.

Denmark: 29–6, Sarugaku-cho, Shibuya-ku (E); *Ambassador:* PER S. GROOT.

Dominican Republic: Sunshine 60 Bldg., 58th Floor, Room 12, 1-1, Higashi-Ikebukuro 3-chome, Toshima-ku (E); *Ambassador:* BOLÍVAR A. GARCÍA JIMÉNEZ.

Ecuador: Azabu Sky Mansion, Room 101, 19-13 Minami-Azabu 3-chome, Minato-ku (E); *Ambassador:* ANDRÉS CRESPO REINBERG.

Egypt: 5-4, Aobadai 1-chome, Meguro-ku (E); *Ambassador:* Dr. SAAD A. F. KHALIL.

El Salvador: Yurakucho Bldg., Room 1019, 10-1, Yurakucho, 1-chome, Chiyoda-ku (E); *Ambassador:* GREGORIO CONTRERAS MORALES.

Ethiopia: 6-21, Akasaka 9-chome, Minato-ku (E); *Ambassador:* Brig.-Gen. AFEWORK ATLABACHEW.

Finland: 2-7, Roppongi 3-chome, Minato-ku (E); *Ambassador:* HENRIK LENNART BLOMSTEDT.

France: 11-44, Minami-Azabu 4-chome, Minato-ku (E); *Ambassador:* XAVIER DAUFRESNE DE LA CHEVALERIE.

Gabon: 16-2, Hiroo 2-chome, Shibuya-ku (E); *Ambassador:* ANDRÉ MANGONGO N'ZAMBI.

German Democratic Republic: Akasaka Mansion, 5-16 Akasaka 7-chome, Minato-ku; *Ambassador:* HORST BRIE.

Germany, Federal Republic: 5-10, Minami-Azabu 4-chome, Minato-ku (E); *Ambassador:* GÜNTER DIEHL.

Ghana: Mori Bldg., 11th Floor, 16-13, Nishi-Azabu 4-chome, Minato-ku (E); *Ambassador:* VICTOR ESEM WOOD.

Greece: 4th Floor, Green Fantasia Bldg., 11-11, Jingumae 1-chome, Shibuya-ku (E); *Ambassador:* JEAN C. CAMBIOTIS.

Guatemala: 58th Floor, Sunshine 60 Bldg., 1-1, Higashi-Ikebukuro, Toshima-ku (E); *Ambassador:* CARLOS ENRIQUE MOLINA MUÑOZ.

Guinea: Daishodaini Bldg., 18-2, Roppongi 5-chome Minato-ku (E); *Ambassador:* MANDIOU TOURÉ.

Haiti: 604 Aoyama Mansions No. 1, 4-14 Akasaka 8-chome, Minato-ku; *Chargé d'affaires:* GÉRARD FRITZ VILLAIN.

Honduras: 2-25, Minami-Azabu 4-chome, Minato-ku (E); *Ambassador:* CÉSAR MOSSI SORTO.

Hungary: 3-1, Aobadai 2-chome, Meguro-ku (E); *Ambassador:* Dr. PÉTER KÓS.

India: 2-11, Kudan-Minami 2-chome, Chiyoda-ku (E); *Ambassador:* AVTAR SINGH.

Indonesia: 2-9, Higashi Gotanda 5-chome, Shinagawa-ku (E); *Ambassador:* Lt.-Gen. ANTONIUS JOSEF WITONO SARSANTO.

Iran: 10-32, Minami-Azabu 3-chome, Minato-ku (E); *Ambassador:* Dr. GHASSEM SALEHKOU.

Iraq: Rms. 1 and 5, Greenleaves Hill, 17-12 Sarugaku-cho, Shibuya-ku (E); *Chargé d'affaires:* MOHAMMED M. AL-AMILI.

Ireland: Kowa Bldg., No. 25, 8-7 Sanban-cho, Chiyoda-ku (E); *Ambassador:* CHARLES V. WHELAN.

Israel: 3, Niban-cho, Chiyoda-ku (E); *Ambassador:* AMNON BEN-YOHANAN.

Italy: 5-4, Mita 2-chome, Minato-ku (E); *Ambassador:* BORIS BIANCHERI.

Ivory Coast: No. 38 Kowa Bldg. 7F, 12-24, Nishi-Azabu 4-chome, Minato-ku (E); *Ambassador:* PIERRE N. COFFI.

Jordan: 4A, B, Chiyoda House, 17-8 Nagatacho 2-chome, Chiyoda-ku (E); *Ambassador:* ZUHAIR AL-MUFTI.

Kenya: 24-25 Nishi-Azabu 3-chome, Minato-ku; *Ambassador:* KEFA ONYONI.

Korea, Republic: 2-5 Minami-Azabu 1-chome, Minato-ku (E); *Ambassador:* CHOI KYONG-NOK.

Kuwait: 13-12, Mita 4-chome, Minato-ku (E); *Ambassador:* AHMAD GAITH ABDULLAH.

Laos: 3-21, Nishi-Azabu 3-chome, Minato-ku (E); *Ambassador:* SALI KHAMSI.

Lebanon: 6th Floor, Chiyoda House, 17-8 Nagata-cho 2-chome, Chiyoda-ku (E); *Ambassador:* JOSEPH NAFFAH.

Liberia: Odakyu Minami Aoyama Bldg., 6th Floor, 8-1 Minami Aoyama 7-chome, Minato-ku; *Ambassador:* C. ANSUMANA COOPER.

Libya: 5-36-21 Shimouma, Setagaya-ku; People's Bureau.

Madagascar: 3-28 Moto-Azabu 2-chome, Minato-ku (E); *Ambassador:* APOLINAIRE ANDRIATSIAFAJATO.

Malaysia: 20-16, Nanpeidaimachi, Shibuya-ku (E); *Ambassador:* Datuk JAMALUDDIN BIN Haji ABU BAKAR.

Mali: Moscow, U.S.S.R. (E).

Mexico: 15-1, Nagata-cho 2-chome, Chiyoda-ku (E); *Ambassador:* XAVIER IGNACIO OLEA MUÑOZ.

Mongolia: Pine Crest Mansion, 21-4 Shoto, Kamiyama-cho, Shibuya-ku (E); *Ambassador:* DENZENGIYN TSERENDENDOV.

Morocco: 5th and 6th Floors, Silver Kingdom Mansion, 16-3 Sendagaya 3-chome, Shibuya-ku (E); *Ambassador:* ABDELSAM TADLAOUI.

Nepal: 16-23, Higashi Gotanda 3-chome, Shinagawa-ku (E); *Ambassador:* SUNDAR NATH BHATTARAI.

Netherlands: 6-3, Shibakoen 3-chome, Minato-ku (E); *Ambassador:* Dr. JOHAN KAUFMANN.

New Zealand: 20-40, Kamiyama-cho, Shibuya-ku (E); *Ambassador:* RODERICK MACALISTER MILLER.

Nicaragua: 2-3, Roppongi 4-chome, Minato-ku (E); *Ambassador:* Maj.-Gen. JULIO U. GUTIÉRREZ RIVERA.

Nigeria: 2-19-7 Uehara, Shibuya-ku (E); *Ambassador:* BALARABE ABUBAKAR TAFAWA BALEWA.

Norway: 12-2, Minami-Azabu 5-chome, Minato-ku (E); *Ambassador:* BJØRN BLAKSTAD.

Pakistan: 14-9, 2-chome, Moto-Azabu, Minato-ku; *Ambassador:* QAMAR UL ISLAM.

Panama: 58th Floor, Sunshine 60 Bldg., 1-1, Higashi-Ikebukuro 3-chome, Toshima-ku (E); *Ambassador:* ALBERTO A. CALVO PONCE.

Papua New Guinea: Room 313, 3rd Floor, Mita Kokusai Bldg., 1-4-28 Mita, Minato-ku, 108; *Ambassador:* J. K. NOMBRI.

Paraguay: Asahi Kamiosaki Bldg., 5th Floor, 5-8 Kamiosaki 3-chome, Shinagawa-ku (E); *Ambassador:* MARCOS MARTÍNEZ MENDIETA.

Peru: Higashi 4-4-27, Shibuya-ku; *Ambassador:* CÉSAR ESPEJO-ROMERO.

Philippines: 11-24, Nampeidai-cho, Shibuya-ku (E); *Ambassador:* CARLOS J. VALDES.

Poland: 13-5, Mita 2-chome, Meguro-ku (E); *Ambassador:* (vacant).

Portugal: Olympia Annex Apt. 306, 31-21, Jingumae 6-chome, Shibuya-ku (E); *Ambassador:* FRANCISCO MOITA.

Qatar: Hiroo Towers, 1-12, Minami-Azabu 4-chome, Minato-ku (E); *Ambassador:* HAMAD MANSOUR AL HAJIRI.

Romania: 16-19, Nishi Azabu 3-chome, Minato-ku (E); *Ambassador:* RADU IOAN BOGDAN.

Saudi Arabia: 6-2, Hiroo 2-chome, Shibuya-ku (E); *Ambassador:* Sheikh ZEIN AL-ABIDEEN DABBAGH.

Senegal: 3-4 Aobadai 1-chome, Meguro-ku (E); *Ambassador:* ASSANE BASSIROU DIOUF.

Singapore: 12-3 Roppongi 5-chome, Minato-ku (E); *Ambassador:* WEE MON CHENG.

Spain: 3-29, Roppongi 1-chome, Minato-ku (E); *Ambassador:* Don JOSÉ ARAGONES.

Sri Lanka: 14-1, Akasaka 1-chome, Minato-ku (E); *Ambassador:* SUSANTA DE ALWIS.

Sudan: Yada Mansion, 6-20 Minami-Aoyama 6-chome, Minato-ku (E); *Ambassador:* EL-BAGHIR ABDEL-MUTAAL.

Sweden: 10-3, Roppongi 1-chome, Minato-ku (E); *Ambassador:* BENGT ODEVALL.

Switzerland: 9-12, Minami-Azabu 5-chome, Minato-ku (E); *Ambassador:* FRITZ R. STAEHELIN.

Syria: 12-6 Roppongi 5-chome, Shibuya-ku; *Ambassador:* ABDUL WADOUD ATASSI.

Tanzania: 21-9, Kamiyoga 4-chome, Setagaya-ku (E); *Ambassador:* AHMED HASSAN DIRIA.

Thailand: 14-6, Kami-Osaki 3-chome, Shinagawa-ku (E); *Ambassador:* PAYONG CHUTIKUL.

Trinidad and Tobago: New Delhi, India (E).

Tunisia: 29, Ichiban-cho 2-chome, Chiyoda-ku (E); *Ambassador:* HABIB BEN YAHIA.

Turkey: 33-6, Jingumae 2-chome, Shibuya-ku (E); *Ambassador:* NAZIF CUHRUK.

Uganda: 2-2 Shoto 2-chome, Shibuya-ku; *Ambassador:* DAVID A. W. NSUBUGA BARLOW.

U.S.S.R.: 2-1-1 Azabudai, Minato-ku (E); *Ambassador:* VLADIMIR PAVLOV.

United Arab Emirates: Kotsu Anzen Kyoiku Centre Bldg., 24-20 Nishi Azabu 3-chome, Minato-ku (E); *Ambassador:* AHMED SALIM AL-MOKARRAB.

United Kingdom: 1, Ichiban-cho, Chiyoda-ku (E); *Ambassador:* Sir HUGH CORTAZZI, K.C.M.G.

U.S.A: 10-5, Akasaka 1-chome, Minato-ku (E); *Ambassador:* MICHAEL MANSFIELD.

Uruguay: 38 Kowa International Bldg., Room 908, 12-24, Nishi-Azabu 4-chome, Minato-ku (E); *Ambassador:* ALBERTO RODRÍGUEZ NIN.

Vatican City: 9-2, Sanbancho, Chiyoda-ku (Pro-Nunciature); *Apostolic Pro-Nuncio:* Archbishop MARIO PIO GASPARI.

Venezuela: 11-23, Minami-Azabu 3-chome, Minato-ku (E); *Ambassador:* Dr. MANUEL PLIDO TAMAYO.

Viet-Nam: 50-11 Moto Yoyogi-Cho, Shibuya-ku (E); *Ambassador:* NGUYEN TIEN.

Yemen, People's Democratic Republic: Rm. 301, Akasaka Heights, 5-26, Akasaka 9-chome, Minato-ku (E); *Chargé d'affaires a.i.:* MOHAMED ALI BASURAH.

Yugoslavia: 7-24, Kitashinagawa 4-chome, Shinagawa-ku (E); *Ambassador:* SELMO HASIMBEGOVIC.

Zaire: 5th Floor, Odakyu Minami-Aoyami Bldg., 8-1, Minami-Aoyama 7-chome, Minato-ku (E); *Ambassador:* LOMBO LO MANGAMANGA.

Zambia: 3-19-8, Takanawa, Minato-ku (E); *Ambassador:* MORRIS KATOWA CHIEF MAPANZA.

Japan also has diplomatic relations with Albania, Angola, the Bahamas, Bahrain, Barbados, Benin, Botswana, Burundi, Cameroon, Cape Verde, the Comoros, the Congo, Cyprus, Djibouti, Fiji, The Gambia, Grenada, Guinea-Bissau, Guyana, Iceland, Jamaica, Kiribati, Lesotho, Luxembourg, Malawi, Maldives, Malta, Mauritania, Mauritius, Mozambique, Nauru, Niger, Oman, Rwanda, San Marino, São Tomé and Príncipe, Seychelles, Sierra Leone, Solomon Islands, Somalia, South Africa, Suriname, Swaziland, Togo, Tonga, Tuvalu, Upper Volta, Vanuatu, Western Samoa, the Yemen Arab Republic and Zimbabwe.

JUDICIAL SYSTEM

The basic principles of the legal system are set forth in the Constitution, which lays down that the whole judicial power is vested in a Supreme Court and in such inferior courts as are established by law, and enunciates the principle that no organ or agency of the Executive shall be given final judicial power. Judges are to be independent in the exercise of their conscience, and may not be removed except by public impeachment, unless judicially declared mentally or physically incompetent to perform official duties. The justices of the Supreme Court are appointed by the Cabinet, the sole exception being the Chief Justice, who is appointed by the Emperor after designation by the Cabinet.

The Court Organization Law, which came into force on May 3rd, 1947, decreed the constitution of the Supreme Court and the establishment of four types of inferior court —High, District, Family (established January 1st, 1949), and Summary Courts. The constitution and functions of the courts are as follows:

THE SUPREME COURT

This court is the highest legal authority in the land, and consists of a Chief Justice and fourteen associate justices. It has jurisdiction over the following matters:

(1) **Jokoku** (appeals).
(2) **Kokoku** (complaints), prescribed specially in codes of procedure.

It conducts its hearings and renders decisions through a Grand Bench or three Petty Benches. Both are collegiate bodies, the former consisting of all justices of the Court, and the latter of five justices. A Supreme Court Rule prescribes which cases are to be handled by the respective Benches. It is, however, laid down by law that the Petty Bench cannot make decisions as to the constitutionality of a statute, ordinance, regulation, or disposition, or as to cases in which an opinion concerning the interpretation and application of the Constitution or of any laws or ordinances is at variance with a previous decision of the Supreme Court.

Chief Justice: Takaaki Hattori.

Secretary-General: Koichi Yaguchi.

INFERIOR COURTS

High Court

A High Court conducts its hearings and renders decisions through a collegiate body, consisting of three judges, though for cases of insurrection the number of judges must be five. The Court has jurisdiction over the following matters:

(1) **Koso** appeals from judgments in the first instance rendered by District Courts, from judgments rendered by Family Courts, and from judgments concerning criminal cases rendered by Summary Courts.

(2) **Kokoku** complaints against rulings and orders rendered by District Courts and Family Courts, and against rulings and orders concerning criminal cases rendered by Summary Courts, except those coming within the jurisdiction of the Supreme Court.

(3) **Jokoku** appeals from judgments in the second instance rendered by District Courts and from judgments rendered by Summary Courts, except those concerning criminal cases.

(4) Actions in the first instance relating to cases of insurrection.

District Court

A District Court conducts hearings and renders decisions through a single judge or, for certain types of cases, through a collegiate body of three judges. It has jurisdiction over the following matters:

(1) Actions in the first instance, except offences relating to insurrection, claims where the subject matter of the action does not exceed 300,000 yen, and offences liable to a fine or lesser penalty.

(2) **Koso** appeals from judgments rendered by Summary Courts, except those concerning criminal cases.

(3) **Kokoku** complaints against rulings and orders rendered by Summary Courts, except those coming within the jurisdiction of the Supreme Court and High Courts.

Family Court

A Family Court handles cases through a single judge in case of rendering judgments or decisions. However, in accordance with the provisions of other statutes it conducts its hearings and renders decisions through a collegiate body of three judges. A conciliation is effected through a collegiate body consisting of a judge and two or more members of the conciliation committee selected from among citizens.

It has jurisdiction over the following matters:

(1) Judgment and conciliation with regard to cases relating to family as provided for by the Law for Adjudgment of Domestic Relations.

(2) Judgment with regard to the matters of protection of juveniles as provided for by the Juvenile Law.

(3) Actions in the first instance relating to adult criminal cases of violation of the Labour Standard Law, the Law for Prohibiting Liquors to Minors, or other laws especially enacted for protection of juveniles.

Summary Court

A Summary Court handles cases through a single judge, and has jurisdiction in the first instance over the following matters:

(1) Claims where the value of the subject matter does not exceed 300,000 yen (excluding claims for cancellation or change of administrative dispositions).

(2) Actions which relate to offences liable to fine or lesser penalty, offences liable to a fine as an optional penalty, and certain specified offences such as habitual gambling and larceny.

A Summary Court cannot impose imprisonment or a graver penalty. When it deems proper the imposition of a sentence of imprisonment or a graver penalty, it must transfer such cases to a District Court, but it can impose imprisonment with hard labour not exceeding three years for certain specified offences.

A Procurator's Office, with its necessary number of procurators, is established for each of these courts. The procurators conduct searches, institute prosecutions and supervise the execution of judgments in criminal cases, and act as representatives of the public interests in civil cases of public concern.

RELIGION

The traditional religions in Japan are Shintoism and Buddhism. Neither is exclusive, and many Japanese subscribe at least nominally to both. Since the war a number of new religions based on an amalgamation of Shinto, Buddhist, Daoist, Confucian and Christian beliefs have grown up.

SHINTOISM

Shintoism is an indigenous cult of nature and ancestor worship. It is divided into two cults: national Shintoism, which is represented by the shrines; and sectarian Shintoism, which developed towards the end of the Tokugawa Shogunate. In 1868, Shinto was designated a national religion, and all Shinto shrines acquired the privileged status of a national institution. After the adoption of the present constitution in 1947, however, complete freedom of religion was introduced, and state support of Shinto was banned. There are an estimated 81,000 shrines, 101,000 priests and approximately 90,000,000 adherents.

BUDDHISM

World Buddhist Fellowship: Rev. Riri Nakayama, Hozenji Buddhist Temple, 1115, 3-chome, Akabanecho, Kita-ku, Tokyo.

CHRISTIANITY

In 1978 the number of Christians in Japan was estimated at 1,358,882. Twenty-two universities are maintained by Christian communities.

The following are the largest groups:

Roman Catholic Church: Archdiocese of Tokyo: Sekiguchi, 3-chome, 16-15, Bunkyo-ku, Tokyo 112; Archbishop of Tokyo Mgr. Peter Seiichi Shirayanagi; Archdiocese of Nagasaki: Catholic Center, 10-34 Uenomachi, Nagasaki; Archbishop of Nagasaki Cardinal Joseph A. Satowaki; Archdiocese of Osaka: 1-55, Nishinomiyashi, Hyogo-ken; Archbishop of Osaka Mgr. Paul Hisao Yasuda; 387,205 adherents (Dec. 1978).

United Church of Christ in Japan: Japan Christian Center, Room 31, 3-18 Nishi Waseda 2-chome, Shinjuku-ku, Tokyo 160; f. 1941; union of 34 Presbyterian, Methodist, Congregational, Reformed and other denominations; 191,831 mems. (March 1981); Moderator Rev. Toshio Ushiroku; Vice-Moderator Rev. Yoichi Kishimoto; Gen. Sec. Rev. John M. Nakajima.

Japanese Orthodox Church: Holy Resurrection Cathedral (Nicolai-Do), 1-3, 4-chome, Surugadai, Kanda, Chiyoda-ku, Tokyo 101; Primate H.E. Most Rev. Theodosius, Archbishop of Tokyo and Metropolitan of All Japan; 24,783 adherents.

Nippon Sei Ko Kai (*Holy Catholic Church in Japan*): 4-21, Higashi 1-chome, Shibuya-ku, Tokyo 150; in Communion with the Church of England; est. as Province of the Anglican Communion 1887; 55,569 mems. (1980); Primate Rt. Rev. Titus Yoshio Nakamichi (Bishop of Kobe); 10 other diocesan bishops.

OTHER RELIGIONS

There are an estimated 5,000,000 adherents of other religions, with 1,200 shrines and temples and 15,000 priests.

The "New Religions"

Many new cults have grown up in Japan since the end of World War II. Collectively these are known as the New Religions (*Shinko Shukyo*). The most important are as follows:

Soka Gakkai: 32 Shinano-machi, Shinjuku-ku, Tokyo; f. 1930; the lay society of Nichiren Shoshu (Orthodox Nichiren Buddhism); membership 7.9 million households (1982); Buddhist group aiming at individual happiness and world peace; Hon. Pres. Daisaku Ikeda; Pres. Einosuke Akiya.

Rissho Kosei-kai: 2-11-1, Wada Suginami-ku, Tokyo 166; f. 1938; Buddhist laymen; Pres. Rev. Nikkyo Niwano; 5 million mems. in Japan, the Republic of Korea, the U.S.A., Australia and Brazil (1981).

THE PRESS

The average circulation of Japanese dailies is the highest in the world after the U.S.S.R. and the U.S.A., and the circulation per head of population is highest at about 575 copies per thousand inhabitants. The two newspapers with the largest circulations are the *Asahi Shimbun* and *Yomiuri Shimbun*. Other influential papers include *Mainichi Shimbun*, *Nihon Keizai Shimbun*, *Chunichi Shimbun* and *Sankei Shimbun*. A notable feature of the Japanese press is the number of weekly news journals.

Technically the Japanese press is highly advanced, and the major newspapers are issued in simultaneous editions in the main centres.

PRINCIPAL DAILIES

Tokyo

Asahi Evening News: 8-5, Tsukiji 7-chome, Chuo-ku, 104; f. 1954; evening; English language; Man. Editor I. Ebitsubo; circ. 37,860.

Asahi Shimbun: 3-2, Tsukiji 5-chome, Chuo-ku, 104; f. 1879; Exec. Dir. (Editorial Affairs) M. Itoh; circ. morning 3,773,242, evening 2,576,364.

Business JAPAN: Sankei Bldg., 7-2, 1-chome, Otemachi, Chiyoda-ku; f. 1955; Pres. T. Masaki; Editor-in-Chief Shozo Hochi; circ. 63,000.

Daily Sports: 1-1-17, Higashi-Shinbashi, Minato-ku; f. 1948; morning; Man. Editor Jiro Ohishi; circ. 367,420.

The Daily Yomiuri: 7-1, 1-chome, Otemachi, Chiyoda-ku; f. 1955; English; morning; Editor Tatsu Okuyama; circ. 37,600.

Dempa Shimbun: 11-15, Higashi Gotanda 1-chome, Shinagawa-ku; f. 1950; morning; Man. Editor H. Ninomiya; circ. 200,000.

Hochi Shimbun: 1-1, 2-chome, Hirakawa-cho, Chiyoda-ku; f. 1872; morning; Man. Editor T. Aoki; circ. 1,000,000.

The Japan Times: 5-4, 4-chome, Shibaura, Minato-ku, 108; f. 1897; morning; English; Chair. Shintaro Fukushima; Editor K. Murata; circ. 49,856.

Komei Shimbun: 17 Minami-motomachi, Shinjuku-ku; organ of the Komeito political party; circ. 850,000, Sunday edition 1,400,000.

The Mainichi Daily News: 1-1-1 Hitotsubashi, Chiyoda-ku, 100; f. 1922; English; morning; Man. Editor A. Konishi; circ. 17,534.

Mainichi Shimbun: 1-1, 1-chome, Hitotsubashi, Chiyoda-ku, 100; f. 1872; Man. Editor K. Ueda; circ. morning 1,932,282, evening 1,059,279.

Naigai Times: 14-14, 7-chome, Ginza, Chuo-ku, 104; f. 1949; evening; Man. Editor T. YOSHIKAWA.

Nihon Keizai Shimbun: 9-5, 1-chome, Otemachi, Chiyoda-ku, 100; f. 1876; morning, evening and weekly (English editions: The Japan Economic Journal); economic news; Man. Editor Y. TAKEYAMA; circ. morning 1,116,944, evening 756,263.

Nihon Kogyo Shimbun: 7-2, 1-chome, Otemachi, Chiyoda-ku, 100; f. 1933; morning; business and financial; Pres. T. MASAKI; Man. Editor K. SEKI; circ. 425,000.

Nihon Nogyo Shimbun (*Agriculture*): 2-3 Akihabara, Taito-ku, 110; f. 1928; morning; Man. Editor M. ARAI; circ. 417,694.

Nikkan Kogyo Shimbun (*Industrial Daily News*): 8-10, 1-chome, Kudan-kita, Chiyoda-ku; f. 1945; morning; Man. Editor T. FUJIYOSHI; circ. 269,500.

Nikkan Sports: 5-10, 3-chome, Tsukiji, Chuo-ku, 104; f. 1946; morning; Man. Editors F. OKAZAKI, K. TSUKAMOTO; circ. 617,100.

Nikkan Suisan Keizai Shimbun (*Fisheries*): 6-8-19, Roppongi, Minato-ku, 106; f. 1948; morning; Man. Editor S. SASAGO; circ. 52,000.

Sankei Shimbun: 7-2, 1-chome, Otemachi, Chiyoda-ku, 100; f. 1950; Man. Editor K. FUJIMURA; circ. morning 844,349, evening 387,920.

Sankei Sports: 7-2, 1-chome, Otemachi, Chiyoda-ku, 100; f. 1963; morning; Man. Editor R. WASHINO; circ. 317,400.

Seikyo Shimbun: 18 Shinano-machi, Shinjuku-ku 160; f. 1951; organ of Soka Gakkai Buddhist movement; Principal Officer EINOSUKE AKIYA; circ. 4,540,000.

Shipping and Trade News: Tokyo News Service Ltd., Tsukiji Hamarikyu Bldg., 3-3 Tsukiji 5-chome, Chuo-ku, 104; f. 1949; English; Man. Editor K. JANARA; circ. 14,400.

Sports Nippon: Palace Side Bldg., 1-1, 1-chome, Hitotsubashi, Chiyoda-ku, 100; f. 1949; morning; Man. Editor J. EGUMA; circ. 765,217.

Tokyo Shimbun: 3-13, 2-chome, Konan, Minato-ku, 108; f. 1942; Man. Editor M. OZAKI; circ. morning 824,921, evening 620,401.

Tokyo Sports: 5-10, 3-chome, Tsukiji, Chuo-ku, 104; f. 1959; evening; Man. Editor G. TAKAHASHI; circ. 693,280.

Tokyo Times: 1-16, 1-chome, Higashi-Shimbashi, Minato-ku, 105; f. 1946; morning; Man. Editor M. YOSHIDA; circ. 162,350.

Yomiuri Shimbun: 7-1, 1-chome, Otemachi, Chiyoda-ku, 100; f. 1874; Man. Editor K. MITUKAMI; circ. morning 5,225,232, evening 3,094,280.

Yukan Fuji: 7-2, 1-chome, Otemachi, Chiyoda-ku, 100; f. 1969; evening; Man. Editor Y. HOSOYA; circ. 1,172,292.

OSAKA DISTRICT

Asahi Shimbun: 2-4, 3-chome, Nakano-shima, Kita-ku; f. 1879; Man. Editor K. KUWADA; circ. morning 2,176,965, evening 1,351,776.

Daily Sports: 1-18-11, Edobori, Nishi-ku; f. 1948; morning; Editor T. MAEDA; circ. 527,600.

Hochi Shimbun: 2-22-17, Honjo-Nishi, Oyodo-ku; f. 1964; morning; Man. Editor S. SUZUKI; circ. 186,831.

Kansai Shimbun: 1-9-3 Hirano-cho, Higashi-ku; f. 1950; evening; Man. Editor T. KIMURA; circ. 110,500.

The Mainichi Daily News: 1-6-20, Dojima, Kita-ku; f. 1922; English; morning; Man. Editor T. SHIMIZU; circ. 30,100.

Mainichi Shimbun: 1-6-20, Dojima, Kita-ku; f. 1882; Man. Editor N. OHTAKA; circ. morning 1,611,061, evening 1,010,500.

Nihon Keizai Shimbun: 1-1, Kyobashi-maeno-cho, Higashi-ku; f. 1950; Man. Editor T. INOUE; circ. morning 503,816, evening 342,447.

Nikkan Sports: 92-1, 5-chome, Hattori-kotubuki-cho, Toyonaka City 561; f. 1950; morning; Editor S. FUKOUKA; circ. 391,100.

Osaka Nichi-nichi Shimbun: 1-5-13, Kitadori, Edobori, Nishi-ku; f. 1946; evening; Man. Editor K. KISHIMOTO; circ. 89,000.

Osaka Shimbun: 2-4-9 Umeda, Kita-ku; f. 1922; evening; Man. Editor S. HIRAYOSHI; circ. 163,349.

Osaka Sports: 4th Floor, Osaka-ekimae Daiichi Bldg., 1-3-1-400, Umeda, Kita-ku; f. 1964; evening; Editor S. OKADA; circ. 335,530.

Sankei Shimbun: 2-4-9 Umeda, Kita-ku; f. 1933; Man. Editor T. HIGASHIYAMA; circ. morning 1,169,687, evening 714,716.

Sankei Sports: 2-4-9 Umeda, Kita-ku; f. 1955; morning; Editor H. KAGAWA; circ. 323,500.

Shin Osaka: 1-10-1, Minami-horie, Nishi-ku; f. 1946; evening; Man. Editor K. YANO; circ. 29,100.

Sports Nippon: 3-2-25, Oyodo-minami, Oyodo-ku; f. 1949; morning; Man. Editor M. HIGO; circ. 497,100.

Yomiuri Shimbun: 8-10, Nozaki-cho, Kita-ku; f. 1952; Pres. G. SAKATA; Man. Editor G. SAKATA; circ. morning 2,298,344, evening 1,477,500.

Yukan Fuji: 2-4-9, Umeda, Kita-ku; f. 1969; evening; Editor Y. HOSOYA; circ. 330,640.

KANTO DISTRICT
(Outside Tokyo)

Chiba Nippo (*Chiba Daily News*): 4-14-10 Chuo, Chiba City 280; f. 1957; morning; Man. Editor K. TSURUOKA; circ. 111,043.

Ibaraki: 2-15 Kitami-machi, Mito City 310; f. 1891; morning; Man. Editor I. MUROFUSHI; circ. 126,421.

Jyomo Shimbun: 90 Furuichi-machi, Maebashi City 371; f. 1887; morning; Man. Editor R. USUDA; circ. 181,000.

Kanagawa Shimbun: 23, 2-chome, Otomachi, Naka-ku, Yokohama City 231; f. 1942; morning; Man. Editor R. UCHIYAMA; circ. 188,799.

Shimotsuke Shimbun: 1-8-11, Showa, Utsunomiya City 320; f. 1884; morning; Man. Editor M. LIZUKA; circ. 220,013.

Tochigi Shimbun: 45, Shimo-tomatsuri 1-chome, Utsunomiya City 320; f. 1950; morning; Editor Y. SHIBUYA; circ. 106,321.

TOHOKU DISTRICT
(Northeast Honshu)

Akita Sakigake Shimpo: 2-6, 1-chome, O-machi, Akita-shi, Akita 010; f. 1874; Man. Editor S. WASHIO; circ. morning 225,802, evening 225,802.

Daily Tohoku: 3 Ban-cho, Hachinohe, Aomori; f. 1945; morning; Editor R. SHIBATA; circ. 78,300.

Fukushima Mimpo: 13-17, Ohta-machi, Fukushima City 960; f. 1892; Man. Editor K. Hoshi; circ. morning 241,610, evening 14,299.

Fukushima Minyu: 9-9, Naka-Machi, Fukushima City 960; f. 1895; Man. Editor S. Ito; circ. morning 152,107, evening 10,580.

Iwate Nippo: 3-7, Uchimaru, Morioka City 020; f. 1938; Man. Editor G. Murata; circ. morning and evening each 203,682.

Kahoku Shimpo: 2-28, 1-chome, Itsutsubashi, Sendai City 980, Miyagi; f. 1897; Man. Editor A. Kyogoku; circ. morning 410,755, evening 166,715.

Tooh Nippoh: 2-11, 2-chome, Shin-machi, Aomori City 030; f. 1888; Man. Editor Y. Iwabuchi; circ. morning 230,430, evening 225,887.

Yamagata Shimbun: 5-12, 2-chome Hatago-cho, Yamagata City 990; f. 1876; Man. Editor R. Tanaka; circ. morning and evening each 216,755.

Chubu District (Central Honshu)

Asahi Shimbun: 3-3, 1-chome, Sakae, Naka-ku, Nagoya City 460; f. 1935; Editor S. Saeki; circ. morning 489,505, evening 264,299.

Chubu Keizai Shimbun: 4-4-12, Meieki, Nakamura-ku, Nagoya City 450; f. 1946; morning; Man. Editor T. Hirata; circ. 112,184.

Chukyo Sports: Chukei Bldg., 4-4-12, Meieki, Nakamura, ku, Nagoya City 450; f. 1968; evening; Man. Editor T. Hirano; circ. 158,270.

Chunichi Shimbun: 6-1, 1-chome Sannomaru, Naka-ku, Nagoya City 460; f. 1942; Editor S. Nakayama; circ. morning 1,857,753, evening 825,411.

Chunichi Sports: 6-1, 1-chome, Sannomaru, Naka-ku, Nagoya City 460; f. 1954; evening; Dir. S. Nakayama. circ. 430,000.

Gifu Nichi-nichi Shimbun: 9 Imakomachi, Gifu City 500; f. 1879; Pres. M. Sugiyama; Man. Editor K. Muto; circ. morning 119,839, evening 30,309.

Mainichi Shimbun: 4-7-35, Mcieki, Nakamura-ku, Nagoya; f. 1935; Man. Editor T. Ikeoa; circ. morning 249,812, evening 114,576.

Nagoya Times: 3-10, 1-chome, Marunouchi, Naka-ku, Nagoya City 460; f. 1946; evening; Man. Editor I. Kimi; circ. 133,811.

Shinano Mainichi Shimbun: 657 Minamiagata-cho, Nagano City 380; f. 1873; Man. Editor N. Shinohara; circ. morning 369,144, evening 63,406.

Shizuoka Shimbun: 1-1, 3-chome, Toro, Shizuoka City 422; f. 1941; Man. Editor K. Nagahashi; circ. morning 595,195, evening 595,255.

Yamanashi Nichi-Nichi Shimbun: 6-10, 2-chome, Kitaguchi, Kofu City 400, f. 1872; morning; Man. Editor N. Mitsui; circ. 142,015.

Hokuriku District (North Coastal Honshu)

Fukui Shimbun: 1-14, 1-chome, Haruyama, Fukui City 910; f. 1889; morning; Man. Editor T. Kato; circ. 137,123.

Hokkoku Shimbun: 5-1, 2-chome, Korinbo, Kanazawa City 920; f. 1893; Man. Editor S. Arai; circ. morning 240,047, evening 85,351.

Hokuriku Chunichi Shimbun: 7-15, 2-chome, Korinbo, Kanazawa City 920; f. 1960; Editor T. Enomoto; circ. morning 94,337, evening 17,646.

Kita Nihon Shimbun: 2-14 Yasuzumi-cho, Toyama-shi, Toyama City 930; f. 1940; Man. Editor I. Saito; circ. morning 186,744, evening 32,705.

Niigata Nippo: 189-3 Ichiban-cho, Higashinaka-dori Niigata City 951; f. 1942; Editor S. Harada; circ. morning 392,444, 98,881 evening.

Yomiuri Shimbun: 4-5 Shimonoseki-machi, Takaoka City 933; f. 1961; Man. Editor M. Nagahara; circ. morning 136,045, evening 11,541.

Kinki District (West Central Honshu)

Ise Shimbun: 34-6, Hon-cho, Tsu City 514; f. 1878 morning; Man. Editor M. Mizuno; circ. 95,000.

Kobe Shimbun: 1-1, 7-chome, Kumoidori, Chuo-ku, Kobe City 651; f. 1898; Man. Editor S. Danjyo; circ. morning 447,957, evening 266,817.

Kyoto Shimbun: 239 Shoshoi-machi Ebisugawa-kitairu, Karasuma-dori, Nakakyo-ku, Kyoto 604; f. 1879; Man. Editor J. Nishimura; circ. morning 440,553, evening 357,601.

Nara Shimbun: 606 Sanjo-machi, Nara City 630; f. 1946; morning; Man. Editor T. Watanabe; circ. 76,000.

Chugoku District (Western Honshu)

Chugoku Shimbun: 7-1 Dobashi-cho, Naka-ku, Hiroshima City; f. 1892; Pres. A. Yamamoto; Man. Editor T. Ogata; circ. morning 588,597, evening 111,906.

Okayama Nichi-nichi Shimbun: 6-30, Hon-cho, Okayama 70; f. 1946; evening; Man. Editor K. Mori; circ. 48,535.

San-In Chuo Shimpo: 4-24, Sodeshi-machi, Matsue; f. 1942; morning; Man. Editor S. Kowata; circ. 122,963.

Sanyo Shimbun: 1-23, 2-chome, Yanagi-cho, Okayama; f. 1879; Man. Editor M. Yamamoto; circ. morning 377,872, evening 82,478.

Yamaguchi Shimbun: 1-1-7, Higashi-Yamato-cho, Shimonoseki 750; f. 1946; morning; Pres. K. Ogawa; Editor I. Fujii; circ. 36,000.

Shikoku Island

Ehime Shimbun: 12-1, 1-chome, Otemachi, Matsuyama, 790; f. 1941; Man. Editor J. Yamaoka; circ. morning 211,579, evening 26,771.

Kochi Shimbun: 2-15, 3-chome, Honcho, Kochi City 780; f. 1904; Man. Editor S. Hashii; circ. morning 193,462 evening 114,044.

Shikoku Shimbun: 15-1, Nakono-machi, Takamatsu 760; f. 1889; Man. Editor K. Matsuoka; circ. morning 166,532 evening 19,869.

Tokushima Shimbun: 6, 1-chome, Saiwai-cho, Tokushima 770; f. 1941; Man. Editor Y. Ibata; circ. morning 205,233, evening 45,758.

Hokkaido Island

Asahi Shimbun: 1-1, 1-chome, Nishi, Kita Nijo, Sapporo 060; f. 1959; Man. Editor Jyosui Setoguchi; circ. morning 166,931, evening 113,527.

Hokkai Times: 6, 10-chome, Nishi Minami-Ichijo, Chuo-ku, Sapporo 060; f. 1946; Man. Editor T. Fushikida; circ. morning 93,664, evening 43,453.

Hokkaido Shimbun: 6, 3-chome, Odori-Nishi, Sapporo 060; f. 1942; Editor N. Tatebe; circ. morning 500,573, evening 434,167.

Mainichi Shimbun: 1, Nishi 6, Kita-Nijo, Sapporo 060; f. 1959; Rep. TATSUO MANIWA; circ. morning 116,444, evening 59,259.

Nikkan Sports: Times Bldg., 10-6, Nishi, Minami-Ichijo, Chuo-ku, Sapporo 060; f. 1962; morning; Man. Editor T. AKASAKA; circ. 134,860.

Yomiuri Shimbun: 1, 4-chome, Kita-Shijyo, Chuo-ku, Sapporo 060; f. 1959; Editor A. MITSUHASHI; circ. morning 244,829, evening 131,032.

KYUSHU ISLAND

Asahi Shimbun: 12-1, 1-chome, Sunatsu, Kokura Kita-ku, Kita-Kyushu City 802; f. 1935; Man. Editor M. AOYAMA; circ. morning 863,385, evening 245,672.

Fukunichi: 2-1, 1-chome, Imaizumi, Chuo-ku, Fukuoka 810; f. 1946; morning; Man. Editor I. ISHIHARA; circ. 137,771.

Kagoshima Shimpo: 7-28 Jonan-cho, Kagoshima 892; f. 1959; morning; Man. Editor N. TOKONAMI; circ. 55,329.

Kumamoto Nichi-nichi Shimbun: 2-33, Kamidori-machi, Kumamoto 860; f. 1942; Editor T. MURAKAMI; circ. morning 292,652, evening 94,478.

Kyushu Sports: Fukuoka Tenjin Centre Bldg., 2-14-8, Tenjin, Chuo-ku, Fukuoka 810; f. 1966; morning; Man. Editor S. KOBIKI; circ. 199,260.

Mainichi Shimbun: 13-1, Konya-machi, Kokura Kita-ku, Kitakyushu 802; f. 1935; Rep. S. MAKIUCHI; circ. morning 642,131, evening 173,274.

Minami Nihon Shimbun: 1-2 Yasui-cho, Kagoshima-shi, Kagoshima 892; f. 1881; Man. Editor S. FUKUISHI; circ. morning 302,233, evening 29,179.

Miyazaki Nichi-nichi Shimbun: 1-33, 1-chome Takachiho-dori, Miyazaki 880; f. 1940; Man. Editor S. HIRASHIMA; morning; circ. 175,630.

Nagasaki Shimbun: 3-1, Mori-machi, Nagasaki 852; f. 1889; Man. Editor H. IWANAGA; circ. morning 150,659; evening 50,136.

The Nihon Keizai Shimbun: 3-1, 2-chome, Sumiyoshi, Hakata-ku, Fukuoka City; f. 1964; Chief S. TAKEI; circ. morning 143,108, evening 58,842.

Nishi Nippon Shimbun: 4-1, 1-chome, Tenjin, Chuo-ku, Fukuoka 810; f. 1877; Man. Editor H. MIYATA; circ. morning 700,347, evening 223,562.

Oita Godo Shimbun: 9-15, 3-chome, Fudai-cho, Oita 870; f. 1886; Man. Editor S. NANRI; circ. morning 181,867, evening 182,085.

Okinawa Times: 2-2-2, Kumoji, Naha City, Okinawa; f. 1948; Man. Editor A. ARAKAWA; circ. morning 167,040, evening 161,112.

Ryukyu Shimpo: 1-10-3, Izumisaki, Naha City, Okinawa; f. 1893; Man. Editor H. ICHIMURA; circ. morning 161,884, evening 161,884.

Saga Shimbun: 3-18, 1-chome, Matsubara, Saga City 840; f. 1884; morning; Man. Editor S. INADA; circ. 100,460.

Sports Nippon: 4-1, 1-chome, Kiyotaki, Moji-ku, Kitakyushu 801; f. 1955; morning; Man. Editor T. DOI; circ. 151,100.

Yomiuri Shimbun: 1-11 Meiwa-machi, Kokurakita-ku, Kitakyushu 802; f. 1964; Man. Editor M. WATAI; circ. morning 836,214, evening 158,126.

WEEKLIES

Asahi Graphic: Asahi Shimbun Publishing Co., Tsukiji, Chuo-ku, Tokyo; f. 1923; pictorial review; Editor YUKO HATSUYAMA; circ. 200,000.

Asahi Journal: Asahi Shimbun Publications Dept., Tsukiji, Chuo-ku, Tokyo 104; f. 1959; review; Editor SHOJI TAKASE.

Economist: 1-1-1, Hitotsubashi, Chiyoda-ku, Tokyo; f. 1923; published by the Mainichi Newspapers; Editorial Chief MOTOI GOTO; circ. 117,000.

The Gijitsu Journal: 8-10 Kudan kita, 1-chome, Chiyoda-ku, Tokyo; f. 1959; industrial technology.

Nihon Shogyo: Tokyo; f. 1895; Exec. Dir. SHIGETOSHI MATSUNAGA; circ. 35,000.

Shukan Asahi: Asahi Shimbun Publishing Co., Tsukiji, Chuo-ku, Tokyo; Editor TETSUAKI HATAKEYAMA; circ. 600,000.

Shukan Bunshun: 3 Kioi-cho, Chiyoda-ku, Tokyo; f. 1959; general; circ. 550,000.

Shukan Daiyamond: Diamond Inc., 4-2, 1-chome, Kasumigaseki, Chiyoda-ku, Tokyo; Editor KAZUYA TSUBAKI.

Shukan Gendai: Kodansha Co. Ltd., 12-21, 2-chome, Otowa, Bunkyo-ku, Tokyo; Editor TOMIO SUZUKI.

Shukan Post: Shogakukan Publishing Co. Ltd., 3-1, 2-chome, Hitotsubashi, Chiyoda-ku, Tokyo; Editor SUSUMU SEKINE.

Shukan Sankei: 7-2, 1-chome, Otemachi, Chiyoda-ku, Tokyo; general; Editor TAKAO YAMURA.

Shukan Shincho: 71 Yarai-cho, Shinjuku-ku, Tokyo; general; Editor HIKOYA YAMADA; circ. 910,000.

Shukan Toyo Keizai: 1-4 Hongkoku-cho, Nihonbashi, Chuo-ku, Tokyo; f. 1895; economics; Editor SASABURO SATO; circ. 60,000.

Shukan Yomiuri: 7-1, 1-chome, Otemachi, Chiyoda-ku, Tokyo; Editor KENJI SAKAI; general.

Student Times: Japan Times Inc., 4-5-4 Shibaura, Minato-ku, Tokyo; English and Japanese.

Sunday Mainichi: 1-1-1 Hitotsubashi, Chiyoda-ku, Tokyo; Editor HIROSHI SHIKATA; circ. 500,000.

Tenji Mainichi: 2-36 Dojima, Kita-ku, Osaka; f. 1922; in Japanese braille; Editor MICHITOSHI ZENIMOTO; circ. 12,000.

PERIODICALS

Airview: 601 Kojun Bldg., 6-8-7 Ginza, Chuo-ku, Tokyo; f. 1946; monthly; Editor T. MIZUNO.

All Yomimono: 3, Kioi-cho, Chiyoda-ku, Tokyo; f. 1930; popular fiction; monthly; Editor TAKUJI SUZUKI.

Alpinist: 3-13, 2-chome, Konan, Minato-ku, Tokyo; f. 1942; circ. 100,000; Editor K. MOMOSE; monthly.

Asahi Camera: Tsukiji, Chuo-ku, Tokyo 104; f. 1926; photography; monthly; Editor TERUO OKAI; circ. 200,000.

Asia Pacific Community: The Asian Club, P.O.B. 71, Trade Center, Tokyo; f. 1978; political, economic, cultural, social, etc.; quarterly (Jan., April, July, Oct.) in English; Editor HIDEO UENO; Man. Editor JOHEI TACHIBANA; circ. 6,000.

Bijutsu Techô: Bijutsu Shuppan-sha, Inaoka Bldg., 2-36 Kanda, Jinbo-cho, Chiyoda-ku, Tokyo; f. 1948; monthly; fine arts.

Bungaku (*Literature*): Iwanami Shoten, 2-5-5, Hitotsubashi, Chiyoda-ku, Tokyo; f. 1933; monthly; Editor YOSHIYA TAMURA.

Bungei-Shunju: 3 Kioi-cho, Chiyoda-ku, Tokyo; f. 1923; popular monthly; general.

Chuo Koron: 8-7, Kyobashi 2-chome, Chuo-ku, Tokyo; f. 1886; monthly; political, economic, scientific and literary; Chief Editor MASAMI AOYAGI.

Fujin Koron: Chuo Koron-sha, 8-7, Kyobashi 2-chome, Chuo-ku, Tokyo; women's literary monthly; Editor KAZUO MATSUMURA.

Fujin-Seikatsu: 19-5, Yusima 2-chome, Bunkyo-ku, Tokyo; f. 1947; women's; monthly; Editor TOYOHEI HONJO.

Geijitsu Shincho: 71 Yarai-cho, Shinjuku-ku, Tokyo; f. 1950; monthly; fine arts, music, architecture, drama and design; Editor-in-Chief SHOZO YAMAZAKI.

Gendai: 12-21, Otowa 2-chome, Bunkyo-ku, Tokyo; f. 1966; cultural and political; monthly; Editor TOSHIO ITO.

Gengo-Seikatsu: Chikuma-shobo, Chiyoda-ku, Tokyo; f. 1951; language and life monthly; Editor MINEO NAKAJIMA; circ. 20,000.

Gunzo: 12-21, Otowa 2-chome, Bunkyo-ku, Tokyo; f. 1946; literary monthly; Editor YUJI HASHINAKA.

Horitsu Jiho: 14 Sugamachi, Shinjuku-ku, Tokyo; f. 1929; law journal; monthly.

Ie-no-Hikari (*Light of Home*): 11 Funagawara-cho, Ichigaya, Shinjuku-ku, Tokyo; f. 1925; monthly; rural and general interest; Pres. YASUO OGUSHI; Editor IWAO OHTANI; circ. 1,300,000.

Iwa-To-Yuki (*Rock and Snow*): 1-1-33, Shiba Daimon, Minato-ku, Tokyo; every 2 months; mountaineering.

The Japan Architect: 31-2, Yushima 2-chome, Bunkyo-ku, Tokyo 113; f. 1956; monthly; international edition of *Shinkenchiku*; Editor SHOZO BABA; Publisher YOSHIO YOSHIDA; circ. 17,000.

Japan Company Handbook: 1-4, Hongoku-cho Nihonbashi, Chuo-ku, Tokyo; English, published by *The Oriental Economist*; 2 a year; Editor SEI KAGAWA.

Japan Quarterly: Asahi Shimbun, 5-3-2, Tsukiji, Chuo-ku, Tokyo; f. 1954; English; Exec. Editor YUICHIRO KOMINAMI.

Jitsugyo No Nihon: 3-9, Ginza 1-chome, Chuo-ku, Tokyo; f. 1897; semi-monthly; economic and business; Editor NOBUYOSHI YOSHIDA; circ. 100,000.

Journal of Electronic Engineering: 11-15, Higashi Gotanda 1-chome, Shinagawa-ku, Tokyo; f. 1950; monthly; circ. 72,000.

Journal of the Electronics Industry: 11-15, Higashi Gotanda 1-chome, Shinagawa-ku, Tokyo 141; f. 1954; monthly; circ. 108,500.

Kagaku (*Science*): Iwanami Shoten, 2-5-5, Hitotsubashi, Chiyoda-ku, Tokyo; f. 1931; Editor KAZUO OTSUKA.

Kagaku Asahi: 5-3-2, Tsukiji, Chuo-ku, Tokyo; f. 1941; scientific; monthly; Editor KEI NOZAURA.

Kagakushi-Kenkyu: History of Science Society of Japan, Centre for Humanities and Social Sciences, Tokyo Institute of Technology, 2-12-1, Ookayama, Méguro-ku, Tokyo 152; f. 1941; quarterly Journal of the History of Science Society of Japan; Editor HIROSHI ISHIYAMA.

Kaisha Shikiho: 1-4, Hongoku-cho, Nihonbashi, Chuo-ku, Tokyo; f. 1936; economic; quarterly; circ. 600,000.

Keizai Hyoron: 14 Sugamachi, Shinjuku, Tokyo; economic review.

Keizaizin: Kansai Economic Federation, Nakanoshima Center Bldg., 6-2-27, Nakanoshima, Kita-ku, Osaka; economics; monthly; Editor I. MORIGUCHI.

Kokka: Kokka-sha, 7F Hamariyyu Bldg., 5-3-3, Tsukiji, Chuo-ku, Tokyo; f. 1889; Far Eastern art; monthly; Chief Editor YOSHIHO YONEZAWA.

Mizue: Bijutsu Shuppan-sha, Inaoka Bldg., 2-36 Kanda, Jimbo-cho, Chiyoda-ku, Tokyo 101; f. 1905; monthly; fine arts.

Nogyo Asahi: 2-3, Yuraku-cho, Chiyoda-ku, Tokyo; monthly; scientific.

Ongaku No Tomo (*Friends of Music*): Ongaku No Tomo Sha Corpn., Kagurazaka 6-30, Shinjuku-ku, Tokyo; classical music; monthly; circ. 96,000.

Oriental Economist: 1-4, Hongoku-cho, Nihonbashi, Chuo-ku, Tokyo; f. 1934; economic and political monthly; English edn.; Pres. YASUJI TABUCHI; Editor ATSUO TSURUOKA.

Sekai: Iwanami Shoten, 5-5, 2-chome, Hitotsubashi, Tokyo; f. 1946; review of world and domestic affairs; monthly; Editor RYOSUKE YASUE; circ. 100,000.

Shincho: 71, Yarai-cho, Shinjuku-ku, Tokyo; literary; monthly; Editor SHOHEI TANIDA; circ. 30,000.

Shinkenchiku: 31-2, Yushima 2-chome, Bunkyo-ku, Tokyo 113; f. 1924; monthly architectural journal; Editor SHOZO BABA; Publr. YOSHIO YOSHIDA; circ. 48,000.

Shiso (*Thought*): Iwanami Shoten, 2-5-5, Hitotsubashi, Chiyoda-ku, Tokyo; f. 1921; philosophy, social sciences and humanities review; monthly; Editor ATSUSHI AIBA.

Shizen (*Nature*): Chuo Koron Sha, 1, 2-chome, Kyobashi, Chuo-ku, Tokyo; scientific monthly; Editor AKIHIKO OKABE.

Shosetsu Shincho: Shincho-sha Publishing Co., 71 Yarai; cho, Shinjuku-ku, Tokyo; f. 1945; monthly; literature-Chief Editor REIKO KAWANO.

Shukan FM: Ongaku No Tomo Sha Corpn., 6-30, Kagurazaka, Shinjuku-ku, Tokyo; guide to music broadcasts; every 2 weeks; circ. 330,000.

So-en: Bunka Publishing Bureau, 1-22, Yoyogi 3-chome, Shibuya-ku, Tokyo; fashion monthly; Chief Editor FUMIKO NIMURA; circ. 400,000.

Statistics Monthly (*Toyo Keizai Tokei Geppo*): published by *The Oriental Economist*, 1-4, Hongoku-cho, Nihonbashi, Chuo-ku, Tokyo; f. 1895.

Stereo: Ongaku No Tomo Sha Corpn., 6-30, Kagurazaka, Shinjuku-ku, Tokyo; records and audio; monthly; circ. 140,000.

Sûgaku (*Mathematics*): Mathematical Society of Japan, 25-9-203, Hongo 4-chome, Bunkyo-ku, Tokyo 113; f. 1947; quarterly.

Tenbo: Chikuma-Shobo, 2-8, Kanda Ogawamachi, Chiyoda-ku, Tokyo; f. 1964; general; monthly; Editor MITSUMASA KATSUMATA; circ. 50,000.

Yama-To-Keikoku (*Mountain and Valley*): 1-1-33, Shiba-Daimon, Minato-ku, Tokyo; monthly; mountain climbing.

Zosen: Tokyo News Service Ltd., Tsukiji Hamarikyu Bldg., 3-3, Tsukiji 5-chome, Chuo-ku, Tokyo 104; monthly, English; shipbuilding; Editor ISAO SATO; circ. 7,500.

NEWS AGENCIES

Foreign Press Centre: 6th Floor, Nippon Press Centre Bldg., 2, 2-1 Uchisaiwai-cho, Chiyoda-ku, Tokyo; f. 1976; sponsored by Japan Newspaper Publishers and Editors Association and the Japan Federation of Economic Organizations; provides services to the foreign Press; Dir. KINJI KAWAMURA; Pres. SHIZUO SAITO.

Jiji Tsushin-Sha (*Jiji Press*): 1-3 Hibiya Park, Chiyoda-ku, Tokyo 100; f. 1945; Pres. TADAYOSHI OHATA.

Kyodo Tsushin (*Kyodo News Service*): 2-2-5 Toranomon, Minato-ku, Tokyo 105; f. 1945; Pres. TAKEJI WATANABE; Man. Dir. SHINJI SAKAI; Man. Editor Y. INUKAI.

Radiopress Inc.: Fuji TV Bldg., 7 Ichigaya Kawada-cho, Shinjuku-ku, Tokyo 162; f. 1945; provides news from China, U.S.S.R., North Korea, Viet-Nam etc. to the Press and govt. offices; Pres. JIRO INAGAWA; publ. *China Directory* (annually).

Sun Telephoto: Palaceside Bldg., 1-1, 1-chome, Hitotsubashi, Chiyoda-ku, Tokyo 100; f. 1952; Pres. K. MATSUOKA; Man. Editor Y. YAMAMOTO.

FOREIGN BUREAUX

Tokyo

Agence France-Presse (AFP): Asahi Shimbun Bldg., 11th Floor, 3-2 Tsukiji 5-chome, Chuo-ku, 104; Bureau Chief FÉLIX BOLO.

Agencia EFE (*Spain*): c/o U.P.I., Palaceside Bldg., 1-1-1 Hitotsubashi, Chiyoda-ku, 100; P.O.B. 665; Correspondent DAVID CORRAL BRAVO.

Agentstvo Pechati Novosti (APN) (*U.S.S.R.*): 3-9-13, Higashi-gotanda, Shinagawa-ku 141; Correspondent MIKHAIL AFIMOV.

Agenzia Nazionale Stampa Associata (ANSA) (*Italy*): 9th Floor, Kyodo Tsushin Kaikan, 2 Akasaka, Aoi-cho, Minato-ku, 107; Correspondent MARIA ROMILDA GIORGIS.

Allgemeiner Deutscher Nachrichtendienst (ADN) (*German Democratic Republic*): 9-9, 4-chome, Jingu-mae, Shibuya-ku, 150; Correspondents Dr. ANDREAS KABUS, HELGA KABUS.

Antara (*Indonesia*): 9th Floor, Kyodo Tsushin Bldg., 2-2-5 Toranomon, Minato-ku, 107; Correspondent GANDHI SUKARDI.

Associated Press (AP) (*U.S.A.*): Asahi Shimbun Bldg., 3-2, Tsukiji, 5-chome, Chuo-ku; Bureau Chief ROY K. ESSOYAN.

Bulgarian Telegraph Agency (BTA): Room 802, Daiichi Aoyama Mansion, 1-10, 5-chome, Minami Aoyama, Minato-ku, 107; Correspondent IVAN A. GAYTANDJIEV.

Central News Agency Inc. (*Taiwan*): Room 503, Kyowa Bldg., 5-6 Iidabashi, 1-chome, Chiyoda-ku; Bureau Chief CHIA LEE.

Deutsche Presse-Agentur (dpa) (*Federal Republic of Germany*): Shisei Kaikan, Room 202, Hibiya Park, Chiyoda-ku, 100; Bureau Chief HANS-JÜRGEN KAHL.

Keystone Press Agency (*U.K.*): Kaneda Bldg., 3-17-2 Shibuya, Shibuya-ku, 150; Pres. JUNZO SUZUKI.

Magyar Távirati Iroda (MTI) (*Hungary*): 3-10-2 Kakinokizaka, Meguro-ku, 152; Correspondent ISTVAN FLESCH.

Prensa Latina (*Cuba*): 36-6, 3-chome, Nozawa, Setagaya-ku 154; Correspondent CARLOS IGLESIAS CELESTRIN.

Reuters (*U.K.*): Kyodo Tsushin Bldg., 2-2-5 Toranomon, Minato-ku.

Tanjug News Agency (*Yugoslavia*): 3-1-10, Takanawa, Minato-ku, 108; Correspondent ŽARKO MODRIĆ.

Telegrafnoye Agentstvo Sovietskogo Soyuza (TASS) (*U.S.S.R.*): 5-1, 1-chome, Hon-cho, Shibuya-ku, 151; Correspondent VICTOR ZATSEPINE.

United Press International (UPI) (*U.S.A.*): Palaceside Bldg., 1-1, Hitotsubashi 1-chome, Chiyoda-ku, 100; Correspondent TOSHIYUKI AIZAWA.

Xinhua (New China News Agency) (*People's Republic of China*): 35-23, 3-chome, Ebisu, Shibuya-ku, 150; Dir. KONG MAI; Correspondents WU XUE-WEN, LIU WENUOU, YU YIGUO.

Yonhap (United) News Agency (*Republic of Korea*): Kyodo Tsushin Bldg., 2-2-5 Toranomon, Minato-ku, 105; f. 1945; Bureau Chief LEE SANG-KWON.

PRESS ASSOCIATIONS

Nihon Shinbun Kyokai (*Japan Newspaper Publishers and Editors Association*): Nippon Press Center Bldg., 2-1, Uchisaiwai-cho 2-chome, Chiyoda-ku, Tokyo 100; f. 1946; mems. include 165 companies, including 114 daily newspapers, 4 news agencies and 47 radio and TV companies; Pres. SEIKI WATANABE; Man. Dir. SUSUMU EJIRI; Sec.-Gen. TOSHIE YAMADA; publs. *The Japanese Press* (annual), *Shimbun Kenkyu* (monthly), *Shimbun Kyokai Ho* (weekly), *Nihon Shimbun Nenkan* (annual), *Shimbun Insatsu Gijutsu* (quarterly), *Shimbun Keiei* (quarterly), *NSK News Bulletin* (quarterly), *Shimbun Kokoku Ho* (monthly).

Japan Magazine Publishers' Association: 7, 1-chome, Kanda Surugadai, Chiyoda-ku, Tokyo; f. 1945; 59 mems.; Pres. GENZO CHIBA; Sec. JEIJI JANUMA.

PUBLISHERS

(In Tokyo unless otherwise indicated)

Akane Shobo Co. Ltd.: 3-2-1, Nishikanda, Chiyoda-ku; f. 1949; science, literature, juvenile; Pres. MUTSUTO OKAMOTO.

Akita Publishing Shoten Co. Ltd.: 2-10-8, Iidabashi, Chiyoda-ku; f. 1948; social science, history, juvenile; Man. Dir. SADAMI AKITA.

Baifukan Co. Ltd.: 3-12, Kudan Minami 4-chome, Chiyoda-ku; f. 1924; mathematics, natural and social science, technology; Pres. KENJI YAMAMOTO.

Bijutsu Shuppan-Sha: 6th Floor, Inaoka Bldg., 2-36, Kanda Jimbo-cho, Chiyoda-ku; f. 1905; art and architecture; Pres. ATSUSHI OSHITA.

Chikuma Shobo Publishing Co. Ltd.: 2-8, Kanda Ogawamachi, Chiyoda-ku; f. 1940; general fiction and non-fiction; Rep. KAKUZAEMON NUNOKAWA.

Chuokoron-Sha Inc.: 2-8-7, Kyobashi, Chuo-ku; f. 1886; philosophy, history, sociology, literature, fine arts and magazines; Pres. HOJI SHIMANAKA.

Froebel-Kan Co. Ltd.: 3-1, Kanda Ogawa-machi, Chiyoda-ku; f. 1907; juvenile, educational, music; Pres. SHIROMI WATANABE.

Fukuinkan Shoten: 1-1-9, Misaki-cho, Chiyoda-ku; f. 1952; juvenile; Pres. TADASHI MATSUI.

Gakken Co. Ltd.: 4-40-5, Kamiikedai, Ohta-ku, 145; f. 1946; fiction, juvenile, education, art, history, reference, encyclopaedias, dictionaries, language; Pres. HIDETO FURUOKA.

Hakusui-Sha: 3-24, Kanda Ogawa-machi, Chiyoda-ku, f. 1915; general literature, science and languages; Pres. SUEO NAKAMORI.

Heibonsha: 5, Sanbancho, Chiyoda-ku; f. 1914; encyclopaedias, art, history, geography, Japanese and Chinese literature, etc.; Pres. KUNIHIKO SHIMONAKA.

Hirokawa Publishing Co.: 3-27-14, Hongo, Bunkyo-ku; f. 1926; science, medicine, textbooks; Pres. GENJI HIROKAWA.

The Hokuseido Press: 12, Nishikicho 3-chome, Kanda, Chiyoda-ku, 101; f. 1914; regional non-fiction, text books; Pres. JUMPEI NAKATSUCHI.

Ie-No-Hikari Association: 11 Funagawara-cho, Ichigaya, Shinjuku-ku; f. 1925; social science, industry; Pres. YASUO OGUSHI; Man. Dir. MAREKI KURUBA.

Iwanami Shoten: 2-5-5, Hitotsubashi, Chiyoda-ku; f. 1913; natural and social sciences, literature, history, geography; Chair. YUJIRO IWANAMI; Pres. TORU MIDORIKAWA.

Jimbun Shoin: Takakura-Nishi-iru, Bukkoji-dori, Shimogyo-ku, Kyoto; f. 1922; literary, philosophy, history, fine art; Pres. MUTSUHISA WATANABE.

Kanehara & Co. Ltd.: 31-14, Yushima 2-chome, Bunkyo-ku; f. 1875; medical, agricultural, engineering and scientific; Pres. HIDEO KANEHARA.

Kodansha Ltd.: 2-12-21, Otowa, Bunkyo-ku; f. 1909; art, education, children's picture books, fiction, cookery, encyclopaedias, natural science, paperbacks in Japanese, various magazines; Pres. KOREMICHI NOMA.

Kyoritsu Shuppan Co. Ltd.: 4-6-19, Kobinata, Bunkyo-ku; f. 1926; scientific and technical; Pres. MASAO NANJO.

Maruzen Co. Ltd.: 3-10, Nihonbashi 2-chome, Chuo-ku; f. 1869; general; Pres. SHINGO IIZUMI; Exec. Dir. TAKEMI EGUCHI; Man. Dir. KUMAO EBIHARA.

Minerva Shobo Co. Ltd.: 1 Tsutsumidani-cho, Hinooka, Yamashina-ku, Kyoto 607; f. 1948; general non-fiction and reference; Pres. NOBUO SUGITA.

Misuzu Shobo Publishing Co.: 3-17-15, Hongo, Bunkyo-ku; f. 1947; general, philosophy, history, literature, science, art; Pres. TAMIO KITANO; Man. Dir. TOSHITO OBI.

Nanzando Co. Ltd.: 4-1-11, Yushima, Bunkyo-ku; medical reference, paperbacks; Man. Dir. KIMIO SUZUKI.

Obunsha Co. Ltd.: 55 Yokodera-cho, Shinjuku-ku; f. 1931; textbooks, reference books, general science and fiction; magazines; encyclopaedias; audio-visual aids; Pres. YOSHIO AKAO.

Ohmsha Ltd.: 1-3, Kanda Nishiki-cho, Chiyoda-ku, 101; f. 1914; engineering, technical and scientific; Pres. SEIKOH MITSUI; Exec. Dir. S. SATO.

Ongaku No Tomo Sha Corp.: 6-30, Kagurazaka, Shinjuku-ku; f. 1941; folios, music copyrights, music books and magazines; Pres. SUNAO ASAKA.

Risosha: 46 Akagishita-machi, Shinjuku-ku, 162; f. 1927; philosophy, religion, social science; Pres. TETSUO SHIMOMURA.

Sankei Shimbun Shuppankyoku Co.: 3-15, Kanda Nishikicho, Chiyoda-ku; f. 1950; history, social sciences, politics, juvenile; Man. Dir. MASASHI ONODA.

Sanseido Publishing Co.: 2-22-14, Misakicho, Chiyoda-ku; f. 1881; dictionaries, education, languages, science, sociology; Pres. HISANORI UENO.

Seibundo-Shinkosha Publishing Co. Ltd.: 1-5, Kanda Nishiki-cho, Kanda, Chiyoda-ku; f. 1912; technical and scientific, agriculture, flowers, hobbies, electronics, audio, commerce; Pres. and Man. Dir. SHIGEO OGAWA.

Shinkenchiku-Sha Ltd.: 31-2, Yushima 2-chome, Bunkyo-ku; f. 1925; architecture; Editor SHOZO BABA; Publr. YOSHIO YOSHIDA.

Shogakukan Publishing Co. Ltd.: 2-3-1, Hitotsubashi, Chiyoda-ku; f. 1922; juvenile, education, geography, history, encyclopaedias, dictionaries; Pres. TETSUO OHGA.

Shokokusha Publishing Co. Ltd.: 25 Saka-machi, Shinjuku-ku; f. 1932; architectural, technical and fine art; Chair. and Pres. GENSHICHI SHIMOIDE; Man. Dir. TAISHIRO YAMAMOTO.

Shufunotomo Co. Ltd.: 6, Kanda Surugadai 1-chome, Chiyoda-ku; f. 1916; domestic science, juvenile, fine art, gardening, handicraft, cookery; monthly women's magazines; Pres. HARUHIKO ISHIKAWA.

Shunju-Sha Co. Ltd.: 2-18-6, Soto-kanda, Chiyoda-ku; f. 1918; philosophy, religion, literary, economics, music, etc.; Pres. HIROKICHI TANAKA; Man. O. KANDA.

Taishukan Shoten: 3-24, Kanda Nishiki-cho, Chiyoda-ku; f. 1918; reference, Japanese and foreign languages, Buddhism, audio-visual aids, dictionaries; Man. Dir. TOSHIO SUZUKI.

Tokyo News Service Ltd.: Tsukiji Hamarikyu Bldg., 10th Floor, 3-3, Tsukiji 5-chome, Chuo-ku, 104; f. 1947; shipping and shipbuilding; Pres. T. OKUYAMA.

University of Tokyo Press: 7-3-1, Hongo, Bunkyo-ku, 113; f. 1951; natural sciences, social sciences and humanities; academic journals; Japanese and English; Man. Dir. KAZUO ISHII.

Yama-kei Publishing Co. Ltd.: 1-1-33, Shiba-Daimon, Minato-ku; f. 1930; natural science, geography, mountaineering; Pres. YOSHIMITSU KAWASAKI.

Yuhikaku Publishing Co. Ltd.: 2-17, Kanda Jimbo-cho, Chiyoda-ku; f. 1877; social sciences, law, economics; Pres. TADAATSU EGUSA; Chair. SHIRO EGUSA.

Zoshindo Juken Kenkyusha: 2-19-15, Shinmachi, Nishi-ku, Osaka 550; f. 1890; educational, juvenile; Pres. SHIGETOSHI OKAMOTO.

PUBLISHERS' ASSOCIATIONS

Japan Book Publishers' Association: 6 Fukuro-machi, Shinjuku-ku, Tokyo 162; Dir.-Gen. TOSHIYUKI HATTORI; Man. Dir. SHIGESHI SASAKI.

Publishers Association for Cultural Exchange: 1-2-1, Sarugaku-cho, Chiyoda-ku, Tokyo 101; 135 mems.; Pres. SHOICHI NOMA; Dir. SHOICHI NAKAJIMA.

RADIO AND TELEVISION

Nippon Hoso Kyokai, N.H.K. (*Japan Broadcasting Corporation*): Broadcasting Centre, NHK Hoso Centre, 2-2-1, Jinnan, Shibuya-ku, Tokyo 150; f. 1925; Chair. Board of Govs. T. HARA; Pres. TOMOKAZU SAKAMOTO.

Nippon Hoso Kyokai is a non-commercial public corporation whose Governors are appointed by the Government. Five (2 TV and 3 radio) networks and 7,170 stations cover the country, the TV ones equipped for colour broadcasting, equally divided between general and educational networks; central stations at Tokyo, Osaka, Nagoya, Hiroshima, Kumamoto, Sendai, Sapporo and Matsuyama. The Overseas Service broadcasts in 21 languages.

National Association of Commercial Broadcasters in Japan (MINPOREN): Bungei Shunju Bldg., 3, Kioi-cho. Chiyoda-ku, Tokyo 102; Pres. YOSHIYUKI YAMANISHI; Exec. Dir. NAGATO IZUMI; Sec.-Gen. SEIGO NAGATAKE; association of 116 companies (98 TV companies, 18 radio companies. Among the TV companies, 36 operate radio and TV) with 204 radio stations and 5,078 TV stations. They include:

Asahi Hoso-Asahi Broadcasting Corp.: 2-2-48, Oyodo-Minami, Oyodo-ku, Osaka 531; Chair. TSUNEJIRO HIRAI; Pres. KIYOSHI HARA.

Bunka Hoso-Nippon Cultural Broadcasting, Inc.: 1-5, Wakabo, Shinjuku-ku, Tokyo 160; f. 1952; Chair. YOSHIO AKAO; Pres. MASATOSHI IWAMOTO.

Nippon Hoso-Nippon Broadcasting System, Inc.: 1-9-3, Yuraku-cho, Chiyoda-ku, Tokyo 100; f. 1954; Chair. N. SHIKANAI; Pres. T. ISHIDA.

Nihon Tanpa Hoso-Nihon Short-Wave Broadcasting Co.: 9-15, Akasaka 1-chome, Minato-ku, Tokyo 107; Pres. S. ANDO.

Okinawa Televi Hoso-Okinawa Television Broadcasting Co. Ltd.: 2-32-1, Kume, Naha 900, Okinawa; f. 1959; Pres. Y. YAMASHIRO.

Ryukyu Hoso-Ryukyu Broadcasting Corporation Ltd.: 2-3-1, Kumoji, Naha 900, Okinawa; f. 1954; Pres. TSUGUHIRO TOHMA.

Tokyo Hoso-Tokyo Broadcasting System, Inc.: 5-3-6, Akasaka, Minato-ku, Tokyo 107; f. 1951; Chair. HIROSHI SUWA; Pres. YOSHIYUKI YAMANISHI.

There are also 92 commercial television stations operated by Asahi Broadcasting Co., Nippon TV Network Co., Fuji Telecasting Co. and others, including:

Televi Asahi—Asahi National Broadcasting Co. Ltd.: 4-10, 6-chome Roppongi, Minato-ku, Tokyo 106; f. 1959; Chair. YOSHIO AKAO; Pres. MAKOTO TAKANO.

Yomiuri Televi Hoso—Yomiuri Telecasting Corporation: 1-8-11, Higashi-Tenma, Kita-ku, Osaka 530; f. 1958; 18 hrs. broadcasting a day, of which 62 hrs. per week in colour; Chair. MITSUO MUTAI; Vice-Pres. HIDEO TACHIBANA.

Regular colour television transmissions started in 1960.

TELEVISION NEWS AGENCIES

Asahi Video Projects Ltd.: 6-4-10 Roppongi, Minato-ku, Tokyo; f. 1958; Pres. K. SAMEJIMA.

Kyodo Television News: 7 Kawata-cho, Ichigaya, Shinjuku-ku, Tokyo; f. 1958; Pres. AKIRA HONMA.

There were an estimated 91 million radio receiving sets and 28,887,000 television sets in 1981.

FINANCE

BANKING

(cap.=capital; p.u.=paid up; dep.=deposits; m.=million; amounts in yen)

Japan's central bank and note-issuing body is the Bank of Japan, founded in 1882. More than half the credit business of the country is handled by 76 commercial banks (13 city banks and 63 regional banks), seven trust banks and three long-term credit banks, collectively designated "All Banks". The most important of these are the city banks, some of which have a distinguished history, reaching back to the days of the *zaibatsu*, the private entrepreneurial organizations on which Japan's capital wealth was built up before the Second World War. Although the *zaibatsu* were abolished as integral industrial and commercial enterprises during the Allied Occupation, the several businesses and industries which bear the former *zaibatsu* names, such as Mitsubishi, Mitsui and Sumitomo, continue to flourish and to give each other mutual assistance through their respective banks and trust corporations. Among the commercial banks, one, the Bank of Tokyo, specializes in foreign exchange business, while the Industrial Bank of Japan provides a large proportion of the finance for capital investment by industry. The Long-Term Credit Bank of Japan and Nippon Credit Bank Ltd. also specialize in industrial finance; the work of these three privately-owned banks is supplemented by the government-controlled Japan Development Bank.

The Government has established a number of other specialized organs to supply essential services not performed by the private banks. Thus the Japan Export-Import Bank advances credits for exports of heavy industrial products and imports of raw materials in bulk. A Housing Loan Corporation assists firms building housing for their employees, while the Agriculture, Forestry and Fisheries Finance Corporation gives loans to the named industries for equipment purchases. Similar services are provided for small businesses by the Small Business Finance Corporation.

An important part is played in the financial activity of the country by co-operatives, and by the many small enterprise institutions. Each prefecture has its own federation of co-operatives, with the Central Co-operative Bank of Agriculture and Forestry as the common central financial institution. This Central Co-operative Bank also serves as an agent for the Government's Agriculture, Forestry and Fisheries Finance Corporation.

There are also three types of private financial institutions for small business. The 71 Sogo Banks (Mutual Loan and Savings Banks) are now similar to commercial banks. There are 461 Credit Associations and 479 Credit Co-operatives, which loan only to members. The latter also receive deposits.

The commonest form of savings is through the government-operated Postal Savings System, which collects petty savings from the public by means of the post office network. Total deposits stood at 65,862,020 million yen in September 1981. The funds thus made available are used as loan funds by the Government financial institutions, through the Government's Trust Fund Bureau.

Clearing houses operate in each major city of Japan, and total 177 institutions. The largest are those of Tokyo and Osaka.

CENTRAL BANK

Nippon Ginko (*Bank of Japan*): 2-1, Nihonbashi Hongoku-cho 2-chome, Chuo-ku, Tokyo; f. 1882; cap. 100m.; Gov. HARUO MAEKAWA; Deputy Gov. SATOSHI SUMITA.

PRINCIPAL COMMERCIAL BANKS

Bank of Tokyo Ltd.: 6-3, Nihonbashi Hongoku-cho 1-chome, Chuo-ku, Tokyo; f. 1946; specializes in foreign exchange business; cap. p.u. 80,000m., dep. and debentures 8,561,620m. (Sept. 1981); Chair. SOICHI YOKOYAMA; Pres. YUSUKE KASHIWAGI; 80 brs.

Bank of Yokohama Ltd.: 47, Honcho 5-chome, Naka-ku, Yokohama; f. 1920; cap. p.u. 30.000m., dep. 3,868,452m. (Sept. 1981); Pres. JIRO YOSHIKUNI; 169 brs.

Dai-Ichi Kangyo Bank Ltd.: 1-5, Uchisaiwai-cho 1-chome, Chiyoda-ku, Tokyo; f. 1971; cap. p.u. 96,000m., dep. 15,693,602m. (Sept. 1981); Chair. SHOJIRO NISHIKAWA; Pres. SHUZO MURAMOTO; 337 brs.

Daiwa Bank Ltd.: 21, Bingomachi 2-chome, Higashi-ku, Osaka; f. 1918; cap. p.u. 60,000m. (Feb. 1982), dep. 7,432,485m. (Sept. 1981); Chair. SUSUMU FURUKAWA; Pres. ICHIRO IKEDA; 170 brs.

Fuji Bank Ltd.: 5-5, Otemachi 1-chome, Chiyoda-ku, Tokyo; f. 1880; cap. p.u. 111,375m., dep. 14,199,633m. (Sept. 1981); Chair. TAKUJI MATSUZAWA; Pres. YOSHIRO ARAKI; 247 brs.

Hokkaido Takushoku Bank Ltd.: 7 Nishi 3-chome, Odori, Chuo-ku, Sapporo; f. 1900; cap. 30,000m., dep. 3,594,856m. (Sept. 1981); Chair. TAKEI TOJO; Pres. AKIRA GOMI; 178 brs.

Kyowa Bank Ltd.: 1-2, Otemachi 1-chome, Chiyoda-ku, Tokyo 100; f. 1948; cap. 42,000m., dep. 5,484,553m. (Sept. 1981); Pres. TETSUO YAMANAKA; Chair. YOSHIAKA IROBE; 234 brs.

Mitsubishi Bank Ltd.: 7-1 Marunouchi, 2-chome, Chiyoda-ku, Tokyo 100; f. 1880; cap. 111,375m., dep. 13,452,648m. (Sept. 1981); Chair. TOSHIO NAKAMURA; Pres. HAJIME YAMADA; 223 brs.

Mitsui Bank Ltd.: 1-2, Yuraku-cho 1-chome, Chiyoda-ku, Tokyo; f. 1876; cap. p.u. 76,000m., dep. 9,983,470m. (Sept. 1981); Chair. MASAHIKO SEKI; Pres. TOSHIO KUSABA; 183 brs.

Saitama Bank Ltd.: 4-1, Tokiwa 7-chome, Urawa City, Saitama Prefecture; f. 1943; cap. 30,000m., dep. 4,816,056m. (Sept. 1981); Chair. KYOSUKE NAGASHIMA; Pres. TSUNESHIRO OHKI; 174 brs.

Sanwa Bank Ltd.: 4-10, Fushimi-cho, Higashi-ku, Osaka; f. 1933; cap. 111,375m., dep. 13,059,412m. (Sept. 1981); Chair. DAIGO MIYADOH; Pres. TOSHIO AKASHI; 250 brs.

Sumitomo Bank Ltd.: 22, Kitahama 5-chome, Higashi-ku, Osaka; f. 1895; cap. 111,375m., dep. 14,001,454m. (Sept. 1981); Chair. KYONOSUKE IBE; Pres. ICHIRO ISODA; 225 brs.

Taiyo Kobe Bank Ltd.: 56 Naniwa-cho, Chuo-ku, Kobe; f. 1936; cap. p.u. 70,000m., dep. 8,641,988m. (Sept. 1981); Chair. SHINICHI ISHINO; Pres. TADAO SHIOTANI; 341 brs.

Tokai Bank Ltd.: 21-24 Nishiki, 3-chome, Naka-ku, Nagoya; f. 1941; cap. p.u. 75,000m., dep. 9,858,034m. (March 1981); Chair. SHIGEMITSU MIYAKE; Pres. RYUICHI KATO; 240 brs.

PRINCIPAL TRUST BANKS

Chuo Trust and Banking Co. Ltd: 7-1 Kyobashi, 1-chome, Chuo-ku, Tokyo 104; f. 1962; cap. p.u. 5,000m., total assets 3,374,101m. (Sept. 1981); Chair. HISAO FUKUDA; Pres. TAKESHI SEKIGUCHI; 49 brs.

Mitsubishi Trust and Banking Corporation: 4-5, Marunouchi, 1-chome, Chiyoda-ku, Tokyo; f. 1927; cap. 37,500m., total assets 8,847,792m. (Sept. 1981); Pres. TADASHI YASUI; 51 brs.

Mitsui Trust and Banking Co. Ltd.: 1-1 Nihonbashi Muromachi, 2-chome, Chuo-ku, Tokyo 103; f. 1924; cap. 37,500m., total assets 7,522,477m. (Sept. 1982); Pres. SEIICHIRO YAMANAKA; 50 brs.

Sumitomo Trust and Banking Co., Ltd.: 15, Kitahama 5-chome, Higashi-ku, Osaka; f. 1925; cap. 37,500m., total assets 7,908,520m. (Sept. 1981); Pres. TAKESHI TASHIRO; 51 brs.

Toyo Trust and Banking Co. Ltd: 4-3, Marunouchi 1-chome, Chiyoda-ku, Tokyo; f. 1959; cap. p.u. 26,000m. (Oct. 1979); total assets 4,753,032m. (Sept. 1981); Pres. CHIGAZO MORITA; 49 brs.

Yasuda Trust and Banking Co. Ltd.: 2-1 Yaesu, 1-chome, Chuo-ku, Tokyo; f. 1925; cap. 30,000m., total assets 5,842,313m. (Sept. 1981); Pres. YOSHIO YAMAGUCHI; 52 brs.

LONG-TERM CREDIT BANKS

The Long-Term Credit Bank of Japan Ltd.: 2-4 Otemachi, 1-chome, Chiyoda-ku, Tokyo; f. 1952; cap. p.u. 100,000m., dep. and debentures 9,646,602m. (Sept. 1981); Chair. BINSUKE SUGIURA; Pres. KANBEI YOSHIMURA; 22 brs.

Nippon Credit Bank Ltd.: 13-10 Kudan-Kita 1-chome, Chiyoda-ku, Tokyo; f. 1957; cap. p.u. 78,500m., dep. and debentures 5,924,132m. (Sept. 1981); Chair. TATSUO SHODA; Pres. SHICHIRO YASUKAWA; 19 brs.

Nippon Kogyo Ginko (*The Industrial Bank of Japan, Ltd.*): 3-3, Marunouchi 1 chome, Chiyoda-ku, Tokyo 100; f. 1902; medium- and long-term financing; cap. p.u. 103,680m., dep. and debentures 11,515,128m., loans and discounts 7,939,390m. (Sept. 1981); Chair. ISAO MASAMUNE; Pres. KISABURO IKEURA; 25 brs.

PRINCIPAL GOVERNMENT CREDIT INSTITUTIONS

Agriculture, Forestry and Fisheries Finance Corporation: 9-3, Otemachi 1-chome, Chiyoda-ku, Tokyo; f. 1953; finances plant and equipment investment; cap. 168,233m. (Sept. 1982); Pres. KAZUHITO NAKANO; Vice-Pres. SHIRO ODAMURA.

Central Co-operative Bank for Commerce and Industry (*Shoko Chukin Bank*): 10-17, Yaesu 2-chome, Chuo-ku, Tokyo 104; f. 1936 to provide general banking services to facilitate finance for smaller enterprise co-operatives and other organizations formed mainly by small- and medium-scale enterprises; issues debentures; cap. 1,332,000m.; dep. and debentures 6,091,000m. (Dec. 1981); Pres. EIJI KAGEYAMA; Vice-Pres. HIROMI TOKUDA; publs. *Shoko Kinyu* (Commerce-Industry Financing, monthly), *Chukin Dayori* (monthly newspaper).

Central Co-operative Bank for Agriculture and Forestry (*Norinchukin Bank*): 8-3, Otemachi 1-chome, Chiyoda-ku, Tokyo; f. 1923; apex organ of financial system of agricultural, forestry and fisheries co-operatives; receives deposits from individual co-operatives, federations and agricultural enterprises; extends loans to these and to local government authorities and public corporations; adjusts excess and shortage of funds within co-operative system; issues debentures, invests funds and engages in other regular banking business; 11,129 mems.; cap. p.u. 30,000m., dep. and debentures 12,503,000m. (Dec. 1981); Pres. OSAMU MORIMOTO; Vice-Pres. TSUNEMASA SUZUKI.

The Export-Import Bank of Japan: 4-1, Otemachi 1-chome, Chiyoda-ku, Tokyo; f. 1950 to supplement or encourage the financing of exports, imports and overseas investment by ordinary financial institutions; cap. p.u. 952,300m. (March 1982); Pres. MICHIO TAKEUCHI.

Housing Loan Corporation: 4-10, Koraku 1-chome, Bunkyo-ku, Tokyo; f. 1950 to provide long-term capital for the construction of housing at low interest rates; cap. 97,200m. (March 1981); Pres. ON OHTSURU; Vice-Pres. YOSHIRO IWASE.

The Japan Development Bank: 9-1, Otemachi 1-chome, Chiyoda-ku, Tokyo; f. 1951; provides long-term loans;

subscribes for corporate bonds; guarantees corporate obligations; invests in specific projects; borrows funds from Government and abroad; issues external bonds and notes; cap. 233,971m.; loans outstanding 5,658,400m. (Sept. 1981); Gov. SHIGEYA YOSHISE; Deputy Gov. TATSUO TAJIMA.

Medical Care Facilities Finance Corporation: 2-2, Nibancho, Chiyoda-ku, Tokyo; f. 1960; cap. 11,500m. (Sept. 1982); Principal Officer RIKIO KITAGAWA.

The Overseas Economic Co-operation Fund: Takebashi Godo Bldg., 4-1, Otemachi 1-chome, Chiyoda-ku, Tokyo 100; f. 1961 to provide long-term loans or investments for projects in developing countries; cap. 840,244m.; Pres. TAKASHI HOSOMI; Deputy Pres. SHINZO AOKI.

People's Finance Corporation: 9-3, Otemachi 1-chome, Chiyoda-ku, Tokyo; f. 1949 to supply business funds particularly to very small enterprises among those sections of the population who are not in a position to obtain loans from banks and other private financial institutions; cap. p.u. 24,000m.; 4,800 mems.; Gov. MASATAKA OKURA; Deputy Gov. KEIICHI TSUJI.

Small Business Finance Corporation: 9-3, Otemachi 1-chome, Chiyoda-ku, Tokyo; f. 1953 to lend plant and equipment funds and long-term operating funds to small businesses (capital not more than 100m., or not more than 300 employees) which are not easily secured from other financial institutions; cap. p.u. 29,200m. (Sept. 1981) wholly subscribed by Government; Gov. MASAMICHI FUNAGO; Vice-Gov. MASAMI SUZUKI.

PRINCIPAL FOREIGN BANKS

Algemene Bank Nederland N.V. (*Netherlands*): Fuji Bldg., 2-3, Marunouchi 3-chome, Chiyoda-ku, Tokyo 100, C.P.O.B. 374; brs. in Kobe, Osaka, Fukuoka; Man. J. J. W. ZWEEGERS.

American Express International Banking Corpn. (*U.S.A.*) Toranomon Mitsui Bldg., 8-1, Kasumigaseki, 3-chome Chiyoda-ku, Tokyo 100; brs. in Naha, Okinawa; Vice-Pres. and Gen. Man. R. C. ARSENAULT.

Amro Bank (*Netherlands*): Yurakucho Denki Bldg., 7-1; Yuraku-cho 1-chome, Chiyoda-ku, Tokyo.

Bangkok Bank Ltd. (*Thailand*): Mitsui Bldg. No. 6 Annex, 8-11, Nihonbashi Muromachi 2-chome, Chuo-ku, Tokyo; 1 br.

Bank of America NT & SA: Tokyo Kaijo Bldg., 2-1, Marunouchi 1-chome, Tokyo; brs. in Yokohama, Osaka and Kobe; Exec. Vice-Pres. J. P. MISCOLL.

Bank of India: Mitsubishi Denki Bldg., 2-3, Marunouchi 2-chome, Chiyoda-ku, Tokyo; Chief Man. K. C. CHAKRABERTTI; br. in Osaka.

Bank Indonesia: Hibiya Park Bldg., 8-1, Yuraku-cho 1-chome, Chiyoda-ku, Tokyo.

Bank Negara Indonesia 1946: Kokusai Bldg., Room 117-118, 1-1, Marunouchi 3-chome, Chiyoda-ku, Tokyo; Gen. Man. WINARTO SOEMARTO.

Bankers Trust Co. (*U.S.A.*): Kishimoto Bldg., 2-2-1, Marunouchi 2-chome, Chiyoda-ku, Tokyo; Vice-Pres. and Gen. Man. R. PAUL FUKUDA.

Banque de l'Indochine et de Suez (*France*): French Bank Bldg., 1-2, Akasaka 1-chome, Minato-ku, Tokyo 107; Gen. Man. YVES A. MAX; br. in Osaka.

Banque Nationale de Paris (*France*): Yusen Bldg., 3-2, Marunouchi 2-chome, Chiyoda-ku, Tokyo 100; Gen. Man. MICHEL LE LAY.

Banque de Paris et des Pays-Bas (*France*): Yurakucho Denki Bldg., 7-1, Yuraku-cho 1-chome, Chiyoda-ku, Tokyo 100; Gen. Man. ROBERT TALLON.

Barclays Bank International Ltd. (*U.K.*): Mitsubishi Bldg., 5-2, Marunouchi 2-chome, Chiyoda-ku, Tokyo, (C.P.O.B. 466); Chief Man. E. A. K. STAINES.

Bayerische Vereinsbank (*Federal Republic of Germany*): Togin Bldg., 4-2, Marunouchi 1-chome, Chiyoda-ku, Tokyo 100; Gen. Mans. Dr. PETER P. BARON, PETER KERSTEN-THIELE.

Chartered Bank (*U.K.*): Fuji Bldg., 2-3, Marunouchi 3-chome, Tokyo; brs. in Kobe and Osaka; Man. T. G. LIGHTFOOT.

Chase Manhattan Bank, N.A. (*U.S.A.*): AIU Bldg., 1-3, Marunouchi 1-chome, Chiyoda-ku, Tokyo 100; Vice-Pres. and Gen. Man. TIMOTHY MCGINNIS; br. in Osaka.

Chemical Bank (*U.S.A.*): Mitsubishi Shoji Bldg. Annex, 3-1, Marunouchi 2-chome, Chiyoda-ku, Tokyo; Vice-Pres. and Gen. Man. D. S. SMITH, III.

Citibank N.A. (*U.S.A.*): 2-1, Otemachi 2-chome, Chiyoda-ku, Tokyo 100; brs. in Osaka, Yokohama, Nagoya; Sr. Vice-Pres. TATSUO UMEZONO.

Commerzbank AG (*Federal Republic of Germany*): Nippon Press Center Bldg., 2-1, Uchisaiwai-cho 2-chome, Chiyoda-ku, Tokyo; Gen. Mans. Dr. AXEL SMEND, ALBRECHT STAERKER, TAKAYOSHI MURAYAMA.

Continental Illinois National Bank and Trust Company of Chicago (*U.S.A.*): Mitsui Seimei Bldg., 2-3, Otemachi 1-chome, Chiyoda-ku, Tokyo; Vice-Pres. J. H. LERCH; 1 br.

Deutsche Bank AG (*Federal Republic of Germany*): Yurakucho Denki Bldg., S., 7-1, Yurakucho 1-chome, Chiyoda-ku, Tokyo 100; Gen. Mans. Dr. H. J. BECK, T. YASUI.

Dresdner Bank AG (*Federal Republic of Germany*): Tokyo branch: Mitsubishi Bldg., 5-2, Marunouchi 2-chome, Chiyoda-ku, Tokyo; Sr. Mans. ERNST REIMERS, KAZUHIKO NAGASO, KARL GRUTSCHNIG.

First National Bank of Chicago (*U.S.A.*): Time Life Bldg., 3-6, Otemachi 2-chome, Chiyoda-ku, Tokyo; Vice-Pres. and Gen. Man. KATSUHIKO YAMAMOTO.

Grindlays Bank p.l.c. (*U.K.*): 8F Yanmar Tokyo Bldg., 1-1, Yaesu 2-chome, Chuo-ku,Tokyo; Gen. Man. P. D. HAND.

Hongkong and Shanghai Banking Corporation (*Hong Kong*): 1-2, Marunouchi 2-chome, Chiyoda-ku, Tokyo; Chief Exec. R. E. HALE; 1 br.

International Commercial Bank of China (*Taiwan*): Togin Bldg., 4-2, Marunouchi 1-chome, Chiyoda-ku, Tokyo 100; Sr. Vice-Pres. and Man. THEODORE S. S. CHENG; 2 brs.

Korea Exchange Bank (*Republic of Korea*): New Kokusai Bldg., 4-1, Marunouchi 3-chome, Chiyoda-ku, Tokyo 100; Gen. Man. CHUN KEUN-OH; 3 br.

Lloyds Bank International Ltd. (*U.K.*): Yurakucho Denki Bldg., 7-1, Yurakucho 1-chome, Chiyoda-ku, Tokyo 100 (C.P.O.B. 464); Man. B. R. MACILWAINE.

Manufacturers Hanover Trust Co. (*U.S.A.*): 21st Floor, Asahi Tokai Bldg., 6-1, Otemachi 2-chome, Chiyoda-ku, Tokyo; Vice-Pres. and Man. KEITH K. KANEKO.

Marine Midland Bank (*U.S.A.*): Kokusai Bldg., 1-1, Marunouchi 3-chome, Chiyoda-ku, Tokyo; Vice-Pres. and Gen. Man. HOWARD J. BOYER.

Mercantile Bank Ltd. (*Hong Kong*): 5-15, Nishiki 1-chome, Naka-ku, Nagoya; Man. T. UESUGI.

Midland Bank p.l.c. (*U.K.*): Togin Bldg., 4-2, Marunouchi 1-chome, Chiyoda-ku, Tokyo 100; Man. MARK A. BYNG.

Morgan Guaranty Trust Co. (*U.S.A.*): Shin Yurakucho Bldg., 12-1, Yurakucho 1-chome, Chiyoda-ku, Tokyo 100; Vice-Pres. and Gen. Man. OSAMU TOBA.

National Bank of Pakistan: 20 Mori Bldg., 7-4, Nishi Shinbashi 2-chome, Minato-ku, Tokyo; f. 1949; Man. SHAH NAWAZ.

National Westminster Bank Ltd. (*U.K.*): Mitsubishi Bldg., 5-2, Marunouchi 2-chome, Chiyoda-ku, Tokyo; Regional Gen. Man. (Japan) I. N. F. POWELL.

Oversea-Chinese Banking Corpn. (*Singapore*): 128 Shin Tokyo Bldg., 3-1, Marunouchi 3-chome, Chiyoda-ku, Tokyo 100; Man. CHAN CHONG HOW.

Security Pacific National Bank (*U.S.A.*): Yurakucho Bldg., 10-1, Yurakucho 1-chome, Chiyoda-ku, Tokyo; Vice-Pres. and Gen. Man. DAVID M. PROCTOR, III.

Société Générale (*France*): Hibiya Chunichi Bldg., 1-4, Uchisaiwai-cho 2-chome, Chiyoda-ku, Tokyo; Gen. Man. GILBERT W. GREY.

State Bank of India: South Tower 352, Yurakucho Denki Bldg., Yurakucho 1-7-1, Chiyoda-ku, Tokyo 100; Chief Man. CHARLES ABRAHAM.

Swiss Bank Corpn.: Furukawa Sogo Bldg., 6-1, Marunouchi 2-chome, Chiyoda-ku, Tokyo; Sr. Vice-Pres. and Man. R. A. CAVELTI.

Union Bank of Switzerland: Yurakucho Bldg., 10-1, Yurako-cho 1-chome, Chiyoda-ku, Tokyo; Vice-Pres. and Man. PETER NIEDERHAUSER.

Union de Banques Arabes et Françaises UBAF (*France*): Mitsui Annex, 3-7, Muromachi 3-chome, Nihonbashi, Chuo-ku, Tokyo 103; Man. MAXIME ROCHE.

Westdeutsche Landesbank Girozentrale (*Federal Republic of Germany*): Kokusai Bldg., 1-1, Marunouchi 3-chome, Chiyoda-ku, Tokyo; Gen. Mans. ERHARD PASCHER, KLAUS R. SCHROEDER.

BANKERS' ASSOCIATIONS

Federation of Bankers' Associations of Japan: 3-1, Marunouchi 1-chome, Chiyoda-ku, Tokyo 100; f. 1945; 72 mem. associations; Chair. YOSHIRO ARAKI; Vice-Chair. DAIZO HOSHINO, ICHIRO ISODA; publs. *Kinyu* (Finance) (monthly), *Banking System in Japan*, *Zenkoku Ginko Zaimu-Shohyo Bunseki* (Analysis of Financial Statements of All Banks) (twice a year), *Statistical Supplement to Banking System In Japan* (every two years).

Tokyo Bankers' Association Inc.: 3-1, Marunouchi 1-chome, Chiyoda-ku, Tokyo 100; f. 1945; 82 mem. banks; conducts the above Federation's routine business; Chair. YOSHIRO ARAKI; Vice-Chair. DAIZO HOSHINO, TOSHIRO KUSABA, KANBEI YOSHIMURA.

Regional Banks Association of Japan: 3-1-2 Uchikanda, Chiyoda-ku, Tokyo 101; f. 1936; 63 member banks; Chair. JIRO YOSHIKUNI.

STOCK EXCHANGES

Tokyo Stock Exchange: 6, 1-chome, Nihonbashi-Kabuto-cho, Chuo-ku, Tokyo; f. 1949; 83 mems.; Pres. HIROSHI TANIMURA; publs. *Securities* (monthly), *TSE Monthly Statistics Report*, *Annual Statistics Report*.

Fukuoka Stock Exchange: 2-14-12, Tenjin, Chuo-ku, Fukuoka.

Hiroshima Stock Exchange: 14-18, Kanayama-cho, Hiroshima; f. 1949; 15 mems.; Principal Officer SHIGERU AKAGI.

Nagoya Stock Exchange: 3-17, Sakae-Sanchome, Naka-ku, Nagoya; f. 1949; Pres. JUNICHIRO KUMADA; Man. Dir. ICHIRO KAWAI.

Osaka Securities Exchange: 2-chome, Kitahama, Higashi-ku, Osaka; f. 1949; 51 regular mems. and 3 Nakadachi mems.; Pres. NAOYUKI MATSUI; Chair. MUNEKAZE YANO.

Sapporo Stock Exchange: 5-14-1, Nishi, Minami Ichijo, Naka-ku, Sapporo.

There are also Stock Exchanges at Kyoto and Niigata.

INSURANCE

The principal companies are as follows:

LIFE

Asahi Mutual Life Insurance Co.: 7-3, Nishishinjuku 1-chome, Shinjuku-ku, Tokyo 160; f. 1888; Pres. RYUHEI TAKASHIMA.

Chiyoda Mutual Life Insurance Co.: 19-18, Kamimeguro 2-chome, Meguro-ku, Tokyo 153; f. 1904; Chair. YUKICHI KADONO; Pres. YASUTARO KANZAKI.

Daido Mutual Life Insurance Co.: 23-101, Esakacho 1-chome, Suita-shi, Osaka 564; f. 1902; Chair. TAKESHI MASUMURA; Pres. EIJI FUKUMOTO.

Daihyaku Mutual Life Insurance Co.: 34-1, Kokuryocho 4-chome, Chofu-shi, Tokyo 182; f. 1914; Chair. DAIJIRO KAWASAKI; Pres. MINORU KAWASAKI.

Dai-ichi Mutual Life Insurance Co.: 13-1, Yurakucho 1-chome, Chiyoda-ku, Tokyo 100; f. 1902; Chair. RYOICHI TSUKAMOTO; Pres. SHIN-ICHI NISHIO.

Fukoku Mutual Life Insurance Co.: 2-2, Uchisaiwaicho 2-chome, Chiyoda-ku, Tokyo 100; f. 1923; Pres. TETSUO FURUYA.

Heiwa Life Insurance Co. Ltd.: 2-16, Ginza 3-chome, Chuo-ku, Tokyo 104; f. 1907; Pres. TADAYOSHI TAKEMOTO.

INA Life Insurance Co. Ltd.: Shinjuku Centre Bldg. 48F, 1-25-1 Nishi-Shinjuku, Shinjuku-ku, Tokyo 160; Pres. SHINSAKU KUDO.

Kyoei Life Insurance Co. Ltd.: 2, Nihonbashi Hongokucho 4-chome, Chuo-ku, Tokyo 103; f. 1947; Hon. Chair. and Dir. of Bd. SABURO KAWAI; Pres. MASAYUKI KITOKU.

Meiji Mutual Life Insurance Co.: 1-1, Marunouchi 2-chome, Chiyoda-ku, Tokyo 100; f. 1881; Chair. HIROSHI YAMANAKA; Pres. TERUMICHI TSUCHIDA.

Mitsui Mutual Life Insurance Co.: 2-3, Otemachi 1-chome, Chiyoda-ku, Tokyo 100; f. 1927; Chair. TAKAHIRO TAJIMA; Pres. MASAMI ONIZAWA.

Nippon Dantai Life Insurance Co. Ltd.: 1-2-19, Higashi, Shibuya-ku, Tokyo 150; f. 1934; Chair. TAKEO HIRAKURA; Pres. SAKAE SAWABE.

Nippon Life Insurance Co.: 7, Imabashi 4-chome, Higashi-ku, Osaka 541; f. 1889; Pres. GEN. HIROSE.

Nissan Mutual Life Insurance Co.: 6-30, Aobadai 3-chome, Meguro-ku, Tokyo 153; f. 1909; Chair. MASAO FUJIMOTO; Pres. YASUNORI YAZAKI.

Seibu Allstate Insurance Co. Ltd.: 37th–39th Floors, Sunshine Sixty Bldg., 1-1, Higashi Ikebukuro 3-chome, Toshima-ku, Tokyo 170; f. 1975; Chair. SEIJI TSUTSUMI; Pres. SHIGEO IKUNO.

Sony Prudential Life Insurance Co. Ltd.: 1-1, Minami-Aoyama 1-chome, Minato-ku, Tokyo 107; Pres. TATSUAKI HIRAI.

Sumitomo Mutual Life Insurance Co.: 2-5, Nakanoshima 2-chome, Kita-ku, Osaka 530; f. 1926; Chair. MASAAKI ARAI; Pres. KENJI CHISHIRO.

Taisho Life Insurance Co. Ltd.: 9-1, Yurakucho 1-chome, Chiyoda-ku, Tokyo 100; f. 1913; Pres. TOSHIYUKI KOYAMA.

Taiyo Mutual Life Insurance Co.: 11-2, Nihonbashi 2-chome, Chuo-ku, Tokyo 103; Chair. MAGODAYU DAIBU; Pres. KYOJIRO NISHIWAKI; Vice-Chair. TAKUO KOIZUMI.

Toho Mutual Life Insurance Co.: 15-1, Shibuya 2-chome, Shibuya-ku, Tokyo 150; f. 1898; Chair. (vacant); Pres. SHINTARO OTA.

Tokyo Mutual Life Insurance Co.: 5-2, Uchisaiwaicho 1-chome, Chiyoda-ku, Tokyo 100; f. 1895; Chair. HAJIME MATSUMOTO; Pres. TOSHIO SHIBAYAMA.

Yamato Mutual Life Insurance Co.: 5-1, Yaesu 2-chome, Chuo-ku, Tokyo 104; f. 1911; Pres. YASUNOSUKE KAMONO.

Yasuda Mutual Life Insurance Co.: 9-1, Nishi-shinjuku 1-chome, Shinjuku-ku, Tokyo 160; f. 1880; Chair. HAJIME YASUDA; Pres. MORIO MIZUNO.

NON-LIFE

Asahi Fire and Marine Insurance Co. Ltd.: 6-2, Kajicho 2-chome, Chiyoda-ku, Tokyo; f. 1951; Pres. MICHINOSUKE TANAKA.

Chiyoda Fire and Marine Insurance Co. Ltd.: Kyobashi Chiyoda Bldg., 1-9, Kyobashi 2-chome, Chuo-ku, Tokyo 104; f. 1898; Chair. SADAZO YAMAMOTO; Pres. TADAO KAWAMURA.

Daido Fire and Marine Insurance Co. Ltd.: 14-8, 1-chome, Kumoji, Naha-shi, Okinawa; f. 1971; Pres. YUSHO UEZU.

Dai-ichi Mutual Fire and Marine Insurance Co.: 5-1, Nibancho, Chiyoda-ku, Tokyo; f. 1949; Pres. NAOKADO NISHIHARA.

Dai-Tokyo Fire and Marine Insurance Co. Ltd.: 1-6, Nihonbashi 3-chome, Chuo-ku, Tokyo; f. 1918; Pres. SEIICHI SORIMACHI.

Dowa Fire and Marine Insurance Co. Ltd.: 15-10, Nishitenma 4-chome, Kita-ku, Osaka; f. 1944; Pres. TOMOYOSHI TSUJINO.

Fuji Fire and Marine Insurance Co. Ltd.: 22-10, 5-chome Toyokawa, Ibaraki City, Osaka; f. 1918; Chair. ISAMU WATANABE; Pres. HIROSHI KUZUHARA.

Japan Earthquake Reinsurance Co. Ltd.: 6-5, 3-chome, Kanda Surugadai, Chiyoda-ku, Tokyo; f. 1966; Pres. KEN-ICHI MAEKAWA.

Koa Fire and Marine Insurance Co. Ltd.: 7-3, 3-chome, Kasumigaseki, Chiyoda-ku, Tokyo; f. 1944; Pres. SHIGEO MAETANI.

Kyoei Mutual Fire and Marine Insurance Co.: 18-6, 1-chome, Shimbashi, Minato-ku, Tokyo; f. 1442; Pres. HIDEYUKI TAKAGI.

Nichido Fire and Marine Insurance Co. Ltd.: 3-16, 5-chome, Ginza, Chuo-ku, Tokyo; f. 1914; Chair. TORAJIRO KUBO; Pres. HIDERO NAKANE.

Nippon Fire and Marine Insurance Co. Ltd.: 2-10, Nihonbashi 2-chome, Chuo-ku, Tokyo 103; f. 1892; Chair. YASUTARO UKON; Pres. SCICHISABURO KAWASAKI.

Nissan Fire and Marine Insurance Co. Ltd.: 9-5, 2-chome, Kita-Aoyama, Minato-ku, Tokyo; f. 1911; Chair. MICHIYOSHI SHIROISHI; Pres. SEIICHI HONDA.

Nisshin Fire and Marine Insurance Co. Ltd.: 5-1, 1-chome, Otemachi, Chiyoda-ku, Tokyo; f. 1908; Pres. TATSUO FUJISAWA.

Sumitomo Marine and Fire Insurance Co. Ltd.: 3-5, Yaesu 1-chome, Chuo-ku, Tokyo; f. 1944; Chair. KIYOTOSHI ITOH; Pres. SUMAO TOKUMASU.

Taisei Fire and Marine Insurance Co. Ltd.: 2-1, 4-chome, Kudankita, Chiyoda-ku, Tokyo; f. 1950; Pres. TOKIO NODA.

Taisho Marine and Fire Insurance Co. Ltd.: 1-6-20, Kyobashi, Chuo-ku, Tokyo; f. 1918; Pres. AKIO HIRATA.

Taiyo Fire and Marine Insurance Co. Ltd.: 26-6, Higashigotanda 5-chome, Shinagawa-ku, Tokyo; f. 1951; Chair. TAMOTSU YOKOTA; Pres. KIYOSHI ENDO.

Toa Fire and Marine Reinsurance Co. Ltd.: 6-5, 3-chome, Kanda Surugadai, Chiyoda-ku, Tokyo; f. 1940; Chair. YUZO YASUDA; Pres. MOKUJI KASHIWAGI.

Tokio Marine and Fire Insurance Co. Ltd. (*Tokio Kaijo*): 2-1, Marunouchi 1-chome, Chiyoda-ku, Tokyo; f. 1879; Chair. MINORU KIKUCH; Pres. FUMIO WATANABE.

Toyo Fire and Marine Insurance Co. Ltd.: 4-7, 1-chome, Honcho Nihonbashi, Chuo-ku, Tokyo 103; f. 1950; Chair. TSUNEKAZU SAKANO; Pres. CHIZUKA NAKATA.

Yasuda Fire and Marine Insurance Co. Ltd.: 26-1, 1-chome, Nishi-shinjuku, Shinjuku-ku, Tokyo; f. 1887; Chair. TAKEO MIYOSHI; Pres. YASUO MIYATAKE.

In addition to the commercial companies, the Post Office runs life insurance and annuity schemes.

INSURANCE ASSOCIATIONS

Life Insurance Association of Japan (*Seimei Hoken Kyokai*): New Kokusai Bldg., 4-1, Marunouchi 3-chome, Chiyoda-ku, Tokyo 100; f. 1908; 21 mem. cos.; Chair. RYUHEI TAKASHIMA; Vice-Chair. and Exec. Dir. MASANORI YAMANOUCHI; Man. Dir. YOSHIKATA NAKAOJI.

Marine and Fire Insurance Association of Japan: Non-Life Insurance Bldg., 9, Kanda Awajicho 2-chome, Chiyoda-ku, Tokyo; f. 1917; 22 mems.; Pres. AKIO HIRATA; Vice-Pres. and Exec. Dir. YOSHIKAZU HANAWA.

Fire and Marine Insurance Rating Association of Japan: Non-Life Insurance Bldg., 9, Kanda Awajicho 2-chome, Chiyoda-ku, Tokyo 101; f. 1948; Pres. SHIGEO MAETANI; Exec. Dir. KENJIRO YAMAZAKI.

TRADE AND INDUSTRY

CHAMBERS OF COMMERCE AND INDUSTRY

The Japan Chamber of Commerce and Industry (*Nippon Shoko Kaigi-sho*): 2-2, 3-chome, Marunouchi, Chiyoda-ku, Tokyo; f. 1922; mems. 478 local chambers of commerce and industry; the central organization of all chambers of commerce and industry in Japan; Pres. SHIGEO NAGANO, K.B.E.; publs. *Standard Trade Index of Japan* (annual), *Japan Commerce and Industry* (bi-annual), *Japan New Products and Marketable Commodities* (annual), *Japan Chamber of Commerce and Industry's Business Guide.*

Principal chambers include:

Kobe Chamber of Commerce and Industry: Kobe CIT Center Bldg., 1-14, Hamabe-dori 5-chome, Chuo-ku, Kobe 651; f. 1878; 7,300 mems.; Pres. KENKICHI TOSHIMA; Man. Dir. SHOICHI YAMADA; publs. *Kobe Directory* (annual), *Current Economic Survey of Kobe* (annual), *The Bulletin* (weekly).

Kyoto Chamber of Commerce and Industry: 240, Shoshoicho, Ebisugawa-agaru, Karasumadori, Nakakyo-ku, Kyoto 604; f. 1882; 7,795 mems.; Pres. HIROMU MORISHITA; Man. Dir. KUNIO SHIMADZU.

Nagoya Chamber of Commerce and Industry: 10-19, Sakae 2-chome, Naka-ku, Nagoya, Aichi 460; f. 1881; 1,121 mems.; Pres. KOTARO TAKEDA; Man. Dir. YOSHIHISA HARADA.

Naha Chamber of Commerce and Industry: 2-2-0, Kume Naha, Okinawa; f. 1950; 2,856 mems.; Pres. KOTARO KOKUBA.

Osaka Chamber of Commerce and Industry: 58-7, Uchi-hommachi Hashizume-chome, Higashi-ku, Osaka; f. 1878; 24,360 mems.; Pres. ISAMU SAHEKI; Sr. Man. Dir. TAKEHISA IZUCHI; publs. *Chamber* (Japanese, monthly), *Osaka Economy* (English, quarterly), *List of Members* (Japanese), *Daisho Shimbun* (Japanese newspaper), *Osaka Business Directory* (English), *List of Overseas Chambers of Commerce and Industry, Economic Organizations* (English), *Yearbook of Osaka Economy* (Japanese) and *White Paper on Wages in Osaka* (Japanese).

Tokyo Chamber of Commerce and Industry: 2-2, Marunouchi 3-chome, Chiyoda-ku, Tokyo; f. 1878; 20,030 mems.; Pres. SHIGEO NAGANO; Man. Dir. SATOSHI SASAKI; publs. *Your Business Opportunities* (annual), *The Economic and Industrial Organizations in Japan.*

Yokohama Chamber of Commerce and Industry: 2, Yamashita-cho, Naka-ku, Yokohama; f. 1880; 10,797 mems.; Pres. YUTAKA UYENO; Gen. Sec. MASAO KAWAMURA; publs. *Yokohama Economic Statistics* (Japanese and English, annually).

FOREIGN TRADE ORGANIZATIONS

Council of All-Japan Exporters' Association: Kikai Shinko Kaikan Bldg., 5-8, Shibakoen 3-chome, Minato-ku, Tokyo.

Japan Association for the Promotion of International Trade: Nippon Bldg., 5th Floor, No. 2-6-2, Otemachi, Chiyoda-ku, Tokyo; for the promotion of private trade with the People's Republic of China, the Democratic People's Republic of Korea, Albania and Viet-Nam; handles 90 per cent of Sino-Japanese trade; Pres. A. FUJIYAMA; Chair. TAKAMARU MORITA.

Japan External Trade Organization—JETRO: 2-5, Toranomon 2-chome, Minato-ku, Tokyo 105; f. 1958; information for foreign firms, investigation of foreign markets, exhibition of Japanese commodities abroad, import promotion, etc.; Pres. HISASHI MURATA; Vice-Pres. ISAMU IKOMA; publ. *Focus Japan* (monthly).

Japan Foreign Trade Council, Inc. (*Nippon Boeki-Kai*): 6th Floor, World Trade Center Bldg., 4-1, 2-chome, Hamamatsu-cho, Minato-ku, Tokyo 105; f. 1947; 410 mems.; Pres. TATSUZO MIZUKAMI; Exec. Man. Dir. ZENJI KYOMOTO; Man. Dirs. YASUO OKI, KIKUO KUNUGI, TOSHIO SUZUKI.

TRADE ASSOCIATIONS

Fertilizer Traders' Association: Daiichi Saegusa Bldg. 10-5, Ginza 5-chome, Chuo-ku, Tokyo.

Japan Agricultural Products Exporters' Association: Ikeden Bldg., 12-5, 2-chome, Shimbashi, Minato-ku, Tokyo.

Japan Canned Foods Exporters' Association: New Kokusai Bldg., 4-1, Marunouchi 3-chome, Chiyoda-ku, Tokyo.

Japan Cement Exporters' Association: Hattori Bldg., 10-3, Kyobashi 1-chome, Chuo-ku, Tokyo.

Japan Chemical Exporters' Association: Tokyo.

Japan General Merchandise Exporters' Association: 4-1, Hamamatsu-cho 2-chome, Minato-ku, Tokyo; f. 1953; 400 mems.; Pres. TOKISHIRO SHIINA.

Japan Hardwood Exporters' Association: Matsuda Bldg. 9-1, 1-chome, Ironai, Otaru, Hokkaido 047.

Japan Iron and Steel Exporters' Association: 3-2-10, Nihonbashi-Kayabacho, Chuo-ku, Tokyo.

Japan Lumber Importers' Association: Yushi Kogyo Bldg., 13-11, Nihonbashi 3-chome, Chuo-ku, Tokyo 103; f. 1950; 118 mems.; Pres. S. OTSUBO.

Japan Machinery Exporters' Association: Kikai Shinko Kaikan Bldg., 5-8, Shiba Koen 3-chome, Minato-ku, Tokyo; Exec. Dir. SAKICHI YOSHIKAWA.

Japan Machinery Importers' Association: Koyo Bldg., 2-11, Toranomon 1-chome, Minato-ku, Tokyo; f. 1957; 600 mems.; Pres. TAIICHIRO MATSUO.

Japan Paper Importers' Association: 9-11, Ginza 3-chome, Chuo-ku, Tokyo; f. 1981; 67 mems.; Chair. TAKESI IZUTA.

Japan Paper-Products Exporters' Association: Tokyo; f. 1959; Exec. Dir. KIYOSHI SATOH.

Japan Pearl Exporters' Association: 122 Higashi-machi, Chuo-ku, Kobe; Tokyo branch: 6-15, 3-chome Kyobashi, Chuo-ku; f. 1954; Pres. ATSUSHI KANAI.

Japan Pharmaceutical, Medical and Dental Supply Exporters' Association: 3-6, Nihonbashi-Honcho 4-chome, Chuo-ku, Tokyo 103; f. 1953; 174 member firms; Pres. TAKEO ISHIGURO; Man. Dir. MITSUO SASAKI.

Japan Ship Exporters' Association: Senpaku-Shinko Bldg., 1-15-16, Toranomon, Minato-ku, Tokyo 105.

Japan Sugar Import and Export Council: Ginza Gas-Hall, 9-15, 7-chome, Ginza, Chuo-ku, Tokyo.

Japan Tea Exporters' Association: 81-1, Kitaban-cho, Shinzuoka, Shinzuoka Prefecture.

TRADE FAIR

Tokyo International Trade Fair Commission: 7-24, Harumi 4-chome, Chuo-ku, Tokyo 104; C.P.O. Box 1201.

PRINCIPAL INDUSTRIAL ORGANIZATIONS

GENERAL

Industry Club of Japan: 4-6, Marunouchi, 1-chome, Chiyoda-ku, Tokyo; f. 1917 to develop closer relations between industrialists at home and abroad and promote expansion of Japanese business activities; *c.* 1,600 mems.; Pres. TOSHIO DOKO; Exec. Dir. GINICHI YAMANE.

Japan Commercial Arbitration Association: Tokyo Chamber of Commerce and Industry Bldg., 2-2, 3-chome, Marunouchi, Chiyoda-ku, Tokyo; f. 1950; 1,180 mems.; provides facilities for mediation, conciliation and arbitration in international trade disputes; Pres. SHIGEO NAGANO; publs. monthly (Japanese) and quarterly (English) journals.

Japan Committee for Economic Development (*Keizai Doyukai*): Kogyo Club Bldg., 1-4-6, Marunouchi, Chiyoda-ku, Tokyo; an influential group of business interests concerned with national and international economic and social policies; Chair. TADASHI SASAKI.

Japan Federation of Economic Organizations—KEIDANREN (*Keizaidantai Rengo-Kai*): 9-4, Otemachi 1-chome, Chiyoda-ku, Tokyo, 100; f. 1946; private non-profit association to study domestic and international economic problems; mems. 110 industrial organizations, 820 corporations (Jan. 1982); Chair. YOSHIHIRO INAYAMA; Exec. Vice-Chair. NIHACHIRO HANAMURA; publ. *KEIDANREN REVIEW*.

Japan Federation of Smaller Enterprises: 2-4 Nihonbashi, Kayabacho, Chuo-ku, Tokyo 103.

Japan Productivity Centre (*Nihon Seisansei Honbu*): 3-1-1 Shibuya, Shibuya-ku, Tokyo; f. 1955; 10,000 mems.; concerned with management problems; Chair. KOHEI GOSHI; Man. Dir. MASAICHIRO MUTO; publ. *Japan Productivity News* (weekly).

Nihon Keieisha Dantai Renmei—NIKKEIREN (*Japan Federation of Employers' Associations*): 4-6, Marunouchi 1-chome, Chiyoda-ku, Tokyo; f. 1948; 101 mem. associations; Dir.-Gen. HOSHIN MATSUZAKI; Sec.-Gen. YUICHI NAKAMIYA.

CHEMICALS

Federation of Pharmaceutical Manufacturers' Associations of Japan: 9, 2-chome, Nihonbashi Hon-chu, Chuo-ku, Tokyo.

Japan Perfumery and Flavouring Association: Nitta Bldg., 8, 8-chome, Ginza, Chuo-ku, Tokyo.

Japan Chemical Industry Association: Tokyo Club Bldg., 2-6, 3-chome, Kasumigaseki, Chiyoda-ku, Tokyo; f. 1948; 230 mems.; Pres. YOSHIO MARUTA.

Japan Cosmetic Industry Association: Hatsumei Bldg., 9-14, Toranomon 2-chome, Minato-ku, Tokyo; f. 1959; 450 mem. cos.; Representative Dir. KICHIBEI YAMAMOTO; Man. Dir. KAORU MIYAZAWA.

Japan Gas Association: 15-12, 1-chome Toranomon, Minato-ku, Tokyo 105; f. 1922; Pres. HIROSHI ANZAI; Vice-Pres. YOSHIMITSU SHIBASAKI.

Japan Inorganic Chemical Industry Association: Sanko Bldg., 1-13-1, Ginza Chuo-ku, Tokyo; f. 1948; Pres. KOZO HATANAKA.

Japan Urea and Ammonium Sulphate Industry Association: Hokkai Bldg., 1-3-13, Nihonbashi, Chuo-ku, Tokyo.

The Photo-Sensitized Materials Manufacturers' Association: 2, Kanda Nishiki-cho 2-chome, Chiyoda-ku, Tokyo.

FISHING AND PEARL CULTIVATION

Japan Fisheries Association (*Dai-nippon Suisan Kai*): Sankaido Bldg., 9-13, Akasaka 1, Minato-ku, Tokyo; Pres. TOMOYOSHI KAMENAGA.

Japan Pearl Export and Processing Co-operative Association: 7, 3-chome, Kyobashi, Chuo-ko, Tokyo; f. 1951; 130 mems.

National Federation of Medium Trawlers: Toranomon Chuo Bldg., 1-16 Toranomon 1, Minato-ku, Tokyo; f. 1948.

PAPER AND PRINTING

Japan Paper Association: Kami-Parupu Kaikan Bldg., Ginza 3-chome, 9-11 Chuo-ku, Tokyo; f. 1946; 88 mems.; Chair. F. TANAKA; Pres. T. HASHIMOTO.

Japan Paper-Products Manufacturers' Association: Tokyo; f. 1949; Exec. Dir. KIYOSHI SATOH.

Japan Printers' Association: 1-16-8, Shintomi, Chuo-ku, Tokyo; Pres. YOSHINORI HIGUCHI; Exec. Dir. TOSHIKATA NAKAGAWA; publ. *Graphic Arts Japan* (annual).

MINING AND PETROLEUM

Asbestos Cement Products Association: Takahashi Bldg., 10-8, 7-chome, Ginza, Chuo-ku, Tokyo; f. 1937; Chair. KOSHIRO SHIMIZU.

Cement Association of Japan: Hattori Bldg., 10-3, Kyobashi 1-chome, Chuo-ku, Tokyo 104; f. 1948; 22 mem. cos.; Chair. T. HARASHIMA; Exec. Man. Dir. H. KUROSAWA.

Japan Coal Association: Hibiya Park Bldg., 1-8, Yurakucho 1-chome, Chiyoda-ku, Tokyo.

Japan Mining Industry Association: Shin-hibiya Bldg., 3-6, Uchisaiwai-cho 1-chome, Chiyoda-ku, Tokyo 100; f. 1948; 79 mem. cos.; Pres. T. NISHIDA; Dir.-Gen. S. ICHIJO.

Petroleum Producers' Association of Japan: Keidanren Kaikan, 9-4, 1-chome, Otemachi, Chiyoda-ku, Tokyo; f. 1961; Pres. SOHEI MIZUNO.

METALS

Japan Brass Makers' Association: 12-22, 1-chome, Tsukiji, Chuo-ku, Tokyo; f. 1948; 30 mems.; Pres. D. TOYAMA; Man. Dir. T. WADA.

Japan Iron and Steel Federation: Keidanren Kaikan, 1-9-4, Otemachi, Chiyoda-ku, Tokyo; f. 1948; Chair. E. SAITO.

Japan Light Metal Association: Nihonbashi Asahiseimei Bldg., 1-3, Nihonbashi 2-chome, Chuo-ku, Tokyo 103; f. 1947; 177 mems.; publs. *Aluminium* (monthly), *JLMA Letter* (monthly), *Magnesium* (monthly).

Japan Stainless Steel Association: Tekko Kaikan Bldg., 2-10, Nihonbashi Hayaba-cho 3-chome, Chuo-ku, Tokyo 103; Pres. NOBUYOSHI TERANISHI; Exec. Dir. HIROSO TAGAWA.

The Kozai Club: 3-2-10, Nihonbashi Hayaba-cho, Chuo-ku, Tokyo; f. 1947; mems. 32 manufacturers, 89 dealers; Chair. EISHIRO SAITO.

Steel Castings and Forgings Association of Japan (JSCFA): Tekko Bldg., 8-2, 1-chome, Marunouchi, Chiyoda-ku, Tokyo 100; f. 1972; mems. 78 cos., 90 plants; Exec. Dir. MINORU IMAMURA.

MACHINERY AND PRECISION EQUIPMENT

Electronic Industries Association of Japan: Tosho Bldg., 2-2, 3-chome, Marunouchi, Chiyoda-ku, Tokyo; f. 1948; mems. 580 firms; Pres. SADAKAZU SHINDOH; publs. *Denshi* (Electronics) (monthly), *Electronic Industries Association of Japan Membership List* (annual, English), *Electronic Industry in Japan* (annual, English).

Japan Camera Industry Association: Mori Bldg. Ninth, 2-2, Atago 1-chome, Minato-ku, Tokyo 105; f. 1954; Pres. SHIGEO KITAMURA.

Japan Clock and Watch Association: Nomura Bldg., 2-1-1, Otemachi, Chiyoda-ku, Tokyo.

Japan Electric Association: 1-7-1, Yurakucho, Chiyoda-ku, Tokyo 100; f. 1921; 4,341 mems.; Pres. SEIZO YOSHMULA; publs. *Daily Electricity, Journal of the Japan Electric Association, Production and Electricity, Monthly Report on Electric Power Statistics* (Japanese).

Japan Electrical Manufacturers' Association: 4-15, 2-chome, Nagata-cho, Chiyoda-ku, Tokyo; f. 1948; mems. 250 firms; Pres. M. IMAI; Exec. Dir. F. YANASE.

The Japan Machinery Federation: Kikai Shinko Bldg., 5-8-3, Shiba-Koen, Minato-ku, Tokyo 105; f. 1952; Exec. Vice-Pres. YASUFUMI BABA; publs. *Nikkiren Geppo* (monthly), *Nikkiren Shuho* (weekly).

Japan Machine Tool Builders' Association: Kikai Shinko Bldg., 3-5-8, Shiba-Koen, Minato-ku, Tokyo 105; f. 1951; 113 mems.; Exec. Dir. S. ABE.

Japan Measuring Instruments Federation: Japan Metrology Bldg., 1-25, Nando-cho, Shinjuku-ku, Tokyo.

Japan Microscope Manufacturers' Association: c/o Olympus Optical Co. Ltd., 43-2, Hatagaya, 2-chome, Shibuya-ku, Tokyo; f. 1946; mems. 23 firms; Chair. S. KITAMURA.

Japan Motion Picture Equipment Industrial Association: Kikai-Shinko Bldg., 5-8, Shiba-Koen 3-chome, Minato-ku, Tokyo 105.

Japan Optical Industry Association: Kikai-Shinko Bldg., 3-5-8, Shiba-Koen, Minato-ku, Tokyo 105; f. 1946; 200 mems.; Exec. Dir. M. SUZUKI; publ. *Guidebook of Japanese Optical Precision Instruments.*

Japan Power Association: Uchisaiwai Bldg., 1-4-2, Uchisaiwai-cho, Chiyoda-ku, Tokyo; f. 1950; 69 mems.; Pres. (vacant); Sec. SACHIO TANAKA; publ. *Power* (quarterly).

Japan Society of Industrial Machinery Manufacturers: Kikai-Shinko Kaikan, 3-5-8, Shiba-Koen, Minato-ku, Tokyo; f. 1948; 307 mems.; Chair. GAKUJI MORIYA.

The Japan Textile Machinery Association: Room No. 310, Kikai Shinko Bldg., 3-5-8 Shiba-Koen, Minato-ku, Tokyo; f. 1951; Pres. NOBUYOSHI NOZAKI.

TEXTILES

Central Raw Silk Association of Japan: 7, 1-chome, Yurakucho, Chiyoda-ku, Tokyo.

Japan Chemical Fibres Association: Mitsui Bekkan, 3-3, Nihonbashi Muromachi, Chuo-ku, Tokyo 103.

Japan Cotton and Staple Fibre Weavers' Association: 8-7, Nishi-Azabu 1-chome, Minato-ku, Tokyo.

Japan Knitting Industry Association: 1-16-7, Misuji, Taito-ku, Tokyo 111.

Japan Silk Association, Inc.: 25-2, 3-chome Shinjuku-ku, Tokyo; f. 1959; 11 mem. asscns.; Pres. TADASHI ARITA.

Japan Silk and Rayon Weavers' Association: 15-12, Kudankita 1-chome, Chiyoda-ku, Tokyo.

Japan Silk Spinners' Association: Mengyo Kaikan Building, 8, 3-chome, Bingo Machi, Higashi-ku, Osaka; f. 1948; 95 member firms; Chair. ICHIJI OHTANI.

Japan Textile Council: Sen-i-Kaikan Bldg., 9, 3-chome, Nihonbashi Honcho, Chuo-ku, Tokyo; f. 1948; mems. 24 asscns.; publs. *Textile Yearbook*, *Textile Statistics* (monthly), *Textile Japan* (annual in English).

Japan Wool Spinners' Association: Sen-i-Kaikan 9, 3-chome, Nihonbashi Honcho, Chuo-ku, Tokyo; f. 1958; Chair. K. MIZUTANI; publ. *Statistical Data on the Wool Industry in Japan* (monthly).

Japan Worsted and Woollen Weavers' Association: Sen-i-Kaikan 9, 3-chome, Nihonbashi Honcho, Chuo-ku, Tokyo; f. 1948; Chair. S. OGAWA; Man. Dir. K. OHTANI.

TRANSPORT MACHINERY

Japan Association of Rolling Stock Industries: Daiichi Tekko Bldg., 8-2, Marunouchi 1-chome, Chiyoda-ku, Tokyo.

Japan Auto Parts Industries Association: 1-16-15, Takanawa, Minato-ku, Tokyo 108; f. 1948; mems. 390 firms; Chair. S. TSURU; Sr. Exec. Dir. Y. NAKAMURA; publs. *Auto Parts* (monthly, Japanese), *JAPIA Buyer's Guide* (annually, English).

Japan Automobile Manufacturers Association, Inc.: Otemachi Bldg., 6-1, Otemachi 1-chome, Chiyoda-ku, Tokyo; f. 1967; mems. 13 firms; Pres. T. ISHIHARA; Man. Dir. T. NAKAMURA.

Japan Bicycle Industry Association: 9-15, Akasaka 1-chome, Minato-ku, Tokyo.

Japanese Shipowners' Association: Kaiun Bldg., 6-4, Hirakawa-cho 2-chome, Chiyoda-ku, Tokyo.

Shipbuilders' Association of Japan: Senpaku Shinko Bldg., 1-15-16, Toranomon, Minato-ku, Tokyo 105; f. 1947; 50 mems.; Pres. TSUNESABURO NISHIMURA; Man. Dir. TAKASHI NAKASO.

The Ship-Machinery Manufacturers' Association of Japan: Sempaku-Shinko Bldg., 1-15-16, Toranomon, Minato-ku, Tokyo; f. 1956; 300 mems.; Pres. TOMIO NOJIMA.

The Society of Japanese Aerospace Companies Inc. (SJAC): Hibiya Park Bldg., Suite 518, 8-1, Yurakucho 1-chome, Chiyoda-ku, Tokyo 100; f. 1952; reorganized 1974 as Corporation aggregate; 112 mems., 21 assoc. mems.; Chair. EIICHI OHARA; Vice-Chair. OSAMU NAGANO, RYOJI UENISHI, MASATAKA OKUMA; Exec. Dir. SATOSHI MINOWA; publs. *Aerospace Japan* (English), *Year Book of Japanese Aerospace Industry* (Japanese, annual), etc.

MISCELLANEOUS

Communication Industries Association of Japan: Sankei Bldg. (annex), 1-7-2, Otemachi, Chiyoda-ku, Tokyo 100; f. 1948; Chair. KATSUSHIGE MITA; Pres. HARUO OZAWA; 201 mems.; publs. *Tsushin-Kogyo* (monthly in Japanese), *Communications and Electronics Japan*, *Outline of Communication Industry*.

Japan Canners' Association: Marunouchi Bldg., 4-1, Marunouchi 2-chome, Chiyoda-ku, Tokyo.

Japan Construction Materials Association: Kenchiku Kaikan Bldg., 19-2, 3-chome, Ginza, Chuo-ku, Tokyo; f. 1947; Pres. KENTARO ITO; publ. *Construction Material Industry* (monthly).

Japan Fur Association: Ginza-Toshin Bldg., 3-11-15, Ginza, Chuo-ku, Tokyo; f. 1950; Chair. KIYOJI NAKAMURA; Sec. NORIHIDE SATOH; publ. *Kegawa Shimpo* (Newspaper).

Japan Plastics Industry Association: Tokyo Club Bldg., 2-6, Kasumigaseki 3-chome, Chiyoda-ku, Tokyo.

Japan Plywood Manufacturers' Association: Meisan Bldg., 18-17, 1-chome, Nishishinbashi, Minato-ku, Tokyo; f. 1965; 176 mems.; Pres. HIROSHI INOUE.

Japan Pottery Manufacturers' Federation: 32, Nunoikecho, 39-18 Daikan-cho, Higashi-ku, Nagoya.

Japan Rubber Manufacturers Association: Tobu Bldg., 1-5-26, Moto Akasaka, Minato-ku, Tokyo; f. 1950; 180 mems.; Pres. KANICHIRO ISHIBASHI.

Japan Spirits and Liquors Makers Association: Koura Dai-ichi Bldg., 7th Floor, 1-6, Nihombashi-Kayabacho 1-chome, Chuo-ku, Tokyo 103.

Japan Sugar Refiners' Association: 5-7, Sanbancho, Chiyoda-ku, Tokyo; f. 1949; 18 mems.; Man. Dir. SACHIO AIGA; publs. *Sato Tokei Nenkan* (Sugar Statistics Year Book), *Kikan Togyoshiho* (Quarterly Sugar Journal).

Motion Picture Producers' Association of Japan: Sankei Bldg., 7-2, 1-chome, Otemachi, Chiyoda-ku, Tokyo 100; Pres. SHIGERU OKADA.

Tokyo Toy Manufacturers Association: 4-16-3, Higashi-Komagata Sumida-ku, Tokyo 130.

TRADE UNIONS

A feature of Japan's trade union movement is that the unions are in general based on single enterprises, embracing workers of different occupations in that enterprise.

PRINCIPAL FEDERATIONS

Nihon Rodo Kumiai Sohyogikai—SOHYO (*General Council of Trade Unions of Japan*): Sohyo Kaikan Bldg., 2-11, Kanda Surugadai 3-chome, Chiyoda-ku, Tokyo; f. 1950; 4,550,522 mems. (1980); Pres. MOTOFUMI MAKIEDA; Sec.-Gen. MITSUO TOMIZUKA.

Major Affiliated Unions

Tokyo

Federation of Telecommunications Electronic Information and Allied Workers (*Dentsuroren*): Zendentsu Kaikan Bldg., 6, Kanda Surugadai 3-chome, Chiyoda-ku; 332,249 mems.; Pres. K. OIKAWA.

General Federation of Private Railway Workers' Unions (*Shitetsusoren*): Shitetsu Kaikan Bldg., 3-5, Takanawa 4-chome, Minato-ku; 202,948 mems.; Pres. T. KUROKAWA.

Japan Federation of National Public Service Employees' Unions (*Kokkororen*): Tsukasa Bldg., 6-2, Nishi-shinbashi 3-chome, Minato-ku; 91,603 mems.; Pres. S. UTSUNOMIYA.

Japan Postal Workers' Union (*Zentei*): Zentei Kaikan Bldg., 2-7, Koraku 1-chome, Bunkyo-ku; 188,420 mems.; Pres. K. OOTA.

Japan Teachers' Union (*Nikkyoso*): Kyoiku Kaikan Bldg., 6-2, Hitotsubashi 2-chome, Chiyoda-ku; 672,393 mems.; Pres. M. MAKIEDA.

Japanese Federation of Iron and Steel Workers' Unions (*Tekko Roren*): 6-5, Higashi Oi 3-chome, Shinagawaku; 221,193 mems.; Pres. T. NAKAMURA.

National Council of General Amalgamated Workers' Unions (*Sohyo Zenkoku Ippan*): 5-6, Misakicho 3-chome, Chiyoda-ku; 121,196 mems.; Pres. Y. KURAMOCHI.

National Council of Local and Municipal Government Workers' Unions (*Jichiro*): Jichiro Kaikan Bldg., 1 Rokubancho, Chiyoda-ku; 1,253,917 mems.; Pres. Y. MARUYAMA.

National Federation of Chemical and Synthetic Chemical Industry Workers' Unions (*Gokaroren*): Senbai Bldg., 26-30, Shiba 5-chome, Minato-ku; 127,160 mems.; Pres. G. TACHIBANA.

National Metal and Machine Trade Union (*Zenkoku Kinzoku*): 15-11, Sakuragaoka, Shibuya-ku; 165,682 mems.; Pres. K. TAKAYAMA.

National Railway Workers' Union (*Kokuro*): Kokuro Kaikan Bldg., 11-4, Marunouchi 1-chome, Chiyoda-ku; 250,270 mems.; Pres. M. MORIKAGE.

Zen Nihon Rodo Sodomei—DOMEI (*Japanese Confederation of Labour*): 20-12, Shiba 2-chome, Minato-ku, Tokyo; f. 1964; 2.2 million mems. (1981); affiliated to ICFTU; Pres. TADANOBU USAMI; Gen. Sec. YOSHIKAZU TANAKA.

Major Affiliated Unions

Tokyo

(20-12, Shiba 2-chome, Minato-ku, unless otherwise stated)

All-Japan Postal Labour Union (*Zenyusei*): 20-6, Sendagaya 1-chome, Shibuya-ku; 59,675 mems.; Pres. HIDEMASA FUKUI.

All-Japan Seamen's Union (*Kaiin Kumiai*): 15-26, Roppongi 7-chome, Minato-ku; 149,744 mems.; Pres. KAZUKIYO DOI.

Federation of Electric Workers' Unions of Japan (*Denryokuroren*): 7-15, Mita 2-chome, Minato-ku, 108; 135,358 mems.; Pres. KOICHIRO HASHIMOTO.

Federation of Japan Automobile Workers' Unions (*Jidosharoren*): 4-26, Kaigan 1-chome, Minato-ku; 207,152 mems.; Pres. ICHIRO SHIOJI.

Japan Confederation of Shipbuilding and Engineering Workers' Unions (*Zosenjukiroren*): 177,025 mems.; Pres. HIDENOBU KANASUGI.

Japan Federation of Transport Workers' Unions (*Kotsuroren*): 99,637 mems.; Pres. CHUKICHI MATSUDA.

Japan Railway Workers' Union (*Tetsuro*): 49,729 mems.; Pres. SHIGEYUKI TSUJIMOTO.

Japanese Federation of Chemical and General Workers' Unions (*Zenkadomei*): f. 1951; 98,937 mems.; Pres. YOSHIKAZU TANAKA.

Japanese Federation of Textile, Garment, Chemical, Distributive and Allied Industry Workers' Unions (*Zensen Domei*): 8-16, Kudan Minami 4-chome, Chiyoda-ku; f. 1946; 1,308 affiliates; 460,018 mems.; Pres. TADANOBU USAMI; Gen. Sec. JINNOSUKE ASHIDA.

Japanese Metal Industrial Workers' Union (*Zenkin Domei*): f. 1951; 300,586 mems.; Pres. SOICHIRO ASANO.

National Federation of General Workers' Unions (*Ippan Domei*): 112,623 mems.; Pres. KAZUO MAEKAWA.

Churitsu Rodo Kumiai Renraku Kaigi — CHURITSU ROREN (*Federation of Independent Unions of Japan*): 3rd Floor, Denkiroren Kaikan Bldg., 10-3, 1-chome, Mita, Minato-ku, Tokyo; f. 1956; 1,357,979 mems. (1981); Pres. TOSHIFUMI TATEYAMA.

Major Affiliated Unions

Tokyo

Japanese Federation of Electrical Machine Workers' Unions (*Denki Roren*): Denkiroren Kaikan Bldg., 10-3, 1-chome, Mita, Minato-ku; f. 1964; 530,889 mems.; Pres. TOSHIFUMI TATEYAMA.

Japanese Federation of Food and Allied Workers' Unions (*Shokuhin Roren*): Hiroo Office Bldg., 3-18, Hiroo 1-chome, Shibuya-ku; f. 1954; 70,000 mems.; Pres. SHIGERU OKAMURA.

National Federation of Construction Workers' Unions (*Zenkensoren*): 7-15, Takadanobaba 2-chome, Shinjuku-ku; f. 1960; 289,252 mems.; Pres. RISAKU EGUCHI.

National Federation of Life Insurance Workers' Unions (*Seihororen*): Hiroo Office Bldg., 3-18, Hiroo 1-chome, Shibuya-ku; 333,896 mems.; Pres. RYOJI TAJIMA.

Zenkoku Sangyobetsu Rodo Kumiai Rengo—SHINSAMBETSU (*National Federation of Industrial Organizations*): Takahashi Bldg., 9-7, Nishi Shinbashi 3-chome, Minato-ku, Tokyo; 62,286 mems.; Pres. TETSUZO OGATA.

Major Affiliated Unions

Tokyo

Kyoto-Shiga-block Workers' Federation (*Keijichiren*): Kyoto Rodosha Sogokaikan Bldg., 30-2, Mibusennen-cho, Nakagyo-ku, Kyoto-shi; 10,615 mems.; Pres. MEIWA IKEDA.

National Machinery and Metal Workers' Union (*Zenkikin*): Takahashi Bldg., 9-7, Nishi Shinbashi 3-chome, Minato-ku; 31,789 mems.; Pres. TETSUZO OGATA.

National Organization of All Chemical Workers (*Shinkagaku*): 9-7, Nishi Shinbashi 3-chome, Minato-ku; 11,526 mems.; Pres. AKIHIRO KAWAI.

MAJOR NON-AFFILIATED UNIONS

Tokyo

All-Japan Federation of Transport Workers' Unions (*Unyu Roren*): Zennittsu-Kaikan Bldg., 3-5, Kasumigaseki 3-chome, Chiyoda-ku; 150,000 mems.; Pres. JIRO TAI.

Confederation of Japan Automobile Workers' Unions (*Jidoshasoren*): Kokuryu Shibakoen Bldg., 6-15, Shiba-Koen 2-chome, Minato-ku; f. 1962; 596,417 mems.; Pres. ICHIRO SHIOJI.

Federation of City Bank Employees' Unions (*Shiginren*): Ida Bldg., 3-8, Yaesu 1-chome, Chuo-ku; 176,897 mems.; Pres. MASATOSHI ANZAI.

Japan Council of Construction Industry Employees' Unions (*Nikkenkyo*): Sendagaya Bldg., 30-8, Sendagaya 1-chome, Shibuya-ku; f. 1954; 60,554 mems.; Pres. MASANORI OKAMURA.

Japan Federation of Commercial Workers' Unions (*Shogyororen*): 2-23-1, Yoyogi, Shibuya-ku; 90,682 mems.; Pres. KENSHO SUZUKI.

National Federation of Agricultural Mutual Aid Societies Employees' Unions (*Zennokyororen*): Shinjuku Nokyo Kaikan Bldg., 5-5, Yoyogi 2-chome, Shibuya-ku; 91,718 mems.; Pres. HIDEO GOTO.

NATIONAL COUNCILS

Co-ordinating bodies for unions whose members are in the same industry or have the same employer.

All-Japan Council of Traffic and Transport Workers' Unions (*Zen Nippon Kotsu Unyu Rodo Kumiai Kyogi-kai—*

Zenkoun): c/o Kokutetsu Rodo Kaikan, 11-4, Marunouchi 1-chome, Chiyoda-ku, Tokyo; f. 1947; 858,316 mems.; Pres. TAKESHI KUROKAWA; Gen. Sec. ICHIZO SAKAI.

Council of Public Corporations and National Enterprise Workers' Unions (*Korokyo*): Sohyo Kaikan, 2-11, Kanda Surugadai 3-chome, Chiyoda-ku, Tokyo; 870,000 mems.; Gen. Sec. TOMIJI TAKAHASHI.

Council of SOHYO-affiliated Federations in the Private Sector (*Sohyo Minkan Kaigi*): Sohyo Kaikan, 2-11, Kanda Surugadai 3-chome, Chiyoda-ku, Tokyo; 1,547,920 mems.; Gen. Sec. SIZUO MISHIMA.

ICFTU Japanese Affiliates' Liaison Council (*Nihon Kameisoshiki Renraku Kyogikai*): Oikawa Bldg., 2-12-18 Shinbashi, Minato-ku, Tokyo; f. 1977; 2,210,000 mems.; Chair. ICHIRO SHIOJI, KIYOJI OHTA.

Japan Council of Metalworkers' Unions (*Zen Nihon Kinzoku Sangyo Rodokumiai Kyogikai*): Santoku Yaesu Bldg., 6-21, Yaesu 2-chome, Chuo-ku, Tokyo 104; f. 1964; 1,898,720 mems.; Chair. YOSHIJI MIYATA; Gen. Sec. ICHIRO SETO; publ. monthly newspaper.

Japan Council of Public Service Workers' Unions (*Nihon Komuin Rodo Kumiai Kyoto Kaigi*): Sohyo Kaikan, 2-11, Kanda Surugadai 3-chome, Chiyoda-ku, Tokyo; 2,374,684 mems.; Gen. Sec. YASUO MARUYAMA.

National Council of Dockworkers' Unions (*Zenkokukowan*): c/o All Japan Dockworkers' Union (Zenkowan), 31-4, Sanno 2-chome, Ota-ku, Tokyo 143; f. 1972; 65,000 mems.; Chair. TOKUJI YOSHIOKA.

Trade Union Council for Policy Promotion (*Seisaku Suishin Roso Kaigi*): c/o Denryokuroren, 7-15, Mita 2-chome, Minato-ku, Tokyo 108; 5,000,000 mems.; Gen. Secs. KOICHIRO HASHIMOTO, TOSHIFUMI TATEYAMA.

Trade Union Council for Multi-national Companies (*Takokuseki-Kigyo Mondai Taisaku Roso Renraku Kaigi*): c/o IMF-JC, Santoku Yaesu Bldg., 6-21, Yaesu 2-chome, Chuo-ku, Tokyo 104; 2,920,000 mems.; Chair. ICHIRO SHIOJI.

CO-OPERATIVE ORGANIZATION

National Federation of Agricultural Co-operative Associations—ZENNOH: 8-3, Otemachi 1-chome, Chiyoda-ku, Tokyo; purchasers of agricultural materials and marketers of agricultural products.

MAJOR INDUSTRIAL COMPANIES

The following are the leading 75 industrial companies in Japan based on 1979 sales. The information is compiled from the companies themselves, the *Diamond Japan Business Directory* and *The Fortune Directory*. Unless otherwise indicated, data refer to 1979.

Ajinomoto Co. Inc.: 5-8 Kyobashi 1-chome, Chuo-ku, Tokyo 104; f. 1909; net sales $1,759.3m. (1980); cap. surplus $79.9m.

Manufacture and distribution of seasonings, oil products, convenience foods, amino acids, speciality chemicals etc.

Numerous subsidiaries and overseas offices; Chair. SABUROSUKE SUZUKI; Pres. BUNZO WATANABE; employees: 5,422.

Asahi Chemical Industry Co. Ltd.: Tokyo Kaijo Bldg., 2-1, Marunouchi 1-chome, Chiyoda-ku, Tokyo; f. 1931; sales $2,243,2m.; cap. and res. $563.9m.

Manufacture and sale of synthetic fibres, chemical fibres, acrylonitrilemonomer, plastics, synthetic rubber, explosives, construction materials, foods and fine chemicals.

Pres. KAGAYAKI MIYAZAKI; employees: 22,507.

Asahi Glass Co. Ltd.: 1-2, Marunouchi 2-chome, Chiyoda-ku, Tokyo; f. 1907; sales $1,745.9m.; cap. and res. $705.5m.

Manufacture and sale of flat glass, TV bulbs, alkali and other chemicals, and refractories.

Associated and subsidiary companies in India, Indonesia, Singapore, Thailand and the U.S.A.; Pres. HIDEAKI YAMASHITA; employees: 11,942.

Bridgestone Tire Co. Ltd.: 1 Kyobashi 1-chome, Chuo-ku, Tokyo; f. 1931; sales $2,393.4m.; cap. and res. $753.1m.

Manufacture of all kinds of rubber tyres and tubes, transmission and conveyor belts and hoses, foam rubber, polyurethane foam, golf balls.

Chair. KANICHIRO ISHIBASHI; Pres. SHIGEMICHI SHIBAMOTO; employees: 30,134.

Daido Steel Co. Ltd.: 11-18 Nishiki 1-chome, Naka-ku, Nagoya; sales $1,114.9m.; cap. and res. $108.7m.

Metal refining, steel etc., employees: 10,970.

Daikyo Oil Co. Ltd.: 4-1 Yaesu 2-chome, Chuo-ku, Tokyo; sales 993,000m. yen (1980).

Importing of petroleum, refining, sales and distribution of petroleum products and related activities.

Chair. HIROTAKA MITSUDA; Pres. YOSHIRO NAKAYAMA; employees: 1,974.

Dainippon Printing Co.: 12, Ichigaya Kaga-cho 1-chome, Shinjuku-ku, Tokyo 162; f. 1876; sales $2,342.4m. (1981); cap. and res. $624.1m.

Printing, packaging, paper products, precision electronic products.

Pres. ORIE KITAJIMA; employees: 9,897.

Fuji Heavy Industries Co. Ltd.: 7-2, Nishi-Shinjuku 1-chome, Shinjuku-ku, Tokyo; sales $1,173.4m.; cap. and res. $155.5m.

Motor vehicles.

Employees: 13,258.

Fuji Photo Film Co. Ltd.: 26-30, Nishi Azabu 2-chome, Minato-ku, Tokyo 106; f. 1934; sales 520,096m. yen (1981); cap. 16,792.6m. yen.

Films and photographic materials, magnetic tapes, carbonless copying paper.

Pres. MINORU OHNISHI; employees: 15,329.

Fujitsu Ltd.: Furukawa Sogo Bldg., 6-1, Marunouchi 2-chome, Chiyoda-ku, Tokyo 100; f. 1935; sales $2,099.6m.; cap. and res. $541.5m.

Manufacture and sale of electronic computers and data processing equipment, telephone equipment, etc.

Pres. TAIYU KOBAYASHI; employees: 32,257.

Furukawa Electric Co. Ltd.: 6-1 Marunouchi 2-chome, Chiyoda-ku, Tokyo; f. 1896; sales $1.933,9m. (1981); cap. $101.1m.

Manufacture and sale of electric wires and cables, non-ferrous metal products.

Pres. MASAO FUNAHASHI; employees: 5,442.

Hino Motors Ltd.: 1-1, Hinodai 3-chome, Hino-shi, Tokyo 191; f. 1942; sales $1,156m.; cap. and res. $184.7m.

Diesel trucks and buses, cars.

Chair. MASANOBU MATSUKATA; Pres. MASASHI ARAKAWA; employees: 7,985.

Hitachi Ltd.: New Marunouchi Bldg. 5-1, Marunouchi 1-chome, Chiyoda-ku, Tokyo; f. 1910; sales $12,259.6m.; cap. and res. $3,606.5m.

Manufacture and sale of electric utility apparatus and electrical equipment, consumer products, communications and electronics equipment, measuring instruments, industrial machinery, rolling stock, wire, cable and other products.

Pres. HIROKICHI YOSHIYAMA; employees: 141,132.

Hitachi Zosen Corporation: 1-1-1 Hitotsubashi, Chiyoda-ku, Tokyo; f. 1881; sales 1,672.5m. (1981); cap. and res. $263.7m.

Shipbuilding, ship repairing, remodelling and scrapping; manufacture of diesel engines and turbines, marine auxiliary machinery and fittings. Manufacture of industrial machinery and plant for chemicals, paper, petroleum, sugar, cement and iron, steel bridges and steel structures, environmental equipment, offshore equipment.

Thirty subsidiary companies at home; Pres. MASAO KINOSHITA; employees: 17,000.

Honda Motor Co. Ltd.: 27-8, 6-chome, Jingumae, Shibuya-ku, Tokyo; f. 1948; sales $7,980m. (1981); cap. and res. $1,605.7m.

Manufacture of automobiles, motorcycles, power tillers general purpose engines, and portable generators.

Sixteen foreign subsidiaries in 12 countries; Pres. KIYOSHI KAWASHIMA; Vice-Pres. HIDEO SUGIURA, SHIGERU SHINOMIYA, NOBORU OKAMURA; employees: 38,481.

Idemitsu Kosan Co. Ltd.: 1-1, Marunouchi 3-chome, Chiyoda-ku, Tokyo; f. 1911; sales $5,504.1m.; cap. and res. $176.4m.

Manufacture and sale of petroleum products and petrochemicals and related enterprises.

Chair. KEISUKE IDEMITSU; Pres. MASAMI ISHIDA; employees: 10,519.

Ishikawajima-Harima Heavy Industries Co. Ltd.: 4 Otemachi, 2, Chiyoda-ku, Tokyo; f. 1889; sales $3,538.6m.; cap. and res. $411.2m.

Shipbuilding and ship repair service; manufacture, sale of and repair service for ship turbines and boilers, aircraft gas turbines, atomic power equipment, hauling equipment, iron and steel manufacturing plant, mining and civil engineering machinery, hydro- and thermal electric generating equipment, pneumatic and hydraulic machinery, chemical plant, steel structures.

Pres. TAIJI UBAKAEA; employees: 27,000.

Isuzu Motors Ltd.: 22-10 Minami-oi 6-chome, Shinagawa-ku, Tokyo; f. 1937; sales $2,660.4m.; cap. and res. $432.2m.

Manufacture and sale of trucks, buses, special purpose vehicles, passenger cars and internal combustion engines.

Pres. TOSHIO OKAMOTO; employees: 20,500.

Kanebo Ltd.: Osaka Ekimae Daini Bldg., 2-2 Umeda 1-chome, Kita-ku, Osaka; f. 1887; sales $1,037m. (1980); cap. and res. $158.9m.

Manufacture, bleaching, dyeing, processing and sale of cotton yarns, cloth and thread, worsted and woollen yarns, woollen fabrics, nylon and polyester yarns and fabrics, carpets, spun silk yarns, silk thread spun from waste, silkworm eggs, silk fabrics, rayon staple, spun rayon yarns and fabrics, synthetic resins; cosmetics, pharmaceuticals and industrial materials.

Chair. IKURO AOKI; Pres. JUNJI ITOH; employees: 5,395.

Kawasaki Heavy Industries Ltd.: Nissei-Kawasaki Bldg., 16-1 Nakamachidori 2-chome, Ikuta-ku, Kobe; f. 1896; sales $2,445.9m.; cap. $489.4m.

Manufacture and sale of shipbuilding, rolling stock, aircraft, machinery, engines and motorcycles, plant engineering.

Chair. KIYOSHI YOTSUMOTO; Pres. ZENJI UMEDA; employees: 33,993.

Kawasaki Steel Corporation: New Yurakucho Bldg., 1-12-1, Yurakucho, Chiyoda-ku, Tokyo 100; f. 1950; sales $4,602m.; cap. and res. 981.0$m. (1980).

Manufacture and sale of plates, sheets, structural steels, tubular products, castings and forgings, welding electrodes, prefabricated products and iron powder; manufacturing, engineering and construction services.

Chair. ICHIRO FUJIMOTO; Pres. EIRO IWAMURA; employees: 30,276.

Kirin Brewery Co. Ltd.: 6-26-1, Jingumae, Shibuya-ku, Tokyo; f. 1907; sales $4,178m. (1981); cap. and res. $721.1m.

Production and sale of beer, soft drinks and dairy foods.

Chair. YASUSABURO SATO; Pres. SHUJI KONISHI; employees: 7,763.

Koa Oil Co. Ltd.: Nihon Bldg., 6-2, Ohtemachi 2-chome, Chiyoda-ku, Tokyo; sales $1,213.5m.; cap. and res. $76m.

Petroleum products.

Chair. AWASHI JOCHI; Pres. TERUO NOGUCHI; employees: 1,395.

Kobe Steel Ltd.: Tekko Bldg., Marunouchi 1-chome, Chiyoda-ku, Tokyo; f. 1905; sales $5,412m. (1981); cap. $410m.

Manufacture and sale of iron, steel, aluminium and copper, new metals such as titanium, plant machinery, chemical equipment, robots, construction machinery, cast and foreign products, cutting tools, welding electrodes and plant engineering.

Pres. KOKICHI TAKAHASHI; employees: 31,500.

Komatsu Ltd.: 3-6, Akasaka 2-chome, Minato-ku, Tokyo; f. 1921; sales $3,199m. (1981); cap. and res. 1,266.9m.

Manufacture construction equipment and industrial machinery including bulldozers, motor graders, shovel loaders, dump trucks, hydraulic excavators, presses, dozer shovels, machine tools and welding robots.

Pres. RYOICHI KAWAI; employees: 23,609.

Kubota Ltd.: 2-47, Shikitsuhigash 1-chome, Naniwa-ku, Osaka; f. 1890; sales $2,648. (1981).

Manufacture and sale of cast iron pipes, steel ingot moulds, general castings, internal combustion engines, machine tools, measuring instruments, tractor, tiller, planting machine and general farming equipment, home and utilities, asbestos sheet, manufacturing, sale and installation of plant, flood gates and other steel structures, building materials.

Pres. KEITARO HIRO; employees: 17,000.

Maruzen Oil Co. Ltd.: 3, 1-chome, Nagahoribashi-suji, Minami-ku, Osaka; f. 1933; sales $3,430.5m.; cap. and res. $82.5m.

Import, refining and sale of petroleum; production and sale of petro-chemicals.

Chair. KAZUO MIYAMORI; Pres. SANAE HONDA; employees: 4,260.

Matsushita Electric Industrial Co. Ltd.: 8-2, Hamamatsu-cho 4-chome, Minato-ku, Tokyo; f. 1918; sales $10,020.6m.; cap. and res. $4,247.7m.

Manufacture and sales of electrical and electronic home appliances, including radio, television receivers and parts, communication equipment, medical equipment, batteries, electric light bulbs, and electric motors.

Ten major subsidiary companies in Japan; manufacturing and sales companies in 26 countries; Chair. ARATORO TAKAHASHI; Pres. MASAHARU MATSUSHITA; employees: 95,487.

Matsushita Electric Works Ltd.: 1048, Oaza Kadoma, Kadoma-shi, Osaka 571; sales $2,267.3m. (1981); cap. and res. $717.7m.; lighting equipment and housing and building materials, electrical construction materials, electric appliances and plastic materials.

Chair. MASAHARU NIWA; Pres. KAORU KOBAYASHI; employees: 12,585.

Mitsubishi Chemical Industries Ltd.: 5-2 Marunouchi 2, Chiyoda-ku, Tokyo; f. 1950; sales $2,993.3m.; cap. and res. $356.2m.

Manufacture and sale of coke and coal-tar derivatives, dyestuffs and intermediates, caustic soda, organic solvents and chemicals, reagents, ammonia derivatives, inorganic chemicals, pesticides and herbicides, fertilizers, food additives and pharmaceutical intermediates.

Pres. EIJI SUZUKI; employees: 15,280.

Mitsubishi Electric Corporation: Mitsubishi Building, 2-3, Marunouchi, 2-chome, Chiyoda-ku, Tokyo; f. 1921; sales $6,085.2m. (1981); cap. and res. $1,080.1m. (1981).

Manufacturing and sales of electrical machinery and equipment (for power plant, mining, ships, locomotives and other rolling stock, aircraft), domestic electric appliances, radio communication equipment, radio and television sets, meters and relaying equipment, fluorescent lamps, lighting fixtures, refrigerators, lifts, electric tools, sewing machines.

Chair. SADAKAZU SHINDO; Pres. NIHACHIRO KATAYAMA; employees; 47,875.

Mitsubishi Heavy Industries Ltd.: 5-1, Marunouchi, 2-chome, Chiyoda-ku, Tokyo; f. 1959; sales $9,200.5m.; cap. and res. $917.7m.

Shipbuilding, ship repairing, prime movers, chemical plant and machinery, industrial machinery, heavy machinery, rolling stock, precision machinery, steel structures, construction machinery, refrigerating and air-conditioning machinery, engines, aircraft, special purpose vehicles, space systems.

Principal subsidiary companies in Japan and Brazil and other countries; Chair. GAKUJI MORIYA; Pres. MASAO KANAMORI; employees: 102,112.

Mitsubishi Oil Co. Ltd.: 1-2-4, Toranomon, Minato-ku, Tokyo; f. 1931; sales $2,502.8m.; cap. $98.4m.

Refining, import and marketing of petroleum products and petrochemicals.

Pres. TATSUO MABUCHI; employees: 3,036.

Mitsubishi Petrochemical Co. Ltd.: 5-2, Marunouchi 2-chome, Chiyoda-ku, Tokyo; sales 404,183m. yen (1980); cap. and res. 22,249m. yen.

Plastics and chemicals.

Pres. MASAKI YOSHIDA; employees: 3,778.

Mitsui Engineering & Shipbuilding Co. Ltd.: 6-4, Tsukiji 5-chome, Chuo-ku, Tokyo 104; f. 1937; sales $1,205.8m.; cap. and res. $318m.

Shipbuilding and industrial machinery.

Pres. ISAMU YAMASHITA; employees: 14,847.

Mitsui Toatsu Chemicals Inc.: Kasumigaseki Bldg., 2-5, Kasumigaseki 3-chome, Chiyoda-ku, Tokyo; f. 1933; sales $1,818m. (1981); cap. and res. 166.1m.

Industrial chemicals, fertilizers, dyestuffs, fine chemicals, agricultural and pharmaceuticals, adhesives, electric materials and resins, etc.

Pres. YUICHIRO KASAMA; employees: 6,201.

Nippon Electric Co. Ltd.: 33-1, Shiba 5-chome, Minato-ku, Tokyo 108; f. 1899; sales $2,731.4m.; cap. and res. $390.3m.

Manufacture and sale of telephone switching systems, carrier transmission and terminals, radio and satellite communications, broadcasting electronic data processing and industrial electronic systems, electron devices and consumer electronic products.

Chair. KOJI KOBAYASHI; Pres. TADAO TANAKA; employees: 59,774.

Nippon Gakki Co. Ltd.: 10-1 Nakazawa-cho, Hamamatsu, Shizuoka; sales $1,137.5m., cap. and res. $329.7m.

Musical instruments; employees: 18,672.

Nippon Kokan K.K.: 1-1-2, Marunouchi, Chiyoda-ku, Tokyo 100; f. 1912; sales $4,837.1m.; cap. and res. $146,281m.

Manufacture and sale of pig iron, steel ingots, tubes plates, sheets, bars and shapes, special steels and ferro-alloys, coal derived chemicals, chemical fertilizers, refractories and slag wool; engineering and construction of pipelines, steel plants, steel structures, water treatment plants, diesel engines; shipbuilding, tankers, bulk carriers, cargo ships, container ships, chemical carriers.

Pres. MINORU KANAO; employees: 43,858.

Nippon Mining Co. Ltd.: 10-1, Toranomon 2-chome, Minato-ku, Tokyo; f. 1905; sales 1,306,954m. yen; cap. 35,670m. yen (1981).

Mining, refining, smelting, manufacture and sale of non-ferrous metals; refining and sale of petroleum and petrochemical products; general chemical production; non-ferrous metal and special alloy fabrication, production of electronics and speciality metals.

Chair. SHONOSUKE NIWANO; Pres. TAKANOBU SASAKI; employees: 5,875.

Nippon Steel Corporation: Shin Nittetsu Bldg., 6-3 Otemachi 2-chome, Chiyoda-ku, Tokyo 100; f. 1970; sales $9,521.9m.; cap. and res. $1,864.9m.

Chair. EISHIRO SAITO; Pres. YUTAKA TAKEDA; employees: 80,600.

Nippon Suisan Kaisha Ltd.: 6-2, Otemachi 2-chome, Chiyoda-ku, Tokyo; f. 1911; sales $1,980m. (1980); cap. and res. $158.3m.

Marine fisheries and fish products; food processing; cargo and tanker services.

Pres. SHUNICHI OHKUCHI; employees: 6,300.

Nippondenso Co. Ltd.: 1-1 Showa-cho, Kariya-shi, Aichi-ken; f. 1949; sales 517,360m. yen (1980); cap. 14,442m. yen.

Car electrical equipment, air conditioners, radiators, fuel injection pumps, instruments, sparking plugs, etc.

Chair. TAKEAKI SHIRAI; Pres. FUBITO HIRANO; employees: 25,147.

Nissan Motor Co. Ltd.: 17-1, Ginza 6-chome, Chuo-ku Tokyo; f. 1933; net sales 2,738,868m. yen (1980); cap. p.u. 76,690m. yen.

Manufacture and sale of automobiles, rockets, textile machinery, other machines and appliances and parts.

Chair. KATSUJI KAWAMATA; Pres. TAKASHI ISHIHARA; employees: 60,400.

Nissan Shatai Co. Ltd.: 10-1, Amanuma, Hiratsukashi, Kanagawa-ken 254; f. 1949; sales $1,245.2m.; cap. and res. 129m.

Auto-bodies for passenger cars and small trucks.

Chair. KATSUJI KAWAMATA; Pres. MATSANOBU AOKI; employees: 7,182.

Nisshin Steel Co. Ltd.: Shin Kokusai Bldg., 4-1, Marunouchi 3-chome, Chiyoda-ku, Tokyo; f. 1928; sales $1,160.9m.; cap. and res. $213m.

Manufacture of ordinary steel, stainless steel, special steel and various secondary products.

Pres. NOBUO KANEKO; employees: 11,362.

Oji Paper Co. Ltd.: 7-5, Ginza 4-chome, Chuo-ku, Tokyo 104; f. 1949; sales $1,196.3m.; cap. and res. $213.1m.

Newsprint, packing paper and printing paper.

Pres. FUMIO TANAKA; employees: 7,883.

Sanyo Electric Co. Ltd.: 18 Keihan Hon-dori, 2-chome, Moriguchi City, Osaka-ken; f. 1947; sales $3,023.2m.; cap. and res. $708.4m.

Manufacture and sale of electrical and electronic machinery and appliances—refrigerators, washing machines, electric fans, television and radio sets, bicycle dynamos, bicycle accessories, dry batteries, flashlights, etc.

Pres. KAORU IUE; employees: 17,685.

Sanyo-Kokusaku Pulp Co. Ltd.: 4-5 Marunouchi 1-chome, Chiyoda-ku, Tokyo; f. 1946; sales 275,722m. yen (1981); cap. and res. 25,283m. yen.

Paper, pulp, wood products and chemicals.

Chair. SHUNICHIRO IKEDA; Pres. MASAYOSHI NINOMIYA. Publs. *Nihonkeizai Shinbun, Sankei Shinbun.* Employees: 5,086.

Sekisui Chemical Co. Ltd.: 2 Kinugasa-cho, Kita-ku, Osaka; sales $1,148.5m., cap. and res. $104.4m.

Chemicals, building materials etc., employees: 6,000.

Sharp Corporation: 22-22 Nagaike-cho Abeno-ku, Osaka 545; f. 1912; sales $1,311.9m.; cap. and res. $244.6m.

Manufacture and sale of TV sets, acoustic equipment, domestic electrical appliances, industrial machines and medical equipment.

Chair. TOKUJI HAYAKAWA; Pres. AKIRA SAEKI; employees: 15,699.

Shiseido Co. Ltd.: 5-5, Ginza 7-chome, Chuo-ku, Tokyo; sales $1,123m.; cap. and res. $469.7m.

Cosmetics and toiletries.

Pres. KICHIBEE YAMAMOTO; employees: 12,949.

Showa Denko K.K.: 13-9, Shiba Daimon 1-chome, Minato-ku, Tokyo 105; f. 1939; sales 384,490m. yen (1981); cap. 43,730m. yen.

Manufacture and sale of bulk and speciality chemicals, plastics, fertilizers, ferro-alloys, electrodes and abrasives.

Chair. HARURO SUZUKI; Pres. YASUNOBU KISHIMOTO; employees: 9,476.

Showa Oil Co. Ltd.: Tokyo Bldg., 7-3 Marunouchi 2-chome, Chiyoda-ku, Tokyo; sales $2,129.4m.; cap. and res. 121.4m.

Petroleum; employees: 2,077.

Snow Brand Milk Products Co. Ltd.: 13 Honshio-cho, Shinjuku-ku, Tokyo; f. 1950; sales $2,356.9m.; cap. and res. $141.2m.

Manufacture of liquid milk, condensed and powdered milk, butter, cheese, ice-cream, infant foods, instant foods, margarine, fruit juices, frozen foods, imported wine distribution.

Chair. YOSHIICHI KODAMA; Pres. YOICHI YAMAMOTO; employees: 16,722.

Sony Corporation: 7-35, Kita Shinagawa 6-chome, Shinagawa-ku, Tokyo 141; f. 1946; sales $4,821.3m. (1981); cap. and res. 1,943.6m.

Manufacture and sale of videotape recorders, radios, television sets, radios, tape recorders, etc.

Chair. AKIO MORITA; Pres. KAZUO IWAMA; employees: 38,555.

Sumitomo Chemical Co. Ltd.: 15, 5-chome, Kitahama Higashi-ku, Osaka; f. 1913; sales $2,911.2m. (1981); cap. $340m.

Manufacture and sale of chemical fertilizers, dyestuffs, pharmaceuticals, agricultural chemicals, intermediates, organic and inorganic industrial chemicals, synthetic resins, finishing resins, synthetic rubber and rubber chemicals.

Several subsidiary companies; Chair. NORISHIGE HASEGAWA; Pres. TAKESHI HIJIKATA; employees: 9,429.

Sumitomo Electric Industries Ltd.: 15, Kitahama 5-chome, Higashi-ku, Osaka; f. 1911; sales $1,550.1m.; cap. and res. $233.5m.

Manufacture of electric wires and cables, high carbon steel wires; sintered alloy products; rubber and plastic products; disc brakes; radio-frequency products.

Chair. ISAMU SAKAMOTO; Pres. MASAO KAMEI; employees: 18,682.

Sumitomo Heavy Industries Ltd.: New Ohtemachi Bldg., 2-1, Ohtemachi 2-chome, Chiyoda-ku, Tokyo; f. 1934; sales $1,161m.; cap. and res. $279m.

Industrial machinery and shipbuilding.

Pres. TSUNESABURO NISHIMURA; employees: 12,600.

Sumitomo Metal Industries Ltd.: 5-15, Kitahama, Higashiku, Osaka; f. 1897; cap. 118,912m. yen (1981).

Manufacture and sale of pig iron, steel ingots, steel bars, shapes, wire rods, tubes, pipes, castings, forgings, rolling stock parts, engineering.

Fifty-four subsidiary companies in Japan; 12 offices abroad; Chair. HOSAI HYUGA; Pres. YOSHIFUMI KUMAGAI; employees: 29,675 (1981).

Suzuki Motor Co. Ltd.: 23-2 Daikyo-cho, Shinjuku-ku, Tokyo; sales $1,149.4m., cap. and res. $158.1m.

Motor vehicles; employees: 12,196.

Taiyo Gyogyo (Taiyo Fishery) Co. Ltd.: 1-5-1 Marunouchi, Chiyoda-ku, Tokyo; f. 1880; sales $4,518.3m.; cap. and res. $127.4m.

Fishing, processing and sale of agricultural marine and meat products; canned and frozen salmon, crab, etc.; food processing, marine transport, export and import; refrigeration, ice production and cold storage; manufacture and sale of pharmaceuticals, organic fertilizers and sugar; culture and sale of pearls; breeding and sale of mink.

Pres. TOJIRO NAKABE; employees: 13,750.

Takeda Chemical Industries Ltd.: 27 Dosho Machi 2-chome, Higashi-ku, Osaka; f. 1925; sales $1,360.3m.; cap. and res. $717.9m.

Manufacture and distribution of pharmaceuticals, industrial chemicals, cosmetics, food additives; enriched foods and drinks, agricultural chemicals, fertilizers.

Chair. KANZABURO MORIMOTO; Pres. SHINBEI KONISHI; employees: 13,146.

Teijin Ltd.: 1-1, Uchisaiwai-cho 2-chome, Chiyoda-ku, Tokyo, and 11, Minami Hommachi 1-chome, Higashi-ku, Osaka; f. 1918; sales $1,230.8m.; cap. and res. $340.6m.

Manufactures of fibres, yarns and fabrics from polyester, fibres (Teijin Tetoron), nylon, polyvinyl chloride fibre

(Teijin Teviron), acetate, acrylic fibre (Teijin Beslon), polycarbonate resin (Panlite), acetate resin (Tenex), petro-chemicals, pharmaceuticals.

Seventy-nine subsidiary companies; Pres. SHINZO OHYA; employees: 10,346.

Toa Oil Co. Ltd.: Shin Otemachi Bldg., 2-1, Otemachi 2-chome, Chiyoda-ku, Tokyo 100; f. 1924; sales $1,244m.; cap. and res. $3.6m.

Petroleum products.

Chair. MASAYUKI ECHIGO; Pres. ICHIHEI KISHIDA; employees: 866.

ToaNenryo Kogyo Kabushiki Kaisha: 1-1 Hitotsubashi 1-chome. Chiyoda-ku, Tokyo; f. 1939; sales $2,953.2m.; cap. and res. $554.3m.

Petroleum refining.

Principal subsidiary companies: Nichimo Sekiyu, Tonen Sekiyu, Kagaku Co. Ltd.; Chair. MASAJI NAMBU; Pres. AKIRA MATSUYAMA; employees: 3,927.

Toppan Printing Co. Ltd.: 5-1, Taito 1-chome, Taito-ku, Tokyo 110; f. 1900; sales $1,627.6m. (1980); cap. and res. $496.9m.

General printing.

Pres. KAZUO SUZUKI; employees: 8,360.

Toray Industries Inc.: 2-chome, Nihonbashi-Muromachi, Chuo-ku, Tokyo 103; f. 1926; sales $1,893.8m.; cap. and res. $595.4m.

Manufacturers of nylon, Toray Tetoron (polyester fibre), Toraylon (acrylic fibre), Torayca (carbon fibre), plastics and chemicals.

Chair. KIZO YASUI; Pres. TSUGUHIDE FUJIYOSHI; employees: 24,866.

Toshiba Corporation: 1-6, Uchisaiwaicho 1-chome, Chiyoda-ku, Tokyo; f. 1904; cap. sales $5,755.5m.; cap. and res. $751.5m.

Manufacture, sale and export of electric appliances, apparatus and instruments; heavy electric machinery, Overseas offices in 24 countries; Chair. KEIZO TAMAKI. Pres. KAZUO IWATA; employees: 100,000.

Toyo Kogyo Co. Ltd.: 3-1 Shinchi, Fuchu-cho, Aki-gun, Hiroshima 730-91; f. 1920; sales 1,163,078m. yen (1981); cap. and res. 38,811m. yen (April 1982).

Manufacturing and sale of "Mazda" passenger cars and commercial vehicles; "Toyo" rock drills, machine tools, gauge block and coated sand. Agreement with Perkins Engines (diesel) of U.K.

Seven subsidiary companies at home; subsidiaries in Australia, Belgium, the U.S.A., Canada, Thailand and the Federal Republic of Germany; Pres. YOSHIKI YAMASAKI; employees 27,897.

Toyo Seikan Kaisha Ltd.: 3-1 Uchisaiwai-cho, 1-chome, Chiyoda-ku, Tokyo; sales $1,347.8m., cap. and res. $282.9m.

Metal products; employees: 11,094.

Toyobo Co. Ltd.: 2-8 Dojima Hama, 2-chome, Kita-ku, Osaka 530; f. 1882; sales 446,007m. yen (1981); cap. and res. 47,667m. yen.

Manufacture and dyeing, bleaching, printing, finishing and sale of cotton yarns and fabrics, woollen and worsted yarns and fabrics, polyester yarns and fabrics and various artificial fibres; manufacture and sale of films, resins and biochemicals.

Chair. ICHIJI OHTANI; Pres. OSAMU UNO; employees: 17,425.

Toyota Motor Co. Ltd.: 1, Toyota-cho, Toyota, Aichi; f. 1937; sales $12,768.8m.; cap. and res. $3,937.4m.

Manufacture of passenger cars, trucks and parts.

Pres. EIJI TOYODA; employees: 60,846.

Ube Industries Ltd.: 7-2 Kasumigaseki 3-chome, Chiyoda-ku, Tokyo 100; f. 1942; sales $1,473m.; cap. and res. $222m.

Mining, production, processing and sale of coal, iron ore, limestone, silica, clay, chemical fertilizers, tar products, sulphuric acid, nitric acid, oxalic acid, ammonium nitrate, ammonia, pharmaceuticals, cement, caprolactam, high pressure polyethylene, industrial machinery and equipment, cast steel products, cast iron products, iron and steel bars.

Pres. KANICHI NAKAYASU; Vice-Pres. TOYOZO FUJIMOTO employees: 15,623.

Yamaha Motor Co. Ltd.: 1280 Nakajyo, Hamana-gun Shizuoka; sales $1,321.7m., cap. and res. $165.5m.

Manufacture of motorcycles; employees: 12,900.

TRANSPORT

RAILWAYS

Japanese National Railways (J.N.R.): 1-6-5, Marunouchi, Chiyoda-ku, Tokyo; f. 1949; very high speed Shinkansen line: Tokaido between Tokyo and Shin Osaka (515 km.), Sanyo between Shin Osaka and Hakata (554 km.), Tohoku between Omiya and Morioka (465 km.), Joetsu between Omiya and Niigata (270 km.), and sections between Omiya and Tokyo and Tokyo and Narita under construction; 21,322 km. of track, 8,414 electrified; Pres. FUMIO TAKAGI; Vice-Pres. KAZUMASA MAWATARI; Vice-Pres. Engineering KOJI TAKAHASHI.

PRINCIPAL PRIVATE COMPANIES

Hankyu Corporation: 8-8, Kakuta-cho, Kita-ku, Osaka 530; f. 1907; links Osaka, Kyoto, Kobe and Takarazuka; Pres. SADAO SHIBATANI.

Hanshin Electric Railway Co. Ltd.: 3-19, Umeda 2-chome, Kita-ku, Osaka; f. 1899; Pres. TAKAZO TANAKA.

Keihan Electric Railway Co. Ltd.: 47-5, 1-chome, Kyobashi, Higashi-ku, Osaka; Pres. SEITARO AOKI.

Keihin Kyuko Electric Express Railway Co. Ltd.: 20-20, Takanawa 2-chome, Minato-ku, Tokyo; Pres. MICHIO IIDA.

Keio Teito Electric Railway Co. Ltd.: 3-1-24, Shinjuku, Shinjuku-ku, Tokyo; Pres. MADOKA MINOWA.

Keisei Electric Railway Co. Ltd.: 10-3, 1-chome, Oshiage, Sumida-ku, Tokyo; f. 1909; Pres. MITSUO SATO.

Kinki Nippon Railway Co. Ltd.: 1-55, 6-chome, Uehommachi, Tennoji-ku, Osaka; f. 1910; Pres. YOSHINORI UEYAMA.

Nagoya Railroad Co. Ltd.: 2-4, 1-chome, Meieki, Nakamura-ku, Nagoya-shi; Pres. KOTARO TAKEDA.

Nankai Electric Railway Co. Ltd.: 1-60, 5-chome, Nanba, Minami-ku, Osaka; Pres. DEN KAWAKATSU.

Nishi Nippon Railroad Co. Ltd.: 1-11-17 Tenjin-cho, Chuo-ku, Fukuoka; serves northern Kyushu; Pres. GENKEI KIMOTO.

Odakyu Electric Railway Co. Ltd.: 8-3, 1-chome, Nishi Shinjuku, Shinjuku-ku, Tokyo; f. 1948; Pres. TATSUZO TOSHIMITSU.

Seibu Railway Co. Ltd.: 16-15, 1-chome, Minami-Ikebukuro, Toshima-ku, Tokyo; f. 1912; Pres. YOSHIAKI TSUTSUMI.

Tobu Railway Co. Ltd.: 1-2, 1-chome, Oshiage, Sumida-ku, Tokyo; Pres. KAICHIRO NEZU.

Tokyu Corporation: 26-20, Sakuragaoka-cho, Shibuya-ku, Tokyo; f. 1922; Pres. NOBORU GOTOH.

SUBWAYS AND MONORAILS

Subway service is available in Tokyo, Osaka, Kobe, Nagoya, Sapporo, Yokohama, Kyoto and Fukuoka with a combined network of about 380 km. Most new subway lines are directly linked with existing J.N.R. or private railway terminals which connect the cities with suburban areas.

Japan started its first monorail system on a commercial scale in 1964 with straddle-type cars between central Tokyo and Tokyo International Airport, a distance of 13 km. In 1982 the total length of monorail was 27.5 km. Work started in 1971 on the 54-km. Seikan Tunnel (electric rail only) linking Honshu island with Hokkaido, and is scheduled to be completed in 1985.

Kobe Municipal Rapid Transit: 5-1, Kanocho Chuoku, Kobe; Dir. TOSHITO YAMANAKA; 5.7 km. open; 7.5 km. under construction; 9.3 km. planned for construction.

Nagoya Underground Railway: Nagoya Municipal Transportation Bureau, City Hall Annexe, 1-1, Sannomaru 3-chome, Naka-ku, Nagoya; 54.4 km. open (1982); Gen. Man. MASATAKA OSAWA.

Osaka Underground Railway: Osaka Municipal Transportation Bureau, 11-53, 1-chome, Kujo Minami-dori, Nishi-ku, Osaka; f. 1903; 89.1 km. open; in 1981 the 6.6 km. computer-controlled "New Tram" service began between Suminoekoen and Nakafuto; Gen. Man. KAZUO OTA.

Sapporo Rapid Transit: Municipal Transportation Bureau, Sapporo, Hokkaido; 31.6 km. open; 8.1 km. under construction; Dir. M. OGUNI.

Tokyo Underground Railway: Teito Rapid Transit Authority, 19-6, 3-chome Higashi Ueno, Taito-ku, Tokyo; f. 1941; Pres. AKIYOSHI YAMADA; 131.8 km. open; and Transportation Bureau of Tokyo Metropolitan Government, 2-10-1 Yurako-cho, Chiyoda-ku, Tokyo; f. 1960; Dir.-Gen. TOMOSABURO SUGIMURA; 54.9 km. open; combined length of underground system 186.7 km. (1982).

Yokohama Rapid Transit: Municipal Transportation Bureau, Yokohama; 2 lines of 11.5 km.; Dir.-Gen. S. ISHIWATARI.

ROADS

In March 1980 Japan's road network extended to 1,113,387 km., including 2,579 km. of automobile highways. Plans have been made to cover the country with a trunk automobile highway network with a total length of 7,600 km., of which 3,500 km. were expected to be completed by 1982.

There is a national omnibus service, 57 publicly operated services and 297 privately operated services.

SHIPPING

Shipping in Japan is not nationalized but is supervised by the Ministry of Transport. On June 30th, 1981, the merchant fleet had a total displacement of 40,836,000 gross tons. The main ports are Yokohama, Nagoya and Kobe.

PRINCIPAL COMPANIES

Daiichi Chuo Kisen Kaisha: 5-15, Nihonbashi 3-chome, Chuo-ku, Tokyo; f. 1960; fleet of 15 vessels; liner and tramp services; Pres. K. MORITA.

Japan Line Ltd.: Kokusai Bldg., 1-1, Marunouchi 3-chome, Chiyoda-ku, Tokyo; f. 1948; fleet of 40 vessels; container ship, tanker, liner, tramp and specialized carrier services; Chair. (vacant); Pres. TAKESHI KITAGAWA.

Kansai Kisen Kaisha: 7-15, Benten 6-chome, Minato-ku, Osaka; f. 1942; fleet of 11 vessels; domestic passenger services; Pres. J. JINNO.

Kawasaki Kisen Kaisha (*K Line*): 8 Kaigan-dori, Chuo-ku, Kobe; f. 1919; fleet of 55 vessels; cargo, tankers and bulk ore carrying services worldwide; Pres. K. OKADA.

Mitsui O.S.K. Lines Ltd.: 2-1, Toranomon, Minato-ku, Tokyo; f. 1942; 87 vessels; world-wide container, liner, tramp and specialized carrier and tanker services; Pres. SHIZUO KONDO.

Nippon Yusen Kabushiki Kaisha: 3-2, Marunouchi 2-chome, Chiyoda-ku, Tokyo 100; 122 vessels; world-wide container, cargo, tanker and bulk carrying services; Chair. S. KIKUCHI; Pres. S. ONO.

Nissho Shipping Co. Ltd.: 33 Mori Bldg., 8-21, Toranomon 3-chome, Minato-ku, Tokyo; f. 1943; Pres. D. MINE.

Ryukyu Kaiun Kaisha: 2-24, 1-chome Nishi, Naha City, Okinawa; fleet of 11 vessels; cargo and passenger services on Japanese domestic routes; Pres. EITOKU YAMASHIRO.

Sanko Steamship Co. Ltd.: Shinyurakucho Bldg., 12-1, Yurakucho 1-chome, Chiyoda-ku, Tokyo; f. 1934; fleet of 33 vessels; overseas tramping (cargo and oil); Pres. HIROSHI YOSHIDA.

Sankyo Kaiun Co. Ltd.: Miki Bldg., No. 12-1, 3-chome, Nihonbashi, Chuo-ku, Tokyo; f. 1959; fleet of 12 vessels; liner and tramp services; Pres. K. KAMOI; Man. Dirs. K. KIKUOKA, Y. YAMAZAKI.

Shinwa Kaiun Kaisha Ltd.: Fukokuseimei Bldg., 2-2, 2-chome, Uchisaiwai-cho, Chiyoda-ku, Tokyo; f. 1950; fleet of 35 vessels; ore carrying, cargo and tanker services; Pres. KAZUO KIMURA.

Showa Line Ltd.: 2-3, 2-chome, Uchisaiwai-cho, Chiyoda-ku, Tokyo; f. 1944; 36 vessels; cargo, tanker, tramping and container services world-wide; Chair. TOSHIHARU MATSUE; Pres. SOTARO YAMADA.

Taiheiyo Kaiun Co. Ltd. (*The Pacific Transportation Co. Ltd.*): Marunouchi Bldg., 4-1, 2-chome, Chiyoda-ku, Tokyo; f. 1951; fleet of 7 vessels; cargo and tanker services; Pres. S. YAMAJI.

Yamashita-Shinnihon Steamship Co., Ltd.: 1-1, Hitotsubashi, 1-chome, Chiyoda-ku, Tokyo 100; f. 1917; fleet of 44 vessels, liner, tramp and tanker services worldwide; Pres. T. HORI.

CIVIL AVIATION

There are three international airports at Tokyo, Osaka and Narita.

Japan Air Lines—JAL (*Nihon Koku Kabushiki Kaisha*): 7-3, 2-chome, Marunouchi, Chiyoda-ku, Tokyo 100; f. 1951; operates domestic and international service, from Tokyo to Australia, Brazil, Canada, People's Republic of China, Denmark, Egypt, Fiji, France, Federal Republic of Germany, Greece, Guam, Hong Kong, India, Indonesia, Iran, Iraq, Italy, the Republic of Korea, Kuwait, Malaysia, Mexico, Netherlands, New Zealand, Northern Marianas, Pakistan, the Philippines, Saudi Arabia, Singapore, Spain, Switzerland, Thailand, U.S.S.R., United Arab Emirates, the U.K. and the U.S.A.; Pres. YASUMOTO TAKAGI; fleet of 2 Boeing 727, 39 Boeing 747, 25 DC-8, 17 DC-10.

Japan Asia Airways Co.: Yurakucho Denki Bldg., 7-1, Yurakucho 1-chome, Chiyoda-ku, Tokyo 100; f. 1975; wholly-owned subsidiary of JAL; operates international services to Hong Kong, the Philippines and Taiwan; Pres. TOSHIO ITAKURA; fleet of 2 DC-10, 3 DC-8.

All Nippon Airways Co. Ltd.: 2-5, Kasumigaseki 3-chome, Chiyoda-ku, Tokyo; f. 1952; operates domestic passenger and freight services; charter services to Hong Kong, the Philippines, the People's Republic of China, Singapore and Thailand; Pres. MASAMICHI ANZAI; fleet of 22 Boeing 727, 15 Boeing 737, 13 Boeing 747, 20 TriStar, 25 YS-11, 4 Jet Ranger, 1 Aerospacial AS350.

Nihon Kinkyori Airways Co. (*Nihon Kinkyori Koku KK*): 6-2, 3-chome, Toranomon, Minato-ku, Tokyo; f. 1974; operates domestic services; Pres. KANICHI MARUI; fleet of 9 YS-11, 3 Twin Otter.

Southwest Airlines Co. Ltd. (*Nansei Koku KK*): 3-1, Yamashita-cho, Naha City, Okinawa; f. 1967; subsidiary of JAL; operates inter-island service in Okinawa; Pres. MASAO MASUMO; fleet of 6 YS-11, 4 Twin Otter, 4 Boeing 737.

Toa Domestic Airlines Co.: 18 Mori Bldg., 9-1, 1-chome, Haneda-kuko, Ota-ku, Tokyo 105; f. 1964; domestic services to 39 cities; Pres. ISAMU TANAKA; Senior Vice-Pres. TOSHIHIKO KUBOTA, YOSHITAKA OHKI, SHOGO UCHIYAMA; fleet of 19 DC-9-41, 3 A300B2-201, 6 DC-9-81, 40 YS-11, 5 Kawasaki Hughes 369HS, 4 Fuji Bell 204B, 3 Bell 314B, 4 Kawasaki Bell KH4.

FOREIGN AIRLINES

The following international airlines also serve Japan: Aeroflot (U.S.S.R.), Air France, Air India, Air Nauru, Air New Zealand, Alitalia, British Airways, CAAC (People's Republic of China), Cathay Pacific Airways (Hong Kong), China Airlines (Taiwan), Continental Airlines Inc./Air Micronesia (U.S.A.), CP Air (Canada), EgyptAir, Flying Tiger Line (U.S.A.), Garuda Indonesian Airways, Iran Air, Iraq Airways, KLM (Netherlands), Korean Air Lines (Republic of Korea), Lufthansa (Federal Republic of Germany), MAS (Malaysia), North-west Orient Airlines (U.S.A.), Pan Am (U.S.A.), PAL (Philippines), PIA (Pakistan), Qantas (Australia), Sabena (Belgium), SAS (Sweden, Norway, Denmark), SIA (Singapore), Swissair, Thai Airways International, TMA (Lebanon), UTA (France), and VARIG (Brazil).

TOURISM AND CULTURE

Japan National Tourist Organization: Tokyo Kotsu Kaikan Bldg., 2-10-1 Yuraku-cho, Chiyoda-ku, Tokyo; Pres. YOSHINARI TEZUKA.

Japan Travel Bureau Inc.: 6-4, Marunouchi 1-chome, Chiyoda-ku, Tokyo; f. 1912; approx. 11,000 mems.; Chair. H. TSUDA; Pres. T. NAGASE.

Department of Tourism: 2-1-3 Kasumigaseki, Chiyoda-ku, Tokyo 100; f. 1946; inner department of the Ministry of Transport; Dir.-Gen. YASUO NISHIMURA.

THEATRES

Kabukiza Theatre: Ginza-Higashi, Tokyo; national Kabuki theatre centre.

National Theatre of Japan (*Kokuritsu Gekijo*): 4-1 Hayabusa-cho, Chiyoda-ku, Tokyo 102; f. 1966; Pres. HIDEMI KOHN; Dir.-Gen. TADASHI INUMARU.

Nissei Theatre: 1-1-1 Yuraku-cho, Choyosa-ku, Tokyo; f. 1963; drama, opera and concerts; mems. 300; Gen. Dir. ICHIRO YAMAMOTO.

MUSIC FESTIVAL

Osaka International Festival: New Asahi Bldg., 3-18, Nakanoshima 2-chome, Kita-ku, Osaka 530; joined European Asscn. of Music Festivals 1966.

ATOMIC ENERGY

Twenty-two nuclear power stations were in operation by April 1981 and 13 more are expected to become operational by 1985, with a combined capacity of 27,881 MWe.

Projected generating capacity (1990): 51,000–53,000 MW.

Japan Atomic Energy Commission (JAEC): 2-2-1 Kasumigaseki, Chiyoda-ku, Tokyo; f. 1955; policy board for research, development and peaceful uses of atomic energy; Chair. ICHIRO NAKAGAWA.

Japan Nuclear Safety Commission (JNSC): 2-2-1 Kasumigaseki, Chiyoda-ku, Tokyo; f. 1978; responsible for all matters relating to safety regulations; Chair. KEISUKE MISONOO.

Atomic Energy Bureau (AEB): Science and Technology Agency, 2-2-1 Kasumigaseki, Chiyoda-ku, Tokyo; f. 1956; administers and controls research and development; Dir. TAKAO ISHIWATARI.

Nuclear Safety Bureau (NSB): Science and Technology Agency, 2-2-1 Kasumigaseki, Chiyoda-ku, Tokyo; f. 1976; administrative agency for nuclear safety and regulatory matters; Dir. NOBUHISA AKABANE.

Japan Atomic Energy Research Institute (JAERI): Fukokuseimei Bldg., 2-2-2 Uchisaiwaicho, Chiyoda-ku, Tokyo; f. 1956; all aspects of nuclear research: water reactor safety, fusion, HTR and utilization of radiation; Pres. TSUNEO FUJINAMI.

Power Reactor and Nuclear Fuel Development Corporation (PNC): 1-9-13 Akasaka, Minato-ku, Tokyo; f. 1967; research and development of FBR, ATR and fuel cycle technologies; Pres. MASAO SEGAWA.

Japan Nuclear Ship Research and Development (JNSRD): 1-15-16 Toranomon, Minato-ku, Tokyo; f. 1963; research and development of nuclear ship; Pres. KEIJIRO INOUE.

Japan Atomic Industrial Forum Inc. (JAIF): 5-4, Otemachi 1-chome, Chiyoda-ku, Tokyo 100; f. 1956; non-profit-making organization representing some 750 organizations involved in atomic energy development in Japan and some 100 overseas mems.; aims to promote the peaceful use of atomic energy and the acceptance of nuclear power among the public; carries out field surveys related to those activities; Chair. HIROMI ARISAWA; Exec. Man. Dir. KAZUHISA MORI.

DEFENCE

Self-Defence Forces and Equipment (March 1981): Total 270,184: Ground Self Defence Forces (army) 180,000; Maritime Self Defence Force (navy) 43,897; Air Self Defence Force 46,204; Joint Staff Council 83. The ground forces are equipped with Japanese-made weapons including medium tanks, AA guns, 8 surface-to-air missiles (SAM) groups. The maritime force has 13 submarines and a guided missile destroyer as well as a number of frigates, mine-sweepers, torpedo boats, landing craft and other vessels. There is also a naval air component comprising 190 combat aircraft. The Air Self Defence Force has 400 combat aircraft plus trainers, helicopters and 6 missile groups. With the reversion of Okinawa to Japan in May 1972, a total of 2,059 Japanese military personnel were deployed there in December. By June 1973 an air control and warning group was stationed there together with Hercules and Hawk air defence missiles. The systems formerly under U.S. control were transferred to Japanese control when it assumed responsibility for Okinawa's air defence in July 1973.

Military Service: Voluntary.

Defence Expenditure: Defence Budget 1982/83: 2,586,100 million yen.

Chairman of the Joint Staff Council, Defence Agency: Gen. TSUGIO YADA.

EDUCATION

The standard of literacy among the Japanese has been almost 100 per cent since before the turn of the century.

Before the Government Order of Education in 1872, the form of education for commoners was based on Buddhist temple schools called *terakoya*. Around the middle of the 19th century, there were nearly 16,000 terakoya schools. The noble families had their own form of education by private tutors and governesses. But in 1886 four years' primary education was made compulsory and by the turn of the century, higher education beyond the age of 18 was made available. In 1908 the primary school course was made compulsory for six years. By 1920 more than 90 per cent of the school-age children were attending primary schools.

Immediately after World War II, with the introduction of democratic ideas into Japanese education, the educational system and policies underwent extensive reforms including the adoption of the 6-3-3-4 system. The Fundamental Law of Education of 1947 sets forth the central aims of education as follows: the bringing up of self-reliant citizens with respect for human values and equality of educational opportunity based on ability.

The law prohibits discrimination based on race, creed, sex, social status, economic position or family background. Co-education is authorized under the state education system. It also emphasizes political knowledge and religious tolerance, and prohibits any link between political parties or religious groups and state education. The school year lasts from April to March and is divided into three terms.

One of the striking features of education in Japan today is the increased competition to enter good universities. Though the standards vary, the system is on a dual basis with both private and public schools from primary level to university. The general standards of education in Japan are very high, especially in mathematics and foreign languages.

The Ministry of Education, Science and Culture administers education at all levels and provides guidance, advice and financial assistance to local authorities. In each of the forty-seven prefectures and over three thousand municipalities, boards of education are responsible, in the former, for upper secondary schools, and special schools; while municipal boards maintain public elementary and lower secondary schools. About 11 per cent of the budget was allocated to education and science for the financial year 1980/81. Each level of government provides for its own education with funds derived from its own revenue including taxes. The central government may also grant subsidies where appropriate.

The government offers a scholarship system to promising poor students. Approximately 320,000 students in upper secondary schools, colleges, and universities are currently receiving financial assistance, and are expected to return the money in 20 years after graduation.

Steadily increasing numbers of young people from Asian countries are coming to Japan for technical training at scientific and technological institutes and at factories.

Pre-School Education

There were 13,489 kindergartens in 1976. There were 18,238 day nurseries for children between the age of 3 and 5 in 1975 in which 3,512,712 children were enrolled; about 60 per cent of the former are mainly run privately whilst the latter are operated by local authorities.

Elementary and Lower School Education

All children between 6 and 15 are required to attend six-year elementary schools (Shogakko) and three-year lower secondary schools (Chugakko). All children are provided with text-books free of charge, while children of needy families are assisted in paying for school lunches and educational excursions by the government and the local bodies concerned. There is almost 100 per cent enrolment; 11,826,574 pupils in 24,945 primary and 5,094,402 pupils in 10,779 lower secondary schools in 1980.

Secondary Education

There are three types of course available: full-time, part-time and correspondence. The first lasts three years and the other two both last four years. In 1980 there were 5,208 upper secondary schools in Japan, with an enrolment of 4,621,936.

Higher Education

There were 436 universities and graduate schools, and 579 junior and technical colleges in 1980. The universities offer courses extending from 3 to 4 years and in most cases postgraduate courses for a master's degree in 2 years and a doctorate in 3 years. Junior colleges offer 2- or 3-year courses, credits for which can count towards a first degree. The technical colleges admit lower secondary school students for 5 years. The number of students in universities and graduate schools in 1980 was 1,835,304, and in junior and technical colleges, 417,473.

Teacher Training

Teacher training is offered in both universities and junior

colleges. The total number of students enrolled in faculties of education in 1976 was 211,707.

Special Education

In 1976 there were 603 schools for the handicapped, of which there are 106 for the deaf, 77 for the blind, at kindergarten, primary, secondary and high school levels. Primary and secondary education for the blind, the deaf, the mentally retarded and the physically handicapped are also compulsory.

BIBLIOGRAPHY

GENERAL

BEASLEY, W. G. (ed.) Modern Japan: Aspects of History, Literature and Society (Allen & Unwin, London, 1975).

BUNCE, W. K. Religions in Japan (Tuttle, Tokyo).

EARLE, ERNEST. The Kabuki Theatre (Secker & Warburg, London, 1956).

GUILLAIN, ROBERT. The Japanese Challenge (Hamish Hamilton, 1970).

ISHIDA, R. Geography of Japan (Kokusai Bunka Shinkokai, Tokyo, 1961).

MUNSTERBERG, H. The Arts of Japan (Tuttle, Tokyo).

NAKANE, C. Japanese Society (Weidenfeld & Nicholson, London, 1970).

NORMAN, E. H. Japan's Emergence as a Modern State (Institute of Pacific Relations, New York, 1940).

REISCHAUER, EDWIN O. The Japanese (Harvard University Press, Cambridge, Mass., 1977).

SANSOM, G. B. Japan, A Short Cultural History (Cresset Press, London, 1946).

SMITH, BRADLEY. Japan, History in Art (Weidenfeld & Nicolson, London, 1964).

THOMSEN, H. The New Religions of Japan (Tuttle, Tokyo, 1963).

TSUNODA DE BARY, KEENE. Sources of the Japanese Tradition (Columbia University Press, New York, 1958).

YANAGA, Dr. CHITOSHI. Big Business in Japanese Politics (Yale University Press, New Haven, Conn., 1971).

YAMAMOTO, Y. Approach to Japanese Culture (Kokusai Bunka Shinkokai, Tokyo).

HISTORY

ALLEN, GEORGE C. A Short Economic History of Modern Japan (George Allen & Unwin, London, revised edition, 1972).

ALLEN, LOUIS. The End of the War in Asia (Hart-Davis, MacGibbon, London, 1976).

BEASLEY, WILLIAM G. The Meiji Restoration (Oxford University Press, London, 1973).

BLACKER, CARMEN. The Japanese Enlightenment (Cambridge University Press, Cambridge, 1964).

DORE, RONALD P. (ed.) Aspects of Social Change in Modern Japan (Princeton University Press, Princeton N.J., 1967).

DOWER, JOHN W. Origins of the Modern Japanese State (Pantheon Books, New York, 1975).

DUUS, PETER. The Rise of Modern Japan (Houghton Mifflin, Boston, 1976).

HALL, JOHN W. Japan: From Prehistory to Modern Times (Weidenfeld and Nicolson, London, 1970).

HAVENS, THOMAS R. H. Valley of Darkness: The Japanese People and World War Two (W.W. Norton, New York, 1978).

HIRSCHMEIER, JOHANNES and YUI, TSUNEHIKO. The Development of Japanese Business, 1600–1973 (George Allen & Unwin, London, 1975).

JANSEN, MARIUS B. (ed.) Changing Japanese Attitudes Towards Modernization (Princeton University Press, Princeton, N.J., 1965).

LEHMANN, JEAN-PIERRE. The Image of Japan 1850–1905: From Feudal Isolation to World Power (George Allen & Unwin, London, 1978).

LIVINGSTON, JON, MOORE, JOE, OLDFATHER, FELICIA. (eds.) The Japan Reader 1: Imperial Japan: 1800–1945 (Penguin Books, Harmondsworth, Middlesex, 1976).

The Japan Reader 2: Postwar Japan 1945 to the Present (Penguin Books, Harmondsworth, Middlesex, 1976).

LOCKWOOD, WILLIAM W. The State and Economic Enterprise in Japan (Princeton University Press, Princeton, N.J., 1965).

MORLEY, JAMES W. Dilemmas of Growth in Prewar Japan (Princeton University Press, Princeton, N.J., 1971).

NISH, IAN. The Story of Japan (Faber, London, 1968).
Japanese Foreign Policy, 1869–1942: Kasumigaseki to Miyakezaka (Routledge & Kegan Paul, London, 1977).

REISCHAUER, EDWIN O. Japan Past and Present (Duckworth, London, 1964).

SANSOM, GEORGE B. The Western World and Japan (Cresset Press, London, 1950)
A History of Japan (Cresset Press, London, 1958–64).

SHILLONY, BEN-AMI. Revolt in Japan: The Young Officers and the February 26, 1936 Incident (Princeton University Press, Princeton, N.J., 1973).

SHIVELY, DONALD H. (ed.) Tradition and Modernization in Japanese Culture (Princeton University Press, Princeton, N.J., 1971).

STORRY, RICHARD. A History of Modern Japan (Penguin, London)
Japan and the Decline of the West in Asia 1894–1943 (Macmillan Press, London, 1979).

WARD, ROBERT E. Political Development in Modern Japan (Princeton University Press, Princeton, N.J., 1967).

POLITICS

MAKI, JOHN M. Government and Politics in Japan (Frederick A. Praeger, New York).

MARUYAMA, MASAO. Thought and Behaviour in Modern Japanese Politics (Oxford University Press, London, 1963).

MCNELLY, THEODORE. Contemporary Government of Japan (Allen & Unwin, London, 1964).

PEMPEL, T. J. (ed.) Policymaking in Contemporary Japan (Cornell University Press, Ithaca, N.Y., 1977).

REISCHAUER, E. O. The United States and Japan (Harvard University Press, Cambridge, Mass.).

NISH, IAN. Japanese Foreign Policy 1869–1942: Kasumigaseki to Miyakezaka (Routledge and Kegan Paul, London, 1977).

SCALAPINO, R. A. Parties and Politics in Contemporary Japan.

STEPHAN, JOHN J. The Kuril Islands: Russo-Japanese Frontier in the Pacific (Clarendon Press, Oxford, 1975).

STOCKWIN, J. A. A. Japan: Divided Politics in a Growth Economy (Weidenfeld & Nicholson, London, 1975).

YANAGA, CHITOSHI. Japanese People and Politics (John Wiley, New York).

YOSHIDA, SHIGERU. Japan's Decisive Century (Praeger, New York, 1967).

ECONOMICS

ALLEN, G. C. Japan's Economic Expansion (Oxford University Press, London, 1965).

ASIA KYOKAI. The Co-operative Movement in Japan (Maruzen, Tokyo).

BIEDA, K. The Structure and Operation of the Japanese Economy (John Wiley & Sons, Sydney, 1970).

BOLTHO, ANDREA. Japan: An Economic Survey 1953–1973 (Oxford University Press, 1976).

COHEN, JEROME B. Japan's Postwar Economy (Indiana University Press, Bloomington, Ind.).

International Aspect of Japan's Situation (Council of Foreign Relations, London, 1957).

FRANK, ISAIAH. (ed.) The Japanese Economy in International Perspective (Johns Hopkins University Press, Baltimore and London, 1975).

HEDBERG, H. The Japanese Challenge (Pitman, London, 1970).

Japan's Revenge (Pitman, London, 1972).

KAHN, H. The Emerging Japanese Superstate, Challenge and Response (Prentice-Hall, Englewood Cliffs, N.J., 1970).

KITAMURA, HIROSHI. Choices for the Japanese Economy: National and International Implications of Economic Growth (Chatham House Books, Calder and Boyars, Ltd.).

KOJIMA, KIYOSHI. Japan and a New World Economic Order (Croon Helm, London, 1977).

LEVINE, S. B. Industrial Relations in Postwar Japan (University of Illinois Press, Urbana, Ill.).

MARSH, ROBERT and MANNARI, HIROSHI. Modernization and the Japanese Factory (Princeton University Press, N.J., 1977).

OKITA, SABURO. The Rehabilitation of Japan's Economy and Asia (Ministry of Foreign Affairs, London, 1956).

PATRICK, HUGH, and MEISSNER, LARRY. (eds.) Japanese Industrialization and its Social Consequences (University of California Press, for the Social Sciences Research Council, Berkeley and London, 1977).

PATRICK, H., and ROSOVSKY, H. (eds.) Asia's New Giant: How the Japanese Economy Works (The Brookings Institution, 1976).

TSURU, S. The Mainsprings of Japanese Growth: A Turning Point? (The Atlantic Institute for International Affairs Paris, 1976).

VOGEL, F. EZRA. Japan as Number One (Harvard University Press, Cambridge, 1979).

YOSHIHARA, KUNIO. Japanese Economic Development: A Short Introduction (Oxford University Press, 1980)

Kampuchea

PHYSICAL AND SOCIAL GEOGRAPHY

C. A. Fisher

(Revised for this edition by Harvey Demaine)

Kampuchea occupies a relatively small and compact area of 181,035 square kilometres (69,898 square miles), between Thailand to the west, Laos to the north, and Viet-Nam to the east.

PHYSICAL FEATURES

Apart from the Cardamom and related mountains in the south which tend to shut it off from its short southern coastline, the greater part of the country consists of a shallow lacustrine basin, centred on Tonlé Sap ("the Great Lake") which was formerly much more extensive than it is today. This lowland drains eastwards, via the Tonlé Sap river, to the Mekong, which flows through the eastern part of the lowlands from north to south before swinging eastwards into Viet-Nam and so to the sea.

Throughout its course through Kampuchea, the Mekong averages over a mile in width but is interrupted by serious rapids at Kratié, and by even more serious falls at Khone along the Laotian border. Moreover, its flow varies widely from season to season, and during the period of greatest volume between June and October, a substantial portion of its floodwaters is diverted up the Tonlé Sap river (whose flow is thus reversed) into the Great Lake itself, which comes to occupy an area at least twice as great as it does during the dry season in the early months of the year.

RESOURCES AND POPULATION

With relatively good alluvial soils, abundant irrigation water, and a tropical monsoon climate not marred by excessive rainfall, Kampuchea has a considerable agricultural potential and could undoubtedly support both a wider area and a greater intensity of cultivation than it does at present. This would be particularly the case if the water resource potential of the Mekong River could be harnessed. It has been estimated that some 360,000–375,000 hectares of land could be developed for further cultivation of rice if dams were to be completed upstream, and possible hydroelectric sites within Kampuchea could furnish some 3,600 MW. of electricity.

In 1975 Kampuchea had an estimated 7,100,000 inhabitants and an average population density of 39 per square kilometre; by 1981 it was estimated that the population may have fallen to as little as 5,500,000, owing to warfare, famine and migration, giving a density of only 30 per square kilometre. The capital city, Phnom-Penh, had a population of 450,000 in 1968, which was increased enormously in the early 1970s by refugees. In 1975, however, the majority of the urban population was evacuated to the countryside and in 1978 Phnom-Penh's population was estimated at only 20,000; but by 1981 the resurgence of internal trade may have restored the numbers to their 1968 level.

HISTORY

Michael Leifer

Modern Kampuchea traces its origins to historical legend. It is told that an Indian Brahmin named Kaundinya arrived in the River Mekong delta and married Soma the daughter of the Naga (serpent deity) king known as the Lord of the Soil. Their physical union which symbolized the fertility of the kingdom was to enjoy a central place in Khmer cosmology. This legend derived from Indian cultural influences which took root in Indochina at the beginning of the Christian era and gave rise there to distinctive political forms.

PRE-COLONIAL HISTORY

The legend of political foundation relates more strictly to the Indianized predecessor of Kambuja known as Fu-nan by its Chinese chroniclers. Fu-nan, the earliest of the great Indianized Kingdoms of Indochina is believed to have been established in the middle of the third century A.D. and located to the south-west of the delta of the River Mekong. It came to occupy a dominant position in the peninsula for five centuries although its immediate pre-Kambuja form, the State of Chen-la was to exist in partitioned condition, while its political centre of gravity moved northwards up the Mekong to the eastern end of the Cambodian plain. Khmer cultural and political traditions in the glorious Angkor period derive directly from the heritage of Fu-nan. For example, it was from Fu-nan that there originated the Indian cult of divine kingship in which the person of the monarch was associated with the unity and prosperity of the kingdom. The early kings of Kambuja looked to Fu-nan as the source of their ancestry and also as the fount of their claim to royal title.

The actual beginnings of the post-Fu-nan Cambodian state are somewhat clouded. Nonetheless, it is believed that in the seventh century during the Chen-la period the Shailendra dynasty of Java came to exercise some form of suzerainty. Jayavarman II who is known as the founder of the Khmer Kingdom and who claimed ties of ancestry from Fu-nan returned from exile or captivity in Java at the beginning of the ninth century. He achieved immediate political success after which he sought to legitimize his position through a cult practice which served similar purpose in a Java subject also to Indian influence. He arranged his enthronement as King at the hands of a Brahmin priest at a ceremony which was to symbolize the independence of his newly-founded kingdom from Javanese overlordship. Jayavarman II, who reigned from A.D. 802 to 850, established his capital north of the Great Lake close to the site where the complex of monumental temples were to rise over the next centuries. His dynasty saw the development of an advanced system of agricultural hydraulics which served the rice fields upon which the prosperity of the kingdom and the large population depended. A successor and distant relative, Indravarman (877–89), began the practice of temple building which demonstrated the architectural and artistic genius of the Khmers which reached its apogee with the wondrous Angkor Wat built by Suryavarman II in the early part of the twelfth century.

Following the death of Suryavarman II in approximately 1150, internal revolt and administrative neglect weakened the kingdom for a number of decades; in 1177 Angkor was invaded and sacked by the kingdom of Champa which lay to the east. In 1181, however, a fifty-year-old prince gained the throne and took the title Jayavarman VII. He extended the Khmer empire to an unprecedented dominion which ranged from the Annamite chain in the north to the Malay peninsula in the south. He also established a reputation as a builder of hospitals, hostels and roads and immortalized himself through the awe-inspiring Bayon, the centre-piece of his architectural legacy; the temple complex of Angkor Thom. But if his achievement was great, it lacked the artistic quality of the Angkor Wat period. He sustained Indian politico-religious forms but replaced Hindu deities with Mahayana Buddhism in a manner which continued to express the sacral qualities of the royal being. Under Jayavarman VII, Kambuja reached its political apogee; following his death in 1218 the empire went into progressive decline, never again to return to former glories.

The twelfth century had provided signs of strain within the Khmer empire. These signs were to become more evident in succeeding centuries. Territorial expansion and monumental construction works had placed an unbearable burden on a population increasingly alienated from the court religions. It was at this stage that the dependencies of empire not only began to loosen the bonds of Khmer dominion but also to intrude in the direction of the seat of the Khmer State. From about the middle of the thirteenth century the movement eastwards of Thai (Siamese) peopes began to erode the Khmer position. Between 1350 and 1430 there ensued a state of almost permanent war between the two peoples. This constant warring caused a diversion of labour from construction projects to military purposes and as a consequence temple building came to a halt, never to be resumed. The Thai brought with them a new religion, a Sinhalese reform of Theravada Buddhism which monks from Ceylon (now Sri Lanka) had taken initially to Burma at the end of the twelfth century. Its simple and austere message had a popular appeal which contrasted with the remote religion which underpinned state organization. This challenge to orthodoxy assisted the crumbling of the empire which was hastened by internal dissension and by the excessive burden of royal extravagance. The failure of the hydraulics system as a consequence of neglect and Thai depredations eventually made the capital site untenable and unsuitable for its purposes and in 1431 Angkor was abandoned to the Thai.

By 1434 the Court had re-established itself on the site of the modern capital of Kampuchea, Phnom-Penh, where a replica of the cosmological temple mountain was constructed. During the reign of a king who called himself Suryavarman, the Cambodian state underwent a period of limited revival which was interrupted in 1473 by Siamese military success as a result of which the reigning monarch, the second son of Suryavarman was taken prisoner. However, a third son rallied the Khmers, ejected the invaders and ushered in a century in which intervention from the west was successfully resisted. The capital was then moved, first to Lovek, half-way between Phnom-Penh and the lower end of the Great Lake, and later on to Angkor itself. In 1593 the Siamese returned to the attack and probing as far as Lovek drove the royal family into exile in Laos. This invasion and defeat led to a period of internal disturbance marked by usurpation and assassination of monarchical incumbents. When a king was finally restored to the throne of Cambodia in 1603 it was through the good offices of Siam which released a captured prince to be crowned as a vassal.

In 1618 the capital site was again moved; this time to Oudong situated between Lovek and Phnom-Penh. Two years later Siamese suzerainty was removed as a result of a royal marriage with a daughter of the Nguyen dynasty of Annam (Viet-Nam). One important consequence of this union was an authorization by the Cambodian king, Jayajetta, for the Vietnamese to establish a custom-house at Prei Kor, the site of the modern Ho Chi Minh City. This concession was to facilitate extensive settlement by Vietnamese in the Mekong delta at Cambodian territorial expense.

In the early 1640s the Cambodian monarch, Chan, the son of Jayajetta, converted to Islam and encouraged the settlement of Malay and Javanese migrants. In 1658 the apostate king was successfully challenged by an alliance of two of his brothers with Vietnamese support. The eighteenth century was to see a continuation of civil strife, and both Siam and Annam took territorial advantage of Cambodia's debilitated state. At the end of the century, Cambodia was to lose its western provinces of Battambang and Siemreap. The King, Ang Eng, was even to be crowned in Bangkok. His son, Ang Chan, was enthroned in similar fashion but also paid tribute to the Vietnamese who had encroached throughout what was to become known as Cochinchina. By the beginning of the nineteenth century, Cambodia, territorially reduced, was wedged between competing neighbours who exercised a form of dual suzerainty.

THE COLONIAL PERIOD

In an attempt to halt the erosion of Cambodian territory by its neighbours, Ang Duong sought in 1854 to solicit French protection. This initiative failed because of French mishandling and Siamese obstruction. When, however, in June 1862 the Emperor of Annam ceded to France the three easterly provinces of what became known as the Colony of Cochinchina, the French sought to protect this acquisition by further expansion westward. In July 1863 the French Governor of Cochinchina, Admiral de la Grandière persuaded Ang Duong's son and successor, Norodom, to accept a protectorate which would permit France to control the external affairs of the country and to install a resident-general in the capital. Despite Siamese efforts to forestall formal ratification, the accord came into effect the following year. And in July 1864 the formal coronation of Norodom took place at Oudong with the crown, retrieved from Bangkok, being received from the hands of a French plenipotentiary. Siam, the former suzerain power, was to be appeased at this change of overlordship through a treaty of 1867 whereby France ceded formally on behalf of its ward the westerly provinces of Battambang, Siemreap and Sisiphon. However, the French were instrumental in restoring these territories to Cambodia in 1907.

In 1884 Cambodia entered into a second agreement with France which established a more complete imperial relationship and in 1887 the protectorate was amalgamated into the wider French *Union Indochinoise*. Colonial rule, although somewhat harsh, did not unduly dislocate the Cambodian state. The façade of monarchical authority was maintained although colonial control was exercised over the matter of royal succession. There were two significant but minor uprisings in the nineteenth century but little that might be regarded as a security problem. The elements of nationalist sentiment were not to be displayed until the 1930s.

The fall of France in June 1940 made possible a revival of Thai territorial ambitions. Under Japanese sponsorship the government in Bangkok reasserted a claim to the westerly provinces which had returned to Cambodia in 1907. After military clashes Japan intervened and forced an agreement in Thailand's favour signed in March 1941. The Japanese now enjoyed a dominant position in Indochina exploiting the peninsula for the prosecution of the war effort but leaving undisturbed the French administration. However, by the end of 1944 they became concerned over the allegiance of the French civic authorities and in March the following year moved with force to displace the colonial administration. On the twelfth of the month, King Norodom Sihanouk was persuaded to proclaim his country's independence.

The surrender of Japan in August 1945 and the return of the French in force soon after, saw a restoration of the colonial relationship. It saw also the arrest of Son Ngoc Thanh, the Japanese-sponsored Prime Minister, together with the emergence of a dissident anti-French resistance movement, the *Khmer Issarak*, formed in part of supporters of Thanh. The King sought initially to negotiate Cambodia's independence from France recognizing that his country was not in any position to wage armed struggle for this end. However, the limited political concessions that the French were willing to make compromised the position of the King who came under challenge for being too compliant. In 1946 the absolute monarchy had been abolished and in 1947 a constitution introduced which permitted popular political activity. And it was from the elected members of the National Assembly as well as the *Khmer Issarak* resistance, led by Thanh after his release in 1951, that the King encountered fierce criticism. In June 1952 in an attempt to ensure political stability and to accelerate progress towards independence he dismissed the National Assembly and assumed governmental powers for three years. In February the following year he set off on a diplomatic mission to try and force the hand of the French then facing serious difficulty in Viet-Nam and Laos. Through a series of public statements in Western capitals together with a venture into self-imposed exile in Bangkok, at a time when France was concerned about a popular drift away from the throne and towards the Cambodian associates of the communist-directed Viet-Minh, Sihanouk triumphed. His initiative at a propitious time led to French concessions and the declaration of Cambodian independence on November 9th, 1953. The following July at the Geneva Conference on Indochina this independence was accorded Great Power recognition.

INDEPENDENT CAMBODIA

King Norodom Sihanouk had come to the throne in 1941 at the age of 18. He was not the son of the late king but owed his accession to the throne to a French-instituted method of selection. Under this arrangement Ang Duong's son had been succeeded by his brother. In 1941 the French returned to the senior branch of the royal family to suit their political purpose. It was believed that the young and inexperienced Prince Sihanouk would be a compliant monarch serving as an instrument of colonial rule. In practice Sihanouk was to become a national leader using his throne to great advantage. In 1955, however, Sihanouk's throne was to prove a serious obstacle to his personal exercise of political authority. Under the terms of the Geneva Agreements on Indochina of July 1954, Cambodia had pledged itself to a free and open political process to be demonstrated through elections to be conducted under the terms of the 1947 constitution. This constitution restricted the political role of the monarchy and there was every prospect that governmental office would be resumed by those politicians (from the Democratic Party) whom the King regarded as factious and self-seeking. In March 1955, to escape from the constricting cloak of the constitution under which he would reign more but rule less, Norodom Sihanouk announced his abdication from the throne in favour of his father, Norodom Suramarit. Now free, as Prince Sihanouk, to enter the political lists, the former king founded a political movement, the *Sangkum Reastr Niyum* (Popular Socialist Community), within which he sought to embody all streams of political opinion. *Sangkum* served as a popular national front based on coincident loyalty to Sihanouk and the nation. It trounced all opposition; in the elections of September 1955 *Sangkum* won every seat in the National Assembly. It repeated this performance in the three subsequent elections, held in 1958, 1962 and 1966. In April 1960 King Norodom Suramarit died but a constitutional and political crisis was averted in June when Norodom Sihanouk became Head of State without ascending the throne.

As Head of State, Prince Sihanouk became literally the voice of Cambodia. He articulated its hopes and fears within the country and to the outside world. He ruled through a cabinet and parliament but never relinquished his recourse to popular appeal and sanction for his policies. He appeared a popular figure revered especially in the rural areas as the father figure of his country. However, his authority came under challenge from within the Cambodian élite, especially following the general elections of 1966. Increasing resentment of his personal political style and of his handling of the economy found expression in August 1969 with the assumption to office of an administration headed by the former Army Commander-in-Chief, Lt.-Gen. (later Marshal) Lon Nol. It was this administration which on March 18th, 1970, master-minded Sihanouk's removal from office as Head of State through a unanimous decision of the country's legislature. At the time, Prince Sihanouk was out of the country, in Moscow, on the point of departing for a visit to the People's Republic of China.

After going into exile in China, Prince Sihanouk and his supporters formed an alliance with their former enemies, a Marxist insurgent movement known as the *Khmer Rouge* who had launched an uprising against him in 1967. Sihanoukists and the *Khmer Rouge* formed the National United Front of Cambodia (FUNC) in March 1970 and members of both groups participated in the Royal Government of National Union of Cambodia (GRUNC) set up in 1970 in Peking.

A precipitating circumstance of Sihanouk's deposition was the revealed presence in Cambodia of Vietnamese communist military formations using the sanctuary of the neutral country from which to prosecute the war in South Viet-Nam. During Prince Sihanouk's absence in Paris in March 1970, Vietnamese communist diplomatic missions in Phnom-Penh were sacked. He refused to support these actions which were portrayed as a protest against the Vietnamese communist presence, and the consequence was a series of bitter exchanges which culminated in his deposition. The sacking of the Vietnamese communist diplomatic missions was followed by a demand by the Cambodian Government that the Vietnamese communist military units leave the country. This demand, however, caused the Vietnamese communists to move against the pitifully weak and ill-equipped Cambodian army. Towards the end of April 1970, the capital, Phnom-Penh, was in peril and only the military intervention of South Viet-Nam and the U.S.A. at the beginning of May checked the advance. Protracted conflict continued, however, with the *Khmer Rouge* assuming an increasingly heavy burden of military responsibility. Cambodia succumbed to the brutalizing experience of Viet-Nam with the Government of Marshal Lon Nol under serious challenge by insurgent forces supporting the cause of Prince Sihanouk, in exile in Beijing (Peking).

In October 1970 the name Cambodia was formally changed to the Khmer Republic, thus ending twenty-four years of constitutional monarchy. In March 1972 Lon Nol declared himself President, an act approved by referendum in April. His governments were marked by factional conflict, ineptitude and corrupt practice. The January 1973 peace settlement for Viet-Nam did not have any effect in Cambodia as GRUNC saw little reason to negotiate. Lon Nol's Government was reduced to controlling urban enclaves in the face of *Khmer Rouge* assaults which stopped just short of overrunning the capital, partly because of intensive U.S. bombing which was halted in 1973. From January 1975, however, by changing tactics aimed at cutting communications, and thus food and military supply, the defence perimeter of the capital, Phnom-Penh, was reduced progressively, sustained only by American airlifts. On April 1st President Lon Nol left Phnom-Penh en route for the U.S.A., and on the 17th of that month the capital fell without resistance to the *Khmer Rouge* forces.

In the immediate wake of the *Khmer Rouge* military victory, the country was subjected to a pre-arranged programme of radical social change in which members of the former governing class were either liquidated or directed into forced labour. The population at large was coerced into the rural areas where they were put to work on a collectivist basis. Many hundreds of thousands died from brutal treatment, starvation and disease.

Prince Sihanouk was restored as Head of State, though he remained outside Cambodia until the end of 1975, except for a brief visit to the country in September. In December a National Congress approved a draft constitution establishing a republican form of government. The constitution, promulgated in January 1976, officially named the country "Democratic Kampuchea". Elections were held in March for a 250-member People's Representative Assembly, the seats being contested by 515 candidates of approved "revolutionary" standing. In April Prince Sihanouk resigned as Head of State and GRUNC was dissolved. The new Assembly chose Khieu Samphan as Head of State and appointed a new Council of Ministers in which the Prime Minister was Pol Pot. In September

1977 Pol Pot revealed the existence of the Communist Party of Kampuchea, the founding date of which was given as September 1960, and made known that he was the Secretary of its Central Committee. He also confirmed his political leadership after a period of intra-party factional conflict and purges.

In its new constitution, Kampuchea was described as neutral and non-aligned. However, it became clear that a measure of alignment did exist and that relations with the People's Republic of China had a special importance. By contrast, tensions were evident between Kampuchea and Viet-Nam. Border clashes which had been reported since May 1975, erupted into a full-scale war at the end of 1977. The Kampuchean Government made this conflict public knowledge on December 31st, 1977, when it severed diplomatic relations with Viet-Nam, which it charged with seeking to incorporate Kampuchea within an Indochinese federation. Viet-Nam's determination to overthrow Pol Pot's Government became apparent following the formation of a Kampuchean National United Front for National Salvation (KNUFNS) on December 2nd, 1978. On December 25th Vietnamese regular forces and Kampuchean rebels launched an invasion and by January 7th, 1979, had occupied the capital. On January 11th the People's Republic of Kampuchea was proclaimed, with Heng Samrin as President of the newly-formed People's Revolutionary Council. A treaty of peace, friendship and co-operation was concluded between Kampuchea and Viet-Nam on February 18th and in March the presence of Vietnamese troops was admitted. The People's Republic of Kampuchea secured only limited international recognition, while the ousted Democratic Kampuchean government retained the Kampuchean seat at the United Nations. A military challenge to the Vietnamese-maintained government in Phnom-Penh was posed by the *Khmer Rouge* guerrilla army, which enjoyed access to sanctuary and supplies (including international relief aid) across the border with Thailand. Khieu Samphan, then head of state of the ousted government, assumed the office of Prime Minister in December 1979, while the Kampuchean Communist Party was dissolved in December 1981. However, Pol Pot remained Commander-in-Chief of the *Khmer Rouge* army. By the middle of 1982, that army had sustained an ability to harass the Vietnamese expeditionary force of some 200,000 but they were unable to loosen its grip on the country. Negotiations between Communist and non-Communist Khmer resistance groups concluded an agreement on June 22nd, 1982, to form a coalition government-in-exile. Prince Sihanouk is President, Khieu Samphan is Vice-President, with responsibility for foreign affairs, and former premier Son Sann is Prime Minister. Four co-ordinating committees will replace cabinet ministers. The existing political parties retain their independence, but all decisions must be taken by consensus. The coalition is backed by ASEAN, and military pressure will now be increased on the Vietnamese troops in Kampuchea.

In May 1981 national elections were held for 117 seats in the National Assembly. They were contested by 148 candidates, all of whom had been approved by the electoral committee of the KNUFNS. Later in the month, the first Congress of the ruling People's Revolutionary Party of Kampuchea was held since the Vietnamese invasion. Defence Minister Pen Sovan appeared to confirm his position as the leading political figure in the country with his appointment as Secretary-General of the party and Chairman of the Council of Ministers. In December 1981, however, he was relieved of his posts, ostensibly on the grounds of ill health, and replaced as party leader by the Head of State, Heng Samrin. The episode demonstrated the influence of Viet-Nam and its resentment of Pen Sovan's disposition towards the U.S.S.R.

In July 1981 the United Nations sponsored an international conference on Kampuchea in New York. Its final declaration called for the withdrawal of Vietnamese forces and the holding of free elections. The conference was boycotted by Viet-Nam and the U.S.S.R.; the Government in Phnom-Penh was not invited. The final declaration has not been implemented.

ECONOMIC SURVEY

Michael Leifer

The Kampuchean peace-time economy is based almost entirely on agriculture with a small industrial sector. The staple crop is rice which is grown on approximately 3,080,000 acres or 80 per cent of land suitable for cultivation. Although the lowland soil of the Khmer plain is not of remarkable fertility and restricts yield, seasonal flooding by the Mekong and Tonlé Sap makes wet-rice cultivation possible. An abundance of fish from the many waterways and a supply of fresh vegetables provide in addition an ample subsistence diet for the predominantly rural population. The average per caput income before 1970 was calculated at U.S. $130.

At the time of independence in 1953, Cambodia had an exceedingly small industrial base. There were a number of latex plants operated by French-controlled rubber companies together with a few factories which processed agricultural and forest products. During the 1950s and 1960s there was a manifold increase in the scale of industrial enterprise as indicated by the production of 150 million kWh. of electricity in 1973. In principle, the aim of the former Cambodian Government was to eschew the grandiose in economic development and to concentrate on a limited range of enterprises to meet an increasing local demand and thus to save foreign exchange by reducing imports.

The programme of industrial development was initiated in the mid-1950s through the benefaction of the People's Republic of China. In June 1956 China granted Cambodia equipment valued at U.S. $22.4

million. Further agreements with China led to the completion of a second textile mill in 1967 and the construction of a glass plant. Of the other Communist countries, Czechoslovakia has provided plants for tractor assembly and tyre production as well as a sugar refinery, all on a loan basis.

Prior to 1970, positive achievements were made in the development of infrastructure and social equipment. During the colonial period Cambodia was dependent on the River Mekong and the port of Saigon for its trading needs. The dependence on Saigon was reduced somewhat after the Second World War when the French developed Phnom-Penh as a port to receive ocean-going vessels. With independence, the Cambodian Government became only too painfully aware of the stranglehold that South Viet-Nam could exercise over the Mekong lifeline. In order to circumvent this situation of dependence, the Cambodian Government with major French assistance developed a port on the Gulf of Siam known as Sihanoukville (renamed Kompong-Som). This port was opened in 1960 in order to give Cambodia complete autonomy over its trade outlets. At the time that the construction of Sihanoukville began, the United States, for reasons of self-interest as well as benevolence, constructed a highway linking the port with the capital. In spite of serious erosion and subsidence along the road, due to the use of inappropriate materials, repair work kept the road functioning as a major artery. The Cambodians, however, with French and West German assistance also constructed a railway line from the port to Phnom-Penh to facilitate the speedy transportation of goods.

Prior to 1975 Cambodia received project aid and loans from China, the Soviet Union, Yugoslavia, Czechoslovakia, France, West Germany, Japan and Australia. Foreign economic assistance was, however, of moderate proportions and the Cambodian emphasis was on self-help and project-sharing which produced the French-sponsored oil refinery and truck assembly plant at Sihanoukville. Up to the end of 1963 the bulk of economic assistance came from the United States but in November of that year this was terminated at the insistence of the Cambodian Government. Between 1955 and 1962 economic and military assistance from the United States totalled more than U.S. $350 million. The bulk of this aid was not deployed in a way that its visible effect was easily demonstrated, much being allocated to public health, agricultural development and education. The cessation of this aid was to cause serious repercussions within the Cambodian economy. At first the cessation of aid was softened by good harvests, French credits and borrowing from the Cambodian central bank. But from 1966 onwards serious financial difficulties arose from the Government's inability to adjust expenditure to income. U.S. aid, particularly in the form of budgetary support and provision for the financing of the armed services, enabled a level of expenditure and a style of urban living well beyond the real means of the country. Crop output in rice, cotton and jute together with smuggling was such that a budget deficit, though reduced in 1967 to 1,056 million riels through a cut in imports, remained a pressing problem. The state of world markets in primary products did not help Cambodia's trading and financial position. An additional difficulty which followed from government action in 1963 was the associated decision to nationalize the export and import trades. This move had the effect of freezing Chinese business interests and of inhibiting trade and commerce in general. However, another decision to nationalize banking had more successful consequences. Although foreign policy considerations inhibited Cambodia from participating in any of the recent attempts at regional co-operation in South-East Asia, it was involved in the attempt by the United Nations Economic Commission for Asia and the Far East to develop the water resources of the Lower Mekong basin. However, an important project within Cambodia (the Prek Thnot tributary project) had been delayed due to Cambodian suspicions about the source of finance. In September 1968 at a meeting in Phnom-Penh, administrative arrangements for the Prek Thnot Power and Irrigation Development Project were agreed between ten donor countries, Cambodia and UN representatives. The outbreak of war, however, interrupted work on the project which was scheduled for completion in 1972.

The onset of war in Cambodia completely disrupted the economy. Military activity had a devastating effect on the latex plants and rubber production came to a virtual halt. In addition, the extent of Communist activity and the American bombing disrupted road and rail communications. In effect, the Khmer Republic reverted to a subsistence existence while public expenditure increased dramatically because the army grew from 35,000 to over 200,000 men. A resumption of U.S. economic and military aid served to assist with budgetary difficulties. The country remained on a war footing and, with much of its social and economic equipment destroyed and productive processes disrupted, became totally dependent on external financial assistance for its defence efforts. By April 1975, there was not a Cambodian economy, only the importation of foodstuffs financed by the United States Government.

With the assumption of *Khmer Rouge* control, the first priority was declared to be the restoration of the national economy. Partly to this end, the urban centres, including the capital, were cleared of their inhabitants who were driven into the rural areas to work on the land and in other tasks of economic reconstruction. The initial rigours of the collectivization of agriculture were sustained at great human cost.

In September 1977 Pol Pot, the Prime Minister, announced that the entire population lived "under a collective regime through a communal support system" and that the annual rice ration was 312 kilogrammes per person. However, reports from refugees indicated a harsh regime with a rice ration which seldom rose above 90 kilogrammes. The central feature of the economy was a strict doctrine of self-reliance. Visiting foreign diplomats confirmed the absence of money in circulation and of shops, public transport, internal telecommunications and postal services. The Government claimed to have overcome its basic economic difficulties and the high incidence of malaria, and had 200,000 tons of rice available for export in 1978.

Emphasis was placed on the provision of irrigation systems to boost agricultural production. Industrial development was seen by the authorities as of secondary importance to agriculture, and projects were undertaken only as increased agricultural production provided sufficient capital. By mid-1978 factories producing farm implements and machinery, rubber products, textiles and fertilizers were reported to be in operation.

In the wake of the Vietnamese invasion at the end of 1978, economic activity was brought to a virtual halt, especially in the countryside which was beset by war and a massive movement of population. Agricultural production was a major casualty, with a failure to plant sufficient rice before the onset of the monsoon. Country-wide famine was alleviated only through the efforts of international relief agencies, which despatched essential foodstuffs from September 1979, either directly to Kampuchean ports (as well as to the airport at Phnom-Penh) or across a "land bridge" on the Thai border. During 1980 the spectre of famine was lifted from the country, which came to enjoy near self-sufficiency in food production by the end of the year. It returned in 1982, after a poor harvest, brought about by a combination of alternating flood and drought. The commercial life of the major urban centres, however, has been resumed, but the country will continue to rely on relief aid, which was a promised total of $7,800,000 for 1982.

STATISTICAL SURVEY

Note: Some of the statistics below represent only sectors of the economy controlled by the government of the former Khmer Republic. During the years 1970–75 no figures were available for areas controlled by the *Khmer Rouge*. Almost no official figures are available for the period since April 1975.

AREA AND POPULATION

Area	Population				
	April 17th, 1962 (census)	mid-1969 (official estimate)	UN estimates (mid-year)		
			1975	1979	1980
181,035 sq. km*.	5,728,771	6,701,000	7,098,000	6,746,000	6,747,000

* 69,898 square miles.

CIA population estimates (*Kampuchea: A demographic catastrophe*, 1980): 6,191,000 in 1976; 5,160,000 in 1979.

Capital: Phnom-Penh, population 393,995 in 1962; 200,000 in 1979 (estimate).

Births and Deaths: Average annual birth rate 39.9 per 1,000 in 1970–75, 30.9 per 1,000 in 1975–80; death rate 22.5 per 1,000 in 1970–75, 29.4 per 1,000 in 1975–80 (UN estimates).

ECONOMICALLY ACTIVE POPULATION

(ILO estimates, '000 persons at mid-year)

	1960			1970		
	Males	Females	Total	Males	Females	Total
Agriculture, etc.	1,033	853	1,887	1,248	979	2,227
Industry	62	18	81	90	30	120
Services	243	94	337	353	149	502
Total	1,338	966	2,304	1,691	1,158	2,849

Source: ILO, *Labour Force Estimates and Projections, 1950–2000.*

AGRICULTURE

LAND USE

('000 hectares)

	1967	1968	1969	1970
Arable land	2,832	2,900*	2,987	2,900*
Land under permanent crops . .	152	150*	146	146*
Permanent meadows and pastures . .	580	580	580	580*
Forests and woodland . . .	13,372	13,372	13,372	13,372
Other land	716	650	567	654
Inland water	452	452	452	452
TOTAL AREA . . .	18,104	18,104	18,104	18,104

* FAO estimate.

1971-79: Land use as in 1970 (FAO estimates).

Source: FAO, *Production Yearbook.*

PRINCIPAL CROPS

(FAO estimates)

	AREA HARVESTED ('000 hectares)			PRODUCTION ('000 metric tons)		
	1978	1979	1980	1978	1979	1980
Rice (paddy)	1,400	853	1,200*	1,500	850*	1,000
Maize	65	90	130*	80	70	100
Sweet potatoes	2	2	2	19	14	15
Cassava (Manioc)	19	22	25*	133	143	150
Dry beans	28	20	24	17	12	14
Groundnuts (in shell) . . .	13	10	10	14	10	13
Sesame seed	7	5	5	4	3	4
Coconuts	n.a.	n.a.	n.a.	36	26	30
Copra				6	5	6
Sugar cane	3	2	3	165	15	130
Tobacco (leaves)	11	8	9	6	4	5
Natural rubber	n.a.	n.a.	n.a.	18*	10*	10

* Unofficial estimates.

Source: FAO, *Production Yearbook.*

FRUIT AND VEGETABLES

(FAO estimates, production in '000 metric tons)

	1977	1978	1979	1980
Vegetables and melons .	450	380	270	320
Oranges	32	28	20	22
Mangoes	15	10	7	8
Pineapples	9	7	5	6
Bananas	92	78	55	65

Source: FAO, *Production Yearbook.*

LIVESTOCK

(FAO estimates, 'ooo head, year ending September)

	1978	1979	1980
Horses	10	8	8
Cattle	900	750*	810
Buffaloes	400	350*	400
Pigs	680	500	600
Chickens	4,000	3,600	4,000
Ducks	1,400	1,200	1,400

* Unofficial estimate.

Source: FAO, *Production Yearbook.*

LIVESTOCK PRODUCTS

(FAO estimates, 'ooo metric tons)

	1978	1979	1980
Beef and veal	14	10	11
Buffalo meat	6	6	6
Pig meat	28	20	26
Poultry meat	12	12	14
Cows' milk	15	12	14
Hen eggs	2.5	2.2	2.4
Other poultry eggs	2.2	2.0	2.1
Cattle and buffalo hides	4.4	3.4	3.6

Source: FAO, *Production Yearbook.*

FORESTRY

ROUNDWOOD REMOVALS

(FAO estimates, 'ooo cubic metres, excl. bark)

	1977	1978	1979
Coniferous:			
Sawlogs etc.	5	5	5
Non-coniferous:			
Sawlogs etc.	105	105	105
Other industrial wood	430	443	457
Fuel wood	4,300	4,430	4,565
TOTAL	4,840	4,983	5,132

1980: Production as in 1979 (FAO estimates).

Source: FAO, *Yearbook of Forest Products.*

SAWNWOOD PRODUCTION

('ooo cubic metres, all non-coniferous)

	1969	1970*	1971*	1972*
Sawnwood (incl. boxboards)	223	32	38	43
Railway sleepers	3	3	3	—
TOTAL	226	35	41	43

* FAO estimates.

1973-80: Annual production as in 1972 (FAO estimates).

Source: FAO, *Yearbook of Forest Products.*

FISHING

(FAO estimates, 'ooo metric tons, live weight)

	1977*	1978	1979
Inland waters	73.9	30.1	10.1
Pacific Ocean	10.8	10.8	10.8
TOTAL	84.7	40.9	20.9

* Assumed to be unchanged since 1973.

1980: Catch as in 1979 (FAO estimates).

Source: FAO, *Yearbook of Fishery Statistics.*

MINING

('ooo metric tons)

	1977	1978	1979
Salt (unrefined)*	30	12	5

* Estimates by U.S. Bureau of Mines.

Source: UN, *Yearbook of Industrial Statistics.*

INDUSTRY

SELECTED PRODUCTS

		1969	1970	1971	1972	1973
Distilled alcoholic beverages	'000 hectolitres	143	96	45	55	36
Beer	,, ,,	57	55	26	23	18
Soft drinks	,, ,,	248	98	25	25*	25*
Cigarettes	million	3,807	3,874	3,413	2,510	2,622
Cotton yarn (pure and mixed)	metric tons	1,139	1,171	1,068	1,094	415
Bicycle tyres and tubes	'000	539	186	208	200*	200*
Rubber footwear	'000 pairs	2,760	2,230	1,292	1,000*	1,000*
Soap	metric tons	1,788	756	469	400*	400*
Naphtha	'000 metric tons	17	16	—	—	—
Motor spirit (petrol)	,, ,, ,,	44	30	2	—	—
Kerosene	,, ,, ,,	24	19	—	—	—
Jet fuel	,, ,, ,,	14	24	—	—	—
Distillate fuel oils	,, ,, ,,	146	111	11	—	—
Residual fuel oils	,, ,, ,,	132	76	14	—	—
Cement	,, ,, ,,	57	38	44	53	78
Electric energy†	million kWh.	128	133	148	166	150

Other products (1969): Jute bags 4.2 million; Paper 4,164 metric tons.

* Estimate. † Production by public utilities only.

FINANCE

100 sen = 1 new riel.

Coin: 5 sen.

Notes: 10, 20 and 50 sen; 1, 5, 10, 20 and 50 riels.

Approximate exchange rates (June 1982): £1 sterling = 6.93 riels; U.S. $1 = 4.00 riels.

100 new riels = £14.43 = $25.00.

Note: The riel was introduced in January 1955, replacing (at par) the Indochinese piastre. From May 1953 the piastre's value was 10 old French francs. The initial exchange rate was thus U.S. $1 = 35 riels (1 riel = 2.857 U.S. cents). Except for exchange transactions in U.S. dollars and sterling, the riel was linked to French currency, with a value of 10 French centimes after the introduction of the new French franc in January 1960. In August 1969 the multiple exchange rate system ended when the riel was devalued (in line with the French franc) to 16 milligrammes of gold, worth 1.8004 U.S. cents ($1 = 55.542 riels) until August 1971. In October 1971 the official rate became inoperative except for specified official transfers and a flexible "floating" rate was established, initially at $1 = 140 riels. Thus the riel's link to the French franc was effectively broken and the currency devalued. The "floating" rate was later adjusted upwards, reaching $1 = 120 riels in January 1972, but thereafter the currency was frequently devalued. The exchange rate was $1 = 187 riels at the end of 1972; and $1 = 275 riels at the end of 1973. In September 1974 the currency was devalued by 65 per cent, with the exchange rate altered from $1 = 420 riels to $1 = 1,200 riels. By the end of 1974 the rate was $1 = 1,650 riels. In terms of sterling, the exchange rate was £1 = 98 riels before November 1967; £1 = 84 riels from November 1967 to August 1969; and £1 = 133.30 riels from August 1969 to October 1971. Since April 1975 almost no information about the exchange rate has been available. However, a rate of $1 = 1,200 riels was quoted in 1977 and 1978 and it has also been reported that a floating exchange rate ($1 = 1,610 riels in 1977 and 1978) was available for foreign visitors. Domestically, the use of currency was abolished in 1975. Money was reintroduced in March 1980 and the exchange rate is reported to be approximately U.S. $1 = 4 new riels. The value of the new riel was 1 kg. of rice.

EXTERNAL TRADE

(U.S. $ million)

	1974	1975	1976*	1977*	1978*	1979*
Imports	273	92	8	22	21	140–150
Exports	14	6	3	3	2	1–2

* Estimates.

Source: Economist Intelligence Unit, *Annual Supplement* 1980.

PRINCIPAL COMMODITIES

(million old riels)

Imports	1972	1973
Agricultural and food products	3,461.0	7,720.6
Mineral products	341.3	1,667.6
Textiles	781.7	1,814.2
Metals and metal manufactures	765.2	1,272.2
Pharmaceuticals	641.3	1,395.5
Chemicals	272.4	329.9
TOTAL (incl. others)	6,262.9	14,200.1

Exports	1972	1973
Rice	99.1	14.0
Rubber	233.3	2,544.1
Haricot Beans	236.7	120.3
Sesamum	65.0	54.0
TOTAL (incl. others)	634.2	2,732.5

Source: Banque Nationale du Cambodge, *Bulletin Mensuel.*

PRINCIPAL TRADING PARTNERS*

(U.S. $'000)

Imports	1970	1971	1972
Australia	n.a.	2,627	1,735
France	12,546	9,042	6,120
Germany, Fed. Repub.	1,666	1,120	1,736
Hong Kong	2,510	1,645	6,331
Japan	4,108	2,732	7,565
Singapore	3,794	4,120	2,261
Switzerland	3,112	770	227
Thailand	n.a.	n.a.	7,041
United Kingdom	2,643	2,606	1,344
U.S.A.	3,199	765	4,301
TOTAL (incl. others)	41,927	28,056	42,599

Exports	1970	1971	1972
France	5,570	167	298
Hong Kong	5,480	1,124	1,347
Italy	1,135	n.a.	3
Japan	1,161	553	303
Netherlands	1,172	41	19
Senegal	n.a.	1,653	n.a.
Singapore	1,970	789	749
United Kingdom	1,432	43	46
U.S.A.	1,030	38	122
Viet-Nam, South	n.a.	n.a.	4,024
TOTAL (incl. others)	34,144	6,488	7,347

* Imports by country of production; exports by country of last consignment.

Source: UN, *Yearbook of International Trade Statistics.*

TRANSPORT

RAILWAY TRAFFIC

	1971	1972	1973
Passenger-kilometres (million)	91	56	54
Freight ton-kilometres (million)	10	10	10

ROAD TRAFFIC

(motor vehicles in use*)

	1971	1972	1973
Passenger cars	26,400	27,200	n.a.
Commercial vehicles†	11,100	11,100	11,000

* Including vehicles no longer in circulation.
† Excluding tractors and semi-trailer combinations.

INTERNATIONAL SEA-BORNE SHIPPING

(freight traffic in '000 metric tons)

	Goods Loaded			Goods Unloaded		
	1971	1972	1973	1971	1972	1973
Phnom-Penh	95	34	29	308	416	420
Kompong-Som (Sihanoukville)	122	14	21	101	81	163
TOTAL	217	48	50	409	497	583

CIVIL AVIATION
(scheduled services)

	1970	1971	1972	1973	1974
Kilometres flown ('000)	1,056	1,030	1,000	1,100	1,000
Passengers carried ('000)	41	107	112	140	129
Passenger-kilometres (million)	30.8	32.5	34	51	48
Freight ton-kilometres ('000)	400	658	700	500	500

EDUCATION

	Teachers		Students	
	1969	1972	1969	1972
Primary	23,964	20,374	989,464	479,616
Secondary: general	5,292	2,544	119,988	99,936
vocational	n.a.	309	5,798	3,483
teacher-training	n.a.	n.a.	1,005	n.a.
Higher	916*	1,164	6,154*	9,988

* 1970.

THE CONSTITUTION

In June 1981 a new constitution was approved by the National Assembly. It consists of a Preamble and ten chapters, divided into 93 Articles. A summary of the main points follows:

Political System: the People's Republic of Kampuchea is an independent sovereign state, gradually advancing towards socialism.

Economic System: the national economy is under the direction of the state, and comprises three sectors, the state-run, the collective and the family-run economy. Foreign trade is the monopoly of the state.

National Assembly: the supreme organ of state power and the sole legislative organ. Its deputies are elected by the principle of universal secret ballot and its term of office is five years. It has the power to adopt and revise the constitution and laws, to control their implementation, to adopt economic policies and the state budget, to elect or remove the Chairman, Vice-Chairman or Secretary from the National Assembly, the Council of State and the Council of Ministers, to control the activities of the Council of State and the Council of Ministers.

Council of State: the representative organ of the country and a standing organ of the National Assembly. Its members are elected from the National Assembly deputies. The Chairman of the Council of State is Supreme Commander of the Armed Forces and Chairman of the National Defence Council, to be set up when necessary. Its duties include promulgating laws, deciding on the appointment or removal of members of the Council of Ministers, creating and abolishing ministries, ratifying or rejecting international treaties except when it is deemed necessary to refer them to the National Assembly.

Council of Ministers: the government and organ of direct management of society, responsible to the National Assembly.

Local People's Committees: the territory of Kampuchea is divided into provinces and municipalities, under the direct administration of central authority. People's committees are established in all provinces, municipalities, districts, communes and wards, and are responsible for local administration, public security and social order.

Judiciary and Courts: the judicial organs of Kampuchea are the people's courts and military tribunals.

THE GOVERNMENT

(July 1982)

COUNCIL OF STATE

President of the Council: HENG SAMRIN.

Vice-President: SAY PHOUTHANG.

Secretary-General: CHAN VEN.

Members of the Council: MEN CHAN, KHAM LEN, HENG TEAV, VANDY KAON.

COUNCIL OF MINISTERS

Chairman: CHAN SI.

Vice-Chairman and Minister of Foreign Affairs: HUN SEN.

Vice-Chairman and Minister of Planning: CHEA SOTH.

Vice-Chairman and Minister of Defence: BOU THANG.

Minister of the Interior: KHANG SARIN.

Minister of Agriculture: KONG SAMOL.

Minister of Industry: (vacant).

Minister of Communications, Transport and Posts: KHUN CHHY.

Minister of Trade: TANG SAROEM.

Minister of Finance: CHAN PHIN.

Minister of Justice: OUK BUN CHOEUN.

Chairman of Nat. Bank of Kampuchea: CHA RIENG.

Chairman of the State Control Committee: SIM KA.

Minister of Education: PEN NAVOUTH.

Minister of Health: Dr. YIT KIM SENG.

Minister of Information, Press and Culture: CHHENG PHON.

Director of the Cabinet: UNG PHAN.

Vice-Ministers:

Vice-Ministers of Foreign Affairs: HOR NAM HONG, KONG KORM, PRACH SUN.

Vice-Ministers of Defence: SOY KEO, TEA BANH, MEAS KROCH, DI PHIN.

Vice-Minister for Social Affairs: DOUANG CHOUM.

Vice-Ministers for Health: CHEA THANG, NUT SAVOEUN, Mrs. CHEY KANH NHA.

Vice-Minister of Education: (vacant).

Vice-Ministers of the Interior: SOEM SONG, SIM SONG.

Vice-Minister of Communications and Posts: CHIM SENG.

Vice-Ministers of Trade: THONG CHAN, POUN PONLE.

Vice-Minister of Industry: NUON SARETH.

Vice-Ministers of Agriculture: NHEM HENG, MAT LY.

Vice-Minister of Agriculture (Fisheries): MAU PHAUK.

Vice-Minister of Planning: TI YAV.

The United Nations recognizes the following government:

GOVERNMENT OF DEMOCRATIC KAMPUCHEA

(Coalition government formed June 22nd, 1982)

President: Prince NORODOM SIHANOUK.

Vice-President in charge of Foreign Affairs: KHIEU SAMPHAN.

Prime Minister: SON SANN.

Chairman of Committee for Finance and Economic Affairs: IENG SARY.

Chairman of Committee for Defence: SON SEN.

Chairman of Committee for Health and Social Affairs: Dr. THIOUAN THIOEN.

Chairman of Committee for Education and Culture: THUNC RIEN.

LEGISLATURE

NATIONAL ASSEMBLY

The Assembly has 117 members, serving a five-year term. Elections were held on May 1st, 1981.

Chairman: CHEA SIM.

Vice-Chairmen: MAT LY, Venerable TEP VONG, NU BENG.

Secretary-General: Mrs. PHLEK PIROUN.

POLITICAL ORGANIZATIONS

Kampuchean People's Revolutionary Party (KPRP): Phnom-Penh; f. 1951; pro-Soviet communist party; 8-mem. Politburo, 21-mem. Cen. Cttee.; Gen. Sec. of Politburo HENG SAMRIN; Chair. of Org. Cttee. SAY PHOUTHANG.

Kampuchean United Front for National Construction and Defence (KUFNCD): Phnom-Penh; f. 1978; an 80-member National Council and a seven-member honorary Presidium were elected in December 1981; Chair. of National Council CHEA SIM, Sec.-Gen. YOS POR; Chair. of Presidium HENG SAMRIN.

Khmer People's National Liberation Front (KPNLF): f. March 1979 in France and formally established in Kampuchea in October; Pres. SON SANN; distributes newsletter.

DIPLOMATIC REPRESENTATION

EMBASSIES ACCREDITED TO KAMPUCHEA

(In Phnom-Penh)

Bulgaria: *Ambassador:* SIMEONOV DIMITROV.

Cuba: *Ambassador:* HÉCTOR GALLO.

Czechoslovakia: *Ambassador:* (vacant).

German Democratic Republic: Monivong East; *Ambassador:* GÜNTER HORN.

Hungary: Monivong East; *Ambassador:* ALFRED ALMASI.

India: *Chargé d'affaires:* NIGAM PRAKASH.

Laos: *Ambassador:* KAMPHAN VILACHIT.

Mongolia: Hanoi, Viet-Nam.

Poland: Monivong East; *Ambassador:* SERGIUSZ MILULICZ.

U.S.S.R.: *Ambassador:* OLEG BOSTORIN.

Viet-Nam: *Ambassador:* NGO DIEN.

Yemen, People's Democratic Republic: Beijing, People's Republic of China.

Kampuchea also has diplomatic relations with Ethiopia, Grenada, Guinea, Guyana, the Democratic People's Republic of Korea, Seychelles and Yugoslavia.

JUDICIAL SYSTEM

The judical system comprises People's Courts and Military Tribunals. People's Assessors participate in judgement, and have the same rights as judges.

RELIGION

BUDDHISM

The principal religion of Kampuchea is Theravada Buddhism (Buddhism of the Little Vehicle), the sacred language of which is Pali. Before April 1975 there were more than 2,500 monasteries throughout the land and nearly 20,000 Bonzes (Buddhist priests).

Patriotic Kampuchean Buddhists' Association: Phnom-Penh; mem. of KUFNCD; Pres. LONG SIM.

THE PRESS

NEWSPAPER

Kaset Kangtoap Padivoat (*Revolutionary Army*): f. 1979; army newspaper.

NEWS AGENCY

Saporamean Kampuchea (SPK) (*Kampuchea Information Agency*): f. 1978; information service of the KUFNCD; Dir.-Gen. CHEY SAPHON; publ. *Kampuchea* (weekly; circ. 122,000).

ASSOCIATION

Association of Kampuchean Journalists: f. 1979; member of KUFNCD; Chair. CHEY SAPHON; Vice-Chair. UN DARA; Sec.-Gen. KHIEU KANHARITH.

RADIO

Samleng Pracheachon Kampuchea (*Voice of the Kampuchean People*): 28 Ave. Sandech Choun Nath, Phnom-Penh; f. 1978; service of the KUFNCD; broadcasts 10 hours daily in English, French, Lao and Thai; Dir.-Gen. UN DARA; Deputy Dir.-Gen. SOM KIM SUOR.

FINANCE

The former government of Pol Pot abolished banks and withdrew all currency from circulation. The regime established in January 1979 announced the formation of a national bank in November. In March 1980 currency was reintroduced and the National Bank of Kampuchea announced the establishment of a Foreign Trade Bank to expand trade, provide international loans and assist in currency control.

National Bank of Kampuchea: Phnom-Penh; f. 1980; Chair. CHA RIENG.

TRADE AND INDUSTRY

All means of production were nationalized after 1975, but no detailed information on the organization of trade and industry is available. By December 1980 some 67 factories had resumed activities and the following organizations were reported to be operating:

National Trade Commission: Pres. TANG SAROEM.

KAMPEXIM: Phnom-Penh; f. 1979; handles Kampuchea's impoıts and exports and the receipt of foreign aid.

TRADE UNION

Trade Unions for the Salvation of Kampuchea (TUSK): Phnom-Penh; Vice-Chair. HENG TEAV.

TRANSPORT

Railways: Moha Vithei Pracheathippatay, Phnom-Penh. Before April 1975 the total length of railway track was 1,370 km. Lines linked Phnom-Penh with the Thai border via Battambang and with Kompong-Som. A new line between Samrong Station and Kompong Speu was under construction in 1978. By November 1979 the 260-km. Phnom-Penh-Kompong Som line, and by February 1980 the Phnom-Penh-Battambang line, had been restored.

Roads: Before 1975 there were nearly 11,000 km. of motorable roads and tracks, of which about 2,000 km. were asphalted. In 1981 a newly-repaired section of the National Highway One, which runs from the Vietnamese border to Phnom-Penh, was formally opened.

Inland Waterways: The major routes are along the Mekong River, and up the Tonlé Sap River into the Tonlé Sap (Great Lake) covering in all about 1,400 km. The inland ports of Neak Luong, Kompong Cham and Prek Kdam have been supplied with motor ferries and the ferry crossings have been improved.

Shipping: The main port is Kompong-Som on the Gulf of Thailand, which can handle vessels up to 10,000 tons; the total number of berths was raised to 10 in 1970 at a cost of U.S. $50 million. Phnom-Penh port, currently undergoing reconstruction, lies some distance inland. Steamers of up to 4,000 tons can be accommodated.

Civil Aviation: There is an international airport at Pochentong, near Phnom-Penh. In September 1979 flights between Phnom-Penh, Ho Chi Minh City and Hanoi began, operated twice weekly by Vietnamese aircraft, and in March 1980 scheduled flights between Phnom-Penh and Vientiane began functioning.

DEFENCE

There are some 200,000 Vietnamese troops in Kampuchea (July 1981).

Commander-in-Chief of the Kampuchean People's Revolutionary Armed Forces: HENG SAMRIN.

Chief of General Staff of the Army: SOY KEO.

EDUCATION

Since 1979, under the new regime, child and youth educational policy is aimed at the study of general knowledge. Adult education is directed at persons between 15 and 50 years of age with the intention of eradicating illiteracy and enhancing the professionalism of cadres, combatants and personnel throughout the country. It is claimed that each co-operative has an elementary school and since February 1979 many primary schools in rural areas have been reopened. Official sources have stated that primary school enrolment in 1981 was 1.4 million. There is no university although there are plans to build new schools and universities in due course. In 1980 the Faculty of Medicine and Pharmacy was reopened, and over 80 doctors and pharmacists graduated. It is also reported that a Teacher Training College and some secondary vocational schools have been opened.

BIBLIOGRAPHY

ARMSTRONG, J. P. Sihanouk Speaks (New York, 1964).

BARRON, JOHN, and PAUL, ANTHONY. Peace with Horror: The Untold Story of Communist Genocide in Cambodia (Hodder and Stoughton, London, 1977).

BRIGGS, L. P. The Ancient Khmer Empire (Transactions of the American Philosophical Society, Philadelphia, 1951).

BRODRICK, A. H. Little Vehicle; Cambodia and Laos (London).

CADY, J. F. Thailand, Burma, Laos and Cambodia (Prentice-Hall Inc., Englewood Cliffs, New Jersey, 1966).

COEDES, G. Les Etats hindouisés d'Indochine et d'Indonésie (F. de Boccard, Paris, 1948).

COUR, CLAUDE-GILLES. Institutions Constitutionelles et Politique du Cambodge (Paris, 1965).

DELVERT, J. Le Paysan Cambodgien (Paris and the Hague, 1961).

FITZSIMMONS, T. (ed.). Cambodia, its People, its Society, its Culture (HRAF Press, New Haven, Conn., 2nd edn., 1959).

GROSLIER B. Angkor et le Cambodge au XVIe siècle (Paris, 1958).

HERTZ, M. F. A Short History of Cambodia from the days of Angkor to the Present (Stevens and Sons, London, 1958).

KIRK, DONALD. Wider War: The Struggle for Cambodia, Thailand and Laos (Praeger, N.Y., 1971).

LEIFER, M. Cambodia—The Search for Security (Pall Mall Press, London, 1967).

Conflict and Regional Order in South-East Asia (Adelphi Papers No. 162, International Institute for Strategic Studies, London, 1980).

MACDONALD, M. Angkor (Cape, London, 1958).

MIGOT, A. Les Khmers (Paris, 1960).

NATIONAL GEOGRAPHIC (Volume 161, no. 5, May 1982, pp. 548–623).

OSBORNE, M. E. The French Presence in Cochinchina and Cambodia: Rule and Response, 1859–1905 (Ithaca, New York, 1969).

Politics and Power in Cambodia (Camberwell, Victoria 1973).

Before Kampuchea, Preludes to Tragedy (Allen and Unwin, London, 1979).

PONCHAUD, FRANÇOIS. Cambodge; Année Zéro (Julliard, Paris, 1977; publ. in transl. as Cambodia Year Zero, Penguin Books, Harmondsworth, 1978).

PRESCHEZ, PHILIPPE. Essai sur la Démocratie au Cambodge (Paris, 1961).

SHAWCROSS, WILLIAM. Sideshow (André Deutsch, London, 1979).

SIHANOUK, NORODOM. War and Hope: the Case for Cambodia (Sidgwick and Jackson, London, 1980).

SMITH, ROGER M. Cambodia (in Governments and Politics of Southeast Asia, Edited by G. McT. Kahin) (Ithaca, New York, 1964).

Cambodia's Foreign Policy (Ithaca, New York, 1965).

THIERRY, S. Les Khmers (Paris, 1964).

WILLMOTT, WILLIAM E. The Chinese in Cambodia (Vancouver, 1967).

See also Laos and Viet-Nam.

Korea

PHYSICAL AND SOCIAL GEOGRAPHY

John Sargent

(Revised by the Editor, 1981–82)

The total area of Korea is 220,766 square kilometres (85,238 square miles), including North and South Korea and the demilitarized zone between them. North Korea has an area of 120,538 square kilometres (46,540 square miles), and South Korea an area of 98,966 square kilometres (38,211 square miles). The demilitarized zone covers 1,262 square kilometres (487 square miles).

The Korean peninsula is bordered to the north by the People's Republic of China, and has a very short frontier with the U.S.S.R. in the north-east.

PHYSICAL FEATURES

Korea is predominantly an area of ancient folding, although in the south-east, where a relatively small zone of recent rocks occurs, a close geological similarity with Japan may be detected. Unlike Japan, the peninsula contains no active volcanoes, and earthquakes are rare.

Although, outside the extreme north, few mountains rise to more than 1,650 metres, rugged upland, typically blanketed in either pine forest or scrub, predominates throughout the peninsula. Cultivated lowland forms only 20 per cent of the combined area of North and South Korea.

Two broad masses of highland determine the basic relief pattern of the peninsula. In the north, the Changpai Shan and Tumen ranges form an extensive area of mountain terrain, aligned from south-west to north-east, and separating the peninsula proper from the uplands of eastern Manzhou (Manchuria). A second mountain chain runs for almost the entire length of the peninsula, close to, and parallel with, the eastern coast. Thus, in the peninsula proper, the main lowland areas, which are also the areas of maximum population density, are found in the west and south.

The rivers of Korea, which are short and fast-flowing, drain mainly westwards into the Huang Hai (Yellow Sea). Of the two countries, North Korea, with its many mountain torrents, is especially well endowed with opportunities for hydro-electric generation. Wide seasonal variations in the rate of flow, however, tend to hamper the efficient operation of hydroelectric plants throughout the year.

In contrast with the east coast of the peninsula, which is smooth and precipitous, the intricate western and southern coasts are well endowed with good natural harbours, an asset which, however, is partly offset by an unusually wide tidal range.

CLIMATE

In its main elements, the climate of Korea is more continental than marine, and is thus characterized by a wide seasonal range in temperature. In winter, with the establishment of a high pressure centre over Siberia and Mongolia, winds are predominantly from the north and north-west. North Korea in winter is extremely cold, with January temperatures falling, in the mountains, to below −13°C. (8°F.). Owing to the ameliorating influence of the surrounding seas, winter temperatures gradually rise towards the south of the peninsula, but only in the extreme southern coastlands do January temperatures rise above freezing point. Winter precipitation is light, and falls mainly in the form of snow, which, in the north, lies for long periods.

In the southern and western lowlands, summers are hot and humid, with July temperatures rising to 26°C. (80°F.). In mid-summer, violent cloudbursts occur, often causing severe soil erosion and landslides. In the extreme north-east, summers are cooler, and July temperatures rarely rise above 17°C. (64°F.).

Annual precipitation, over half of which falls in the summer months, varies from below 63.5 cm. (25 in.) in the north-east to over 152 cm. (60 in.) in the south.

NATURAL RESOURCES

Although 70 per cent of the total area of Korea is forested, high quality timber is virtually limited to the mountains of North Korea, where extensive stands of larch, pine, and fir provide a valuable resource. Elsewhere, excessive felling has caused the forest cover to degenerate into poor scrub.

Korea is fairly well provided with mineral resources, but most deposits are concentrated in the north, where large-scale mining operations were begun by the Japanese before the Second World War. In North Korea, the main iron mining areas are found south of Pyongyang, and in the vicinity of Chongjin in the extreme north-east.

Throughout Korea, many other minerals, including copper, lead, zinc, tungsten, gold, silver and asbestos, are mined.

POPULATION

At mid-1980 the estimated population of North Korea was 17,892,000, while that of South Korea (at the October 1980 census) was 37,448,836, giving a combined total of more than 55 million. The population of Korea has grown rapidly since 1954, when the combined total was 30 million, with an increase of 25 million in 25 years.

Population density in 1980 was higher in South Korea (378 per square kilometre) than in North Korea

(148 per square kilometre), but mean density figures conceal the crowding of population on the limited area of agricultural land, which is a salient characteristic of the geography of South Korea.

In 1970, 40 per cent of the population of South Korea was concentrated in cities with populations of 100,000 and over. Seoul, the capital of South Korea, had a population of 8,366,756 in 1980; Pusan, with 3,160,276, was the second largest city, followed by Taegu with 1,607,458 and Inchon with 1,084,730.

According to 1976 estimates, the population of Pyongyang, the capital of North Korea, was 1,500,000. That of Chongjin, the leading port of the north-east coast, was 300,000. The other two principal cities are Hungnam, with a population of 260,000, and Kaesong, with 240,000.

HISTORY

Andrew C. Nahm

FROM EARLY TIMES TO 1945

The Tungusic people, with their Ural-Altaic tongue, shamanic religion and a paleolithic culture, made a southward move from eastern Siberia into Manzhou (Manchuria) and Korea about 30,000 years B.C. They were a vigorous, hardy people with a strong ethnic and tribal indentity. In 2333 B.C. Tan'gun is said to have united the tribal groups in north-western Korea and adjacent Manzhou and formed a "Korean kingdom".

Bronze tools and weapons introduced from China, initiated the Sinification of the Korean peninsula. A warrior from southern Manzhou, named Wiman, extended his domination into the fertile river basin surrounding present-day Pyongyang in 190 B.C. Meanwhile, contacts between Korea and China increased. Finally, in 108 B.C., Emperor Wu of the Han dynasty of China invaded Korea and established four Chinese commandaries, overthrowing the kingdom Wiman. The most important of the Chinese commandaries was Lo-lang (Nangnang in Korean) in the north-western plain of Korea, with its capital near Pyongyang.

The Three Kingdom Period

The Puyo tribesmen of the peninsula and Manzhou managed to retain an independent existence. In 37 B.C. these tribes were welded into the Kingdom of Koguryo, a kingdom which steadily incorporated the territories which China had controlled, and they then moved into Korea. In A.D. 313 the end of Chinese domination in Korea came with the destruction of Lo-lang by Koguryo. Perhaps to ward off this northern threat, the tribes in the southern half of Korea forged themselves into three loosely organized federations, Chin-Han, Ma-Han and Pyon-Han. (The present-day name of the Republic of Korea, which is Tae-Han Minguk, or Hanguk, traces its origin to these federations.) In 18 B.C. the tribal federation in the central part was transformed into the Kingdom of Paekche. In 57 B.C. the Kingdom of Silla rose in the south-eastern part of Korea, with its capital at Kyongju. The Paekche kingdom moved its capital to Puyo.

Facing the growing power of Koguryo, Paekche and Silla formed an alliance in the early fifth century A.D., and they managed to check the aggressive move on the part of Koguryo for a while. However, the alliance was soon broken and the power struggle grew intense among the three kindgoms. It was during this period of conflict that Paekche nurtured a Buddhist civilization in Japan. Meanwhile, the warriors of Koguryo managed successfully to defeat the invading forces of the Sui dynasty of China. The Tang dynasty, which succeeded the Sui in 618, suffered similar defeats. But Koguryo was weakened and Silla, seizing the opportunity, allied itself with the Tang and destroyed first Paekche in 663, and then Koguryo five years later, thus unifying Korea.

The Three Kingdom period was the most important epoch in the development of Korea as a distinct nation and people. During this period, not only rapid political transformation occurred, but also an agricultural economy and a new pattern of social life of the people developed. Buddhism, an important unifying force, contributed greatly to the development of art, architecture, literature and technology in Korea. At the same time, the secular culture of China (Confucian, Daoistic and other thoughts and systems) exerted a great influence on the development of ideas and literature as well as the political and social institutions of Korea.

The Unified Silla and Koryo Periods

The Kingdom of Silla lasted 270 years following the unification of Korea, the first 150 years constituting a golden age in Korean history. But, as warring clans created political havoc, political decline set in. Abuses of political power, misuse of funds, exploitation of the peasants and usurpation of privilege by members of the aristocracy brought about peasant revolts. In 892 a small state, called Later Paekche, was set up by rebels, while a monk named Kungye established Later Koguryo in 1901. Wang Kon, one of the officers of Kungye, removed the monk from power, and founded in 918 a new dynasty of his own named Koryo, with its capital at Kaesong. In 935 the last king of Silla submitted to Wang Kon, and Later Paekche was destroyed by Wang Kon the following year.

The Koryo dynasty, from which the Western name for Korea was derived, lasted until 1392. The dynasty's bureaucracy was strengthened with the creation of a new, closed hereditary aristocracy which monopolized political power, despite the introduction of the Chinese system of civil service examinations.

The Sinicized bureaucracy was manned by a salaried officialdom. The people were stratified into two large units below the officialdom: the tax-paying commoners and the landless peasants and slaving population called the "lowborn".

Although the manufacturing of the renowned Koryo celadon ware flourished, commerce failed to develop, as international trade declined almost completely. Buddhism became the state religion, and the monastic movement and Buddhist culture made great strides. The rise of Buddhist study witnessed the construction of magnificent temples, as well as the invention (or improvement) of printing.

With the increase of Chinese cultural influence, scholarship in historical studies grew. As a result, such important historical sources as *History of the Three Kingdoms* and *Memorabilia of the Three Kingdoms* were produced by Korean scholars in the twelfth and thirteenth centuries, respectively.

Koryo was beset by external problems. The Mongols, the Khitans and the Jurchens to the north steadily increased their pressure, and Koryo suffered the first disaster when the Khitans descended upon Koryo in the 990s. In order to strengthen its northern defences. Koryo constructed a "great wall" across its northern border, excluding the north-eastern portion of the Korean peninsula.

Discontent began festering among the military leaders as power struggles within the ruling class began. In 1170 warfare among military leaders broke out, joined by slave rebellions. Finally, in 1199, the military dictatorship of the Ch'oe family was established and lasted until 1256.

During its political and social turmoil Koryo was invaded by the Mongols, and in 1231 the Mongols forced the Koreans to capitulate. Not satisfied with Koryo's attitudes, the Mongols invaded Korea again in 1259, and forced Mongol suzerainty upon Korea. During the Mongol domination, which lasted a century, new cultural horizons were opened up, bringing Korea into contact with knowledge of astronomy, mathematics and other sciences, as well as the arts of those areas of western Asia. Meanwhile, Neo-Confucianism was introduced to Korea.

The anti-Mongol sentiment grew stronger as the Mongol empire began to crumble. Some twenty years after the overthrow of the Mongol rule by the founder of the Ming dynasty in 1368, Yi Song-gye put the Koryo dynasty completely under his control, and instituted ambitious economic and social reforms while pursuing a pro-Ming foreign policy. Opposition to General Yi's land policy grew, and the power struggle within the Government continued. But in 1392 he overthrew the Koryo dynasty and established the Yi dynasty. He named his kingdom Choson ("The Land of the Morning Calm"), resurrecting the ancient name of Korea.

The Yi Dynasty

The Yi dynasty, with its new capital at Seoul, ruled Korea for 518 years. For the first time the entire Korean peninsula, divided into eight provinces, came under the rule of a single government in Seoul. The major organs of Government were a State Council, a Royal Secretariat and six ministries. Five other important state organs were two offices of Censors, the Office of Special Counsellors, the Office of the Royal Lecturers and the Office of Superintendent of Education.

The new land policy of the Yi dynasty marked the beginning of a modern landlordism when land became taxable. Although some tax-free estates existed, the era of large tax-free estates ended as the size of landlord holdings became modest and the number of landholders increased. The bulk of the farming population possessed no land. The Buddhist church was deprived of any rights to hold agricultural lands.

The class structure also changed. The scholar-gentry class, high-ranking members of the officialdom who were landholders, constituted the aristocracy. Beneath it were petty government functionaries and professional specialists; the "common people", which included tenant farmers, artisans and merchants; and the "lowborn", which included farm hands, domestic servants and slaves.

The adoption of the Neo-Confucianism of Chu-hsi as the state creed brought about strong anti-Buddhist policy, and Buddhist monks and nuns moved to Korea's remote regions. Meanwhile, the strengthening of the civil service examination system nurtured the growth of educational institutions and scholarship. A Confucian university, four official schools in the capital, and official schools in provincial capitals were the centres of learning. Private schools and the Royal Library (*Kyujanggak*), established in the eighteenth century, played a significant role in the advancement of the intellectual movement in Korea.

One of the most outstanding cultural achievements of the Yi period was the institutionalization in 1446 of Korean script commonly called *Han'gul* ("Korean Letters"), by King Sejong. Volumes of legal compendiums were compiled, and historical studies resulted in the publication of such valuable sources as *Essential History of Koryo* and *General Outline History of Korea* during the fifteenth century.

Towards the end of the fifteenth century, the Court was torn by a struggle for power, as well as ideological conflicts. As a result, there were four great purges of hundreds of *literati* between 1491 and 1545. Internal turmoil, caused by battling officials and scholars, and the Japanese invasions of 1592 and 1597, under Toyotomi Hideyoshi, inflicted a mortal wound from which the Korean society never recovered. The aftermath of the seven-year war, with a period of intermittent peace negotiations, was a weakening of the social fabric and a decrease in population as a vast number of artisans and technicians were forcibly taken to Japan by the invaders.

In 1627 the Manzhous invaded Korea and forced the Korean Government to accept vassalage, and to supply food, soldiers and labourers. The Yi dynasty turned against them, resulting in the second invasion by the Manzhous in 1637. Korea remained a tributary state to the Manzhous, who conquered China and established the Qing (Ch'ing) dynasty in 1644.

With the introduction of Roman Catholicism to Korea in the late eighteenth century, interest in Western religion and science grew. Subsequently, a Chinese and several French missionaries entered Korea illegally and spread Christianity, giving birth to two significant intellectual movements, the *Sohak* ("Western Learning") and the *Sirhak* ("Practical Learning"). But Korea's "Western Learning" failed to promote modern and scientific studies, manufacturing technology or social transformation. Moreover, with no ports open to the West, Korea was not exposed to the civilization of the West.

The school of "Practical Learning" emerged during the mid-eighteenth century when scholars with a nationalistic and progressive outlook came forward, advocating political and educational reform, social justice, and economic reconstruction. Such scholars as Chong Yak-yong (pen-name Tasan), a leading figure in the "Western Learning" movement, attacked corrupt and inefficient government and bureaucrats, while criticizing the "empty learning" of Neo-Confucianists. They emphasized the study of Korea's traditional culture and the strengthening of its own identity and independence. They also insisted that the primary function of the Government was the promotion of the people's welfare and the maintenance of order. The *Sirhak* painters initiated a new movement when they produced a genre of art that depicted Korean life of the times.

The conservative Government refused to adopt proposals made by the *Sirhak* scholars, and the Yi dynasty was unable to lessen the Government's weaknesses or social decay. The economic situation worsened, with population increase and a rising tax burden.

The worsening economic and social conditions, coupled with the misuse of power by corrupt Confucian officials, gave impetus to peasant rebellions in the late eighteenth and early nineteenth centuries. The *Tonghak* ("Eastern Learning") group, which emerged around 1860, criticized political corruption, economic mismanagement and social injustice, and, while preaching salvation through faith in the "Eastern Learning", opposed "Western Learning". In 1863 the Government arrested its founder (who was later executed) and many of his followers. The "Eastern Learning" sect, however, grew steadily among the poverty-stricken peasant population in the southern provinces, and was destined to create more serious problems for the Government in later years.

Korea encountered increasing foreign problems as Western mercantilism spread rapidly in Asia in the nineteenth century. The persecutions of Christians in 1865-66, which resulted in the deaths of French priests and a French invasion, the destruction of an American merchant ship in 1866, and the subsequent American invasion of 1871, created serious international complications while promoting anti-foreign sentiments among Koreans. Korea proclaimed its isolationistic policy in 1871.

Japan, where a revolution had overthrown the Tokugawa Shogunate in 1867, made several requests to the Korean Government for the renewal of diplomatic and commercial relations, suspended almost completely since the Japanese wars of 1592 and 1597. The Korean refusal brought about a Japanese military threat which the Korean Government was unable to repel and it concluded a treaty and commercial agreements in 1876.

The Demise of the Korean Nation

Korea, under unimaginative and inefficient pro-Chinese conservatives, with its weak social and economic foundation, an ill-prepared military and ever-increasing discontent among the masses, was destined to encounter growing danger to national survival as well as domestic crisis. Queen Min and her allies successfully ousted the reform-minded and nationalistic Regent (*Taewon'gun*), and established absolute domination over King Kojong and his Government. Meanwhile, conflict between China and Japan grew over Korea's sovereignty: Japan recognized Korea's sovereignty in the 1876 treaty, but China did not. The growing economic strength of the Japanese in Korea only aggravated the Sino-Japanese relations.

The Chinese intervened in Korea in 1882 to crush the military insurrection in which the deposed Regent attempted to regain power. The Chinese military intervention, however, stimulated the rise of nationalistic sentiment in Korea, particularly among the progressive scholars such as Kim Ok-kyun and Pak-Yong-hyo, who sought assistance not only from Japan, but also from the United States, which concluded a treaty with Korea in 1882.

The harder the progressives (who were known as the *Kaehwadang*, or the "Party of Modernization") attempted to bring about urgently needed reforms, the stronger the opposition grew. They managed to gain the support of the Japanese minister to Korea, and in order to bring about political, economic and social reforms, they carried out a palace coup in December 1884. A second Chinese military intervention quickly crushed the new Government. The majority of the progressives were killed but a handful fled to Japan and the U.S.A.

The Japanese leaders regarded the re-assertion of Chinese direct suzerainty over Korea as intolerable, for they were fearful that it would lead to the domination of Korea by a Western power such as Russia. The opinion of the Japanese leaders was that Korea's safe existence was the guarantee for Japan's security. Japanese antagonism toward China grew, leading to the Sino-Japanese War of 1894–95, from which Japan emerged a victor.

Although the treaty ending the war stated that Korea was an independent nation, Korea did not secure complete independence, as the military occupation by the Japanese during the war led to increased Japanese domination of Korea. King Kojong's so-called *Kabo* Reform of 1894–95 was more or less a reluctant gesture to accommodate heavy pressure which the Japanese brought upon him.

The Triple Intervention of Russia, Germany and France in 1895 forced Japan to cancel the agreement in which China agreed to lease the Liaodong territory to Japan for 25 years. The weakened Japanese stand against the European powers prompted the rise of a pro-Russian group supported by Queen Min. The Japanese minister to Korea was determined to maintain the position which Japan had gained. He had Queen Min assassinated and forced the Korean Government to restore a pro-Japanese cabinet. The killing of the queen by Japanese only strengthened the Koreans' anti-Japanese sentiment. King Kojong was spirited out of his palace to the nearby Russian Legation in 1896, and a Korean-Russian alliance was formed against Japan.

At this point a new group of young reform advocates emerged, preaching national salvation through self-strengthening and the enlightenment of the people. Its leader, Dr. So Chae-p'il (Philip Jaisohn), who had fled to the United States in 1884, returned to Korea and formed the Independence Club in co-operation with young progressives. Meanwhile, other groups also arose and advocated national reconstruction.

An awakening of intellectuals, accompanying the ever-increasing number of newspapers, journals, and reform societies, marked the opening of a new chapter in Korean history. The voices of reform advocates grew louder as the cultural influence of the West increased and more modern schools were built, but a strong reaction against the Independence Club developed among conservative officials. Finally, Dr. Jaisohn was forced to leave Korea again while other members were imprisoned in 1898.

The growth of Russian influence and of the nationalistic spirit in Korea aroused Japanese concern. As a result, the Anglo-Japanese Alliance was formed in 1902 and Japanese attitudes toward Russia stiffened. Meanwhile, the Russians pursued an equally determined policy to extend their influence and control in Asia. This rivalry led to the Russo-Japanese War of 1904–05, which was disastrous for Korea. Under Japanese military occupation, Korea helplessly concluded a series of agreements with Japan during the war. Although the treaty ending the war guaranteed Korea's independence, Japan's *de facto* control over Korea, and an understanding between the U.S.A. and Japan in 1905, led to the establishment of a Japanese protectorate over Korea. The Japanese enthroned a new Korean emperor in 1907, and forced the last ruler of Korea to sign the treaty by which Japan annexed the country on August 22nd, 1910.

The Japanese Colonial Period, 1910-45

Although the Japanese imperial decree issued at the time of Japan's annexation of Korea stated that the Koreans would be treated in the same way as Japanese subjects, the Korean people were subjected to military rule and deprived of rights and privileges constitutionally guaranteed to the Japanese. The Government-General of Korea in Seoul was headed by army generals, except from 1919 to 1931, and oppressive police rule drove the people into virtual slavery. The Koreans lost their freedom and rights, and their lands were also taken away by the Japanese.

During the period of colonial rule, Korean people at home and abroad launched an independence movement, culminating in the celebrated March First movement of 1919. On March 1st that year the Declaration of Independence of the Korean people was proclaimed. The peaceful independence movement, however, was met with brutal retaliation by the Japanese military and police. The uprising lasted over a month as it spread into the remotest corners of the country, but it did not remove the Japanese imperialistic rule from Korea. Other efforts made by the Koreans to regain their freedom and independence were likewise fruitless.

The Japanese aims in Korea were threefold: the use of human and natural resources in Korea to aid the economic development of Japan, the assimilation of the Koreans into Japanese culture, and the construction of a strong basis for continental expansion. With these objectives, the Japanese developed the Korean economy and expanded educational facilities to train "loyal, obedient, and useful subjects" of the Japanese emperor. The Korean economy was dominated by the Japanese, and Korea remained the chief supplier of food and manpower to Japan. The development of higher and secondary education was kept to a minimum, and training programmes were aimed at the production of cheap labourers with limited skills. The cultural assimilation programme was aimed at the destruction of the Korean cultural heritage. The use of the Korean language was first discouraged, and then forbidden; Christianity was allowed to exist only under severe restrictions. Koreans were forced to abandon Korean names and adopt Japanese names.

The industrialization and modern economic development of Korea came only after the Japanese launched their aggression in Manzhou in 1931 and a war against China in 1937, leading to the greater exploitation of Korea by the Japanese. The Second World War only intensified Japanese control and exploitation of Korea.

In Shanghai (and later in Chongqing) the Provisional Government of the Republic of Korea in exile, which was established in April 1919 under the presidency of Dr. Syngman Rhee, led the national restoration movement of the rightist nationalists, while the nationalists who turned to Communism maintained their struggle against the Japanese near the north-eastern regions of Korea as well as in the border regions of Manzhou and the Soviet Union. The *Singanhoe* ("New Shoot Society") and other rightist and leftist organizations in Korea made gallant, but futile, efforts against Japanese rule.

The Liberation from Japan and the Division of Korea

On August 15th, 1945, the Japanese surrendered to the Allies. The Cairo Declaration of December 1943, issued by the British and American leaders and Chiang Kai-shek of China, had stated that "in due course Korea shall become free and independent". The

Soviet leader, Josef Stalin, accepted the Cairo agreement, but proposals made by the Americans in 1945 led to the division of Korea into two military zones: the area south of the 38th parallel line under American occupation and the northern area under Soviet occupation.

The Japanese governor-general in Korea persuaded Yo Un-hyong, a prominent left-wing nationalist (Socialist), to form a political body to maintain law and order at the end of the Japanese colonial rule. The Committee for the Preparation of the National Construction of Korea was thus organized. After Japan's surrender, Korean political prisoners were freed and the Committee began to function as a government. Provincial, district and local committees were organized to maintain law and order. On September 6th, two days before the arrival of American occupation forces, the Committee called a "National Assembly" and established the People's Republic of Korea, claiming jurisdiction over the whole country. Meanwhile, Soviet troops which entered Korea in early August quickly moved southward as they crushed Japanese resistance, and within a month the entire northern half of Korea came under Soviet occupation.

The American occupation authority accepted the surrender of Korea from the Japanese governor-general, but, unlike the Soviet general in the north, refused to recognize the legitimacy of either the People's Republic or the Provisional Government of Korea in exile in China, waiting to return to Korea. The United States Army Military Government in Korea (USAMGIK) was established and lasted until August 1948.

Exiled political leaders returned to Korea toward the end of 1945, Dr. Rhee from the United States, Kim Ku and Dr. Kim Kyu-sik from China, and Kim Il-sung and other Communists from the Soviet Union and China. Pak Hon-yong, a Communist who had been released from the Japanese prison, quickly formed the Korean Communist Party in South Korea. Freedom of political activity permitted by the American military government resulted in a proliferation of political parties and social organization of all political orientation, each vying for prominence. The military government attempted vainly to bring about a coalition of moderate nationalists and non-communist leftists.

In December 1945 representatives of the United Kingdom, the United States and the Soviet Union entered into the Moscow Agreement, providing for a five-year trusteeship for Korea under a four-power regime (China was the fourth power), with the view to establish an independent and united nation of Korea. Despite violent anti-trusteeship demonstrations, the Allied occupation authorities resolved to implement the Moscow plan. Then, suddenly, the Communists throughout Korea changed their stand in favour of the Moscow plan, splitting the Korean people into two opposing camps.

In South Korea left-wing political and labour organizations created serious political and economic problems. Communist-directed labour strikes became widespread, and terrorism of both right-wing and left-wing organizations became rampant. The severe winter of 1945 hit the people hard, with commodity shortages and high unemployment.

A Joint U.S.-U.S.S.R. Commission was formed to establish a national government of Korea in consultation with Korean political and social organizations. The first session of the Joint Commission was held in Seoul in March–May 1946. The Soviet delegate insisted that only "democratic" organizations should participate and that only organizations which supported the Moscow Agreement were "democratic". It became clear that the Soviet Union intended to establish a national government of Korea dominated by Communists.

In May 1947 the second session of the Joint Commission in Pyongyang similarly failed to achieve any agreement and in June the Commission's business was suspended indefinitely.

Realizing that the establishment of the Korean unity and its national government was a remote possibility, the American occupation authority adopted new plans for South Korea. The Soviet occupation authority likewise proceeded to establish its puppet regime under Kim Il-sung. All anti-Soviet and anti-communist organizations were either broken up or put under communist leadership. A communist monolithic state began to emerge in the north as Kim Il-sung formed his own party in defiance of Pak Hon-yong, head of the Korean Communist Party, whose headquarters were in Seoul.

In South Korea the Americans established the South Korean Interim Legislative Assembly in late 1946, and in May 1947 the South Korean Interim Government was created, both under moderate nationalists. These actions were bitterly criticized by conservative right-wing leaders such as Dr. Syngman Rhee and Kim Ku. The relationship between the Americans and the right-wing nationalists worsened while terrorist activities created an extremely uneasy situation. Several prominent right-wing leaders, as well as Yo Un-hyong, were assassinated. Neither the Interim Legislative Assembly nor the Interim Government was effective, for both of them were regarded by the conservative nationalists as American puppets attempting to prolong the American military occupation of Korea. Meanwhile, the economic hardships of the people grew worse.

In September 1947 the United States Government placed the Korean question before the United Nations and discarded the Moscow plan. The United Nations General Assembly formed the UN Temporary Commission on Korea in November and authorized it to conduct a national election in Korea to create a national government for the whole country.

The UN decision was welcomed by the Americans and by most people in South Korea. The Soviet occupation authority and the Korean Communists in the north, however, rejected the UN plan, and did not allow the UN Temporary Commission to visit North Korea. It soon became apparent that the UN plan would not work in the whole of Korea, and the Commission adopted an alternative plan to hold elections in those areas where it was possible, namely in South Korea only. It was assumed by the Commission that UN-sponsored and supervised elections would be held in the north in the near future, that a national assembly created by the first democratic elections in Korea would represent the entire country, that the Government to be established would be that of all Korea, and that the people in the north would elect their representatives to the national assembly later.

Whereas the right-wing nationalists welcomed such an alternative plan, the moderate and progressive nationalists, such as Kim Kyu-sik, the head of the Democratic Independence Party, as well as an extreme right-wing nationalist, Kim Ku, vehemently opposed it, fearing that it would turn the temporary division of Korea into a permanent political partition. They visited North Korea and talked with Kim Il-sung and other Communists, but failed to achieve their objective.

The Soviet authorities in the north had already begun to transfer power to the Supreme People's Assembly and the Central People's Committee, both established in early 1947, Dr. Rhee's society advocated the immediate independence of South Korea. The bitter controversy over the new UN plan divided the people in the south as tension rose.

The UN-sponsored elections held in the south in May 1948 created a National Assembly, heavily dominated by conservative right-wing members. About 7.5 million people, or 75 per cent of the electorate elected 198 of 210 representatives from the south, while 100 unfilled seats in the 310-member National Assembly were to be occupied by the north Korean representatives later.

The National Assembly in South Korea drew up a democratic constitution for the Republic of Korea. Dr. Rhee was elected by the National Assembly to be the first President of the Republic of Korea, whose legitimacy was immediately recognized by the United Nations. On August 15th, 1948, the Republic of Korea was inaugurated, and the American occupation came to an end.

In August 1948 the communists in the north held an election and established the new 527-member Supreme People's Assembly of the Democratic People's Republic of Korea (D.P.R.K.), proclaimed on September 9th, 1948.

THE KOREAN WAR, 1950-53*

American forces were withdrawn from South Korea in June 1949, leaving only a small advisory group. South Korea's own forces were weaker than those of the north, which had been built up with Soviet help. Tension and rivalry between the North and the South culminated in the Korean War, when a North Korean force of over 60,000 troops, supported by Soviet-built tanks, crossed the 38th parallel and invaded the south on June 25th, 1950. Four days later the North Koreans captured Seoul, the South Korean capital. American forces, whose assistance was requested by the Seoul Government, arrived on June 30th.

In response to North Korea's attack, the United Nations mounted a collective defence action in support of South Korea. Armed forces from 16 UN member states, attached to a unified command under the U.S.A., were sent to help repel the invasion. Meanwhile, the North Koreans continued their drive southwards, advancing so strongly that they soon occupied most of South Korea, leaving UN troops confined to the south-east corner of the peninsula. Following sea-borne landings by UN forces at Inchon, near Seoul, in September 1950, the attackers were driven back and UN troops advanced into North Korea, capturing Pyongyang, the capital, in October and reaching the Chinese frontier on the Yalu River in November.

In October 1950 the People's Republic of China sent in troops to assist North Korea and 200,000 Chinese crossed the Yalu River into Korea, forcing the evacuation of South Korean and UN troops. The Chinese advanced into South Korea but were driven back by a UN counter-attack in April 1951.

Peace negotiations began in July 1951 but hostilities continued until an armistice agreement was made on July 27th, 1953. The war caused more than 800,000 casualties in South Korea and enormous damage to property. The 1953 ceasefire line, roughly along the 38th parallel, remains the boundary between North and South Korea, with a narrow demilitarized zone separating the two countries.

SOUTH KOREA

The First Republic, 1948-60

The foundation of the Republic was hardly settled when a Communist-inspired military rebellion broke out in October 1948. The rebellion was crushed, but it demoralized the nation and increased the suppressive character of the Government. The democratic aspirations and trends of the pre-Korean War period diminished as the Government became more autocratic during and after the Korean War. Political and social conditions became chaotic as economic hardships multiplied.

South Korea's politics were turbulent, and there was a series of crises. President Rhee and his Liberal Party (created in 1952) acted high-handedly towards their opponents, and a series of constitutional amendments were forcibly pushed through the National Assembly. In July 1952 the National Assembly adopted a constitutional amendment to elect the president by popular vote, and the election, conducted under a Martial Law, was won by Dr. Rhee. In 1954 the National Assembly adopted another series of amendments, including the exemption of the incumbent president from the two-term constitutional limitation in office, and the abolition of the post of Prime Minister.

In the 1956 presidential election, a new opposition Democratic Party, founded in 1955, nominated candidates for the offices of President and Vice-President. The sudden death of the presidential candidate of the opposition party assured victory for Dr. Rhee,

* This section on the Korean War was contributed by the Editor.

but the Democratic candidate, Chang Myon, defeated the Liberal Party candidate for the vice-presidency.

As corruption among government officials and members of the Liberal Party, and repression by the police, increased, a widespread desire for change grew, particularly among the urban voters. The voters in rural districts remained "captives" of the Liberal Party, but in the 1958 National Assembly elections, the Democratic Party increased its seats substantially. Aware of the danger of losing its absolute control, the Liberal Party-dominated National Assembly repealed local autonomy laws, and passed a new national security law.

In the fourth presidential elections held in March 1960, Dr. Rhee and Yi Ki-bung ran as the presidential and vice-presidential candidates of the Liberal Party. Three weeks before the election, the Democratic Party presidential candidate, Dr. Cho Pyong-ok, died, assuring the election of Dr. Rhee. However, the election of Yi Ki-bung as Vice-President was somewhat uncertain. Popular reaction against the corrupt and fraudulent practices of the administration and the Liberal Party grew, and fierce student riots erupted throughout the country.

The student uprising of April 19th forced President Rhee and his cabinet to resign on April 26th. A caretaker government was set up under Ho Chong, and in mid-June the National Assembly adopted a constitutional amendment establishing a strong parliamentary system, reducing the presidency to a figurehead chief of state, and resurrecting the office of Prime Minister. In August the National Assembly named Yun Po-son as President and Chang Myon as Prime Minister responsible to the lower house of the Assembly; and the Second Republic emerged.

With the exception of the Land Reform Law of 1949, the First Republic recorded no positive success in the economic field. In the post-Korean War period a degree of economic recovery was achieved with aid from UNKRA and the U.S.A., but South Korea remained economically backward, suffering shortages of power, fuel, food and consumer goods.

The Second Republic, 1960-61

The Second Republic was handicapped from the start: it had no mandate from the people and both President Yun Po-son and Prime Minister Chang lacked fortitude and practical tactics. The Chang administration was indecisive in dealing with former leaders of the Rhee regime and seemed too tolerant toward left-wing radicals. It was unable to deal effectively with ideological and social cleavage between political and sectional groups, while gaining no new support or the loyalty of the people.

The ruling Democratic Party was badly split, and it had no suitable solutions to economic and social problems. With the exception of the stillborn Five-Year Plan, the Chang administration failed to tackle the country's serious economic problems. Meanwhile, new demonstrations erupted as the influence of the communists among the students grew. Agitation by students for direct negotiations with North Korean students, aimed at reunification of the country, created anxiety and turmoil. Stronger party discipline was finally achieved in early spring of 1961, but the danger to national security increased as food and job shortages worsened.

Military Rule, 1961-63

On May 16th, 1961, a military revolution, led by a small group of young army officers headed by Maj.-Gen. Park Chung Hee, overthrew the Chang administration. The military junta dissolved the National Assembly, forbade all political activity, and declared martial law, banning student demonstrations and censoring the press. Lt.-Gen. Chang Do-yong, the Army Chief of Staff, became chairman of the Supreme Council for National Reconstruction which they created. President Yun remained in office, but the Government was in the hands of the military. Pledges by the revolutionaries were issued, upholding anti-communism and adherence to the United Nations, and calling for stronger ties with the United States and the free world, the eradication of corruption and graft, the extinction of street violence and social evils, rejuvenation of national spirit, and the construction of a self-supporting economy, a solid foundation for a new and truly democratic republic, as well as the restoration of civilian rule.

The Supreme Council acted as a legislative body, and a National Reconstruction Extraordinary Measures Law was adopted as a substitute for the constitution. In July 1961, when Gen. Chang was arrested for alleged anti-revolutionary conspiracy, Gen. Park took over the chairmanship of the Supreme Council. In August Gen. Park announced that political activity would be permitted in early 1963 to pave the way for the restoration of a civilian government. A constitutional amendment was passed by national referendum in December 1962, restoring a strong presidential system while limiting presidential office to two four-year terms. When President Yun resigned in March 1962, Gen. Park was appointed acting President.

In January 1963 the revolutionaries formed the Democratic Republican Party and nominated Gen. Park as its presidential candidate. In mid-March a plot to overthrow the military government was allegedly uncovered and the acting President announced that a plebiscite would be held on a four-year extension of military rule. The reaction was strongly negative, and in July civilian government within a year was promised. In August Gen. Park retired from the army and became an active presidential candidate of the Democratic Republican Party. Freedom of political activity was restored for those not charged with past political crimes.

The opposition forces were badly split. Former President Yun eventually emerged as the candidate of the Civil Rule Party. The election in October gave Gen. Park victory by a narrow margin and National Assembly elections, held in November, gave a major victory to the Democratic Republican Party. Civilian constitutional rule was restored on December 17th, 1963, with the inauguration of President Park and the convening of the Assembly.

The Third Republic, 1963-72

Although a civil Government was established in 1963, all important positions in the Government were occupied by ex-military men, and the National Assembly was completely controlled by the Democratic Republican Party, headed by President Park. Although considerable economic development was achieved under the two Five-Year Plans (1962–66 and 1967–71), the Third Republic faced many difficulties at home. In March 1964 large student demonstrations broke out in Seoul, protesting against the negotiations with Japan to establish a normal relationship between the two countries. Despite demonstrations in opposition, the Government dispatched troops to South Viet-Nam in co-operation with the U.S.A., declared martial law in June 1965 in the Seoul area, and concluded the treaty which established normal relations with Japan as more troops were sent to South Viet-Nam.

In order to promote a parliamentary democracy, if not to weaken the power of the ruling party, minor parties formed a coalition party named the New Democratic Party in January 1967. However, in the May 1967 presidential election, the incumbent president defeated Yun Po-son, nominee of the New Democratic Party, again by a large margin, and the ruling party won a substantial majority of seats in the National Assembly. When election irregularities involving the ruling party in the presidential and National Assembly elections were uncovered, the opposition New Democratic Party demanded the nullification of the election results and called for a new election. Failing in that, its members refused to participate in Assembly action.

The popularity of the New Democratic Party grew steadily in urban areas, which contained the more educated voters, and the threats from North Korea increased considerably. Due to these factors and the realization that more time was needed for President Park to achieve the aims of "national regeneration", the ruling party proposed a constitutional amendment in order to allow the incumbent President to serve another (third) term of office. Consequently, in September 1969, while the members of the opposition party were boycotting the session, the National Assembly adopted an amendment to the constitution, allowing for a third term of office by President Park. A national referendum held in October approved the amendment. In the seventh presidential election, held in April 1971, President Park defeated Kim Dae-jung, nominee of the New Democratic Party, by a narrow margin.

In 1971 the Government launched the New Community Movement, aiming at the development of rural areas. Its plans were to improve the economy, promote social movement and elevate the living standards of people in rural areas. It accomplished much in the modernization of villages, economic growth of farm population, transport and sanitation in rural regions, and the increase of scientific knowledge for farming. A drive to achieve the "green revolution" also accompanied the Movement.

On July 4th, 1972, Seoul and Pyongyang simultaneously issued a statement which announced the opening of dialogue between North and South to achieve national unification by peaceful means without outside intervention. The announcement stunned the people, but their hopes for the restoration of the unity of the divided country rose. The North-South Co-ordinating Committee was established for the purpose.

The Fourth Republic, 1972-79

The two Five-Year Plans (1962–71) had laid a good foundation, and the economic future of the nation seemed brighter. The sudden changes in the international situation, due to the Sino-American détente and new developments in North-South relations since 1972, provided the ruling party with convenient pretexts to perpetuate, if not prolong, President Park's rule. As a result, the Government proclaimed martial law in October 1972, dissolved the National Assembly, and suspended the 1962 constitution in order to pave the way for Park's continued rule. A new constitution was proposed by the Extraordinary State Council and approved by the people in November, in a national referendum in which 91 per cent of the voters participated.

The new constitution, known as the *Yusin* (Revitalizing Reform) Constitution, gave the President greatly expanded powers, authorizing him to issue emergency decrees and establish the National Conference for Unification (NCU) as an electoral college. In December 1972 the NCU, with 2,359 members, was established, and it elected Park to serve a new six-year term. Thus the Fourth Republic emerged.

The elections held in February 1973 elected 146 members of the new National Assembly to serve a six-year term. The ruling Democratic Republican Party took 71 seats while 52 candidates of the New Democratic Party and 21 independent candidates were elected. Meanwhile, a new political movement named *Yujonghoe* (Political Fraternity for the Revitalizing Reform) was set up as a sister organization of the ruling party, and 73 of its members were elected by the NCU on the President's recommendation to serve a three-year term in the National Assembly. Thus, President Park was assured of an absolute majority of 144 legislators who were loyal to him in the National Assembly.

South Korea witnessed a tremendous economic growth during the period of the Third Five-Year Plan (1972–76) and the Fourth Five-Year Plan (which began in 1977), accompanied by rapid industrialization and an increase in per caput income. It also brought about a remarkable educational and cultural development. The South Koreans called their economic achievement the "Miracle on the Han River".

However, the ever-growing autocracy and bureaucratism of the Government, coupled with corruption, irregularities and favouritism on the part of the Government and the ruling party, caused the democratic movement to suffer as freedom of speech and the press and other civil rights were repressed or violated. Consequently, frustration mounted and the number of political dissidents increased.

The Fourth Republic encountered an increasing amount of domestic and foreign problems. In July 1973 a group of dissidents publicly advocated the end of the "dictatorial government" for the sake of democracy, and in October students held a rally and demanded an end to "fascist intelligence rule and government infringement of basic human rights". In 1973 the kidnapping of Kim Dae-jung, the 1971 presidential candidate who had been campaigning against Park in the U.S.A. and Japan, from Tokyo to Korea by agents of Korean CIA created serious problems for Seoul with Tokyo and Washington.

Anti-government agitation and demands for the abolition of the 1972 *Yusin* Constitution continued to cause political instability in 1974 and after. To cope with the situation, the Government proclaimed four emergency decrees in the spring of 1974, banning all anti-government activities and agitation for constitutional reform, making the political situation only more unstable. In the tense situation, President Park's wife was killed in August in an assassination attempt against Park by a North Korean agent from Japan. In the following two months, the four emergency decrees were repealed, but the opposition NDP and others relentlessly pressed for constitutional reform and the release of political prisoners.

The Presidential Emergency Measure for Safeguarding National Security, which was proclaimed in May 1975, only antagonized the dissidents more, although it was ostensibly proclaimed to strengthen national security against a mounting threat of aggression from North Korea, following the fall of South Viet-Nam. The new measure imposed further prohibition on opponents of the 1972 constitution, banned student demonstrations, and outlawed public defamation of the current Emergency Measure and the Government.

The Fourth Republic successfully completed the Third Five-Year Plan (1972–76) and the Fourth Five-Year Plan for 1977–81 was announced. A new Ministry of Energy and Resources was created in 1977, and the economy of the Republic, despite the fuel shortage and growing inflationary trends, seemed promising. However, political turbulence lingered on as the hopes of the people for more freedom and rights grew dim in a tightly controlled political situation. More voices were heard in favour of constitutional reform and the end of autocratic rule. Many dissidents were imprisoned.

In March 1978 the three major dissident political leaders issued a joint statement, demanding the abolition of the 1972 constitution and the restoration of complete human rights. This was followed by a series of student demonstrations. The re-election in May 1978 of President Park to serve another six-year term, by the new members of the NCU, only made the situation worse as the restlessness of young college students, supported by the opposition party, caused greater political turmoil. The popularity of President Park and the ruling party rapidly declined despite their economic accomplishments.

In the elections held in December 1978 for 154 of the 231 members of the National Assembly, the DRP managed to elect 68 members, but the opposition NDP narrowed the gap by electing 61 assemblymen. The DRP received only 31.7 per cent of the votes while the NDP received 32.9 per cent, but the election of 22 independent candidates was a clear display of the voters' displeasure with both major parties. Being aware of the growing political and economic problems, President Park carried out a major Cabinet reshuffle in December 1978, and in that month and in May 1979 he released 1,004 prisoners, many of whom were violators of the emergency measures, including Kim Dae-jung. Some 2,870 prisoners received a reduction of their prison terms. However, the voice of the dissidents grew louder in March and May 1979.

From June 1979 until the complete military takeover of the Government in May 1980, South Korea encountered critical political, social and economic problems. In July the opposition NDP elected Kim Young-sam as its new president, and he in turn accelerated anti-government activities and increased his demand for human rights. Kim's anti-government speeches and press interviews led to the suspension of his presidency, and then to his expulsion from the National Assembly. All the NDP legislators tendered their resignations in protest in October. A power struggle within the NDP ensued, although the resignation notices were returned. Some conciliatory steps taken by President Park, such as the release of more political and "model" prisoners in the summer of 1979, did not satisfy the dissidents and students, who intensified their demands for constitutional reform.

The student protests led to a serious uprising in Pusan and other southern cities in mid-October. The situation became more critical as college students in Seoul prepared for a large-scale uprising towards the end of October. In the midst of the crisis, Kim Chae-kyu, director of the Korean CIA, shot and killed President Park on October 26th. The country faced an unprecedented national crisis for the first time in 20 years. Prime Minister Choi Kyu-ha was named acting President as martial law was proclaimed. Kim Jong-pil took over the presidency of the ruling DRP. The cancellation of Emergency Decree No. 9 was carried out in December, and the termination of the *Yusin* rule was effected. Some 1,640 more prisoners were pardoned in December.

On the diplomatic front, the Fourth Republic encountered serious problems with the U.S.A. and Japan: the kidnapping of Kim Dae-jung in 1973 and the suppression of basic human rights by the Government constituted the main causes. The visit to Korea by President Gerald Ford in November 1974 improved the relations between the two nations somewhat as it boosted the morale of the Korean Government. Negotiations between Seoul and Tokyo toward the end of 1974, in connection with the kidnapping of Kim, relaxed tension. However, basic issues between Seoul, Tokyo and Washington were not solved.

The election of President Carter in 1976 and his stand for human rights revived tension between Seoul and Washington. The announcement made in 1977 by the Carter administration of its intention to withdraw all U.S. ground troops from South Korea within four or five years created serious problems. To make matters worse, the exposure of a bribery scandal, involving the former Korean Ambassador to the U.S.A. and a Korean rice dealer in Washington, strained U.S.-Korean relations further. The "Koreagate" issues made American critics more hostile to Seoul as U.S. Congressional investigations into them were carried out. The matter was not settled until 1978. However, the movement of anti-South Korean critics in the U.S.A. did not stop until the death of President Park.

The establishment of normal diplomatic relations between the U.S.A. and the People's Republic of China, together with the participation in April 1979 of a U.S. team in an international table tennis tournament in Pyongyang (in which South Korea could not participate because of North Korea's refusal to issue visas), created tension between Seoul andWashington. However, Carter's visit to Seoul in June 1979, and the assurance given by the American Government regarding the suspension of the troop withdrawal, led to a relaxation of tension. Be that as it may, American criticism of the lack of human rights in South Korea, and of the ways in which the Seoul Government dealt with the rebels in the southern part of Korea, continuously troubled the Government, as did anti-government activities by pro-North Korean Japanese.

The Interim Period, 1979-81

The NCU elected Choi Kyu-ha as the new President of the Republic on December 6th, 1979, and a new Cabinet, headed by Shin Hyun-hwack, emerged. President Choi stated in his inaugural address that a new constitution would be offered to the people for their approval as soon as possible, and that he had no intention of running for the presidency under the new constitution.

The assassin Kim and his accomplices were given death sentences by a military court martial, and they were executed in May 1980. Meanwhile, a power struggle within the DRP, as well as within the military, developed. Within the military this erupted into a coup on December 12th, led by Lt.-Gen. Chun Doo-hwan, Commander of the Defence Security Command, who removed the martial law commander and made himself a new "strong man" in the country. The ex-Army Chief, Gen. Chong Sung-hwa, was imprisoned and Kim Kye-won, who was formerly secretary to President Park and was implicated in the President's murder, was imprisoned for life.

The cry for an immediate adoption of a new constitution grew strong as the demoralized DRP, under the leadership of Kim Jong-pil, made attempts to maintain its power. Kim Young-sam, who resumed the presidency of the NDP, made various efforts to win the support of Kim Dae-jung, who was freed from prison, regained full citizenship in February and once again became actively involved in politics. However, Kim Dae-jung refused to return to the NDP, and announced that he would form a new political party, and run for the presidency against the other two Kims—Kim Jong-pil and Kim Young-sam.

Both the opposition NDP and students became impatient with the slow progress in political reform, causing chaos at nearly all college campuses. Conditions further deteriorated in April as rallies became more disorderly, with more violent anti-government agitation by the students and the NDP. The appointment of Gen. Chun Doo-hwan as acting director of the Korean CIA in April only inflamed them more. Kim Dae-jung and Kim Young-sam issued a joint statement demanding the immediate end of martial law.

More campus rallies followed in early May, demanding the immediate end of martial law, the adoption of a new constitution without delay, and the resignation of Gen. Chun. Tens of thousands of students marched into the streets in mid-May, clashing with the police. Troops were mobilized, and on May 17th martial law was extended to the entire country as Decree No. 10 was proclaimed. Under this, some 30 political leaders, including Kim Jong-pil and Kim Dae-jung, were arrested for interrogation. Kim Young-sam was put under house arrest and the National Assembly was closed, as were colleges, while all political activities, assemblages and public demonstrations were banned. In spite of these restrictions, the rebellious students and dissidents in the city of Kwangju in South Cholla Province (the home province of Kim Dae-jung) took over the city on May 19th, after a few days of bloody clashes with paratroopers and police. They demanded the immediate lifting of martial law and the resignation of Gen. Chun.

On May 20th all the members of the Cabinet tendered their resignations, and a new Cabinet, headed by Acting Prime Minister Park Choong-hoon, emerged in an extremely unstable situation. The newly arrived troops stormed the city of Kwangju on May 27th and recaptured it from the rebels after brief fighting. Meanwhile, as riots spread to other cities in South Cholla Province, the Martial Law Command brought charges against Kim Dae-jung for alleged seditious activities and a plot to overthrow the Government by force. He was also accused of instigating student uprisings and the Kwangju rebellion.

As an aftermath of the closing of the National Assembly, a council known as the Special Committee for National Security Measures (SCNSM) was formed on May 31st. President Choi became its chairman but real power was in the hands of Gen. Chun and 15 other army generals, appointed by him to the SCNSM. With the establishment of the SCNSM, Gen. Chun resigned as acting director of the Korean CIA but, as chairman of the standing committee of the SCNSM, he exercised absolute power. Under tight political control and stern social "purification" measures by the SCNSM, stability began to return as students remained inactive. However, anti-government sentiment among reform-minded people remained strong as economic problems grew. The rate of unemployment rose, as did the price of commodities.

President Choi suddenly stepped down on August 16th "to put an end to the unhappy political history by establishing the precedent of peaceful transfer of power", and "to provide a historic turning point for the building of a new, happy community of stability, morality and prosperity". Immediately after his resignation, the movement to elect Gen. Chun, who had recently retired from active military duty after being promoted to the rank of four-star general, began. On August 27th, 1980, the electoral college (NCU) elected Chun to be the next president, and on September 2nd he was inaugurated. On that day an all-civilian Cabinet, headed by Nam Duck-woo, emerged. President Chun pledged that he would build a "democratic welfare society" in the 1980s under a new "efficient Constitution", and thereby made it known that it was his intention to run for the presidency under the new constitution. Meanwhile, Kim Dae-jung was given a death sentence. In the middle of September, all colleges and universities which had been closed since May were re-opened in an uncertain political climate.

The National Assembly, which had long been closed, held its final session in late September, when, after approving the appointment of Premier Nam, it went out of existence. On September 30th the Government made public the draft of the new constitution and on October 22nd a national referendum was held to approve it. Meanwhile, the Legislative Council for National Security was created, replacing the National Assembly which, with the SCNSM, was dissolved. All members of the new Council were appointed by President Chun.

To "purify" politics and remove politicians who were regarded as responsible for political turmoil in the past, the Government carried out intensive investigations and purged some 835 politicians in November. About 250 of them were exonerated but a large number of former leaders of the two parties were not. Some key political leaders of both parties, such as Kim Jong-pil and Kim Young-sam, were not only deprived of rights to participate in the political process, but were jailed during the investigation period. They were released only after they agreed to give up their properties, which were regarded as profits of corruption and irregularities. Although released from jail, they were put under house arrest.

The popularity of President Chun rose following his statement on January 12th, 1981, when he invited Kim Il-sung of North Korea to visit South Korea and indicated that he would visit North Korea without any conditions if he were invited by Kim Il-sung. His visit to the United States, immediately after the inauguration of President Ronald Reagan, also increased his popularity among the people. Whereas his campaigns against political corruption, bribery, favouritism and social evils were welcomed by the people, the announcement made by the Reagan administration during Chun's visit, regarding the cancellation of the American plan to withdraw U.S. ground troops from South Korea, lifted his prestige further as well as raising the spirit of the nation.

The Fifth Republic, 1981-

The partial lifting of martial law was announced on January 10th, 1981. With this, new political parties were organized and a new electoral college of 5,278 members was created by popular election in February. On February 25th the new electoral college elected the incumbent President as the 12th President of the Republic, to serve a single seven-year term of office under the new constitution, which banned re-election.

On March 3rd President Chun was inaugurated, and the Fifth Republic emerged. In his inaugural address, he re-affirmed his pledge to build a "democratic welfare society", and he promised that he would do his utmost to free the people and the nation from what he called "three great evils": the threats of war, political repression and abuse of power, and poverty. A new Cabinet was formed, but Dr. Nam remained Prime Minister. A new Ministry of Labour was established in April, and a major reorganization of radio-TV networks, newspaper presses and large corporations was carried out under the direction of the new President.

Elections were held on March 25th, electing 276 legislators of the new National Assembly. The Democratic Justice Party, a government party headed by President Chun, won 151 seats and became the majority party, while the Democratic Korea Party won 81 seats. With the establishment of the new National Assembly, which held its special session in early May, the Legislative Council for National Security was dissolved. The South Korean CIA was renamed the Agency for National Security Planning in April 1981. Meanwhile, a large-scale replacement of old judicial officials at all levels by younger men was carried out in May. Nearly all judges who had been closely associated with the previous regimes were replaced.

The future seemed bright for the Fifth Republic as signs of economic recovery appeared in the spring. The G.N.P. growth in 1981 was 5 per cent, compared with less than 6 per cent in 1980. President Chun's visits to the five member nations of ASEAN in July strengthened the ties between South Korea and the South-East Asian nations, and the selection of Seoul as the site for the 1988 Olympic Games added to the prestige of the new Government. The Fifth Five-Year Economic Development Plan was announced in August, with the aim of achieving an average annual G.N.P. growth of 7.6 per cent between 1982 and 1986.

The confidence and expectations of the people in the new Government increased somewhat, but the Republic faced many problems. Inflation grew worse and new economic problems arose as economic recession abroad led to a decline in exports. Student riots, accompanied by some violence, erupted in October and November.

Facing these problems, the Government carried out a Cabinet reshuffle in January 1982, when Yoo Chang-soon, a former politician, became Premier and four ministers were replaced. Some accommodations to the wishes of the students and others were made by the Government. In January and March of 1982, the regulations for hair style and uniforms for students were abolished and the 36-year-old midnight curfew was lifted, except in the area near the demilitarized zone and along the coasts, in early January. In March, some 2,860 prisoners were granted amnesty, including the reduction of the life term for Kim Dae-jung to a 20-year term. However, political restrictions on former politicians were not lifted, nor were concrete measures taken to relax the campus atmosphere, or to promote stronger support of the people for the new administration.

The political climate became turbulent again in the spring of 1982. In March a small group of students burned down the American Cultural Center in Pusan as an expression of anti-American feelings, and students in Seoul and other cities carried out anti-government and anti-American demonstrations in April, May and June. In April the Korean Christian Action Organization, a joint body of Catholic and Protestant clergymen, issued a protest note against the Government, including a demand for the recall of the U.S. ambassador and the commander of the U.S. Armed Forces in Korea. Be that as it may, the centennial of the signing of the first American-Korean treaty in 1882 was widely celebrated, both in South Korea and America.

A policeman who ran amok and killed some 56 villagers in the southern part of the country in April, and a financial scandal involving relatives of the wife of President Chun, precipitated a serious political crisis in May. As a result, the Home Minister was replaced in April, followed by a large-scale Cabinet reshuffle in May, in which 11 ministers were replaced. In June the Director of the National Security Planning and the Foreign Minister, along with top leaders of the ruling Democratic Justice Party, were replaced. Meanwhile, Kim Young-sam, former leader of the now defunct New Democratic Party, who predicted the fall of President Chun by the Autumn of 1982, was put under house arrest in early June.

The visit to Seoul of U.S. Vice-President George Bush in late April boosted the morale of the government somewhat, but it faced an increasing number of domestic and foreign problems as the confidence of the people in the Government declined sharply as a result of the biggest financial scandal in the history of the Republic. The inability of the Government to secure a $600 million loan from Japan for the recently announced fifth Five-Year Economic Development Plan, together with general discontent among the people, caused a decline in the popularity of the new Government.

Editorial Note: In a Cabinet reshuffle on June 24th, 1982, President Chun dismissed the Prime Minister, Yoo Chang-soon, and replaced him by Kim Sang-hyup, President of Korea University.

NORTH KOREA

Strong nationalist leadership with potentially large popular support was at hand in North Korea when the Second World War ended. It consisted chiefly of democratically-inclined, Western missionary-educated individuals, of whom the most outstanding leader was Cho Man-sik. In August 1945, the Japanese governor in Pyongyang handed over control to Cho and a newly-formed Provincial People's Committee. In August Soviet troops reached Pyongyang, accepted the legitimacy of the Committee, and approved Cho as chairman of the Five Provinces Administrative Bureau, set up to act as the indigenous government organ for North Korea.

In September, Kim Il-sung, a young communist, who had led a guerrilla group of Korean communists in south-eastern Manzhou, returned to Korea with Soviet troops. Kim, however, had to cope with the "domestic" communists who challenged his "Kapsan" or "partisan" faction. In the early power struggle among the communists, Hyon Chun-hyok, the leader of the "domestic" faction, was assassinated in September 1945.

Three groups of communists returned to North Korea after the liberation from Japan: one associated with the Soviet Army known as the "Soviet" faction, one known as the "Kapsan" or "partisan" faction, and one from Yanan, in China, under the leadership of Kim Tu-bong of the Korean Independence League. In early October, Kim Il-sung formed the North Korean Central Bureau of the Korean Communist Party in order to build his political position. A Marxist, known to and apparently trusted by the Soviet occupation authority, Kim was given covert Soviet support.

Cho Man-sik organized the Korean Democratic Party which received the backing of the majority of the people, but his uncompromising stand against the Moscow plan for a five-year trusteeship of the Allied powers, however, led to his downfall in January 1946. He was promptly placed under house arrest. Many members of the Korean Democratic Party fled to South Korea.

After the departure of the nationalists, a North Korean Provisional People's Committee was established in February 1946 with Kim Il-sung as Chairman and Kim Tu-bong as Vice-Chairman. The Soviets gave government status to the Committee. Kim Tu-bong formed the New People's Party in March to expand his power base, and managed to increase his party's membership. In July 1946 the North Korean Central Bureau of the Korean Communist Party and the New People's Party merged to form the North Korean Workers' Party, with Kim Tu-bong as its Chairman and Kim Il-sung as its Vice-Chairman. Real power, however, was in the hands of the latter.

In the spring of 1947 the Supreme People's Assembly was established as the highest legislative organ in North Korea, and the Assembly in turn established an executive branch called the Central People's Committee. The Committee's first major act was to direct land reforms. No real attempts were made to establish collective farms and the land which was distributed to landless peasants became the private property of the cultivators. It was not until the end of the Korean War in 1953 that the agricultural "co-operativization" programme was inaugurated. Land reform was followed by the nationalization of industry, transport, communications and financial institutions.

In early 1948 Pak Hon-yong and leaders of his South Korean Workers' (Communist) Party, fled from the south when the party was outlawed by the American occupation authority. Pak Hon-yong, who had been enjoying strong support from the "domestic" faction felt that he, instead of Kim Il-sung, should lead the movement in Korea. However, he was unable to achieve his objectives, and he grudgingly accepted a subordinate position to that of Kim Il-sung.

The Democratic People's Republic of Korea

After refusing to allow the United Nations Temporary Commission on Korea to visit North Korea and conduct elections, Kim Il-sung established a separate pro-Soviet state there. In August elections were held in the north for a new Supreme People's Assembly. The newly created Assembly drafted a constitution, ratified it on September 8th, and proclaimed the Democratic People's Republic of Korea (DPRK) on September 9th. Kim Il-sung was named Premier, while Pak Hon-yong was made Vice-Premier and Minister for Foreign Affairs.

In June 1949 the merger of the North Korean Workers' Party and the South Korean Workers' Party brought about a unified communist party, the Korean Workers' Party, with Kim Il-sung as its Chairman and Pak Hon-yong as its Vice-Chairman.

The establishment of the DPRK made the temporary military division of Korea a permanent political partition. The Soviet Union announced the withdrawal of its troops from North Korea, completing the process in December 1949. However, a large number of Soviet advisers in various fields remained.

During 1950 North Korea substantially increased the size and strength of its armed forces with Soviet supplies. In June 1950 the North Korean invasion of the south initiated the bloody Korean War (*see* above), inflicting great damage on both sides. During and after the unsuccessful attempt to conquer South Korea, Kim Il-sung purged many of his enemies, including Pak Hon-yong.

Conflict among the surviving communist leaders, however, did not end and Kim Tu-bong, who survived a series of purges, remained a formidable figure. Kim Il-sung's economic reconstruction programme, which emphasized the development of heavy industry, met strong opposition. The debate lasted until 1956, when Tu-bong fell from power. Meanwhile, the Yanan faction attacked the personality cult of Kim Il-sung; he counter-attacked, forcing some Yanan communists to flee to China. China and the U.S.S.R. effected a temporary reconciliation, but leaders of the Yanan faction were systematically relegated to less important posts or eased entirely out of power. By 1958 it ceased to pose any further threat.

Following the announcement of the 1972 Joint North-South agreement to open dialogue for peaceful unification of the country, the Korean Workers' Party proposed amendments to the constitution. General elections were held in December to choose deputies to the Fifth Supreme People's Assembly. The newly elected representatives adopted a socialist constitution and elected Kim Il-sung and Kim Il as President and Premier respectively. For the first time, the North Korean Constitution stated that the capital was Pyongyang and not Seoul. It also created the Central People's Committee, headed by the President, as the highest organ of state, and the State Administrative Council, headed by the Premier.

In 1973 North Korea gained observer status at the United Nations. The observer status nullified both the branding of North Korea as an aggressor in 1950 and the view that the Government of South Korea was the only lawful government in Korea. Both Koreas were invited to the UN General Assembly in November 1973 for a debate on the Korean question. North Korea was also given membership in the United Nations Conference on Trade and Development in May 1973.

In February 1974 the Central Committee of the Korean Workers' Party launched the "Three Great Revolutions": ideological, technical and cultural. It emphasized the promotion of a self-orientated, self-reliant and independent ideology, or *Juche* thought. Kim Il-sung's birthday was declared a new national holiday. The Supreme People's Assembly, meeting in March, proposed in a letter to the U.S. Congress the conclusion of a peace treaty between the U.S.A. and North Korea to replace the Korean Armistice Agreement of 1953. It also advocated the removal of all foreign troops from South Korea.

The Korean Workers' Party reorganized the structure of the cabinet and reshuffled its membership twice in 1974. The seventh vice-premiership went to Ho Dam, concurrently Minister for Foreign Affairs. Kim Yong-ju, brother of Kim Il-sung, who had been regarded as heir apparent, was demoted in the party hierarchy, while Kim Il-sung's only surviving son, Kim Chong-il, rose in rank as a possible successor to his father. Significantly, a military leader, Gen. O Chin-u, also rose in rank within the party.

One of North Korea's major objectives in 1975 was the intensification of diplomatic activity to strengthen ties between non-aligned nations. In early 1975, Kim Il-sung visited Beijing, but failed to gain China's encouragement for his aggressive plan against South Korea. Subsequent visits by Kim to Mauritania, Bulgaria and Yugoslavia consolidated the DPRK's diplomatic objectives but no invitation from Moscow was received. The ministerial conference of the non-aligned nations in Lima, Peru, voted to accept North Korea's application for participation.

In 1976 the Pyongyang regime suffered a series of embarrassments, when narcotics trade and widespread usurpation of diplomatic privileges by North Korean diplomatists in Scandinavia and elsewhere were exposed. As a result, a number of North Korean diplomatists were expelled from Denmark, Sweden, Norway and the Soviet Union. Moreover, many creditor-nations threatened to cut trade links and refused to make more loans to North Korea, when it was unable to pay even interest on loans. Pyongyang's efforts to secure loans and aid from the Soviet Union had only a limited success.

Internal power struggles, the mysterious deaths of a few key leaders, and the naming of Kim Il-sung's son, Chong-il, as his successor, were widely reported. Kim Il-sung appointed two new vice-premiers in December 1976. Pyongyang rejected a proposal by

Dr. Henry Kissinger, then U.S. Secretary of State, for a "phased approach" to solve the Korean problem. However, it increased its efforts to establish a peace treaty and relations with the United States. Meanwhile, it refused to re-open the North-South dialogue.

The political turbulence which developed in 1976 continued to cause serious domestic problems in 1977. An unconfirmed newspaper report said that in September 1977 there had been an attempt to assassinate Kim Chong-il. He had not been seen between July 1977 and July 1978. A large-scale purge of anti-Kim Chong-il elements, including Gen. Yi Yong-mu, former Secretary of the Political Bureau of the Ministry of Defence, was reported to have been carried out.

North Korea announced in September 1975 that the Six-Year Plan (1971–76) had been completed ahead of schedule, but it was not until 1977 that most of its targets were met. Economic problems, particularly the inability to make payments on foreign loans, commercial credits, and interests, together with the shortage of imported and domestically produced raw materials, troubled the Pyongyang regime. A critical shortage of food and commodities was reported. In 1977, North Korea signed a new trade pact with China, and an economic and technical co-operation agreement with the U.S.S.R. It was reported that the Soviet Union had made large shipments of military goods to North Korea and had sent technical advisers in 1977.

The adoption in September 1977 of the Theses on Socialist Education by the Central Committee of the Korean Workers' Party was a clear indication that efforts which it had made to indoctrinate the youth with Kim Il-sung's *Juche* ideology had not brought about satisfactory results. The new plan was reported to have been adopted to strengthen the loyalty to Kim Il-sung and the Party.

North Korea welcomed the U.S. plan to withdraw its troops from South Korea, but when it became known that the intention was to withdraw only ground troops within four or five years, and to reinforce South Korean military and U.S. air strength in South Korea, Kim Il-sung launched bitter attacks against it. The shooting down of an unarmed U.S. Army helicopter in July 1977 by North Korean troops at the eastern end of the demilitarized zone created a serious war threat in Korea. However, although the apologies and regrets between U.S. President Carter and Kim Il-sung, and the prompt return of the three dead and one wounded American crewmen to the UN Command, settled the immediate issue, North Korea resumed its anti-U.S. campaign. A new military code of conduct was adopted, and in August 1977, North Korea announced the establishment of a 50 nautical mile (93 km.) military sea boundary and a 200 nautical mile (370 km.) economic zone in the surrounding seas.

Following the election for 579 members of the Supreme People's Assembly in November 1977, the cabinet structure was revised. The number of Vice-Presidents was increased from two to three; Lee Jong-ok, an economist, was named Premier; former Premier Pak Sung-chul was promoted to Vice-President; and the number of members of the Central People's Committee was reduced from 28 to 15.

The new Seven-Year Plan (1978–84) was adopted by the Central Committee of the Korean Workers' Party in January 1978 and promulgated by the Supreme People's Assembly in April. The Party designated April 25th as the new founding day of the People's Army, and published an open letter to party members, urging them to increase the nation's productive capacities and strengthen their loyalty to the Party. Changes in the Party ranks were reported in September 1978, including the appointment of Kang Hui-wun, a relative of Kim Il-sung, as a Vice-Premier.

The most important ideological-political campaign of 1978 was for the strengthening of *Juche* thought. A renewed drive to promote the Three Revolutions (ideological, technical, and cultural) was reportedly led by Kim Chong-il. A new Socialist Labour Law was promulgated in April 1978 which called for a new way of life for the workers—eight hours of work, eight hours of rest, and eight hours of study of Kim Il-sung's *Juche* thought.

Under an ordinance of the Central People's Committee in April 1979, North Korea carried out a monetary reform, whereby all old monies issued at the time of the first monetary reform in 1959 must be exchanged for new monies of the same value, and all surplus funds of individuals and organizations must be deposited in the government banks. The reform was designed to increase bank deposits, thereby enabling the Government to have additional funds without issuing more currency, and to readjust and control commodity prices. The new trade agreements which North Korea signed with the Soviet Union, China and other socialist countries in 1978 and early 1979 were aimed at supplementing the Soviet assistance given to the new Seven-Year Plan, the aims of which are to expand the production of electricity, aluminium and steel, trucks and cargo vessels, and heavy machinery at the Taean plant near Pyongyang.

Despite economic difficulties, North Korea increased its military spending and expanded its ground forces. The officially stated military budget for 1979 was U.S. $1,500 million, or 15.2 per cent of the total budget of $9,600 million. However, intelligence sources estimated that North Korea's 1979 military expenditure would exceed $3,000 million. Reliable sources indicated that North Korea's ground troops increased from 430,000 in 1978 to 600,000 by the spring of 1979, and that the number of tanks increased from 1,950 in 1978 to 2,600 in early 1979. It was reported also that North Korea was to receive over 20 Soviet MiG 23s, and some 100 North Korean pilots have been trained in Libya to handle the new Soviet fighter planes.

The Pyongyang visits of China's Premier Hua Guofeng and Vice-Premier Deng Xiaoping in 1978 and the new trade agreement between Pyongyang and Beijing seem to have improved Sino-North Korean ties. China reportedly promised to supply more petroleum and greater economic assistance. Pyongyang dealt cautiously with the new Sino-American relationship and, while criticizing the Vietnamese invasion of Kampuchea, eschewed any comments on China's punitive war against Viet-Nam.

The new trade agreement between Moscow and Pyongyang, Vice-President Pak Sung-chul's visit to Moscow in January 1979, and increasing contacts between Soviet and North Korean military leaders seemed to indicate a growing solidarity between the two countries. North Korea provided special privileges to the Soviet Union in the port of Najin on the north-eastern coast of the Japan Sea, making it a Soviet "leased" territory and a Soviet naval base.

The 19th session of the Fifth Party Congress of the Korean Workers' Party was held in December, and it adopted a resolution to convene the Sixth Party Congress in October 1980. The plan to hold the next Congress that soon led to the rise of speculation that some significant changes would be made in the autumn of 1980. A woman was named Finance Minister by the fourth session of the Sixth Supreme People's Assembly, which met in April 1980.

In August 1980 the State Council was reorganized into seven committees and 31 ministries, with the creation of five new ministries in economic and scientific fields. The military training programme for students was expanded and the number of student-soldiers at college level grew to 960,000. Efforts made by Pyongyang to gain more support from the Soviet Union and the People's Republic of China failed. Meanwhile, North Korea's diplomatic relations with Iraq, Syria and Libya were severed after Pyongyang supported Iran when the Iran-Iraqi war broke out.

After conducting intense campaigns to select reliable and loyal supporters of Kim Il-sung's son as delegates, the 6th Congress of the Korean Workers' Party, attended by 3,220 full delegates and half that number of candidate delegates, met in early October 1980 for the first time since 1970. After accepting various reports submitted by the Party leaders, it made many significant structural and personnel changes in the Party hierarchy. Although Kim Chung-il, son of Kim Il-sung, was not officially designated as successor to his father as anticipated, he became a key member of many crucial committees in the Party.

A new five-member Standing Committee of the Political Committee (Politburo) of the Central Committee of the Party was established, and Kim Il-sung became its chairman, thus strengthening the concentration of power in the hands of a few. Many new members of the Central Committee and its sub-committees were the supporters of Kim Chung-il, and it was reported that those who opposed his succession to power were removed from other key positions in the Party, Government and military. The Party Congress approved the appointment of Kim Chung-il in several key committees, in which he was the youngest member.

In April 1981 elections were held for members of provincial, city and county People's Assemblies in the usual manner: one candidate named by the Party for each position and a 100 per cent turnout of voters.

In February 1982, 615 new members of the Supreme People's Assembly were elected, and the seventh Assembly emerged in early April. It approved the re-appointment of the president, three vice-presidents, premier and 13 vice-premiers, but, contrary to expectations, it failed to name Kim Il-sung's son, Kim Chung-il, as vice-president to be his 70 year-old father's future successor.

Shortly before the convening of the Supreme People's Assembly, the Central Committee of the Korean Workers' Party met, followed by a joint conference of the Central Committee of the Party and the Supreme People's Assembly in the middle of April. Both meetings failed to solve the succession question. Meanwhile, the power struggle between the supporters of Kim Chung-il (40) and the backers of Kim Pyung-il (28), who is the only son of Kim Il-sung's current wife, became intense. Kim Chung-il's Red Guards were said to been have formed.

While the political turmoil surrounding the succession question increased instability in North Korea, several armed clashes between the military and workers occurred in Chongjin, in the north-east, in September 1981, followed in June 1982 by civil disturbances in Namp'o, near Pyongyang, involving Koreans who went to North Korea from Japan. Some 500 workers were reported to have been killed in the clashes in the north-eastern regions while many fled into Soviet territory. It was reported that an estimated 105,000 political dissidents were held at several concentration camps. Of these, some 23,000 were Koreans who went to North Korea from Japan some years ago.

The relationship between Moscow and Pyongyang seemed to have deteriorated since June 1979, when the Soviet Union stopped its petroleum supplies to North Korea for unknown reasons. Then in February 1980 North Korea, along with Yugoslavia and Romania, refused to sign a communiqué of the Sofia meeting of the communist states, urging solidarity with the Afghan Government which had been installed with Soviet backing. North Korea, along with the People's Republic of China, disapproved of the invasion of Afghanistan by Soviet troops and of Soviet intervention in the internal affairs of that nation. The Communist Parties of North Korea and Italy had reaffirmed that they would pursue an independent policy line in January, and a delegation of the Italian Communist Party visited Pyongyang in February 1980. However, Kim Il-sung, who attended Marshal Tito's funeral, met Soviet President Leonid Brezhnev in Belgrade in May.

The relationship between Beijing and Pyongyang also became somewhat strained following the pressure which Beijing had exerted on North Korea in the wake of the death of President Park of South Korea. It was reported that Beijing warned Pyongyang that, if North Korea took any aggressive actions against the south and caused any difficulties between Beijing and Washington, China would cut off its petroleum supplies to North Korea. Pyongyang refrained from taking any provocative military actions against the south, but its official announcements and government-sponsored mass rallies gave their support to those rebellious anti-government movements of radical students and dissidents in the south who created a serious situation in April and May 1980.

For the first time in six years, North Korea's Premier visited Beijing in January 1981, seeking China's economic aid for the completion in 1984 of the second Seven-Year Plan that began in 1978. Beijing, like Moscow, failed to send its delegation to Kim Il-sung's 70th birthday celebration in April 1982. The failure of China and the Soviet Union to send their delegations was regarded as a rebuff to Kim Il-sung's attempts to make his son, Kim Chung-il, his successor and establish a dynastic rule in a communist state.

North-South Relations since 1972

The joint statement issued by both Seoul and Pyongyang on July 4th, 1972, did not bring about any tangible results in terms of paving the way for a peaceful unification or toward the relaxation of tension between them, although a few meetings were held between their representatives from July 1972. In 1973, however, Pyongyang unilaterally suspended the talks between North and South, and North Korean hostility towards the South and the United States revived, to become more intense. In 1975 the North Korean leader even attempted to secure assistance from the Chinese Communists and others to launch another invasion against South Korea in order to achieve what the North Vietnamese had accomplished in South Viet-Nam.

Meanwhile, North Korea made vain efforts to lead the United States to conclude a peace treaty with it, aiming at the replacement of the armistice agreement of 1953 to drive a wedge between the U.S.A. and South Korea, and removing American troops from the South. At the same time, North Korea took advantage of various opportunities to advocate its plan for the formation of a confederation of the two Korean states without outside help.

The killing of two American army officers by North Korean soldiers at Panmunjom in August 1976, North Korea's dispatch of several armed ships and commandoes into South Korea since 1974, the discovery (by UN forces) of three tunnels which North Koreans had dug under the demilitarized zone to facilitate rapid military infiltrations into the South, their refusal to issue visas to the South Korean table tennis team in 1979, the abduction of South Korean fishing vessels by the North Korean navy, the discovery of several underground pro-North Korean organizations and spy rings and the arrest of their leaders in 1979, 1980, and 1981, and the increased anti-South Korea agitations of North Korea all worsened the situation in the Korean peninsula.

North Korea rejected all appeals made by Seoul for the renewal of political talks, including those made in January 1979 by President Park. Efforts made in 1979 by the UN Secretary-General, Dr. Kurt Waldheim, also failed to change the attitudes of the North Koreans. In January 1980, however, North Korean Premier Li Jong-ok sent a letter to his counterpart in the South in which he called the Republic of Korea by its official name, proposing the earliest possible contacts between them. His letter was followed by others sent by North Korea's Vice-President Kim Il to South Korean political leaders, proposing the beginning of dialogue between the leaders of the two Korean states. A series of meetings, held at Panmunjom from March onwards by representatives of the two Governments to arrange the meetings of the premiers, failed to accomplish their objectives when the North Koreans presented certain unacceptable conditions to South Korea. Meanwhile, North Korea vainly attempted to instigate more violence and even a revolution in South Korea in 1980, in order to annex the South. In 1980 the rise of Kim Il-sung's son, who advocates a hard line against the South, made even more remote the chance of a renewal of talks, if not the relaxation of tension in the Korean peninsula. Pyongyang flatly rejected the proposal made by President Chun on January 12th, 1981, to visit North Korea and for Kim Il-sung to visit South Korea.

Meanwhile, South Korea experienced various provocations. The most serious case was the plot to assassinate South Korea's President Chun by pro-Pyongyang Koreans and their hired assassins in Canada during Chun's forthcoming visit to Canada. The plot was uncovered by the Canadian police in April 1982. Pyongyang denied any connections with the assassination plot but, since the main plotter fled from Canada to North Korea (and he and his father have been staunch and vocal supporters of Kim Il-sung), the assassination plot was reported to have been approved and financed by Pyongyang.

North Korea steadfastly refused to accept various proposals of the South Korean government for a peaceful solution of the Korean question suggested by President Chun in January 1982, as well as those of the Minister of Unification of South Korea in February. The South Korean proposals included, among others, the convening of a top-level meeting either in Seoul or in Pyongyang; the opening of the Seoul–Pyongyang highway; the opening of scenic areas along the east-central coast in North and South Korea for tourism; trade and the exchange of journalists between the north and south; and the establishment of a sports arena in the demilitarized zone to be used by both, as well as a joint fishing ground along the east-central coast. Meanwhile, the North Koreans proposed a conference of 100 overseas Koreans, and themselves named 50 "South Korean representatives".

ECONOMIC SURVEY OF NORTH KOREA

T. M. Burley

The land area of the Democratic People's Republic of Korea, 120,538 square kilometres, represents just over half the total area of Korea: its population, at 17.9 million in 1980, is thought to be growing by 2.4 per cent a year. About 75 per cent of the country is mountainous, and in 1979 the cultivable area was only 2,228,000 hectares or 18 per cent of the total. Farmland per household averages 1.6 hectares and a generally harsh climate restricts agriculture to one crop each year. The country's work force is greatly affected by the presence of some 600,000 persons in the armed forces (very few nations in the world have a bigger military deployment). The work force in 1980 was estimated at 6.3 million, of which rural activities account for about 40 per cent.

North Korea possesses most of the peninsula's minerals and a trained and notably energetic workforce. Yet, in his 1978 New Year broadcast, the President found it necessary to extol workers to "reject easy life and indolence". This seems to have had the required effect, since indications are that the economy is now performing better. Economic activity is also benefiting from past efforts to improve the nation's infrastructure, notably transport, to raise output of raw materials and to install modern manufacturing equipment.

It was officially claimed that per caput G.N.P. had reached U.S. $1,920 in 1979. This seems unlikely since the World Bank estimate for 1979 is only U.S. $1,130. Most statistics pertaining to North Korea have to be treated with caution, since they may be distorted for propaganda purposes.

AGRICULTURE

Arable land is concentrated in the relatively flat western provinces; on the east coast the mountains come close to the sea. By January 1959 "the individual peasant economy had been eliminated and one million peasants' households organized into 3,800 co-operatives". North Korean agriculture was now to embark on a revolution of Chinese origin, chiefly designed to raise yields and reduce the area sown to food crops, and comprising a combination of irrigation schemes, mechanization and electrification, deep ploughing, close planting and heavy use of fertilizers.

In 1976 paddy rice covered 760,000 hectares or 36 per cent of the arable area, compared with 27 per cent in 1960. In 1979, despite a drought, the grain harvest is claimed to have exceeded 8 million tons, with wheat yields in the range of 6–12 tons per hectare, and rice yields 7–10 tons per hectare. A record grain harvest of 8.5 million tons was claimed for 1977, with slightly less produced in 1978. For 1979 the cereal harvest was claimed to be 9 million tons—thanks to excellent yields of both rice and maize, the principal crops.

Among lesser crops, North Korea is now self-sufficient in vegetables, with some available for export. The aims are now to diversify output, further to improve productivity, and generally to make production increasingly sophisticated. Emphasis is also being placed on fruit production, involving an area of 300,000 hectares which lies mainly in South Hwanghae Province. The target is to produce an annual crop of 1.5 million tons of stone fruit, grapes, apples, etc.

Agricultural output in 1980 included 4.8 million tons of rice, much the same as in 1979, but 2.2 million tons of maize, 250,000 tons more than in 1979. The leading non-cereal crops comprise potatoes, soyabeans and pulses. Output of meat and dairy produce continued to advance in 1980. The livestock population includes nearly 1 million cattle and over 2 million pigs.

Irrigation has a key role to play in agricultural progress. An important project, the Ujidon irrigation system, was opened in 1961: it comprises the Suhjeung reservoir, said to be the largest in the country and able to irrigate 38,000 hectares of land in South and North Hwanghae provinces. The other most important irrigation projects include those at Pyongnam, Kiyang, Amnok-gang and Chungdan. More recently, irrigation projects have centred on the Kiyang, Singye and Aprok Rivers and Lakes Yongpung-ho and Yontan.

Mechanization has also received high priority. By 1977 it was claimed that there were 5–6 tractors per 100 hectares of farmland and in 1980 collective farms were stated to be in possession of 8–10 tractors per 100 hectares. Large numbers of rice transplanting machines also exist and rice production is claimed to be largely mechanized on some collective farms.

Land reclamation is being given priority and some 25,000 hectares have already been brought into production in this way; current efforts include the largest single project ever attempted in Asia, involving an 8-km. dam across the Taedong river. Overall, the aim is to reclaim 300,000 hectares, of which some 200,000 hectares are scheduled for agricultural use. Most reclaimed land will be used to grow rice, but fish-ponds will also be created. Aquaculture is considered to have a key role to play in meeting the target production level for aquatic items of 5 million tons per year by the end of the 1980s: about 1.2 million tons were produced in 1979. Deep-sea fishing continues to be the subject of much new investment, both onshore and afloat: the fleet includes 10,000-ton mother ships and 3,750-ton stern trawlers. Timber is in short supply; substantial quantities are imported from the Soviet Far East. Past extensive deforestation is being reversed but it is a slow process, as over 3 million hectares are involved.

MINING

The regime estimates North Korea's coal deposits at nearly 10,000 million metric tons, of which 70 per cent is anthracite. The principal collieries are found north of Pyongyang, but during the 1970s much investment was made into developing resources to the south. Thus the Government was able to announce that in 1976 output had exceeded 50 million tons (roughly double the 1970 total) and that in 1980, with output at 60 million tons, the country was in a position to export modest quantities of coal.

All oil and petroleum products have to be imported, but North Korea has signed a tentative agreement with a Singapore firm to explore for oil off-shore, probably in the Gulf of Chihli.

North Korea produces about 10 million tons of iron ore (gross weight) annually. The mines at Musan, Unryul, Toksong, Tokhyon, Chaeyong and Hasong have benefited from substantial investments. New mines are being opened up at Toksong and Sohaeri. The country's reserves total about 2,000 million tons of low-grade ore.

North Korea claims to lead the world in magnesite deposits; mines in Kanyo province support a large refractory industry. About 50,000 tons of concentrates are imported annually to feed a copper smelter. Lead, zinc, tungsten, mercury, phosphates, gold, silver and sulphur are mined in large quantities. In recent years exploration activity has focused on non-ferrous minerals in the northern provinces of Yanggang and Chagang. Zinc ore is smelted within the country and part of the lead ore is shipped abroad for smelting. Domestic smelting facilities are to be found at Tanchon and also at Nampo, Haeju and Mungyong.

An aluminium smelter with an annual capacity of 20,000 tons was recently established; three small aluminium plants are in production at Hungnam, Chinnampo and Tasado. Under a long-term barter agreement North Korea is supplying substantial quantities of barytes to the Soviet Union. Cement is of increasing importance; several new plants have been built, including one (at Sunchon) with an ultimate capacity of 5 million tons; at present it has a capacity of 3 million tons, roughly one-third of the total capacity of the industry (that embraces seven major and 50 minor facilities).

Coal supplies about half of the nation's energy needs. Two petroleum refineries exist: one, at Unggi, processes Soviet crude oil for the nearby 200MW power station; the other at Bonghwa was built with Chinese aid and produces petrol and industrial oils.

MANUFACTURING

During the 1971–76 Plan industrial output recorded an average annual increase of 16.3 per cent. By 1977 the engineering industry was responsible for one-third of this output. The greater publicity now being given to industrial output performance suggests that real progress has been made of late. Concern now centres on the need to secure the necessary capital and technological expertise to sustain recent advances. Significantly, compared with the 1970s, there is now increased emphasis on light industry to help meet the planned rise in consumer goods.

Metallurgy

Production of steel in 1978 reportedly exceeded 5 million metric tons, but South Korean sources claim that only 3.77 million tons were produced in 1979. The Hwanghae Iron Works has been displaced as the country's biggest iron and steel centre by "the world's leading metallurgical centre" at the Kim Chaek Iron Works. Kim Chaek's annual capacity is put at 1.5 million tons, compared with 1.2 million tons for Hwanghae. Other steel plants are located at Kangson (capacity 540,000 tons), Songjin (260,000 tons), Kaechon, Sinulju and Kaesong. Construction of a new steelmaking plant is planned for 1982 at Songjin, as part of the country's seven-year plan target of some 7.5 million tons per year by 1984, and an eventual capacity of some 15 million tons per year.

Machine Building

The industry currently manufactures large-size machines, such as 6,000-ton presses, 50,000-kW. generators, 25-ton trucks, tractors, excavators, 300-h.p. bulldozers, electric and diesel locomotives and ships of up to 20,000 tons, as well as aggregate plant for power stations and metallurgical and chemical factories. Some 30,000 15-h.p. tractors were produced in 1976. By 1978 the country was claimed to be 98 per cent self-sufficient in machinery.

Chemicals

This industrial sector, and especially fertilizers, has received much attention. In 1979 production of chemical fibres increased by 36 per cent but the output of synthetic resins rose by only 12 per cent. Recent developments include a fertilizer factory with an annual capacity of 1 million tons and a 360,000-ton urea plant. The chemical fertilizer industry's annual capacity is put at 3 million tons. A French-built petrochemical complex north of Pyongyang is designed to produce ethylene, polyethylene and acrylo-nitrite. The crude petroleum needed by the plant will come from nearby refineries built by the Soviet Union. In 1974 the plant was able to produce a wide range of synthetic resins. Reflecting the importance of this sector to a country short of natural raw materials and committed to an urban-industrial strategy, plants have recently been constructed for the production of vinylchloride, urea, polyethylene and orlon. A new chemical base, centred upon a caustic soda plant, is planned for the western coast.

Textiles

The industry, based mainly on synthetics, was given priority in the 1960s and the resultant investment enabled output of textile fabrics to exceed 500 million metres by the mid-1970s. More recent investment has seen a shift of emphasis to end-products. For example, during the Six-Year Plan period (1971–76), new garment-producing equipment, with a capacity of 15 million dresses, and other knitting equipment was installed to augment the production capacity 6-fold for sweaters and jackets, 1.6-fold for underwear and 1.8-fold for socks and stockings. The Second Seven-Year Plan period (1978–84) is expected to witness a 1.7-fold increase in the production of knitwear, in particular a rapid growth in the production of various knitted goods with home-made orlon.

INFRASTRUCTURE

Transport

Transportation difficulties were a cause for official concern in the 1970s since they were partially nullifying mining and manufacturing progress. Most items transported are bulky, and large-scale renovation and expansion of the transport system are required to cope with such movements. For example, the country's five international trading ports (Nampo and Haeju on the west coast and Najin, Chongjin and Wonsan on the east coast) have been the subject of major modernization schemes in an effort to eliminate bottlenecks.

In 1974 only about one half of the rail system of 4,380 km. had been electrified, but by 1981 it was claimed that all the major trunk routes had been electrified and that 87.5 per cent of all railway haulage was by electric traction. As a result of the completion of the circle rail system linking the eastern and western parts of the country, the rail network now exceeds 5,000 km. Supplementing the network are extensive lengths of pipeline, cableway and belt conveyors, notably the largescale Musan-Chongjin pipeline for transporting concentrated ores and the long-distance belt conveyor line at the Unryul mine.

Power

Production of electric power in 1976 was estimated at 30,000 million kWh., compared with 16,500 million kWh. in 1970. The 1970 production came mainly from a network of over 1,000 newly-built medium-sized and small power stations, but the construction of a number of large power plants raised installed electricity capacity to 40,000 million kWh. by the mid-1970s. Further large power plants have been built or are under construction at Taedonggang, Chongchankang and Chongjin. The 1,200-MW. plant at Pukchang is being expanded. All the large plants appear to use fossil fuel (coal), not atomic power, although several sizeable hydro-electric plants have been erected on a joint basis with the Chinese in the region of the Yalu river; one unit, Sup'ng, is able to generate 700 MW. The absence of a national grid means that local needs have to be met through many small and medium units, utilizing hydraulic, thermal and tidal power, which is generally readily available. Reflecting the advances made in raising industrial output, and those planned for the future, renewed efforts are being made to step up the rate of expansion of power production. The aim is to produce up to 60,000 million kWh. by 1984 and 100,000 million kWh. by the end of the decade.

FOREIGN TRADE

Trade links with the capitalist world have been severely affected by the country's inability to pay past debts, totalling some U.S. $2,000 million. Yet trade is essential if North Korea is to secure the high technology needed to modernize its industry. Recognizing this, "export goods are to be given priority in all fields of national economy", according to President Kim. The American Central Intelligence Agency estimates the value of total trade in 1979 at U.S. $1,900 million. According to the Economist Intelligence Unit, exports to North Korea's twenty leading markets rose 43 per cent to U.S. $711.3 million in 1979, while imports from the same countries rose by 39 per cent to US. $851.4 million.

It was a combination of low prices for North Korea's exports, transport difficulties and soaring import prices, including the cost of petroleum bought from the Soviet Union and China, that precipitated the balance of payments crisis. The balance with Western trading partners had been transformed from a surplus of U.S. $18 million in 1970 to a $430 million deficit in 1974. The trade deficit in 1975 was put at $362 million, and the cumulative deficit for the 1970–75 period amounted to $1,800 million. As of October 1979 the principal debtors were believed to be the U.S.S.R. ($700 million), Japan ($400 million) and the Federal Republic of Germany ($150 million).

At the end of 1979 the problem of trade debts entered a new phase. Agreement was reached with the Japanese on a 10-year repayment period running through to 1989. As a result, the value of Japanese goods imported rose from U.S. $257 million in 1979 to U.S. $380 million in 1980; the corresponding increase in exports to Japan was U.S. $136 million to U.S. $191 million. Conspicuous amongst Japanese products, increasing in sales, were trucks, machinery in general, industrial chemicals and other intermediate industrial materials. North Korean products growing in sales were chiefly mineral products, notably zinc ore.

Japan is the principal non-communist trading partner; West Germany is also a major export market but, with Singapore (its rival for the position of second most important supplier), it sells to North Korea goods to a value of only one-tenth of those bought from Japan. Two-way trade with the principal communist partner, the U.S.S.R., is estimated at $232 million for 1978, excluding commodity and foreign aid. On a more comprehensive basis, South Korean sources estimate two-way trade with the U.S.S.R. at $754 million in 1979, representing 51 per cent of total two-way trade with communist bloc countries. A sizeable portion of the balance (30 per cent) was represented by trade with China. Modest export sales have been achieved with Romania but a new major trading partner is Saudi Arabia: petroleum imports from that country soared in value from $23 million in 1976 to $171 million in 1978.

FINANCE

For 1973 both expenditure and revenue were estimated to be 8,544.0 million won. Of the 1973 expenditure, 15 per cent was allocated to national defence, compared with 30 per cent in 1970. Total expenditure in 1976 was officially estimated at 12,513 million won, a 10.1 per cent increase over 1975 (for the previous year the increase was 17.7 per cent). Defence spending was expected to total 2,065 million won. In 1975 revenues were 15.4 per cent higher than in 1974, at 11,367 million won. For 1976 they were expected to rise by 8 per cent to match expenditure. The 1977 budget allocated marginally smaller proportions of expenditure (from a total of 13,349 million won) for defence (15.4 per cent instead of 16.7 per cent) and social and cultural affairs. In 1978 revenue totalled 15,657 million won whilst expenditure amounted to 14,744 million won: 59.4 per cent of expenditure was allocated to the people's economy, 23.2 per cent to social and cultural affairs, 15.4 per cent to defence and 2.0 per cent to management. The 1979 budget was provisionally balanced at 17,301 million won but, in fact, government revenue in 1979 reached 17,480 million won, marginally greater than was planned. A financial reserve of 505 million won was then able to be carried over into 1980.

For 1980 the budget envisaged expenditure totalling 18,800 million won, 11.3 per cent up on 1979. Defence was to receive 14.5 per cent of the total allocation, compared with 15.1 per cent in 1979. Investment for economic advancement was dominated by the 37.1 per cent share allocated to the mining sector. The biggest increase in investment (70 per cent) was for fishing. The 1981 budget, at 20,480 million won, represents a rise of 7.0 per cent on 1980. Defence spending is expected to take 14.7 per cent of the total, compared with 14.6 per cent in 1980. Overall, the budget projects an 8.7 per cent increase in expenditure. Further efforts to raise output in the fishing industry and investment to raise electricity production were prominent features.

South Korean sources put per caput consumption at U.S. $160 in 1975. The domestic savings rate was 35 per cent. Defence expenditure accounted for 13.9 per cent of the G.N.P. and per caput investment was $110.

PLANNING

The Seven-Year Plan (1961–67) arrived at an industrial output in 1967 3.2 times greater than that of 1960, representing an average annual increase of 18 per cent, compared with the 36.6 per cent claimed for 1957–60. Soviet aid seems to have been suspended in 1963–64. In 1966 the Plan was extended for three years to 1970, in view of the need to build up armaments, and new construction projects were "frozen".

In late 1971 the Government announced a Six-Year Plan (1971–76) which envisaged a rise in output of textiles of 50–60 per cent, of paper production by 80 per cent, processed meats by 400 per cent, processed vegetables by 1,370 per cent, aluminium products by 180 per cent, glassware by 420 per cent, porcelain by 130 per cent, and clocks and watches by 150 per cent. An overall increase over the six-year period of 160 per cent was expected. Specific targets included 70 million shoes, 126,000 refrigerators, 27,000 machine tools, 2.9 million tons of fertilizers, 8 million tons each of cement and iron ore, 51 million tons of coal and 3.9 million tons of steel.

Although in December 1976 it was stated that the Six-Year Plan had been successfully concluded, speculation that this was not the case was heightened by the designation of 1977 as a year of "readjustment", and not the start of another plan period. It was officially admitted that the country had been strained by the Plan, with key problems cited as being that "transportation fails to keep pace with fast growing production", and "the mining industries do not keep decisively ahead of the processing industries".

Kim Il-sung has stated that no foreign capital would be introduced during the 1978–84 Seven-Year Economic Development Plan. This was a tacit recognition of the country's inability to borrow from abroad because of existing debts. However, without such assistance, the modest aims of the Plan (often below the targets of the previous Six-Year Plan) are proving difficult to achieve. Overall, the aim is to expand industrial output by 12.1 per cent a year, compared with the 16.3 per cent target for the Six-Year Plan ending in 1976, or just under the 12.6 per cent growth claimed for the 1960s and the 14 per cent for 1971–76.

Following the decision to give priority to exports, the hoped-for increase in high technology imports has prompted the announcement of ambitious goals for the 1984–91 Seven-Year Plan. (These need to be seen in the context of a claimed increase in industrial production between 1970 and 1979.) The nine principal goals include increasing production of electricity, coal, steel, grain, textile fabrics, cement, chemical fertilizers, aquatic products and non-ferrous metals.

ECONOMIC SURVEY OF SOUTH KOREA

T. M. Burley

South Korea is one of the most densely populated countries of Asia, with an average population density which is the third highest among major countries (after Bangladesh and Taiwan). Nearly one-third of the total population lives in the two biggest cities: the capital, Seoul, and Pusan. The rural population, which accounted for 55 per cent of the national total in 1965, had declined to about 30 per cent by 1980.

Economic growth has been rapid in recent years: labour is abundant, diligent and with high educational standards. The per caput income recorded an average annual increase in real terms of 8 per cent in the 1970s; it was estimated at U.S. $1,520 in 1980.

Growth has been very much an export-led phenomenon but the benefits of economic progress have spread into the domestic economy, leading to the emergence of a middle class with considerable buying power. Any diversion of resources from the export sector will not be easy because of the ever increasing burden of petroleum imports. It was this burden, plus the need to maintain the competitive strength of the export industries in the face of the world recession, that prompted the 1980 currency devaluation and a concomitant dampening down of economic activity.

During 1979 the economy, with its reliance on export-led growth, had become increasingly under pressure through the influence of various factors: the soaring price of petroleum and other raw materials whose importation is essential for the export industries; a lower level of world trade and associated protectionism as the world recession intensified; rising labour rates, further accentuated by inflationary pressures; a general lack of new export markets to be exploited and reduced opportunities in Iran. The planners had foreseen most of these trends but they were surprised by their severity, which produced a nil volume growth in merchandise exports for 1979 and a drop in annual G.N.P. growth from 11.6 per cent to 7.1 per cent. The outcome was a reappraisal of the short-term economic strategy centring on a 16.6 per cent devaluation of the won in January 1980.

Further oil shocks and the continuing world recession meant that the devaluation and related measures were not given a proper chance to take effect. Bad weather hit agricultural production (and a cholera scare hit the tourist trade) so that the trade balance and inflation worsened significantly. As a result, G.N.P. fell (by 5.7 per cent) for the first time since the late 1950s. Business confidence was further affected by ill-conceived attempts by the new Government at wholesale reorganization of various industrial sectors, notably motor vehicles and heavy engineering. However heavy Government support, channelled through the banking system, has enabled most companies to avoid the worst effects of inflation, recession and the weak won.

The depreciation of the won, apart from exacerbating the impact of imported inflation (notably through the price of oil), upset Government plans to revitalize industry through increased investment in advanced foreign machinery and production equipment. Instead emphasis has shifted to enhancing the profitability of exports by realistic pricing: for example, underbidding to secure Middle East construction contracts is being discouraged, and by greater product sophistication and enhanced marketing expertise.

Despite these difficulties, most of the advances attained during the 1960s and 1970s are still enjoyed by the general public. In the period 1961–80, the average South Korean increased his spending on food three-fold while he spent four times as much on clothing (and consumed four times as much electricity) in 1980 than in 1961. In the 1970s rice consumption fell slightly, but in contrast, per caput consumption of other foods more than compensated for this, in particular far more meat is eaten: 3.4 times more than in 1961. On the other hand, housing, water supply, education, social welfare and industrial safety are seriously deficient, considering the level of economic development so far attained.

AGRICULTURE

About a quarter of the land area is cultivated and a further two-thirds is classified as forest land. Soil erosion, resulting from indiscriminate felling, has caused considerable damage to croplands and irrigation reservoirs. South Korea's agriculture is mainly concentrated along river basin areas, with rice as the principal crop.

The priority given to urban industrial development has forced many farmers off the land but population pressures still necessitate fragmentation of land holdings to an average of about 0.9 of a hectare per farm household. The rural environment is not particularly conducive to increased productivity through mechanization but output has been stimulated by government subsidies, and the somewhat authoritarian *Saemaul Undong* (New Community) movement. Grain and fertilizer subsidies are a major inflationary force but one so far considered justifiable in the light of the strategic and political importance of the rural sector.

Only two agricultural products, raw silk and tobacco, are important export earners so food items (rice, barley, wheat, soybeans and potatoes) dominate agricultural output. Nevertheless, substantial imports of wheat and sugar are necessary each year. Small quantities of rice were exported in 1977 but subsequent government policy has been to divert surpluses into its emergency stockpile. In fact, there was less rice available in 1978 and 1979, despite a notable shift into higher yielding varieties, as a result of very poor growing conditions (which were repeated in

1981). An over-enthusiastic switch to high-yielding varieties not entirely suited to local conditions, as well as a lack of labour to exact proper crops management, has not helped either. In this regard, too, the government scheme to narrow income differences between agricultural and non-agricultural sectors of the economy by setting generous purchasing prices for rice has proved counter-productive.

The Government's efforts to halt the decline in cattle numbers, by providing incentives for livestock rearing, have proved successful. Although still low in comparison with Japan, consumption of meat is growing at a faster rate and requires a high level of imports: eight times as much beef was imported in 1978 as in 1977, for example. To reduce imports, a 40,000-hectare cattle-raising project is to be established on Cheju Island. When fully operational in 1986, there will be a herd of 50,000 milk cows and 50,000 beef cattle. Government loans and tax benefits are available for would-be livestock farmers. Such schemes, however, increase the pressure for a greater output of oilseeds which is far from satisfying domestic food or feed needs.

During the fifth Five-Year Plan period, the country's land will be divided into 10 major farming areas in consideration of weather conditions and geographical features, to establish an effective crop planting system which will encourage the growing of crops suitable for each farming area. In order to develop new sources for additional incomes, the plan selected malting barley, groundnuts, garlic, sesame seed and six other crops as 10 major strategic crops to be raised intensively during the Plan period. It also called for the breeding of 50,000 head of cattle and the import of 20,000 cattle per year to meet the growing meat demand and stabilize beef prices. Other highlights of the Five-Year Plan include the modernization of the distribution channels of farm and marine products, the introduction of an insurance system to reduce flood and drought damage, and the diversification of import sources for feed grains.

Fisheries

In recent years South Korea has emerged as one of the world's leading ocean-fishing nations. Activity centres on a deep-sea fishing base at Ulsan, with its associated fish-processing plants designed to handle 150,000 tons annually, and on Masan port, which has the ability to handle 2,000 tons of fish at any one time.

The establishment of exclusive fishing zones by countries throughout the world, and particularly by the U.S.S.R. and the U.S.A., threatens virtually to halve Korea's deep-sea catch. On-shore fishing is hampered by pollution but progress is being made with fish culture in controlled conditions.

Forest Products

Timber resources have been depleted in the past by indiscriminate felling. Afforestation and related soil erosion schemes have arrested the devastation but the forestry sector currently makes only a small contribution to timber supplies. However, the country is the world's principal exporter of hardwood plywood. This is achieved by the fact that the country's modern plywood and veneer plants rely primarily on logs imported from Indonesia and the Philippines. Paper production comes mostly from twelve large-scale plants; the main raw material is waste paper, as domestic pulp supplies are limited.

MINING

South Korea has about 50 different kinds of mineral resources but still needs to import iron ore, coal, copper and lead in substantial quantities. Conspicuous by its absence is petroleum. South Korea has ambitious plans for petroleum exploration in its off-shore areas, and Gulf, Caltex and Shell have each contracted to explore and develop areas off the west or south coasts. Off-shore boundary disputes with Japan and China prevent further leasing, however, but an agreement with Japan awaits ratification. A national oil company was set up in 1974 to oversee exploration activities.

Coal

Mostly in the form of anthracite, coal is one of the leading mineral resources in South Korea. Geological surveys show that there are about 1,400 million tons of coal deposits, of which about one-quarter is exploitable. In 1982, however, it was reported that a new coalfield with reserves of 62 million tons had been discovered in Kangura Province. In an effort to increase domestic output, under-sea deposits may be mined. At present, supplies are drawn from a variety of state and privately owned mines, mostly small in size.

Domestic consumption is currently rising by some 1 million tons per year. As a result, domestic output has to be augmented by imports. Coking coal has had to be imported in substantial quantities for the iron and steel industry since 1978.

Metallic mineral products

Iron ore reserves are estimated to be about 120 million tons, mostly of magnetite. Copper ore reserves are put at 100,000 tons (copper content) and a similar amount of tungsten exists. The metal content of the lead-zinc deposit at Yeonwha approaches 125,000 tons. The tungsten mine at Sangdong is the second largest in the world; more tungsten and molybdenum ore bodies are known to exist nearby. Other mines work gold-silver ore deposits.

Non-metallic mineral products

South Korea is one of the principal sources of natural graphite, with estimated reserves of amorphous graphite of 30 million tons and reserves of crystalline graphite of 2.6 million tons. There are about 40 operating fluorite mines and it is estimated that there are 1.8 million tons of fluorite deposits in terms of 70 per cent concentrate. Limestone is abundant and cement is produced in large quantities; by 1978, the capacity of the cement industry had exceeded 15 million tons. Kaolin production is substantial. Several uranium ore bodies have been discovered.

MANUFACTURING INDUSTRY

When South Korea launched its First Five-Year Economic Development Plan in 1962, high priority was given to development of manufacturing industry. This priority has been consistently maintained but many of the major industrial projects are close to or below the minimum efficient size, and thus are high-cost producers. The Government is aware of this and is prepared to subsidize output where necessary to maintain producers' competitive strength against foreign suppliers. Indeed, although the country's rapid industrial growth has been basically the result of private entrepreneurship, it is actively promoted and guided by the Government's credit policy and fiscal incentives. While foreign investment has been encouraged, no more than a 50-50 joint venture arrangement has been permitted. However, the new emphasis on high technology industries has forced a relaxation of this policy to permit even 100 per cent foreign investment in selected manufacturing activities.

During the First Five-Year Plan (1962–66) the Government's industrial development efforts concentrated on promoting export industries, but the Second Five-Year Plan (1967–71) emphasized import substitution and large-scale investment in iron and steel, petrochemicals, fertilizers and cement. In recent years import substitution has been overshadowed by an all-out export drive. The economic stabilization plan, introduced in 1979, marked a watershed in industrial growth, with its intention to increase the relative importance of domestic market-oriented light industry. Unfortunately, the economic crisis later in the same year forced a change of priority on the government.

Less than a year after the heralding of the country's "second industrial revolution", both the domestic market emphasis and high technology industrial growth strategy were drastically revamped to allow for the soaring cost of energy, the need to curb capital investment, export market sales difficulties and inflationary pressures. Projects already in the pipeline escaped the economy drive but the moratorium imposed on new projects means that consolidation, rather than expansion, is now to be the keynote. While large-scale industry faces a less buoyant future, small and medium-scale operators (frequently neglected in the past) will benefit from a one-third increase, to 400,000 million won, in the special support funds available to this sector.

As a result of these developments, exports from the heavy industries did not perform as well as planned. In 1980, for example, 52.4 per cent of exports came from light industries, with 29 per cent emanating from the textile industry alone. In contrast, the leading product of heavy industry, electronic goods, contributed only 12 per cent; many such industries, notably motor vehicles, were operating well below capacity.

Textiles

Textiles have been a cornerstone of economic growth. They account for about one-quarter of employment in the country's manufacturing industries, contribute about one-fifth of G.N.P., and provide 30 per cent of exports. The industry seems destined to remain the leading source of exports well into the 1980s, following the problems faced by heavy industry. Recognizing this, the Government allocated a further U.S. $180 million in 1981 to be spent over the following four years on modernization projects. Increasing product sophistication is causing the industry to seek more highly-skilled labour. Also, the female workforce, upon which the industry depends for two-thirds of its employees, is decreasing and is less willing to accept the low wages offered. At the same time, within South Korea's export markets there is a growing challenge from protectionism and low quality supplies from rival products. Diversification of markets and products as well as modernization and expansion of production facilities and technology are seen as the way forward.

A key role is to be played by what is claimed to be the world's largest cotton spinning and weaving plant at Chongbu. The capacity of the country's synthetic fibre factories is about 900 tons per day, or one-quarter that of Japan, but this is rising to nearly 1,500 tons a day as the Yochon petrochemical complex becomes operational. However, these advances have underlined the fact that much equipment (perhaps one-third) in the older factories is out-dated, especially dyeing facilities (new dyeing complexes are to be built in Seoul, Taegu and Pusan).

The related footwear industry, based upon cheap canvas shoes, has been adversely affected by trade restrictions in its main export markets, notably the U.S.A. In volume terms, both production and exports fell in 1980.

Petroleum Refining

Petroleum increased its share of South Korea's energy demand from one-tenth to one-third between 1965 and 1975, and the import bill for crude oil rose by over 500 per cent. Petroleum imports represent one-fifth of total net imports. Rising demand, reflecting primarily the expanding needs of industry for fuel oil, is met from local refineries. To protect future requirements, the Government is to embark upon a U.S. $1,000 million scheme to stockpile 60 days' supply of oil.

Chemicals

The industry was established in the 1960s through plants producing chemical fertilizers and several basic chemicals (soda ash, ammonia and methanol). The output of chemical products has increased in quantity and sophistication in the 1970s, as a result of expanded production of polyvinylchloride, carbide, dyestuffs, pharmaceuticals, cosmetics, telephatic acid, para-xylene, etc.

The focal point of activities is the Ulsan petrochemical complex. It is based on a naphtha-cracking centre which produces 150,000 tons of ethylene a year. Downstream facilities include a caprolactam plant, an aceta-idehyde plant and an ethanol plant to be built at Kwanyang in South Cholla Province. The second major chemical complex, at Yochon on the southern coast, includes an ethylene production capacity of 350,000 tons a year and major facilities for the production of caustic soda, chlorine, polyethylene, vinyl chloride, ethylene dichloride, polypropylene and ethylene glycol.

Metallurgy

The country's first integrated steel-making plant, at Yongil Bay, was inaugurated in 1973: its production capacity was doubled in 1976, and rose to 8.5 million tons in 1980. The operator, the Pohang Iron and Steel Company (POSCO), now plans to spend U.S. $314 million to raise capacity to 9.6 million tons. Three other steelworks projects are planned for the 1980s, including one completely new integrated plant. Most of the iron ore and coal needed for steel production has to be imported, but imports of products are now confined largely to special steels, with this cost partially offset by increasing exports of lower-grade bars and plates.

There are refineries for the production of copper, tungsten, gold and lead. Non-ferrous refineries include facilities for zinc at Onsan and Sukpo, and for aluminium at Ulsan. A copper smelter, with a capacity of 80,000 tons, is located at Onsan.

Machine Building

Machine building in the 1960s was limited to light machinery products, light agricultural machinery and equipment, and simple metal-working machinery, such as lathes and cotton gins. During the Second Plan period, the construction of new plants made possible the production of industrial machinery, metal-working machinery, communications equipment, motor vehicles, ships and other transport equipment, and internal combustion engines.

Led by the electronic sector the production of electrical machinery and appliances soared in the 1970s. The resultant heavy burden of machinery imports has led government planners to initiate a shift of emphasis from light to heavy industry: by the end of the Fourth Plan it was planned to manufacture 70 per cent of machinery, excluding shipbuilding and electronics, locally.

The country's recent economic difficulties have not only reduced business for heavy machinery, but the level of investment in new plans (notably at the Changwon complex) has had to be cut back. Government efforts at radical reorganization have not helped either; it could take until the mid-1980s to achieve economic viability in some instances: motor vehicles, chemical and heavy electrical machinery, in particular, face a long period of readjustment.

The motor vehicle industry, in particular, was drastically curtailed by the economic crisis; instead of producing 280,000 vehicles in 1980, output fell to merely 123,000, less than one-third of the industry's capacity. Despite this, the aim is to produce 1,000,000 vehicles in 1986, of which 312,000 would be exported.

Plans to expand the nation's shipbuilding capacity to almost 6 million d.w.t., making South Korea one of the 10 largest shipbuilding nations in the world have been frustrated by the world recession and capacity is being restricted to half the original targets. Hyundai Shipbuilding Co.'s shipyard at Ulsan, with a capacity of about 1.5 million d.w.t., has been augmented by the Okpo shipyard of Daewo Heavy Industries. This 1.2 million d.w.t. facility is located on Koje Island. The Government had planned no fewer than four separate shipbuilding complexes there during the 1980s.

Now the emphasis has shifted to enlarging ship repair facilities.

INFRASTRUCTURE

Transport

Already the principal freight mode, road transportation of passengers has now outstripped the railways. However, the oil burden has enhanced the priority given to the debt-ridden railways under the Fourth Plan transport investment programme, now that the road building programme has achieved a network of all-weather paved highways between major population centres. Special priority has been given to expanding Seoul's mass transit system. In the 10 years from the mid-1960s, the capacity of South Korea's ports increased fivefold to 50 million tons a year. Between the mid-1970s and mid-1980s, annual capacity is planned to increase to 230 million tons. In tune with these objectives, an entirely new port has been created at Pukpyong on the east coast.

Under the Fifth Plan's transport investment programme, the Government will invest more than 10,000,000 million won in the expansion of transport facilities. The total length of the railways will be extended from the current 6,007 km. to 6,599 km. by 1986, and that of underground lines from the present 22.1 km. to 143.2 km. The programme also projects an increase in the number of road motor vehicles in use from the current 528,000 to 1,148,000; of ocean-going vessels from the present 5,200,000 tons to 9,400,000 tons; and of guest rooms in tourist hotels across the country from 19,104 to 30,000.

Energy

Energy usage is the equivalent of 45 million tons of petroleum per year. It is derived mainly from petroleum (62 per cent), which is entirely imported, most of it under long-term contracts with Saudi Arabia, Kuwait and Iran. The other energy sources are coal (25 per cent), firewood (8 per cent), nuclear power and hydro-electricity. This balance is scheduled to change: in an effort to cut the oil import bill, alternative sources of energy, notably nuclear power and coal, are being encouraged; energy conservation, too, has priority (with such success that consumption is rising at a rate only 80 per cent of G.N.P. growth). Joint venture projects in overseas coal mining represent another effort to cut oil imports.

The revised energy development plan for 1974–81 provided for 19 new hydro-electric power stations (total capacity 1,460 MW.), four nuclear plants (2,395 MW.) and seven thermal stations (1,860 MW.). The energy development programme for 1982–86 estimates the growth in the country's energy demand at an annual average of 7.2 per cent from 44 million tons of coal equivalent in 1980 to 67 million tons by 1986. The programme envisages that the country's oil demand will grow by an annual average of 5.6 per cent from 198 million to 261 million tons. Meanwhile, coal production is expected to increase by 2.5 per cent annually from 19 million to 21.5 million tons, and the country's power generation capacity should rise from 9 million to 18 million kW. The Government will construct five more nuclear power stations by 1986, in addition to the one already in operation, to increase capacity to 4,770,000 kW of electricity. In order to supply more liquefied natural gas (LNG) to households, as well as to industrial establishments, the Government will also construct a large-scale LNG terminal, with an annual processing capacity of 1 million tons, by 1983.

Industrial estates

In an effort to stimulate exports, the Government has established a number of industrial estates, several of which are especially designed for foreign companies. The latest, at Asan Bay, will include an international-level port. The largest, at Pukpyong, covers 16.5 square kilometres and has a modern port able to handle vessels of up to 50,000 gross tons. The next largest (180 hectares) is the Masan Free Export Zone (MAFEZ). The zone is a 100 per cent bonded area and, in addition to normal investment incentives, all duties and taxes are waived.

Nearby at Changwon, a new industrial city is under construction. In contrast to the export-oriented light industries of Masan, Changwon is to be a centre of heavy machine building, capable of making South Korea into one of the world's leading producers. The site includes 20 sq. km. of factory sites and provision for a population of 500,000. By 1980, 80 of the anticipated 120 companies had been granted entry and 70 were operational. The level of activity was hard hit by the depressed economic conditions prevailing in that year, but Changwon is now functioning more effectively, albeit on a less grandiose scale.

INTERNATIONAL TRADE

In 1977 South Korea achieved its first current account surplus for many years. This proved to be a false dawn, however, and a major economic crisis was precipitated by the inability to raise the volume of exports in 1979. To foster exports of capital goods, an export-import bank has been established, and in 1975 special privileges were granted to 13 giant export-oriented conglomerates, or General Trading Corporations (GTCs). By 1978 they were responsible for 30 per cent of Korean exports.

A major problem for South Korean exporters in recent years is that other newly industrialized nations in the area, notably Taiwan, have become more competitive. Using a labour cost index of 100, based on 1975, South Korean costs had jumped to 197 by mid-1979, whereas the index for Taiwan had fallen to 94. On the import side, the weakness of the won, combined with the oil burden, added to the balance of payments problem. Export-led growth is the cornerstone of economic planning, but this is currently prejudiced by the high level of inflation and the fact that the rate of growth of imports exceeds that of exports.

Exports

Korea's exports grew by an annual average of nearly 40 per cent between 1962 and 1978, as a result of the change in the Government trading policy from import substitution to an export drive. However, in 1979 exports recorded a mere 16 per cent increase and gave only a marginally better performance in 1980; a 21.4 per cent increase was recorded for 1981. The devaluation of the won is claimed to have restored exports to the same level of competitiveness as in 1976; moreover, the cost of exports in 1980 are calculated to have risen by only 5 per cent, compared with a world average increase of about 10 per cent. In order to capitalize on these advantages, and generally to boost exports, greater attention is to be paid to product sophistication, brand images and marketing generally, and further to penetrating markets in the developing world. For example, exports of electronic products now emphasize colour television sets and cooking ranges instead of black and white televisions and radios.

Sales to Japan and the U.S.A. together account for about one-half of the goods exported but otherwise a great diversity of markets is tapped. Significantly, "Third World" nations figure prominently: for example, Saudi Arabia takes more South Korean goods than Italy, and Indonesia takes more than France. Panama, as a market for ships, is a special case but, overall, between one-quarter and one-third of all exports now go to Third World nations where, in most cases, South Korea is competing on equal terms with the world's developed industrial nations.

Imports

Until 1975 mounting demand for imports was generated to supply necessary raw materials for the rapidly growing production of export commodities. It was further stimulated by increasing domestic demand, activated by both liberalization of imports and income growth. The industrial growth of recent years has required further imports. For 1975, however, a combination of export stagnation and domestic austerity briefly contained this upward trend. Then imports surged forward again, at annual rates in excess of 20 per cent up to 1978, when the falling value of the U.S. dollar, to which the won is linked, caused an acceleration to nearly 40 per cent in that year and in 1979. The 1980 devaluation was largely responsible for an 81.5 per cent increase in the oil import bill, but the total import bill increased by only 9.6 per cent as a downturn in the economy slashed imports across the board. Over U.S. $1,000 million had to be spent on rice imports in 1981 to offset the poor domestic crop, but the stability in world oil prices helped to contain the total import bill (indeed, crude oil imports' share fell from 25.3 to 24.4 per cent). Nonetheless, the value of imports rose by 17.2 per cent.

Invisible Trade

Although receipts exceeded $6,000 million in 1981 (made up largely of $3,400 million from construction work and related services overseas and $460 million from tourism), such trade was in deficit to the tune of nearly $1,250 million. Such a massive deficit first appeared in 1980; it arose primarily from higher outflows of investment income, largely interest payments on the country's foreign debt.

Overseas contracts are of very substantial dimensions: in 1977 there were 187,000 South Koreans working in foreign countries, including 57,000 in the Middle East and 19,000 in Europe. By 1981 the numbers in the Middle East had risen to 160,000 or roughly 1 per cent of the country's work force. In that year South Korean contractors secured business worth $13,600 million in the construction field alone. Civil engineering, shipping and nursing are some of the main avenues of activity. In 1980 construction contracts, valued at a then record $8,250 million, were secured by South Korean companies, operating in the Middle East and elsewhere. Remittances from such contracts (excluding workers' remittances) totalled $1,600 million in 1980. As competition intensifies, contracts are becoming less profitable; indeed, fears have been expressed that the contribution of profits to invisible exports will fall to only nominal levels, leaving workers' remittances as the central source of foreign exchange. Between 1977 and 1981 average foreign exchange earnings per project were halved and in 1981 the net profit per project was barely 5 per cent.

Korea's accessibility, relatively low prices and aggressive promotion of its scenic and other attractions has stimulated a major tourist industry: over one million visitors arrive each year, of whom over half are Japanese. There were over 15,000 hotel rooms at the end of 1978, with a further 5,000 under construction, but occupancy rates fell sharply in 1979, reflecting rising prices and the adverse impact of the assassination of the President. A cholera scare in 1980 added to the depressed state of the industry but it recovered in 1981 to earn some $450 million in foreign exchange.

Being essentially a trading nation, costs and revenues associated with international trade figure prominently in the overall picture of invisible trade. With costs approaching $2,000 million in 1981, prominence is being given to the Government's determination that the bulk of trade will be carried on South Korean vessels. The national fleet was to be doubled to 6.2 million d.w.t. by 1981, when it was hoped that Korean vessels would be carrying one-half of the nation's international trade. Already, South Korea has exceeded the 40 per cent target for seaborne cargo carried in national vessels set in the UNCTAD liner code. In 1981 the aggressive marketing of the services provided by the 500-plus vessels in the fleet resulted in freight receipts of around $1,500 million or nearly one-quarter of the total value of invisible earnings.

FINANCE

Fiscal Policy

In an effort to cut domestic demand for funds and to encourage savings by drastically raising interest rates, the central bank used market forces more than in the past when it acted in the wake of the Janaury 1980 devaluation. The measures included the elimination of much of the subsidy on exports and those capital-intensive industries favoured by cheap money for machinery purchase. Exporters benefited, however, in that their support loans incur interest at a comparatively low rate. In fact, a major reason why South Korean business emerged relatively unscathed from the pre-1981 high inflation and recession was the heavy Government support through the banking system.

Nevertheless, the new (i.e. post-1979) approach to economic policy-making has been taken much further by the present regime, resulting in a total, if temporary, reversal of the basic priorities which governed economic policy from the early 1960s to the late 1970s. Previously, it was assumed that inflation was "endemic" to the economy and must be tolerated in the interests of growth. The attitude of the new government, however, is that inflation must be suppressed if the economy is to achieve sustainable growth in the future.

One result of this change has been an effort to create a "bottom-up" decision-making process, on the Japanese model, and to decontrol the banking system. For the time being, at least, government economic policy is not delivering the regular improvements in living standards that came to be taken for granted under President Park. The real income of South Korean industrial workers, for example, fell sharply in both 1980 and 1981. At best, they may remain stable in 1982 if current policies remain unchanged.

Even allowing for the "defence surtax" levied on all incomes, South Korea's ratio of tax burden to G.N.P. is still relatively low compared with that of developing countries. In 1977 an overall tax reform plan became operative, with value added tax replacing eight indirect taxes. In the long term, the introduction of value added tax should bring the much needed restructuring of the country's archaic distribution system. In a bid to modernize economic and financial institutions, the Government is to allow foreign insurance companies to operate in the domestic market. However, any foreign participation in the financial markets, as in commercial banking, is closely controlled by the Government: such participation is seen only as a catalyst to draw in capital and develop trade. Similarly the local commercial banks are used by the Government as a conduit for policy loans. In like manner, foreign investors are being permitted only a toe-hold in the securities market. Initially they are to be allowed to buy only beneficial certificates issued by investment trusts, known as SITS (Securities Investment Trusts), which are, in effect, open-ended unit trusts.

Foreign Indebtedness

The mid-1970s saw a growing awareness by the Government of a need to be more self-reliant; hence, the effort to accelerate the growth in domestic savings and the relatively conservative Fourth Plan targets.

Even so, the Fourth Plan (1977–81) anticipated that $10,000 million in foreign funds would be required, the bulk of it through IECOK (The International Economic Consultative Organization of Korea) which comprises major nations and multilateral finance institutions with a stake in South Korea. Greater reliance on the Eurodollar market as a source of funds was also planned. South Korea's debt to foreign commercial banks amounted to about $17,000 million by the end of 1980; it was only about $6,500 million at mid-1978.

Capital investment averaged 28 per cent of G.N.P. in the 1970s, but domestic savings averaged only 22 per cent. As a result 24 per cent of investment was financed by foreign capital. The Japanese are the dominant foreign investors, however, with over 300 Japanese-affiliated enterprises. At the end of 1978 Japan was responsible for 64.3 per cent of all approved foreign investment, a cumulative total of $699 million compared with $177 million from the U.S.A., the cumulative total at the end of 1980 was about $1,200 million. At the end of 1980 the country's foreign debt was $27,200 million. While the debt ratios are not exceptional, the volume of interest and amortization payments ($2,636 million in 1979) constitutes a substantial and increasing burden.

Money Supply

The Government's rigid control of the monetary sector, while suited to fostering industrial growth, means that action to control either inflation or consumption spending is inhibited or else rebounds upon industry. The measures imposed in January 1980 were particularly traumatic for industry, in part because of their severity, but also because it has not recovered from the detrimental consequences for export financing arising out of the widespread irregularities that were behind the bankruptcy of the Yulsan GTC.

Five banks, all partially owned by the State, represent more than half the country's banking market in terms of deposits. Special banks, wholly owned by the State, exist to serve major development areas, such as housing, medium industry and agriculture. Authority over the banking community technically lies with the Bank of Korea, but it is virtually subordinate to the Ministry of Finance. The Government normally imposes its monetary policy by detailed instruction on lending, rather than by intervention in the money market.

The money market in Korea is characterized by its dual structure: an organized market and an unorganized one, commonly known as the "kerb market". The former covers official financial institutions regulated and controlled by the Government; and it is still limited in its operations. Most short-term financing has been provided by the banks as direct loans. Discounting of bills is comparatively very small in volume while commercial papers were issued only by the commercial banks and bought by the Bank of Korea. There had been, therefore, a lack of an intermediary link between investors having short-term idle funds and enterprises in need of short-term financing. The kerb market is essentially a short-term money market, since the majority of loans mature in less than three months. Because of their anonymous and discreet nature, the magnitude of kerb market operations has never been accurately quantified but it could be worth over $5,000 million per year; if so, it would account for 40 per cent of funds available for loan in the country. It is particularly active on urban housing estates; its existence reflects the absence of a well-organized finance company network. The market probably provides around 10 per cent of available credit, at a cost normally twice that of bank finance. In an effort to restrict the kerb market, the Government has taken advantage of the fact that inflation has pushed the domestic interest rate structure out of gear to keep bank deposit rates high, thus drawing some funds back to the organized banking sector. Despite being involved in a corruption scandal in 1982, the kerb market continues to prosper since domestic savings have been boosted by workers' nervousness about the upward trend in unemployment.

In 1972 when the Government acted to freeze all outstanding debts, the private money lenders' system came to an end. This led to the creation of Short Term Finance Companies (S.T.F.C.s), which provided the market with its first major form of trading securities. More recently, the role of the commercial banks and the S.T.F.C.s has been augmented by Diversified Financial Institutions (D.F.I.s). These are in effect merchant banks and they are the nearest that foreign financial institutions have got to the South Korean domestic market. Most are 50 per cent foreign-owned. Originally set up to develop fee-based corporate activity, they are now allowed to participate in the profitable short-term money market. The main participants in this market are the 11 finance companies, dealing mainly in commercial paper.

The Government is seeking to widen the spread of asset ownership, make the capital market a better medium for encouraging domestic savings and broaden the capital base of local companies. A Securities and Exchange Commission has been established for this purpose. Because of controls on capital movements, foreign portfolio investment remains conspicuous by its absence. In 1978 new money raised on the stock market was a record 325,000 million won but in 1979 this fell sharply to only 196,000 million won and not a single new name was added to the equity lists. The volatility of the equity market discourages serious investment. Investment in property is also highly speculative, a capital gains tax discourages activity, leaving little option for savers but to patronize the two money markets. The exceptional conditions prevailing in 1980 thus created excessive liquidity at the banks with the inflow of domestic savings being augmented by government-subsidized bank loans to industry, and by the fact that the current account deficit is absorbing part of the foreign exchange reserve base.

Wages and Prices

Inflation has become a source of major concern, not least to the workforce, whose new-found affluence is threatened. Until recently, inflation was regarded by the Government as a price to be paid for economic growth, but now its containment is central to government policy. The country can no longer be regarded as a cheap-labour nation, so its export competitiveness is threatened (including the dominance of the labour-intensive Middle East construction business and the ability of the Export Zones to attract foreign investors).

The real increase in wages averaged only 8.8 per cent a year over the period 1970/78; the comparable increase in productivity was about 10 per cent. However, the temporary slowing down of inflation in 1976 gave unions the opportunity to secure big gains in real wages. The high productivity of Korean workers justified such increases initially, but by the end of the decade wage rises were out of step with productivity. Many Korean workers now earn more than their counterparts in rival exporting nations such as Hong Kong and the many workers employed by the big companies profit also enjoy wide-ranging fringe benefits.

With skilled workers securing proportionately greater wage increases, the issue of wage differentials is likely to come increasingly to the fore. However, out of a potential union strength of 3.7 million, only about 0.6 million workers belong to a union. The likely trend towards less labour intensive industries will change the roll of unions; also the employee-management councils, resulting from legislation that became effective in 1981, could undermine this role, though the present purpose of the councils is to improve the position of workers in non-union factories.

Inflationary pressures re-emerged in 1977 due to the money supply difficulties. Concern over the resultant boom in consumer spending led to appeals for workers to adopt a frugal life style and to increase savings in the national interest. Fears that the upsurge in consumer spending could jeopardize the target of the economic planners were highlighted in 1978, for example, when expenditure on consumer durables rose by 32 per cent, even after allowing for price increases. By 1980 inflation pressures were intense. In that year the devalued won floated further downwards to give an overall decline of 36 per cent against the already weak U.S. dollar. This was a major factor in pushing up wholesale prices by 44 per cent and consumer prices by 35 per cent. Unemployment rose, too, including 5 per cent of the work force, despite a strategy designed to reduce overtime instead of releasing workers.

In 1981 the pace of inflation moderated to 12.6 per cent and the value of the won fell by only 5.4 per cent. Real incomes fell by 3.4 per cent; the 20.3 per cent increase in consumer expenditure was, in fact, equivalent to a 2.5 per cent fall in real terms.

PLANNING

Scarcely three months after launching the Fourth Five-Year Plan in January 1977, the Government felt constrained to revise the basic framework of its targets, calling for their achievement one year earlier than originally envisaged. The basic reasoning behind such radical revision was the increased indigenous defence burden resulting from the planned early withdrawal of U.S. forces that called for an upward revision of the annual growth target from 9.2 per cent to more than 10 per cent. To this end, the annual investment ratio needed to be increased from 26 to 31 per cent, domestic savings from 24 to 27 per cent and overseas savings from 3.4 per cent to between 4 and 5 per cent.

The Fourth Five-Year Plan aimed to increase capacity and production, to create more jobs and to improve the infrastructure. It called for annual average G.N.P. growth of 9 per cent compared with almost 10 per cent for the Third Plan, 10.5 per cent in the Second Plan and 7.7 per cent in the First Plan.

The strategy of industrial development revolved around substantial fiscal support, private initiatives strongly supported by the Government's various measures, expansion of social overhead capital investment so as to smooth out the flow of economic activities, a dynamic balance of payments policy including activated flows of foreign capital into productive investments, rapid export expansion particularly of manufactured goods, and considerably fewer restrictive import schemes to cope with the rapid economic changes in both internal and the external sectors.

The Fourth Plan differed from previous ones in its added emphasis on social development. This programme was designed to facilitate more equitable distribution of wealth, and called for more government spending on housing, education, public health, medical care and insurance programmes. During the Third Plan, spending for this purpose accounted for 17.3 per cent of total investment. The figure was to rise to 20.6 per cent during the Fourth Plan.

The economic stabilization plan, announced in April 1979, sought to place investment in the heavy and chemical industries on a more selective basis, enabling some funds to be diverted into light industry. New investment was to be split on a 60:40 basis between heavy and light industry, instead of the present 70:30. Also, government spending, mainly in construction, would be curtailed. These measures aimed to reduce the rate of real economic growth from 11 to 9 per cent, an effort to check unwanted features of the economy, notably inflationary pressures, in order to provide a stable base upon which the ambitious long-term developments can be built.

The Fifth Five-Year Economic and Social Development Plan, covering the years 1982–86, assumes that structural readjustment is essential to further economic growth and that fundamental reforms across a broad area of the economy need to be implemented by 1983 in preparation for "another take-off" in the latter half of the Plan period. It is intended that tax revenue shall rise (from 18.4 per cent of G.D.P. in 1981 to 22.0 per cent in 1986) while preferential exemptions from (and rebates on) corporate taxes, import tariffs, etc. will be gradually reduced. In the monetary field, interest rates will be kept positive in real terms, policy preference loans at subsidized interest rates will be curtailed; short-term export credit will also be curtailed but there will be more credit to finance export sales on deferred terms. Government intervention in banking will be kept to a minimum. These commitments amount to a decisive withdrawal from detailed government control over bank lending policies, which made it extremely difficult for a company to move in a direction that the government did not favour. The plan also promises to liberalize imports further, to lower prohibitively high tariffs, to increase the opportunities and incentives for foreign investment, and to take domestic policy measures designed to remove obstacles to competition.

The overall Plan target is an average G.N.P. growth rate of 7.6 per cent, measured in constant 1980 prices. As in the past, exports are to provide the main driving force, with a target growth rate of 11.4 per cent annually in real terms (compared with one of 8.4 per cent for imports). Investment, too, is to show an above-average annual growth rate, of 8.8 per cent, which would leave it accounting for 32.4 per cent of G.N.P. in 1986. Domestic savings would account for 29.6 per cent of G.N.P. in that year. In output terms, an average rate of increase of 10.8 per cent is foreseen for manufacturing and mining, which would leave them producing 35.0 per cent of G.N.P. in 1986, compared with 30.7 per cent in 1980. The heavy and chemical industries would average a 12.2 per cent growth rate, and light industry one of 9.5 per cent. It is expected that employment will grow by 3 per cent annually but the labour force by only 2.8 per cent, so that unemployment would fall over the five years to 4 per cent in 1986. Inflation is expected to moderate, the G.N.P. deflator being reduced from 27.7 per cent in 1980 to 9.5 per cent in 1986.

Although the Plan anticipates a moderate reduction in the trade deficit and the current account deficit, it envisages a gross foreign capital requirement of $46,500 million over five years, of which 44.7 per cent is required to finance the current deficit, 34.2 per cent for debt amortization and the rest to finance exports on deferred terms and to increase the exchange reserves. Loan capital would provide 71.6 per cent of the total and foreign currency bond issues 3.7 per cent. The remaining 24.7 per cent includes direct investment and, perhaps, portfolio investment. On the assumption that the debt structure is improved by heavier reliance on long-term borrowing from international agencies, it is planned that the debt servicing ratio should fall slightly, from 13.3 per cent in 1980 to 11.0 per cent in 1986.

Two of the key international assumptions of the Plan are that the volume of world trade will grow by an average of 5 per cent annually during the Plan period and that oil prices will rise, in nominal terms, by 10 per cent a year. If criticisms that these assumptions are too optimistic should be substantiated, the export prospects will not be fulfilled. It is also possible that the Plan underestimates domestic growth potential.

DEMOCRATIC PEOPLE'S REPUBLIC OF KOREA

STATISTICAL SURVEY

AREA AND POPULATION

Area*	Population					
	Official Estimates‡		UN Estimates (mid-year)			
	Dec. 31st, 1960	Oct. 1st, 1963	1977	1978	1979	1980
120,538 sq. km.†	10,789,000	11,568,000	16,657,000	17,063,000	17,475,000	17,892,000

* Excluding the demilitarized zone between North and South Korea, with an area of 1,262 square kilometres (487 square miles).

† 46,540 square miles.

‡ *Source:* Institute of Economics of the World Socialist System, Moscow.

PRINCIPAL CITIES
(estimated population 1976)

Pyongyang (capital)	1,500,000
Chongjin	300,000
Hungnam	260,000
Kaesong	240,000

Source: Far Eastern Economic Review, *Asia 1977 Yearbook*.

Births and deaths: Average annual birth rate 35.7 per 1,000 in 1970–75, 32.5 per 1,000 in 1975–80; death rate 9.4 per 1,000 in 1970–75, 8.3 per 1,000 in 1975–80 (UN estimates).

LABOUR FORCE
(ILO estimates, '000 persons at mid-year)

	1960			1970		
	Males	Females	Total	Males	Females	Total
Agriculture, etc.	1,334	1,620	2,954	1,483	1,794	3,278
Industry	705	405	1,110	1,073	584	1,657
Services	478	225	703	683	375	1,058
Total	2,517	2,250	4,767	3,239	2,753	5,993

Source: ILO, *Labour Force Estimates and Projections, 1950–2000.*

Mid-1980 (estimates in '000): Agriculture etc. 3,670; Total 8,002 (*Source:* FAO, *Production Yearbook*).

AGRICULTURE

LAND USE, 1979
(FAO estimates, '000 hectares)

Arable land	2,140
Land under permanent crops	90
Permanent meadows and pastures	50
Forests and woodland	8,970*
Other land	791
Inland water	13
Total Area	12,054

* Including rough grazing. Data taken from the world forest inventory carried out by the FAO in 1958.

Source: FAO, *Production Yearbook.*

PRINCIPAL CROPS
(FAO estimates)

	Area Harvested ('000 hectares)			Production ('000 metric tons)		
	1978	1979	1980	1978	1979	1980
Wheat	150	150	155	350	370	380
Rice (paddy)	780	780	800	4,500	4,800	4,800
Barley	170	200	210	350	380	380
Maize	360	370	380	1,850	1,950	2,200
Rye	33	33	34	55	55	50
Oats	70	80	80	125	130	130
Millet	410	415	420	430	440	440
Sorghum	120	120	120	120	130	130
Potatoes	118	120	125	1,450	1,500	1,550
Sweet potatoes	26	27	28	365	370	375
Pulses	325	327	330	274	280	280
Soybeans	300	300	300	320	330	340
Cottonseed	} 15	15	15	6	6	6
Cotton (lint)				3	3	3
Tobacco	34	35	36	42	43	45
Hemp fibre	8	8	8	2	2	3

Source: FAO, *Production Yearbook.*

LIVESTOCK
(FAO estimates, '000 head, year ending September).

	1978	1979	1980
Horses	35	36	37
Asses	3	3	3
Cattle	900	925	950
Pigs	1,900	2,000	2,100
Sheep	280	285	290
Goats	220	230	240

Source: FAO, *Production Yearbook.*

LIVESTOCK PRODUCTS
(FAO estimates, metric tons)

	1978	1979	1980
Beef and Veal	29,000	30,000	31,000
Mutton and Lamb	1,000	1,000	1,000
Goats' Meat	1,000	1,000	1,000
Pigmeat	96,000	106,000	115,000
Poultry Meat	31,000	32,000	32,000
Cows' Milk	42,000	50,000	57,000
Hen Eggs	92,500	99,500	105,000
Raw Silk	2,400	2,550	2,700
Cattle Hides	3,990	4,137	4,305

Source: FAO, *Production Yearbook.*

FORESTRY

ROUNDWOOD REMOVALS
(FAO estimates, '000 cubic metres, excluding bark)

	Coniferous (soft wood)			Broadleaved (hard wood)			Total		
	1978	1979	1980	1978	1979	1980	1978	1979	1980
Industrial wood	400	400	400	200	200	200	600	600	600
Fuel wood	3,416	3,500	3,585	1,708	1,750	1,750	5,124	5,250	5,335
Total	3,816	3,900	3,985	1,908	1,950	1,950	5,724	5,850	5,935

Sawnwood production ('000 cubic metres): 280 (coniferous 185, broadleaved 95) per year (FAO estimates).

Source: FAO, *Yearbook of Forest Products.*

FISHING

(FAO estimates, 'ooo metric tons, live weight)

	1975	1976	1977	1978	1979	1980
Inland waters	50	56	60	60	66	70
Pacific Ocean	1,000	1,064	1,130	1,200	1,264	1,330
TOTAL CATCH	1,050	1,120	1,190	1,260	1,330	1,400

Source: FAO, *Yearbook of Fishery Statistics.*

MINING

(estimated production)

		1976	1977	1978	1979
Anthracite	'ooo metric tons	33,000	34,000	35,000	35,000
Bituminous coal and lignite	" " "	9,000	10,000	10,500	10,000
Iron ore*	" " "	3,800	3,902	4,003	4,003
Copper ore*	" " "	15	15	15	15
Lead ore*	" " "	110	110	105	105
Magnesite	" " "	1,500	1,500	1,500	n.a.
Tungsten concentrates*	metric tons	2,700	2,700	2,700	2,700
Zinc ore*	'ooo metric tons	150	150	140	140
Salt	" " "	540	540	540	540
Phosphate rock	" " "	450	500	500	500
Sulphur†	" " "	245	250	255	255
Graphite	" " "	75	75	75	75
Silver	metric tons	50	50	50	50
Gold	kilogrammes	5,000	5,000	5,000	5,000

Note: No recent data are available for the production of molybdenum ore and asbestos.

* Figures relate to the metal content of ores and concentrates.

† Figures refer to the sulphur content of iron and copper pyrites, including pyrite concentrates obtained from copper, lead and zinc ores.

Source: U.S. Bureau of Mines.

INDUSTRY

(estimated production—'ooo metric tons)

	1976	1977	1978	1979
Nitrogenous Fertilizers (*a*)*	370	440	540	550
Phosphate Fertilizers (*b*)*	127	127	127	127
Coke†	2,500	2,500	2,650	2,750
Cement†	7,000	7,000	7,000	8,000
Pig Iron and Ferro-alloys†	3,000	3,500	4,000	4,000
Crude Steel†	3,000	3,500	4,000	4,000
Refined Copper (unwrought)†	25	25	25	25
Lead (primary metal)†	78	70	75	75
Zinc (primary metal)†	135	135	130	130

* Figures for fertilizer production are unofficial estimates quoted by the FAO. Output is measured in terms of (*a*) nitrogen or (*b*) phosphoric acid.

† *Source:* U.S. Bureau of Mines.

FINANCE

100 chon (jun) = 1 won.

Coins: 1, 5 and 10 chon.

Notes: 50 chon; 1, 5, 10, 50 and 100 won.

Exchange rates (June 1982): £1 sterling = 1.724 won (basic rate) or 3.686 won (non-commercial rate), U.S. $1 = 97.15 chon (basic rate) or 2.128 won (non-commercial rate). 100 won = £58.02 = $102.93 (basic rates).

Note: The new won, equal to 100 old won, was introduced in February 1959. From 1958 the basic exchange rate was U.S. $1 = 120 old won. The initial basic rate of $1 = 1.20 new won (1 won = 83.33 U.S. cents) remained in force until August 1971. From December 1971 to February 1973 the basic rate was $1 = 1.105 won (1 won = 90.48 U.S. cents). In terms of sterling, the basic rate was £1 = 2.88 won from November 1967 to June 1972. In January 1961 a commercial exchange rate was established for foreign trade transactions. This was fixed at £1 = 6.16 won, equal to $1 = 2.20 won until November 1967. The commercial rate, tied to sterling, was $1 = 2.567 won from November 1967 to August 1971; and $1 = 2.364 won from December 1971 to June 1972. The commercial rate was abolished in June 1972, when sterling was "floated". Since February 1973 the non-commercial rate has been $1 = 2.128 won. The basic rate is linked to the Soviet rouble at a parity of 1 rouble = 1.34 won.

BUDGET
(million won)

	1976	1977	1978	1979	1980*
Revenue	12,513.2	13,789.0	15,657.3	17,477.9	18,893.6
Expenditure	12,513.2	13,349.2	14,743.6	16,972.6	18,893.6

* Provisional.

1981 (estimate): 20,480 million won.

SEVEN-YEAR PLAN, 1978–84

		1984 TARGETS
Electricity	million kWh.	56,000–60,000
Coal	million metric tons	70–80
Iron ore	,, ,, ,,	16
Non-ferrous metal ores	,, ,, ,,	1
Pig iron, granulated iron, blister steel	,, ,, ,,	6.4–7.0
Steel	,, ,, ,,	7.4–8.0
Rolled steel	,, ,, ,,	5.6–6.0
Cement	,, ,, ,,	12–13
Engineering products	,, ,, ,,	5
Machine tools	number	50,000
Tractors	,,	45,000
Textiles	million metres	800
Sugar	metric tons	300,000
Aquatic products	million metric tons	3.5
Grain	,, ,, ,,	10
Fruit	,, ,, ,,	1.5
Meat	metric tons	800,000–900,000

EXTERNAL TRADE

APPARENT EXPORTS OF SELECTED MINERAL COMMODITIES*

(metric tons)

	1972	1973	1974	1975
Iron ore and concentrate	527,081	423,348	304,533	202,705
Pig iron and cast iron	135,702	107,139	106,220	148,384
Steel, semi-manufactures	93,600	101,108	112,818	125,642
Lead metal and alloys, all forms	36,109	37,840	42,168	62,620
Zinc:				
Ore and concentrate	3,508	2,822	51,795	52,299
Metal and alloys, all forms	52,221	65,729	48,320	56,169
Cement	428,000	495,290	345,000	500,000
Clay products, refractory	341,800	n.a.	n.a.	n.a.
Magnesite	522,777	524,901	576,868	629,946
Coal and coal briquettes	61,667	46,056	236,764	36,938

* Compiled from import data of partner countries.

Source: U.S. Department of the Interior, *Bureau of Mines Minerals Yearbook*, 1973–76.

SELECTED TRADING PARTNERS

(U.S. $ million at Dec. 1979 rates)

	Exports		Imports	
	1979	1980	1979	1980
Austria	1.32	0.55	6.92	4.55
Belgium/Luxembourg	1.12	0.32*	0.75	0.42*
Denmark	0.12	0.23	0.61	0.24
Federal Republic of Germany	76.81	173.51	35.67	30.31
France	30.31	17.69	8.45	4.42
Hong Kong	21.37†	28.05†	1.71	1.17
Ireland	n.a.	0.19*	n.a.	0.08*
Italy	8.99	13.27*	9.82	7.28*
Japan	135.68	190.92‡	256.84	379.39‡
Netherlands	0.90	0.22*	4.69	3.76*
Norway	1.11	0.08	n.a.	0.09
Singapore	8.76	9.39*	38.33	38.51*
Sweden	0.84	1.37*	2.05	7.56*
Switzerland	16.21	45.75	11.09	8.51
United Kingdom	2.14	0.94	1.80	2.35
U.S.S.R.	398.14	n.a.	365.53	n.a.

* Estimate.

† Re-exports to Korea (U.S. $ million): 36.46 (1979); 57.49 (1980).

‡ Nov. 1979/Nov. 1980.

Source: Country Survey: North Korea, Ostasiatischer Verein EV, Hamburg.

TRANSPORT

INTERNATIONAL SEA-BORNE SHIPPING

(estimated traffic, '000 metric tons)

	1973	1974	1975
Goods loaded	854	1,100	1,300
Goods unloaded	1,210	1,850	2,000

Source: United Nations, *Statistical Yearbook.*

EDUCATION

(1966–67)

	Schools	Teachers	Pupils
Primary	4,064	22,132	1,113,000†
Middle	3,335	30,031	704,000†
Technical	1,207	12,144	285,000†
Higher Technical	500*	5,862	156,000†
University and Colleges	129*	9,244	200,000*

* 1970. † 1964–65.

1974: (Estimates): schools 10,000; pupils 3,000,000 (primary 1,500,000, secondary 1,200,000, tertiary 300,000).

THE CONSTITUTION

(adopted December 27th, 1972)

The following is a summary of the main provisions of the Constitution.

Articles 1-6: The Democratic People's Republic is an independent socialist State (Art. 1); the revolutionary traditions of the State are stressed (its ideological basis being the *Juche* idea of the Workers' Party of Korea) as is the desire to achieve national reunification by peaceful means on the basis of national independence.

Articles 7-10: National sovereignty rests with the working people who exercise power through the Supreme People's Assembly and People's Assemblies at lower levels, which are elected by universal, secret and direct suffrage.

Articles 11-17: Defence is emphasized as well as the rights of overseas nationals, the principles of friendly relations between nations based on equality, mutual respect and non-interference, proletarian internationalism, support for national liberation struggles and due observance of law.

Articles 18-48: Culture and education provide the working people with knowledge to advance a socialist way of life. Education is free and there are universal and compulsory one-year pre-school and ten-year senior middle school programmes in being.

Articles 49-72: The basic rights and duties of citizens are laid down and guaranteed. These include the right to vote (for those over the age of 17), to work (the working day being eight hours), to free medical care and material assistance for the old, infirm or disabled, to political asylum. National defence is the supreme duty of citizens.

Articles 73-88: The Supreme People's Assembly is the highest organ of State power, exercises exclusive legislative authority and is elected by direct, equal, universal and secret ballot for a term of four years. Its chief functions are: (i) to adopt or amend legal or constitutional enactments; (ii) to determine State policy; (iii) to elect the President, Vice-President, Secretary and members of the Central People's Committee (on the President's recommendation); (iv) to elect members of the Standing Committee of the Supreme People's Assembly, the Premier of the Administration Council (on the President's recommendation), the President of the Central Court and other legal officials; (v) to approve the State Plan and Budget; (vi) to decide on matters of war and peace. It holds regular and extraordinary sessions, the former being twice a year, the latter as necessary at the request of at least one-third of the deputies. Legislative enactments are adopted when approved by more than half of those deputies present. The Standing Committee is the permanent body of the Supreme People's Assembly. It examines and decides on bills; amends legislation in force when the Supreme People's Assembly is not in session; interprets the law; organizes and conducts the election of Deputies and judicial personnel.

Articles 89-99: The President as Head of State is elected for four years by the Supreme People's Assembly. He convenes and presides over Administrative Council meetings, is the Supreme Commander of the Armed Forces and chairman of the National Defence Commission. The President promulgates laws of the Supreme People's Assembly and decisions of the Central People's Committee and of the Standing Committee. He has the right to issue orders, to grant pardons, to ratify or abrogate treaties and to receive foreign envoys. The President is responsible to the Supreme People's Assembly.

Articles 100-106: The Central People's Committee comprises the President, Vice-President, Secretary and Members. The Committee exercises the following chief functions: (a) to direct the work of the Administration Council as well as organs at local level; (b) to implement the constitution and legislative enactments; (c) to establish and abolish Ministries, appoint Vice-Premiers and other members of the Administration Council; (d) to appoint and recall ambassadors and defence personnel; (e) to confer titles, decorations, diplomatic appointments; (f) to grant general amnesties, make administrative changes; (g) to declare a state of war. It is assisted by a number of Commissions dealing with Internal Policy, Foreign Policy, National Defence, Justice and Security and other matters as may be established. The Central People's Committee is responsible to the Supreme People's Assembly's Standing Committee.

Articles 107-114: The Administration Council is the administrative and executive body of the Supreme People's Assembly. It comprises the Premier, Vice-Premiers and such other Ministers as may be appointed. Its major functions are the following: (i) to direct the work of Ministries and other organs responsible to it; (ii) to work out the State Plan and take measures to make it effective; (iii) to compile the State Budget and to give effect to it; (iv) to organize and execute the work of all sectors of the economy as well as transport, education and social welfare; (v) to conclude treaties; (vi) to develop the armed forces and maintain public security; (vii) to annul decisions and directives of State administrative departments which run counter to those of the Administration Council. The Administration Council is responsible to the President, Central People's Committee and the Supreme People's Assembly.

Articles 115-132: The People's Assemblies of the province (or municipality directly under central authority), city (or district) and county are local organs of power. The People's Assemblies or Committees exercise local budgetary functions, elect local administrative and judicial personnel and carry out the decisions at local level of higher executive and administrative organs.

Articles 133-146: Justice is administered by the Centra Court—the highest judicial organ of the State, the loca Court, the People's Court and the Special Court. Judges and other legal officials are elected by the Supreme People's Assembly. The Central Court protects State property, Constitutional rights, guarantees that all State bodies and citizens observe State laws and executes judgements. Justice is administered by the court comprising one judge and two people's assessors. The Court is independent and judicially impartial. Judicial affairs are conducted by the Central Procurator's Office which exposes and institutes criminal proceedings against accused persons. The Office of the Central Procurator is responsible to the Supreme People's Assembly, the President, and the Central People's Committee.

Articles 147-149: These articles describe the national emblem, the national flag and designate Pyongyang as the capital.

THE GOVERNMENT

HEAD OF STATE

President: Marshal KIM IL SUNG (took office December 28th, 1972; re-elected December 1977).

Vice-Presidents: KIM IL, KANG RYANG UK, PAK SUNG CHUL.

CENTRAL PEOPLE'S COMMITTEE

Members:

Marshal KIM IL SUNG
KIM IL
KANG RYANG UK
CHOE HYON
PAK SUNG CHUL
Gen. O JIN U
SO CHOL
LI JONG OK
O BAEK RYONG
KIM HWAN
HONG SI HAK
KIM MAN GUM
PAK YONG SOK

Secretary: HO CHUNG SUK

ADMINISTRATION COUNCIL

(January 1982)

Premier: LI JONG OK.

Vice-Premiers:

KYE UNG TAE
HO DAM
CHONG JUN GI
KANG SONG SAN
CHOE KWANG
SO GWAN HI
KIM HOE IL
KONG JIN TAE
KIM DU YONG
JO SE UNG
CHOE JAE U
KIM GYONG RYON
KIM BOK SIN

Secretary: KIM YUN HYOK.

Minister of People's Armed Forces: Gen. O JIN U.

Minister of Foreign Affairs: HO DAM.

Minister of Public Security: LI JIN SU.

Chairman of the State Planning Commission: HONG SONG RYONG.

Chairman of the Agricultural Commission: SO GWAN HI.

Minister of Mining Industry: CHO CHANG DOK.

Minister of Metal Industry: KIM YOUN HYOK.

Minister of Power Industry: LI JI CHAN.

Minister of Machine Industry: (vacant).

Minister of Chemical Industry: WON DONG GU.

Minister of Construction: JO CHOL JUN.

Chairman of the State Construction Commission: KIM UNG SANG.

Minister of Building Materials Industry: KIM JONG SONG.

Chairman of the Light Industry Commission: HO SUN.

Minister of Railways: KANG SONG SAN.

Minister of Land and Sea Transportation: LI CHOL BONG.

Minister of Fisheries: KIM YUN SANG.

Chairman of the People's Service Commission: RIM HYONG GU.

Chairman of the Education Commission: CHOE TAE BOK.

Minister of Materials Supply: KIM TAE GUK.

Minister of Communications: KIM YONG CHAE.

Minister of Culture and Art: LI CHANG SON.

Minister of Finance: YOUN KI JONG.

Minister of Foreign Trade: KYE UNG TAE.

Minister of External Economic Affairs: JONG SONG NAM.

Minister of Labour Administration: CHAE HUI JONG.

Chairman of the State Scientific and Technological Commission: CHU HWA JONG.

Minister of Public Health: PAK MYONG BIN.

Minister of Territorial Administration: CHOE WON IK.

LEGISLATURE

CHOE KO IN MIN HOE UI

(*Supreme People's Assembly*)

The 579 members of the Sixth Supreme People's Assembly were elected unopposed for a four-year term on November 11th, 1977. New elections were scheduled for February 28th, 1982.

STANDING COMMITTEE

Chairman: HWANG JANG YOP.

Vice-Chairmen: HO JONG SUK, HONG GI MUN.

Secretary: (vacant).

Members:

KIM YONG NAM
CHONG DONG CHOL
YUN GI BOK
KIM GWAN SOP
KIM GI NAM
KIM BONG JU
CHANG YUN PIL
KIM SONG AE
SON SONG PIL
CHON SE BONG

POLITICAL PARTIES

The Democratic Front for the Reunification of the Fatherland: Pyongyang; f. 1949; a united national front organization embracing patriotic political parties and social organizations for reunification of North and South Korea; Sec.-Gen. Ho Jong Suk.

Members of the Presidium:

Kang Ryang Uk, Han Duk Su, So Chol, Chong Du Hwan.

The component parties are:

The Workers' Party of Korea: Pyongyang; f. October 10th, 1945; the ruling party; leads Democratic Front for the Reunification of the Fatherland; the guiding principle is the *Juche* idea, based on the philosophy that man is the master of all things; Gen. Sec. of the Central Committee: Kim Il Sung; Presidium of the Politburo: Kim Il Sung, Kim Il, Gen. O. Jin U, Kim Jong Il, Li Jong Ok; publs. *Rodong Sinmun* (newspaper), *Kunroja* (theoretical journal).

Chondoist Chongu Party: Pyongyang; f. 1945; supports policies of Workers' Party; Chair. Jong Sin Hyok.

Korean Social-Democratic Party: Pyongyang; f. 1945; supports policies of the Workers' Party; Chair. Kang Ryang Uk.

DIPLOMATIC REPRESENTATION

EMBASSIES ACCREDITED TO THE DEMOCRATIC PEOPLE'S REPUBLIC OF KOREA

(In Pyongyang unless otherwise stated)

Albania: *Ambassador:* Miltiadh Bode.

Algeria: Munsudong; *Chargé d'affaires a.i.:* Laredj Abdelfettah.

Australia: Beijing, People's Republic of China.

Austria: Beijing, People's Republic of China.

Bangladesh: Beijing, People's Republic of China.

Benin: Beijing, People's Republic of China.

Bulgaria: *Ambassador:* Kristo Kelchev.

Burma: *Ambassador:* U Aung Win.

Burundi: Beijing, People's Republic of China.

Chad: Beijing, People's Republic of China.

China, People's Republic: *Ambassador:* Lu Zhixian.

Congo: Beijing, People's Republic of China.

Cuba: *Ambassador:* Wilfredo Rodríguez Cardenas.

Czechoslovakia: *Ambassador:* Josef Hadravek.

Denmark: Beijing, People's Republic of China.

Egypt: *Ambassador:* Muhammad Abdel Rahman Abdel Salam.

Equatorial Guinea: Beijing, People's Republic of China.

Ethiopia: Beijing, People's Republic of China.

Finland: Beijing, People's Republic of China.

Gabon: *Ambassador:* Ignace Vane.

German Democratic Republic: Munsudong; *Ambassador:* Hermann Schwiesau.

Guinea: Beijing, People's Republic of China.

Guyana: Beijing, People's Republic of China.

Hungary: *Ambassador:* Sándor Etre.

India: *Ambassador:* (vacant).

Indonesia: 5 Foreigners' Bldg., Moon Sol Dong Tai, Dong Kang District; *Ambassador:* R. Djundjunan Kusumahardja.

Iran: *Ambassador:* Asghar Nahavandian.

Jordan: *Ambassador:* Hani al-Khasawinah.

Laos: Beijing, People's Republic of China.

Libya: *Secretary of People's Bureau:* Abdulmaged Kashkusha.

Madagascar: Beijing, People's Republic of China.

Mali: Beijing, People's Republic of China.

Mexico: *Ambassador:* Eugenio Anguiano Roch.

Mongolia: *Ambassador:* Tse. Demiddagva.

Nepal: Beijing, People's Republic of China.

Nigeria: Beijing, People's Republic of China.

Norway: Beijing, People's Republic of China.

Pakistan: Munsudong; *Ambassador:* Ghulam Rabbani.

Poland: *Ambassador:* Leon Tomaszewski.

Portugal: *Ambassador:* António Eduardo de Carvalho Ressano Garcia.

Romania: *Ambassador:* Constantin Iftodi.

Rwanda: Beijing, People's Republic of China.

Senegal: Beijing, People's Republic of China.

Sierra Leone: Beijing, People's Republic of China.

Somalia: Beijing, People's Republic of China.

Sri Lanka: Beijing, People's Republic of China.

Sudan: Beijing, People's Republic of China.

Sweden: Beijing, People's Republic of China.

Syria: *Chargé d'affaires a.i.:* Anwar Wahbi.

Tanzania: Beijing, People's Republic of China.

Thailand: Beijing, People's Republic of China.

Togo: Beijing, People's Republic of China.

Tunisia: Beijing, People's Republic of China.

Uganda: Beijing, People's Republic of China.

Upper Volta: *Ambassador:* Dah Monvel Michel.

U.S.S.R.: *Ambassador:* G. A. Kriulin.

Viet-Nam: *Ambassador:* Le Trung Nam.

Yemen Arab Republic: Beijing, People's Republic of China.

Yemen, People's Democratic Republic: Beijing, People's Republic of China.

Yugoslavia: *Ambassador:* Ljupčo Tavčiovski.

Zaire: *Ambassador:* Tuma Waku Dia Bazika.

Zambia: Beijing, People's Republic of China.

The Democratic People's Republic of Korea also has diplomatic relations with Afghanistan, Angola, Argentina, Barbados, Botswana, Cape Verde, the Central African Republic, the Comoros, Costa Rica, Dominica, Fiji, The Gambia, Ghana, Grenada, Guinea-Bissau, Iceland, Jamaica, Kampuchea, Kenya, Lebanon, Lesotho, Liberia, Malawi, Malaysia, Maldives, Malta, Mauritania, Mozambique, Nauru, Nicaragua, Niger, Papua New Guinea, Saint Lucia, São Tomé and Príncipe, Seychelles, Singapore, Switzerland, Vanuatu, Venezuela, Western Samoa and Zimbabwe.

JUDICIAL SYSTEM

The judicial organs include the Central Court, the Court of the Province (or city under central authority) and the People's Court. Each court is composed of judges and people's assessors.

Central Court: Pyongyang; the Central Court is the highest judicial organ and supervises the findings of all courts.

President: PANG HAK SE.

Central Procurator's Office: supervises work of procurator's offices in provinces, cities and counties.

Procurator-General: (vacant).

Procurators supervise the ordinances and regulations of all ministries and the decisions and directives of local organs of state power to see that they conform to the Constitution, laws and decrees, as well as to the decisions and orders of the Cabinet. Procurators bring suits against criminals in the name of the state, and participate in civil cases to protect the interests of the state and citizens.

RELIGION

The traditional religions are Buddhism, Confucianism, Shamanism and Chundo Kyo, a religion peculiar to Korea combining elements of Buddhism and Christianity.

BUDDHISM

Korean Buddhist Federation: Pyongyang; Chair. PAK TAE HO.

THE PRESS

PRINCIPAL NEWSPAPERS

Jokook Tongil: Pyongyang; organ of the Committee for the Peaceful Unification of Korea.

Joson Inmingun (*Korean People's Army*): Pyongyang; f. 1948.

Kyowen Shinmoon: Ministry of General Education.

Minjoo Chosun: Pyongyang; government organ; 6 issues per week; Editor-in-Chief CHAE JUN BYONG.

Nongup Keunroja: Pyongyang; Central Committee of the Korean Agricultural Working People's Union.

Pyongyang Shinmoon: Pyongyang; general news.

Rodong Chongyon: Pyongyang; organ of the Central Committee of the Socialist Working Youth League of Korea; 6 issues per week.

Rodong Sinmun (*Labour Daily*): Pyongyang; f. 1946; organ of the Central Committee of the Workers' Party of Korea; daily; Editor-in-Chief KIM GI NAM; circ. 700,000.

Rodongja Shinmoon: Pyongyang; General Federation of Trade Unions of Korea.

Saenal: Pyongyang; League of Socialist Working Youth of Korea.

Sonyon Sinmun: Pyongyang; League of Socialist Working Youth of Korea.

Tongil Sinbo: Pyongyang; non-affiliated.

PRINCIPAL PERIODICALS

Chollima: Pyongyang; popular magazine; monthly.

Choson (*Pictorial*): Pyongyang; social, economic, political and cultural; monthly.

Choson Munhak: Pyongyang; organ of the Central Committee of the Korean Writers' Union; monthly.

Choson Yesul: Pyongyang; organ of the Central Committee of the General Federation of Literature and Arts of Korea; monthly.

Hwahakkwa Hwahak Kongop: Pyongyang; organ of the Hamhung branch of the Korean Academy of Sciences; every two months.

Kunroja: 1 Munshin Dong, Tongdaewon, Pyongyang; f. 1946; organ of the Central Committee of the Workers' Party of Korea; monthly; circ. 300,000.

Kwahakwon Tongbo: Pyongyang; organ of the Standing Committee of the Korean Academy of Sciences; every two months.

Munhwaohaksup: Pyongyang; published by the Publishing House of the Academy of Social Sciences; quarterly.

Punsok Hwahak: Pyongyang; organ of the Central Analytical Institute of the Korean Academy of Sciences; quarterly.

Ryoksagwahak: Pyongyang; published by the Academy of Social Sciences; quarterly.

Sahoekwahak: Pyongyang; published by the Academy of Social Sciences; every two months.

Suhakkwa Mulli: Pyongyang; organ of the Physics and Mathematics Committee of the Korean Academy of Sciences; quarterly.

FOREIGN LANGUAGE PUBLICATIONS

The Agricultural Working People of Korea: Pyongyang; English, French and Russian; every two months.

The Democratic People's Republic of Korea: Foreign Languages Publishing House, Pyongyang; illustrated news; English, French and Spanish; monthly.

Foreign Trade: Foreign Trade Publishing House, Potonggang District, Pyongyang; economic developments and export promotion; English, French, Japanese, Russian and Spanish; monthly.

Korea: Pyongyang; pictorial in Chinese, English, French, Spanish and Russian; monthly.

Korea Today: Foreign Languages Publishing House, Pyongyang; current affairs; Chinese, English, French, Russian and Spanish; monthly.

Korean Nature: Pyongyang; English; quarterly.

Korean Stamps: Pyongyang; English and French; published by the Philatelists' Union of the DPRK; every 2 months.

The Korean Trade Unions: Pyongyang; English and French; every two months.

Korean Women: Pyongyang; English and French; quarterly.

Korean Youth and Students: Pyongyang; English and French; every two months.

New Korea: Pyongyang; Russian and Chinese.

The Pyongyang Times: Pyongyang; English and French; weekly.

NEWS AGENCIES

Korean Central News Agency (KCNA): Potonggang-dong 1, Potonggang District, Pyongyang; f. 1946; sole distributing agency for news in the DPRK; Gen. Dir. KIM SONG GOL; publs. *Choson Chungang Tongsin* (daily), *Chamgo Tongsin* (morning and evening), *Choson Chungang Nyongam* (Korean Central Yearbook), *Telephoto* (daily) and daily bulletins in English, Russian, French and Spanish.

FOREIGN BUREAUX

Agentstvo Pechati Novosti (APN) (*U.S.S.R.*): Pyongyang; Correspondent ALEXANDER B. DENISOVICH.

TASS (U.S.S.R.) and Xinhua (People's Republic of China) are also represented.

PUBLISHERS

PYONGYANG

Academy of Sciences Publishing House: Central District, Nammundong; f. 1953; publs. *Kwahakwon Tongbo* (Journal of the Academy of Sciences of the Democratic People's Republic of Korea) bi-monthly; *Kwahakgwa Kwahakgoneop* (Journal of Chemistry and the Chemical Industry) bi-monthly; also quarterly journals of Geology and Geography; Metals; Biology; Analytical Chemistry; Mathematics and Physics; and Electricity.

Academy of Social Sciences Publishing House.

Agricultural Books Publishing House: Pres. LI HYUN U.

Economic Publishing House.

Educational Books Publishing House.

Foreign Languages Publishing House: Pres. L. RYANG HUN.

Foreign Trade Publishing House: Oesong District.

Higher Educational Books Publishing House: Acting Pres. SHIN JONG SUNG.

Industry Publishing House.

Korean Workers' Party Publishing House.

Mass Culture Publishing House.

Medical Science Publishing House.

Photo Service.

Publishing House of the General Federation of Literary and Art Unions.

Transportation Publishing House: f. 1952; Acting Editor PAEK JONG HAN.

RADIO AND TELEVISION

Korean Central Broadcasting Committee: Pyongyang; programmes relayed nationally with local programmes supplied by local radio committees. Loudspeakers are installed in factories and in open spaces in all towns. Home broadcasting hours: 0500 to 0200 hrs. Foreign broadcasts are in Russian, Chinese, English, French, Spanish, Arabic and Japanese; Chair. YI YONG IK; Vice-Chair. CHA SUNG-SU.

There were an estimated 175,000 radio receivers in 1968.

A television network covers most of the country. Colour television is available in Pyongyang.

FINANCE

BANKING

CENTRAL BANK

Korean Central Bank: Nammundong, Central District, Pyongyang; f. 1946; sole issuing and control bank.

Foreign Trade Bank of the Democratic People's Republic of Korea: Nammundong, Central District, Pyongyang; f. 1959 as dept. of Central Bank, name changed to the above in 1963; state bank; operates payments with foreign banks and control of foreign currencies; Pres. BANG KI YONG.

Korean Industrial Bank: Pyongyang; f. 1964; operates short-term loan, savings, insurance work, guidance and control of financial management of co-operative farms and individual remittance.

INSURANCE

State Insurance Bureau: Pyongyang; handles all life, fire, accident, marine, hull insurance and reinsurance as the national enterprise.

Korea Foreign Insurance Co. (*Chosunbohom*): Potonggang District, Pyongyang; branches in Chongjin, Hungnam, Nampo, Haeju and Rajin, and agencies in foreign ports; handles all foreign insurance.

TRADE AND INDUSTRY

Korean Committee for the Promotion of International Trade: Central District, Pyongyang; Sec.-Gen. PAK SE CHAN.

Korean Council of the Central Federation of Consumption Co-operative Trade Union: Pyongyang.

Korean General Merchandise Export and Import Corporation: Pyongyang.

TRADING CORPORATIONS

PYONGYANG

Korea Building Materials Export and Import Corpn.: Central District; chemical building materials, woods, timbers, cement, sheet glass, etc.

Korea Chemicals Export and Import Corpn.: Central District; petroleum and petroleum products, raw materials for the chemical industry, rubber and rubber products, fertilizers, etc.

Korea Daesong Trading Corpn.: Potonggang District; machinery and equipment, chemical products, textile goods, agricultural products, etc.

Korea Ferrous Metals Export and Import Corpn.: Central District; steel products.

Korea Film Export and Import Corpn.: Central District; feature films, cartoons, scientific and documentary films.

Korea Foodstuffs Export and Import Corpn.: Central District; cereals, wines, meat, canned foods, fruits, cigarettes, etc.

Korea Hyopdong Trading Corporation: Oesong District; fabrics, glass products, ceramics, chemical goods, building materials, foodstuffs, machinery, etc.

Korea Jangsu Trading Co.: Potonggang District; medicinal products and clinical equipment.

Korea Jei Equipment Export Corporation: Central District; machine plant and irrigation equipment.

Korea Jei Equipment Import Corporation: Central District; hydro-power and thermal-power plants, machine building plants, transport and communication equipment.

Korea Jeil Equipment Export and Import Corpn.: Central District; ferrous and non-ferrous metallurgical plants, building materials, mining plants.

Korea Jesam Equipment Export and Import Corpn.: Central District; chemical, textile, pharmaceutical and light industry plant.

Korea Kwangmyong Export and Import Corporation: Central District; handicrafts, agricultural produce, marine products; Dir. CHOE KWAN SU.

Korea Light Industry Goods Export and Import Corpn.: Central District; drinking glasses, ceramics, handbags, pens, plastic flowers, musical instruments, etc.

Korea Machinery Export and Import Corpns.: Central District; metallurgical machinery and equipment, electric machines, building machinery, farm machinery, diesel engines, etc.

Korea Maibong Trading Corporation: Central District; non-ferrous metal ingots and their products, non-metallic minerals, agricultural and marine products.

Korea Manpung Trading Corpn.: Central District; chemical and agricultural products, machinery and equipment.

Korea Marine Products Export and Import Corporation: Central District; canned, frozen, dried, salted and smoked fish, fishing equipment and supplies.

Korea Minerals Export and Import Corpn.: Central District; minerals, solid fuel, graphite, precious stones, etc.

Korea Namheung Trading Co.: Tongdaewon District; fertilizers, rayon yarns and other chemical products.

Korea Okyru Trading Corpn.: Central District; agricultural and marine products, household goods, clothing, chemical and light industrial products.

Korea Ponghwa General Trading Corpn.: Central District; machinery, metal products, minerals and chemicals.

Korea Publications Export and Import Corpn.: Oesong District; export and import of books, periodicals, postage stamps and records; Dir. KIM GI ZUN.

Korea Pyongchon Trading Co.: Oesong District; axles, springs, spikes, bolts and bicycles.

Korea Pyongyang Trading Co. Ltd.: Central District; P.O.B. 550; one-side and barter trade; pig iron, steel, magnesia clinker, textiles etc.

Korea Rungrado Export and Import Corporation: Tongdaewon District; one-side, barter and triangular trade; food and animal products, machinery.

Korea Ryongsong Trading Co.: Tongdaewon District; drilling and grinding machines, sewage and centrifugal pumps and other machinery.

Korea Senbong Trading Corpn.: Central District; ferrous and non-ferrous metals, rolled steels, mineral ores, chemical and other products.

Korea Somyu Hyopdong Trading Co.: Oesong District; clothing and textiles.

Korea Songhwa Trading Corpn.: Oesong District; ceramics, glass, hardware, leaf tobaccos, fruit and wines.

Korea Technical Corpn.: Central District; scientific and technical co-operation.

Korea Unha Trading Corpn.: Central District; clothing and fibres.

Korea Vegetables Export Corporation: Oesong District; vegetables, fruit and their products.

TRADE UNIONS

General Federation of Trade Unions of Korea: Pyongyang; f. 1945; total membership (1970) 2,200,000; 9 affiliated unions; Chair. KIM BONG JU; publs. *Rodongja Shinmoon, Rodongja, Korean Trade Unions.*

General Federation of Literature and Arts of Korea: Pyongyang; f. 1961; 7 branch unions; Pres. of Central Committee LI KI YONG.

General Federation of Agricultural and Forestry Technique of Korea: Chung Ku-yuck Nammundong, Pyongyang; f. 1946; 523,000 mems.; publ. *Nong-oup Kisyl* (monthly journal of technical information on agriculture).

General Federation of Industrial Technology of Korea: Pyongyang; f. 1946; 523,000 mems.

Korean Agricultural Working People's Union: Pyongyang; f. 1965 to replace former *Korean Peasants' Union*; 2,400,000 mems.; Chair. Central Committee CHANG YUN PIL.

Korean Architects' Union: Pyongyang; f. 1954; 500 mems.; Chair. KIM JUNG HI.

Korean Democratic Lawyers' Association: Pyongyang; f. 1954; Pres. CHOE MIN SIN.

Korean Democratic Scientists' Association: Pyongyang; f. 1956.

Korean Journalists' Union: Pyongyang; f. 1946; Chair. Central Cttee. KIM KI NAM.

TRANSPORT

RAILWAYS

In 1981 it was estimated that at least 500 km. of the rail system of 4,400 km. had been electrified. Electrification of the 140 km. link between Kilchu and Hyesan was reported to have been completed in 1978 and the electrification of the Motga–Rimyongsu, Pyongyang–Nampo and Kocham–Sinmyongchon lines in 1979. Further improvements are being undertaken.

There is an underground railway system in Pyongyang.

ROADS

A motorway connects Pyongyang and Wonsan.

INLAND WATERWAYS

Yalu and Daidong, Dooman and Ryesung are the most important commercial rivers. Regular passenger and freight services: Manpo–Chosan–Soopoong; Chungsoo–Shinuijoo–Dasado; Nampo–Jeudo; Pyongyang–Nampo.

SHIPPING

Korea Chartering Corporation: Central District, Pyongyang; arranges cargo transportation and chartering.

Korea Foreign Transportation Corpn.: Central District, Pyongyang; arranges transportation of export and import cargoes (transit goods and charters).

Korean-Polish Maritime Brokers Co. Ltd.: Moranbong District, Pyongyang; maritime trade with a number of foreign ports.

Korea Tonghae Shipping Co.: Oesong District, Pyongyang; arranges transportation by Korean vessels.

CIVIL AVIATION

Civil Aviation Administration of the Democratic People's Republic of Korea: Chosonminhang, Sunan District, Pyongyang; internal flights and external services to Beijing and Khabarovsk, U.S.S.R.; extensions are planned to Moscow, Shanghai, Hong Kong, Hanoi and Tokyo; fleet: two Tupolev Tu 154B, Il-14, Il-18, An-24.

FOREIGN AIRLINES

Services are also provided by Aeroflot (U.S.S.R.) and CAAC (People's Republic of China).

TOURISM

Korean International Tourist Bureau: Central District, Pyongyang.

DEFENCE

Armed Forces and Equipment (July 1981 estimates): Total 782,000; army 700,000; navy 31,000; air force 51,000. The army is equipped with Soviet material including medium and heavy tanks, AA guns and surface-to-surface and surface-to-air missiles. The navy has 19 ex-Chinese and ex-Soviet submarines and a number of motor, torpedo and patrol boats, some armed with missiles. The air force has 700 combat aircraft, largely Soviet MiGs. In addition to the above forces, there are also 38,000 security and border guards and a People's Militia.

Military Service: Army 5 years, navy 5 years, air force 3/4 years.

Defence Expenditure: Defence spending for 1981 was estimated at 3,010 million won.

Chief of the Korean People's Army (KPA): Gen. O Kuk Yol.

EDUCATION

Free and compulsory 11-year education in state schools was introduced in 1975. In 1980 there were 10,000 primary and senior middle schools. There is one university and about 170 other higher education institutions. English is compulsory as a second language at the age of 14.

REPUBLIC OF KOREA

STATISTICAL SURVEY

AREA AND POPULATION

Area*	Population (census results)				
	October 1st, 1970	October 1st, 1975	October 1st, 1980		
			Total	Male	Female
98,966 sq. km.†	31,465,654	34,678,972	37,448,836	18,764,130	18,684,706

* Excluding the demilitarized zone between North and South Korea, with an area of 1,262 sq. km. (487 sq. miles.)

† 38,211 sq. miles. The figure indicates territory under the jurisdiction of the Republic of Korea on December 31st, 1977, surveyed on the basis of land register.

PRINCIPAL TOWNS

(population at 1980 census)

Seoul (Soul—capital)	8,366,756	Ulsan	418,415	Mokpo	221,856
Pusan (Busan)	3,160,276	Masan	386,773	Jinju (Jingu)	202,753
Taegu (Daegu)	1,607,458	Seongnam	376,447	Cheju (Jeju)	167,546
Inchon (Incheon)	1,084,730	Chonchu (Jeonju)	366,997	Gunsan	165,318
Kwangchu (Gwangju)	727,627	Suweon	310,757	Yeosu	161,009
Taejon (Daejon)	651,642	Cheongju	252,985	Chuncheon	155,247

Births and Deaths: Average annual birth rate 28.8 per 1,000 in 1970–75, 25.3 per 1,000 in 1975–80; death rate 8.8 per 1,000 in 1970–75, 8.1 per 1,000 in 1975–80 (UN estimates).

ECONOMICALLY ACTIVE POPULATION*

(1981 Average)

	Males	Females	Total
Agriculture, forestry and fishing	2,707,000	2,098,000	4,806,000
Mining and quarrying	115,000	9,000	124,000
Manufacturing	1,750,000	1,121,000	2,871,000
Construction	806,000	69,000	875,000
Services	3,307,000	2,064,000	5,372,000
Total in employment	8,687,000	5,361,000	14,048,000
Unemployed	526,000	135,000	661,000
Total labour force	9,213,000	5,496,000	14,710,000

* Excluding armed forces.

AGRICULTURE

LAND USE, 1979
('000 hectares)

Arable land	2,069
Land under permanent crops	138
Permanent meadows and pastures	45*
Forests and woodland	6,571
Other land	996
Inland water	29
TOTAL AREA	9,848

* FAO estimate.

Source: FAO, *Production Yearbook.*

PRINCIPAL CROPS
('000 metric tons)

	1978	1979	1980	1981
Wheat	36	42	92	57.1
Barley	555	584	354	329.4
Naked Barley	792	924	457	529.2
Maize	100.2	148.9	154.1	145.3
Foxtail (Italian) Millet	6.7	3.5	3.6	4.7
Rice (paddy)	5,979.1	5,545.8	3,529.5	5,039.6
Potatoes	304.1	355.7	446.1	554.3
Sweet Potatoes and Yams	1,627.2	1,387	110.3	1,108.5
Onions	165	393.1	274.9	281.4
Tomatoes	35	56.4	49.2	74.4
Cabbages	26	87	73	58.6
Cucumbers and Gherkins	83	144.1	112.6	99.4
Melons	152	198.2	158.9	133.4
Water Melons	213	306.5	334.6	290.7
Apples	428	443.7	410.0	523.1
Pears	68	65.4	59.6	71.6
Peaches	91	92.4	88.7	88.7
Grapes	56	53.9	56.8	71.7
Soybeans	292.8	257.1	216.3	256.9
Tobacco	134.9	110.6	92.5	87.0

LIVESTOCK
(recorded numbers at December)

	1977	1978	1979	1980	1981
Cattle	1,492,036*	1,624,301	1,562,591	1,379,508	1,506,000
Pigs	1,481,889*	1,719,364	2,843,163	1,761,124	1,832,000
Goats	216,331	244,274	225,446	200,502	197,000
Sheep	6,974	7,900	8,181	6,233	4,000
Horses	6,847	5,696	4,641	3,894	4,000
Rabbits	1,047,495	1,042,308	816,708	548,540	523,000
Chickens	30,224,309*	40,753,249	41,120,822	39,231,861	42,999,000
Ducks	543,361	559,919	493,895	403,882	388,000
Geese	7,758	6,925	6,361	4,776	5,000
Turkeys	7,617	40,867	176,910	35,340	16,000
Beehives	181,465	238,356	260,102	244,764	315,000

* Preliminary.

LIVESTOCK PRODUCTS
(metric tons)

	1976	1977‡	1978‡	1979‡	1980‡
Beef and Veal*	74,533	87,000	74,000	90,000	97,000†
Pig Meat	113,620	146,000	172,000	219,000	231,000
Poultry Meat	60,885	74,000	83,000	91,000	96,000
Other Meat	5,790	4,000	4,000	3,000	4,000
Cows' Milk	199,556	254,000	320,000	380,000	452,000
Goats' Milk	815	1,000	n.a.	1,000§	1,000†
Hen Eggs	167,660	213,120	225,744	253,860§	321,000§
Honey	1,950	1,912	2,177	2,917	2,100
Raw Silk	5,157	5,121	3,792	3,821	4,100†
Fresh Cocoons	41,704	n.a.	n.a.	n.a.	n.a.
Cattle Hides	8,487†	10,541†	9,485	11,214†	11,970†

* Inspected production only, i.e. from animals slaughtered under government supervision.

† FAO estimate. ‡ *Source:* FAO, *Production Yearbook.* § Unofficial estimate.

FORESTRY

ROUNDWOOD REMOVALS
(FAO estimates, 'ooo cubic metres, excluding bark)

	Coniferous (soft wood)			Broadleaved (hard wood)			Total		
	1977	1978	1979	1977	1978	1979	1977	1978	1979
Sawlogs, veneer logs and logs for sleepers	1,595	461	1,320	1,127	1,815	372	2,722	2,276	1,692
Pitprops (mine timber)	514	592	592	20	25	25	534	617	617
Pulpwood	166	223	173	75	90	60	241	313	233
Other industrial wood	100	100	100	78	78	78	178	178	178
Fuel wood	24,700*	25,000*	25,700*	37,549	38,239	38,933	62,249	63,239	64,633
Total	27,075	26,376	27,885	38,849	40,247	39,468	65,924	66,623	67,353

* Unofficial estimate.

1980 ('ooo cubic metres): Fuel wood 65,627 (Coniferous 26,000, Broadleaved 39,627); Industrial wood as in 1979 (FAO estimates).

Source: FAO, *Yearbook of Forest Products.*

SAWNWOOD PRODUCTION
('ooo cubic metres, incl. boxboards)

	1974	1975	1976*	1977	1978	1979	1980
Coniferous	1,042	846	846	1,668	1,740	2,048	1,570
Broadleaved	867	1,396	1,396	1,277	1,557	1,025	1,407
Total	1,909	2,242	2,242	2,945	3,297	3,073	2,977

* FAO estimate.

Source: FAO, *Yearbook of Forest Products.*

FISHING

('ooo metric tons)

	1976	1977	1978	1979	1980
Fish	1,614.0	1,578.6	1,604.9	1,580	1,497.8
Shellfish	318.9	356.6	316.3	378.5	381.6
Sea plants	287.5	333.6	258.9	257.2	317.2
Others	186.5	152.5	173.5	207.4	213.7
Total	2,406.9	2,421.3	2,353.6	2,422.2	2,410.3

MINING

		1978	1979	1980	1981
Anthracite	'ooo metric tons	18,054	18,208	18,543	19,854
Iron ore	,, ,, ,,	587	459	489	494
Copper ore*	metric tons	4,459	2,888	5,967	7,614
Lead ore	,, ,,	30,348	24,858	21,203	22,892
Zinc ore	,, ,,	132,536	124,398	112,300	113,049
Molybdenum ore	,, ,,	297	233	293	577
Tungsten ore	,, ,,	4,685	4,628	4,629	4,761
Gold (refined)	kg.	828	733	1,191	1,264
Silver (refined)	,,	64,319	87,780	72,743	97,926

* The copper content is estimated at 15 per cent.

INDUSTRY

SELECTED PRODUCTS

		1978	1979	1980	1981
Wheat flour	'ooo metric tons	1,184.1	1,242	1,472	1,439
Refined sugar	,, ,, ,,	511.0	625	758	691
Beer	'ooo hectolitres	4,442.7	6,406	5,790	5,992
Cigarettes	million	62,812	64,391	70,351	72,139
Cotton yarn (pure and mixed)	metric tons	189,173	244,519	266,088	245,057
Woven cotton fabrics (pure)[1]	'ooo sq. metres	273,391	317,160	358,136	402,968
Woven silk fabrics (pure)	,, ,, ,,	17,050	13,846	11,311	18,665
Yarn of synthetic fibres	metric tons	286,100	308,909	334,985	362,978
Synthetic fabrics	'ooo sq. metres	645,945	664,376	790,236	988,627
Plywood	'ooo cubic metres	2,742.2	2,510	1,693	1,671
Newsprint	metric tons	163,199	173,905	214,764	236,402
Rubber tyres[2]	'ooo	6,905.2	10,025	12,328	9,102
Sulphuric acid	metric tons	1,461,399	1,644,797	1,683,322	1,294,345
Caustic soda	,, ,,	75,539	75,675	148,038	189,818
Soda ash	,, ,,	176,090	203,792	221,920	202,063
Urea fertilizer	,, ,,	1,185,969	1,165,612	972,876	1,070,089
Liquefied petroleum gas	million litres	521.9	510	607	645
Naphtha	,, ,,	3,296.2	3,570	3,805	3,906
Kerosene	,, ,,	1,079.7	1,417	1,401	1,292
Distillate fuel oil	,, ,,	5,476.2	6,050	6,073	6,228
Bunker C oil	,, ,,	12,731.3	13,320	13,653	13,154
Residual fuel oil	,, ,,	934.1	1,169	778	618
Cement	'ooo metric tons	15,133	16,413	15,631	15,617
Pig iron	,, ,, ,,	2,741.1	5,063	5,577	7,928
Crude steel	,, ,, ,,	n.a.	n.a.	57,902	n.a.
Radio receivers	'ooo	4,767.7	4,772	4,143	5,126
Television receivers	,,	4,826.5	5,867	6,819	7,697
Passenger cars (assembly)	number	92,331	112,400	57,037	72,132
Lorries and trucks (assembly)	,, ,,	58,326	78,585	n.a.	n.a.
Electric energy	million kWh.	29,532	35,600	37,239	40,207

[1] After undergoing finishing processes.
[2] Tyres for passenger cars and commercial vehicles.

FINANCE

100 chun (jeon) = 10 hwan = 1 won.
Coins: 1, 5, 10, 50 and 100 won.
Notes: 1, 5, 10, 50, 100, 500, 1,000, 5,000 and 10,000 won.
Exchange rates (June 1982): £1 sterling = 1,282.5 won; U.S. $1 = 740.5 won.
10,000 won = £7.80 = $13.50.

Note: The new won was introduced in June 1962, replacing the hwan at the rate of 1 new won = 10 hwan. The hwan had been introduced in February 1953, replacing the old won at the rate of 1 hwan = 100 old won. The official exchange rate was initially U.S. $1 = 100 hwan but subsequently the hwan was frequently devalued. From February 1961 the exchange rate was $1 = 1,300 hwan. The initial rate of $1 = 130 new won (£1 sterling = 364 new won) remained in force until May 1964, after which the won's value was allowed to fluctuate in a free market. The official buying rate was $1 = 255 won (£1 = 714 won) from May 1964 to March 1965. For the next three years the rate was around 270 to 275 won per U.S. dollar, declining to 281 won per dollar (£1 = 674 won) by the end of 1968 and then to more than 300 won per dollar by November 1969. Depreciation of the won continued and in June 1971 the currency was officially devalued, the new buying rate being $1 = 370 won (£1 = 888 won). Further depreciation followed, despite the devaluation of the U.S. dollar in December 1971, and the buying rate was $1 = 400 won by June 1972. Thereafter the won's value held steady at around that rate (but unchanged by a further dollar devaluation in February 1973) until December 1974, when a new rate of $1 = 484 won was introduced. This remained in force until January 1980, when a rate of $1 = 580 won was established. In February 1980 the direct link between the won and the U.S. dollar was broken and the currency was tied to the IMF's Special Drawing Right. The average market rates of won per U.S. dollar were: 398.3 in 1973; 400.4 in 1974; 607.4 in 1980; 681.0 in 1981.

BUDGET
(million won, fiscal years)

Revenue	1977	1978	1979	1980*
Internal taxes	1,926,384	2,596,724	3,669,414	4,073,590
Customs duties	476,299	775,538	732,294	988,478
Monopoly profits	220,000	280,000	360,000	425,000
Contribution from government enterprises (net)	221,075	206,838	360,850	787,771
Other receipts	383,800	54,498	951,684	593,176
Total	3,227,557	3,913,598	6,074,242	6,868,015

* Estimates.

Expenditure	1977	1978	1979	1980*
National defence	958,810	1,228,680	1,539,492	2,167,134
General expenditures	1,417,739	1,836,412	2,842,592	3,211,852
Fixed capital formation	462,949	535,457	786,754	1,328,886
Other expenditures	286,840	173,602	167,994	554,090
	3,126,338	3,774,151	5,336,832	7,261,962
Net lending	36,633	44,474	72,787	73,409
Total	3,162,971	3,818,625	5,409,619	7,335,371

* Estimates.

1981: Total budget 7,537,124 million won (estimate).

FOURTH FIVE-YEAR ECONOMIC PLAN 1977–81
(In 1975 constant '000 million won)

	1975		1977		1981		Average Annual % Growth Rate (1977–81)
	Amount	Percentage Composition	Amount	Percentage Composition	Amount	Percentage Composition	
G.N.P.	9,080.3	100.0	11,486.6	100.0	16,214.3	100.0	9.2
Agriculture, forestry and fishing	2,302.8	25.4	2,562.6	22.3	2,997.8	18.5	4.0
Mining and manufacturing	2,697.1	29.7	4,005.5	34.9	6,631.0	40.9	14.2
Social, overhead and other services	4,080.4	44.9	4,918.5	42.8	6,585.5	40.6	7.6
Consumption	7,444.4	82.0	8,954.5	78.0	11,983.3	73.9	7.8
Gross investment	2,478.4	27.3	3,097.9	27.0	4,219.9	26.0	7.8
Exports	2,847.7	31.4	4,803.7	41.8	8,474.3	52.3	16.8
Imports	3,870.7	42.6	5,369.5	46.7	8,463.2	52.2	13.0

INTERNATIONAL RESERVES

(U.S. $ million at December 31st)

	1979	1980	1981
Gold	30.6	30.8	32.2
IMF Special Drawing Rights . . .	24.7	12.6	63.9
Reserve position in IMF . . .	24.8	—	—
Foreign exchange .	5,628.1	6,528.1	6,795.0
TOTAL . . .	5,708.3	6,571.4	6,891.0

MONEY SUPPLY

('000 million won at December 31st)

	1979	1980	1981
Currency outside banks	1,604.0	1,856.4	2,025.4
Demand deposits at deposit money banks .	1,648.0	1,920.0	1,972.0

BALANCE OF PAYMENTS

(U.S. $ million)

	1976	1977	1978	1979	1980	1981
Merchandise exports f.o.b. . .	7,814	10,046	12,711	14,705	17,214	20,886
Merchandise imports f.o.b. . .	−8,404	−10,523	−14,491	−19,100	−21,598	−23,871
TRADE BALANCE . . .	−590	−477	−1,780	−4,395	−4,384	−2,985
Exports of services . . .	1,643	3,027	4,450	4,825	5,363	6,618
Imports of services . . .	−1,709	−2,761	−4,226	−5,020	−6,749	−8,626
BALANCE OF GOODS AND SERVICES	−656	−211	−1,556	−4,590	−5,770	−4,993
Private unrequited transfers (net) .	193	170	434	399	399	435
Government unrequited transfers (net)	153	53	37	40	50	80
CURRENT BALANCE . . .	−310	12	−1,085	−4,151	−5,321	−4,478
Direct capital investment (net) .	75	73	61	16	−7	82
Other long-term capital (net) . .	1,257	1,327	2,050	3,055	1,994	3,513
Short-term capital (net) . .	534	−10	18	2,282	3,983	1,090
Net errors and omissions . .	−243	−32	−313	−328	−338	−536
TOTAL (net monetary movements)	1,312	1,369	731	874	312	−329
Allocation of IMF Special Drawing Rights	—	—	—	22	22	22
Valuation changes (net) .	1	−14	−21	—	16	63
CHANGES IN RESERVES .	1,313	1,355	710	896	350	−244

Source: IMF, *International Financial Statistics.*

EXTERNAL TRADE

(U.S. $ million)

	1975	1976	1977	1978	1979	1980	1981
Imports c.i.f.	7,274.4	8,773.6	10,810.5	14,971.9	20,338.6	22,291.7	26,131.4
Exports f.o.b.	5,081.0	7,715.1	10,046.5	12,710.6	15,055.5	17,504.9	21,253.8

PRINCIPAL COMMODITIES

(U.S. $'000)

Imports	1978	1979	1980	1981
Wheat and meslin (unmilled)	235,354	299,077	366,617	405,091
Rice	610	69,367	328,428	1,085,488
Raw sugar	143,172	165,163	491,907	427,242
Crude rubber	163,068	235,364	276,825	241,778
Wood	658,751	975,075	876,810	676,312
Pulp	121,156	175,490	225,802	247,501
Raw cotton	447,454	461,623	604,066	623,620
Artificial fibres	24,192	43,003	38,833	49,652
Petroleum and petroleum products	2,312,088	3,415,571	6,163,536	6,917,779
Organic chemicals	559,366	960,015	949,975	996,843
Plastic materials	273,573	422,969	256,441	297,043
Textile yarn and thread	123,051	121,808	110,427	166,840
Textile fabrics (woven)	167,550	198,369	192,406	212,775
Iron and steel ingots	416,541	503,170	487,013	380,506
Iron and steel plates and sheets	205,713	194,944	185,049	233,694
Power generating machinery	373,702	648,453	451,151	563,677
Textile machinery	248,650	336,010	162,302	186,115
Electric power machinery	356,957	492,689	357,090	438,304
Telecommunications apparatus	213,880	256,157	317,992	461,915
Thermionic valves, tubes, etc.	385,720	468,023	527,006	611,637
Aircraft	206,100	395,346	356,943	419,652
Ships and boats (excl. warships)	401,849	315,795	472,029	872,978
Total (incl. others)	14,971,930	20,338,611	22,291,663	26,131,421

Exports	1978	1979	1980	1981
Fish (fresh, chilled or frozen)	420,262	548,676	434,957	530,286
Crustacea and molluscs	123,326	173,828	161,194	197,051
Tobacco (unmanufactured)	111,464	91,327	83,978	101,815
Raw silk (not thrown)	61,003	40,122	19,010	293
Rubber tyres and tubes	213,808	325,036	477,372	459,641
Plywood	346,102	388,218	303,976	322,726
Textile yarn and thread	337,669	443,697	623,608	568,225
Cotton fabrics (woven)	104,782	127,332	148,858	143,180
Textile fabrics	965,754	1,018,125	1,248,145	1,532,027
Cement	142,265	113,982	234,668	339,071
Iron or steel sheets	298,196	447,117	557,922	564,354
Electrical machinery	1,254,540	1,684,491	1,928,009	1,004,800
Transport equipment	1,123,974	1,097,627	1,153,736	2,056,322
Textile clothing (not knitted)	1,249,029	1,501,516	1,588,038	2,060,272
Outer garments (knitted)	522,866	451,440	498,697	686,361
Footwear	686,171	728,911	874,397	1,024,101
Wigs and false beards	60,174	54,344	55,547	53,085
Total (incl. others)	12,710,642	15,055,453	17,504,862	21,253,757

PRINCIPAL TRADING PARTNERS

(U.S. $'000)

Imports	1978	1979	1980	1981
Australia	463,765	599,043	680,019	909,964
Canada	204,033	326,348	378,429	530,660
France	442,377	356,779	190,810	279,804
Germany, Federal Republic	490,905	843,634	636,603	671,799
Indonesia	407,828	591,988	484,525	384,792
Japan	5,981,487	6,656,699	5,857,810	6,373,553
Kuwait	746,533	1,155,822	1,753,192	1,572,862
Malaysia	227,913	383,272	471,563	643,178
Saudi Arabia	1,280,673	1,585,365	3,288,408	3,561,364
Taiwan	152,619	209,941	313,336	353,191
United Kingdom	211,497	499,382	303,589	397,860
U.S.A.	3,042,950	4,602,581	4,890,248	6,049,664
Total (incl. others)	14,971,930	20,338,611	22,291,663	26,131,421

Exports	1978	1979	1980	1981
Australia	148,828	156,967	230,370	293,567
Belgium	94,443	118,940	139,020	176,420
Canada	327,173	387,643	343,446	483,501
Germany, Federal Republic	662,884	845,340	875,488	804,487
Hong Kong	384,686	530,668	823,318	1,154,680
Indonesia	102,992	195,095	365,637	370,396
Iran	164,482	185,659	107,555	n.a.
Japan	2,627,266	3,353,028	3,039,408	3,502,785
Netherlands	307,287	330,694	349,506	327,932
Singapore	143,630	196,693	266,281	305,631
Taiwan	140,079	161,407	216,322	262,310
United Kingdom	393,029	541,605	572,531	705,012
U.S.A.	4,058,345	4,373,929	4,606,625	5,660,593
Total (incl. others)	12,710,642	15,055,453	17,504,862	21,253,757

TOURISM

	1977	1978	1979	1980	1981
Visitors*	949,667	1,079,396	1,126,099	976,415	1,093,214

* Including Koreans residing abroad: 113,939 in 1977; 135,058 in 1978.

TRANSPORT

RAILWAYS

('000)

	1977	1978	1979	1980	1981
Passengers	301,592	371,012	423,657	430,773	441,430
Freight (metric tons)	47,631	49,654	50,879	49,009	48,761

ROAD TRAFFIC
(motor vehicles in use)

	1979	1980	1981
Passenger Cars	241,422	249,102	267,605
Trucks	206,822	226,940	243,828
Buses	37,697	42,463	50,595

SEA-BORNE SHIPPING*
(freight traffic in '000 metric tons)

	1979	1980	1981
Goods loaded	36,587	41,534	48,134
Goods unloaded	91,751	90,204	100,861

* Including coastwise traffic loaded and unloaded.

CIVIL AVIATION

	Domestic Services			International Services		
	1979	1980	1981	1979	1980	1981
Passengers	1,812,000	1,481,000	1,555,220	2,989,000	2,922,000	3,228,696
Freight (kg.)	13,681,000	12,495,000	17,239,325	150,342,800	183,333,500	200,751,945
Mail (kg.)	237,000	268,000	333,108	7,122,000	8,067,555	8,172,543

EDUCATION
(1981)

	Schools	Teachers	Pupils
Kindergarten	3,465	5,877	166,369
Primary schools	6,681	124,312	5,465,401
Middle schools	2,199	58,823	2,660,849
High schools	1,408	57,891	1,889,159
Junior vocational colleges	127	5,098	206,205
Junior teachers' colleges	11	482	11,040
Universities	97	18,668	515,780
Graduate schools	169	247	63,326

Source (unless otherwise indicated): National Bureau of Statistics, Economic Planning Board, Seoul.

THE CONSTITUTION

A new constitution was approved by national referendum in October 1980. The main provisions are summarized below.

THE GOVERNMENT

The President: The President is to be elected by the Presidential Electoral College for one term of seven years. In times of national emergency and under certain conditions the President shall have power to take necessary emergency measures in all matters of State. He shall notify the National Assembly of these measures and obtain its concurrence, or they shall lose effect. He may, in times of war, armed conflict or similar national emergency, declare martial law in accordance with the provisions of law. He shall lift the emergency measures and martial law when the National Assembly so requests with the concurrence of a majority of the members. He is authorized to take directly to the people important issues through national referenda, and may dissolve the National Assembly but not within one year of its formation. A general election shall be held within 30 to 60 days from the date of dissolution. The President shall appoint public officials.

The State Council: The State Council shall be composed of the President, the Prime Minister and no more than 30 and no fewer than 15 others appointed by the President, and shall deliberate on policies that fall within the power of the executive.

The National Assembly: The National Assembly shall be composed of more than 200 members, two-thirds of whom are elected for four years by universal, equal, direct and secret ballot, the remaining third proportioned to the parties as determined by law. A regular session shall be held once a year and extraordinary sessions shall be convened upon request of the President or one-third of the Assembly's members. The period of regular sessions shall not exceed 90 days and of extraordinary sessions 30 days. The legislative power shall be vested in the National Assembly. It has the power to recommend to the President the removal of the Prime Minister or any other Minister. The National Assembly shall have the authority to pass a motion for the impeachment of the President or any other public official.

The Constitution Committee: The Constitution Committee shall be composed of nine members appointed by the President, three of whom shall be appointed from persons selected by the National Assembly and three from persons nominated by the Chief Justice. The term of office shall be six years. It shall pass judgment upon the constitutionality of laws upon the request of the Court, matters of impeachment and the dissolution of political parties. In these judgments the concurrence of six members or more shall be required.

THE JUDICIARY

The courts shall be composed of the Supreme Court, which is the highest court of the State, and other courts at specified levels (for further details *see* Judicial System, page 753). When the constitutionality of a law is a prerequisite to a trial the Court shall request a decision of the Constitution Committee. The Supreme Court shall have the power to pass judgment upon the constitutionality or legality of administrative decrees, and shall have final appellate jurisdiction over military tribunals.

POLITICAL PARTIES

The establishment of political parties shall be free and the plural party system guaranteed. However, a political party whose aims or activities are contrary to the basic democratic order may be dissolved by the Constitution Committee.

AMENDMENTS

A motion to amend the Constitution shall be proposed by the President or by a majority of the total members of the National Assembly. Proposed amendments to the Constitution shall be put before the public by the President for 20 days or more. Within 60 days of the public announcement, the National Assembly shall decide upon the proposed amendments, which require a two-thirds majority of the National Assembly. They shall then be submitted to a national referendum not later than 30 days after passage by the National Assembly and shall be determined by more than one-half of votes cast by more than one-half of voters eligible to vote in elections for members of the National Assembly. If these conditions are fulfilled, the proposed amendments shall be finalized and the President shall promulgate them without delay.

FUNDAMENTAL RIGHTS

Under the constitution all citizens are equal before the law. Freedom of speech, press, assembly and association are guaranteed, as are freedom of choice of residence and occupation. No state religion is to be recognized and freedom of conscience and religion is guaranteed. Citizens are protected against retrospective legislation, and may not be punished without due process of law.

Besides legal limitations on certain of these rights as provided for in specific provisions of the constitution, there is a general clause stating that rights and freedoms may be restricted by law when this is deemed necessary for the maintenance of national security, order or public welfare.

THE GOVERNMENT

President: Chun Doo-Hwan (took office September 2nd, 1980, re-elected February 25th, 1981).

STATE COUNCIL

(July 1982)

Prime Minister: Kim Sang-Hyup.

Deputy Prime Minister and Minister of Economic Planning Board: Kim Joon-Sung.

Minister of Foreign Affairs: Lee Bum-Suk.

Minister of Home Affairs: Rho Tae-Woo.

Minister of Finance: Kang Kyung-Shik.

Minister of Justice: Pae Myung-In.

Minister of National Defence: Yun Sung-Min.

Minister of Education: Lee Kyu-Ho.

Minister of Agriculture and Fisheries: Park Chong-Mun.

Minister of Commerce and Industry: Kim Dong-Whie.

Minister of Energy and Resources: Lee Sun-Ki.

Minister of Construction: Kim Chong-Ho.

Minister of Health and Social Affairs: Mrs. Kim Chung-Rye.

Minister of Labour: Chung Han-Soo.

Minister of Transportation: Lee Hui-Sung.

Minister of Communications: Choi Soon-Dal.

Minister of Culture and Information: Lee Chin-Ui.

Minister of Government Administration: Park Chan-Keung.

Minister of Science and Technology: Lee Chong-Oh.

Minister of National Unification Board: Sohn Jae-Shik.

Minister of Sports: Lee Won-Kyung.

First Minister of State: Oh Se-Ung.

LEGISLATURE

KUK HOE

(National Assembly)

Election, March 25th, 1981*

	Elected Representatives	Proportional Representatives	Total Seats
Democratic Justice Party	90	61	151
Democratic Korea Party	57	24	81
Korea National Party	18	7	25
Civil Rights Party	2	—	2
Democratic Socialist Party	2	—	2
New Political Party	2	—	2
Others	13	—	13
Total	184	92	276

* Two-thirds of the Assembly's seats were filled by direct election, with each of the 92 districts electing two members (although no party could present more than one candidate per district). Of the additional one-third of the seats, 61 were allocated to the party gaining most votes by direct election, with the remaining 31 for other parties in proportion to seats won directly.

POLITICAL PARTIES AND ORGANIZATIONS

All political parties were dissolved in October 1980 by the new constitution. New political parties were established prior to the presidential election held on February 25th, 1981.

Democratic Justice Party (DJP): 155–2 Kwanhoon-dong, Chongno-ku, Seoul; f. 1981; Government party; Pres. Chun Doo-Hwan; Chair. Lee Chai-Hyung; Sec.-Gen. Kwon Chung-Dal.

Democratic Korea Party (DKP): 1–643 Yoido-dong, Yongdeungpo-ku, Seoul; f. 1981; main opposition party; Pres. Yoo Chi-Song; Sec.-Gen. You Han-Yul.

Korea National Party (KNP): 11–3 Chung-dong, Chung-ku, Seoul; Pres. Kim Chong-Chul.

Civil Rights Party (CRP): 170 Insa-dong, Chongno-ku Seoul; Pres. Kim Eui-Taek.

Democratic Socialist Party (DSP): 340, 2-ka, Taepyong-ro, Seoul; merged with former New Political Party, March 1982; Pres. Koh Jung-Hoon; Chair. Kim Kap-Su.

DIPLOMATIC REPRESENTATION

EMBASSIES ACCREDITED TO THE REPUBLIC OF KOREA

(In Seoul unless otherwise stated)

Argentina: 135-53, Itaewon-dong, Yongsan-ku; *Ambassador:* Ricardo H. Videla.

Australia: 5th–7th Floors, Kukdong-Shell House, 58-1 Shinmun-ro, 1-ka, Chongno-ku; *Ambassador:* Edward Robert Pocock.

Austria: Tokyo, Japan.

Bangladesh: Tokyo, Japan.

Belgium: 1–65, Dongbinggo-dong, Yong San-ku; *Ambassador:* Charles Winterbeeck.

Bolivia: Tokyo, Japan.

Brazil: Rm. 301/306, New Korea Bldg., 192-11, 1-ka, Ulchiro, C.P.O.B. 2164, Chung-ku; *Ambassador:* Frederico Carlos Carnauba.

Burma: Tokyo, Japan.

Canada: 10th Floor, Kolon Bldg., 45 Mugyo-Dong, Chung-ku; *Ambassador:* W. E. Bauer.

Central African Republic: Tokyo, Japan.

Chile: 142-5, Itaewon-dong, Yongsan-ku; *Ambassador:* Jorge Paredes W.

China (Taiwan): 83, 2-ka, Myong-dong, Chung-ku; *Ambassador:* Ding Mou-shih.

Colombia: Rm. 1405, Kukdong Bldg., 60-1 Chungmu-ro, 3-ka, Chung-ku; *Ambassador:* Dr. Virgilio Olano B.

Costa Rica: A-402 Namsan Village Apt., Itaewon-dong, Yongsan-ku; *Ambassador:* Jaime Botey Brenes.

Denmark: Suite 701, Namsong Bldg., Namsan Kwankwang Rd., Itaewon-dong; *Ambassador:* Jørgen Holm.

Dominican Republic: Tokyo, Japan.

Ecuador: Tokyo, Japan.

El Salvador: Tokyo, Japan.

Ethiopia: Tokyo, Japan.

Finland: Suite 604, Kyo Bo Bldg., 1-1, 1-ka Chongno, Chongno-ku; *Ambassador:* Henrik Blomstedt.

France: 30 Hap-dong, Seodaemun-ku; *Ambassador:* André Baeyens.

Gabon: 43–2, Nonhyoun-dong, Dae Young Bldg., Kang Nam-ku; *Ambassador:* M. Megner-Mbo.

Germany, Federal Republic: 4th Floor, Daehan Fire and Marine Insurance Bldg., 51-1 Namchang-dong, Chung-ku; *Ambassador:* Wolfgang Eger.

Ghana: Tokyo, Japan.

Greece: Tokyo, Japan.

Guatemala: A-206, Namsan Village Apt., Itaewon-dong, Yongsan-ku; *Ambassador:* JOAQUÍN D. S. MONTENEGRO.

Honduras: Tokyo, Japan.

India: 1–48, Dongbinggo-dong, Yongsan-ku; *Ambassador:* V. V. PARANJPE.

Indonesia: 1-887, Yoido-dong, Yongdeungpo-ku; *Ambassador:* KAHARUDDIN NASUTION.

Iran: 726-116, Hannam-dong, Yongsan-ku; *Chargé d'affaires a.i.:* HASSAN TAHERIAN.

Israel: Tokyo, Japan.

Italy: 1-169, 2-ka, Shinmun-ro, Chongno-ku; *Ambassador:* EMANUELE COSTA.

Ivory Coast: Tokyo, Japan.

Japan: 18-11 Chunghak-dong, Chongno-ku; *Ambassador:* TOSHIKAZU MAEDA.

Jordan: Tokyo, Japan.

Liberia: Tokyo, Japan.

Libya: *Secretary of People's Bureau:* ASHUR BEN KHAYALNI.

Madagascar: Washington, D.C., U.S.A.

Malaysia: 726-115 Hannam-dong, Yongsan-ku; *Ambassador:* (vacant).

Mexico: 142 Namsan Village, New Itaewon-dong, Yongsan-ku; *Ambassador:* FRANCISCO JAVIER ALEJO LÓPEZ.

Morocco: Tokyo, Japan.

Nepal: Tokyo, Japan.

Netherlands: 1-48 Dongbinggo-dong, Yongsan-ku; *Ambassador:* DR. ROLAND VAN DEN BERG.

New Zealand: 2nd Floor, Publishers' Bldg., 105-2 Sagan-dong, Chongno-ku; *Ambassador:* EDWARD FARNON.

Nicaragua: Tokyo, Japan.

Niger: Washington, D.C., U.S.A.

Norway: 124-12 Itaewon-dong, Yongsan-ku, P.O.B. 555; *Ambassador:* NILS AXEL KJAERGAARD NISSEN.

Panama: No. 1201 Garden Tower, 98–78 Wooni-dong, Chongno-ku; *Ambassador:* JUAN DEL BUSTO.

Paraguay: Taipei, Taiwan.

Peru: House 132, Namsan Village, Itaewon-dong, Yongsan-ku; *Ambassador:* GABRIEL GARCÍA-PIKE.

Philippines: 559-510, Yeoksam-dong, Kangnam-ku; *Ambassador:* Col. NICANOR T. JIMENEZ.

Portugal: Tokyo, Japan.

Qatar: Tokyo, Japan.

Saudi Arabia: 1–35, 2-ka, Shinmun-ro, Chongno-ku; *Ambassador:* SHEIKH ZEIM A. DABBAGH.

Senegal: Tokyo, Japan.

Singapore: Tokyo, Japan.

Spain: Garden Tower Apt., 1802, Wooni-dong, Chongno-ku; *Ambassador:* LUIS CUERVO.

Sri Lanka: Tokyo, Japan.

Sudan: Tokyo, Japan.

Sweden: C.P.O.B. 3577, UN Village, 1–9 Hannam-dong, Yongsan-ku; *Ambassador:* KARL WÄRNBERG.

Switzerland: 32-10 Songwol-dong, Chongno-ku; *Ambassador:* CARLO JAGMETTI.

Thailand: House 133, Namsan Village, Itaewon, Yongsan-ku; *Ambassador:* ASA BOONYAPRATUANG.

Tunisia: Tokyo, Japan.

Turkey: 330-294, Sungbuk-dong, Sungbuk-ku; *Ambassador:* ERDIL K. AKAY.

Tuvalu: *Ambassador:* IONATANA IONATANA.

Uganda: Tokyo, Japan.

United Kingdom: 4 Chung-dong, Chung-ku; *Ambassador:* J. A. L. MORGAN.

U.S.A.: 82 Sejong-no, Chongno-ku; *Ambassador:* RICHARD WALKER.

Uruguay: 506–29, Changchon-dong, Sodaemun-ku; *Ambassador:* ADOLFO SILVA DELGADO.

Vatican City: 2 Kungjung-dong, Chongno-ku; *Apostolic Pro-Nuncio:* Archbishop LUCIANO ANGELONI.

Venezuela: Tokyo, Japan.

Zaire: Tokyo, Japan.

The Republic of Korea also has diplomatic relations with Afghanistan, Antigua and Barbuda, Bahrain, Barbados, Benin, Botswana, Cameroon, Chad, the Comoros, Djibouti, Dominica, Equatorial Guinea, Fiji, The Gambia, Guinea, Guyana, Haiti, Iceland, Iraq, Jamaica, Kenya, Kiribati, Kuwait, Lebanon, Lesotho, Luxembourg, Malawi, Maldives, Mauritania, Mauritius, Nauru, Nigeria, Oman, Papua New Guinea, Rwanda, Saint Lucia, Sierre Leone, Solomon Islands, Suriname, Swaziland, Tonga, the United Arab Emirates, Upper Volta, Vanuatu, Western Samoa and Zambia.

JUDICIAL SYSTEM

Supreme Court: this is the highest court consisting of no more than 13 Justices including the Chief Justice. The Chief Justice is appointed by the President with the consent of the National Assembly for a term of five years. Other Justices of the Supreme Court are appointed for five years by the President on the recommendation of the Chief Justice. It is empowered to receive and decide on appeals against decisions of the Appellate courts in civil and criminal cases. It is also authorized to act as the final tribunal to review decisions of courts-martial and to try election cases.

Appellate Courts: three courts situated in Seoul, Taegu and Kwangchu with three chief, 39 senior and 91 other judges. Has appellate jurisdiction in civil and criminal cases and can also pass judgment on administrative litigation against government decisions.

District Courts: established in all major cities with 12 chief, 119 senior and 410 other judges. Exercise jurisdiction over all civil and criminal cases in the first instance.

Family Court: there is one Family Court, in Seoul, with a Chief Judge and Judges and Probation Officers. This deals with domestic relations and juvenile delinquency.

Courts-Martial: these exercise jurisdiction over all offences committed by members of the armed forces and their civilian employees. Also authorized to try civilians accused of military espionage or interference with the execution of military duties.

THE SUPREME COURT

Chief Justice: YOO TAE-HEUNG.

Justices:

LEE IL-KYU	LEE JUNG-UH
KANG WOO-YOUNG	YUN IHL-YOUNG
KIM JUNG-SEOH	KIM DEOK-JU
CHUNG TAE-KYUN	SHIN JEONG-CHUL
LEE SEONG-YUL	LEE HOI-CHANG
CHUN SANG-SUK	KIM YONG-CHUL

Minister of Court Administration: Justice KIM YONG-CHUL.

RELIGION

The traditional religions are Buddhism, Confucianism, Daoism and Chundo Kyo, a religion peculiar to Korea combining elements of Buddhism and Christianity.

RELIGIONS
(1980)

	Temples or Churches	Priests	Believers
Buddhism	7,244	22,260	12,329,720
Confucianism	232	11,828	5,182,902
Protestantism	21,243	31,740	7,180,627
Roman Catholicism	2,342	4,529	1,321,293
Chundo Kyo	249	3,264	1,153,677
Taejong Kyo	80	85	316,591
Won Buddhism	333	3,921	947,993
Others	791	5,833	2,382,184

Buddhism: Korean Buddhism has 18 denominations. The Chogye-jong is the largest Buddhist order in Korea, being introduced from China in 372 A.D. The Chogye Order accounts for over half the 12,329,720 Korean Buddhists. It has also more than 1,500 out of 7,244 Buddhist temples and there are 22,260 monks. Leader: The Most Venerable LEE SUNG-CHUL, Haein-sa, Hapchon-kun, Kyungnam Privince.

Roman Catholicism: Archbishop of Seoul: H.E. Cardinal STEPHEN SOU-HWAN KIM, Archbishop's House, 2-Ka 1, Myong-dong, Chung-ku, Seoul.

Protestantism: Bishop of Seoul: Rt. Rev. PAUL C. LEE, D.D., LL.D., C.B.E., 3 Chong-dong, Chung-ku, Seoul 100; Bishop of Taejon: Rt. Rev. MARK PAE, P.O.B. 22, Taejon 300; Bishop of Pusan: Rt. Rev. WILLIAM CH'OE, P.O.B. 18, Pusan 600.

THE PRESS

NATIONAL DAILIES

Chosun Ilbo: 61, 1-ka, Taepyong-ro 1, Chung-ku, Seoul; f. 1920; morning, weekly and children's editions; independent; Publr. BANG WOO-YOUNG; Editor YOO KUN-HO; circ. (morning edn.) 405,000.

Dong-A Ilbo (*The Oriental Daily News*): 139 Sechong-ro, Chongno-ku, Seoul; f. 1920; evening; independent; Publr. KIM SANG-MAN; circ. 800,000.

Hankook Ilbo: 14 Chunghak-dong, Chongno-ku, Seoul; f. 1954; morning; independent; Publr. CHANG KANG-JAE; Editor HONG YU-SUN; circ. 700,000.

Hankook Kyungje Shinmun (*The Korea Economic Daily*): 441 Chungrim-dong, Seoul; f. 1964; economics and business; Publr. LEE KYU-HAENG; Editor HO YOUNG-JIN.

Ilgan Sports (*The Daily Sports*): 14 Chunghak-dong, Chongno-ku, Seoul; f. 1969; Publr. CHANG KANG-JAE; Man. Editor YOO YONG-CHONG; circ. 403,000.

Joong-ang Ilbo: 58-9 Seosomun-dong, Seosomun-ku, Seoul; f. 1965; evening; Chair. HONG JIN-KI; Pres. LEE CHONG-KI; circ. 1,200,000.

The Korea Herald: 11-3, 3-ka, Hoehyundong, Chung-ku, Seoul; f. 1953; English; morning; independent; Pres. HAN JONG-WOO; Editor KIM YONG-SOO.

The Korea Times: 14 Chunghak-dong, Chongno-ku, Seoul; f. 1951; morning; English; independent; Publr. CHANG KANG-JAE; Editor YU IL-YON; circ. 120,000.

Kyunghyang Shinmun: 22 Chong-dong, Seoul; f. 1946; evening; independent; Editor LEE HWAN-EY; circ. 300,000.

Seoul Shinmun: 31-3, 1-ka, Taepyong-ro, Chung-ku, Seoul; f. 1945; morning; independent; Pres. MUN TAE-KAP; Editor KIM CHONG KYU; circ. 480,000.

Sonyon Dong-A: 139 Seijong-ro, Chongno-ku, Seoul; f. 1964; children's; Publr. LEE DONG-WOOK; Editor PARK KWON-SANG; circ. 280,000.

LOCAL DAILIES

Cheju Shinmoon: 1280, 1-dong, 1-do, Cheju; f. 1945; Publr. KIM SUN-HI; Editor CHOI HYUN-SIK.

Chungchung Ilbo: 81, 2-ka Nammoon-ro, Cheongju; f. 1946; Publr. LEE SUK-HOON; Editor LEE SANG-HOON.

Jeonbuk Shinmoon: 148, 1-ka, Kosa-dong, Chonchu; f. 1973; Publr. SEO JUNG-SANG; Editor LEE CHI-BACK.

Kangwon Ilbo: 53, 1-ka, Chungang-ro, Chuncheon; f. 1945; Publr. KANG PYO-WON.

Kwangchu Ilbo: 78 Kwang Sang-dong, Kwang-ju.

Kyeonggi Shinmun: 136, Kyo-dong, Suweon; f. 1973; Publr. HONG DEA-KUN; Editor LIM SANG-KYU.

Kyungnam Ilbo: 184 Bonsung-dong, Jinju; f. 1909; Publr. KIM YOON-YANG; Editor SON KANG-HO.

Kyungnam Maeil Shinmun: 18 BI-42, Hapsang-dong, Masan; f. 1946; Publr. KIM BOO-HYUN; Editor LEE KWANG-SUK.

Maeil Shinmun: 138 Namil-dong, Chung-ku, Taegu; f. 1950; Publr. CHUN DAL-CHUL; Editor AN DUK-HWAN.

Pusan Ilbo: 53-17, 4-ka, Jungang-dong, Chung-ku, Pusan; f. 1946; Publr. WANG HACK-SOO; Editor KWON O-HYN.

Taegu Maeil Shinmun: 71 2-ka, Kae San-dong, Chung-ku, Taegu.

Taejon Ilbo: 77-2 Jung-dong, Taejon; f. 1950; Publr. AN SE-YOUNG; Editor AN YOUNG-JIN.

SELECTED PERIODICALS

Donghwa News Graphic: 43-1, 1-ka, Pil-dong, Chung-ku, Seoul; f. 1960; Publr. CHUNG JAE-HO.

Han Kuk No Chong (*FKTU News*): Federation of Korean Trade Unions, FKTU Bldg., 1–117, Yoido-dong, Yongdeungpo-ku, Seoul; labour; f. 1958; Publr. KIM YOUNG-TAE; circ. 15,000.

Hyundae Munhak: 136-46 Yeunji-dong, Chongno-ku, Seoul; f. 1955; literature; Chief Editor YUN HYUN-CHO; circ. 115,000.

Korea Newsreview: 2nd Floor, FKI Bldg., 1-124 Yoido-dong, Yongdeungpo-ku, Seoul; weekly; English; Publr. KIM TAE-DONG; Editor KIM MYONG-WHAI.

Korean Business Review: 1-124, FKI Bldg., Yoido-dong, Yongdeungpo-ku, Seoul; organ of the Federation of Korean Industries; quarterly.

Shin Dong-A (*New East Asia*): 139 Sejong-ro, Chongno-ku, Seoul; f. 1931; general; Publr. KIM SANG-KEE; Editor KWON O-KIE; circ. 95,000.

Weekly Chosun: 61 Taepyong-ro 1, Chung-ku, Seoul; circ. (weekly) 170,000 (*see under* Dailies).

The Weekly Hankook: 14 Chunghak-dong, Chongno-ku, Seoul; f. 1964; Editor HONG YOO-SUN; circ. 400,000.

Wolkan Joong-ang (*Monthly Joong-ang*): 58-9 Seosomun-dong, Seodaemun-ku, Seoul.

Women's Weekly: 14 Chunghak-dong, Chongno-ku, Seoul.

Yosong Dong-A (*Women's Far East*): 139 Sejong-ro, Chung-ku, Seoul; f. 1933; women's magazine; Publr. LEE DONG-WOOK; Editor KIM SONG-HWAN; circ. 213,000.

NEWS AGENCIES

Naewoe Press: 42-2, Chuja-dong, Chung-ku, Seoul.

Yonhap (United) News Agency: 98-5, Woani-dong, Chongno-ku, Seoul; f. 1945; Pres. KIM SONG-CHIN; Man. Dir. HONG IL-HAE.

FOREIGN BUREAUX

Agence France-Presse (AFP): c/o Yonhap News Agency, Samwhan Bldg., 98–5 Wooni-dong, Chongno-ku, Seoul; Bureau Chief P. K. MINN.

Agencia EFE (*Spain*): Jin-Ju Apt., C-dong, 11-05 Yoido-dong, Yongdeungpo-ku, Seoul; Corr. MARÍA DEL PILAR PÉREZ VALERO.

Associated Press (AP) (*U.S.A.*): Samwhan Bldg., 98–5 Wooni-dong, Chongno-ku, Seoul; Correspondent K. C. HWANG.

Central News Agency of China (*Taiwan*): Hapdong Bldg., 108–4 Susong-dong, Chongno-ku, Seoul; Correspondent LI TAI-FANG.

Deutsche Presse-Agentur (dpa) (*Federal Republic of Germany*): c/o Yonhap News Agency, 108-4 Susong-dong, Chongno-ku, Seoul; Correspondent JAI CHANG CHOI.

Jiji Tsushin-Sha (*Japan*): Joong-ang Daily News Bldg., 58–9, Seosomun-dong, Chung-ku, Seoul; Chief Corr. KATSUMI MUROTANI.

Kyodo Tsushin (*Japan*): Rm. 1006, Samwhan Bldg., Wooni-dong, Chongno-ku, Seoul; Corr. KATSUHIRO KURODA.

Press Trust of India: 50, Unjung-dong, Songnam, Kyonggi Prov.

Reuters (*U.K.*): Samwhan Bldg., 98–5 Wooni-dong, Chongno-ku, Seoul.

United Press International (UPI) (*U.S.A.*): Room 916, Samwhan Bldg., Wooni-dong, Chongno-ku, Seoul; Correspondent JAMES KIM.

PRESS ASSOCIATIONS

The Korean Newspaper Editors Association: 31, 1-ka, Taepyong-ro, Chung-ku, Seoul; f. 1957; 416 mems.; Pres. YOO KUN-HO.

The Korean Newspapers Association: Room 201, The Press Centre of Korea, 31, 1-ka, Taepyong-ro, Chung-ku, Seoul; 21 mems.; Pres. MUN TAE-KAP.

PUBLISHERS

Bak Yeong Sa: 184 Kwanchul-dong, Chongno-ku, Seoul 110; f. 1952; Pres. AHN WON-OK; sociology, philosophy, literature, social sciences.

Beopmun Sa: 1-48 Chung-dong, Chung-ku, Seoul 111; f. 1957; Pres. KIM SUNG-SOO; law, economics, sociology, psychology, education, business administration.

Chang-Jo Publishing Co.: 92 Shinmun-ro 2-ka, Chongno-ku, Seoul 110; f. 1963; Pres. CHOI DEOK-KYO; literature.

Dongwha Publishing Co. Ltd.: 130-4 Wonhyoro 1-ka, Yongsan-ku, Seoul 140; f. 1968; Pres. LIM IN-KYU; literature, fine arts, history.

Eul-yoo Publishing Co. Ltd.: 46-1 Susong-dong, Chongno-ku, Seoul 110; f. 1945; Man. Dir. CHOUNG CHIN-SOOK; sociology, literature, history, philosophy.

Hae Dong Publishing Co.: 437-26, Gongdug-dong, Mapo-ku, Seoul 120; f. 1973; Pres. LEE TAEK-HWAN; educational, reference, juvenile.

Hollym Corporation: 14-5 Kwanchul-dong, Chongno-ku, Seoul; f. 1963; Pres. RHIMM IN-SOO; fiction, literature, biography, history, children's books.

Hyong Sol Publishing Co.: 18-8, Kwanchul-dong, Chongno-ku, Seoul 110; f. 1962; Pres. CHANG JI-IK; literature, language, engineering.

Il Cho Kak: 9 Gongpyung-dong, Chongno-ku, Seoul 110; f. 1953; Pres. HAN MAN-NYUN; history, literature, sociology, linguistics.

Il Ji Sa: 46-1 Chunghak-dong, Chongno-ku, Seoul 110; f. 1956; Dir. KIM SEONG-JAE; literature, fine arts.

Jeongeumsa Publishing Co.: 22-5 Chungmuro 5-ka, Chung-ku, Seoul 110; f. 1950; Pres. CHOI CHUL-HAE; language, fine arts, literature.

Kye Mong Sa: 12-23 Kwanchul-dong, Seoul 110; f.1950; Pres. KIM CHOON-SIK; juvenile literature.

Korea University Press: 1, 5-ka, Anam-dong, Sungbuk-ku, Seoul 132; f. 1956; Pres. KIM SANG-HYUP; philosophy, history, language, literature, sociology, education, psychology, social science, natural science, engineering, agriculture.

Kwang Myong Publishing Co.: 62–7 1-ka Manri-dong, Jung-ku, Seoul; f. 1967; Pres. LEE HAK-SOO; social sciences, fine arts, sciences.

Kyelim Publishing Co.: 84-7, Kwanhun-dong, Chongno-ku, Seoul 110; f. 1970; Pres. LIM EUI-HEUM; juvenile, school reference, sociology.

Minjungseorim: 1-48, Jeong-dong, Chung-ku, Seoul 100; f. 1979; Pres. KIM MYUNG-HWAN; dictionaries.

Panmun Book Co. Ltd.: 40 Chongno 1-ka, Chongno-ku, Seoul 110; f. 1955; Pres. LIU IK-HYUNG; dictionaries, sociology, economics, medicine, pharmacy.

Sam Joong Dang: 244-5 Huam-dong, Yongsan-ku, Seoul 140; f. 1950; Pres. SEO KUN-SUK; literature.

Samsung Publishing Co.: 43-7, Kwanchul-dong, Chongno-ku, Seoul 110; f. 1958; Pres. KIM BONG-KYU; literature, history, juvenile, dictionaries.

Seomun Dang: 121–155 Dangsan-dong, Yongdeungpo-ku, Seoul 150; f. 1968; Pres. CHOI SUK-RO; literature, fine arts, history, philosophy.

Seoul National University Press: 56-1 Shinrim-dong, Kwanark-ku, Seoul 151; Chair. YOON CHUN-JOO; text-books, magazines, journals.

Tamgu Dang Book Centre: 101-1 Kyungwoon-dong, Chongno-ku, Seoul 110; f. 1950; Pres. HONG SUK-WOO; language, fine arts.

PUBLISHERS' ASSOCIATION

Korean Publishers Association: 105-2 Sagan-dong, Chongno-ku, Seoul 110; f. 1947; Pres. MIN YOUNG-BIN; Vice-Pres. LIM IN-KYU, MOON JONG-SUNG, HONG YOUN-HEE; Sec.-Gen. LEE DOO-YOUNG; publs. *Newsletter on New Books* (fortnightly, Korean), *The Korean Publishers Association Journal* (monthly, Korean), *Korean Publication Yearbook*, *Books from Korea* (every 2 years, English).

RADIO AND TELEVISION

RADIO

Korean Broadcasting System (KBS): Apt. 1, Yoido-dong, Yongdeungpo-ku, Seoul; f. 1927; publicly-owned corporation; overseas service in Korean, English, Arabic, Indonesian, Chinese, Japanese, French, Spanish and Russian; Pres. LEE WON-HONG.

Munhwa Broadcasting Corporation (MBC) Network: 22 Chong-dong, Chung-ku, Seoul; f. 1961; commercial; 14 TV networks, 19 FM and 21 AM stations; Pres. LEE JIN-HIE.

Radio Station HLAZ: C.P.O.B. 3939, Seoul; f. 1973; religious, educational station operated by Far East Broadcasting Co.; programmes in Korean, Chinese, Russian, Japanese and English; Dir. Rev. BILLY KIM.

Radio Station HLKX: C.P.O.B. 5255, Seoul; f. 1956; religious, educational station operated by Far East Broadcasting Co.; programmes in Korean, Chinese, Russian and English; Dir. Rev. BILLY KIM.

Christian Broadcasting System (CBS): 136-46 Yonchi-dong, Chongno-ku, Seoul; f. 1954; independent religious station with five network stations in Seoul, Taegu, Pusan, Kwangchu and Iri; programmes in Korean; Pres. KIM KWAN-SUK.

American Forces Korea Network: Head Office: Seoul; Mil. Address: A.P.O. San Francisco, Calif. 96301, U.S.A.; f. 1950; 7 originating AM stations and 8 relay AM stations; 1 originating and 11 relay FM stations broadcast 24 hours a day; Commanding Officer JOSEPH P. HOLLIS., LTC.

There were an estimated 10,100,000 radio receivers in 1981.

TELEVISION

Korean Broadcasting System (KBS): Apt. 1, Yoido-dong, Yongdeungpo-ku, Seoul; f. 1961; publicly-owned corporation with nine local broadcasting and 248 relay stations; Pres. LEE WON-HONG.

Munhwa Broadcasting Corporation (MBC)-TV Network: 22 Chong-dong, Chung-ku, Seoul; f. 1969; station in Seoul and 6 throughout country; Pres. LEE JIN-HIE.

American Forces Korea Network: Head Office: Seoul; Mil. Address: A.P.O. San Francisco, Calif. 96301, U.S.A.; f. 1957; key station in Seoul; 18 rebroadcast transmitters and translators; 100 hours weekly (*see* above, Radio).

In 1981 there were an estimated 6,280,000 television sets.

FINANCE

BANKING

(cap.=capital; p.u.=paid up; dep.=deposits; res.=reserves; m.=million; amounts in won, unless otherwise stated)

CENTRAL BANK

Bank of Korea: 110, 3-ka, Namdaemun-ro, Chung-ku, Seoul; f. 1950; 14 domestic brs., 8 overseas offices; Gov. HAH YEUNG-KI; Deputy Gov. KIM GUN; publs. *Annual Report, Quarterly Economic Review*, etc.

COMMERCIAL BANKS

Bank of Seoul and Trust Co.: 10-1 Namdaemun-ro, 2-ka, Chung-ku, Seoul 100; f. 1959 as Bank of Seoul, merged with Korea Trust Co. in 1976; cap. 92,150m.; dep. 2,971,541m. (Dec. 1981); Pres. KIM YONG-WOON; Vice-Pres. LEE HUN-SEUNG.

Cho Heung Bank: 14, 1-ka, Namdaemun-ro, Chung-ku, Seoul; f. 1879; cap. p.u. 75,000m., dep. 1,662,886m. (June 1981); Chair. and Pres. LIM JAE-SOO; Dir. and Deputy Pres. SHIN YEONG-CHEOL.

Commercial Bank of Korea Ltd.: 111-1, 2-ka, Namdaemun-ro, Chung-ku, Seoul 100; f. 1899; cap. p.u. 65,000m., dep. 1,744,103m. (July 1981); Pres. KONG DUK-CHONG; Vice-Pres. PARK WOO-SUH; 96 domestic brs., 7 overseas brs.

Hanil Bank: 130, 2-ka, Namdaemun-ro, Chung-ku, Seoul; f. 1932; cap. p.u. 75,000m., dep. 1,412,649m. (July 1981); Pres. AHN YOUNG-MO.

Korea First Bank: 53-1, 1-ka, Chungmu-ro, Chung-ku, Seoul 100, P.O.B. 2242; f. 1929; cap. p.u. 90,000m., dep. 2,223,110m. (Dec. 1981); Chair and Pres. LEE PIL-SUN; Dir. KIM SE-WON.

DEVELOPMENT BANK

Korea Long Term Credit Bank: 1–60 Yoido-dong, Youngdeungpo-ku, Seoul, 150; f. 1967; assists in the development of private enterprises by medium- and long-term financing (including loans, guarantees and purchases of equities) and contributes to the development of the Korean capital market by issuing bank debentures; cap. p.u. 50,000m.; dep. 8,999m. (July 1981); Chair. KIM BONG-EUN; Pres. HAHM TAE-YONG.

SPECIALIZED BANKS

Citizen's National Bank Ltd.: 9-1, 2-ka, Namdaemun-ro, Chung-ku, Seoul 100; f. 1963; cap. p.u. 30,000m., dep. 1,090,097m. (July 1981); Pres. SONG BYOUNG-SOON; Vice-Pres. KIM SANG-CHAN.

Export-Import Bank of Korea (Korea Eximbank): 541, 5-ka, Namdaemun-ro, Chung-ku, Seoul 100; f. 1976; cap. 244,855m. (October 1981); Pres. LEE TAE-HO; Vice-Pres. HA KOOK-WHAN; 7 overseas brs.

Korea Development Bank: 140-1, 2-ka, Namdaemun-ro, Chung-ku, Seoul 100, C.P.O.B. 28; f. 1954; cap. p.u. 505,300m., dep. 39,079m. (July 1981); Gov. HAH YEUNG-KI; Deputy Gov. JOON PARK; 6 overseas brs.

Korea Exchange Bank: 10 Kwanchul-dong, Chongno-ku, Seoul 110; f. 1967; cap. p.u. 300,000m., dep. 2,327m. (July 1981); Pres. CHUNG CHOON-TAIK; Vice-Pres. CHOO INN-KI, KIM WON-DON.

Korea Housing Bank: 61-1, 1-ka, Taepyong-ro, Chung-ku, Seoul; f. 1967; cap. p.u. 12,000m., dep. 786,854m. (Dec. 1981); Pres. RYU DON-WOO; Exec. Vice-Pres. LEE SANG-HOON.

National Agricultural Co-operatives Federation: 75, 1-ka, Chungjeung-ro, Seodaemun-ku, Seoul 120; cap. p.u. 16,182m., dep. 1,130,830m. (July 1981); Pres. RHEE DUCK-YONG.

National Fishers Federation of Co-operatives: 88 Kyongwoon-dong, Chongno-ku, Seoul 100; cap. p.u. 11,989m., dep. 153,248m. (July 1981); Pres. LEE DONG-YONG.

Small and Medium Industry Bank: 36–1, 2-ka, Ulchiro, Chung-ku, Seoul; f. 1961; cap. p.u. 107,060m., dep. 1,087,931m.; Pres. Kim Sun-Kil; Vice-Pres. Suh Won-Suk.

Provincial Banks

Bank of Pusan Ltd.: 25-2, 4-ka Jungang-dong, Pusan; f. 1967; cap. p.u. 20,000m., dep. 353,202m. (July 1981); Pres. Park Tae-Joo; Vice-Pres. Kim Tae-Sung.

Chungbuk Bank: 86-3, Young-dong, Cheongju; f. 1971; cap. p.u. 3,000m., dep. 56,196m. (July 1981); Pres. Park Chung-Suh; Vice-Pres. Nam Chung-Yoon.

Chungchong Bank: 48-1 Eunhyaeng-dong, Taejon; f. 1968; cap. p.u. 5,000m., dep. 100,549m. (July 1981); Pres. Kim Kwan-Soo; Vice-Pres. Song Hee-Bin.

Daegu Bank Ltd.: 20-3 Namil-dong, Chung-ku, Daegu 630, P.O.B. 122; f. 1967; cap. p.u. 20,000m., dep. 221,715m. (May 1981); Pres. Jeong Dal-Yong; Vice-Pres. Roh Yong-Son.

Gwangchu Bank: 1-11, 3-ka Kumnamro, Dong-ku, Kwangchu; f. 1968; cap. p.u. 5,000m., dep. 88,028m. (July 1981); Pres. Moon Bang-Heum; Vice-Pres. Kim Young-Mo.

Jeonbuk Bank: 103, 1-ka Kyungwan-dong, Jeonju; f. 1969; cap. p.u. 5,000m., dep. 55,400m. (July 1981); Pres. Lee Ye-Chul; Vice-Pres. Lee Yong-Man.

Kangwon Bank: 72-3 Unkyo-dong, Chuncheon, Kwangwon 200, P.O.B. 200; f. 1970; cap. p.u. 3,000m., dep. 62,816m. (July 1981); Pres. Lee Tae-Sung; Vice-Pres. Chung Guk-Jin.

Kyungki Bank Ltd.: 9-1 Sa-dong, Chung-ku, P.O.B. 6, Inchon; f. 1969; cap. 10,000m., dep. 204,113m.,total assets 302,804m. (Dec. 1981); Pres. Sung Seung-Mo.

Kyungnam Bank: 172 Chang-dong, Masan; f. 1970; cap. p.u. 10,000m., dep. 140,087m. (July 1981); Pres. Hong Sung-Hwan; Vice-Pres. Yoo Sang-Won.

The Bank of Cheju Ltd.: 1349, 2-Do, 1-Dong, Cheju City, Cheju-Do; f. 1969; cap. p.u. 2,500m., dep. 40,609m. (July 1981); Pres. Han Suk-Hwan; Dir. and Deputy Pres. Cho Nam-June.

Foreign Banks

Algemene Bank Nederland (*Netherlands*): Daewoo Centre Bldg., Room 1818, 541, 5-ka, Namdaemun-ro, Chung-ku, C.P.O.B. 3035, Seoul; f. 1979; Man. H. W. E. Riedlin.

American Express International Banking Corpn. (*U.S.A.*): 20th Floor, Daewoo Centre, 541, 5-ka, Namdaemun-ro, Chung-ku, C.P.O.B. 8251, Seoul; Vice-Pres. and Gen. Man. William C. Brown.

Bank of America (*U.S.A.*): C.P.O.B. 3026, Dong-bang Bldg., 250, 2-ka, Taepyung-ro, Chung-ku, Seoul 100; Man. R. A. Fuller.

Bank of Credit and Commerce International (Overseas) Ltd. (*Cayman Islands*): 801 Daewoo Centre, 541, 5-ka Namdaemun-ro, Chung-ku, Yangsan P.O.B. 117, Seoul 100; Gen. Man. Krishan Murari.

Bank of Montreal (*Canada*): 17-7, 4-ka, Namdaemun-ro, Chung-ku, Seoul; Man. Y. J. P. Bourdeau.

Bank of Nova Scotia (*Canada*): 22nd Floor, Daewoo Centre, 286 Yang-dong, Chung-ku, Seoul 100; Man. E. G. Bernard.

Bank of Singapore: Suite 2215, Daewoo Centre, 286 Yang-dong, Chung-ku, Seoul 100; Man. Cheok Cheng Kiat.

Bank of Tokyo (*Japan*): 25-1 Mugyo-dong, Chung-ku, Seoul; Gen. Man. Masayasu Otsuki.

Bankers Trust Co. (*U.S.A.*): Center Bldg., 91-1 Sokong-dong, Chung-ku, Seoul; Vice-Pres. and Gen. Man. Dong H. Choi.

Banque Indosuez (*France*): 360-1, 2-ka, Taepyong-ro, Chung-ku, C.P.O.B. 158, Seoul; Man. Charles Rey-bet-Degat.

Banque de Paris et des Pays-Bas (*France*): 1-1, 1-ka, Chongno, Chongno-ku, Seoul 110; Man. Denis Antoine.

Banque Nationale de Paris (*France*): 18F Samsung Main Bldg., 250, 2-ka, Taepyong-ro, Chung-ku, Seoul; Man. Gérard Muguet.

Barclays Bank International Ltd. (*U.K.*): C.P.O.B. 3010, 23rd Floor, Daewoo Centre, 541, 5-ka, Namdaemun-ro, Chung-ku, Seoul 100; Chief Man. A. J Addis.

Chartered Bank (*U.K.*): 108–110 Samsung Bldg., 50 1-ka, Ulchiro, Chung-ku, Seoul; P.O.B. Kwangwhamun 259, Seoul; Man. J. R. Medley.

Chase Manhattan Bank, N.A. (*U.S.A.*): 50, 1-ka, Ulchiro, Chung-ku, C.P.O.B. 2249, Seoul 100; Vice-Pres. and Gen. Man. Roger F. R. Griffin.

Chemical Bank (*U.S.A.*): 18F, Samsung Main Bldg., 250, 2-ka, Taepyung-ro, Chung-ku, Seoul 100; Vice-Pres. and Gen. Man. James L. Rawn.

Citibank (*U.S.A.*): 1-1, 1-ka, Chongno, Chongno-ku, Seoul; Vice-Pres. and Gen. Man. Thomas J. Charters; br. in Pusan.

Continental Illinois National Bank & Trust Co. of Chicago (*U.S.A.*): 18th Floor, Daewoo Centre, 541 Namdaemun-ro 5-ka, Chung-ku, Seoul 100; Vice-Pres. and Gen. Man. Frank J. Dictus.

Crédit Lyonnais (*France*): 17F, Daewoo Centre, 541, 5-ka, Namdaemun-ro, Chung-ku, Seoul 100; Gen. Man. Jacques Bertholier.

Crocker National Bank (*U.S.A.*): 14f. Dong-bang Bldg., 250, 2-ka, Taepyung-ro, Chung-ku, Seoul 100; Man. Ho Yang.

Dai-Ichi Kangyo Bank Ltd. (*Japan*): KAL Bldg., 118, 2-ka, Namdaemun-ro, Chung-ku, Seoul; f. 1972; cap. U.S. $1.7m., dep. $12.0m.; Gen. Man. Akio Sano.

Development Bank of Singapore: 541, 5-ka, Namdaemun-ro, Chung-ku, Seoul; Man. Lim Yin Kiat.

European Asian Bank (*Federal Republic of Germany*): Ground and First Floors, Daehan Fire and Marine Insurance Bldg., 51–1, Namchang-dong, Chung-ku, C.P.O.B. 8904, Seoul; Man. Kevin H. Cain.

First Interstate Bank of California (*U.S.A.*): 1-1, 1-ka, Chongno, Chongno-ku, Seoul; Man. Donald J. Huse.

First National Bank of Chicago (*U.S.A.*): 2nd Floor, Daewoo Centre, 286 Yang-dong, Chung-ku, Seoul 100; Vice-Pres. and Gen. Man. John R. G. Pansons.

Fuji Bank Ltd. (*Japan*): Daeil Bldg., 18, 1-ka, Namdaemun-ro, Chung-ku, Seoul 100; Gen. Man. Murayama Ryoich.

Grindlays Bank Ltd. (*U.K.*): C.P.O.B. 9051, Suite 936/7 Daewoo Centre, 541 Namdaemun-ro, 5-ka, Chung-ku, Seoul; Gen. Man. R. H. Prendergast.

Indian Overseas Bank: 3rd Floor, Daeyungak Bldg., 25-5, 1-ka, Chungmu-ro, Chung-ku, Seoul 100; Man. S. K. Balakrishnan.

International Bank of Singapore Ltd.: Daewoo Centre Bldg., 541, 5-ka, Namdaemun-ro, Chung-ku, Seoul; Man. Cheng Kiat Cheok.

Lloyds Bank International Ltd. (*U.K.*): C.P.O.B. 8111, Samsung Main Bldg., 250, 2-ka, Taepyong-ro, Chung-ku, Seoul; Man. H. Frederick.

Manufacturers Hanover Trust Co. (*U.S.A.*): 11F. Daewoo Centre, 541, 5-ka, Namdaemun-ro, Chung-ku, Seoul; Man. E. W. Young.

Marine Midland Bank (*U.S.A.*): 1-1, 1-ka, Chongno, Chongno-ku, Seoul; Man. James C. Spakman.

Mitsubishi Bank Ltd. (*Japan*): 188-3, 1-ka, Ulchiro, Chung-ku, Seoul; Man. Tosho Morita.

Morgan Guaranty Trust Co. of New York (*U.S.A.*): 15F, Samsung Main Bldg., 250, 2-ka, Taepyong-ro, Chung-ku, Seoul 100; Vice-Pres. and Gen. Man. T. R. Mills.

Union de Banques Arabes et Françaises (*France*): 18F. Dong-bang Bldg., 250, 2-ka, Taepyung-ro, Chung-ku, Seoul 100; Man. M. Harmafi.

Banking Association

Bankers' Association of Korea: 4, 1-ka, Myung-dong, Chung-ku, Seoul; mems. 26 financial institutions; Chair. and Pres. Hah Yeung-Ki (Gov. Bank of Korea); Exec. Vice-Pres. Lee Chan-Sup.

INSURANCE

Principal Companies

Life

Daehan Kyo Yuk Life Insurance Co. Ltd.: 1, 1-ka, Chongno, Chongno-ku, Seoul; f. 1958; Pres. Park Sung-Bok.

Daehan Life Insurance Co. Ltd.: 34-17 Yang-dong, Chung-ku, C.P.O.B. 290, Seoul 100; f. 1946; Pres. Choi Soon-Young.

Dong Bang Life Insurance Co. Ltd.: 250, 2-ka, Taepyong-ro, Chung-ku, Seoul 100; f. 1957; Pres. Ko Sang-Kyum.

Dong Hae Life Insurance Co. Ltd.: 25-5, 1-ka, Chungmu-ro, Chung-ku, Seoul; f. 1973; cap. 1,000m. won; Pres. Wooh Jae-Ku; Exec. Vice-Pres. Ha O-Soo, Kim Bong-Seon.

Hung Kuk Life Insurance Co. Ltd.: 94-151, Yongdeongpo-ku, Seoul 150; f. 1958; cap. 500m. won; Pres. Chey Woo-Jik; Chair. Lee Eam-Yong; publ. *The Life Insurance* (monthly).

Je Il Life Insurance Co. Ltd.: 58-3, Seocho-dong, Kangnam-ku, Seoul; f. 1954; cap. 500m. won, dep. 3,244m. won; Pres. Park Soo-Kee.

Non-Life

Ankuk Fire and Marine Insurance Co. Ltd.: 7th Floor, Samsung Main Bldg., 50, 1-ka, Ulchiro, Chung-ku, C.P.O.B. 469, Seoul 100; f. 1952; Pres. Sohn Kyung-Shik.

Daehan Fire and Marine Insurance Co. Ltd.: 51-1 Nam-chang-dong, Chung-ku, Seoul; f. 1946; Pres. Hwang Pil-Joo; Vice-Pres. Kim Seong-Du.

Eastern Marine and Fire Insurance Co. Ltd.: 92-3, 2-ka, Myung-dong, Chung-ku, Seoul; f. 1955; Chair. and Pres. Cho Wal-Byuk.

First Fire and Marine Insurance Co. Ltd.: 12-1 Seosomun dong, Chung-ku, C.P.O.B. 530, Seoul; f. 1949; Pres. Kim Young-Chull.

Haedong Fire and Marine Insurance Co. Ltd.: 185-10, 2-ka, Chungjeong-ro, Seodaemun-ku, C.P.O.B. 1821, Seoul 120; f. 1953; Pres. Chung Young-Kook.

International Fire and Marine Insurance Co. Ltd.: International Insurance Bldg., 120, 5-ka, Namdaemun-ro, Chung-ku, Seoul; f. 1947; Pres. Lee Kyung-Suh.

Korea Automobile Insurance Co.: 21-9 Cho-dong, Chung-ku, Seoul; f. 1962; Pres. Kim Young-Dong.

Korea Fidelity and Surety Co.: 136-74 Yeunji-dong, Chongno-ku, Seoul; f. 1969; cap. p.u. 1,000m. won (March 1982); Pres. Pyoun Kyu-Su.

Korean Reinsurance Company: 7-8th Floor, Kukdong Bldg., 60-1, 3-ka, Chungmu-ro, Chung-ku, C.P.O.B. 1438, Seoul 100; f. 1963; Chair and Pres. Sim Yoo-Sun; Vice-Pres. Chi Se-Hyun.

Koryo Fire and Marine Insurance Co. Ltd.: 145 Naesoo-dong, Chongno-ku, Seoul; f. 1948; Pres. Yoon Han-Chae.

Oriental Fire and Marine Insurance Co. Ltd.: 19, 1-ka, Taepyong-ro, Chung-ku, P.O.B. 230, Kwanghwamoon, Seoul 100; f. 1922; Pres. Kang Yun-Kook.

Pan Korea Insurance Co.: 77 Sogong-dong, Chung-ku, Seoul 100; f. 1959; Pres. Cho Tae-Ho; Man. Dir. Rhee Jae-Hee.

Shindong-A Fire and Marine Insurance Co. Ltd.: 43, 2-ka, Taepyong-ro, Chung-ku, Seoul; f. 1946; cap. p.u. 567m. won; Chair. and Pres. Moon Sang-Chul; Vice-Pres. Ahn Soon-Jip, Choi Soon-Kwang.

Insurance Associations

Life Insurance Association of Korea: 16th Floor, Kukdong Bldg., 60-1, 3-ka, Chungmu-ro, Chung-ku, Seoul 100; f. 1950; mems. 6 companies; Chair. Chang Sung-Tae.

Korea Non-Life Insurance Association: 9th Floor, K.F.P.A. Bldg., 1-614 Yeoyido-dong, Yongdeungpo-ku, Seoul; Yeoyido P.O.B. 43; f. 1946; Chair. Kim Sang-Hee; publ. *Korea Non-Life Insurance* (English).

TRADE AND INDUSTRY

CHAMBER OF COMMERCE AND INDUSTRY

Korea Chamber of Commerce and Industry: 111 Sogong-dong, Chung-ku, Seoul; f. 1894; total mems. over 500,000; 42 local chambers; promotes development of the nation's economy and international economic co-operation; Pres. Chung Soo-Chang; publs. *Korean Business Directory, Korea Chamber Quarterly News*, etc.

FOREIGN TRADE ORGANIZATIONS

Korea Export Industrial Corporation: 188-5 Kuro-dong, Yongdeungpo-ku, Seoul; f. 1964; encourages industrial exports, provides assistance and operating capital, market surveys; Chair. Choi Myung-Hun.

Korea Trade Promotion Corporation (KOTRA): C.P.O.B. 1621, 10-1, 2-ka, Huehyun-dong, Chung-ku, Seoul; f. 1962; 86 overseas brs.; Pres. Yoon Ja-Joong; publ. *Korea Trade.*

Korea Cotton Textiles Export Association: 10-1, 2-ka, Hoehyun-dong, Chung-ku, Seoul; f. 1965; overseas br. Brussels; Pres. Baek Young-Ki.

Korean Hair Goods Export Association: 10-1, 2-ka, Hoehyun-dong, Chung-ku, Seoul; f. 1966; Pres. Kim Pok-Ki.

Korean Knitted Goods Exporters Association: 10-1, 2-ka, Hoehyun-dong, Chung-ku, Seoul; f. 1965; overseas brs. New York, Rotterdam; Pres. Kim Woo-Chong.

INDUSTRIAL ORGANIZATIONS

Agriculture and Fishery Development Corporation—AFDC: 65-228, 3-ka, Hangang-ro, Yongsan-ku, C.P.O.B. 3213, Seoul 140; f. 1968 to develop principal producing areas for various agricultural and fisheries produce, to develop and encourage processing, preservation and marketing of such products, to make loans and promote investment and to give technical assistance and managerial guidance; thereby to elevate income levels of farming and fishing communities; principal exports: canned mushrooms, oysters, tomato juice, white peaches, tobacco, silk; cap. U.S. $20m.; Pres. BONG HYUN CHIN; Exec. Vice-Pres. MOO CHAE LEE.

Electronic Industries Association of Korea: Room 1101, World Trade Center, 10-1, 2-ka, Hoehyon-dong, Chung-ku, Seoul 100; f. 1970; mems. 350 companies; Pres. Dr. WAN HEE KIM; publs. *Catalog of Korea Electronics* (annually), *Directory of Korea Electronics Exporters* (annually), *Electronics Industry* (annually), *Journal of Korean Electronics* (monthly).

Federation of Korean Industries: 2nd Floor, FKI Bldg., 1-124 Yoido-dong, Yongdeungpo-ku, Seoul; f. 1961; conducts research and survey work on domestic and overseas economic conditions and trends; makes recommendations on important economic matters to the government and other interested parties; exchange of economic and trade missions with other countries with a view to exploring markets and fostering economic co-operation; sponsoring of regular business conferences with friendly countries; mems. 423 companies and 71 business asscns.; Chair. CHUNG JU-YUNG; Man. Dir. YOON TAI-YEOP; publs. *Korean Business Review* (quarterly), *Chunkyunryun* (monthly), *Korean Economic Yearbook, FKI Membership Director* (every two years), etc.

Korean Economic Development Association: 340, 2-ka, Taepyong-ro, Chung-ku, Seoul; f. 1965; economic research; mems. 38 companies; Pres. KWON TAEK-SANG.

Korea Productivity Centre: 10, 2-ka, Pil-dong, Chung-ku, Seoul 100; f. 1957; business consultancy services, economic research; mems. 173 companies; Pres. RHEE EUN-BOK; Chair LEE EUN-POK; publ. *Journal* (monthly).

Korea Traders Association: World Trade Center, Korea Bldg., 10-1, 2-ka, Hoehyon-dong, Chung-ku, Seoul; f. 1946; Pres. SHIN BYONG-HYUN; Vice-Chair. KAY BONG-HYUK; publs. *Statistical Yearbook of Foreign Trade, Monthly Statistics of Foreign Trade, Korean Trade Directory*, etc.

Construction Association of Korea: Construction Bldg., 31-23, 1-ka, Taepyong-ro, Chung-ku, Seoul 100; f. 1959; national licensed contractors' association; mems. 504 companies (May 1981); Pres. CHOI CHONG-WHAN; Vice-Pres. YOON HAE-BONG (acting); publs. *The Construction Industry* (monthly), *The Construction Materials Prices* (monthly), *Construction News Service* (daily).

Daehan Coalmines Association: 88 Kyongun-dong, Chung-ku, Seoul; f. 1949; Pres. KIM YOUNG-SAENG.

Korea Food Industry Association Inc.: Room 304/5 Chinyang Apt., 125-1, 4 ka, Chungmu-ro, Chung-ku, Seoul 100; f. 1969; mems. 35 companies; Pres. CHUNG TAEK-SUH.

Korea Petroleum Association: 59-22, 3-ka, Chungmu-ro, Chung-ku, Seoul 100; f. 1956; mems. 76 companies; Chair. HAHM SUNG-YONG.

Korea Sericultural Association: 15-1 Kwanchul-dong, Chongno-ku, Seoul 110; f. 1946; improvement research and promotion of sericulture; Pres. KIM WON-TAE.

Korea Shipowners Association: Room 1002, Baejae Bldg., 55-4 Seosomun-dong, Chung-ku, Seoul 100; f. 1960; mems. 72 shipping companies; Pres. LEE MAENG-KEE; publ. *KSA Bulletin* (weekly).

Korea Steel Industry Association: Seoul; Pres. PARK TAE-JOON.

Mining Association of Korea: 35-24 Tongui-dong, Chongnu-ku, Seoul 110; f. 1918; mems. 139 companies; Pres. BAHNG HEE.

Spinners' and Weavers' Association of Korea: 43-8 Kwanchul-dong, Chongno-ku, Seoul 110; f. 1947; mems. 21 companies; Pres. BAI DUCK-CHIN.

CO-OPERATIVES

National Agricultural Co-operative Federation (N.A.C.F.): 75, 1-ka, Chunjung-ro, Chung-ku, Seoul; f. 1961; purchase, marketing, utilization and processing, mutual insurance, banking and credit services, education and guidance, research and surveys, international co-operation; Pres. RHEE DUCK-YONG; Vice-Pres. LEE POO-YUNG, SHIN JUNG-SOO; cap. 50,548 million won (Dec. 1980); publs. *Agricultural Co-operative Yearbook, Annual Report, Monthly Review, New Farmer* (monthly), *Farmers' Newspaper* (weekly), etc.

Central Federation of Fisheries Co-operatives: 88, Kyeongun-dong, Chongno-ku, Seoul; f. 1962; Pres. KIM DUK-YUP.

Federation of Korea Knitting Industry Co-operatives: 48, 1-ka, Shinmun-ro, Chongno-ku, Seoul 110; f. 1962; mems. 9 regional co-operatives composed of 1,224 manufacturing firms; Chair. KIM SUK-NAM.

Korea Woollen Spinners and Weavers Co-operative: 129-1 Chungrim-dong, Chung-ku, Seoul; f. 1964; Pres. LEE JANG-WOO.

National Federation of Medium Industry Co-operatives: 138-1 Kongpyong-dong, Chongno-ku, Seoul; f. 1962; Chair. KIM BONG-JAI; Vice-Chair. YONGWOON WON; publ. *Medium Industry News*.

EMPLOYERS' ASSOCIATION

The Korean Employers' Association: 10, Kwanchul-dong, Chongno-ku, Seoul 110; f. 1970; mems. 170 companies and 23 associations; Pres. KIM YONG-JOO.

TRADE UNIONS

Federation of Korean Trade Unions (FKTU): 1-117, Yeouido-dong, Yongdeungpo-ku, Seoul; f. 1961; Pres. CHUNG HAN-JOO; Gen. Sec. LEE YONG-JOON; 16 unions are affiliated with a membership of 922,317; affiliated to ICFTU; publs. *FKTU News* (monthly), *Foreign Labor News* (monthly); major affiliated unions are:

Federation of Foreign Organization Employees' Unions: 17-1, Kalwol-dong, Yongsan-ku, Seoul; f. 1961; Pres. KWON YONG-SO; 18,625 mems.

Federation of Korean Automobile Workers' Unions: 32, 2-ka, Bomoon-dong, Seongbuk-ku, Seoul; f. 1963; Pres. LEE SANG-WON; 78,493 mems.

Federation of Korean Chemical Workers' Unions: 106-1, Yeonhi-dong, Seodaemun-ku, Seoul; f. 1961; Pres. KIM CHANG-YOON; 156,592 mems.

Federation of Korean Metal Workers' Unions: 18-2, Hangang-ro, Yongsan-ku, Seoul; f. 1961; Pres. PAENG JONG-CHOOL; 108,928 mems.

Federation of Korean Mine Workers' Unions: 78, Changsin-dong, Chongno-ku, Seoul; f. 1961; Pres. KIM KYU-BAIK; 55,315 mems.

Federation of Korean Printing Workers' Unions: 543, Chunglim-dong, Chung-ku, Seoul; f. 1963; Pres. HWANG TAE-SOO; 6,456 mems.

Federation of Korean Textile Workers' Unions: 382-31, Hapjung-dong, Mapo-ku, Seoul; f. 1961; Pres. KIM HONG-DO; 156,959 mems.

Korea Communication Workers' Union: 18, 1-ka, Chungmu-ro, Chung-ku, Seoul; f. 1958; Pres. PARK SOO-KEUN; 46,883 mems.

Korea Monopoly Workers' Union: 48-2, Inui-dong, Chongno-ku, Seoul; f. 1960; Pres. KIM DONG-JIN; 13,163 mems.

Korea Seamen's Union: 335, Chunglim-dong, Chung-ku, Seoul; f. 1961; Pres. BANG HAE-RANG; 54,581 mems.

Korean Federation of Bank & Financial Workers' Unions: 1-508, Yeouido-dong, Yongdeungpo-ku, Seoul; f. 1961; Pres. KIM JAE-YONG; 58,943 mems.

Korean Federation of Port & Transport Workers' Unions: 2-5, 1-ka, Do-dong, Yongsan-ku, Seoul; f. 1980; Pres. KIM DONG-IN; 39,770 mems. (Federation of Port Workers' Unions and Federation of Transport Workers' Unions were combined).

Korean National Electrical Workers' Union: 2, Chungdam-dong, Kangnam-ku, Seoul; f. 1961; Pres. CHANG HWAL-SOO; 16,495 mems.

Korean National United Workers' Federation: 43-22, Dongja-dong, Yongsan-ku, Seoul; f. 1961; Pres. KIM IN-KEUN; 67,720 mems.

Korean Tourist Industry Workers' Federation: 749, 5-ka, Namdaemoon-ro, Chung-ku, Seoul; f. 1970; Pres. LEE MOO-WOONG; 10,796 mems.

Railway Workers' Union: 40, 3-ka, Hangang-ro, Yongsan-ku, Seoul; f. 1947; Pres. PARK JOON-HONG; 32,598 mems.

MAJOR INDUSTRIAL COMPANIES

The following are some of Korea's major industrial groups and companies, arranged by sector:

MAJOR INDUSTRIAL GROUPS

Hanjin Group: Seoul; Korea's largest business conglomerate; involved in transportation, construction, petroleum distribution, hotels, fishing, import-export, mining, securities, insurance; Chair. CHO CHOONG-HOON.

Hyundai Group: 178 Sejong-ro, Chongno-ku, Seoul; nine member companies; involved in construction, heavy industry, shipbuilding, cement manufacture, manufacture of automobiles, etc.; Chair. CHUNG JU YUNG.

The Lucky Group: 537 Namdaemoon-ro, 5, C.P.O.B. 1088, Seoul; f. 1947; 20 member companies, insurance, construction, engineering, oil refining, etc.

Samsung Group: C.P.O. Box 1144, Seoul; 40,000 employees; 25 member companies; involved in construction, petrochemicals, heavy industry, electronics, shipbuilding, telecommunications, food, textiles, paper, broadcasting, insurance, retailing; Chair. LEE BYUNG-CHULI.

CEMENT

Asia Cement Manufacturing Co. Ltd.: 120-23 Seosomun-dong, Chung-ku, C.P.O.B. 5278, Seoul; f. 1957; cap. p.u. 5,000m. won; manufactures and exports Portland cement, sulphate resistant cement, construction materials, plywood, steel products, etc.; Pres. LEE BYUNG-MOON; Man. Dir. LEE BYUNG-MOO; employees: 1,042.

Hanil Cement Manufacturing Co. Ltd.: 64-5, 2-ka, Chungmu-ro, Chung-ku, C.P.O.B. 5339, Seoul; f. 1961; cap. 1.53m. won; sells and exports Portland cement with an annual capacity of one million tons; Pres. KIM YONG-JOO; Vice-Pres. LEE JOON-GIU; employees: 557.

Hyundai Cement Co. Ltd.: 178 Sejong-ro, Chongno-ku, Seoul; f. 1964; manufacture of Portland cement and various building materials; Pres. YUNG CHUNG-SUN.

Ssangyong Cement Industrial Co. Ltd.: 24, 2-ka, Zuh-dong, Chung-ku, Seoul; f. 1962; cement manufacturers; mine excavating, exporting and importing, civil engineering; Rep. SEO SEONG-TAEK; employees: 7,550.

Tongyang Cement Manufacturing Co. Ltd.: 1 Euijuro, 1-ka, Chung-ku, Seoul; f. 1957; manufactures and sells Portland cement (annual capacity of 3,800,000 tons), ready-mixed concrete (annual capacity 600,000m³); Pres. KEE TONG-NAM.

CHEMICALS AND FERTILIZERS

Chinhae Chemical Co. Ltd.: 65-228, 3-ka, Hangang-ro. Yongsan-ku, Seoul; f. 1965; manufacturers of urea and various NPK complex fertilizers with annual production capacity of about 300,000 tons; Pres. CHOI SE-IN; Exec. Vice-Pres. K. E. NIELSON; employees: 700.

Korea Explosives Co. Ltd.: 34 Seosomun-dong, Seodaemun-ku, Seoul; f. 1952; manufacturers of dynamite and other explosives, safety fuses, electric detonators, mineral products and chemicals; Pres. SHIN HYEON-GI.

Korea Oil Corpn.: 10-1, 2-ka, Namdaemoon-ro, Chung-ku, Seoul; gasoline, kerosene, fuel oil, ethylene, etc.; Rep. CHEY JONG-HYON.

Korea Petrochemical Industrial Co. Ltd.: 95-1, 3-ka, Namdaemun-ro, Seoul; f. 1970; cap. p.u. U.S. $23,000,000; manufacturers of polypropylene resin and high density polyethylene resin with an annual capacity of 105,000 metric tons and 70,000 metric tons respectively; Pres. LEE CHUNG-HO; Vice Pres. KANG SU-CHEUL; employees: 392.

Nanhae Chemical Corpn.: 343 Nakpo-ri, Samil-up, Yechungun, Junnam Prov.; C.P.O.B. 3259, Seoul; manufacturers and sellers of fertilizers and chemicals with an annual capacity of 700,000 metric tons and 2,238,000 metric tons respectively; Pres. PARK HEE-DONG.

Tong Shin Chemical Products Co. Ltd.: 984, Shi Heung-dong, Koo-ro-ku, Seoul; f. 1935; manufacturers of rubber products, zinc ingots; Rep. LEE DONG-JOO.

ELECTRICAL AND ELECTRONICS

Gold Star Co. Ltd.: 337 Namdaemoon-ro, 5, Chung-ku, Seoul (International P.O.B. 2530, Seoul); f. 1958; manufacturer and exporter of electric and electronic products; Pres. HUH SHIN-KOO; employees: 9,000.

Hyosung Heavy Industries Ltd.: 4-5-ka, Dangsan-Dong, Yeongdeungpo-ku, Seoul, P.O.B. 78; f. 1962; manufacturers of electrical apparatus, transformers, motors, pumps, etc.; Pres. CHOI JONG-WAN; employees: 2,300.

Samsung Electronics Co. Ltd.: 250, 2-ka, Taepyong-ro, Chung-ku, Seoul; f. 1969; manufacturers of wide range of electronic goods, including TV, radio, calculators, tape recorders, refrigerators; Pres. KANG JIN-KU; employees: 4,500.

Taihan Electric Wire Co. Ltd.: 194-15, 1-ka, Hoehyun-dong, Chung-ku, Seoul; f. 1955; manufacturers of electric wires and cables, consumer electronic components; Chair. SULL WON-RYANG; Pres. CHOI HYUNG-KYU.

IRON AND STEEL

Boo-Kook Steel and Wire Co. Ltd.: 1179 Hwamyung-dong, Pusanjin-ku, Pusan, P.O.B. 277; f. 1956; cap. p.u. U.S. $3m.; manufacturers and exporters of high carbon steel wire, steel wire rope, aircraft cable etc. with monthly production capacity of 4,000 tons; Pres. KIM YOUNG-SOO; employees: 800.

Donkguk Steel Mill Co. Ltd.: 50 Suha-dong, Chung-ku, Seoul; f. 1954; manufactures iron and steel; Pres. CHANG SANG-TAI.

Inchon Heavy Industry Co. Ltd.: 16, 1-ka, Ulchi-ro, Chung-ku, Seoul; f. 1962; manufacturers of steel goods; Rep. LEE DONG-CHOON.

Inchon Iron and Steel Co. Ltd.: 5th Floor, Pukyang Bldg., Banp-dong, San 2-ka, Kang Nam-ku, Seoul; f. 1964; manufacturers iron and steel products; Pres. CHUNG MONG-PIL.

Pohang Iron & Steel Co. Ltd.: 3 Deungchon-dong, Pohang, Kyung Sang Book Do; state-owned; Pres. KIM SANG-JUN.

POWER AND TRANSPORT

Hanjin Transportation Co. Ltd.: 51 Sokong-dong, Chung-ku, Seoul; f. 1945; transporting and stevedoring; Rep. KIM HYEONG-BAE.

Hyundai International Inc.: San 2, Chungdam-dong, Kangnam-ku, Seoul; f. 1962; exporters and importers, shipbuilding, construction, engineering; Rep. CHUNG IN-YUNG.

Hyundai Motor Co.: 140-2, Ke-dong, Chongno-ku, Seoul; f. 1967; assembling and manufacture of passenger cars, trucks, buses, etc.; Rep. YUNG CHUNG-SE.

Korea Electric Company: 5, 2-ka, Namdaemun-ro, Chung-ku, Seoul; f. 1961; generation, transmission and distribution of electric power, and development of electric power sources; output: 19,620 kWh. sold in 1976; Pres. KIM YUNG-JOON; employees: 14,942.

Saehan Motor Co. Ltd.: 62-10 Choong Moo-ro, 2-ka, Choong-ku, Incheon; f. 1972; manufacturers buses, jeeps, cars and parts; Pres. RHOO SEOK-HEE.

TEXTILES, SILK AND SYNTHETIC FIBRES

Cheil Wool Textile Industrial Co. Ltd.: 250, 2-ka, Taepyong-ro, Chung-ku, Seoul; f. 1954; production of worsted and spun synthetic fibres; import and export; Chair. LEE SOO-BIN.

Chonbang Co. Ltd.: 10 Kwan Chul-dong, Chong-ro-ku, Seoul; f. 1952; manufacturers of cotton and blended yarns and fabrics; garments; Pres. KIM CHANG-SUNG.

Daewoo Industrial Co. Ltd.: 286 Yang-dong, Chung-ku, Seoul; f. 1967; manufacture of clothes, sporting and leather goods; Pres. KIM WOO-CHONG.

Dainong Co. Ltd.: Chinyang Bldg., 125-1, 4-ka, Chung-mu-ro, Chung-ku, Seoul; f. 1955; manufacturers of cotton and synthetic fibre products; import and export; Pres. PARK YOUNG-IL.

Hanil Synthetic Fibre Ind. Co. Ltd.: 58-7 Seosomun-dong, Seodaemun-ku, Seoul; f. 1964; manufacturers and exporters of synthetic fibre; Pres. KIM HAN-SOO.

Ilshin Spinning Co. Ltd.: 20-23 Seosomun-dong, Chung-ku, Seoul, Korea; f. 1961; cotton spinning and production of yarn and fabrics; one subsidiary company in Korea with dyeing and finishing factories; import and export; Chair. HYUNG N. KIM; Pres. CHANG H. KIM; employees: 2,500.

Korea Nylon (Kolon) Company Ltd.: 35-34 Tongeu-dong, Chongno-ku, Seoul; f. 1957; manufacturers of nylon filament yarn; Rep. LEE DONG-CHAN.

Korea Silk Co. Ltd. 11th Floor, Korea Automobile Bldg., 21-9 Cho-dong, Chung-ku, Seoul; f. 1946; manufacturers and exporters of raw silk, silk products and garments, electric products, chemical and plastic products, footwear, luggage, etc.; Pres. KIM YOUNG-WOO.

Sunkyong Ltd.: Sunkyong Bldg., 5-3, 2-ka, Namdaemun-ro, Chung-ku, Seoul; f. 1953; textile piece goods, garments, machinery and steel products, electrical equipment, chemicals, etc.; import and export; Pres. CHOI MOO-HYUN.

Tae Kwang Industrial Co. Ltd.: Tae Kwang Bldg., 162-1, 2-ka, Jangchung-dong, Chung-ku, P.O.B. 1173, Seoul; f. 1961; manufacturers, exporters and importers of fabrics, blankets, acrylic yarns and knitwear; Chair. LEE EAM-YONG; Pres. LEE KI-HWA.

MISCELLANEOUS

Chunusa Co. Ltd.: 81 Sokong-dong, Chung-ku, Seoul; f. 1947; exporters, importers and marine transportation services; dealers in tyres, machinery, chemicals, foodstuffs, clothing, etc.; Pres. CHUN HYUN-CHAI.

Daelim Industrial Co. Ltd.: 146-12 Susong-dong, Chongno-ku, Seoul; f. 1939; general contractor for all construction fields, engineering; Pres. LEE JOON-YONG.

Dai Han Coal Corporation: Changseong-ri, Changseong-gun, Kangweon Prov.; f. 1950; 13,789 mems.; Pres. LEE HOON-SUP.

Hanil Development Co. Ltd.: 118, 2-ka, Namdaemoon-ro, Chung-ku, Seoul; f. 1968; construction, electrical work, mining, gas and petroleum transport; Pres. CHO CHOONG-KUN.

Hankuk Glass Industry Co. Ltd.: Yeoevido, P.O.B. 88, Seoul; f. 1957; cap. U.S. $2.4m. (650m. won); manufacturers of flat glass, figured glass and tube glass, Seoul and Pusan; output: U.S. $6.18m. (including exports); one subsidiary company in Korea; Pres. HONG DAE-SHIK; employees: 900.

Hyundai Construction Co. Ltd.: 178 Sejong-ro, Chongno-ku; Seoul; f. 1950; design and construction of industrial plants, power plants, water resources development, highways, bridges, tunnels, railways, subways, building, dredging, harbour development, airports, and steel fabrication, shipbuilding and repairing, manufacture and sale of ship products; Chair. CHUNG JU-YUNG; employees: 51,534.

Keang Nam Enterprises Ltd.: 151, 2-ka, Inhyun-dong, Chung-ku, Seoul; f. 1951; construction, marine and land transport, vehicle maintenance, labour service, manufacture of souvenirs; Rep. SHIN KI-SOO.

Korea Marine Industry Development Corporation: Baeje Bldg., 55-4 Seosomun-dong, Chung-ku, Seoul; f. 1963; owns and operates 163 fishing boats engaged in deep-sea fishing (tuna) with annual catches of about 68,700 metric tons; Pres. CHAE HANG-SUCK; employees: 2,989.

Korea Shipbuilding and Engineering Corporation: 1-1, 1-ka, Chongno-ku, Seoul; f. 1937; private; Korea's major shipbuilder, yards at Pusan and Mokpo; vessels up to 1m. d.w.t., steel structures, rolling stock; Chair. RYUN NAMKOONG; Pres. HO NAMKOONG.

Kumyang Trading Co. Ltd.: Central P.O.B. 160, 93-33 Bookchang-dong, Chung-ku, Seoul; f. 1949; manufacturers of socks, sporting goods; exporters and importers; Pres. KIM CHO-SOON; Dirs. SONG BONG-SUNG, KIM YOUNG-JOON; employees: 380.

Lotte Moolsan Co. Ltd.: 516-2, Doksan-dong, Yong-deungpo-ku, Seoul; f. 1968; manufactures aluminium foil, import and export; Pres. SHIN KYUK-HO.

Oriental Brewery Co. Ltd.: 582 Youngdeungpo-dong, Youngdeungpo-ku, Seoul; f. 1952; cap. p.u. 10,000m. won; manufacturers and exporters of beer and wine; Pres. KIM HAK-BAE; employees: 1,500.

Whashin Industrial Co. Ltd.: 21-9 Cho-dong, Chung-ku, Seoul; f. 1926; cap. 2,000m. won; exporters, importers, domestic sales of textiles, electrical consumer products, commercial air-conditioning equipment and other merchandise; 8 subsidiary companies; Pres. PARK HEUNG-SIK; Vice-Pres. KIM JOONG-KIL; employees: 5,500.

TRANSPORT

Ministry of Transportation: 168, 2-ka, Bongrae-dong, Chung-ku, Seoul; Administrator KIM JAE MYEONG.

RAILWAYS

Korean National Railroad: 168, 2-ka, Bongrae-dong, Chung-ku, Seoul; f. 1963; operates all railways under the supervision of the Ministry of Transportation; total track length of 6,045.3 km. (1982); Administrator AHN CHANG-HWA; Deputy Administrator KIM YOUNG-KWAN.

Seoul Metropolitan Rapid Transit: 60-1, Taepyong-ro, Chung-ku, Seoul; length of 58.34 km. including 48.8 km. under construction in 1979; the network will eventually extend to 142 km.; Dir. WOO MYUNG KU.

ROADS

In 1980 there were 46,951 km. of roads of which 15,599 km. were paved. A network of motorways (1,225 km. in 1980) links all the principal towns, the most important being the 428 km. Seoul-Pusan motorway. The 201 km. Yeongdong motorway, linking Seoul and Kangneung, and the 32-km. Donghae motorway, connecting Kangneung and Mukho, opened in 1976. The 85 km. Gu-Ma motorway, linking Taegu and Masan, opened in 1977.

Korea Highway Corporation: 293-1 Geumto-dong, Seognam, Gyeonggido; f. 1969; responsible for construction, maintenance and management of toll roads; Pres. YOON PILL-YONG.

SHIPPING

In 1980 South Korea had a merchant fleet of 4.9 million tons. Chief ports include Pusan, Inchon, Mukho, Masan, Yeosu, Gunsan, Mokpo, Pohang, Ulsan, Cheju, Sogcho, Samcheonpo.

Korea Maritime and Port Authority: 263 Yeunji-dong, Chongno-ku, Seoul; f. 1976; operates under the Ministry of Transportation; supervises all branches of shipping; Administrator LEON BEOM JUN.

PRINCIPAL COMPANIES

Asia Merchant Marine Co. Ltd.: 485-1 Sinsa-dong, Kangnam-ku, Seoul; tanker bulk carrier and car carrier; Pres. P. J. CHO.

Cho Yang Shipping Co. Ltd.: 1001 New Kal Bldg., 51 Siking-dong, Chung-ku, Seoul; f. 1961; Korea/Japan, Korea/Australia, Far East/Europe and Mediterranean liner services and world-wide tramping with 26 vessels; Rep. PARK NAM-KYU.

Far Eastern Marine Transport Co. Ltd.: 55-4 Seosomun-dong, Seodaemun-ku, Seoul; f. 1952; 4 cargo vessels; Pres. NAM KOONG-RYUN.

Korea Shipping Corporation Ltd.: 188-3, 1-ka, Ulchiro, Chung-ku, Seoul 100 (C.P.O.B. 1164, 131); f. 1950; 16 cargo vessels; world-wide transportation service and shipping agency service in Korea; Chair. YOON SUK-MIN; Pres. YOUNG GUN HWANG.

Korea United Lines, Inc.: 50-10, 2-ka, Chungmu-ro, Chung-ku, Seoul; f. 1967; world-wide transportation with bulk carriers; Pres. PARK YONG-HAK; Chair. LEE CHUNG-NIM.

Pan Ocean Bulk Carriers Ltd.: Han Yang Investment Bldg., 9-10, 2-ka, Ulchiro, Chung-ku, Seoul (C.P.O.B. 3051); f. 1966; 29 bulk carriers, 13 tankers; transportation of petroleum products, L.N.G., dry cargo; Pres. HAN SANG-YEON; Chair. PARK KEN-SUK.

Ships of U.S., British, Japanese, Dutch and Norwegian lines call at South Korea's principal ports.

CIVIL AVIATION

Korean Air Lines: P.O.B. 864 Central, Seoul; No. 118, 2-ka, Namdaemun-ro, Chung-ku, Seoul; f. 1962 by the Korean Government; transferred 1969 to the *Hanjin Group*; the only scheduled airline in the Republic of Korea, serves 8 major domestic cities and flies to Baghdad, Bahrain, Federal Republic of Germany, France, Hong Kong, Japan, Kuwait, Libya, the Netherlands, the Philippines, Saudi Arabia, Singapore, Sri Lanka, Switzerland, Taiwan, Thailand, United Arab Emirates and the U.S.A.; Pres. CHO CHOONG-HOON; fleet: 7 B-747-200B, 4 B-747-200F, 6 B-727, 7 B-707-320, 8 A300 B4, 5 DC-10-30, 1 F-27, 2 B-747SP.

FOREIGN AIRLINES

The following foreign airlines also serve Seoul: Cathay Pacific Airways (Hong Kong), China Airlines (Taiwan), JAL (Japan), MAS (Malaysia), Northwest Orient Airlines (U.S.A.), SIA (Singapore) and Thai Airways International.

TOURISM

Korea National Tourism Corporation: Kukdong Bldg., 60-1, 3-ka, Chungmu-ro, Chung-ku, Seoul 100; f. 1962 as Korea Tourist Service; Pres. HWANG IN-SUNG.

Korea Tourist Association: Room 303 Hanil Bldg., 132-4, Pongnae-dong, Chung-ku, Seoul 100; f. 1963; Pres. KIM IL-HWAN.

In 1980 there were 976,415 visitors to South Korea.

ATOMIC ENERGY

Korea's first atomic power plant at Gori went into operation in 1978 with a generating capacity of 587 MW. Five further plants are under construction.

Atomic Energy Commission: Ministry of Science and Technology, Seoul 110; responsible for fundamental plans and policies, furtherance of research and training of personnel; Chair. Dr. LEE CHUNG-OH; Vice-Chair. LEE EUNG-SUN; Standing Commissioners Dr. LEE BYONG-WHIE, Dr. LIM YONG-KYU.

Atomic Energy Bureau: Ministry of Science and Technology, Seoul 110; f. 1973, reorganized 1979; administrative agency comprising three divisions: Atomic Energy Planning, Research and Development and International Co-operation; Dir.-Gen. Dr. KANG BAK-KWANG.

Nuclear Regulatory Bureau: Ministry of Science and Technology, Seoul 110; f. 1979; comprises four divisions responsible for the implementation of nuclear power plant safety regulations; Dir.-Gen. PARK SHU YOHL.

DEFENCE

Armed Forces (July 1981): Total strength 601,600: army 520,000, navy 49,000 and a marine corps of 24,000, air force 32,600. There are also para-military forces, i.e. a local defence militia, the Homeland Reserve Defence Force, totalling about 2,800,000. In 1977 U.S. President Carter announced plans for the gradual withdrawal of the 33,000 American ground troops from South Korea. In 1978 the withdrawal was delayed, and this policy was reaffirmed in 1979, following a reassessment of North Korean military strength. In mid-1979 30,500 American troops remained.

Equipment: The army is equipped with American material including medium and heavy tanks; armoured personnel carriers and armoured cars; up to 203mm. guns and surface-to-surface and surface-to-air missiles. The navy has mostly destroyers, frigates, landing ships, patrol boats and other escort and coastal vessels (some equipped with ship-to-ship missiles). The air force has some 378 combat aircraft, some equipped with missiles.

Military Service: Army/Marines, 2 years 6 months; Navy and Air Force 3 years.

Defence Expenditure: Estimated defence spending for 1981 was 2,953,000 million won.

Chief of Staff ROK Army: Gen. HWANG YUNG-SI.

Chief of Staff Air Force: Gen. KIM SANG-TAE.

Chief of Naval Operations: LEE EUN-SOO.

EDUCATION

During the second half of the nineteenth century western ideas and education were introduced into Korea by foreign missionaries. As a result, the Government adopted a more modern education system, and after 1885 established various types of modern school. During the Japanese colonial period many more modern schools were established, though educational opportunities for Koreans were strictly limited, and only 30 per cent of school-aged Korean children attended elementary school. Japanese was the official language, and the speaking, reading and writing of Korean was discouraged and finally in 1941 forbidden in all schools. Consequently at independence 78 per cent of the population was illiterate.

Thus in 1945, when Korea regained its independence, there were only 19 institutes of higher education, 2,834 elementary and 165 secondary schools. A modern system of education was formulated, providing six years' free elementary education, and was embodied in the Constitution of the Republic of Korea in 1948. Although elementary education was stated to be compulsory it was impossible to achieve this fully owing to the overwhelming problems of shortage of funds, teachers and school facilities. During the Korean War, 1950–53, over 50 per cent of the educational facilities were destroyed and once again the educational system had to be rebuilt. The basic needs were to rebuild and repair school facilities, to train teachers, to continue the programme for the eradication of illiteracy, and to introduce a vocational education programme as an aid to the economy. With public participation, and the help of welfare organizations such as UNESCO much has been done.

Elementary Education

Elementary education consists of kindergartens, civic schools, and elementary schools:

Kindergartens are for children between the ages of three and six and cover one to two years. In 1980 there were 901 kindergartens, but all but forty were privately owned though subject to some governmental control; 66,433 children were enrolled, which represents only a limited number of the total children eligible.

As a result of the government's five-year plan of educational development launched in 1962, the attendance rate of the total school-aged population was raised to 99.8 per cent. The criteria for the curriculum of all elementary schools, both public and private, are established by the Ministry of Education though local authorities are encouraged to develop curricula that will meet the needs of individual communities. Korean language, arithmetic, social studies, Korean history, natural science, music, art, moral education and physical education are taught in classes during 22–31 hours a week. In 1981, there were 6,517 elementary schools.

Civic schools are for children who are beyond the compulsory attendance age and for illiterate adults. There are two separate classes, the children's education being a three-year course covering in condensed form the basic requirements of the elementary six-year course, while the adult course covers 200 hours or more. The number of civic schools has decreased with the implementation of the six-year course.

Secondary Education

Secondary education is divided into two three-year units, middle and high school, which are generally administered as separate institutions. They are fee-paying and therefore not compulsory, and are generally segregated. The Ministry of Education has abolished the compulsory entrance examination to middle schools. Since independence the number of secondary schools has greatly increased: in 1981 there were 3,551 secondary schools with 4,428,874 pupils.

Middle Schools: In 1981 there were 2,174 middle schools, with 2,573,945 pupils and 57,838 teachers. The basic curriculum includes moral education, the Korean language, Korean history, mathematics, social studies, natural science, art, music, physical education, foreign languages including English, and vocational training.

High Schools: In 1981 there were 1,402 high schools, with 1,823,039 students (twice as many boys as girls). In the past the curriculum has been largely limited to the courses required for entrance into the various colleges, and the prestige of a particular school was in proportion to the number passing the entrance examination. But now increasing emphasis is laid on a well-rounded curriculum with a wide variety of subjects. Many high schools have evening sessions for students who work an eight-hour day and then start school at five o'clock.

Vocational Education

Much emphasis is placed on vocational education, particularly in the light of the country's economic needs. Elementary vocational education begins in middle school and for children who cannot afford a secondary education there are technical trade and higher technical trade schools at middle and high school level which offer vocational training; they are nearly all private and offer one- to three-year courses. There are also higher civic schools for elementary school leavers. In middle schools, five hours a week are spent in vocational training. The eventual ratio of academic to vocational schools will be 4 : 6. Comprehensive schools have been set up as a means of solving this problem and they have become increasingly popular since they provide courses in academic subjects, general machine shops, home economics, agriculture and science.

Higher Education

The first modern institutions of higher education were established at the end of the nineteenth century with the arrival of foreign missionaries. The founding of Yonhui College (Chosun Christian College) in Seoul in 1905 and Soong Sil College in Pyongyang in 1906 marked the beginning of modern college education, and were followed by others after the annexation of Korea by Japan in 1910, though higher education for Koreans was discouraged. In 1945 there were 19 institutes of higher education in Korea.

There are three types of higher institution: the junior vocational college which provides two-year courses, and colleges and universities which provide four- or six-year courses. A university consists of three or more colleges, one of which must be a college of natural sciences and another a graduate school. With the exception of about 20 universities and colleges for women, higher education in Korea is co-educational.

The Ministry of Education sets minimum standards for the curricula, teaching staff, physical facilities and equipment. The colleges are free to formulate their own curricula, which are then subject to ministerial approval. However, all colleges teach some subjects of general culture; they include the Korean language, at least two foreign languages, outline of philosophy, cultural history, outline of natural science and physical training, which have to total one-third of the number of required subjects. Physical education plays a very important role at all levels of Korean education and is one of the main requirements in the national examinations.

Colleges and universities have expanded rapidly during recent years, though often at the expense of planning and quality. Reforms are now being made and government regulations are strictly enforced. The Ministry of Education proposes to improve the facilities at national universities, to extend financial subsidies for private institutions, and to create ties between universities and industrial corporations for co-ordination in research. Until recently the majority of enrolments have been in the liberal arts faculties, but since the restoration of civilian rule in 1963 greater emphasis has been placed on technical and scientific education; 50–60 per cent of university enrolments are now in natural and applied sciences.

Higher Technical Education: With the task of rebuilding the economy after the period of Japanese rule, there was a great demand for artisans, engineers, businessmen, experts in fishery and agriculture as well as technicians in all fields. At present there are 41 engineering and professional colleges, most of them attached to universities and situated in the capital. There are also fourteen colleges of agriculture and ten colleges of commerce, several of which include departments of public and business administration.

Teacher Training: In 1961 there were three types of teacher training institution, the normal schools for elementary teachers, the two-year teachers' colleges and the four-year colleges of education, for secondary school teachers. In 1962 in order to improve the quality of teachers the normal schools were up-graded to two-year colleges, and the two-year colleges for secondary school teachers were abolished. There are plans to upgrade the junior teachers' colleges into four-year colleges, and this was implemented in 1981 in Seoul, Pusan and Kwangchu, the remaining colleges to be converted by 1985. There are now 11 two-year colleges and 28 four-year colleges of education, of which 18 are private. Tuition is free and monthly allowances are allocated to students of national teaching colleges on condition that they teach in a national school for a period equal to the duration of their training. In 1980 there were 47,586 students under training.

Social Education

Before 1970 social education was divided into education for illiterates and training courses in trades and vocations. Since 1970 emphasis has been on technical education and mental development. Owing to the success of the Third Economic Development Plan and the growth of national income, the Government is changing its social education policy towards strengthening the moral education of the nation, in particular that of the younger generation.

BIBLIOGRAPHY

GENERAL

ALLEN, HORACE N. Korea: Fact and Fancy (Methodist Publishing House, 1904).

BRANDT, VINCENT S. R. A Korean Village between Farm and Sea (Harvard University Press, Cambridge, Mass., 1971).

CHANG, NEDRA, and LUERAS LEONARD, (eds.). Korea (Apa Productions' Insight Guides, Singapore, 1981).

HAKWONSA. Korea, its Land, People and Culture of All Ages (Seoul, 1960).

HENDERSON, GREGORY. Korea: The Politics of the Vortex (Harvard University Press, Cambridge, Mass., 1960).

LEE, PETER. Korean Literature: Topics and Themes (University of Arizona Press, Tucson, 1965).

MCCUNE, EVELYN. The Arts of Korea: An Illustrated History (Charles E. Tuttle, Tokyo and Rutland, 1962).

NAHM, ANDREW C. (ed.) Studies in the Developmental Aspects of Korea (The Center of Korean Studies, Western Michigan University, Kalamazoo, 1969).

Korea and the New Order in East Asia (The Center for Korean Studies, Western Michigan University, Kalamazoo, 1974).

North Korea: Her Past, Reality, and Impression (The Center for Korean Studies, Western Michigan University, Kalamazoo, 1978).

OSGOOD, CORNELIUS. The Koreans and their Culture (Ronald Press, New York, 1951).

HISTORY

BERGER, CARL. The Korea Knot: A Military-Political History (University of Pennsylvania Press, Philadelphia, 1957).

CHO, SOO SUNG. Korea in World Politics 1940–1950 (University of California Press, Berkeley, Los Angeles and London, 1967).

CHUNG, CHIN O. Pyongyang Between Peking and Moscow: North Korea's Involvement in the Sino-Soviet Dispute 1958–75 (University of Alabama Press, 1978).

CHUNG, HENRY. The Case of Korea (F. H. Revell Co., New York, 1921).

CONROY, F. H. The Japanese Seizure of Korea, 1868–1910 (University of Pennsylvania Press, Philadelphia, 1960).

DEUCHLER, MARTINA. Confucian Gentlemen and Barbarian Envoys: The Opening of Korea 1875–1885 (University of Washington Press, Seattle, Wash., 1978).

HAN, SUNGJOO. The Failure of Democracy in South Korea (University of California Press, Berkeley, Los Angeles and London, 1974).

HAN, WOO KEUN. A History of Korea (Eulyoo Publishing Co., 1972).

HARRINGTON, FRED H. God, Mammon and the Japanese (The University of Wisconsin Press, Madison, Wisconsin, 1944).

HELLER, FRANCIS H. (ed.) The Korean War: A 25-Year Perspective (Regents Press, Lawrence, Kansas, for the Harry S. Truman Library for National and International Affairs, 1977).

HENTHORN, WILLIAM E. A History of Korea (The Free Press, New York, 1971).

HULBERT, HOMER B. The Passing of Korea (Doubleday, Page and Co., New York, 1906).

History of Korea (Routledge, London, 1962).

KEON, MICHAEL. Korea Phoenix, A Nation from the Ashes (Prentice-Hall International, Englewood, Calif., 1977).

KIM, C. I. EUGENE, and KIM, HAN-KYO. Korea and the Politics of Imperialism, 1876–1910 (University of California Press, Berkeley, Los Angeles and London, 1970).

KIM, C. I. EUGENE, and MORTIMORE, D. E. (eds.) Korea's Response to Japan: The Colonial Period 1910–45 (The Center for Korean Studies, Western Michigan University, Kalamazoo, 1977).

KIM, HAN K. (ed.) Reunification of Korea: 50 Basic Documents (Institute for Asian Studies, Washington, D.C., Monography 2, 1972).

KIM SE JIN. The Politics of Military Revolution in Korea (University of North Carolina Press, Chapel Hill, 1971).

(ed.) Korean Unification: Source Materials with an Introduction (Research Center for Peace and Unification, Seoul, 1976).

KIM, SE-JIN, and SUK-RYUL YE. (eds.) Documents on Korean-American Relations 1943–1976 (Research Center for Peace and Unification, Seoul, 1976).

LEE, CHONG-SIK. The Politics of Korean Nationalism (University of California Press, Berkeley, Los Angeles and London, 1963).

MCCORMACK, G., and GITTINGS, J. Crisis in Korea (Spokesman Books, 1978).

MCKENZIE, F. A. Korea's Fight for Freedom (Fleming H. Revell, New York, 1920; reprint, Yonsei University Press, Seoul, 1969).

The Tragedy of Korea (reprint, Yonsei University Press, Seoul, 1969).

MEAD, E. G. American Military Government in Korea (King's Crown Press, New York, 1951).

NAHM, ANDREW C. (ed.) Korea Under Japanese Colonial Rule (The Center for Korean Studies, Western Michigan University, Kalamazoo, 1973).

North Korea: Her Past, Reality, and Impression (The Center for Korean Studies, Western Michigan University, Kalamazoo, 1978).

NELSON, M. F. Korea and the Old Orders in Western Asia (Louisiana State University Press, Baton Rouge, 1945).

OH, JOHN K. C. Korea: Democracy on Trial (Cornell University Press, Ithaca, N.Y., 1968).

RUTT, RICHARD. James Scarth Gale and his History of the Korean People (Royal Asiatic Society, Korea Branch, Seoul, 1972).

SCALAPINO, ROBERT A. and LEE, CHONG-SIK. Communism in Korea (University of California Press, Berkeley, Los Angeles, London, 1972).

SOHN, POW-KEY, et al. The History of Korea (Korean National Commission for UNESCO, Seoul, 1970).

SUH, DAE-SOOK. The Korean Communist Movement 1918–1948 (Princeton University Press, New Jersey, 1967).

SUH, SANG-CHUL. Growth and Structural Changes in the Korean Economy, 1910–40 (Harvard University Press, Cambridge, Mass., 1978).

THOMAS, R. C. W. The War in Korea 1950–53 (Gale & Polden, Aldershot, 1954).

WRIGHT, EDWARD R. (ed.) Korean Politics in Transition (University of Washington Press, Seattle, Wash. 1975).

ECONOMICS AND GEOGRAPHY

BANG, SUNG-HWAN. The Long-Run Productivity Growth in Korean Agricultural Development: 1910–1968 (University of Minnesota Press, Minneapolis, 1971).

CHOI, HOCHIN. The Economic History of Korea (The Freedom Library, Seoul, 1971).

CHUNG, JOSEPH SANG-HOON. The North Korean Economy: Structure and Development (Hoover Institution Press, Stanford University, 1974).

COLE, D. C., and LYMAN, P. N. Korean Development: The Interplay of Politics and Economics (Harvard University Press, Cambridge, Mass., 1971).

FRANK, CHARLES R., KIM, KWANG SUK, and WESTPHAL, LARRY. Foreign Trade Regimes and Economic Development: South Korea (Columbia University Press for the National Bureau of Economic Research, New York, 1977).

HAN, KEE CHUN, and PAK, KI HYUK. An Analysis of Food Consumption in the Republic of Korea (Yonsei University, Seoul, 1969).

HAN, KEE CHUN, et al. A Study of Land Tenure in Korea (Korea Land Economics Research Center, Seoul, 1966).

HASAN, PARVEZ. Korea: Problems and Issues in a Rapidly Growing Economy (Johns Hopkins University Press, Baltimore, Md., for the World Bank, 1977).

KOO, JAE-SUH. A Study of the Regional Characteristics of Korean Agriculture (Korea University Press, Seoul, 1967).

KUZNETS, PAUL W. Economic Growth and Structure in the Republic of Korea (Yale University Press, New Haven, Conn., 1977).

MCCUNE, SHANNON. Korea's Heritage: A Regional and Social Geography (Charles E. Tuttle, Tokyo and Rutland, 1966).

REEVE, W. D. The Republic of Korea: A Political and Economic Study (Oxford University Press, London, 1963).

ROSSMILLER, G. E., et al. Korean Agricultural Sector Analysis and Recommended Development Strategies 1971–1985 (Department of Agricultural Economics, Michigan State University, E. Lansing, 1972).

RUDOLPH, P. North Korea's Political and Economic Structure (Institute of Pacific Relations, New York, 1959).

Laos

PHYSICAL AND SOCIAL GEOGRAPHY

C. A. Fisher

(Revised for this edition by Harvey Demaine)

Laos covers an area of 236,800 square kilometres (91,400 sq. miles) consisting almost entirely of rugged upland, except for the narrow floors of the river valleys. Of these rivers much the most important is the Mekong, which forms the western frontier of the country for much of its length.

In the northern half of Laos the deeply dissected plateau surface exceeds 1,500 metres over wide areas, and although the average level of the Annamite Chain which occupies most of the southern half is somewhat lower, its rugged and more densely forested surface makes it no less inhospitable. While on the plateau and in the Annamite Chain the tropical temperatures are considerably mitigated by altitude, the more habitable lowlands experience tropical conditions throughout the year, and receive a total annual rainfall of about 125 cm., most of which falls between May and September.

The natural resources of Laos have not been fully surveyed. It is estimated that some 60 per cent of the country is covered with forest which could support an annual production of up to 2 million cubic metres of timber. Mineral resources may also be extensive. Tin deposits in Khammouane province have been worked for some time and three is certainly scope for expansion, while recent surveys in the Phu Nhouan area of Xieng Khouang province have suggested iron ore reserves estimated at "hundreds of millions of tons". In addition, the Mekong River offers substantial potential for fisheries, irrigation and hydroelectricity.

Laos had an estimated population of 3,721,000 at mid-1980, although refugee migration, arising from continuing problems of internal security and government policies, may well make this figure an over-estimate. About 60 per cent of the population are ethnic Lao, living mainly in the western valleys. A further 35 per cent belong to various hill tribes, although the important Meo (Hmong) group has been particulary affected by the fighting. The remainder are either Vietnamese (who also keep an army estimated at 50,000 in the country) or Chinese. Vientiane, the administrative capital, is the only large town. Its population was 176,637 in 1973, but was estimated to be more than 200,000 in 1981.

HISTORY

Ralph Smith

The country known in the twentieth century as Laos was formally the creation of French imperialism, and in particular of treaties between France, Thailand and Britain in the years 1893–96 which recognized French control of the east bank of the Mekong. There had previously existed in that area a number of kingdoms or principalities which had gradually been absorbed into the Thai sphere of influence, but which were ethnically Lao and which were related to one another by traditions of dependency (or sometimes enmity) going back to the fourteenth century and probably earlier. The ethnic term "Lao" refers to the lowland population of the region, and extends also to part of the population of northern and north-eastern Thailand. In addition modern Laos includes large tracts of hill country inhabited by other ethnic groups, notably the Yao and Meo who migrated there in relatively recent times from south-western China. It is not surprising that the history of Laos has been somewhat complicated over the centuries, and even now we do not have a complete picture of all its phases.

Pre-Colonial Laos

Before the middle of the fourteenth century, hardly anything is known about this region except that it appears to have been dominated in some way by the powerful Khmer kings of Angkor. The Lao chronicles trace back the history of Luang Prabang (also known as Lan Chang) to 1353, when the kingdom of Muang Swe was conquered by Fa Ngum and then ruled by him until he was himself deposed in 1373. He is said to have brought the Prabang image to the city and to have been responsible for the spread of Theravada Buddhism, which has been the predominant religion of Laos ever since. The descendants of Fa Ngum ruled at Luang Prabang during the next two centuries, and for much of the time were able to dominate also the principalities of Vieng Chan (Vientiane) and Chiang Khuang (Xieng Khuang, known to the Vietnamese as Tran Ninh). In 1479 the Vietnamese made their first major incursion into Laos and sacked Luang Prabang, but they were subsequently driven out. By this period the kingdom probably also had relations with Ayudhya, capital of Siam.

A new phase of Lao history begins in the sixteenth century with the reigns of Photisarath (1520–48) and Setthathirat (1548–71). Vieng Chan was becoming more important both as a trading and as a religious centre, and, after being an occasional royal residence for some decades, it was made the principal capital by Setthathirat in 1563. In the meantime the kings of

Lan Chang became involved in the politics of Chigan Mai (now in northern Thailand), where Photisarath imposed his own solution on a succession dispute in 1546. Domination of Chiang Mai could not, however, be sustained after the conquest of that kingdom by the Burmese in 1556. By the 1560s Burmese expansion was beginning to impinge on the more easterly Lao states, and in 1570 the Burmese king Bayinnaung made an unsuccessful attack on Vieng Chan itself. There followed a period of crisis and disunity in which Setthathirat was deposed, and finally the Burmese took Vieng Chan in 1575; they attempted to rule through a vassal king until 1592, but could not prevent the spread of anarchy. The kingdom (Vieng Chan and Luang Prabang) was eventually reunified and again independent under Nokeo Koumane (1591–96) and Thammikarath (1596–1622). The seventeenth century saw a "golden age" of peace and prosperity, notably under King Souligna Vongsa (1637–88). During his reign both Dutch merchants (1641–42) and Jesuit missionaries (1642–47) visited Laos; but on the whole it remained beyond the range of the early phases of European expansion in South-East Asia.

At the end of the seventeenth century internal conflict led to a further period of disunity and also the first serious involvement of outsiders in Laotian politics since 1592. Possibly following a coup in Vieng Chan, one party appealed for aid to the Vietnamese ruler of Hué, and with his help was able to recover control of the central part of Laos. But he failed to subdue the north, where a grandson of Souligna Vongsa secured Luang Prabang and refused to recognize the supremacy of Vieng Chan. Meanwhile in the south another virtually independent kingdom was established at Champassak in the early eighteenth century. Thus by about 1720 there were three separate kingdoms, centred on Luang Prabang, Vieng Chan and Champassak; and a fourth, Chiang Khuang, was loosely dependent upon Vieng Chan. It is noticeable that Inthasom of Luang Prabang (1727–76) established a direct tributary relationship with China from 1729, which did not affect the other kingdoms. Vieng Chan sometimes sent tribute to Hué, whilst Champassak probably had closer links with Siam.

The revival of Burmese expansion in the second half of the eighteenth century brought further trouble to Laos, so that by 1764 both Luang Prabang and Vieng Chan were once again under Burmese domination. Three years later Ayudhya was sacked, and in the 1770s Viet-Nam was torn apart by the Tay-Son rebellion. But the recovery of the Thai came quickly and in 1778 they were able to capture Vieng Chan in turn; it was on this occasion that the famous "Emerald Buddha" was taken from there to Bangkok, and the ruler became a vassal of Siam. Luang Prabang also established good relations with Bangkok and in return was protected against an intervention by the king of Vieng Chan in 1791. The final phase of Thai domination over Vieng Chan came in 1827–28, when King Chao Anou rebelled and attempted to get Vietnamese assistance to invade Siam itself. He failed, and in 1828 Vieng Chan was captured and sacked by a Thai army. This time its territory was annexed, and the city remained largely unoccupied until its revival as the French administrative capital, Vientiane. The king of Luang Prabang responded to this by making overtures to Viet-Nam in 1831–33, but by 1836 he was obliged to submit to Thai supremacy and himself became a vassal. The Vietnamese secured domination over only one portion of Laos at this time, Chiang Khuang (Tran Ninh). In the 1870s, northern Laos was invaded by Chinese rebels and the Vietnamese could not prevent them from dominating Tran Ninh. From there they threatened Luang Prabang until 1885–86, when Bangkok sent an army north to pacify the region and to establish a virtual protectorate over northern Laos.

French Rule

French interest in Laos stemmed from two sources. As early as 1867–68, after France's annexation of southern Viet-Nam and establishment of a protectorate over Cambodia, the French sent an expedition to explore the Mekong route to China, and despite the difficulties they kept that idea alive during the next two decades. Secondly, after the establishment of a French protectorate over central and northern Viet-Nam in 1884, they began to explore Vietnamese claims to suzerainty over various parts of Laos. In 1886–87 France made an agreement with Siam to appoint a French vice-consul at Luang Prabang, and from then until 1892 the French representative, Auguste Pavie, made a series of explorations and scientific studies of Laos. By 1893 the French were seeking to lay claim to the whole area east of the Mekong, and the British decided to take no action against them except to try, unsuccessfully, to create a buffer zone between French and British (Burma) territory on the upper Mekong. Siam was obliged to sign a treaty ceding its territories east of the Mekong to France, whereupon they were added to the Union of Indochina.

For the next half-century Laos was ruled as a French protectorate, with a *résident-supérieur* and major government offices situated in Vientiane, while the king was allowed to remain in the palace at Luang Prabang and to exercise very limited powers in the northern provinces. The survival of the monarchy, even within these constraints, probably contributed to the relative political stability of the colonial period, as well as to the form taken by Lao nationalism when it first emerged in the 1940s. A small French-educated Lao élite developed, but for the most part government was in the hands of either Frenchmen or Vietnamese brought in from outside. At Vientiane, trade was in the hands of either Vietnamese or Chinese immigrants. Apart from a small area of tin-mining, there was little significant development of resources by the French. There was, however, a demand for opium in the modern cities of the Far East, and some of it was already being grown in northern Laos in this period. The trade was not yet illegal and the drug could not yet command the high prices of later years.

Colonial rule continued in Laos relatively undisturbed by the events of the Second World War, despite the presence of Japanese armies in Indochina as a whole. Neither Thailand nor Indochina became embroiled in serious fighting before 1945, and even then operations were on a small scale. Change came in the spring of 1945, following the seizure of direct control in Indochina by the Japanese in March. In Vientiane the French were quickly interned, but northern Laos was the one area where French forces were able to mount a short-lived resistance (with a small amount of aid from British air-drops, but a conspicuous lack of American support). It was not until April 5th, 1945, that a Japanese column got through to Luang Prabang, and three days later King Sisavang Vong proclaimed the "independence" of Laos. In fact, he merely exchanged French for Japanese protection, and had to send his heir (Prince Savang Vatthana) to Saigon as a virtual hostage. After the surrender of Japan the following August, the king rallied to the French; but not all members of the royal family agreed.

On September 1st, 1945, a new declaration of Laotian independence was made in Vientiane by Prince Phetsarath, and on September 15th he announced the reunification of the northern and southern provinces. The king refused to follow this lead and in October tried to dismiss the Phetsarath government. But at this stage (in accordance with the Potsdam agreement on who should receive the Japanese surrender) the northern and central areas of Laos (including Vientiane) were being occupied by Chinese Nationalist forces; the French controlled only the south. It was not until March 1946 that the French were entitled to advance northwards, under the Chungking Agreement. In April 1946 the Phetsarath Government had to flee from Vientiane as the French returned, and proceeded to regroup as the Lao Issara movement in Thailand; the French went on to reoccupy Luang Prabang in May. The nationalist attempt to resist the French advance was probably aided by the Viet-Minh, which may well represent the effective start of Viet-Minh involvement in the Laotian conflict.

The French now aimed to create a semi-independent kingdom of Laos, which would accept its place within the reconstructed French Union and would therefore be partly subject to French control of policy. To this end, elections were held the following year, and on May 11th, 1947, a constitution was promulgated. But the details of forming a Laotian government remained to be worked out, and this was delayed by events in Viet-Nam. It was not until July 1949 that a French-Laotian Convention established an "independent" state, on the lines of the 1947 Constitution. Meanwhile in Bangkok, the Lao Issara leaders had formed a government-in-exile under the leadership of Phetsarath, which also included his brother and half-brother, Prince Souvanna Phouma and Prince Souphanouvong. The latter was inclined to sympathize with the Viet-Minh and took charge of the military side of the Lao Issara movement. In May 1949 he was expelled from the Government. Later in the year he went to the "liberated area" of northern Tongkin to join the Viet-Minh leaders and was probably behind the claim that a Lao National Assembly had proclaimed a Democratic Republic of Laos, somewhere inside Viet-Nam, in August 1949. This was the communist response to the Franco-Laotian Convention, and was in effect the origin of the "Pathet Lao". Finally in October 1949 the Lao Issara government was dissolved. Phetsarath remained in Bangkok but the other ministers, led by Souvanna Phouma, returned to Vientiane and many of them joined the new Royal government being formed there.

During the later stages of the Indochina war between the French and the Viet-Minh the French became concerned lest the Vietnamese forces mount an attack on Luang Prabang, which was within their power by then. At the end of 1953 and the beginning of 1954 it seemed as though that would happen, and the French resigned themselves to losing control of northern Laos. However, in late February 1954, when the decision was taken internationally to discuss Indochina at a conference in Geneva, the Viet-Minh leaders appear to have changed their minds and concentrated their whole strength on assaulting Dien-Bien-Phu. Earlier, in April 1953, Prince Souphanouvong had established a Pathet Lao headquarters in Laos itself; and later that year the French agreed to give the kingdom of Laos full independence. A full-scale war between the two regimes was averted at that time only by the 1954 Geneva Conference. A communist attempt to seat the Pathet Lao at the conference table, alongside the Viet-Minh, was abandoned as merely a bargaining counter, and in July 1954 an armistice agreement for Laos was signed without any French recognition of the Pathet Lao as a distinct entity. It was, however, agreed that the communists would regroup in the northern provinces of Phong Saly and Sam Neua, whilst the French and Royal Laotian Army would regroup farther south. In due course the country would be reunified under a coalition government. In the meantime, the remainder of the country was placed under the control of the government in Vientiane, whose independence was formally completed at the end of 1954 with the abrogation of the Indochinese customs union and other joint arrangements.

Division, Neutrality and War

During 1955 the kingdom of Laos became a recognized member of the international community and was admitted to the United Nations in December of that year. It became economically associated with Thailand by a commercial agreement of July 1955. Unable to secure any co-operation from the Pathet Lao, the leaders in Vientiane went ahead with elections to a National Assembly in December 1955, followed by the formation of a new government in March 1956, with Souvanna Phouma as Prime Minister. By this time the United States had assumed responsibility for the development of a non-communist state in South Viet-Nam and during the next few years they gradually took over from the French as the principal Western power in the region.

The next two years (from March 1956 to May 1958) were taken up by a long process of negotiation between Vientiane and the Pathet Lao, which progressed very slowly towards the goal of reintegrating the Pathet Lao provinces into a unified administration, their forces into a unified army, and their leaders into a coalition government; the Pathet Lao were to participate in the political life of a united Laos through their political party, the Lao Patriotic Front (*Neo Lao Haksat*). Agreement on a coalition was reached in November 1957, leading to new elections the following May, for 21 seats in the National Assembly. The Communists won nine of these seats and another four went to the Peace Party of the left-wing neutralist Quinim Pholsena. This alarmed the rightists led by Phoui Sananikone and Gen. Phoumi Nosavan, who in June 1958 formed (with American encouragement) the Committee for the Defence of National Interests. The Government of National Union formed the previous November collapsed in late July 1958 and gave way to one headed by Phoui Sananikone, in which the Pathet Lao were no longer included. In January 1959 there was a further move to the right with the admission to the government of Gen. Phoumi Nosavan, and the way was opened to a closer relationship with the U.S.A. This meant that responsibility for carrying out the agreement on reintegrating the Pathet Lao provinces and armed forces lay with a pro-American, anti-communist government. The result was that in May 1959 a key battalion of Pathet Lao troops refused to integrate and withdrew to the Plain of Jars, whereupon the Government placed Souphanouvong and other Communist leaders under house arrest. This incident may be taken as marking the end of attempts at coalition and the start of the war in Laos which continued until 1975.

Inevitably, as the war progressed, the two sides became more and more dependent on their outside allies, the Americans and the North Vietnamese; but American claims that there was an actual Vietnamese "invasion" of Laos in August 1959 were probably exaggerated in order to justify their own increasing involvement. Throughout the next fifteen years there was continued reluctance on the part of American officials to admit to the scale of United States military involvement, and the full extent of it became apparent only in the 1970s.

In December 1959 differences of opinion between Phoui and Gen. Phoumi Nosavan led to a government crisis which was resolved by a military coup at the end of the year. A new government was formed by Kou Abhay in January 1960, in which the dominant voice was that of Phoumi Nosavan and the Committee for the Defence of National Interests. The latter was able to secure a majority of seats in the Assembly in new elections held in April, and continued in power until the neutralist coup by Captain Kong Lae in August 1960. Kong Lae hoped to return Laos to the middle path which it had abandoned since the summer of 1958. The immediate outcome was another neutralist government formed by Souvanna Phouma, with Quinim Pholsena as Minister of the Interior. Phoumi Nosavan responded by rallying the rightists in the south and forming a counter-coup committee, but after fighting in September, a joint U.S.-British-French statement expressed support for the government of Souvanna Phouma, who was then free to go ahead and resume negotiations with the Pathet Lao. The latter took advantage of the new situation to recover their position in the northern provinces and also to receive more assistance from North Viet-Nam. In October 1960, pursuing his neutralist policy, Souvanna Phouma received a Soviet ambassador in Vientiane. A Soviet airlift enabled him to survive a blockade imposed by Thailand. But the situation was transformed yet again in mid-December 1960 when Phoumi Nosavan was strong enough (with unofficial American assistance) to recover control of Vientiane and to force Kong Lae to withdraw. Souvanna Phouma also withdrew to Cambodia, while the Western powers recognized a new rightist government at Vientiane under Boun Oum.

A communist offensive began in March 1967, in which the Pathet Lao made significant gains, but it became clear that the major world powers (except for China) did not wish to see an escalation of the conflict in Laos. A ceasefire was implemented on May 3rd and a fortnight later a new Geneva Conference was convened to discuss Laotian neutrality. In June a meeting in Zurich between Boun Oum, Souvanna Phouma and Souphanouvong laid down broad lines of agreement, but then progress was interrupted by a new crisis in American-Soviet relations in July 1961. Progress towards a settlement was resumed late in the year after a further meeting of the three Laotian leaders in October, but serious disagreement continued. In May 1962, with still no agreement in sight, a new Pathet Lao offensive culminated in the fall of Nam Tha, which was seen by the United States as a threat to Thailand. It led directly to the agreement which permitted American troops to be based in Thailand. Finally in June there was yet another ceasefire and progress was made towards creating a new Government of National Unity under Souvanna Phouma, so that on July 21st, 1962, it was possible for the Geneva Conference to proclaim the neutrality of Laos.

The failure of this second Geneva agreement to resolve permanently the conflict in Laos will probably always be a matter of controversy, with the Americans and the communists each holding the other responsible. During 1963 and 1964 growing American involvement in South Viet-Nam made it unlikely that a permanent solution to the Laotian problem would be found while that of Viet-Nam remained unresolved. Moreover as the Viet-Nam War escalated it became increasingly important for the North Vietnamese to maintain sufficient control of the whole eastern side of Laos to be able to infiltrate their forces along the "Ho Chi Minh Trail" into South Viet-Nam. It is not surprising, therefore, that when fresh fighting occurred in central Laos in April-May 1963 the powers took no action to try to stop it. Direct American involvement, which had been reduced after the Geneva Agreement, was again stepped up after the coup of April 19th, 1964, had sabotaged new contacts between Vientiane and the Pathet Lao and had forced a reconstruction of the Laotian Government along rightist lines. Phoumi Nosavan was now less important, however, and, after several attempts to return to power in early 1965, he retired to Bangkok; the neutralist leader Kong Lae also went into exile in 1966, and his forces were reintegrated into the Royal Laotian Army. By that time, although the forms of neutrality were preserved by Souvanna Phouma, the conflict was essentially one between the U.S.A. and North Viet-Nam (as supporters of the Pathet Lao). It was characterized by American use of airpower on an increasing scale, both for reconnaissance and heavy bombing raids, and also by the involvement of the CIA in creating special ground forces such as the army of Meo tribesmen commanded by Gen. Vang Pao. On the communist side, it was a guerrilla war with limited anti-aircraft power, run from Pathet Lao hideouts in the caves of northern Laos.

An important area of conflict was the Plain of Jars, control of which changed hands several times. Some of the heaviest fighting there came between 1969 and 1972, when it became clear that the Royalist forces could occupy the plain in the rainy season (June-November) but would then lose it again to the Communists during the dry season (December-May). Also during those years there was fighting around Luang Prabang in the north and on the Bolovens plateau in the south. In February and March 1971 a frontal invasion of southern Laos occurred when South Vietnamese forces (with American backing) moved west across the border and briefly captured the town of Tchepone before retreating in disarray. The government in Vientiane was unable to take any action against what was clearly an intrusion into its territory; it had in practice allowed the United States a free hand in attacking the Ho Chi Minh Trail both on the ground and from the air. By this time, indeed, the outcome of the war in Laos was completely bound up with that in Viet-Nam, even though the origins of the two conflicts had been distinct.

The Emergence of a People's Democratic Republic

The signing of a ceasefire agreement for Viet-Nam in Paris in January 1973 made possible a new stage of negotiations between the two sides in Laos, this time in a situation where further escalation of the war was no longer a serious alternative. They were able to reach a simple ceasefire agreement on February 21st, 1973, but then began the long-drawn-out process of creating another coalition government which would now be expected to operate effectively. Enough progress had been made to permit the neutralization of Vientiane and Luang Prabang by the end of 1973, and this allowed the Pathet Lao to emerge into the open and to move nearly 2,500 of their men into the two capitals. Joint administration and policing of the two cities was agreed on in February 1974, but it was not until April 5th that everything was ready for the King to sign a decree actually establishing the coalition government. Souvanna Phouma remained Premier, but with a Pathet Lao Deputy Premier and Minister of Foreign Affairs, Phoumi Vongvichit, and a number of other leftist ministers. Prince Souphanouvong, returning to a hero's welcome in Vientiane, was made head of the Joint National Political Council, which was to become the instrument of eventual Communist takeover. Within sixty days of the formation of this government all foreign forces were to leave Laos; by early June it was reported that all unauthorized American personnel had left and that the North Vietnamese troops had withdrawn to duties concerned solely with keeping open the Ho Chi Minh Trail. The war in Viet-Nam had not yet ended, even though American forces had withdrawn.

The coalition Government held power for about a year, during which it seemed as though there might be a long and gradual transition towards a Laotian form of socialism. But with the final communist victories in Cambodia and South Viet-Nam in April 1975, events in Laos began to move more rapidly. In a further bout of fighting in mid-April the Royalists lost ground and had to abandon a strategic road junction north of Vientiane: as the Pathet Lao advanced down the road to Vientiane it became clear that no military action could save the day for the Royalists, and there was panic among the rightists in the capital. Many of them fled to Thailand or beyond, especially after the anti-American demonstrations in May which led to the dismissal of five rightist ministers and a number of generals (including Vang Pao, who also fled to Thailand). On May 19th Pathet Lao forces occupied Thakhek and other towns in the south, and two days later demonstrators in Vientiane attacked the U.S. AID headquarters and demanded an end to its operations. By mid-August all American economic and military aid to Laos was completely at an end. The Government was reconstructed in June, with moderates replacing the rightist ministers, and this was followed by an increase in the number of Pathet Lao officials appointed at lower levels of the administration. This stage of the Lao revolution ended on August 23rd, when Vientiane was declared completely liberated and most communications with the outside world were cut. The army was re-formed and a number of people were sent for political re-education.

The final stage of the communist takeover came in December 1975, when a National Congress of People's Representatives accepted the abdication of King Savang Vatthana and declared Laos a People's Democratic Republic. The coalition Government was dismissed, giving way to a regime in which the dominant role was played by the (communist) Lao People's Revolutionary Party, which is now known to have been founded in 1955. Souphanouvong became President, while the Council of Ministers was headed by Kaysone Phomvihane, Secretary-General of the Party; the key Ministry of Finance went to his colleague Nouhak Phoumsavanh. The socialist revolution now began in earnest and involved both political re-education of the old élite (those of its members who had not fled to Thailand) and the mobilization of the masses behind new leaders. Economically and politically the new regime sought to move closer to Viet-Nam, but it had to recognize that for some time it would remain partly dependent on supplies coming through

Thailand. Relations with the latter were moderately good during most of 1976, despite occasional friction and the partial closure of the border by the Thais. But in October 1976 the fall of the civilian Government in Bangkok and the virtual restoration of military rule was immediately denounced by the Laotians as a "fascist" move engineered by the U.S.A. Tension between the two countries became increasingly serious during 1977, as did the communist-led guerrilla war in northern Thailand. By March 1977 there were reports of rebel activity within Laos itself (said to be directed from Thailand), and the government in Vientiane responded by arresting the ex-King and former Crown Prince and (it was rumoured) sending them to a political re-education centre in a part of the country remote from the Thai border. Serious resistance in the lowlands decreased during the remainder of 1977, but there were reports of continuing guerrilla activity by dissident Meo groups in 1978. The Three-Year Plan (1978–80) was hampered by serious floods in 1978 as well as by security problems in the north, but some initial progress was made towards development of resources, with the Laotian economy becoming increasingly tied to the Vietnamese.

Internationally, Laos became firmly established as part of the communist world. From 1976 the Prime Minister, Kaysone Phomvihane, made a number of visits to the Soviet Union, Eastern Europe, and also Cuba. Relations with Viet-Nam were especially close, and in July 1977 they were cemented by a treaty of friendship, signed in the course of a visit to Vientiane by Le Duan and Pham Van Dong. It was estimated in 1978 that there were 40,000 Vietnamese regular troops in Laos. However, close relations with Viet-Nam made it increasingly difficult to maintain friendly contacts with the People's Republic of China, as Sino-Vietnamese relations deteriorated after mid-1978. The Chinese withdrew their technicians from northern Laos in September; relations with France were broken at about the same time. However, France and Laos restored diplomatic relations early in 1982 and both embassies were re-opened.

The dispute with China led ultimately to conflict within the Laotian ruling party, and arrests of officials reported in 1979-80 probably indicated a major purge. The editor of the Party organ, *Siang Pasason*, was said to have "defected" to China in mid-1979. Possibly in order to restore national unity, the Party introduced economic reforms in November 1979 which slowed down the pace of "socialist transformation". Shortly afterwards a number of non-communist "technicians" were appointed to government positions to improve the regime's efficiency. However the primacy of the Party was not in doubt, and Kaysone's control of the leadership was confirmed when it held its Third Congress in Vientiane at the end of April 1982. A Soviet delegation was led by Grigori Romanov, while Troung Chinh represented the Vietnamese Communist Party.

During 1980 a crisis in relations with Thailand led to the closing of the Mekong border between mid-June and late August, and during the heightened tension the Lao Government moved even closer to Viet-Nam. In the course of the year, Hanoi imposed what amounted to a common foreign policy on Laos and Kampuchea, expressed through periodic meetings of the three Foreign Ministers. Direct Lao-Soviet relations also continued to develop, with frequent visits by Soviet delegations and a further visit by Kaysone to the U.S.S.R. Conversely, relations with China deteriorated further, and by September 1980 the Chinese were encouraging the formation of a Lao People's National Liberation United Front—designed to bring together former neutralist and rightist leaders as well as pro-Beijing leftists. In the absence of detailed reporting, however, it remained difficult for outsiders to assess whether the Front presented a serious challenge to Vientiane. Short of a new "armed struggle", the new political pattern in Laos seemed to be well-established.

ECONOMIC SURVEY

T. M. Burley

In economic terms, Laos is thought to be potentially the richest of the Indochinese countries, based on its abundant agricultural, forestry and mineral reserves and its hydroelectric potential. However, this potential remains largely untapped, owing to the political turmoil and national disasters (both flood and drought). Per caput G.N.P. in 1979 was estimated at only U.S. $95 but it passed $100 soon after, following an above-average performance by the economy in both 1980 and 1981.

Progress towards a planned economy along socialist lines saw the initial emphasis placed on improving inter-village communications and the distribution of goods, eliminating profiteering middlemen and setting up more government shops. Subsequent efforts focused on self-sufficiency in food, primarily by raising rice output. This and the "socialist transformation" of the economy were the prime objectives of the 1979–80 Plan and will also be central to the 1981–85 Plan. Soviet aid is a key factor: the U.S.S.R. is to assist with over 50 projects in the new Plan, including a cement works, oil pipeline and two large bridges.

The 1981–85 Plan seeks to achieve self-sufficiency in food, further development of exports, improvements in productivity and a better standard of living. More co-operatives and greater efficiency in the state enterprises are seen as the means of attaining these basic objectives. Rice culture, livestock rearing and forestry operations have priority in the agricultural sector. Efforts are to be made to introduce large-scale manufacturing operations; overall, priority is to be given to electricity, machine repair, construction materials, chemicals, agricultural product processing and handicrafts. Although a "capitalist role" will be maintained, it is to be phased out; state enterprises will take over all export and import business, for example.

In 1978 economic problems centred upon food shortages brought about by severe flooding. Half the land area under rice was lost and, despite some subsequent food aid, near famine conditions prevailed. The road transport system was also badly affected. In 1979, 1980 and 1981 an absence of major climatic disorders enabled useful progress to be made, both in respect of crop and livestock production and also the formation of agricultural co-operatives and the expansion of irrigated areas. Indeed, in 1981 little or no imports of food were required since the output of rice increased by 13 per cent and that of other cereals by 25 per cent.

Although some two-thirds of Laos is forested, agriculture is the basis of the economy and employs about 80 per cent of the work force of some 1.6 million people (90 per cent if subsistence farming is included). Efforts to increase the cultivable area under irrigation are bearing fruit: some 25 per cent of rice fields were irrigated in 1980, compared with only 10 per cent in 1979. In 1981 the amount of rice sold to the state was double that of 1980. This development reflects both the impact of the steep increase in produce prices, initiated by the Government in 1980, and the favourable growing conditions. It meant that no scarce foreign exchange had to be expended on rice imports to feed the ever-growing number of city dwellers. The population of the capital, Vientiane, increased by one-fifth between 1973 and 1981.

AGRICULTURE AND FORESTRY

Land tenure in the valleys still reflects the traditional pattern where land ownership is nominally vested in the state but farmers possess rights of usufruct and inheritance. The land is worked mainly on a family basis but in the more heavily populated districts near the towns there is some share-cropping, often organized on an intra-family or intra-community basis. Being primitive in structure, and also very vulnerable to the vagaries of the weather, agricultural crops are rarely abundant—the largest urban areas cannot rely on domestic supplies and have to resort to importation. Thus, country markets in Laos are on a very small scale. Farmers can sell rice on the free market as well as to the state; the same applies to cattle, pigs and poultry. Certain products—timber, coffee and opium, for example—are prohibited in private trade, and all private traders must be licensed.

Through the system of mutual aid teams, the Government hopes eventually to move towards full collectivization. By late 1979 Laos had 2,696 co-operatives with 129,569 hectares of cultivated land and 97,943 draught animals. These co-operatives embraced 22.4 per cent of the farm population (the end-year target was 30–35 per cent). Co-operatives are designed to embrace 30–35 families; if a village is larger than this, more than one co-operative can be established. An important objective of the scheme is to raise productivity by the simple expedient of greater involvement by individuals (in building irrigation facilities, crop drying areas, etc.): the target is to raise the average number of working days per farmer from 100 to 200. The co-operatives also make it easier for machinery to be effectively employed. Although such schemes will no doubt improve agricultural production, resentment over the effectively forced direction of labour has resulted in absenteeism and unattended paddy fields.

The Lao farmer relies heavily on fish for protein and the fish and rice diet is supplemented by domestic fowls, eggs and pork and many varieties of vegetables and fruit. Fishpond farming is being encouraged and the recently constructed Nam Ngum reservoir also supplements traditional sources, notably the Mekong River.

The forestry industry was particularly hard hit by the war: it has been estimated that the area of best quality timber covers only 11 million hectares (in the 1960s it was about 20 million hectares). Exports of timber, and also forest products such as benzoin, have declined: in 1976/77 only 30,000 cubic metres of timber was produced, and exports earned U.S. $1.4 million, compared with a production of 160,000 cubic metres and exports worth about $7 million in 1974. Output is claimed to be back to pre-war levels, doubtless helped by the substantially higher procurement prices for timber that came into effect in 1980. Revitalization of the industry is accorded high priority and tree planting schemes have been introduced in various parts.

However, both the major timber processing companies have been nationalized and the resultant loss of confidence on the part of foreign investors has put in jeopardy scope for development of potentially valuable rosewood veneer production.

Rice dominates agricultural activities but, despite this, substantial quantities usually have to be imported, both legally and illegally, across the Mekong River from Thailand. Wet rice growing is practised along the middle Mekong and in certain other valley areas in north and north-east Laos such as Luang Prabang. Until recently, few sophisticated irrigation techniques were employed and farmers relied on simple methods of rainfall and flood conrol. Rice mills, too, lacked proper equipment or maintenance. In the hill regions dry rice is grown by means of the "slash and burn" technique which involves the periodic clearing and re-clearing of forest land to maintain fertility. This has caused serious deforestation in north and north-east Laos, and on the Bolovens plateau in the south. Ironically, much of the surplus of rice achieved by the six southern provinces has been exported to Thailand, from which the rice deficit provinces secure their imports. Production of rice reached 1.2 million tons and is expected to increase by 21 per cent by 1985.

Considerable emphasis has been placed on the reclamation of waste land as a means of expanding rice fields; in 1976, for example, local peasants were able to reclaim more than 40,000 hectares of waste land. Most success was recorded in Savannakhet province where 18,269 hectares of waste land was reclaimed and 11,321 hectares of new rice fields tilled. Although emphasis has also been given to improving irrigation, the most significant boost to rice production is likely to come from double-cropping through the growing of winter-spring rice.

Other principal crops are coffee, cotton, medicinal oils, spices and tobacco, and the Meo hill peoples produce maize as a food in addition to rice. It was government policy to diversify from rice to other products, especially animal feeds, cattle, poultry and vegetables, but diversification was held back by the war and has been confined mainly to accessible areas close to the capital. Opium is grown in upper Laos which forms part of the notorious "Golden Triangle".

Non-traditional crops are being experimented with in an effort to increase production. Agricultural experimental stations have planted grain, pigeon peas (dal), cassava, maize, soybeans and green peas. Particular emphasis is being placed on cassava, sweet potato and maize. The state is encouraging improvements in agricultural techniques, ranging from the establishment of animal breeding stations to increased output of agricultural tools. Government ministries have had to participate in this agricultural drive and are expected to set up farming communities producing vegetables, fruit, oxen, buffaloes, pigs, poultry and fish. Stress also is being placed on agricultural training, which is to be augmented by Soviet aid: 2,000 Lao workers and specialists are to undergo training in the U.S.S.R. and the local agricultural college is to be rebuilt.

MANUFACTURING

Most manufacturing activities are confined to the processing of domestic raw materials and the production of handicrafts and basic consumer goods. Such activities are responsible for less than 5 per cent of G.D.P. They are dominated by saw-milling, accounting for 80 per cent of the principal factories. Small-scale operations are almost universal, and only a handful of sizeable factories exist. Despite the state's efforts to increase the availability of credit for industry and to increase supplies of petroleum, other raw materials and spare parts, the level of industrial activity remains far from satisfactory. However, it has improved since the first half of 1977, for example, when truck wreckage and other metal scrap was the raw material from which 750,000 small farm tools were made by small smithy units.

Manufacturing is focused in the Vientiane area. Small plants, employing an estimated 2,500 workers, produce a variety of items such as tobacco products, lumber, matches and rubber shoes. Brewing, detergents and corrugated iron plants appear to be recording the best performance. State ownership is not universal: factories whose management was willing to follow government production guidelines have been allowed to continue. In these mixed ventures the state and the private sector share profits in accordance with the size of their shareholding.

Although lacking fossil fuel, energy for industry is freely available for the Nam Ngum dam, which provides both irrigation facilities and hydroelectric power. Indeed, when this first stage came into operation, Laos became a net exporter of electricity to Thailand. The completion of the second stage of the dam, in 1978, means that annual production of electricity is of the order of 600 million kWh., compared with the 90 million kWh. produced in 1974. Nam Ngum power will play an important role in the integrated rural development schemes planned along the Mekong and in the interior, and in boosting earning of foreign exchange. Over 90 per cent of output is exported to Thailand; under a 10 year agreement, Thailand will purchase 600 million units each year.

MINING

Laos possesses a variety of minerals, one of the most important being tin. After initial surveys, proven reserves were put at 65,000 metric tons, with an average tin content of between 0.5 per cent and 1 per cent. It seems likely that real reserves may be as high as 700,000 tons.

A gypsum mine is now operating in Savannakhet province. Laos also has deposits of lead, zinc, coal, potash and iron ore. A number of veins of lead-zinc ore, containing small quantities of gold, have been discovered in the Capaban, Chepon and Vientiane regions. There are proven deposits of lead containing some zinc and silver near Chepon, and coal near Saravane and north of Vientiane. Alluvial gold and silver were found some years ago in the Toraminh region of Kuing Khong. There is some small-scale mining of precious stones but much of the production is smuggled out of the country. There are huge iron ore deposits located 170 kilometres north-east of Vientiane. Reserves are estimated at several thousand million tons averaging 65 per cent iron content. However, potash mining seems to offer the greatest potential for expansion. The discovery of high-grade sylvite mineralization was one of the final contributions of the United States Agency for International Development (U.S. AID) before it was expelled from Laos. The U.S.S.R., the German Democratic Republic, and Canada have already shown interest in exploiting these deposits which lie 11 kilometres from the capital, Vientiane. Since the deposits could contain more than 1,000 million tons, they will probably have to be developed by foreign interests.

TRANSPORT

Transport presents major difficulties. Laos, which is completely land-locked, is not a natural unit as far as communications are concerned. Since the mid-1950s most international trade has been conducted via Thailand but goods have had to be transported by a Thai government transport company. They suffered delays, theft and often exorbitant dues, both official and unofficial, all of which had to be carried by the Lao consumer.

Despite their rapids and waterfalls, the Mekong River and its principal tributaries comprise important internal routes of communication. Navigable waterways total approximately 4,600 km. and are particularly significant due to the lack of railways and roads, and the limited internal air services.

The building of new roads and the up-grading and repair of existing highways has high priority. Various state and mixed road transport companies exist but substantial quantities of goods are still transported on rivers. Various internal air routes have been opened, relying heavily on Soviet techncial and financial assistance. Under the present regime the main air links are with Canton and Hanoi rather than with tourist centres such as Hong Kong. However, a slow growth in tourism can be expected now that regular flights to Bangkok are permitted.

FINANCE AND PRICES

According to a United Nations report, G.D.P. in real terms was nearly U.S. $300 million in 1980. However, the foreign debt was an estimated U.S. $250 million and the current account deficit was U.S. $128 million. Most economic indicators improved in 1980 over 1979 (G.D.P. rose by 10 per cent, for example) and the UN is optimistic that further advances are possible, given a continuation of the better performance in agriculture and exploitation of the country's forest resources. The good support now being given to the balance of payments by sales of electricity will also make an important contribution.

The Lao monetary system is composed of two institutions, the Banque Nationale du Laos (B.N.L.), the central bank, and the Banque du Commerce Extérieur Lao (B.C.E.L.), a subsidiary of the B.N.L. The B.N.L. concerns itself mostly with domestic banking activities. Since 1980 the B.N.L. is the sole issuer of the national currency, the kip. It is the major source of credit and is also the holder of all Government accounts in kips.

The B.C.E.L., as the holder of official reserves, is involved mostly in international transactions. It contracts foreign loans, and registers most official foreign debt in its balance-sheet as well as residents' foreign currency loans and deposits. Since 1980, in order to improve financial management, financial magnitudes and policies are being set within the framework of a cash plan which identifies areas in which action can be taken to influence the money demand of private cash holders.

The public sector consists of the central Government and 13 provincial administrations (*Khueng*). There are also several public enterprises and a few joint ventures. The budget comprises the financial transactions of the central Government, including budgetary grants to provincial administrations and subsidies to, and transfers from, public enterprises. Equipment (except military hardware), materials and food financed through foreign loans and grants are recorded in the budget. The budget is prepared by the Ministry of Finance in co-operation with the National Planning Committee and the National Bank; thereafter, it is approved by the Council of Ministers and subsequently submitted to the Supreme People's Assembly along with the annual plan. In theory, the budget is the financial reflection of the plan, but the link between the budget and the plan has so far been loose, as current expenditures are excluded from the plan and only part of the budgeted capital outlays are included in the plan.

All financial transactions of state enterprises are managed by the National Bank. In order to strengthen control over their operations and ensure more realistic costing of capital, effective in the 1980 budget year the entire amount needed as working capital is to be provided at an interest charge by the National Bank. All fixed capital, however, continues to be provided by the Government; these advances are repaid to the budget by depreciation allowances. Operating losses of enterprises are offset by budgetary allocations at the end of the year.

Between 1977 and 1979, domestic revenue increased at a faster rate than total expenditures. The improvement in the financial situation during the period under review reflected various measures including improvement in financial management, reductions in less essential expenditures, and tax reforms. Bank financing of the budget was reduced from 76 per cent to 10 per cent of the money stock at the beginning of these respective years. In terms of G.D.P., the overall deficit (before foreign aid) gradually declined from 21 per cent in 1977 to 12 per cent in 1979. In 1980 and 1981, however, the budget deficit grew again, exceeding U.S. $100 million in both years.

Most government revenue is derived from customs duties and other indirect taxation but an agricultural tax and revenue from state-run shops augment government funds. Efforts to collect government revenue are often frustrated, however. The collection of taxes from industry was reportedly 60–70 per cent short of expectations and it was claimed that food aid received from abroad was being diverted to feed Vietnamese soldiers. In order to tap alternative sources of funds, a savings campaign has been started: its aim is that each province should provide from savings 25 per cent of its total capital expenditure. But savings have not been made compulsory so targets are unlikely to be attained: the population has little confidence that money saved in this way will be returned to them or that the interest offered compensates for the risk.

Neither the old kip nor the new liberation kip was ever stable in the 1970s, so in December 1979 another drastic currency reform occurred. The liberation kip was replaced by a "new" kip worth 100 old kips and the former was devalued by 75 per cent against the U.S. dollar. This unheralded move was aimed at speculators but it also had the effect of bringing the official currency rate in line with the "black market" rate, with adverse consequences for the Thai traders engaged in clandestine cross-border business.

In effect, a programme of economic liberalization was initiated. Prices of goods increased following the Government price re-structuring (state purchase prices were raised by 300–500 per cent) but increases in salaries (up to 170 per cent) improved purchasing power. As a result of these measures, increased food supplies became available and, despite periodic dislocation, greater supplies of consumer goods were permitted to enter the country from Thailand. In a parallel move, a licensing system was introduced to encourage private traders to export commodities (other than the state-controlled items—tin, coffee, timber and opium).

Although the high level of inflation has not been appreciably eased by changes in the distribution system, business confidence has been boosted and the bureaucracy has been revitalized (public sector workers did have preferential access to state collective shops but they still were forced to spend up to 70 per cent of their income on the free market).

INTERNATIONAL AID AND TRADE

The U.S.A. used to be the most important donor but, since the end of the war, communist bloc countries and international agencies have become the most important sources of aid. In fact, Laos is critically dependent on foreign aid to maintain such momentum as its economy currently generates. Both budget and balance of payments deficits are consistently large and can be covered only by aid funds. Periodically, too, substantial food aid was necessary to avert famine arising from the twin perils of flood and drought. Virtually all efforts at economic advancement are assisted by foreign aid as are many social aspects. The flow of aid took a little while to regain momentum following the inception of the new regime but in the period 1977–79 total financial aid amounted to over $100 million; additionally, substantial quantities of technical assistance and other difficult-to-quantify aid were received. For the period 1979–82 the value of project aid alone is forecast to total over $400 million.

By virtue of its political affiliations, Laos may soon become a full member of the Council for Mutual Economic Assistance (OMEA), thus gaining access to the facilities of the International Bank for Economic Co-operation and the International Investment Bank. To date, a wide variety of bilateral aid has been received from the U.S.S.R., Viet-Nam and East European CMEA members. Chinese and North Korean aid has, however, stopped; it had amounted to some $8 million. Bilateral aid is also received from many nations in the developed and developing world. The IMF can be regarded as the country's most important aid donor, since the nation would be bankrupt without its financial support. It has been IMF guidance, rather than outright aid, which has been important in the sense of encouraging other donors to support Laos. However, Laos has also received direct financial support through the IMF's compensatory financing scheme; the chief sources of development finance are the International Development Association (IDA), an arm of the World Bank, and the Asian Development Bank (ADB).

The National Mekong Committee, which acts as the state organ representing the Lao Government on the Mekong Interim Committee, has started 20 projects under foreign aid programmes; with investments due to total eventually $17.6 million. The projects include the improvement of the waterway (river) and the construction of two dredges, a shipyard, a meteorological station, 51 pumping stations in Vientiane and a ferry at Keng Kabao (Savannakhet province). A further 11 projects were due to be started in 1980, with eight others under consideration.

The so-called socialist nations have been an important source of aid since independence. Not surprisingly, the U.S.S.R. has been dominant in this regard, especially since late 1978, when all bilateral assistance from China (and North Korea) was suspended. Like the U.S.S.R, East Germany, Hungary and Czechoslovakia have been prominent in providing fellowships to enable Lao students to acquire a variety of skills through technical or university training. Other East European countries are also involved in this aspect of aid, which has high priority because of its combined direct and indirect benefits. Initially, aid priorities focused on basic needs, but the U.S.S.R. also made available a loan of 32 million roubles to replace contributions from the now defunct Foreign Exchange Operations Fund. In a parallel development, Viet-Nam made available 17 million dông to finance supplies of food, medicine, consumer goods and basic needs. Similar, unspecified aid was also received from China. More recently, transport infrastructure, in particular, has benefited from the activities of the U.S.S.R. and the Vietnamese.

Non-food project aid comes in roughly equal proportions from non-communist countries, international organizations and communist countries. Although total disbursed debt at the end of 1980 was nearly U.S. $250 million, or 85 per cent of G.D.P., it was on highly concessional terms with long maturity. Although the debt servicing ratio is low (below 10 per cent of export value), the country's deficit on international trade is restrained only by strict controls on imports and on donated commodity supplies.

The leading exports are timber, electricity, coffee and tin. Imports are dominated by petroleum products, equipment, raw materials and consumer goods. To finance such deficits, Laos has made periodic compensatory finance drawing from its IMF quota. This facility, together with parallel loans from the U.S.S.R. and other socialist partners, is designed to help to finance purchases of essential imports.

Several communist countries now have trade representatives in Vientiane and have signed various trade and economic co-operation agreements with Laos. Most trade, however, is with capitalistic nations, notably Japan and Thailand.

STATISTICAL SURVEY

AREA AND POPULATION

Area	Mid-Year Population (UN estimates)†							
	1973	1974	1975	1976	1977	1978	1979	1980
236,800 sq. km.*	3,159,000	3,229,000	3,303,000	3,381,000	3,462,000	3,546,000	3,633,000	3,721,000

* 91,400 square miles.

† Estimates are based on the results of an administrative count made in May 1958, adjusted upwards by 30 per cent.

Population (official estimate): 3,427,000 at December 31st, 1977.

PRINCIPAL TOWNS
(population in 1973)

Vientiane (capital)	176,637	Luang Prabang	44,244
Savannakhet	50,690	Saya Bury	13,775
Pakse	44,860	Khammouane	12,676

Births and Deaths: Average annual birth rate 46 per 1,000; death rate 23 per 1,000 (official estimates). Average annual birth rate 44.6 per 1,000 in 1970–75, 44.1 per 1,000 in 1975–80; death rate 22.8 per 1,000 in 1970–75, 20.3 per 1,000 in 1975–80 (UN estimates).

LABOUR FORCE
(ILO estimates, '000 persons at mid-year)

	1960			1970		
	Males	Females	Total	Males	Females	Total
Agriculture, etc.	544	540	1,084	618	560	1,178
Industry	36	15	51	52	26	78
Services	111	59	170	151	87	238
Total	691	613	1,305	821	674	1,495

Source: ILO, *Labour Force Estimates and Projections, 1950–2000.*

Mid-1979 (estimates in '000): Agriculture, etc. 1,289; Total 1,734 (*Source:* FAO, *Production Yearbook*).

AGRICULTURE

LAND USE, 1979
('000 hectares)

Arable land	845*
Land under permanent crops	20*
Permanent meadows and pastures	800†
Forests and woodland	13,000†
Other land	8,315
Inland waters	600
Total	23,680

* FAO estimate. † Unofficial figure.

Source: FAO, *Production Yearbook.*

PRINCIPAL CROPS

	Area ('000 hectares)			Production ('000 metric tons)		
	1978	1979	1980	1978	1979	1980
Rice (paddy)	665†	689	690†	796†	925†	1,000
Maize	32†	23	38*	46†	48*	52*
Potatoes	4*	4*	4*	28†	31*	34*
Sweet potatoes and yams	2*	3*	3*	22†	25*	28*
Cassava (Manioc)	4*	4*	5*	55†	60*	68*
Pulses	9*	10*	10*	15*	16*	17*
Soybeans	5*	4	6*	5*	6*	6*
Groundnuts (in shell)	7*	11	12*	7*	8	9*
Cottonseed	4	7	7*	6†	6*	6*
Cotton (lint)				3†	3*	3*
Vegetables and melons	n.a.	n.a.	n.a.	164*	174*	184*
Sugar cane	2*	2*	3*	9*	9*	10*
Coffee	8†	5	8*	4†	4	4*
Tobacco	12†	13*	14*	7†	8*	9*

*FAO estimate. † Unofficial figure.

Source: FAO, *Production Yearbook.*

LIVESTOCK

(FAO estimates, '000 head, year ending September)

	1978	1979	1980
Horses	28	30	32
Cattle	350	373*	399
Buffaloes	620	682*	756
Pigs	700	786*	843
Goats	27	30	35
Chickens	12,500	13,000	15,000
Ducks	190	200	210

Domestic elephants: 892 recorded in 1971.

* Unofficial figure.

Source: FAO, *Production Yearbook.*

LIVESTOCK PRODUCTS

('000 metric tons—FAO estimates)

	1978	1979	1980
Beef and veal	3	3	4
Buffalo meat	7	8	8
Pig meat	25	28	30
Poultry meat	10	11	13
Cows' milk	6	6	6
Hen eggs	18.8	19.8	20.2
Cattle and buffalo hides	3.4	3.4	3.6

Source: FAO, *Production Yearbook.*

FORESTRY

ROUNDWOOD REMOVALS

('000 cubic metres, all non-coniferous)

	1973*	1974*	1975*	1976*	1977*	1978	1979	1980*
Sawlogs, veneer logs and logs for sleepers	132	190	131	95	95	139	130	130
Other industrial wood	80	81	83	85	87	89*	91*	93
Fuel wood	2,351	2,403	2,459	2,517	2,577	2,640*	2,704*	2,770
Total	2,563	2,674	2,673	2,697	2,759	2,868	2,925	2,993

* FAO estimates.

Source: FAO, *Yearbook of Forest Products.*

SAWNWOOD PRODUCTION

('000 cubic metres, all non-coniferous)

	1972*	1973*	1974*	1975*	1976*	1977*	1978	1979
Total (incl. boxboards) .	48	66	92	63	44	46	56	41

* FAO estimate.

1980: Production as in 1979 (FAO estimate).

Source: FAO, *Yearbook of Forest Products.*

Fishing: Total catch 20,000 metric tons of freshwater fishes per year (FAO estimate).

MINING

		1975	1976*	1977*	1978*	1979*
Tin concentrates (metal content) .	metric tons	518	576	600	600	600

* Estimate.

Source: International Tin Council, London.

INDUSTRY

SELECTED PRODUCTS

		1969	1970	1971	1972	1973
Distilled alcoholic beverages .	'000 hectolitres	18	18	9	15	24
Cigarettes	million	381	361	381	375	628
Washing powder	metric tons	n.a.	7,000	2,880	2,880	n.a.
Rubber footwear	'000 pairs	864	1,152	1,889	161	180
Clay building bricks . . .	million	27	27	—	137	n.a.
Electric energy	million kWh.	21	12	16	228	245*

* Estimate.

Cigarettes (million): 850 in 1974; 900 in 1975; 1,000 in 1976; 1,100 per year in 1977–79 (estimates by U.S. Department of Agriculture).

Electric energy (million kWh.): 255 in 1974; 350 in 1975; 400 in 1976; 450 in 1977; 500 in 1978; 600 in 1979 (estimates).

Source: mainly United Nations, *Statistical Yearbook* and *Yearbook of Industrial Statistics.*

FINANCE

100 at (cents) = 1 new kip.

Notes: 1, 5, 10, 20 and 50 new kips.

Exchange rates (June 1982): £1 sterling = 17.3 new kips; U.S. $1 = 10.0 new kips.

100 new kips = £5.77 = $10.00.

Note: **The kip was introduced in January 1955, replacing (at par) the Indo-Chinese piastre. From May 1953 the piastre's value was 10 old French francs. The initial exchange rate was thus U.S. $1 = 35 kips (1 kip = 2.857 U.S. cents). In October 1958 the currency was devalued by 56 per cent, the new exchange rate being $1 = 80 kips (1 kip = 1.25 U.S. cents). This rate remained in force until the end of 1963. From January 1964 to November 1971 the official exchange rate was $1 = 240 kips (1 kip = 0.417 U.S. cent), although a free market rate also operated officially at around 500 kips to the dollar. In November 1971 this official free rate was fixed at $1 = 600 kips (1 kip = 0.167 U.S. cent) and this became the rate used to convert the value of foreign trade transactions. The official basic rate of $1 = 240 kips was abolished in April 1972, when the basic and free rates were unified at $1 = 600 kips. A financial (selling) rate of $1 = 840 kips was introduced in May 1972. The currency was devalued in March 1975, when the rates were fixed at $1 = 750 kips (buying) or 1,200 kips (selling). In June 1976 the** liberation kip was introduced, replacing the former currency at the rate of 1 liberation kip = 20 kips. However, the currency was devalued by 70 per cent so that the exchange rate became $1 = 200 liberation kips. This remained in force until May 1978, when a rate of $1 = 400 liberation kips was introduced. In December 1979 the liberation kip was replaced by a new "kip national", worth 100 of the former units. At the same time the currency was devalued by 75 per cent, so that the exchange rate was set at U.S. $1 = 16 new kips. In January 1980 the rate was adjusted to $1 = 10 new kips. In terms of sterling, the exchange rate was £1 = 576 kips (official) from November 1967 to August 1971; and £1 = 1,563.43 kips (free market) from December 1971 to June 1972.

BUDGET
(million kips)

Revenue	1979	1980	1981
Private sector taxes	48.4	98.3	140.0
State enterprises	200.2	567.8	700.0
Other	19.4	82.1	90.0
Total Domestic Revenue	268.0	748.2	930.0

Expenditure	1979	1980	1981
Current expenditure	393.9	1,028.0	1,210.0
Capital expenditure	242.1	748.9	950.0
Total	636.0	1,776.9	2,160.0

INTERNATIONAL RESERVES*
(U.S. $ million)

1976	1977	1978	1979	1980
12.4	7.8	21.5	26.1	14.0

* Comprising gold, IMF Special Drawing Rights and foreign exchange.

MONEY SUPPLY
(million old kips at December 31st)

	1968	1969	1970	1971	1972	1973	1974
Bank Deposits	1,068	1,327	1,141	1,231	1,731	3,213	2,900
Money in Circulation	11,294	12,497	14,215	17,723	21,743	23,449	33,800

COST OF LIVING

Consumer Price Index, Vientiane

(base: 1970=100)

	1967	1968	1969	1971	1972	1973	1974	1975*
Food	99.8	105.5	107.5	100.6	135.8	190.7	289.9	450.0
Clothing	90.0	93.7	97.2	101.4	121.9	146.5	228.4	333.8
Rent, fuel and light	87.9	89.2	94.2	102.5	108.6	128.6	185.4	246.1
All Items	92.0	96.5	99.6	101.3	126.8	165.7	248.1	368.3

* January to August. The index of all items for the whole year was 457.3 (food index 544.9).

Source: International Labour Office, mainly *Year Book of Labour Statistics.*

EXTERNAL TRADE

(U.S. $ million)

	1977	1978	1979	1980
Imports (c.i.f.)	59.1	76.3	94.3	130.1
Exports (f.o.b.)	9.6	11.8	35.2	30.5

PRINCIPAL COMMODITIES

(million new kips)

Exports	1976	1977	1978	1979*
Timber	0.70	0.91	2.70	2.40
Tin	1.34	0.93	0.82	0.12
Coffee	3.15	3.08	1.06	1.22
Wood products	0.57	0.45	0.17	0.09
Electricity	1.65	1.85	1.88	1.90
Others	0.07	1.38	2.20	1.25
Total	7.48	8.60	8.83	6.98

* January to May.

Source: Economist Intelligence Unit, *Annual Supplement* 1980.

PRINCIPAL TRADING PARTNERS
(million old kips)

Imports	1970	1971	1972
France	2,194.9	1,377.4	1,125.8
Germany, Federal Republic	177.6	341.6	327.9
Hong Kong	398.4	363.6	513.6
Indonesia	4,173.0	2,113.3	2,097.1
Japan	3,925.8	3,843.5	2,469.9
Singapore	1,529.0	1,823.2	1,025.7
Taiwan	266.1	269.0	396.0
Thailand	5,622.8	5,086.0	12,353.7
United Kingdom	675.0	366.2	366.2
U.S.A.	6,647.9	3,143.0	4,298.4
Others	1,718.6	1,012.9	1,231.1
Total	27,329.1	19,739.7	26,205.4

Exports	1970	1971	1972	1973*
Hong Kong	44.0	25.5	19.7	73.8
Singapore and Malaysia	689.2	773.7	1,027.2	910.5
Thailand	472.6	634.6	457.0	1,987.3
South Viet-Nam	18.6	0.2	—	0.4
Total (incl. others)	1,726.7	1,485.4	1,540.1	3,044.6

* Provisional.

TRANSPORT

ROAD TRAFFIC
(motor vehicles in use*)

	1970	1971	1972	1973
Cars	10,969	12,054	12,765	13,611
Trucks	1,694	2,060	2,230	2,369
Motor cycles	10,365	11,068	12,105	13,162
Total	23,028	25,182	27,100	29,142

* Excluding official vehicles.

1974: Passenger cars 14,100; Commercial vehicles 2,500 (*Source:* UN, *Statistical Yearbook*).

CIVIL AVIATION
Scheduled Services
(million)

	1976	1977	1978
Kilometres flown	0.8	0.4	0.2
Passengers carried ('000)	45	30	12
Passenger-kilometres	22	10	6
Freight tonne-kilometres	0.5	0.1	0.1
Total tonne-kilometres	2	1	1

Source: UN, *Statistical Yearbook*.

Tourism (1973): 12,378 visitors.

EDUCATION
(1978/79)

	Pupils
Elementary	451,800
Secondary	60,400
Senior high schools	7,800
University	1,684

Source (unless otherwise indicated): Service National de la Statistique, Vientiane.

THE CONSTITUTION

Following the change of regime in December 1975 and the abolition of the monarchy, it was announced that a new constitution would be prepared by the Supreme People's Assembly.

THE GOVERNMENT

HEAD OF STATE

President: Souphanouvong (took office December 4th, 1975).

SUPREME PEOPLE'S ASSEMBLY

President: Souphanouvong.

Vice-Presidents: Sisomphone Lovanxay, Faydang Lobliayao, Khamsouk Keola.

Secretary-General: Khamsouk Keola.

Vice Secretary-Generals: Xay Phetrasy, Souvannarath.

COUNCIL OF MINISTERS

(July 1982)

Prime Minister: Kaysone Phomvihane.

Vice-Prime Minister and Minister of Finance: Nouhak Phounsavanh.

Vice-Prime Minister and Minister of Education, Sport and Religion: Phoumi Vongvichit.

Vice-Prime Minister and Minister of Foreign Affairs: Phoun Sipraseuth.

Vice-Prime Minister and Minister of Defence and Supreme Commander of the Lao People's Liberation Army: Gen. Khamtay Siphandone.

Vice-Prime Minister and Chairman of the National Planning Committee: Saly Vongkhamsao.

Ministers to the Prime Minister's Office: Chanmy Douagboudy, Maychantan Sengmani, Thongsavat Khaykhamphithoune.

Minister of the Interior: Sisavat Keobounphanh.

Minister of Information, Propaganda, Culture and Tourism: Sisana Sisan.

Minister of Justice: Kou Souvannamethi.

Minister of Communications, Public Works and Transport: Sanan Southichak.

Minister of Health: Tiao Soukvongsak.

Minister of Agricultural Production, Forestry and Irrigation: Khamsouk Saignaseng.

Minister of Industry and Commerce: Maysouk Saysompheng.

Minister of Posts and Telecommunications: Thammasin Saikhamphan (acting).

Counsellor to the Government: Souvanna Phouma.

There are a further 23 members in the Council of Ministers: 18 Vice-Ministers, the Governor of the National Bank and the respective Chairmen of the National Committees for Social Security and War Veterans, Science and Technology, Labour and Wages, and Nationalities.

LEGISLATURE

NATIONAL CONGRESS

A National Congress of People's Representatives, comprising 264 delegates elected by local authorities, was convened in December 1975. The Congress appointed the Supreme People's Assembly to draft a new constitution.

POLITICAL ORGANIZATIONS

Phak Pasason Pativat Lao (*Lao People's Revolutionary Party—LPRP*): Vientiane; f. 1975 in succession to the People's Party of Laos (f. 1955); communist; Sec.-Gen. KAYSONE PHOMVIHANE; Deputy NOUHAK PHOUNSAVANH; publ. *Siang Pasason.*

Politburo:

Seven full members:

KAYSONE PHOMVIHANE
NOUHAK POUNSAVANH
SOUPHANOUVONG
PHOUMI VONGVICHIT
Gen. KHAMTAI SIPHANDON
PHOUNE SIPASEUTH
SISOMPHON LOVANSAY

Secretariat:

Nine full members:

KAYSONE PHOMVIHANE
NOUHAK PHOUNSAVANH
PHOUNE SIPASEUTH
Gen. KHAMTAI SIPHANDON
SISOMPHON LOVANSAY
SALI VONGKHAMSAO
SISAVAT KEOBOUNPHANH
SAMAN VIGNAKET
MAYCHANTAN SENGMANI

Lao Front for National Reconstruction: Vientiane; f. 1979 to replace the former Lao Patriotic Front; comprises representatives of various political and social groups, of which the LPRP is the most important; aims to increase national solidarity and to assist the development of the economy and socialism; 76-mem. Central Cttee.; Chair. Pres. SOUPHANOUVONG; Vice-Chair. FAYDANG LOBLIAYAO, KHAMSOUK KEOLA, BOLANG.

DIPLOMATIC REPRESENTATION

EMBASSIES ACCREDITED TO LAOS

(In Vientiane unless otherwise stated)

Albania: Hanoi, Viet-Nam.

Algeria: Hanoi, Viet-Nam.

Australia: rue Pandit J. Nehru, Quartier Phone Xay, B.P. 292; *Ambassador:* PHILIP F. PETERS.

Austria: Bangkok, Thailand.

Belgium: Bangkok, Thailand.

Bulgaria: *Ambassador:* JETCHO PETROV RADOUNOV.

Burma: *Chargé d'affaires:* U MINN HLAING.

Canada: Bangkok, Thailand.

China, People's Republic: *Chargé d'affaires:* WANG PAO MIN.

Cuba: *Ambassador:* LUIS REYES MAS.

Czechoslovakia: 5 rue Thadeua, B.P. 508; *Ambassador:* LADISLAV KOCSIS.

Denmark: Bangkok, Thailand.

Egypt: *Ambassador:* Dr. AHMAD EL MASRY.

Finland: Hanoi, Viet-Nam.

France: rue Sethathirath; *Ambassador:* JEAN-NOËL DE BOUILLANE.

German Democratic Republic: rue Sok Paluang, B.P. 1102; *Ambassador:* DIETER DOERING.

Germany, Federal Republic: P.O.B. 314, rue Pandit J. Nehru; *Ambassador:* HERMANN FLENDER.

Hungary: B.P. 733, Quartier Sisangvone; *Ambassador:* JÁNOS ZEGNAL.

India: *Ambassador:* P. R. SOOD.

Indonesia: Phone Keng Ave., P.O.B. 277; *Ambassador:* PUDJO PRASETJO.

Iran: Bangkok, Thailand.

Iraq: Hanoi, Viet-Nam.

Italy: Bangkok, Thailand.

Japan: rue Sisangvone; *Ambassador:* YOSHINA ODAKA.

Kampuchea: *Ambassador:* NAO SAMOM.

Korea, Democratic People's Republic: *Ambassador:* YOUN DJEUNG SEUP.

Malaysia: *Chargé d'affaires:* M. SANTHANANABAN.

Mexico: Hanoi, Viet-Nam.

Mongolia: *Ambassador:* ORSOOGIYN NYAMAA.

Nepal: *Ambassador:* KHAGAJEET BARAL.

Netherlands: Bangkok, Thailand.

New Zealand: Bangkok, Thailand.

Pakistan: Hanoi, Viet-Nam.

Philippines: 4 Thadeua Rd.; *Ambassador:* JOSÉ M. EVANGELISTA.

Poland: Place That Luang, B.P. 1106; *Ambassador:* MAREK CZURLEJ.

Romania: Hanoi, Viet-Nam.

Spain: Beijing, People's Republic of China.

Sri Lanka: Rangoon, Burma.

Sweden: rue Sok Paluang, P.O.B. 800; *Chargé d'affaires:* MATS ÅBERG.

Switzerland: Hanoi, Viet-Nam.

Thailand: *Ambassador:* SUNTHON KHONG SAK.

Turkey: Bangkok, Thailand.

U.S.S.R.: *Ambassador:* VLADIMIR F. SOBCHENKO.

United Kingdom: rue Pandit J. Nehru, P.O.B. 224; *Ambassador:* W. B. J. DOBBS.

U.S.A.: *Chargé d'affaires:* WILLIAM W. THOMAS.

Viet-Nam: *Ambassador:* NGUYEN XUAN.

Yemen, People's Democratic Republic: Beijing, People's Republic of China.

Laos also has diplomatic relations with Afghanistan, Angolia, Argentina, Benin, Ethiopia, Grenada, Guinea, Lebanon, Libya, Madagascar, Mozambique, Nicaragua, Singapore, Tanzania and Yugoslavia.

JUDICIAL SYSTEM

There is no formal judicial system in operation yet.

RELIGION

The principal religion of Laos is Buddhism.

BUDDHISM

The Venerable Phra Maha THONGKHOUNE ANANTASUNTHONE, Wat That Luang, Vientiane.

Lao Unified Buddhists' Association: Maha Kudy, That Luang, Vientiane; f. 1964; Pres. Phra Maha THONGKHOUNE ANANTASUNTHONE; Sec. Gen. Rev. SIHO SIHAVONG.

CHRISTIANITY

Roman Catholic: Vicar Apostolic: Mgr. THOMAS NANTHA, B.P. 113, Mission Catholique, Vientiane.

THE PRESS

Heng Ngan: Vientiane; organ of the Federation of Lao Trade Unions; monthly.

Meying Lao: Vientiane; f. 1980; women's magazine established to commemorate International Women's Day; monthly; Editor-in-Chief KHAMPHON PHIMMASENG; circ. 4,000.

Noum Lao (*Lao Youth*): Vientiane; f. 1979; organ of the Lao People's Revolutionary Youth Union; fortnightly; Editor DOUANGDY INTHAVONG; circ. 6,000.

Siang Pasason (*Voice of the People*): P.O.B. 110, 80 Sethathirat, Vientiane; f. 1975; organ of the Central Cttee. of the LPRP; Editor CHANTHY DEUANSAVANE (acting); circ. 10,000.

Suksa May: Vientiane; organ of the Ministry of Education; monthly.

Valasan Houpphab Pathet Lao: Vientiane; illustrated; circ. 7,000.

Viengchane May (*New Vientiane*): P.O.B. 989, Vientiane; f. 1975; morning daily; organ of the Party Cttee. of Vientiane province and city; Editor SICHANE (acting); circ. 2,500.

There is also a newspaper published by the Lao People's Liberation Army while several provinces have their own newsletters.

NEWS AGENCIES

Khao San Pathet Lao (KPL): B.P. 122, Vientiane; organ of the Ministry of Information; daily bulletins in Lao, French, teletype transmission in English; Dir. CHANTHY DEUANSAVANE (acting).

Foreign Bureaux

Agentstvo Pechati Novosti (APN) (*U.S.S.R.*): P.O.B. 626, Vientiane.

Viet-Nam News Agency (VNA): Vientiane; Chief DO VAN PHUONG.

Tass (U.S.S.R.) also has an office in Laos.

Association

Lao Journalists' Association: Vientiane; Sec.-Gen. CHANTHY DEUANSAVANE.

PUBLISHERS

Khoualuang Kanphim: 2-4-6 Khoualouang Market, Vientiane.

Lao Printing Office: Samsenthai Rd., Vientiane.

Pakpassak Kanphim: 9–11 Quai Fa-Ngum, Vientiane.

RADIO

Radio Diffusion Nationale Lao: B.P. 310, Vientiane; f. 1951; government-owned; programmes in Lao, French, English, Thai, Khmer and Vietnamese (news only); domestic and international services; Dir.-Gen. CHALEUN VONGSAMANG; number of radio sets (1974) 102,000.

In addition there are several local radio stations.

FINANCE

BANKING

(cap.=capital; p.u.=paid up; dep.=deposit; m.=million)

Central Bank

Banque Nationale du Laos: rue Yonnet, P.O.B. 19, Vientiane; f. 1955; central bank; cap. p.u. 290m. old kips; dep. 44,842m. old kips (Dec. 1974); Gov.-Gen. SOT PHETLASI.

Banque pour le Commerce Extérieur Lao: Vientiane; performs as executive agent for the central bank; Dir. Miss KHEMVIENG.

TRADE AND INDUSTRY

Responsibility for foreign trade lies with the Department of Foreign Trade, Ministry of Industry and Commerce, Vientiane.

Lao Import-Export Company: Vientiane; Dir. SISAVAT SISAN.

Lao National Planning Committee: Vientiane; Chair. SALY VONGKHAMSAO.

DEVELOPMENT ORGANIZATION

National Office for Agriculture and Livestock: Vientiane; public enterprise; imports and markets agricultural commodities; produces and distributes feed and animals.

CO-OPERATIVES

Central Level Committee to Guide Agricultural Co-operatives: Vientiane; f. 1978; to help organize and plan regulations and policies for co-operatives; by the end of 1979 there were 2,696 agricultural co-operatives in Laos, farming 129,569 hectares of paddy fields; Chair. SALY VONGKHAMSAO.

TRADE UNION ORGANIZATION

Federation of Lao Trade Unions: Vientiane; Pres. SANAN SOUTTHICHAK; Vice-Pres. BOUNTHAM KHOUNLAPVISETAKHOM; publ. *Heng Ngan* (monthly).

TRANSPORT

There are no railways in Laos.

ROADS

There are about 1,300 km. of all-weather roads. The main routes link Vientiane and Luang Prabang with Ho Chi Minh City (Saigon) (south Viet-Nam), north Viet-Nam and the Kampuchean border, Vientiane with Savannakhet, Phong Saly to the Chinese border, Vientiane with Luang Prabang and Khammouane with Ha Tink (north Viet-Nam). In 1981 work commenced on the improvement of Route 9, the main road linking Savannakhet to Da Nang in Viet Nam. Several other highways are also being improved, including Route 13, the north-south link.

INLAND WATERWAYS

The River Mekong, which forms the western frontier of Laos for much of its length, is the country's greatest traffic artery. There are about 4,600 km. of navigable waterways.

CIVIL AVIATION

Lao Civil Aviation Department: Vientiane; Dir. PHOUN KHAMMOUNHUANG.

Lao Aviation: 2 rue Pang Kham, B.P. 119, Vientiane; f. 1976; state airline, operates internal services and international services to Hanoi, Phnom-Penh and Bangkok; 6 Antonov An-24V, 1 Viscount 700, 3 Fairchild Provider, 1 An-2M.

FOREIGN AIRLINES

The following foreign airlines also serve Vientiane: Aeroflot (U.S.S.R.), Air Viet-Nam and Thai Airways.

TOURISM

Lao National Tourism Department: B.P. 122, Samsenthai Rd., Vientiane; administered by an Executive Committee.

DEFENCE

Armed Forces (July 1981): Total strength 55,700; army 46,000; navy 1,700; air force 8,000; there is a system of conscription in operation.

Defence Expenditure (1979): 15,150 million kips (U.S. $37.9 million).

Commander-in-Chief: Gen. KHAMTAY SIPHANDONE.

Chief of the General Staff: SISAVAT KEOBOUNPHANH.

EDUCATION

Schooling in Laos is compulsory for six years. The age of entry into primary school is six. Primary education lasts for five years and the duration of the secondary school course is three years, with an additional senior high school course of three years. Lao is the medium of instruction in schools and a new type of school based on a comprehensive school system has been introduced.

During 1978–79 there were 451,800 pupils at primary schools, 60,400 at secondary schools, 7,800 at senior high schools and 1,684 students at the only university. In 1982 about 4,000 students were studying abroad, mainly in the U.S.S.R.

BIBLIOGRAPHY

(*See* also Kampuchea and Viet-Nam.)

CONDOMINAS, G. Essai sur la société lao de la région de Vientiane (Commissariat des affaires rurales, Vientiane).

DOMMEN, A. J. Conflict in Laos: The Politics of Neutralization (Pall Mall Press, London, 1964).

LANCASTER, D. The Emancipation of French Indo-China (Oxford University Press, London, 1961).

LANGER, P. F., and ZASLOFF, J. J. North Vietnam and the Pathet Lao (Harvard University Press, Cambridge, Mass., 1970).

LE BAR, F. M., and SUDDARD, A. Laos, its People, its Society, its Culture (HRAF Press, New Haven, 1960).

McCOY, A. W. The Politics of Heroin in Southeast Asia (Harper & Row, New York, 1972).

TOYE, H. Laos—Buffer State or Background (Oxford University Press, London).

UN AID TO LAOS. Annual Statistical Report.

ZASLOFF, J. J. The Pathet Lao: Leadership and Organisation (Heath, Lexington, Mass., 1973).

Macau

Frank H. H. King

(Revised by the Editor, 1982)

GEOGRAPHY

Macau has an area of 15.5 square kilometres, comprising the peninsula of the Chinese district of Fo Shan and the two small islands of Taipa and Colôane which together lie some 64 kilometres west across the Guangzhou (Canton) River estuary from Hong Kong. The climate is sub-tropical.

The population was estimated at more than 350,000 in 1981, of whom 2,000 to 3,000 are Portuguese. With Chinese immigration reaching a rate of 500 people a day and with Chinese refugees from Viet-Nam held off with difficulty, the situation is both unstable and of grave concern to the Government.

HISTORY

The territory was established as one of several trading posts by the Portuguese as early as 1537; records of continuous settlement begin in 1557. Driven by trade and missionary zeal, the Portuguese developed Macau as a base for their operations both in China and Japan, and penetration during Japan's "Christian century" involved close relations with Macau. However, sovereignty remained vested in China, the Chinese residents remained subject to a Chinese official, and Macau's Portuguese administration, virtually autonomous for the first two hundred years, concerned itself with the governance of the Portuguese and, until the establishment of Hong Kong, with the growing presence of other European trading nations. The Portuguese paid an annual rent to China.

Macau was an uncertain base for an expanded China trade. The Catholic administration was unfriendly to Protestants, the Chinese authority was too close and restrictive, and the opium question and growing restlessness of the "private" merchants undermined a system which had developed during the years of controlled and relatively limited "company" trade.

The ceding of Hong Kong to Britain in 1842 revealed China's weakness and in 1845 Portugal declared Macau a free port. In the consequent disputes the Macau Governor, Ferreira do Amaral, was assassinated, Portugal drove out the Chinese officials, and the settlement was proclaimed Portuguese territory. This unilateral declaration was recognized by China in 1887 in return for provisions intended to facilitate the enforcement of its customs laws, particularly in regard to opium, by the Imperial Maritime Customs.

However, Macau's establishment as a colony did not restore prosperity. With the silting of its harbour, the diversion of its trade to Hong Kong, and the opening of the treaty ports as bases of trade and missionary work, Macau was left to handle the local distributive trade, while developing a reputation as a base for smuggling, gambling and other unsavoury activities. With the closing of the Hong Kong–China border in 1938, Macau's trade boomed, but this prosperity was short-lived as the colony soon became isolated as the only European settlement on the China coast not occupied by the Japanese during the Second World War.

In 1951 Macau was declared an overseas province of Portugal and elected a representative to the Portuguese legislature. Macau's economic prosperity depended largely on the gold trade, illegal in Hong Kong, on gambling and tourism, and on an entrepôt business with China.

Recent political developments

Macau's tranquility was disrupted by communist riots in 1966–67, inspired by the Cultural Revolution in mainland China. These were contained only after the Macau Government signed an agreement with Macau's Chinese Chamber of Commerce outlawing the activities of Chinese loyal to the Taiwan regime, which Portugal continued to recognize, paying compensation to the families of Chinese killed in the rioting, and refusing entry to refugees from China.

But the nature of the settlement made it clear that China wished the Portuguese administration to continue, and on admission to the United Nations the Beijing (Peking) Government affirmed that it regarded the future of both Hong Kong and Macau as an internal matter.

After the military coup in Portugal in April 1974 Macau's was the only governor of an overseas territory retained in office. China refused to discuss the future of Macau with Portugal and the revolutionary leaders became convinced that there was no demand for an independence which China would not, in any case, have tolerated. Nevertheless the revolution caused considerable political activity in Macau. The Centro Democrática de Macau (CDM) was established to press for radical political reform and the purging of those connected with the former regime. The conservative Association for the Defence of the Interests of Macau (ADIM) was established and in April 1975 defeated the CDM's candidate for Macau's representative to the Lisbon assembly. The Macau electorate reaffirmed its conservative bias when, under the constitutional arrangements, over 65 per cent voted for right-wing parties in the Lisbon constituency.

Colonel Garcia Leandro, who succeeded Nobre de Carvalho at the end of his much-extended term as Governor in late 1974, correctly assessed China's position while being sufficiently flexible to recognize that Macau needed capitalism and was not ready for socialism. He initiated policies which, in effect, insulated Macau from the direct influence of a series of Portuguese regimes which contained elements sympathetic to the Soviet Union and which might have disrupted the delicate balance necessary for the continuation of Macau's existence. Thus, Leandro, who had at first dealt with the CDM, expelled many of its supporters, effectively assuring the success of the ADIM in elections to the Legislative Assembly in July 1976. Leandro also backed legislation in Portugal which, in February 1976, appeared to give Macau virtual political autonomy. Meanwhile, all Portuguese military units were withdrawn and replaced by local security forces, while plans were made for a central bank which, it was promised, could provide Macau with a separate economic policy.

Macau had thus become a special territory of Portugal with a Governor of ministerial rank appointed by the President of the Portuguese Republic, to whom he is responsible. The Governor is the executive authority and may issue decrees, a subject of continuing controversy, and he remains independent of the Legislative Assembly with the right to veto legislation not passed by a two-thirds majority. The composition of the Assembly reflects Macau's social and political structure, which is still divided into Chinese and "Portuguese", the latter self-determined on the basis of culture, language and religion—not on place of origin. Of the 17 members, six are elected on a proportional basis, six are elected indirectly by designated organizations, and five are appointed by the Governor.

These elections confirmed Macau's conservative preference, with the ADIM receiving 55 per cent of the 2,700 votes cast and winning four of the six seats. A group of young independents, including civil servants, stood as the GEDEC (Grupo de Estudos para o Desenvolvimento Comunitário de Macau) and, with 17 per cent of the vote, elected Jorge Rangel, director of tourism, while the radical and once dominant CDM trailed but also elected a member. The Governor appointed the key figure of Ho Yin, President of the Chamber of Commerce and representative of the Chinese community. His role in the exchange of views between the Guangdong (Kwangtung) provincial authorities and Macau is of great significance to the territory's stability. Other appointees and those indirectly elected created an Assembly which was still recognizably Portuguese, confirming the Portuguese nature of the government and avoiding the anomalous position of a Chinese population voting for non-Communist parties on China's very borders. Of the officially estimated 263,350 residents in mid-1976, only some 3,500 electors, almost all "Portuguese", registered, and electoral politics have remained the virtual monopoly of those culturally identified with Portugal.

By 1978, however, Macau's political position required reinterpretation. Disassociation from Portugal in the first months of the revolution and during any period of likely pro-Soviet orientation was sound policy, but with improving relations with China, culminating in recognition in 1979, Macau's rationale depended on its Portuguese connection. The trend towards "autonomy" had to be reversed and political links with Portugal reforged. This last took such forms as fulfilment of the potential relationship between Macau's ADIM and Portugal's Partido do Centro Democrático Social (CDS), and the inclusion in late 1978 of a section on Macau in the new Lisbon Government's programme. Unfortunately lack of political stability in Lisbon has prevented these developments from maturing.

Governor Leandro, who correctly appraised Macau's needs in 1974, was frustrated in his desire to obtain greater local Chinese political participation, and his efforts to have the Macau population involved in the nomination of his successor were ineffective. His four-year administration was, however, marked by a more realistic planning orientation, marred in execution by administrative problems, dreams of an autonomous central bank, and inherited problems with economic overheads. He did, however, change patterns of thinking, set in motion basic economic reforms, and see through legislation which has resulted in a sounder taxation system and improvements for the local civil service.

A change in governors, however, also means a change in top staff or "cabinet" level officers, none of whom has had actual experience in Macau. The new Governor, General Melo Egídio, and his staff arrived only in late February 1979. The Governor appeared to favour a quiet approach with an apparent reliance on Portugal. The new cabinet spent the rest of 1979 studying the general situation.

The Legislative Council members were to stand for re-election in late 1979 but in June the Legislative Assembly extended the term of the seven elected representatives for another year. This temporarily averted the Constitutional crisis facing the Governor in 1980 when the four-year-old Organic Law was to come up for review. A delegation of the representatives had visited Lisbon to discuss proposals to revise the 1976 Organic Law with politicians in the Portuguese parliament. Their proposals, which were to give the local population a greater say in the running of Macau, included enlarging the Legislative Assembly from 17 to 21 members. All of these would be elected, thus reducing the Governor to a merely titular status. (At present five members are appointed by the Governor, six are elected directly and six indirectly.) In March 1980, when General Melo Egídio visited Beijing on the first official visit by a Governor of Macau since its establishment as a Portuguese colony in 1557, the Chinese leader Deng Xiaoping, while expressing his approval of the stability of Macau, also made it clear that the Chinese opposed any change in the Organic Law. His views were echoed by the local population in Macau, who feel close ties with Beijing. Ninety-seven per cent of the population do not speak Portuguese, they run their own schools, take very little part in political life and are largely unaffected by the Portuguese administration.

There have been significant cultural developments, however, in Macau. With grants from the Calouste Gulbenkian Foundation and continued government support, drastic reconstruction and redevelopment of Macau's important Luis de Camoes museum is under-way. The well preserved archives are being professionally catalogued for the first time under the direction of Portugal's leading historian of the overseas empire, Fr. Dr. António da Silvo Rego. The new University of Macau, re-christened the University of the Far East, was inaugurated on March 28th, 1981, and was to admit its first students in October 1981. Funded by Hong Kong, it is to provide higher education for those qualified but unable, through restrictions on intake, to attend either of Hong Kong's universities.

International relations. The People's Republic of China regards Macau as Chinese territory under a Portuguese administration. In Western legal terms Macau is a territory and Portugal is sovereign. In both interpretations Macau has no international personality itself and its relations are subject to the *de jure* approval of the President of Portugal and the *de facto* tolerance of China. In April 1978, while negotiations had begun on the establishment of diplomatic relations between Beijing and Lisbon, the Chinese authorities, acting on a long-standing request of Governor Leandro, invited him to visit several cities (not including Beijing) of the People's Republic. It was the first visit by a Governor of Macau since the Communist revolution but, while interpreted as confirmation of China's acceptance of Macau's present status, the visit was seen in the context of China's overall policy rather than as an endorsement of Leandro himself. Meanwhile, leaders of the Chinese community continued to participate in political events in China, including attendance at the National People's Congress in Beijing in March 1978.

Diplomatic relations with Portugal were established in February 1979 with statements countering ill-founded rumours that Macau's status might be changed. Recognition has been accompanied by exchange visits of junior officials but the full impact of the change has yet to be determined. Macau has negotiated trade agreements with the EEC and, as a member of the GATT Multi-Fibre Arrangement, has agreements with other European countries, but Macau has not as yet attempted to establish itself in any regional associations.

The appointment in 1981 of Commodore (later Rear-Admiral) Vasco Almeida e Costa as Governor was evidence of an unspoken agreement between Beijing and Lisbon not to alter the legal status of Macau. Although the Chinese disapprove of Portuguese colonialism, it is not in their interest to oust the Portuguese, since they rely not only on Macau for trade with the West, but even more so on Hong Kong. Portuguese officials believe that Beijing's policy is to leave Macau alone in order not to alarm Hong Kong about its own future.

ECONOMIC SURVEY

In 1976 Macau's economy recovered fully from the 1974–75 recession but the rate of growth could not be sustained in 1977 and 1978. Although the tourism and construction industries continued buoyant, official statistics suggest that overall industrial production declined. Exports increased by only 4 per cent in 1978 while imports grew by 10 per cent, but a favourable trade balance was nevertheless maintained, and sustained in 1979. Although Macau is a member of the Multi-Fibre Arrangement, the EEC has restricted the annual growth of the territory's textile exports to a maximum of 6 per cent. Many small factories, which had taken advantage of Macau's previous quota position, have closed and textile workers have found employment mainly in the construction industry. Diversification is seen as the solution but, as usual, there are no clear policies on how this could be achieved.

Overall economic buoyancy was reflected in the continued strong position of the Macau pataca and in the increased level of expenditures planned in the 1978 budget. However, few large projects were initiated due to lack of planning approval, continued problems with the electricity supply, and a shortage of water on Taipa and Colôane islands where, since construction of the bridge from Macau in 1974, much of the development planning is focused.

Nevertheless, Macau continues to present an attractive front. Tax reform measures have been passed, the gambling industry is on a sound base, and a Business Centre has been established in the private sector. By 1981 a construction boom was in progress.

Tourism

Despite efforts to diversify the economy, Macau remained heavily dependent on tourism and the related gambling industry, with clientele coming mainly from Hong Kong at weekends. During 1978 an average of 8,095 visitors arrived in Macau daily, a total of 2.95 million for the year. Macau now prefers to calculate its tourists excluding Hong Kong "visitors", but even so the total figure for 1978 exceeded half a million, a 4.5 per cent increase over 1977. Some 38 per cent of tourists came from Japan, compared with 45 per cent the previous year, followed by tourists from the United Kingdom, the U.S.A. and Australia. There is also a significant number of Thai tourists. In 1979 there were 3.7 million visitors to Macau, including 2.5 million Hong Kong Chinese, and the figures for 1980 and 1981 were over 4 million.

There may, however, be more chance for Macau to diversify within this sector. One-day tours to the People's Republic of China, necessitating overnight stops in Macau, had become a regular activity by 1981 and programmes to restore and develop historic Macau offer visitors opportunities for cultural insights perhaps lost in Hong Kong.

In 1976 a new six-year contract was made with the Sociedade de Turismo e Diversoes de Macau (STDM), a syndicate controlling gambling in Macau and its biggest source of income, employing 10,000 people in a wide range of activities including all the big hotels. Under the new contract, which came into effect in June 1976, the syndicate's annual rent to the Government was increased from HK $9 million to HK $30 million and it was also obliged to invest HK $30 million annually in the economy.

The STDM's contribution to the budget may be as high as 30 per cent, while its overall contribution to the economy equals that of the ordinary budget as officially recorded. Efforts are being made to broaden the base of the tourist industry, to encourage longer stays and to bring visitors from overseas to visit the territory's historical and religious monuments. Nevertheless, there are plans for resort developments on Taipa and Colôane, the more modest of which may soon be implemented.

Finance

In April 1977 the link with the escudo was ended and a new parity of HK$1 = 1.075 patacas was established, an appreciation of about 38 per cent. Exporters have been required to surrender 50 per cent of their growing foreign exchange earnings to the official Exchange Fund which therefore had sufficient resources to maintain the value of the pataca, which is now floating with the Hong Kong dollar.

A state-owned Issuing Institute was founded in 1980, taking over the issuing function of the Banco Nacional Ultramarino, which, however, remains the government's banker of the territory.

Trade

Macau's once flourishing gold trade disappeared with the 1974 legalization in Hong Kong and the focus changed to manufactures, which as late as 1969 were virtually confined to fireworks and matches. There has recently been a spillover from Hong Kong industrialists who have established textiles, plastics and other manufacturing enterprises.

The appreciation of the pataca in terms of the escudo and the removal by Portugal of a 30 per cent tax on imports from the territory regularized their trade relations and removed a potential political problem. As noted, the agreement with the EEC on textiles was restrictive and Macau's negotiations with other countries were not encouraging. However, Macau recorded only a small deficit on visible trade in 1980, with exports rising by 36.1 per cent in value while imports increased by 52.9 per cent. Macau had recovered from the 1976 recession but could not be expected to sustain that year's record growth rate of 68 per cent. Exports of clothing and knitwear in 1980 totalled 2,063 million patacas or 75.2 per cent of the total.

Hong Kong continued to be Macau's principal supplier, with the People's Republic of China ranked second. These two countries accounted for some 81 per cent of Macau's imports. In 1976 Macau lost its markets in Portuguese Africa, but in 1977 and 1978 there was a significant revival in its exports to Angola, although they fell slightly again in 1977. Exports to the U.S.A. almost doubled in 1977 and reached almost five times their 1976 level in 1980 (537 million patacas).

Industry and Power

With the emigration of trained professionals and others in unsettled 1974 and 1975, skilled labour is at a premium and the lack of water on the islands reinforces the view that industrial development must now be selective, with government priority for more sophisticated manufacturing such as electronics. The chronic electricity shortage was temporarily solved with the installation of three 15 kW. diesel generators, but the technical problems which delayed the installation of two 25 MW. steam-operated generators have been overcome and they came into operation in late 1978, in the first stage of a long-term development. At least one further 25 MW. generator was due to be installed by 1981 and the STDM's franchise agreement requires annual investment in the electricity company. In March 1981 Macau officials signed an agreement to buy electricity from China.

Industrial production declined in 1977, particularly in the footwear industry, where production fell by 35 per cent. The production of knitwear fell by 2 per cent to 6,840 metric tons and clothing output fell by 12 per cent to 14,368 metric tons. While footwear production continues to fall, the production of knitwear rose to 10,770 metric tons in 1980 and clothing output rose to 21,211 metric tons. The construction industry, however, flourished and in 1978 136 private buildings were completed compared with 93 in 1977. At the end of 1977 there were 29,175 people employed in registered establishments, most of them of the small, traditional type, indicating a source of potential manpower should investment permit the expansion of the modern sector. Macau actively seeks new markets with official trade delegations, but is more selective in attracting direct investment due to the restraints previously discussed.

Development

Ambitious plans have been drawn up, and in some cases contracts signed, for the construction of a container pier, a luxury hotel complex on Colôane, a trotting race course on Taipa, various housing developments, and a new pier at the outer harbour. Port development depends on China's intended use of Macau as an entrepôt for shipments to and from the neighbouring areas of Guangdong, on the development of joint-venture enterprises, which could result in new land reclamation, and on the much-needed industrial diversification. After the initial euphoria it is now recognized that China's enthusiasm for modernization is tempered by an acceptance of financial realities. Local China-controlled interests, the Nam Kwang Trading Company for example, are redeveloping, giving some basis for local optimism.

Other projects await final planning approval, but all are dependent on water. Plans to build or improve the capacity of reservoirs within the territory exist but are limited by geographical and other considerations. Discussions continue on the piping of water from nearby Chinese islands but, more immediately, Macau awaits the completion of a reservoir some

13 kilometres from the Chinese border. The territory could then receive an additional daily supply of 10 million gallons, but piping of this from Macau to the water-starved islands would still have to be undertaken; furthermore the supply from China is not guaranteed, especially in regional dry periods affecting rainfall in all the relevant catchment areas. Progress is undoubtedly being made on some projects, including the more practically conceived hotel and housing complex on Taipa, but press reports are sometimes overly optimistic or confuse statements of intent with the commencement of work.

In August 1979 the Egídio administration announced that it had prepared a land-use plan. The master plan was based on a massive land reclamation scheme which required soil from China. However, none of the feasibility studies was made in consultation with the Chinese, thus undermining the plan's validity. Nevertheless, in March 1980 General Egídio visited China and was able to secure Chinese approval for Macau's two most ambitious projects: its own airport and a first-class road into China. China's agreement to supply more water and to sell electricity to Macau is helping the colony over its most serious development difficulties. China is also to open up 185,806 square metres of land on the frontier with Macau for a large housing project after a similar venture was agreed with Hong Kong.

As a result of the establishment of diplomatic relations between Portugal and China in February 1979 and the subsequent growth of confidence in the territory, there has been a considerable property boom in Macau. Land sold by the Portuguese administration a few years ago to encourage residential development had more than quadrupled in value by 1981. Office rents have escalated, hotels and flats are being built, many of the latter being sold to Hong Kong businessmen. It is clear that the growing shortage of land for development purposes is becoming a serious problem.

Communications

The bulk of Macau's trade must be routed via Hong Kong with transhipment, although satellite container service has already been inaugurated. Some trade takes place directly with the neighbouring counties of Guangdong Province in the People's Republic of China, and considerable local exchange, both of products and of people, occurs. However, the bulk of Macau's visitors arrive from Hong Kong on one of the half-hourly hydrofoils, an augmented fleet of jetfoils, now the world's largest, or the three ferryboat services.

There is continued discussion of a helicopter service from Hong Kong. China's previous hesitation may not now be the final impediment, but the new night jetfoil service could well eliminate the demand for an air service under prevailing conditions. Any major developments would depend on China's determining to use Macau as a major transhipment point in its modernization programme and with special reference to the area between Guangzhou and the Portuguese territory. There is much speculation but as yet no hard information to support more than the vaguest rumours in this direction, but such are nevertheless frequently heard.

Editorial Note: In 1982 Macau's Governor, Rear-Admiral Almeida e Costa, announced his administration's plans for the colony: telecommunications, airport and harbours, housing, textiles and light industry are to be given priority. Some of these plans are already being put into practice, notably the development of Macau's telecommunications network. Plans also include revitalizing the banking sector, with a view possibly to turning Macau into a financial centre.

STATISTICAL SURVEY

AREA AND POPULATION

Area	Population 1970 Census	1981 Estimate
15.5 sq. km.	248,636	350,000

There are between 2,000 and 3,000 Portuguese living in Macau.

	Births	Marriages	Deaths
1977 . .	2,532	786	1,424
1978 . .	2,407	802	1,360
1979 . .	3,019	880	1,504
1980 . .	3,784	1,016	1,555

AGRICULTURE

MEAT PRODUCTION
(metric tons, slaughter weight)

	1977	1978	1979	1980
Cattle . . .	577	648	462	365
Buffaloes . .	482	463	687	820
Pigs . . .	4,853	5,873	7,245	7,825
Total .	5,912	6,984	8,394	9,010

Fishing (1980): Total catch 6,624 metric tons.

INDUSTRY

(metric tons)

	1977	1978	1979	1980
Wine	1,706	1,497	1,187	1,421
Woven fabrics and textiles . . .	34	n.a.	237	359
Knitwear	6,840	6,443	8,567	10,770
Footwear	675	526	467	299
Clothing	14,368	15,109	18,968	21,211
Furniture	463	345	680	1,060
Explosives and pyrotechnic products .	892	876	1,076	816
Optical articles	137	199	253	244
Electric energy (million kWh.)* . .	143.7	158.5	182.5	202.2

* Consumption.

FINANCE

100 avos=1 pataca.
Coins: 5, 10 and 50 avos; 1, 5 and 20 patacas.
Notes: 5, 10, 50, 100 and 500 patacas.

Exchange rates (June 1982): £1 sterling=10.70 patacas; U.S. $1=6.18 patacas.
100 patacas=£9.35=$16.19.

Note: From January 1968 to February 1973 the pataca was valued at 4.80 Portuguese escudos. The exchange rate was U.S. $1=5.990 patacas from January 1968 to August 1971; and $1=5.677 patacas from December 1971 to February 1973. In terms of sterling, the rate was £1=14.375 patacas from January 1968 to August 1971; and £1=14.793 patacas from December 1971 to June 1972. From February 1973 to April 1977 the official exchange rate was 1 pataca=5.00 escudos but the pataca's value in terms of most other currencies was fixed in relation to its rate against the Hong Kong dollar, which was frequently adjusted. In April 1977 the link with the escudo was ended and the currency was tied to the Hong Kong dollar, initially at a parity of HK $1=1.075 patacas. Exchange rates against other currencies are determined by reference to rates against the Hong Kong dollar, which also circulates freely in Macau.

BUDGET

('000 patacas)

Revenue	1980
Ordinary	361,022
Current revenue:	
Direct taxes	132,089
Indirect taxes	86,018
Taxes, fines and other penalties	2,746
Income from property	2,310
Transfers	16,173
Sale of durable goods	12
Sale of non-durable goods and services	14,208
Other current revenue	6,521
Capital revenue:	
Sale of investment goods	25,600
Transfers	388
Financial assets	303
Refunds	400
Transitory accounts	74,254
Extraordinary	125,000
Current revenue:	
Transfers	—
Other current revenue	—
Capital revenue:	
Transfers	55,000
Financial liabilities	—
Other capital revenue	70,000
Total	486,022

Expenditure	1980
Ordinary	7,021
General services	4,292
Civil administration	21,596
Education	50,622
Health and welfare	100,555
Finance	4,868
Economy	10,024
Public works and transport	7,202
Navy	71,466
Security forces	81,628
Other	1,748
Budgetary balance	
Extraordinary	125,000
Total	486,022

CURRENCY IN CIRCULATION

('000 patacas at December 31st)

	1976	1977	1978	1979	1980
Notes	122,645	139,621	159,702	188,420	206,894
Coins	23,437	25,142	27,946		
Total	146,082	164,763	187,648	188,420	206,894

EXTERNAL TRADE

(million patacas)

	1976	1977	1978	1979	1980
Imports (retained)	977.1	1,102.4	1,252.3	1,817.9	2,779.9
Exports (excluding re-exports)	1,146.2	1,221.5	1,302.9	2,014.3	2,741.9

PRINCIPAL COMMODITIES

('000 patacas)

IMPORTS	1977	1978	1979	1980
Pigs	38,855	41,505	51,709	61,910
Eggs	9,661	10,884	11,713	13,951
Fresh fruit	18,733	19,774	81,684	160,348
Rice	24,041	21,187	32,938	38,455
Canned meat	12,229	15,695	26,223	23,142
Tobacco (manufactured)	27,804	32,486	42,682	50,949
Marble	6,206	14,602	7,735	4,351
Cement (incl. clinker)	9,750	12,266	20,749	24,211
Plastic materials	7,279	8,563	10,063	17,210
Carded wool yarn	23,216	14,025	41,410	86,046
Woven cotton fabrics	129,399	161,992	395,635	459,882
Woven fabrics of cellulose fibres	35,853	29,366	46,540	56,685
Clothing	11,040	13,870	23,588	37,387
Passenger cars	13,292	21,859	31,214	50,244
Fuel oil	65,333	64,252	71,800	139,110
Medicines	5,405	5,547	8,429	14,372
Wood, wood products and charcoal	15,159	18,606	31,364	45,274
Paper and cardboard	10,529	9,752	15,207	77,317
Ceramic products	56,999	29,807	50,616	88,330
Casting and soft iron; steel	20,270	25,836	41,634	50,042
Machinery and apparatus	39,342	56,353	105,886	190,680
TOTAL (incl. others)	1,102,437	1,252,358	1,817,891	2,779,922

EXPORTS	1977	1978	1979	1980
Fresh fish	12,570	13,768	5,289	2,724
Shrimps	24,600	23,558	23,200	21,541
Pyrotechnic products	3,427	3,624	3,997	4,162
Leather manufactures	6,181	14,704	21,639	24,976
Woven fabrics of cellulose fibres	10	22	17	43
Knitwear and other made-up goods, elastic, without rubber	399,023	399,270	596,084	882,880
Clothing	577,706	646,312	981,305	1,180,288
Handkerchiefs	20,469	14,763	17,794	22,271
Clothes for bed, table and other domestic uses	45,064	30,947	60,707	110,898
Footwear	4,274	5,520	5,960	5,345
Porcelain ware	14,365	14,994	17,353	24,926
Optical articles	9,147	11,746	14,429	10,542
TOTAL (incl. others)	1,221,518	1,302,905	2,014,302	2,741,987

PRINCIPAL TRADING PARTNERS

('000 patacas)

IMPORTS	1977	1978	1979	1980
China, People's Republic	287,271	330,054	536,058	730,769
Hong Kong	678,914	774,559	929,755	1,520,588
Japan	25,953	40,868	102,325	182,560
Portugal	5,377	3,884	12,416	12,448
United Kingdom	10,830	25,797	37,837	44,608
U.S.A.	30,831	48,021	74,513	113,605
TOTAL (incl. others)	1,102,437	1,252,358	1,817,891	2,779,922

continued on next page]

PRINCIPAL TRADING PARTNERS—*continued*]

EXPORTS	1977	1978	1979	1980
Angola	3,198	3,529	2,635	2,155
Belgium-Luxembourg	31,780	18,495	22,467	30,396
France	192,794	204,968	316,563	422,842
Germany, Federal Republic	240,470	256,207	333,512	511,001
Hong Kong	119,131	146,196	270,172	343,299
Italy	64,077	44,681	95,158	166,327
Japan	19,761	15,606	30,231	37,384
Mozambique	4,016	103	—	—
Netherlands	58,898	45,846	62,840	86,840
Portugal	45,777	35,863	50,683	84,945
Sweden	39,721	27,331	34,598	51,265
United Kingdom	75,951	95,196	169,269	220,688
U.S.A.	209,155	296,869	466,972	537,012
TOTAL (incl. others)	1,221,518	1,302,905	2,014,302	2,741,987

TRANSPORT

ROAD TRAFFIC

(Vehicles in use)

	1977	1978	1979	1980
Passenger cars	7,739	8,845	10,308	12,573
Trucks and buses	1,992	2,247	2,638	3,241
Motor cycles	9,169	9,344	9,332	9,123

SHIPPING

	1977	1978	1979	1980
Vessels entered:				
Number	24,815	24,479	21,311	27,769
'000 g.r.t.	7,151	7,618	8,182	8,252
Freight (metric tons):				
Unloaded	508,915	456,279	566,457	651,519
Loaded	592,368	646,614	780,631	516,370
Passengers:				
Embarked	2,591,544	2,730,556	3,305,102	3,407,461
Disembarked	2,591,510	2,719,852	3,284,688	3,393,413

EDUCATION

(1979/80)

	SCHOOLS	TEACHERS	STUDENTS
Kindergarten	50	307	8,041
Primary	44	787	33,687
Secondary:			
High schools	37	564	12,681
Technical schools (commercial and industrial)	4	20	281
Other*	11	47	1,980

* Including one school of arts and five training schools for public staff.

Schools are run by the Chinese, outside the Portuguese administration. The new University of the Far East, situated in Macau, was inaugurated on March 28th, 1981, and was to admit 500 students in October 1981. There are expected to be 2,000 students by 1984.

Source: Serviços de Estatística, Macau.

THE CONSTITUTION

The constitution of Macau is embodied in an organic statute of Portugal promulgated in February 1976.

Macau, comprising the town of Nome de Deus de Macau (God's Name of Macau) and the Taipa and Coloane islands, has administrative, economical, financial and legislative autonomy.

The sovereign organs of Portugal, except the Law Courts, are represented in the territory by the Governor. In foreign relations and international agreements or conventions, Macau is represented by the President of Portugal who may delegate to the Governor if the matters concern the territory only.

The judicial power is independent and it is regulated by legislation enacted in Portugal.

The Governor

The Governor is nominated after the local population is consulted, through the Legislative Assembly, and dismissed by the President of Portugal, to whom he is responsible politically. He has a rank similar to a Minister of Government in Portugal.

The Secretaries-Adjunct

The Secretaries-Adjunct, up to five in number, are nominated and dismissed by the President of Portugal on the Governor's proposal. Each has a rank similar to a Secretary of State of Government in Portugal.

They exercise the executive powers which have been delegated by the Governor.

The Superior Council of Security

The Superior Council of Security works in conjunction with the Governor who presides over it. It comprises the Secretaries-Adjunct, the Commander, Second-Commander and Chief of General Staff of the Security Forces, and three deputies elected by the Legislative Assembly. Its duties are to settle and to co-ordinate directives relating to the security of the territory.

The Legislative Assembly

The Legislative Assembly comprises 17 deputies with a mandate of three years. Five deputies are appointed by the Governor from among residents of recognized reputation, six are elected by direct and universal suffrage and six elected by indirect suffrage.

The President of Portugal can dissolve the Assembly in the public interest on the Governor's recommendation.

The Consultative Council

The Consultative Council is presided over by the Governor and has five elected members (two elected by the members of the administrative bodies and from among them, one by organizations representing moral, cultural and welfare interests, and two by associations with economic interests; three statutory members (the Secretary-Adjunct for the Civil Administration Services, the Attorney of the Republic and the Chief of Finance Services); and two members nominated by the Governor.

Judicial System

Ordinary justice is administered directly from Portugal.

Under the superintendence of the Attorney of Portugal are the Delegate of the Attorney of the Republic, the Delegation of the Attorneyship of the Republic, the Services of Registries and of Notarial Affairs, the Judiciary Police, and the Cabinet of the Government's Juridical Consultation.

Finance

Macau draws up its own budget, which is annual and unitary.

Money issue is guaranteed through the Issuing Institute of Macau, while the Government's banker of the territory remains the Banco Nacional Ultramarino.

The annual public accounts of the territory must be submitted to the judgment of the Administrative Law Court.

THE GOVERNMENT

(July 1982)

Governor: Rear-Admiral Vasco Almeida e Costa.

Secretaries: Dr. Adelino Augusto do Amaral Marques Lopes (Administration).
Col. Eng. João Manuel Soares de Almeida Viana (Development).
Dr. Jorge Alberto da Conceiçao Hagedorn Rangel (Tourism, Education and Culture).
Dr. João António Morais da Costa Pinto (Economic Co-ordination).
Dr. José Augusto Roque Martins (Social Welfare).

The Cabinet comprises five secretaries who are appointed and relieved by the President of Portugal on the Governor's advice. There is a consultative committee of *ex officio* and nominated members representing the Chinese community.

LEGISLATIVE ASSEMBLY

Seventeen members, five appointed by the Governor, six elected directly and six indirectly, serve for three years.

The Assembly elects its President from among its members, by secret vote.

President: Dr. Carlos d'Assumpção.

POLITICAL GROUPS

There are no political parties but a number of civic associations exist. The three represented in the Legislative Assembly are: the Associação para a Defesa dos Interesses de Macau (ADIM), the Centro Democrático de Macau (CDM) and the Grupo Independente de Macau (GIMA).

JUDICIAL SYSTEM

Courts of First Instance. These administer the Legal Code of Metropolitan Portugal. Cases may be finally referred to the Court of Second Instance and the Supreme Court in Lisbon.

RELIGION

ROMAN CATHOLIC

There are 6 parishes and 3 missions for the 20,000 Catholics.

Bishop of Macau: Most Rev. D. ARQUIMÍNIO RODRIGUES DA COSTA, C.P. 324, Macau.

The majority of the Chinese residents probably profess Buddhism, and there are numerous Chinese places of worship.

THE PRESS

PORTUGUESE LANGUAGE

Boletim Oficial: C.P. 33, Macau; f. 1838; weekly government publication; Dir. ALEXANDRE DA SILVA.

O Clarim: Rua Central 26, Macau; f. 1948; twice weekly; Dir. TOMÁS DA ROSA PEREIRA (acting).

Confluência: Rua Francisco Xavier Pereira, Edificio Vila Verde, Macau; twice monthly; Dir. HENRIQUE DE SENNA FERNANDES.

Democracia em Marcha: Sede do CDM, Avenida da República, Macau; irregular; Dir. JOSÉ DA SILVA MANEIRAS.

Diário de Macau: Infante D. Henrique 37, Macau; f. 1979; daily; Dir. LEONEL BORRALHO.

Luso-Chinês: f. 1978; weekly; Dir. ALBERTINO ALVES DE ALMEIDA.

CHINESE LANGUAGE

Jornal "Va Kio": 7–9 Rua da Alfândéga, Macau.

Ou Mun: Rua Almirante Sérgio, 30–32, Macau.

Seng Pou: Travessa da Caldeira, 11, Macau.

Si Man: Avda. Almeida Ribeiro 107–1°, Macau.

Tai Chung: Rua dos Mercadores, 136–2°, Macau.

RADIO AND TELEVISION

Emissora de Radiodifusão de Macau (*Radio Macau*): P.O.B. 446, Macau; government public service.

Emissora Vila Verde: Rua Francisco Xavier Pereira 123, Macau; private commercial station; programmes in Chinese; Dir. HO YIN.

In 1979 there were 50,000 television sets in Macau. Macau is served by the Hong Kong television stations.

FINANCE

BANKING

(cap.=capital; dep.=deposits; m.=million; amounts in patacas)

ISSUING INSTITUTE

Instituto Emissor de Macau, E.P. (*Issuing Institute of Macau*): Avenida da República 6, Macau; f. 1980; state-owned, issues local currency; Man. Dir. Dr. JOSÉ ANTÓNIO IGLÉSIAS TOMÁS; Gen. Man. Dr. MÁRIO DÚLIO NEGRÃO.

COMMERCIAL BANKS

Banco de Cantão, S.A.R.L.: Rua de Cinco de Outubro 136, P.O.B. 165, Macau; f. 1937; cap. 5m.; dep. 66.1m. (Dec. 1980); Man. C. Y. CHING.

Banco Comercial de Macau, S.A.R.L.: Rua da Praia Grande 16, Macau; f. 1974; cap. 10m.; dep. 180m.; Chair. COLIN STEVENS; Gen. Man. RUI FERNANDO C. DO AMARAL BARATA.

Banco Hang Sang, S.A.R.L.: Avda. Almeida Ribeiro 56 r/c, Macau; f. 1973; cap. 25m.; dep. 194.3m. (Dec. 1981); Chair. AU CHONG KIT STANLEY.

Banco Nacional Ultramarino: f. 1864; est. in Macau 1902; Head Office: Rua do Comércio 84, P.O.B. 2069, 1100 Lisbon; Avenida Almeida Ribeiro 2, Macau.

Banco do Oriente, S.A.R.L.: Avda. da Amizade, Edifício Sintra, P.O.B. 515, Macau; f. 1973; cap. 10m.; dep. 183.9m. (Dec. 1981); Man. Dir. CARLOS A. W. DE MENDONÇA; Gen. Man. AFONSO DELGADO LUÍS.

Banco do Pacifico, S.A.R.L.: 67–67B Avda. da Amizade. Edifício Kam Va Kok, Macau; f. 1974; cap. 10m.; dep. 1,376m. (Dec. 1981); Mans. WONG CHUNG HO, KHOO YEN SENG.

Banco Seng Heng, S.A.R.L.: Avda. Almeida Ribeiro 142, Macau; f. 1972; cap. 5m.; dep. 39.1m. (Dec. 1977); Man. Dir. LOU TOU-VO.

Banco Tai Fung, S.A.R.L.: Avda. Almeida Ribeiro 3 Macau; f. 1961; cap. 20m.; Pres. HO YIN.

Banco Weng Hang, S.A.R.L.: Avda. Almeida Ribeiro 21, Macau; f. 1973; cap. 5m.; dep. 135m. (Dec. 1977); Man. Dir. FUNG YIU-WANG.

Luso International Banking Ltd.: 1 Rua Henrique de Macedo, Macau; f. 1974; cap. 100m.; dep. 462m. (Dec. 1981); Chair. and Pres. GEORGE M. K. LEE.

Nam Tung Bank Ltd.: Avda. Almeida Ribeiro 1, Macau; f. 1950; cap. HK $25m. (Dec. 1977).

FOREIGN BANKS

Banco do Brasil, S.A. (*Brazil*): Rua da Praia Grande 39, Macau; f. 1980; Gen. Man. C. RODRIGUES.

Banque Nationale de Paris (*France*): Rua da Praia Grande 25, Macau; f. 1979; Gen. Man. EDWARD F. KMIEC.

Hongkong and Shanghai Banking Corporation (*Hong Kong*): Apt. 476, Rua da Praia Grande, 2 (Edifício Montepio), Macau; Man. D. E. DA ROZA.

Overseas Trust Bank Limited (*Hong Kong*): Avda. do Infante D. Henrique, 51–53, Macau; Man. DOMINIC K. M. CHEUNG.

There are also seven registered dealers in foreign exchange.

INSURANCE

The following Portuguese companies are represented in Macau:

Companhia de Seguros Bonança, E.P.: Agents: H. Nolasco & Cia. Ltd., P.O.B. 223, 20 Avda. Almeida Ribeiro, Macau.

Companhia de Seguros de Crédito, E.P.: Rua da Praia Grande 41-41d-r/c-D; Dir. MANUEL ESTEVAO.

Companhia de Seguros Império: Rua de P.N. Silva, 43-1-A; Dir. FERNANDO ANTUNES.

Companhia de Seguros Tagus, S.A.R.L.: Agents: F. Rodrigues (Suc. Res.) Lda., Rua da Praia Grande 71, P.O.B. 2, Macau.

TRADE AND INDUSTRY

CHAMBERS OF COMMERCE

Associação Comercial de Macau: Pres. HO YIN.

Associação dos Exportadores de Macau: Pres. Union Trading.

Associação Industrial de Macau: Travessa da Praia Grande 11-1; f. 1959; Pres. PETER PAN.

Associação das Agências de Turismo de Macau: Pres. PEDRO HYNDMAN LOBO.

TRANSPORT

ROADS

There were approximately 90 km. of roads in 1981. In the same year plans were announced for the building of a 240-km. toll road linking Macau with Guangzhou (Canton) and Shenzhen, near Hong Kong.

SHIPPING

There are representatives of shipping agencies for international lines in Macau.

Hydrofoils, jetfoils and ferry-services operate a regular service during daylight between Macau and Hong Kong; a jetfoil night service was introduced in 1980.

TOURISM

Direcção dos Serviços de Turismo: Travessa do Paiva 1, P.O.B. 461, Macau; Dir. Dr. MARINHO DE BASTOS; there were 4,719,612 visitors to Macau in 1981; publs. *Macau Travel Talk* (monthly).

Gabinete de Comunicação Social (*Government Information Services*): Rua da Praia Grande 31-10E, C.P. 706, Macau; Dir. BELTRÃO COELHO; publs. *Sábado* (weekly magazine), *Macau* (bimonthly), *Anurário de Macau* (Yearbook).

DEFENCE

The official Portuguese garrison has been replaced by the *Comando de Forças de Segurança* (Comforseg) of 1,800 men, which consists of a paramilitary force of about 150 men and the fire brigade and the police force. Military service lasts for one year and is voluntary only for Chinese residents.

BIBLIOGRAPHY

BOXER, C. R. The Portuguese Seaborne Empire (Hutchinson and Co., London, 1969).

BRAGA, J. M. Macau: a Short Handbook (Department of Information and Tourism, Macau, 1970).

O primeiro acordo Luso-Chinês (Macau, 1939).

The Western Pioneers and their Discovery of Macau (Macau, 1949).

CLEMENS, J. Discovering Macau, A Visitor's Guide (Macmillan, Hong Kong, 1972).

COATES, AUSTIN. A Macao Narrative (Heinemann Educational Books (Asia) Ltd., Hong Kong, 1979).

DA SILVA, E. T. A Brief Guide to the Macau Economy (Macau Business Centre, Macau, revised annually).

GOMES, L. G. Bibliografia Macaense (Imprensa Nacional Macau, 1973).

JESUS, C. A. MONTALDO DE. Historic Macau (Salesean Printing Press, Macau, 1926).

JONES, P. H. M. The Golden Guide to Hong Kong and Macau (Far Eastern Economic Review, Hong Kong, 1969).

LJUNGSTEDT, A. An Historical sketch of the Portuguese Settlements in China (Boston, 1936).

LOBO, P. J. Bases e Processos da Economia de Macau (Macau, 1953).

MACAU, GOVERNMENT OF. Anuário de Macau (Centro de Informação e Turismo, Imprensa Nacional, Macau, annual).

Anuário Estatístico (Serviços de Estatística, Imprensa Nacional, annual).

NG, ELIZABETH. (ed.) Directory of Research on Asian Topics 1977, with an Appendix on Macau (Centre of Asian Studies, Hong Kong, 1977).

WESLEY-SMITH, P. "Macao" in Albert P. Blaustein, ed. Constitutions of Dependencies and Special Sovereignties, Vol. III (Oceana Press, New York, 1977).

Malaysia

PHYSICAL AND SOCIAL GEOGRAPHY

C. A. Fisher

(Revised for this edition by HARVEY DEMAINE)

Malaysia covers a total of 330,433 square kilometres (127,581 square miles), comprising Peninsular Malaysia, with an area of 131,587 square kilometres (50,806 square miles), and Sarawak and Sabah, in northern Kalimantan (Borneo), with areas of, respectively, 124,449 square kilometres (48,050 square miles) and 74,397 square kilometres (28,725 square miles).

While Peninsular Malaysia, Sabah and Sarawak lie in almost identical latitudes between 1° and 7° N. of the Equator, and have characteristic equatorial climates with uniformly high temperatures and rain at all seasons, there is nevertheless a fundamental difference in their geographical position. For Peninsular Malaysia forms the southern tip of the Asian mainland, and on its western side, facing the sheltered and calm waters of the Straits of Malacca, flanks one of the oldest and most frequented maritime highways of the world, whereas Sabah and Sarawak lie off the track of the main shipping routes, along the northern fringe of the remote island of Kalimantan.

PHYSICAL FEATURES

Structurally, both parts of Malaysia form part of the old stable massif of Sunda-land, though whereas the dominant folding in the Malay peninsula is of Mesozoic age that along the northern edge of Kalimantan dates from Tertiary times. In Peninsular Malaysia the mountain ranges, whose summit levels reach 1,200–2,100 metres (4,000–7,000 ft.), run roughly north to south and their granitic cores have been widely exposed by erosion. The most continuous of these is the Main Range which over most of the peninsula marks the divide between the relatively narrow western coastal plain draining to the Straits of Malacca, and the much larger area of mountainous interior and coastal lowland which drains to the South China Sea.

Because of the much greater accessibility of the western lowlands to the main sea-routes, and also of the existence of extensive areas of alluvial tin in the gravels deposited at the break of slope in the western foothills of the Main Range, the strip of country lying between the latter and the western coast of Peninsular Malaysia has been much more intensively developed than the remaining four-fifths of the country. For although tin has long taken second place to rubber, the planting of the latter became concentrated in the vicinity of the roads, railways and other facilities originally developed in connection with the former. In contrast to the placid waters of the west coast, the east coast is open to the full force of the N.E. monsoon during the period from October to March, and the difficulties which this situation has presented to small craft have reinforced the remoteness of the eastern side of the peninsula from the main stream of commercial activity.

In many respects Sabah and Sarawak display similar basic geographical characteristics to eastern Peninsular Malaysia, but in a more extreme form. Thus, the lowlands are mostly wider, the rivers longer and even more liable to severe flooding, the coastline is exposed to the N.E. monsoon and avoided by shipping, and the equatorial forest cover appears even denser and more continuous than that of the peninsula. Moreover, while in general the mountains of Sabah and Sarawak are of comparable height to those in Peninsular Malaysia, there is one striking exception in Mount Kinabalu, a single isolated horst which towers above the Croker Range of Sabah to an altitude of 4,101 metres (13,455 ft.).

NATURAL RESOURCES

Malaysia is endowed with an extremely rich natural resource base. The country's tin deposits may still be the largest in the world, following the discovery of further large reserves in reservation land at Kuala Langat, and the Peninsula has small deposits of iron ore and other minerals. As further surveys have been carried out and as accessibility has improved, moreover, significant deposits of minerals are being shown to exist in East Malaysia, with copper mining already established in Sabah and bauxite and coal discovered in Sarawak.

East Malaysia's main wealth remains, however, the coastal and off-shore deposits of hydrocarbons. Petroleum production from the original Miri field, in onshore Sarawak, has now ceased, but discoveries off-shore in the 1960s have maintained production. Some 90,000 barrels per day (b.p.d.) now derive from the Sarawak coast, mainly from the West Lutong and Baram fields, while some 70,000 b.p.d. are being produced from the Sabah coastal zone. More recently, however, the focus has shifted to the waters off the east coast of Peninsular Malaysia, where new discoveries have raised the estimates of reserves to some 2,500 million barrels. The petroleum is complemented by natural gas deposits now estimated at 850,000 million cubic metres, mainly in the West Lutong field off Sarawak (170,000 million cubic metres) and off the coast of Trengganu.

Until the rise of petroleum, Malaysia's main economic resource has been the agricultural potential of the Peninsula. This derived not so much from the inherent superiority of its soils—indeed, those of Sarawak and Sabah are similar—but rather from its accessibility for commercial enterprise. Rubber and, more recently, oil palm have flourished in this environment, although both are again showing some expansion in the eastern wing, particularly in Sabah, which to date has relied heavily upon its vast wealth in tropical timbers, which currently make Malaysia the world's largest exporter.

POPULATION AND CULTURE

The total population of Malaysia at the 1980 census was 13,435,588, of whom 11,138,227 were in Peninsular Malaysia, giving it an average density of 102.1 per square kilometre, 1,002,608 were in Sabah (13.5 per square kilometre) and 1,294,753 in Sarawak (10.4 per square kilometre).

However, the difference in density is not the only difference in the populations of the two wings of Malaysia. In Peninsular Malaysia the indigenous population, apart from some 50,000 or so primitive animist peoples, consists of Muslim Malays, though these form only 54 per cent of the total population, which also includes 35 per cent Chinese and a further 10 per cent Indians (an ethnic term which applies to people from India, Pakistan or Bangladesh). In Sabah and Sarawak, on the other hand, Malays and other Muslim peoples are confined mainly to the coastal zone while various other ethnic groups occupy the interior. Nevertheless, there is also a large Chinese element, amounting to 30 per cent of the 1979 estimate in Sarawak and 18 per cent of the 1978 figure for Sabah, so that in Malaysia as a whole Malays constituted 47 per cent, Chinese 33 per cent, Indians 9 per cent, Borneo indigenes 9 per cent and others 2 per cent of the population in 1977.

Finally, the contrast between the two parts of the country shows up most sharply of all in respect of urbanization, for while Peninsular Malaysia has at least ten towns of over 50,000 people (including Kuala Lumpur, the national capital, which had a population of 451,986 in 1970), Sarawak has only one, namely Kuching, the capital (with a population of 63,535 in 1970), and the largest town in Sabah is not the capital, Kota Kinabalu (formerly Jesselton, whose population was 41,061 in 1970), but Sandakan (42,249).

HISTORY

J. M. Gullick

The state of Malaysia was established as recently as 1963 but its long history is a significant factor in its present situation. In prehistoric times it was populated by successive waves of migrants from the north. On the arrival of the Malays about five thousand years ago the earlier settlers retreated to the remoter highland areas where they are now represented by small groups of aborigines who still live mainly as hunters and collectors. The first Malays developed a simple agriculture on the lowland and riverine areas. Because of its position across the sea route from India to the Far East, the Malay Peninsula was always exposed to contact with foreign traders but their influence was felt on the coast and at the northern isthmus of Kra (part of modern Thailand) and it did not penetrate to the uninhabited interior. The northern part of Borneo was more isolated but subject to the same factors to a lesser extent. In the first millennium of the Christian era contact with India introduced to the Malay culture a number of elements of Indian civilization, including the Hindu religion. At this time there was a series of kingdoms in South-East Asia whose economy was based on trade rather than agriculture. In the area of the Straits of Malacca the centre of power shifted in the fifteenth century from the east coast of Sumatra to Malacca where a Malay Sultanate was established about A.D. 1400. Malacca was the last and one of the greatest indigenous kingdoms of South-East Asia and its traditions shaped the Malay States of later centuries.

THE MALAY POLITICAL SYSTEM

Malacca began as an offshoot of another centre of power. According to the "Malay Annals", a classic of Malay literature, a Malay prince from Tumasik (the modern Singapore) established himself at Malacca, then an obscure and unimportant area, at the beginning of the fifteenth century. The new port flourished mightily; its earliest rulers were converted to Islam through contacts with traders from India and the Persian Gulf; they also sent trade missions to the imperial court of China to secure recognition.

The Sultans of Malacca were drawn from a patrilineal royal dynasty and combined in their office attributes of indigenous South-East Asian, Hindu and Islamic royal prerogatives and symbolism. In the government of the state the Sultan was assisted by high officers, to whom were given titles such as Bendahara (Chief Minister), Temenggong (Minister of War and Police) and Shahbandar (Minister of Ports and Trade). These officers were drawn from families of aristocratic but not royal pedigree though, on occasion, the Sultans took wives from these families. Inevitably, there was intrigue and competition for power but the ruling aristocracy as a whole was a caste set above and apart from their subjects. Unlike its successor states Malacca was essentially a centre of power based on regional and foreign trade. To the port of Malacca came traders from other parts of South-East Asia such as Acheh in northern Sumatra and the Celebes, and also merchants from India, the Middle East and China. Their common purpose was to sell the cargoes which they had brought and to purchase from others cargoes for the return voyage. The half-yearly change of prevailing winds under the monsoon climate made this inflow and outflow possible and predictable. The polyglot population of the thriving port was administered through headmen appointed from the main groups. Malacca had influence over many lesser ports on both sides of the Straits but did not possess a territorial empire. The rural population was sparse and agriculture of secondary importance. In its last decades Malacca was weakened by conflict within the ruling class and by disputes with the foreign traders who filled the town. The disaffection of the latter contributed to the fall of Malacca to the Portuguese.

PORTUGUESE, DUTCH AND BRITISH INTERVENTION

Now that the colonial period in South-East Asia fades into historical perspective it can be seen as "the Vasco da Gama Epoch of Asian History" (the sub-title of K. M. Pannikar's *Asia and Western Dominance*). It was an episode prolonged and important but less decisive than perhaps it once seemed in shaping modern South-East Asia. The main effects of European control were, firstly, to break the sequence of indigenous kingdoms and to disrupt the trade system upon which they had been based; secondly, to delimit colonial spheres of influence and thereby to fix the subsequent boundaries of the national states which are heirs to colonial rule; and lastly to promote economic development and establish the infrastructure of government and other services which that development required; mass immigration from India and China was an incidental consequence of economic development. However, the culture, institutions, values and traditions of the region persisted even in a context of alien cultural and political domination.

First of the European powers to attempt to dominate the region were the Portuguese who came to Malacca as traders in 1509 and as aggressors in 1511.

The seventeenth century saw the arrival of the Dutch as the leading European trading power in South-East Asia. In 1641 Malacca fell to the Dutch and their Johore Malay allies. Although Malacca was always an important link in Dutch communications and trade, the main centre of their power was further east in Java. The Dutch pursued the same objectives as the Portuguese before them but by more methodical and systematic means. By diplomacy and the show of force they endeavoured to control the trade of the region. Like the Portuguese, they encountered much resistance and evasion. In particular during the early years of the eighteenth century the Dutch came into conflict with the Bugis, a people from the Celebes who for centuries had sailed their ships on trading voyages through the narrow seas of modern Indonesia and Malaysia.

The Bugis were to play a prominent part in the Malay resistance to the Dutch but they were latecomers. On the fall of Malacca to the Portuguese in 1511 the Malacca dynasty removed itself to the southern tip of the Malay peninsula and founded the kingdom of Johore. But the rulers of Johore, harassed during the sixteenth century both by the Portuguese and by the Achehnese of north Sumatra, could never regain the wealth and power of their Malacca predecessors. They were, however, the recognized successors of Malacca. In northern Malaya a branch of the same dynasty had established itself in Perak, destined later to be the major tin-producing area of the peninsula; other Malay states emerged in the north and east; in northern Borneo the long domination of the Malay rulers of Brunei had begun. But these were scattered centres of power lacking a common leadership and sense of purpose. The Bugis leaders took control of the weak and divided Johore, reducing its Malay rulers to puppets and installing themselves as "under kings". Further north in the mid-eighteenth century Bugis established settlements on the west central coast of Malaya and eventually became Sultans of a new State of Selangor. Their attempts to establish a similar hegemony of the small states between Selangor and Malacca were resisted, however, under the leadership of Malay Rajas invited over from the Menangkabau region of Sumatra; thus began the Negri Sembilan confederacy. There had been an offshoot of the Johore dynasty on the Pahang River since the sixteenth century and, further still up the east coast, the Malay States of Trengganu and Kelantan were within the sphere of influence of Siam. The modern pattern of the peninsular Malay States was emerging but the intervention of European powers prevented any coalescence of Malay States into a confederacy or centre of power without providing an effective European integration of the area.

In the latter part of the eighteenth century Dutch power waned; the British, victorious in India, turned eastwards to South-East Asia and in particular to trade with China. During the period of the Napoleonic War, Malacca and then Java passed temporarily from Dutch to British control and Stamford Raffles, with his vision of an imperial mission, made his appearance. In the settlement which followed the war, maritime South-East Asia was in effect divided by the Anglo-Dutch treaty of 1824 into two spheres of influence. Britain took or retained the island of Penang (first acquired from Kedah in 1786), Malacca and also Singapore (acquired from Johore in 1819). These three positions along the west coast of Malaya formed the Straits Settlements; the hinterland of the Malay Peninsula as far north as the undetermined southern boundary of Siamese influence was also within the British sphere. There was also some ambiguity over the line of division in Borneo but in the event James Brooke in Sarawak and the Borneo Company in modern Sabah acquired substantial parts of the territories of the Sultanate of Brunei as the century went on.

Information is fragmentary on the condition of the Malay States as they entered the period of British influence and eventual direct control. Until 1874 it was the object of British policy to avoid involvement in the Malay States; there was no systematic reporting on their condition. Some common features can, however, be discerned. None of the States was a major centre of trade or production; without the essential sinews of public revenue the rulers tended to impotence. The Malay population of the entire peninsula was probably well below half a million and of that total a considerable part was in the Siamese sphere of influence to the north and east. The population was dispersed in small villages along the coasts and up the rivers. The villagers lived by rice cultivation, fishing and the collection of jungle produce such as rattans, gutta percha, sago and fruit. Effective power was in the hands of district chiefs drawn from the ruling aristocracy. The chief might bear some title of office in the Malacca tradition such as Temenggong or Shahbandar but the duties of the office no longer existed. His position was that of a medieval baron ruling his fief rather than that of an officer of a royal government. When the office of Sultan fell vacant the ensuing struggle for power might lead to civil war and similar competition arose over the remunerative position of district chief. Along the west coast of the Malay peninsula mining of alluvial tin deposits was becoming the most important source of wealth. From about 1830 mining passed from Malay to Chinese control since the immigrant Chinese were better organized for sustained and large-scale operations. The expansion of Chinese tin mining drew in considerable numbers of labourers imported from China under arrangements made by Chinese merchants in the ports of the Straits Settlements. First Lukut (now in Negri Sembilan), then central Selangor and the Larut tinfields of Perak attracted Chinese in their thousands for lucrative but laborious and crude mining operations. Thus the multi-racial society of western Malaya had its real beginning though, until well into the twentieth century, most of the Chinese were temporary immigrants who eventually returned to China. The expansion of tin mining in the nineteenth century had two significant effects on the Malay States. First, competition for the right to work the most productive tinfields led to fighting between rival groups of Chinese organized under "secret society" leadership and also between Malay rulers and chiefs whose tax revenues increasingly came from this source. Secondly, commercial interests in the Straits Settlements, including some European as well as Chinese entrepreneurs, became involved in mining investments in the western Malay States and were accordingly at risk on the outcome of local struggles for power. These conflicts threatened the whole political and economic stability of the western Malay States in the 1860s and early 1870s. The official British policy of non-intervention came increasingly under pressure by interested parties. Elsewhere in eastern Malaya and northern Borneo the absence of these economic stresses permitted a more stable situation to continue.

Apart from the objective of non-involvement in the Malay States, British policy also required that no foreign power should intervene in a territory which stood at the "back door" of the Straits ports. In the second quarter of the nineteenth century the main concern of the British authorities in the Straits Settlements was to hold in check Siamese aspirations to extend or consolidate their suzerainty in north-western Malaya. In mid-century there was growing concern among the merchants in the Straits ports about the continuing viability of their position. In its earliest period Singapore had attracted trade from far afield. The establishment of Hong Kong in 1842 and the appearance of the French and Spanish in Indo-china and the Philippines shut out Singapore in the north of the region. Nearer home the Dutch were consolidating their hold on what was to become the Netherlands East Indies and in so doing introducing mercantilist policies to the detriment of Singapore trade. There were fears also that Germany, a formidable competitor and a growing imperial power, might intervene in the British sphere. These factors, added to the increasing impracticability of maintaining peace in the Malay States by remote control, led to demands for a "forward policy" which would bring the economically most important parts of the peninsula under direct British control. In northern Borneo there was at the same time a completely separate but bitter rivalry between Sarawak and the Borneo Company over claims to what remained of the territories of the Sultan of Brunei.

British policy changed abruptly at the end of 1873. Within a few months the troubled and economically important States of west-central Malaya had come under a British protectorate. It was the first step in a sequence of events which was to bring the entire peninsula under direct British rule.

BRITISH RULE IN THE MALAY STATES

The basis of British administration in the Malay States was to be found in the key passage of the Treaty of Pangkor, 1874, whereby, under the Residential system, British rule was exercised through British Officers, whose advice must be asked and acted upon by the Malay States in all matters other than those touching Malay religion and custom. In the circumstances of the Malay States in 1874, this was unworkable and the British attempted then to exert a stronger rule in the Malay States. Resentment against British rule led to disturbances in Perak, Selangor and Negri Sembilan and to a Malay revolt in 1875. Nevertheless, the Residential system became the basis for British administration until the Second World War. The Residential system was extended from Perak to Selangor, Negri Sembilan and Pahang and together they formed the Federated Malay States (F.M.S.) in 1896.

There remained two zones of Malaya outside the sphere of British rule. The four States of Kedah, Perlis, Kelantan and Trengganu in the north were within the Siamese sphere of influence. Though the British were anxious to extend northwards to carry their boundary up to the narrow Kra Isthmus, Anglo-French rivalry in and around Siam prevented the achievement of this policy. However, by 1909, the European differences were resolved and the four northern States accepted British advisers but did not enter the centralized administration of the F.M.S., i.e. they became known as the Unfederated Malay States (U.M.S.). Johore remained independent and avoided becoming a formal protectorate until 1914 when some defects in local administration resulted in the acceptance of a permanent British Adviser in Johore. With this, the unification of the Malay peninsula under British rule was complete.

Under the British, the Malay political system was preserved though there were minor modifications. The basic framework of political power was maintained though the Sultans and the chiefs felt the loss of national dignity and the forced obedience to law. But the Malay ruling class was reconciled to the Residential system by the scrupulous insistence of the British advisers in distinguishing between the constitutional basis of power and executive control. The Residential system meant government in the name of the Sultan of the State. In addition to the consultative machinery of the State Councils, the early British residents conferred with the Malay rulers, and treated them with due deference as royalty. The unemployed or frustrated aristocrats were converted into civil servants. Malay chiefs were appointed to the honorific sinecure of "Malay Magistrates" in the districts. The young generation of Malay aristocrats was given English education, the main purpose of which was to train them for appointment to the administrative branch of the civil service. The local headman (*Penghulu*) became the main instrument of rural government and was essentially a government servant with a host of administrative chores. Also, the British devised inexpensive means of governing the Malay peasant class. Local police forces were raised to keep order and the police rank and file were recruited almost entirely from the Malay peasantry.

British rule in the Straits Settlement and the Malay States encouraged the immigration of non-Malay communities, particularly the Chinese, into Malaya. By 1921, the Chinese in Malaya numbered 1.2 million, and they formed more than 50 per cent of the total population in Selangor and Perak. At the apex of the Chinese community were the relatively small number of wealthy Chinese merchants in the major ports who financed tin-mining in the Malay States and who imported their countrymen from China to work in the mines. The institutional framework which embraced the community was the "secret society", at one time the dominant form of association among the Malayan Chinese. The secret society provided them with welfare services, economic management, local government and leadership but it also enabled the merchants to dominate, intimidate and exploit the immigrants.

The British administrators were unable to cope with the problems presented by the secret societies primarily because they did not understand the language and customs of the Chinese. An attempt to solve the problem was the establishment of the Chinese Protectorate in 1877, staffed by officers who could speak Chinese. A further move was made in 1889 by the enactment of a Societies Ordinance, which outlawed the secret societies. But though their political power was broken, remnants of the secret societies persisted as undercover criminal organizations. Later, Chinese nationalism in the form of the Kuomintang replaced the secret society as the *imperium in imperio* of the Malayan Chinese community.

NATIONALISM AND PLURALISM

The creation of the State Council was the first move in the evolution of the Malay States towards constitutional monarchy and representative government. It provided contact between the Chinese and the Anglo-Malay regime and was a step towards the acceptance of the non-Malays as Malayans. However, the transfer of power from the States to the new federal executive of the F.M.S. in 1895 deprived the State Councils of their usefulness and it left them merely to approve proposals handed down to them from a federal secretariat. Subsequently, the establishment of a Federal Council for the F.M.S. in 1909 was an attempt to restore the balance. When the Council was enlarged in the 1920s to take in Malay unofficial members, it became a political body in which the force of public opinion could be mobilized on local issues to influence the federal bureaucracy. From 1925, various measures of decentralization were proposed, designed to restore to the State governments of the F.M.S. some of the powers and functions which they had lost. Nominated Malay unofficial members of aristocratic status were included in the Federal Council. However, the concept of a larger federation proved unattainable and this was the position until 1941.

The Straits Settlements were governed under a Crown Colony system. There were no Malay rulers and therefore no Anglo-Malay dyarchy. Between the World Wars the educated members of the Chinese and Eurasian communities were admitted to the administrative service but on terms inferior to those of British members. Demands for an elected unofficial majority in the local legislatures of the Straits Settlements were dismissed on the ground that the majority of the population were transient aliens who showed no interest in their government. The U.M.S. remained essentially Malay States in the political sense, subject to British influence rather than control.

The existence of the various communities with conflicting interests and different viewpoints prevented the emergence of a united nationalist movement in the period up to 1942. To the Malays the colonial regime was a bulwark against the economic strength and sheer numbers of the immigrant communities. The Chinese and Indians were preoccupied with their own material interests and in the political developments of their ancestral homelands. Moreover, the Malay aristocracy, which still commanded the loyalty of the mass of the peasantry, was distrustful of the minority of the Malay religious and social reformers. The Chinese middle class gave its support to the Kuomintang (KMT), an externally orientated nationalist movement, but the KMT was circumscribed both by British restrictions on its activities and the communist penetration of the working class.

Under the British there was an intensive Malay preoccupation with Islamic affairs; a new establishment of religious officials appeared both in the capitals and villages. Steamer services made possible the pilgrimage to Mecca to a greater number of the peasantry and they brought back the ideas prevalent in the Middle East of reinvigoration of the Islamic peoples through religious reforms. The Malay upper class and the new religious "establishment" opposed such ideas as dangerous. In the period between the two World Wars incipient Malay nationalism took on a secular form and lost its pan-Islamic flavour. This was attributed to the presence of some Indonesian nationalists in the late 1920s and the emergence of a politically conscious group among the Malays. At this time, the Sultan Idris Training College was the main forum of Malay intellectual discussion. It produced an articulate generation of village schoolmasters together with a minority of left-wing political activists. Together with the English-educated Malay civil servants, the Malay society was acquiring a new middle stratum which included the village headmen, the Islamic clergy, landowners, the schoolmasters and the retired civil servants.

The first Malay communal body of a semi-political character was the Singapore Malay Union formed in 1926; in the Straits Settlements the Malays were a small minority without the protection of being subjects of a Malay ruler but they were better educated and more sophisticated than their rural brethren. In the Malay peninsula between 1937–39 local bodies sprang up under the leadership of Malay public figures and senior civil servants. The first pan-Malayan conference of local Malay associations was held in 1939. They were the origin of the Malay national party after the war. At the same time, the pan-Malaysian left-wing group formed the Union of Young Malays (*Kesatuan Melayu Muda*—KMM). The anti-British tone of the KMM resulted in their leaders' arrest under defence regulations in 1940.

In the 1920s the Kuomintang government of China extended its influence among the overseas Chinese in order to gain financial support from the latter. In their drive for members and contributions among the Malayan Chinese, the local KMT leaders enlisted the support of the old secret societies and until 1927 they admitted communists to the party. The effect of these KMT activities was to spread among the immigrant Chinese a sense of national solidarity in opposition to European rule. After the split in 1927 within the KMT, the communists broke away to form in April 1930 the Malayan Communist Party. The third group among the Malayan Chinese community was the small but influential group of Straits Chinese. Through the Straits Chinese British Association they sought recognition of their position as a Malayan-domiciled community. They had Western education and experience in the consultative procedures of government. The renewed Japanese attack on China in 1937 evoked strong patriotic feelings which the MCP was able to exploit, and this brought about the rapprochement between the MCP, KMT supporters and the government.

Up to 1942, the forces of tradition in Malaya were rather stronger than in many other Asian countries then under colonial rule. The British regime managed a satisfactory accommodation both with the aristocratic leaders of the Malay community and the influential Chinese merchant class. There was no educated middle class in revolt against these forces. With the important exception of the MCP, no radical or left-wing group had achieved significant influence with the mass of the people. The status quo, however, was upset by the Japanese defeat of the British, which altered the balance between conservatism and change.

THE INDEPENDENCE OF MALAYA

This flow of change led Malaya to eventual independence. The Japanese victory in 1942 and the ensuing occupation (1942–45) was both a traumatic and a catalytic experience. The British had failed to defend the country from foreign attack; their credentials as the protecting power were destroyed. Each of the major communities looked forward to some new regime in which there would no longer be a British umpire between them. Yet relations between the communities deteriorated owing to Japanese discrimination. The Japanese encouraged Malay and Indian nationalism so long as they could harness it to their own war effort; they encountered resistance from the Chinese led by the communist Malayan People's Anti-Japanese Army (MPAJA). In these years when British policy-makers were cut off from Malaya the British Government became committed to two new objectives for Malaya. First, it was necessary to complete the territorial unification of the whole Malay peninsula (excluding Singapore which was regarded as a distinct and special problem); the second objective was to put all the communities on an equal basis, thus abandoning the distinction between the indigenous Malay population and the other communities with their recent history of immigration and their existing links with the countries of their origin. As soon as the Japanese surrender of September 1945 reopened communications the new plan was promulgated in the form of a "Malayan Union", a unitary State in which the Malay States and their sovereign Malay Rulers would lose all title to constitutional identity; all persons who had made Malaya their home (by various tests of local birth, residence or parentage) were to be citizens of the new state regardless of their origin. The high-handed manner in which these reforms were introduced added to the deep Malay resentment and dislike of the whole concept of the Malayan Union. Opposition galvanized the nascent Malay political associations into the immediate formation of the United Malay National Organization (UMNO) which since 1946 has been the dominant Malay communal party and since 1956 the main government party in office. In face of this opposition the British Government withdrew its Malayan Union proposals and negotiated a Federation of Malaya with the Malay Rulers and political leaders. The Federation (established on February 1st, 1948) was still a union of the whole peninsula (including the former Straits Settlements of Penang and Malacca but not Singapore) under a strong central government. But it also recognized the continued sovereignty of the Malay Rulers in their States and preserved what came to be called the "special position" of their Malay subjects as the indigenous people of the country with appropriate rights.

The Chinese and other non-Malay communities had had no part in these Anglo-Malay negotiations. Their opposition to the Federation of Malaya was predictable but ineffectual. In part this was because the opposition group comprised every element of opinion from conservative to communist but it lacked political organization. The Chinese were less interested in political matters than the Malays; indeed many did not yet fully identify themselves with Malays rather than China as their homeland. If they continued to follow a constitutional path of co-operation or moderate opposition they were unlikely to secure the equality with the Malays which the shortlived Malayan Union had offered them. Many were therefore tempted to follow the more extreme leadership of the Malayan

Communist Party (MCP) which at this time was a legal and important political organization. The MPAJA as the military wing of the MCP had led Chinese opposition to the Japanese and in 1945 it was still an effective cadre with arms prudently dumped in jungle hideouts. The communist victory in China in 1949 further increased the prestige of the movement as the expression of Chinese nationalist feeling—for the same reason communism made little appeal to the Malays. To follow communist leadership was for the Malayan Chinese to commit themselves to extreme policies and to isolate themselves from co-operation with the Malays. The communist leadership itself was sharply divided on the choice of strategy to adopt, i.e. whether to take full advantage of its high standing with non-communist bodies and manipulate a "united front" for communist purposes or whether, following the example of Mao Zedong (Mao Tse-tung), to launch a direct military attack as a bid for power, beginning from the periphery and moving in to the centre of power at the end.

In 1948 the choice was made of the second alternative and so began the long struggle known in Malaya as "the Emergency". In this campaign small bodies of armed communists operating from jungle hideouts made raids and laid ambushes designed to destroy government control of the remoter parts of the country which were to become "liberated areas" and bases for further extension of communist control. The raiders were much assisted by the supplies and information provided, from fear or loyalty, by Chinese "squatters" settled along the fringe of the jungle zone. After several years of intense effort by numerically superior security forces, the resettlement of squatters in "New Villages" where they could be protected and controlled, and the development of a much improved intelligence system, the government was able to destroy much of the communist forces and to drive the remainder into refuge on the inaccessible border zone between Thailand and northern Malaya. As the communist movement cut itself off by open resistance from the mainstream of legal political activity the main body of the Malayan Chinese grouped itself with some hesitation behind the Malayan Chinese Association (MCA), whose leaders were drawn mainly from the world of Chinese business, traditionally the spokesmen of the community. In 1956 the MCP had the opportunity of negotiating a settlement with the new Alliance Government but lost it by asking for too much. The Emergency was formally ended in 1960.

In 1952 the leaders of UMNO and MCA entered into an "Alliance" (to which the Malayan Indian Congress (MIC) was later admitted). Thus a limited coalition of moderate leaders of the three major communities prepared the way for self-government. Throughout the period 1948–56 there was a wholly nominated central legislature (the Federal Legislative Council) in which appointed unofficial members (in fact chosen on the advice of political and other representative bodies) outnumbered but rarely outvoted the government official members. The British High Commissioner was advised in his function of head of the government executive by an Executive Council in which from 1950 onwards certain quasi-ministerial responsibilities were discharged by Malay, Chinese and Indian leaders. It was an embryo cabinet based on a dyarchy in which power was shared between local leaders and the British authorities. In the States there were somewhat similar arrangements under which the Malay Ruler acted as a constitutional monarch and executive power was exercised by a Malay Chief Minister (with slight modifications in the former Settlements of Penang and Malacca). The qualifications for citizenship admitted virtually all Malays and a majority of the adult non-Malay population (on criteria of local birth, parentage, residence and proficiency in the Malay language). The first elections held in 1955 to choose members of the federal and state councils, yielded an overwhelming victory to the Alliance which won 51 out of 52 seats in the federal council and a majority in nine out of eleven state councils. In the ensuing twenty years it has at all times had a similar preponderance. A new constitution whose complexity reflected the issues of inter-communal relationships was introduced. In 1957 the government, which had had powers of internal self-government since 1955, assumed the powers of a fully independent state. The first Prime Minister was Tunku Abdul Rahman, President of UMNO and architect of the inter-communal Alliance coalition. His deputy and eventual successor (in 1970) was Tun Abdul Razak.

Apart from its unsuccessful attempt to come to terms with the MCP the new Alliance government tackled a number of other difficult issues. The Malayan education system was reorganized with a view to the greater integration of the different community schools and the more extended use of the Malay language. Much effort and money was put into a "rural development" programme, and also the opening up of new land for settlement; both were designed to improve the economic position of the Malay community whose sense of their own weakness as compared with the Chinese was one of the basic causes of inter-communal tension. British civil servants, who at independence held two-thirds of the senior posts, were phased out and replaced by local men.

FORMATION OF MALAYSIA

In the late 1950s the future of Singapore was a matter of increasing concern to the Malayan Government. In the reconstruction after the war Singapore had been excluded from the newly united Malaya because it was felt that Singapore with its preponderance of Chinese population and its concentration of economic power would upset the delicate communal balance in Malaya. Accordingly, Singapore progressed as a separate state by stages to a system of elected legislature and internal self-government (in 1956). But Singapore showed itself politically unstable; its economic survival as a separate state was doubted at this time (wrongly as later events have shown). The Malayan Government came to the view that its own problems of Sino-Malay relations would be eased rather than aggravated if Singapore joined the Federation on terms which gave it reduced representation in the federal parliament but extended local powers of government (as compared with the Malay States). Participation on these terms was welcomed by the People's Action Party (PAP) Government of Singapore headed by Lee Kuan Yew. The British Government, which shared power in Singapore in uneasy partnership with the PAP, also welcomed the scheme and proposed that its remaining territories in northern Borneo, i.e. Sabah and Sarawak (Crown colonies since 1945), and the protected state of Brunei should also join the enlarged federation. To the Malayan Government it seemed—over-optimistically as it turned out—that the Borneo territories with their agricultural populations, some of whom were Malay or at least Malay-speaking Muslims, would fit easily into the enlarged state and counterbalance Singapore. There was considerable opposition from Indonesia and the Philippines (*see* below "International Relations") but Malaysia was formed in September 1963 to include the eleven States of Malaya, Singapore, Sarawak and Sabah. Brunei at a late stage decided to stay out.

Indonesia then attempted by military means ("Confrontation") to bring down the new and enlarged state but failed. Following the fall from power of President Sukarno a reconciliation was effected in 1966. Singapore proved a disturbing influence on the internal politics of Malaysia as its slogan of "Malaysian Malaysia" afforded a rallying point for those who opposed the Malay predominance in the political system. In August 1965 Singapore was compelled to withdraw from Malaysia as its government saw no other way of avoiding severe communal friction. Relations between the central government of Malaysia and the State governments of Sabah and Sarawak also proved difficult but here the disparity of power led to the supersession of local opponents by more accommodating State governments.

EVENTS SINCE 1965

The ending of Confrontation, the withdrawal of Singapore and the settlement of disputes in northern Borneo seemed to afford to Malaysia a period of calm and progress. The country had continued to make satisfactory economic progress; its internal government machinery was working reasonably well; the Alliance government had been re-elected in 1964 with a larger majority than it had obtained in the previous elections of 1959. Inter-communal friction has largely been avoided through a compromise, based on the understanding that over a period of time the Malays are to have a greater share in the economy of the country and the Chinese are to move nearer to equality of political rights, i.e. the "special rights" of the Malays are to be diminished. The delicate balance of this compromise seemed to be in danger in the election campaign of May 1969, when it appeared that the MCA was losing ground among its Chinese electorate to parties disposed to demand a more rapid end to Malay predominance. Malay anxiety at this trend was increased by provocative behaviour. In the end there was serious rioting in which it is believed that several hundred people lost their lives.

In this crisis the constitution was suspended for over a year while the government framed measures to remedy the situation and to prevent recurrence of the disorder. It was at this point that Tunku Abdul Rahman, whose anguish at the disaster had impeded his ability to deal with it effectively, gave way to Tun Abdul Razak as Prime Minister. The Sedition Act was amended to prohibit any public advocacy of changes which would diminish the sovereignty of the Malay Rulers, which since the withdrawal of the Malayan Union in 1947 has been the sheet anchor of the Malay position, or reduce the special rights of the Malays and (in Borneo) other indigenous groups and the citizenship rights of any ethnic group. As an essay in more positive nation building a written National Ideology (*Rukunegara*) was submitted to Parliament for approval. These principles included belief in God, loyalty to King and country, respect for the Constitution, the rule of Law and good behaviour and morality. The next five-year economic development plan (1971–75) included a twenty-year objective, to be attained by 1990, of raising the ownership by indigenous communities (*bumiputra*) to at least 30 per cent of national wealth. In the political sphere the old Alliance coalition was widened to absorb most of the former opposition parties into a National Front. The purpose here was presumably to harness the energies of the opposition to constructive aims and to bring disputes within the framework of a political coalition rather than let them find expression in open conflict. The two opposition parties (since 1978) are the Democratic Action Party (DAP), which is a radical movement drawing support mainly from the Chinese electorate, and Partai Islam (PI—formerly PMIP), which, as the name suggests, is a partly Islamic movement which appeals to the more conservative element of the Malay rural electorate. Neither could ever combine with the other and so there is no alternative government to replace the ruling NF regime. The latest federal elections (held in April 1982) increased still further the preponderance of the NF in the House of Representatives. The risks to which the NF is, as before, exposed are fission within the coalition or its individual parties and popular discontent if the remarkable momentum of economic growth should slacken in the present world recession.

Dr. Mahathir Mohamad took over as Prime Minister in July 1981; he had previously been deputy leader. He first came to notice as a controversial backbencher in the crisis of 1969. On becoming Prime Minister, he soon imprinted his personal ideology on government policy. Its main feature is a more forceful drive to bring foreign, especially British, enterprises in Malaysia into Malaysian ownership. This policy requires that these businesses shall come under *bumiputra* (i.e. Malay rather than Chinese) control. Mahathir rejects the tacit "special relationship" with Britain which was maintained by his predecessors. He therefore instituted a policy of positive discrimination against British firms in the award of government contracts. He sees the economic future of Malaysia in closer association with other Asian countries such as Japan (and, of course, the ASEAN group).

INTERNATIONAL RELATIONS

Malaysia has been a significant factor in South-East Asia, being the focal point in the international politics of the Straits of Malacca area since the 1950s. As a primary producer and a developing country, Malaysia was oriented very much towards the United Kingdom and the rest of the Commonwealth for trade and assistance. Between 1948 and 1960 and again between 1963 and 1966, when Malaysia was faced with the threats of local communism and Indonesian aggression, it had to rely on the British, Australian and New Zealand military power to deter them successfully.

Malaysia's general orientation in foreign policy until 1970 was one of alliance with the Western Powers and opposition to the Communist bloc. Hence Malaysia supported the United States' involvement in Viet-Nam and became a member of the anti-communist group, the Asian and Pacific Council. It had no diplomatic relations with any communist countries, including the Soviet Union and the People's Republic of China. Within South-East Asia, Malaysia attempted to initiate regional co-operation and was able to establish the Association of South-East Asia or ASA with Thailand and the Philippines in 1961. Two years later, Malaysia, together with the Philippines and Indonesia, formed Maphilindo. But these groupings were aborted primarily due to the conflicts in the area, and manifestations of these were seen in the hostile policies of the Philippines and Indonesia toward Malaysia; the Philippines pursued a claim over the Malaysian territory of Sabah, and Indonesia wanted the break-up of the federation.

A shift in Malaysia's foreign policy occurred in 1970. International developments, such as the Western military withdrawal and the détente within the South-East Asian region, resulted in a re-examination of the efficacy of the policy of alignment. The British decision to withdraw east of Suez and the American decision to reduce its land forces in Viet-Nam reflected the trend towards a new international order in East Asia. The subsequent re-emergence of China and Japan as the additional power-centres in the region was another decisive factor. Within the region, Malaysia negotiated the end of the Indonesian Confrontation, effected the resumption of diplomatic relations with the Philippines and accepted the independence of Singapore. The Malaysia-Philippines dispute over Sabah was eventually resolved but Malaysia-Singapore relations continued to become strained from time to time.

Malaysia's foreign policy during the 1970s was based on regional co-operation within the framework of the Association of South East Asian Nations (ASEAN), founded in 1967 by Malaysia, Indonesia, the Philippines, Singapore and Thailand to replace ASA. Such modest progress as ASEAN has made has been mainly in the field of economics; it is not a military defence group, but it has represented its members' political solidarity in opposing the Vietnamese occupation of Kampuchea. There is a programme of industrialization on a regional basis which makes only slow progress. Negotiations with the developed nations and associations such as the EEC are conducted by ASEAN as a group. Amid the welter of inconclusive international discussion of commodity stabilization schemes, Malaysia has been able to promote a considerable advance towards achieving a stabilization scheme for natural rubber. Malaysia is, of course, the world's largest single producer of natural rubber.

In 1974 Malaysia established normal diplomatic relations with the People's Republic of China. There is apparently a mutual understanding that China will not seek to interfere, as the KMT regime used to between the wars, in the delicate process of Sino-Malay adjustment in Malaysia. The developments of 1941–45 showed to what extent maritime South-East Asia can be threatened by events in the area which now comprises Kampuchea, Laos and Viet-Nam. The massive flow of refugees, mainly ethnic Chinese, from Viet-Nam which began in late 1978 persisted during 1980–81. However, Malaysian external policy, like that of its ASEAN partners, continues to be dominated by the instability of the Indo-China region which, to some extent, represents the conflict of interests between the U.S.S.R. and China in the region.

ECONOMIC SURVEY

Linda Seah (based on an essay by Helen Moody)

Malaysia, with an estimated G.N.P. per capita of M$3,902 at current prices in 1981, has one of the highest living standards among the developing countries in Asia. In 1981 its real G.N.P. was sustained at a relatively favourable rate of 7 per cent, compared with 8.6 per cent in the previous year and 8.5 per cent in the Third Malaysia Plan period (1976–80). The country is basically rural, with a 1980 population of 13,435,588, of whom 82.9 per cent lived in Peninsular Malaysia, 9.6 per cent in Sarawak and 7.5 per cent in Sabah. Between 1957 and 1970 the urban proportion of Peninsular Malaysia's total population increased only slightly, from 27 to 29 per cent. Since 1970 urban growth has been much faster, and the urban population in 1976 was about 32 per cent of the total. In Sarawak and Sabah the proportion of rural inhabitants is higher, consisting of hunters as well as peasants.

The Malaysian economy is highly dependent on agricultural exports and in 1981 the sector contributed 23 per cent of the G.D.P. and employed about 2,100,000 people or 39.6 per cent of the working population. The agricultural sector remained the leading source of export earnings, although its share of total export receipts had been declining steadily, from 55.8 per cent in 1977 to 42.8 per cent in 1981. The sector also accounts for the highest incidence of poverty in Malaysia. A major aim of recent Government five-year plans (discussed in detail below) has been the implementation of programmes and projects in the agricultural sector with the aim of redressing this poverty and spreading the increases in the G.N.P. much more widely into the rural areas. The incidence of poverty in households in Peninsular Malaysia declined from 49.3 per cent in 1970 to 29.2 per cent in 1980. The Fourth Malaysia Plan (FMP) for the period 1981–85 optimistically projects that this figure will fall to 15 per cent by 1990.

The Malaysian export-based economy is also highly dependent on the mining sector, notably tin and, increasingly, petroleum. The manufacturing sector, which stagnated in the early 1970s, was the focus of considerable attention in the Third Malaysia Plan (TMP), 1976–80. One of the major problems facing the Malaysian Government in recent years, in common with the governments of most developing countries, has been rising rates of unemployment and underemployment, particularly in Peninsular Malaysia, where unemployment in 1981 was 5.2 per cent, and a major aim of government economic planning is to reduce this unemployment rate.

AGRICULTURE, FORESTRY AND FISHING

Export Sector

Malaysia has traditionally relied on its export products, particularly rubber, although the composition of exports is changing. Growth in exports was more rapid during the 1976–80 period, when it expanded by 9.4 per cent per annum, compared with the rate of growth of 5.9 per cent per annum during 1971–75. The stronger growth during 1976–80 was brought about generally by the higher export volume of all commodities except tin. Commodity exports also benefited from higher world prices, so that exports in current prices grew at the rate of 18.6 per cent during 1971–80. Export demand will continue to be the major factor determining growth.

Rubber. Malaysia is the world's leading producer of natural rubber, with an estimated 2,030,700 hectares planted with rubber trees in 1981. Peninsular Malaysia accounted for 84.5 per cent of the total area. Rubber has been the mainstay of the economy since British colonial times and, although acreage has been declining and production has stagnated in recent years, rubber is expected to remain the main export earner for some time, although other resources are beginning to challenge its pre-eminence.

The huge rubber acreage is concentrated on the west coast of Peninsular Malaysia, with the bulk occupied by rubber smallholders and a small portion by rubber estates. The declining acreage has been largely in the plantation sector, due to the better returns obtainable from palm oil and other crops, difficulties in recruiting adequate labour in the estate sector, as well as the disincentive posed by declining prices and sluggish international demand in the face of escalating costs. On the whole, rubber production in Peninsular Malaysia declined by 0.8 per cent to 1,474,000 metric tons in 1981, while output in Sabah and Sarawak fell by 22.7 per cent and 22.9 per cent to 23,800 and 27,200 tons respectively. The decline in rubber output occurred in both the estate and smallholding sectors. Production on estates fell by 3.8 per cent to 598,300 tons in 1981, while smallholder output declined by 0.4 per cent to 926,700 tons. The entire fall in output in the smallholding sector reflected the fall in production in Sabah and Sarawak since production by smallholders in Peninsular Malaysia increased marginally. For the country as a whole, output by the smallholding sector continued to predominate, accounting for 60.8 per cent of total production. The average yield on smallholdings was smaller than that for estates, the main reasons being low productivity and the inadequate size of the holdings. Export receipts from rubber in 1981 declined by 19.7 per cent after five successive years of growth, reflecting both the fall of 2.8 per cent in export volume as well as depressed prices, the export unit value having declined by 17.3 per cent during the year. Nevertheless, rubber continued to be the nation's second largest export earner, although its share of total export receipts was reduced to 14.4 per cent from 16.4 per cent in 1980.

A major challenge for the Government is to improve the income of smallholders and estate labourers, who are amongst the poorest groups in the country. It was estimated that in 1975 rubber smallholders represented 28 per cent of the total households in poverty in Peninsular Malaysia and that 234,000 rubber smallholding households were below the officially established poverty line. Since these households represent a potential political, as well as an economic problem, an important element of the TMP and FMP is to improve their condition. The principal means of reducing this poverty is seen as accelerated replanting with high-yielding stock, and replanting grants for rubber smallholders were raised in October 1980 and January 1981. But, lacking the advantage of economies of scale, advanced technology, efficient management, large capital resources and a well-developed infrastructure, the progress of smallholders is likely to be slow.

A major problem for the Government is that of ensuring sufficient rubber supplies to meet growing world demand in the face of declining acreage and output. This is being attempted largely through replanting and some chemical stimulation of trees. Another major problem in the past was the constant and sometimes extreme fluctuations in rubber prices, which resulted in the initiation of both a national and an international price stabilization scheme. The persistent decline in rubber prices during the year is reflected in poor sales, due to global recession, especially the sharp downturn in the automobile and tyre industries in the major industrial countries. Other contributory factors include inadequate support by the International Natural Rubber Organisation (INRO), of which Malaysia is a member, and the difficulties of getting the International Natural Rubber Agreement into force definitively. Rubber, then, remains the mainstay of the economy, but with increasing diversification and higher returns now being provided by other crops, the industry is not without some problems.

Palm Oil. Since the early 1960s, when the Government first attempted to diversify agriculture away from rubber, palm oil production has increased spectacularly. Unlike rubber and timber, palm oil weathered the 1974/75 recession and played a key role in balancing the budget, due to favourable price trends and a steady growth in the volume of exports, so that the share of palm oil and palm kernel oil rose to 12.4 per cent of total value added by agriculture in 1975, third only to rubber and sawlogs.

The total area cultivated with oil palm stood at an estimated 1,059,900 hectares at the end of 1981, an increase of 7.7 per cent over 1980's area. Of this total oil palm area, 89 per cent or 942,600 hectares were in Peninsular Malaysia, while Sabah and Sarawak accounted for the remaining 117,300 hectares. Output of crude palm oil in Peninsular Malaysia in 1981 rose by 10.5 per cent to 2,647,200 metric tons, to account for a higher share (93.7 per cent) of total output. In contrast, output in Sabah and Sarawak declined by 0.1 per cent and 6.0 per cent respectively during the year.

As in previous years, the increase in both output and area planted with oil palm reflected mainly new planting by the various land development agencies, especially the Federal Land Development Authority (FELDA) which is the largest single producer of palm oil. In 1981, production by FELDA rose by 12.3 per cent to 663,600 metric tons, compared with a much higher rate of 28.3 per cent in 1980. By the end of the year, FELDA had developed a total of 352,800 hectares, representing about one-third of the total area planted with oil palm in the country. Many of the new oil palm estates were converted from old rubber estates. Malaysia became the world's largest producer of palm oil in 1972, supplying nearly one-half of the total world output. As in rubber production, Peninsular Malaysia accounts for the bulk (90 per cent) of palm oil output.

With favourable weather conditions, additional hectares of harvested area and improved yields, output of crude palm oil rose by 17.4 per cent to 2,824,200 metric tons in 1981. Since 1975 the Government had intervened in the industry to broaden its emphasis from planting and exporting crude palm oil to producing, refining, manufacturing and selling oil-based products. In line with the continued emphasis of the Government to process further crude palm oil into more downstream products, domestic consumption of crude palm oil continued to increase in 1981 by 10.5 per cent to 2,698,200 metric tons to account for 95.5 per cent of the total palm oil production in the country. For export receipts from oil palm products, comprising crude and processed palm oil as well as palm kernel oil, growth increased by 7.9 per cent, the only major agricultural commodity to record a growth in export earnings during the year. As in 1980, the increased earnings were entirely due to the higher export volume since the unit value continued to decline. With the increased earnings, export receipts from palm oil products accounted for 12.2 per cent of total export proceeds in 1981, compared with 10.4 per cent in 1980. Palm oil remained the third largest earner of foreign exchange (after petroleum and rubber), having replaced sawlogs since 1980.

The major buyers of processed palm oil from Malaysia continued to be India, Singapore and Pakistan, which accounted for 17.8, 17.6 and 8.9 per cent respectively in 1981. During the year, Pakistan re-emerged as the largest buyer of refined palm oil, followed by the EEC, India and the U.S.S.R. For palm kernel oil, the two major buyers in 1981 continued to be the U.S.A. and the Netherlands.

Malaysia remains concerned that consumer countries, particularly the U.S.A., will impose import restrictions. The sector is also expected to be unfavourably affected as overall world demand for oils and fats slackens with lower growth rates in the populations of industrialized countries. Considerable emphasis has therefore been placed on research to improve both the quality and the end uses of the oil. Another growing concern has been the realization that palm oil development has possibly moved too fast at the expense of rubber, coupled with the recognition that, as rubber is considerably more labour-intensive, the shift to oil palm has added to unemployment problems, particularly among Indian estate labourers.

Forestry. Timber production is an increasingly important sector of the economy, especially in Sabah, from where logs accounted for 65.7 per cent of total export receipts in 1981. The Government is concerned both to increase the value of timber exports and to broaden the export market, and to encourage the greater use of timber in the domestic market. Hence, many projects under the TMP encourage the greater use of timber, particularly for the construction of low-cost housing. Output of sawlogs expanded at 1.6 per cent per annum during 1971–75 and 5.2 per cent per annum during 1976–80, giving an annual average growth of 3.4 per cent for the decade. In 1981, production of sawlogs increased by 4.9 per cent to 29.3 million cubic metres, compared with a growth rate of 1.6 per cent in 1980. In Sabah, output expanded by 29.4 per cent to 11.7 million cubic metres, reflecting higher production associated with the clearing of forests for agricultural development. As a result, Sabah's share of the total sawlog output in the country rose from 32.5 per cent in 1980 to about 40 per cent in 1981. In contrast, production declined by 11.1 per cent to 9.3 million cubic metres in Peninsular Malaysia, owing mainly to the depletion of timber resources and the Government's forest conservation policy. As a result of rapid rates of exploitation and export of sawlogs in past years, the wood products industry had suffered a shortage of logs, which led to a gradual restriction on the export of logs, commencing in 1972, and the adoption of a National Forest Policy in 1978 for the orderly and effective management and utilization of forest resources. Efforts at forest conservation have also been undertaken in Sabah and Sarawak in recent years. To encourage reafforestation, the Government introduced various tax incentives in 1980. However, the timber industry was badly hit in 1974 and 1975 by a large drop in prices, resulting in cut-backs in production. In 1976 the renewed demand for timber led to shortages of timber for processing, but 1977 was a bad year. Export earnings from sawlogs and timber rose sharply in 1979, but declined in 1980. The decline in export earnings accelerated in 1981, with an overall drop of 12.2 per cent to M$3,493 million during the year, compared with a decline of 5.7 per cent in 1980. The lower export receipts reflected the sharp decline in prices, although the volume of exports was also depressed by the continued slack in building and construction in major industrial countries, particularly the U.S.A. and Japan.

Japan remained the largest buyer of sawlogs, accounting for more than one-half of the total export volume. Singapore and the EEC remained the two largest markets for Malaysia's sawn timber, accounting for 28.8 per cent and 27 per cent respectively of the total volume of sawn timber exports in 1981.

Concern over the rate of forest exploitation is also linked with the likely adverse effects on timber supply, water resources, soil conservation and wild life. In 1981, plans to reafforest land which had been logged continued to be actively pursued to ensure an adequate supply in the future. At the current rate of exploitation of about 373,100 hectares per year, Malaysia could well run out of prime logs by 1990. A new comprehensive programme of reafforestation to meet the country's anticipated timber requirements over the next 15 years is expected to be implemented by 1982.

Subsistence agriculture

The principal subsistence crop in Malaysia is rice although fishing is an important occupation in coastal areas, and hunting an important activity among the indigenous people in the inland of Sarawak and Sabah. The bulk of rice production is from irrigated paddy fields, and is concentrated in Peninsular Malaysia, estimated in 1981 to have produced 86 per cent of the total rice output (2,010,100 metric tons), while Sarawak and Sabah supplied the rest. In 1981, paddy production declined in Peninsular Malaysia, Sabah and Sarawak by 0.6, 6.6 and 1.6 per cent respectively to 1,727,700, 95,300 and 187,100 metric tons.

At independence in 1957 Malaysia imported 45 per cent of its rice requirements, and since then there has been a continued drive for rice self-sufficiency. Since independence vast resources have been spent on drainage and irrigation projects, the introduction of double-cropping and high-yielding varieties of rice, and the Government's Guaranteed Minimum Price Scheme to achieve self-sufficiency. In 1981 78.5 per cent of domestic needs were met, compared with 88.5 per cent in 1980. Thailand provided three-fifths of Malaysia's total imports with the balance supplied mainly by the People's Republic of China and the Philippines. The total area planted with paddy in 1981 was 766,300 hectares, of which 97 per cent was wet paddy. Paddy production on the whole has increased owing to continued favourable weather conditions, the more intensive application of fertilizers under the Government's fertilizer scheme and the greater use of high-yielding varieties of paddy. Double-cropping has also been practised.

Malaysian post-independence rice policy has pursued an income redistribution goal along with that of self-sufficiency. It can be argued that, while self-sufficiency is being approached, the net redistributive gain of the programme, although positive, has probably not been large. Next to rubber smallholders, paddy cultivators remain the largest group in poverty in Peninsular Malaysia. The incidence of poverty among paddy farmers declined only marginally from 77 per cent in 1975 to about 74 per cent in 1978. One cause of this poverty is the small size of holdings: about 55 per cent of all holdings are under three acres and 80 per cent are under five acres, whereas the TMP estimates that an owner-operated double-cropped holding of between 3 and 4 acres is needed if a poverty-line income is to be earned. Other causes of such poverty are the lack of drainage and irrigation facilities for double-cropping and low yields (despite the enormous expenditure to extend these facilities), and the prevalence of tenancy.

A large part of paddy production in Sarawak, and to a lesser extent in Sabah, is hill or dry paddy. Sarawak has about 70 per cent of the country's dry paddy. Such paddy is grown as a subsistence crop by shifting indigenous cultivators. Because of low yields the incidence of poverty amongst this group is particularly high.

Despite Government policy, there is evidence that many resulting benefits have accrued to the wealthier part of the rural community, the landlords and the large farm operators. It is argued that major land reform is the only solution to large scale poverty amongst farmers. However, government efforts, in the form of aid and subsidies for farmers, continue. The maintenance of government subsidies on rice prices is regarded as necessary, since rice production in Malaysia is very price responsive. The Government increased the minimum paddy or support prices in 1979 and 1980. The encouragement of resettlement on public land schemes is another aspect of government policy, in order to increase the size of holdings.

Other farming activities

Fishing, livestock, horticulture, cocoa and coconut production are still small, although they are regarded as having a potential for the diversification of the agricultural base, and the promotion of mixed farming. Production of these minor agricultural crops, including marine fish landings, showed a mixed performance in 1981. Only outputs of cocoa and coconut oil and landings of marine fish increased during the year, while other minor crops recorded lower output levels. Despite the persistent decline in world prices, production of cocoa beans continued to expand sharply, particularly in Sabah, and the returns continued to be favourable compared with other crops. Pepper is a significant export crop, 95 per cent of total output being exported, and 90 per cent of it being grown in Sarawak, with the remainder in Johore in Peninsular Malaysia. Pepper output, however, continued to decline in 1981 because of depressed prices, causing many smallholders to abandon their harvests.

Under the FMP, the two-pronged approach for agricultural development through *in situ* and new land development will continue. During 1981–85 agricultural value added is projected to grow at a rate of 3 per cent per annum and to continue to decline in its contribution to G.D.P. to 17.8 per cent in 1985. A more integrated approach towards agricultural development has increasingly been adopted and a national agricultural policy is envisaged under the FMP. The agricultural programmes are to meet the objectives of the New Economic Policy (NEP) and to enable the rural population to enjoy the basic infrastructure and essential services which were not previously available.

MINERAL, FUEL AND POWER RESOURCES

Tin

Tin used to be one of the twin pillars of the Malaysian economy, together with rubber, and second only to rubber as a foreign exchange earner. Now it has fallen behind timber and petroleum. In 1977 it was also superseded by palm oil. Most tin is produced in the west coast states of Perak and Selangor, with the dredges still owned largely by Europeans, although the gravel pump mines are increasingly owned by Malaysians.

Malaysian production of tin still constitutes about 32 per cent of total world output and 60 per cent of world trade in the metal. Tin production was severely hit by the 1974–75 recession and began to increase only in 1978. Production of tin-in-concentrates declined over the period 1970–75 while the export value of tin increased only slightly over the same period. Some 100 marginal mines were closed down during the recession period. Mine production of tin concentrates fell from 76,833 metric tons (metal content) in 1972 to 58,703 tons in 1977 (its lowest level since 1962), and mining and quarrying's share of the G.D.P. fell from 5.7 per cent in 1970 to 4.0 per cent in 1975. Output of tin-in-concentrates in the TMP period (1976–80) fell at an average annual rate of 0.9 per cent. Gravel pump mines as a group accounted for 55.5 per cent of the total production of 59,900 metric tons in 1981, while dredges accounted for 29 per cent. The total number of gravel pump mines in operation declined by 153 to 593 by the end of 1981, while the number of dredges in operation increased by six to 60. With the closure of gravel pump mines, the number of persons employed in the tin mining industry fell by 3,800 to 35,200, representing 1.7 per cent of total employment at the end of 1981. The industry faced serious problems in 1981, with rising costs of machinery and energy and the rapid depletion of high-grade tin-bearing areas. Mines continued to be compelled to install equipment with greater capacity in order to work the lower grade areas. The Government had tried to boost the industry in the period 1978–81 by giving concessions with respect to the tin export duty and the tin profits tax. However, continuing depletion is the main problem unless new commercial ore deposits are found.

Petroleum

While Malaysia still plays only a small part in world petroleum production, crude oil has emerged as the second largest export earner (after rubber) since 1976. The rapid expansion in the production of crude oil, which rose at an average annual rate of 33.6 per cent in the period 1976–78, caused the high growth rate of the whole mining sector of 11.0 per cent per annum, exceeding the TMP target of 5.7 per cent per annum. In 1978 average daily output was 229,000 barrels, compared with 96,000 barrels in 1975. In 1980, however, for the first time since the sharp expansion of production in the 1970s, output of crude petroleum declined by 2.6 per cent to 100.6 million barrels, or the equivalent of 275,000 barrels per day. This reflected the implementation of the National Depletion Policy in June 1980, aimed at slowing down the rate of exploitation in order to conserve crude oil reserves. In 1981, output of crude petroleum declined further by 6.4 per cent to 258,100 barrels per day, reflecting both the slack international oil situation and the Government's oil conservation policy. Of the total production, 42.9 per cent was from Peninsular Malaysia offshore fields while Sabah and Sarawak accounted for 37.7 and 19.4 per cent respectively. Active exploitation for oil and gas continued to be conducted off the coasts of both West and East Malaysia. In 1981 an additional oilfield offshore of Sabah commenced production, bringing the total number of producing fields to 16. The number of wells drilled declined from 103 in 1980 to 97 in 1981. Export receipts from crude petroleum rose by only 3.3 per cent to M$6,911 million in 1981, mainly because of the dampening impact of softening crude oil prices. As in previous years, Japan, the U.S.A. and Singapore continued to be the major buyers of crude oil, accounting for 38, 36 and 11 per cent respectively of total crude oil exports.

Other minerals and quarrying

Other minerals which are exported include copper, bauxite and iron. Bauxite and iron ore production and exports declined substantially over the Second Plan period and prices stagnated. However, in May 1975 the Mamut copper mine in Sabah, jointly operated by Japanese and Malaysians, started operations and produced 20,900 metric tons of copper. This mine holds estimated reserves of 77 million tons with a 0.61 per cent copper content. On reaching the planned full production level at the mine, the output of copper concentrates increased from 13,300 tons in 1975 to 113,000 tons in 1980. In 1981, production of copper concentrates reached 120,400 tons, while export receipts amounted to M$162 million. Bauxite production, which had been declining continuously since 1974, increased sharply in 1980 by 138.1 per cent to 920,400 metric tons, while bauxite export receipts rose by 47.8 per cent to

M$19.8 million, owing largely to increased overseas demand, particularly from Japan. In 1981, however, production of bauxite declined by 14 per cent to 791,900 metric tons. Iron ore production has declined substantially since the closure of mines in Trengganu and Pahang in 1970. As a consequence of declining output and stagnant prices, the value of production decreased from M$198 million in 1970 to M$9 million in 1981. Export receipts for iron in 1981 amounted to only M$2 million.

Being very capital-intensive, the mining sector provides little employment. The whole mining and quarrying sector accounted for only 1.7 per cent of total employment in 1981. Ownership of share-capital in the sector continues to be mainly held by foreign interests, although the Government gives preference to Malaysians in the granting of mineral rights. During the FMP period (1981–85), value added in the mining sector is projected to grow by 5.8 per cent per annum, generating 2,300 jobs.

Gas and electricity

Large commercial deposits of off-shore natural gas have been discovered off Sarawak and off the coast of Peninsular Malaysia. Reserves have been estimated at 17,000,000 million cubic feet. In mid-1976 deliveries of liquefied natural gas from Sarawak were approximately one million cubic metres a day to Japan. Public supplies of electricity are provided mainly by the National Electricity Board, and are generated mainly by thermal stations. Energy consumption in 1971–80 grew an at annual rate of 9 per cent. The demand for electricity in Peninsular Malaysia showed an annual rate of growth of about 12.7 per cent over the same period. Under the FMP, a comprehensive national energy policy is being formulated and the main targets include the reduction of the country's dependence on petroleum for electricity generation and an increase in the coverage of electricity supply to rural households.

INDUSTRY AND INVESTMENT

Although, like most developing countries, Malaysia at independence had only a rudimentary manufacturing industrial sector, Chinese entrepreneurship and a vigorous encouragement of foreign private investment led to a rapid growth of the sector during the 1960s and early 1970s, so that by 1975 the sector contributed 14.4 per cent of the G.D.P., with the value of manufactured exports reaching M$2,100 million, or 20 per cent of export revenue.

Since 1960 the manufacturing sector has been a major source of growth and, since the Second Plan, industrial development has been given a central role in the overall development as well as a source of greater employment opportunities for the Malays. Until the late 1960s the strategy of import substitution was used, which changed to one of export-orientation and resource-based industries to use rubber, timber and palm oil processing, electronics and textiles, in particular, as the basis for expansion. Peninsular Malaysia, especially the states of Perak and Selangor, accounts for about 90 per cent of manufacturing output in the country. The manufacturing sector became the leading growth sector in the economy, with its share of the G.D.P. rising from 12.2 per cent in 1970 to 16.4 per cent in 1975 and 19.0 per cent in 1978. It contributed about 28.6 per cent of the output growth in 1978. Over the period 1976–78, value added in the sector grew in real terms by 14.3 per cent per annum, exceeding the whole Third Plan period's target of 12.0 per cent per annum. The year 1976 was the best for growth, as 1977 and 1978 saw some slackening of external demand conditions and protectionist tendencies in the industrialized countries. Manufacturing output in 1980 increased by only 12.1 per cent, compared with 15.5 per cent in 1979. In 1981, output growth in the manufacturing sector slackened to 6 per cent in response to a general softening in domestic, as well as overseas, demand.

The Third Plan envisaged that employment opportunities in the sector would grow at a rate of 7.4 per cent per annum. This was exceeded during the period 1976–78, when employment grew by 9.4 per cent per annum from 448,000 jobs to 587,300 jobs. This represented 29.4 per cent of the total new jobs created. Labour productivity grew by 4.5 per cent per annum over the same period. Despite the slowdown in 1980–81, the manufacturing sector continued to generate the largest number of new jobs in the economy. In 1981 employment in the sector rose at a slightly lower rate of 5.8 per cent (6.4 per cent in 1980) to account for 16.2 per cent of total employment.

While not as buoyant as in 1979, the increase in manufacturing output in 1980 and 1981 continued to be broadly based, although the growth rates for many industries moderated. The slowdown in manufacturing output was most pronounced in those branches of industry which engaged in off-estate processing and in the production of electrical machinery, appliances and supplies, food, textiles, non-metallic mineral products and transport equipment. The few industries which recorded higher levels of production in 1981 were those producing wood, rubber and chemical products. Exports of manufactured goods, which had been rising since 1972 and rose by 26.4 per cent in 1980, declined by 17.3 per cent to M$5,051 million in 1981, under the impact of recession in the world economy and growing protectionism in a number of industrialized countries. The share of manufacturing goods in gross export earnings fell significantly from 21.7 per cent in 1980 to 19.6 per cent in 1981.

The Malaysian Industrial Development Authority (MIDA) provides a one-stop agency for industrial development. Various incentives, such as tax relief, investment tax credit and special export allowances, are offered. In this sector, private investment is favoured under the TMP, where some 60 per cent of the total investment target of M$44,200 million is expected to come from the private sector. In contrast, under the SMP, the main role was played by the public sector. The industrialization strategy under the TMP will, however, continue to be geared to meet the New Economic Policy (NEP) objectives of eradicating poverty and restructuring the society in the context of an expanding economy. The strategy of encouraging the growth of labour-intensive industries, both agro-based and export-orientated, is linked with the aim of dispersing such industries to the less developed states.

Under the FMP, the manufacturing sector will continue to be the leading growth sector, but is projected to grow at 11 per cent per annum, compared with the growth rate of 12.5 per cent during 1971–80. Its share of G.D.P. is projected to increase from 20.5 per cent in 1980 to 23.9 per cent in 1985, overtaking the agricultural sector (expected to decline to 17.8 per cent of G.D.P. by 1985). Sources of growth will continue to come from both external and domestic demand. The value of exports of manufactured goods is expected to increase from M$7,158 million in 1980 to M$19,823 million in 1985, representing 25.2 and 31.4 per cent respectively of total merchandise exports. Manufacturing employment is expected to account for 18.0 per cent of total employment in 1985.

TRADE

Malaysia's heavy dependence on exports has led to a corresponding reliance on foreign trade. Exports currently account for about one-half of the G.N.P. As in previous years, the agricultural sector continued to be the leading source of export earnings, although its share of total export receipts declined from 55.8 per cent in 1977 to 42.8 per cent in 1981. Rubber, which had been the country's largest export earner over the past 20 years, became second to crude petroleum since 1980. Its share of total exports fell from 16.6 per cent in 1980 to 14.4 per cent in 1981. Exports of sawlogs and palm oil, including processed palm oil, formed 9.2 per cent and 11.0 per cent respectively of total exports in 1981. Exports of minerals accounted for another 36.2 per cent, of which petroleum formed 26.8 per cent, while exports of manufactures took 19.6 per cent. Gross exports totalled M$25,738 million in 1981 while gross imports were recorded at M$26,504 million. All categories of imports rose but the sharpest growth was recorded in the import of consumer goods (18.8 per cent), followed by intermediate goods (12.7 per cent), the latter reflecting largely the rapid expansion of output of both the manufacturing and construction sectors. For investment goods, the rate of growth was 9.5 per cent.

Like most developing countries, Malaysia's main export outlets are in developed countries. The EEC, Japan, the U.S.A. and the ASEAN countries are the most important trading partners, together accounting for about 75 and 72 per cent of Malaysia's exports and imports, respectively, in 1981. Within ASEAN, Singapore, which accounted for 85.7 and 73.1 per cent of Malaysia's intra-ASEAN exports and imports respectively in 1981, is by far the most important trading partner.

While exports of primary and raw materials face problems of fluctuating prices and demand conditions, manufactured exports, too, have difficulties related to high tariffs and very restrictive non-tariff barriers, especially in countries like Australia, the U.S.A., Japan and the EEC countries. Diversification to other non-traditional export markets is thus pursued via trade-cum-investment missions overseas. On the whole, Malaysia's balance of payments, like that of many other primary producing countries, was adversely affected in 1981 by the prolonged recession in the major industrial countries. The merchandise account, the traditional source of strength in Malaysia's balance of payments, recorded a deficit (of M$735 million) for the first time in 1981, owing largely to a significant deterioration in terms of trade.

FINANCE AND BANKING

Since 1967 the currency has been the ringgit or Malaysian dollar, and in recent years it has been strong in relation to major world currencies. It appreciated to a record level against the U.S. dollar in early 1975, although it fell towards the end of the year. It climbed steadily throughout 1976 and the first half of 1977, gaining 12 per cent against the currencies of its major trading partners since 1971. In 1980 the value of the ringgit was, on average, 2.2 per cent above the conceptual par value of its official 'basket' or composite of currencies of Malaysia's trading partners. Inflation, which soared in 1974 to 17.4 per cent but fell to 4.5 per cent in 1975 and 2.6 per cent in 1976, stabilized at around 5 per cent in the period 1977–79. In 1980 the increase in the consumer price index for Peninsular Malaysia (1967 = 100) accelerated to average an annual rate of 6.7 per cent as against only 3.6 per cent in 1979. In 1981 the rate shot up to 9.6 per cent. The underlying factors were the continuing sharp increase in import prices and the moderate expansion of real aggregate demand, which had been sustained since 1975. For Sabah and Sarawak, the average annual inflation rates were 10.7 and 11.1 per cent respectively in 1981, compared with 6.8 and 7.7 per cent respectively in 1980.

In 1977 the stagnation in investment, despite the commodity boom and a buoyant economy, manifested itself in increasing bank deposits, leading to over-liquidity. Interest rates were cut by 1 per cent in an attempt to reactivate loan demand and to stimulate investment. Although these measures had little effect in 1977, they began to succeed by the second half of 1978. In 1979 a number of monetary changes took place to induce a market-oriented financial system which can respond more flexibly and efficiently to changing market conditions. These included the changing of the system of determining bank interest rates to a regime that is market-oriented, reform of the liquidity requirements to be maintained by financial institutions, bringing the merchant banks within the ambit of the Banking Act, and the introduction of two new monetary instruments, namely bankers' acceptances and negotiable certificates of deposit in May 1979. As a further step to add depth and breadth to the money market, the central bank (Bank Negara Malaysia) issued its own securities in 1980.

In 1981 the stance of monetary policy remained basically unchanged in the pursuit of its stabilization goals. The limited extent of central bank accommodation for the banking system during the second half of the year provided ample scope for market factors to activate a self-adjusting process towards stability. Within this environment of a selectively restrictive monetary policy aimed at restraining inflation while promoting economic growth, growth in money and credit moderated in 1981. Money supply, comprising currency and demand deposits of the private sector, rose by 12.8 per cent, compared with 15 per cent in 1980.

Monetary policy has thus emerged as an important aspect of economic management in Malaysia, with the rapid expansion in the external reserves held by the central bank and the commercial banks, and with the growth in the money and capital markets. Strong central control by Bank Negara is a feature of monetary policy, with, for example, the central bank exercising control over the commercial bank's lending policies, and over the operations of merchant banks. About 35 commercial banks operate in Malaysia, half of which are locally incorporated, and no foreign government-owned bank is allowed to operate. Foreign banks still account for slightly more than half the total deposits with commercial banks.

TRANSPORT

Road and rail communications are more highly developed in Peninsular Malaysia than in Sabah and Sarawak. Sarawak is particularly poorly provided with roads. Most road systems in the peninsula run north-south, and efforts are being made to improve the east-west communications with an east-west highway, from Kota Bahru to Penang, although security problems have interrupted the construction programme. Increases in the number of motor vehicles grew steadily at annual rates of over 10 per cent in the 1970s, matched by the expansion of the road system. But as the TMP drew to a close in 1980, it was apparent that the infrastructure was becoming inadequate to meet the rate of economic expansion envisaged for the 1980s. Under the FMP, there are plans to expand and modernize airports, including the international airport at Kuala Lumpur, and similar plans are being made for roads and ports.

The Malaysian Airlines System (MAS) was formed in 1971, after Malaysia Singapore Airlines (MSA) split into two airlines, and provides domestic and international services.

The major seaports of Peninsular Malaysia are those at Penang and Port Kelang, which has recently been extensively expanded, and the main ports in Sarawak are at Kuching, Sibu and Miri, while Labuan is the main port of Sabah. The national shipping line, the Malaysian International Shipping Corporation, had 32 vessels in operation in 1981. By 1985 an estimated 46 vessels are to be added to the fleet to achieve a target carrying capacity of 2.5 million d.w.t.

DEVELOPMENT AND PLANNING

Since independence, Malaysia has launched five development plans: the First Malayan Plan (1956–60), the Second Malayan Plan (1961–65), the First Malaysia Plan (1966–70), the Second Malaysia Plan (SMP) (1971–75) and the Third Malaysia Plan (TMP) (1976–80). The Third Malaysia Plan, published in mid-1976, provides a useful basis for analysis of past and future planning, and of the Malaysian development process. In March 1979 the Government published a mid-term review of this Plan. A Fourth Malaysia Plan (FMP) for the period 1981–85 was officially launched in March 1981.

A basic feature of the Malaysian economy is the concentration of Malays and other indigenous people in the traditional sectors of the economy (i.e. in subsistence agriculture), with other races, notably the Chinese, having the major role in the modern rural and urban sectors. In order to change this balance, the SMP, and to some extent the TMP, have been based on the New Economic Policy (NEP), which was inaugurated in 1970 in the aftermath of racial riots. The two main aims of the NEP (and of the SMP) are: to reduce and eventually eradicate poverty by raising income levels and by increasing employment opportunities for all Malaysians, irrespective of race; and to accelerate the process of restructuring Malaysian society to correct economic and geographical imbalances, thereby reducing and eventually eliminating, the identification of race with economic function. The period 1971–80 represents the first decade of the Outline Perspective Plan (OPP) 1971–90, within which the objectives of the NEP are to be realized.

In the TMP, this Malayanization process under the NEP continued, but an overriding policy of unity to combat the communist threat was emphasized as well. As with the three previous plans, the broad objectives of the FMP, which inaugurates the second decade of the OPP, are to achieve greater agricultural and industrial production, balanced socio-economic development and improved standards of living for Malaysia's people. While considerable progress has been made since 1971, especially in the generating of employment and the eradication of poverty, there has been a shortfall in the attainment of the restructuring target. In the plan period, Malaysia hopes to achieve an annual real growth rate of 7.6 per cent in G.D.P. and to keep domestic inflation between 6 and 7 per cent. While this projected G.D.P. growth rate is lower in real terms than that achieved during the TMP, it represents a significant expansion, given the constraints, both external and internal, to be faced during the plan period. The agricultural sector, currently the largest contributor to G.D.P., will expand by 3 per cent per annum while the manufacturing sector will experience the fastest rate of growth, at 11 per cent per annum, thereby becoming progressively more important in terms of income and employment. Underlying the average annual G.D.P. growth of 7.6 per cent in real terms, or 14 per cent in current prices, is the expectation that economic growth will slacken up to 1983, but increase more rapidly until 1985 in line with the expected recovery of the world economy from low growth and inflation. The plan provides for a public sector outlay of M$42,800 million and assigns an even greater role for the private sector, which is expected to invest M$74,100 million or 72.2 per cent of the targeted total investment of various projects, including oil. The M$42,800 million public development project is M$6,000 million more than the revised TMP outlay of M$36,700 million.

RECENT DEVELOPMENTS

Malaysia felt the full impact of the world recession between 1973 and 1975, with a consequent decline in its export earnings, hence in its general economic situation, and a slowing down of economic growth, to an annual average real increase in the G.N.P. of 4.9 per cent, and an increase in inflation and unemployment. In 1976 the economy made a significant and unexpected recovery, with exports rising by 43 per cent, a real growth in the G.N.P. of about 8.5 per cent and a 13 per cent improvement in the terms of trade.

Employment in 1976 increased by 3.5 per cent compared with 1975, mainly in the export-oriented and labour-intensive sectors of the economy, by 3.3 per cent in 1977, and by 3.6 per cent in 1978. Manufacturing employment increased by 12 per cent in 1976, although the rise declined to 7 and 10 per cent in 1977 and 1978 respectively. Overall unemployment declined steadily from 7 per cent in 1975 to around 5.2 per cent in 1981.

After the impressive recovery of 1976, the pace of growth slowed in 1977 and 1978, when G.N.P. grew in real terms by 7.6 and 7.2 per cent respectively. The growth rate increased to 8.5 per cent in 1979, moving down again to 8.0 per cent in 1980 and 6.5 per cent in 1981. Reasons for these slower growth rates include the drought and resultant smaller harvests, the consequent deterioration in export growth, and the unsatisfactory growth rate of private investment. While exports grew, in value terms, by 11.4 per cent in 1977 and 8.3 per cent in 1978, the increase was only 3.4 per cent in volume terms in 1978, a cause of some concern. Rubber continued to be one of the main foreign exchange earners, despite a decline in production. It is significant that, with the switch by estates from rubber to palm oil and other crops, rubber is becoming a smallholders' crop. Palm oil, on the other hand, remains largely an estate crop, in that smallholders cannot afford the resources to mill their crop. Palm oil has become the second largest agricultural export earner.

Despite falls in production, Malaysia remains the world's largest tin producer, and high prices have cushioned the impact of the fall in output. The Government recognizes the need for improved processes for land leasing, fiscal incentives, better surveys and higher technology to halt the decline, while the tin companies are pressing for action on land and taxation in particular. The mining sector's contribution to economic output in 1977 and 1978 reflected the considerable increase in petroleum production. The oil bonanza has begun in Malaysia, but there is a growing consciousness that oil reserves are limited, and a debate on the merits of a conservationist versus a rapid exploitation policy has begun.

With the fall in rice production in 1977 and 1978, the subsistence sector was not very healthy, and there is evidence that the growth of average incomes among the poorest agricultural households has been so slow that the gap between rich and poor is widening.

It would seem, then, that recent economic worries have centred upon the fall in agricultural production and the unsatisfactory growth rate of private investment. Fortunately for Malaysia, the effect of these factors has been partially cushioned by the high prices received for the main export commodities, and the rapid growth of the petroleum industry. However, it is some cause for concern that the TMP emphasis on the private sector as a vehicle of growth has not worked, and this has resulted in a larger than anticipated growth in state ownership and public spending.

However, it would still seem that, within the limitations imposed by the NEP, Malaysia is attempting to remain a predominantly free-enterprise, trade-oriented economy that intends to fight both communism and poverty with capitalism. The trading and commodity outlook remains healthy and the FMP was launched in a decade of broad-based consolidated economic strength.

The modest projected real growth rate of 7.6 per cent for the next five years under the FMP demonstrates an optimism that, despite challenges from the sluggish international economic community, the Malaysian economy will stay on a path of steady growth. The economy could withstand a short recession easily with net international reserves of the central bank sufficient to finance about 5½ months of retained imports at the 1980 level, though a more prolonged downturn affecting world trade and commodity prices would test the economy severely. Malaysia has benefited from the windfall gains of generally firm commodity prices throughout the 1970s, diversified its agricultural base significantly, as well as exploiting other revenue earners such as oil and natural gas. The question which is taking on increasing economic and political importance, if international economic trends continue to falter, would be whether the nation's planners have maximized the opportunities of these favourable influences. There also appears to be the conflict between the objectives of redistribution of national wealth between the *bumiputras* (indigenous Malays) and the non-*bumiputras* and creating national wealth. The Government recognizes the economic need for the country to square its racial contradictions and unite all ethnic groups behind a common development strategy to meet the challenges of external economic forces.

The economy ended 1981 on a significantly weaker note than at the beginning of the year. While the 1982 budget continued to be counter-cyclical and had set the stage for continuing high government development expenditure, its impact on overall economic activity is likely to be limited unless private sector spending strongly supports the Government's efforts. There is concern over the widening current account deficit, which reached a record high in 1981, and it is expected to widen further in 1982, owing to the continued slump in commodity and oil prices. By April 1982 the Government noted that some of the ambitious development programmes under the FMP may have to be reviewed in the face of an economic downturn. Thus, amid weak commodity prices (together with the growing uncertainty of a firm recovery in the major industrial countries), stable economic growth for Malaysia in 1982 will depend critically on the extent to which existing policies of financial prudence (especially those affecting the growth of money and credit) and the financing of the Government deficit will be maintained in order to contain domestic inflation and dampen further inflationary expectations. Equally important will be the need to take stock and consolidate after a period of prolonged rapid real growth, in order to prepare the economy to take full advantage of the international revival when it comes.

STATISTICAL SURVEY

Note: Unless otherwise indicated, statistics refer to Peninsular Malaysia only.

AREA AND POPULATION

	Area (sq. miles)	Population (Census, Aug. 1970)	Population (Census, 1980)*			1980 Density (per sq. mile)
			Males	Females	Total	
Peninsular Malaysia	50,806	8,809,557	5,570,198	5,568,029	11,138,227	219.2
Sabah	28,725	653,604	524,319	478,289	1,002,608	34.9
Sarawak	48,050	976,269	653,449	641,304	1,294,753	26.9
Total	127,581†	10,439,430	6,747,966	6,687,622	13,435,588	105.3

* Excluding transients afloat. † 330,433 sq. km.

PRINCIPAL RACES

(Estimated as at December 31st, 1979)

	Peninsular Malaysia	Sabah*	Sarawak
Chinese	3,876,532	178,469	383,504
Malays	6,050,361	49,937	244,990
Indians and Pakistanis	1,158,680	—	—
Land Dyak	—	—	110,966
Malanau	—	—	66,630
Kadazan	—	238,046	—
Bajau	—	109,108	—
Murut	—	39,282	—
Ibans	—	—	354,158
Other Indigenous	—	176,777	64,122
Other	83,004	189,925	12,058

* 1978 figures.

STATES

	Area (sq. miles)	Population* (1980 Census)	Capital	Population* (1980 Census)
Johore	7,330	1,601,504	Johore Bahru	249,880
Kedah	3,639	1,102,200	Alor Star	71,682
Kelantan	5,765	877,575	Kota Bahru	170,559
Malacca	637	453,153	Malacca Municipality	88,073
Negri Sembilan	2,565	563,955	Seremban	136,252
Pahang	13,886	770,640	Kuantan	136,625
Penang and Province Wellesley	399	911,586	George Town	250,578
Perak	8,110	1,762,288	Ipoh	300,727
Perlis	307	147,726	Kangar	12,956
Sabah	28,460	1,002,608	Kota Kinabalu	59,500
Sarawak	48,049	1,294,753	Kuching	74,229
Selangor	3,074	1,467,445	Shah Alam	24,138
Trengganu	5,002	542,280	Kuala Trengganu	186,608
Federal Territory	94	937,875	Kuala Lumpur†	937,875

* Preliminary figures.

† Kuala Lumpur, the capital of Malaysia, was designated a separate federal territory on February 1st, 1974. A new capital for Selangor was established at Shah Alam in 1977.

ECONOMICALLY ACTIVE POPULATION

(1970 census)

	Peninsular Malaysia*			Sabah	Sarawak	Malaysia
	Males	Females	Total	Total	Total	Total
Agriculture, forestry, hunting and fishing	772,886	451,689	1,224,575	125,777	228,951	1,579,303
Mining and quarrying	48,203	7,073	55,276	889	1,108	57,273
Manufacturing	178,881	73,058	251,939	7,079	17,003	276,021
Construction	55,624	4,238	59,862	6,230	5,341	71,433
Electricity, gas, water and sanitary services	18,732	1,024	19,756	1,395	1,410	22,561
Commerce	224,993	49,611	274,604	11,770	17,316	303,690
Transport, storage and communications	93,852	4,117	97,969	6,923	6,090	110,982
Services	332,158	140,468	472,626	32,326	38,369	543,321
Activities not adequately described	152,417	127,331	279,748	20,325	30,421	330,494
Total	1,877,746	858,609	2,736,355	212,714	346,009	3,295,078

* Excluding persons seeking work for the first time, numbering 134,594 (80,542 males, 54,052 females).

1977: Peninsular Malaysia's economically active population was 3,988,200 (males 2,609,300; females 1,378,900).

AGRICULTURE

LAND USE
('000 hectares)

	Peninsular Malaysia		Sabah		Sarawak		Total‡	
	1971	1976	1971	1976	1971	1976	1971	1976
Arable land	593	625*	62	79	2,423†	2,435*	3,078	3,139
Land under permanent crops	2,260	2,310*	180	250	265*	305*	2,705	2,865
Permanent meadows and pastures	30	30*	7	8	15†	15†	52	53
Forests and woodland	7,874	6,850*	6,050†	6,050	9,433	9,433	23,357	22,333
Other land	2,402	3,344	1,072	984	189	137	3,663	4,465
Inland water	—	—	—	—	120	120	120	120
Total Area	13,159	13,159	7,371	7,371	12,445	12,445	32,975	32,975

* FAO estimate. † Unofficial estimate. ‡ Including FAO and unofficial estimates.

Source: FAO, *Production Yearbook*.

1979 (FAO estimates for all Malaysia, '000 hectares): Arable land 995; Land under permanent crops 3,305; Permanent meadows and pastures 27; Forests and woodland 22,630; Other land 5,898; Inland water 120.

PRINCIPAL CROPS
(metric tons, unless otherwise stated)

	1976	1977	1978	1979
Rubber	1,563,658	1,536,784	1,530,146	1,528,100
Rice	1,135,600	1,060,000	798,700	1,170,120
Palm oil (crude)	1,260,608	1,483,591	1,640,044	2,032,900
Palm kernels	256,015	310,637	339,816	441,040
Copra	21,446	21,369	18,617	105,178
Coconut oil	85,442	79,560	61,357	65,310
Copra cake	47,050	41,508	33,582	37,210
Tea	3,206	3,239	2,993	3,197

Sabah* (1980—metric tons): Rubber 30,824, Copra 43,167, Palm oil (crude) 143,604.

Sarawak* (1980—metric tons): Rubber 35,209, Sago flour 26,355, Pepper 30,709.

* Export figures only.

LIVESTOCK
('000 head)

	1977	1978	1979	1980
Cattle	428	455	462	481
Buffalo	211	216	200	199
Goats	332	324	322	312
Sheep	52	55	63	59
Pigs	1,186	1,202	1,217	1,393

Source: Veterinary Division, Ministry of Agriculture, Malaysia.

FORESTRY

TIMBER PRODUCTION

		1976	1977	1978	1979	1980*
Sawlogs	'000 cu. metres	10,003	10,476	9,551	10,402	9,282
Poles	,, ,, ,,	66	72	66	101	99
Charcoal	,, ,, ,,	4,722	2,537	1,852	513	459
Firewood	,, ,, ,,	106	101	26	57	72
Sawn timber	,, ,, ,,	4,789.8	5,104.7	4,672.8	5,389.9	4,953.9

* Provisional figures.

Sabah ('000 cu. ft.): (1973) 392,575 of logs; (1974) 276,028 of logs; (1975) 322,430 of logs; (1976) 446,252 of logs; (1977) 420,793 of logs; (1978) 463,182 of logs.

Sarawak (Hoppus tons): (1973) 1,803,325 of logs; (1974) 1,568,032 of logs; (1975) 1,393,100 of logs; (1976) 2,448,670 of logs (1977) 2,706,954 of logs; (1978) 3,315,723 of logs; (1979) 4,167,331 of logs.

Source: Forestry Department.

FISHING

('000 metric tons, live weight, excluding freshwater catch)

	1975	1976	1977	1978	1979	1980
Peninsular Malaysia	375.2	411.0	498.0	564.9	570.9	623.9
Sabah	33.5	31.7	36.2	41.6	41.9	34.5
Sarawak	64.2	73.2	83.3	77.5	82.3	77.1
TOTAL	472.9	515.9	617.5	684.0	695.1	735.5

Source: Fisheries Division, Ministry of Agriculture, *Annual Fisheries Statistics.*

MINING

PRODUCTION

		1975	1976	1977	1978	1979	1980
Tin-in-concentrates	metric tons	64,364	63,401	58,703	62,650	62,995	61,404
Iron ore	,, ,,	348,200	308,184	329,971	320,034	350,498	371,186
Gold (raw)	troy oz.	2,484	3,574	4,172	6,252	6,335	5,000
Ilmenite concentrate*	metric tons	112,243	179,996	153,673	166,643	199,819	189,121
Bauxite	,, ,,	703,561	660,235	616,214	615,060	386,520	920,356
Crude petroleum	'000 U.S. barrels	35,780	60,547	66,984	79,171	n.a.	n.a.

* Exports.

Source: Department of Statistics and Department of Mines, Kuala Lumpur.

INDUSTRY

SELECTED PRODUCTS

		1978	1979	1980
Rubber:				
Crepe Rubber	metric tons	30,302	25,020	18,348
Ribbed Smoked Sheets	,, ,,	39,755	82,454	76,005
Foam Rubber (excl. mattresses)	,, ,,	2,584	2,728	3,717
Foam Rubber Mattresses	,, ,,	3,745	3,904	3,848
Rubber Compound	,, ,,	10,140	10,881	12,172
Tubing and Hoses*	,, ,,	892	1,147	1,047
Inner Tubes	,, '000	5,793	6,099	6,169
Footwear	'000 pairs	31,414	29,086	31,929
Cement	metric tons	2,196,496	2,264,000	2,349,000
Cigars, Cigarettes, Cheroots and other Manufactured Tobacco	,, ,,	13,543	14,573	14,711
Tin Metal (primary)	,, ,,	71,953	73,068	71,318

* Wholly of rubber or reinforced.

FINANCE

(Malaysia)

100 sen = 1 ringgit or Malaysian dollar (M$).

Coins: 1, 5, 10, 20 and 50 sen.

Notes: 1, 5, 10, 50, 100 and 1,000 ringgits.

Exchange rates (June 1982): £1 sterling = M$4.10; U.S. $1 = M$.2.37

M$100 = £24.39 = U.S. $42.26.

Note: The Malaysian dollar was introduced in June 1967, replacing (at par) the Malayan dollar. From September 1949 the Malayan dollar was valued at 2s. 4d. sterling (£1 = M$8.5714) or 32.667 U.S. cents (U.S. $1 = M$3.0612). This valuation in terms of U.S. currency remained in effect until August 1971. Between December 1971 and February 1973 the Malaysian dollar was valued at 35.467 U.S. cents (U.S. $1 = M$2.8195). From February to June 1973 the Malaysian dollar's value was 39.407 U.S. cents (U.S. $1 = M$2.5376). In terms of sterling, the exchange rate was £1 = M$7.347 from November 1967 to June 1972. The Malaysian dollar was interchangeable with the Singapore and Brunei dollars until May 1973. Since June 1973 the Malaysian dollar has been allowed to "float". From September 1975 the Malaysian dollar's link with the U.S. dollar was ended and its value determined by changes in a weighted "basket" of currencies of the country's main trading partners. In June 1976 the Malaysian dollar was officially renamed the ringgit. The average market exchange rate (ringgits per U.S. dollar) was: 2.443 in 1973; 2.407 in 1974; 2.402 in 1975; 2.542 in 1976; 2.461 in 1977; 2.316 in 1978; 2.188 in 1979; 2.177 in 1980; 2.304 in 1981.

ORDINARY BUDGET

(million M$/ringgits)

Revenue	1977	1978*	1979†
Tax revenue	7,070	8,006	8,285
Direct taxes	2,946	3,323	3,907
Indirect taxes	4,124	4,683	4,378
Non-tax revenue	580	665	638
Service fees	168	179	173
Interest	243	294	285
Licences	111	123	116
Others	58	69	64
Non-revenue receipts	109	156	126
From government agencies	37	49	42
Others	72	107	84
Total	7,759	8,827	9,049

Expenditure	1977	1978*	1979†
Defence	973	1,090	1,190
Internal security	544	650	737
Health	532	560	660
Education	1,750	1,800	1,945
Grants, subsidies, investments, interest payments, sinking fund contributions, pensions and other transfers General public administration and economic services	3,599	3,928	5,378
Total	7,398	8,028	9,910

* Estimated actual outturn. † Estimates.

Source: Federal Financial Statements and Federal Budgets.

1981: Revenue M$15,243 million; Expenditure M$14,790 million (operating), M$9,190 million (development).

1982: Revenue M$17,683 million; Expenditure M$17,320 million (operating), M$10,663 million (development).

DEVELOPMENT BUDGET

(expenditure in million M$/ringgits)

	1975	1976	1977	1978	1979†
Peninsular Malaysia	1,875	2,126	2,910	3,778*	4,029
Sabah	161	117	166	187	265
Sarawak	160	143	180	201*	226
TOTAL	2,196	2,386	3,256	4,166‡	4,520‡

* Revised estimates. † Estimates. ‡ Excluding M$400 million under contingency.

PUBLIC DEVELOPMENT EXPENDITURE, 1971–85

(million M$/ringgits)

	SECOND MALAYSIA PLAN (1971–75) (estimates)	THIRD MALAYSIA PLAN (1976–80) (revised allocation)	FOURTH MALAYSIA PLAN (1981–85) (estimates)
Agriculture and rural development	2,129	7,585	8,359
Commerce and industry	1,618	3,205	5,433
Transport	1,781	5,017	4,116
Utilities and energy	931	3,444	3,249
Other economic services	641	2,251	1,607
Social services	1,348	5,561	6,388
General administration	349	1,229	805
Security	1,024	3,784	9,372
TOTAL	9,821	32,076	39,330

INTERNATIONAL RESERVES

(U.S. $ million at December 31st)

	1979	1980	1981
Gold	98	104	95
IMF Special Drawing Rights	115	125	146
Reserve position in IMF	89	149	136
Foreign exchange	3,711	4,114	3,816
TOTAL	4,013	4,491	4,193

Source: IMF, *International Financial Statistics*, and Department of Statistics, Kuala Lumpur.

MONEY SUPPLY

(million M$/ringgits at December 31st)

	1979	1980	1981
Currency outside banks	4,094	4,758	5,100
Demand deposits at commercial banks	4,251	4,875	5,714

Source: IMF, *International Financial Statistics.*

BALANCE OF PAYMENTS

(million M$/ringgits)

	1976	1977	1978	1979	1980	1981
Merchandise exports f.o.b.	13,330	14,854	16,932	23,977	28,060	25,609
Merchandise imports f.o.b.	−9,608	−11,116	−13,242	−17,397	23,284	26,344
TRADE BALANCE	3,722	3,738	3,690	6,580	4,776	−735
Exports of services	1,578	1,984	2,323	3,084	4,094	5,007
Imports of services	−3,726	−4,570	−5,668	−7,259	−9,270	−9,925
BALANCE ON GOODS AND SERVICES	−1,574	1,152	345	2,405	400	−5,653
Private unrequited transfers (net)	−121	−113	−157	−143	−155	−145
Government unrequited transfers (net)	21	35	53	24	32	40
CURRENT BALANCE	1,474	1,074	241	2,286	−523	−5,758
Direct capital investment (net)	967	999	1,083	1,448	2,129	3,065
Other long-term capital (net)	597	618	418	712	310	2,909
Short-term capital (net)	−242	−982	18	−1,492	799	187
Net errors and omissions	−744	−954	−1,099	−1,165	−1,713	−1,496
TOTAL (net monetary movements)	2,054	755	625	1,789	1,002	−1,093
Allocation of IMF Special Drawing Rights	—	—	—	74	76	73
IMF resources	265	−265	—	—	—	510
CHANGES IN RESERVES, ETC.	2,319	490	625	1,863	1,078	−510

Source: Department of Statistics, Malaysia, Inter-Agency Planning Group and Bank Negara.

EXTERNAL TRADE

(Malaysia—million M$/ringgits)

	1974	1975	1976	1977	1978	1979	1980
Imports	9,891.2	8,530.4	9,713.3	11,164.7	13,690.1	17,161.1	23,539.1
Exports	10,194.7	9,230.9	13,442.0	14,959.2	17,094.2	24,218.9	28,201.3

PRINCIPAL COMMODITIES

(million M$/ringgits)

IMPORTS	MALAYSIA		
	1978	1979	1980
Food and live animals	1,981.1	2,053.2	2,449.7
Beverages and tobacco	186.1	185.0	221.5
Crude materials, inedible, excluding fuels	722.4	842.2	1,047.1
Mineral fuels, lubricants and related materials	1,470.4	2,063.8	3,538.5
Animal and vegetable oils and fats	26.0	30.1	30.5
Chemicals	1,228.1	1,772.9	2,035.1
Basic manufactures	2,263.8	2,955.5	3,910.5
Machinery and transport equipment	4,945.9	6,327.5	9,080.8
Miscellaneous manufactured articles	723.9	793.7	1,002.4
Other commodities and transactions	142.4	137.2	223.0
TOTAL	13,690.1	17,161.1	23,539.1

[*continued on next page*

PRINCIPAL COMMODITIES—*continued*]

EXPORTS	MALAYSIA		
	1978	1979	1980
Food and Live Animals	887.3	1,082.0	1,014.2
Beverages and Tobacco	16.1	20.8	29.2
Crude Materials, inedible, excluding fuels	6,363.5	9,026.6	9,128.4
Logs and timber	2,466.2	4,097.4	3,800.6
Rubber	3,600.8	4,482.3	4,617.4
Mineral Fuels, Lubricants and related materials	2,343.0	4,339.4	6,905.6
Petroleum	2,247.0	4,209.9	6,709.0
Animal and Vegetable Oils and Fats	2,105.8	3,015.6	3,131.3
Palm oil	1,828.6	2,387.8	2,615.2
Chemicals	103.4	132.5	172.4
Basic Manufactures	2,820.9	3,315.2	3,688.1
Tin	2,021.5	2,315.8	2,505.2
Machinery and Transport Equipment	1,820.3	2,538.9	3,238.4
Miscellaneous Manufactured Articles	495.8	600.6	738.1
Other Commodities and Transactions	138.1	147.3	155.6
TOTAL	17,094.2	24,218.9	28,201.3

PRINCIPAL TRADING PARTNERS

(million M$/ringgits)

IMPORTS	MALAYSIA		
	1978	1979	1980
Australia	878.9	1,039.1	1,289.9
China, People's Republic	509.4	486.9	550.9
Germany, Federal Republic	842.8	1,018.8	1,276.1
Indonesia	108.2	166.3	175.9
Japan	3,169.0	3,840.3	5,373.1
Singapore	1,166.6	1,580.4	2,750.2
Thailand	576.3	617.0	696.9
United Kingdom	1,018.0	1,096.2	1,274.1
U.S.A.	1,902.5	2,565.3	3,556.6
TOTAL (incl. others)	13,690.1	17,161.1	23,539.1

EXPORTS	MALAYSIA		
	1978	1979	1980
ASEAN	3,172.1	4,861.7	6,306.4
Singapore	2,761.6	4,225.9	5,393.7
Australia	304.5	424.3	402.8
China, People's Republic	250.8	397.3	620.9
Eastern Europe	628	936.0	1,007.9
Japan	3,703.0	5,668.2	6,447.7
U.S.A.	3,182.9	4,182.5	4,609.1
Western Europe	3,412	4,666.5	5,178.4
Germany, Federal Republic	617.4	885.7	1,017.4
Netherlands	963.1	1,356.7	1,691.7
United Kingdom	821.9	943.4	779.0

TRANSPORT

RAILWAYS

Peninsular Malaysia

('000)

	1976	1977	1978	1979	1980
Freight tons	3,294	3,789	4,144	4,190	3,608
Net ton-mileage freight	615,745	739,355	790,878	829,656	730,622
Passengers	6,400	6,388	5,998	6,764	7,068
Passenger-miles	706,994	791,082	788,771	851,919	985,969

Sabah

	1975	1976	1977	1978	1979	1980
Passenger-km. ('000)	681.4	706.5	691.7	700.8	659.1	592.7
Freight ton-km. ('000)	286.9	223.1	287.9	290.1	305.9	280.1

ROAD TRAFFIC

REGISTERED VEHICLES IN USE

	1975	1976	1977	1978	1979	1980
Private motor cycles	722,309	830,834	951,080	1,079,020	1,183,391	1,391,899
Private motor cars	398,014	436,939	491,933	555,358	595,600	714,742
Buses	8,688	9,735	10,545	11,589	12,094	13,079
Lorries and vans	92,207	101,610	112,025	122,543	131,723	154,533
Taxis	9,004	10,116	10,907	11,587	12,034	13,644

Sabah: Licensed motor vehicles: 129,478 (1980).

Sarawak: Licensed motor vehicles: 130,929 (1980).

SHIPPING

FOREIGN TRADE

(vessels over 75 net registered tons)

	Entered		Cleared	
	No. of vessels	'000 net registered tons	No. of vessels	'000 net registered tons
1976	5,417	26,295	5,396	26,205
1977	5,725	29,773	5,731	29,501
1978	5,721	32,727	5,691	32,567
1979	5,399	34,103	5,408	34,090
1980	5,611	34,132	5,558	34,072

Sabah (1980): Tonnage entered 10,977,427; tonnage cleared 12,032,060.

Sarawak (1980): Tonnage entered 8,897,160; tonnage cleared 8,915,935.

Coastal Trade
(vessels over 75 net registered tons)

	Entered		Cleared	
	No. of vessels	Net registered tons	No. of vessels	Net registered tons
1976	4,211	2,070,137	4,199	2,077,308
1977	5,071	2,450,153	5,052	2,451,478
1978	6,210	3,456,833	6,172	3,424,286
1979	7,736	4,025,503	7,740	4,024,196
1980	5,889	3,239,437	5,868	3,258,686

CIVIL AVIATION

	No. of Landings/ Take-Offs	No. of Passengers		Total Freight Handled ('000 kilogrammes)		Total Mail Handled ('000 kilogrammes)	
		Embarked	Disembarked	Landed	Despatched	Landed	Despatched
1975	66,834	815,782	854,303	8,174	5,607	2,050	1,146
1976	71,818	988,422	1,013,727	10,250	7,953	2,249	1,395
1977	69,597	885,169	904,007	9,177	6,505	1,796	1,186
1978	67,355	957,243	979,667	7,434	5,894	2,325	1,491
1979	73,048	1,264,109	1,222,513	10,024	6,624	2,758	1,292
1980	95,069	1,612,237	1,644,841	13,041	7,901	2,032	1,566

Sabah (1980): Total passengers embarked 954,229; total passengers disembarked 936,468.

Sarawak (1980): Total passengers embarked 287,927; passengers disembarked 296,655.

TOURISM

	1977	1978	1979
Tourist arrivals*	1,289,000	1,399,100	1,462,000
Tourist receipts (U.S. $ million)	169.1	204.0	246.0

* Excluding visitors from Singapore by road through Johore Bahru, as the majority are seasonal workers.

Source: Asian Development Bank, *Annual Report* 1980.

COMMUNICATIONS MEDIA

	1978	1979	1980
Television sets licensed	692,017	818,664	1,002,480
Radio sets licensed	246,511	208,890	185,599

EDUCATION
(1981)

	Establishments	Teachers	Students
Schools:			
Malay medium primary	4,488	49,043	1,350,495
Chinese medium primary	1,387	19,563	609,795
Tamil medium primary	579	3,741	73,513
Government-assisted secondary	970	49,315	1,100,967
Vocational and professional	45	5,721	62,004
Private secondary	464	3,021	90,324
Teacher training	26	1,198	13,028
Total	7,959	131,602	3,300,126

Sabah (1981): *Primary:* schools 821, pupils 148,280; *Secondary:* schools 95, pupils 61,261.

Sarawak (1981): *Primary:* schools 1,276, pupils 210,183; *Secondary:* schools 99, pupils 96,252.

Source: Ministry of Education, Kuala Lumpur.

Source (unless otherwise stated): Departments of Statistics, Kuala Lumpur, Kuching and Kota Kinabalu.

THE CONSTITUTION

(Promulgated August 31st, 1957, subsequently amended)

Supreme Head of State

The Yang di-Pertuan Agong (King or Supreme Sovereign) is the Supreme Head of Malaysia.

Every act of government flows from his authority although he acts on the advice of Parliament and the Cabinet. The appointment of a Prime Minister lies within his discretion, and he has the right to refuse to dissolve Parliament even against the advice of the Prime Minister. He appoints the Judges of the Federal Court and the High Courts on the advice of the Prime Minister. He is the Supreme Commander of the Armed Forces. The Yang di-Pertuan Agong is elected by the Conference of Rulers, and to qualify for election he must be one of the nine Rulers. He holds office for five years or until his earlier resignation or death. Election is by secret ballot on each Ruler in turn, starting with the Ruler next in precedence after the late or former Yang di-Pertuan Agong. The first Ruler to obtain not fewer than five votes is declared elected. A Deputy Supreme Head of State (the Timbalan Yang di-Pertuan Agong) is elected by a similar process. On election the Yang di-Pertuan Agong relinquishes, for his tenure of office, all his functions as Ruler of his own State and may appoint a Regent. The Timbalan Yang di-Pertuan Agong exercises no powers in the ordinary course, but is immediately available to fill the post of Yang di-Pertuan Agong and carry out his functions in the latter's absence or disability. In the event of the Yang di-Pertuan Agong's death or resignation he takes over the exercise of sovereignty until the Conference of Rulers has elected a successor.

Conference of Rulers

The Conference of Rulers consists of the Rulers and the heads of the other States. Its prime duty is the election by the Rulers only of the Yang di-Pertuan Agong and his deputy. The Conference must be consulted in the appointment of judges, the Auditor-General, the Election Commission and the Services Commissions. It must also be consulted and concur in the alteration of State boundaries, the extension to the federation as a whole, of Islamic religious acts and observances, and in any bill to amend the Constitution. Consultation is mandatory in matters affecting public policy or the special position of the Malays and natives of Sabah and Sarawak. The Conference also considers matters affecting the rights, prerogatives and privileges of the Rulers themselves.

Federal Parliament

Parliament has two Houses—the Dewan Negara (Senate) and the Dewan Rakyat (House of Representatives). The Senate has a membership of 58, made up of 26 elected and 32 appointed members. Each State Legislature, acting as an electoral college, elects two Senators; these may be members of the State Legislative Assembly or otherwise. The Yang di-Pertuan Agong appoints the other 32 members of the Senate. Members of the Senate must be at least 30 years old. The Senate elects a President and a Deputy President from among its members. It may initiate legislation, but all money bills must be introduced in the first instance in the House of Representatives. All bills must be passed by both Houses of Parliament before being presented to the Yang di-Pertuan Agong for the Royal Assent in order to become law. A bill originating in the Senate cannot receive Royal Assent until it has been agreed to by the House of Representatives, but the Senate has delaying powers only over a bill originating from and approved by the House of Representatives. Senators serve for a period of six years, but the Senate is not subject to dissolution. Parliament can by statute increase the number of Senators elected from each State to three. The House of Representatives consists of 154 elected members. Of these, 114 are from Peninsular Malaysia, 24 from Sarawak and 16 from Sabah. Members are returned from single-member constituencies on the basis of universal adult franchise. The life of the House of Representatives is limited to five years, after which time a fresh general election must be held. The Yang di-Pertuan Agong may dissolve Parliament before then if the Prime Minister so advises.

The Cabinet

The Yang di-Pertuan Agong appoints a Cabinet to advise him in the exercise of his functions, consisting of the Prime Minister and an unspecified number of Ministers who must all be members of Parliament. The Prime Minister must be a citizen born in Malaysia and a member of the House of Representatives who, in the opinion of the Yang di-Pertuan Agong, commands the confidence of that House. Ministers are appointed on the advice of the Prime Minister. A number of Deputy Ministers (who are not members of the Cabinet) are also appointed from among Members of Parliament. The Cabinet meets regularly under the chairmanship of the Prime Minister to formulate policy.

Public Services

The Public Services, civilian and military, are non-political and owe their loyalty not to the party in power but to the Yang di-Pertuan Agong and the Rulers. They serve whichever government may be in power, irrespective of the latter's political affiliation. To ensure the impartiality of the service, and to protect it from political interference, a number of Services Commissions are established under the Constitution to select and appoint officers, to place them on the pensionable establishment, to decide as to promotion, and to maintain discipline.

The States

The heads of nine of the thirteen States are hereditary Rulers. The Ruler of Perlis has the title of Raja and that of Negri Sembilan, Yang di-Pertuan Besar. The rest of the Rulers are Sultans. The heads of the States of Malacca, Penang, Sabah and Sarawak are each designated Yang di-Pertua Negeri and do not participate in the election of the Yang di-Pertuan Agong. Each of the 13 States has its own written Constitution, and a single Legislative Assembly. Every State Legislature has powers to legislate on matters not reserved for the Federal Parliament. Each State Legislative Assembly has the right to order its own procedure, and the members enjoy parliamentary privilege. All members of the Legislative Assemblies are directly elected from single-member constituencies. The head of the State acts on the advice of the State Government, which advice is tendered by the State Executive Council or Cabinet in precisely the same manner as the Federal Cabinet tenders advice to the Yang di-Pertuan Agong.

The Legislative authority of the State is vested in the head of the State in the State Legislative Assembly. The executive authority of the State is vested in the head of the State but executive functions may be conferred on other persons by law. Every State has an Executive Council or Cabinet to advise the head of the State, headed by a Chief Minister (in Malacca, Penang, Sabah and Sarawak) or Menteri Besar (in other States), and collectively responsible to the State legislature. Each State in Peninsular Malaysia is divided into administrative districts under a District Officer. Sabah is divided into four residencies: West Coast, Interior, Sandakan and Tawau with headquarters at Kota Kinabalu, Keningua, Sandakan and Tawau respectively. The island of Labuan is administered by a District Officer responsible direct to the State Secretary in Kota Kinabalu. Sarawak is divided into five Divisions, each in charge of a Resident—the First Division, with headquarters at Kuching; the Second Division, with headquarters at Simanggang; the Third Division, with headquarters at Sibu; the Fourth Division, with headquarters at Miri; the Fifth Division, with headquarters at Limbang.

Amendments

From February 1st, 1974, the city of Kuala Lumpur, formerly the seat of the Federal Government and capital of Selangor State, is designated the Federal Territory of Kuala Lumpur. It is administered directly by the Federal Government and returns five members to the Dewan Rakyat.

An amendment passed in April 1981 empowers the Yang di-Pertuan Agong to declare a state of emergency on the grounds of imminent danger of a breakdown in law and order or a threat to national security.

THE GOVERNMENT

THE SUPREME HEAD OF STATE

(His Majesty the Yang di-Pertuan Agong)

His Majesty Tuanku Haji AHMAD SHAH AL-MUSTAIN BILLAH IBNI AL-MARHUM Sultan ABU BAKAR RI'AYATUDDIN AL-MU'ADZAM SHAH (Sultan of Pahang); elected April 26th, 1979; installed July 10th, 1980.

Deputy Supreme Head of State

(Timbalan Yang di-Pertuan Agong)

His Royal Highness Tunku JA'AFAR IBNI AL-MARHUM Tuanku ABDUL RAHMAN (Yang di-Pertuan Besar of Negri Sembilan)

THE CABINET

(July 1982)

Prime Minister and Minister of Defence: Datuk Seri Dr. MAHATHIR MOHAMAD.

Deputy Prime Minister and Minister of Home Affairs: Datuk MUSA HITAM.

Minister of Works and Public Utilities: Datuk S. SAMY VELLU.

Minister of Transport: Dato LEE SAN CHOON.

Minister of Science, Technology and Environment: Datuk AMAR STEPHEN YONG.

Minister of Trade and Industry: Tengku AHMAD RITHAUDDEEN BIN TENGKU ISMAIL.

Minister of Land and Regional Development: Datuk RAIS BIN YATIM.

Minister of Welfare Services: Datin Paduka Hajjah AISHAH BINTI Haji ABDUL GHANI.

Minister of the Federal Territory: Datuk PENGIRAN OTHMAN BIN Haji PENGIRAN RAUF.

Minister of Foreign Affairs: Tan Sri Haji MUHAMMAD GHAZALI BIN SHAFIE.

Minister of Housing and Local Government: Datuk Dr. NEO YEE PAN.

Minister of Education: Datuk SULAIMAN BIN Haji DAUD.

Minister of Finance: Tengku Tan Sri RAZALEIGH HAMZAH.

Minister of Culture, Youth and Sports: Dato MOKHTAR BIN HASHIM.

Minister of Health: Tan Sri CHONG HON NYAN.

Minister of Agriculture: Datuk ABDUL MANAN BIN OTHMAN.

Minister of Information: Encik ADIB ADAM.

Minister of Labour and Manpower: Dato MAK HON KAM.

Minister of Primary Industries: Datuk PAUL LEONG KHEE SEONG.

Minister of Public Enterprises: Datin PADUKA RAFIDAH AZIZ.

Minister of Energy, Telecommunications and Posts: Datuk LEO MOGGIE ANAK IROK.

Minister of National and Rural Development: SANUSI BIN JUNID.

Ministers without Portfolio: Dato Haji MOHAMED NASIR, Dato ABDULLAH BIN Haji AHMAD.

LEGISLATURE

PARLIAMENT

DEWAN NEGARA

(Senate)

58 members, 26 elected, 32 appointed. Each State Assembly elects two members. The Monarch appoints the other 32 members.

DEWAN RAKYAT

(House of Representatives)

154 elected members, 114 from Peninsular Malaysia, 16 from Sabah and 24 from Sarawak.

Speaker: Datuk MOHAMED ZAHIR ISMAIL.

DEWAN RAKYAT

(General Election, April 22nd, 1982)

PARTY	SEATS
National Front*	132
Democratic Action Party	9
Pan-Malayan Islamic Party	5
Independent†	8

*See under Political Parties.

† Including one member aligned to the National Front.

THE STATES

JOHORE

(Capital: Johore Bahru)

Sultan: His Royal Highness Tunku MAHMOOD ISKANDAR IBNI AL-MARHUM Sultan ISMAIL.

Menteri Besar: ABDUL AJIB AHMED.

STATE ASSEMBLY
(Elected April 1982)

PARTY	SEATS
National Front	32
TOTAL	32

KEDAH

(Capital: Alor Star)

Sultan: His Royal Highness Tunku Haji ABDUL HALIM MU'ADZAM SHAH IBNI AL-MARHUM Sultan BADLISHAH, D.K., D.K.H., D.K.M., D.M.N., D.U.K., D.K. (Kelantan), D.K. (Pahang), S.P.M.K.

Menteri Besar: Datuk SYED NAHAR BIN Tun SYED Sheikh SHAHABUDDIN.

STATE ASSEMBLY
(Elected April 1982)

PARTY	SEATS
National Front	24
Pan-Malayan Islamic Party . . .	2
TOTAL	26

KELANTAN

(Capital: Kota Bahru)

Sultan: His Royal Highness Tengku ISMAIL PETRA IBNI AL-MARHUM Tuanku Sultan YAHAYA PETRA.

Menteri Besar: Datuk Haji MOHAMED BIN YAACOB, P.M.K., S.M.T.

STATE ASSEMBLY
(Elected April 1982)

PARTY	SEATS
National Front.	26
Pan-Malayan Islamic Party . . .	10
TOTAL	36

MALACCA

(Capital: Malacca)

Yang di-Pertua Negeri: His Excellency Tun SYED ZAHIRUDDIN BIN SYED HASSAN, S.M.N., P.S.M., D.P.M.P., J.M.N.

Chief Minister: ABDUL RAHIM THAMBY CHIK.

STATE ASSEMBLY
(Elected April 1982)

PARTY	SEATS
National Front	18
Democratic Action Party . . .	2
TOTAL	20

NEGRI SEMBILAN

(Capital: Seremban)

Yang di-Pertuan Besar: His Royal Highness Tunku JA'AFAR IBNI AL-MARHUM Tuanku ABDUL RAHMAN, D.M.N., D.K. (Brunei), D.K. (Kelantan).

Menteri Besar: Encik ISA SAMAD.

STATE ASSEMBLY
(Elected April 1982)

PARTY	SEATS
National Front	22
Democratic Action Party . . .	2
TOTAL	24

PAHANG

(Capital: Kuantan)

Regent: His Royal Highness Tengku ABDULLAH IBNI Sultan Haji AHMAD SHAH.

Menteri Besar: Datuk Najib ABDUL RAZAK.

STATE ASSEMBLY
(Elected April 1982)

PARTY	SEATS
National Front.	31
Democratic Action Party . . .	1
TOTAL	32

PENANG

(Capital: George Town)

Yang di-Pertua Negeri: His Excellency Datuk Dr. AWANG BIN HASSAN, S.P.M.J.

Chief Minister: Dr. LIM CHONG EU.

STATE ASSEMBLY
(Elected April 1982)

PARTY	SEATS
National Front	25
Democratic Action Party . . .	2
TOTAL	27

PERAK

(Capital: Ipoh)

Sultan: His Royal Highness Sultan IDRIS AL-MUTAWAKIL ALLAHI SHAH IBNI AL-MARHUM Sultan ISKANDAR SHAH KADDASALLAH, D.K., D.M.N., S.P.M.P., D.K. (Johore), P.K.J., C.M.G., D.K. (Pahang), S.P.C.M.

Menteri Besar: Datuk Seri WAN MOHAMED BIN Haji WAN TEH.

STATE ASSEMBLY
(Elected April 1982)

PARTY	SEATS
National Front	38
Democratic Action Party	4
TOTAL	42

PERLIS

(Capital: Kangar)

Raja: His Royal Highness Tuanku SYED PUTRA IBNI AL-MARHUM SYED HASSAN JAMALULLAIL, D.K., D.M.N., S.M.N., S.P.M.P., D.K. (Selangor), D.K. (Kelantan), D.K. (Brunei), S.P.D.K. (Sabah).

Menteri Besar: TUAN Haji ALI BIN AHMAD.

STATE ASSEMBLY
(Elected April 1982)

PARTY	SEATS
National Front	11
Pan-Malayan Islamic Party	1
TOTAL	12

SABAH

(Capital: Kota Kinabalu)

Yang di-Pertua Negeri: His Excellency Tun MOHAMAD ADNAN ROBERT.

Chief Minister: Datuk HARRIS SALLEH.

STATE ASSEMBLY
(Elected April 1981)

PARTY	SEATS
Berjaya (elected)	44
Berjaya (nominated)	6
USNO	3
SCCP	1
TOTAL	54

SARAWAK

(Capital: Kuching)

Yang di-Pertua Negeri: His Excellency Tan Sri Datuk Patinggi Abdul Rahman YA'KUB.

Chief Minister: Datuk Amar TAIB MAHMOOD.

STATE ASSEMBLY
(Elected September 1979)

PARTY	SEATS
National Front	45
Independents	3
TOTAL	48

SELANGOR

(Capital: Shah Alam)

Sultan: His Royal Highness Sultan SALAHUDDIN ABDUL AZIZ SHAH IBNI AL-MARHUM Sultan HISAMUDDIN ALAM SHAH Haji, D.K., D.M.N., S.P.M.S.

Menteri Besar: Datuk AHMAD RAZALI ALI.

STATE ASSEMBLY
(Elected April 1982)

PARTY	SEATS
National Front	31
Democratic Action Party	1
Independent	1
TOTAL	33

TRENGGANU

(Capital: Kuala Trengganu)

Sultan: His Royal Highness Tengku MAHMOOD IBNI AL-MARHUM Tuanku Sultan ISMAIL NASIRUDDIN SHAH.

Menteri Besar: Datuk WAN MOKHTAR BIN AHMAD, K.M.N. J.P., P.J.K.

STATE ASSEMBLY
(Elected April 1982)

PARTY	SEATS
National Front	23
Pan-Malayan Islamic Party	5
TOTAL	28

POLITICAL PARTIES

The National Front: a multiracial coalition of eleven parties; Sec.-Gen. ABDUL GHAFAR BABA. The component parties of the National Front are:

United Malay National Organization (UMNO): UMNO Bldg., 399 Jalan Tunku Abdul Rahman, Kuala Lumpur; f. 1946; Pres. Dr. MAHATHIR BIN MOHAMAD; Sec.-Gen. ABDUL GHAFAR BABA.

Barisan Jama'ah Islamiah Semalaysia (BERJASA) (*Front Malaysian Islamic Council*) (*FMIC*): 4960 Jalan Bayam (Dusun Muda), Kota Bahru, Kelantan; f. 1977 in opposition to the PAS; pro-Islamic policies;Pres. Dato Haji MOHAMAD NASIR; Sec.-Gen. ISMAIL ALI TAIB.

Berjaya (*Sabah People's Union*): 1st Floor, Natikar Building, P.O.B. 2130, Kota Kinabalu, Sabah; f. 1975; Pres. Datuk HARRIS SALLEH; Sec.-Gen. Haji MOHAMMED NOOR MANSOR.

Malaysian Chinese Association: P.O.B. 626, 163 Jalan Ampang, Kuala Lumpur, Pres. Datuk LEE SAN CHOON.

Malaysian Indian Congress (MIC): Wisma Tan Sri Manickavasagam, 1 Jalan Rahmat, off Jalan Tun Ismail, Kuala Lumpur; f. 1946; Pres. Datuk S. SAMY VELLU.

Parti Gerakan Rakyat Malaysia (GERAKAN): c/o Chief Minister's Office, Bungunan Tunku Syed Putra, Panang; f. 1968; Pres. Dr. LIM KENG YAIK.

Parti Pesaka Bumiputra Bersatu (PPBB) (*United Bumiputra Party*): Jalan Satok, Kuching, Sarawak; Pres. Datuk Pattingi Tan Sri ABDUL RAHMAN YA'KUB; Vice-Pres. Datuk AMAR Haji TAIB MAHMUD.

People's Progressive Party of Malaysia (PPP): 23 Jalan Bandar Raya, Ipoh, Perak; f. 1955; Pres. (vacant).

Sarawak National Party (SNAP): 304–305 Mei Jun Bldg., Rubber Rd., P.O.B. 2960, Kuching, Sarawak; f. 1961; Pres. Datuk JAMES WONG KIM MIN; Sec.-Gen. Y. B. Encik JOSEPH BALAN SELING.

Sarawak United People's Party (SUPP): 7 Central Rd., P.O.B. 454, Kuching, Sarawak; f. 1959; Pres. Tan Sri ONG KEE HUI.

United Sabah National Organization (USNO): Kota Kinabalu, Sabah; Pres. Tun Datu Haji MUSTAPHA BIN Datu HARUN.

Democratic Action Party: 27 Road 20/9, Petaling Jaya, Selangor; f. 1966; largest Opposition party in Parliament; advocates multi-racial Malaysia based on democratic socialism; Chair. Dr. CHEN MAN HIN; Sec.-Gen. LIM KIT SIANG.

Kesatuan Insaf Tanah Ayer (KITA) (*National Consciousness Party*): 41 Jalan Pasar, Taiping, Perak; Sec.-Gen. Encik SAMSURI MISU.

Kongres Indian Muslim Malaysia (KIMMA): 97-4 Jalan Pekeliling, Kuala Lumpur; f. 1976; aims to unite Malaysian Indian Muslims politically; Pres. BADRUL ZAMAN; Sec.-Gen. A. AHMAD TAJUDIN BIN ABDUL MAJID.

Pajar: Sarawak; f. 1978; Leader ALI KAWI.

Parti Islam Semalaysia (PAS) (*Pan-Malayan Islamic Party*): 28A Jalan Pahang, Kuala Lumpur; f. 1951; seeks to establish the Islamic system in society; Pres. Dato Haji MOHAMED Asri BIN Haji MUDA; Sec.-Gen. Mohd. NAPI NAKHAIE Haji AHMAD.

Parti Keadilan Masyarakat (PEKEMAS) (*Social Justice Party*): Kuala Lumpur; f. 1971; Chair. SHAHARYDDIN DAHALAN.

Parti Sosialis Rakyat Malaya (PSRM): 94C Jalan Bangsar, Kuala Lumpur; f. 1955; Chair. Encik KASSIM AHMAD (detained Nov. 1976); Sec.-Gen. ABDUL RAZAK AHMAD.

Pertubuhan Rakyat Sabah Bersatu (*United Sabah People's Organization* (*USPO*)): Tingkat 3, 9 Jalan Bendahara, Berjaya, Kg. Air, P.O.B. 993, Kota Kinabalu, Sabah.

Sabah Chinese Consolidated Party (*SCCP*): P.O.B. 704, Kota Kinabalu, Sabah; f. 1964; Sec.-Gen. CHAN TET ON.

Sarawak People's Organization (SAPO): Miri; mainly Chinese support; Sec.-Gen. RAYMOND SEZTU.

DIPLOMATIC REPRESENTATION

HIGH COMMISSIONS AND EMBASSIES ACCREDITED TO MALAYSIA

(In Kuala Lumpur unless otherwise stated)

(HC) High Commission; (E) Embassy.

Algeria: New Delhi, India (E).

Argentina: Bangkok, Thailand (E).

Australia: 6 Jalan Yap Kwan Seng (HC); *High Commissioner:* C. G. WOODARD.

Austria: 7th Floor, MUI Plaza Bldg., Jalan Parry, P.O.B. 154 (E); *Ambassador:* FRANZ PALLA.

Bangladesh: 204-1 Jalan Ampang (HC); *High Commissioner:* MUSTAFIZUR RAHMAN.

Belgium: 4th Floor, Wisma Bunga Raya, 152 Jalan Ampang, Kuala Lumpur 04-07 (E); *Ambassador:* JEAN J. L. DAVAUX.

Bolivia: 4th Floor, Suite 423, Kompleks Antarabangsa, Jalan Sultan Ismail (E); *Chargé d'affaires:* JORGE QUIROGA LUIZAGA.

Brazil: Hilton Hotel, Rooms 1003-1005, Jalan Sultan Ismail (E); *Ambassador:* SERGIO F. GUARISCHI BATH.

Bulgaria: 6 Jalan Taman U Thant, P.O.B. 1080 (E); *Ambassador:* MATEY KARASIMEONOV (resident in Jakarta).

Burma: 7 Jalan Taman U Thant (E); *Ambassador:* U MYINT AUNG.

Canada: 5th Floor, AIA Bldg., Jalan Ampang, P.O.B. 990 (HC); *High Commissioner:* G. F. G. HUGHES.

Chile: Jakarta, Indonesia (E).

China, People's Republic: 229 Jalan Ampang (E); *Ambassador:* YE CHENGZHANG.

Cuba: Tokyo, Japan (E).

Cyprus: New Delhi, India (HC).

Czechoslovakia: 32 Jalan Mesra, off Jalan Ampang (E); *Ambassador:* Dr. MILAN MACHA (resident in Jakarta).

Denmark: 3rd Floor, Denmark House Annexe, 86 Jalan Ampang, P.O.B. 908 (E); *Ambassador:* POUL H. KRYGER.

Egypt: 28 Lingkungan U Thant, P.O.B. 2004 (E); *Ambassador:* MAHMOUD EL-TOHAMY.

Ethiopia: Tokyo, Japan (E).

Fiji: Canberra, A.C.T., Australia (HC).

Finland: Wisma Angkasa Raya, 10th Floor, Jalan Ampang, P.O.B. 909 (E).

France: 210 Jalan Bukit Bintang, P.O.B. 700 (E); *Ambassador:* MARIE-THÉRÈSE CORBIE.

German Democratic Republic: 2A Pesiaran Gurney, P.O.B. 2511 (E); *Ambassador:* KLAUS MÄSER.

Germany, Federal Republic: 3 Jalan U Thant, P.O.B. 23 (E); *Ambassador:* Dr. HAUS FERDINAND LINSSER.

Ghana: Canberra, A.C.T., Australia (HC).

Greece: New Delhi, India (E).

Hungary: Jakarta, Indonesia (E).

India: United Asian Bank Bhd. Bldg., 19 Malacca St., P.O.B. 59 (HC); *High Commissioner:* PRAKASH SHAH.

Indonesia: 233 Jalan Pekeliling, P.O.B. 889 (E); *Ambassador:* MAKMUN MUROD.

Iran: (E); *Ambassador:* SADEGH AYOTOLLAHI.

Iraq: 2 Jalan Langgak Golf, off Jalan Pekeliling, P.O.B. 2022 (E); *Ambassador:* WAHBI ABDEL-RAZZAQ FATAN.

Ireland: New Delhi, India (E).

Italy: 11th Floor, Kompleks Kewangan, Jalan Raja Chulan; *Ambassador:* Dr. MARCELLO SPATAFORA.

Japan: 6th Floor, AIA Bldg., Jalan Ampang (E); *Ambassador:* TAKEO ARITA.

Jordan: Islamabad, Pakistan (E).

Korea, Democratic People's Republic: 203 Jalan Ampang (E); *Ambassador:* HO GYONG.

Korea, Republic: 422 Jalan Pekeliling (E); *Ambassador:* HO-JOONG CHOI.

Kuwait: Tokyo, Japan (E).

Laos: Bangkok, Thailand (E).

Lebanon: Islamabad, Pakistan (E).

Libya: 6 Jalan Madge, off Jalan U Thant.

Mexico: Jakarta, Indonesia (E).

Mongolia: Tokyo, Japan (E).

Morocco: Islamabad, Pakistan (E).

Nepal: Rangoon, Burma (E).

Netherlands: 3rd Floor, Denmark House Annexe, 86 Jalan Ampang, P.O.B. 543 (E); *Ambassador:* J. B. VAN HOEVE.

New Zealand: 193 Jalan Pekeliling, P.O.B. 2003 (HC); *High Commissioner:* M. MANSFIELD.

Norway: Jakarta, Indonesia (E).

Pakistan: 132 Jalan Ampang (E); *Ambassador:* Maj.-Gen. M. RAHIM KHAN.

Papua New Guinea: Jakarta, Indonesia (HC).

Philippines: 1 Cangkat Kia Peng (E); *Ambassador:* YUSUP R. ABUBAKAR.

Poland: 8B Jalan Ampang Hilir (E); *Ambassador:* JANUSZ SWITKOWSKI.

Portugal: Bangkok, Thailand (E).

Qatar: Islamabad, Pakistan (E).

Romania: 23 Jalan Mayang (E); *Ambassador:* ION COTOŢ (resident in Jakarta, Indonesia).

Saudi Arabia: 251 Jalan Pekeliling (E); *Ambassador:* Sheikh MOHAMED AL-HAMAS AL-SHUBAILI.

Singapore: 209 Jalan Pekeliling (HC); *High Commissioner:* WEE KIM WEE.

Somalia: Islamabad, Pakistan (E).

Spain: Bangkok, Thailand (E).

Sri Lanka: 29 Jalan Yap Kwan Seng, P.O.B. 717 (HC); *High Commissioner:* C. R. DIAS DESINGHE.

Sudan: New Delhi, India (E).

Sweden: 6th Floor, Wisma Angkasa Raya, Jalan Ampang, P.O.B. 239 (E); *Ambassador:* BENGT RÖSIÖ.

Switzerland: 16 Pesiaran Madge, P.O.B. 2008 (E); *Ambassador:* JEAN-PIERRE KEUSCH.

Syria: Jakarta, Indonesia (E).

Thailand: 206 Jalan Ampang (E); *Ambassador:* NISSAI VEJJAJIVA.

Turkey: 30 Jalan Inai, off Jalan Inibi (E); *Ambassador:* TEUFIK UNAYDIN.

U.S.S.R.: 263 Jalan Ampang (E); *Ambassador:* BORIS TROMIFOVICH KULIK.

United Kingdom: Wisma Damansara, 5 Jalan Semantan, P.O.B. 1030 (HC); *High Commissioner:* WILLIAM BENTLEY, C.M.G.

U.S.A.: AIA Bldg., Jalan Ampang (E); *Ambassador:* RONALD D. PALMER.

Viet-Nam: 4 Pesiaran Stonor (E); *Ambassador:* VU BACH MAI.

Yugoslavia: 353 Jalan Ampang, P.O.B. 2357 (E); *Ambassador:* LAZAR MUSICKI.

Malaysia also has diplomatic relations with Afghanistan, Albania, Guyana, Iceland, Jamaica, Maldives, Oman, Senegal and Trinidad and Tobago.

JUDICIAL SYSTEM

The two High Courts, one in Peninsular Malaysia and the other in Sabah and Sarawak, have original, appellate and revisional jurisdiction as the federal law provides. Above these two High Courts is a Federal Court which has, to the exclusion of any other court, jurisdiction in any dispute between States or between the Federation and any State; and has special jurisdiction as to the interpretation of the Constitution. There is also a right of appeal from the High Courts to the Federal Court and limited right of appeal from the Federal Court to the Yang di-Pertuan Agong who may refer appeals in certain civil matters to the Judicial Committee of the Privy Council in the United Kingdom. The High Courts each consist of the Chief Justice and a number of Judges. The Federal Court consists of the Lord President together with the two Chief Justices of the High Courts and six Federal Judges. The Lord President and Judges of the Federal Court, and the Chief Justices and Judges of the High Courts, are appointed by the Yang di-Pertuan Agong on the advice of the Prime Minister, after consulting the Conference of Rulers.

The Sessions Courts, which are situated in the principal urban and rural centres, are presided over by a President, who is a member of the Federation Legal and Judicial Service and is a qualified barrister or a Bachelor of Law from any of the recognized universities. Their criminal jurisdiction covers the less serious indictable offences, excluding those which carry penalties of death or life imprisonment. Civil cases are heard without a jury. Civil jurisdiction of a President's Sessions Court is up to M$25,000. The Presidents are appointed by the Yang di-Pertuan Agong.

The Magistrates' Courts are also found in the main urban and rural centres and have both civil and criminal jurisdiction, although of a more restricted nature than that of the Sessions Courts. The Magistrates consist of officers from either the Federation Legal and Judicial Service or are seconded from the administration to the Judicial Department for varying periods up to three years. They are appointed by the heads of the States in which they officiate on the recommendation of the Chief Justice.

Lord President of the Federal Court of Malaysia: Hon. Mr. Justice Tun MOHAMED SUFFIAN BIN HASHIM, S.S.M., D.I.M.P., J.M.N. (Brunei), P.J.K., M.A., LL.B.

Chief Justice of the High Court in Peninsular Malaysia: Hon. Mr. Justice Tan Sri RAJA AZLAN SHAH.

Chief Justice of the High Court in Sabah and Sarawak: Hon. Mr. Justice Tan Sri Datuk LEE HUN HOE.

Attorney-General: Tan Sri Datuk ABU TALIB BIN OTHMAN.

RELIGION

Islam is the established religion but freedom of religious practice is guaranteed. All Malays are Muslims. A small minority of Chinese are Christians but most Chinese follow Buddhism, Confucianism or Daoism. Of the Indian community, about 70 per cent are Hindu, 20 per cent Muslim, 5 per cent Christian and 2 per cent Sikh. In Sabah and Sarawak there are many animists.

ISLAM

President of the Majlis Islam: Datuk AMAR Haji ABANG IKHWAN ZAINI, Kuching, Sarawak.

CHRISTIANITY

ANGLICAN

Bishop of West Malaysia: The Rt. Rev. Tan Sri J. G. SAVARIMUTHU, P.S.M., B.D., Bishop's House, 14 Pesiaran Stonor, Kuala Lumpur 04-08.

Bishop of Sabah: Rt. Rev. LUKE CHHOA HENG SZE, Bishop's House, P.O.B. 811, Kota Kinabalu, Sabah.

Bishop of Kuching: Rt. Rev. Datuk BASIL TEMENGONG, Bishop's House, P.O.B. 347, Kuching, Sarawak.

ROMAN CATHOLIC

Archbishop of Kuala Lumpur: Rt. Rev. Tan Sri DOMINIC VENDARGON, 528 Jalan Bukit Nanas, Kuala Lumpur 04-01.

Archbishop of Kuching: Rt. Rev. PETER CHUNG HOAN TING, St. Peter's Seminary, P.O.B. 327, Kuching, Sarawak.

METHODIST

Bishop for Malaysia: Rev. C. N. FANG, Tingkat 8, Wisma Methodist, Lorong Hang Jebat, Kuala Lumpur 05-05; the Church has 85,000 members.

THE PRESS

PENINSULAR MALAYSIA

DAILIES

ENGLISH LANGUAGE

Business Times: 31 Jalan Riong, Kuala Lumpur 22-03; f. 1976; Editor HENRY CHANG; circ. 9,500.

Malay Mail: 31 Jalan Riong, P.O.B. 250, Kuala Lumpur 22-03; f. 1896; afternoon; Editor AHMAD SEBI; circ. 51,714 in all states of Malaysia.

National Echo: P.O.B. S-55, Sentul, Kuala Lumpur; f. 1903; morning; Group Editor Dato MOHAMED SOPIEE; circ. 33,000.

New Straits Times: 31 Jalan Riong, P.O.B. 250, Kuala Lumpur 22-03; f. 1945; morning; Editor LIM THOU BOON; circ. 185,670 in all states of Malaysia.

The Star: 13 Jalan 13/6, Petaling Jaya, P.O.B. 2474, Selangor; f. 1971; morning and evening; Chief Editor HUNG-YONG H'NG; circ. 98,000 (weekdays), 80,000 (Sunday).

CHINESE LANGUAGE

Chung Kuo Pao (*China Press*): 2 Market St., Kuala Lumpur; f. 1946; morning; Publisher NG HON YUEN; Editor-in-Chief WONG SIEW HOON; circ. 42,357.

Kin Kwok Daily News: 6 Jalan 13/6, Petaling Jaya, Selangor; f. 1940; morning; Editor PUAH YOU LAI; circ. 60,000.

Kwong Wah Yit Poh: 2-4 Chulia St., Chaut, Penang; f. 1910; morning; Chief Editor CHUNG SHING FONG; circ. 20,000 (weekdays), 25,000 (Sunday).

Malayan Thung Pau: 40 Jalan Lima, off Jalan Chan Sow Lin, Kuala Lumpur; f. 1959; Chief Editor LIM THOONG KWONG; circ. 47,716.

Nanyang Siang Pau (Malaysia): 80 Jalan Riong, Kuala Lumpur; f. 1923; morning; Editor-in-Chief CHU CHEE CHIAN; circ. 119,000.

Shin Min Daily News: 19–19C Jalan Murai Dua, Batu 3, Jalan Ipoh, P.O.B. 920, Kuala Lumpur; f. 1966; morning and evening; Editor-in-Chief PAUL CHIN; circ. 100,000.

Sin Chew Jit Poh Malaysia: 19 Jalan Semangat, P.O.B. 367, Jalan Sultan, Petaling Jaya; f. 1929; morning; Editor-in-Chief LIEW CHEN CHUAN (acting); circ. 66,000 (daily), 72,000 (Sunday).

Sing Pin Jih Pao: 8 Leith St., Penang; f. 1939; morning; Publr. FOO YEE FONG; Editor-in-Chief CHEAH SEE KIAN; circ. 39,900.

TAMIL LANGUAGE

Tamil Nesan: 37 Jalan Ampang, P.O.B. 299, Kuala Lumpur; f. 1924; morning; Editor V. VIVEKANANTHAN; circ. 25,000 (daily), 45,400 (Sunday).

Tamil Osai: 336-B Jalan Ipoh, Sentul, Kuala Lumpur; Editor ATHI KUMANAN; circ. 10,000 (daily), 23,000 (Sunday).

Thinamani: 9 Jalan Murai Dua, Batu Complex, Jalan Ipoh, Kuala Lumpur; Editor S. NACHIAPPAN; circ. 18,000 (daily), 45,000 (Sunday).

MALAY LANGUAGE

Berita Harian: 31 Jalan Riong, P.O.B. 250, Kuala Lumpur 22-03; f. 1957; morning; Editor Encik SALIM KAJAI; circ. 190,000 in all states of Malaysia.

Bintang Timur: 216 Penang Road, Penang; Editor-in-Chief KADIR AHMAD; circ. 20,000.

Mingguan Perdana: 48 Jalan Siput Akek, Taman Billion, Kuala Lumpur; Group Chief Editor KHALID JAFRI.

Mengguan Tanahair: 246-A Jalan Ipoh, Kuala Lumpur; Chief Editor IKHWAN NASIR.

Utusan Malaysia: 46M Jalan Chan Sow Lin, P.O.B. 671, Kuala Lumpur; f. 1965; morning; Editor-in-Chief MAZLAN NORDIN; circ. 215,000.

Utusan Melayu: 46M Jalan Chan Sow Lin, P.O.B. 671, Kuala Lumpur; f. 1939; morning; Editor-in-Chief MAZLAN NORDIN; circ. 201,000.

PUNJABI LANGUAGE

Malaya Samachar: 265 Jalan Brickfields, Kuala Lumpur; f. 1965; evening; Editor TIRLOCHAN SINGH; circ. 2,500.

Navjiwan Punjabi News: 52 Jalan 8/81, Jalan Taman, Petaling Jaya; Associate Editor TARA SINGH.

SUNDAY PAPERS

ENGLISH LANGUAGE

National Sunday Echo: 216 Penang Rd., Penang; f. 1930; morning; Group Editor K. C. CHIEN; circ. 45,000.

New Sunday Times: 31 Jalan Riong, P.O.B. 250, Kuala Lumpur 22-03; f. 1845; morning; Editor P. C. SHIVADAS; circ. 242,000 in all states of Malaysia.

Sunday Mail: 31 Jalan Riong, P.O.B. 250, Kuala Lumpur 22-03; f. 1896; morning; Editor JOACHIN S. P. NG; circ. 90,000 in all states of Malaysia.

Sunday Star: 13 Jalan 13/6, Petaling Jaya, P.O.B. 2474, Selangor; f. 1971; Editor-in-Chief HUNG-YONG H'NG; circ. 120,000.

MALAY LANGUAGE

Berita Minggu: 31 Jalan Riong, P.O.B. 250, Kuala Lumpur 22-03; f. 1957; morning; Editor Encik SUTAN SHAHRIL LEMBANG; circ. 191,651 in all states of Malaysia.

Mingguan Malaysia: 46M Jalan Chan Sow Lin, P.O.B. 671, Kuala Lumpur; f. 1964; Sunday; Editor-in-Chief MAZLAN NORDIN; circ. 242,848.

Mingguan Timur: 216 Penang Rd., Penang; f. 1951; Editor MOHD. YUSOFF SHARIFF; circ. 20,000.

Utusan Zaman: 46M Jalan Chan Sow Lin, P.O.B. 671, Kuala Lumpur; f. 1939; Editor MUSTAFA FADULA SHUHAIMI; circ. 57,175.

PERIODICALS

ENGLISH LANGUAGE

Fanfare: Balai Berita, 31 Jalan Riong, Kuala Lumpur 22-03; f. 1969; monthly; Editor AYESHA HARBEN; circ. 11,000.

Galaxie: 6 Jalan Travers, Kuala Lumpur; f. 1974; weekly; Editor Mr. S. F. YONG; circ. 30,000.

Her World: Balai Berita, 31 Jalan Riong, Kuala Lumpur 22-03; monthly; Editor AYESHA HARBEN; circ. 17,000.

Malaysia Warta Kerajaan Seri Paduka Baginda (H.M. Government Gazette): Kuala Lumpur; fortnightly.

Malaysian Agricultural Journal: Ministry of Agriculture, Jalan Mahameru, Kuala Lumpur; f. 1901; twice yearly.

Malaysian Forester: Forest Research Institute, Kepong, Selangor; f. 1931; Editors N. MANOKARAN, WONG TUCK MENG.

New Straits Times Annual: Balai Berita, 31 Jalan Riong, Kuala Lumpur; Editor Miss NG POH TIP; circ. 7,900.

The Planter: 29, 31 & 33 Jalan Taman U Thant, P.O.B. 262, Kuala Lumpur 01-02; f. 1919; Incorporated Society of Planters; monthly; Editor M. RAJADURAI; circ. 3,500.

CHINESE LANGUAGE

Mister Magazine: 2 Jalan 19/1, Petaling Jaya, Selangor; f. 1976; monthly; Editor CHEW SUNG; circ. 60,000.

New Life Post: 2 Jalan 19/1, Petaling Jaya, Selangor; f. 1972; bi-weekly; Editor GOH TUCK HAI; circ. 120,000.

New Tide Magazine: 2 Jalan 19/1, Petaling Jaya, Selangor; f. 1974; every three weeks; Editor CHEONG SAW LAN; circ. 68,000.

MALAY LANGUAGE

Dewan Masyarakat: Dewan Bahasa dan Pustaka, Jalan Wisma Putra, P.O.B. 803, Kuala Lumpur; f. 1963; current affairs; monthly; Chief Editor M. NOOR AZAM; circ. 45,000.

Dewan Pelajar: Dewan Bahasa dan Pustaka, Jalan Wisma Putra, P.O.B. 803, Kuala Lumpur 08-08; f. 1967; children's magazine; monthly; Editor SALEH DAUD; circ. 45,000.

Jelita: Balai Berita, 31 Jalan Riong, Kuala Lumpur 22-03; monthly; family magazine; Editor ZAHARAH NAWAWI; circ. 36,500.

Mastika: 46M Jalan Chan Sow Lin, Kuala Lumpur; Malayan illustrated magazine; monthly; Editor AZIZAH ALI; circ. 40,000.

Pengasoh: Majlis Ugama Islam, Kota Bahru, Kelantan; f. 1918; monthly; Editor YUSOFF ZAKY YACOB; circ. 15,000.

Sinar Zaman: Jalan Tun Perak, Kuala Lumpur; produced by the Federal Information Services; Editor ABDUL AZIZ MALIM.

Utusan Filem dan Feshen: 46M Jalan Chan Sow Lin, Kuala Lumpur; cinema; fortnightly; Editor MUSTAFA BIN ABDUL RAHIM; circ. 34,656.

Utusan Radio dan TV: 46M Jalan Chan Sow Lin, Kuala Lumpur; fortnightly; Editor NORSHAH TAMBY; circ. 89,380.

Wanita: 46M Jalan Chan Sow Lin, Kuala Lumpur; women; weekly; Editor NIK RAHIMAH HASSAN; circ. 107,008.

Watan Harian Nasional: 12 Jalan Murai, Batu Complex, Jalan Ipoh, Kuala Lumpur 04-09; f. 1977; Malay and English; weekly; Editor MOKHTAR SHUIB; circ. 25,000.

TAMIL LANGUAGE

Janobahari: Ipoh, Perak; f. 1946; monthly; produced by Information Services; Editor C. V. KUPPUSAMY; circ. 25,000.

PUNJABI LANGUAGE

Navjiwan Punjabi News: 52 Jalan 8/18, Petaling Jaya, Selangor; f. 1970; weekly; Associate Editor TARA SINGH; circ. 8,500.

SABAH

DAILIES

Api Siang Pau (*Kota Kinabalu Commercial Press*): 24 Lorong Dewan, P.O.B. 170, Kota Kinabalu; f. 1954; Chinese; morning; Editor Datuk LO KWOCK CHUEN; circ. 3,000.

Daily Express: P.O.B. 139, 75 Gaya St., Kota Kinabalu; f. 1963; English and Malay; morning; Editor-in-Chief JOSEPH M. FERNANDEZ; circ. 15,000.

Hwa Chiaw Jit Pao (*Overseas Chinese Daily News*): P.O.B. 139, 9 Gaya St., Kota Kinabalu; f. 1936; Chinese; morning; Editor HII YUK SENG; circ. 27,925.

Kinabalu Sabah Times: P.O.B. 525, 76 Gaya St., Kota Kinabalu; f. 1952; English, Malay and Kadazan; Editor YAHAYA ISMAIL; circ. 15,481.

Merdeka Daily News: P.O.B. 332, Sandakan; f. 1968; Chinese; morning; Editor-in-Chief KWAN KUH HANG; circ. 18,600.

SARAWAK

DAILIES

Berita Petang Sarawak: LOT 163, Chan Chin Ann, Kuching; f. 1972; Chinese; evening; Chief Editor LAI SHIANG; circ. 9,500.

Borneo Post: Borneo Post Sendirian Bhd., Kuching; English; Chief Editor Encik SOO YEE HIE.

Chinese Daily News: P.O.B. 138, Kuching; f. 1945; Chinese; Editor SOW THAI SHOOK; circ. 5,000.

International Times Daily: Lot 200, Jalan Abell, Kuching; f. 1968; Chinese; morning; Editor TAY HIANG BOON; circ. 10,000.

Malaysia Daily News: 7 Island Rd., P.O.B. 237, Sibu; f. 1968; Chinese; morning; Editor WONG SENG KWONG; circ. 26,500.

Miri Daily News: Piasau Industrial Estate, P.O.B. 377, Miri; f. 1957; Chinese; morning; Editor CHAI SZE-VOON; circ. 17,000.

Sarawak Siang Pau: 4 Ole St., Sibu; f. 1966; Chinese; daily; Editor CHEE GUAN HOCK; circ. 5,000.

Sarawak Tribune and Sunday Tribune: Jalan Nipah, off Jalan Abell Utara, P.O.B. 138, Kuching; f. 1945; English; Editor B. R. ADAI; circ. 15,200.

See Hua Daily News: 11 Island Rd., Sibu; f. 1952; Chinese; morning; Editor SIA KAT DIENG; circ. 18,600.

Utusan Sarawak: Abell Rd., Kuching; f. 1949; Malay; Editor JAMIL BIN Haji BUSRAH; circ. 1,500.

PERIODICALS

Dewan Perintis: Dewan Bahasa dan Pustaka Cawangan Sarawak, P.O.B. 1390, Kuching; f. 1978; Bahasa Malaysia and English; monthly; aims to promote use of Bahasa Malaysia; Chief Editor OTHMAN ISMAIL.

Pedoman Ra'ayat: Malaysian Information Service, Kuching; f. 1956; Malay; monthly; Editor Haji MOHD. RAKAWI BIN TAN SRI IKHWAN; circ. 6,000.

Pemborita: Malaysian Information Office, Kuching; f. 1956; Iban and Chinese; monthly; Editor DUNSTAN MELLING; circ. 6,000.

Sarawak Gazette: Govt. Printing Office, Kuching; f. 1870; English; quarterly; Editor-in-Chief Datuk AMAR ABANG Haji YUSUF PUTEH; circ. 1,000.

Sarawak by the Week: Malaysian Information Services, Mosque Rd., Kuching; f. 1961; weekly; Malay and Dayak; circ. 2,700.

NEWS AGENCIES

Bernama (*Malaysian National News Agency*): 42 Jalan Syed Putra, P.O.B. 24, Kuala Lumpur 01-02; f. 1967; general and foreign news service and economic feature, photo and radio teletype services; daily output in Malay and English; Gen. Man. AHMAD MUSTAPHA.

FOREIGN BUREAUX

Agence France-Presse (AFP): P.O.B. 2627, Kuala Lumpur; Correspondent G. NAIR.

Associated Press (AP) (*U.S.A.*): China Insurance Bldg., 174 Jalan Tuanku Abdul Rahman, P.O.B. 2219, Kuala Lumpur; Correspondent HARI SUBRAMANIAM.

Reuters (*U.K.*): 3rd Floor, Wisma Ng Goon Han, 33/35 Jalan Klyne, P.O.B. 841, Kuala Lumpur; Representative LUIZ WORSDELL.

Tass (*U.S.S.R.*): 297-C Jalan Ampang, Kuala Lumpur; Representative G. M. SHMELYOV.

Thai News Agency: 124-F Burmah Rd., Penang; Kuala Lumpur; Representative SOOK BURANAKUL.

UNICOM News (UCN) (*U.S.A.*): Wisma Teck Choon, 2nd Floor, 70–72 Jalan Tun Perak, Kuala Lumpur 01-19; Representative K. LIM.

Xinhua (*People's Republic of China*) also has a bureau in Kuala Lumpur.

NEWSPAPER ASSOCIATION

Persatuan Penerbit-Penerbit Akhbar Malaysia (*Malaysian Newspaper Publishers' Association*): 3rd Floor, Wisma Socfin, Jalan Semantan, Damansara Heights, Kuala Lumpur 23-03; Chair. Encik NIK IBRAHIM BIN KAMIL.

PUBLISHERS

Kuala Lumpur

Berita Publishing Sdn. Bhd.: Balai Berita, 31 Jalan Riong; romances, children's and school books, newspapers and periodicals; Man. Dir. AYOUB Dato ISMAIL.

Dewan Bahasa Dan Pustaka: P.O.B. 803, Kuala Lumpur 08-08; f. 1956; textbooks, literature, general books and children's books; Dir.-Gen. TUAN HJ HASSAN AHMAD.

Longman Malaysia Sdn. Bhd.: 2nd Floor, Wisma Damansara, Jalan Semantan, P.O.B. 63; textbooks, general books, educational materials; Dir. J. B. HO.

Marican and Sons (Malaysia) Sdn. Bhd.: 321 Jalan Tuanku Abdul Rahman; publishers and booksellers.

M. S. Geetha Publishers: 13A Jalan Kouil Hilir Batu 2½, Jalan Ipoh, Sentul, Kuala Lumpur 13-05; history, education, reference and textbooks; Man. Dir. SETHU.

University of Malaya Press Ltd.: University of Malaya, Lembah Pantai, Kuala Lumpur 22-11; f. 1954; general fiction, literature, economics, history, medicine, politics, general and social science; Man. Dir. HARUN Haji ABDULLAH.

Negri Sembilan

Bharathi Press: 23-24 Jalan Tuan Sheikh, Seremban, P.O.B. 74; f. 1939; Partners C. RAMASAMY, M. R. N. MUTHURENGAM, M. SUBRAMANIA BHARATHI.

Penang

Kwong Wah Yit Poh Press Bhd: 2–4 Chulia St., Ghaut, P.O.B. 31; f. 1910; daily news; Man. Dir. OON CHOO KHYE.

Sino Malay Publishing Co. Ltd.: 272-D Jalan Ayer Hitam, Penang.

Perak

Charles Grenier Sdn. Bhd.: 37/39 Station Rd., P.O.B. 130, Ipoh; Man. Dir. Dato Seri J. E. S. CRAWFORD.

Selangor

Federal Publications Sdn. Bhd.: Lot 8238, Jalan 222, Petaling Jaya; educational books; Man. H. S. KHOO.

FEP International Sdn. Bhd.: Lot 8246 Jalan 225, P.O.B. 1091, Petaling Jaya; textbooks and reference books; Man. Dir. LIM MOK HAI.

Oxford University Press: 3 Jalan 13/3, Petaling Jaya; f. 1957; educational and general, dictionaries and reference books; S.-E. Asia Gen. Man. M. SOCKALINGAM.

RADIO AND TELEVISION

Radio Television Malaysia (RTM): Department of Broadcasting, Angkasapuri, Kuala Lumpur 22-10; f. 1946 (television 1963); Dir.-Gen. Datuk ABDULLAH MOHAMAD; Dir. News TAMIMUDDIN KARIM; supervises radio and television broadcasting in Malaysia.

SABAH

Radio Television Malaysia (Sabah): Jalan Tuavan, P.O.B. 1016, Kota Kinabalu; f. 1955; incorporated as a department of Radio Malaysia 1963 (television introduced 1971); broadcasts programmes 244 hours a week in Malay, English, Chinese (2 dialects), Kadazan, Murut, Dusun, Bajau and Tagalog (*Voice of Malaysia*); Dir. TAMIMUDDIN ABDUL KARIM.

SARAWAK

Radio Television Malaysia (Sarawak): Broadcasting House, Jalan Satok, Kuching; f. 1954; incorporated as a department of Radio Malaysia 1963; broadcasts in Malay, English, Chinese, Iban, Bidayuh, Melanau, Kayan/Kenyah, Bisayah and Murut; Dir. Haji MOKHTAR DAUD.

RADIO

PENINSULAR MALAYSIA

Radio Malaysia: Department of Broadcasting, Angkasapuri, Kuala Lumpur 22-10; f. 1946; domestic service; operates 6 networks; broadcasts in Bahasa Malaysia, English, Chinese (Mandarin and other dialects) and Tamil; Controller of Programmes ISMAIL HASHIM.

Suara Malaysia (*Voice of Malaysia*): overseas service in Arabic, Burmese, English, Indonesian, Chinese (Mandarin), Bahasa Malaysia, Tagalog and Thai; Head of Overseas Service AZIZ WOK.

Rediffusion (Malaya) Sdn. Bhd.: P.O.B. 570, Kuala Lumpur; f. 1949; 2 programmes; Man. Dir. M. J. BLEECK; 33,953 subscribers in Kuala Lumpur; 13,240 subscribers in Penang; 11,928 subscribers in Ipoh.

In 1980 there were 290,150 radio receivers in use.

TELEVISION

Television Malaysia: Angkasapuri, Kuala Lumpur 22-10; operates 4 television networks; Controller of Programmes ZAINAL ABU.

In 1980 there were 965,953 licensed television receivers in Peninsular Malaysia. Colour television transmissions began in December 1978.

FINANCE

BANKING

(cap. = capital; p.u. = paid up; dep. = deposits; m. = million; brs. = branches; M$ = Malaysian dollars/ringgits; Bhd. = Berhad)

CENTRAL BANK

Bank Negara Malaysia: Jalan Kuching, P.O.B. 922, Kuala Lumpur 01-02; f. 1959; bank of issue; cap. p.u. M$100m., dep. M$5,038.4m. (Dec. 1980); Gov. Dato ABDUL AZIZ BIN Haji TAHA, J.M.N.; Deputy Gov. Dr. LIN SEE YAN; 6 brs.

COMMERCIAL BANKS

Peninsular Malaysia

Ban Hin Lee Bank Bhd.: 43 Beach St., P.O.B. 232, Penang; f. 1935; cap. p.u. M$100m., dep. M$242.9m. (Dec. 1981); Chair. YEAP TEIK LEONG; Chief Exec. GOH ENG TOON; 9 brs.

Bank Bumiputra Malaysia Bhd.: P.O.B. 407, Menara Bumiputra, Jalan Melaka, Kuala Lumpur 01-18; f. 1965; cap. p.u. M$476m., dep. M$9,264m. (Dec. 1981); Exec. Chair. Dr. NAWAWI BIN MAT AWIN; Exec. Dir. MOHD. HASHIM SHAMSUDIN; 84 brs.

Bank Buruh (Malaysia) Bhd.: 2-8 Jalan Gereja, P.O.B. 591, Kuala Lumpur 01-17; f. 1975; cap. p.u. M$16.4m., dep. M$63.5m. (June 1981); Chair. P. P. NARAYANAN; Senior Vice-Chair. S. J. H. ZAIDI.

Bank of Commerce Bhd.: 11th Floor, Wisma Stephens, Jalan Raja Chulan, P.O.B. 566, Kuala Lumpur; cap. p.u. M$10m., dep. M$143m. (Dec. 1980); Chair. Datuk JUNUS SUDIN; Exec. Dir. P. J. BOLAND; 3 brs.

Development and Commercial Bank (Ltd.) Bhd.: 18 Jalan Silang, P.O.B. 145, Kuala Lumpur 01-02; f. 1966; cap. p.u. M$30.0m., dep. M$768m. (Dec. 1980); Chair. Tun Sir HENRY H. S. LEE; Gen. Man. Sen. ALEXANDER Y. L. LEE; 21 brs.

Kwong Yik Bank Bhd.: 75 Jalan Bandar, P.O.B. 135, Kuala Lumpur; f. 1913; cap. p.u. M$12m., dep. M$370.1m. (Dec. 1981); Chair. Dato JAFFAR HUSSEIN; Exec. Dir. ABDUL GHANI AHMAD; 15 brs.

Malayan Banking Bhd.: 92 Jalan Bandar, P.O.B. 2010, Kuala Lumpur 01-20; f. 1960; cap. p.u. M$180m., dep. M$6,800m. (Nov. 1981); Chair. Datuk JAFFAR HUSSEIN; Exec. Dir. RAJA BADROL AHMAD; 157 brs.

Oriental Bank Bhd.: P.O.B. 243, 111 Jalan Bukit Bintang, Kuala Lumpur 01-25; f. 1936; cap. p.u. M$5m., dep. M$363.9m. (Dec. 1980); Chair. Dato BORHAN BIN KUNTOM; Gen. Mans. MOHAMED MAZLAN BIN IDRIS, CHEE ENG TONG; 12 brs.

Pacific Bank Bhd.: Wisma Hangsam, Jalan Hang Lekir, P.O.B. 43, Kuala Lumpur; f. 1963; cap. p.u. M$9.0m., dep. M$282m. (1981); Chair. Tun TAN SIEW SIN; Gen. Man. MARK C. BLACKER.

Perwira Habib Bank Malaysia Bhd.: 1st Floor, MUI Plaza, Jalan Parry, P.O.B. 459, Kuala Lumpur; f. 1975; cap. p.u. M$25m., dep. M$743.0m. (Dec. 1981); Chair.

Gen. Tan Sri Datuk IBRAHIM BIN Datuk ISMAIL; Exec. Dir. Datuk MOHD. SALLEH YUSOF.

Public Bank Bhd.: Bangunan Public Bank, 6 Jalan Sulaiman, P.O.B. 2542, Kuala Lumpur 01-33; f. 1965; cap. p.u. M$25m., dep. M$1,172m. (June 1981); Exec. Chair. Datuk TEH HONG PIOW; 16 brs.

Southern Banking Bhd.: 2 Jalan Raja Chulan, Kuala Lumpur; f. 1963; cap. p.u. M$20m., dep. M$416m. (March 1982); Chair. Datuk SAW CHOO THENG; Gen. Man. Tan HOCK SENG; 13 brs.

United Asian Bank Bhd.: 12 Jalan Tuanku Abdul Rahman, P.O.B. 753, Kuala Lumpur; f. 1973; cap. p.u. M$50.8m., dep. M$1,035.6m. (Dec. 1979); Chair. Y. A. M. Tengku IBRAHIM IBNI Sultan Sir ABU BAKAR; Chief Exec. Dir. M. SUPPIAH; 29 brs.

United Malayan Banking Corporation Bhd.: Bangunan UMBC, Jalan Sultan Sulaiman, P.O.B. 2006, Kuala Lumpur; f. 1960; cap. p.u. M$45m., dep. M$1,410m. (Dec. 1979); Chair. ABDUL RAHMAN BIN ABDUL HAMID; Exec. Dir. BOON KOK CHENG; 50 brs.

Sabah

Hock Hua Bank (Sabah) Bhd.: subsidiary of Hock Hua Bank Bhd. (Sarawak); 59/61 Jalan Tiga, Sandakan; f. 1961; cap. p.u. M$10m., dep. M$151.7m. (March 1982); Chair. Datuk AMAR LING BENG SIEW, P.N.B.S.; Exec. Dirs. LAU HIENG ING, JOHN TING; 4 brs.

Sabah Bank Bhd.: Lot 4-6, Block K, Sinsuran Shopping Complex, W.D.T. 132, Kota Kinabalu; f. 1980; cap. p.u. M$10m., dep. M$304m. (Dec. 1980); Chair. Tan Sri Datuk THOMAS JAYASUIRYA; Gen. Man. C. N. AZIZ.

Sarawak

Bank Utama (Malaysia) Bhd.: Jalan Tun Haji Openg, P.O.B. 2049, Kuching; f. 1976; cap. p.u. M$5.0m., dep. M$67.7m. (Dec. 1980); Chair. Haji BIDARI BIN Tan Sri Datuk Haji MOHAMED.

Hock Hua Bank Bhd.: Head Office: 3 Central Rd., Sibu; f. 1951; cap. p.u. M$10.6m., dep. M$329.8m. (Dec. 1981); Chair. Datuk AMAR LING BENG SIEW, D.A., P.N.B.S.; Man. Dir. Datuk TING LIK HUNG, O.B.E., P.B.S., P.N.B.S.; 8 brs.

Kong Ming Bank Bhd.: Head Office: 82 Market Road, P.O.B. 656, Sibu; f. 1963; cap. p.u. M$5m., dep. M$176.1m. (Dec. 1981); Chair. Datuk LING BENG SUNG; Man. Dir. LING BENG KING; 8 brs.

Kwong Lee Bank Bhd.: Head Office: 30 Main Bazaar, P.O.B. 33, Kuching; f. 1923; cap. p.u. M$10m., dep. M$144.2m. (Dec. 1979); Chair. Y. A. M. Tunku OSMAN IBNI Tunku TEMENGGONG AHMAD; Exec. Dirs. LAWRENCE LAM KWOK FOU, Dato TEO AH KHIANG; 8 brs.

Wah Tat Bank Bhd.: 15 Bank Rd., P.O.B. 87, Sibu; f. 1929; cap. p.u. M$2.0m., dep. M$59.9m. (Dec. 1981); Chair. Dr. CHEW PENG HONG; Man. Dirs. CHEW PENG ANN, CHEW PENG CHENG; 2 brs.

MERCHANT BANKS

Association of Merchant Banks in Malaysia:

Malaysian International Merchant Bankers Bhd. (Chairman Bank): 5th Floor, Bangunan Yee Seng, Jalan Raja Chulan, P.O.B. 2250, Kuala Lumpur 05-02; Chair. GEH IK CHEONG.

UDA Merchant Bankers Bhd. (Secretary Bank): 17th Floor, Plaza See Hoy Chan, Jalan Raja Chulan, Kuala Lumpur 05-10.

Amanah-Chase Merchant Bank Bhd: 19th Floor, Bangunan Kompleks Kewangan, 82 Jalan Raja Chulan, P.O.B. 2492, Kuala Lumpur 01-02; Gen. Man. MOHD IBRAHIM ZAIN.

Arab-Malaysian Development Bank Bhd.: Bangunan Dato Zainal, Jalan Melaka, P.O.B. 233, Kuala Lumpur 01-02; Exec. Dir. GHAZALI BIN Dato YUSOFF.

Aseambankers Malaysia Bhd.: 15th Floor, MUI Plaza, Jalan Parry, P.O.B. 1057, Kuala Lumpur 01-02; f. 1973; Man. Dir. IZHAM MAMUD.

Asian International Merchant Bankers Bhd.: 5th Floor, Bangunan UMBC, Jalan Sulaiman, P.O.B. 988, Kuala Lumpur 01-33; Gen. Man. WONG HENG WOOI.

Asiavest Merchant Bankers (M) Bhd.: 9th Floor, Wisma Budiman, Persiaran Raja Chulan, Kuala Lumpur 05-01; Man. Dir. and Chair. Dr. SYED MAHMOOD BIN SYED HUSSAIN.

Bumiputra Merchant Bankers Bhd.: 12th Floor, Menara Bumiputra, Jalan Melaka, P.O.B. 890, Kuala Lumpur 01-18.

Chartered Merchant Bankers Malaysia Bhd.: 7th Floor, Chartered Bank Bldg., 2 Jalan Ampang, P.O.B. 1001, Kuala Lumpur 01-16; Gen. Man. DAVID BERRY.

D. & C. Nomura Merchant Bankers Bhd.: 10th Floor, MUI Plaza, Jalan Parry, Kuala Lumpur 04-01; f. 1974; Chair. Tun Sir HENRY HAU SHIK LEE.

Pertanian Baring Sanwa Bhd.: 8th Floor, Bangunan Bank Pertanian, Jalan Leboh Pasar Besar, P.O.B. 2362, Kuala Lumpur 01-02; a joint venture between Bank Pertanian Malaysia, Baring Bros. & Co. Ltd. (U.K.), and Sanwa Bank Ltd. (Japan).

Rakyat First Merchant Bankers Bhd.: 5th Floor, Bangunan Angkasa Raya, Jalan Ampang, P.O.B. 2346, Kuala Lumpur.

CO-OPERATIVE BANK

Bank Kerjasama Rakyat Malaysia Bhd.: Bangunan Bank Rakyat, Jalan Tangsi, P.O.B. 1024, Kuala Lumpur 10-01; Chair. Tan Sri Dato IBRAHIM SALLEH; Man. Dir. ABDUL AZIZ ABDUL RAHMAN.

DEVELOPMENT BANKS

Industrial Development Bank of Malaysia: Kuala Lumpur; f. 1979; government-owned; finances long-term, high-technology projects; auth. cap. U.S. $100m., of which U.S. $20m. is paid up.

Sabah Development Bank: Ground Floor, Berjaya H.Q. Bldg., P.O.B. 2172, Kota Kinabalu, Sabah; f. 1977; wholly owned by State Government of Sabah; auth. cap. M$100m., of which M$45m. is paid up; Man. Dir. RICHARD W. MANING.

FOREIGN BANKS

Algemene Bank Nederland N.V. (*Netherlands*): Wisma Sachdev 16-2, Jalan Raja Laut, P.O.B. 94, Kuala Lumpur; f. 1888; dep. M$22.4m. (Dec. 1977); Man. JAN ELZINGA.

Bangkok Bank Ltd. (*Thailand*): 105 Jalan Bandar, P.O.B. 734, Kuala Lumpur 01-22; f. 1959; dep. M$113.3m. (Dec. 1979); Gen. Man. BOOM SERMSUKSKUL.

Bank of America N.T. and S.A. (*U.S.A.*): P.O.B. 950, Kompleks Antarabangsa, Jalan Sultan Ismail, Kuala Lumpur; f. 1963; dep. M$74.0m. (Dec. 1976); Man. PHILIP J. HORAN.

Bank of Canton Ltd. (*Hong Kong*): 16-20 Leboh Pudu, P.O.B. 980, Kuala Lumpur 01-22; f. 1957; dep. M$29.5m. (Dec. 1977): Man. LEOW BOCK LIM.

Bank of Nova Scotia (*Canada*): 41 Jalan Melayu, Bangunan Safety Insurance, P.O.B. 1056, Kuala Lumpur; f. 1973; dep. M$69.6m. (Oct. 1981); Man. D. H. STEWART.

Bank of Tokyo Ltd. (*Japan*): 22 Medan Pasar, P.O.B. 959, Kuala Lumpur; f. 1959; dep. M$63.9m. (March 1980); Gen. Man. KORETSUGU KODAMA.

Banque de l'Indochine et de Suez (*France*): French Bank Bldg., P.O.B. 69, 11-A Jalan Raja Chulan, Kuala Lumpur; f. 1958; dep. M$146.3m. (Dec. 1980); Man. R. BEYLOT.

Chartered Bank (*U.K.*): 2 Jalan Ampang, P.O.B. 1001, Kuala Lumpur 01-16; f. 1875; dep. M$1846.4m. (Dec. 1979); Chief Man. N. H. GREEN; 35 brs.

Chase Manhattan Bank, N.A. (*U.S.A.*): Wisma Stephens, 88 Jalan Raja Chulan, P.O.B. 1090, Kuala Lumpur 01-17; f. 1964; dep. M$230m. (June 1980); Gen. Man. PETER D. LEE.

Chung Khiaw Bank Ltd. (*Singapore*): 10–11 Medan Pasar, Lee Wah Bank Bldg. (2nd Floor), Kuala Lumpur 01-23; f. 1950; dep. M$620.3m. (Dec. 1981); Gen. Man., Malaysia YOONG YAN PIN; 16 brs.

Citibank N.A. (*U.S.A.*): 28 Medan Pasar, P.O.B. 112, Kuala Lumpur; f. 1959; dep. M$143.8m., (Dec. 1977); Vice-Pres. PHILIP MARKERT.

European Asian Bank (*Federal Republic of Germany*): Bangunan Yee Seng, 15 Jalan Raja Chulan, P.O.B. 2211, Kuala Lumpur; f. 1972; dep. M$110.4m. (Dec. 1981); Man. HOLGER F. DES COUDRES.

Hongkong and Shanghai Banking Corporation (*Hong Kong*): 2 Leboh Ampang, P.O.B. 244, Kuala Lumpur 01-02; f. 1860; Man. DAVID JACQUES; 36 brs.

Lee Wah Bank Ltd. (*Singapore*): 10-12 Medan Pasar, Lee Wah Bank Bldg., Kuala Lumpur; f. 1950; dep. M$311m. (Dec. 1981); Chair. WEE CHO YAW; 9 brs.

Oversea-Chinese Banking Corpn. Ltd. (*Singapore*): Wisma Lee Rubber, Jalan Melaka, P.O.B. 197, Kuala Lumpur; f. 1959; dep. M$3,110m. (Dec. 1979); Chair. Tan Sri TAN CHIN TUAN; 25 brs.

Overseas Union Bank Ltd. (*Singapore*): OUB Bldg., Leboh Pasar Besar, P.O.B. 621, Kuala Lumpur 01-23; f. 1959; dep. M$348.4m. (Dec. 1979); Gen. Man. (Malaysia) ROBERT WONG KIN THONG; 12 brs.

Tokai Bank (*Japan*): Suite 502, 15th Floor, Plaza See Hoy Chan, Jalan Raja Chulan, Kuala Lumpur; Chief Rep. KAZUHIRO SUZUKI.

United Overseas Bank Ltd. (*Singapore*): Block 37, Lot 1, Jalan Perpaduan, P.O.B. 1202, Kampong Air, Kota Kinabalu, Sabah; f. 1966; dep. M$34m. (Dec. 1977); Man. YONG KON FAH.

BANKERS' ASSOCIATIONS

Association of Banks in Malaysia: 23rd Floor, West Wing, Bangunan Dato Zainal, Jalan Melaka, Kuala Lumpur; Chair. Datuk JAFFAR HUSSEIN.

Association of Merchant Banks of Malaysia: 4th Floor, Wisma Methodist, Jalan Hang Jebat, Kuala Lumpur; Chair. Malaysian International Merchant Bankers Bhd.; Sec. UDA Merchant Bankers Bhd.

STOCK EXCHANGE

Kuala Lumpur Stock Exchange Bhd.: 4th Floor, Block C, Damansara Heights, Kuala Lumpur; f. 1976; 97 mems.; Chair. Tengku NOONE; publ. *Gazette*.

INSURANCE

Malaysia National Insurance Sdn. Bhd.: 9th Floor, Wisma Yakin, Jalan Melayu, P.O.B. 799, Kuala Lumpur; state-run company handling life and general insurance; auth. cap. M$10m.; Chair. Dato A. RAHMAN HAMIDON

TRADE AND INDUSTRY

PENINSULAR MALAYSIA

CHAMBERS OF COMMERCE

The National Chamber of Commerce and Industry of Malaysia: 23rd Floor, Dato Zainal Bldg., P.O.B. 2529, Kuala Lumpur; f. 1962; 5 mems.: The Malay Chamber of Commerce and Industry of Malaysia, the Associated Chinese Chambers of Commerce and Industry of Malaysia, the Associated Indian Chambers of Commerce of Malaysia, Malaysian International Chamber of Commerce and Industry and the Federation of Malaysian Manufacturers; Pres. Tan Sri KAMARUL ARIFFIN; Hon. Sec.-Gen. Encik MOHD. RAMLI KUSHAIRI.

Associated Chinese Chambers of Commerce and Industry of Malaysia: Chinese Assembly Hall, Ground Floor, 1 Jalan Birch, Kuala Lumpur 08-02.

Penang Chinese Chamber of Commerce: 2 Penang St., Penang; f. 1903; Pres. SAW HUN ENG, D.S.P.N., K.M.N., P.J.K., J.P.; CHOY MENG FOOK, A.M.N., P.B.; 1,644 mems.; publ. monthly bulletin.

Perak Chinese Chamber of Commerce: 35-37 Jalan Banda Raya, Ipoh, P.O.B. 220; f. 1908; Pres. Dato TAN KIM SENG; Gen. Sec. CHAN SWEE CHIN; 821 mems.

Selangor Chinese Chamber of Commerce: Chinese Assembly Hall, 1st Floor, Jalan Birch, Kuala Lumpur 08-02; Pres. Tan Sri LEE YAN LIAN, P.S.M., J.M.N., D.P.M.S.; Exec. Sec. POA SOON TEONG.

Associated Indian Chambers of Commerce of Malaysia: 18 Jalan Tun Perak, P.O.B. 675, Kuala Lumpur 01-03; f. 1950; Pres. Sen. Tan Sri S. O. K. UBAIDULLA; Sec. Dato G. S. GILL; six branches:

Johore Indian Chamber of Commerce: 55/56 Jalan Ibrahim, Johore Bahru, Johore.

Kelantan Indian Chamber of Commerce: P.O.B. 61, Kota Bahru, Kelantan.

Malacca Indian Chamber of Commerce: 39 Jalan Temenggong, Malacca.

The Malaysian Indian Chamber of Commerce: State of Penang, 119-B Penang St., Penang.

Perak Indian Chamber of Commerce: 17 Lahat Ave., P.O.B. 279, Ipoh, Perak.

Selangor Indian Chamber of Commerce and Industry: 116 (1st Floor), Jalan Tuanku Abdul Rahman, Kuala Lumpur.

Federation of Malaysian Manufacturers: 8th Floor, Angkasa Raya Bldg., Jalan Ampang, P.O.B. 2194, Kuala Lumpur; f. 1968; 725 mems.; Pres. Tunku Tan Sri MOHAMED BIN TUNKU BESAR BURHANUDDIN; Exec. Dir. TAN KEOK YIN.

Malay Chamber of Commerce and Industry of Malaysia: 23rd Floor (East Wing), Dato Zainal Bldg., 23 Jalan Melaka, Kuala Lumpur; Chair. Tan Sri KAMARUL ARIFFIN.

Malacca Chamber of Commerce: 8-H Jalan Panjang, Malacca; f. 1948; Pres. CHAN LEONG CHENG, B.K.T.

Malaysian International Chamber of Commerce and Industry (MICCI) (*Dewan Perniagaan dan Perindustrian Antarabangsa Malaysia*): 8th Floor, Wisma Damansara, Jalan Semantan, P.O.B. 192, Kuala Lumpur; f. 1907 as Selangor Chamber of Commerce; 382 mem. companies; Pres. A. P. O. THOMAS; Exec. Dir. D. C. L. WILSON.

Penang Branch: Chartered Bank Chambers, P.O.B. 331, Penang; f. 1837 as Penang Chamber of Commerce; Chair. J. ARMSTRONG; Secs. EVATT & Co.

Perak Branch: 20A Market Street, P.O.B. 136; Ipoh; f. 1911 as Perak Chamber of Commerce, Chair. B. J. HOULSTON; Secs. EVATT & Co.

DEVELOPMENT ORGANIZATIONS AND PUBLIC CORPORATIONS

Federal Agricultural Marketing Authority (FAMA): Bangunan Wisma Yan, 17–19 Jalan Selangor, Petaling Jaya, Selangor; f. 1965 to supervise, co-ordinate and improve existing markets and methods of marketing agricultural produce and to seek and promote new markets and outlets for agricultural produce; Chair. Y. B. Encik SHAMSURI BIN MOHD. SALEH, A.M.N., J.P.; Dir.-Gen. Tuan Hj. MOHD. HARIRI BIN ABU TAIF.

Federal Land Development Authority (FELDA): Jalan Maktab, Kuala Lumpur; f. 1957; quasi-governmental corporation formed to raise the productivity and income of low income groups and to eradicate rural poverty; in 1981 had developed 1.4 million acres of land; involved in rubber, oil palm, cocoa and sugar cane cultivation; Chair. RAJA Tan Sri MUHAMMAD ALIAS BIN RAJA MUHAMMAD ALI; Dir.-Gen. ALLADIN HASHIM.

Fisheries Development Authority (Malaysia): Tingkat 7, Wisma PKNS, Jalan Raja Laut, Kuala Lumpur; Chair. NIK HASSAN BIN Haji WAN ABDUL RAHMAN.

Kumpulan FIMA Bhd.: 3rd & 4th Floors, Main Tower Block, Wisma MCIS, Jalan Barat, Petaling Jaya, Kuala Lumpur; f. 1972; government corporation to promote food and related industry through investment on its own or by joint ventures with local or foreign entrepreneurs; oil palm, cocoa and fruit plantation developments; manufacturing and packaging, trading, supermarkets and restaurants; Chair. Dato Haji BASIR B. ISMAIL; Man. Dir. MOHAMAD RAMLI KUSHAIRI.

Lembaga Perindustrian Kayu Malaysia (*Malaysian Timber Industry Board*): 5th Floor, Wisma Bunga Raya, Jalan Ampang, P.O.B. 887, Kuala Lumpur; f. 1968; to promote, regulate and control the export of timber and timber products from Peninsular Malaysia; Chair. Tan Sri G. K. RAMA IYER; Dir. Gen. Encik ABDUL LATIF BIN NORDIN; publs. *Timber Trade Review, Maskayu, Commercial Timber of Peninsular Malaysia, Directory of Timber Trade, Malayan Grading Rules for Sawn Hardwood* (English and Chinese editions), Timber trade leaflets.

Majilis Amanah Rakyat (MARA) (*Council of Trust for the People*): Pertama Complex, Jalan Tuanku Abdul Rahman, Kuala Lumpur; f. 1965 to promote, stimulate, facilitate and undertake economic and social development; to participate in industrial and commercial undertakings and joint ventures; Chair. Dr. NAWAWI BIN MAT AWIN; Dir.-Gen. MOHD. RIDZUAN BIN ABD. HALIM.

Malaysia Export Credit Insurance Bhd.: 2nd Floor, Wisma Damansara, Kuala Lumpur; joint government and private sector venture to provide insurance for exporters of locally manufactured products; Gen. Man. B. M. SIDWELL.

Malaysian Agricultural Development Authority (MADA): Alor Setar; Chair. Dato Seri SYED NAHAR SHAHABUDDIN.

Malaysian Industrial Development Authority (MIDA): Wisma Damansara, P.O.B. 618, Kuala Lumpur; f. 1967; Chair. Dato JAMIL BIN MOHAMED JAN; Dir.-Gen. Dato ABDUL RAHMAN BIN Haji YUSOF.

Malaysian Industrial Development Finance Bhd.: P.O.B. 2110, Kuala Lumpur; f. 1960 by the Government, Banks, Insurance Companies; shareholders include International Finance Corporation, Commonwealth Development Finance Co.; provides capital for industry, marketing services and builds factories; cap. M$80m. (1978); Chair. Tan Sri ISMAIL MOHAMED ALI; Gen. Man. H. F. G. LEEMBRUGGEN.

National Land Finance Co-operative Society Ltd.: 2 Jalan Seleiman, Bangunan Tun Sambanthan, P.O.B. 2133, Kuala Lumpur; f. 1960 to mobilize capital from rubber industry workers and others to purchase rubber estates; 60,000 mems.; owns 19 rubber, tea, oil palm, cocoa and coconut plantations; cap. p.u. M$26.3m.; Pres. Y. B. Datuk SERI S. SAMY VELLU, D.P.M.J., D.P.M.S., A.M.N., P.C.M.; Chair. TOH PUAN UMASUNDARI SAMBANTHAN; Sec. Encik K. R. SOMASUNDARAM, A.M.N., J.P.

Palm Oil Registration and Licensing Authority (PORLA): 4th Floor, Block B, Damansara Office Complex, Damansara Heights, Jalan Dungan, P.O.B. 2184, Kuala Lumpur; f. 1977 to regulate and promote all aspects of the palm oil industry; Dir.-Gen. TOH AH BAH.

Perbadanan Nasional Bhd. (PERNAS): Kompleks Antarabangsa, Jalan Sultan Ismail, P.O.B. 493, Kuala Lumpur; f. 1969; a government-sponsored company established to promote trade, banking, property and plantation development, construction, mineral exploration, steel manufacturing, inland container transportation, mining, insurance, industrial development and engineering services; auth. cap. M$500m.; cap. p.u. M$116.25m.; has 10 wholly-owned subsidiary companies, over 60 jointly-owned subsidiaries and 18 associated companies; Chair. Tunku Dato SHAHRIMAN BIN TUNKU SULAIMAN; Man. Dir. Dato A. RAHMAN BIN HAMIDON.

Petronas (National Oil Company): 136 Jalan Pudu, P.O.B. 2444, Kuala Lumpur 05-03; f. 1974; Chair. Tan Sri ABDULLAH SALLEH.

INDUSTRIAL AND TRADE ASSOCIATIONS

All-Malaya Chinese Mining Association.

Federation of Malaysian Manufacturers: 8th Floor, Angkasa Raya, Jalan Ampang, P.O.B. 2194, Kuala Lumpur; Pres. Y. M. Tunku Tan Sri MOHAMED BIN Tunku BESAR BURHANUDDIN; Exec. Dir. Tan KEOK YIN.

Federation of Rubber Trade Associations of Malaysia: 138 Jalan Bandar, Kuala Lumpur.

Malaysian Employers' Federation: Wisma Perdana, 2nd Floor, Jalan Dungun, P.O.B. 1026, Kuala Lumpur 23-04; Exec. Dir. K. A. MENON, K.M.N.; private sector organization incorporating:

Malayan Agricultural Producers' Association: Bangunan Angkasa Raya (19th Floor), Jalan Ampang, P.O.B. 1063, Kuala Lumpur; f. 1980; 444 mem. estates and 63 factories; Pres. Tunku MANSUR YAACOB, K.M.N., A.D.K.; Dir. S. J. CHELLIAH.

Malayan Mining Employers' Association: 6th Floor, Ming Bldg., Jalan Bukit Nanas, P.O.B. 2560, Kuala Lumpur; Pres. CHAN WAN CHOON.

Malayan Commercial Banks' Association: P.O.B. 2001, Kuala Lumpur.

Commercial Employers' Association of Peninsular Malaysia: 123 Jalan Ampang, P.O.B. 247, Kuala Lumpur; Pres. B. J. COLUMBUS.

The Motor Vehicle Assemblers' Association, West Malaysia: 86 Jalan Ampang, Kuala Lumpur.

The States of Malaya Insurance Association: P.O.B. 1026, Kuala Lumpur; Pres. K. PADMANABHAN.

The Malayan Pineapple Industry Board: P.O.B. 35, Batu 5, Jalan Scudai, Johore Bahru; Acting Chair. WONG KUM CHOON.

Malaysian Oil Palm Growers' Council: 3rd Floor, Wisma Bunga Raya, Jalan Ampang, P.O.B. 747, Kuala Lumpur 01-02; f. 1953.

The Malaysian Rubber Products Manufacturers' Association: c/o The Malaysian Rubber Research and Development Board, 150 Jalan Ampang, Bunganan Getah Asli, P.O.B. 508, Kuala Lumpur 01-02.

Malaysian Rubber Research and Development Board: 150 Jalan Ampang, P.O.B. 508, Kuala Lumpur 04-06; f. 1959; plans and determines policies and programmes of natural rubber research, technical development and promotion work nationally and worldwide; co-ordinates all research activities; Controller of Rubber Research and Chair. of the Board and its subsidiary units Tan Sri Dr. B. C. SEKHAR; publs. *Malaysian Rubber Review* (irregular), *Natural Rubber News* (monthly), *Getah Asli* (quarterly), *Rubber Developments* (quarterly), *NR Technology* (quarterly), *Planters Bulletin*, *Annual Report of the Board*, and occasional monographs.

National Tobacco Board: P.O.B. 198, K. Bahru, Kelantan.

Rubber Trade Association of Ipoh: 1-3 Jalan Chua Cheng Bok, Ipoh.

Rubber Trade Association of Malacca: 128A Wolferston Rd., Malacca.

Rubber Trade Association of Penang: 16 Anson Rd., Penang; f. 1919; 169 mems.; Pres. Datuk KOH PEN TING; Hon. Sec. HWANG SING LUE; Hon. Treas. Datuk TAN HOAY EAM.

Rubber Trade Association of Selangor and Pahang: 138 Jalan Bandar, Kuala Lumpur.

States of Malaya Chamber of Mines: 6th Floor, Ming Bldg., Jalan Bukit Nanas, P.O.B. 2560, Kuala Lumpur; f. 1914; Pres. ABDUL RAHIM AKI; Vice-Pres. Haji MOKTY BIN Datuk MAHOOD, J.S.M., P.M.P.; Sec.-Gen. DAVID WONG; 251 mems.

Timber Trade Federation of the Federation of Malaysia: 2 Lorong Haji Taib Satu, Kuala Lumpur 02-07.

Tin Industry Research and Development Board: 6th Floor, Ming Bldg., Jalan Bukit Nanas, P.O.B. 2560, Kuala Lumpur; Chair. ABDUL RAHIM AKI.

TRADE UNIONS

Malaysian Trades Union Congress: Bangunan Buruh, 19 Jalan Barat, Petaling Jaya, P.O.B. 38, Selangor; f. 1949; 111 affiliated unions, 382,000 mems.; Pres. Dr. P. P. NARAYANAN; Sec.-Gen. V. DAVID; publ. *Suara Buroh* (monthly).

Principal affiliated union:

National Union of Plantation Workers in Malaya: 2 Jalan Templer, P.O.B. 73, Petaling Jaya, Selangor; f. 1954; about 125,000 mems.; Gen. Sec. P. P. NARAYANAN.

INDEPENDENT FEDERATIONS

Amalgamated Union of Employees in Government Clerical and Allied Services: 23A Jalan Marsh, Brickfields, Kuala Lumpur; about 6,000 mems.; Pres. Haji YUNUS BIN MAARIS; Gen. Sec. A. H. PONNIAH.

Federation of Government Medical Services Unions: General Hospital, Panang Rd., Kuala Lumpur; 9 affiliates.

Federation of Indian School Teachers' Unions: 5 affiliates.

CO-OPERATIVES

There are a total of 1,450 registered co-operatives involved in housing, agriculture and industry in Malaysia, with over 1 million members. In March 1980 the Government allocated M$25 million to assist in their development.

SABAH

CHAMBERS OF COMMERCE

Chinese Chamber of Commerce: P.O.B. 100, Beaufort; P.O.B. 63, Kota Kinabalu; P.O.B. 14, Keningau; P.O.B. 31, Labuan; P.O.B. 32, Lahad Datu; P.O.B. 28, Papar; P.O.B. 161, Sandakan; P.O.B. 12, Semporna; P.O.B. 164, Tawau; P.O.B. 6, Tenom; P.O.B. 37, Tuaran.

Sabah Chamber of Commerce and Industry: P.O.B. 1204, Sandakan; Pres. T. H. WONG.

Sabah Chamber of Commerce and Industry: P.O.B. 609, Kota Kinabalu.

Sabah United Chinese Chamber of Commerce: P.O.B. 89, Kota Kinabalu.

TRADE UNIONS AND ASSOCIATIONS

Chinese School Teachers' Association: P.O.B. 10, Tenom; f. 1956; 74 mems.; Sec. VUN CHAU CHOI.

Employees' Trade Union: Sandakan; f. 1955; 40 mems.; Sec. LOUIS L. QUYN.

The Incorporated Society of Planters, (North-East) Sabah Branch: P.O.B. 1209, Sandakan, f. 1962; 64 mems.; Chair. A. J. RITCHIE.

Kota Kinabalu Teachers' Association: P.O.B. 282, Kota Kinabalu; f. 1962; 258 mems.; Sec. K. J. JOSEPH.

Sabah Civil Service Union: P.O.B. 175, Kota Kinabalu; f. 1952; 1,356 mems.; Pres. J. K. K. VOON; Sec. STEPHEN WONG.

Sabah Commercial Employees' Union: P.O.B. 357, Kota Kinabalu; f. 1957; 1,750 mems.; Gen. Sec. SEVIAR GOPAL.

Sandakan Tong Kang Association: 120 Mile ½, Leila Rd., Sandakan; f. 1952; 86 mems.; Sec. LAI KEN MIN.

SARAWAK

CHAMBERS OF COMMERCE

The Associated Chinese Chamber of Commerce: 86 Main Bazaar, P.O.B. 608, Kuching; f. 1920; Pres. WEE BOON PING; Sec. Gen. SIM TECK KUI; publs. *Trade Directory* and *Quarterly Chamber's Magazine*.

Bumiputra Chamber of Commerce: P.O.B. 2983, Kuching; f. 1953; Pres. Y. B. Haji WAN HABIB BIN SYED MAHMUD; Vice-Pres. Haji HUSEN BIN SHEIKH MOHAMAD.

Sarawak Chamber of Commerce: c/o Ernst & Whinney, 301–303 Wisma Bukit Mata Kuching, Jalan Tunku Abdul Rahman, Kuching; f. 1950; Chair. Datuk MOHD. AMIN BIN Haji SATEM; Vice-Chair. MAGNUS STIRLING.

South Indian Chamber of Commerce of Sarawak: 37-C India St., Kuching; f. 1952; Pres. ABDUL MAJEED; Vice-Pres. SYED AHMAD.

United Chambers of Commerce and Industry of Sarawak: c/o Ernst & Whinney, 301–303 Wisma Bukit Mata Kuching, Jalan Tunku Abdul Rahman; Kuching; f. 1966; Pres. Datuk MOHD. AMIN BIN Haji SATEM; Vice-Pres. SYED AHMAD.

DEVELOPMENT ORGANIZATIONS

Borneo Development Corporation Sdn. Bhd.: Head Office: Electra House, P.O.B. 342, Power St., Kuching, Sarawak; Sabah Office: P.O.B. 721, 1st Floor, Lot 6, Wisma Yakim, Jalan Haji Saman, Kota Kinabalu; f. 1958; shareholders: State Governments of Sarawak and Sabah; Gen. Man. FRANK APAU; Sec. BOHARI BIN OSMAN; Man. (Sarawak) ALI TREADY.

Sarawak Economic Development Corporation: 1st Floor, Bangunan Yayasan Sarawak, Jalan Masjid, P.O.B. 400, Kuching; f. 1972; statutory organization responsible for commercial and industrial development in Sarawak either on its own or jointly with foreign and local entrepreneurs; responsible for the management and development of industrial estates in the state; Chair. Encik EFFENDI NORWAWI; Deputy Chair. Encik AZIZ HUSAIN.

MAJOR INDUSTRIAL COMPANIES

The following is a selected list of some of the major industrial organizations in Malaysia:

Aluminium Company of Malaysia Bhd.: Jalan 13/6, P.O.B. 47, Petaling Jaya, Selangor; manufacturers of aluminium sheet and extruded products; Chair. Tunku Tan Sri MOHAMED BIN Tunku BESAR BURHANUDDIN; Man. Dir. DONAL P. CRILLY; 705 employees.

Associated Pan Malaysia Cement Sdn. Bhd.: 20th Floor, Plaza See Hoy Chan, Jalan Raja Chulan, P.O.B. 613, Kuala Lumpur 05-10; cement manufacturers; Man. Dir. SAW EWE SENG; 950 employees.

Bata (Malaysia) Bhd.: P.O.B 38, 3¼ Mile Kapar Rd., Kelang, Selangor; manufacturers, retailers, wholesalers and exporters of leather, canvas and plastic shoes; Man. Dir. U. K. HOCKE; 1,838 employees.

Berger Paints (Malaysia) Sdn. Bhd.: 4, Jalan 205, P.O.B. 1, Petaling Jaya, Selangor; paint manufacturers; Man. Dir. J. D. BRUGGEN; 140 employees.

Carrier International Sdn. Berhad: 5 Jalan Kemajuan, Petaling Jaya, Selangor; manufacturers of room air-conditioners, packaged equipment, split systems and air handling units; Gen. Man. OOI KIM SWEE; 383 employees.

Chemical Company of Malaysia Bhd.: 11th Floor, Wisma Damansara, Jalan Semantan, P.O.B. 284, Kuala Lumpur; manufactures concentrated fertilizers and a number of chemicals including chlorine, caustic soda and hydrochloric acid; Chair. S. A. RIDGEWELL; 600 employees.

Cold Storage (Malaysia) Bhd: P.O.B. 401, 12th Floor, Komplek Kewangan, Jalan Raja Chulan, Kuala Lumpur; f. 1903; aerated drinks, cordials, sterilized flavoured milks, still drinks, sterilized milk, butter, ghee, margarine, bread, bread products, ice, ice cream, bacon, ham, sausages, halal and non-halal processed meat products; Man. Dir. R. J. BARTON; 800 employees.

Cycle and Carriage Bintang Sdn. Bhd.: Wisma MCIS, 6th Floor Main Tower, Jalan Barat, Petaling Jaya, Selangor; franchise holders for Mercedes Benz commercial and passenger vehicles; Deputy Gen. Man. Ecnik JAFFAR MOHDALI; 703 employees.

Dunlop Malaysian Industries Bhd.: P.O.B. 66, 4 Jalan Tandang, Petaling Jaya, Selangor; f. 1961; cap. p.u. M$50.0m.; manufacturers of a complete range of Dunlop tyres and tubes, Dunlopillo and chemical products, sports goods; Man. Dir. M. J. H. MOFFETT; 2,074 employees.

Esso Malaysia Bhd.: Kompleks Antarabangsa, Jalan Sultan Ismail, P.O.B. 601, Kuala Lumpur; refiners and marketers of all classes of petroleum products, lubricating oils, gas and ammonia; Chair. G. F. COX; 728 employees.

Fraser & Neave (Malaya) Sdn. Bhd.: P.O.B. 55, Kuala Lumpur; manufacturers of soft drinks and mineral waters; Gen. Man. JORDAN YIN; 2,000 employees.

Glaxo Malaysia Sdn. Bhd.: Jalan 51A/221, Petaling Jaya, Selangor; manufacturers of pharmaceuticals, specialized foods and antibiotic preparations; Dir. and Gen. Man. J. B. ROUTLEDGE; 181 employees.

Goodyear Malaysia Bhd.: P.O.B. 49, Shah Alam, Selangor; manufacturers of passenger car, motorcycle, scooter, truck and tractor tyres and tubes; Man. Dir. J. F. FIEDLER; 910 employees.

Guinness Malaysia Bhd.: P.O.B. 144, Petaling Jaya; cap. p.u. M$72m.; brewing, bottling and distribution of Guinness Stout and shandy; Man. Dir. H. A. NOWELL; 847 employees.

Hargill Malaysia Sdn. Bhd. (Engineering Division): Syah Alam Industrial Estate, P.O.B. 50, Sungei Renggam, Selangor; f. 1968; subsidiary of Syarikat Harper Gilfillan Bhd.; manufactures products for mining, transport, the oil industry; Deputy Chair. G. K. WINES; 150 employees.

Hume Industries (Malaysia) Bhd.: P.O.B. 21, Petaling Jaya, Selangor; manufacturers of asbestos cement products, steel and concrete pipes, pre-stressed concrete beams and piles, tanks, electrical conduits and other moulded products, pressure vessels, autoclaves and lift gates; Man. Dir. R. W. HICKS; 1,364 employees.

ICI Paints (Malaysia) Sdn. Bhd.: Jalan 205, Petaling Jaya, manufacturers of a variety of paints; Chair. Dr. S. A. RIDGEWELL; 294 employees.

Kris Metal (M) Sdn. Bhd.: 12 Jalan 13/4, Section 13, Petaling Jaya, Selangor; manufacturers of metal window frames, sliding doors, sunscreens, etc.; Man. Dir. MICHAEL NG; 255 employees.

Lam Soon Oil & Soap Mfg. Sdn. Bhd.: P.O.B. 8, Jalan 205, Petaling Jaya, Selangor; manufacturers of soap, detergents, cooking oil and margarine, copra cakes, crude glycerine, coconut oil, canned foodstuffs, soft drinks, etc.; Man. Dir. SAMUEL KAM; 839 employees.

Lever Brothers (Malaysia) Sdn. Bhd.: 12th Floor, Wisma Damansara, 5 Jalan Semantan, P.S. 1015, Kuala Lumpur 23-03; manufacturers of soaps, detergents, edible products and toilet preparations; Chair. D. R. MCCARTHY; 1,172 employees.

Malayan Breweries (Malaya) Sdn. Bhd.: P.O.B. 55, Kuala Lumpur; manufacturers of beer and stout; Man. F. H. SCHERMERS; 450 employees.

Malayan Cables Bhd.: 10 Jalan Tandang, P.O.B. 4, Petaling Jaya; f. 1957; cap. p.u. M$12.9m.; manufactures a wide range of cables; Dir./Gen. Man. D. M. WARREN; Sales Man. OOI PHAIK HONG; 402 employees.

Malaysia Mining Corp. Bhd. (MMCB): f. 1981 following the merger of Malayan Tin Dredging Co. and Malaysia Mining Corp.; the world's largest tin mining group with interests in the exploration, mining, smelting and marketing of tin and also plantation and diamond exploration; Chair. Encik MOHAMED DESA BIN PACHEE.

Malaysian Oxygen Bhd.: 13 Jalan 222, Petaling Jaya, Selangor; cap. p.u. 30.7m. ringgit; manufactures industrial and medical gases and electrodes, supplies welding, safety, marine, medical and fire-fighting equipment; Man. Dir. D. W. E. STAFFERTON; 555 employees.

Malaysian Tobacco Co. Bhd.: 178-3 Jalan Sungai Besi, Kuala Lumpur 07-01; cigarette manufacturers; Chair. A. R. J. CHRISTODOLO; 1,716 employees.

Metal Box Malaysia Bhd.: 1 Jalan 221, Petaling Jaya, Selangor; manufacturers and lithographers of cans, tin boxes, screw caps, aluminium tubes, etc.; Dir. M. G. ALDERSON; 1,000 employees.

Paper Products (Malaya) Bhd.: 1½ Ms. Jalan Sungei Chua, Kajang, Selangor; manufacturers of paper bags, tissue paper, etc.; Gen. Man. LIM GUAN TEIK; 600 employees.

Petronas: 136 Jalan Pudu, Kuala Lumpur; state oil company; Chair. Tan Sri ABDULLAH SALLEH.

Rothmans of Pall Mall (Malaysia) Bhd.: Virginia Park, Jalan University, Petaling Jaya, Selangor; cigarette manufacturers; Man. Dir. G. VESSEY; 1,862 employees.

Shell Refining Company (Fed. of Malaysia) Bhd.: Port Dickson, Negri Sembilan; refiners of all classes of petroleum products; Gen. Man. M. LEE.

Sissons Paints (East) Sdn. Bhd.: P.O.B. 14, 2 Jalan Kemajuan, Petaling Jaya; f. 1959; manufacture a variety of paints; Man. Dir. R. S. BAYLOCK.

Tamco Cutler-Hammer Sdn. Bhd.: Lot 9D, 12/18 Jalan Kemajuan, P.O.B. 156, Petaling Jaya, Selangor; f. 1965; cap. p.u. M$3.5m.; manufacturers of telecommunications equipment; Man. Dir. G. W. ANGUS; 250 employees.

Tropical Veener Co. Bhd.: 6th Floor, Johore Tower, 15 Jalan Gereja, Johore Bahru, Johore; f. 1969; cap. p.u. M$5.5m.; manufacturers and exporters of various species of wood; Chair. Tan Sri GAN TECK YEOW; Man. Dir. ONG CHIN KUN, S.M.T.; 513 employees.

United Engineers (M) Bhd.: P.O.B. 115, Jalan Sungei Besi, Kuala Lumpur; iron, steel and non-ferrous founders; mechanical, electrical, civil, structural and telecommunication engineers for contract and project schemes; Gen. Man. C. S. MITCHELL; 627 employees.

RUBBER PRODUCERS AND PROCESSORS

Associated Estates Agencies Sdn. Bhd.: P.O. Box 1021, Kuala Lumpur.

Barlow Boustead Estates Agency Sdn. Bhd.: P.O. Box 295, Kuala Lumpur.

Dunlop Estates Bhd.: P.O. Box 55, Malacca.

East Asiatic Co. (M) Bhd.: Estates Department, P.O. Box 354, Kuala Lumpur.

Eastern Plantation Agency (Johore) Sdn. Bhd.: P.O. Box 705, Johore Bahru, Johore.

Harrisons & Crosfield (M) Sdn. Bhd.: Estates Department, P.O. Box 1007, Kuala Lumpur.

Kuala Lumpur Kepong Bhd.: Ladang, Pinji, Lahat, P.O.B. 633, Ipoh, Perak.

Kumpulan Guthrie Sdn. Bhd.: Wisma Guthrie, P.O. Box 2516, Kuala Lumpur 01-02.

Plantation Agencies Sdn. Bhd.: P.O. Box 706, Penang.

Sime Darby Plantations: 54A Jalan Imbi, P.O.B. 157, Kuala Lumpur; Chair. D. PARK.

Socfin Co. Bhd.: Wisma SOCFIN, Jalan Semantan, P.O. Box 330, Kuala Lumpur 01-02; f. 1930.

Taiko Plantations Sdn. Bhd.: Ladang Pinji, Lahat, Perak.

Uniroyal Malaysian Plantations Sdn. Bhd.: P.O. Box 350, Penang.

Wilkinson Process Rubber Co. Ltd.: 5¾ miles, Jalan Ipoh, Batu Caves, Kuala Lumpur.

Linatex Far East Division: Manufacturers and suppliers of linatex lined pumps, valves and auxiliary equipment, abrasion and corrosion resistant linings.

TRANSPORT

RAILWAYS

PENINSULAR MALAYSIA

Malayan Railway Administration: Jalan Sultan Hishamuddin, P.O.B. 1, Kuala Lumpur; f. 1885; Gen. Man. Dato ISHAK BIN TADIN.

The main line, 787 km. long, follows the west coast and extends from Singapore in the south to Butterworth (opposite Penang Island) to the north.

From Bukit Mertajam, close to Butterworth, the line branches off to the Thai border at Padang Besar where connection is made with the State Railway of Thailand.

The East Coast Line, 526 km. long, runs from Gemas to Tumpat (near Kota Bahru). A 21-km. branch line from Pasir Mas, which is 27 km. south of Tumpat, connects with the State Railway of Thailand at the border station of Sungei Golok.

Branch lines serve railway-operated ports at Port Dickson and Telok Anson as well as Port Kelang and Jurong (Singapore).

Express Rakyat rail services are operated between Butterworth and Singapore in addition to the normal express services between Butterworth, Kuala Lumpur and Singapore. In March 1980 the Express K.M.T. began operating between Singapore and Kuala Lumpur.

SABAH

Sabah State Railways: Kota Kinabalu; the length of the railway was 140 km. in 1979. The line is of metre gauge and runs from Kota Kinabalu to Tenom serving part of the west coast and the interior; diesel trains are used; Gen. Man. DANIEL WONG THIEN SUNG (acting).

ROADS

PENINSULAR MALAYSIA

In 1979 there were an estimated 21,768 kilometres of roads in Peninsular Malaysia. The Federal highway links Kuala Lumpur with Poh Kelang. Work is expected to commence in 1982 on a 13.5-km. bridge between Penang Island and Peninsular Malaysia, at a cost of M$525 million. It will form the last link of the east-west highway which connects Kota Baru and Penang, due to be completed in 1982.

SABAH

The Public Works Department maintains a network of trunk, district and local roads comprising 470 km. of bitumen, 1,495 km. of metal (gravel) and 595 km. of earth surface, making a total of 2,560 km. (1968).

SARAWAK

The State Government maintains about 225 km. of hard-surfaced roads, 590 km. of gravelled and 80 km. of earth roads. In addition local authorities maintain some 545 km. of roads. The first connecting road between Sabah and Sarawak was opened in 1981.

SHIPPING

PENINSULAR MALAYSIA

The principal ports, which have undergone considerable extension, are Penang, Port Kelang, Malacca, Port Dickson, Kuantan, Kuching, Sibu, Kota Kinabalu and Sandakan. A major port expansion programme, costing M$120m. was launched under the Second Malaysia Plan (1971–75). The Pasir Gudang port at Johore Bahru became fully operational in 1976.

Malaysian International Shipping Corpn. Bhd. (*National Shipping Line of Malaysia*): Wisma MISC, 2 Jalan

Conlay, P.O.B. 371, Kuala Lumpur 04-09; f. 1968; fleet of 32 vessels; regular sailings between Far East, Australia and Europe; Exec. Chair. Tengku Tan Sri Datuk NGHA MOHAMED; Man. Dir. LESLIE EU PENG MENG.

Syarikat Perkapalan Kris Sdn. Bhd. (*The Kris Shipping Company of Malaysia*): Bangunan NUPCIW, Jalan 8/1E, Petaling Jaya; coastal fleet of 1 tanker and 8 dry cargo vessels; domestic services; Dirs. Dato Seri SYED NAHAR SHAHABUDDIN, R. ST. JOHN STEVENS, Datin Seri NIK MAIMUNAN YAHYA, Tan Sri ARIFF BIN DARUS, KHONG CHAI SENG, MOHAMED BIN Haji ABDUL RAHMAN; Sec. ROHANY TALIB; Gen. Man. MOHD. BIN Haji ABDUL RAHMAN.

SABAH

The chief ports are Labuan, Sandakan, Kota Kinabalu, Kudat, Tawau, Sempoma and Lahad Datu. The operation of all ports, except Labuan, is carried out by the Sabah Ports Authority. A new port at Tawau, Sabah, costing M$64 million, was begun in 1980 and was scheduled to be completed in 1982.

Many international shipping lines serve Sabah. Local services are maintained by smaller vessels.

SARAWAK

Under the Second Malaysia Plan (1971–75), work started on a new port at Pending Point, near Kuching. In 1979 the construction of a new deepwater port at Bintulu commenced and is due for completion in 1983.

CIVIL AVIATION

Malaysia has five international airports at Kuala Lumpur, Kota Kinabalu, Penang, Johore Bahru and Kuching. In addition there are airports catering for domestic services at Alor Star, Ipoh, Kota Bahru, Kota Trengganu, Kuantan and Malacca in Peninsular Malaysia, Sibu and Miri in Sarawak and Sandakan, Tawau and Labuan in Sabah. There are also numerous smaller airstrips all over Malaysia.

Under the Fourth Malaysia Plan the Government has allocated about M$500 million for the further development of the following airports to cater for heavier air traffic and larger aircraft: Bintulu, Sibu, Tawau, Kuching, Kota Bahru, Trengganu, Miri and Sandakan.

Malaysian Airline System (MAS) Bhd.: UMBC Bldg., 4 Jalan Sulaiman, Kuala Lumpur 01-33; f. 1971 as the Malaysian successor to the Malaysia Singapore Airlines (MSA); Chair. Raja Tan Sri MOHAR BIN Raja BADIOZAMAN; Gen. Man. (vacant); operates a fleet of 9 Boeing 737, 2 Boeing 747, 11 F-27, 3 DC-10, 4 BN-2, one 737-200C and 4 Airbus A-300 to 37 domestic and 21 international destinations. Its network consists of flights from Kuala Lumpur to Australia, Brunei, France, Dubai, the Federal Republic of Germany, Hong Kong, India, Indonesia, Japan, the Republic of Korea, Kuwait, the Netherlands, the Philippines, Saudi Arabia, Singapore, Taiwan, Thailand and the United Kingdom.

FOREIGN AIRLINES

The following foreign airlines serve Malaysia: Aeroflot (U.S.S.R.), Air India, Biman (Bangladesh), British Airways, Cathay Pacific Airways (Hong Kong), China Airlines (Taiwan), ČSA (Czechoslovakia), Garuda (Indonesia), Iraqi Airways, JAL (Japan), KLM (Netherlands), PIA (Pakistan), Qantas (Australia), Sabena (Belgium), SAS (Sweden), SIA (Singapore), Thai International.

TOURISM

Tourist Development Corporation of Malaysia: 17th & 18th floors, Wisma MPI, Jalan Raja Chulan, Kuala Lumpur; f. 1972; responsible for the co-ordination of activities relating to tourism; formulating recommendations thereon and for promoting tourism overseas; overseas information centres in London, Frankfurt, San Francisco, Sydney, Tokyo, Hong Kong, Bangkok and Singapore; Chair. Tan Sri PHILIP KUOK.

Sabah Tourist Association: P.O.B. 946, Kota Kinabalu; f. 1962; 52 mems.; semi-governmental promotion organization; Chair. ROBERT DE SOUZA; Exec. Sec. BENEDICT TOPIN; publ. *Guide to Sabah* and others.

Sarawak Tourist Association: Sarawak Museum Gardens, Jalan Tun Haji Openg, P.O.B. 887, Kuching; Chair. Encik AHMAD Haji EBON; Hon. Sec. Encik ABDUL MURAT ABDULLAH; publ. *Welcome to Sarawak*, *Sarawak on Your Own*.

DEFENCE

Armed Forces (July 1981): Total strength 102,000; army 90,000, navy 6,000, air force 6,000; military service is voluntary. Paramilitary forces of 90,000 include Police Field Force of 19,000; People's Volunteer Corps of over 350,000.

Equipment: The army and navy have mainly British equipment while the air force has Australian fighter-bombers and French helicopters. Under agreements concluded in 1975 and 1976 the U.S.A. was to supply 6 S-61A and 5 Bell 206B helicopters to Malaysia.

Defence Budget: The budget estimate for 1982 is M$3,560 million.

CHIEFS OF STAFF

Chief of the Armed Forces Staff: Gen. Tan Sri Datuk MOHAMAD GHAZALI BIN MOHAMAD SETH.

Army: Gen. Tan Sri Datuk ZAIN MAHMUD BIN HASHIM.

Navy: Rear-Admiral MOHAMAD ZAIN BIN MOHAMAD SALLEH.

Air Force: Maj.-Gen. Datuk MOHAMMED BIN TAIB.

EDUCATION

The education scheme provides six years of free education between the ages of 6 and 11. The Government recognizes two types of schooling: assisted schools, and private schools, which receive no financial aid from the Government and are allowed to operate provided they observe the statutory requirements applicable to assisted schools.

The Government spends over 20 per cent of the total annual budget on education, amounting to an estimated M$1,942 million in 1979. Total school enrolment in assisted schools in 1981 was 3,152,194. No school fees are charged in assisted primary schools or in any of the Malay-medium secondary schools, but in other assisted secondary schools fees of between M$7.50 and $15.00 a month are charged per pupil, though up to 10 per cent may receive free places. Scholarships are awarded at all levels and there are many scholarship holders studying at universities and other institutes of higher education at home and abroad. In 1982 there were 49,000 Malaysians studying abroad.

Primary Education

Primary education is provided in Malay, Chinese and Tamil; this is intended to preserve the main cultures of

Malaysia and at the same time to establish a national system of education in which the national language gradually becomes the main medium of instruction. As stated in the 1961 Education Act, the Government aimed to make Malay the sole official language ten years after independence. Two-thirds of the total of the primary school enrolment is in national schools where Malay is used and the remainder in national-type primary schools where Tamil or Chinese is used. By 1971 all Standard One pupils in national-type English primary schools were using the national language, Bahasa Malaysia, in all subject classes. By 1980 the national language was in use in all secondary schools. Common content syllabuses are used in all schools.

A place in primary school is now assured to every child from the age of 6 onwards, and parents are free to choose the language medium. The total primary school enrolment in 1976 was 1,602,638 in 4,331 schools. The primary school course lasts for six years.

Secondary Education

Children automatically proceed from primary to secondary school to begin a three-year course of comprehensive education culminating in the Lower Certificate of Education examination. This enables pupils to select the type of further education to which they are most suited, either academic, technical or vocational. Admission to a two-year course leading to the Higher Certificate of Education, the qualifying examination for university entrance, is according to the performance of pupils in the Malaysian Certificate of Education examination taken in the fifth year of the secondary course. There has been a considerable increase since 1960 in the number of schools. In that year there were only 209; by 1976 the number had increased to 702. There has also been a correspondingly large increase in the number of trained teachers, rising from 4,390 in 1971 to 27,901 in 1976.

Secondary Vocational Schools provide a two-year course and are open to children who have completed the three-year lower secondary course. In 1977 there were 23 such schools, with an enrolment of 8,891. Pupils are selected on the results of the Lower Certificate of Education.

Secondary Technical Schools: Pupils are selected on the basis of the Lower Certificate of Education. The school provides an initial technical education which will enable them to take up a technical career. In 1977 there were nine technical schools, with an enrolment of 4,863 students. In addition, there are two polytechnics, at Ipoh and Kuantan respectively.

In 1980 there were 32 vocational and professional schools, with a total enrolment of 15,547.

Higher Education

Teacher Training: There are 26 teacher training colleges in Peninsular Malaysia, three in Sarawak and three in Sabah. The basic course lasts two years and the colleges together produce 600 trained teachers annually.

Universities: In 1982 Malaysia had five universities, with over 26,000 students.

Further Education

The Government provides further education for adults in the form of evening classes.

SABAH AND SARAWAK

Both states now come under the Federal Ministry of Education and are subject to central government financial controls, but still retain a certain degree of control over policy and administration.

Sabah

The policy is to provide a place at school for every child of primary school age. In 1980 there were 814 primary schools with an enrolment of 138,973 pupils. There were 87 secondary schools with an enrolment of 59,822 pupils.

Sarawak

Primary schools are run by the State Government, missionary bodies and a large group by Chinese Committees. Apart from the latter that employ Mandarin, all primary schools use English as the language medium. However, in 1977 a programme to convert all English medium primary schools to the use of Malay was launched. By 1987 it is expected that Malay will be used in all secondary schools. The primary school course, which is not compulsory, lasts six years starting at the age of 6. In 1980 there were 1,270 primary schools with 184,509 pupils, and 90 secondary schools with an enrolment of 91,808.

BIBLIOGRAPHY

GENERAL

FISHER, C. A. South-East Asia, A Social, Economic and Political Geography (Methuen, London, 1966).

GINSBURG, N., and ROBERTS, C. F. Malaya (University of Washington Press, Seattle, Wash., 1958).

HODDER, B. W. Man in Malaya (University of London Press, London, 1959).

PURCELL, V. Malaysia (Thames & Hudson, London, 1965).

RYAN, N. J. The Cultural Heritage of Malaya (Longman Malaysia, Kuala Lumpur, 1971).

SMITH, T. E. Population Growth in Malaya (Royal Institute of International Affairs, London, 1952).

SMITH, T. E., and BASTIN, J. Malaysia (Oxford University Press, London, 1967).

WANG, G. (ed.) Malaysia—a Survey (Pall Mall Press, New York and London, 1964).

PEOPLES OF MALAYSIA

ALI, H. S. Peasant Society and Leadership (Oxford University Press, London, 1977).

ARASARATNAM, S. Indians in Malaysia and Singapore (Oxford University Press, Singapore, 1979).

FIRTH, R. W. Malay Fishermen, their Peasant Economy (Routledge & Kegan Paul, London, 1966).

FREEDMAN, M. Chinese Family and Marriage in Singapore (HMSO, London, 1957).

JONES, L. W. The Population of Borneo (Athlone Press, London, 1966).

NEWELL, W. H. Treacherous River; a Study of Rural Chinese in North Malaya (Oxford University Press, Kuala Lumpur, 1962).

PURCELL, V. The Chinese in South East Asia (Oxford University Press, London, 1965).

SANDHU, K. S. Indians in Malaya 1786–1957 (Cambridge University Press, Cambridge, 1969).

SWIFT, M. G. Malay Peasant Society in Jelebu (Athlone Press, London, 1965).

HISTORY

BASTIN, J., and WINKS, R. W. Malaysia—Selected Historical Readings (Oxford University Press, London, 1979).

BLYTHE, W. The Impact of Chinese Secret Societies in Malaya (Oxford University Press, London, 1969).

CHAPMAN, F. S. The Jungle is Neutral (Chatto & Windus, London, 1949).

COWAN, C. D. Nineteenth Century Malaya (Oxford University Press, London, 1961).

EMERSON, R. Malaysia, a Study in Direct and Indirect Rule (University of Malaya Press, Kuala Lumpur, 1964).

GULLICK, J. M. Malaysia and its Neighbours (Routledge & Kegan Paul, London, 1967).
Malaysia (Benn, London, 1981).

HAHN, E. James Brooke of Sarawak (Arthur Barker, London, 1953).

HALL, D. G. E. A History of South East Asia (Macmillan, London, 1981).

JONES, S. W. Public Administration in Malaya (Royal Institute of International Affairs, London, 1953).

KENNEDY, J. A. A History of Malaya 1400–1959 (Macmillan, London, 1962).

KHOO KAY KIM. The Western Malay States 1850–1873 (Oxford University Press, Kuala Lumpur, 1972).

LOH, F. S. P. The Malay States 1877–95 (Oxford University Press, Singapore, 1969).

MILLER, H. The Story of Malaysia (Faber & Faber, London, 1967).

MILLS, L.A. British Rule in Eastern Asia (Oxford University Press, London, 1942).
British Malaya 1824–1967 (Oxford University Press, London, 1968).

PARKINSON, C. N. A Short History of Malaya (Singapore, 1954).
British Intervention in Malaya 1867–77 (University of Malaya Press, Kuala Lumpur, 1960).

PRINGLE, R. Rajahs and Rebels: the Iban of Sarawak under Brooke rule 1841–1941 (Macmillan, London, 1971).

PURCELL, V. The Chinese in Malaya (Oxford University Press, Oxford, 1971).

RUNCIMAN, S. The White Rajahs (Cambridge University Press, Cambridge, 1960).

ROFF, W. The Origins of Malay Nationalism (Yale University Press, New Haven, Conn., 1967).

SADKA, E. The Protected Malay States 1874–95 (University of Malaya Press, Kuala Lumpur, 1968).

SHORT, A. The Communist Insurrection in Malaya 1948–1960 (Frederick Muller, London, 1975).

SIMANDJUNTAK, B. Malayan Federalism 1945–63 (Oxford University Press, Kuala Lumpur, 1969).

SWETTENHAM, F. A. British Malaya (Allen & Unwin, London, 1948).

TREGONNING, K. G. A History of Modern Sabah 1881–1963 (Oxford University Press, Oxford, 1965).

TURNBULL, C. M. The Straits Settlements 1826–67 (Athlone Press, London, 1972).

WINSTEDT, R. O. Malaya and its History (Hutchinson, London, 1949).

WURTZBURG, C. E. Raffles of the Eastern Isles (Hodder & Stoughton, London, 1954).

POLITICS

ARIFF, M. O. The Philippines Claim to Sabah (Oxford University Press, Singapore, 1970).

CROUCH, H., LEE, K. H. and ONG, M. Malaysian Politics and the 1978 Election (1980).

ESMAN, M. J. Administration and Development in Malaysia (Cornell University Press, Ithaca, N.Y., 1972).

GOH, C. T. The May Thirteenth Incident and Democracy in Malaysia (Oxford University Press, Kuala Lumpur, 1971).

GOULD, J. W. The United States and Malaysia (Harvard University Press, Cambridge, Mass., 1969).

MAHATHIR, MOHAMAD. The Malay Dilemma (Asia Pacific Press, Singapore, 1970, re-published 1981).

MEANS, G. P. Malaysian Politics (Hodder & Stoughton, London, 1976).

MILNE, R. S. Government and Politics in Malaysia (Houghton Miflin, Boston, Mass., 1967).

PURCELL, V. Malaya Communist or Free (Gollancz, London, 1954).

RATNAM, K. J. Communalism and the Political Process in Malaya (University of Malaya Press, Kuala Lumpur, 1965).

ROFF, M. C. The Politics of Belonging: Political Change in Sabah and Sarawak (Oxford University Press, London, 1975).

SCOTT, J. C. Political Ideology in Malaysia: Reality and Beliefs of an Elite (University of Malaya Press, Kuala Lumpur, 1968).

SILCOCK, T. H., and AZIZ. Nationalism in Malaya (in *Asian Nationalism and the West*, ed. W. L. HOLLAND, Allen & Unwin, London, 1953).

STOCKWELL, A. J. British Policy and Malay Politics during the Malayan Union Experiment 1942–48 (Malaysian Branch of the Royal Asiatic Society, Kuala Lumpur, 1979).

ECONOMICS

ALLEN, G. C., and DONNITHORNE, A. G. Western Enterprise in Indonesia and Malaya (Allen & Unwin, London, 1957).

BARLOW, C. The Natural Rubber Industry (Oxford University Press, Kuala Lumpur, 1978).

BAUER, P. T. The Rubber Industry (Longmans Green, London, 1948).

CHAI, H. C. The Development of British Malaya 1896–1909 (Oxford University Press, Kuala Lumpur, 1964).

COWAN, C. D. (ed.) The Economic Development of South East Asia (Allen & Unwin, London, 1964).

DRABBLE, J. H. Rubber in Malaya 1876–1922 (Oxford University Press, London, 1973).

EDWARDS, C. T. Public Finances in Malaya and Singapore (Australian National University Press, Canberra, A.C.T., 1970).

HILL, R. D. Rice in Malaya: A Study in Historical Geography (Oxford University Press, Kuala Lumpur, 1977).

INTERNATIONAL BANK FOR RECONSTRUCTION AND DEVELOPMENT. The Economic Development of Malaya (Johns Hopkins Press, Baltimore, Md., 1955).

KANAPATHY, V. The Malaysian Economy: Problems and Prospects (Asia Pacific Press, Singapore, 1970).

KHERA, H. S. The Oil Palm Industry of Malaysia: An Economic Study (Penerbit Universiti Malaya, Kuala Lumpur, 1976).

LEE, H. L. Household Saving in West Malaysia and the Problem of Financing Economic Development (Faculty of Economics and Administration, University of Malaya, Kuala Lumpur, 1971).

Public Policies and Economic Diversification in West Malaysia, 1957–70 (University of Malaya Press, Kuala Lumpur, 1978).

LIM, C. Y. Economic Development of Modern Malaya (Oxford University Press, Kuala Lumpur, 1967).

LIM, T. G. Peasants and their Agricultural Economy in Colonial Malaya 1874–1941 (Oxford University Press, Kuala Lumpur, 1977).

McGEE, T. G. The Urbanization Process in the Third World (Bell, London, 1971).

MALAYSIA: ECONOMIC PLANNING UNIT. Second Malaysia Plan 1971–75 (Government Press, Kuala Lumpur, 1971).

Third Malaysia Plan 1976–80 (Government Press, Kuala Lumpur, 1976).

Fourth Malaysia Plan 1981–85 (Government Press, Kuala Lumpur, 1981).

NESS, G. D. Bureaucracy and Rural Development in Malaysia (University of California Press, Berkeley, Calif., 1967).

OOI, J. B. Land, People and Economy in Malaya (Longmans, London, 1963).

SILCOCK, T. H. (ed.) Readings in Malayan Economics (Eastern Universities Press, Singapore, 1961).

SILCOCK, T. H., and FISK, E. K. (eds.) The Political Economy of Independent Malaya (Eastern Universities Press, Singapore, 1963).

SNODGRASS, D. R. Inequality and Economic Development in Malaysia (Oxford University Press, Kuala Lumpur, 1980).

YIP, Y. H. The Development of the Tin Mining Industry in Malaya (University of Malaya Press, Singapore, 1969).

Maldives

PHYSICAL AND SOCIAL GEOGRAPHY

B. H. Farmer

The Republic of Maldives comprises a group of 1,196 islands, strung out from north to south about 670 km. south-west of Sri Lanka, and stretching from just north of the Equator to about 8° North latitude. Of these islands, 203 are inhabited. At the census of December 31st, 1977, the population was 142,832, of whom 29,555 lived in the capital, Malé. The estimated population at mid-1981 was 157,000.

Maldives rests on a submarine ridge, which may be volcanic in origin. The islands are grouped into 19 atolls (rings of coral islands, each ring encircling a lagoon: the word *atoll* is itself, in fact, Maldivian). All of the islands are built entirely of coral, coral sand, and other coral detritus. The climate is similar to that of Colombo (*see* under Sri Lanka). Most of the islands are covered with coconut palms.

The Maldivians are thought to be of mixed descent, deriving from South Indians (Dravidians), Sinhalese and Arabs. The language they speak, Dhivehi, is related to Sinhala. Their religion is Islam.

HISTORY

It was in the twelfth century that the islanders adopted the Muslim religion, and the fourteenth century saw the first description of conditions there, recorded by Ibn Batutah, an Arab traveller and historian. The ruler was then a Sultan of the ad-Din (Didi) dynasty. However, long before the extinction of the Sultanate in 1968, the Didi rank had been receding in importance in respect of the leadership of the country. The Portuguese, in their rapid and widespread colonization during the sixteenth century, established themselves on the islands in 1558, but were driven out in 1573. In the seventeenth century the islands came under the protection of the Dutch rulers of Ceylon (now Sri Lanka). When the British took possession of Ceylon in the late eighteenth century, they extended their protection to the Maldive Islands, and this was formally recorded in an agreement in 1887.

In 1948, when Ceylon became independent, a new agreement between the United Kingdom and the Maldive Islands provided that the United Kingdom should control the foreign affairs of the islands but should not interfere internally. The Sultan undertook to provide necessary facilities to British forces for the defence of the islands.

In 1956 the Maldivian and British Governments agreed to the establishment of a British Royal Air Force staging post on Gan, an island in the southernmost atoll, Addu. The Maldivian Government accorded free and unrestricted use by the United Kingdom Government of Gan Island and of 110 acres of Hittadu Island, for a radio station. Another agreement was signed in 1960, under which the Maldivian Government entrusted Gan and the demarcated area on Hittadu as a free gift to the United Kingdom, together with the free use of Addu lagoon and the adjacent territorial waters, for 30 years—this period to be extendable by agreement.

Independence

The Maldive Islands achieved full independence on July 26th, 1965, becoming a full sovereign state with all rights to conduct its own external relations. When the islands became independent, the British Government retained those facilities in Addu Atoll accorded to them in 1960 for purposes of Commonwealth defence. The British Government also undertook to pay the Maldivian Government £100,000, with a further £750,000 spread over five years or more, for economic development. In 1975, however, the British Government decided to close the air force base. With the evacuation of Gan by the British forces completed in March 1976, the 30-year agreement was terminated, creating a large commercial and military gap.

In October 1977 President Nasir rejected a U.S.$1 million offer from the U.S.S.R. to lease the former base on Gan, on the grounds that he did not want to lease the island to a superpower. In 1981 President Gayoom announced plans to set up an international business complex on Gan and said that two schemes to set up garment factories had already been approved. Approximately £1,500,000 would be needed to make the airport on Gan fully operational. However, Maldives seeks to maintain and develop strong and varied foreign relations in order to obtain more aid and to ensure a peaceful Indian Ocean area.

The Republic of Maldives

Until 1968, apart for the period between January 1953 and February 1954, when the islands became temporarily a republic, an elected Sultan was head of state. In a referendum held throughout Maldives in March 1968 over 80 per cent of those who voted approved a proposal to establish a republic in place of the sultanate. The Republic of Maldives was proclaimed on November 11th, 1968. Amir Ibrahim Nasir, who had been Prime Minister since 1954, was elected President.

The new Constitution, promulgated in 1968, vested considerable powers in the President, including the right to appoint and dismiss the Prime Minister and the Cabinet. In March 1975 President Nasir dismissed the Prime Minister, Ahmed Zaki, who was banished to a remote atoll, and the post of Prime Minister was abolished. However, Nasir unexpectedly announced that he would not stand for re-election at the end of his second five-year term in 1978. Maumoon Abdul Gayoom, a little-known member of Nasir's Cabinet and a former Permanent Representative of Maldives to the UN, was nominated by the *Majilis* (Parliament) and succeeded Nasir as President in November 1978. Gayoom's Government claims to have restored freedom to the republic—freedom of the press, for instance—and is undertaking investigations into the activities of former Government officials, notably Nasir's Public Safety Minister, Amir Abdul Hannan, who is charged with political persecution. Nasir himself, now living in Singapore but still with considerable business interests in Maldives, would face trial for misuse of Government funds if he returned to Maldives and in November 1980 it was announced that he would stand trial in his absence on these and other charges. In April 1980 the President confirmed an attempted coup against the Government, and implicated Nasir in the alleged plot. In April 1981 Ahmed Naseem, former deputy fisheries minister and brother-in-law of Nasir, was sentenced to life imprisonment for plotting to overthrow the President. Nasir himself has flatly denied any involvement in the coup and attempts to extradite him from Singapore have been unsuccessful.

In July 1982, Maldives became the 47th member of the Commonwealth.

ECONOMIC SURVEY

The majority of the population lives in tiny villages on remote atolls and, in the main, subsists by fishing and collecting coconuts. Malé has traditionally maintained a higher standard of living by levying an indirect tax on these products. Arable land is minimal and, while small amounts of coconuts, millet, sorghum, maize and yams are grown, virtually all the main food staples have to be imported. An estimate of per caput national income in 1978 was U.S. $158, growing at 6.2 per cent a year, but there is an increasing disparity of wealth on the islands. The working population at the December 1977 census was 60,259 (42.2 per cent of the total population). The Government is trying to diversify the economy by developing the shipping and tourist industries.

Fishing

The economy of Maldives is almost entirely dependent on fisheries for its export earnings. The catch consists mainly of tunas which were traditionally exported to Sri Lanka in a dried form known as "Maldive fish". However, the Sri Lankan Government has gradually reduced its quota since 1972 and by 1978 had ceased importing "Maldive fish". In 1979 an agreement was concluded whereby these fish imports would be resumed. In 1972 the Maldivian Government concluded an agreement with the Marubeni Corporation of Japan for the export of fresh fish and in 1978 the first factory for canning and processing fish was opened outside Malé. In 1979 the Maldivian Government announced the formation of the Maldives Fisheries Corporation "to exploit the fisheries resources in the most profitable manner for the benefit of the country". In 1980 Maldives and Iraq signed agreements on economic and technical co-operation, and on setting up a fishing company financed by Iraq. Raw and fresh fish now make up the bulk of fish exports.

There are several thousand fishing boats built in the country out of coconut wood, each boat taking about a dozen fishermen. Using sails they go out to a distance of fifteen to twenty miles from the shores, depending on the prevailing winds and currents. Provided a good shoal is encountered, the daily catch per boat exceeds 500 and may be as much as 1,500. Under a 50-year loan of U.S. $3.2 million from the IDA, the fishing fleet is being mechanized, diesel engines replacing sails, and five more maintenance and repair centres are being built.

Shipping

The second largest commercial industry of Maldives is the shipping industry, which began in 1958. Two ships were then in operation. By reinvesting the profits the country has been able to build up a sizeable fleet of ships, and today the profits of Maldives Shipping Ltd., with 40 ships, are contributing substantially to the settlement of the heavy cost of imports. The Government is trying to develop the shipping industry as much as possible by the training of technical personnel to replace the foreigners presently engaged in this field, and by increasing the total tonnage of the fleet. In June 1981 the ADB approved a $1 million loan to Maldives to help provide the country's first reliable, scheduled shipping services between Malé and the atolls.

Tourism

Tourism is another industry which brings considerable foreign exchange to Maldives, with its white sandy beaches, clear water and multi-coloured coral formations. Since 1972 tourist facilities have been developed by local private enterprises, and by 1980 27 individual islands had been developed for tourists, with a capacity of 1,748 beds. In 1978 the Government announced plans for tourist resorts with over 20 beds to become state-controlled by 1980. The number of tourists visiting Maldives rose from 1,799 in 1972/73 to 33,140 in 1979. One result of this increase in tourism is the Government's effort to improve the infrastructure. Telephones were installed on several resort islands for the first time in 1977 and a Tourist Advisory Board was set up in 1981 to expand the industry yet further.

Other Economic Activities

Coconut and coconut oil production is the fourth largest commercial industry of Maldives. Another major occupation is coir yarn weaving, in which only women are engaged. In spite of several centuries of continued production of this commodity, the methods in use have not undergone much change; the women do the work in their own homes.

Collecting cowries is another occupation in which only women take part. Cowries and other varieties of shells are a natural product meant solely for export, and not generally used for any domestic purpose. Many varieties of shells in demand by collectors are found in Maldives, including some of the rarest in the world.

Mat weaving is another small-scale cottage industry, principally for women. Mats are woven out of a particular type of reed and then dried in the sun; most of the mat weaving is done in the three southernmost atolls of the archipelago. Beautiful colours are incorporated and some of the mats have commercial value abroad.

There is a small-scale cottage industry, which prevails throughout the islands, of applying lacquer as a design on vases and other containers. Finally, cadjan weaving is quite common in the islands; both men and women are engaged in this work. Cadjan is much in demand because of its value for roofing purposes, the heat of the tropical sun being reduced considerably by its use.

STATISTICAL SURVEY

AREA AND POPULATION

Area	Population (census results)						Density (per sq. km.)
	June 1972	June 1974	December 31st, 1977			Mid-1981 (estimate)	1981
			Males	Females	Total		
298 sq. km.*	122,673	128,697	75,224	67,608	142,832	157,000	527

* 115 sq. miles.

Capital: Malé, population 29,555 (excluding foreigners) at December 31st, 1977.

Births and Deaths: (1979) 6,610 registered births; 2,067 registered deaths (including stillbirths).

Labour force: 60,259 (Dec. 1977).

AGRICULTURE

LAND USE

(FAO estimates, 'ooo hectares)

	1979
Arable land	} 3*
Land under permanent crops	
Permanent meadows and pastures	1
Forests and woodland	1
Other land	25
Total Area	30

* Unofficial estimate.

Source: FAO, *Production Yearbook.*

PRINCIPAL CROPS

(metric tons)

	1975	1976	1977	1978
Coconuts ('000 nuts)	10,736	7,139	13,267	8,542
Finger millet	1,731.7	66.3	35.8	18.9
Arica nuts	2.2	10.1	1.9	0.5
Maize	46.1	13.9	12.6	7.8
Italian millet	311.9	63.8	33.0	0.0
Cassava	15.7	4.1	5.5	5.1
Taro	925.8	1,210.9	865.4	358.0
Alocasia	77.8	54.0	45.2	16.3
Sweet potatoes	118.5	25.0	26.3	7.4
Onions	21.9	0.8	6.5	1.2
Chillies	1.9	3.0	2.7	2.4

SEA FISHING

('000 metric tons, live weight)

	1975	1976	1977	1978	1979	1980
Frigate and bullet tunas	3.9	2.7	3.1	1.9	1.8	2.0
Skipjack tuna (Oceanic skipjack)	16.0	19.9	14.4	13.8	17.9	24.0
Yellowfin tuna	4.2	4.8	4.3	3.7	4.3	4.2
Other marine fishes	3.8	4.9	4.5	6.4	3.7	3.3
TOTAL CATCH	27.9	32.3	26.3	25.8	27.7	33.5

Source: FAO, *Yearbook of Fishing Statistics.*

FINANCE

100 laaris (larees) = 1 rufiyaa (Maldivian rupee).

Notes: 1, 2, 5, 10, 50 and 100 rufiyaa.

Exchange rates (June 1982): £1 sterling = 13.08 rufiyaa; U.S. $1 = 7.55 rufiyaa.

100 rufiyaa = £7.647 = $13.245.

Note: Prior to August 1971 the official value of the Maldivian rupee (renamed the rufiyaa in July 1981) was 21 U.S. cents ($1 = 4.76 rupees). From December 1971 to February 1973 the exchange rate was $1 = 4.375 rupees. In February 1973 a new official rate of $1 = 3.93 rupees was established. This remained in operation until the end of 1974, since when the rupee's value has been frequently adjusted. The average exchange rate (rupees per U.S. dollar) was: 5.856 in 1975; 8.469 in 1976; 8.779 in 1977; 8.956 in 1978; 7.446 in 1979.

BUDGET

(million rufiyaa)

	1977	1978	1979
Government revenue	20.7	11.7	16.4
Government expenditure	38.4	41.2	39.5

EXTERNAL TRADE

('000 rufiyaa)

	1976	1977	1978	1979
Imports	21,498.1	35,819.7	51,361.8	86,630.0
Exports	11,755.3	13,750.2	16,133.3	23,009.8

PRINCIPAL COMMODITIES

('000 rufiyaa)

IMPORTS	1978	1979
Food and live animals	10,624.4	35,438.7
Beverages and tobacco	4,070.6	5,956.2
Crude materials (inedible) except fuels	1,804.2	1,694.4
Mineral fuels, lubricants, etc.	4,669.6	9,656.6
Animal and vegetable oils and fats	29.0	24.8
Chemicals	2,582.7	2,829.4
Basic manufactures	15,441.7	12,792.2
Machinery and transport equipment	3,814.5	7,535.8
Miscellaneous manufactured articles	8,325.1	10,701.9
TOTAL	51,361.8	86,630.0

EXPORTS	1978	1979
Maldive fish	817.9	246.8
Dried salt fish	2,647.9	8,375.7
Fresh fish	10,342.0	12,908.5
Dried shark fins	1,348.8	573.3
Tortoise shells	181.2	347.3
Cowrie shells	89.7	45.6
Red coral	12.0	18.7
Black ambergris	533.5	463.2
Other marine products	160.1	30.7
TOTAL	16,133.1	23,009.8

TRANSPORT

INTERNATIONAL SHIPPING
(freight traffic in metric tons)

	1977	1978	1979
Goods loaded . .	1,077	634	1,940
Goods unloaded .	30,227	18,695	37,842

TOURISM

	1978	1979	1980*
Tourist arrivals .	29,265	33,140	22,793
Number of hotel beds	1,278	1,674	1,748
Number of resorts .	16	25	27

* Figures to July 31st.

Receipts from tourism in 1979 (rufiyaa): 2,601,078.8.

COMMUNICATIONS

Radio licences issued: 3,526 in 1978; 6,351 in 1979.

EDUCATION

(1979)

	Schools	Pupils	Teachers
Primary . .	73	13,483	179
Secondary . .	4	3,859	105
Vocational . .	1	32	8

Source: (unless otherwise stated) Department of Information and Broadcasting, Malé.

THE CONSTITUTION

The main provisions of the 1968 republican Constitution are:

1. The Head of State is the President and he is vested with full executive powers.
2. The President is elected by a popular vote every five years.
3. The President appoints a Cabinet.
4. The members of the Cabinet are individually responsible to the *Majilis*, or Citizens' Council.
5. The *Majilis* has 48 members, including 40 elected for five years by universal adult suffrage (two by the National Capital Island and two from each of the 19 atolls) and eight appointed by the President.
6. The powers of the President, the Cabinet and the legislature are laid down in the Constitution.
7. Within the provisions of Islam, freedom of "life movement", speech and development are guaranteed as basic rights of the people.

THE GOVERNMENT

President and Head of State: Maumoon Abdul Gayoom (took office November 11th, 1978).

THE CABINET

(July 1982)

President: Maumoon Abdul Gayoom.

Minister of Agriculture: Ahmed Hilmy Didi.

Minister of External Affairs: Fathulla Jameel.

Minister of Education: Mohamed Zahir Hussain.

Minister of Health: Mohamed Musthafa Hussain.

Minister of Provincial Affairs: Abdulla Hameed.

Minister of Fisheries: Abdul Satter Moosa Didi.

LEGISLATURE

MAJILIS

Comprises 48 members, of whom 8 are nominated by the President, 2 elected by the people of Malé and 2 elected from each of the 19 atolls.

Speaker: Ahmed Shathir.

POLITICAL PARTIES

There are no political parties in Maldives.

DIPLOMATIC REPRESENTATION

EMBASSIES ACCREDITED TO MALDIVES

India: Maafannuaage, Malé; *Ambassador:* Brij Kumar.

Iraq: Maagiri, Henveiru, Malé; *Chargé d'affaires:* Ali Salman.

Libya: Guleyseemuge, Maafannu, Malé; *Secretary of People's Bureau*: Mohamed Abdul Salam Treiki.

Pakistan: 2 Moonimaage, Galolhu, Malé; *Chargé d'affaires:* S. S. Quresh.

Sri Lanka: Muraka, Maafannu, Malé; *Ambassador:* W. M. G. Abeyaratne.

Maldives also has diplomatic relations with Argentina, Australia, Austria, Bahrain, Bangladesh, Belgium, Burma, Canada, the People's Republic of China, Cuba, Czechoslovakia, Egypt, France, the German Democratic Republic, the Federal Republic of Germany, Hungary, Indonesia, Iran, Italy, Japan, Jordan, the Democratic People's Republic of Korea, the Republic of Korea, Kuwait, Malaysia, Mali, Mexico, Nepal, the Netherlands, New Zealand, Oman, the Philippines, Romania, Saudi Arabia, Seychelles, Singapore, Spain, Sudan, Sweden, Switzerland, Thailand, Turkey, the U.S.S.R., the United Arab Emirates, the United Kingdom, the U.S.A., Viet-Nam and Yugoslavia. In most cases the missions are in Sri Lanka.

JUDICIAL SYSTEM

The administration of justice is carried out according to the Shari'ah, the sacred law of Islam, through a body appointed by the President. In 1980 the Maldives High Court was established. There are Island Courts in every inhabited island and a Police Court in Malé.

HIGH COURT

Chief Justice: Moosa Fathy.

Judges: Ahmed Adam, Ibrahim Rameez.

Attorney-General: Hussain Abdul Rahman (acting).

CITIZENS' SPECIAL MAJILIS

This is a special council set up to deal with matters concerning the Constitution, financial activities and the protection of citizens' rights and includes any law changing the administrative structure or related to the leasing of land to foreigners. It is composed of all the members of the Citizens' Majilis, the Cabinet and 48 elected members (two from each atoll, two from Malé and eight nominated by the President).

Chairman: Ibrahim Shibab.

RELIGION

Islam is the State religion. The Maldivians are Sunni Muslims.

THE PRESS

Aafathis: Malé; Dhivehi and English; daily; Editor Abdul Shakoor.

Faiythoora: Malé; Dhivehi; monthly magazine; Editor Hon. Uz Mohamed Jameel Didi.

Hafthaa: Malé; Dhivehi and English; weekly; Editor Ahmed Zahir.

Haweeru: Malé; Dhivehi and English; daily; Editor Faarooq Hassan.

RADIO AND TELEVISION

Department of Information and Broadcasting: Faashanaa Bldg., Marine Drive, Malé; Dir. Hassan Ahmed Maniku; Deputy Dir. Mohamed Waheed.

Voice of Maldives: Hadhuvaree Higun, Malé; radio broadcasting began in 1962; home service in Dhivehi and English; Asst. Dirs. Ibrahim Maniku, Badrul Naseer.

TV Maldives: Buruzu Magu, Malé; television broadcasting began in 1978; Deputy Dir. Hussain Shihab; Man. Ali Ibrahim.

In 1981 there were 9,169 radio receivers.

In 1981 there were 1,148 television receivers.

FINANCE

CENTRAL BANK

Maldives Monetary Authority (MMA): Malé; f. 1981; issues currency, fixes the value of the rufiyaa in relation to other currencies; acts as an advisory body to the Government on fiscal and economic matters; Gov. Maumoon Abdul Gayoom; Deputy Gov. Ismail Fathy.

COMMERCIAL BANK

Bank of Maldives: Beach Crescent Building, Marine Drive, Malé; f. 1982; operates in conjunction with Bangladesh International Finance and Investment Company; Chair. Ahmed Adam; Dirs. Ahmed Mujuthaba; Moosa Ismail; Ali Shareef.

The State Bank of India (f. 1974), the Bank of Ceylon (office f. 1981), and Habib Bank Ltd. (Pakistan, office f. 1976) have offices in Malé.

TRADE AND INDUSTRY

State Trading Organization (STO): Malé; Government-sponsored commercial and financial organization; imports staple foods and other consumer items; Man. Dir. Ilyas Ibrahim; Dir. Ali Shareef.

INDUSTRIAL ORGANIZATIONS

Insulectra Maldives Ltd.: Malé; a subsidiary of Insulectra Ltd. of Hong Kong; manufactures and exports electronic components; Man. Dir. Kisto Kumar Saha.

Maldive Nippon Corporation: Fasmeeru H., Marine Drive, Malé; exports skipjack and yellowfin tuna; in 1978 opened canning factory on Feliwaru Island, Lhaviyani Atoll; Chair. K. Gomyoh.

Maldives Fisheries Corporation: Malé; f. 1979; state-owned commercial enterprise incorporated under Presidential decree to carry out the activities of fishing, fish purchasing, processing, export and import and to deal with marine fishery resources; took over Faadhippolhu fish canning factory in 1982; Man. Dir. Hussain Manikfan; Asst. Mans. Ahmed Nazeer, Mohamed Kamal.

TRANSPORT

Maldives Transport and Contracting Company: Malé; f. 1981; 60 per cent public and 40 per cent government owned; Man. Dir. Ahmed Adam.

SHIPPING

Maldives Shipping Ltd.: MSL Building, Orchid Magu, Malé; f. 1965; 100 per cent government-owned; operates fleet of 40 vessels: 34 general cargo ships (one of 500 d.w.t., one of 20,000 d.w.t., 11 of 15,000 d.w.t. and others 1,000 to 14,000 d.w.t.), two tugs, three tankers (1,000 d.w.t.); and one passenger liner; also manages four general cargo ships (one of 20,000 d.w.t. and others 1,000–5,000 d.w.t.); sole shipping operator; brs. in Bombay, London, Karachi, Colombo and Singapore; Dir. Ahmed Mujuthaba.

Vessels operate between Maldives and Sri Lanka at frequent intervals. They also call at places in India, Pakistan, Burma, Singapore, Malaysia, Bangladesh, Thailand, Indonesia, Japan, Korea, Europe, Brazil, Canada, Africa, the Middle East and Adriatic ports.

CIVIL AVIATION

The Department of Civil Aviation, set up in 1979, handles all activities connected with air transport. The existing airport on Hululé island was expanded and improved to international standard with financial assistance from Kuwait, Abu Dhabi, Saudi Arabia and OPEC and, as Malé International Airport, was officially opened in November 1981. Charter flights from Europe have subsequently begun operation.

Air Maldives: operates a twice weekly internal air service between Malé International Airport and Gan.

Maldive International Airlines (MIA): Malé International Airport, Marine Drive, Malé; f. 1977 jointly by Maldives Government and Indian Airlines; services to India and Sri Lanka; 1 Boeing 737-200; operates daily flights between Malé and Colombo and three flights a week to Trivandrum in southern India; Man. MOHAN RAO.

Indian Airlines and Air Lanka flights also serve Maldives.

TOURISM

Department of Tourism and Foreign Investment: Malé; Dir. AHMED MUJTHABA.

Tourist Advisory Board: Malé; f. 1981 to establish standards of service in tourist resorts and hotels, formulate uniform prices and to expand the tourist industry; Chair. of Bd. FATULLAH JAMEEL.

EDUCATION

Education has been centred largely on the capital, Malé, until very recently. In 1976 the 16 schools in existence were all in Malé and catered mainly for primary school age. UNICEF in particular has contributed to provincial development and in 1978 the first school opened outside Malé, on Baa atoll. There are further plans for expansion with UN assistance, but the nature of the country and the scattered population impede progress. The Government is looking into the possibilities of educational broadcasting to overcome these problems. In 1980 a Basic Education Programme was launched and an estimated 10,000 adults attended the classes during that year.

There are three types of formal education: traditional Koranic schools (*Makthab*), Dhivehi-medium primary schools (*Madhrasa*) and English-medium primary and secondary schools. The latter are the only ones equipped to teach a standard curriculum. In 1979 there were 78 schools, with 17,374 pupils, and it was estimated that less than half of the school-age population attended school. The first school outside Malé was opened in 1978. In 1975, with the assistance of the UNDP and the ILO, a full-time vocational training centre was opened in Malé, and in 1979 the Science Education Centre was opened with the help of UNICEF, UNESCO and the UNDP.

Mongolia

PHYSICAL AND SOCIAL GEOGRAPHY

Charles Bawden

(Revised by Alan Sanders since 1977)

The Mongolian People's Republic occupies an area of 1,565,000 square kilometres in east central Asia. It is bordered by only two other states, the U.S.S.R. along its northern frontier (3,005 km.) and China along the considerably longer southern frontier (4,673 km.).

PHYSICAL ENVIRONMENT

For the purpose of geographical description Mongolia may be divided into five regions. In the west is the Altay area, where peaks covered with eternal snow reach up to over 4,300 metres. To the east of this lies a great depression dotted with lakes, some of salt water and some of fresh. Some of these, such as Uvs nuur (3,350 square km.) and Hövsgöl nuur (2,620 square km.), the latter being quite important for navigation, reach a considerable size. Thirdly, the north-central part of the country is occupied by the Hangay-Hentiy mountain complex, enclosing the relatively fertile and productive agricultural country of the Selenge-Tuul basin. This has always been the focus of what cultural life existed in the steppes of north Mongolia: the imperial capital of Karakorum lay here and the ruins of other early settlements are still to be seen. To the east again lies the high Mongolian plateau reaching to the Chinese frontier, and to the south and east stretches the Gobi or semi-desert.

Water is unevenly distributed. In the mountainous north and west of the country large rivers originate, draining into either the Arctic or the Pacific. A continental watershed divides Mongolia, and the much smaller rivers of the south drain internally into lakes or are lost in the ground.

Climate

The climate shows extremes of temperature between the long cold dry winter and the short hot summer during which most of the year's precipitation falls. In Ulan Bator the July temperature averages 16.5°C and the January temperature −22.5°C. Annual precipitation is variable but light. Ulan Bator's average is 312 mm., with 9 cm. of snow in December. However, rain is liable to fall in sudden heavy showers or more prolonged outbursts in mid-summer, particularly in July, with severe flooding and damage to towns and bridges. The bitter winter weather is relieved by the almost continuous blue sky and sunshine. Mongolia is liable to severe earthquakes, especially in mountainous regions, but the population is too widely scattered for heavy losses to be caused.

POPULATION

Mongolia is very sparsely inhabited. The population was 1,594,800 at the January 1979 census, or just over one person per square km. It is not correct to regard the Mongols as essentially nomadic herdsmen, though stock-movement (*otor*), sometimes covering large distances, is a regular feature of rural life. Of the total population, over 45 per cent live in towns, more than half of these in the capital Ulan Bator (Ulaanbaatar). Moreover, there is a definite shift towards living in permanent settlements in the rural areas, which it is national policy to encourage through capital investment in rural building. There are some 300 such settlements, inhabited by about 22 per cent of the population. The population is, relatively speaking, homogeneous. Some 87 per cent of the people are Mongols, and of these the overwhelming majority belong to the Khalkha (Halh) group. The only important non-Mongol element in the population is that of the Kazakhs, a Turkish-speaking people dwelling in the far west, and representing slightly over five per cent of the whole. The population has grown steadily over recent years: since 1963 it has increased by about 50 per cent. As a result there is a preponderance of young people: 65.6 per cent of the population is aged 30 or under. The official language is Mongol, written nowadays in an adaptation of the Cyrillic script. Mongol is quite different from both Russian and Chinese, its geographic neighbours, but does show certain similarities, perhaps fortuitous, to Turkish, Korean and Japanese. Several Mongol dialects beside the dominant Khalkha are spoken in the Republic, and in the Kazakh province of Bayan-ölgiy Kazakh is the first language, most people being bi-lingual in Mongol.

HISTORY

Charles Bawden

(Revised by Alan Sanders since 1977)

Today only a minority of Mongols live in the Mongolian People's Republic (M.P.R.), the one independent Mongol state. Apart from the related Buryat and Kalmyk peoples who are to be found within the U.S.S.R. in their own autonomous republics near Lake Baikal and on the lower Volga respectively, many true Mongols dwell outside the M.P.R., most of them in the Nei Monggol (Inner Mongolia) Autonomous Region of the People's Republic of China and adjacent areas—Heilongjiang (Heilungkiang), Jilin (Kirin), Liaoning, Gansu (Kansu), Ningxia (Ninghsia) and Xinjiang (Sinkiang). This division came about in the following way. In the early seventeenth century the Manzhous (Manchus), expanding southwards from Manzhou (Manchuria) towards their ultimate conquest of all China, passed through what came to be called Nei Monggol, which lay across their invasion routes. Many of the Mongol princes allied themselves with the Manzhous, sometimes cementing such alliances by marriages, others submitted voluntarily to them, while yet others were conquered. In 1636, after the death of Ligdan Khan, the last Mongol emperor, the subordination of these princes to the new rising dynasty was formalized. The princes of Khalkha or Outer Mongolia maintained a sort of client relationship towards the Manzhous for a further half-century, but in their turn lost their independence at the Convention of Dolonnor in 1691. The Manzhous had, in 1688, entered Khalkha to expel Galdan, the ruler of the west Mongol Oirats, who was both terrorizing the Khalkhas and challenging the Manzhous for supremacy in this area. With Galdan defeated, the three great princes of Khalkha, and the Javdzandamba Hutagt, or Living Buddha of Urga, the head of the lamaist church in Mongolia, had to accept Manzhou overlordship.

Outer Mongolia was administered by the Manzhous as a separate area from Nei Monggol. A fourth princedom (*aymag*) was created in addition out of the existing three in 1725 and soon afterwards the princedoms were renamed Leagues and removed from the jurisdiction of the hereditary princes to be administered by Mongol League Heads appointed by the Li Fan Yuan or Colonial Office in Beijing (Peking). Within the League organization Mongolia was divided into about a hundred banners and a number of temple territories, while the Living Buddha owned a huge number of serfs scattered about here and there. This state structure survived the fall of the Manzhous in 1911 and lasted until the foundation of the M.P.R. in 1924. In spite of their dependence on Beijing, however, the Mongols always considered themselves allies of the Manzhous, not subjects on the same level as the Chinese, and made good use of this distinction when the Manzhou dynasty lost the throne of China.

Autonomous Mongolia

The beginnings of the existence of contemporary Mongolia can be traced back to 1911. In that year the fall of the Manzhous enabled the Mongols to terminate their association with China. With some political and military support from Russia a number of leading nobles proclaimed Mongolia an independent monarchy, and the throne was offered to the Living Buddha. The new government, in an unrealistic excess of euphoria, invited all Mongols everywhere to adhere to the new state, but this involved them in conflict with China, which held on to Nei Monggol. Nor did they obtain much useful support from Russia which was bound by secret treaties with Japan not to obstruct the latter's interests in Nei Monggol, and which in any case was reluctant to engage in a doubtful pan-Mongolist adventure. An inconclusive war with China dragged on for a couple of years until in 1915 Russian, Chinese and Mongol representatives, meeting at Kyakhta (Hiagt) on the Russo-Mongol border, agreed to the reduction of Mongolia's state of independence to one of autonomy under Chinese suzerainty. At this time autonomous Mongolia consisted more or less of the present territory of the M.P.R., the only substantial difference being the accession of Dariganga in the south-east at the time of the 1921 revolution. Nei Monggol, Barga and the Altay district of Xinjiang were to remain under Chinese control, while Tannu Tuva, after a brief period of independence as a "People's Republic" was annexed by the U.S.S.R. during the Second World War.

Autonomous Mongolia was a theocratic monarchy, and during the few years of its existence very little happened to change the conditions inherited from Manzhou times. Russian advisers did begin to modernize the Mongol army and to bring some sort of order into the fiscal system. Some primary schools and a secondary school were opened, some children, including the future dictator Choybalsan, were sent to study in Russia, and the first newspaper appeared. But the state structure, the feudal organization of society and the administration of justice remained more or less as they had been, while the church managed to consolidate and enhance its position of privilege. Though legally subject to Chinese suzerainty, Mongolia was, in fact, a Russian protectorate. When Russian power and prestige in Central Asia were sapped by the collapse of the Tsarist empire and the outbreak of revolution, this dependence of Mongolia became very apparent, and China lost no time in reasserting its authority. By mid-1919 the abrogation of autonomy was being discussed by the Mongol Government and the Chinese resident in Urga, the capital, but the process was brutally accelerated by the arrival in Mongolia of General Xu Shuzeng who, with a large military force at his disposal, forced the capitulation of the Mongols in early 1920.

The Revolutionary Movement

Towards the end of 1919 two revolutionary clubs

had been founded in Urga: the next year these amalgamated to form the Mongol People's Party. There was no long-standing revolutionary tradition in Mongolia, which perhaps explains how it was that the Mongol revolution fell so completely under Soviet control. The members of the clubs included men of varied social origin, lamas such as Bodoo the Premier of 1921 who was liquidated in 1922, government servants, workers, soldiers such as Sühbaatar, and returned students from Russia, such as Choybalsan. They had the sympathy of several prominent nobles through whom they were able to approach the King, while at the same time they acquired some knowledge of Marxism from their acquaintance with left-wing Russian workers in Urga. The first real contacts with Soviet Russia took place in early 1920 when a Comintern agent, Sorokovikov, came to Urga to assess the situation. It is therefore not surprising to find that the aims of the revolutionaries were at this time fairly moderate. First of all they desired national independence from the Chinese, then an elective government, internal administrative reforms, improved social justice, and the consolidation of the Buddhist faith and church. With Sorokovikov's approval they planned to send a delegation to Russia to seek help against the Chinese. They obtained the sanction of the King, and carried with them a letter authenticated with his seal. They were, in fact, authorized only to obtain advice from the Russians, not to negotiate actual intervention.

In their absence from Mongolia the situation was complicated by the incursion into the country of White Russian forces under Baron Ungern Sternberg. At first the Mongol authorities and the people welcomed the White Russians who dislodged the oppressive Chinese, and with the help of Ungern, the King was restored to the throne. However, Ungern's brutalities soon turned the Mongols against him. More important, the Soviet agents dealing with the Mongol delegation were able to use Ungern's apparent ascendancy over the Urga regime to extract far-reaching concessions. They made the offer of help conditional upon the establishment in Urga later of a new government friendly to them. In March 1921 the first congress of the Mongol People's Party was held at Kyakhta on Soviet territory, and a provisional revolutionary government was also set up there in opposition to the legal authorities in Urga who had sponsored the delegates who now abandoned them. This provisional government gathered a small band of partisans who, with much more significant Soviet forces, entered Mongolia, defeated Ungern, and then marched on Urga. Here, in July 1921, a new government was proclaimed, under the restored King. The monarchy existed now, however, in name only. Mongolia came more and more under Soviet direction. A secret police force was set up and in 1922 the first of a long series of political purges took place. In 1924 the People's Party was renamed the People's Revolutionary Party (M.P.R.P.); the King died, and a People's Republic was proclaimed, with a Soviet-style constitution.

The Mongolian People's Republic

Mongolia was now in name a People's Republic, the second socialist state in the world, but its primitive stage of development posed daunting problems. An unproductive church which commanded deep loyalty from the people weighed heavily on the economy and was a powerful ideological opponent of communism. Local separatism, especially in the far west, took years to overcome, and in some outlying parts local government could not be established till 1928 or 1929. Moreover, it was easy for disillusioned herdsmen to trek with their herds over the frontiers into China, and there were considerable losses of population by emigration. The country suffered from almost total illiteracy, and of those who could read and write, many were in fact lamas whose skill was in Tibetan and not Mongol. The country's economy depended exclusively on extensive animal herding. Trade and crafts were in the hands of foreigners, almost all of them Chinese. There was no banking system, no national currency, no industry and no medical service in the modern sense. Finally, most of those men who were politically experienced and capable of running the local administration were lamas or nobles, two classes whom the revolutionary regime aimed at annihilating in time.

Thus the stage of economic, social and intellectual development which Mongolia had reached was far below the U.S.S.R.'s, and its capacity for independent action was practically nil against its one international partner, the immeasurably more powerful U.S.S.R. It was willy-nilly caught up with Soviet interests and developments and its history over the next two decades shows the same progression of events as characterized Stalin's U.S.S.R. At first, until 1928, there ensued a few years of semi-capitalist development, during which the privileges of the nobility and clergy were not gravely tampered with. In international contacts, too, the Mongols reached out to France and Germany. However, parallel with the rise of Stalin and the swing to the left in the U.S.S.R. there developed in Mongolia what came to beknown as the "leftist deviation". All foreign contacts except with the U.S.S.R. were cut off. The U.S.S.R. monopolized Mongolia's trade in which it had hitherto had only a modest share. Between 1929 and 1932 an unprepared programme of collectivization ruined the country's economy, stocks of cattle dropping by at least one-third. A vicious anti-religious campaign did much to turn people against the Party, and in 1932 uprisings broke out which, particularly in west Mongolia, reached the proportions of civil war, and necessitated the intervention of the Soviet army. Thousands of Mongols deserted the country with their herds. This disastrous course was reversed only on the direct instructions of the Soviet Communist Party in June 1932. Leaders who until then had been enthusiastic leftists, such as Genden who became Premier and was later "unmasked" as a "Japanese spy" and liquidated by Choybalsan, now swung to a more moderate line, and under what was termed the "New Turn Policy" private ownership of cattle and private trade were again encouraged, and the Church was treated more gently. However, from 1936 onwards Mongolia fell under the dictatorship of Marshal Choybalsan (died 1952), whose methods were indistinguishable from those of Stalin. The lamaist church was utterly destroyed with much loss of life and property, and most of the old guard of revolutionaries, politicians, high military officers and intellectuals were liquidated on charges, usually of treasonable plotting with the Japanese, which have since been acknowledged to have been quite false. Thus Choybalsan declared in 1940 that Mongolia could begin the transition from "democratic revolution" to "socialism". Party and government were now staffed by a new body of very young men, protégés of Choybalsan, some of whom, such as the present leader, Yumjaagiyn Tsedenbal, have continued uninterruptedly in office until today.

The progress made by 1940 had been mostly negative, consisting in the elimination of old social groupings and the redistribution of wealth confiscated from the former nobles, liquidated in and after 1929, and the Church. A certain amount of reconstruction had been achieved, in the fields of education, medical services, communications and industry, but it was not until well after the Second World War that any drastic programme of modernization was to be attempted in Mongolia. One reason for this tardiness was the threat posed by the Japanese in Manzhou, which meant that most of the Soviet expenditure in Mongolia was devoted to a military build-up. It is significant that the only railway to be built in pre-war years served the base of Choybalsan in east Mongolia. Only after the war was Mongolia's main economic region, the centre, around Ulan Bator, to be connected with the Trans-Siberian line.

Post-War Political Developments

Mongolia escaped the worst of the Second World War, though suffering some effects. The Japanese in Manzhou had for some years been probing the defences of Mongolia, and in the summer of 1939 they provoked a series of battles on the Khalkha River (Halhyn Gol) in which they were heavily defeated by Soviet and Mongol troops. From then on a truce reigned until August 1945 when Mongolia followed the U.S.S.R. in declaring war on Japan. Mongol forces advanced as far as the Pacific coast of China, but were soon afterwards withdrawn, and the only advantage Mongolia drew from its belated participation in the war was the labour of a number of Japanese prisoners. On the debit side, imports from the U.S.S.R. almost dried up during the war years, and Mongolia itself made a heavy contribution to the Soviet war-effort, though it was never at war with Germany. As a result there was practically no economic progress. The one important event in Mongolia's history at this time was the recognition of its independence by China in January 1946 after a plebiscite the previous October had called for confirmation of the status quo. However, Mongolia's international position of isolation in unique dependence on the U.S.S.R. did not change until the communization of eastern Europe and the success of the Communists in China provided it with a new and ready-made field of diplomatic activity. Between October 1948 and March 1950 it exchanged diplomatic recognition with all the then existing communist states except Yugoslavia (1956), and thereafter with a number of non-aligned countries such as India, Burma and Indonesia. The United Kingdom was the first Western European state to recognize Mongolia. Mongolia was admitted to the United Nations in 1961.

Mongolia still looks mainly to the U.S.S.R. for guidance and help in its affairs in spite of its wider international contacts. In 1946 the traditional alphabet was abandoned in favour of a form of the Cyrillic script. Russian is the most widely known foreign language. Most of those students who study abroad do so in the U.S.S.R., while many textbooks are translated from Russian. But most important, Mongolia's party and state structure, public institutions, educational system, journalism and publications are clearly based on the Soviet model, while economic planning proceeds in close consultation with Soviet experts. Mongolia's alignment with the U.S.S.R. in the Sino-Soviet dispute was predictable, and the official press continues to adopt a sharp anti-Beijing line. China is accused, among other things, of carrying out a colonialist policy in its minority areas, including Nei Monggol (Inner Mongolia), and, in Tsedenbal's words, of openly preparing for war with the U.S.S.R. and Mongolia. Soviet troops are stationed in the M.P.R. at the Mongolian Government's request, because of the "real threat" of Chinese "great-power expansion".

The partial thaw which was initiated in the U.S.S.R. by Nikita Khrushchev was imitated in Mongolia, where the cult of personality was denounced in 1956 and again in 1962, and several of the leaders put to death in the 1930s were rehabilitated. Contacts with non-communist foreigners were permitted, a small tourist industry was built up and controls on publications somewhat relaxed. An individual feature of this period has been the reassertion of feelings of Mongolian nationalism, which for twenty years had been repressed. Since 1936 the existence of pre-revolutionary culture in Mongolia had been systematically denied. Nothing was taught of old Mongol literature in schools, no old books were reprinted, and party agents went round the countryside collecting and destroying old manuscripts as being contrary to contemporary ideology. After 1956 this policy was modified. School curricula, while still insisting that children be given a communist education which was to convince them of the inevitable victory of communism, were liberalized so far as to include extracts from ancient literature once more. The Committee of Sciences (from 1961, Academy) was able to begin quite an ambitious programme of research and publication in the fields of literature, history and linguistics, and to organize in 1959 the First International Congress of Mongolists. This was the first, and so far only occasion on which scholars from the Western world, the Soviet bloc and China have conferred together in Mongolia. This renascence of national sentiment has been rebuffed from time to time when it clashed with Soviet requirements of greater international communist conformity, as in 1962 when the Mongols celebrated the 800th anniversary of the birth of Genghis Khan. The event was translated into the international sphere since the Chinese, for reasons of their own, also celebrated this event in Inner Mongolia. The enthusiasm provoked in

Mongolia was seen by Moscow, and in more orthodox quarters in Mongolia itself, as manifesting excessive feelings of nationalism at the expense of "proletarian internationalism", and the celebrations were abruptly called off. Early in 1963 an ideological conference was held in Ulan Bator with the participation of a strong Soviet delegation, in order to reassert the correct political line. On four occasions during the 1960s high party and government officials, hitherto respected comrades, were "unmasked" and dismissed on multiple charges of inefficiency, arrogance, dishonesty, corruption and so on.

In June 1974, Premier Yumjaagiyn Tsedenbal became Head of State, succeeding Jamsrangiyn Sambuu who had died in May 1972. The new Premier, Jambyn Batmönh, was a comparative newcomer to political life. Tsedenbal has been concurrently First Secretary of the M.P.R.P. Central Committee since 1958, and was General Secretary of the party for most of the 18 years before then.

In his address to the 17th congress of the M.P.R.P. in June 1976, Tsedenbal called for tighter discipline and higher political vigilance. He said it was very important to intensify the process of Mongolia's "drawing together" with the Soviet Union, on the basis of integrating the Mongolian economy with the Soviet economy, so as to equalize the level of economic development in the socialist countries.

On his 60th birthday (September 17th, 1976), Tsedenbal was said by the party press to enjoy "great authority, trust and affection" among the Mongolian people as their "universally recognized leader". Tsedenbal is also a Marshal of the M.P.R.—the highest rank in the Mongolian People's Army.

At the general elections to the People's Great Hural in June 1977 a 99.99 per cent vote for the official candidates was recorded. The Hural re-elected Tsedenbal as Chairman of the Presidium (President of the M.P.R.) for a new four-year term. New legislation introduced at the beginning of 1978 imposed severe restrictions on internal travel to halt the drift of population into the towns, and put a firm limit on the number of personal livestock that may be kept by individuals.

Following the 18th Congress of the MPRP in May 1981, the new Central Committee approved a proposal that Tsendenbal's title should change from First Secretary back to General Secretary, without any change in his functions. For the first time, a public security chief joined the top leadership of the Mongolian party, with the election of Bugyn Dejid to candidate membership of the Politburo and the chairmanship of the Party Control Committee, responsible for checking on implementation of party instructions. This followed a pattern continued in the Soviet Central Asian republics during their party congresses earlier in the year.

Namsrayn Luvsanravdan was removed from the Politburo. The MPRP Secretariat was joined by Mangaljavyn Dash, a former Minister of Agriculture. The congress had emphasized the need for a great improvement in agricultural production, and had encouraged the opening up of auxiliary farms at factories, and the cultivation of private plots.

At the first session of the 10th People's Great Hural, held soon after the general elections of June 1981 (another 99.99 per cent vote for official candidates), Namsrayn Luvsanravdan was replaced by Nyamyn Jagvaral as one of two Deputy Chairmen of the Hural Presidium (Vice-Presidents of the MPR).

ECONOMIC SURVEY

Charles Bawden

(Revised by Alan Sanders since 1977)

From 1948 the Mongol economy has been developed under a series of Five-Year Plans with large-scale assistance from other communist countries, principally the countries now forming the Council for Mutual Economic Assistance (CMEA). The two salient features of post-war development have been the completion of the transition to the socialist system of production, and a rate of economic expansion very much faster than was achieved in the first thirty years of the Republic.

Agriculture: Collective and State Farms

After the catastrophe of the period of leftist deviation, animal herding, the mainstay of Mongolia's economy, had reverted to private enterprise, and apart from taking compulsory deliveries of produce during the war years the Government had kept its hands off the herds. Small-scale mutual help in carrying out certain tasks was practised, and some herdsmen joined together in small producers' associations, but under the New Turn Policy the formation of co-operatives was discouraged. By 1952 the existing co-operatives contained only 280,000 animals out of a national stock of nearly 23 million. However, collectivization of herding had by 1947 again become a matter of policy and in that year the Central Committee of the Party was given the task of examining the situation. Although collectivization is said to have been carried out voluntarily by the herdsmen, the initiative came from the Party, and propaganda and economic compulsion were widely used to persuade people to join. Thus, state loans were granted to newly-formed co-operatives, discriminatory rates of taxation were imposed on individuals who owned large herds and similarly differential norms of compulsory deliveries of produce were set. The collectivization programme reached its peak in 1958 and by April 1959 all but a tiny minority of herdsmen had been collectivized. Great attention was paid to the Soviet *kolkhoz* system in organizing the Mongol co-operatives.

These are quite different in character from the earlier producers' associations. They are of considerable size, and are units of local administration as well as economic units. Labour is regulated by means of work books issued to each member, who receives pay according to his work. All families are allowed to retain a certain number of private animals. Produce is purchased by the state which also grants loans to the co-operatives. Internally, each co-operative is organized into a number of permanent brigades, each with its own territory and headquarters and its own special tasks. The brigade in its turn contains a number of bases, each base consisting usually of two households living in felt tents and looking after a number of animals.

An innovation in the Mongolian rural economy has been the development of large-scale agriculture. This did not affect any previous pattern of economic activity, and from the start was organized as a direct state venture. Ten state farms existed in 1940 and 60 state farms and "fodder farms" in 1980. In and after 1959 the area ploughed up increased sharply as large tracts of virgin land were opened, but the sown area was smaller in 1970 than in 1965. By 1978, 1 million hectares of virgin land had been put to the plough. Annual grain production now averages 300,000 to 400,000 metric tons. Increasing attention is to be paid to mechanization and the introduction of scientific methods. The division of activity between the 255 herding co-operatives and the 60 state farms is not a strict one. Co-operatives also engage in field work, especially fodder growing, and in craft work, while state farms are also expected to supply good breeding animals. The principal crops produced by the state farms are cereals, potatoes and vegetables. An apparently successful innovation has been the establishment of 17 inter-cooperative production enterprises in which neighbouring co-operatives pool efforts to specialize in particular farm-related activities.

Though still of major importance, Mongolia's rural economy, and in particular its main sector, animal-herding, continues to lag, as was stressed by President Tsedenbal in a speech in December 1976. Although the catastrophic losses of animals suffered in 1967 and 1968 through *dzud* (spring starvation when the winter-weakened beasts fail to break through the hard snow-cover to reach the available grazing) are said to have been made good by mid-1973, a new decline in livestock numbers began in 1976. The carelessness and neglect of 1976 was then compounded by the particularly harsh winter of 1976–77. The number of livestock surviving from birth in 1977 was about 7.2 million, some 2.1 million fewer than planned. Tsedenbal was obliged to warn party officials that pessimism about the prospects for animal husbandry was "extremely harmful" and deserved "resolute condemnation". The Mongolian press made repeated reference to Tsedenbal's appeals for the livestock losses of 1976 and 1977 to be made up by 1980.

Tsedenbal's personal Directive No. 14 said it was imperative to draw the appropriate conclusions from the "considerable harm done to the national economy by the loss of many livestock during the temporary weather difficulties, as a result of shortcomings in the countryside". At the end of the year, it was officially confirmed that in 1977, 2.6 million animals had died from cold, starvation, thirst and neglect. The party has again recently complained that some herdsmen exchange good animals from public herds for their own sick stock, and that, through lack of attention, publicly-owned stock produce fewer young. These losses were partly offset by a record 9.3 million survivals from birth in 1978. In the spring of 1980, however, at least 500,000 livestock were killed in blizzards in the eastern provinces.

A new theme, and one repeatedly developed in the press in the 1970s, is that of the importance of nature conservancy. This problem is assuming critical importance even in Mongolia's under-developed territory. Two aspects especially are stressed—forest protection and control of hunting. Proper methods of forestry are regularly urged and much reafforestation has been achieved, but good intentions are too often frustrated by local indifference and laziness. Woods are cleared in wholesale fashion and not replanted, young wood is cut for fuel, cut wood is left to rot unused, and negligence leads to bad forest and pasture fires. New laws concerning water and forests were promulgated in July 1974.

Industry

Large-scale industry has developed only since the revolution. Before the revolution most manufactured requisites had been imported or were made locally, chiefly by Chinese craftsmen. In the 1920s technicians from Western Europe were engaged to help develop Mongolia's infant industry. In particular they built a power station and a brickworks. But after the swing to the left in 1929 only Soviet aid and expertise were welcome, and in pre-war years industrial growth was slow. Only one enterprise of any size was commissioned, the Industrial Combine in Ulan Bator, which commenced production in 1934 of leather goods and felts. Industry has developed in two channels. Co-operative industry has a much smaller output than state industry. It produces many items needed for domestic use, as well as providing repair services. Since the war, the state-operated industry has expanded rapidly, given Mongolian conditions, and many new enterprises have been commissioned.

Mongolia has received enormous aid from its political allies, without which its industrial advance, modest though it is in world terms, could not have been envisaged. For a while, in the 1950s, it seemed as if China was hoping to challenge the U.S.S.R.'s leading position in Mongolia, using the weapon of economic aid. A first gift of 160 million roubles in 1955 was followed by the dispatch of Chinese labourers to help Mongolia's inadequate and under-trained labour force. Exact numbers are not available, but in the peak years of 1959 and 1960 several thousands of Chinese were working on diverse projects, building apartment blocks, laying roads and irrigation systems, and so on. Many had their families with them. As the Sino-Soviet rift widened, the Chinese labourers began to leave Mongolia, till by mid-1964 most had gone home. To some extent the loss of these workers has been made good by the supply of Soviet construction troops, working principally in Ulan Bator, the Darhan area and Choybalsan, where a third industrial area is planned. However, the break with China had other adverse effects. Chinese consumer goods, in particular silk and cloth, which were plentiful in 1959, were, by 1968, no longer available. The drastic drop in railway through-goods traffic between the U.S.S.R. and China also meant a considerable loss of state revenue.

For purposes of immediate and long-range economic planning, the M.P.R. is considered as comprising three economic regions—Central, Western and Eastern, of which the first is the most significant. There are also a number of sub-regions.

The principal centres of industry in Mongolia are both in the central economic region, at Ulan Bator and Darhan, half-way between the capital and the Soviet frontier. Both centres are situated in the area of densest population and have direct road and rail communication with the U.S.S.R. Both have their own coal supplies also, Ulan Bator at Nalayh, and Darhan at an open cast mine at Sharyn Gol, to which it is linked by a new rail spur. Light producing and service industries are to be found elsewhere in the country: coal is mined in each of the provinces, for example, and an important vehicle repair station has been opened in Hovd. A large new open cast mine has been opened at Baga nuur, east of Ulan Bator, and linked to the Trans-Mongolian railway. However, the two centres mentioned account for most of Mongolia's production in terms of electric power, capital materials such as cement, bricks and wall panels, and consumer goods—food, drink, leather goods, china, sweets, soap and so on.

Perhaps the most important development in Mongolia's economy in recent years has been the joint Soviet-Mongol exploitation of copper and molybdenum deposits at Erdenet in Bulgan province. The deposits are located near Hangal sum, about two hours' journey by road to the west of Darhan, and thus accessible to transport routes. A town to house 40,000 workers is under construction. The Salhit-Erdenet railway line, linking the new complex with the main rail system, went into operation in October 1975, and the ore concentrator in December 1978. A joint Mongol-Soviet enterprise, "Mongol-sovtsvetmet" has been set up to mine gold and fluorspar.

Mongolia has no single major industry. It continues to rely heavily on imports from abroad to satisfy both capital construction and consumer demand. Nevertheless, home production increases annually, in a race, as it were, with the rapidly rising population. But to judge from a reading of the press, underuse of machinery, waste of energy and raw materials, poor deployment of labour, and inefficient application of technology and scientific knowledge, as well as what is termed slack labour discipline, appear to be a chronic drag on the progress of the economy. In 1978, Tsedenbal called on Mongolians to preserve and guard as something sacred, "first, public property, and second, honest labour—the source of socialist property". He added: "Everybody from an early age must become scrupulously economical, sparing and thrifty, and must with a sharp eye protect at every step each minute grain of socialist property and respect labour reverently." In 1979 he called for a national campaign to study and learn the skills of leading workers.

Starting in 1968 a number of enterprises have been going over to what is termed the "new system of planning and economic incentive". Press articles on this topic stress that the Mongol system is much indebted to Soviet and Hungarian experience in this field. The "new system" aims at increased output, higher productivity and profitability, etc., to be promoted by the "scientific organization of labour", and by material rewards and incentives which take account not only of quantitative plan fulfilment as previously, but also of considerations of quality, economy in use of raw materials, discovery and use of "concealed resources", reduction in unnecessary movement and in wasted hours, and so on. The new system is being applied not only to industrial enterprises but to others as well.

A drive for increased initiative was begun in 1971 jointly by the State Committee for Labour and Wages and the State Commission for New Initiatives. Prizes have been awarded to individuals who submitted new ideas for innovations in work processes, but difficulty has been experienced in translating some of the accepted ideas into action. As part of this system, and in an effort to improve accounting procedures, information-flow, internal work-evaluation and price-fixing, etc., Mongolia is experimenting with "industrial production associations" (*üyldverleliyn negdel*) which appear to be groupings of enterprises within an industry. Soviet experience is being drawn upon.

Foreign Trade

Trade is almost entirely with the countries of the "socialist bloc" but concrete figures are not available. Progress is being made towards economic integration within the CMEA. Mongolia exports mainly primary products and imports industrial goods and equipment. In 1975 some 35 per cent of its exports consisted of raw materials, including hides, furs and wool. Raw foodstuffs and food products, including livestock, meat and meat products, account for another 28 per cent. Industrial consumer goods, including leather goods, make up only 9 per cent. The main imports are consumer goods (33 per cent), machinery and equipment (35.8 per cent), fuels, minerals and metals (10.3 per cent), and food products (7.3 per cent). Apart from this, the Mongol armed forces are equipped from Soviet bloc countries.

Power and Transport

Fuel of many types is used in Mongolia. At one end of the scale is the new thermal power station at Darhan, built with Soviet help and designed to serve the north-central region through a power line stretching from Sühbaatar to Ulan Bator. *Aymag* (provincial) centres may have thermal power stations or diesel generators, and in smaller rural centres small diesel generators are the rule. Domestic heating in apartment blocks in Ulan Bator is by central town-heating from the power station. Elsewhere wood, roots, bushes and dried animal dung are used for domestic firing. Transport shows a similar range of sophistication. Ulan Bator is linked with the U.S.S.R. (Moscow direct and via Irkutsk) and distant provincial centres by turbo-prop aircraft. The direct Trans-Siberian rail route from Moscow to Beijing traverses Mongolia, and there is another link between the Trans-Siberian and the town of Choybalsan. Otherwise long-distance transport is mainly by lorry or Soviet-built *gazik* (jeep-type vehicle), but horse, ox and camel carts are still widely used, even in Ulan Bator, and camels are employed as beasts of burden. Water transport is not of great significance. A fuel-saving campaign was launched in 1979 under the slogan "A drop will save a tonne".

Plan Fulfilment

The Fifth Five-Year Plan for 1971-75 was published in the form of proposals in April 1971 and confirmed by the 16th Party Congress which was held in June. During 1975, the final year of the Fifth Plan, considerable attention was being paid to the problem of increasing production while effecting economies. This was to be achieved partly through the promotion and development of the familiar device of "socialist competition" and also through the further device of "augmented plans" (*ugtvar tölövlögöö*). The latter appear to be a formalization of the tasks assumed by an enterprise in addition to its normal obligations. Many *aymags* published their additional targets early in 1975. Extra production was to be achieved within the limits of material and labour resources authorized for the original level. In connection with the recently promulgated Labour Law, but also with the aim of engaging workers more fully in the implementation of the state plan, regulations for trades union committees, made in 1960, were replaced by a new set in July 1974. Among the duties allotted to these bodies was the direction of the "local courts", primary-level local elective courts which deal with minor offences, and which are also intended to persuade, in a friendly manner, individuals with backward or anti-communist views, to change their attitudes. There are now over 1,000 of these courts, first introduced under a decision of the Great Hural of 1960.

The basic directive for the Sixth Five-Year National Economic and Cultural Plan for 1976–80 was published by the Central Committee of the Mongol People's Revolutionary Party in April 1976, preparatory to discussion later in the year at the 17th plenary meeting of the Party. The basic aims of the new plan were to increase the social product, to raise profitability, to improve quality in all branches of economy and culture, and on this basis to improve the material conditions and raise the cultural level of the population. There was thus no fundamental change in the national policy of the Fifth Five-Year Plan, and the main interest of the plan resided in its more detailed provisions. In the rural economy great emphasis was laid on the development of agriculture, with a sharp increase in the production of grain, potatoes and vegetables forecast. To achieve this, it was intended to bring 230,000 hectares of virgin land under cultivation, and to establish eleven new state farms, together with other new agricultural enterprises. The area of irrigated farmland was to be increased by at least two and a half times by 1980. A range of measures was also proposed to increase the numbers of livestock and to raise productivity. In industry, the main aims were to increase reserves of power, to improve product quality and to raise productivity with the intention of providing a better domestic supply of goods and increasing exports. Geological prospecting and exploitation of mineral resources would be developed and zinc deposits at Salhit in the Central Region would be exploited. The Baga nuur coal mine and the Erdenet enterprise, which were referred to in the Plan, have now both come into operation. According to the Plan, output at the Baga nuur mine was estimated at some 2 million tons by 1979. Industrial production as a whole would rise by up to 65 per cent, with labour productivity rising by up to 38 per cent. There would be an increase of 25 per cent in the number of hospital beds, no doubt in part a reflection of Mongolia's rapidly growing population. Emphasis was laid upon measures to be taken for the closer integration of Mongolia's economy within the CMEA. In particular, the question of the exploitation of Mongolia's mineral wealth, within the linked plan for socialist economic integration, was to be elaborated in association with interested member countries of the CMEA. Further co-operation with socialist countries in the fields of education, health, culture, art and sport, was planned.

The procedure in 1981 for adopting guidelines for the Seventh Five-Year Plan (1981–85) was similar to that for the Sixth. The Statistical Survey contains a table, showing how far the basic targets of the Sixth Plan were attained, and listing the basic targets of the Seventh Plan.

STATISTICAL SURVEY

Revised by A. J. K. Sanders

AREA AND POPULATION

Area	Estimated Population (at January 1st each year)				
	1977	1978	1979†	1981	1982
1,565,000 sq. km.*	1,512,400	1,553,600	1,594,800	1,685,400	1,732,400

* 604,250 square miles. † Census of January 5th.

ADMINISTRATIVE DIVISIONS

(January 1st, 1981)

Province (Aymag)	Area ('000 sq. km.)	Provincial Districts (sum)	Population ('000)	Provincial Centre
Arhangay	55	17	79.3	Tsetserleg
Bayanhongor	116	19	65.3	Bayanhongor
Bayan-ölgiy	46	12	74.5	Ölgiy
Bulgan	49	14	43.5	Bulgan
Dornod (Eastern)	123.5	14	61.9	Choybalsan
Dornogov' (East Gobi)	111	13	44.9	Saynshand
Dundgov' (Central Gobi)	78	15	40.8	Mandalgov'
Dzavhan	82	22	81.7	Uliastay
Gov'-altay	142	17	58.0	Altay
Hentiy	82	18	55.6	Öndörhaan
Hovd	76	16	64.5	Hovd
Hövsgöl	101	19	91.1	Mörön
Ömnögov' (South Gobi)	165	14	34.1	Dalandzadgad
Övörhangay	63	18	86.0	Arvayheer
Selenge	42.8	16	69.9	Sühbaatar
Sühbaatar	82	12	44.6	Baruun urt
Töv (Central)	81	25	44.4	Dzuun mod
Uvs	69	18	74.8	Ulaangom

PRINCIPAL TOWNS

(January 1980)

	Area ('000 sq. km.)	Urban Districts	Population ('000)
Ulan Bator	2.0	8	435.4
Darhan	0.2	4	56.4
Erdenet	n.a.	4	38.7

Births and Deaths (1980): Birth rate: 37.9 per 1,000; death rate: 10.4 per 1,000.

Expectation of life: males 59.1 years; females 62.3 years (1969).

EMPLOYMENT

(socialized sector)

	1977	1978	1979	1980
Industry*	57,400	59,700	63,900	66,200
Building	20,700	21,600	22,100	22,600
State agriculture	29,300	31,400	34,600	37,500
Transport and communications	28,500	31,900	33,300	33,600
Trade, services, procurement	31,500	32,400	33,600	34,100
Total	274,200	288,900	305,000	315,100

* Mining, manufacturing, electricity and water.

AGRICULTURE

SOWN AREAS
(hectares)

	1980
Cereals	557,500
Vegetables (incl. potatoes) .	9,800
Fodder	136,700
	704,000

Total for 1981: 664,000.

PRINCIPAL CROPS
(metric tons)

	1978	1979	1980	1981
Wheat	279,300	239,600	206,900	343,800 (Wheat, Barley, Oats, Other cereals)
Barley	48,600	55,000	31,800	
Oats	25,900	34,600	17,600	
Other cereals . .	1,100	1,500	2,200	
Potatoes . . .	48,500	72,400	39,300	41,100
Other vegetables .	24,600	23,500	26,000	26,300
Fodder	141,100	200,300	102,800	257,600
Hay	1,032,600	1,067,700	1,125,400	1,102,100

LIVESTOCK

	1978	1979	1980
Sheep . .	14,152,700	14,400,200	14,230,700
Goats . .	4,704,600	4,714,900	4,566,700
Horses . .	2,078,400	2,078,900	1,985,400
Cattle . .	2,481,500	2,476,900	2,397,100
Camels . .	608,600	613,700	591,500
TOTAL .	24,025,800	24,284,600	23,771,400
Pigs . .	28,500	34,500	33,900
Poultry . .	261,900	264,900	249,300

Livestock raised from birth in 1979 totalled 8.6 million, against a target of over 9 million. In April 1980 about 500,000 animals died in blizzards in eastern Mongolia. Livestock raised from birth totalled 8,507,700, against a target of 9.2 million, in 1980, and 9,100,000 in 1981, to give a total of 24,262,400 at the 1981 winter census.

LIVESTOCK PROCUREMENT

		1978	1979	1980
Cattle . .	metric tons	65,700	68,600	65,600
Sheep . .	,, ,,	111,600	113,000	105,400
Goats . .	,, ,,	22,700	22,000	24,500
Horses . .	head	160,700	105,000	101,200
Milk . .	million litres	96	96.8	92.4

PROCUREMENT OF WOOL, HIDES AND SKINS

		1978	1979	1980
Sheep's wool . . .	metric tons	19,800	20,500	20,000
Camels' wool . . .	,, ,,	3,100	3,000	3,100
Goats' wool . . .	,, ,,	1,000	1,000	900
Goats' hair . . .	,, ,,	1,200	1,300	1,300
Cattle hides . . .	units	400,000	405,600	442,500
Horse hides . . .	,,	154,600	114,500	117,100
Camel skins . . .	,,	25,600	26,000	26,200
Sheep skins . . .	,,	3,382,500	3,595,300	3,510,400
Goat skins . . .	,,	1,118,800	1,119,500	1,186,900
Marmot pelts . . .	,,	933,300	837,100	n.a.
Squirrel skins . . .	,,	30,700	15,100	n.a.
Wolf skins . . .	,,	4,700	3,900	n.a.
Fox skins* . . .	,,	—	—	n.a.

* Fox protected in 1978 and 1979.

MINING

(metric tons)

	1977	1978	1979	1980	1981†
Coal and lignite	3,324,000*	3,798,400	4,114,000	4,376,100	4,301,700
Fluorspar	334,900	454,900	567,000	603,500	595,000

* Coal 240,000 tons, lignite 3,084,000 tons.

† Provisional.

1977: Salt production 15,000 metric tons.

INDUSTRY

SELECTED PRODUCTS

		1978	1979	1980	1981†
Electricity	MWh.	1,174,000	1,290,400	1,634,700	1,652,700
Bricks	units	102,700,000	104,600,000	110,100,000	108,668,700
Lime	metric tons	56,200	45,900	63,800	79,680
Cement	,, ,,	165,500	185,400	177,900	n.a.
Sawn timber	cubic metres	527,300	576,700	559,400	556,600
Felt	metres	603,700	611,700	614,600	615,200
Leather shoes	pairs	1,717,400	1,961,600	2,104,900	1,940,700
Matches	boxes	30,200,000	30,800,000	21,400,000	n.a.
Woollen cloth	metres	953,300	955,400	963,500	962,500
Flour	metric tons	112,000	141,400	83,400	125,700
Meat	,, ,,	57,700	59,700	57,300	68,000
Fish	,, ,,	493.5	537.1	n.a.	n.a.
Butter	,, ,,	3,700	3,900	n.a.	n.a.
Alcohol	litres	2,443,300	2,567,000	n.a.	n.a.
Vodka	,,	5,306,800	5,873,500	n.a.	(+6.5%)
Beer	,,	8,139,200	8,900,000	9,816,700	10,062,100

† Provisional

FINANCE

100 möngö = 1 tögrög (tughrik).

Coins: 1, 2, 5, 10, 15, 20 and 50 möngö; 1 tögrög.

Notes: 1, 3, 5, 10, 25, 50 and 100 tögrög.

Exchange rates (June 1982): £1 sterling = 5.46 tögrög; U.S. $1 = 3.15 tögrög.
100 tögrög = £18.33 = $31.75.

Note: The tögrög's value is fixed at 22.5 Soviet kopeks (1 rouble = 4.444 tögrög). Prior to August 1971 the basic exchange rate was U.S. $1 = 4.00 tögrög (1 tögrög = 25 U.S. cents). Between December 1971 and February 1973 the rate was $1 = 3.684 tögrög (1 tögrög = 27.14 U.S. cents). In terms of sterling, the basic exchange rate from November 1967 to June 1972 was £1 = 9.60 tögrög. The rates of tögrög per U.S. dollar at December 31st were: 3.18 in 1973; 3.36 in 1974; 3.38 in 1975; 3.33 in 1976; 3.26 in 1977; 3.00 in 1978; 2.90 in 1979; 2.85 in 1980; 3.15 in 1981.

BUDGET

(million tögrög)

Revenue	1980	1981*	1982*
Turnover tax	2,738.6	2,985.3	3,173.1
Deductions from profits	644.3	724.3	951.1
Tax on funds	244.5	262.6	300.3
Income tax from agricultural co-operatives	12.9	14.1	n.a.
Social insurance	153.6	158.6	164.0
Taxes and dues	30.2	32.1	34.3
Local dues	10.6	—	
Forestry and hunting	32.4	199.7	201.6
Other revenue	135.6		
Total	4,002.7	4,362.6	4,824.4

* Estimates.

[*continued on next page*

BUDGET—*continued from previous page*]

EXPENDITURE	1980	1981	1982
National economy	1,530.3	1,614.9	1,870.2
Social and cultural measures	1,643.3	1,827.6	1,934.6
Administration and other expenditure	817.0	823.5	1,009.6
of which: Defence*	589.7	630.0	802.6
TOTAL	3,990.6	4,266.0	4,814.4

* Estimate.

SIXTH AND SEVENTH FIVE-YEAR PLANS

(% growth over five years)

	SIXTH PLAN 1976–80		SEVENTH PLAN 1981–85 Target	
	Target	Result	Provisional	Revised
Capital investment	80–100	120	23–26	n.a.
Gross social product	40–44	35	41–45	n.a.
National income	37–41	30.9	38–41	41
Real per capita income	16–18	14	10–12	11
Average monthly wage	7–9	4	4–6	4.8
Average annual herdsman's income	14–17	13	20–23	22
Gross industrial production	60–65	58	52–58	60
Industrial productivity	34–38	20	24–26	n.a.
Average annual gross agricultural production	26–30	6.3	22–26	23
Retail trade turnover	32–35	30	27–31	27.6
Freight turnover	30–35	60	30–32	n.a.
Foreign trade	40–45	50	50–55	60

(selected production figures)

	SIXTH PLAN 1976–80		SEVENTH PLAN 1981–85 Target	
	Target	Result	Provisional	Revised
(output in fifth year)				
Electricity (million kWh)	1,440.0	1,430.0	2,431.0–2,717.0	2,400.0
Coal (million metric tons)	4.5–4.9	4.4	6.8–7.2	6.8
(five-year total)				
Housing ('000 sq. metres)	730–760	740	830–860	830
(five-year average)				
Grain ('000 metric tons)	500–530	347	580–640	600
Meat ('000 metric tons, live weight)	94.5–97.7	89.2	93.6–94.5	n.a.

EXTERNAL TRADE

(million roubles)

	1976	1977	1978	1979	1980
Imports	226.8	276.3	285.2	326.3	367.0
Exports	174.6	171.0	191.6	224.6	269.9

COMMODITIES
(%)

	Exports			Imports		
	1975	1979	1980	1975	1979	1980
Machinery and equipment . . .	0.3	0.3	0.3	35.8	30.0	33.1
Fuels, minerals, metals	2.5	16.9	26.4	10.3	22.5	24.1
Chemical products, fertilizers, rubber .	0.1	0.0	—	5.2	5.7	6.3
Construction materials	0.3	0.5	0.4	2.6	2.3	1.9
Raw materials (excl. foodstuffs) . .	34.9	31.8	30.9	1.5	3.2	2.4
Raw materials for food production . .	27.2	16.5	13.4	3.0	5.6	2.9
Food products	21.6	23.8	19.0	7.3	10.0	8.4
Industrial consumer goods . . .	9.1	10.1	9.6	33.4	20.7	20.9

TRADING PARTNERS
(%)

	1975	1979	1980
Exports			
to Socialist Countries .	99.3	98.6	98.4
including:			
CMEA	96.4	96.4	96.5
Others	2.9	2.2	1.9
to Capitalist Countries .	0.7	1.4	1.6
Imports			
from Socialist Countries .	98.5	98.9	98.5
including:			
CMEA	96.0	97.2	96.8
Others	2.5	1.7	1.7
from Capitalist Countries	1.5	1.1	1.5

MONGOLIAN-SOVIET TRADE*
(million roubles)

	1977	1978	1979	1980	1981
Mongolian exports	126.1	147.0	177.2	207.3	248.6
Mongolian imports	550.4	596.1	594.4	676.3	787.3

* Soviet figures, including credit trade not recorded in Mongolian statistics.

PRINCIPAL COMMODITIES IN MONGOLIAN-SOVIET TRADE
(million roubles)

IMPORTS	1978	1979
Power generating equipment	36.176	66.093
Coal mining equipment	32.285	55.066
Ore mining equipment	36.911	74.170
Well drilling equipment	12.477	12.979
Buildings and services	123.080	112.658
Agricultural machinery	8.746	8.623
Tractors	3.192	2.916
Lorries	9.129	4.869
Spares and garage equipment	8.546	12.625
Oil and oil products	44.690	51.535
Rolled ferrous metals	6.820	7.200
Fertilizer	3.700	4.843
Seeds	2.059	5.966
Tea	2.265	2.301
Flour	4.652	7.764
Sugar	8.188	8.018
Cotton textiles	9.761	10.757
Domestic appliances	1.448	1.907

EXPORTS	1978	1979
Minerals*	13.255	16.738
Timber	8.892	9.320
Wool	25.795	27.795
Beef cattle (slaughtered)	37.829	35.667
Cattle	10.747	8.811
Sheep and goats	13.193	14.697
Horses for meat	13.889	12.159
Meat (canned)	41.900	46.546
Meat (frozen)	40.290	44.386
Carpets	1.234	1.604
Leather (clothing)	3.901	4.364

* Copper concentrate exports in 1980 were worth more than 40,000,000 roubles.

TRANSPORT

FREIGHT TURNOVER
(million metric ton/km.)

	1978	1979	1980
Rail	2,738.2	3,125.9	3,449.4
Road	1,299.4	1,342.1	1,528.7
Water	5.4	5.4	4.8
Air	3.9	4.8	4.5
TOTAL	4,046.9	4,478.2	4,987.4

PASSENGER TURNOVER
(million passenger/km.)

	1977	1978	1979	1980
Rail	226.6	244.8	267.1	296.6
Road	382.9	409.1	454.5	497.2
Air	142.4	189.5	206.3	213.3
TOTAL	785.9	843.4	927.9	1,007.1

COMMUNICATIONS MEDIA

	1978	1979	1980	1981
Telephones ('000)	35.7	37.7	39.8	41.5
Radio sets ('000)	140.4	150.3	164.3	171.3
Television sets ('000)	40.9	46.4	52.9	57.9

EDUCATION

	INSTITUTIONS			TEACHERS			STUDENTS		
	1975	1979	1980/81	1975	1979	1980/81	1975	1979	1980/81*
General schools	555	570	571	11,200	13,600	13,883	322,500	363,500	394,400
Vocational-Technical	34	37	37	—	—	—	13,500	2 20,200	22,100
Special secondary	22	24	25	800	1,000	1,100	13,500	18,000	18,700
Higher	6	7	7	800	1,000	1,100	13,600	1,100	23,200

* Total for 1981/82 (all schools): 466,500.

THE CONSTITUTION

The Mongolian People's Republic is a sovereign democratic state of working people. All land, natural resources, factories, transport and banking organizations are state property. In addition to state ownership the people have co-operative ownership of public enterprises, especially in livestock herding. A limited degree of private ownership is also permitted.

The supreme state power is the People's Great Hural (Assembly), which was elected every four years by universal, direct and secret suffrage of all citizens over the age of 18. The term was extended to five years after the June 1981 elections. It has the power to amend the Constitution (by a two-thirds majority), adopting laws, formulating the basic principles of policy and approving the budget and economic plans. Its Presidium consists of a Chairman (who is Head of State), two Vice-Chairmen, a Secretary and five members. The functions of the Presidium are to interpret legislation and issue decrees, ratify treaties and appoint or dismiss (with the approval of the People's Great Hural) the members of the Council of Ministers.

The Council of Ministers is the highest executive power and consists of the Chairman, First Vice-Chairmen, Vice-Chairmen, Ministers and Chairmen of State Commissions.

Local government is exercised by Hurals and their executive committees at Aymag (Province) and Somon (County) levels.

THE GOVERNMENT

HEAD OF STATE

Chairman of the Presidium of the People's Great Hural: Yumjaagiyn Tsedenbal (took office June 11th, 1974).

COUNCIL OF MINISTERS

(July 1982)

Chairman: Jambyn Batmönh.

First Deputy Chairmen: Damdinjavyn Maydar (Chairman, State Committee for Science and Technology), Tümenbayaryn Ragchaa.

Vice-Chairmen:

Chairman, State Planning Commission Dumaagiyn Sodnom.

Chairman, Commission for CMEA Affairs Myatavyn Peljee.

Chairman, People's Control Committee Tsendiyn Molom.

Dondogiyn Tsevegmid, Minister of Culture.

Chairman, State Committee for Construction Architecture and Technical Control Choynoryn Süren.

Minister of Agriculture: Sürenhoriyn Sodnomdorj.

Minister of Fuel and Power Industry: Punsalmaagiyn Ochirbat.

Minister of Geology and Mining Industry: Uthany Mavlyet.

Minister of Light and Food Industries: Gombojavyn Naydan.

Minister of Construction and Building Materials Industry: Orony Tleyhan.

Minister of Forestry and Woodworking Industry: Damdingiyn Tseden.

Minister of Transport: Dogoyn Yondonsüren.

Minister of Water Supply: Bavuudorjiyn Bars.

Minister of Communications: Irvüüdziyn Norovjav.

Minister of Trade and Procurement: Chuvaandorjiyn Molom.

Minister of Foreign Trade: Yondongiyn Ochir.

Minister of Finance: Erdeniyn Byambajav.

Minister of Foreign Affairs: Mangalyn Dügersüren.

Minister of Defence: Col.-Gen. Jarantayn Avhia.

Minister of Public Security: Col.-Gen. Sonomyn Luvsangombo.

Minister of Education: Chimidiyn Sereeter.

Minister of Health: Dar'sürengiyn Nyam-osor.

Minister of Culture: Dondogiyn Tsevegmid.

Minister of Communal Economy and Services: (vacant).

Minister of Justice: Origiyn Jambaldorj.

Head, Central Statistical Directorate: Damiranjavyn Dzagasbaldan.

Chairman of Board of State Bank: Gochoogiyn Hüderchuluun.

President, Academy of Sciences: Choydogiyn Tseren.

Chairman, State Committee for Physical Culture and Sport: Gombyn Damdin.

Chairman, State Committee for Labour and Social Security: Ravjaagiyn Dagvadorj.

Chairman, State Committee for Information, Radio and Television: (Vacant).

Chairman, State Committee for Prices and Standards: Dashiyn Byambasüren.

Director of Administration, Council of Ministers: Baldangiyn Badarch.

First Deputy Chairman, State Planning Commission (Minister), Chairman, State Committee for Material and Technical Supply: Byambyn Rinchinpeljee.

Chairman, State Committee for Foreign Economic Relations (Minister): Dangaasürengiyn Saldan.

First Deputy Chairman, State Planning Commission (Minister): Puntsagiyn Jasray.

First Deputy Chairman, People's Control Committee (Minister): Öldziyhutagiyn Ganhuyag.

LEGISLATURE

PEOPLE'S GREAT HURAL

At the June 1981 elections, 370 deputies were elected to serve a five-year term. Every deputy was elected unopposed.

PRESIDIUM

Chairman: YUMJAAGIYN TSEDENBAL.

Vice-Chairmen: SAMPILYN JALAN-AAJAV, NYAMYN JAGVARAL.

Secretary: TSEDENDAMBYN GOTOV.

Members: GOMBOJAVYN OCHIRBAT, SONOMYN UDVAL, LODONGIYN TÜDEV, BANDZRAGCHIYN LAMJAV.

Chairman of the People's Great Hural: B. ALTANGEREL.

Chairman of the Executive Committee of the Parliamentary Group: SH. BIRA.

POLITICAL PARTY

Mongolian People's Revolutionary Party (MPRP): Ulan Bator; f. 1921; total membership 76,240 (June 1981).

The Central Committee elected at the XVIIIth Congress in May 1981 had 91 members and 71 candidate members.

General Secretary of the Central Committee: YUMJAAGIYN TSEDENBAL.

Members of the Political Bureau and Secretaries of the Central Committee: DAMDINY GOMBOJAV, SAMPILYN JALAN-AAJAV, DEMCHIGIYN MOLOMJAMTS.

Members of the Political Bureau: BAT-OCHIRYN ALTANGEREL, JAMBYN BATMÖNH, DAMDINJAVYN MAYDAR, TÜMENBAYARYN RAGCHAA, YUMJAAGIYN TSEDENBAL.

Candidate members of the Political Bureau: BUGYN DEJID (also Chairman of the Party Control Committee), NYAMYN JAGVARAL, SONOMYN LUVSANGOMBO.

Secretaries of the Central Committee: GELEGIYN AD'YAA, PAAVANGIYN DAMDIN, MANGALJAVYN DASH.

Director of the Institute of Social Sciences: BADAMYN LHAMSÜREN.

Director of the Higher Party School: GOMBYN MIYEEGOMBO.

First Secretary, Mongolian Revolutionary Youth League (over 200,000 members): LODONGIYN TÜDEV.

DIPLOMATIC REPRESENTATION

EMBASSIES ACCREDITED TO MONGOLIA

(In Ulan Bator unless otherwise stated)

Afghanistan: *Ambassador:* ASSADULLAH SARWARI.

Algeria: Beijing, People's Republic of China.

Argentina: Moscow, U.S.S.R.

Australia: Moscow, U.S.S.R.

Austria: Moscow, U.S.S.R.

Bangladesh: Moscow, U.S.S.R.

Belgium: Moscow, U.S.S.R.

Bulgaria: *Ambassador:* KRISTYN YEVTIMOV.

Burma: Moscow, U.S.S.R.

Canada: Moscow, U.S.S.R.

China, People's Republic: *Ambassador:* MENG YING.

Cuba: *Ambassador:* ANGEL FERRAS MORENO.

Cyprus: Moscow, U.S.S.R.

Czechoslovakia: *Ambassador:* VALENTIN RUZIČ.

Denmark: Moscow, U.S.S.R.

Egypt: Moscow, U.S.S.R.

Finland: Moscow, U.S.S.R.

France: *Ambassador:* PHILIPPE LEGRAIN.

German Democratic Republic: *Ambassador:* HEINZ BAUER

Germany, Federal Republic: Tokyo, Japan.

Greece: Moscow, U.S.S.R.

Guinea: Moscow, U.S.S.R.

Hungary: *Ambassador:* JANOS TARABA.

Iceland: Moscow, U.S.S.R.

India: *Ambassador:* GONDKER NARAYANA RAO.

Indonesia: Moscow, U.S.S.R.

Iran: Moscow, U.S.S.R.

Italy: Moscow, U.S.S.R.

Japan: *Ambassador:* MITSUTAKA AKIHO.

Kampuchea: *Ambassador:* KONG KORM.

Korea, Democratic People's Republic: *Ambassador:* PAK SI-KWON.

Laos: Moscow, U.S.S.R.

Luxembourg: Moscow, U.S.S.R.

Malaysia: Moscow, U.S.S.R.

Mali: Moscow, U.S.S.R.

Mauritania: Moscow, U.S.S.R.

Mexico: Moscow, U.S.S.R.

Nepal: Moscow, U.S.S.R.

Netherlands: Moscow, U.S.S.R.

New Zealand: Moscow, U.S.S.R.

Norway: Moscow, U.S.S.R.

Pakistan: Moscow, U.S.S.R.

Poland: *Ambassador:* STANISŁAW STAWIARSKI.

Portugal: Moscow, U.S.S.R.

Romania: *Ambassador:* CONSTANTIN MINDREANU.

Spain: Moscow, U.S.S.R.

Sri Lanka: Beijing, People's Republic of China.

Sweden: Moscow, U.S.S.R.

Switzerland: Moscow, U.S.S.R.

Thailand: Moscow, U.S.S.R.

Turkey: Moscow, U.S.S.R.

U.S.S.R.: *Ambassador:* A. I. SMIRNOV.

United Kingdom: 30 Enh Tayvny Gudamj (G.P.O. Box 703); *Ambassador:* JAMES PATERSON.

Viet-Nam: *Ambassador:* CAO KIEN THIET.

Yemen, People's Democratic Republic: Moscow, U.S.S.R.

Yugoslavia: *Ambassador:* RADOVAN SMILJANIĆ.

Mongolia also has diplomatic relations with Angola, Benin, Cape Verde, the Central African Republic, the Congo, Costa Rica, Ethiopia, Ghana, Grenada, Guinea-Bissau, Guyana, Iraq, Jordan, Kuwait, Liberia, Libya, Madagascar, Malta, Morocco, Mozambique, Nicaragua, Nigeria, Papua New Guinea, the Philippines, Saint Lucia, São Tomé and Príncipe, Senegal, Seychelles, Singapore, Somalia, Sudan, Syria, Tanzania, Tunisia, Zaire and Zambia.

JUDICIAL SYSTEM

Justice is administered by the Supreme Court, the City Court of Ulan Bator, 18 aymag (provincial) courts and local somon (county) courts. The Chairman and members of the Supreme Court are elected by the People's Great Hural for a term of five years; other judges are elected by local Hurals for terms of three years. The Procurator of the Republic is also appointed by the People's Great Hural for a term of five years. A Ministry was set up in 1972.

Minister of Justice: ORIGIYN JAMBALDORJ.

Chairman of the Supreme Court: BYARAAGIYN CHIMID.

Procurator of the Republic: RAVDANGIYN GÜNSEN.

RELIGION

Religious freedom is guaranteed by the Constitution Traces survive of Buddhism of the Tibetan variety.

Chairman of Council of Religious Affairs: D. BALJINNYAM

Hamba Lama: Ulan Bator; Head of the Gandantegchinlen Monastery (the only active temple of Mongolia): HARHÜÜGIYN GAADAN.

THE PRESS

The following are the most important newspapers and periodicals:

NEWSPAPERS

Ünen (*Truth*): Nayramdlyn Gudamj 24, Ulan Bator; f. 1920; organ of the Central Committee of the Mongolian People's Revolutionary Party and M.P.R. Council of Ministers; Tuesday to Sunday; Editor-in-Chief TSENDIYN NAMSRAY; circ. (1981) 145,000.

Ediyn Dzasag (*Economics*): Ulan Bator; f. 1974; organ of the Central Committee of the MPRP; 52 issues a year; Editor D. SÜRENJAV.

Hödölmör (*Labour*): Ulan Bator; f. 1928; organ of the Central Council of Trade Unions; 144 issues a year; Editor-in-Chief N. MYAGMAR.

Pionyeriyn Ünen (*Pioneers' Truth*): Ulan Bator; f. 1943; organ of the Central Council of the D. Sühbaatar Pioneers' Organization of the Central Committee of the Revolutionary Youth League; 84 issues a year; Responsible Editor Ts. DASHDONDOV; circ. 175,000.

Sotsialist Hödöö Aj Ahuy (*Socialist Agriculture*): Nayramdlyn Gudamj 24, Ulan Bator; f. 1961; weekly; circ. 14,000.

Ulaan Od (*Red Star*): Ulan Bator; f. 1930; paper of the Ministries of Defence and Public Security; 144 issues a year; Editor-in-Chief A. BAYARMAGNAY.

Utga Dzohiol Urlag (*Literature and Art*): Ulan Bator; f. 1954; organ of the Writers' Union and Ministry of Culture; weekly; Editor-in-Chief D. TARVA.

Dzaluuchuudyn Ünen (*Young People's Truth*): Ulan Bator; f. 1924; organ of the Central Committee of the Revolutionary Youth League; 144 issues a year.

Shine Hödöö (*New Countryside*): Ulan Bator; f. 1970; published by the Ministry of Agriculture; weekly.

There are also 18 provincial newspapers, published biweekly by provincial Party and executive committees, including one in Kazakh (**Jana Ömir** (*New Life*) in Bayan-ölgiy Aymag). Ulan Bator, Nalayh, Erdenet and Darhan cities and the Ulan Bator Railway also have their own newspapers. **Ulaanbaataryn Medee** (*Ulan Bator News*) was founded in 1954 and has 208 issues a year. Its editor is H. ARSAD.

PERIODICALS

Ajilchin (*Worker*): Ulan Bator.

Akademiyn Medee (*Academy News*): 2 Leniniy Gudamj, Ulan Bator; f. 1961; journal of the Mongolian Academy of Sciences.

Anagaah Uhaan (*Medicine*): Ulan Bator; published by the Ministry of Health; quarterly.

Ardyn Armi (*People's Army*): Ulan Bator; 6 issues a year.

Ardyn Tör (*People's Government*): Ulan Bator; f. 1950; organ of the Presidium of the People's Great Hural; 6 issues a year; Editor Ts. GOTOV; circ. 11,000.

Barilgachin (*Builder*): Ulan Bator; published by Ministry of Construction and Building Materials Industry; 4 issues a year; Editor A. DAVAA.

BNMAU—yn Huul', Dzarlig Togtoolyn Emhetgel (*Collection of M.P.R. Laws, Decrees and Regulations*): Ulan Bator; f. 1926; irregular; Editor-in-Chief B. BADARCH.

Büteegdehüüniy Chanar, Standarchillyn Asuudal (*Questions of Product Quality and Standardization*): Ulan Bator; f. 1982; 6 issues a year.

Dorno Dahiny Sudlalyn Asuundal (*Questions of Oriental Studies*): Ulan Bator; published by the Institute of Oriental Studies of the Mongolian Academy of Sciences; 2 issues a year; Editor SH. BIRA.

Dürsleh Urlag (*Fine Arts*): Ulan Bator; published by Union of Mongolian Artists; 4 issues a year.

Dzalgamjlagch (*Successor*): Ulan Bator; 6 issues a year.

Dzaluu Dzohion Büteegch (*Young Designer*): Ulan Bator; quarterly.

Dzaluu Üye (*Young Generation*): Ulan Bator; 6 issues a year; Editor H. BATAA.

Ediyn Dzasgiyn Asuudal (*Economic Questions*): Ulan Bator; 6 issues a year; Editor-in-Chief D. SÜRENJAV.

Erüül Enhiyn Tölöö (*For Health*): Ulan Bator; published by the Ministry of Health and the Mongolian Red Cross Society; weekly.

Erüül Mend (*Health*): Ulan Bator; 4 issues a year.

Holboochin (*Communications Worker*): Ulan Bator; organ of the Ministry of Communications.

Hödöö Aj Ahuy (*Agriculture*): Ulan Bator; 6 issues a year.

Hödöö Aj Ahuyn Dzuragt Huudas (*Agriculture Illustrated*): Ulan Bator; 16 issues a year.

Hudaldaaniy Medeelel (*Trade Information*): Ulan Bator; published by Ministry of Trade and Procurement; 4 issues a year; Editor-in-Chief J. CHULUUNBAATAR.

Hüühdiyn Hümüüjil (*Children's Education*): Ulan Bator; published by Ministry of Education; 6 issues a year; Editor N. TSEVGEE; circ. 23,400.

Jargalan (*Happiness*): Ulan Bator; illustrated annual on child care published by the Mongolian Red Cross Society.

Kino Medee (*Cinema News*): Ulan Bator; organ of Mongol Kino.

MAHN—yn Töv Horoony Medee (*MPRP Central Committee News*): Ulan Bator; published by MPRP Central Cttee.

Malchdad Dzövlölgöö (*Advice to Herdsmen*): Ulan Bator; illustrated monthly published by the Ministry of Agriculture.

Medeelel HTsHUH (*Information from the State Committee for Labour and Wages*): Ulan Bator; quarterly.

Mongolyn Anagaah Uhaan (*Mongolian Medicine*): Ulan Bator; quarterly.

Mongolyn Emegteychüüd (*Mongolian Women*): Ulan Bator; f. 1925; 4 issues a year; Editor-in-Chief E. OYUUN.

Mongolyn Hudaldaa (*Mongolian Trade*): Ulan Bator; 4 issues a year.

Mongolyn Üyldverchniy Evlel (*Mongolian Trade Unions*): Ulan Bator; published by Central Council of Mongolian Trade Unions; 6 issues a year; Editor N. MYAGMAR.

Namyn Am'dral (*Party Life*): Ulan Bator; f. 1923; organ of the Central Committee of the Mongolian People's Revolutionary Party; 12 issues a year; Editor-in-Chief GOMBO-OCHIRYN CHIMID; circ. 22,600.

Nayramdal (*Friendship*): Ulan Bator; organ of the Mongolian-Soviet Friendship Society.

Oyuun Tülhüür (*Key to Knowledge*): Ulan Bator; 8 issues a year.

Pionyeriyn Udirdagch (*Pioneer Leader*): Ulan Bator; f. 1980; published by Central Council of Pioneers' Organization; quarterly.

Sanhüü Dzeel Bürtgel (*Financial Credit Accounting*): Ulan Bator; f. 1981; quarterly.

Setgüülch (*Journalist*): Ulan Bator; f. 1982; published by Ünen and Mongolian Journalists' Union; quarterly.

Shinjleh Uhaan Am'dral (*Science and Life*): Mongolian Academy of Sciences, Ulan Bator; f. 1935; magazine published by the Society for the Dissemination of Scientific Knowledge; 6 issues a year; Editor-in-Chief L. JAMBALDORJ; circ. 14,400.

Sotsialist Ahuy (*Socialist Economy*): Ulan Bator; quarterly.

Sotsialist Huul' Yos (*Socialist Law*): Ulan Bator; journal of the Procurator's Office, Supreme Court and Ministry of Justice; 4 issues a year; Editor S. BÜDRAGCHAA.

Sportyn Medee (*Sports News*): Ulan Bator; published by Central Council of Mongolian Physical Culture and Sport Society; 104 issues a year; Editor J. SHAGDAR.

Soyol (*Culture*): Ulan Bator; f. 1945; published by Ministry of Culture; 4 issues a year; Editor Y. DORJSÜREN.

Surgan Hümüüjüülegch (*Educator*): Ulan Bator; published by Ministry of Education; 6 issues a year; Editor N. TSEVGEE.

Tarialanchdad Dzövlölgöö (*Advice to Farmers*): Ulan Bator; illustrated monthly published by the Ministry of Agriculture.

Teevriyn Medeelel (*Transport Information*): Ulan Bator; published by Ministry of Transport; quarterly.

Tonshuul (*Woodpecker*): Nayramdlyn Gudamj 24, Ulan Bator; f. 1935; humorous magazine published by the editorial office of *Ünen*; 24 issues a year; Responsible Editor M. GÜRSED; circ. 80,000.

Tsog (*Spark*): Ulan Bator; f. 1944; political and literary magazine of the Union of Writers; 6 issues a year; Responsible Editor D. TARVA.

Tyehnik, Tyehnologiyn Medee (*News of Techniques and Technology*): Ulan Bator; published by Council of Ministers' State Cttee. for Prices and Standards; 4 issues a year; Editor D. TSERENDORJ.

Uhuulagch (*Agitator*): Ulan Bator; f. 1931; published by MPRP Central Cttee.; 18 issues a year; Editor P. PERENLEY; circ. 31,000.

Yaam, tusgay gadzryn normativ aktyn medeelel (*Information about normative acts of ministries and special offices*): Ulan Bator; f. 1981; published by Ministry of Justice.

FOREIGN LANGUAGE PUBLICATIONS

Foreign Trade of Mongolia: Nayramdlyn Gudamj 24, Ulan Bator; annual; published by the Ministry of Foreign Trade; English and Russian; Editor-in-Chief N. BAVUU.

Monggu Xiaozibao (*News of Mongolia*): Ulan Bator; Chinese; weekly.

Mongolia: Ulan Bator; published by State Committee for Information, Radio and Television; English; 6 issues a year; Editor-in-Chief B. YONDON.

Mongoliya (*Mongolia*): Ulan Bator; published by State Committee for Information, Radio and Television; Russian; 12 issues a year; Editor-in-Chief B. YONDON.

News from Mongolia: Ulan Bator; information bulletin published by Montsame's Foreign Service, Sühbaataryn Talbay 9; 52 issues a year.

Les Nouvelles de Mongolie: Ulan Bator; French edition of *News from Mongolia*.

Novosti Mongolii (*News of Mongolia*): Sühbaataryn Talbay 15, Ulan Bator; f. 1942; Russian; published by Montsame; 104 issues a year; Editor-in-Chief LHAGVADULAM.

NEWS AGENCIES

Montsame (Mongol Tsahilgaan Medeeniy Agentlag) (*Mongolian Telegraph Agency*): Sühbaataryn Talbay 9, Ulan Bator; f. 1957; government owned; Gen. Dir. (vacant).

FOREIGN BUREAUX

Agentstvo Pechati Novosti (APN) (*U.S.S.R.*): Ulan Bator; Correspondent IVAN NIKOLAYEVICH ZHARSKYI.

Allgemeiner Deutscher Nachrichtendienst (ADN) (*German Democratic Republic*): P.O.B. 709, Ulan Bator; Correspondents ANGELA and RAINER KOHLER.

TASS (U.S.S.R.) is also represented.

PUBLISHERS

State Publishing Committee: Ulan Bator; f. 1921; in overall charge of all publishing; Editor-in-Chief T. SODNOMDARJAA.

There are also publishing houses in each province, and other publishing organs in Ulan Bator.

RADIO AND TELEVISION

RADIO

Ulan Bator Radio: State Committee for Information, Radio and Television, P.O.B. 365, Ulan Bator; programmes in Mongolian (two), Russian, Chinese, English, French and Kazakh; Chair. of the State Committee (vacant); Head of Foreign Service Relations Dept. B. DAGVA.

There were 143,000 loudspeakers and 171,300 radio sets in 1981.

TELEVISION

A television centre has been built by the U.S.S.R. at Ulan Bator, and a television service was opened in November 1967. Daily transmissions, comprising locally-originated material and/or relays of Moscow programmes via the Molniya satellite and the Orbita ground station. Moscow television is received in several provincial centres via the Ekran satellite system. A 1,900 km. radio relay line from Ulan Bator to Altay and Ölgiy provides STD telephone links and television services for Western Mongolia. Dir. of Television SAMBUUGIYN GONCHIG.

There were 57,900 television sets in 1981.

FINANCE

State Bank of the Mongolian People's Republic: Oktyabriyn Gudamj 6, Ulan Bator; f. 1924; 65 brs.; Chair. of Board GOCHOOGIYN HÜDERCHULUUN.

Insurance is covered by a non-contributory scheme administered by the State Directorate for Insurance of the Ministry of Finance; Head J. PÜREVDORJ.

TRADE AND INDUSTRY

All trade and industry is concentrated in the hands of the state, either through direct state ownership or through co-operatives.

Ministry of Trade and Procurement: Ulan Bator; Minister CHUVAANDORJIYN MOLOM.

Central Council of Mongolian Trade Unions: Ulan Bator; branches throughout the country; Chair. BAT-OCHIRYN LUVSANTSEREN; Head of Foreign Department Dz. DEJEE; 425,000 mems. (1982); affiliated to WFTU.

CO-OPERATIVES

Federation of Agricultural Production Associations (Co-operatives): Ulan Bator; body administering the 255 agricultural co-operatives throughout the country; Chair. of Council: Minister of Agriculture (*ex officio*); Sec. D. RINCHINSANGI.

Industrial co-operatives have now been absorbed into the state industrial structure. Industrial production associations are gradually being established under various ministries; they are not co-operatives but groupings of allied enterprises (flourmilling, leather processing, etc.)

FOREIGN TRADE

The Mongolian People's Republic has trading relations with over 20 countries. The Ministry of Foreign Trade is responsible for the foreign trade monopoly and controls the operations of several importing and exporting companies.

There are four specialized import and export organizations dealing in trade with foreign countries.

Mongoleksport: Export of Mongolian goods.

Mongolraznoimport: Import of consumer goods and medicines.

Mongoltekhnoimport: Import of machinery and equipment, other than motor vehicles, fuels and lubricants.

Avtonefteimport: Import of motor vehicles, fuels and lubricants.

Kompleksimport: Imports sets of equipment for the mining industry and power stations, and production lines for light and food industry enterprises.

Mongol Nom: Export of Mongolian publications.

Chamber of Commerce of the Mongolian People's Republic: Nayramdlyn Gudamj 24, Ulan Bator; f. 1960; is responsible for establishing economic and trading relations, contacts between trade and industrial organizations both at home and abroad and assists foreign countries; organizes commodity inspection, press information and international exhibitions and fairs at home and abroad; Pres. D. HISHGEE; Gen. Sec. S. TIMUR.

TRANSPORT

RAILWAYS

Ulan Bator Railway: Ulan Bator; Dir. S. I. SOLOVYEV; Deputy Dir. N. TSERENNOROV.

External Lines: from the Soviet frontier at Naushki Sühbaatar (connecting with the Trans-Siberian Railway) to Ulan Bator on to the Chinese frontier at Dzamyn-üüd/Erhlien and connecting with Beijing (total length 1,115 km.).

Branches: from Darhan to Sharyn Gol coalfield (length 68 km.); branch from Salhit near Darhan westwards to Erdenet (Erdenetiyn-ovoo open-cast copper mine) in Bulgan Province (length about 170 km.); from Maan't to Baga nuur coal-mine south-east of Ulan Bator (about 120 km.).

Eastern Railway: Choybalsan; from the Soviet frontier at Borzya/Ereentsav to Choybalsan (length 237 km.).

Mongolia's railways account for over 75 per cent of total freight turnover.

ROADS

Main roads link Ulan Bator with the Chinese frontier at Dzamyn üüd/Erhlien and with the Soviet frontier at Altanbulag/Kyakhta. A road from Chita in the U.S.S.R. crosses the frontier in the east at Mangut/Onon (Öldziy) and branches for Choybalsan and Öndörhaan. In the west and north-west, roads from Biysk and Irkutsk in the U.S.S.R. go to Tsagaannuur, Bayan-ölgiy Aymag, and Hanh, on Lake Hövsgöl, respectively. The total length of these and other main roads is about 8,600 km. The length of asphalted roads is now approaching 1,600 km., almost entirely in towns. The first section of a hard-surfaced road between Ulan Bator and Bayanhongor was completed in

1975. The road from Darhan to Erdenet is also to be surfaced. Inter-provincial and intra-provincial traffic goes across country in most cases.

There are bus services in Ulan Bator and other large towns, and lorry services throughout the country on the basis of motor transport depots, mostly situated in provincial centres.

INLAND WATERWAYS

Water transport plies Lake Hövsgöl and the River Selenge (474 km. navigable) in the northern part of the country. Tugs and barges on Lake Hövsgöl transport goods brought in by road to Hanh from the U.S.S.R. to Hatgal on the southern shore.

CIVIL AVIATION

Mongolian Civil Air Transport (MIAT): Ulan Bator; f. 1956; internal services to most provincial centres and many county centres; service from Ulan Bator (Buyant-Uhaa) to Irkutsk; fleet of 20 An-24, three Il-14, and also several An-2, Mil-4 and Yak-12; Dir. of Civil Aviation LHAGVASÜRENGIYN LHAGVAA.

Mongolia is also served by Aeroflot (U.S.S.R.).

TOURISM

Juulchin: Ulan Bator; f. 1960; the official foreign tourist service bureau, managed by the Ministry for Foreign Trade; Dir. B. DELGERSÜREN.

There were 8,000 foreign tourists in 1981.

DEFENCE

Armed Forces and Equipment (July 1981): Total strength 33,100: army 30,000, air force 3,100. There are also about 36,000 militia, frontier guards and internal troops. Military service is for 2 years. The armed forces have Soviet equipment comprising, in the case of the army, medium tanks, armoured personnel carriers, heavy artillery including howitzers and AA guns. The air force has 12 MiG 21 and also uses transport, trainers and helicopters in support of the army. It also has some Guideline surface-to-air missiles.

Defence Expenditure: Estimated defence spending for 1982 was 802 million tögrög.

Chief of Staff of the Mongolian People's Army: Lieut.-Gen. CHOYNDONGIYN PÜREVDORJ.

EDUCATION

The organization and administration of education in the Mongolian People's Republic is the responsibility of the Ministry of Education and the State Committee for Higher, Special Secondary and Technical-Vocational Education.

Kindergartens

Some 38,000 children aged 3 to 7 attend kindergartens, of which there were 554 in the 1976/77 school year.

General Education Schools

General education schools offer primary (4 years), incomplete secondary (7 years) or complete secondary education (10 years). In 1974, it was planned to ensure incomplete secondary education for all children of school age, and provide such schools in 80 per cent of Mongolia's counties (somons). In the 1977/1978 school year, general education schools had a total teaching staff of over 11,000. In 1980/81 there were 585 general education schools with 377,000 pupils. Many of these schools have two shifts.

Boarding Schools

In 1974, 18 boarding schools for nearly 11,000 rural children were to be built, raising the number of children of nomadic herdsmen going to school to 47,700, 45.6 per cent of the total. In 1975, another 30 boarding schools were to be built, for 50,700 herdsmen's children. A 10 per cent increase in funds for feeding boarding school children was approved in 1975.

Special Secondary and Technical Schools

Special secondary schools (25) and vocational technical schools (37), which had over 32,300 pupils in 1981, train personnel for the service industries, and vehicle drivers and machine operators for industry and agriculture.

Higher Education

In 1979, 19,700 students were studying at the Mongolian State University and at six other tertiary institutions. Higher education also is provided at special colleges for Party cadres and army officers, and at the Mongolian Teacher Training College. The Mongolian State University has nine faculties: physics and mathematics, natural sciences, engineering and economics, building engineering, social sciences, philology, economics, geology and geography, and energy and mechanics. The technical colleges train doctors, veterinary surgeons, and agricultural specialists. In 1974, of 24,600 graduates of general education schools, 1,900 were accepted by higher education establishments and 3,000 by technical colleges. In 1975, it was planned to accept a total of 6,000 from among 28,500 graduates.

Education Abroad

Each year, some 1,000 Mongolian students study abroad, mostly at Soviet universities, colleges and technical colleges.

BIBLIOGRAPHY

GENERAL

JAGCHID, S. and HYER, P. Mongolia's Culture and Society (Wm. Dawson and Sons Ltd., Folkestone, 1979).

PUNTSAGNOROV, T. 50 Years of People's Mongolia (MPR State Publishing House, Ulan Bator, 1971).

RUPEN, R. A. How Mongolia is Really Ruled (Hoover Institution Press, Stanford University, California 1971).

SANDERS, A. J. K. The People's Republic of Mongolia: A General Reference Guide (Oxford University Press, London, 1968).

HISTORY

BAWDEN, C. R. The Modern History of Mongolia (Weidenfeld and Nicolson, London, and Praeger, New York, 1968).

BOYLE, J. A. The Mongol World Empire 1206–1370 (Variorum Reprints, London, 1977).

BROWN, W. A. and ONON, U. History of the Mongolian People's Republic (Harvard University Press, Cambridge, Mass. 1976). *English translation, with extensive footnotes, of Vol. 3 of Mongolia's official history.*

DE RACHEWILTZ, I. Papal Envoys to the Great Khans (Faber and Faber, London, 1971).

EWING, E. E. Between the Hammer and the Anvil? Chinese and Russian Policies in Outer Mongolia 1911–21 (Indiana University, Bloomington, 1980).

HEISSIG, W. A. Lost Civilisation (Thames and Hudson, London, 1964).

LATTIMORE, OWEN. Nationalism and Revolution in Mongolia (E. J. Brill, Leiden, 1955). *English translation of the official life of the revolutionary leader, Sühbaatar, with introduction.*

Nomads and Commissars (Oxford University Press, London, 1962).

Studies in Frontier History, Collected Papers 1929–58 (Oxford University Press, London, 1962).

MURPHY, G. G. S. Soviet Mongolia (University of California, 1966).

ONON, U. (Trans.) Mongolian Heroes of the 20th Century (AMS Press, New York, 1976).

RUPEN, R. A. Mongols of the Twentieth Century, Vol. 1 (History), Vol. 2 (Bibliography) (Indiana University and Mouton and Co., The Hague).

The Mongolian People's Republic (Hoover Institution Studies, Stanford, 1966).

SAUNDERS, J. J. The History of the Mongol Conquests (Routledge and Kegan Paul, London, 1971).

TRAVEL, ETC.

BISCH, J. Mongolia, Unknown Land (Allen and Unwin, London, 1963).

HASLUND, H. Tents in Mongolia (London, 1935).

Mongolian Journey (Routledge and Kegan Paul, 1949).

JISL, L. Mongolian Journey (Batchworth Press, London, 1960).

LATTIMORE, OWEN. Mongol Journeys (Cape, 1941).

MONTAGU, I. Land of Blue Sky (Dennis Dobson, London, 1956).

Nepal

PHYSICAL AND SOCIAL GEOGRAPHY

B. H. Farmer

Nepal is situated between the high Himalayas and the Ganges Plains, between India and China's Tibetan territory. It occupies 141,059 square kilometres (54,463 square miles) and extends from 26° 20′ to 30° 10′ north latitude, and from 80° 15′ to 88° 15′ east longitude.

PHYSICAL FEATURES

Nepal's southernmost physical region is the Terai which, like the similar region in India, is a belt of low-lying plain, highly liable to flooding during the monsoon. North of it rises the Himalayas system, the world's greatest mountain range. With the associated Karakoram, Hindu Kush and Pamir ranges, the Himalaya system contains all but two of the 86 mountains over 7,500 metres (24,606 ft.) above sea-level. The world's highest peak, Mount Everest (known as Sagarmatha to the Nepalese), rises to 8,848 metres (29,028 ft.) and lies on Nepal's frontier with Xizang (Tibet), in the People's Republic of China. A series of transverse or more complex valleys breaks up the simple pattern of parallel ranges, and one of these, the Valley of Nepal, contains the capital, Kathmandu.

CLIMATE

It is difficult to be at all precise about the climate in the absence of accurate data. It would seem, however, that it exemplifies two main tendencies. In the first place, temperatures, for obvious reasons, decrease as one moves from the Terai through the foothills and internal valleys to higher Himalayan ranges. At Kathmandu, 1,337 metres (4,388 ft.) above sea level, average monthly temperatures are 10°C. (50°F.) in January and 23°C. (73°F.) in May. In January the average daily maximum is 18°C. (65°F.) and the average minimum 2°C. (35°F.). In the highest Himalaya, of course, air temperatures are always below freezing point. In the second place, rainfall, other things being equal, tends to decrease from east to west, as it does, of course, in the Indian plains below. Eastern Nepal receives about 250 cm. (100 inches) per year; Kathmandu 142 cm. (56 inches); and western Nepal about 100 cm. (40 inches).

SOILS AND NATURAL RESOURCES

There is little reliable scientific information on soils. As in corresponding parts of the Indian Himalayas, soils are likely to be skeletal, thin and poor on steep slopes (except where improved artificially under terraced cultivation); and better soils are probably confined to valley bottoms and interior basins, and to the Terai.

There has been a great deal of clearing for cultivation in the Terai, in interior valleys like the Valley of Nepal, and on lower hillsides. But in some areas text-book examples of altitudinal zonation may be seen: tropical moist deciduous forests to 1,200 metres (4,000 ft.) or so; moist hill pine forests from 1,200 to 2,600 metres (8,500 ft.) or so; coniferous forests from 2,600 to 3,350 metres (11,000 ft.), alpine vegetation beginning at the latter altitude.

In Nepal, the only mineral so far discovered in significant quantities is mica, mined east of Kathmandu. There are local workings of lignite in the outermost range of mountains, and small deposits of copper, cobalt and iron ore. Raw materials exist for cement manufacture.

POPULATION AND ETHNIC GROUPS

According to the census of June 1981, Nepal had a population of 14,179,301. The population is unevenly distributed, with fairly dense clusters and ribbons along the valleys and in the Terai, a scatter of isolated upland settlements, and great empty spaces at high altitude.

In Nepal there are a number of tribes of Mongoloid appearance speaking Tibeto-Burman languages, for example Gurungs, Magars and Bhotiyas. There are also Gurkhas who claim Rajput origin, Newars in the Valley of Nepal and recent Indian immigrants in the Terai.

HISTORY

Geography has dictated the history of this independent state, 880 km. long and 160 km. broad, a rectangle lying slantwise across the Himalayas on the north-east frontier of India. It is the only practicable gateway from Tibet to the Indo-Gangetic plains, and a pattern of political non-alignment has been imposed by the fact that its borders are both with India and the People's Republic of China.

The unification of such a country was clearly a problem. The inaccessibility of the country and its people retarded the development of a national unity which is still only a veneer in the more remote areas. The word *Nepal* appeared for the first time only in A.D. 879 and means the beginning of a new era. Although ancient Nepalese history is still only partially documented, it is assumed that from about the year 700 B.C. the Kirantis ruled. They are mentioned in Vedic literature and the Mahabharata. They are the ancestors of ancient Nepalese groups including the Newars, Rais, Limbus, Thamangs and Sunwars. During the rule of the Kirantis, Buddha was born in 560 B.C. in the small town of Lumbini in the Terai, near the Indian border. It is still a centre of pilgrimage for Buddhists all over the world, although the infiltration of Tantricism, Hinduism and Brahmanism has transformed both doctrine and practice. Between the ninth and the fourteenth centuries, the Nepal Valley, then, as now, the most important part of the country, was invaded from India until Jaya Sthithi Malla, a Southern Indian, began the Malla dynasty. Jaksha Malla, most able of the Malla Kings, extended his power far beyond the Valley. He divided his kingdom among his four heirs in 1488; Kathmandu, Bhatgaon, Patan and Banepa remained intact until the Gurkha conquest. The Gurkhas were originally a warlike tribe of the Rajput Kshatriyas who were driven out of India in 1303 by the Sultan, Alau-d-din. They escaped into the hills of central Nepal and gradually spread out into the region of Gorakhnath where they settled in about 1559. At this time the country was divided into small principalities and therefore vulnerable to the adventurous and energetic Gurkha, Prithvinarayan Shah.

The Gurkhas

Prithvinarayan Shah is the acknowledged maker of modern Nepal. He conceived the idea of carving out a viable Kingdom in the Himalayas by conquering neighbouring territories. His idea was to conquer the Valley of Nepal and from there to expand in all directions. The *Gorkha Vamsavali* describes in vivid detail how he ordered a general mobilization. By a series of campaigns ending in 1767 he was in control of the territories which today constitute Nepal. Just before his death in 1775, he was planning to annex Sikkim as he wanted to make his boundary continuous with Bhutan.

But Prithvinarayan Shah's contribution to the history of Nepal was not only that he gave it an entity but that he preserved it in its earliest days from the foreigner. He was excessively anti-foreign; he wanted to encourage the enterprise of all the castes and sects and he advised his countrymen to support native industries. His reign coincided with Great Britain's efforts to open up trade with Tibet and China. In 1768 the Secretary to the Board of Directors of the East India Company instructed their representative in Calcutta "to obtain the best intelligence you can whether trade can be opened with Nepal and whether cloth and other European commodities may not find their way thence to Tibet, Lhasa and Western parts of China". The Gurkha King was adamant; he prohibited the entry of certain British traders to Kathmandu and advised the authorities in Lhasa not to be tempted by a British offer of establishing new relations between Bengal and Tibet. In short, had the Gurkha King been a less determined man, Nepal might well have become just another Princely State of British India. As it is, the Shah dynasty which he founded remains to this day.

The central figure in Nepal during the vital years 1786–94 was Bahadur Shah. Like his Gurkha predecessors he was determined to extend the area of his country; his armies occupied states of the Baisis and Chaubisis and Kumaon and Garhwal in the west and Sikkim in the east. A portion of Tibetan Kachhar also was taken. His policy was even more vigorously pursued when his nephew, Rana Bahadur, then only 20, took over power in 1796. He outraged public sentiment by marrying a Brahmin girl, and subsequently the country fell apart into two warring families, the Pandes and Thapas. A revolt on the part of the Brahmins and hostile courtiers forced him to abdicate. When he regained the throne in 1804, he dismissed his Prime Minister, Damodar Pande, who had signed a treaty with the East India Company allowing it the right to appoint a British Resident in Nepal. He was succeeded by one of the most famous Prime Ministers in Nepalese history—Bhim Sen Thapa.

Bhim Sen Thapa continued an expansionist policy which brought him into conflict with British India, and, finally, to the Anglo-Nepalese war of 1814-16. He sued for peace in March 1816. Sir David Ochterlony, the United Kingdom's representative, replied: "You must take either a Resident or war", a phrase which long embittered the martial Nepalese. The Treaty of Segauli (March 4th, 1816) gave the United Kingdom the right to appoint a Resident and the cession of the hills of Kumaon, Garhwal, Nainital Simla, and a great portion of the Terai. The United Kingdom was also compelled to withdraw from Sikkim.

Rana Autocracy

Bhim Sen Thapa's authority remained virtually unchallenged until the young King Rajendra Vikram Shah came of age and decided to take control himself. Bhim Sen Thapa was dismissed in 1837 and imprisoned. He killed himself two years later. Out of the complete confusion, massacres and intrigues which followed, another outstanding figure emerged—Jung Bahadur Rana, and another chapter began in Nepalese history which lasted until 1950. He was astute and ruthless. He proclaimed himself Prime Minister and Commander-in-Chief of the Army. He assumed the title of Rana and, independently of the ruling Monarchy, distributed power among his own relations and made his own and their positions hereditary. He reversed the policy of his predecessors by allying himself with the United Kingdom and offering support in its war against the Sikhs. His strategic value was recognized when he visited the United Kingdom in 1848. And his offer to place troops at Her Majesty's disposal was redeemed at the time of the Indian Mutiny when he personally commanded a second army which besieged Lucknow. He substantially helped Lord Canning in his difficult task of suppressing the Mutiny.

The Rana family now had a complete monopoly of power in every walk of life. From his birth a Rana could become a General or Colonel and from his fifteenth year he could pass as the Director of Education. The British encouraged the Ranas to follow an isolationist policy. The country remained backward industrially and intellectually. It was a recruiting ground for the British armies in which Gurkha regiments became famous for their toughness and loyalty. When the First World War started, the British Government demanded and received permission for the free recruitment of Gurkha soldiers. The Rana Chandra Shamsher behaved like the ruler of a Princely State. He had his reward in 1923 when the Treaty of Segauli was revised. The Nepalese wanted an unequivocal declaration of their independence, but the British Government insisted on retaining those clauses which limited Nepal's external relations to those with the United Kingdom. A change in the designation of the British Resident was made; he was henceforth to be called officially *His Majesty's Minister Plenipotentiary and Envoy Extraordinary*. The King was now to be called *His Majesty* instead of *His Royal Highness*, and the Prime Minister, *His Highness the Maharajah of Nepal*. British titles were generously distributed on leading Ranas. An annual contribution of one million rupees was arranged to be remitted by the Indian Exchequer to the Nepalese ruler.

During Chandra Shamsher's reign (1901-29) the question of Nepal's foreign relations arose. The Treaty of 1792 had placed Nepal in an undefined position of satellite to China, and, until 1900, the Nepalese had sent a goodwill mission to Beijing (Peking) every twelfth year. In 1911, when the revolution in China confused international relations, the time came for the next mission. But when the Chinese High Commissioner at Lhasa raised the question of Nepal's vassalage under the old treaty, the Delhi authorities advised Chandra Shamsher to refuse to send it. By implication, Nepal unilaterally repudiated the 1792 Treaty.

In internal affairs, Chandra Shamsher made a small chink in Nepal's wall of isolation and there was some movement of social ideas. Under pressure from the enlightened world, Chandra Shamsher abolished slavery in 1926, freeing some 60,000 people at a cost of 3.7 million rupees.

As long as British rulers remained in India, the Ranas felt secure. But the new ideas which swept India in the 1930s, and which were realized in 1947 with the coming of Indian independence, influenced the 3 million Nepalese who lived in the frontier provinces of Bengal, Bihar and Uttar Pradesh and in turn spread into the Valley of Nepal.

In 1950 the Nepali National Congress was merged with the Nepali Democratic Congress, which had a similar programme, to form the Nepali Congress. The Nepali Congress, secretly helped by the monarch, King Tribhuvan, himself, went ahead with its plans to overthrow the Rana regime and an armed struggle was organized. All power was vested in the President, M. P. Koirala.

The Chinese occupation of Tibet in October 1950 brought matters to a head, for both India and Nepal. It undoubtedly influenced the timing of King Tribhuvan's dramatic challenge to the position of the Ranas; in November 1950 he refused to sign death warrants of alleged plotters against the Rana regime and took political asylum in the Indian embassy. The Indian Government sent two aircraft to bring him to Delhi. Local Nepalese greeted him enthusiastically. Along the border the insurgents struck, captured Nepal's second largest town, Birganj, and proclaimed a rival Government.

In this trial of strength between the Nepali Congress and the Rana regime, the decisive factor was where did the army stand? It soon became clear that it was loyal to the regime. In these circumstances, some modus vivendi between the King, the Ranas and the Nepali Congress was necessary. The Prime Minister of India, Jawaharlal Nehru, and his colleagues stood firm in their support for the King, and the Nepalese Government finally accepted India's proposals on January 7th, 1951. They provided for the return of the King to the throne, an amnesty for the insurgents if they laid down their arms, elections by 1952, and the formation of an interim Cabinet of 14 Ministers on the basis of parity between the Ranas and popular representatives. The Royal Family and the Nepali Congress leaders made a triumphal return to Kathmandu on February 15th, 1951. Three days later the new Ministry was sworn in—it had been reduced from 14 to 10. Mohun Shumshere Jang Bahadur Rana was the Prime Minister and B. P. Koirala (half-brother of M. P. Koirala) took the vital Home Ministry. It was the end of Ranarchy, and the beginning of an experiment in democracy.

Parliamentary Government

The experiment soon ran into difficulty. The Ranas fought a rear-guard action. They were not reconciled to the loss of their century-old absolute power. Nepali Congress leaders were divided and broke up into factions on a personal or an ideological basis, sometimes on both. King Tribhuvan declared a state of emergency in the country in January 1952 and armed the Prime Minister with emergency powers. Extreme parties of Right and Left (the Rashtriya Mahasabha and the Communists) were declared illegal and political meetings banned indefinitely. Yet an Advisory Assembly of 40 people was set up and opened by the King in July. Its powers were limited; it could not discuss foreign policy nor the King's personal behaviour and it could not pass a vote of no confidence in him. It lasted only two months; the King disagreed with his Ministers and they could not agree among themselves.

Once more King Tribhuvan tried to form an Advisory Assembly. It consisted of 112 members, but on its opening day in May 1954, the Nepali Congress boycotted it on the grounds that as the largest party it should have the right to form a government and command a majority in the Assembly. Internal rivalries, widespread corruption and nepotism combined to prevent the working of any Assembly. The Communists, working in front organizations since their party was illegal, made considerable headway especially among the younger generation of disillusioned intellectuals in Kathmandu.

Matters came to a head when King Tribhuvan died in March 1955. From his deathbed he dissolved the Royal Council of State and vested all Royal powers in the Crown Prince. The new King Mahendra Bir Birkram Shah Deva was tough, resolute, immensely hard-working and pragmatic. He made no pretence of believing in parliamentary democracy. In a

National Day broadcast he said: "Some people say that democracy in Nepal is in its infancy. But infants do not indulge in corruption and bribery". He did not disguise his contempt for most politicians, but royal dictatorship, even of an energetic, intelligent, and dedicated nationalist, did not give his country stability or prosperity.

In December 1957 he announced that elections would be held in February 1959. They were held a week after the King had given Nepal its first Constitution providing for a Senate (Mahasabha), consisting of 36 members of whom 18 would be elected by the Lower House and 18 nominated by the King, and a Lower House (Pratinidhi Sabha), which would consist of 109 members elected from single-member territorial constituencies. In a country where 96 per cent of the population were illiterate, the elections were held with surprising success. People voted in some of the most remote areas, showing independence and responsibility. Most candidates gave priority to the abolition of the *Birta* system, by which landlords, mostly Ranas, held land tax-free; to the nationalization of the zamindari system; to irrigation; to co-operative farming; to cottage industries, and to government-supported medium industries. Most parties subscribed to this programme, though the Nepali Congress seemed the most likely to carry it out if elected. Its top echelons had subscribed to socialist ideas for many years.

This is clearly what was in the minds of the masses who gave the Nepali Congress 38 per cent of the total votes cast. This gave 74 seats in the Lower House out of the 109. On the right, the Gorkha Parishad won 19 seats or 17.1 per cent of the votes cast while the Communists won 4 seats, or 7.4 per cent. When the King appointed B. P. Koirala as Prime Minister and the first popularly elected Parliament of Nepal was opened in July 1959, it seemed as if the long road towards democracy was firmly established. Yet the Constitution providing for a parliamentary government and civil rights left sovereignty in fact, not only in form, with the King. He could, for example, force the Prime Minister to resign; he could suspend the Cabinet and rule directly or with newly appointed ministers; he could prorogue Parliament or call for a special sitting; he had a veto over all legislation and constitutional amendments. This fundamental limitation of the democratic process at the core was a major cause of B. P. Koirala's frustration. Yet the overwhelming majority which his Party had secured was prepared to support him in his schemes for land reform. He gave greater security to tenants and redistributed some of the large estates owned by the Ranas. The Ranas themselves fought a rear-guard action which Koirala could still have won but for a growing tension between himself and the young King Mahendra. This clash of personalities came to a head on December 15th, 1960, when King Mahendra staged a coup, and jailed B. P. Koirala and most of the top cadres of the Nepali Congress. He suspended rights guaranteed by the Constitution and dissolved Parliament, substituting his own hand-picked Council of Ministers. The royal coup demonstrated the loyalty of the army to King Mahendra.

The Panchayat System

The King, who had a built-in disbelief in all party politics and politicians, worked immensely hard to create a "partyless Panchayat democracy". This panchayat system, proclaimed in 1961 and promulgated under the Constitution the following year, is a four-tier administrative pyramid. At the apex is the King, who appoints the Prime Minister. This office was filled successively by Dr. Tulsi Giri (1962–65), Surya Bahadur Thapa (1965–69) and Kirti Nidhi Bista (1969–70). King Mahendra himself was Prime Minister from April 1970 to April 1971, when Bista was reappointed. Bista resigned as Prime Minister in July 1973 and was succeeded by Nagendra Prasad Rijal.

In September 1967 the tenth session of the Rashtriya Panchayat (National Assembly) adopted a far-reaching programme based on a "Back to the Village" campaign, and a detailed scheme for panchayat administration. The decision of Nepali Congress leaders in May 1968 that they would co-operate with King Mahendra in the panchayat system led to the release of B. P. Koirala and his colleagues in October 1968; they subsequently went into self-exile in India. But in April 1969, 175 workers of the outlawed Nepali Congress Party, who had been in exile since the royal coup in 1960 and convicted in absentia, were released and allowed to return to civilian life, but not to any party political life. The King and his Council of Ministers introduced well-known Royalist figures into the Cabinet and emphasized the fact that there could be no politics whatsoever except within the panchayat system.

King Mahendra died on January 31st, 1972, and was succeeded by his son as King Birendra Bir Bikram Shah Dev, whose coronation eventually took place in February 1975. King Birendra had been educated at Eton and Harvard and at his accession hopes were aroused that he might relax the late king's rather autocratic rule. In 1975 a Royal Commission was set up to examine the panchayat system and discovered that many people thought that the electoral base should be widened. A group of 18 members of the Rashtriya Panchayat then issued a seven-point statement which included demands for the appointment of the Prime Minister by the Rashtriya Panchayat, the formation of political parties, full adult franchise, rural representation and increased political rights. Since such demands went beyond the Commission's mandates, the Government convened a meeting of the presidents of the 75 districts of Nepal and persuaded them to denounce the statement. Changes in Nepal's political system still seemed unlikely.

In December 1975 Dr. Tulsi Giri became Prime Minister, despite opposition to his appointment from Kirti Nidhi Bista. During 1976 Giri nominated supporters of the banned Nepali Congress Party and ex-communists as members of the Rashtriya Panchayat and there was renewed demand for political change. Numerous amendments to the Constitution were adopted which allowed for a widening of the franchise and more frequent elections to the Rashtriya Panchayat, but in no way were the King's powers eroded; he could, if he so wished, consult the Rashtriya Panchayat and the "Back to the Village" Campaign Central Committee, but was not obliged to act on their advice.

In December 1976 B. P. Koirala returned to Nepal from exile in India, but was arrested on arrival and it was announced that he would be tried for treason. However, six months later, under pressure from India, he was released and left the country. In September 1977 Giri resigned as Prime Minister, primarily because of differences with King Birendra over Koirala's detention. Giri had also been accused of corrupt practices and a number of Rashtriya Panchayat members had put pressure on him to resign in order to save Nepal from economic chaos and political disorder. Kirti Nidhi Bista was re-appointed Prime Minister.

By late 1977 B. P. Koirala had been acquitted of five charges of treason and in March 1978 returned to Nepal to spearhead a renewed campaign for political change. He claimed to have the support of other banned opposition groups, including the Communist Party of Nepal. He also had the open sympathy of certain elements in the Rashtriya Panchayat which resulted in a purge of the Panchayat by the King and a strengthening of the State Council (Raj Sabha), the King's personal advisory body.

However, rioting and student unrest continued and some members of the Congress Party lost patience with Koirala's insistence on co-operation with the King and urged a nationwide "non-violent movement" against the authorities. But this was clearly out of the question while the King retained the support of the army and police force. In February 1979 two Congress Party activists were executed for "sedition and treason", in April Koirala was put under house arrest and numerous other Congress members were reported to have been detained. Demonstrations in April and May were suppressed with considerable violence by the police.

In April 1979 Bista offered his resignation as Prime Minister after five people were reported killed in the disturbances. The King eventually accepted his resignation and with it the by now very apparent need for political concessions. After widespread unrest, the arrest of a number of political leaders and allegations of alleged misrule by Panchayat authorities, King Birendra announced at the end of May that a national referendum would be held to choose between the Panchayat system and a multi-party system. All the members of the "Back to the Village" Campaign Central Committee then resigned and in June a new Cabinet was formed by the liberal former Prime Minister, Surya Bahadur Thapa. A National Election Committee was set up to supervise the referendum and a general amnesty was granted to political prisoners and exiles so that all eligible adults could vote in the May 1980 poll. Out of 4,813,486 voters, 54.8 per cent supported the Panchayat system, with reforms, whereas 45.2 per cent favoured a multi-party system.

On December 15th, 1980, King Birendra issued a decree under which amendments to the Constitution were made (*see* Constitution). Under these new provisions, elections were held on May 9th, 1981, the first of their kind since 1959, although still on a non-party basis. Despite calls by B. P. Koirala to boycott the polling on the grounds that it was "inadequate and undemocratic", 1,096 candidates contested the 112 elective seats in the Rashtriya Panchayat. Only 35 of the 93 pro-government candidates obtained seats while newcomers, pledged to eliminate corruption, improve the economy and reduce unemployment, won a majority.

Surya Bahadur Thapa was unanimously re-elected by the Rashtriya Panchayat as Prime Minister on June 14th and the King installed a 28-member Council of Ministers, comprising 10 Cabinet Ministers, six Ministers of State and 12 Assistant Ministers.

ECONOMIC SURVEY

The Nepalese economy has always been handicapped by the fact that the country is landlocked and that communications within the country itself are still in need of development. Until the 1950s there were virtually no roads at all. Since then, largely with Chinese, Indian and U.S. aid, Nepal has built up a network of roads of over 4,000 kilometres. However, inflation, due to the increase in petroleum prices, has had a serious impact on development projects: road construction, in particular, has suffered serious delays in many projects. The largest allocation of the fourth Five-Year Development Plan (1970–75) went towards the improvement of communications, and almost 30 per cent of the outlay of the fifth Five-Year Plan (1975–80) was likewise allocated to transport and communications. Under the sixth Plan, an estimated 21 per cent of the total allocation is to be spent on transport and communications.

This emphasis on infrastructure in the development strategy has, however, meant a relative lack of investment in direct production, with a consequent slow rate of growth. Nepal is one of the 25 least developed nations on the World Bank scale. Between 1970 and 1979 the average annual real growth in Nepal's G.N.P. per capita (U.S. $130 in 1979) was only 0.3 per cent. In 1978/79 G.N.P. grew by less than 1 per cent, against a target of 3.5 per cent, and industrial production showed little change.

Agriculture and Forestry

Agriculture is the largest productive sector, employing about 90 per cent of the labour force. The principal crops are rice, maize, barley, millet, wheat, sugar cane, tobacco, potatoes and oilseeds, but development has been slow owing to shortages of fertilizers, improved seed, irrigation and storage facilities and agricultural credit. Recent crops, moreover, have been disappointing and the Government has had to import grains.

The Government declared 1975/76 "Agriculture

Year" and allocated 20 per cent of development funds to agriculture. Most of the money was spent on chemical fertilizers. Nepal produced a bumper food crop in 1976 with a total food grain output of 3.9 million metric tons. However, adverse weather conditions in three successive years caused a fall in food grain production to an estimated 3.2 million metric tons in 1979/80. Production rose to 3.9 million metric tons in 1980/81.

Forestry is a major source of income. However, in recent years deforestation has become a problem. The World Bank has approved a Rs. 216 million loan for a five-year project to combat deforestation, while a longer-term project to help stop soil erosion and deforestation was launched with substantial international aid. The Panchayat forest development programme aims to plant trees on private land and to protect some 40,000 hectares of forest. In 1980 an estimated 4.8 million hectares of land was forested.

Industry

The most important modern industries in Nepal include brick and tile manufacture, construction materials, paper, food grain processing and oil extraction, sugar refining and a brewery. Over one million workers are employed in traditional industries such as basket making, cotton fabrics, edible oil, etc. Government policy is to encourage new industries using domestic raw materials and there are plans to promote import-substitution industries, such as textiles and paper, with the help of credit and tax benefits. In general these policies have been effective and the industrial sector has been growing at an average annual rate of 9 per cent. Chinese aid financed the construction of a cotton factory at Hetauda, which started production in 1978 with an annual capacity of 11 million metres of cloth. Nepal and India have agreed to establish a joint company to build a cement plant with an annual capacity of over one million tons.

Mica is mined east of Kathmandu and there are also small deposits of lignite, copper, cobalt and iron ore. Nepal's rivers are being exploited for hydro-electric power production. Two hydro-electric projects are under way, costing over U.S. $1,000 million in international aid. The projects are expected to go into production in the late 1980s. Amongst the possible power projects, the Karnali project would have the potential to provide enough generating capacity to enable large-scale exports of hydro-electric power to India.

Trade

The landlocked nature of the country has made it difficult for Nepal to diversify its foreign trade, more than 80 per cent of which is with India. Its chief exports are grains, jute, papier mâché, wood and cane products. Some problems of exporting were alleviated by the second Trade and Transit Treaty, signed with India in August 1971, under which India provided road transport facilities, warehouse space at Calcutta and port facilities. At its expiry in 1976 the Trade and Transit Treaty was extended, and then replaced in 1977 by two separate treaties allowing Nepal to expand its trade with other countries. Nepal has established trade links with the People's Republic of China, North Korea, Bangladesh, Egypt and Sri Lanka, but diversification has been frustrated by India's persistant refusal to grant transit rights. Following the visit by a Tibetan trade delegation in 1980, 21 trade routes were opened up along the Nepal-Tibetan frontier.

Nepal's trade deficit increased by more than four times between 1970/71 and 1974/75. The situation improved in 1975/76, due to the bumper food crop, and rice, the principal export, was sold to China, Bangladesh and Sri Lanka. The trade gap widened again in 1976/77 and 1977/78, principally because of the fall in rice production and reduced foreign demand, especially from India. In 1978 the export shortfall forced the Government to purchase the equivalent of SDRs 9.5 million under the International Monetary Fund's compensatory financing facility. In 1979 the trade deficit grew by almost 20 per cent, mainly as a result of a rise in imports, and in 1980 the deficit increased by a further 13 per cent.

Foreign Aid

Foreign aid has played a large part in financing development and was to finance 45 per cent of the total outlay of the fifth Five-Year Plan. The largest individual contributors are the People's Republic of China and India, although the World Bank and the Asian Development Bank were jointly responsible for an estimated 84 per cent of total foreign loan assistance in 1978/79. Foreign aid has declined since 1978/79. The strategic situation of Nepal has resulted in an element of competition between these large powers over aid to the country. China's contribution to Nepal's economy is expanding rapidly, and in 1978 Japan was committed to a major expansion of its aid to Nepal.

Finance

Nepal's official foreign exchange reserves have, in general, increased annually, based on the balance of payments position, which is marginally favourable, taking into account invisible earnings such as receipts from tourism, interest on short-term foreign investment, foreign cash grants and loans and the savings and pensions of Gurkha soldiers, which can make them relatively rich men in Nepalese terms. Holdings of Indian currency, to which much importance is attached, have, however, been falling, following the cessation of the export of grains to that country.

The basic draft of the sixth Five-Year Plan (1980–85) aims at an ambitious average annual increase of 5 per cent in the G.N.P. The Plan envisages heavy investment in agriculture (31 per cent of total expenditure) and aims to provide irrigation for 25 per cent of cultivated land in hill districts and 40 per cent in lowland areas. It provides for continued growth of new industries, such as cotton textiles, vegetable oil and paper and pulp. The Government expects to make basic health and education facilities available throughout the country by the end of the Plan period.

STATISTICAL SURVEY

AREA AND POPULATION

Area	Population (census results)					
	June 22nd, 1971			June 22nd, 1981†		
	Males	Females	Total	Males	Females	Total
141,059 sq. km.*	5,817,203	5,738,780	11,555,983	7,132,424	7,046,877	14,179,301

* 54,463 square miles. † Preliminary results.

Capital: Kathmandu, population 393,494 (1981 preliminary census results).

Births and Deaths: Birth rate 38.59 per 1,000 in 1981; death rate 18.41 per 1,000 in 1981 (estimates).

ECONOMICALLY ACTIVE POPULATION
(1971 census)

	Males	Females	Total
Agriculture, hunting, forestry and fishing	3,187,307	1,392,245	4,579,552
Mining and quarrying	31	5	36
Manufacturing	45,391	6,511	51,902
Electricity, gas and water	1,570	26	1,596
Construction	4,876	140	5,016
Trade, restaurants and hotels	55,708	7,852	63,560
Transport, storage and communications	9,322	315	9,637
Financing, insurance, real estate and business services	3,331	315	3,466
Community, social and personal services	126,752	11,007	137,759
Total	3,434,288	1,418,236	4,852,524

Source: Central Bureau of Statistics.

Mid-1980 (estimates in '000, based on ILO data): Agriculture, etc. 6,264; total 6,766 (*Source:* FAO, *Production Yearbook*).

AGRICULTURE

LAND USE
('000 hectares)

Forest	4,823
Perpetual snow	2,112
Cultivated	2,326
Pasture	1,786
Water	400
Residential area and road	30
Waste land	2,629
Total	14,106

Source: Central Bureau of Statistics.

PRINCIPAL CROPS
(year ending July 15th)

	AREA HARVESTED ('000 hectares)			PRODUCTION ('000 metric tons)		
	1978/79	1979/80	1980/81*	1978/79	1979/80	1980/81*
Paddy rice	1,263	1,254	1,275	2,339	2,060	2,464
Maize	454	432	457	743	554	743
Millet and barley	149	149	149	155	142	145
Wheat	374	367	381	454	440	482
Oil seeds	144	118	122	92	62	77
Sugar cane	23	23	25	379	384	479
Tobacco	8	8	7	5	5	5
Jute	45	58	49	66	68	59
Potatoes	51	51	51	268	278	295

* Provisional.

Source: Economic Survey 1980/81, Ministry of Finance.

LIVESTOCK
(FAO estimates, '000 head, year ending September)

	1978	1979	1980
Cattle	6,750	6,850	6,900
Buffaloes	4,100	4,150	4,200
Pigs	340	350	355
Sheep	2,350	2,360	2,360
Goats	2,450	2,480	2,500
Poultry	21,000	21,500	22,000

Source: FAO, *Production Yearbook.*

LIVESTOCK PRODUCTS
(FAO estimates, '000 metric tons)

	1978	1979	1980
Beef and veal	4	4	5
Buffalo meat	18	19	19
Mutton and lamb	8	8	8
Goats' meat	10	10	10
Pig meat	5	5	5
Poultry meat	21	22	22
Cows' milk	213	215	216
Buffaloes' milk	470	475	480
Goats' milk	31	31	32
Butter and ghee	8.5	8.7	8.8
Hen eggs	14.0	14.5	14.8
Wool: greasy	4.2	4.2	4.2
clean	2.3	2.3	2.3

Source: FAO, *Production Yearbook.*

FORESTRY

ROUNDWOOD REMOVALS
(FAO estimates, '000 cubic metres, excluding bark)

	CONIFEROUS (soft wood)			BROADLEAVED (hard wood)			TOTAL		
	1978	1979	1980	1978	1979	1980	1978	1979	1980
Industrial wood*	20	20	20	540	540	540	560	560	560
Fuel wood	100	100	100	12,250	12,531	12,816	12,350	12,631	12,916
TOTAL	120	120	120	12,790	13,071	13,356	12,910	13,191	13,476

* Assumed to be unchanged since 1972.

Source: FAO, *Yearbook of Forest Products.*

SAWNWOOD PRODUCTION
('000 cubic metres, including boxboards)

	1967	1968	1969	1970	1971	1972*
Coniferous	7	7	10	10*	10*	10
Broadleaved	205	207	210	210	210	210
TOTAL	212	214	220	220	220	220

* FAO estimates.

1973–80: Annual production as in 1972 (FAO estimates).
Source: FAO, *Yearbook of Forest Products.*

Fishing (inland waters): Total catch of freshwater fishes 3,700 metric tons (1980).

INDUSTRY

SELECTED PRODUCTS
(twelve months ending July 15th)

		1977/78	1978/79	1979/80	1980/81*
Jute	metric tons	12,152	15,520	14,777	n.a.
Sugar	,, ,,	24,272	27,200	14,158	10,481
Tea	,, ,,	405	326	387	150
Cement	,, ,,	38,080	21,019	28,892	19,436
Beer	hectolitres	6,040	11,811	1,310	n.a.
Cigarettes	million	1,149	2,068	16,424	12,282
Shoes	pairs	43,631	55,779	70,299	68,214
Cotton textiles	'000 metres	3,889	2,264	3,489	3,270
Synthetic textiles	,, ,,	1,717	1,775	2,190	1,652

* Figures for the first nine months only.

Source: Economic Survey 1980/81, Ministry of Finance.

FINANCE

100 paisa (pice) = 1 Nepalese rupee (NR).
Coins: 1, 5, 10, 25 and 50 paisa; 1 rupee.
Notes: 1, 5, 10, 100, 500 and 1,000 rupees.
Exchange rates (June 1982): £1 sterling = NRs 22.86; U.S. \$1 = NRs 13.20.
1,000 Nepalese rupees = £43.74 = \$75.76.

Note: Between August 1958 and April 1960 the Nepalese rupee was valued at 14 U.S. cents (U.S. \$1 = 7.143 rupees). In April 1960 the rupee was devalued by 6.25 per cent to 13.125 U.S. cents (\$1 = 7.619 rupees) and this valuation remained in force until June 1966. From June 1966 to December 1967 the rupee's value was 13.13 U.S. cents (\$1 = 7.616 rupees). Between December 1967 and February 1973 the exchange rate was \$1 = 10.125 rupees (1 rupee = 9.8765 U.S. cents). The rate was \$1 = 10.56 rupees (1 rupee = 9.47 U.S. cents) from February 1973 to October 1975; \$1 = 12.50 rupees (1 rupee = 8 U.S. cents) from October 1975 to March 1978. A new basic rate of \$1 = 12.00 rupees (1 rupee = 8.33 U.S. cents) was introduced in March 1978. At the same time a "second" rate, initially set at \$1 = 16.00 rupees, was effective for some transactions. The "second" rate was adjusted to \$1 = 14.00 rupees in February 1980. The two-tier system was ended in September 1981, when a unified rate of \$1 = 13.20 rupees was established. In terms of sterling, the exchange rate was £1 = 21.333 rupees from April 1960 to June 1966; £1 = 21.325 rupees from June 1966 to November 1967; £1 = 24.30 rupees from December 1967 to August 1971; and £1 = 26.383 rupees from December 1971 to June 1972.

BUDGET

(NRs million—Twelve months ending July 15th)

Revenue†	1980/81*	1981/82‡
Customs	849.1	1,079.5
Excise	236.0	306.8
Land revenue	92.8	101.7
Forests	82.8	102.4
Taxes	792.8	1,023.7
Registration	126.5	140.7
Irrigation and water	1.3	1.9
Communications	21.8	22.8
Transport	21.0	27.3
Electricity	7.0	7.9
Interest, principal and dividend	125.8	182.8
Civil administration	32.1	52.3
Miscellaneous	37.1	50.2
Foreign and internal loans, cash reserves	904.7	2,612.8
Foreign aid	855.5	1,400.4
Total	4,186.3	7,113.2

Expenditure	1980/81*	1981/82‡
Constitutional bodies	65.5	62.7
General administration	62.2	85.2
Revenue administration	37.1	46.1
Economic administration	39.9	49.6
Judicial administration	19.7	26.7
Foreign service	48.0	50.7
Defence	425.8	471.7
Education	385.1	557.6
Social services (excl. education)	458.2	1,095.7
Agriculture	747.9	1,486.2
Transport	618.0	962.5
Other economic services	804.2	1,537.9
Loans and investments	11.2	14.3
Loan repayment and interest	218.5	336.5
Miscellaneous	245.0	339.8
Total	4,186.3	7,113.2

* Revised. † Includes mint. ‡ Estimate.

Source: Ministry of Finance.

FIFTH FIVE-YEAR PLAN (1975–80)

Proposed Expenditure

(NRs million)

	Minimum Programme	Maximum Programme
Agriculture, land reform, irrigation, forestry and rehabilitation, etc.	3,167.0	3,970.8
Industry, commerce, electricity and mining	1,799.9	2,040.4
Transport and communication	2,527.1	3,385.4
Education, health, drinking water and other social services	1,703.0	2,007.4
Total	9,197.0	11,404.0

SIXTH FIVE-YEAR PLAN (1980–85)

Allocation of Resources

(NRs million at 1979/80 prices)

Agriculture, land reform, irrigation, soil conservation, forestry, etc.	10,570
Industry, commerce, electricity, mining and tourism	8,810
Transport and communication	5,870
Education, health, drinking water, housing and other social services	8,690
Total	33,940

OFFICIAL RESERVES

(NRs million at July 15th)

	1977	1978	1979	1980	1981
Gold bullion and coins	69.8	73.4	74.7	76.0	76.0
IMF gold tranche	—	—	38.3	46.7	81.8
IMF Special Drawing Rights	29.2	19.9	29.3	43.5	10.5
Foreign exchange	1,710.3	1,579.7	1,996.8	2,057.1	2,097.1
Total	1,809.3	1,673.0	2,139.1	2,223.3	2,216.2

Source: Nepal Rastra Bank.

MONEY SUPPLY*

(NRs million at July 15th)

	1975	1976	1977	1978	1979	1980	1981
Currency outside banks	916.5	963.5	1,193.2	1,351.9	1,615.2	1,814.1	2,148.0
Private sector deposits with monetary authorities	80.8	101.4	139.9	131.5	164.0	229.4	224.0
Demand deposits at commercial banks	340.4	387.6	519.8	577.2	725.7	876.8	1,014.9
TOTAL MONEY	1,337.7	1,452.5	1,852.9	2,060.6	2,504.9	2,920.3	3,386.9

* Excluding Indian currency in circulation.

Source: Nepal Rastra Bank.

COST OF LIVING

NATIONAL CONSUMER PRICE INDEX

(year ending July; base: 1972/73=100)

	1977/78	1978/79	1979/80	1980/81
Food and beverages	156.4	158.8	176.2	210.1
Non-food and services	156.2	167.8	180.7	211.9
Clothing and sewing services	145.5	150.8	160.1	175.1
Housing	172.3	194.0	214.0	153.7
Fuel, light and water	179.5	213.5	240.6	299.0
ALL ITEMS	156.4	161.8	177.6	210.6

Source: Nepal Rastra Bank.

NATIONAL ACCOUNTS

GROSS DOMESTIC PRODUCT BY ECONOMIC ACTIVITY

(NRs million at current market prices, year ending July 15th)

	1976/77	1977/78	1978/79	1979/80
Agriculture, hunting, forestry and fishing	10,389	11,616	13,365	13,520
Mining and quarrying	26	25	34	42
Manufacturing*	736	794	848	936
Electricity, gas and water	39	42	48	60
Construction	1,020	1,338	1,559	1,570
Wholesale and retail trade	553	604	635	786
Restaurants and hotels	83	103	89	103
Transport, storage and communications	852	1,093	1,248	1,541
Finance, insurance, real estate and business services	1,412	1,534	1,613	1,833
Community, social and personal services	1,145	1,277	1,340	1,495
G.D.P. AT FACTOR COST	16,255	18,426	20,779	21,886
Indirect taxes, *less* subsidies	1,025	1,306	1,436	1,465
G.D.P. IN PURCHASERS' VALUES	17,280	19,732	22,215	23,351

* Including cottage industries.

Source: Central Bureau of Statistics.

FOREIGN AID RECEIVED

(NRs million, year ending July 15th)

	Grants			Loans			Total		
	1978/79	1979/80	1980/81*	1978/79	1979/80	1980/81*	1978/79	1979/80	1980/81*
Bilateral	1,030.6	696.8	825.3	151.3	149.6	179.1	1,181.9	846.4	1,004.4
Multilateral	163.8	108.8	124.1	1,071.6	385.3	819.8	1,225.4	394.1	1,043.9
Total	1,194.4	805.6	1,049.4	1,222.9	534.9	998.9	2,417.3	1,340.5	2,048.3

* Estimates.

Source: Ministry of Finance.

EXTERNAL TRADE

(NRs million, year ending July 15th)

	1976/77	1977/78	1978/79	1979/80	1980/81*
Imports	2,008.0	2,469.6	2,884.6	3,512.7	3,795.6
Exports	1,164.8	1,046.1	1,296.8	1,040.8	987.9

* Provisional.

Source: Nepal Rastra Bank.

PRINCIPAL COMMODITIES

(NRs million, year ending July 15th)

Imports	1977/78	1978/79	1979/80	1980/81*
Food and live animals	323.1	292.0	359.4	388.8
Beverages and tobacco	44.2	35.7	17.4	11.3
Crude materials (inedible) except fuels	53.1	61.4	86.5	76.4
Mineral fuels, lubricants, etc.	250.2	232.4	405.6	490.2
Animal and vegetable oils and fats	30.8	22.4	21.4	69.3
Chemicals	254.9	297.5	420.2	474.4
Basic manufactures	819.2	1,084.8	1,123.8	1,133.6
Machinery and transport equipment	483.1	574.6	772.9	766.6
Miscellaneous manufactured articles	201.0	275.0	294.5	270.5
Other commodities and transactions	9.9	8.9	10.9	14.5
Total	2,469.6	2,884.7	3,512.7	3,795.6

* Provisional.

Exports	1977/78	1978/79	1979/80	1980/81*
Food and live animals	405.3	488.2	275.6	347.2
Beverages and tobacco	11.2	13.7	1.8	0.4
Crude materials (inedible) except fuels	441.2	491.7	403.4	309.9
Mineral fuels, lubricants, etc.	0.2	0.7	0.5	0.1
Animal and vegetable oils and fats	6.0	17.1	22.1	44.6
Chemicals	3.6	0.8	1.2	3.5
Basic manufactures	123.3	229.1	289.0	191.6
Machinery and transport equipment	2.7	2.9	3.3	1.2
Miscellaneous manufactured articles	51.2	52.4	43.5	88.8
Other commodities and transactions	1.5	0.2	0.4	0.6
Total	1,046.1	1,296.8	1,040.8	987.9

* Provisional.

Source: Nepal Rastra Bank.

Trade with India (NRs million): Imports totalled 1,534.1 in 1977/78; 1,581.8 in 1978/79; 1,799.1 in 1979/80; 1,876.8 in 1980/81 (provisional). Exports totalled 498.1 in 1977/78; 650.1 in 1978/79; 434.3 in 1979/80; 614.5 in 1980/81 (provisional).

TRANSPORT

ROAD TRAFFIC

(vehicles in use at December 31st)

	1976	1977	1978
Private cars	11,526	12,679	14,201
Buses and coaches	1,484	1,662	2,001
Goods vehicles	5,848	6,608	7,987
Motorcycles and scooters	6,485	7,523	9,521

Source: International Road Federation, *World Road Statistics*.

CIVIL AVIATION

ROYAL NEPAL AIRLINES CORPORATION

(year ending July 15th)

	1978/79	1979/80	1980/81†
Passengers	397,000	400,350	320,153
Freight (metric tons)*	1,860	2,036	2,114

* Excluding mail.

† Provisional.

TOURISM

	1978	1979	1980
Tourist arrivals	156,123	162,276	162,897
Number of hotel beds*	4,888	5,018	5,109

* Recognized by Department of Tourism.

Source: Department of Tourism.

COMMUNICATIONS MEDIA

	1977
Radio receivers	200,000
Telephones in use	9,700
Newspapers	24*
Total circulation	365,000*

* 1975 figure.

EDUCATION

('000 students)

	1975/76	1976/77	1977/78	1978/79	1979/80
Primary	459	777	883	921	1,068
Lower Secondary	174	232	277	334	391
Secondary	67	84	93	111	121
Higher	23	21	26	31	54
TOTAL	723	1,114	1,279	1,397	1,634

Source: Ministry of Education.

Source (unless otherwise stated): National Planning Commission Secretariat, Kathmandu.

THE CONSTITUTION

(Promulgated December 1962, amended in 1967, 1976 and 1980)

GOVERNMENT

The Constitution of Nepal comprises a constitutional monarchy with executive power vested in the King but ordinarily exercised on the recommendation of a Cabinet led by a Prime Minister, selected by the King from among the membership of the Rashtriya Panchayat (National Assembly). The Cabinet is responsible to the Rashtriya Panchayat but the King has power to grant or withhold assent to Bills at his discretion.

STATE COUNCIL

The Constitution also provides for a State Council or Raj Sabha which will declare upon the succession or appoint a Regency Council besides giving advice to the King in times of emergency.

LEGISLATURE—RASHTRIYA PANCHAYAT

The Rashtriya Panchayat, which is at the apex of the partyless Panchayat system of democracy, is the supreme national unicameral legislature, comprising 135 members, 112 of whom are elected from among the members of the Anchal Sabhas (Zonal Councils), who in turn are elected from among the members of Zilla Sabhas (District Councils) who, again in turn, are elected from the Gaon Sabhas (Village Councils). In other words, membership of the Rashtriya Panchayat is based on the popular election of Local Panchayat (which is the basic unit of the four-tiered Panchayat system), from each of which members choose from among themselves representatives for District Panchayats. They may advance by similar stages to the zonal and then to the Rashtriya Panchayat. The remaining members are nominated by the Crown according to the Constitution.

The Rashtriya Panchayat is a perpetual body whose members are elected from Zonal Councils and serve a fixed term of five years. House proceedings are open to the public. A summary record of the proceedings of every meeting of the House or its committees is published.

Bills to the House are presented by the Committees of the House, in consultation with Ministers. The annual budget is submitted to the House for consideration, deliberation and adoption. In order that these legislative tasks be conducted with becoming dignity and efficiency, the members of the House fully enjoy the privilege of freedom from arrest for anything spoken in the House or the manner in which voting is exercised.

CITIZENS' RIGHTS AND DUTIES

Besides enumerating a number of fundamental rights, including the right against exile, the Constitution lays down a series of fundamental duties of the citizen.

AMENDMENTS

Amendments to the 1962 Constitution, adopted in 1967 and 1976, include the following: Prime Minister to be appointed by the King who may, if he wishes, consult the Rashtriya Panchayat; Ministers to be collectively and individually responsible to the King; King to appoint directly the Zonal Commissioners who are to enjoy greater powers than the Chairmen of Zonal Panchayat; Speaker of the House to be appointed by at least two-thirds of Rashtriya Panchayat; associations for non-political purposes allowed but political parties continue to be banned; provision for appointment of an independent Election Commission; the country to be divided into four areas for electoral purposes, with elections for all elective bodies every four years on a rotational basis; elected members of Rashtriya Panchayat can be recalled. Following the national referendum of May 1980, the King formed an 11-member Constitutional Reforms Commission to recommend reforms to the system.

Amendments to the Constitution of December 1980: direct elections to be held every five years for 112 of the 140 seats in the Rashtriya Panchayat; the remaining 28 seats to be nominated by the King; the Prime Minister to be elected by members of the Rashtriya Panchayat; the Council of Ministers to be appointed by the King (on the recommendation of the Prime Minister) and to be responsible to the Rashtriya Panchayat; the establishment of Nepal as a "zone of peace" to be included as a directive principle in the Constitution.

THE GOVERNMENT

HEAD OF STATE

H.M. King BIRENDRA BIR BIKRAM SHAH DEV (succeeded to the throne January 31st, 1972; crowned February 24th, 1975).

COUNCIL OF MINISTERS

(July 1982)

Prime Minister, Minister of Palace and Foreign Affairs: SURYA BAHADUR THAPA.

Minister of Local Development, Health and Panchayat Affairs: NAVA RAJ SUBEDI.

Minister of Forests and Land Conservation: RAMANANDA PRASAD YADAV.

Minister of Home Affairs: NAIN BAHADUR SWANR.

Minister of Defence and Industry: BALA RAM GHARTIMAGAR.

Minister of Agriculture: HEM BAHADUR MALLA.

Minister of Education and Culture: NAYAN DUTTA BHATT.

Minister of Water Resources: LAL BAHADUR KHADAYAD.

Minister of Finance, Commerce and Supplies: YADAV PRASAD PANT.

Minister of Works and Transport: KASHI NATH GAUTAM.

State Minister of Land Reform: HARI BAHADUR THAPA CHHETRI.

State Minister of Tourism: DRON SHUMSHER J. B. RANA.

State Minister of General Administration: BHIM PRASAD GAUCHAN.

State Minister of Labour and Social Welfare: BHADRA KUMARI GHALE.

State Minister of Communications: FATEH SINGH THARU.

State Minister of Law and Justice: BISHNU MADEN.

Assistant Minister of Water Resources: DAYAN BAHADUR RAI.

Assistant Minister of Home Affairs: NARA BAHADUR GURUNG.

Assistant Minister of Land Reform: NARAYA MALLA.

Assistant Minister of Works and Transport: MOTI PRASAD PAHADI.

Assistant Minister of Forest and Land Conservation: DEEP BAHADUR SINGH.

Assistant Minister of Health: SOM NATH BASTOLA.

Assistant Minister of Agriculture: RAGHAVENDRA PRATAP SHAH.

Assistant Minister of Industry: KRISHANA CHARAN SHRESTHA.

Assistant Minister of Finance: (vacant).

Assistant Minister of Tourism: DEEPAK BOHARI.

Assistant Minister of Education and Culture: KESHAR BAHADUR BISTA.

Assistant Minister of Labour and Social Welfare: TEELAK BAHADUR NEGI LAMA.

LEGISLATURE

RASHTRIYA PANCHAYAT

The Rashtriya Panchayat (National Assembly) is the supreme legislative body of Nepal under the Panchayat system (*see* under Constitution). It has 140 members, of whom 112 are directly elected for 5 years and 28 nominated by the King.

Chairman of the Rashtriya Panchayat: MARICH MAN SINGH.

POLITICAL PARTIES

Under the Panchayat system there are no political parties.

DIPLOMATIC REPRESENTATION

EMBASSIES ACCREDITED TO NEPAL

(In Kathmandu unless otherwise stated)

Afghanistan: New Delhi, India.
Argentina: New Delhi, India.
Australia: New Delhi, India.
Austria: New Delhi, India.
Bangladesh: Naxal Bhagwati Bahal; *Ambassador:* HARUNUR RASHID.
Belgium: New Delhi, India.
Brazil: New Delhi, India.
Bulgaria: New Delhi, India.
Burma: Krishna Galli, Pulchowk, Patan; *Ambassador:* Dr. KHIN MAUNG WIN.
Canada: New Delhi, India.
Chile: New Delhi, India.
China, People's Republic: Baluwatar; *Ambassador:* MA MUMING.
Cuba: New Delhi, India.
Czechoslovakia: New Delhi, India.
Denmark: New Delhi, India.
Egypt: Pulchowk, Patan; *Ambassador:* FAWZY MAHBOUB.
Finland: New Delhi, India.
France: Lazimpat; *Ambassador:* FRANCIS DELOCHE DE NOYELLE.
German Democratic Republic: Tripureshwar; *Ambassador:* WALTER SCHMIDT.
Germany, Federal Republic: Kantipath; *Ambassador:* Dr. HANS HENNING WOLTER.
Greece: New Delhi, India.
Hungary: New Delhi, India.
India: Lainchaur; *Ambassador:* Shri N. P. JAIN.
Indonesia: Rangoon, Burma.
Iran: New Delhi, India.
Iraq: New Delhi, India.
Israel: Lazimpat; *Ambassador:* SHAUL KARIV.
Italy: Baluwatar; *Chargé d'affaires:* FRANCESCO FEDELI (Ambassador resident in New Delhi, India).
Japan: Panipokhari; *Ambassador:* KENICHIRO NISHIZAWA.
Korea, Democratic People's Republic: Lalitpur; *Ambassador:* HWANG DU HO.
Korea, Republic: Keshar Mahal, Thamel, P.O.B. 1058; *Ambassador:* KIM HYUNG-SOO.
Laos: New Delhi, India.
Lebanon: New Delhi, India.
Malaysia: New Delhi, India.
Mongolia: New Delhi, India.
Morocco: New Delhi, India.
Netherlands: New Delhi, India.
New Zealand: New Delhi, India.
Norway: New Delhi, India.
Oman: New Delhi, India.
Pakistan: Panipokhari, P.O.B. 202; *Ambassador:* ABDUL FAZL.
Philippines: New Delhi, India.
Portugal: New Delhi, India.
Romania: New Delhi, India.
Saudi Arabia: Dacca, Bangladesh.
Singapore: New Delhi, India.
Spain: New Delhi, India.
Sri Lanka: New Delhi, India.
Sweden: New Delhi, India.
Switzerland: New Delhi, India.
Syria: New Delhi, India.
Thailand: Jyoti Kendra Bldg., Thapathali; *Ambassador:* PONG BUA-IAM (resident in New Delhi, India).
Turkey: New Delhi, India.
U.S.S.R.: Dilli Bazar; *Ambassador:* ABDUL RAKHMAN KHALIL OGLY VEZIROV.
United Kingdom: P.O.B. 106, Lainchaur; *Ambassador:* JOHN B. DENSON, C.M.G., O.B.E.
U.S.A.: Panipokhari; *Ambassador:* CARLETON S. COON, Jr.
Viet-Nam: Rangoon, Burma.
Yugoslavia: New Delhi, India.

Nepal also has diplomatic relations with Albania, Algeria, Bahrain, Costa Rica, Cyprus, Ethiopia, Jordan, Kenya, Kuwait, Libya, Luxembourg, Maldives, Mexico, Nigeria, Peru, Poland, Qatar, Sudan, Tanzania and the United Arab Emirates.

JUDICIAL SYSTEM

There is one Supreme Court, four Regional, 15 Zonal and 75 District Courts. These have both civil and criminal jurisdiction.

The Supreme Court: The Constitution of Nepal provides for a Supreme Court which shall have a Chief Justice and not more than six other Justices unless otherwise specified by law. The Supreme Court is to hold appellate as well as original jurisdiction, and may function as a court of review. The Supreme Court protects the fundamental rights of the people and guarantees the Rule of Law.

Chief Justice: Rt. Hon. NAYAN BAHADUR KHATRI.

RELIGION

At the 1971 census 89.4 per cent of the population professed Hinduism (the religion of the Royal Family), while 7.5 per cent were Buddhists and 3.0 per cent Muslims.

In 1976 it was estimated that 60 per cent of the population were Hindus, 33 per cent Buddhists and 7 per cent Muslims.

BUDDHISM

Nepal Buddhist Association: Rev. BHIKKHU AMRITANANDA, Ananda Kuti, Kathmandu.
Young Buddhist Council of Nepal: Rev. AMRITANANDA.

THE PRESS

DAILIES

Commoner: Naradevi, Kathmandu; English; Editor GOPAL DAS SHRESTHA; circ. 7,000.

Dainik Nepal: Anu Printing Press, 5/82 Jhochhen, Kathmandu; Nepali; Editor INDRAKANT MISHRA; circ. 1,000.

Gorkha Patra: Dharma Path, Kathmandu; f. 1901; Nepali; Editor GOKUL PRASAD POKHREL; circ. 35,000.

Hamro Desh: Sharada Printing Press, Nhasal, Dharma Path, Kathmandu; Nepali; Editor KIRAN PRASAD PANDEY.

Himali Bela: Bhawani Printing Press, Tripureswar, Kathmandu; English; Editor S. S. RAJBHANDARI.

Jana Jivan: Gorakha Printers, Rani Pokhari, Kathmandu; Nepali; Editor S. R. BHANDARI.

Jandoot: Matribhoomi Pres. Ghantaghar, Kathmandu; Nepali; Editor GOVIND BIYOGI.

The Motherland: P.O.B. 1184, Kathmandu; English; Editor MANINDRA RAJ SHRESTHA; circ. 5,000.

Naya Nepal: Naya Nepal Chhapakhana, Bhrahma Tole, Kathmandu; Nepali; Editor GOBINDA PRADHAN.

Naya Samaj: Roopayan Press, Dhoka Tole, Kathmandu; f. 1957; Nepali; Editor BAL MUKUND DEV PANDEY; circ. 3,000.

Nepal Bhasha Patrika: Singh Press, Kilagal, Kathmandu; Newari; Chief Editor FATEH BAHADUR SINGH; circ. 1,200.

Nepal Samachar: Sagarmatha Press, Ramshah Path, Kathmandu; Nepali; Editor NARENDRA VILAS PANDEY; circ. 900.

Nepali: P.O.B. 49, Kathmandu; f. 1958; Hindi; evening; Editor UMA KANT DAS; circ. 12,500.

The New Herald: Kathmandu; English; Editor RAMESH NATH PANDEY; circ. 20,000.

The Rising Nepal: Dharma Path, Kathmandu; f. 1965; English; Editor MANA RANJAN JOSSE; circ. 20,000.

Sahi Aawaj: Bhotebahal, Kathmandu; Nepali; Editor SURYA LALAPIDIT.

Samaj: National Printing Press, Dilli Bazar, Kathmandu; Nepali; Editor MANI RAJ UPADHYAYA; circ. 2,100.

Samaya: Kamal Press, Ramshah Path, Kathmandu; Nepali; Editor MANIK LAL SHRESTHA; circ. 18,000.

Swatantra Samachar: Vina Bhadranalya, Chhetrapati, Kathmandu; Nepali; Editor MADAN SHARMA.

SELECTED PERIODICALS

Arpan: P.O.B. 285, Kohity Bahal, Kathmandu; Nepali; weekly; f. 1964; Chief Editor and Publr. MANJU RATNA SAKYA; Associate Editors Mrs. SUBHA LUXMI SAKYA, MEWA KAZI KANSAKAR; circ. 16,000.

Commerce: P.O.B. 171, 7/358 Kohity Bahal, Kathmandu; f. 1971; English; monthly; Chief Editor and Publr. MANJU RATNA SAKYA; Editor Mrs. SUBHA LUXMI SAKYA; circ. 10,000.

The Everest: Gorkha Printers, Rani Pokhari, Kathmandu; English; weekly; Publr. and Editor S. R. BHANDARI.

Foreign Affairs Journal: 5/287 Lagon, Kathmandu; f. 1976; articles on Nepalese foreign relations and calendar of main news events; three times a year; Editor and Publr. BHOLA BIKRUM RANA; circ. 5,000.

Janmabhumi: Janmabhumi Press, Tahachal, Kathmandu; Nepali; weekly; Publr. and Editor GANESH BALLAV PRADHAN.

Madhuparka: Dharma Path, Kathmandu; Nepali; monthly; literary; Editor GOKUL PRASAD POKHAREL; circ. 3,000.

Matribhoomi: Matribhoomi Press, Ghantaghar, Kathmandu; Nepali; weekly; Editor GOVIND BIYOGI.

Naya Sandesh: Dilli Bazar, Maitidevi, Kathmandu; Nepali; weekly; Editor RAMESH NATH PANDEY; circ. 40,000.

Nepal Post: c/o Vibid Sewa Kendra, Kamalpokhari, Kathmandu; f. 1973; Nepali; weekly; Publr. and Editor DEVENDRA GAUTAM; Associate Editor ROCHAK GHIMIRE; circ. 5,500.

Rooprekha: Dhoka Tole, Kathmandu; Nepali; monthly; literary; Editor and Publr. UTTAM KUMAR.

Tark: Madhuri Printing Press, Bagabazar, Kathmandu; Nepali; weekly; Publr. and Editor KRISHNA PRASAD BASKOTA.

Vashudha: Makhan, Kathmandu; English; monthly; articles on Nepalese social, political and economic affairs; Editor and Publr. T. L. SHRESTHA.

Viswadoot: Jyabahal, Kathmandu; Nepali; weekly; Publr. and Editor AMBIKA PRASAD MAINALI.

NEWS AGENCIES

Rastriya Samachar Samiti (R.S.S.): P.O.B. 220, Panchayat Plaza, Kathmandu; f. 1962; Chair. and Gen. Man. R. S. BISTA.

FOREIGN BUREAUX

Agence France-Presse (AFP): G.P. Box 402, Hansa Marga, Bhote Bahal, Kathmandu; Man. KEDAR MAN SINGH.

Associated Press (AP) (*U.S.A.*): Thapathali Panchayan, P.O.B. 513, Kathmandu; Correspondent BINAYA GURUBACHARYA.

Deutsche Presse-Agentur (dpa) (*Federal Republic of Germany*): 561 Tebahal Tole, Kathmandu 7101; Correspondent SHYAM BAHADUR, K.C.

Kyodo Tsushin (*Japan*): c/o Rastriya Samachar Samiti, Baneshwar; Correspondent MADHAV ACHARYA.

Reuters (*U.K.*): P.O.B. 224, Dilli Bazar, Kathmandu.

Telegrafnoye Agentstvo Sovietskogo Soyuza (TASS) (*U.S.S.R.*): Tangal Camp, Kathmandu; Correspondent YURI ROGIONOV.

United Press International (UPI) (*U.S.A.*): P.O.B. 802, Kathmandu; Correspondent BHOLA BIKRAM RANA.

Xinhua (*People's Republic of China*): Balram Bhawan, Kathmandu; Correspondent HAO GHEYIN.

PRESS ASSOCIATIONS

Nepal Journalists Association (NJA): P.O.B. 285, Tripureswar, Kathmandu; 1,500 mems.; Pres. MANJU RATNA SAKYA; Sec. S. S. RAJBHANDARI.

Press Council: Panchayat Plaza, Kathmandu; f. 1969; Pres. Justice B. SHARMA; Sec. KALI PRASAD RIJAL.

PUBLISHERS

Department of Information: Ministry of Communications, Kathmandu.

Educational Enterprise: Mahankalsthan, Kathmandu; education.

La Kaul Press: Palpa Tansen.

Mahabir Singh Chiniya Main: Makhan Tola, Kathmandu.

Mandas Sugatdas: Kambachi, Kathmandu.

Ratna Pustak Bhandar: P.O.B. 98, Bhotahity, Tole, Kathmandu; Propr. RATNA PRASHAD SHRESTHA.

Royal Nepal Academy: Kamalandi, Kathmandu; history, literature, art, sciences.

Sajha Prakhashan: Pulchowk, Kathmandu; f. 1966; educational and general; Chair. Shri KSHETRA PRATAP ADHIKARY.

RADIO

Radio Nepal: Dept. of Broadcasting, His Majesty's Govt. of Nepal, P.O.B. 634, Singhadurbar, Kathmandu; f. 1951; broadcasts on short and medium wave in Nepali and English; stations at Jawalakhel and Khumaltar; Dir.-Gen. B. P. SHAH.

In 1981 there were an estimated 96,000 radio receiving sets. There is no television.

FINANCE

BANKING

(cap.=capital; p.u.=paid up; auth.=authorized; dep.= deposits; m.=million; NRs=Nepali Rupees; brs.= branches).

CENTRAL BANK

Nepal Rastra Bank: Lalita Niwas, Baluwatar, Kathmandu; f. 1956; state bank of issue; cap. p.u. NRs 10m., total assets NRs 3,757m. (July 1979); 14 brs.; Gov. and Chair. KUL SHEKHAR SHARMA.

COMMERCIAL BANKS

Nepal Bank Ltd.: Dharmapath, Juddha Rd., Kathmandu; f. 1937; cap. p.u. NRs 15m., dep. NRs 2,853m. (Feb. 1982); 157 brs.; Chair. NARAKANTA ADHIKARI; Gen. Man. BHARAT LAL RAJBHANDARI; publ. *Nepal Bank Patrika* (12 a year).

Rastriya Banijya Bank (*National Commercial Bank*): Tangal, Kathmandu; f. 1966; cap. p.u. NRs 20m., dep. NRs 1,691m. (Oct. 1981); 117 brs.; 4 regional offices; Chair. SURYA PRASHAD SHRESTHA; Gen. Man. PUNYA KESHARI UPADHAYA (acting); publs. *Quarterly Statistical Bulletin, Balance Sheet.*

DEVELOPMENT BANKS

Agricultural Development Bank: Ramshah Path, Panchayat Plaza, Kathmandu; f. 1968; specialized agricultural credit institution providing credit to co-operatives, individuals and associations in agricultural development; receives deposits from individuals, co-operatives and other associations to generate savings in the agricultural sector; will act as government's implementing agency for small farmers' group development project, assisted by the Asian Development Bank and financed by the UN Development Programme; operational networks include 10 zonal offices, 14 brs., 69 sub-brs., 50 depots and 54 Small Farmers' Development Projects; there are plans to develop 30 Small Farmers' Projects in 1982/83; auth. cap. NRs 150m. Chair. and Gen. Man. AKRUR NARSINGH RANA.

Nepal Industrial Development Corporation (NIDC): NIDC Bldg., P.O.B. 10, Durbar Marga, Kathmandu; f. 1959; state-owned; has shares in 20 industrial enterprises, has financed 338 loans to industrial enterprises (July 1980), offers financial and technical assistance to private sector industries; cap. NRs 250m.; Chair. and Gen. Man. SHIVA NARAYAN DAS; publs. *Nepal Industrial Digest* (annually), *Annual Report, Audyegik Jagat* (Industrial Magazine) and various brochures.

INSURANCE

There is one insurance company:

Rastriya Beema Sansthan (*National Insurance Corporation*): P.O.B. 527, Kathmandu; f. 1967; Gen. Man. NARA PRATAP, K.C.

TRADE AND INDUSTRY

National Planning Commission: P.O.B. 1284, Singh Durbar, Kathmandu; Chair. The Prime Minister; Vice-Chair. Hon. Dr. RATNA S. J. B. RANA; Sec. Dr. DEBYA DEO BHATT.

Agriculture Inputs Corporation: Teku, Kuleshwor, Kathmandu, P.O.B. 195; f. 1972; government undertaking; sole dealer of agriculture inputs for agricultural development (procuring and distribution of chemical fertilizers, improved seeds, agricultural tools and plant protection material) at national level; conducts seed multiplication programme (paddy, wheat and maize); seed processing plants at Hetauda, Nepalgunj, Bhairahawa, Janakpur and Ittahari; Chair. BED BAHADUR KHADKA; Gen. Man. RAMESHWAR BAHADUR SINGH.

National Trading Ltd.: P.O.B. 128, Teku, Kathmandu; f. 1962; government undertaking; imports and distributes construction materials and raw materials for industry, machinery, vehicles and consumer goods; operates bonded warehouse, duty-free shop and related activities; brs. in all major towns; Exec. Chair. and Gen. Man. MANA MOHAN LAL SINGH.

Nepal Resettlement Company: Kathmandu; f. 1963; government undertaking; engaged in resettling people from the densely-populated hill country to the western Terai plain.

Salt Trading Corporation Ltd.: P.O.B. 483, Kalimanti, Kathmandu; f. 1963 as a joint venture of the public and private sectors (30 and 70 per cent respectively) to manage the import and distribution of salt in Nepal; now also deals in sugar, edible oils and wheat flour throughout Nepal; Chair. A. M. SHERCHAN; Gen. Man. H. B. MALLA.

CHAMBERS OF COMMERCE

Federation of Nepalese Chambers of Commerce and Industry: P.O.B. 269, Meera Home, Khichapokhari, Kathmandu; f. 1965; Pres. I. B. SHRESTHA; Vice-Pres. HULAS CHAND GOLCHHA; Sec.-Gen. MADHAV MANI RAJBHANDARI; publ. *Udyog Banijya Patrika* (fortnightly).

Nepal Chamber of Commerce: Nepal Bank Bldg. No. 2, P.O.B. 198, Kathmandu; f. 1952; non-profit making organization devoted to cause of industrial and commercial development in Nepal and to the service of its members; about 2,500 mems.; publ. *Chamber Patrika* (Nepali, fortnightly).

TRANSPORT

Ministry of Works and Transport: Babar Mahal, Kathmandu; Sec. GYAN PRASAD SHARMA.

Nepal Yatayat Sansthan (*Nepal Transport Corporation*): P.O.B. 309, Teku, Kathmandu; responsible for the operation of road transport facilities, railways, ropeway, trucks, trolley buses and autobuses; Exec. Chair. KRISHNA RAJ PANDEY.

RAILWAYS

Janakpur Railway: Khajuri; f. 1937; 53 km. open, linking Jayanagar (India) with Janakpurdham and Bijalpura; Man. PRADHAN BHUVAN BAHADUR.

Nepal Railway: Birganj; f. 1927; 49 km. linking Raxaul to Amlekhganj, of which the 6 km. between Raxaul and Birgunj are used for goods traffic; Man. DEVENDRA SINGH, K.C.

Provision has been made in the sixth Five-Year Plan (1980–1985) for the construction of a railway line between Udaipur Garhi in eastern Nepal and Calcutta, India.

ROADS

There are over 4,600 kilometres of roads, of which about 1,900 are metalled. Around Kathmandu there are short sections of motorable roads and there is a 28 km. ring road round the valley. A mountain road, Tribhuwana Rajpath, links the capital with the Indian railhead at Raxaul. The Siddhartha Highway, constructed with Indian assistance, connects the Pokhara Valley in mid-west Nepal with Sonauli on the Indian border in Uttar Pradesh. A British-built section of 40 km. links Butwal with Batghat. Mahendra Highway will have a total length of 922 km. Construction of the 400 km. Pokhara-Surkhet road began in 1974, with Chinese help, and this will eventually be linked to the 149 km. all-weather highway which stretches from Dhangadhi to Dedelhura in the west. The 65 km. Dharan–Dhankuta road is being constructed with British help.

A fleet of container trucks operates between Calcutta and Raxaul and other points in Nepal for transporting exports to, and imports from, third countries. Trolley buses provide a passenger service over the 13 km. between Kathmandu and Bhaktapur.

ROPEWAY

A 42-kilometre ropeway links Hetauda and Kathmandu and can carry 25 tons of freight per hour throughout the year. Food grains, construction goods and heavy goods on this route are transported by this ropeway.

SHIPPING

Royal Nepal Shipping Corpn.: Kanti Path, Kathmandu; f. 1971, became operational in May 1972; Resident Dir. Brig.-Gen. R. S. RANA.

Royal Nepal Shipping Line: f. 1971, became operational in May 1972; Man. Dir. Dr. J. JHA.

CIVIL AVIATION

Royal Nepal Airlines Corporation: RNAC Bldg., Kanti Path, Kathmandu; f. 1958; scheduled services and charters to 36 domestic stations and international flights to India, Sri Lanka and Thailand; fleet of 2 Boeing 727, 3 Avro HS-748, 8 Twin Otters, 3 Pilatus Porters; Chair. G. N. RIMAL.

FOREIGN AIRLINES

The following foreign airlines operate services to Nepal: Bangladesh Biman, BAC (Burma), Indian Airlines, Thai International.

TOURISM

Department of Tourism: His Majesty's Government of Nepal, Kathmandu; Dir.-Gen. Dr. SASHI NARAYAN SHAH.

DEFENCE

Armed Forces (July 1981): 25,000 army; there is no air force; the Army Flight Department operates the aircraft; military service is voluntary.

Defence Expenditure (1981/82 estimate): NRs 471.7 million.

Chief of Staff: Gen. SINGHA PRATAP SHAH.

EDUCATION

After the overthrow of the Ranas in 1951 there was a rapid expansion of teaching facilities in Nepal. Some 8,000 pupils attended the country's 321 primary schools in 1950; in 1979/80 1,068,000 children had primary school places. The number of secondary schools rose from two in 1950 to 2,952 in 1977, when there were 308,797 pupils at this level.

The Ministry of Education supervises the finance, administration, staffing and inspection of government schools, and makes inspection of private schools receiving government subsidies. In other respects, private schools are autonomous. The National Educational Planning Commission recommends educational curricula, and in some cases these have been adopted by the private schools.

Both primary and secondary education is provided by English schools set up during the period of British influence in the nineteenth century. There has been a rapid expansion of government schools since 1951, especially at lower secondary level where the number of schools rose from 1,062 in 1973 to 2,400 in 1977. In 1975 the Government began to provide free primary education for five years and use Nepali as the medium of instruction. Vernacular schools give secular education to villagers in local dialects, while, in addition to Buddhist and Hindu religious establishments, there are a number of Basic schools, on the pattern set in India, which concentrate on handicrafts and agriculture.

The oldest of the colleges of higher education in Nepal is Tri Chandra School in Kathmandu, set up in 1918, which gives four-year arts courses. The only other advanced college set up before the 1951 revolution was the Sanskrit College in Kathmandu, founded in 1948. A single College of Education was established in 1956 for the training of secondary school teachers and other educational personnel. There are also five Primary Teacher Training Centres at Birgunj, Kathmandu, Pokhara, Dharan and Palpa, which organize various kinds of in-service training courses.

BIBLIOGRAPHY

BARAL, L. S. Political Development of Nepal (C. Hurst, London, 1980).

BHOOSHAN, B. S. The Development Experience of Nepal (Concept Publishing, Delhi, 1979).

CAPLAN, L. Land and Social Change in East Nepal (Routledge & Kegan Paul, London, 1970).

GAIGE, FREDERICK H. Regionalism and National Unity in Nepal (University of California Press, Berkeley, 1975).

GORDON, EUGENE. Nepal, Sikkim and Bhutan (Oak Tree Press, London, 1972).

HAGEN, TONI, WAHLEN, F. T., and CORTI, W. R. Nepal: The Kingdom in the Himalayas (Kummerly and Frey, Berne, 1961).

HAIMENDORF, C. VON F. Himalayan Traders (Murray, London, 1975).

HAMILTON, F. An Account of the Kingdom of Nepal (Constable, Edinburgh, 1819).

JAIN, GIRILAL. India Meets China in Nepal (Asia Publishing House, New York, 1959).

KARAN, P. P. Nepal: A Cultural and Physical Geography (University of Kentucky Press, 1960).

KARAN, P. P., and JENKINS, W. M. The Himalayan Kingdoms: Bhutan, Sikkim and Nepal (Van Nostrand, Princeton, 1963).

KUMAR, SATISH. Rana Polity in Nepal: Origin and Growth (Asia Publishing House for the Indian School of International Studies, 1968).

LANDON, PERCIVAL. Nepal (Constable, London, 1928).

MACFARLANE, A. Resources and Population: A Study of the Gurungs of Nepal (Cambridge University Press, Cambridge, 1976).

MIHALY, EUGENE B. Foreign Aid and Politics in Nepal (Oxford University Press for Royal Institute of International Affairs, London, 1965).

MORRIS, JOHN. A Winter in Nepal (Hart-Davis, London, 1963).

PANT, Y. P. Development of Nepal (Kitab Mahal, Allahabad, 1968).

PETECH, LUCIANO. Medieval History of Nepal (Istituto Italiano per il Medio ed Estremo Oriente, 1958).

RAMAKANT. Nepal, China and India (Abhinar, Delhi, 1976).

REGMI, D. R. Ancient Nepal (Mukhopadhyay, Calcutta, 1960).

Modern Nepal: Rise and Growth in the Eighteenth Century (Mukhopadhyay, Calcutta, 1961).

ROSE, LEO E. Nepal: Strategy for Survival (California University Press, 1971).

SEDDON, D. (ed.) Peasants and Workers in Nepal (Avis and Phillips, Warminster, 1979).

SHAHA, RISHIKESH. Nepali Politics: Retrospect and Prospect (Oxford University Press, 1977).

SITWELL, SACHEVERELL. Great Temples of the East (Oblensky, New York, 1962).

SNELLGROVE, D. Himalayan Pilgrimage (Bruno Cassirer, Oxford, 1961).

TUCKER, FRANCIS. Gorkha: The Story of the Ghurkas of Nepal (Constable, London, 1957).

WHEELER, J. T. A Short History of the Frontier States of Afghanistan, Nepal and Burma (Colliers, New York, 1894).

WOODMAN, DOROTHY. Himalayan Frontiers: a political review of British, Chinese, Indian and Russian rivalries (Barrie and Jenkins, London, 1969).

WRIGHT, DANIEL. (ed.) History of Nepal (Cambridge University Press, 1877).

New Zealand

PHYSICAL AND SOCIAL GEOGRAPHY

A. E. McQueen

New Zealand lies 1,600 kilometres (1,000 miles) south-east of Australia. It consists of two main islands, North Island with an area of 114,500 square kilometres (44,200 square miles) and South Island with an area of 150,700 square kilometres (58,170 square miles), plus Stewart Island to the south, with an area of 1,750 square kilometres (625 square miles), and some smaller islands. North and South Islands are separated by Cook Strait, which is about 30 kilometres (20 miles) wide at the narrowest point. The total area of New Zealand is 269,057 square kilometres (103,883 square miles).

CLIMATE

There are three major factors affecting the climate of New Zealand, particularly so far as pasture growth is concerned.

The first is the country's situation in the westerly wind belt which encircles the globe. The main islands lie between 34° S. and 47° S., and are therefore within the zone of the eastward moving depressions and anti-cyclones within this belt. The second factor is the country's location in the midst of a vast ocean mass, which means that extremes of temperature are modified by air masses passing across a large expanse of ocean. It also means that abundant moisture is available by evaporation from the ocean, and rainfall is considerable and fairly evenly distributed throughout the year. The mean annual rainfall varies from 33 cm. (13 in.) east of the Southern Alps to ver. 762 cm. (300 in.) west of the Alps, but the averago for the whole country lies between 63.5 and 152.5 ecm (25 and 60 in.).

The third factor is more of local significance: the presence of a chain of mountains extending from south-west to north-east through most of the country. The mountains provide a barrier to the westward moving air masses, and produce a quite sharp climatic contrast between east and west. The rain shadow effect of the mountains produces in certain inland areas of the South Island an almost continental climate, although no part of New Zealand is more than 130 km. (80 miles) from the sea.

Because of this generally "maritime" influence the temperature range is fairly small; the annual range of mean monthly temperatures in western districts of both islands is about 8°C. (15°F.), elsewhere from 9°C. (17°F.) to 11°C. (20°F.) except in inland areas of the South Island where it may be as high as 14°C. (25°F.). The mean temperatures for the year vary from 15°C. (59°F.) in the far north to 12°C. (54°F.) about Cook Strait and 9°C. (49°F.) in the south. With increasing altitude, mean annual temperatures fall about 1°C. per 180 metres.

Snow is rare below 615 metres (2,000 ft.) in the North Island, and falls for only a few days a year at lower altitudes in the South Island. Rainfall and temperature combine to give a climate in which it is possible to graze livestock for all the year at lower altitudes in all parts of the country, and at higher altitudes, even in the South Island, for a considerable part of each year. Pasture growth varies according to temperature and season, but varies from almost continual growth in North Auckland to between 8 and 10 months in the South Island.

PHYSICAL FEATURES

Altitude and surface configuration are important features affecting the amount of land which is readily available for farming. Less than one-quarter of the land surface lies below 200 metres (650 ft.); in the North Island the higher mountains, those above 1,250 metres (4,000 ft.), occupy about 10 per cent of the surface, but in the South Island the proportion is much greater. The Southern Alps, a massive chain including 16 peaks over 3,100 metres (10,000 ft.), run for almost the entire length of the island. The economic effect of the Southern Alps as a communications barrier has been considerably more than in the case of the North Island mountains; their rain-shadow effect is also significant for land use, as the lower rainfall, while giving a reduced growth rate, also produces the dry summers of the east coast plains which are major grain-growing areas. In addition, the wide expanses of elevated open country of lower rainfall have led to the development of large-scale pastoral holdings, and it is the South Island high country which produces almost all New Zealand's fine wools, particularly from the Merino sheep.

Other natural phenomena with economic significance include rivers, lakes and earthquakes. Most New Zealand rivers are of little use for navigation but they are of vital importance for hydroelectric power production, with their high rate of flow and reliable volume of ice-free water. Many of the larger lakes of both islands, most of which are situated at quite high altitudes, are also important in power production, acting as reservoirs for the rivers upon which the major stations are situated. Earthquakes are a particular risk along a zone west of the Southern Alps, through Wellington and thence north-east to Napier and Wairoa. Their economic significance lies in the extra strengthening which must be incorporated into buildings, particularly larger commercial structures, and the risk to main communication lines. The degree of earthquake activity in New Zealand is often regarded as roughly similar to that in California, but very much less intense than in Japan or Chile.

NATURAL RESOURCES

In general geological terms, New Zealand is part of the unstable circum-Pacific Mobile Belt, a region where, in parts, volcanoes are active and where the earth's crust has been moving at a geologically rapid rate. Such earth movements, coupled with rapid erosion, have formed the sedimentary rocks which make up about three-quarters of the country. New Zealand also includes in its very complex geology schist, gneiss, and other metamorphic rocks, most of which are hundreds of millions of years old, as well as a number of igneous rocks. In such a geologically mobile country the constant exposure of new rock has led to young and generally fertile soils.

Within this broad pattern a variety of minerals has been found, many of them, however, in only very small deposits. Non-metallic minerals, such as coal, clay, limestone and dolomite are today both economically and industrially more important than metallic ores; but new demands from industry, and a realization that apparently small showings of more valuable minerals may well indicate much larger deposits, have led to a surge of prospecting since the early 1960s. One of the most successful results so far has been the proving of iron sand deposits on the west coast of the North Island. This development, along with the discovery of a satisfactory method of processing the sands, has paved the way to the founding of an iron and steel industry which began production in 1969. But knowledge of New Zealand's economic geology is still far from complete; in many respects the concentration upon farming had led the nation to believe that there were no economically attractive mineral resources, and the exploration and prospecting at present being carried out by both local and overseas firms is only now testing the assumption that the nation's only worthwhile natural resource is its climate and soil. A particularly notable discovery in 1970 was a large natural gas field, off the South Taranaki coast. Further drilling is now taking place in the same area and pipelines to bring the gas to major centres have been constructed. Approval has recently been given to start building major plants to convert this gas into synthetic petrol and methanol.

When the first European settlers came to New Zealand they found two-thirds of the land's surface covered by forest. Today only about one-fifth of that forest remains, most of it kept as reserve or as national parks. The rest has been felled, much of it with little regard for land conservation principles. Out of today's total forested area of over 7 million hectares, about 6 million are still in indigenous forest, much of it unmillable protection forest; it is towards the 800,000 hectares of man-made exotic forest that New Zealand now looks as the major source of building timber and raw material for rapidly developing pulp and paper and other forest product industries. These activities are based largely on the extensive exotic forests of the Bay of Plenty—Taupo region, near the centre of the North Island, but extensive planting has taken place in other regions for eventual use in newly-developed processing plants. New paper producing plants are being considered for Nelson, North Auckland and Otago.

POPULATION

At the last census, in March 1981, New Zealand's population was 3,175,737, an increase of only 1.5 per cent since the previous census in 1976. By March 1982 the population was 3,190,100. About 80 per cent of the population live in cities, boroughs or townships with populations greater than 1,000. In terms of international comparison, the population is small, density (11.9 per sq. km. in 1982) is low, the growth rate is currently negligible or even negative, and the degree of urbanization is high.

The majority of the population is of European origin; in December 1980 there were 290,100 indigenous Maoris.

Between 1926 and 1945 an average annual increase in population of 1.1 per cent was recorded, one of the lowest rates in the country's history. Between 1945 and 1970, however, the rate of population growth was maintained at a high level—a trend supported by both a high level of natural increase and immigration. A high post-war birth rate, which reached a peak of 26.99 per thousand in 1961 but which has since fallen steadily to 15.11 per thousand in 1981, contrasts with an average death rate of 8.2 per thousand in the mid-1970s, one of the lowest in the world. This high rate of increase was complemented by a steady influx of immigrants, some of them assisted to New Zealand by the Government. The total number of immigrants increased annually until 1952/53, since when there have been large variations in the immigration rate. Although the net increase for 1973/74 was 27,000, that for 1975/76 was only 5,000. In 1977/78 there was a net migration loss of nearly 27,000 and in 1978/79 the net loss reached over 40,000. The loss fell to 34,400 in 1979/80 and to 24,800 in 1980/81. A major factor influencing the level of immigration is the level of economic activity; when prosperity declines, the number of government-assisted and privately sponsored immigrants falls sharply.

The processes of economic development have dictated a steadily increasing concentration of population, farm products processing, and industrial output in the major cities, especially within the North Island. Larger towns contain more of the population than other urban areas. In 1901 10 per cent of the population lived in towns of over 25,000; in 1921, 24 per cent; and in 1981, about 70 per cent of the population lived in urban areas with populations over 25,000. Conversely, the relative importance of towns with less than 5,000 people has declined steadily since 1901, and the number of people living in rural areas has steadily diminished as a proportion of the total population.

HISTORY

E. J. Tapp

COLONIZATION

In 1642 the islands of New Zealand were discovered and named by the Dutch navigator, Abel Tasman. He found and left them in possession of the Maoris, a neolithic Polynesian people who came, it is thought, from tropical Oceania several centuries before. After Tasman's visit they remained for a century and a quarter undisturbed and secure in their tribal lives until 1769 when they were rediscovered by Captain James Cook. He reported so favourably upon their lands that when a penal colony was established in New South Wales free settlers lost little time in making trading contact with them in search of timber and flax. They were soon followed by sealers and whalers who found the adjacent waters rich hunting grounds. From the consequent fugitive contacts that were made white settlement developed in the far northern district of the Bay of Islands. There the licentious and unscrupulous conduct of traders and whalers gave New Zealand a sinister reputation while traffic in firearms wrought terrible havoc among the natives in their hitherto comparatively harmless tribal warfare.

Concern for the welfare of the natives led in 1814 to the establishment of an Anglican mission in the Bay of Islands by the senior chaplain at Port Jackson (Australia), the Reverend Samuel Marsden. So precarious was its position that for years it exercised little influence. Finally, after repeated appeals from missionaries and traders the British Government in 1833 appointed a Resident for New Zealand. But so inadequate were his authority and power that "the man of war without guns", as the Maoris contemptuously called him, was quite unable to maintain law and order. In the meantime, trade and settlement increased, and in England sufficient interest was aroused to cause Edward Gibbon Wakefield, the systematic colonizer, to establish the New Zealand Company for planned settlement in the islands. Its dispatch of settlers, fear of the French and repeated representation from missionaries and merchants, finally forced the British Government to abandon its policy of minimum intervention and to empower Captain James Hobson to take possession of New Zealand as Lieutenant-Governor under the Government of New South Wales. Accordingly, in 1840 Hobson landed in the Bay of Islands and concluded the Treaty of Waitangi with Maori chiefs. By this treaty the natives were confirmed in their right to their lands, of which in return for the Queen's protection they gave her the exclusive right of purchase. By such prompt action Hobson checked unbridled land speculation and restricted a French colonizing venture to settlement at Akaroa, in the South Island, under the British flag. After a brief foster-father connection with New South Wales, New Zealand in 1842 became a separate colony with Hobson its first Governor.

Meanwhile, undue haste by New Zealand Company settlers to lay claim to a valley in the north of the South Island led to a disastrous clash with its native inhabitants. At the same time Maoris in the far north, fearing for their lands and their way of life, openly rebelled against the *pakeha* (European). Until Captain George Grey arrived as Governor attempts at suppression were abortive. But by vigorous attack and with a promise to uphold the Treaty of Waitangi, he not only ended the war but won the esteem of the Maoris.

Elsewhere, largely through the activities of the New Zealand Company, colonization went on apace. Several hundred West of England farmers landed in Taranaki to found the settlement of New Plymouth. In the South Island, where there were but few Maoris, a Scottish Free Church colony was established in 1848, and two years later a Church of England settlement was made on the Canterbury Plains. Assuming that such colonists would expect this, the British Government in 1846 passed an Act conferring representative institutions on New Zealand. But, thinking the Act premature, the autocratic Governor Grey delayed until 1852 the introduction of self-government, which provided for a General Assembly for the whole of New Zealand and for six Provincial Councils. Four years later the colony secured responsible government, but for twenty years it was in most matters controlled by the Provincial Councils.

THE YEARS 1850-1918

During the first two decades of the period the North Island was troubled by war with the Maoris. In 1860 European ignorance of the nature of the tribal ownership of land provoked bitter fighting in Taranaki which spread over much of the island. Under astute leadership the Maoris drew together to present a united front to *pakeha* encroachment. In spite of its pacific overtures the Government was for suppressing the Maoris, and even the return of Grey for a second term of office failed to restore peace. At every turn the natives harassed soldier and settler alike until by about 1870, their resources at an end, organized resistance gradually ceased.

In the South Island, meanwhile, the English and Scottish settlements, untroubled by war, made rapid progress. The discovery of gold in 1861 in Otago and on the West Coast in 1865 greatly quickened the pace of development. More important in the long run was the impact made by tens of thousands of gold diggers from Australia and North America. Politically their influence was of particular significance, for, free of regional attachments, they encouraged a national rather than a narrow provincial outlook. This tendency was assisted by better communications, inter-island steamship service and the telegraph. By 1870 the prosperity of the South and the pacification of the North Island made a bold policy of economic expansion uniquely opportune. With supreme confidence and foresight Julius Vogel, the Colonial Treasurer (who was to become Premier in 1872-75) borrowed from London nearly £20 million during the next ten years for an extensive scheme of public works. An unwitting pioneer of the social welfare state, Vogel established the Government Life Insurance and the Public Trust organization. In the 1860s and 1870s, independently of the Government, the Bank of New Zealand and several large mercantile companies had already been established.

In the wake of capital came about 100,000 migrants to build roads and railways and to open up the country, especially the Canterbury plains for wheat. Pioneering in the backblocks entailed much privation and hardship, but determined settlers were soon pasturing sheep and laying the foundations of much of New Zealand's future prosperity. In all this development Vogel and the entrepreneurs were favoured by high prices for their exports. Moreover, so disruptive of parochial loyalties were the economic advances and the centripetal forces set up so weakened the Provincial Councils that in 1876 Vogel abolished them.

By 1878 the Vogel boom was over, the spending spree ended. Instead, the high cost of public works and falling export prices combined to bring New Zealand to the brink of disaster. Only a policy of stringent economy tided the colony through the long depression of the 1880s. Of a population that had grown to half a million, thousands left to enjoy the prosperous conditions in Australia. Recovery came slowly, but with more settled conditions in the North Island primary production increased steadily. To this revival nothing gave such a fillip as did the commercial application in 1882 of refrigeration, an invention which not only helped to rescue the colony from its financial predicament but which shaped the whole pattern of New Zealand's future development.

In politics hard times had fostered radicalism and ousted the Conservatives from office in favour of the Liberals with their concern for the artisan and small farmer. This tendency was strengthened by the failure of the great Australasian maritime strike of 1890 and the subsequent recourse of labour to the ballot box for reform. With its support the Liberal Government not only stepped in to save the Bank of New Zealand from collapse but embarked upon an era of unprecedented social activity. Strongly influenced by the Fabian socialism of William Pember Reeves, the Premier, R. J. ("Dick") Seddon, a rugged pragmatist, introduced such far-reaching reforms as to make the New Zealand worker the best protected in the world. Within a few years Seddon carried through legislation which provided for better factory conditions, accident compensation, shorter working hours and payment for overtime, compulsory conciliation and arbitration in industrial disputes, and finally, in 1898, old age pensions. In addition land hunger was appeased by legislation which made possible subdivision of large holdings and which imposed a graduated tax on unimproved land values. Such empirical humanitarianism earned for New Zealand a reputation as an advanced social laboratory. By the end of the century it had in fact so outdistanced the Australian colonies in social legislation as to make it little disposed to accept the invitation to join the Commonwealth of Australia. With urban development fostering secondary industries to supplement the main agricultural and pastoral activities of the people, including the Maoris, whose self-confidence was rapidly being restored, few saw any merit in union with Australia.

Foreign Affairs

So absorbed had it become with its own domestic problems that New Zealand had taken little interest in external affairs. For a few brief years it had, under the audacious imperialism of Vogel, espoused a policy of "Oceania for the Anglo-Saxons", but with little encouragement from the United Kingdom, enthusiasm for it died. From the very beginning it had with unquestioning loyalty placed implicit trust in the Mother Country for protection. After 1887 it contributed regularly towards the British navy and sent a volunteer contingent to the South African War. At the outbreak of the First World War it gave Britain immediate and generous support. At home the war made little difference to the life of the average New Zealander. The Labour Party opposed the introduction of conscription for military service. High prices for primary exports and the stimulus that the war gave to their production greatly strengthened the economy.

Generally the war quickened New Zealand's maturity in more ways than one. Separate representation at the Peace Conference and independent membership of the League of Nations enhanced its international prestige. From the spoils of war it gained the mandate over ex-German Western Samoa and shared with Australia and the United Kingdom the mandate for the phosphate island of Nauru. For all that, it took little interest in imperial or foreign affairs and preferred to remain as close as possible to the United Kingdom.

THE INTER-WAR PERIOD

After the war, under conditions of general prosperity and full employment, New Zealand resumed a selective assisted migration policy which increased the population by nearly 70,000 by 1928 when the intake temporarily ceased. As trade conditions hardened the Government intervened more and more to control the nation's economy. It offered expert advice and financial assistance to step up production. The many dairy farmers who had banded together to establish co-operative butter and cheese factories were content to let the Government organize the marketing of their produce overseas. Increasingly too did the public turn to the Government for aid when in 1928 the first signs of depression appeared. To meet the growing unemployment and unfavourable balance of trade the leader of the United Party, Sir Joseph Ward, proposed to borrow £70 million with which to prime the economy. But, although elected to office, the party was unable to cope with a deteriorating situation. Far from raising tens of millions, the Government was put to the less spectacular tasks of setting up relief works and of rationalizing the rail and road transport system to effect economies. A coalition Government of United and Reform Parties proceeded on orthodox lines to reduce expenditure on defence and to halt railway construction. Faced with a mounting army of unemployed, the Government imposed emergency taxes of a direct and indirect nature and also reduced salaries and wages of public servants. It also declared a moratorium on war debts and converted many of its bonds at lower rates of interest. Along with the other Dominions New Zealand committed itself to the Ottawa Agreement of 1932 in its search for economic recovery, and for the benefit of the primary producer depreciated the New Zealand pound by 25 per cent.

But in spite of all these palliatives the depression grew worse instead of better. Trade had so contracted that in 1931 income from exports fell by 40 per cent. Confidence in the Government was badly shaken, for by 1935 the number of unemployed had risen to 70,000. Disorder and rioting broke out in the major cities, and labour unrest was rife throughout the country. The working classes and small farmers complained that the Government failed to consider welfare as against wealth. In 1935 small farmers combined with the working classes to return the Labour Party to power with a substantial majority.

It was a radical political change which only desperate conditions could have provoked. Nevertheless, with the increase in urban development, the Labour Party had steadily gained in strength until it had become the official parliamentary opposition. Extremist elements, which had made an unsuccessful bid for party leadership, had mellowed with the years to play a prominent part in the Labour Government. Imbued with much of the idealism of the old Liberal Party, the Government was now eager to take over where Seddon had left off. Under its leader, Michael Savage, prices of essential commodities were fixed. The dairy farmer was given a guaranteed price for his butter and cheese which were marketed by the Government both at home and abroad. The scourge of unemployment was tackled by the introduction of large-scale public works such as road and railway construction. The State offered the right to work at a fixed basic wage and made trade union membership compulsory. Salary and wage cuts were restored and a forty-hour week was introduced to increase the demand for labour. To cope with the acute housing shortage the Government set up a special department to undertake a most ambitious and exemplary building programme. These various and extensive undertakings were financed by means of increased taxation and public loans. In 1936 the Government bought out the private shareholders of the Reserve Bank, which had been set up two years previously, and thus secured control over currency and exchange rates.

Out of the privately controlled National Mortgage Corporation it built up the State Advances Corporation, but otherwise it interfered little with secondary industry. Partly because of the vigorous and successful government attacks on the evils of the depression, and partly because of the general improvement in trading conditions in all countries, at the end of three years Colin Clark, the eminent economist, could point to New Zealand farmers as the "best off" in the world; and he further declared that "no other country has made such a bold departure from the old fashioned fatalistic outlook towards depression or taken such positive steps to promote and maintain employment and income".

It was no undeserved tribute; and, when in 1937 the Labour Government went to the country seeking a mandate for advanced social legislation, a grateful public granted it willingly. The Government then began to build upon the social legislation of the 1890s to complete the welfare state. In 1938 a Social Security Act provided for free general practitioner services, medicine, hospital treatment and maternity benefits, and for family allowances and increased old age pensions. To finance such comprehensive insurance a special tax was levied on all incomes and supplemented by grants from ordinary revenue. Fortunately, these were years of prosperity with high prices for exports. But although its economic recovery was real enough, New Zealand was so prodigal of its funds that by 1939 they had become so depleted by heavy withdrawals to meet overseas commitments and by the flight of private capital that to stave off a crisis the Government restricted imports and controlled the export of capital.

THE PERIOD SINCE 1939

Such attempts to insulate New Zealand against forces inimical to the welfare state were aided by the advent of the Second World War, which intensified the demand and raised prices for exportable products. The war itself was accepted with fatalistic fortitude by a people who had become progressively disillusioned by the failure of the League of Nations to keep the peace. With a sober appraisal of New Zealand's position in the Pacific its Government had invited Australia and the United Kingdom to a defence conference before hostilities began. The Mother Country's declaration of war in 1939 was felt to be as binding on New Zealand as it had been in 1914. A special war cabinet was formed on the basis of a coalition of all parties. The Premier, Peter Fraser, concentrated the economic policy around the objective of stabilization, and in this he was largely successful. Conscription was introduced for overseas service, essential commodities were rationed and the country's resources were mobilized for the war effort. But the rationalizing of manpower in 1942 provoked a crisis in the coal mining industry and caused the Government to take over the mines. Incensed at what it regarded as the Government's capitulation to the coal miners, the National Party withdrew from the war cabinet. With the entry into the war of Japan the country quickly responded to meet the dire threat of imminent invasion, but even after the attack on Pearl Harbor it did not recall its troops from the Middle East. The forty-hour week was suspended and in 1943 thousands of men were released from the armed forces to increase food and factory production and thereby assist the United States in its overall Pacific campaign.

Political Developments since 1945

After the war the Government immediately tackled problems of rehabilitation and reconstruction. Although rationing of butter and meat continued for many years, most controls were soon removed. In 1945 the Labour Government, in spite of much opposition, nationalized the Bank of New Zealand, the Dominion's largest trading bank. But at the 1946 elections it lacked the vote of the small farmers and only the support of the four Maori electorates, which Labour had sedulously cultivated, enabled it to live another day and make minor additions to its social security programme. In the face of widespread industrial troubles which it was powerless to subdue, and embarrassed by a Communist splinter group, Labour at the 1949 elections lost office to the National Party under Sydney Holland.

Astute enough to realize that no government dare tamper with the social security legislation, the Prime Minister contented himself with removing artificial brakes on prices and imports. With the full approval of the Labour opposition the Government abolished the Legislative Council, which as a council of review had gradually declined in importance. It returned the coal mines to private ownership and withdrew subsidies on certain commodities. But attempts to peg prices failed to prevent inflation. In the consequent social unrest extremists refused to abide by the principle of compulsory arbitration, and the Government brought in troops to break a prolonged waterfront strike. Public feeling ran high over the Prime Minister's handling of the crisis, but at a surprise election in 1951 he secured an unequivocal endorsement of his policy.

So little now separated the two major parties that public interest in politics declined. At the 1954 general elections the Labour Party was unable to defeat the National Party with its more liberal policy towards private enterprise. Growing dissatisfaction with both parties was evident in the surprising support (11 per cent of the votes cast) given to the newly formed Social Credit Party. In 1955 import controls were relaxed only to be replaced a year later by credit restrictions to limit spending. At the general elections in 1957 the Labour Party, by outbidding its opponents on income tax rebates and larger security payments, gained a narrow victory under its veteran leader, Walter Nash.

Almost immediately the Labour Government was embarrassed by pressing economic problems. Falling prices for meat and dairy produce led to an adverse balance of trade and an alarming depletion of the country's overseas reserves. To avert a crisis and to stave off unemployment the Government re-imposed import licensing and exchange control and raised over £30 million in London and Australia and another £20 million internally. Although these measures arrested the decline, the Government's "black budget" of 1958, a further attempt to restore economic balance, sealed the fate of Labour and at the elections in 1960 the National Party under Mr. (later Sir) Keith Holyoake regained the Treasury benches. Among the more important changes that followed was the appointment in 1962 of a Parliamentary Commissioner (Ombudsman) to enquire into public complaints arising from administrative decisions of the Government. Relatively stable economic conditions enabled the National Party to be returned to power in 1966. At the next General Election in 1969 Keith Holyoake, although managing to retain office, lost ground to Labour. Neither the paternalism and sober conservatism of John Marshall, who succeeded Sir Keith Holyoake when he stepped down from office in February 1972 after twelve years as Prime Minister, nor the advent of a new Values Party prevented a major swing in November 1972, when Labour swept into office under Norman Kirk. His vigorous and forthright leadership, especially in the field of foreign policy, was, however, cut short in August 1974 by his untimely death. His successor, Wallace (Bill) Rowling, who found himself opposed by a new leader of the National Party, Robert Muldoon, in place of the deposed Mr. (later Sir) John Marshall, continued his predecessor's policy but less forcefully.

Playing on fears of national disaster consequent on Labour's heavy overseas borrowing policy with its inflationary effects, the opposition leader, Robert Muldoon, campaigned on the promise of a more attractive and egalitarian superannuation policy than that offered by the Government. The much rejuvenated National Party roundly defeated the less well organized and positive Labour Government at the general elections of November 1975. In an almost unprecedented, surprising and disastrous swing against it, Labour lost 23 seats, including those of 5 Cabinet members.

The National Government, under Robert Muldoon, immediately undid much of the previous government's legislation. It replaced the Labour superannuation policy with a more liberal scheme and simplified a newly erected broadcasting structure by setting up a single Broadcasting Council to cover television and radio. Not only was the new Government unable to combat inflation due to overseas economic pressures, but its failure to fulfil election promises and the abrasive style of leadership of the Prime Minister resulted in loss of credibility with the general public.

Meanwhile, humiliated, disorganized and later embarrassed by the alleged misconduct of two of its senior members, the Labour Party was slow to recover its equilibrium. Confidence was partly restored by success at two by-elections and at the 1978 Labour Party Conference, when the Federation of Labour closed ranks with the Parliamentary Labour Party under Bill Rowling, whose leadership was heartily endorsed. However, in the November 1978 general elections the National Party was returned to power in a Parliament enlarged by five extra seats to 92, but its majority was reduced to 11, owing largely to the unpopularity of the Prime Minister, Robert Muldoon. The Labour Party, on the other hand, won 41 seats and the greatest number of votes, while the Social Credit

Party, with 16 per cent of the votes, secured only one seat, that of its leader, Bruce Beetham. With no firm basis of appeal, the Values Party fared poorly. To stabilize the parliamentary representation of the South Island, which has been losing population relative to the North Island for many years, its number of seats has been fixed at 25. Yet even this did not prevent a movement in the South Island calling for some measure of self-government in 1979. All this, however, had been forgotten with the growing popularity of the Social Credit Party and its surprising gain of a previously safe National seat at a by-election in 1980. In a hard-fought campaign in November 1981, the National Party, under Robert Muldoon, narrowly retained office with a bare working majority of two seats, but with fewer votes than the Labour Party. The Social Credit League again polled remarkably well at the expense of both National and Labour, taking 20 per cent of the votes, but gained only two seats.

International Relations

In world affairs New Zealand has become very conscious of its position as a Pacific Power. Apart from its activities as a member of the Commonwealth, its first major step in independent policy was made in 1944 with the signing of the Canberra Pact, a mutual security agreement with Australia. In 1974 New Zealand finally adopted the Statute of Westminster, which gave it complete autonomy and freedom of action in international affairs. As a strong supporter of the UN, in 1950 it sent troops to join the UN Command in Korea. Although not without misgivings at the exclusion of the United Kingdom, in 1952 it joined Australia and the United States in the ANZUS defence treaty, and two years later became a member of the South East Asia Treaty Organization (SEATO). To give effect to its treaty commitments, New Zealand sent a military unit to Malaya in 1955 and combined with Australia in an ANZAC unit in Viet-Nam. Along with Australia, it also sent troops to Singapore and Malaysia to combine with remaining British forces in safeguarding the political *status quo* of the region.

New Zealand has played an increasingly important role in the Pacific since it joined the South Pacific Commission as a founder member in 1947. It administered the UN Trust Territory of Western Samoa until 1962, when those islands became independent, and in 1965 it assisted the Cook Islands towards self-government in free association with New Zealand. When Fiji became independent in 1970, New Zealand helped to establish the University of the South Pacific in Suva.

With widened and new horizons, New Zealand no longer looked so much to Britain for a lead in foreign policy. In 1971 it joined the five-power (Australia, Malaysia, New Zealand, Singapore and the United Kingdom) arrangements for the external defence of Malaysia and Singapore which replaced the Anglo-Malaysian Defence Agreement, and also that year joined the South Pacific Forum, established to promote economic and political co-operation in the region. When the Labour Party took office in 1972, New Zealand began to assert an even greater measure of independence, especially in Asia where, with a critical interest in the maintenance of peace and prosperity, it established stronger diplomatic links. Since the Second World War, relations with Japan and the Republic of Korea have been especially close, mainly for economic reasons, and recently, since the normalization of relations in 1972, New Zealand's contacts with the People's Republic of China have been increasing. However, while retaining the ANZUS treaty as its chief platform of defence, New Zealand has begun to phase out its military commitments under SEATO, to concentrate more on non-military objectives for, as the Prime Minister aptly said, "Trade is our foreign policy". New Zealand has therefore sought access to the European Economic Community and has become a member of the Organisation for Economic Co-operation and Development. With Eastern Europe, too, its contacts have grown, especially with the U.S.S.R., where it established an embassy in 1973. New Zealand had little contact with Middle Eastern countries until they became its chief source of petroleum and it established resident missions in Iran and Iraq in 1972 and in Bahrain in 1977. In deference to President Carter's call for assistance in the crisis created by the Iranians' seizure of American hostages at the U.S. embassy in Teheran in 1979, it has curtailed relations with Iran to a politic minimum. As part of the general protest against the Soviet intervention in Afghanistan, New Zealand severed diplomatic relations with the U.S.S.R. In the Middle East it contributed towards an international peace-keeping force in Sinai. In 1982, with even greater alacrity, Prime Minister Muldoon promised aid to the United Kingdom in its efforts to recapture the Falkland Islands after their illegal seizure by Argentina: a frigate was provided to release a British vessel from peace-time duties in the Indian Ocean and a boycott was placed on Argentine goods.

Although it has no diplomatic representation in the continent of Africa, New Zealand supported Britain in 1967 in applying sanctions against Rhodesia's unilateral declaration of independence and later, in 1980, it sent a contingent of troops to help police the elections leading to the declaration of an independent Zimbabwe. Meanwhile, with so much in common with Australia, social and demographic contacts have continued to grow, thus reinforcing efforts for closer economic relations. In addition, diplomatic representation was at long last established in a virtually unknown South America, with Chile in 1972 and Peru in 1974. A trade boycott imposed on Chile by the labour unions after the fall of the Allende Government in 1973 was expected to be lifted in late 1982. Even with a low profile in international affairs, New Zealand budgeted for $NZ 550 million in defence expenditure in 1981/82, with a further $NZ 38 million for bilateral aid to Oceania and south-east Asia.

Domestic Affairs

In its response to the needs of the barely viable economies of the South Pacific islands, New Zealand has, since 1962, admitted over 170,000 of their inhabitants, mainly from the Cook Islands, Tonga and Fiji. Of that number, over 55,000 have settled permanently, for the most part in Auckland, where job opportunities are more readily available. Unfortunately, lack of education and preparation for a new and more sophisticated environment has led to social problems and a more restricted island immigration policy. In addition to Polynesians, about 1,600 refugees from Viet-Nam and Kampuchea have been allowed to settle in New Zealand since 1977. The native Maori people, while continuing to intermarry freely with the *pakeha* (whites) and becoming an integral part of the work force and of society generally, have begun to show signs of unrest and disaffection at what many regard as the failure of the Government to honour the Treaty of Waitangi of 1840 in respect of their land. Such discontent, manifest in protest movements, has been greatly accentuated by the drift of Maoris to the cities, especially in the North Island, where they have become alienated from their tribes and native way of life and, more than the *pakeha*, have become victims of unemployment and have fallen too often into crime and gang violence. Among the most recent signs of Maori unrest have been vigorous protest over alleged infringement of their land rights on Bastion Point in Auckland and more recently the resignation of a former Government minister from the Labour Party to form a separate political Maori Party.

Other social and political issues have also divided New Zealanders. Although they are a people much given to outdoor sports, with rugby union the most popular game and almost a secular religion, there has been much controversy over the question of allowing the national team (the "All Blacks") to play against the "Springboks" from South Africa. In 1973 the Labour Prime Minister, Norman Kirk, refused the Springboks entry and since then New Zealand has approved the Gleneagles Agreement of 1977 which committed Commonwealth countries to the boycott of sporting contacts with South Africa because of its apartheid policy. However, in the face of considerable and widespread protest, the Government refused to prevent the Springboks from making a rugby tour of New Zealand in September 1981. In consequence, African members caused the Commonwealth meeting of Finance Ministers to be transferred in 1981 from Auckland to Trinidad, and New Zealand only narrowly averted a boycott by African countries of the 1982 Commonwealth Games in Brisbane, Australia. Earlier, almost all New Zealand athletes had boycotted the 1980 Olympic Games in Moscow in protest against the U.S.S.R.'s intervention in Afghanistan.

Of even greater public concern have been two major health issues. In the face of sectional protests, the Government passed a Contraception, Sterilization and Abortion Bill, mainly to prevent abortion on demand, and this has had the effect of driving hundreds of young women to New South Wales, where there are few restrictions on abortion. Of more general public concern has been the rising consumption of alcohol and the related increase in road deaths.

The recent stagnant and depressed state of the economy has, however, generally been responsible for the most worrying problems. Unemployment gradually increased from about 15,000 in 1971 to about 46,000 in 1982, and this in spite of the exodus of some 42,000 young and skilled workers, Maori and *pakeha* alike, mainly to Australia. In recent years widespread unrest has infected the labour movement, with its most serious outbreak in 1980 at the forest product plant at Kinleith, North Island. Although generally undisturbed in their relative prosperity, even farmers had to seek government relief from drought in 1978 in some parts of the North Island and from floods in Southland in 1979, South Otago in 1980 and North Auckland and the Hauraki Plains in 1981. There has also been much concern for some of the public institutions whose services have been reduced out of economic necessity. In particular, the long-established Karitane infant hospitals have been closed and public hospitals have been subject to financial cuts. Educational facilities have also been severely curtailed. In the media and communications there have been important changes: the national broadcasting system has been reorganized and the country's two major airlines have been amalgamated to form Air New Zealand.

Generally, however, in spite of the vicissitudes of nature and economic recession, the comfortable and relaxed life-style of most New Zealanders remains unaffected, with an increasing emphasis being put on recreational activities.

Two major problems concern the public around the shores of New Zealand. Along with Australia, New Zealand has opposed French nuclear testing at Mururoa atoll in the South Pacific, and many city dwellers have objected to the berthing of U.S. nuclear-powered ships in their ports. Both countries, in fact, have striven for a nuclear-free zone in the South Pacific. New Zealand also declared a fishing limit of 200 nautical miles (370 km.) around its coasts in 1977, allowing it to grant fishing rights within those limits to countries such as Japan, the Republic of Korea and the U.S.S.R. for trade bargaining purposes.

To exploit the scenic and recreational facilities of New Zealand's attractive countryside, the Government is assisting private enterprise to develop the tourist industry, especially the skiing grounds in the mountains of both islands. On the other hand, conservation bodies, such as the Wild Life Protection Society, are increasingly active in order to meet the threat that tourism (which brought more than 460,000 visitors in 1981) and industry are making to the native forests and their unique bird life.

ECONOMIC SURVEY

J. W. Rowe

Despite being a country of moderate affluence by international standards, New Zealand shares a number of important structural features with developing countries, notably in external dependence characteristics. Historically there has been a concentration on a relatively narrow range of farm exports whose production has been favoured by a benign climate supported by a highly scientific approach to the improvement of soil productivity and of stock breeding and management.

Exports and imports of goods and services have averaged about 25 per cent of gross domestic product (G.D.P.) in recent years. Farm products—chiefly wool, dairy produce, lamb, mutton and beef—comprise about 75 per cent of merchandise exports. Thus, agricultural exports provide the great bulk of foreign exchange upon which manufacturing industry relies for raw materials and capital equipment. The relatively great distances separating New Zealand from all other countries of any size (except Australia) add a high transport cost component to international trade operations. In recent years, rises in the costs of processing and shipping farm products have been out of proportion to market returns.

Growth of exports has, none the less, taken place despite protection applying in New Zealand's export markets, including the EEC, and the depressed state of the world economy. Exports have been diversified successfully in recent years, both as regards commodity composition (horticultural products, venison, frozen fish, timber and paper products, and casein and other dried milk products) and geographical composition (lamb to the Middle East, wool and mutton to the U.S.S.R.). New Zealand has a comparative advantage internationally in the production of high-quality pastoral products and has an established and skilled infrastructure on which to base further growth.

PRIMARY INDUSTRY

Agriculture

Farming and associated processing industries play a far greater part in the New Zealand economy than in most developed countries because of their export orientation. In 1980 there were 8.5 million cattle, including 2 million dairy cows, and 69 million sheep. Grasslands have been developed to the point where good dairy farms carry more than one cow per acre throughout the year, without winter stabling and with minimal supplementation of grass in the diet. This high carrying capacity is sustained only by intensive use of artificial fertilizers, mainly phosphates. Sheep farming is fairly evenly distributed but dairying is concentrated in the North Island, particularly in its upper half which has two-thirds of New Zealand's cows.

Sheep account for two-fifths of gross agricultural output, cattle for a sixth, dairy products a quarter and all other farm products another fifth. Domestic consumption accounts for about 40 per cent of New Zealand's output of beef and mutton, 20 per cent of butter and cheese, and 10 per cent of lamb and wool.

Cropping, fruit growing, horticulture and miscellaneous farming activities are of increasing importance. New Zealand is virtually self-sufficient in wheat, while barley, maize, peas and potatoes are other significant crops, mainly for the lôcal market. Seeds are grown in quantity mainly for export, and apple, pear and kiwifruit (Chinese gooseberry) production is also export-oriented. Tobacco cultivation has long been fostered as a means of import substitution so that New Zealand now produces half its needs. Hop production is also substantial and extensive planting of vineyards has boosted wine production.

There has been virtually no increase in the area of land used for farming since the early twentieth century. Numbers employed in farming have hardly increased for 70 years, although total population has more than trebled. The volume of agricultural exports, nevertheless, has outpaced population because of increasing investment in land improvement, farm machinery and better livestock. The continuing high level of inflation in farm input prices, which averaged 22 per cent annually in 1978–81, has reduced the cash surplus available for re-investment on farms. This is likely to slow up the increase in stock numbers and farm output. Wool production increased by 26 per cent between 1977 and 1981 but weakening demand, caused by the world-wide economic recession, resulted in a drop in real prices. Meat marketing is presenting a challenge but market outlets for dairy products are adequate.

Forestry

The forestry industry is now using about 1,000,000 cubic metres of exotic logs per year, providing direct full-time employment for over 40,000 people (3 per cent of the labour force) and contributing 9 per cent of New Zealand's export earnings. In especially favourable growing conditions, the main exotic species, Monterey pine (*Pinus radiata*), takes only 25 to 30 years to produce logs suitable for milling. Over 450,000 hectares of exotic forests were planted between 1966 and 1981, and land and capital continue to be attracted to forestry at a steady rate. Rapid acceleration of production will, therefore, begin in the 1990s, when the new plantations are expected to be capable of producing 15 million cubic metres of wood per year.

Fishing

New Zealand has a wide variety of fish in waters around her coastline, and many of these are now recognized to be commercially valuable species. An important factor in the recent growth of the fishing industry was the enactment of the Territorial Sea and Exclusive Economic Zone Act in 1978, which gave New Zealand control over the fisheries resources in approximately 1.2 million square nautical miles (4.1 million sq. km.) of sea surrounding New Zealand territory.

Joint ventures with foreign partners have contributed particularly to the development of the industry, especially in the trawl fisheries in deeper waters. The joint-venture catch expanded threefold during 1980 to a level of 120,000 metric tons. There has also been continuing expansion of the domestic finfish industry, and during the 1970s the volume of wetfish exports increased by 27 per cent on average per year.

Mining

Mining of metallic minerals is very limited except for titanomagnetic ironsands from the West Coast of the North Island, exports of which reached 3.3 million tons, with a value of $NZ 31 million, in 1980; mining for local steel production totalled nearly 200,000 tons, valued at $NZ 1.6 million.

Production of coal in 1980 totalled 2.16 million tons, valued at over $NZ 50 million. Most of this was for New Zealand's use, but 147,000 tons were exported to Japan. By 1990 coal exports of as much as 1 million tons per year may be achieved, earning over $NZ 65 million annually at current international prices. Expansionary developments up to 1986 are expected to centre on the Waikato coalfields, but significant mining could be revived in the Greymouth coal region to meet export opportunities.

Natural gas has become economically important, especially now that the on-shore supply has been supplemented by off-shore gas from the large Maui field which has an expected life of 30 years.

SECONDARY INDUSTRY

Manufacturing contributes more than 25 per cent of G.D.P. and employs about the same proportion of the labour force. In recent years output has been growing at an average annual rate of 5 to 6 per cent. Processing primary products accounts for about one-fifth of manufacturing, the remainder covering a wide range of activities, characterized by orientation towards the domestic market, reliance on imports and small-scale operations. Only about one-half of manufacturing output comes from factories employing more than 100 workers and those employing more than 500 workers account for only one-fifth. Furthermore, many of the latter are in the primary products processing sector. Prices for domestic manufactures often exceed corresponding import prices by 50 per cent, and domestic costs of production are sometimes twice those in advanced industrial countries.

Two of New Zealand's largest industrial enterprises are N.Z. Forest Products Ltd. and Fletcher Challenge Corporation. Both produce large quantities of sawn timber and chemical pulp; the former also produces kraft and other coarse papers and the latter newsprint and mechanical (groundwood) pulp. They are largely responsible for exports of timber (mainly to Japan) and pulp and paper (mainly to Australia). More recently two large ground wood mills have been established by Japanese-New Zealand consortiums, again almost entirely for export.

Another large enterprise is New Zealand Steel Ltd., which is exploiting iron sand deposits with the benefit of a secure domestic market. It plans to produce the bulk of New Zealand's steel requirements by the mid-1980s in association with Pacific Steel Ltd. An Australian-Japanese consortium operates a large aluminium smelter based on power from a state-owned hydro-electric station and using Queensland alumina. The great bulk of the resulting metal is exported to assured markets in Australia and Japan. Aluminium fabrication and semifabrication have also expanded substantially in recent years.

Between 1976 and 1981 the volume of manufactured goods, excluding food but including forestry products other than logs and pulp, increased on average by 17 per cent annually, and these goods constituted 16 per cent of export receipts in 1981. Exports of forestry products have also expanded steadily and contributed 9 per cent of export receipts in 1981.

The increasing independence of the Australian and New Zealand economies has led the governments of both countries to explore a basis for a closer economic relationship (CER). The broad outline has been accepted and, if specific issues can be settled, an agreement could become operative in 1983. The main objective of a new trans-Tasman relationship is to encourage the development of economically strong productive structures in both countries.

TERTIARY INDUSTRY

Construction

The construction industry in New Zealand has three distinct parts: dwelling construction, predominantly of timber in single units; commercial and industrial construction, notably of middle-rise office buildings; and heavy engineering associated with major development projects, many of them related to the provision of energy resources. Since the mid-1960s the industry as a whole, and especially its residential component, has been subject to marked cyclical fluctuations about a slowly falling trend, with a recent sharp fall-off in housing as a result of migration changes and a halt to population growth.

Transport

It is estimated that the transport industry provides employment for more than 9 per cent of the labour force, and that the cost of moving goods and people is over $NZ 2,000 million each year. Central government holds fixed assets valued at over $NZ 550 million in the transport services through its involvement in the Railways Corporation, the Shipping Corporation and Air New Zealand; in addition, it has a large administrative function through the operations of the National Roads Board and road transport licensing.

GROWTH AND EMPLOYMENT

Attaining the twin objectives of economic growth and full employment has been frustrated in recent years by a continuing current deficit on the balance of payments. New Zealand's imported oil bill trebled between 1973 and 1975 and rose again by almost the same proportion between 1979 and 1981 (years ending in June). Although this problem was shared by all countries, few experienced coincidentally such sharp downward fluctuations in the terms of trade as New Zealand encountered. The policy response was to reduce the level of domestic activity, particularly in 1976/77, in order to protect the balance of payments. Substantial overseas borrowing was undertaken to facilitate a gradual adjustment process, based on the use of monetary and fiscal policy to restrain domestic demand and the use of the exchange rate plus export incentives to encourage an expansion of export volumes.

The net result of these and other events was that the balance of payments deficit declined from its peak of 13.6 per cent of G.D.P. in 1974/75 to 2.7 per cent of G.D.P. in 1978/79, rising only marginally to just over 3 per cent in 1980/81, despite the second major oil price increase. An adjustment of this order was not achieved without some sacrifice: there was little real growth in the economy from 1975 to 1980 and unemployment rose to a level which, by New Zealand standards, was regarded as fairly high (as a proportion of the labour force, registered unemployed rose to nearly 4 per cent ,while persons on job creation projects constituted a further 2 per cent).

The major redeeming features of the prospective economic situation are that export volumes are now expanding at a reasonable rate and a marked increase in real investment is likely during the 1980s as a result of the series of major new industrial projects now being undertaken. This will assist, directly and indirectly, in providing employment for growing numbers of persons seeking work, but it will not necessarily see a reduction in unemployment, the rate of which is lower than that of most other countries. In the near future unemployment may well remain at its present level despite a rise in the number of persons actually in employment. Growth will have to be steady to create the extra 30,000 jobs per year needed by school-leavers and married women returning to the labour force. Following recent employment patterns, most of the additional jobs will need to be created in the services sector.

Despite its high import content, the ambitious energy-oriented investment programme—together with continued investment in agriculture and further progress towards restructuring in manufacturing industries—is expected to generate in the 1980s a rate of economic growth sufficient to induce a gradual decline in the rate of unemployment.

ENERGY POLICY

Power Supply

Abundant rainfall and a mountainous terrain associated with large lakes give New Zealand a big hydroelectric potential. Electricity output is about 20,000 million kWh. per year, with hydroelectricity contributing 15,000 million kWh. The main thermal stations are fired by coal and oil/gas. There is also a large geothermal station with a capacity comparable with that of both the main thermal stations. The two main islands are linked by two-way direct current cables so virtually the whole country is served by the grid.

Oil consumption and electricity generation both increased greatly between the mid-1960s and mid-1970s, the latter doubling and the former more than doubling. Following the 1973 increase in oil prices, it was decided to fire future thermal power stations with natural gas or coal.

Energy Strategy

Events have forced a complete re-evaluation of energy strategy. National priorities have been set by the Government, namely:

to reduce New Zealand's dependence on petroleum; to increase diversity in the energy supply system; to ensure that energy is used efficiently through the reduction of waste and by using appropriate energy types; to transfer energy supplies from non-renewable sources in the long term; and to establish a framework for energy planning which provides for changing economic and social circumstances.

Major decisions taken in 1980 involve building a plant that will turn natural gas into petrol (to provide about 30 per cent of the New Zealand demand), another plant to produce 1,200 metric tons of chemical methanol per day and a plant to produce ammonia-urea fertilizer from natural gas. In addition, the Marsden Point oil refinery is to be expanded to enable more crude petroleum, rather than refined products, to be imported. Steps are also being taken to promote the use of compressed natural gas and liquefied petroleum gas as vehicle fuels.

As a result of this policy, the share of imported oil in meeting total energy demand is expected to fall from 50 per cent in 1981 (60 per cent in 1973) to about 25 per cent by 1987. Additional hydroelectric capacity is being installed to provide power for energy-intensive industries, while coal production will expand into the 1990s. For the 1981–90 period, investment in large-scale energy and energy-based projects is tentatively estimated to amount to $NZ 5,000 million at 1980 prices, about one-fifth of 1980 G.D.P. It is expected that, by 1986, the resulting savings will contribute to a strengthening in the trade balance of an amount equal to 2 per cent of annual G.D.P.

INTERNATIONAL TRADE AND PAYMENTS

In 1950 the United Kingdom took nearly two-thirds of New Zealand's exports; in 1981 it accounted for only 13 per cent and was overtaken by Australia, Japan and the U.S.A. Similarly for imports, the importance of the market share of the United Kingdom has greatly diminished, from 60 per cent in 1950 to 14 per cent in 1981, which places it behind Australia (with nearly 20 per cent) and only slightly ahead of the U.S.A. and Japan. The relative importance of Australia, Japan and the U.S.A. has increased since 1950 but that of Japan, with which there was virtually no trade in 1950, has grown most spectacularly.

Primary producers have a major say in the marketing of their products. The Dairy Board regulates the internal marketing of butter and cheese and both acquires and markets all exports of dairy products, being particularly concerned in the last few years to market these more widely. The Meat Producers' Board controls grading of export meat, negotiates shipping freights, allocates cargo space and organizes shipments. It has also taken the initiative in promoting sales in non-traditional markets. Through its efforts and otherwise, a greater range of meat products is now more widely marketed, very recent developments being the opening up of markets for mutton in the Middle East. The New Zealand Wool Board fixes minimum prices for various types of wool and participates in auctions to ensure that these prices are maintained. It may also trade on its own account. An Apple and Pear Marketing Board buys all such fruit grown in New Zealand and markets the crops both internally and externally. There are similar authorities for honey, eggs, potatoes, citrus fruit and milk for local consumption.

Receipts from tourism are equivalent to about one-half of the amount of travel payments in overseas exchange. More than one-half of the visitors come from Australia, with the U.S.A. the next most important country of origin, and the number of Japanese tourists has increased considerably in recent years.

In the late 1960s there were misgivings about export prospects, especially for products sold mainly in the United Kingdom, because of the likelihood that Britain would sooner or later join the agriculturally protectionist European Economic Community. These misgivings returned in 1974, following Britain's entry into the EEC in 1973, but in between there was a remarkable surge of export income, attributable to a temporary shortage of most farm products. Prices for all major exports rose in 1971-74 but more recently most of New Zealand's major exports slumped in price until a recovery in 1979. However, similar increases in import prices have resulted in a continuation of the adverse terms of trade.

Since the oil crisis at the end of 1973, the New Zealand economy has been faced with a fundamental change in the relationship between export prices and the cost of imports. This has resulted in a massive shortage of foreign exchange. The purchasing power of exports in overseas markets is still little more than four-fifths of what was enjoyed before the onset of the oil crisis. Protectionist lobbies in some of the principal markets continue their pressures, with some political success. With the assistance of heavy overseas borrowing, private as well as public, New Zealand has been able to cover its external deficit without having to deflate the economy too severely.

The New Zealand dollar's fixed relationship with the U.S. dollar was ended in July 1973 when a trade-weighted daily "float" was introduced, involving the currencies of New Zealand's main trading partners. Subsequently, the New Zealand dollar was revalued in September 1973 but has been devalued from time to time since then.

OVERALL ECONOMIC PERFORMANCE

The overall performance of the New Zealand economy in recent years has been unimpressive, with a record of slow growth in real terms, high inflation and recurring balance of payments difficulties. Real per caput G.D.P. rose by less than 2 per cent a year on average from the mid-1950s to the mid-1970s. The OECD, in its annual review of New Zealand's economy, has estimated that the Government programme to stimulate the economy generated a 2.25 per cent expansion in real G.D.P. in 1981/82, compared with 0.6 per cent growth in 1980/81, but that G.D.P. growth could settle back to 1.5 per cent in 1982/83 if investment lags. The Reserve Bank agrees that growth will be constrained in 1982/83 because of continuing poor terms of trade, but foresees a rise in the growth rate to 2.5 per cent in the year to March 1984. Allowance for depressed terms of trade further reduces the rate of growth in effective terms.

Because New Zealand has a relatively large external trade sector and most of its exports are subject to major price fluctuations, the terms of trade have always been a key variable. Furthermore, prices of imports and exports tend to be determined externally, with New Zealand having little influence on them. In 1974/75 the terms of trade deteriorated very sharply to a level lower than any since the 1930s. Since then the terms of trade have remained depressed, though there was a mild recovery in 1979/80, with improved prices for beef and wool.

Export, as well as import, prices greatly influence internal prices because most export commodities are also consumed internally and the export market determines prices. In addition, the attempt by organized labour to increase its share of national income in the early 1970s markedly accelerated the rate of inflation. From the mid-1950s consumer prices rose by an average of 5 per cent per annum. However, in the 1970s inflation more than doubled. For the 12 months to June 1976 the consumer price index rose by almost 17 per cent but this reflected in part fiscal measures which should have been taken earlier. Since then inflation has slowed to 10 per cent in 1978/79, jumped to 18 per cent in 1979/80 and dropped back to 15 per cent in 1980/81 and 1981/82. It is an objective of the Government to bring down the rate of inflation to the world level, that is to about 12 or even 10 per cent.

Inflation and the high tax rate are creating tensions which tend to reduce productivity. Trade unions have become restive as rising prices have put pressure on single-income families. There is a danger that worsening industrial relations fostered by militant unions will further diminish the country's standard of living.

In recent years the proportion of total private

income going to salary and wage-earners has risen sharply, mainly at the expense of farmers but to some extent at the expense of capital returns.

There has been a relative increase in the public sector's claim on the private sector on account of current expenditure. Within the public sector itself central government was increasingly obliged to transfer resources to territorial and other local authorities because the latter lack the automatically increasing flow of funds which a progressive (personal) income tax structure so conveniently provides. At the same time there is a tendency for local or regional authorities to assume responsibility for a greater proportion of total public sector expenditure.

Government expenditure approached 40 per cent of G.D.P. in 1981/82. The origins of this expansion lay in the rapid growth of nominal incomes during the early 1970s, reflecting first a commodity boom and a real wage explosion and subsequently the world-wide acceleration of prices and incomes following the 1973 oil price rise. This growth brought with it an even more rapid expansion of government revenues as the wave of accelerating incomes was partly absorbed by a progressive tax structure whose parameters were fixed in nominal terms. There developed an even faster growth in government expenditure, partly because of the higher wage content. Also, long-standing commitments put upward pressure on government expenditure which could not quickly be reduced. The growth of current outlays in real terms was brought back to 4 per cent in the 1979–81 period. However, a number of offsetting influences have prevented any broad reduction in the overall fiscal deficit. Social welfare transfers have continued to rise strongly in real terms, the growth in unemployment benefits replacing some slowing down in super-annuation and other benefits. Interest payments in the public departments, both domestic and overseas, have grown rapidly in real terms as both the level of debt and interest rates have increased. As with other countries, deficit budget financing has had to be adopted. Despite efforts at economy, the deficit before borrowing in 1981/82 is likely to be about 7.5 per cent of estimated G.D.P. This is relatively lower than the record deficit for 1975/76, which was 8.7 per cent of G.D.P. but is recognized to be a level which is higher than desirable. Meanwhile, taxation reform is under intensive study and a Task Force on Tax Reform made a number of recommendations in its report in April 1982.

The Government recognizes that continued restraint in its expenditure is essential if its economic policies are to be successful, despite continuing pressures to increase the level and scope of such expenditure. In 1981/82 the growth in staff levels continued to be strictly limited and a requirement that proposed new programmes be funded by compensatory savings in existing departmental functions was rigorously applied.

ECONOMIC POLICY

Steps towards a more effective fiscal policy were taken in 1968, only to be retracted in the excitement of the external and internal boom of the early 1970s which roughly coincided with the brief return to power of the Labour Government (1972–75). Monetary policy remained static until early 1976, when interest rates were allowed to rise significantly on government stock and most other controlled securities, and a good deal of freedom was restored to the financial system and the trading banks in particular. In mid-1976 the indications were that the reforms were having the desired effects, uncontrolled interest rates having first gone up but later receded a little. The yield on government stock was still too low to attract willing lenders but since September 1978 this has changed with new government stock being issued at competitive interest rates. A major aim of the exercise is to slow down the growth of financial institutions on the fringe of the controlled institutions, and thereby increase the ambit of effective government control. It is, however, likely that the New Zealand monetary and financial system will remain more subject to detailed regulation than in most Western countries.

Economics and politics are inseparable, such are the effects of inflation and wide swings in the terms of trade. In particular, organized labour appears to be endeavouring consciously to obtain and retain a greater share of national resources. This effort coincides with slow productivity growth. It is also unfortunate, but perhaps equally inevitable, that a much wider range of social demands are being made of central and local government, many of which are inimical to economic growth. Thus, although the economy's capacity to sustain rising material living standards is increasingly in doubt, claimants are becoming more demanding. The outlook for the economy, therefore, depends heavily on the future course of salary and wage payments. The National Government decided on a return to free wage bargaining in 1977 after a period of wage restraint with indifferent success since 1970, but in 1979 the Government moved on several occasions to counter pending pay agreements which were likely to have serious flow-on effects for the economy generally. Efforts are continuing in an attempt to hammer out an acceptable wages policy on a tripartite basis, if possible combining income tax reductions with reduced wage rate increases, with a commitment by all parties to minimize the impact of inflation.

STATISTICAL SURVEY

AREA AND POPULATION

Area	Population (census results)		
	March 23rd, 1971	March 23rd, 1976	March 1981
269,057 sq. km.*	2,862,631	3,129,383	3,175,737

* 103,883 square miles.

Estimated population: 3,190,100 at March 31st, 1982.

CHIEF CENTRES OF POPULATION

(Census of 1981)

Wellington (capital)	343,982	Hamilton	160,215
Auckland	829,519	Dunedin	114,033
Christchurch	321,720		

BIRTHS, MARRIAGES AND DEATHS

	Live Births*		Marriages		Deaths*	
	Number	Rate (per '000)	Number	Rate (per '000)	Number	Rate (per '000)
1977	54,179	17.3	22,589	7.2	25,961	8.3
1978	51,029	16.3	22,426	7.2	24,669	7.9
1979	52,279	16.7	22,326	7.2	25,340	8.1
1980	50,542	16.1	22,981	7.3	26,676	8.5
1981	50,794	16.09	n.a.	n.a.	25,150	7.97

* Data for births and deaths are tabulated by year of registration rather than by year of occurrence.

IMMIGRATION AND EMIGRATION*

(April 1st to March 31st)

	1973/74	1974/75	1975/76	1976/77	1977/78	1978/79	1979/80	1980/81
Long-term immigrants	69,815	65,900	48,460	37,020	36,972	40,808	41,607	44,965
Long-term emigrants	42,338	43,461	43,160	56,092	63,680	81,008	76,024	69,790

* Figures refer to persons intending to remain in New Zealand, or New Zealand residents intending to remain abroad, for 12 months or more.

ECONOMICALLY ACTIVE POPULATION

('000 persons at February 1981)

	Males	Females	Total
Agriculture, hunting, forestry and fishing	113.9	28.0	141.9
Mining and quarrying	4.5	0.3	4.8
Manufacturing industry	223.1	80.7	303.8
Electricity, gas and water	15.0	1.9	16.9
Construction	81.4	5.9	87.3
Wholesale and retail trade	127.8	102.5	230.3
Transport, storage and communications	84.4	25.5	109.9
Finance, insurance, real estate, etc.	48.6	41.1	89.7
Community, social and personal services	130.6	150.1	280.7
Total in Industry	829.3	436.1	1,265.3
Armed Forces in New Zealand	9.6	1.1	10.7
Registered unemployed	28.6	20.8	49.4
Total Labour Force	867.5	457.9	1,325.4

AGRICULTURE

LAND USE

('000 hectares in 1976)

Arable land	726
Land under permanent crops	11
Permanent meadows and pastures	12,847
Forests and woodlands	7,403
Other land	5,880
Inland waters	1
Total Area	26,868

PRINCIPAL CROPS

(April 1st to March 31st)

	Area ('000 hectares)			Production ('000 metric tons)		
	1977/78	1978/79	1979/80	1977/78	1978/79	1979/80
Wheat	91	87	86	329	295	306
Oats	16	18	19	52	58	62
Barley	71	78	67	259	264	228
Maize	25	22	19	174	179	157
Peas	21	23	24	59	63	69
Potatoes	9	8	8	237	203	214

LIVESTOCK

('000 head at January 31st)

	1977	1978	1979	1980*
Dairy cows in milk	2,074	2,053	2,040	1,999
Total cattle	9,472	9,129	8,499	8,131
Breeding ewes	42,782*	44,515*	46,108*	48,245
Total sheep	59,105	62,163	62,894	68,772
Total pigs	536	539	503	434

* As at June 30th.

LIVESTOCK PRODUCTS

('000 metric tons)

	1976/77	1977/78	1978/79	1979/80	1980/81
Beef[1]	529.9	533.7	490.5	478.8	480.8
Veal[1]	27.8	27.8	21.1	16.9	17.3
Mutton[1]	156.2	159.6	162.8	168.5	200.5
Lamb[1]	341.5	342.0	351.1	391.2	425.7
Pig meat[1]	39.0	38.2	35.7	34.5	32.5
Other meat[1]	58.0	58.8	58.1	61.0	50.6
Liquid milk (million litres)[2]	6,442	5,892	6,176	6,499	6,356
Butter (creamery)[2]	277.1	233.6	252.1	259.6	264.9
Cheese[2]	81.0	78.3	90.3	105.7	84.3
Preserved milk*[2]	307.08	271.44	277.11	285.62	309.9
Casein[2]	56.95	57.0	66.9	67.0	59.6
Wool: greasy[3]	302.5	310.8	320.6	356.5	n.a.
clean[3]	221.7	225.6	234.3	263.8	n.a.

* Skim-milk powder, condensed and powdered whole-milk, butter-milk powder.

[1] Year ended September 30th.
[2] Year ended May 31st.
[3] Year ended June 30th.

FORESTRY

ROUNDWOOD REMOVALS

('000 cubic metres, excluding bark)

	Coniferous (soft wood)			Broadleaved (hard wood)			TOTAL		
	1978	1979	1980	1978	1979	1980	1978	1979	1980
Sawlogs, veneer logs and logs for sleepers	4,697	5,079	5,730	484	79	86	5,181	5,158	5,816
Pitprops (mine timber)	12	—	—	2	—	—	14	—	—
Pulpwood	2,871	3,184	3,345	145	152	155	3,016	3,336	3,500
Other industrial wood	538	476	611	4	4	4	542	480	615
Fuel wood	125	n.a.	n.a.	125	n.a.	n.a.	250	380	692
TOTAL	8,243	n.a.	n.a.	760	n.a.	n.a.	9,003	9,354	10,623

Source: New Zealand Forest Service.

SAWNWOOD PRODUCTION

('000 cubic metres, April 1st to March 31st)

SPECIES	1974/75	1975/76	1976/77	1977/78	1978/79	1979/80
Rimu and miro	271.6	265.7	242.2	185.3	152.5	137.0
Matai	17.1	19.7	15.5	9.3	2.7	2.6
Douglas fir	147.3	153.8	161.2	141.1	131.6	163.5
Kahikatea	28.9	32.1	31.5	21.4	13.7	9.6
Exotic pines	1,541.8	1,427.5	1,662.2	1,521.8	1,478.8	1,608.9
TOTAL (incl. others)	2,085.6	2,003.3	2,211.6	1,961.4	1,865.5	2,010.5

Source: New Zealand Forest Service.

FISHING

('000 metric tons)

	1975	1976	1977	1978	1979
Marine fish	38.0	52.8	60.0	77.6	84.1
Oysters	9.9	10.0	10.8	10.1	10.1
Rock lobster	3.3	3.7	3.5	3.8	4.0
Other	12.0	9.3	8.6	7.0	6.3
TOTAL	63.2	75.8	82.9	98.5	104.5

Source: Fisheries Management Division, Ministry of Agriculture and Fisheries.

MINING

		1978	1979	1980
Hard coal	'000 metric tons	2,032	1,737	1,953.2
Lignite	,, ,, ,,	151	209	208.0
Gold	kilogrammes	219.1	217.7	187.0
Silver	,,	62.6	51.0	23.2
Petroleum (crude)	'000 cu. metres	724	477	419
Natural gas	million cu. metres	2,124.65	1,307.46	1,069.1
Liquid petroleum gas	'000 cu. metres	—	—	26.8
Iron sands	'000 metric tons	3,946	3,527	3,389.5
Silica sand	,, ,, ,,	128	137	135.9
Limestone	,, ,, ,,	3,390	3,618	2,793.1
Salt	,, ,, ,,	65	55	n.a.

INDUSTRY

SELECTED PRODUCTS

		1979	1980	1981
Canned meat†	metric tons	3,025	n.a.	n.a.
Flour	,, ,,	213,997	222,931	223,632
Refined sugar	,, ,,	133,441	133,401	124,953
Biscuits	,, ,,	23,900	25,065	25,719
Jam*	,, ,,	5,670	5,379	6,466
Canned fruit*	,, ,,	16,842	20,689‡	24,061
Canned vegetables*	,, ,,	20,922	23,604‡	25,230
Quick frozen vegetables	,, ,,	54,226	53,565	44,339
Solid detergents	,, ,,	11,067	10,986	n.a.
Beer and stout	'000 litres	375,308	378,297	382,566
Wool yarn	metric tons	18,119	18,696	n.a.
Woollen and worsted piece goods	'000 sq. metres	2,724	2,837	n.a.
Refrigerators	number	196,603	176,134	n.a.
Washing machines	,,	67,300	61,650	n.a.
Lawn mowers	,,	93,727	94,653	91,575
Radio receivers	,,	200,347	n.a.§	n.a.§
Tobacco	metric tons	645	616	622
Cigarettes	million	6,406	6,276	6,191
Chemical fertilizers	'000 metric tons	2,285	2,251	1,985
Cement	,, ,, ,,	752	720	759
Passenger cars	number	70,469	73,353	95,458
Lorries, vans and buses (assembled)	,,	13,816	17,366	20,133

* Year ending June.

† Year ending September.

‡ Includes bottled and dehydrated products.

§ No longer being surveyed.

FINANCE

100 cents = 1 New Zealand dollar ($NZ).

Coins: 1, 2, 5, 10, 20 and 50 cents.

Notes: 1, 2, 5, 10, 20 and 100 dollars.

Exchange rates (June 1982): £1 sterling = $NZ 2.3365; U.S. $1 = $NZ 1.351.

$NZ100 = £42.80 = U.S. $74.02.

Note: The New Zealand dollar was introduced in July 1967, replacing the New Zealand pound at the rate of £NZ1 = $NZ2 From October 1961 the New Zealand pound had a value of U.S. $2.78, so the initial value of the New Zealand dollar was U.S. $1.39 (U.S. $1 = 71.9 NZ cents). This remained in force until November 1967, after which the exchange rate was $NZ1 = U.S. $1.12 (U.S. $1 = 89.3 NZ cents) until August 1971. From December 1971 to February 1973 the par value of the New Zealand dollar was U.S. $1.216 (U.S. $1 = 82.2 NZ cents), though the effective mid-point rate was $NZ1 = U.S. $1.195. From February to July 1973 the exchange rate was $NZ1 = U.S. $1.351 (U.S. $1 = 74.0 NZ cents). In terms of sterling, the exchange rate was £1 = $NZ2.143 ($NZ1 = 9s. 4d. or 46.67p.) from November 1967 to December 1971; and £1 = $NZ2.180 from December 1971 to June 1972. The fixed relationship with the U.S. dollar was ended in July 1973, since when the basis for the New Zealand dollar's valuation has been a weighted "basket" of currencies of the country's main trading partners. In September 1973 the New Zealand dollar was revalued by 10 per cent against this "basket" (becoming equivalent to U.S. $1.478) but in September 1974 it was effectively devalued by about 6.2 per cent, and in August 1975 by 15 per cent. In November 1976 the currency was devalued by 7 per cent against the U.S. dollar but this was partially reversed in December. A 5 per cent devaluation was announced in June 1979. The average value of the New Zealand dollar was: U.S. $1.363 in 1973; U.S. $1.401 in 1974; U.S. $1.215 in 1975; 99.6 U.S. cents in 1976; 97.1 U.S. cents in 1977; U.S. $1.038 in 1978; U.S. $1.023 in 1979; 97.3 U.S. cents in 1980; 87.0 U.S. cents in 1981.

BUDGET
($NZ million, April 1st to March 31st)

Income	1980/81
Income Tax	5,299
Estate and Gift Duty	39
Land Tax	12
Total Direct Taxation	5,350
Customs Duty	349
Beer Duty	64
Sales Tax	776
Motor Spirits Tax	139
Racing Duty	46
Other Stamp Duties	54
Energy Resources Levy	20
Other	63
Total Indirect Taxation	1,512
Total Taxation Receipts, Consolidated Revenue Account	6,861
Highways Tax	189
Total Taxation	7,051
Interest, Profit and Miscellaneous Receipts	558
Borrowing	1,525
Total	9,133

Expenditure	1980/81
Administration	786
Defence	446
Foreign Affairs	131
Development of Industry	797
Education	1,292
Social Services	2,590
Health	1,356
Transport and Communications	333
Debt Services and Miscellaneous Investment Transactions	1,402
Total Net Expenditure	9,133
Total	9,133

OVERSEAS RESERVES
($NZ million at March 31st)

	Assets of N.Z. Banking System	Overseas Securities		Gold	IMF		Total Reserves
		Treasury-held	Other Government-held		Reserve Position	Special Drawing Rights	
1977	390.7	284.2	23.9	0.7	—	21.2	720.6
1978	471.7	424.3	23.9	1.6	13.8	48.3	983.6
1979	424.8	264.5	30.0	0.7	43.5	48.5	812.0
1980	464.8	238.8	41.9	0.7	—	37.4	783.6
1981	379.0	253.4	49.0	0.7	35.9	28.5	746.5

MONEY SUPPLY
($NZ million at end of year)

	1975	1976	1977	1978	1979	1980	1981
Currency outside banks	352.2	418.3	459.9	536.3	590.0	577.2	682.7
Demand deposits at trading banks	1,244.6	1,385.1	1,369.6	1,637.4	1,741.0	1,876.1	2,129.3

COST OF LIVING

Consumers' Price Index
(Base: Oct.–Dec. 1980 = 100)

	1974	1975	1976	1977	1978	1979	1980	1981
Food	39.2	43.3	51.4	60.1	66.5	78.1	94.0	103.6
Housing	50.2	58.7	64.8	71.9	78.5	84.8	94.8	103.3
Household operation	41.1	45.8	54.9	64.4	72.6	83.2	95.7	101.6
Apparel	42.7	49.0	56.2	65.8	75.7	84.4	95.7	101.3
Transportation	35.5	43.1	53.3	59.6	67.2	77.5	94.6	104.4
Miscellaneous	37.9	43.5	51.5	59.5	68.0	78.9	94.4	103.2
All Items	41.4	47.5	55.6	63.6	71.2	80.9	94.8	103.1

NATIONAL ACCOUNTS

($NZ million at current prices, year ending March 31st)

National Income and Product

	1975/76	1976/77	1977/78	1978/79	1979/80*	1980/81*
Compensation of employees	6,401	7,184	8,227	9,604	11,214	13,412
Operating surplus	3,425	4,464	4,604	5,296	6,579	6,887
Domestic Factor Incomes	9,826	11,648	12,831	14,900	17,793	20,299
Consumption of fixed capital	947	1,086	1,198	1,321	1,464	1,603
G.D.P. at Factor Cost	10,773	12,734	14,029	16,221	19,257	21,902
Indirect taxes	1,103	1,299	1,466	1,725	2,002	2,356
Less Subsidies	391	241	277	442	351	338
G.D.P. in Purchasers' Values	11,484	13,792	15,217	17,504	20,908	23,920
Net factor income from abroad	−165	−263	−337	−421	−467	−537
Gross National Product	11,319	13,529	14,880	17,083	20,441	23,383
Less Consumption of fixed capital	947	1,086	1,198	1,321	1,464	1,603
National Income in Market Prices	10,372	12,443	13,682	15,761	18,977	21,780

Expenditure on the Gross Domestic Product

	1975/76	1976/77	1977/78	1978/79	1979/80*	1980/81*
Government final consumption expenditure	1,732	1,953	2,377	2,898	3,336	4,191
Private final consumption expenditure	7,147	8,313	9,332	10,502	12,342	14,624
Increase in stocks	356	698	636	292	1,587	1,169
Gross fixed capital formation	3,125	3,448	3,346	3,546	3,718	4,250
Statistical discrepancy	−82	−196	−202	122	221	−116
Total Domestic Expenditure	12,278	14,316	15,489	17,360	21,204	24,118
Exports of goods and services	2,692	3,824	4,197	4,788	6,070	7,081
Less Imports of goods and services	3,486	4,248	4,467	4,644	6,366	7,279
G.D.P. in Purchasers' Values	11,484	13,792	15,217	17,504	20,908	23,920
G.D.P. at Constant 1975/76 Prices	11,484	11,501	11,187	11,443	11,575	11,484

* Provisional figures.

BALANCE OF PAYMENTS

(U.S. $ million)

	1976	1977	1978	1979	1980	1981
Merchandise exports f.o.b.	2,779	3,099	3,613	4,407	5,383	5,556
Merchandise imports f.o.b.	−2,825	−2,826	−2,991	−3,653	−4,614	−5,285
TRADE BALANCE	−46	273	622	754	769	271
Exports of services	432	568	640	739	846	1,439
Imports of services	−1,070	−1,510	−1,695	−2,079	−2,425	−2,791
BALANCE ON GOODS AND SERVICES	−684	−669	−433	−586	−810	−1,081
Private unrequited transfers (net)	51	39	40	43	131	66
Government unrequited transfers (net)	−2	3	0	−5	−5	−41
CURRENT BALANCE	−635	−627	−393	−548	−684	−1,056
Direct capital investment (net)	179	163	0	47	77	−16
Other long-term capital (net)	150	−71	18	−74	−617	−699
Short-term capital (net)	−141	−105	−33	53	250	−135
Net errors and omissions	20	46	−34	47	41	554
TOTAL (net monetary movements)	−428	−594	−442	−475	−932	−1,352
Allocation of IMF Special Drawing Rights	—	—	—	31	32	30
Valuation changes (net)	−101	78	−29	−75	−4	107
Loans to Government and Reserve Bank	464	509	523	667	1,089	1,707
CHANGES IN RESERVES	−65	−7	52	148	185	492

Source: IMF, *International Financial Statistics.*

EXTERNAL TRADE

($NZ '000)

Twelve months ending June 30th.

	1975/76	1976/77	1977/78	1978/79	1979/80	1980/81
Imports c.i.f.	2,961,598	3,537,982	3,276,655	3,840,507	5,172,607	6,023,628
Exports f.o.b.	2,386,854	3,228,692	3,313,496	4,067,378	5,152,212	6,065,277

PRINCIPAL COMMODITIES

($NZ '000)

IMPORTS (current domestic value)	1978/79	1979/80	1980/81
Food and live animals, beverages and tobacco	186,647	246,866	260,662
Crude materials, inedible (except fuels); animal, vegetable oils and fats	201,409	225,601	269,465
Mineral fuels, lubricants and related materials	502,228	944,182	1,247,680
Chemicals	453,451	603,339	611,933
Machinery and electrical equipment	686,636	862,065	978,304
Transport equipment	468,570	572,544	843,160
Iron, steel and non-ferrous metals	300,327	356,800	336,754
Textiles, clothing and footwear	275,832	353,485	334,652
Other manufactures and miscellaneous	499,040	644,744	704,713
TOTAL	3,574,139	4,809,625	5,587,323

[*continued on next page*

PRINCIPAL COMMODITIES—*continued*]

EXPORTS (f.o.b., excluding re-exports)	1978/79	1979/80	1980/81
Meat and meat preparations	1,094,018	1,192,282	1,520,865
Butter	277,212	360,607	398,004
Cheese	75,472	105,861	137,714
Fruit and vegetables	103,790	128,735	170,017
Hides, skins and pelts	181,804	180,121	129,856
Wool	683,322	930,760	892,602
Sausage casings	30,181	33,481	46,807
Tallow	41,132	42,194	46,732
Casein	62,629	112,522	117,235
Pulp, paper and paper board	176,167	243,400	370,346
TOTAL (incl. others)	3,945,961	5,012,453	5,830,031

Re-exports ($NZ'000): 1978/79 121,417; 1979/80 139,759; 1980/81 211,671*.

* Provisional.

PRINCIPAL TRADING PARTNERS

($NZ '000)

IMPORTS (current domestic value)*	1978/79	1979/80	1980/81
Australia	798,513	914,802	1,043,556
Bahrain	46,735	68,433	61,786
Belgium	20,279	23,318	22,566
Canada	85,417	95,329	125,387
France	44,866	54,209	48,427
Germany, Federal Republic	231,044	223,848	160,558
Hong Kong	52,313	65,037	59,944
Iran	41,214	50,656	136,458
Italy	47,115	70,616	60,504
Japan	495,154	605,593	833,698
Netherlands	48,272	61,338	57,950
Saudi Arabia	86,239	218,522	286,710
Singapore	67,753	273,247	311,462
United Kingdom	542,819	692,599	584,934
U.S.A.	489,562	649,687	984,883
TOTAL (incl. others)	3,574,139	4,809,625	5,587,323

* Excludes specie and gold.

[*continued on next page*

PRINCIPAL TRADING PARTNERS—*continued*]

EXPORTS*	1978/79	1979/80	1980/81
Australia	501,190	634,057	814,725
Belgium	44,533	51,998	45,369
Canada	101,350	98,000	132,260
China, People's Republic	78,849	118,351	172,804
Fiji	55,019	71,142	86,653
France	94,513	126,691	94,734
Germany, Federal Republic	102,480	116,245	149,468
Italy	107,973	128,341	83,298
Japan	600,583	635,229	785,031
Netherlands	65,741	84,165	94,532
Philippines	42,275	69,541	80,506
U.S.S.R.	129,134	250,921	225,876
United Kingdom	676,733	714,917	760,225
U.S.A.	632,176	721,423	769,183
TOTAL (incl. others)	3,985,201	5,022,483	6,065,277

* Excluding ships' stores, specie and gold; including re-exports.

TOURISM

('000 visitors, year ending March 31st)

FROM	1978/79	1979/80	1980/81
Australia	217.8	214.5	215.5
U.S.A.	58.9	70.2	75.3
United Kingdom	28.6	34.7	35.3
Canada	13.5	17.0	17.8
Japan	13.6	17.5	20.5
Western Europe	14.4	18.7	21.5
Other countries	71.9	72.6	77.6
TOTAL	418.7	445.2	463.5

TRANSPORT

RAILWAYS

(year ending March 31st)

	1975/76	1976/77	1977/78	1978/79	1979/80	1980/81
Passenger journeys ('000)	20,035	18,588	16,402	16,749	16,011	14,934
Freight ('000 metric tons)	13,197	13,603	12,577	11,722	11,755	11,344
Freight metric ton-km. (million)	3,650	3,603	3,402	3,281	3,226	3,139

ROAD TRAFFIC

(Vehicles licensed at June 30th)

	1979	1980	1981
Passenger cars	1,280,837	1,322,493	1,363,077
Trucks (lorries)	256,577	261,891	273,270
Contract vehicles	1,283	1,409	1,287
Buses and service cars	3,453	3,436	3,573
Trailers and caravans	380,967	387,293	392,915
Motor cycles and power cycles	115,332	135,525	148,262
Other vehicles	107,052	107,742	105,807
TOTAL	2,145,501	2,219,789	2,288,191

SHIPPING

	Entered				Cleared			
	Overseas		Coastal		Overseas		Coastal	
	Vessels	Net Tonnage ('000)	Vessels	Net Tonnage ('000)	Vessels	Net Tonnage ('000)	Vessels	Net Tonnage ('000)
1978	3,251	23,134	6,741	10,506	3,261	23,186	6,740	10,521
1979	3,438	25,199	6,782	11,440	3,433	25,313	6,772	11,431
1980	2,705	12,970	7,406	22,265	2,710	13,079	7,379	22,213

CIVIL AVIATION

(Scheduled Services)

	1977	1978	1979	1980
Domestic				
Passengers carried ('000)	2,408	2,520	2,628	2,478
Passenger kilometres ('000)	1,123,101	1,179,101	1,234,457	1,171,884
Freight carried (metric tons)	63,800	61,000	63,400	47,200
Freight metric ton-km. ('000)	29,216	28,050	31,558	24,714
Mail metric ton-km. ('000)	1,531	1,496	1,624	1,668
International				
Passengers carried ('000)	1,286	1,415	1,682	1,814
Freight carried (metric tons)	41,684	49,209	57,373	62,276
Mail carried (metric tons)	2,286	2,366	2,666	2,890

COMMUNICATIONS MEDIA

TV Sets Licensed	913,559*
Daily Newspapers	43†
Telephones per 100 people	56.9‡

* At September 1981.
† At November 1981.
‡ At March 1981.

EDUCATION

(1981)

	Institutions	Pupils	Teachers (full-time)
Pre-school	1,208	55,992	1,126
Primary (state and private)	2,526	487,679	20,243
Area*	34	8,816	489
Secondary (state and private)	360	222,287	13,695
Technical	21	140,706	2,298
Teacher training	8	5,901	562
University	7	52,988	3,043

Source: Department of Education, Wellington.

* Area schools provide both primary and secondary education.

Source (unless otherwise specified): Department of Statistics, Wellington 1.

THE CONSTITUTION

Head of State

Executive power is vested in the Queen and is exercisable by her personal representative, the Governor-General.

In the execution of the powers and authorities vested in him the Governor-General must be guided by the advice of the Executive Council; but if in any case he sees sufficient cause to dissent from the opinion of the Council, he may act in the exercise of his powers and authorities in opposition to the opinion of the Council, reporting the matter to the monarch without delay, with the reasons for his so acting.

Executive Council

The Executive Council consists of the Governor-General and all the Ministers. Two members, exclusive of the Governor-General or the presiding member, constitute a quorum. The Governor-General appoints the Prime Minister and, on the latter's recommendation, the other Ministers.

House of Representatives

Parliament comprises the Crown and the House of Representatives.

The number of members constituting the House of Representatives is 92: 88 drawn from general seats and four from Maori seats. They are designated "Members of Parliament". Parliaments sit for three-year terms.

Everyone over the age of 18 years may vote in the election of members for the House of Representatives. Since August 1975 any person, regardless of nationality, ordinarily resident in New Zealand for 12 months or more and resident in an electoral district for three months or more is qualified to be registered as a voter. Compulsory registration of all electors except Maoris was introduced at the end of 1924; it was introduced for Maoris in 1956.

There are 88 European electoral districts and four Maori electoral districts. As from August 1975 any person of the Maori race, which includes any descendant of such a person, who elects to be considered as a Maori for the purposes of the Electoral Act may enrol on the Maori roll for that particular Maori electoral district in which that person resides.

By the Electoral Amendment Act, 1937, which made provision for a secret ballot in Maori elections, Maori electors were granted the same privileges, in the exercise of their vote, as general electors.

In local government, with some minor exceptions, there is a wider electoral franchise, non-residential rate payers also being eligible to vote.

THE GOVERNMENT

Head of State: H.M. Queen ELIZABETH II.

Governor-General and Commander-in-Chief: The Hon. Sir DAVID STUART BEATTIE, G.C.M.G., G.C.V.O., Q.C. (took office November 6th, 1980).

CABINET

(July 1982)

Prime Minister, Minister of Finance and Minister in charge of the Legislative Department, the Audit Department and the Security Intelligence Service: Rt. Hon. ROBERT D. MULDOON, C.H.

Deputy Prime Minister, Minister of Agriculture, Minister of Fisheries and Minister in charge of the Rural Banking and Finance Corporation: Rt. Hon. DUNCAN MACINTYRE, D.S.O., O.B.E., E.D.

Minister of State and of State Services, Minister of Defence, Minister in charge of War Pensions and Rehabilitation: Hon. DAVID S. THOMSON, M.C., E.D.

Minister of Energy, National Development and Regional Development: Hon. WILLIAM F. BIRCH.

Minister of Labour: Hon. JAMES B. BOLGER.

Minister of Transport, of Civil Aviation and Meteorological Services and Minister of Railways: Hon. GEORGE F. GAIR.

Minister of Trade and Industry: Hon. HUGH C. TEMPLETON.

Minister of Foreign Affairs and Minister of Overseas Trade: Hon. WARREN E. COOPER.

Minister of Customs, Minister in charge of the Government Life Insurance Office, the State Insurance Office and of the Earthquake and War Damage Commission, and Associate Minister of Trade and Industry: Hon. KEITH ALLEN.

Attorney-General and Minister of Justice: Hon. JAMES K. MCLAY.

Minister of Works and Housing: Hon. TONY FRIEDLANDER.

Minister of Social Welfare, Minister in charge of the Public Trust Office and of the Government Printing Office: Hon. VENN S. YOUNG.

Minister of Internal Affairs, Minister of Local Government, Minister of Recreation and Sport, Minister of Civil Defence and Minister for the Arts: Hon. D. ALLAN HIGHET.

Minister of Education: Hon. MERVYN L. WELLINGTON.

Minister of Police and Maori Affairs: Hon. M. BENJAMIN R. COUCH.

Minister of Immigration and Minister of Health: Hon. ANTHONY G. MALCOLM.

Minister for the Environment, Minister of Science and Technology and Minister of Broadcasting: Dr. The Hon. IAN J. SHEARER.

Minister of Tourism, Minister in charge of Publicity and Postmaster-General: Hon. ROBERT L. G. TALBOT.

Minister of Lands, of Forests and Minister in charge of the Valuation Department: Hon. JONATHAN H. ELWORTHY.

Minister of Statistics, Minister in charge of the Inland Revenue Department and of Friendly Societies, Associate Minister of Finance: Hon. JOHN H. FALLOON.

LEGISLATURE

HOUSE OF REPRESENTATIVES

Speaker: Hon. Sir RICHARD HARRISON, E.D.

Chairman of the Committees J. F. LUXTON.

Leader of the House: Hon. DAVID S. THOMSON, M.C., E.D.

Leader of the Opposition: Rt. Hon. WALLACE E. ROWLING.

Clerk of the House: C. P. LITTLEJOHN.

GENERAL ELECTION, November 28th, 1981

Party	Votes	Votes (per cent)	Seats
National Party	698,507	38.65	47
Labour Party	702,601	38.89	43
Social Credit	372,097	20.59	2
Others	24,649	1.36	—
Informal	8,985	0.50	—

POLITICAL PARTIES

Communist Party of New Zealand: 37 St. Kevin's Arcade, Auckland; pro-Chinese; 300 mems.; Gen. Sec. VICTOR WILCOX; publ. *People's Voice* (weekly).

Labour Party: P.O.B. 6146, Te Aro, Wellington; f. 1916; the policy of the Party is the maximum utilization of the Dominion's resources for organizing an internal economy to distribute goods and services so as to guarantee to every person able and willing to work an adequate standard of living; New Zealand Pres. J. P. ANDERTON; Gen. Sec. J. F. WYBROW; Parliamentary Leader Rt. Hon. WALLACE E. ROWLING.

New Zealand National Party: 35–37 Victoria St., Wellington 1; f. 1936; the National Party represents the Conservative and Liberal elements in New Zealand politics; it stands for maintenance of democratic government, and the encouragement of private enterprise and competitive business, coupled with maximum personal freedom; Pres. Sir GEORGE CHAPMAN; Parliamentary Leader Rt. Hon. ROBERT D. MULDOON; Gen. Dir. and Sec. P. B. LEAY.

New Zealand Values Party: P.O.B. 137, Wellington; f. May 1972; socialist ecologist party; Leaders JANET ROBORGH, ALAN WILKINSON, JON MAYSON; Gen. Sec. DANNY ASHWORTH; publ. *Linkletter*.

Social Credit Political League: Le Normandie Arcade, World Trade Centre, 116 Cuba St., P.O.B. 11–174, Wellington 1; f. 1954; aims to reform the monetary system through restoring the ownership and use of the nation's financial credit to the people through a national credit authority; 35,000 mems.; Pres. J. S. LIPA; Leader BRUCE C. BEETHAM; publ. *Social Credit New Guardian* (monthly).

Socialist Unity Party: P.O.B. 1987, Auckland; f. 1966; Marxist socialist; Press. G. H. ANDERSEN; Sec. GEORGE E. JACKSON; publs. *New Zealand Tribune* and *Socialist Politics*.

DIPLOMATIC REPRESENTATION

EMBASSIES AND HIGH COMMISSIONS ACCREDITED TO NEW ZEALAND

(In Wellington unless otherwise stated)

(HC) High Commission

Australia: 72–78 Hobson St., Thorndon, 1, Private Bag (HC); *High Commissioner:* Hon. J. J. WEBSTER.

Austria: Canberra, A.C.T., Australia.

Bangladesh: Canberra, A.C.T., Australia (HC).

Belgium: Robert Jones House, 1–3 Willeston St., P.O.B. 3841; *Ambassador:* LÉON L. C. OLIVIER.

Brazil: Canberra, A.C.T., Australia.

Burma: Canberra, A.C.T., Australia.

Canada: ICI House, Molesworth St., 1, P.O.B. 12049 (HC); *High Commissioner:* C. O. ROGER ROUSSEAU.

Chile: 12th Floor, Robert Jones House, Jervois Quay, P.O.B. 3861; *Ambassador:* SERGIO FUENZALIDA.

China, People's Republic: 2–6 Glenmore St.; *Ambassador:* QIN LIZHEN.

Colombia: Beijing, People's Republic of China.

Cyprus: Canberra, A.C.T., Australia (HC).

Czechoslovakia: 12 Anne St., Wadestown, 1, P.O.B. 2843; *Ambassador:* Dr. MILAN MACHA (resident in Jakarta, Indonesia).

Denmark: Canberra, A.C.T., Australia.

Ecuador: Tokyo, Japan.

Egypt: 13th Floor, Dalmuir House, The Terrace, 1, P.O.B. 10-386; *Ambassador:* ABDEL RAHMAN MAREI.

Fiji: 2nd Floor, Robert Jones Bldg., P.O.B. 3940 (HC); *High Commissioner:* JOSEPH D. GIBSON, C.B.E.

Finland: Canberra, A.C.T., Australia.

France: 14th Floor, Robert Jones House, 1–3 Willeston St., P.O.B. 1695; *Ambassador:* JACQUES BOURGOIN.

German Democratic Republic: Canberra, A.C.T., Australia.

Germany, Federal Republic: 90-92 Hobson St., P.O.B. 1687; *Ambassador:* Dr. HANS A. STEGER.

Greece: Canberra, A.C.T., Australia.

Hungary: Yarralumla, A.C.T., Australia.

India: 10th Floor, Princess Towers, 180 Molesworth St., 1 (HC); *High Commissioner:* A. K. BUDHIRAJA.

Indonesia: 9 and 11 Fitzherbert Terrace, Thorndon, 1, P.O.B. 3543; *Ambassador:* SUKAMTO SAYIDIMAN.

Iran: Canberra, A.C.T., Australia.

Iraq: Canberra, A.C.T., Australia.

Ireland: Canberra, A.C.T., Australia.

Israel: 13th Floor, Williams City Centre, Plimmer Steps, P.O.B. 2171; *Ambassador:* YAAKOV MORRIS.

Italy: 38 Grant Rd., Thorndon, 1, P.O.B. 463; *Ambassador:* Dr. GIORGIO DE ANDREIS.

Japan: 7th and 8th Floors, Norwich Insurance House, 3–11 Hunter St., P.O.B. 6340, Wellington 1; *Ambassador:* TAKASHI OYAMADA.

Korea, Republic: 12th Floor, Williams Centre, P.O.B. 12115; *Ambassador:* YOUNGHUN HAHM.

Laos: Canberra, A.C.T., Australia.

Lebanon: Canberra, A.C.T., Australia.

Malaysia: Chase-NBA House, 163–165 The Terrace, P.O.B. 9422 (HC); *High Commissioner:* M. M. SATHIAH.

Mexico: Canberra, A.C.T., Australia.

Mongolia: Tokyo, Japan.

Nepal: Tokyo, Japan.

Netherlands: 10th Floor, Investment Centre, cnr. Featherston and Ballance Sts., P.O.B. 840; *Ambassador:* Baron ROBERT S. N. VAN DER FELTZ.

Nigeria: Canberra, A.C.T., Australia (HC).

Norway: Canberra, A.C.T., Australia.

Pakistan: Canberra, A.C.T., Australia.

Papua New Guinea: Construction House, 82 Kent Terrace, 1, P.O.B. 9746, Courtenay Place (HC); *High Commissioner:* BRIAN K. AMINI.

Peru: Southern Cross Building, 22 Brandon St., P.O.B. 10-398; *Chargé d'affaires a.i.:* CARLOS GONZALES.

Philippines: Level 30, Williams City Centre, P.O.B. 11-243; *Ambassador:* PACIFICO EVANGELISTA.

Poland: Canberra, A.C.T., Australia.

Portugal: Canberra, A.C.T., Australia.

Romania: 100 Evans Bay Parade; *Chargé d'affaires a.i.:* RADU IRIMIA.

Singapore: 17 Kabul St., Khandallah, P.O.B. 29-023 (HC); *High Commissioner:* A. RAHIM ISHAK.

Spain: Canberra, A.C.T., Australia.

Sri Lanka: Canberra, A.C.T., Australia (HC).

Sweden: 8th Floor, Greenock House, 39 The Terrace, P.O.B. 1800; *Ambassador:* GUNNAR GERRING.

Switzerland: Panama House, 22–24 Panama St., P.O.B. 386; *Chargé d'affaires a.i.:* ERICH WIRTH.

Thailand: 2 Burnell Avenue, 1, P.O.B. 2530; *Ambassador:* SAKOL VANABRIKSHA.

Turkey: Canberra, A.C.T., Australia.

U.S.S.R.: 57 Messines Rd., Karori; *Chargé d'affaires a.i.:* VLADIMIR I. AZARUSHKIN.

United Kingdom: British High Commission, Reserve Bank Bldg., 2 The Terrace, P.O.B. 1812 (HC); *High Commissioner:* R. J. STRATTON, C.M.G.

U.S.A.: 29 Fitzherbert Terrace, Private Bag; *Ambassador:* H. MONROE BROWNE.

Uruguay: Canberra, A.C.T., Australia.

Vatican City: Apostolic Nunciature, 112 Queen's Drive, Lyall Bay, Wellington 3, P.O.B. 14044; *Apostolic Pro-Nuncio:* The Most Rev. ANTONIO MAGNONI.

Venezuela: Canberra, A.C.T., Australia.

Viet-Nam: Canberra, A.C.T., Australia.

Western Samoa: 1A Wesley Rd., Kelburn, P.O.B. 1430 (HC); *High Commissioner:* FEESAGO S. (GEORGE) FEPULEA'I.

Yugoslavia: 24 Hatton St., Karori; *Ambassador:* NIKOLA KRAJINOVIĆ.

New Zealand also has diplomatic relations with Bahrain, Barbados, Costa Rica, El Salvador, Guyana, Iceland, Jamaica, Kiribati, Luxembourg, Maldives, Malta, Nauru, Saudi Arabia, Solomon Islands, Tanzania, Tonga, Tuvalu and Vanuatu.

JUDICIAL SYSTEM

The Judicial System of New Zealand comprises a Court of Appeal, a High Court (previously the Supreme Court), an Arbitration Court and a Compensation Court. There are also District Courts, having both civil and criminal jurisdiction. Final appeal is to the Judicial Committee of the Privy Council in the United Kingdom.

As from May 1st, 1981, District Courts have jurisdiction in most criminal matters and specified District Court Judges are empowered to sit with juries. As from October 1st, 1981, Family Courts are constituted as Divisions of District Courts to deal with dissolution of marriage, separation, maintenance, custody and other family law matters.

Chief Justice: Rt. Hon. Sir RONALD DAVISON, G.B.E., C.M.G.

THE COURT OF APPEAL

President: Rt. Hon. Sir OWEN WOODHOUSE, K.B.E., D.S.C.

Registrar: WILLIAM L'ESTRANGE.

Judges:

Rt. Hon. Sir RONALD DAVISON, G.B.E., C.M.G. (*ex officio*)
Rt. Hon. Sir ROBIN BRUNSKILL COOKE
Rt. Hon. IVOR LLOYD MORGAN RICHARDSON
Rt. Hon. DUNCAN WALLACE MCMULLIN.
Rt. Hon. EDWARD JONATHAN SOMERS.

THE HIGH COURT

Judges:

Rt. Hon. Sir RONALD DAVISON, G.B.E., C.M.G.
Hon. LESTER FRANCIS MOLLER
Hon. CLINTON MARCUS ROPER
Hon. JAMES PETER QUILLIAM
Hon. JOHN BARRY O'REGAN
Hon. MUIR FITZHERBERT CHILWELL
Hon. MAURICE EUGENE CASEY
Hon. JOSEPH AUGUSTINE ONGLEY
Hon. RICHARD IAN BARKER
Hon. JOHN FRANCIS JEFFRIES
Hon. MAXWELL HELIER VAUTIER
Hon. JAMES BAYNE SINCLAIR
Hon. GORDON ELLIS BISSON
Hon. ALAN DOUGLAS HOLLAND
Hon. THOMAS MURRAY THORP

Hon. LAURENCE MURRAY GREIG
Hon. JOHN PHILIP COOK, O.B.E., E.D.
Hon. RICHARD CHRISTOPHER SAVAGE
Hon. MICHAEL HARDIE BOYS
Hon. EVAN MURRAY PRICHARD
Hon. JOHN HAMILTON WALLACE

ARBITRATION COURT

Chief Judge: J. R. P. HORN

Judges:
N. P. WILLIAMSON
D. S. CASTLE

RELIGION

ANGLICAN
(Province of New Zealand)

Archbishop: Most Rev. P. A. REEVES, Bishop's House, 2 Arney Crescent, Remuera, Auckland 5; 895,000 mems.; publ. *Anglican News*.

Provincial Secretary: Mrs. JENNY COTTRELL, P.O.B. 320, Christchurch.

ROMAN CATHOLIC CHURCH

Archbishop of Wellington: Most Rev. THOMAS STAFFORD WILLIAMS; P.O.B. 198, Wellington 1; at the 1981 census there were 449,660 Catholics in New Zealand.

OTHER DENOMINATIONS

Baptist Union of New Zealand: 185–187 Willis St., P.O.B. 27–390, Wellington 1; f. 1882; Pres. of Union Rev. L. S. ARMSTRONG; Gen. Sec. Rev. Dr. S. L. EDGAR; 19,934 mems.

Churches of Christ in New Zealand (Associated): 90a Mount St., Nelson; 3,000 mems.; Gen. Sec. T. G. TODD; publ. *N.Z. Christian*.

Congregational Churches (*The Congregational Union of New Zealand*): c/o 29 Alexander Rd., Raumati Beach; f. 1883; Chair. Rev. J. B. CHAMBERS, O.B.E.; Treasurer D. L. PROUT; Sec. Mrs. J. B. CHAMBERS; 381 mems.

Methodist Church of New Zealand: Connexional Office, P.O.B. 931, Christchurch 1; 24,800 communicant mems.; Gen. Sec. Rev. A. K. WOODLEY; Gen. Sec. Overseas Division Rev. W. G. TUCKER (Auckland).

Presbyterian Church of New Zealand: Dalmuir House, P.O.B. 10-000, The Terrace, Wellington 1; Moderator The Rt. Rev. L. R. HAMPTON; Assembly Exec. Sec. Rev. W. A. BEST; Moderator of Maori Synod Rev. R. KOIA; 70,000 communicant mems.; publ. *The Outlook* (monthly).

Maori Denominations: there are several Maori Churches in New Zealand with a total membership of over 30,000—Ratana Church of New Zealand, Ringatu Church, Church of Te Kooti Rikirangi, Absolute Maori Established Church, United Maori Mission.

THE PRESS

NEWSPAPERS AND PERIODICALS

MAJOR DAILIES

Auckland Star: Shortland St., P.O.B. 3697, Auckland 1; f. 1870; evening; Man. Dir. N. P. WEBBER; Editor KEITH AITKEN; circ. 116,000.

Bay of Plenty Times: P.O.B. 648, Tauranga; f. 1872; evening; Man. Dir. A. F. SHERSON; Editor ERNEST F. T. BEER; circ. 16,699.

Christchurch Star: P.O.B. 1467, Christchurch; f. 1868; independent; evening; Gen. Man. E. P. D. COONEY; Editor P. H. OSBORNE; circ. 60,330.

The Daily News: P.O.B. 444, New Plymouth; f. 1857; morning; Gen. Man. R. J. AVERY; Editor DENIS GARCIA; circ. 22,500.

The Daily Post: P.O.B. 1442, Rotorua; f. 1885; evening; Man. Dir. J. B. GEDDIS; Editor M. A. BERRY; circ. 15,517.

Daily Telegraph: P.O.B. 343, Napier; f. 1871; evening; Man. Dir. J. B. GEDDIS; Editor M. A. BERRY; circ. 19,108.

The Dominion: Press House, Willis St., Box 1297, Wellington; f. 1907; morning; Gen. Man. W. J. KELSO; Editor E. G. A. FROST; circ. 63,000.

Evening Post: Press House, Willis St., P.O.B. 3740, Wellington; f. 1865; Gen. Man. W. J. KELSO; Editor D. R. CHURCHILL; circ. 92,835.

Evening Standard: P.O.B. 3, Palmerston North; f. 1880; evening; Man. Dir. P. G. HENSON; Editor P. R. CAVANAGH; circ. 30,000.

Gisborne Herald: P.O.B. 1143, Gisborne; f. 1874; evening; Man. Dir. M. C. MUIR; Editor IAIN GILLIES; circ. 11,685.

The Hawke's Bay Herald Tribune: Karamu Rd., Box 180, Hastings; f. 1857; independent conservative; evening; Man. Dir. K. J. STINSON; Editor L. E. ANDERSON; circ. 20,100.

Nelson Evening Mail: P.O.B. 244, Nelson; f. 1866; evening; Man. Dir. W. D. LUCAS; Editor R. S. NEVILLE; circ. 18,500.

New Zealand Herald: P.O.B. 32, Auckland; f. 1863; morning; Man. Dir. H. M. HORTON; Editor ALLAN V. COLE; circ. 239,800.

Northern Advocate: Water St., P.O.B. 210, Whangarei; f. 1875; evening; Man. Dir. G. C. BEAZLEY; Editor C. R. ASHBY; circ. 17,900.

Otago Daily Times: Stuart St., P.O.B. 517, Dunedin; f. 1861; morning; Man. Dir. J. C. S. SMITH; Editor KEITH EUNSON; circ. 54,500.

The Press: Cathedral Square, Box 1005, Christchurch; f. 1861; morning; Gen. Man. R. A. BARKER; Editor E. B. LOCK; circ. 80,000.

Southland Times: P.O.B. 805, 67 Esk St., Invercargill; f. 1862; morning; Man. Dir. I. L. GILMOUR; Editor P. M. MULLER; circ. 33,361.

Taranaki Herald: P.O.B. 444, New Plymouth; f. 1852; evening; Gen. Man. R. J. AVERY; Editor GEORGE K. KOEA; circ. 11,250.

Timaru Herald: Sophia St., P.O.B. 46, Timaru; f. 1864; morning; Man. Dir. E. G. KERR; Editor M. J. VANCE; circ. 17,539.

Waikato Times: Tasman St., P.O.B. 444, Hamilton; f. 1872; independent; evening; Editor B. M. MARTIN; Gen. Man. A. W. GOLDFINCH; circ. 39,962.

Wanganui Chronicle: P.O.B. 433, Wanganui; f. 1856; morning; Gen. Man. A. P. BATES; Editor GEORGE V. ABBOTT; circ. 11,185.

Wanganui Herald: P.O.B. 433, Wanganui; f. 1867; evening; Gen. Man. A. P. BATES; Editor GEORGE V. ABBOTT; circ. 9,710.

WEEKLY AND OTHER NEWSPAPERS

Best Bets: P.O.B. 1327, Auckland; horse-racing and trotting; Editor LEX NICHOLS; circ. 54,000.

Economic News: N.Z. Economic News Ltd., 7 Bowen St., P.O.B. 1026, Wellington; f. 1954; Editor A. P. KEMBER.

8 O'Clock: P.O.B. 3697, Auckland; sports results and features, weekend news, etc.; Saturday evening; Editor NEIL ANDERSON; circ. 102,400.

Mercantile Gazette of New Zealand: 8 Sheffield Cres., P.O.B. 20-034, Christchurch; f. 1876; economics, finance, management, stock market, politics; Editor Mrs. R. RICHARDS; circ. 24,000.

New Zealand Gazette: Dept. of Internal Affairs, Private Bag, Wellington; f. 1840; Thursday; circ. 1,550.

New Zealand Tablet: 64 Vogel St., P.O.B. 1285, Dunedin; f. 1873; Wednesday; Roman Catholic; Editor J. P. KENNEDY, O.B.E.; circ. 11,000.

New Zealand Times: Press House, Willis St., Wellington; f. 1981; Editor R. C. FOX; circ. 122,000.

New Zealand Truth: Press House, Willis St., P.O.B. 1122, Wellington; f. 1904; Tuesday; international and local news and comment; sports; finance; women's interests; Editor R. S. GAULT; circ. 172,000.

New Zealand Woman's Weekly: P.O.B. 1409, Auckland; f. 1934; Monday; family magazine, general interest; Editor JEAN WISHART; circ. 245,000.

North Shore Times Advertiser: P.O.B. 33-235, Takapuna, Auckland 9; twice weekly; Editor Mrs. P. M. GUNDRY; circ. 50,250.

Taieri Herald: P.O.B. 105, Mosgiel; Editor J. F. FOX; circ. 5,000.

Waihi Gazette: Seddon St. Waihi; Editor RON DALLY.

Wairarapa News: P.O.B. 18, Carterton; f. 1869; Editor J. G. DRAPER; circ. 3,100.

Waitara Times: West Quay, Waitara; f. 1960; Editor B. L. OLDFIELD.

Weekend Star: Box 2651, Christchurch; Saturday evening; Editor A. DONEY; circ. 37,000.

Zealandia: P.O.B. 845, Auckland; f. 1934; Tuesday; Roman Catholic; Editor Rev. DENNIS J. HORTON; circ. 15,000.

OTHER PERIODICALS

Better Business: Private Bag, Dominion Rd., Auckland; f. 1938; monthly; Editor DAVID PARDON; circ. 17,000.

Friday Flash: P.O.B. 1034, Wellington; weekly; horse-racing; circ. 30,000.

Journal of the Polynesian Society: c/o Dept. of Anthropology, University of Auckland, Private Bag, Auckland; f. 1892; Editors Dr. G. J. IRWIN, Dr. R. S. OPPENHEIM; circ. 1,500.

Landfall: 113 Victoria St., Christchurch; quarterly; literary; published by Christchurch Caxton Press Ltd.; Editor DAVID DOWLING.

Management: P.O.B. 3159, Auckland; f. 1954; business; monthly; Editor SHANE C. NIBLOCK; circ. 7,000.

Monthly Abstract of Statistics: Dept. of Statistics, Private Bag, Wellington; f. 1914; Editor and Dir. of Information Services J. V. LERMIT.

Motorman: Fourman Holdings Ltd., P.O.B. 883, Wellington; f. 1957; motoring monthly; Editor DAVID HALL.

Nation: P.O.B. 957, Wellington; f. 1911; monthly; current topics; Editor M. W. LEAMAN; circ. 30,000.

New Zealand Architect: P.O.B. 2182, Wellington; f. 1905; bi-monthly; journal of the New Zealand Institute of Architects; Man. Editor G. D. MOLLER; circ. 2,300.

New Zealand Dairy Exporter: P.O.B. 1001, Wellington; Man. Editor J. D. McGILVARY; circ. 22,000.

The New Zealand Farmer: P.O.B. 1409, Auckland 1; f. 1882; twice monthly; Editor NEIL RENNIE; circ. 30,000.

The New Zealand Financial Review: P.O.B. 1367, Wellington; f. 1982; finance, investment, business; Editor DENIS WEDERELL; cire. 8,000.

New Zealand Gardener: Private Bag, Petone; monthly; Editor Mrs. J. GRACE; circ. 22,000.

New Zealand Journal of Agriculture: Private Bag, Petone; f. 1910; monthly; Editor MATTHEW BIRD; circ. 20,000.

New Zealand Journal of Science: Department of Scientific and Industrial Research, P.O.B. 9741, Wellington 1; f. 1958; chemistry, engineering, mathematics, meteorology, nutrition, physics, soil science; quarterly; Editor N. HAWCROFT.

New Zealand Law Journal: Butterworths of New Zealand Ltd., 33-35 Cumberland Place, P.O.B. 472, Wellington; monthly.

New Zealand Listener: Broadcasting Corporation of N.Z., P.O.B. 98, Wellington; f. 1939; weekly; broadcasting topics, political and social commentary, literature, arts; Editor PETER STEWART; circ. 370,000.

New Zealand Medical Journal: P.O.B. 5441, Dunedin; f. 1887; twice monthly; Editor Prof. R. G. ROBINSON, G.M., CH.M., F.R.C.S.; circ. 4,900.

New Zealand Motor World: P.O.B. 1, Wellington; f. 1936; bi-monthly; official organ of 12 automobile associations, 6 caravan clubs; Man. Editor R. A. HOCKING; circ. 88,000.

New Zealand Official Yearbook: Dept. of Statistics, Private Bag, Wellington; f. 1892; Editor N. G. KILLICK.

New Zealand Science Review: P.O.B. 1874, Wellington; f. 1942; science policy, social responsibilities of scientists; every 2 months; Editor J. G. GREGORY.

New Zealand Sports Digest: P.O.B. 1034, Wellington; f. 1949; fortnightly; Editors P. A. CAVANAGH, R. C. FOX; circ. 14,000.

New Zealand Wings: Aeronautical Press, P.O.B. 305, Fielding; f. 1932; Editor ROSS MCPHERSON; circ. 18,000.

New Zealand Woman: P.O.B. 957, Dunedin; circ. 32,500.

N.Z. Company Director and Executive: 8 Sheffield Cres., P.O.B. 20-034, Christchurch; economics, management, politics; Editor Mrs. R. RICHARDS; circ. 5,700.

Otago Farmer: P.O.B. 45, Balclutha; fortnightly; Editor A. MOORE; circ. 5,200.

Pacific Islands Trade News: 4 Kingdon St., Newmarket 1; circ. 22,000.

Pacific Viewpoint: Victoria University, Private Bag, Wellington; f. 1960; Editor Prof. R. F. WATTERS; circ. 1,050.

Public Service Journal: P.O.B. 5108, Wellington; monthly; Editor JOHN MILNE; circ. 65,000.

Reader's Digest: P.O.B. 3372, Auckland; monthly; Editor DENIS WALLIS; Advertising Man. BARRIE N. MASON; circ. 165,000.

Southland Farmer: P.O.B. 45, Balclutha; fortnightly; Editor A. MOORE; circ. 5,500.

Straight Furrow: P.O.B. 715, Wellington; f. 1933; fortnightly; Editor H. BROAD; circ. 37,000.

Tu Tungata: Dept. of Maori Affairs, Private Bag, Wellington; f. 1979; Maori and English; every 2 months; Editor PHILIP WHAANGA; circ. 10,000.

Turf Digest Racetrack: P.O.B. 1034, Wellington; weekly; circ. 60,000.

World Affairs: UN Asscn. of N.Z., Box 1011, Wellington; f. 1945; quarterly; Editor Miss G. E. RYAN.

NEWS AGENCIES

New Zealand Press Association: Newspaper House, 93 Boulcott St., P.O.B. 1599, Wellington; f. 1879; non-political; Chair. J. M. ROBSON; Gen. Man. G. W. JENKINS.

South Pacific News Service (SOPAC): P.O.B. 5026, Lambton Quay, Wellington; f. 1948; Man. Dir. E. W. BENTON; Editor N. N. MCMILLAN.

FOREIGN BUREAUX

Agentstvo Pechati Novosti (APN) (*U.S.S.R.*): Wellington; Correspondent: c/o P.O.B. 27-246, Wellington.

Reuters (*U.K.*): New Zealand Press Association, Newspaper House, 93 Boulcott St., P.O.B. 1599, Wellington.

PRESS COUNCIL

New Zealand Press Council: P.O.B. 1066, Wellington; f. 1972; Chair. Rt. Hon. Sir THADDEUS MCCARTHY, K.B.E.; Sec. H. L. VERRY, C.B.E.

PRESS ASSOCIATIONS

Newspaper Publishers' Association of New Zealand (Inc.): Newspaper House, P.O.B. 1066, 93 Boulcott St., Wellington; f. 1898; 45 mems.; Pres. R. F. SMITH; Exec. Dir. D. J. PATTEN; Sec. T. CONNOLLY-BROWN.

Commonwealth Press Union (New Zealand Section): P.O.B. 444, New Plymouth; Chair. P. MULLER; Sec. D. J. PATTEN.

PUBLISHERS

Associated Book Publishers (N.Z.) Ltd.: 61 Beach Rd., Auckland; publishers of New Zealand books under Methuen New Zealand imprint, and representatives and wholesalers for a range of U.K. and U.S. publishers; incorporates Sweet and Maxwell (N.Z.) Ltd., legal books.

Auckland University Press: Private Bag, University of Auckland, Auckland; f. 1966; Man. Editor R. D. MCELDOWNEY.

Butterworths of New Zealand Ltd.: 33-35 Cumberland Place, P.O.B. 472, Wellington; legal, commercial, medical, scientific, technical.

Christchurch Caxton Press Ltd.: P.O.B. 25088, 113 Victoria St., Christchurch 1; f. 1936; poetry, art, history, prose, gardening; Man. Dir. BRUCE BASCAND.

Collins (William) Publishers Ltd.: P.O.B. 1, Auckland; Man. Dir. B. D. PHILLIPS.

Dunmore Press Ltd.: P.O.B. 5115, Palmerston North; f. 1975; history, general, university; Chair. and Dir. JOHN DUNMORE; Editor PATRICIA CHAPMAN.

Heinemann Publishers (N.Z.) Ltd.: P.O.B. 36-064, Auckland; f. 1980; educational, technical, academic, general, reference; Chair. A. R. BEAL; Man. Dir. D. J. HEAP.

Hodder and Stoughton Ltd.: P.O.B. 3858, Auckland; Man. Dir. R. J. COOMBES.

Hutcheson, Bowman and Stewart Ltd.: P.O.B. 9032, 15-19 Tory St., Wellington.

Hutchinson Group (N.Z.) Ltd.: P.O.B. 40-086, Glenfield, Auckland 10; f. 1977; general and educational books; Chair. J. POTTER; Man. Dir. K. C. POUNDER; Dirs. C. CLARK, B. PERMAN, J. MOTTRAM, S. MCCLOUD.

Longman Paul Limited: G.P.O. Box 4019, Auckland 1; f. 1968; educational; Dirs. ROSEMARY STAGG, N. J. RYAN, B. J. SPRUNT, G. D. BEATTIE.

John McIndoe Ltd.: P.O.B. 694, Dunedin; f. 1893; fiction, reference, art, history, music, science, medicine, university; Man. Dir. J. H. MCINDOE.

New Zealand Council for Educational Research: P.O.B. 3237, Wellington; f. 1934; scholarly books, research monographs, bulletins, educational tests, research summaries, academic journal; Chair. Prof. R. S. ADAMS; Dir. J. E. WATSON.

Oxford University Press: 1st Floor, 28 Wakefield St., P.O.B. 5294, Auckland 1; Editor WENDY HARREX.

Pegasus Press Ltd.: 14 Oxford Terrace, P.O.B. 2244, Christchurch; f. 1948; publishers and printers; fiction, poetry, history, biography, etc. by New Zealand authors; Man. Dir. DONALD H. WALLACE; Editor ROBIN MUIR.

Pelorus Press Ltd.: 22-24 Olive Rd., Penrose, Auckland; f. 1947; Dirs. T. J. ANSTIS, R. A. SIMPSON.

Reed, A. H. and A. W. Ltd.: 68-74 Kingsford-Smith St., Wellington 3; f. 1907; general; Man. Dir. P. M. BRADWELL.

University of Otago Press: P.O.B. 56, Dunedin; f. 1958.

Whitcoulls Ltd.: 111 Cashel St., Christchurch; N.Z. general and educational books; Man. Dir. P. E. BOURNE.

Wise, H., and Co. (New Zealand) Ltd.: 27 St. Andrew St., Dunedin; f. 1865; publishers of maps and street directories, N.Z. Guide and N.Z. Post Office Directories; Man. J. A. DECOURCY.

RADIO AND TELEVISION

The Broadcasting Corporation of New Zealand (BCNZ), established in 1977, supervises the independent operating Services, Radio New Zealand (RNZ) and Television New Zealand (TVNZ), and provides transmission facilities for them. Revenue for public broadcasting is derived from radio and television advertising and from the television licence fee. Colour broadcasting began in 1973.

Broadcasting Corporation of New Zealand (BCNZ): Bowen State Bldg., Bowen St., P.O.B. 98, Wellington; f. 1977; nine member board; supervises public radio and television in New Zealand; Chair. IAN R. CROSS.

RADIO

Radio New Zealand: P.O.B. 2092, Wellington; f. 1975; 2 non-commercial networks. Both non-commercial and commercial networks broadcast 24 hours a day; Dir.-Gen. GEOFFREY F. WHITEHEAD.

Commercial radio has been operating in New Zealand since 1937. In 1976 there were seven privately-owned commercial radio stations, depending entirely on commercial revenue but operating under the supervision of the Broadcasting Tribunal.

TELEVISION

Television New Zealand: Centrecourt Bldg., Queen St., P.O.B. 3819, Auckland; f. 1980; the television service is responsible for the production of programmes for the two TV networks and for the sale of all local productions. The networks are commercial for 5 days a week and transmit in colour. One network (TV 1) covers the entire population, and the other (TV 2) has some 95 per cent coverage, with extensions planned to match the first. Both networks transmit afternoon and evening, seven days a week, and about 40 per cent of programme content is produced in New Zealand; Dir.-Gen. A. W. MARTIN.

In January 1982 there were 915,564 licensed television sets, including 725,649 colour sets.

FINANCE

BANKING

(cap.=capital; p.u.=paid up; subs.=subscribed; dep. =deposits; m.=million; $NZ=$ New Zealand)

CENTRAL BANK

Reserve Bank of New Zealand: P.O.B. 2498, 2 The Terrace, Wellington; f. 1934; became State-owned institution 1936; bank of issue; dep. (demand) $NZ594.1m. (March 1981); Gov. D. L. WILKS; Deputy Gov. Dr. R. S. DEANE.

COMMERCIAL BANKS

ANZ Banking Group (New Zealand) Ltd.: 27–35 Mercer St., Wellington; incorporated 1979; a partly owned subsidiary of Australia and New Zealand Banking Group Ltd. of Melbourne, Australia; subsidiary companies: ANZ Savings Bank (New Zealand) Ltd., UDC Group Holdings Ltd.; cap. p.u. $NZ53.0m.; Gen. Man. D. NICOLSON.

Bank of New Zealand: Cnr. of Lambton and Customhouse Quays, P.O.B. 2392, Wellington; f. 1861; cap. $NZ41.5m.; dep. $NZ3,755m. (March 1981); Chair. L. N. ROSS, C.M.G.; Gen. Man. and Chief Exec. WILLIAM J. SHAW.

National Bank of New Zealand Ltd.: 170–186 Featherston St., P.O.B. 1791, Wellington 1; f. 1873; cap. p.u. $NZ16.1m.; res. $NZ119.6m.; dep. $NZ2,045.9m. (Oct. 1981); Chair. Sir JOHN MARSHALL, G.B.E., C.H.; Chief Exec. S. T. RUSSELL; 145 brs. in New Zealand and the Cook Islands.

FOREIGN BANKS

Westpac Banking Corporation (*Australia*): 318 Lambton Quay, Wellington 1; f. 1982, following merger of Bank of New South Wales and Commercial Bank of Australia Ltd.

SAVINGS BANKS

Bank of New Zealand Savings Bank Ltd.: Cnr. of Lambton and Customhouse Quays, P.O.B. 2392, Wellington; f. 1964; cap. subs. and p.u. $NZ2m.; dep. $NZ404m. (March 1981); Chair. L. N. ROSS, C.M.G.; Gen. Man. and Chief Exec. W. J. SHAW.

Post Office Savings Bank: 49 Willis St., Wellington 1.

STOCK EXCHANGES

Auckland Stock Exchange: No. 1 Bldg., C.M.L. Centre, Queen St., Auckland; Chair. H. J. NISBET; See. D. S. WRIGHT.

Christchurch Invercargill Stock Exchange Ltd.: P.O.B. 639, Christchurch; Chair. D. S. DOTT; Sec. P. F. MAPLES.

Dunedin Stock Exchange: P.O.B. 483, Dunedin; Chair. K. J. ELSOM; Sec. K. R. SELLAR.

Wellington Stock Exchange: P.O.B. 767, Govt. Life Insurance Bldg., Brandon St., 1; Chair. J. E. ABURN; Sec. G. H. GOSS.

ASSOCIATION

New Zealand Stock Exchange Association: P.O.B. 2959, Wellington; Exec. Dir. ROGER B. W. GILL.

INSURANCE

Government Life Insurance Office: P.O.B. 590, Wellington 1; f. 1869; Commissioner H. D. PEACOCK.

State Insurance Office: Lambton Quay, Wellington 1; f. 1905; Gen. Man. G. D. PRINGLE.

A.A. Mutual Insurance Company: P.O.B. 1348, Wellington; f. 1928; Chair. J. C. BATES; Sec. P. G. DESMOND.

A.M.P. Fire and General Insurance Company (N.Z.) Ltd.: 86/90 Customhouse Quay, Wellington; f. 1958; Chair. DOUGLAS A. SMITH; Man. A. D. BOWLES; fire, accident, marine, general.

Colonial Mutual Life Assurance Society Ltd.: Customhouse Quay, P.O.B. 191, Wellington; Man. I. C. CURRY; life, accident, sickness, staff superannuation.

Commercial Union General Insurance Company Ltd.: 142 Featherston St., P.O.B. 2797, Wellington; Gen. Man. W. S. MANSFIELD; fire, accident, marine, engineering.

Export Guarantee Office: Box 5037, Wellington 1; f. 1964; Gen. Man. G. D. PRINGLE; Dir. D. R. IRVINE; export credit insurers.

Farmers' Mutual Insurance Group: 138 Queen St., P.O.B. 1943, Palmerston North; comprises Farmers' Mutual Insurance Association and The Primary Industies Insurance Company Ltd.; Gen. Man. J. D. WILDE; fire, accident, motor vehicle, marine, life.

Metropolitan Life Assurance Company of N.Z. Ltd.: 139 Albert St., P.O.B. 1117, Auckland 1; f. 1962; life; Chair. D. ST. CLAIR BROWN; Chief Exec. Dir. A. W. TILLS; Gen. Man. R. G. THOMAS.

The National Insurance Company of New Zealand, Ltd.: 300 Princes St., Dunedin; f. 1873; Chair. C. D. BAKER; Gen. Man. J. S. HODGKINSON; Sec. R. HENDRY.

National Mutual Group of Companies: National Mutual Centre, 70 The Terrace, P.O.B. 1692, Wellington; Man. G. M. J. HOSKINS; life, disability, superannuation, estate planning, business assurance.

New Zealand Counties' Co-operative Insurance Company Limited: Local Government Bldg., Lambton Quay, P.O.B. 5034, Wellington; f. 1942; Chair. M. E. GROOME; Sec. B. P. GRESHAM; fire, accident, fidelity guarantee, motor.

The New Zealand Municipalities Cooperative Insurance Company Ltd.: Local Government Bldg., 114–118 Lambton Quay, Wellington; f. 1960; Chair. Sir MICHAEL FOWLER; Gen. Man. C. H. ARCHER; Sec. K. F. J. BRYANT; fire, motor vehicle, all risks, accident.

The New Zealand South British Group Ltd.: South British Bldg., Shortland St., Auckland; f. 1981; Chair. Sir ALAN HELLABY; Chief Exec. Officer D. N. CHALMERS.

Norwich Union Life Insurance Society: cnr. Hunter and Victoria Sts., Wellington 1.

Phoenix Assurance Co. of New Zealand Ltd.: 125–127 Featherston St., P.O.B. 894, Wellington; Group Gen. Man. A. W. HALL, F.C.I.I.; fire, accident, marine.

Provident Life Assurance Company Ltd.: 125–127 Featherston St., P.O.B. 894, Wellington, C.1; f. 1904; a subsidiary of Phoenix Assurance Co.; Gen. Man. R. A. JESSUP, B.SC., F.I.A.

Prudential Assurance Co. Ltd.: 332–340 Lambton Quay, P.O.B. 291, Wellington; Mans. C. C. HOUGH, D. MAIN; life, fire, accident, marine.

Queensland Insurance Co. Ltd.: Huddart Parker Bldg., Wellington 1.

S.I.M.U. Mutual Insurance Association: 29–35 Latimer Square, Christchurch; f. 1926; Chair. T. J. CHAMBERLAIN; Gen. Man. E. B. MCKESSAR.

TRADE AND INDUSTRY

CHAMBERS OF COMMERCE

New Zealand Chambers of Commerce: Molesworth St., Thorndon, P.O.B. 1071, Wellington 1; Exec. Vice-Pres. A. R. SIMM; publ. *New Zealand Commerce* (monthly).

Wellington Chamber of Commerce: Commerce House, 126 Wakefield St., Wellington, P.O.B. 1590, Wellington; f. 1856; Pres. J. A. HAZLETT; Exec. Dir. A. P. CUMING; Sec. R. J. F. AIREY; 1,050 mems.; publs. *Voice of Business* (monthly), *Information and Trade Enquiry Bulletin* (monthly), *Annual Report*.

DEVELOPMENT ORGANIZATIONS

Development Finance Corporation of New Zealand: P.O.B. 3090, Wellington; f. 1973 as a wholly government-owned corporation to provide finance, especially medium- and long-term finance, and advisory services to industry and commerce. Its major functions are to assist the expansion of exports and to encourage efficient import substitution, to contribute to increased productivity and the development of engineering and technical skills, and to assist the growth of key industries and planned regional development. It also administers the Applied Technology Programme, a scheme of incentives for industrial research and development, and the Small Business Agency; cap. p.u. $NZ 25m. (1979); Gen. Man. J. M. HUNN.

New Zealand Export-Import Corporation: Robert Jones House, 1 Willeston St., P.O.B. 11332, Wellington; f. 1974; undertakes export and import of goods and services and trade promotion activities; advisory service; may act as buying and selling agent for government and undertake trade transactions on its behalf; cap. $NZ2m.; Gen. Man. C. B. STANWORTH; Sec. D. L. PAETZ.

The New Zealand Bureau of Importers and Exporters (Inc.): Parnell House, 470 Parnell Rd., Auckland; f. 1938.

OVERSEAS DEVELOPMENT

ENEX of New Zealand Inc.: P.O.B. 2585, Wellington 1; f. 1969; a private organization of 80 member firms promoting New Zealand expertise in South-East Asia and the Pacific; membership includes consultants, contractors and manufacturers; publ. *ENEX Review*.

MANUFACTURERS' ORGANIZATIONS

The Auckland Manufacturers' Association: P.O.B. 28-245, Remuera, Auckland 5; f. 1886; Pres. R. G. ALEXANDER; Dir. J. WHATNALL; 1,150 mems.

Canterbury Manufacturers' Association: P.O.B. 13-152, Armagh, Christchurch; f. 1879; Dir. I. D. HOWELL; 675 mems.

New Zealand Manufacturers' Federation (Inc.): Industry House, Courtenay Place and Allen St., Wellington 1; f. 1898; Dir.-Gen. I. G. DOUGLAS; publ. *Manufacturer* (fortnightly).

Otago Southland Manufacturers' Association Inc.: P.O.B. 5118, Moray Place, Dunedin; Pres. J. A. AITKEN; Dir. W. R. MAY; 200 mems.

Wellington Manufacturers' Association: P.O.B. 9234, Wellington; f. 1895; Pres. G. W. SALMOND; Dir. W. L. GARDNER; 800 mems.

PRODUCERS' ORGANIZATIONS

Federated Farmers of New Zealand: 7th Floor, Commercial Union House, Featherston St., P.O.B. 715, Wellington, C.1; f. 1945; Pres. W. R. STOREY; Chief Exec. R. D. MCLAGAN; 32,000 mems.; publ. *Straight Furrow* (fortnightly).

Meat Producers' Board: P.O.B. 121, Wellington 1; f. 1922; Chair. ADAM BEGG; Sec. M. W. CALDER; 9 mems.; publ. *Meat Producer* (monthly).

National Beekeepers' Association of New Zealand (Inc.): P.O.B. 4048, Wellington 1; f. 1913; 1,000 mems.; Pres. W. A. CLISSOLD; Sec. L. J. JONES; publ. *N.Z. Beekeeper.*

New Zealand Animal By-Products Exporters' Association: P.O.B. 1087, 95–99 Molesworth St., Wellington; 27 mems.; Sec. J. G. MCCARTHY.

New Zealand Berryfruit Growers' Federation (Inc.): Securities House, 126 The Terrace, P.O.B. 10050, Wellington; 900 mems.; Pres. J. J. DEKKER; Exec. Officer T. S. JOHNSON.

New Zealand Dairy Board: Pastoral House, Lambton Quay, P.O.B. 417, Wellington 1; f. 1961; statutory board of 14 mems.; Chair. J. T. GRAHAM; Sec. J. P. MCFAULL.

The New Zealand Fruitgrowers' Federation Ltd.: Huddart Parker Bldg., P.O.B. 882, Wellington, C.1; f. 1916; Gen. Man. J. A. DEYELL; publ. *The Orchardist of New Zealand.*

New Zealand Poultry Board: P.O.B. 379, Wellington 1; f. 1933; Chair. A. J. HARVEY; Gen. Man. G. G. KERMODE; Sec. L. A. MCKINNON; 8 mems. (3 Government and 5 producer); publ. *Poultry Forum* (monthly).

New Zealand Vegetable and Produce Growers' Federation (Inc.): Securities House, The Terrace, Wellington 1; 4,400 mems.; Pres. J. L. CLAYTON; Chief Exec. Officer R. H. F. NICHOLSON.

New Zealand Wool Board: 139–141 Featherston St., Private Bag, Wellington; amalgamated with Wool Marketing Corporation 1977; Chair. J. D. MCILRAITH; Man. Dir. H. L. M. PEIRSE; Sec. G. H. DREES.

Pork Industry Council: P.O.B. 4048, Wellington; Chair. D. H. LEPPER; Chief Exec. Officer R. H. F. NICHOLSON; publ. *Pork Industry Gazette*; circ. 2,500.

PRINCIPAL EMPLOYERS' ASSOCIATIONS

New Zealand Employers' Federation (Inc.): 95-99 Molesworth St., P.O.B. 1786, Wellington; f. 1902; links district employers' associations and other national industrial organizations; Pres. S. W. B. DUNCAN; Exec. Dir. J. W. ROWE.

New Zealand Engineering Employers Federation: 95–99 Molesworth St., Wellington; 316 mems.; Industry Man. (Engineering) K. COLE; Sec. J. W. ROWE.

New Zealand Fruitgrowers I.U. of Employers: Huddart Parker Bldg., Wellington; 800 mems.; Sec. C. D. STORY.

New Zealand Master Builders' Federation (Inc.): 80–82 Kent Terrace, P.O.B. 1796, Wellington; Exec. Dir. L. B. STREET.

New Zealand Retailers Federation (Inc.): P.O.B. 12–086, 101–103 Molesworth St., Wellington; f. 1920; direct membership over 5,000 stores, affiliated membership 4,700; Pres. K. J. TREACY; Exec. Dir. BARRY I. PURDY; publ. *Retail News* (monthly).

New Zealand Sawmillers' Federation (Inc.): P.O.B. 12017, Wellington; 300 mems.; Man. W. F. COADY.

New Zealand Sheepowners: Commercial Union House, 140–144 Featherston St., P.O.B. 715, Wellington; 350 mems.; Pres. M O'B. LOUGHNAN; Sec. O. SYMMANS.

New Zealand Timber Industry Employers' Union (Inc.): 95–99 Molesworth St., Wellington; 250 mems.; Man. W. F. COADY.

TRADE UNIONS

The New Zealand Federation of Labour: F.O.L. Bldg., Lukes Lane, P.O.B. 6161, Te Aro, Wellington 1; f. 1937; Pres. W. J. KNOX; Sec. K. G. DOUGLAS; affiliated to ICFTU; publ. *Bulletin.*

PRINCIPAL AFFILIATED UNIONS

National Union of Railwaymen: P.O.B. 858, Wellington; f. 1886; 11,800 mems.; Pres. G. FINLAYSON; Gen. Sec. D. C. GOODFELLOW; publ. *N.Z. Railway Review* (monthly).

New Zealand Boilermakers' Federation: P.O.B. 11123, Wellington; Pres. J. FINLAY; Sec. C. DEVITT.

New Zealand Carpenters and Related Trades Industrial Union of Workers: P.O.B. 11356, Wellington; 10,928 mems.; Pres. E. BURGESS; Sec. A. RUSS; publ. *Building Worker.*

New Zealand Clerical Employees' Association: Nashua House, 163 Vivian St., Wellington; f. 1938; 44,162 mems.; Pres. M. SKIFFINGTON; Sec. and Treasurer JOHN SLATER; publ. *Paper Clip.*

New Zealand Dairy Factories and Related Trades Union: P.O.B. 6077, Hamilton; f. 1937; 6,505 mems.; Sec. R. MCMILLAN.

New Zealand Drivers' Federation: P.O.B. 6394, Wellington; Pres. E. H. SOPER; Sec. H. S. MCCAFFLEY.

New Zealand Engineering, Coachbuilding, Aircraft, Motor and Related Trades Industrial Union of Workers: 37–39 Majoribanks St., P.O.B. 9450, Wellington; f.1945; 51,300 mems.; Nat. Pres. T. F. KEANE; Nat. Sec. E. W. J. BALL; publ. *Metal.*

New Zealand Federated Hotel and Related Trades Workers' Association: P.O.B. 68255, Newton, Auckland; 50,000 mems.; Pres. Mrs. I. TIRIA-STEWART; Sec. L. SHORT.

New Zealand Food Processing and Chemical Union: 314 Willis St., P.O.B. 27361, Wellington 1; 5,250 mems.; Sec. G. FRASER.

New Zealand Labourers' Union: P.O.B. 9124, Wellington; 17,500 mems.; Pres. G. BRINSDON; Sec. C. B. CLAYTON.

New Zealand Meat Workers and Related Trades Union: Trade Union Centre, 199 Armagh St., P.O.B. 13032, Christchurch; 24,494 mems.; Sec. A. J. KENNEDY; publ. *Meat Worker.*

New Zealand Printing and Related Trades Industrial Union of Workers: 27 Marion St., P.O.B. 6413, Te Aro, Wellington; f. 1862; 12,000 mems.; Pres. W. H. CLEMENT; Nat. Sec. C. A. CHILES; publ. *Imprint.*

New Zealand Shop Employees Association: P.O.B. 6394, Wellington; *c.* 29,000 mems.; Nat. Sec. H. S. MCCAFFLEY.

New Zealand Timber Workers' Union: P.O.B. 93, Rotorua; 11,056 mems.; Pres. R. RICHARDSON; Sec. R. HAMILTON.

New Zealand Waterside Workers' Federation: P.O.B. 27-004, 220 Willis St., Wellington 1; 5,600 mems.; Gen. Sec. S. P. JENNINGS.

New Zealand Workers' Union: P.O.B. 11,761, Central Chambers, 3 Eva St., Wellington; 17,000 mems.; membership includes workers in shearing and agriculture, forestry and highway and power construction; Gen. Sec. D. J. DUGGAN; publ. *N.Z. Worker* (every three months).

North Island Electrical and Electronic Workers' Union: P.O.B. 6367, Wellington; 10,400 mems.; Pres. C. T. LYNCH; Sec. A. J. NEARY; publ. *Power.*

United Mine Workers of New Zealand: P.O.B. 2054, Huntly; 1,320 mems.; Pres. N. TVRDEIC; Sec. M. J. BASSICK.

New Zealand Public Service Association: PSA House, 11 Aurora Terrace, P.O.B. 5108, Wellington 1; 69,000 mems.; Pres. DAVID THORP; Gen. Sec. BARRY TUCKER; publ. *PSA Journal.*

MAJOR INDUSTRIAL COMPANIES

The following are the major industrial enterprises in New Zealand, selected on the basis of ordinary paid-up capital:

CONSTRUCTION AND CEMENT

Ceramco Ltd.: Private Bag, Auckland 7; f. 1929; cap. p.u. $NZ20m. (1981).

Manufacturers of ceramic products: bricks, crockery, pipes, china clay, etc. Heavy engineering: boilers, cranes. Engineers' supplies. Distribution and service activities.

Eighty subsidiaries; Chair. J. C. FAIR; Man. Dir. T. E. CLARK.

Golden Bay Cement Co. Ltd.: Third Floor, Conference Chambers, Farish St., Wellington; f. 1909; cap. p.u. $NZ11.1m. (December 1976).

Manufacturers of cement.
Chair. A. S. PATERSON; employees: 450.

New Zealand Cement Holdings Ltd.: P.O.B. 6040, Christchurch; f. 1888; cap. p.u. $NZ9.7m. (1979).

Cement manufacturers.
Two subsidiaries; Chair. P. H. SCOTT; Man. Dir. D. M. WILSON.

Winstone Ltd.: Eden House, 44 Khyber Pass Rd., Auckland; f. 1864; cap. p.u. $NZ29.2m. (1980).

Holding company for over 20 subsidiaries in the supply and manufacture of materials for the construction industry; quarry owners and processors of metal aggregates and sands; glass merchants; land developers; residential housing developers; forestry owners and timber pulp and chip processors.

Branches in London, Sydney, Hong Kong and Papua New Guinea; Chair. A. H. WINSTONE; Man. Dir. B. D. BAMFIELD; employees: 2,703.

FOOD AND DRINK

Ballins Industries Ltd.: P.O.B. 619, Christchurch; f. 1936; cap. p.u. $NZ9.7m. (1980).

Wine and spirit merchants, soft drink manufacturers, industrial caterers, hotel proprietors, tobacco merchants.

Twenty-six subsidiaries; Chair. W. WILSON.

Dominion Breweries Ltd.: "Waitemata House", cnr. Albert and Wyndham Sts., Auckland 1; f. 1930; cap. p.u. $NZ32.6m. (1981).

Brewers, bottlers, wine and spirit merchants, hotel proprietors.

Chair. H. G. GALLAM, C.M.G.; Man. Dir. J. R. FLETCHER.

Goodman Group Ltd.: P.O.B. 593, Wellington.

Lion Breweries Ltd.: 15–17 Murphy St., P.O.B. 211, Wellington, N.1; f. 1923; cap. p.u. $NZ41.6m. (March 1979).

Brewers, bottlers and hotelkeepers. Branches in Auckland, Palmerston North, Wellington, Christchurch, Hamilton and Dunedin.

Six associated companies; Chair. Sir RALPH THOMPSON; Man. Dir. J. MACFARLANE.

Southland Frozen Meat Ltd.: 8 Esk St., Invercargill; f. 1882; cap. p.u. $NZ16.1m. (June 1980).

Freezing works proprietors. Manufacturers of frozen meat, sliped wool, pickled pelts, hides, tallow, casings, meat meal.

Chair. Rt. Hon. J. B. GORDON; employees: 2,900.

Waitaki NZ Refrigerating Ltd.: 58 Kilmore St., P.O.B. 1472, Christchurch 1; f. 1881; cap. p.u. $NZ28.6m. (1976).

Producers and exporters of lamb, mutton, beef, fancy meats, wool, pelts, hides, tallow, casings, liver meal, meat and bone meal, blood and bone, dried blood and neatsfoot oil.

Chair. R. P. THOMPSON; Vice-Chair. J. A. VALENTINE; employees: 3,800.

Wattie Industries Ltd.: Fitzroy Ave., Hastings; f. 1934; cap. p.u. $NZ52.9m. (1981).

Food processing and industrial supplies.

Holding company for Wattie Group comprising: J. Wattie Canneries Ltd., General Foods Corpn. (N.Z.) Ltd., Cropper—NRM Ltd. and subsidiaries.

Chair. W. T. MORRISS; Man. Dir. J. O. HAWORTH; employees: 8,000.

FORESTRY, PULP AND PAPER

Carter Holt Holdings Ltd.: P.O.B. 8532, Auckland; f. 1971; cap. p.u. $NZ10m. (1978).

Holding company with interests in sawmilling, pulp and paper, builders' supplies, forestry.

Chair. K. C. A. CARTER.

N.Z. Forest Products Ltd.: O'Rorke Rd., Penrose, Auckland; f. 1935; cap. p.u. $NZ80.4m. (1981).

Company has at Penrose two wallboard mills and associated remanufacturing and woodgrain printing departments, a mineral fibre plant, two multiwall paper bag factories, a paper mill and a polyethene extrusion plant. At Kinleith are timber mills, two kraft pulp mills, a semi-chemical pulp mill, chemical extraction systems, paper machines, a paper recovery plant and a plywood mill. At Whakatane is a timber mill, a kraft digester and three paperboard machines. At Mataura are two paper machines.

Nineteen subsidiary companies; Chair. L. N. ROSS; Man. Dir. D. O. WALKER; employees: 9,100.

STEEL

New Zealand Steel Ltd.: Private Bag, Auckland; cap. p.u. $NZ32m. (1982).

Manufacturers of iron-sand concentrate, sponge iron steel, galvanized sheet and pipe.

Chair. Sir ALAN HELLABY; Man. Dir. J. H. INGRAM.

Steel and Tube Holdings Ltd.: Wakefield House, 90 The Terrace, Wellington; cap. p.u. $NZ14.2m. (1980).

Holding company.

Twenty subsidiary companies; Chair. F. H. KEMBER; Chief Exec. D. C. THURSTON.

MISCELLANEOUS

Alex Harvey Industries Ltd. Private Bag, Auckland; f. 1886; cap. p.u. $NZ48.0m. (1982).

Manufacturers of domestic and commercial glassware and lightingware, metal and tin containers, aerosol cans, pails and drums, closures, injection and blow moulded bottles, vials, industrial bulk containers, mouldings and extrusions, plastic closures, plastic, polythene and rigid PVC pipe, rigid plastic sheet, polythene bags and film, gummed tape, reinforced aluminium foil insulation, corrugated and solid fibres containers, boxes, fibreglass wool insulation, aluminium sliding doors and windows, domestic insect screens, roof tiles, garage roll and tilt doors, vitreous enamelled steel bathroomware, office equipment, shelving, kitchen hardware and utensils, commercial and stationery printers; skifield operators.

Seventy-four operating units; Chair. H. N. AVERY; Man. Dir. S. D. PASLEY.

Cable Price Downer Ltd.: C.P.D. House, 108 The Terrace, Wellington, C.1; f. 1854; cap. p.u. $NZ17.6m. (1980).

Holding company for the Cable Price Downer Group of Companies.

Chair. R. W. STEELE.

Dalgety New Zealand: P.O.B. 1397, Wellington; cap. p.u. $NZ24.7m. (December 1978).

Stock and station agents; importers and exporters.

Man. Dir. E. MILLAR; Gen. Man. (International Trade) R. V. MCPHAIL.

EMCO Group Ltd.: P.O.B. 2599, Wellington; cap. p.u. $NZ20m. (December 1981).

Motor assembly and distribution, television rentals, construction equipment, fabrication and engineering, bus and vehicle bodies.

Feltex New Zealand Ltd.: 145 Symonds St., P.O.B. 4278, Auckland; cap. p.u. $NZ35.2m. (1981).

Manufacturers of carpets, underlays, mattresses, pillows, tyres, tubes, retreads, general rubber goods, footwear, wooden furniture, wools and yarns, elastic, laces, polyester ropes, webbings, steel furniture, moulded and extruded plastic products and sports equipment.

Chair. H. G. CALLAM; Man. Dir. H. M. TITTER; employees: 6,400.

Fletcher Challenge Ltd.: 105–109 The Terrace, P.O.B. 1696, Wellington; f. 1981; cap. p.u. $NZ129.7m.

Forestry, sawnwood, kraft pulp, newsprint, particle board, doors, livestock, wool, grain and seed, farm merchandise, stud stock, automobile assembly and distribution, low pressure gas distribution, engineering services, fishing, commercial and industrial development and construction, housing, property management, consumer finance, merchant banking, credit cards, computer services, insurance broking, steel processing and merchandising, building products manufacturing, wire manufacturing, motor mowers, bicycles, concrete, retail builders' supplies, aluminium, energy and mineral resources.

Fifty-six subsidiary companies in Australia and south east Asia; sixty associated companies; Pres. Sir JAMES FLETCHER; Chair. and Chief Exec. R. R. TROTTER; Man. Dir. H. A. FLETCHER; employees: 18,100.

ICI New Zealand Ltd.: ICI House, Molesworth St., Wellington (P.O.B. 1592); f. 1935; cap. p.u. $NZ17.5m. (1979).

Importers and manufacturers of chemical and related products including industrial and agricultural chemicals, metal stampings and specialized containers, plastic polymers, polythene and PVC piping, packaging film, nylon and polyester fibres, wood-bonding resins, dyes and pigments, paints and coatings, wallpapers, zip fasteners, sporting ammunition, pharmaceuticals, medical disposables and animal remedies.

Six subsidiary companies in New Zealand; Chair. and Man. Dir. P. R. DEMAINE; employees: 2,000.

New Zealand Farmers' Fertilizer Co. Ltd.: 81 Carlton Gore Rd., Newmarket, Private Bag, Auckland; f. 1916; cap. p.u. $NZ18.9m. (1979).

Manufacturers of fertilizers, sulphuric acid, copper sulphate, sulphate of alumina, chrome sulphate, agricultural chemicals, pharmaceutical products. Distributors of medical, dental and scientific supplies.

Thirty-eight subsidiaries; Chair. J. L. B. STEVENS; Man. Dir. P. G. RIDDELL; Gen. Man. K. M. HOGGARD; employees: 744.

N.Z. News Ltd.: Private Bag, UBD Centre, 360 Dominion Rd., Auckland 3; f. 1870; cap. p.u. $NZ8.6m. (1977).

Newspaper proprietors. Branches in Auckland, Christchurch, New Plymouth and Oamaru.

Chair. G. T. UPTON; Man. Dir. N. P. WEBBER.

New Zealand Refining Co. Ltd.: P.O.B. 44, Whangarei; f. 1961; cap. p.u. $NZ24m. (1977).

The company operates Whangarei Refinery at Marsden Point, which refines petrol, diesel oils, fuel oils and bitumen.

Gen. Man. F. JACOMBS; employees: 330.

Rothmans Industries: P.O.B. 3281, Auckland; cap. p.u. $NZ12.4m. (December 1980).

Manufacturers of cigarettes, cigars, pipe and fine cut tobacco; manufacturers and distributors of table, sparkling and fortified wines; electronic equipment manufacturers; laminators and specialist printers; computer management, data processing and systems consultants; finance and property investment; manufacturers and distributors of sun and rain umbrellas.

U.E.B. Industries Ltd.: 1–11 Short St., P.O.B. 37, Auckland 1; f. 1948; cap. p.u. $NZ28.2m. (1978).

Manufacturers of tufted and woven carpets and carpet yarn. Also manufacturers of cardboard containers and cartons, packaging lines, polystyrene, wood-wool and cement slabs, steel-framed furniture, etc.

Eight subsidiary companies in New Zealand, three abroad; Man. Dir. G. R. J. TEDCASTLE; employees: 4,000.

TRANSPORT

RAILWAYS

New Zealand Railways Corporation: Private Bag, Wellington 1; rail, road and ferry services; 4,536 km. open (at March 31st, 1980); Gen. Man. T. M. HAYWARD; Deputy Gen. Man. H. G. PURDY.

ROADS

National Roads Board: P.O.B. 12-041, Wellington North; f. 1953; Chair. Hon. TONY FRIEDLANDER, Minister of Works; Sec. R. K. THOMSON.

The Board consists of ten members nominated to represent various interests; it is advised by District Roads Councils. New Zealand is divided into 22 geographical Roads Districts, each of which is administered by a Roads Council. The Board and Councils are responsible for the administration of State Highways. Maintenance and construction expenditure of these highways is met in full from the National Roads Fund. Expenditure from the National Roads Fund for 1982/83 was estimated at $NZ281m.

Rural roads and Borough streets are the full responsibility of County, Borough and City Councils, which are assisted in meeting expenditure on maintenance and construction by the National Roads Board.

There were 92,850 km. of roads in 1982.

SHIPPING

New Zealand Ports Authority: P.O.B. 10059, Wellington; f. 1968 to foster an integrated and efficient ports system for New Zealand; Chair. Hon. Sir DONALD McKAY; Chief Exec. Officer K. J. GILLIGAN; Sec. W. H. Cox.

PRINCIPAL COMPANIES

The Shipping Corporation of New Zealand Ltd.: Pastoral House, 98 Lambton Quay, Wellington; f. 1973.

Trades: container, bulk, general; routes: worldwide; fleet of 8 ships totalling 93,531 g.r.t. Several subsidiary companies; Chair. Sir THOMAS SKINNER; Gen. Man. C. H. SPEIGHT.

Union Steam Ship Company of N.Z. Ltd.: 36 Customhouse Quay, P.O.B. 1799, Wellington; f. 1875; cargo services between New Zealand and Australia; also cargo services on New Zealand and Australian coast; conventional cargo vessels, 7 roll-on/roll-off cargo vessels; Chair. Sir PETER ABELES.

Other major shipping companies operating services to New Zealand include Farrell Lines Inc. and Sofrana-Unilines, which link New Zealand with Australia, the Pacific Islands and the U.S.A.

CIVIL AVIATION

There are international airports at Auckland, Christchurch and Wellington. The latter two are used for flights to Australia and internal flights only.

Air New Zealand Ltd.: 1 Queen St., Auckland 1; f. 1978 following a merger of Air New Zealand Ltd. and New Zealand National Airways Corporation; operates services to Australia, Fiji, Western Samoa, Tonga, the Cook Islands, Tahiti, New Caledonia, Norfolk Island, Hong Kong, Singapore, Japan, Honolulu, the United Kingdom and the U.S.A. (Los Angeles), as well as regular daily services to 24 cities and towns in New Zealand; Chair. C. W. MACE; Chief Exec. NORMAN GEARY; fleet of 3 Boeing 747, 6 DC-10, 2 DC-8, 1 DC-8 Freighter, 10 Boeing 737 and 15 Friendship F-27 (October 1981).

Mount Cook Line Airline Division: 47 Riccarton Rd., Christchurch; f. 1920; domestic services throughout New Zealand; Man. Dir. P. S. PHILLIPS; Man. M. L. JERVIS; fleet of 5 HS-748, 2 Pilatus Turbo Porter, 6 NB-2A Islanders, 16 Cessna, 8 FU-24, 2 Thrush, 1 Bell helicopter.

Safe Air Ltd.: P.O.B. 244, Blenheim; f. 1951; operates non-scheduled passenger and cargo services; Chief air freight carrier in N.Z.; Pres. J. SAWERS; Chair. A. A. WATSON; Gen. Man. D. P. LYNSKEY; fleet of 2 Argosy 200, 7 Bristol Freighters 31.

FOREIGN AIRLINES

The following foreign airlines serve New Zealand: Air Pacific (Fiji), British Airways, JAL (Japan), Pan Am (U.S.A.), Qantas (Australia), UTA (France).

TOURISM AND CULTURE

New Zealand Tourist and Publicity Department: Private Bag, Wellington; f. 1901; National Tourist Office; Gen. Man. W. N. PLIMMER; offices in Auckland, Wellington, Christchurch, Dunedin, Invercargill, Rotorua and Queenstown; 11 offices overseas.

CULTURAL ORGANIZATIONS

Music Federation of New Zealand (Inc.): 126 Wakefield St., P.O.B. 3391, Wellington; f. 1950; arranges about 250 concerts a year, about one-quarter by overseas groups, for its 43 affiliated organizations and in educational institutions; educational work includes a nationwide school music contest, an individual teaching programme for advanced students etc.; mems. approx. 6,500; Gen. Man. ELISABETH AIREY.

The New Zealand Ballet: P.O.B. 6682, Wellington; f. 1953; Chair. W. N. SHEAT, O.B.E.; Gen. Man. CHRIS MANGIN; Artistic Dir. HARRY HAYTHORNE; publ. *Pointe* (quarterly).

New Zealand Symphony Orchestra: 132 Willis St., P.O.B. 11-440, Wellington; a division of the Broadcasting Corporation of New Zealand; public and broadcast concerts throughout New Zealand; 90 mems.; Gen. Man. PETER NISBET.

Queen Elizabeth II Arts Council: P.O.B. 6040, Te Aro, Wellington; f. 1964; a statutory body which administers state aid to the arts; Chair. JOAN G. E. KERR; Dir. MICHAEL VOLKERLING.

ATOMIC ENERGY

New Zealand Atomic Energy Committee: c/o D.S.I.R., Private Bag, Lower Hutt; responsible to the Minister of Science for advising Government on the development of peaceful uses of atomic energy in New Zealand; Chair. C. K. STONE; Exec. Sec. W. N. MACQUARRIE.

DEFENCE

Armed Forces (1981): Total strength 12,913: army 5,675 (excluding 5,934 active Territorials), navy 2,843, air force 4,395. Military service is voluntary.

Equipment: The army has medium tanks, armoured personnel carriers, and artillery. The navy has a small number of frigates armed with surface-to-air missiles; other craft include a hydrographic vessel, a research ship, patrol craft and inshore survey vessels. The air force has 33 combat aircraft and 20 helicopters.

Defence Expenditure: Defence expenditure for 1980 was $NZ 442.8 million (U.S. $426 million).

Chief of the Defence Staff: Vice-Admiral Sir NEIL ANDERSON, K.B.E., C.B.

Chief of Staff (Army): Maj.-Gen. B. M. POANANGA, C.B., C.B.E.

Chief of Staff (Navy): Rear-Admiral K. M. SAULL.

Chief of Staff (Air Force): Air Vice-Marshal D. E. JAMIESON, C.B., O.B.E.

EDUCATION

Education in New Zealand is free and secular in State schools and compulsory for all children aged 6 to 15 years, although in practice about 98 per cent start at the age of 5 years.

The central administrative body is the Department of Education, headed by the Director-General of Education, which is responsible for administering the 1964 Education Act. The Department inspects all schools to ensure standards are maintained, issues curricula, conducts the School Certificate examination, grants secondary school bursaries and arranges school transport. It also directly controls departmental special schools and the Correspondence school.

Elementary Education

Pre-school

Local kindergartens and play centres are maintained and controlled by voluntary associations to which the Government gives substantial assistance including grants, subsidies and free sites. In 1981 about 55,000 children of three and four years of age were attending kindergartens and play centres and nearly 24,000 were attending other pre-school services.

Primary Education

Virtually all children start school when they turn five, though six is the legal starting age. All state primary schools are co-educational and provide a six-year course. In 1981 there were 493,856 pupils at state primary and private primary schools. There were 70 special primary schools, 2,028 primary schools and 279 private primary schools. The state primary schools are all co-educational. After the six-year primary course the pupils complete the final two years of primary school education either at the same school, at an *intermediate school* or, in country districts, at a form 1–7 or an area school. An intermediate school is a centrally situated school usually holding 300 to 600 pupils between eleven and thirteen years of age. In 1981 there were 73,383 pupils at 149 intermediate schools and intermediate departments.

Secondary Education

At about the age of 13, children go to secondary school where they are obliged to stay until they are fifteen; all children are entitled to free secondary education until the end of their nineteenth year. At secondary level all form one to seven schools and three-quarters of the state secondary schools are co-educational, while the remaining quarter and nearly all the private secondary schools are single-sex. In 1980 a total of 224,926 pupils received secondary education. The majority of pupils leave school at the end of their third or fourth year. The School Certificate examination is taken at the end of the third or fourth year of secondary school. Pupils who pass subjects in this examination may go on to a year in the sixth form. At the end of the sixth form year they may obtain the Sixth Form Certificate, and pass University Entrance examination either by examination or accrediting. Pupils intending to go on to university usually spend a further year in the seventh form to obtain a Higher School Certificate which is awarded without examination and provides a higher bursary. They may also sit examinations for university bursaries and entrance scholarships.

Rural Education

In order to give children in country districts the advantage of special equipment and the more specialized teaching of larger schools, the consolidation of the smaller rural schools has been undertaken wherever this is practicable. In certain cases boarding allowances are granted to pupils living in areas where there are no convenient transport services enabling them to attend school. In small rural districts area schools provide primary and secondary education for all pupils in the immediate vicinity and education from the first to the seventh form is provided in larger districts in separate schools.

Correspondence School

This school serves students who cannot attend school because they live in remote areas, because of illness or other causes. It also provides courses for pupils who wish to study subjects not offered at their local school, and adults who do not have access to secondary school classes.

Education of Maori and Pacific Island students

There is a continued increase in Maori enrolment, particularly at secondary school level, and a steady increase in the numbers of Maori children attending pre-school institutions. The period of stay of Maori secondary pupils remains considerably shorter than that for other pupils. In 1981 there were 112,266 Maori children receiving primary and secondary education, of whom 29,939 were pupils at secondary school level. Recognized play centres provided for 1,841 Maori and Pacific Island children out of a total enrolment of 16,198 in July 1981, and kindergartens for 5,949 out of a total of 38,768. In addition, 481 Maori and Pacific Island pre-school children were enrolled in primary schools for special pre-school programmes.

Groups such as the National Advisory Committee on Maori Education have been instrumental in the appointment of a Director of Maori and Islands Education within the Department of Education, in transferring Maori schools to board control and in fostering the growth of Maori language teaching in schools. Special in-service training courses are now being run for teachers of Maori students, universities and teachers' colleges offer Maori studies courses, and teams of advisers throughout the country are developing English language and Maori studies programmes for all pupils. Bilingual schooling has begun in some districts. Schools with a high proportion of Maori pupils are provided with counsellors and extra teachers.

In 1961 the Maori Education Foundation was set up to provide financial assistance to Maori students, and it has also been active in other areas, notably pre-school education. A Pacific Island Polynesian Education Foundation was also established in 1972.

The Technical Institute System

The technical institute system comprises community colleges, technical institutes and senior technical divisions of secondary schools. Some technical institutes have adopted the name of Polytechnic or Institute of Technology. In spite of the difference in nomenclature, all are legally technical institutes and offer both technical and practical training for apprentices and technicians.

In 1982 there were 12 technical institutes, six community colleges, two senior technical divisions of secondary schools and the Technical Correspondence Institute. This last is the largest technical institute in the country, serving the needs of an estimated 30,000 students from apprentices to professional accountants.

In 1981 there were 2,295 full-time staff in the technical institute system and 6,915 full-time and 35,849 part-time students.

Universities

The six universities and one agricultural college are autonomous bodies with their own councils. Eighty per cent of the universities' funds are provided from the quinquennial Government block grant, which is distributed by the University Grants Committee. The remainder of the funds comes from tuition fees. The Committee also advises the Government on the need for university education and research, and reviews the expenditure of grants.

The University Entrance Board is responsible for maintaining a common standard for admission, and for prescribing examination conditions. A university education is open to anyone with University Entrance (UE). Those without this qualification may be admitted if they are over 21 years and are judged to stand a good chance of success. All students with UE receive a fees bursary which pays 75 per cent of their costs, and those with higher school Certificate are entitled to an allowance above this. A tertiary assistance grant is paid to full-time students and supplements for hardship may be added to this. Scholarships and bursaries may be held in conjunction with these. About 11 per cent of pupils leaving secondary school go to university. The number of first-year students in New Zealand universities each year is over 11,000 while the approximate number of graduates is 8,000. In 1981 there were 52,988 students enrolled at the universities, of whom 8,028 were external students and 224 were attending short courses. There was a teaching staff of 3,043 full-time teachers.

Teacher Training

In 1981 there were 5,901 students undergoing early childhood, primary and secondary teacher training in eight teachers' colleges. Most primary teacher trainees follow a three-year course leading to the Teacher's Certificate; those for early childhood education have a two-year course. University graduates take a course lasting one year. In 1981 there were 38,385 full-time teachers in all schools.

BIBLIOGRAPHY

GENERAL

BEST, E. The Maori as he was (Government Printer, Wellington, 1974).

CUMBERLAND, K. B., and WHITELAW, J. S. New Zealand (Longman, London, 1970).

FRANCES SMITH, R. V., JACOBS, W., and BILLING, G. The New Zealanders (Golden Press, Auckland, 1975).

HOLCROFT, M. H. The Shaping of New Zealand (Hamlyn, Auckland, 1974).

JACKSON, W. K. New Zealand: Politics of Change (Reed, Wellington, 1973).

LARKIN, T. C. New Zealand's External Relations (Oxford University Press, London, 1962).

MCLINTOCK, A. H. (ed.) An Encyclopaedia of New Zealand (Government Printer, Wellington, 1966).

METGE, J. The Maoris of New Zealand (Routledge, London, 1967).

NEW ZEALAND OFFICIAL YEARBOOK (Government Printer, Wellington).

OXFORD NEW ZEALAND ENCYCLOPAEDIA (Oxford University Press, 1965).

ROWE, J. W., and ROWE, M. A. New Zealand (E. Benn, London, 1967).

SCHWIMMER, E. G. The World of the Maori (Reed, Wellington, 1974).

SIERS, J., and HENDERSON, J. The New Zealanders (Millwold Press, Wellington, 1975).

THOMPSON, K. W., and TRLIN, A. D. (eds.) Contemporary New Zealand; Essays on the Human Resources, Urban Growth and Problems of Society (Hicks Smith, Wellington, 1973).

WARDS, I. (ed.). New Zealand Atlas (Government Printer, Wellington, 1977).

WATTERS, R. F. (ed.) Land and Society in New Zealand (Reed, Wellington, 1965).

HISTORY

ADAMS, P. W. T. Fatal Necessity: British Intervention in New Zealand (Auckland University Press, 1977).

BEAGLEHOLE, J. C. The Discovery of New Zealand (Oxford University Press, London, 1960).

Conflict and Compromise. Essays on the Maori since Colonization (Reed, Wellington, 1975).

COWAN, J. The New Zealand Wars (Government Printer, Wellington, 1955).

DALTON, B. J. War and Politics in New Zealand 1855–1870 (Sydney University Press, Sydney, 1967).

HALL, D. The Golden Echo: Some Aspects of New Zealand Social History (Collins, Auckland, 1971).

LLOYD PRICHARD, M. F. An Economic History of New Zealand until 1939 (Collins, Auckland, 1970).

MCCLYMONT, W. G. The Exploration of New Zealand (Oxford University Press, Wellington, 1959).

New Zealand in World Affairs, Vol. I (Price Milburn, Wellington, 1977).

OLIVER, W. H. The Story of New Zealand (Faber, London, 1963).

OLIVER, W. H., and WILLIAMS, B. R. The Oxford History of New Zealand (Oxford University Press, 1981).

SIMMONS, D. R. The Great New Zealand Myth (Reed, Wellington, 1976).

SINCLAIR, K. The Origins of the Maori Wars (Auckland University Press, Auckland, 1962).

A History of New Zealand (rev. edn., Penguin Books, Harmondsworth, 1969).

Walter Nash (Auckland University Press, Auckland, 1976).

SUTCH, W. B. The Quest for Security in New Zealand (Oxford University Press, Wellington, 1966).

TAPP, E. J. Early New Zealand: Relations with Australia (Melbourne University Press, 1958).

WARD, A. A Show of Justice: Racial Amalgamation in Nineteenth Century New Zealand (Auckland University Press, Auckland, 1974).

WARDS, I. The Shadow of the Land (Government Printer, Wellington, 1968).

ECONOMY

BLYTH, C. A. Inflation in New Zealand (New Zealand Institute of Economic Research, Wellington, 1977).

BLYTH, C. A. (ed.) The Future of Manufacturing in New Zealand (Oxford University Press, London, 1964).

BRIGHT, T. N. Banking Law and Practice in New Zealand (Sweet and Maxwell, Wellington, 1969).

BURTT, D. J. Trans-Tasman Development and Trade (New Zealand Institute of Economic Research, Wellington, 1977).

Franklin, C. H. Trade, Growth and Anxiety: New Zealand Beyond the Welfare State (Methuen, Wellington, 1976).

Holmes, F. W. (ed.) New Zealand at the Turning Point—Report of the Task Force in Social and Economic Planning (Government Printer, Wellington, 1976).

Lane, P. A. Economy in the Balance; An Introduction to the New Zealand Economy (Methuen, Wellington, 1976).

Lloyd Prichard, M. F. Economic Practice in New Zealand, 1954–55 to 1967–68 (Collins, Auckland, 1970).

McLean, I. The Future for New Zealand Agriculture: Economic Strategies for the 1980s (Fourth Estate Books, Wellington, 1978).

Marris, E. C. New Zealand Investment Guide (New Zealand Financial Times, Wellington, rev. edn., 1970).

Monitoring Group of the New Zealand Planning Council. Occasional Publication (1978–).

New Zealand Department of Statistics. Official Yearbook (Government Printer, Wellington).

New Zealand, Town and Country Planning Division. National Resources Surveys, Parts I–VII (Government Printer, Wellington, 1959–71).

Organisation for Economic Co-operation and Development. New Zealand (OECD, Paris, 1979).

Rimmer, J. O. (ed.) Marketing in New Zealand (Hicks Smith, Wellington, 1972).

The Pacific Islands

	Page
THE PACIFIC ISLANDS—PHYSICAL, SOCIAL AND ECONOMIC GEOGRAPHY	867
AMERICAN SAMOA	871
COOK ISLANDS	873
CORAL SEA ISLANDS TERRITORY	876
FIJI	877
FRENCH POLYNESIA	888
GUAM	891
HAWAII	894
JOHNSTON ISLAND	896
KIRIBATI	897
MIDWAY ISLANDS	900
NAURU	901
NEW CALEDONIA	904
NIUE	908
NORFOLK ISLAND	910
NORTHERN MARIANA ISLANDS	912
PAPUA NEW GUINEA	914
PITCAIRN ISLANDS	927
SOLOMON ISLANDS	928
TOKELAU	935
TONGA	937
TRUST TERRITORY OF THE PACIFIC ISLANDS	940
TUVALU	944
VANUATU	947
WAKE ISLAND	951
WALLIS AND FUTUNA ISLANDS	951
WESTERN SAMOA	952
BIBLIOGRAPHY	957

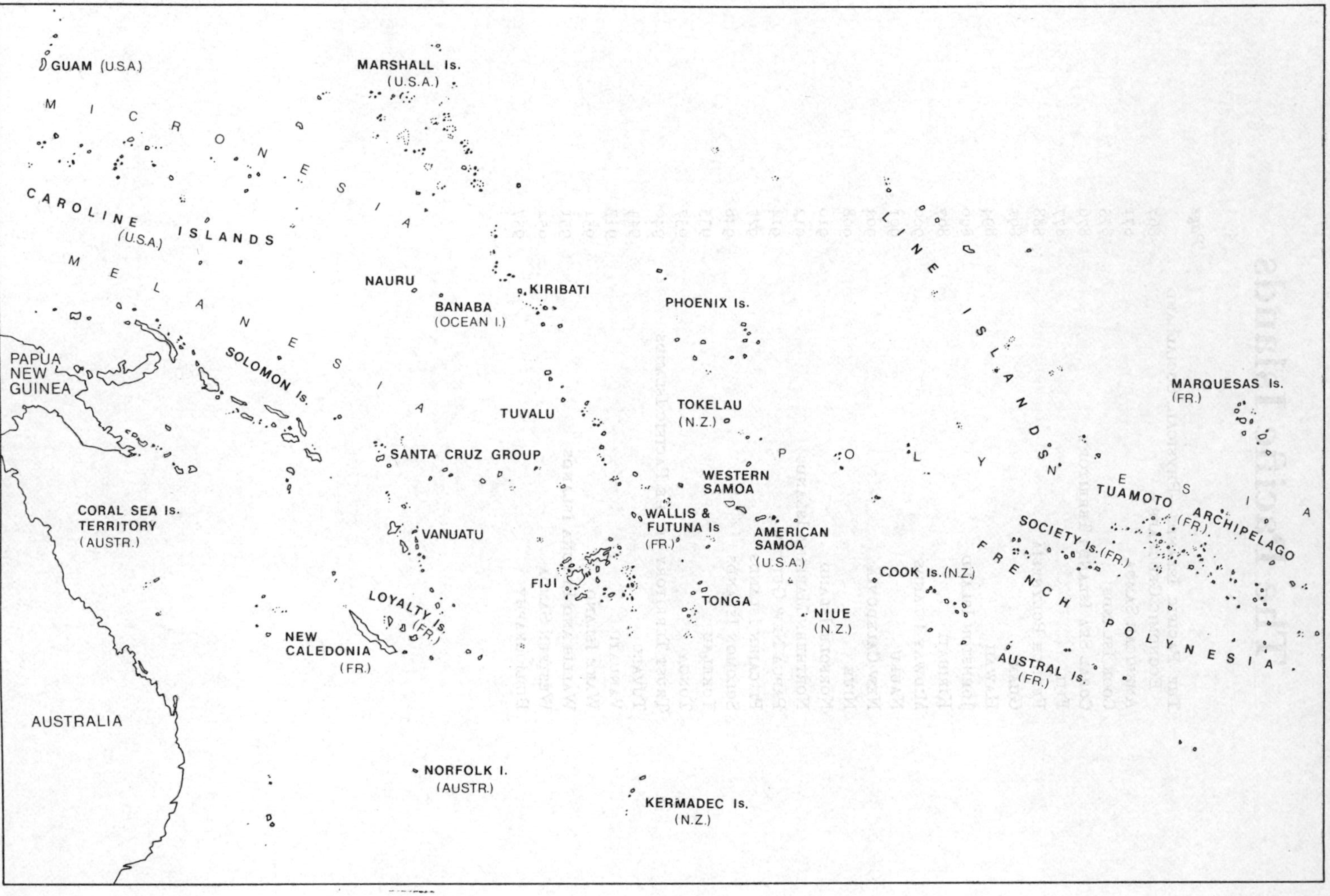

The Pacific Islands

The Pacific Islands

Bryant J. Allen

The Pacific Ocean occupies a third of the earth's surface. Within it are located many thousands of islands, more than in all the rest of world's seas combined. The numerousness of Pacific islands, and their widespread distribution, gives rise to a great variety of physical, social and economic environments. Their location relative to the continents and larger islands which border the Pacific and which include North and South America, Japan, China, the Philippines, Indonesia, Australia and New Zealand, continues to influence political and economic conditions in them. Their small size and physical isolation has rendered them vulnerable to influences from the rest of the world. Rapid and often traumatic ecological, social, economic and political changes have occurred throughout the Pacific following penetration by European and Asian explorers and colonists, a process which is still under way, as improved communications and the neo-colonialism of mining, investment and tourism bring the area closer to the modern world.

A number of broad classifications of Pacific Islands exist. The islands may be divided into continental islands, high islands, low islands and atolls. The people of the Pacific may be divided into Melanesians, Polynesians and Micronesians. Melanesians occupy the larger islands in the south-west, Irian Jaya and Papua New Guinea, Solomon Islands, Vanuatu, Fiji and New Caledonia. Polynesians live on islands which are located over an immense area from Hawaii in the north to Easter Island in the south-east to New Zealand in the south-west. In the central Pacific, Polynesians occupy the major groups of Tonga, Samoa, the Society Islands including Tahiti, and the Cook Islands, as well as numerous small atolls. The Micronesians live in the north, central and west Pacific in the Mariana, Caroline, Marshall, Gilbert, Phoenix and Line groups.

The islands may be also divided into politically dependent and independent states. The dependent states are governed wholly or partially by colonial administrations owing allegiance to the United Kingdom, France, the U.S.A., Australia and New Zealand. Islands which fall into this category are the Pitcairn Islands (the United Kingdom); New Caledonia, the Society Islands, the Tuamotu, Austral, Gambier and Marquesas groups, Wallis and Futuna (France); Tokelau, the Cook Islands and Niue (New Zealand); Norfolk Island (Australia); the Caroline, Marshall and Northern Mariana Islands, Guam and American Samoa (U.S.A.); and Hawaii, a state of the United States.

Former dependencies which have achieved political independence are Western Samoa (from New Zealand in 1962); Nauru (from the United Nations and Australia in 1968); Tonga (from the United Kingdom in 1970); Fiji (from the United Kingdom in 1970); Papua New Guinea (from Australia in 1975); Tuvalu (from the United Kingdom in 1978); Solomon Islands (from the United Kingdom in 1978); Kiribati (from the United Kingdom in 1979); and Vanuatu (from the United Kingdom and France in 1980). Irian Jaya, the western half of the island of New Guinea, is a province of Indonesia and will not be considered in this section; New Zealand and the Philippines are also excluded.

The most important regional organization is the South Pacific Forum. A grouping of independent and self-governing nations, it grew out of a dissatisfaction with the South Pacific Commission (SPC) which includes non-independent countries and the former colonial powers. The Forum has an administrative and economic arm, the South Pacific Bureau for Economic Co-operation (SPEC).

An important trade agreement was made between Australia, New Zealand and the Forum countries in January 1981. Known as the South Pacific Regional Trade and Economic Cooperation Agreement (SPARTECA), it was designed to ease import restrictions on island goods into Australia and New Zealand, in an attempt to adjust the massive trade imbalance which exists. Island leaders have been critical of some features of the agreement, in particular those which require goods to contain 50 per cent content from island countries, and lists of unrestricted goods which cannot be produced in the islands.

The 21st SPC conference was held at Port Vila, Vanuatu, in October 1981. The conference elected a new Secretary-General, Mr. Francis Bugotu of Solomon Islands. Major items of discussion included a 10 per cent budget increase, a regional technical seminar, a planned women's resources bureau, nuclear testing and the dumping of nuclear waste, a proposed regional price stabilization scheme for agricultural produce, and the establishment of a regional development fund. The problem of two regional organizations and proposals to integrate the SPC and SPEC were also debated. The Republic of Palau, in the Caroline Islands, was admitted to the SPC as a full member.

PHYSICAL GEOGRAPHY

No agreement exists on the origin of the Pacific basin. One hypothesis suggests that the basin is the result of shrinkage and depression of the earth's crust, while another argues that the gradual expansion of the earth, the emergence of new rocks on the ocean floors and the drift of continental land masses on great plates, has created the great oceans of the world, of which the Pacific is the largest.

The physical features of the Pacific basin are better known. The basin is from four to six kilometres deep and roughly circular in shape. The boundary is in most places the continental margin, but elsewhere it is obscured in a jumble of island arcs and fragmented continental blocks. The northern half of the basin forms one relatively deep unit between five and six kilometres deep, and the southern half another shallower one. The north is characterized by a number of enormous volcanoes and numerous clusters of smaller ones. The crust here is broken by very long faults. The south is deformed by a series of very long broad arches or rises with associated block and wrench faulting. Island arcs and deep trenches occur along the margins of the basins and parallel to them, archipelagoes of volcanic islands and clusters of submarine volcanoes occur in all parts of the basins but most are in the west and south-west.

These structures give rise to a number of characteristic island types. West of the so-called andesite-line, representing the farthest eastward limit of the continental blocks of Asia and Australia, are islands formed on the broken edges of the continental blocks. These continental islands have foundations of ancient folded and metamorphosed sediments which have been intruded by granites. Vulcanism has overlaid these rocks with lavas, tuff and ash, and transgressions by the ocean have laid down softer and younger marine sediments. Erosion has resulted in plains, deltas and swamps along the modern coastline. New Guinea* is the best example of these continental islands; it is dominated by a massive central cordillera within which lie dissected and flat-floored montane valleys. The highest peak in the island is over 5,000 metres. Active volcanoes exist along the north coast and in the New Guinea islands. North and south of the central mountains are broken hills and vast swamps. The coastal pattern is one of small coastal plains alternating with low river terraces, high marine terraces, coastal hills and steep mountain slopes plunging straight into the sea. The largest rivers of all the Pacific Islands are found here. The Fly is navigable by motorized vessels for about 800 kilometres and the Sepik for 500. Other continental islands are Fiji, Solomon Islands, Vanuatu and New Caledonia.

The high islands of the central Pacific are composed almost entirely of volcanic materials, together with reef limestone and recent sediments. The islands are the peaks of the largest volcanoes in the world. The Hawaiian volcano of Mauna Loa, for example, rises nine kilometres from the ocean floor and is over 200 kilometres in diameter. Characteristic landforms of the high islands are striking peak and valley forms, with old volcanic cores often eroded to form fantastic skylines. Waterfalls, cliff faces and narrow beaches, with fringing coral reefs complete the pattern. High islands in the Pacific include Hawaii, the Samoas, Tahiti and the Marquesas, Rarotonga in the Cook Islands, and Ponape and the Northern Mariana Islands.

Low islands are of two types: some are volcanic islands which have been eroded, while others are raised atolls, which resemble sea-level reefs, but which are now elevated above modern sea-level. Caves and sinkholes occur widely. Small pockets of soil occur within the limestone rocks. Surface water is uncommon. Examples of low volcanic islands include Aitutaki in the Cook Islands and Wallis Island. Raised coral islands include some of the islands of the Tuamotu, Society, Cook, Line, Tokelau, Marshall, Caroline and Kiribati groups. Low islands with raised reefs are also common. One of the best examples is Mangaia in the Southern Cook group, which has a central core of volcanic rock 180 metres high surrounded by an unbroken kilometre wide band of coral limestone raised 70 metres above the present sea-level. A new fringing reef now surrounds the island.

The fourth island form are the atolls, roughly circular reefs of coral limestone, partly covered by sea water on which there are small islands made up of accumulations of limestone debris, and within which there occurs a lagoon of calm water. Atoll islets are commonly less than three metres above the high-tide level. It is generally agreed that atolls have developed on the tops of volcanoes which now no longer protrude above sea-level. Atolls vary in size from Rose Island (American Samoa), an atoll about 3 kilometres by 3 kilometres, to the Kwajalein Atoll in the Marshall Islands which is over 60 kilometres long. Sources of fresh water are rain and a freshwater lens which is frequently found floating on salt groundwater beneath the islets. Hurricanes and typhoons frequently sweep over atolls, partially or completely destroying islets.

Climate

Five atmospheric circulation regions have been identified in the Pacific. A middle latitude area is characterized by the occurrence of extra-tropical cyclones with characteristic distinctive frontal weather systems. The Marianas and the western Hawaiian Islands sometimes receive this type of weather in the northern winter. The trade winds regions where at least 60 per cent of prevailing winds are from the north-west in the northern hemisphere and the south-east in the southern hemisphere, lie in an arc from the west coast of Mexico through Hawaii to the Marshall Islands in the north, and from the west coast of South America across the Marquesas and Tuamotus to the Society Islands. In these areas distinct wet and dry zones appear on larger islands, Hawaii being a good example. The monsoon area occurs to the far west and influences few of the Pacific Islands. The weather of Papua New Guinea is influenced, however, and a wet season and a dry season are distinguishable, although they are by no means as sharp as the term "monsoon" implies. A doldrums area occurs in a poorly defined band south of the equator in an arc extending east from Solomon Islands to the Phoenix Islands. Finally, a hurricane zone exists in the northern Pacific west from Panama in an arc which includes the Marshall, Caroline and Mariana Islands. A similar zone occurs in the south extending from the Tuamotus west across the Cooks, the Samoas, Tonga and Fiji to the north-east Australian coast.

Rainfall in the Pacific is geographically most variable; some islands are semi-arid while others are very wet. In the northern Pacific, for example, Mid-

* Comprises Papua New Guinea, Irian Jaya and surrounding islands.

way receives a mean annual rainfall of 1,194 mm. and Honolulu 550 mm. Further south Yap receives 3,023 mm., Palau 3,900 mm., Ponape 4,700 mm. and Fanning 2,054 mm. In the eastern Pacific near the equator islands are frequently barren. Rainfall decreases from west to east along the equator: Nauru receives 2,050 mm., Ocean Island 1,930 mm. and Christmas Island 950 mm. Further south in an arc extending east from New Guinea to the Society Islands in the Central Pacific average annual rainfall varies from between 3,500 mm. in the west to 2,000 mm. in the east. In Papua New Guinea altitude and local relief influence climate. Areas exposed to the north-west and south-east winds receive over 5,000 mm. of rain, while inland areas cut off from moist air masses may receive less than 1,500 mm. On the south-eastern coast east and west of Port Moresby average annual rainfall is less than 1,000 mm.

Soils, minerals, vegetation

Geology, soil, altitude, landforms, location and climate are all combined in the creation of the widely varying physical environments of Pacific islands. Continental islands exhibit the widest range of environments, from high alpine grasslands, through montane forest, and lowland rainforest to savannah and mangrove swamps. They also contain the richest deposits of minerals: nickel, chrome and manganese are mined in New Caledonia, gold and copper in New Guinea. The high volcanic islands contain no known minerals of commercial value. Terrain is frequently a limit to cultivation, although soils are in general heavily leached and of low fertility, with low mineral and humus content. Raised coral islands lack groundwater and soils are shallow and often scattered in pockets. Phosphate deposits are mined from the coraline limestone on Nauru and Banaba (Ocean Island), and were formally mined on Makatea in the Society Islands. The atolls contain only sparse resources. Soil development is often nil, fresh water difficult to obtain and foodplants other than coconuts and pandanus nuts difficult to cultivate. Special techniques are used to cultivate taro, but storms or high sea-levels frequently destroy gardens. The atolls provide the most tenuous existence for man in the Pacific.

The flora and fauna of the Pacific Islands are unbalanced in comparison with the continents in that many major categories of plants have not reached the islands. A few ancestral immigrants have given rise to the entire endemic biota. Lack of ecological competition appears to have resulted in genera developing many more species than plants on continental land masses have been able to produce.

PREHISTORY, CULTURE AND SOCIETY

The continental and oceanic Pacific islands were never linked by land bridges to the Asian continent and the Indonesian islands east of Bali and west of New Guinea form a frontier zone between a realm of placental mammals and marsupial mammals, the Wallace Line. Prehistorians argue therefore that man, a placental mammal, is an intruder in the Pacific. The first men to immigrate across the Wallace Line are believed to have been *Homo sapiens* approaching the modern form. The people of the interior of New Guinea are classified as Australoid populations which are thought to have begun moving into the area from Indonesia about 30,000 years ago. Until 5,000 years or so ago, archaeological evidence points to the Pacific east of the Bismarck Archipelago being devoid of human settlement. Between 4,000 and 2,000 years ago, people who are thought to have lived in north-eastern Indonesia and the Philippines, and who had descended from a Mongoloid stock, spread into the Pacific and along the coasts of the continental islands, intermarrying with the existing Australoid populations of eastern Indonesia and New Guinea. Modern Melanesians, Polynesians and Micronesians are thus to varying degrees the outcome of the mixing of these early Australoid and Mongoloid stocks.

Thus the Melanesians who inhabit the island chains from Solomon Islands eastwards to Fiji are basically an Australoid group, while the Fijians are a more intermediate group. Polynesians tend towards the Mongoloid end of the continuum and Micronesians more so. The actual pattern, however, is far more complex than this simple description.

Origins of the three groups may also be evidenced in their cultures. The Polynesians are culturally and linguistically the most homogenous. Polynesian societies are basically patrilineal and genealogically ranked, with elaborate hierarchical systems of rank and class, best developed on the Hawaiian, Tongan and Society Islands. Micronesian societies are mainly matrilineal, with the exception of Yap and Kiribati. Melanesia is culturally the most diverse area of all. Hereditary ranking occurs in Fiji, but in many areas, especially in Papua New Guinea, status is achieved rather than inherited. Most groups are patrilineal, but matrilineal societies occur in New Guinea, Solomon Islands and Vanuatu.

Throughout the Pacific, the pre-contact subsistence economy was based on the vegetative propagation of root and tree crops, together with fishing and some pig husbandry and hunting. The only domesticated animals were dogs, pigs and fowls but all three were not present everywhere in the region. The major root crops, taro and yam,have Asian origins, but one, the sweet potato which was grown in New Guinea, Hawaii, Marquesas, Society and Easter Island groups prior to European contact, has a South American origin. Shifting cultivation was the main agricultural technique in most areas, although the intensity of land use and the periodicity of cycles varied widely in relation to population densities. In New Caledonia and parts of Polynesia, notably Hawaii, Tahiti and the Cook Islands, taro was cultivated in relatively elaborate, terraced, irrigated gardens.

Short distance ocean voyaging was well-established in Polynesia and Micronesia before European contact, with large double-hulled canoes and navigation based on stars, wave patterns, bird flights and inherited geographical knowledge. Large ocean-going and coastal canoes were also used in Papua New Guinea and Fiji.

Over 1,000 different languages are spoken in the

Pacific Islands, more than 700 being found in Papua New Guinea and Solomon Islands. They belong to two groups, the non-Austronesian phyla found in Papua New Guinea (and in scattered pockets in Indonesia), and the Austronesian phyla, which are spoken in coastal Papua New Guinea, most of island Melanesia, all of Polynesia and Micronesia (as well as in parts of Indonesia, the Philippines, South-East Asia and Madagascar).

To summarize, existing evidence suggests that Papua New Guinea was already settled over 30,000 years ago by ancestral Australoid populations who were followed about 3,000 years ago by Austronesian speakers of Mongoloid stock who probably brought pottery, horticulture and pigs to Papua New Guinea. Intermixing occurred, followed by further movements east to New Caledonia and Vanuatu. Fiji was then settled by people who carried with them a pottery technology previously established in Papua New Guinea and islands to the east, and further movements into the Pacific Ocean took place. During the last 2,500 years further intermixing has occurred in Melanesia while Polynesian and Micronesian populations have had less interaction.

American Samoa

PHYSICAL AND SOCIAL GEOGRAPHY

American Samoa comprises the seven islands of Tutuila, Tau, Olosega, Ofu, Aunuu, Rose and Swains. They lie in the South Central Pacific along latitude 14° S. at about longitude 170° W., some 3,700 kilometres south-west of Hawaii. Swains Island lies 340 kilometres to the north-west of the main group. They are high volcanic islands with rugged interiors and little flat land except along the coasts.

In 1980 the population was estimated at 32,395, of whom 30,226 lived on Tutuila, where the capital, Pago Pago, is situated.

The islands are peopled by Polynesians and are thought to have been the origin of many of the people who now occupy islands further east. The Samoan language is believed to be the oldest form of Polynesian speech in existence. Samoan society developed an intricate hierachy of graded titles comprising titular chiefs and orator chiefs. One of the striking features of modern Samoa is the manner in which these titles and the culture before European contact remains a dominant influence. Most of the population are Christians.

HISTORY AND ECONOMY

The Samoan islands were first visited by Europeans in the 1700s, but it was not until 1830 that missionaries from the London Missionary Society settled there. In 1878 the then independent Kingdom of Samoa gave the United States the right to establish a naval base at Pago Pago. Britain and Germany were also interested in the island, but Britain withdrew in 1899 leaving the Western islands for Germany to govern until 1914. The chiefs of the eastern islands ceded their lands to the United States in 1904 and the island officially became an American territory in 1922.

Until 1978 American Samoa was administered by a Governor, appointed by the United States, and a legislature comprising a Senate and a House of Representatives. In November 1977, the first ever gubernatorial elections were held and in January 1978, Peter Coleman was inaugurated as Governor and Tufele Li'a as Lieutenant-Governor. Both were re-elected to a second term in the elections of November 1980. There is much emigration to the U.S.A., California and Hawaii in particular, and many Samoans have become permanent American mainland residents. The American Samoan economy and urban life is oriented strongly towards the United States. A tuna canning plant was built at Pago Pago in 1953 and processes fish from Taiwanese and Korean vessels. Tourism is also an important industry and Pago Pago is a major mid-Pacific stop-over for large passenger aircraft.

STATISTICAL SURVEY

Area: 194.8 square kilometres (76.1 square miles).

Population (census of April 1st, 1980): Total 32,395; Manu'a Islands (Ofu, Olosega and Tau) 1,740; Aunuu 400, Swains 29, Tutuila (including Pago Pago, capital) 30,226.

Births and Deaths (1980): 1,084 live births (33.5 per 1,000); 151 deaths (4.7 per 1,000).

Agriculture (1980—metric tons, FAO estimates): Coconuts 12,000, Roots and tubers 16,000, Bananas 4,000. Papayas, pineapples and breadfruit are also grown.

Livestock (1980—FAO estimates): Chickens 43,000, Pigs 8,000, Goats 8,000.

Sea Fishing (catch in metric tons): 113 in 1976; 352 in 1977; 377 in 1978; 383 in 1979; 398 in 1980.

Industry: Canned Fish U.S. $120,277,671 (1980); Electricity 72.6 million kWh. worth $6.1 million (1980).

Currency: 100 cents = 1 United States dollar (U.S. $).
Coins: 1, 5, 10, 25 and 50 cents; 1 dollar.
Notes: 1, 2, 5, 10, 20, 50 and 100 dollars.
Exchange rates (June 1982): £1 sterling = $1.73; U.S. $100 = £57.74.

Budget (1980—U.S. $'000): Local Revenue $24,751; Congressional grants and direct appropriation $17,309; Other Federal grants $16,943; Total receipts $59,003.

External Trade ($ million, year ending June 30th): Imports 54.9 in 1976/77, 73.3 in 1977/78, 95.1 in 1980; Exports 82.1 in 1976/77, 104.2 in 1977/78, 127.1 in 1980.

Transport (1980): *Roads:* Motor vehicles 3,435; *Shipping:* Ships entered 1,002; cleared 1,001; *Civil Aviation* (1981): Aircraft arriving at Pago Pago airport 10,622, Passenger arrivals and departures 213,440.

THE CONSTITUTION

American Samoa is administered by the United States Department of the Interior. According to the 1966 constitution executive power is vested in the Governor. The Governor's authority extends to all operations within the territory of American Samoa. He has veto power with respect to bills passed by the Fono (Legislature). The Fono consists of a Senate and a House of Representatives, with a President and a Speaker presiding over their respective divisions. The Senate is composed of 18 members elected according to Samoan custom from local chiefs, or *matai*. The House of Representatives consists of 20 members elected by popular vote. The Fono meets twice a year, in February and July, for not more than 45 days and at such special sessions as the Governor may call. The Governor has the authority to appoint heads of departments with the approval of the Senate. Local government is carried out by indigenous officials. In August 1976 a referendum on the popular election of a Governor and Lt.-Governor resulted in an affirmative vote. On September 13th, 1977, the Secretary of the Interior issued an order which provided for gubernatorial elections every four years. The first of these elections was held on November 8th, 1977.

THE GOVERNMENT

(July 1982)

Governor: PETER TALI COLEMAN.

Lieutenant-Governor: High Chief TUFELE LI'A.

JUDICIAL SYSTEM

High Court: Consists of three Divisions: Appellate, Trial, and Land and Titles. The Appellate Division has limited original jurisdiction and hears appeals from the Trial Division, the Land and Titles Division and from the District Court when it has operated as a court of record. The Trial Division has general jurisdiction over all cases. The Land and Titles Division hears cases involving land or *matai* titles.

Chief Justice: RICHARD I. MIYAMOTO.

Associate Justice: THOMAS W. MURPHY.

District Court: Hears misdemeanours, infractions (traffic and health), civil claims less than $3,000, small claims, Uniform Reciprocal Enforcement of Support cases, and *de novo* trials from Village Courts.

Judge: CHARLES ALAILIMA.

Judge: MICHAEL F. KRUSE (temporary).

Village Court: Hears matters arising under uniform village regulations.

Judges: MULIPOLA F. H. SCANLAN; TAGO SEVA'AETASI.

RELIGION

The population is largely Christian.

Roman Catholic: under the jurisdiction of Bishop of Samoa and Tokelau: H.E. Cardinal PIO TAOFINU'U (Cardinal's Residence, Box 532, Apia, Western Samoa).

Protestant Churches: denominations active in the Territory include the Congregational Christian Church, the Methodist Church, the Church of Jesus Christ of the Latter-Day Saints, Assemblies of God, Church of the Nazarene, Seventh Day Adventists and Jehovah's Witnesses.

THE PRESS

News Bulletin: Office of Information, American Samoa Government, Pago Pago; English; daily; Editor PHILIP SIVETT; circ. 3,600.

Samoa News: P.O.B. 57, Pago Pago; twice a week; Editor JAKE KING; circ. 6,500.

RADIO AND TELEVISION

RADIO

Radio Samoa: P.O.B. 2567, Pago Pago; former government-administered station leased to Radio Samoa Ltd. in 1975; programmes in English and Somoan; 24 hours a day; Gen. Man. RICK PETRI.

In 1978 there were 30,000 radio sets.

TELEVISION

KVZK: Pago Pago; f. 1964; government-owned; programmes in English and Samoan; operates Channels 2, 4 and 5, broadcasting for 18 hours on weekdays and 12 hours on Saturdays and Sundays; Gen. Man. PAUVEUVEN FULI FULI.

In 1978 there were 7,100 television sets.

FINANCE

BANKING

(cap.=capital; dep.=deposits; m.=million; amounts in U.S. $)

Bank of Hawaii: P.O.B. 69, Pago Pago 96799; f. 1897; cap. $93m., dep. $1,400m.; Chair. and Chief Exec. Officer WILSON P. CANNON, Jr.; Man. ROGER E. O'CONNOR.

Development Bank of American Samoa: P.O. Box 9, Pago Pago; f. 1969; cap. $6.5m. (1981); a government-owned non-commercial undertaking; Chair. and Pres. AUINA TO'OTO'O.

INSURANCE

G.H.C. Reid and Co. Ltd.: P.O.B. 1269, Pago Pago; general merchants, household goods movers, agents for Lloyd's of London.

Burns Philp (SS) Company Ltd.: P.O.B. 129, Pago Pago.

National Pacific Insurance Ltd.: Pago Pago.

Oxford Pacific Insurance Management: Pago Pago.

TRADE AND INDUSTRY

DEVELOPMENT ORGANIZATIONS

American Samoa Development Corporation: Pago Pago; f. 1962; financed by Samoan private shareholders.

Division of Agricultural Development and Extension Services: f. 1973 out of other departments to co-ordinate agricultural development on behalf of the Department of Agriculture.

Office of Economic Development and Planning: Government of American Samoa, Pago Pago; Dir. JOSEPH PEREIRA.

Territorial Planning Commission: Pago Pago; f. 1969.

TRANSPORT

ROADS

There are about 150 km. of paved and 200 km. of secondary roads.

Non-scheduled commercial buses operate a service over 350 km. of main and secondary roads.

SHIPPING

There are various passenger and cargo services from the U.S. Pacific coast, Japan, Australia (mainly Sydney) and New Zealand, that call at Pago Pago. The Pacific Forum Line, Daiwa Lines, Farrell Lines, Pacific Navigation of Tonga, Kyowa Line, Union Steam Ship Co., General Steamship Corpn., Warner Pacific Line and Pacific Islands Transport Line are amongst the shipping companies which operate regular cargo services to American Samoa. Inter-island boats operate frequently between Western and American Samoa.

CIVIL AVIATION

Samoa Airlines: Pago Pago; f. 1982; operates service to Honolulu (Hawaii) using 1 B-707.

American Samoa is also served by Air Pacific Ltd. (Fiji), Polynesian Airlines (Western Samoa) and South Pacific Islands Airways (Tonga).

EDUCATION

Education is compulsory from the age of 6 to 18. The education system is based on the American pattern of 8 years' elementary school and 4 years' high school. The Government maintains 25 consolidated elementary schools, 4 senior high schools and 1 community college. It also operated in 1977 135 village early childhood education centres. There are 4 private elementary schools and 2 private high schools. In 1978/79 total enrolment in elementary and secondary public schools was 7,526 pupils, with a total staff of 427 teachers. The community college had 856 students in late 1979 and at that time there were altogether nearly 1,400 students in higher education. Total educational enrolment in 1979 was over 13,000.

Cook Islands

PHYSICAL AND SOCIAL GEOGRAPHY

The 13 inhabited and two uninhabited islands of the Cook Islands are located midway between Samoa and Tahiti. The Cooks form two groups: the Northern Cooks which are all atolls, and include Pukapuka, Rakahanaga and Manihiki, and the Southern Cooks, including Aitutaki, Mangaia and Rarotonga, which are all volcanic islands. The total area of all the islands is 234 square kilometres. Total population at the 1981 census was, provisionally, 17,695. The capital is Avarua on Rarotonga.

HISTORY

The Cook Islands were proclaimed a British Protectorate in 1888 and a part of New Zealand in 1901. On August 4th, 1965, they became a self-governing territory in free association with New Zealand. Recent economic difficulties have caused speculation about the political future of the islands and the possibility of full integration with New Zealand has been suggested by some groups, although rejected by the Government. The people are British subjects and New Zealand citizens. The Premier elected in 1965, Albert Henry (later Sir Albert Henry), leader of the Cook Islands Party, retained power until July 1978, when the Democratic Party, under Dr. (later Sir) Thomas Davis, took power after Albert Henry was removed for electoral malpractice. Constitutional changes approved in 1981 will extend the life of the Legislative Assembly from four to five years, revise the electoral system to "one man, one vote", and increase the membership of the Assembly from 22 to 23. Other changes will abolish the Land Court, change public service conditions and the national anthem and ensign.

ECONOMIC SURVEY

Economic and agricultural development on the Cook Islands has always suffered from isolation and smallness. All forms of exports, but in particular fresh fruit, oranges, bananas, tomatoes and pineapples, have been hindered by lack of shipping and inadequate marketing in New Zealand metropolitan centres.

The islands receive a large proportion of their revenue in the form of aid from New Zealand and remittances sent back to the islands by migrants.

Most of the working population are engaged in agriculture, service and commerce, with the Government as a major employer. There are two clothing factories, a fruit canning factory and four factories making handicraft products, as well as a developing tourist industry.

During 1976 the economic situation on the islands worsened noticeably. Emergency funds, in addition to the $NZ3 million a year grant, were obtained from New Zealand to meet shortfalls in local revenue caused by falling agricultural production. On Rarotonga orange growers have failed to replant ageing orchards and on Mangaia pineapple production has fallen well below expectations. A threat to close down a New Zealand-owned canning factory in Rarotonga was averted in 1977 when the Government acquired a 51 per cent interest in the company, thus safeguarding an important market for citrus and pineapple producers.

A feature of island life since 1945 has been the pattern of migration from the outer islands to Rarotonga and from there to New Zealand. In 1978 there were 18,610 Cook Islanders living in New Zealand, more than in the Cook Islands. Population declined by 2.4 per cent between 1976 and 1981.

Following the change of Government in July 1978, the Cook Islands First Development Plan was announced. The main aims are to stimulate the economy, through the private sector wherever possible, by offering incentives and developing infrastructure, negotiating joint ventures with "distant water" fishing nations and attracting qualified Cook Islanders back from New Zealand. An Asian Development Bank survey in 1979 saw the future of the Cook Islands being one of closer links with New Zealand, greater tourist flows and more frequent movement of Cook Islanders between the two countries.

Developments in 1981 included a fishing agreement with Taiwan worth U.S. $90,000, a proposed Norwegian research project in offshore fishing, and a $NZ90,000 project to develop a fishing industry on Rakahanga and Palmerston Islands, where all other economic opportunities are lacking. In March 1982, in connection with the country's Second Development Plan (1982–85), the ADB approved a loan of U.S. $1.5 million to the Cook Islands Development Bank for distribution throughout the economy. Offshore banking was established in the islands in May 1982.

STATISTICAL SURVEY

AREA

Total area: 234 square km. (90.3 square miles).

POPULATION*

At the census of December 1st, 1981 the population totalled 17,695.

Rarotonga†	9,477	Manuae	12
Aitutaki	2,348	Nassau	134
Atiu	1,225	Palmerston	51
Mangaia	1,364	Penrhyn	608
Manihiki	405	Pukapuka	797
Mauke	684	Rakahanga	269
Mitiaro	256		

Suwarrow and Takutea are uninhabited.

* All figures are provisional.

† Including the capital, Avarua.

Births and Deaths (1979): birth rate 25.7 per 1,000; death rate 6.8 per 1,000.

Labour force (1976 census): 5,384.

AGRICULTURE

PRINCIPAL CROPS

		1978	1979	1980	1981
Copra*	metric tons	642	1,608	943	997
Citrus fruit*	,, ,,	2,863	2,611	1,435	2,671
Pineapples*	,, ,,	1,124	1,251	1,870	44
Bananas .	,, ,,	171	1,106	2,076	2,422
Pawpaw† .	kilogrammes	110,042	106,656	202,078	261,326
Capsicums† .	,,	59,219	75,376	62,027	28,397
Beans† .	,,	50,800	41,293	41,553	32,651
Aubergines† .	,,	23,802	—	—	—
Courgettes† .	,,	24,147	32,115	30,540	14,204
Avocados† .	,,	15,434	11,205	20,366	18,916

* Processed and exported quantities.

† Production from Rarotonga only, air freighted and sold on the New Zealand market.

LIVESTOCK
(Rarotonga only)

	1971	1977	1978*
Cattle . .	208	207	250
Pigs . .	5,002	6,498	8,500
Goats . .	950	1,098	1,050

* Estimates.

Total Livestock (1978 estimates): Cattle 350; Pigs 16,500; Goats 2,700; Poultry 50,000; Horses 850.

Source: Government of the Cook Islands, Rarotonga.

Fishing (catch in metric tons): 1,091 in 1978; 830 in 1979.

FINANCE

New Zealand and local currency are both legal tender.

New Zealand currency: 100 cents = 1 New Zealand dollar ($NZ).

Coins: 1, 2, 5, 10, 20 and 50 cents.
Notes: 1, 2, 5, 10, 20 and 100 dollars.

Cook Islands currency: 100 cents = 1 Cook Islands dollar ($CI).

Coins: 1, 2, 5, 10 and 50 cents; $1.

Also minted are a $100 gold coin, and silver coins for $2, $2.50, $5, $7.50, $25 and $50.

Exchange rates (June 1982): £1 sterling = $NZ2.3365; U.S. $1 = $NZ1.351; $NZ100 = £42.80 = U.S. $74.02.

Note: For details of previous changes in the exchange rate, *see* the chapter on New Zealand.

BUDGET
($NZ'000)

	1978/79	1979/80	1980/81
Revenue . .	13,862	15,887	19,436
Expenditure . .	14,701	16,414	18,751

Principal sources of revenue: Import and export duties sales tax, stamp sales, income and welfare tax, turnover tax. The Cook Islands also receive budgetary aid from New Zealand ($NZ8.4 million in 1981/82).

Principal items of expenditure: Education, public health, public works.

CONSUMER PRICE INDEX
(base: 1970 = 100)

	1978	1979	1980	1981
Food .	301.1	335.7	378.7	462.1
General .	292.2	324.9	369.5	446.5

EXTERNAL TRADE

($NZ '000)

	1979	1980	1981
Imports c.i.f. . .	22,458	23,610	n.a.
Exports f.o.b. .	3,778	4,190	5,015

Principal imports: Foodstuffs, timber, fuel and cement.

Principal exports: Fruit juices, canned fruit, tomatoes, mother-of-pearl, copra, citrus fruits, clothing and handicrafts.

Trade is chiefly with New Zealand, the EEC, Japan, the U.S.A., Hong Kong and Australia.

Tourism: Number of visitors in 1978: 17,913; 1979: 19,722; 1980: 21,051; 1981: 18,498.

EDUCATION

(1982)

	Institutions	Pupils
Pre-school . . .	11	525
Primary . . .	27	4,137
High schools . .	2	198
Colleges. . . .	7	3,058

THE CONSTITUTION

A new constitution was proclaimed in 1965, under which the Cook Islands have complete control over their own affairs in free association with New Zealand, but they can at any time move into full independence by a unilateral act if they so wish.

Executive authority is vested in the British monarch, who is Head of State, and exercised through her official representative. The New Zealand Government is represented by the New Zealand representative, who resides on Roratonga.

Executive Government is carried out by a Cabinet consisting of a Premier and six Ministers including a Deputy to the Premier. The Cabinet is collectively responsible to the Legislative Assembly.

The Legislative Assembly consists of 23 members elected by universal suffrage every five years, one member being elected by voters living overseas, and is presided over by a Speaker. The Upper House or House of Ariki, consisting of up to 15 members who are hereditary chiefs, can advise the Legislative Assembly but has no legislative powers.

Each of the main islands has an Island Council.

THE GOVERNMENT

THE CABINET

(July 1982)

Prime Minister, Minister for Finance, Immigration, External Affairs, Police and Marketing: Dr. Sir THOMAS (TOM) R. A. H. DAVIS.

Deputy Prime Minister, Minister for Health, Telecommunications, Public Service and Northern Group, and Postmaster General: Hon. PUPUKE ROBATI.

Minister for Education, Cultural Development, Library and Museums: Hon. TANGAROA TANGAROA.

Minister for Economic Development, Planning, Attorney General, Minister for Civil Defence, Civil Aviation, Labour and Consumer Affairs and Correctional Services: Hon. VINCENT INGRAM.

Minister for Agriculture, Fisheries, Kia Orana Food Corporation and Legislative Service: Hon. TANGATA SIMIONA.

Minister for Internal Affairs, Justice and Tourism: Hon. IAVETA SHORT.

Minister for Works, Survey, Energy Resources, Building and Housing and Electric Power Supply: Hon. PAPAMAMA PAKINO.

LEGISLATIVE ASSEMBLY

Speaker: DAVID HOSKING.

At December 1979 the Democratic Party held 16 seats against the Cook Islands Party's 6 seats. In May 1981 a 23rd seat was created for a member representing Cook Islanders living overseas, but the vacancy was not filled immediately.

HOUSE OF ARIKI

President: PA TEPAERU ARIKI.

POLITICAL PARTIES

Cook Islands Party: Rarotonga; Leader G. A. HENRY.

Democratic Party: P.O.B. 202, Rarotonga; f. 1971; Leader Dr. Sir THOMAS DAVIS.

JUDICIAL SYSTEM

The judiciary comprises the Privy Council, the Court of Appeal and the High Court.

The High Court exercises jurisdiction in respect of civil, criminal and land titles cases throughout the Cook Islands. The Court of Appeal hears appeals against decisions of the High Court. The Privy Council, sitting in the United Kingdom, is the final appellate tribunal for the country.

Chief Justice of the High Court: GRAHAM DAVID SPEIGHT.

Judge of the High Court: J. D. DILLON.

RELIGION

Main groups are Cook Islands Christian Church (Congregational), to which 75 per cent of the population belong, Roman Catholic, Latter-Day Saints and Seventh Day Adventists.

Roman Catholic: Bishop of Rarotonga (Cook Islands and Niue): Most Rev. DENIS G. BROWNE; P.O.B. 147, Rarotonga. There are about 2,200 Catholics in the Cook Islands and Niue; publ. *The Torea* (six a year).

THE PRESS

Akatauira: Rarotonga; f. 1979; Cook Islands Party weekly.

Cook Islands News: P.O.B. 126, Avarua, Rarotonga; daily government newspaper; Editor ARTHUR TARIPO; circ. 2,000.

The Weekender: P.O.B. 322, Rarotonga; f. 1975; privately owned; weekly.

RADIO

Cook Islands Broadcasting and Newspaper Corporation: P.O.B. 126, Avarua, Rarotonga; broadcasts in English and Maori 06.00h. to 23.00h. seven days a week; Gen. Man. ROBERT PFEIFFER.

Radio Ikurangi: Rarotonga; f. 1979; broadcasts on FM.

There were 7,100 radio sets in 1978.

FINANCE

BANKING

The National Bank of New Zealand has a branch on Rarotonga and the government Post Office Savings Bank also operates in the islands.

Cook Islands Development Bank: P.O.B. 113, Rarotonga; f. 1978 to replace National Development Corporation; set up to finance development projects in all areas of the economy and to help islanders establish small businesses and industries by providing loans and management advisory assistance; cap. p.u. U.S. $1,684,700; total assets U.S. $2,641,565 (March 1982); Gen. Man. J. M. ROWLEY.

TRADE AND INDUSTRY

There is a chamber of commerce on Rarotonga and in 1978 the Primary Marketing Board was established.

TRANSPORT

ROADS

On Rarotonga a 33 km. sealed road encircles the island's coastline.

SHIPPING

Ships from New Zealand, the United Kingdom, Japan and the U.S.A. call at Rarotonga. The Shipping Corporation of New Zealand Ltd. operates services between the Cook Islands, Niue, French Polynesia and Auckland, New Zealand. Kyowa Line and Daiwa Lines operate monthly services linking the Cook Islands with Hong Kong, Taiwan, the Republic of Korea, Japan and various Pacific islands.

CIVIL AVIATION

An international airport was opened at Rarotonga in 1974.

Air New Zealand: Rarotonga; passenger and cargo flights between Rarotonga, New Zealand, Fiji, French Polynesia and the U.S.A. (Los Angeles) operated with B737 and DC10 aircraft.

Air Rarotonga: P.O.B. 79, Rarotonga; privately owned; operates internal service between the Cook Islands; Dirs. EWAN F. SMITH, IAN R. RHODES.

Cook Islands Airways: Rarotonga; owned by Air New Zealand and the Cook Islands Government; operates an internal air service between Rarotonga, Mauke, Aitutaki, Mitiaro, and Atiu.

The Cook Islands are also served by Polynesian Airlines (Western Samoa) operating between Rarotonga, American Samoa, Western Samoa and Tahiti (French Polynesia).

EDUCATION

In 1977 there were 23 government schools, four of which were high schools. There were also 4 private primary schools and 2 private colleges. Total enrolment was 7,172 pupils.

Free secular education is compulsory for all children between the ages of 6 and 15.

Secondary education is provided at Tereora College in Rarotonga and junior high schools on Aitutaki, Mangaia and Atiu. Under the New Zealand Training Scheme, the New Zealand Government offers education and training in New Zealand, Fiji and Western Samoa for secondary and tertiary education, career training and short-term in-service training.

Coral Sea Islands Territory

The Coral Sea Islands Territory, a dependency of Australia, was created in May 1969. It comprises several islands east of Queensland between the Great Barrier Reef and 157° 10′ E. The islands had been acquired by the Commonwealth by acts of sovereignty over a number of years. All are very small and they include Cato Island, Chilcott Islet in the Coringa Group, and the Willis Group. Three members of the Commonwealth Bureau of Meteorology are stationed on one of the Willis Group, but the remainder of the islands are uninhabited.

The Act constituting the Territory did not establish an administration on the islands but provides means of controlling the activities of those who visit them. The possibility of exploration for oil on the continental shelf and the increasing range and scope of international fishing enterprises made desirable such an administrative framework and system of law. The Governor-General of Australia is empowered to make ordinances for the peace, order and good government of the Territory and, by ordinance, the laws of the Australian Capital Territory apply. The Supreme Court and Court of Petty Sessions of Norfolk Island have jurisdiction in relation to the Territory. The Minister for Home Affairs and Environment is responsible for matters affecting the Territory.

Fiji

PHYSICAL AND SOCIAL GEOGRAPHY

The total area of Fiji, including the Rotuma group, is 18,376 square kilometres. The Fiji group comprises four main islands, Viti Levu, Vanua Levu, Tavenui and Kadavu; in addition there are numerous smaller islands, atolls and reefs, numbering in all about 400, of which fewer than 100 are inhabited.

Fiji is characterized by racial diversity. The indigenous Fijian population fell sharply during the 1850s due to measles and influenza epidemics in which thousands died. Only in the 1950s did it begin to recover and by the 1970s was increasing at over 3 per cent a year. The Indian population, originally brought to Fiji as labour for the canefields from 1879, has always increased rapidly.

Figures issued by the Bureau of Statistics for June 1980 estimated a population of 634,151. In 1980 about 50 per cent were Indians and 45 per cent Fijians. The annual growth rates in 1979 were estimated at 2.1 per cent for Fijians and 1.9 per cent for Indians.

HISTORY

The first documented sighting of the islands by a European was that of Abel Tasman in 1643. The first Europeans to settle on the islands were sandalwood traders, missionaries and shipwrecked sailors. Under their influence local fighting and jealousies reached unprecedented heights, until by the 1850s, one chief, Thakombau, had gained a tenuous influence over the whole of the western islands. Thakombau ran foul of American interests during the 1850s and turned to the British for assistance, unsuccessfully at first, but in 1874 Britain agreed to a second offer of cession, and Fiji was proclaimed a British possession. Fiji became independent in October 1970.

The racial diversity, compounded by actions of the past colonial administrations, presents Fiji with one of its most difficult problems. The colonial government consistently favoured the Fijian population, protecting them from exploitation and their land from alienation but allowed the importation of foreign labour. Approximately 80 per cent of the islands are owned by Fijian communities, but over 90 per cent of the sugar crop, Fiji's largest export, is produced by Indians usually on land leased from Fijians. Until recently, Indians were poorly represented politically, while Fijians had their own administrative and judicial systems.

During the early 1970s signs of racial tension and unrest had been minimal but in 1974 a breakaway movement from the Alliance Party led by Sakiasi Butadroka formed the Fijian National Party (FNP). The FNP campaigned during the 1977 general election on a "Fiji for the Fijians" platform with the stated intention of splitting the indigenous Fijian vote, on which the Alliance Party relies, in order that this might foster nationalist feeling. In 1982 campaigning for a July election, the FNP adopted, even more vigorously, a similar platform, calling for the restoration of special seats for ethnic Fijians, and the return of all Crown and freehold land to Fijians. With the FNP supported by a new Fijian nationalist party, the Western United Front, and a disagreement between the ruling Alliance Party and the Indian Alliance which formerly supported the Prime Minister, Ratu Sir Kamisese Mara, the outcome of the July poll was unpredictable. In the event, the Government's 16-seat majority was reduced to four with the Alliance Party winning 28 seats and a coalition of the National Federation Party and the Western United Front winning 24.

ECONOMIC SURVEY

The economy is basically agricultural, with sugar as the main crop. The instability of the international sugar market seriously affected the Fijian economy in the mid-1970s but, as a signatory of the Lomé Convention since 1975, Fiji benefits from the Convention's subsidies and trade provisions. The International Sugar Agreement, in force from January 1978, was also expected to boost the industry. However, Fiji's quota of sugar exports to the U.S.A. has been reduced from 119,000 metric tons in 1979 to almost nil in the year ending June 1983. The loss of this important market has been partly compensated for by an agreement under which the People's Republic of China will take 120,000 tons of Fiji's sugar between 1982 and 1985. Fiji's principal trading partners are Australia, Japan, New Zealand, Singapore, the United Kingdom and the U.S.A. Tourism is developing with some difficulty but is still the second largest source of foreign exchange earnings, accounting for receipts of $F108 million in 1980. Next in importance are gold and coconut products.

In an effort to diversify the economy and reduce the growing trade deficit ($F271 million in 1981), domestic industries such as cement, timber, cigarettes and tuna canning are being encouraged by income tax concessions and export incentive reliefs. The Seventh Five-Year Development Plan (1976–80) aimed to expand production and develop the infra-structure, and gave priority to agriculture. In 1978 an Australian aid project involving an estimated investment of $A7.5 million over ten years was launched. It aims to bring 324,000 hectares of hilly and largely undeveloped land into production by establishing 103 individual farm holdings with an emphasis on livestock and grazing. In 1977 agreement was reached by the Government, employers and trade unions on the need for a policy of wage restraint to combat inflation, which stood at 11.6 per cent in 1981, after falling from 13.7 per cent in 1975 to 6.1 per cent in 1978. In 1980 G.D.P. fell by 1 per cent, compared with a 12 per cent rise in 1979.

Under Fiji's Eighth Five-Year Development Plan (1981–85), sugar production and tourism are to remain the dominant industries, but the development of cocoa, coffee, ginger, citrus fruits, timber, beef, goat meat, fish and dairy farming should diversify the economy. Reliance on petroleum products is to be reduced by the development of hydroelectricity (the important scheme at Monasavu was due to be completed in 1981) and by the processing of sugar cane into ethanol. Fishing and exploration for petroleum and other minerals should continue to expand following the declaration in 1977 of an economic zone extending for 200 nautical miles (370 km.) from the coasts of the Fijian group.

STATISTICAL SURVEY

AREA AND POPULATION

Area*	Census Population				Estimated Population (mid-year)	Density (per sq. km.)
	Sept. 12th, 1966	Sept. 13th, 1976			1980	1980
		Males	Females	Total		
18,376 sq. km.†	476,727	296,950	291,118	588,068	634,151	34·5

* Includes the Rotuma group.

† 7,095 sq. miles.

ETHNIC GROUPS

	1976 (Census)	1980 (Estimates, mid-year)
Fijians	259,932	281,954
Indians	292,896	317,385
Part Europeans	10,276	11,200
Rotumans	6,822	7,761
Other Pacific Islanders	7,291	6,412
Chinese	4,652	4,618
Europeans	4,929	3,945
Others	1,270	876
Total	588,068	634,151

Suva (Capital): population 66,018 in 1979.

Births and Deaths: Birth rate 32.6 per 1,000 (1980); death rate 5.7 per 1,000 (1979).

ECONOMICALLY ACTIVE POPULATION
(1976 census)

	Males	Females	Total
Agriculture, hunting, forestry and fishing	70,037	6,849	76,886
Mining and quarrying	1,592	70	1,662
Manufacturing	11,277	1,762	13,039
Electricity, gas and water	1,579	49	1,628
Construction	11,037	149	11,186
Trade, restaurants and hotels	12,938	4,434	17,372
Transport, storage and communications	8,445	594	9,039
Financing, insurance, real estate and business services	2,476	1,042	3,518
Community, social and personal services	18,785	10,349	29,134
Activities not adequately described	8,149	4,172	12,321
Total	146,315	29,470	175,785

AGRICULTURE

PRINCIPAL CROPS
(metric tons)

	1978	1979	1980
Sugar cane	2,849,000	4,058,000	3,360,000
Coconuts	245,000	205,000	229,000
Cassava	92,000	92,000	92,000
Copra	26,000	21,822	22,802
Rice (paddy)	16,000	18,712	17,846
Sweet potatoes	8,000	8,000	8,000
Bananas	4,000	4,000	4,000
Green ginger	1,845	1,701	1,462

Livestock (1980—FAO estimates): Cattle 151,000, Pigs 23,000, Goats 55,000, Poultry 977,000, Horses (1979 estimate) 39,000.

Fishing (metric tons): Total catch 9,176 in 1978; 20,420 in 1979; 18,650 in 1980.

MINING

		1978	1979	1980	1981
Gold	grammes	872,920	992,965	773,503	960,000
Silver	,,	326,680	325,996	207,940	260,000
Limestone	metric tons	2,522	1,308	n.a.	n.a.
Crushed metal	cu. metres	233,451	205,071	n.a.	n.a.

INDUSTRY

SELECTED PRODUCTS

		1978	1979	1980	1981
Beef	metric tons	2,722	3,616	3,525	5,394
Sugar	,, ,,	347,000	473,000	396,000	470,000
Copra	,, ,,	26,313	21,822	22,802	20,520
Coconut oil	,, ,,	16,519	14,947	14,631	13,936
Soap	,, ,,	5,229	5,970	6,010	5,601
Cement	,, ,,	86,800	87,400	82,900	92,200
Paint	'000 litres	1,702	1,722	1,799	1,788
Beer	,, ,,	16,206	17,830	17,995	18,246
Soft drinks	,, ,,	5,179	5,482	4,307	4,162
Cigarettes	million	551	560	549	643
Timber	'000 cu. metres	181	180	233	205
Matches	'000 gross boxes	169	178	173	207

FINANCE

100 cents=1 Fiji dollar ($F).
Coins: 1, 2, 5, 10, 20 and 50 cents.
Notes: 1, 2, 5, 10 and 20 dollars.

Exchange rates (June 1982): £1 sterling=$F1.619; U.S. $1=93.5 Fiji cents.
$F100=£61.78=U.S. $107.00.

Note: The Fiji dollar was introduced in January 1969, replacing the Fiji pound at the rate of £F1=$F2. From November 1967 the exchange rate was £1 sterling=£F1.045 (£F1=U.S. $2.2966) so the new rate was £1 sterling=$F2.09, with the Fiji dollar valued at U.S. $1.1483 (U.S. $1=87.08 Fiji cents) until August 1971. The link with sterling was maintained and the exchange rate was $F1=U.S. $1.2467 (U.S. $1=80.21 Fiji cents) from December 1971 to June 1972, when the British currency was allowed to "float". The Fiji dollar also "floated", the exchange rate continuing at £1=$F2.09 until October 1972. The rate was £1=$F1.98 from October 1972 to September 1973; and £1=$F1.89 from September 1973 to February 1974. In February 1974 the link with sterling was broken and a new exchange rate of $F1=U.S. $1.25 (U.S. $1=80 Fiji cents) was established. This remained in effect until April 1975, since when the Fiji dollar has been valued in relation to a weighted "basket" of the currencies of the country's main trading partners. The average value of the Fiji dollar was U.S. $1.213 in 1972; U.S. $1.260 in 1973; U.S. $1.244 in 1974; U.S. $1.215 in 1975; U.S. $1.111 in 1976; U.S. $1.090 in 1977; U.S. $1.181 in 1978; U.S. $1.197 in 1979; U.S. $1.223 in 1980; U.S. $1.172 in 1981.

BUDGET
($F'000)

Revenue	1980	1981	Expenditure	1980	1981
Customs duties and port dues	73,632	78,012	Public debt charges	35,395	39,189
Income tax and direct revenue	106,700	118,406	Pension and gratuities	5,505	6,069
Interest	554	602	Works annually recurrent	21,429	26,958
Income from property and entrepreneuring	41,274	41,643	Departmental expenditure	160,742	167,366
Total	227,160	238,663	Total	223,071	239,582

CURRENCY IN CIRCULATION
($F'000 at end of year)

1975	1976	1977	1978	1979	1980	1981
27,335	30,702	34,022	38,790	45,241	44,052	48,725

CONSUMER PRICE INDEX
(Base: January 1974=100)

	1978	1979	1980*	1981*
Food	146.4	155.2	115.3	130.1
Housing	167.6	180.4	104.4	116.6
Household operation	158.1	172.1	114.0†	119.3†
Clothing and footwear	171.6	181.1	116.3	128.5
Transport	177.4	198.6	120.6	132.6
Miscellaneous	137.4	151.5	115.7	124.1
All Items	155.3	167.3	114.5	127.3

* Base: 1979=100. † Refers to durable household goods.

NATIONAL ACCOUNTS

Gross Domestic Product by Economic Activity

($F million at constant 1977 factor cost)

	1978	1979	1980	1981
Agriculture, forestry and fishing	139.5	163.4	152.8	170.8
Mining and quarrying	0.4	0.4	0.3	0.4
Manufacturing	74.3	87.7	80.7	88.9
Electricity, gas and water	6.1	6.5	6.5	6.8
Building and construction	44.5	50.5	51.4	53.8
Distribution (incl. tourism)	108.7	117.3	117.3	123.9
Transport and communications	57.6	66.9	66.8	70.6
Finance and insurance	80.2	83.1	85.6	88.9
Government and other services	121.3	122.9	124.1	125.3
Less imputed bank service charges	−16.6	−18.4	−18.5	−15.9
TOTAL	616.6	690.9	668.5	710.9

Gross Domestic Product by Expenditure

($F million at current prices)

	1978	1979*	1980*
Final consumption expenditure	539.7	618.5	743.1
Private	424.6	490.0	153.2
Government	115.1	128.5	589.9
Gross fixed capital formation	149.4	221.6	247.1
Private	85.3	127.6	126.8
Public	64.2	94.0	120.3
Net change in stocks	26.0	40.0	56.7
Exports of goods and services	299.5	385.8	470.1
Less imports of goods and services	330.5	432.2	518.6
G.D.P. at Current Market Prices	684.1	833.8	917.1
Less net indirect taxes	59.2	72.8	81.3
G.D.P. at Factor Cost	624.9	761.0	835.8

* Provisional.

EXTERNAL TRADE

($F'000)

	1976	1977	1978	1979	1980	1981
Imports	238,040	281,014	299,997	392,863	458,753	540,072
Exports	122,523	164,316	166,493	215,043	305,559	268,764

PRINCIPAL COMMODITIES
($F'000)

IMPORTS	1980	1981*
Machinery and electrical goods	n.a.	74,237
Transport equipment	25,940	43,802
Fabrics	19,488	20,339
Iron and steel	20,413	21,111
Food	64,934	76,551
Fuel	105,711	138,500
Clothing	5,424	6,492
Tape recorders	1,432	1,704
Watches	4,540	4,581

EXPORTS	1979	1980	1981*
Sugar	116,962	174,175	131,561
Gold	6,492	12,410	11,640
Coconut oil	11,683	6,528	6,355
Molasses	7,363	11,989	9,620
Coconut meal	234	42	—
Green ginger	1,021	1,087	2,036
Veneer sheets	868	807	1,655
Biscuits	769	759	835
Prepared fish	11,551	8,570	16,328
Cement	236	145	69
Lumber	1,634	4,083	1,756
Silver	53	41	41

* Provisional.

($F'000)

RE-EXPORTS	1979	1980	1981
Fuel	25,332	46,658	51,981
Fish	1,564	6,146	3,003
Textile yarns and fabrics	2,617	3,103	3,146
Clothing	724	620	610

PRINCIPAL TRADING PARTNERS
($F'000)

IMPORTS	1980	1981
Australia	140,267	194,069
Canada	2,707	2,804
Germany, Federal Republic	5,002	6,963
Hong Kong	7,027	8,910
India	4,938	4,964
Japan	65,174	86,344
Netherlands	1,030	2,676
New Zealand	67,543	75,056
Singapore	50,514	37,836
United Kingdom	33,337	29,537
U.S.A.	29,923	38,782

EXPORTS	1980	1981
Australia	20,685	19,480
Canada	20,731	10,656
Germany, Federal Republic	200	848
Japan	31,577	19,319
New Zealand	31,188	21,866
Singapore	5,131	9,052
Tonga	7,430	11,307
United Kingdom	61,593	67,409
U.S.A.	30,917	27,597
Western Samoa	6,449	5,824

TRANSPORT

ROAD TRAFFIC
('000 motor vehicles registered at December 31st)

	1977	1978	1979	1980	1981
Passenger cars	19.4	20.4	21.9	23.4	25.2
All other vehicles	16.2	18.9	21.2	23.9	26.8

SHIPPING

(sea-borne freight traffic)

	1978	1979	1980	1981
International shipping:				
Vessels entered:				
Number	558	542	542	524
Displacement ('000 net reg. tons)	2,613	2,556	2,463	2,359
Vessels cleared:				
Number	558	542	542	524
Displacement ('000 net reg. tons)	2,613	2,556	2,462	2,359
Freight ('000 metric tons):				
Loaded	567	691	735†	n.a.
Unloaded	801	857	826	n.a.
Coastwise shipping:*				
Freight ('000 metric tons):				
Loaded	59	n.a.	n.a.	n.a.
Unloaded	34	n.a.	n.a.	n.a.

* Suva only. † Provisional.

CIVIL AVIATION

	1977	1978	1979	1980
Passengers arriving	196,807	208,087	214,076	219,112
Passengers departing	196,580	209,490	215,146	218,453
Transit passengers	183,414	135,536	129,449	129,735

TOURISM

	1978	1979	1980	1981
Number of visitors	184,063	188,740	189,996	189,915
Receipts ($F'000)	86,000	104,000	108,200	n.a.

EDUCATION

(1981)*

	SCHOOLS	STUDENTS
Primary	661	116,190
Secondary	137	45,844
Vocational and Technical	37	2,426
Teacher Training	4	367
Medical	1	294

* Provisional.

Source (unless otherwise stated): Bureau of Statistics, Suva.

THE CONSTITUTION

The Constitution is set out in the Fiji (Independence) Order of 1970. It contains provisions relating to the protection of fundamental rights and freedoms, the powers and duties of the Governor-General, the Cabinet, the House of Representatives, the Senate, the Judiciary, the Public Service and finance.

It provides that every person in Fiji regardless of race, place of origin, political opinion, colour, creed or sex is entitled to the fundamental rights of life, liberty, security of the person and protection of the law, freedom of conscience, expression, assembly and association; protection of the privacy of his home and other property and from the deprivation of property without compensation. The enjoyment of these rights, however, is subject to the proviso that they do not prejudice the rights and freedom of others, or the public interest.

EXECUTIVE

H.M. the Queen appoints a Governor-General as her representative in Fiji.

The Cabinet consists of the Prime Minister, the Attorney-General and any other Minister whom the Governor-General might appoint on the advice of the Prime Minister. The Governor-General appoints as Leader of the Opposition in the House of Representatives either the leader of the largest Opposition party or, if there is no such party, the person whose appointment would be most acceptable to the leaders of the Opposition parties in the House.

PARLIAMENT

The Fiji Parliament consists of a Senate and a House of Representatives. The Senate has 22 members: 8 nominated by the Council of Chiefs, 7 nominated by the Prime Minister, 6 nominated by the Leader of the Opposition and one nominated by the Council of the Island of Rotuma. Their appointments are for a six-year term. The President and Vice-President of the Senate are elected from members who are neither Ministers nor Assistant Ministers. The House of Representatives has 52 members: 27 elected on the communal roll and 25 on the national roll (a cross-voting system by which all races vote together). The House elects a Speaker and a Deputy Speaker from among its non-ministerial members.

PROVINCIAL GOVERNMENT

There are thirteen provinces, each headed by a provincial council.

THE GOVERNMENT

Head of State: H.M. QUEEN ELIZABETH II.

Governor-General: Ratu Sir GEORGE CAKOBAU, G.C.M.G., G.C.V.O., O.B.E., J.P. (took office 1973).

THE CABINET

(July 1982)

Prime Minister: Rt. Hon. Ratu Sir KAMISESE KAPAIWAI TUIMACILAI MARA, P.C., K.B.E., M.A.

Deputy Prime Minister, Minister for Fijian Affairs and Rural Development: Ratu Sir PENAIA GANILAU, K.B.E., C.M.G., C.V.O., D.S.O., E.D.

Minister of Finance: CHARLES WALKER.

Minister for Education: Dr. AMAD ALI.

Minister for Economic Planning and Development: Ratu DAVID TOGANIVALU.

Minister for Lands, Local Government and Housing: MILITONI LEWENIQILA.

Minister for Transport and Civil Aviation: EDWARD BEDDOWES.

Minister of Employment and Industrial Relations: MOHAMMED RAMZAN, M.B.E.

Minister of Agriculture and Fisheries: JONATI MAVOA.

Minister for Works and Communications: SEMESA SIKIVOU, C.B.E.

Minister for Home Affairs: Ratu WILLIAM TOGANIVALU.

Minister for Foreign Affairs and Tourism: MOSESE QIONIBARAVI.

Minister for Energy and Mineral Resources: PETER STINSON.

Minister for Health and Social Welfare: Dr. APENISA KURUISAQILA.

Minister of State for Forests: Ratu JOSAIA TAVAIQIA, O.B.E.

Minister of State for Co-operatives: LIVAI NASTIVATA.

Minister of State without Portfolio: APISAI TORA.

Attorney-General: MANIKAM V. PILLAI, M.B.E.

LEGISLATURE

PARLIAMENT

THE SENATE

Twenty-two appointed members.

President: Sir ROBERT L. MUNRO.

Vice-President: Ratu LIVAI VOLAVOLA.

HOUSE OF REPRESENTATIVES

Speaker: MOSESE QIONIBARAVI, C.M.G.

Deputy Speaker: HARISH SHARMA.

Leader of the Opposition: JAI RAM REDDY.

At the general election held in July 1982 the Alliance Party won 28 seats, and the National Federation and the Western United Front won 24.

POLITICAL PARTIES

Alliance Party: Suva; multi-racial; government party; Leader Rt. Hon. Ratu Sir KAMISESE K. T. MARA, P.C., K.B.E., M.A.

National Federation Party: P.O.B. 228, Suva; f. 1963; fusion of two parties: the Federation, which was mainly Indian but multi-racial, and the National Democratic Party, a purely Fijian party; Pres. RAM SAMI GOUNDAR.

Fijian Nationalist Party: Suva; f. 1974; seeks more representation for Fijians in Parliament and for general reforms in their favour; Leader SAKIASI BUTADROKA.

National Labour and Farmers' Party: Suva; f. 1982; Pres. GURUBUX SINGH.

Western United Front: Suva; Leader Ratu OSEA GAVIDI.

DIPLOMATIC REPRESENTATION

EMBASSIES AND HIGH COMMISSIONS ACCREDITED TO FIJI

Australia: Dominion House, P.O.B. 214, Suva; *High Commissioner:* COLIN MCDONALD.

Bangladesh: Canberra, A.C.T., Australia (HC).

Belgium: Wellington, New Zealand.

Canada: Wellington, New Zealand (HC).

Chile: Wellington, New Zealand.

China, People's Republic: 49 Cakobau Rd., Suva; *Ambassador:* SHEN ZHIWEI.

Denmark: Canberra, A.C.T., Australia.

Egypt: Canberra, A.C.T., Australia.

France: 1st Floor, Dominion House, Suva; *Ambassador:* ROBERT PUISSANT.

German Democratic Republic: Canberra, A.C.T., Australia.

Germany, Federal Republic: Wellington, New Zealand.

India: P.O.B. 405, Suva; *High Commissioner:* CHITILENCHERY PATHIYIL RAVINDRANATHAN.

Indonesia: Wellington, New Zealand.

Israel: Canberra, A.C.T., Australia.

Italy: Canberra, A.C.T., Australia.

Korea, Republic: Canberra, A.C.T., Australia.

Malaysia: Suva; *High Commissioner:* Encik ABDUL KARIM MARZUKI.

Mexico: Canberra, A.C.T., Australia.

Netherlands: Wellington, New Zealand.

New Zealand: 8th Floor, Ratu Sukuna House, P.O.B. 1378, Suva; *High Commissioner:* MICHAEL POWLES.

Pakistan: Canberra, A.C.T., Australia.

Papua New Guinea: 6th Floor, Ratu Sukuna House, P.O.B. 2447, Suva; *High Commissioner:* NAIME DOKO.

Philippines: Canberra, A.C.T., Australia.

Singapore: Canberra, A.C.T., Australia (HC).

Sweden: Wellington, New Zealand.

Thailand: Canberra, A.C.T., Australia.

Turkey: Canberra, A.C.T., Australia.

Tuvalu: Suva; *High Commissioner:* KAMUTA LATASI.

U.S.S.R.: Canberra, A.C.T., Australia.

United Kingdom: Civic Centre, Stinson Parade, P.O.B. 1355, Suva; *High Commissioner:* ROBERT A. R. BARLTROP.

U.S.A.: 31 Loftus St., P.O.B. 218, Suva; *Ambassador:* FRED J. ECKERT.

Fiji also has diplomatic relations with Argentina, Cyprus, Finland, Greece, Jamaica, Japan, Kiribati, the Democratic People's Republic of Korea, Nauru, Norway, Romania, Senegal, Spain, Tonga, Vanuatu, the Vatican City, Western Samoa and Yugoslavia.

JUDICIAL SYSTEM

Justice is administered by the Fiji Court of Appeal, the Supreme Court and the Magistrates' Courts. The Supreme Court of Fiji is the superior court of record presided over by the Chief Justice, who is also the President of the Fiji Court of Appeal. The Fiji Court of Appeal hears appeals from the Supreme Court and the High Courts of Solomon Islands and Tuvalu.

Chief Justice: Hon. Sir TIMOCI TUIVAGA, K.B.E.

Puisne Judges: Hon. G. MISHRA, Hon. J. T. WILLIAMS, Hon. R. G. KERMODE, Hon. G. O. L. DYKE, Hon. T. MADHOJI.

Chief Registrar: M. D. SCOTT.

RELIGION

Most Fijians are Christians, mainly Protestant. The Indians are mostly Hindus, and there is also a Muslim and a Sikh community.

Anglican: Bishop in Polynesia: Rt. Rev. JABEZ LESLIE BRYCE; Bishop's House, 7 Disraeli Rd., P.O.B. 35, Suva.

Methodist Church: P.O.B. 357, Suva; Pres. Rev. INOKE NABULIVOU; Sec. Rev. T. KANAILAGI.

Roman Catholic Church: Archbishop: Most Rev. PETERO MATACA; Archbishop's House, P.O.B. 393, Suva.

THE PRESS

Fiji Times and Herald Ltd.: P.O.B. 1167, Suva; f. 1869; largest newspaper publishers; also printers and publishers of books and magazines; Gen. Man. GARRY BARKER.

Coconut Telegraph: P.O.B. 249, Savusavu, Vanua Levu; f. 1975; monthly; serves widely-scattered rural community; Editor Mrs. LEMA LOW.

Fiji: Ministry of Information, Suva; f. 1978; English; every two months; current events; Editor K. T. VUIKABA.

Fiji Beach Press: published by News (South Pacific) Ltd., P.O.B. 5176, Raiwaqa, Suva; tourist paper; weekly in English, twice annually in Japanese; Editor PETER TIFFANY.

Fiji Fantastic: Newspapers of Fiji Ltd., Suva; f. 1978; English; monthly; Editor BRENDA WENDT; circ. 25,000.

Fiji Holiday: P.O.B. 1167, Suva; f. 1968; published by Fiji Times and Herald Ltd.; monthly; Editor ASHA LAKHAN; circ. 22,000.

Fiji Royal Gazette: Printing Department, P.O.B. 98, Suva; f. 1874; Fridays.

Fiji Sun: Newspapers of Fiji Ltd., Suva; f. 1974; English daily; Editor ADISHWAR PADARATH; circ. 26,312.

Fiji Times: P.O.B. 1167, Suva; f. 1869; published by Fiji Times and Herald Ltd.; English; daily; Gen. Man. GARRY BARKER; circ. 27,000.

Jai Fiji: P.O.B. 109, Lautoka; f. 1959; Hindi; Thursdays; Editor K. P. MISHRA; circ. 8,000.

Na Davui: Ministry of Information, Suva; f. 1978; Fijian; monthly; Editor ADI CAKAU COCKBURN; circ. 6,000.

Nai Lalakai: P.O.B. 1167, Suva; f. 1962; published by Fiji Times and Herald Ltd.; Fijian; weekly; Editor DALE TONAWAI; circ. 18,000.

Shankh: Ministry of Information, Suva; f. 1978; Hindi; monthly; Editor R. N. SHARMA; circ. 6,000.

Shanti Dut: P.O.B. 1167, Suva; f. 1935; published by Fiji Times and Herald Ltd.; Hindi; weekly; Editor G. D. SHARMA.

Siga Rarama: Newspapers of Fiji Ltd., Suva; f. 1974; Fijian; weekly; Editor ESALA RASOVO; circ. 10,500.

South Pacific Islands Business News: published by News (South Pacific) Ltd., P.O.B. 5176, Raiwaqa, Suva; f. 1980; monthly; circ. 2,500.

Sunsport: Newspapers of Fiji Ltd., Suva; f. 1979; English; weekly; Publr. P. V. HARKNESS; Editor PETER LOMAS; circ. 18,500.

Sunday Sun: Newspapers of Fiji Ltd., Suva; f. 1974 English; weekly; Editor A. PADARATH; circ. 31,600.

Sunday Times: Fiji Times and Herald Ltd., P.O.B. 1167, Suva; English; weekly; Gen. Man. GARRY BARKER.

RADIO

Fiji Broadcasting Commission (Radio Fiji): P.O.B. 334, Broadcasting House, Suva; f. 1954; broadcasts from ten AM and one FM station in two national networks, Radio Fiji One and Radio Fiji Two; in English, Fijian and Hindustani; Chair. N. MAHARAJ; Gen. Man. HUGH LEONARD.

The number of radio sets in 1978 was 300,000.

FINANCE

BANKING

(cap.=capital; res.=reserves; m.=million; brs.=branches)

Central Monetary Authority of Fiji: P.O.B. 1220, Suva; f. 1973; arbiter on banking affairs in Fiji; carries out all usual central banking functions; cap. $F2m. (Sept. 1980); Chair. D. J. BARNES; Gen. Man. S. SIWATIBAU.

Fiji Development Bank: P.O.B. 104, Suva; f. 1967; finances the development of natural resources, agriculture, transportation and other industries and enterprises; statutory body; cap. and res. $F13.0m. (June 1981); Chair. LEN G. USHER; Man. Dir. GLEN CAMPBELL FORGAN.

National Bank of Fiji: P.O.B. 1166, Suva; 6 brs.

FOREIGN BANKS

Australia and New Zealand Banking Group Ltd.: P.O.B. 179, Suva; Chief Man. (Fiji) T. D. SULLIVAN.

Bank of Baroda (*India*): P.O.B. 57, Suva; Man. for Fiji branches K. C. CHOKSHI.

Westpac Banking Corporation (*Australia*): 1 Thomson St., P.O.B. 238, Suva; Chief Man. G. YATES; 8 brs.

Bank of New Zealand: Private Mail Bag, Suva; Man. for Fiji A. R. HANNAY; 7 brs.

Barclays Bank International Ltd. (*U.K.*): Dominion House, Thomson St., P.O.B. 30, Suva; Man. R. W. WHITE.

INSURANCE

Colonial Mutual Life Assurance Society Ltd.: Private Bag, Suva; f. 1876; Gen. Man. B. E. LAWS.

Fiji Insurance Co. Ltd.: Stinson Bldg., Walu Bay, P.O.B. 1080, Suva; f. 1966; Gen. Man. J. O. BRYANT.

GRE Insurance Ltd.: Honson Bldg., 68 Thomson St., Suva.

New Zealand Insurance Co. Ltd.: Ratu Sukuna House, Suva.

TRADE AND INDUSTRY

DEVELOPMENT CORPORATIONS

Commonwealth Development Corpn.: Regional Office for Pacific Islands, P.O.B. 161, Suva; Regional Controller DAVID LINCOLN-GORDON, O.B.E.

Fijian Development Fund Board: P.O.B. 122, Suva; f. 1951; the Fund was established at the request of the Fijian Provincial Council and the Council of Chiefs (now the Great Council of Chiefs); funds derived from payments of $F20 a ton from the sales of copra by indigenous Fijians only; deposits credited to the producing group or individual at 2½ per cent interest; funds used only for Fijian development schemes; dep. $F875,025 (Dec. 1980); Chair. Ratu Sir PENAIA GANILAU; Sec. VUKICEA TAMANILO.

Fiji Development Company Ltd.: P.O.B. 161, Suva; f. 1960; subsidiary of the Commonwealth Development Corporation; Man. P. DAYAL.

Land Development Authority: c/o Ministry of Agriculture and Fisheries, P.O.B. 358, Suva; f. 1961 to co-ordinate development plans for land and marine resources; Chair. Rt. Hon. JOSAIA TAVAIQIA.

CHAMBER OF COMMERCE

Suva Chamber of Commerce: 7th Floor, Honson Bldg., Thomson St., P.O.B. 337, Suva; f. 1902; 101 mems.

MARKETING ORGANIZATIONS

Fiji Pine Commission: P.O.B. 521, Lautoka; f. 1976; development of forest and wood conversion industry, and marketing forest products; Gen. Man. E. GREGOR. Sec. W. TERWIEL.

Fiji Sugar Corporation Ltd.: P.O.B. 283, Suva; nationalized 1974; buyer of sugar cane and raw sugar manufacturer; Chair. C. NARSEY; Man. Dir. RASHEED A. ALI.

Fiji Sugar Marketing Co. Ltd.: P.O.B. 1402, Suva; Man. Dir. ERIC JONES.

National Marketing Authority: P.O.B. 5085, Raiwaqa, Suva; f. 1971; a statutory body set up to develop markets for agricultural and marine produce; exporters of fresh fruit and vegetables, fish,. fresh, syruped and crystallized ginger; Gen. Man. D. M. KERR.

CO-OPERATIVES

In 1977 there were 922 registered co-operatives.

EMPLOYERS' ORGANIZATIONS

Fiji Employers' Consultative Association: P.O.B. 575, Suva; represents 132 of the principal employers in Fiji; Pres. GERALD W. S. BARRACK; Dir. JACK MAYER.

Fiji Manufacturers' Association: 7th Floor, Honson Bldg., Thomson St., Suva; f. 1902; 90 mems.

TRADE UNIONS

Fiji Trades Union Congress: 298 Waimanu Rd., P.O.B. 1418 Suva; f. 1951; affiliated to ICFTU and ICFTU-ARO; 34 affiliated unions; over 35,000 mems.; Pres. JALE TOKI, M.B.E.; Nat. Sec. JAMES R. RAMAN; publ. *Fiji Labour Sentinel* (monthly).

Largest affiliated unions:

Fiji Public Service Association: 298 Waimanu Rd., P.O.B. 1405, Suva; 5,970 mems.; Pres. Dr. T. U. BAVADRA; Gen. Sec. M. P. CHAUDHRY.

Fiji Sugar and General Workers' Union: P.O.B. 330, Lautoka; Gen. Sec. CHIRAG ALI SHAH; 3,300 mems.

Fiji Teachers' Union: P.O.B. 3582, Samabula; f. 1930; 3,000 mems.; Pres. S. CHARAN; Gen. Sec. PRATAP CHAND.

Fiji Waterfront Workers' and Seamen's Union: f. 1947; Gen. Sec. TIMOCI MATAI KUKU.

National Union of Factory and Commercial Workers: P.O.B. 989, Suva; 4,500 mems.; Gen. Sec. JAMES R. RAMAN.

Public Employees' Union: P.O.B. 781, Suva; 8,640 mems.; Gen. Sec. JOVECI GAVOKA, M.B.E.

Other significant unions are the Building Workers' Union, the Fiji Hotel and Catering Employees' Union, the Fiji Bank Officers' Association, the Fiji Sugar Tradesmen's Union and the Fijian Mineworkers' Union. In April 1979 44 trade unions were registered.

MAJOR INDUSTRIAL COMPANIES

Burns Philp (South Seas) Co. Ltd.: P.O.B. 355, Suva; f. 1920; general merchants, vehicle supplies, shipping and travel; Man. Dir. B. R. PERRY.

Carlton Brewery (Fiji) Ltd.: P.O.B. 696, Suva; f. 1957; Gen. Man. J. PICKERING.

Central Manufacturing Co. Ltd.: P.O.B. 560, Suva; f. 1955; manufacture and distribution of cigarettes and tobacco; Man. T. V. RAJU.

Cope Allman (South Pacific) Ltd.: P.O.B. 359, Suva; f. 1922; manufacture of soap and cleaning preparations, plastic products and biscuits; Man. Dir. K. A. J. ROBERTS; includes The Pacific Biscuit Co., Union Soaps, Viti Plastics.

Crest Mills (Fiji) Ltd.: P.O.B. 83, Nausori; f. 1965; manufacture of prepared animal food; Gen. Man. J. CAMPBELL.

Eddie Hin Industries Ltd.: P.O.B. 98, Marine Drive, Lautoka; f. 1949; manufacture of non-alcoholic beverages; Man. Dir. EDDIE WONG, M.B.E., J.P.

Emperor Gold Mining Co. Ltd.: Vatukoula; f. 1935; gold mining and processing, and timber milling; subsidiary of Emperor Mines Ltd.; assoc. companies Tavua Power Ltd. and Emperor Timber Industries Ltd.; Chief Exec. Dir. J. REID.

Flour Mills of Fiji Ltd.: P.O.B. 977, Suva; f. 1971; Man. Dir. SHARDHA NAND; Man. VIJAY SINGH.

Kiwi United (South Pacific) Ltd.: P.O.B. 427, Suva; f. 1965; manufacture of matches, paper and paperboard containers, boxes, bags, paper towels, serviettes, toilet tissue, wax paper and polythene bags; Dir. S. C. ISRAEL.

P. A. Lal & Co. Ltd.: P.O.B. 1242, Suva; f. 1946; builders of buses, trucks, trailers, coaches, furniture and fibreglass work; Dir. FRANCIS G. LAL.

Shell Fiji Ltd.: P.O.B. 168, Suva; f. 1928; petroleum stations and distribution of petroleum; Gen. Man. S. L. CHRISTIAN.

TRANSPORT

RAILWAYS

Fiji Sugar Corporation Railway: P.O.B. 283, Suva; 644 km. of permanent track and 225 km. of temporary track, serving cane-growing areas at Ba, Lautoka and Penang on the island of Viti Levu; also Labasa on the island of Vanua Levu.

ROADS

Fiji has almost 3,300 km. of roads, of which 1,200 are all-weather links. A 500-km. highway circles the main island of Viti Levu.

SHIPPING

There are ports of call at Suva, Lautoka and Levuka. The main port, Suva, handles more than 800 ships a year, including large passenger liners. Lautoka handles more than 300 vessels and liners and Levuka mainly handles commercial fishing vessels.

Savusavu Shipping Co. Ltd.: P.O.B. 936, Suva, and P.O.B. 227, Savusavu; f. 1978; Man. Dir. L. B. SMITH.

Transcargo Express Fiji Ltd.: P.O.B. 936, Suva; f. 1974; Man. Dir. LEO B. SMITH.

Williams Taoniu Shipping Co. Ltd.: P.O.B. 1270, Suva; inter-island shipping.

The main foreign companies serving Fiji are: Karlander (Aust.) Pty. Ltd., Sofrana-Unilines (Fiji Express Line), Pacific Forum Line, and Pacific Navigation of Tonga operating cargo services between Australia and Fiji; Union Steam Ship Co. of New Zealand from New Zealand; Blue Star Line Ltd. and Crusader Shipping Co. Ltd. calling at Fiji between North America and New Zealand, and P. & O. between the U.S.A. and Australia; Nedlloyd operates to Fiji from New Zealand, the U.K. and Northern Europe; Bank Line Ltd. from the U.K. and the Netherlands; NYK Line and Daiwa Lines from Japan; Kyowa Shipping Co. Ltd. from Hong Kong, Taiwan, the Republic of Korea and Japan.

CIVIL AVIATION

There is an international airport at Nadi, a domestic airport at Nausori and 13 other airfields.

Air Pacific Ltd.: Air Pacific House, Corner of MacArthur and Butt Streets, Suva; f. 1951; domestic services and regional services to Western Samoa, Tonga, Solomon Islands, Kiribati, Vanuatu, New Caledonia, French Polynesia, American Samoa, Australia and New Zealand; fleet of 2 BAC 1 11/475, 1 B737/200, 4 EMB-110P1, Chair. M. ISRAEL; Gen. Man. A. SAVU.

Fiji Air Ltd.: 219 Victoria Parade, P.O.B. 1259, Suva; domestic airline operating over 200 scheduled services a week to 20 destinations; 90,500 passengers carried in 1981; charter operations, aerial photography and surveillance also conducted; partly owned by the Fijian Government; fleet of 3 DHC6 Twin Otters, 1 Britten Norman Islander, 1 King Air Super 200, 1 Beech Baron C55; Man. Dir. M. C. D. TYLER.

Fiji is also served by Air New Zealand, Canadian Pacific, Continental (U.S.A.), JAL (Japan), Pan American and Qantas (Australia).

TOURISM

Fiji Visitor's Bureau: P.O.B. 92, Suva; Chair. MAHENDRA PATEL; Gen. Man. MALAKAI GUCAKE.

DEFENCE

The Royal Fiji Military Forces consist of men in the regular army, the Naval Squadron, the conservation corps and the territorials. The conservation corps was created in 1975 to make use of unemployed labour in construction work. Fiji is contributing a battalion to the UN peacekeeping force in Lebanon.

Armed Forces (July 1981): Total strength 2,051 (army 1,924, navy 127), excluding the conservation corps.

Commander of the Royal Fiji Military Forces: Brig. ROBERT IAN THORPE, C.B.E.

EDUCATION

Education is not free but is heavily subsidized by the Government. Free primary education was introduced in Class 1 in 1973 and is being extended to cover the first six years of education. Some grants are given in case of hardship at all levels and all basic textbooks are provided free at primary school level. Secondary education lasts for 4 or 5 years and leads to the Fiji Junior Certificate examination in the second year, the New Zealand or Cambridge School Certificate examination in the third or fourth year and the New Zealand University Entrance examination in the fourth or fifth year. Higher education is provided at the University of the South Pacific.

In 1978, 165,593 pupils, about 96 per cent of children, attended school. In 1981 there were 116,190 children in the 661 primary schools and 45,844 in the 137 secondary schools. There were six private primary schools and two private secondary schools in 1974. In 1976 the Government employed 4,000 teachers and there were 80 teachers in private schools.

There are four teacher training colleges. In 1981 there were 37 vocational and technical institutions, including the Fiji Institute of Technology in Suva, with 444 full-time and 1,982 part-time students, the Fiji School of Medicine in Suva, with 294 students, and the Fiji College of Agriculture at Koronivia, with 136 students. The University of the South Pacific was established in 1968 and by 1979 had 1,448 full-time students. The students included 796 holders of Fiji Government Scholarships in 1979.

Government expenditure on education in 1981 was $F47.9 million, the largest expenditure in the budget.

French Polynesia

PHYSICAL AND SOCIAL GEOGRAPHY

French Polynesia is an Overseas Territory of France containing six island groups: Society, Tuamotu, Austral, Gambier, Marquesas and Rapa. The Society Islands comprise the Windward group to the south-east, including Tahiti and Moorea, and the Leeward group about 160 km. north-west, which includes Huahine, Raiatea, Borabora and Maupiti. The Tuamotu Archipelago comprises 78 islands scattered east of the Society group in a line stretching north-west to south-east for about 1,500 km. The Gambier Islands, 1,600 km. south-east of Tahiti, are made up of the islands of Mangareva, Taravai and two others. The Austral or Tubuai group, 640 km. south of Tahiti, include Rurutu, Tubuai and Raevaevae. Rapa is 770 km. south-east of Tubuai. The Marquesas Islands are 1,450 km. north-east of Tahiti and comprise a northern group, which includes Nuku Hira, and a southern group.

The total population at the census of April 29th, 1977, was 137,382, including 62,735 in the capital, Papeete (on Tahiti). The estimated total in 1981 was 143,800.

HISTORY

The islands of French Polynesia were first visited by Europeans during the sixteenth century by Spanish and Portuguese explorers. Dutch and British explorers followed during the 1700s. Descriptions of Tahiti and other Society Islands by Wallis, who first visited in 1767, and Captain James Cook and his officers, gave rise in Europe to a vision of a new Arcadia in the South Pacific, the "islands of love", a romantic view which has drawn Europeans to the islands. In fact, European discovery dealt the Tahitian and other island groups' populations a severe blow. Disease caused rapid declines in population and inter-island and inter-group warfare killed many others.

Tahiti was made a French protectorate in 1842 and a colony in 1880. The other groups were all annexed during the last 20 years of the nineteenth century. The islands were governed from France under a decree of 1885 until 1957, when it became an Overseas Territory with a Governor in Papeete, the capital on Tahiti. A Council and members of a Territorial Assembly were elected in five *circonscriptions* to assist the Governor.

Moves towards more local autonomy began in 1977 and new statutes creating a fully elected local executive were approved in Paris in May 1977. Increasing criticism of France's role in the Pacific coincided with a visit of the French President, Giscard d'Estaing, to French Polynesia, New Caledonia and the New Hebrides (now Vanuatu) in July 1979. On Tahiti the President stressed "Polynesia's French future". The elections of May 1982 to the Territorial Assembly lent considerable local support to this policy, the new coalition led by Gaston Flosse seeking greater, but not full independence from France, especially in economic matters.

France has been testing nuclear weapons at Mururoa Atoll, in the Tuamotu Archipelago, since 1966. Further nuclear tests were carried out in 1981 and 1982, despite strong protests by Papua New Guinea and New Zealand.

In 1981 French workers on Mururoa released a document reporting widespread nuclear contamination on the atoll, which was confirmed by the French Government for the first time since testing began.

ECONOMIC SURVEY

The influx of large numbers of French military personnel and the creation of many more employment and commercial opportunities has severely distorted the economy, to the extent that many islanders believe a French withdrawal from Tahiti would cause an economic disaster. Migration into Tahiti and the military bases from outer islands has created a larger group of people who no longer have the subsistence skills of previous generations. In addition, since the loss of France's African colonies, more than 15,000 civilian settlers have migrated to Tahiti. Tourism, which was the island's major industry before the nuclear tests, will not be able to maintain the economy in its present state without massive outside investment.

Copra, vanilla and mother-of-pearl production are the main traditional economic activities but these have been declining in the 1970s to make way for new trochus shell, fresh fruit and cultured pearl projects. Exports of cultured pearls were valued at 121 million francs CFP in 1978, a 570 per cent increase over 1977.

STATISTICAL SURVEY

Area: 4,200 sq. km.

Population (1981): 143,800; Papeete (capital, 1977) 62,735.

Agriculture (1980—metric tons): Copra 15,986 (1981), Vegetables 3,102, Roots and tubers 19,000 (FAO estimate), Fresh fruit 4,000 (FAO estimate).

Livestock (1980—FAO estimates): Cattle 7,000, Horses 2,000, Pigs 22,000, Goats 3,000, Sheep 3,000, Chickens 477,000, Ducks 34,000.

Fishing (catch in metric tons): 2,826 in 1976; 699 in 1977; 2,987 in 1978; 2,987 in 1979 (FAO estimate); 2,380 in 1980.

Industry (1979): Coconut oil 9,880 metric tons (1981); Beer 95,000 hectolitres; Printed cloth 200,000 metres; Japanese sandals 600,000 pairs; Electric energy (Tahiti) 151.7 million kWh. (1981).

Currency: 100 centimes = 1 franc de la Communauté française du pacifique (franc CFP or Pacific franc). Coins: 50 centimes; 1, 2, 5, 10, 20 and 50 francs CFP. Notes: 100, 500, 1,000 and 5,000 francs CFP. Exchange rates (June 1982): 1 franc CFP = 5.5 French centimes; £1 sterling = 216.45 francs CFP; U.S. $1 = 125.000 francs CFP; 1,000 francs CFP = £4.62 = $8.00.

Budget (1982—estimates): 28,069 million francs CFP.

Consumer Price Index (at Jan. 1st; Base: Nov. 1st, 1972 = 100): 151.0 in 1976; 163.0 in 1977; 172.9 in 1978; 184.5 in 1979; 205.3 in 1980; 226.9 in 1981.

Aid from France (1981—million francs CFP): 37,300; also subsidies to local authorities, of which 660 to general expenses, 381 to FIDES, 2,500 (1978) to public funds; loans at low interest rates 2,500.

External Trade (1981—million francs CFP): *Imports:* 54,843 (mainly cereals, petroleum products, metal manufactures), principal suppliers: France 25,512, U.S.A. 11,425; *Exports:* 2,816.3 (mainly coconut oil, cultured pearls, trochus shells, vanilla, fresh fruit), principal customer: France.

Tourism (1981): 96,826 visitors, excluding cruise passengers and excursionists.

Shipping (1981): ships entered 2,096, net registered tons 1,476,071; goods loaded 19,093 metric tons, unloaded 456,059 metric tons (international freight); passenger arrivals 63,490, departures 75,462.

Civil Aviation (Faaa airport, Papeete—1981): aircraft arrivals and departures 36,654, freight handled 5,265 metric tons, passenger arrivals 351,489, passenger departures 338,006.

Education (1981/82: Pupils: Kindergarten 9,744; Primary 29,371; Secondary 10,451; Technical 2,855; Teachers (total): 2,613.

THE GOVERNMENT

(July 1982)

High Commissioner: PAUL NOIROT-COSSON.

Secretary-General: JACQUES FOURNET.

COUNCIL OF GOVERNMENT

(July 1982)

President: The High Commissioner.

Vice President: GASTON FLOSSE.

Councillors (elected by the Territorial Assembly): GASTON FLOSSE (Vice-President), TERII SANFORD, JACQUES TEHEIURA, ALEXANDRE LEONTIEFF, CHARLES TETARIA, BORIS LEONTIEFF, SYLVAIN MILLAUD.

TERRITORIAL ASSEMBLY

Elected every five years on the basis of universal suffrage.

President: EMILE VERNAUDON.

(Election May 1982)

Party	Seats
Tahoeraa Huiraatira ((RPR)*	13
Ai'a Api*	3
Pupu Here Ai'a	6
Ia Mana Te Nunaa	3
Taatiraa Polynesia	1
Te E'a Api	1
Others	3

*Member party of ruling coalition.

French Polynesia elects two delegates to the French National Assembly, one delegate to the French Senate and one Economic and Social Councillor on the basis of universal adult suffrage.

Deputies to the French National Assembly: GASTON FLOSSE, JEAN JUVENTIN.

Representative to the Senate: DANIEL MILLAUD.

Economic and Social Councillor: RAYMOND DESCLAUX.

POLITICAL PARTIES

Ai'a Api: Papeete; f. 1981; Leader EMILE VERNAUDON.

Ia Mana Te Nunaa: rue du Commandant Destrémau, B.P. 1223, Papeete; f. 1976; socialist; Sec.-Gen. JACQUES DROLLET; publs. *Te Ve'a Hepetoma* (weekly), *Ia Mana* (monthly).

Papu Here Ai'a: Papeete; f. 1965; advocates autonomy; 7–8,000 mems.; Pres. JOHN TEARIKI.

Pupu Taina (*Rassemblement des Libéraux*): B.P. 169, rue Cook, Papeete; f. 1976; advocates retaining close links with France and the French UDF party; Leader MICHEL LAW.

Taatiraa Polynesia: B.P. 283, Papeete; f. 1976; Leader ARTHUR CHUNG.

Tahoeraa Huiraatira: rue du Commandant Destrémeau, B.P. 471, Papeete; f. 1958; affiliated to the French *Rassemblement pour la République*; Pres. GASTON FLOSSE.

Te Autahoeraa: Papeete; Leader CHARLES TAUFA.

Te E'a Api (United Front Party): Papeete; Leader FRANCIS SANFORD.

JUDICIAL SYSTEM

Supreme Court of Appeal: Papeete; Pres. THIERRY CATHALA; Procurator of the Republic JEAN BARON.

Court of the First Instance: Papeete; Pres. HENRI RENAUD DE LA FAVERIE; Procurator of the Republic JEAN-DOMINIQUE SARCELET; Clerk of the Court GEORGES REID.

RELIGION

About 50 per cent of the population are Protestant and about 34 per cent Roman Catholics.

Protestant: President du Conseil Supérieur de l'Eglise Evangélique MARURAI UTIA; B.P. 113, Papeete.

Roman Catholic: B.P. 94, Papeete; Archbishop of Papeete Mgr. MICHEL COPPENRATH.

There are also small Sanito, Mormon, Adventist and Jehovah's Witness missions.

THE PRESS

La Dépêche de Tahiti: Société Polynésienne de Presse, B.P. 50, Papeete; f. 1964; daily; Dir. MICHEL ANGLADE.

Les Nouvelles: B.P. 629, Papeete; f. 1956; daily; Editor G. PUGIN.

Tahiti Sun Press: B.P. 887, Papeete; f. 1980; weekly; English; Man. Editor G. WARTI; circ. 3,500.

FOREIGN BUREAUX

Agence France-Presse (AFP): B.P. 2679, Papeete.

Associated Press (AP) (*U.S.A.*): B.P. 912, Papeete; Corresp. AL PRINCE.

Reuters (*U.K.*): B.P. 50, Papeete.

United Press International (UPI) (*U.S.A.*): B.P. 50, Papeete.

PUBLISHER

Les Editions du Pacifique: 10 ave. Bruat, B.P. 1722, Papeete; f. 1971; travel, natural science, history, non-fiction; Dir. ALBERTO MANGUEL.

RADIO AND TELEVISION

Radio-Télé-Tahiti: B.P. 125, 410 rue Dumont d'Urville, Papeete; f. 1951 as Radio-Tahiti, television service began 1965; run by France Régions 3, Paris; daily programmes in French and Tahitian; Dir. JEAN-PIERRE LANNES.

In 1980 there were 80,000 radio receivers and 25,000 television sets, of which about 1,500 were colour sets.

FINANCE

BANKING

(cap.=capital; dep.=deposits; m.=million; brs.=branches; frs.=francs)

Banque de l'Indochine et de Suez S.A. (*France*): 2 place Notre-Dame, Papeete; brs. in Papeete, Faaa, Pirae and Uturoa; Dir. YVES CEVAER.

Banque de Polynésie: B.P. 530, Papeete; Pres. JACQUES DE MALVILLE; Gen. Man. MICHEL OTTAVIANI.

Banque de Tahiti S.A.: B.P. 1602, rue Paul Gauguin, Papeete; f. 1969; affiliated to Bank of Hawaii, Honolulu, and Crédit Lyonnais, Paris; cap. 400m. frs. CFP; Pres. CHARLES GIORDAN; Dirs. CORNELIS J. GROEN, ROBERT SABATIER.

TRADE AND INDUSTRY

Chambre de Commerce et d'Industrie de la Polynésie Française: B.P. 118, Papeete; f. 1880; 27 mems.; Pres. CHARLES T. POROÏ; publ. *C.C.I. Bulletin*.

Chambre d'Agriculture et d'Elevage (CAEP): Route de l'Hippodrome, B.P. 5383, Pirae; f. 1886; 10 mems.; Pres. SYLVAIN MILLAUD.

EMPLOYERS' ORGANIZATIONS

Union Patronale: B.P. 317, Papeete; f. 1948; 34 mems.; Pres. HENRY DEVAY.

Chambre Syndicale des Entrepreneurs du Bâtiment et des Travaux Publics (*Building and Public Works*): B.P. 2218, Papeete; Pres. CLAUDE GUTIERREZ.

Fédération Polynésienne de l'Hôtellerie et des Industries Touristiques: B.P. 118, Papeete; Pres. CHARLES POROÏ.

Syndicat des Importateurs et des Négociants (*Importers and Businessmen*): B.P. 1607, Papeete; Pres. JULES CHANGUES.

Union Interprofessionnelle du Tourisme de la Polynésie Francaise: B.P. 1588, Papeete; f. 1973; 1,200 mems.; Pres. PAUL MAETZ; Sec.-Gen. JEAN CORTEEL.

TRADE UNIONS

Papeete

Cartel des Syndicats des Dockers Polynésiens: B.P. 3366, Papeete; Pres. FELIX COLOMBEL.

Centrale des Travailleurs Autonomistes Polynésiens: B.P. 451, Papeete; Pres. NINO SCARANTO.

Fédération Polynésienne de l'Agriculture et de l'Elevage: Papara, Tahiti; Pres. MICHEL LEHARTEL.

Fédération des Syndicats de la Polynésie Française: B.P. 1136; Pres. MARCEL AHINI.

Syndicat Autonome des Travailleurs de Polynésie: Douanes, Papeete; Pres. MAURICE LEHARTEL.

Syndicat des Cadres de la Fonction Publique: B.P. 2016, Papeete; Pres. JEAN-MARIE SIMON.

Union des Syndicats Autonomistes Polynésiens: B.P. 3366, Papeete; LAWRENCE TUHEIAVA.

Union Territoriale des Syndicats Démocratiques: B.P. 2335, Papeete; Pres. ROBERT SALVANAYAGAM.

TRANSPORT

ROADS

There are 243.8 km. of bitumen-surfaced and 497 km. of stone-surfaced roads.

SHIPPING

Papeete

Agence Tahiti Poroi: B.P. 83; f. 1958; commission agents, exporters and importers.

Compagnie Générale Maritime: ave. du Général de Gaulle, P.O.B. 96; shipowners and agents; freight services between Europe and most international ports; agents in Papeete for Shell, Chevron Shipping, Morflot, Cunard Line and Sitmar Cruise.

Pacific Islands Transport Line: Agents: Agence Maritime Internationale Tahiti, B.P. 274; services every six weeks to American Samoa, the U.S.A. and Western Samoa.

Other companies operating services to, or calling at, Papeete are: Daiwa Line, Karlander, Hamburg-Sued, China Navigation Co., Nedlloyd, Shipping Corporation of New Zealand Ltd., Bank Line, Kyowa Line and Polynesia Line Ltd.

CIVIL AVIATION

There is one international airport, Faaa airport, on Tahiti and there are about 40 smaller airstrips.

Air Polynésie: B.P. 314, Papeete; f. 1953; inter-islands services to Anaa, Makemo, Hao, Gambier-Mangareva, Ua Pou, Matahiva, Tikehau, Huahine, Raiatea, Bora Bora, Rangiroa, Manihi, Ua-Huka, Moorea, Maupiti, Tubuai, Takapoto, Rurutu, Napuka, Apataki, Hiva-oa, Kaukura, Nuku Hiva, Fakarava, Pukarua, Tatakoto, Raiao and Nuku Tavake; Dir.-Gen. MICHEL NOUAILLE; fleet of 2 Fairchild FH-227, 3 Fairchild F-27J, 2 Twin Otter DHC-6, 2 BN-2A Islander.

Air Tahiti: B.P. 6019, Papeete; operates internal services between Tahiti and Moorea Island and some inter-territorial services; Dir. Gen. JEAN GILLOT.

The following international airlines also serve Tahiti: Air New Zealand, Air Pacific (Fiji), Air Tungaru (Kiribati), LAN-Chile, Polynesian Airlines (Western Samoa), Qantas (Australia), South Pacific Island Airways (Hawaii) and UTA (France).

TOURISM

Office de développement du Tourisme de la Polynésie Française: B.P. 65, Papeete; f. 1966; Chair. JANINE LAGUESSE; Man. Dir. PATRICK LEBOUCHER.

Syndicat d'Initiative de la Polynésie Française: B.P. 326, Papeete; Pres. Mme PIU BAMBRIDGE.

EDUCATION

Education is compulsory up to the age of 14. It is free of charge in the government schools for day pupils. Primary education is financed by the territorial budget, while secondary and technical education is conducted with State funds. There are 175 government primary schools and kindergartens, and secondary education is provided by both government and church schools. In 1981/82 the total number of children attending school and kindergartens was 50,373, including 11,319 in private schools and 39,054 in government schools. There were also 558 students in private and 2,492 in government-run technical schools.

Guam

Guam, the largest of the Mariana Islands, was ceded to the U.S.A. by Spain in 1898. It is situated about 1,500 miles south-east of the Philippines.

HISTORY

Magellan discovered the islands in 1521 and they were colonized by Spain in 1668. When Spain ceded Guam to the U.S.A. it sold the other Mariana Islands to Germany. Japan obtained a League of Nations mandate over the German islands in 1919. In 1941 it seized Guam but the island was retaken by American forces in 1944.

Guam is under the jurisdiction of the U.S. Department of the Interior. In 1970 the island elected its first Governor and in 1972 a new law gave Guam one delegate to the U.S. House of Representatives. The delegate may vote in Committee but not on the House floor. In September 1976 an island-wide referendum decided that Guam should maintain close ties with the U.S.A., but that negotiations should be held to improve the island's status. In a further referendum in 1982, in which only 38 per cent of voters chose to take part, the status of commonwealth was the most favoured of six options, polling 48 per cent of the votes cast. Guam remains an important strategic military base for the U.S.A. with about 10,000 U.S. servicemen stationed there in 1980.

ECONOMIC SURVEY

The economy is based on the export of copra, fish and handicrafts. Industries, including an oil refinery, a brewery, and textile and garment firms, were established in the early 1970s, in addition to existing smaller-scale manufacturing of soft drinks and watches. Tourism is expanding rapidly, with over 300,000 tourists, 80 per cent of whom are Japanese, visiting the island each year. Annual tourist expenditure is estimated at over $150 million, and 20 per cent of government revenue is derived from this source.

STATISTICAL SURVEY

Area: 541 sq. km.

Population (census of April 1st, 1980): 105,979. Servicemen and dependants, *c.* 21,500. Capital: Agaña.

Births and Deaths (1980): 3,003 live births (25.0 per 1,000); 422 deaths (3.5 per 1,000).

Agriculture: Production (1981): Fruit and vegetables 1,570,000 lb.; Eggs 1,904 dozen; Pork 1,012,000lb.; Beef 54,000 lb.; Poultry 196,000 lb.

Sea Fishing (catch in metric tons): 95 in 1976; 125 in 1977; 316 in 1978; 182 in 1979; 100 in 1980; 74 in 1981.

FINANCE

100 cents = 1 United States dollar (U.S. $).
Coins: 1, 5, 10, 25 and 50 cents; 1 dollar.
Notes: 1, 2, 5, 10, 20, 50 and 100 dollars.
Exchange rates (June 1982): £1 sterling = $1.73; U.S. $100 = £57.74.

BUDGET

(U.S. $ million, year ending September 30th)

Revenue	1979
General fund	204.9
Special funds	17.0
Semi and autonomous agencies	60.2
Capital projects, federal grants and other funds	56.1
Total Revenue	338.2

Expenditure	1979
Departments Agencies	133.0
Special funds	20.0
Semi and autonomous agencies	67.0
Capital projects	4.4
Encumbrances	1.1
Legislative and judicial branches	7.2
Total Expenditure	232.7

1980 (U.S. $ million): Total revenue 128.7; Total expenditure 140.1.

COST OF LIVING

CONSUMER PRICE INDEX
(1978=100)

	1976	1977	1979	1980	1981
Food	83.6	84.4	116.8	139.2	178.0
Housing	88.1	91.3	111.3	137.3	163.0
Clothing and upkeep	83.8	94.7	105.7	118.7	128.1
Transport	84.6	89.1	115.0	150.1	183.3
Medical care	88.6	83.9	109.0	123.9	147.3
Entertainment		93.6	106.1	104.0	133.2
Other goods and services		92.0	103.7	117.1	130.4
ALL ITEMS	85.8	88.6	112.1	134.0	161.4

External Trade (1980): Imports $544.2 million; Exports $61.0 million.

Shipping (1978): Vessels entered 827; Freight entered 818,300 tons, cleared 512,700 tons, in transit 226,800 tons.

Tourism: No. of visitors ('000) (1976) 201.3; (1977) 240.5; (1978) 232.0; (1979) 264.3; (1980) 291.1; (1981) 312.9.

Sources (unless otherwise stated): Department of Commerce, Government of Guam, P.O.B. 682, Agaña, Guam 96910; United States Department of the Interior, Office of the Secretary, Washington, D.C.

THE CONSTITUTION

Guam is governed under the Organic Act of Guam of 1950, which gave the island statutory local power of self-government and made its inhabitants citizens of the United States, although they cannot vote in national elections. Their delegate to the House of Representatives is elected every two years. Executive power is vested in a civilian Governor, first elected in 1970. Elections for the governorship occur every four years. The Government has 15 executive departments, whose heads are appointed by the Governor with the consent of the Guam Legislature. The Legislature consists of 21 members elected by popular vote every two years. It is empowered to pass laws on local matters, including taxation and fiscal appropriations.

THE GOVERNMENT

Governor: PAUL MCDONALD CALVO.

Lieutenant-Governor: JOSEPH F. ADA.

LEGISLATURE

Speaker: THOMAS TANAKA.

In the November 1980 elections the Republican Party won 11 seats and the Democratic Party 10 seats.

JUDICIAL SYSTEM

District Court of Guam: Judge appointed by the President. The court has the jurisdiction of a district court of the United States in all cases arising under the law of the United States. Appeals may be made to the Court of Appeals for the Ninth Circuit and to the Supreme Court of the United States.

Presiding Judge: Hon. CRISTOBAL C. DUENAS.

Clerk of Court: EDWARD L. G. AGUON.

The Superior Court of Guam has jurisdiction over other cases arising in Guam.

There are also the Police Court, Traffic Court, Juvenile Court and the Small Claims Court.

RELIGION

About 93 per cent of the population are Roman Catholic, although other Christian denominations are represented.

Roman Catholic: Bishop's House, Cuesta San Ramon, Agaña 96910; Bishop of the Diocese of Agaña Most Rev. FELIXBERTO CAMACHO FLORES, O.F.M.CAP.

THE PRESS

Pacific Daily News and **Sunday News:** P.O.B. DN, Agaña; f. 1950; Publisher ROBERT E. UDICK; Exec. Editor JOHN M. SIMPSON; Editor JOSEPH C. MURPHY; circ. 18,000 on weekdays and 17,000 on Sunday.

Pacific Voice: P.O.B. 2553, Agaña; Sunday; Editor Fr. BRIGIDO U. ARROYO; circ. 6,000.

RADIO AND TELEVISION

RADIO

Radio Guam (KUAM): P.O.B. 368, Agaña 96910; f. 1954; affiliated to CBS and NBC; operates on AM and FM 24 hours a day; Pres. LAWRENCE S. BERGER; Gen. Man. GREG PEREZ.

Trans World Radio (TWR): P.O.B. 3518, Agaña; broadcasts religious programmes on stations KTWG at 801 kHz AM, covering Guam and nearby islands, and KTWR, which operates four 100 kW. short-wave transmitters reaching most of Asia and the Pacific.

K-Stereo: P.O.B. 20249, GMF, 96921; operates on FM 24 hours a day; Pres. EDWARD POPPE.

KGUM: P.O.B. GM, Agaña; Gen. Man. J. ANDERSON.

There were 88,000 radio receivers in 1978.

TELEVISION

Guam-Agaña (KUAM-TV): P.O.B. 368, Agaña 96910. f. 1956; affiliated to CBS and NBC programme networks; operates colour service; Pres. LAWRENCE S. BERGER; Gen. Man. GREG PEREZ.

Guam Cable TV: 530 West O'Brien, Agaña 96910.

KGTF: P.O.B. 21449 GMF, Agaña 96921-0117; f. 1970; educational programmes; Station Man. BETTY BENNETT-LYON.

There were 140,000 television receivers in 1978.

FINANCE

BANKING

(m.=million; brs.=branches)

American Savings and Loan Association (*U.S.A.*): P.O.B. 811, Agaña; 3 brs.; total assets $40m. (December 1977); Exec. Vice-Pres. JOHN MICKELSON.

Bank of America National Trust and Savings Association (*U.S.A.*): P.O.B. BA, Agaña; 2 agencies; Pres. JAMES LAHERTY; Man. R. E. BAUM.

Bank of Guam: P.O.B. BW, Agaña; total assets U.S. $115.9 million (1981); 2 brs.; Pres. JESUS S. LEON GUERRERO.

Bank of Hawaii (*U.S.A.*): P.O.B. BH, Agaña; 3 brs.; Vice-Pres. and Man. M. D. SCHOCHET.

Bank of the Orient (*U.S.A.*): P.O.B. E1, Agaña, 96910; 1 br.; Man. WILFRED K. YAMAMOTO.

California First Bank (*U.S.A.*): P.O.B. 7809, Tamuning 96911; Man. MASAO KUWANO.

California Overseas Bank (*U.S.A.*): P.O.B. 24881, GMF 96921; 1 br.; Man. MANUEL C. CASTRO.

Chase Manhattan Bank, N.A. (*U.S.A.*): P.O.B. AE, O'Hara St., Agaña; Man. JOSEPH E. HOSIE.

Citibank N.A. (*U.S.A.*): P.O.B. FF, Agaña; 1 br.; Vice-Pres. B. P. SANTOS.

First Commercial Bank (*U.S.A.*): P.O.B. 2461, Agaña Gen. Man. CHIN TIAO LAI.

First Hawaiian Bank (*U.S.A.*): P.O.B. AD, Agaña; 2 brs.; Vice-Pres. and Man. (Agaña br.) JOHN K. LEE.

Guam Savings and Loan Association: P.O.B. 2888, Agaña 96910; 3 brs.; Pres. PHILIP FLORES.

Hongkong and Shanghai Banking Corporation: P.O.B. 27C, Agaña; Man. RICHARD CROMWELL.

Metropolitan Bank and Trust (*U.S.A.*): 414 Soledad Ave., GCIC Agaña; Man. JOSE GUEVARA, Jr.

National Bank of Fort Sam Houston (*U.S.A.*): P.O.B. 4356, Yigo, 96912; 2 brs.; Man. DAVID D. EVENSON.

TRADE AND INDUSTRY

DEVELOPMENT

Guam Economic Development Authority (GEDA): P.O.B. 3280, Agaña, Guam 96910.

TRADE UNIONS

Many workers belong to trade unions based in the U.S.A. such as the American Federation of Government Employees, the American Postal Workers' Union and the Operating Engineers. About 4,000 of the island's 31,000 workforce belong to unions.

Guam Federation of Teachers: P.O.B. 2301, Agaña; f. 1965; Pres. BETH MCCLURE; 2,400 mems.; publ. *Union*.

EMPLOYERS' ORGANIZATION

Guam Employers' Council: Suite 106, Ada Plaza Center, P.O.B. BV, Agaña, 96910; f. 1966; private, non-profit-making association for consultants on personnel and labour relations; conducts twice-yearly wage and benefit surveys; publs. reports and opinions on laws regarding employment.

TRANSPORT

ROADS

There are 674 kilometres of modern all-weather roads.

SHIPPING

Atkins Kroll: P.O.B. 6428, Tamuning 96911; Pres. LANE LASTAIRE.

Pacific Navigation System: P.O.B. 7, Agaña; f. 1946; Pres. KENNETH T. JONES, Jr.

Trans-Pacific Freighting: P.O.B. 37, Agaña; Pres. GEORGE G. MELAH.

Tucor Services Inc.: P.O.B. 6128, Tamuning, Guam 96911; General Agents for numerous tankers, dry cargo, passenger and fishery companies; Gen. Man. BOB KENT.

Monthly cargo services are operated by Kyowa Line vessels, calling at Guam en route from Hong Kong, Taiwan, the Republic of Korea and Japan to various Pacific islands, and by Daiwa Line vessels, linking Guam with Japan and Pacific islands including Fiji, New Caledonia and American and Western Samoa.

CIVIL AVIATION

Guam is served by Air Micronesia (Northern Mariana Islands), Air Nauru, Continental Airlines (U.S.A.), JAL (Japan), Northwest (U.S.A.), Pan Am (U.S.A.) and several air taxi operators.

TOURISM

Guam Visitors Bureau: P.O.B. 3520, Agaña, Guam 96910; Chair. JOSE D. DIEGO; Gen. Man. JOSEPH CEPEDA.

Micronesian Regional Tourism Council: 6th floor, ITC Bldg. (Tamuning), P.O.B. 682, Agaña, 96910; f. 1976 to promote tourism in the region; composed of government and independent representatives from Micronesia, Saipan and Guam; Exec. Dir. GORDON W. TYDINGCO.

There were 312,862 tourists in 1981. Total expenditure was about $155 million.

EDUCATION

There were 37 public and 18 private schools operating on the island in 1980, including six senior high schools. Total school enrolment was over 34,364, including 18,697 elementary school pupils. School attendance is compulsory from 6 to 16 years of age.

Hawaii

PHYSICAL AND SOCIAL GEOGRAPHY

The Hawaiian Islands of the central northern Pacific are comprised of volcanic and coral islands formed by the peaks of huge undersea volcanoes, covering a total land area of 16,642 sq. km. There are eight major islands and 124 minor islands which form a chain from Hawaii in the south-east (10,456 sq. km.) through Maui (1,886 sq. km.), Molokai (676 sq. km.), Oahu (1,535 sq. km.) to Kauai (1,421 sq. km.) in the north-west. Further west a series of small islands including Midway, the only inhabited island, which lies just east of the International Date Line, complete the chain (the Midway Islands are not legally part of the State of Hawaii). Active volcanoes are the outstanding physical feature of the Hawaiian Islands.

The Hawaiian population is multi-racial. The Polynesian population was estimated to be 142,050 in 1823. This had fallen to 56,900 by 1872. In 1980 the total resident population of the islands was 964,691. Organized immigration of non-Polynesian groups into Hawaii began in the 1890s with Portuguese from Madeira and the Azores. They were followed by other Europeans, Americans, Puerto Ricans, Indians, Chinese, Japanese, Koreans and Filipinos. Caucasian, Japanese, Chinese, Filipino, Korean and Hawaiian are major identifiable present day groups.

HISTORY

The Hawaiian Islands were probably the last of the Pacific Islands to be settled by Polynesians. Oral history suggests that until about A.D. 1300 contacts were maintained between Tahiti and Hawaii. There followed, however, a long period of isolation in which the Hawaiian Polynesian culture developed its own characteristic features.

Captain James Cook is the first documented European to have visited the islands. He landed at Waimea on Kauai Island in 1778, but was killed at Kealakekua on Hawaii during a return visit in 1779. Hawaiian history from contact until June 1900, when it became officially a United States Territory, is one of the virtual destruction of the indigenous Polynesian culture by missionary, commercial and political intervention by outsiders and the sharp reduction of the indigenous population by disease. Russian, Spanish, British, French and American interests all vied for favours with the islands' rulers during the 1800s, while independent traders and entrepreneurs supplied arms to various chiefs in an attempt to gain a foothold for their enterprises. The four chiefdoms in existence in 1782 had been unified under Kamehameha I by 1810. Kamehameha's first wife became a nominal Christian in 1823 and Christianity rapidly became a national religion, which increased the disintegration of the old society. Gradually United States influence became entrenched. Internal insurrections and unrest in the 1890s led to annexation by the United States in 1900.

Hawaii was admitted to the United States as the 50th state in 1959. Hawaiians are United States citizens and may move freely between Hawaii and the mainland.

ECONOMIC SURVEY

The most important early commercial activities in the islands were sandalwood trading and whaling. Sugar, the most important agricultural export, was first cultivated for sale in 1802, but became important during the 1870s. By 1930 over one million metric tons per year were being exported and this rate is maintained in the 1980s. The sugar is grown on intensive plantations, many of which are irrigated. Pineapples were first cultivated commercially in the 1900s. In 1980 more than 18 million cases of canned fruit and juice were produced by three major companies The industry employs over 12,000 people, including those hired for the summer canning season, and provides work for about 4,900 persons throughout the year. Other agricultural products include livestock, coffee, cut flowers, bananas, macadamia nuts, papayas, taro and various nursery products. Fishing and fish processing is a well developed industry. Secondary industries are largely linked to Hawaii's important agricultural base and include fertilizer and canning plants and two oil refineries. A handicraft industry has developed in response to the tourist industry. Tourism is the most important industry in the islands with almost 4 million visitors a year, earning about U.S. $3,200 million in 1981, more than all agricultural exports together. Hawaii is also the centre for the unified command of all United States Armed Forces in the Pacific, an activity which contributes significantly to the economy.

STATISTICAL SURVEY

AREA AND POPULATION

Total Area	Population (at April 1st)	
	1970 Census	1980 Census
16,707 sq. km.*	769,913	964,691†

* 6,450 sq. miles.

† Includes 61,019 members of the armed forces and 64,023 military dependants.

MAIN TOWNS

(1980 census)

Honolulu District (capital)	365,017	Kailua (Oahu)	35,812
Pearl City	42,575	Hilo	35,269

FINANCE

100 cents = 1 United States dollar (U.S. $).
Coins: 1, 5, 10, 25 and 50 cents; 1 dollar.
Notes: 1, 2. 5, 10, 20, 50 and 100 dollars.
Exchange rates (June 1982): £1 sterling = $1.73; U.S. $100 = £57.74.

BUDGET
(1980)

Revenue: U.S. $1,760,187,000.
Expenditure: U.S. $1,815,855,000.

CONSUMER PRICE INDEX
Honolulu
(1967 = 100)

	1979	1980*
Food	239.8	259.9
All items . . .	204.6	228.5

* Provisional

EXTERNAL TRADE
(U.S. $ million)

	1979	1980
Imports	1,239	1,721
Exports	176	174

TRANSPORT

	1980	1981
Registered motor vehicles .	617,571	649,350

TOURISM

	1980	1981
Visitors ('000) . . .	3,930	3,934

EDUCATION

	Pupils	
	1980	1981
Government schools, primary and secondary	165,094	162,805
Private schools, primary and secondary	37,878	38,039
Higher education . . .	49,871	52,197

Source: Department of Planning and Economic Development, Honolulu.

THE CONSTITUTION

Under Hawaii's State Constitution, drawn up in 1950 and modified in 1968 and 1978, executive powers are vested in Governor and a Lt.-Governor elected for four-year terms. There is a bicameral Legislature which is composed of a House of Representatives, with 51 members elected from 25 Districts for two-year terms, and a Senate with 25 members elected from eight Districts for four-year terms. The Legislature meets annually in Honolulu. As a State, Hawaii elects a delegation to the U.S. Congress. Local government is vested in one combined city-county (Honolulu, comprising the island of Oahu and several outlying islets), three non-metropolitan counties (Hawaii, Kauai and Maui) and one area (Kalawao County) administered by the State Department of Health.

THE GOVERNMENT

Governor: George R. Ariyoshi.

Lieutenant-Governor: Jean King.

LEGISLATURE

HOUSE OF REPRESENTATIVES

Speaker: Henry H. Peters.

SENATE

President: Richard S. H. Wong.

JUDICIAL SYSTEM

The State Judiciary includes a five-member Supreme Court, an intermediate Court of Appeal and four Circuit Courts, with judges appointed by the Governor with the consent of the State Senate. The State also has four District Courts whose judges are appointed by the Chief Justice of the State Supreme Court.

Chief Justice: Hon. William S. Richardson, Supreme Court, 417 South King St., Honolulu, Hawaii 96813.

RELIGION

There are many different religions in Hawaii, including Christianity, to which belong 68 per cent of the population professing a religion (31 per cent Roman Catholic, 34 per cent Protestant, 3 per cent other), Chinese Confucianism, Daoism and Buddhism, various forms of Japanese Mahayana Buddhism and Shintoism. About 12 per cent of the population are Buddhist. The first Jewish synagogue was established in 1950.

The following are some of the principal churches:

PROTESTANT

The Episcopal Church in Hawaii: Queen Emma Sq., Honolulu, Hawaii 96813; Bishop Rt. Rev. Edmond L. Browning.

Hawaii Baptist Convention: 2042 Vancouver Drive, Honolulu, Hawaii 96822; Head Dr. Edmond Walker.

Hawaii Conference of the United Church of Christ: 2103 Nuuanu Ave., Honolulu, Hawaii 96817; Conference Minister The Rev. Teruo Kawata.

United Methodist Church: 1000 S. Beretania St., Honolulu, Hawaii 96814; Head of Hawaii District Rev. David Harada.

ROMAN CATHOLIC

Bishop of Honolulu: Most Rev. John J. Scanlan, 1184 Bishop St., Honolulu, Hawaii 96813.

In 1978 there were 220,000 Roman Catholics.

OTHER RELIGIONS

Church of Jesus Christ of Latter-Day Saints: 1500 South Beretania St., Honolulu 96826; Exec. Admin. Elder Adney Y. Komatsu.

Honpa Hongwanji Mission of Hawaii: 1727 Pali Highway, Honolulu, Hawaii 96813; Head Rev. YOSHIAKI FUJITANI.

Judaism: Temple Emanu-El, 2550 Pali Highway, Honolulu, Hawaii 96817; 380 mems.; Pres. LEONARD M. RAND; Rabbi ARNOLD J. MAGID.

THE PRESS

In 1982 there were two major daily newspapers, several language newspapers and numerous magazines and other periodicals.

Honolulu Advertiser: 605 Kapiolani Blvd., Honolulu, Hawaii 96813; mail: P.O.B. 3110, Honolulu 96802; f. 1856; daily; Editor-in-Chief GEORGE CHAPLIN; circ. 83,720.

Honolulu Star-Bulletin: 605 Kapiolani Blvd., Honolulu, Hawaii 96813; f. 1912; evening; Exec. Editor JOHN SIMONDS; circ. 115,815.

Sunday Star-Bulletin and Advertiser: 605 Kapiolani Blvd., Honolulu, Hawaii 96813; mail: P.O.B. 3110, Honolulu 96802; f. 1962; Sundays; Editor-in-Chief GEORGE CHAPLIN; circ. 201,300.

RADIO AND TELEVISION

Hawaiian Association of Broadcasters: c/o KHOM-TV, 1170 Auahi St., Honolulu 96814; Pres. RICHARD SCHALLER.

In 1981 there was 1 educational and 36 commercial radio stations and 10 commercial and two educational television stations in Hawaii; there were 1 million radio receivers and 293,500 households had television sets.

FINANCE

BANKING

(cap.=capital; dep.=deposits; m.=million)

Bank of Hawaii: 111 South King St., Honolulu, Hawaii 96813; f. 1897; cap. U.S. $93.1m.; dep. U.S. $1,458.4m. (Dec. 1978); Chair. and Chief Exec. WILSON P. CANNON, Jr.; Pres. FRANK J. MANAUT.

First Hawaiian Bank: 165 South King St., Honolulu, Hawaii 96813; f. 1858; cap. U.S. $103.4m.; dep. U.S. $1,732m. (Dec. 1981); Chair. and Chief Exec. JOHN D. BELLINGER.

TRADE AND INDUSTRY

Chamber of Commerce of Hawaii: 735 Bishop St., Honolulu, Hawaii 96813.

Department of Planning and Economic Development: P.O.B. 2359, Honolulu, Hawaii 96804.

TRANSPORT

SHIPPING

More than two dozen passenger and cargo steamship companies operate through Honolulu. Hawaii has seven deep-water ports including the naval shipyard and base at Pearl Harbor. The ports have a wide range of services, and terminal facilities are equipped to handle bulk, conventional and container cargo.

CIVIL AVIATION

Aloha Airlines Inc.: P.O.B. 30028, Honolulu International Airport, Hawaii 96820; f. 1946; inter-Hawaiian island services; Chair. HUNG WO CHING; Pres. EDWARD E. SWOFFORD; fleet of 11 Boeing 737s.

Hawaiian Airlines Inc.: P.O.B. 30008, Honolulu International Airport, Honolulu, Hawaii 96820; f. 1929; operates scheduled passenger and cargo services between Honolulu and the islands of Kauai, Molokai, Maui, Lanai and Hawaii and occasionally charter cargo services on the U.S. mainland; Pres., Chair. and Chief Exec. JOHN H. MAGOON Jr.; fleet of 13 Douglas DC-9s, 8 Electra freighters, 2 Shorts SD3-30s.

The following airlines also serve Hawaii: Air Micronesia Inc. (N. Mariana Islands), Air New Zealand, Air Niugini, American Airlines Inc. (U.S.A.), Braniff International (U.S.A.), China Airlines (Taiwan), Continental Airlines (U.S.A.), CP Air (Canada), JAL (Japan), Korean Air Lines, Northwest Airlines Inc. (U.S.A.), Pan Am (U.S.A.), PAL (Philippines), Qantas (Australia), Singapore Airlines, South Pacific Island Airways, United Airlines Inc. (U.S.A.), Western Airlines Inc. (U.S.A.) and World Airways (U.S.A.).

TOURISM

Hawaii Visitors Bureau: 2270 Kalakaua Ave., Honolulu, Hawaii 96815; Vice-Pres. (Marketing) GENE COTTER.

DEFENCE

Hawaii is the headquarters of the U.S. Pacific Command and is responsible for all U.S. military bases and forces in the Pacific Ocean area, the Indian Ocean, Southern Asia, the Aleutian Islands chain and a portion of the Arctic Ocean. The U.S. Pacific fleet is the largest force based at Hawaii, with about 240 ships and 2,000 aircraft.

U.S. Armed Forces based in Hawaii (1980): Total strength 61,521; navy 23,815.

Federal Defence Expenditure in Hawaii (1981): U.S. $1,449.3 million.

EDUCATION

Hawaii has a statewide public school system operated by the State Department of Education, and an elected Board of Education formulates school policy and supervises its application. In 1981/82 162,805 pupils from kindergarten through secondary level attended 225 regular and 5 special State schools and 36,300 attended 141 private schools. The University of Hawaii had 20,629 students at its main campus in Honolulu and 3,478 at Hilo in 1981, and in 1981 20,949 students were enrolled at the six State community colleges offering two-year courses. There are also two private universities with 4,250 students, two private colleges and several technical schools.

Johnston Island

Johnston Island lies in the Pacific, about 1,130 km. west-south-west of Hawaii. It has an area of less than 1.5 sq. km. and in 1978 had a population of 378. It is administered by the Defense Nuclear Agency, Washington, D.C.

Kiribati

PHYSICAL AND SOCIAL GEOGRAPHY

Kiribati comprises 33 atolls, in three principal groups, scattered over about 5 million square kilometres of ocean and extending about 3,780 km. from east to west and 2,050 km. from north to south. There are 16 islands in the main group, 8 Phoenix Islands, 8 Line Islands and Banaba. The people are mainly Micronesians.

HISTORY

In 1892 the United Kingdom established a protectorate over the 16 atolls of the Gilbert Islands and the nine Ellice Islands (now Tuvalu). The two groups were administered together under the jurisdiction of the Western Pacific High Commission (WPHC), which was based in Fiji until its removal to the British Solomon Islands (now Solomon Islands) in 1953. The phosphate-rich Ocean Island (now Banaba), west of the Gilberts, was annexed by the United Kingdom in 1900. The Gilbert and Ellice Islands were annexed in 1915, effective from January 1916, when the protectorate became a colony. Later in 1916 the new Gilbert and Ellice Islands Colony (GEIC) was extended to include Ocean Island and two of the Line Islands, far to the east. Christmas Island (now Kiritimati), another of the Line Islands, was added in 1919 and the eight Phoenix Islands (then uninhabited) in 1937. The Line and Phoenix Islands, south of Hawaii, were also claimed by the U.S.A. A joint British-U.S. administration for two of the Phoenix group, Canton (now Kanton) and Enderbury, was agreed in April 1939.

During the Second World War the GEIC was invaded by Japanese forces, who occupied the Gilbert Islands in 1942–43. Tarawa Atoll, in the Gilbert group, was the scene of some of the fiercest fighting in the Pacific between Japan and the U.S.A.

To prepare the GEIC for self-government, an Advisory Council and an Executive Council were established in 1963. In 1967 a House of Representatives was formed, with 23 elected members and up to seven others. The Executive Council was replaced by a Governing Council, with up to 10 members, including five chosen by the elected members of the House. In 1970 these two bodies were in turn replaced by a Legislative Council (33 members, including 28 elected) and an Executive Council (10 members, including a Leader of Government Business elected by the Legislative Council). In January 1972 a Governor of the GEIC was appointed to assume almost all the functions previously exercised in the colony by the High Commissioner. At the same time the five uninhabited Central and Southern Line Islands, previously administered directly by the High Commissioner, became part of the GEIC. In May 1974 the Legislative Council was replaced by a House of Assembly, with 28 elected members and three official members. A Chief Minister, Naboua Ratieta, was elected by the House and chose between four and six other Ministers.

On October 1st, 1975, the Ellice Islands were allowed to break away from the GEIC to form a separate territory, named Tuvalu. The remainder of the GEIC was renamed the Gilbert Islands and the House of Assembly's membership was reduced.

In 1975 the British Government refused to recognize as legitimate an independence move by the people of Ocean Island (Banaba) who had been in litigation with the British Government since 1971 over revenues derived from exports of phosphate. The discovery of the guano deposits on the 600 hectare island was a prime motive in Britain's annexation of the island. Since 1920 the British Phosphate Commissioners, a consortium of the British, Australian and New Zealand governments, have been mining phosphate for use as a fertilizer in Australia and New Zealand. Open-cast mining so adversely affected the island's environment that the Banabans, who were removed from the island during the Second World War, were resettled on Rabi Island, 2,600 kilometres away in the Fiji group, and became citizens of Fiji in 1970. They remain the landowners on Banaba.

The Banabans rejected the British Government's argument that phosphate revenues should be spread over the whole Gilbert Islands group and in 1973, despite winning 50 per cent of the revenues, continued with litigation. They claimed unpaid royalties from the British Government and damages for the destruction of the island's environment against both the Government and the British Phosphate Commissioners. The Banabans took these two cases to the British High Court in London. In 1976, after a lengthy hearing, their claim for royalties was dismissed but that for damages upheld. In May 1977 the British Government offered them an *ex gratia* payment of $A10 million without admitting liability for damages and on condition that no further appeal would be made to the Courts. The offer was not accepted. The Banaban emissary to London, the Rev. Tebuke Rotan, was unsuccessful in pressing the case for the constitutional separation of the island.

In November 1977 the Rabi Council of Leaders met with Gilbertese ministers at Bairiki, Tarawa, and drew up 11 "Bairiki Resolutions". It was proposed that, prior to the forthcoming constitutional conference to decide the question of the independence of the Gilbert Islands, a referendum would be held to determine the status of Banaba. The British Government agreed to abide by the results of the proposed referendum, but refused to increase the offer of compensation made to the Banabans in May 1977.

The Gilbert Islands obtained internal self-government on January 1st, 1977. Later in 1977 the number of elected members in the House of Assembly was increased to 36. This was subsequently adjusted to 35, with the remaining seat to be filled by a nominee of the Rabi Council of Leaders. Following a general election in February 1978, Ieremia Tabai, Leader of the Opposition in the previous House of Assembly, was elected Chief Minister in March. In December 1978 the Banabans were represented at a conference on the independence of the Gilbert Islands but, when the conference decided that Banaba should remain within the Gilbert Islands after independence, the Banaban delegation walked out. On July 12th, 1979, the Gilbert Islands became an independent republic, within the Commonwealth, under the name of Kiribati. Ieremia Tabai became the country's first President. In September Kiribati signed a treaty of friendship with the U.S.A., which relinquished its claim to the Line and Phoenix Islands, including Kanton and Enderbury. In April 1981 the Banaban community on Rabi accepted the British Government's earlier *ex gratia* offer of $A10 million in compensation together with the interest accrued ($A14.58 million in total), although they continued to seek self-government. In May 1982 Tabai was re-elected President for a second term.

ECONOMIC SURVEY

Until 1979 phosphate rock, derived from rich deposits of guano, was mined on Banaba by the British Phosphate Commission for export to Australia and New Zealand, where it was used for fertilizer. The ending of phosphate production has had a devastating effect on the economy since earnings from phosphate accounted, on average, for about 80 per cent of total export earnings and 50 per cent of government taxation revenue. Gross Domestic Product has fallen from about $750 per caput to $350.

Apart from Banaba, Kiribati is composed of coral atolls with poor quality soil. Most of them are covered with coconut palms, which provide the only agricultural export in the form of copra. A government-owned company operates a coconut plantation on Kiritimati and there are commercial plantations on two other atolls in the Line Islands. Most islanders are fully engaged in subsistence activities. Bananas, pandanus, breadfruit and paw paw are grown as food crops. Fishing is an important local activity and considerable hopes are placed on the development of marine resources, particularly skipjack tuna fishing around the Phoenix Islands.

The islands rely heavily on foreign aid. The United Kingdom gave Kiribati about A$8 million per year in 1979–82, as well as additional aid in the form of training programmes and technical projects, including the re-development of Banaba. Kiribati has also received a $A1.75 million loan from the Asian Development Bank and was to receive $A4 million from Australia, $A0.6 million from New Zealand, $A3 million from Japan, $A0.7 million from the UN and $A4.15 million from the European Development Fund between 1980 and 1982.

STATISTICAL SURVEY

Area: Land area: 711 sq. km.

Population (census results): 51,929 at December 8th, 1973; 56,213 at December 12th, 1978.

Capital: Tarawa (population 20,148 at 1978 census).

Employment (1978): Government service and private enterprise 6,005, phosphate mining in Banaba and Republic of Nauru and other employment outside Kiribati 988.

Agriculture (1980): Copra 6,003 metric tons.

Livestock (1980—FAO estimates): 10,000 pigs, 166,000 chickens.

Sea Fishing (catch in metric tons): 17,936 in 1978; 18,338 in 1979; 18,925 in 1980.

Mining: Phosphate mining at Banaba ceased at the end of 1979.

Finance: Australian currency: 100 cents = 1 Australian dollar ($A). Coins: 1, 2, 5, 10, 20 and 50 cents, Notes: 1, 2, 5, 10, 20 and 50 dollars. Exchange rate (June 1982): £1 sterling=$A1.6925; U.S. $1=97.9 Australian cents; $A100=£59.08=U.S. $102.17.

Note: For details of previous changes in the exchange rate, *see* the chapter on Australia.

Budget (1982): revenue $A15,907,793; expenditure $A15,704,163; Development Programme $A13,189,600; Reserve Fund $A67,230,000.

Consumer Price Index (Base 1975=100): Jan.–March 1982: Food 185.9 Clothing 176.7, Housing and Household 271.2, General Index 186.6.

External Trade (1980): Imports $A16,848,457 (32.3 per cent food); Exports $A2,425,623 (89.2 per cent copra, 9.9 per cent fish).

Trade is mainly with Australia, New Zealand, the United Kingdom, Papua New Guinea and Fiji.

Transport: *Roads*: There are about 640 km. suitable for motor vehicles. *Shipping:* The Government and the Kiribati Shipping Corporation maintain a fleet of six passenger/freight vessels for administrative business. During 1980 71 overseas vessels called at the islands.

THE CONSTITUTION

A new constitution was promulgated at independence on July 12th, 1979. The main provisions are set out below.

The Constitution states that Kiribati is a sovereign democratic Republic and that the Constitution is the supreme law. It guarantees protection of all fundamental rights and freedoms of the individual and provides for the determination of citizenship.

The President, known as the Beretitenti, is Head of State and Head of the Government and presides over the Cabinet which consists of the Beretitenti, the Kauoman-ni-Beretitenti (Vice-President), the Attorney-General and not more than eight other ministers appointed by the Beretitenti from an elected parliament known as the Maneaba ni Maungatabu. Executive authority is vested in the Cabinet which is directly responsible to the Maneaba ni Maungatabu. The Constitution also provides for a Council of State consisting of the Chairman of the Public Services Commission, the Chief Justice and the Speaker.

Legislative power resides with the single-chamber Maneaba ni Maungatabu, composed of 35 members elected for four years, one nominated member (*see* below) and the Attorney-General as an *ex officio* member if he is not elected. The Maneaba is presided over by a Speaker, who is elected by the Maneaba from among persons who are not members of the Maneaba. The 35 elected members of the pre-independence House of Assembly took office as members of the first Maneaba.

One chapter makes special provision for Banaba and the Banabans, stating that one seat in the Maneaba is reserved for a nominated member of the Banaban community. The Banabans' inalienable right to enter and reside in Banaba is guaranteed and, where any right over or interest in land there has been acquired by the Republic of Kiribati or by the Crown before independence, the Republic is required to hand back the land on completion of phosphate extraction. A Banaba Island Council is provided for and also the establishment of an independent Commission of Inquiry three years after Independence Day to review the provisions relating to Banaba.

The Constitution also makes provision for finance, for a Public Service and for an independent judiciary (*see* Judicial System).

THE GOVERNMENT

HEAD OF STATE

President (Beretitenti): IEREMIA T. TABAI, C.M.G. (took office July 12th, 1979).

Vice-President (Kauoman-ni-Beretitenti): TEATAO TEANNAKI.

THE CABINET

(July 1982)

President and Minister of Foreign Affairs: IEREMIA T. TABAI, C.M.G.

Vice-President and Minister of Home Affairs: TEATAO TEANNAKI.

Minister of Health and Family Planning: ATARAOTI BWEBWENIBURE.

Minister of Communications: TAOMATI T. IUTA.

Minister of Works and Energy: BAITIKA TOUM.

Minister of Trade, Industry and Labour: BOANAREKE BOANAREKE.

Minister of Finance: TIWAU AWIRA.

Minister of Natural Resource Development: BABERA KIRATA, O.B.E.

Minister of Education: TEWEE AROBATI.

Minister of the Line and Phoenix Groups: IEREMIA TATA.

Attorney-General: R. L. DAVEY.

LEGISLATURE

MANEABA NI MAUNGATABU

(*House of Assembly*)

Unicameral body comprising 35 elected members and one nominated representative of the Banaban community.

Speaker: MATITA TANIERA.

DIPLOMATIC REPRESENTATION

EMBASSIES AND HIGH COMMISSIONS ACCREDITED TO KIRIBATI

(HC) High Commission.

Australia: P.O.B. 77, Bairiki, Tarawa (HC); *High Commissioner:* R. H. WRIGHT (acting).

Belgium: Wellington, New Zealand.

Canada: Wellington, New Zealand (HC).

Chile: Wellington, New Zealand.

China, People's Republic: Suva, Fiji.

Germany, Federal Republic: Wellington, New Zealand.

Japan: Suva, Fiji.

Korea, Republic: Suva, Fiji.

Netherlands: Wellington, New Zealand.

New Zealand: Suva, Fiji (HC).

Papua New Guinea: Suva, Fiji (HC).

United Kingdom: P.O.B. 61, Bairiki, Tarawa (HC); *High Commissioner:* D. H. G. ROSE.

U.S.A.: Suva, Fiji.

Kiribati also has diplomatic relations with Fiji and Solomon Islands.

JUDICIAL SYSTEM

The High Court of Kiribati is a superior court of record and consists of the Chief Justice and other judges as may be prescribed, appointed by the Beretitenti. The High Court has jurisdiction to supervise any civil or criminal proceedings before any subordinate court and appeals from it lie with the Court of Appeal for Kiribati. This, also, is a court of record and consists of the Chief Justice and other qualified persons appointed by the Beretitenti.

Chief Justice: J. R. JONES, C.B.E.

RELIGION

Anglican, Methodist, Roman Catholic, Seventh-Day Adventist, Baha'i and Church of God communities are represented.

Roman Catholic: P.O.B. 79, Bairiki, Tarawa; Bishop of Tarawa, Nauru and Funafuti, Most Rev. PAUL MEA KAINEA.

Protestant: P.O.B. 80, Bairiki, Tarawa; f. 1968; Moderator Pastor ROBUTI RIMON.

THE PRESS

Te Itoi ni Kiribati: P.O.B. 79, Tarawa; f. 1914; Roman Catholic Church newsletter; monthly; circ. 1,650.

Te Kaotan te Ota: f. 1915; Protestant Churches newspaper; monthly.

Te Uekera: Broadcasting and Publications Authority, Tarawa; English and I-Kiribati (Gilbertese); weekly.

RADIO

Radio Kiribati: P.O.B. 78, Bairiki, Tarawa; f. 1954; statutory body; station T3KI broadcasting on one MW transmitter; programmes in I-Kiribati and English; Man. TOMASI K. TARAU.

In 1978 there were 7,636 radio receivers.

FINANCE

BANKING

Westpac Banking Corporation (*Australia*): P.O.B. 66, Bairiki, Tarawa; f. 1982 (incorporating the *Government Savings Bank*;) Man. IAN HURRELL.

TRADE AND INDUSTRY

CO-OPERATIVE SOCIETIES

Co-operative societies dominate trading in Tarawa and have an almost complete monopoly outside the capital, except for Banaba and Kiritimati. In April 1982 there were 29 co-operative societies.

The Kiribati Copra Co-operative Society Ltd.: Betio, Tarawa; f. 1976; the sole exporter of copra; nine committee mems.; 22 member Co-operative Societies; Chair. IAONEABA IOBI; Sec. BINATAAKE TAWAIA.

TRADE UNION

The Kiribati General Workers' Federation: P.O.B. 40, Bairiki, Tarawa; f. 1979 after federation of three former unions; membership open to all employees, unestablished government employees as well as local contractors; 2,700 mems.; Pres. AWIU TAARAM; Gen. Sec. ETERA TEANGANA.

TRANSPORT

ROADS

Wherever practicable, roads are built on all atolls and connecting causeways between islets are also being built as funds and labour permit.

SHIPPING

United Kingdom cargo ships call at Tarawa every four months. Ships call at Tarawa to collect copra every two or three months, and at Kiritimati, Tabuaeran (Fanning) and Teraina (Washington) twice a year. There is an irregular service from Tarawa to Suva, Fiji, by Government vessels. Ships owned by the Karlander Line operate a container service from New Zealand and Australia to Kiribati via New Caledonia and Solomon Islands; Pacific Forum line vessels call at Tarawa, and tankers bring fuel from Fiji and occasionally from Nouméa in New Caledonia.

Kiribati Shipping Corporation: Tarawa; maintains, with the Government, a fleet of six passenger/freight vessels for administrative business.

CIVIL AVIATION

There are 18 airfields in Kiribati.

Air Tungaru Corporation: P.O.B. 274, Bikenibeu, Tarawa; f. 1977; national airline; operates scheduled passenger services between Tarawa's Bonriki Airport and Abaiang, Abemama, Aranuka, Arorae, Beru, Butaritari, Maiana, Makin, Marakei, Nikunau, Nonouti, Onotoa, North Tabiteuea, South Tabiteuea and Tamana; also flies to Funafuti, Honolulu and Papeete; fleet of 2 Trislander, 1 Riley Heron, 1 Boeing 727-100C; Chief Exec. (vacant).

Kiribati is also served by Air Nauru.

EDUCATION

In 1981 there were 103 primary schools of which 99 were operated by the Government and 4 were private institutions. There are 5 secondary schools, 1 maintained by the Government to sixth form standard and 4 by church missions to lower standards. Two community high schools enrolled a total of 674 students in 1981. The Government also maintains a Teacher Training College, a Technical Institute and a Marine Training School which trains about 200 seamen each year for employment by overseas shipping companies. The Protestant Church has a theological college on Tarawa.

In 1981 enrolment figures were 13,383 in primary schools and 979 in secondary schools. The total number of teachers in all establishments was 592. Kiribati participates in the University of the South Pacific, based in Fiji.

Midway Islands

The Midway Islands consist of Sand Island and Eastern Island in the North Pacific, 1,850 kilometres north-west of Hawaii. They have an area of about five square kilometres and in 1975 had an estimated population of 2,256. The islands are administered by the U.S. Navy Department.

Nauru

PHYSICAL AND SOCIAL GEOGRAPHY

The Republic of Nauru is a small island in the Central Pacific. Lying about 4,000 km. north-east of Sydney, Australia, and 4,160 km. west of Hawaii, Nauru has a tropical climate, with a westerly monsoon season from November to February. At the 1977 census the population was 7,254, including 4,174 Nauruans.

HISTORY

Nauru was annexed by Germany in 1888. In 1914, shortly after the outbreak of the First World War, the island was captured by Australian forces. It continued to be administered by Australia under a League of Nations mandate (granted in 1920) which also named the United Kingdom and New Zealand as co-trustees. Between 1942 and 1945 Nauru was occupied by the Japanese. In 1947 the island was placed under United Nations Trusteeship, with Australia as the administering power on behalf of the Governments of Australia, New Zealand and the United Kingdom. The UN Trusteeship Council proposed in 1964 that the indigenous people of Nauru be resettled on Curtis Island, off the Queensland coast. This offer was made in anticipation of the progressive exhaustion of the island's phosphate deposits. The Nauruans elected to remain on the island and studies were put in train in 1966 for the shipping of soil to the island to replace the phosphate rock. Nauru received a considerable measure of self-government in January 1966, with the establishment of Legislative and Executive Councils, and proceeded to independence on January 31st, 1968.

The Head Chief of Nauru, Hammer DeRoburt, was elected President in May 1968 and re-elected in 1971 and 1973. Subsequent to elections in December 1976 a political crisis arose when the President refused to make changes in his cabinet in favour of younger men. After losing a vote of no confidence he was succeeded by Bernard Dowiyogo. In April 1978, however, Bernard Dowiyogo was defeated on a Bill dealing with phosphate royalties and replaced by Lagumot Harris. He resigned after three weeks and DeRoburt was again elected to the Presidency. He was re-elected in a poll in December 1980. A new ESCAP Liaison Office for the Pacific was opened on Nauru in October 1980.

ECONOMIC SURVEY

The island's economy is based on the extraction of phosphate rock, derived from rich deposits of guano, which constitutes about four-fifths of the area. Phosphate mining is manned largely by indentured labour. Exports of phosphate rock were 2.0 million tons in 1977/78 but deposits are expected to be exhausted by 1995, by which time, it is hoped, Nauru will be able to derive economic security from its shipping and civil aviation services and from its proposed role as a tax haven for international business.

Although Nauru accounts for only 0.5 per cent of world exports of phosphates, the revenue gained is very high: some $A120 million in 1974, a boom year. The revenue from phosphate sales is shared between the Government (which takes about half the profits), the Nauruan landowners, a royalties long-term trust fund and the Nauru Local Government Council. Under the latter's auspices, the Government opened a 53-storey office block in Melbourne in 1977 and in June 1982 agreed to contribute 40 per cent of the cost of a U.S. $205 million fertilizer plant in India. Also due to the phosphate revenues, the Government is able to provide an extensive welfare system.

STATISTICAL SURVEY

Area: 20.9 sq. km. (8.1 sq. miles).

Population (1977 census): Total 7,254 (Nauruan 4,174, Other Pacific Islanders 1,890, Chinese 616, Caucasians—mainly Australians and New Zealanders—564).

Employment (1966): 2,473 (Administration 845, Phosphate Mining 1,408, Other activities 220).

Agriculture and Livestock (1980–FAO estimates): Coconuts 2,000 metric tons; Pigs 2,000.

Mining (exports in '000 metric tons, year ending June 30th): Phosphate rock 2,288 in 1973/74; 1,534 in 1974/75; 755 in 1975/76; 1,146 in 1976/77; 1,999 in 1977/78 (*Source:* International Phosphate Industry Association).

Finance: Australian currency: 100 cents=1 Australian dollar ($A). Coins: 1, 2, 5, 10, 20 and 50 cents. Notes: 1, 2, 5, 10, and 50 dollars.

Exchange rates (June 1982): £1 sterling=$A1.6925; U.S. $1=97.9 Australian cents. $A100=£59.08=U.S. $102.17.

Note: For details of previous changes in the exchange rate, *see* chapter on Kiribati.

Budget ($A'000, 1981/82): Estimated revenue: 109,500; Estimated expenditure: 85,600.

Imports ($A, 1976/77): Total 14,190,000.

Exports (1976/77—metric tons, Phosphate only): 929,142; to Australia 474,297, New Zealand 377,677, Japan 44,338, Republic of Korea 32,830.

Education (1978): Primary schools: 3, with 1,500 pupils. Secondary schools: 2, with 600 pupils. There were an estimated 130 teachers. Nauruans studying at secondary and tertiary level overseas (1975 total): 92.

THE CONSTITUTION

(Promulgated in 1968)

The Constitution protects the fundamental rights and freedoms and provides for a Cabinet responsible to a popularly elected Parliament. The President of the Republic is elected by Parliament from among its members. The Cabinet is composed of five or six members including the President, who presides. There are 18 members of Parliament, including the Cabinet. Voting is compulsory for those over 20 years of age, except in certain specified instances.

The highest judicial organ is the Supreme Court and there is provision for the setting up of subordinate courts with designated jurisdiction.

There is a Treasury Fund from which monies may be taken by Appropriation Acts.

A Public Service is provided for with the person designated as the Chief Secretary being the Commissioner of the Public Service.

Special mention is given to the allocation of profits and royalties from the sale of phosphates.

THE GOVERNMENT

HEAD OF STATE

President: HAMMER DEROBURT, O.B.E. (elected May 11th, 1978).

CABINET

(July 1982)

President, Minister for Internal Affairs, External Affairs, Island Development, Industry, Civil Aviation and Public Service: HAMMER DEROBURT, O.B.E.

Minister for Health and Education: LAWRENCE STEPHEN.

Minister for Finance: KENAS AROI.

Minister for Works and Community Services and Minister Assisting the President: ROBIDOK BURARO DETUDAMO.

Minister for Justice: JOSEPH DETSIMEA.

LEGISLATURE

PARLIAMENT

Comprises 18 members.

Speaker: Hon. REUBEN KUN.

In the November 1977 elections the Nauru Party won 9 seats and the Opposition won 8 seats. In May 1978 one Nauru Party member transferred his allegiance and the Nauru Party Government resigned.

POLITICAL PARTY

Nauru Party: f. 1976; Leader BERNARD DOWIYOGO.

DIPLOMATIC REPRESENTATION

EMBASSIES AND HIGH COMMISSIONS ACCREDITED TO NAURU

(HC) High Commission.

Australia: Civic Centre, Nauru; *High Commissioner:* O. J. CORDELL.

Belgium: Wellington, New Zealand.

France: Suva, Fiji.

India: Suva, Fiji (HC).

Japan: Canberra, Australia.

United Kingdom: Suva, Fiji (HC).

U.S.A.: Canberra, Australia.

Nauru also has diplomatic relations with Fiji, the German Democratic Republic, the Democratic People's Republic of Korea, the Republic of Korea, New Zealand, Taiwan and Western Samoa.

JUDICIAL SYSTEM

The Chief Justice presides over the Supreme Court, which exercises both original and appellate jurisdiction. The Resident Magistrate presides over the District Court, and he also acts as Coroner under the Inquests Act 1977. The Supreme Court and the District Court are courts of record. The Family Court consists of three members, one being the Resident Magistrate as Chairman, and two other members drawn from a panel of 10 Nauruans.

SUPREME COURT

Chief Justice: His Honour Mr. Justice IAN ROY THOMPSON.

DISTRICT COURT

Resident Magistrate: SUSHIL CHANDRA CHATURVEDI.

FAMILY COURT

Chairman: SUSHIL CHANDRA CHATURVEDI.

RELIGION

About 43 per cent of Nauruans are adherents of the Nauruan Protestant Church. The Sacred Heart of Jesus Mission (Roman Catholic) is also represented.

THE PRESS

Bulletin: Local and overseas news in Nauruan and English; fortnightly; Editor A. D. DEIYE; circ. 750.

The Nauru Post: weekly; Editor R. J. T. KUN.

RADIO

Radio Nauru: f. 1968; government-owned and not used for commercial purposes; broadcasts in English and Nauruan; Man. DAVID AGIR; Broadcasts Officer REGINALD AKIRI.

There were 3,600 radio sets in 1978.

FINANCE

BANKING

(auth.=authorized; cap.=capital; dep.=deposits; m.=million).

Bank of Nauru: P.O.B. 289, Nauru; f. 1976; government-owned; cap. and res. $A5.5m.; dep. $A56.5m. (June 1980); Chair. Hon. R. B. DETUDAMO, M.P.; Dirs. Hon. J. A. BOP, M.P., P. D. COOK, K. CLODUMAR, G. DEGIDOA, L. STEPHEN; Gen. Man. and Sec. R. H. DEVENISH.

INSURANCE

Nauru Insurance Corporation: P.O.B. 82, Nauru; f. 1974; sole licensed insurer and reinsurer in Nauru.

TRADE AND INDUSTRY

Nauru Co-operative Society: Civic Centre; f. 1925; operated by the Nauru Local Government Council; the major retailer in Nauru; Man. Dir. HAMMER DEROBURT.

Nauru Fishing Corporation: Aiwo District; f. 1976; owned by Nauru Local Government Council; two 600-ton purse-seine vessels; Chair. HAMMER DEROBURT.

Nauru Phosphate Corporation: Aiwo; f. 1969; Chair. Hon. J. A. BOP; Gen. Man. R. H. FLOYD; the Corporation operates the phosphate industry of the Republic of Nauru on behalf of the Nauruan people. It is responsible for the mining and marketing of phosphate.

TRADE UNIONS

The Nauruan Workers' Organization: f. 1974 to represent the interests of a substantial section of Nauru's employees; Chair. BERNARD DOWIYOGO; Sec. DETONGA DEIYE.

The Phosphate Workers' Organization: f. 1953.

TRANSPORT

RAILWAYS

There are 5.2 km. of 3 ft. gauge railway to serve the phosphate workings.

ROADS

A sealed road, 19 km. long, circles the island, and another serves Buada District. Registered vehicles (1977): 1,761.

SHIPPING

Nauru has no wharves, so passenger and cargo handling is carried out by barge.

Nauru Pacific Line: Civic Centre; f. 1969; five vessels; owned by Nauru Local Government Council; operates fortnightly services to Melbourne, Australia, and the Trust Territory of the Pacific Islands, and other cargo and passenger services; Man. Dir. HAMMER DEROBURT.

CIVIL AVIATION

Air Nauru: Department of Civil Aviation, Yaren; f. 1972; operates services to Apia, Auckland, Guam, Hong Kong, Honiara, Kagoshima, Majuro, Manila, Melbourne, Nadi, Nouméa, Okinawa, Ponape, Saipan, Singapore, Suva, Taipei, Tarawa, Tonga and Vila; fleet of 3 Boeing 727, 2 Boeing 737; Dir. VINCI N. CLODUMAR.

EDUCATION

Education is free and compulsory for children between the ages of 4 and 16. In 1978 the island had three primary schools, with 1,500 pupils, and two secondary schools with 600 pupils; there were an estimated 130 teachers.

New Caledonia

PHYSICAL AND SOCIAL GEOGRAPHY

The territory of New Caledonia comprises one large island and several smaller islands with a total land area of 19,103 sq. km., south and slightly west of Vanuatu. The main island, New Caledonia, is long and narrow, and has a total area of 16,750 sq. km. The nearby Loyalty Islands, which are administratively part of New Caledonia, are 2,353 sq. km. in area. The third group of islands is the uninhabited Chesterfield Islands, which lie about 400 km. north-west of the main island. Rugged mountains divide the west of the main island from the east and there is little flat land.

The population on January 1st, 1980, was estimated to be 139,600. Melanesians numbered 60,500 (43 per cent), Europeans, mainly French, 49,700 (36 per cent), Wallisians and Tahitians 17,600 (13 per cent) and others, mainly Asians, 11,800 (8 per cent). The capital is Nouméa.

HISTORY

New Caledonia became a French Territory in 1853 when the island was annexed as a dependency of Tahiti. In 1884 a separate administration was established, and in 1946 it became an Overseas Territory of the French Republic. From 1856 to 1946 two separate administrations existed for Melanesians and expatriates. In 1956 the old Conseil Générale was replaced by an Assemblée Territoriale of 30 members elected by universal adult suffrage. The Governor retains control of all French national departments and the Gendarmerie Nationale but otherwise there is substantial self-government.

Early European settlers on New Caledonia quickly set about alienating Melanesian land, which involved iniquitous legislation and physical violence in putting down rebellions by Melanesians, the last of which took place in 1917. Further seizures of land followed as punishment. Cattle grazing practised by the Europeans disrupted indigenous agriculture and today large areas of formerly irrigated taro terraces lie abandoned.

In 1974 there were demonstrations and unrest against metropolitan France. A general strike was held in October 1974 for greater local control of the mines (largely owned by the Société le Nickel, the major mining consortium) and further strikes took place in December 1977 and in June and July 1978. New Caledonian demands for a measure of self-government were answered in December 1976 by a new statute for the territory which increased the size of the Council of Government and gave it responsibility for certain internal affairs.

The French Government dismissed the Council of Government in March 1979, following its failure to support a proposal for a ten-year contract between France and New Caledonia because the plan did not acknowledge the possibility of New Caledonian independence. The territory was then placed under the direct authority of the High Commissioner. A new electoral law, recommended by the French Minister for Overseas Departments and Territories, ensured that minor political parties were not represented in the Assembly following the July general election. Consequently mainly the Melanesian-supported, pro-independence groups were excluded, and the elections resulted in the two "national" parties loyal to France winning 22 of the 36 seats in the Assembly. During his visit in July 1979, the French President, Giscard d'Estaing, criticized entrenched conservative elements who were unable to accept Melanesian involvement in the governing of the territory.

Tension grew sharply in September 1981 after the assassination of Pierre Declercq, Secretary-General of the pro-independence party *Union Calédonienne*, and in November 1981 President Mitterrand called an urgent meeting of ministers in Paris to discuss the situation. Recognizing the need for major reforms, Henri Emmanelli, French Secretary of State for Overseas Departments and Territories, outlined in December the most immediate aims of the French Government, including fiscal reform (income tax was introduced in January 1982), equal access for all new Caledonians to positions of authority, land reforms, the wider distribution of mining revenue and the fostering of Melanesian cultural institutions. To help effect these reforms, the French Government simultaneously announced that it would rule by decree for a period of a year. In June 1982, accusing its partner in the ruling coalition of "active resistance to evolution and change" in New Caledonia, the *Fédération pour une Nouvelle Société Calédonienne* joined with the opposition *Front Indépendantiste* to form a government more favourable to the proposed reforms. The anti-independence deputy to the French National Assembly, Jacques Lafleur, immediately resigned to seek re-election, to show that the new government was "unrepresentative".

ECONOMIC SURVEY

Since the first local discovery of nickel in 1867, and of cobalt and chrome in 1875, New Caledonia has been strongly influenced by the presence of large-scale mining enterprises. Because local labour proved too unreliable, large numbers of New Hebrideans, Japanese, Vietnamese and Javanese were imported to work the mines. By 1921 4,000 Asians were resident.

After 1946, Melanesians began to move into the towns and to the mines, where heavy capitalization increased productivity. Further expansion absorbed more labour from rural areas and the high wages paid to nickel workers threatened all forms of rural production and eliminated chrome and cobalt mining, removing almost all forms of non-urban employment, particularly in the northern part of the island. New Caledonia possesses the world's largest known nickel deposit and has the third largest nickel production, after the U.S.S.R. and Canada. The vulnerability of such a narrowly based economy was demonstrated in 1973 when, after enjoying a boom from 1969, nickel exports and revenues fell, resulting in a sharp depression and public unrest. Diversification of the Territory's economic activities and enterprises producing import substitutes are encouraged by grants, subsidies and tax concessions. Major projects in 1982 sought to increase the production of rice and fruit. France has declared nickel a strategic material and maintains strict control over mining.

STATISTICAL SURVEY

Area: 19,103 sq. km.

POPULATION

	Census (April 23rd, 1976)	1980 Estimate
Melanesians	55,598	59,800
Europeans	50,757	49,200
Wallisians	9,571	17,400
Polynesians	6,391	
Others	10,916	11,600
Total	133,232	138,000

Nouméa (capital): 74,335 (1976 census).

ECONOMICALLY ACTIVE POPULATION
(1976 census)

Agriculture	13,564
Services	11,338
Banking, real estate and business	6,458
Industry	5,469
Building and public works	4,475
Transport and telecommunications	2,632
Mining	2,110
Water and electricity	547
Other	96
Total	46,689

Agriculture (1980—metric tons): Maize 1,550, Wheat 250, Sorghum 1,420, Potatoes 3,000, Copra 979, Coffee 597, Sweet Potatoes 500, Bananas 230, Fresh Vegetables 3,530, Fruit 7,608.

Livestock ('000 head, 1980—FAO estimates): Horses 10, Cattle 125, Pigs 37, Sheep 5, Goats 20, Poultry 210.

Fishing (catch in metric tons): 900 in 1975, 1,000 in 1976, 1,425 in 1977, 2,324 in 1978, 1,921 in 1979.

MINING
(metal content, metric tons)

	1977	1978	1979	1980
Nickel ore	113,319	65,171	80,464	86,592

FINANCE

For currency and exchange rates, *see* French Polynesia.

BUDGET
(million francs CFP)

Revenue	1980
Taxation	9,602
Other ordinary receipts*	7,606
Extraordinary receipts	2,091
Total	19,299

Expenditure	1980
Ordinary expenditure	16,187
Extraordinary expenditure	2,092
Total	18,279

* Direct aid from France: 5,217 million francs CFP.

COST OF LIVING
(Index at December 31st each year; base: August 1975=100)

1975	1976	1977	1978	1979	1980
100.87	107.35	113.90	121.30	133.36	149.42

Aid from France (francs CFP, FIDES 1980): Local section 246 million; General section 697 million.

External Trade (1980—million francs CFP): *Imports:* 35,041 (of which 33.7 per cent from France); *Exports:* 30,805 (of which 59.6 per cent to France).

Road Traffic (1980): Motor Vehicles 39,650, Motor Cycles 3,440, Tractors 770.

Shipping (1980): Vessels entered 413, Freight entered 841,700 metric tons, Freight cleared 2,210,100 metric tons.

Civil Aviation (La Tontouta airport, Nouméa—1979): Freight entered 4,841 metric tons, Freight cleared 1,526 metric tons, Postal traffic handled 667,000 metric tons.

Passengers by air and sea (1980): arrivals 108,930, departures 108,631.

Tourism (1980): 65,507 visitors.

EDUCATION

(1981)

	Schools	Teachers	Pupils
Primary	262	1,516	34,281
Secondary	33	545	9,366
Technical	12	315	3,961
Higher	4	60	421
Total	311	2,436	48,029

Source (unless otherwise stated): Service de la Statistique, B. P. 823, Nouméa.

THE GOVERNMENT

Chef du Territoire: Christian Nucci.

Secretary-General: Alain Christnacht.

COUNCIL OF GOVERNMENT

(July 1982)

The Council of Government is composed of seven members elected by the Territorial Assembly, either from its own members or, in certain circumstances, from outside. It is elected every five years, after the elections for the Territorial Assembly. The President of the Council is the High Commissioner and does not vote. All proposals to be submitted to debate by the Territorial Assembly or its Standing Committee are drawn up by the Council. The Council is in charge of all legislation over land matters.

President: Christian Nucci.

Members:

Jean-Marie Tjibaou.
André Gopea.
Henri Bailly.
Yvonne Hnada.
Stanley Camerlynck.
Gaston Morlet.
Henri Wetta.

TERRITORIAL ASSEMBLY

The Territorial Assembly is composed of 36 members elected by direct universal suffrage for a five-year term on the basis of proportional representation. According to the new electoral law in force at the 1979 elections, all parties gaining less than 7.5 per cent of the votes lose their deposits.

President: Jean Pierre Aïfa (FNSC).

(General Election, July 1979)

Party	Seats
Rassemblement pour la Calédonie dans la République	15
Front Indépendantiste	14
Fédération pour une Nouvelle Société Calédonienne	7
Total	36

Deputies to the French National Assembly: Roch Pidjot (one post vacant).

Representative to the Senate: Lionel Cherrier.

Economic and Social Councillor: André Caillard.

POLITICAL PARTIES

Parties in favour of retaining the status quo or of New Caledonia's becoming a department of France:

Rassemblement pour la Calédonie dans la République (RPCR): Nouméa; f. 1978; Leader Jacques Lafleur; a coalition of the *Union pour la Renaissance de la Calédonie, Sociaux Démocrates Chrétiens* (*see* below) and the three following parties. All five parties have retained their own identity:

Rassemblement pour la Calédonie: Nouméa; f. 1977; Leaders Jacques Lafleur, Roger Laroque.

Rassemblement de la République: Nouméa; f. 1977; Leader Dick Ukeiwe.

Mouvement Liberal Calédonien: Nouméa; f. 1971; Leader Jean Leques.

Union pour la Démocratie Française en Calédonie: f. 1979; a coalition of:

Union pour la Renaissance de la Calédonie: Nouméa; f. 1977; Sec.-Gen. Jean Louis Mir.

Sociaux Démocrates Chrétiens/Entente Toutes Ethnies: f. 1979; Leader Dr. Raymond Mura.

Parties in favour of internal autonomy:

Fédération pour une Nouvelle Société Calédonienne (FNSC): Nouméa; f. 1979; Leader Jean Pierre Aïfa; a coalition of the following parties:

Mouvement Wallisien et Futunien: f. 1979; Pres. Finau Melito.

Parti Républicain Calédonien (PRC): Nouméa; f. 1979; Leader Lionel Cherrier.

Union Démocratique (UD): Nouméa; f. 1968; Leader Gaston Morlet.

Union Jeunesse Calédonienne (UJC): Leader Jean-Paul Belhomme.

Union Nouvelle Calédonienne (UNC): Nouméa; f. 1977; Leader Jean Pierre Aïfa.

Parties in favour of independence:

Front Indépendantiste (FI): Nouméa; f. 1979 as a grouping of the following pro-independence parties:

Front Uni de Libération Kanak (FULK): Nouméa; f. 1974; Leader Yann Céléné Uregei.

Libération Kanak Socialiste: Nouméa.

Parti de Libération Kanak (PALIKA): Nouméa; f. 1975; Leader Nidoish Naisseline.

Parti National Calédonien: Nouméa; Leader Georges Chatenay.

Parti Socialiste Calédonien (PSC): Nouméa; f. 1975; Leader M. Violette.

Union Calédonienne (UC): Nouméa; f. 1952; Leader Roch Pidjot.

Union Progressiste Mélanésienne (UPM): Nouméa; f. 1974; Leader André Gopea.

JUDICIAL SYSTEM

Court of Appeal: Palais de Justice, B.P. F4, Nouméa; First Pres. PIERRE DEROURE; Procurator-General Y. MICOUIN.

Court of the First Instance: Nouméa; Pres. E. DEBUC; Procurator of the Republic J. GAUTHIER.

RELIGION

The population is Christian, Roman Catholics comprising over 65 per cent. There is a substantial Protestant minority.

Roman Catholicism: B.P. 3, Nouméa; the Archdiocese of Nouméa comprises New Caledonia and the Loyalty Islands; Archbishop of Nouméa Most Rev. MICHEL CALVET; publ. *Eglise de Nouvelle-Calédonie.*

THE PRESS

L'Avenir Calédonien: 10 rue Gambetta, Nouméa; organ of the Union Calédonienne; Dir. PAÏTA GABRIEL.

Corail: 5 rue Gallieni, Nouméa; f. 1980; weekly; Dir. D. TARDIEU; circ. 5,000.

Eglise de Nouvelle-Calédonie: B.P. 170, Nouméa; f. 1976; official bulletin of the Catholic Church in New Caledonia; weekly; circ. 450.

Les Nouvelles Calédoniennes: 34 rue de la République, Nouméa; daily; Dir. J. P. LEYRAUD; circ. 15,000.

30 Jours: B.P. 370, Nouméa; f. 1981; Dir. HUBERT CHAVELET.

RADIO AND TELEVISION

Radio Nouméa: B.P. G3, Nouméa; f. 1942; France Régions 3; 16 hours of daily programmes in French; Dir. HENRI SIRE.

Télé Nouméa: B.P. G3, Nouméa; f. 1965; transmits for 6 hours a day.

In 1978 there were 65,000 radio receivers and 28,000 television sets.

FINANCE

BANKING

Banque de l'Indochine et de Suez (*France*): rue de l'Alma et ave. Foch, B.P. G5, Nouméa.

Banque Nationale de Paris Nouvelle Calédonie (*France*): 60 ave. de la Victoire, B.P. K3, Nouméa; 6 brs.

Banque de Paris et des Pays-Bas (Nouvelle-Calédonie): 33 rue de l'Alma, B.P. J3, Nouméa.

Banque de Nouvelle-Calédonie (B.N.C.)/Crédit Lyonnais: 73 rue de Sébastopol, B.P. L3, Nouméa; f. 1974; cap. 150m. fr. CFP (Sept. 1974); Dir. MICHEL GENADINOS.

Société Générale Calédonienne de Banque: 56 ave. de la Victoire, B.P. G2, Nouméa.

TRADE AND INDUSTRY

Chambre d'Agriculture: B.P. 111, Nouméa; f. 1909; 18 mems.; Pres. ROGER PENE.

Chambre de Commerce et d'Industrie: B.P. 10, Nouméa; f. 1879; 20 mems.; Pres. ARNOLD DALY; Vice-Pres. JEAN LANCHON, G. LAVOIX; Sec. Treas. H. BOISSERY; publ. *Bulletin de la C.C.I.*

EMPLOYERS' ORGANIZATION

Fédération Patronale de Nouvelle-Calédonie et Dépendances: 13 rue de Verdun, B.P. 466, Nouméa; f. 1936; groups the leading companies of New Caledonia for the defence of professional interests, co-ordination, documentation and research in socio-economic fields; Pres. DIDIER LEROUX; Sec.-Gen. ANNIE BEUSTES.

TRADE UNIONS

Confédération des Travailleurs Calédoniens: Nouméa; Sec.-Gen. R. JOYEUX; grouped with:

Fédération des Fonctionnaires: Nouméa; Sec.-Gen. GILBERT NOUVEAU.

Syndicat Général des Collaborateurs des Industries de Nouvelle Calédonie: Sec.-Gen. H. CHAMPIN.

Union des Syndicats Ouvriers et Employés de Nouvelle-Calédonie: Nouméa; Sec.-Gen. GUY MENNISSON.

TRANSPORT

ROADS

In 1980 there was a total of 5,496 km. of roads in New Caledonia, of which 766 km. were bitumen-surfaced, 589 km. unsealed, 1,618 km. stone-surfaced and 2,523 km. tracks; the outer islands had a total of 470 km. of roads and tracks.

SHIPPING

Most traffic is through the port of Nouméa. Passenger and cargo services are regular and frequent.

Shipping companies operating cargo services to New Caledonia include Hamburg-Sued, Nedlloyd and Bank Line (which connect Nouméa with European ports), Kyowa Line (with Hong Kong, Taiwan, the Republic of Korea and Japan), Somacal (with Sydney, Australia), Sofrana-Unilines (with various Pacific islands and ports on the west coast of Australia), Daiwa Line (with Sydney, Australia, Japan, and various Pacific Islands), Compagnie des Chargeurs Calédoniens (with Sydney, Australia, and both European and Mediterranean ports) and the China Navigation Company (with New Zealand, Fiji and Japan).

CIVIL AVIATION

Air Calédonie: Aérodrome de Magenta; f. 1955; services throughout New Caledonia and to the Loyalty Islands; fleet of four Twin Otters, two Islanders, one Piper Navajo, one C. 310; Man. Dir. DANNYS FAMIN.

Foreign airlines serving New Caledonia are: Air Nauru, Air New Zealand, Air Pacific Ltd. (Fiji), Qantas (Australia), Thai Airways International and UTA (France).

TOURISM

Office Territorial du Tourisme de Nouvelle-Calédonie: 25 av. Maréchal Foch, B.P. 688, Nouméa; f. 1960; Dir. MICHEL DOPPLER.

EDUCATION

Schools are operated by both the state and churches under the supervision of the Department of Education. The French Government finances the state secondary system. In 1981 there were 262 primary schools, 33 secondary schools and 16 technical and higher institutions. Total enrolment was 48,029 pupils. Work began in 1981 on a new University of Technology in Nouméa, due eventually to serve 1,500 students. About 100 students attend universities in France.

Niue

PHYSICAL AND SOCIAL GEOGRAPHY

Niue is a coral island of 259 square kilometres, located about 480 kilometres east of Tonga and 930 kilometres west of the Southern Cook Islands. The island is mainly covered with bush and forest and, because of the rocky and dense nature of the terrain, fertile soil is not plentiful. Agriculture is further made difficult because there are no running streams or surface water. The restricted nature of local resources has led many islanders to migrate to New Zealand. The population declined from 5,194 in September 1966 to 3,578 in March 1979.

HISTORY

The first European to discover Niue was Captain James Cook in 1774. Missionaries visited the island throughout the nineteenth century and in 1900 Niue was declared a British protectorate. In 1901 Niue was formally annexed to New Zealand as part of the Cook Islands but was made a separate administration in 1904. In 1974 Niue attained the status of "self-government in free association with New Zealand". New Zealand is constitutionally responsible for Niue's defence and external affairs and continues to provide budgetary support as well as development assistance. Niueans retain New Zealand citizenship and more than 5,600 Niueans are resident in New Zealand; about twice as many Niueans live in New Zealand as on Niue.

ECONOMIC SURVEY

The majority of the population is engaged in subsistence farming. The main subsistence crops are taro, yams, tapioca and kumara. Limes, passion fruit, copra, pawpaw and honey are cash crops grown for export. About 51,000 of the island's 64,000 acres are used for agriculture and over 13,000 acres are merchantable forest. Niue supplies about one-third of New Zealand's passion fruit market and approximately 50 acres are given over to passion fruit production.

Vegetables, fruit, copra and handicrafts are exported to New Zealand. New Zealand aid is being employed to establish a bee industry, to develop poultry, dairy and beef cattle farming for local consumption and to provide a deep-sea fishing boat and gear and training for the crew. A small forestry project is also being undertaken. An Australian mining company spent five years prospecting for economic bauxite and uranium deposits and in 1977 drilled the first test bores to determine the quantity and grade of uranium discovered earlier that year.

STATISTICAL SURVEY

Area: 259 sq. km. (100 sq. miles).

Population (Mini-census of March 10th, 1979): Total 3,578 (Males 1,823, Females 1,755).

Births and Deaths (1980): 105 live births (birth rate 32.3 per 1,000); 32 deaths (death rate 9.8 per 1,000).

Agriculture (1976—metric tons): Copra 236, Passion fruit and pulp 273, Limes 133, Honey 31, Beef 12.

FINANCE

Currency: 100 cents=1 New Zealand dollar ($NZ). For details, *see* the Cook Islands.

BUDGET

($NZ, April 1st to March 31st)

	Revenue	Expenditure	New Zealand Subsidy
1976/77	2,506,305	4,836,889	2,620,000
1977/78	3,139,830	6,309,719	2,800,000
1978/79	4,236,649	3,218,638	3,600,000
1979/80*	4,078,414	4,012,714	2,800,000

* Estimate.

1980/81: Budget revenue $NZ5,000,000.

Revenue is raised mainly from import and export duties, sale of postage stamps, court fines and income tax. Niue's contribution to the budget from local revenue is increasing.

CONSUMER PRICE INDEX

(Jan.–March each year; base: Jan.–March 1976=100)

	1977	1978	1979	1980
Food	128.4	150.8	172.0	197.8
Clothing	116.0	140.3	135.2	169.4
General Index	120.6	139.1	158.0	178.8

EXTERNAL TRADE

($NZ '000)

	1976	1977	1978	1979
Imports	1,752	2,109	2,317	2,087
Exports	153	255	240	373

Export items include copra, plaited ware, honey, passion fruit and limes.

New Zealand takes most of Niue's exports (97.6 per cent in 1979) and provides a large part of the island's imports (79.9 per cent in 1979). The main imports in 1978 were food and live animals, manufactured goods, machinery, fuels, lubricants, chemicals and drugs.

THE CONSTITUTION

In October 1974 Niue gained self-government in free association with New Zealand. The latter, however, remains responsible for Niue's defence and external affairs and will continue economic and administrative assistance. Executive government in Niue is through the Premier, assisted by three Ministers. Legislation is carried out by the Niue Assembly but New Zealand, if called upon to do so by the Assembly, will also legislate for the island. There is a New Zealand representative in the territory.

THE GOVERNMENT

New Zealand Representative: Dr. Malcolm McNamara.

THE CABINET

(July 1982)

Premier and Minister of Finance, Inland Revenue, Customs and Trade, Transport (Shipping and Aviation), Government Administration, Housing, Information Services, Police and Immigration: Hon. ROBERT R. REX, O.B.E., C.M.G.

Minister of Economic Development, Works, Justice, Lands and Survey and Local Affairs: Hon. Dr. ENETAMA LIPITOA.

Minister of Education, Forestry, Post Office, Telecommunications and Tourism: Hon. FRANK FAKAOTIMANAVA LUI.

Minister of Health, Fisheries, Agriculture, Youth, Cultural Affairs and Sport: ROBERT R. REX, Jr.

Secretary to the Government: T. M. CHAPMAN.

ASSEMBLY

Speaker: S. P. E. TAGELAGI.

JUDICIAL SYSTEM

The High Court: exercises civil and criminal jurisdiction in Niue.

The Land Court: is concerned with litigation over land and titles.

Land Appellate Court: hears appeals over decisions of the Land Court.

The Chief Justice of the High Court and the Land Court Judge visit Niue quarterly. Appeals against High Court judgments are heard in the Appeal Court of New Zealand.

RELIGION

Seventy-five per cent of the population belong to the Ekalesia Niue, which is closely related to the London Missionary Society, a Protestant organization. The Latter-Day Saints, Roman Catholics, Jehovah's Witnesses, Seventh Day Adventists and Church of God of Jerusalem are also represented.

THE PRESS

Tohi Tala Niue: Information and Broadcasting Services, Central Office, P.O.B. 67, Alofi; weekly; English and Niuean.

RADIO

Radio Sunshine Niue ZK2ZN: Information and Broadcasting Services, Central Office, P.O.B. 67, Alofi; government-controlled; broadcasts in Niuean and English; Sec. T. M. CHAPMAN.

There were more than 1,000 radio sets in 1981.

TRANSPORT

ROADS

There are 123 kilometres of all-weather roads and 106 kilometres of access and plantation roads. At March 31st, 1979, there were 1,009 registered motor vehicles, of which 612 were motor cycles, 264 cars, 59 trucks, 5 buses and 69 other vehicles.

SHIPPING

The best anchorage is an open roadstead at Alofi, the largest of Niue's 13 villages. A shipping service operated by the Shipping Corporation of New Zealand Ltd. (cargo only) is maintained with New Zealand via the Cook Islands on a regular monthly basis.

CIVIL AVIATION

Hanan International Airport has a total sealed runway of 1,650 metres, capable of taking most types of aircraft except modern jet aircraft. The island is served by three weekly commercial passenger and freight services operated by Polynesian Airlines (Western Samoa).

EDUCATION

There are 8 bilingual (Niuean/English) primary schools and 1 secondary. Education is free and compulsory between the ages of six and fourteen. In 1979 there were 1,063 children attending school. A significant number of High School leavers take up tertiary education mainly in the Pacific region, and to a small extent in New Zealand. Education policy emphasizes education relevant to Niue.

Norfolk Island

Norfolk Island lies off the eastern coast of Australia, about 1,400 km. east of Brisbane. It is about 8 km. long and 4.8 km. wide and was discovered by Captain Cook in 1774. The island was used as a penal settlement from 1788 to 1813 and again from 1825 to 1855. It was a separate Crown Colony until 1897, when it became a Dependency of New South Wales. In 1913 it was transferred to the Australian Government.

Under the Norfolk Island Act 1979, Norfolk Island progressed to responsible legislative and executive government, enabling it to run its own affairs to the greatest practicable extent. Wide powers are exercised by the nine-member Norfolk Island Legislative Assembly (the first elections for which were held on January 27th, 1982) and by an Executive Council comprising the executive members of the Legislative Assembly who have ministerial-type responsibilities. The Act preserves the Commonwealth's responsibility for Norfolk Island as a Territory under its authority, with the Minister for Home affairs and Environment as the responsible Minister. The Act indicates Parliament's intention that consideration would be given to an extension of the powers of the Legislative Assembly and the political and administrative institutions of Norfolk Island within five years.

About 405 hectares are arable. The main crops are Kentia palm seed, cereals, vegetables and fruit. Some flowers and plants are grown commercially. The Administration is increasing the area devoted to Norfolk Island pine and hardwoods. Seed of the Norfolk Island pine is exported. Tourism is the island's main industry.

STATISTICAL SURVEY

Area: 3,455 hectares.

Population (Census June 30th, 1981): 2,175 (including visitors).

Budget (year ending June 30th, 1981): Revenue $A3,288,338; Expenditure $A2,810,673.

Imports (year ending June 30th, 1981): $A13,354,676, mainly from Australia.

Exports (year ending June 30th, 1981): $A1,767,513.

Tourism (1980/81): 22,878 visitors.

THE GOVERNMENT

The Administrator is appointed by the Governor-General of Australia and is responsible to the Minister for Home Affairs and Environment. A form of responsible legislative and executive government was extended to the island in 1979, as outlined above.

Administrator: Air Vice-Marshal R. E. TREBILCO, A.O., D.F.C.

EXECUTIVE COUNCIL

Executive Member for Administration, Education and Health: DAVID BUFFETT.

Executive Member for Planning, Tourism and Environment: JOHN BROWN.

Executive Member for Finance and Commerce: ED HOWARD.

LEGISLATIVE ASSEMBLY

President: DAVID BUFFETT.

JUDICIAL SYSTEM

Supreme Court of Norfolk Island: appeals lie to the **Federal Court of Australia.**

Judges: The Hon. Mr. Justice R. W. FOX (Chief Judge), The Hon. Mr. Justice E. A. DUNPHY, The Hon. Mr. Justice P. G. EVATT.

THE PRESS

Norfolk Island Government Gazette: Kingston; weekly.

Norfolk Islander: "Greenways Press", P.O.B. 150, Norfolk Island 2889; f. 1965; weekly; circ. 1,100; Co-Editors Mr. and Mrs. THOMAS LLOYD.

RADIO

Norfolk Island Broadcasting Service: Administration of Norfolk Island; broadcasts 106 hours of programmes a week; Broadcasting Officer Mrs. K. M. LECREN.

There were estimated to be 1,500 radio receivers in 1982.

FINANCE

BANKING

There are branches of the Commonwealth Trading Bank (Australia), the Commonwealth Savings Bank of Australia, the Bank of New South Wales Trading Bank (Australia) and the Bank of New South Wales Savings Bank (Australia).

TRADE

Norfolk Island Chamber of Commerce: P.O.B. 370; f. 1966; affiliated to the Australian Chamber of Commerce, Canberra, A.C.T.; 64 mems.; Pres. G. BENNETT; Sec. JUDIE JARVIS; publs. monthly newsletter and *Shopping and Tourist Guide*.

TRANSPORT

ROADS

There are about 80.5 km. of roads, including 53 km. of sealed road.

SHIPPING

The Compagnie des Chargeurs Calédoniens operates cargo services from Sydney, Australia, and Auckland, New Zealand. A small tanker from Nouméa (New Caledonia) delivers petroleum products to the Island and another from Australia delivers liquid propane gas.

CIVIL AVIATION

Norfolk Island has one airport, with two runways of 1,700 and 1,550 metres, capable of taking the smaller modern aircraft.

Norfolk Island Airlines: P.O.B. 226, Norfolk Island 2899; f. 1973; operates regular flights to Brisbane and Lord Howe Island; and charters throughout Australia and the South Pacific; Chair. JOHN BROWN; fleet of Beechcraft Super King Air 200s.

Norfolk Island is also served from Sydney by East-West Airlines (Australia) and from Auckland by Air New Zealand.

TOURISM

Norfolk Island Government Tourist Bureau: Burnt Pine, P.O.B. 211, Norfolk Island 2899.

EDUCATION

Education is free and compulsory for all children between the ages of 6 and 15. Pupils attend the government school from infant to secondary level. Students wishing to follow higher education in Australia are eligible for bursaries and scholarships.

Northern Mariana Islands

The Commonwealth of the Northern Mariana Islands comprises 16 islands (all the Marianas except Guam) in the Western Pacific, 5,300 km. west of Honolulu (Hawaii). Six islands, including the three largest, Saipan, Tinian and Rota, are inhabited; the chief settlement and administrative centre are on Saipan.

Formerly part of the Trust Territory of the Pacific Islands, the islands voted for separate status as a U.S. commonwealth territory in June 1975, and in March 1976 President Ford signed the Northern Marianas Commonwealth Covenant. In October 1977 President Carter approved the constitution of the Northern Mariana Islands, which provides that from January 1978 the former Marianas District is internally self-governing. In December 1977 elections were held for a bicameral legislature, a governor and a lieutenant-governor. The residents of the islands are not expected to obtain full citizenship of the U.S.A. until negotiations to decide the future status of the Trust Territory of the Pacific Islands are completed and the trusteeship is ended.

Military land on Tinian is to be leased to the U.S. Government for U.S. $19 million, and the islands will also receive $14 million in direct aid for each of the seven years after 1978. Additional income is expected to come from U.S. federal welfare and development programmes.

Serious damage was caused by Typhoon Dinah on November 22nd, 1980, and the sudden eruption of a volcano in May 1981 forced the inhabitants of the island of Pagan to flee.

STATISTICAL SURVEY

Area: 479 sq. km.; Saipan 122 sq. km., Tinian 101 sq. km., Rota 83 sq. km.

Population (Census 1981): 16,862; Saipan 14,585, Tinian 899, Rota 1,274, Northern islands 104.

External Trade (1981): Exports: vegetables 180,000 lb.; beef and pork 443,000 lb.

Tourism (1981): 119,370 visitors.

(For other figures, *see* the chapter on the Trust Territory of the Pacific Islands.)

THE GOVERNMENT

(July 1982)

Governor: Pedro P. Tenorio.

LEGISLATURE

Legislative authority is vested in the Northern Marianas Commonwealth Legislature, a bicameral body consisting of a Senate and a House of Representatives. There are nine senators elected for four-year terms and 14 members of the House of Representatives elected for two-year terms.

Senate President: Olympio T. Borja.

Speaker of the House: Benigno R. Fitial.

RELIGION

The population is predominantly Christian, mainly Roman Catholic.

THE PRESS

The Commonwealth Examiner: P.O.B. 1074, Saipan; f. 1979; weekly; independent; English and Chamorro.

Marianas Variety News and Views: P.O.B. 231, Saipan, C.M. 96950; f. 1972; weekly; independent; English and Chamorro; Mans. Abed and Paz Younis; circ. 1,600.

Pacific Daily News: P.O.B. 822, Saipan, C. M. 96950; f. 1970; daily; English; Editor Mark Cook.

RADIO AND TELEVISION

RADIO

Station KSAI: Saipan; non-commercial station owned by Far Eastern Broadcasting Co.; 10 kW.; broadcasts on 936 kHz.

Station WSZE: Navy Hill, Saipan; commercial station owned by Micronesian Broadcasting Corpn.; 1 kW.; broadcasts on 1053 kHz.

TELEVISION

Saipan Cable TV: P.O.B. 1015, Saipan; 12-channel commercial station broadcasting 24 hours a day; U.S. programmes and local and international news; 2,300 subscribers; Man. Ray D. Motley.

There were approximately 5,000 television sets in the Northern Mariana Islands in 1980.

FINANCE

BANKING

American Savings Bank (*U.S.A.*): Chalan Kanoa, Saipan.

Bank of Guam (*U.S.A.*): P.O.B. 678, Saipan 96950; Man. Karl T. Reyes; brs. in Truk and Majuro, Marshall Islands and Guam.

Bank of Hawaii (*U.S.A.*): P.O.B. 566, "Nauru Bldg.", Saipan.

California First Bank (*U.S.A.*): Saipan 96950.

INSURANCE

Micronesian Insurance Underwriters: P.O.B. 206, Saipan.

The New Zealand Insurance Co. Ltd. Microl Corporation: P.O.B. 267, Saipan, CM 96950; general agents.

ToKio Marine and Fire Insurance Co.: P.O.B. 168, Saipan.

TRADE AND INDUSTRY

CO-OPERATIVES

The Mariana Islands Co-operative Association, Rota Producers and Tinian Producers Association operate in the islands.

TRANSPORT

SHIPPING

Saipan Shipping Co.: P.O.B. 8, Saipan; services to Guam, Micronesia and the Far East.

Nauru Pacific Line operates a regular container service from Melbourne, Australia, to Saipan and the Trust Territory, and Kyowa Line vessels call at Saipan en route from Hong Kong, Taiwan, the Republic of Korea, Japan and Guam to the Trust Territory. Additional cargo services are provided by Daiwa Line vessels and the Philippines, Micronesia and Orient Navigation Co.

CIVIL AVIATION

Air Micronesia Inc.: P.O.B. 138, Saipan; f. 1966; owned by United Micronesia Development Association, Continental Airlines and Aloha Airlines; provides internal and some external services; Chair. CARLTON SKINNER; Pres. DONALD PECK; Gen. Man. DANIEL H. PURSE; fleet of three Boeing 727.

The Northern Mariana Islands are also served by Air Nauru, JAL (Japan) and Island Air Airways.

TOURISM

Marianas Visitors Bureau: P.O.B. 861, Saipan, CM 96950; Exec. Dir. J. M. GUERRERO.

The Micronesian Regional Tourism Council, based in Guam (*q.v.*), promotes tourism in the Northern Mariana Islands.

Papua New Guinea

PHYSICAL AND SOCIAL GEOGRAPHY

Papua New Guinea lies east of Indonesia and north of the north-eastern extremity of Australia. It comprises the eastern part of the island of New Guinea, the western section of which (Irian Jaya) is part of Indonesia, and some smaller islands including the Bismarck Archipelago (mainly New Britain, New Ireland and Manus) and the northern part of the Solomon Islands (mainly Bougainville and Buka). It covers a total area of 462,840 square kilometres. The climate is hot and humid throughout the year, with an average maximum temperature of 33°C. and an average minimum of 22°C.

A census in September 1980 recorded a population of 3,006,799 (provisional total). The rate of increase between 1971 and 1980 is between 2.1 and 2.3 per cent per annum.

HISTORY

New Guinea was divided in 1828. The west was administered until 1949 as part of the Netherlands East Indies and from 1949 until 1962 as the Nederlands Nieuw Guinea. In 1963, after military action by Indonesia, the territory became provisionally Daerah Irian Barat and became part of Indonesia by an "act of free choice" in August 1962. It is known as Irian Jaya, a province of Indonesia.

The southern part of the eastern end of New Guinea became British New Guinea in 1906 after the establishment of a British Protectorate in 1884 and annexation in 1886. Australia administered what became the Territory of Papua until 1949, when it was joined, under one administration, with New Guinea. The northern part of the eastern end of the island became Schutzgebiet Kaiser-Wilhelmsland und Bismarck-archipel in 1884, part of the Schutzgebiet Deutsch Neu-Guinea in 1899, the Mandated Territory of New Guinea in 1919 and the Trust Territory of New Guinea in 1946. Australian troops invaded Rabaul in 1914 and relieved the Germans of the territory. Australia administered the area until 1942 when much of it fell under Japanese administration until 1945. In December 1973 the Territory of Papua New Guinea became internally self-governing and on September 16th, 1975, became the independent nation of Papua New Guinea.

A House of Assembly (renamed the National Parliament at independence) was elected in February 1972. It had 102 members elected by universal adult suffrage. There were 20 ministers including the Prime Minister, Michael Somare, and an inner Cabinet of 10 ministers. The Government was formed from a loose coalition of three main political parties with the opposition made up of one main party and a number of independents supporting both sides.

Although broad cultural similarities occur among groups in the Papuan Coastal, New Guinea Highlands, New Guinea Coastal, New Guinea Islands and Bougainville regions, local group sympathies are strong and in rural areas where approximately two million of the 2,959,800 indigenous population live, understanding of national issues is low or non-existent.

The Papua New Guinea Government inherited from Australia a highly bureaucratic, centralized administration unsuited to a country in which transport is so difficult and national awareness so low. Strong pressure from some provinces during 1975 and 1976 resulted in the Government reintroducing into the constitution provisions for decentralized provincial governments. In 1976 leaders of a group calling itself the Independent Republic of the North Solomons on Bougainville island threatened to break away from the rest of Papua New Guinea, but, after months of negotiations, Bougainville was granted Provincial Government status and became self-governing in July 1976, and by 1978 all 20 provinces had been granted Provincial Government status. The constitutional and administrative implications of this decentralization of power remain, as yet, uncertain.

Within the provinces 160 local government councils operate. The first were established in the 1950s by the Australian administration. The councils are empowered to levy taxes and make rules. However, many councils are too small to operate efficiently and rely heavily on funds and administrative assistance from the central government. Councils are finding increasing difficulty collecting personal taxes.

On March 12th, 1980, the opposition succeeded in a motion of "no confidence" in the Prime Minister, Michael Somare, and the Government changed hands. Sir Julius Chan, a part-Chinese former Finance Minister and leader of the People's Progress Party (PPP), became Prime Minister. Somare became Leader of the Opposition.

National elections were held in June 1982. Somare's Pangu Pati won 41 seats in the 102-member Parliament, and in August 1982 Parliament chose Somare to be Prime Minister. Sir Julius Chan's People's Progress Party won only 12 seats, while the Deputy Prime Minister, Iambakey Okuk, lost his seat and his National Party won only nine seats. The election was fought against accusations of increasing bribery and corruption at high levels. In 1980 Somare failed to introduce into Parliament a Leadership Code which would require all political and public service leaders to declare their assets and sources of income. The major issues to emerge during the election involved the economic management of the country in the face of depressed commodity prices.

During 1982 several incursions of Indonesian troops across the border occurred. Indonesia claimed that they were mistakes, but it seems that Indonesian troops were attempting to rescue people kidnapped in 1981 by Free West Papua (OPM) fighters. These people escaped into Papua New Guinea early in 1982. Previous border disturbances have also coincided with national elections in Papua New Guinea.

ECONOMIC SURVEY

The Papua New Guinea economy comprises five major components: the non-market or subsistence sector, primary agricultural exports (coffee, cocoa, copra, timber and fish), secondary and tertiary industries, Bougainville Copper Limited (which owns the huge Panguna mine, the fourth largest in the world), and the Government sector.

The G.D.P. in 1978 was $A1,684 million. Of this, the subsistence sector was estimated to contribute $A235 million or 14 per cent. However, this sector is difficult to assess in terms of market prices and, moreover, it supports about 72 per cent of all the working population.

The primary export sector contributed 15 per cent of G.D.P. in 1978. Most important were coffee ($A150 million), fish ($A90 million), cocoa ($A67 million), coconut products ($A42 million), forest products ($A35 million), palm oil ($A28 million), tea ($A12 million) and rubber ($A9 million).

Bougainville Copper contributed $A269 million to the 1978 G.D.P. and is a critical sector in the economy. Fluctuations in the price of copper are alleviated by a Mineral Resources Stabilization Fund.

The manufacturing sector is small and weak, limited by the small internal market, the low purchasing power of the population and the lack of an integrated transport network. The tertiary sector is large for the size of the economy, a carry-over from colonial times, and is unlikely to grow in the immediate future. Together, these sectors contributed $A555 million (33 per cent) of the 1978 G.D.P. The G.D.P. in 1980 was K1,738.1 million.

The government sector is financed from three main sources: internal revenue, loans and overseas aid. Total expenditure exceeds internal revenue by about 45 per cent, although this proportion is falling. The Australian Government is pledged to provide support of $A241.2 million in 1981/82.

Papua New Guinea is a member of the Asian Development Bank and the World Bank and has received substantial long-term loans from both organizations. Two major schemes involve agricultural and infrastructural projects in the East Sepik and Southern Highland Provinces. In addition, loans from the World Bank and the Asian Development Bank are being used on extending the national highway network, with the ultimate object of a trans-national highway linking Port Moresby with the Highlands and the north coast.

In an effort to co-ordinate development planning, the Government instituted the National Public Expenditure Plan in 1977 and set out major planning objectives for the next five years. The Expenditure Plan combines aid and internal funds for projects submitted by Provinces and Government Departments. Projects for 1980–81 included agricultural, health, population control, education and improved administration schemes.

Telecommunications are highly developed. Broadcasting is the principal means of mass communication. The National Broadcasting Commission operates a national service in English and local services in the two main *lingua franca*, Pidgin and Hiri Motu, as well as local languages. Television is to be introduced in 1985.

High rainfall and relief give Papua New Guinea the potential to generate large amounts of hydro-electricity. The Ramu River project stage I has been completed at a cost of K30 million and has a capacity of 45 MW. Eventually this project will generate 255 MW. A feasibility study is being undertaken on the Purari River at Wabo by Japanese and Australian interests for a 1,500 MW. power station and dam estimated to cost about K700 million.

Forestry is a sizeable activity and exports of sawn timber are growing steadily. The Vanimo timber project in West Sepik Province, which was awarded to a Philippine company, Hetura Meja, in May 1982, promises to be of major importance to Papua New Guinea's economy.

Development has begun of the Ok Tedi and associated copper deposits in the Telefomin area of the West Sepik and Western Provinces. Exploration was begun by the Kennecott Corporation which discovered an ore body of up to 300 million metric tons averaging 0.9 per cent copper at Ok Tedi, and other lower grade deposits nearby. The area is 800 km. from the coast (by river), 2,700 metres above sea level and receives over 10,000 mm. of rain a year, so severe engineering and transport problems must be overcome before any extraction is possible. Gold mining is due to start at Ok Tedi in 1984 and copper mining in 1986. The potential of another large gold deposit at nearby Porgera was being assessed in 1982.

Towns in Papua New Guinea grew at an annual rate of around 14 per cent between 1971 and 1980, mainly as a result of rural-urban migration. Employment in the towns is not available to many who seek it, and urban services cannot cope with the migrants when they arrive. Migrant "shanty" towns are already a feature of all the major urban areas. Services are being extended to these settlements and materials and loans for housing improvement are being made available. Existing forecasts suggest towns will grow by an average of 9.4 per cent between 1971 and 1986, which will alter the present rural-urban population distribution from 11 per cent in urban areas in 1971 to 23 per cent in 1986. One serious problem facing all towns is lack of land, and the unwillingness of village owners to sell land to the government for urban development.

As yet no clearly stated political ideology has emerged in Papua New Guinea. Foreign investment is sought and encouraged on the one hand, but fears of neo-colonialism and domination of the economy by overseas interests are frequently expressed. Rural development is a government aim, but most government spending per head of population occurs in towns, which are growing rapidly, and it is in urban areas that the best living conditions, services and educational facilities are to be found. A marked rural-urban migration pattern has developed, with the best educated people being drawn from the villages into the towns where they are fast forming an urban élite. Papua New Guinea enjoys one advantage that many developing countries do not: about 80 per cent of the population are employed in the subsistence, non-monetarized sector of the economy to varying degrees, and provide themselves with almost all their daily requirements of food, clothing and shelter. However, even this advantage is being rapidly whittled away by rapid population growth. A sharp fall in export earnings occurred in 1981 and, coupled with inflation, a high demand for internal credit and government overspending outside the 1980 and 1981 budget caused concern.

STATISTICAL SURVEY

AREA AND POPULATION

Area (sq. km.)			Estimated Population (1982)		
Mainland	Islands	Total	Citizen	Non-citizen	Total
395,730	67,110	462,840*	3,097,000	33,000	3,130,000

* 178,704 square miles.

Administrative Capital: Port Moresby, with an estimated population of 138,500 (including 12,000 non-nationals) in 1982.

Births and Deaths: Average annual birth rate 45.1 per 1,000; death rate 14.9 per 1,000 (National Health Plan, 1979 estimate).

EMPLOYMENT*
(Census of July 1971)

Agriculture, forestry and fishing	294,143
Mining and quarrying	5,742
Manufacturing	17,741
Building and construction	27,321
Transport, storage and communications	14,847
Commerce	16,582
Community and business services	39,924
Personal service (hotels, cafés and amusements)	17,286
Others (incl. activities not adequately described)	24,905
Total	458,491

* Those engaged in paid employment only. The total economically active population was 1,080,347 (males 661,929, females 418,418).

AGRICULTURE

PRINCIPAL CROPS
('000 metric tons)

	1978	1979	1980
Rice (paddy)	1	2*	2*
Sorghum	4	4*	4*
Sweet potatoes*	430	436	440
Cassava (Manioc)*	90	92	94
Other roots and tubers*	552	559	572
Pulses*	21	21	22
Groundnuts (in shell)*	3	4	5
Coconuts*	800	870	780
Copra	143	144	140
Palm kernels*	13.3	13.4	13.4
Vegetables*	237	240	242
Sugar cane*	375	379	382
Pineapples*	8	8	8
Bananas*	880	889	898
Coffee (green)	46	49	50†
Cocoa beans	31	26	30
Tea	6	8	8*
Natural rubber	3	4	5*

* FAO estimates. † Unofficial figure.

Source: mainly FAO, *Production Yearbook*.

LIVESTOCK
(FAO estimates, '000 head, year ending September)

	1978	1979	1980
Cattle	130	135	140
Pigs	1,740	1,750	1,760
Goats	15	15	15
Chickens	1,102	1,119	1,137
Ducks	3	3	3

Source: FAO, *Production Yearbook*.

LIVESTOCK PRODUCTS
(FAO estimates, '000 metric tons)

	1978	1979	1980
Pig meat	22	22	22
Other meat	18	18	19
Cows' milk	1	1	1
Hen eggs	1.7	1.7	1.7

Source: FAO, *Production Yearbook*.

FORESTRY

ROUNDWOOD REMOVALS
('000 cubic metres)

	1974	1975	1976	1977	1978	1979	1980
Industrial wood:							
Coniferous (soft wood)	80	84	87	86	93	103	115
Broadleaved (hard wood)	884	1,022	1,237	1,050	1,263	807	1,103
Fuel wood (all broadleaved)	4,639*	4,753*	4,870*	4,995*	5,122*	4,832	10,936
TOTAL	5,603	5,859	6,194	6,131	6,478	5,742	12,154

* FAO estimates.

Source (1974–78): FAO, *Yearbook of Forest Products*.

SAWNWOOD PRODUCTION
('000 cubic metres, including boxboards)

	1974	1975*	1976	1977	1978	1979	1980
Coniferous	28	24	29	25	34	47	54
Broadleaved	114	113	123	113	139	102	133
TOTAL	142	137	152	138	173	149	187

* FAO estimates.

Source (1974–77): FAO, *Yearbook of Forest Products*.

FISHING

	1972	1973	1974	1975	1976	1977	1978	1979
Total catch ('000 metric tons)	27.2	45.4	50.1	34.8	50.9	26.4	52.6	29.8

Source: FAO, *Yearbook of Fishery Statistics*.

MINING*

		1975	1976	1977†	1978†	1979†	1980†
Copper concentrates	'000 metric tons	172.5	176.5	182.3	198.6	170.8	146.8
Silver	metric tons	42	45	47	52.5	44.6	36.9
Gold	kilogrammes	19,574	20,770	23,419	23,367	19,703	14,050

* Figures refer to the metal content of ores and concentrates mined.
† Provisional.

INDUSTRY

SELECTED PRODUCTS

		1975	1976	1977	1978	1979	1980
Palm oil	'000 metric tons	31	49	53	55	80	n.a.
Beer	'000 litres	36,160	37,194	46,277	49,266	48,164	51,828
Electric energy*	million kWh.	982	974	1,015	1,187	1,215	1,249

* Twelve months ending June 30th of the year stated.

FINANCE

100 toea = 1 kina (K).
Coins: 1, 2, 5, 10 and 20 toea; 1 kina.
Notes: 2, 5, 10 and 20 kina.

Exchange rates (June 1982): £1 sterling = 1.282 kina; U.S. $1 = 74.0 toea.
100 kina = £78.01 = $135.12.

Note: The kina was introduced in April 1975, replacing (at par) the Australian dollar ($A). Australian currency remained legal tender until December 31st, 1975. The kina maintained its parity with the Australian dollar until July 1976, when a new exchange rate of 1 kina = $A1.05 was established. This remained in effect until November 1976, when the kina was revalued against the Australian dollar (to $A1.181) but devalued against other currencies. The November devaluation was partially reversed in December 1976 and the exchange rate was later adjusted again. The average value of the kina in U.S. dollars was: 1.310 in 1975; 1.262 in 1976; 1.264 in 1977; 1.412 in 1978; 1.405 in 1979; 1.492 in 1980; 1.487 in 1981. For details of previous changes in the exchange rate, *see* the chapter on Australia.

BUDGET
(K '000)

Revenue	1980	1981†	Expenditure	1980	1981
Customs and excise	108,950	115,534	Departmental	298,027	659,043 (combined)
Other taxation	130,701	144,270	Capital works and services	56,433	
Foreign Government grant*	174,599	184,348	Other expenditure	235,962	
Loans	60,590	57,178			
Other revenue	104,163	127,545			
Total	579,003	628,875	Total	590,422	659,043

* Mainly Australia. † Provisional.

DEVELOPMENT ASSISTANCE
($A million)

	1980–82	1982/83	1983/84	1984/85	1985/86
Australian commitment	242	253	265	277	298

CONSUMER PRICE INDEX
(Average for urban areas, June quarter. Base: 1977 = 100)

	1978	1979	1980	1981
Food	103.0	106.0	124.6	136.6
Drink, tobacco and betel nut	100.9	110.1	117.6	130.5
Clothing and footwear	108.0	111.3	118.2	122.3
Rents, council charges, fuel and power	102.9	121.6	150.3	157.1
Total (incl. others)	104.1	109.5	123.4	134.2

BALANCE OF PAYMENTS
(K million)

	1977	1978	1979	1980
Merchandise exports f.o.b.	536.6	532.6	720.3	660.9
Merchandise imports f.o.b.	−442.3	−474.2	−557.8	−671.1
Balance of Trade	94.4	58.4	162.5	−10.2
Net invisibles	−157.1	−169.6	−220.0	−272.3
Net transfers	148.2	117.9	112.0	108.6
Balance on Current Account	85.5	6.8	54.5	−173.8
Balance on capital account	15.3	11.5	26.8	68.9
Net errors and omissions	−0.4	−20.1	−3.7	61.2
Changes in Reserves	110.4	−1.8	77.6	−54.4

EXTERNAL TRADE*

(K million, July 1st to June 30th)

	1973/74	1974/75	1975/76	1976/77	1977‡	1978‡	1979‡	1980‡	1981‡
Imports†	228.9	357.4	346.4	393.2	448.3	478.3	561.6	684.2	n.a.
Exports f.o.b.	482.1	420.1	361.8	515.1	571.4	550.4	686.9	691.7	568.1

* Figures include outside packaging and migrants' and travellers' dutiable effects but exclude gold, some parcel post and arms, ammunition and other equipment for military use.

† Imports are valued f.o.b. or at current domestic value in the exporting country, whichever is higher.

‡ Year ending December 31st.

PRINCIPAL COMMODITIES

(K '000)

Imports	1974/75	1975/76*	1980†
Food and live animals	71,364	73,088	133,176
Beverages and tobacco	5,597	5,810	8,690
Crude materials, except fuel	1,246	1,109	2,117
Mineral fuels, lubricants etc.	38,292	47,220	117,863
Animal and vegetable oils and fats	805	846	1,870
Chemicals	22,939	18,945	36,584
Basic manufactures	61,631	48,051	91,607
Machinery and transport equipment	112,151	109,192	206,330
Miscellaneous manufactured articles	30,117	27,992	52,891
Miscellaneous commodities and transactions	9,278	10,748	33,044

Exports	1979†	1980†	1981†
Copra	38,162	24,594	19,476
Cocoa beans	60,785	46,493	34,135
Coffee	125,003	118,643	74,217
Rubber	3,498	3,751	3,403
Tea	7,982	8,507	7,131
Timber (logs)	20,884	29,979	31,517
Plywood	3,293	2,520	3,000
Tuna	14,337	24,656	19,974
Crayfish and prawns	6,209	6,560	6,851
Copra oil	20,599	16,610	12,508
Palm oil	14,442	11,956	14,223
Copper ore and concentrates	288,064	313,264	292,977
Timber (lumber)	7,548	6,155	3,897

* Figures for 1977–79 are not available.

† Year ending December 31st.

PRINCIPAL TRADING PARTNERS

(K '000)

Imports	1975/76*	1980†
Australia	161,413	279,194
Germany, Fed. Republic	4,956	9,326
Hong Kong	8,959	15,282
Japan	49,980	123,481
Singapore	40,557	104,451
United Kingdom	18,327	28,673
U.S.A.	24,365	44,079

* Figures for 1977–79 are not available.

Exports (incl. gold)	1980†	1981†
Australia	104,552	65,192
Germany, Fed. Republic	173,429	125,082
Japan	241,428	211,714
Spain	25,092	31,280
United Kingdom	28,709	28,705
U.S.A.	22,713	19,649

† Year ending December 31st.

TRANSPORT

ROAD TRAFFIC

(licensed vehicles)

	1978	1979	1980
Cars and station wagons	17,150	17,730	18,481
Commercial vehicles	22,548	25,135	27,142
Motor cycles	2,892	2,860	2,351
Tractors	1,728	1,711	1,796

SHIPPING FREIGHT

		1976/77	1977/78	1978/79	1979†	1980†
Vessels entered	'000 gross reg. tons	4,788	4,205	4,661	4,266	4,964
Vessels cleared	,, ,, ,, ,,	4,455	4,188	4,701	4,222	4,966
Cargo unloaded	'000 metric tons	1,505*	n.a.	n.a.	n.a.	n.a.
Cargo loaded	,, ,, ,,	1,711*	n.a.	n.a.	n.a.	n.a.

* Figures for the calendar year ending December 31st, 1977.
† Figures for the calendar year ending December 31st.

CIVIL AVIATION

Internal Flights	1980	1981
Scheduled Services:		
Passengers embarked	229,530	223,605
Freight carried (kg.)	5,864,862	6,179,199
Mail carried (kg.)	747,854	703,404
Charter Services:		
Passengers embarked	1,483	1,590
Freight carried (kg.)	749,029	24,103
Mail carried (kg.)	5,099	483

Overseas Flights	1980	1981
Passengers embarked	87,226	85,070
Freight carried (kg.)	1,635,967	1,822,747
Mail carried (kg.)	236,046	299,876

EDUCATION

(1981)

	Schools	Pupils	Teachers
Community	2,118	299,588	9,507
Secondary	102	37,987	1,485
Technical	9	3,293	230
Vocational and other	133	15,675	788

Source (unless otherwise stated): Papua New Guinea Bureau of Statistics.

THE CONSTITUTION

A new constitution came into effect on September 16th, 1975, when Papua New Guinea became independent.

PREAMBLE

The national goals of the Independent State of Papua New Guinea are: integral human development, equality and participation in the development of the country, national sovereignty and self-reliance, conservation of natural resources and the environment and development primarily through the use of Papua New Guinean forms of social, political and economic organization.

BASIC RIGHTS

All people are entitled to the fundamental rights and freedoms of the individual whatever their race, tribe, places of origin, political opinion, colour, creed or sex. The individual's rights include the right to freedom, life and the protection of the law, freedom from inhuman treatment, forced labour, arbitrary search and entry, freedom of conscience, thought, religion, expression, assembly, association and employment, and the right to privacy. Papua New Guinea citizens also have the following special rights: the right to vote and stand for public office, the right to freedom of information and of movement, protection from unjust deprivation of property and equality before the law.

THE NATION

Papua New Guinea is a sovereign, independent state. There is a National Capital District which shall be the seat of government.

The Constitution provides for various classes of citizenship. The age of majority is 19 years.

HEAD OF STATE

Her Majesty the Queen of Great Britain and Northern Ireland is Queen and Head of State of Papua New Guinea. The Head of State appoints and dismisses the Prime Minister on the proposal of the National Parliament and other ministers on the proposal of the Prime Minister. The Governor-General, Chief Justice and members of the Public Services Commission are appointed and dismissed on the proposal of the National Executive Council. All the privileges, powers, functions, duties and responsibilities of the Head of State may be had, exercised or performed through the Governor-General.

GOVERNOR-GENERAL

The Governor-General must be a citizen who is qualified to be a member of Parliament or who is a mature person of good standing who enjoys the respect of the community. No one is eligible for appointment more than once unless Parliament approves by a two-thirds majority. No one is eligible for a third term. The Governor-General is appointed by the Head of State on the proposal of the National Executive Council in accordance with the decision of Parliament by simple majority vote. He may be dismissed by the Head of State on the proposal of the National Executive Council in accordance with a decision of the Council or of an absolute majority of Parliament. The normal term of office is six years. In the case of temporary or permanent absence, dismissal or suspension he may be replaced temporarily by the Speaker of the National Parliament until such time as a new Governor-General is appointed.

THE GOVERNMENT

The Government comprises the National Parliament, the National Executive and the National Judicial System.

National Parliament

The National Parliament, or the House of Assembly, is a single-chamber legislature of members elected from single-member open or provincial electorates and not more than three nominated members who are appointed on a two-thirds absolute majority vote of Parliament. The National Parliament has 109 members elected by universal adult suffrage. The normal term of office is five years. There is a Speaker and a Deputy Speaker, who must be members of Parliament and must be elected to these posts by Parliament. They cannot serve as Ministers concurrently.

National Executive

The National Executive comprises the Head of State and the National Executive Council. The Prime Minister, who presides over the National Executive Council, is appointed and dismissed by the Head of State on the proposal of Parliament. The other ministers, of whom there shall be not fewer than six nor more than a quarter of the number of members of the Parliament, are appointed and dismissed by the Head of State on the proposal of the Prime Minister. The National Executive Council consists of all the ministers, including the Prime Minister, and is responsible for the executive government of Papua New Guinea.

National Judicial System

The National Judicial System comprises the Supreme Court, the National Court and any other authorized courts. The judiciary is independent.

The Supreme Court consists of the Chief Justice, the Deputy Chief Justice and the other judges of the National Court. It is the final court of appeal. The Chief Justice is appointed and dismissed by the Head of State on the proposal of the National Executive Council after consultation with the Minister responsible for justice. The Deputy Chief Justice and the other judges are appointed by the Judicial and Legal Services Commission. The National Court consists of the Chief Justice, the Deputy Chief Justice and no less than four nor more than six other judges.

The Constitution also makes provision for the establishment of the Magisterial Service and the establishment of the posts of Public Prosecutor and the Public Solicitor.

THE STATE SERVICES

The Constitution establishes the following State Services which, with the exception of the Defence Force, are subject to ultimate civilian control.

National Public Service

The Public Service is managed by the Public Services Commission which consists of not fewer than four members appointed by the Head of State on the proposal of the National Executive Council. The Commission is responsible to the National Executive Council.

Police Force

The Police Force is subject to the control of the National Executive Council through a Minister and its function is to preserve peace and good order and to maintain and enforce the law.

Papua New Guinea Defence Force

There shall be no office of Commander-in-Chief of the Defence Force. The Defence Force is subject to the superintendence and control of the National Executive Council through the Minister of Defence. The functions of the Defence Force are to defend Papua New Guinea, to provide assistance to civilian authorities in a civil disaster, in the restoration of public order or during a period of declared national emergency.

The fourth State Service is the Parliamentary Service.

The Constitution also includes sections on Public Finances, the office of Auditor-General, the Public Accounts Commission and the Ombudsman Commission, and the declaration of a State of National Emergency.

THE GOVERNMENT

Head of State: H.M. Queen Elizabeth II.

Governor-General: Sir Tore Lokoloko, G.C.M.G., O.B.E. (took office March 1st, 1977).

NATIONAL EXECUTIVE COUNCIL

(August 1982)

Prime Minister: Michael Somare.

Deputy Prime Minister and Minister for Primary Industry and National Planning: Pius Wingti.

Minister for Transport and Civil Aviation: Matthew Bendum.

Minister for Foreign Affairs and Trade: Rabbie Mamalui.

Minister for Decentralization: John Milkare.

Minister for Education: Barry Hollowe.

Minister for Labour and Employment: Caspar Anggua.

Minister for Works and Supply: PATO KAKARAYA.

Minister for Correction Services and Liquor Licensing: PUNDIA KANGE.

Minister for Health: MARTIN TOVADEK.

Minister for Finance: PHILLIP BOURAGA.

Minister for Lands: BEBES KOROWARO.

Minister for Forests: LUCAS WAKA.

Minister for Police: JOHN GIHENA.

Minister for Urban Development: KALA SWOKIM.

Minister for Justice: TONY BAIS.

Minister for Defence: EPEL TITO.

Minister for the Media: BOYAMO SALI.

Minister for Home Affairs: ROY EVARA.

Minister for Culture and Tourism: MCKENZIE JAVOPA.

Minister for Religion, Youth and Recreation: TOM AWASA.

Minister for State Responsible for Parliamentary Service: Sir PITA LUS.

Minister for Public Utilities: MICHAEL PONDROS.

Minister for Commerce and Industry: KARL KITCHENS-STACK.

Minister for Environment and Conservation: HARALU MAI.

Minister of State responsible for Public Services: TONY SIAGURU.

Minister for Minerals and Energy: FRANCIS DIDIMAN.

LEGISLATURE

NATIONAL PARLIAMENT

Speaker: DENNIS YOUNG.

Nominated Members: None appointed (the Papua New Guinea Act provides for the appointment of up to 3).

Elected Members: 109 (89 represent open electorates and 20 represent provincial electorates). The last elections were held in June 1982.

POLITICAL PARTIES

Melanesian Alliance (MA): Port Moresby; f. 1978; socialist; Leaders Fr. JOHN MOMIS, JOHN KAPUTIN.

Melanesian People's Party: Port Moresby.

National Party (NP): Port Moresby; f. 1979; formerly People's United Front; Leader IAMBAKEY OKUK.

Pangu Pati: P.O.B. 623, Port Moresby; f. 1967; urban-based; Leader MICHAEL SOMARE.

Papua Action Party: Port Moresby; f. 1982; Leader SERE PETRI.

Papua Besena (PB): Port Moresby; republican; Leader GEREGA PEPENA.

Papuan National Alliance (PANAL): Port Moresby; f. 1980; regionally-based party whose objectives are to be reached within a united Papua New Guinea; Leader Mrs. CLOWES.

People's Christian Alliance: Port Moresby; f. 1981; Leader TOM KORAEA.

People's Progress Party (PPP): Port Moresby; f. 1970; Leader Rt. Hon. Sir JULIUS CHAN, P.C., K.B.E.; National Chair. HUDSON AREK.

United Party (UP): Port Moresby; f. 1969; was opposed to early independence and stands for retaining links with Australia; Leader RAPHAEL DOA; Parliamentary Leader ROY EVARA.

The Papuan republican movement comprises two major organizations: Papua Besena and the Eriwo Development Association, led by Simon Kaumi. Associated with the movement are the Papua Black Power Movement and the Socialist Workers' Party.

DIPLOMATIC REPRESENTATION

EMBASSIES AND HIGH COMMISSIONS ACCREDITED TO PAPUA NEW GUINEA

(HC) High Commission.

Australia: P.O.B. 9129, Hohola; *High Commissioner:* ROBERT N. BIRCH.

Austria: Canberra, A.C.T., Australia.

Belgium: Wellington, New Zealand.

Canada: Canberra, A.C.T., Australia (HC).

China, People's Republic: P.O.B. 1351, Boroko; *Ambassador:* GAO GUANGJUN.

Costa Rica: Tokyo, Japan.

Cyprus: Canberra, A.C.T., Australia (HC).

Denmark: Jakarta, Indonesia.

France: P.S.A. Building, Waigani, P.O.B. 3155, Port Moresby; *Ambassador:* ANTOINE COLOMBANI.

Germany, Federal Republic: P.O.B. 73, Port Moresby; *Ambassador:* B. OETTER.

Ghana: Canberra, A.C.T., Australia (HC).

Greece: Canberra, A.C.T., Australia.

Indonesia: P.O.B. 7165, Boroko; *Ambassador:* ABDUL AZIZ BUSTAM.

Israel: Canberra, A.C.T., Australia.

Japan: P.O.B. 3040, Port Moresby; *Ambassador:* TAKASHI SENGOKU.

Korea, Democratic People's Republic: Canberra, A.C.T., Australia.

Korea, Republic: P.O.B. 381, Port Moresby; *Ambassador:* CHU WONG WOON.

Luxembourg: Jakarta, Indonesia.

Malaysia: Jakarta, Indonesia (HC).

Mexico: Jakarta, Indonesia.

Netherlands: Wellington, New Zealand.

New Zealand: P.O.B. 1144, Boroko, Port Moresby; *High Commissioner:* TIM HANNAH.

Nigeria: Canberra, A.C.T., Australia (HC).

Norway: Canberra, A.C.T., Australia.

Pakistan: Jakarta, Indonesia.

Philippines: P.O.B. 5916, Boroko; *Chargé d'affaires a.i.:* LUIS G. MAGBANUA.

Singapore: Jakarta, Indonesia (HC).

Solomon Islands: Canberra, A.C.T., Australia (HC).

Thailand: Jakarta, Indonesia.

Turkey: Canberra, A.C.T., Australia.

United Kingdom: United Church Bldg., 3rd Floor, Douglas St., P.O.B. 739, Port Moresby; *High Commissioner:* ARTHUR J. COLLINS, O.B.E.

U.S.A.: P.O.B. 3492, Port Moresby; *Ambassador:* VIRGINIA SCHAFER.

Vatican City: P.O.B. 98, Port Moresby; *Apostolic Pro-Nuncio:* Mgr. FRANCESCO DE NITTIS.

Yugoslavia: Jakarta, Indonesia.

Papua New Guinea also has diplomatic relations with Argentina, Czechoslovakia, Egypt, Fiji, Finland, the German Democratic Republic, Hungary, India, Italy, Kiribati, Laos, Mongolia, Romania, Spain, Sweden, Switzerland, Tanzania, Tuvalu and the U.S.S.R.

JUDICIAL SYSTEM

Supreme Court of Papua New Guinea: Chief Justice The Hon. Sir BURI KIDU.

Registrar: HUBERT A. AOAE.

The Supreme Court is the highest judicial authority in the country. Appeals to it may be made from decisions of a single judge sitting as the National Court. District Courts deal with summary and non-indictable offences. In addition, Local Courts deal with minor offences, including matters regulated by native custom and are open to all races. They have limited jurisdiction in land matters. Wardens' Courts have jurisdiction over civil cases respecting mining or mining lands and offences against mining laws. Cases involving land are heard by the Land Titles Commission from which appeals lie to the National Court. Children's Courts deal with cases involving minors.

RELIGION

The belief in magic or sorcery is universal even among the significant proportion of the population that has adopted Christianity. The indigenous population is mainly pantheistic. There are many Missionary Societies.

ANGLICAN

Archbishop of Papua New Guinea: Most Rev. G. DAVID HAND, Box 806, Port Moresby.

ROMAN CATHOLIC

Archbishop of the Highlands: Most Rev. GEORGE BERNARDING.

Archbishop of Madang: Most Rev. LEO ARKFELD, C.B.E., Archbishop's Residence, P.O., Alexishafen, Madang.

Archbishop of Port Moresby: Most Rev. PETER KURONGKU, P.O.B. 82, Port Moresby.

Archbishop of Rabaul: Most Rev. Fr. ALBERT BUNDERVOET, M.S.C., Archbishop's House, P.O.B. 414, Rabaul.

UNITED CHURCH

The United Church in Papua New Guinea and Solomon Islands: P.O.B. 1401, Port Moresby; f. 1968 by union of the Methodist Church in Melanesia, the Papua Ekalesia and United Church, Port Moresby, a branch of the United Church of North Australia; Moderator Rev. ALBERT TO BURUA; 110,000 communicant mems.

LUTHERAN

Bishop of the Evangelical Lutheran Church of Papua New Guinea: Rt. Rev. GETAKE S. GAM; P.O.B. 80, Lae; 550,000 mems.; publ. *Niugini Luteran.*

Bishop of the Gutnius Lutheran Church of Papua New Guinea: Dr. T. W. WAESA; Good News Lutheran Church of Papua New Guinea, P.O.B. 111, Wabag, Enga Province; f. 1948; 57,000 mems.; Gen. Sec. MARK YAPAO; publs. *Enga News, Church Reports* (monthly).

SEVENTH-DAY ADVENTIST

Papua New Guinea Union Mission of the Seventh-day Adventist Church: P.O.B. 86, Lae; Pres. Pastor D. E. G. MITCHELL; Sec. Pastor C. M. WINCH; 86,500 adherents.

THE PRESS

Arawa Bulletin: P.O.B. 86, Arawa; weekly.

Education Gazette: Department of Education, Port Moresby; Editor LORRAINE WARD; circ. 8,000.

Hiri: Office of Information, P.O.B. 2312, Konedobu; monthly; official magazine of the PNG Government; in English; Editor RIC LARDIZABAL; circ. 4,000.

New Nation: P.O.B. 1982, Boroko; f. 1977; monthly magazine; English; readership mainly under 30; Publr. KEVIN WALCOT; Editor MARGARET KITCHEN; circ. 45,000.

Niugini Nius: P.O.B. 759, Lae; f. 1979; daily except Sat., Sun. and Mon.; English; Editor CHARLES CEPILUS; circ. 16,500.

Niugini Nius Weekender: P.O.B. 759, Lae; f. 1980; Sat.; English; Editor CHARLES CEPILUS; circ. 14,800.

Our News: Office of Information, Prime Minister's Department, P.O.B. 2312, Konedobu; f. 1958; fortnightly; Editor UME OFOI; in English, circ. 33,000; Pidgin, circ. 12,000; Hiri Motu, circ. 6,500.

Papua New Guinea Post-Courier: P.O.B. 85, Port Moresby; f. 1969; independent; daily; Gen. Man. WAYNE GRANT; Editor LUKE SELA; circ. 27,000.

The Times of Papua New Guinea: P.O.B. 1982, Boroko NCD; f. 1980; weekly; in English; Publr. KEVIN WALCOT; Editor FRANZALBERT JOKU; circ. 12,500.

Wantok: P.O.B. 1982, Boroko; f. 1970; weekly in New Guinea Pidgin; mainly rural readership; Publr. KEVIN WALCOT; Editor JIM FRANKS; circ 14,500.

There are numerous newspapers and magazines published by government departments, statutory organizations, missions, sporting organizations, local government councils and provincial governments. They are variously in English, Pidgin, Motu and vernacular languages.

PUBLISHERS

Gordon and Gotch (PNG) Pty. Ltd.: P.O.B. 3395, Port Moresby.

Scripture Union of Papua New Guinea: P.O.B. 280, University of Papua New Guinea; Bible reading notes.

Word Publishing Co. Pty. Ltd.: P.O.B. 1982, Boroko; f. 1970; Man. Dir. JOHN H. BEVERLEY; Editor-in-Chief ROWAN CALLICK.

RADIO

National Broadcasting Commission of Papua New Guinea: P.O.B. 1359, Boroko; f. 1973; broadcasting in English, Pidgin, Motu and 14 major vernaculars; Chair. LEO MORGAN.

The Papua New Guinea Service of Radio Australia is also received.

There were 125,000 radio sets in 1978.

FINANCE

BANKING

(cap.=capital; dep.=deposits; m.=million; brs.=branches; K=kina; p.u.=paid up)

CENTRAL BANK

Bank of Papua New Guinea: P.O.B. 121, Douglas St., Port Moresby; f. 1973; bank of issue; cap. K5m.; dep. K245m. (Dec. 1977); Gov. Sir HENRY TOROBERT; Deputy Gov. R. L. KNIGHT; Sec. L. KATIT (acting).

COMMERCIAL BANKS

Australia and New Zealand Banking Group (PNG) Limited: P.O.B. 3152, Port Moresby; Chief Man. M. J. FRENCH; 7 brs., 2 agencies.

Westpac Bank (P.N.G.) Ltd.: 5th Floor, Moguru Moto Bldg., Champion Parade, P.O.B. 706, Port Moresby; cap. p.u. K4.45m.; dep. K119.4m. (Sept. 1981); Chief Man. R. L. FROST; 17 brs.

Bank of South Pacific Ltd.: P.O.B. 173, Douglas St., Port Moresby; f. 1974; subsidiary of the National Bank of Australasia; cap. K2.3m.; Chair. Sir ROBERT LAW-SMITH, C.B.E., A.F.C.; Chief Man. E. K. FULWOOD; 7 brs.

Papua New Guinea Banking Corporation: P.O.B. 78, Port Moresby; f. 1974; cap. K10m.; dep. K219m. (May 1982); Man. Dir. H. G. EWING; Exec. Dir. H. T. FABILA; 19 brs.; publ. *Trends* (quarterly).

DEVELOPMENT BANK

Papua New Guinea Development Bank: P.O.B. 6310, Boroko; f. 1967; government statutory agency; cap. $A25.7m.; Chair. MEL TOGOLO; Man. Dir. VAI REVA.

SAVINGS AND LOAN SOCIETIES

Registry of Savings and Loan Societies: P.O.B. 121, Port Moresby; 119 savings and loan societies; 118,495 mems.; total funds K37,589,039, loans outstanding K28,128,080, investments K6,582,647 (Dec. 1980).

INSURANCE

There are branches of several of the principal Australian and United Kingdom insurance companies in Port Moresby, Rabaul, Lae and Kieta.

TRADE AND INDUSTRY

INDUSTRIAL AND DEVELOPMENT ORGANIZATIONS

Bougainville Copper Ltd.: Panguna, North Solomons Province; subsidiary of the Rio Tinto-Zinc group; Chair. D. C. VERNON.

Cocoa Industry Board of Papua New Guinea: P.O.B. 532, Rabaul; f. 1974.

Coffee Industry Board: P.O.B. 137, Goroka; Chair. ALBERT LLOYD HURRELL, C.M.G.

Copra Marketing Board: Port Moresby; markets all copra in Papua New Guinea; consists of a chairman and members representing producers, and the Department of Primary Industry; Chair. JIM GROSE.

Department of Commerce: P.O. Wards Strips, Waigani; f. 1971; government body to promote and assist the development of business and small-scale industrial activities by Papua New Guineans.

Department of Primary Industry: Port Moresby; aims to improve and to provide technical assistance for agriculture, fisheries and marine products, forestry and animal husbandry; also to encourage production of commodities for export.

Food Marketing Corporation Pty. Ltd.: P.O.B. 1811, Lae; f. 1976; Government-owned; handles distribution of fruit and vegetables throughout the country; 6 brs.; auth. cap. K5 million.

Higaturu Oil Palms Ltd.: P.O.B. 28, Popondetta, Northern Province; f. 1976; jointly owned by The Commonwealth Development Corpn. (U.K.) and the Papua New Guinea Government; major producer of palm oil.

Investment Corporation: Hunter St., P.O.B. 155, Port Moresby; f. 1975; government body formed to support local enterprise and to purchase shares in foreign businesses operating in Papua New Guinea.

National Investment and Development Authority (NIDA): f. 1975; a statutory body charged with the promotion, supervision and regulation of foreign investment; the first contact point for foreign investors for advice on project proposals and approvals of applications for registration to carry on business in the country; NIDA contributes to planning for investment and recommends priority areas for investment to the Government; also co-ordinates the evaluation and registration of investment proposals; Chair. MEKERE MORAUTA; Exec. Dir. JOSEPH AUNA.

New Britain Palm Oil Development Ltd.: Kimbe, West New Britain; f. 1967; jointly owned by the Government and Harrisons and Crosfield (London); major producer and processor of palm oil and supplier of high quality oil palm seed; Gen. Man. J. A. VUGTS.

Pita Lus National Silk Institute: Kagamuga, Mt. Hagen; f. 1978; Government silk-producing project.

CHAMBERS OF COMMERCE

Port Moresby Chamber of Commerce and Industry: P.O.B. 1764, Port Moresby.

Papua New Guinea Chamber of Commerce and Industry: P.O.B. 265, Lae.

TRADE UNIONS

The Industrial Organizations Ordinance requires all industrial organizations which consist of no fewer than twenty employees or four employers to register. In 1977 there were 56 registered industrial organizations, including a general employee group registered as a workers' association in each province and also unions covering a specific industry or profession.

Papua New Guinea Trade Union Congress: P.O.B. 1103, Lae; Pres. TONY ILA, M.P.; Sec. PAUL WANI.

The following are amongst the major occupational organizations:

Bougainville Mining Workers' Union: P.O.B. 777, Panguna, North Solomons Province; Pres. HENRY MOSES.

Central Province Building and Construction Industry Workers' Union: P.O.B. 265, Port Moresby.

Central Province Transport Drivers' and Workers Union: P.O.B. 265, Port Moresby.

Employers' Federation of Papua New Guinea: P.O.B. 490, Port Moresby; f. 1963; Pres. D. N. HARVEY; Exec. Dir. M. W. WELLS, M.B.E.; 80 mems.; publ. *Monthly Bulletin*.

Papua New Guinea Journalists' Association: P.O.B. 1359, Boroko; f. 1977; Pres. TARCISSIUS BOBOLA; Sec. JOHN HARANGU.

Papua New Guinea Teachers' Association: P.O.B. 6546, Boroko; f. 1971; Pres. P. KEAGA; Nat. Sec. M. BOLA; 10,500 mems., publs. *Teacher* and a newsletter.

Papua New Guinea Waterside Workers' and Seamen's Union: Port Moresby; f. 1979 as a result of the amalgamation of four unions.

Police Association of Papua New Guinea: P.O.B. 903, Port Moresby; f. 1964; Pres. Sergeant Maj. SEMEL BUKA; Gen. Sec. JOHN A. SHIELDS; 4,596 mems.; publ. *Kumul*.

Port Moresby Council of Trade Unions: P.O.B. 265, Boroko; Gen. Sec. JOHN KOSI.

Port Moresby Miscellaneous Workers' Union: P.O.B. 265, Boroko.

Printing and Kindred Industries Union: Port Moresby.

Public Employees Association: P.O.B. 6091, Boroko; f. 1974; 28,000 mems.; Pres. NAPOLEON LIOSI; Gen. Sec. KAPIA ARIA.

MAJOR INDUSTRIAL COMPANIES

GENERAL

Kagamuga Natural Products Co. Pty. Ltd.: P.O.B. 74, Mt. Hagen; pyrethrum extract, soft drinks.

Port Moresby Freezing Co. Ltd.: P.O.B. 4105, Badili; aerated water, cordials, fruit juice extracts, soft drinks, sausages and small food goods; ice; joinery products.

Steamships Trading Co. Ltd.: P.O.B. 1, Port Moresby; ship repairs; steel fabrications, tanks, sheet metal products, refrigeration, industrial gases; milled timber, joinery products; coffee processing, aerated water, soft drinks, hotels, department stores, food wholesale and retail, stevedoring, shipping and road transport.

Watkins PNG Ltd.: P.O.B. 1393, Boroko; aluminium extruded shapes and buildings; concrete blocks; milled timber, joinery products; household furniture, furnishings, floor coverings.

FOOD, DRINK AND TOBACCO

Associated Mills Ltd.: P.O.B. 1906, Lae; flour milling.

W. R. Carpenter & Co. Estates: P.O.B. 94, Mount Hagen; cocoa, coffee and tea processing.

San Miguel (PNG) Ltd.: P.O.B. 6022, Boroko; f. 1972; beer; Man. Dir. P. TELESCO.

South Pacific Brewery Ltd.: P.O.B. 6550, Boroko; lager.

Star-Kist PNG Pty. Ltd.: P.O.B. 1341, Rabaul; fish processing.

Tanubada Dairy Products Pty. Ltd.: P.O.B. 6203, Boroko; reconstituted milk, ice cream, ice confection, orange drinks.

W. D. & H. O. Wills (PNG) Ltd.: P.O.B. 50, Port Moresby; cigarettes and tobacco.

MINERALS AND HEAVY ENGINEERING

Barclay Bros. (NG) Pty. Ltd.: P.O.B. 277, Lae; all types of civil engineering and building construction.

Bougainville Copper Ltd.: (*see* Industrial and Development Organizations above).

Monier (PNG) Ltd.: P.O.B. 328, Port Moresby; concrete pipes, masonry blocks and roofing tiles, cement supplies, pre-cast concrete, sand and gravel; paints; fibreglass and plastic products.

Naco (N.G.) Pty. Ltd.: P.O.B. 707, Port Moresby; aluminium windows and sliding doors, louvre windows and metal blades.

N.G.I. Steel: P.O.B. 672, Lae; pre-fabricated buildings, bridges, tubular fabrications, plant hire.

TIMBER AND PALM OIL

ANG Timbers Pty. Ltd.: P.O.B. 1984, Boroko; milled timber, mouldings, scantling, flooring, pre-cut buildings, joinery products; electric power generation; ice and oxygen.

Higaturu Oil Palms Pty. Ltd.: P.O.B. 28, Popondetta; palm oil.

Jant Pty. Ltd.: P.O.B. 714, Madang; wood chips, milled timber.

Mosa Oil Mill Pty. Ltd.: (*see* New Britain Palm Oil Development Ltd. under Industrial and Development Organizations).

Open Bay Timber Pty. Ltd.: P.O.B. 1020, Rabaul; milled timber, mouldings, scantlings.

PNG Forest Products Pty. Ltd.: P.O.B. 89, Lae; plywood, mouldings, milled timber, furniture.

CHEMICALS

C.I.G. New Guinea Pty. Ltd.: P.O.B. 93, Lae; industrial gases, carbon dioxide dry ice, solid carbon dioxide, compressed or liquefied oxygen, acetylene gas, nitrogen, anaesthetic; germicides, disinfectants, water treating compounds.

ICI New Guinea Pty. Ltd.: P.O.B. 1105, Lae; industrial, agricultural and domestic chemicals, public health products.

Melanesian Soap Products Pty. Ltd.: P.O.B. 981, Lae; soap.

Shell Papua New Guinea Pty. Ltd.: P.O.B. 169, Port Moresby; fuel, agricultural and industrial chemicals.

TRANSPORT

ROADS

In 1981 there were 18,500 km. of roads in Papua New Guinea, of which 4,800 km. were classified as highways or trunk roads and 1,020 km. as urban roads. Work was in progress in 1981 to complete a transnational highway linking Port Moresby with the Highlands and the north coast. The 1978 budget provided K16.08 million for roads.

SHIPPING

Papua New Guinea has 16 major ports and a coastal fleet of about 300 vessels.

New Guinea Australasia Line Pty. Ltd.: P.O.B. 145, James Building, Corner of Stanley Esplanade and Cuthbertson St., Port Moresby; operates regular container services from Australia to Papua New Guinea and Solomon Islands; Chair. E. J. R. SCOTT.

Papua New Guinea Shipping Corporation: f. 1977; Government-owned; operates two PNG Line (PNGL) vessels, providing a container service to the West coast of North America calling at Honiara (Solomon Islands) and Tarawa (Kiribati); two-monthly service to Darwin, Australia; owns P.N.G. Mainport Liner Services Pty. Ltd., operating four coastal semi-container cargo liners, and P.N.G. Offshore Tug & Salvage; managing agents for Pacific Forum Line in P.N.G.; Chair. G. T. BLACKER, M.B.E.; Man. Dir. Capt. P. H. KING; Gen. Man. (Coastal) T. MILLER-MCCALL.

Papua Shipping and Stevedoring Co.: operates a shipping service, stevedoring and the delivery of cargo between Papua New Guinea, the Pacific region and other overseas ports.

Shipping companies operating container/break bulk services to Papua New Guinea include NGAL/PNGL/CONPAC consortium every 9 days from Australia and Solomon Islands; Niugini Express Lines (2 a month) and Karlander New Guinea Line (monthly) from Australia; Bank Line, which operates 28-day services from the U.K. and Continent via Pacific Islands and returning via Mediterranean; China Navigation Co., which operates a monthly service from the Philippines, Hong Kong, Taiwan and Singapore to several Pacific islands; Sofrana-Unilines, which connects Papua New Guinea with Solomon Islands and New Zealand; Pacific Forum Lines, monthly from New Zealand via Fiji; NYK Line and Mitsui-OSK operates a 20-day service from Japan; Daiwa Line operates a monthly service from Australia and Pacific Islands.

CIVIL AVIATION

There is an international airport at Port Moresby and over 400 other airports and airstrips throughout the country.

Air Niugini: P.O.B. 7186, Boroko; f. 1973; the national airline, owned by the Government; operates scheduled internal cargo and passenger services from Port Moresby to 19 destinations in Papua New Guinea and international services to Brisbane, Cairns and Sydney (Australia), Tokyo (Japan), Irian Jaya (Indonesia), Solomon Islands,the Philippines, Hong Kong and Singapore; Chair. B. SABUMEI; Gen. Man. J. J. TAUVASA; fleet of 4 Boeing 707-338C, Fokker F-27, 4 Fokker F-28, 3 de Havilland DHC-7; publ. *Paradise* (monthly).

Douglas Airways Pty. Ltd.: P.O.B. 1179, Boroko; internal services; Man. Dir. DENNIS DOUGLAS; fleet of 10 Britten Norman, 3 Beech Baron, 2 Partenaria, 2 Nomad, 1 Cessna 206, 1 Beech Queenair.

Talair Pty. Ltd.: P.O.B. 108, Goroka; f. 1952; regular services to 267 destinations in Papua New Guinea; Man. Dir. R. D. BUCHANAN, M.B.E.; Gen. Man. Capt. H. O. TSCHUCHNIGG, M.B.E.; fleet of 4 Embraer Bandeirante, 8 Twin Otters, 1 Queenair, 10 Cessna 402, 9 Beech-Barons, 22 BN2 Islanders, 3 Cessna 207, 6 Cessna 206, 1 Cessna 185, 1 Pilatus Porter.

FOREIGN AIRLINES

Papua New Guinea is also served by PAL (Philippines), Qantas (Australia) and Solair (Solomon Islands).

TOURISM AND CULTURE

National Cultural Council: P.O.B. 7144, Boroko; Chair. JOHN KASAIPWALOVA.

National Theatre Company: P.O.B. 239, University, N.C.D.; f. 1977; Dir. ARTHUR JAWODIMBARI.

DEFENCE

On March 6th, 1975, the Papua New Guinea Government assumed responsibility for defence from the Australian Government. In July 1981 the Papua New Guinea Defence force had a total strength of 3,500.

The fully integrated units consist of a land element with three battalions. The maritime element is equipped with five Attack class patrol boats. The air element has six DC-3 and two Nomad aircraft.

Commander of Papua New Guinea Defence Force: (vacant).

EDUCATION

Education from pre-school to tertiary level is available in Papua New Guinea although facilities are still inadequate and unevenly distributed. In 1981 there were 2,118 community schools, 102 secondary schools and 142 technical, vocational and other schools. There are two universities.

Children attend school from the age of seven. At the age of thirteen they move from Community schools to Provincial High Schools for a further three years and are then eligible to spend another two years at the National High Schools where they are prepared for entrance to tertiary education. Originally schooling was free but in recent years fees and charges for equipment have been introduced.

An average of 58 per cent of primary school age children attend school. In some areas, such as East New Britain and Port Moresby, almost all children attend school whereas in others, such as the Highlands provinces, as few as 34 per cent do. Access to higher education ranges from 7 per cent in the Eastern Highlands to almost 50 per cent in East New Britain.

Estimated expenditure on education in 1982 was K101.1 million. In 1976 a Five-Year Education Plan was adopted which provides for six years of primary and four to six years of secondary schooling.

Pitcairn Islands

The Pitcairn Islands consist of Pitcairn Island and three uninhabited islands, Henderson, Ducie and Oeno. Pitcairn, situated at 25°04'S. and 130°06'W. and about halfway between Panama and New Zealand, has an area of 4.5 sq. km. (1.75 sq. miles) and a population of 54 in 1982. The economy is based on subsistence agriculture, fishing, handicrafts and the sale of postage stamps. New Zealand currency is used. The Pitcairn Islands are administered by the British High Commission in New Zealand, with the High Commissioner acting as Governor, in consultation with an Island Council of four elected, five nominated and one *ex officio* members.

THE GOVERNMENT

(July 1982)

Governor: R. J. STRATTON, C.M.G. (British High Commissioner in New Zealand).

ISLAND COUNCIL

Island Magistrate: IVAN CHRISTIAN.

Island Secretary (*ex officio*): BEN CHRISTIAN.

Members: CHARLES CHRISTIAN, VULA YOUNG, THELMA BROWN, STEVE CHRISTIAN, JAY WARREN, TOM CHRISTIAN, Pastor T. PETTY, A. K. COX.

PRESS

There is one monthly four-page mimeographed news sheet, *Pitcairn Miscellany*, first published in 1959 and edited by the Education Officer. Circulation was 800 in 1982.

TRANSPORT

There are approximately 6.4 km. each of dirt road suitable for four-wheeled vehicles and of dirt track suitable for two-wheeled vehicles. In 1982 there were 25 motor cycles, three light jeeps and two tractors; traditional wheelbarrows are still used occasionally.

EDUCATION

Education was made compulsory for all children from 5 to 15 years in 1838. A New Zealand teacher is appointed for a two-year term as Education Officer. Bursaries enable students of post-primary age to attend school in New Zealand if they wish.

Solomon Islands

PHYSICAL AND SOCIAL GEOGRAPHY

Solomon Islands (formerly the British Solomon Islands Protectorate) is a scattered Melanesian archipelago in the south-western Pacific Ocean, east of Papua New Guinea. The country includes most of the Solomon Islands (those to the north-west being part of Papua New Guinea), Ontong Java Islands (Lord Howe Atoll), Rennell Island and the Santa Cruz Islands, about 500 km. (300 miles) to the east. There are 21 large islands and many small ones. The principal islands, all in the main group, are Choiseul, Santa Isabel, New Georgia, Malaita, Guadalcanal and San Cristobal. The climate is equatorial, with small seasonal variations governed by the trade winds. Much of the territory remains under dense tropical rainforest; extensive tracts of native and introduced grassland cover the northern plains of Guadalcanal. The total population at the 1976 census was 196,823, including 1,359 Europeans, 452 Chinese, 2,753 Micronesians resettled from Kiribati, formerly the Gilbert Islands, and 7,821 Polynesians from the Polynesian "outliers" in the western Pacific near the Solomons. The rate of population growth is estimated to be over 3 per cent per year. The capital is Honiara on the island of Guadalcanal.

HISTORY

First European contacts with the island economy in the 1500s caused little change. It was not until the nineteenth century that traders, whalers and missionaries began to establish outposts on the main islands. Forcible recruiting of labour spread from the New Hebrides (now Vanuatu) to the Solomon Islands during the 1860s.

The northern Solomon Islands became a German protectorate in 1885 and the southern Solomons a British protectorate in 1893. Rennell Island and the Santa Cruz Islands were added to the British protectorate in 1898 and 1899. Germany ceded most of the northern Solomons and Ontong Java Islands to the United Kingdom between 1898 and 1900. The whole territory, known as the British Solomon Islands Protectorate, was placed under the jurisdiction of the Western Pacific High Commission (WPHC), with its headquarters in Fiji. The High Commissioner for the Western Pacific was represented locally by a Resident Commissioner.

The Solomon Islands were invaded by Japan in 1942 but, after a fierce battle on Guadalcanal, most of the islands were recaptured by U.S. forces in 1943. After the Second World War the protectorate's capital was moved from Tulagi Island to Honiara. In January 1953 the headquarters of the WPHC also moved to Honiara. Meanwhile, elected local councils were established on most of the islands and by 1966 almost the whole territory was covered by such councils.

Under a new constitution, introduced in October 1960, a Legislative Council and an Executive Council were established for the protectorate's central administration. Initially, all members of both bodies were appointed but from 1964 the Legislative Council included elected members and the elective element was gradually increased. Another constitution, introduced in March 1970, established a single Governing Council of 17 elected members, three *ex officio* members and (until the end of 1971) up to six public service members. A new Governing Council of 24 directly elected members was formed in 1973, when a ministerial system was introduced.

A further new constitution, adopted in April 1974, instituted a single Legislative Assembly with 24 members who chose a Chief Minister with the right to appoint his own Council of Ministers. A new office of Governor of the Protectorate was also created to assume almost all the functions previously exercised in the territory by the High Commissioner for the Western Pacific. Solomon Mamaloni, leader of the newly founded People's Progress Party, was appointed the first Chief Minister in August 1974. The territory was officially renamed the Solomon Islands in June 1975, although it retained protectorate status.

In January 1976 the Solomon Islands received internal self-government, with the Chief Minister presiding over the Council of Ministers in place of the Governor. In June elections were held for an enlarged Legislative Assembly and in July the Assembly elected one of its new members, Peter Kenilorea, to be Chief Minister. Following a constitutional conference in London in September 1977, Solomon Islands (as it was restyled) became an independent state, within the Commonwealth, on July 7th 1978. The Legislative Assembly became the National Parliament and designated Kenilorea the first Prime Minister.

After re-election in 1980, Kenilorea resigned and was replaced by Solomon Mamaloni in August 1981. Mamaloni proposed a Programme of Action which includes a study aimed at turning the country into a republic, the formation of a Melanesian Alliance with Papua New Guinea and Vanuatu, the expansion of the defence force, and the establishment of a central bank to replace the monetary authority.

ECONOMIC SURVEY

About 90 per cent of the population depend on subsistence agriculture, the main crops being coconuts, sweet potatoes, taro, yams, cassava, garden vegetables and fruit. Fishing is also a traditional subsistence activity. The principal commercial agricultural product is copra, which was for many years the islands' main export. About 70 per cent of the country's copra production comes from smallholders and co-operatives, and the rest from plantations. A record crop of 33,673 metric tons was produced in 1981. Rice is also exported.

Since the 1960s the economy has been successfully diversified away from dependence on copra exports. In 1980 fish accounted for 38 per cent of total export earnings while timber contributed almost 25 per cent, copra 17 per cent and palm oil a further 9 per cent. By 1978 the British Government had provided $A7.5 million to enable the Solomon Islands Government to buy shares in the Commonwealth Development Corporation oil palm project and in the Japanese skipjack tuna fishing, freezing and canning company, Solomon Taiyo Limited, operating in the islands. The Government also had its own fishing project, the National Fisheries Development Company. A U.S. company has invested U.S. $8 million is a wet rice project and a large rice mill on the North Guadalcanal Plains.

A heavy mineralized area at Betilonga and in the Sutakiki Valley, on Guadalcanal, has been investigated for gold, silver and copper, and there have been surveys of phosphate deposits, estimated at 10 million metric tons, on Bellona Island and of deposits of asbestos at Kumboro, on Choiseul, and high-grade bauxite on Rennell and Vaghena Islands.

Until independence, aid was mainly from the United Kingdom, Australia, and New Zealand, although Solomon

Islands also received multilateral aid from the Asian Development Bank, the European Development Fund, the UN and its agencies and the IMF which increased after 1978. The British Government agreed to provide a £23 million post-independence financial settlement over four years.

The islands' transport facilities are seriously inadequate, which hampers agricultural and economic development, but the Government is trying to minimize these problems by emphasizing decentralized rural development to prevent a population drift to the capital. In the 1975–79 Development Plan, the Government allocated almost half of public capital expenditure to economic infrastructure projects. These were mainly road construction, the expansion and modernization of the Government shipping fleet and the construction of wharves and telecommunications, as well as a hydro-electric scheme on the Lungga River on Guadalcanal. The 1980–84 Development Plan also gave priority to the country's infrastructure, as well as to education and to general rural development.

STATISTICAL SURVEY

AREA AND POPULATION

Area	Population							Density (per sq. km.)
	Census results				Official estimates (mid-year)			
	Feb. 7th, 1970	Feb. 7th, 1976						
		Males	Females	Total	1979	1980	1981	1981
27,556 sq. km.*	160,998	102,808	94,015	196,823	221,000	228,000	234,000	8.5

* 10,639 square miles.

Capital: Honiara, population 18,346 at census of October 1979; 1981 estimate: 20,842.

ETHNIC GROUPS
(Population at 1976 Census)

Melanesians	183,665	Europeans	1,359
Polynesians	7,821	Chinese	452
Micronesians	2,753	Others	773

EMPLOYMENT
(wage-earners only, 1980)

Agriculture, forestry and fishing	6,833
Mining and manufacturing	2,082
Electricity and water	254
Construction	1,824
Wholesale and retail trade	1,863
Transport and communications	1,439
Financial services	303
Social and personal services	5,767
Total	20,365

AGRICULTURE

PRINCIPAL CROPS
(metric tons)

	1978	1979	1980
Copra	27,529	33,616	29,169
Cocoa	235	309	346
Rice (paddy)	7,658	10,224	14,256
Palm oil	10,911	13,010	14,228

LIVESTOCK
(head)

	1978	1979	1980
Cattle	25,185	22,584	22,995

FORESTRY

ROUNDWOOD REMOVALS
('000 cubic metres, excluding bark)

	1977	1978	1979
Industrial wood:			
Coniferous	13	16	6
Broadleaved	273	233	296
Fuel wood (all broad-leaved)*	198	204	210
TOTAL	484	453	512

* FAO estimates.

Source: FAO, *Yearbook of Forest Products.*

1980: Industrial wood 299,000 cubic metres.

SEA FISHING

('000 metric tons, live weight)

	1977	1978	1979
Skipjack tuna	13.0	17.5	23.8
Other marine fishes	2.3	2.9	3.8
Other aquatic animals	0.4	0.3	0.4
TOTAL CATCH	15.8	20.7	28.0

Source: FAO, *Yearbook of Fishery Statistics.*

FINANCE

100 cents=1 Solomon Islands dollar (SI$).
Coins: 1, 2, 5, 10 and 20 cents; 1 and 10 dollars.
Notes: 2, 5, 10 and 20 dollars.

Exchange rates (June 1982): £1 sterling=SI$1.620; U.S. $1=93.5 SI cents.
SI$100=£61.74=U.S. $106.93.

Note: The Solomon Islands dollar was introduced in October 1977, replacing (at par) the Australian dollar. The average value of the Solomon Islands dollar was: U.S. $1.1089 in 1977; U.S. $1.1446 in 1978. The parity with Australian currency was maintained until May 1979, when the Solomon Islands dollar was revalued to $A1.05. The direct link with Australian currency was ended in October 1979, since when the value of the Solomon Islands dollar has been determined in relation to a weighted "basket" of the currencies of the country's principal trading partners. Its average value was: U.S. $1.1545 in 1979; U.S. $1.1955 in 1980. For details of previous changes in the exchange rate, *see* the chapter on Australia.

BUDGET
(SI$ million)

	1978	1979	1980	1981*
Revenue	15.2	22.5	27.0	34.8
Overseas aid	13.6	11.0	13.0	23.5
Expenditure	30.6	37.3	45.1	61.3

* Revised estimates.

DEVELOPMENT EXPENDITURE
(SI$ '000)

	1979	1980
Development Sector:		
Natural resources	5,500	6,500
Commerce and industry	1,800	4,500
Economic infrastructure	13,300	14,200
Social Sector:		
Education	4,300	5,100
Health	3,000	4,100
Culture and welfare	500	900
Administrative sector	8,900	9,900
TOTAL	37,300	45,100

COST OF LIVING

Consumer Price Index for Honiara

(Base: 1977=100)

	1978	1979	1980	1981
Food . . .	107.4	115.9	133.4	160.0
Housing and utilities	103.2	108.4	119.4	130.6
Clothing . . .	102.1	104.0	108.7	115.8
All Items . .	107.0	114.8	129.7	151.1

EXTERNAL TRADE

(SI$ '000)

	1977	1978	1979	1980	1981
Imports f.o.b.	25,753	30,879	50,574	61,545	66,000
Exports f.o.b.	29,614	32,960	59,260	60,797	57,600

PRINCIPAL COMMODITIES

(SI$'000)

Imports	1979	1980
Food and live animals .	6,400	6,600
Beverages and tobacco	1,900	1,800
Crude materials (inedible) except fuels	200	400
Mineral fuels, lubricants, etc.	6,500	9,900
Animal and vegetable oils and fats	600	400
Chemicals	3,300	3,200
Basic manufactures	8,800	10,200
Machinery and transport equipment	18,900	24,100
Miscellaneous manufactured articles	3,700	4,700
Other commodities and transactions	200	200
Total	50,600	61,500

Exports	1978	1979	1980
Fish . .	7,296	16,900	23,200
Copra . .	7,856	16,100	10,500
Timber (logs) . .	6,837	14,700	14,900
Sea shells . .	165	178	326
Cocoa	596	600	600
Tobacco	94	67	132
Rice and rice products	n.a.	1,000	1,500
Gold	n.a.	200	600
Palm oil and kernels .	5,074	7,200	7,100
Others . . .	2,669	2,600	2,400
Total .	30,594	59,300	60,800

EDUCATION

(1980)

	Schools	Pupils
Primary:		
Government	299	25,153
Private	71	3,717
Secondary	15	3,547
Overseas centres	—	245*

* Figure is for 1979.

Source (unless otherwise stated): Statistics Office, Honiara.

THE CONSTITUTION

A new constitution came into effect on July 7th, 1978, when Solomon Islands became independent.

The main provisions are that Solomon Islands is a constitutional monarchy with the British sovereign (represented locally by a Governor-General, who must be a Solomon Islands citizen) as Head of State, while legislative power is vested in the unicameral National Parliament composed of 38 members, elected by universal adult suffrage for four years (subject to dissolution), and executive authority is effectively held by the Cabinet, led by the Prime Minister. The Governor-General is appointed for up to five years, on the advice of Parliament, and acts in almost all matters on the advice of the Cabinet. The Prime Minister is elected by and from members of Parliament. Other Ministers are appointed by the Governor-General, on the Prime Minister's recommendation, from members of Parliament. The Cabinet is responsible to Parliament. Emphasis is laid on the devolution of power to proposed provincial governments, and traditional chiefs and leaders have a special role within these arrangements.

The constitution contains comprehensive guarantees of fundamental human rights and freedoms, and provides for the introduction of a "leadership code" and the appointment of an Ombudsman and a Public Solicitor. It also provides for "the establishment of the underlying law, based on the customary law and concepts of the Solomon Islands people". Solomon Islands citizenship was automatically conferred on the indigenous people of the islands and on other residents with close ties with the islands upon independence. The acquisition of land is reserved for indigenous inhabitants or their descendants.

THE GOVERNMENT

Head of State: H.M. Queen ELIZABETH II.

Governor-General: Sir BADDELEY DEVESI, G.C.M.G. (took office July 7th, 1978).

THE CABINET
(July 1982)

Prime Minister and Minister for Provincial Affairs (Guadalcanal): Hon. SOLOMON MAMALONI (PAP).

Deputy Prime Minister and Minister for Home Affairs and National Development: Hon. KAMILO TEKE (PAP).

Minister for Finance: Hon. BARTHOLOMEW ULUFA'ALU (NADEPA).

Minister for Police and Justice: Hon. PAUL KEYAUNI (PAP).

Minister for Education and Training and Acting Minister for Foreign Affairs and International Trade: Hon. MICHAEL EVO (Independent).

Minister for Land, Energy and Natural Resources: Hon. PETER SALAKA (Independent).

Minister for Employment, Youth and Social Development: Hon. GEORGE MILTON TALASASA (PAP).

Minister for Transport, Communications and Government Utilities: Hon. JOHN NGINA (PAP).

Minister for Health and Medical Services: Hon. GEORGE SURI (Independent).

Minister for Provincial Affairs (Western): (vacant).

Minister for Provincial Affairs (Malaita): Hon. ADRIAN BATAIOFESI (NADEPA).

Minister for Provincial Affairs (Central Islands and Ysabel): Hon. RICHARD HARPER (PAP).

Minister for Provincial Affairs (Makula and Temotu): Hon. ATABAN TROPA (PAP).

LEGISLATURE

NATIONAL PARLIAMENT

The 38-member National Parliament, established following independence in July 1978, succeeded the former Legislative Assembly. Elections are held every four years. In the August 1980 elections for the National Parliament the majority of candidates stood as independents. A majority of those elected chose Peter Kenilorea to be Prime Minister, but in August 1981 voted to replace him by Solomon Mamaloni. The Government is a coalition of the People's Alliance Party, the National Democratic Party and the Independents.

Speaker: MAEPEZA GINA, C.B.E.

Leader of the Official Opposition: Sir PETER KENILOREA, K.B.E.

Leader of the Independent Members: FRANCIS BILLY HILLY.

POLITICAL PARTIES

Political parties are not very influential in Solomon Islands politics. The following parties represent the main groupings:

National Democratic Party (NADEPA): Honiara; f. 1976; Leader BARTHOLOMEW ULUFA'ALU.

People's Alliance Party (PAP): P.O.B. 722, Honiara; f. 1979; a coalition of the People's Progressive Party and the Rural Alliance Party; Leader SOLOMON MAMALONI; Sec. E. KINGMELE.

Solomon Islands United Party (SIUPA): Honiara; f. 1979; Leader Sir PETER KENILOREA, K.B.E.

DIPLOMATIC REPRESENTATION

EMBASSIES AND HIGH COMMISSIONS ACCREDITED TO SOLOMON ISLANDS

(HC) High Commission.

Australia: Hongkong and Shanghai Bank Bldg., Mendana Ave., P.O.B. 589, Honiara; *High Commissioner:* TREVOR SOFIELD.

Belgium: Wellington, New Zealand.

Canada: Canberra, A.C.T., Australia (HC).

France: Port Vila, Vanuatu.

Germany, Federal Republic: Port Moresby, Papua New Guinea.

Japan: Port Moresby, Papua New Guinea.

Korea, Republic: Canberra, A.C.T., Australia.

New Zealand: Honiara; *High Commissioner:* MARY CHAMBERLIN.

Papua New Guinea: Honiara; *High Commissioner:* JACOB KAIRI.

Sweden: Canberra, A.C.T., Australia.

Turkey: Canberra, A.C.T., Australia.

United Kingdom: Soltel House, Mendana Ave., P.O.B. 676, Honiara; *High Commissioner:* GEORGE N. STANSFIELD.

U.S.A.: Port Moresby, Papua New Guinea.

Solomon Islands also has diplomatic relations with Kiribati.

JUDICIAL SYSTEM

The High Court is a Superior Court of Record with jurisdiction and powers as prescribed by the Solomon Islands Constitution or by any law for the time being in force in Solomon Islands. The Judges of the High Court are the Chief Justice, resident in Solomon Islands and employed by its government, and Puisne Judges, who are non-resident and visit the territory as and when necessary. Appeals from this Court go to the Fiji Court of Appeal.

In addition there are Magistrates' Courts staffed by qualified and lay magistrates exercising limited jurisdiction in both civil and criminal matters. There are also Local Courts staffed by elders of the local communities which have jurisdiction in the areas of established native custom, petty crime and local government by-laws. In 1975 Customary Land Appeal Courts were established to hear land appeals from local courts.

Chief Justice of the High Court: Hon. FRANCIS DALY.

Registrar of the High Court: DAVID CROME.

RELIGION

Over 95 per cent of the people are Christian, and the remainder follow traditional beliefs. According to the census of 1976, about 33 per cent of the population adhered to the Church of Melanesia (Anglican), 19 per cent were Roman Catholics, 17 per cent belonged to the South Seas Evangelical Church, 11 per cent to the United Church and 10 per cent supported the Seventh-Day Adventists.

Assembly of God: Honiara; f. 1971; Gen. Superintendent Rev. S. MAKINI.

Christian Fellowship Church: Church, Paradise, P.O. Munda, Western Province; f. 1960; over 4,800 mems. in 24 villages; runs 5 primary schools; Leader: Holy Mama (SILAS ETO).

Church of Melanesia (Anglican): P.O.B. 19, Honiara; Archbishop of the Province of Melanesia: The Most Rev. N. K. PALMER, C.M.G., M.B.E.

Roman Catholic: Archdiocese of Honiara, P.O.B. 237, Honiara; Archbishop of Honiara: His Grace Archbishop DANIEL STUYVENBERG, C.B.E.

Seventh Day Adventist: Honiara; Pres. of Western Pacific Region Pastor REX V. MOE.

South Sea Evangelical Church: Honiara; Gen. Superintendent Rev. JOASH FILOA.

United Church of Papua New Guinea and Solomon Islands: Munda, New Georgia, Western District; f. 1968; Bishop of Solomon Islands Region: Rev. J. PRATT.

THE PRESS

Agricola: Ministry of Agriculture and Lands, P.O.B. 11, Honiara; quarterly; Editor MARTIN TODD.

Solomons News Drum: P.O.B. 718, Honiara; f. 1975; Government Information Service; weekly; circ. 3,000.

Solomons Toktok: P.O.B. 599, Honiara; f. 1977; independent weekly with monthly news magazine *The Observer*; Editor/Publr. GEORGE ATKIN; circ. 2,000.

RADIO

Solomon Islands Broadcasting Corporation: P.O.B. 654, Honiara; f. 1976; daily transmissions are mainly in Pidgin with some English news bulletins and programmes; broadcasts total 116 hours per week; Chair. W. BENNETT, M.B.E., M.M.; Gen. Man. ASHLEY B. WICKHAM; Chief Engineer G. RICHARDSON.

In 1982 there were about 25,000 radio receivers.

FINANCE

BANKING

Solomon Islands Monetary Authority: P.O.B. 634, Honiara; f. 1976; Central Bank, with sole right of currency issue; Chair. A. V. HUGHES.

Development Bank of Solomon Islands: P.O.B. 760, Honiara; f. 1978; cap. and dep. U.S. $9.2m.; Gen. Man. KEVIN MISI.

National Bank of Solomon Islands Ltd.: P.O.B. 37, Honiara; f. 1981; 49 per cent owned by the Solomon Islands Government, 51 per cent by The Commonwealth Trading Bank of Australia; cap. SI$2m. (1981); Gen. Man. L. G. M. LATIMER.

FOREIGN BANKS

Australia and New Zealand Banking Group Ltd.: P.O.B. 10, Honiara.

Hongkong and Shanghai Banking Corporation: Mendana Ave., P.O.B. 12, Honiara.

INSURANCE

About ten major British insurance companies maintain agencies in the territory.

TRADE AND INDUSTRY

Cattle Development Authority (CDA): P.O.B. 525, Honiara; Gen. Man. R. K. FINNIMORE.

Solomon Islands Chamber of Commerce: P.O.B. 64, Honiara; Chair. W. TSHE.

Solomon Islands Copra Board: P.O.B. 54, Honiara; sole exporter of copra; agencies at Honiara and Yandina; Gen. Man. S. Ilala.

Solomon Islands Plantations Ltd.: P.O.B. 350, Honiara; established by the Commonwealth Development Corporation (CDC); major exporter of palm oil and kernels; second largest employer in Solomon Islands.

Trading Company (Solomons) Ltd.: Mendana Ave., P.O.B. 114, Honiara; f. 1947; wholesalers, retailers, motor vehicle distributors, duty free goods, shipping and travel agents, Port Authority agents, Lloyds agents.

CO-OPERATIVE SOCIETIES

In 1979 there were 230 primary co-operative societies working mostly outside the capital. There are two associations running and aiding co-operative societies in Solomon Islands: the Central Co-operative Association (CCA) and the Western General Co-operative Association (WGCA).

TRADE UNION

Solomon Islands General Workers' Union: Honiara; Pres Joses Taungenga.

TRANSPORT

ROADS

There are about 1,300 km. of roads maintained by the central and provincial governments; in 1976, main roads covered 455 km. In addition, there are 800 km. of privately maintained roads mainly for plantation use. Road construction and maintenance is difficult because of the nature of the country, and what roads there are serve as feeder roads to the main town of an island. Honiara now has a main road running about 65 kilometres each side of it along the north coast of Guadalcanal, and Malaita has a road 157 kilometres long running north from Auki and around the northern end of the island to the Lau Lagoon, where canoe transport takes over; and one running south for 35 kilometres to Masa. On Makira a road has been built linking Kira Kira and Kakoranga, a distance of 35 kilometres. Before it abandoned mining investigations in 1977, the Mitsui Mining and Smelting Company built 40 kilometres of road on Rennell Island.

SHIPPING

Regular shipping services (mainly cargo) exist between Solomon Islands and Australia, New Zealand, Papua New Guinea, Hong Kong, Japan, Singapore, European ports and various Pacific Islands, including Fiji, Tonga and New Caledonia. In 1981 internal shipping was provided by 34 ships of the government marine fleet and about 106 commercial vessels. The three main ports are at Honiara, Yandina and Gizo but a new deep-sea harbour is being planned for Noro on New Georgia to replace the port at Gizo. The ports are controlled by the Solomon Islands Ports Authority.

Solomon Islands Ports Authority: P.O.B. 307, Honiara; Chair. A. B. Wickham; Gen. Man. James Vaukei; Sec. N. J. Constantine; Chief of Port Operations John Kwaeota (acting); Harbourmaster Captain J. Murdoch.

Shipping companies operating freight services to Solomon Islands include Sofrana-Unilines, Kyowa Line, Ocean Pacific Line, P.N.G. Shipping Corporation, Kambara Kisen Line, Chief Container Service, China Navigation Service, Columbus Line, the Bank Line and Warner Pacific Line. Solomon Islands joined the Pacific Forum Line in 1977. P&O and Sitmar Cruises are amongst the companies which operate passenger services to the islands.

CIVIL AVIATION

Three airports are open to international traffic and a further 20 take internal flights.

Solomon Islands Airways Ltd. (Solair): P.O.B. 23, Honiara; f. 1968; internal scheduled and charter services to 24 airstrips and water ports, and scheduled services between Honiara and Kieta (Papua New Guinea) and Espiritu Santo (Vanuatu); Gen. Man. K. J. Witt; fleet of 2 Beechcraft Baron, 2 Britten-Norman Islander, 1 Beechcraft Queen-Air, 1 Metro II.

International air services are also provided by Air Pacific Ltd. (Fiji), Air Nauru and Air Niugini (Papua New Guinea).

TOURISM

Solomon Islands Tourist Authority: P.O.B. 321, Honiara; f. 1972; Chair. Jack Barley; Sec./Man. Bartholemew Buchanan.

EDUCATION

About two-thirds of school-age children receive formal education, mainly in state schools. In 1976 and 1977 eight "New Secondary Schools" were opened to provide courses of a practical and local nature, mainly in agriculture and development studies. In 1980, 28,870 children attended primary schools and 3,547 children attended secondary schools. There are two teacher-training schools and a technical institute. Scholarships are available for higher education at various universities overseas. In 1977 the Solomon Islands Centre of the University of the Pacific opened in Honiara.

Tokelau

Tokelau consists of three atolls, Atafu, Nukunonu and Fakaofo, which lie about 480 kilometres north of Western Samoa. The total population in 1979 was 1,615.

HISTORY

The territory became a British protectorate in 1877. At the request of the inhabitants Britain annexed the islands in 1916 and included them within the Gilbert and Ellice Islands Colony. In 1925 the United Kingdom Government transferred administrative control to New Zealand. In 1946 the group was officially designated the Tokelau Islands and in 1948 sovereignty was transferred to New Zealand. From 1962 until the end of 1971 the High Commissioner for New Zealand in Western Samoa was also the Administrator of the Tokelau Islands. In November 1974 the administration of the Tokelau Islands was transferred to the Ministry of Foreign Affairs in New Zealand. In 1977 the Tokelau Islands were officially redesignated Tokelau.

ECONOMIC SURVEY

Tokelau's soil is thin and infertile. Apart from some copra production, agriculture is of a basic subsistence nature. Food crops include coconuts, pulaka, breadfruit, pawpaw and bananas. Livestock consists of pigs and poultry. Ocean and lagoon fish and shellfish are staple constituents of the islanders' diet.

STATISTICAL SURVEY

AREA

(acres)

Atafu	Nukunonu	Fakaofo	Total
860	1,150	980	2,990

POPULATION

(census of October 25th, 1979)

	Males	Females	Total
Atafu .	284	293	577
Nukunonu .	191	183	374
Fakaofo .	323	341	664
Total .	798	817	1,615

1981 (estimated population): Atafu 562, Nukunonu 361, Fakaofo 631; Total 1,554.

Births and deaths (1980): 45 live births; 12 deaths.

AGRICULTURE

FAO estimates (metric tons): Coconuts 4,000 (1980), Copra 1,000 (1980).

FINANCE

Currency: 100 cents=1 New Zealand dollar ($NZ). For details, *see* the Cook Islands.

Western Samoan currency is also used.

BUDGET

($NZ—April 1st to March 31st)

	1980/81
Revenue	246,000
Expenditure	1,906,665
New Zealand Subsidy	1,605,000

Revenue is derived mainly from copra export duty, import duty, and sale of postage stamps, coins and handicrafts. Expenditure is devoted mainly to the provision of social services, particularly health, education, agriculture and communications, and also to public works.

EXTERNAL TRADE

In 1976/77 copra exports totalled $NZ13,001. There were no other exports. The main imports are foodstuffs, building materials and fuel.

THE GOVERNMENT

The administration of Tokelau is the responsibility of the Minister of Foreign Affairs of New Zealand, who is empowered to appoint an Administrator to the territory. In practice, most of the Administrator's powers are delegated to the Official Secretary, Office of Tokelau Affairs. The islands are self-governing in many respects, and are serviced by the Tokelau Public Service. By agreement with the Government of Western Samoa, the Office of Tokelau Affairs is based in Apia.

Administrator: F. H. Corner.

Official Secretary, Office of Tokelau Affairs: J. P. Larkindale.

LOCAL GOVERNMENT

Each village has a Council of Elders or *Taupulega* which comprises the heads of family groups together with the *Faipule* and the *Pulenuku*. The *Faipule* represents the village in its dealings with the administering power and the public service, and presides over the Council and the court. The *Pulenuku* is responsible for the administration of village affairs. Both are democratically elected by universal adult suffrage every three years.

JUDICIAL SYSTEM

The High Court of Niue has civil and criminal jurisdiction, and the Supreme Court of New Zealand has original and appellate jurisdiction. There is provision for a Tokelauan Commissioner on each of the islands to deal with civil proceedings and criminal offences.

RELIGION

On Atafu all inhabitants are members of the Congregational Christian Church of Samoa; on Nukunonu all are Roman Catholic, while both denominations are represented on Fakaofo.

FINANCE

In February 1977 a savings bank was set up on each island; commercial and savings banking facilities are available in Apia, Western Samoa.

TRADE AND INDUSTRY

A village co-operative store was established on each island in 1977. Local industries are copra production, wood work and plaited craft goods.

TRANSPORT

The territory is visited about ten times per year by vessels under charter. An irregular seaplane service links Tokelau and Western Samoa.

EDUCATION

Education is free, and attendance is almost 100 per cent. There are three schools, one on each atoll. In 1980 there were 40 qualified Tokelauan teachers on the islands. The New Zealand Department of Education provides advisory services and some educational equipment. Schools receive daily radio broadcasts from the Western Samoan Education Department. Scholarships are awarded for secondary and tertiary education and vocational training in Western Samoa, Fiji, Niue, the Cook Islands and New Zealand.

Tonga

PHYSICAL AND SOCIAL GEOGRAPHY

The Kingdom of Tonga, which is located in the central South Pacific about 400 miles east of Fiji and south of Samoa, comprises 171 islands, totalling 748 square kilometres in area. The islands lie in two lines, those to the west being volcanic and those to the east being coral islands. They are divided into three groups, Vava'u in the north, Ha'apai and Tongatapu in the south. Only 36 of the islands are permanently inhabited. In 1981 the population of Tonga was 98,915. More than half of the population are resident on Tongatapu, where the capital, Nuku'alofa, is situated. The inhabitants of the islands are Polynesians.

HISTORY

From about the 10th century Tongan society developed a lineage of sacred chiefs, who gradually became effective rulers. Since European contact the chiefs have become known as kings. The Kingdom of Tonga adopted its first constitution in 1875, during the reign of King George Tupou I. As a result of increasing internal difficulties Tonga negotiated a treaty with the United Kingdom in 1900, whereby it became a British Protectorate.

Queen Salote Tupou III came to the throne in 1918 and ruled Tonga until her death in December 1965. She was succeeded by her son, Prince Tupouto'a Tungi, who had been Prime Minister since 1949. He took the title of King Taufa'ahau Tupou IV and appointed his brother, Prince Fatafehi Tu'ipelehake, to be Prime Minister. In 1958 a treaty of friendship was signed between Tonga and the United Kingdom providing for the appointment of a British Commissioner and Consul to be responsible to the Governor of Fiji, who held the office of British Chief Commissioner for Tonga. Tonga gained increased control over internal affairs in 1967 and became fully independent, within the Commonwealth, on June 4th, 1970. Elections held on May 1st, 1981, brought a surprise loss to the People's Representatives group, the new Assembly being dominated by traditionalist conservatives. In March 1982 the Finance Minister, Mahe Tupouniua, resigned at the King's request after refusing him travel funds above those budgeted for.

In May 1981 and in March and June 1982, Tonga was struck by cyclones which caused extensive damage.

ECONOMIC SURVEY

The economy is based mainly on agriculture, the two principal crops, coconuts and bananas, accounting for the bulk of Tonga's exports. Vanilla has also been introduced as a cash crop and in 1979 it was the third most important export. Two five-year development plans, for 1965–70 and 1970–75, both aimed at stimulating coconut production and tourism. The third Five-Year Plan (1976–80) aimed to continue directing investment to the productive sector of the economy and at expanding the existing infrastructure. Every adult male is allotted 3.3 hectares of land in which to garden, plus a building site in his village, although all land remains the property of the Crown. Alienation of land is forbidden.

There is a high rate of migration to New Zealand and Australia. Unemployed Tongans in New Zealand and illegal immigrants in Australia have caused both countries to restrict the entry of Tongans to those with return tickets or guaranteed employment. A marked imbalance in the Tongan population and a lack of skilled labour in the islands have been secondary outcomes of these movements. The Tongan Government has sought to establish a shipping service and a regional banking operation, but both have proved unsuccessful.

STATISTICAL SURVEY

Area: 748 sq. km. There are 171 islands.

Population (1981 estimates): 98,915 (50,519 males, 48,396 females); Tongatapu 63,108, Vava'u 16,543, Ha'apai 11,865, 'Eua 4,881, Niuas 2,518; Nuku'alofa (capital—1980 estimate) 19,882.

Agriculture (1980, metric tons, FAO estimates): Coconuts 75,000, Sweet Potatoes 80,000, Cassava 13,000, Copra 9,000, Bananas 3,000, Oranges 3,000, Tomatoes 2,000.

Livestock (1978): Pigs 95,718, Horses 10,090, Cattle 9,588, Goats 11,272, Poultry 125,463.

Sea Fishing (catch in metric tons): 1,019 in 1976; 1,197 in 1977; 1,143.6 in 1978; 2,000 in 1979; 1,993 in 1980.

Currency: 100 seniti (cents) = 1 pa'anga (Tongan dollar, \$T). Coins: 1, 2, 5, 10, 20 and 50 seniti; 1 and 2 pa'anga. Notes. 50 seniti; 1, 2, 5 and 10 pa'anga. Exchange rates (June 1982): £1 sterling = \$T1.6925; U.S. \$1 = 97.9 Tongan cents. \$T100 = £59.08 = U.S. \$102.17. The pa'anga is at par with the Australian dollar.

Budget (\$T, 1980/81): Revenue 12,428,900, Expenditure 11,757,600; (1981/82 estimate): Revenue 14,744,200, Expenditure 14,735,800.

External Trade (1981): *Imports:* \$T34,998,766 (mainly food and machinery); *Exports:* \$T6,550,465 (mainly copra and desiccated coconut). Trade is chiefly with other members of the Commonwealth.

Transport: *Roads* (1980): Commercial Vehicles 1,294, Private Vehicles 1,082, Motor Cycles 188; *Shipping* (1980): Vessels entered 1,132,877 tons, vessels cleared 1,087,065 tons; *Civil Aviation* (1980): Aircraft arriving 936.

Tourism (1981): 59,210 visitors.

Education (1981): Primary: 97 government schools, 13 church schools, 17,364 pupils; Secondary: 44 church, 1 private and 3 government schools, 14,283 pupils; Technical and vocational: 6 church and 4 government colleges, 658 pupils; 1 teacher-training college, 182 pupils; 174 students overseas (in 1980).

THE CONSTITUTION

The Constitution of Tonga is based on that granted in 1875 by King George Tupou I. It provides for a government consisting of the Sovereign; a Privy Council, which is appointed by the Sovereign and consists of the Sovereign and the Cabinet; the Cabinet, which consists of a Prime Minister, a Deputy Prime Minister, other Ministers and the Governors of Ha'apai and Vava'u; a Legislative Assembly and a Judiciary. Limited law-making power is vested in the Privy Council and any legislation passed by the Executive is subject to review by the Legislative Assembly.

THE GOVERNMENT

The Sovereign: H.M. King TAUFA'AHAU TUPOU IV, G.C.M.G., G.C.V.O., K.B.E. (succeeded to the throne December 15th, 1965).

CABINET

(July 1982)

Prime Minister, Minister of Agriculture, Marine Affairs and Telegraphs and Telephones: H.R.H. Prince FATAFEHI TU'IPELEHAKE, K.B.E.

Deputy Prime Minister and Minister of Lands: Hon. TUITA, C.B.E.

Minister of Foreign Affairs and Defence: Crown Prince TUPOU TOA.

Minister of Finance: Hon. CECIL COCKER (acting).

Minister of Police: Hon. 'AKAU'OLA.

Minister of Education and Works: Hon. Dr. S. LANGI KAVALIKU.

Minister of Industries, Commerce, Labour and Tourism: Hon. the Baron VAEA.

Minister of Health: Hon. Dr. SIONE TAPA.

Governor of Ha'apai: Hon. VA'EHALA.

Governor of Vava'u: Hon. MA'AFU TUPOU.

LEGISLATURE

The Legislative Assembly consists of the Speaker, the members of the Cabinet, seven nobles elected by the 33 Nobles of Tonga, and seven representatives elected by literate taxpayers over the age of 21. There are elections every three years and the Assembly must meet at least once every year.

Speaker and President of the Legislative Assembly: Hon. MA'AFU.

DIPLOMATIC REPRESENTATION

EMBASSIES AND HIGH COMMISSIONS ACCREDITED TO TONGA

(HC) High Commission.

Belgium: Wellington, New Zealand.

Canada: Wellington, New Zealand (HC).

Chile: Wellington, New Zealand.

China (Taiwan): P.O.B. 842, Nuku'alofa; *Ambassador:* CLEMENT A. K. TSIEN.

Denmark: Canberra, A.C.T., Australia.

France: Suva, Fiji.

Germany, Federal Republic: Wellington, New Zealand.

India: Suva, Fiji (HC).

Israel: Canberra, A.C.T., Australia.

Italy: Wellington, New Zealand.

Korea, Republic: Wellington, New Zealand.

Netherlands: Wellington, New Zealand.

New Zealand: Tungi Arcade, Taufa'ahau Rd., Nuku'alofa; *High Commissioner:* J. R. BRADY.

Sweden: Wellington, New Zealand.

Turkey: Canberra, A.C.T., Australia.

U.S.S.R.: Wellington, New Zealand.

United Kingdom: P.O.B. 56, Nuku'alofa; *High Commissioner:* BERNARD COLEMAN.

U.S.A.: Suva, Fiji.

Tonga also has diplomatic relations with Australia, Fiji, Japan, Libya and Spain.

JUDICIAL SYSTEM

There are Magistrates' Courts, a Land Court and a Supreme Court from which appeals lie to the Privy Council.

There are nine Magistrates, and appeals from the Magistrates' Courts are heard by the Supreme Court. In cases which come before the Supreme Court the accused, or either party in a civil suit, may elect for a jury trial. The Chief Justice is resident in Tonga and appeals from the Supreme Court are heard by the Privy Council as a Court of Appeal. The Puisne Judge is Judge of the Supreme Court and of the Land Court in which he sits with a Tongan assessor.

Chief Justice and Puisne Judge: HENRY HUBERT HILL, M.C.

RELIGION

The Tongans are Christian, 77 per cent belonging to sects of the Wesleyan faith. There is also a small number of Roman Catholics, Anglicans and Mormons. Fourteen denominations are represented in total.

Anglican: P.O.B. 157, Bishop's House, Nuku'alofa; Bishop FINE HALAPUA.

Free Church of Tonga: Pangai; f. 1928; a branch of Methodism; 8,000 mems.; Pres. SELU PEPELIMAFI.

Free Wesleyan Church: P.O.B. 57, Nuku'alofa; f. 1826; 34,009 mems.; Pres. Rev. Dr. SIONE 'AMANAKI HAVEA; Sec. Rev. SIONE LEPA TO'A; publ. *Ko e Tohi Fanongonongo*; circ. 5,400.

Roman Catholic: P.O.B. 1, Nuku'alofa; Bishop of Tonga Most Rev. PATELISIO PUNOU-KI-HIHIFO FINAU, S.M.

Church of Jesus Christ of Latter-day Saints (*Mormon*): Mission Centre, P.O.B. 58, Nuku'alofa; 26,272 mems.; Pres. PITA F. HOPOATE.

THE PRESS

Tonga Chronicle: weekly newspaper, sponsored by the Government; f. 1964; Acting Editor PAUA MANUATA; circ. (Tongan) 4,300, (English) 1,200.

There is a regular issue of Church newspapers by the various missions.

RADIO

Tonga Broadcasting Commission: P.O.B. 36, Nuku'alofa; f. 1961; independent statutory body; commercially-operated; programmes in English and Tongan; Man. S. TAVAKE FUSIMALOHI.

In 1979 there were over 50,000 radio receivers.

FINANCE

BANKING

Bank of Tonga: P.O.B. 924, Nuku'alofa; f. 1974; owned by Government of Tonga, Bank of Hawaii, Bank of New Zealand and Bank of New South Wales; dep. $T18.5 million (1981); Man. and Chief Exec. K. G. JOWETT.

Tongan Development Bank: Nuku'alofa; f. 1977; Man. Dir. LISIATE 'ALOVEITA 'AKOLA.

TRADE AND INDUSTRY

DEVELOPMENT ORGANIZATION

Commodities Board: P.O.B. 27, Nuku'alofa; f. 1974; non-profit-making organization; Chair. H.R.H. Prince FATAFEHI TU'IPELEHAKE, K.B.E.; Dir. S. HURRELL.

Copra Division: f. 1941; non-profit-making board controlling the export of coconut and all coconut products; Chair. H.R.H. Prince Tu'ipelehake, K.B.E.; Gen. Man. S. 'Amanaki.

Construction Division: P.O.B. 28, Nuku'alofa; f. 1958 to carry out the construction programme of the Commodities Board as well as those of government, local bodies and private concerns; commission agents for imports and exports; Chair. H.R.H. Prince Tu'ipelehake, K.B.E.; Gen. Man. Tevita T. Havili (acting).

Produce Division: P.O.B. 84, Nuku'alofa; non-profit-making organization controlling the export of all agricultural produce on behalf of growers; Chair. H.R.H. Prince Tu'ipelehake, K.B.E.; Gen. Man. Nomani S. Vaka.

CO-OPERATIVES

In April 1978 there were 54 registered co-operative societies, including the first co-operative registered under the Agricultural Organization Act.

TRANSPORT

ROADS

There are about 192 km. of all-weather metalled roads on Tongatapu and 70 km. on Vava'u. Total road length, including fair-weather-only dirt roads, is 433 km.

SHIPPING

The chief ports are Nuku'alofa, and Neiafu on Vava'u.

Shipping Corporation of Polynesia Ltd.: P.O.B. 453, Nuku'alofa; regular inter-island passenger and cargo services; Gen. Man. V. Pahl.

Cargo services to Tonga are provided by Karlander (Australia) Pty. Ltd., which operates a monthly service from Melbourne and Sydney, Australia, by Bank Line vessels en route to European ports, by the Union Steam Ship Co. of New Zealand, which operates a fortnightly service from Auckland, New Zealand, by Warner Pacific Line to the Samoas, and by the Pacific Forum Line, calling at Tonga, Fiji, the Samoas, New Zealand and Australia.

CIVIL AVIATION

Tonga is served by Fua'amotu Airport, 22 km. from Nuku'alofa, limited seaplane facilities at Nuku'alofa and airstrips at Vava'u, Ha'apai and 'Eua.

South Pacific Islands Airways: P.O.B. 215, Nuku'alofa; f. 1967; operates internal services to the Vava'u, 'Eua, Ha'apai and Tongatapu islands, and connects Tonga with American Samoa and Western Samoa; Pres. George Wray; Man. Dir. John Lemoto.

Tonga Air Lines Ltd.: Nuku'alofa; f. 1978; inter-island services; fleet of 1 Beechcraft B-50, 1 De Havilland Dove, 1 Britten-Norman Islander.

Air Nauru, Air New Zealand, Air Pacific Ltd. (Fiji) and Polynesian Airlines (Western Samoa) also serve Tonga.

TOURISM

Tonga Visitors' Bureau: Vuna Rd., P.O.B. 37, Nuku'alofa; Dir. S. Taumoepeau.

EDUCATION

Free state education is compulsory between the ages of 6 and 14 and the Government and other Commonwealth countries offer scholarships for higher education abroad. In 1981 there were 158 schools, about two-thirds of which were government schools and the rest mission schools, with 31,647 pupils. There are also 8 technical and vocational colleges and one teacher training college.

Estimated government expenditure on education in 1977/78 was $T1,261,976.

Trust Territory of the Pacific Islands

PHYSICAL AND SOCIAL GEOGRAPHY

The U.S. Trust Territory of the Pacific Islands consists of over 2,000 islands covering about 1,300 square kilometres of land and scattered over 7,500,000 square kilometres of ocean. The Territory lies within the area (which includes Kiribati, Tuvalu and other territories) known as Micronesia. Most of the islands lie in a band which begins about 800 kilometres east of the Philippines and stretches 4,800 kilometres east across the Pacific towards Hawaii. In the far west are the Palau group, with Yap and Ulithi slightly to the north and east, comprising together the Western Caroline Islands. Further east, Truk and Ponape form the Eastern Carolines. The Marshall islands lie further east again.

Only 84 of the islands are large enough to be inhabited. The population of the Trust Territory was estimated at 120,000 in 1978. Most live on the largest islands in the districts of Palau, Truk, Yap and Ponape.

HISTORY AND ECONOMY

First European contacts were Iberian. Magellan sailed through the islands in the 1500s and the Spanish maintained a presence in the Mariana Islands from 1700 until the Spanish-American war in 1898. The indigenous population was all but completely destroyed by disease and violent conquest and the modern population is made up from an intermixing of the Spanish and native Chamorro population.

In the Caroline Islands intensive contacts did not begin until the 1800s and in some areas, notably the Palau group, until the early 1900s.

In 1885 Germany took over control of the Marshall Islands and in 1898 bought the rest of the territory, except Guam, from Spain. German administration ended in 1914 when Japan occupied the islands. In 1920 Japan received a mandate from the League of Nations to administer the islands, and remained in control until being forcibly ejected by United States military forces in 1944 and 1945.

Under the Germans, and more so under the Japanese, a policy of colonization and exploitation of natural resources was followed. Fishing and agriculture, in particular copra and sugar production, were encouraged and sugar mills and fish processing plants were established. The Micronesians were involved mainly as labourers in most enterprises, but many moved out of subsistence production completely.

After the 1942-45 war, almost all of the Japanese were repatriated. Their colonial towns and almost the whole of their pre-war economy disappeared and many islanders were forced to revert to subsistence farming or rely on United States aid. The Mariana islanders were removed to Saipan where, with no access to fishing or agricultural resources, they lived in poverty.

Between 1947 and 1951 the islands were administered by the U.S. Navy. Bikini and Eniwetok in the Marshall Islands were used for nuclear bomb experiments in 1946 and 1948. Early in 1977 the islanders were given back parts of Eniwetok although some areas remain contaminated by radioactivity and some islanders are still suffering from diseases commonly associated with radiation. In 1978 the 139 inhabitants of Bikini Island were evacuated because of a rise in radioactive material in their bodies.

In 1951 the Trust Territory administration was set up to administer the islands, although the Marianas remained under military rule until 1962. The civil administration operated under an inadequate budget and little development occurred until 1962. Apart from subsistence agriculture and fishing, the only money-earning activities were government employment and the sale of vegetables, copra, trochus shell and scrap metal left over from the war. Immigration and visits by outsiders were severely restricted. In 1962 the islands' budget was doubled and further increased in following years. Schools, hospitals, housing, roads, airstrips and port facilities were built or upgraded. Public services were expanded and incomes rose, although the greater part was provided by the U.S.A.

Since 1970, tourism has overtaken copra and sugar to become the most important industry. About half of all tourists come from the U.S.A. and a third from Japan.

Since 1965 there have been increased demands for local autonomy. In that year the Congress of Micronesia was formed, and in 1967 a commission to examine the future political status of the islands was established. In 1970 it declared Micronesians' rights to sovereignty over their own lands, self-determination, the right to form their own constitution and to revoke any form of free association with the United States. In May 1977, after eight years of negotiations, President Carter announced that his administration intended to take steps to terminate the Trusteeship Agreement by 1981.

On January 9th, 1978, the Marianas District achieved separate status as the Commonwealth of the Northern Mariana Islands. It remains legally part of the Trusteeship until the future status of the Trust Territory is decided. The Marshall Islands District drafted its own constitution, which came into effect on May 1st, 1979. The four districts of Yap, Truk, Ponape and Kosrae ratified a new constitution and became the Federated States of Micronesia on May 10th, 1979. In the Palau District a referendum in July 1979 approved a local Constitution which came into effect on January 1st, 1981, when the islands became the Republic of Palau.

On October 31st, 1980, leaders from the Marshall Islands and the Federated States of Micronesia initialled agreements providing for self-government. On November 17th the Republic of Palau signed a similar agreement. Under the agreements the four states (including the Northern Mariana Islands) would be independent of each other and would manage their internal and foreign affairs separately. The United States would be responsible for defence and security. These agreements are known as the Compact of Free Association. The Compact was to become effective following approval by the legislatures of each territory, the holding of a plebiscite and approval by the United States. After further discussion and a "review" of the Carter agreement by President Reagan's administration, which further delayed its ratification, the Marshall Islanders were due to vote to accept or reject the Compact on August 17th, 1982. Failure by either country to ratify the Compact was to result in full independence for the islands, for the trusteeship of the Marshall Islands was due to end in any case on October 1st, 1982. Under the Compact, the U.S.A. was to retain its military bases in the Marshall Islands for at least 15 years and, over the same period, was to provide $2,000 million in aid.

STATISTICAL SURVEY

Area: 1,300 sq. km. (land only); the largest islands are Babelthuap (367 sq. km.) in Palau and Ponape Island (330 sq. km.) in Ponape District.

Population (Census of September 1980): Total 116,974; Marshall Islands 31,041, Palau 12,177, Ponape 22,319, Truk 37,742, Yap 8,172, Kosrae 5,522.

Agriculture: The chief crops are coconuts, breadfruit, bananas, taro, yams, cocoa, pepper and citrus. Subsistence crop production predominates and, except for copra, little is marketed. Production (1980—metric tons, FAO estimates): Coconuts 270,000, Copra 37,000, Cassava 9,000, Sweet Potatoes 3,000.

Livestock (1980—FAO estimates): Pigs 24,000, Cattle 9,000, Goats 5,000, Poultry 184,000.

Fishing (total catch in metric tons): 6,342 in 1976; 6,261 in 1977; 11,299 in 1978; 6,504 in 1979; 5,377 in 1980.

FINANCE

United States currency: 100 cents=1 U.S. dollar (U.S. $).

Coins: 1, 5, 10, 25 and 50 cents; 1 dollar.

Notes: 1, 2, 5, 10, 20, 50 and 100 dollars.

Exchange rates (June 1982): £1 sterling=U.S. $1.73; $100=£57.74.

BUDGET

(U.S. $, year ending September 30th)

Revenue	1979/80
Direct U.S. Appropriation	1,187,000
Reimbursements and Other Operating Income	10,698,000
Grant from U.S. Congress	112,701,000
Total Funds Available	124,586,000

Expenditure	1979/80
Resources and Development	4,881,700
General Administration	5,481,100
Construction	57,700,000
Legal and Public Safety	2,445,600
Health	7,581,000
Education	11,735,100
Public Works	11,566,100
Other	8,037,000
Total	109,427,600

EXTERNAL TRADE

(including the Northern Mariana Islands)

1977: *Imports:* $44.22 million (estimate including foodstuffs and beverages $20.2 million, building materials $6.1 million). *Exports:* $10.9 million (including coconut products $5.9 million, fish $3.5 million, handicrafts $248,100).

TRANSPORT

(including the Northern Mariana Islands)

Road Traffic (vehicles in use, 1977): Trucks 273; pickups 2,038; sedans 4,002; jeeps 335; motorcycles, etc. 468; other motor vehicles 107.

Shipping (1977): Passengers 12,631 (TransPacific Lines Inc.); Freight 196,838 tons; other American vessels also entered and cleared in external trade.

Civil Aviation (1976): Passengers flown 147,904; Passenger miles flown 87,323,000. Freight flown 8,104,949 lb.; freight ton miles flown 2,973,991.

EDUCATION

(1976/77)

(including the Northern Mariana Islands)

	Schools	Pupils
Elementary	248	30,923
High School	31	7,707
MOC* (Secondary Programme)	1	323
COM (Community College)	1	231

* Micronesian Occupational College. Also provides post-secondary and adult education. During the 1976/77 academic year 1,468 Micronesian students were pursuing post-secondary courses outside the Trust Territory.

THE CONSTITUTION

The Trust Territory of the Pacific Islands is a United Nations Trusteeship administered by the U.S.A. Executive and administrative authority is exercised by a High Commissioner, appointed by the President of the U.S.A. with the consent and approval of the U.S. Senate. The High Commissioner is under the direction of the Secretary of the Interior.

On May 1st, 1979, the locally drafted Constitution of the Marshall Islands became effective. The Constitution provides for a parliamentary form of government with legislative authority vested in the 33-member Nitijela. On May 10th, 1979, the locally drafted Constitution of the Federated States of Micronesia, incorporating the four districts of Kosrae, Yap, Ponape and Truk, became effective. Each of the four districts has its own legislature. A locally drafted Constitution for Palau came into effect on January 1st, 1981, and the islands became known as the Republic of Palau.

With the establishment of duly constituted Micronesian governments, the role of the High Commissioner, as the chief executive of the Trust Territory, was altered to provide for the maximum permissible amount of local self-government. The High Commissioner retains only that authority necessary to carry out the obligations and responsibilities of the U.S.A. under the terms of the 1947 Trusteeship Agreement and other treaties, laws and regulations generally applicable in the Trust Territory.

Local governmental units are the municipalities and villages. Elected Magistrates and Councils govern the municipalities. Village government is largely traditional.

THE GOVERNMENT

(July 1982)

TRUST TERRITORY GOVERNMENT

High Commissioner: JANET McCOY.

Deputy High Commissioner: JUAN SABLAN.

Department of Administrative Services: N. NEIMAN CRALEY (Administrator).

Department of Community Services: RESIO MOSES (Administrator).

Department of Developmental Services: LAZARUS SALII (Administrator).

Attorney-General: DANIEL HIGH.

MARSHALL ISLANDS GOVERNMENT

President: AMATA KABUA.

Minister of Finance: ATJANG PAUL.

Minister of Internal Affairs: WILFRED KENDALL.

Minister of Internal Security: ATAJI BALOS.

Minister of Public Works: KUNAR ABNER.

Minister of Health: JETON ANJAIN.

Minister of Education: TOM KIJINER.

Minister of Transportation and Communications: RUBEN ZACKHRAS.

Minister of Resources and Development: KESSAI NOTE.

Minister of Social Welfare: JINA LAVIN.

Secretary of Foreign Affairs: ANTON DEBRUM.

Attorney-General: ROBERT GREEN (acting).

FEDERATED STATES OF MICRONESIA GOVERNMENT

President: TOSIWO NAKAYAMA.

Secretary of the Department of External Affairs: ANDON AMARAICH.

Secretary of the Department of Resources and Development: BERNARD HELGENBERGER.

Secretary of the Department of Finance: ALOYSIUS TUUTH.

Secretary of the Department of Social Services: YOSIWO GEORGE.

Attorney-General: FRED RAMP.

REPUBLIC OF PALAU GOVERNMENT

President: HARUO I. REMELIIK.

Vice-President: ALFONSO OITERONG.

LEGISLATURES

THE MARSHALL ISLANDS NITIJELA

Speaker: ATLAN ANIEN.

CONGRESS OF THE FEDERATED STATES OF MICRONESIA

Speaker of the House of Representatives: Hon. BETHWEL HENRY.

PALAU NATIONAL LEGISLATURE

(*Olbiil era Kelulau*)

President of the Senate: KALEB UDUI.

Speaker of the House of Delegates: CARLOS H. SALII.

STATE LEGISLATURES

Kosrae State Legislature: unicameral body of 14 members serving for four years; Governor JACOB NENA.

Ponape State Legislature: 24 representatives elected for four years (terms staggered); Governor LEO FALCAM.

Truk State Legislature: 28 members, serving for four years; Governor ERHART ATEN.

Yap State Legislature: 10 members, 6 elected from the Yap Islands proper and 4 elected from the Outer Islands of Ulithi and Woleai, for a four-year term; Governor JOHN MANGEFEL.

JUDICIAL SYSTEM

The Trust Territory laws derive from the Trusteeship Agreement, certain applicable laws of the United States and Executive Orders of the President, Secretarial Orders of the Secretary of the Interior, laws and regulations of the Government of the Trust Territory, enactments of the legislative bodies, and municipal ordinances. Recognized customary law has full force where it does not conflict with aforementioned laws.

High Court: Appellate and Trial Divisions; Chief Justice Hon. HAROLD W. BURNETT; Associate Justice Hon. ERNEST GIANOTTI.

District Courts: one each in Marshall Islands, Palau, Ponape, Truk and Kosrae.

Yap State Court: replaced Yap District Court in 1982; Chief Justice EDWARD C. KING.

Community Courts: a number in each District; 103 judges.

RELIGION

The population is predominantly Christian, mainly Roman Catholic. In the Marshall Islands the Assembly of God, Jehovah's Witnesses, Seventh-day Adventists, Mormons, Baptists and the Bahá'í Faith are also represented.

Roman Catholic Church: The Bishop of the Caroline and Marshall Islands, Most Rev. Bishop MARTIN JOSEPH NEYLON, P.O.B. 250, Truk, Caroline Is. 96942.

Protestant Church: Marshall Islands and Eastern Caroline Islands: under the auspices of the United Church Board for World Ministries (475 Riverside Drive, New York, N.Y. 10115, U.S.A.); Pacific Regional Sec. Rev. PAUL GREGORY.

Western Carolines: under auspices of the Liebenzell Mission of Germany and the U.S.A.; Rev. PETER ERMEL, Truk, Caroline Islands 96942.

THE PRESS

Marshall Islands Journal: P.O.B. 14, Majuro, Marshall Islands; f. 1964; five times weekly; Editor DANIEL C. SMITH; circ. 2,500.

The National Union: FSM Information, P.O.B. 490, Kolonia, Ponape, Eastern Caroline Islands 96941; twice a month; circ. 5,000.

Tia Belau: P.O.B. 569, Koror, Palau, W. Caroline Is.; f. 1972; bi-weekly; independent; Editor MOSES ULUDONG; circ. 1,000.

RADIO AND TELEVISION

RADIO

Station WSZA: Colonia, Yap, W. Caroline Is. 96943; programmes in English and Yapese; 1 kW.; Man. A YUG.

Station WSZB: Koror, Palau, W. Caroline Is. 96940; member of the Micronesian Broadcasting System; broadcasts American, Japanese and Micronesian music; broadcasts 18 hours a day on weekdays and 16 hours on Sundays; Man. SANTOS IKLUK.

Station WSZC: Moen, Truk, E. Caroline Is. 96942; programmes in English and Trukese; Man. L. HAUK.

Station WSZD: Kolonia, Ponape, E. Caroline Is. 96941; programmes in English, Kusaiean and Ponapean; 10 kW.; Man. FRANCES ZARRED.

Station WSZO—Radio Marshalls: Majoro, Marshall Islands 96960; programmes in English and Marshallese; Station Man. SAMUEL J. JORDAN.

In 1978 there were 9,500 radio receivers (including the Northern Mariana Islands).

TELEVISION

Cable television started in Majuro, Marshall Islands, in 1975.

Station KPON: Kolonia, Ponape; commercial.

Station WAAB: Colonia, Yap; state-owned.

Station WTKK: Moen, Truk; commercial.

FINANCE

BANKING

Bank of Guam (*U.S.A.*): brs. in Truk and Majuro, Marshall Islands.

Bank of Hawaii (*U.S.A.*): brs. in Kwajalein (Marshall Is.), Koror, Ponape, Saipan, Yap, Midway.

Marshall Islands First Commercial Bank: Majuro; Pres. CLARENCE S. B. TAN.

Banking services for the rest of the territory are available in Guam, Hawaii and on the U.S. mainland.

INSURANCE

Micronesian Insurance Underwriters Inc.

CO-OPERATIVES

Palau: Palau Fishermen's Co-operative, Palau Boatbuilders' Association, Palau Handicraft and Woodworkers' Guild.

Marshall Islands: Ebeye Co-op, Farmers' Market Co-operative, Kwajalein Employees' Credit Union, Marshall Islands Credit Union, Marshall Islands Fishermen's Co-operative, Marshall Islands Handicraft Co-operative.

Ponape: Ponape Federation of Co-operative Associations (P.O.B. 100, Ponape, E. Caroline Is. 96941), Ponape Handicraft Co-operative, Ponape Fishermen's Co-operative, Uh Soumwet Co-operative Association, Kolonia Consumers' and Producers' Co-operative Association, Kitti Minimum Co-operative Association, Kapingamarangi Copra Producers' Association, Metalanim Copra Co-operative Association, PICS Co-operative Association, Mokil Island Co-operative Association, Ngatik Island Co-operative Association, Nukuoro Island Co-operative Association, Kosrae Island Co-operative Association, Pingelap Consumers' Co-operative Association.

Truk: Truk Co-operative, Faichuk Cacao and Copra Co-operative Association, Pis Fishermen's Co-operative, Fefan Women's Co-operative.

Yap: Yap Co-operative Association, P.O.B. 159, Colonia, Yap, W. Caroline Is. 96943; f. 1952; Pres. JOACHIM FALAMOG; 1,200 members.

Co-operative organizations have been set up for the sale of school supplies and sundries, one at the Truk High School and one at the Ponape High School.

TRANSPORT

ROADS

Macadam and concrete roads are found in the more important islands. Other islands have stone and coral-surfaced roads and tracks. By 1976 there were about 200 kilometres of paved road and 550 kilometres of unpaved.

SHIPPING

There are seven commercial docks; one on each of the major inhabited islands.

Most shipping in the Territory is government-organized. (*See* the chapter on the Northern Mariana Islands.) However, Nauru Pacific Line operates a regular container service from Melbourne (Australia) to Truk, Ponape, Kosrae and Majuro and other services from San Francisco (U.S.A.) and Honolulu (Hawaii) to Majuro, Ponape and Truk. The Kyowa Line operates a monthly service from Hong Kong, Taiwan, the Republic of Korea and Japan to Truk and Ponape. Other commercial carriers which serve the Marshall Islands include Philippine Micronesia and Orient Navigation (PM & O), Tiger Line, Nippon Yusen Kaisha, and Matson Line.

CIVIL AVIATION

Airline of the Marshall Islands, based in Majuro, provides an internal service for the Marshall Islands. The Trust Territory is also served by Air Micronesia (Northern Mariana Islands. JAL (Japan) and Air Nauru operate occasional services to the territory.

Tuvalu

PHYSICAL AND SOCIAL GEOGRAPHY

Tuvalu is a scattered group of nine small atolls, extending 560 km. from north to south, in the western Pacific Ocean. Its nearest neighbours are Fiji to the south, Kiribati to the north and Solomon Islands to the west. The climate is warm and pleasant, with a mean annual temperature of 30°C (86°F), and there is very little seasonal variation. The average annual rainfall is 3,500 mm. (140 inches). The population was 7,349 in 1979. The capital is on Funafuti atoll.

HISTORY

Tuvalu was formerly known as the Ellice (or Lagoon) Islands. Between about 1850 and 1875 many of the islanders were captured by slave-traders and this, together with European diseases, reduced the population from about 20,000 to 3,000. In 1877 the United Kingdom established the Western Pacific High Commission (WPHC), with its headquarters in Fiji, and the Ellice Islands and other groups were placed under its jurisdiction. In 1892 a British protectorate was declared over the Ellice Islands and the group was linked administratively with the Gilbert Islands to the north. In 1916 the United Kingdom annexed the protectorate, which was renamed the Gilbert and Ellice Islands Coloney (GEIC). During the Japanese occupation of the Gilbert Islands in 1942–43, the administration of the GEIC was temporarily moved to Funafuti in the Ellice Islands. (For more details of the history of the GEIC, *see* chapter on Kiribati, p. 897.)

A series of advisory and legislative bodies prepared the GEIC for self-government. In May 1974 the last of these, the Legislative Council, was replaced by a House of Assembly, with 28 elected members (including eight Ellice Islanders) and three official members. A Chief Minister was elected by the House and chose between four and six other Ministers, one of whom had to be from the Ellice Islands.

In January 1972 the appointment of a separate GEIC Governor, who assumed most of the functions previously exercised by the High Commissioner, increased the long-standing anxiety of the Ellice Islanders over their minority position as Polynesians in the colony, dominated by the Micronesians of the Gilbert Islands. In a referendum held in the Ellice Islands in August and September 1974, over 90 per cent of the voters favoured separate status for the group, and in October 1975 the Ellice Islands, under the old native name of Tuvalu ("eight standing together"), became a separate British dependency. The Deputy Governor of the GEIC took office as Her Majesty's Commissioner for Tuvalu. The eight Ellice representatives in the GEIC House of Assembly became the first elected members of the new Tuvalu House of Assembly. They elected one of their number, Toaripi Lauti, to be Chief Minister. Tuvalu was completely separated from the GEIC administration in January 1976. The remainder of the GEIC was renamed the Gilbert Islands and achieved independence, under the name of Kiribati, in July 1979.

Tuvalu's first separate elections were held in August 1977, when the number of elective seats in the House was increased to 12. An independence constitution was finalized at a conference in London in February 1978. After five months of internal self-government. Tuvalu became independent on October 1st 1978, with Lauti as the first Prime Minister. Like Nauru, Tuvalu is a "special member" of the Commonwealth and is not represented at meetings of Heads of Government.

In April 1979 it was reported that Tuvalu had signed a treaty of friendship with the U.S.A., which renounced its claim, dating from 1856, to the four southernmost atolls. Following elections to the House of Assembly in September 1981, Dr. Tomasi Puapua became Prime Minister. The main election issue was the lack of information about government funds entrusted to a Californian businessman for investment in the U.S.A. soon after independence.

ECONOMIC SURVEY

Tuvalu is composed of coral atolls with poor quality soil. Most of the land is covered with coconut palms, which provide the only export in the form of copra. There is subsistence farming of coconuts, pigs and poultry. Fishing is carried out on a small scale but it is hoped that the exploitation of fish resources can be developed to form the basis of the economy. Foreign exchange is earned from the sale of postage stamps and remittances sent home by Tuvaluans working abroad, mainly in the phosphate industry on Nauru, or on foreign ships.

The United Kingdom agreed to continue financial assistance after independence with a $A4.7 million special development grant, $A4.9 million general development aid for three years and $A1.7 million budgetary aid for 1979/80. General development aid was extended in 1980 and budgetary aid of $A810,000 for 1981 and $A900,000 for 1982 was agreed. A seaplane service provided by a New Zealand company began in 1980, linking six of Tuvalu's islands.

STATISTICAL SURVEY

Land Area: 26 square km. (10 square miles).

Population: 7,349 at census of May 1979. In addition, there were about 2,000 Tuvaluans living overseas.

Labour Force: In 1979 there were 936 people in paid employment, 50 per cent of them in government service. In 1979 114 Tuvaluans were employed by the Nauru Phosphate Co., with a smaller number employed in Kiribati and about 255 on foreign ships.

FINANCE

Australian currency: 100 cents=1 Australian dollar ($A). Coins: 1, 2, 5, 10, 20 and 50 cents. Notes: 1, 2, 5, 10, 20 and 50 dollars.

In January 1977, Tuvaluan coinage of denominations 1, 2, 5, 10, 20 and 50 cents and 1 dollar was introduced. A 5-dollar piece was added in 1981. Australian notes and coins continue to circulate.

Exchange rates (June 1982): £1 sterling=$A1.6925; U.S. $1=97.9 Australian cents. $A100=£59.08=U.S. $102.17.

Note: For details of previous changes in the exchange rate, *see* the chapter on Australia.

Budget (1981): Expenditure $A2,820,390, of which $A810,000 was British grant-in-aid. The remainder, $A2,010,390, was expected to comprise personal tax revenue of $A160,000, customs duties of $A450,000, shipping fares and freights $A180,000 and philately $A515,600.

Development (1981): $A4.3 million derived from grant and loan funds from the United Kingdom, New Zealand, Australia, Canada, Japan, the Federal Republic of Germany, the EDF and UNDP.

In 1982 the Government planned to spend $A156,140 on social services and education, $A948,166 on commerce and natural resources, $A180,022 on communications and works.

EXTERNAL TRADE

COPRA EXPORTS

	1977	1978	1979	1980
Quantity (metric tons) . .	139	153	517	282
Value ($A) . .	55,636	36,933	237,412	62,659

THE CONSTITUTION

A new Constitution came into effect on October 1st, 1978, when Tuvalu became independent. The main provisions are set out below:

The Constitution states that Tuvalu is a democratic sovereign state and that the Constitution is the Supreme Law. It guarantees protection of all fundamental rights and freedoms and provides for the determination of citizenship.

The British sovereign is represented by the Governor-General who must be a citizen of Tuvalu and is appointed on the recommendation of the Prime Minister. The Prime Minister is elected by Parliament, and up to four other Ministers are appointed by the Governor-General from among the members of Parliament, after consultation with the Prime Minister. The Cabinet, which is directly responsible to Parliament, consists of the Prime Minister and the other Ministers whose functions are to advise the Governor-General upon the government of Tuvalu. The Attorney-General is the principal legal adviser to the Government. Parliament is composed of 12 members directly elected by universal adult suffrage for four years, subject to dissolution, and is presided over by a Speaker elected by the members. The Constitution also provides for the operation of a Judiciary (*see* Judicial System) and for an independent Public Service.

THE GOVERNMENT

HEAD OF STATE

H.M. Queen ELIZABETH II.

Governor-General: Sir FIATAU PENITALA TEO, G.C.M.G., I.S.O., M.B.E. (took office October 1st, 1978).

CABINET

(July 1982)

Prime Minister, Minister for Civil Service Administration and Local Government and Minister for Foreign Affairs: Dr. TOMASI PUAPUA.

Deputy Prime Minister and Minister for Finance: HENRY F. NAISALI.

Minister for Social Services: FALAILE PILITATI.

Minister for Commerce and Natural Resources: LALE SELUKA.

Minister for Works and Communications: METIA TEALOFI.

LEGISLATURE

PARLIAMENT

There are 12 elected members presided over by the Speaker. Elections were held in September 1981. There are no political parties.

DIPLOMATIC REPRESENTATION

EMBASSIES AND HIGH COMMISSIONS ACCREDITED TO TUVALU

(HC) High Commission.

Australia: Suva, Fiji (HC).
Belgium: Wellington, New Zealand.
Canada: Wellington, New Zealand (HC).
Chile: Wellington, New Zealand.
China (Taiwan): Nuku'alofa, Tonga.
France: Wellington, New Zealand.
Germany, Federal Republic: Wellington, New Zealand.
Japan: Suva, Fiji.
Korea, Republic: Wellington, New Zealand.
New Zealand: Suva, Fiji (HC).
Papua New Guinea: Suva, Fiji (HC).
Turkey: Canberra, Australia.
United Kingdom: Suva, Fiji (HC).
U.S.A.: Suva, Fiji.

Tuvalu also has diplomatic relations with Bangladesh, Fiji and Switzerland.

JUDICIAL SYSTEM

The Supreme Law is embodied in the Constitution. The High Court is the superior court of record, presided over by the Chief Justice, and has jurisdiction to hear appeals from judgments of the Magistrates' Courts and the Island Courts. Appeals from the High Court lie with the Court of Appeal in Fiji or, in the ultimate case, with the Judicial Committee of the Privy Council in the United Kingdom.

There are eight Island Courts with limited jurisdiction in criminal and civil cases.

RELIGION

Church of Tuvalu: Funafuti; f. 1861 derived from the Congregationalist foundation of the London Missionary Society; embraces about 97 per cent of the population; Chair. Rev. PANAPA MAKINI; publ. *Te Lama.*

There are small groups of Seventh-day Adventists, Jehovah's Witnesses and Bahá'i.

THE PRESS

Tuvalu Newsheet: Broadcasting and Information Division, Vaiaku, Funafuti; fortnightly; circ. 250.

RADIO

Radio Tuvalu: Vaiaku, Funafuti; f. 1975; broadcasts daily, 27 hours per week; Broadcasting and Information Officer PUSINELLI LAFAI.

FINANCE, TRADE AND INDUSTRY

National Bank of Tuvalu: Vaiaku; Funafuti; f. 1980; Gen. Man. ANDREW HOPE-MORLEY. brs. on all islands.

Retail trade is almost exclusively in the hands of island co-operative societies which are supplied by the

Tuvalu Co-operative Society Ltd.: Funafuti; f. 1979 after amalgamation of the eight island Societies; Co-operatives Officer ITIBO P. TOFIGA.

Tuvalu Copra Co-operative Society Ltd.: Funafuti; f. 1979.

TRANSPORT

Shipping: There is a deep-water lagoon at the port of entry, Funafuti, and irregular shipping services connect Tuvalu with Fiji and elsewhere. The Government operates one inter-island ship.

Civil Aviation: Air Tungaru (Kiribati) operates a weekly service between Tarawa and Funafuti. Sea Bee Air Ltd. of Auckland (New Zealand) operates, on behalf of the Government, an amphibian service between Funafuti and Nukulaelae, Nukufetau, Vaitupu, Nui and Nanumea.

EDUCATION

In 1979 there were eight primary schools with a total enrolment of 1,298 children. The one secondary school at Motufoua, Vaitupu, has 236 pupils. There were about 20 private and officially sponsored students undertaking tertiary education abroad, especially at the University of the South Pacific.

Vanuatu

PHYSICAL AND SOCIAL GEOGRAPHY

The Republic of Vanuatu (formerly the New Hebrides) comprises an archipelago of some 70 islands, including the Banks and Torres Islands, stretching from south of Solomon Islands to Hunter and Matthew Islands, east of New Caledonia, 900 kilometres in all. The islands range in size from 12 hectares to 3,600 square kilometres. The islands have rugged mountainous interiors with narrow coastal strips where most of the inhabitants dwell. Three islands have active volcanoes on them. The census of January 1979 recorded a population of 112,700, of whom over 90 per cent were New Hebrideans. Other races represented include Europeans, Chinese and Polynesian migrants. The capital is Vila.

HISTORY

The New Hebrides were governed until 1980 by an Anglo-French Condominium which was established in 1906. Under this arrangement there were three elements in the structure of administration: the British National Service, the French National Service and the Condominium (Joint) Departments. Each power was responsible for its own citizens and other non-New Hebrideans who chose to be "*ressortissant*" of either power. Indigenous New Hebrideans were not permitted to claim either British or French citizenship. The result of this was two official languages, two police forces, three public services, three courts of law, three currencies, three national budgets, two resident commissioners in Vila, the capital, and two district commissioners in each of the four Districts.

Local political initiatives began after the Second World War and originated in New Hebridean concern over the alienation of native land. More than 36 per cent of the New Hebrides was owned by foreigners. Na-Griamel, one of the first political groups to emerge, had its source in cult-like activities. In 1971 Na-Griamel leaders petitioned the United Nations to prevent more land sales at a time when land was being sold to American interests for development as tropical tourist resorts. In 1972 the New Hebrides National Party was formed with support from Protestant missions and covert support from British interests. In response French interests formed the Union des Communautés Néo-Hébridaises in 1974. Discussions in London in 1974 resulted in the replacement of the Advisory Council, set up in 1957, by a Representative Assembly of 42 members, of whom 29 were directly elected, but this did not satisfy nationalist aspirations.

The Representative Assembly was dissolved in early 1977 following a boycott by the National Party, which had changed its name to the Vanuaaku Party (VP) in 1976. However, the VP succeeded in reaching an agreement with the Condominium powers for new elections for the Representative Assembly to be held, based on universal suffrage for all seats.

In July 1977 it was announced at a conference in Paris between British, French and New Hebrides representatives, that the islands would become independent in 1980 following a referendum and elections. The VP boycotted this conference on the grounds that they demanded immediate independence. The VP also boycotted the elections held in November and declared a "People's Provisional Government".

Nevertheless, a reduced Assembly of 39 members was elected and a measure of self-government was introduced early in 1978. A Council of Ministers and the office of Chief Minister were created, and the French, British and Condominium Services were being replaced by a single New Hebrides Public Service. The VP declined to participate in the new Government at first but in December 1978 a Government of National Unity was formed with Father Gérard Leymang, a Catholic priest, as Chief Minister.

In September 1979 a Conference was held to draw up a constitution. Agreement was reached, after considerable difficulties, over electoral systems and the role of the Head of State. British and French rivalries did little to help the deliberations but independence was finally scheduled for July 30th, 1980. On November 14th, 1979, new elections were held which resulted in the VP's winning 26 of the 39 seats in the Assembly. The outcome brought about a riot by Na-Griamel supporters on Espiritu Santo who threatened non-Santo "foreigners". British and French police commissioners could not agree on the use of police but individual officials spoke with the Na-Griamel leader, Jimmy Stevens. On November 29th, 1979, Walter Lini, leader of the Vanuaaku Party, was elected Chief Minister.

In June 1980 Jimmy Stevens declared Santo independent of the rest of the New Hebrides, styling it the "Independent State of Vemarana". On July 30th the New Hebrides became independent as Vanuatu, and Walter Lini sought assistance from Papua New Guinea to deal with the rebellion on Santo. Papua New Guinea, with support from Australia and New Zealand, sent 300 troops to Vanuatu. They landed on Santo and quickly arrested the leaders of the rebellion, and many French and mixed-race supporters. A number of deaths occurred. All but two of the people taken prisoner during the rebellion were released in November 1981.

In February 1981 the French ambassador to Vanuatu was expelled following the deportation from New Caledonia of the VP Secretary-General, who was due to attend an assembly of the New Caledonian Independence Front. France immediately withdrew aid to Vanuatu but, when relations between the countries improved in March, a $A6.9 million aid agreement was signed and a new ambassador appointed. In September 1981 Vanuatu became the 155th member of the United Nations.

ECONOMIC SURVEY

The native population is mainly engaged in peasant agriculture, producing both subsistence and cash crops. In 1979 French copra planters still occupied about 80 per cent of the islands' good arable land and the majority of New Hebridean adult males were occupied as full-time subsistence gardeners. The production of copra, frozen fish and beef are the three most important industries. Cocoa and coffee are also grown in small quantities. Secondary industry is on a small scale, catering almost exclusively for local consumption but in 1978 a new abattoir was opened in Santo which began exporting frozen meat to France. It will also operate as a meat cannery in addition to the small existing meat cannery. There is a small fish freezing works and in 1979 it was planned to expand the oil mill to increase the proportion of copra processed domestically. Manganese has been mined since 1961 and is exported to Japan.

STATISTICAL SURVEY

Area: 4,700 sq. miles (12,190 sq. km.).

Population (Census of January 15th, 1979): 112,700; Port Vila (capital) 14,880.

Agriculture: 95,000 hectares are cultivated; there are 16,000 hectares of forest. Production (1980—metric tons, FAO estimates): coconuts 346,000, copra 50,000, meat 4,000.

Livestock (1980—FAO estimates): Cattle 90,000, Pigs 67,000, Goats 7,000, Poultry 150,000.

Fishing (catch in metric tons): 2,825 in 1978; 2,819 in 1979; 2,796 in 1980.

Mining (exports in '000 metric tons): Manganese ore (metal content): 18.5 in 1976; 11.3 in 1977; 10.1 in 1978; 5.0 in 1979.

Finance: 100 centimes = 1 vatu, formerly the New Hebrides franc (franc néo-hébridais or FNH). Coins: 1, 2, 5, 10, 20, 50 vatu. Notes: 100, 500, 1,000 vatu. Exchange rates (June 1982): £1 sterling = 169.16 vatu; U.S. $1 = 97.67 vatu; 1,000 vatu = £5.91 = $10.24.

Note: Until the end of 1980 the FNH and Australian currency were both legal tender. On January 1st, 1981, the FNH was renamed the vatu and became the sole official currency. The FNH was linked to French currency and from August 1969 had a value of 6.1875 French centimes. This valuation remained in effect until September 1981, when the link with French currency was ended and the vatu was tied to the IMF Special Drawing Right at a rate of 1 SDR = 106.2 vatu.

Budget: (1982 estimate): *Expenditure* 2,472 million vatu. More than one-quarter of this was allocated to education. *Revenue* 2,415 million vatu from local sources and in aid from France and the U.K. Locally raised revenue was expected to total 1,730 million vatu, more than 50 per cent of it from custom duties. There are no direct or company taxes.

EXTERNAL TRADE

(million vatu)

	1979	1980	1981
Imports c.i.f. . .	5,029	4,922	5,123
Exports f.o.b. .	3,236	2,449	2,883

PRINCIPAL COMMODITIES

(million vatu, preliminary)

Exports	1979	1980	1981
Copra . . .	1,505	592	1,070
Fish . . .	831	1,056	826
Beef . . .	139	75	159
Total (incl. others)	3,236	2,449	2,883

Imports: Food and drink, manufactured goods and petroleum products are the principal imports.

Transport (1981): *Roads:* 4,948 vehicles; *Shipping:* 340 ships called at Vanuatu ports; *Aviation:* 1,014 aircraft landed at Port Vila.

TOURISM

	1979	1980	1981
Number of visitors .	30,454	21,973	22,092

Education (1981): 289 primary schools, 10 secondary schools, 1 technical institute and 1 teacher-training college.

THE CONSTITUTION

A new Constitution came into effect on July 30th, 1980, when Vanuatu achieved independence. The main provisions are described below.

The Republic of Vanuatu is a sovereign democratic state, of which the Constitution is the supreme law. Bislama is the national language and the official languages are Bislama, English and French. The Constitution guarantees protection of all fundamental rights and freedoms and provides for the determination of citizenship.

The President, as head of the Republic, symbolizes the unity of the Republic and is elected for a five-year term of office by secret ballot by an electoral college consisting of Parliament and the Presidents of the Regional Councils.

Legislative power resides in the single-chamber Parliament consisting of members elected for four years on the basis of universal franchise through an electoral system which includes an element of proportional representation to ensure fair representation of different political groups and opinions. Parliament is presided over by a Speaker elected by the members. Executive power is vested in the Council of Ministers which consists of the Prime Minister (elected by Parliament from among its members) and other Ministers (appointed by the Prime Minister from among the members of Parliament). The number of Ministers, including the Prime Minister, may not exceed a quarter of the number of members of Parliament.

Special attention is paid to custom law and to decentralization. The Constitution states that all land in the Republic belongs to the indigenous custom owners and their descendants. There is a National Council of Chiefs, composed of custom chiefs elected by their peers sitting in District Councils of Chiefs. It may discuss all matters relating to custom and tradition and may make recommendations to Parliament for the preservation and promotion of the culture and languages of Vanuatu. The Council may be consulted on any question in connection with any bill before Parliament. Each region may elect a regional council and the Constitution lays particular emphasis on the representation of custom chiefs within each one.

The Constitution also makes provision for public finance, the Public Service, the Ombudsman, a leadership code and the judiciary (*see* Judicial System).

THE GOVERNMENT

HEAD OF STATE

President: Ati George Sokomanu, M.B.E. (took office July 30th, 1980).

COUNCIL OF MINISTERS

(July 1982)

Prime Minister: Hon. Fr. Walter Hayde Lini, C.B.E.

Minister for Home Affairs and Deputy Prime Minister: Hon. F. Timakata.

Minister of Education: Hon. DONALD KALPOKAS.

Minister of Finance: Hon. KALPOKOR KALSAKAU.

Minister of Agriculture, Forestry and Fisheries: SETHY REGENVANU.

Minister of Health: Hon. WIVIE KORISA.

Minister of Transport, Communications and Public Works: Hon. JOHN NAUPA.

LEGISLATURE

PARLIAMENT

Vanuatu's first Parliament was formed by the pre-independence Representative Assembly. After the elections in December 1979, the Vanuaaku Pati held 26 of the 39 seats.

Speaker: MAXIME CARLOT.

Leader of the Opposition: VINCENT BOULEKONE.

POLITICAL PARTIES

Vanuaaku Pati (VP): Port Vila; f. 1972 (formerly the National Party); Government party; Pres. Father WALTER LINI.

Vanuatu Alliance Party: Port Vila; f. 1982; Leaders THOMAS SERU, GEORGE WOREK, KALMER VOCOR.

DIPLOMATIC REPRESENTATION

EMBASSIES AND HIGH COMMISSIONS ACCREDITED TO VANUATU

(HC) High Commission.

Australia: Melitco House, P.O.B. 111, Port Vila (HC).

Belgium: Wellington, New Zealand.

Canada: Canberra, A.C.T., Australia (HC).

Fiji: Suva, Fiji; *roving ambassador*.

France: Port Vila; *Ambassador:* MARC MENGUY.

Germany, Federal Republic: Port Moresby, Papua New Guinea.

Japan: Suva, Fiji.

Korea, Republic: Canberra, Australia.

New Zealand: Honiara, Solomon Islands (HC).

Spain: Canberra, A.C.T., Australia.

United Kingdom: Melitco House, rue Pasteur, P.O.B. 567, Port Vila (HC); *High Commissioner:* R. B. DORMAN.

Vanuatu also has diplomatic relations with the People's Republic of China, India, Italy, the Democratic People's Republic of Korea, the Netherlands, Nigeria, Switzerland and Viet-Nam.

JUDICIAL SYSTEM

The Supreme Court has unlimited jurisdiction to hear and determine any civil or criminal proceedings. It consists of a Chief Justice, appointed by the President of the Republic after consultation with the Prime Minister and the leader of the opposition, and three other judges who are appointed by the President of the Republic, one being nominated by the President of the National Council of Chiefs, and one being nominated by the Presidents of the Regional Councils.

The Court of Appeal is constituted by two or more judges of the Supreme Court sitting together.

Persons knowledgeable in custom may sit with the judges of the Supreme Court or the Court of Appeal and take part in the proceedings.

The Constitution of 1980 states that "Parliament shall provide for the establishment of village or island courts with jurisdiction over customary and other matters and shall provide for the role of chiefs in such courts".

RELIGION

Most of the inhabitants are Christian. Eight churches and groups are represented, including Presbyterian, Anglican, Seventh Day Adventist and Churches of Christ. The Roman Catholic Church is also well established.

Church of Melanesia: Anglican; Bishop of Vanuatu: Rt. Rev. HARRY S. TEVI, Luganville, Santo.

Roman Catholic: Bishop of Port Vila: Most Rev. FRANCIS LAMBERT, S.M.; P.O.B. 59, Port Vila.

THE PRESS

There are no independent daily or weekly newspapers.

Le Melanésien: Port Vila; in French.

Tam-Tam: Government Information Dept., Port Vila; f. 1980; fortnightly; Bislama, English and French; circ. 1,000.

Voice of Vanuatu: Port Vila; in English.

RADIO

Radio Vanuatu: P.O.B. 49, Port Vila; f. 1966; government-owned; broadcasts in English, French and Bislama; Man. J. CARLO.

In 1978 there were 15,500 receivers.

FINANCE

The republic has no personal income tax nor tax on company profits and is therefore developing rapidly as a finance centre and "tax haven".

BANKING

There are eight commercial banks in the capital.

DEVELOPMENT BANKS

Development Bank of Vanuatu: P.O.B. 241, Port Vila; f. 1979; government-owned; cap. 200m. vatu (1982); Gen. Man. CAMILLE BASTIEN.

Caisse Centrale de Coopération Economique (*France*): Port Vila; provides finance for certain types of project.

FOREIGN BANKS

Banque INDOSUEZ (*France*): rue Higginson, P.O.B. 29, Port Vila.

Barclays Bank International Ltd. (*U.K.*): P.O.B. 123, Port Vila; Man. E. J. CRUTCHLEY.

Westpac Banking Corporation (*Australia*): rue Higginson, Port Vila.

Australia and New Zealand Banking Group Ltd. and Hongkong and Shanghai Banking Corpn. (Hong Kong) also have branches in Vanuatu.

TRADE AND INDUSTRY

MARKETING BOARD

Vanuatu Commodities Marketing Board: Port Vila; f. 1982.

CO-OPERATIVES

There are more than 300 co-operative primary societies in Vanuatu and at least 85 per cent of the distribution of goods in the islands is done by co-operative organizations. Almost all rural ni-Vanuatu are members of a co-operative society (through family membership), as are many urban dwellers also.

Co-operative Federation: Port Vila; the principal apex society; alone handles 75 per cent of consumer goods distribution in the outer islands as well as operating a large shipping service and a savings bank.

TRANSPORT

ROADS

In 1980 there were about 1,000 km. of roads, 35 km. of which were sealed.

SHIPPING

The principal ports are Port Vila and Santo.

Vanua Navigation SARL: Port Vila; f. 1977 by the Co-operative Federation and Sofrana Unilines.

The following services call regularly at Vanuatu: Compagnie Générale Maritime, Daiwa Line and Pacific Navigation of Tonga from Sydney and other Pacific Islands; China Navigation Co. from Australia, Hong Kong, Taiwan and Singapore; Kyowa Shipping Co. from Hong Kong, Japan and the Republic of Korea; Sofrana-Unilines from New Caledonia and Solomon Islands; Bank Line from the United Kingdom, the Netherlands and the Federal Republic of Germany. Royal Viking Line and P. & O. cruises also call at Vanuatu.

CIVIL AVIATION

The principal airports are Bauerfield (Efate) and Pekoa (Santo).

Air Melanesiae: Air Melanesiae House, P.O.B. 72, Port Vila; f. 1966; operates scheduled flights to 21 destinations within the archipelago; charters and aerial scenic tours are available on request; Gen. Man. Capt. H. O. Tschuchnigg; fleet of 4 Britten Norman Islanders, 1 Trislander and 1 De Havilland Twin Otter Series 300.

Air Vanuatu: Air Melanesiae House, Kumul Highway, Port Vila; f. 1981; flies from Port Vila to Sydney; operates 1 DC-9.

Vanuatu is also served by Air Nauru, Air Pacific Ltd. (Fiji) and UTA (France).

EDUCATION

The Education Department supervises 249 primary schools; in 1981, there were some 10,800 pupils enrolled in French-speaking primary schools and 13,300 in English-speaking primary schools. Primary education is not free but only nominal fees are charged and primary education is available for most children. Forty primary schools are maintained by missions and voluntary agencies.

In addition, there are 10 secondary schools, with a total of 1,880 students, a technical institute, with 229 students, and a teacher-training college with 83 students.

Wake Island

Wake Island and its neighbours, Wilkes and Peale Islands, lie in the Pacific on the direct route from Hawaii to Hong Kong about 3,200 km. west of Hawaii and 2064 km. east of Guam. The group is 7.2 km. long, 2.4 km. wide and covers less than 8 sq. km. In 1970 the population was 1,647. The U.S.A. took formal possession in 1899 and the group has been administered since 1972 by the U.S. Air Force.

Wallis and Futuna Islands

This self-governing French Overseas Territory comprises two groups: the Wallis Islands, including Wallis Island (also known as Uvea) and 22 islets on the surrounding reef, and, to the southeast, Futuna (or Hooru), comprising the two small islands of Futuna and Alofi. The islands are located north of Fiji and west of Samoa. The total area is 274 square kilometres and in 1976 the total population of the islands was 9,192. The inhabitants are Polynesians.

A French Protectorate since 1888, the islands chose by referendum in December 1959 to become an Overseas Territory. In July 1961 they were granted this status.

Copra, which formerly provided the main cash income for the islands, has been seriously affected by rhinoceros beetle. Most monetary income on the island is derived from government employment and remittances sent home by islanders employed in New Caledonia. Yams, taros, bananas, arrowroot and other food crops are also cultivated.

STATISTICAL SURVEY

Area (sq. km.): Wallis Island 159, Futuna Island and Alofi Island 115, total of all islands 274.

Population (census of March 26th, 1976): 9,192; Wallis Island 6,019 (chief town Mata-Utu), Futuna Island 3,173; Alofi Island uninhabited; about 11,000 Wallisians and Futunians live on New Caledonia and in Vanuatu.

Livestock: (FAO estimates): 4,000 pigs (1980); 11,000 goats (1979).

Currency: *see* French Polynesia.

Budget (1981): 13,290,000 French francs.

External Trade (1980): *Imports:* 540 million francs CFP; *Exports:* n.a.

Aid from France (1981): 50,000,000 French francs.

Transport: *Civil Aviation*, Wallis Island—1980: aircraft arrivals and departures 581, freight handled 171 metric tons, passenger arrivals 4,555, passenger departures 4,300, mail loaded and unloaded 72 metric tons.

Education (1978): 3,000 pupils in 9 State-financed primary and lower secondary schools.

THE GOVERNMENT

The territory is administered by a French Administrateur Supérieur who is assisted by a 20-member Territorial Assembly. The Assembly, together with a senator and a deputy to the French Parliament, are elected locally on a common roll.

Administrateur Supérieur: Robert Thil.

President of the Territorial Assembly: Manuelo Lisiahi.

Representative to the National Assembly: Benjamin Brial.

Representative to the Senate: Sosefo Makape Papillo.

RELIGION

The entire population is nominally Catholic; Bishop of Wallis and Futuna Mgr. Lolesio Fuahea.

RADIO

In 1979 a radio station was opened on Wallis Island, broadcasting in Wallisian and French for 6 hours each day.

TRANSPORT

SHIPPING

Services to Nouméa (New Caledonia), Suva (Fiji), Port Vila and Santo (Vanuatu), are operated by the Compagnie des Chargeurs Calédoniens.

CIVIL AVIATION

UTA (France) operates three flights a week from Wallis to Futuna and external services. Air Nauru also serves Wallis Island.

Western Samoa

PHYSICAL AND SOCIAL GEOGRAPHY

Western Samoa comprises the two large islands of Savai'i and Upolu and seven small islands, five of which are uninhabited. Their total area is 2,835 square kilometres. These high volcanic islands, with rugged interiors and little flat land except along the coasts, lie in the South Pacific 2,400 kilometres north of New Zealand.

At mid-1981 the estimated population of Western Samoa was 156,893, including 33,784 in the capital, Apia, on the island of Upolu. At the 1976 census about 72 per cent of the population lived on Upolu.

HISTORY

The islands are peopled by Polynesians and are thought to have been the origin of many of the people who now occupy islands further east. The Samoan language is believed to be the oldest form of Polynesian speech in existence. Samoan society developed an intricate hierarchy of graded titles comprising titular chiefs and orator chiefs. One of the striking features of modern Samoa is the manner in which these titles and pre-contact culture remain a dominant influence. Most of the population have become Christians.

The Samoan islands were first visited by Europeans in the 1700s but it was not until 1830 that missionaries from the London Missionary Society settled there. The eastern islands (now American Samoa) were ceded to the United States in 1904 but Western Samoa, a former German colony, was occupied by New Zealand in 1914 and the League of Nations granted a mandate over the territory to New Zealand in 1920. In 1946 the United Nations assumed responsibility for the Territory of Western Samoa through its Trusteeship Council, with New Zealand as the administering power. From 1954 measures of internal self-government were gradually introduced, culminating in the adoption of an independence constitution in October 1960. This was approved by a UN-supervised plebiscite in May 1961 and the islands became independent on January 1st, 1962. The office of Head of State was to be jointly held by two of the Paramount Chiefs but, upon the death of his colleague in April 1963, Malietoa Tanumafili II became sole Head of State for life.

Despite independence, Western Samoa still has strong links with New Zealand, where many Samoans now live and where many others received their secondary and tertiary education. Western Samoa joined the Commonwealth in August 1970 and the UN in December 1976.

Western Samoa has had a legislative assembly since 1947. Since independence in 1962, the islands have been governed under a parliamentary system, with a Prime Minister and Cabinet. The 1973 elections were won by Fiame Mata'afa Fuamui Mulinuu, who was first elected Prime Minister in 1959 but who lost the position in 1970 to Tupua Tamasese Lealofi. Fiame Mata'afa Mulinuu became Prime Minister again in 1973, remaining in office until his death in 1975, when Tupua Tamasese Lealofi was recalled to complete the term of office. Tupuola Taisi Efi was elected Prime Minister in March 1976 and re-elected in February 1979. The elections held in February 1982 resulted in a win for the opposition Human Rights Protection Party, which gained 24 of the 47 seats in the *Fono*. Va'ai Kolone was elected Prime Minister. Serious political problems to emerge from the elections are petitions against the result in 13 seats, alleging bribery, and the ruling of the Chief Justice that the present electoral law is discriminatory and unconstitutional because only *matai* (chiefs) and those on the Individual Voters Roll (i.e. non-Samoans) may vote. The government has appealed against this judgment.

ECONOMIC SURVEY

Western Samoa's main exports are copra, cocoa, desiccated coconut and bananas, which are shipped to New Zealand, Australia and the United Kingdom. A serious economic slump, which began in 1976, was eased in early 1977 by the rising price of copra and the fluctuating price of cocoa. New Zealand accounted for about 33 per cent of external trade in 1980. Australia, the U.S.A., Japan, Fiji and the Federal Republic of Germany are also important trading partners.

A number of small industrial enterprises have been established in recent years. These are principally concerned with the processing of foodstuffs but there are also plans to develop the timber industry by large-scale exploitation of forest resources on the islands of Savai'i and Upolu. In 1982 work began in Apia on a copra mill which is expected to process the country's entire copra production.

STATISTICAL SURVEY

AREA AND POPULATION

	Area (sq. km.)	Population (Census results)				Density (per sq. km.) 1976
		Sept. 25th, 1961	Nov. 21st, 1966	Nov. 3rd, 1971	Nov. 3rd, 1976	
Savai'i*	1,714	31,948	36,159	40,581	42,218	24.8
Upolu*	1,121	82,479	95,218	106,046	109,765	97.8
Total . . .	2,835†	114,427	131,377	146,627	151,983	53.7

* Including adjacent small islands. † 1,095 square miles.

Estimated population: 156,893 (July 1st, 1981).

Capital: Apia (population 32,099 in 1976; estimate for July 1st, 1981: 33,784).

Births and deaths (1980): 2,558 live births (birth rate 16.4 per 1,000); 475 deaths (death rate 3.1 per 1,000).

EMPLOYMENT

	1971	1976
Agriculture, forestry and fishing	25,410	23,373
subsistence	22,850	n.a.
cash	2,560	n.a.
Manufacturing and construction	2,440	2,525
Trade and commerce	2,420	2,407
Transport and communications	1,250	2,058
Government and services	6,230	7,215
Others	n.a.	671
TOTAL	37,740	38,249

AGRICULTURE

PRINCIPAL CROPS
('000 metric tons)

	1977	1978	1979	1980
Taro (Coco yam)	32.0*	26.4	26.4	n.a.
Coconuts	215.0†	207.0	226.0	210.0*
Copra	16.9	13.3	20.4	23.2
Bananas	36.0*	20.3	20.5	20.0*
Cocoa beans	2.0	2.2	2.2	2.0†

*FAO estimate. † Unofficial figure.

Sources: Western Samoa Department of Statistics, Apia; FAO, *Production Yearbook*.

Livestock (1980—FAO estimates): Pigs 60,000, Cattle 27,000, Horses 10,000, Poultry 500,000.

Fishing (catch in metric tons): 1,000 in 1975; 1,100 in 1976; 1,250 in 1977; 1,090 in 1978.

FINANCE

100 sene (cents) = 1 tala (Western Samoan dollar—WS$).

Coins: 1, 2, 5, 10, 20 and 50 sene.

Notes: 1, 2, 5, 10 and 20 tala.

Exchange rates (June 1982): £1 sterling = 2.120 tala; U.S. $1 = 1.224 tala.

100 tala = £47.17 = $81.70.

Note: The tala was introduced in July 1967, replacing the Western Samoan pound at the rate of £WS1 = 2 tala. This changeover coincided with a similar move in New Zealand. The Western Samoan pound had been introduced in January 1962, replacing (at par) the New Zealand pound. From October 1961 the pound was valued at U.S. $2.78 so the initial value of the tala was $1.39 ($1 = 71.9 sene). The market rate was fixed at 1 tala = U.S. $1.387 (U.S. $1 = 72.11 sene). This valuation remained in effect until August 1971. From December 1971 to February 1973 the central rate was 1 tala = $1.51 ($1 = 66.24 sene) and the market rate originally 1 tala = $1.478 and later 1 tala = $1.485. From February 1973 to October 1975 the central rate was 1 tala = $1.677 ($1 = 59.62 sene) and the market rate 1 tala = $1.649 ($1 = 60.66 sene). Since October 1975 the tala's direct link with the U.S. dollar has been broken and it is pegged to a "basket" of currencies (as used by New Zealand). The average value of the tala in U.S. dollars was: 1.5853 in 1975; 1.2547 in 1976; 1.2706 in 1977; 1.3586 in 1978; 1.2205 in 1979; 1.0876 in 1980. In terms of sterling, the central exchange rate between November 1967 and June 1972 was £1 = 1.727 tala.

BUDGET
('000 tala)

REVENUE	1978*	1979	1980
Tax on income	3,791	4,144	4,150
Customs	10,237	11,804	13,810
Other tax revenue	198	141	140
Other receipts	5,694	—	—
TOTAL	19,920	16,089	18,100

EXPENDITURE	1978*	1979	1980
Economic services	3,104	3,563	3,622
Social services	5,898	6,967	7,623
Other current expenditure	5,292	6,319	7,821
Investments	22,800	n.a.	n.a.
TOTAL	37,094	n.a.	n.a.

* Revised.

INTERNATIONAL RESERVES
('000 tala at December 31st)

	1977	1978	1979	1980
IMF Special Drawing Rights	24	35	5	—
Foreign Exchange	1,151	600	608	429
TOTAL	1,175	635	613	429

CURRENCY IN CIRCULATION*

('000 tala)

	1975	1976	1977	1978	1979	1980
Coins	209.7	237.9	243	281	338	379
Notes	1,227.1	1,506.5	1,610	2,289	3,283	3,490

* Figures up to 1977 relate to the Bank of Western Samoa. Figures from 1978 cover the Bank of Western Samoa and the Pacific Commercial Bank Ltd.

CONSUMER PRICE INDEX

(Base: August 1971–July 1972=100)

	1977	1978	1979	1980*	1981*
Food	207.9	207.9	236.6	320.2	389.9
Clothing and footwear	194.8	194.8	238.4	258.1	349.2
Household	186.1	200.2	206.3	281.2	374.3
Miscellaneous	140.2	155.8	161.3	177.2	278.1
All Items	193.3	197.5	219.4	291.9	366.2

* Provisional.

EXTERNAL TRADE

('000 tala)

	1975	1976	1977	1978	1979	1980
Imports c.i.f.	23,111	23,627	32,254	38,567	60,946	57,438
Exports f.o.b.	4,541	5,447	11,577	8,170	14,981	15,828

PRINCIPAL COMMODITIES

(distribution by SITC, '000 tala)

Imports c.i.f.	1978	1979	1980*
Meat and meat preparations	2,525.6	3,166.3	2,855.8
Cereals and cereal preparations	1,824.8	2,557.4	3,070.2
Fish and fish preparations	787.2	2,066.1	1,404.9
Sugar, sugar preparations and honey	1,124.0	1,512.0	1,839.6
Beverages	1,031.9	463.4	386.5
Tobacco and tobacco manufactures	1,156.3	1,264.3	1,094.8
Petroleum and petroleum products	2,839.7	5,739.1	9,551.7
Rubber manufactures	583.5	982.1	809.3
Paper, paperboard and manufactures	1,051.9	1,587.9	1,858.6
Textile yarn, fabrics and manufactured articles	1,213.5	1,419.2	1,609.9
Iron and steel	802.6	1,796.3	2,127.9
Non-electric machinery*	3,005.8	3,964.6	5,736.4
Electrical machinery*	3,341.4	2,367.1	3,280.4
Transport equipment*	3,524.5	15,586.5	2,691.7
Miscellaneous manufactured articles*	3,545.4	3,613.2	3,808.6
Total (incl. others)	38,566.8	60,946.3	57,437.9

* Provisional.

Exports f.o.b.†	1978	1979	1980*
Copra	3,535.9	8,018.4	8,404.8
Cocoa	2,637.8	3,468.4	3,012.6
Bananas	108.2	266.1	439.8
Taro and taamu	993.7	1,512.2	1,048.3
Timber	142.9	291.0	324.6
Other food and beverages	431.3	971.4	1,539.4
Coconut cream	251.1	427.2	580.8
Other non-food	337.1	453.8	1,058.8
Total	8,186.9	14,981.3	15,828.3

† Including re-exports.

PRINCIPAL TRADING PARTNERS
('000 tala)

	1977		1978		1979		1980	
	Exports	Imports	Exports	Imports	Exports	Imports	Exports	Imports
Australia	289	5,445	219	5,891	187	10,125	312	11,704
Fiji	17	1,825	13	1,705	147	1,707	19	1,856
Germany, Fed. Rep.	5,267	2,714	1,725	733	4,208	12,193	1,677	1,147
Japan	800	4,709	507	7,437	1	6,717	767	5,346
New Zealand	2,028	9,419	2,836	12,837	3,199	15,030	4,068	18,478
Singapore	—	1,484	17	2,187	2	3,460	—	6,306
United Kingdom	299	1,055	382	1,099	98	1,516	75	3,344
U.S.A.	1,128	2,795	301	3,614	1,342	5,266	947	4,934

TRANSPORT

ROAD TRAFFIC
(vehicles registered)

	1978	1979	1980
Taxis and buses	532	558	523
Private cars and lorries	1,362	1,433	1,489
Motor cycles	118	114	121
Pick-ups	1,639	1,564	1,628

TOURISM

Visitors: 24,418 (1976), 26,214 (1977), 25,379 (1978), 25,778 (1980; figure for 1979 is not available).

COMMUNICATIONS

Telephones: 2,755 subscribers, 4,298 receivers (1978); 3,268 subscribers, 5,497 receivers (1979); 3,361 subscribers; 5,762 receivers (1980).

Radio receivers: 50,000 (1974, estimate).

EDUCATION

(1980)

	Government	Mission	Total
Pupils:			
Primary	28,492	4,520	33,012
Intermediate	7,092	1,440	8,532
Secondary*	6,154	4,613	10,767
Teachers:			
Primary and intermediate	1,253	185	1,438
Secondary*	268	207	475

* Including Secondary Vocational schools.

Source (unless otherwise indicated): Western Samoa Department of Statistics, Apia.

THE CONSTITUTION

(adopted by a Constitutional Convention on October 28th, 1960)

HEAD OF STATE

The office of Head of State is held by His Highness Malietoa Tanumafili II, who will hold this post for life. After that the Head of State will be elected by the Legislative Assembly for a term of five years.

EXECUTIVE

Executive power lies with the Cabinet, consisting of a Prime Minister, supported by the majority in the Legislative Assembly, and eight Ministers selected by the Prime Minister. Cabinet decisions are subject to review by the Executive Council, which is made up of the Head of State and the Cabinet.

LEGISLATURE

Since the General Election of February 25th, 1967, the Legislative Assembly has consisted of 47 members, two of whom are elected from the individual voters' roll. It has a three-year term and the Speaker is elected from among the members. Samoans and non-Samoans have separate electoral rolls; two members from the individual voters' roll are elected by universal adult suffrage and the other 45 members by *Matai* (elected clan leaders) in 41 traditional electoral constituencies.

The plebiscite on the constitution, held in May 1961, resulted in clear acceptance of *Matai* suffrage.

THE GOVERNMENT

HEAD OF STATE

O le Ao o le Malo: H.H. MALIETOA TANUMAFILI II, C.B.E. (took office as joint Head of State January 1st, 1962; became sole Head of State April 5th, 1963).

CABINET

(July 1982)

Prime Minister, Minister of Foreign Affairs, of Internal Affairs, of the Cabinet, of Legislative Affairs, of Police and Prisons, of the Public Service Commission and of Immigration, and Attorney-General: VA'AI KOLONE.

Deputy Prime Minister and Minister of Finance and of Customs and Inland Revenue: TOFILAU EPI.

Minister of Justice: TALIAOA MAOAMA.

Minister of Health: LAVEA LIO.

Minister of Economic Affairs, of Fisheries, of Statistics and of Transport: LAUOFO METI.

Minister of Lands, of Labour, of Broadcasting and of the Post Office: LE MAMEA ROPATI.

Minister of Education: (vacant).

Minister of Works: TAUA LATU LOME.

Minister of Agriculture and Forests: JACOB OLAF NETZLER.

LEGISLATURE

FONO

(*Legislative Assembly*)

Speaker: NONUMALO L. SOFARA.

Deputy Speaker: ATIIFALE FISO.

Matai Members: 45 representing 41 territorial constituencies.

Individual Members: 2.

POLITICAL PARTY

Human Rights Protection Party: Apia; Western Samoa's first formal political party; f. 1979 to oppose the leadership of Tupuola Taisi Efi; won the elections of February 1982; Leader VA'IA KOLONE.

Vaega o le Tautua: Apia; f. 1981; seeks to encourage industrialization and private enterprise; Leader MAPUILESUA PELENATO.

DIPLOMATIC REPRESENTATION

EMBASSIES AND HIGH COMMISSIONS ACCREDITED TO WESTERN SAMOA

(HC) High Commission.

Australia: Beach Rd., Apia; *High Commissioner:* A. DEACON.

Belgium: Wellington, New Zealand.

Canada: Wellington, New Zealand (HC).

Chile: Wellington, New Zealand.

China, People's Republic: Matautu-uta, Apia; *Ambassador:* ZHANG ZHANWU.

Egypt: Wellington, New Zealand.

France: Wellington, New Zealand.

Germany, Federal Republic: Wellington, New Zealand.

India: Suva, Fiji (HC).

Israel: Canberra, A.C.T., Australia.

Japan: Wellington, New Zealand.

Korea, Republic: Wellington, New Zealand.

Netherlands: Wellington, New Zealand.

New Zealand: Beach Rd., Apia; *High Commissioner:* DAVID CAFFIN.

Philippines: Wellington, New Zealand.

Sweden: Wellington, New Zealand.

Thailand: Wellington, New Zealand.

U.S.S.R.: Wellington, New Zealand.

United Kingdom: Wellington, New Zealand (HC).

U.S.A.: Wellington, New Zealand.

Yugoslavia: Wellington, New Zealand.

Western Samoa also has diplomatic relations with Fiji, Indonesia, the Democratic People's Republic of Korea and Nauru.

JUDICIAL SYSTEM

The Supreme Court is presided over by the Chief Justice. It has full jurisdiction for both criminal and civil cases. Appeals lie with the Court of Appeal.

Chief Justice: Hon. J. CALLANDER (acting).

Secretary for Justice: FALEFATU SAPOLU.

The Court of Appeal consists of a President (the Chief Justice of the Supreme Court), and of such persons possessing qualifications prescribed by statute as may be appointed by the Head of State. Any three judges of the Court of Appeal may exercise all the powers of the Court.

The Magistrates Court consists of two Magistrates and three senior Samoan Judges, assisted by seven junior Samoan Judges.

Magistrates: P. A. MACALEVEY, S. L. THOMSEN.

The Land and Titles Court has jurisdiction in respect of disputes over Samoan land and succession to Samoan titles. It consists of a President (who is also Chief Justice of the Supreme Court) assisted by Samoan associate judges and assessors; P.O.B. 33, Apia.

Registrar: TAPUSATELE KELI TUATAGALOA.

RELIGION

The population is almost entirely Christian.

PROTESTANT CHURCHES

Anglican Church: Rev. V. T. TOHI; P.O.B. 16, Apia.

Church of Jesus Christ of Latter-Day Saints: Pres. R. CARL HARRIS, Samoa Mission, P.O.B. 197, Apia.

Congregational Christian Church in Samoa: Tamaligi, P.O.B. 468, Apia; Chair. TUUAU SAO.

Congregational Church of Jesus in Samoa: Rev. SOLOMONA SIULAGI, Fataogo, American Samoa.

Methodist Church in Samoa: P.O.B. 199, Apia; f. 1828; 30,146 mems.; Pres. Rev. FAATAUVAA TAPUAI; Sec. Rev. SIONE U. TAMAALII.

Seventh-day Adventist Church: Box 600, Apia; f. 1895; mission territory constituted by American Samoa and Western Samoa; adherents (1981 est.) 3,577; Pres. Pastor C. S. ADAMS; publ. one bi-monthly magazine.

ROMAN CATHOLIC CHURCH

Bishop of Samoa and Tokelau: H.E. Cardinal PIO TAOFINU'U, Cardinal's Residence, Box 532, Apia.

THE PRESS

The Observer: P.O.B. 1572, Apia; f. 1979; weekly; English and Samoan; Editor SANO MALIFA; circ. 4,500.

The Samoa Times: P.O.B. 1160, Apia; f. 1967; weekly; independent bilingual newspaper; Publr. FATA PITO FAALOGO; Editor LEULU FELISE VAA; circ. 5,000.

Samoa Sun: Apia; f. 1980; weekly; bilingual; Editor FALA MANULELEUA.

Samoa Weekly: Saleufi Apia; f. 1977; weekly; independent; bilingual; Editor LIKI CRICHTON; circ. 4,500.

Savali: P.O.B. 193, Apia; government publication; fortnightly; Samoan edition f. 1904; Editor FALESEU L. FUA; circ. 10,000; English edition f. 1977; circ. 2,000.

South Seas Star: Box 800, Apia; f. 1971; weekly (Wed.); Man. Editor TAGALOA LEOTA PITA; Editor FOFOA; circ. 5,000.

Tusitala Samoa: Apia; f. 1979; weekly; Samoan; Editor MATAIO SAROA.

RADIO AND TELEVISION

Western Samoa Broadcasting Service: Broadcasting Dept., P.O.B. 200, Apia; f. 1948; government-controlled with commercial sponsorship; broadcasts on two channels in English and Samoan between 6 a.m. and 11 p.m. (1700 hrs.–1000 hrs. G.M.T.); Dir. J. W. MOORE.

In 1981 there were 100,000 radio sets in use.

The American Samoan television service, KVZK TV, is widely received in Western Samoa, linking in with American television networks. In 1981 there were estimated to be 5,000 television sets in use in Western Samoa.

FINANCE AND TRADE

BANKING

(cap.=capital; p.u.=paid up; dep.=deposits; amounts in tala)

Bank of Western Samoa: Apia; f. 1959; cap. p.u. 1,500,00; dep. 26,059,659 (Dec. 1981); Chair. L. N. ROSS, C.M.G.; Man. R. T. NEWTON.

Development Bank of Western Samoa: P.O.B. 1232, Apia; f. 1974 by Parliamentary legislation to foster economic and social development; cap. p.u. 3,600,120; dep. 240,000 (1982); Gen. Man. S. G. LEUNG WAI.

Pacific Commercial Bank Ltd.: P.O.B. 192, Apia; first independent bank; f. 1977; affiliated with Bank of New South Wales, Australia, and the Bank of Hawaii, U.S.A.; cap. p.u. 500,000; Chair. FRANK J. MANAUT; Dirs. ERIC C. TAIT, WILLIAM KEIL; Man. JOHN R. MARSH.

INSURANCE

Western Samoan Life Assurance Corporation: P.O.B. 494, Apia; f. 1977; Gen. Man. D. D. DAVIS.

CO-OPERATIVES

In 1966 there were 8 registered co-operatives, and 13 credit unions.

TRANSPORT

Public Works Department: Apia; Dir. of Works L. TONE.

ROADS

In 1982 there were 396 km. of main roads on the islands, of which 228 km. are bitumen surfaced; 69 km. of urban roads, of which 32 km. are bitumen surfaced; 440 km. of unsealed secondary roads and about 730 km. of improved plantation roads. Major road construction in 1981 included coastal roads on the island of Savai'i.

SHIPPING

There are deep-water wharves at Apia and Asau.

Pacific Forum Line: Headquarters, Apia; monthly liner services from Australia and New Zealand to the South and Central Pacific; Gen. Man. GEORGE W. FULCHER.

There are regular cargo services linking Western Samoa with Australia, New Zealand, American Samoa, Fiji, New Caledonia, Solomon Islands, Tonga, U.S. west coast ports and various ports in Europe. Shipping companies operating regular cargo services to Western Samoa include The Pacific Forum Line, Bank Line, Warner Pacific Line, Pacific Islands Transport Lines, Polynesia Shipping Line, Kyowa Line, Bali Hai Shipping Line, Columbus Line.

CIVIL AVIATION

Polynesian Airlines Ltd.: P.O.B. 599, Beach Rd., Apia; international services to American Samoa, Fiji, Niue, Rarotonga (Cook Is.), Tonga, Tahiti (French Polynesia) and New Zealand; domestic services between islands of Upolu and Savai'i; fleet of 1B737-200, 2 Britten Norman Islanders, 1 Nomad 12; Chair. E. ANNANDALE; Gen. Man. J. L. CARLOS.

Services between Western Samoa and other Pacific territories are also run by Air Pacific Ltd. (Fiji), Air Nauru and South Pacific Island Airways (Tonga).

EDUCATION

The education system is divided into primary, intermediate and secondary and is based on the New Zealand system. In 1971 there were 159 primary, 39 intermediate and 15 secondary schools. In 1980 there were 52,311 children attending school. There are also a trades' training institute, a teacher's training college and a college for tropical agriculture. Western Samoa has also joined other Governments in the area in establishing the regional University of the South Pacific.

BIBLIOGRAPHY

AMARSHI, A., GOOD, K., and MORTIMER, R. Development and Dependency: The Political Economy of Papua New Guinea (Oxford University Press, 1979).

BAIN, K. R. The Friendly Islanders (Hodder and Stoughton, London, 1967).

BALL, I. M. Pitcairn (Gollancz, London, 1973).

BARROW, T. Art and Life in Polynesia (Phaidon Press, London, 1972).

BELLWOOD, P. S. Man's Conquest of the Pacific (Collins, London, 1977).

BORDEN, C. A. South Sea Islands (Robert Hale, London, 1963).

BROOKFIELD, H. C. Melanesia, a Geographical Interpretation of an Island World (Methuen, London, 1971).

Colonialism, Development and Independence; the Case of the Melanesian Islands in the South Pacific (Methuen, London, 1972).

The Pacific in Transition: a Geographical Perspective on Adaptation and Change (Australian National University, Canberra, 1973).

CARMICHAEL, P., and KNOX-MAWER, J. A World of Islands (Collins, London, 1968).

COPPELL, W. G. A Bibliography of the Cook Islands (Australian National University, Canberra, 1970).

CORRIS, P. R. Passage, Port and Plantation: A History of Solomon Islands Labour Migration 1870–1914 (Melbourne University Press, 1973).

Cranstone, B. A. L. Melanesia (British Museum, London, 1961).

Davidson, J. W. Samoa Mo Samoa: the Emergence of the Independent State of Western Samoa (Oxford University Press, Melbourne, 1967).

Daws, G. Shoal of Time. A History of the Hawaiian Islands (University of Hawaii, Honolulu, 1968).
A Dream of Islands (Jacaranda, Queensland, 1980).

Day, A. G. Pacific Islands Literature (University of Hawaii, Honolulu, 1971).

Diolé, P. The Forgotten People of the Pacific (Cassell, London, 1976).

Doumenge, F. L'Homme dans le Pacifique Sud; Etude Géographique (Société des Océanistes, Paris, 1966).

Feher, J. Hawaii: A Pictorial History (Bishop Museum, Honolulu, 1969).

Fields, J. and D. South Pacific (Kodasha, California, 1972).

Finney, B. R. A New Kind of Sugar: Tourism in the Pacific (East-West Center, University of Hawaii, Honolulu, 1974).

Fisk, E. K. (ed.) New Guinea on the Threshold (Australian National University, Canberra, 1966).

Ford, E. (ed.) Papua New Guinea Resource Atlas (Jacaranda Press, 1974).

Gill, W. W. Cook Islands Customs (University of the South Pacific and the Ministry of Education, Cook Islands, 1979).

Griffin, J., Nelson, H., and Firth, S. Papua New Guinea: A Political History (Heinemann Educational, Australia, 1980).

Grimble, Sir Arthur. A Pattern of Islands (London, 1952).
Return to the Islands (London, 1957).
Migrations, Myth and Magic from the Gilbert Islands, edited by Rosemary Grimble (Routledge and Kegan Paul, London, 1972).

Gunson, W. N. (ed.). The Changing Pacific: Essays in Honour of H. E. Maude (Oxford University Press, Melbourne, 1978).

Hastings, P. (ed.) Papua New Guinea (Angus and Robertson, London, 1971).

Heyerdahl, T. Sea Routes to Polynesia (Allen and Unwin, London, 1968).

Howells, W. The Pacific Islanders (Reed, Wellington, 1973).

Institute of Pacific Studies, U.S.P., and Ministry of Education, Training and Culture, Kiribati. Kiribati: Aspects of History (1979).

Joesting, E. Hawaii (W. W. Norton, New York, 1972).

Kennedy, T. F. A Descriptive Atlas of the Pacific Islands (A. H. and A. W. Reed, Wellington, 1967).

Kent, J. The Solomon Islands (Stockpole, Harrisburg, Pa., U.S.A., 1973).

Kiki, Sir Albert. Ten Thousand Years in a Lifetime: a New Guinea Autobiography (Cheshire, Melbourne, 1968).

Lewis, D. The Voyaging Stars—Secrets of the Pacific Island Navigators (Collins, Sydney and London, 1978).

Latukefu, S. Church and State in Tonga (Australian National University, Canberra, 1974).

Lieber, M. D. (ed.) Exiles and Migrants in Oceania (University of Hawaii, Honolulu, 1977).

Löffler, E. Geomorphology of Papua New Guinea (Australian National University, Canberra, 1977).

Maude, H. E. Of Islands and Men (Oxford University Press, Melbourne, 1968).

Moorehead, A. The Fatal Impact: The Invasion of the South Pacific 1767–1840 (Hamish Hamilton, London, 1966).

Newbury, C. Tahiti Nui (University of Hawaii, Honolulu, 1980).

Nicolson, R. B. The Pitcairners (Angus and Robertson, Sydney, 1965).

Nordyke, E. C. The Peopling of Hawaii (University of Hawaii, Honolulu, 1977).

O'Reilly, P. G. F. Bibliographie méthodique, analytique et critique de la Nouvelle-Calédonie (Société des Oceanistes, Paris, 1955).
Bibliographie méthodique, analytique et critique des Nouvelles-Hébrides (Société des Océanistes, Paris, 1958).

O'Reilly, P. G. F., and Reitman, F. Bibliographie de Tahiti et de la Polynésie française (Musée de l'Homme, Paris, 1967).

Pearce, G. L. The Story of the Maori People (Collins, Auckland and London, 1968).

Read, K. E. The High Valley (George Allen and Unwin, London, 1960).

Rose, R. G. Hawaii: The Royal Isles (Honolulu, Bishop Museum, 1980).

Roth, G. K. Fijian Way of Life (edited by G. B. Milner, Oxford University Press, Melbourne, revised, 1973).

Snow, P. A. Best Stories of the South Seas (Faber and Faber, London, 1967).
Bibliography of Fiji, Tonga and Rotuma (Australian National University, Canberra, and Miami University Press, 1969).

Snow, P. A., and Waine, S. The People from the Horizon: an Illustrated History of the Europeans among the South Sea Islanders (Phaidon Press, Oxford, 1979).

Somare, M. T. Sana, an Autobiography (Niugini Press, Port Moresby, 1975).

Souter, G. New Guinea. The Last Unknown (Angus and Robertson, London, 1964).

Steinbauer, F. Melanesian Cargo Cults (University of Queensland Press, 1978).

Todd, I. Island Realm (Angus and Robertson, Sydney, 1974).

Trumbull, R. Tin Roofs and Palm Trees (University of Washington, Seattle, 1977).

Tudor, J. (ed.) Pacific Islands Year Book and Who's Who (Pacific Publications, Ltd., Sydney, 1968).

Viviani, N. Nauru (Australian National University, Canberra, 1970).

Ward, R. G. (ed.). Man in the Pacific Islands: Essays on Geographical Change in the Pacific Islands (Clarendon Press, 1972).

Wenkam, R. Maui: The Last Hawaiian Place (Friends of the Earth, San Francisco, 1970).

Wenkam, R., and Baker, B. Micronesia (University of Hawaii, Honolulu, 1971).

Woodcock, G. South Sea Journey (Faber, London, 1976).

Pakistan

PHYSICAL AND SOCIAL GEOGRAPHY

B. H. Farmer

Pakistan has an area of 803,943 square kilometres (310,403 square miles), excluding Jammu and Kashmir, which is disputed with India. It stretches between 23° 45′ and 36° 50′ North latitude and between 60° 55′ and 75° 30′ East longitude, and is bounded to the west, north-west and north by Iran and Afghanistan (a narrow panhandle in the high Pamirs separates it from direct contact with the U.S.S.R.), to the east and south-east by India and by Jammu and Kashmir, and to the south by the Arabian Sea.

Pakistan, like India, became independent on August 15th, 1947, and inherited, generally speaking, those contiguous districts of the former Indian Empire that had a Muslim majority. Its former eastern wing became the independent People's Republic of Bangladesh after the Indo-Pakistan war of December 1971.

PHYSICAL FEATURES

Much of Pakistan is mountainous or, at any rate, highland. Its northernmost territories consist of the tangled mountains among which the western Himalayas run into the high Karakoram and Pamir ranges. From these the mighty River Indus breaks out through wild gorges to the plains. West of the Indus lies Chitral, a territory of hill ranges, deep gorges and high plateaux. South of this, on the Afghan border, structures are simpler, consisting essentially of a series of mountain arcs like the Safed Koh, Sulaiman and Kirthar Ranges, less complex in geological structure and lower in height than the Himalayas, Pamirs or Karakoram, breached by famous passes like the Khaibar and Bolan, and enclosing belts of plateau country. Baluchistan, the westernmost part of West Pakistan's territory, is essentially a region of plateaux and ranges which run over the border into Iran.

Contrasting strongly with all this high and often mountainous terrain is the plain country to the south-east. Part of the great Indo-Gangetic Plain, this consists for the most part of the alluvium brought down by the Indus and its tributaries, of which by far the most important are the five rivers of the Punjab, the Jhelum, Chenab, Ravi, Beas and Sutlej (part of whose course lies, however, in Indian or Kashmiri territory). The southern part of the Indian border runs through the waterless wastes of the Thar Desert.

CLIMATE

The Pakistan plains, like those of northern India, have an annual cycle of three seasons. The "cool season" (December to February) has relatively low average temperatures (Lahore, 12°C. January) but warm days. Karachi, farther south and on the coast, is rather warmer (18°C. January average). This season is dry, apart from rain brought by northwesterly disturbances. The "hot season" (March to May) builds up to very high temperatures (Lahore, 31.5°C. May average, but up to 48.5°C. by day, and even hotter in that notorious hot-spot, Jacobabad; but rather cooler, 29.5°C. May average, in Karachi); this season is dry. From June to September the south-west monsoon brings more wind, lower temperatures, and rains that are everywhere relatively light (34.3 cm. in four months at Lahore) and that fall off to little or nothing westward into Baluchistan and southward into Sind and the Thar Desert. Much of Pakistan would, in fact, be unproductive agriculturally if it were not for irrigation.

The mountains of Pakistan have a climatic regime modified by altitude and with a winter maximum of rainfall (such as it is) in the north-west, but, again, widely characterized by aridity.

SOILS

The soils of the plains of Pakistan, like those in similar physiographic circumstances in India, exhibit considerable variety. Those of the Thar desert tend to be poor and sandy, and there is a good deal of natural salinity in the more arid tracts, especially in Sind. More fertile alluvium follows the main rivers and also spreads more widely in the Punjab, but there is, again as in India, the danger of man-induced salinity and alkalinity with the spread of irrigation, and consequent rise in the water-table and capillary ascent of salts to the surface. Indeed, large areas of land have gone out of cultivation for just this reason. The hill areas of Pakistan tend to have poor, skeletal mountain soils, though better conditions prevail in some intermont valleys.

VEGETATION

In the distant past, much of the plains area of Pakistan was probably covered with tropical thorn forest, degenerating into semi-desert or even true desert in the Thar. Similar dry types of vegetation may well have covered the western hills and plateaux, though there was dry evergreen forest on the Sulaiman and other relatively high ranges. The northern mountains, in Chitral and adjacent areas, showed a more complex altitudinal zonation, including pine forest.

Now, after centuries if not millennia of occupation by man and his animals, there is very little "natural" vegetation left, except for poor, semi-desert scrub in uncultivated portions of the plains of Pakistan (such as part of the Thal, between the Indus and Jhelum) and in Baluchistan, and montane forests in parts of the western and northern hills (notably the Sulaimans). Even this surviving vegetation has been degraded by man: for instance, by the practice of pastoralism in Baluchistan and elsewhere in the western hills and plateaux.

Not surprisingly, Pakistan is desperately short of timber, and has actually planted irrigated forests, especially of shisham (*Dalbergia sissoo*) in the Thal and elsewhere.

MINERALS

Most of the mineral wealth is concentrated in the mountainous regions of Pakistan and difficulty of access retarded exploration. Twenty types of mineral were known to exist at the time of partition, but only coal (sub-bituminous and non-coking), rock salt, chromite, gypsum and limestone were mined. Fire-clay, silica sand, celestite, ochres and iron ore are now also commercially exploited, and there may be commercial deposits of copper, manganese, bauxite and phosphates. Small oil and gas fields have been found.

POPULATION

According to the latest census, the population on March 15th, 1981, was 83,782,000. The average annual rate of increase between 1972 and 1981 was 2.92 per cent.

Pakistan has densities of over 300 per square kilometre in well-watered districts like Lyallpur, but an overall average of only 104 per square kilometre (1981).

Pakistan also has sizeable conurbations in Karachi (population 3,498,634 at the 1972 census) and Lahore (population 2,165,372 in 1972).

ETHNIC GROUPS

There are considerable contrasts of race within Pakistan. Tall, relatively fair and blue-eyed Pathans of the western hills contrast with darker, brown-eyed (though also often tall) "plainsmen"—itself a heterogeneous category.

Although the population of Pakistan is overwhelmingly Muslim, it is divided, not only by race but also by linguistic and by tribal differences. Punjabi, Baluchi and Pashtu (the language of the Pathans) are spoken. Tribal divisions are most noticeable in the western hills, but also affect the plains where there are Janglis (former lawless nomads, now largely cultivators), Thiringiuzars (camel-herders) and other "tribes".

HISTORY*

Sharif al Mujahid†

Pakistan as a separate political entity came into being on August 15th, 1947, primarily as a result of the efforts of the 100 million Muslims of the Indian sub-continent under the dynamic leadership of Muhammad Ali Jinnah, popularly known as *Quaid-i-Azam* ("Great Leader"). The State of Pakistan was set up under the June 3rd Partition Plan, often referred to as the Mountbatten Plan, which was accepted by the three main Indian parties—the Indian National Congress, the Muslim League and the Akali Dal, representing the Sikhs. The Indian Independence Act of July 1947, which was based on the Partition Plan, endowed the new state with its constitutional and legal sanction.

THE PROBLEMS OF PARTITION

From its very inception, Pakistan suffered from certain handicaps and was faced with almost insurmountable problems. Some of these were inherent in the nature and logistics of its birth while others were created by forces hostile to its very existence.

Firstly, Pakistan was divided into two disparate halves. East Pakistan (the province of East Bengal), comprising only about one-seventh of the area, contained four-sevenths of the population, while West Pakistan (the provinces of Punjab, Sind, North-West Frontier Province (N.W.F.P.) and Baluchistan), comprising six-sevenths of the area, had only three-sevenths of the population. This difference was to create anomalies in the application of the federal principle in subsequent years. Secondly, the two wings of Pakistan were a thousand miles apart, separated by India. This led to an interwing communication problem, especially in view of India's traditional hostility. Thirdly, the most populous provinces, Bengal and the Punjab, were themselves partitioned, thus creating several problems for the newly created provinces. East Bengal lost both the capital and the chief port (Calcutta), and Punjab lost the water headworks to Eastern Punjab (India), turning vast tracts of its agricultural land into desert. East Bengal had to set up a make-shift capital at Dacca, and trade through the undeveloped port at Chittagong. Fourthly, Pakistan did not inherit a central government, a capital, an administrative core, or an organized defence force. Karachi, with its extremely limited facilities, was the only city available to house the new nation's capital, and an improvised central government was set up. The number of Muslims in the higher civil service was disappointingly low. Even the armed forces had to be built up out of those who had opted for Pakistan, many of whom were either in India or abroad at the time of partition.

Moreover, the social and administrative resources of the country were poor: there was little equipment and even fewer statistics. The Punjab communal holocaust had caused extensive disruption. This, together with the mass migration of the Hindu and Sikh entrepreneurial and managerial classes, had left

* Since 1947 (for the pre-1947 history, *see* the chapter on *India*).

† This article is in part a revision of an earlier version by Mahmud Husain.

the economy almost shattered. On top of this, the still unorganized nation was called upon to feed some eight million refugees who had fled from the insecurities of the north Indian plains. But, even despite this, Pakistan's economic prospects would have looked unpromising. Although it comprised about one-fifth of the sub-continent's area and population, Pakistan had less than one-tenth of the sub-continent's factories and industries. Its principal cash crops were jute in the East and cotton in the West; but all the jute and cotton mills were located in India. Also, Pakistan lacked both capital and the technical know-how for industrial development.

Politically, however, the situation did not seem too bleak initially. In Jinnah, it had a trusted and experienced leader, who fulfilled the nation's desperate need for imaginative, constructive and charismatic leadership at that time, but he died within thirteen months of independence. His chief lieutenant, Prime Minister Liaquat Ali Khan, was assassinated in 1951, and this time there was no political heir to fill the void. This dismal situation was compounded by the failure of the Muslim League to provide imaginative leadership capable of giving political coherence and direction in the formative stage. It did not have the time to build up its organization and structure and a deep-seated loyalty among its followers in the way in which its chief rival, the Indian National Congress in India, had. The Muslim League soon became divided and politically weak. Moreover, the political vacuum following Liaquat's assassination led to the rise of too many claimants for leadership, to frequent squabbles and conspiracies, and, in the end, to political instability.

Indo-Pakistan Disputes

Other problems were the result of the Radcliffe Boundary Commission's award and the peculiar nature of Indo-Pakistan relations. The Kashmir question and the dispute over the canal waters were a corollary of the award. The state of Jammu and Kashmir had a large Muslim majority and was contiguous to Pakistan, with all its economic interests and communications being linked with Pakistan. But for the award which gave the Muslim majority district of Gurdaspur to India, India would not have had physical access to it at all. India succeeded in annexing the state when the Hindu ruler's position was threatened by internal unrest and invasion by Pakistan tribesmen. Kashmir has since then poisoned relations between India and Pakistan. The award also broke up the irrigation system of the Punjab by awarding the headworks of the Punjab canals at Madhopur and Ferozepur to India. This gave India a lever which it could and did use against Pakistan. As early as April 1948 water supply was cut off and Pakistan had to conclude an agreement under duress by which it surrendered essential riparian rights and agreed to make a payment to India for the use of water. Constant bickerings followed until the matter was taken up at an international level culminating in an agreement arrived at through the good offices of, and a substantial loan from, the World Bank (*see* chapter *Indus Waters Treaty*).

India also withheld payment of Pakistan's share of the assets of the Reserve Bank of India. This led to a serious financial crisis within months of independence, pushing the new state to the verge of bankruptcy. It was only after Mahatma Gandhi's intervention that the Government of India released a portion of Pakistan's share of the assets.

POLITICAL AND CONSTITUTIONAL DEVELOPMENTS

Pakistan, which had become an independent Dominion under the Indian Independence Act 1947, was administered initially under the Government of India Act 1935, as adapted in Pakistan. The Indian Independence Act had abolished the special powers of the Governor-General which he had exercised ever since the time of Cornwallis (1786). Moreover, a sovereign Constituent Assembly replaced the Indian Legislative Assembly which had been set up under the Government of India Act of 1919, and whose measures the Governor-General could veto or overrule. Yet, because of the unusual situation, the Governor-General was still armed with special powers to adapt the Government of India Act. Many arrangements which had yet to be made between the two Dominions consequent on partition and the new responsibility for the defence of the country made these powers necessary. But they were to be exercised by the Governor-General on the advice of the Cabinet. Hence these were essentially different from the powers of the Governor-General in the past.

The Constituent Assembly, to which power was transferred formally by Earl Mountbatten on August 14th, 1947, was a small house elected indirectly by the provincial legislatures on the basis of one member for a population of one million. Initially comprising only 69 members, the number was later raised to 79, of whom 44 represented East Bengal.

Quaid-i-Azam Muhammad Ali Jinnah was the first Governor-General. He derived his power not so much from the office he held as from the position he occupied amongst the people as the father of the nation. He was also President of the Constituent Assembly and presided over Cabinet meetings. But, although he was only titular head, he wielded immense power. After his death in September 1948 Prime Minister Liaquat Ali Khan became the chief executive and Khwaja Nazimuddin was appointed Governor-General.

The Drafting of a Constitution

Constitution-making was delayed in Pakistan for many reasons. Apart from the various problems which demanded solution, a constitution incorporating the principles of Islam was something new and not easy to devise. The only notable steps towards constitution-making during Liaquat Ali Khan's regime were the passing of the *Objectives Resolution* (1949) and the presentation of the *Interim Report of the Basic Principles Committee* (1950).

On Liaquat Ali Khan's assassination in October 1951, the Governor-General, Khwaja Nazimuddin, became Prime Minister, but the focus of power now shifted to the new Governor-General, Ghulam

Muhammad. Exploiting public discontent over food shortage, he dismissed Khwaja Nazimuddin in April 1953, even though the latter enjoyed the fullest confidence of the Assembly, and replaced him with Muhammad Ali Bogra, until then Pakistan's Ambassador in Washington. This dismissal represented the first authoritarian thrust into Pakistan's body-politic, and signalled Pakistan's entry into an era of "palace" intrigues.

Renewed efforts towards constitution-making were more successful, however. A Constitution was prepared on the basis of the Muhammad Ali Formula, under which the majority of the Lower House was to come from East Pakistan on the basis of population and of the Upper House from the four units of West Pakistan, but the number was fixed in such a way that in a joint session of the two Houses the members from each wing numbered 175 (East Pakistan 165+10, and West Pakistan 135+40). The two Houses were given equal powers and in case of conflict the joint House was to decide the issue. A bill was required to be supported by at least 30 per cent of the members from each wing to become law. Votes of confidence in the Government and the election of the President of Pakistan were also to be decided in joint session. The question of representation between the Eastern and Western wings was thus settled. When the Constitution was about to be passed as law, the Constituent Assembly was dissolved by the Governor-General in October 1954, presumably because the Constitution had sought to curtail the Governor-General's powers.

Ghulam Muhammad's idea was to present a Constitution to his liking without bothering to create another Constituent Assembly. But the Federal Court, which declared valid Ghulam Muhammad's action in dissolving the Constituent Assembly, also declared that the Constitution could be framed only by a Constituent Assembly, which should be elected on the same basis as the first one, i.e. indirectly by the Provincial Legislatures. Because of the radical change which had occurred in the membership of the Provincial Legislatures, the East Pakistan Assembly in particular, the newly elected Constituent Assembly was a very different body from the first one. Although the Muslim League was still the largest party in the new Assembly, it did not have an overall majority. The new Assembly had six parties represented, compared with only two parties in the earlier Assembly.

The Constitutions of 1956 and 1962

The new Constituent Assembly first amalgamated the four provinces of West Pakistan into one single province. Then, in March 1956, the Constitution was finally drawn up, passed by the Assembly and authenticated by the Governor-General. It set up a federal republic of two provinces only, namely East and West Pakistan, with much decentralization, and established a parliamentary form of government. It recognized the principle of parity of representation for the two provinces and provided for only one House. It also incorporated several Islamic provisions amongst the directive principles. The Head of State was to be a Muslim and, although Islam was not declared the state religion, no law which went against the teachings of Islam was to be promulgated. In addition, the existing laws were to be brought into conformity with Islam. The rights and personal laws of the non-Muslims were, however, respected. The question of joint versus separate electorates was put aside to be settled by the Legislatures. Urdu and Bengali were both recognized as state languages, though English was retained for official purposes until further decision.

However, this 1956 Constitution was not given a fair trial. For one thing, the political parties were weak and not well organized, and for another, the Governor-General, Iskandar Mirza, did not believe in parliamentary government or any kind of democracy in Pakistan. When the parliamentary system had become discredited—a situation to which he himself had substantially contributed—Iskandar Mirza abrogated the Constitution (October 7th, 1958), dismissed the cabinet, abolished the legislatures, banned political parties and promulgated martial law under Gen. Ayub Khan, the Commander-in-Chief. Not being a popular leader, Mirza had realized that he had no chance of being elected President under the 1956 Constitution.

On October 27th Ayub Khan removed Iskandar Mirza, and himself became President. Martial law continued until a new Constitution was promulgated in June 1962. Its most important feature was the institution of Basic Democracies, which, as local governmental institutions, had been in existence since 1959. The Constitution provided for a presidential system of government. All executive power and a good deal of legislative power was concentrated in the hands of the President. Once elected, he was practically irremovable during his five-year term. Unlike the 1956 Constitution, the 1962 Constitution tended towards centralization of power in the hands of the chief executive. The powers of the legislatures were limited, even in regard to finance. The system of election was indirect. Direct elections were, however, provided at the lowest level, the Basic Democrats (40,000 in East Pakistan and 40,000 in West Pakistan, later raised to 60,000 each) being elected by the vote of all registered voters. All the councils at the *Tehsil*, district and division levels were indirectly elected, one after the other. For the election of the Provincial and Central Assemblies and the President, the entire body of Basic Democrats formed an Electoral College.

The Overthrow of Ayub Khan

In 1968 the regime made the costly mistake of celebrating the tenth anniversary of President Ayub's seizure of power as the "Decade of Reforms". Instead of popularizing the regime, the celebrations created just the opposite effect and brought to the surface all the hitherto submerged opposition. What had been privately felt about corruption, nepotism and autocratic controls now began to be said in public. Religious elements and students took the lead in anti-Ayub agitation. Disturbances took place on a large scale and urban workers and peasants became involved so that the regime was shaken to its very foundations. President Ayub made one concession after another to public opinion and to the political parties and held a Round Table Conference with political leaders in February 1969, but all to no avail. Thus, when in March 1969 it became impossible to maintain law and order, he decided—or rather was forced—to surrender power to his Commander-in-Chief, General Agha Muhammad Yahya Khan. Martial Law was once more proclaimed. The new President and Chief Martial Law Administrator, however, lost no time in announcing that general elections would be held in October 1970, later postponed to December 1970.

Thus the whole question of the constitution of Pakistan was once more re-opened. But certain important constitutional issues were settled by the President. Under one of his orders the new Assembly was to be elected on the basis, not of parity, but of the population of the various provinces, which meant that 56 per cent of seats were to go to East Pakistan. One Unit was dissolved and the provinces of Punjab, N.W.F.P., Sind (including Karachi) and Baluchistan actually started functioning separately from July 1970. The system of Basic Democracies was abandoned and the new Constitution was to provide direct elections and a parliamentary system of government. The main issues that remained to be settled by the National Assembly were the extent of provincial autonomy in a federal set-up and the content of the Islamic element in the Constitution.

However, following postponement of the formation of a Constituent Assembly, events took a serious turn in the Eastern Wing. Internal turmoil, followed by India's invasion, resulted in the secession of East Pakistan as Bangladesh in December 1971. Military defeat thoroughly exposed and discredited the military dictatorship. Yahya Khan fell, and Zulfiqar Ali Bhutto, the founder and Chairman of the Pakistan People's Party (PPP), took over as President.

The National Assembly started meeting and a consensus was soon achieved among the leaders of all the parties represented in the Assembly (October 1972). A federal parliamentary system of government was agreed upon, with four units and two houses of legislature. The Prime Minister, answerable to the lower house, was to be the chief executive, while the President, elected by both houses voting together, was visualized as a constitutional head. Quite a few subjects were assigned to the federal centre which would make it sufficiently effective, though considerable authority was still left in the hands of the four federal units. On the basis of the principles agreed upon, the Constitution Committee of the National Assembly prepared a draft for the consideration of the Assembly. In April 1973 Pakistan at long last acquired a democratic Constitution, framed by a directly elected assembly, which came into force on August 14th, 1973. At the inauguration of the Constitution the President, Zulfiqar Ali Bhutto, became the Prime Minister of Pakistan.

POLITICAL PARTIES

A few years before the partition of India, the Muslim League, which had been founded in 1906, had become for all practical purposes the only party of the Muslims. In the same way, the Indian National Congress represented almost all Hindus. However, in the final phase of the freedom struggle, the Muslim League was not a mere political party but a nationalist coalition comprising diverse interests among Muslims, which had joined together in the national struggle for independence. That diverse elements should come under the banner of the League was a source of strength while the struggle for Pakistan lasted. But once the goal was achieved, the presence of heterogeneous elements in the League became a cause of weakness. Even so, the achievement of Pakistan had endowed the League with tremendous prestige and was responsible for discrediting other parties which had opposed the country's creation. Only the Congress survived among the Hindus of East Bengal.

Thus in the first Constituent Assembly (1947–54), there were initially only two parties: the Muslim League Assembly Party and a small opposition of twelve Hindus belonging to the Congress. The League practically dictated terms, but the absence of a strong opposition was not a healthy phenomenon. When, through secessions from the League itself, new groups and parties were started, the League adopted an unreasonable attitude. Thus, opposition to the League was considered opposition to Pakistan and those opposed to the League were termed enemies of Pakistan.

Gradually new parties were founded by men who had been former members of the League. Mamdot founded the Jinnah Muslim League in West Pakistan, and Suhrawardy the Awami Muslim League in East Bengal. Their programmes were, however, no different from the League's. The two parties later amalgamated to form the Jinnah Awami Muslim League, which won nineteen seats in the Punjab elections in 1951. However, within a short time the two leaders parted company and the Suhrawardy group reverted to its original nomenclature of Awami Muslim League. Four years later, in 1955, the "Muslim" was dropped under pressure from Maulana Abdul Hamid Khan Bhashani, the party chief in East Bengal. The party opened its doors to non-Muslims and functioned under the joint leadership of Suhrawardy and Bhashani, one exercising considerable influence over the educated classes and the other over the peasantry. A secession within the Constituent Assembly brought into being the Azad Pakistan Party in the Punjab in 1950/51.

When elections took place to the Provincial Assembly in East Bengal in 1954, four parties opposed to the League constituted a United Front under the leadership of Fazlul Haq. The Pakistan National Congress was also closely allied with the United Front. The United Front evolved a programme consisting of twenty-one points with emphasis on provincial autonomy. It also demanded the dissolution of the first Constituent Assembly and the quashing of the *Basic Principles Committee Report*. The United

Front obtained 222 seats out of 309 while the League won only 9 seats.

Soon, however, a rift developed between the component elements, particularly between Fazlul Haq and the Awami League. Later, when, upon becoming Prime Minister in September 1956, Suhrawardy advocated a pronounced pro-Western policy, Bhashani first challenged Suhrawardy within the party and then, failing to carry the party with him, left it and formed his own National Awami Party (NAP) in 1957. In West Pakistan, though the Muslim League had won the provincial elections of 1951 in the Punjab, and subsequent elections in N.W.F.P. and Sind, a number of small parties continued to exist, and the League's *débâcle* in East Bengal in 1954 inspired them with new life. Of particular importance was Maulana Maududi's Jamaat-i-Islami, which advocated an Islamic constitution and the revival of Islamic values. It was a small but well organized party with a large number of devoted and sincere workers. The Muslim League split in 1956 over the nomination of Dr. Khan Sahib, who was the N.W.F.P. Chief Minister at the time of partition, a Congressite and opposed to the creation of Pakistan, to the Chief Ministership of the newly constituted West Pakistan province. Dr. Sahib's supporters launched the Republican Party under his leadership and with the backing of Governor-General Iskander Mirza in April 1956.

Since political parties were not well organized and their leadership was not very effective, ambitious civil servants could easily manipulate and dominate the political scene. Several of them had been given political posts by Muhammad Ali Jinnah, Liaquat Ali Khan and Khwaja Nazimuddin. They played off one party against another and undermined their solidarity, thus bringing about political instability. They also inspired the creation of the Republican Party in 1956.

When the army took over in October 1958 political parties were banned. They were allowed to function again, though with certain restrictions, only after the promulgation of a new constitution in 1962. The first elections to the Basic Democracies had taken place in 1959, long before the new Constitution came into force and before the ban on parties was lifted. At that time the Basic Democrats (BDs) were viewed as instruments of local self-government only. These BDs were to confirm President Ayub in office in February 1960.

The Revival of Parties

In the process of revival, in the wake of the 1962 Constitution, a schism occurred in the Muslim League. The old guard of the League was opposed to President Ayub and the 1962 Constitution, while some of the League members in the lower echelons had joined Ayub's presidential cabinet in June 1962. They ultimately chose Ayub Khan as chief of their party, which came to be called Convention Muslim League. The original League party, which was revived through the convoking of the 1958 League council, came to be known as Council Muslim League and was led by Khwaja Nazimuddin, a veteran League leader and a former Governor-General and Prime Minister.

In East Pakistan a move not to revive parties but to fight unitedly for the restoration of democracy and against the 1962 Constitution brought into being the National Democratic Front (NDF), with Nurul Amin, Ataur Rahman Khan, Hamidul Haq Choudhry and Abu Hussain Sarkar as leaders. But though the Front was never dissolved it lost much of its significance when several parties of East Pakistan were revived, the more important among them being the Awami League, led by Sheikh Mujibur Rahman (after the death of Suhrawardy), the National Awami Party of Maulana Bhashani, and the Nizam-i-Islam.

When the time came for the election to the Basic Democracies in 1964 under the new Constitution, five opposition parties joined to form a Combined Opposition Party (COP): the Council Muslim League, the Awami League, the NAP, the Nizam-i-Islam and the Jamaat-i-Islami. The National Democratic Front also gave its general support to the COP. Thus the election was fought between the COP presidential candidate, Miss Fatima Jinnah, the ageing sister of Muhammad Ali Jinnah, and President Muhammad Ayub Khan, the candidate of the Convention Muslim League. Initially Miss Jinnah made a great impression, but no one could possibly win against a candidate so powerfully entrenched as Field-Marshal Ayub Khan, under a system strongly favouring the incumbent. Miss Jinnah's main contribution was that she demonstrated for the first time that the authority of Ayub Khan could be challenged.

A new party, the Pakistan People's Party (PPP), professing socialistic ideals, was formed in December 1967 by Zulfiqar Ali Bhutto, who had been an enthusiastic supporter of President Ayub for eight years and served him as his minister. However, Bhutto's influence remained confined to West Pakistan. The NAP was split, one section led by Wali Khan in West Pakistan and the other by Bhashani in the East. In late 1968 certain non-political figures like Air Marshal Asghar Khan also entered the political arena. In March 1969 the latter founded the Justice Party, which later merged with certain other parties to form the Pakistan National Democratic Party (PDP), led by Nurul Amin, a former Chief Minister of East Bengal.

Later, Asghar Khan left the PDP and founded the Tehrik-i-Istiqlal. Another Muslim League under Khan Abdul Qayyum Khan was also formed so that there were three Muslim Leagues: the Council Muslim League, the Convention Muslim League and the Qayyum Muslim League.

Ulama or Muslim religious scholars had also been politically active. Not only the Jamaat-i-Islami but also the Jamiat-i-Ulamae-i-Islam (JUI) were working for the establishment of the Islamic order and against socialism. Another organization of Sunni Ulama with more or less similar aims, Jamiatul-Ulema-e-Pakistan (JUP), was formed to put up candidates in the elections. There was also a section of the Ulama (the Hazarvi Group) which had leanings towards socialism and which worked in co-operation with the PPP during the elections.

In East Pakistan the party which made real headway was the Awami League under Mujibur Rahman. Bhashani also had a considerable following of his own, particularly among the peasants.

The parties were far from well-disciplined. They had no democratic base and regular membership did not exist; at best it was mostly fictitious. There were, of course, working committees, organizing committees, co-ordination committees and conveners but they were seldom elected by the party membership at large. For instance, the Awami League, in its long, chequered history, never held any party elections, nor did the PPP, although it has been in existence for over a decade. The party membership itself is indeterminate. Leaders were mostly self-appointed for all practical purposes. In Pakistan, therefore, regular membership of a party provides no clue to its influence.

Most parties except the Muslim League were in effect regional or provincial parties. However, for a long time the Muslim League had been a house divided against itself and in any case had lost its glamour. The most popular party in West Pakistan was the Pakistan People's Party (PPP) and in East Pakistan the Awami League.

ELECTIONS

The 1970 Elections and After

The first ever general elections were held in December 1970. At the elections only two parties achieved overwhelming success, the Awami League in East Pakistan and the PPP in two of the largest provinces of West Pakistan—the Punjab and Sind. The Awami League had fought the elections on the basis of Six Points which were aimed at an extreme form of provincial autonomy and decentralization of authority.

The Awami League, having secured nearly all the seats from East Pakistan, obtained an absolute majority in the Central Legislature. In the normal course, the largest party had the right to form the central government, but in this case it was not a workable proposition because of the federal character of Pakistan as a state and the exclusively provincial character of the party concerned. The Awami League seemed inclined to coalesce with some of the smaller parties of West Pakistan but the PPP chief vehemently opposed the idea. He sought assurances on certain constitutional issues before the calling of the session of the National Assembly. As the PPP was the second largest party in the Assembly, the President postponed the session to give the two largest parties an opportunity for arriving at a consensus on some of the remaining constitutional issues. Negotiations among the political parties themselves and between the President and the Awami League leader, Mujibur Rahman, followed. However, while the negotiations continued, the situation in East Pakistan took an ugly turn. The Awami League, instead of making any concession on the Six Points, adopted a much more uncompromising stand and virtually advocated independence for East Pakistan, a very different proposition from provincial autonomy on the basis of which elections had been won.

The administration of the province was paralysed and an intense hate campaign was launched, not only against West Pakistan but also against all those inhabitants of East Pakistan itself whose mother tongue was not Bengali. Finally, on March 23rd, Pakistan Day, the Bangladesh flag was hoisted and the stage set for secession. It was in these circumstances that the Government decided to take action, claiming that it was necessary to put a stop to massacres and to save the integrity of the country. Mujibur Rahman was arrested and brought over to West Pakistan.

When the Pakistan Army came into action, many Bengalis fled to India, some in sympathy with secession, others under duress or out of fear. The Pakistan Government claimed that India was the base for Bengali insurgents' training and incursions into East Pakistan. There followed border clashes between Indian and Pakistani troops and finally, in November 1971, an invasion of East Pakistan by the Indian armed forces. However, the war did not remain confined to the East but spread to West Pakistan as well. It was a short but decisive war in which India achieved quick success, bringing about the surrender of Pakistan troops in the East, and a ceasefire in the West.

In the aftermath of the war, Bhutto's Government embarked on the task of writing a new Constitution. The Constitution proposed in 1972 seemed to have the support of all parties. In early 1973, however, opposition parties of the right and left formed a United Democratic Front (UDF) to demand further amendments which would create "a truly Islamic, democratic and federal constitution". Their fears that the Constitution would give too much power to the Prime Minister and the central government were strengthened by events in Baluchistan where tribal fighting was followed, in February 1973, by the imposition of direct presidential rule and the invocation of emergency powers. The amended Constitution came into force in August 1973 with Bhutto as Prime Minister. The situation in Baluchistan remained grave and although the Government offered an amnesty for political opponents, fighting continued in the province. In addition, dissident movements became more active in the other provinces during 1974.

The National Awami Party was banned in February 1975 and many of its leading members were arrested, following the murder of the N.W.F.P.'s most senior minister, Hayat Mohammed Sherpao. In the same month, although boycotted by the opposition parties, the National Assembly adopted a constitution bill empowering the Government to extend the state of emergency beyond six months without parliamentary approval.

The Government's decision to ban the NAP was referred to the Supreme Court under the Political Parties Act of 1962. The Court's proceedings were boycotted by the NAP but the Court upheld the Government's decision. Following the Court's ruling in October 1975, the Political Parties Act was amended in January 1976 to provide that any official of a dissolved political party at the national and provincial level would be disqualified from being a member of Parliament or a provincial assembly and from being elected to them for a period of five years.

Meanwhile, a new party, the National Democratic Party (NDP), was launched in November 1975, with Sherbaz Khan Mazari, leader of the Independent Group in the National Assembly, as leader. It claimed the adherence of most of the former NAP leaders.

The 1977 Elections and After

In the wake of the announcement, in January 1977, that national elections would be held on March 7th, 1977, nine opposition parties formed a broad-based opposition front, called the Pakistan National Alliance (PNA). The parties forming the Alliance were Air-Marshal (retd.) Asghar Khan's Tehrik-i-Istiqlal (TI), Mian Tufail Muhammad's Jamaat-i-Islami (JI), Maulana Mufti Mahmud's Jamiatul-Ulema-e-Islam (JUI), Maulana Shah Ahmed Noorani's Jamiatul-Ulema-e-Pakistan (JUP), Pir Pagara's Pakistan Muslim League (PML), Sherbaz Khan Mazari's National Democratic Party (NDP), Nawabzada Nasrullah Khan's Pakistan Democratic Party (PDP), Khan Muhammad Ashraf Khan's Khaksar Tehrik (KT), and Sardar Abdul Qayyum's Azad Kashmir Muslim Conference (AKMC). Although some other minor parties like the Qayyam Muslim League and Pakhtoon Khwa, chiefly in the N.W.F.P. and Baluchistan respectively, and a considerable number of independents contested the elections, the main contest was between the newly formed PNA and the ruling Pakistan People's Party (PPP) led by Bhutto. While Bhutto based his appeal on "socio-economic reforms" introduced by him, the "political stability" and "economic prosperity" achieved during his previous term and his achievements in foreign affairs and other fields, the opposition Alliance concentrated on what they termed the gradual erosion of fundamental rights and of the authority and dignity of the courts, the concentration of power in the hands of the executive, and the "undemocratic" and "authoritarian" nature of the PPP regime. Electioneering was intense, strident, and, for the most part, characterized by charges and counter charges. Domestic issues dominated the election debate, with the person of Bhutto himself, his achievements and failures, being the main theme.

The elections gave the PPP an overwhelming majority in the National Assembly: it won 155 seats, conceding only 36 seats to the PNA and one to the Qayyum Muslim League. But the opposition front accused the Government of rigging the elections. It called for the boycott of the provincial assembly polls scheduled for March 9th and for a countrywide strike on the following day. It demanded fresh elections under the supervision of the judiciary and the armed forces, the resignation of the Chief Election Commissioner and the constitution of a new impartial Election Commission. It also decided to launch a movement of countrywide civil disobedience from March 14th onwards to buttress its demands for fresh elections, lifting of the emergency and restoration of fundamental rights.

Although the rigging charge was later confirmed by the Chief Election Commissioner and the Election Commission's findings, Bhutto denied the charges, but tried to soften opposition resentment by offering to hold the provincial polls again and by giving more power to the Election Commission. However, these concessions were to no avail, and the PNA launched the civil disobedience movement as scheduled. Within a week most of its leaders were in gaol, but the movement, though mostly confined to urban centres, continued to gain momentum, causing a breakdown of law and order in several places and of economic life in the principal industrial centres. So serious was this breakdown that the armed forces had to be called in at several places, a curfew had to be imposed for various periods in at least seven places and martial law had to be imposed in Karachi, Lahore and Hyderabad, continuing until June 7th. Official sources put the death toll at 275 and the injured at 2,000, but the unofficial figures were over a thousand dead and several thousand injured. Some 40,000 people were arrested.

Meanwhile, the new National Assembly met on March 26th and re-elected Bhutto as the leader of the House. He formed a new cabinet. Subsequently, the newly elected provincial assemblies in all the four provinces were called to session, and new provincial governments were constituted. The Government was obviously trying to ease the situation and bring it back to normalcy, while the opposition seemed bent upon keeping the civil disobedience movement alive by weekly strike calls, processions, and attempts to break the curfew and violate martial law regulations.

The deepening crisis induced some Muslim countries, particularly Saudi Arabia, to mediate and finally bring the two sides to the negotiating table in early June. The civil disobedience movement was suspended, martial law, curfew and press censorship were withdrawn, and there was a gradual release of most detainees. Four weeks of protracted negotiations resulted in an accord whereby the PNA withdrew its demand for Bhutto's resignation and Bhutto, for his part, accepted the PNA's original demands for fresh elections, the lifting of the emergency, and the restoration of fundamental rights and of the power of the judiciary. Elections were scheduled for October 7th. However, before the accord was formally signed, serious differences developed over the machinery being set up to ensure free and fair elections, and this resulted in a further deadlock which seemed insoluble. Meanwhile, armed clashes had occurred between PPP and PNA supporters, and the country seemed on the verge of civil war.

At this stage, the armed forces stepped in on July 5th, taking the top echelons of both the PPP and the PNA leadership (including Bhutto) into "temporary protective custody". Martial law was imposed, the national and provincial assemblies and the Senate were disbanded, the federal and provincial cabinets were dismissed, and the armed forces took over the administration of the country. The Constitution was not abrogated, but some of its clauses were put in abeyance. The incumbent President was allowed to remain as Head of State, but Provincial Governors were replaced by Chief Justices of the High Courts in the four provinces. General Mohammad Zia ul-Haq, Chief of the Army Staff, became Martial Law Administrator, and a four-member military council (comprising the chiefs of the three services and Chairman of the Joint Chiefs of Staff) was constituted. Political activity was banned for a month, but elections were promised for October as originally stipulated in the PPP–PNA accord. General Zia gave assurances that he had no personal political ambitions and that the army take-over was solely motivated by the desire to avert a civil war and to transfer power to the elected representatives of the people.

The PPP and PNA leaders were released in August and elections were announced for October 20th. The state of emergency was lifted on September 15th and the election campaign officially began three days later. However, on October 1st Gen. Zia postponed elections indefinitely, for, as "classified" information became available to the martial law authorities, it was decided that elections would be meaningless unless those holding public offices during the past seven years were first made accountable for their deeds and misdeeds.

The accountability process was for the main part limited to misdemeanours on two counts – amassing of wealth through official position, and misuse of public office. Thus candidates for the postponed elections were called upon to file declarations of their assets. Also, inquiries were instituted against a number of previous ministers and others holding public office, and those found guilty of corruption were likewise debarred. In both cases special tribunals were constituted for the purpose, and the accountability process is still continuing.

Several cases were instituted against former Prime Minister Bhutto and a number of his ministers who had been arrested in September 1977. In particular, Bhutto was charged with the instigation of the murder of a party dissident in 1974. In the murder attempt on a former PPP member which followed several such attempts on him since 1972, his father, Nawab Muhammad Ahmad Khan, was killed. The Lahore High Court convicted Bhutto and four others and sentenced them to death in March 1978. The appeal against Bhutto's conviction was heard by the Supreme Court, headed by the Chief Justice of Pakistan, Syed Anwarul Haq, for some nine months, and the court confirmed the earlier conviction by a majority decision in February 1979. After the dismissal of a review petition by the same court, Gen. Zia's regime, despite mercy appeals from numerous Heads of State, decided to uphold the court's decision, and Bhutto was hanged on April 4th, 1979. Bhutto's hanging led to commotion and disturbances in the major cities, but the situation was firmly under control within three days.

Since its inception, the martial law administration had decided to review cases instituted against political opponents and dissidents by the Bhutto regime. Some 11,000 political prisoners were released, including the NAP leaders, in detention since 1975; in addition, a general amnesty was declared in Baluchistan in an attempt to conciliate the "aggrieved" province. Although the official ban on political activity continued, limited political activity was allowed.

In January 1978 Gen. Zia appointed a council of 16 advisers, comprising generals, senior civil servants and retired politicians, to act as departmental ministers. However, the existing military council, which consisted of Gen. Zia, the commanders of the Air Force and Navy and the chairman of the committee of joint chiefs of staff, was to remain supreme. In July Gen. Zia formed a Cabinet, comprising 22 members of ministerial rank. Like the advisory council, it included generals, businessmen and technocrats. Politicians who were appointed were all members of the right-wing Muslim League, the only party which had formally decided to join the cabinet if asked. At the end of June, Gen. Zia announced that he had abandoned the idea of forming a national government with the co-operation of the political parties, but, following the PNA's decision to participate in government, he formed a 22-member civilian Cabinet in August 1978. Apart from 15 PNA members, it contained only some independents and technocrats. At its request, the PNA members were relieved of their office in April 1979 and a new Cabinet comprising five army generals and 10 civilians (independents, technocrats and businessmen) was installed. Meanwhile, President Fazal Elahi Chaudhri resigned in September 1978, for "health reasons", and Gen. Zia became President.

Gen. Zia ul-Haq has embarked upon the task of bringing the country's laws into conformity with Islamic laws. In July 1978 he announced that he was seeking the advice of religious experts from Saudi Arabia and Egypt on Islamic measures to be taken to transform Pakistani society. In February 1979 Gen. Zia announced the enforcement of Islamic penal laws with immediate effect, and the introduction of *zakat* (poor-tax at the rate of 2½ per cent on banks' deposits and savings accounts) from July 1979, and of *ushr* (tax on agricultural produce at the rate of 5 per cent) from October 1979. *Zakat* was charged on 11 categories of assets, and, under instructions from the Government, banks deducted the poor-tax from all savings accounts on June 21st, 1980, for credit to the Central *Zakat* Fund. *Zakat* funds were established at the central, provincial and local levels, which would be utilized for providing assistance to the needy and the poor. Likewise, *ushr* is to be collected for the first time on a compulsory basis from land-owners during 1980. The regime is also pledged to initiate measures designed to make the economy interest free; the process is due to be completed by 1982. As a first step, interest-free banking was introduced from January 1st, 1981.

A Federal Shariat Court, replacing the Shariat Benches of the High Courts, was set up in May 1980, and a Chairman was appointed in June. The Court would associate three religious scholars (*ulama*) and is expected to ensure speedy justice. The Council of Islamic Ideology has been broadened and reconstituted, and it has been assigned the task of drafting an Islamic system of government in Pakistan since, according to Gen. Zia, implementation of Islamic values cannot be assured without such a system. Meanwhile, the religious scholars have formulated a 21-point programme for accelerating the pace of the Islamization process.

The political situation continued to be fluid, however. Neither the Pakistan National Alliance (PNA) nor the PPP presented a united front. The Tehrik-i-Istiqlal (TI) left the opposition Alliance in November 1977, as did the Jamiatul-Ulema-e-Pakistan (JUP) and the National Democratic Party (NDP), two other PNA components, in July and August 1978, the latter upon the PNA's decision to join Gen. Zia's civilian cabinet. When the NDP left the Alliance, the Baluch leaders joined the NDP, only to leave it in April 1979 and form a splinter group called the Pakistan National Party (PNP). Headed by Ghaus Bakhsh Bizenjo, a former leader of the defunct NAP and a former Governor of Baluchistan, the PNP has some nominal support in the three other provinces; it stands for "four nationalities" and greater provincial autonomy. The Qayyum League, which was incorporated into the Pakistan Muslim League headed by Pir Pagaro, has left it and revived its independent existence. The Pakistan Muslim League itself was split into two factions—the Pagaro and the Chatta groups—and several attempts to heal the split have proved abortive. After much reluctance, the PNA recognized the Pagaro group as the original component, and it has since joined the PNA deliberations. But relations between Pir Pagaro and the Jamaat-i-Islami (JI), the most well-organized component of the PNA, have soured since 1978, with Pagaro openly condemning it and associating himself with the JUP, which is deadly opposed to the JI. Most of the PPP leadership, which had been in gaol or under house arrest since March 1978 for repeated attempts to organize demonstrations for Bhutto's release, was released after Bhutto's hanging, and the PPP is being reorganized under the leadership of Benazir Bhutto, the daughter of the deceased leader. Surprisingly, the PPP has not disintegrated, despite the loss of its founder-chairman, and there is a strong degree of cohesion among its leaders. A PPP faction, styling itself as the Liberal PPP and launched by Maulana Kausar Niazi, a close associate of Bhutto, has failed to get off the ground and has made no serious inroads into the strength of the PPP.

Elections to the local bodies, which aroused considerable misgivings among various political parties, were finally held on a non-party basis in September 1979. They were boycotted by the PNA, but the PPP was shrewd enough to set up candidates unofficially as "independents".

The clamour of all the political parties for elections had earlier forced Gen. Zia to announce national elections for November 17th, 1979. However, in order to "tame" the parties and make them "behave" during the elections, Gen. Zia announced a series of amendments to the Political Parties Act of 1962. These amendments made it mandatory for all parties (i) to hold annual elections at every level within a specified period; (ii) to submit their accounts for audit to the Election Commission; and (iii) to register themselves with the Election Commission. Failure to fulfil any of these obligations was to render the parties ineligible for participation in the elections. All the major parties protested against the amendments, arguing that they empowered the Government to blacklist or ban any party under various pretexts, and vehemently opposed the registration clause.

General Zia also promulgated a presidential order by which elections to the national and provincial assemblies were proposed to be held under the system of proportional representation (PR), as against the plurality-vote system which was in vogue since independence.

By September 30th, the deadline for the registration of political parties, 56 parties had registered themselves with the Election Commission, and 44 had submitted their accounts; but those granted registration totalled only 16, including three major parties—TI, JUP and JI. Four major parties—the PPP, PNA (except JI), NDP and PNP—refused to register, but their candidates, except for the PNA's, nevertheless filed nomination papers. Prolonged manoeuvres to induce the PNA to participate in the elections having failed, and with NDP and PNP refusing to register, Gen. Zia finally announced on October 16th the indefinite postponement of elections, the dissolution of all the political parties, and the reinforcement of martial law. Simultaneously, censorship was imposed, some pro-PPP newspapers and periodicals were banned, and leaders of various political parties were either detained or put under house arrest, to pre-empt any attempt at organizing agitation against the reinforced martial law.

In view of a rash of petitions in the courts against detention of political workers and against martial law regulations and orders, Article 199 of the Constitution was amended in May 1980. The amendment debarred High Courts from making an order relating to the validity or effect of the martial law regulations or orders; this has obviously caused a good deal of disaffection in the legal community, which had earlier welcomed the replacement of the Bhutto regime by the military one. The amendment has since been challenged in the high courts of all four provinces, and the decision of the Sind High Court, upholding the amendment, is under appeal in the Supreme Court. Meantime, the Baluchistan High Court has given an adverse decision against the presidential amending order.

On March 27th, 1981, the Government promulgated a Provisional Constitutional Order which retained 119 articles, either wholly or in part, of the 1973 Constitution. The new Order provides for one or two Vice-Presidents, a *Majlis-i-Shura* (Consultative Committee/Council), and a framework for the functioning of political parties. The Lahore High Court has since ruled that the Provisional Constitutional Order was not a new legal order.

Contacts between the various political parties finally resulted in the setting up of a common platform, called the Movement for the Restoration of

Democracy (MRD), and the movement was officially launched on March 2nd, 1981. However, the hijacking of a PIA plane to Kabul by PPP activists that same afternoon caused widespread public resentment against opposition activities, leading to the disbandment of the MRD by seven of its nine components. On March 13th, in a move to blunt the political parties' demand for democratization, a new 23-member Federal Cabinet was sworn in, comprised chiefly of civilians and technocrats. This was closely followed by the setting up of provincial cabinets in the N.W.F.P., the Punjab and Sind. The setting up of a 200-member Federal Council, promised in 1980, is, however, still awaited.

While General Zia has ruled out the holding of elections at the present time, he is pledged to establish a government of people's representatives who are chosen through the "Islamic mode". The form of government best suited to Pakistan continues to be debated, with most political leaders opting for the parliamentary form of government about which the regime has some serious reservations. Meanwhile, the Federal Cabinet is reportedly engaged in formulating a viable political framework to associate the people in the decision-making process at the highest level, and the Council of Islamic Ideology is occupied with the task of drafting an Islamic system of government.

Since 1979 there has been considerable improvement in the economic sector. With an inflation rate of only 8.5 per cent, the price level has been kept under control. The denationalization of certain industries has given a boost to the private sector, the Karachi Steel Mill has started production, the Guddu Thermal Power Project has been inaugurated, a massive new dam on River Indus has been initiated, some coal reserves (about 55 million tons) have been discovered near Hyderabad, and petroleum exploration has been stepped up. Agreements for joint enterprise have been signed with Saudi Arabia and Libya, and for economic collaboration in various fields with a number of other countries. The World Bank Aid to Pakistan Consortium pledged $1,080 million for 1980/81 and $1,170 million for 1981/82; a further $110 million has been earmarked for Afghan refugees in Pakistan. The World Bank has also agreed to the rescheduling of Pakistan's debts, and the U.S.A. to debt relief. Preliminary census statistics put Pakistan's population at 84 million in 1980 and a National Council of Population has been set up to check overpopulation.

FOREIGN POLICY

The foreign policy of Pakistan has been conditioned very largely by Indo-Pakistan relations. This is not surprising. When the idea of Pakistan was mooted, **it evoked great hostility on the part of the** Hindus of **India irrespective of the party to which they belonged. And even when Pakistan was accepted by the Congress this acceptance was not genuine, as is evident** from the resolution of the All-India Congress Committee which approved the June 3rd Plan: "Geography and the mountains and the seas fashioned India as she is and no human agency can change that shape. . . . Economic circumstances and the insistent demands of international affairs make the unity of India still more necessary. . . ." Even after partition the Indian Prime Minister Jawaharlal Nehru said: "Both the dominions will unite into one country"; and the Deputy Prime Minister, Vallabhbhai Patel, expressed "full hope and confidence that sooner or later we shall be again united in common allegiance to one country". Such thoughts were not only expressed in the beginning but continued to be reiterated by Pandit Nehru and others. Keith Callard observed in 1959: "Many Indians feel that the creation of Pakistan was a tragic mistake which might still be corrected, at least so far as East Bengal is concerned."

Pakistan was thus confronted from the very beginning with the problem of survival. India's territory and population were over four times those of Pakistan; its industrial potential was at least ten times as great and its armed forces, even before the massive military aid began to flow into India in the wake of the Indo-Chinese clashes of 1962, were three times those of Pakistan (the ratio of armed strength has been disturbed lately to the disadvantage of Pakistan). Moreover, since Pakistan was divided into two wings, one thousand miles apart, the ratio worked further to Pakistan's disadvantage. This explains why, from Jinnah to Muhammad Ayub Khan, Pakistan made many attempts to come to some arrangement by which the two countries, instead of dissipating their energies against each other, would come to some clear and friendly understanding and settle the disputes by peaceful means. Jinnah spoke of a mutually evolved "Monroe Doctrine". Liaquat Ali Khan made a proposal for the settlement of disputes between the two countries by means of arbitration. Ayub Khan suggested an understanding on "common defence" to which Pandit Nehru's retort was "common defence against whom?". This was not long before the Indo-Chinese flare-up of 1962. Once Nehru threatened Pakistan with "other methods" and on another occasion he mooted loudly the idea of "police action" in East Pakistan.

Being relatively so weak, Pakistan could not afford to belittle the importance of the anti-Pakistan feelings in India nor to consider the pronouncements of Indian leaders as empty threats, particularly since India had a record of settling territorial problems by the use of force, as in Kashmir, Jungadh, Hyderabad and Goa.

The basic difficulty in Indo-Pakistan relations seemed to be the very existence of Pakistan and so the problems between the two countries remained unsolved. Among the causes which created estrangement were the position of minorities and the question of evacuee property. The Canal Water dispute and the dispute over some of the boundaries also proved difficult, but certain adjustments were made with regard to them. India's construction of the Farakka Barrage in West Bengal was a later move which created dissatisfaction in Pakistan. Then there was the vital Kashmir question, to which a solution has not yet been found. Last but not least was the Bangladesh issue which attained such vast proportions, due to India's involvement. The result has been that there have been occasions when the two countries have fought local wars, as in Kashmir (1947–48) and the Rann of Kutch (1965), and two fully-fledged wars in 1965 and 1971. Yet there are no two countries whose defence, security and prosperity make it more imperative that they should be friends and allies, rather than enemies.

Since the war of 1971 and its tragic outcome, feeling has been growing in favour of an understanding with India on the basis of "live and let live". Moreover, Bhutto had also advocated *rapprochement* with India. Partial success in this policy resulted in the Simla Agreement of July 1972, which provided for the withdrawal of Indian and Pakistani troops from occupied territory. But the Simla Agreement did not have an altogether smooth passage, the return of prisoners being held up for more than a year until the signing of another Indo-Pak agreement in August 1973. The return of prisoners of war was completed in May 1974.

Linked with the problem of relations with India was the question of the recognition of Bangladesh. Pakistan's recognition of Bangladesh came in February 1974. Bhutto had insisted that Bangladesh give up plans for the trial of certain prisoners of war as a condition for normalizing relations. This was rejected by Sheikh Mujib, who also refused to attend the Islamic Summit Conference due to be held in Lahore in February 1974. A mission of foreign ministers of the Islamic countries, sent to Dacca, helped to break the deadlock between them, and Bangladesh was finally recognized a few hours before the opening of the conference. This enabled Mujib to attend the Islamic Summit in Lahore. Although Bhutto returned the visit the following summer, relations between the two countries remained rather cool until the toppling of the Mujib regime in August 1975. Pakistan was the first country to recognize the new regime headed by Khondakar Mushtaq Ahmed, and also persuaded the West Asian Muslim countries to extend aid to Bangladesh. In late 1975 the two countries agreed to establish diplomatic relations, and the exchange of envoys took place in January 1976. The President of Bangladesh, General Ziaur Rahman, visited Islamabad in December 1977, and relations between the two countries were strengthened further.

Relations with India, however, deteriorated further after the latter's nuclear test in May 1974. Further tension between the two countries was created in July as a result of alleged troop movements by India and Afghanistan on Pakistan's borders. Nevertheless, after assurances by India that the provisions of the Simla Agreement would be observed and that there would be no threat of the use of force in settling differences, an agreement was reached by both countries in September, restoring communication and travel facilities which had been broken off at the time of the 1971 war. In January 1975 trade agreements and an agreement on the resumption of shipping services were also concluded. In May 1976 India and Pakistan agreed to exchange ambassadors in July, and in June an agreement was reached on restoring severed air links.

A goodwill visit by Indian External Affairs Minister Atal Behari Vajpayee to Pakistan in February 1978 resulted in further normalization. It also paved the way for an accord on the Salal Dam, after eight years of negotiations. The agreement, signed in New Delhi in April 1978, sought to safeguard Pakistan's vital interests in the flow of the Chenab waters, while ensuring benefits to India. The accord was hailed in both New Delhi and Islamabad as a step forward in increasing mutual understanding.

New Delhi's posture since Indira Gandhi's return to power in January 1980 has caused a setback to the trend towards normalization and increasing mutual understanding. As against the rest of the non-communist world, Mrs. Gandhi not only refused to condemn Soviet intervention in Afghanistan (*see* below) but also did not consider it a threat to Pakistan's security. Second, New Delhi reacted adversely to the U.S. offer of military aid to Pakistan, designed to bolster the country's defences in view of the Soviet threat. Third, while protesting vehemently against Pakistan's nuclear programme for peaceful purposes, India has officially affirmed its right to produce nuclear weapons, and has developed and successfully launched in July a four-stage rocket of its own design to place a satellite into orbit. India's nuclear and aero-space programme is viewed in Pakistan in the context of India's prepossession with military power, which includes large arms purchases from the Soviet Union and vast expansion of its armament industry in recent years. India also protested to the U.S.A. when it became known that the new Reagan administration has offered to help Pakistan in meeting its normal defence requirements. Mrs. Gandhi termed Pakistan's efforts to acquire modern equipment as a threat to India. On the other hand, Pakistan has stoutly defended its sovereign right to acquire arms to meet its defence requirements. However, as a concession to India, Pakistan has suggested that the parameters of the two countries' defence requirements be fixed and that the ratio of arms levels be maintained by both sides. These two principles were finally agreed upon by both countries during the visit of India's External Affairs Minister in June 1981. The visit, which generated goodwill on both sides, has been considered significant in the context of regional security and bilateral relations between the two South Asian neighbours. Of particular significance is the Indian Minister's reiteration of his country's commitment to Pakistan's independence.

Relations Beyond the Sub-Continent

Relations with India have largely influenced the relations of Pakistan with other nations. Pakistan felt in its early years that the Commonwealth was not a particularly useful instrument for the resolution of its disputes with India. As to the two major blocs into which the world was divided, Pakistan, without allying itself definitely with one, was inclined towards the West for some years and tried to come closer to the U.S.A., particularly from 1954 onwards when a Mutual Defence Assistance Agreement was concluded. In the same year Pakistan became a member of SEATO. In 1955 it joined the Baghdad Pact with the

United Kingdom, Turkey, Iraq and Iran. When Iraq left in 1958 this pact came to be known as CENTO. To reinforce CENTO a further bilateral agreement was concluded with the United States in 1959.

India's annexation of Goa was a turning-point in the foreign policy of Pakistan, which then started looking towards nations other than those belonging to the Western Bloc and established closer relations with China. Pakistan received a bigger shock when, after the Indo-Chinese border skirmishes in 1962, the Western Powers, particularly the U.S.A., started giving massive military aid to India, thereby disturbing the entire balance of armed strength in the subcontinent. Pakistan tried further to develop relations with China and for the first time made serious efforts to bring about normalcy in its relations with the Soviet Union. This led to a deterioration in relations with the United States and affected the economic and military aid which Pakistan had been receiving from that source. Closer relations with Turkey and Iran had been developed since 1964, and the policy has paid dividends. When India and Pakistan were at war in 1965 and again during the East Pakistan crisis of 1971, China, along with certain Muslim powers, proved to be the only supporter of Pakistan.

The secession of East Pakistan and its aftermath created misgivings in Pakistan against both the U.S.A. and the U.S.S.R., the latter having openly sided with Bangladesh and India, while the former was believed to have done the same surreptitiously. Many people in West Pakistan believed that the U.K. was a centre of anti-Pakistan propaganda and in January 1972 Pakistan withdrew from the Commonwealth. Since 1979, however, Pakistan has shown interest in rejoining the Commonwealth, but India is reportedly barring its re-entry.

Relations with the U.S.A. improved when the U.S. ban on arms sales to Pakistan was lifted after official visits by Bhutto in 1973 and 1975. Pakistan withdrew from SEATO in 1972, but continued to attend CENTO ministerial council meetings. However, from 1976 relations with the U.S.A. worsened in the wake of U.S. opposition to the sale of a nuclear reprocessing plant by France to Pakistan and the Carter Administration's refusal to sell A-7 bombers. Bhutto also accused the U.S.A. of hatching a conspiracy to topple him, and threatened to leave CENTO. Relations with the U.S.A. have since improved, but in August 1978 the Carter administration announced that it would suspend all economic aid to Pakistan for 1978–79 in response to Islamabad's intended purchase of the reprocessing plant. The threatened suspension of economic aid came in April 1979 in the wake of Bhutto's hanging, on the suspicion that Pakistan was secretly working towards producing an atomic bomb. All this has somewhat soured Pakistan-U.S. relations. Pakistan also refused to participate in any military pact with the U.S.A. Further talks during 1981 resulted in a Pakistan-U.S. accord on a $3,000 million, five-year package programme of economic supporting funds, development assistance, and loans for foreign military sales in June 1981. Pakistan desires that the U.S.A. sell arms at concessional prices, as is done by the Soviet Union to India. By the new agreement, the U.S.A. has agreed to sell F-16 aircraft, to assist Pakistan in improving its air defence capabilities, and to the early delivery of selected defence equipment, urgently needed by Pakistan. Pakistan, which earlier ruled out military ties with the U.S.A., insists that the deal does not compromise the principles and purposes of the Non-Aligned Movement and the Organization of the Islamic Conference.

Following the revolution in Iran in early 1979 and in consultation with the new regime, Pakistan left CENTO in March 1979. Iran and Turkey also left and CENTO was disbanded following their withdrawal. Further deterioration in Pakistan-U.S. relations came in the wake of reports in the American press in late 1979 of U.S. plans to destroy Pakistani nuclear installations through commando action, and of the burning down of the American Embassy in Islamabad and the Information Centre in Lahore in November 1979 by a rally, protesting against the sacrilege of the Holy Ka'aba in Mecca, Saudi Arabia. The U.S.A. demanded full reparation for the damage caused. However, the Soviet intervention in Afghanistan in late December, which posed a common threat to the national interests of both Pakistan and the U.S.A., helped to overcome mutual acrimony and bitterness, and the two countries, along with others, tried to evolve a common policy to curb Soviet adventurism in the region. The U.S.A. showed a growing concern for Pakistan's security and offered $400 million in economic and military aid over the next two years. However, Gen. Zia turned down the offer, saying that the volume of aid offered was "peanuts"—that is, extremely disproportionate to the requirements of the situation.

Meantime, Pakistan was admitted to the Non-Aligned Movement (NAM) at the sixth summit conference of the non-aligned nations at Havana, which was attended by Gen. Zia. The conference endorsed the Pakistani position regarding the right of all states to acquire nuclear technology for peaceful purposes and denounced the use of aid by developed countries to pressurize them into abandoning some of their sovereign rights.

Pakistan has had difficulties with Afghanistan since the beginning, the point at issue being "Pakhtunistan", which has been championed by Afghanistan but consistently regarded by Pakistan as an interference in its internal affairs. With the overthrow in July 1973 of King Zahir Shah and the establishment of a new regime in Afghanistan, under Lt.-Gen. Daud, which revived the Afghan claims to the areas of Pakistan inhabited by Pathans, relations between both countries greatly deteriorated. After 1975, however, relations between the two countries were somewhat normalized by exchange meetings and talks between Bhutto, and later Gen. Zia, and President Daud of Afghanistan. However, after the April 1978 coup in Afghanistan, the Taraki regime in Kabul reverted to the traditional refrain about "Pakhtunistan", the alleged desire of Pathans in the North-West Frontier Province for an independent homeland. The internal revolt in Afghanistan has led some 125,000

Afghans to take refuge in the N.W.F.P. and Baluchistan province of Pakistan. Both Kabul and Moscow have repeatedly accused Pakistan of providing shelter, ammunition and training facilities to Afghan guerrillas waging a war of attrition against the Soviet-backed regime; but Pakistan claims that these refugees have been accommodated purely on humanitarian grounds and that no training camps exist on its territory. The UN High Commissioner for Refugees, who has inspected the refugee camps and their environs, has said that he did not find any traces of guerrilla training camps in the region. Pakistan's efforts to work out a *modus vivendi* with Kabul finally resulted in a visit to Islamabad by the Afghan Deputy Minister for Foreign Affairs in June 1979.

The easing of the tension between the two countries following talks at Foreign Minister level, however, did not last long. Before the Pakistan Adviser on Foreign Affairs returned the visit, the Soviet intervention in Afghanistan in late December 1979 caused an unprecedented deterioration in Pakistan-Afghan relations. Pakistan was obviously gravely concerned at this new development along its north-western frontier, and felt that the Soviet move violated the UN Charter and the Bandung principles. Along with other non-aligned countries, it sponsored a resolution in the UN Security Council demanding an "immediate and unconditional withdrawal from Afghanistan"; on being blocked by the Soviet veto, the resolution was moved and adopted in the General Assembly on January 14th, 1980, by an overwhelming majority. Subsequently, an emergency session of the Islamic Foreign Ministers' Conference was called at Islamabad in late January to discuss the Afghanistan issue. The conference denounced the Soviet intervention and called for its withdrawal; suspended the membership of Afghanistan until such time as the Soviet intervention ended; declared complete solidarity with the Afghan *mujahideen* (freedom fighters) in their struggle to safeguard their faith, independence and territorial integrity, and with the neighbouring Islamic countries against any threat to their security; and urged a boycott of the Olympic Games in Moscow. This resolution was reaffirmed at the 11th Islamic Foreign Ministers' Conference, also held at Islamabad, in May 1980. In an effort to find a political solution to the Afghanistan issue, the conference constituted a three-member committee comprising the Foreign Ministers of Iran and Pakistan and the Secretary-General of the Islamic Conference Organization. However, because of the negative attitude adopted by both Moscow and Kabul, the committee could not make any progress until late July. In order to break the deadlock, the Pakistan Foreign Minister went so far as to concede that the interests and aspirations of the Afghan people as a whole can be reconciled with the security interests of the Soviet Union. He said that, while Pakistan was also prepared to give all reasonable guarantees to the U.S.S.R., it was not in a position either to control the rebels or to bring about a cease-fire in Afghanistan. For a long while, both Moscow and Kabul have accused Pakistan of providing military training to Afghan *mujahideen* and refugees. However, Pakistan has consistently denied this charge and has justified the assistance provided to the refugees on humanitarian grounds. By April 1982, there were 2,700,000 registered Afghan refugees in Pakistan. The cost of their upkeep for 1982 is estimated at about £121 million of which Pakistan is contributing half.

ECONOMIC SURVEY

Kevin Rafferty

At independence in 1947, Muhammad Ali Jinnah, the country's founder and first Governor-General, was handed a "moth-eaten Pakistan". In 1971 it was torn apart again and more than half its population was detached to form the independent state of Bangladesh. Pakistan was thus cut off from its biggest foreign exchange earner, jute, and its industrialists lost a captive market of about 70 million people. The loss of Bangladesh cost Pakistan only 55,000 of its 365,000 square miles.

In spite of all these difficulties, Pakistan should have been in the best position of all the countries of the sub-continent. It had a good base in both agriculture and industry, affording enormous potential for economic growth. Even promising reserves of petroleum had been discovered. Its population, estimated at 87 million at mid-1982, does not create the same pressures on the land as those in India or Bangladesh, though the Pakistan growth rate is a dangerously high 3 per cent a year. However, in the 1970s Pakistan again became preoccupied with political problems which called into question the very roots of its survival. In July 1977, after riots, strikes, disruptions and stoppages estimated to have cost up to U.S. $1,000 million, the army intervened and overthrew the Prime Minister, Zulfiqar Ali Bhutto. His conviction for murder and his hanging in April 1979 kept the political turmoil to the fore and pushed the numerous economic problems into the background. General Zia ul-Haq, Pakistan's President, promised elections but postponed them and diverted his energies towards turning Pakistan into a fully Islamic state. First steps were actively taken in January 1981 with the setting-up of an Islamic banking system, which is interest-free, and a new profit-sharing company system to run alongside traditional western-style economic methods. By the early 1980s Zia had given Pakistan stability and several years of growth at about 6 per cent annually. However, there were still the problems of a country living beyond its means internationally and trying new economic systems in an uncertain atmosphere.

HISTORY

At partition in August 1947 Pakistan was inferior in every way to India, being without a natural capital, without much industry to speak of, or experienced industrialists, and without a major port. Moreover, the upheavals and bloodshed following the division of the Punjab and Bengal, and the award of part of each to India and Pakistan, brought a huge colony of displaced migrants from India to Pakistan. The division of the Punjab led to a dispute with India over vital irrigation water supplies and this was not settled until the early 1960s, and only then through the assistance of the World Bank and the promise of massive aid to allow Pakistan to build the Mangla and Tarbela dams. The manner of the 1947 partition and the war over Kashmir produced constant tensions between India and Pakistan, encouraging both countries to spend vast sums on defence which they could ill afford.

Pakistan was fortunate in its early years to have guaranteed foreign exchange earnings from jute, all of which came from the East Wing. These earnings allowed imports and the build-up of an infant industry, at least in basic goods like cotton textiles, food processing and engineering. During the 1960s Ayub Khan gave both stable government and encouragement to private industry. Growth rates in West Pakistan were impressive: 10 per cent a year in industry and 5 per cent in agriculture. However, the gap between East and West Pakistan grew, and so did the ill-feeling. This was particularly so after the cyclone in East Pakistan in November 1970, when possibly 500,000 Bengalis died and the rest felt neglected by the Islamabad rulers. So East Pakistan's voters overwhelmingly elected the Awami League, dedicated to more autonomy for the East than the West was prepared to allow. A break was inevitable.

One inheritance of the years of Ayub Khan's rule was an administrative apparatus which strongly supported the status quo. Little was done to examine the underlying causes of poverty and lack of development, or to do anything about them. Banking and industrial assets became concentrated in the hands of a small number of businessmen. Some land reforms were introduced but the upper limit on land holdings remained high and the most stringent measures could be evaded. The measures had little impact on the problem of landlessness.

Zulfiqar Ali Bhutto took over as President of Pakistan after the fall of the military government in December 1971. He started by attacking the so-called "22 families" whom an eminent economist, Dr. Mahbub ul Haq, had accused of controlling two-thirds of Pakistan's industry and 80 per cent of its banking and insurance business.

Within a month of taking over and using his powers as a martial law President, Bhutto took over 11 groups of industries, including basic metals, heavy engineering, electrical goods, chemicals, electricity, gas, cement and the manufacturing and assembling of cars and tractors, installing new boards of directors to subject them to government control. Businessmen protested that the government measure was equivalent to nationalization without compensation; eventually these industries were nationalized. Labour reforms (giving more rights to industrial workers), education reforms (extending free education for all to the matriculation level), and new land reforms were introduced. Economically, the effect was unsettling. Pakistan's economy began to run into problems. Savings and investment began to fall.

Industrialists did not invest because they feared that new industries might be taken over.

Much more successful was the devaluation of the Pakistani rupee from 4.76 per U.S. dollar to 11.0 per dollar in May 1972. That measure, which had been urged by the international monetary agencies for some time, replaced a complicated system of exchange rates in which bonus vouchers were issued for certain categories of exported goods and could then be used. The more realistic rate gave a great impetus to exports when the world was still moving through boom and there were great opportunities for Pakistan.

Pakistanis seized these opportunities. Exports of cotton and goods made of cotton increased substantially. Goods which would have been sold to the captive market of East Bengal found a good sale elsewhere for foreign currency. World foodgrain production in 1972 was poor and Pakistan was able to sell rice, which would normally have gone to East Pakistan, on the international market. As a result, the value of Pakistan's exports increased from U.S. $698 million in 1972 to $958 million in 1973. Although imports rose even more, trade was almost balanced.

However, recession in the industrialized world coincided in 1974 with the exposure of persistent internal economic problems. Bad weather, problems of supply and distribution of essential agricultural inputs and political uncertainty succeeded one another, and at the same time Pakistan was having to pay more for its imports. Pakistan's terms of trade deteriorated.

The world recession and the increase in oil prices meant that Pakistan's trade account went wildly into deficit. Its exports rose steadily to reach about $1,310 million by 1977/78 but imports soared to reach almost $2,800 million. Pakistan had a trade deficit of more than $1,000 million for the first time in 1974/75 and in succeeding years the gap grew to $1,500 million. The situation was alleviated only by the inflow of remittances, reaching $1,000 million a year by 1977, from Pakistanis working abroad. These economic problems resulted in little improvement in the standard of living. Economists calculated that, in constant prices, per capita income had risen from $105 in 1947 to only $170 in 1977. With the coming of the military regime and better luck with the weather, economic growth began to pick up and, according to government figures, averaged a steady 6 per cent a year under Gen. Zia. Per capita income had reached $300 by the end of 1981. Even so, the economy remained weak, with many problems still unsolved, especially on the external account. These were so bad that, at the end of 1980, Pakistan received what was then the largest ever loan made to a developing country by the International Monetary Fund. In addition, it received substantial debt relief from traditional Western aid donors, yet the Government still said that it would have huge problems concerning payments until at least 1983. As a token of this, Pakistan had to take expensive loans from the international commercial markets. The question was whether Pakistan could avoid a trade deficit of $3,000 million, with the gap being bigger than total exports.

AGRICULTURE

Agriculture is still the most important contributor to Pakistan's economy, accounting for about 35 per cent of the nation's G.D.P. It is also responsible for the employment of 56 per cent of the labour force and directly and indirectly provides the majority of the country's exports. Because of unfavourable weather and other factors, agriculture fared badly after 1970. Having grown at an annual rate of 5 per cent between 1961 and 1970, the growth rates slumped to 0.3 per cent between 1971 and 1975, and in 1974/75 there was a 2 per cent decline in output. There were some improvements in the three subsequent years but these were somewhat marred by the see-sawing of cotton and food production—as one went up, the other fell. Not until 1979/80 did production of wheat and cotton properly recover, again reaching record levels.

Pakistan's agricultural potential is high but it has not fulfilled its promise. John Cool, then the Ford Foundation representative in the country, estimated that cereal production of 3 metric tons per acre could be achieved on two-thirds of the cultivated area. In other words, total production could reach 100 million metric tons a year. Pakistan should be the world's main rice exporter; instead it is usually the U.S.A. One of the obvious problems is that great effort and money are invested in the large projects, such as irrigation, but little in management, where the lack of performance really shows through.

The most important crop is wheat, production of which fell to less than 8.3 million tons in 1977/78, compared with 8.8 million in 1976/77, and the lowest since 1974/75. Self-sufficiency had been achieved in 1976/77 but in the following year, instead of being in a position to export wheat, Pakistan imported more than 2 million tons. However, with better weather and the use of Tarbela Dam waters, a record 11.5 million tons of wheat was produced in 1980/81, bringing self-sufficiency almost within reach again. The other major food crop is rice, much of which is exported, although sales of rice have not compensated for money spent on wheat imports. Production of milled rice has risen but in recent years has fluctuated with the weather. The 3.3 million tons of 1979/80 remained a record, as poor weather took a toll of the rice harvest in the following years. One of Pakistan's specialities is the production of aromatic *basmati* rice. Other food crops are maize and sugar cane. The cane crop reached 30 million tons in 1977/78 but then fell in successive years to about 27 million tons.

The main non-food crop is cotton, production of which has traditionally been of the order of 4 million bales. In 1975/76, production fell to below 3 million bales because of weevils and heavy rains and floods which made replanting necessary in the Punjab. Cotton production in 1976/77 fell even lower to 2.4 million bales. The loss of such a large part of the cotton crop was a severe blow to Pakistan's export earnings. However, in 1977/78 there was some recovery to about 3.2 million bales. In 1979/80 production passed 4 million bales to reach 4.2 million, a new record.

In terms of climate and irrigation facilities, Pakistan is similar to Egypt and the eastern Punjab of India, but it has done less well than either with its agricultural production. Yields for Pakistan's wheat are about 1,000 lb. per acre, compared with 2,000 lb. in the east Punjab and 2,600 lb. in Egypt. Pakistan's rice yield is just below that of the east Punjab but only just over half the 3,000 lb. per acre produced by Egypt, and far from the 4,800 lb. per acre produced in Japan, the world's most efficient rice producer. Pakistan's maize production is below 1,000 lb. per acre whereas the Indian Punjab's is just above that and Egypt's is 3,500. In production of cotton, Pakistan achieves only 40 per cent of Egyptian yields of 2,000 lb. per acre and once more falls below the standards set by the Punjab India, which produces 1,000 lb. per acre.

In 1976/77 Pakistan was able to start using water from the giant Tarbela Dam, the largest earth-filled dam in the world. Fertilizer and water are the key to better yields with the new varieties of seeds. It appears, however, that the "green revolution" in Pakistan has reached a critical point now that the easiest benefits have been obtained.

Besides its crops, Pakistan has large herds of livestock. Taking five sheep or goats as equivalent to one head of cattle or one buffalo, Pakistan has about the same number of animals per person as the United States. Yet average production for each animal unit in Pakistan is only 10 per cent of the U.S. figure. The major reasons for this lack of productivity in Pakistan are inadequate cattle feed and poor management.

MINING AND POWER

Pakistan has a good range of minerals, including petroleum, natural gas, coal, iron ore, uranium, chromite gypsum and limestone. The government-owned Resource Development Corporation reported reserves of over 330 million tons of copper ore in 1977, with 63 million tons containing gold in significant value. Coal in Pakistan is too sulphurous to be transformed into coke for industry. Although annual production has reached 1.5 million metric tons, coal imports are still necessary.

Mining has not been greatly developed commercially, except for mining of chromite, exports of which go to the U.S.A. Reasons for the slow development of mining range from the inaccessibility of some of the areas of Baluchistan to the heavy costs of infrastructure and expertise in setting up mining. For all its contacts with the West, Pakistan has never gone out of its way to seek foreign private investment. However, deposits of both graphite and limestone, discovered during 1977, were expected to provide a surplus for export, and it was also planned to increase annual production of sulphur to 21,000 tons in the next few years.

Pakistan is also looking at hydro-electric power projects. The Tarbela Dam began generating electric power in June 1977. It will have a power generating capacity of 2,000 MW. when fully developed. Pakistan has other mountain streams but the cost of turning them to hydropower would be expensive.

One of the most significant events in the mid-1970s was the discovery of petroleum. For years the Sui natural gasfield in Baluchistan had been important in supplying fuel to Karachi, but Pakistan oilfields were small and ageing and could not increase production to cope with the damage done to the economy by higher oil prices. However, there was enough interest among the oil companies to tempt Gulf, one of the major companies, to explore the potential for joint work with Pakistan in looking for petroleum, although negotiations were slowed down by the political turmoil and changes of regime. The World Bank was also interested enough to look at the prospects of assisting the development. In 1978, the Oil and Gas Development Corporation announced that it intended to spend Rs. 3,720 million on the implementation of the development plan over the subsequent five years, and envisaged drilling 10 more wells at Tut, 14 at Dhodak and six at Meyal. High expectations of the domestic oil industry were slow to be fufilled. At the end of 1981, domestic oil production had fallen slightly on the previous year and was only 500,000 tons. Spending on oil imports had risen to $1,500 million, a threefold increase in three years.

INDUSTRY

Textiles, which form the bulk of manufacturing exports and are the mainstay of manufacturing industry, were badly affected by the 1975 recession and are still faring badly, hampered by restrictions imposed by the developed countries. Within the manufacturing sector, there are wide variations in the size of enterprises and the scale of their activities. They range from large family concerns, which have many interlinked interests, and big engineering works run by the Government to very small-scale factories and even individual workshops. One of the more important decisions of Bhutto's rule was to take the important industries involving large-scale investment into the public sector. During the 1970s that decision and the world recession have done much to create uncertainty. Private industrialists were frightened that Bhutto might be tempted to take over more industries and so they held back on investment, although, in September 1977, it was announced that all rice-husking and cotton-ginning factories nationalized in 1976 were to be returned to their former owners. In constant prices (based on 1969/70), private industrial investment fell from Rs.1,358 million in 1970/71 to Rs.650 million in 1976/77. Public sector industrial investment rose from Rs.65 million to Rs.1,563 million, but the wisdom of such heavy investment could be questioned. Few private industrialists regarded the then President, later Prime Minister, as a socialist, but they thought that socialism might be an election winner. The industries taken over were themselves troubled and only under the stricter financial regime of Rafi Raza, Minister of Production until 1977, did they begin to function efficiently. One problem was that the Government's choice of the original industries taken over was decided as much by political considerations as by the needs of the coherent organization of industry.

The new government of Gen. (later President) Zia set out to reassure investors and private entrepreneurs. Some industries were handed back to private enterprise, others were opened up and concessions were given to encourage industrialists. Yet even so, one of the biggest criticisms made by the IMF, on providing its $1,700 million three-year loan, was that inefficient public-sector industries were draining precious reserves and bank credit.

In general, Pakistan's industry did not have the good start of Indian industry. The areas now comprising Pakistan were too much on the outer edges of the British Indian Empire and the great industries were run by Hindus. Pakistan has had some help from abroad. Contractors from the People's Republic of China built a heavy engineering complex near Taxila. A $200 million steel mill, built near Karachi by the U.S.S.R., was opened in August 1980, long behind schedule and thought by foreigners to be too expensive. Industry is still unsophisticated. Textiles, for example, are concentrated at the cheaper end of the scale, largely turning out grey cloth. For all that, many economists have been impressed by the enterprise of Pakistanis.

That enterprise shows clearly in small-scale industries which have been much more successful than their larger counterparts, so much so that organizations such as the World Bank recommend that more encouragement should be given to smaller-scale industries. This sector has recorded some notable success stories, for example the sports goods industries around Sialkot, in the Punjab, and the carpet makers who have contributed greatly to Pakistan's export drive. In 1978, the Pakistan government proposed to set up two free industrial zones, one in Karachi and one in Lahore. Legislation is complete and an authority has been established to administer the areas. Only export industries will be allowed, and preference is to be given to industries based on raw materials from Pakistan. Already about 40 foreign concerns have expressed a desire to establish industries within these zones. However, other countries of the sub-continent have a headstart in establishing such export zones.

TRADE AND PAYMENTS

The international account is the most obvious weak link, particularly trade. Even though exports rose under Gen. Zia, imports rose faster. Exports reached $2,800 million in 1980/81, but began to slump badly in the first half of the next year because of falls in raw cotton, yarn, rice and carpet exports. At one time it was feared that the trade gap might even reach $4,000 million or more and the payments deficit might be $500 million. But then trade improved (thanks to a devaluation of the rupee), import prices rose more slowly than expected and earnings from remittances increased to alleviate the strain. Exports were nevertheless expected to be flat in the 1981/82 year at $2,700 million.

Exports are dominated by raw cotton, cotton products (yarn and cloth) and rice, together making up about 60 per cent of Pakistan's exports. Attempts have been made to diversify export destinations, and goods going to the Middle East have risen from almost nothing in the 1960s to about 25 per cent of total exports at the end of the 1970s; yet Pakistan has a large deficit with the Middle East because of petroleum purchases.

It is unlikely that Pakistan will find it easy to cut imports, especially given the heavy cost of POL; expansion of exports will not be easy either. In the areas where its industrialists are experts, they face restrictions and protection. However, a bigger problem is that Pakistan's industrialists have not developed a broad enough base to take advantage of any expansion of world trade. The real spirit has been shown by smaller industrialists who lack technology and resources. Bigger industrialists have been affected by the political uncertainty and threats against them.

The Government has managed to cover its successive enormous trade gaps by heavy borrowings from Western donors and OPEC countries. Immediately after the oil price rise, Pakistan's particular Islamic friendships with the Middle East nations meant that it was able to cover the vast trade gap more easily than had been expected. In 1973/74 Pakistan received more loans from OPEC ($610 million) than from Western aid donors ($539 million). Aid from the West has continued to increase and some time ago topped $1,000 million. Yet demands for aid have increased as the trade gap widened.

Debt payments were pressing. At the end of 1981 Pakistan's long term outstanding debt had risen to $8,775 million. Repayments were more than $600 million a year, or more than 20 per cent of export earnings. But Pakistan had the cushion of remittances from Pakistanis working abroad. These sums were expected to reach $2,200 million or more by 1982. In the past, the United Kingdom was the most important source of funds from Pakistanis abroad. Since 1970, however, as the U.K. closed its doors and the oil boom began, other countries have experienced the massive emigration of Pakistanis, including Canada and the U.S.A., but most especially the Middle East. There are estimated to be more than a million Pakistanis working abroad, with the annual rate of emigration reaching 100,000. Indeed, in some of the smaller Gulf states, Pakistanis outnumber the local population. The exodus of workers has had other damaging effects on the rest of the economy.

Late in 1980 Pakistan received a large measure of relief in the shape of a $1,700 million three-year loan from the International Monetary Fund. The terms attached to it were a good commentary on the plight of Pakistan's economy. The country promised to liberalize imports of raw materials and machinery, to cut deficit financing by reduction of food subsidies, to start on income tax reforms to make the tax a useful revenue earner and to attempt to make state industries more productive. Even so, the IMF money was not considered to be enough to enable Pakistan's balance of payments to go back into surplus. The Government asked the Western aid consortium for debt relief of $280 million per year for three years, but instead it was granted $233 million to last for 18 months. The Government had claimed that it would have a payments deficit of $400 million until 1983.

In early January 1982 Pakistan allowed the rupee to "float" instead of being pegged to the U.S. dollar. In the next few months the currency slipped by about 10 per cent against the dollar and 8 per cent overall. This was a start which allowed Pakistan's exports, previously overpriced as they rose with the dollar, to regain some ground. Some economists thought that a more comprehensive devaluation of the order of 20 per cent or more was what was needed, and some observers claimed that that was what the IMF also wanted. But suggestions of a deal with the IMF were denied by Pakistan's Finance Minister, Ghulam Ishaq Khan.

One of the factors which worries Western aid donors is that the amount of the regular budget spent on defence has risen steadily and reached about 50 per cent. In 1981 Pakistan's defence forces received a boost in the form of a $2,500 million largely military aid package from the U.S.A., and immediately India gave indications that it would have to respond by increasing arms spending, triggering fears of another damaging round of military expenditure.

ECONOMIC GROWTH

The rapid economic growth of the 1960s was accomplished without any major changes in the lives or prospects of the majority of Pakistanis. In spite of land reforms, the "ceiling" on land holdings remains high and the problem of landlessness has grown. In spite of politicians' promises, anything like socialism remains a long way off from real-life Pakistan today. Pakistan has a great deal of poverty but nothing as extreme as in Bangladesh or as concentrated as in the great metropolitan areas of India.

In his Budget speech in late June 1980, Ghulam Ishaq Khan, the Finance Minister, scored political points, making much of the fact that economic growth under Gen. Zia had been a long way ahead of the 3.7 per cent average of the seven Bhutto years, but he was also frank enough to admit the fragile base. He said: "We have only partly recovered the ground lost during a fairly long period of mismanagement". However, the Government was also imposing its own extra strains on the weak economy. The Budget speech was full of references to the goodness of Allah in that "He provided us the guidance and gave us the courage to live by His precepts and in His bountiful mercy He also rewarded us with encouraging results during the year." The Finance Minister also reiterated the Zia Government's intention of introducing a fully Islamic financial system.

An important step was taken on June 21st when Pakistanis with bank savings accounts found that 2.5 per cent had been taken away from them as their contribution to the Islamic *zakat* tax, the proceeds of which are distributed among the needy. Even staunch Muslims pointed out that the procedure was a reversal of tradition, under which the *zakat* is paid first to poor members of the family, then to servants and only then, if anything is left, to the State treasury. In spite of the grumbles, President Zia planned to move over to an interest-free system of banking. Some banks opened a "second window" for interest-free accounts but pointed out that the whole campaign might make it difficult for Pakistan to attract capital and to borrow in dealing with a hard-faced world outside, which did not believe in Islamic precepts. One banker commented: "The Saudis are helping Pakistan to push the Islamic system, but I think they are glad that the experiments are being conducted here, not in Saudi Arabia."

Pakistan's banks, which were nationalized in 1974 after complaints that they were controlled by the famous "22 families", opened their interest-free windows at the beginining of 1981 and quickly collected Rs.2,000 million or just over 3 per cent of total deposits. The new style of accounts were on a profit and loss basis as it was held that, although Islam frowns on interest, it does not frown on profit. The majority of investors clearly wanted to wait and see whether the profit and loss system would yield profits or losses. A new law also allowed *modarba* (profit-sharing) companies, using the funds collected in the new banking windows. Funds channelled through the banks were going mainly to finance commodity trade, public sector exports and loans for house-building. Initial claims were that the returns on the Islamic deposits were earning more than conventional funds.

Meanwhile, more conventional criticism of Pakistan's economy came from the noted West German economist and former Finance Minister, Karl Schiller. He urged a 20 per cent devaluation of the Pakistani rupee to make exports more competitive and improve the balance of payments. The immediate reaction to this from the authorities was that, with the oil bill mounting, a devaluation would be risky. Schiller also proposed a number of other controversial measures in a private report to the Government. These included proposals that the Government should encourage exports, cut the size of the government-owned sector and merge it into a market economy within five years, end the system of allocating bank credit by sectors (which, he said, favoured the big public enterprises), liberalize imports and investments, reduce deficit financing and retain high interest rates to combat inflation, which in 1980 topped 12 per cent. Many of the proposals overlapped those from the IMF. Schiller said that the Pakistan economy was over-controlled. Yet officials said that any changes would have to take into account the move towards an Islamic system.

In 1978 the fifth development plan, covering the five years from July 1st, 1978, to June 30th, 1983, was announced. It involves a development outlay of Rs.210,000 million, with more than 75 per cent of it to be financed from domestic resources and national savings, and the remainder to be financed by foreign assistance. Rs. 148,000 million are to be spent in the public sector and Rs. 62,000 million in the private. Priority has been given to agriculture and rural development, a target growth rate of 6 per cent a year in the agricultural sector being proposed, as against an average annual growth rate of 1.8 per cent over the previous eight years. The plan also envisages an increase in the average growth rate of the industrial sector, to 10 per cent, as a result of improved utilization of major projects in the public sector and more favourable private investment.

In 1982 Mahbub ul-Haq returned from a senior post with the World Bank in Washington to become Minister of Planning in Islamabad. While away from Pakistan he had acquired a reputation as a radical at least in the theory of economic development. It remains to be seen whether he will be able to translate any of his ideas into practical benefit.

DEVELOPMENT PROBLEMS

The problems involved in modernizing Pakistan's agriculture are enormous. In spite of land reforms and rent reforms, 60 per cent of the country's farmers are tenants or partial tenants and mostly share-croppers. Under this system, the owner provides inputs, pays the taxes and water charges, and receives half of the output. Such a system does not provide sufficient incentive to the farmer to adopt new techniques. In November 1975 the Government announced the restructuring of land taxes to make the system more progressive. Then in January 1977 further land reforms were introduced and the land recovered from individual owners was distributed free to the peasants cultivating it. At the same time the land revenue system was replaced by an agricultural income tax system.

Something must also be done about the need for improved water control. Foreign experts have calculated that only a third of the water actually reaches the crops. This has two effects. The more obvious is that crops are denied water and yields are much lower than necessary. The other is that spilling the water leads to waterlogging and salinity. This is already apparent in a number of places.

In industry, it would be worth the Government's while to give greater encouragement to private industrialists working on a very small scale. Although small-scale industry provides only 20 per cent of the value added, it gives jobs to 85 per cent of the manufacturing labour force. Moreover, the investment for each additional job in small-scale industry is only 3,000 rupees, compared with 80,000 rupees in large-scale industry. In addition to this, small-scale industry has done well at exporting in areas like carpets, surgical instruments and sporting goods, and foreign studies have shown that the small businessmen make as good as or better profit than larger concerns in spite of receiving fewer subsidies and facing more competition and higher interest rates.

One of the most obvious difficulties is that the Government spends large amounts of money on prestige projects, such as the steel mill at Karachi, the new Port Mohammad bin Qasim and the massive water projects. There are often insufficient controls over spending and high costs which increase as time schedules over-run. Many of Pakistan's aid-donors consider that the money could be better spent on smaller projects, such as the development of cottage and small-scale industries.

Another vital problem facing Pakistan is to establish a proper balance between the provinces. The Punjab, which has more than half of Pakistan's population, is far ahead of, and far richer than, the other three, Sind, the North-West Frontier Province and Baluchistan. The large amount of time spent by Bhutto in ensuring that his own Pakistan People's Party was master in each of the four provinces set back development. One of the most difficult issues is apportioning revenues between the centre and the provinces. Baluchistan's remoteness means that money will have to be spent on infrastructure. The North-West Frontier Province has often complained that Islamabad takes benefits from its tobacco and other crops and does not put equivalent sums into development.

Whatever happens, Pakistan has an enormous population problem. Although it is impressive that Pakistan's workers and their skills are sought all over the Middle East, it should cause the Government to stop and think that its skilled men prefer (or need) to work outside the country. It should also be remembered that for every person who goes, there are many others who never have the chance or whose energies are completely untapped, and who remain underemployed, if they are employed, in the local villages. One of the results of the exodus of skilled labour to the more lucrative Middle East was that it was denying Pakistan itself many much-needed workers in key areas. By 1981 the drain of workers included soldiers. It was estimated that there were 22 Pakistani military contingents abroad, with 10,000 Pakistanis, apart from those in Saudi Arabia. In 1981 Indian experts estimated that Pakistanis in Saudi Arabia numbered 20,000 troops, though the Pakistan President had insisted in 1980 that talks then going on with Saudi Arabia would result in the dispatch of only an extra 600 to 700 troops to that country.

Meanwhile, at home, officials estimated that, even with a labour force of 26.1 million people in June 1983, Pakistan would have a shortage of 165,000 craftsmen, such as plumbers, fitters, carpenters and electricians. There would also be a shortfall of 2,000 doctors and nearly 2,000 engineers and technicians. At the same time there would be a surplus of 300,000 agricultural workers, 92,000 clerks and 11,000 administrative workers. Bridging the gap would be difficult because of widespread illiteracy. It is estimated that 77 per cent of the 1981 labour force of 24 million Pakistanis is illiterate.

STATISTICAL SURVEY

AREA AND POPULATION*

AREA	CENSUS POPULATION				ESTIMATED POPULATION (mid-year)		
	September 16th, 1972‡			March 15th, 1981‡			
	Male	Female	Total		1979	1980	1981
310,403 sq. miles†	34,417,000	30,475,000	64,892,000	83,782,000	79,760,000	82,140,000	84,580,000

* Excludes data for the disputed territory of Jammu and Kashmir. The Pakistan-held parts of this region are known as Azad ("Free") Kashmir, with an area of 4,494 sq. miles (11,639 sq. km.) and an estimated population of 1,700,000 in 1977, and Northern Areas, with an area of 28,000 sq. miles (72,520 sq. km.) and an estimated population of 500,000 in 1977. Also excluded are Junagardh and Manavadar.

† 803,943 sq. kilometres.

‡ Provisional figures. Revised total or 1972 is 64,979,732.

Source: Pakistan Statistical Yearbook.

ADMINISTRATIVE DIVISIONS
(estimated population in March 1981)

Provinces:	
Baluchistan	4,305,000
North-West Frontier Province	10,885,000
Punjab	47,116,000
Sind	18,966,000
Federally Administered Tribal Area	2,175,000
Federal Capital Territory: Islamabad	335,000
TOTAL	83,782,000

Source: Ministry of Finance, Planning and Development.

POPULATION OF PRINCIPAL CITIES

	1961 CENSUS	1972 CENSUS		1961 CENSUS	1972 CENSUS
Islamabad (capital)	—	77,318	Peshawar	218,691	268,368
Karachi	1,912,598	3,498,634	Sialkot	164,346	203,779
Lahore	1,296,477	2,165,372	Sargodha	129,291	201,407
Faisalabad (Lyallpur)	425,248	822,263	Sukkur	103,216	158,87(
Hyderabad	434,537	628,310	Quetta	106,633	156,000*
Rawalpindi	340,175	615,392	Jhang	95,000	135,722
Multan	358,201	542,195	Bahawalpur	84,000	133,956
Gujranwala	196,154	360,419			

* Provisional.

Population (March 1981): Karachi 5,103,000, Lahore 2,922,000, Faisalabad 1,092,000, Rawalpindi 928,000, Hyderabad 795,000, Multan 730,000, Gujranwala 597,000, Peshawar 555,000, Sialkot 296,000, Sargodha 294,000, Quetta 285,000, Islamabad 201,000.

Births and Deaths: Annual average birth rate 44.2 per 1,000 in 1970–75, 43.1 per 1,000 in 1975–80; death rate 16.5 per 1,000 in 1970–75, 15.0 per 1,000 in 1975–80 (UN estimates).

ECONOMICALLY ACTIVE POPULATION

(sample surveys, '000 persons at January 1st)

	1978	1979	1980	1981
Agriculture, hunting, forestry and fishing	12,018	12,383	12,754	13,124
Mining and quarrying	33	34	35	36
Manufacturing	2,989	3,080	3,172	3,264
Electricity, gas and water	107	111	114	117
Construction	919	946	976	1,005
Trade, restaurants and hotels	2,432	2,506	2,581	2,656
Transport, storage and communications	1,068	1,100	1,133	1,166
Financing, insurance, real estate and business services	147	151	156	160
Community, social and personal services	2,145	2,210	2,276	2,342
Activities not adequately described	72	75	77	79
TOTAL EMPLOYED	21,930	22,596	23,274	23,949
Unemployed	378	390	n.a.	413
TOTAL LABOUR FORCE	22,308	22,986	n.a.	24,362

Source: International Labour Office, *Year Book of Labour Statistics.*

AGRICULTURE

LAND USE

(unofficial estimates, '000 hectares)

	1973	1976	1979
Arable land	19,191	19,508	19,900*
Land under permanent crops	190*	252	275*
Permanent meadows and pastures	5,000*	5,000*	5,000*
Forests and woodland	2,853	2,860	2,810
Other land	50,638	50,252	49,887
Inland water	2,522	2,522	2,522
TOTAL AREA	80,394	80,394	80,394

* FAO estimate.

Source: FAO, *Production Yearbook.*

PRINCIPAL CROPS

(July 1st to June 30th)

	AREA ('000 acres)			PRODUCTION ('000 long tons)		
	1976/77	1977/78	1978/79	1978/79	1979/80	1980/81
Rice (milled)	4,322.7	4,692.9	5,005.5	3,220.0	3,272.0	3,119.5
Wheat	15,790.5	15,716.2	16,546.2	9,787.5	10,587.7	11,302.8
Cat-tail millet (Bajra)	1,601.3	1,584.0	1,627.5	312.5	272.8	214.4
Sorghum (Jowar)	1,104.3	1,283.7	n.a.	248.0	246.6	233.5
Maize	1,542.0	1,621.3	1,606.0	785.8	861.5	946.5
Barley	430.7	411.9	436.9	127.1	116.2	n.a.
Chick-peas (Gram)	2,704.6	2,716.0	3,025.6	529.3	308.5	n.a.
Other pulses	1,081.7	n.a.	n.a.	n.a.	194.0	n.a.
Rape and mustard	1,282.0	1,018.8	1,037.6	238.8	246.1	n.a.
Sesame	74.9	78.0	91.0	14.0	17.2	18.3
Cotton: production seed	4,607.9	4,554.5	4,674.2	934.6	4,095.8*	714.4
Cotton: production lint				2,670.0*		n.a.
Groundnuts	111.4	125.3	90.2	44.8	49.6	n.a.
Sugar cane	1,946.7	2,032.5	1,859.6	26,895.2	27,325.5	32,157.0
Tobacco	124.8	131.7	118.4	67.5	76.5	n.a.

* Production in thousand bales. One bale of cotton weighs 392 lb. (177.8 kg.).

LIVESTOCK
('000 head)

	1978	1979	1980
Cattle	14,946	14,992	15,083
Buffaloes	11,069	11,305	11,547
Sheep	22,291	24,185	26,239
Goats	25,597	27,804	30,203
Chickens	42,144	48,872	56,672
Ducks	931	1,079	1,251
Horses	466	480	494
Asses	2,298	2,371	2,447
Mules	64	66	68
Camels	819	835	850

Source: FAO, *Production Yearbook*.

LIVESTOCK PRODUCTS
('000 metric tons)

	1978	1979	1980
Beef and veal	166	167	167
Buffalo meat	169	173	177
Mutton and lamb	115	124	135
Goats' meat	151	164	178
Poultry meat	34	40	46
Other meat	10	10	10
Cows' milk	2,176	2,183	2,189
Buffaloes' milk	6,119	6,250	6,383
Sheep's milk	31	34	36
Goats' milk	344	374	406
Butter and ghee*	209.5	213.1	216.8
Hen eggs	71.1	82.4	95.7
Other poultry eggs	1.9	2.2	2.6
Wool: greasy	36.2	39.3	42.6
clean	22.2	24.0*	26.0*
Cattle and buffalo hides*	78.1	79.1	80.2
Sheep skins*	25.8	28.0	30.4
Goat skins*	30.3	33.0	35.8

*FAO estimate.

Source: FAO, *Production Yearbook*.

FORESTRY

ROUNDWOOD REMOVALS
('000 cubic metres)

	Coniferous (soft wood)			Broadleaved (hard wood)			Total		
	1977	1978*	1979*	1977	1978	1979	1977	1978	1979
Sawlogs, veneer logs and logs for sleepers	121	121	121	131*	131*	131*	252	252*	252*
Other industrial wood	15	16	16	241	249	257	256	265	273
Fuel wood	452*	466	482	16,230*	16,760*	17,308*	16,682	17,226	17,790
Total	588	603	619	16,602	17,140	17,696	17,190	17,743	18,315

* FAO estimate.

Source: FAO, *Yearbook of Forest Products*.

SAWNWOOD PRODUCTION
(FAO estimates, '000 cubic metres)

	1975	1976	1977	1978	1979
Coniferous sawnwood*	71	15	45	45	45
Broadleaved sawnwood*	5	—	—	—	—
	76	15	45	45	45
Railway sleepers	3	15	15	15	15
Total	79	30	60	60	60

* Including boxboards.

Source: FAO, *Yearbook of Forest Products*.

FISHING

('000 metric tons, live weight)

	1971	1972	1973	1974	1975	1976	1977	1978	1979
Inland waters	26.2	26.3	26.6	26.2	27.2	28.5	33.1	35.2	40.7
Indian Ocean	148.4	185.0	209.1	163.3	167.8	177.2	236.8	257.8	259.7
TOTAL CATCH	174.6	211.3	235.7	189.5	195.0	205.7	270.0	293.0	300.4

Source: FAO, *Yearbook of Fishery Statistics.*

MINING

(July 1st to June 30th)

	PRODUCTION (tons)				
	1977/78	1978/79	1979/80	1980/81	1981/82
Chromite	9,470	4,885	3,835	1,181	1,000
Limestone	3,699,504	3,298,000	3,269,000	3,467,000	2,427,000
Gypsum	273,991	284,000	364,000	554,000	252,000
Fireclay	50,471	52,387	56,503	60,000	46,000
Silica sand	61,744	84,000	104,000	84,000	44,000
Celestite	446	548	357	295	159
Ochres	15,153	790	267	445	1,687
Rock salt	428,877	48,600	495,000	514,000	385,000
Coal and lignite ('000 metric tons)	1,196	1,279	1,504	1,597	1,236
Crude petroleum ('000 barrels)	3,529	3,733	3,649	3,560	2,750
Natural gas (million cubic metres)	5,834	6,300	7,534	8,500	6,800

INDUSTRY

SELECTED PRODUCTS

(July 1st to June 30th)

		1977/78	1978/79	1979/80	1980/81
Cotton cloth	'000 sq. metres	391,347	339,352	342,335	307,882
Cotton yarn	metric tons	297,894	327,798	362,862	374,947
Art silk and rayon cloth	'000 metres	15,585	13,996	n.a.	n.a.
Sugar	'000 tons	860.8	607.0	586	851.3
Vegetable ghee	,, ,,	360.3	422.3	451	504.9
Sea salt	,, ,,	215.1	163.5	197.1	218.8
Cement	,, ,,	3,223.3	3,022.0	3,343	3,538.0
Urea	,, ,,	594.9	620.0	641	962.9
Superphosphate	,, ,,	75.0	97.8	101	101.8
Ammonium sulphate	,, ,,	95.6	97.0	99	96.6
Sulphuric acid	,, ,,	46.6	56.4	57	56.9
Soda ash	,, ,,	68.8	71.3	79	96.4
Caustic soda	,, ,,	31.1	35.9	40	38.5
Chlorine gas	,, ,,	4.9	7.8	9	8.3
Cigarettes	million	31,304	32,537	34,647	35,791

* '000 sq. yards.

FINANCE

100 paisa = 1 Pakistani rupee.
Coins: 1, 2, 5, 10, 25 and 50 paisa; 1 rupee.
Notes: 5, 10, 50 and 100 rupees.
Exchange rates (June 1982): £1 sterling = 21.09 rupees; U.S. $1 = 12.18 rupees.
1,000 Pakistani rupees = £47.41 = $82.12.

Note: From July 1955 to May 1972 the par value of the Pakistani rupee was 21 U.S. cents (U.S. $1 = 4.7619 rupees). Between May 1972 and February 1973 the central exchange rate was U.S. $1 = 11.00 rupees and the market rate $1 = 11.031 rupees. In February 1973 a new central rate of $1 = 9.90 rupees was established. In January 1982 the link with the U.S. dollar was ended and the rupee was pegged to a trade-weighted "basket" of currencies. In terms of sterling, the central exchange rate was £1 = 11.43 rupees from November 1967 to August 1971, and £1 = 12.41 rupees from December 1971 to May 1972.

CENTRAL GOVERNMENT BUDGET
(million rupees, July 1st to June 30th)

Revenue	1980/81	1981/82	1982/83
Taxes on income	6,145	8,449	8,602
Customs duties	13,750	15,000	17,470
Excise duties	11,070	12,400	13,365
General turnover tax	3,000	3,250	3,750
Other taxes and surcharges	1,437	835	1,165
Other receipts	8,951	10,958	12,834
Total	44,353	50,892	57,186
Less transfer to Provinces	7,172	9,232	9,980
Net Revenue	37,181	41,660	47,206

Expenditure	1980/81	1981/82	1982/83
Non-development expenditure:			
Interest on public debt	8,016	9,107	12,384
National defence	14,083	19,593	22,095
Education and health	1,233	855	1,063
Transfers to provinces Grants	1,103	1,576	2,306
Other current expenditure on administration	4,337	3,124	3,773
Subsidies	2,577	1,074	1,362
Other non-development expenditure	5,832	2,754	4,418
Unallocable	—	6	6
Five per cent economy	—	—	500
Total	37,181	38,089	47,907

PLANNED DEVELOPMENT EXPENDITURE*
(million rupees, July 1st to June 30th)

	1980/81	1981/82	1982/83
Sectoral Programme:			
Agriculture	3,165.6	2,861	2,474
Water	2,605.0	3,301	3,503
Power	4,015.7	4,848	5,650
Industry	3,967.2	2,750	2,932
Fuels	1,500.0	1,719	2,070
Minerals	83.7	138	137
Transport and Communication	4,147.5	4,824	4,973
Physical Planning and Housing	561.7	723	811
Mass media	111.5	149	137
Education and training	491.0	713	756
Social Welfare	7.7	21	24
Health	413.7	494	446
Population Planning	160.0	190	190
Manpower and employment	13.1	—	—
Rural Development	65.5	75	67
Relief and Construction Programme	72.0	56	25
Special Programme for Women	40.0	68	60
Culture and sports	162.8	171	110
Total Sectoral Programme	21,574.0	23,101	24,365

* In 1978 the Fifth Development Plan was announced, covering the years from July 1st, 1978, to June 30th, 1983. Development outlay is 210,000 million rupees, of which over 150,000 million rupees is to be financed from domestic resources.

† Revised.

STATE BANK RESERVES

(U.S. $ million, last Thursday of the year*)

	1974	1975	1976	1977	1978	1979	1980
Gold	67	67	68	68	332	728	1,188
IMF Special Drawing Rights	24	29	37	35	40	45	29
Foreign Exchange	368	311	429	414	368	168	467
TOTAL	459	407	534	517	740	941	1,684

* Prior to 1977, figures refer to the last Friday of the year.

Source: IMF, *International Financial Statistics.*

MONEY SUPPLY

(million rupees, last Thursday of the year*)

	1974	1975	1976	1977	1978	1979	1980
Currency outside banks	11,427	11,884	13,853	17,349	21,040	26,447	32,476
Demand deposits at Scheduled Banks	10,614	13,107	19,519	21,926	25,887	29,981	33,926
TOTAL MONEY†	22,518	25,621	34,044	39,966	47,194	56,829	66,893

* Prior to 1977, figures refer to the last Friday of the year.
† Including also private sector deposits at the State Bank.

Source: IMF, *International Financial Statistics.*

COST OF LIVING

Consumer Price Index for industrial, commercial and government employees
(base: 1969/70=100)

	1976/77	1977/78	1979/80*	1980/81†	1981/82‡
Food, beverages and tobacco	255.2	270.9	316.7	398.6	395.47
Clothing	242.9	262.2	306.9	347.3	406.25
Housing and household expenditure	221.9	234.8	315.6	367.9	368.32
Miscellaneous	226.7	247.9	355.2	415.9	431.95
ALL ITEMS	242.9	n.a.	322.4	391.2	n.a.

* Based on figures for June 1980.
† Based on figures for September 1981.
‡ Based on figures up to March 1982.

Source: Government of Pakistan, Ministry of Finance, Planning and Economic Affairs, *Statistical Yearbook*; Development Advisory Centre, Karachi.

NATIONAL ACCOUNTS

(million rupees at current prices, year ending June 30th)

National Income and Product

	1976/77	1977/78	1978/79	1979/80	1980/81
Domestic factor incomes*	128,230	147,389	167,781	199,471	233,393
Consumption of fixed capital	7,456	9,782	11,020	13,000	15,645
Gross Domestic Product at Factor Cost	135,686	157,171	178,801	212,471	249,038
Indirect taxes	15,650	19,604	24,058	30,151	34,751
Less Subsidies	1,884	3,110	6,987	7,099	6,974
G.D.P. in Purchasers' Values	149,452	173,665	195,872	235,523	276,815
Net factor income from abroad	5,480	12,139	14,514	18,187	26,094
Gross National Product	154,932	185,804	210,386	253,710	303,909
Less Consumption of fixed capital	7,456	9,782	11,020	13,000	15,645
National Income in Market Prices	147,476	176,022	199,366	240,710	288,264

* Compensation of employees and the operating surplus of enterprises.

Expenditure on the Gross Domestic Product

	1976/77	1977/78	1978/79	1979/80	1980/81
Government final consumption expenditure	15,816	17,977	19,177	22,551	26,200
Private final consumption expenditure	118,965	141,683	164,499	196,752	230,851
Increase in stocks	1,000	1,000	1,750	2,000	2,800
Gross fixed capital formation	26,421	28,976	31,427	39,275	43,829
Total Domestic Expenditure	162,202	189,636	216,853	260,578	303,680
Exports of goods and services	13,991	16,629	21,529	29,535	35,311
Less Imports of goods and services	26,741	32,600	42,510	54,590	62,176
G.D.P. in Purchasers' Values	149,452	173,665	195,872	235,523	276,815
G.D.P. at Constant 1959/60 Prices	45,583	49,150	51,103	55,360	58,587

Gross Domestic Product by Economic Activity

(at factor cost)

	1976/77	1977/78	1978/79	1979/80	1980/81
Agriculture and livestock	42,842	48,403	56,165	64,202	73,634
Forestry and logging	292	411	445	486	547
Fishing	552	708	801	1,034	1,444
Mining and quarrying	1,196	1,234	1,378	2,226	2,865
Manufacturing	22,234	25,201	28,133	34,796	42,006
Electricity and gas	1,916	2,448	3,397	4,789	5,627
Construction	7,376	8,291	9,336	11,762	13,755
Wholesale and retail trade	19,769	23,106	26,033	30,782	37,127
Transport, storage and communications	9,252	11,260	13,044	15,451	18,712
Banking and insurance	3,573	4,273	4,931	5,356	6,035
Ownership of dwellings	4,931	5,460	6,082	7,000	8,255
Public administration and defence	10,371	13,155	13,898	16,858	18,732
Other services	11,382	13,221	15,158	17,729	21,299
Total	135,686	157,171	178,801	212,471	249,038

BALANCE OF PAYMENTS
(U.S. $ million)

	1975	1976	1977	1978	1979	1980
Merchandise exports f.o.b.	1,049	1,167	1,121	1,397	1,948	2,567
Merchandise imports f.o.b.	−2,207	−2,191	−2,487	−3,220	−4,289	−5,454
TRADE BALANCE	−1,158	−1,024	−1,366	−1,823	−2,341	−2,887
Exports of services	301	307	343	440	580	733
Imports of services	−596	−609	−702	−856	−1,104	−1,240
BALANCE ON GOODS AND SERVICES	−1,453	−1,326	−1,725	−2,239	−2,865	−3,394
Private unrequited transfers (net)	275	434	885	1,419	1,579	2,229
Government unrequited transfers (net)	128	110	119	99	167	236
CURRENT BALANCE	−1,050	−782	−721	−721	−1,119	−929
Direct capital investment (net)	25	8	16	27	62	57
Other long-term capital (net)	426	433	612	455	458	613
Short-term capital (net)	92	61	37	181	272	37
Net errors and omissions	−13	−16	−3	−11	67	−14
TOTAL (net monetary movements)	−520	−296	−59	−69	−260	−236
Allocation of IMF Special Drawing Rights	—	—	—	—	38	39
Valuation changes (net)	18	−22	−9	−29	−10	30
IMF Subsidy Account grants	—	3	7	7	6	5
Other grants	—	30	—	—	—	53
IMF Trust Fund loans	—	—	29	91	—	172
Other loans	308	301	10	—	100	100
Official financing (net)	—	—	—	—	25	270
CHANGES IN RESERVES	−194	16	−22	−0	−101	433

Source: IMF, *International Financial Statistics.*

EXTERNAL TRADE
(million rupees, July 1st to June 30th)

	1976/77	1977/78	1978/79	1979/80	1980/81
Imports	23,012.2	26,010.2	36,390.5	46,931.7	53,543.7
Exports	11,436.0	13,016.6	17,098.7	23,714.6	29,279.5

PRINCIPAL COMMODITIES
(million rupees)

IMPORTS	1977/78	1978/79	1979/80	1980/81
Chemicals	3,345.4	5,147.4	5,778.3	7,342.2
Drugs and medicines	513.4	600.9	750.9	936.2
Dyes and colours	363.0	310.8	392.2	461.8
Chemical fertilizers	1,047.9	2,807.6	2,711.1	3,537.3
Electrical goods	1,594.0	1,698.8	1,804.3	1,915.3
Machinery, non-electrical	4,146.5	4,251.0	5,589.9	5,686.4
Transport equipment	1,635.0	2,474.0	5,902.9	3,989.2
Paper, board and stationery	377.5	658.4	589.0	718.8
Tea	1,257.9	999.9	953.5	1,183.7
Sugar, refined	1.0	2.9	410.5	378.3
Art-silk yarn	16.5	96.0	138.3	179.2
Iron and steel and manufactures thereof	2,660.3	2,305.7	2,790.9	2,607.6
Non-ferrous metals	343.9	327.7	483.9	581.7
Oil minerals (including greases)	4,918.3	5,247.0	10,684.6	15,199.3
Oil vegetables	1,553.6	3,279.9	2,294.9	2,625.3
Grain, pulses and flour	1,338.6	3,507.6	1,050.1	637.0
TOTAL (incl. others)	27,814.7	36,388.1	46,929.1	53,543.7

PRINCIPAL COMMODITIES—*continued*]

EXPORTS	1977/78	1978/79	1979/80	1980/81
Fish and fish preparations	342.4	342.4	530.5	559.2
Rice	2,408.5	2,408.5	4,179.3	5,601.6
Hides and skins	—	—	53.5	23.0
Raw wool	72.8	99.9	106.3	80.2
Raw cotton	1,093.6	655.4	3,321.0	5,203.4
Leather	636.5	1,247.4	1,264.4	891.9
Cotton waste	16.1	14.9	18.6	18.7
Cotton yarn	1,059.5	1,957.2	2,038.0	2,044.0
Cotton thread	70.7	57.4	70.1	100.6
Cotton fabics	1,741.2	2,135.4	2,416.6	2,389.6
Petroleum and products	625.9	607.9	1,764.2	1,675.2
Synthetic textiles	154.0	65.3	57.8	1,272.3
Footwear	71.6	97.0	105.8	100.8
Animal casings	26.4	30.7	410.8	60.0
Cement and products		—	—	—
Guar and products	202.6	271.3	332.6	286.3
Oil cakes	98.9	71.3	41.4	34.3
Paints and varnishes	7.6	7.9	2.0	14.1
Tobacco, raw and products	126.1	100.9	80.6	53.7
Ready-made garments and hosiery	397.3	999.9	731.1	745.1
Drugs and chemicals	138.7	122.8	751.0	224.9
Surgical instruments	160.5	210.9	140.2	264.0
Carpets and rugs	1,170.6	1,762.2	2,198.4	2,245.7
Sports goods	194.9	211.8	244.6	312.3
Others	2,164.0	3,446.6	2,551.3	5,078.3
TOTAL	12,980.4	16,925.0	23,410.1	29,279.5

PRINCIPAL TRADING PARTNERS

('000 rupees)

	IMPORTS			EXPORTS		
	1978/79	1979/80	1980/81	1978/79	1979/80	1980/81
Australia	806,032	905,712	501,928	130,517	129,576	252,389
Bahrain	14,296	114,850	942,382	86,424	175,160	111,189
Belgium and Luxembourg	379,204	596,650	597,080	164,593	323,485	232,352
Canada	768,866	825,313	618,984	97,771	137,312	137,579
China, People's Republic	980,721	1,463,850	1,765,431	142,669	1,441,688	3,570,827
France	1,061,191	2,148,851	1,509,162	423,362	581,189	623,251
Germany, Federal Republic	2,083,454	2,368,698	2,693,989	1,036,779	1,429,629	1,260,246
Hong Kong	283,792	227,719	259,014	1,394,002	1,841,226	1,141,001
India	208,847	129,671	21,850	166,668	962,317	478,895
Indonesia	447,187	496,017	244,801	75,406	151,541	73,365
Italy	1,254,215	1,813,715	1,690,296	678,389	881,804	750,112
Japan	4,148,695	5,422,357	6,187,846	1,669,840	1,812,707	1,877,254
Kuwait	2,310,324	4,738,891	4,276,193	215,113	486,621	510,044
Malaysia	830,090	1,291,280	1,506,381	15,507	23,727	41,491
Netherlands	1,862,006	1,093,531	1,040,949	334,660	376,153	375,193
Saudi Arabia	1,962,017	3,235,203	6,868,693	944,883	1,269,131	1,742,784
Sri Lanka	423,041	442,890	419,319	423,422	381,380	300,282
Sudan	10,219	3,714	992	64,504	212,673	122,633
United Kingdom	2,278,986	2,877,972	3,296,736	1,289,162	1,127,905	1,163,198
U.S.A.	5,790,714	5,219,278	5,850,820	1,164,308	1,201,136	1,769,588

TRANSPORT

RAILWAYS

(July 1st to June 30th)

	1978/79	1979/80	1980/81
Number of passengers ('000)	145,998	144,328	123,200
Passenger-kilometres (million)	16,712	17,308	16,311
Freight ('000 tons)	11,958	11,853	11,400
Net freight ton-kilometres (million)	9,375	8,598	—

ROAD TRAFFIC

(motor vehicles in use)

	1975	1976	1977	1978	1979
Passenger cars (incl. taxis)	203,325	221,564	227,262	262,516	303,738
Buses and coaches	36,370	38,991	41,650	43,358	47,618
Goods vehicles	58,197	61,864	56,898	60,424	66,537
Motorcycles (incl. rickshaws)	233,979	276,443	314,256	369,810	469,131
Others	43,287	57,542	75,972	94,086	128,837
TOTAL	575,558	656,404	716,038	830,194	1,015,861

SHIPPING

(port of Karachi)

	1976/77	1977/78	1978/79	1979/80	1980/81
Vessels ('000 net reg. tons):					
Entered	7,203	8,767	9,707	9,840	10,246
Cleared	7,085	8,764	10,566	9,899	10,193
Goods ('000 long tons):					
Loaded	2,374	2,811	3,038	3,398	3,617
Unloaded	7,215	8,918	11,987	11,259	11,037

CIVIL AVIATION

(domestic and international flights, July to June—'000)

	1976/77	1977/78	1978/79	1979/80	1980/81
Kilometres flown	35,490	42,710	58,443	50,298	48,962
Passenger-kilometres	3,751,925	4,408,559	4,799,355	5,180,272	6,039,971
Freight ton-kilometres	144,432	180,029	211,838	228,404	245,395
Mail ton-kilometres	4,218	4,762	5,070	5,225	6,489

TOURISM

	1976	1977	1978	1979	1980
Tourist arrivals	197,323	220,448	291,358	318,558	299,012

Receipts from tourism (U.S. $ million): 41 in 1976; 61 in 1977; 82 in 1978; 95 in 1979.

EDUCATION
(1979/80)

	TEACHERS	STUDENTS
Primary . . .	139,300	7,090,000
Middle . . .	52,400	1,448,000
Secondary . . .	63,200	548,000
Higher:		
Arts and science colleges .	13,435	248,500
Professional* . .	3,563	72,479
Universities . . .	2,880	28,280

* Including Educational Colleges.

Source (unless otherwise stated): Development Advisory Centre, Karachi.

THE CONSTITUTION

The Constitution was promulgated on April 10th, 1973, and amended in 1974, 1975, 1976, 1977, 1978, 1979, 1980 and 1981.

GENERAL PROVISIONS

The Preamble upholds the principles of democracy, freedom, equality, tolerance and social justice as enunciated by Islam. The rights of religious and other minorities are guaranteed.

The Islamic Republic of Pakistan consists of four provinces—Baluchistan, North-West Frontier Province, Punjab and Sind—and the tribal areas under federal administration. The provinces are autonomous units.

Fundamental rights are guaranteed and include equality of status (women have equal rights with men), freedom of thought, speech, worship and the press and freedom of assembly and association. No law providing for preventive detention shall be made except to deal with persons acting against the integrity, security or defence of Pakistan. No such law shall authorize the detention of a person for more than one month.

PRESIDENT

The President is Head of State and acts on the advice of the Prime Minister. He is elected at a joint sitting of the Federal Legislature to serve for a term of five years. He must be a Muslim. The President may be impeached for violating the Constitution or gross misconduct.

FEDERAL LEGISLATURE

The Federal Legislature consists of the President, a lower and an upper house. The lower house, called the National Assembly, has 200 members elected directly for a term of five years, on the basis of universal adult suffrage, while the upper house, called the Senate, has 63 members who serve for four years, half retiring every two years.*

* Although the Constitution provides for a Senate of 63 members, the number in 1977, when the Senate was dissolved, was still 45, the same as before the promulgation of the Constitution in 1973.

Each Provincial Assembly is to elect 14 Senators. The tribal areas are to return five and the remaining two are to be elected from the Federal Capital Territory by members of the Provincial Assemblies. Six seats in the National Assembly are reserved for minorities and for a period of 10 years from 1973 women are to get 10 seats, raising the strength of the Assembly to 216.

There shall be two sessions of the National Assembly and Senate each year, with not more than 120 days between the last sitting of a session and the first sitting of the next session.

The role of the Senate in an overwhelming majority of the subjects shall be merely advisory. Disagreeing with any legislation of the National Assembly, it shall have the right to send it back only once for reconsideration. In case of disagreement in other subjects, the Senate and National Assembly shall sit in a joint session to decide the matter by a simple majority.

GOVERNMENT

The Constitution provides that bills may originate in either house, except money bills. The latter must originate in the National Assembly and cannot go to the Senate. A bill must be passed by both houses and then approved by the President, who may return the bill and suggest amendments. In this case, after the bill has been reconsidered and passed, with or without amendment, the President must give his assent to it.

PROVINCIAL GOVERNMENT

In the matter of relations between Federation and Provinces, the Federal Legislature shall have the power to make laws, including laws bearing on extra-territorial affairs, for the whole or any part of Pakistan, while a Provincial Assembly shall be empowered to make laws for that Province or any part of it. Matters in the Federal Legislative List shall be subject to the exclusive authority of the Federal Legislature, while the Federal Legislature and a Provincial Assembly shall have power to legislate with regard to matters referred to in the Concurrent Legislative List. Any matter not referred to in either list may be subject to laws made by a Provincial Assembly alone, and not by the Federal Legislature, although the latter shall have exclusive power to legislate with regard to matters not referred to in either list for those areas in the Federation not included in any Province.

Four provisions seek to ensure the stability of the parliamentary system. First, the Prime Minister shall be elected by the National Assembly and he and the other Ministers shall be responsible to it. Secondly, any resolution calling for the removal of a Prime Minister shall have to name his successor in the same resolution which shall be adopted by not less than two-thirds of the total number of members of the lower house. The requirement of two-thirds majority is to remain in force for 15 years or three electoral terms, whichever is more. Thirdly, the Prime Minister shall have the right to seek dissolution of the legislature at any time even during the pendency of a no-confidence motion. Fourthly, if a no-confidence motion is defeated, such a motion shall not come up before the house for the next six months.

All these provisions for stability shall apply *mutatis mutandis* to the Provincial Assemblies also.

A National Economic Council, to include the Prime Minister and a representative from each province, shall advise the Provincial and Federal Governments.

There shall be a Governor for each Province, appointed by the President, and a Council of Ministers to aid and advise him, with a Chief Minister appointed by the Governor. Each Province has a provincial legislature consisting of the Governor and Provincial Assembly.

The executive authorities of every Province shall be required to ensure that their actions are in compliance with the Federal laws which apply in that Province. The Federation shall be required to consider the interests of each Province in the exercise of its authority in that Province. The Federation shall further be required to afford every Province protection from external aggression and internal disturbance, and to ensure that every Province is governed in accordance with the provisions of the Constitution.

To further safeguard the rights of the smaller provinces, a Council of Common Interests has been created. Comprising the Chief Ministers of the four provinces and four Central Ministers to decide upon specified matters of common interest, the Council is responsible to the Federal Legislature. The constitutional formula gives the net proceeds of excise duty and royalty on gas to the province concerned. The profits on hydro-electric power generated in each province shall go to that province.

OTHER PROVISIONS

Other provisions include the procedure for elections, the setting up of an Advisory Council of Islamic Ideology and an Islamic Research Institute, and the administration of tribal areas.

AMENDMENTS

Amendments to the Constitution shall require a two-thirds majority in the National Assembly and endorsement by a simple majority in the Senate.

In 1975 the Constitution (3rd Amendment) Bill abolished the provision that a State of Emergency may not be extended beyond six months without the approval of Parliament and empowered the Government to detain a person for three months instead of one month.

In July 1977, following the imposition of martial law, several provisions, including all fundamental rights provided for in the Constitution, were suspended.

An amendment of September 1978 provided for separate electoral registers to be drawn up for Muslims and non-Muslims.

In October 1979 a martial law order inserted a clause in the Constitution establishing the supremacy of military courts in trying all offences, criminal and otherwise.

On May 26th, 1980, the President issued a Constitution Amendment Order, which amended Article 199, debarring High Courts from making any order relating to the validity of effect of any judgment or sentence passed by a military court or tribunal granting an injunction; from making an order or entering any proceedings in respect of matters under the jurisdiction or cognizance of a military court or tribunal, and from initiating proceedings against the Chief Martial Law Administrator or a Martial Law Administrator.

By another amendment of the Constitution, the Federal Shariat Court will replace the Shariat Benches of the High Courts. The Shariat Court, on the petition of a citizen or the Government, may decide whether any law or provision of law is contrary to the injunction of Islam as laid down in the Holy Koran and the Sunnah of the Holy Prophet.

In March 1981 the Government promulgated Provisional Constitutional Order 1981, whereby provision is made for the appointment of one or more Vice-Presidents, to be appointed by the Chief Martial Law Administrator, and a Federal Council (*Majlis-i-Shura*) consisting of persons nominated by the President. All political parties not registered with the Election Commission on September 13th, 1979, will be dissolved and their properties made forfeit to the Federal Council. Any party working against the ideology, sovereignty or security of Pakistan may be dissolved by the President.

The proclamation of July 1977, imposing martial law, and subsequent orders amending the Constitution and further martial law regulations shall not be questioned by any court on any grounds.

All Chief Justices and Judges shall take a new oath of office. New High Court benches for the interior of the provinces shall be set up and retired judges are debarred from holding office in Pakistan for two years. The powers of the High Courts shall be limited for suspending the operation of an order for the detention of any person under any law provided for preventative detention, or release any person on bail, arrested under the same law.

The Advisory Council of Islamic Ideology (headed by Mr. Justice Tanzihur Rehman), which was asked by the Government to suggest procedures for the election and further Islamization of the constitution, has recommended non-party election, separate electorates, Islamic qualifications for candidates and a federal structure with greater devolution of power by changing the present divisions into provinces.

THE GOVERNMENT

HEAD OF STATE

President: Gen. MOHAMMAD ZIA UL-HAQ (assumed office September 16th, 1978).

CABINET

(May 1982)

Chief Martial Law Administrator, responsible for Science and Technology, Cabinet Division, Establishment Division, and Chairman of the Planning Commission: Gen. MOHAMMAD ZIA UL-HAQ.

Minister of Defence: ALI AHMAD TALPUR.

Minister of Housing and Works: Air Marshal INAMUL HAQ UL KHAN.

Minister of Finance and Economic Affairs: GHULAM ISHAQ KHAN.

Minister of Education: MOHAMMAD ALI KHAN HOTI.

Minister of Food, Agriculture and Co-operatives: Vice-Adm. MOHAMMAD FAZIL JANJUA.

Minister of Industries: ILLAHI BUKHSH SOOMRO.

Minister of Local Government and Rural Development: FAKHAR IMAM.

Minister of Labour, Manpower and Overseas Pakistanis: GHULAM DASTGIR KHAN.

Minister of Kashmir Affairs and Northern Affairs: Maj.-Gen. (retd.) JAMAL DAR.

Minister without Portfolio: ALHAJ ABBAS KHAN ABBASI.

Minister of Health and Social Welfare: Dr. NASIR UD DIN JOGEZAI.

Minister of Water and Power: RAJA SIKANDAR ZAMAN.

Minister of Petroleum and Natural Resources: Maj.-Gen. (retd.) RAO FARMAN ALI KHAN.

Minister of Production Division, Railways and National Logistic Board: Lt.-Gen. SAEED QADIR.

Minister of Information and Broadcasting: RAJA MOHAMMAD ZAFARUL HAQ.

Minister of Interior: MAHMOUD A. HAROON.

Minister for Law and Parliamentary Affairs: Attorney-General S. SHARIFUDDIN PIRZADA.

Minister of Communications: MOHYUDDIN BALUCH.

Minister of Culture, Sports and Tourism: NIAZ MOHAMMAD ARBAB.

Minister for Foreign Affairs: Lt.-Gen. (retd.) SAHIBZADA YAKUB KHAN.

Minister of Planning: MAHBUB UL-HAQ.

Minister of State for Social Welfare: Begum AFIFA MAMDOT.

Minister of State and Chairman of the National Council of Social Welfare: MAHMUD ALI.

Minister of Religious and Minorities Affairs: ALHAJ MOHAMMAD ABBAS KHAN ABBASI.

ADVISERS WITH THE RANK OF FEDERAL MINISTER

Adviser on Foreign Trade and Chairman of the Export Promotion Bureau: HAMID D. HABIB.

Adviser on Overseas Pakistanis: MUAZZAM ALI.

Adviser on Shipping: MUSTAFA K. GOKAL.

Adviser on Business Co-ordination and Internal Trade: Sheikh ISHRAT ALI.

ADVISERS WITH THE RANK OF MINISTER OF STATE

Adviser on Population Welfare: Dr. ATTIYA INAYATULLAH.

Adviser on Health: Dr. BASHARAT JAZBI.

Adviser on Science and Technology: M. A. KAZI.

Adviser on Higher Education: Dr. MOHAMMAD AFZAL.

Chairman, Pakistan Tourist Development Corporation: Begum VIQARUN NISA NOON.

Adviser on Natural Medicine: HAKIM MOHAMMAD SAID.

MILITARY COUNCIL

On July 5th, 1977, the Government was overthrown in a bloodless military coup. A Military Council was formed to assist the President and Cabinet in the administering of the country until general elections are held.

Chief of Military Council: Gen. MOHAMMAD ZIA UL-HAQ, Commander-in-Chief of the Armed Forces.

Members of the Military Council:

Gen. MOHAMMAD IQBAL KHAN, Chairman of the Joint Chiefs of Staff Committee.

Admiral KARAMAT RAHMAN NIAZI, Chief of Naval Staff.

Air Chief Marshal MOHAMMAD ANWAR SHAMIM, Chief of Air Staff.

General SAWAR KHAN, Vice-Chief of Army Staff.

Lt.-Gen. MOHAMMAD ARIF, Chief of Staff to the President.

FEDERAL LEGISLATURE

Under the 1973 Constitution, the Federal Legislature comprises a lower house (the National Assembly) and an upper house (the Senate).

NATIONAL ASSEMBLY

The National Assembly is elected for five years. It comprises 200 directly elected members and 10 women members elected by the Assembly. Six seats are reserved for minorities. The National Assembly which came into existence after the March 1977 elections was dissolved in July 1977, following the imposition of martial law.

SENATE

The Senate serves for four years. In 1973, when the new Constitution came into effect, the Senate comprised 45 members. The Constitution provides for an increase to 63 members, including 56 elected by the provincial assemblies. The Senate was dissolved in July 1977, following the imposition of martial law.

MAJLIS-I-SHURA

The Consultative Committee/Council was established in 1982 and acts in an advisory capacity to evolve a democratic system in accordance with the requirements of Islam, to advise the Government on possible legislation, to discuss Five-Year plans and budgets, etc.; 350 nominated mems. (maximum); Chair. KHWAJA MOHAMMAD SAFDAR; Vice-Chair. QARI SAEED-UR-REHMAN (Punjab), AGHA SADRUDDIN (Sind), KHAN FIDA MOHAMMAD KHAN (North-West Frontier Province), MIR JAM GHULAM QADIR KHAN (Baluchistan).

PROVINCES

Pakistan comprises the four provinces of Sind, Baluchistan, Punjab and the North-West Frontier Province, plus the Federal capital and "tribal areas" under federal administration.

Governors:

Sind: Lt.-Gen. S. M. ABBASI.
Baluchistan: Lt.-Gen. RAHIMUDDIN KHAN.
Punjab: Lt.-Gen. GHULAM GILANI KHAN.
North-West Frontier Province: Lt.-Gen. FAZLE HAQ.

POLITICAL PARTIES

Note: Political activities were suspended from July 1977, following the imposition of martial law, although some political activity was subsequently allowed. In October 1979, following the postponement of the general elections scheduled for November, all political activity was banned.

Nine parties joined to form the **Pakistan National Alliance (PNA)**, with the late MAULANA MUFTI MAHMUD as President, in January 1977. Tehrik-i-Istiqlal originally formed part of the Alliance, but broke away in 1977, as did the Jamiatul-Ulema-e-Pakistan and the National Democratic Party in 1978. The Jamaat-i-Islami was expelled in 1979.

All Pakistan Jammu and Kashmir Conference: f. 1948; advocates free plebiscite in the whole of Kashmir; Pres. SARDAR SIKANDAR HAYAT KHAN.

Jamiatul-Ulema-e-Islam: advocates constitution in accordance with Islamic teaching; Pres. MAULANA FAZLUR RAHMAN.

Pakistan Democratic Party (PDP): f. 1969; aims to uphold "democratic and Islamic values"; Leader NAWABZADA NASRULLAH KHAN; Sec.-Gen. Sheikh NASIM HASAN.

Pakistan Khaksar Party: f. during British rule, dissolved 1947, later revived; upholds Islamic values but emphasizes military training for all persons; Pres. MOHAMMAD ASHRAF KHAN.

Pakistan Muslim League: Muslim League House, 33 Davis Rd., Lahore; split into two groups in 1979; Pres. PIR SAHIB PAGARO (Pagaro group), KAWAJA KHAIRUDDIN (Chatta group).

Jamaat-i-Islami: Mansoorah, Multan Rd., Lahore; f. 1941; aims at the establishment of the Islamic state; Pres. MIAN TUFAIL MUHAMMED; Sec.-Gen. QAZI HUSSAIN AHMAD.

Jamiatul-Ulema-e-Pakistan: f. 1968; advocates legislation in accordance with Islamic teaching; Pres. SHAH AHMAD NOORAIN; Sec.-Gen. MAULANA ABDUS SATTAR NIAZI.

National Democratic Party (NDP): f. 1975 after ban on National Awami Party; demands civil liberties; Pres. SHERBAZ KHAN MAZARI; Sec.-Gen. ZAHORUL HEQUE.

Pakistan Musawat Party: f. 1978; advocates rule of the people; Chair. HANIF RAMAY.

Pakistan National Party (PNP): Karachi; f. 1979 from breakaway group of the NDP; advocates higher degree of decentralization; Chair. MIR GHAUS BAKHSH BIZENJO; Sec.-Gen. SYED QASWAR GARDEZI.

Pakistan People's Party (PPP): f. 1967; Islamic socialism, democracy and an independent foreign policy; Chair. Begum NUSRAT BHUTTO; Sec.-Gen. Dr. GHILAM HUSAIN.

Progressive People's Party: f. 1978 after breaking away from the PPP; Chair. MAULANA KAUSAR NIAZI.

Tehrik-i-Istiqlal (*Solidarity Party*): f. 1968; upholds democratic and Islamic values; Acting Pres. ASHAF VARDAG; Sec.-Gen. MUSHEER ÀHMAD PESH IMAM.

DIPLOMATIC REPRESENTATION

EMBASSIES ACCREDITED TO PAKISTAN

(In Islamabad unless otherwise stated)

Afghanistan: 176 Shalimar 7/3; *Ambassador:* (vacant).

Albania: Cairo, Egypt.

Algeria: 72, St. 26, Shalimar F-6/2; *Ambassador:* ABDERRAHMANE SETTOUTI.

Argentina: 7, St. 17, Shalimar 6/2; *Ambassador:* Dr. RAUL DESMARAS-LUZURIAGA.

Australia: Plot No. 17, Sector G-4/4, Diplomatic Enclave No. 2; *Ambassador:* W. P. HANDMER.

Austria: 13, 1st St., Shalimar 6; *Ambassador:* Dr. EGON LIBACH.

Bangladesh: House 21, St. 88, G-6/3; *Ambassador:* Maj.-Gen. GHOLAM DASTGIR.

Belgium: 40, St. 12, Shalimar 6; *Ambassador:* GUY COPPAT.

Brazil: 194 Embassy Rd., Ramna 6/3; *Ambassador:* ANTÔNIO CARLOS DINIZ DE ANDRADA.

Bulgaria: 66 Attaturk Ave., Shalimar G-6/3; *Ambassador:* ASEN STANEV YANKOV.

Burma: 368, Shalimar 6/3; *Ambassador:* MAUNG MAUNG NYUNT.

Canada: Diplomatic Enclave, Sector G-5, P.O.B. 1042; *Ambassador:* WILLIAM T. WARDEN.

China, People's Republic: 23–24, Shalimar 6/4; *Ambassador:* WANG CHUANBIN.

Czechoslovakia: House No. 49, 27th St., Shalimar F-6/2; *Ambassador:* PETER KADLEC.

Denmark: P.O.B. 1118, 121, 90th St., Ramna 6/3; *Chargé d'affaires a.i.:* MOGENS PREHN (Ambassador resident in Teheran, Iran).

Egypt: 449-F, Sector Ramna 6/4; *Ambassador:* MOHAMMAD EZELDIN SHARIF.

Finland: Teheran, Iran.

France: 217-C, 54th St., Shalimar 7/4; *Ambassador:* JEAN GORY.

German Democratic Republic: Shalimar 6/3, St. 3, House 218; *Ambassador:* KURT MEIER.

Germany, Federal Republic: Ramna 5, Diplomatic Enclave, P.O.B. 1027; *Ambassador:* Dr. KLAUS TERFLOTH.

Ghana: H. No. 178, St. 88, Shalimar; *Ambassador:* WILLIAM WALDO KOFI VANDERPUYE.

Greece: Teheran, Iran.

Guinea: Beijing, People's Republic of China.

Guyana: Washington, D.C., U.S.A.

Hungary: 164, Shalimar 6/3; *Ambassador:* JÓZSEF FERRÓ.

India: 42a-F, SectorD 6/4; *Ambassador:* KRISHNA DAYAL SHARMA.

Indonesia: 10-12, Shalimar 6/3; *Ambassador:* FOUZI ABDUL RENI.

Iran: 36–37 Attaturk Ave., Ramna 6; *Ambassador:* AGHA ABBAS AGHA ZAMANI ABU SHARIF.

Iraq: House 1, St. 15, Sector F/7-2; *Ambassador:* AHMED ZAFAR AL-GAILANI.

Italy: 448, Shalimar 6/3; *Ambassador:* Dr. PAOLO TORELLA DI ROMAGNANO.

Japan: Plot Nos. 53-70, Ramna 5/4; *Ambassador:* TATEO SUZUKI.

Jordan: 435, Ramna 6/4; *Ambassador:* Maj.-Gen. (retd.) MAJID HAJJ HASSAN.

Korea, Democratic People's Republic: 9, 89th St., Ramna 6/3; *Ambassador:* YU SONG CHIN.

Kuwait: 148-G, Attaturk Ave., Ramna 6/3; *Ambassador:* MOHAMMAD IBRAHIM AL-NAJRAN.

Laos: Bangkok, Thailand.

Lebanon: 24, Khayaban-e-Iqbal, Shalimar F-6/3; *Ambassador:* SOUHEIL FREIJY.

Libya: P.O.B. 1024, 20 Hill Rd., Shalimar 6/3; *Ambassador:* (vacant).

Malaysia: 224, Shalimar 7/4; *Ambassador:* DALI BIN MAHMUD HASHIM.

Mauritania: Beijing, People's Republic of China.

Mauritius: 532-F, Ramna 6/4; *Ambassador:* (vacant).

Mexico: Ankara, Turkey.

Mongolia: Beijing, People's Republic of China.

Morocco: 19, 87th St., Ramna 6/3; *Ambassador:* (vacant).

Nepal: 506, 84th St., Attaturk Ave., Ramna 6/4; *Ambassador:* GOVIND PRASAD LOHANI.

Netherlands: 5, 61st St., Shalimar 6/3; *Ambassador:* B. C. PEYRA.

New Zealand: Teheran, Iran.

Nigeria: 6, 22, Shalimar 6/2; Ambassador: Alhaji MAHMUD AHMED.

Norway: Teheran, Iran.

Oman: 440 Bazar Rd., Ramna 6/4; *Ambassador:* (vacant).

Paraguay: Tokyo, Japan.

Philippines: 11, St. 26, Shalimar 6/2; *Ambassador:* PEDRO ANGARA-ARAGON.

Poland: 172, St. 88, Ramna 6/3; *Ambassador:* WŁADYSŁAW NENEMAN.

Portugal: 8, 90th St., Ramna 6/3; *Ambassador:* (vacant).

Qatar: 201 Masjid Rd., Shalimar 6/4; *Ambassador:* AHMED ALI AL-ANSARI.

Romania: 10, St. 90, Ramna 6/3; *Ambassador:* CONSTANTIN BURADA.

Saudi Arabia: Plot 436-F, Ramna 6/4; *Ambassador:* Sheikh SAMIR ALI SHIHABI.

Senegal: Beirut, Lebanon.

Sierra Leone: Beijing, People's Republic of China.

Singapore: Cairo, Egypt.

Somalia: 174 Margalla Rd., F-7/3; *Ambassador:* ADAM ISAAK AHMED.

Spain: P.O.B. 1144, 180-G, Ramna 6/3; *Ambassador:* VICTOR SANCHEZ MESAS.

Sri Lanka: 28, Street 28, Shalimar F6/1; *Ambassador:* Lieut.-Col. L. E. OSCAR DE LIVERA.

Sudan: 203, Ramna 6/3; *Ambassador:* MOHAMAD EL MOKKI IBRAHIM.

Sweden: 6-A, Agha Khan Rd., Markaz Shalimar 6, P.O.B 1100; *Ambassador:* CARL-JOHAN GROTH.

Switzerland: 11, 84th St., Ramna 6; *Ambassador:* PAUL WIPFLI.

Syria: 343, Shalimar 6/3; *Ambassador:* SAIFI HAMWI.

Thailand: 23, St. 25, Shalimar 6/2; *Ambassador:* PRAMOM KONGSAMUT.

Tunisia: 426, St. 2, Shalimar F-6/3; *Ambassador:* JAMELEDDINE GORDAH.

Turkey: 125-H, Ramna 6/3; *Ambassador:* AYHAN KAMAL.

U.S.S.R.: Diplomatic Enclave, Ramna 4; *Ambassador:* V. S. SMIRNOV.

United Arab Emirates: 228, 1st St., Shalimar 6/3; *Ambassador:* SAEED ALI AL-NOWAIS.

United Kingdom: Diplomatic Enclave, Ramna 5, P.O.B. 1122; *Ambassador:* OLIVER G. FORSTER, C.M.G., M.V.O.

U.S.A.: Diplomatic Enclave, Ramna 4; *Ambassador:* RONALD L. SPIERS.

Vatican City: P.O.B. 1106, Diplomatic Enclave (Apostolic Nunciature); *Pro-Nuncio:* Mgr. EMMANUEL GERADA.

Viet-Nam: 60 Embassy Rd., Ramna 6/3

Yugoslavia: 14, St. 87, Ramna 6/3; *Ambassador:* SLOBODAN MARTINOVIC.

Pakistan also has diplomatic relations with Angola, Bahrain, Benin, Bolivia, Cameroon, the Central African Republic, Chad, Chile, Colombia, the Congo, Costa Rica, Cyprus, Djibouti, El Salvador, Ethiopia, The Gambia, Guinea-Bissau, Iceland, Ireland, the Ivory Coast, Jamaica, Kenya, the Republic of Korea, Liberia, Luxembourg, Madagascar, Maldives, Mali, Malta, Mozambique, Nicaragua, Niger, Panama, Papua New Guinea, Peru, Suriname, Tanzania, Togo, Trinidad and Tobago, Uganda, Upper Volta, Uruguay, Venezuela, the Yemen Arab Republic, the People's Democratic Republic of Yemen, Zambia and Zimbabwe.

JUDICIAL SYSTEM

SUPREME COURT

Rawalpindi

Chief Justice: Mr. Justice MOHAMMAD HALIM (acting).

HIGH COURT OF BALUCHISTAN

Chief Justice: Mr. Justice ZAKAULLAH LODHI (acting).

HIGH COURT OF LAHORE (PUNJAB)

Chief Justice: Mr. Justice SHAMIM HUSSAIN QADRI.

HIGH COURT OF PESHAWAR (NORTH-WEST FRONTIER PROVINCE)

Chief Justice: Mr. Justice USMAN ALI SHAH.

HIGH COURT OF KARACHI (SIND)

Chief Justice: Mr. Justice ABDUL HAYEE KURESHI.

FEDERAL SHARIAT COURT

Chief Justice: Mr. Justice AFTAB HUSAIN.

RELIGION

ISLAM

Islam is the state religion. The majority of the population are Sunni Muslims, while about one-tenth of the total population are of the Shi'a sect.

HINDUISM

Hindus make up 1.6 per cent of the population.

CHRISTIANITY

There is a small minority of Christians, including about 423,762 Catholics in 1978.

THE PRESS

In 1980 there were 115 daily newspapers and 327 weeklies and bi-weeklies. The first Urdu-language newspaper, the daily *Urdu Akhbar*, was founded in 1836. After 1947, with the establishment of Pakistan and the introduction of modern equipment, the more influential English newspapers, such as *Dawn* and *The Pakistan Times*, were firmly established, while several new Urdu newspapers, for example *Nawa-i-Waqt* and *Daily Jang*, became very popular. The Urdu Press comprises 797 newspapers, with *Daily Jang*, *Musawat* (under suspension), *Imroze*, *Nawa-i-Waqt*, *Jasarat* and *Mashriq* being the most influential. The largest daily is *Daily Jang* (circulation *c.* 290,000). Although the English-language Press reaches only 2 per cent of the population and totals 128 publications, it is influential in political, academic and professional circles.

The Press has always been subject to Government scrutiny and "guided reporting", especially in political matters. After the July 1977 coup the martial law administration closed down two daily papers. In October 1979 press censorship was imposed and publication of *Musawat*, *Sadaqat* and other opposition papers was suspended. In December 1981 censorship was lifted from literary and educational books and magazines, and in January 1982 pre-censorship on daily newspapers was also lifted. Pre-censorship continued, however, on political, semi-political and non-literary weeklies, monthlies and periodicals.

PRINCIPAL DAILIES

RAWALPINDI

Daily Jang: Edwards Rd.; f. 1937; published simultaneously in Quetta, Karachi and Lahore; Urdu; independent national; Editor MIR JAVED REHMAN; circ. (Rawalpindi) 65,000.

Daily Ta'Meer: Jamia Masjid Rd.; f. 1949; Urdu; independent; Editor BASHIRUL ISLAM USMANI.

Daily Wifaq: 7/A Commercial Area, Satellite Town; f. 1959; simultaneous edns. in Lahore, Rawalpindi, Sargodha and Rahimyar Khan; Urdu; Editor MUSTAFA SADIQ.

KARACHI

Aghaz: Preedy St., 11 Japan Mansion, Saddar, Karachi 2, f. 1963; Urdu; evening; Editor M. A. FARUQI; circ. 25,000.

Amn: Akhbar Manzil, off I. I. Chundrigar Rd.; Urdu; Editor AFZAL SIDDIQI.

Business Recorder: Recorder House, Business Recorder Road, Karachi 0509; f. 1965; English; Editor M. A. ZUBERI.

Daily Jang: H.O. Printing House, I. I. Chundrigar Rd., P.O.B. 52; f. 1937; Urdu; morning; editions also in Quetta, Rawalpindi and Lahore; Editor-in-Chief MIR KHALIL-UR-RAHMAN; circ. 367,000 (weekdays), 482,000 (Friday).

Daily News: Printing House, I. I. Chundrigar Rd., f. 1962; evening; English; Editor WAJID SHAMSUL HASAN; circ. 43,000.

Dawn: Haroon House, Dr. Ziauddin Ahmed Rd., Karachi 4; f. 1947; English, Gujarati; Chief Exec. MAHMUD HAROON; Editors AHMAD ALI KHAN (English edn.), GHULAM NABI MANSURI (Gujarati edn.); circ. 70,000.

Hilal-e-Pakistan: 2nd Floor, Court View Bldg., M. A. Jinnah Rd.; Sindhi; Editor (vacant).

Hurriyet: Haroon House, Dr. Ziauddin Ahmed Rd.; Urdu; Editor MOHAMMAD AHMAD.

Inqilab: Grand Hotel Bldg., I.I. Chundrigar Rd.; Editor ABDUL MAJID.

Jasarat: Everready Chambers, Mohammad bin Qasim Rd.; Urdu; Editor MOHAMMAD SALAHUDDIN; circ. 50,000.

Leader: 191 Altaf Hussain Rd., Karachi 2; f. 1958; English; independent; Editor MANZARUL HASAN; circ. 11,100.

Millat: 191 Altaf Hussain Rd., Karachi 2; f. 1946; Gujarati; independent; Editor INQUILAB MATRI; circ. 17,400.

Morning News: Saifee House, Dr. Ziauddin Ahmed Rd., P.O.B. 2804; f. 1942; English; Editor RAFIQ JABIR.

Star: Haroon House, Dr. Ziauddin Ahmed Rd., Karachi 4; evening; English; Editor G. N. MANSURI.

Vatan: Haroon House, Dr. Ziauddin Ahmed Rd.; f. 1942; Gujarati; Editor N. J. M. NOOR; circ. 12,000.

LAHORE

Imroze: Rattan Chand Rd.; f. 1948; morning; Urdu; Editor HAROON SAAD; circ. 48,000 (Lahore), 17,000 (Multan).

Mahgribi Pakistan: Beadon Rd.; Urdu; Editor M. SHAFAAT.

Mashriq Daily: 46 Nishet Rd.; f. 1963; Urdu; simultaneous editions in Karachi, Peshawar and Quetta; Chief Exec. IQBAL AHMAD ZUBERI; circ. 140,000.

Nawa-i-Waqt Daily: 4 Shar-e-Fatima Jinnah, Lahore; f. 1940; English, Urdu; simultaneous editions in Lahore, Karachi, Rawalpindi and Multan; Editor MAJID NIZAMI; circ. 200,000.

Pakistan Times: Rattan Chand Rd., P.O.B. 223; f. 1947; English; liberal; simultaneous edition in Rawalpindi; Chief Editor Z. A. SULERI; circ. 40,000.

Sadaqat: Nairobi Mansion, Napier Rd.; Editor Prof. M. I. QURESHI.

Sayasat: 6-C Data Darbar Market, Lahore.

Tijarat: 14 Abbot Rd., opp. Nishat Cinema; Urdu; Editor JAMIL ATHAR.

Wifaq: Shahrah-i-Quaid-e-Azam, 3A Shahdin Bldg.; Urdu; simultaneous editions in Rawalpindi, Sargodha and Rahimyar Khan; Editor MOSTAFA SADIQ.

OTHER TOWNS

Aftab: Risala Rd., nr. Circular Bldg., Hyderabad; Sindhi; also published from Multan; Editor SHEIKH ALI MOHAMMAD.

Al Falah: Al Falah Bldg., Saddar Rd., Peshawar; f. 1939; Urdu and Pashtu; Editor S. ABDULLAH SHAH.

Al-Jamiat-e-Sarhad: Kocha Gilania Chakagali, Karimpura, Peshawar; f. 1941; Urdu and Pashtu; Editor S. M. HASSAN GILANI.

Baluchistan Times: Jinnah Rd., Quetta; Editor SYED FASIH IQBAL.

Daily Meezan: Meezan Chambers, Prince Rd., Quetta; Urdu; Editor JAMIL UR-REHMAN.

Daily Rehbar: Bahawalpur Office, 17/B-East Trust Colony, Bahawalpur; f. 1952; Urdu; Chief Editor MALIK MOHAMMAD HAYAT, T.K.; circ. 9,970.

Jehad: 15A Islamia Club Bldg., Khyber Bazar, Peshawar; also in Karachi and Lahore; Editor SHARIF FAROOQ.

Kaleem: Queen's Rd., P.O.B. 88, Sukkur; Urdu; Editor MEHR ELAHI SHAMSHI.

Khyber Mail: Saddar Bazar, Peshawar; f. 1932; English; independent; Editor SH. ZAKAULLAH; circ. 5,000.

Maghribi Pakistan: Sukkur; Urdu; Editor JAVED ASHRAF.

The Muslim: 9 Hameed Chambers, Aabpara, Islamabad; f. 1979; English; independent; Pres. and Editor-in-Chief AGHA MURTAZA POOYA; Editor MUSHAHID HUSSAIN.

Punjab News: Kutchery Bazar, Faisalabad.

Sarhad: New Gate, Peshawar.

Sind News: P.O.B. 289, Garikhata, Hyderabad; Editor SALIM AKBAR QAZI.

Sind Observer: Garikhata, Hyderabad; English; Editor SALIM AKBAR QAZI.

Watan: 10 Nazar Bagh Flat, Peshawar.

Zamana: Jinnah Rd., Quetta; Urdu; Editor SYED FASIH IQBAL; circ. 5,000.

SELECTED WEEKLIES

Afro-Asia: 42 Commercial Bldg., Shahrah-i-Quaid-e-Azam, Lahore; Editor ABDUL QADIR HASAN.

Akhbar-e-Jehan: Printing House, off I.I. Chundrigar Rd., Karachi; f. 1967; Urdu; independent national; illustrated family magazine; Editor MIR JAVED RAHMAN; circ. 82,000.

Al Wahdat: Peshawar; Urdu and Pashtu; Editor NURUL HAQ.

Amal: Aiwan-a-Abul Kaif, Abul Kaif Rd., Shah Qabool Colony, Peshawar; f. 1958; Urdu; Editor AQAI ABUL KAIF KAIFI SARHADDI.

Awam: Iftikhar Chambers, Altaf Husain Rd., Karachi 2; f. 1958; Urdu; political; Editor ABDUL RAUF SIDDIQI; circ. 3,000.

Badban: Nai Zindagi Publications, Rana Chambers, Old Anarkali, Lahore; Editor MUJIBUR REHMAN SHAMI.

Chatan: 88 McLeod Rd., Lahore; f. 1948; Urdu; Editor MASUD SHORISH.

Current: Shaikha House, Faiz Mohammad Fateh Ali Rd., nr. Haqqani Chowk, Karachi; English; Editor ZAHID ALI.

Dawn Overseas: Haroon House, Dr. Ziauddin Ahmed Rd., Karachi.

Fanoos Digest: 689-C, Central Commercial Area, Allama Iqbal Rd., Karachi; Chief Editor RUKHSANA SEHAM MIRZA.

Hilal: Hilal Rd., Rawalpindi; f. 1951; Urdu; Sunday; Illustrated Services journal; Editor MUMTAZ IQBAL MALIK; circ. 40,000.

Insaf: P-929, Banni, Rawalpindi; f. 1955; Editor MIR ABDUL AZIZ.

Lahore: 113B Balwant Mansion, Beadon Rd., Lahore 5; f. 1952; Editor SAQIB ZEERVI; circ. 8,200.

Mahwar: D23, Block H, North Nazimabad, Karachi; Editor SHAHIDA NAFIS SIDDIQI.

Meyar: 110K Block 2, P.E.C.H.S. 29; f. 1976; Editor MAHMUD SHAM; circ. 15,000.

Memaar-i-Nao: 39 K.M.C. Bldg., Leamarket, Karachi; Labour magazine; Urdu; Editor M. M. MUBASIR.

Nairang Khayal: 8 Mohammadi Market, Rawalpindi; f. 1924; Urdu; Chief Editor SULTAN RASHK.

Nigar Weekly: Victoria Mansion, Abdullah Haroon Rd., Karachi; Editor ILYAS RASHIDI.

Noor Jehan Weekly: Kohinoor Cinema Bldg., Marston Rd., Karachi; f. 1948; film journal; Urdu; Editor SAEED CHAWLA; circ. 16,000.

Ofaq: 20 Press Chamber, I. I. Chundrigar Rd., Karachi; f. 1978; Editor WAHAJ UDDEEN CLINTI; circ. 2,000.

Pakistan and Gulf Economist: P.O.B. 10449, 2nd Floor, Shafi Court, Mereweather Rd., Karachi 4; f. 1960; English; Editor AKHTAR ADIL RAZVI; circ. 20,000.

Pak Kashmir: Pak Kashmir Office, Soikarno Chowk, Liaquat Rd., Rawalpindi; f. 1951; Urdu; Editor MUHAMMED FAYYAZ ABBAZI.

Parbat: Nawabshah; Editor WAHAB SIDDIQI.

Parsi Sansar and Loke Sevak: Marston Rd., Karachi; f. 1909; English and Gujarati; Wed. and Sat.; Editor MEHERJI P. DASTUR.

Parwaz: Madina Office, Bahawalpur; Urdu; Editor MUSTQA AHMED.

Pictorial: Jamia Masjid Rd., Rawalpindi; f. 1956; English; Editor MUHAMMAD SAFDAR.

Qallandar: Peshawar; f. 1950; Urdu; Editor M. A. K. SHERWANI.

Quetta Times: Albert Press, Jinnah Rd., Quetta, Baluchistan; f. 1924; English; Editor S. RUSTOMJI; circ. 4,000.

Rahbar-e-Sarhad: Peshawar; f. 1956; Urdu; Editor M. SHABIR AHMAD.

Sahafat: 38 Multan Rd., Lahore; Editor RIAZ SHAHID.

Shahab-e-Saqib: Shahab Saqib Rd., Maulana St., Peshawar; f. 1950; Urdu; Editor S. M. RIZVI.

Shah Jahan: Akber Manzil, I. I. Chundrigar Rd., Karachi; Editor ZAKI USMANI.

Shkbar-e-Khwateen: 42/8/6 P.E.C.H.S., Karachi 28; Editor IRSHAD AHMAD.

The Statesman: 260-C Central Commercial Area, P.E.C.H.S., Karachi 29; f. 1955; English; Editor MOHAMMAD OWAIS.

Tanvir: Bazar Qissa Khani, Peshawar; independent; Urdu and Pashtu; Editor AMIR SIDDIQI.

Tarjaman-i-Sarhad: Peshawar; Urdu and Pashtu; Editor MOHAMMAD SHAFI SABIR, M.A.

Viewpoint: 4 Lawrence Rd., Lahore; English; Editor MAZHAR ALI KHAN.

SELECTED PERIODICALS

(Karachi unless otherwise stated)

Aalami Digest: B-1, Momin Square, Rashid Minhas Rd., Gulshan-e-Iqbal; Urdu; monthly; Editor Mrs. ZAHEDA HINA.

Adabarz: Misbat Rd., Lahore; monthly; Editor IBNE WAHSHI MAHREHARVI.

Afkar: Robson Rd.; f. 1945; Urdu; art, literature; monthly; Editor SAHBA LUCKNAVI.

Ahang: 4th Floor, Qassim Manzil, Randle Rd.; fortnightly; Urdu; Chief Editor SABIH MOHSIN.

Akhbar-e-Watan: Noor Mohammed Lodge, 444 Dr Ziauddin Ahmed Rd.; monthly.

Albalagh: Darul Uloom, Karachi 14; monthly; Editor MOHAMMED TAQI USMANI.

Al-Ma'arif: Institute of Islamic Culture, Club Rd., Lahore 3; f. 1954; Urdu; monthly; Editor M. ISHAQ BHATTI; Dir. Prof. M. SAEED SHEIKH.

Anchal: 24 Saeed Mansion, I. I. Chundrigar Rd.; monthly

Bayanat: New Town, Karachi 5; monthly; Editor MAULANA MOHAMMED ASAD BANORI.

Chand: Nisbet Rd., Lahore; monthly; Editor PIR JUNGLI.

Defence Journal: 16-B, 7th Central St., Defence Housing Authority; f. 1975; English; monthly; Editor Brig. (retd.) A. R. SIDDIQI; circ. 2,000.

Director: 42 Commercial Bldgs., Shahrah-i-Quaid-e-Azam, Lahore; f. 1948; Urdu; monthly; films, literature and the arts; Editor M. FAZALHAQ; circ. over 21,000.

Dosheeza: 689, C-Central Commercial Area, Allama Iqbal Rd., P.E.C.H.S.; Urdu; monthly; Editor RUKHSANA SEHAM MIRZA.

Eastern Message: Pakistan Union Store, Jamia Masjid Rd., Mipur Khas; f. 1959; English; quarterly; Editor Sultan AHMAD ANSARI.

Economic Review: Al-Masiha, 3rd Floor, 47 Abdullah Haroon Rd., P.O.B. Box 7843, Karachi 3; f. 1969; monthly; Pakistan's economic development; Editor IQBAL HAIDARI; circ. 10,000.

Engineering Review: P.O.B. Box 807; English; fortnightly.

Flyer International: P.O.B. 8034, 187/3-B2, P.E.C.H.S., Karachi 29; f. 1966; aviation and tourism; Man. Editor BASHIR A. KHAN; Editor AZAM ALI; circ. 9,750.

Ghuncha: Aurangzeb Market; monthly; Editor MAZHAR YUSUFZAI.

Hamdard-i-Sehat: Institute of Health and Tibbi Research, Hamdard Foundation Pakistan, Nazimabad, Karachi 18; f. 1933; Urdu; monthly; Editor HAKIM MOHAMMED SAID; circ. 2,750.

Hamdard Islamicus: Hamdard Foundation Pakistan, Nazimabad, Karachi 18; f. 1978; English; quarterly; Editor HAKIM MOHAMMED SAID; circ. 2,000.

Hamdard Medicus: Hamdard Foundation Pakistan, Nazimabad, Karachi 18; f. 1957; quarterly; Editor HAKIM MOHAMMED SAID; circ. 2,000.

Hamdard Naunehal: Hamdard Foundation Pakistan, Nazimabad, Karachi 18; f. 1952; Urdu; quarterly; Editor MASOOD AHMED BARAKATI; circ. 25,000.

The Herald: Haroon House, Dr. Ziauddin Ahmed Road, Karachi 4; f. 1970; English; monthly; Editor RAZIA BHATTI; circ. *c.* 10,000.

Hikayat: 26 Patiala Ground, Link McLeod Rd., Lahore; monthly; Editor INAYATULLAH.

Hoor: Hoor St., Nishtar Rd., Lahore; monthly; Editor AMMATULLAH QURESHI.

Islami Jumhuria: Laj Rd., Old Anarkali, Lahore; monthly; Editor NAZIR TARIQ.

Islamic Studies: Islamic Research Institute, P.O.B. 1035, Islamabad; f. 1962; quarterly; Editor MAZHERUDDIN SIDDIQI.

Journal of the Pakistan Historical Society: 30 New Karachi Housing Society; f. 1950; English; quarterly; Editor Dr. MOINUL HAQUE.

Jugnoo: Adabi Market, Chowk Anarkali, Lahore; monthly; Editor ARSHAD NIAZ.

Karan: 37 Urdu Bazaar; Editor MAHMUD BABAR FAISAL.

Khel-Ke-Duniya: 6/13 Alyusaf Chamber.

Khwateen Digest: Urdu Bazar, M. A. Jinnah Rd.; Urdu; monthly; Editor MAHMUD RIAZ.

Kiran Digest: 37 Urdu Bazar, M. A. Jinnah Rd.; monthly.

Mah-i-Nau: P.O.B. 183, Pakistan Publications; f. 1948; illustrated cultural; Urdu; monthly; circ. 14,000.

Medicus: Pakistan Chowk, Dr. Ziauddin Ahmed Rd., Karachi 1; f. 1950; English; medical journal; monthly; Editor M. S. QURESHI.

Naey-Ufaq: 24 Saeed Mansion, I. I. Chundrigar Rd.; fortnightly.

Naqqad: Bander Rd.; Editor AZHAR NIAZI.

Naya Daur: Pakistan Cultural Centre Society, Karachi 6; quarterly.

Pakeeza Digest: Frere Market; monthly.

Pakistan Digest: 4 Amil St., off Robson Rd., Karachi 1; f. 1974; English; monthly; Editor AMEEN TAREEN.

Pakistan Exports: Export Promotion Bureau; f. 1950; English; monthly; Editor MOHAMMAD HUSAIN.

Pakistan Journal of Scientific and Industrial Research: Pakistan Council of Scientific and Industrial Research, 39 Garden Rd., Karachi 0310; f. 1958; English; 6 times a year; Editor A. H. KHAN.

Pakistan Management Review: Pakistan Institute of Management, Shahrah Iran, Clifton, Karachi 6; f. 1960; English; quarterly; Editor ZARRAR R. ZUBAIR.

Pakistan Medical Forum: 15 Nadir House, I. I. Chundrigar Rd., Karachi 2; f. 1966; English; monthly; Man. Editor M. AHSON.

Pallak: Chowk Anarkali, Lahore; monthly; Editor ARSHAD NIAZ.

Pasban: Faiz Modh Rd., Quetta; Urdu; fortnightly; Editor MOLVI MOHD. ABDULLAH.

Printer: Alyusaf Chambers, First Floor, Shahrah-e-Liaquat; f. 1981; Urdu; monthly; Editor MOHAMMAD IRFAN QURESHI.

Qaumi Digest: Rana Chamber, Old Anarkali, Lahore; monthly; Editor MUJIBUR REHMAN SHAMI.

Sayyarah: Zaildar Park Ichhra, Lahore 12; monthly; Editor NAEEM SIDDIQI.

Sayyarah Digest: c/o Paradise Book Stall, Hameed Nizami Rd., Lahore; Urdu; monthly; Editor ATTASH DURRANI.

Seep: Alam Market, Block No. 16, Federal B Area; quarterly; Editor NASIM DURRANI.

Sehar: Shaikh Bldg., Royal Park, Lahore; fortnightly; Editor ASIM JILANI.

Sind Quarterly: 36-D Karachi Administrative Co-operative Housing Society, Off Shaheed-e-Millat Rd., Karachi 8; Editor SAYID GHULM MUSTAFA SHAH.

Subrang Digest: 47–48 Press Chambers, I. I. Chundrigar Rd., Karachi 1; f. 1970; Urdu; monthly; Editor SHAKEEL ADIL ZADAH; circ. 150,000.

Taj: Jamia Tajia, Street 13, Sector 14/B, Buffer Zone, Karachi 36; P.O.B. 18084; monthly; Editor BABA ANWAR SHAH TAJI.

Talimo Tarbiat: Ferozons Ltd., 60 Shahrah-i-Quaid-e-Azam, Lahore; f. 1941; children's monthly; Urdu; Chief Editor A. SALAM; circ. 40,000.

Tot Batot: 110K Block 2, P.E.C.H.S., Karachi 29; f. 1978; children's monthly; Editor MAHMUD SHAH; circ. 10,000.

Trade Chronicle: Altaf Husain Rd.; f. 1953; English; monthly; trade and economics; Editor ABDUL RAUF SIDDIQI; circ. 5,500.

Turjamaney Ahle Sunnat: Mohammadi Mansion, Marston Rd.; monthly; Editor RAZA AL MUSTAFA AZHARI.

UNESCO Payami: Hamdard Foundation, Pakistan, Nazimabad, Karachi 18; f. 1977; Urdu; monthly; Editor HAKIM MOHAMMED SAID; circ. 2,000.

Universal Message (*Journal of the Islamic Research Academy*): 10/C/163, Mansurah, Federal "B" Area, Karachi 3805; f. 1979; literature, politics, religion; English; monthly; Editor KHALID F. RAHMAN.

Urdu Digest: 5 Main Rd., Samnabad, Lahore; Urdu; monthly; Editor ALTAF HUSSAN QURESHI.

Voice of Islam: Jamiyat-ul-Falah Bldg., Akbar Rd., Saddar, P.O.B. 7141; f. 1952; English; monthly; Chief Editor Dr. MANZOOR AHMAD; Man. Editor Prof. SYED LUTFULLAH.

Yaqeen International: Mujahidabad, Hub River Rd., Karachi 1; f. 1952; English and Arabic; Islamic organ; Editor M. M. ANSARI.

NEWS AGENCIES

Associated Press of Pakistan (APP): House 7, St. 45, Shalimar 6/1, Islamabad; f. 1948; Dir.-Gen. MUKHTAR ZAMAN.

Pakistan Press International (PPI): Assembly Bldg., Karachi; f. 1956; Editor FAZAL QURESHI.

United Press of Pakistan: 1 Victoria Chambers, Abdullah Haroon Rd., Karachi; f. 1949; Man. Dir. MAHMUDUL AZIZ.

FOREIGN BUREAUX

Agence France-Presse (AFP): P.O.B. 1276, Islamabad; Chief Rep. ALAIN FAUDEUX.

Agenzia Nazionale Stampa Associata (ANSA) (*Italy*): P.O.B. 263, Rawalpindi; Chief Corresp. ABSAR H. RIZVI.

Associated Press (AP) (*U.S.A.*): 32, Mirza Kalegbeg Rd., Karachi 3; Corresp. ZAMIR SIDDIQI.

Deutsche Presse-Agentur (dpa) (*Federal Republic of Germany*): c/o Pakistan Press Institute, R. A. Bazar, Rawalpindi; Bureau Chief ANWAR MANSURI.

Reuters (*U.K.*): No. 149, 19th St., Shalimar 6, Islamabad.

United Press International (UPI) (*U.S.A.*): c/o 4-A Mrs. Davis' Hotel, Rawalpindi; Corresp. ASRAR AHMED.

TASS (U.S.S.R.) and Xinhua (People's Republic of China) also have offices in Pakistan.

PRESS ASSOCIATIONS

All Pakistan Newspaper Employees Confederation: Karachi Press Club, M. R. Kayani Rd., Karachi; f. 1976; confederation of all press industry trade unions; Chair. MINHAJ BARNA; Sec.-Gen. HAFEEZ RAQIB.

All Pakistan Newspapers Society: 3rd Floor, 32 Farid Chambers, Abdullah Haroon Rd., Karachi 3; f. 1949; Pres. MAJID NIZAMI.

Council of Pakistan Newspaper Editors: c/o Daily Jang, I. I. Chundrigar Rd., Karachi; Pres. S.A. ZUBERI.

Pakistan Federal Union of Journalists: *Dawn* Bureau, Lahore; f. 1950; objectives: better working conditions and freedom of the Press: Pres. (Barna Group) NISAR USMANI, Pres. (Bashid Group) RASHID SIDDIQI.

PUBLISHERS

Aina-e-Adab: Chowk Minar, Anarkali, Lahore; f. 1957; general fiction; Proprietor ABDUS SALAM.

Anjuman Tarraqqi-i-Urdu Pakistan: Baba-i-Urdu Rd., Karachi 1; f. 1903 in pre-partitioned India; literature, religion, textbooks, Urdu dictionaries, specializes in Urdu literature and criticism; publs. *Qaumi Zaban* (monthly), *URDU* (quarterly); Pres. AKHTAR HUSAIN; Sec. JAMILUDDIN A'ALI.

Barque and Co.: Barque Chambers, Barque Sq., Shahrah-e-Liaqat Ali Khan, Lahore; f. 1930; trade directories, Who's Who, periodicals; Man. Dir. A. M. BARQUE.

Camran Publishers: Jalaluddin Hospital Bldg., Circular Rd., Lahore; f. 1964; general, technical, textbooks; Proprietor ABDUL HAMID.

Chronicle Publications: Iftikhar Chambers, Altaf Husain Rd., Karachi; reference books, directories; Dir. ABDUR RAFAY.

Crescent Publications: Urdu Bazar, Lahore.

Daira-i-Moinul Maarif: 30, New Karachi Housing Society, Karachi 29; f. 1958; general literature, religion, history; Pres. Dr. S. MOINUL HAQ.

Economic and Industrial Publications: Al-Masiha, 47 Abdullah Haroon Rd., Karachi 3; f. 1965; industrial research service on Pakistan's specific industries, weekly investors' service on corporate companies in Pakistan and fortnightly labour research service.

Elite Publishers Ltd.: 16/A, Mohammad Ali Housing Society, Karachi; Chair. JAMIL AHMAD MIRZA.

Ferozsons Ltd.: 60 Shahrah-i-Quaid-e-Azam, Lahore; f. 1894; books, periodicals, maps, atlases; Man. Dir. A. HAMEED KHAN.

Frontier Publishing Co.: Urdu Bazar, Lahore.

Ghulam Ali and Sons: Adabi Market, Chowk Anarkali, Lahore; f. 1887; general, religion, technical, textbooks; Partner NIAZ AHMAD.

Government Publications: Manager of Publications, Central Publications Branch, Government of Pakistan, Block University Rd., Karachi.

Idara Taraqqi-i-Urdu: S-1/363 Saudabad, Karachi 27; f. 1949; general literature, technical and professional books and magazines; Proprietor IKRAM AHMED.

Ilmi Kitab Khana: Kabeer St., Urdu Bazar, Lahore; f. 1948; technical, professional, historical and law; Proprietor Haji SARDAR MOHAMMAD.

Islamic Book Centre: P.O.B. 1625, 25-B Masson Rd., Lahore 29; religion in Arabic, Urdu and English; Islamic and historical reprints; Man. Dir. ROZINA NIGHAT.

Islamic Publications Ltd.: 13-E Shahalam Market, Lahore 7; Islamic literature in Urdu and English; Man. Dir. ASHFAQUE MIRZA.

Jamiyat-ul-Falah Publications: Jamiyat-ul-Falah Bldg., Akbar Rd., Saddar, P.O.B. 7141, Karachi 1; f. 1952; Islamic history and culture and monthly English journal; Sec.-Gen. Prof. SYED LUTFULLAH.

Kazi Publications: 121 Zulqarnain Chambers, Ganpat Rd., Lahore; f. 1978; Islamic literature, religion, law, biographies; Man. MUHAMMAD IKRAM SIDDIQI; Chief Editor MUHAMMAD IQBAL SIDDIQI.

Lark Publishers: Urdu Bazar, Karachi 1; f. 1955; general literature, magazines; Proprietor MAHMOOD RIAZ.

Lion Art Press Ltd.: 112 Shahrah-i-Quaid-e-Azam, Lahore; f. 1919; general publications in English; Dir. KHALID A. SHEIKH.

Maktabe-i-Darut Tasnif: Shahrah-e-Liaquat, Karachi 3; f. 1965; Koran and Islamic literature; Dir. RIAZ AHMAD.

Malik Sons: Karkhana Bazar, Faisalabad.

Medina Publishing Company: M. A. Jinnah Rd., Karachi 1; f. 1960; general literature, textbooks; Proprietor HAKIM MOHAMMAD TAQI.

Mercantile Guardian Press and Publishers: 81–83 Shahrah-i-Quaid-e-Azam, Lahore; f. 1949; trade directories, etc.; Editor MAHMOOD AHMAD MIR.

Mina Press and Publishing House Ltd.: D-152, S.I.T.E., Manghopir Rd., Karachi; Dir. MOHAMMAD DIN SHAMSI.

Mohammad Hussain and Sons: Kashmiri Bazar, 17 Urdu Bazar, Lahore 2; f. 1941; religion, textbooks; Partners: MOHAMMAD HUSSAIN, AZHAR ALI SHEIKH, PERVEZ ALI SHEIKH.

Muhammad Ashraf: 7 Aibak Rd., New Anarkali, Lahore; f. 1923; books on all aspects of Islam in English; Chief Literary Adviser M. ASHRAF DARR.

Pakistan Law House: Pakistan Chowk, P.O.B. 90, Karachi; f. 1950; importers and exporters of legal books; Partners M. NOORANI, K. NOORANI.

Pakistan Publication: Shahrah-e-Iraq, P.O.B. 193, Karachi 1; general interest and literary books and magazines about Pakistan in English, Urdu and Arabic, etc.

Pakistan Publishing House: Victoria Chambers 2, A. Haroon Rd., Karachi 3; f. 1959; Man. Dir. M. NOORANI; Gen. Man. MATIN M. KHAN.

Peco Ltd.: P.O.B. 70, Lahore; f. 1936; Koran and Islamic literature; Man. Dir. JAMEEL MAZHAR.

Pioneer Book House: 1 Avan Lodge, Bunder Rd., P.O.B. 37, Karachi; periodicals, gazettes, maps and reference works in English, Urdu and other regional languages.

Publishers International: Bandukwala Bldg., 4 I. I. Chundrigar Rd., Karachi; f. 1948; reference books, advertising; Man. Dir. KAMALUDDIN AHMAD.

Publishers United Ltd.: 176 Anarkali, Lahore; textbooks, technical, reference, military and general books.

Punjab Religious Books Society: Anarkali, Lahore 2; educational, religious, law and general.

Sindhi Adabi Board (*Sindhi Literary and Publishing Organization*): P.O.B. 12, Hyderabad, Sind; f. 1951; history, literature, culture of Sind, in Sindhi, Urdu, English, Persian and Arabic; translations into Sindhi, especially of literature and history; Chair. Prof. MAULANA GHULAM MUSTAFA QASMI; Sec. GHULAM RABBANI A. AGRO.

M. Siraj-ud-Din & Sons: Kashmiri Bazar, Lahore 8; f. 1905; religious books in many languages; Man. M. SIRAJ-UD-DIN.

Taj Company Ltd.: P.O.B. 530, Karachi; f. 1929; religious books; Man. Dir. SH. ENAYATULLAH.

Times Press: Mansfield St., Saddar, Karachi 3; f. 1948; Government printers (security and confidential division) and registered publishers of Quran and text books; Man. Dir. SHUJADDIN.

Urdu Academy Sind: 16 Bahadur Shah Market, M. A. Jinnah Rd., Karachi; f. 1947; brs. in Hyderabad and Lahore; reference books, general and textbooks; Man. Partner A. D. KHALID.

West-Pak Publishing Co. Ltd.: 56-N, Gulberg, Lahore; f. 1932; textbooks; government printers; Man. Dir. S. M. SHAH.

PUBLISHERS' ASSOCIATION

Pakistan Publishers' and Booksellers' Association: Y.M.C.A. Bldg., Shahrah-i-Quaid-e-Azam, Lahore; Chair. NIAZ AHMAD; Sec. SALAH-UD-DIN.

RADIO AND TELEVISION

RADIO

Pakistan Broadcasting Corpn.: Broadcasting House, Constitution Ave., Islamabad; f. 1947 as Radio Pakistan, incorporated 1972; Chair. Maj.-Gen. MUJIB-UR-REHMAN KHAN; Dir.-Gen. Q. A. SAEED; Dir. (Programmes) A. F. KALIMULLAH; Dir. (Finance) EJAZ AHMAD.

National broadcasting comprises fourteen stations in Bahawalpur, Dera Ismail Khan, Gilgit, Hyderabad, Islamabad, Karachi, Khaipur Mir, Khuzder (Baluchistan), Lahore, Multan, Peshawar, Quetta, Rawalpindi, Skardu and Turbat. Home service 220 hrs. daily in 21 languages; external services 31 hrs. daily in 18 languages.

There were 1.56 million radio licences issued in 1980.

TELEVISION

Pakistan Television Corporation Ltd.: Federal TV Complex, Constitution Ave., P.O.B. 1221, Islamabad; f. 1967; Chair. Maj.-Gen. MUJIB-UR-REHMAN KHAN; Man. Dir. ZIA NISAR AHMAD.

Programmes daily 16.30–23.00 hours (winter), 17.00–23.30 (summer). Extended transmissions on Fridays.

Colour television was launched in December 1976.

In 1981/82 there were 850,000 television receivers in use.

FINANCE

BANKING

(cap. = capital; p.u. = paid up; dep. = deposits; m. = million; Rs. = rupees; brs. = branches)

In January 1974 all Pakistani banks were nationalized. Foreign banks were not affected, but were not permitted to open any new branches in Pakistan. By March 1979 there were 45 foreign banks operating in Pakistan. Since nationalization the number of commercial bank branches has risen from 3,000 to 7,128 (June 1981), while deposits have risen to 69,041.1m. (June 1981).

Central Bank

State Bank of Pakistan: Central Directorate, P.O.B. 4456, I. I. Chundrigar Rd., Karachi; f. 1948; bank of issue; controls and regulates currency and foreign exchange; cap. p.u. Rs. 100m., dep. Rs. 19,743m. (June 1981); Gov. and Chair. A. G. N. Kazi.

Commercial Banks

Allied Bank of Pakistan Ltd.: Jubilee Insurance House, I. I. Chundrigar Rd., Karachi; f. 1942; cap. p.u. Rs. 132.208m., res. 40.99m., dep. Rs. 390m. (Dec. 1981); 698 brs. in Pakistan and three overseas; Pres. Khadim H. Siddiqi.

Habib Bank Ltd.: Habib Bank Plaza, I. I. Chundrigar Rd., Karachi 21; f. 1941; cap. p.u. Rs. 542m., res. Rs. 496m., dep. Rs. 31,004m. (Dec. 1980); 1,845 brs. throughout Pakistan and 78 overseas brs.; Pres. Abdul Jabbar Khan.

Muslim Commercial Bank Ltd.: Adamjee House, I. I. Chundrigar Rd., Karachi 2; f. 1948; cap. p.u. Rs. 262m., dep. Rs. 10,881m. (Dec. 1981); 1,341 brs. in Pakistan and 24 brs. overseas; Pres. M. Ajmal Khalil.

National Bank of Pakistan: NBP Building, I. I. Chundrigar Rd., P.O.B. 4937, Karachi; f. 1949; cap. p.u. Rs. 561m., res. Rs. 189m., dep. Rs. 17,301m. (Dec. 1980) over 1,625 brs. in Pakistan and 27 brs. overseas; Pres. Mohammad Nawaz Khan; publs. weekly and monthly economic newsletters, quarterly economic journal.

United Bank Ltd.: State Life Bldg. No. 1, I. I. Chundrigar Rd., Karachi; f. 1959; cap. p.u. and res. Rs. 531m., dep. Rs. 23,317m. (June 1981); 1,674 brs. in Pakistan and 70 brs. overseas; Pres. Sadiq Dar.

Principal Foreign Banks

Algemene Bank Nederland, N.V. (*Netherlands*): P.O.B. 4096, Mackinnon's Bldg., I. I. Chundrigar Rd., Karachi; f. 1948; Man. J. H. van Dijk.

American Express International Banking Corpn. (*U.S.A.*): Standard Insurance House, P.O.B. 4847, I. I. Chundrigar Rd., Karachi; f. 1950; Asst. Vice-Pres. and Man. Majid Husain; 3 brs.

Bank of America National Trust and Savings Association (*U.S.A.*): 4th Floor, Jubilee Insurance House, I. I. Chundrigar Rd., Karachi; f. 1961; Man. Ronald A. Mathias; 3 brs.

Bank of Credit and Commerce International (Overseas) Ltd. (*Cayman Islands*): 19 Muhammadi House, I. I. Chundrigar Rd., Karachi 2; cap. (U.S. $) 220m., total assets (U.S. $) 370m.; Gen. Man. E. A. Garda; 3 brs.

Bank of Dubai (*United Arab Emirates*): No. 4, Old Bandukwala Bldg., I. I. Chundrigar Rd., P.O.B. 6776, Karachi; Gen. Man. Anver Majid; 2 brs.

Bank of Oman: Variava Bldg., P.O.B. 930, I. I. Chundrigar Rd., Karachi; Man. Rahat H. Khan; 2 brs.

Bank of Tokyo Ltd. (*Japan*): Qamar House, M. A. Jinnah Rd., P.O.B. 4232, Karachi; Gen. Man. H. Hirano.

Banque de l'Indochine et de Suez (*France*): I. I. Chundrigar Rd., P.O.B. 6942, Karachi.

Chartered Bank (*U.K.*): P.O.B. 4896, I. I. Chundrigar Rd., Karachi 2; Man. D. R. Scotchmer; 4 brs.

Chase Manhattan Bank: Shaheen Building, M. R. Kayani Rd., Karachi.

Citibank, N.A. (*U.S.A.*): State Life Bldg., I. I. Chundrigar Rd., P.O.B. 4889, Karachi; f. 1961; Vice-Pres. Robert S. Eichfeld; 3 brs.

European Asian Bank (*Federal Republic of Germany*): P.O.B. 4925, Unitowers, I. I. Chundrigar Rd., Karachi; f. 1962; Man. R. Mueller.

Grindlays Bank p.l.c. (*U.K.*): P.O.B. 5556, I. I. Chundrigar Rd., Karachi 2; Gen. Man. L. M. W. Hendry; 14 brs.

Middle East Bank Ltd. (*United Arab Emirates*): Nadir House, I. I. Chundrigar Rd., Karachi; Gen. Man. Sultanali E. Merchant; 3 brs.

Rupali Bank (*Bangladesh*): I. I. Chundrigar Rd., Karachi; f. 1976; Asst. Gen. Man. D. H. Choudhury; Sub. Man. Ashafud Daullah.

Union Bank of the Middle East Ltd. (*United Arab Emirates*): Nadir House, I. I. Chundrigar Rd., Karachi; Gen. Man. Husain Lawai; 3 brs.

Co-operative Bank

Federal Bank for Co-operatives: P.O.B. 1218, Islamabad; f. 1976; owned jointly by the Federal Government, the Provincial Governments and the State Bank of Pakistan; provides credit facilities to each of four provincial co-operative banks and regulates their operations; supervises policy of provincial co-operative banks and of multi-unit co-operative societies; assists Federal and Provincial Governments in formulating schemes for development and revitalization of co-operative movement; carries out research on rural credit, etc.; cap. p.u. Rs. 200m., res. Rs. 81.5m.; Chair. A. G. N. Kazi.

Under legislation passed in 1976 all existing co-operative banks were dissolved and given the option of becoming a branch of the appropriate Provincial Co-operative Bank or of reverting to a credit society.

Development Finance Organizations

Agricultural Development Bank of Pakistan: Faisal Ave., P.O.B. 1400, Islamabad; f. 1961; provides credit facilities to agriculturists and cottage industrialists in the rural areas and for allied projects; cap. auth. Rs. 400m.; total loans p.u. Rs. 2,503m. (June 1980); Chair. A. Jamil Nishtar; Exec. Dir. Amjad Ali Qureshi; 18 regional offices and 172 field offices.

Bankers Equity Ltd.: State Life Bldg. No. 3, Dr. Ziauddin Ahmed Rd., Karachi; f. 1980 to centralize rupee and foreign currency investment in large- and medium-scale projects in the private sector; cap. p.u. Rs. 250m.; Man. Dir. D. M. Qureshi.

House Building Finance Corporation: Shaikh Sultan Trust Bldg., 10 Beaument Rd., Karachi; provides construction loans; Man. S. Azamali.

Industrial Development Bank of Pakistan: State Life Bldg., I. I. Chundrigar Rd., Karachi; f. 1961; provides credit facilities in Pakistani and foreign currencies for establishment of new industrial units and to meet needs of existing industrial enterprises; cap. p.u. Rs. 50m.; Man. Dir. S. Aftab Ahmad Zaidi (acting); 10 brs.

Investment Corporation of Pakistan: National Bank Bldg., I. I. Chundrigar Rd., P.O.B. 5410, Karachi 2; f. 1966 by the Government "to encourage and broaden the base of investments and to develop the capital market"; auth. cap. Rs. 200m., cap. p.u. Rs. 100m.; Chair. AKHTER HUSAIN; Man. Dir. M. W. FAROOQUI.

National Development Finance Corporation: N.S.C. Bldg., Tamizuddin Khan Rd., P.O.B. 5094, Karachi; f. 1973; sanctions loans for industrial development; shareholders equity Rs. 350m., dep. Rs. 1,327m; Chair. ZAFAR IQBAL; 10 brs.

National Investment (Unit) Trust: 6th Floor, National Bank of Pakistan Bldg., I. I. Chundrigar Rd., Karachi; f. 1962; mobilizes domestic savings to meet the requirements of growing economic development and enables investors to share in the industrial and economic prosperity of the country; total assets over Rs. 1,200m. (June 1981); 69,500 Unit holders; Man. Dir. N. H. JAFARY.

Pakistan Industrial Credit and Investment Corporation Limited (P.I.C.I.C.): State Life Bldg. 1, I. I. Chundrigar Rd., Karachi 2; f. 1957 as an industrial development bank to provide financial assistance for the establishment of new industries and balancing modernization of existing ones in the private sector; in 1979 approved the financing of 22 industrial projects, sanctioning loans equivalent to Rs. 350.5m. in foreign currencies; auth. cap. Rs. 150m.; cap. p.u. Rs. 91.63m.; public joint stock company with 65 per cent and 35 per cent shareholdings of local and foreign investors respectively; Chair. N. M. UQUAILI; Man. Dir. M. I. A. HANAFI; publ. *PICIC News* (quarterly); 5 brs.

BANKERS' ASSOCIATION

Pakistan Banks' Association: National Bank of Pakistan Bldg., P.O.B. 4937, I. I. Chundrigar Rd., Karachi 2; Chair. M. NAWAZ KHAN; Sec. Sheikh LAL JANI.

STOCK EXCHANGES

Karachi Stock Exchange Ltd.: Stock Exchange Bldg., Stock Exchange Rd., Karachi 2; f. 1947; 200 mems.; Pres. MOHAMMED BASHEER JAN MOHAMMED.

Lahore Stock Exchange Ltd.: 17 Bank Square, Lahore; f. 1970; 119 mems.; publs. daily quotation and analysis reports; Pres. MIAN TAJAMMAL HUSSAIN.

INSURANCE

Department of Insurance: Hajra Mansion, Zaibun-Nisa St., Saddar, Karachi; f. 1948; a government department attached to the Ministry of Commerce; regulates insurance business; Controller of Insurance A. M. KHALFE.

LIFE INSURANCE

In 1972 all life insurance companies and the life departments of composite companies were nationalized and merged into the State Life Insurance Corporation of Pakistan.

State Life Insurance Corporation of Pakistan: State Life Bldg. No. 2, P.O.B. 5725, I. I. Chundrigar Rd., Karachi 2; f. 1972; life and group insurance and occupational pension schemes; Chair. N. A. JAFAREY.

Postal Life Insurance Organization: Tibet Centre, M. A. Jinnah Rd., Karachi.

GENERAL INSURANCE

Adamjee Insurance Co. Ltd.: Adamjee House, 6th Floor, I. I. Chundrigar Rd., P.O.B. 4850, Karachi; f. 1960; Man. Dir. MOHAMMED CHOUDHURY.

Alpha Insurance Co. Ltd.: State Life Bldg. No. 1-B, State Life Sq., off I. I. Chundrigar Rd., Karachi 2; f. 1951; Man. Dir. V. C. GONSALVES.

Asia Insurance Co. Ltd.: Karachi; f. 1980; Man. Dir. ZAFAR IQTAL SHEIKH.

Central Insurance Co. Ltd.: Dawood Centre, P.O.B. 3988, Karachi 4; Chair. N. M. UQUAILI; Man. Dirs. and Gen. Mans. KHURSHID MINHAS, S. JAWAD GILLANI.

Co-operative Insurance Society of Pakistan Ltd.: Co-operative Insurance Bldg., P.O.B. 147, Shahrah-i-Quaid-e-Azam, Lahore; Gen. Man. MAZHAR ALI KHAN.

Crescent Star Insurance Co. Ltd.: Nadir House, I. I. Chundrigar Rd., P.O.B. 4616, Karachi; Gen. Man. MUNIR AHMAD.

Eastern Federal Union Insurance Co. Ltd.: Qamar House, M. A. Jinnah Rd., P.O.B. 5005, Karachi 2; f. 1932; Pres. SULTAN AHMAD; Chair. ROSHEN ALI BHIMJEE; Man. Dir. NAWAB HASAN.

Eastern General Insurance Co. Ltd.: Nadir House, I. I. Chundrigar Rd., Karachi; Chair. and Dir. HUSSAIN AFTAB.

Habib Insurance Co. Ltd.: P.O.B. 5217, Insurance House, No. 1 Habib Sq., M. A. Jinnah Rd., Karachi; f. 1942; Chair. YUSUF A. HABIB; Chief Gen. Man. M. H. MAHOMED; Gen. Man. R. N. DUBASH.

International General Insurance Co. of Pakistan Ltd.: Finlay House, 1st Floor, I. I. Chundrigar Rd., Karachi 2; f. 1953; Gen. Man. and Sec. YUSUF J. HASWARY.

Khyber Insurance Co. Ltd.: 719-726 Muhammadi House, I. I. Chundrigar Rd., Karachi; f. 1961; Dir. SUHAIL ZAHEER LARI; Man. HALIM AHMED FARUQUI.

Mercantile Fire and General Insurance Co. of Pakistan Ltd.: 17 Chartered Bank Chambers, I. I. Chundrigar Rd., Karachi 2; f. 1958; Man. Dir. FAKHRUDDIN A. LOTIA.

The Muslim Insurance Co. Ltd.: 3 Bank Sq., The Mall, Lahore; f. 1934; brs. throughout Pakistan; Chair. YUSUF H. SHIRAZI.

National Insurance Corporation: Shafi Court, Mereweather Rd., Karachi; Chair. N. A. QAZI.

National Security Insurance Co. Ltd.: 3rd Floor, Aiwan-e-Auqaf, P.O.B. 671, Lahore; f. 1963; Gen. Man. M. SARWAR SHEIKH.

New Jubilee Insurance Co. Ltd.: Jubilee Insurance House, I. I. Chundrigar Rd., P.O.B. 4795, Karachi; f. 1953; Pres. and Man. Dir. MASOOD NOORANI.

Pakistan General Insurance Co. Ltd.: P.O.B. 1364, Bank Sq., Shahrah-i-Quaid-e-Azam, Lahore; f. 1948; Gen. Man. ALAUDDIN HONY; Chair. AAMIR HAYAT KHAN (acting); Man. Dir. SHEIKH MOHAMMAD ASHRAF.

Pakistan Guarantee Insurance Co. Ltd.: Serai Rd., P.O.B. 5436, Karachi 2; Gen. Man. FAZAL REHMAN.

Pakistan Insurance Corporation: Pakistan Insurance Bldg., M. A. Jinnah Rd., P.O.B. 4777, Karachi 2; f. 1953; handles all classes of reinsurance except life; majority of shares held by the Government; Chair. M. YAKUB.

The Pakistan Mutual Insurance Co. Ltd.: 17/B Shah Alam Market, Lahore; f. 1946; Chair. Alhaj SIDDIQ UL HASSAN; Man. Dir. FATEH MUHAMMAD; Gen. Man. ALI AHMED KHAN.

Pioneer Insurance Co. Ltd.: 311–313 Qamar House, M. A. Jinnah Rd., P.O.B. 5117, Karachi 3; Man. Dir. ABID ZUBERI.

Premier Insurance Co. of Pakistan Ltd.: Wallace Rd., off I. I. Chundrigar Rd., P.O.B. 4140, Karachi 2; f. 1952; Chair. MOHAMMED BASHIR.

Raja Insurance Co. of Pakistan Ltd.: Panorama Centre, Saddar, Karachi 3; Chair. RAJA ABDUL RAHMAN.

Shalimar General Insurance Co. Ltd.: Nadir House, 3rd Floor, I. I. Chundrigar Rd., Karachi; Dir. MANZOOR HUSAIN.

Standard Insurance Co. Ltd.: 9th Floor, Muhammadi House, I. I. Chundrigar Rd., Karachi; Man. Dir. SHAMIM-UR-REHMAN.

Sterling Insurance Co. Ltd.: 26 The Mall, P.O.B. 119, Lahore; f. 1949; 250 mems.; Man. Dir. S. A. RAHIM.

Union Insurance Co. of Pakistan Ltd.: 9th Floor, Adamjee House, I. I. Chundrigar Rd., Karachi; Chair. MIAN MOHAMMED AYUB.

United Insurance Co. of Pakistan Ltd.: Valika Chambers, Altaf Husain Rd., Karachi 2; Chair. KAMRUDDIN VALIKA.

Universal Insurance Co. Ltd.: 63 The Mall, P.O.B. 539, Lahore; Chair. Lt.-Gen. (retd.) M. HABIBULLAH KHAN.

INSURANCE ASSOCIATIONS

Insurance Association of Pakistan: Jamshed Katrak Chambers, Machi Miani, P.O.B. 4932, Karachi 2; f. 1948; membership comprises 40 cos. (Pakistani and foreign) transacting general insurance business in Pakistan; issues tariffs and establishes rules for insurance in the country; brs. in Lahore; Chair. M. CHOUDHURY; Vice-Chair. SHARAFUL ISLAM KHAN; Sec. M. MAROOF.

Pakistan Insurance Institute: Shafi Court, 2nd Floor, Mereweather Rd., Karachi 4; f. 1951 to encourage insurance education; Sec. A. E. ISMAIL.

TRADE AND INDUSTRY

CHAMBERS OF COMMERCE

Federation of Pakistan Chambers of Commerce and Industry: St. 28, Block 5, Share Firdousi, Clifton, Karachi 6; f. 1950; 80 mems.; Pres. (vacant); Sec.-Gen. AZIZ Y. SIDDIQUI.

The Islamic Chamber of Commerce, Industry and Commodity Exchange: NBP Bldg., Kahkashan, Clifton Rd., Karachi; Pres. Sheikh ISMAIL ABU DAWOOD; Sec.-Gen. SAMI CANSEN ONARAN.

SELECTED AFFILIATED CHAMBERS

Chamber of Commerce and Industry, Karachi: Aiwan-e-Tijarat, P.O.B. 4158, Karachi 2; f. 1960; 5,621 mems.; Pres. HAJI RAZAK JANOO; Sec. M. NAZIR ALI.

Chamber of Commerce and Industry, Quetta: D-5/2(7) Ingle Rd., P.O.B. 117, Quetta; Pres. AGHA SYED SAID MOHAMMAD; Sec. UMAR HAYAT MALIK.

Faisalabad Chamber of Commerce and Industry: Muslim Commercial Bank Bldg., 5th Floor, Circular Rd., Faisalabad; Pres. SYED NAZAR HUSAIN SHAH; Sec. M. M. SIDDIQI.

Gujranwala Chamber of Commerce and Industry: 499-B Satellite Town, Gujranwala; Pres. MAULVI MUHAMMAD ANWAR; Sec. RAJA ASMAT ULLAH.

Hyderabad Chamber of Commerce and Industry: 526 Shahrah-i-Quaid-e-Azam, P.O.B. 99, Cantonment, Hyderabad; Pres. MOHAMMAD AMIN KHATRI; Sec. A. U. MALIK.

Lahore Chamber of Commerce and Industry: P.O.B. 597, 11 Race Course Rd., Lahore; f. 1923; 5,000 mems.; Pres. ABDUL QAYYUM BHATTY; Sec. IKRAM H. SYED.

Mirpur Azad Jammu and Kashmir Chamber of Commerce and Industry: P.O.B. 12, Mirpur, A.k.; Pres. Brig. (retd.) M. DILAWAR KHAN.

Multan Chamber of Commerce and Industry: P.O.B. 90, Kutchery Rd., Multan; Pres. Mian Mughis A. SHAIKH; Sec. G. A. BHATTI.

Rawalpindi Chamber of Commerce and Industry: Chamber House, 108 Adamjee Rd., Rawalpindi; Pres. PERVEZ ASLAM; Sec. MUSHTAQ AHMAD.

Sarhad Chamber of Commerce and Industry: Sarhad Chamber House, Panj Tirath, G.T. Rd., Peshawar; f. 1958; 800 mems., including five Trade Groups and two Town Associations; Pres. NOOT MOHD; Sec. S. MOHAMMAD NAWAZ KHAN.

Sukkur Chamber of Commerce and Industry: New Cloth Market, Sukkur; Pres. MUNAWWAR KHAN; Sec. MIRZA IQBAL BEG.

GOVERNMENT-SPONSORED ORGANIZATIONS

Baluchistan Development Authority: Civil Secretariat, Block 7, Quetta; created for economic and industrial development of Baluchistan; exploration and exploitation of mineral resources; establishment of industries, development of fish harbours, water resources, etc.; Chair. ABU SHAHMIM M. ARIFF.

Cotton Board: Dr. Abbasi Clinic Bldg., 76 Strachan Rd., Karachi 1; f. 1950; Chair. HAMID D. HABIB; Deputy Sec. MUKHTAR AHMED KHAN.

Cotton Export Corporation of Pakistan Ltd.: State Life Bldg. No. 3, Dr. Ziauddin Ahmed Rd., P.O.B. 3738, Karachi; f. 1973; handles raw cotton exports exclusively in the public sector; Chair. NUSRAT HASAN.

Export Promotion Bureau: Press Trust Bldg., I. I. Chundrigar Rd., Karachi; Chair. HAMID D. HABIB.

Federal Chemical and Ceramics Corporation Ltd.: 15th Floor, N.S.C. Bldg., Karachi; Chair. Dr. M. H. CHAUDHRY.

Ghee Corporation of Pakistan Ltd.: 5 Bank Sq., Lahore; Chair. HYDER ALI SHORO.

Karachi Electricity Supply Corporation: Abdullah Haroon Rd., Karachi; Chair. M. D. PARVEZ AHMAD BUTT.

Mechanized Construction of Pakistan Ltd.: 39 Main Gulberg, Lahore; operating infrastructure projects worth U.S. $307 million (1980), including the Simly Dam and tunnel, Indus River training works, projects in Iraq, also land reclamation and irrigation projects.

National Design & Industrial Services Corporation: Hotel Ambassador Bldg., 7 Davis Rd., Lahore; Chair. RIYAZ H. BOKHARI.

National Economic Board: f. 1979 by the President as an advisory body to review and evaluate the state of the economy and to make proposals, especially to further the adoption of the socio-economic principles of Islam; Chair. Pres. ZIA UL-HAQ; Vice-Chair. GHULAM ISHAQ KHAN.

National Economic Council: supreme economic body with the President as Chairman; the Governors and Chief Ministers of the four Provinces and Federal Ministers in charge of economic Ministries are its members; senior Federal and Provincial officials in the economic field are also associated.

National Fertilizer Corporation of Pakistan Ltd.: Alfalah, Shahrah-i-Quaid-e-Azam, P.O.B. 1730, Lahore; Chair. RIYAZ H. BOKHARI.

National Power Construction Corporation Ltd.: 46 Main Gulberg, Lahore; Man. Dir. M. AJAZ MALIK; Man. (contracts and planning) TAUQIR A. SHARIFI.

Oil and Gas Development Corporation: 4th Floor, Shafi Chambers, Club Rd., Karachi 4; f. 1961; Chair. SYED MAHMUDEL HASAN RIZVI; Admin. Dir. S. M. A. SUBZWARI.

Overseas Employment Corporation: P.O.B. 861, Red Crescent Bldg., Dawood Pota Rd., Karachi.

Pakistan Automobile Corporation (PACO): 6th Floor, N.S.C. Bldg.; f. 1972; Chair. Maj.-Gen. (retd.) MOHAMMAD JALALUDDIN.

Pakistan Industrial Development Corporation (PIDC): P.I.D.C. House, Dr. Ziauddin Ahmad Rd., Karachi; f. 1962 by Act of Parliament; semi-autonomous; manufacturers of woollen and cotton textiles, carpets, sugar; gas distributors; Chair. M. A. G. M. AKHTAR.

Pakistan Industrial Technical Assistance Centre (PITAC): Maulana Jalal-ud-Din Roomi Rd., Lahore 16; f. 1962 by the Government to provide technical assistance to industry by the production of tools, moulds, jigs, dies and fixtures; also provides training in the metal trades, foundry practice and design protective coating techniques; Chair. IMTIAZ AHMAD CHAUDHRY; Gen. Man. Brig. M. A. FARUQI.

Pakistan Mineral Development Corporation: P.I.D.C. House, Dr. Ziauddin Ahmed Rd., Karachi 4; Man. A. A. MALIK.

Pakistan Steel Mills Corporation Ltd.: P.O.B. 5429, Pipri, Karachi; f. 1968 to implement all activity connected with iron and steel manufacturing; responsible for steel mill project at Bin Qasim near Karachi with an initial annual capacity of 1.1 million tons, which started partial production in 1981 and is expected to achieve full production by 1984; Chair. HAQ NAWAZ AKHTER.

Pakistan Water and Power Development Authority: WAPDA House, Shahrah-i-Quaid-e-Azam, Lahore; f. 1958; for development of irrigation, water supply and drainage, building of replacement works under the World Bank sponsored Indo-Pakistan Indus Basin Treaty; flood-control and watershed management; reclamation of waterlogged and saline lands; inland navigation; generation of hydroelectric and thermal power and its transmission and distribution; Chair. Maj.-Gen. GHULAM SAFDAR BUTT; publs. *Indus* (English, monthly), *Barqab* (Urdu, monthly), *WAPDA News* (fortnightly), *Annual Report* (English).

Punjab Seed Corporation: 4 Lytton Row, Lahore.

Rice Export Corporation of Pakistan: State Life Bldg., No. 1 (3rd Floor), I. I. Chundrigar Rd., Karachi; f. 1974; procures, mills, cleans, stores, packs and sells rice for export on monopoly basis and implements government policy on ensuring maximum exports of standard quality rice; Chair. RIAZ AHMAD NAIK.

Sind Sugar Corporation Ltd.: 6th Floor, Shaikh Sultan Trust Bldg., Beaumont Rd., Karachi 3.

State Cement Corporation of Pakistan Ltd.: P.E.C. Bldg., 97-A/B-D Gulberg III, Lahore; Chair. ASLAM IQBAL.

State Engineering Corporation Ltd.: 10th Floor, P.N.S.C. Bldg., Karachi 2; f. 1979; Chair. JAWAID AHMAD MIRZA.

State Petroleum, Refining and Petro-Chemical Corporation: 4th Floor, Karim Chambers, Merewether Rd., Karachi; Chair. MOHAMMAD SALIM.

Textile Machinery Corporation of Pakistan Ltd.: 5th Floor, P.I.D.C. House, Karachi.

Trading Corporation of Pakistan: Press Trust House, I. I. Chundrigar Rd., Karachi; f. 1967; sole importer of country's total requirements in bulk ferrous and non-ferrous metals, coal, coke, quicksilver, edible oil and sugar from world-wide sources, and for guaranteed quality exports of miscellaneous commodities; Chair. AFTAB AHMAD.

EMPLOYERS' AND TRADE ASSOCIATIONS

All-Pakistan Textile Mills Association: Muhammadi House, 3rd Floor, I. I Chundrigar Rd., P.O.B. 5446, Karachi 2; Chair. AFTAB AHMED; Sec. S. M. USMAN.

Karachi Cotton Association: The Cotton Exchange, I. I. Chundrigar Rd., Karachi; Chair. TAHIR SHAFIQUE; Sec. N. A. SYED.

Pakistan Automobile Spare Parts Importers' and Dealers' Association: 8 Masjid Al-Sattar, M. A. Jinnah Rd., Karachi; Chair. S. M. IDREES.

Pakistan Carpet Manufacturers' and Exporters' Association: PIIA Bldg., 2nd Floor, Strachan Rd., Karachi; Chair. KHAWAJA ZUBAIR AHMAD; Sec. S. N. AHMAD SHAH GILANI.

Pakistan Cotton Ginners' Association: Bungalow 159, Block 'C', Unit 2, Shah Latifabad, Hyderabad; Chair. MUNAWWAR KHAN; Sec. SYED ABBAS HUSSAIN.

Pakistan Film Producers' Association: Regal Cinema Bldg., Shahrah-i-Quaid-e-Azam, Lahore; Chair. A. MAJEED; Sec. MUSHTAQ AHMAD (acting).

Pakistan Hardware Merchants' Association: Mandviwala Bldg., Serai Rd., Karachi; Chair. MOHAMMED ARSHAD; Sec. M. A. SIDDIQUE.

Pakistan Iron and Steel Merchants' Association: 2nd Floor Writers' Chambers, Dunolly Rd., Karachi; Pres. MALIK AHMAD; Gen. Sec. S. Z. ISLAM.

Pakistan Paint Manufacturers' Association: ST/6-A, Block 14, Federal 'B' Area, Karachi 38; f. 1953; Chair. ABDULLAH ISMAIL; Sec. S. ABDUR RAHMAN.

Pakistan Shipowners' Association: c/o Pakistan National Shipping Corporation, P.N.S.C. Bldg., Moulvi Tamizuddin Khan Rd., Karachi; Chair. (vacant); Sec. D. J. PATEL.

Pakistan Silk and Rayon Mills' Association: 10 Bank House, No. 3 Habib Sq., M. A. Jinnah Rd., Karachi 2; f. 1974; Chair. JAMIL MEHBOOB; Sec. M. H. K. BURNEY.

Pakistan Steel Re-rolling Mills' Association: Rashid Chambers, 6-Link McLeod Rd., Lahore; Chair. Mr. SHAHNAWAZ; Sec. Lt.-Col. (retd.) S. H. A. BOKHARI.

Pakistan Sugar Mills' Association: 329 Alfalah Bldg., Shahrah-i-Quaid-e-Azam, Lahore; Chair. TAJ MUHAMMAD KHANZADA; Sec.Gen. C. H. M. SHAFFI GILL.

Pakistan Vanaspati Manufacturers' Association: 404 Muhammadi House, I. I. Chundrigar Rd., Karachi.

Pakistan Wool and Hair Merchants' Association: 27 Idris Chambers, Talpur Rd., Karachi; Pres. MIAN MOHAMMAD SIDDIQ KHAN; Sec. KHALID LATEEF.

Employers' Federation of Pakistan: 2nd Floor, State Life Bldg., No. 2, off Wallace Rd., off I. I. Chundrigar Rd., Karachi 2; P.O.B. 4338; Pres. Rear-Adm. M. I. ARSHAD; Sec. MOHAMMED MUSTAFA SHARIF.

TRADE UNIONS

Pakistan National Federation of Trade Unions: 406 Qamar House, M.A. Jinnah Rd., Karachi; f. 1962; 270 unions with total of 130,000 mems.; Pres. MOHAMED SHARIF; Sec.-Gen. RASHID MOHAMMAD; Publ. *PNFTU News*.

The principal affiliated federations are:

All Pakistan Federation of Labour: Hotel Peshawar, Karachi; about 50 affiliates; Pres. RAHMATULLAH KHAN DURRANI; Gen. Sec. RAHMATULLAH CHAUDHRY.

All Pakistan Federation of Trade Unions: 28 Nisbat Rd., Lahore; *c.* 150,000 mems.; Pres. BASHIR BAKHTIAR; Gen. Sec. KHURSHID AHMED.

National Labour Federation: Pak Colony, nr. Bara Board, Karachi.

Pakistan Central Federation of Trade Unions: 220 Alnoor Chambers, M. A. JINNAH Rd., Karachi.

Pakistan Railway Employees' Union (PREM): Karachi; Sec. ABDUL JABBAR QURESHI.

Pakistan Trade Union Federation: Khamosh Colony, Karachi; Pres. Mrs. KANIZ FATIMA; Gen. Sec. SALEEM RAZA.

Pakistan Transport Workers' Federation: 110 McLeod Rd., Lahore; 17 unions; 92,512 mems.; Pres. MEHBOOB-UL-HAQ; Gen. Sec. CH. UMAR DIN.

United Workers' Federation: Labour Welfare Centre, Shershah, Karachi; *c.* 150,000 mems.; Pres. NAYAB H. NAQVI; Gen. Sec. NABI AHMED.

MAJOR INDUSTRIAL COMPANIES

The following is a selection of the major industrial companies in Pakistan:

AUTOMOBILES

Awami Autos Ltd.: West Wharf, Karachi.

National Motors Ltd.: Hub Chauki Rd., S.I.T.E., P.O.B. 2706, Karachi 28; state enterprise; manufactures trucks, assembles buses and land cruisers.

Naya Daur Motors Ltd.: State Life Bldg. No. 3, Dr. Ziauddin Ahmed Rd., Karachi 4.

Republic Motors Ltd.: D-2, S.I.T.E., Karachi.

CEMENT

Associated Cement: 3rd Floor, WAPDA House, Lahore.

Javedan Cement Ltd.: 2nd Floor, Al-Haroon, Garden Rd., Karachi.

Maple Leaf Cement Factory Ltd.: 2nd Floor, Haroon House, Dr. Ziauddin Ahmed Rd., Karachi 4.

White Cement Industries Ltd.: 2nd Floor, Haroon House, Dr. Ziauddin Ahmed Rd., Karachi 4.

Zeal Pak Cement Factory Ltd.: Haroon House, Dr. Ziauddin Ahmed Rd., Karachi 4.

CHEMICALS

Antibiotics (Private) Ltd.: Iskandarabad (Daudkhel), Dist. Mianwali.

DDT Factory: Amangarh, Nowshera.

ICI (Pakistan) Manufacturers Ltd.: 5 West Wharf, P.O.B. 4731, Karachi 2.

Ittehad Chemicals: G. T. Rd., Kala Shah Kaku.

Ittehad Pesticides: Kala Shah Kaku, Sheikhupura, P.O.B. 886, Lahore.

Kurram Chemical Company Ltd.: Sihala Rd., P.O.B. 40, Rawalpindi; f. 1951; manufacturing chemists; Chair. Dr. M. H. CHAUDHRY, Sen. Man. M. SHAMSUL HAQ KHAN.

M & B Pakistan Ltd.: G. T. Rd., Wah Cantt; f. 1977; cap. Rs. 9.7m.; Chair. Dr. M. H. CHOUDHURY; Man. Dir. I. A. KHAN.

Pak Chemicals Ltd.: Hakimsons Bldg., West Wharf Rd., P.O.B. 4739, Karachi 2; f. 1950.

Pak Dyes and Chemicals Ltd.: Iskandarabad (Daudkhel) Dist. Mianwali.

Pakistan PVC Ltd.: 4th Floor, Al-Haroon, Garden Rd., Karachi.

Ravi Rayon Ltd.: P.O.B. 830, Lahore; factory G. T. Rd., Kala Shah Kaku, District Sheikhupura.

Sind Alkalis Ltd.: State Life Bldg. No. 1-A, I. I. Chundrigar Rd., Karachi.

ENGINEERING

Bela Engineers Ltd.: 207/H Block 11, P.E.C.H.S., Off Tariq Rd., P.O.B. 2038, Karachi; manufacturers of multi-purpose Bela diesel engines.

Heavy Mechanical Complex: Taxila; f. 1971; production of sugar, chemical and cement plants, boilers, road-rollers, steel structures, etc.

Lahore Engineering and Foundry Ltd.: Hotel Ambassador Bldg., Davis Rd., Lahore.

Northern Foundry and Engineering Works Ltd.: P.O.B. 1104, Kot Lakhpat, Lahore.

Nowshera Engineering Company Ltd.: P. O. Ferozsons Laboratory, Amangarh, Nowshera, Peshawar; f. 1959; Principal Officer SYED PHOOL BADSHAH.

Pakistan Engineering Co. Ltd.: 6 Ganga Ram Trust Bldg., Shahrah-i-Quaid-e-Azam, Lahore; nationalized and renamed 1972; lathes, machine tools, diesel engines, centrifugal pumps (irrigation), deep well turbines, automatic power looms, concrete mixers, rolled material, electric motors, iron and steel castings, steel structures.

Sind Engineering Ltd.: West Wharf, Karachi.

FERTILIZERS

Dawood Hercules Chemicals Ltd.: Box 1294, 35-A Empress Rd., Lahore; Man. Dir. M. HUSSAIN DAWOOD.

Esso (Pakistan) Fertilizer Company Ltd.: Daharki, District Sukkur; Manufacturing Man. I. A. SHAH.

Lyallpur Chemical & Fertilizers (Lyallpur) Ltd.: Lahore Rd., Faisalabad; also in Jaranwala.

Natural Gas Fertilizer Factory: Khanewal Rd., Multan.

Pak-American Fertilizers Ltd.: Iskandarabad, Mianwali Dist.

Pak Arab Fertilizers Ltd.: Multan.

Paksaudi Fertilizers Ltd.: Mirpur Mathelo, Sukkur Dist., Lahore.

GAS

Indus Gas Company: Hyderabad.

Karachi Gas Company Ltd.: Premier Insurance Bldg., Wallace Rd., Karachi.

Sui Gas Transmission Company Ltd.: State Life Bldg. 3, Dr. Ziauddin Ahmed Rd., P.O.B. 540, Karachi 4; natural gas purification and transmission; design, engineering and construction of high-pressure pipelines, compression facilities, gas purification and dehydration plants, cathodic protection systems and telecommunication facilities.

Oil and Petroleum

Attock Refinery Ltd.: Rawalpindi; petroleum refining; operates the country's largest producing field at Meyal; Chief Exec. Usman Aminuddin.

National Refinery Ltd.: 7B Korangi Industrial Area, Korangi, P.O.B. 3964, Karachi 31; capacity of 48,500 BSD; products: naphtha, Kerosene, diesel oil, JP-1, JP-4, motor gasoline, high octane blending component, fuel oil, L.P.G., lubricating oil base stocks, jute batching oil, process oil, asphalt, benzene, toluene, xylene.

Pakistan Oilfields Ltd. (POL): Refinery P.O., Rawalpindi; exploration, drilling and production firm of Attock Oil Co.; Attock owns 53.7 per cent, the Government 34.7 per cent, the International Finance Corpn. 6.2 per cent and the public 5.3 per cent; Chair. Afzal Khan.

Pakistan Petroleum Ltd.: 4th Floor, P.I.D.C. House, Dr. Ziauddin Ahmed Rd., Karachi; oil and gas exploration and production; 29 per cent government-owned.

Pakistan Refinery Ltd.: Korangi, Karachi.

Pakistan State Oil Company Ltd.: Dawood Centre, Moulvi Tamizuddin Khan Rd., Karachi; incorporated 1976; prospect, manufacture, import, export, storage, distribution, marketing, refining and blending of all kinds of petroleum, petroleum products and chemicals; Man. Dir. Saeed Ibrahim.

Textiles

Adamjee Industries Ltd.: Adamjee House, I. I. Chundrigar Rd., Karachi; cotton textiles, fashion fabrics, cotton yarn and thread.

Ahmed Abdul Gani Textile Mills: A/46, S.I.T.E., Manghopir Rd., Karachi.

Allawasaya Textile & Finishing Mills Ltd.: P.O.B. 42, Mumtazabad Industrial Area, Vehari Rd., Multan.

Bawany Industries Ltd.: 2nd Floor, Hakimsons Bldg., 19 West Wharf Rd., P.O.B. 6060, Karachi 2.

Burewala Textile Mills Ltd.: 403-405, Alfalah Building, Shahrah-i- Quaid-e-Azam, Lahore.

Cofcot Textiles Ltd.: Variawa Bldg., I. I. Chundrigar Rd., Karachi.

Dawood Cotton Mills Ltd.: Dawood Centre, Dr. Ziauddin Ahmed Rd., Karachi 4.

Jubilee Spinning & Weaving Mills Ltd.: 3rd Floor, Finlay House, P.O.B. 5674, I. I. Chundrigar Rd., Karachi.

Kohinoor Textile Mills Ltd.: Peshawar Rd., Rawalpindi; mills in Faisalabad and Mianwali.

Lyallpur Cotton Mills: Factory Area, Samundri Rd., P.O.B. 17, Faisalabad.

Usman Textile Mills Ltd.: 8th Floor, Adamjee House, I. I. Chundrigar Rd., Karachi.

TRANSPORT

RAILWAYS

Department of Railways: Islamabad; f. 1974 to ensure proper functioning of the Pakistan Railways; Sec. H. Zaheer.

Pakistan Railways: Lahore; state-owned; 12,607 km. of track in 1981; six divisions (Karachi, Lahore, Multan, Quetta, Rawalpindi and Sukkur); Chair. M. Siddiq.

ROADS

The total length of main roads in June 1980 was 38,385 km., while secondary roads totalled 62,049 km. In 1978 the 800-km. Karakoram highway was opened, linking Xinjiang province in the People's Republic of China with Havelian, north of Islamabad, after being under construction for 20 years. In 1980 the 106-km. Karachi–Ormara coastal highway was completed at a cost of Rs. 5 million.

Government assistance comes from the Road Fund, financed from a share of the excise and customs duty on sales of petrol and from development loans.

Karachi Transport Corporation: 3 Modern Housing Society, Dright Rd., Karachi 8; Man. Dir. Brig. (retd.) S.S.A. Qasim.

Punjab Road Transport Board: Transport House, 11-A Egerton Rd., Lahore.

Punjab Urban Transport Corporation: 37-E-3 (1st Floor) Liberty Market, Gulberg III, Lahore; Man. Dir. Brig. Naeem Khawaja.

Sind Urban Transport Corporation: 3-Modern Housing Society, Dright Rd., Karachi 8; Man. Dir. Brig. (retd.) Qasim.

SHIPPING

The chief port is Karachi. A second port, Port Mohammad bin Qasim, started partial operation in July 1980. In 1974 the Government took control of maritime shipping companies.

National Tanker Company Ltd.: f. 1981 with the joint participation of the Pakistan National Shipping Corpn., the State Petroleum Refinery and the Petrochemical Corpn. Ltd.; auth. cap. Rs. 100m.; aims to make Pakistan self-reliant in the transport of crude oil and petroleum products; Chair. Rear-Adm. Abdul Waheed Bhombal.

Pakistan National Shipping Corporation: Head Office: P.N.S.C. Bldg., Moulvi Tamizuddin Khan Rd., Karachi 2; f. 1979 by the merger of the National Shipping Corporation of Pakistan and the Pakistan Shipping Corporation; Chair. Rear-Adm. Abdul Waheed Bhombal; Sec. Rafiq A. Zuberi; 45 vessels; 608,593 d.w.t. (1981).

CIVIL AVIATION

The Department of Civil Aviation comes under the Ministry of Defence; Dir.-Gen. N. H. Hanafi.

Karachi, Lahore and Rawalpindi have international airports.

Pakistan International Airlines Corpn. (PIA): PIA Bldg., Karachi Airport; f. 1955; operates domestic services and international services to Afghanistan (suspended October 1981), Bahrain, Bangladesh, the People's Republic of China, Egypt, India, Iran, Iraq, Japan, Jordan, Kenya, Kuwait, Libya, Malaysia, Nigeria, Oman, the Philippines, Qatar, Saudi Arabia, Singapore, Somalia, Sri Lanka, Syria, Tanzania, Thailand, the United Arab Emirates, the U.S.A., Zimbabwe and Europe; cargo service to Switzerland and Hong Kong; fleet of 4 Boeing 747, 3 DC-10-30, 3 Boeing 720B, 6 Boeing 707, 9 Fokker F-27, on order: 1 Airbus A-300; Chair. Maj.-Gen. (retd.) M. Rahim Khan; Man. Dir. and Chief Exec. M. M. Salim.

Foreign Airlines

The following foreign airlines serve Pakistan: Aeroflot (U.S.S.R.), Air France, Air India, Air Lanka, Alia (Jordan), Biman (Bangladesh), British Airways, CAAC; EgyptAir, Garuda (Indonesia), Gulf Aviation Ltd. (Bahrain), Indian Airlines, Inter Flug; Iranian Airways, Iraqi Airways, Japan Airline, KLM (Netherlands), Kenya Airlines, Kuwait Air; Libyan Airlines, Lufthansa (Federal Republic of Germany), Pan Am (U.S.A.), Romanion Air Transport; Saudia, Swissair, Syrian Arab Airlines, Thai Airways International, Turkish Airlines.

TOURISM AND CULTURE

Pakistan Tourism Development Corpn.: 177A Sarwar Rd., Rawalpindi; f. 1970; Chair. Begum VIQARUNNISA NOON; Man. Dir. AFTAB AHMED KHAN; publ. *Focus on Pakistan* (2 a year).

CULTURAL ORGANIZATIONS

Karachi Arts Council: R. Kayani Rd., Karachi; Exec. Dir. IRFAN HUSAIN.

National Institute of Folk and Traditional Heritage: P.O.B. 1184, Islamabad; Dir.-Gen. KHALID SAEED.

National Institute of Sports and Culture: Kashmir Highway, Islamabad.

Pakistan National Council of Arts: 73-F6/2, Islamabad.

ATOMIC ENERGY

Pakistan Atomic Energy Commission: P.O.B. 1114, Islamabad; responsible for (i) harnessing nuclear energy for economic development and development of nuclear technology as part of the nuclear power programme; KANUPP and power station planned at Kundian; (ii) establishing research centres; PINSTECH; (iii) promoting peaceful use of atomic energy in agriculture, medicine, industry and hydrology; (iv) search for indigenous nuclear mineral deposits; (v) training engineers, scientists, technicians for manning projects; Chair. Dr. MUNIR AHMAD KHAN; publs. *Nucleus* (quarterly), *PakAtom* (monthly).

Pakistan Institute of Nuclear Science and Technology (PINSTECH): Nilore, Rawalpindi; f. 1961; centre for nuclear studies and research; controlled by the Pakistan Atomic Energy Commission; equipped with 5 MW. swimming-pool-type reactor (critical 1966); Dir. Dr. NAEEM AHMAD KHAN.

There also exist several institutes for nuclear research in the fields of agriculture, food stuffs and medicine.

DEFENCE

Armed Forces: (July 1981) Total strength 450,600; army 408,000, navy 13,000, air force 17,600. There is also a para-military force of 109,100 men. Military service is voluntary.

Defence Budget: The defence budget for 1982/83 is U.S. $1,900 million (47 per cent of total budget).

CHIEFS OF STAFF

Commander-in-Chief of the Armed Forces: Gen. MOHAMMAD ZIA UL-HAQ.

Chief of Air Staff: Air Chief Marshal MOHAMMAD ANWAR SHAMIM.

Chief of Naval Staff: Admiral KARAMAT RAHMAN NIAZI.

EDUCATION

At independence in 1947 Pakistan retained the education system which had been designed by the colonial British Government in India. Efforts to introduce educational reforms and to expand educational facilities were hampered by lack of finances. However, in 1972 the Pakistan Government formulated a new Education Policy which envisaged the enforcement of elementary education and an adult literacy programme, and emphasized the study of Islamiat —the ideological basis for the existence of Pakistan—and the introduction of an agro-technical bias in school education. All institutions except missions were nationalized and most colleges and universities became co-educational, although there do exist coeglles that admit females only.

The total development and non-development expenditure on education amounted to Rs. 3,582.6 million in 1979/80, Rs. 1,007.52 million in 1980/81 and an estimated Rs. 1,409.1 million for 1981/82 (7 per cent of the G.N.P.).

Curriculum

The Education Policy envisaged that the study of Islamiat (study of Islam) should be "woven into the entire warp and woof of our educational fabric". The National Bureau of Curriculum, set up in 1972, prepared a ten-year course in Islamiat, which includes study of the Koran, the life of Muhammad and the general code for a Muslim. Children of the Sunni and the Shia sects follow the same course for the first eight years. In classes nine and ten they are divided to study separately the rituals of the two sects. Islamiat and Deeniat (theology) are compulsory subjects throughout the ten years.

Agro-technical subjects are introduced in the seventh and eighth years of schooling.

Primary Education

Universal and free primary education is a constitutional right. The Education Policy's original aim of providing free primary education to all boys by 1980 has been revised to 1983 for boys and 1987 for girls. In 1981/82 there were an estimated 62,580 primary schools, and 147,000 teachers and enrolment at primary stage increased to 6,590,000. In 1981/82 1145 Mosque and 834 Mohalla schools were opened. With the assistance of the World Bank, a Primary Education Project has been launched to increase educational facilities and improve the quality of instruction.

Secondary Education

There were an estimated 6,100 middle schools and 3,567 high schools in 1981/82. Enrolment in 1981/82 was estimated at 1.5 million in middle schools and 575,000 in high schools.

Higher Education

In 1981 there were 440 arts and science colleges and 100 professional colleges. Enrolment increased to 243,000 in arts and science colleges and 77,662 in professional colleges. Five new universities are planned, in addition to the 15 already existing. There were 57,000 enrolments in 1981/82. The Open University has been set up with the technical support of the British Open University.

Technical Education

With the assistance of the Asian Development Bank, 11 polytechnic institutes and a national teacher-training college are being established by the Federal Government. Training is to be provided for teachers at polytechnic, commercial and vocational institutes.

Female Education

According to the 1972 census, the female population had a literacy rate of 11.6 per cent: 41.5 per cent in urban areas and 14.3 per cent in rural areas. There were 13,744 educational institutes exclusively for women in 1970/71 (27.4 per cent of the total). This number is expected to increase to 28.8 per cent of the total. Co-education exists in a number of primary schools, professional colleges and universities.

Third Education Project

To develop education in professional fields, Pakistan launched two joint ventures with the help of the World Bank in 1964 and 1970 for improving facilities and expertise at the Agricultural University, Faisalabad and Dawood Engineering College, Karachi. The Third Education Project was launched in 1977 with the assistance of the International Development Association for the extension and reconstruction of various agricultural institutions. Several teachers have been sent abroad for higher training. Under this project, an adult functional literacy programme is to be set up, providing television coverage for educational institutions.

RELATED TERRITORIES

The status of Jammu and Kashmir has remained unresolved since the 1949 cease-fire, whereby the area was divided into sectors administered by India and Pakistan separately. Pakistan administers Azad (Free) Kashmir and the Northern Areas as *de facto* dependencies, being responsible for foreign affairs, defence, coinage, currency and the implementation of UN resolutions concerning Kashmir.

AZAD KASHMIR

Area: 11,639 sq. km. (4,494 sq. miles).

Population: 1,980,000 (1981 census).

Administration: Government is based on the Azad Jammu and Kashmir Interim Constitution Act of 1974. There are four administrative districts: Kotli, Mirpur, Muzaffarabad and Poonch.

Legislative Assembly: consists of 42 members: 40 directly elected and two women nominated by the other members.

Azad Jammu and Kashmir Council: consists of the President of Pakistan as Chairman, the President of Azad Kashmir as Vice-Chairman, five members nominated by the President of Pakistan, six members by the Legislative Assembly, and the Pakistan Minister of Kashmir affairs and Northern affairs (*ex officio*): Brig. MUHAMMAD HAYAT KHAN.

NORTHERN AREAS

Area: 72,520 sq. km. (28,000 sq. miles).

Population: 562,000 (1981 census).

Administration: There are three administrative districts: Baltistan, Diamir and Gilgit. The Northern Areas Council consists of 16 elected members, headed by a Commissioner who is appointed by the Pakistan Government.

BIBLIOGRAPHY

GENERAL

AHMAD, AZIZ. Studies in Islamic Culture in the Indian Environment (Oxford University Press, Karachi, 1970).

AHMAD, KAZI S. A. Geography of Pakistan (Oxford University Press, London, 1972).

AZIZ, K. K. The Making of Pakistan (National Book Foundation, Karachi, 1976).

BOLITHO, HECTOR. Jinnah: Creator of Pakistan (John Murray, London, 1954).

CHEEMA, PERVAIZ. A Select Bibliography of Periodical Literature on India and Pakistan 1947–70 (National Commission on Historical and Cultural Research, Islamabad, 1976).

GUSTAFSAN, ERIC (ed.). Pakistan and Bangladesh: Bibliographic Essays in Social Science (University of Islamabad Press, Islamabad, 1976).

JAIN, NARESH KUMAR. Muslims in India: A Biographical Dictionary; Vol. I (A–J) (Manohar, New Delhi, 1979).

JALAL, HAMID, et al (eds.). Pakistan Past and Present (Stacey International, London, 1977).

JOHNSON, B. L. C. Pakistan (Heinemann, London, 1979).

KHURSHID, ANIS. Quaid-i-Azam Mohammad Ali Jinnah: An Annotated Bibliography; Vol. I, Western Languages; Vol. II, Eastern Languages (Quaid-i-Azam Academy, Karachi, 1978–79).

KORSON, J. HENRY. Contemporary Problems of Pakistan (Brill, Leiden, 1974).

MAHAR, J. M. India and Pakistan, a Critical Bibliography (University of Arizona Press, Tucson, Ariz., 1964).

MALIK, HAFEEZ (ed.). Iqbal: Poet-Philosopher of Pakistan (Columbia University Press, New York, 1975).

Muslim Nationalism in India and Pakistan (Public Affairs Press, Washington D.C., 1964).

MOHAMMAD ALI, CHAUDHRI. The Emergence of Pakistan (Columbia University Press, New York, 1967).

MUJAHID, SHARIF AL (ed.). Ideological Orientation of Pakistan (National Book Foundation, Karachi, 1976).

Quaid-i-Azam Jinnah: Studies in Interpretation (Quaid-i-Azam Academy, Karachi, 1980).

NAIM, C. M. (ed.) Iqbal, Jinnah and Pakistan: The Vision and the Reality (Maxwell Graduate School of Citizenship and Public Affairs, Syracuse, N.Y., 1979).

QURESHI, ISHTIAQ HUSAIN. The Muslim Community of the Indo-Pakistan Subcontinent (Ma'aref, Karachi, 2nd edn., 1977).

SAIYID, M. H. Mohammad Ali Jinnah: A Political Study (Ashraf, Lahore, 1953).

SAYEED, KHALID BIN. Pakistan, the Formative Phase (Pakistan Publishing House, Karachi, 1960).

STEPHENS, IAN. The Pakistanis (Oxford University Press, London, 1967).

WASTI, S. RAZI. Biographical Dictionary of South Asia (Publishers United, Lahore, 1980).

HISTORY AND POLITICS

AFZAL, R. Political Parties in Pakistan 1947–58 (National Commission on Historical and Cultural Research, Islamabad, 1976).

AHMAD, AZIZ. Islamic Modernism in India and Pakistan (1857–1964) (Oxford University Press for Chatham House, London, 1967).

AYUB KHAN, MOHAMMAD. Friends not Masters: A Political Autobiography (Oxford University Press, London, 1967).

AZIZ, K. K. Party Politics in Pakistan 1947–1958 (National Commission on Historical and Cultural Research, Islamabad, 1976).

BHUTTO, Z. A. The Great Tragedy (Pakistan People's Party, Karachi, 1971).

Politics of the People (Pakistan Publications, Karachi, 3 vols., 1975).

If I am Assassinated . . . (Vikas Publishing House Pvt. Ltd., New Delhi, 1978).

BINDER, LEONARD. Religion and Politics in Pakistan (University of California Press, Berkeley, Calif., 1961).

BRINES, R. The Indo-Pakistan Conflicts (Pall Mall Press, New York, 1968).

CALLARD, KEITH. Pakistan, A Political Study (Allen & Unwin, London, 1957; Lawrence Verry, Mystic, Conn., 1965).

Foreign Policy of Pakistan (Institute of Pacific Relations, New York, 1959).

CHOUDHURY, G. W. Constitutional Development in Pakistan (Longmans, Lahore and London, 1959; Institute of Pacific Relations, New York, 1959).

The Last Days of United Pakistan (Indiana University Press, Bloomington, 1974).

FELDMAN, HERBERT A. Revolution in Pakistan: A Study of the Martial Law Administration (Oxford University Press, London and New York, 1967).

From Crisis to Crisis: Pakistan 1962–1969 (Oxford University Press, London and Karachi, 1972).

The End and the Beginning: Pakistan 1969–1971 (Oxford University Press, London and Karachi, 1976).

LAPORTE, R., Jr. Power and Privilege: Influence and Decision Making in Pakistan (University of California Press, Los Angeles, 1976).

MALIK, HAFEEZ. Muslim Nationalism in India and Pakistan (Public Affairs Press, Washington, D.C., 1964).

RAZVI, M. The Frontiers of Pakistan: a Study of Frontier Problems in Pakistan's Foreign Policy (National Publishing House, Karachi, 1971).

RAHMAN, MAITUR. Second Thoughts on Bangladesh (News and Media Ltd., London, 1979).

SALIK, SIDDIQ. Witness to Surrender (Oxford University Press, Karachi, 1977).

SAYEED, KHALID BIN. The Political System of Pakistan (Allen & Unwin, London, 1967).

SHERWANI, L. A. (ed.). Pakistan Resolution to Pakistan (National Publishing House Ltd., Karachi, 1969).

Pakistan: The Nature and Direction of Change (Praeger, New York, 1980).

SIDDIQUI, KALIM. Conflict, Crisis and War in Pakistan (Macmillan, London, 1972).

Functions of International Conflict: A Socio-economic Study of Pakistan (Royal Book Company, Karachi, 1975).

SINGHAL, DAMODAR P. Pakistan (Prentice-Hall, Englewood Cliffs, New Jersey, 1972).

STEPHENS, IAN. Pakistan (Ernest Benn, London, 3rd edn., 1967).

VON VORYS, K. Political Development in Pakistan (Princeton University Press, New Jersey, 1965).

WILCOX, W. A. Pakistan: Consolidation of a State (Columbia University Press, New York, 1964).

WILLIAMS, L. F. R. Pakistan Under Challenge (Stacey International, London, 1975).

WRIGGINS, H. (ed.). Pakistan in Transition (University of Islamabad, Islamabad, 1975).

YUSUF, HAMID. Pakistan in Search of Democracy 1947–77 (Afrasia Publications, Lahore, 1980).

ZIRING, LAWRENCE. The Ayub Khan era: politics in Pakistan 1958–69 (Syracuse University Press, New York, 1971).

Pakistan: The Enigma of Political Development (1980).

ZIRING, LAWRENCE, BRAIBANTI, RALPH, and WRIGGINS, H. (eds.). Pakistan: The Long View (Duke University Center for Commonwealth and Comparative Studies, Durham, N.C., 1977).

ECONOMY

DONALDSON, G. F., and MCINERNEY, J. P. The Consequences of Farm Tractors in Pakistan (World Bank Paper No. 210, 1975).

GARIFFIN, KEITH, and KHAN, AZIZUR RAHMAN. Growth and Inequality in Pakistan (Macmillan, St. Martin's Press, London, 1972).

LEWIS, STEPHEN R. Economic Policy and Industrial Growth in Pakistan (Allen & Unwin, London, 1969).

MICHEL, A. A. The Indus Rivers: a study of the effect of Partition (Yale University Press, New Haven, Conn., 1967).

NULTY, L. The Green Revolution in West Pakistan (Praeger, New York.)

PAPANEK, GUSTAV F. Pakistan's Development: Social Goals and Private Incentives (Harvard University Press, Cambridge, Mass., and Oxford University Press, London, 1967).

RASHID, AMJAD. Industrial Concentration and Economic Power in Pakistan (Punjab University Press, Lahore, 1974).

WHITE, L. J. Industrial Concentration and Economic Power in Pakistan (1974).

FOREIGN RELATIONS

BARNDS, W. J. India, Pakistan and the Great Powers (Praeger, for the Council on Foreign Relations, New York, 1972).

BHUTTO, Z. A. The Myth of Independence (Oxford University Press, Karachi, 1969).

BURKE, S. M. Pakistan's Foreign Policy: An Historical Analysis (Oxford University Press, London, 1973).

Main Springs of Indian and Pakistani Foreign Policies (Oxford University Press, 1975).

CHOUDHURY, G. W. Pakistan's Relations With India (Praeger, New York, 1968).

India, Pakistan, Bangladesh and the Major Powers (The Free Press, New York and Collier Macmillan, London, 1975).

HASAN, MASUMA (ed.). Pakistan in a Changing World (Pakistan Institute of International Affairs, Karachi, 1978).

KHAN, M. ASGHAR. Indo-Pakistan War: The First Round (Islamic Information Service, London, 1979).

LAMB, A. Asian Frontiers: Studies in a Continuing Problem (Pall Mall Press, London, 1968).

RAZVI, M. The Frontiers of Pakistan: A Study of Frontier Problems in Pakistan's Foreign Policy (National Publishing House, Karachi, 1971).

SHERWANI, L. A. India, China and Pakistan (Council for Pakistan Studies, Karachi, 1967).

Pakistan, China and America (Council for Pakistan Studies, Karachi, 1980).

SHERWANI, L. A., CHAUDHRI, M. A., MUJAHID, S. AL, and HASAN K. Foreign Policy of Pakistan (Allies Book Corporation, Karachi, 1964).

SYED, ANWAR HUSAIN. China and Pakistan: Diplomacy of Entente Cordiale (University of Massachusetts Press, London, 1975).

WILCOX, W. A. India, Pakistan and the Rise of China (Walter, New York, 1964).

The Philippines

PHYSICAL AND SOCIAL GEOGRAPHY

C. A. Fisher

(Revised for this edition by HARVEY DEMAINE)

The combined surface area of the 7,100 islands which make up the Philippines amounts to 300,000 square kilometres (115,831 square miles). With the intervening seas, most of which rank as Philippines territorial waters, the country extends over a considerably larger area, from above 18° N. to below 6° N. latitude, lying between the South China Sea and the Pacific Ocean.

Of its multitudinous islands, some 880 are inhabited and 462 have an area of one square mile (2.6 square kilometres) or more, though the two largest, namely Luzon in the north, covering 104,688 square kilometres (40,420 square miles), and Mindanao in the south, with an area of 94,630 square kilometres (36,537 square miles), account for 66.4 per cent of its territory, and this figure is raised to 92.3 per cent if the next nine largest (Samar, Negros, Palawan, Panay, Mindoro, Leyte, Cebu, Bohol and Masbate) are also included.

PHYSICAL FEATURES

Structurally, the Philippines forms part of the vast series of island arcs which fringe the East Asian mainland and also include Japan, the Ryukyus and Taiwan to the north, and extend into Sulawesi, Irian and other Indonesian islands to the south. Two main and roughly parallel lines of Tertiary folding run roughly north–south through Luzon, swing approximately north-west–south-east through the smaller islands surrounding the Sabayan, Visayan and Mindoro seas, and resume a north–south trend in Mindanao. In addition to these two, a less pronounced north-east–south-west pair extend from the central Philippines through Panay and the smaller islands of the Sulu archipelago, ultimately linking up with the similar Tertiary structures of the north-eastern tip of Borneo.

These major lines of folding largely determine the broad pattern of relief throughout the country. Over most of the islands Tertiary sediments and Tertiary-Quaternary eruptives predominate, and over a dozen major volcanoes are still in the active stage. Nearly all the larger islands have interior mountain ranges, attaining heights typically of 1,200–2,400 metres (4,000–8,000 ft.), but apart from narrow strips of coastal plain few have any extensive lowlands. This is the greatest natural liability from which the country suffers, and it is largely because the central plain of Luzon represents such a significant exception that this island has assumed the dominant role in the life of the country as a whole.

CLIMATE

Because of its mountainous character and its alignment across the south-west monsoon and the north-east trade winds, the Philippines shows considerable regional variation in both the total amount and the seasonal incidence of rainfall. Thus, in general, the western side of the country gets most of its rain during the period of the south-west monsoon (late June–late September) whereas on most of the eastern side the wettest period of the year is from November to March when the influence of the north-east trades is at its greatest, though here, in contrast to the west, there is no true dry season. These differences can be seen by comparing Manila (on the west side of Luzon) which, out of an annual total of 210 cm. (82 in.), receives 110 cm. (47 in.) in July–September and only 15 cm. (6 in.) in December–April, with Surigao (in the north-east of Mindanao) which receives an annual total of 356 cm. (140 in.), 223 cm. (88 in.) of it between November and March inclusive, but with no monthly total falling below the August figure of 12 cm. (4.8 in.). In some sheltered valleys, however, totals may be as low as 102 cm. (40 in.) which, in association with mean annual sea-level temperatures rarely much below 26.7°C. (80°F.) anywhere in the country, makes farming distinctly precarious. On the other hand, a different kind of climatic hazard affects many of the more exposed parts of the country as a result of their exposure to typhoons, which are commonest in the later months of the year, and tend to be most severe in eastern Luzon and Samar.

NATURAL RESOURCES

As has already been implied, the central lowlands of Luzon provide by far the best major food-producing region within the country, and although many of the smaller lowlands are also intensively cultivated, their soils are in most cases of only average fertility. From the 1940s the only substantial areas of lowland offering scope for any important extension of cultivation have been in the southern island of Mindanao. Once aptly described as the frontier of the Philippines, even this island is now filling up steadily and the once extensive resources of tropical hardwoods have been disappearing rapidly in recent years.

While, as elsewhere in South-East Asia, rice forms the most important single item in the country's agricultural system, its predominance is less marked than in other parts of the region and indeed in several of the islands, partly because of their relatively low rainfall, and partly because of the close cultural link with Latin America, maize is the leading food crop. So far as export crops are concerned the emphasis has hitherto been mainly on sugar, coconuts, bananas and pineapples.

The Philippines has a fairly wide range of metallic mineral deposits, the most important of which are copper, mainly found on Cebu and at Marinduque, chromite and nickel. The country has been, on the other hand, sadly deficient in energy minerals and increasing costs of oil imports have led to a frantic search for domestic energy supplies in recent years. Oil has now been discovered off the island of Palawan, but quantities appear to be scarcely economically viable and perhaps greater scope lies with hydro-electric power and geothermal energy, both the product of the youthful landscape and unstable geological structure of the archipelago.

POPULATION AND CULTURE

With a population growth rate of at least 2.4 per cent per annum, the Philippines has already added over two million people to its total population of 47,914,017 recorded at the May 1980 census. It had then an average population density of 160 per square kilometre (414 per square mile), which was nearly double the South-East Asian average and exceeded only by those of northern Viet-Nam and Singapore. The shortage of lowland means that much the greater part of the population is concentrated in a relatively small area and, particularly in the lowlands of central Luzon, the resultant pressure is now a serious problem and likely to become increasingly severe owing to the exceptionally high rate of population growth.

Despite the existence of several regional languages spoken by the lowland Filipinos, the latter, who form the great majority of the population, share a basically common culture which is much influenced by Catholicism. In recent decades considerable progress has been made in developing Tagalog, the language of central Luzon, as a national language (Pilipino) though, particularly among the largely mestizo élite elements, English is widely used.

Other than the Christian Filipinos, the only large indigenous group comprises the Muslim Moros inhabiting the southern and southwestern peripheries of the country, who form about 5 per cent of the total population. But there are also several much smaller communities of animist hill peoples, mainly in the remoter parts of Luzon and Mindanao, who together form perhaps 6 per cent of the total. By comparison with other parts of South-East Asia, the Chinese population in the Philippines is very small, accounting for only about 1 per cent of the total.

Largely because of its long history of colonial rule and its archipelagic nature, the Philippines now has a widespread scatter of small administrative and market towns. Manila is the nation's capital, with a population of 1,626,249 at the 1980 census. However, this figure misleads, since the boundaries of the new administrative unit of Metropolitan Manila encompass a large number of former towns and districts, including Quezon City (1980 population 1,165,990), and contain a total population of at least 4,500,000. Other macro-regions of the country also have their urban foci, however, with Cebu (489,208) in the Visayas, Davao (611,311) in south-east Mindanao and Zamboanga City (344,275) in south-west Mindanao being the largest.

HISTORY

Renato Constantino

PRE-COLONIAL SOCIETIES

The autonomous communities that the Spanish *conquistadores* encountered in the sixteenth century were communities in transition from a primitive communal state to some form of Asiatic feudalism. The social unit was the *barangay*. While there were some large *barangays* most were small, scattered communities of 100 to 500 persons. They were kinship groups, with only informal contacts with other villages.

Primitive economic units with a system of subsistence agriculture, the *barangay* had no class structure although there were social stratifications. Such stratifications were more marked in the more advanced Muslim communities of the south. *Barangay* chiefs, freemen and "debt peons" were the main strata, but this stratification was not rigid, for chiefs could be deposed, freemen could be reduced to dependence and "debt peons" became freemen after paying their debts.

Pre-Spanish settlements had houses of renewable materials, usually aligned along a riverbank or on a shore. Travel was principally by water; there were no roads nor wheeled vehicles. Agriculture was the principal occupation. There was no separate artisan class. Syllabic writing was confined to the more advanced coastal communities and was used for sending messages rather than for recording purposes. There were no houses of stone and no public buildings. Trade between communities and with Muslim and Chinese traders was on the whole accidental and irregular. The fairly low level of political and social organization made it easy for the Spaniards to conquer the native population and impose their own culture and values.

SPANISH COLONIALISM

Spanish intrusion into the islands, which would later be named Filipinas in honour of Felipe II, began in 1521, when Ferdinand Magellan attempted unsuccessfully to implant Spanish sovereignty. This Spanish adventure was in implementation of the mercantilist policies of Spain which like its rival, Portugal, had embarked on a search for colonies to extract gold and to control the spice trade.

It was not until 1565 that another expedition, headed by Miguel López de Legazpi, arrived from Mexico and finally established a foothold in Manila on the island of Luzon. Spanish control was rapidly extended over the entire country, with the exception of Muslim territory in Mindanao and Sulu and certain mountain communities of Northern Luzon which successfully resisted domination to the end of Spanish rule.

Disappointed in their mercantilist objective of finding rich deposits of gold and silver and a fortune in spices, the Spaniards adopted other means of extracting wealth from their colony. They imposed tributes, conscripted labour, levied on communities assessments of rice and other produce for the needs of the government and the army. Thousands of young men were impressed into the Spanish navy and army.

Until the middle of the eighteenth century, Spanish colonialism was mainly extractive. The economic development of the country was given little importance. Agriculture was neglected. Instead, the main economic activity of the Spanish community was the profitable galleon trade. But, since Manila was merely a transshipment port through which Chinese goods were shipped to Mexico and Mexican silver to the Chinese coast, the galleon trade had practically no effect on the native economy. No Philippine products were developed for export.

Church and State

Although the economy was largely stagnant, profound changes were being effected in the lives of the people, mainly by the Church. The theocratic nature of the Spanish state gave the religious a pre-eminent position in colonial administration. In fact, to bring the light of Christianity to the heathen was solemnly declared to be the primary motivation for Spanish colonization.

Because of the union of church and state and the small number of Spanish colonial officials, the friars from the start took on administrative duties that eventually made them an important part of the exploitative colonial establishment. The friars almost single-handedly effected the resettlement of the scattered *barangays* into more compact and therefore more easily controlled communities, with the church as the physical and psychological centre. Since in most of the smaller towns the friar was the only Spaniard, he assumed so many administrative functions that he had a say in almost every aspect of community life.

To their spiritual and administrative control over the people the friars soon added a third factor: economic power. The religious orders acquired vast landed estates and also profitably engaged in the galleon trade and in internal commerce. As a result of this economic ascendancy, the Church was transformed from a colonial accessory to the principal apparatus of colónial appropriation and exploitation.

A by-product of friar control was cultural poverty. Until the mid-nineteenth century, education was mainly religious instruction under the supervision of the parish priests. Art was purely religious imagery and public entertainment centred on the feast days of patron saints. Spanish was not taught.

Pattern of Resistance

Despite the control over the native mind through religion, the material fact of colonial exploitation urged the people to rise in many unsuccessful revolts. Although these were localized actions at different times and in different areas, two evolving historical threads may be perceived: first, the development and transformation of revolts with religious content and, second, the rise and ebb of élite participation in the people's uprisings.

The religious thread started as nativism, an assertion of the power of the old pagan gods against the Catholic god. Because of the prominence of the Church in the colonial enterprise, the people's protest against their material deprivation and physical oppression was expressed in a rejection of the Catholic religion and a return to their old gods. But, as Catholicism made further inroads, later revolts, while still exhibiting nativistic characteristics and rejecting the friars, adopted more and more of the beliefs and rituals of Catholicism.

The other historical thread began to unfold with the emergence of the local élite. Spanish colonialism gradually transformed the *barangay* chieftains into adjuncts of colonial rule. Administrative responsibilities gave the chiefs colonial privileges as well as opportunities to participate in the exploitation of the people. The chiefs and ex-chiefs and their families constituted the *principales* (principals) of a community, a prospering upper stratum with colonial sanction.

Thus, the middle of the seventeenth century saw the emergence of a new pattern of native resistance in which *principales* took advantage of mass unrest to advance their own interests. Some exploited the grievances of their followers to extract concessions for themselves from the Spaniards. Others led uprisings to expel the Spaniards from their region so that they could rule in their stead.

Except for the Bohol* revolt, which was sustained for 85 years due to a fortuitous combination of circumstances, the numerous uprisings lasted only briefly. They were conceived and conducted as local revolts triggered by local grievances and they had neither the ideology, the resources nor the organization to wage a prolonged resistance. But, over the years, two aspects of Spanish colonialism stimulated a trend toward unification of the country; the administrative structure and the uniform oppression which developed a growing awareness of common grievances. However, these were not enough to spark a national revolution for there could be no nation and no national consciousness to wage such a struggle until certain economic developments had occurred to produce a national economy, better communications facilities, and a group of articulators who could project the common grievances and crystallize the aspirations of the people.

Economic Transformation, 1750–1850

Spanish colonialism underwent vital changes after the Seven Years' War with Great Britain. The British occupied Manila from 1761 to 1764. Spain's Latin American colonies revolted and Spain itself was gripped by liberal revolutions. British interests penetrated the Spanish colony. European and American firms also started coming in during the latter part of the eighteenth century. The Philippines was gradually

* Island province in East Visayas.

opened to world trade. Spain, responding to the imperatives of an expanding world capitalism, liberalized its former restrictive economic policies. The demand for agricultural products for export, particularly sugar, indigo, tobacco, hemp, rice and coffee quickly fostered the regionalization of production.

The British linked the country to world capitalism but it was the Chinese who acted as the economic catalysts in the hitherto stagnant interior, for it was they who gathered the agricultural crops for the foreign traders and sold to the people the goods these same traders brought into the country. When a majority of the Chinese was expelled or killed during the last two of the periodic purges by the Spaniards, the Chinese *mestizos* (sons of Chinese fathers and native mothers but brought up as natives and Catholics) replaced them. The Chinese *mestizos* later relinquished their trading activities to the Chinese when the latter were again allowed to return and operate in the provinces but by this time the Chinese *mestizos* were already rich enough to shift to agriculture. They merged with, or took over from, the old native *principales* as community leaders and landowners.

The educational reforms of 1863 opened the doors of higher institutions of learning to the natives. Children of prosperous Chinese *mestizo* and native families studied in Manila; the wealthier families sent their sons to Spain. From these youths emerged the *ilustrados* (the enlightened ones) who were to become the disseminators of Spanish culture and liberal thought and eventually the articulators of the intellectual ferment in the colony.

Reform Movement

Ferment sprang from diverse sectors of the population and was spurred by economic development and the dissemination of liberal ideas. The *creoles* or Españoles-Filipinos (Spaniards born in the Philippines) resented the preferential treatment given to the *peninsulares* (Spaniards born in Spain) in government employment and in the army. They gravitated toward the *ilustrados* who, having prospered, were chafing under the restrictions which the Government continued to impose on them and which inhibited further economic ascendancy. The *ilustrados* also demanded social equality, civil rights and a voice in government.

Economic progress and the liberalized policies on education had increased the number of native priests. Discriminated against by the Spanish friars who monopolized the more lucrative parishes, the native clergy made common cause with the *creole* clergymen in demanding Filipinization of the clergy. This demand became one of the rallying cries of the steadily growing sentiment of nationality, with *creoles* accepting the educated natives as Filipinos.

The growth of the concept of nationhood was coterminous with the development of the concept of Filipino. From a term with narrow racial and élitist connotation (only for Spaniards born in the Philippines), the term Filipino began to include Chinese *mestizos* and urbanized natives whose economic ascendancy in the eighteenth and nineteenth centuries gave them the opportunity to acquire education and Hispanic culture. This made them socially acceptable to the *creoles*, especially since progress had given both groups a common economic base to protect. Later, the *ilustrados*, offsprings of this rising local élite, wrested the term Filipino from the *creoles* and infused it with national meaning to include the entire people. From then on, the term Filipino would refer to the inhabitants of the Philippine archipelago regardless of racial strain or economic status.

The National Revolution of 1896

Progress inevitably produced economic dislocations. Many small landholders lost their lands, the people suffered from rising prices, aggravated by unemployment in those areas where native production could not compete with imported goods. Economic development produced better communications and a national market, both of which made for greater cohesiveness and facilitated the dissemination of protest, thus increasing its scope and intensity. The particular grievances of Philippine-born Spaniards, of the native clergy, of the Chinese *mestizos* and of the indigenous élite swelled the stream of general discontent which finally found more or less systematic articulation in the writings of the *ilustrados*.

The *ilustrados* were reformists. They agitated for better treatment of the colony and its eventual assimilation as a province of Spain. The foremost leader of what is now called the Propaganda Movement was José Rizal. But, although the people revered Rizal and the other reformists, the revolutionary spirit that had been nurtured in centuries of struggle made them decide in favour of revolution rather than reform and separation rather than assimilation.

The people's revolution was launched by the *Katipunan** under the leadership of Andres Bonifacio in August 1896 and quickly spread to the rest of the country. Military successes in Cavite† catapulted to prominence Captain (later General) Emilio Aguinaldo and aroused the ambitions of the Cavite élite who wrested the leadership of the Revolution from Bonifacio. The *Katipunan* organization was discarded and General Aguinaldo was elected President of the revolutionary government. Aguinaldo and his group eventually compromised the national struggle by consenting to stop hostilities in return for a monetary settlement and exile to Hong Kong.

A few months later, the Spanish-American war broke out and Gen. Emilio Aguinaldo returned to the Philippines. The people had continued their revolution against Spain even after Aguinaldo had abandoned the struggle. With American backing, Aguinaldo reassumed leadership of the movement and proclaimed Philippine independence on June 12th, 1898, placing the country's independence under American protection.

THE FIRST PHILIPPINE REPUBLIC

The Filipino people pressed their fight against the Spaniards until they were in control of the whole country except Cavite and Manila, which passed to

* "Association of the Sons of the People".

† Province in Southern Luzon.

American hands. The Americans made arrogant demands on their supposed allies and colluded with the Spaniards to stage a sham battle so that Manila could be surrendered to the Americans alone. Despite many ominous signs, Aguinaldo continued to declare his faith in the United States.

Aguinaldo was inaugurated President of the Philippine Republic at Malolos in January 1898. But the Malolos Government was a completely *ilustrado* government. Wealthy Manilans, who had shunned Bonifacio's *Katipunan*, had joined the Revolution when it looked as if it just might succeed. Aguinaldo appointed the élite to his cabinet and they dominated the Congress.

AMERICAN OCCUPATION

In the Treaty of Paris of December 1898 Spain ceded the Philippines to the United States for $20 million. The American expansionists now had a free hand to subdue their new colony. Aguinaldo's forces were no match for the American army; after a series of retreats Aguinaldo was captured in March 1901. But the hostilities did not end. New leaders emerged and the resistance continued into the second decade of the century, although brutally suppressed by the Americans. All political activity was banned.

Despite fierce resistance, American colonial administrators established a civil government. In this the Americans were able to use quite a number of *ilustrados* who declared their acceptance of American rule. These *ilustrados* had occupied prominent positions under the Spanish regime. That Aguinaldo had appointed many of them to his cabinet made them all the more valuable to the Americans as exhibits of Filipino acceptance of the American regime. These men were rewarded with high office in the new dispensation while news of resistance was suppressed.

Colonial Policy

The principal agent of Americanization was the public school system, and the master stroke of educational policy was the adoption of English as the medium of instruction. A people who had long been denied educational facilities under Spain welcomed this development. However, the use of English made possible the introduction of the American public school curriculum, with its American culture and values which had the effect of gradually dissipating the intense feelings of nationalism that had animated the people during the Revolution and the resistance to American occupation. A quasi-American society was eventually established which bore the imprint of the institutions, values and outlook of the colonizing power. The American colonial technique finally earned for the United States the loyalty of millions of Filipinos.

American economic policies in the Philippines represented a compromise between two clashing economic forces in the United States: those interested in trade and economic holdings overseas and those interested in protecting local agricultural production and labour from foreign competition. The first enthusiastically supported colonization; the second opposed it and subsequently agitated for independence for the colony. The agricultural sector, however, concerned itself with colonial policy only when its interests were involved; otherwise, official policy was dictated by the requirements of American commercial and industrial interests.

Exploitation of the colony involved development of the import-export trade and investment principally in the extractive industries. The various economic legislations culminating in the establishment of free trade were all designed to produce an economic climate attractive to American traders and investors and to transform the colony into a source of cheap raw materials and a market for American manufactured goods.

American land policy favoured the traditional landed élite. Agricultural lands were undertaxed and agricultural products exempted from tax assessments in order to encourage export-crop production. Demand for their products under free trade conditions stimulated landowners to enlarge their holdings. The *hacienda* system was therefore strengthened and the tenancy problem worsened.

Colonial Politics

The Filipinization policy which was conceived as a pacification measure but was presented as a policy in pursuance of the American desire to train the Filipinos in the art of self-government gave political power to the landed élite. With the help of property restrictions on suffrage which the Americans imposed, this landed élite acquired political control in the municipal elections of 1905 and emerged in full force in the Philippine Assembly of 1907. Although suffrage was subsequently extended, the élite never lost political power, exercising it either directly or through middle-class professionals whom they sponsored or co-opted. Subsequent gains in Filipinization, a Senate, to take the place of the American-dominated Philippine Commission, and Filipino cabinet members and bureau heads, did not diminish élite control.

The Nacionalista Party, under the leadership of Sergio Osmeña (later supplanted by Manuel L. Quezon), retained a virtual monopoly of political power from the start. All other political groups died away or were absorbed by this party. Fierce political battles occurred only when personal ambition caused a temporary split in Nacionalista ranks.

These basic factors determined the peculiar characteristics of Philippine colonial politics: on the one hand, a colonial master that gave its wards a semblance of democratic power but kept for itself the substance of that power, and on the other, a people still resolute in their desire for independence. In the middle were the Filipino leaders who owed their positions to an electorate faithful to the old goal of independence, and their powers and prerogatives to the colonizer. The political battle-cry was still for "immediate, complete and absolute independence" and many independence missions were sent to the United States but mainly for political effect inasmuch as the idea of immediate and absolute independence had long been tacitly discarded.

Filipino leaders and the class they represented wanted independence eventually but having accepted the concept of tutelage and allowed the development of an economy dependent upon free entry of its raw materials into the U.S. market, they became increasingly reluctant to trade their prosperous dependence for the uncertainties of freedom and preferred to postpone it whenever it appeared to be within reach.

The Philippine Commonwealth (1935–46)

It was therefore more as a result of the agitation of American farm and labour groups that the United States moved to give the Philippines its independence. By 1932 American farm and dairy interests, hard hit by the deep economic crisis, renewed their clamour for immediate Philippine independence so that free trade could be abandoned and tariffs imposed for their protection. The American Federation of Labor, which wanted to exclude cheap Filipino labour, applied pressure. The result was the passage in 1934 of a law which established a Commonwealth and provided for the recognition of Philippine independence after a ten-year transition period. The Philippine Commonwealth was inaugurated on November 15th, 1935, with Manuel L. Quezon as president and Sergio Osmeña as vice-president.

Social Unrest

The masses, although temporarily quiescent after their resistance to American occupation had been crushed, remained faithful to the revolutionary dream of freedom. Poverty, usury, oppressive treatment by landlords, the dispossession of poor farmers, fraudulent titling and other legal trickeries produced a new upsurge of peasant unrest in the 1920s. Ideologically confused and poorly organized, the revolutionary peasant movements of this period were easily suppressed by the Philippine Constabulary which the Americans had organized to police the country.

Unrest was not confined to the rural areas. Urban workers joined labour unions, some of which became increasingly radical. The economic crisis of the late 1920s and early 1930s intensified unionization as well as peasant organization. Large peasant unions based in Central Luzon joined unions of urban workers to form a militant Confederation. Although peasants and workers directed their strikes and other mass actions primarily against their own exploiters, their radical leadership began to project the interrelationship between their economic demands and the national goal of independence. A number of these radical leaders, headed by Crisanto Evangelista, established the Communist Party of the Philippines in 1930.

Another group called *Sakdal* (Accusation), despite a leadership that was eventually exposed as opportunistic and fascist-inclined, contributed to the politicization of the people. *Sakdal* staged a violent uprising in 1935 which was quickly suppressed, thus ending a movement whose surprising electoral victories had sparked hopes that a real opposition party might emerge.

President Quezon tried to counter unrest with his Social Justice Program. While some constructive legislation was passed, the programme was essentially intended to placate the masses while reassuring the landowners. In 1938 the Communist Party and the Socialist Party merged. In 1940 this group joined other progressive and left-wing elements to form the Popular Front which won some modest victories in the provincial and municipal elections of that year.

But as the Second World War was extended to Asia, left-wing groups joined other organizations in a united front against fascism. Growing class animosities were temporarily set aside, although by no means obliterated, as the Pacific War broke out.

JAPANESE INTERLUDE

The outbreak of the Pacific war altered the course of domestic developments. Contrary to the hopes of most Filipinos, who were sure that the Americans would trounce the Japanese in a matter of weeks, the American forces were driven out of the country after a few months of resistance. The Japanese instituted a new apparatus of control over the Philippines.

The Filipinos eventually resigned themselves to a period of enemy occupation, confident that it was to be temporary. They regarded America's war as their own. While the Filipino people resented the new colonialism, it served only to deepen their loyalty to the U.S.A., upon whom, after the initial shock of seeing it defeated by Japan, they pinned their hopes for their liberation.

Spanish religious prejudices and Americanization had developed in the Filipinos an attitude of superiority toward the Japanese and Asians in general. Filipino prejudices were subsequently confirmed and exacerbated by the cruelties inflicted on the Filipinos by Japanese soldiers.

The Japanese military administration immediately put into operation plans to integrate the Philippines into Japan's "Greater East Asia Co-prosperity Sphere." A segment of the old colonial leadership, left behind by Quezon, was harnessed for this task. Other segments continued their resistance as guerrilla groups or as supporters of resistance groups waiting for the return of U.S. forces. The Commonwealth officials, led by Quezon and his vice-president, Sergio Osmeña, lived in exile in Washington.

Military Rule

The Japanese imposed a very severe form of military rule. Arms were confiscated; civil liberties were curtailed; censorship was established. Only media licensed by the military were allowed to operate. Neighbourhood associations were established for closer control of the population and to facilitate the rationing of basic commodities. Production was geared to the needs of the military. With the Philippines isolated from the rest of the world, with production facilities and agriculture at less than peak performance and with the Japanese occupation forces having first preference and even exporting Philippine produce to Japan, there were severe shortages of vital items for the civilian population.

An aggravating factor was the Japanese attempt to reorient the country's economy to contribute to Japan's war effort and to be finally integrated into the autarchic scheme of the Japanese empire. Sugar production was limited; instead of being used for export, excess sugar was utilized for the manufacture of alcohol and butanol to fuel Japanese vehicles. A programme was initiated to convert part of the sugar lands into areas for growing cotton for Japan's textile mills. New lands were opened to expand grain production. The military took over the management of public utilities and other firms vital to the war effort, and labour conscription was initiated.

Filipino Collaboration

In early 1942 the Japanese organized an executive commission to carry on the government functions. This commission was drawn from the ranks of former politicians and high-ranking bureaucrats led by Jorge Vargas, Quezon's executive secretary. The native constabulary was reorganized and its ranks bolstered by former prisoners of war. A civico-political organization called *Kalibapi** was organized. This was headed by Benigno Aquino, Sr., a senator of the old regime. The organization was vocally anti-American and aided the Japanese in mobilizing public support for Japanese policies.

On October 14th, 1943, one year and a half after the occupation had begun, the Japanese granted the Philippines independence. The puppet republic joined the East Asia Co-prosperity Sphere. The new Philippine Republic was headed by Jose P. Laurel who had been instructed by Quezon to remain and deal with the occupying forces to protect the people. While on the whole he acquiesced to Japanese demands, he was at the same time trying to protect the people from Japanese abuses. For one thing, he was able to prevent the conscription of Filipinos to fight with the Japanese. Documents would later reveal that Laurel had liaison with some of the guerrilla groups.

Resistance

Soon after the fall of Bataan†, various guerrilla groups were formed, most of them under the leadership of former USAFFE‡ officers, American and Filipino. The resistance of these groups was confined to sporadic skirmishes with Japanese patrols. They held their forces in reserve until instructed by the American command to attack the Japanese in preparation for the American landings.

Only one guerrilla group, the *Hukbalahap*, had a different orientation. Operating in Central and Southern Luzon, its forces fought the enemy throughout the occupation. Coming from the ranks of militant peasants who had been on the verge of revolt just before the Pacific war, and led by Communists and Socialists, the "Huks" were both anti-Japanese and anti-landlord. They did not, however, have clear-cut goals of opposing the return of the Americans. Their struggle was premised on the return of the Commonwealth government.

With the successive defeats of the Japanese in the mid-Pacific, the economic situation in the Philippines quickly deteriorated. Increasingly severe shortages and high inflation made life progressively more miserable. Thousands suffered from malnutrition and in the cities many starved. Economic conditions, the brutality of the army of occupation as well as the popular bias in favour of the Americans and against the Japanese made it impossible for the puppet Republic to gain any acceptance among the people.

During the occupation there was an attempt to eradicate American culture and values. The use of the national language was encouraged and its importance vis-à-vis English was stressed. Filipinos were constantly exhorted to remember that they were Asians. But none of this made a strong impression on most Filipinos because of their hatred for the Japanese and because their minds were focused on the return of the Americans. American forces entered Manila in February 1945. The war ended officially when Japan surrendered in September 1945.

Return of the Commonwealth, 1945

The return of the Americans was received with nationwide rejoicing. The government-in-exile, headed by Sergio Osmeña who had succeeded Manuel Quezon after the latter's death in 1944, returned to resume the Commonwealth rule. Osmeña faced insurmountable problems. On the one hand, there was the problem of rehabilitation and reconstruction which required unity and concentrated effort, and on the other the problem of collaborators which was dividing the nation and distracting its attention from pressing economic and financial problems.

Meanwhile, in Washington, rehabilitation funds were being provided for in a Philippine Rehabilitation Bill. A companion bill defined the trade relations between the Philippines and the United States. This bill provided for free trade for a period of eight years and a graduated tariff schedule for the next 20 years. It also granted Americans parity rights with Filipinos in the exploitation, disposition and utilization of natural resources and the operation of public utilities. This was to be the framework of Philippine-American relations after the grant of independence. The Rehabilitation Act contained a condition that no payment in excess of $500 would be given as war damage unless an agreement was reached by the presidents of the United States and of the Philippines regarding trade relations. But acceptance of this condition would require amendment of the Constitution to give Americans rights that the constitution had reserved only for Filipino citizens. Osmeña was forced into an alliance with the Left, led by the Democratic Alliance (DA). The DA was a non-traditional group, a united front of liberals, leftists and anti-collaborationist elements. Besides being strongly anti-collaborationist, the DA stood for a more independent posture vis-à-vis the United States. Osmeña lost the elections of April 1945 and Manuel Roxas, who had been

* Kapisanan sa Paglilingkod sa Bagong Pilipinas (Association in the Service of the New Philippines).

† Peninsula in western Luzon.

‡ United States Armed Forces in the Far East.

supported by the returning Americans, became the last president of the Commonwealth and on July 4th, 1946, the first President of the new Philippine Republic.

In one sense, Roxas' victory represented a break in the monopoly of power of the Nacionalista party which had held sway since the early period of colonial politics. Sections of this party had broken away in the past only to wither away or be re-absorbed once more. Roxas' Liberal Party was also a splitting wing of the Nacionalista Party, but from then on it achieved co-equal status to establish an orthodox two-party system in the Philippines. In a more fundamental sense, however, the two parties merely represented two sections of the same ruling group. Proof of this were the frequent shifts by political figures from one to the other party.

THE PHILIPPINE REPUBLIC, 1946–79

Roxas clearly delineated the direction of the new republic. A proud product of the American public school system, with a long career in colonial politics, and the head of a country economically prostrate and still euphoric over its American "liberation", Roxas firmly placed his country "in the glistening wake of America".

Roxas went all out for American parity rights. To secure the amendment of the Constitution, he had to have a 75 per cent vote of Congress. This was attained by unseating the Democratic Alliance Congressmen for alleged election frauds and terrorism. Parity became a reality with the approval of the amendment in a plebiscite held in 1947. A military bases agreement was also concluded, giving the Americans a 99-year lease on areas of Philippine territory. The collaboration issue was buried when Roxas issued an amnesty for all collaborators in 1948. In March 1948 Roxas outlawed the *Hukbalahap*.

Dissidence and Economic Difficulties

Dissidence in Central Luzon spread as the "Huks", now seeing no possibility of working within the existing framework, stepped up their organizational activities and began combating government forces in a long-range programme to seize power.

Roxas died in April 1948. Vice-President Elpidio Quirino succeeded Roxas and immediately tried, unsuccessfully, to solve the dissidence problem. He was no more successful with the vast economic problems he had inherited and which were to continue to plague each succeeding president. The war damage payments and other payments from the United States were quickly dissipated in an orgy of spending on non-essentials. The old colonial set-up was restored under parity. Faced with an exchange crisis, the country had to adopt import and exchange controls, limiting importation and the expenditure of foreign exchange. This institution, however, was wracked by corruption although it was able to produce a group of entrepreneurs who would in the future demand more nationalistic policies.

Quirino ran for re-election in 1949 against Jose Laurel, the war-time collaboration leader. Quirino won but wholesale frauds and terrorism further disillusioned the people and brought new strength to the dissident movement led by the Partido Komunista ng Pilipinas (PKP). In 1950 Quirino was able to arrest almost the entire leadership of the PKP. This feat was credited to his defence secretary, Ramon Magsaysay. The problem in Central Luzon was defused and many dissidents were either resettled or kept under interdiction.

Magsaysay's star was rising. He was considered by his American backers to be ready to challenge Quirino. When Quirino insisted on running for re-election in 1953, Magsaysay left the Liberal Party to become the standard bearer of the Nacionalistas, whose leaders accepted him due to American pressure. With the backing of the Americans, Ramon Magsaysay became the next President.

Magsaysay did not conceal the fact that he was an American puppet. It was during his term that the South East Asia Treaty Organization (SEATO) was established and Magsaysay was among the first presidents to recognize the regime of Ngo Dinh Diem, his counterpart in South Viet-Nam.

The Nationalist Crusade

It was during Magsaysay's term that the parity provisions were extended to the realm of business under the Laurel-Langley Agreement. One of Magsaysay's vote-catching gimmicks, "an artesian well in every barrio", dramatized the American aim of keeping the Philippine economy principally agricultural. This was opposed by proponents of nationalist industrialization led by Senator Claro M. Recto.

Recto started a nationalist campaign and exposed Magsaysay's pro-American policies. This campaign reached its climax in the presidential elections of 1957, in which Recto was a contender. Magsaysay, however, died in a plane crash a few months before the elections. He was succeeded by his Vice-President, Carlos P. Garcia, who won the election in a four-cornered presidential battle. Garcia's administration was characterized by the adoption of nationalistic policies, the principal expression of which was the "Filipino First" policy. This policy was the result of the pressures of the Recto campaign and also of the emergence of a new group of indigenous entrepreneurs who had benefited from controls.

The Trade-Loan Devaluation Cycle, 1961–72

Graft and corruption and the various scandals that rocked the Garcia administration led to its defeat in 1961. The new President, the Liberal Party's Diosdado Macapagal, scrapped controls in return for stabilization loans urged on him by the U.S. Treasury Department and the International Monetary Fund (IMF). Among the conditions of the loan was the devaluation of the peso. Decontrol and devaluation initiated a period of unbalanced neo-colonial trading where deficits in the balance of payments were always remedied by new loans to aid the peso. Devaluation crippled infant Filipino industries and scuttled plans for nationalist industrialization. Many floundering local industries were bought by American corporations.

Senate President Ferdinand E. Marcos, who left the Liberal Party ranks to become the Nacionalista Party standard bearer, defeated President Macapagal in the elections of November 1965. Marcos' administration has been credited with massive infrastructure programmes. But the trade-loan devaluation cycle, started during the Macapagal administration, continued to take its toll well into the Marcos administration, and its effects have been responsible for many contemporary developments. In February 1970 the peso was allowed to float. Marcos' term saw an increase in American investments covering vital and strategic areas. Many of these investments started as joint venture projects in anticipation of the end of parity in 1974. The deterioration of the economy also featured recurrent shortages in the production of rice. Worldwide inflation adversely affected the country, whose economic and financial policies were geared mainly to strictures by the U.S.A. and the IMF.

Marcos' second term, beginning in 1969, was marked by demonstrations and protests on issues ranging from American bases to rural feudalism on the part of the left, while right-wing and moderate reformist forces attacked corruption and the excesses of oligarchies. These groups a found common denominator in their opposition to the Marcos administration.

During the early 1970s, conditions deteriorated further. There were bombings and reports of attempted assassinations. Armed clashes occurred between government troops and the New People's Army and clashes between Christians and Muslims in Mindanao increased in frequency and magnitude.

Throughout this period the Constitutional Convention was meeting to draft a new constitution for the country. It became the arena for the conflicts that were agitating the country: the conflicts between the nationalists and the anti-nationalists, between those who wanted an end to the Marcos regime after 1973 and those who wanted him or his wife to continue in office, between those who wanted reforms and those who opposed them.

Martial Law

In September 1972, Marcos declared martial law. Leading members of the opposition, from right to left, and journalists critical of the administration were arrested and detained.

Martial law was the first departure in a history of parliamentary government that lasted nearly seven decades. Congress was not convened but work on the new constitution was allowed to continue until its completion. This constitution was submitted to the people in a referendum in 1973. Opponents of the Marcos government questioned the legality of the referendum which they claimed was not free.

During this period there were constant agitations for the lifting of martial law and the release of detained prisoners. But these expressions of opposition were muted because of continued constraints on the media, despite some liberalization compared with the early days of martial law.

The martial law government became the agent for the implementation of the new World Bank development policies that emphasized export orientation, the lowering of tariff barriers, generous incentives to foreign investors and cheap and docile labour. Multinational corporations responded favourably and their investments rose rapidly. The tourist industry was being promoted as a dollar earner and local banking institutions merged and/or entered into joint ventures with foreign banking giants. Some sectors demanded a review of the country's policies on foreign investment. Japanese and American investors were criticized for taking advantage of local credit instead of bringing in capital, and for remitting profits to their home countries.

The administration still faces armed opposition from various sectors which range from NPA elements to the Muslim autonomy movement. While continuing military operations against these dissenting forces, the Government initiated various steps to bring about what it calls "normalization".

On April 7th, 1978, the Philippines held its first elections under martial law. Despite its criticism of government restrictions, the opposition participated. The government party, Kilusan Bagong Lipunan (KBL or New Society Movement), won overwhelmingly amid charges of rampant irregularities. An interim Legislative Assembly was thus constituted, which, despite charges that it is merely a "rubber stamp", is expected to be a first stage in the gradual transition to parliamentary government. The Assembly was convened in June 1978 and President Marcos was confirmed as Prime Minister.

On January 30th, 1980, local elections were held. Again, the KBL was victorious but the opposition exposed widespread cheating and terrorism. These electoral exercises were the Government's response to local and foreign pressures to lift martial law. Marcos abolished martial law on January 17th, 1981, but, with the prior passage of a National Security Code and a Public Order Act, his powers have remained intact.

On April 7th, 1981, a plebiscite approved amendments to the Constitution, replacing the parliamentary form with a mixed presidential-parliamentary government. The most important amendment to the Constitution was the provision for an executive committee that would take over the powers of the president in the event of the latter's incapacity or demise. This solved the succession issue and assured foreign investors of an orderly and stable transition. In the election of June 16th, 1981, Marcos won a new term of six years. His opponent was Alejo Santos, representing one wing of the Nacionalista Party while the other wing, under Speaker José B. Laurel, boycotted the elections. Marcos appointed Finance Minister César Virata as Prime Minister. He reorganized his cabinet giving technocrats the key positions of Finance, Industry, Trade, Investments, Natural Resources and the Budget.

Since his inauguration, Marcos has openly endorsed the World Bank programmes of development and has entered into various agreements covering economic programmes as well as educational drives. New export processing zones were opened and he launched the National Livelihood Movement (KKK), which dovetails with transnational corporation goals of popularizing subcontracting as a way of utilizing cheap labour, insulating themselves from labour problems and minimizing equity investments. These projects billed as livelihood programmes are essentially geared to the export market.

An indication that there has been an accommodation on all sides is the fact that Marcos is getting more World Bank funding and has now secured the explicit support of the Reagan administration.

ECONOMIC SURVEY

T. M. Burley

The Philippines, an archipelago of over 7,000 islands, has a land area of 30 million hectares, of which about 12.5 million hectares are reserved as permanent forests. Economic, especially non-rural, activity is still concentrated on the island of Luzon, and in the vicinity of the capital, Manila, in particular. Increasingly, however, development planning seeks to generate economic activity elsewhere, and especially on the southernmost island of Mindanao.

The economy is based largely on agriculture, forestry and fishing, which provide one-third of the Gross Domestic Product and employ about half the labour force. The major food-producing area is the central lowland of Luzon. Rice forms the most important single item in the agricultural system, but its predominance is less marked than in other South-East Asian countries, and in some of the islands maize is a leading food crop. Coconut and coconut products, sugar, bananas and pineapples are other significant crops. The country is widely forested and timber products provide an important export commodity. Mineral deposits include copper, iron ore, manganese, molybdenum, zinc and lead. Gold and silver are also to be found. In the manufacturing sector food and beverage products, chemicals, textiles, tobacco and footwear are the main products. There has been a determined effort to increase the amount of domestic processing of raw materials, particularly timber, copper and copra.

The introduction of measures designed to create a more favourable climate for business and industry and to attract foreign investment were a feature of the the 1970s. These included the creation of the National Economic and Development Authority (NEDA), to determine priorities and incentives for economic growth, and an overhaul of the tariff, customs and taxation codes. The activities of NEDA, and the Board of Investments (BOI), have necessarily involved greater government interference in the private sector, and this has caused some concern among foreign investors and in domestic business circles. However, the net effect of government intervention has been to rationalize and co-ordinate a generally inefficient commercial and industrial structure, and hence to promote confidence and investment Revision of the Internal Revenue Code was undertaken to cover a broad range of changes in taxes on income, and on domestic transactions, consumption and transfers. Measures were also taken to attract foreign capital.

During the mid-1970s the economy expanded at a fairly constant rate, with the annual increase in Gross National Product averaging 6 per cent. In 1977, as in previous years, good performance in some sectors offset the poor performance of others; manufacturing and mining fared well, but the performance of exports was poor (due to low prices) and new construction activity levelled off. The mining sector was boosted by the opening of new copper and nickel mines and was reinforced by increased production of chromite and other metals. There were substantial gains in a variety of manufacturing sectors: wood. chemicals, beverages and food products, for example, In 1978 adverse trading conditions, coupled with lower productivity in the agricultural and manufacturing sectors, resulted in a disappointing export performance. Mining recorded further gains while renewed activity in government housing boosted the construction sector. Despite the disappointing performance of exports, progress was made in diversifying both the commodities exported and the markets in which they were sold. Economic activity in 1979 slowed down in the face of tight credit, high inflation and the ever-increasing oil price burden. Less favourable overseas markets for export commodities, notably coconut products and copper, exacerbated the situation in 1980. Even the traditionally high level of public expenditure was affected. With real wages and incomes remaining depressed, increasing concern was expressed over such consequences as malnutrition and crime.

Martial law was officially ended in January 1981, but within days the economy was rocked by the precipitate departure overseas of a leading industrialist, Dewey Dee, leaving behind debts of 635 million pesos, much of which was unsecured. This prompted a strengthening of the Central Bank's regulatory powers, but could not prevent considerable financial difficulties for a number of leading industrial and investment companies. To counter this, and the associated further tightening of business credit, the Government had to set up a fund of 1,500 million pesos to lend to private companies with liquidity problems. Generally though, 1981 was a year of modest progress. Many economic indicators exhibited favourable trends in spite of continuing difficulties in respect of exports due to weak commodity prices and the impact of bad weather on agricultural output.

AGRICULTURE

Arable activities are generally highly intensive, with double-cropping widely practised. Rice occupies some 40 per cent of the cultivated area, and maize a further one-third. The next most extensively cultivated crop is the coconut palm, which occupies over 2 million hectares.

The weather is a major influence. In particular, typhoons, such as those occurring in 1972 and 1977, can cause severe damage. In 1981 typhoon damage was exacerbated by drought in some rice-growing areas.

Government subsidies on fertilizers and generous credit schemes for the purchase of new seed, pesticides and fertilizers are aimed at improving yields. Other government measures include a major effort to improve the country's rural infrastructure, particularly irrigation and roads.

Reflecting the successes achieved in boosting output, emphasis has now been changed to multi-cropping and agro-business ventures to raise farm incomes. The Government is seeking to encourage investment in agriculture through a combination of technological, credit and marketing support. World Bank aid to strengthen agricultural extension services and the introduction of very early-maturing rice continues the stress on raising productivity.

The prime emphasis in Philippine agriculture remains the achievement of self-sufficiency in food-grain production, particularly rice. A complementary target is to eliminate malnutrition. In order to meet domestic food requirements, agricultural output will have to grow at an average annual rate of 4 per cent, according to World Bank estimates for the ten-year period to 1985. This growth will have to come primarily from an increase in the area farmed or from an increase in yields. As the cultivated area is unlikely to expand annually by more than 1.5 per cent over the period, yields will have to increase by at least 2.5 per cent a year. In order to achieve these increases in output, technological development, expanded irrigation networks and improved supporting services are needed. The National Irrigation Administration has embarked on a ten-year programme to irrigate an additional 1.3 million hectares of harvested land by 1985; the programme, which has attracted considerable foreign aid support, also calls for the rehabilitation of systems servicing some 300,000 hectares.

Rice

Despite the introduction of higher-yield strains of rice, the Philippines is still some way from achieving its full potential for rice production as irrigation water is available to only a third of the rice area, farmers have insufficient capital and yields are still too low. In 1974 the Government ordered all large corporations to produce rice for their workers, and by 1977 over 250 corporations were engaged in rice-growing, having developed 63,000 hectares of previously idle land. By employing mostly irrigated, large-scale mechanized operations, yields double those of traditional operations have been recorded. Since 1977 it has not been necessary to import rice.

Sugar

The sugar industry is of major importance to the country, occupying about half a million hectares and employing a similar number of people, although over one-third are seasonal workers employed for planting and harvesting only. Exports, formerly sent almost exclusively to the U.S.A., now enter a diversity of markets. Recent depressed world market conditions have led to official encouragement to convert marginal sugar land into other crops such as maize, soybeans and sorghum. This reverses earlier plans for a massive boost to the sugar area which had been encouraged by high prices in 1974/75. The Government has become increasingly involved in the industry and in 1977 the Philippine Sugar Commission was formed to control and co-ordinate the sugar trade and prices, and policy matters. It has not always been successful in its operations but has helped the industry to adjust to the restrictions imposed on exports by the International Sugar Agreement. It has also facilitated government efforts to alleviate the oil price burden through its "alcogas" programme whereby sugar cane and other agricultural raw materials are processed to extract their alcohol content for blending with petroleum.

Coconuts

The Philippines accounts for almost three-quarters of world exports of coconut products. A rapid rise in production, resulting from new planting, has resulted in marked advances in the quantity and quality of exports, though their value has suffered from depressed world prices. Paralleling this, Europe became a market equally as important to the Philippines as the U.S.A. Increasingly, exports are in the form of coconut oil rather than copra, following increased investment in processing facilities. Coconut oil exports exceeded 1 million tons for the first time in 1978 and accounted for over 50 per cent of exports of coconut products. However, over-investment in processing has led to the formation of a quasi-governmental body, the United Coconut Oil Mills Corporation, to co-ordinate the resources of the industry, a task it has not always coped with adequately.

Other Crops

Bananas have followed pineapples in displacing abaca (Manila hemp) and tobacco as foreign exchange earners (though not in area cropped). Coffee, cotton and rubber have also obtained increasing prominence. Efforts are now being made to develop oil palm on a commercial estate basis, thus involving the state-owned National Development Company, the only local firm allowed to own more than 1,000 hectares of land. Easily the most important product, however, is maize, whose value as a staple food, particularly in less productive rice areas, is now augmented by demand arising from the burgeoning needs of the poultry and livestock industries. By encouraging the use of high-yielding varieties, fertilizers, credit, etc., the Masagana development scheme has brought the Philippines close to self-sufficiency but inadequate technology and slowness in providing credit continue to thwart further progress. Sweet potatoes and cassava are widely grown as secondary food crops.

Other Rural Occupations

Meat production continues to lag behind domestic demand, though, on the basis of the country's modest per caput nutritional levels, it is only beef that is in deficit. Only 10 per cent of milk requirements, however, is met by domestic output. Fishing production also lags behind domestic demand and about a third of local requirements are met by imports, despite the potential of Philippine waters. A $70 million project, aided by the World Bank, aims to develop fisheries training on a large scale. The Asian Development Bank has also become heavily involved in supporting a variety of fisheries projects.

Philippine forests carry an estimated stand of 465 million board feet of valuable hardwoods; at present less than 7 million hectares are available for commercial exploitation and less than 200 of the 1,000 commercially useful species of trees are currently being marketed. Moreover, the country's forest resources have been rapidly depleted (by an estimated 40 per cent since 1945), mainly owing to shifting cultivation, illegal cutting and inadequate reafforestation. In the late 1970s the Government acted to conserve forest resources by restricting logging and log exports so that by 1980 earnings from wood products exports exceeded those from logs for the first time. Exports go mainly to Japan and the U.S.A. The local plywood and furniture industries, with a view to expanding lines and increasing production capacity have increasingly sought to integrate their operations.

Land reform

In 1972 a Presidential Decree proclaimed the whole country a land reform area to enable the emancipation of the tenant-farmers of rice and/or maize. This was to be effected by transferring to them ownership of the land on the basis that the tenant-farmer shall be deemed owner of a portion constituting a family-size farm of five hectares if not irrigated and three hectares if irrigated (existing holdings of smaller areas were not affected). Landowners were to be paid for land given to their tenants based on a pre-determined value and time period while the Government would provide all possible technical and financial assistance to the tenant-farmers for all phases of farming operations.

The programme was expected to affect an estimated 915,000 farmers and 1.4 million hectares. A succession of new rulings on this highly sensitive issue have made the guidelines on land reform too complex to be administered easily and it appears that only about half of the original 915,000 farmers affected will secure their own land and also that the stated area of a family-style farm represents the maximum, not the norm. As of mid-1977, some 250,000 tenants tilling 425,000 hectares had received Certificates of Land Transfer: these entitle the tenant to receive land, but not until he completes payment, usually over a 15-year period. Ultimately, some 400,000 tenants tilling some 750,000 hectares are likely to benefit.

MINING

The Philippines has extensive deposits of gold, silver, copper, nickel, iron, lead, manganese, limestone and chrome and the Government has given high priority to the development of minerals. As a result, mining has been one of the fastest-growing productive sectors in recent years. In addition to mining development, the Government is encouraging mineral processing ventures. These include copper and aluminium smelting, iron sintering and gold refining. A new, giant nickel plant started operation at Surigao in 1974.

Copper is the leading product but the output of iron, nickel, chromite, coal and gold is substantial. Lesser but still important products include silver, zinc, cobalt and manganese. Cement and salt are also produced in large quantities. It is estimated that less than 10 per cent of the country's mineral deposits has been tapped and developed. Metallic ore reserves are estimated at 12,200 million tons (including nickel reserves of 1,220 million tons, iron ore reserves of 1,110 million tons and copper ore reserves of 3,650 million tons), while non-metallic deposits (principally limestone for cement manufacture) are placed at 24,000 million tons.

Unfortunately, proven deposits are often too small in extent, inferior in quality or too inaccessible for profitable exploitation on a regular basis. Many existing operations, too, are marginal in the sense that they may operate profitably only when prices are favourable, and this is far from being the case in the 1980s. Gold mining is notorious in this respect (although much gold is a by-product of copper mining). Another major problem facing the mining industry is the increasing cost of operations, which is exacerbated by governmental, financial and pollution controls. The copper industry has been so badly hit that the Government has had to establish a 200 million pesos copper stabilization fund to help distressed producers.

Energy

Fuel sources have been subject to intense study. Only 81 per cent of the country's requirements are now derived from imported oil, compared with over 90 per cent in the 1970s. The Government wants to reduce this figure drastically to 45 per cent by 1986, but this target seems unattainable, especially now that it plans to boost geothermal, oil and gas, and that alcogas energy sources have been trimmed to help control the Government's investment expenditure. In 1977 commercial petroleum deposits were found off Palawan and further off-shore oil finds were made in 1978. In March 1979 a consortium of oil companies began the first commercial oil production in the Philippines, at an average rate of 11,000 barrels per day; subsequently it exceeded 40,000 barrels per day but this level was not maintained due to operational difficulties. The second commercial oil field was opened in 1981, at Cadlao. By mid-1981, domestic contribution to oil demand had fallen to two per cent, after peaking at nine per cent. The exploitation of geothermal resources has been actively pursued: there are 10 plants, with an installed capacity of 444.5 MW., a total exceeded only by the U.S.A. and Italy. Considerable resources remain to be tapped: some estimates suggest the total potential exceeds 35,000 MW. It had been thought that recoverable coal reserves did not warrant exploitation, but proven reserves are now estimated at 186 million tons; output is expanding rapidly with the cement and mining companies as principal consumers. To further reduce dependence on imported oil, a 620 MW. nuclear power plant is under construction. Wood burning power generation units are also planned.

Generating capacity exceeds 4,100 MW., with nearly one-quarter coming from hydroelectric sources. Geothermal sources supply a further 5 per cent, leaving over two-thirds of capacity based on petroleum. With capacity increases and associated distribution systems hard pressed to keep up with rising demand, power cuts have been a feature of urban life. Despite efforts to establish an electric co-operative system for every province, power is available to less than two million of the rural population. In all, nearly 8 million people have access to electric power and this total should be boosted considerably (by over 400,000) through the current $220 million rural electrification programme.

MANUFACTURING

There has been a noticeable change in the composition of industrial activities since the mid-1960s. Initially, the food component accounted for about a third of total value-added for manufacturing. Later, a movement towards intermediate processing activities became apparent. This was most pronounced in the manufacture of textiles, concrete products, glassware, electrical machinery and related products. There were marked increases also in the output of cement, chemicals, machine and base metal manufactures. Nonetheless, the current degree of industrial development is only equivalent to that achieved by neighbouring Taiwan and South Korea in the 1960s.

Current priorities focus upon the creation of domestically efficient, export-competitive industries. Development strategy has to allow for the fact that most activities continue to be high cost operations: blame is placed upon the high cost of fuel and materials and the under-utilization of capacity, exacerbated by protective tariffs which deter an interest in exporting (exceptions are textiles, electronics and handicrafts, all requiring large inputs of labour, which is readily available in the Philippines). The dismantling of protective barriers is now part of government policy. This, allied to a combination of fiscal incentives and selective lending, is seen as the best way to influence the direction of industrial development.

The processing of primary products remains the mainstay of secondary industry, but the 1970s saw a marked growth in the number of assembly plants basically dependent on imported components, although a number of components are now being produced locally under protective tariffs. The structure of industry is still heavily weighted toward the production of consumer goods, and lacks capital goods capacity. Manila is the principal manufacturing centre, producing one quarter of the sector's contribution to the G.N.P. However, the first two export processing zones, established at Mariveles (Luzon) and at Misamis Oriental (Mindanao), have proved so successful that 10 more are to be established by 1985.

Current investment plans indicate a move towards large import substitution projects such as steel, fertilizers, other petrochemicals, pulp and paper, and shipbuilding. However, because of financing difficulties, supply problems and depressed world markets, the only major projects likely to be in effective production by 1985 are a copper smelter, a phosphate fertilizer plant, diesel engine manufacturing facilities and a coco-chemicals plant.

These projects alone involve an investment in excess of U.S. $1,000 million. To enable effective participation by the Government, the National Development Company has been expanded to make it the largest government corporation in the country. Small- and medium-scale industries should benefit from a partnership programme between the Government and the commercial banks designed to make available £10 million in venture capital for each qualifying firm, half being in the form of a concessional loan from the Government.

The new projects are not expected to generate significant direct employment opportunities. However, the further industrialization permitted by the output of these industries is expected to result in many new jobs. It is hoped that less than 15 per cent of the demand for industrial goods will be met by imports in the mid-1980s, compared with 24 per cent in 1974 and 19 per cent projected for 1980. Most of the imports will be goods that cannot be manufactured locally because of the lack of technological capability or the limited size of the home market. It is also planned that the industrial sector will expand the value of its exports by about 16 per cent a year between 1975 and 1985.

INFRASTRUCTURE

Development spending on infrastructure has been substantial in recent years. As a result, the Government is now favouring efforts to improve production capacity. Investment in new roads, bridges, ports, etc. is continuing but at a slower pace. For example, the budget for the Public Highways Ministry in 1981 was set at £2,100 million, compared with £3,600 million two years previously.

Transport

Over one million road vehicles of all types were registered for the first time in 1978 but only one-fifth of the 125,000 km. road network is surfaced. To save on energy consumption, renewed interest has been shown in the railway system. Outstanding in this respect is the Manila rapid transit system, an elevated light rail line of 15 km., being built with Belgian aid from Caloocan in the north to Pasay in the south. Meanwhile, the standard guage single track south from Manila is being extensively renovated. Harbours and ports developments stress the improvement of selected national ports by providing adequate berthing and storage facilities and dredging work. This will enable a more efficient handling of increases in the volume of maritime traffic and changes in vessel characteristics whilst meeting the requirements of an accelerated programme of regional development. Coal is likely to be prominent and its development alone will require the construction of eight terminals and five outloading ports. A fleet of 12 colliers will be added to the already large inter-island fleet currently benefiting from a major refurbishment programme. Maintenance and repair facilities for marine craft have also been expanded with government incentives, including a major yard at Subic Bay designed to secure international business.

The airports programme centres on improving existing airports rather than building new ones. Emphasis is being placed on the international airports of Mactan (Cebu), Laoag, Tacloban, Puerto Princesa, Zamboanga and Davao, in co-ordination with the tourism programme. Manila now possesses a new international airport designed to cope with the traffic expected through to the end of the century.

POPULATION AND EMPLOYMENT

Transcending the needs for infrastructural improvements is a need for a solution to the population and employment problems. Success in slowing population growth and creating wider employment opportunities accessible to a greater number of people is vital to the nation's economic programme: the population growth rate remains one of the highest in the world. Densities are high too: the 1980 average was 161 persons per square kilometre, but much higher values have been recorded in the principal agricultural areas. A very high fertility among Filipino child-bearing women, a tradition of large families and a culture of children-loving people has contributed immensely to the fast growth of population. A rapid and well supported health development programme by both the Government and private sector has also influenced the population boom to a great extent.

Job creation is not keeping up with demand for jobs. Officially, the unemployment rate was 14.6 per cent in 1980, but unofficial estimates put it close to 20 per cent. Over 150,000 jobs are expected to be created through the development of manufacturing activities but population growth requires that over 500,000 new jobs be created annually. Half the labour force remains engaged in rural occupations, compared with one in ten in manufacturing. However, in agriculture, forestry and fishing, employment from May to August is largely seasonal.

FINANCE

Successive budgets in the 1970s were characterized by rapidly rising government expenditure to maintain the pace of the infrastructure development programme and, subsequently, to pay for the cost of combating the Muslim secessionist movement in the south. Meanwhile the Government's revenue position improved as the result of higher prices for most exports in the mid-1970s. At the same time, however, the growth in the money supply accelerated due to the continuing substantial deficit on current fiscal transactions. However, the budget deficit was reduced at the end of the 1970s, reflecting a rise in import duty receipts due to a boom in import spending (the related sharp deterioration in the foreign trade account also reduced the growth in the money supply).

At the end of the 1970s events in Iran caused the Government to order a cutback in public expenditure and the 1980 budget provided for only a minimal increase in spending in real terms, largely through a cutback in work on infrastructure and utilities. Subsequent budgets have maintained this policy.

Monitoring of the economy by the IMF under its Extended Fund Facility programme has prompted changes in monetary and fiscal policy. For example, rebates have been scrapped on import duties offered to manufacturers as an incentive to investment. However, tariff barriers and related devices still make local industry in the Philippines one of the most protected (and hence inefficient) and high-cost operations in Asia.

Despite the inherent weaknesses of its economy, the Philippines enjoys a relatively high standing in the eyes of foreign investors; they look with favour upon the influence exerted by the technocrats in the Government, and the resultant pragmatic debt-management methods. Two-thirds of approved foreign investment originates from the U.S.A. and Japan. Foreign investors have concentrated their investments in manufacturing, injecting over one-half of the total into the sector and a further one-fifth into financial institutions.

Government policy is to encourage firms to rely on such forms of borrowing as suppliers' credits rather than short-term cash loans. It also aims to increase regular savings deposits and create a strong secondary market in government bonds and securities (the stock market remains predominantly mining and petroleum oriented, with speculators outnumbering investors).

The balance of payments deficit, which reached U.S. $560 million in 1981, has been financed by foreign borrowing: the total external debt at the end of 1981 totalled U.S. $13,767 million. The massive rise in foreign borrowing that occurred in the late 1970s was subsequently regulated by the IMF, as a condition of its participation in the management of the economy, through a stand-by facility and a supplemental financing facility, which is to extend through to 1982.

Banking

Following the Central Bank's restructuring of the financial system, five universal banks had been created by the end of 1981. Each bank, operating under a licence from the Monetary Board, may engage in the full range of banking activities. Their creation represents a logical extension of the variety of regulations that have raised the aggregate capital base of the private commercial banks, thus reducing the dominance of the government-owned Philippine National Bank (PNB). Many problems remain. In particular, that the facilities provided are unevenly distributed. Outside the main cities, and more particularly outside Manila, branches are few. In part this gap has been filled by the creation of 600 rural banks designed to facilitate the availability of credit to farmers. Other sources of long-term finance are the PNB, the Private Development Corporation of the Philippines and the National Investment Development Corporation. A floating rate policy for interest charges has been adopted to encourage savings and allow more efficient financial intermediation, thus making available more long-term capital.

Following success in the Government's efforts to attract the regional offices of multinational companies to Manila by generous operational incentives, regulations were issued in 1976 to permit the operation of an off-shore banking system. These terms are more generous than those offered by a number of other such centres in the region. This new attempt to establish Manila as a rival to Hong Kong and Singapore started encouragingly with 18 banks being granted approval to operate in mid-1979. Such operations, however, are expected to complement existing off-shore banking systems in the region as the tax and other incentives offered and the low cost of labour and accommodation in Manila cannot wholly compensate for the complex and sophisticated banking facilities offered by Hong Kong and Singapore. In fact, while generating deposits of U.S. $736 million in 1977, the system suffered a net loss of U.S. $1 million.

The Government plans to fix the peso against a "basket" of currencies which would initially include the U.S. dollar, the yen and the Deutsche Mark. At present there is an informal link with the U.S. dollar, with the Central Bank intervening in the foreign exchange market to keep the peso in line with the dollar within a narrow band (1 per cent either way in the last three years). The new arrangement would more adequately reflect the importance of Japan as a source of imports and foreign investment and would make the exchange rate a more flexible instrument of policy.

Wages and Prices

The cost of living doubled in the five years ending 1977. The highest price rises occurred in 1974, with food prices rising by 42 per cent and with the general index rising by 51 per cent. Subsequently, the Government's price stabilization policy and several subsidies extended to food related industries helped dampen consumer prices movements. However, official indices are believed to understate the situation through their emphasis on basic food items which have maintained relatively stable prices, although recently the Government has freed a number of essential items and increased price ceilings for others. The continuing pressure of rising petroleum costs was the underlying factor in the 20 per cent annual increases in prices recorded in the late 1970s and in 1980. Inflationary pressures moderated in 1981 which brought the rate down to 11 per cent, have given rise to the prospect of single-figure inflation in 1982.

Average earnings rose faster than prices in only one year (1979) in the past decade, leading to claims that real wages for skilled labour have fallen to less than three-quarters of their 1972 levels; for unskilled labour a decline of over one-third has occurred. The resultant erosion of purchasing power has, it is claimed, increased the number of households below the poverty line. According to indicators drawn up by the Development Academy of the Philippines, 80 per cent of the population live below the poverty line; in contrast, the highest 5 per cent of income earners now share one-third of the national income. It is not surprising, therefore, that Filipino labour is now the cheapest in South-east Asia, matched only by that of Indonesia. This is in line with Government strategy to employ many people, even at low wages, rather than a few at high minimum wages.

INTERNATIONAL TRADE

The Philippines' trade pattern over the past few years has been characterized by sluggish and erratic export behaviour, the latter reflecting variations in world prices for the country's export commodities. However, it is increasingly the oil price burden which has caused substantial trade deficits every year, except 1973, thanks to the boom in world commodity prices then. Central Bank borrowing, including the use of IMF compensatory financing facilities and short-term credits, has protected the country's foreign exchange reserves. This policy has increased pressure on the debt service ratio; to keep it below the IMF ceiling (20 per cent of the previous year's export earnings) reserves have been run down to the equivalent of only four months imports.

The dominance of the U.S.A. and Japan in the Philippines' international trade, is slowly being eroded as a result of the Government's trade diversification policies and the cost of importing petroleum from the Middle East. For example, the EEC accounts for 15 per cent of all trade (with the United Kingdom the largest supplier and the Netherlands the largest purchaser). Receipts from Filipino workers abroad, particularly in the Middle East, are another element of the changing pattern of trade but the country has yet to benefit from the creation of ASEAN, whose members account for less than 5 per cent of total trade with the Philippines. A trade agreement with the U.S.A., signed in late 1979, means that over half of the Philippines' sales will receive tariff cuts, averaging a 65 per cent reduction for all exports to the U.S.A.; the corresponding reduction on imports from the U.S.A. will be a mere 5.7 per cent. Paralleling this, the Government announced two new sets of export incentives, these being mainly a liberalization of existing incentives, but also new measures to encourage import substitution industries to develop overseas sales.

Exports

In 1980 the Government directed that firms which use a substantial amount of foreign currency must earn their own cash to finance purchases of raw materials or supplies. They will need to set up trading companies, with government assistance, through which exporters, particularly of non-traditional items, will channel their foreign sales.

Since the early 1970s the Philippines has been putting a great deal of effort into expanding non-traditional exports. A number of these, including nickel, electronics, bananas, garments and handicrafts, have made impressive strides: for 1979 the combined value of exports of non-traditional manufactured goods exceeded the value of coconut product exports. However, appearances can be deceptive: nickel, bananas and handicrafts now face marketing problems due to world over-supply, while many manufactured exports represent the re-export of semi-processed goods brought to the Philippines from Japan and the U.S.A. to take advantage of its low labour costs.

The bulk of export revenue is derived from primary products. Their relative importance fluctuates from year to year, depending on world market prices, but in the late 1970s coconut products were pre-eminent; normally though, sugar is the leading export commodity. Copper and timber products are other major foreign exchange earners, as is gold. Efforts to increase the value of export commodities have focused upon greater domestic processing, notably the conversion of copra into coconut oil and logs into sawn timber, plywood or veneer. Future efforts are likely to focus on the smelting of copper and other minerals but it is to be hoped that this does not result in a repetition of the over-investment that characterized agricultural product processing.

Imports

Mineral fuels, non-electric machinery, transport equipment and base metals are the major imports, with mineral fuels responsible for one-third of the total. In 1981 imported crude oil alone represented 26 per cent of the import bill, a share double that of the peak contribution made before the 1973 oil price increase.

The burden of oil imports has to some degree inhibited the growth of other imports in recent years especially raw materials for industry and capital goods. The build-up in domestic oil production will have only a small initial impact on the balance of payments because the oil companies have secured fast cost recovery terms.

Efforts to create import substitution industries have had only modest success—only in the case of cereals has there been a major decrease in imports, reflecting the progress of rice and maize-sufficiency programmes. Despite a rapid expansion of domestic manufacturing facilities, imports of transport equipment continue to soar, giving added urgency to government plans to initiate diesel engine manufacture.

"Invisible" Trade

Earnings from services and transfers have flourished in recent years, with two sources pre-eminent: remittances from Filipinos working in the Middle East and elsewhere, and an increasing number of tourists to the Philippines. The advance in tourist arrivals was checked in 1981, but an estimated 500,000 workers repatriated U.S. $1,000 million in that year. However, at least 40 per cent of this did not go through the banking system and is therefore on the black market. The majority of visitors are Japanese, Americans and overseas Filipinos (*Balikbayans*). A government-encouraged increase in hotel building in the mid-1970s, associated with the construction of the International Convention Centre (the latter representing a total investment of around U.S. $500 million), has an important role to play in attracting visitors to Manila.

PLANNING

The 1974–78 Five-Year Development Plan was the successor of the 1972–76 Plan, revised to take into account more recent developments in the national economy, particularly the major social and economic reforms which have drastically altered the framework in which economic development proceeds. In addition to the general development goal of improving the standards of living of the greater mass of the population, this Plan set forth the following objectives: (1) promotion of employment; (2) maximum economic growth feasible; (3) more equitable income distribution; (4) regional development and industrialization; (5) promotion of social development; and (6) maintenance of acceptable levels of price and balance of payments stability.

Three basic agricultural development programmes were envisioned to raise agricultural productivity attain self-sufficiency in food production, and raise the level of rural income; namely, agrarian reform, food production, and co-operatives development. For the industrial sector, a programme aimed at promoting employment opportunities, diversifying and expanding manufactured exports, and increasing efforts at regional development was laid out. Notably, the development of export-oriented industries and of medium- and small-scale industries was given top priority. To sustain the overall development effort, the infrastructure programme provided for the setting up of an efficient system of roads, ports, railways and airports, as well as of power-generating, telecommunication and water resource facilities. The well-being of individuals through education, employment, housing, social welfare, community development and health services was also to be improved. Moreover, in view of the growth imbalance among regions, more emphasis was to be given to regional development and industrialization. Thus, in addition to the correction of policies which artificially favour a few select areas, the integrated approach to regional development was to be utilized. This approach called for the integration of physical development with the economic, social administrative and financial aspects of development into a common plan for a given area.

The Five-Year Plan for 1978–82 extended its economic planning goals to the year 2000 and called for rural development and agrarian reform, expansion of industry and accelerated investment in irrigation, water supply, power, transport, communications, education and housing. The Plan states that income inequality, unemployment and underemployment, population growth, external balance of payments deficits, price instability and energy constraints are the Philippines' most critical problems. The long-term strategy is to spread development over a wider geographical area, and to modify the present uneven distribution of income within and among the regions. To counter income inequality, the Government plans to spend more on socio-economic projects, particularly those favouring the poor, and to disperse new industries to various regions.

According to the Plan, the country's G.N.P. will grow at an average annual rate of 8 per cent, reaching almost 1,000,000 million pesos (at constant 1975 prices) by the year 2000. The share of agriculture in the total net domestic product will drop from 29 per cent in 1975 to 14 per cent in 2000, while the share of industry will increase from 27 per cent to 43 per cent. Manufacturing will increase its share to 33 per cent during the 25-year period and exports will account for 31 per cent of the G.N.P.

The Plan states that the industrial sector will provide the major thrust in the national growth strategy until 2000. This strategy calls for the establishment of a wider industrial base through the encouragement of small- and medium-scale industries and the establishment of heavy industries. With the gradual movement away from light manufacturing towards heavy manufacturing industries, the share of heavy manufacturing goods in the total output of the economy is expected to reach about 60 per cent by the year 2000. NEDA expects that the manufacturing sector will account for half of total exports by 1987. This, in effect, will result in a substantial change in the commodity structure of the country's exports from a basically primary product to a predominantly industrial product orientation by the year 2000.

Export objectives will be realized through a package of fiscal and financial policies, and a restructuring of the present tariff system to provide protective rates on finished products will be implemented to benefit primarily the export-oriented, non-traditional, small- and medium-scale industries. More export processing zones in various areas of the country will also be established. These will favour labour-intensive and export-oriented firms. The Plan also envisages that export markets will shift away from heavy dependence on the U.S.A. and Japan towards such areas as the Middle East, the EEC and ASEAN.

The agriculture sector will continue to pursue self-sufficiency in food and diversification of agricultural exports. Self-sufficiency in staple cereals and feed-grains should be attained by the year 2000 through the expansion of the present intensification programmes. Similarly, expansion in the production of major traditional export commodities such as copra, abaca and sugar is also anticipated. The cultivated area of arable land is expected to increase by 20 per cent by the year 2000. Intensive land use and improved cropping patterns will be emphasized.

The Plan recognizes that the successful implementation of its socio-economic development programme is dependent on maintaining energy supplies. By 1985, the demand for energy should more than double and should further increase between six- and sevenfold by the year 2000. Electric energy will be derived from hydro, geothermal and nuclear resources and half of the non-electric energy supplies will be provided by petroleum. 1990 is the target year for the electrification of the whole country.

The Plan projects an annual average population growth of about 2 per cent until almost the end of the century. The labour force is expected to grow by about 3 per cent a year and it is planned to create an average of about 300,000 new jobs a year between 1975 and 1985 and 350,000 a year between 1985 and 2000.

The broad principles of the 1978–82 Plan also dominate the Plan for 1983–87. It aims to sustain growth of the economy and to ensure equitable distribution of the benefits of economic progress. Its priority is to increase production through a more efficient use of investments and updated technology. The leading objectives are increasing food production, generating more job opportunities in the rural areas and progressively reducing the country's dependence on imported oil or energy.

The private sector will remain the major source of economic growth under the Plan. However, this does not preclude the public sector from involvement in the creation of needed infrastructure and improvements in the social services. The Government will push through the much-debated 11 major industrial projects: copper smelter, phosphatic fertilizer factory, aluminium smelter, integrated steel mill, alcogas programme, heavy engineering industries, integrated pulp and paper complex, petrochemical complex, diesel engine manufacturing, cement industry expansion, and coconut industry rationalization.

Other points in the Government's industrial development programme enunciated in the Plan include support, other than tariff protection, to domestic enterprises with new ventures turned away from sectors already overcrowded, to ensure market viability of production, new incentives to encourage industries to disperse to the countryside, especially the less economically developed areas in the Visayas and Mindanao (Central and Southern Philippines), which will be aligned with government policy for the promotion of exports and generation of more employment opportunities and less government intervention in the private sector phase of industrial development.

In the context of an annual average growth rate (real terms) in G.N.P. of 6.5 per cent, government expenditures are expected to record an annual average increase of 14.5 per cent during 1983–87. Expenditures would account for about 60 per cent of the total, with average growth at 14.8 per cent. Adequate fund allocation will be made for the maintenance of infrastructure projects completed during the 1970s with those undertaken in the interim peaking in 1983, with the Government thereafter reducing investments. The Plan also provides for a graduated increase in allocations for pay of government employees and in the interest payments of economic development loans obtained abroad.

In essence, the food industry and energy dominate the Philippine development plan for 1983–87. Economic planners envisage a well-fed population manning a growing industrial sector fuelled largely by domestic energy sources. While the Plan aims at expanding agricultural yields, it places special emphasis on food production for the "nutritionally at-risk and deprived population group". The Plan looks to an improved and stable income for farmers as the best incentives to raise yields. This necessarily requires low production costs and the Plan aspires to achieve both through the expansion—plus rationalization—of existing agricultural infrastructure projects and credit activities. Meanwhile, agrarian reform will be accelerated in order to increase the number of owner-cultivators, who are assumed to be more productive than tenant farmers or sharecroppers. The system of buying and marketing agricultural produce is also to be rationalized. The Plan also recognizes the problem that more and more agricultural land is being converted for commercial and industrial uses and sees that much more land will have to be put under the plough as the population grows. It aims to ensure the eventual cultivation of all land suitable for agriculture.

The Plan's industrial strategy is to stimulate manufacturing for exports. Philippine industry is to be made internationally competitive on three fronts: existing import-substituting industries are to be modernized and expanded to raise efficiency; small- and medium-scale industries are to be encouraged since they contribute significantly to increased employment and the dispersal of industries to rural areas (but to qualify for government incentive ventures they must strive to export part of their output); capital-intensive basic industries are to be established to provide links with existing extractive and light manufacturing industries.

On energy, the Plan's target is to build up the country's domestic resources, eventually reduce the country's dependence on imported oil, and ultimately provide secure and less expensive energy industries. The Ministry of Energy is accelerating the development and production of domestic fuel sources especially for industrial use. Coal is foremost of these; cement plants are to be used as pilot projects for oil-to-coal conversion. The Industry Ministry plans to extend coal use to more industries, including textiles and other energy-intensive plants. To reduce power costs further, more power plants fuelled by coal or geothermal energy will be built so that oil-fired thermal plants can gradually be retired.

The Plan's ultimate goal is to raise annual per capita income from the current 1,700 pesos by 1987. The Plan admits that the "differences in income and development among regions throughout the country are alarming". To alleviate this situation, the KKK (Kilusang Kabuhayan at Kaunlaran) or National Livelihood Programme has been set up to finance small rural development projects to be owned and managed by villagers and financed by a Government fund through private institutions.

New fiscal dating

In 1977 the official fiscal year was re-set to begin on January 1st instead of July 1st. The 1975/76 fiscal period was consequently extended to the end of 1976, with current spending in the extra six months up to 50 per cent of the programmed or actual levels in the twelve-month period. The Government's aim is to make development planning easier.

STATISTICAL SURVEY

AREA AND POPULATION

AREA OF ISLANDS
(sq. km.)

Luzon	Mindanao	Samar	Negros	Palawan	Panay	Mindoro	Leyte	Cebu	Bohol	Masbate	Others
104,688	94,630	13,080	12,705	11,785	11,515	9,735	7,214	4,422	3,865	3,269	23,092

Total area: 300,000 sq. km. (115,831 sq. miles).

Source: National Census and Statistics Office.

POPULATION

Census Results				Official Estimates (mid-year)			Density (per sq. km.)
May 1st, 1975	May 1st, 1980*						
	Males	Females	Total	1978	1979	1980	1980
42,070,660	24,028,523	23,885,494	47,914,017	45,500,000	46,580,000	48,400,000	161.3

* Preliminary results, excluding adjustment for underenumeration.

Source: National Census and Statistics Office.

PRINCIPAL TOWNS
(population at May 1980, preliminary census results)

Manila (capital)*	1,626,249	Cagayan de Oro City	228,409
Quezon City*	1,165,990	Angeles City	185,995
Davao City	611,311	Butuan City	172,404
Cebu City	489,208	Iligan City	165,742
Caloocan City*	471,289	Olongapo City	156,312
Zamboanga City	344,275	Batangas City	143,554
Pasay City*	286,497	Cabanatuan City	138,297
Bacolod City	266,604	San Pablo City	131,686
Iloilo City	244,211	Cadiz City	128,839

* Part of Metropolitan Manila.

Source: National Census and Statistics Office.

Births and Deaths: Average annual birth rate 38.3 per 1,000 in 1970–75, 36.2 per 1,000 in 1975–80; death rate 10.0 per 1,000 in 1970–75, 8.6 per 1,000 in 1975–80 (UN estimate).

EMPLOYMENT

(persons aged 10 years and over, excluding armed forces)

	1976 (Aug.)	1977* (3rd quarter)	1978* (2nd quarter)
Agriculture, forestry and fishing	8,126,000	7,474,000	8,054,000
Mining and quarrying	56,000	52,000	80,000
Manufacturing	1,680,000	1,515,000	1,755,000
Construction	491,000	484,000	506,000
Electricity, gas and water supply	46,000	42,000	51,000
Commerce	1,864,000	1,355,000	1,660,000
Transport, storage and communications	550,000	681,000	658,000
Services	2,570,000	2,636,000	2,885,000
Other activities	44,000	96,000	50,000
TOTAL	15,427,000	14,335,000	15,699,000

* Persons aged 15 years and over.

Source: National Census and Statistics Office.

AGRICULTURE

LAND USE, 1979

(FAO estimates, '000 hectares)

Arable land	7,050
Land under permanent crops	2,850
Permanent meadows and pasture	1,000
Forest and woodland	12,500
Other land	6,417
TOTAL LAND	29,817
Inland water	183
TOTAL AREA	30,000

Source: FAO, *Production Yearbook.*

PRINCIPAL CROPS

	AREA HARVESTED ('000 hectares)			PRODUCTION ('000 metric tons)		
	1978	1979	1980	1978	1979	1980
Rice (paddy)	3,469	3,379	3,450*	7,198	7,236	7,431*
Maize	3,222	3,327	3,281	2,855	3,167	3,117
Sweet potatoes	228	238	230†	1,037	1,120	1,050†
Cassava (Manioc)	182	192	185†	1,782	2,249	1,900†
Other roots and tubers	54	55	58†	205	217	220†
Pulses	72	71	72†	49	50	53†
Groundnuts (in shell)	48	54	55†	38	50	50†
Coconuts	n.a.	n.a.	n.a.	10,072	9,154	9,575
Copra	n.a.	n.a.	n.a.	2,133	1,910*	2,000*
Vegetables (incl. melons)	n.a.	n.a.	n.a.	1,586	1,648	1,729†
Sugar cane	472	424*	450†	20,273†	19,397†	20,917†
Mangoes	n.a.	n.a.	n.a.	335	359	330†
Pineapples	n.a.	n.a.	n.a.	465	605	600†
Bananas	n.a.	n.a.	n.a.	2,886*	3,862*	3,800†
Plantains	n.a.	n.a.	n.a.	270*	280†	280†
Coffee (green)	76	84	85†	105	122	125†
Cocoa beans	4	5	5†	3	4	4†
Tobacco (leaves)	74	67	75†	57	51	60†
Natural rubber	n.a.	n.a.	n.a.	54	55†	55†

* Unofficial figure. † FAO estimate.

Source: FAO, *Production Yearbook.*

LIVESTOCK

('000 head, year ending September)

	1978	1979	1980
Cattle	1,820	1,833	1,885*
Pigs	6,910	7,445	7,590*
Buffaloes	2,959	2,803	2,760*
Horses†	325	325	325
Goats*	1,410	1,430	1,450
Sheep†	30	30	30
Chickens	58,892	60,000†	65,000†
Ducks	5,365	5,338	6,000†
Turkeys†	190	200	210

* Unofficial figure. † FAO estimate.

Source: FAO, *Production Yearbook.*

LIVESTOCK PRODUCTS

('000 metric tons)

	1978	1979	1980
Beef and veal*	78	76	78
Buffalo meat*	49	48	49
Pigmeat*	366	377	408
Poultry meat†	173	179	184
Cows' milk	15	13†	13†
Buffalo milk†	18	18	18
Hen eggs†	183	190	200
Other poultry eggs†	11.0	11.5	12.0
Cattle and buffalo hides†	18.2	17.8	18.2

* Unofficial figure. † FAO estimate.

Source: FAO, *Production Yearbook.*

FORESTRY

('000 cubic metres, all broadleaved)

ROUNDWOOD REMOVALS

(excluding bark)

	1978	1979	1980
Sawlogs, etc.	7,169	6,578	6,352
Pulpwood*	810	820	820
Other industrial wood*	1,871	1,927	1,985
Fuel wood*	24,495	25,289	26,056
TOTAL	34,345	34,614	35,213

* FAO estimates.

SAWNWOOD PRODUCTION

	1978	1979	1980
Total (incl. boxboards)	1,781	1,262	1,529

Source: FAO, *Yearbook of Forest Products.*

FISHING

('000 metric tons, live weight)

	1978	1979	1980
Milkfish	128.2	140.2	173.3
Threadfin-breams	36.8	32.5	37.4
Ponyfishes (Slipmouths)	68.2	70.4	60.4
Scads (Decapterus)	142.7	146.3	132.0
Bigeye scad	46.5	47.0	47.2
Sardinellas	149.7	106.4	117.3
Rainbow sardine	35.8	24.0	34.1
"Stolephorus" anchovies	76.1	70.5	80.2
Frigate and bullet tunas	50.9	79.9	96.9
Kawakawa	36.3	23.1	24.7
Skipjack tuna	49.7	45.1	31.2
Yellowfin tuna	47.6	49.2	48.0
Other fishes	435.6	388.9	n.a.
Crustaceans	47.1	51.8	n.a.
Freshwater molluscs	103.2	159.4	179.8
Marine molluscs	39.9	38.5	n.a.
Other sea creatures	0.3	1.4	n.a.
TOTAL CATCH	1,494.6	1,475.2	1,556.6

Source: FAO, *Yearbook of Fishery Statistics.*

MINING

		1975	1976	1977	1978	1979
Coal	'000 metric tons	105	121	285	255	367
Iron ore*: gross weight .	,, ,, ,,	1,351	571	—	1,747‡	2,957‡
metal content .	,, ,, ,,	839	354	—	1,089	n.a.
Chromium ore (dry)† .	,, ,, ,,	188.8	157.8	162.1	101.8	134.8
Copper ore† . . .	,, ,, ,,	225.8	237.6	267.1	263.4	300.5
Manganese ore† . .	,, ,, ,,	—	4.3	20.9	3.9	4.9
Zinc concentrates† . .	,, ,, ,,	10.5	16.6	14.9	9.5	10.7
Salt (unrefined) . . .	,, ,, ,,	202	203	213	225.6	338.5
Phosphate rock . . .	,, ,, ,,	5	12	10	1	1
Mercury†	metric tons	8	—	—	—	n.a.
Nickel ore†	,, ,,	9,364	15,239	30,666	29,528	28,762
Gold†	'000 troy ounces	502.6	501.3	558.3	586.6	561.1
Silver†	,, ,, ,,	1,612.9	1,480.8	1,621.1	1,637.4	1,830.2

* Iron mining was temporarily suspended in July 1976.

† Figures refer to the metal content of ores and concentrates.

‡ Lump ore in dry weight.

Source: Bureau of Mines.

INDUSTRY

SELECTED PRODUCTS

		1973	1974	1975	1976	1977
Raw sugar	'000 metric tons	2,093	2,656	2,672	2,984	2,624
Cement	,, ,, ,,	4,059	3,482	4,351	4,229	4,112
Manufactured tobacco* .	metric tons	906	1,031	743	1,933	n.a.
Cigarettes*	million	51,194	41,454	47,688	50,950	n.a.
Cotton yarn†	metric tons	32,225	29,401	35,675	32,618	30,756
Cotton fabrics . . .	'000 metres	222,304	183,748	192,330	204,032	202,517

* Twelve months ending June 30th of year stated.

† Excluding yarn made from waste.

1978 ('000 metric tons): Raw sugar 2,273; Cement 4,197.

FINANCE

100 centavos = 1 Philippine peso.

Coins: 1, 5, 10, 25 and 50 centavos; 1 and 5 pesos.

Notes: 2, 5, 10, 20, 50 and 100 pesos.

Exchange rates (June 1982): £1 sterling = 14.644 pesos; U.S. $1 = 8.455 pesos.
100 Philippine pesos = £6.83 = $11.83.

Note: Prior to January 1962 the official exchange rate was U.S. $1 = 2.00 pesos but other rates were effective for certain transactions. The multiple exchange rate system was ended in January 1962, when a free market was introduced. In May 1962 the free rate stabilized at $1 = 3.90 pesos (1 peso = 25.64 U.S. cents) and this became the par value in November 1965. In February 1970 a free market was re-introduced and the peso "floated" downward. The average market rate (pesos per U.S. dollar) was 6.432 in 1971; 6.671 in 1972; 6.756 in 1973; 6.788 in 1974; 7.248 in 1975; 7.440 in 1976; 7.403 in 1977; 7.366 in 1978; 7.378 in 1979; 7.511 in 1980; 7.900 in 1981. In terms of sterling, the exchange rate between November 1967 and February 1970 was £1 = 9.36 pesos.

BUDGET*
(million pesos)

Revenue	1976	1977	1978†
Taxes on income	4,167.0	4,683.0	5,300.0
Import duties	4,251.7	4,268.4	4,337.6
Export duties	696.8	598.6	662.4
Excises	3,284.9	2,739.1	3,964.6
Other taxes	3,386.9	4,734.9	7,734.0
Other receipts	1,966.9	1,042.9	2,210.3
Total	17,754.2	18,066.9	24,208.9

Expenditure‡	1976	1977	1978†
Education	2,448	3,190	3,900
Other social services	1,552	2,310	3,400
Agriculture and natural resources	1,191	882	2,000
Transport and communications	7,188	5,047	10,000
Other economic services	6,421	6,071	6,400
National defence	3,700	5,100	4,800
Total	22,500	22,600	30,500

* Consolidated transactions of the General, Special, Fiduciary and Bond Funds.

† Estimates.

‡ Figures are rounded. Totals (in million pesos) were: 22,488 in 1976; 22,597 in 1977; 30,464 in 1978.

Source: Budget Commission.

1980 expenditure (million pesos): Economic services 15,500; Social services 11,000; Defence 4,100; General public services 6,000; Debt servicing and interest payments 3,200.

1981 expenditure: 54,800 million pesos.

1982 expenditure: 59,000 million pesos.

1983 expenditure: 65,000 million pesos.

CENTRAL BANK RESERVES
(U.S. $ million at December 31st)

	1978	1979	1980	1981
Gold	118	166	294	508
IMF Special Drawing Rights	17	34	—	2
Foreign exchange	1,746	2,216	2,846	2,197
Total	1,881	2,416	3,140	2,707

Source: IMF, *International Financial Statistics.*

MONEY SUPPLY
(million pesos at December 31st)

	1978	1979	1980	1981
Currency outside banks	8,135	9,182	10,178	11,630
Demand deposits at commercial banks	8,811	9,662	12,363	11,900
Total Money	16,946	18,844	22,541	23,530

Source: IMF, *International Financial Statistics.*

NATIONAL ACCOUNTS
(million pesos at current prices)

National Income and Product

	1976	1977	1978	1979	1980
Domestic factor incomes*	108,802	125,986	144,182	175,262	212,420
Consumption of fixed capital	12,873	15,637	16,759	20,538	26,291
Gross Domestic Product at Factor Cost	121,675	141,623	160,941	195,800	238,711
Indirect taxes	12,821	14,400	} 17,662	23,326	27,833
Less Subsidies	568	392			
G.D.P. in Purchasers' Values	133,928	155,631	178,603	219,126	266,544
Factor income from abroad	1,767	2,243	} −536	−863	−2,279
Less Factor income paid abroad	2,983	3,594			
Gross National Product (G.N.P.)	132,712	154,280	178,067	218,263	264,265
Less Consumption of fixed capital	12,873	15,637	16,759	20,538	26,291
National Income in Market Prices	119,839	138,643	161,308	197,725	237,974
Other current transfers from abroad	1,972	1,950	} 1,915	1,847	2,137
Less Other current transfers paid abroad	83	102			
National Disposable Income	121,728	140,491	163,223	199,572	240,111

* Compensation of employees and the operating surplus of enterprises.

Expenditure on the Gross Domestic Product

	1976	1977	1978	1979	1980
Government final consumption expenditure	14,050	14,489	16,564	18,259	21,424
Private final consumption expenditure	87,120	102,626	118,846	144,143	177,991
Increase in stocks	8,300	7,929	9,178	11,381	13,165
Gross fixed capital formation	32,753	36,322	42,528	53,932	67,460
Statistical discrepancy	298	−366	1,251	3,070	1,247
Total Domestic Expenditure	142,521	161,000	188,367	230,785	281,287
Exports of goods and services	23,248	29,306	31,557	41,461	54,181
Less Imports of goods and services	31,841	34,675	41,321	53,120	68,924
G.D.P. in Purchasers' Values	133,928	155,631	178,603	219,126	266,544
G.D.P. at Constant 1972 Prices	72,962	78,000	82,800	87,700	92,800

Gross Domestic Product by Economic Activity

	1976	1977	1978	1979	1980
Agriculture and livestock	27,668				
Forestry and logging	3,305	41,668	47,334	55,516	61,598
Fishing	6,368				
Mining and quarrying	2,128	2,488	3,333	5,810	8,095
Manufacturing	32,545	39,318	44,404	54,689	68,181
Electricity, gas and water	1,231	1,415	1,699	2,124	2,763
Construction	9,784	11,356	12,525	15,822	20,751
Wholesale and retail trade	19,075	24,220	28,636	36,164	45,322
Restaurants and hotels	1,676				
Transport, storage and communications	6,072	8,583	9,894	12,377	16,444
Owner-occupied dwellings	3,337				
Finance, insurance, real estate and business services	8,105	26,583	30,778	36,624	43,390
Government services	7,267				
Other services	5,367				
G.D.P. in Purchasers' Values	133,928	155,631	178,603	219,126	266,544

BALANCE OF PAYMENTS
(U.S. $ million)

	1974	1975	1976	1977	1978	1979	1980
Merchandise exports f.o.b.	2,694	2,263	2,517	3,078	3,423	4,602	5,789
Merchandise imports f.o.b.	−3,144	−3,459	−3,633	−3,916	−4,733	−6,141	−7,726
Trade Balance	−450	−1,196	−1,116	−838	−1,310	−1,539	−1,937
Exports of services	833	907	872	1,088	1,427	1,575	2,079
Imports of services	−867	−953	−1,128	−1,332	−1,593	−1,954	−2,621
Balance on Goods and Services	−484	−1,242	−1,372	−1,082	−1,476	−1,918	−2,479
Private unrequited transfers (net)	123	165	148	146	194	230	299
Government unrequited transfers (net)	154	153	120	116	120	126	135
Current Balance	−207	−924	−1,104	−820	−1,162	−1,562	−2,045
Direct capital investment (net)	4	97	126	210	164	73	40
Other long-term capital (net)	224	420	1,011	655	834	1,134	939
Short-term capital (net)	625	577	60	123	1,140	909	2,290
Net errors and omissions	−70	−182	−147	−213	−171	−239	−318
Total (net monetary movements)	576	−12	−54	−45	805	315	906
Monetization of gold	—	—	—	—	33	42	127
Allocation of IMF Special Drawing Rights	—	—	—	—	—	28	29
Valuation changes (net)	—	—	−30	−20	−35	−7	22
Loans from IMF Trust Fund	—	—	—	19	60	61	52
Changes in Reserves	576	−12	−84	−46	863	439	1,136

Source: IMF, *International Financial Statistics.*

EXTERNAL TRADE

(U.S. $ million)

	1975	1976	1977	1978	1979	1980	1981
Imports (f.o.b.)	3,459.2	3,633.5	3,915.0	4,638.0	5,540.0	6,380.0	8,400.0
Exports (f.o.b.)	2,294.5	2,573.7	3,150.9	3,424.9	3,780.0	4,660.0	5,910.0

PRINCIPAL COMMODITIES

(U.S. $'000)

Imports	1974	1975	1976	1977	1978
Textile fibres (raw)	88,685	77,625	80,303	86,709	101,158
Mineral fuels and lubricants	653,378	769,886	890,675	993,217	1,030,175
Non-electric machinery	424,015	654,871	625,264	588,990	737,245
Base metals	295,669	212,786	245,259	304,923	382,666
Transport equipment	265,330	301,591	276,099	295,057	389,089
Dairy products	74,465	61,789	55,016	70,097	60,059
Cereals	154,946	175,410	157,711	121,699	121,357
Textile fibres	88,685	77,625	80,303	86,709	n.a.
Electric machinery	105,335	156,944	187,185	134,704	203,253
Explosives and miscellaneous chemicals	113,777	109,282	115,307	137,918	151,631

Exports	1977	1978	1979	1980	1981*
Bananas	73,595	84,775	97,906	140,160	145,620
Desiccated coconut	90,047	81,888	n.a.	102,060	107,820
Canned pineapple	55,908	n.a.	n.a.	76,390	67,530
Raw sugar	506,360	196,904	211,554	n.a.	n.a.
Oil-seed cake and meal	58,469	69,059	n.a.	68,670	68,630
Copra	200,525	135,684	89,128	66,490	48,160
Logs and lumber	200,413	230,059	348,465	311,600	258,460
Iron ore (excl. pyrites)	57,047	103,967	120,016	n.a.	n.a.
Copper concentrates	267,801	250,387	440,637	678,930	543,890
Silver	58,766	n.a.	103,280	n.a.	n.a.
Coconut oil	412,238	620,572	742,513	512,190	553,310
Chemicals	52,033	61,614	112,751	n.a.	n.a.
Veneers, plywood boards, etc.	63,110	100,470	152,178	83,760	109,490
Nickel metal	77,096	55,095	91,660	153,570	98,630
Machinery and transport equipment	53,153	68,606	83,260	n.a.	n.a.
Clothing (excl. footwear)	113,711	160,115	217,299	n.a.	n.a.

* Preliminary.

Source: Central Bank of the Philippines.

PRINCIPAL TRADING PARTNERS

(U.S. $'000)

	Imports (f.o.b.)			Exports (f.o.b.)		
	1978	1979	1980	1978	1979	1980
Australia	167,246	206,002	214,965	75,402	93,809	97,893
Belgium and Luxembourg	26,152	34,942	32,894	18,983	26,984	34,433
Canada	42,427	54,411	68,470	42,664	61,923	64,143
France	101,220	171,779	88,790	53,672	122,340	94,917
Germany, Federal Republic	184,106	276,106	323,356	142,875	226,475	255,061
Hong Kong	107,895	152,887	194,152	90,410	157,979	191,653
India	9,777	12,625	11,064	1,072	4,119	16,205
Indonesia	148,200	182,497	178,035	90,424	46,007	107,152
Italy	31,015	52,525	65,490	33,222	39,950	66,665
Japan	1,285,105	1,397,929	1,531,183	818,381	1,201,003	1,533,333
Korea, Republic	52,687	90,151	136,929	66,372	141,147	202,553
Malaysia and Singapore	56,655	171,348	284,660	107,888	120,487	206,903
Netherlands	71,907	98,313	112,730	280,011	359,851	365,768
Spain	9,321	7,873	951	14,994	29,927	2,423
Switzerland	40,565	39,491	45,292	11,978	7,728	10,196
Taiwan	131,817	175,261	182,666	41,276	69,314	100,555
United Kingdom	171,685	195,007	180,446	90,082	136,451	146,609
U.S.A.	994,966	1,400,151	1,784,815	1,142,819	1,371,592	1,576,405

Source: National Census and Statistics Office.

TRANSPORT

RAILWAYS

	1977	1978	1979	1980	1981
Passengers ('000)	12,796	9,582	n.a.	7,423	7,808
Passenger-kilometres (million)	692	621	n.a.	490	353
Freight ('000 metric tons)	244	159	145	142	116
Ton-kilometres (million)	49	39	39	37	32

Source: National Census and Statistics Office.

ROAD TRAFFIC

(motor vehicles in use)

	1973	1974	1975	1976	1977
Passenger Cars	332,233	397,603	403,481	402,328	440,466
Commercial Vehicles	239,114	272,689	281,731	290,619	327,146

Source: Land Transportation Commission.

CIVIL AVIATION

(Philippine Airlines only—'000)

	1973	1974	1975	1976	1977
Kilometres flown	27,395	33,671	42,040	42,033	41,057
Passenger-kilometres	1,587,953	2,389,944	2,753,262	2,993,145	3,010,100
Revenue freight-ton-kilometres	43,089	59,208	94,139	121,689	132,612
Mail ton-kilometres	3,100	3,231	3,606	4,065	3,078

Source: Civil Aeronautics Board.

INTERNATIONAL SEA-BORNE SHIPPING

('000 metric tons)

	1973	1974	1975	1976	1977
Vessels entered	10,081	8,707	7,415	7,189	10,626
Vessels cleared	9,941	8,893	7,352	7,126	10,563
Goods loaded	16,760	14,532	12,943	11,202	14,819
Goods unloaded	13,923	12,964	15,051	16,428	19,543

Source: Philippine Coast Guard.

TOURISM

	1975	1976	1977	1978	1979
Number of visitors ('000)	502	615	730	859	950
Average stay (days)	7.8	8.1	8.1	n.a.	n.a.
Estimated spending (U.S. $'000)	155,217	235,175	300,842	355,000	400,000

Source: Department of Tourism and Asian Development Bank, *Annual Report* 1980.

1980: 1,100,000 visitors; U.S. $500 million estimated spending.

COMMUNICATIONS MEDIA

	1979
Radio sets	2,000,000
Television sets	1,000,000
Telephones	567,000
Daily newspapers	24*
Total circulation	1,196,239*

* 1974 figures.

Sources: Bureau of Posts, Bureau of Telecommunications, Print Media Council and Philippine Mass Communications Research Society.

EDUCATION

(1979/80)

	Institutions	Pupils
Elementary schools	31,404	8,670,613
Secondary schools	5,144	3,397,740
Universities, colleges and vocational schools	1,098	1,288,197

Source: Bureau of National and Foreign Information.

Source (unless otherwise stated): Statistical Co-ordination Office, National Economic and Development Authority.

THE CONSTITUTION

(Proclaimed January 17th, 1973; amended October 1976; amended April 1981)

Note: When President Marcos proclaimed the ratification of the new Constitution, he also announced the suspension of the interim National Assembly originally envisaged by the Constitution and the continuation of martial law, in force since September 1972. In a referendum held in July 1973 a majority voted that President Marcos should continue in office after 1973 and complete the reforms he had initiated under martial law, and in further referenda, held in February 1975 and October 1976, a majority voted that martial law should be continued. The October 1976 referendum also approved amendments to the transitional provisions of the Constitution. In January 1981 martial law was lifted, although Marcos retained many of his former powers to rule by decree. In April 1981 the Constitution was amended after a national plebiscite.

The following is a summary of the main features of the Constitution.

BASIC PRINCIPLES

Sovereignty resides in the people; defence of the State is a prime duty and all citizens are liable for military or civil service; war is renounced as an instrument of national policy; the State undertakes to strengthen the family as a basic social institution, promote the well-being of youth, maintain adequate social services, promote social justice, assure the rights of workers and guarantee the autonomy of local government.

Other provisions guarantee the right to life, liberty and property, freedom of abode and travel, freedom of worship, freedom of speech, of the press and of petition to the Government, the right of *habeas corpus* except in cases of invasion, insurrection or rebellion, and various rights, before the courts.

THE PRESIDENT

The President is elected from among the members of the National Assembly for a six-year term, by a majority vote; he shall be Head of State and Chief Executive of the Republic and shall formulate the guidelines of national policy; he ceases to be a member of the Assembly or of any political party; he must be at least 50 years of age; he may not receive any emolument other than that entitled to as the President; he can dissolve the National Assembly, call general elections and, when appropriate, recommend and accept the resignation of the Cabinet; during his tenure he shall be immune from lawsuit.

THE NATIONAL ASSEMBLY

Legislative power is vested in the National Assembly (*Batasang Pambansa*), which shall be composed of not more than 200 members; members are elected for six years and must be natural-born citizens, over 25 years of age, literate and registered voters in their district. All citizens of the Philippines over the age of 18 years, not disqualified by law, resident in the Philippines for at least one year and in their voting district for at least six months, are eligible to vote.

Regular elections are to be held on the second Monday of May; the Assembly convenes on the fourth Monday of July for its regular session; it elects a Speaker from among its members; the election of the President and Prime Minister precedes all other business following the election of the Speaker.

Various provisions define the procedures of the Assembly and the rights of its members, among them that the Assembly may withdraw its confidence in the Prime Minister by a majority vote; that no bill shall become law until it has passed three readings on separate days; that every bill passed by the Assembly shall be presented to the Prime Minister for approval, upon the withholding of which, the Assembly may reconsider a bill and, by a majority vote of two-thirds, enable it to become law.

THE PRIME MINISTER AND CABINET

Executive power is exercised by the Prime Minister with the assistance of the Cabinet; the Prime Minister is nominated by the President, and elected from the members of the National Assembly by a majority vote; he appoints the members of the Cabinet. The President may nominate a Deputy Prime Minister who shall be elected by the National Assembly.

The Prime Minister is Commander-in-Chief of the armed forces; he may suspend the writ of *habeas corpus* and proclaim martial law; the President shall have control of the Ministries, and the Prime Minister shall have supervision over them; there shall be an Executive Committee composed of the Prime Minister and not more than 14 other members, at least half of whom shall be members of the National Assembly, to be designated by the President.

THE JUDICIARY

The Supreme Court is composed of a Chief Justice and 14 Associate Justices, and may sit *en banc* or in two divisions.

LOCAL GOVERNMENT

The National Assembly shall enact a local government code which shall establish a more responsive and accountable local government structure.

CONSTITUTIONAL COMMISSIONS

These are the Civil Service Commission, the Commission on Elections and the Commission on Audit. The Commission on Elections enforces and administers all laws relating to the conduct of elections and registers and accredits political parties.

THE NATIONAL ECONOMY

The National Assembly shall establish a National Economic Development Authority which shall recommend co-ordinated social and economic plans to the National Assembly and all appropriate governmental bodies. Various provisions relating to the public interest in economic matters are set forth.

AMENDMENTS

Amendments and revisions to the Constitution may be proposed by the National Assembly upon a vote of three-quarters of its members, or by a constitutional convention. Any amendment or revision is valid when ratified by a majority of votes cast in a plebiscite.

THE GOVERNMENT

HEAD OF STATE

President: FERDINAND EDRALIN MARCOS (inaugurated December 30th, 1965; re-elected November 1969, term of office extended by referendum July 1973; re-elected June 1981).

THE CABINET

(July 1982)

Prime Minister and Minister of Finance: CÉSAR E. A. VIRATA.

Deputy Prime Minister and Minister of Local Government: JOSE A. ROÑO.

Minister of Foreign Affairs: CARLOS P. ROMULO.

Minister of Justice: RICARDO PUNO.

Minister of Agriculture: ARTURO R. TANCO, Jr.

Minister of Education and Culture: Dr. ONOFRE CORPUZ.

Minister of Labor: BLAS F. OPLE.

Minister of National Defense: JUAN PONCE ENRILE.

Minister of Health: Dr. JESUS AZURIN.

Minister of Agrarian Reform: CONRADO F. ESTRELLA.

Minister of Tourism: JOSE D. ASPIRAS.

Minister of Industry, Trade and Investment: ROBERTO ONGPIN.

Minister for Public Works and Highways: JESUS S. HIPOLITO.

Minister of Natural Resources: TEODORO PENA.

Minister of Energy: GERONIMO Z. VELASCO.

Minister of Human Settlements and Ecology: IMELDA R. MARCOS.

Minister of Social Services and Development: SYLVIA P. MONTES.

Minister of Transportation and Communications: JOSE DANS.

Officials with Cabinet Rank:

Director of Public Information: GREGORIO CENDAÑA.

Director-General of National Economic Development Authority: PLACIDO MAPA.

Chairman of the National Science Development Board: EMIL JAVIER.

Budget Commissioner: MANUEL ALBA.

Presidential Executive Assistant: JUAN C. TUVERA.

Commissioner for Islamic Affairs: Rear Adm. ROMULO ESPALDON.

Presidential Assistant on National Minorities: MANUEL ELIZALDE, Jr.

Solicitor General: ESTELITO P. MENDOZA.

LEGISLATURE

BATASANG PAMBANSA

Under the amended transitional provisions of the 1973 constitution, an interim National Assembly, with some members elected and some appointed by the President, was convened in June 1978 following elections held in April 1978. Elections for a full National Assembly are due to be held in 1984.

Speaker: QUERUBE MAKALINTAL.

Seats at General Election, April 7th, 1978.

New Society Movement	149
Pusyon Bisaya Party	13
Others	2
Representatives of Sectoral Organizations	14
Cabinet Ministers (appointed)	10
TOTAL	188

POLITICAL PARTIES

After the proclamation of martial law in September 1972 no political parties were authorized to operate. The ban was lifted in January 1978 and elections for an interim National Assembly (*Batasang Pambansa*) were held in April. Taking part were the New Society Movement, Lakas Ng Bayan-Laban and Pusyon Visaya Party. A presidential election held in June 1981 after the lifting of martial law was partially boycotted by the opposition.

Lakas Ng Bayan—Laban (*People's Power Movement—Fight*): opposition grouping comprising many members of the former Liberal Party and other anti-Marcos elements, led by BENIGNO AQUINO, Jr.; boycotted the 1980 provincial, municipal and local elections in protest against martial law; Chair. LORENZO TANADA.

Liberal Party: Manila; f. 1946; represents the centre-liberal opinion of the old *Partido Nacionalista*, which split in 1946; boycotted the 1980 provincial, municipal and local elections in protest against martial law; Pres. (vacant).

Mindanao Alliance: Cagayan de Oro; regional party; led by Governor HOMOBONO ADAZA.

Nacionalista Party: Manila; f. 1907; represents the right wing of the former *Partido Nacionalista*, which split in two in 1946; split into two factions in 1981, led by JOSE ROY and JOSE B. LAUREL respectively.

National Union for Liberation (NUL): f. 1979; Leader DIOSDADO MACAPAGAL.

New Society Movement (*Kilusan Bagong Lipunan*): formed in early 1978 by supporters of the former Nacionalista Party and the Marcos Administration; led by FERDINAND E. MARCOS.

Pilipino Democratic Party (PDP): f. 1981 by former members of the Mindanao Alliance and other parties; led by AQUILINO PIMENTEL.

Pusyon Visaya Party: won 13 seats in the Visayas region of the Central Philippines in 1978 elections; split into two factions in 1981, led by BARTOLOME CABANGBANG and MARIANO LOGARTA respectively.

Social Democratic Party: f. 1981 by members of the *Batasang Pambansa* allied to the Nacionalista (Roy faction), Pusyon Visaya and Mindanao Alliance parties; led by MARIANO LOGARTA, FRANCISCO TATAD and REUBEN CANOY.

DIPLOMATIC REPRESENTATION

EMBASSIES ACCREDITED TO THE PHILIPPINES

(In Metropolitan Manila unless otherwise stated)

Afghanistan: Tokyo, Japan.

Argentina: 408–411 Oledan Bldg., 131–133 Ayala Ave., Makati; *Ambassador:* HUGO CARLOS BENNET.

Australia: 3rd and 5th Floor, China Bank Bldg., Paseo de Roxas, Makati; *Ambassador:* RICHARD ARTHUR WOOLCOTT.

Austria: Jakarta, Indonesia.

Bangladesh: *Ambassador:* Maj.-Gen. MOINUL HUSSAIN CHOWDURY.

Belgium: 6th Floor, Don Jacinto Bldg., cnr. de la Rosa and Salcedo Sts., Legaspi Village, P.O.B. 968, Makati; *Ambassador:* Dr. WILFRIED DE PAUW.

Brazil: 3rd Floor, Dominga Bldg., 162 Legaspi St., Legaspi Village, Makati; *Ambassador:* LAURO SOUTELLO ALVES.

Bulgaria: 1212 Tamarind Rd., Dasmariñas Village, Makati; *Ambassador:* TODOR PETKOV DICHEV.

Burma: 4th Floor, DAO II, Alvarado St., Legaspi Village, Makati; *Ambassador:* U LA WOM.

Canada: 4th Floor, Cibeles Bldg., 6780 Ayala Ave., Makati; *Ambassador:* EDWARD L. BOBINSKI.

Chile: 7th Floor, F. & M. Lopez Bldg., cnr. Legaspi and Herrera Sts., Legaspi Village, Makati; *Ambassador:* (vacant).

China, People's Republic: 4896 Pasay Rd., Dasmariñas Village, Makati; *Ambassador:* MO YANZHONG.

Colombia: Cristina Condominium, Room 204, Legaspi Village, Makati; *Ambassador:* VIRGILIO OLANO.

Cuba: 51 Paseo de Roxas, Urdaneta Village, Makati; *Ambassador:* JOSÉ ARTEAGA Y HERNÁNDEZ.

Czechoslovakia: 14 La Salle St., Greenhills Village, San Juan, Metro Manila; *Ambassador:* Ing. KAREL HOUSKA.

Denmark: Citibank Center, 10th Floor, 8741 Paseo de Roxas; *Ambassador:* ANTHON CHRISTIAN KARSTEN.

Dominican Republic: Taipei, Taiwan.

Egypt: 13th Floor, Cibeles Bldg., Ayala Ave., Makati; *Ambassador:* MOHAMED FAROUK EL-HENNAWY.

Ethiopia: Tokyo, Japan.

Finland: 14th Floor, PAL Bldg., Ayala Ave., Makati; *Ambassador:* KLAUS SNELLMAN.

France: 2nd Floor, Filipinas Life Assurance Bldg., 6786 Ayala Ave., Makati; *Ambassador:* ALBERT TRECA.

Gabon: 2nd Floor, Zeta Bldg., 191 Salcedo St., Legaspi Village, Makati; *Ambassador:* THÉOPHILE P. A. ISSEMBE.

German Democratic Republic: Jakarta, Indonesia.

Germany, Federal Republic: 5th Floor, Citibank Center, Paseo de Roxas, Makati; *Ambassador:* HILDEGUNDE FEILNER.

Greece: Tokyo, Japan.

Guatemala: Tokyo, Japan.

Hungary: Tokyo, Japan.

India: 3rd Floor, Casmer Bldg., Salcedo St., Legaspi Village, Makati; *Ambassador:* R. K. JERATH.

Indonesia: Indonesian Embassy Bldg., Salcedo St., Legaspi Village, Makati; *Ambassador:* Lt.-Gen. LEO LOPULISA (*recalled January, 1982*).

Iran: 4th Floor, Don Jacinto Bldg., cnr. Salcedo and de la Rosa Sts., Legaspi Village, Makati; *Chargé d'affaires:* SAIID ZIBAKALAM MOFRAD.

Iraq: Kuala Lumpur, Malaysia.

Israel: Metropolitan Bank Bldg., 6813 Ayala Ave., Makati; *Ambassador:* JAKOB AVIAD.

Italy: 6th Floor, Zeta Bldg., 191 Salcedo St., Legaspi Village, Makati; *Ambassador:* GIULIANO BERTUCCIOLI.

Japan: L.C. Bldg., 375 Buendia Ave. Ext., Makati; *Ambassador:* HIDEHO TANAKA.

Jordan: Tokyo, Japan.

Korea, Republic: 3rd Floor, ALPAPI Bldg., 140 Alfaro St., Salcedo Village, Makati; *Ambassador:* SONG KWANG-JUNG.

Laos: Bangkok, Thailand.

Lebanon: Tokyo, Japan.

Libya: 4928 Pasay Rd., Dasmariñas Village, Makati; *Ambassador:* MOUSTAFA M. DREIZA.

Malaysia: 2nd and 3rd Floors, Republic Glass Bldg., cnr. Gallardo and Tordesillas Sts., Salcedo Village, Makati; *Ambassador:* Datuk ISMAIL BIN MOHAMAD.

Malta: 1 Narra Ave., Forbes Park, Makati; *Ambassador:* ERNESTO LAGDAMEO.

Mexico: 814 Pasay Rd., San Lorenzo Village, Makati; *Ambassador:* JOAQUIN BERNAL.

Mongolia: Tokyo, Japan.

Nepal: Tokyo, Japan.

Netherlands: Metropolitan Bank Bldg., 6813 Ayala Ave., Makati; *Ambassador:* CHRISTIANUS T. F. THURKOW.

New Zealand: 10th Floor, Bankmer Bldg., 6756 Ayala Ave., Makati; *Ambassador:* DAVID G. HOLBOROW.

Nigeria: 4th Floor, Fortune Bldg., 160 Legaspi St., Legaspi Village, Makati; *Ambassador:* ALHAJI AHMED KYARI MOHAMMAD.

Norway: 6th Floor, ERECHEM Bldg., cnr. Salcedo and Herrera Sts., Legaspi Village, Makati; *Ambassador:* PETER MOTZFELDT.

Pakistan: 3rd Floor, CMI Bldg., 6799 Ayala Ave., Makati; *Ambassador:* (vacant).

Panama: Taipei, Taiwan.

Papua New Guinea: Ground Floor, Pacific Bank Bldg., 6776 Ayala Ave., Makati; *Ambassador:* THOMAS B. RITAKO.

Peru: 6th Floor, F & M Bldg., Legaspi St. cnr. Herrera St., Legaspi Village, Makati; *Ambassador:* GUILLERMO HEREDIA.

Poland: Tokyo, Japan.

Romania: 1268 Acacia Rd., Dasmariñas Village, Makati; *Ambassador:* (vacant).

Saudi Arabia: 8th Floor, Insular Life Bldg., 6781 Ayala Ave., Makati; *Ambassador:* FAWZI ABDUL MAJID SHOBOKSKI.

Senegal: Tokyo, Japan.

Sierra Leone: Beijing, People's Republic of China.

Singapore: 6th Floor, ODC International Plaza Bldg., 219 Salcedo St., Legaspi Village, Makati; *Ambassador:* Dr. KWAN SAI KHEONG.

Somalia: Beijing, People's Republic of China.

Spain: 2515 Leon Guinto, cnr. Estrada St.; *Ambassador:* CLEOFE LIQUINIANO ELGORIAGA.

Sri Lanka: 4th Floor, Sarmiento Bldg., Ayala Ave., Makati; *Ambassador:* FRANCIS W. WANIGASEKERA.

Sweden: 15th Floor, Citibank Center, 8741 Paseo de Roxas, Makati; *Ambassador:* BO KÄLFORS.

Switzerland: 5th Floor, V. Esguerra Bldg., 140 Amorsolo St., Makati; *Ambassador:* J. RICHARD GAECHTER.

Thailand: 6th Floor, Oledan Bldg., 131 Ayala Ave., Makati; *Ambassador:* CHAO SAICHEUA.

Turkey: Tokyo, Japan.

U.S.S.R.: 1245 Acacia Rd., Dasmariñas Village, Makati; *Ambassador:* VALERIAN VLADIMIROVICH MIKHAILOV.

United Kingdom: Electra House, 115–117 Esteban St., cnr. Herrera St., Legaspi Village, Makati; *Ambassador:* M. H. MORGAN, C.M.G.

U.S.A.: 1201 Roxas Bldv.; *Ambassador:* MICHAEL H. ARMACOST.

Uruguay: Seoul, Republic of Korea.

Vatican City: 2140 Taft Ave. (Apostolic Nunciature); *Apostolic Nuncio:* Mgr. BRUNO TORPIGLIANI.

Viet-Nam: 554 Vito Cruz, Malate; *Ambassador:* HOANG HOAN NGHINH.

Yugoslavia: 7th Floor, ODC International Plaza, 219 Salcedo St., Legaspi Village, Makati; *Ambassador:* JOKAS BRAJOVIĆ.

The Philippines also has diplomatic relations with Algeria, Bolivia, Costa Rica, Cyprus, Ecuador, El Salvador, Fiji, Guinea, Honduras, Iceland, Ireland, Kuwait, Liberia, Maldives, Monaco, Nicaragua, Niger, Oman, Portugal, Qatar, the United Arab Emirates, Venezuela, Western Samoa, and the People's Democratic Republic of Yemen.

JUDICIAL SYSTEM

Supreme Court: Composed of a Chief Justice and 14 Associate Justices. The Court sits *en banc* and in two divisions. Cases involving the constitutionality of a treaty, law or executive agreement are decided *en banc*. To declare a treaty, law or executive agreement unconstitutional, or to impose the death penalty, at least ten Justices must concur. In other cases heard *en banc*, the concurrence of at least eight Justices is required for a decision. Cases heard by division are decided by the concurrence of at least five Justices; if the required number is not obtained, the Chief Justice sits with the division concerned.

The Court's powers include the supervision of the administration of all courts and their personnel; the promulgation of rules on pleading, practice and procedure in all courts; admission to the practice of law and the integration of the Bar which, however, may be repealed, altered or supplemented by the National Assembly.

Chief Justice: ENRIQUE M. FERNANDO.

Intermediate Appelate Court: Consists of a Presiding Justice and 49 Associate Appelate Justices.

Presiding Justice: RAMON GAVIOLA.

In August 1981 the Court of Appeals and lower courts were abolished and replaced by special trial and new appeal courts. President Marcos was given the power to appoint new judges.

RELIGION

Iglesia Filipina Independiente (*Philippine Independent Church*): 1500 Taft Ave., P.O.B. 2484, Ermita, Metro Manila; f. 1902; 3.9 million mems.; The Most Rev. ABDIAS R. DE LA CRUZ, Head Bishop; publ. *Aglipayan Review*.

Iglesia ni Cristo: Central Ave., Diliman, Quezon City, Metro Manila; f. 1914; Brother ERAÑO G. MANALO, Exec. Minister; publ. *Pasugo*.

ROMAN CATHOLIC CHURCH

Roman Catholicism is the predominant religion of the Philippines.

Metropolitan See of Manila: Archbishop's House, Villa San Miguel, 438 Shaw Blvd., Mandaluyong, Metro Manila; H. E. Cardinal JAIME L. SIN, D.D.

Metropolitan See of Cebu: Archbishop's House, Cebu City 6401; Most Rev. RICARDO J. VIDAL, D.D.

Metropolitan See of Cotabato: P.O.B. 186, Cotabato City 9301; Most Rev. PHILIP SMITH, O.M.I., D.D.

Metropolitan See of Nueva Segovia: Archbishop's House, Vigan, Ilocos Sur 0401; Most Rev. JOSE T. SANCHEZ, D.D.

Metropolitan See of Caceres: Archbishop's House, Naga City 4701; Most Rev. TEOPISTO V. ALBERTO, D.D.

Metropolitan See of Lingayen-Dagupan: Archbishop's House, Dagupan City 0701; Most Rev. FEDERICO G. LIMON, S.V.D., D.D.

Metropolitan See of Jaro: Archbishop's House, Jaro, Iloilo City; Most Rev. ARTEMIO G. CASAS, D.D.

Metropolitan See of Cagayan de Oro: Archbishop's House, Cagayan de Oro City; Most Rev. PATRICK H. CRONIN, D.D.

Metropolitan See of Zamboanga: Archbishop's House, Box 1, Zamboanga City 7801; Most Rev. FRANCISCO R. CRUCES, D.D.

Metropolitan See of Lipa: Archbishop's House, Lipa City 4216; Most Rev. MARIANO G. GAVIOLA, J.C.D.

Metropolitan See of Capiz: Archbishop's House, Roxas City 5701; Most Rev. ANTONIO F. FRONDOSA, D.D.

Metropolitan See of Davao: Archbishop's House, P.O.B. 138, Davao City; Most Rev. ANTONIO LL. MABUTAS, D.D.

Metropolitan See of San Fernando (Pampanga): Archbishop's Residence, San Fernando, Pampanga 2001; Most Rev. OSCAR V. CRUZ, D.D.

Metropolitan See of Tuguegarao: Archbishop's House, Tuguegarao, Cagayan 1101; Most Rev. TEODULFO S. DOMINGO, D.D.

PROTESTANT CHURCHES

Union Church of Manila: cnr. Rada-Legaspi, Legaspi Village, Makati, Metro Manila; Pastor ALEXANDER B. ARONIS.

United Church of Christ in the Philippines: P.O.B. 718, Manila; Gen. Sec. Bishop ESTANISLAO Q. ABAINZA; 300,000 mems.; publ. *United Church Letter*.

ISLAM

Imam: Hadji MADKI ALONTO, Governor of Lanao del Sur.

There are about 2,800,000 Muslims in the southern Philippines.

OTHERS

There are about 43,000 Buddhists and 400,000 Animists and persons of no religion.

THE PRESS

The Philippines had a large and diverse press, with about 15 metropolitan dailies and 175 weeklies, before the imposition of martial law by President Marcos in September 1972, when all newspapers and radio stations were shut down. A number of reporters, editors and publishers were arrested, and before publication could be resumed the Government's Mass Media Council had to screen staff and give its authorization. The strict controls on content and comment were gradually relaxed, and the Mass Media Council was replaced in May 1973 by a Media Advisory Council, composed of representatives of the various media. In November 1974 controls were further relaxed with the abolition of the Media Advisory Council and its replacement by the all-civilian Philippine Council for Print Media (P.C.P.M.). In January 1981 this too was abolished, coinciding with the lifting of martial law. Newspapers are expected to publish only what the President described as news of "positive national value" and to eschew sensationalism.

METRO MANILA

DAILIES

Balita: 2249 Pasong Tamo, Makati; f. 1972; morning; Pilipino; published by Liwayway Publishing Inc.; Editor DOMINGO M. QUIMLAT; circ. 136,701.

Bulletin Today: Bulletin Publishing Corpn., Muralla St., Recoletos, Intramuros; f. 1972; English; Publisher HANS M. MENZI; Editor BEN F. RODRIGUEZ; circ. 273,039.

Business Day: 113 West Ave., Quezon City; f. 1967; 5 a week; English; Editor RAUL L. LOCSIN; circ. 26,250.

Evening Express: 371 Bonifacio Drive, Port Area; English; Man. Editor AUGUSTO P. SANTA ANA; circ. 16,010.

Manila Evening Post: 20th St. and Bonifacio Drive, Port Area; English; published by Oriental Media Inc.; Editor RAMON FRANCISCO; circ. 70,000.

The Orient News: Railroad and 13th St., Port Area; f. 1974; English and Chinese; published by The Orient Media Inc.; Editor GEORGE CHEN; circ. 25,500.

People's Journal: Journal Bldg., Railroad St., cnr. 19th and 20th Sts., Port Area; English and Pilipino; published by Philippines Journalists Inc.; Editor AUGUSTO B. VILLANUEVA; circ. 507,967.

Philippines Daily Express: 371 Bonifacio Drive, Port Area; f. 1972; English and Pilipino editions; magazine supplement *Weekend*; Editor ENRIQUE P. ROMUALDEZ; circ. 119,603.

Pilipino Express: 371 Bonifacio Drive, Port Area; Pilipino; Editor ANTONIO S. MORTEL; circ. 17,697.

The Times Journal: The Times Journal Bldg., Railroad St., cnr. 19th and 20th Sts., Port Area; English; magazine supplement, *Parade*; published by Philippine Journalists Inc.; Editor-in-Chief JOSE LUNA CASTRO; circ. 151,000.

United Daily News: 818 Benavides St., Binondo; f. 1973; Chinese and English; published by United Daily News Corporation; Editor SY YINCHOW; circ. 21,600.

SELECTED PERIODICALS

Weeklies

Ang Pahayagang Malaya: 784 Units B & C, Ground Floor, RMS Bldg., Quezon City; Publisher and Editor JOSE G. BURGOS; circ. 15,000.

Bannawag: Liwayway Bldg., 2249 Pasong Tamo, Makati; f. 1934; Ilocano; published by Liwayway Publishing Inc.; Editor DIONISIO S. BULONG; circ. 45,000.

Bisaya: Liwayway Bldg., 2249 Pasong Tamo, Makati; f. 1934; Cebu-Visayan; published by Liwayway Publishing Inc.; Editor NAZARIO BAS; circ. 55,000.

Focus Philippines: 200 Second St., Port Area; f. 1972; English; general interest magazine; Editor KERIMA POLOTAN TUVERA; circ. 70,000.

Liwayway: Liwayway Bldg., 2249 Pasong Tamo, Makati; f. 1922; Pilipino; Editor BIENVENIDO RAMOS; circ. 159,000.

Observer: Journal Bldg., Railroad St., cnr. 19th and 20th Streets, Port Area; English and Pilipino; published by Times Journal; circ. 20,000.

Philippine Panorama: Recoletos St., Intramuros; f. 1968; English; Publr. HANS MENZI; Editor DOMINI TORREVILLAS SUAREZ; circ. 330,000.

Sports News: 1526 Constancia St., Sampaloc, Manila; f. 1975; Editor RUDY NAVARRO; circ. 50,000.

WE Forum: 784 Units B & C, Ground Floor, RMS Bldg., Quezon Ave., Quezon City; Publisher and Editor JOSE G. BURGOS; circ. 25,000.

Who: 2249 Pasong Tamo, Makati; Editor CIELO BUENAVENTURA; circ. 34,000.

Woman's Home Companion: 70 8th Ave., Quezon City; English; Editor COOKIE GUERRERO; circ. 75,116.

Women's Journal: Chronicle Bldg., Meralco Ave., Tektite Rd., Pasig; English; Editor LUISA H. A. LINSANGAN; circ. 79,749.

Monthlies

Asia Mining: 7514 Bagtikan, cnr. Pasong Tamo, Makati; English; Editor ERNESTO O. RODRIGUEZ; circ. 13,900.

Farming Today: Room 306, Catalina Bldg., New York St., Cubao, Quezon City; f. 1974; English; Editor BERNARDITA AZURIN QUIMPO; circ. 10,000.

National Observer: 407 Leyba Bldg., Dasmariñas.

Philippine Law Gazette: 13 Mapayapa, U.P. Village, Diliman, Quezon City; Editor VICENTE B. FOZ.

Sunburst: 2nd Floor, 215 Buendia Ave., Makati; f. 1973; English; Publr. J. NOBLE SORIANO; circ. 138,000.

SELECTED REGIONAL PUBLICATIONS

BICOL REGION

Naga Times: 801 Ojeda IV, Naga City; f. 1959; weekly; English; Editor RAMON S. TOLARAM; circ. 5,200.

Sorsogon Today: 2nd Floor, Gabarda Bldg., Sorsogon; f. 1977; weekly; Publisher and Editor MARCOS E. PARAS, Jr.; circ. 1,600.

CAGAYAN VALLEY

Cagayan Star: Arellano St., Tuguegarao; Sunday.

The Valley Times: Clavarall St., Ilagan, Isabela; f. 1962; weekly; English and Ilocano; Editor DIOGENES M. FALLARME; circ. 4,500.

CENTRAL LUZON

Palihan: Diversion Rd., cnr. Sanciangco St., Cabanatuan City; f. 1966; weekly; Pilipino; Editor FIEL JARLEGO; circ. 2,000.

The Tribune: Maharlika Highway, Cabanatuan City; f. 1960; weekly; English and Pilipino; Editor ORLANDO M. JARLEGO; circ. 5,000.

ILOCOS REGION

Baguio Midland Courier: 16 Kisad Rd., P.O.B. 50, Baguio City; English and Ilocano; Editor SINAI C. HAMADA.

MINDANAO

Mindanao Star: 44 Kolambagohan-Capistrano St., Cagayan de Oro City; Saturday; Editor ROMULFO SABAMAL.

Mindanao Today: Newslane, Baliwasan, Zamboanga City; three times a week; Editor-in-Chief E. RENE R. FERNANDEZ.

The Pagadian Times: Margosatubig and Brueg, Zamboanga del Sur; Monday; Editor JACINTO LUMBAY.

The Voice of Islam: P.O.B. 407, Davao City; f. 1973; English and Arabic; Editor MUHAMMAD AL'RASHID.

Zamboanga Times: Campaner St., Zamboanga City; 3 a week; Man. RENE FERNANDEZ.

SOUTHERN TAGALOG

Bayanihan Weekly News: P. Guevara Ave., Santa Cruz, Laguna; f. 1966; Pilipino and English; Editor ARTHUR A. VALENOVA; circ. 3,000.

The Quezon Times: 180 Quezon Ave., Lucena City; English; Editor VEN ZOLETA.

VISAYAS

The Aklan Reporter: 1227 Rizal St., Kalibo, Aklan; f. 1971; Wednesday; English and Aklanon; Editor ROMAN A. DE LA CRUZ; circ. 2,350.

Ang Bag-ong Kasanag: Bonifacio Drive, Iloilo City; Publr. MARIANO M. DILOSA; Editor DOUGLAS K. MONTERO.

Bohol Chronicle: 56 Mabini St., Tagbilaran City, Bohol; f. 1954; weekly; English and Cebuano; Editor ZOILO DEJARESCO; circ. 4,200.

Cebu Advocate: 158 Pelaez St., Cebu City; daily; Editor E. C. AVELLANOSA; circ. 3,750.

Cebu Daily Times: 135 P. Gonzales St., Cebu City; Editor WILFREDO VELOSO.

The Kapawa News: 10 Jose Abad Santos St., P.O.B. 365, Bacolod City; f. 1966; weekly (Saturday); Hiligaynon and English; Editor NATALIA V. SITJAR; circ. 3,000.

Morning Times: V. Gullas and D. Jacosalem Sts., P.O.B. 51, Cebu City; f. 1942; daily (except Monday); English and Visayan; Editor PEDRO D. CALOMARDE; circ. 7,500.

The Visyan Tribune: 826 Iznart St., Iloilo City; weekly (Monday); English; Editor NOBERTO C. BAYLEN; circ. 1,200.

The Weekly Negros Gazette: Broce St., San Carlos City, Negros Occidental, 6033; f. 1956; weekly; Editor NESTORIO L. LAYUMAS, Sr.; circ. 5,000.

Weekly Scope: 28 Rosario St., Bacolod City; Man. AURELIO SERVANDO, Jr.

NEWS AGENCIES

Philippines New Agency: National Press Club, Magallanes Drive, Intramuros, Manila; f. 1973; Chief Editor LORENZO J. CRUZ.

FOREIGN BUREAUX

Agence France-Presse (AFP): 5th Floor, VIP Bldg., cnr. Roxas Blvd. and Plaza Ferguson, P.O.B. 1019, Ermita, Manila; Chief of Bureau TEODORO C. BENIGNO.

Associated Press (AP) (*U.S.A.*): ITT-Globe Mackay Bldg., 689 United Nations Ave., Ermita, Manila; Chief of Bureau DAVID BRISCOE.

Far East News Agency (FENA) (*Taiwan*): Veterans Bank Bldg., Bonifacio Drive, Metro Manila; Bureau Chief NELSON CHUNG.

Jiji Tsushin-sha (*Japan*): Room 403, Katigbak Bldg., 1000 A Mabini St., Ermita, Metro Manila; Correspondent SHUJI ONOSE.

Kyodo News Service (*Japan*): Room 277 Manila Hilton Hotel, United Nations Ave., Ermita, Manila; Bureau Chief TATSUO SAITOH.

Reuters (*U.K.*): Room 277 Manila Hilton Hotel, United Nations Ave., Ermita, Manila.

Tass (*U.S.S.R.*): 1821 Suntan St., Dasmariñas Village, Makati, Metro Manila; Correspondent ALEX PETROV.

United Press International (UPI) (*U.S.A.*): Veterans Bank Bldg., 8th Floor, Bonifacio Drive, Port Area, Manila; Bureau Chief FERNANDO DEL MUNDO.

Xinhua (*People's Republic of China*): 2008 Roxas Blvd., Metro Manila; Chief Correspondent CHANG CHIEH.

Agencia EFE (Spain) also has a bureau in Manila.

PRESS ASSOCIATIONS

National Press Club of the Philippines: Magallanes Drive, Intramuros, Manila; f. 1952; Pres. OLAF GIRON; 934 mems.

Manila Overseas Press Club: HRAP Restaurant, Philtrade Exhibits, CCP Complex, Roxas Blvd., Manila.

PUBLISHERS

Abiva Publishing House Ind.: 851 G. Araneta Ave., Quezon City; f. 1949; history, religion, reference and textbooks; Chair. L. Q. ABIVA, Jr.

Associated Publishers Inc.: 63 Quezon Blvd. Ext., Quezon City, P.O.B. 449, Manila; f. 1952; law, medical and educational books; Pres. J. V. ROXAS.

Bustamente Press Inc.: 155 Panay Ave., Quezon City; f. 1949; textbooks on English, sciences and mathematics; Pres. PABLO N. BUSTAMENTE, Jr.

Capitol Publishing House Inc.: 54 Don Alejandro A. Roces Ave., Quezon City.

Editorial Associates Ltd.: 48 West Ave., Quezon City; publishing services.

R. P. Garcia Publishing House: 903 Quezon Ave. Ext., Quezon City; f. 1936; printer and publisher of textbooks for Philippine schools; Pres. and Gen. Man. ROLANDO M. GARCIA.

Liwayway Publishing Inc.: 2249 Pasong Tamo, Makati, Metro Manila; magazines.

G. Miranda & Sons: 844 N. Reyes St., Manila; textbooks, comics, reprints; Pres. ELISA D. MIRANDA.

Mutual Books Inc.: 425 Shaw Blvd., Mandaluyong, Metro Manila; f. 1959; college textbooks on accounting, management and economics; Pres. ALFREDO S. NICDAO, Jr.; Sec. and Treas. FRANCISCO F. GONZALEZ IV.

Philippine International Publishing Co.: 1789 A. Mabini St., Ermita, Manila.

Regal Publishing & Printing Co.: 1729 J. P. Laurel St., San Miguel, Manila 2804; f. 1958; Philippine literature; Vice-Pres. CORINNA BENIPAYO MOJICA.

Sinag-Tala Publishers Inc.: Quezon City; educational textbooks; business, professional and religious books.

PUBLISHERS' ASSOCIATIONS

Philippine Educational Publishers' Asscn.: 927 Quezon Ave., Quezon City; Pres. JESUS ERNESTO R. SIBAL; Vice-Pres. ESTHER A. VIBAL.

Publishers' Association of the Philippines Inc.: Bulletin Today Bldg., Muralla St., Intramuros, Manila; f. 1974; a non-profit-making corporation composed of all newspaper, magazine and book publishers in the Philippines; Pres. HANS MENZI; Sec.-Treas. MARIANO B. QUIMSON; Exec. Dir. ROBERTO M. MENDOZA.

RADIO AND TELEVISION

National Telecommunications Commission: Panay Ave., cnr. Scout Reyest St., Quezon City; exercises maximum control and regulation of all public telecommunications (common carriers; safety and special aid broadcast series) in the Philippines; Chair. Gen. CEFERINO S. CARREON.

Telecommunications Control Bureau: 5th Floor, De los Santos Bldg., 100 Quezon Blvd., Quezon City 3008; supervises and enforces policies, rules and regulations involving telecommunications, including operation of radio stations and other telecommunications facilities; Dir. Gen. CEFERINO S. CARREON.

RADIO

There are 270 broadcasting radio stations (commercial and non-commercial). The following are the principal operating networks:

Banahaw Broadcasting Corporation: Broadcast City, Capitol Hills, Diliman, Quezon City; 14 stations; Pres. ALEX LUKBAN.

Far East Broadcasting Company: P.O.B. 1, Valenzuela, Metro Manila; f. 1948; 27 stations; operates a home service 23 hours a day, a classical music station, an overseas service throughout Asia in 90 languages; Pres. BOB BOWMAN; Dir. FRED M. MAGBANUA, Jr.; publ. *The Signal* (quarterly).

Manila Broadcasting Co.: Elizalde Bldg., 141 Ayala Ave., Makati, Metro Manila; 10 stations; Pres. MANUEL ELIZALDE, Sr.; Gen. Man. EDUARDO L. MONTILLA.

Nation Broadcasting Corporation: Jacinta Bldg., 914 Pasay Rd., Makati, Metro Manila; 25 stations; Pres. and Gen. Man. ABELARDO L. YABUT, Sr.

Newsounds Broadcasting Network: 2406 Nobel cnr. Edison St., Makati, Metro Manila; 10 stations; Pres. REGELIO FLORETE; Consultant MIGUEL C. ASIGNACION.

Office of Media Affairs Radio Network: BSP Bldg., Cóncepcion St., Manila; 21 stations; domestic broadcasts; Head of Office GREGORIO S. CENDAÑA.

Philippines Broadcasting Service (PBS): Office of Media Affairs, BSP Bldg., Cóncepcion St., Manila; overseas service of Bureau of Broadcasts, Ministry of Public Information; Officer-in-Charge GREGORIO S. CENDAÑA.

Philippine Federation of Catholic Broadcasters: 2307 Pedro Gil, Santa Ana, P.O.B. 2722, Manila 2802; 19 radio stations and one TV channel; Pres. Bishop JULIO XAVIER LABAYEN, O.C.D.; publ. *Intercom* (twice a month).

Radio Mindanao Network: Suites 411–413 Chateau Makati Bldg., F. Zobel St., Makati, Metro Manila; 36 stations; Pres. HENRY R. CANOY; Chair. TEODORO F. VALENCIA.

Radio Philippines Network: Broadcast City, Capitol Hills, Diliman, Quezon City; 15 stations; Pres. JOSE MONTALVO; Gen. Man. FELIPE G. MEDINA, Jr.

Radio-Republic Broadcasting System: E. de los Santos Ave., Diliman, Quezon City; Chair. FELIPE L. GOZON; Pres., Exec. Officer and Dir. MENARDO R. JIMENEZ.

Tinig ng Pilipinas: National Media Production Center, Philcomcen Bldg., Ortigas Ave., Pasig, Metro Manila; Dir. GREGORIO CENDAÑA.

In 1979 there were 2 million radio receivers in use.

TELEVISION

There are five major television networks operating in the country with 19 carrying and 7 relay stations. The following are the principal operating television networks:

Banahaw Broadcasting Corporation: Broadcast City Complex, Capitol Hills, Quezon City; Gen. Man. Ms. KITCHIE BENEDICTO.

GMA Radio Television Arts: E. de los Santos Ave., Diliman, Quezon City; Chair. FELIPE L. GOZON; Pres., Exec. Officer and Dir. MENARDO JIMENEZ.

Intercontinental Broadcasting Corporation: Broadcast City, Capitol Hills, Diliman, Quezon City; 19 stations; Gen. Man. JOSE JALANDOON.

Kanlaon Broadcasting System, Inc.: Broadcast City, Capitol Hills, Diliman, Quezon City; manages the Banahaw Broadcasting Corporation and the Radio Philippines Network; Pres. SYKE GARCIA; Gen. Man. FELIPE MEDINA, Jr.

Maharlika Broadcasting System: Media Center, Bohol Ave., Quezon City; jointly operated by the Bureau of Broadcasts and the National Media Production Center; Dir. GREGORIO CENDAÑA.

In 1979 there were 1 million television sets.

ASSOCIATION

Kapisanan ng Mga Brodkaster Sa Pilipinas (KBP) (*Association of Broadcasters in the Philippines*): 4th Floor, L&F Bldg., Aguirre St., Legaspi Village, Makati, Metro Manila; Pres. ANTONIO C. BARREIRO; Chair. TEODORO VALENCIA.

FINANCE

BANKING

(cap.=capital; p.u.=paid up; dep.=deposits; m.=million; brs.=branches; amounts in pesos)

The Central Bank of the Philippines supervises the entire financial system.

The financial structure consists of: (1) the banking system: commercial banks, thrift banks (savings and mortgage banks, stock savings and loan associations and private development banks), regional unit banks (rural banks), and specialized and unique government banks such as the Development Bank of the Philippines, and the Land Bank of the Philippines; (2) non-bank financial intermediaries: investment houses and companies, securities dealers, financing companies, fund managers, pawnshops and lending investors. Legislation passed in September 1976 permitted the establishment of off-shore banks in the Philippines. By mid-1980 20 foreign banks had been authorized to operate off-shore banking units.

CENTRAL BANK

Central Bank of the Philippines: A. Mabini cnr. Vito Cruz, Malate, Metro Manila; f. 1949; cap. 10m.; dep. 29,222m. (March 1981); Gov. and Chair. (Monetary Board) JAIME LAYA.

GOVERNMENT BANKS

Philippine National Bank (PHILNABANK): P.O.B. 1844, PNB Bldg., Escolta, Metro Manila; f. 1916; government-controlled; cap. p.u. 1,622m.; dep. 15,704m. (March 1981); Pres. and Acting Chair. P. O. DOMINGO; 183 brs.

Philippine Veterans Bank: Bonifacio Drive, Port Area, Metro Manila; f. 1964; cap. p.u. 100.0m.; dep. 2,122m. (March 1981); Chair. ALEJO SANTOS; Pres. ESTEBAN B. CABANOS; 25 brs.

PRINCIPAL COMMERCIAL BANKS

Allied Banking Corporation: Allied Bank Centre, 6754 Ayala Ave., cnr. Legaspi St., Makati, Metro Manila, P.O.B. 2009; f. 1977; cap. p.u. 441m.; dep. 4,621m. (Dec. 1981); Chair. LUCIO C. TAN; Pres. ROMEO Y. CO.

Bank of the Philippine Islands: P.O.B. 1827 MCC, Makati, Metro Manila; f. 1851; cap. p.u. 300.0m.; dep. 3,947.9m. (March 1981); Pres. ENRIQUE ZOBEL; 129 brs.

China Banking Corporation: cnr. Dasmariñas and Juan Luna Sts., P.O.B. 611, Metro Manila; f. 1920; cap. p.u. 248.9m.; dep. 1,583m. (March 1981); Chair. Pres. ROBERT DEE SE WEE; 7 brs.

Far East Bank and Trust Co.: Far East Bank Bldg., Muralla St., Intramuros, Metro Manila (P.O.B. 1411); f. 1960; cap. p.u. 328m.; dep. 2,813m. (Dec. 1980); Chair. JOSÉ B. FERNANDEZ, Jr.; Pres. AUGUSTO M. BARCELON; 48 brs.

Metropolitan Bank and Trust Co.: Metrobank Plaza, Buendia Ave. Ext., Makati, Metro Manila; f. 1962; cap. and res. 353.9m.; dep. 3,559.9m. (Dec. 1980); Chair. GEORGE S. K. TY; Pres. ANDRES V. CASTILLO; 122 brs.

Pacific Banking Corporation: 460 Quintin Paredes St., Metro Manila; f. 1955; cap. p.u. 140.4m.; dep. 1,784.7m. (March 1980); Chair. S. ANTONIO ROXAS CHUA, Jr.; Pres. and Chief Operating Officer JOSE F. UNSON; 43 brs.

Philippine Commercial and Industrial Bank: Legaspi St., Legaspi Village, Makati, Metro Manila; f. 1960; cap. p.u. 190.7m.; dep. 2,280m. (March 1980); Chair. EMILIO ABELLO; Pres. ANTONIO H. OZAETA; 67 brs.

Philtrust Bank (Philippine Trust Co.): United Nations Ave., cnr. San Marcelino St., Metro Manila; f. 1916; cap. p.u. 165.0m.; dep. 623m. (March 1982); Pres. ALBERTO F. DE VILLA-ABRILLE; Chair. EMILIO T. YAP; 19 brs.

Pilipinas Bank: MSE Bldg., Ayala Ave., Makati, Metro Manila; cap. p.u. 320m.; dep. 328.5m. (March 1981); Chair. PANFILO O. DOMINGO; Pres. CONSTANTINO T. BAUTISTA.

Rizal Commercial Banking Corpn.: 333 Buendia Ave. Ext., Makati, Metro Manila; f. 1963; cap. p.u. 141m.; dep. 1,999.4m. (Oct. 1981); Chair. A. T. YUCHENGCO; Pres. DAVID B. SYCIP; 41 brs.

RURAL BANKS

Small private banks established with the encouragement and assistance (both financial and technical) of the Government in order to promote and expand the rural economy in an orderly manner. Conceived mainly to stimulate the productive capacities of small farmers, small merchants and small industrialists in rural areas, and to combat usury, their principal objectives are to place within easy reach and access of the people credit facilities on reasonable terms and, in co-operation with other agencies of the Government, to provide advice on business and farm management and the proper use of credit for production and marketing purposes. The nation's rural banking system consisted of 1,000 units in December 1979.

SPECIAL BANKS

Development Bank of the Philippines: DBP Bldg., cnr. Makati and Buendia Aves., Makati, Metro Manila; f. 1947; government-owned; provides long-term loans for agricultural and industrial developments; cap. 3,050.2m.; dep. 3,697.4m. (March 1980); Chair. RAFAEL A. SISON.

Land Bank of the Philippines: 6th Floor, Palacio del Gobernador, Aduana St., Intramuros, Metro Manila; f. 1963; provides financial support in all phases of the Government's agrarian reform programme; cap. 1,549.3m.; dep. 2,275.3m. (March 1982); Chair. CESAR E. A. VIRATA; Pres. BASILIO ESTANISLAO; 21 brs.

In addition there are 24 private development banks.

FOREIGN BANKS

Bank of America: BA-Lepanto Bldg., 8747 Paseo de Roxas, Makati, Metro Manila D-708; dep. 698.1m. (March 1980); Vice-Pres. and Man. LARRY DEAN HARTWIG.

Chartered Bank (*U.K.*): 7901 Makati Ave., Makati, Metro Manila; cap. p.u. 143.5m.; dep. 338.8m. (Sept. 1980); Man. R. O. YOUNG.

Citibank (*U.S.A.*): 8741 Paseo de Roxas, Makati, Metro Manila; dep. 634,843.9m. (Sept. 1981); Sen. Vice-Pres. JAMES J. COLLINS.

Hongkong and Shanghai Banking Corporation (*Hong Kong*): PAL Bldg., Ayala Ave., Makati, Metro Manila; dep. 417.7m. (March 1980); Sen. Exec. Vice-Pres. D. G. HARRISON.

MAJOR OFF-SHORE BANKS

American Express International Banking Corpn. (*U.S.A.*): 3rd Floor, Corinthian Plaza, Paseo de Roxas, Makati, Metro Manila; f. 1977; Vice-Pres. and Gen. Man. VICENTE CHUA.

The Bank of California (*U.S.A.*): 2nd Floor, Corinthian Plaza, Paseo de Roxas, Makati, Metro Manila; f. 1977; Man. JONES M. CASTRO, Jr.

Bank of Nova Scotia (*Canada*): 2nd Floor, Pioneer House, 108 Paseo de Roxas, Makati, Metro Manila; f. 1977; Man. A. F. LEUNG.

The Bank of Tokyo (*Japan*): 3rd Floor, Corinthian Plaza, Paseo de Roxas, Makati, Metro Manila; f. 1977; Gen. Man. TATSUHIKO ENDO.

Banque de l'Indochine et de Suez (*France*): Ground Floor, Corinthian Plaza, Paseo de Roxas, Makati, Metro Manila; f. 1977; Man. JEAN MALLET.

Banque Nationale de Paris (*France*): 7th Floor, Citibank Center, 8741 Paseo de Roxas, Makati, Metro Manila; f. 1977; Gen. Man. PIERRE GRANDAMY.

Barclays Bank International Ltd. (*U.K.*): National Life Bldg., 6762 Ayala Ave. (P.O.B. 1939 MCC), Makati, Metro Manila; f. 1977; Sen. Vice-Pres. and Man. GERALD S. SHELTON.

The Chase Manhattan Bank (*U.S.A.*): 18th Floor, Filinvest Financial Centre, Ayala Ave., Makati, Metro Manila; f. 1977; Vice-Pres. and Man. MILES G. ARMSTRONG.

Crocker National Bank (*U.S.A.*): 5th Floor, Pacific Bank Bldg., 6776 Ayala Ave., Makati, Metro Manila; f. 1977; Vice-Pres. and Man. LYNN E. KUCKUCK.

European Asian Bank (*Federal Republic of Germany*): 17th Floor, Filinvest Financial Center Bldg., 8753 Paseo de Roxas Ave., Makati, Metro Manila; f. 1977; Man. T. L. HOOPER.

International Bank of Singapore: Bancom III Bldg., cnr. Rada and Legaspi Sts., Legaspi Village, Makati, Metro Manila; f. 1977; Man. LEOW MIN SIONG.

Lloyds Bank International (*U.K.*): 6813 Ayala Ave., (P.O.B. 2174 MCC), Makati, Metro Manila; f. 1977; Man. JORGE O. JAMES.

Manufacturers Hanover Trust Co. (*U.S.A.*): 4th Floor, Corinthian Plaza, Paseo de Roxas, Makati, Metro Manila; f. 1977; Vice-Pres. and Man. JOSEPH A. LONGOBARDI.

Rainier National Bank (*U.S.A.*): 2nd Floor, Corinthian Plaza, Paseo de Roxas, Makati, Metro Manila; f. 1977; Vice-Pres. and Man. MARK D. EHLINGER.

Security Pacific National Bank (*U.S.A.*): 11th Floor, Metrobank Plaza, Buendia Ave., Makati, Metro Manila; f. 1977; Gen. Man. JOHN C. GETZELMAN.

United California Bank (*U.S.A.*): 12th Floor, Metrobank Plaza, Buendia Ave., Ext. Makati, Metro Manila; f. 1977; Vice-Pres. and Man. ALAN F. SMITH.

BANKING ASSOCIATION

Bankers' Association of the Philippines: Room S-314, 3rd Floor, Secretariat Bldg., CCP Complex, Roxas Blvd., Manila; Pres. EDWARD S. GO.

STOCK EXCHANGES

Makati Stock Exchange: Makati Stock Exchange Bldg., Ayala Ave., Makati, Metro Manila; f. 1963; Pres.-Gov. EDUARDO LIM.

Manila Stock Exchange: Manila Stock Exchange Bldg., Muelle de la Industria and Prensa Sts., Binondo, Manila; f. 1927; 54 mems.; Pres. SIMPLICIO J. ROXAS; Sec. IGNACIO B. GIMENEZ; publs. *MSE Weekly Letter, MSE Monthly Review, MSE Investment Guide Yearbook, MSE Investor's Information Series, MSE Oil Guidebook*.

Metropolitan Stock Exchange: 2nd Floor, Padilla Arcade, Greenhills Commercial Center, San Juan, Metro Manila; f. 1974; Pres. TEOPHILO REYES, Jr.; 36 mems.

Securities Exchange Commission: Manila; Chair. ANGEL LIMJOCO.

INSURANCE

Capital Insurance and Surety Co. Inc.: P.O.B. 1613, Escolta, Manila; f. 1949; Pres. J. G. GARRIDO; Chair. J. MUÑOZ; fire, casualty, marine, life.

Central Surety & Insurance Co.: 2nd Floor, Universalre Condominium Bldg., 106 Paseo de Roxas St., Legaspi Village, Makati, Manila; f. 1949; Pres. CONSTANCIO T. CASTAÑEDA, Jr.; bonds, fire, marine, casualty, motor car.

Commonwealth Insurance Co.: Warner Barnes Bldg., 2900 Faraday, cnr. South Expressway, Makati, Metro Manila; f. 1935; Pres. JUAN DE IBAZETA.

Co-operative Insurance System of the Philippines: Room 300, Delta Bldg., Intramuros, Manila; Chair. ORLANDO J. SACAY; Gen. Man. EDUARDO T. MALINIS.

Domestic Insurance Company of the Philippines: Domestic Insurance Bldg., Port Area, Manila; f. 1946; Pres. A. L. ACHAVAL; Man. J. J. CRUZ.

Empire Insurance Co.: 4th and 5th Floors, Kalaw-Ledesma Condominium, 117 Gamboa St., Legaspi Village, Makati, Metro Manila; f. 1949; Chair. SERGIO CORPUZ; fire, bonds, marine, accident, extraneous perils.

Equitable Insurance Corporation: 4th Floor, Equitable Bank Bldg., 262 Juan Luna St., Binondo, P.O.B. 1103, Manila; f. 1950; Pres. GEORGE L. GO; Exec. Vice-Pres. ERNESTO C. MAURICIO; fire, marine, personal, accident, car, bond.

FGU Insurance Corporation: Insular Life Bldg., 6781 Ayala Ave., Makati, Metro Manila; f. 1963; Pres. ENRIQUE CLEMENTE, Jr.

First Continental Assurance Co. Inc.: Licaros Bldg., Intramuros, Manila; f. 1960; Pres. G. B. LICAROS, Jr.; fire, marine, motor car, accident, workmen's compensation, bonds.

First National Surety & Assurance Co. Inc.: Insurance Center Bldg., 633 Gen. Luna St., Intramuros, Manila; f. 1950; Pres. DANIEL L. MERCADO, Sr.; general insurance.

Insular Life Assurance Co. Ltd.: Insular Life Bldg., 6781 Ayala Ave., Makati, P.O.B. 128, Metro Manila; f. 1910; Pres. VICENTE R. AYLLÓN.

Malayan Insurance Co. Inc.: 4th Floor, Yuchengo Bldg., 484 Quintin Paredes St., Manila; f. 1948; Pres. ALFONSO YUCHENGCO; industrial and commercial.

Manila Surety & Fidelity Co. Inc.: 66 P. Florentino, Quezon City; f. 1945; Pres. Dr. PRECIOSO S. PEÑA; Vice-Pres. Dr. ELISA V. PEÑA.

Metropolitan Insurance Company: Elizalde Bldg., 141 Ayala Ave., Makati, Metro Manila; f. 1933; Pres. MANUEL ELIZALDE; Exec. Vice-Pres. and Man. G. A. REEDYK; non-life.

National Life Insurance Company of the Philippines: National Life Insurance Bldg., 6762 Ayala Ave., Makati, Metro Manila; f. 1933; Pres. BENJAMIN L. DE LEON; Sr. Vice-Pres. JOSE L. BURGOS.

Paramount Surety and Assurance Co. Inc.: 3rd Floor, Paramount Bldg., 434 Quintin Paredes St.,Binondo, Metro Manila; f. 1950; Pres. HERNAN P. SAN LUIS; fire, marine, casualty, car.

People's Surety & Insurance Co. Inc.: 1111 Trinidad Bldg., cnr. A. Mabini and UN Aves., Manila; f. 1950; Pres. and Chair. CONCHITA L. DE BENITEZ; non-life, surety, fidelity.

Philippine American General Insurance Co. Inc.: Philamlife Centre, UN Ave., Ermita, Manila; f. 1939; Pres. B. M. ARAGON; Chair. M. CAMPOS; all classes of general insurance.

Philippine Prudential Life Insurance Co. Inc.: Insurance Center Bldg., 633 Gen. Luna St., Intramuros, Manila; f. 1963; Pres. D. L. MERCADO; life, health and accident.

Philippine Reinsurance Corporation: 2nd Floor, Asian Reinsurance Bldg., cnr. Gamboa and Salcedo Sts., Legaspi Village, Makati, Metro Manila; f. 1958; Pres. ATTY. NICANOR JACINTO, Jr.; reinsurance in all branches.

Pioneer Insurance and Surety Corpn.: Pioneer House, 108 Paseo de Roxas, Makati, Metro Manila; f. 1954; Pres. and Chief Exec. JOSE HALILI.

Reinsurance Company of the Orient Inc.: 2nd Floor, Rico House, 126 Amorsolo St., Legaspi Village, Makati, Metro Manila; f. 1956; Pres. CARMELINO G. ALVENDIA; all classes.

Rico General Insurance Corporation: 2nd Floor, Rico House, 126 Amorsolo St., Legaspi Village, Makati, Metro Manila; f. 1964; Chair. and Pres. Justice ESPERANZA P. ALVENDIA; Gen. Man. FELICISIMO G. ALVENDIA.

Rizal Surety and Insurance Co.: 4th and 5th Floors, Kalaw-Ledesma Condominium, 117 Gamboa St., Legaspi Village, Makati, Metro Manila; f. 1939; Pres. and Chair. SERGIO CORPUS; fire, bond, marine, motor car, accident.

Standard Insurance Co. Inc.: 5th Floor, Cardinal Bldg., cnr. F. Agoncillo and Herran Sts., Manila; f. 1958; Pres. LOURDES T. ECHAUZ.

State Bonding & Insurance Co. Inc.: 2nd and 3rd Floors, Jacinto Bldg., 352 T. Pinpin cnr. Escolta, Manila; f. 1949; Pres. and Gen. Man. NICANOR JACINTO, Jr.

Tabacalera Insurance Co. Inc.: 900 Romualdez St., Paco Manila; f. 1937; Pres. ALEJANDRO ROS DE LACOUR; Chair. MANUEL P. MANAHAN.

Universal Reinsurance Corpn.: Universalre Bldg., 106 Paseo de Roxas, Legaspi Village, Makati, Metro Manila; f. 1971; Chair. JAIME ZOBEL DE AYALA; Pres. ANGEL B. GABRIEL.

World-Wide Insurance & Surety Co. Inc.: 4th Floor, Cardinal Bldg., cnr. Pedro Gil and F. Agoncillo Sts., Ermita, Manila; f. 1950; affiliated with Standard-Cardinal Life Insurance Companies; Pres. EDUARDO T. ECHAUZ; fire, marine, motor car, accident, workmen's compensation, loans, mortgages, bonds, aviation.

The majority of the larger British, American and Canadian insurance companies are represented in Manila.

TRADE AND INDUSTRY

CHAMBERS OF COMMERCE AND INDUSTRY

Philippine Chamber of Commerce and Industry: Chamber of Commerce Foundation Bldg., Magallanes Drive, Intramuros, Manila 2801; f. 1977 following the merger of the Chamber of Commerce of the Philippines and the Philippine Chamber of Industries; Pres. FRED J. ELIZALDE; Dir.-Gen. Dr. FELIX MARAMBA, Jr.

Chamber of Agriculture and Natural Resources of the Philippines: 5th Floor, Rico House, Amorsolo St., Legaspi Village, Makati, Metro Manila; Pres. ALFREDO MONTELIBANO.

Chamber of International Trade: Room 914, L&S Bldg. No. 2, 1515 Roxas Blvd., Ermita, Metro Manila; Pres. JOVITO A. RIVERA.

European Chamber of Commerce of the Philippines Inc.: P.O.B. 763, 6th Floor, Jardine Davies Bldg., 222 Buendia Ave., Makati, Metro Manila; f. 1898; 171 mems.; Pres. H. J. SCHUMACHER; Vice-Pres. R. O. YOUNG.

Federation of Filipino-Chinese Chambers of Commerce and Industry Inc.: P.O.B. 23, 6th Floor, Federation Center, Muelle de Binondo, Manila; Pres. RALPH NUBLA.

There are local chambers affiliated to Philippine Chambers of Commerce in all the more important towns and seaports.

TRADING CORPORATIONS

Philippine Cement Corpn. (Philcemcor): Manila; State trading firm in cement.

Philippine International Trading Corporation (PITC): 3rd Floor, ITC Bldg., 337 Buendia Ave. Ext., Makati, Metro Manila; f. 1973; government-owned stock corporation to conduct bulk trade in general merchandise, agri-based products, industrial and construction goods, raw materials, semi-finished and finished goods; Pres. DOMINADOR I. LIM.

Philippine Sugar Commission: Quezon City; f. 1977; government organization conducting research into, and development and marketing of, sugar; Chair. of Board of Commrs. ROBERTO S. BENEDICTO; Vice-Chair. JOSE A. UNSON; publs. *Philsucom Journal, The Cane Point, Factory Performance Audit.*

Wenagro Industrial Corporation: Manila; producer and exporter of Philippine products; took over Philippine Exporters Trading Corporation (PETCOR) 1980; Man. Dir. FRANCISCO C. WENCESLAO.

DEVELOPMENT ORGANIZATIONS

National Economic and Development Authority (NEDA): Quezon City Complex, E. de los Santos Ave., Diliman, Quezon City; f. 1973; central planning and policy formulation body of the Philippines, to ensure the optimum utilization of scarce resources and to increase economic efficiency; Dir.-Gen. GERARDO P. SICAT.

Agricultural Credit Administration (ACA): 2544 Taft Ave., Manila; wholly government-owned corporation; provides crop production credit to farmers and marketing and facility loans to agricultural co-operatives; Administrator TEOFILO T. AZADA.

National Development Company (NDC): Goodland Bldg., 377 Buendia Extension Ave., Makati, Metro Manila; f. 1919; wholly government-owned corporation engaged in the organization, financing and management of subsidiaries and corporations including commercial, industrial, mining, agricultural and other enterprises which may be necessary or contributory to the economic development of the country, including joint industrial ventures with other ASEAN countries; Chair. ROBERTO V. ONGPIN; Gen. Man. ANTONIO L. CARPIO.

Private Development Corporation of the Philippines (PDCP): PDCP Bldg., Ayala Ave., Makati, Metro Manila; f. 1963 with World Bank assistance; assists private enterprise development in the Philippines, especially of capital markets and managerial skills; Chair. ROBERTO T. VILLANUEVA; Pres. VICENTE R. JAYME.

EMPLOYERS' ASSOCIATIONS

Employers' Confederation of the Philippines: Chamber of Commerce Foundation Bldg., Magallanes Drive, Intramuros, Manila 2801; f. 1975; Pres. AURELIO PERIQUET, Jr.; Exec. Dir. CONSTANTE C. ROLDAN.

Filipino Shipowners' Association: Magsaysay Bldg., T. M. Kalaw St., Ermita, Metro Manila; f. 1950; 33 mems.; Pres. MIGUEL A. MAGSAYSAY; Exec. Sec. HERMELO E. CABAUATAN.

Philippine Cigar and Cigarette Manufacturers' Association: Metro Manila; Pres. RALPH NUBLA.

Philippine Coconut Producers' Federation, Inc.: 2nd and 3rd Floors, Lorenzo Bldg., cnr. Taft Ave. and Vito Cruz, Metro Manila; Pres. MARIA CLARA L. LOBREGAT.

Philippine Copra Exporters' Association Inc.: 943 Gabaldon Bldg., J. Llanes Escoda St., Ermita, Metro Manila; Pres. MANUEL J. IGUAL.

Philippine Sugar Association: Rm. 1111, National Life Insurance Bldg., Ayala Ave., Makati, Metro Manila; f. 1922; 16 mems.; Pres. MANUEL ELIZALDE; Exec. Vice-Pres. and Treas. EDGARDO F. Q. YAP.

Pulp and Paper Manufacturers' Association Inc.: Room 704, Katigbak Bldg., A. Mabini cnr. T. M. Kalaw Sts., Ermita, Manila; f. 1959; Pres. FRANCISCO P. MONGE.

Sugar Producers' Co-operative Marketing Association, Inc.: 7th Floor, Kalayaan Bldg., Corner Salcedo and De la Rosa Sts., Makati, P.O.B. 3839, Manila; Pres. A. U. BENEDICfo; Sec., Dir. CIRO LOCSIN.

Textile Mills Association of the Philippines, Inc. (TMAP): Alexander House, 132 Amorsolo St., Legaspi Village, Makati, Metro Manila; f. 1956; 34 mems.; Pres. RAMON L. SIY.

Textile Producers' Association of the Philippines, Inc.: Rm. 513, Downtown Center Bldg., 516 Quintin Paredes St., Binondo, Metro Manila; Pres. ALFREDO ESCAÑO; Exec. Sec. ROBERT L. TAN.

TRADE UNIONS

FEDERATIONS

Associated Marine Officers and Seamen's Union of the Philippines (AMOSUP): Transport Hall, Port Area, Manila; f. 1976; 23 affiliated unions and 13,876 mems.; Pres. GREGORIO S. OCA.

Confederation of Citizens Labor Unions (CCLU): 312 Forum Bldg., Rizal Ave., cnr. Lope de Vega St., Sta. Cruz, Manila; f. 1951; 49 affiliated unions and 45,766 mems.; Pres. LEON O. TY.

Federation of Free Farmers (FFF): 41 Highland Drive, Blue Ridge, Quezon City; f. 1953; 200,000 mems.; Pres. JEREMIAS MONTEMAYOR.

Federation of Free Workers (FFW): 4th Floor, Cuevas Bldg., cnr. Pedro Gil and Taft Ave., P.O.B. 163, Manila; f. 1950; affiliated to the Brotherhood of Asian Trade Unionists and the WCL; 480 affiliated unions and 300,000 mems ; Pres JUAN C. TAN; Exec. Vice-Pres. EFREN P. ARANZAMENDEZ.

National Association of Trade Unions (NATU): Suite 401, San Luis Terraces, T.M. Kalaw St., Ermita, Manila; f. 1954; 56 affiliated unions and 13,261 mems.; Pres. MARCELINO LONTOK Jr.,

Philippines Association of Free Labour Unions (PAFLU): 1233 Tecson cnr. J. Abad Santos Ave., Tondo, Manila; f. 1977; 43 affiliated unions and 27,143 mems.; Pres. ONOFRE P. GUEVARA; Exec. Sec. WILFRIDO GUEVARA.

Katipunang Manggagawang Pilipino (KMP-TUCP) (*Trade Union Congress of the Philippines*): 7th Floor, Cardinal Bldg., 999 Pedro Gil cnr. F. Agoncillo, Ermita, Manila; f. 1975; 1.25 million mems.; Pres. DEMOCRITO T. MENDOZA; Sec.-Gen. ANDRES L. DINGLASAN, Jr.; publs. *TUCP Bulletin* (monthly), *Research Center Memo* (monthly), *Philippine Labor Research Bulletin* (every two months); 27 affiliates including:

National Congress of Unions in the Sugar Industry of the Philippines (NACUSIP): 7th St., Cap Subitoldivision, Bacolod City; 18 affiliated unions and 25,062 mems.; Pres. ZOILO V. DELA CRUZ, Jr.

National Labour Union Inc.: 3199 Magsaysay Blvd., Manila; f. 1929; Pres. EULOGIO R. LERUM; Sec. ANTONIO V. POLICARPIO; 106 affiliated unions and 43,270 mems.; publ. *National Labor Unionist* (quarterly).

Philippine Congress of Trade Unions (PHILCONTU): 2357 Leon Guinto St., Malate, Manila; 13 affiliated unions and 444,713 mems.; Pres. DEMOCRITO MENDOZA.

Philippine Transport and General Workers' Organization-ITF (PTGWO-ITF): 13th and Boston Sts., Port Area, Manila; 99 affiliated unions and 44,447 mems.; Pres. ROBERTO M. OCA, Jr.; Sec. PACIFICO V. CULVA.

Philippines Trade Union Council (PTUC): Suite 528, FEMII Bldg., Aduana St., Intramuros, Manila; f. 1954; 10 affiliated federations and 291,952 mems.; affiliated to ICFTU; Pres. AURELIO S. INTERTAS; Gen. Sec. GABRIEL M. GATCHALIAN.

Trade Unions of the Philippines and Allied Services (TUPAS): 514-518 FEMII Bldg., Aduana St., Intramuros, Manila; 515 affiliated unions and 250,000 mems.; Pres. NAPOLEON MACULADA; Sec.-Gen. BONIFACIO TUPAS.

MAJOR INDUSTRIAL COMPANIES

CEMENT

Bacnotan Consolidated Industries Inc.: 4th Floor, PHINMA Bldg., 166 Salcedo St., Legaspi Village, Makati, Metro Manila; f. 1957; manufacture of cement and G. I. sheets; cap. 41.7 million pesos; 473 employees; Chair. E. O. ESCALER; Pres. R. V. DEL ROSARIO.

Northern Cement Corporation: 10th Floor, National Life Insurance Bldg., Ayala Ave., Makati, Metro Manila, Pres. EDUARDO COJUANGCO, Jr.

Union Industrial Inc.: 1350 Ermita Center Bldg., Roxas Blvd., Ermita, Manila; Pres. ALEJANDRO B. TY.

COCONUT PRODUCTS

International Copra Export Corpn.: Manila; net sales 1,241.3 million pesos (1977).

Legaspi Oil Co.: Manila; f. 1929; processors of coconut oil; net sales 708.1 million pesos (1977); six subsidiaries.

Lu Do and Lu Ym Corporation: P.O.B. 18, Tupas St., Cebu City; f. 1896; manufacturer of crude coconut oil, refined edible oil, and copra meal pellets; assets 145 million pesos, net sales 902 million pesos (1979); 425 employees; Pres. C. LU.

Philippine Refining Co., Inc.: 1351 United Nations Ave., Manila; f. 1927; detergents, toilet preparations, and food manufacturers; processors of coconut oil; net sales 850 million pesos (1979); Pres. JAMES S. TAGGART.

Procter and Gamble Philippe Manufacturing Corpn.: Sarmiento Bldg., Ayala Ave., Makati, Metro Manila; f. 1935; processors of coconut oil; toilet preparations and detergents; food manufacturers; net sales 546.6 million pesos (1977); Pres. and Gen. Man. RAFAEL A. NUÑEZ.

CONSTRUCTION

Construction Consultants Corpn.: Room 58, Zeta II Bldg., Salcedo St., Makati, Metro Manila; Pres. TEODORO GENER.

Construction and Development Corpn. of the Philippines: Tierra Factors Bldg., 355 Buendia Ave. Ext., Makati, Metro Manila; f. 1966; construction; heavy machinery; agriculture; mining; hotels; refrigeration; net sales 1,012.9 million pesos (1977); Pres. RODOLFO M. CUENCA.

MINING

Acoje Mining Co., Inc.: 5th Floor, RFM Bldg., Pioneer Mandaluyong, Metro Manila; Pres. WALTER W. BROWN.

Atlas Consolidated Mining and Development Corpn.: A. Soriano Bldg., 8776 Paseo de Roxas, cnr. Ayala Ave., Makati, Metro Manila; f. 1953; mining of copper ore and recovery of copper concentrate and by-products of gold, silver and pyrite; net sales 2,057.6 million pesos (1981); 10,686 employees; Chair./Pres. ANDRES SORIANO, Jr.; Sec. A. R. INFANTE.

Benguet Consolidated Inc.: 2259 Pasong Tamo Ext., Makati, Metro Manila; f. 1903; principal primary gold producer; cap. 50 million pesos; Pres. JAIME V. ONGPIN.

Consolidated Mines Inc.: Consolidated Mines Incorporated Bldg., Makati, Metro Manila.

Marcopper Mining Corporation: V. Madrigal Bldg., Ayala Ave., Makati, Metro Manila; net loss 21 million pesos (1981); Pres. GARTH S. JONES.

Marinduque Mining and Industrial Corpn.: nickel, copper and cement production; net sales 1,609.8 million pesos (1981); Chair. and Pres. JESUS S. CABARRUS.

OIL

Caltex (Philippines) Inc.: 540 Padre Faura, Metro Manila; net sales 2,347.5 million pesos (1977); Pres. and Man. Dir. RODERICK J. O'CONNOR.

Getty Oil (Philippines) Inc.: Keystone Bldg., Buendia Ave., Makati, Metro Manila; net sales 610.1 million pesos (1977); Pres. SAMMUEL O. ABELLERA.

Mobil Oil (Philippines) Inc.: Doña Narcisa Bldg., Paseo de Roxas, Makati, Metro Manila; net sales 2,026.3 million pesos (1977); Pres. NORMAN FARR.

Petrophil Corpn.: Petrophil Bldg., 7901 Makati Ave., Makati, Metro Manila; national oil company; net sales 6,712.4 million pesos (1979); Pres. GERONIMO VELASCO.

Pilipinas Shell Petroleum Corpn.: Lopez Bldg., Ortigas Ave., Pasig, Metro Manila; part of the First Philippines Holdings Corpn.; petroleum refining; net sales 2,418 million pesos (1977).

POWER

Manila Electric Company (Meralco): Lopez Bldg., Meralco Center, Pasig; f. 1903; supplies electric power to Manila and six provinces in Luzon; net sales 4,982.2 million pesos (1981); Pres. MARIO COMACHO.

National Power Corporation: 161 Bonifacio Drive, Port Area, Manila; (Anda Circle, Port Area, Manila—after Dec. 1981); f. 1936; state-owned corporation supplying electric and hydro-electric power to the whole country; Pres. GABRIEL ITCHON; Gen. Man. CESAR DEL ROSARIO.

SUGAR

Binalbagan Sugar Co., Inc.: SGV Bldg., Ayala Ave., Makati, Metro Manila.

Central Azucarera de la Carlota: 141 Ayala Ave., Makati, Metro Manila.

Hawaiian-Philippine Company: 222 Buendia Ave., Makati, Metro Manila; f. 1918; raw sugar production and molasses; cap. 50 million pesos; 870 employees; Pres. E. G. VORSTER; Man. S. Y. HILADO.

Southern Negros Development Corpn.: Femii Bldg., Intramuros, Manila.

Victorias Milling Co., Inc.: 4th Floor, Bank of P.I. Bldg., Ayala Ave., Makati, Rizal; P.B. 762 or C.C.P.O.B. 1211, Makati, Metro Manila.

TEXTILES

Central Textile Mills: E. de los Santos Ave., Balintawak, Quezon City; Pres. WILLY CO.

Floro and Sons Inc.: Caniogan Pasig, Metro Manila; Pres. ERNESTO FLORO.

General Textiles Inc.: E. Rodriguez Ave., Ext. Libis, Quezon City; Pres. JESUS S. YUJUICO.

Herditex Mills Inc.: 180 Salcedo St., Legaspi Village, Makati, Metro Manila; Pres. DELFIN PENGSON, Jr.

Imperial Textile Mills Inc.: 917 Juan Luna St., Metro Manila; Pres. LUCIANO SALAZAR.

Industrial Textile Mfg. Co. of the Philippines, Inc. (ITEMCOP): P.O.B. 942, Manila; manufacturer of polypropylene woven bags and cloth.

Lirag Textile Mills: Tinajeros, Malabon, Metro Manila; Pres. BASILIO LIRAG.

Litton Textile Mills: c/o CFC Corpn., P.O.B. 4447, Manila; Pres. JOHN GOKONGWEI, Jr.

Ramie Textiles Inc.: 5th Floor, Combank Bldg., 6764 Ayala Ave., Makati, Metro Manila; Pres. RAOUL E. KAHN.

Riverside Mills Corporation: Bo. Rosario, Pasig, Metro Manila; Pres. ERNESTO TANCHI, Sr.

Universal Textile Mills Inc.: Barranca, Marikina, Metro Manila.

TOBACCO

Columbia Tobacco Co., Inc.: 307 Jose Rizal St., Mandaluyong, Metro Manila.

La Perla Industries, Inc.: Chengt-saijun Bldg., Quirino Ave., Parañaque, Metro Manila.

La Suerte Cigar and Cigarette Factory: South Super Highway, Parañaque, Metro Manila; net sales 929.3 million pesos (1977).

WOOD AND WOOD PRODUCTS

Aguinaldo Development Corporation: Adecor Bldg., U.N. Ave., corner Romualdez St., Manila.

Insular Lumber Company (PHIL.), Inc.: P.O.B. 3377, Manila; 19th floor, B. A. Lepanto Bldg., Paseo de Roxas, Makati, Metro Manila; Hinoba-an, Negros Occidental (Mills); f. 1904 (U.S.A.), 1966 inc. in Philippines; wood processing, major exporter of mahogany, sawn lumber and lumber products; cap. 75 million pesos; 1,600 employees; Chair. CARLOS PALANCA, Jr.; Vice-Chair. A. M. VELAYO; Pres. RAMON A. RECTO.

L. S. Sarmiento & Co., Inc. and Sarmiento Industries, Inc.: Sarmiento Bldg., 2 Pasong Tamo Extension, Makati, Metro Manila; manufacturers and exporters of plywood and panels, lumber and woodwork products.

Sta. Clara Lumber Co. Inc.: Diadem Bldg., Cnr. Herrera and Ormaza Sts., Legaspi Village, Makati, Metro Manila; f. 1924; logs, lumber, veneers/corestock, plywood, blockboards and uniply; Pres. and Chair. RENATO AREVALO.

Zamboanga Wood Products Inc.: Room 55, 5th Floor, GPL Bldg., 219 Buendia Ave., Makati, Metro Manila.

MISCELLANEOUS

Aboitiz & Co., Inc.: P.O.B. 65, 183 J. Luna St., Cebu City 6401; f. 1920; exporters of hemp, importers of general merchandise, industrial and agricultural machinery; construction; banking, power distribution; cap. 150 million pesos; Pres. LUIS ABOITIZ, Jr.

Atlantic Gulf and Pacific Co. of Manila. Inc.: AG&P House, 345 Buendia Ave. Ext., Makati, Metro Manila; engineering, heavy industrial construction, fabrication and castings, air conditioning and refrigeration, wood preserving, off-shore oil platform and marine structures, industrial manufacturing and machinery sales.

Bataan Refining Corpn.: Manila; net sales 4,186 million pesos (1977).

Commonwealth Foods, Inc.: Comfoods Bldg., Buendia Ave., Makati, Metro Manila; cocoa, coffee and biscuits.

Delta Motor Corpn.: Manila; vehicle assembly; net sales 750.3 million pesos (1977).

Engineering Equipment Inc.: 110 E. Rodriguez Jr. Ave., Ortigas Industrial Estate, Quezon City, Metro Manila 3120; f. 1931; heavy machinery; steel fabrication; industrial construction; 10,324 employees; Chair. and Chief Exec. JAIME V. ONGPIN.

Paper Industries Corporation of the Philippines: UPRC Bldg., 389 Buendia Extension, Makati, Metro Manila; net sales 1,072.5 million pesos (1981).

Planters Products Inc.: Planters Products Bldg., Esteban St., Legaspi Village, Makati, Metro Manila; fertilizers; net sales 840.1 million pesos (1979).

RFM Corporation: Pioneer St., Mandaluyong, Metro Manila; f. 1958; food processing, flour mills and poultry farms; 1,000 employees; Pres. and Chief Exec. Officer J. CONCEPCION, Jr.; Chair. B. J. SERVER.

TRANSPORT

RAILWAYS

Philippine National Railways: 943 Claro M. Recto Ave., Metro Manila; f. 1892; government-owned; over 1,028 km. of tracks (1982); the northern line runs from Manila to San Fernando, La Unión, and the southern line from Manila to Camalig, Albay; a Camalig-Legaspi deviation line is under construction; Chair. Col. SALVADOR T. VILLA; Gen. Man. JUAN N. DE CASTRO.

Panay Railways Inc.: P.O.B. 300, Lapuz, Iloilo City; f. 1906 (known as Phividec since 1975); 116 km.; operates an isolated line from Iloilo to Roxas on Panay Island; Chair. ROBERTO S. BENEDICTO; Gen. Man. CARLOS V. SIBUG.

ROADS

In June 1979 there were 127,150 km. of roads in the Philippines of which 48,277 km. were unsurfaced.

Ministry for Public Highways: Manila; Minister JESUS S. HIPOLITO.

Philippine Motor Association: 4071 R. Magsaysay Blvd., Sta. Mesa, P.O.B. 999, Manila; f. 1931; Pres. CONRADO R. AYUYAO; Vice-Pres. ANDRES NARVASA; Treas. NOEL ARANETA; publ. *Philippine Motor Review*.

SHIPPING

Philippine Ports Authority (PPA): BF Condominium, Aduana St., Intramuros, Metro Manila; f. 1977; supervises all 94 national ports, 496 municipal ports and 247 registered private ports in the Philippines; Gen. Man. E. S. BACLIG, Jr.

NATIONAL LINES

Botelho Bulk Transport Corpn.: 8th Floor, Antonino Bldg., 540 T. M. Kalaw St., Ermita, Manila; f. 1966; 4 vessels, services world-wide; Pres. LUISITA P. BOTELHO; Exec. Vice-Pres. and Man. Dir. HROAR OLSEN.

Eastern Shipping Lines, Inc.: ESL Bldg., Anda Circle, Port Area, Manila; inc. 1957; owners/managers of 11 vessels; services to Japan; brs. in Tokyo, Yokohama, Kobe and Osaka; Pres. JAMES L. CHIONGBIAN; Exec. Vice-Pres. ERWIN L. CHIONGBIAN; Vice-Pres. and Gen. Man. Capt. AMADO V. ROMILLO.

Galleon Shipping Corp.: Alco Bldg., 391 Buendia Ave., Makati, Manila; 9 cargo vessels; services to U.S.A.; Vice-Pres. and Operations Captain MARIO K. ALFELOR.

Luzteveco (Luzon Stevedoring Corpn.): Tacoma and Second Sts., Port Area, P.O.B. 582, Manila; f. 1909; 4 brs.; towage, salvage, chartering and oil drilling support services; fleet of 71 tugs and 167 barges; Pres. RODOLFO M. CUENCA; Vice-Pres. RODOLFO B. SANTIAGO.

Maritime Company of the Philippines: 105 Dasmariñas St., Binondo, Metro Manila; 8 cargo liners, 8 reefer ships; Chair. and Pres. JOSE P. FERNANDEZ; Vice-Pres. and Gen. Man. WILLIAM R. PALOU.

Northern Lines Incorporated: Femii Bldg., Advana St., Intramuros, Manila; 10 bulk carriers and conventional vessels; services worldwide; Gen. Man. JESUS C. MARTINEZ.

Philippine Ace Lines Inc.: P.O.B. 3567, Ground Floor, Mary Bachrach Bldg., Port Area, Metro Manila; 5 vessels; cargo and liner services to Japan, Europe, South America and the U.S.A.; Pres. RUFINO GUY SU SIM; Vice-Pres. and Gen. Man. LOPE O. ANGANGCO.

Philippine Internal Shipping Corpn. (PISC): f. 1978; ASEAN co-operative venture by 18 companies; 6 cargo vessels; Pres. GEORGE U. LIM.

Philippine President Lines, Inc.: PPL Bldg., 1000–1046 United Nations Ave., Manila; 10 cargo vessels; services; Chartering, U.S.A., Japan, Europe; Chair. EMILIO T. YAP; Pres. EMILIO C. YAP, Jr.

Transocean Transport Corpn.: 8th Floor, Magsaysay Bldg., 520 T. M. Kalaw St., Ermita, Manila; 9 vessels; Pres. and Gen. Man. MIGUEL A. MAGSAYSAY; Vice-Pres. EDUARDO U. MANESE.

United Philippine Lines, Inc.: UPL Bldg., Santa Clara St., Aduana, Metro Manila; services to Japan, Hong Kong and U.S.A.; Pres. RENATO TANSECO.

William Lines, Inc.: Pier 14, North Harbor, Manila; 11 brs.; passenger and cargo inter-island service; 16 pass./cargo vessels; Asst. Vice-Pres. ESPIRITU P. TAN.

CIVIL AVIATION

Bureau of Air Transportation: Manila International Airport, Pasay City, Metro Manila D-3110; in charge of technical and operational side of aviation, establishes policies, rules and regulations for the efficient operation and control of the country's civil aviation activities; Dir.-Gen. JESUS Z. SINGSON.

In 1980 there was a total of 84 airports in the Philippines. In addition to the international airports at Manila and Mactan (Cebu), there are five alternative international airports: Laoag, Ilocos Norte; Tacloban, Leyte; Davao City; Zamboanga City; Puerto Princesa, Palawan.

Philippine Airlines Inc. (PAL): PAL Bldg., Legaspi St., Legaspi Village, Makati, P.O.B. 954, Metro Manila; f. 1946; domestic and international services to Australia, Bahrain, the People's Republic of China, Hawaii, Hong Kong, Indonesia, Japan, People's Republic of Korea, Malaysia, Papua New Guinea, Singapore, Taiwan, Thailand, U.K., U.S.A., the Federal Republic of Germany, Greece, Italy, the Netherlands and Pakistan; Chair. and Pres. ROMAN CRUZ, Jr.; fleet of 4 DC-10-30, 7 HS-748, 12 BAC 1-11-500, 8 Nihon YS-11, 4 B-747, 2 B-727, 3 A-300; publ. *Mabuhay*.

FOREIGN AIRLINES

The following foreign airlines serve the Philippines: Air France, Air India, Air Nauru, Air Niugini (Papua New Guinea), Alia (Jordan), Alitalia (Italy), British Airways, Canadian Pacific Airlines, Cathay Pacific Airlines (Hong Kong), China Air Lines (Taiwan), Civil Aviation Administration of China (People's Republic of China), EgyptAir, Garuda (Indonesia), Gulf Air (Bahrain), JAL (Japan), Japan Asia Airways (Japan), KLM (Netherlands), Korean Air Lines (Republic of Korea), Kuwait Airways, Lufthansa (Federal Republic of Germany), Malaysian Airlines, Northwest Orient Airline (U.S.A.), Pan American Airways (U.S.A.), PIA (Pakistan), Qantas (Australia), Royal Brunei (Borneo), Sabena World Airways (Belgium), SAS (Sweden), Saudia (Saudi Arabia), SIA (Singapore), Swissair, Thai International, Trans Mediterranean Airways (Lebanon) and VARIG (Brazil).

TOURISM AND CULTURE

Ministry of Tourism: Agrifina Circle, Rizal Park, Manila, P.O.B. 3451; Minister JOSE D. ASPIRAS.

PRINCIPAL THEATRE COMPANIES

Bayanihan Philippine Dance Company: Philippine Women's University, Taft Ave., Manila; f. 1957; regular programmes; efforts towards a folk dance revival and the emergence of a native dance tradition; occasional subsidies from the Ministry of Tourism, government grants for foreign tours; Pres. Dr. HELENA Z. BENITEZ; Exec. Dir. Dr. LETICIA P. DE GUZMAN.

Filipinescas Dance Company: 41 Timog (South) Ave., Quezon City; f. 1957; private company; folkloric ballets in native dance styles; Founder-Dir. Madame LEONOR OROSA GOQUINGCO.

PNC Barangay Folk Dance Troupe: Philippine Normal College, Taft Ave., Manila; f. 1946; research, study and propagation of Philippine folk dances, songs and games; formal and informal folk dance courses within a teacher training curriculum; television appearances, national and international performances; Founder-Dir. Dr. PAZ-CIELO A. BELMONTE; Man. RAMON D. BELMONTE.

PRINCIPAL ORCHESTRAS

CCP Philharmonic Orchestra: 3rd Floor, Cultural Center of the Philippines, Roxas Blvd., Metro Manila; f. 1973; regular symphony concerts, opera and ballet programmes; Senior Conductor OSCAR YATCO; Assoc. Conductors BASILIO C. MANALO, FRANCISCO F. FELICIANO.

The Manila Symphony Orchestra: P.O.B. 664, Manila; f. 1926; regular symphonic, opera and ballet programmes; encourages young artists; Music Dir. and Conductor SERGIO ESMILLA, Jr.; Pres. CONCHITA SUNICO.

National Philharmonic Orchestra: Acea Compound, Tindalo St., Makati, Metro Manila; f. 1960; seasonal symphony concerts; sponsors international operas and ballets; privately financed; Pres., Musical Dir. and Conductor REDENTOR ROMERO.

ATOMIC ENERGY

Philippine Atomic Energy Commission: Don Mariano Marcos Ave., Diliman, Quezon City, D-505; f. 1958; the official body dealing with nuclear energy activities in the Philippines, under the office of the Prime Minister. It has a 1,000-kW. swimming pool reactor for research, training and production of radioisotopes. Its research centre conducts studies in agriculture, biology, medicine, chemistry, physics and nuclear engineering. It provides technical services utilizing nuclear techniques to research agencies, educational institutions and hospitals. Technical assistance is received mainly from International Atomic Energy Agency, United States Agency for International Development, Colombo Plan and through bilateral agreements with other nations. Commissioner ZOILO M. BARTOLOME; Deputy Commissioner ALEJANDRO V. ALBANO.

The Philippines' first nuclear power station is under construction at Bagac (Bataan Province), and is scheduled for completion in 1984.

DEFENCE

Armed Forces: Total strength (1981) 112,800: army 70,000, navy 26,000, air force 16,800; military service is compulsory for all able-bodied men over the age of 21 years; the constabulary numbers 43,500 and the local self-defence force 65,000.

Equipment: The army, navy and air force have American and Japanese equipment and there are U.S. military bases in the country.

Defence Expenditure: Defence budget (1981): 6,600 million pesos.

CHIEFS OF STAFF

Chief of Staff of the Armed Forces: Gen. FABIAN VER.

Army: Maj.-Gen. JOSEPHUS RAMAS.

Navy: Rear-Admiral SIMEON ALEJANDRO.

Air Force: Brig.-Gen. PETRONIO LAPEÑA.

Constabulary: Maj.-Gen. FIDEL B. RAMOS.

EDUCATION

The 1973 Constitution provides for free compulsory public education at elementary level and in some areas education is free up to secondary level. The organization of education is the responsibility of the Minister of Education and Culture. The department under him is responsible for the development and implementation of programmes based on policies formulated by the National Board of Education (NBE). A 10 year development programme for elementary education will run from 1981–90.

There are both government and non-government schools. The non-government or private schools are either sectarian or non-sectarian. In 1975 the existing administrative bureaux were abolished and replaced by the Bureau of Elementary Education, the Bureau of Secondary Education and the Bureau of Higher Education.

Education in the Philippines is divided into four stages: pre-school (from the age of 3), elementary school (for 8 years), secondary or high school (for 4 or 5 years) and higher education (normally 4 years). The public schools offer a general secondary curriculum and there are private schools which offer more specialized training courses. There is a common general curriculum for all students in the first and second years and more varied curricula in the third and fourth years leading to either college or technical vocational courses. In 1979 the National College Entrance Examination (NCEE) was taken by 370,369 students.

The education budget for 1982 was 4,300 million pesos, about 7.3 per cent of the total national budget. Total enrolment in 1979/80 was 12.2 million as against 4.3 million in 1963/64. In 1979/80, 8,670,613 students were enrolled at elementary level, 3,397,740 at secondary level and 1,288,197 were enrolled in vocational courses and the professions. A total of 50,658 adults attended functional literacy courses in 1975.

From 1945 to 1979 the number of public school teachers at elementary, secondary and college levels increased from 46,864 to approximately 330,850. The number of private school teachers increased from 1,006 to 62,010. In 1980, there were 31,404 elementary schools, 5,144 higher schools, 1,055 colleges and vocational schools and 43 universities.

At the primary level instruction is in English or Pilipino. At the secondary and college levels English is the usual medium, although Pilipino is sometimes used.

BIBLIOGRAPHY

GENERAL

BOOK OF THE PHILIPPINES (Aardvark Associates, Manila, 1976).

BURLEY, T. M. The Philippines. An Economic and Social Geography (G. Bell and Sons Ltd., London, 1973).

CORPUZ, O. The Philippines (Prentice-Hall, Englewood Cliffs, 1965).

CUTSHALL, A. The Philippines: Nation of Islands (D. Van Nostrand Co., Princeton, N.J., 1964).

GOWING, P. G. and SCOTT, W. H. (eds.). Acculturation in the Philippines: Essays in Changing Societies (New Day Publishers, Quezon City, 1971).

GUTHRIE, G. M. (Ed.). Six Perspectives on the Philippines (Bookmark Inc., Manila, 1971).

THE PHILIPPINE ATLAS (Fund for Assistance to Private Education, Manila, 1975).

PHILIPPINE YEARBOOK (NEDA, Manila).

SAITO, SHIRO. The Philippines: A Review of Bibliographies (University of Hawaii, Honolulu, 1966).

WERNSTEDT, F. L. and SPENCER, J. E. The Philippine Island World: A Physical, Cultural and Regional Geography (University of California, Berkeley and Los Angeles, 1967).

HISTORY

AGONCILLO, TEODORO A. Malolos, the Crisis of the Republic (University of the Philippines, Quezon City, 1960).
The Fateful Years (R. M. Garcia, Quezon City, 1965).

ALFONSO, OSCAR M. Theodore Roosevelt and the Philippines, 1897–1908 (University of the Philippines, Quezon City, 1970).

BLOUNT, J. H. The American Occupation of the Philippines, 1898–1912 (Malaya Books, Quezon City, 1968).

CONSTANTINO, R. Identity and Consciousness: The Philippine Experience (Malaya Books Inc., Quezon City, 1974).
History of the Philippines: From the Spanish Colonization to the Second World War (MR Press, New York and London, 1976).

CONSTANTINO, R., and CONSTANTINO, L. R. The Philippines: The Continuing Past (The Foundation for Nationalist Studies, Quezon City, 1979).

DE LA COSTA, HORACIO. The Jesuits in the Philippines, 1581–1768 (Harvard University Press, Mass., 1961).

FELIX, ALFONSO (ed.). The Chinese in the Philippines (2 vols.), (Solidaridad Publishing House, Manila, 1966).

GEORGE, T. J. S. Revolt in Mindanao: The Rise of Islam in Philippine Politics (Oxford University Press, 1980).

QUIASON, SERAFIN D. English "Country Trade" with the Philippines, 1644–1765 (University of the Philippines, Quezon City, 1966).

ROSENBERG, DAVID A. (ed.). Marcos and Martial Law in the Philippines (Cornell University Press, Ithaca and London, 1979).

SCHIRMER, D. B. Republic or Empire: American Resistance to the Philippine War (Schenkman Publishing Co. Inc., Mass., 1972).

ECONOMICS

BALDWIN, R. E. Foreign Trade Regimes and Economic Development: The Philippines, Vol. V (National Bureau of Economic Research, New York, 1975).

CONSTANTINO, R. The Nationalist Alternative (Foundation for Nationalist Studies, Quezon City, 1979).

FAST, JONATHAN and RICHARDSON, JIM. Roots of Dependency (Foundation for Nationalist Studies, Quezon City, 1980).

GOLAY, F. H. The Philippines: Public and National Economic Development (Cornell University Press, Ithaca, N.Y., 1961).

HARTENDORP, A. V. H. History of Industry and Trade of the Philippines (American Chamber of Commerce of the Philippines Inc., Manila, 1958).

HUKE, R. E. Shadows on the Land: An Economic Geography of the Philippines (Bookmark Inc., Manila, 1963).

LICHAUCO, A. The Lichauco Paper (Monthly Review Press, New York, 1973).

MEARS, L. et al. Rice Economy of the Philippines (University of the Philippines, Quezon City, 1974).

OFFRENEO, RENE. Capitalism in Philippine Agriculture (Foundation for Nationalist Studies, Quezon City, 1980).

THE PHILIPPINE ECONOMY IN THE 1970S (Institute of Economic Development and Research, University of the Philippines, Quezon City, 1972).

THE PHILIPPINES: PRIORITIES AND PROSPECTS FOR DEVELOPMENT (The World Bank, Washington, D.C., 1976).

POWER, J. H. and SICAT, G. P. The Philippines: Industrialization and Trade Policies (Oxford University Press, London, 1971).

SPENCER, J. E. Land and People in the Philippines: Geographic Problems in Rural Economy (University of California, Berkeley, 1952).

POLITICS AND GOVERNMENT

ABUEVA, J. V. Filipino Politics and Emerging Ideologies (Modern Book Co., Manila, 1975).

CANOY, REUBEN R. The Counterfeit Revolution: Martial Law in the Philippines (Manila, 1980).

CONSTANTINO, R. The Making of a Filipino (Malaya Books Inc., Quezon City, 1969).
Dissent and Counter-Consciousness (Malaya Books Inc., Quezon City, 1970).

CORPUZ, O. D. The Bureaucracy in the Philippines (University of the Philippines, Institute of Public Administration, Manila, 1957).

GOWING, PETER G. Muslim Filipinos: Heritage and Horizon (New Day Publishers, Quezon City, 1979).

GREGORIO ARANETA MEMORIAL FOUNDATION. Lectures on Constitutional Reforms (Manila, 1970).

KERKVLIET, B. Political Change in the Philippines: Studies of Local Politics Preceding Martial Law (University of Hawaii Press, Honolulu, 1974).

LANDE, CARL H. Leaders, Factions and Parties: The Structure of Philippine Politics (Yale University Press, Southeast Asia Studies, Monograph Series No. 6).

MEYER, MILTON W. A Diplomatic History of the Philippine Republic (University of Hawaii Press, Honolulu, 1965).

Singapore

PHYSICAL AND SOCIAL GEOGRAPHY

C. A. Fisher

(Revised for this edition by Harvey Demaine)

The Republic of Singapore is an insular territory of 618 square kilometres (238 square miles) lying to the south of the Malay peninsula to which it is joined by a causeway carrying a road, a railway and a water pipeline across the intervening Straits of Johore.

Singapore Island, which is situated less than 1½° north of the equator, occupies a focal position at the turning point on the shortest sea-route from the Indian Ocean to the South China Sea.

PHYSICAL FEATURES

The mainly granitic core of the island, which rises in a few places to summits of over 100 metres, is surrounded by lower land, much of it marshy, though large areas are now intensively cultivated. Singapore City has grown up on the firmer ground adjacent to the Mt. Faber ridge, whose foreshore provides deep water anchorage in the lee of two small offshore islands, Pulau Blakang Mati and Pulau Brani. In recent years suburban growth has been rapid towards the north and along the eastern foreshore, and since 1961 a large expanse of mangrove swamp to the west of the dock area has been reclaimed to provide the Jurong industrial estate.

POPULATION

The population at the June 1980 census totalled 2,413,945, giving a population density of 3,906 per square kilometre, one of the highest in the world. Of the total, 1,856,200 were Chinese, 351,500 Malay and 154,600 Indian. Forty per cent of the population are under 19 years old.

HISTORY

C. Mary Turnbull

Singapore, the world's second busiest port, became an independent republic only in 1965.

ORIGINS AND EARLY DEVELOPMENT

The island has a record of human habitation going back possibly some 2000 years, but its early history is obscure, and the very name of Singapura (Sanskrit for Lion City) is unexplained, since the lion is not native to the region. According to the earliest historical chronicle, the *Malay Annals*, the city was founded by a Sumatran prince, when he landed on the island and encountered a strange beast, whom he took to be a lion and a creature of good omen.

The original seaport was known as Temasek and may have been part of the great Sumatran maritime empire of Srivijaya but it emerges more clearly out of the decay of that empire in the thirteenth century. The Venetian traveller, Marco Polo, who visited Sumatra in the last decade of the century, makes a hearsay reference to "Chiamassie", possibly Temasek, which he heard was "a very large and noble city". An early fourteenth-century Chinese trader, Wang Ta-yüan, portrayed the settlement and the surrounding seas as a dreaded pirate haunt, but the *Malay Annals* described fourteenth-century Temasek as a prosperous trading centre. About this time it became known as Singapura and came under the rule of a Sumatran adventurer prince. However, the island's prosperity brought it into the sphere of rival expanding empires: Thai Ayuthia and Javanese Majapahit. Claimed and attacked by both and torn further by internal strife, the city was destroyed in the final years of the fourteenth century. The ruler and his followers fled to found a more auspicious settlement at Melaka (Malacca), which became a renowned empire.

After this blood-soaked episode, Singapore remained almost deserted for more than 400 years, home of a few tribes of *orang laut* or boat people, who lived by fishing, piracy and petty trading and owned allegiance to the Malay Riau-Johor empire, centred nearby in the Riau archipelago. Soon all that remained of the old city were a few crumbling ramparts and the neglected graves of its former rulers on the hill above the Singapore River.

While commerce flourished in the region, Singapore itself was an isolated backwater. The main shipping route between Europe and Eastern Asia lay far away to the south through the Sunda Strait which separates Sumatra and Java. From the seventeenth century, international trade was dominated by the Dutch, with their headquarters in Batavia (the modern Jakarta) and their interests primarily in Java and the Moluccas. Riau itself was a prosperous emporium for regional commerce, but Singapore merely battened on the piratical fringe of that trade.

In the early nineteenth century the Melaka Straits and the southern part of the Malay peninsula assumed a new commercial and strategic importance when Britain's East India Company sought bases along the route from India to China to protect its China trade and to challenge the Dutch commercial monopoly in the Malay peninsula and archipelago. In 1819 Sir Stamford Raffles, an East India Company official, obtained permission from the Sultan of Riau-Johor and the local chief, to establish a trading post at the mouth of the Singapore river. Initial Dutch opposition came to an end with the signing of the Anglo-Dutch Treaty of London in 1824, and later that same year the East India Company signed a further treaty with the two Malay chiefs, who ceded the island in perpetuity to the Company and its successors, in return for money payments and pensions.

The Straits Settlements

In 1826 the Company united Singapore with its two other dependencies on the west coast of the Malay peninsula: Penang, acquired in 1786, and Melaka, ceded by the Dutch in 1824. These scattered territories remained one political entity, known as the Straits Settlements, for the next 120 years.

To attract settlers and commerce to Singapore, Raffles laid down from the beginning a policy of unrestricted immigration and free trade, two principles which became cardinal tenets of the Singapore merchants' creed, to be treasured and preserved for more than a century, so that Singapore was the first place in the world to put into practice the principles of Adam Smith and *laissez-faire*.

Under the East India Company's protection, conveniently situated but free from customs duties or restrictions, the new port drew in traders and settlers from all over the region: Malays, Chinese, Indians, Javanese, Sumatrans, Buginese. They came first from the nearby ports of Riau, Melaka and Penang, but soon others began to arrive from further afield in the Indonesian archipelago, and from Thailand, Indo-China, Burma, Borneo, the Philippines, India, China and Europe.

In 1833 the East India Company lost its monopoly of the China trade, after which it had no further use for the Straits Settlements. It continued to administer them but on a "shoestring" budget. The very laxness of government, with its absence of restrictions, served to attract further steady immigration and trade, but the European merchants of Singapore became increasingly dissatisfied with administrative inefficiency and the lack of representative institutions. When the Indian Mutiny broke out in 1857, Singapore's merchants petitioned that the Straits Settlements be separated from India and brought under direct British rule.

As a result, in 1867 the Straits Settlements became a Crown Colony, with a constitution which remained basically unchanged up to the Second World War. A Governor appointed from the United Kingdom ruled with the assistance of an executive and a legislative council, the latter comprising a majority of officials with a few unofficial members nominated by the Governor. The first "unofficials" were all European but a Chinese was appointed to the legislative council in 1869, and over the years the number of unofficial and of Asian councillors increased, so that by the 1920s there were equal numbers of officials and unofficials on the legislative council, with the Governor having the casting vote. By that time some "unofficials" were nominated by the Chambers of Commerce but there were no elected members as such.

The transfer of the Straits Settlements to direct colonial rule was soon followed by two events which gave a boost to Singapore's development: the opening of the Suez Canal in 1869, and the first treaties of protection made between the British and rulers of the Malay states in 1874.

With the opening of the Suez Canal the India-Melaka Straits route replaced the Sunda Straits as the main highway from Europe to the Far East, and on this route Singapore held a dominating position.

The 1874 treaties, whereby the rulers of the west coast Malay states of Perak, Selangor and the Sungei Ujong agreed to accept British Residents at their courts, marked the first step in bringing the whole peninsula under British protection: Pahang accepted a British Resident in 1888; Siam (modern Thailand) transferred the northern states of Kedah, Perlis, Kelantan and Trengganu to British protection in 1909; and finally in 1914 Johor accepted a British Adviser.

The peninsula was not administered as a single unit but was divided into the Straits Settlements Colony; the Federated Malay States of Perak, Selangor, Negri Sembilan and Pahang, which formed a federation in 1895; and the unfederated former Siamese states and Johor. However, Singapore provided a political focal point as the base of the Governor of the Straits Settlements, who was also High Commissioner of the Malay States and the chief authority for the three British protected Borneo states of Sarawak, North Borneo and Brunei.

Singapore also became the centre for the dramatic economic opening-up of the peninsula in the late nineteenth and early twentieth centuries. Peace, stability and a growing network of rail and road communications enabled rapid exploitation of the rich tin resources of the Malay states and the development of commercial agriculture. Successful experiments in growing Brazilian para rubber in the Botanic Gardens in Singapore led to large-scale commercial planting of rubber in the Malay states in the last years of the nineteenth century. Malaya's economic prosperity was based largely on tin and rubber, but Singapore was the commercial and financing centre for these operations, its port the major outlet for exports and the centre of secondary industries in the form of tin smelting and rubber processing.

The island also became the commercial centre for the whole region. Growing western interests in south-east Asia and the expansion of international trade, the liberalizing of Dutch policy in the East Indies, the increasing use of steamships (which from the 1880s replaced sailing ships as the main carriers) and the development of telegraphs all put Singapore, with its fine natural sheltered harbour, at the hub of international trade in south-east Asia, and made it a vital link in the chain of British ports which stretched from Gibraltar, through the Mediterranean Sea and the Indian Ocean, to the Far East.

The 60 years from the opening of the Suez Canal to the onset of the Great Depression in 1929 were a time of unbroken peace, steady economic expansion and population growth in Singapore, with little dramatic incident to ruffle the calm. However, they were years of subtle but significant change, as more sophisticated administration brought the population into the pale of the government and the law courts.

In the early years the different immigrant groups lived in specified districts of the town, largely supervised by their own community leaders or *kapitans*. The majority of immigrants were Chinese, who as early as 1872 were the biggest single community in Singapore and by the beginning of the twentieth century constituted three-quarters of the population, a proportion which remained fairly constant from that time. Most Chinese came from the troubled Guangdong (Kwangtung) and Fujian (Fukien) provinces of southern China, representing a variety of dialect groups, chiefly Fukien, Cantonese, Teochew, Hakka and, in the later years of the century, Hainanese. Most were young adult men who aimed to make money abroad and return to their native China, so that the population throughout the nineteenth and well into the twentieth century was transitory and shifting, with very few women, children or old people.

The Chinese, in particular, were a law to themselves, controlled largely by secret societies, which in the early days were neither secret nor illegal but were tolerated by the Straits authorities since they fulfilled essential functions in organizing the immigration and employment of labour.

In 1877 a Chinese Protectorate was created to take over supervision of Chinese immigration and labour contracts, the protection of women and girls and supervision of the societies, so that over the years the legitimate functions of the secret societies were superseded and in 1889 "dangerous societies" were proscribed.

The character of the population changed in these years. Singapore was still cosmopolitan, still predominantly a male society of transients, but as the years passed more women came to Singapore, and a large number of immigrants married, settled permanently and raised families there. By the early twentieth century there was a large Straits-born Asian community, who were British subjects and sometimes English-educated.

The provision of education expanded slowly. Free Malay schooling was available for the indigenous minority, who made up only 15 per cent of the population by the early twentieth century. There were a few mission and government-subsidized English-language schools at primary and secondary level. The King Edward Medical College was opened in 1905 and the Raffles College of Arts and Sciences in 1928. However, before the 1920s the government did not concern itself with vernacular Chinese or Indian schools, which were left to private enterprise.

Some Straits-born Asians collaborated with the colonial establishment as legislative and municipal councillors or justices of the peace, while at the other end of the social scale others worked as clerks and assistants. In the 1930s the colonial regime created a Straits Civil Service, Straits Legal Service and Straits Medical Service which offered the first openings to Asian British subjects in professional government work, but only at the bottom of the ladder. All senior administrative and technical posts in Singapore were in the hands of British European officials.

There was little interest in local politics. From the mid-1920s, Legislative Councillor Tan Cheng Lock began to call for elected representation on the Legislative Council for those who had made the Straits Settlements their home, but he found little backing even among his fellow Straits Chinese. There was no indigenous nationalist movement or desire for independence and any political interest was directed more to China or India.

Immigration reached a peak in the boom year of 1927, when an all-time record of 360,000 Chinese landed in Singapore. However, the Great Depression of 1929-33 hit Singapore hard, leading to the first restrictions. Although in 1930 an Immigration Restriction Ordinance imposed a quota on Chinese men, it did not affect women for some years, and this also encouraged the trend towards permanent family settlement.

THE SECOND WORLD WAR AND JAPANESE OCCUPATION

After the First World War, Singapore acquired a new strategic significance as a naval and military base. Although the installations were completed in 1938, they did not deter Japan from attacking Malaya in December 1941 as part of a campaign to seize raw materials which it needed from south-east Asia. After a lightning campaign down the Malay peninsula, culminating in a week of fighting on the island itself, Singapore capitulated to the Japanese in February 1942.

Renamed Syonan, or Light of the South, it remained under Japanese occupation for more than three years. The Japanese intended to retain Singapore as a permanent colony and military base, a focal point in its proposed East Asian Co-Prosperity Sphere, but wartime priorities and difficulties precluded the Japanese from developing this concept. Japan destroyed the colonial economy without replacing it by an Asian alternative, and tried to suppress the English language and colonial education without building up Japanese in its place. Japan did nothing to promote indigenous politics in Singapore, although the island for a time became the regional base for the Indian National Army and the Indian Independence League.

The occupation was a time of misery, hunger and fear, which came to an end suddenly in August 1945, when Japan surrendered after atom bombs were dropped on two of its own cities, thus sparing Singapore the ordeal of an Allied invasion.

THE POST-WAR PERIOD

In September 1945 the British set up a temporary military administration in preparation for a return to colonial government. However, Singapore had changed and the British attempted a new government structure. They aimed to rationalize the untidy administration of Crown Colony, federation and unfederated states, and unite the peninsula by creating a Malayan Union comprising all the Malay states, together with Penang and Melaka, but separating Singapore as a crown colony. In April 1946 civil rule was restored, the Straits Settlements were broken up, and the Malayan Union and Singapore Crown Colony came into being.

These decisions were taken because of Singapore's special place as a free port, its importance as a military base and the complications of trying to absorb it into a Malaya embarking on the road to self-government and independence. However, Singapore's separation was not intended to be permanent.

The proposals provoked protest in Singapore, leading in 1945 to the creation of its first political party, the Malayan Democratic Union, which wanted the island's incorporation in a democratic socialist Malayan Union. The party joined other opposition groups in the peninsula to form the All-Malaya Council of Joint Action, which put forward *The People's Constitutional Proposals for Malaya*, calling for the inclusion of Singapore in a Malayan federation. However, this was swept aside by the intensity of peninsular Malay nationalism, reacting against the Malayan Union, the loss of state identity, and the proposed liberal granting of citizenship to immigrants. As a result, in 1948 a Federation of Malaya replaced the Malayan Union. Singapore remained separated, but this time on racial grounds, since the Malay leaders did not want to upset the ethnic balance of the Federation by including a predominantly Chinese Singapore.

Constitutional Development, 1948–65

Meanwhile, Singapore was also groomed for eventual self-government by developing the existing colonial constitutional machinery of executive, legislative and municipal councils and rural boards, and by an expansion of English education. A provisional advisory council was created in 1946, with an unofficial but still nominated majority, but in 1948 the first elections were held for six members of the legislative council. The Malayan Democratic Union, now heavily communist-infiltrated, boycotted the election, and most of the elected seats fell to the Singapore Progressive Party. This upper-middle-class English-educated group supported British plans for gradual constitutional reform while maintaining the economic *status quo*.

There was little popular enthusiasm for this constitutional experiment. Voting was confined to British subjects, registration was voluntary, and the activities of the English-speaking legislative council were remote from the majority of the population, with their problems of poverty, unemployment, bad housing and inadequate vernacular education. There was little redress for their grievances after the outbreak of a Communist Emergency in the Federation of Malaya in 1948, which led to a period of severe repression of all radical politics in Singapore. While the colony was not directly involved in the revolt, the same emergency regulations were enforced. The Malayan Communist Party was proscribed in 1948 and the Malayan Democratic Union disbanded itself.

As the Malayan Emergency was brought under control, the authorities permitted greater political activity in Singapore. In 1955 a new constitution was granted in an effort to speed up constitutional reform and jolt the small apathetic electorate into a sense of real participation and responsibility. The new legislative assembly had an elected majority (25 out of 32 members), voters were registered automatically, and the leader of the largest party in the Assembly, as Chief Minister, would form a Council of Ministers responsible to the Assembly.

Two new left-wing parties were created to fight the election: the Labour Front, headed by lawyer David Marshall, and the People's Action Party (PAP), led by Lee Kuan Yew. The elections produced shock results when the two radical parties routed the Progressives and other conservatives, and David Marshall's moderate Labour Front formed a minority government. However, in 1955–56 the communists, in common cause with the PAP, made a determined bid for power through the trade union movement and Chinese middle schools. For a time they even wrested control of the PAP central executive committee away from Lee Kuan Yew. The Labour Front Government checked them by using emergency regulations to imprison their leaders and by taking steps to remove genuine grievances. A 1957 Education Ordinance gave parity to the four main language streams; in the same year citizenship was offered on generous terms to nearly all residents, and again in 1957 a new Public Services Commission was set up to achieve rapid localization of the civil service. David Marshall had resigned in 1956, following failure to negotiate immediate self-government, and was succeeded as chief minister by Lim Yew Hock. In the following year, terms were agreed for full internal self-government, and at elections held in 1959 to implement this, the PAP was swept to power, winning an outright majority (43 out of 51 seats). Having insisted on the release of the imprisoned PAP extremists, Lee Kuan Yew took office as Prime Minister. Under his leadership, the party has remained in power ever since.

In the face of poverty, unemployment and a soaring birth rate, the new government committed itself to a programme of rapid industrialization and social reform, with ambitious schemes for education and housing. It also aspired within its four-year term to achieve full independence through a merger with the Federation of Malaya, which had itself secured independence in 1957. Such a union was seen as vital to provide the military security and free access to a Malayan market which were considered essential for Singapore's survival. However, the implementation of this policy quickly led to dissension in the party, and to challenges from the extreme left wing, which threatened to tear the party apart and plunge Singapore into chaos.

The Federation of Malaya, which was originally reluctant to draw closer to Singapore because of its large Chinese population and left-wing tendencies, now realized the need to exercise direct control on the near-communist state emerging on its doorstep. To do this, in May 1961 the Malayan Prime Minister, Tunku Abdul Rahman, proposed a closer association between the Federation and Singapore, by bringing in the three Borneo territories to achieve racial equilibrium. The PAP leadership eagerly took up this idea, but the prospect of merging Singapore in a conservative, anti-communist Federation so alarmed members of the party's radical left wing that in July 1961 they made a bid to topple Lee Kuan Yew's government. Having failed by a narrow margin at a dramatic all-night session of the Assembly, the rebels then broke away to form an opposition Barisan Sosialis (Socialist Front).

Lengthy discussions on the proposed merger were hotly disputed by the Barisan Sosialis, but a public referendum in 1962 endorsed Singapore's entry, and in July 1963 the Malaysia Agreement was finally signed, under which Singapore was to join Malaya, Sarawak and Sabah (North Borneo) in forming the Federation of Malaysia on August 31st, 1963.

The implementation was deferred until mid-September to enable United Nations representatives to ascertain that the people of the Borneo states agreed. Singapore took advantage of this delay to declare its own unilateral independence from colonial rule and to call a snap election.

Having survived the 1961 crisis, the moderate element of the PAP had reorganized and strengthened the party, and, profiting from the success of the Malaysia merger, the ruling party secured a comfortable victory, winning 39 seats to the Barisan's 13.

However, the association was strained. "Confrontation" by Indonesia, which objected to the formation of the Malaysian federation, severely damaged Singapore's trade and led to acts of violence by Indonesian saboteurs. Simultaneously the central government and Singapore clashed over what they took to be undue interference in each other's internal affairs. In July and September 1964 communal riots in Singapore further strained relations with Kuala Lumpur, while the ruling Alliance Party in Malaysia objected to the PAP's contesting the 1964 general elections. Finally Lee Kuan Yew's attempts to unite all Malaysian opposition parties brought the crisis to a head, and on August 9th, 1965, the central government forced Singapore to agree to a separation.

REPUBLIC OF SINGAPORE

In this way Singapore became independent against the wishes of its own leaders. It joined the United Nations in September 1965 and was admitted as a member of the Commonwealth the following month. The new republic, established in December 1965, was committed to multi-racial, non-communist, democratic socialist policies, and to co-operation with Malaysia, particularly in economic and defence matters.

Politically, the transition to full independence was smooth. The machinery of government remained almost intact, with small constitutional amendments, notably appointing a non-executive President as Head of State. Effective power lay in the hands of the Prime Minister and his Cabinet, responsible to the single-chamber Parliament (formerly the Legislative Assembly), which was elected for a five-year term by all adult Singapore citizens.

On the recommendation of a constitutional commission, appointed in 1966 to devise safeguards for minority rights, a nominated advisory Presidential Council was created in 1970 (renamed the Presidential Council for Minority Rights in 1973), to draw attention to any discriminatory legislation.

With the expansion of population and migration to new towns, constituencies were redrawn and the number of parliamentary seats was increased to 58 in 1967, to 65 in 1971, to 69 in 1976 and to 75 in 1980. Basically, however, the constitution remained unchanged.

Other adjustments were more painful. Few if any had visualized a separate independent Singapore on the grounds that such a tiny state, with a large population and no natural resources, could neither sustain its economy nor defend itself.

Initially, the British defence "umbrella" continued to shelter Malaysia and Singapore, but in 1966 the United Kingdom decided to withdraw its bases from "east of Suez" in the mid-1970s. Singapore introduced compulsory national service and was working to build up a credible defence force when, in 1968, Britain advanced the pull-out date to 1971.

The accelerated British withdrawal threatened Singapore's economy, since the bases accounted for 20 per cent of the country's Gross National Product, but the government took advantage of the situation to call an election in 1968, when it won a mandate to pass far-reaching labour legislation, curbing trade union activity, to provide the right climate for foreign investment. As hopes for access to the Malaysian market evaporated, Singapore stepped up its efforts to achieve rapid export-oriented industrialization. To attract foreign and local capital and expertise, the government rejected doctrinaire socialism in favour of a mixed economy, largely privately owned and managed but with a sizable public ownership stake used by the government to give impetus and direction to industrialization.

Official policy aimed at improving living standards without creating a welfare state: it encouraged full employment and subsidized education, housing and public health. A vigorous education programme concentrated on bilingual primary and secondary schooling, while developing technical skills tailored to the republic's economy. This was followed in 1980 by the merging of Singapore's two universities to form a national university designed to raise the level of tertiary education.

An energetic programme of urban renewal and the building of new townships meant that in 1981 more than 60 per cent of the population lived in public housing, the majority in owned, not rented, accommodation. Social reform was accompanied by a strict policy of family limitation and population control, together with stringent immigration curbs, including a refusal to accept Vietnamese or other refugees as permanent residents.

With independence suddenly thrust upon it in 1965, Singapore needed to create a sense of nationhood. In the early years this was done by stressing the unique qualities and differences which distinguished Singapore from its neighbours, resulting in an abrasive foreign policy. While the republic was a founder member of the Association of South East Asian Nations (ASEAN), formed in 1967 along with Malaysia, Thailand, Indonesia and the Philippines, at first it paid only lip service to regional co-operation. But the British pullout, the sharp increase in petroleum prices in 1974 (oil refining is Singapore's largest industry), followed by South Viet-Nam's falling to the communists in 1975, induced Singapore to draw closer to its neighbours. It led the way in giving support to ASEAN and the concept of regional solidarity, particularly after the first ASEAN summit meeting in Bali in 1976.

From the beginning, Singapore tried to keep on friendly terms and to forge economic links with all countries: the West, the Third World, Japan, the Middle East, and communist states. In order to play down its image as an ethnic Chinese state, it intended to wait until the last of its ASEAN neighbours, Indonesia, established diplomatic relations with the People's Republic of China before doing so itself. Although Singapore maintains friendly contact with China, it also uses facilities in Taiwan to train its army.

At the time of separation in 1965, Singapore hoped that it would eventually be readmitted to the Federation of Malaysia, but this hope disappeared with the realization of the country's viability as an independent state and the maturing sense of nationhood. After an initial stormy period, in the early 1970s the relationship between the two countries became friendlier as the last formal links were broken: their joint airline in 1972; joint currency arrangements, rubber and stock exchanges, and banking association in 1973. They maintained close co-operation in matters of joint concern: combating subversion and the narcotic drugs trade, protecting the Straits of Melaka and Singapore.

The timing of Singapore's independence was fortunate in that it was followed by eight years of international boom, when Singapore achieved an "economic miracle" in industrialization, in providing full employment and raising standards of living. As the world's third largest refinery centre, Singapore was hit by the 1973 oil crisis but reacted with characteristic vigour to the threat of world recession. By 1976 its economy had recovered momentum, and in 1979 Singapore overtook Yokohama as the second largest port in the world, surpassed only by Rotterdam. That same year the Government launched a "second industrial revolution" aimed at phasing out labour-intensive industries in favour of advanced technology, and creating a new Japanese-style work ethic based on team-work between management and workers. In 1981 the Singapore economy achieved its highest growth rate in eight years.

From 1968 to 1981 the PAP held all parliamentary seats. After the 1961 crisis, the Government pursued a consistently anti-communist policy, using the emergency regulations—a legacy of colonial times—to imprison "hard-core" subversives. The left-wing Barisan Sosialis assemblymen refused to acknowledge Singapore's independence in 1965, boycotted the Parliament and resigned their seats the next year, preferring to oppose the Government by extra-constitutional means. After the communist victories in Indo-China in 1975, the extreme left wing regrouped to attempt a resurgence in Singapore and Malaysia, but the Government arrested leading cadres of the Malayan National Liberation Front, the militant satellite of the Communist Party of Malaya. In the more relaxed political climate of 1980 and 1981, numbers of political prisoners were released, leaving only a small band of committed communist subversives in detention.

Since 1961 the PAP leadership has exhibited a remarkable cohesion which has contributed to the stability of the state. However, it has also tended to stifle all criticism. Radio and television are state-owned. Newspapers require annual licences and incline to self-censorship. The concentration of power and patronage in the hands of one group, and acknowledgement of the considerable achievements and success of its policies, has emphasized the lack of credible alternatives. Seven opposition parties contested the 1980 parliamentary elections, but the ruling party achieved its greatest-ever landslide victory, winning all seats for the fourth successive election and capturing nearly 78 per cent of the votes.

Prime Minister Lee Kuan Yew hailed this prematurely as a "watershed election" since, for the first time, a leading part was played by younger party men, groomed to succeed the "old guard". A number of older members of Parliament stood down in favour of new candidates, and, immediately after the election, four senior Ministers, including founder members of the party's executive, retired to make way for younger leaders. In opening the ranks to younger blood, no attempt was made to recruit any women, and the Singapore Parliament is an all-male institution.

In twenty years of remarkable economic progress Singapore had achieved the second highest per capita income in Asia after Japan, a healthy standard of living and minimal unemployment. But by the latter months of 1981 the growth rate of the economy showed signs of slowing down, and the strains of the Republic's success story began to show.

The victory of the opposition Workers' Party Secretary-General at a parliamentary by-election in October 1981 came as a shock to the ruling PAP, which had enjoyed a monopoly of power for thirteen years. One lone opposition member in the Singapore Parliament posed no serious practical threat to the Government but produced a considerable psychological effect. The days of political complacency by the PAP were over. The Government set out to remove material grievances but also to channel media criticism towards its desired goals by a major restructuring of the newspaper industry in April 1982.

The by-election surprise, attributed in part to the immaturity and inexperience of the new generation of junior leaders of the PAP, has thrown doubt upon Singapore's political future in the post-Lee Kuan Yew era. While Singapore remains one of the world's most prosperous and stable countries, it faces the future with a new sense of uncertainty and challenge.

ECONOMIC SURVEY

David H. B. Lim

(Revised since 1980 by Linda Seah)

Modern Singapore achieved its initial economic success as an entrepôt mainly as a result of its strategic geographic position and excellent natural harbour. Between 1960 and 1973, the economy grew at an average annual rate of about 10 per cent but declined to around 6 per cent after 1974. Although slowed by the worldwide recession of the mid-1970s, Singapore's economic growth has been remarkable. A major factor has been the effective implementation of soundly conceived government policies which from the outset took full account of Singapore's strengths and weaknesses. Other major contributing factors have been the competitiveness of Singapore's export products in the world market, its ability to attract overseas investment, the allocation of resources to investment —especially for infrastructure and human resources rather than consumption—and the development of a highly sophisticated and successful international financial sector.

In 1981 Singapore's G.D.P. increased by 9.9 per cent in real terms, fractionally lower than the 10.2 per cent achieved in 1980. The latter rate had been the first double-digit growth rate since the oil crisis in 1973/74, which had marked the end of the similar rates during the 1960s and early 1970s. In previous years, domestic factors accounted for less than a quarter of the G.D.P. growth. But in 1981, they were as important as external factors in stimulating economic activities in Singapore. The domestic driving force came from the acceleration of capital expenditure by the private sector on buildings and other construction works and a high rate of investment in machinery and equipment. As in 1980, Singapore's real growth in 1981 continued to out pace those of other competitive export-oriented economies like Taiwan (7.5 per cent) and South Korea (7.1 per cent), and was just under Hong Kong's (10 per cent). Though growth in 1981 was achieved at a rate of inflation of 8.2 per cent compared to 4.0 per cent in 1979 and 8.5 per cent in 1980, consumer prices were substantially lower than those of Hong Kong, South Korea and Taiwan, whose inflation rates ranged from 9.5 to 14 per cent and 8.5 per cent in 1980. The growth in 1981, as in previous years, was broadly based, but except for construction, all sectors of the economy grew more slowly than the previous year. The financial and business services sector was the fastest growing sector, at 18 per cent and contributed 27 per cent to the overall increase in G.D.P. in 1981. The other major source of growth came from the manufacturing sector which continued to diversify and upgrade with the establishment of new industries and firms venturing into new product lines. Despite depressed demand in the major industrialized countries, the sector grew by 10 per cent and maintained its position as the second largest contributor to G.D.P. at 22 per cent in 1981. In all, per caput G.N.P. in 1981 rose to S$10,800, compared with S$9,464 in 1980, an increase of 8.5 per cent in real terms. This level of real per capita income was comparable to that of Japan in 1972 and Singapore remains second only to Japan by this criterion in East Asia.

PROBLEMS OF DEVELOPMENT

The major concern of public policy during the 1960s was to accelerate economic growth and the rate of job creation so as to reduce the problem of mounting unemployment and the stagnating entrepôt trade sector which had been the backbone of the economy.

The post-war baby boom of the early 1950s and the flow of immigrants resulted in an average annual population growth rate of 4.4 per cent between 1947 and 1957. The population increased by 507,000 during this ten-year period. In 1957 unemployment stood at around 5 per cent of the labour force and increased steadily to 9.2 per cent in 1966.

Aggravating the situation was the slow rate of income and employment generation by the entrepôt trade sector. With the demise of the European colonial empires in Indonesia, Malaya and Indochina which were once Singapore's protected hinterland, the newly emerging nations, dictated both by economic and political considerations, have attempted to develop trade services and facilities traditionally provided by the Republic. As a result of such a development, the entrepôt functions have diminished in importance to its neighbours.

At the same time, industrial relations were undergoing a turbulent period, and the early 1960s were characterized by industrial unrest and work-stoppages resulting in many man-days lost.

Political instability was further evidenced by the stormy relationships of Singapore with neighbouring countries. In 1963, Indonesia launched a policy of confrontation against the formation of Malaysia, of which Singapore was an original member. Indonesian confrontation meant the loss of an important trading partner for Singapore. However, two years after the establishment of Malaysia, Singapore was separated from the federation due to irreconcilable differences in the political, economic and social policies of Singapore and the mainland.

By the end of the 1960s a new problem had arisen. The British Government announced the withdrawal of its forces from Singapore by 1971, a move which resurrected fears of massive unemployment since British military services constituted the Republic's largest single employer. Moreover, it meant the loss of an important source of foreign exchange. United Kingdom military expenditure had been estimated at more than $400 million a year.

In the early 1970s, the entrepôt function of Singapore for the region was damaged by the end of the war in Viet-Nam and the decline in off-shore oil exploration activities in the mid-1970s. The Viet-Nam war had boosted trade and the oil refining industry in Singapore while regional oil exploration had benefited the shipbuilding and shipping services industries.

In the last few years, a number of serious economic problems have emerged which threaten to affect adversely an economy which is heavily dependent on trade. These are the problems of energy and oil prices, lower external demand, protectionism and slower rates of growth in the 1980s. These increasingly strong protectionistic sentiments of the Western industrialized countries make the upgrading of industries in Singapore more urgent to lessen the adverse effects. As a non-oil producing country, it will join the rest of other developing nations in bearing the bulk of the deficits in current account imbalances which exist between oil and non-oil producing nations and which will worsen as oil prices escalate. The recycling of the petrodollar is also not expected to be fast enough to help the imbalances. The Singapore economy continues to be deeply affected by the deepening recession in the major OECD countries, especially that of the U.S.A.

DEVELOPMENT STRATEGY

The People's Action Party (PAP), in power since 1959, has recognized Singapore's economic strengths and weaknesses and the necessity to adapt to changing circumstances. Since the initiation of the Singapore Development Plan in 1961, the emphasis in development policy has been upon industrialization, in recognition of the limits of growth based on entrepôt trade. However, the basic resources at Singapore's disposal for stimulating economic growth are largely intangibles. The island Republic has very few natural resources and has to obtain almost all its basic requirements, including food, water, and raw materials, from external sources. Further, the population is too small to create a significant domestic market. But the Republic has the advantages of a favourable geographical position and natural harbours, and has an urbanized, highly literate and increasingly well-educated population, which appears to be singularly adaptable. These factors, together with its experience as a trading centre, and political stability, have enabled the Government successfully to redirect the economy towards industrialization and away from its historical reliance on entrepôt trade. The development objectives were to build up a manufacturing sector geared to the export market, to provide suitable and economic infrastructure, to attract foreign and local capital to industry, to develop technical, managerial and marketing expertise and to train and discipline the labour force.

Two important pieces of legislation were enacted in 1968, the Employment Act 1968 and the Industrial Relations (Amendment) Act 1968. Together these two Acts established the ascendancy of the employer and management over the worker and militant unionism and industrial unrest were almost completely eliminated.

The Government enhanced the investment climate through the provision of fiscal incentives. As part of the strategy for selective industrial development, a series of tax incentives were made available through the Economic Expansion Incentives (Relief from Income Tax) Act, 1967. These include tax holidays, accelerated depreciation for capital expenditures, and concessionary tax rates on profits earned from the export of manufactured products.

Between 1960 and 1980, the value of industrial output increased over 21-fold, employment nearly nine-fold, value-added over 48-fold and direct exports over 22-fold. The restructuring and diversification of the economy caused a World Bank team to report that "in 1968 Singapore entered a new phase of accelerated growth with boom conditions in private investment and a decline in unemployment, buoyancy of government investments and a significant build-up of external reserves". But the economy remained vulnerable to adverse external influences.

The economic strategy of the 1970s was to diversify the economy, to upgrade industries to higher skill levels and higher value-added and to develop Singapore into a regional service and international financial centre. In the area of industrial development, more skill-intensive and higher-technology industries are being encouraged. Further incentives were given in 1978 and 1979 under the Economic Expansion Incentives Act through the introduction of an investment credit scheme and an investment allowance scheme. To give the private sector more encouragement to undertake research and development, a number of tax incentives were also given in 1980. The Government has also extended its assistance to other areas such as product development, skills development, drive towards higher productivity and others. The high wage policy adopted since 1979 was geared towards better utilization of scarce manpower resources and upgrading skills and productivity. The Asian Dollar Market has had many tax stimulants since its formation, including the complete removal of foreign exchange controls. In the area of trade development, export promotion continues to be the major policy objective. Entrepôt trade is not consciously inhibited in any way, although it plays a greatly diminished role. In the services sector, the emphasis is on the tourist industry, transportation and warehousing, as well as financial and insurance services.

GROWTH AND EMPLOYMENT

Economic development during the 1950s was characterized by slow growth with intermittent booms and slumps. The Korean War boom of the early 1950s was immediately followed by a mild recession which lasted till 1955 when the foreign trade sector once again was boosted by improved rubber prices. The average annual growth rate of the G.D.P. between 1956 and 1960 has been estimated at 5.4 per cent. The period of political transition in the first half of the 1960s also marked a period of co-ordinated and planned growth for the Singapore economy stimulated by increased public and private expenditure. Rapid growth was sustained at the rate of 12 per cent a year between 1968 and 1974. In the recession period 1974–75, the double-digit growth rates plunged to negligible growth rates but recovery since 1976 has been steady. By 1980, a return to double-digit growth was attained. The six-year period between 1974 and 1980 saw an average annual rate of growth of 7.8 per cent compared to 12 per cent between 1968 and 1974.

The overall growth of the economy was accompanied by growth in employment. The establishment of labour-intensive industries such as textiles and electronics assembly in the earlier stages of industrialization contributed immensely to the rate of labour absorption in the industrial sector. Between 1970 and 1974, employment grew at 5.4 per cent a year while the labour force increased annually by only 4.8 per cent. The unemployment rate was officially estimated at 2.9 per cent of the labour force in 1981, compared with 3.0 per cent in 1980 and 10.4 per cent in 1970. The tight labour market has to be eased by foreign workers imported from traditional Malaysian sources, as well as from Indonesia, Thailand, the Philippines, India and Sri Lanka. Demand for foreign workers is more acute in the industrial and construction sectors.

Accompanying the employment expansion was a change in the pattern of employment, reflecting the restructuring of the economy. In 1981, the manufacturing sector continued to be the leading employer, accounting for 29.3 per cent of total employment (22 per cent in 1970), followed by the trade sector and the community and social services sector which absorbed 22.7 per cent and 20.6 per cent of total employment respectively. With rapid growth in the financial and business services sectors, its share of employment at 7.9 per cent in 1981 was more than double that in 1970. The higher demand for trained manpower reflecting economic restructuring also meant more professional, technical, administrative and managerial workers were employed. In 1981, such workers formed 13.4 per cent of total workers employed and the employment growth for this category of workers at 5.8 per cent was the highest, surpassing those of all other groups. Persons employed in sales, services, clerical and related work formed 40.1 per cent of the total work force, with production and related workers accounting for another 38.8 per cent in 1981. These sectoral and occupational distributions of the work force reflect the activities of the small industrialized service-oriented economy.

Except for the brief recession in 1974–75, Singapore had experienced near full or full employment coupled with labour productivity growth at an average rate of 4 per cent in the 1970s (as measured by real value-added per worker). Since 1972 the National Wages Council (NWC), formed as a tripartite body comprising equal representation from the government, employers and workers, has been formulating wage policies and guiding wage increases. While such NWC recommendations were not mandatory, they have been accepted in full by the public sector (which, as the largest single employer, employed 11.6 per cent of all workers in 1981), and widely followed by the private sector. Between 1972 and 1974, as a result of the NWC's recommendations, the mean earnings of workers grew at an annual average rate of 14 per cent. Such high wage rises were partly to offset the strong inflation which eroded the take-home pay of workers during the period 1973–74, and partly to induce productivity growths. While wages moderated in 1975 with the recession, the NWC in 1979 started a three-year wage corrective policy with the objective of upgrading and economizing on the use of labour. The 1979 wage increase was a hefty 20 per cent rise over 1978's wage level. In 1980 a two-tier wage guideline, consisting of a general wage rise for all workers and an incentive component amounting to 3 per cent of total wages for above-average workers, was recommended. In 1981, the two-tier guideline was continued but with the merit increment of only 2 per cent compared with 1980's 3 per cent. Another change in 1981 was the recommendation by the NWC of a range of increases instead of a fixed quantum to give employers and unions flexibility in their wage negotiations. It would also pave the way for a return to normal collective wage bargaining.

Employment continued to expand but at a slower rate which was more comparable with the indigenous labour supply's growth. Productivity in 1981 stood at 5.4 per cent, more than double that in 1979, making possible faster economic growth with fewer new workers employed. Productivity increases are zealously sought after, given the zero population growth policy and the policy to minimize the economic and social pressures of a large imported work force. The high-wage policy to induce economic upgrading has resulted in the average earnings of workers growing, which in August 1981 was 14 per cent higher than the year before. But as productivity has improved and given Singapore's relatively lower inflation, its labour costs remained competitive. In 1979 the NWC has also recommended a 2 per cent levy on employers, based on their employees' salaries, as an economic tax to be paid into a Skills Development Fund (SDF). The SDF was to provide funds for training of workers and complemented the wage correction policy in encouraging employers to utilize labour more efficiently and restructure their workers' skills. In 1980 the levy was raised to 4 per cent and the usage of the SDF was extended to subsidize interest payments on the purchase of new machinery and equipment required to increase labour productivity and the use of skilled workers. All in all, the wage correction policy appeared to be having its greatest impact on the manufacturing sector whose workers enjoyed the sharpest wage increase in 1981.

INFLATION

The growth of the Singapore economy throughout the 1960s and even until 1972 was achieved with remarkable price stability. Official statistics show that the average annual increase in consumer prices was less than 2 per cent between 1963 and 1972. However, in the 12 months ending December 1973 consumer prices rose by 34.6 per cent, compared with an increase of less than 6 per cent in 1972, largely as a result of worldwide inflation. By March 1974, however, inflation had been brought under control. The Consumer Price Index (CPI) declined by 1.9 per cent in 1976, mainly as a result of falling food prices, and increased by only 3.2 per cent in 1977. In 1978 consumer prices worsened slightly, increasing by 4.8 per cent, but inflation fell to 4.0 per cent in 1979. But as world inflation continued to be severe in 1980, the CPI shot up to 8.5 per cent which, though higher than 1979, was still lower than the rates suffered by many countries. In 1981, the rate eased to 8.2 per cent owing partly to the improvement in productivity and partly to the continued strengthening of the Singapore dollar against major world currencies as well as to the glut in oil supply and general decline in global inflation. The G.D.P. deflator, which measures the movement of the price level of the net output or value added of the economy and provides an indirect and rough indication of average increases in production costs, rose by 5 per cent compared with 6 per cent in 1980. The moderation in the G.D.P. deflator was the result of lower increases in the prices of imported commodities, crude oil and manufactured products. Wage increases were, however, only marginally higher than those in 1980.

Inflation has been due to both imported and domestically generated factors. The Republic, being devoid of raw materials and natural resources, has a high propensity to import, which has been further augmented by the needs of rapid growth and economic development since 1968. It has been estimated that 60 per cent of total consumer expenditure is spent on imported goods and import prices increased by more than 45 per cent in 1974. Total imports over total trade in 1981 stood at a ratio of 0.57. Imported inflationary factors have also taken the form of large capital inflows. Nonetheless, the rise in consumer prices in Singapore in 1981 was lower than those of other ASEAN countries, which ranged from 10 to 14 per cent.

FOREIGN TRADE

Between 1960 and 1980 the value of Singapore's external trade (excluding trade with Indonesia for which official published data are not available) increased over twelve times, from S$7,555 million in 1960 to S$92,797 million in 1980. In 1981, despite economic recessions in the U.S.A. and Europe, total trade grew by 10 per cent to S$102,539 million. This growth rate was, however, the lowest since 1975. Exports grew by only 7 per cent to S$44,291 million, while imports grew almost twice as fast as exports, by 13 per cent to S$58,248 million. The trade deficit thus widened to S$13,957 million, compared with S$9,893 million in 1980. The increase in the volume of imported crude petroleum contributed significantly to the deficit. The composition of exports has also changed since the increased importance of export-orientated industrialization. In 1972, domestic exports accounted for only 35.1 per cent of total exports. The proportion has increased steadily to 66.5 per cent in 1981, reflecting the declining importance of entrepôt trade. The upsurge in domestic exports has resulted from the Government's successful policy of encouraging the establishment of export-oriented industries as well as increased overseas demand for Singapore's goods. Accompanying the growth was the steady widening of Singapore's trade deficit which is characteristic of its trade balance. The cause can be attributed both to the increase in volume and prices of import required for the industrial sector, and to infrastructural development. The wide trade deficit in 1981 in particular was also influenced by the changes in the balance of trade with major trading partners such as Saudi Arabia, Japan, the EEC and the U.S.A.

Direction and Composition of Trade

Singapore's leading trade partners in 1981 were Japan, Malaysia and the U.S.A., together accounting for 41.7 per cent of total trade. The other two major trade partners were Saudi Arabia and the EEC, which absorbed another 21.6 per cent of total trade. Petroleum, machinery and transport equipment, rubber and timber still constituted the bulk of Singapore's total trade in 1981, accounting for 76 per cent of the increase in total trade. Petroleum was the most important item, accounting for one-third of Singapore's total trade, with machinery and transport equipment accounting for another one-quarter.

Growth in exports in 1981 slowed down owing to the economic recessions in the U.S.A. and Europe. The value of exports was reduced by depressed commodity prices, while the sharp appreciation of the Singapore dollar relative to the European currencies could have affected exports to these countries. The economic recessions and trade protectionism also reduced the rate of increase in domestic exports. There were slower growth rates for domestic exports of petroleum products and machinery and transport equipment. Notable increases in exports were, however, recorded for high-value products such as off-shore oil exploration equipment and supplies, electric generators, supply boats and oil rigs. Re-export trade declined by 5 per cent for the first time in six years, affected by the weaker world demand for primary commodities from regional economies, as well as the slowdown in re-export of manufactured and capital goods to these countries. This poorer re-export trade also caused slower growth in imports in 1981.

Terms of Trade

The upsurge in Singapore's external trade in 1976 and 1977 was due to both improved terms of trade as well as substantial increases in volume. In 1974 and 1975, Singapore's terms of trade (1972=100) declined by 1.1 per cent and 2.9 per cent respectively when commodity prices escalated at the height of the period of worldwide inflation. In 1976 the terms of trade index improved by 1.6 per cent and a further 1.5 per cent in 1977. The terms of trade index (exports/ imports) stood at 111.6 in 1981, compared with 109.2 in 1980. The improvement in terms of trade in 1981 was mainly because of the stronger Singapore dollar.

Tourist Trade

In line with economic diversification, the tourist sector has been actively promoted to earn foreign exchange. The industry's contribution to G.D.P. in 1960 was only 1.5 per cent. By 1973, it had risen to 5.8 per cent, and in 1979, the restaurant and hotel sector accounted for about 4 per cent of G.D.P.

In 1981, tourist arrivals rose by 10 per cent to exceed 2.8 million, with half of the increase coming from the ASEAN countries and Japan. Excluding Malaysian visitors embarking direct from Peninsular Malaysia, Indonesian visitors remained the largest group, forming 16.9 per cent of all visitors, followed by Japanese 12.5 per cent, Australians 9.1 per cent, British 5.1 per cent and Americans also 5.1 per cent. Visitors from ASEAN countries as a whole increased by 8.5 per cent in 1981, compared with 14.5 per cent in 1980. Singapore is also an attractive regional and international convention centre and a convenient stopover for visitors bound for the East and Southeast Asian region. The restaurant and hotel industry has thus become a major service industry and many hotels have undertaken expansion projects and upgrading of services to meet the demand. As a result of the buoyant tourist industry in 1981, hotels and restaurants enjoyed a busy year. The average hotel occupancy rate rose to 86 per cent, despite an increase of 1,800 rooms that year.

Balance of Payments

Singapore's balance of payments clearly reflects its small trade-oriented service economy; merchandise trade has regularly shown a deficit, with sizeable earnings from services. The widening trade deficit was clearly the consequence of rapid industrialization which generated an urgent and greater need to import capital goods and raw materials in a period of rising prices. While the overall balance of payments continued to be in surplus in 1981, at S$1,938 million compared with S$1,434 million in 1980, the trade deficit widened from S$9,292 million in 1980 to S$13,289 million in 1981. This wider trade deficit in 1981 was again due to massive infrastructural development and rapid expansion of the productive capacity of the economy. Singapore thus imported more than it exported, as investment in productive capacity proceeded at a higher pace. The trade deficit was partly offset by vastly improved earnings from services which rose from S$5,991 million in 1980 to S$9,706 million in 1981, and came mainly from transportation, tourism and other services. Nonetheless, the current account recorded a larger deficit at S$3,695 million compared with S$3,410 million in 1980. However, as the capital account saw a larger surplus at S$5,335 million compared with S$3,612 million in 1980, its traditional offsetting of current account deficits resulted in the larger overall balance of payments. As in the past years, the bulk of the capital inflow comprised mainly private capital inflow into the non-monetary sector. The amount brought in totalled S$4,070 million in 1981, compared with S$3,353 million in 1980. This reflected the continuing confidence of private foreign investors in Singapore, coupled with more profits retained by foreign firms for re-investment and larger amounts of financing of local branches by their overseas head-offices. Other capital inflow including short-term trade capital inflow and trade credits also remained favourable given the economy's overall performance and strong Singapore dollar. The latter was relatively stable *vis-à-vis* the U.S. dollar and the Japanese yen in 1981. It eased against the yen, but this depreciation was matched by a slight firming against the U.S. dollar. On average, the Singapore dollar appreciated by 16 per cent, 26 per cent and 14 per cent against the pound sterling, the Deutschmark and the Hong Kong dollar respectively. The appreciation of the Singapore dollar had, in so far as it was passed on to consumers in the form of lower prices, softened the impact of imported inflation. It also ameliorated the increase in costs of raw materials and intermediate goods for manufacturing production.

In 1981 total official foreign reserves reached S$15,491.1 million, which can finance 3.2 months of Singapore's current imports of goods and services. Although the amount of official reserves has increased, compared to the amount of S$3,097.9 million in 1970, the latter year's reserves could have financed 4.9 months of imports.

AGRICULTURE, LIVESTOCK AND FISHERIES

This sector accounted for 1.2 per cent of the G.D.P. at 1968 factor cost in 1981. The principal agricultural activities are vegetable growing, pig and poultry farming, and egg and fish production. It was estimated that 13.1 per cent of Singapore's total land area was used for agricultural purposes in 1980. Most of the agricultural establishments are engaged in mixed farming where cultivation of vegetables is carried out together with the rearing of livestock. Local farms supply some 24 per cent of total vegetable consumption. About 80 per cent of poultry meat requirements is produced by local farms while some 26 per cent of the fish consumed is produced locally. Hence, Singapore relies on imports for most of its basic requirements. Two major agricultural exports are quality orchids and aquarium fish.

MANUFACTURING

The drive toward industrialization was initially launched on the basis of tariff protection and import substitution to alleviate a potentially severe unemployment problem. In 1961, the Economic Development Board (EDB) was created to formulate and implement the industrialization programme. Its functions were to promote industrial investment, to develop and manage industrial estates and to provide industrial financing. When the limits of import substitution, given the small domestic market, became evident, policy was redirected toward promoting an export-oriented, labour-intensive industrialization programme. Apart from the provision of fiscal incentives, the Government also created a number of statutory authorities to help implement its industrialization policy. The EDB had formerly provided medium- and long-term financing; this function was taken over in 1968 by the newly created Development Bank of Singapore. Similarly, the function of planning and management of industrial estates was turned over to the Jurong Town Corporation. The EDB concentrated its efforts on investment promotion and counselling, technical assistance and training.

With government stimulus, the manufacturing sector has become the mainstay of Singapore's phenomenal economic growth. Between 1960 and 1980, this sector grew in real terms by 12.4 per cent a year and accounted for 22 per cent of real G.D.P. in 1981. The growth of the manufacturing sector was retarded by the 1974–75 recession but achieved a real growth of 15 per cent in 1979, the highest rate since the recession. In 1981, the real growth rate was only 10 per cent, lower than the 12 per cent of 1980.

Pattern of Industrial Growth

The problem of labour absorption in the mid-1960s was contained to a large extent by the establishment of labour-intensive industries such as textiles, clothing and electronic assembly. With the shift in emphasis to establishing high-technology and more skill-intensive industries, industries such as petroleum products, shipbuilding and repairing, transport equipment, basic metals and metal products and precision instruments have become more important. The contribution of the relatively higher value-added industries to total manufacturing employment and value-added was evident by 1975 when they provided employment for 55 per cent of the industrial workforce and contributed 72 per cent to total value-added in manufacturing.

At the same time, the industrial sector has become increasingly export-oriented. In 1968 the proportion of output absorbed by foreign markets was only 28 per cent, suggesting that early manufacturing growth had depended upon import-substitution and hence the expansion of the domestic market. Export sales surged to account for 39 per cent of total sales in 1970 and 60 per cent by 1974. By 1981 this proportion stood at 60.6 per cent, compared with 65.6 per cent in 1980.

Performance in 1981

The manufacturing sector grew by 10 per cent in 1981, compared with 12 per cent in 1980. The diversity of both industries and markets, together with sharp improvements in productivity, enabled the sector to weather the economic recessions in Western Europe and the U.S.A. for the second year. The better growth rates of the petroleum industry and the shipbuilding and shiprepairing industries helped to offset the slower growth rates of the electrical and electronic industries and the continued decline of the labour-intensive textile and timber industries. Nonetheless, the sector faced difficulties arising from the sharp depreciation of the European currencies against the U.S. and Singapore dollars. Protectionism continued to plague local manufacturers.

The leading growth industry in 1981 was the transport equipment industry, growing by 26 per cent and accounting for over one-third of the growth in value added of the manufacturing sector. The industry had made tremendous advances since its slump in 1977/78 to become a major pillar of the manufacturing sector. Factors contributing to its growth include its diversified base, Singapore's strategic location for the services offered, availability of skilled labour and competitive costs.

The second largest industry was the petroleum industry, which recovered from the decline in 1980 to achieve a high growth rate of 17 per cent in 1981. Other industries which grew include industrial and metal engineering (12 per cent), printing and publishing (10 per cent), fabricated metal products (8 per cent), chemicals (7 per cent) and electricals and electronics (5 per cent). Despite the weaker growth in the last-mentioned industry, very few companies economised on labour costs, as there is expectation of demand from the U.S.A. to pick up in mid-1982.

The industries which recorded negative growth rates were those of textiles, garments and sawn timber and plywood. Weak overseas demand was the main factor for the textiles and garments industries' poor results, while the decline in overseas housing and construction depressed output of the sawn timber and plywood industry.

Reflecting the slower pace of growth in the whole manufacturing sector, as well as the policy of more efficient use of labour, job creation slowed down. The increase in employment was only 1,300, a sharp drop from 26,200 and 16,700 in 1979 and 1980 respectively. But productivity improved significantly by 9.5 per cent, almost double the rate in 1980, because of mechanization, upgrading of production and employment of more skilled workers.

Foreign Investment

Growth in Singapore's manufacturing has depended to a large extent on foreign investment. Despite slow world economic growth, the inflow of foreign investments from developed economies to Singapore was maintained. Gross fixed assets of foreign investments as at June 1981 reached S$8,000 million, 16 per cent more than the previous year. This continued inflow of foreign investments contributed to the systematic development of the manufacturing sector and encouraged greater local participation in joint ventures.

Net new investment commitments from local and foreign sources, excluding the petrochemical complex, increased to S$1,938 million. Foreign investments continued to account for the larger share of total investment commitments. As in previous years, new foreign investments came mainly from the U.S.A., Western Europe and Japan. Together, they accounted for 60 per cent of total commitments. New investment projects committed in 1981 were in technology-intensive and high value-added industries. The petroleum, electrical and electronic, transport equipment, metal products and precision engineering and chemical industries accounted for 75 per cent of total commitments. In 1981 too, fixed investment per worker and expected value added per worker in real terms were about three times those committed in 1979. Prior to 1979, these two ratios had increased at only moderate rates, and their accelerated advance in the last three years coincided with the wage-correction policy and the launching of the economic restructuring programme. The investment commitment of companies with full knowledge of these government policies indicates that such policies had influenced investment decisions in the last three years toward more capital-intensive and higher value-added industries in Singapore.

Industrial Development Schemes

The Government continued to assist industries in export promotion through finance and product development. Overseas investment promotion has also been stepped up. A Bureau for Joint Ventures was established by the EDB to co-ordinate foreign investment interest in Singapore. In 1976, the Export Credit Insurance Scheme, the Ship Financing Scheme, the Capital Assistance Scheme and the Small Industries Finance Scheme were launched. In 1977, a Product Development Assistance Scheme was introduced to help local manufacturing enterprises develop new products or processes related to their existing activities to increase their competitiveness in overseas markets. In 1978, the EDB planned to modify its Capital Assistance Scheme to help the development of local entrepreneurial ability in the manufacturing sector. Current incentives under the Economic Expansion Incentives Act were also further improved by introducing an investment credit scheme in 1978. Under this scheme, a company carrying out an approved manufacturing or related technical servicing project will be allowed an investment credit in respect of its new fixed investment on plant, machinery and factory building. The scheme is meant to complement the existing pioneer status and export incentive schemes available under the Act.

In 1979 the Government announced four new incentives to promote further growth. These are the Investment Allowance Scheme, the Warehousing and Servicing Incentive Scheme, the International Consultancy Incentive Scheme and the International Trade Incentive Scheme. The first scheme enables projects with long generation periods to claim tax exemption on profits. The second scheme is intended primarily to promote the establishment of regional warehousing and servicing operations for engineering products. The scheme cuts the company tax of 40 per cent to 20 per cent on profits derived from export sales or export services for five years. The third scheme is intended to promote the establishment of consultancy services through a five-year tax holiday, with a 20 per cent concessionary tax on export profits. The last incentive is directed at companies that are exporting Singapore-made products or trading in non-traditional commodities. The tax concession is the same as in the second and third incentive schemes.

A new financial scheme called the Fixed Rate Export Finance Scheme was implemented in November 1979 to boost exports of capital goods and provides exporters with medium- and long-term financing at fixed preferential rates of interest for exports that are sold on credit terms for two years or more. This enhances local exporters' competitiveness as their cost of credit is reduced. Only exports which are guaranteed by the Export Credit Insurance Corporation of Singapore (ECICS) are eligible for this scheme. It is administered by the ECICS, with the Monetary Authority of Singapore acting as the agents for the government.

In 1980, attention was given to research and development (R & D), product development and industrial land development. For all companies, tax incentives include double deduction for R & D expenditure, accelerated depreciation over three years for all plant and machinery for R & D, investment allowance of up to 50 per cent of capital equipment in R & D, extension of the initial allowance of 25 per cent and annual allowance of 3 per cent to cover R & D buildings, and capitalization and writing-off of lump sum payments for manufacturing licensing for a period of five years, were given. The year 1980 also saw a revitalization of the Product Development Assistance Scheme started in 1978. Dollar-for-dollar cash grants to be given to local companies undertaking product development under this scheme. The JTC also stepped up industrial land development to meet the demand for more industrial land and factories. In a further move to stimulate R & D, the Government allocated S$50 million in the 1982 budget to finance directed research in the public sector over the five years. This amount was five times larger than that provided for in the previous budget.

CONSTRUCTION

The construction and quarrying industry, which accounted for 5 per cent of G.D.P. in 1981, expanded at a faster rate because of the continued building boom, to emerge as the second fastest growing sector in the economy. Private sector construction activities boomed to cater for the high demand for condominiums, hotels, office complexes and industrial buildings. Growth in public sector construction, however, slowed down, mainly owing to the completion of major projects. With the relaxation of the policy on the recruitment of foreign labour from non-traditional sources, the construction labour market was less tight. The supply of building materials improved following increases in local production and imports. Their price decreases, coupled with the fall in speculative demand in the property market and an increased supply of residential properties, helped to stabilize inflationary trends in the construction industry.

Through the Government's housing development programme, 60 per cent of Singapore's population now live in public low cost housing. The Housing and Development Board, under its Third Five-Year Building Programme (1970–75), built 114,000 dwelling units. The Fourth Programme (1976–80) plans to add another 150,000 housing units. The Government's urban renewal scheme, spearheaded by the newly created Urban Redevelopment Authority, has been aimed at clearing slums and derelict buildings and rebuilding parts of the city to ensure optimum land use. These activities have provided continued impetus in the construction sector.

MONEY, BANKING AND FINANCE

Monetary and Financial Development Policies

The formulation and execution of monetary and financial development policies rest with the Monetary Authority of Singapore (MAS). The MAS is responsible for the administration and supervision of the banking system, foreign exchange regulations and acts as banker and financial agent of the Government. It thus performs all the functions of a central bank except that of currency issue which is undertaken by the Board of Commissioners of Currency of Singapore (BCCS). A decisive move was made in 1980, terminating all preparations for the merger of the MAS and the BCCS to form a central bank. Instead, the BCCS was reorganized to be left with only the task of issue of notes and coins. Its other major role of handling investment of the Government's foreign currencies and assets would be transferred either to the Government Investment Corporation or the MAS. The latter also underwent drastic reorganization to streamline its function. The principal objective of monetary and financial policies in Singapore is the maintenance of monetary stability and the promotion of credit and exchange conditions conducive to the balanced and sustained growth of the economy. Its developmental objective is the improvement and expansion of the financial infrastructure and promoting the growth of Singapore as an international financial centre.

Monetary expansion in 1981, in terms of currency and demand deposits (M_1), was 12 per cent, compared with 14 per cent in 1980. The ratio of money supply (M_1) to G.D.P. at current market prices was 26.5 per cent, compared with 26.1 per cent in 1980. While increased inflow of private capital and more lending by banks to the private sector remained the factors inducing monetary growth in 1981, Government borrowing from the domestic market continued to exert a contracting influence on money supply. The demand for credit, as measured by loans and advances to non-bank customers (including bills financing), grew by 24.9 per cent in 1981, compared with 26.2 per cent in 1980, to reach S$25,229 million. This was induced by increased economic activity and relatively lower domestic interest rates, as compared with external rates. The highest rate of growth of loans and advances was to the building and construction industry, reflecting the latter's rapid pace in 1981. Deposits of non-bank customers, including Singapore Dollar Negotiable Certificates of Deposit, increased by S$3,973m., compared with a rise of S$3,857m. in 1980. The weighted average lending rate of banks increased from 13.6 per cent in 1980 to a peak of 11.8 per cent in 1981.

Singapore as an International Financial Centre

Singapore's development as a financial centre was conceived as part of the Government's plan to diversify the economy away from its dependence on entrepôt trade to developing the manufacturing and services sectors. Among the factors favouring the development of the financial sector in Singapore are its geographical location, political and monetary stability, relatively developed financial infrastructure and its traditional function as a commercial and trading centre.

Singapore has emerged in recent years as a major banking centre, providing a varied range of financial services in South-East Asia and outside the region. Official encouragement for growth has been provided in the following areas: liberalization of exchange control to facilitate international financial transactions; tax incentives to promote the growth of banking activity and the development of money market instruments; relaxation or removal of restrictive practices to encourage healthy competition and growth in the banking and financial system; a selective policy on the entry of foreign banks and financial institutions; and development of training facilities and the adoption of liberal entry requirements for skilled personnel to expand the pool of financial expertise.

The financial sector averaged an annual growth of 14 per cent in the 1970s, making it one of the fastest growing sectors. Total assets/liabilities of commercial banks grew strongly by 35 per cent in 1981, compared with 25 per cent in 1980, to reach S$44,631 million. The number of commercial banks operating in Singapore reached 108 in 1981, with the establishment of 11 more off-shore banks. Of the 1981 total, 13 were local and the rest foreign. Three types of banking licences are issued for commercial banks: full licensed (37 in 1981), restricted (13 in 1981) and off-shore (58 in 1981). The number of representative banking offices increased from eight in 1970 to the present total of 47. The Gold Exchange, which deals with "paper" gold, was established in November 1978.

The Asian Dollar and Bond Markets

The focal point of Singapore's development as an international financial centre has been the Asian Dollar market. The market was launched in 1968 when the local branch of the United States-based Bank of America secured government approval to borrow deposits of non-residents, mainly in foreign currencies and to use them to finance corporate activities in Asia. At that time, expanding economic development in South-East Asia was rapidly increasing the demand for foreign investment funds and the desirability of a regional centre able to carry out the necessary middleman functions was apparent. Singapore offered the ideal location. It also enjoyed a special advantage over Hong Kong and Tokyo with respect to time zones in that the European and Far East money markets remained open while the Singapore market was still operating. The impetus to the creation of the Asian Dollar market in Singapore was provided when the Government decided to abolish the withholding tax on interest on foreign currency deposits earned by non-residents.

The market functions through the Asia Currency Unit (ACU), which is a separate division of a participating bank or other financial institutions licensed by the MAS to accept deposits in foreign currencies and process international investment loans in such currencies. The number of ACUs increased to 131 in 1981 from 19 in 1971. Although the size of the Asian Dollar market is about 6 per cent the size of the Euro-dollar market, its growth has been phenomenal. After Japan, the market is the largest external currency in Asia. Assets grew from U.S. $30.5 million in 1968 to U.S. $85,852 million at the end of 1981. The growth averaged 77.5 per cent annually between 1969 and 1979. U.S. dollars constitute more than 90 per cent of all funds dealt with in the market although some 20 different currencies are dealt with. The market is characterized by interbank activities. Interbank deposits constitute the main source of funds for ACUs. More than 90 per cent of the interbank deposits are from banks abroad or from the ACUs themselves. Deposits from non-bank customers form about 16 per cent of total liabilities. Interbank lending constitutes about 73 per cent of total assets while loans to non-bank customers constitute about 23 per cent. The maturity structure of the ACU funds shows a large concentration of funds of 1 month and 3 months' maturities. Approximately 45 per cent of the deposits are 1 month maturity and another 28 per cent up to 3 months.

The participants in the Asian Dollar market come from a wide geographical region covering Asia, the Middle East, Europe, the U.S.A. and Australia. Generally, the net suppliers of funds are from the United Kingdom, the EEC, the Middle East and the U.S.A., while net users include the ASEAN countries, Hong Kong and Japan. Approximately 60 per cent of the total deposits placed with ACUs originate from outside Asia, but on the users' side, Asian countries, excluding Singapore, absorb about 62 per cent of the funds.

To promote further the growth of Singapore as a financial centre, several measures were implemented in 1977. These included the extension of the 10 per cent concessionary tax on income from Asian Dollar loans to non-residents to cover all off-shore income other than foreign exchange profits and transactions with domestic banking units and residents. The U.S. dollar Negotiable Certificate of Deposit was introduced to add greater depth to the Asian Dollar market. In June 1978 all foreign exchange controls were abolished. ACUs were also to be allowed to open savings accounts and underwrite off-shore debt-security issues. In 1979 and 1980 more fiscal incentives were given to stimulate further the offshore market. For 1980, the concessionary tax rate of 10 per cent was extended to offshore gold transactions by the ACUs. Stamp duty on documents for offshore loans and on Asian dollar bonds was also abolished.

Since its inception in 1968, transactions in the Asian Dollar market have been mainly of a short-term nature. In order to develop the market fully into an effective instrument for mobilizing international funds for long-term development, the complementary long-term aspect of the market was promoted through the establishment of the Asian Dollar Bond market. As in 1976, borrowers obtained longer term funds at lower cost in the bond market. In 1981, 22 Asian Dollar bond issues were floated, making the largest number of issues in a single year since the market was launched in 1971.

Public Sector Finance

Government expenditure and revenue clearly indicate the rising prosperity of Singapore. Total government revenue has risen yearly, largely from transfer receipts of income tax and taxes on production and expenditure. This has been helped to a large extent by the existence of an effective tax collecting machinery as well as the highly monetized character of the economy. Total government revenue amounted to S$7,146.2 million in 1981, an increase of 30.1 per cent over 1980. Traditionally, transfer receipts in the form of taxation constitute more than 70 per cent of total government revenue. In 1981, transfer receipts contributed 73.7 per cent, of which 50 per cent came from taxes on income and the remainder from taxes on production and expenditure (mainly excise duties, import duties and property tax) and other transfer receipts. Government sale of goods and services contributed 19.6 per cent while interest, dividends and other receipts made up the remaining 6.7 per cent.

The most outstanding feature of public finances in recent years has been the extent of expansion of the Government's influence on the course of domestic business activity and the increasing use of fiscal measures to achieve monetary control. Public capital expenditure rose markedly with the initiation of the First Development Plan in 1961. Capital formation by the public sector rose from S$67 million in 1960 to S$367 million in 1970 and reached S$2,879.8 million in 1981 or 25.8 per cent of gross domestic fixed capital formation. As a result of the rapid rise of public capital, the overall pattern and rate of investment in the economy are substantially influenced by the government contribution. Government stimulus has been applied chiefly through public works and building construction, although its participation in other sectors of activity, particularly in industry, has also increased significantly.

Government expenditure increased from S$702 million in 1968 to S$5,798.2 million in 1981. The average annual rate of growth in the period 1969–79 was 18.4 per cent. In 1981, expenditure on social and community services amounted to 19.8 per cent

(S$1,147.7 million) of total current expenditures, of which the bulk went to education, housing and health. Expenditures on defence, justice and police accounted for 23.3 per cent, public debt financing 46.2 per cent, economic services 4.9 per cent and general services 3.1 per cent. About 1.7 per cent was transferred to the Development Fund.

Following the 1974 recession, expansionary budgetary policies of the major statutory boards helped to sustain economic growth. This has been the distinctive feature of public sector financing in Singapore. To enable the Government to carry out long-term economic and social development projects with the minimum of administrative delay, the Government created various statutory bodies and provided the capital funds for their expansion and operation. The seven major statutory boards are the Housing and Development Board, the Jurong Town Corporation, the Public Utilities Board, the Port of Singapore Authority, the Telecommunication Authority of Singapore, the Urban Redevelopment Authority and the Sentosa Development Corporation. The deficit incurred by these boards was S$235 million in 1981. Thus, although the government sector had a surplus of S$306 million in 1981, the overall public sector surplus was reduced to S$71 million compared with a surplus of S$379 million in 1979. The statutory board expenditures are financed partly from income generated by their own operations but mainly through loans from the Government.

To finance the rapid development of economic and social infrastructure, the Government has raised money both domestically and externally. The domestic debt comprises about 95 per cent of total public debt. The remaining 10 per cent comes in official aid, loans from the IBRD and the Asian Development Bank as well as loans raised in international capital markets. It is mainly through the issue of Singapore registered stocks and bonds that the Government mobilizes private savings for financing economic and social development. The gross national savings rate in Singapore in 1981 was 29.8 per cent of the G.N.P., compared with 19.6 per cent in 1968.

The public debt amounted to S$17,138.2 million at the end of 1981 or 64.9 per cent of the G.N.P. at market prices. Total external debt, however, constituted only 6.4 per cent of total government debt. The Government has not had the need to borrow extensively from external sources since domestic sources as well as the inflow of foreign direct investments have been adequate.

STATISTICAL SURVEY

AREA AND POPULATION

Area (1981)	Population†						
	Census results				Official estimates (mid-year)		
	June 22nd, 1970	June 24th, 1980					
		Males	Females	Total	1978	1979	1981
617.9 sq. km.*	2,074,507	1,231,760	1,182,185	2,413,945	2,353,600	2,383,500	2,443,300

* 238.6 square miles. Of the total, Singapore Island is 572.2 sq. km. (220.9 sq. miles) and other islands 45.7 sq. km. (17.6 sq. miles).

† Excluding transients afloat (4,565 in 1970; 5,553 in 1980) and non-locally domiciled military and civilian services personnel and their dependants (47,959 in 1970; 5,187 in 1980).

Capital: Singapore City (population 1,327,500 at June 30th, 1974).

ETHNIC GROUPS
('000 at June 30th, 1981)

Chinese	1,876.9
Malays	357.0
Indians	156.5
Others	52.9
Total	2,443.3

BIRTHS AND DEATHS

	Registered Live Births		Registered Deaths	
	Number	Rate (per 1,000)	Number	Rate (per 1,000)
1975	39,948	17.7	11,447	5.1
1976	42,783	18.7	11,648	5.1
1977	38,364	16.5	11,955	5.1
1978	39,441	16.8	12,065	5.1
1979	40,779	17.1	12,468	5.2
1980	41,217	17.1	12,505	5.3
1981	42,250	17.3	12,863	5.3

EMPLOYMENT
(at June)

	1979*	1980*	1981†
Agriculture, forestry, hunting and fishing	15,182	16,962	12,700
Mining and quarrying	1,518	1,139	1,200
Manufacturing	294,685	324,121	326,100
Construction	54,345	72,346	66,400
Electricity, gas, water and sanitary services	9,817	8,464	9,200
Commerce	237,346	229,759	252,600
Transport, storage and communications	118,902	119,917	127,600
Services	288,488	303,966	314,100
Activities not adequately defined	749	416	2,800
Total	1,021,032	1,077,090	1,112,700

* Employed persons aged 10 years and over.
† Employed persons aged 15 years and over. Preliminary results.

Sources: Labour Force Surveys and Department of Statistics, Singapore.

AGRICULTURE

LAND USE
(1981—square km.)

Built-up*	288.6
Agricultural†	74.9
Cultivable waste	91.4
Forest	28.6
Marsh and tidal waste	22.4
Others‡	112.0
Total	617.9

* Includes new industrial sites.

† Refers to farm holding area of licensed farms excluding land occupied by pure rubber and coconut plantations.

‡ Includes inland water, open spaces, public gardens, cemeteries, non-built up areas in military establishments, rubber and coconut plantations and quarries.

PRINCIPAL CROPS

	AREA (hectares)			PRODUCTION (metric tons)			
	1972	1973	1974	1978	1979	1980	1981
Rubber	3,294	3,160	2,391	—	—	—	—
Coconuts*	2,600	2,400	1,860	6	6	6	5
Fruits	2,588	2,657	2,638	11,060	9,260	9,055	8,065
Mixed vegetables	1,367	1,025	} 851	40,665	37,800	36,839	42,861
Root crops	1,013	790					
Tobacco	243	310	279	596	478	402	133

* Production in million nuts.

LIVESTOCK

(FAO estimates, '000 head, year ending September)

	1978	1979	1980
Cattle	9	9	9
Buffaloes	3	3	3
Pigs	1,100	1,133	1,166
Goats	2	2	2
Chickens	15,000	15,500	15,644
Ducks	2,269	2,336	2,402

Source: FAO, *Production Yearbook.*

LIVESTOCK PRODUCTS

('000 metric tons)

	1978	1979	1980
Mutton and lamb*	2	2	2
Pig meat	53†	42†	43*
Poultry meat*	51	51	53
Cows' milk*	1	1	1
Hen eggs	26.2	26.9	27.3*
Other poultry eggs	3.5†	3.5*	3.5*

* FAO estimate. † Unofficial figure.

Source: FAO, *Production Yearbook.*

FISHING

FISH LANDED AND AUCTIONED*

(metric tons)

1975	1976	1977	1978	1979	1980	1981
65,803	65,976	67,478	66,883	68,299	74,244	85,016

* Including fish landed in Singapore by non-Singapore vessels. The total catch (live weight) of Singapore vessels was 19,236 metric tons in 1974, 17,560 metric tons in 1975, 16,429 metric tons in 1976, 15,105 metric tons in 1977, 16,172 metric tons in 1978, 16,552 metric tons in 1979, 16,043 metric tons in 1980 and 16,111 metric tons in 1981.

INDUSTRY

PETROLEUM PRODUCTS

(estimated production in '000 metric tons)

	1976	1977	1978	1979	1980*
Liquefied petroleum gas	138	141	174	193	161
Naphtha	1,884	2,613	2,748	2,557	1,463
Motor spirit (petrol)	1,084	1,124	1,220	1,223	1,152
Kerosene	1,950	2,730	2,270	2,071	1,236
Jet fuel	1,755	1,875	2,438	2,963	2,473
Distillate fuel oils	5,046	5,569	6,780	6,566	4,619
Residual fuel oil	9,127	10,209	10,154	10,340	6,457
Lubricating oils	429	469	540	600	635
Petroleum bitumen (asphalt)	280	280	335	400	350

* Excluding amounts processed for overseas customers.

Source: UN, *Yearbook of Industrial Statistics.*

SELECTED OTHER PRODUCTS

		1979	1980	1981
Processed rubber	metric tons	150,583	125,233	104,363
Paints	kilolitres	20,856.4	23,777.9	26,476.6
Broken granite	'000 cu. metres	2,507.3	3,185.0	4,484.4
Bricks	'000 units	150,925	166,508	170,618
Cigarettes and cheroots	metric tons	3,278.2	3,146.8	3,203.3
Soft drinks	'000 litres	169,516.5	175,132.2	189,641.7
Coconut oil	metric tons	14,048	20,957	n.a.
Vegetable cooking oil	,, ,,	75,267	95,598	98,179
Animal fodder	,, ,,	319,630	341,578	268,935
Electricity	million kWh.	6,447.9	6,940.4	7,441.9
Gas	,, ,,	597.7	614.1	625.6

FINANCE

100 cents = 1 Singapore dollar (S$).

Coins: 1, 5, 10, 20 and 50 cents; 1 dollar.

Notes: 1, 5, 10, 20, 25, 50, 100, 500, 1,000 and 10,000 dollars.

Exchange rates (June 1982): £1 sterling = S$3.753; U.S. $1 = 2.1665.

S$100 = £26.65 = U.S. $4.6.16

Note: **The Singapore dollar (S$) was introduced in June 1967, replacing (at par) the Malayan dollar (M$). From September 1949 the Malayan dollar was valued at 2s. 4d. sterling (£1 = M$8.5714) or 32.667 U.S. cents (U.S. $1 = M$3.0612). This valuation in terms of U.S. currency remained in effect until August 1971. Between December 1971 and February 1973 the Singapore dollar was valued at 35.467 U.S. cents (U.S. $1 = S$2.8195). From February to June 1973, the Singapore dollar's value was 39.407 U.S. cents (U.S. $1 = S$2.5376). In terms of sterling, the exchange rate was £1 = S$7.347 from November 1967 to June 1972. The formal link with the Malaysian dollar, begun in June 1967, ended in May 1973, but the Brunei dollar rem ains tied to the Singapore dollar. Since June 1973 the Singapore dollar has been allowed to "float". The average exchange rate (Singapore dollars per U.S. dollar) was: 2.809 in 1972; 2.444 in 1973; 2.437 in 1974; 2.371 in 1975; 2.471 in 1976; 2.439 in 1977; 2.274 in 1978; 2.175 in 1979; 2.141 in 1980; 2.113 in 1981.**

ORDINARY BUDGET

(S$ million—estimates for year ending March 31st)

Revenue	1982/83	Expenditure	1982/83
Direct Taxes	3,788.9	General Services	310.2
Indirect Taxes and Taxes on Outlay	1,488.8	Defence and Justice	1,819.2
Reimbursements and Sales on Goods and Services	1,280.9	Social and Community Services	1,562.1
Income from Investments and Property	492.2	Economic Services	444.7
Others	588.0	Public Debt	1,382.0
		Unallocable	72.9
		Add: Transfer to Development Fund	2,047.7
Total	7,638.8	Total	7,638.8

DEVELOPMENT BUDGET

(S$ million—estimates for year ending March 31st)

Expenditure	1979/80	1980/81	1981/82	1982/83
General services	116.07	102.27	252.0	424.9
General administration	105.73	80.20	220.0	380.0
Fiscal administration	—	1.79	7.0	11.6
General economic regulation	0.60	—	1.0	7.5
Conduct of foreign affairs	—	10.00	10.5	12.0
Others	9.74	10.28	13.5	13.8
Defence and justice	111.49	160.77	155.5	164.9
Defence	100.00	150.00	150.0	150.0
Justice and police	11.17	10.33	5.1	14.7
Others	0.32	0.44	0.4	0.2
Social and community services	1,261.75	1,598.75	2,036.7	3,201.9
Community	26.11	39.24	33.6	59.6
Environment	211.07	222.31	201.8	266.1
Education	92.61	116.86	221.6	500.2
Health	89.32	73.36	93.5	96.1
Housing	836.00	1,133.00	1,464.0	2,253.0
Social welfare	—	—	—	—
Others	6.64	13.98	22.2	26.9
Economic services	1,070.90	1,754.84	2,600.0	3,057.7
Land development	94.50	147.50	233.0	445.2
Agricultural and non-mineral resources	21.43	4.68	6.0	9.0
Industrial and commercial development	561.60	1,047.42	2,002.6	2,197.0
Tourism	—	105.60	9.0	4.5
Transport and communications	393.27	429.54	393.3	354.2
Public utilities	—	20.00	—	—
Others	0.10	0.10	10.1	47.8
Total	2,560.21	3,616.63	5,044.2	6,849.4

OFFICIAL FOREIGN ASSETS

(S$ million, valuation at cost, December 31st)

	1978	1979	1980	1981
Gold and Foreign Exchange	11,435.5	12,466.2	13,588.9	15,242.5
Reserve position in the IMF	38.3	61.8	126.1	173.0
SDRs	—	34.4	42.7	75.6
Total	11,473.8	12,562.4	13,757.7	15,491.1

BALANCE OF PAYMENTS

(S$ million—estimates)

	1978	1979	1980	1981*
BALANCE ON CURRENT ACCOUNT	−1,403.5	−2,179.7	−3,409.9	−3,698.1
Imports f.o.b.	27,493.8	35,772.0	47,964.1	54,483.6
Exports f.o.b.	21,694.5	28,994.0	38,672.1	41,194.5
Trade Balance	−5,799.3	−6,778.0	−9,292.0	−13,289.1
Service Payments (net)	4,484.2	4,674.4	5,991.5	9,706.4
Total Goods and Services (net receipts)	−1,315.1	−2,103.6	−3,300.5	−3,582.7
Transfers (net receipts)	−88.4	−76.1	−109.3	−115.4
TOTAL CAPITAL MOVEMENTS	2,915.0	3,317.0	4,843.6	5,636.5
Non-monetary Sector (net)	1,634.9	2,570.0	3,319.9	4,035.8
Private	1,622.6	2,605.1	3,352.6	4,069.6
Official	12.3	−35.1	−32.7	−33.8
Monetary Sector—Commercial banks (net)	668.9	−400.3	291.6	1,299.0
Allocation of IMF Special Drawing Rights	—	14.3	14.5	17.6
Net Errors and Omissions	611.2	1,133.0	1,217.6	284.1
Net Surplus or Deficit	1,511.5	1,137.3	1,433.8	1,938.4

* Preliminary.

EXTERNAL TRADE*

(S$ million)

	1976	1977	1978	1979	1980	1981
Imports c.i.f.	22,404.5	25,521.9	29,601.3	38,334.4	51,344.8	58,248.0
Exports f.o.b.	16,265.9	20,090.3	22,985.5	30,940.1	41,452.3	44,290.8

* Excluding trans-shipments to and from Peninsular Malaysia.

PRINCIPAL COMMODITIES

(distribution by SITC, S$ million)

IMPORTS c.i.f.	1979	1980	1981
Food and live animals	2,552.6	2,915.5	3,270.5
Cereals and cereal preparations	573.2	694.3	754.0
Beverages and tobacco	207.3	276.0	282.2
Crude materials (inedible) except fuels	3,108.2	3,416.9	2,775.5
Crude rubber, etc.	2,017.7	2,163.5	1,659.7
Wood, lumber and cork	461.4	423.6	388.0
Mineral fuels, lubricants, etc.	9,672.7	14,889.2	19,831.1
Petroleum and petroleum products	9,668.0	14,879.5	19,819.2
Animal and vegetable oils and fats	829.4	1,001.0	721.8
Chemicals	2,178.5	2,686.7	2,756.1
Basic manufactures	5,736.7	7,237.2	8,079.7
Textile yarn, fabrics, etc.	1,666.1	1,835.6	1,905.0
Iron and steel	1,461.0	1,854.6	2,360.6
Machinery and transport equipment	11,343.9	15,303.8	16,474.9
Non-electric machinery	4,002.4	5,720.7	6,685.2
Electrical machinery, apparatus, etc.	4,675.5	6,051.7	6,665.7
Miscellaneous manufactured articles	2,194.3	2,951.1	3,413.0
Other commodities and transactions	510.9	667.4	643.2
TOTAL	38,334.5	51,344.8	58,248.0

[*continued on next page*

PRINCIPAL COMMODITIES—*continued*]

EXPORTS f.o.b.	1979	1980	1981
Food and live animals	1,674.5	2,008.2	2,124.8
Coffee, tea, cocoa and spices	597.5	627.4	659.2
Crude materials (inedible) except fuels	4,412.9	4,700.0	3,665.3
Crude rubber, etc.	3,070.2	3,294.1	2,455.4
Mineral fuels, lubricants, etc.	7,414.5	11,965.7	14,175.6
Petroleum and petroleum products	7,337.2	11,828.0	13,980.6
Chemicals	1,124.3	1,418.5	1,556.3
Basic manufactures	2,841.6	3,441.7	3,669.8
Wood and cork manufactures (excl. furniture)	482.5	549.2	539.3
Textile yarn, fabrics, etc.	787.9	793.2	737.0
Machinery and transport equipment	8,216.7	11,089.4	11,779.4
Non-electric machinery	1,958.9	2,662.8	3,119.8
Electrical machinery, apparatus, etc.	5,045.6	6,656.6	6,724.7
Transport equipment	1,212.2	1,770.0	1,934.9
Miscellaneous manufactured articles	2,121.7	2,572.4	2,919.1
Clothing (excl. footwear)	811.0	912.8	990.1
TOTAL (incl. others)	30,940.1	41,452.3	44,290.8

PRINCIPAL TRADING PARTNERS*

(S$ million)

IMPORTS c.i.f.	1979	1980	1981
Australia	843.4	1,162.3	1,207.5
China, People's Repub.	894.1	1,332.1	1,629.8
Germany, Fed. Repub.	1,419.0	1,677.1	1,610.4
Hong Kong	836.5	1,055.1	1,093.0
Iran	561.2	473.7	753.4
Japan	6,530.5	9,162.4	10,957.4
Malaysia			
Peninsular Malaysia	4,605.6	6,179.1	6,164.5
Sabah and Sarawak	787.8	936.6	1,045.0
Saudi Arabia	4,019.9	6,412.3	10,771.8
Thailand	1,086.3	1,019.0	997.6
United Kingdom	1,347.3	1,771.2	1,742.9
U.S.A.	5,489.5	7,237.2	7,356.4

EXPORTS f.o.b.	1979	1980	1981
Australia	1,149.5	1,670.8	1,770.5
France	671.7	906.1	796.4
Germany, Fed. Repub.	1,054.2	1,247.0	1,126.2
Hong Kong	2,088.4	3,195.9	3,881.4
Japan	2,967.7	3,338.3	4,487.6
Malaysia			
Peninsular Malaysia	3,402.8	4,739.5	5,346.5
Sabah and Sarawak	1,024.7	1,478.5	1,560.1
Thailand	1,320.5	1,809.3	1,864.6
United Kingdom	963.8	1,069.2	1,050.6
U.S.A.	4,265.9	5,272.0	5,848.7
Viet-Nam	190.5	n.a.	n.a.

* No figures are available for trade with Indonesia.

TRANSPORT

ROAD TRAFFIC

(registered vehicles)

	1979	1980	1981
Private cars	143,402	152,574	161,692
Motor cycles and scooters	108,051	118,345	127,722
Motor buses	6,217	6,512	6,950
Goods vehicles (incl. private)	67,201	78,020	87,752
Others	13,858	15,890	17,689
TOTAL	338,729	371,341	401,805

SHIPPING

(vessels of over 75 net registered tons)

	Ships Entered	Ships Cleared	Cargo Discharged ('000 metric tons)	Cargo Loaded ('000 metric tons)
1977	20,602	20,616	39,833.8	24,284.8
1978	21,787	21,829	44,832.5	28,506.7
1979	23,704	23,721	48,424.4	31,388.4
1980	24,877	24,820	48,550.0	32,412.5
1981	26,134	26,097	53,598.7	33,745.1

CIVIL AVIATION

	Passengers			Mail (metric tons)		Freight (metric tons)	
	Arrived	Departed	In Transit	Landed	Despatched	Landed	Despatched
1977	2,106,710	2,118,109	899,084	2,040	3,378	35,361	53,142
1978	2,410,255	2,404,128	935,415	2,746	3,267	58,734	64,359
1979	2,720,180	2,710,067	1,064,077	3,619	3,798	78,301	79,786
1980	3,140,723	3,151,032	1,002,794	3,975	4,076	90,713	91,062
1981	3,597,104	3,578,108	976,946	4,291	4,244	100,931	96,172

TOURISM

	1977	1978	1979	1980	1981
Tourist arrivals*	1,681,985	2,047,224	2,247,091	2,562,085	2,828,899
Tourist expenditure (S$ million)	891	1,034	1,379	1,821	2,033†

* Including visitors staying for less than 24 hours.

† Preliminary figures.

In December 1981 there were 69 gazetted tourist hotels, having 13,924 rooms in operation. Another 10,465 rooms are under construction and are expected to be completed by December 1986.

Source: Singapore Tourist Promotion Board.

COMMUNICATIONS MEDIA

(at December 31st)

	1978	1979	1980	1981
Radio licences issued	57,284	58,912	62,294	66,897
Radio and television licences issued	353,248	371,692	397,155	414,535
Rediffusion subscribers	93,175	100,487	107,080	110,792

EDUCATION

(December 1981)

	Institutions*	Students	Teachers†
Primary	327	289,697	11,108
Secondary	145	177,238	8,807
Technical and Vocational Institutes	17	13,001	889
Universities and Colleges	5	24,156	2,226
Total	494	504,092	23,030

* A full school conducting both primary and secondary classes is treated as one primary and one secondary school.

† Including relief teachers but excluding teachers on national service, study leave, scholarship, secondment, etc.

Source (unless otherwise stated): Yearbook of Statistics, Department of Statistics, Singapore.

THE CONSTITUTION

(Promulgated 1958, subsequently amended)

HEAD OF STATE

The Head of State is the President, elected by Parliament for a four-year term. He normally acts on the advice of the Cabinet.

THE CABINET

The Cabinet, headed by the Prime Minister, is appointed by the President and is responsible to Parliament.

THE LEGISLATURE

The Legislature consists of a Parliament of seventy-five members, presided over by a Speaker who may be elected from the members of Parliament themselves or appointed by Parliament although he may not be a member of Parliament. Members of Parliament are elected by universal adult suffrage.

A 21-Member Presidential Council chaired by the Chief Justice examines material of racial or religious significance, including legislation, to see whether it differentiates between racial or religious communities or contains provisions inconsistent with the fundamental liberties of Singapore citizens.

CITIZENSHIP

Under the constitution Singapore citizenship may be acquired either by birth, descent or registration. Persons born when Singapore was a constituent State of Malaysia could also acquire Singapore citizenship by enrolment or naturalization under the constitution of Malaysia.

THE GOVERNMENT

HEAD OF STATE

President: C. V. Devan Nair (elected by Parliament, October 23rd, 1981).

THE CABINET

(July 1982)

Prime Minister: Lee Kuan Yew.

First Deputy Prime Minister and Minister for Education: Dr. Goh Keng Swee.

Second Deputy Prime Minister for Foreign Affairs: Sinnathamby Rajaratnam.

Minister for Finance: Hon Sui Sen.

Minister for the Environment: Ong Pang Boon.

Minister for Law: Edmund William Barker.

Minister for Home Affairs: Chua Sian Chin.

Minister for Communications and Labour: Ong Teng Cheong.

Minister for Defence and Second Minister for Health: Goh Chok Tong.

Minister for National Development: Teh Cheang Wan.

Minister for Health: Howe Yoon Chong.

Minister for Foreign Affairs and Culture: Supphiah Dhanabalan.

Minister for Trade and Industry: Dr. Tony Tan Keng Yam.

Minister Without Portfolio: Lim Chee Onn.

Minister for Social Affairs: Dr. Ahmad Mattar (acting).

LEGISLATURE

PARLIAMENT

Parliament has 75 members and is elected every five years.

The Speaker: Dr. YEOH GHIM SENG, B.B.M., J.P.

In the December 1980 general elections, 75 per cent of the electorate voted for the People's Action Party, which was returned in all 75 constituencies. At a by-election held in October 1981, the Workers' Party gained one seat.

POLITICAL PARTIES

People's Action Party (PAP): 11 Napier Rd., Singapore 1025; f. 1954; first formed the Government of Singapore in 1959; re-elected 1963, 1968, 1972, 1976 and 1980; Chair. ONG TENG CHEONG; Sec.-Gen. LEE KUAN YEW.

There are many small opposition parties. The following are the most important:

Barisan Sosialis (*Socialist Front*): 436-C Victoria St., Singapore 7; f. 1961; left-wing; formerly members of People's Action Party; seeks to abolish national service, provide free medical services for the poor, reduce taxes and relax the citizenship laws; Chair. Dr. LEE SIEW CHOH.

Pertubohan Kebangsaan Melayu Singapura (PKMS) (*Singapore Malays' National Organization*): 218–E, PKM Bldg., Changi Rd., Singapore 1441; reorganized 1967; formerly the United Malays' National Organization in Singapore; seeks to safeguard and work for the implementation of the special rights of Malays in Singapore, as stated in the Constitution, to promote Islam and Malay culture, to encourage democracy and racial harmony; Chair. Hj. RAHMAN ZIN; Sec.-Gen. SAHID SAHOOMAN.

United People's Front (UPF): 715, 7th Floor, Colombo Court, Singapore 0617; f. 1974; a coalition of several small parties; Chair. WOO KONG SENG; Sec.-Gen. HARBANS SINGH.

Workers' Party: Suite 602, Colombo Court, Singapore 0617; f. 1957; seeks to establish a democratic socialist Government with a Constitution which guarantees fundamental citizen's rights; Chair. WONG HONG TOY; Sec.-Gen. J. B. JEYARETNAM.

Other parties include the Singapore Democratic Party (SDP), the Singapore Justice Party and the United Front.

DIPLOMATIC REPRESENTATION

EMBASSIES AND HIGH COMMISSIONS ACCREDITED TO SINGAPORE

(In Singapore City unless otherwise stated)

(HC) High Commission.

Australia: 25 Napier Rd., Singapore 1025; *High Commissioner:* KENNETH MCDONALD.

Austria: Bangkok, Thailand.

Bangladesh: Rangoon, Burma (HC).

Belgium: Unit 824, 8th Floor, International Plaza, 10 Anson Rd., Singapore 0207; *Ambassador:* BALDER A. POSTHUMA.

Brazil: Suites 1503/4, 15th Floor, Tong Bldg., 302 Orchard Rd., Singapore 0923; *Ambassador:* MURILLO GURGEL VALENTE.

Bulgaria: Room 808/9, 8th Floor Thong Teck Bldg., 15 Scotts Rd., Singapore 0922; *Ambassador:* Dr. MATEY KARASIMEONOV (resident in Jakarta, Indonesia).

Burma: 15 St. Martin's Drive, Singapore 1025; *Ambassador:* U KYAW HTOON.

Canada: 7th and 9th Floors, Faber House, 230 Orchard Rd., Singapore 0923; *High Commissioner:* LEONARD MICHAEL BERRY.

Chile: 22nd Floor, Tong Eng Bldg., 101 Cecil St., Singapore 0106; *Chargé d'affaires:* EDUARDO RODRÍGUEZ.

Cyprus: New Delhi, India (HC).

Czechoslovakia: Rangoon, Burma.

Denmark: 8th Floor, Supreme House, Penang Rd., Singapore 0923; *Chargé d'affaires:* KAY RODRIGUEZ DUARLE GAD.

Egypt: 20C and 22C Paterson Rd., Singapore 0923; *Ambassador:* MOHEB MOHD EL SAMRA.

El Salvador: Tokyo, Japan.

Fiji: Canberra, A.C.T., Australia (HC).

Finland: 35B/37B Podium Block, Goldhill Plaza, Newton Rd., Singapore 1130; *Ambassador:* RISTO HYVAERINEN (resident in New Delhi, India).

France: 5 Gallop Rd., Singapore 1025; *Ambassador:* PHILIPPE MARANDET.

German Democratic Republic: Jakarta, Indonesia.

Germany, Federal Republic: 12th Floor, Far East Shopping Centre, 545 Orchard Rd., Singapore 0923; *Ambassador:* Dr. WOLFRAM DUFNER.

Greece: Rooms 707/709, 7th Floor, Robina House, Singapore 0106; *Ambassador:* (vacant) (resident in New Delhi, India).

Hungary: Jakarta, Indonesia.

India: India House, 31 Grange Rd., Singapore 0923; *High Commissioner:* SHRI CHANDRASHEKAR DASGUPTA.

Indonesia: "Wisma Indonesia", 1st Floor, 435 Orchard Rd., Singapore 0923; *Ambassador:* SUDJATMIKO.

Iran: Bangkok, Thailand.

Iraq: Jakarta, Indonesia.

Ireland: New Delhi, India.

Israel: 10th Floor, Faber House, 230K Orchard Rd.; *Ambassador:* NAHUM ESHKOL.

Italy: Room 810–812, 8th Floor, Singapore House, Penang Rd., Singapore 0923; *Ambassador:* Dr. LUIGI DURANTE.

Japan: 16 Nassim Rd., Singapore 1025; *Ambassador:* TOSHIJIRO NAKAJIMA.

Korea, Democratic People's Republic: 37 Stevens Rd., Singapore 1025; *Ambassador:* KANG DAL SON.

Korea, Republic: Rooms 2408-14, 24th Floor, Shaw Centre, Scotts Rd., Singapore 0922; *Ambassador:* (vacant).

Malaysia: 301 Jervois Rd., Singapore 1024; *High Commissioner:* SYED AHMAD BIN SYED MAHMUD SHABA-BUDDIN.

Mexico: Manila, Philippines.

Mongolia: New Delhi, India.

Nepal: Bangkok, Thailand.

Netherlands: Liat Towers, 12th Floor, 541 Orchard Rd., Singapore 0923; *Ambassador:* WILLEM CH. E. A. DE VRIES.

New Zealand: 13 Nassim Rd., Singapore 1025; *High Commissioner:* J. K. CUNNINGHAM.

Norway: 16th Floor, Hong Leong Bldg., 16 Raffles Quay, Singapore 0104; *Ambassador:* FINN KOREN.

Pakistan: 510–511 Shaw House, Orchard Rd., Singapore 0923; *Chargé d'affaires:* MOHD. ZUBAIR KIDWAI.

Papua New Guinea: Jakarta, Indonesia (HC).

Philippines: Rooms 505–506, 5th Floor, Thong Teck Bldg., 15 Scotts Rd., Singapore 0922; *Ambassador:* PRIVADO G. JIMENEZ.

Poland: Suites 2311–12, 23rd Floor, Shaw Towers, 100 Beach Rd., Singapore 0718; *Ambassador:* (vacant).

Portugal: Bangkok, Thailand.

Romania: 64 Sime Rd., Singapore 1128; *Chargé d'affaires:* GHEORGHE MIU.

Saudi Arabia: 10 Nassim Rd., Singapore 1025; *Chargé d'affaires:* ABDUL RAHMAN I AL-TOEIMI.

Spain: Bangkok, Thailand.

Sri Lanka: Rooms 1207–1212, 12th Floor, Goldhill Plaza, Newton Rd., Singapore 1130; *High Commissioner:* CANAGARATNAM GUNASINGHAM.

Sweden: PUB Building, 4th Floor, Somerset Road, Singapore 0923; *Ambassador:* JEAN-CHRISTOPHE OEBERG.

Switzerland: 1703–1704 Liat Towers, 541 Orchard Rd., Singapore 0923; *Chargé d'affaires:* OTTO GRITTI.

Thailand: 370 Orchard Rd., Singapore 0923; *Ambassador:* SANAN PLANGPRAYOON.

Trinidad and Tobago: New Delhi, India (HC).

Turkey: Bangkok, Thailand.

U.S.S.R.: 51 Nassim Rd., Singapore 1025; *Ambassador:* FYODOR POTAPENKO.

United Kingdom: Tanglin Rd., Singapore 1024; *High Commissioner:* Sir PETER MOON.

U.S.A.: 30 Hill St., Singapore 0617; *Ambassador:* HARRY E. T. THAYER.

Vatican City: Bangkok, Thailand.

Yugoslavia: 17H Grange Heights, Block C, St. Thomas Walk, Singapore 0923; *Chargé d'affaires:* BORISLAV PETROVIC (closed temporarily March 1982).

Singapore also has diplomatic relations with Argentina, Iceland, Laos, Luxembourg, Maldives, Panama and the People's Republic of China.

JUDICIAL SYSTEM

A Supreme Court consisting of the High Court, the Court of Appeal and the Court of Criminal Appeal was established by the Supreme Court of Judicature Act. The High Court exercises original criminal and civil jurisdiction and hears appeals from the Subordinate Courts. An appeal from the High Court lies to the Court of Criminal Appeal or the Court of Appeal which exercises appellate jurisdiction. In certain cases, a further appeal lies from the decision of the Court of Criminal Appeal or Court of Appeal, as the case may be, to the Judicial Committee of the Privy Council in the United Kingdom.

The Subordinate Courts consist of Magistrates', Juvenile, Coroners' and District Courts which have limited civil and criminal jurisdiction. There is also an Industrial Arbitration Court to regulate labour relations.

Chief Justice: Mr. Justice WEE CHONG JIN.

Senior Judge: Mr. Justice T. KULASEKARAM.

Puisne Judges: Mr. Justice F. A. CHUA, Mr. Justice T. S. SINNATHURAY, Mr. Justice LAI KEW CHAI, Mr. Justice A. WAHAB GHOWS, Mr. Justice A. P. RAJAH.

RELIGION

The majority of Chinese are Buddhists, Confucians or Daoists. The Malays and Pakistanis are almost all Muslims, while the Europeans and Eurasians are mainly Christian. Most of the Indian community are Hindu. Buddhists are numbered at 1.3 million, Muslims at 400,000, Hindus at 100,000, Roman Catholics and Protestants at 75,000 each and Sikhs at 15,000.

BUDDHISM

The Singapore Buddhist Sangha Organization: Phor Kark See, Bright Hill Drive, off Thomson Rd., Singapore 2057.

The Buddhist Union: 28 Jalan Senyum, Singapore 1441.

The Singapore Buddhist Federation: 50 Lorong 34, Geylang, Singapore 1439.

World Buddhist Society: 40 Pender Rd., Singapore 0409.

CHRISTIANITY

Anglican Church: Diocese of Singapore: Bishop of Singapore and Dean of St. Andrew's Cathedral; The Rt. Rev. DR. MOSES TAY, Bishopsbourne, 4 Bishopsgate, Singapore 1024.

Roman Catholic Church: Archdiocese of Singapore: Archbishop GREGORY YONG SOOI NGEAN, Archbishop's House, 31 Victoria St., Singapore 0718.

Methodist Church in Singapore: 10 Mount Sophia, Singapore 0922; Bishop KAO JIH CHUNG, 50 Barker Rd., Singapore 1130.

Brethren Assemblies: Bethesda Hall, 77 Bras Basah Rd., Singapore 0718; f. 1864; Hon. Sec. LIM TIAN LEONG; Bethesda (Katong) Church, 17 Pennefather Rd., Singapore 1542; Hon. Sec. T. C. KOH.

Presbyterian Church: Minister Rev. JOHN MCKINLAY, "B" & "C" Orchard Rd., cnr. Penang Rd., Singapore 0923; f. 1856; services in English, Mandarin, Dutch, Indonesian and German; 1,000 mems.

HINDUISM

Hindu Advisory Board: c/o Ministry of Social Affairs, Pearl's Hill Terrace, Singapore 0316; Chair. PERIOWSAMY OTHARAM.

ISLAM

Majlis Ugama Islam Singapura: c/o Muslim Religious Council, Ministry of Social Affairs, Empress Place, Singapore 0617; Pres. Hj. ISMAIL MOHD. SAID.

Muslim Missionary Society: 31 Lorong 12 Geyland, Singapore 1439.

THE PRESS

In 1974 the Government passed a bill providing for compulsory government vetting of newspaper management. It obliged all newspaper companies to become public.

DAILIES

ENGLISH LANGUAGE

Business Times: Times Centre, 1 New Industrial Rd., Singapore 1953; f. 1976; Editor R. D. MACKIE; circ. 14,000 (Singapore only).

New Nation: Unit 201-A, Delta House, 2A Alexander Rd., Singapore 0315; f. 1971; Proprs. Singapore Monitor Ltd.; independent; Editor SIA CHEONG YEW; circ. 40,000.

The Straits Times: Times House, 390 Kim Seng Rd., Singapore 0923; f. 1845; Editor CHEONG YIP SENG; circ. 226,000 (Singapore only).

CHINESE LANGUAGE

Kuai Bao: 307 Alexandra Rd., Singapore 0315; evening; Editor MOH LEE KWANG; circ. 25,000 (daily), 45,000 (Sunday).

Min Pao Daily: 62 Bendermeer Rd., Singapore 1233; f. 1960; Chief Editor CHUA TENG HWA; circ. 15,000.

Nanyang Siang Pau: 307 Alexandra Rd., Singapore 0315; f. 1923; morning; Editor MOK LEE KWANG; circ. 98,000 (daily), 118,100 (Sunday).

Shin Min Daily News: 577 Macpherson Rd., Singapore 1336; f. 1967; Editor WONG TUCK WING; circ. 87,000.

Sin Chew Jit Poh: 19 Keppel Rd., Singapore 0208; f. 1929; morning; Editor LOY TECK JUAN; circ. 114,000 (daily).

MALAY LANGUAGE

Berita Harian: Times House, 390 Kim Seng Rd., Singapore 0923; f. 1957; morning; Editor ZAINUL ABIDIN BIN MOHD. RASHEED; circ. 34,000.

MALAYALAM LANGUAGE

Malaysia Malayali: 12 Kinta Rd., Singapore 8; f. 1938; only Malayalam daily outside Kerala State, India; Man. Editor V. P. ABDULLAH; circ. 460 (Singapore and Malaysia).

TAMIL LANGUAGE

Tamil Murasu: 139–141 Lavender St., Singapore 1233; f. 1936; Editor JAYARAM SARANGAPANY; circ. 6,100 (daily), 9,500 (Sunday).

SUNDAY PAPERS

ENGLISH LANGUAGE

Sunday Nation: Unit 201-A, Delta House, 2A Alexandra Rd., Singapore 0315; f. 1974; Editor Miss TAN WANG JOO; circ. 94,000.

Sunday Times: Times House, 390 Kim Seng Rd., Singapore 0923; f. 1931; Editor ZAINUL ABIDIN MOHD. RASHEED; circ. 235,000 (Singapore only).

MALAY LANGUAGE

Berita Minggu: Times House, 390 Kim Seng Rd., Singapore 0923; f. 1957; Editor ZAINUL ABIDIN BIN MOHD. RASHEED; circ. 44,000.

PERIODICALS

About 300 periodicals are published in the various languages. The principal ones only are given here.

ENGLISH LANGUAGE

Asia Research Bulletin: Room 2815, 28th Floor, International Plaza, 10 Anson Rd., Singapore 0207; political and economic monthly; Editor JOHN G. S. DRYSDALE.

Fanfare: Times Periodicals Pte. Ltd., 422 Thomson Rd., Singapore 11; f. 1969; teenage pop magazine; fortnightly; Editor SYLVIA TOH; circ. 25,000.

Female: MPH Magazines (S) Pte. Ltd., Room 5, 3rd Floor, 5 Stadium Walk, Singapore 14; women's fortnightly; Editor NORMA O. MIRAFLOR.

Go Magazine: Times Periodicals Pte. Ltd., 422 Thomson Road, Singapore 1129; f. 1980; entertainment and fashion monthly; Editor PAT CHAN; circ. 20,000.

Her World: Times Periodicals Pte. Ltd., 422 Thomson Rd., Singapore 1129; f. 1960; women's monthly; Editor BETTY L. KHOO.

Living: MPH Magazines (S) Pte. Ltd., Room 5, 3rd Floor, 5 Stadium Walk, Singapore 14; general interest; monthly; Editor NORMA O. MIRAFLOR.

Republic of Singapore Government Gazette: Singapore National Printers (Pte.) Ltd., P.O.B. 485; weekly (Friday).

Singapore Business: Times Periodicals Pte. Ltd., 422 Thomson Rd., Singapore 1129; monthly; Editor ARUN SENKUTTUVAN.

Singapore Medical Journal: Singapore Medical Association, 4A College Rd., Singapore 0316; bi-monthly; Editor Dr. FENG PAO HSII.

Times Annual: Times Periodicals Pte. Ltd., 422 Thomson Rd., Singapore 1129; Editor TERRY TAN.

CHINESE LANGUAGE

Min Chong Pao: People's Association, Kallang, Singapore 14; fortnightly; Editor LIM CHIN TEONG.

Shaonian Yue Kan (*Youth Monthly*): Educational Publications Bureau, Block 162, 3545C Bukit Merah Central, Singapore; monthly; Editor CHONG FUN LIAM.

Singapore Art Magazine: Educational Publications Bureau, Block 162, 3545C Bukit Merah Central, Singapore 0315; quarterly; Editor TEO SONG LENG.

Singapore Literature: Singapore Literature Society, 122B Sims Ave., Singapore 1438; quarterly; Editor SEAH KHOK CHUA.

MALAY LANGUAGE

Harapan: Educational Publications Bureau, 175A–179A Outram Park, Singapore 0316; monthly (Jan.–Oct.).

PUNJABI LANGUAGE

Navjiwan National Punjabi News: 5 Albert House, Albert St., Singapore 0718; f. 1951; fortnightly; Voice of the Sikhs in South-East Asia; Editor DEWAN SINGH RANDHAWA.

NEWS AGENCIES

FOREIGN BUREAUX

Agence France-Presse (AFP): 607 Nehsons Bldg., 24 Peck Seah St., Singapore 0207; Dir. (Singapore and Malaysia) PETER DAVID SPENCE.

Agentstvo Pechati Novosti (APN) (*U.S.S.R.*): 116 University Rd., Singapore 1129; Correspondent ALEXANDER SKORODUMOV.

Agenzia Nazionale Stampa Associata (ANSA) (*Italy*): 37 Grove Lane, Singapore 1027; South-East Asia Correspondent GIULIO PECORA.

Allgemeiner Deutscher Nachrichtendienst (ADN) (*German Democratic Republic*): King's Mansion, 807 Block B, Tanjong Katong Rd., Singapore 1543; Correspondent PETER KOARD.

Associated Press (AP) (*U.S.A.*): Room 1001, Robina House, Shenton Way, Singapore 0106; Chief KENNETH L. WHITING.

Central News Agency (CNA) (*Taiwan*): 52 Valley Mansion, Oxley Rd., Singapore 0923; Correspondent CLIFF LIN CHANG-SONG.

Deutsche Presse-Agentur (dpa) (*Federal Republic of Germany*): 1 Faber Walk, Singapore 0512; South-East Asia Correspondent WILDERICH LOCHOW.

Jiji Press Ltd. (Jiji Tsushin-sha) (*Japan*): Unit 2505, 25th Floor, International Plaza, 10 Anson Rd., Singapore 0207; Correspondent YOSHIMA INADA.

Kyodo News Service (*Japan*): 12th Floor, Marina House, Shenton Way, Singapore 0207; Chief YUJI ITO.

Pan-Asia Newspaper Alliance (PANANEWS): Rooms 12-M and 12-G, Asia Insurance Bldg., Singapore 0207; Correspondent CHIN KAH CHONG.

Reuters (*U.K.*): 12th Floor, Marina House, Shenton Way, Singapore 0207; Regional Man. MARTIN VICKERY.

Telegrafnoye Agentstvo Sovietskogo Soyuza (TASS) (*U.S.S.R.*): 37, A6 Nassim Rd., Singapore 1025; Correspondent VLADIMIR ZAGORODNEV.

United News of India (UNI): P.O.B. 768, Singapore 9015; Correspondent E. M. RASHEED.

United Press International (UPI) (*U.S.A.*): Suite 110, Raffles Hotel, Beach Rd., Singapore 0718; Regional Man. PAUL F. WEDEL, Jr.

PUBLISHERS

ENGLISH LANGUAGE

Apa Productions Pte. Ltd.: 5 Lengkong Satu, Singapore 1441; travel guides and photographic essays; Publ. HANS HOEFER.

Book Emporium (S) Pte. Ltd.: Units 709–712, 7th Floor, Block 3, PSA Multi-Storey Complex, Pasir Panjang Rd., Singapore 0511; Man. Dir. PEH CHIN HUA.

Chopmen Enterprises: 428/429 Katong Shopping Centre, Mountbatten Rd., Singapore 1543; f. 1966; academic, children's and general; Man. Dir. N. T. S. CHOPRA.

Eastern Universities Press Sdn. Bhd.: 112F Boon Keng Rd., P.O.B. 1742, Singapore 1233; f. 1958; biography, history, textbooks, fiction; Man. GOH KEE SEAH.

Educational Publications Bureau Pte. Ltd.: Block 162, 3545C Bukit Merah Central, Singapore 0315; textbooks, general and reference books, English and Chinese; Man. Dir. CHAN FOOK CHUAN.

Federal Publications (S) Pte. Ltd.: 1 New Industrial Rd., Singapore 1953; f. 1957; educational and children's books; Gen. Man. H. H. CHIAM.

FEP International Pte. Ltd.: 348 Jalan Boon Lay, Jurong, Singapore 2261; Man. Dir. DAVID CHEW.

Gunung Agung (S) Pte. Ltd.: Suite 3808, OCBC Centre, Chulia St., Singapore 0104; educational and general; Chair. and Man. Dir. MASAGUNG.

Harper & Row Inc.: 202 Eng Cheong Tower, 5611 North Bridge Rd., Singapore 0719; f. 1817; social sciences, medicines, humanities and general; Area Man. STEVEN GOH.

Heinemann Educational Books (Asia) Ltd.: 41 Jalan Pemimpin, Singapore 2057; educational and general; Gen. Man. CHARLES CHER.

Institute of Southeast Asian Studies: Heng Mui Keng Terrace, Pasir Panjang Rd., Singapore 0511; scholarly publications; Dir. Prof. KERNIAL S. SANDHU.

Longman Malaysia Sdn. Bhd.: 25 First Lok Yang Rd., Jurong Town, Singapore 2262; educational; Man. Dir. JAMES B. HO.

McGraw-Hill International Book Co.: 348 Jalan Boon Lay, Jurong, Singapore 2261; educational books in all fields; Man. Dir. JOHN R. MARTIN.

Macmillan Southeast Asia Pte. Ltd.: 41 Jalan Pemimpin, Singapore 2057; educational and general; Exec. Dir. LOH MUN WAI.

Malayan Law Journal Pte. Ltd.: 1302–1305 Shenton House, 13th Floor, Shenton Way, Singapore 0106; f. 1932; law books, journals and periodicals; Man. Dir. and Man. Ed. AL-MANSOR ADABI; Man. Dir. and Chief Exec. AMIR MALLAL.

Oxford University Press: 4–2 Block A, Tong Lee Bldg., 35 Kallang Pudding Rd., Singapore 1334; educational, academic and general; Representative GOH TEOW HUAT.

Prentice-Hall of Southeast Asia Pte. Ltd.: 4B, 77 Ayer Rajah Industrial Estate, Ayer Rajah Rd., Singapore 0513; f. 1975; educational; Gen. Man. K. C. ANG.

Singapore University Press Pte. Ltd.: National University of Singapore, Kent Ridge, Singapore 0511; scholarly publications; Man. Mrs. MARIAN PAN.

Times Books International: Times Centre, 1 New Industrial Rd., Singapore 1953; general, scholarly and childrens' books, Gen. Man. SHIRLEY HEW.

MALAY LANGUAGE

Malaysia Press Sdn. Bhd. (*Pustaka Melayu*): 745–747 North Bridge Rd., Singapore 0719; f. 1962; educational books; Man. Dir. ABU TALIB BIN ALLY.

Pustaka Nasional Pte. Ltd.: 1211 Shaw Towers, Beach Rd., Singapore 0718; books on Malay literature and Islam; Man. Partner SYED AHMAD BIN MUHAMAD.

CHINESE LANGUAGE

Shanghai Book Co. (Pte.) Ltd.: 81 Victoria St., Singapore 0718; educational and general books; Man. Dir. Madam CHEN MONG HOCK.

Shing Lee Book Store: 79 Block 79 Toa Payoh Central, Singapore 1231; educational and general books; Man. PEH CHIN HUA.

Union Book Co. (Pte.) Ltd.: 303 North Bridge Rd., Singapore 0718; educational and general; Man. CHOW LI-LIANG.

The World Book Co. Pte. Ltd.: 710 Tan Boon Liat Bldg., 315 Outram Rd., Singapore 0316; educational and general books; Man. Dir. CHOU CHENG CHUEN.

RADIO AND TELEVISION

The Singapore Broadcasting Corporation came into operation on February 1st, 1980, taking over all the functions of Radio-Television Singapore, and the collection of radio and television licence fees from the Inland Revenue Department.

RADIO

Radio Singapore: Singapore Broadcasting Corporation, P.O.B. 1902, Singapore; f. 1936; broadcasts in English, Chinese (Mandarin and six dialects), Malay and Tamil, over four networks; each language channel broadcasts over one hundred hours weekly; one multi-language service with 42 hours weekly; one FM stereo service in English and Chinese with 126 hours weekly; Gen. Man. Mrs. WONG-LEE SIOK TIN.

Rediffusion (Singapore) Pte. Ltd.: P.O.B. 608; f. 1949; commercial wired broadcasting service, originating two programmes in Mandarin and English; over 107,000 subscribers; Man. Dir. J. SNOWDEN.

Far East Broadcasting (F.E.B.A. Ltd.): P.O.B. 751, Singapore 9015; f. 1960; Chair. YEO KOK CHENG; Exec. Dir. JOHN B. LIN.

In September 1981 there were 472,370 radio sets.

TELEVISION

Television Singapore: Singapore Broadcasting Corporation, P.O.B. 1902, Singapore; one station with two separate channels started operations in 1963; colour television was introduced in 1974; total weekly average of 115 hours; education service of 9½ hours weekly; services in Malay, Chinese, Tamil and English; Gen. Man. Mrs. WONG-LEE SIOK TIN.

In September 1981 there were 669,413 television licences.

FINANCE

BANKING

(cap.=capital; p.u.=paid up; dep.=deposits; m.= million; S$=Singapore dollars; brs.=branches)

The Singapore monetary system is regulated by the Monetary Authority of Singapore (MAS) and the Ministry of Finance. The Monetary Authority of Singapore performs all the functions of a central bank, except the issuing of currency, a function which is carried out by the Board of Commissioners of Currency. In 1981 the Government Investment Corporation was formed, chaired by Prime Minister LEE KUAN YEW. In May 1981 there were 103 commercial banks (13 local, 90 foreign) and 49 representative offices in Singapore. Thirty-seven banks were fully licensed, 13 had restricted licences and 53 foreign banks had off-shore banking licences. There were also 39 merchant banks.

Board of Commissioners of Currency: Ground Floor, 79 Robinson Rd., Singapore 0106; Chair. First Deputy Prime Minister Dr. GOH KENG SWEE.

Government of Singapore Investment Corporation (GSIC): c/o MAS, SIA Bldg., 77 Robinson Rd., Singapore 0106; Chair. LEE KUAN YEW; Man. Dir. YONG PUNG HOW.

Monetary Authority of Singapore (MAS): SIA Building, 77 Robinson Rd., Singapore 0106; Chair. First Deputy Prime Minister Dr. GOH KENG SWEE; Man. Dir. LIM KIM SAN.

MAJOR COMMERCIAL BANKS

Asia Commercial Banking Corpn. Ltd.: 2 Mistri Rd., Singapore 0207; f. 1959; cap. p.u. S$50m.; dep. $S276.1m. (Dec. 1980); Chair. Datuk ANG KEONG LAN; Gen. Man. YEW CHONG KEW.

Bank of Singapore Ltd.: G2, 101 Cecil St., Singapore 0106; f. 1954; cap. p.u. $S25m.; dep. S$84m. (Dec. 1981); Chair. RUNME SHAW; Vice-Chair. TAN TOCK SAN; Exec. Dir. TEO BENG CHUAN; Gen. Man. ANDREW KOK HUP LEONG.

Chung Khiaw Bank Ltd.: 1 Bonham St., Raffles Place, Singapore 0104; f. 1950; subsidiary of United Overseas Bank Ltd.; cap. p.u. U.S. $75m., dep. U.S. $1,476.7m. (Dec. 1981); Chair. and Man. Dir. WEE CHO YAW; Deputy Chair. ALLAN NG POH MENG.

Far Eastern Bank Ltd.: 156 Cecil St., Singapore 0106; f. 1959; cap. p.u. S$24.4m.; dep. S$263.6m. (Dec. 1980); Chair. Datuk Sri NG QUEE LAM; Man. Dir. NG ENG KIAT; Gen. Man. TAN POH SOON.

Four Seas Communications Bank Ltd.: 57 Chulia St., Singapore 0104; incorporated in Singapore 1906; cap. p.u. S$20m.; dep. S$325m. (Dec. 1981); Chair. LEE HIOK SIANG; Gen. Man. GOH YONG SIANG.

Industrial and Commercial Bank Ltd.: ICB Bldg., 2 Shenton Way, Singapore 0106; f. 1954; cap. p.u. S$50m.; dep. S$614.5m. (Dec. 1981); Chair. TAN PEE CEE; Gen. Man. ANG HONG CHOON.

International Bank of Singapore: IBS Building, 31 Raffles Place, Singapore 0104; f. 1974; cap. p.u. S$50m.; dep. S$429m. (Dec. 1981); Chair. J. Y. M. PILLAY; Gen. Man. MICHAEL WEE SOON LOCK.

Lee Wah Bank Ltd.: UOB Bldg., 1 Bonham St., Raffles Place, Singapore 0104; f. 1920; subsidiary of United Overseas Bank Ltd.; cap. p.u. S$10m.; dep. S$452.5m. (Dec. 1981); Chair. WEE CHO YAW; Vice-Chair. RICHARD EU KENG MUN.

Oversea-Chinese Banking Corporation Ltd.: OCBC Centre, Chulia St., Singapore 0104; f. 1932; cap. p.u. S$210m.; dep. S$3,760m. (Dec. 1980); Chair. Tan Sri TAN CHIN TUAN; Vice-Chair. YONG PUNG HOW; Gen. Mans. CHOI SIEW HONG, TEO CHENG GUAN, TJIO KAY LEON, WONG NANG JANG; 21 brs. in Singapore; 31 overseas brs.

Overseas Union Bank Ltd.: 60 Robinson Rd., Singapore 0106; f. 1947; cap. p.u. S$201m.; dep. S$3,262m. (Dec. 1981); Chair. and Man. Dir. LIEN YING CHOW; Man. Dir. LEE HEE SENG; 52 brs.

Tat Lee Bank Ltd.: Tat Lee Bldg., 63 Market St., Singapore 0104; f. 1973; cap. p.u. S$84m.; dep. S$823.2m. (Dec. 1981); Chair. GOH TJOEI KOK; Pres. GOH SEONG PEK.

United Overseas Bank Ltd.: UOB Bldg., 1 Bonham St., Raffles Place, Singapore 0104; f. 1935; cap. p.u. S$394.5m.; dep. S$5,341.8m. (Dec. 1981); Chair. WEE CHO YAW; Vice-Chair. RICHARD EU KENG MUN; 53 brs. in Singapore, 34 overseas.

DEVELOPMENT BANK

The Development Bank of Singapore Ltd.: DBS Bldg., 6 Shenton Way, Singapore 0106; f. 1968; functions: providing medium- and long-term loans, long-term guarantees, equity participation; working capital financing, short-term loans, import and export (trade) financing, consumer financing; current, saving and time deposit accounts, remittances; negotiable certificates of deposit, Asian Currency Unit facilities, bullion, foreign exchange, Euro and Asian bonds, correspondent banking; management and underwriting of securities, loan syndication, portfolio management, corporate finance advisory services; cap. S$229m.; dep. S$4,622m. (Dec. 1981); Pres. CHUA KIM YEOW; Exec. Vice-Pres. PATRICK YEOH KHWAI HOH.

FOREIGN BANKS

Commercial Banks

Algemene Bank Nederland N.V. (*Netherlands*): 2 Cecil St., Singapore 0104; Man. C. HAGOORT.

American Express International Banking Corpn. (*U.S.A.*): Shing Kwan House, 4 Shenton Way, Singapore 0106; Vice-Pres. and Gen. Man. MICHAEL C. L. JAMES.

ANZ Banking Group (New Zealand) Ltd.: Ocean Bldg., Collyer Quay; Chief Man. P. H. PEATE.

Banca Commerciale Italiana (*Italy*): Shing Kwan House, 4 Shenton Way, Singapore 0106; Man. G. CARAVAGGI.

Ban Hin Lee Bank Bhd. (*Malaysia*): 52A Circular Rd., Singapore 0104; Dir. YEAP TEIK LEONG; Man. TAN BUCK KIN.

Bangkok Bank Ltd. (*Thailand*): 180 Cecil Street, Singapore 0106; Vice-Pres. and Gen. Man. ATHIT WASANTACHAT.

Bank of America National Trust and Savings Association (*U.S.A.*): Clifford Centre, 24 Raffles Place, Singapore 1; Vice-Pres. and Man. CANDIDO BANDUCCI.

Bank of Canton Ltd. (*Hong Kong*): Denmark House, Raffles Quay, Singapore 0104; Man. J. D. CHANG.

Bank of China (*People's Republic of China*): Bank of China Bldg., Battery Rd., Singapore 0104; Gen. Man. HSUEH WENLIN; Sen. Deputy Gen. Man. CHANG CHI-HSIN.

Bank of East Asia Ltd. (*Hong Kong*): 137 Market St., Singapore 1; Dir. and Man. KAN YUET FAI.

Bank of India: 104–108 Robinson Rd., Singapore 0106; Asst. Gen. Man. D. D. AVARI.

Bank Negara Indonesia 1946: 3 Malacca St., Singapore 1; Gen. Man. PINTOR SIREGAR.

Bank of Tokyo Ltd. (*Japan*): Hong Leong Bldg., 16 Raffles Quay, Singapore 1; Gen. Man. S. SHIMIZU.

Banque de l'Indochine et de Suez (*France*): Shenton House, 3 Shenton Way, P.O.B. 246, Singapore 0106; f. 1905; Man. P. CAVARD.

Banque Nationale de Paris (*France*): Overseas Union House, Collyer Quay, Singapore 0104; Chief Man. CLAUDE BLANGERO.

Banque de Paris et des Pays-Bas (*France*): 37th Floor, Hong Leong Bldg., 16 Raffles Quay, Singapore 0104; Gen. Man. P.-Y. LEJEUNE.

Bayerische Landesbank (*Federal Republic of Germany*): 3rd–5th Floors, Tuan Sing Towers, 30 Robinson Road, Singapore 0104; Jt. Chief Execs. J. LANGMAACK, M. KING.

The Chartered Bank (*U.K.*): 21 Raffles Place, P.O.B. 1901, Singapore 0104; Chief Man. C. W. G. ENDACOTT.

Chase Manhattan Bank, N.A. (*U.S.A.*): Shing Kwan House, 4 Shenton Way, Singapore 0106; 3 brs.; Vice-Pres. and Gen. Man. HUGHLYN FIERCE.

Citibank, N.A. (*U.S.A.*): UIC Bldg., 5 Shenton Way, Singapore 1; Vice-Pres. D. THOMAS DUNTON, DANIEL LI, DAVID LEONG.

Commerzbank (South East Asia) Ltd. (*Federal Republic of Germany*): Tower 3902, DBS Bldg., 6 Shenton Way, Singapore 1; f. 1979; Man. Dir. KARLHEINZ SCHROTH.

Crédit Suisse (*Switzerland*): DBS Bldg., 6 Shenton Way, Singapore 0106; First Branch Man. and Vice-Pres. FELIX W. SCHWEIZER.

Deutsche Bank (Asia Credit) Ltd. (*Federal Republic of Germany*): Suite 4301, OCBC Centre, 65 Chulia St., Singapore 0104; f. 1978; Man. Dir. MICHAEL WILKENS.

Dresdner Bank AG (*Federal Republic of Germany*): 17-01 Raffles Tower, 50 Raffles Place, Singapore 0104; Sr. Mans. FRANZ SCHROTT, GAN KOK NGARN.

European Asian Bank (*Federal Republic of Germany*): Overseas Union House, 50 Collyer Quay, Singapore 0104; Jt. Gen. Mans. MARTIN KONRAD, JURGEN ZIELER

First Commercial Bank (*Taiwan*): G2 UIC Bldg., 5 Shenton Way, Singapore 0106; Sr. Vice-Pres. and Gen. Man. LAI YAO NAN.

First National Bank of Chicago: (*U.S.A.*) 150 Cecil St., Singapore 0106; Vice-Pres. and Gen. Man. RICHARD E. STAHL.

Guangdong (Kwangtung) Provincial Bank (*People's Republic of China*): 60 Cecil St., Singapore 0104; Man. LI HE.

Habib Bank Ltd. (*Pakistan*): Ground and Mezzanine Floors, Harapan Bldg., 141 Market Street, Singapore 0104; Sr. Vice-Pres. and Gen. Man. (Far East) CHANDHRI SAJJAD ALI.

Hongkong and Shanghai Banking Corpn. (*Hong Kong*): Ocean Bldg., 10 Collyer Quay, Singapore 0104; Sr. Man. F. P. HUEY.

Indian Bank: 59 Robinson Rd., Singapore 1; Asst. Gen. Man. K. SUBRAMANIAN.

Indian Overseas Bank: 1 and 3 Collyer Quay, Singapore 0104; Asst. Gen. Man. P. R. AHUJA.

Korea Exchange Bank (*Republic of Korea*): Ground Floor, Asia Insurance Bldg., 2 Finlayson Green, Singapore 0104; Gen. Man. NAM YUNG JIN.

Kwong Lee Bank Bhd. (*Malaysia*): 39/41 South Bridge Rd., Singapore 1; Exec. Dir. Dato TEO AH KHIANG.

Malayan Banking Bhd.: Fullerton Square, Singapore 1; Gen. Man. JUN YING LIM.

Mitsubishi Bank Ltd. (*Japan*): Podium G2, DBS Bldg., Shenton Way, Singapore 0106; Gen. Man. SADANORI OKADA.

The Mitsui Bank Ltd. (*Japan*): Hong Leong Bldg., 16 Raffles Quay, Singapore 0104; Gen. Man. KIHEI HIRAI.

Monte dei Paschi di Siena (*Italy*): Suite 1308, Ocean Bldg. 10 Collyer Quay, Singapore 1.

Moscow Narodny Bank Ltd.(*U.K.*): 50 Robinson Road, Singapore 0106; Man. Dir. V. V. GERASCHENKO.

Skandinaviska Enskilda Banken (South-East Asia) Ltd. (*Sweden*): 3901 Hong Leong Bldg., 16 Raffles Quay, Singapore 1; Man. CLAES VON POST.

The Sumitomo Bank Ltd (*Japan*): Podium G9, DBS Bldg., 6 Shenton Way, Singapore 0106; Gen. Man. Y. YUMOTO.

Tokai Bank Ltd. (*Japan*): 2801/2803 Clifford Centre, 24 Raffles Place, Singapore 1; Gen. Man. KAZUAKI OHMORI.

United Commercial Bank (*India*): 140–142 Robinson Rd., Singapore 0106; Man. R. A. BAGARIA.

United Malayan Banking Corporation Bhd.: UMBC Bldg., 22 Malacca St., Singapore 0104; Gen. Man. KONG SIK HUNG.

Major Off-shore Banks

Amsterdam-Rotterdam Bank N.V. (*Netherlands*): Suite 3601, OCBC Centre, 65 Chulia St., Singapore 0104.

Australia and New Zealand Banking Group Ltd. (*Australia*): Suite 601, Ocean Bldg., Collyer Quay, Singapore 0104.

Banco do Brasil SA: 26th Floor, DBS Building, 6 Shenton Way, Singapore 0106.

Banco Urquijo S.A. (*Spain*): Suite 2801, OCBC Centre, 65 Chulia St., Singapore 0104.

Bank Bumiputra Malaysia Bhd. (*Malaysia*): 1st Floor, Wing On Life Bldg., 150 Cecil St., Singapore 0106.

Bank of Montreal (*Canada*): UIC Bldg., 27th Floor, 5 Shenton Way, Singapore 0106.

The Bank of New York (*U.S.A.*): Suite 2202-4 Ocean Bldg., Collyer Quay, Singapore 0104.

Bank of Novia Scotia (*Canada*): Suite 2501, Ocean Bldg., Collyer Quay, Singapore 0104.

Bankers Trust Co. (*U.S.A.*): Suite 506–508, Ocean Bldg., Collyer Quay, Singapore 0104.

Banque de Paris et des Pays-Bas (*France*): 37th Floor, Hong Leong Bldg., 16 Raffles Quay, Singapore 0104.

Barclays Bank International Ltd. (*U.K.*): 21st Floor, Clifford Centre, Collyer Quay, Singapore 0104.

Canadian Imperial Bank of Commerce: Tower 1401, DBS Bldg., 6 Shenton Way, Singapore 0106.

Chemical Bank (*U.S.A.*): Tower 3801, DBS Bldg., 6 Shenton Way, Singapore 1.

The Commercial Bank of Korea Ltd. (*Republic of Korea*): Suite 3105, OCBC Centre, 65 Chulia St., Singapore 0104.

Continental Illinois National Bank and Trust Company of Chicago (*U.S.A.*): 2101 OCBC Centre, Chulia St., Singapore 0104.

Crédit Lyonnais (*France*): Suite 3701, OCBC Centre, 65 Chulia St., Singapore 0104.

The Dai-Ichi Kangyo Bank Ltd. (*Japan*): G2 Hong Leong Bldg., 16 Raffles Quay, Singapore 0104.

Deutsche Genossenschaftsbank (*Federal Rèpublic of Germany*): 10th Floor, Tuan Sing Tower, 30 Robinson Road, Singapore 0104.

First City National Bank of Houston (*U.S.A.*): Suite 2307, Ocean Bldg., Collyer Quay, Singapore 0104.

First National Bank in Dallas (*U.S.A.*): UIC Bldg., 5 Shenton Way, Singapore 0106.

The First National Bank of Boston (*U.S.A.*): 10th Floor, Ocean Bldg., Collyer Quay, Singapore 0104.

Fuji Bank Ltd. (*Japan*): Tower 6001-3, 6th Floor, DBS Bldg., 6 Shenton Way, Singapore 0106.

Grindlays Bank Ltd. (*U.K.*): Tower 2201, DBS Bldg., 6 Shenton Way, Singapore 0106.

Harris Trust and Savings Bank (*U.S.A.*): Suite 2505, OCBC Centre, 65 Chulia St., Singapore 0104.

The Industrial Bank of Japan Ltd. (*Japan*): Tower 1301, DBS Bldg., 6 Shenton Way, Singapore 0106.

Irving Trust Company (*U.S.A.*): 25th Floor, Ocean Bldg., Collyer Quay, Singapore 0104.

Lloyds Bank International Ltd. (*U.K.*): 12th Floor, Shing Kwan House, 4 Shenton Way, P.O.B. 3348, Singapore 0106.

The Long-Term Credit Bank of Japan Ltd. (*Japan*): Suite 2201/4, OCBC Centre, 65 Chulia St., Singapore 0104.

Manufacturers Hanover Trust Co. (*U.S.A.*): 21st Floor, UIC Bldg., 5 Shenton Way, Singapore 1.

Marine Midland Bank, N.A. (*U.S.A.*): 15th Floor, Shing Kwan House, 4 Shenton Way, Singapore 0106.

Midland Bank Ltd. (*U.K.*): Suite 4805, OCBC Centre, 65 Chulia St., Singapore 0104.

National Westminster Bank Ltd. (*U.K.*): Suite 901/7 Shing Kwan House, 4 Shenton Way, Singapore 1.

Nordic Bank Ltd.: P.O.B. 1769, DBS Bldg., 6 Shenton Way, Singapore 0106.

Philippine National Bank (*Philippines*): Suite 801/2, Bangkok Bank Bldg., 180 Cecil St., Singapore 0106.

Rainier National Bank (*U.S.A.*): Suite 2003, CPF Bldg., 79 Robinson Rd., Singapore 0106.

Republic National Bank of Dallas (*U.S.A.*): Suite 1309, Shenton House, 3 Shenton Way, Singapore 0106.

The Royal Bank of Canada: Level 1, PIL Bldg., 140 Cecil St., Singapore 0106.

The Royal Bank of Canada (Asia) Ltd.: Level 16, PIL Bldg., 140 Cecil St., Singapore 0106.

The Saitama Bank Ltd. (*Japan*): Unit 3601, Hong Leong Bldg., 16 Raffles Quay, Singapore 0104.

Sanwa Bank Ltd. (*Japan*): 2501, 1 Raffles Place, Singapore 0104.

Security Pacific National Bank (*U.S.A.*): Suite 1205, OCBC Centre, 65 Chulia St., Singapore 0104.

Société Générale (*France*): Ground Floor, Tuan Sing Towers, 30 Robinson Road, Singapore 0106.

State Bank of India (*India*): Tower 9001, DBS Bldg., 6 Shenton Way, Singapore 0106.

Swiss Bank Corpn.: 1303 Ocean Bldg., Collyer Quay, Singapore 0104.

The Taiyo Kobe Bank Ltd. (*Japan*): Unit 4202, Hong Leong Bldg., 16 Raffles Quay, Singapore 0104.

The Tokai Bank Ltd. (*Japan*): Suite 2801/3, Clifford Centre, 24 Raffles Place, Singapore 0104.

The Toronto-Dominion Bank (*Canada*): Shenton House, 3 Shenton Way, Singapore 0106.

Union Bank of Switzerland (*Switzerland*): Room 1508–12, Shing Kwan House, 4 Shenton Way, Singapore 0106.

United California Bank (*U.S.A.*): 22nd Floor, UIC Bldg., 5 Shenton Way, Singapore 0106.

Wells Fargo Bank (*U.S.A.*): 2 Shenton Way, Singapore 0106.

Westpac Banking Corp. (*Australia*): Suite 4201, OCBC Centre, 65 Chulia St., Singapore 0104.

STOCK EXCHANGE

Stock Exchange of Singapore: 1403 Hong Leong Bldg., Raffles Quay, Singapore 0104; f. 1930; 102 mems.; Chair. Ng Soo Peng; Deputy Chair. Ong Tjin An; Gen. Man. Lim Choo Peng.

INSURANCE

The insurance system is supervised by the Monetary Authority of Singapore (*see* Banking).

Companies

Export Credit Insurance Corpn. of Singapore Ltd.: 3702–3 37th Floor, Tower Block, DBS Bldg., 6 Shenton Way, Singapore 0106; f. 1976; equity participation; 50 per cent state owned, 46 per cent by commercial banks and 4 per cent by all insurance companies; aims to help expand and develop trade with overseas countries by protecting exporters against non-payments or frustration of contracts by overseas buyers; Chief Exec. J. G. Sorbie; Asst. Gen. Mans. Chia Choon Peng, Kwah Thiam Hock.

Life Business Only:

Asia Life Assurance Society Ltd.: Asia Insurance Bldg., Finlayson Green, Maxwell Rd., P.O.B. 76, Singapore 9001; f. 1948; Man. Dir. Ng Aik Huan.

Manulife (Singapore) Pte. Ltd.: 4-316 Merlin Plaza, Beach Rd., Singapore 0719; Man. Dir. Douglas Whitney.

Public Life Assurance Co. Ltd.: 57–61 Robinson Rd., Singapore 0106; f. 1954; Man. Fung Lok Nam.

General Business Only:

Asia Insurance Co. Ltd.: Asia Insurance Bldg., Finlayson Green, Maxwell Rd. P.O.B. 76, Singapore 9001; f. 1923; Man. Dir. Ng Aik Huan.

Cosmic Insurance Corporation Ltd.: 1403–1408 CPF Bldg., 79 Robinson Rd., Singapore 0106; Gen. Man. Teo Kwang Whee.

Industrial and Commercial Insurance Ltd.: ICB Bldg., 2 Shenton Way, Singapore 0106; f. 1958; Chair. Tan Leong Seng; Gen. Man. Tan Teck Bak.

Malayan Motor and General Underwriters (Pte.) Ltd.: 3rd Floor, M & G Centre, 164–170 Clemenceau Ave., Singapore 0923; f. 1954; Chair. H. D. S. Ellis; Dirs. Milton Tan, Tan Bak Nam.

Nanyang Insurance Co. Ltd.: 25–26 Circular Rd., Singapore 0104; f. 1956; Exec. Dir. and Principal Officer Teo Soo Chew.

Overseas Union Insurance Ltd.: 9th, 10th & 12th Floors, UMBC Bldg., 22 Malacca St., Singapore 0104; f. 1956 Gen. Man. Lau Hui Bu.

People's Insurance Co. of Malaya Ltd.: People's Insurance Bldg., 6 Cecil St., Singapore 1; f. 1957; Chair. and Man. Dir. Ng Eng Kiat.

Public Insurance Co. Ltd.: 57–61 Robinson Rd., Singapore 0106; f. 1950; Chair. Datuk Lee Chee Shan; Man. Fung Lok Nam.

Singapore Aviation and General Insurance Co (Pte.) Ltd.: 12th Floor, SIA Bldg., 77 Robinson Rd., Singapore 0106; Gen. Man. Lye Yuen Chew.

Sun Alliance Insurance (Singapore) Ltd.: 1st & 2nd Floors, UOF Bldg., 124/126 Robinson Rd., Singapore 0106; Advisor Hwang Soo Jin.

United Overseas Insurance Ltd.: 1st & 2nd Floors, United Overseas Finance Bldg., 124–126 Robinson Rd., Singapore 0106; Man. Dir. and Principal Officer Hwang Soo Jin.

Life and General Business:

The Great Eastern Life Assurance Co. Ltd.: 18th Floor, OCBC Centre, 65 Chulia St., Singapore 0104; f. 1908; Dir. and Gen. Man. N. N. Handa.

Insurance Corporation of Singapore Ltd.: Podium 416, DBS Bldg., 6 Shenton Way, Singapore 0106; f. 1969; Gen. Man Chew Loy Kiat.

N.T.U.C. Co-operative Insurance Commonwealth Enterprise Ltd. (INCOME): 33rd Floor, Shaw Towers, 100 Beach Road, Singapore 0718; f. 1970; Gen. Man. Tan Kin Lian.

Overseas Assurance Corporation Ltd.: 5 Malacca St., Singapore 0104; f. 1920; Chief Gen. Man. Tan Hoay Gie.

In addition, many foreign insurance companies have offices in Singapore.

TRADE AND INDUSTRY

CHAMBERS OF COMMERCE

Singapore Federation of Chambers of Commerce and Industry: Room 201, 2nd Floor, Chinese Chamber of Commerce Bldg., 47 Hill St., Singapore 0617; f. 1978 by the Singapore Chinese Chamber of Commerce and Industry, the Singapore Malay Chamber of Commerce, the Singapore Indian Chamber of Commerce, the Singapore International Chamber of Commerce and the Singapore Manufacturers' Association; Pres. WEE CHO YAW; Sec.-Gen. LEE ONG PONG.

Singapore Chinese Chamber of Commerce and Industry: 47 Hill St., Singapore 0617; Pres. LIM KEE MING; Exec. Sec. PANG SAY SOK; publ. *Economic Quarterly*.

Singapore Indian Chamber of Commerce: 55A Robinson Rd., Singapore 0106; f. 1937; 504 mems.; Pres. G. RAMACHANDRAN; Sec. GEORGE ABRAHIM. M.A., M.SOC.SC.

Singapore International Chamber of Commerce: Denmark House, Raffles Quay, Singapore 0104; f. 1837; Chair. C. W. ENDACOTT; Exec. Dir./Sec. R. MACLEAN, O.B.E.; publs. *Economic Bulletin* (monthly), *Showcase* (annual), *Investor's Guide*, Annual and other Reports.

Singapore Malay Chamber of Commerce: Suite 1901, 19th Floor, International Plaza, Anson Rd., Singapore 0207; Pres. Haji JALIL HARON; Hon. Sec. SAMAD YUSOF.

DEVELOPMENT ORGANIZATIONS

Economic Development Board: 9th Floor, World Trade Centre, 1 Maritime Sq., Telok Blangah Rd., Singapore 0409; f. 1961; statutory organization planning and implementing Government's industrialization programme; Chair. P. Y. HWANG; Alternative Chair. CHAN CHIN BOCK; Deputy Chair. I. F. TANG; Dir. YEO SENG TECK.

Housing and Development Board: National Development Bldg., Maxwell Rd., P.O.B. 702, Singapore 9014; f. 1960; public housing authority; Chair. MICHAEL FAM; publ. *Our Home*.

Jurong Town Corpn.: Jurong Town Hall Rd., Singapore 2261; f. 1968; statutory organization responsible for developing and maintaining industrial estates in Singapore; Chair. I. F. TANG.

INDUSTRIAL AND TRADE ASSOCIATIONS

Department of Trade: Suite 201, 2nd Floor, World Trade Centre, 1 Maritime Square, Telok Blangah Rd., Singapore 0409; Dir. RIDZWAN DZAFIR.

Malayan Pineapple Industry Board: Suite 2303, Ocean Bldg., Collyer Quay, Singapore 0104; f. 1957; controls pineapple cultivation, canning and marketing; Chair. WONG KUM CHOON.

Rubber Association of Singapore: 12th Floor, Singapore Rubber House, 14 Collyer Quay, Singapore 0104; incorporated Oct. 1967 to support, develop and maintain the rubber industry in general, and to conduct a market in Singapore for the sale and purchase of rubber under the arrangements and regulations formulated by the Corporation; Chair. TAN ENG JOO; Exec. Sec. GNOH CHONG HOCK.

Singapore Association of Shipbuilders and Repairers (SASAR): Tanjong Pagar, P.O.B. 60, Singapore 9108; f. 1968; 30 full mems., 165 assoc. mems.; Pres. LAI PAK ON; Exec. Sec. ONG CHEW LIANG; publs. *Sasar News*, *Directory*.

Singapore Manufacturers' Association: Suite 118, World Trade Centre, 1 Maritime Sq., Telok Blangah Rd., Singapore 0409; f. 1932; Chair. MICHAEL YEO; Deputy Chairs. GOH SENG CHEE, LAM SHEUNG LIM.

CO-OPERATIVES

As at December 31st, 1981, Singapore had 78 co-operative societies classified into 12 types, comprising 40 thrift and credit societies, 8 consumer societies, 17 multi-purpose societies, 3 housing/land-purchase societies, 1 transport society, 2 producer societies, 1 insurance society, 1 medical society, 2 service societies, 2 school co-operative societies and 1 co-operative union. These societies had a combined membership of 273 institutional members and 180,229 personal members with paid-up share capital of S$53,030,112 and a statutory reserve fund of S$10,665,019.

EMPLOYERS' ORGANIZATIONS

The Singapore National Employers' Federation: 23A Amber Mansions, Orchard Rd., Singapore 0923; f. 1980; Pres. JACK CHIA; Exec. Dir. TAN PENG BOO.

Singapore Maritime Employers' Federation: P.O.B. 247, Singapore; f. 1955; Chair. F. D. MURPHY.

TRADE UNIONS

Singapore National Trades Union Congress (SNTUC): Trade Union House, Shenton Way, Singapore 0106; f. 1964; 61 affiliated unions; Pres. PETER VINCENT; Sec.-Gen. LIM CHEE ONN; publs. *Singaporean*, *Fern Toh Pau*.

In January 1982 there were 86 employees' unions (total membership 219,951) and 61 employers' unions (total membership 210,256), affiliated to SNTUC. In 1981 the two largest unions, the Pioneer Industries Employees' Union (PIEU) and the Singapore Industrial Labour Organization (SILO) were completely restructured, forming nine industrial unions.

MAJOR INDUSTRIAL COMPANIES

The following are among the major industrial establishments in Singapore in terms either of employment or capital investment.

BUILDING AND BUILDING MATERIALS

Hume Industries (Singapore) Ltd.: 13.7 km. Bukit Timah Rd., Singapore 2158; f. 1938; cap. S$58m.

Manufacturers of reinforced concrete products, and steel, cast and galvanized iron and PVC products.

Gen. Man. TAY KWANG SENG; 750 employees.

Pilkington (S.E.A.) Pte. Ltd.: 2nd Floor, Haw Par Glass Tower, 180C Clemenceau Ave., Singapore 0923; f. 1971.

Activities include moulding of fibreglass reinforced plastic items such as water tanks and translucent sheets and custom mouldings for architects; responsible for marketing of Pilkington Group products throughout the region.

Man. Dir. J. G. HAMPSON.

Singapore P.E. Pte. Ltd.: 205 Kallang Bahru, Singapore 1233; f. 1961; cap. S$1m.

Manufacturers and converters of polythylene bags; Man. Dirs. C. P. CHIA, H. JIAN; 150 employees.

Electrical and Electronics

Asahi Electronics (S) Pte. Ltd.: 8/8A Block 6, Kallang Place, Singapore 1233; cap. S$1.5m.
Manufacturers of radio cassette tape-recorders; Man. Dir. T. Sano; 1,200 employees.

BBC Brown Boveri (S) Pte. Ltd.: 2 Ayer Rajah Industrial Estate, Singapore 0513; f. 1974; cap. S$5m.
Manufacturers of low voltage switchgear, industrial controls and miniature circuit breakers.
Man. Dir. H. F. Busch; 650 employees.

European Standard Electronics (Pte.) Ltd.: 1F–29F Block 3, Kallang Way, Singapore 1334; f. 1975; cap. S$5.9m.
Manufacturers of tuners, radios, video tapes and television components.
Man. Dir. Daniel Geneste; 1,900 employees.

Fairchild Singapore (Pte.) Ltd.: 11 Lorong 3, Toa Payoh, Singapore 1231; f. 1969.
Manufacturers of integrated circuits and electronic devices.
Man. Dir. Harry Van Winkle; 4,000 employees.

General Electric (U.S.A.) Television & Appliance Pte. Ltd.: 159C Boon Keng Rd., Kallang Industrial Estate, Block 2, Singapore 1233; f. 1970; cap. S$2.3m.
Manufacturers of television components.
Man. Dir. G. T. Scott; 4,230 employees.

Hewlett-Packard Singapore (Pte.) Ltd.: 1150 Depot Rd., Singapore 4; f. 1970; cap. S$240,000.
Manufacturers of electronic calculators, LED displays, analogue meters, oscilloscopes and data cartridges.
Man. Dir. Richard Love; 1,740 employees.

Hitachi Consumer Products (S) Pte. Ltd.: 206 Bedok South, Avenue 1, Singapore 1646; f. 1972; cap. S$16.4m.
Manufacturers of television, radio, tape-recorders, vacuum cleaners and component parts.
Man. Dir. R. Ishikawa; 2,700 employees.

Intersil Singapore (Pte.) Ltd.: 4th Floor, JTC Flatted Factory, 10 Dundee Rd., Singapore 0314; f. 1969; cap. S$1m.
Manufacturers of semi-conductors.
Man. Dir. Rano Sotitriou; 1,000 employeres.

Matsushita Electronics (S) Pte. Ltd.: 202 Bedok South, Avenue 1, Singapore 1646; f. 1979.
Manufacturers of radios, tape-recorders and stereo equipment.
Man. Dir. T. Kuroda; 2,700 employees.

Philips Singapore Pte. Ltd.: Lorong 1, Toa Payoh, P.O.B. 340, Singapore 1231; f. 1951; cap. S$20m.
Manufacturers of television sets, radios, tape-recorders, household appliances, telecommunication equipment, machinery and tools.
Chair. and Man. Dir. B. M. Lap; 5,300 employees.

Sanyo Industries (S) Pte. Ltd.: 4 Wan Lee Rd., Jurong Industrial Estate, Singapore 22; f. 1966; cap. p.u. S$1.5m.
Manufacturers of electrical household appliances.
Man. Dir. Ng Ghit Cheong; 750 employees.

Setron Ltd.: 10 Dundee Rd., Singapore 0314; f. 1966; cap. p.u. S$17.85m.
Manufacturers of television receivers, tuners, amplifiers, radiograms, tape-recorders and related electronic equipment.
Gen. Man. S. K. Huang; 800 employees.

SGS—ATES Singapore (Pte.) Ltd.: Lorong 4 & 6, Toa Payoh, Singapore 1231; f. 1967; cap. S$10m.
Manufacturers of radios, integrated circuits, diodes and thyristors.
Man. Dir. Grudo Zargani; 1,800 employees.

Texas Instruments Singapore Pte. Ltd: 990 Bendemeer Rd., Singapore 1233; f. 1969; cap. S$25,000.
Manufacturers of semi-conductor components.
Man. Dir. G. Culhane; 3,100 employees.

Food and Beverages

Allied Chocolate Industries Ltd.: 481 Tanglin Halt Rd., Singapore 0314; f. 1959; cap. S$9.9m.
Manufacturers of chocolates and cocoa products.
Man. Dir. M. C. Chuang; 313 employees.

Edible Products Ltd.: 255 Jalan Boon Lay, Jurong Town, Singapore 2261.
Vegetable oil refiners.
Man. Dir. Kwok Kian Hai; 176 employees.

Food Specialities Singapore Pte. Ltd.: 50 International Rd., Jurong Town, Singapore 2262.
Producers of sweetened condensed milk, culinary sauces, instant noodles, UHT milk, protomalt extract.
Factory Man. P. Taymans; 200 employees.

Fraser & Neave Ltd.: 475 River Valley Road, Singapore 1024; f. 1964; cap. S$84m.
Producers of soft drinks and cordials.
Group Gen. Man. and Dir. J. D. H. Neill; 1,161 employees.

Khong Guan Biscuit Factory (S) Pte. Ltd.: 338 Jalan Boon Lay, Singapore 2261.
Biscuit manufacturers.
Man. Dir. C. H. Chew; 320 employees.

Malayan Breweries (S) Pte. Ltd.: P.O. Box 853, Singapore 9017; f. 1964; cap. S$81m.
Brewers of beer and stout.
Gen. Man. J. D. H. Neill; 1,683 employees.

Prima Ltd.: 201 Keppel Rd., Singapore 0409; f. 1969; cap. S$30m.
Producers of wheat flour, wheat bran and pollard.
Man. Dir. Tsang man Cheng; 200 employees.

Sugar Industry of Singapore Ltd.: 34 Jurong Port Rd., Jurong Town, Singapore 2261; f. 1963; cap. S$8m.
Sugar refiners.
Man. Dir. Tan Puay Hee; 316 employees.

Yeo Hiap Seng Ltd.: 950 Dunearn Rd., Singapore 2158; f. 1974; cap. S$25m.
Manufacturers of canned foodstuffs, beverages and sauces.
Man. Dir. Alan Yeo; 519 employees.

Metals and Engineering

Far East Levingston Shipbuilding Ltd.: 31 Shipyard Rd., Singapore 2262; f. 1967; cap. S$23m.
Builders of off-shore drilling rigs, vessels and ship repairing.
Man. Dir. Loh Wing Siew; 1,300 employees.

Jurong Shipyard Ltd.: 5 Pulau Samulun, Jurong Town, Singapore 2262.
Shipbuilders and repairers.
Chair. Tan Teck Chwee; Man. Dir. T. Yano; 2,500 employees.

Keppel Shipyard Ltd.: 325 Telok Blangah Rd., Singapore 0409; f. 1968; cap. S$120m.
Shiprepairers.
Chair. G. E. Gogaars; 1,000 employees.

Metal Box Singapore Ltd.: 24 Km. Woodlands Rd., Singapore 2573; f. 1949; cap. S$20m.
Manufacturers and lithographers of cans and tin boxes including aerosol containers, screw caps and closures, etc.

Man. Dir. LIM HONG KEAT; Commercial Man. HWANG SOO CHIN; 700 employees (parent company only); parent company of Metal Box Thailand Ltd. and Secura Singapore Pte. Ltd.

National Iron and Steel Mills Ltd.: 22 Tanjong Kling Road, Singapore 2262; f. 1961; auth. cap. S$100m.
Manufacturers of mild steel bars and wire rods.
Chair. CHUA KIM YEOW; 947 employees.

PETROLEUM

Amoco Far East Oil Co.: 9th Floor, Yen San Bldg., Orchard Rd., Singapore 9.
Petroleum refining and marketing.

B.P. Singapore Pte. Ltd.: P.O.B. 2814, B.P. House, 1 Pasir Panjang Rd., Singapore 0511; f. 1964; cap. S$20m.; Marketing of petroleum products.
Chair. K. R. SEAL; 290 employees.

Burmah Oil Orient (Pte.) Ltd.: Rooms 705–706, 7th Floor, Supreme House, Penang Rd., Singapore 0923; P.O.B. 122, Tanglin Post Office.
Oil extractors.

Castrol (F.E.) Pte. Ltd.: P.O.B. 35, Bukit Panjang Post Office, Singapore 9168.
Manufacturers of lubricating oils, greases, speciality products and brake fluids.

Esso Singapore Pte. Ltd.: Pulau Ayer Chawan, P.O.B. 23, Jurong Town Post Office, Singapore 9161.
Petroleum refining.
Man. Dir. T. E. YOUNG.

Gulf Oil Company South Asia: Ming Court Hotel, P.O.B. 641, Singapore 9012.
Regional administrative company.

Mobil Oil Singapore Pte. Ltd.: 18 Pioneer Rd., Jurong Town, P.O.B. 3025, Singapore 2262.
Manufacturers and marketers of petroleum products.
Chair. ROGER O'NEIL; 415 employees.

Shell Eastern Petroleum (Pte.) Ltd., Shell Singapore (Pte.) Ltd., Shell Eastern Chemicals (Pte.) Ltd., Shell Eastern Lubricants (Pte.) Ltd., Shell Lubricants Blending (S) Pte. Ltd.: 1 Bonham St., Raffles Place, P.O.B. 643, Singapore 0104; 2,300 employees.

Singapore Petroleum Co. Pte. Ltd.: Tower 4101, DBS Bldg., 6 Shenton Way, Singapore 0106.
Petroleum refining and marketing; Chair. TAN BOON TEIK; Vice-Pres. CHENG HOHN KOK.

PHARMACEUTICALS

Beecham Pharmaceuticals Pte. Ltd.: Quality Rd., Jurong Town, Singapore 2261.
Manufacture and sale of pharmaceuticals.

Bristol-Myers (S) Pte. Ltd.: Unit 301–305, 3rd Floor, CIDECO Industrial Complex 1, 50 Genting Lane, Singapore 1334.
Importers, distributors and manufacturers of pharmaceuticals, toiletries and consumer household goods.

Ciba-Geigy S.E. Asia (Pte.) Ltd.: 1 Third Lokyang Rd., Singapore 2262.
Importers, manufacturers, distributors of Ciba-Geigy products (dyestuffs, chemicals, pharmaceuticals, plastics, additives, glues) in Singapore and S.E. Asia.

Drug Houses of Australia: 56 International Rd., Singapore 2261.
Manufacturers and distributors of pharmaceutical products, specializing in sterile production; also contract manufacture of pharmaceuticals, toiletries and cosmetics.

Jack Chia-MPH Limited: Malayan Credit House, 7th Floor, 96 Somerset Rd., Singapore 0923; f. 1927; cap. S$48m.
Holding and investment company; manufacturers and distributors of pharmaceuticals, perfumes, toiletries and confectionery; also owns and operates timber industries, a recreation complex, a hotel and other property; importers and retailers of books and magazines (also publishers), educational toys, stationery and novelties.
Chair. JACK CHIARAPURK; 797 employees.

Roche Pharmaceuticals Pte. Ltd.: Roche Bldg., 30 Shaw Rd., Singapore 1336.
Distributors of pharmaceuticals, fine chemicals, cosmetics, diagnostic reagents and hospital equipment.
Man. Dir. KOH CHOON HUI.

Wellcome (S) Pte. Ltd.: 33 Quality Rd., Jurong Town, P.O.B. 2, Singapore 2261.
Medical and veterinary products, consumer products manufacturers, insecticide products, hygiene service.

TEXTILES AND GARMENTS

Great Malaysia Textiles Mfg. Co. Pte. Ltd.: 1 Tanglin Halt Close, Singapore 3; cap. p.u. S$1.7m.; *c.* 1,200 employees.

Malaysia Garment Manufacturers Ltd.: 407 Chinese Chamber of Commerce Bldg., 47 Hill St., Singapore 0617; cap. S$422,000; 354 employees.

Unitex Singapore Pte. Ltd.: 26 Jalan Tukang, Singapore 2261; cap. S$4m.; 300 employees.

Wing Tai Garment Manufactory (S) Pte. Ltd.: 107 Tampines Rd., Singapore 1953; cap. S$4.2m.; 1,800 employees.

WOOD AND PAPER PRODUCTS

Golden City Plywood Pte. Ltd.: 8 Jalan Papan, Singapore 2261; cap. S$4m.; 720 employees.

Hong Kong Teakwood Works (S) Pte. Ltd.: 19 Kranji Way, Singapore 2513; cap. S$2m.; 1,350 employees.

Jurong Plywood Co. Pte. Ltd.: 28 Penjuru Rd., Singapore 2260; cap. S$15m.; 900 employees.

Kranji Plywood Industrial Co. (Pte.) Ltd.: 11 Kranji Way, Singapore 2513; cap. S$15m.; 770 employees.

Southern Wood Products (Pte.) Ltd.: 34 Penjuru Rd., Singapore 2260; cap. S$8m.; 700 employees.

Starlight Timber Products Co. Ltd.: 4 Jalan Papan, Jurong Town, Singapore 2261; annual sales S$39m.; Sales Man. CHOO EIOW MENG. 600 employees.

United Pulp and Paper Co. Ltd.: 20 Liu Fang Rd., Singapore 2261; cap. S$4.75m.; 200 employees.

Veneer Products Ltd.: Jurong Town, P.O.B. 4, Singapore 2261; cap. S$11.4m.; 450 employees.

MISCELLANEOUS

Singapore Holdings Co.: f. 1981 from Rothmans (Singapore); cap. S$14.35m.; cigarette producers.

TRANSPORT

RAILWAYS

In 1978 there were 26 km. of metre-gauge railway, linked with the Malaysian railways system and owned by the Malayan Railway Administration. The main line crosses the Johore causeway and terminates near Keppel Harbour. Branch lines link it with the industrial estate at Jurong.

ROADS

In September 1981 Singapore had a total of 2,338 kilometres of roads of which 2,030 kilometres were asphalt-paved. The road system includes dual carriage-ways, flyovers and expressways.

SHIPPING

Port of Singapore Authority: P.O.B. 300, Singapore 9005; Chair. LIM KIM SAN; Gen. Man. WONG HUNG KHIM; Dir. Operations LEE CHEE YENG; Dir. Finance LIM TIAN LEONG; Dir. Engineering Services PHILIP NG; Dir. Admin. and Sec. BILLIE CHENG SHAO-CHI.

Container port facilities comprise five main berths totalling 1,554 metres (13.4 metres LWOST), a feeder service berth of 238 metres (10.8 metres LWOST) and a cross berth of 213 metres (10.4 metres LWOST). Construction of another berth totalling 355 metres and conversion of two berths at Keppel Wharves into container berths totalling 535 metres are due to be completed in 1983/84. In addition, there are conventional wharves which include Keppel Wharves (4.8 km.), Telok Ayer Wharves (1.2 km.), Jurong Port (1.7 km.), Pasir Panjang Wharves (2.3 km.), and Sembawang Wharves (0.8 km.).

MAJOR SHIPPING LINES

American President Lines Ltd.: Mercantile Bank Bldg., 21 Raffles Place, Singapore 0104; container services to South-East Asia, the U.S.A., the Persian Gulf and Canada; Man. Dir. M. D. MORRIS.

Barber Wilhelmsen Agencies Pte. Ltd.: 10th Floor, Ocean Bldg., Singapore 0104; services to the U.S.A. and Canada; Man. Dir. KNUT S. BERENTSON.

Ben Line Steamers Ltd.: 18th Floor, Clifford Centre, Raffles Place, Singapore 0104; container services to Japan, Taiwan and Europe; bulk services to Europe; Man. J. B. MATTINSON.

Chip Seng Co. Pte. Ltd.: 9th Floor, Manhattan House, 151 Chin Swee Road, Singapore 0316; services to the U.S.A., Europe, the Persian Gulf and the Caribbean Sea; Gov. Dir. WEE MON-CHENG; Man. Dir. LAWRENCE NG.

Everett Steamship Corpn.: 16th Floor, Clifford Centre, Raffles Place, Collyer Quay, Singapore 0104; cargo services; Gen. Man. CARL BAUMANN.

Guan Guan Shipping Pte. Ltd.: 2nd Floor, Guangdong Provincial Bank Bldg., Singapore 0104; f. 1955; shipowners and agents; passenger/cargo services to East and West Malaysia, Indonesia, Pakistan, Sri Lanka, Bengal Bay ports, Persian Gulf ports, Hong Kong and China; T. E. GOH.

Lian Soon Shipping and Trading Co. Pte. Ltd.: Suite 1101, 11th Floor, CPF Building, Singapore 0106; services to Indonesia, East Malaysia, Sri Lanka, India, Pakistan and the Middle East; Man. Dir. DAVID ONG.

Maersk Line (Singapore) Pte. Ltd.: 20th Floor, UIC Bldg., 5 Shenton Way, Singapore 0106; f. 1974; cargo services on Far East/U.S.A., Far East/Europe, Far East/AP Gulf routes; operates container vessels; Man. Dir. JORGEN LUND.

Nedlloyd EAC Agencies Pte. Ltd.: 1 Finlayson Green, Singapore 0104; f. 1963; agency for Nedlloyd Lines and Scandutch I/S partnership; Gen. Man. J. H. MEIJER.

Neptune Orient Lines Ltd.: Neptune Bldg., 13 Trafalgar St., Singapore 0207; f. 1968; liner containerized services on the Far East/Europe, Far East/U.S.A. West and East Coasts, Straits/Australia, South Asia/Europe and South-East Asia, Far East/Mediterranean routes; tankers and dry cargo vessels on charter; 31 ships in operation (and 10 on order); total tonnage 1,135,000 d.w.t.; Chair. M. WONG PAKSHONG; Man. Dir. LUA CHENG ENG.

Pacific International Lines Pte. Ltd.: PIL Bldg., 140 Cecil St., Singapore 0106; cargo services to East Africa, the Persian Gulf and throughout South-East Asia, container services to Europe and Saudi Arabia; Man. Dir. Y. C. CHANG.

Seven Seas Maritime Co. Pte. Ltd.: Suite 304-305, Ocean Bldg., Collyer Quay, Singapore 0104; services to Europe, Middle East, Africa and South-East Asia; Man. Dirs. WIM H. TIOMENA, T. H. TAN.

Singapore Islands Line: 20th Floor, Ocean Bldg., Collyer Quay, Singapore 0104; services to Middle East; Man. Dir. KUA PEK LONG.

Straits Steamship Co. Ltd.: 14th Floor, Ocean Bldg., Collyer Quay, Singapore 0104; f. 1890; holding company for container shipping agencies and regional and coastal shipping lines; also has interests in distributive trades, food importation, property, data processing, freight forwarding and warehousing, precision engineering, travel and tours, vehicle hire, insurance broking, oilfield support services and industry; Chair. WEE CHO YAW; Sec. CHOO CHIN TECK.

CIVIL AVIATION

Singapore's new international airport at Changi was opened in 1981.

Singapore Airlines Ltd. (SIA): Singapore Changi Airport, P.O.B. 501, Singapore 9181; f. 1972; passenger services to Australia, Bahrain, Belgium, Brunei, Denmark, France, the Federal Republic of Germany, Greece, Hong Kong, India, Indonesia, Italy, Japan, the Republic of Korea, Malaysia, the Netherlands, New Zealand, the Philippines, Saudi Arabia, Sri Lanka, Switzerland, Taiwan, Thailand, the United Arab Emirates, the United Kingdom, and the U.S.A.; fleet of sixteen 747, four 727, three DC-10, six A300B4; Chair. J. Y. M. PILLAY; Man. Dir. LIM CHIN BENG.

FOREIGN AIRLINES

Singapore is also served by the following foreign airlines: Aeroflot (U.S.S.R.), Air India, Air Lanka (Sri Lanka), Air Niugini (Papua New Guinea), Alitalia (Italy), Air Nauru, Air New Zealand, All Nippon Airways (Japan), BAC (Burma), Bangladesh Biman, British Airways, Cargolux Airlines International (Luxembourg), Cathay Pacific (Hong Kong), China Air Lines (Taiwan), ČSA (Czechoslovakia), Flying Tiger Line (U.S.A.), Garuda (Indonesia), JAL (Japan), JAT (Yugoslavia), KLM (Netherlands), Lufthansa (Fed. Repub. of Germany), MAS (Malaysia), Pan Am (U.S.A.), PAL (Philippines), PIA (Pakistan), Qantas (Australia), Royal Brunei Airlines, Sabena (Belgium), SAS (Sweden), Swissair, Tarom (Romania), Thai International, TMA (Lebanon), UTA (France).

TOURISM AND CULTURE

Singapore Tourist Promotion Board: 131 Tudor Court, Tanglin Rd., Singapore 1024; f. 1964; Chair. TAN I TONG; Dir. YUEN KUM CHUEN; publs. *Singapore Travel* (quarterly in English and monthly in Japanese), *Singapore Guidebook* (English), *Singapore Diary of Events, Hotels of Singapore* (English), *Singapore—The Most Surprising Tropical Island on Earth* (English, Japanese, French, German, Indonesian, Chinese, Korean, Thai and Spanish), *Crossroads Singapore* (English), *Travel Agent Manual* (English) and several Special Interest leaflets.

Singapore Convention Bureau: 135 Tudor Court, Tanglin Rd., Singapore 1024; f. 1974; a division of the Singapore Tourist Promotion Board; Dir. JENNIE CHUA; publs. *Singapore Convention News* (English, Japanese), *Singapore Convention Calendar* (English), *Get Together with Us—Singapore* (English, Japanese), *Even More of an Incentive—Singapore* (English), *Convention Facilities Guide* (English).

CULTURAL ORGANIZATIONS

The Singapore Arts Council: c/o National Museum, Stamford Rd., Singapore 0617; aims to promote cultural activities and the integration of the Malay, Chinese, Tamil and English cultures; to maintain and improve standards in all forms of art and to serve as co-ordinating body for all cultural societies and associations in the Republic; Pres. Dr. OW CHIN HOCK, M.P.; Hon. Sec. CHRISTOPHER HOOI.

National Theatre Trust: Clemenceau Ave., Singapore 0923; f. 1963; responsible for the management of the National Theatre and the encouragement and development of culture and cultural exchange; Chair. THAI CHEE KEN, Dr. MICHAEL LOKE.

People's Association: Kallang, Singapore 1439; a statutory corporation set up in 1960 for the organization of leisure, the promotion of youth activities and group participation in social, cultural, educational, vocational and athletic activities; operates a network of 157 community centres, 3 holiday camps, 1 camp site, 4 holiday bungalows and a 30-unit holiday complex.

DEFENCE

Armed Forces (1981): Total strength 42,000: army 35,000, navy 3,000, air force 4,000; military service lasts 2–3 years. Army reserves number 50,000 and para-military forces comprise 7,500 police, marine and Gurkha guard battalions; Home Guard 30,000.

Equipment: The army has French tanks and British guns. The navy has patrol boats and landing craft. The air force has mainly British aircraft, but France, Italy and New Zealand have also provided equipment.

Defence Expenditure: (1980) S$1,260 million.

Chief of General Staff: Brig. WINSTON CHOO.

EDUCATION

Education in Singapore is not compulsory, but all children are entitled to at least six years' free primary education, which may be completed in eight years by less able pupils, under the New Primary Education System implemented in 1979. A place is ensured for every child, though most schools still work a shift system, one functioning in the morning and another in the afternoon.

In January 1981 there were 501 schools, comprising 58 kindergartens, 304 primary schools, 108 secondary schools, 23 full (with primary and secondary classes) schools and 8 junior colleges. The total enrolment was 468,391, of which 3,914 were in pre-primary classes or kindergartens, 299,086 in primary schools and 165,391 in secondary schools or junior colleges.

The policy of bilingualism ensures that children are taught two languages, English and one of the other official languages, Chinese, Malay and Tamil. The option to study French, German or Japanese is offered to interested pupils in secondary schools with linguistic ability as a third language, and as a second language to pupils not of Chinese, Malay or Indian ethnic origin.

After six years of primary schooling, successful candidates proceed to secondary schools which offer four-year courses with a technical, academic or commercial bias, leading to the Singapore-Cambridge General Certificate of Education "Ordinary" Level Examination. Less able pupils are able to complete the four year course over a period of five years. Those who complete this course successfully may follow a 2-year pre-university course leading to the General Certificate of Education "Advanced" Level Examination.

Teacher Training

The Institute of Education conducts both pre-service and in-service teacher training courses. During the 1980/81 academic year, there were 2,473 pre-service students of whom 608 were university graduates. A further 825 teachers also returned to the Institute for a variety of in-service training courses.

Higher Education

As of June 1979 there were 15 technical and vocational institutes, including four government training centres, a hotel and catering training school and a school of printing. There are also two technical colleges, one teacher training institute and the National University of Singapore, formed in April 1980 from an amalgamation of the University of Singapore and the Chinese-orientated Nanyang University. In 1980/81 the total enrolment was 8,634.

Vocational and Industrial Training

The Vocational and Industrial Training Board was formed following the merger of the Adult Education Board and the Industrial Training Board in April 1979. It runs 18 training institutes and centres and is responsible for the basic training of school leavers in industrial, commercial and service skills.

BIBLIOGRAPHY

BEDLINGTON, STANLEY S. Malaysia and Singapore: The Building of New States (Cornell University Press, Ithaca, 1978).

BUCHANAN, IAIN. Singapore in Southeast Asia; An Economic and Political Appraisal (G. Bell, London, 1972).

CHAN, HENG CHEE. Singapore: Politics of Survival 1965–1967 (Oxford University Press, Singapore, 1971).

EMERSON, R. Malaysia, A Study in Direct and Indirect Rule (1937, reprinted, Oxford University Press, Kuala Lumpur, 1966).

GOH, KENG SWEE. The Economics of Modernization and other essays (Asia Pacific Press, Singapore, 1972).

The Practice of Economic Growth (Federal Publications, Singapore, 1977).

HASSAN, RIAZ (ed.). Singapore: Society in Transition (Oxford University Press, Kuala Lumpur, 1976).

JOSEY, ALEX. Lee Kuan Yew: The Struggle for Singapore (Angus & Robertson, Sydney, 1980).

LEE KUAN YEW. The Battle for Merger (Ministry of Culture, Singapore, 1961).

LEE SHENG-YI. Public Finance and Public Investment in Singapore (Institute of Banking and Finance, Singapore, 1978).

MINISTRY OF FINANCE. Economic Survey of Singapore (Singapore National Printers (Pte.) Ltd.).

MONETARY AUTHORITY OF SINGAPORE. Quarterly Bulletin.

NAIR, C. V. DEVAN. Socialism That Works: The Singapore Way (Federal Publications, Singapore, 1977).

NATIONAL LIBRARY, SINGAPORE. Singapore National Bibliography (Government Printing Office, Singapore, 1969).

OOI JIN BEE & CHIANG HAI DING (eds.). Modern Singapore (University of Singapore Press, Singapore, 1969).

OSBORNE, MILTON. Singapore and Malaysia (Data Paper No. 53, Cornell University, New York, U.S.A., 1964).

PANG, CHENG LIAN. Singapore's People's Action Party (Oxford University Press, Singapore, 1971).

SAW SWEE HOCK. Asian Metropolis: Singapore in transition (University of Pennsylvania and Oxford University Press, 1970).

Singapore Trade and Industry Yearbook (Straits Times Press, Singapore).

THIO, EUNICE (ed.). Singapore 1819-1969 (Journal of South-East Asian History, University of Singapore, March 1969).

TURNBULL, C. M. A History of Singapore 1819–1975 (Oxford University Press, 1978).

A Short History of Malaysia, Singapore, and Brunei (Cassells, Australia, 1980 and Graham Brash Singapore, 1981).

The Straits Settlements, 1826–67 (Athlone Press, London, and Oxford University Press, Kuala Lumpur, 1972).

WILSON, DICK. East meets West: Singapore (Times Printers, Singapore, 1971).

WILSON, H. E. Social Engineering in Singapore: Educational Policies and Social Change, 1819–1972 (Singapore University Press, Singapore, 1978).

WONG LIN KEN. The Trade of Singapore, 1819–1869 (Journal of the Malayan Branch, Royal Asiatic Society, 1961).

WURTZBURG, C. E. Raffles of the Eastern Isles (Hodder and Stoughton, London, 1954).

YEO KIM WAH. Political Development in Singapore, 1945–1955 (Singapore University Press, Singapore, 1973).

YOU, POH SENG, and LIM CHONG YAH. The Singapore Economy (Eastern Universities Press, Singapore, 1971).

(*See also* Malaysia.)

Sri Lanka

PHYSICAL AND SOCIAL GEOGRAPHY

B. H. Farmer

Sri Lanka (formerly called Ceylon) consists of one large island and several smaller ones lying east of the southern tip of the Indian sub-continent. It has an area of 65,610 square kilometres (25,332 square miles). The Bay of Bengal lies to its north and east and the Arabian Sea to its west. It is separated from India by the Gulf of Mannar and the Palk Strait, between which there lie, in very shallow water, the string of small islands known as "Adam's Bridge", linking Sri Lanka and India. Sri Lanka stretches from 5° 55′ to 9° 50′ north latitude and from 79° 40′ to 81° 55′ east longitude.

PHYSICAL FEATURES

Sri Lanka consists almost entirely of hard ancient crystalline rocks (though recent work has cast doubt on the age of some of them). Unaltered sedimentary rocks occupy only the Jaffna Peninsula (a raised coral reef) in the north and a strip down the north-west coast. Alluvial spreads follow the main rivers and also occupy infilled coastal lagoons, especially on the east coast.

The highest land in Sri Lanka occupies the south-centre, the "Up-country", and rises to over 1,500 metres (5,000 feet). The highest point is Pidurutalagala (2,524 metres or 8,280 feet). From the Up-country, the land falls by steps to a rolling coastal plain, narrow in the west and south-west, broadest in the north (though even there isolated hills rise above the general level). The rivers, apart from the longest, the Mahaweli Ganga (which has a complicated course), are generally short and run radially outwards from the Up-country.

CLIMATE

Sri Lanka has temperatures appropriate to its near-equatorial position, modified by altitude Up-country. In Colombo, at sea-level, mean monthly temperatures fluctuate only between 25°C. (77°F.) in January and 28°C. (82°F.) in May. At Nuwara Eliya, at 1,889 metres (6,199 feet), temperatures range between 14°C. (57°F.) in January and 16°C. (61°F.) in May.

A fundamental division in Sri Lanka, so far as rainfall and therefore agriculture are concerned, is that between the Wet and Dry Zones. The former occupies the southwestern quadrant of the island, and normally receives rain from both the south-west and north-east monsoons. Colombo, for example, has a mean annual rainfall of 236.5 cm. (93.1 inches): it receives 6.9 cm. (2.7 inches) in February, the driest month, and 37.1 cm. (14.6 inches) in May, the wettest. The Dry Zone, covering the lowlands of the north and east and extending in modified form into the eastern Up-country, has a period of severe drought in the south-west monsoon and most of its rain from the north-east. Trincomalee, for example, with a mean annual rainfall of 164.8 cm. (64.9 inches), receives on average only 6.9 cm. (2.7 inches), 2.8 cm. (1.1 inches) and 5.1 cm. (2 inches) in May, June and July respectively (and mean *expectation* is less than the mean rainfall); but it receives over 35.6 cm. (14 inches) in both November and December. Commercial crops like tea and rubber are almost entirely confined to the Wet Zone.

SOILS AND NATURAL RESOURCES

Sri Lanka is fortunate to have a soil map based on modern scientific methods. The "red-yellow podzolic" soils of most of the Wet Zone and Up-country are not very fertile, but grow tree-crops and give a high response to fertilizers. Young soils are found on steeper slopes. Over a large part of the Dry Zone, especially the north-centre and south-east, "reddish-brown earths" require careful handling but are more fertile than is normal in the Tropics. In the Jaffna Peninsula soils are also, largely through human exertion, relatively fertile; but elsewhere in the Dry Zone, apart from alluvium, soils are generally infertile or difficult or both (although some can be improved).

The Wet Zone and wetter hills must once have been covered with wet evergreen forest akin to tropical rain forest, passing into drier forest on the lowland Dry Zone boundary, and into montane wet evergreen forest in the high hills. Most of this forest cover has disappeared with the advance of cultivation. A fair proportion of the lowland Dry Zone is, however, still covered with dry mixed evergreen forest (producing valuable timbers such as ebony and satin-wood) which is probably secondary, the result of centuries of shifting cultivation. In the drier north-west and south-east this passes into thorn scrub; while in the eastern Dry Zone are patches of savanna-like grassland thought to be due to periodic burning.

Sri Lanka is poor in mineral wealth. There are no known deposits of petroleum or coal; an estimated total of only 2.2 million tons of exploitable iron ore in scattered deposits; and virtually the only workable sources of non-ferrous metals are beach sands yielding ilmenite, rutile, monazite and zircon. Graphite and gem-stones are Sri Lanka's most valuable mineral products. Salt is manufactured by the evaporation of sea water, and useful deposits of limestone and clay (for cement) and kaolin are beginning to be exploited.

POPULATION AND ETHNIC GROUPS

The population at the 1981 census was 14,850,001. The crude birth rate fell from 37 per 1,000 in 1960 to an estimated 27.6 per 1,000 in 1980. The population is very unevenly distributed. The Wet Zone and most of the Up-country have a dense rural population and also contain the principal conurbation, Colombo (population 586,000 at the 1981 census) and a number of other towns, e.g. Kandy (101,000 in 1981). Much of the Dry Zone is still sparsely peopled, in spite of considerable colonization in the last forty years or so.

Sri Lanka has a plural society. The majority group, the Sinhalese, speak a distinctive language related to the Indo-Aryan tongues of north India, and are mainly Buddhist. There are two groups of Tamils: "Ceylon Tamils", the descendants of Tamil-speaking groups who long ago migrated from South India, and "Indian Tamils", comparatively recent immigrants who came over to work on plantations, and their descendants: both are predominantly Hindu. There are also groups of Muslims (called "Moors") and Christians (drawn from the Sinhalese, Tamil and other communities).

HISTORY

Kingsley M. de Silva

ANCIENT CEYLON

Sri Lanka is a plural society whose roots go back more than 2,000 years. The Sinhalese and Tamils, the main component elements in Sri Lanka's plural society, have a common Indian origin but from two "racial" stocks, Aryan and Dravidian. Aryan settlement and colonization in the island began around 500 B.C. while Dravidian-Tamil settlements in Sri Lanka emerged a few centuries later.

The early settlements arose in the Dry Zone of Sri Lanka. The ancient Sinhalese developed a highly sophisticated irrigation system which became the basis of a thriving economy. The introduction of Buddhism to the island around the third century B.C. had an impact on the people as decisive as the development of irrigation technology was in economic activity. Buddhism became the bedrock of the culture and civilization of the island, and the state religion. More importantly, the intimate connection between the land, the "race" and the Buddhist religion foreshadowed the intermingling of religion and national identity which has always had the most profound influence on the Sinhalese.

The ancient Sri Lankan kingdom had many of the attributes of a feudal polity. While the king was, in theory, an absolute ruler, custom and tradition acted as formidable constraints on his absolutism, and thus it was not a highly centralized autocratic state but one in which the balance of political forces incorporated a tolerance of centrifugalism.

The flourishing but highly vulnerable irrigation civilization of Sri Lanka's northern plain proved to be a tempting target for invasion from South India. The Sinhalese contributed to their own discomfiture by calling in Tamil assistance in settling disputed successions and dynastic squabbles. The tensions and conflicts between the Sinhalese and Tamils which emerged from this have been magnified far beyond the reality of historical fact. Folklore and mythology have fed the image of the Tamils as the implacable national enemy. This was especially so with regard to the collapse of Sri Lanka's hydraulic civilization in the thirteenth century A.D. Political instability within the Sinhalese kingdom was just as important a cause of its disintegration as Tamil invasion but it is the latter which is remembered as the crucial factor.

After the thirteenth century, with the establishment of a Tamil kingdom in the north of the island, there was, in fact, a geographical separation between the Sinhalese and the Tamils. The Sinhalese abandoned the north central plains and migrated to the hilly, wetter and forested south-west quarter of the island. Until the beginning of the twentieth century a vast forest belt lay between the two peoples although they were not totally isolated from each other, nor was there a break in the social and economic relations between them.

THE BEGINNINGS OF WESTERN INFLUENCE

Western influence began in the sixteenth century with the Portuguese intrusion into the affairs of the littoral. By 1600 they were well established, but within 60 years they were displaced by the Dutch, who in turn were dislodged by the British at the end of the eighteenth century. During Portuguese and Dutch rule, however, parts of the island, most notably the Kandyan kingdom, remained independent under Sinhalese rule. The fact that neither the Portuguese nor the Dutch were able to conquer the whole island was an important factor in the emergence, in the course of time, of a distinction among the Sinhalese themselves, between those of the south-west littoral, the low-country Sinhalese, and those of the Kandyan areas. This was based on custom and outlook fostered by colonial rule in the one instance and the absence of it in the other.

It was during Portuguese and Dutch rule that Christianity was introduced in all its sectarian variety. Converts to the official or orthodox version of Christianity came to be treated as a privileged group. Moreover, Roman Catholicism under the Portuguese and Calvinism under the Dutch were notable for their intolerance of the traditional faiths while under the Dutch the Roman Catholics too were under great pressure.

The impact of the Portuguese and the Dutch on the island's economy was more significant. By the fifteenth century, cinnamon, which grew wild in the forests of the island's wet zone, had developed into one of the main exports of the island. The Portuguese and the Dutch monopolized the export trade in this valuable commodity, and the profits from it became the mainstay of the revenues they controlled in Sri Lanka. In the late eighteenth century the Dutch began to cultivate cinnamon in plantations. They also introduced other cash crops, such as coffee, sugar, cotton and tobacco, but these were comparatively minor products. It was under the British that the plantation system established itself as the most flourishing sector of the economy.

With the British conquest of the former Dutch possessions in Sri Lanka in 1795–96 the balance of power in the island shifted decisively against the Kandyans. By 1815 the British were masters of the Kandyan kingdom, and their control of it was effectively consolidated when they crushed the Kandyan rebellion of 1817–18. For the first time in several centuries the whole island was under the rule of one power. With the Colebrooke-Cameron reforms of 1832 a single administrative system was established for the island.

THE CONSOLIDATION OF BRITISH RULE

A period of experimentation in plantation crops began in the mid-1830s and within 15 years the success of one of these crops, coffee, radically transformed the economy of the island. When the coffee industry was mortally stricken by a leaf disease in the 1870s the plantation economy demonstrated a remarkable resilience and the three decades 1880 to 1910 saw a sustained growth in the plantation sector which matched, if it did not surpass, that achieved in the coffee era. It was in these years that the pattern was established of an overwhelming dominance in the island's economy of three major plantation crops: tea, rubber and coconuts. British interests were dominant in tea and strong in rubber, but much less so in coconuts; shipping, banks, insurance and the export-import trade were mainly if not entirely controlled by British commercial interests.

The changeover from coffee to the other plantation crops entailed a fundamental change in the character of Sri Lanka's immigrant Indian labour. For whereas labour on the coffee plantations was performed by seasonal migrants, tea and, to a lesser extent, rubber required a permanent and resident supply of labour. Thus Sri Lanka's Indian problem in its modern form emerged.

One of the most far-reaching effects of the development of a capitalist economy on the foundation of plantation agriculture and trade was the growth of a new élite which was largely an indigenous capitalist class. The traditional élite, especially in the low-country, was absorbed into this expanding new élite. Yet they were soon left far behind in the two most important channels of mobility, the acquisition of a Western education and participation in capitalist enterprise. Elite status in fact became much less dependent on hereditary status and the holding of government office. The capitalist class was largely low-country Sinhalese with a sprinkling of Tamils and other minority groups; Kandyan representation was virtually non-existent.

Among the adverse effects of the growth of plantations was the lop-sided development of the economy, and the comparative neglect of traditional agriculture. This was despite the sustained, if not unbroken, effort made in the second half of the nineteenth century to rehabilitate the Dry Zone through a revival of the ancient irrigation works there.

In the 1830s and 1840s every sphere of activity, political, economic and social, had been affected by a passion for reform generated by Evangelicalism, in matters relating to religion and education, and by the secular "creed" of laissez-faire. But by the last quarter of the nineteenth century it was only in plantation enterprise that the old zest and energy was maintained, and the British administration had become much more sympathetic to the conservative forces in Sri Lanka society.

The first notable reversal of policy was with regard to Buddhism. The official attitude changed from neglect and studied indifference to one of according Buddhism a measure of judicious patronage and emphasizing the principle of the Government's neutrality in religious affairs. The change of attitude to the traditional élite was equally decisive: instead of a determined effort to reduce their powers and privileges there was now a policy of aristocratic resuscitation which continued into the first decade of the twentieth century. The motive in both instances was political, to build a counterweight to the more assertive sections of the élite who were seeking a share of political power in the colony.

The last three decades of the nineteenth century mark the first phase in the emergence of nationalism in Sri Lanka. While incipient nationalist sentiment was primarily religious in outlook and content, asserting the need for the primacy of Buddhist values and claiming that Buddhism was in danger, political overtones in it were visible from its inception, especially in the appeal to the native past as against a contemporary situation of foreign domination. The temperance movement, an integral part of the Buddhist revival in the first decade of the twentieth century, was an introduction, tentative but astutely restrained, to political activity and the rallying point of the recovery of national consciousness. However, faith in the permanence of British control over the affairs of the island remained largely unshaken, and nobody in public life at the turn of the century could have imagined that Sri Lanka would be independent within 50 years.

CONSTITUTIONAL REFORM AND TRANSFER OF POWER

In the first two decades of the twentieth century the colonial authorities in the island successfully withstood the pressures of the élite for a share in the administration of the country. Neither the First World War, nor the perverse mishandling of the situation in the island in the wake of the Sinhalese-Muslim riots of 1915, led to a more pronounced radicalization of politics. The keynotes of the reform movement were restraint and moderation. The formation of the Ceylon National Congress in 1919 was evidence of the strength of these attitudes rather than of any notable departure from them.

The 1920s, on the other hand, were characterized by bolder initiatives in politics. There was a significant heightening of working class activity and trade unionism, particularly in Colombo and its suburbs. A more intractable problem was the breakdown of the comparative harmony of interests and outlook which had characterized relations between Sinhalese and Tamil politicians in the first two decades of the twentieth century. Forseeing a transfer of a substantial measure of political power to the indigenous political leadership, minority groups led by the Tamils were increasingly anxious to protect their interests.

The constitutional reforms introduced in 1931 amounted to the first step towards self-government. Equally significant was the introduction of universal suffrage, which was the main determining factor in the re-emergence of "religious" nationalism, that is nationalism intertwined with Buddhist resurgence and its associated cultural heritage. Again, although the massive rural vote easily swamped the working class vote, universal suffrage strengthened the working class movement and opened the way for it to play an independent role in politics. By the early 1930s Marxists had established themselves in the leadership of the indigenous working class movement. On a different level universal suffrage was largely responsible for the broad impulse towards social welfare, especially in the years 1936–47. Among the most constructive achievements of this era was the purposeful programme of restoration of the irrigation schemes of the Dry Zone, and the settlement of colonists there, under the instigation of Stephen Senanayake, Minister of Agriculture and Lands for 15 years. The investment in education, health and food subsidies increased substantially, and this trend continued beyond 1947 to the detriment, it would seem, of economic growth.

The final phase in the transfer of power began under the leadership of Stephen Senanayake, the country's first Prime Minister, who was guided by a strong belief in ordered constitutional evolution to Dominion status on the analogy of constitutional development in the white dominions. In response to the agitation in Sri Lanka the British Government appointed the Soulbury Commission in 1944 to examine the constitutional problem there. The constitution that emerged from their deliberations was based substantially on one drafted for Senanayake in 1944 by his advisers. It gave the island internal self-government while retaining some Imperial safeguards in defence and external affairs, but Sri Lanka's leaders pressed, successfully, for the removal of these restrictions, and the island was granted independence, with Dominion status, on February 4th, 1948. The transfer of power was smooth and peaceful, a reflection of the moderate tone of the dominant strand of the country's nationalist movement. In general the situation in the country seemed to provide an impressive basis for a solid start in nation-building and national regeneration.

INDEPENDENCE AND AFTER, 1948-70

Stephen Senanayake's policies for the transfer of power in the early years of independence were based on his acceptance of the reality of a plural society. He sought the reconciliation of the legitimate interests of the majority and minority ethnic and religious groups within the context of an all-island polity. This held out the prospect of peace and stability in the vital first phase of independence. It was expected that the new Government would be threatened from the left but the Marxist parties were too divided to pose an effective challenge. Within a year of the grant of independence, Stephen Senanayake's United National Party (UNP) stabilized its position in the country and strengthened its hold on Parliament.

The first major challenge to the UNP-dominated Government emerged with Solomon Bandaranaike's formation of the Sri Lanka Freedom Party (SLFP) in September 1951, after he had crossed over to the opposition in July 1951. The SLFP's populist programme, offering social change, social justice and economic independence from foreign powers, emphasized economic development and economic equality. It was directed at the large protest vote that went to the Marxist parties for want of a democratic alternative to the UNP, and at the rural areas which formed the basis of the UNP's hold on political power in the country.

Stephen Senanayake's death in March 1952 seemingly stabilized the equilibrium of political forces he had established. When, in May 1952, his son and successor as Prime Minister, Dudley Senanayake, won a massive electoral victory, the verdict of the electorate was in many ways an endorsement of the life's work of Stephen Senanayake. Nevertheless, by the mid-1950s the UNP's position in the country was being undermined, even though its hold on Parliament appeared to be as strong as ever. The economy was faltering, after a period of prosperity, and an attempt to reduce the budgetary allocation for food subsidies provoked violent opposition, organized by the left-wing parties, in August 1953. Besides, religious, cultural and linguistic issues were gathering momentum and developing into a force too powerful for the existing social and political set-up to accommodate or absorb. Neither the Government nor its left-wing critics showed much understanding of the sense of outrage and indignation of the Buddhists at what they regarded as the historic injustices suffered by their religion under Western rule.

Solomon Bandaranaike successfully channelled this discontent into a massive campaign which swept the UNP out of office in 1956. His decisive victory was a significant point in Sri Lanka's history, for it represented the rejection of the concept of a Sri Lanka nationalism, based on plurality, which Stephen Senanayake had striven to nurture, and the substitution of a more democratic and populist nationalism which was at the same time fundamentally divisive in its impact on the country because it was unabashedly Sinhalese and Buddhist in content. Against the background of the worldwide celebration in 1956 of the 2,500th anniversary of the death of the Buddha an intense religious fervour became the catalyst of a populist nationalism whose explosive effect was derived from its interconnection with language. Language became the basis of nationalism and Sinhala nationalism was consciously or unconsciously treated as being identical with Sri Lanka nationalism, and this the minorities, especially the Tamils, rejected. As a result 1956 saw the beginning of almost a decade of ethnic and linguistic tensions erupting occasionally into race riots and religious confrontation.

With the emergence of this linguistic nationalism there was increased pressure for the close association of the state with Buddhism, and a corresponding decline of Christian influence. On the whole Bandaranaike's Government was much more cautious in handling matters relating to the Christian minority than it was on the language issue. This was a matter of prudence and priorities. The language struggle took precedence over all else, and there was no desire to add to the problems of the Government by taking on an issue which was just as combustible.

At the time of his assassination in September 1959, the culmination of a bitter struggle for power within his own party, Bandaranaike's hold on the electorate was not as strong as it had been in 1956–57. However, his assassination dramatically changed the political situation and, after a few months of drift and regrouping, the SLFP emerged, under the leadership of his widow, Sirimavo Bandaranaike, more powerful than ever before.

Unlike her husband, Sirimavo Bandaranaike was not reluctant to take on two inflammable issues at the same time. As well as pursuing her husband's policy on language, she made a determined bid to bring schools under state control and to secularize education, thus antagonizing the Roman Catholics as decisively as her language policy alienated the Tamils.

A wide variety of economic enterprises, foreign and local, were nationalized. Socialism was viewed as a means of redressing the balance in favour of the Sinhalese-Buddhists and Sri Lanka nationals in a situation in which the island's trade was largely dominated by foreign capitalists and the minorities were disproportionately influential within the indigenous capitalist class. This extension of state control over trade and industry was justified on the grounds that it helped to curtail the influence of foreign interests and the minorities.

Two significant events in 1964 were the Bandaranaike/Shastri pact, which laid the basis for an equitable settlement of Sri Lanka's Indian problem, and the establishment of a coalition Government between the SLFP and the Trotskyist Lanka Sama Samaja Party (LSSP). This shift to the left of the SLFP was designed to stabilize the Government after the political turmoil of the early years of Mrs. Bandaranaike's regime which saw extended periods of rule under emergency powers in the wake of ethnic and religious confrontations, and an abortive plot by high-ranking police, military and naval officers to overthrow the Government. While the dominance of the SLFP in national politics had resulted in a corresponding decline in the electoral fortunes of the Marxist groups, the *apertura a sinistra* was regarded as a necessity for keeping the UNP out of power. In joining the SLFP in a coalition, the LSSP came to accept the SLFP's stand on religion and did so in order to protect its mass base. However, far from stabilizing the Government, the SLFP's shift to the left had the immediate effect of causing a rift which precipitated its fall in December 1964, and contributed to its subsequent defeat in the general elections of March 1965.

Dudley Senanayake's UNP-dominated coalition enjoyed a five-year term of office. A resolute endeavour was made to maximize agricultural productivity, with self-sufficiency in food as the prime objective. The very considerable success achieved in this field gave the whole economy a boost. Yet, while its economic policies achieved substantial success, the Government's popularity was eroded by inflation and its conspicuous failure to solve the problem of educated unemployment. The rising expectations of an increasingly educated population had created an almost unmanageable problem for the Government. Sri Lanka, by now, was very much the example *par excellence* of population explosion.

Dudley Senanayake made ethnic and religious reconciliation the keynote of his policy. Yet his Government was placed on the defensive from the moment the Federal Party opted to join it in coalition. By a virulent campaign of ethnic hostility directed against Senanayake's policy of ethnic and religious reconciliation, the opposition prevented the Prime Minister from implementing some of the key legislative and administrative measures, which would have made his policy effective. The limits of that policy were thus clearly demonstrated.

It was evident that the two Bandaranaikes between them had established a new equilibrium of forces within the country, and that their supporters and associates, the Marxists groups, as well as their opponents had to accommodate themselves to this. The primary feature of the new balance of forces was the acceptance of the predominance of the Sinhalese Buddhists within the Sri Lanka polity, and a sharp decline in status of the ethnic and religious minorities.

THE UNITED FRONT IN POWER, 1970-1977

In their election campaign and their election manifesto of 1970, the parties of Mrs. Bandaranaike's United Front (UF)—the SLFP, the LSSP and the Communist Party (Moscow wing)—held out the distinct assurance of purposeful, systematic and fundamental changes in every sphere of life. However, the rhetorical flourishes indulged in during an acrimonious election campaign proved an embarrassment when economic conditions showed no sign of improvement and the number of unemployed did not decrease. Within a few weeks of their victory they were confronted by precisely the combination of factors that had brought down their predecessor—unemployment, rising prices and scarcities of food items—and the UF Government floundered just as badly as Dudley Senanayake's Government.

More significantly the pace of change and reform in the first ten months (after June 1970) of the Government's tenure of office proved inadequate to satisfy the desires of the more militant and articulate young people whose political aspirations had been whetted by the zest with which they had worked to bring the Government to power. By the middle of March 1971 it was evident that the Government faced a deadly threat from the Janata Vimukti Peramuna (JVP), an ultra-left organization dominated by educated youths, unemployed or disadvantageously employed. The insurrection that broke out in April 1971 was put down with considerable ruthlessness.

Though suppressed, the 1971 insurrection had a marked influence on future developments. It undoubtedly hastened the proceedings begun under the UF in 1970 for an autochthonous constitution for Sri Lanka; and it gave a tremendous impetus to the adoption of a series of radical economic and social changes, the most far-reaching of which were the Land Reform Law of 1972 and the nationalization of the plantations in 1975. During 1970–75 state control in trade and industry was accelerated and expanded to the point where the state had established a dominance of the commanding heights of the economy.

However, the economic situation grew rapidly worse. The serious balance of payments problem, inherited by the UF Government, was aggravated to a grave crisis partly through the operation of external forces beyond the Government's control. The crux of the problem was that the prices of the country's principal imports, particularly its food, rose to unprecedented heights, especially in 1973/74, while there was no corresponding rise in the price of its exports. The Government was compelled to trim food subsidies, which were absorbing too much foreign exchange, and cuts in welfare expenditure, begun in 1971, continued through 1973. The Government was also forced to adopt a strategy of agricultural development and domestic self-sufficiency in rice, which was precisely the one preached for so long and practised with greater sureness of touch by its main challenger, the UNP. With inflationary pressures never greatei and the problem of unemployment as serious as ever, the Government lost public support, as evidenced by its dismal record in by-elections to Parliament (by far the worst of any government since 1948). By the middle of 1972 the UNP had recovered from its *débâcle* at the 1970 polls and re-emerged as a viable democratic alternative to the UF regime.

To save itself from further embarrassment the Government tended to become increasingly authoritarian. No doubt this trend was originally an after-effect of the suppression of the rebellion in 1971, but it continued long after the threat to state security had disappeared.

A new republican and autochthonous constitution was adopted in May 1972 on the initiative of the UF Government. Under this constitution the state power of the republic was vested in the National State Assembly (a unicameral legislature). Thus one of its distinctive features was the absence of meaningful institutional or constitutional checks on executive power. While the new constitution was a notable landmark in the island's recent history, opposition parties were antagonized by two issues stemming from its adoption. Firstly, the ruling coalition gave itself an extended term of two years (to May 1977) beyond the five years for which it was elected in May 1970. Secondly, the adoption of the constitution gave rise to a new phase of communal antagonism in the island especially as regards relations between the Sinhalese and the indigenous Tamils.

A by-product of the increasing alienation of the Tamils has been the conversion of a large section of the Tamils of the north to the idea of a separate Tamil state. The most militant agitators for separatism are the educated unemployed, now a substantial element in Tamil society. In 1974 Mrs. Bandaranaike negotiated the settlement, on a firm and amicable basis, of the vexed question of the status of the Indians in Sri Lanka. Nearly half a million of them would eventually be integrated into the Sri Lanka polity, and Sri Lanka citizenship would confer on them the political legitimacy which, as an ethnic group, they had not had since 1948. But the Government's relations with the leadership of the Ceylon Workers' Congress, the most powerful trade union-cum-political party of the Indians in Sri Lanka, were as unfriendly as those with the leadership of the indigenous Tamils.

By 1975 sharp differences of opinion over the mechanics of the nationalization of foreign-owned plantations on the island triggered off acrimonious bickering between the SLFP and the LSSP, the two major components of the UF, which culminated in October 1975 in the expulsion of the LSSP from the Government. The political consequences were not immediately evident. On the contrary, the Government sought to stabilize its position by exploiting any political advantages to be gained from staging the Non-Aligned Nations Conference in Colombo in August 1976. Indeed, as if to give credence to this theory, the Government retained a parliamentary seat at a by-election in August 1976, its first such success since 1972.

One surprising, but ultimately ineffectual, move begun during the period of the conference was an attempt to secure a postponement of the general elections scheduled for mid-1977 by an amendment of the Constitution. A group of SLFP cabinet ministers opposed it, as did the Communist Party (CP). After a futile bid at a last-minute reconciliation with the Tamil United Liberation Front (TULF), the Government at last faced up to the reality of isolation in its bid to postpone the elections. Worse still, the coalition was disintegrating rapidly. By the end of February 1977 the UF coalition had been dissolved and what remained was a dispirited and demoralized SFLP Government confronting Sri Lanka's worst wave of strikes for 20 years, which had been engineered by its erstwhile coalition partners. For the first time since March 1960 there was no electoral pact against the UNP.

In the general elections the UNP, under the leadership of J. R. Jayawardene, won 140 out of 168 seats in the National State Assembly. Jayawardene, who had twice rebuilt the UNP following defeat in 1956, and again after he took control of it in 1973, appeared to have the prospect of certain victory during the last months of Mrs. Bandaranaike's regime, and more particularly throughout the election campaign.

THE UNP IN OFFICE, 1977 ONWARDS

No defeat in the annals of Sri Lanka's volatile parliamentary history has been quite as comprehensive as that suffered by the rivals of the UNP in July 1977. The SLFP found itself with only nine seats (it had had 90 in 1970), while every candidate of the Marxist left was defeated, many of them quite decisively. As a result of the peculiar demographic profile of the island, with a concentration of the Tamils in the north and, to a lesser extent, in the east of the island, the TULF, with only about one-fifth of the popular vote secured by the SLFP, had more than double the number of seats won by the SLFP and emerged as the main parliamentary opposition party. For the first time since independence a Tamil, Appapillai Amirthalingam, became Leader of the Opposition. This distortion of the electoral process would by itself have given an unusually sharp focus to minority rights since it ensured that, over the life of the new parliament, ethnic and language rights, rather than ideology, would be the basis of opposition to the Government. The outbreak of communal violence between the Sinhalese and Tamils in mid-August 1977, on a scale which bore comparison with the race-riots of the mid-1950s, brought the problem of relations between the two main ethnic groups of the island to the attention of the politicians.

The new Government stopped the conflagration with a mixture of firmness and restraint, and, more significantly, without resort to emergency rule. At the height of the disturbances it announced that a Commission of Inquiry would be appointed to examine the circumstances that had led to the outbreak of violence. On a more practical basis a series of administrative measures were taken to meet some of the long-standing grievances of the Tamils.

If these ethnic conflicts deflected the Government's attention from more pressing issues it was not for very long. High on its list of priorities was a reassessment of Sri Lanka's constitutional framework. In late September 1977 the National State Assembly adopted a constitutional amendment establishing a presidential form of government and the Prime Minister, Junius Jayawardene, became the first executive President of Sri Lanka on February 4th, 1978. The new Constitution, promulgated in September 1978, is a blend of some of the functional aspects of Sri Lanka's previous constitutions and features of the American, French and British systems of government, resulting in a presidential structure designed to meet Sri Lanka's special requirements and drawing on the experience of previous constitutions. One underlying theme was the rejection of many of the authoritarian features of the Constitution of 1972. There was also greater emphasis on the rights of the individual vis-a-vis the state and, even more significant in the context of the current crisis in relations between the Sinhalese and Tamils, on the rights of the minorities. Among other important innovations was the introduction of proportional representation on the list system in place of the "first-past-the-post" principle of representation which had been based on the British model.

The concessions made to the Tamil minority with regard to the status of their language in the Sri Lanka polity were a fulfilment of a pledge given in the Government's first statement of policy in the National State Assembly in August 1977, well before the outbreak of communal disturbances. Article 19 of the Constitution declared that Sinhala and Tamil were to be the national languages of Sri Lanka (with Sinhala remaining the sole official language), a major departure from the language policy established since the mid-1950s. Equally important was the abolition of the distinction between citizens by descent and citizens by registration, such as the Indian Tamils, thus removing the stigma of second-class citizenship attached to the latter. Combined with the lifting, in December 1977, of the bar on plantation workers resident on estates voting in local government elections, which had been in force since the 1930s, this ensured that citizens of Indian origin, in the main plantation workers, were treated on a par with Sri Lanka citizens by descent. The position of the Indians resident in Sri Lanka was further improved by affording to stateless persons the same civil rights guaranteed by the Constitution to citizens of the country.

No previous constitution, not even that of 1946–48, had offered the minorities a more secure position within the Sri Lanka polity. The Indian Tamils responded more positively to these conciliatory gestures than the TULF. When S. Thondaman, leader of the Ceylon Workers' Congress, the main political party cum trade union of the Indian plantation workers, entered the cabinet following the introduction of the new Constitution in September 1978, it marked a major breakthrough in Sri Lanka's politics for it brought the Indian Tamils within Sri Lanka's "political nation" for the first time since the 1930s. The TULF, now very much a party of the indigenous Tamils, had dissociated itself from the constitution-making and is anxious to emphasize its commitment to a separate state for the Tamils. They are all too conscious of the challenge they face from their youth wing, and especially an extremist terrorist group, the Tamil Tiger Liberation Movement, who are the most committed adherents of separatism and whose activities brought the country more than once, in 1979 and 1981, to the brink of another round of communal violence.

The Government averted a potentially dangerous conflagration by a mixture of firmness and conciliation. Special legislation, avowedly modelled on the British Prevention of Terrorism Bill, was rushed through Parliament in early 1979 and simultaneously a state of emergency was declared in the north of the island, with a military commander to co-ordinate security arrangements in Jaffna and to stamp out terrorism there. The emergency remained in force as it was intended to until December 31st, 1979. If these measures appeared to indicate a breakdown in communications between the Government and the TULF, relations between them improved considerably by the first week of August. On August 8th a Parliamentary Select Committee was appointed to investigate allegations made by the TULF, against the police, of atrocities committed in Jaffna in the wake of the recently imposed state of emergency. Then, on August 10th, came a more important decision: the establishment of a 10-member Presidential Commission to report on the decentralization of administration through the device of District Development Councils. Among the members of the Commission was a nominee of the TULF. These measures had the desired effect of restoring law and order in Jaffna, and paving the way for political initiatives, designed to restore communal harmony in the island. The state of emergency was lifted on the due date. The Presidential Commission completed its work in February 1980, and in August Parliament approved legislation establishing Development Councils as a measure of democratic decentralization. Elections were held for seats in these Councils in the 24 districts of the island on June 4th, 1981. The election campaign was orderly and peaceful except in Jaffna where the violence that erupted was quite unprecedented in Sri Lanka's long history of electoral politics. Fortunately the violence was contained within the Jaffna peninsula and did not spread to other parts of the island. More important, the establishment of these councils and their smooth functioning have helped to blunt the edges of separatist aspirations among the Tamils, and has given the restive Jaffna Peninsula what at present appears to be a durable peace.

The Jayawardene Government inherited a stagnant economy ravaged by inefficiency and corruption, and one in which, with the nationalization of the plantations, the state sector is in a position of overwhelming dominance. Unemployment was high and inflation a serious problem. The Government's budgetary policy has been far removed from that of its predecessors, and aims at creating a free market economy after almost 20 years of controls and restrictions. The rate of economic growth has improved quite dramatically since 1977 and the improvement has been sustained since 1978 at a uniformly high level. The key features of the Government's programme of economic activity are: the accelerated Mahaweli multi-purpose project; the establishment of an Export Processing Zone to the north of the city of Colombo; the Greater Colombo Development Scheme and several massive housing projects. Improved economic conditions in the country explain, to a large extent, the Government's success in the management of the "political market", in retaining the initiative in politics, and in keeping its rivals at bay.

In the local government elections in mid-May 1979 (the first to be held since 1969–70) the Government won as decisive a victory as it had achieved in the general elections of July 1977. The SLFP came a poor second, while the "old" left was routed once more. Only the TULF and, to a lesser extent, the "new" left had any significant successes. A similar pattern was discernible in the elections to the Development Councils, held in June 1981, except that, at the last moment, the sharply-divided SLFP leadership opted to boycott them. The traditional "left" had taken the same stand earlier on, but for different reasons. In the three by-elections held since 1979, the UNP retained Galle and wrested the rural Anamaduwa seat from the SLFP in 1980; the third by-election, held in January 1981 for the Kalawana seat, was won by the Communist Party. The UNP, which won the seat in 1977, did not contest it on this occasion. Indeed the *contretemps* over Kalawana caused the Government considerable embarrassment.

The Government has benefited substantially from the continuing disarray of its opponents. The decline of the "old" left is a notable factor in Sri Lanka's political scene. The most conspicuous evidence of this lies in the current state of the LSSP, the oldest of the island's Marxist parties. Just before the elections of 1977 a left-wing group had broken away and proceeded thereafter to wrest control of the main LSSP-led trade unions. In March 1982 yet another group (led this time by two former MP's who had been Cabinet Ministers in the short-lived SLFP-LSSP coalition of 1964) left the party, intent on taking their faction of the LSSP into the SLFP controlled by Mrs. Bandaranaike. The "new" left, with the factionalized JVP in the vanguard, is as hostile to the traditional left and the SLFP as it is to the Government. It is thus vocal and vigorous but not very effective as an anti-government force. Nevertheless, it is now the major left-wing force in the island. Nor is the SLFP yet in a position to mount an effective political challenge to the Government. Its morale was shattered by a dismal performance in the local government elections in 1977, the loss of the Anamaduwa seat in 1980, and a continuing leadership crisis which has been aggravated by Mrs. Bandaranaike's expulsion from Parliament on October 16th, 1980, after a Presidential Commission of Inquiry found her guilty on charges of abuse of power. The party is now split in two, and each of the warring factions, one led by Mrs. Bandaranaike and the other by her erstwhile deputy Maithripala Senanayake, claims to be the official SLFP. In this situation the Government has much greater room for manoeuvre to deal with economic problems, such as inflation and high unemployment, than if it had been faced with a cohesive opposition under a leadership with a reputation untarnished by association with the events of the early and mid-1970s.

ECONOMIC SURVEY

S. W. R. de A. Samarasinghe

In many respects Sri Lanka's economy is typical of that of a "small" developing country. In 1981 income per caput was a modest U.S. $265. About half of those who were gainfully employed were in agriculture. Earnings from the export of three primary products (tea, rubber and coconut) accounted, on average, for about 60 per cent of total visible export earnings and for about one-sixth of the national income during 1979–81. In contrast the country's manufacturing industry contributed only 12 per cent to the national product. Against a backdrop of a doubling of the population from 7.5 million to almost 15.0 million between Independence in 1948 and 1981, the creation of sufficient job opportunities for a rapidly growing labour force has become the single most pressing socio-economic problem.

Ever since Independence the state has played a *dirigisme* role in the economy, both in its capacity as a regulator of private sector activity and as a direct producer in industry and agriculture. However, the United National Party (UNP) Government, elected to office in July 1977, undertook several far-reaching economic reforms in order to reduce state control and to provide greater incentives to the private sector. The main features of the reform programme were the liberalization of imports, reductions in exchange controls, price controls and rationing, the virtual abolition of the state's monopoly in the import of certain key goods, the establishment of a unified (and floating) exchange rate, and lowering of corporate and personal taxes. According to the Minister of Finance and Planning, Ronnie de Mel, the purpose of the reforms was to move the economy away from "inward looking policies (that) had led to . . . a disastrous misallocation of resources (and) to set it on a path that would lead to self-sustained growth and development".

GROSS DOMESTIC PRODUCT

The Gross Domestic Product (G.D.P.) for 1980 at current factor cost prices has been provisionally estimated at Rs. 78,506 million (Rs. 20,706 million at constant 1970 factor cost prices). The composition of real G.D.P. has undergone a moderate change between the early 1970s and the early 1980s. The value of mining and quarrying has risen from 0.8 per cent of G.D.P. in 1970–72 to 1.9 in 1979–81, that of construction from 5.3 to 8.3 per cent and that of banking from 1.2 to 2.9 per cent. The share of transport has fallen from 9.5 per cent to 8.7 and that of trade from 19.9 to 17.4 per cent. However, the shares of agriculture (33 per cent), manufacturing (11 per cent), electricity, gas, water and sanitary services (0.9 per cent) have remained practically unchanged. In each of the two years 1980–81 G.D.P. grew in real terms by 5.8 per cent, which, although higher than the average rate of growth achieved in the early and mid-1970s, was lower than the 8.2 and 6.2 per cent achieved in 1978 and 1979 respectively.

AGRICULTURE

The Sri Lankan economy is dominated by its agriculture. According to the Labour Force and Socio-Economic Survey 1980/81 2.17 million people (45.9 per cent of the labour force) were employed in that sector. It has been the normal practice to divide Sri Lanka's agriculture into an export-oriented plantation sector, specializing in cash crops, and a subsistence-oriented peasant sector specializing in food crops. The agricultural labour force divides itself roughly equally between the two sectors. In Sri Lanka about 1.7 million hectares (25 per cent of the total land area) have been cultivated. Of this amount, about 1.0 million hectares (58 per cent of cultivated land) are under plantation crops and the remainder under food crops. In recent times, however, the distinction between plantation and peasant agriculture has become increasingly blurred. On the one hand, the bulk of the coconut crop and a significant proportion of rubber and tea are produced by "smallholders" who belong to the peasant sector. On the other hand, the peasant sector, growing food crops, has steadily become commercialized.

Export Crops

All three principal export crops are grown largely in the south-west quadrant (Wet Zone) of the island which receives a well-distributed and reliable rainfall of over 190 cm. per year. Tea is grown in elevations ranging from a few hundred metres above sea level to above 2,000 metres, although teas with the best flavours are usually found at elevations above 1,200 metres. Rubber is grown mostly on slopes below 600 metres from sea level, and coconut is concentrated on the western and southern lowlands. In addition to these three staples, Sri Lanka also cultivates a number of minor plantation crops such as cocoa, pepper, cloves, nutmeg, cardamom, cinnamon and citronella. It was estimated that in 1980 about 250,000 hectares were cultivated with tea, 225,000 hectares with rubber, and 450,000 hectares with coconut. The minor plantation crops together accounted for a further 40,000 hectares.

Since 1940 two important changes have occurred in Sri Lanka's plantation sector. The first is the transfer of ownership from European to local interests. Before 1972 this meant the purchase of estates from their European owners by Ceylonese entrepreneurs and, to a lesser extent, by the Government. In 1972 and 1975, under the Land Reform, a large proportion of the estates owned by foreign and local private individuals and all estates owned by public companies were nationalized with compensation. Today about 60 per cent of the tea land, 30 per cent of the rubber, and 10 per cent of the coconut are owned by the state. The second change is the fragmentation of some of the larger estates into smaller units, caused partly by the pressure of population on land, partly by the practice of dividing large estates into smaller units when selling, and partly by the Governments' policy of land redistribution. Nevertheless, the bulk of Sri Lanka's tea (210,000 metric tons in 1981) and around two-thirds of its rubber (124,000 tons in 1981) are produced on estates of 8 hectares or more.

State-aided schemes have been in operation since the 1950s to replant tea and rubber land with high-yielding varieties. This effort has been more successful in rubber, where, by the end of 1981, almost 70 per cent of the total area had been replanted. In tea the proportion was only 16 per cent. Under a state-sponsored crop diversification programme, an effort is also being made to put uneconomical tea and rubber lands to more profitable agricultural uses.

Food Crops

According to the 1981 Census, only an estimated 21.5 per cent of Sri Lanka's population lived in urban areas. No less than 72 per cent lived in rural areas (excluding estates) which is a true measure of the importance of peasant agriculture in the life of the community.

Paddy rice is the pre-eminent crop in peasant agriculture, having about 580,000 hectares—one-third of all cultivated land—under asweddumized conditions, spread throughout the island. However, when adequate irrigation is available, the Dry Zone (i.e. the drier parts of the country outside the south-west quadrant) is considered to be better suited to paddy.

Only about 25 per cent of Sri Lanka's paddy land consists of units of two hectares or more. About 43 per cent consists of units of one hectare or under. Thus the 1972 Land Reform, which fixed a ceiling of 10.1 hectares on paddy holdings per family, left paddy ownership practically untouched. However, the small size of the typical paddy unit reflects the severe pressure on existing land, especially in the densely-populated Wet Zone of the country. The settlement of farming families on undeveloped state-owned land in the Dry Zone (land colonization) has been the Government's answer to this problem. This programme, which began in the mid-1930s, has received a major boost under the Accelerated Mahaweli Diversion Programme. When completed, this is expected to provide irrigation for about 260,000 hectares of new land and a further 100,000 hectares of land already under cultivation. Under its original plan, the Programme was to be completed in 30 years (1969–98). However, the present Government has accelerated its implementation with the help of large amounts of foreign aid—the total estimated cost at 1977 prices was Rs. 22,400 million or 65 per cent of that year's G.N.P.—from the World Bank and other Western donors, and hopes to complete the Programme by 1983.

Since the early 1950s paddy cultivation has shown one of the most impressive growth records in the Sri Lankan economy. The annual output of paddy quadrupled from about 450,000 metric tons in the early 1950s to about 1.8 million metric tons in the late 1970s as a result of both an expansion in area under cultivation and a rise in land productivity under the impact of the "Green Revolution". In 1981, helped by a substantial increase in fertilizer application, favourable prices and good weather, both the total output (2.2 million metric tons) and the average yield (3,014 kg. per hectare) reached record levels, making Sri Lanka about three-quarters self-sufficient in rice.

MINERAL AND POWER RESOURCES

No comprehensive assessment has been made of Sri Lanka's mineral resources. However, the country has a variety of economically useful minerals such as gem stones, graphite, ilmenite, limestone, quartz, mica, industrial clays, salt, titanium, monazite and zircon. There are no known deposits of coal or petroleum, although exploration for the latter is continuing in north-west Sri Lanka.

A few local industries, such as ceramics, cement, glass, salt and bricks, are based on extraction of minerals. Graphite and gem stones are the only two minerals that are extracted in commercially significant quantities for export. In 1980 Sri Lanka exported graphite valued at Rs. 80 million (less than 0.15 per cent of the total value of visible exports). Due to a number of incentives offered by the Government, the production and export of gem stones rose significantly over the 1970s. Although no production figures are available, State Gem Corporation data indicate that the value of exports rose from U.S. $1.5 million in 1972 to U.S. $32.7 million in 1981.

The bulk of Sri Lanka's electricity is generated through hydro-electric power. Since 1979, due to a sharp rise in the demand for electricity, the Government has been forced to supplement hydro-electric power with gas turbines which are more expensive to run than hydro-turbines. At the end of 1981 Sri Lanka's installed capacity in electricity was 501 MW. This is expected to increase substantially and ease the electricity shortage when the various power projects under the Accelerated Mahaweli Programme come on stream.

MANUFACTURING INDUSTRY

In 1958 Sri Lanka's manufacturing sector (including cottage industries) accounted for barely 6 per cent of G.D.P. In the 1960s, with the help of a protected market, it grew at some 6 per cent per annum and by the end of the decade contributed about 10 per cent of G.D.P.

The production of producer goods is less important than the production of consumer goods in Sri Lanka's manufacturing industry. Almost all the large-scale manufacturing units are run by state industrial corporations, of which there were 26 at the end of 1980. The private sector covers a wide range of light consumer goods industries and a few producer goods industries such as machine tools and building materials. Although the Government continues to control the establishment of new industrial units through the Local Investment Approvals Committee (LIAC), the Foreign Investment Approvals Committee (FIAC) and the Greater Colombo Economic Commission (GCEC), the more liberal policies of the present Government have given the private industrialist a freer hand.

The GCEC was established in 1978 to promote investment, especially foreign private investment, in export-oriented industry in an Investment Promotion Zone (IPZ), north of Colombo, covering 518 sq. km. The Commission has statutory powers to grant a wide range of concessions to investors, including tax "holidays" of seven to 10 years. By the end of 1981, 68 firms had signed contracts with the GCEC to establish various industries while 41 firms, with 19,921 employees, were in commercial production. Gross export earnings from the IPZ amounted to Rs. 802 million in 1981.

FOREIGN TRADE AND BALANCE OF PAYMENTS

Sri Lanka has suffered from a chronic deficit in the balance of trade and of payments since the late 1950s. The combined impact of import liberalization coupled with increased economic activity, an adverse movement in the terms of trade, and either stagnant or falling output in the three major exports worsened this situation after 1977. In 1981 Sri Lanka's trade deficit was Rs. 16,200 million (21 per cent of G.N.P.).

In 1980 the U.S.A. was the largest purchaser of Sri Lanka's exports, accounting for about 11 per cent of the total value, followed by Australia and the United Kingdom. Japan was the leading supplier of Sri Lanka's imports, accounting for 13 per cent of the total, followed by Saudi Arabia and the United Kingdom.

Balance of Payments

In 1981, whereas the merchandise account recorded a deficit of Rs. 16,200 million, the services account recorded a small surplus of Rs. 136 million. Receipts from services amounted to Rs. 5,800 million, with tourism contributing Rs. 2,270 million (11.1 per cent of total visible export earnings). However, interest payments on the foreign debt claimed back over one-third of the former sum. Nevertheless the overall deficit in the current account balance was reduced to Rs. 9,000 million with the help of substantial net private and official transfers (Rs. 3,800 and Rs. 3,100 respectively), a large proportion of the former coming from remittances of Sri Lankan workers in West Asia and Africa.

About 60 per cent of the current account deficit of Rs. 9,000 million was financed with project and commodity loans and the balance with credit from banks and several other sources. A noteworthy development was the receipt of Rs. 800 million of foreign private investment in Sri Lanka. A sum of Rs. 400 million from Sri Lanka's external reserves was also used to bridge the deficit. The unsatisfactory external payments situation in 1981 adversely affected the international value of the Sri Lankan rupee, which depreciated on average by about 71 per cent over the year against several major foreign currencies.

FINANCE

Banking

The Central Bank of Ceylon has a monopoly on the issue of the currency and also acts as a financial adviser to the Government and administers monetary policy. In recent years it has also played an important role in helping to develop credit facilities for groups such as peasant farmers, who normally do not enjoy access to established lending institutions.

The commercial banking system of Sri Lanka is dominated by the two state-owned banks, the Bank of Ceylon and the People's Bank, which between them accounted for about 80 per cent of total bank deposits at the end of 1981. By the end of that year there was a bank office for every 16,000 of Sri Lanka's inhabitants, most of the offices being branches of the two state banks. In 1981 alone, 57 new bank offices were established in the country.

In 1979 there were two important new developments in Sri Lanka's banking. One was the decision to allow foreign banks to open branches in Sri Lanka with a view to attracting foreign investment. By the end of 1981 twenty foreign banks had opened branch offices in Colombo. The second was the establishment of the Foreign Currency Banking Units (FCBUs) in commercial banks, as a prelude to the development of an offshore banking centre in Sri Lanka. FCBUs were allowed to deal in foreign currency with non-residents, "approved residents" and firms affiliated to the GCEC. By the end of 1981, 23 such banking units, with total assets amounting to U.S. $366 million, were in operation.

Public Finance

In 1981 total central government expenditure amounted to Rs. 31,000 million and total revenue to Rs. 16,200 million (40 per cent and 21 per cent of G.N.P. respectively). Almost three-fifths (Rs. 8,300 million) of the budget deficit of Rs. 14,800 million was financed with foreign finance and the remainder with funds borrowed from local sources, including the banking system.

The principal sources of government revenue in Sri Lanka are income and profits taxes, business turnover taxes, excise duties, and tariffs on imports and exports. Although government expenditure has risen much faster than revenue in recent years, the growth of revenue itself has kept slightly ahead of the growth of G.N.P.: the revenue-to-G.N.P. ratio having risen from 19.4 per cent in 1977 to 21.1 per cent in 1981.

ECONOMIC DEVELOPMENT

Performance

In broad terms the present Government's export-oriented and liberal economic strategy has led to a revival of economic activity. Between 1978-81 total investment spending has doubled in real terms. Rough estimates suggest that during the same period about 600,000 new jobs were created making a substantial impact on the unemployment situation. In agriculture, paddy output increased by 33 per cent between 1977 and 1981. Manufacturing output increased in real terms by about 6.5 per cent per year over 1978–81 and the value of exports of manufactures (excluding petroleum products) increased five-fold from SDR 31 million to SDR 162 million between 1977 and 1981. Under the public sector housing programmes, the target is to build 132,000 housing units over the period 1978–83. Of this number, 57,000 (43 per cent) had been completed by the end of 1981 and another 24,000 (8 per cent) were under construction.

Problems and Prospects

The deceleration in the rate of growth from 8.2 per cent in 1978 to 5.8 per cent in 1980–81 may be said to be a return to a more normal growth path that is sustainable over a long period. However, the Government is bound to view with concern the fact that in the two year period 1980–81 only 60,000 new jobs were created in the state and the organized private sector (the annual net addition to the labour force is 125,000), compared with about 260,000 in 1978–79. Moreover, several other disturbing features in the economic picture have emerged. The growth of output has been too biased in favour of the construction industry and trade, especially the import trade. In sharp contrast, agriculture has not done too well. Although the production of minor food crops made a recovery in 1980–81, their overall performance has been poor since 1977. A cause for even greater concern is the inability of the export agriculture sector to make a rapid and steady recovery from the sluggish conditions it experienced in the 1970s. Although there was an overall increase of 7.5 per cent in its output in 1981 on account of increases in tea and coconut output, rubber declined to 124 million kg., the lowest in a decade. The poor performance in staple export production together with the deteriorating international commodity terms of trade has worsened Sri Lanka's external payments situation and increased its dependence on foreign aid. In manufacturing, certain industries—such as fabricated metal products, machinery and transport equipment production, handloom textiles—have suffered because of import liberalization. Admittedly, excessive protection in the past has led to the creation of many inefficient industrial units. Nevertheless there is a widely shared belief that there are still some industries with good future potential that should be protected from cheap imports for a further period of time. The pronounced bias in the IPZ towards the textile and garments industry has also invited criticism, chiefly because there is concern that textile manufacturers from the Far East are using the IPZ to "corner" a part of the export quotas allocated to Sri Lanka by Western countries. Moreover, at present the textile and garments industry in the IPZ has a relatively low domestic-value-added and normally does not bring new technology into the country. In 1981 no less than 88 per cent of the gross export earnings of the IPZ were from textiles and garments. However, this situation will probably change in the future because the GCEC has begun to discourage new investment in this field.

The rapid rise in economic activity has also strained the capacity of certain vital sectors to service the economy. The shortage of skilled manpower—aggravated by immigration to West Asia and Africa—is one such example.

The other major concern is inflation, which was running at an annual rate of about 40 per cent in 1980. As a consequence, the real wages of fixed income earners, especially those in government employment, dropped sharply in that year. The Government, partly in response to pressure from the IMF and the World Bank, tried to dampen inflation by cutting public sector investment spending—including spending on the Mahaweli Programme and Urban and Housing Development, which are two "lead" projects—and by applying a "credit squeeze" on bank lending to the private and state corporation sectors. These measures helped to reduce the annual rate of inflation to a figure below 20 per cent in 1981. However, it was also evidence that the cutbacks adversely affected economic growth and employment.

Compared with Singapore, Taiwan and other newly industrializing countries, Sri Lanka was perhaps 15 years too late in embarking on an export-industry-led growth strategy. Today, with "stagflation" and protectionism in the world economy at large, it is that much more difficult to break into world markets. Nevertheless, given Sri Lanka's resources, the country probably has no other viable option.

STATISTICAL SURVEY

AREA AND POPULATION

AREA (including inland water)	POPULATION							DENSITY (per sq. km.)
	Census Results							
	July 8th, 1963	October 9th, 1971			March 17th, 1981†			
		Total	Males	Females	Total	Males	Females	1981†
65,610 sq. km.*	10,582,064	12,689,897	6,531,361	6,158,536	14,850,001	7,539,128	7,310,893	230.0

* 25,332 sq. miles. † Provisional.

Source: Department of Census and Statistics, Colombo.

ETHNIC GROUPS

	1971	1981
Sinhalese	9,131,000	10,986,000
Ceylon Tamil	1,424,000	1,872,000
Indian Tamil	1,175,000	825,000
Ceylon Moors	828,000	1,057,000
Others	132,000	110,000
TOTAL	12,690,000	14,850,000

DISTRICTS

	AREA (sq. km., excl. inland water)	POPULATION * (1981 census)	DENSITY * (persons per sq. km.)
Colombo	652.4	1,698,322	2,603
Gampaha	1,398.8	1,389,490	993
Kalutara	1,606.6	827,189	515
Kandy	2,157.5	1,126,296	522
Matale	1,988.6	357,441	180
Nuwara-Eliya	1,437.2	522,219	363
Galle	1,673.9	814,579	487
Matara	1,246.5	644,231	517
Hambantota	2,593.4	424,102	164
Jaffna	2,072.3	831,112	401
Mannar	2,002.1	106,940	53
Vavuniya	2,645.2	95,904	36
Mullattivu	1,966.1	77,512	39
Batticaloa	2,464.6	330,899	134
Amparai	4,539.2	388,786	86
Trincomalee	2,618.2	256,790	98
Kurunegala	4,772.8	1,212,755	254
Puttalam Chilee	2,976.9	493,344	166
Anuradhapura	7,129.2	587,822	82
Polonnaruwa	3,403.8	262,753	77
Badulla	2,818.2	642,893	228
Moneragala	5,586.9	279,743	50
Ratnapura	3,238.8	796,468	246
Kegalle	1,662.8	682,411	410
TOTAL	64,652.0	14,850,001	230

* Provisional.

Source: Registrar General's Office.

PRINCIPAL TOWNS

(1981 census results)

Colombo (capital)	586,000	Kandy*	101,000
Dehiwala-Mount Lavinia	174,000	Galle	77,000
Jaffna	118,000		

* Provisional.

Source: Department of Census and Statistics, Colombo.

Births and Deaths (1979 provisional): 415,695 births registered (birth rate 28.7 per 1,000); 94,190 deaths registered (death rate 6.5 per 1,000); 1980 provisional: 407,243 births registered (birth rate 27.6 per 1,000); 89,325 deaths registered (death rate 6.1 per 1,000).

Source: FAO, *Production Yearbook.*

AGRICULTURE

PRINCIPAL CROPS

	Area ('000 hectares)			Production ('000 metric tons)		
	1978	1979	1980*	1978	1979	1980*
Rice (paddy)	839	790	999	1,890	1,917	2,383
Maize	25	19	20	20	22	22
Millet	35	26	35	21	16	20
Potatoes	3	4	4	29	38	38
Sweet potatoes	21	16	16	133	149	148
Cassava (Manioc)	74	54	55	586	535	530
Dry beans	13*	13*	13	6*	7*	7
Sesame seed	12	26	25	5	10	10
Coconuts	n.a.	n.a.	n.a.	1,677	1,819	1,550†
Copra	n.a.	n.a.	n.a.	132	166	126
Chillies	50	36	35	39	46	46
Onions	8	9	9	58	68	67
Sugar cane	6*	7*	5	310*	325*	265
Cashew nuts	n.a.	n.a.	n.a.	0.8	0.9	0.9
Coffee	7	7	7	12	10	10
Cocoa beans	9	8	8	2†	2†	2
Tea	243	244	240	199	206	191
Tobacco	11*	11*	11	7*	8*	8
Natural rubber	n.a.	n.a.	n.a.	156	153	155

* FAO estimates. † Unofficial estimates.

Source: FAO, *Production Yearbook.*

LIVESTOCK

('000 head, year ending September 30th)

	1978	1979	1980	1981
Buffaloes	814	844	843	898
Cattle	1,542	1,623	1,644	1,720
Sheep	23	24	28	30
Goats	450	461	493	512
Pigs	41	49	71	93
Chickens	4,912	5,882	6,341	6,296
Ducks	13	16	22	25

Source: Department of Census and Statistics.

LIVESTOCK PRODUCTS

('000 metric tons)

	1978	1979	1980*
Beef and veal	13	12	12
Buffalo meat*	6	6	6
Goats' meat*	1	1	1
Pig meat*	1	1	1
Poultry meat*	10	11	11
Cows' milk	178	167	167
Buffaloes' milk	47	52	53
Goats' milk*	5	6	6
Hen eggs*	16.6	19.9	20.3
Cattle and buffalo hides*	4.8	4.5	4.5

* FAO estimates.

Source: FAO, *Production Yearbook*.

FORESTRY

ROUNDWOOD REMOVALS

('000 cubic metres, all non-coniferous)

	1973	1974	1975	1976	1977	1978	1979
Sawlogs, veneer logs and logs for sleepers	87	92	97	65	53	113	142
Other industrial wood*	400	410	419	428	436	445	454
Fuel wood*	6,306	6,407	6,514	6,627	6,746	6,870	6,995
TOTAL	6,793	6,909	7,030	7,120	7,235	7,428	7,591

* FAO estimates.

Source: FAO, *Yearbook of Forest Products*.

SAWNWOOD PRODUCTION

('000 cubic metres, all non-coniferous)

	1973	1974	1975	1976	1977	1978	1979
Sawnwood (incl. boxboards)	8	18	23	27	21	57	71
Railway sleepers	15	15	15	10	4	4	4
TOTAL	23	33	38	37	25	61	75

* FAO estimates.

Source: FAO, *Yearbook of Forest Products.*

FISHING*

('000 metric tons)

	1976	1977	1978	1979	1980	1981
Inland waters:						
Freshwater fishes	12.5	13.0	16.7	17.3	20.3	27.7
Indian Ocean:						
Marine fishes	123.3	125.7	139.8	151.0	167.4	177.0
Crustaceans and molluscs (cured fish)	8.1	6.7	4.3	6.2	8.7	8.9
TOTAL CATCH	143.9	145.4	160.8	174.5	196.4	213.6

* Excluding (*a*) quantities landed by Sri Lanka craft in foreign ports, and (*b*) quantities landed by foreign craft in Sri Lanka ports.

Source: Ministry of Fisheries.

MINING

		1977	1978	1979	1980	1981
Natural graphite (exports)	metric tons	8,059	11,416	9,491	7,656	7,453
Mica (crude)	,, ,,	n.a.	100.8	367.4	145.0	182.0
Sand, silica and quartz	'000 metric tons	n.a.	4.9†	—		
Salt (unrefined)	,, ,, ,,	46	115*	123.3	114	104

Ilmenite, Rutile and Zircon (metric tons): 50,595 (1978); 71,409 (1979); 44,867* (1980).

* Provisional. † Consumption.

Source: Ceylon Mineral Sand Corporation.

INDUSTRY

SELECTED PRODUCTS

		1978	1979	1980	1981*
Beer	'000 hectolitres	81	71	74	53
Cigarettes	million	5,097	4,637	5,226	5,539
Cotton yarn	'000 metric tons	8.5	8.5	6.5	8.6
Cotton fabrics	million sq. metres	47	46	n.a.	n.a.
Cement	'000 metric tons	575	662	623	706
Raw sugar	,, ,, ,,	26	19	26	25

* Provisional.

FINANCE

100 cents = 1 Sri Lanka rupee.

Coins: 1, 2, 5, 10, 25 and 50 cents; 1 and 2 rupees.

Notes: 2, 5, 10, 20, 50 and 100 rupees.

Exchange rates (June 1982): £1 sterling = 35.99 rupees; U.S. $1 = 20.78 rupees.
1,000 Sri Lanka rupees = £27.78 = $48.12.

Note: Between September 1949 and November 1967 the Ceylon (now Sri Lanka) rupee was valued at 21 U.S. cents (U.S. $1 = 4.7619 rupees). In November 1967 the rupee was devalued by 20 per cent to 16.8 U.S. cents ($1 = 5.9524 rupees) and this valuation remained in effect until August 1971 and from November 1971 to July 1972. In terms of sterling, the exchange rate was £1 = 14.286 rupees from November 1967 to November 1971; and £1 = 15.510 rupees from December 1971 to June 1972. In 1968 a second rate was established, at a large premium over the official rate, through a system of "foreign exchange entitlement certificates" for certain exports and other earners of foreign exchange. From July 1972 to May 1976 the Sri Lanka authorities maintained an official exchange rate against sterling at a mid-point of £1 = 15.60 rupees, thus allowing the rupee's value to fluctuate against other currencies in line with sterling ("floating" since June 1972). In May 1976 the direct link with sterling was ended and the rupee's value has since been determined in relation to a weighted "basket" of currencies of Sri Lanka's trading partners. In November 1977 the two-tier exchange rate system was ended and since then the rupee has been "floating". The average market rate (rupees per U.S. dollar) was 6.405 in 1973; 6.649 in 1974; 7.050 in 1975; 8.459 in 1976; 9.153 in 1977; 15.608 in 1978; 15.569 in 1979; 16.534 in 1980; 19.248 in 1981.

BUDGET

(million rupees)

Revenue	1980	1981*	Expenditure	1980†	1981*
General sales and turnover taxes	1,640.1	2,720.0	Defence	1,088.5	1,077.5
Selective sales taxes	1,877.6	2,005.1	Foreign affairs	149.9	147.9
Import levies	2,924.9	3,100.0	Plan implementation	882.6	725.7
Export levies	3,638.2	3,765.0	Lands and land development	1,045.5	802.1
Receipts from foreign exchange entitlement certificates	0.1	—	Education	1,559.1	1,988.4
			Higher education	306.9	308.5
Income taxes	2,086.0	1,940.0	Power	778.1	533.7
Gross receipts from government trading enterprises	835.8	1,095.7	Public administration	752.8	949.0
Interest, profits and dividends	250.5	156.0	Local government, housing and construction	2,385.3	2,128.1
Sales and charges	208.6	161.5	Industries and scientific affairs	1,214.1	126.2
			Finance and planning	4,912.4	6,866.9
			Transport	2,300.4	1,110.6
			Agricultural development and research	1,016.3	931.1
			Mahaweli development	3,536.0	3,036.2
			Rural industries development	125.9	164.2
			Posts and telecommunications	805.9	668.1
			Health	944.5	997.1
			Food and co-operatives	1,930.6	1,725.3
			Highways	530.5	334.8
Total (incl. others)	14,068.4	15,550.2	Total (incl. others)	28,221.1	26,901.8

* Approved estimates.

INTERNATIONAL RESERVES
(U.S. $ million at December 31st)

	1977	1978	1979	1980
Gold . . .	—	2	3	3
IMF Special Drawing Rights . . .	24	34	29	—
Foreign exchange	269	363	488	246
TOTAL .	293	399	520	249

MONEY SUPPLY
(million rupees at December 31st)

	1977	1978	1979	1980
Currency outside banks	2,792	3,016	3,774	4,181
Demand deposits at commercial banks .	2,526	2,863	3,857	5,139

Sources: Central Bank of Ceylon and IMF, *International Financial Statistics.*

COST OF LIVING
CONSUMER PRICE INDEX, COLOMBO
(base: 1970=100)

	1973	1974	1975	1976	1977	1978	1979	1980	1981
Food . . .	121.7	138.9	149.6	148.0	148.9	173.9	192.8	248.7	292.5
Fuel and light . .	120.8	162.4	174.2	194.9	189.2	192.6	241.4	414.3	564.2
Clothing . . .	135.5	149.0	151.6	154.2	163.0	164.8	168.4	174.7	187.8
Rent	100.0	100.0	100.0	100.0	100.0	100.0	100.0	100.0	100.0
ALL ITEMS .	119.7	134.4	143.5	145.2	147.0	164.8	182.6	230.2	271.6

Source: Department of Census and Statistics.

GROSS DOMESTIC PRODUCT BY ORIGIN
(million rupees at current prices)

	1976	1977*	1978*	1979*
Agriculture, hunting, forestry and fishing .	8,657	11,249	12,736	13,241
Mining and quarrying	639	595	732	947
Manufacturing	5,620	8,023	8,289	10,418
Construction	1,164	1,133	1,965	3,218
Electricity, gas, water and sanitary services .	171	194	239	398
Transport, storage and communications .	2,286	2,723	3,232	4,643
Wholesale and retail trade . . .	5,456	6,239	6,991	8,140
Banking, insurance and real estate . . .	419	542	845	1,243
Ownership of dwellings	468	476	533	1,269
Public administration and defence . .	948	1,177	1,516	1,664
Other services	2,470	2,852	3,257	3,944
G.D.P. AT FACTOR COST	28,498	34,933	40,335	49,125
Net factor income from abroad . . .	−282	−252	−237	−240
G.N.P. AT FACTOR COST	28,216	34,681	40,098	48,885
Indirect taxes, less subsidies	906	1,004	2,060	2,776
G.N.P. AT MARKET PRICES . . .	29,122	35,685	42,158	51,661

* Provisional.

Source: Central Bank of Ceylon.

BALANCE OF PAYMENTS

(U.S. $ million)

	1975	1976	1977	1978	1979	1980
Merchandise exports f.o.b.	555.0	556.4	747.1	845.6	981.3	1,061.7
Merchandise imports f.o.b.	−681.9	−576.3	−644.9	−898.8	−1,304.6	−1,845.1
TRADE BALANCE	−126.9	−19.9	102.2	−53.2	−323.3	−783.4
Exports of services	80.1	76.1	103.3	125.1	192.7	278.4
Imports of services	−142.1	−127.0	−138.8	−216.8	−290.0	−430.8
BALANCE ON GOODS AND SERVICES	−188.9	−70.8	66.7	−144.9	−420.6	−935.8
Unrequited transfers (net): Private	2.7	6.7	10.4	22.0	48.2	136.3
Government	76.9	57.6	58.2	55.6	141.6	136.3
CURRENT BALANCE	−109.3	−6.5	135.3	−67.3	−230.8	−663.2
Direct capital investment (net)	0.1	0.0	−1.0	1.5	47.0	43.0
Other long-term capital (net)	89.2	71.7	71.6	117.2	126.8	165.6
Short-term capital (net)	−3.5	−29.2	−79.4	−32.4	11.9	116.0
Net errors and omissions	−2.3	0.1	14.8	−17.8	51.1	22.8
TOTAL (net monetary movements)	−25.8	36.1	141.3	1.2	6.0	−315.8
Allocation of IMF Special Drawing Rights					16.0	16.3
Valuation changes (net)	−15.8	−14.4	4.5	11.4	−1.0	13.0
IMF Subsidy Account grants	—	0.6	2.0	2.1	2.2	1.8
IMF Trust Fund loans	—	—	—	50.1	38.5	32.5
Official financing (net)	—	2.5	2.5	5.5	−7.3	20.5
CHANGES IN RESERVES	−41.6	24.8	150.3	70.3	54.4	−231.7

Source: IMF, *International Financial Statistics.*

EXTERNAL TRADE

(million rupees, excluding gold)

	1974	1975	1976	1977	1978	1979	1980	1981
Imports c.i.f.	4,554	5,251	4,645	6,007	14,687	22,560	33,637	35,530
Exports f.o.b.	3,472	3,933	4,815	6,638	13,206	15,273	17,273	19,740

Source: Customs Returns of Ceylon.

PRINCIPAL COMMODITIES

(million rupees)

IMPORTS	1979	1980	1981
Rice	884	755	860
Flour	1,691	1,786	25
Sugar	929	1,915	2,662
Petroleum products	4,143	8,681	8,904
Machinery and equipment	2,993	4,941	5,106
Wheat	—	554	1,872
TOTAL (incl. others)	22,560	33,637	35,530

EXPORTS	1979	1980	1981
Tea	5,722	6,170	6,444
Rubber	2,491	2,590	2,895
Coconut oil	509	49	200
Copra	13	5	42
Desiccated coconut	775	701	768
Precious and semi-precious stones	490	664	634
Other exports	5,228	6,999	8,305
TOTAL (incl. re-exports)	15,273	17,273	19,740

Source: Customs, Sri Lanka.

PRINCIPAL TRADING PARTNERS

('000 rupees)

IMPORTS	1979	1980	1981
Australia	1,077,939	653,036	1,067,846
Belgium	141,885	552,201	169,592
Burma	196,112	389,601	467,388
Canada	291,320	402,580	385,971
China, People's Republic	1,039,204	840,220	686,220
France	481,668	1,309,694	769,796
Germany, Federal Republic	1,222,107	1,176,849	1,741,543
India	2,334,369	1,594,163	1,459,640
Iran	739,792	1,814,272	2,349,793
Italy	263,948	233,413	241,339
Japan	3,005,291	4,301,769	4,969,895
Korea, Republic (South)	344,919	583,372	1,556,433
Netherlands	477,017	772,455	398,309
Pakistan	493,013	496,588	328,996
Saudi Arabia	1,569,653	3,527,494	6,192,757
Singapore	1,358,757	1,520,082	1,904,475
U.S.S.R.	167,789	177,397	43,699
United Kingdom	2,014,866	3,206,039	2,139,075
U.S.A.	1,210,995	1,492,614	2,488,590
TOTAL (incl. others)*	22,439,701	33,534,140	35,407,233

* Excludes Re-imports.

EXPORTS	1979	1980	1981
Australia	228,128	189,254	210,920
Canada	226,339	258,173	255,621
China, People's Republic	856,770	848,442	860,738
France	252,747	247,981	322,110
Germany, Federal Republic	902,412	917,953	1,115,319
Iran	326,659	549,476	488,625
Iraq	464,564	613,184	588,376
Italy	426,911	262,885	324,074
Japan	1,037,069	552,020	685,928
Kuwait	327,736	288,709	339,834
Netherlands	484,567	472,964	455,880
Pakistan	686,187	568,026	1,073,681
Saudi Arabia	448,622	606,971	632,328
Singapore	157,209	196,519	457,186
South Africa	259,922	312,638	352,055
U.S.S.R.	476,992	518,903	457,522
United Kingdom	1,230,773	1,278,377	1,290,502
U.S.A.	1,585,184	1,925,276	2,805,562
TOTAL (incl. others)*	13,858,406	15,313,907	17,794,777

* Excludes Re-exports and Bunkers.

Source: Customs return of Ceylon.

TOURISM

FOREIGN VISITORS BY ORIGIN

(excluding cruise passengers and excursionists)

	1977	1978	1979	1980	1981
Western Europe	104,723	128,233	163,206	215,650	245,190
Asia	26,158	35,995	56,187	72,022	87,894
North America	10,134	12,426	13,941	15,408	16,554
Eastern Europe	4,552	6,163	5,595	4,938	5,284
Australasia	5,410	6,511	7,334	8,720	9,570
Others	2,688	3,264	3,901	5,042	6,250
TOTAL	153,665	192,592	250,164	321,780	370,742

Tourist earnings (million rupees): 157.1 (1975); 237.8 (1976); 363.1 (1977); 870.0 (1978); 1,209.4 (1979); 1,830.3 (1980); 2,500.0 (1981)*.

* Provisional.

Sources: Ceylon Tourist Board.

TRANSPORT

RAILWAYS

	1977	1978	1979	1980	1981
Passenger-kilometres (million)	2,792	3,709	4,972	3,798	2,985
Freight ton-kilometres (million)	225	261	285	206	219

Source: Railway Department.

ROAD TRAFFIC

(motor vehicles in use at December 31st)

	1977	1978	1979	1980	1981
Cars and cabs	97,010	103,798	114,453	120,873	126,256
Motor-cycles	24,435	29,643	45,087	79,803	96,851
Buses	14,123	14,994	17,317	20,752	23,092
Lorries and vans*	40,174	45,237	51,665	61,158	68,427
Agricultural tractors and engines†	32,284	38,321†	45,558	54,796	58,826
TOTAL	208,026	231,993	274,080	337,382	373,452

* Including ambulances and hearses. † Including tractors and trailers.

Source: Commissioner of Motor Traffic.

INTERNATIONAL SEA-BORNE SHIPPING

(000 metric tons)

	1977	1978	1979	1980	1981
Vessels:					
Entered	4,104	5,046	4,395	6,165	n.a.
Cleared	3,612	3,513	2,610	3,514	n.a.
Goods:					
Loaded	1,241	1,321	1,324	1,192	1,340
Unloaded	3,571	4,332	3,777	2,495	2,357

Source: Customs returns, Department of Census and Statistics, Colombo.

CIVIL AVIATION

(Air Ceylon domestic services)

	1974	1975	1976	1977
Kilometres flown ('000)	289	371	282	388
Passenger-kilometres ('000)	5,746	8,775	8,795	12,833
Cargo (ton-km.)	580	1,695	4,845	3,994

Source: Central Bank of Ceylon, *Bulletin*, March 1978.

EDUCATION

	1979	1980
Schools	9,626	9,794
Primary	3,834	3,846
Junior secondary	3,994	3,911
Senior secondary	1,509	1,755
Pirivenas	289	282
Pupils*	3,135,716	3,399,776
Teachers*	133,249	136,714
Schools*	9,052	9,117

* Government only.

Source (unless otherwise stated): Department of Census and Statistics, Colombo.

THE CONSTITUTION

(Summary)

The Constitution of the Democratic Socialist Republic of Sri Lanka was approved by the National Assembly on August 17th, 1978, and promulgated on September 7th, 1978.

FUNDAMENTAL RIGHTS

The Constitution guarantees the fundamental rights and freedoms of all citizens, including freedom of thought, conscience and worship and equal entitlement before the law.

THE PRESIDENT

The President is Head of State. He exercises all executive powers including defence of the Republic. He is directly elected by the people for a term of six years, and is eligible for re-election. The President's powers include the right to:

(*a*) choose to hold any portfolio in the Cabinet;
(*b*) appoint or dismiss the Prime Minister or any other minister;
(*c*) preside at ceremonial sittings of Parliament;
(*d*) dismiss Parliament at will;
(*e*) submit to a national referendum any Bill or matter of national importance which has been rejected by Parliament.

LEGISLATURE

The Parliament is the legislative power of the people. It consists of such number of representatives of the people as a Delimitation Commission shall determine. The members of Parliament are directly elected by a system of modified proportional representation. By-elections are abolished, successors to members of Parliament being appointed by the head of the party which nominated the outgoing member at the previous election. Parliament exercises the judicial power of the people through courts, tribunals and institutions created and established or recognized by the Constitution or established or recognized by the Constitution or established by law. Parliament has control over public finance.

OTHER PROVISIONS

Religion. Buddhism has the foremost place among religions and it is the duty of the State to protect and foster Buddhism, whilst assuring every citizen the freedom to adopt the religion of their choice.

Language. The Constitution recognizes two national languages, Sinhala and Tamil. Sinhala remains the official language and all laws must be made or enacted in this language. Either of the national languages may be used by all citizens in transactions with government institutions.

Amendments to the Constitution require a two-thirds majority in Parliament. In February 1979 the Constitution was amended by allowing Members of Parliament who resigned or were expelled from their party to retain their seats, in certain circumstances. In January 1981 Parliament amended the Constitution to increase its membership from 168 to 169.

THE GOVERNMENT

HEAD OF STATE

President: JUNIUS RICHARD JAYAWARDENE (sworn in February 4th, 1978).

CABINET

(July 1982)

President, Minister of Defence, Power and Energy, Higher Education, Janatha (People's) Estate Development, State Plantations and Plan Implementation: JUNIUS RICHARD JAYAWARDENE.

Prime Minister, Minister of Highways, Local Government, Housing and Construction: RANASINGHE PREMADASA.

Minister of Foreign Affairs: A. C. S. HAMEED.

Minister of Posts and Telecommunications: D. B. WIJETUNGA.

Minister of Trade and Shipping: LALITH W. ATHULATHMUDALI.

Minister of Public Administration and Plantation Industries: W. G. MONTAGU JAYAWICKREMA.

Minister of Justice: NISSANKA WIJERATNE.

Minister of Finance and Planning: RONALD J. G. DE MEL.

Minister of Labour: Capt. C. P. J. SENEVIRATNE.

Minister of Industries and Scientific Affairs: C. CYRIL MATHEW.

Minister of Cultural Affairs: E. L. B. HURULLE.

Minister of Fisheries: M. FESTUS W. PERERA.

Minister of Health: Dr. R. K. P. ATAPATTU.

Minister of Parliamentary Affairs and Sports: M. VINCENT PERERA.

Minister of Transport, Transport Boards, Private Omnibus Transport and Muslim Cultural Affairs: H. M. MOHAMED.

Minister of Agricultural Development and Research: GAMANI N. JAYASURIYA.

Minister of Textile Industry: WIJEPALA MENDIS.

Minister of Home Affairs: K. W. DEVANAYAGAM.

Minister of Social Services: ASOKA KARUNARATNE.

Minister of Food and Co-operatives: S. B. HERAT.

Minister of Education, Youth Affairs and Employment: RANIL WICKREMASINGHE.

Minister of Rural Industrial Development: W. E. K. R. S. THONDAMAN.

Minister of Rural Development: I. WIMALA KANNANGARA.

Minister of Land, Land Development and Mahaveli Development: GAMINI DISSANAYAKE.

Minister of Regional Development: C. RAJADURAI.

Minister of State for Tourism, Broadcasting and Information: ANANDA TISSA DE ALWIS.

LEGISLATURE

PARLIAMENT

Speaker: BAKEER MARKAR.

GENERAL ELECTION, JULY 1977*

PARTY	SEATS
United National Party	142
Tamil United Liberation Front	16
Sri Lanka Freedom Party	8
Ceylon Workers' Congress	1
Vacant	1
TOTAL	168

* The distribution of seats in December 1981 was: UNP 143; TULF 16; SLFP 7; Communist Party 1; CWC 1.

POLITICAL PARTIES

The following are the main political parties:

Ceylon Workers' Congress (CWC): 72 Ananda Kumaraswamy Mawatha, Colombo 7; f. 1940; Pres. SAVUMYAMOORTHY THONDAMAN; Gen. Sec. M. S. SELLASAMY; publs. *Congress News* (fortnightly in English), *Congress* (fortnightly in Tamil).

Janatha Vimukti Peramuna (JVP) (*People's Liberation Front*): 14 Cyril C. Perera Mawatha, Colombo 13; outlawed after an attempt to overthrow the Government in 1971, regained legal status in 1977, but is not officially recognized; Leader ROHANA WIJEWEERA.

Sri Lanka Freedom Party (SLFP): 301 Darley Rd., Colombo 10; f. 1951 by the late Solomon Bandaranaike; Socialist; stands for a neutralist foreign policy, nationalization of certain industries, Sinhala as the official language, with safeguards for minorities; Pres. Hon. MAITHRIPALA SENANAYAKE, M.P.; publs. *Dinaya* (Sinhala daily), *Sathiya* (Sinhala weekly).

Tamil United Liberation Front (TULF): 238 Main St., Jaffna; f. 1949; aims to establish a separate autonomous region, known as Eelam, with the right of self-determination; Pres. M. SIVASITHAMPARAM; Sec.-Gen. APPAPILLAI AMIRTHALINGAM; publ. *Udayasurayan*.

All Ceylon Tamil Congress: Congress House, 120 Main St., Jaffna; f. 1944; aims to attain freedom for Tamil-speaking people to establish their right of self-determination; Pres. S. R. KANAGANAYAGAM; Gen. Sec. G. G. PONNAMBALAM; publ. *Thamizhakam* (every two weeks).

Lanka Sama Samaja Party (**LSSP**) (*Equal Society Party*): 457 Union Place, Colombo 2; f. 1935; Trotskyist; stands for nationalization of foreign-owned companies; opposed to communalism; Sec. BERNARD SOYSA; publs. *Sumasamajaya, Samadharmam* and *Samasamajist* (Trotskyist weeklies in Sinhala, Tamil and English respectively).

Democratic Workers' Congress (*Political Wing*): 98A Mohideen Masjed Rd., P.O.B. 1009, Colombo 10; f. 1978; aims to eliminate social and economic exploitation and inequality, represents all-round development of human personality; Leader ABDUL AZIZ; Sec. V. P. GANESAN; publ. *Jananayaga Thozhilali* (fortnightly in Tamil).

Communist Party of Sri Lanka: 91 Cotta Rd., Colombo 8; f. 1943; pro-Moscow; left the ULF in March 1977; Chair. (vacant); Gen. Sec. K. P. SILVA; publs. *Shakthi, Forward* (weeklies in Tamil and English respectively), *Aththa* (Sinhala daily), *Samajawadhaya* (Sinhala periodical).

United National Party (**UNP**): 532 Galle Rd., Colombo 3; f. 1947; Democratic Socialist party; aims at a neutralist foreign policy, Sinhala as the official language and State-aid to denominational schools; Leader JUNIUS RICHARD JAYAWARDENE; publ. *The Journal* (weekly in Sinhala and English).

DIPLOMATIC REPRESENTATION

HIGH COMMISSIONS AND EMBASSIES ACCREDITED TO SRI LANKA

(HC) High Commmission; (E) Embassy.

Afghanistan: New Delhi, India (E).

Argentina: New Delhi, India (E).

Australia: 3 Cambridge Place, P.O.B. 742, Colombo 7 (HC); *High Commissioner:* D. C. RUTTER.

Austria: New Delhi, India (E).

Bangladesh: 207/1 Dharmapala Mawatha, Colombo 7 (HC); *Chargé d'affaires:* Z. S. CHOURDHURY.

Belgium: 7 Race Course Avenue, Colombo 7 (E); *Chargé d'affaires:* T. W. TSAN.

Brazil: New Delhi, India (E).

Bulgaria: 29/9 Jayasinghe Rd., Kirillapoul, Colombo 6 (E); *Chargé d'affaires:* TODOR DIMITROV.

Burma: 23 Havelock Rd., Colombo 5 (E); *Ambassador:* U MAUNG MAUNG GYI.

Canada: 6 Gregory's Rd., Colombo 7 (HC); *High Commissioner:* ROBERT W. CLARK.

China, People's Republic: 191 Dharmapala Mawatha, Colombo 7 (E); *Ambassador:* GAO-E.

Cuba: 109 Kynsey Rd., Colombo 8 (E); *Chargé d'affaires a.i.:* V. D. RAMIREZ PENA.

Cyprus: New Delhi, India (HC).

Czechoslovakia: 47 & 47A Horton Place, Colombo 7 (E); *Ambassador:* JAROSLAV CISAR.

Denmark: New Delhi, India (E).

Egypt: 39 Dickmans Rd., Colombo 4 (E); *Ambassador:* GAMAL ABDUL-OYOUM.

Ethiopia: New Delhi, India (E).

Finland: P.O.B. 1914, 35/2 Guildford Crescent, Colombo 7 (E); *Chargé d'affaires a.i.:* KARI KARANKO.

France: 89 Rosmead Place, Colombo 7 (E); *Ambassador:* FRANÇOIS TOUSSAINT.

German Democratic Republic: 101 Rosmead Place, Colombo 7 (E); *Ambassador:* DIETER PHILIPP.

Germany, Federal Republic: 16 Barnes Place, Colombo 7 (E); *Ambassador:* Dr. GERHARD PEIFFER.

Ghana: New Delhi, India (HC).

Greece: New Delhi, India (E).

Guyana: New Delhi, India (HC).

Hungary: 79/2 Horton Place, Colombo 7 (E); *Ambassador:* Dr. FERENC TURI.

India: 3rd Floor, State Bank of India, Sir Baron Jayatilaka Mawatha, Colombo 1 (HC); *High Commissioner:* THOMAS ABRAHAM.

Indonesia: 10 Independence Ave., Colombo 7 (E); *Ambassador:* SOEDHARMO DJAJADIWANGSA.

Iran: 6 Sir Ernest de Silva Mawatha, Colombo 7 (E); *Chargé d'affaires a.i.:* JAFFAR AZARMGIN.

Iraq: P.O.B. 79, 19 Barnes Place, Colombo 7 (E); *Ambassador:* MAMDOH ABDUL HAMID.

Italy: 586 Galle Rd., Colombo 3 (E); *Ambassador:* FRANCO MICELI DE BIASE.

Japan: 20 Gregory's Rd., Colombo 7 (E); *Ambassador:* KAZUO CHIBA.

Jordan: New Delhi, India (E).

Kenya: New Delhi, India (HC).

Korea, Democratic People's Republic: New Delhi, India (E).

Korea, Republic: 98 Dharmapala Mawatha, Colombo 7 (E); *Ambassador:* MING IL CHUNG.

Kuwait: New Delhi, India (E).

Laos: New Delhi, India (E).

Lebanon: New Delhi, India (E).

Libya: 30 Horton Place, Colombo 7 (E); *Secretary of the Popular Committee:* ALI M. SHONEGY.

Malaysia: 63A Ward Place, Colombo 7 (HC); *High Commissioner:* ANTHONY YEO KEAT SEONG.

Maldives: 25 Melbourne Avenue, Colombo 4 (E); *Chargé d'affaires a.i.:* AHMED ABDULLAH

Mauritius: New Delhi, India (HC).

Mexico: New Delhi, India (E).

Mongolia: New Delhi, India (E).

Morocco: New Delhi, India (E).

Nepal: New Delhi, India (E).

Netherlands: 25 Torrington Ave., Colombo 7 (E); *Chargé d'affaires:* F. P. KUETHE.

New Zealand: Singapore (HC).

Nigeria: New Delhi, India (HC).

Norway: New Delhi, India (E).

Pakistan: 17 Sir Ernest de Silva Mawatha, Colombo 7 (E); *Ambassador:* BAKHITAR ALI.

Philippines: 5 Torrington Place, Colombo 7 (E); *Ambassador:* ROGELIO DE LA ROSA.

Poland: 120 Park Rd., Colombo 5 (E); *Ambassador:* RYSZARD FIJALKOWSKI.

Portugal: New Delhi, India (E).

Qatar: New Delhi, India (E).

Romania: 15 Glifford Ave., Colombo 3 (E); *Ambassador:* Dr. DUMITRU NICULESCU.

Saudi Arabia: New Delhi, India (E).

Senegal: New Delhi, India (E).

Singapore: New Delhi, India (HC).

Spain: New Delhi, India (E).

Sudan: New Delhi, India (E).

Sweden: P.O.B. 1072, 315 Vauxhall St., Colombo 2 (E); *Chargé d'affaires a.i.:* CARL GUSTAV AKESSON.

Switzerland: 80 Kumaratunga Munidasa Mawatha, Colombo 7 (E); *Chargé d'affaires:* CLAUDE OCHSENBEIN.

Syria: New Delhi, India (E).

Thailand: 10 Sir Ernest de Silva Mawatha, Colombo 7 (E); *Ambassador:* ANAT SUWANAWIHOK.

Trinidad and Tobago: New Delhi, India (HC).

Turkey: New Delhi, India (E).

Uganda: New Delhi, India (HC).

U.S.S.R.: 62 Sir Ernest de Silva Mawatha, Colombo 7 (E); *Ambassador:* BORIS YEFREMOVICH KIRNASOVSKY.

United Kingdom: P.O.B. 1433, 190 Galle Rd., Kollupitiya, Colombo 3 (HC); *High Commissioner:* Sir JOHN NICHOLAS, K.C.V.O., C.M.G.

U.S.A.: 44 Galle Rd., Colombo 3 (E); *Ambassador:* JOHN H. REED.

Vatican City: 1 Gower St., Colombo 5 (Apostolic Nunciature); *Pro-Nuncio:* Most Rev. NICOLA ROTUNNO.

Viet-Nam: 2 Dudley Senanayake Mawatha, Colombo 8 (E); *Ambassador:* LE BAO.

Yugoslavia: 32 Cambridge Place, Colombo 7 (E); *Ambassador:* ULADIMUR BABSIK.

Zaire: New Delhi, India (E).

Zambia: New Delhi, India (HC).

Sri Lanka also has diplomatic relations with Albania, Bolivia, Luxembourg, Oman and the United Arab Emirates.

JUDICIAL SYSTEM

Chief Justice: Hon. NEVILLE D. M. SAMARAKOON, Q.C.

The judicial system consists of the Supreme Court, the Court of Appeal, the High Court, District Courts, Magistrates' Courts, Family Courts and Primary Courts. The last five are Courts of the First Instance and appeals lie from them to the Court of Appeal and from there, on a question of law, to the Supreme Court. Appeals also lie from the Court of Appeal if special leave is granted by the Supreme Court. The High Court deals with all criminal cases and the District Courts with civil cases. There are also Labour Tribunals to decide labour disputes.

The Judicial Service Commission consists of the Chief Justice and two judges of the Supreme Court, nominated by the President. All judges of the Courts of First Instance (except High Court Judges) and the staff of all courts are appointed and controlled by the Judicial Service Commission. The Supreme Court consists of the Chief Justice and not fewer than six and not more than ten other judges. The Court of Appeal consists of the President and not fewer than six and not more than eleven other judges.

RELIGION

The distribution of the population by religion, according to the provisional results of the 1981 census ('000):

Buddhists	10,293
Hindus	2,296
Muslims	1,134
Roman Catholics	1,010
Other Christians	102
Others	15
TOTAL	14,850

BUDDHISM

Seventy per cent of the population are Theravada Buddhist. There are 12,000 Buddhist Bhikkhus (monks), living in 6,000 temples on the island.

All Ceylon Buddhist Congress: 380 Bauddhaloka Mawatha, Colombo 7; f. 1919; Pres. Prof. L. G. HEWAGE (acting); Jnt.-Secs. H. L. CALDERA, P. C. CALDERA.

Ceylon Regional Centre of the World Fellowship of Buddhists: 6 Paget Rd., Colombo 5; Sec. W. P. DALUWATTA.

HINDUISM

The majority of the Tamil population are Hindus. The Hindu population numbers over two million.

ISLAM

The total Muslim population is over one million.

CHRISTIAN CHURCHES

About 8 per cent of the population is Christian.

CHURCH OF CEYLON

Bishop of Kurunagala: Rt. Rev. CYRIL LAKSHMAN WICKREMESINGHE; f. of diocese 1950; Bishop's House, Kandy Road, Kurunagala; publ. *Ceylon Churchman*.

Bishop of Colombo: SWITHIN FERNANDO; Bishop's House, 368/3 Bauddhaloka Mawatha, Colombo 7; publ. *Ceylon Churchman*.

CHURCH OF SOUTH INDIA

Bishop: Rt. Rev. D. J. AMBALAVANAR, B.A., B.D., M.TH.; Bishop's House, Jaffna Diocese, Vaddukoddai; the mission was established in Jaffna in 1816 and there are about 6,000 mems. of the Church of South India in Sri Lanka.

METHODIST CHURCH IN SRI LANKA

President of Conference: Rev. S. K. PERERA, B.D., H.M.; Methodist Headquarters, Colombo 3.

THE PRESBYTERY OF SRI LANKA

The Dutch Reformed Church in Sri Lanka.

Moderator: Rev. C. N. JANSZ, G.TH.

ROMAN CATHOLIC CHURCH

In 1981 there were 1,010,000 Roman Catholics in Sri Lanka.

Archbishop: The Most Rev. NICHOLAS MARCUS FERNANDO, B.A., D.D., Metropolitan Archdiocese; Archbishop's House, Gnanarthapradeepaya Mawatha, Colombo 8.

THE PRESS

NEWSPAPERS

Newspapers are published in Sinhala, Tamil and English. There are four main newspaper publishing groups:

Associated Newspapers of Ceylon Ltd.: P.O.B. 248, Lake House, D. R. Wijewardene Mawatha, Colombo 10; f. 1926; nationalized 1973; Publr. of five dailies, incl. *Ceylon Daily News, Evening Observer* and *Dinamina*, three Sunday papers, incl. *Silumina* and seven periodicals; Chair. R. BODINAGODA; Sec. R. H. M. CHANDRASEKERA.

Express Newspapers (Ceylon) Ltd.: 185 Grandpass Rd., Colombo 14; Publr. of *Mithran, Virakesari* (dailies) and *Mithran Varamalar, Virakesari Vaaraveliyeedu* (Sunday); Chief Editor K. SIVAPIRAGASAM.

Independent Newspapers Ltd.: 5 Gunasena Mawatha, Colombo 12; closed down by the Government in 1974, restored to private ownership 1977; Publr. of *Dawasa, Dinapathi* and *Sun* (dailies), *Riviresa, Weekend, Chintamani* and *Iranama* (weeklies) and *Sri* (monthly); Chair. PERCY GUNASENA.

The Times of Ceylon Ltd.: 3 Bristol St., Colombo 1; closed down by the Government in 1973, reopened as a Government undertaking 1977; Publr. of the dailies *Ceylon Daily Mirror* and *Lankadipa*, two Sunday papers *Sunday Times* and *Sri Lankadipa* and *Vanithavithi* (fortnightly); Competent Authority: Associated Management Services Ltd.; Dirs. D. C. WIJESEKERA, D. S. PORAGE.

Upali Newspapers Ltd.: 223 Bloemendhal Rd., Colombo 13; f. 1981; Publr. of the *Island, Divaina* (dailies), two Sunday papers, *Sunday Island* and *Divaina*; Man. Dir. UPALI WIJEWARDENE.

DAILIES

Aththa: 91 Cotta Rd., Colombo 8; f. 1965; Sinhala; progressive; Editor B. A. SIRIWARDENE; circ. 28,000.

Ceylon Daily Mirror: 3 Bristol St., Colombo 1; f. 1961; morning; English; publ. by Times of Ceylon Ltd.; independent; Acting Editor ELMO GUNARATNE; circ. 30,000.

Ceylon Daily News: P.O.B. 248, Lake House, D. R. Wijewardene Mawatha, Colombo 10; f. 1918; morning; English; publ. by the Associated Newspapers of Ceylon Ltd.; Editor MANIK DE SILVA; circ. 65,000.

Dawasa: P.O.B. 226, 5 Gunasena Mawatha, Colombo 12; f. f. 1961; morning; Sinhala; publ. by Independent Newspapers Ltd.; Editor C. A. SEELAWIMALA; circ. 108,000.

Dinamina: P.O.B. 248, Lake House, D. R. Wijewardene Mawatha, Colombo 10; f. 1909; morning; Sinhala; publ. by the Associated Newspapers of Ceylon Ltd.; Editor W. B. METTANANDA; circ. 140,000.

Dinapathi: P.O.B. 226, 5 Gunasena Mawatha, Colombo 12; f. 1966; morning; Tamil; publ. by Independent Newspapers Ltd.; Editor S. T. SIVANAYAGAM; circ. 41,200.

Eelanaadu: P.O.B. 49, 63 Sivan Kovil West Rd., Jaffna; f. 1959; morning; Tamil; Man. Editor S. PERUMAL; circ. 12,000.

Evening Observer: P.O.B. 248, Lake House, D. R. Wijewardene Mawatha, Colombo 10; f. 1834; evening (5 days) and Sunday morning; publ. by the Associated Newspapers of Ceylon Ltd.; Editor HAROLD J. M. PIERIS; circ. 10,000 (evening), 84,000 (Sunday).

Janadina: 47 Jayantha Weerasekera Mawatha, Colombo 10; f. 1965; morning; Sinhala; publ. by Suriya Publishers Ltd.; Editor-in-Chief SARATH NAWANA; circ. 30,000.

Janatha: P.O.B. 248, Lake House, D. R. Wijewardene Mawatha, Colombo 10; f. 1953; evening; Sinhala; publ. by the Associated Newspapers of Ceylon Ltd.; Editor U. L. D. CHANDRATILAKE; circ. 6,000.

Lankadipa: 3 Bristol St., Colombo 1; f. 1947; morning; Sinhala; publ. by Times of Ceylon Ltd.; Editor ELMO GOONERATNE; circ. 67,000.

Mithran: 185 Grandpass Rd., Colombo 14; f. 1966; morning; Tamil; publ. by Express Newspapers (Ceylon) Ltd.; Editor K. SIVAPIRAGASAM; circ. 17,500.

Sun: 5 Gunasena Mawatha, Colombo 12; f. 1964; morning; English; publ. by Independent Newspapers Ltd.; Editor REX DE SILVA; circ. 17,500.

The Island: Colombo; f. 1981; morning and Sunday; English and Sinhala; publ. by Upali Newspapers; Publr. UPALI WIJEWARDENE.

Thinakaran: P.O.B. 248, Lake House, D. R. Wijewardene Mawatha, Colombo 10; f. 1932; morning; Tamil; publ. by the Associated Newspapers of Ceylon Ltd.; Editor R. SIVAGURUNATHAN; circ. daily 13,800.

Virakesari: 185 Grandpass Rd., P.O.B. 160, Colombo 14; f. 1930; morning; Tamil; publ. by Express Newspapers (Ceylon) Ltd.; Editor K. SIVAPIRAGASAM; circ. 35,000.

SUNDAY PAPERS

Chintamani: 5 Gunasena Mawatha, Colombo 12; f. 1966; Tamil; publ. by Independent Newspapers Ltd.; Editor R. ARIARATNAM; circ. 38,000.

Janasathiya: 47 Jayantha Weerasekara Mawatha, Colombo 10; f. 1965; Sinhala; publ. by Suriya Publishers Ltd.; Editor SARATH NAWANA; circ. 50,000.

Mithran Varamalar: 185 Grandpass Rd., Colombo; f. 1969; Tamil; publ. by Express Newspapers (Ceylon) Ltd.; Editor K. SIVAPIRAGASAM; circ. 24,000.

Riviresa: 5 Gunasena Mawatha, Colombo 12; f. 1961; Sinhala Weekly; publ. by Independent Newspapers Ltd.; Editor ROHANA GAMAGE; circ. 316,650.

Silumina: P.O.B. 248, Lake House, D. R. Wijewardene Mawatha, Colombo 10; f. 1930; Sinhala; publ. by the Associated Newspapers of Ceylon Ltd.; Editor W. B. METHANANDA; circ. 253,914.

Sri Lankadipa: 3 Bristol St., Colombo 1; f. 1947; Sinhala; publ. by Times of Ceylon Ltd.; Editor ELMO GOONERATNE; circ. 173,000.

Sunday Times: P.O.B. 159, 3 Bristol St., Colombo 1; f. 1923; independent; English; publ. by Times of Ceylon Ltd.; Editor RITA SEBASTIAN; circ. 40,000.

Thinakaran Vaaramanjari: P.O.B. 248, Lake House, D. R. Wijewardene Mawatha, Colombo 10; f. 1948; Tamil; publ. by the Associated Newspapers of Ceylon Ltd.; Editor S. SIVAGURUNATHAN; circ. 21,100.

Viraksari Vaaraveliyeedu: 185 Grandpass Rd., Colombo 14; f. 1931; Tamil; publ. by Express Newspapers (Ceylon) Ltd.; Editor K. SIVAPIRAGASAM; circ. 45,000.

Weekend: 5 Gunasena Mawatha, Colombo 12; f. 1965; English; publ. by Independent Newspapers Ltd.; Editor REX DE SILVA; circ. 56,000.

PERIODICALS

(weekly unless otherwise stated)

Ceylon Medical Journal: 6 Wijerama Mawatha, Colombo 7; f. 1887; quarterly; Editors Dr. LAKSHMAN RANASINGHE, Dr. C. G. URAGODA.

Chitta Dharma Vidya: 150 Dutugemunu St., Dehiwala; f. 1978; Sinhala; fortnightly; science of the mind; Editor SUMANADASA SAMARASINGHE; circ. 6,000.

Exponews Bulletin: Trade and Shipping Information Service, P.O.B. 1525; f. 1981; publ. by the Trade and Shipping Information Service of the Ministry of Trade and Shipping; Editor Dir. of Trade and Shipping Information Service.

The Financial Times: P.O.B. 330, 323 Union Place, Colombo 2; quarterly; commercial and economic affairs; Man. Editor CYRIL GARDINER.

Gnanarathapradeepaya: Colombo Catholic Press, 956 Gnanarathapradeepaya Mawatha, Borella, Colombo 8; Sinhala; National Catholic paper; Chief Editor HECTOR WELGAMPOLA; circ. 26,000.

Honey: 5 Gunasena Mawatha, Colombo 12; f. 1976; illustrated family magazine; English; publ. by Independent Newspapers Ltd.; Editor JEANNE PINTO; circ. 27,000.

Janakavi: 47 Jayantha Weerasekera Mawatha, Colombo 10; Sinhala; fortnightly; Associated Editor KARUNARATNE AMERASINGHE.

Mihira: Lake House, D. R. Wijewardene Mawatha, Colombo 10; Sinhala children's magazine; Editor M. N. PINTO; circ. 145,000.

Navalokaya: Gampaha, W.P.; f. 1941; Sinhala; monthly; publ. by Communist Party; articles on literature, art, politics, education, science, etc.

Navayugaya: Lake House, D. R. Wijewardene Mawatha 1, Colombo 10; f. 1956; literary fortnightly; Sinhala; Editor EDWIN ARIYADASA; circ. 56,800.

Pathukavalan: P.O.B. 2, Jaffna; f. 1876; Tamil; publ. by St. Joseph's Catholic Press; Editor Rev. Fr. ANTON MATTHIAS; circ. 5,000.

Priyavi: 5 Gunasena Mawatha, Colombo 12; f. 1976; teenage pop scene; Sinhala; publ. by Independent Newspapers Ltd.; Editor W. WATUREGAMA; circ. 37,000.

Public Opinion: 723 Maradana Rd., Colombo 10; monthly; Editor N. G. L. MARASINGHE.

Rasavahini: 3 Bristol St., Colombo 1; f. 1956; Sinhala monthly; Editor SAMAN TILAKASIRI.

Sarasaviya: P.O.B. 248, Lake House, D. R. Wijewardene Mawatha, Colombo 10; f. 1963; Sinhala; circ. 55,800; Editor GRANVILLE SILVA.

Sinhala Bauddhaya: Maha Bodhi Mandira, 13 Maligakanda Rd., Colombo 10; f. 1906; publ. by The Maha Bodi Society of Ceylon; Editor-in-Chief RAJA V. EKANAYAKA; circ. 25,000.

Sri Lanka Government Gazette: P.O.B. 500, Government Press, Colombo; f. 1802; official government publication; circ. 54,360.

Sri Lanka News: P.O.B. 248, Lake House, D. R. Wijewardene Mawatha, Colombo 10; f. 1938; digest of news and features from Sri Lanka; publ. by the Associated Newspapers of Ceylon Ltd.; Editor NEVILLE DE SILVA.

Sri Lanka Today: Government Department of Information, 7 Sir Baron Jayatilaka Mawatha, Colombo 1; English; quarterly.

Subasetha: P.O.B. 248, Lake House, D. R. Wijewardene Mawatha, Colombo 10; f. 1967; astrological and native medicine news; Sinhala; Editor JAYATILAKA AMBUWANGALA; circ. 80,000.

Sutantiran: 15 Mahatma Gandhi Rd., Jaffna; f. 1947; Tamil; twice a week; Editor KOVAI MAHESHAN.

Tharuni: P.O.B. 248, Lake House, D. R. Wijewardene Mawatha, Colombo 10; f. 1969; women's journal; Sinhala; Editor SUMANA SAPARAMADU; circ. 117,000.

Tribune: 43 Dawson St., Colombo 2; f. 1954; English; review of news in Sri Lanka and abroad; Editor S. P. AMARASINGAM.

Vanitha: Times Bldg., Colombo; f. 1957; Sinhalese women's magazine; Editor CHANDRA RANASINGHE; circ. 7,100.

NEWS AGENCIES

Lankapuvath (National News Agency of Sri Lanka): 54 Chatham St., Colombo 1; Chair. ESMOND WICKREMASINGHE; Chief Editor J. P. PATHIRANA.

Press Trust of Ceylon: P.O.B. 131, Negris Bldg., Colombo 1; Chair. R. BODINAGODA; Sec. and Gen. Man. A. W. AMUNUGAMA.

Sandesa News Agency: 23 Canal Rav, Colombo 1; f. 1968; Dir. GAMINI NAVARATNE.

FOREIGN BUREAUX

Agence France-Presse (AFP): 20, 1/1 Regent Flats, Parsons Rd., Colombo 2; Corr. NEVILLE DE SILVA.

Associated Press (AP) (*U.S.A.*): 9/1 Charles Way, Colombo 3; Corr. MANIK DE SILVA.

Deutsche Presse-Agentur (dpa) (*Federal Republic of Germany*): 31 Raymond Rd., Nugegoda; Corr. REX DE SILVA.

Iraqi News Agency: Dinakara, 301 Darley Rd., Colombo 10; Corr. SARATH COORAY.

Novinska Agencija Tanjug (*Yugoslavia*): 53/25A Torrington Ave., Colombo 7; Corr. LADISLAV BRUNER.

Press Trust of India (PTI): 20–22 Regent Flats, Colombo 2; Corr. K. DHARMARAJAN.

Reuters (*U.K.*): P.O.B. 131, 1st Floor, National Mutual Building, Chatham St., Colombo 1; Corr. DALTON DE SILVA.

United Press International (UPI) (*U.S.A.*): 3/6 Pagoda Rd., Nugegoda; Corr. IQBAL ATHAS.

Xinhua (*People's Republic of China*): 21 Anderson Rd., Colombo; Corr. LI ZHENG.

The following are also represented: Prensa Latina (Cuba), TASS (U.S.S.R.), Tanjug (Yugoslavia).

PUBLISHERS

W. E. Bastian: P.O.B. 10, 23 Canal Row, Fort, Colombo 1; f. 1904; art, literature, technical; Man. Prop. W. D. E. BASTIAN.

H. W. Cave: P.O.B. 25, 81 Sir Baron Jayatilaka Mawatha, Colombo 1; f. 1876; history, arts, law, medicine, technical, educational; Man. Dir. B. J. L. FERNANDO.

Colombo Catholic Press: 956 Gnanarathapradeepaya Mawatha, Borella, Colombo 8; f. 1865; liturgical books; publishers of *The Messenger*, *The Gnanarathapradeepaya*, *The Weekly;* Man. Dir. Rev. Fr. BENEDICT JOSEPH.

Cultural Council: Ministry of Cultural Affairs, P.O.B. 307, 135 Dharmapala Mawatha, Colombo 7; f. 1971; literature, religion, art, culture; Dir. R. L. WIMALADHARMA.

M. D. Gunasena and Col Ltd.: P.O.B. 246, 217 Olcott Mawatha, Colombo 11; f. 1913; educational and general; stationers and paper merchants.

Hansa Publishers Ltd.: Hansa House, Clifford Ave., Colombo 3; general.

Lake House Printers and Publishers Ltd.: P.O.B. 1458, 41 W.A.D. Ramanayake Mawatha, Colombo 2; f. 1965; commercial and security printing; Chair. R. S. WIJEWARDENE; Company Sec. UPALI K. SALGADO.

Saman Publishers Ltd.: 49/16 Iceland Bldgs., Colombo 3.

K. V. G. de Silva and Sons (Colombo) Ltd.: 415 Galle Rd., Colombo 4; f. 1898; Chair. and Gov. Dir. K. V. J. DE SILVA; Man. Ms. VIMALA SENEVIRATNE.

The Union Press: P.O.B. 362, 169 Union Place, Colombo 2; f. 1942; Man. Dir. A. H. DHAS.

PUBLISHERS' ASSOCIATION

Sri Lanka Publishers' Association: 61 Sangaraja Mawatha, Colombo 10; Sec.-Gen. EAMON KARIYAKARAWANA.

RADIO AND TELEVISION

Sri Lanka Broadcasting Corporation: P.O.B. 574, Torrington Square, Colombo 7; f. 1967; under Ministry of State for Broadcasting and Information; controls all broadcasting in Sri Lanka; radio stations at Amparai, Anuradhapura, Diyagama, Galle, Jaffna, Maho, Puttalam, Senkadagala, Weeraketiya, Welikada, Seeduwa and Matara; Home Service in English, Sinhala and Tamil; Foreign Service also in Arabic, Hindi, Japanese, Kannada, Malayalam, Marathi, Nepali, Telugu and Urdu; 671 broadcasting hours per week: 283 hours on Sinhala Channels I, II, III, All-India Hindi Service and Middle East Service, 186 hours on English Channels I, II, Asia and South-east Asia service, 108 hours on Tamil Channels I and II; Education services comprise 40 hours; Chair. EAMON KARIYAKARAWANA; publs. *Guvan Viduli Sangarawa, Radio Times, Vanoli Mangari* (fortnightly).

Trans World Radio: P.O.B. 364, Colombo; f. 1978; missionary radio station; broadcasts 2½ hours every morning and 3½ hours each evening to Indian sub-continent; Field Dir. A. H. REMTEMA.

In 1981 there were an estimated 705,000 radio receivers.

Experimental television, broadcasting within a 50-km-radius of Colombo, began in April 1979 and was taken over by the Government in June 1979. It was expected that transmissions would be extended to the entire island by February 1982.

FINANCE

(cap. p.u.=capital paid up; auth.=authorized; dep.=deposits; Rs.=rupees; m.=million; brs.=branches)

BANKING

All domestic banks were nationalized in 1975.

CENTRAL BANK

Central Bank of Ceylon: P.O.B. 590, 34–36 Janadhipathi Mawatha, Colombo 1; f. 1950; cap. Rs. 15m.; dep. Rs. 5,342.5m. (Dec. 1980); Gov. and Chair. of the Monetary Board Dr. WARNASENA RASAPUTRAM; Sec. P. WATTEGAMA.

NATIONAL BANKS

Bank of Ceylon: 41 Bristol St., Colombo 1; f. 1939; cap. p.u. Rs. 250m.; dep. Rs. 11,894m. (1981); Chair. NISSANKA WIJEWARDENE; Gen. Man. L. PIYADASA; 633 brs.

Commercial Bank of Ceylon Ltd.: P.O.B. 148, 57 Sir Baron Jayatilaka Mawatha, Colombo 1; f. 1969; cap. Rs. 30m.; dep. Rs. 1,370m. (Dec. 1981); Chair. V. MANICAVASAGAR; Man. Dir. W. S. CHANDRARATNE; 11 brs.

Hatton National Bank Ltd.: P.O.B. 98, 16 Janadhipathi Mawatha, Colombo 1; f. 1970; cap. p.u. Rs 10m.; dep. Rs. 1,458m. (Dec. 1981); Chair. H. L. E. COORAY; Man. Dir. M. DHARMARAJA; 28 brs.

People's Bank: Sir Chittampalam Gardiner Mawatha, Colombo 2; f. 1961; cap. auth. Rs. 1,000m.; dep. Rs. 11,475m. (1981); Chair. Dr. S. T. G. FERNANDO; Gen. Man. P. B. RATNAYAKE; 298 brs.

STATE DEVELOPMENT BANKS

Agricultural and Industrial Credit Corpn. of Ceylon: P.O.B. 20, 292 Galle Rd., Colombo 3; f. 1943; loan cap. Rs. 30m.; Chair. V. P. VITTACHI; Gen. Man. H. S. F. GOONEWARDENA.

Development Finance Corpn. of Ceylon: P.O.B. 1397, 9 Horton Place, Colombo 7; f. 1955; Chair. W. TENNEKOON; Gen. Man. Dir. and Chief Exec. M. R. PRELIS.

The National Development Bank of Sri Lanka: P.O.B. 1825, 6th Floor, Ceylinco House, Janadhipathi Mawatha, Colombo 1; provides long-term finance for projects, equity financing and merchant banking services.

State Mortgage and Investment Bank: 91 Horton Place, Colombo; f. 1979; Chair. L. PIYASENA; Gen. Man. D. L. FERNANDO.

FOREIGN BANKS

Algemene Bank Nederland N.V. (*Netherlands*): P.O.B. 317, 30 Sir Baron Jayatilaka Mawatha, Colombo 1; Man. W. H. M. STRUYCKEN.

Amro Bank (*Netherlands*): P.O.B. 1329, 90 Chatham St., Colombo 1; f. 1981 in Sri Lanka.

Bank of America (*U.S.A.*): P.O.B. 308, 324 Galle Rd., Colombo 3.

Bank of Credit and Commerce International (Overseas) Ltd. (*Cayman Islands*): P.O.B. 410, 52 Mudalige Mawatha, Colombo 1; f. 1979; Man. Y. H. ABEDI.

Banque Indosuez (*France*): P.O.B. 303, Ceylinco Bldg., 69 Janadhipathi Mawatha, Colombo 1; f. 1979; Man. G. LOUBEYRE.

Chartered Bank (*U.K.*): P.O.B. 27, 17 Janadhipathi Mawatha, Colombo; f. 1853; Man. A. H. DEVERELL.

Citibank N.A. (*U.S.A.*): P.O.B. 888, Iceland Building, Colombo 3; Vice-Pres. PHILIP M. BROWN; Asst. Vice-Pres. NORMAN J. WILDING.

Grindlays Bank Ltd. (*U.K.*): P.O.B. 112, 493/1 Darley Rd., Colombo 10; f. 1881; Gen. Man. P. COLVIL.

Habib Bank Ltd. (*Pakistan*): P.O.B. 1088, 163 Keyzer St., Colombo; f. 1951; Man. H. KHAN.

Hongkong and Shanghai Banking Corporation (*Hong Kong*): 24 Sir Baron Jayatilaka Mawatha, Fort, Colombo 1; Man. R. THAMBIAH.

Indian Bank (*India*): P.O.B. 624, 81, 91, 93 Main St., Colombo 11; Man. M. G. GOEL.

Indian Overseas Bank (*India*): P.O.B. 671, 139 Main St., Overseas Bank Bldg., Colombo 11; Man. T. R. KALLAPIRAN.

Overseas Trust Bank Ltd. (*Hong Kong*): Y.M.C.A. Bldg., 39 Bristol St., Colombo 1.

State Bank of India: P.O.B. 93, 16 Sir Baron Jayatilaka Mawatha, Fort, Colombo 1; f. 1955; Chief Man. K. B. SRITHARAN.

Union Bank of the Middle East Ltd.: P.O.B. 358, 69 Chatham St., Colombo 1; Gen. Man. A. N. R. MCHARG.

STOCK EXCHANGE

The Colombo Brokers' Association: P.O.B. 101, 59 Janadipathi Mawatha, Colombo; f. 1904; produce and share brokers.

INSURANCE

Insurance Corporation of Sri Lanka: Rakshana Mandiraya, No. 21 Vauxhall St., Colombo 2; f. 1961; all classes of insurance; Chair. R. CHANAKA D. DE SILVA.

TRADE AND INDUSTRY

CHAMBERS OF COMMERCE

Ceylon Chamber of Commerce: P.O.B. 274, 127 Lower Chatham St., Colombo; incorp. 1895; Chair. P. A. SILVA; Sec. S. S. JAYAWICKRAMA; publs. *Sri Lanka in brief* (annually), *Annual Review of Business and Trade*, *Directory of Exporters* (annually), *Directory of Garment Manufacturers/Exporters* (annually), *Register of Members*.

Ceylon Moor Chamber of Commerce: 14 China St., Colombo 11; Pres. Sir RAZIK FAREED, O.B.E.; Admin. Sec. A. I. L. MARIKAR.

Chamber of Commerce of Ceylonese by Descent: 78 First Cross St., Colombo 11; f. 1964; Pres. GNANASEKARA SENANAYAKE; Admin. Sec. E. L. DE SOYZA.

The National Chamber of Commerce of Sri Lanka: P.O.B. 1375; 2nd Floor, YMBA Bldg., Main St., Colombo 1; f. 1950; Pres. A. D. E. DE S. WIJEYERATNE; Admin. Sec. T. SENEVIRATNE; publ. *Ceylon Commerce*.

Sinhala Chamber of Commerce: Colombo; f. 1937; 2,500 mems.; Pres. K. A. G. PERERA.

Sri Lanka National Council of the International Chamber of Commerce: 17 Alfred Place, Colombo 3; Chair. S. AMBALAVANER; Hon. Sec. H. E. P. COORAY.

TRADE AND INDUSTRIAL ORGANIZATIONS

Industrial Development Board of Ceylon: 615 Galle Rd., Katubedde, Moratuwa; f. 1969 under Ministry of Industries and Scientific Affairs for the encouragement and development of industries in Sri Lanka; Chair. NAUFEL ABDUL RAHMAN; Gen. Man. N. SENANAYAKE; publ. *Karmantha*.

All Ceylon Trade Chamber: 212/45, 1/3 Gas Works St., Colombo 11.

Ceylon Association of Manufacturers: c/o Ceylon Chamber of Commerce, P.O.B. 274, 127 Lower Chatham St., Colombo; f. 1955; Chair. L. NAMASIVAYAM; Sec. S. S. JAYAWICKRAMA.

Ceylon Hardware Merchants' Association: 449 Old Moor St. Colombo 12; Pres. S. H. M. ALLIAR.

Ceylon Merchants' Chamber: de Mel Bldg., Chatham St., Colombo; f. 1926.

Ceylon National Chamber of Industries: 20, 1st Floor, Galle Face Court, Colombo 3; f. 1960; 350 mems.; Chair. A. R. P. WIJEYESEKERA; Chief Exec. P. KASI LINGAM; publ. *Industrial Ceylon* (annually).

Ceylon Planters' Society: P.O.B. 46, Kandy; f. 1936; 1,667 mems; 20 branch organizations; Chair. D. P. Z. LEANAGE; Sec. A. R. RAJENDRAM, J.P.

Coconut and General Products Exporters' Association: c/o The Ceylon Chamber of Commerce, P.O.B. 274, 127 Lower Chatham St., Colombo; f. 1925; Chair. S. C. SIRIMANNE; Sec. J. B. WICKREMARACHCHI.

Coconut Marketing Board: 11 Duke St., Colombo 1; f. 1972; Board appointed under statute by Minister of Plantation Industries; Chair. D. A. P. KAHAWITA; Gen. Man. J. EDIRISINGHE.

Colombo Rubber Traders' Association: c/o Ceylon Chamber of Commerce, P.O.B. 274, 127 Lower Chatham St., Colombo; f. 1918; Chair. H. S. DE SILVA; Sec. J. B. WICKREMARACHCHI.

Colombo Tea Traders' Association: c/o Ceylon Chamber of Commerce, P.O.B. 274, 127 Lower Chatham St., Colombo; f. 1894; 100 mems.; Chair. R. L. JURIANZ; Sec. K. VINAYAGA MUDALI.

Greater Colombo Economic Commission (GCEC): Investment Promotion Division, P.O.B. 1768, 14 Sir Baron Jayatilaka Mawatha, Colombo 1; f. 1978 to promote investment in the Export Processing Zone; runs apprenticeship schemes; Dir.-Gen. (vacant).

Low-Country Products Association of Ceylon: 40 1/1 Upper Chatham St., Colombo 1; f. 1908; 75 mems; Chair. U. DIAS.

Mercantile Chamber of Commerce of Ceylon: 2nd Floor, 99-2/62 Gaffoor Bldg., Main St., Colombo 1; f. 1930; 350 mems.; Pres. A. H. RAJKOTWALA.

Sri Lanka Export Development Board: 310 Galle Rd., Colombo 3.

Sri Lanka Importers, Exporters and Manufacturers' Association: P.O.B. 1050, 26 Reclamation Rd., Colombo 11; f. 1955; Pres. J. OLIVER PERERA, J.P.; Hon. Gen. Sec. HERBERT R. PERERA, J.P.

Sri Lanka Pharmaceutical Traders' Association: P.O.B. 875, Colombo 12; Pres. J. CAMILLUS.

Sri Lanka State Trading (Consolidated Exports) Corporation: P.O.B. 263, 68-70 York St., Colombo 1; f. 1971; largest government export organization; exports products manufactured, grown and mined in Sri Lanka.

Sri Lanka Tea Board: P.O.B. 1750, 574 Galle Rd., Colombo 3; f. 1976 for development of tea industry through research and promotion in Sri Lanka and in world markets; Chair. I. O. K. G. FERNANDO; Dir.-Gen. Dr. R. L. DE SILVA.

Tea Research Institute of Sri Lanka: St. Coombs, Talawakele; f. 1925 to research into all aspects of tea production and manufacture, and to provide and publish information derived from this research; 5 brs.; 70 research workers; Dir. Dr. P. SIVAPALAN.

Trade and Shipping Information Service: P.O.B. 1525, 31 Galle Face Court 2, Colombo 3; f. 1981 to collect and disseminate commercial information and to provide advisory services to exporters; Dir. HENRI DE SARAM.

THE CO-OPERATIVE MOVEMENT

The most important organizations on the consumer side are the Wholesale Stores Unions, which handle all foodstuffs and miscellaneous goods supplied by the Co-operative Wholesale Establishment, as well as running a large number of retail stores. The Co-operative Wholesale Establishment is at the head of the consumer co-operative movement. It was founded in 1943 and is administered by an autonomous Board of Directors.

EMPLOYERS' ORGANIZATION

Employers' Federation of Ceylon: P.O.B. 858, 30 Sulaiman Ave., Colombo 5; f. 1928; mem. International Organization of Employers; 193 mems.; Chair. D. S. JAYASUNDERA; Vice-Chair. H. L. E. COORAY; Sec. S. R. DE SILVA; publs. newsletter, handbook.

TRADE UNIONS

All Ceylon Federation of Free Trade Unions (ACFFTU): 94, 1/6 York Bldg., York St., Colombo 1; 6 affiliated unions; 65,000 mems.; Pres. W. K. WIJEMANNE; Gen. Sec. ANTONY LODWICK.

Ceylon Federation of Labour (CFL): 457 Union Place, Colombo 2; f. 1957; 16 affiliated unions; 155,969 mems.; Pres. Dr. COLVIN R. DE SILVA; Gen. Sec. R. WEERAKOON.

Ceylon Trade Union Federation (CTUF): 123 Union Place, Colombo; f. 1941; 24 affiliated unions; 35,271 mems.; Sec.-Gen. L. W. PANDITHA.

Ceylon Workers' Congress (CWC): 72 Ananda Kumaraswamy, Mawatha, Colombo 7; f. 1960; mainly plantation workers; 362,329 mems.; Pres. S. THONDAMAN; Gen. Sec. M. S. SELLASAMY; publs. *Congress News* (fortnightly in English), *Congress* (fortnightly in Tamil).

Democratic Workers' Congress (DWC): 98A Mohideen Masjed Rd., Maradana, Colombo 10; f. 1962; 168,285 mems. (1981); Pres. ABDUL AZIZ; Gen. Sec. V. P. GANESAN.

Government Workers' Trade Union Federation (GWTUF): 457 Union Place, Colombo 2; 52 affiliated unions; 100,000 mems.

Jathika Sevaka Sangamaya (JSS): 532 Galle Rd., Colombo 3; f. 1959; 317,000 mems.; largest multi-representative Trade Union in South Asia, which represents over 60 per cent of the unionized white and blue collar workers of Sri Lanka; Pres. C. CYRIL MATHEW; Sec. SIRINAL DE MEL.

Lanka Jathika Estate Workers' Union (LJEWU): 532 Galle Rd., Colombo 3; f. 1958; 303,107 mems.; Pres. GAMINI DISSANAYAKE; Gen. Sec. RAJAH SENEVIRATNE.

Public Service Workers' Trade Union Federation (PSWTUF): P.O.B. 500, Colombo; 100 affiliated unions; 100,000 mems.

Sri Lanka Independent Trade Union Federation (SLITUF): 213 Dharmapala Mawatha, Colombo 7; f. 1960; 35 affiliated unions; 65,132 mems.; affiliated to Sri Lanka Freedom Party; Pres. HERBERT WICKRAMASINGHE; Gen. Sec. ANANDA DASSANAYAKE.

Union of Post and Telecommunication Officers: P.O.B. 15, 11/4 Duke St., Colombo 1; f. 1945; Pres. UPALI S. JAYASEKERA; Gen. Sec. JAYASIRI GUNASEKERA; publ. *U.P.T.O. News*.

MAJOR INDUSTRIAL COMPANIES

STATE CORPORATIONS

The following are government-sponsored, profit-making corporations:

Ceylon Ceramics Corporation: Thumbowila, Piliyandala; factories at Piliyandala and Negombo; makes entire range of domestic crockery, sanitary ware, electrical insulators, mosaic tiles, refractories, scouring powder; refines its own kaolin and supplies refined kaolin to other industries; mines ball clay, dolomite and feldspar; nineteen factories; exports ceramic mosaic tiles and domestic crockery; subsidiaries: Lanka Porcelain Ltd., Rattora and Lanka Wall Tiles Ltd., Balangoda.

Ceylon Fisheries Corporation: Rock House Lane, Mutwal, Colombo 15; f. 1964; main harbours at Mutwal and Galle; exports fish and fish products.

Ceylon Galvanising Industries Ltd.: Lady Catherine Drive, P.O.B. 35, Ratmalana; f. 1967; cap. p.u. Rs. 4.5m.; manufactures galvanized steel sheets; Man. Dir. V. BALASUBRAMANIAM; 50 employees; Sales (1979) Rs. 27.9m.

Ceylon Hotels Corporation: P.O.B. 259, 63 Janadhipathi Mawatha, Colombo 1; Chair. NIMALASIRI SILVA; Gen. Man. SAMPAT SRI NANDALOCHANA.

Ceylon Leather Products Corporation: 141 Church Rd., Mattakkuliya, Colombo 15; manufacture and export of footwear, sports goods and leather goods; Chair. L. R. WATAWALA.

Ceylon Mineral Sands Corporation: 167 Sri Vipulasena Mawatha, P.O.B. 1212, Colombo 10; ilmenite, rutile, zircon and monazite plants at Pulmoddai, rutile/zircon plant at China Bay.

Ceylon Oils and Fats Corporation: Seeduwa; f. 1958; manufacturers and exporters of mixed fatty acids, crude glycerine and compounded animal feeds.

Ceylon Petroleum Corporation: 113 Galle Rd., Colombo 3; terminal at Kolonnawa, Colombo; refinery at Sapugaskanda.

Ceylon Plywoods Corporation: 420 Bauddhaloka Mawatha, Colombo 7; factory at Gintota, woodwork complex at Kosgama, timber extraction project at Kanneliya.

Ceylon Silks Ltd.: 50/22 Mayura Place, P.O.B. 132, Colombo 6; f. 1962; cap. Rs. 12m.; manufacture of rayon and synthetic textiles; Competent Authority SARATH GUNARATNE; Gen. Man. P. M. D. GUNASEKERA; 800 employees.

Ceylon State Hardware Corporation: H.O. Yakkala; factory at Yakkala, Cast Iron Foundry at Enderamulle.

Ceylon Steel Corporation: Office and Works, Oruwala, Athurugiriya; f. 1961; steel rolling; manufacture of wire products, steel castings, machine tools; welding electrodes; soldering lead; metallographic work and testing, etc.; cap. Rs. 282m. (1979); Chair. and Man. Dir. (vacant); Gen. Man. D. T. ABEYSIRI.

Ceylon Tea Export Corporation: f. 1971; handles exports to Communist countries.

Government of Sri Lanka (Ceylon) Successor to the Business Undertaking of British Ceylon Corporation Ltd.: P.O.B. 281, Huttsdorf Mills, Colombo; manufacturers and shippers of coconut oil, household and toilet soaps etc.

National Paper Corporation: 356 Union Place, Colombo 2; paper boards, printing, pulp; Chair. and Man. Dir. Y. G. EDWARD; Gen. Man. K. M. KARUNARATNE; factories at Valaichchenai and Embilipitiya.

National Salt Corporation: 110 Sir James Peiris Mawatha, Colombo 2; sea urns at Hambantotta and Mannar.

National Small Industries' Corporation: 181 Sir James Peiris Mawatha, Colombo 2.

National Textile Corporation: 16 Gregory's Rd., Colombo 7; factories at Veyangoda, Thulhiriya, Mattegama, Minneriya and Pugoda.

Paranthan Chemicals Corporation: P.O.B. 1489, 10 Chelsea Gdns., Colombo 3; factory at Paranthan.

Sri Lanka Ceylon Cement Corporation: 302 Galle Rd., Colombo 4; factory at Kankesanturai and another at Puttalam; grinding and packing plant at Galle; combined capacity of factories meets country's requirements and provides for export.

Sri Lanka Fertilizer Corporation: P.O.B. 841, 294 Galle Rd., Colombo 3.

Sri Lanka State Flour Milling Corporation: 7 Station Rd., Colombo 3; mill at Mutwal, Colombo 15.

Sri Lanka Sugar Corporation: 651 Alvitigala Mawatha, Colombo 5; factories at Kantalai and Hingurana.

Sri Lanka Tyre Corporation: P.O.B. No. 8, Kelaniyae factory at Kelaniya.

State Engineering Corporation: 130 W. A. D. Ramanayake Mawatha, P.O.B. 194, Colombo 2.

State Fertilizer Manufacturing Corporation: P.O.B. 1344, Colombo; Sapugaskanda, Kelaniya; f. 1966; Chair. D. P. ABEYSIRI GUNAWARDANA; Works Man. A. R. MUNASINGHE.

State Gem Corporation: 25 Galle Face Terrace, Colombo 3; export of gems.

State Timber Corporation: 7 Vajira Lane, Colombo 5; f. 1968; extraction of timber, saw milling, running of timber sales depots, exploration of possibilities of increased timber exploitation, timber seasoning, preservation, import of timber and special projects connected with timber industry, afforestation, re-forestation, scientific management of forests and forest plantations and agricultural production.

STATE-OWNED COMPANIES

United Motors Ltd.: P.O.B. 697, 100 Hyde Park Corner, Colombo 2; government acquired 1972; assembles and markets motor vehicles, manufactures motor spares, construction equipment, agricultural machinery, generators, tyres and batteries; Competent Authority A. N. SENANAYAKE; Gen. Man. S. D. LIYANAGE; 486 employees; Sales (1981) Rs. 132.5m.

Wellawatte Spinning and Weaving Mills: 324 Havelock Rd., Colombo 6; government acquired 1976; textiles.

PRIVATE COMPANIES

The following are among the major private manufacturing companies in Sri Lanka, arranged alphabetically:

Aitken, Spence and Co. Ltd.: Lloyd's Bldgs., P.O.B. 5, Colombo; f. 1871; Lloyd's agents for shipping principals, insurance principals (local and foreign), airlines, charter tour operators and container principals, hoteliers, engineers, printers and carton manufacturers, garment manufacturers and exporters, car hirers, hotel managing agents; Man. Dir. C. P. DE SILVA; 2,000 employees; Sales (1981) Rs. 150m.

Allied Industries Ltd.: Third Floor, Chartered Bank Bldg., Janadhipathi Mawatha, Colombo 1; coated stainless and carbon steel razor blades, paper clips, hair pins and clips; Chair. and Man. Dir. M. P. S. WIJAYAWARDENA.

Asbestos Cement Industries Ltd.: 175 Armour St., Colombo 12; cap. Rs. 9.5m.; asbestos cement products; Chair. T. C. A. DE SOYSA; Man. Dir. M. GANESAN.

Asian Electrical and Mineral Industries Ltd.: P.O.B. 1091, 411 Ferguson Rd., Colombo 15; f. 1969; manufactures Tungsram electric bulbs; Chair. RAY DE COSTA; Accountant/Chief Exec. D. E. G. ARULANANTHAM; 110 employees.

Associated Battery Manufacturers (Ceylon) Ltd.: P.O.B. 42, Mount Lavinia; f. 1960; manufactures batteries, battery components and antimonial lead; Dir. and Gen. Man. T. C. B. KELAART; 150 employees; Sales (1982) Rs. 53m.

Associated Motorways Ltd.: 185 Union Place, Colombo 2; f. 1951; tyre rebuilding, rubber goods and rubber compounds; factories at Kalutara; Chair. V. T. DE ZOYSA; Man. Dir. CHULA DE ZOYSA.

Browns Group Industries Ltd.: P.O.B. 20, Mount Lavinia; air conditioners, ceiling fans, spring bed frames, agricultural trailers and implements, hardware, plastic goods etc.; Exec. Dir. WIMAL PREMARATNE.

Ceylon Cold Stores Ltd.: P.O.B. 220, Colombo; manufacturers, wholesalers, retailers of food and beverages; exports sea food, spices, essential oils, fruit juices and processed meats; brs. at Kandy and Trincomalee.

Ceylon Cycle Industry Ltd.: Hokandara, Pannipitiya; bicycles.

Ceylon Pencil Company Ltd.: 96 Parakrama Rd., Peliyagoda; pencils and ball-point pens; exporters of lead slips; Chair. D. S. MADANAYAKE.

Ceylon Synthetic Textile Mills Ltd.: 752 Baseline Rd., Colombo 9; synthetic textiles, exports to Europe, Africa and Japan.

Contracts and Supplies Co.: P.O.B. 487, Colombo; f. 1960; importers of electrical and mechanical plant and equipment; engineers for water supply projects; 16 agencies; Man. Prop. R. CUMARASAMY; Imports Man. T. KANESHALINGAM; 85 employees; Sales (1978/79) Rs. 9.2m.

Contracts and Supplies (Mfg.) Ltd.: f. 1974; govt. approved manufacturing of CEYGMA water pumps; Man. Dir. R. CUMARASAMY; Exports Man. T. KANESHALINGAM; 112 employees; Sales (1978/79) Rs. 11.7m.

Glaxo Ceylon Ltd.: P.O.B. 1653, Colombo 1; infant milk foods and pharmaceuticals; Chair. M. R. TEMPLE; Gen. Man. C. M. PIACHAUD.

Hayleys Ltd.: 400 Deans Rd. and 25 Foster Lane, Colombo 10; f. 1952, originally Chas. P. Hayley and Co. f. 1878; processing and packing coir fibre for export; export of coir yarn and twine, essential oils, spices, charcoal and coconuts; imports and indenting business; inland distribution of locally-manufactured products; subsidiary and associate companies involved in manufacture of agricultural machinery and implements, manufacture and export of activated carbon, formulation of crop protection and household chemicals, manufacture of industrial and household brushes and rubber gloves; Dirs. D. S. JAYASUNDERA, G. C. BOBBIESE, M. T. L. FERNANDO, Dr. P. R. THIAGARAJAH, S. MENDIS, S. KRISHNANTHAN, M. J. C. AMARASURIYA.

H. Don Carolis & Sons Ltd. and Parquet (Ceylon) Ltd.: P.O.B. 48, Keyzer St., Colombo 11; f. 1860; exporters of wooden furniture, handicrafts and tea, and exporters of parquet flooring.

Hentley Garments Ltd.: 10 Old Airport Rd., Ratmalana; f. 1953; manufactures and exports clothes; Man. Dir. R. N. CHOKSY; Dir. K. C. VIGNARAJAH; 2,300 employees.

Hirdaramani Industries Ltd.: 65 Chatham St., Colombo 1; clothing.

Indo-Ceylon Leather Company Ltd.: 80 Prince St., Colombo 2; tanners.

Jinasena Group: P.O.B. 196, 4 Hunupitiya Rd., Colombo 2; f. 1905; comprises Jinasena Ltd., Jinasena Electric Motors Ltd., Jinasena Seals Ltd. and Royal Lotus Hotel; manufactures agricultural machinery, water pumps, internal combustion engines, paddy threshers, foundry castings, ladies garments, carbon seals, electric motors; Man. Dir. T. N. JINASENA; Finance Dir. R. T. JINASENA; 1,000 employees; Sales (1981/82) Rs. 120m.

Jonaliver and Co. Ltd.: 28 Rajamalwatta Rd., Colombo 15; f. 1946; manpower consultants; Man. Dir. J. OLIVER PERERA.

Lever Bros. (Ceylon) Ltd.: 258 Grandpass Rd., Colombo 14; f. 1938; soaps, cosmetics, toilet preparations, margarine, oils and fats; Chair. and Man. Dir. T. G. S. MAXWELL.

Maliban Biscuit Manufacturers Ltd.: 389 Galle Rd., Ratmalana.

Max International: 27–14 Rajalamawaata Rd., Colombo 15; importers, exporters and manufacturers' representatives.

Mercantile Motors and Industries Ltd.: 28 Sunethra Devi Rd., Kohuwela Nugegoda; f. 1969; automobile and general engineers, used car dealers; Chair. G. ONDAATJIE; Man. Dir. V. ONDAATJIE; 75 employees.

Modern Confectionery Works (The): 663 Prince of Wales Ave., Colombo 14; f. 1945.

Reckitt and Colman of Ceylon Ltd.: Borupana Ferry Rd., Ratmalana; f. 1962; manufactures pharmaceuticals, cosmetics and household products; Man. Dir. F. R. SAMARAWEERA; 225 employees.

Richard Pieris and Co. Ltd.: 69 Hyde Park Corner, Colombo 2; goods from rubber latex foam, expanded polystyrene polyurethane and PVC cloth.

Rio Paint Industries Ltd.: Main Rd., Attidiva, Dehiwala; f. 1965; manufactures paint; Man. Dir. U. G. G. PERERA; Sales (1971–72) Rs. 500,000.

D. Samson Industries Ltd.: 97 First Cross St., Colombo 11; f. 1962; manufactures and exports footwear, rubber beach sandals, microcellular rubber sheets; Chair. D. SAMSON RAJAPAKSA; Man. D. K. RAJAPAKSA; 320 employees.

Sri Lanka Distilleries Ltd.: Wadduwa; f. 1945; distils arrack, gin and rectified spirits; Chair. Dr. M. P. M. COORAY; Man. Dir. G. A. R. COORAY; Sec. J. C. W· SILVA; 60 employees.

United Garments International Ltd.: Head Office: c/o Sellamuttu's, 128–130 2nd Cross Street, Colombo 11; manufactures and exports clothing; Chair. and jnt. Man. Dir. SELLAMUTTU SIVANATHAN; jnt. Man. Dir. W. SELLAMUTTU.

Usha Industries Ltd.: 68 Attidiya Rd., Ratmalana; f. 1961; engaged in manufacture of sewing machines and electric fans; Chair. Y. D. GUNDEVIA; Exec. Dir. D. M. J. DISSANAYEDA; 265 employees; Sales (1980/81) Rs. 14.8m.

TRANSPORT

RAILWAYS

Sri Lanka Government Railway: P.O.B. 355, Colombo 10; operates a network of 1,519.6 km. of track, of which 59.2 km. is narrow gauge and 1,460.4 km. broad gauge (incl. 100.8 km. of double track); there are 10 railway lines across the country and 269 stations (1981); Gen. Man. G. P. S. WEERASOORIYA.

ROADS

There are approximately 81,000 km. of roads in Sri Lanka, just over 30 per cent of which were maintained by the Department of Highways. The remainder, about half of which are bridle paths and earth roads, are the responsibility of other agencies such as local authorities and other government departments. In 1979 road passenger transport was opened to the private sector, which operates about 1,500 vehicles with the approval of the Ministry of Private Omnibus Transport.

Department of Highways: Ministry of Highways, P.O.B. 1720, Lower Chatham St., Colombo 1; the Ministry maintains 25,292 km. of roads, almost all of which are motorable.

Sri Lanka Central Transport Board: P.O.B. 1435, 200 Kirula Rd., Colombo 5; f. 1958; nationalized organization responsible for road passenger transport services consisting of a Central Transport Board and nine Regional Transport Boards; operates a fleet of 7,525 buses from 96 depots (1981); Chair. WIMAL PREMARATNE; Sec. MAHINDA D'ALWIS; publs. *Transport News* and *Transport Management.*

SHIPPING

Colombo is one of the most important ports in Asia and is situated at the junction of the main trade routes. The other main ports of Sri Lanka are Trincomalee, Galle and Jaffna. Trincomalee is the main port for shipping out tea.

Ceylon Association of Steamer Agents: 101 Vinayalankara Mawatha, Colombo 10; f. 1966; primarily a consultative organization; represents members in dealings with Government Authorities; 57 mems.; Chair. M. L. MACK; Hon. Sec. A. R. ROCHE.

Sri Lanka Ports Authority: P.O.B. 595, 19 Church St., Colombo 1; f. 1979 (formerly Ports (Cargo) Corpn. f. 1958); responsible for all cargo handling operations in the ports of Colombo, Galle and Trincomalee and harbour maintenance; Chair. WIMAL AMARASEKERA; Gen. Man. K. S. C. DE FONSEKA.

SHIPPING COMPANIES

Ceylon Ocean Lines Ltd.: P.O.B. 1276, 95 Wijerama Mawatha, Colombo 7; agents for Polish, Russian, East German, Romanian, Chinese and Bulgarian lines; also charter vessels; Chair. L. G. GUNASEKARA, B.A., LL.B.; Sec. N. N. GUNEWARDENE.

Ceylon Shipping Corporation: P.O.B. 1718, No. 6 Sir Baron Jayatilaka Mawatha, Colombo 1; f. 1971 as government corporation; operates fully containerized service to the U.K. and the Continent and other services to the Red Sea, the Arabian Gulf, the Far East and China; fleet of 8 vessels; Chair. M. L. D. CASPERSZ.

Ceylon Shipping Lines Ltd.: P.O.B. 891, Sir Baron Jayatilake Mawatha, Colombo 1; subsidiary of Ceylon Shipping Corporation Ltd.; operates coastal shipping service with four chartered vessels; Chair. M. L. D. CASPERSZ; Man. Dir. H. M. CHANDRASENA.

Colombo Dock Yard Ltd.: Colombo; 75 per cent owned by the Ceylon Shipping Corporation, 25 per cent owned by a Hong Kong company; dry-docking and repair of ships of up to 30,000 d.w.t.

INLAND WATERWAYS

There are over 160 km. of canals open for traffic.

CIVIL AVIATION

The control of Civil Aviation is in the hands of the Department of Civil Aviation.

There are airports at Batticaloa, Colombo (Ratmalana Airport), Gal Oya, Jaffna, Katunayake (International Airport) and Trincomalee.

Air Lanka: Greater Colombo Economic Commission Bldg., 14 Sir Baron Jayatilaka Mawatha, Colombo 1; f. 1979; domestic flights and international services to Europe, the Middle East, Far East, and West and South-East Asia; Chair. Capt. RAKHITA WIKRAMANAYAKE; Chief International Officer VIRACHAI VANNAKUL; Chief Operating Officer PETER SWIFT; fleet of 1 Boeing 737, 3 Lockheed Tristar L1011-1, 1 L1011.

FOREIGN AIRLINES

The following foreign airlines serve Sri Lanka: Aeroflot (U.S.S.R.), Balkan (Bulgaria), British Airways, Garuda (Indonesia), Gulf Air (Bahrain), Indian Airlines, KLM (Netherlands), Kuwait Airways, MIA (Maldives), PIA (Pakistan), Royal Nepal Airlines, SIA (Singapore), Swissair, Thai International Airways, UTA (France).

TOURISM AND CULTURE

Ceylon Tourist Board: P.O.B. 1504, 228 Havelock Rd., Colombo 5; f. 1966; Chair. H. P. SIRIWARDHANA; Dir. Gen. H. M. S. SAMARANAYAKE.

CULTURAL ORGANIZATIONS

Cultural Council of Sri Lanka: Department of Cultural Affairs, 135 Dharmapala Mawatha, Colombo 7; f. 1971, Admin. Trustee P. A. ABEYWICKRAME.

National Theatre Trust: Department of Cultural Affairs, 135 Dharmapala Mawatha, Colombo 7; promotes development of theatre; Pres. K. H. M. SUMATHIPALA; Sec. H. H. BANDARA; publ. monthly bulletin of theatre news in Sinhala.

DEFENCE

Armed Forces (July 1981): Total strength 14,840: army 10,000, navy 2,740, air force 2,100; there are also para-military forces of 23,000. Military service is voluntary.

Defence Expenditure: The estimated defence budget for 1980 was Rs. 984.4m.

CHIEFS OF STAFF

Commander-in-Chief of the Sri Lanka Army: Maj.-Gen. J. E. D. Perera.

Commander-in-Chief of the Sri Lanka Navy: Rear-Admiral Alfred Perera.

Commander-in-Chief of the Sri Lanka Air Force: Air Vice-Marshal W. D. H. S. W. Goonetilleke.

EDUCATION

The formulation of educational policy is the responsibility of the Minister of Education who is assisted by his Permanent Secretary, the Director-General of Education, the central authority under legislation now in force. He in turn is assisted by an additional Permanent Secretary and three Deputy Directors-General each of whom is responsible for elementary, secondary and higher education respectively. The administration and management of the school system is divided into 15 regions each in charge of a Regional Director. Government expenditure allocated to education at all levels has grown considerably over the last twenty-five years, from Rs. 120,012 million in 1952 to Rs. 954,400 million by 1977. Enrolment at elementary (Level I) stage represented 89 per cent of the total population in the age range 5–11 and 33 per cent of those of school age (12–17) at secondary (Level II) stage in 1970.

Since 1947 education has been free. In 1975 some 2.5 million pupils and students attended 9,435 schools, where the teachers numbered 102,223. Sri Lanka has a literacy rate of 82 per cent.

School attendance is now compulsory between the ages of 5 and 13 and each year about 350,000 new children start school. Until recent years schools were streamed according to the language medium used, either Sinhala, Tamil or a small minority of English. Government policy has sought to abandon English progressively as the medium of instruction. In 1960 all denominational schools were brought under state control.

Elementary Education (*Level* I)

This lasts seven years from 5 to 13. The first phase of Elementary Education is organized as Kindergarten classes. Total enrolment in 1970 was 2,100,000 in 8,000 State schools with about 70,000 teachers.

Secondary Education (*Level* II)

The secondary course lasts for four years from 13 to 17. A new system of public examinations, the National Certificate of General Education (NCGE), came into effect in 1975 to replace the British examination system. A comprehensive post-primary education programme of four years (Grades VI–IX) open to everyone was set up, terminating in the public examination for the NCGE at the end of Grade IX.

The NCGE places emphasis on practical subjects such as mathematics, science, health and physical education, social studies and pre-vocational studies. Admission to *Junior Technical Institute* is open to those with the NCGE and arrangements were being made by the Ministry of Education to organize vocational and technical courses after NCGE as well as for earlier school drop-outs. The Higher National Certificate of Education (HNCE), introduced in 1977, is more employment-oriented. The *pre-university course* is being revised to benefit not merely the 10 per cent who enter university but also those who seek employment on terminating the course.

Technical and Vocational Education

Courses are provided, for which the entry requirement is six passes in the G.C.E. (or in the new NCGE), at technical institutes and colleges. Two-year full-time courses in engineering, industry, commerce and agriculture are available which may include a year of job experience. Vocational technical education to develop occupational skills begins after eight years of general education and includes two-year full-time craft or trade courses some of which may also be part-time. Total enrolment for all types of courses was about 7,600 in 1970.

Universities

The University of Sri Lanka was founded in 1972 as a single institution with 6 campuses. These, however, developed a high degree of autonomy and, under the Universities Act of 1978 which came into force on January 1st, 1979, became six independent universities. The Act also established a University Grants Commission to supervise and administer all aspects of higher education.

Teacher Training

Training courses normally last about two years. About 7,240 students were under training in 27 colleges in 1971.

BIBLIOGRAPHY

GENERAL

Arasaratnam, S. Ceylon (Prentice-Hall, Englewood Cliffs, N.J., 1964).

Cooray, L. J. M. An Introduction to the Legal System of Ceylon (Lake House Investments Ltd., Colombo, 1972).

de Silva, Daya, and de Silva, C. R. Sri Lanka (Ceylon) Since Independence, 1948–1976; A Bibliographical Survey of the Literature in the Field of Social Sciences in Sri Lanka (Institute of Asian Affairs, Hamburg, 1978).

de Silva, K. M. (ed.). Sri Lanka, A Survey (C. Hurst & Co., London, 1977).

Farmer, B. H. Ceylon (in O. H. K. Spate and A. T. A. Learmonth, *India and Pakistan*, 3rd edn., Methuen, London, 1967).

Jayasuriya, J. E. Education in Ceylon Before and After Independence 1939–1968 (Associated Educational Publishers, Colombo, 1969).

Johnson, B. L. C. and Scrivenor, M. le M. Sri Lanka, Land People and Economy (Heinemann, London, 1981).

Ludowyk, E. F. C. The Story of Ceylon (Faber and Faber, London, 1962).

Malalgoda, K. Buddhism in Sinhalese Society, 1750–1900 (University of California Press, Berkeley, 1976).

Paranavitana, S. Art of the Ancient Sinhalese (Lake House Investments Ltd., Colombo, 1972).

Pieris, Ralph. Sinhalese Social Organisation (University of Ceylon Press, Colombo, 1956).

Raghavan, M. D. Tamil Culture in Ceylon (Kalai Nilayam Ltd., Colombo, 1972).

RAHULA, BHIKKHU. History of Buddhism in Ceylon: The Anuradhapura Period (Gunasena, Colombo, 1956).

REYNOLDS, C. H. B. (ed). An Anthology of Sinhalese Literature up to 1815 (translated by W. G. Archer *et al*) (Allen and Unwin, London, 1971).

SARATHCHANDRA, Dr. E. R. Folk Drama of Ceylon (Dept. of Cultural Affairs, Colombo, 1966).

HISTORY AND POLITICS

DE SILVA, COLVIN R. Ceylon Under the British Occupation (2 vols., Colombo Apothecaries Press, Colombo, 1950).

DE SILVA, K. M. (ed.). The University of Ceylon, *History of Ceylon*, Vol. 3 (University of Ceylon Press, Colombo, 1973).

DE SILVA, K. M. A. History of Sri Lanka (C. M. Hurst, London, 1982).

JIGGINS, J. Caste and Family in the Politics of the Sinhalese (Cambridge University Press, 1979).

JUPP, J. Sri Lanka, Third World Democracy (Frank Cass, London, 1978).

KEARNEY, R. N. Communalism and Language in the Politics of Ceylon (Duke University Press, Durham, N.C., 1967).

The Politics of Ceylon (Sri Lanka) (Cornell University Press, Ithaca and London, 1973).

LUDOWYK, E. F. C. The Modern History of Ceylon (Weidenfeld & Nicolson, London, 1966).

MENDIS, G. C. Early History of Ceylon (Colombo, 4th edn., 1946).

NICHOLAS, C. W., and PARANAVITANA, S. A Concise History of Ceylon (University of Ceylon Press, Colombo, 1961).

PARANAVITANA, S. (ed.). The University of Ceylon, *History of Ceylon*, Vol. I (Parts 1 & 2) (University of Ceylon Press, Colombo, 1959–60).

WILSON, A. J. Politics in Sri Lanka, 1947–1973 (Macmillans, London, 1974).

Electoral Politics in an Emergent State: The Ceylon General Elections of May 1970 (Cambridge University Press, 1975).

WILSON, A. J. The Gaullist System in Asia, The Constitution of Sri Lanka, (1978) (Macmillan, London, 1980).

WOODWARD, C. A. The Growth of a Party System in Ceylon. (Brown University Press, Providence, Rhode Island, 1969).

WRIGGINS, W. HOWARD. Ceylon: Dilemmas of a New Nation (Princeton University Press, N.J., 1960).

ECONOMY

CENTRAL BANK OF CEYLON. Review of the Economy (Central Bank of Ceylon, Colombo, Annual).

FARMER, B. H. Pioneer Peasant Colonization in Ceylon (Royal Institute of International Affairs, London, 1957).

GUNASEKERA, H. A. DE S. From Dependent Currency to Central Banking in Ceylon (G. Bell & Sons, London, 1962).

KAPPAGODA, NIHAL and PAINE, SUZANNE. The Balance of Payments Adjustment Process (Marga Institute, Colombo, 1981).

KARUNATILAKA, H. N. S. Central Banking and Monetary Policy in Sri Lanka (Lake House, Colombo, 1973).

Economic Development in Ceylon (Praeger, New York and London, 1971).

OBEYSEKERA, G. Land Tenure in Village Ceylon (Cambridge University Press, 1967).

PYATT, G., ROE, A., and others. Social Accounting for Development Planning with Special Reference to Sri Lanka (Cambridge, 1977).

RICHARDS, P., and GOONERATNE, W. Basic Needs, Poverty and Government Policies in Sri Lanka (International Labour Office, Geneva, 1980).

SAMARASINGHE, S. W. R. DE A. (ed.). Agriculture in the Peasant Sector of Sri Lanka (Ceylon Studies Seminar, Peradeniya, 1977).

SNODGRASS, D. Ceylon: An Export Economy in Transition (Richard D. Irwin, Inc., Homewood, Ill., 1966).

Thailand

PHYSICAL AND SOCIAL GEOGRAPHY

C. A. Fisher

(Revised for this edition by Harvey Demaine)

Thailand, which was formerly known as Siam, occupies the centre of the South-East Asian mainland, between Burma to the west, Laos and Kampuchea to the east, and Peninsular Malaysia to the south. Its total area is 542,373 square kilometres (209,411 square miles).

Of this territory much the greater part lies to the north of the Bight of Bangkok, and hence well removed from the main shipping routes across the South China Sea between Singapore and Hong Kong, though peninsular Thailand, extending south to the Malayan border approximately at latitude 6° N., has a coastline some 960 km. long facing the Gulf of Siam, and a somewhat shorter one facing the Andaman Sea. Between these two the peninsula narrows at the isthmus of Kra to a straight-line distance of only 56 km. between salt water on both sides, and at various times during the last hundred years the possibility has been considered of cutting a canal here to link the Indian Ocean with the South China Sea, thus by-passing Singapore.

PHYSICAL AND CLIMATIC ENVIRONMENT

Apart from peninsular Thailand, which except in the far south consists of mainly narrow coastal lowlands backed by low and well-wooded mountain ranges, the country comprises four main upland tracts—in the west, north, north-east and south-east—surrounding a large central plain drained by the principal river, the Menam Chao Phraya. Because of its central position within mainland South-East Asia, Thailand, while experiencing tropical temperatures throughout its entire area, receives relatively less rainfall than either Burma to the west or most parts of the Indochinese lands to the east. In general, rainfall is highest in the south and south-east, and in the uplands of the west and to some extent in the higher hills in the north, but most of the rest of the country in effect constitutes a rain-shadow area where the total annual fall is below 150 cm. (60 inches).

The western hills are formed by a series of N.–S. ridges, thickly covered by tropical monsoon forest with much bamboo, and drained by the Kwei Noi and Kwei Yai rivers. Although summit levels here are only of the order of 600–900 metres (2,000–3,000 feet), the ridge and furrow pattern makes this generally inhospitable country. In the northern uplands, which represent the southernmost portion of the great Yunnan-Shan-Laos plateau, altitudes are higher than in the west, reaching an upper limit of about 1,500 metres (5,000 feet), and the upland surface is fairly well forested, though the natural cover has clearly deteriorated in many areas as a result of shifting cultivation. But in the four parallel valleys of the Ping, Wang, Yom and Nan rivers, which flow through these uplands and subsequently converge farther south to form the Chao Phraya, there are relatively broad lowlands with a more open vegetation now largely cleared for rice cultivation.

The northeastern plateau, also known as the Korat plateau, is mostly of much lower altitude than the two uplands just described. For while on its western and southern edges it presents a continuous rim usually exceeding 300 metres (1,000 feet) and in places much higher than that, elsewhere it consists of a relatively low and undulating surface, draining eastwards via the Nam Si and the Nam Mun to the Mekong, which flows along its entire northern and eastern edge.

In contrast to most of the other uplands, including the small southeastern area of steep and rugged hills which lie along the northern shore of the Gulf of Siam, and are very heavily forested, the Korat plateau is an area of barely adequate rain, which during the dry season presents a barren and desiccated appearance. Since the main rivers flowing across it rise within this same area of low rainfall, Korat is less favourably placed in respect of irrigation water than the central plain, which, though likewise receiving an annual rainfall of less than 150 cm. (60 inches), is well watered by the Chao Phraya system.

Because of its focal position, its fertile alluvial soils, and the well developed system of natural waterways, the central plain forms by far the most important single region within the country. And within this region, the delta, which begins about 190 km. from the coast, enjoys all these advantages to a more pronounced extent, and it is here that both the former capital, Ayudhya, and the present capital, Bangkok, are situated, and that the highest densities of rural population also occur.

NATURAL RESOURCES

As the above remarks imply, Thailand's main natural resources lie in its agricultural potential, and in particular in the capacity of the central plain (and to a lesser extent the Korat plateau) to produce a substantial surplus of rice. In addition, since the late 1950s substantial areas of upland have been opened up in these areas for the cultivation of maize, cassava (tapioca), kenaf (upland jute), beans and, more recently, cotton and pineapple. The more humid and more truly equatorial coastal plains of the southern peninsular of Thailand have similarly expanded their production of rubber. Unfortunately this expansion has been very much at the expense of the country's timber resources, which are estimated to have contracted to less than 20 per cent of the total area, with the once famous teak of the northern hills now in extremely short supply.

Thailand is not especially well endowed for minerals, with the southern tin deposits, an extension of those in Peninsular Malaysia, for long the most im portant Mining has now extended off-shore into the An daman Sea. Nevertheless various other minerals, including tungsten, lead, fluorite and lignite are being worked and the country is beginning to make inroads into its serious deficit of energy supplies since the discovery of natural gas in the Gulf of Thailand. Reserves of natural gas are estimated at 328,000 million cubic metres and these now promise to be supplemented by discoveries of oil in the north central plain province of Kampaengphet. In addition, massive rock-salt and potash deposits are known to underly the Khorat Plateau.

POPULATION AND ETHNIC GROUPS

The population in 1982 was estimated at some 48,490,000, up from registration estimates of 46,961,388 at the end of 1980, when the average density was 89 per square kilometre. Although average densities fall to between a quarter and a half of this in the west and north, the total area of really sparsely populated upland is small, and in general the population is much less unevenly distributed than in most other countries in South-East Asia. Similarly, the proportion formed by indigenous minority peoples is low, and apart from some 700,000 Muslim Malays in the far south, a smaller number of Kampucheans near the eastern borders, and a total of 300,000 scattered hill peoples—Meo, Lahu, Yao, Lisu, Lawa, Lolo and Karen—mainly in the far north and west, virtually the entire indigenous population belongs to the Thai ethnic group (which also includes the Shan and Lao) and subscribes to Theravada Buddhism. However, it should be added that the inhabitants of the north-east tend to be closer in speech and custom to the Lao populations on the other side of the Mekong than to those of central Thailand and this sense of difference is aggravated by the lower standards of living in the former area.

Excluding the Lao groups, the largest minority in Thailand may be said to be the ethnic Chinese. However, estimates as to their proportion of the total population vary and many Chinese have been assimilated into the Thai culture. Most are now entitled to be, and have become, Thai citizens and in 1970 only 311,000 still remained Chinese citizens.

As an overwhelmingly agricultural country Thailand so far shows only a relatively limited degree of urbanization. The urban scene is totally dominated by the single great complex of Bangkok-Thonburi which had an estimated population of 5,153,902 in December 1980. This metropolis dwarfs other centres of which the biggest are Chiangmai (100,146), Haad Yai (98,091) and Khonkaen (94,019).

HISTORY

David K. Wyatt

When groups of the Thai people began to move into the area of present-day Thailand towards the tenth century, most of the region was under the rule of the Khmer Empire of Angkor. After a number of attempts, one such group at Sukhothai on the northern edge of the great central plain succeeded in asserting its independence early in the thirteenth century, and by the end of that century had extended its rule far down the Malay Peninsula, westwards into lower Burma, and into northern Laos. The region's political centre of gravity, however, shifted towards the south, and in 1350 a rival Thai kingdom was established at Ayudhya which soon gained a dominant position by conquering Angkor in 1369 and 1389 and reducing Sukhothai to vassalage by the end of that century. During the reign of the great King Borommatrailokanat (1448–88), the kingdom's constitution was formalized. The absolute monarchy, imbued with the authority and sanctity of the god-king of classical Indian tradition, lay under the rule of the moral principles of Theravada Buddhism; while the civil and military bureaucracy was firmly established and placed under the central control of the capital. On these institutional foundations the kingdom grew and prospered.

One theme prominent in the history of the Kingdom of Ayudhya is the manner in which it was compelled to come to terms with the world which lay around and outside it. Early conflict with Cambodia (now Kampuchea) over territory to the east and north-east, and with the northern Thai kingdom of Chiangmai over the mountainous lands to the north, was gradually extended further afield, until the Thai came into conflict with Burma, and suffered the first sack of Ayudhya in 1569, after which Chiangmai remained under Burmese control for a further two centuries. The growth and development of international trade brought to Ayudhya the Portuguese early in the sixteenth century and Western commercial rivalries in the seventeenth, which grew into an abortive Franco-Siamese alliance during the reign of King Narai the Great (1657–88), when the French, having won to their side the Greek adventurer who was Narai's prime minister, attempted to dominate the kingdom but were expelled after a revolution in 1688. Out of regional conflict and the development of international trade came a strengthening of Ayudhya's control over its export-producing provinces in the south, west, and south-east, and a growing dependence on foreign trade which survived the withdrawal of European traders after 1688. Conflict with the Burmese, however, resumed in the middle of the eighteenth century, and brought about the utter destruction of the Kingdom of Ayudhya in 1767.

Reconstruction

The kingdom was re-constituted militarily by King Taksin, the half-Chinese usurper who reigned at

Thonburi from 1767 until his overthrow in 1782; and it was reconstructed politically and economically by the first of the Bangkok kings, Rama I (1782–1809). Increasingly, the kingdom's attention was engaged by a situation of regional conflict which for the first time caught the Thai kingdom between two major powers, Burma and a resurgent Viet-Nam. At issue were Thai hegemony in Laos and Cambodia to the east, and in Chiangmai in the north. In addition, Thai interests in the northern Malay states, especially Kedah, threatened further to bring the Thai into conflict with the British East India Company. The Thai responded to these difficulties with great sensitivity to changes in international politics, strong military measures in the east and south in the reign of King Rama III (1824–51), and timely concessions to the British in a treaty of 1826 which opened Bangkok to a limited Western trade. In the later years of the reign of Rama III there grew up at court an influential group of men whose interests were closely involved with foreign trade and who were remarkably well-informed of events outside their own country, receptive to Western innovations and learning and intelligent and practical realists in their attitudes to foreign relations. One of the leaders of this group was the Buddhist monk and royal prince Mongkut, who became King Rama IV in 1851. His party was able to force the country's acceptance of Western demands that Thailand should open its ports to free commercial intercourse with the West; and the modern history of Thailand begins with the Anglo-Siamese Treaty of 1855 which was at once the springboard of rapid economic development, founded on the rice trade, and the signal for a dramatic intensification of colonial threats to Thai independence.

MODERN HISTORY

The policies of King Rama IV and his son King Rama V (Chulalongkorn, 1868–1910) to counter these threats were threefold. First, they attempted by diplomacy carefully to play against each other the Western powers, particularly the United Kingdom and France. Secondly, they worked to integrate more securely into the kingdom outlying provinces and dependent states, as in the north, the north-east, Laos, and northern Malaya, lest the local rulers of these areas either defect or by their actions provide the Western powers with excuses for intervention. Thirdly, they worked to modernize the financial, judicial, and administrative institutions of the kingdom both so as to strengthen its ability to resist the West and to meet the standards of justice and efficiency expected of it by the West. Mainly for political reasons, progress in meeting these objectives was painfully slow, and it was not until the late 1880s that fundamental reorganization of the machinery of state could be undertaken. By the death of King Rama V in 1910, these policies had been proven successful by the kingdom's survival; yet survival had been purchased at a high price. National integration had been undertaken too late to prevent the loss of Thai suzerainty over Cambodia (1863–67) and the provinces of Laos to France after the Franco-Siamese conflict of 1893, when Anglo-French rivalry failed to work in Thailand's favour. Likewise, release from some of the most onerous provisions of the treaties with the Western powers, particularly extraterritoriality, could be gained only by further territorial cessions in Laos and Cambodia to France (1904–07) and in Malaya to the United Kingdom (1909). The loss could have been much worse; and the fact that it was not is due largely to the great reforms of 1889–1910, which gave the kingdom a unified and centralized provincial administration, a modern revenue and financial system, improved communications, and a modern system of education.

King Rama V handed on to his son Vajiravudh, who ascended the throne as King Rama VI in 1910, the basic structure of a modern state. That structure, however, had been created rapidly, and the society's accommodation to it was still imperfect. Economic development had been uneven: large areas of the country, such as the impoverished north-east, were largely untouched by it; and large-scale Chinese immigration had created by 1910 a distinct Chinese community numbering about 800,000 which held a dominant position in the economy. In addition, the growth of modern education and the creation of a national bureaucracy brought into being a new class of men who increasingly demanded a degree of political power which the absolute monarchy did not give them. King Rama VI fostered the development of a modern nationalist feeling and enlarged the role of the new bureaucratic élite in the government. His younger brother Prajadhipok, King Rama VII (1925–35), who succeeded to the throne unexpectedly, lacked his predecessors' political skills and tended to be dominated by his uncles, the brothers of Rama V. He wished to grant his kingdom a constitution, but was dissuaded from doing so. By 1930, financial retrenchment still further weakened his support in the bureaucracy, and hastened the formation of a coalition of conservative civil servants, and young military officers, civil servants, and professionals trained abroad, which on June 24th, 1932, staged a coup; this ended the absolute monarchy and inaugurated a constitutional regime which the king first accepted and then rejected by abdicating in 1935.

Army Rule: 1933–45

The "Promoters" of the coup of 1932, who called themselves the People's Party, included in their number widely diverse elements. Young civilian radicals, led by a university law lecturer, Pridi Phanomyong attempted to commit their party to radical economic reform, and they were forced out of the government in April 1933. When conservative and royalist forces appeared to be using this move to strengthen their own power, the military wing of the party led by Phraya Phahon Phonphayuhasena and Luang Phibunsongkhram, staged another coup in June 1933, which firmly established the predominance of the army; and their position was further strengthened when they overcame a royalist counter-coup led by Prince Boworadet in October. The Constitution of 1932 provided for a National Assembly of which half the members were appointed by the People's Party and half were elected in a general election in November 1933. As Prime Minister, Phraya Phahon steered the government along a course which was moderate and progressive, particularly in the fields of education and social welfare. At the same time, the importance of the military to the People's Party required that the Assembly grant substantial funds to the army, although these budgets could be justified first in terms of internal and then of external threats to the government's existence. At the end of 1938, amidst growing fears of Japanese expansionism, a rising nationalist feeling directed against the Chinese community, and the growing prestige of authoritarian governments elsewhere in the world, Phraya Phahon lost a vote of confidence in the National Assembly and was succeeded as Prime Minister by Luang Phibunsongkhram, his Minister of Defence since 1934.

The extreme nationalism of Phibun's first government, from 1938 to 1944, was characterized by aggressively anti-Chinese and anti-Western measures, and by the assertion of irredentist claims on the territories lost to France between 1867 and 1907. Taking advantage of France's prostration in 1940, these claims were pressed on the government of French Indochina, and a short war broke out which was settled to Thailand's advantage by Japanese mediation early in 1941, when the Thai were awarded Lao territories on the west bank of the Mekong River and a portion of western Cambodia. The further extension of Thai claims eastwards was forestalled by Japan's virtual occupation of French Indochina in July. When Japanese troops without warning landed at Thai ports on the Gulf of Siam on December 8th, 1941, Prime Minister Phibun was forced to commit his government fully to the Japanese war effort in order to retain for his country a maximum degree of independence. Small forces of Japanese troops were stationed in Thailand throughout the war, but as allied forces rather than as occupying troops. After Thailand declared war on the United Kingdom and the U.S.A. in January 1942, the Japanese attempted to gain further Thai support by handing over the four Malay states ceded to the United Kingdom in 1909 and two of the Shan States of Burma, in November 1943. By this time, however, the prospects of a Japanese victory were increasingly dim. Pridi Phanomyong, who at this time was acting as Regent for the boy-king Ananda (Rama VIII, 1935–46), who was at school in Switzerland, was actively working with the anti-Japanese *Free Thai* underground, which was in direct contact with the Allied powers. In August 1944, the resignation of Phibun's government was forced by an adverse vote in the National Assembly. The military clique within the old People's Party was discredited by the reverses of its wartime ally, and a government led by a civilian politician, Khuang Aphaiwong, was installed under the aegis of Pridi.

The Post-War Period

At the close of the war it was vitally necessary for Thailand to avoid being treated as a defeated belligerent. It was to this end that the authoritarian military regime was swept away and a semblance of parliamentary democracy restored. Seni Pramoj, who as Thai Ambassador in Washington during the war had refused to present Thailand's declaration of war to the U.S. government and who had co-operated in establishing Allied links with the Thai underground, replaced Khuang as Prime Minister in September 1945. He skilfully utilized American support and goodwill to moderate the extreme British and French demands for compensation, and the immediate crisis in Thailand's foreign relations passed with the signing of peace treaties with the United Kingdom and France in 1946, restoring Thailand's pre-war status; but internal politics quickly heated up. A new Constitution, promulgated in May 1946, introduced a bicameral legislature, the lower house of which was fully elected while the upper house was elected by the lower. In the developments which led up to this further change in the internal balance of power, Pridi was forced to come out from behind the scenes and accept office as Prime Minister in March 1946. Pridi was in an exposed position. Some of the concessions which he had to make to regain for Thailand a respectable place in the world community were unpalatable at home; Thailand's international trade had not recovered from the war; and inflation and rampant rice smuggling brought increased official corruption and a weakening of national morale. The death of the boy-king Ananda on June 9th, 1946, an event never fully explained, rebounded against Pridi, who soon had to resign; and he was replaced by a conservative independent, Luang Thamrong Nawasawat, who lacked a secure political following and was unable to act firmly. As successive parliamentary governments showed a continuing inability to deal with mounting problems of corruption and inflation, a return to authoritarian military rule might have been expected; yet the memory of the recent past and the delicacy of Thailand's international relations made the army extremely reluctant to resume an active political role. Finally in November 1947, an army conspiracy seized power, abrogated the Constitution, and experimented briefly with a new government of Khuang Aphaiwong, who had led the parliamentary opposition to Pridi. In April 1948, however, Khuang was forced from office and Field Marshal Phibunsongkhram again became Prime Minister.

The years 1948–51 were a period of extreme political uncertainty, due partly to considerations of foreign affairs and partly to the fragmentation of the Thai political élite. The civilian, liberal politicians were split: Pridi's radicals had been routed after the death of the King, while the Democrat Party resented the high-handed manner in which Khuang, their leader, had been treated. The armed forces were divided both on service lines and within the army itself, younger elements within the latter still distrustful of Phibun's leadership. The government was in need of external support, yet fearful of American disapproval of an avowedly military regime. As the war in Indochina became more intense and Thailand appeared to be the only haven of relative stability in South-East Asia, American economic and military aid was forthcoming. Phibun could afford to ignore the parliament, which through these years was dominated by Khuang's disheartened Democrat Party; but his authority was not sufficiently strong to avert a major split within his own forces. After four abortive coups between 1948 and 1951, Phibun's military rivals were reduced to two men: General Phao Siyanon, Director-General of the para-military Police Department, and General Sarit Thanarat, Commander of the Army in Bangkok Phibun was caught between these two of his aides, and power began to slip from his hands.

Both external threats to the country's security and internal political instability worked to strengthen the army. Viet-Minh gains in Viet-Nam, Cambodia, and Laos early in 1954 and the prospects of continued subversion on Thailand's frontiers after the execution of the Geneva agreements made the Thai fearful for their safety. They were enthusiastically receptive to the conclusion of the SEATO pact in 1954, and thereafter benefited substantially from increased U.S. military and economic aid. But while Phibun's foreign policy successes grew, his political position at home was still further eroded as the wilful and arbitrary acts of General Phao discredited his regime, and public criticism of the government mounted. On his return from a visit to Europe and the U.S.A. in 1955, Phibun made a dramatic attempt to rally the nation in his favour by legalizing political parties, holding press conferences, and lifting restraints on free speech, in preparation for general elections scheduled for early 1957. The campaign of the massive government party, pledged to Phibun's support, was managed by General Phao, while the chief opposition came from Khuang's Democrat Party and smaller leftist parties based in the North-East. In February 1957, the government barely won a majority of the seats contested, despite flagrant electoral corruption and mismanagement. General Sarit, who had managed to avoid identification with Phibun and Phao, became the rallying point for national discontent, and in September 1957 staged a bloodless military coup which ended the long political career of Phibun.

After new elections in December, an experimental parliamentary government under Sarit's deputy, General Thanom Kittikachorn, was inaugurated while Sarit went abroad for urgent medical attention. The political pressures on the government, however, were great: its supporters and members represented interests too diverse for accommodation and the government was unable to act decisively on the many economic and foreign policy problems facing it. In October 1958 Sarit returned suddenly from abroad and restored military rule. Field Marshal Sarit's five-year rule was not, however, a return to the politics of the Phibun era. He commanded broad support which was not confined to the armed forces, brought into his government professional civil servants, and enhanced his authority by encouraging King Bhumibol Adulyadej to play a greater role in the public life of the nation. At the same time, he exercised his authority by acting decisively on the serious problems facing the country.

The achievements of the military governments of Field Marshal Sarit and of Field Marshal Thanom Kittikachorn, who took power on Sarit's death in 1963, were in many ways impressive. Ambitiously planned economic development raised the G.N.P. at a real annual rate of almost 8 per cent in the 1960s, and major programmes for the improvement of communications and social services, particularly education, were successful. Foreign investment and aid contributed substantially to this development, but the key to its success was a leadership hitherto lacking. New stimulus was lent to government efforts by events in neighbouring Indochina. The dominant fear of the Thai Government in the early and mid-1950s centred on what was felt to be the subversive potential of Thailand's Chinese minority. Some substance was lent to this fear by the creation of a Thai Communist opposition in China with which the exiled Pridi became associated in 1954, and by the creation of a Thai Patriotic Front in China in 1965, as well as by vociferous Chinese support for North Viet-Nam and for insurgent movements in Laos and Cambodia.

Thailand has particularly strong and historic interests in Laos and Kampuchea (Cambodia). Its frontiers with both are to some extent artificial, and across them movement by hostile or subversive forces could be easy. The Thai consistently viewed Laotian and Cambodian neutrality as weakness and a threat to Thailand's security. During the Laotian crisis of 1960–62, when Thai-supported rightist forces were losing control, the Thai demanded strong action from the U.S.A., and acquiesced in the Geneva neutralist solution of 1962 only after U.S. troops were sent to North-East Thailand and the U.S. Government secretly pledged further support for the defence of Thailand. As the Viet-Nam war intensified and spread into Laos and then Cambodia by the early 1970s, Bangkok felt that Thailand's fate rested on the outcome. Thanom firmly committed his nation to the U.S. cause by sending Thai military units to fight in Laos and South Viet-Nam, by allowing U.S. aircraft to bomb North Viet-Nam and Laos from bases in Thailand, and by providing support for government forces in Cambodia and Laos.

Period since the War in Indochina

The withdrawal after 1973 of U.S. forces from the war in Indochina, followed by the collapse of the Thieu and Lon Nol governments in 1975, brought the Thai to a fundamental re-examination of their foreign policy. Carefully correct relations were established with the new Laos coalition and the new Khmer Rouge Government, the Thai officially requested that all U.S. military personnel leave Thailand by mid-1976, and diplomatic relations were resumed with the People's Republic of China in July 1975.

Through this critical period in the early 1970s successive Thai governments were plagued by a rising tide of internal pressures. Insurgency within Thailand, which began in the North-East region in the early 1960s, by the 1970s was endemic in several provinces.

What proved to be even stronger pressure came from Thailand's burgeoning educated urban classes, who forced Thanom's government to experiment briefly with a restoration of parliamentary rule in 1969–71, which failed because of the military's alarm over student agitation, growing insurgency, economic decline, and the course of events in Indochina. Thanom's government, under a new interim constitution restoring military dominance, came under heavy

attack by mass demonstrations involving mainly students in 1973. These culminated in massive demonstrations and pitched battles between students and police in mid-October 1973. The country's military, unwilling to move against strong popular opinion, refused to step in to save the government, and Thanom and his deputies were forced to flee the country and were replaced by an interim civilian government led by a university rector, Dr. Sanya Dharmasakti.

The events of 1973 and 1974 suggested that fundamental changes were taking place in the political life of the kingdom. Popular demonstrations occurred in nearly every province on a scale and with an intensity never before seen in Thailand. Marching students were joined by urban labourers and even by disgruntled farmers. Much political energy was channelled into the formation of numerous political parties that contested the elections to the House of Representatives in January 1975. No single party gained a working majority, and several attempts were made to form governments. Seni Pramoj's Democratic Party, in a coalition with two leftist parties, formed a Government in February 1975 but it lasted only two weeks. Seni was succeeded by his brother Kukrit and a 17-party coalition led by the Social Action Party. Kukrit initially won the approval of demonstrating students for his actions to eliminate the American military presence and for negotiating the resumption of diplomatic relations with the People's Republic of China. His government fell in January 1976 over his insistence on a complete U.S. withdrawal, which many Thai regarded as seriously weakening Thailand's defences at a time of great international uncertainty.

New parliamentary elections held in April 1976 returned Seni Pramoj to power, and initially seemed to have strengthened and stabilized the political scene. Seni's Democratic Party won 114 of the 279 seats in the House of Representatives and his coalition, with four other parties of the right and centre, gave him a total of 207 seats. The representation of the Socialists, and other parties on the left, fell from 37 to 6 seats. Seni's coalition, however, proved unworkable. Its inclusion and representation of interest groups and leaders of the right and extreme right prevented the Government from making any progress towards urgently-needed reforms demanded both by moderates and by the vocal university students.

The strikes, demonstrations and attempts to bring about reform, in which the university students had played such an active role since 1973, slowly provoked a powerful counter-reaction on the right. With the support of elements of the military, police, commercial and aristocratic élite, and sympathetic coverage by some newspapers and radio stations, powerful organizations arose to challenge the new political institutions and political parties associated with the growing instability. These organizations brought a frightening degree of political violence to Thai daily life by 1976, which included political assassinations and violent harassment of electioneering by parties of the centre and left, and turned the demonstrations of university students into pitched battles, abetted by the authorities. Thai society rapidly became polarized in a manner unprecedented in Thai history, and the explosion of feelings, when it came, was violent.

Former Prime Minister Thanom returned from exile in Singapore to be ordained as a Buddhist monk in Bangkok's most prominent royal monastery in September 1976. This action, clearly encouraged and supported by prominent politicians of the right and by the royal family, incensed the university students, particularly at Thammasat University in central Bangkok, which traditionally had taken a leading role in political opposition. Demonstrations on the university grounds had been proceeding for several days when, on October 5th, a leading right-wing newspaper published a doctored photograph purporting to show students hanging the Crown Prince in effigy and an Army radio station called upon "patriots" to take action against the students. Village Scouts, Red Gaurs and other members of patriotic organizations joined with police in an assault on the university precincts which met virtually defenceless university students. Students were lynched, burned alive and brutally beaten. Officially, 40 were killed, several hundred injured, and 3,000 arrested; but the actual totals may have been much higher.

Later that day, Thailand's latest experiment in constitutional rule was ended by military intervention. The Constitution was suspended, Parliament was abolished, political meetings were banned, and many thousands of people were arrested on suspicion of subversion. The "Administrative Reform Council" appointed a former Justice of the Supreme Court, Thanin Kraivixien, to be Prime Minister while the military factions behind the coup began a jockeying for power that promised continuing instability.

Prime Minister Thanin instituted a government more authoritarian and more repressive than many of his military predecessors, and quickly alienated even the military factions that had brought him to power. Following an abortive army coup in March, a narrowly-based group of officers led by General Kriangsak Chomanan engineered Thanin's dismissal on October 20th, 1977. Kriangsak formally succeeded him as Prime Minister in November, and promised to hold elections for a new attempt at constitutional government by April 1979.

While by mid-1979 the extreme right had been brought under control, some freedom of speech had been restored, and some concessions had been made to moderate demands for reform, Gen. Kriangsak's political base was too insecure, and his position too threatened by military rivals, for him to be able to formulate and execute aggressive policies for urgent social and economic reform, or to attempt seriously to curb rampant official corruption. Rural insurgency is chronic in some parts of the Kingdom and a Marxist critique of the existing order is gaining strength among students and intellectuals.

Developments in Indochina during 1978–79 rendered Thailand's international and domestic situation even more difficult. The Vietnamese invasion of Kampuchea heightened Thai fears of Vietnamese power and influence in the region and encouraged closer relations with the People's Republic of China, whose troops invaded Viet-Nam in early 1979, and with the fugitive Pol Pot regime. With neither of these relationships were the Thai military leaders completely comfortable. Furthermore, the steady flight of refugees from Laos, Kampuchea and Viet-Nam who crossed into Thai territory placed an intolerable strain on Thai resources and security forces. The refugees posed a continuing problem until the point was reached when Thailand refused to accept any more, repatriated thousands, and by early 1982, only 3 refugee camps remained.

The elections of April 1979 brought no clear resolution to Thailand's chronic political problems. No single party won sufficient seats in the 301-seat House of Representatives to challenge Kriangsak's continued rule, and by forging a coalition of independents and smaller parties Kriangsak was able to form a new government. Former Prime Minister Kukrit Pramoj's Social Action Party emerged as the largest opposition party, with 82 seats.

General Kriangsak's government faced mounting difficulties through 1979 that came to a head early in 1980, with controversy over economic policies which finally forced his resignation. He was succeeded in March by a government headed by General Prem Tinsulanonda that included representatives of most of the active political parties. However, one year later, the coalition government collapsed as a result of a dispute between the SAP and the Thai Action Party over alleged corruption concerning oil contracts. Thirteen ministers resigned and Gen. Prem formed a new coalition government excluding the SAP. Yet this coalition faltered, over ineffective management of economic policy and in April 1981 a faction of young army officers mounted a coup against him. Prem fled to army headquarters in the north-east, where he was joined by the Royal Family; and with their support, returned to power two days later. In the wake of the coup, observers judged the unity of the military élite to have been seriously damaged, while civilian politicians showed no consistent ability to take the lead in managing the affairs of the state.

In September 1981, Gen. Kriangsak set up a strong challenge to the Government by forming the National Democracy Party and in December Gen. Prem carried out a ministerial reshuffle reincorporating the SAP in order to strengthen the coalition against this new political threat.

A certain patriotic euphoria swept the country on the bicentennial of the Chakri dynasty in April 1982, but many could not help but worry over relatively sluggish growth and continuing double-digit inflation. While the level of anti-government insurgency in the provinces had dropped off markedly, Thailand continued to work with its ASEAN neighbours to defuse the tense situation in Kampuchea with its occupation by Vietnamese troops.

ECONOMIC SURVEY

Christopher J. Dixon

Although never legally a colony, Thailand was incorporated into the world economy from the 1850s under Western domination. In 1896 an Anglo-French treaty reserved the kingdom as a field for British trade and investment. British advisers exerted some control over Thai finances until 1950, although their power had been reduced by successive treaty revisions, notably in 1927.

After the Second World War, United States influence became more important, and from 1963 to 1978 the Thai baht was tied to the U.S. dollar. In the 1950s a large volume of American loans, grants and direct investment flowed into Thailand to finance infrastructure developments, many with strategic implications. Early in the 1960s American aid was reduced, due in part to the growth of the Thai economy in the general world boom. However, from the middle of the 1960s growth rates began to slow down in line with world trends. Increasing insurgency, especially in the North-East region, and Thailand's strategic position for the Viet-Nam war, brought more U.S. aid and military presence. After the defeat of the U.S.A. in Viet-Nam in 1975, both the aid and the bases were rapidly withdrawn, causing serious problems of readjustment in a period of deepening national and international economic difficulties.

Between 1961 and 1980 Thailand's G.D.P. increased at an average annual rate of 6.6 per cent at constant prices, but this growth was extremely erratic and also slowed considerably after 1970. While the growth rate averaged 7.4 per cent in the period before 1970, it averaged only 6.4 per cent from 1970 to 1980. In sectoral terms, the pattern of growth has been even more irregular, with a growth rate for the agricultural sector, which accounts for over a quarter of the G.D.P., varying, for example, from a growth of 9.4 per cent in 1978 to a decline of 1.9 per cent in 1979. Generally speaking, the growth rates of sectors such as mining, manufacturing, electricity and water, and trade have fallen but there has been expansion in construction, transport, banking and public administration and defence.

Regional disparities have also increased rapidly as the economy as a whole has grown, certainly since the appearance of adequate regional figures in 1961. The Bangkok and Central Plain regions have sharply increased their share of the national G.D.P., as well as their levels of per caput income, which reached 246.6 and 149.2 per cent of the national average by 1979. In contrast, the North-East has fallen further behind, with a per caput income only 43.4 per cent of the national average. Although data for personal incomes are less reliable, income disparities seem to have widened also since the early 1960s.

The National Economic Development Board was established in 1959 to co-ordinate and stimulate development, and the First Economic Development Plan was implemented from 1961 to 1966. This was the only Plan to achieve either overall or sectoral targets, and subsequent Plans, although based on sounder statistics and more sophisticated techniques, have fallen short of expectations.

In the Second and Third Plans, regional elements became more important, with particular emphasis placed on the North-East with its extreme poverty and increasing communist insurgency. Under the Third Plan (1972–76), separate regional plans were drawn up but, because of the shortage of funds, failure to complete the infrastructure projects of the Second Plan and widespread unrest, greater emphasis was placed on low-cost self-help schemes in rural areas. A shift of expenditure to social projects was matched by a change of name for the planning body to the National Economic and Social Development Board.

These trends were continued in the Fourth Plan (1977–81) drafted under the more liberal civilian regime. This Plan was implemented under the very different political conditions which prevailed after the 1977 *coup d'état* and amid a rapidly worsening economic situation. The social measures were largely abandoned and by 1981, not only were many of the targets of the Fourth Plan not realized, but a number from the Third Plan remained uncompleted.

Since 1978 the increasingly apparent rural poverty and associated discontent have caused the Government to emphasize the rural sector. In 1980 a programme of rural job creation was initiated with a budget of 3,500 million baht. This project was intended to generate employment in the most impoverished rural areas and to reduce migration to urban areas. Additional funds have been allocated to agricultural credit schemes, extension services and small-scale irrigation schemes.

Serious problems of accelerating inflation, falling direct investment from overseas, a worsening balance of payments and escalating foreign debt were the experience of Thailand in the late 1970s and have continued into the 1980s. The recession was particularly sharply felt in Thailand in 1980 and the expected recovery in 1981 did not occur, owing mainly to depressed world prices for agricultural produce. Despite efforts to diversify the economy, the country remains dependent on a narrow range of exports prone to price fluctuations and unreliable production levels over which the Government has little control. More than 30 years of attempts to plan and co-ordinate development have not produced an even pattern of growth, and personal and regional income disparities have increased.

AGRICULTURE, FORESTRY AND FISHING

Agriculture dominates the Thai economy in terms of employment and is the largest single contributor to the G.D.P. and to export earnings. In 1980 agriculture and livestock accounted for 22.6 per cent of the G.D.P. Nevertheless, the contribution of agriculture has declined steadily during the 1970s.

Rice

Rice exports have declined in volume and value relative to other commodities, and the poorest areas of the kingdom and the most impoverished groups are those solely dependent on rice cultivation, with little or no off-farm employment or other cash crops to supplement incomes. The poverty of rice growers results from world price fluctuations and the low farm-gate prices, which are kept down by the Government's rice premium. This is in effect an export tax designed to keep internal prices up to 35 per cent below international prices. A high degree of monopsony reduces the farmers' bargaining position, and a cycle of low prices and low inputs (fertilizers, mostly imported, are relatively expensive) leads to low output, which in turn limits incomes on all but the largest farm units in the most favoured areas of the Central Plain. Thai rice yields remain among the lowest in South-East Asia and production levels are the most variable.

Unreliable rainfall, especially in the planting months, and a mere 20 per cent of the land classed as "irrigable", combine to produce considerable variations in the area planted each year, and this combines with crop damage and variable yields to create great fluctuations in the total output. The North-East region has the most unpredictable growing conditions, the lowest level of irrigation provision and the largest proportion of people directly dependent on agriculture.

Despite marked annual variations in production, due to unfavourable weather conditions, the long-term trend is one of gradual expansion. The volume of exports, while always varying with production levels, has since the late 1960s become more variable as the international rice market has become more volatile. Since the poor harvest of 1977, which reduced exports in 1978 to 1.6 million metric tons, rice exports have remained relatively high at 2.8 million metric tons in 1979, 2.65 million metric tons in 1980 and a record 3.06 million in 1981. In 1981 the Ministry of Commerce reduced the level of required domestic reserves, simplified export procedures and lowered the export premium. These measures succeeded in increasing the level of exports, particularly that of high-grade rice. Export prices for rice were 12 per cent higher in 1981 than in 1980 and the value of rice exports rose by 32.9 per cent. The rice sector's percentage share of export value rose from 13.5 per cent in 1980 to 17.2 per cent in 1981.

Since the late 1950s upland cash crops such as maize, cassava (tapioca) and kenaf (upland jute) have replaced rice on land unsuited to, or marginal to, rice. These crops are mainly for export, and in 1981 amounted to 16.7 per cent of total export earnings.

Cassava (Tapioca)

The production of cassava has expanded considerably since 1967, displacing kenaf over much of the North-East. In 1978 the value of cassava exports exceeded that of rice exports, and a record 6,287,965 metric tons were shipped during the year. Most is sent to Europe, principally to the Netherlands, but also to France, Belgium and the Federal Republic of Germany, in the form of pellets for cattle food. The boom in cassava has resulted in some inferior products reaching the market, and occasional shipments have been rejected because they exceeded the 3 per cent impurity standard. Since 1979 the Thai Tapioca Traders Association in conjunction with the Thai Board of Trade, have attempted to enforce purity standards.

Heavy investment in cassava processing plants has resulted in some over-capacity, particularly in flour mills, as the demand for flour in Japan fell after 1975, and, to a lesser extent, in pellet mills. Prices fell from 1976 to 1979 but output continued to expand. A poor crop in 1979 resulted in increased prices, the closure of a number of flour mills due to a shortage of roots, and a reduction of exports to 3,975,000 metric tons. The 1980 and 1981 crops both reached the 1978 level and exports were 6,212,495 metric tons and an estimated 6,300,000 metric tons respectively. In the period 1979–81 cassava ranked second to rice as an export earner, contributing 11 per cent of earnings in 1980 and 11.7 per cent in 1981. Farmers are attracted by prices which are higher and more stable than those of other crops, and by the lower labour inputs needed. However, the crop is demanding of soil nutriment and yields on poor soils fall sharply after only one or two years' cultivation. Soil exhaustion and erosion have been reported in parts of the North-East. The Government is concerned, too, about over-production. In late 1981 and early 1982 there were signs of a fall in exports and prices. Government measures to stimulate exports have so far proved unsuccessful.

Kenaf

During the 1960s the crop which was expanding most rapidly in cultivation was kenaf, a low-grade fibre like jute. In 1966 kenaf exports represented 11.5 per cent of exports by value, but production and exports declined subsequently, and in 1980 kenaf accounted for only 0.1 per cent of exports. The low quality of the fibre, unreliable price levels and a general fall in world demand for hard fibres, together with the potential for growing cassava on the same land, explain this decline. The low quality of Thai kenaf has caused the domestic gunny sack industry to import increasing amounts of fibre. Since December 1979 imports have been restricted in an attempt to protect the local growers. Production and exports increased slightly in 1979 and 1980, exports reaching 64,000 and 144,000 metric tons respectively. The depression in international hard fibre prices in 1981 is hastening the long-term decline of Thai kenaf; provisional figures suggest that production and exports in 1981 were well below 1981 levels.

Maize

Maize, like kenaf, spread widely as a cash crop in the late 1950s and 1960s, and from 1959 until the early 1970s it was the most valuable agricultural export after rice and rubber. It is grown principally in the northern parts of the Central Plain. The domestic market is small, with the main trade as cattle fodder for Japan and, to a lesser extent, Singapore, Malaysia, Hong Kong and Taiwan. Falling prices and falling Japanese demand stimulated a change to cassava. Exports in 1977 and 1978 were markedly lower than in previous years, and the area under maize contracted. Since 1979, both production and exports have increased as a result of more stable prices and the guaranteeing of export markets, the result of new trading agreements with Hong Kong. Production has increased from 2.8 million metric tons in 1978 to 3.7 million in 1981. In 1981, following a bumper crop, a record 2.6 million metric tons were exported, indicating that the fall in prices and the level of exports that occurred in early 1981 have been overcome, largely as a result of a reduction in export costs. The regulations governing maize exports have been simplified, the quota system has ended and export taxes reduced.

Sugar

Sugar cane production has fallen sharply, from 29.1 million metric tons in 1976 to 12.6 million in 1980. Price rises in 1980 brought the figure up slightly, to 13.7 million. A disturbing feature of Thai sugar production is the drastic fall in yields. Production dropped from 50.2 metric tons per hectare in 1976 to 26.4 metric tons in 1981, a result of less intensive cultivation in the face of low and uncertain price levels. The use of fertilizer has declined and there are now serious signs of soil exhaustion.

There are 44 operating sugar mills in Thailand. All exports are channelled through the Thai Sugar Trading Corporation or the Thai Sugar Producers' Association, which in 1981 handled respectively 51 per cent and 49 per cent of exports. In 1980 0.75 million metric tons of sugar were exported. Improved world market conditions in 1981 raised exports to 1.12 million metric tons. The share of export earnings derived from sugar rose from 3.1 per cent in 1980 to 5.9 per cent in 1981.

Rubber

Since the late 1920s, rubber has been a major crop and significant export. Until challenged by maize, cassava and sugar in the 1970s, it was the kingdom's second most important export earner. Production is mainly in the south, on smallholdings often with old, low-yielding trees. The small scale of the operations, both for growing and processing, has resulted in problems of quality, but replanting and reorganization in the 1970s, against a background of rising costs for oil-based synthetic rubber, are overcoming these problems. The Rubber Replanting Aid Fund, in operation since 1961, was revitalized by the injection of Commonwealth Development Corporation and World Bank funds between 1977 and 1980, resulting in the replanting of 16 per cent of stands. Thai rubber has now replaced the Malaysian rubber formerly imported by international companies for local motor tyre manufacture. Since 1971 Thailand has increased production at an average annual rate of 5.95 per cent, faster than any other major producer, and by 1979 had become the world's third largest producer. In 1980 rubber represented 9.6 per cent of export earnings. Despite an increase in the volume of exports of 3.5 per cent to 471,249 metric tons, falling prices have reduced the value of exports by 13.8 per cent. As a result, rubber's share of export earnings fell to 7.1 per cent in 1981.

Other crops

In the 1970s, in spite of agronomic problems and an initial shortage of processing facilities, oil-seed crops, notably soya beans, groundnuts and muang beans, were more widely grown. Fruit crops, too, have increasingly found export markets; pineapples account for a large proportion of a growing fruit-canning industry in the southern provinces, and a substantial percentage of the world supply. The boom in pineapple production and canning has attracted considerable foreign and domestic investment since the early 1970s. By 1979 a world glut had appeared which, despite cutbacks in production, was still present in 1981. Several canning factories under construction in 1979 have been left unfinished and six approved projects have been shelved indefinitely. In 1981 the seven main plants were working at 75 per cent capacity and were investigating the possibility of canning a wide range of Thai produce.

Despite the development of canning and, more recently, freezing of fruit, the majority of Thai crops are exported after only very simple processing.

Livestock

Sales of livestock consistently contributed between 2.9 and 3.9 per cent of the G.D.P. during the 1970s, but there is little specialist livestock rearing. The North-East supplies roughly a third of the pigs and half the cattle and buffaloes for the domestic meat market, as well as draught animals for the more intensive arable areas of the Central Plain.

In many of the subsistence or near-subsistence areas the size of the herd follows the fortunes of the rice harvest, as animals are bought in good years and sold or slaughtered in bad years; pigs and poultry are fed on rice when the price is low. Export and slaughtering quotas are designed to protect the stock of draught and breeding animals in this situation.

Exports of hides and skins, although variable, have generally fallen since the early 1970s. In 1980 only 563 metric tons were exported, compared with 9,603 in 1972. The export of live animals, although similarly variable, increased from 28,924 cattle and buffalo in 1976 to 41,796 in 1977 and 50,523 in 1978. Disease and consequent restrictions on imports from Thailand have made expansion of this sector of the economy difficult. Since 1978 the establishment of a disease-free zone in the south and the reduction of restrictions on exports should have markedly improved the prospects for this sector, but the international recession has seriously affected the meat and livestock trade. In 1979 Thai cattle exports fell to 46,882 head and to 19,520 in 1980. Breeding programmes, especially for cattle, and the introduction of Brahmin stock have been implemented, particularly in the North-East and the South, during the 1970s, and have shown localized improvements in quality. Relatively little meat is processed for export, although since 1979 the export of frozen chickens has been one of the fastest growing sectors, the main market being Japan.

Fishing

Fishing, a substantial contributor to the Thai diet, has slowly expanded on a commercial basis, with modest growth in the small fresh-water sector which accounted for 6.7 per cent of the catch sold in 1978. The main development has come from stocking and fishing of the larger irrigation reservoirs. The volume of subsistence fishing in rivers, lakes, ponds and paddy fields is impossible to estimate, but it is vital to rural protein supply.

Serious concern has arisen about claims by neighbouring countries for territorial waters extending 200 nautical miles (370 km.) from their coasts. This development and the depletion of stocks by overfishing led to concern over future production levels. Despite the development of distant fisheries, for example the agreement reached with Bangladesh early in 1980, marine catches have stagnated since 1975. Increased exports are occurring at the expense of the domestic market where high quality produce is becoming prohibitively expensive.

For the Thai market, much fish is dried, salted, fermented or turned into paste or sauce for preservation. Since 1975 the development of canning and freezing facilities has greatly expanded the export of seafood, particularly shrimps, prawns and squid. The primary market is currently Japan, but Thai exports are experiencing increased competition from cheaper Chinese produce. In 1980, 56,666 metric tons were exported and in 1981 an estimated 61,000 metric tons, representing 2.3 per cent and 2.4 per cent respectively of total export earnings.

Forestry

From the late nineteenth century, teak was exported by European companies, and around the turn of the century timber accounted for over 10 per cent of goods sold overseas. In 1951 it accounted for a mere 3.3 per cent, and the volume of timber as well as its relative share of export earnings has declined consistently since then. In 1969 wood accounted for 1.1 per cent of export earnings, and in 1980 only 0.01 per cent.

Heavy cutting and widespread clearance for agriculture (particularly now there are commercial crops which can use the land not suited for the traditional subsistence staples), local construction and fuel, with an absence of planting by the mainly foreign forestry firms, all mean that the stock of trees has been depleted. Cutting of other hardwoods, especially yang, has increased as the shortage of teak has been felt first. Vast areas are designated as forest reserves under the jurisdiction of the Royal Thai Forestry Department, but no effective control is exercised over much of them. Satellite photographs are now able to provide an accurate assessment of the country's timber resources, and it is clear that timber will remain of little economic significance.

Thailand is now facing a timber shortage and since 1978 has been a net importer. In response to the situation, the Government has announced a 50 per cent reduction in the output of the national forests and a replanting programme of 17,000 hectares per annum. This has generally been dismissed as "too little and too late".

MINING AND MANUFACTURING

Mining for precious stones and metals (tin, tungsten, lead, antimony, manganese, copper and zinc) is on a small scale, with the exception of tin. Although less important now than in the past, tin accounted for 82 per cent of mineral production and 8.0 per cent of the value of exports in 1980. The steady climb in tin prices between 1978 and 1980 revived the industry. However, from early 1981 soaring operating costs and falling world prices have brought the closure of over 200 small mines. Provisional figures suggest that in 1981 production has fallen from the 1980 peak of 46,547 metric tons of tin concentrates to 45,000 metric tons.

The industrial sector is dominated by the processing of primary produce in small-scale plants. Although a wide range of products are now made in Thailand, traditional agricultural processes, rice milling, tapioca chipping and sawmills, still attract the largest number of new investments.

Textiles were a major growth industry of the 1960s, first for the internal market and later for export. The industry was severely affected by the world recession between 1974 and 1976. Most plants were in full production again by 1978, and since 1977 the export market for Thai textiles has been relatively buoyant. In 1978 the value of exports grew by 52.8 per cent, a reflection of increased U.S.A. and EEC quotas for Thai textiles and reductions in quotas for Taiwan, Japan and South Korea. Expansion was slowed by the refusal of the EEC to increase the Thai quota in 1979 and 1980, and only marginal increases by the U.S.A. In 1981, the devaluation of the baht made Thai textiles more competitive on the world market. As a result, the EEC increased the quota for Thai textiles and new markets in the Middle East, Eastern Europe and South Africa. The value of exports grew by 22.1 per cent, compared to 1980. The textile factories import silk and cotton yarn from Japan, illustrating the failure of the newer types of Thai industry to substitute entirely for imports. The stagnation of domestic cotton production and the increased cost of imported yarn, particularly synthetics, are likely to increase production costs sharply and place increased strain on the industry. Thailand remains a peripheral textile producer and is likely to suffer severely during the current recession and the move to higher degrees of protection in Western Europe and the U.S.A.

Construction was a major growth sector in the late 1970s. In 1979 construction grew by 14 per cent, representing 13 per cent of non-agricultural G.D.P. Shortages of cement and timber are placing increased constraints on the industry, reflected in a fall in growth to 11.2 per cent in 1980 and to 8.6 per cent in 1981. From 1978 to 1980 the main growth was in public projects and the rapidly expanding Bangkok private housing sector. In 1981, virtually no new public projects were initiated and the housing boom has collapsed.

Industry's contribution to the G.D.P. doubled between 1951, when it was 10 per cent, and 1980, when it was 20.8 per cent, and although the growth has not been dramatic, it has been steady. Labour force figures are unreliable and not always collected on the same basis, but an impression of the increase in industrial employment can be gained from official statistics. In 1947, 2.2 per cent of the work force was employed in industry, and by 1979 the figure was 6.4 per cent. There is widespread under-registration of small operations, to avoid safety and minimum wage legislation as well as taxes, and it is reasonable to assume that both G.D.P. and employment statistics underestimate the growth of the industrial sector.

Government policy has been directed at stimulating investment, particularly from abroad, through the Board of Investment, founded in 1959. Emphasis has been given to concerns which would substitute local manufacture for imported goods.

Few major multinational developments have taken place in Thailand because there have hitherto been more attractive and secure areas for investment in South-East Asia. Between 1959 and 1969 only 647 firms were issued with the 'promotional certificates' which exempt them from restrictions on repatriating profits and capital and on foreign ownership of land, import duties and taxes on equipment, as well as giving guarantees against nationalization or competition from state enterprises and other tax or tariff advantages. The number of certificates issued and implemented increased gradually from 48 in 1977 to 70 in 1980, but fell to 62 in 1981. In general, although new foreign firms are larger in terms of investment than domestic concerns (foreign investment averaged 23.6 million baht in 1980) they are small by multinational standards.

ENERGY

Thailand is facing a severe energy crisis. Government measures to restrict consumption, the closure of bars and restaurants during certain hours and a ban on Sunday driving according to licence-plate numbers have been ineffective. Currently petroleum and fuel oil prices are subsidised to the extent that domestic prices are 20 per cent below the international level. In 1980 oil and oil product imports represented 31.1 per cent of the total import bill, having risen sharply from 22 per cent in 1978 and 23 per cent in 1979. Stable oil prices in 1981 and the substitution of off-shore natural gas for oil have kept the increase in expenditure on imports down to 10.7

per cent. This has reduced oil imports to 30 per cent. The proportion of oil refined in Thailand has fallen steadily from 97 per cent in 1972 to 80 per cent in 1978 and is expected to be little more than 50 per cent in the early 1980s. The three domestic refineries are running at well below capacity and acute shortages of particular refined products have resulted, these being met mainly by irregular high-cost purchases in the "spot market".

The refining industry is privately organized and mainly multinational. Profitability in the refining industry is hard to establish; Thai Oil reported losses in 1977/78 and predicted heavier losses for 1978/79. The pledge of the Government to expand refinery capacity will be hard to fulfil without foreign investment. Since 1972 there has been no investment in new refineries. All development has been concentrated in off-shore oil and gas exploration in the Gulf of Thailand.

In 1977 the Natural Gas Organization of Thailand was set up to co-ordinate exploitation and development. Gas began to come ashore from the Gulf of Thailand in 1981 via the world's longest (265 miles) underwater pipeline, and by early 1982 90 million cubic feet per day were being utilized. By the end of 1982 production is expected to be 200 million cubic feet per day, equivalent to 14.2 per cent of oil consumption in 1981. Conversion of electricity generating plants from oil to gas is planned, and this is expected to make a major contribution to Thai energy demand in the 1980s.

The Government has begun the construction of a gas separation plant at Ban Mabtaput in Rayong Province, which should commence production in 1984. An ethylene cracking plant is also planned. To encourage private and largely overseas investment in gas-associated industries, major infrastructure projects are planned. These include the development of a containerized port at Laem Chalang, the upgrading of the port facilities at Sattahip and the construction of railway links from the east coast to the north and north-east. Work has begun on the first private development, a fertilizer plant at Ban Mabtaput. This represents an investment of U.S. $350 million and should come into production in 1984. Its capacity is 900,000 metric tons of urea and phosphates per annum.

Given the present economic situation and continued uncertainty over the security of investment in Thailand, large-scale foreign investment in chemicals and heavy industry is unlikely. The Thai Government is also likely to find the financing of the various public projects extremely difficult.

INVESTMENT

Direct foreign investment in Thailand fell from 1,565 million baht in 1976 to 1,244 million baht in 1977, 1,109 million baht in 1978 recovering to 1,412 million baht in 1979 and 3,020 million baht in 1980. Investment remains at a low level, as the international recession and anxieties about Thailand's long-term future continue. There are no signs that the change of government in March 1980 has altered the prospects for investment. Government investment plans received a serious setback in August 1979 when the attempt to float a U.S. $48.45 million loan on the Tokyo stock market failed.

Foreign investment has become more broadly based, with less interest in textiles and mining, and increasing sums of money for electronics assembly and gas exploration. Much direct investment recently has taken the form of expansion of existing plants, notably by Firestone and Goodyear tyres. A relative boom in construction after 1976, mainly of government infrastructure projects, has increased demand for funding for the Portland cement works, and since 1978 13 major developments have been planned but none implemented due to uncertainty over future domestic and export markets. The expected large-scale investment associated with the development of off-shore gas reserves has not yet occurred.

Foreign investors are mostly Japanese but there are secondary roles for the U.S.A., Taiwan and the United Kingdom, in that order. Japanese investors have been particularly cautious, and a number of major projects have been postponed or cancelled. Domestic investment continues at a low level, and surplus capital has, since 1976, found outlets in speculation in stocks and commodity futures, both on the Securities Exchange of Thailand and via complicated brokerage arrangements on the Hong Kong and Singapore exchanges. Similarly, foreign money has been involved in speculation on the Thai exchange. Measures initiated in 1978 and 1979 to control and increase the taxation on the activities of the Securities Exchange of Thailand have met with limited success.

Economic growth was restricted in the 1960s and 1970s by the lack of direct investment on a large scale and the shortage of government funds to promote projects. The Thai Plans have been increasingly financed by domestic sources and foreign loans. Under the 1961–66 Plan, 27.6 per cent of expenditure came from foreign grants, under the Second Plan, 13.9 per cent, and under the Third, 16.9 per cent. The proportion of foreign loans in the first three Plans was 39.6, 30.8 and 58.8 per cent respectively, but in the Fourth Plan (1977–81) they are expected to account for a mere 13.4 per cent, showing the lack of investment confidence and the cuts in foreign aid.

FOREIGN TRADE AND FINANCE

An adverse balance of payments first appeared in 1953 and, except in 1955 and 1956, has consistently increased. Since the early 1950s the import bill for such items as consumer goods, raw materials, machinery and particularly petroleum has grown enormously, while the earnings from exports has failed to keep pace. As with all oil-importing developing countries, the steep rise in the price of petroleum products in the 1970s increased the trade deficit substantially. The terms of trade have declined steadily from 87.6 per cent in 1977 to 80 per cent in 1981.

The severing of the link between the baht and the U.S. dollar in favour of valuation against a "basket" of currencies, and the revaluation of the baht by 1 per cent, were also aimed at improving the balance of payments, for 90 per cent of imports, and the entire bill for imported petroleum, are paid in dollars. New banking legislation to strengthen the role of the Ministry of Finance and the Central Bank of Thailand, as well as daily fixing of the exchange rate, open the way to more dramatic government intervention in the future.

Since 1977, when the external trade deficit increased by 90 per cent, successive governments have attempted to reduce imports by a variety of measures, including import quotas, higher duties and prohibitions on the import of a number of items including motor cars. None of these measures have proved effective. In 1980 the balance of payments deficit rose to a record 10 per cent of G.D.P. The widening gap is being met increasingly by the use of foreign currency reserves and short-term loans. In 1971 18 per cent of the balance of payments deficit was financed by foreign loans, a figure which had risen to over 60 per cent by 1980. Longer terms are becoming increasingly hard to obtain. As a result, Thailand's foreign debt and the cost of servicing it are increasing rapidly. Between 1970 and 1980 foreign debt as a proportion of G.N.P. increased from 5.39 to 11.9 per cent. In 1980 and 1981 the World Bank and other international creditors expressed concern over the rate of increase of Thailand's debts, and the kingdom's ability to continue to service them.

The rapid deterioration of the balance of payments in the last months of 1979 brought Thailand to the verge of a financial crisis. A stand-by credit of U.S. $600 million was agreed with the IMF but this involved the surrendering of most of the country's economic sovereignty until 1982. The rise in world prices for a number of key Thai exports late in 1979 and early in 1980 has temporarily avoided this situation. During the first half of 1981 falling world prices resulted in a rapid deterioration in the balance of payments. During this period the value of imports increased by 20.1 per cent, while that of exports went up by only 8.6 per cent. A series of measures were implemented to ease export regulations, quotas were removed for a number of commodities and export taxes were reduced. In May 1981 the baht was devalued by 1.08 per cent against the U.S. dollar. This proved to be ineffective and a further devaluation, of 8.7 per cent, took place in August. A number of Thai and foreign observers have been highly critical of this action, suggesting that long-term economic prospects will suffer. However this measure has been successful in respect of the balance of payments. Provisional figures indicate that the growth of imports for 1981 was restricted to 13.9 per cent and that exports revived to grow at 14.4 per cent. The balance of payments deficit on current account was 54,760 million baht compared to the mid-year estimate of 97,000 million baht.

The composition of exports has changed, away from tin, rice, rubber and teak, which together accounted for over 80 per cent of exports in the period before 1950. These commodities accounted for only 50 per cent of export earnings by 1969 and only 30.1 per cent in 1981. They have been replaced by new crops, mainly maize and cassava, and, to a lesser extent, by manufacturing and earnings from tourism, but none of the industrial developments are in a position to replace the dependence on agricultural products which are both prone to variations in production, due to rainfall, and vulnerable to international price fluctuations.

Textile exports, a success of the 1960s, slumped in the early 1970s and, although most of the surplus capacity was re-utilized in the period 1976–78, the future of the industry remains heavily dependent on the level of import quotas set by the U.S.A. and EEC. Portland cement, in which Thailand has been self-sufficient for many years, was exported, mainly to Indonesia and the Middle East, on an increasing scale from 1967 (33,000 metric tons) to 1974 (919,536 metric tons), when it represented 1.3 per cent of export earnings. By 1977, however, it accounted for only 0.3 per cent of exports, both because of growing domestic industries in the Middle East and because of international economic difficulties. During 1978 exports ceased altogether and since 1979 Thailand has been a net importer.

Protectionism on the part of traditional trading partners has encouraged a search for new destinations for exports, and trade missions were sent in 1978 and 1979 to the People's Republic of China, Iran, Romania, Hungary, the Republic of Korea, the Democratic People's Republic of Korea and the EEC. There have been increasing sales to the oil-rich Middle East countries, such as Kuwait and Saudi Arabia as well as Eastern Europe, but Japan and the U.S.A. remain the major supplier of imports and the purchasers of exports.

DEVELOPMENT AND FUTURE PROSPECTS

In 1981 the Thai economy faced serious problems, including rapid inflation, an increasingly adverse balance of payments, escalating foreign debt and declining confidence on the part of international creditors. Early in 1981 there were optimistic forecasts of economic recovery, but they have not materialized. The rate of inflation fell to 12 per cent in 1981 and oil prices were relatively stable, but falling prices for most Thai exports and the steeply rising costs of non-oil imports cancelled out any gain for the economy. Economic growth did not accelerate. The Government's anti-inflationary measures meant high interest rates and tight monetary control which discouraged investment. The various measures introduced by governments since 1978 to increase control over the economy have met with little success. Late in 1980 the IBRD produced a dismal economic report on the Thai economy and recommended a five-year programme of 'structural readjustment'. According to the IBRD, the continuation of present trends and government policy would result in the increase of overseas debts from U.S. $3,800 million to $20,300 million between 1980 and 1985, and a rise in the debt service ratio from 15.4 to 25.1 per cent. The main IBRD policy recommendations were: to raise domestic energy prices to the international level; the development of a strongly deflationary monetary and fiscal policy; an end to the import substitution policy for industry and emphasis to be placed on export-orientated industries; reduction of import tariffs and the removal of all export restrictions and taxes; increased and more effective personal taxation; an end to restrictions on the level of domestic interest rates; and a comprehensive review of government organization and expenditure in order to eliminate waste.

At the meeting of the Thai aid group in February 1981, an agreement was reached to provide loans to the kingdom of U.S. $1,200 million in 1981, an increase of 41 per cent over 1980 and equivalent to over half the estimated public borrowing needs. The receipt of these funds has been made conditional on the implementation of the IBRD policy recommendations.

The Fifth Plan (1982–86) shifts the emphasis from national and regional planning as solutions to developmental problems to the development of heavy industry in association with the exploitation of the Eastern Seaboard gas reserves. Overseas and private domestic sources will provide most of the funding for these projects. In 1981 the Eastern Seaboard Development Committee allocated U.S. $13 million for preparatory work on 3,360 hectares of land in Rayong Province, where most of the initial development is planned. It is hoped that the gas developments, with low Thai labour costs, will attract the foreign investment which to date has been reluctant to come to Thailand.

Rural development is to be concentrated in the most backward and politically unstable areas. Initially, 246 districts have been singled out for special attention in an effort to reduce poverty. A co-ordinated defence and development programme will also be applied to 4,000 "self-defence" villages in areas of marked poverty and communist activity.

The role of the private sector in agricultural development is to be highlighted. Rural areas have been divided into three types: backward, where development will be government-financed; more advanced, where combined government and private development will be fostered; advanced, which will be left entirely to the private sector.

Since 1979, foreign investment in Thailand has recovered to the level of the early 1970s. However, the scale of investment remains low, and Thailand has never been recognized as a secure and attractive area for investment. Largely because of poor international transport facilities, other than air transport, the Thai manufacturing industry does not have the cost advantages of, for example, Taiwan, South Korea or Singapore. Overseas enterprise and investment has been discouraged by continued uncertainty over the country's political future. Future prospects are heavily dependent on the level of investors' confidence in the Government's resistance to communist revolution.

A long-term problem of escalating insurgency is behind the priority given to rural development in the designation of 1979 as the "year of the farmers", for, like its predecessors over the last 20 years, the Government regards economic advance as the best "counter-insurgency measure". However, since 1978 expenditure on defence and internal security has increased rapidly, reaching 26.1 per cent of the national budget in 1979.

Nevertheless, shortage of funds, vested interests and unwieldy administration seriously limit the impact of such policies as the rice price support scheme for farmers, rural credit and water supply and land reform. In many rural areas, land is acutely short, with much landlessness, illegal forest clearance, and cultivation of unsuitable land, some on watersheds prone to soil erosion. The ambitious land improvement scheme drawn up in 1976 has met with little success. By 1980, work on little more than two million rai (0.33 million hectares) had been completed. In 1980, the IBRD recommended that much scrubland currently classified as forest could be released for agriculture but the productivity of such land is likely to be extremely low. Most of the more ambitious plans, such as free health facilities, initiated under civilian governments between 1974 and 1976 have been abandoned or subjected to severe cash limits, both because of budgetary difficulties and through realization that they are inadequate at removing rural discontent.

The rice price support scheme operating since 1979 is intended to benefit farmers by guaranteeing a minimum price and making subsidized rice available to poor urban workers. Poor organization, financial constraints and inadequate storage space have severely limited the impact of the scheme. Since 1978 rice exporters must sell half a metric ton of rice to the Government's Warehouse Organization for every metric ton exported, at an average of 14 per cent below the wholesale price, and the rice bought in this way is issued at low prices to schools, civil servants and others, as well as being sold to the government export trade. Since 1955 the rice premium has operated to keep the internal price below the international price, thus depressing the price which farmers receive in order to lower the urban cost of living. Only a large injection of government funds would ensure a rice marketing system which would benefit both rural producers and urban interests.

The annual rate of inflation reached a peak of 24 per cent in 1974 and, although subsequently lower, rose steadily from 1976 to reach 19.7 per cent in 1980, declining again to 12.7 per cent in 1981. Higher oil prices are a major contributor to rising prices over a wide range of goods. After a virtual wage freeze from 1974, governments have agreed to annual increases in the minimum wage of 25 per cent in 1978 and 1979, and 30 per cent in 1980, recognizing both the high inflation and the demands of an increasingly vocal labour movement. In 1981 the increase in minimum wages was higher outside Bangkok, reflecting the Government's policy of reducing migration from rural areas. Although strikes were illegal from 1977 to 1981, industrial disputes were seen to disrupt production in a number of sectors since 1977, and since the overthrow of the Thanom regime no Thai government can afford to ignore industrial unrest.

The IBRD has been reluctant to fund large-scale infrastructural projects such as the proposed new port at Laem Chabang, and has given preference to lower-cost short-term projects, such as the extension of existing port facilities at Bangkok and Sattahip. Clearly the IBRD itself is hesitant over the long-term security of investment in Thailand and the ability of the country to undertake repayment of large loans.

New planning measures—including axes of development linking key centres, industrial estates and new towns around Bangkok such as Navo Nakorn—are unlikely to progress without the expenditure of large sums. Increased stability and growth depend on investment but the ability to withstand the revolutionary tide depends on that same growth and investment. Several government officials expressed concern about the political and economic situation, and some even spoke of time periods as short as two or three years in which, without a radical alteration in the economic prospect, revolution seemed inevitable.

STATISTICAL SURVEY

AREA AND POPULATION

Area	Census Population†		Estimated Population (mid-year)				Density (per sq. km.) 1982
	April 1st, 1970	Dec. 31st, 1979	1979	1980	1981	1982	
542,373 sq. km.*	34,397,374	46,113,756	45,460,000	46,455,000	47,488,000	48,490,000	89

* 209,411 square miles.

† Excluding adjustment for underenumeration. For 1970 this was 2.01 per cent, giving an adjusted census total of 35,103,000.

Principal towns (1970 census): Bangkok (capital) 2,157,303; Thonburi 920,058. Bangkok Metropolis (including Thonburi): 5,153,902 (Dec. 1980).

Source: National Statistical Office, Ministry of Interior, Chulalongkorn University Institute of Population Studies.

BIRTHS, MARRIAGES AND DEATHS*

	Registered Live Births		Registered Marriages		Registered Deaths	
	Number	Rate per '000	Number	Rate (per '000)	Number	Rate (per '000)
1973	1,167,272	29.3	176,166	4.4	239,151	6.0
1974	1,185,869	29.1	199,258	4.9	246,459	6.0
1975	1,132,806	27.1	266,934	6.3	237,018	5.7
1976	1,166,292	27.1	270,415	6.2	237,062	5.5
1977	1,156,504	26.3	281,111	6.4	236,783	5.4
1978	1,101,634	24.4	291,501	6.6	233,217	5.2
1979	1,130,907	24.5	285,461	6.2	235,094	5.1

* Registration is incomplete. Average annual rates estimated by the United Nations are: Births 37.9 per 1,000 in 1970–75, 32.3 per 1,000 in 1975–80, 28.4 per 1,000 in 1981; Deaths 10.5 per 1,000 in 1970–75, 8.9 per 1,000 in 1975–80, 7.7 per 1,000 in 1981.

Source: Department of Local Administration, Ministry of the Interior.

ECONOMICALLY ACTIVE POPULATION*

(labour force sample survey, 'ooo persons aged 11 and over)

	January–March 1978			July–September 1978		
	Males	Females	Total	Males	Females	Total
Agriculture, forestry, hunting and fishing	6,180.2	4,295.3	10,475.5	8,183.9	7,833.1	16,017.0
Mining and quarrying	31.8	11.9	43.7	23.3	6.3	29.6
Manufacturing	1,046.4	702.7	1,749.1	858.4	618.1	1,476.5
Construction, repair and demolition	394.4	54.2	403.6	270.8	41.7	312.5
Electricity, gas, water and sanitary services	44.8	7.3	52.1	50.1	7.9	58.0
Commerce	829.5	901.4	1,730.9	772.0	866.6	1,638.6
Transport, storage and communications	394.0	35.6	429.6	363.2	23.7	386.9
Services	1,028.2	779.3	1,807.5	985.2	826.5	1,811.7
Activities not adequately described	0.2	0.0	0.2	2.7	3.0	5.7
Total in Employment (incl. others)	9,905.3	6,788.5	16,693.9	11,509.6	10,226.9	21,736.5
Unemployed	121.9	67.9	189.9	104.7	52.1	156.8
Total Labour Force	10,027.3	6,856.4	16,883.8	11,614.3	10,279.0	21,893.3

* Excluding unpaid family workers who worked less than 20 hours during the survey week.

1980: Total labour force 21,030,000 (incl. 1,140,000 unemployed).

Source: Report of the Labour Force Survey, National Statistical Office.

AGRICULTURE

LAND USE, 1979

('ooo hectares)

Arable land	16,250*
Land under permanent crops	1,700*
Permanent meadows and pastures	308†
Forest and woodland	16,330†
Other land	16,589
Total Land	51,177
Inland water	223
Total	51,400‡

* FAO estimate. † Unofficial estimate.

‡ Other sources give the area as 54,237,000 hectares.

Source: FAO, *Production Yearbook*.

PRINCIPAL CROPS

	Area Harvested ('000 hectares)			Production ('000 metric tons)		
	1978	1979	1980	1978	1979	1980
Rice (paddy)	8,288	8,651	9,145*	17,530	15,758	18,000*
Maize	1,386	1,509	1,562	2,791	3,300	3,150
Sorghum	176	230*	270*	216	260*	350*
Sweet potatoes	36†	36†	36	330†	350†	358†
Cassava (manioc, tapioca)	1,323	858*	1,015*	18,399	11,100*	13,500*
Dry beans	418	418†	425†	262	260†	275†
Soybeans	155†	130†	135†	159	102*	105*
Groundnuts (in shell)	105†	100†	120†	128	109*	130*
Cottonseed	} 74	81*	132*	54*	66*	98*
Cotton (lint)				27	33†	49*
Coconuts	} n.a.	n.a.	n.a.	860*	688*	900*
Copra				46†	42†	51†
Water melons	40†	40†	40†	500†	500†	510†
Sugar cane	480*	480*	416*	20,561	20,244*	12,612*
Bananas	n.a.	n.a.	n.a.	2,000*	2,000†	2,000†
Kenaf (mesta)	197†	197†	197†	368	290†	250†
Natural rubber	n.a.	n.a.	n.a.	467	547*	510*
Pineapples	n.a.	n.a.	n.a.	1,400†	1,500†	1,500†
Onions (dry)	23*	21*	23*	140*	137*	140*
Tobacco	152*	152*	152*	83*	83*	86*
Castor beans	42†	42†	38†	43*	37*	26*

* Unofficial figure. † FAO estimate.

Source: FAO, *Production Yearbook*.

LIVESTOCK
('000 head, year ending September)

	1978	1979	1980
Horses*	167	167	167
Cattle	4,706	4,850†	5,000†
Buffaloes	6,562	6,000†	6,250†
Pigs	4,943	5,386†	5,547*
Sheep*	55	58	61
Goats*	31	31	31
Chickens	56,306	65,324	70,000†
Ducks	9,991	9,013	9,500†

* FAO estimates. † Unofficial figures.

Source: FAO, *Production Yearbook*.

LIVESTOCK PRODUCTS
('000 metric tons—FAO estimates)

	1978	1979	1980
Beef and veal	138	140	142
Buffalo meat	71	71	72
Pigmeat	220	235	240
Poultry meat	150	163	172
Cows' milk	5	5	5
Buffalo milk	7	7	7
Hen eggs	99.5	99.0	105.0
Other poultry eggs	95.4	97.2	100.2
Cattle and buffalo hides	39.4	40.0	40.3

Source: FAO, *Production Yearbook*.

FORESTRY

ROUNDWOOD REMOVALS
('000 cubic metres, all non-coniferous)

	1973*	1974*	1975	1976	1977	1978	1979	1980
Sawlogs, veneer logs and logs for sleepers	3,517	3,517	3,090	3,210	3,340	2,609	3,101	2,425
Other industrial wood	1,790	1,849	1,911	1,974*	2,040*	2,107*	3,122	2,453
Fuel wood*	24,541	25,260	25,997	26,753	27,526	28,319	29,132	29,966
Total	29,848	30,626	30,998	31,937	32,906	33,035	35,355	34,844

* FAO estimate.

Source: FAO, *Yearbook of Forest Products*.

SAWNWOOD PRODUCTION

('000 cubic metres, all non-coniferous)

	1974	1975	1976	1977	1978	1979	1980
Sawnwood (incl. boxboards)	1,500	1,659	1,659*	1,737	1,565	1,550	1,214
Railway sleepers	19	13	11	7	7	8	17
TOTAL	1,519	1,672	1,670	1,744	1,572	1,558	1,231

* FAO estimate.

Source: FAO, *Yearbook of Forest Products.*

FISHING

('000 metric tons)

	1973	1974	1975	1976	1977	1978	1979
Freshwater	120.9	158.9	160.7	147.3	122.4	150.0	160.0
Sea	1,538.0	1,351.6	1,394.6	1,551.8	2,067.5	1,957.0	2,055.0
TOTAL	1,658.9	1,510.5	1,555.3	1,699.1	2,189.9	2,107.0	2,215.0

Source: Department of Fisheries: Fisheries Record of Thailand.

MINING

(production in metric tons)

	1975	1976	1977	1978	1979
Brown coal and lignite	462,801	680,343	438,570	638,942	1,356,468
Iron ore*	32,476	25,000	63,470	88,121	103,101
Rock salt	2,600	5,575	12,570	11,839	n.a.
Antimony ore*	7,372	8,637	5,774	6,759	6,941
Lead concentrates*	3,608	2,127	1,190	3,945	20,515
Manganese ore*	24,914	50,225	76,962	72,221	35,175
Tin concentrates*	22,397	27,921	33,044	41,210	46,547
Tungsten concentrates*	3,441	3,986	4,276	6,182	3,556
Zinc concentrates*	14,000	—	—	—	—

* Figures refer to the gross weight of ores and concentrates. The estimated metal content (in metric tons) was:

Iron: 18,000 in 1975; 14,000 in 1976; 36,000 in 1977; 50,000 in 1978.
Antimony: 3,244 in 1975; 3,800 in 1976; 2,527 in 1977; 2,970 in 1978.
Lead: 1,400 in 1975; 900 in 1976; 500 in 1977; 1,600 in 1978.
Manganese: 8,700 in 1975; 17,600 in 1976; 26,900 in 1977; 25,300 in 1978.
Tin: 16,406 in 1975; 20,453 in 1976; 24,205 in 1977; 30,186 in 1978; 33,962 in 1979.
Tungsten: 2,005 in 1975; 2,233 in 1976; 2,464 in 1977; 3,780 in 1978.
Zinc: 3,200 in 1975.

Source: Department of Mineral Resources and National Statistical Office, Bangkok.

Crude petroleum (estimated production in '000 metric tons): 6 in 1975; 8 in 1976; 8 in 1977; 8 in 1978.
Phosphate rock ('000 metric tons): 6 in 1975; 7 in 1976; 3 in 1977.

INDUSTRY

SELECTED PRODUCTS

		1976	1977	1978	1979
Sugar[1]	'000 metric tons	1,604	2,212	1,584	1,795
Beer[2]	'000 hectolitres	749.9	1,030.1	1,083.7	1,562.1
Cigarettes[1]	metric tons	22,642	23,477	23,905	27,160
Cotton yarn	,, ,,	73,300	n.a.	n.a.	n.a.
Woven cotton fabrics[1]	million sq. metres	585	615	n.a.	n.a.
Non-cellulosic continuous filaments[3]	metric tons	25,800	31,700	34,700	n.a.
Non-cellulosic discontinuous fibres[3]	,, ,,	29,400	38,100	43,600	n.a.
Woven fabrics of man-made fibres	million sq. metres	437.5	469.0	n.a.	n.a.
Rubber tyres	'000	1,214	1,608	n.a.	n.a.
Sulphuric acid[1]	'000 metric tons	41.8	48.2	60.2	48.1
Hydrochloric acid[1]	,, ,, ,,	59.5	71.8	66.6	76.2
Caustic soda (100%)[1]	,, ,, ,,	61.3	65.3	62.1	66.8
Nitrogenous fertilizers (N content)	,, ,, ,,	6.9	8.9	3.5	n.a.
Liquefied petroleum gas[4]	,, ,, ,,	127	137	125	143
Naphtha[5]	,, ,, ,,	230	220	230	n.a.
Motor spirit (petrol)[4]	,, ,, ,,	1,408	1,568	1,254	1,567
Kerosene[4]	,, ,, ,,	237	228	212	258
Jet fuel[4]	,, ,, ,,	680	609	612	633
Distillate fuel oils[4]	,, ,, ,,	2,216	2,435	2,241	2,412
Residual fuel oils[4]	,, ,, ,,	2,458	2,697	2,968	3,313
Petroleum bitumen (asphalt)[5]	,, ,, ,,	141	140	156	n.a.
Cement[1]	,, ,, ,,	4,422.1	5,062.7	5,044.5	5,203.7
Crude steel	,, ,, ,,	281	300	314	n.a.
Tin (unwrought): primary	metric tons	20,337	23,102	28,945	n.a.
Passenger motor cars (assembly)[1]	'000	15.3	17.9	n.a.	21.6
Commercial motor vehicles (assembly)[1]	,,	32.3	47.3	44.6	30.9
Electric energy[4]	million kWh.	10,295	11,691	13,204	14,067

[1] *Source:* Industrial Economics and Planning Division, Ministry of Industry.
[2] *Source:* The Boonrawd Brewery Co. Ltd. and Thai Amarit Brewery Co. Ltd.
[3] *Source:* Textile Economics Bureau, Inc. (New York).
[4] *Source:* National Energy Administration, Office of the Prime Minister.
[5] *Source:* Bureau of Mines, U.S. Department of the Interior.

FINANCE

100 satangs = 1 baht.

Coins: ½, 1, 5, 10, 20, 25 and 50 satangs; 1 and 5 baht.

Notes: 50 satangs; 1, 5, 10, 20, 100 and 500 baht.

Exchange rates (June 1982): £1 sterling = 39.84 baht; U.S. $1 = 23.00 baht.

1,000 baht = £25.10 = $43.48.

Note: From October 1963 to July 1973 the official exchange rate was U.S. $1 = 20.80 baht (1 baht = 4.8077 U.S. cents). In July 1973 the par value of the baht was fixed at 5 U.S. cents ($1 = 20.00 baht) but in March 1978 the direct link with the U.S. dollar was ended and the baht pegged to a "basket" of the currencies of Thailand's main trading partners. The market rate was fixed at $1 = 20.375 baht (1 baht = 4.9080 U.S. cents) until October 1975 and at $1 = 20.40 baht (1 baht = 4.9020 U.S. cents) from November 1975 to August 1978. Thereafter the rate was adjusted frequently, although remaining fairly stable, until July 1981, when the currency was devalued from 21.0 to 23.0 per U.S. dollar. The average rate (baht per U.S. dollar) was: 20.379 in 1975; 20.336 in 1978; 20.419 in 1979; 20.476 in 1980; 21.820 in 1981. In terms of sterling, the exchange rate was £1 = 49.92 baht from November 1967 to August 1971; and £1 = 54.20 baht from December 1971 to June 1972.

BUDGET ESTIMATES

(million baht, October 1st to September 30th)

Revenue	1979/80	1980/81	1981/82*
Taxation	75,778.1	102,683.5	118,566.1
Sale of property and services	2,229.7	2,808.1	3,244.5
State enterprises	4,101.8	5,153.3	6,826.3
Others	2,790.4	4,605.1	4,530.1
New taxes and tax revisions	3,100.0	4,750.0	6,833.0
Total Revenue	88,000.0	120,000.0	140,000.0
Total borrowing	17,500.0	16,000.0	19,000.0
Treasury reserves	3,500.0	4,000.0	2,000.0
Total Receipts	109,000.0	140,000.0	161,000.0

Expenditure	1979/80	1980/81	1981/82
Economic services	22,823.7	32,189.2	33,058.8
Education	22,583.4	27,944.5	32,630.3
Defence	22,349.9	27,708.0	31,395.3
Internal security	6,046.7	7,270.0	8,197.2
Public Health	4,539.5	15,120.6 (Public Health and Public utilities)	6,234.0
Public utilities	7,682.9		10,268.9
General administration	3,490.2	4,746.8	4,127.7
Debt services	12,392.9	17,530.9	21,008.5
Others	7,090.8	7,488.0	14,079.3
Total	109,000.0	140,000.0	161,000.0

* Preliminary figures.

Source: Bank of Thailand.

1982/83: Budget estimate: 177,000 million baht.

NATIONAL ACCOUNTS

Gross National Product

(million baht at current prices)

	1974	1975	1976	1977	1978	1979
Agriculture, etc.	84,735	94,063	104,657	110,929	131,167	145,616
Crops	62,229	69,666	77,509	79,069	99,342	109,082
Livestock	10,583	11,473	12,354	14,409	12,724	16,860
Fishing	7,273	8,454	9,792	12,456	14,103	14,584
Forestry	4,650	4,470	5,002	4,995	4,998	5,090
Mining and quarrying	4,530	4,062	5,174	8,139	10,604	13,798
Manufacturing	49,359	53,910	63,025	74,676	87,657	108,865
Construction	10,704	12,873	15,784	20,251	25,863	31,471
Electricity and water	2,789	3,290	3,745	4,384	5,168	5,730
Transport and communications	15,966	18,764	21,828	24,706	29,793	35,312
Wholesale and retail trade	53,964	54,681	59,391	74,931	94,631	112,964
Banking, insurance and real estate	12,835	14,559	16,075	19,537	25,300	31,372
Ownership of dwellings	4,174	4,415	4,840	5,272	5,868	6,875
Public administration and defence	10,533	12,321	13,571	14,810	17,943	21,292
Other services	21,779	25,878	29,545	35,395	43,347	51,136
Gross Domestic Product (G.D.P.)	271,368	298,816	337,635	393,030	477,341	564,431
Net factor income from abroad	798	−219	−1,261	−2,014	−3,712	−7,652
Gross National Product	272,166	298,597	336,374	391,016	473,629	556,779

Source: Bank of Thailand and National Accounts Division, National Economic and Social Development Board.

BALANCE OF PAYMENTS
(U.S. $ million)

	1976	1977	1978	1979	1980	1981
Merchandise exports f.o.b.	2,959	3,454	4,045	5,234	6,449	6,900
Merchandise imports f.o.b.	−3,145	−4,247	−4,913	−6,787	−8,352	−8,910
TRADE BALANCE	−186	−793	−868	−1,553	−1,903	−2,010
Exports of services	686	724	1,088	1,428	2,125	2,333
Imports of services	−963	−1,068	−1,413	−2,021	−2,509	−3,009
BALANCE ON GOODS AND SERVICES	−463	−1,137	−1,193	−2,146	−2,287	−2,686
Unrequited transfers (net)	23	40	40	60	209	163
BALANCE ON CURRENT ACCOUNT	−440	−1,097	−1,153	−2,086	−2,078	−2,523
Direct investment (net)	79	106	50	51	187	285
Other long-term capital (net)	240	322	520	1,246	1,824	1,995
Short-term capital (net)	221	617	715	499	−63	143
Net errors and omissions	−19	43	−232	20	−172	89
TOTAL (net monetary movements)	81	−9	−100	−270	−302	−11
Allocation of IMF Special Drawing Rights	—	—	—	24	25	23
Valuation changes (net)	45	95	161	−11	−33	−99
IMF Trust Fund loans	—	17	52	53	45	1
Official financing (net)	—	—	—	—	—	−1
CHANGES IN RESERVES	126	103	113	−204	−265	−87

Source: IMF, *International Financial Statistics.*

EXTERNAL TRADE
(million baht)

	1974	1975	1976	1977	1978	1979	1980	1981
Imports c.i.f.	64,044	66,835	72,877	94,177	108,899	146,161	188,686	216,246
Exports f.o.b.	50,245	45,007	60,797	71,198	83,065	108,179	133,197	153,030

PRINCIPAL COMMODITIES
(million baht)

IMPORTS	1974	1975	1976	1977	1978	1979
Food	1,812	1,952	2,281	2,503	2,846	3,909
Beverages and tobacco	676	753	656	1,043	1,013	1,213
Crude materials	4,276	3,977	5,225	7,404	7,316	11,408
Mineral fuels and lubricants	12,571	14,233	16,695	20,889	22,851	32,650
Animal and vegetable oils and fats	124	108	163	292	272	473
Chemicals	9,318	9,122	10,505	13,356	14,979	21,791
Basic manufactures	12,015	10,560	11,984	15,409	18,479	25,794
Machinery	20,467	23,125	21,424	27,982	33,636	38,346

[*continued on next page*

PRINCIPAL COMMODITIES—*continued*]

EXPORTS	1976	1977	1978	1979	1980	1981
Rice	8,603	13,383	10,425	15,592	19,508	26,352
Rubber	5,297	6,163	8,030	12,351	12,351	10,838
Tin metal	2,973	4,542	7,229	9,252	11,347	9,099
Kenaf and jute	579	418	448	391	n.a.	n.a.
Maize	5,677	3,345	3,975	5,644	7,300	8,328
Teak and other woods	853	613	348	126	n.a.	n.a.
Tapioca products	7,528	7,720	10,892	9,891	14,866	16,433
Sugar	6,842	7,445	3,970	4,797	2,975	9,571

Source: Department of Customs.

PRINCIPAL TRADING PARTNERS
(million baht)

IMPORTS	1976	1977	1978	1979	1980*
Australia	1,560	1,882	2,457	3,268	n.a.
France	934	1,239	1,420	2,524	n.a.
Germany, Federal Republic	3,469	5,194	6,300	7,936	8,237
Hong Kong	756	1,086	1,230	1,546	1,792
Italy	940	1,184	1,305	2,182	n.a.
Japan	23,649	30,469	33,461	37,636	39,985
Kuwait	1,577	1,305	1,604	1,498	n.a.
Malaysia	397	897	1,367	2,491	3,383
Saudi Arabia	5,538	7,789	6,076	9,403	n.a.
Singapore	1,836	2,789	4,419	6,848	12,262
Taiwan	1,759	2,336	3,650	4,027	3,793
United Kingdom	2,623	3,808	4,164	4,708	5,033
U.S.A.	9,739	11,570	14,831	22,754	27,206

EXPORTS	1976	1977	1978	1979	1980*
Germany, Federal Republic	1,979	2,491	3,441	4,391	5,507
Hong Kong	3,036	3,342	4,436	5,260	6,754
Indonesia	3,136	4,281	1,394	3,862	n.a.
Japan	15,686	14,029	16,866	22,901	20,098
Malaysia	2,552	3,769	4,296	4,769	5,990
Netherlands	8,064	9,564	12,185	12,260	n.a.
Singapore	4,114	4,505	6,723	9,222	10,202
Taiwan	1,871	3,167	1,147	1,365	1,953
United Kingdom	980	1,017	1,283	1,989	2,493
U.S.A.	6,098	6,939	9,153	12,106	16,833

* Preliminary figures.

Source: Department of Customs.

TRANSPORT

RAILWAYS
('000)

	1975	1976	1977	1978	1979
Passenger-kilometres	5,704,073	5,531,239	5,792,607	6,067,460	7,592,317
Freight (ton-kilometres)	2,339,509	2,630,465	2,877,833	2,630,149	2,850,770
Freight tons carried	5,052	5,545	6,363	6,045	6,477

Source: The State Railway of Thailand.

ROAD TRAFFIC
(motor vehicles in use)

	1974	1975	1976	1977	1978
Cars	286,225	266,135	293,541	325,078	358,712
Lorries and buses	245,723	244,198	312,801	354,068	400,549
Motor cycles	442,636	456,467	498,125	593,463	727,486
Others	26,046	29,435	30,262	36,462	46,343

Source: Licences Division, Police Department.

SHIPPING
(Port of Bangkok)

	Vessels Entered (number)	Net Registered Tonnage (in ballast)	Vessels Cleared (number)	Net Registered Tonnage (in ballast)	Cargo Tons Unloaded	Cargo Tons Loaded
1975	3,002	3,422,338	2,993	4,350,679	11,315,427	8,782,837
1976	3,284	4,889,248	3,270	4,591,569	12,941,520	11,782,292
1977	3,630	5,413,829	3,618	6,157,554	15,072,049	12,230,508
1978	3,718	5,690,160	3,617	7,183,492	15,822,841	12,138,942
1979	3,850	4,252,048	3,674	7,392,734	17,886,653	12,185,785

Source: Department of Customs.

CIVIL AVIATION

	Kilometres* Flown	Total Load Ton/ Kilometres*	Passengers Carried		Freight Carried	
			Number	Passenger kilometres	Tons	Ton/ kilometres
1975	26,909,192	82,879,431	1,159,910	2,585,089,479	19,759.5	77,977,258
1976	30,657,242	95,905,692	1,235,070	3,182,484,527	22,473.9	91,533,280
1977	31,476,345	109,094,931	1,283,112	3,393,633,780	24,643.8	104,623,661
1978	32,416,919	139,646,507	1,774,467	3,938,745,336	36,062.7	134,448,631
1979	35,714,988	170,223,263	2,088,876	4,475,443,707	46,589.9	163,560,376

* Includes mail carried.

Source: Thai Airways Co. Ltd. and Thai Airways International Ltd.

TOURISM

	1979	1980	1981
Number of visitors	1,591,455	1,858,801	2,015,615
Receipts(million baht)	11,232	17,765	n.a.

Source: Tourist Authority of Thailand.

COMMUNICATIONS MEDIA

	1978	1979
Radio receivers	5,883,943	5,900,000
Television receivers	765,000	1,000,000

EDUCATION

(1978)

	SCHOOLS	TEACHERS	STUDENTS
Kindergarten	75	2,471	68,565
Elementary (Ministry of Education)	444	7,468	146,291
Elementary (Provincial Authority)	29,343	225,124	5,805,754
Municipal	829	19,849	431,481
Secondary (Public)	1,275	54,883	1,160,435
General Education (Private)	2,327	46,423	1,119,528
Vocational	187	8,638	160,589
Teacher Training	48	4,904	88,670

Source: Ministry of Education and National Statistical Office.

Source: (unless otherwise stated) National Statistical Office, Bangkok.

THE CONSTITUTION

The Constitution of Thailand was promulgated on December 22nd, 1978, and consists of 11 provisions and 206 sections. A summary of the main provisions follows.

The King

Thailand is a Kingdom, one and indivisible. The King is Head of State and is head of the armed forces. Sovereignty rests with the people and the King exercises such power only in conformity with the provisions of the Constitution. The King exercises legislative power through the National Assembly, executive power through the Council of Ministers and judicial power through the courts. The person of the King is sacred and shall not be violated, accused or sued in any way. The King appoints the President of the Privy Council and not more than 14 other Privy Councillors. The Privy Council has the duty to advise the King on all matters pertaining to his functions.

The National Assembly

The National Assembly has the duty to consider and approve Bills. The Assembly is a bicameral legislature, with 225 members of the Senate appointed by the King on the recommendation of the incumbent Prime Minister and 301 members of the House of Representatives elected by the people. A Senator must have Thai nationality by birth and be 35 years of age or older and his term of office is six years. A Senator must not be a member of any political party. A Representative must be a Thai national by birth and be 25 years of age or older and a member of a political party. His term of office is four years. The King may dissolve the House of Representatives for a new election of members to the House. Members of the Senate and the House of Representatives are immune from prosecution in voting or expressing opinions during sittings of the National Assembly. At a sitting of the Senate or the House of Representatives, the presence of not less than one-half of the total number of members of each House is required to constitute a quorum. The President of the Senate acts as President of the National Assembly. The Assembly is vested with the power to control the administration of state affairs.

The Council of Ministers

The King appoints a Prime Minister, the Royal Command being countersigned by the President of the National Assembly. He also appoints not more than 44 Ministers to constitute the Council of Ministers on the advice of the Prime Minister. The King may remove a Minister on the advice of the Prime Minister. The Prime Minister and Ministers may not hold a permanent position in the National Assembly nor hold any position in a private undertaking which operates its business for profit. The Prime Minister and Ministers may speak at meetings of the National Assembly but may not vote.

Emergency Powers

The King may enact Royal Decrees which are not contrary to law. All laws and royal commands relating to state affairs must be countersigned by the Prime Minister or a Minister. In case of an emergency when there is an urgent necessity to maintain national or public safety or national economic security or to avert public calamity, the King may issue an emergency decree which shall have the force of an Act. The emergency decree shall be submitted by the Council of Ministers to the National Assembly as soon as possible. If it is approved, it shall continue in force; if not, it shall lapse.

Other Provisions

Judges are independent in the trial and adjudication of cases in accordance with the law. In the case where there is a dispute on the jurisdiction between the Court of Justice and any other Court, or between other Courts, the Constitutional Tribunal shall decide it.

THE GOVERNMENT

HEAD OF STATE

King BHUMIBOL ADULYADEJ (King RAMA IX), succeeded to the throne June 1946.

PRIVY COUNCIL

SANYA DHARMASAKTI (President).
SRISENA SOMBATSIRI.
Gen. LUANG SURANARONG.
PRAKOB HUTASINGH.
Police Maj.-Gen. ARTHASIDHI SIDHISUNTHORN.
M. C. VONGSANUWAT DEVAKUL.
Gen. SAMRAN PHAETYAKUL.
GUL ISARASENA.
CHAOVANA NA SILAWAN.
CHINTA BUNYA-AKOM.
M. C. CHAKRABANDHU PENSIRI CHAKRABANDHU.
KITTI SIHANOND.
CHARUNPHAN ISARANGKUN NA AYUTHAYA.
M. L. CHIRAYU NAVAWONGS.
THANIN KRAIVIXIEN.

COUNCIL OF MINISTERS

(July 1982)

Prime Minister and Minister of Defence: Gen. PREM TINSULANONDA.

Deputy Prime Ministers: Maj.-Gen. PRAMARN ADIREKSARN, Gen. SERM NA NAKORN, Dr. (Special Col.) THANAT KHOMAN, Gen. PRACUAB SUNTHARANGKUL, THONGYOD CHITTAVERA.

Ministers to the Prime Minister's Office: Lt.-Gen. CHARN ANGSUCHOTE, Pol. Lt. CHARN MANOOTHAM, SULEE MAHASANTANA, MEECHAI RUCHUPAN.

Deputy Ministers of Defence: Admiral SAMUT SAHANAVIN, Air Chief Marshal PANIENG KANTARAT.

Minister of Finance: SOMMAI HOONTRAKOOL.

Deputy Minister of Finance: SUTHEE SINGHASENEH.

Minister of Foreign Affairs: Air Chief Marshal SIDDHI SAVETSILA.

Deputy Minister of Foreign Affairs: Dr. ARUN PANUPONG.

Minister of Agriculture and Co-operatives: CHUAN LEEKPAI.

Deputy Ministers of Agriculture and Co-operatives: NARONG WONGWAN, BOON-UA PRASERTSUWAN, PRIDA PATTANATABUTR.

Minister of Communications: Admiral AMORN SIRIGAYA.

Deputy Ministers of Communications: VEERA MUSIKAPONG, MONTRI PONGPANICH, CHUMPOL SILAPAARCHA.

Minister of Commerce: Dr. PUNNAMEE PUNSRI.

Deputy Ministers of Commerce: PRAPASS LIMPABANDHU, THAWEE KRAIGUPTA.

Minister of the Interior: Gen. SITTHI CHIRAROTE.

Deputy Ministers of the Interior: KOSOL KRAIRIKSH, VICHIEN VEJSAWAN, BANYAT BANTHADTHARN.

Minister of Justice: MARUT BUNNAG.

Minister of Science, Technology and Energy: Wing Commdr. THINAKORN BHANDHUGRAVI.

Minister of Education: Dr. KASEM SIRISUMPUNDH.

Deputy Minister of Education: KHUNTONG PHUPHIEWDUAN.

Minister of Public Health: Dr. SEM PRINGPUANGKAEW.

Deputy Minister of Public Health: AMNUAY YOSSUK.

Minister of Industry: Maj.-Gen. CHATICHAI CHOONHAVAN.

Deputy Ministers of Industry: BAROM TANTHIEN, JIRAYU ISSARANGKUL NA AYUDHAYA.

Minister of Bureau of University Affairs: Dr. KASEM SUWANAGUL.

LEGISLATURE

NATIONAL ASSEMBLY

THE SENATE

Speaker and President of the National Assembly: Air Chief Marshal HARIN HONGSAKUL.

Deputy Speakers: Air Chief Marshal KAMOL DEJATUNGKA SANONG TUCHINDA.

The 225 members of the Senate are appointed by the King on the nomination of the incumbent Prime Minister. The Senators appointed in 1979 were almost all military officers.

HOUSE OF REPRESENTATIVES

Speaker and Vice-President of the National Assembly: BOONTHENG THONGSAWAS (Social Action Party).

Deputy Speakers: SA-ARD PIYAWAN (Chart Thai Party), THIEM CHAINANT (Democratic Party).

ELECTIONS TO THE HOUSE OF REPRESENTATIVES

Party	Seats: General Elections, April 22nd, 1979	Seats: After By-elections, Nov. 29th, 1981
Social Action Party	82	69
National Democracy Party	—	50
Chart Thai Party	38	40
Democratic Party	32	32
Prachakorn Thai	32	32
Pracha Rasdr	—	31
Seritham Party	21	—
Siam Democratic Party	—	22
Other parties	33	19
Independents	63	6

POLITICAL PARTIES

Chart Thai (*Thai Nation*): Bangkok; right-wing with elements of former United Thai People's Party; Leader Maj.-Gen. PRAMARN ADIREKSAN; Deputy Leader Maj.-Gen. SIRI SIRIYOTHIN; Sec.-Gen. Maj.-Gen. CHARTICHAI CHOONHAVAN.

Democratic Party: Bangkok; f. 1946; the oldest political party; liberal; Leader PICHAI RATTAKUL.

National Democracy Party: Bangkok; f. 1981; Leader Gen. KRIANGSAK CHOMANAN.

New Force Party: Bangkok; left of centre; advocates a wide range of reforms along social democratic lines; Leader (vacant).

Pracha Rasdr: Bangkok; Leader CHAISIRI RUANGKANCHANASET.

Prachakorn Thai (*Thai Citizens Party*): Bangkok; right-wing, monarchist; Leader SAMAK SOONTORNVEJ.

Seritham Party: Bangkok; liberal; Leader BUNYING NANDAPHIYAT.

Siam Democratic Party: right-wing; Leader Col. POL RERNGPRASERTWIT.

Social Action Party (SAP): Bangkok; conservative; Leader KUKRIT PRAMOJ.

Social Agrarian Party: Bangkok; right-wing; Leader SAWAT KHAMPRAKORB.

Social Democratic Party (formerly Socialist Party of Thailand): Bangkok; left-wing; Leader KLAEW NORAPATI.

DIPLOMATIC REPRESENTATION

EMBASSIES ACCREDITED TO THAILAND

(In Bangkok unless otherwise stated)

Afghanistan: New Delhi, India.

Argentina: 5th Floor, Thaniya Bldg., 62 Silom Rd.; *Ambassador:* MIGUEL CARLOS MARÍA AUGUSTO DE MARTINI.

Australia: 37 South Sathorn Rd.; *Ambassador:* G. A. JOCKEL, C.B.E.

Austria: 14 Soi Nandha, off Soi Athakarnprasit; *Ambassador:* RUDOLF BOGNER.

Bangladesh: 6-8 Charoenmitr, 63 Sukhumvit Rd.; *Ambassador:* Maj.-Gen. QUAIZ GOLAM DASTGIR.

Belgium: 44 Soi Phya Phipat, Silom Rd.; *Ambassador:* PIERRE BRANCART.

Bolivia: Kuala Lumpur, Malaysia.

Brazil: 8/1 Sukhumvit Rd. 15; *Ambassador:* OVIDIO DE ANDRADE MELO.

Bulgaria: 11 Soi Lampetch, Hua Mark; *Ambassador:* BOGDAN BORISOV ALEXIEV.

Burma: 132 Sathorn Nua Rd.; *Ambassador:* U SOE MYINT.

Canada: Boonmitr Bldg., 138 Silom Rd., Bangkok 5; *Ambassador:* FRED BILD.

Chile: 15, Sukhumvit 61; *Ambassador:* FERNANDO GONZALEZ.

China, People's Republic: 1371 Paholyothin Rd.; *Ambassador:* SHEN PING.

Cuba: Manila, Philippines.

Czechoslovakia: 7th Floor, Silom Bldg., 197 Silom Rd.; *Ambassador:* JOSEF BOZEK (resident in Burma).

Denmark: 10 Soi Attakarn Prasit, Sathorn Tai Rd.; *Ambassador:* W. MCILQUHAM SCHMIDT.

Dominican Republic: Taipei, Taiwan.

Egypt: 49 Soi Ruam Rudee, Ploenchit Rd.; *Ambassador:* MOHSEN FALMY YOUSSEF.

Finland: 3rd Floor, Vithayu Place, 89-17 Wireless Rd.; *Ambassador:* TUURE MENTULA.

France: Custom House Lane, Off Charoen Krung Rd.; *Ambassador:* ANDRE ARNAUD.

German Democratic Republic: Kuala Lumpur, Malaysia.

Germany, Federal Republic: 9 Sathorn Tai Rd.; *Ambassador:* JOHANN CHRISTIAN LANKES.

Greece: New Delhi, India.

Hungary: 28 Soi Sukjai, 42 Sukhumvit Rd.; *Ambassador:* JÁNOS VERES.

Iceland: 55 Oriental Avenue; *Ambassador:* PETUR THORSTEINSSON.

India: 46 Soi Prasaranmitr, 23 Sukhumvit Rd.; *Ambassador:* A. B. GOKHALE.

Indonesia: 600–602 Phetchburi Rd.; *Ambassador:* SOEBAMBANG.

Iran: Shell Bldg., 140 Wireless Rd., 9th Floor; *Chargé d'affaires a.i.:* HASSAN SEBGHATI.

Iraq: 47 Pradipat Rd., Samsen Nai, Phya Thai; *Ambassador:* AHMED ABDUL QADIR AL-SHAWI.

Ireland: New Delhi, India.

Israel: 31 Soi Lang Suan, Ploenchit Rd.; *Ambassador:* AVRAHAM COHEN.

Italy: 92 Sathorn Nua Rd.; *Ambassador:* Dr. FRANCESCO RIPANDELLI.

Japan: 1674 New Phetchburi Rd.; *Ambassador:* MOTOO OGISO.

Jordan: New Delhi, India.

Korea, Democratic People's Republic: Rangoon, Burma.

Korea, Republic: 25/1 Surasak Rd., Silom; *Ambassador:* TAE WOONG KWON.

Laos: 193 Sathorn Tai Rd.; *Ambassador:* KHAMPHAM SIMMALAVONG.

Lebanon: New Delhi, India.

Libya: Kuala Lumpur, Malaysia.

Malaysia: 35 Sathorn Tai Rd.; *Ambassador:* Datuk SAHHUDDIN BIN MOHAMED TAIB.

Mongolia: Vientiane, Laos.

Nepal: 189 Soi Puengsuk, Sukhumvit Rd.; *Ambassador:* KHELENDRA PRASAD PANDEY.

Netherlands: 106 Wireless Rd.; *Ambassador:* PIET-HEIN HOUBEN.

New Zealand: 93 Wireless Rd.; *Ambassador:* R. L. JERMYN.

Nigeria: New Delhi, India.

Norway: 20th Floor, Chokechai Bldg., 690 Sukhumvit Rd.; *Ambassador:* PETER M. MOTZFELDT.

Pakistan: 31 Soi Nana Nua, Sukhumvit Rd.; *Ambassador:* KAMAL MATINUDDIN.

Papua New Guinea: Jakarta, Indonesia.

Peru: Tokyo, Japan.

Philippines: 760 Sukhumvit Rd.; *Ambassador:* Lt.-Gen. RAFAEL M. ILETO.

Poland: 61 Soi Prasanmitr, (23) Sukhumvit Rd.; *Ambassador:* Dr. JAN MAJEWSKI.

Portugal: 26 Bush Lane, Charoen Krung Rd.; *Ambassador:* JOSÉ EDUARDO DE MELLO GOUVEIA.

Romania: 39 Soi, 10 Sukhumvit Rd.; *Ambassador:* JOSIF CHIRU.

Saudi Arabia: 10th Floor, 138 Silom Rd.; *Chargé d'affaires:* GHALEB A. SAMMAN.

Singapore: 129 Sathorn Tai Rd.; *Ambassador:* CHI OWYANG.

Spain: 104 Wireless Rd.; *Ambassador:* NICOLÁS REVENGA DOMÍNGUEZ.

Sri Lanka: 7th Floor, Nai Lert Bldg., 87 Sukhumvit Rd.; *Ambassador:* Mrs. IRANGANI MANEL ABEYSEKERA.

Sweden: 11th Floor, Boonmitr Bldg., 138 Silom Rd.; *Ambassador:* AXEL EDELSTAM.

Switzerland: 35 North Wireless Rd., P.O.B. 821; *Ambassador:* WALTER RIESER.

Turkey: 153/2 Soi Mahadlek Luang, 1 Rajdamri Rd.; *Ambassador:* REHA AYTAMAN.

U.S.S.R.: 108 Sathorn Nua Rd.; *Ambassador:* YURI IVANOVICH KUZNETSOV.

United Kingdom: Wireless Rd., *Ambassador:* H. A. J. STAPLES, C.M.G.

U.S.A.: 95 Wireless Rd.; *Ambassador:* JOHN GUNTHER DEAN.

Uruguay: Tokyo, Japan.

Vatican: 217/1 Sathorn Tai Rd., P.O.B. 12-178; *Apostolic Pro-Nuncio:* Archbishop RENATO RAFFAELE MARTINO.

Viet-Nam: 83/1 Wireless Rd.; *Ambassador:* (vacant).

Yugoslavia: 15 Soi 61, Sukhumvit Rd.; *Ambassador:* DUŠAN GASPARI.

Thailand also has diplomatic relations with Algeria, Bahrain, Cyprus, Ethiopia, Fiji, Gabon, Grenada, Guatemala, the Ivory Coast, Kenya, Kuwait, Liberia, Luxembourg, Maldives, Mali, Mauritania, Mexico, Monaco, Nicaragua, Niger, Oman, Paraguay, Qatar, Senegal, Sudan, Tunisia and Western Samoa.

JUDICIAL SYSTEM

Ministry of Justice: Rajinee Rd., Bangkok 2.

COURTS OF FIRST INSTANCE

Magistrates' Courts (*Sarn Kwaeng*): Function is to dispose of small cases with minimum formality and expense. Judges sit singly.

Juvenile Courts (*Sarn Kadee Dek Lae Yaowachon*): original jurisdiction over juvenile delinquency and matters affecting children and young persons. One judge and one woman associate judge form a quorum. There are four courts in Bangkok, Songkla, Nakhon Ratchasima and Chiangmai.

Civil Court (*Sarn Paeng*): Court of general original jurisdiction in civil and bankruptcy cases in Bangkok and Thonburi. Two judges form a quorum.

Criminal Court (*Sarn Aya*): Court of general original jurisdiction in criminal cases in Bangkok. Two judges form a quorum.

Provincial Courts (*Sarn Changvad*): Exercise unlimited original jurisdiction in all civil and criminal matters, including bankruptcy, within its own district which is generally the province itself. Two judges form a quorum. At each of the five Provincial Courts in the South of Thailand where the majority of the population are Muslims (i.e. Pattani, Yala, Betong, Satun and Narathiwat), there are two Dato Yutithum or Kadis (Muslim judges). A Kadi sits with two trial judges in order to administer Islamic laws and usages in civil cases involving family and inheritance where all parties concerned are Muslims. Questions on Islamic laws and usages which are interpreted by a Kadi are final.

There is also a Labour Court to rule in cases of labour disputes.

COURT OF APPEALS

Sarn Uthorn: Appellate jurisdiction in all civil, bankruptcy and criminal matters; appeals from all the Courts of First Instance throughout the country come to this Court. Two judges form a quorum.

SUPREME COURT

Sarn Dika: The final court of appeal in all civil, bankruptcy and criminal cases. The quorum in the Supreme Court consists of three judges. The Court sits in plenary session occasionally to determine cases of exceptional importance, when the judges disagree or cases where there are reasons for reconsideration or overruling of its own precedents. The quorum for the full Court is half the total number of judges in the Supreme Court.

Chief Justice: Prof. BANYAT SUCHIVA.

RELIGION

Buddhism is the prevailing religion. Besides Buddhists, there are some Muslim Malays. Most of the immigrant Chinese are Confucians.

There is also a small number of Christians, mainly in Bangkok and Northern Thailand.

BUDDHIST

Supreme Patriarch of Thailand: Somdej Phra ARIYAVONGSAKHATAYAN (Wasana Mahathera).

The Buddhist Association of Thailand: 41 Phra Aditya St., Bangkok; under royal patronage; f. 1934; 4,183 mems.; Pres. SANYA DHARMASAKTI.

ROMAN CATHOLIC

Bangkok: Archbishop: Most Rev. MICHAEL MICHAI KITBUNCHU, Assumption Cathedral, Bangrak, Bangkok 10500.

Tharé and Nonseng: Archbishop's House, Tharé, Sakonnakhon 47230; Archbishop: Most Rev. LAWRENCE KHAI SAEN PHON-ON.

Catholic Association of Thailand: 57 Soi Bulapa Bangrak Rd., Bangkok.

PROTESTANT

The Church of Christ in Thailand: 14 Pramuan Rd., Bangkok; f. 1934; 30,000 communicant mems.; Moderator VIBUL PATTARATHAMMAS; Gen. Sec. Rev. SAMRAN KUANGWAEN; 27 organizations have missionaries or ecumenical personnel assigned to the Church of Christ in Thailand; member of WARC, Christian Conference in Asia and WCC.

THE PRESS

(In Bangkok unless otherwise stated)

DAILIES

THAI LANGUAGE

Ban Muang: 1 Soi Pluemmanee, Vibhavadi Rangsit; f. 1972; Editor MANA PRAEPHAN; circ. 200,000.

Daily Mirror: 528/6–7 Pathoomwan; Editor AMNART SUTHIPAN; circ. 49,000.

Daily News: 114 Viphavadu Rangsit Rd.; f. 1964; Editor PRACHA HETRAKUL; circ. 450,000.

Dao Siam: 60 Mansion 4, Rajdamnern Ave.; f. 1974; Editor CHAMNONG ROONGRUENKUL; circ. 140,000.

Khao Panich (Daily Trade News): Khao Panich Printing House, 78/13 Pradipat Sq., Rama VI Rd.; f. 1950; Editor SOMSAKDI RUGSASOOK; circ. 30,000.

Khao-Sod: 861/3 New Rd., Bangkok 1; Editor VACHARIN NARAPHORN; circ. 70,000.

Mati Chon: 117/119–2 Fuengnakorn; Editor KHANCHAI BUNPAN; circ. 50,000.

Matupoom: 18/1 Prachatipatai Rd., Bangkok 2; Editor CHOOP MANITHAPHO; circ. 21,000.

Naewna: 18/40 Soi Pleummanee, Vibhavadee Rangsit Rd., Bangkok 2; Editor PHADEJ PUREEPATIPAN; circ. 50,000.

Siam Rath: 12 Mansion 6, Rajdamnern Ave.; f. 1950; Editor SOMBATI BHUKANCHANA; circ. 120,000.

Siang Puang Chon (Voice of the People): 531/7 Muay Kwang; Editor RUANG-NAM RUANG VOOTH; circ. 93,000.

Tavan Siam: 52/3–8 Trok Ban Panthom, Banglampoo, Bangkok 2; Editor CHALERM SIBOONRUENG; circ. 90,000.

Thai Rath: 1 Vibhavadi Rangsit; f. 1958; Editor THUNG THOT VAIDAYANOND; circ. 600,000.

Thailand Times: 45/1 Soi Saen Sabai, Rama IV Rd., Bangkok 11; Editor SOMDEJ SORNJITTIYOTHIN; circ. 30,000.

ENGLISH LANGUAGE

Bangkok Post: 3rd Floor, U-Chuliang Bldg., 968 Rama IV Rd.; f. 1946; Man. Editor PETER R. FINUCANE; circ. 26,000.

Bangkok World: 3rd Floor, U-Chuliang Bldg., 968 Rama IV Rd.; evening paper; Man. Editor PETER R. FINUCANE; circ. 10,000.

The Nation Review: 8/3–5 Soi 42, Sukhumvit Rd.; f. 1971; Editor SUNIDA PANYARATABANDHU; circ. 26,000.

CHINESE LANGUAGE

The New Chinese: 1022–1030 Charoen Krung Rd., Talad Noi; Editor KRIANGKRAI RIDTHONGPITAK; circ. 20,000.

Sing Sian Yit Pao Daily News: 267 Charoen Krung Rd.; f. 1950; Editor TANUNG TUANGLAKTHAM; circ. 85,000.

Sirinakorn: 108 Suapa Rd.; f. 1959; Editor PRASIT SIRIWARIWET; circ. 80,000.

Thai Shang Yig Pao: 970/31 Charoen Krung, Talad Noi; f. 1977; evening paper; Editor CHAN-LIANG; circ. 100,000.

Tongfua Daily News: 877/879 Charoen Krung Rd., Talad Noi; Editor CHART PAYONITHIKARN; circ. 50,000.

Universal Daily News: 21/1 Charoen Krung Rd.; Editor BOON OUNG SAELEE; circ. 25,000.

WEEKLIES

THAI LANGUAGE

Bangkok Weekly: 533–539 Sriayuthaya Rd.; Editor VICHIT ROJANAPRABHA.

Darunee (Lady): 7/2 Soi Watanawonge, Makasan; f. 1953; Editor WEERAWAN SUWANVIPATH; circ. 150,000.

Nakorn Thai: 13–22 Soi Wat Hiranruchee, Prachatipok Rd.

Phadung Silp: 163 Soi Thesa, Rajborpit Rd.; Editor AKSORN CHUAPANYA.

Satri Sarn: 83–86 Arkarntrithosthep 2, Prachathipatai Rd.; f. 1948; women's magazine; Editor Miss NILAWAN PINTONG.

See Ros: 612 Luke Luang Rd.; Editor MANI CHINDANONDH.

Siam Rath Weekly Review: Mansion 6, Rajdamnern Ave.; Editor SAMRUEY SINGHADET.

Skul Thai: 58 Soi 36, Sukhumvit Rd.; Editor PRAYOON SONGSERM-SWASDI.

ENGLISH LANGUAGE

Financial Post: Mansion 4, Rajdamnern Ave.

FORTNIGHTLIES

THAI LANGUAGE

Dara Thai: 91 Soi Sriaksorn, Tung Mahamek; Editor SURAT PUKAVES.

Pharp Khao Taksin: 226 Samsen Rd.; Editor LUAN VIRAPHAT.

Saen Sook: 553/9 Sriayuthya Rd.; Editor SUCHATI AMONKUL.

Sena Sarn: Army Auditorium, Ministry of Defence; Editor Lt.-Col. FUEN DISYAVONG.

MONTHLIES

Chaiya-Pruek: 599 Maitrichit Rd.; f. 1953; Thai; Editor WARAPANJA WONGPUKAHUTA.

Chao Krung: Mansion 6, Rajdamnern Ave.; Thai; Editor NOPPHORN BUNYARIT.

The Dharmachaksu (*Dharma-vision*): Foundation of Mahãmakut Rãjavidyãlaya, Phra Sumeru Rd., Bangkok 2; f. 1894; Thai; Buddhism and related subjects; Editor Group Capt. MEGH AMPHAICHARIT; circ. 5,000.

The Investor: The Investment Publications Co. Ltd., 101 Nares Rd.; f. 1968; English language; business, industry, finance and economics; Editor TOS PATUMSEN; circ. 6,000.

Kasikorn: Dept. of Agriculture, Bangkhen, Bangkok 9; f. 1928; Thai; agriculture and agricultural research; Man. JINDA LIAMURAI; Editor JINDA JAN-ORN.

The Lady: 77 Rama V Rd.; Editor Princess NGARMCHITR PREM PURACHATRA.

Satawa Liang: 689 Wang Burapa Rd.; Thai; Editor THAMRONGSAK SRICHAND.

Villa Wina Magazine: 3rd Floor, Chalerm Ketr Theatre Bldg.; Thai; Editor BHONGSAKDI PIAMLAP.

NEWS AGENCIES

FOREIGN BUREAUX

Agence France-Presse (AFP): Panavongs Bldg., 104 Surivongse Rd., P.O.B. 1567, Bangkok; Correspondent XAVIER BARON.

Associated Press (AP) (*U.S.A.*): P.O.B. 775, Bangkok; Correspondent DENNIS D. GRAY.

Central News Agency Inc. (CNA) (*Taiwan*): 17 Soi St., Louis 2, Sathorn South Rd., Bangkok; Chief of Bureau CONRAD LU.

Jiji Tsushin-sha (*Japan*): Jiji Press, 8th Floor, Boonmitr Bldg., 138 Silom Rd., Bangkok; Correspondent AKIRA KANAI.

Kyodo Tsushin (*Japan*): 2nd Floor, U Chuliang Bldg., 968 Rama IV Rd., Bangkok; Correspondent HIDEKI IKEUCHI.

Reuters (*U.K.*): P.O.B. 877, Prinya Bldg., 544/11 Ploenchit Rd., Bangkok.

United Press International (UPI) (*U.S.A.*): U Chuliang Bldg., 968 Rama IV Rd., Bangkok; Man. SYLVANA FOA.

Antara (Indonesia) also has a bureau in Bangkok.

PRESS ASSOCIATION

Press Association of Thailand: 299 Nakorn Rassima North Rd., Bangkok; f. 1941; Pres. WASANT CHOOSAKUL.

There are other regional Press organizations and two journalists' organizations.

PUBLISHERS

Advance Media: U Chuliang Foundation Bldg., 968 Rama IV Rd., Bangkok; Man. PRASERTSAK SIVASAHONG.

Barnakich Trading: 34 Nakorn Sawan Rd., Bangkok; Thai novels, school textbooks; Man. SOMSAK TECHAKASHEM.

Chalermnit Press: 108 Sukhumvit Soi 53, Bangkok; f. 1957; dictionaries, history, literature, guides to Thai language, books on Thailand; Mans. M. L. M. JUMSAI and Mrs. JUMSAI.

Dhamabuja: 5/1–2 Asadang Rd., Bangkok; religious books; Man. VIROCHANA SIRI-ATH.

Prae Pittaya Ltd.: P.O.B. 914, 716–718 Wang Burapa Palace, Bangkok; general Thai books; Man. CHIT PRAEPANICH.

Prapansarn: Siam Sq., Soi 2, Rama 1 Rd., Bangkok; Thai pocket books; Man. Dir. SUPHOL TAECHATADA.

Ruamsarn (1977): 864 Burapa Palace, Bangkok 2; f. 1951 fiction, poetry, literature, philosophy, religion and textbooks; Man. PIYA TAWEWATANASARN.

Ruang Silpa: 663 Samsen Nai Rd., Bangkok; Thai pocket books; Propr. DHAMNOON RUANG SILPA.

Sermmitr Barnakarn: 222 Nakorn Kashem, Bangkok; general Thai books; Man. PRAVIT SAMMAVONG.

Suksapan Panit (*Business Organization of Teachers' Institute*): Mansion 9, Rajdamnern Ave., Bangkok; f. 1950; general books, textbooks, children's books, pocket books; Man. KAMTHON SATHIRAKUL.

Thai Watana Panit: 599 Maitrijit Rd., Bangkok; children's books, school textbooks.

Watana Panit: 216–222 Bamrungmuang Rd., Bangkok 2; school textbooks and children's books; Foreign Business Man. W. VINIT.

ASSOCIATION

Publishers' and Booksellers' Association of Thailand: 20 Rajprasong Trade Centre, Bangkok 10502; Pres. DHAMNOON RUANG SILPA; Sec.-Gen. PIYA TAWEWATANASARN RUAMSARN.

RADIO AND TELEVISION

RADIO

Radio Thailand (Thai National Broadcasting Station): Government Public Relations Department, Rajdamnern Ave., Bangkok 2; f. 1930; under Government control; educational, entertainment, cultural and news programmes; Dir.-Gen. of Public Relations Dept. KAMJAT KEEPANICH; Dir. of Radio Thailand MANIT VARIN.

Home Service: 60 affiliated stations in Bangkok and 49 provinces; operates three programmes; Dir. PRASONG DHAMMATHITI.

External Services: In Thai, English, French, Vietnamese, Khmer, Japanese, Burmese, Lao, Malay and Mandarin; Dir. RAMYONG SAKORNPAN.

Ministry of Education Broadcasting Service: Centre for Educational Innovation and Technology, Ministry of Education, Bangkok; f. 1954; evening programmes for general public; daytime programmes for schools; Dir. of Centre NAPA BHONGBHIBHAT.

Pituksuntiradse Radio Stations: one at Bangkok, Nakorn Rachasima, Chiangmai, Pitsanuloke and Songkla; programmes in Thai; Dir.-Gen. PAITOON WAIJANYA.

Voice of Free Asia: Broadcasting Division, Information Department, Ministry of Foreign Affairs, Savanrom Palace, Bangkok 2; f. 1968; under the Ministry of Foreign Affairs; programmes in Thai and English.

In 1980 there were an estimated 6.7 million radio sets.

TELEVISION

Television of Thailand (TVT): Government Public Relations Department, Rajdamnern Ave., Bangkok; operates 5 black and white stations (Lampang, Khonkhaen, Surat Thani, Phuket and Haadyai/Songkla). A new colour station in Buriram was opened in December 1981.

The Mass Communications Organization of Thailand (Channel 9): 222 Asoke Din, Daeng Rd., Bangkok 10; f. 1954 as Thai Television Co. Ltd.; colour service; Dir. PRAMUT SUTABUTR.

Royal Thai Army HSA-TV: Phaholyothin St., Sanam Pao, Bangkok; f. 1958; operates channels in Bangkok, Nakorn Sawan and Nakorn Rachasima; Dir.-Gen. Maj.-Gen. CHALERM KARANYAWATH.

In 1980 there were about 1.6 million TV receivers in use.

FINANCE

(cap.=capital; p.u.=paid up; dep.=deposits; m.=million; res.=reserves; brs.=branches; amounts in baht).

BANKING

CENTRAL BANK

Bank of Thailand: 273 Samsen Rd., P.O.B. 154, Bangkok 2; f. 1942; government-owned; cap. p.u. 3,000m., dep. (Government, banks and others) 50,966m. (April 1982); Gov. Dr. NUKUL PRACHUABMOH; publs. *Monthly Bulletin, Annual Economic Report.*

COMMERCIAL BANKS

Bangkok

Asia Trust Bank Ltd.: 80-82 Anuwongse Rd., P.O.B. 195; f. 1965; cap. p.u. 400m., dep. 5,048m. (Dec. 1981); Chair. and Pres. WALLOB TARNVANICHKUL; 25 brs.

Bangkok Bank Ltd.: 333 Silom Rd., P.O.B. 95; f. 1944; cap. p.u. 2,000m., dep. 103,269m. (Dec. 1981); Pres. CHATRI SOPHONPANICH; Chair. CHIN SOPHONPANICH; 264 brs.

Bangkok Bank of Commerce Ltd.: 171 Surawongse Rd.; f. 1944; cap. p.u. 175m., dep. 14,955m. (Dec. 1981); Chair. M. R. KUKRIT PRAMOJ; Man. Dir. THANIT BISALPUTRA; 130 brs.

Bangkok Metropolitan Bank Ltd.: 2 Chalermkhet IV Rd., Suam Mali; f. 1950; cap. p.u. 200m., dep. 12,031m. (Dec. 1981); Chair. UDANE TEJAPAIBUL; Pres. UTHORN TEJAPAIBUL; 83 brs.

Bank of Asia Ltd.: 601 Charoen Krung Rd., P.O.B. 122; f. 1939; cap. p.u. 248m., dep. 6,082m. (Dec. 1981); Chair. CHAROON EUARCHUKIATI; Pres. YOS EUARCHUKIATI; 38 brs.

Bank of Ayudhya Ltd.: 550 Ploenchit Rd., P.O.B. 491; f. 1945; cap. p.u. 500m., dep. 14,489m. (Dec. 1981); Chair. Police Gen. PRASERT RUCHIRAVONGS; Man. Dir. WIT VIRIYATRATAIKIT; 138 brs.

First Bangkok City Bank Ltd.: 20 Yukhon 2 Rd., Suan Mali; f. 1934 as Thai Development Bank; cap. p.u. 900m., dep. 8,531m. (Dec. 1981); Chair. SUNTHORN SATHIRATHAI; Man. Dir. CORO TEJAPAIBUL; 50 brs.

Krung Thai Bank Ltd. (*State Commercial Bank of Thailand*): 260 Jawaraj Rd., Bangkok; f. 1966; government-owned; cap. p.u. 1,200m., dep. 40,589m. (Dec. 1981); Chair. CHANCHAI LEETAVORN; Pres. TAMCHAI KHAMBHATO; 177 brs.

Leam Thong Bank Ltd.: 289 Surawongse Rd., P.O.B. 131; f. 1948; cap. 50m., dep. 1,779m. (Dec. 1981); Chair. PAYAP SRIKARNCHANA; Man. Dir. SOMBOON NANDHABIWAT; 4 brs.

Siam City Bank Ltd.: 13 Anuwongse Rd.; f. 1941; cap. p.u 300m., dep. 10,049m. (Dec. 1981); Chair. CHALERM CHEO-SAKUL; Man. Dir. VISIDTHA SRISOMBOON; 100 brs.

Siam Commercial Bank Ltd.: 1060 Phetchburi Rd., P.O.B. 15, Bangkok 10400; f. 1906; cap. p.u. 275m., dep. 16,719m. (Dec. 1981); Chair. POONPERM KRAIRIKSH; Pres. and Exec. Officer PRACHITR YOSSUNDARA; 134 brs.

Thai Danu Bank Ltd.: 393 Silom Rd.; f. 1949; cap. p.u. 150m , dep. 2,740m. (Dec. 1981); Chair. POTE SARASIN; Pres. CHALERM PRACHUABMOH; 16 brs.

Thai Farmers Bank Ltd.: 142 Silom Rd., P.O.B. 1366, Bangkok 5; f. 1945; cap. p.u. 646m., dep. 40,912m. (Dec. 1981); Pres. BANYONG LAMSAM; Chair. BANCHA LAMSAM; 238 brs.

Thai Military Bank Ltd.: 34 Phayathai Rd.; f. 1957; cap. p.u. 10m., dep. 9,226m. (Dec. 1981); Pres. PRAYOON CHINDAPRADIST; Gen. Man. ANUTHRA ASAWANONDA; 79 brs.

Union Bank of Bangkok Ltd.: 624 Yawaraj Rd., P.O.B. 2114; f. 1949; cap. p.u. 100m., dep. 4,672m. (Dec. 1981); Chair. Gen. KRITCHA PUNNAKANTA; Pres. BANJURD CHOLVIJARN; 74 brs.

Wang Lee Bank Ltd.: 1016 Rama IV Rd., P.O.B. 2731, Bangkok 5; f. 1933; cap. p.u. 40m., dep. 1,067m. (Dec. 1981); Chair. TAN SIEW TING WANGLEE; Pres. SUVIT WANGLEE; 9 brs.

Government Savings Bank of Thailand: 470 Phaholyothin Rd., Bangkok 4; f. 1913; cap. 2,321m., dep. 27,163m. (Dec. 1981); Chair. PANAS SIMASATHIEN; Dir.-Gen. DUSDEE SVASDI-XUTO; 389 brs.

FOREIGN BANKS

Bank of America N.T. and S.A. (*U.S.A.*): 297 Surawongse Rd., P.O.B. 158, Bangkok 5; dep. 846m. (Dec. 1981); Man. ALFRED ANLERS.

Bank of Canton Ltd. (*Hong Kong*): 197/1 Silom Rd., Bangkok 5; dep. 140m. (Dec. 1981); Man. SUN CHEN YA.

Bank of Tokyo Ltd. (*Japan*): 62 Thaniya Bldg., Silom Rd., Bangkok; dep. 762m. (Dec. 1981); Gen. Man. IWANE YAMAMOTO.

Banque de l'Indochine et de Suez S.A. (*France*): 142 Wireless Rd., P.O.B. 303, Bangkok 5; dep. 440m. (Dec. 1981); Man. M. COURET.

Bharat Overseas Bank (*India*): 221 Rajawongse Rd., Bangkok; dep. 297m. (Dec. 1981); Chief Man. C. ROJAGOPALAN.

The Chartered Bank (*U.K.*): 1–3 Rama IV Rd., P.O.B. 320, Bangkok; dep. 832m. (Dec. 1981); Man. D. MELLOR.

Chase Manhattan Bank, N.A. (*U.S.A.*): 965 Rama I Rd., P.O.B. 525, Bangkok; dep. 963m. (June 1981); Man. E. J. Cooper.

European Asian Bank (*Federal Republic of Germany*): 28/1 Surasak Rd., P.O.B. 1237, Bangkok; dep. 142m. (Dec. 1981); Man. Rainer Mueller.

Four Seas Communications Bank Ltd. (*Singapore*): 231 Rajawongse Rd., Bangkok 1; dep. 136m. (Dec. 1981); Man. Chanin Pongchaiyaraeke.

Hongkong and Shanghai Banking Corporation (*Hong Kong*): Siam Center, 965 Rama I Rd., Bangkok 5; dep. 603m. (Dec. 1981); Man. C. J. A. Chubb.

International Commercial Bank of China (*Taiwan*): 95 Suapa Rd., Bangkok; dep. 183m. (Dec. 1981); Man. James C. C. Cheng.

Mercantile Bank Ltd. (*U.K.*): 64 Silom Rd., Bangkok; dep. 220m. (Dec. 1981); Man. Tanong Purananda.

Mitsui Bank Ltd. (*Japan*): 138 Silom Rd., Bangkok; dep. 1,115m. (Dec. 1981); Man. Wohimitsu Tomotsu.

United Malayan Banking Corpn. Ltd. (*Malaysia*): 149 Suapa Rd., P.O.B. 2149, Bangkok; dep. 208m. (Dec. 1981); Man. Loh Kum-Choon.

Development Finance Organizations

Bank for Agriculture and Agricultural Co-operatives (BAAC): 469 Nakhonsawan Rd., Bangkok; f. 1966 to provide credit for agriculture; cap. 2,296m., dep. 10,646m. (Dec. 1981); Chair. Sommai Hoontrakool; Man. Chamlong Tohtong.

Board of Investment (BOI): 28 Mansion 2, Rajdamnern Ave., Bangkok; Chair. Gen. Prem Tinsulanonda; Sec.-Gen. Somporn Punyagupta.

Government Housing Bank: 77 Rajdamnern Ave., Bangkok; f. 1953 to provide housing finance; cap. 639.6m., dep. 5,890m. (Dec. 1981); Chair. Kraisri Chatikavanit; Man. Kitti Patpongpibul.

Industrial Finance Corporation of Thailand (IFCT): 1770 New Petchburi Rd., Bangkok 10310; f. 1959 to assist in the establishment, expansion or modernization of industrial enterprises in the private sector; organizes pooling of funds and capital market development; makes medium- and long-term loans, underwriting shares and securities and guaranteeing loans; cap. p.u. 400m. (Dec. 1981); loans granted 8,399m. on 606 projects (Dec. 1981); Chair. Sommai Hoontrakool; Pres. Sukri Kaocharern.

Small Industries Finance Office (SIFO): 16 Mansion 6, Rajdamnern Ave., Bangkok; f. 1964 to provide finance for small-scale industries; cap. 54m. (Dec. 1981); Chair. Kaset Pitakpaivan; Acting Man. Puangthip Tantiratana.

STOCK EXCHANGE

Securities Exchange of Thailand (SET): 965 Rama I Rd,. Bangkok; f. 1975; 30 mems.; 82 listed firms; 5 authorized firms; Pres. Mrs. Sirilak Ratanakorn; Chair. Bandit Bunyapana.

INSURANCE

In 1981 there were 58 domestic insurance companies operating in Thailand (4 life, 41 non-life, 6 life and non-life, 6 health and 1 reinsurance). There were also 8 foreign companies (1 life, 6 non-life, 1 life and non-life).

Selected Domestic Insurance Companies
Bangkok

Bangkok Insurance Co. Ltd.: The Bangkok Insurance Bldg., 302 Silom Rd.; f. 1947; non-life insurance; Pres. Chai Sophonpanich.

Bangkok Union Insurance Co. Ltd.: 175–177 Surawongse Rd.; f. 1962; non-life; Chair. Porn Liewparath; Man. Dir. Malinee Liewparath.

China Insurance Co. (Siam) Ltd.: 95 Suapa Rd.; f. 1948; non-life; Chair. Daeng Phupat; Man. Dir. Lee An-Kiet.

INTERLIFE Co. Ltd.: 364/29 Sri-Ayudhaya Rd.; f. 1951; life insurance; Chair Suti Nopakun; Man. Dir. Paiboon Samranputi.

International Assurance Co. Ltd.: 488/7–9 Henri Dunant Rd.; f. 1952; non-life, fire, marine, general; Chair. Pichai Kulavanich; Man. Dir. Somchai Mahasantipiya.

Ocean Insurance Company Ltd.: 1666 Krung Kasem Rd.; f. 1949; life and non-life; Chair. Choti Assakula; Man. Dir. Saiyud Tavipat.

Shiang Ann Insurance Co. Ltd.: Orient Bldg., 68/1 Silom Rd.; f. 1923; non-life; Chair. Thong Assarat; Pres. Vanich Chaiyawan.

South-East Insurance Co. Ltd. (*Arkanay Prakan Pai Co. Ltd.*): South-East Insurance Bldg., 315 Silom Rd.; f. 1946; life and non-life; Chair. Payap Srikanchana; Man. Dir. Athorn Tittiranonda.

Syn Man Kong Insurance Co. Ltd.: 12/7–9 Plabplachai Rd.; f. 1951; fire, automobile and personal accident; Chair. Supasit Mahakun; Man. Dir. Thanavit Dusadeesurapote.

Thai Commercial Insurance Co. Ltd.: 133/19 (6th Floor) Rajdamri Rd.; f. 1940; fire, marine and casualty; Chair. Thana Posayanond; Man. Dir. Surajit Wanglee.

Thai Health Insurance Co. Ltd.: 968 Rama IV Rd., f. 1979; Chair. Vanich Chaiyawan; Pres. Kopr Kritayakirana.

Thai Insurance Co. Ltd.: Thai Danu Bldg., 393 Silom Rd.; f. 1938; non-life; Chair. Pote Sarasin; Man. Dir. Chalor Thongsuphan.

Thai Life Insurance Co. Ltd.: 968 Rama IV Rd.; f. 1942; life; Chair. Aniwat Kritayakirana; Man. Dir. Kopr Kritayakirana.

Thai Prasit Insurance Co. Ltd.: 82 Soi 62 Sukhumvit Rd., f. 1947; life, fire, marine and automobile; Chair. and Man. Dir. Sura Chansrichawala.

Wilson Insurance Co. Ltd.: 5th Floor, Bangkok Bank, Ratchawong Branch Bldg., 245–249 Rajawongse Rd.; f. 1951; fire, marine; Chair. Chin Sophonpanich; Man. Dir. Choomporn Rungsopinkul.

Associations

General Insurance Association: 223 Soi Ruamrudee, Wireless Rd., Bangkok.

Thai Life Assurance Association: 36/1 Soi Spankoo, Rama IV Rd., Bangkok.

TRADE AND INDUSTRY

CHAMBERS OF COMMERCE

Thai Chamber of Commerce: 150 Rajbopit Rd., Bangkok 2; f. 1946; 909 mems., 51 assoc. mems. (March 1981); Pres. Dr. SOMPHOB SUSSANGKARN; Vice-Pres. CHAROON RUANGVISESH, BOONTOM YENMANOJ, PREECHA TANPRASERT; publs. *Thailand Business Review* (monthly), *Thai Chamber of Commerce Directory*, twice weekly bulletin.

Chiangmai Chamber of Commerce: 81 Rajavithi Rd., Chiangmai.

Chiangrai Chamber of Commerce: Uttrakit Rd., Chiangrai.

Nongkai Chamber of Commerce: 896/3 Prasia Rd., Nongkai.

GOVERNMENT ORGANIZATIONS

Forest Industry Organization: 76 Rajdamnern Nok Ave., Bangkok 2; f. 1947; has wide responsibilities concerning all aspects of Thailand's forestry and wood industries; Man. Dir. CHERN NILVISES.

Petroleum Authority of Thailand (PTT): 14 Lim Chareon Bldg., Vibhavadi Rangsit Rd., Bangkok 10900; f. 1978; has since merged with National Gas Organization of Thailand (NGOT) and the Oil and Fuel Organization; government organization responsible for supervising all activities relating to the production and distribution of petroleum and gas; Chair. Gen. PREM TINSULANONDA; Gov. Dr. TONGCHAT HONGLADAROMP.

Rubber Estate Organization: Rajdamnern Nok Ave., Bangkok 2; Man. Dir. THAVON VISESJINDA.

Thai Sugar Organization: Luang Rd., Bangkok 1.

INDUSTRIAL AND TRADE ASSOCIATIONS

The Association of Thai Industries: 394/14 Samsen Rd. Tambol Dusit, Bangkok; f. 1967; 300 mems.; Pres. Dr. THAWORN PHORNPRAPHA PONG SARASIN, CHUMSAI HASDIN, ANAND PANYARACHUN.

Bangkok Rice Millers' Association: 952 Sathorn Tai Rd., Bangkok.

Board of Trade of Thailand: 150 Rajbopit Rd., Bangkok 2; f. 1955; Pres. Dr. SOMPHOB SUSSANGKARN.

Jute Association of Thailand: 52/3 Suriwongse Rd., Bangkok 5.

Mineral Industry Association of Thailand: c/o Department of Mineral Resources, Rama VI Rd., Bangkok 4.

Pharmaceutical Manufacturers' Association of Thailand: 175–177 Surawongse Rd., Bangkok.

Rice Exporters' Association of Thailand: 120 N. Sathorn Rd., Bangkok 5; Chair. SAMARN OPHASWONGSE.

Rice Mill Association of Thailand: 333 South Sathorn Rd., Bangkok 5.

Sawmills Association: 350 Visuthykasat Rd., Bangkok 2.

Thai Food Processors' Association: Kasetsart University, Paholyothin Rd., Bangkok.

Thai Jute Association: 52/3 Thai Laithong Bldg., Suriwongse Rd., Bangkok.

Thai Lac Association: 66 Chalerm Khetr 1, Bangkok 1.

Thai Maize and Produce Traders' Association: 52/16-18 Suriwongse Rd., Bangkok 5.

Thai Rubber Traders' Association: 57 Rong Muang 5 Rd., Bangkok 10500; Pres. VICHIT UPATISRING.

Thai Silk Association: c/o Dept. of Industrial Promotion, Rama VI Rd., Bangkok.

Thai Sugar Producers' Association: 49 Sukhumvit 64 Rd., Bangkok.

Thai Tapioca Trade Association: U-Chuliang Foundation Bldg., 968 Rama IV Rd., Bangkok 5; Pres. SURAPHOL ASVASIRAYOTHIN.

Thai Textile Manufacturing Association: 454–460 Sukhumvit Rd., Bangkok 11.

Thai Timber Exporters' Association: 462/1-5 4th Floor, Union Bldg., Siphya Rd., Bangkok 5; f. 1949; 52 mems.; Chair. VIBUL VASAVAKUL.

Timber Traders' Association: 7/2 Pipat Lane, Silom Road, Bangkok.

Union Textile Merchants' Association: 252–254 Mahachak Rd., Bangkok 1.

TRADE UNIONS

Labour Council of Thailand: Petchaburi Rd., Bangkok; represents 87 labour unions and 300,000 individual mems.; Pres. AHMAD KHAMTHESTHONG Sec.-Gen. SUWAT LOOKDOD.

National Congress of Thai Labour.

MAJOR INDUSTRIAL COMPANIES

American Standard Sanitary Ware (Thailand) Ltd.: 392 Sukhumvit 18, Bangkok 11.

Atlantic Laboratories Corpn. Ltd.: 2038 Sukhumvit Rd., Bangkok 11; manufacturers of pharmaceutical and veterinary supplies.

Boonrawd Brewery Co. Ltd.: 999 Samsen Rd., Bangkrabue, Bangkok 3.

The Jalaprathan Cement Co. Ltd.: 2974 New Petchburi Rd., Bangkok 10.

Sahaviriya Panich Co. Ltd.: 33/1 Soi Chonglom, Naglingi Rd., Bangkok 1.

Siam Cement Co. Ltd.: 814 Techavanich Rd., Bangkok 8.

Siam Food Products Co. Ltd.: 283 Silom Rd., Sibunruang Bldg., Bangkok 5.

Siam Yamaha Co. Ltd.: 1 Din-Dang Rd., Samseannai, Phyathai, Bangkok 4; f. 1966; sale and production of motorcycles; Man. Dir. KASEM NARONGDEJ.

Siriwiwat (2515) Co. Ltd.: 988–90 Sukhumvit Rd., Bangkok 11; Chair. and Man. Dir. SOMJET WATANASIN.

Srimaharaja Co. Ltd.: 36 Mansion 5, Rajdamnern Ave., Bangkok 2.

Tanin Industrial Co. Ltd.: 52 Soi Udomsuk, Sukhumvit Rd., Bangna, Bangkok; manufactures and assembles radio and television sets.

Thai Amarit Brewery Ltd.: 369/1 Pracharas Rd., Bangkok 3.

Thai Asahi Glass Co. Ltd.: 1016 Rama IV Rd., Bangkok 5.

Thai Oil Refinery Co. Ltd.: 14 Surasak Rd., Bangkok 5.

Thai Pineapple Canning Industry Co. Ltd.: 87 Sukhumvit Rd., 7th Floor, Nai Lert Bldg., Bangkok 11.

Thai Plywood Co. Ltd.: 6 Rajdamnern Ave., Bangkok 2.

Thai Seri Cold Storage Co. Ltd.: 1575 Charoennakorn Rd., Bangkok 6; producers and exporters of seafood products.

Thai Tejin Co. Ltd.: 6th Floor, Thai Airways Bldg., Lanluang Rd., Bangkok 1.

Thailand Sugar Corporation Ltd.: 624 Jawarad Rd., Bangkok 1.

Yuasa Battery (Thailand) Co. Ltd.: 937–9 Sukhumvit 51, Bangkok 10110; f. 1963.

TRANSPORT

RAILWAYS

State Railway of Thailand: Yodse Rd., Bangkok 10500; f. 1891; 3,825 km. of track in 1981; Chair. Lt.-Gen. THIENCHAI SIRISAMPAN; Gen. Man. DHAWAT SANGPRADAB; Sec. MANI HINSHIRANAN; publ. *Khaorotfai* (Thai, 2 a month), *Information Booklet* (English, annually), *Annual Report* (English and Thai).

ROADS

Total length of primary and secondary roads at the end of 1981 was 44,052 km. Under Thailand's Second Highway Project it is planned to build approximately 90 km. of a new two-lane highway to the east of the Nan River and possibly to improve 475 km. of feeder roads in the area.

Department of Highways: Sri Ayudhaya Rd., Bangkok 10400; Dir.-Gen. SEREE SUEBSANGUAN.

Department of Land Transport: Phaholyothin Rd., Bangkok 10900; Dir.-Gen. CHAMLONG SALIGUPTA; publ. *Thailand Transportation Journal* (Thai, monthly).

Express Transportation Organization (ETO): Sri Ayudhaya Rd., Bangkok 10400; Chair. Maj.-Gen. SUDSAI HUSDIN; publ. *Bulletin* (Thai, monthly).

Bangkok Mass Transit Authority (BMTA): Petchburi Rd., Bangkok 10400; controls Bangkok's local transport system; Chair. Lt.-Gen. SAK BOONTHRAKUL.

SHIPPING

Harbour Department: Yotha Rd., Bangkok 10100; Dir.-Gen. Rear-Admiral PRAKIT PRACHUABMOH.

Office of the Mercantile Marine Promotion Commission: 19 Phra-Atti Rd., Bangkok 10200; f. 1979; Sec.-Gen. KAMOL SANDHIKHETRIN.

Port Authority of Thailand: Klong Yoi, Bangkok 10110; 31 vessels; Chair. Admiral SOMBOON CHUAPHIBUL, R.T.N.; publ. *Bulletin* (Thai); Dir.-Gen. Capt. LAPO ISRANGKURA NA AYUDHYA, R.T.N.

Bangkok United Mechanical Co. Ltd.: 144 Sukhumvit Rd., Bangkok; coastal services; Pres. P. PRASARTTONG ORSOTH; Man. C. W. CHAIKOMIN; 1 tanker.

CP Co. Ltd.: 197/1 Silom Bldg., Silom Rd., Bangkok 10500; coastal tanker services to Singapore; 20 vessels; Chair. and Man. Dir. Rear-Admiral CHANO PHENCHART.

Jutha Maritime Co. Ltd.: 197/1 Silom Bldg. 2nd Floor, Silom Rd., Bangkok 10500; services between Bangkok and Japanese ports; 3 vessels; Chair. and Man. Dir. CHANO PHENCHART.

Thai International Maritime Enterprises Ltd.: 5th Floor, Sarasin Bldg., 14 Surasak Rd., Bangkok 10500; services from Bangkok to Japan; 7 vessels; Chair. CHOW CHOWKWANYUN; Man. Dir. SUN SUNDISAMRIT.

Thai Maritime Navigation Co. Ltd.: 59 Charoenkrung Rd., Yannawa, Bangkok 12; services from Bangkok to Japan and ASEAN countries; 4 vessels; Chair. Admiral TIAM MAKARANDA, R.T.N.; Dir.-Gen. Lt. Commdr. PHET SIRIYONG, R.T.N.

Thai Mercantile Marine Ltd.: Bangkok Bank Bldg., 4th Floor, P O B. 905, 300 Silom Rd., Bangkok 10500; f. 1967; 2 vessels; services between Japan and Thailand; Chair. CHIN SOPHONPANICH; Man. Dir. VARI VIRANGKURA.

Thai Petroleum Transports Co. Ltd.: Air France Bldg., 3 Patpong Rd., Bangkok; coastal tanker services; Chair. C. CHOWKWANYUN; Man. Capt. N. J. M. CARD; 5 tanker vessels.

United Thai Shipping Co. Ltd. (UNITHAI): 7th Floor, Central Bldg., 306 Silom Rd., Bangkok 10500; regular containerized services to Europe; 5 vessels; Chair. Admiral TIAM MAKARANANDA, R.T.N.; Man. Dir. SUN SUNDISAMRIT.

CIVIL AVIATION

Don Muang, Chiangmai, Haadyai and Phuket airports are of international standard. U-Tapao is an alternative airport.

Airports Authority of Thailand: Bangkok Int. Airport, Vibhavadi Rangsit Rd., Bangkhen, Bangkok 10210; f. 1979; Man. Dir. Air Marshal SAWAI CHUANGSUVANISH.

Department of Aviation: Soi Ngarmduplee, Thungmahamak, Bangkok 10120; Dir.-Gen. SRIBHUMI SUKHANETR; publ. *Annual Report* (English).

Thai Airways International Ltd. (THAI): 89 Vibhavadi Rangsit Rd., Bangkok 10900; f. 1959; international services from Bangkok to Australia, Bahrain, Bangladesh, Burma, People's Republic of China, Denmark, France, Federal Republic of Germany, Greece, Hong Kong, India, Indonesia, Italy, Japan, Republic of Korea, Kuwait, Malaysia, Nepal, the Netherlands, New Caledonia, Pakistan, the Philippines, Saudi Arabia, Singapore, Sri Lanka, Taiwan, the United Kingdom and U.S.A.; Chair. Air Chief Marshal PANIENG KANTARAT; Pres. Air Chief Marshal BANCHA SUKHANUSASNA; fleet of 3 DC-8-63, 1 DC-8-62, 2 DC-10-30, 5 B747-200, 10 A300B4; publs. *Khaogalbinthai* (English and Thai, monthly), *Sawasdee* (English, fortnightly).

Thai Airways Co. Ltd.: 6 Larn Luang Rd., Bangkok 10200; f. 1951; operates domestic services and also flies to Laos and Malaysia; Chair. Air Chief Marshal PANIENG KANTARAT; Man. Dir. Air Marshal PRAYUTE PRACHUABMOH; fleet of 7 HS-748, 4 Boeing 737.

FOREIGN AIRLINES

Thailand is also served by the following airlines: Aeroflot (U.S.S.R.), Air France, Air India, Air Lanka, Alia (Jordan), Alitalia, BAC (Burma), Bangladesh Biman, British Airways, CAAC (People's Republic of China), Cathay Pacific Airways (Hong Kong), China Airlines (Taiwan), EgyptAir, Finnair (Finland), Garuda Indonesian Airways, Gulf Air (Bahrain), Hang Khong Vietnam, Iraqi Airways, JAL (Japan), KLM (Netherlands), Korean Airlines (Republic of Korea), Kuwait Airways, Lao Aviation, LOT (Poland), Lufthansa (Federal Republic of Germany), MAS (Malaysia), PAL (Philippines), Pan Am (U.S.A.), PIA (Pakistan), Qantas (Australia), Royal Brunei Airlines, Royal Nepal Airlines, Sabena (Belgium), SAS (Sweden), Saudia, SIA (Singapore), Swissair, TAROM (Romania), TMA (Lebanon).

TOURISM

The Tourist Authority of Thailand (TAT): Head Office: 4 Ratchadamnoen Nok Ave., Bangkok 1; f. 1960 as the Tourist Organization of Thailand; Gov. Col. SOMCHAI HIRANYAKIT; Deputy Govs. DHARMNOON PRACHUABMOH, SEREE WANGPAICHITR and PHAIROTE THAMMAPIMUK; publs. *Holiday Time in Thailand* (monthly, English), *Anusarn Or. Sor. Tor.* (monthly, Thai).

Tourist Association of North Thailand: 135 Praisanee Rd., A. Muang, Chiangmai; Pres. Mrs. CHAMCHIT LAOHAVAD

DEFENCE

Armed Forces (1981): Total strength 238,100: army 160,000, navy 35,000, air force 43,100; military service lasts for two years and is compulsory; Para-military forces number 44,500.

Equipment: The armed forces are mainly American-equipped, recent additions to the air force have been T-6 Air Tourer trainers from New Zealand, F-53 fighters and A37B "Skyraider" from the U.S.A.

Defence Expenditure: The amount allocated to defence in 1981 was 26,200 million baht.

Supreme Commander of the Armed Forces: Gen. SAIYUD KERDPHOL.

Commander-in-Chief of the Air Force: Air Chief Marshal TAKLAEW SUSILAVORN.

Commander-in-Chief of the Army: Gen. PRAYUTH CHARUMANEE.

Commander-in-Chief of the Navy: Admiral SOMBOON CHUAPIBUL.

EDUCATION

Education in Thailand is free and compulsory for six years. All education is state controlled. There are four types of schools: (1) Government schools established and maintained by government funds; (2) Local schools which are usually financed by the Government; however, if they are founded by the people of the district, funds collected from the public may be used in supporting such schools; (3) Municipal schools, a type of primary school financed and supervised by the municipality; (4) Private schools set up and owned by private individuals under the provisions of the 1954 Private Schools Act. The National Scheme of Education provides for education on four levels: (1) Pre-School Education (nursery and kindergarten), which is not compulsory and aims at preparing children for elementary education; (2) Elementary Education; (3) Secondary Education; (4) Higher Education.

Elementary Education

Starts at the age of 7 and lasts for six years. From 1955 on the Ministry of Education made an annual provision in the budget so that every district would have at least one primary extension school. These efforts have now spread to the villages, resulting in the opening of about a hundred schools of this type every year.

Secondary Education

Aims at providing knowledge and skills to enable pupils to carry out an occupation or to prepare them for further education. Secondary education is divided into the lower and upper schools, each having no more than three grades. There are three streams: the first, general, stream is designed to give instruction in theoretical subjects and is not concerned directly with occupational skills. The second, vocational, stream is designed to prepare students with knowledge and skills for directly taking up specific occupations. There is also a teacher-training stream at secondary level.

Higher Education

In 1979 there were fourteen universities in Thailand, offering both undergraduate and graduate courses in all fields. There remains a shortage of university places, although university enrolment increased to approximately 50,000 in 1973. The enrolment of women, although small, increased faster than that of men. Other higher education establishments include the various Military and Police Academies providing a standard of training equivalent to that of civil establishments, and teacher-training establishments. In 1974 it was announced that a number of educational institutions which previously offered only post-secondary diploma programmes were to be allowed to award degrees. This would double the number of universities and degree-awarding colleges in Thailand.

Rural Education

Expansion of rural education has been an important project to stem the increasing flow of students to the cities, especially Bangkok. For this purpose the Ministry of Education set up the Regional Education Development Project, including higher education in its terms of reference. The Education Broadcasting Service has been functioning since 1954 to give schoolchildren and teachers as well as the public general education and educational news. In 1958 school broadcasting was begun, covering such subjects as civics, music and English. In 1977 about 7,000 schools made use of this service, which it is hoped to extend, especially to schools in remoter areas.

Much has been done for the improvement in both quality and quantity of vocational training throughout the country. Short-term vocational courses are given in more rural areas, and new multi-vocational mobile schools have been tried out giving such courses as dressmaking, hairdressing, cooking, etc. Another innovation is the Special Agricultural School for the self-help settlements, designed to give such settlers a basic knowledge of agriculture.

BIBLIOGRAPHY

GENERAL

BASCHE, J. Thailand: Land of the Free (Taplinger, New York, N.Y., 1971).

BLANCHARD, W. Thailand: Its People, Its Society, Its Culture (Human Relations Area Files, New Haven, Conn., 1958).

CRIPPS, F. The Far Province (Hutchinson, London, 1965).

DE YOUNG, J. E. Village Life in Modern Thailand (University of California Press, Berkeley, Calif., 1955).

DONNER, W. Five Faces of Thailand (C. Hurst, London, 1978).

EVERS, H. D. Loosely Structured Social Systems: Thailand in Comparative Perspective (Yale University Press, New Haven, Conn., 1969).

HO, R., and CHAPMAN, E. C. (eds.). Studies of Contemporary Thailand (Australian National University, Canberra, A.C.T., 1973).

KRULL, G. Bangkok: Siam's City of Angels (Robert Hale, London, 1964).

NACH, J. Thailand in Pictures (Oak Tree Press, London, 1963).

SEIDENFADEN, E. The Thai Peoples (The Siam Society, Bangkok, 1963).

SHARP, L., and HANKS, L. Bang Chan: Social History of a Rural Community in Thailand (Cornell University Press, Ithaca, N.Y., 1978).

SKINNER, G. W. Chinese Society in Thailand (Cornell University Press, Ithaca, N.Y., 1957).

SRISVASDI, B. C. The Hill Tribes of Siam (Khun Aroon, Bangkok, 1963).

WATSON, J. W. Thailand: Rice Bowl of Asia (Garrad Publishing Co., Ill., 1966).

HISTORY

CADY, J. F. Thailand, Burma, Laos and Cambodia (Prentice-Hall Inc., Englewood Cliffs, N.J., 1966).

CHAKRABONGSE, Prince CHULA. Lords of Life: the Paternal Monarchy of Bangkok, 1782–1932 (Taplinger, New York and Alvin Redman, London, 1960).

FISTIE, P. L'Evolution de la Thailande Contemporaine (Paris, 1967).

NUECHTERLEIN, D. E. Thailand and the Struggle for South-East Asia (Cornell University Press, Ithaca, N.Y., 1965).

PENDLETON, R. L., and KINGSBURY, R. C. Thailand: Aspects of Landscape and Life (Duell, Sloan & Pearce, New York, 1962).

WOOD, W. A. R. A History of Siam (Chalermnit, Bangkok, 1959).

ZIMMERMAN, C. Siam: First Rural Survey (Times Press, Bangkok, 1931).

ECONOMICS AND POLITICS

CALAVAN, M. Decisions against Nature: an Anthropological Study of Agriculture in Northern Thailand (Northern Illinois Centre for Southeast Asian Studies, 1977).

CALDWELL, J. A. American Economic Aid to Thailand (Lexington Books, 1974).

ELLIOTT, D. Thailand: Origins of Military Rule (Zed, London, 1978).

GIRLING, J. L. S. Thailand: Society and Politics (Cornell University Press, Ithaca, N.Y. and London, 1981).

INGRAM, J. C. Economic Change in Thailand 1850–1970 (Stanford University Press, Stanford, Calif., 2nd edn., 1971).

MARZOUK, G. A. Economic Development and Policies (Rotterdam University Press, Rotterdam, 1972).

MORELL, D. and CHAI-ANAN SAMUDVANIJ. Thailand: Reform, Reaction and Revolution (Oelgeschlager, Gunn and Hain, Cambridge, Mass., 1981).

MUSCAT, R. J. Development Strategy in Thailand: A Study of Economic Growth (Pall Mall Press, London, 1966).

NEHER, C. D. Modern Thai Politics: From Village to Nation (Schenkman, Cambridge, Mass., 1979).

RIGGS, F. W. Thailand: The Modernization of a Bureaucratic Polity (East-West Center Press, Honolulu, Hawaii, 1966).

SATO, T. Field Crops of Thailand (Kyoto University South East Asia Centre, 1966).

SIFFIN, W. J. The Thai Bureaucracy: Institutional Change and Development (East-West Center Press, Honolulu, Hawaii, 1966).

SILCOCK, T. H. (ed.). Thailand: Social and Economic Studies in Development (Australian National University Press, Canberra, 1967).

The Economic Development of Thai Agriculture (Cornell University Press, Ithaca, N.Y., 1970).

THAK CHALOEMTIARANA. Thailand: The Politics of Despotic Paternalism (Social Science Association of Thailand, Bangkok, 1979).

Thailand Into the 80s (Office of the Prime Minister, Kingdom of Thailand, Bangkok, 1979).

UNPHAKORN, P. *et al*. Finance, Trade and Economic Development in Thailand (Bangkok 1973).

VAN ROY, E. Economic Systems of Northern Thailand (Cornell University Press, Ithaca, N.Y., 1971).

WATABE, T. Glutinous Rice in North Thailand (Kyoto University, 1967).

WILSON, D. A. Politics in Thailand (Cornell University Press, Ithaca, N.Y., 1962).

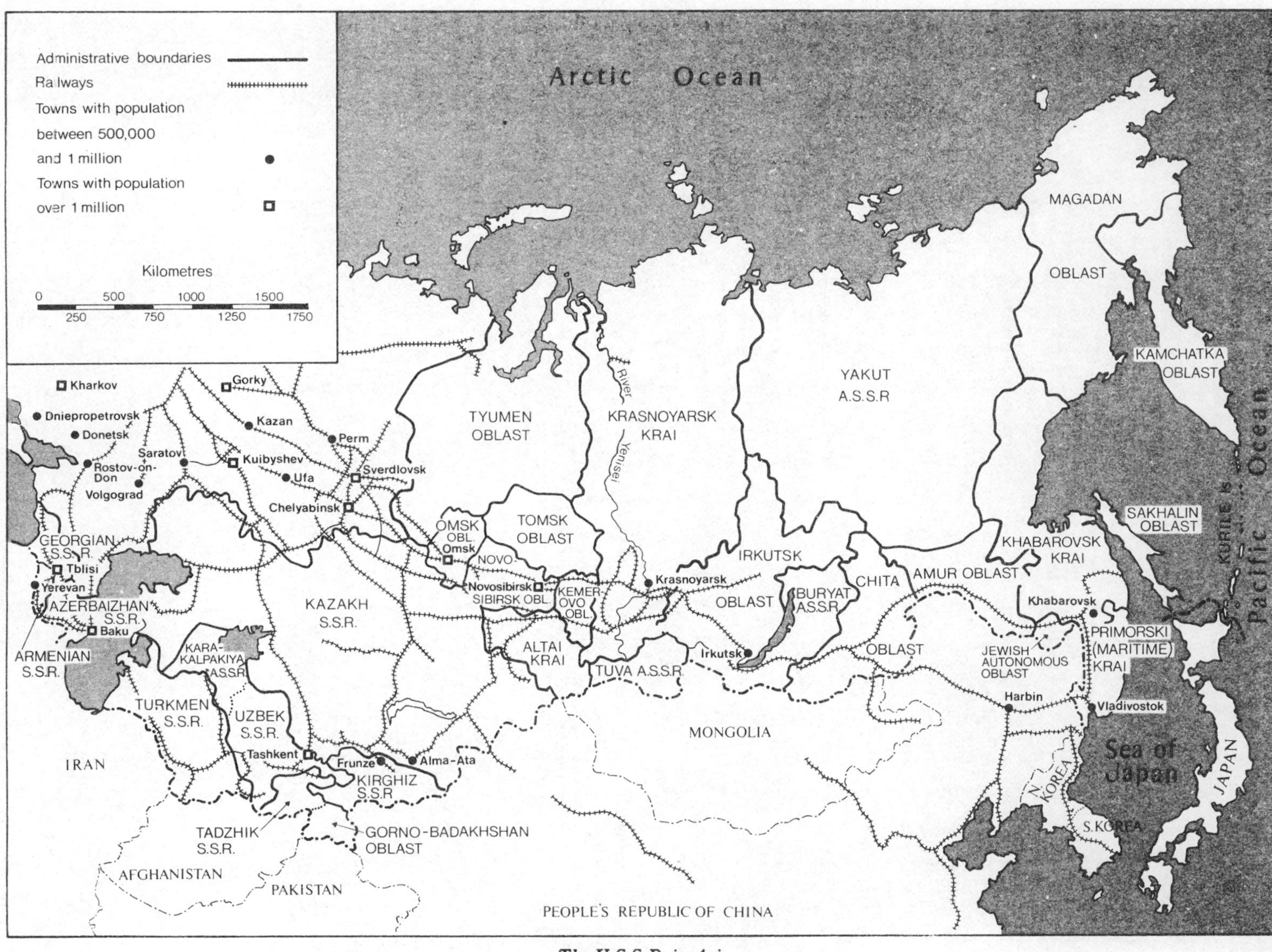

The U.S.S.R. in Asia.

The U.S.S.R. in Asia

SOVIET CENTRAL ASIA

G. E. Wheeler

(Revised by Ann Sheehy, 1977–82)

PHYSICAL AND SOCIAL GEOGRAPHY

Soviet Central Asia is the term now usually applied to the territory occupied by the Kazakh, Uzbek, Tadzhik, Kirghiz and Turkmen S.S.Rs. (Soviet Socialist Republics). Soviet writers, however, include only the last four in this term, the Kazakh S.S.R. being regarded as a separate region. The whole area is bounded on the north by Western Siberia, on the south by Iran and Afghanistan, on the east by the Xinjiang Uygur (Sinkiang Uighur) Autonomous Region of China, and on the west by the Caspian Sea.

Physically, Soviet Central Asia can be divided into four regions: the *steppe*, consisting of the northern part of the Kazakh S.S.R.; the *semi-desert* consisting roughly of the rest of the Kazakh S.S.R.; the *desert region* lying to the south of the semi-desert and reaching the Iranian frontier in the west and the Chinese frontier in the east; and the *mountain region* of which the main features are the Pamirs and the Tien-shan. Vegetation is sparse, being confined to a belt of wooded steppe in the north-east, the grasslands of the Kazakh S.S.R., hardy perennials such as saxaul in the deserts, and a variety of trees and plants along the river valleys and in the piedmont zones. In proportion to the vast areas of desert and mountains, the area of cultivated and populated land is very small.

CLIMATE

The climate is "continental", with hot summers and cold winters. In the north of the Kazakh S.S.R. January temperatures may fall as low as minus 50°C., while in the extreme south the climate is sub-tropical with average shade temperatures reaching 40°C. Precipitation is low throughout the whole region: in the semi-desert most of the rain falls in summer, while in the south most rain falls in March. Heavy falls of snow are uncommon except in the mountainous districts.

POPULATION

In January 1982 the total population of the region was nearly 43 million. Asians, comprising chiefly the indigenous Muslim peoples, constitute just over two-thirds of the population, a proportion that has recently been growing because of their very high birth rates. The remaining third is made up of European (predominantly Slav) settlers who have arrived during the past 100 years. Before the coming of the Russians, the most meaningful distinction for the indigenous population was not as between nationalities or even ethnic groups, but as between nomad and settled peoples. The nomads were in fact exclusively of Turkic origin speaking closely related Turkic languages—Kazakhs, Kirghiz and, to a lesser extent, Turkmens. The settled peoples contained both Turkic (Uzbek and Turkmen) and Iranian (Tadzhik) elements. Until the first half of the nineteenth century there was a marked difference in the way of life followed by the nomad and settled elements, urban culture being entirely confined to the settled people occupying the oases and valleys. During the last 60 years, however, the nomads have been to a large extent stabilized and cultural differences have tended to become much less. Anthropologically, with figures for 1979, the peoples of Central Asia may be grouped as follows. The Uzbeks (12.5 million) and the Tadzhiks (2.9 million) belong to the Caucasoid race; they are brachycephalic, of medium height and have dark hair and eyes. Some Mongoloid features can be found among them. The Kazakhs (6.6 million) and the Kirghiz (1.9 million) belong to the South Siberian type formed as a result of the mingling of the Central Asian Mongoloids with the ancient Caucasoid population of the Kazakh Steppe. The Karakalpaks (303,000) occupy a position between the Uzbeks and Kazakhs, somewhat closer to the latter. The Turkmens (2.0 million) are in a somewhat different class. They have predominantly Caucasoid physical features, but they are dolichocephalic and considerably taller than the Uzbeks and Tadzhiks.

There are a number of other smaller Asian communities including Uygurs, Dungans (Chinese Muslims),—whose numbers increased from 95,000 to 211,000 and from 22,000 to 52,000 respectively between 1959 and 1979, partly as a result of an influx in the early 1960s from Xinjiang—Koreans, Arabs and Baluchis. The large but scattered Tatar community of 1,154,000 includes Crimean Tatars expelled from the Crimea in 1944. The Jewish community, embracing both European and Bukharan Jews, numbers about 150,000. The non-Asian population totals roughly 12 million, of whom the Russians, numbering 9.3 million, are the most numerous and indeed the most numerous of all the nationalities living in the region after the Uzbeks (12.4 million in the five republics). The remaining non-Asians include 1,200,000 Ukrainians, over one million Germans, mainly in the Kazakh, Kirghiz and Tadzhik S.S.Rs., 156,000 Byelorussians and some 50,000 Poles in the Kazakh S.S.R.

In spite of the very large number of non-Muslims living side by side with the local population there has been remarkably little inter-marriage and in general the two communities keep apart from each other during their leisure hours.

HISTORY

Little is known of the history of Soviet Central Asia before the 8th century, when the Arabs extended their conquest of Iran to Transoxania, the land between the Amu-Dar'ya and Syr-Dar'ya rivers. During the 9th century most of Transoxania became part of the Persian Samanid empire. After the downfall of the Samanids in 999, the desert and oasis regions were mainly ruled by various Turkic Muslim dynasties, the most important being the Seljuks and the Khorezm Shahs. From 1137 to 1212 Transoxania and the region to the west of the Syr-Dar'ya were dominated by a Tungusic people, the Kara-Kitays. During the whole of this period the Kazakh Steppe remained in possession of Turkic nomads who were never conquered by the Arabs. The Mongol invasion, which began in 1220, included the whole of the desert and semi-desert regions and part of the Kazakh Steppe. By the middle of the 14th century all the Mongol rulers had become Turkicized and embraced Islam. Thenceforward, the whole region remained under the rule of various Turkic Muslim dynasties until the coming of the Russians. The principal of these dynasties was that of Timur (Tamerlane) which dominated the whole of the southern part of the region until, at the beginning of the 16th century, it was overthrown by the Uzbek dynasty of Shaibani. This came to an end in 1655 when it broke up into various khanates of which the principal were Kokand, Bukhara and Khiva.

The Russians began to encroach on the Kazakh Steppe in the first half of the eighteenth century, establishing a fortified line along its northern and eastern fringes as far as the Chinese frontier. But the Steppe was not physically incorporated in the Tsarist Empire until the first half of the nineteenth century. The Russians then continued their advance southwards, capturing the city of Tashkent in 1865. During the next 20 years Russian rule was extended to the frontiers of Afghanistan and Iran; the whole of the khanate of Kokand was annexed and the khanates of Bukhara and Khiva reduced to a state of vassalage. Samarkand, Timur's ancient capital, was annexed to Russia in 1868. The warlike Turkmens were finally subdued after the battle of Geok Tepe in 1881. Although essentially military in character, Tsarist rule was not oppressive and it brought peace and security to the whole region. Roads and railways were built and economic conditions greatly improved. Little was done in the way of education: compulsory primary education was not introduced, nor were any universities established. Religion and existing local traditions and customs were not interfered with, the official view being that, faced with the superior Russian civilization, Islamic culture would eventually die of inanition. The main defects of the Tsarist administration were first that it made no provision for the eventual grant of self-government to the local population and consequently made no attempt to train an indigenous civil service or armed forces. Secondly, it allowed, and indeed encouraged, large-scale settlement of Russian and Ukrainian peasants without any proper organization or regard for the local population.

During the chaos which followed the collapse of the Imperial administration in 1917, attempts were made by the local population to set up national governments. These were unsuccessful owing to their lack of administrative experience and armed forces and to the presence of over two million Russian and Ukrainian settlers. By 1924, the new Soviet regime had re-established military control over the whole region and in the same year embarked on a fundamental reorganization of the administrative system. This involved the final liquidation of the semi-independence of the former khanates of Bukhara and Khiva and the eventual creation of the existing five Soviet Socialist Republics.

ADMINISTRATION

According to the U.S.S.R. Constitution, the five Republics are regarded as fully sovereign states forming part of the U.S.S.R. but with the theoretical right of secession. Each Republic is named after the majority indigenous nationality. In 1979 the latter accounted for between 68 per cent (Turkmen S.S.R.) and 36 per cent (Kazakh S.S.R.) of the total population. The system of Republican administration is uniform throughout the U.S.S.R., each Republic having a President, a Council of Ministers and an elected Supreme Soviet or Parliament. Each Republic has representatives in both Chambers of the U.S.S.R. Supreme Soviet in Moscow. Paramount control of all political, economic and cultural activities, and of defence and foreign policy is exercised by the Communist Party. All the Republics have their own Communist Parties, but these are integral parts of the "indivisible" Communist Party of the Soviet Union. While the First Secretary of each Republican Party is a native, the Second is a non-native, usually a Russian. The Republics are subdivided into oblasts and rayons; the Autonomous Soviet Socialist Republic of Kara-Kalpakiya is included in the Uzbek S.S.R. and the Autonomous Oblast of Gorno-Badakhshan (the Pamirs) in the Tadzhik S.S.R. There are no national military formations: conscription into the Soviet Armed Forces is universal, and conscripts are liable for service anywhere in the Soviet Union or abroad.

PUBLIC WORKS

The Imperial Russian Government had established good road, railway and telegraph systems and adequate port facilities in the Caspian and Aral Seas. They had founded a number of towns in the Kazakh Steppe where none had been before, and they had developed and modernized those in the southern part of the region. All these achievements were inherited and further developed by the Soviet regime, which in addition successfully expanded the modern irrigation system, a field in which the Tsarist government had made little progress. Major works of railway construction undertaken by the Soviet regime include the Turksib Railway connecting the Central Asian and Trans-Siberian systems, the Mointy-Chu stretch west of Lake Balkhash, the Amu-Dar'ya Valley line from Chardzhou to Kungrad, recently extended to Makat on the Gur'yev-Kandagach line, and the so-called Friendship Railway from Aktogay on the Turksib to the Chinese frontier, where it was designed to connect with a Chinese railway. In 1982, however, the Chinese section was still unfinished. A large number of entirely new towns has been built, including the capitals of the Tadzhik and Kirghiz S.S.Rs., Dushanbe (formerly Stalinabad) and Frunze. The irrigation works undertaken in Central Asia by the Soviet Union are among its greatest material achievements. One of the many major projects completed or under construction in the region is the Kara-Kum canal, which already stretches for more than 1,000 km. across the desert west from the Amu-Dar'ya river to beyond Ashkhabad and will eventually extend to Krasnovodsk on the Caspian Sea. With a shortage of water expected to hamper both industrial and agricultural development in the region in the future and with the need to provide employment for the rapidly burgeoning population, studies are currently in progress on the possible diversion of some of the waters of the Siberian rivers south towards the Aral Sea along a 2,500 km. canal.

SOCIAL CONDITIONS

The process of modernization and westernization which has affected most of Muslim Asia during the past 50 years has been greatly speeded up in Soviet Central Asia by the energetic and often arbitrary steps taken by the Soviet Government. Most of these steps have had a beneficial effect on material living conditions, particularly in the urban areas. In respect of standard of living, public health, employment, education and equality of opportunity, the Muslim peoples of Central Asia are undoubtedly still better off than those of the adjoining non-Soviet Muslim countries. Owing to travel restrictions on foreigners, impartial observation of conditions in the rural areas is difficult and Soviet reporting provides evidence that these are still fairly primitive in certain districts.

The old tribal and clan social structure of the local inhabitants is tending to disappear, although it is often observed that members of a single enterprise such as a collective farm belong to one tribe or clan. The political organization of the people into national republics, although originally artificial and evidently intended by the authorities to remain so, is now showing signs of crystallization.

RELATIONS WITH NEIGHBOURING COUNTRIES

During the Tsarist regime there was considerable freedom of movement across the frontiers between Russian Central Asia and the adjoining countries of Iran, Afghanistan and China, in all of which countries live large numbers of people of the same nationalities. For example, in Afghanistan there are over two million Tadzhiks and over one million Uzbeks; in the Xinjiang Uygur Autonomous Region of China there are half a million Kazakhs and smaller communities of Tadzhiks, Kirghiz and Uzbeks; and in Iran there are over 200,000 Turkmens. In the early years of the Soviet regime some attempt was made to attract these elements into the newly formed Soviet Republics. These attempts were unsuccessful and were abandoned. At present, the frontiers are closely guarded by a special force maintained for the purpose. However, since the April 1978 "revolution" in Afghanistan (which brought that country more firmly within the Soviet orbit), contacts between the adjacent Central Asian republics and Afghanistan have increased. Since the Sino-Soviet dispute assumed serious proportions in 1960, numerous frontier violations and incidents have been reported by both Soviet and Chinese governments. According to Soviet reports, in 1962 some 60,000 Kazakhs and Uygurs migrated into Soviet territory from the Ili district of the Xinjiang Uygur A.R. After armed clashes on the Sino-Soviet frontier in Central Asia and the Far East in 1969 frontier negotiations were started in Beijing (Peking) and have been carried on intermittently since then, but no progress has been made.

CULTURE AND EDUCATION

After the Arab Muslim conquests of the 8th century Islamic culture spread rapidly throughout the settled districts of the region and more gradually and less effectively among the nomad elements. The main effects of Islam were on law, social customs and language. Such education as there was before the Russian invasion was exclusively in the hands of the Muslim clergy and was mainly conducted in Arabic. Before the Mongol conquests of the 13th century, the written official language had been Arabic and to a minor extent Persian, but during the 13th and 14th centuries a written Turkic language called Chaghatay was developed. This used the Perso-Arabic script and a large Persian and Arabic loan vocabulary. Chaghatay served as a kind of written *lingua franca*, but the spoken languages remained fairly distinct and had considerable oral literatures.

The Tsarist government interfered little in religious and cultural matters. The Soviet regime, on the other hand, pursued from the beginning an active policy of cultural regimentation. Apart from the development of a complete primary, secondary and higher educational system from which religious instruction was completely excluded, it instituted and maintains a propaganda campaign against the belief and practice of Islam and against all customs and traditions directly or indirectly associated with it. Efforts have been made to develop the arts (literature, music, painting and sculpture) on socialist-realist lines. In 1930, the Perso-Arabic script in which all local languages were formerly written was abolished in favour of a Latin script, and this, in 1940, was changed to a series of cyrillic scripts. The aim has been to modernize and enrich the languages so as to suit them for modern cultural and scientific requirements. Some success has been achieved in this direction, but it remains to be seen whether the Soviet regime's current campaign to promote universal knowledge of Russian among the native population will hamper further development of the vernacular languages. The effect of the language reforms on literature has been very great. Poetry, once the main literary medium, has largely lost its place to prose-writing on Soviet Russian lines. The press has been greatly developed and every republic has a large number of newspapers and periodicals in Russian and the vernacular languages. All are extensively used as vehicles for official propaganda. The republics have their own radio and television stations as well as television channels which carry programmes beamed by satellite from Moscow.

The development of education is one of the main Soviet achievements in Central Asia. In 1917 the proportion of literates did not exceed five per cent. It is now claimed that over 90 per cent of the population are literate, having completed four years at school. While this may be an exaggeration, there can be no doubt that the standard of literacy and of higher and technical education in Soviet Central Asia is far higher than that of any other Muslim country in the world, and indeed, higher than any Asian or African country with the exception of Japan and Israel. With the introduction of compulsory primary education in 1930, the old Muslim schools (*mektebs*) and higher educational establishments (*medresehs*) disappeared. In 1943 a single *medreseh* was opened in Bukhara for the purpose of training clerical functionaries, and another has recently been re-opened in Tashkent. These are the only establishments of their kind in the Soviet Union. The capital of each of the Republics, including the Autonomous Republic of Kara-Kalpakiya, has its own university, Uzbekistan and Kazakhstan having additional ones in Samarkand and Karaganda respectively. Each Republic also has its own Academy of Sciences. In the late 1950s the Muslim nationalities were still markedly under-represented in higher education in the Soviet Union, but the gap narrowed appreciably in the 1960s, and any differences today are due largely to the fact that there are proportionately fewer women of the Muslim nationalities among the student body. Standards, however, are still not as high as in the European part of the Soviet Union.

In spite of strenuous Soviet efforts to eliminate Islamic culture, there are many indications that Islam remains the predominant cultural influence in the whole area.

ECONOMIC SURVEY

Before the Revolution the economy was almost exclusively agricultural, industry being confined to a small amount of cotton ginning and to the extraction of copper, coal and petroleum. Since the Revolution there has been a great expansion of industry, particularly since the Second World War when a large number of factories with their trained personnel were evacuated to Central Asia from the West. However, mineral extraction and primary processing of raw materials continue to be the main industrial activities.

Cotton still dominates the agricultural economy of the three southernmost republics (Uzbek, Tadzhik and Turkmen). Together with the Azerbaidzhan S.S.R., the Central Asian republics supply all the U.S.S.R.'s domestic needs and a substantial surplus for export. In spite of early failures in organization and susceptibility to drought, the Virgin Lands of Kazakhstan, brought under the plough in the mid-1950s, are proving a useful additional source of wheat for the whole Soviet Union. Animal husbandry, particularly sheep-breeding, is of considerable importance. The deposits of copper, lead, zinc and chrome in the Kazakh S.S.R., and of such rare metals as mercury and antimony in the Kirghiz S.S.R., are the largest in the Soviet Union and make it almost self-sufficient in these respects. The Kazakh S.S.R. also possesses one-sixth of Soviet coal stocks as well as considerable iron ore mines and reserves of petroleum. The whole area has one-fifth of the Soviet Union's hydro-energy resources, and Uzbekistan is a major producer of both gold and uranium. In addition, Turkmenistan and Uzbekistan account for about one-third of the Soviet Union's natural gas output. The long-established Turkmen oil industry, on the other hand, is declining because of failure to discover new commercial deposits. Local natural gas and phosphates support chemical and fertilizer industries. Engineering includes textile, agricultural and mining machinery. Apart from heavy industry, such light industries as textile manufacture and the canning of food products have been considerably expanded, although the cotton textile industry is still small relative to the output of raw cotton and does not yet even meet local demand.

The economic organization of Central Asia has varied from complete centralization under Stalin to a substantial measure of decentralization favoured by Khrushchev. After the latter's downfall in 1964, the former centralized administration of industry and planning was restored but with a somewhat greater degree of flexibility than before. All decisions on investment, prices and so on are made in Moscow.

As a result of the demographic explosion among the indigenous peoples in the last 25 years, the region has considerable reserves of labour. The labour force in the heavy and extractive industries is predominantly immigrant, while the indigenous population remains largely agricultural. Efforts are being made to attract some of the surplus manpower to the labour-deficient areas of Siberia and the European part of the Soviet Union, but so far with very limited success.

THE KAZAKH SOVIET SOCIALIST REPUBLIC

INTRODUCTION

The Kazakh Republic was formed as an Autonomous Republic within the Russian Federation on August 26th, 1920, and reconstituted as a Union Republic on December 5th, 1936. It has an area of 2,717,300 sq. km. and a population of 15,045,000 (January 1st, 1981). Of these, 36 per cent are Kazakhs, 40.8 per cent Russians, 6.1 per cent Ukrainians and 2.1 per cent Tatars. The population density is 5.5 persons per sq. km. Alma-Ata, the capital, has a population of 975,000 (1981). In size the Kazakh Republic (Kazakhstan) is second only to the Russian Federation. It extends from the Volga to the Altai Mountains and from the Western Siberian plains to the Central Asian deserts. Kazakhstan has a frontier with the People's Republic of China to the south-east.

The number of towns and industrial communities in Kazakhstan has increased greatly in recent years. The Kazakh settlement of Baikonur, in the heart of the Steppe, is the launching place of the Soviet spaceships.

STATISTICS

POPULATION

BIRTHS AND DEATHS

	Birth Rate (per '000)	Death Rate (per '000)
1975	24.3	7.2
1976	24.5	7.2
1977	24.2	7.2
1978	24.4	7.4
1979	24.0	7.7
1980	23.8	8.0

AGRICULTURE

Agriculture in Kazakhstan is varied and intensive. It is one of the most productive regions of the U.S.S.R. in grain and other agricultural crops.

Besides sheep and horses, cows, camels, goats, pigs and poultry are raised. Kazakhstan produced 11.8 per cent of the Soviet Union's total yield of grain, 6.7 per cent of meat and 4.7 per cent of milk in 1978.

In 1978 there were 1,472,000 persons engaged in agriculture on 418 collective farms and 2,035 state farms.

CROP PRODUCTION

('000 tons)

	1975	1976	1977	1978
Grain	12,007	29,826	17,727	27,891
Wheat	8,421.2	21,497	12,137.7	18,851
Maize	286	382	406	449
Rice	283.4	447.3	522.0	478
Cotton	284	310	324	260
Sugar beet	1,959	2,140	1,687	2,624
Sunflower	75	87	99	103
Potatoes	1,728	1,747	2,189	1,728
Other vegetables	918	885	893	n.a.
Grapes	88	133	111	190
Other fruit	196	294	232	n.a.

1979: Grain 34,519,100 tons.

LIVESTOCK

('000)

	1977	1978	1979	1980
Cattle	7,645	7,804	8,017	8,334
of which: Cows	2,626	2,716	2,819	2,908
Pigs	2,218	2,648	2,857	3,105
Sheep and goats	34,438	33,503	34,166	35,067
Poultry	39,050	42,200	45,457	47,560

ANIMAL PRODUCTS

('000 tons)

	1976	1977	1978	1979	1980
Meat	893	1,004	1,041	1,023	1,056
Milk	4,055	4,343	4,415	4,441	4,570
Eggs (million)	2,913	3,147	3,254	3,352	3,368
Wool (greasy)	102.1	103.7	105.6	104.9	111.4

INDUSTRY AND MINING

PRODUCTION

		1972	1973	1974	1975
Pig Iron	'000 tons	3,366	3,500	3,408	3,634
Steel	" "	4,024.0	4,800.0	4,829.6	4,907.3
Petroleum	" "	18,000	20,300	22,308	23,889
Coal	" "	74,500	79,800	86,972	92,225
Metal-Cutting Lathes	number	2,500	2,600	2,700	2,399
Natural Gas	million cu. metres	3,500	4,800	5,372	5,119
Electric Power	million kWh.	41,300	44,000	48,700	52,452
Mineral Fertilizers	'000 tons	3,300	4,200	5,334	5,822
Cement	" "	6,100	6,300	6,491	6,712
Cotton Fabrics	million sq. metres	79.8	82.1	94.0	96.7

1976: Electric power 55,623 million kWh.; Mineral fertilizers 5,835,000 tons.

1977: Electric power 58,266 million kWh.; Mineral fertilizers 6,496,000 tons.

1978: Coal 103,476,000 tons; Metal-cutting lathes 2,623; Electric power 59,218 million kWh.; Mineral fertilizers 6,589,000 tons.

1979: Electric power 59,700 million kWh; Coal 106.2 million tons; Metal-cutting lathes 2,774; Mineral fertilizers 6,372,200 tons.

1980: Electric power 61,500 million kWh.; Mineral fertilizers 6,549,000 tons.

EDUCATION

The literacy of the population of Kazakhstan between the ages of 9 and 49 is 99.7 per cent. According to the census of 1970, 52.2 per cent of people over the age of 9 have received higher or secondary education.

(1980/81)

	Institutions	Students
Secondary Schools	8,700	3,300,000
Secondary Specialized Schools	236	265,400
Higher Schools (incl. Universities)	55	260,000

GOVERNMENT

SUPREME SOVIET

Chairman: K. U. Medeubekov.

Presidium President: Sattar N. Imashev.

COUNCIL OF MINISTERS

Chairman: Baiken A. Ashimov.

POLITICAL ORGANIZATIONS

Kazakh Communist Party: Alma Ata; 724,000 mems. (1980); First Secretary of the Central Committee Dinmukhammed A. Kunayev.

Komsomol Leninist Young Communist League of Kazakhstan: Alma Ata; 2.1 million mems. (1980); First Sec. K. Sultanov.

JUDICIAL SYSTEM

Chairman of the Supreme Court: G. B. Elemisov.

Procurator: U. S. Seitov.

THE PRESS

There are 424 newspapers published in the Kazakh S.S.R. in Kazakh, Russian, Uygur, German and Korean. There are 114 periodicals, including 31 in Kazakh.

PRINCIPAL NEWSPAPERS

Kazakhstanskaya Pravda (*Pravda of Kazakhstan*): Alma Ata; f. 1920; organ of the Central Committee of the Kazakhstan Communist Party, Supreme Soviet and Council of Ministers; six times weekly; in Russian; Editor I. D. Spivakov.

Leninshil Zhas (*Leninist Youth*): Alma Ata; f. 1921; organ of the Central Committee of the Leninist Young Communist League of Kazakhstan; five times weekly; in Kazakh; Editor S. Berdikulov.

Leninskaya Smena (*Leninist Rising Generation*): Alma Ata; f. 1922; organ of the Central Committee of the Leninist Young Communist League of Kazakhstan; five times weekly; in Russian; Editor S. Podgorbunsky.

Sotsialistik Kazakhstan (*Socialist Kazakhstan*): Alma Ata; f. 1919; organ of the Central Committee of the Kazakh Communist Party, Supreme Soviet and Council of Ministers; six times weekly; in Kazakh; Editor S. B. Baizhanov.

SELECTED PERIODICALS

(Published monthly unless otherwise indicated)

Ara-Shmel (*Bumble-bee*): Alma Ata; f. 1956; published by the Publishing House of the Central Committee of the Kazakh Communist Party; in Kazakh and Russian; satirical.

Baldyrgan (*Sprout*): Alma Ata; f. 1958; journal of the Central Committee of the Leninist Young Communist League of Kazakhstan, illustrated; for pre-school and first grades of school; in Kazakh.

Bilim zhane enbek (*Knowledge*): f. 1960; journal of the Central Committee of the Leninist Young Communist League of Kazakhstan; popular science and technology; in Kazakh.

Kazakh Adebieti: Alma Ata; f. 1934; organ of the Kazakh Union of Writers; weekly; in Kazakh; Editor Sh. Murtasaev.

Kazakhstan Aielderi (*Women of Kazakhstan*): Alma Ata; f. 1925; journal of the Central Committee of the Kazakh Communist Party; popular women's magazine; in Kazakh.

Kazakhstan Kommunisi (*Communist of Kazakhstan*): Alma Ata; f. 1921; published by the Publishing House of the Central Committee of Kazakhstan Communist Party; in Kazakh.

Kazakhstan Mektebi (*Kazakh School*): Alma Ata; f. 1925; journal of the Ministry of Education of the Kazakh S.S.R.; organization of public education; in Kazakh.

Kazakstannyn Auyl Sharuashylygy (*Agriculture of Kazakhstan*): Alma Ata; f. 1936; journal of the Central Committee of the Communist Party of Kazakhstan; organization of work on collective farms; in Kazakh.

Madamiet zhane Turmys (*Culture and Life*): Alma Ata; f. 1958; published by the Kazakhstan Publishing House; journal of the Kazakh S.S.R. Ministry of Culture; popular illustrated; in Kazakh.

Narodnoe khozyaistvo Kazakhstana (*National Economy of Kazakhstan*): Alma Ata; f. 1926; journal of the State Planning Committee of the Council of Ministers of the Kazakh S.S.R.; theory and practice of planning and managing of the national economy of the Republic; in Russian.

Partiinaya Zhizn Kazakhstana (*Party Life of Kazakhstan*): Alma Ata; f. 1931; published by the Publishing House of the Central Committee of the Kazakhstan Communist Party; political; in Russian.

Prostor (*Wide Horizons*): Alma Ata; f. 1935; journal of the Kazakh S.S.R. Union of Writers; fiction; in Russian.

Russkiy Yazyk v Kazakhskoy Shkole (*Russian Language in the Kazakh School*): Alma Ata; f. 1962; journal of the Ministry of Education of the Kazakh S.S.R.; linguistic problems; in Russian.

Vestnik Selskokhozyaistvennoy Nauki (*Herald of Agricultural Science*): Alma Ata; f. 1958; published by the "Kaynar" (Spring) Publishing House; journal of the Ministry of Agriculture of the Kazakh S.S.R.; problems of agriculture in different zones of Kazakhstan; in Russian.

Zhuldyz (*Star*): Alma Ata; f. 1928; published by the Publishing House of the Central Committee of the Kazakh Communist Party; journal of the Kazakh S.S.R. Union of Writers; fiction; in Kazakh.

Zhurnal Mod (*Fashion Magazine*): Alma Ata; f. 1958; published by the "Dom Modely Odezhdy" (Fashion House) Publishing House; twice a year; everyday fashions; in Russian.

NEWS AGENCY

KazTAG (*Kazakh Telegraph Agency*): Alma Ata, Kommunistichesky 75.

PUBLISHERS

Kainar (Spring) Publishing House: Alma Ata, Ul. Abaya 93; books and booklets about agriculture; Dir. Kh. A. Tlemisov.

Kazakhskoi Sovetskoi Entsiklopedii (*Kazakh Soviet Encyclopaedia*): Alma Ata, Ul. Sovetskaya 50; Chief Editor M. K. Kozybayev.

Kazakhstan Publishing House: Alma Ata 9, Ul. Abaya 93; political and popular editions; Dir. E. Kh. Syzdykov.

Mektep: Alma Ata, Ul. Abaya 93; educational textbooks; Dir. Sh. E. Esmurzayev.

Nauka (*Science*): Alma Ata, Ul. Shevchenko 28; Dir. T. T. Muliar.

Oner: Alma Ata, Ul. Abaya 93; art books; Dir. M. A. Aubakirov.

Zhalyn: Alma Ata, Ul. Abaya 93; fiction by young writers; Dir. K. N. Naimanbayev.

Zhazushy (Writer) Publishing House: Alma Ata, Ul. Abaya 93; fiction; Dir. A. Zh. Zhumabayev.

RADIO

Kazakh Radio: Alma Ata 480413, Ul. Mira 175-A; broadcasts in Kazakh, Russian, Uygur and German.

Kazakh Television: Alma Ata, Ul. Mira 175; broadcasts in Kazakh and Russian.

CULTURE

PRINCIPAL THEATRES

Kazakh State Academic Drama Theatre: Alma Ata; Dir. and Producer A. Mambetov.

Kazakh Academic Opera and Ballet Theatre: Alma Ata, Kalinina 112; Dir. T. Uzbekov.

Koreiskii Muzykalno-Dramaticheskii Teatr (*Korean Musical-Dramatic Theatre*): Alma Ata; Dir. Te Den Gu.

Russian Academic Dramatic Theatre: Alma Ata; Dir. P. Kuznetsov.

Teatr Yunikh Zritelei (TYuZ) (*Youth Theatre*): Alma Ata; Dir. S. Turlymyratov.

Uigurskii Muzykalno-Dramaticheskii Teatr (*Uygur Musical-Dramatic Theatre*): Alma Ata; Dir. I. Masimov.

ORCHESTRAS

Filarmoniya (*Philharmonic Orchestra*): Alma Ata; Dir. T. Ibrayev.

Kazakhkontsert (*Kazakh Concert Orchestra*): Alma Ata; Dir. A. Bekbayev.

THE KIRGHIZ SOVIET SOCIALIST REPUBLIC

INTRODUCTION

Kirghizia was made an Autonomous Republic on February 1st, 1926, and attained the status of a Union Republic on December 5th, 1936. It has an area of 198,500 sq. km. and a population of 3,655,000 (January 1st, 1981). Of these, 43.8 per cent are Kirghiz, 29.2 per cent Russians, 10.6 per cent Uzbeks, 4.1 per cent Ukrainians and 2.4 per cent Tatars (1970 census). Frunze, the capital, has a population of 552,000 (1981). The Kirghiz Republic is situated at the junction of two gigantic mountain systems, the Tien-shan and the Pamirs, and is noted for its severe natural beauty and amazing range of climate. In the south-east there is a frontier with the People's Republic of China

STATISTICS

POPULATION

BIRTHS AND DEATHS

	Birth Rate (per '000)	Death Rate (per '000)
1975	30.4	8.1
1976	31.3	8.2
1977	30.2	8.2
1978	30.4	8.1
1979	30.1	8.3
1980	29.6	8.4

AGRICULTURE

The Kirghiz were formerly wandering herdsmen. They have now settled on the land, taken up agriculture and built up their own industry. Kirghizia produces wheat, cotton, tobacco, southern hemp, kenaf, essential oil plants and poppy. Grape- and fruit-growing and silkworm breeding also have an important place in the economy.

Livestock raising is the main branch of agriculture. The wealth of the Republic is made up of its herds of cattle, flocks of fine-fleece sheep and droves of horses.

In 1974 there were 329,000 people engaged in agriculture on 225 collective farms and 121 state farms.

CROP PRODUCTION
('000 tons)

	1974	1975	1976	1977
Grain	1,087	1,055	1,360	1,134
Rice	1.2	1.7	n.a.	1.0
Cotton	211	202	208	215
Sugar beet	1,799	1,799	1,768	1,803
Potatoes	324	280	268	273
Other vegetables	332	310	308	323
Grapes	46	56	62	64
Other fruit	110	188	182	186

1978: Grain, 1,502,000 tons.

LIVESTOCK
('000)

	1975	1976	1977	1978
Cattle	973	942	940	948
of which: Cows	375	366	366	367
Pigs	290	216	220	263
Sheep	9,688	9,654	9,712	9,819
Poultry	7,900	7,800	8,500	9,300

ANIMAL PRODUCTS
('000 tons)

	1975	1976	1977	1978	1980*
Meat	157	141	151	152	158
Milk	611	615	634	640	681
Eggs (million)	361	393	408	398	410
Wool	32.1	31.4	31.6	n.a.	34.1

* 1979 figures not available.

INDUSTRY AND MINING
PRODUCTION

		1972	1973	1974	1975
Steel	'000 tons	6.1	6.9	8.3	8.9
Petroleum	,, ,,	277	243	235	230
Coal	,, ,,	3,827	3,910	3,980	4,079
Metal-Cutting Lathes	number	2,292	2,479	2,518	2,564
Natural Gas	million cu. metres	395	396	323	285
Electric Power	million kWh.	4,060	4,270	4,400	4,400
Cars	number	15,710	16,100	17,100	17,700
Cement	'000 tons	1,029.1	1,048	1,075	1,131

Electric power (million kWh.): 4,800 in 1976; 4,900 in 1977; 6,900 in 1978; 7,800 in 1979; 9,200 in 1980.

EDUCATION

The literacy of the population of Kirghizia between the ages of 9 and 49 is 99.7 per cent. According to the census of 1970, 50.9 per cent of people over the age of 9 have received higher or secondary education.

(1980/81)

	INSTITUTIONS	STUDENTS
Secondary Schools	1,700	900,000
Secondary Specialized Schools	41	49,400
Higher Schools (incl. Universities)	10	55,400

GOVERNMENT

SUPREME SOVIET

Chairman: Z. Dzhamashev.

Presidium President: Temirbek Koshoyev.

COUNCIL OF MINISTERS

Chairman: A. D. Duysheyev.

POLITICAL ORGANIZATIONS

Kirghiz Communist Party: Frunze: 126,000 mems.: First Secretary of the Central Committee T. U. Usubaliev.

Komsomol Leninist Young Communist League of Kirghizia: Frunze; 364,300 mems.; First Sec. Tashtemir Aitbayev.

JUDICIAL SYSTEM

Chairman of the Supreme Court: Z. Dzhamashev.

Procurator: A. M. Satarov.

THE PRESS

There are 101 newspapers published in the Kirghiz S.S.R. including 56 published in Kirghizian. The daily circulation is 1,196,000 copies (732,000 in Kirghizian). Sixty-seven periodicals are published, including 20 in Kirghizian, with a total circulation of 30,700,000 copies (8,700,000 in Kirghizian).

PRINCIPAL NEWSPAPERS

Komsomolets Kirghizii (*Member of the Leninist Young Communist League of Kirghizia*): Frunze; f. 1938; organ of the Central Committee of the Leninist Young Communist League of Kirghizia; three times weekly; Editor I. Novitsky.

Leninchil Zhash (*Leninist Youth*): Frunze; f. 1926; organ of the Central Committee of the Leninist Young Communist League of Kirghizia; three times weekly; in Kirghizian; Editor K. Osmonaliev.

Sovettik Kyrghyzstan (*Soviet Kirghizia*): Frunze; f. 1924; organ of the Central Committee of the Kirghiz Communist Party, Supreme Soviet and Council of Ministers; six times weekly; in Kirghizian; Editor G. G. Tursunov.

Sovietskaya Kirghizia (*Soviet Kirghizia*): Frunze; f. 1925; organ of the Kirghiz Communist Party, Supreme Soviet and Council of Ministers; six times weekly in Russian and Kirghizian; Editor V. G. Shepel.

SELECTED PERIODICALS

(Published monthly unless otherwise indicated.)

Ala-Too (*Ala-Too Mountains*): Frunze; f. 1931; published by the "Ala-Too" Publishing House; journal of the Kirghiz S.S.R. Union of Writers and Ministry of Culture; novels, short stories, plays, poems of Kirghizian authors and translations into Kirghizian; in Kirghizian.

Chalkan (*Stinging-nettle*): Frunze; f. 1955; published by the "Ala-Too" Publishing House; in Kirghizian; satirical.

Kommunist (*Communist*): Frunze; f. 1926; published by the "Ala-Too" Publishing House; in Kirghizian; political.

Kyrgyzstan Ayaldary (*Women of Kirghizia*): Frunze; f. 1951; journal of the Central Committee of the Kirghiz Communist Party; popular; in Kirghizian.

Kyrgystandyn Ayyl Charbasy (*Agriculture of Kirghizia*): Frunze; f. 1955; published by the "Ala-Too" Publishing House; journal of the Ministry of Agriculture of the Kirghiz S.S.R.; progressive system of farming; in Kirghizian.

Literaturnyi Kirghizstan (*Literature of Kirghizia*): Frunze; f. 1955; published by the "Ala-Too" Publishing House; journal of the Central Committee of the Leninist Young Communist League and Union of Writers of Kirghiz S.S.R.; fiction; bi-monthly; in Russian.

Sovetskoe Zdravookhranenie Kirgizii (*Soviet Public Health System of Kirghizia*): Frunze; f. 1938; published by the "Ala-Too" Publishing House; journal of the Ministry of Public Health of the Kirghiz S.S.R.; medical experimental work; bi-monthly; in Russian.

NEWS AGENCY

KIRTAK (*Kirghiz Telegraph Agency*) Frunze.

PUBLISHER

Kirghizstan Publishing House: Frunze, Ul. Sovetskaya 170; political and fiction; Dir. S. D. Jetymyshev.

RADIO

Dom Radio: 720885 Frunze 10, pr. Molodoi Gvardii; broadcasts in Kirghizian and Russian.

CULTURE

PRINCIPAL THEATRES

State Drama Theatre: Frunze; Dir. T. Tokoldashev.

Russian Drama Theatre: Frunze; Dir. N. K. Angarov.

Academic Opera and Ballet Theatre: Frunze, Dubovy Park; Dir. S. U. Usupov.

THE TADZHIK SOVIET SOCIALIST REPUBLIC

INTRODUCTION

The Tadzhik Republic was formed as an Autonomous Republic on October 14th, 1924, and attained the status of a Union Republic on October 16th, 1929. It has an area of 143,100 sq. km. and a population of 4,009,000 (January 1st, 1981). Of these, 56.2 per cent are Tadzhiks, 23 per cent Uzbeks, 11.9 per cent Russians and 2.4 per cent Tatars (1970 census). Dushanbe, the capital, has a population of 510,000 (1981). The Tadzhik Republic (Tadzhikistan) includes the Gorno-Badakshan Autonomous Region (Khorog). It is a mountainous region including the greater part of the Pamirs where the tallest peaks in the Soviet Union are located. Afghanistan lies to the south.

STATISTICS

BIRTHS AND DEATHS

	Birth Rate (per '000)	Death Rate (per '000)
1976	38.2	8.5
1977	36.5	8.8
1978	37.5	8.3
1979	37.8	7.7
1980	37.0	8.0

AGRICULTURE

Large irrigation projects have been carried out, making it possible to cultivate cotton, vegetables, hemp, kenaf, groundnuts, sugar-beet and essential oil crops in addition to rice, wheat and maize, the main grain crops. Sheep-breeding is the most developed branch of animal husbandry.

In 1974 there were about 340,000 people working on 251 collective farms and 123 state farms.

CROP PRODUCTION
('000 tons)

	1975	1976	1977	1980
Grain	227	305	238	244
Rice	31.4	n.a.	24.0	27.1
Cotton	836	847	861	1,010
Potatoes	113	110	123	152
Other vegetables	284	298	329	377
Grapes	147	167	132	158
Other fruit	276	203	301	215

1978: Grain 336,000 tons.

Note: Other figures for 1978 and 1979 are not available.

LIVESTOCK
('000 head at January 1st)

	1976	1977	1978	1981
Cattle	1,095	1,101	1,115	1,213
of which:				
Cows	403	403	412	456
Pigs	86	99	116	136
Sheep	2,369	2,376	2,416	2,318
Poultry	4,100	4,600	4,800	6,311

Note: Figures for 1979 and 1980 are not available.

ANIMAL PRODUCTS
('000 tons)

	1975	1976	1977	1978	1980
Meat	84	86	89	90	94
Milk	383	408	425	431	490
Eggs (million)	236	261	279	285	325
Wool	5.3	5.4	5.5	n.a.	5.7

Note: Figures for 1979 are not available.

INDUSTRY AND MINING

PRODUCTION

		1973	1974	1975	1980
Petroleum	'000 tons	226	242	274	390
Coal	,, ,,	900	932	868	832
Natural Gas	million cu. metres	520	496	419	221
Electric Power	million kWh.	3,779	3,900	4,700	13,518
Mineral Fertilizers	'000 tons	373	387	406	390
Cement	,, ,,	975	993	1,010	1,052
Cotton Fabrics	million sq. metres	108.0	109.4	113.1	95.2
Silk Fabrics	,, ,, ,,	49.2	49.2	54.0	59.1

1976: Electric power 5,200 million kWh.; Mineral fertilizers 401,000 tons.

1977: Electric power 7,300 million kWh.; Mineral fertilizers 405,000 tons.

1978: Electric power 8,500 million kWh.; Mineral fertilizers 400,000 tons.

1979: Electric power 10,600 million kWh.; Mineral fertilizers 379,000 tons.

Note: Other figures for 1976-79 are not available.

EDUCATION

The literacy of the population of Tadzhikistan between the ages of 9 and 49 is 99.6 per cent. According to the census of 1970, 49 per cent of people over the age of 9 have received higher or secondary education.

(1980/81)

	INSTITUTIONS	STUDENTS
Secondary Schools	3,071	1,063,000
Secondary Specialized Schools	38	40,100
Higher Schools (incl. Universities)	10	56,762

GOVERNMENT

SUPREME SOVIET

Chairman: USMAN KHASANOV.

Presidium President: M. KHOLOV.

COUNCIL OF MINISTERS

Chairman: KAKHAR MAKHKAMOVICH MAKHAMOV.

POLITICAL ORGANIZATIONS

Tadzhik Communist Party: Dushanbe; 97,000 mems.; First Secretary of the Central Committee RAKHMAN NABIYEV.

Komsomol Leninist Young Communist League of Tadzhikistan: Dushanbe; 313,100 mems.; First Sec. SH. M. SULTANOV.

JUDICIAL SYSTEM

Chairman of the Supreme Court: S. KURBANOV.

Procurator: A. A. SHCHELOCHININ.

THE PRESS

There are 59 newspapers published in the Tadzhik S.S.R., including 49 published in Tadzhik. The daily circulation is 1,319,000 copies (1,074,000 in Tadzhik).

There are 64 periodicals published, including 17 in Tadzhik, with a total circulation of 16.2 million copies (9.2 million in Tadzhik).

PRINCIPAL NEWSPAPERS

Kommunist Tadzhikistana (*Tadzhik Communist*): Dushanbe; f. 1929; organ of the Tadzhik Communist Party, Supreme Soviet and Council of Ministers; six times weekly; in Russian; Editor B. N. PSHENICHNY.

Komsomolets Tadzhikistana (*Member of the Leninist Young Communist League of Tadzhikistan*): Dushanbe; f. 1938; organ of the Central Committee of the Leninist Young Communist League of Tadzhikistan; three times weekly; in Russian; Editor V. SCHASTNEV.

Komsomoli Tochikistoni (*Member of the Leninist Young Communist League of Tadzhikistan*): Dushanbe; f. 1930; organ of the Central Committee of the Leninist Young Communist League of Tadzhikistan; three times weekly; in Tadzhik; Editor A. KHADZHIEV.

Tochikistoni Sovieti (*Soviet Tadzhikistan*): Dushanbe; f. 1925; organ of the Tadzhik Communist Party, the Supreme Soviet and the Council of Ministers; six times weekly in Tadzhik; Editor I. FAIZULLAYEV.

SELECTED PERIODICALS

(Published monthly unless otherwise indicated.)

Khochgii Kishloki Tochikiston (*Agriculture of Tadzhikistan*): Dushanbe; f. 1947; journal of the Ministry of Agriculture of the Tadzhik S.S.R.; problems of agriculture; in Tadzhik.

Khorpushtak (*Hedgehog*): Dushanbe; f. 1953; journal of the Central Committee of the Tadzhik Communist Party; in Tadzhik; fortnightly; satirical.

Kommunisti Tochikiston (*Communist of Tadzhikistan*): Dushanbe; f. 1936; published by the Publishing House of the Central Committee of the Tadzhik Communist Party; in Tadzhik; political.

Maktabi Soveti (*Soviet School*): Dushanbe; f. 1930; journal of the Ministry of Public Education of the Tadzhik S.S.R.; theory of pedagogical science; in Tadzhik.

Mashal (*Torch*): Dushanbe; f. 1952; journal of the Central Committee of the Leninist Young Communist League and Republican Council of the Pioneer Organization named after V. I. Lenin of the Tadzhik S.S.R.; fiction for 10–15 years; in Tadzhik.

Sadon Shark (*The Voice of the East*): Dushanbe; f. 1924; journal of the Tadzhik S.S.R. Union of Writers; fiction in Tadzhik.

Zanoni Tochikiston (*Women of Tadzhikistan*): Dushanbe; f. 1951; journal of the Central Committee of the Tadzhik Communist Party; popular; in Tadzhik.

Zdravookhranenie Tadzhikistana (*Tadzhikistan Public Health System*): Dushanbe; f. 1954; journal of the Ministry of Public Health of the Tadzhik S.S.R.; problems of improvement of medical help; bi-monthly; in Russian.

NEWS AGENCY

TADZHIKTAG (*Tadzhik Telegraph Agency*): Dushanbe.

PUBLISHER

Irfon (Light of Knowledge) Publishing House: Dushanbe, Ul. Shevchenko 10; political and fiction.

RADIO AND TELEVISION

Radio Dushanbe: 734025 Dushanbe, Ul. Ordzhonikidze 17; broadcasts in Russian, Tadzhik, Persian and Uzbek.

Tadzhik Television: Dushanbe; broadcasts on four channels in three languages.

CULTURE

PRINCIPAL THEATRES

Lakhuti Academic Drama Theatre: Dushanbe; Dir. K. M. MIRZAEV.

Mayakovsky Russian Drama Theatre: Dushanbe; Dir. A. A. EROSHENKO.

State Academic Opera and Music Theatre: Dushanbe, pl. Moskvy; Dir. Q. R. VALAMATZADE.

THE TURKMEN SOVIET SOCIALIST REPUBLIC

INTRODUCTION

The Turkmen Republic was formed on October 27th, 1924. Turkmenia, the southernmost republic in the Soviet Union, is situated in the south-west of Central Asia. It is bounded on the north by the Kazakh S.S.R., on the east by the Uzbek S.S.R., on the south by Iran, and the south-east by Afghanistan. To the west lies the Caspian Sea. The Republic has an area of 488,100 sq. km. and a population of 2,972,000 (January 1st, 1982). Of these, 68.4 per cent are Turkmen, 12.6 per cent Russians, 8.5 per cent Uzbeks and 2.9 per cent Kazakhs (1979 census).

The Kara-Kum, one of the largest Central Asian deserts, occupies more than four-fifths of the territory and irrigation is therefore of prime importance to this desolate land. The capital, Ashkhabad, has a population of 325,000 (1981).

The average population density of the Republic is five persons per sq. km. The most densely populated areas, with up to 300 inhabitants per sq. km., are the valley of the river Murgab where over a quarter of the population is concentrated, the oases in the foothills of Kopet-Dag, the strip adjoining the railway running across the south of the Republic through the oases of Ashkhabad and Tedzen, and also the lower reaches of the Amu-Dar'ya including the oasis of Tashauz. The population is extremely sparse in the vast desert lands. However, the discovery of rich deposits of petroleum, natural gas, sulphur, mineral salts and other industrial raw materials has caused many settlements to develop even in the most arid districts.

STATISTICS

POPULATION

BIRTHS AND DEATHS

	Birth Rate (per '000)	Death Rate (per '000)
1975	34·4	7·8
1976	34·7	7·7
1977	34·2	7·7
1978	34·4	8·0
1979	34·9	7·6
1980	34·3	8·3

AGRICULTURE

Agricultural areas occupy almost half of the territory. By mid-1979 more than 1,000 km. of the Great Kara-Kum Canal had been completed, from the Amu-Dar'ya river to beyond Ashkhabad. It supplies water for Ashkhabad and has already provided irrigation for more than 463,000 hectares of desert land; it is also used for shipping. Thanks to its special climatic conditions, Turkmenia is able to grow large quantities of long-staple cotton. Other important crops grown are melons and gourds, grapes and other fruit. Sowing and cultivating are fully mechanized. Turkmenia also specializes in the breeding of astrakhan sheep and the production of raw silk.

In 1979 there were 393,800 people engaged in agriculture on 317 collective farms and 108 state farms.

CROP PRODUCTION
('000 tons)

	1977	1978	1979	1980
Grain	205	264	281	274
Rice	19.0	20	24	30
Cotton	1,170	1,027	1,215	1,258
Potatoes	13	16	18	12
Other vegetables	231	283	284	267
Grapes	42	57	63	45
Other fruit	37	n.a.	n.a.	n.a.

LIVESTOCK
('000)

	1978	1979	1980	1981
Cattle	573	583	610	626
of which: Cows	217	219	228	223
Pigs	135	148	160	168
Sheep	4,095	4,368*	4,543*	4,483*
Poultry	4,500	n.a.	n.a.	n.a.

* Figure includes goats.

ANIMAL PRODUCTS
('000 tons)

	1976	1977	1978	1979	1980
Meat	73	72	76	76	78
Milk	259	265	269	313	313
Eggs (million)	192	224	235	258	259
Wool	14.0	13.5	15.9	16.0	16.0

INDUSTRY AND MINING

PRODUCTION

		1972	1973	1974	1975
Petroleum	'000 tons	15,941	16,171	15,857	15,577
Natural Gas	million cu. metres	21,313	28,645	39,272	51,776
Electric Power	million kWh.	1,830	2,500	3,900	4,500
Cement	'000 tons	463	534	510	584
Cotton Fabrics	'000 sq. metres	19,000	19,700	20,300	20,400

1976: Electric power 5,200 million kWh.; Mineral fertilizers 430,000 tons.

1977: Electric power 5,700 million kWh.; Mineral fertilizers 428,000 tons.

1978: Electric power 6,200 million kWh.; Mineral fertilizers 403,000 tons.

1979: Electric power 6,400 million kWh.; Mineral fertilizers 381,000 tons.

1980: Electric power 6,700 million kWh.; Mineral fertilizers 384,000 tons.

EDUCATION

The literacy of the population of Turkmenia between the ages of 9 and 49 is 99.5 per cent. According to the 1970 census, 49.6 per cent of people over the age of 9 have received higher or secondary education.

(1980/81)

	Institutions	Students
Secondary Schools	1,900	700,000
Secondary Specialized Schools	35	34,000
Higher Schools (incl. Universities)	7	35,800

GOVERNMENT

SUPREME SOVIET

Chairman: O. OVEZGELDYEV.

Presidium President: BALLI YAZKULIYEV.

COUNCIL OF MINISTERS

Chairman: CH. S. KARRYEV.

POLITICAL ORGANIZATIONS

Turkmen Communist Party: Ashkhabad; 87,638 mems. (1981); First Secretary of the Central Committee M. G. GAPUROV.

Komsomol Leninist Young Communist League of Turkmenia: Ashkhabad; 432,059 mems. (1981); First Sec. Dz. K. CHARYEVA.

JUDICIAL SYSTEM

Chairman of the Supreme Court: B. M. MUKHAMEDKULIEV.

Procurator: V. I. ARININ.

THE PRESS

There are 68 newspapers published in the Turkmen S.S.R., including 52 published in Turkmenian. Thirty-one periodicals are published, including 14 in Turkmenian.

PRINCIPAL NEWSPAPERS

Komsomolets Turkmenistana (*Member of the Leninist Young Communist League of Turkmenia*): Ashkhabad; f. 1938; organ of the Central Committee of the Leninist Young Communist League; three times weekly; in Russian; Editor B. GAFUROV.

Soviet Turkmenistani (*Soviet Turkmenia*): Ashkhabad; f. 1920; organ of the Turkmen Communist Party, Supreme Soviet and Council of Ministers; six times weekly in Turkmenian; Editor B. KERIMI.

Turkmenskaya Iskra (*Turkmenian Spark*): Ashkhabad; f. 1924; organ of the Turkmen Communist Party, Supreme Soviet and Council of Ministers; six times weekly; in Russian; Editor YE. N. KURYLEV.

Yash Kommunist (*Young Communist*): Ashkhabad; f. 1925; organ of the Central Committee of the Young Communist League of Turkmenia; three times weekly; in Turkmenian; Editor KH. DIVANKULIEV.

SELECTED PERIODICALS

(Published monthly unless otherwise indicated.)

Ashkhabad (*City of Ashkhabad*): Ashkhabad; journal of the Turkmen S.S.R. Union of Writers; popular; bimonthly; in Russian; Editor V. F. RYBIN.

Edebiyat ve Sungat (*Literature and Art*): Ashkhabad; f. 1958; published by the Ministry of Culture and the Union of Writers of the Turkmen S.S.R.; twice a week; in Turkmenian; Editor K. BERDYEV.

Pioner (*Pioneer*): Ashkhabad; f. 1926; journal of the Republican Council of the V. I. Lenin Pioneer Organization of the Turkmenian S.S.R.; fiction for 10–15 years; in Turkmenian; Editor A. B. SEITKULIEVA.

Soviet Turkmenistanyn Ayallary (*Women of Soviet Turkmenia*): Ashkhabad; f. 1952; journal of the Central Committee of the Turkmenian Communist Party; popular; in Turkmenian; Editor K. M. MAMIEVA.

Tokmak (*Beetle*): Ashkhabad; f. 1925; journal of the Central Committee of the Turkmenian Communist Party; satirical; in Turkmenian; Editor B. DZHUTDIEV.

Turkmenistan Kommunisti (*Communist of Turkmenia*): Ashkhabad; f. 1925; published by the Central Committee of the Turkmen Communist Party; in Turkmenian; Editor KH. DURDYEV.

Turkmenistanyn oba Khozhalygy (*Agriculture of Turkmenia*): Ashkhabad; f. 1957; journal of the Ministry of Agriculture in the Turkmen S.S.R.; in Turkmenian; Editor K. KURBANNEPESOV.

NEWS AGENCY

Turkmen Information Agency: Ashkhabad; Dir. A. M. MAMEDOV.

PUBLISHERS

Turkmenistan Publishing House: Ashkhabad, Ul. Gogolya 17A; political and fiction; Dir. A. KHOMMADOV.

Magaryf Publishing House: Ashkhabad; Dir. A. M. DZHANMURADOV.

Ylym Publishing House: Ashkhabad; science; Dir. D. BERDYEV.

RADIO AND TELEVISION

State Committee for Television and Radio Broadcasting: Ashkhabad; Pres. C. A. ANNAKURBANOV.

Turkmenian Radio: Ashkhabad; broadcasts local programmes and programmes from Moscow in Turkmenian and Russian.

Turkmenian Television: Ashkhabad; broadcasts local programmes and programmes from Moscow in Turkmenian and Russian.

CULTURE

PRINCIPAL THEATRES

Mollanepes Academic Drama Theatre: Ashkhabad; Dir. and Producer S. M. MYRADOVA.

A. Kulmamedova Turkmen Young Spectator Theatre: Ashkhabad; Dir. N. N. KESHIKOV.

Pushkin Russian Dramatic Theatre: Ashkhabad; Dir. B. A. LEVIN.

Makhtumkuly Opera and Ballet Theatre: Ashkhabad, Engelsa 93; Dir. K. A. ALLANUROV.

There are three philharmonic orchestras.

THE UZBEK SOVIET SOCIALIST REPUBLIC

INTRODUCTION

The Uzbek Republic was formed on October 27th, 1924. It has an area of 447,400 sq. km. and a population of 16,161,000 (January 1st, 1981). Of these, 65.5 per cent are Uzbeks, 12.5 per cent Russians, 4.9 per cent Tatars, 4.0 per cent Kazakhs, 3.8 per cent Tadzhiks and 2.0 per cent Kara-Kalpaks (census 1970). Tashkent, the capital, has a population of 1,858,000 (1981). The Autonomous Soviet Socialist Republic of Kara-Kalpakiya (capital Nukus) is part of the Uzbek Republic. Uzbekistan is situated in the south-eastern part of the Soviet Union, in the heart of Central Asia, and has a short frontier with Afghanistan in the south. Turkmenia lies to the south west, Kazakhstan to the north, Kirghizia to the east and Tadzhikistan to the south.

STATISTICS

POPULATION

BIRTHS AND DEATHS

	Birth Rate (per '000)	Death Rate (per '000)
1975	34.5	7.2
1976	35.3	7.1
1977	33.7	7.1
1978	33.9	6.9
1979	34.4	7.0
1980	33.8	7.4

AGRICULTURE

Cotton holds the leading place in agriculture with two-thirds of all land under cotton. Sugar beet and groundnuts are grown under irrigation while the main grain crops are rice, wheat and maize.

In 1974 there were 1,540,000 persons engaged in agriculture on 1,009 collective farms and 445 state farms.

CROP PRODUCTION
('000 tons)

	1976	1977	1979	1980
Wheat	n.a.	243	n.a.	n.a.
Maize (grain only)	n.a.	925	1,052	1,251
Rice	n.a.	363.0	455.4	503.6
Cotton	5,335	5,680	5,762	6,237
Potatoes	190	208	228	242
Other vegetables	1,710	1,844	2,241	2,429
Grapes	390	344	n.a.	n.a.
Other Fruit	595	751	n.a.	n.a.

Note: Figures for 1978 are not available.

LIVESTOCK
('000)

	1977	1978	1980	1981
Cattle	3,217	3,227	3,414	3,506
of which: Cows	1,230	1,229	1,305	1,348
Pigs	317	330	423	521
Sheep	7,428	7,521	8,650*	8,907*
Poultry	17,400	19,900	n.a.	n.a.

* Figure includes goats.

Note: Figures for 1979 are not available.

ANIMAL PRODUCTS
('000 tons)

	1976	1977	1978	1979	1980
Meat	263	271	292	302	323
Milk	1,857	1,844	1,992	2,107	2,271
Eggs (million)	1,238	1,231	1,314	1,411	1,458
Wool	24.9	24.0	n.a.	29.1	28.5

INDUSTRY AND MINING
PRODUCTION

		1972	1973	1974	1975
Steel	'000 tons	399.0	403.0	408.2	409.0
Cement	,, ,,	3,360	3,439	3,480	3,586
Coal	,, ,,	3,907	4,275	4,722	5,263
Mineral Fertilizers	,, ,,	4,920	5,531	5,801	6,132
Petroleum	,, ,,	1,921	1,318	1,395	1,352
Natural Gas	million cu. metres	33,700	37,100	37,064	37,211
Electric Power	million kWh.	23,000	26,200	30,000	33,600
Tractors	number	17,600	19,100	21,600	23,000
Cotton Fabrics	million sq. metres	212.0	215.7	217.7	223.1
Silk Fabrics	,, ,, ,,	69.5	75.2	86.2	94.2

Electric power (million kWh): 35,100 in 1976; 34,900 in 1977; 33,800 in 1978; 33,700 in 1979; 33,900 in 1980.

Mineral fertilizers ('000 tons): 5,840 in 1976; 5,879 in 1977; 6,004 in 1978; 6,450 in 1979; 6,511 in 1980.

Tractors: 23,900 in 1979; 24,200 in 1980.

EDUCATION

The literacy of the population of Uzbekistan between the ages of 9 and 49 is 99.7 per cent. According to the 1970 census, 53.8 per cent of people over the age of 9 have received higher or secondary education.

(1980/81)

	Institutions	Students
Secondary Schools	9,445	4,047,200
Secondary Specialized Schools	222	237,700
Higher Schools (incl. Universities)	43	278,100

GOVERNMENT

SUPREME SOVIET

Chairman: Asadilla Ashrapovich Khodzhayev.

Presidium President: I. B. Usmankhodzhayev.

COUNCIL OF MINISTERS

Chairman: Narmakhonmadi D. Khudaiberdyev.

POLITICAL ORGANIZATIONS

Uzbek Communist Party: Tashkent; 489,000 mems.; First Secretary of the Central Committee Sharaf R. Rashidov.

Komsomol Leninist Young Communist League of Uzbekistan: Tashkent; 2 million mems.; First Sec. E. G. Gafurdzhanov.

JUDICIAL SYSTEM

Chairman of the Supreme Court: Kh. M. Mukhitdinova.

Procurator: M. Burikhodzhayev.

THE PRESS

There are 257 newspapers published in the Uzbek S.S.R., including 169 published in Uzbek. The daily circulation is 4,405,000 copies (3,338,000 in Uzbek). One hundred and forty-one periodicals are published, including 34 in Uzbek, with a total circulation of 134,400,000 (about 97 million in Uzbek).

PRINCIPAL NEWSPAPERS

Esh Leninchil (*Young Leninist*): Tashkent; f. 1925; organ of the Central Committee of the Leninist Young Communist League of Uzbekistan; five times weekly; in Uzbek; Editor R. Shogulomov.

Komsomolets Uzbekistana (*Member of the Leninist Young Communist League of Uzbekistan*): Tashkent; f. 1926; organ of the Central Committee of the Leninist Young Communist League of Uzbekistan; five times weekly; in Russian; Editor A. Fitz.

Pravda Vostoka (*Eastern Truth*): Tashkent; f. 1917; organ of the Uzbek Communist Party, Supreme Soviet and Council of Ministers; six times weekly; in Russian; Editor N. Timofeyev.

Soviet Uzbekistoni (*Soviet Uzbekistan*): Tashkent; f. 1918; organ of the Uzbek Communist Party, Supreme Soviet and Council of Ministers; six times weekly; in Uzbek; Editor M. Koriev.

SELECTED PERIODICALS

(Published monthly unless otherwise indicated.)

Fan va Turmush (*Science and Life*): Tashkent; f. 1939; published by the Fan (Science) Publishing House; journal of the Uzbek S.S.R. Academy of Sciences; popular scientific; in Uzbek.

Gulistan (*Flourishing Area*): Tashkent; f. 1967; journal of the Central Committee of the Communist Party of the Uzbek S.S.R.; fiction; in Uzbek.

Gulkhan (*Bonfire*): Tashkent; f. 1952; journal of the Central Committee of the Leninist Young Communist League, Ministry of Education and Republican Council of the V. I. Lenin Pioneer Organization of the Uzbek S.S.R.; illustrated fiction; for ages 10–14 years; in Uzbek.

Guncha (*Small Bud*): Tashkent; f. 1958; journal of the Central Committee of the Leninist Young Communist League and the Republican Council of the Pioneer Organization of the Uzbek S.S.R.; illustrated; for ages 5–10 years; in Uzbek.

Mushtum (*Fist*): Tashkent; f. 1923; published by the Soviet Uzbekistoni newspaper; satirical; in Uzbek; fortnightly.

Obshchestvennie nauki v Uzbekistane (*Social Sciences in Uzbekistan*): Tashkent; f. 1957; published by the Fan (Science) Publishing House of the Uzbek S.S.R. Academy of Sciences; history, oriental studies, archaeology, economics, ethnology, etc.; in Russian.

Partiya Turmushi (*Party Life*): Tashkent; f. 1958; published by the Publishing House of the Central Committee of the Uzbek Communist Party; political; in Uzbek and Russian.

Saodat (*Happiness*): Tashkent; f. 1950; journal of the Central Committee of the Uzbek Communist Party; popular for women; in Uzbek.

Shark Yulduzi (*Star of the East*): Tashkent; f. 1933; journal of the Uzbek Union of Writers; fiction; in Uzbek.

Sovet Maktabi (*Soviet School*); Tashkent; f. 1925; published by the Uchitelj (Teacher) Publishing House; journal of the Ministry of Education of the Uzbek S.S.R.; improvements to the educational system; in Uzbek.

Uzbek tili va adabieti (*Uzbek Language and Literature*): Tashkent; f. 1958; published by the Fan (Science) Publishing House; journal of the Uzbek S.S.R. Academy of Sciences; articles on history and modern development of the Uzbek language, folk-lore, etc.; in Uzbek; twice monthly.

Uzbekiston (*Uzbekistan*): Tashkent; published by the Publishing House of the Central Committee of the Uzbek Communist Party; journal of the Central Committee of the Uzbek Communist Party; popular; illustrated; in Uzbek.

Uzbekiston Kishlok Khuzhaligi (*Agriculture of Uzbekistan*): Tashkent; f. 1925; journal of the Ministry of Agriculture of the Uzbek S.S.R.; cotton-growing, cattle-breeding, forestry; in Uzbek.

Uzbekiston Kommunisti (*Communist of Uzbekistan*): Tashkent; f. 1925; published by the Publishing House of the Central Committee of the Uzbek Communist Party; political; in Uzbek and Russian.

Zvezda Vostoka (*Star of the East*): Tashkent; f. 1933; published by the Publishing House of the Central Committee of the Uzbek Communist Party; fiction; Russian translations from Arabic, Hindi, Turkish, Japanese, etc.

NEWS AGENCY

UZTAG (*Uzbek Telegraph Agency*): Tashkent.

PUBLISHERS

Esh Gvardiya (Young Guard) Publishing House: Tashkent, Ul. Navoi 30; books and journals for the young; Dir. A. V. Vakhabov.

Fan (Science) Publishing House: Tashkent, Ul. Gogolya 70; books and journals in all fields of science; Dir. Kh. Bektemirov.

Gafur Gulyam Publishing House: Tashkent, Ul. Navoi 30; fiction; Dir. D. Dzhabarov.

Meditsina (Medicine) Publishing House: Tashkent, Ul. Navoi 30; all branches of medical sciences; Dir. U. G. Saipov.

Uzbekistan Publishing House: Tashkent, Ul. Navoi 30; various; Dir. N. G. Gaibov.

RADIO

Radio Tashkent: Tashkent, Khorezmskaya 49; broadcasts in Uzbek, English, Urdu, Hindi, Farsi and Arabic.

CULTURE

PRINCIPAL THEATRES

Academic Drama Theatre: Tashkent; Dir. E. Musabekov.

State Academic Opera and Ballet Theatre: Tashkent, Ul. Pravdy Vostoka 31; Dir. M. R. Rachmanov.

Russian Dramatic Theatre: Tashkent; Dir. S. R. Leikina.

PRINCIPAL ORCHESTRA

State Symphony Orchestra: Tashkent; Conductor Z. V. Shakhnazakov.

THE SOVIET FAR EAST AND SIBERIA

E. Stuart Kirby

The term Siberia is applied to the whole of the U.S.S.R. beyond the Urals, excluding Soviet Central Asia. It extends 8,000 kilometres from the Ural mountains to the Pacific and over 3,000 kilometres from its southern borders to the Arctic—an area of 12.8 million square kilometres, 57 per cent of the Soviet Union.

This vast expanse is, however, fully incorporated into one huge political and cultural unit, the Russian Soviet Federative Socialist Republic (R.S.F.S.R.). Western Siberia, Eastern Siberia and the Soviet Far East (S.F.E.) are major economic planning regions of the U.S.S.R. Administrative sub-divisions are oblast', krai, national districts (okrug) for minority peoples, and also the Autonomous Soviet Socialist Republics (A.S.S.R.). The entire structure is governed, planned and administered on an extremely centralized bureaucratic basis from Moscow. Statistical and other data are often given only for the R.S.F.S.R. as a whole.

CLIMATE

Climate is extreme: Arctic winters and short, hot summers. The widespread impression that conditions are humanly impossible is, however, exaggerated; they resemble those in Canada or Alaska. The zone of permafrost is extensive. Some areas are subject to earthquakes, while Kamchatka has large volcanoes.

NATURAL RESOURCES

Siberia is the world's greatest untapped area of natural resources, notably coal, petroleum, natural gas and timber, but with other vital minerals (metals and rare earths). The main geographical analogy is with Canada, which shows broadly the same layout—from steppe, prairie or cereal-growing lands in the south through forest, lake or muskeg country to the tundra in the north and in the high mountains. Geologically, the two great sub-continents contain an essentially similar pattern of mineral reserves. However, Siberia is much larger than Canada. In the future, Siberia may be of great importance to the world as a major source of basic materials that are being depleted elsewhere.

POPULATION

Siberia's population was 28.3 million in 1980, showing a continuing increase. Siberia is thus far from unpeopled; its population is about half that of the United Kingdom and one-eighth that of the United States. Certainly the overall density is very low, averaging just over two persons per square kilometre, which was only a sixth of the average for the U.S.S.R. as a whole, but showing an increase of 10 per cent since 1968. Large areas are uninhabited but over 75 per cent of the population is urban. The leading cities are very large and modern. Among the fastest growing are Novosibirsk (population 1,328,000 in 1980, a 14 per cent increase since 1970), Omsk (1,028,000, 25 per cent more than in 1970), Krasnoyarsk (807,000, a 25 per cent increase) and Vladivostok (558,000, 27 per cent larger than 1970). Other cities include Irkutsk (561,000 in 1980), Khabarovsk (538,000), Tomsk (431,000), Komsomolsk-on-Amur (269,000) and Blagoveshchensk (177,000). Yakutsk, far to the north, had 155,000 inhabitants in 1980 (a 45 per cent increase since 1970) and the remote mining centre of Noril'sk about 173,000, an increase of 28 per cent over 1970. The population is mainly in the less cold and more developed south. Few live in the outer settlements of the Arctic and sub-Arctic zones.

The natural growth rate of population has fallen since 1960 and the decline in the birth rate continues. This decrease is general throughout the U.S.S.R., but is least marked in outlying, less developed areas (especially the ethnically Asian ones) such as Yakutia, Buryatia and Tuva. It is notable that there is (as shown in the table) a considerable eastward migra-

AREA AND POPULATION

	Area ('000 sq. km.)	Population 1968 '000	1968 Density per sq. km.	1978 '000	1978 Density per sq. km.	Percentage increase in the population (1968–80)
Western Siberia	2,428 (14%*)	12,201 (9.5%†)	5.0	13,008 (9.5%†)	5.4	6.6
Eastern Siberia	4,124 (24%*)	7,321 (5.7%†)	1.8	8,255 (6.0%†)	2.0	12.8
Soviet Far East	6,216 (36%*)	5,709 (4.4%†)	0.9	6,927 (5.0%†)	1.1	21.3
Total	12,766 (74%*)	25,231 (19.6%†)	2.0	28,270 (20%†)	2.2	12.0

* Percentage of the total area of the R.S.F.S.R.

† Percentage of the total population of the R.S.F.S.R.

tion. Siberia's population has a somewhat transient character, insofar as young people in Western Russia may be drawn to "go east" temporarily for adventure or higher rewards, but there is strong counter-attraction for young and old Russians in the east to move in the other direction to the more metropolitan, warmer and more "sophisticated" or "European" west of the Soviet Union.

The indigenous peoples of Siberia are a small rural minority. Siberia is a distinctly Russian land (including considerable numbers of Ukrainians, Byelorussians, Balts and others from Russia-in-Europe besides the dominant Great Russians or Muscovites). The other races have a significance equivalent to that of the Indians and Eskimos in North America. Their societies are mostly on a tribal basis, extremely diverse and dispersed. One difference is that throughout history the Russians have widely intermarried with them; pure strains are quite rare.

The largest indigenous groups, the Yakuts and the Buryats (a branch of the Mongols), constitute Autonomous Soviet Republics of their own with populations in each case of about 900,000 as do the Tuvinians (260,000), but, even in those areas, massive influxes of Russians in the Soviet period have made the latter a numerical majority as well as politically and culturally dominant. Even in the Far North, there are about two million Russians in an area counting only a few tens of thousands of the minor Siberian "nationalities", all largely assimilated (in various senses of the term) to Soviet Russianism. The complexity of the question may be illustrated as follows: 27 groups of "native peoples" of Siberia are enumerated in the Soviet censuses; in 1970 they totalled just over a million, of whom 30 per cent were Buryats, another 30 per cent Yakuts and 20 per cent Tuvinians. The remaining 20 per cent were thus of twenty-four nationalities, ranging in size from 65,000 Khakasy in the Krasnoyarsk area down to 400 Aleuts in the north Pacific.

MANPOWER PROBLEMS

Labour shortage is the main overall problem in Siberia, accentuated by the mobility of workers both within Siberia and between it and the rest of the Soviet Union. Wages in Siberia are double or treble those in European Russia. Though prices are also higher and many consumer goods still scarcer, there are some real or supposed net advantages for the Siberians who still have some pride in their "frontier" way of life—in the sense the word was used in America a century or more ago. Mobility, both social and geographical, and the "demonstration effect" have been greatly intensified by the tremendous development of education and communications—including the most extensive airways network in the world, hydrofoil services on the rivers and comprehensive television and telephone facilities. Fluidity and restlessness, even more than shortfall in the labour supply, disturb the elderly Soviet leadership.

HISTORY

The history of Siberia has striking parallels—and no less striking differences—with and from the history of North America. In the 1580s the Cossack Yermak defeated the Tatars in Western Siberia, whose capital Sibir' gave its name to the whole area. Some etymologists construe the word to mean "the Sleeping Land". Yermak, and many other Russian adventurers in the following century, moved swiftly across the whole continent, easily subduing the small and mostly primitive tribes they encountered. Settlements followed on the pattern of colonial expansion, with prospectors, merchants, farmers, exiles and prisoners, as well as bandits and pirates, coming irregularly in fairly considerable numbers into the promising lands. Western historians have emphasized the importance of the fur trade in earlier times and the Russian Empire's need to reach an ice-free littoral. Direct gain and the lack of any insuperable barrier—except China, which at once, in the seventeenth century, diverted the Russian movement far to the north-eastward—seem to have been the most proximate reasons. A chain of Russian forts (*ostrog*), which became also trading posts and administrative and tax bases for the collection of tribute, reached to the coast of Okhotsk as early as 1639. This Russian line extended to the Upper Amur, then swung far to the north of the present frontier with China. Much earlier (from 1441) China had pre-empted southerly parts of what is now the Soviet Far East as far north as the Yablonoi mountains and the mouth of the Amur.

This point is relevant to the present-day Sino-Soviet dispute, as the People's Republic of China demands discussion of claims to that area. Moscow's reply is that China's presence in or possession of those lands was nominal or ineffectual, without substantial Chinese settlement or more than remote control, in contrast to systematic Russian settlement or use on a more "progressive" basis. In other words, a true assimilation of the area (*osvoyenie*). As China's power shrank behind its Great Wall, the Russians established settlements on the Amur, though their main drive was further to the north-east, towards Kamchatka. In 1683–85 the Manzhou (Manchu) dynasty of China attacked and destroyed the Russian settlements on the Amur, deployed a large force as far west as Nerchinsk and dictated a treaty confining the Russians to the north of a line leaving all the present-day Maritime and Amur provinces, the southern half of Khabarovsk, and Sakhalin within the Chinese domain. The Manzhous had desired all the territory up to Lake Baikal and the river Lena, while the Russians wished the Amur to be the boundary. Subsequently the Russians increased their strength and their interest in the caravan trade and missionary links with China. In the Kiakhta treaty of 1727 they obtained the cession of nearly 40,000 square miles of territory from China, bringing the frontier roughly to the present one between the U.S.S.R. and the Mongolian People's Republic. It is well known that in the eighteenth century Russian expansion carried right over into

Alaska, with one outpost as far away as Fort Ross near San Francisco. This was evidently an over-reaching of the Russian capacity at that time, however, and Alaska was sold to the United States in 1867 in the cheapest large-scale land-deal in history, at one dollar per acre. The Russian Empire was thereby retrenching on its over-extension into America, in order to concentrate more effectively on Siberia and the Far East.

In the nineteenth century China fell into decline while Russia modernized. Bold Russian leaders repossessed the Amur lands (about 185,000 square miles) and, under the Peking treaty of 1860, gained not only 135,000 square miles beyond the Ussuri which became Russia's Maritime province, but also rights in Sakhalin. In 1919 Lenin's Soviet government, on extending its power to most of Siberia, repudiated "unequal treaties" and Tsarist seizures of alien territory. But the issue still lives; latter-day Soviet spokesmen have asserted that Lenin himself stipulated reservations about the meaning of these terms and as to which territories were actually in question.

In 1905 Japan defeated Russia in Manzhou and the Western powers concurred in a division of Manzhou into spheres of influence between Japan in the south and Russia in the north. In 1931 the Japanese established their puppet Empire of Manchoukuo as a main base for their wars in China, East Asia and the Pacific. The Soviet Union sold its rights in the Chinese Eastern Railway which traverses northern Manzhou. From the late 1920s Soviet Russia made enormous efforts to develop Siberia by every means including forced labour. Exile and corrective labour camps still exist, though some, at least, of the worst abuses of earlier years have ceased to be in evidence.

In the very last days of the Second World War, after the atomic bombs had sealed the final defeat of Japan, Soviet forces swiftly occupied Manzhou, Japanese Sakhalin, North Korea and the Kurile Islands. This well-organized campaign, together with the Russians' low evaluation of China's political and material strength, contributes, at least among the less well-informed Soviet public, to Russian confidence that they can deal effectively with anything the Chinese might do against Russia. Mao Zedong's (Mao Tse-tung) forces took Manzhou in the wake of the Soviet army. Ten honeymoon years followed in Sino-Soviet relations, with political and economic co-operation in outward harmony. However, at the end of the 1950s there was a dramatic divorce. The estrangment became open in 1962–63 at the time of the Cuban crisis when Beijing denounced Khrushchev for capitulating to the U.S.A. and Moscow accused the Maoists of "adventurism" in distant areas contrasting with China's hypocrisy in not "liberating" Taiwan, Hong Kong and Macau. The Chinese Communist Party brought the Soviet Far East into this dispute by demanding a general discussion of all territorial issues.

RELATIONS WITH FOREIGN COUNTRIES

Siberia, the S.F.E. and their components are not represented abroad in their own right but only through the U.S.S.R. and R.S.F.S.R. as a whole, except occasionally or *ad hoc* in such matters as trade contacts and cultural promotions.

The frontier question persists, even though since 1963 the Soviet Government has asserted that all territorial issues are closed and rejected Chinese suggestions that all such problems (involving any country) should be discussed together. Sporadic local and partial agreements on practical matters such as river navigation have been interspersed with armed clashes, such as the serious incident on the Ussuri in 1978, and continued rumours both of conciliatory moves and of further fighting, with little substantive evidence from the remote and secret areas concerned. The Soviet frontier all through Asia is longer and more complex than its border with Western Europe, and apparently at least as heavily armed. Access to the major naval port of Vladivostok and many other localities is restricted not only to foreigners but to most Russians. A tourist's camera is regarded with suspicion, rather absurdly, in an age when the whole surface of the earth is being surveyed in fine detail by satellites.

The Sino-Soviet dispute is pivotal in a much wider sense than claims to territorial areas. While some observers are hopeful that reconciliation may be possible, others stress that the antagonism is fundamental, for such reasons as the following. The quarrel has the deep bitterness of a "religious" war—a contest for leadership and control of the Communist faith, the aim of World Liberation, between its established "Vatican" in comparatively opulent Moscow and a "Protestant" (or puritan) leadership in Peking. It is a confrontation between a developed and a developing country, the former industrialized on a technologically Western basis, the latter a culturally proud Asian country modernizing, on a still largely peasant basis, with a different interpretation of the Marxist and Leninist doctrines. Populous China, aspiring to rapid industrialization, desires resources for that purpose which are closely to hand in Siberia. The exchanges have become more and more ideologically vituperative in recent years, each side accusing the other of being reformist or reactionary, non- or anti-Marxist-Leninist, expansionist or imperialist. The Chinese now bluntly denounce Soviet "Social imperialism" as the greatest danger to the whole world. Currents of racial antagonism must also be regrettably noted.

In 1979 overall tension increased with the Chinese invasion of Viet-Nam, considered to be a Soviet protégé, and support of Kampuchea, and in 1980 Soviet intervention in Afghanistan alarmed the whole world. Soviet influence on India rose again with Mrs. Gandhi's return to power in January 1980, after the cooling of relations under the preceding Indian Government. Some revival of Sino-Soviet trade has recently occurred, but it remains very small in relation to the past links and the potential.

The U.S.S.R.'s economic relations with Japan are more substantial, but it refuses to discuss the return of the southern Kurile Islands which it occupies, formerly Japanese and only a few miles from the Japanese home islands, and has developed military bases there. Communist propaganda denies Japan's economic "miracle" and portrays that country as at least partly "feudal" and "revanchist", under the dominance of the United States which steers it in those directions. The U.S.S.R. has, on the other hand, encouraged the participation of Japanese capitalists in the development of Siberia and with substantial results: Japanese investments in Siberia since the 1960s in petroleum, natural gas, pipelines, port works, communications and other areas have been in the order of one thousand million dollars. This is, however, about one-fifth of the total projects canvassed. The financial and other aspects of negotiation and operation are complex. The very considerable Japanese interest in Siberian development in the 1960s has now largely subsided.

China now offers Japan oil in particular and great possibilities of collaboration in general, uses a more suave political tone and appeals to Japanese cultural affinities with China with the result that Japan has increasingly turned its attention to China. The late 1970s saw a boom of Japanese interest in the development of China, but disappointments and difficulties have been encountered there too. However, China plays the greater role in Japan's calculations and expectations, especially since China concluded a peace treaty with Japan, leaving the U.S.S.R. as the only country which has not "cleared the slate" with Japan with regard to World War II. An instance is the construction of the new Baikal-Amur Mainline Railway (BAM) running from the Upper Lena to Komsomolsk-on-Amur and passing to the north of Lake Baikal, with links to the existing trunk line, thus tapping areas with vast material resources. Japanese participation in this project was initially envisaged but was withdrawn in view not only of practical problems but also of China's sensitivity to the strategic implications. The Soviets are now vigorously proceeding with this difficult undertaking themselves, expecting to have completed it by 1985.

ECONOMIC SURVEY

Development

The enormous distance in Siberia between sources of supply, markets and the locus of bureaucratic decisions (down to matters of detail) in Moscow, make Siberian development laborious and expensive. Facilities and incentives have to be provided to get workers into the outlands. The climate renders the upkeep of all installations—roads, bridges, water-pipes, railways, telecommunications, vehicles, airfields, buildings and everything else—similarly exacting and costly. Siberia is, nevertheless, mostly a relatively high-income area with earnings often more than compensating for the high prices. Wages range from double to treble (in northern Siberia) the levels in European Russia.

Siberia has had a slightly rising share of the U.S.S.R.'s total capital investment after the Second World War: 14 per cent in 1941–50 (the same proportion as in 1918–40), raised to 15 per cent in 1950–60, over 16 per cent in 1961–70 and 17 per cent from 1971. In more recent years, including some national allocations not regionally allocated and a large increase in military installations, Siberia has received a fifth or a quarter of all the capital investment in the Soviet Union. The proportion is certainly raised to the latter figure if not only the joint investment with the Japanese is included, but also the cost of the Baikal-Amur Railway construction.

In the 1960s overall industrial output in the U.S.S.R. increased by just over 50 per cent. Western Siberia showed the same ratio but Eastern Siberia was some 10 per cent above it. In contrast, the S.F.E. showed a growth of 59 per cent in 1961–65 but 49 per cent in 1966–70. The 1971–75 Five-Year Plan concentrated distinctly on consolidating past achievements rather than initiating large new ventures. More recently, new major projects are in progress, especially in connection with the Baikal-Amur Railway. It has been officially admitted, however, that in the last few years output per worker has been increasing at only two per cent per year.

Mining and Power

Throughout the Soviet period, a major objective has been the provision of plentiful electricity; it is proposed to apply this also to agriculture, by using it to warm the soil as well as to drive the machinery. Abundant electricity could certainly bring about a prodigious transformation of the conditions of life and work in Siberia. The necessary power is fortunately available, in considerable quantities at present, possibly in abundance in the future. Siberia is extremely rich in coal, hydro-electric potential and even in firewood, not to mention the existence of less traditional sources of power, like geothermal (volcanic) sites and tidal energy, which are under continued study and development. That nothing is unconsidered or impossible is instanced by the construction of an isolated atomic-power plant at Bilibino, a remote mining area in western Chukotia in the far north-east.

The Kuznetsk basin in Western Siberia, with an estimated output of 135 million tons of bituminous coal in 1975, one-third greater than in 1965, represents some 16 per cent of all Soviet coal production and is second only to the great Don basin in the Ukraine; but it has about four times the reserves of the latter, and produces at about half the cost.

Eastern Siberia has vast tracts of inferior but useful lignite in the Kansk-Achinsk fields, supplying other industrial districts: Cheremkhovo (which in turn supplies the Angarsk area) and Noril'sk, far to the north, which furnishes hard coal and coking coal for the industrial complex there. The significance of these is, however, changing, as oil displaces coal and nearly all the Trans-Siberian Railway has been electrified. The Soviet Far East has prodigious reserves of coal but they are remote and expensive to mine. Existing workings are, in large part, open-cast. The Raichikhinsk brown coals in the Amur province account for nearly 40 per cent of the output in the Soviet Far East. A similar proportion, some of it harder coal, has come from the Maritime province. Some of the older fields around Suchan near Vladivostok are exhausted but new supplies are coming in from the Ussuri area. The biggest reserves of coal (about one-third of all the U.S.S.R.'s, said to be the largest potential coalfield in the world, containing over 2,500 million tons) are in the vast but remote and difficult terrain of the northern hinterland of Yakutia, particularly around Chul'man, and include coking coal, hitherto obtained in comparatively minor quantities from Sakhalin.

Petroleum has become of major significance. Western Siberia has proven reserves of 1,000 million tons; its annual output is approaching 100 million tons. Soviet enthusiasts expect this to become one of the world's leading oilfields. The sedimentary areas which may bear oil extend all the way from just north of Tyumen' and Tomsk northward to the Arctic Ocean. A similar deposit extending from a point about 200 kilometres north of Markovo, a similar distance west of the northern tip of Lake Baikal, for about 500 kilometres northwards is already a centre of activity. There is another, even more inaccessible deposit about 300 kilometres from north to south and 150 kilometres wide, straddling the Arctic Circle about 300 kilometres north of the last-mentioned area. Beyond the Arctic Circle, farther east in an even more remote and inhospitable region, there is a third and much larger area reaching some 500 kilometres inland from the 1,000 kilometres of Arctic coast between the Yana and Kolyma rivers. Yet another potential "sweep" of the same kind covers both the east and west coasts of Kamchatka and reaches northwards to the area of Anadyr.

Of all these, only the area north of Tyumen' has yet been substantially developed but the exploitation of a similar area, some 900 kilometres across from east to west and 500 kilometres from north to south, around Ust' Vilyui, north of Yakutsk, already worked for the production especially of natural gas, has recently begun. These areas are possible major sources of natural gas and petroleum. Developed for many years for the latter, and recently for the former, is a much smaller area at the northern end of Sakhalin, where new off-shore prospecting is being carried out. The remote Urengoi field, the largest in the world, lies over 1,000 kilometres north-west of Novosibirsk, and is estimated to contain 5,000 million million cubic metres of natural gas.

To utilize and consolidate what has been developed, a network of oil and gas pipelines already exists in Western Siberia, linking it also with European Russia to the west and Irkutsk to the east, while more are under construction and planned. One from Western Siberia all the way to Khabarovsk and Vladivostok was proposed a few years ago and another is proposed from the Ust' Vilyui field to the same destinations. Usefully functioning is the double oil pipeline and single gas pipeline from northern Sakhalin to Komsomolsk on the upper Amur.

Current outputs

All outputs continue to increase. The secrecy and the complexity of the issues make it undesirable to present many figures without lengthy discussion for which there is no space here. The output of energy continues to rise: 85 million tons of petroleum were produced in Western Siberia in 1973, 120 million in 1975, three million in Sakhalin in 1973, 10,000 million cubic metres of natural gas in Western Siberia and 1,000 million in Sakhalin in 1970.

The generation of electric power was: in Western Siberia 44,000 million kWh. in 1970 and 70,000 million in 1975, in Eastern Siberia 74,000 million in 1970 and 97,000 million in 1975, in the S.F.E. 14,000 million in 1970 and 22,000 million in 1975. The output of timber in 1975 (in thousand million cubic metres) was: in Western Siberia 33, in Eastern Siberia 69, in the S.F.E. 33.

Large and increasing quantities of iron ore and non-ferrous metals are produced. A notable potential source of copper, for example, is in the Udokan range some 600–700 kilometres north-west of Chita, said to be larger than the fields of southern Africa. This is a remote permafrost area but an annual output of half a million tons of copper ore is claimed. There are nickel, tin, tungsten, bauxite (an annual output of a million tons of aluminium is claimed), cobalt, lead and zinc. The Soviet Union is one of the world's largest producers of gold, mainly from Siberia. The figures are highly secret, both for production and stocks, which are known also to be high. Diamonds are a matter of equal secrecy but Siberia now claims to be a much larger producer than South Africa. Despite the

Meat Production
('000 tons, deadweight)

	1965	1970	1979	Increase, 1965/1979 (%)
Western Siberia . .	326	391	506	55
Eastern Siberia . .	194	216	296	53
S.F.E. . .	50	82	151	200
Total, Siberia .	570	689	953	68
Total, R.S.F.S.R. .	2,830	3,693	4,759	68

Labour Cost and Prices for Farm Products

	MAN-HOURS OF LABOUR REQUIRED TO PRODUCE 100 kg.					PRICE (roubles* per kg.)				
	Grain	Sugar-beet	Vege-tables	Wool	Milk	Grain	Sugar-beet	Vege-tables	Wool	Milk
R.S.F.S.R.	1.4	1.4	7.1	244	10	8.1	4.4	9.3	599	2.8
West Siberia	1.0	1.6	10.1	192	8	8.4	4.8	7.6	654	2.7
East Siberia	1.2	—†	9.1	201	10	8.2	—†	12.1	533	3.1
S.F.E.	1.1	—†	5.5	111	9	11.8	—†	15.6	249	4.3

* One rouble was equivalent to U.S. $1.308 in June 1981.
† Not produced in that region.

*Production of Canned Foods**
(all kinds, in millions of standard tins)

	1965	1970	1976	1979
R.S.F.S.R.	3,019	4,500	5,900	6,300
of which:				
West Siberia	192	243	329	304
East Siberia	109	139	179	171
of which:				
Krasnoyarsk	66	99	129	122
Buryat A.R.	39	36	42	39
TOTAL West and East Siberia	301	382	508	n.a.
TOTAL S.F.E.	285	437	786	n.a.

* Figures given for canned foods are unsatisfactory in that they do not specify the kinds of products and packages, but they do furnish a broad indication of production.

extreme political differences between the two countries, the U.S.S.R. and South Africa have certainly had contacts, and are believed to collaborate *de facto* regarding gold, diamonds and platinum. Siberia is also endowed with vanadium, beryllium and a number of other minerals essential to aerospace, electronics and other advanced technologies.

Agriculture

Siberia, in its southern parts only, is suited to dairying, wheat and other crops. In the S.F.E. soya beans and rice are produced. Siberia produces (mainly in West Siberia) one-fifth of the R.S.F.S.R.'s output of meat, and (mainly in the S.F.E.) nearly a third of the whole country's supply of fish. Most of this is exported to the Western U.S.S.R., a small proportion abroad.

In some basic crops Siberia has an advantage in terms of the labour required but this is offset by higher cost and price, as the official figures (*see* above) illustrate.

Siberia increased its output in this mixed category of canned foods much more than did the rest of the R.S.F.S.R., particularly the Soviet Far East (contributing very mainly fishery products) which nearly trebled its output between 1965 and 1977, while that of the whole Federation doubled. Western Siberia, the next contributor in this category (furnishing mainly meat products), meanwhile raised its output by only 75 per cent. The S.F.E. contributed 9 per cent of the Federation's total in 1965 and 14 per cent in 1977; the corresponding figures for Western Siberia are 6 per cent for both years, Eastern Siberia's about 3 per cent.

The S.F.E. contributes substantially to the stocks of canned goods in the rest of the R.S.F.S.R. which produced as a whole only about 25 cans of foodstuffs per head of its population in 1965, rising to about 45 in 1977 while the Soviet Far Easterners greatly exceeded that national average, producing four times as many (assorted) cans per head of their own population in 1965 and three times as many in 1977. But the serious fall-off in production in 1977–79 in Siberia and the Soviet Far East is immediately notable.

Forestry and Paper

Recently Western commentators have stressed current difficulties in the Soviet economy which has been experiencing a faltering of economic growth. This is instanced by the figures for the lumber industry which also features the continued shift of the "centre of gravity" towards the east.

Siberia accounts for one-quarter of the Soviet Union's production of paper, the Urals for another quarter, the North-West (Leningrad, Karelia and

Output of Sawn Timber
(million cubic metres)

	1940	1976	1977	1979
R.S.F.S.R.	28.8	90.8	89.0	81.4
Western Siberia	2.8	8.8	8.9	8.3
of which:				
Tyumen'	0.5	2.1	2.2	2.3
Tomsk	0.7	2.0	2.0	1.7
Kemerovo	0.4	1.7	1.7	1.6
Altai	0.5	1.2	1.1	1.2
Novosibirsk	0.6	0.8	0.8	0.7
Omsk	—	0.1	0.1	1.7
Eastern Siberia	2.8	17.5	17.2	16.7
of which:				
Irkutsk	1.0	8.0	7.6	7.4
Krasnoyarsk	1.4	6.7	7.0	6.6
Buryat A.R.	0.2	1.4	1.3	1.1
Chita	0.2	1.1	1.2	1.4
Tuva A.R.	—	0.2	0.2	0.2
Soviet Far East	2.5	6.7	6.5	6.5
of which:				
Khabarovsk	1.4*	2.4	2.2	2.3
Maritimes	0.6	1.7	1.6	1.6
Amur	0.3	0.8	0.8	0.8
Sakhalin	0.1	0.7	0.7	0.6
Kamchatka	n.a.*	0.2	0.2	0.2
Magadan	0.1	0.2	0.2	0.2
Yakut A.R.	0.1	0.6	0.6	0.7

* Figure for Kamchatka included with that for Khabarovsk.

Paper Products, R.S.F.S.R.
(percentage of total paper output)

	1965	1976
Newsprint	28	31
Typographical	9	12
Wrapping	15	13
Bag-paper	11	13
Writing paper	7	5
Offset paper	3	4
Packet and box	3	4
Others	24	18

Paper production, R.S.F.S.R. and Siberia

	1965 ('000 tons)	1970 ('000 tons)	1979 ('000 tons)	Increase 1970–1979 (per cent)
TOTAL R.S.F.S.R.	2,659	3,476	4,401	27
Western Siberia (Novosibirsk)	2	2.5	1.9	−24
Eastern Siberia	94	121	132	9
of which:				
Krasnoyarsk	94	108	120	11
Irkutsk		13	12	−8
Soviet Far East	167	195	249	28
of which:				
Sakhalin	158	183	236	29
Khabarovsk	9	9	9	—
Amur	—	4	4	—
TOTAL SIBERIA	263	318	383	20

Stock of Housing Space in Representative Cities

	Total (million square metres) 1966	1978	Increase (per cent)	Square Metres Per Head (approx.) 1966	1978
Moscow	78.5	124.5	59	11	16
Siberia:					
Blagoveshchensk	1.0	1.9	90	11	10
Chita	1.8	3.1	76	10	11
Irkutsk	3.9	6.7	72	11	13
Khabarovsk	4.0	6.8	71	12	13
Krasnoyarsk	5.1	9.4	83	12	12
Magadan	0.7	1.3	90	11	11
Vladivostok	3.8	6.6	74	13	12

Value of Retail Trade (State and Co-operative)
(Total in thousand million roubles)

	1965	1970	1975	1979
R.S.F.S.R.	63	91	122	146
West Siberia	5.4	7.7	11.0	13.1
East Siberia	3.6	5.0	7.0	8.3
S.F.E.	3.6	5.3	7.4	9.0

Archangel) for a half. The total national output increased from nearly 2,700 million metric tons in 1965 to nearly 4,500 million in 1976, with a marked shift towards printing papers. The increase in Siberian paper production, due largely to a rise in the output of Sakhalin, is much less than that attained in European Russia.

Living Standards and Amenities

Housing is a principal difficulty. Despite much construction, it does not do significantly more than keep up with the increase in population. By Western standards the scale is low: total living-space per person has risen little in recent years, from around eleven to around thirteen square metres, which now compares unfavourably with Moscow. Although amenities have been increasingly provided, investment in them remains geared very much to industrial purposes—and a vast military deployment—rather than to raising levels of personal accommodation.

The levels of consumer goods generally, though rising, are similarly low by Japanese and Western standards (and those of some South-East Asian countries). For the official figures on the total turnover in retail trade, *see* table above.

It must be remembered that prices in the easternmost part of the Soviet Union are much higher than in the European "centre"—roughly speaking, double—and that there are many inadequacies and irregularities in distribution. Per caput figures are a mere average: the Soviet Union is far from being a society with equal rewards for every citizen. Ordinary consumer goods, produced cheaply in vast quantities elsewhere in East Asia and the world, are far from abundant in Siberia which must draw for them on the other parts of the Soviet Union, themselves not

The Academy of Sciences of the U.S.S.R. in Siberia and the Soviet Far East

	Institutions	Academic Personnel							
		Doctors		Masters		Others		Total	
		1977	1978	1977	1978	1977	1978	1977	1978
Siberian Section (Novosibirsk)	30	270	294	1,388	1,430	790	864	2,448	2,588
Buryat Branch	4	15	15	145	147	125	119	285	281
Yakut Branch	6	20	21	220	224	271	296	511	541
Eastern Siberian Branch (Irkutsk)	9	53	54	467	503	548	547	1,068	1,104
Far East Centre (Vladivostok)	19	78	78	762	779	1,136	1,142	1,976	1,999
Total	68	436	462	2,982	3,083	2,870	2,968	6,288	6,513

Higher Education in the R.S.F.S.R.

	1968		1978		
	'000 Students	Per cent of total population	'000 Students	Increase 1968–78 per cent	Per cent of total population
Western Siberia	226	1.8	277	23	2.2
Eastern Siberia	124	1.6	157	27	1.9
Soviet Far East	93	1.6	123	32	1.8
Total R.S.F.S.R.	2,513	2.0	2,955	18	2.2

overstocked with goods. For example, in the 1970s production of knitwear articles in Siberia rose slightly from just about one item of underwear to two items per person of the population in Siberia, while that of outerwear remained just over one item for each inhabitant and that of leather footwear continued at about one and a half pairs per person per year. Siberia's production of furniture, given in value terms (with rising prices) was 10 roubles (say £7 or $16) per head of population in 1970 and 16 roubles (say £11 or $26) in 1977. In the local climate and rough conditions, and after two generations of shortage, these are hardly more than replacement levels.

Culture and education

Siberia is by no means a cultural desert. It is, broadly speaking, no less well served than other parts of the Soviet Union (except for the most metropolitan cities) in all general facilities such as radio and television, the cinema, sports facilities and the like. Libraries are correspondingly available though not generally so well stocked. Efforts continue to expand and improve education, with the usual Soviet bias towards technical education. The scholastic system is topped by the Academy of Sciences of the U.S.S.R. which has in Siberia, among other expanding centres' "Academic Cities" in Novosibirsk, Irkutsk and Vladivostok.

It is interesting to note the revival, in particular, of the Far East Centre (which specializes in the study of the East Asian nations and which had been closed down in the Stalin period), when seen in the light of recent declining activity in higher education and industry in the Soviet Union as a whole. In higher education more generally there are greater rates of expansion than in the R.S.F.S.R. as a whole, rising from West to East although, in the eastern regions, the rate of expansion is less than that of the area's population. Siberia's importance in this field is, however, clearly increasing. The increase in the proportion of science students doing part-time jobs as well as studying is a notable feature.

Future outlook

The natural resources of Siberia in their great quantity and variety, including many scarce and indispensable ones, are coming increasingly into effective use. Siberia will become correspondingly more important in future as a potential supplier and a market, primarily for Japan and East Asia, but also for the world in general. Siberian development, always a main Russian aim, is a slow process. Living standards in Siberia compare unfavourably with those achieved in Alaska, Canada and Scandinavia. This lag has been ascribed to the strict and centralized political control exercised by the Soviet system in its pursuit of autarky. The extent to which the system is responsible for the comparatively slower progress of Siberia remains, however, controversial. Meanwhile, there has been an alarming military build-up in the area on land, at sea and in the field of aero space. The possibilities of international participation in Siberia evidently remain limited in relation to the theoretical potentials. However, in the Soviet scheme of things, Siberia is of very great and vital importance; and, on the background of current difficulties for the Soviet Union as a whole, there has recently been some new thinking in that country, as noted in the following section.

Realistic planning—in face of economic difficulties

In the last issue of this Yearbook (pp. 1165–66) a full account was given of the sweeping proposals prominently stressed at that time for major long-term schemes to transform the whole economic geography of Siberia by diverting the flow of a number of its great rivers from their northward course, to irrigate the extensive dry lands in the south. As often (or usually) happens with the great "drives" in Soviet policy and propaganda, this emphasis has been largely dropped in the subsequent period, to give way to other urgencies and to more realistic perspectives for the nearer future.

This is enforced to a large extent by the present state of the Soviet economy, the performance of which is admittedly grossly unsatisfactory in all the basic respects: production, distribution, efficiency and quality are all well below the levels demanded of them. There are malfunctions in the social as well as the economic system, internally; to which are added external difficulties such as the world depression and the situations in Poland and Afghanistan.

The effects are broadly reflected in the current Five Year Plan of the U.S.S.R., for 1981–85, which was presented by Mr. Brezhnev and Prime Minister N. A. Tikhonov in March 1981, but only filled out in detail during the following twelve months by subsequent comments, statements, explanations and amendments. The aspects relating especially to Siberia and the Soviet Far East (hereinafter, for short, SIBFE) are considered especially below.

So far as the major river-diversion schemes are concerned, the new Plan envisages only "preparatory" work on "part" of the flow. Some actual operations may start during these five years on the Pechama-Kama-Volga sector (envisaged for a very long time past), but only continued "studies" on the Ob' and Yenisei schemes. However, a number of other great undertakings in Siberia continue to be pressed forward; and there is a shift rather than diminution of emphasis on the key importance of Siberia for the future security, development and prosperity of the U.S.S.R. as a whole—seen always as an integrated national task, not one of coordinating development on a regional basis. There are evident stresses on rationalization and modernization, the production of oil and gas, transport, electric power and social questions, as outlined below.

Rationalization and modernization

The current Plan's stress on these problems has been supplemented recently by a great deal of academic and technical research, analysis and publication on the same themes in the U.S.S.R., giving much solid analysis of past results and current problems. Typically, this material is more detailed about past decades than about present problems and requirements, on which it is more reticent or discreet, though still emphatic. There are strong and frank allusions to the following aspects: the general technical inefficiency of industries outside European Russia (itself no paragon in that respect), the need to make better use of plant in general and to improve small plants as well as large-scale installations.

The high capital cost of big investments in new up-to-date facilities is widely emphasized; connectedly there is a broad consensus among technical and economic analysts that the era of "extensive" development of Russia has come to an end and intensive development, with stricter efficiency, is now the order of the day. The official predilection still tends to be, nonetheless, for the gigantic and the ultra-modern; major "territorial industrial complexes" already in existence are to be notably enlarged, namely West Siberia, Southern Yakutia and Bratsk-Ilimsk. West Siberia was described in the draft of the Plan as "the greatest", but this superlative was dropped in the final version. The rising cost of all these large-calibre industrial clusters was noted, but accepted as a necessity.

Oil and gas

The northwest Siberian oil- and gas-field in the Tyumen' and Tomsk Provinces has leapt into truly great significance in the last few years. It is well known that West Europe is now preparing to receive enormous quantities of gas from that area, through an elaborate and costly pipeline scheme—with evident strategic and general implications, and tremendous practical and other difficulties still in evidence in mid-1982. In 1980 the area produced 52 per cent of the U.S.S.R.'s oil and 36 per cent of its gas (i.e. in the order of ten per cent of the output of the whole world). The plans call for this to be increased to between 60 and 64 per cent of the U.S.S.R.'s oil output and between 52 and 62 per cent of its gas production; or in quantitative terms $385–395 \times 10^6$ metric tons of oil and $330–370 \times 10^9$ cubic metres of gas.

The rises in the Northwest Siberian region are to be much above the national average; and two areas within it are given very much the leading role. The Urengoi area is to produce half of the Northwest Siberian output of gas, more than doubling its production. Mr. Brezhnev declared this to be "of the first economic and political importance". The local Party representative for Tyumen' responded boldly to this, asserting that his Province should produce 500×10^9 cubic metres in 1990—and ultimately 1000×10^9 per year. Gas deposits are being opened up in the Yamal Peninsula in the Arctic Ocean some 1,000 miles or 1,700 kilometres north by east of Sverdlovsk; but that is a comparatively inaccessible area, the Tyumen' fields being, though also in wild and difficult country, only about half that distance from developed centres.

For oil, in regard to which Samotlor, some 350 miles or 600 kilometres from Sverdlovsk, is the "star" field, the expectations are less spectacular, though still large. Oil production is to increase in the U.S.S.R. as a whole by 1985 between three and seven per cent; and Premier Tikhonov noted that "great and complicated tasks were" involved in this increase, which would fall very largely on Northwest Siberia. Some surprise is expressed at the lack of mention of offshore exploration in the Kara Sea (to the north of the Yamal Peninsula), which is believed to be an outstanding possibility.

Transport

Major railway, river and other works essential to these oil and gas prospects continue. There was also reference in the Plan and in contingent discussions to the Northern Sea Route round the Arctic coast of the U.S.S.R., on the western sector of which "year-round navigation" is to be established by 1985. In 1980 and 1981 passages were indeed maintained almost throughout the year through the southwest Kara Sea to the Yenisei; apparently this function is to be "secured" rather than extended. On the eastern sector "punctual deliveries of freight to the Far North and Far East are to be secured"—they have been by no means punctual during the last few years—and a build-up of capacity is indicated.

The Northern Sea Route is to increase its turnover of freight by 40 per cent, while the increase for the entire merchant marine of the U.S.S.R. is to be only eight or nine per cent. If the season is extended, the number of trips per vessel can be increased; connectedly at least five more icebreakers are planned (one atom-powered, built in the Soviet Union, and four diesel-engined built in Finland) and some freighters specially constructed for Arctic Ocean use. This traffic would serve especially the development of mineral resources.

By far the most important transport project remains, however, the Baikal-Amur Railway (BAM). It is to be "fully opened" during the current period of the 11th Five Year Plan (i.e. by 1985), but that expression is not closely defined. During the course of the formulation of the current Five Year Plan, between its first draft and the final decree, there was an added stress that the development of forest and mineral resources along the route of the new railroad should begin with immediate effect. A practical addition to that effect was the added direction to make a real beginning on the construction of a line to Yakutsk, which has long been projected (from Berkakit via the Chul'man iron-ore field to Yakutsk). The line is of course being built in sections (including spurs), not sequentially from west to east or vice versa, and sectoral completions will be proclaimed from time to time.

Steps were taken to consolidate and improve the administration, notably by the appointment of Sergei Bashilov, head of the Construction Department in the State Planning Office GOSPLAN, to lead a new "Ministry of Construction in the Far East and Transbaikal" to coordinate the building of the new railway with other construction works and economic development in general in the whole Region. The spectre of "cost-overrun" is haunting this sector, like all the others; cost-projections are rising alarmingly, but it is avowed that they must be met and endured.

Electricity

The generation of electricity is to be expanded as usual. In this sphere also there were some interesting adjustments between the original draft of the Plan and its final version. Work is to continue on building thermal stations at Neryungri in southern Yakutia, at Boguchany on the Angara and Sinegor'ye on the Kolyma, but a projected second thermal plant at Yakutsk was dropped during the elaboration of the Plan. The famous nuclear plant at Bilibino far away in the northeast of Siberia is to be extended. The use of tidal power and small rivers was also indicated—the former actually as an addition, not featured in the original draft. The great emphasis on hydroelectric power, sustained from the beginning of the Soviet period, is by no means dropped but is currently somewhat diminished.

Social problems

Labour shortage remains the largest and most acute problem, with shortfalls occurring in both quantity and quality. Under the new Plan incentive payments will be increased for workers in SIBFE, embodied in higher wage scales in that part of the country, plus "regional coefficients" equivalent to cost of living allowances. The indigenous peoples of Siberia were mentioned, to emphasize how greatly the Soviet system had benefited them—tending to the conclusion that they have now advanced so greatly, conditions having improved for all Soviet citizens equally, that the minorities now require no special provisions or treatment in their favour. Nevertheless the need was emphasized to develop further and better the areas inhabited by the indigenous peoples, and it was declared that help would be given to the reindeer industry. Problems of environmental degradation are not specifically noted in the Plan, but have been canvassed by a number of writers and speakers.

Business relations with Japan

While the oil and gas development at the western end of SIBFE has been prodigious, forging a new and powerful (though not yet complete or assured) connection between Siberia and Western Europe, the once equally impressive hopes for a "joint-venturing" collaboration of Japan in the development of SIBFE reached a "stalemate" in 1982. At that time, just twenty years after the first efforts in that direction, Japanese business and official circles were pessimistic about the prospects.

A twentieth anniversary should have been celebrated, since major Soviet plans for development in Siberia on large-scale and technically modern lines date in fact to 1962; and at that time the Japanese saw that a large and substantial basis existed for joint working in SIBFE. It is thus timely to review the whole experience of those two decades; and that is being widely done in Japan.

In 1965 the Soviet Union made a formal offer, on the basis of a great ferment of interest in Japan. A "Japan-Soviet Economic Development Committee" was formed in each of the two countries; they met together in 1966 and launched three projects, one in timber, another the construction of a new harbour in Wrangel Bay (near Nakhodka, not far from Vladivostok), the third a project to develop wood-pulp production. In the late 1960s another four projects were added: oil development in Tyumen', natural gas in Yakutia, and offshore oil in Sakhalin.

Under the so-called "production-sharing method", each project was to go through three phases: (a) Japan would provide financial and technical means, through credits from the Export–Import Bank of Japan and commercial banks, to be used for furnishing capital goods; (b) the Soviets would then develop the project using Japanese machinery, equipment and know-how; whereafter (c) the U.S.S.R. would export the natural resources thus produced to Japan, in repayment.

The first three projects were successfully completed in the 1970s, and negotiations advanced substantially on the next batch of four projects. There was a "boom" of interest in Siberia in Japan in 1973. The Tyumen' oilfield then became the basic and prestigious model. It postulated Japan's provision of U.S. $2,400 million to be spent on equipment, including a 4000-kilometre pipeline from Tyumen' to Nakhodka. From 1981 Japan would purchase the crude oil; a minimum of 25 million tons of it and a maximum of 40 million tons. This was not effected.

The natural gas project, calculated to require U.S. $3,400 million from Japan and acquiring similar importance to the oil project, has also fallen into a condition of no real progress. The reasons are various. Owing to worldwide inflation, project costs doubled or quadrupled. The Soviet Union is not exempt from this; the costs involved in the Yakut gas project more than doubled, from U.S. $3,400 million to over $7,000 million. The Soviet Union announced unilaterally that it would supply only the minimum (25 million tons) of Tyumen' oil, not the maximum (of 40 million). This was just after the first international "oil shock" of 1973, which hit Japan harder than any of the other industrialized nations.

The Soviets then committed themselves to the construction of BAM, the second Siberian Railway from the north end of Lake Baikal to the lower Amur at Komsomolsk, in lieu of the scheme for a grand pipeline. This move was also to the heavy displeasure of China, for strategic reasons, at a time when the Japanese had high hopes of large-scale friendly and profitable links with China. So the Japanese withdrew from their contemplated participation in the construction of the new railway (while the Soviets apparently preferred, and felt able, to construct it themselves). Japanese business circles and professional economic analysts are, however, self-critical about their own side in these dealings. Contrary to the Western image of a concerted or highly collaborative business strategy in Japan, they allege a disorderly confusion among sectional interests.

There was a "rush" in Japan—spurred from the 1960s by recession leading to a quest for new markets—in a highly competitive or even emotive spirit, to "get into" China and Russia in particular. China, in the throes of the Cultural Revolution, was the reverse of responsive (subsequently it has become highly open and cooperative towards foreign offers of collaboration, but difficulties and disappointments have ensued). At the same time the Soviet Union appeared to be canvassing large tenders on the basis of the major development of SIBFE in general, with a marked focus on specific items the large industries of Japan were eager to provide, such as great pipelines, harbour works, communications equipment, lumbering and mining gear (though, as noted above, some of these "baits" were subsequently withdrawn). Many Japanese firms incurred losses.

This may be an over-simplification of a complicated state of affairs, but it seems generally true that every possibility raised, even some very tentative ones, attracted a large number of Japanese firms, competing widely and sharply among themselves; and the Soviet authorities, on their side "monolithic", were able to take advantage of this, especially where the middle- and smaller-sized Japanese enterprises were involved. It is also useful to note the diversity of interests among the Japanese. In the business sector these have not, as is sometimes supposed, been predominantly the ones interested in acquiring raw materials, minerals, etc. from Russia; though that interest naturally existed, it was evinced later when the matter gathered momentum, rather than intrinsically or at the outset.

Thus in the 1960s or early 1970s hardly any petroleum or coal interests in Japan participated, though they joined in later. The impetus has come rather from Japanese concerned to sell to the U.S.S.R. The Japan–Soviet Economic Committee was presided over from its conception by the former head of the Japan Steel Company, Mr. Nagano, while its other leaders have been directors of firms in manufacturing, heavy machinery, bulldozers, mining gear, communications equipment and other machinery and, for the rest, trading companies. It is interesting to note that another former chairman of Japan Steel, Mr. Inayama, President also of the Employers' Federation (Keidanren) was similarly the leader in relations with China, as President of the Japan–China Economic Committee.

On that background, the role and interests of the Japanese Government must be fully considered. It had to provide or underwrite the billions of dollars of credits involved. It would pay a high price for an improvement in the nation's supply-situation in respect of the raw materials, and especially fuels, on which Japan so vitally depends; but it could not or would not pay an excessive price for this in terms of diplomatic or other losses. Under that heading would come loss of the goodwill of China, the United States or other countries. The Japanese Government has worked, in effect, for trilateral or multilateral bases of progress; for instance, in bringing the United States into the schemes for Siberian development.

Naturally, while keen on Siberian development as such, the Japanese Government must try to use it for leverage on the U.S.S.R. in such respects as the failure of the latter to conclude a peace treaty with Japan, thirty-seven years after the end of the War, or to negotiate concerning the disputed northern islands occupied by the Soviet Union which the Japanese wish to have returned to them. The present lack of progress may be illustrated by the comparative silence and inertia with which new Soviet proposals, advanced late in 1979, have been received in Japan, including the construction of a steel mill in the Soviet Far East, the development of the huge but remote copper deposits at Udokan east of Lake Baikal and the development of asbestos mining in Eastern Siberia. There has been some successful collaboration in the development of offshore gas in Sakhalin; but efforts in such directions were also threatened, as of mid-1982, by the United States embargo on the passing of advanced technical equipment and knowledge to the U.S.S.R. The Japanese imposed sanctions on the Soviet Union after the invasion of Afghanistan; these have been relaxed, but the pulse of Japanese interest in Siberian development, though far from extinct, appears feeble in comparison with its feverish state in the 1960s and 1970s.

Prospects and problems

This summary of Japan's recent relations with Siberia is of more than historical or academic interest; it exemplifies on the one hand the difficulties of dealing with that large and potentially rich area, but on the other hand the fact that, even under the heavy rule of Soviet autarchism, SIBFE is not isolated from the outside world and its pressures, and must sooner or later become an important part of the world economy in general and of East Asia and the Pacific area in particular. Meanwhile the case of Japan, in the Siberian connection, is of marked interest to other countries requiring or wishing to have major relations with the Soviet Union.

Siberia is a huge and complex area, on which only broad conclusions are possible in a brief review. It is much affected by the problems and difficulties of the Soviet Union as a whole—with which it is, in the fullest sense of the term, completely bound up—though showing some local differences, displaying the same striking achievements as the rest of the Soviet Union, in various ways.

From an international point of view, SIBFE remains a vast storehouse of potential resources for the future, locked up in the autarchy of the Soviet system, while the U.S.S.R. expands in overall strength as a Superpower. Its self-containedness is sealed especially by the antagonism between the U.S.S.R. and China and the inability to effect substantial relations with Japan and other countries to which Siberia's resources could be so greatly complementary. In contrast, Western Siberia is linking with west Europe, to supply gas to it.

The contrast is deepened by the state of activity around the rest of the Pacific perimeter, where many of the countries are showing high growth rates and all are internationally active; meanwhile all of them are seeking improved connections and increased economic and other exchanges, on a better coordinated basis, between each other and with other parts of the world, to the extent that there is a vigorous movement for the development of the "Pacific Basin", including advocacy of forming an actual Pacific Economic Community. In comparison with this dynamism, the situation of Siberia appears static and unlikely to change rapidly or significantly, from an international point of view, though continuing to record large industrial achievements on its own Soviet basis.

BIBLIOGRAPHY

HISTORY

ARMSTRONG, T. E. Russian Settlement in the North (Cambridge University Press, 1975).

BECKER, S. Russia's Central Asian Protectorates: Bukhara and Khiva 1865–1925 (Harvard University Press, Cambridge, Mass., 1967).

CAROE, O. Soviet Empire (Macmillan, London, 1953).

CURZON, N. The Russians in Central Asia (Longmans, London, 1889).

HAMBLY, G. (ed.). Central Asia (in the Universal History Series) (Weidenfeld & Nicolson, London, 1970).

HOLDSWORTH, M. Turkestan in the Nineteenth Century (Central Asian Research Centre, London, 1959).

KERNER, R. J. The Urge to the Sea. The Course of Russian History: The Role of Rivers, Portages, Ostrogs, Monasteries and Furs (California University Press, Berkeley and Los Angeles, 1946).

LANTZEFF, G. V. Siberia in the Seventeenth Century (California University Press, Berkeley, 1943).

LANTZEFF, G. V., and PIERCE, R. A. Eastward to Empire (Queen's University Press, Montreal and London, 1973).

PARK, A. Bolshevism in Turkestan 1917–1927 (Columbia University Press, New York, 1957).

PIERCE, R. Russian Central Asia 1867–1917 (California University Press, Berkeley, 1960).

PIPES, R. The Formation of the Soviet Union (Harvard University Press, Cambridge, Mass., 1954).

SEMYONOV, Y. The Conquest of Siberia (Routledge, London, 1944).

WHEELER, G. E. The Modern History of Soviet Central Asia (Weidenfeld and Nicolson, London, 1964).

ECONOMY

CONOLLY, V. Beyond the Urals (Oxford University Press, London, 1967).
Siberia Today and Tomorrow (Collins, London, 1975).

CONQUEST, R. Kolyma (the Arctic Death Camps) (Macmillan, London, 1978).

DIBB, P. Siberia and the Pacific: a Study of Economic Development (Praeger, New York, 1972).

MATHIESON, R. S. Japan's Role in Soviet Economic Growth: Transfer and Technology since 1965 (Praeger, New York, 1979).

MAX, A. The Siberian Challenge (Prentice-Hall Inc., Engelwood Cliffs, N.J., 1977).

MOZHIN, V. P. (Ed.). Ekonomicheskoye razvitie Sibiri i Dal'nego Vostoka (Economic Development of Siberia and the Far East) (Nauka, Moscow, 1980).

NATO, Division of Economic Affairs, Report of Round Table on the Exploitation of Siberia's Natural Resources (Brussels, 1974).

NOVE, A., and NEWTH, J. A. The Soviet Middle East (Allen & Unwin, London, 1967).

SHABAD, T. Geography of the U.S.S.R.: A Regional Survey (Columbia University Press, New York, 1961).
Basic Industrial Resources of the U.S.S.R. (Columbia University Press, New York, 1969).

SHABAD T. and MOTE V. L. Gateway to Siberian Resources (The Baikal-Amur Railway) (Halsted, New York, 1977).

SWEARINGEN, R. The Soviet Union and Postwar Japan (Stanford University Press, Stanford, Calif., 1978).

U.S.S.R. GOVERNMENT. Narodnoe Khoz'aistvo RSFSR (Economy of the R.S.F.S.R.) (Moscow, annually).

GENERAL

BENNIGSEN, A., and QUELQEJAY, C. Islam in the Soviet Union (Pall Mall Press, London, 1967).

CARRÈRE D'ENCAUSSE, HÉLÈNE. L'empire éclaté (Flammarion, Paris, 1978). *English translation:* Decline of an Empire: the Soviet Republic in Revolt (Newsweek, New York, 1980).

KIRBY, E. S. The Soviet Far East (Macmillan, London, 1971).
Russian Studies of China: Progress and Problems of Soviet Sinology (Macmillan, London, 1975).
Russian Studies of Japan (Macmillan, London, 1980).

KOLARZ, W. The Peoples of the Soviet Far East (George Philip, London, 1954).
Religion in the Soviet Union (St. Martin's Press, New York, 1962).

RAKOWSKA-HARMSTONE, T. Russia and Nationalism in Central Asia: the case of Tadzhikistan (Johns Hopkins Press, 1970).

SALISBURY, H. E. The Coming War between Russia and China (Pan Books, London, 1969).
To Peking and Beyond (Arrow, London, 1973).

STEPHAN, J. J. Sakhalin: A History (Oxford University Press, 1971).
The Kuril Islands; Russo-Japanese Frontiers in the Pacific (Oxford University Press, 1974).

WHEELER, G. E. The Modern History of Soviet Central Asia (Weidenfeld and Nicolson, London, 1964).

Viet-Nam

PHYSICAL AND SOCIAL GEOGRAPHY

C. A. Fisher

(Revised for this edition by HARVEY DEMAINE)

Viet-Nam covers a total area of 329,566 square kilometres (127,246 square miles) and lies along the western shore of the South China Sea, bordered by the People's Republic of China to the north, by Laos to the west and by Kampuchea (formerly Cambodia) to the south-west.

PHYSICAL FEATURES

The fundamental geographical outlines of the country are determined by the deltas and immediate hinterlands of the Mekong and Songkoi (Red River) which are linked by the mountain backbone and adjacent coastal lowlands of Annam.

Of the two rivers which are thus of major significance in the geography of Viet-Nam, the Songkoi, rising like the Mekong in southwestern China, is much the shorter, and its delta, together with that of a series of lesser rivers, forms a total area of some 14,500 square kilometres, which is less than half that of the great Mekong delta in the south. Besides the delta, north Viet-Nam also includes a much more extensive area of rugged upland, mainly in the north and west, which represents a southward continuation of the Yunnan and adjacent plateaux of southwestern China, and forms an inhospitable and sparsely populated divide, some 900 to 1,500 metres high, between north Viet-Nam and northern Laos.

Both the Songkoi and its main right-bank tributary, the Songbo (Black River), flow in parallel N.W./S.E. gorges through this upland before their confluence some 100 kilometres above the apex of the delta, while a third main river, the Songma, also follows a parallel course still farther to the south, beyond which rises the similarly N.W./S.E. trending Annamite Chain or Cordillera. This, in relief if not in structure, constitutes a further prolongation of the massive upland system already described, and extends without a break to within about 150 kilometres of the Mekong delta.

With an average breadth of 150 kilometres, and an extremely rugged and heavily forested surface, at many points exceeding 1,500 metres in altitude, the Annamite Chain, which lies mainly in southern Viet-Nam, provides an effective divide between the Annam coast and the middle Mekong valley of southern Laos and eastern Kampuchea. Moreover from the Porte d'Annam (lat. 18° N.) southwards, the Chain not only reaches to within a few miles of the coast, but also sends off a series of spurs which terminate in rocky headlands overlooking the sea. Thus, along the 1,000-kilometre stretch of coast between latitudes 18° and 11° N., the continuity of the coastal plain is repeatedly interrupted and it dwindles to an average width of less than 16 km. and often to less than half that figure. But thereafter it broadens out to merge with the vast deltaic plain of the Mekong and its associated natural waterways, the whole forming an almost dead flat surface covering some 37,800 square kilometres.

CLIMATE

In forming the western hinterland of the South China Sea virtually from the tropic of Cancer to within 9° N. of the equator, Viet-Nam might be assumed to be wholly within the zone of the tropical monsoon climate. But while the greater part of the country does merit such a designation, and Hué, practically at the mid-point of the coastal zone, has a mean monthly temperature range from 20°C. in January to 30°C. in August, and a total rainfall of 260 cm., of which 165 cm. falls during September–November inclusive, the Songkoi delta in the north is not strictly tropical in the climatological sense. For owing to its exposure to cold northern air during the season of the N.E. monsoon, it experiences a recognizable cool season from December to March, and in both January and February the mean monthly temperatures in Hanoi are only 17°C. This fact is of great practical importance since the cooler weather gives greater effectiveness to the 13–15 cm. of rain which fall during these months, and so makes it possible to raise a "winter" as well as a summer crop of rice in this part of the country.

NATURAL RESOURCES

In terms of agricultural potential, the two deltas are of overwhelming importance.

The uplands offer far less opportunity for supporting population and have been almost completely avoided, not only because of the extremely restricted prospects they afford for wet rice cultivation but also because of their intensely malarial character. These facts are in part inter-related, for the anopheles mosquito, which carries malaria, does not flourish in the muddy water of paddy fields. In respect of mineral wealth, on the other hand, the uplands, particularly in the north, contain a wide variety of lesser metallic ores, and also some useful apatite (a source of phosphates), though economically the most important mineral is in the anthracite field of Quang-Yen, which occurs in an area of Mesozoic folding immediately to the north-east of the Songkoi delta. Petroleum has been discovered off-shore in the north and the south of the country.

POPULATION AND ETHNIC GROUPS

The total population of Viet-Nam was estimated to be 54,900,000 at mid-1981, up from the October 1979 census figure of 52,741,766, which gave an average population density of 160 per square kilometre. This average, however, is very misleading, firstly because the great majority of the population (and practically all of the Vietnamese proper) live within the lowlands, and secondly because the lowlands comprise rather more than one-third of the total area of southern Viet-Nam, but barely one-sixth of that of northern Viet-Nam. Thus, whereas most of the vast Mekong delta supports rural densities varying from 40 to 200 to the square kilometre, the comparable figures for the Songkoi delta are between four and five times as great. On the other hand it is the south which shows the higher degree of urbanization. In 1979 the largest town in Viet-Nam was Ho Chi Minh City, in the south, with a population of 3,419,978, whereas the largest towns in the north, the capital Hanoi and its port, Haiphong, had populations of only 2,570,905 and 1,279,067 respectively. The distribution of population in Viet-Nam is likely to change a good deal in the next few years owing to a vast planned resettlement programme.

Vietnamese, who are ethnically close kinsfolk of the southern Chinese, form the overwhelming majority of the population, some 80 per cent in all. The country contains, however, some significant minority groups, notably the Tai in the north (numbering some 2 million), some 750,000 Meo (Hmong) and related groups and a number of smaller groups of people in the Central Highlands, usually known as "Montagnards" and also numbering up to 1 million. In addition there are perhaps 600,000 Kampucheans along the country's south-western border and a now uncertain number of Chinese, still primarily concentrated in the southern city of Cholon, but much reduced in numbers by migration since the deterioration in Sino-Vietnamese relations.

HISTORY

Ralph Smith

EARLY HISTORY

The Vietnamese trace their history back to the Hung Vuong kings who are said to have ruled in what is now northern Viet-Nam during the third or second millennium B.C. For a long time it was thought that such a dynasty was purely legendary, but recent archaeological work suggests that Viet-Nam had at least some kind of distinctive bronze age civilization, perhaps by 1000 B.C. The earliest written evidence records that a country called Au-Lac in that area was conquered by the first Chinese emperor and founder of the Qin (Ch'in) dynasty, about 214 B.C. But its relationship to China at that period was probably rather distant, and its material culture shows closer affinities with that of Yunnan. After a period of dependence on the south Chinese kingdom of Nam-Viet from 207 to 112 B.C., the present northern Viet-Nam became incorporated into the Chinese Han empire and remained effectively a province of China for about a thousand years.

An anti-Chinese revolt led by the Trung Sisters in A.D. 41 was followed by a tightening of control by the Han. Likewise the revolt of Ly Bon in 542 was followed by the Tang period (618–907), when the province of Annam ("pacified South") was absorbed even more firmly into the Chinese cultural sphere. During these centuries of Han and Tang rule, there occurred a gradual fusion of Vietnamese and Chinese ideas and institutions. The Chinese language was introduced, although it did not entirely supplant Vietnamese. The Chinese religions of Daoism, Confucianism and Mahayana Buddhism also took deep root.

When the Tang empire broke up early in the tenth century South China came under the rule of the independent dynasty of Nan-Han, which in 902 extended its control to Viet-Nam. But that control was not easy to maintain; the Nan-Han army was defeated in 931 and 938, and it is from the latter year, when Ngo Quyen became king, that the Vietnamese usually date their independence from Chinese rule. In 981 the new Song dynasty of China tried to take advantage of internal Vietnamese conflicts to reimpose Chinese rule, but it too was defeated. During the next four centuries Viet-Nam (or Dai-Viet) gradually developed into a strong and fairly centralized state, with a capital in Hanoi and institutions modelled on those of China. It was not yet wholly "Confucianized" however; Mahayana Buddhism played an important part in the life of court and people, and twentieth-century Vietnamese Buddhists look back to the eleventh and twelfth centuries as the golden age of their religion. Thus, under the dynasties of the Ly (1009–1225) and Tran (1225–1400), Dai-Viet was strong enough to resist further Chinese attempts at reconquest: by the Song in 1075–77, and by the Yuan (Mongols) in the years 1282–88. In the late fourteenth and early fifteenth centuries the kingdom went through a period of difficulties, and when a new Chinese attack came in 1407 it succumbed. But not for long; after twenty years the Chinese were once more driven out by Le Loi, founder of the Le dynasty (1428–1789).

Meanwhile, in what is now Central Viet-Nam there flourished the kingdom of Champa, with a culture strongly influenced by Hinduism; as was that of the Khmer (Cambodian) kingdom, to which the whole of the Mekong delta then belonged (though the Cambodians later adopted Theravada Buddhism). The remains of Cham temples dating from the ninth to the thirteenth centuries, very Indian in appearance, still survive along the central Vietnamese coast. The

Chams were frequently at war with the Vietnamese, from the tenth century onwards, but on the whole were the losers in most campaigns. Dai-Viet annexed areas of Cham territory in 1070, 1306 and 1470; by the latter year Champa was reduced to a small principality, which was finally extinguished altogether in 1695. But as the Vietnamese kingdom expanded, it found increasing difficulty in maintaining its own unity.

CONFLICTS, DIVISION AND UNIFICATION

The fifteenth century, and especially the reign of Le Thanh Tong (1459–97), was the "golden age" of Confucian culture in Viet-Nam and a period of general stability. But in the early sixteenth century the kingdom began to break up under the stress of conflict between rival clans, one of which established the Mac dynasty (1527–92) but failed to keep control of the whole country. Later the Le were restored to the throne, but not to power. After the intermittent civil war of the sixteenth century, the seventeenth saw a more lasting division of Viet-Nam between two powerful clans: the Trinh in the north and the Nguyen in the south (i.e. central Viet-Nam). The latter resisted a series of Trinh attempts to conquer them (1627–73) and maintained their independence down to 1775. It was the Nguyen who led the way in a further southward expansion. A series of wars with Cambodia beginning about 1658 enabled them to annex much of the lower Mekong delta by 1760, thus establishing their control over the greater part of what is now southern Viet-Nam.

In the 1770s, however, the Nguyen were overthrown by a combination of the Tay-Son rebellion, which broke out at Qui-Nhon in 1773, and a new invasion by the Trinh. The whole country was now thrown into a state of civil war, for although the Tay-Son proved capable of establishing a new dynasty and of repelling a Chinese invasion in 1789, they could not bring new stability. The last Nguyen survivor returned to recapture Saigon in 1789, and from there went on to conquer the centre and north by 1802. He proclaimed himself emperor at Hué, with the title Gia-Long, and for the first time in its history the present area of Viet-Nam was brought under the control of a single ruler. It was under Gia-Long (1802–20) and Minh-Mang (1820–41) that Hué acquired the status and the architectural adornments of an imperial capital.

Under Gia-Long the new unity was precarious, and the governors of Tonking and Cochinchina were allowed considerable independence. Minh-Mang, more orthodox a Confucian than his father, was also more ambitious. When Le Van Duyet, governor of Saigon, died in 1832, the emperor sought to impose a more uniform administrative structure. The immediate consequence was a serious revolt in Cochinchina, lasting from 1833 to 1835 but once it was suppressed Minh-Mang was able to have his way, and for a few years even extended his control to embrace much of Cambodia. At the time of his death, Viet-Nam had the widest extent in the whole of its history. His successor, Thieu-Tri (1841–47), soon lost Cambodia, though he maintained the power of Hué over Viet-Nam itself. But the trend towards centralization and administrative development suffered a set-back with the succession conflict that followed his death, which led to the elevation to the throne of a much younger ruler, Tu-Duc (1847–83). It was in his reign that the Vietnamese came face-to-face with the challenge of imperialist France.

Gia-Long, who had used French advisers in his campaigns before 1802, was willing to tolerate Christianity. Minh-Mang was not, and by 1833 he had instituted a persecution as severe as any the missionaries had faced since they first came to Viet-Nam in the seventeenth century. It was because of this that when Minh-Mang chose to send an embassy to France in 1840, it was refused an audience by the king. The persecution continued under Thieu-Tri and Tu-Duc, and in the meantime French embassies to Hué were brushed aside. Finally, in 1858, a Franco-Spanish fleet attacked Tourane (Da Nang). The following year the same force directed its attentions to Saigon, and by the end of 1860 the French were virtually in possession of three provinces of Cochinchina. After some hesitation they decided to hold on to them, and their annexation was formally recognized by Tu-Duc in 1862. But relations with the Europeans continued to be bad, and in 1867 the French annexed another three provinces. In 1873 a French force attacked Hanoi and captured the citadel, but then withdrew on orders from home. A new Franco-Vietnamese treaty was signed in 1874, recognizing French possession of all Cochinchina and permitting the French to trade in Tongking (Tonkin). It was not until 1882–83 that the French finally occupied Tonking again, and imposed a treaty of "protection" on the Vietnamese empire. Two years later, after a border war with China, the French secured Chinese recognition of their Protectorate. For although Viet-Nam had been independent of China for the past nine hundred years, it had recognized Chinese overlordship by sending regular tribute for most of that time.

FRENCH RULE AND VIETNAMESE OPPOSITION

Thus by 1885 the whole of Viet-Nam was under French colonial rule: Cochinchina, in the south, as a directly administered colony; Tongking and Annam (the north and centre) as protectorates. In 1887 they were united with Cambodia to form the Indochinese Union, to which Laos was added in 1893. The government-general of the Union was at first somewhat nebulous, but in the years 1897-1901 it was transformed by Paul Doumer into an effective central authority with financial control over the whole of Indochina. The French administration promoted economic development in certain spheres, such as the mining of coal and minerals in Tongking, the cultivation of rubber and other plantation crops in the hill areas, the export of rice from Cochinchina, and the construction of several railways. They also created several new towns, notably Saigon and Hanoi, which for a time were alternate capitals of the Union and which attracted the growth of a small urban, French-educated élite amongst the Vietnamese population. In the countryside, on the other hand, the peasantry did not benefit much from French rule. Their taxes were increased several times from about 1897, without very much attention being paid to helping them to raise productivity. During the 1930s, with the economic slump followed by a new inflation, the economic condition of the peasantry declined seriously and many of the poor and landless villagers became permanently indebted to their richer neighbours. The political developments of the 1930s and 1940s must be seen against this background of social conflict. At the same time the development of French education tended to undermine traditional values and to make economic inequalities more transparent.

Opposition to French rule was essentially "traditional" before about 1900: a long sequence of local risings led by scholars or military men who had had some status in the old society, but who had no effective means of defeating the new regime. The period produced several celebrated heroes: notably Truong Cong Dinh, Phan Dinh Phung and Hoang Hoa Tham. During the first decade of the twentieth century a new opposition movement began, characterized by political associations strongly influenced by the model of Japanese modernization and by Chinese revolutionary aspirations. But an anti-taxation revolt and a nationalist education movement in 1907–08 were both suppressed by the French. The two most prominent leaders of this period spent long years in exile. Phan Chau Trinh, at first imprisoned after the events of 1908, was obliged to live in France and returned only when he was dying in 1926. Phan Boi Chau, who wrote many revolutionary and nationalist pamphlets, lived for a time in China and also visited Japan; he was arrested in Shanghai in 1925 and spent the rest of his life under confinement at Hué.

The growth of constitutionalist opposition to Western colonial rule throughout Asia, from about 1916, was reflected in Viet-Nam by the Constitutionalist Party founded in Cochinchina in 1917. The party participated in elections for the Colonial Council, but was not allowed to operate outside Cochinchina: the French did not permit an all-Indochina constitutional opposition movement comparable to the Congress Party in India. Consequently from about 1925 Vietnamese nationalism began to produce revolutionary organizations, some of which became Communist. In 1930 it also found expression in a number of open revolts. A rising known as the Yen-Bay mutiny, started by the Nationalist Party in Tongking in February 1930, was quickly suppressed; so too was a strike movement in certain areas at the beginning of May. But a peasant movement which developed in summer 1930 in parts of Cochinchina and in Nghe-An, Ha-Tinh and other parts of Annam, reached more serious proportions. It was organized largely by the Indochinese Communist Party, which had grown out of a number of organizations developing from 1925 onwards and was formally founded in 1930. The movement lasted into 1931 and is generally known as the "Nghe-Tinh Soviets". It was the first occasion when the French used air power to maintain control, and it was suppressed with some ferocity. As a result many Communist leaders, including several members of the North Vietnamese politburo after 1954, spent the years 1930–36 in prison.

Political life in the early 1930s was somewhat subdued, but no serious efforts were made towards constitutional advancement until 1936, when the Popular Front government in France allowed an amnesty of political prisoners and a measure of press freedom and open political activity. Among those who took advantage of it to organize meetings and to write articles were Pham Van Dong, Vo Nguyen Giap and Dang Xuan Khu (now known as Truong Chinh). In the meantime the Communist Party held its first National Congress at Macau in 1935 and a clandestine leadership was created by Le Hong Phong, who had trained in Moscow. Also during this period a Trotskyist movement grew up, with a strong following in Cochinchina, under the leadership of Ta Thu Thau. They joined with the pro-Comintern (Stalinist) Communists and the Socialist group of Nguyen An Ninh, to devise an all-Indochina Congress in 1937, but it was quickly suppressed. With the outbreak of war in Europe in 1939, the various left-wing groups were again banned. The Trotskyist and some Stalinist leaders were imprisoned, and Pham Van Dong and Vo Nguyen Giap escaped eventually to southern China. But in the north, at least, the Communists managed to maintain a secret network of cells throughout the war period under the leadership of Truong Chinh.

A different type of political movement which developed in the south during the 1920s and 1930s was associated with a number of religious sects whose beliefs were partly apocalyptic and partly spiritualistic. The Caodaists, formally established in 1926, founded a "holy see" at Tay-Ninh, although they subsequently split up into a number of smaller sects. The Hoa-Hao Buddhists, who traced their origins back to the Buu-Son Ky-Huong secret society movement of 1913–16, were reorganized by a new leader in 1939. These groups tended to look towards Japan for political inspiration and support. Also during the 1930s there was a revival of more orthodox Mahayana Buddhism in all regions of Viet-Nam, although it did not play an active role in politics until the 1960s. In addition, Catholicism made considerable progress under the French, so that by 1954 there were probably over two million Vietnamese Catholics.

REVOLUTION, WAR AND PARTITION

It is to the period 1941–46 that we must look for the events which have shaped the recent history of Viet-Nam. In 1940 the Japanese obliged the French to allow them to use military facilities in northern Indochina, and in July 1941 they advanced in strength into southern Indochina. Administrative control, however, was left in French hands, with Admiral Decoux acting as governor and accepting the authority of Vichy France. Among the Vietnamese, pro-Japanese groups gained ground, notably the Cochinchinese sects and the new Dai-Viet (Great Viet-Nam) Party. The Japanese finally overthrew the French administration and disarmed its forces in

March 1945, in order to prevent their playing any role that would assist the allies in the closing stages of the war. At Japanese behest, the Emperor Bao-Dai revoked the treaties of 1884–85 which had made Annam and Tongking into protectorates, and proclaimed his independence. It was not until August, however, that he was permitted to revoke the treaties concerning Cochinchina, signed in 1862 and 1874. In April 1945, Bao-Dai appointed a new government headed by the pro-Japanese Tran Trong Kim, which made some effort to institute reforms. But in war conditions, with most communications destroyed by American bombing, it was unable to control the country effectively and could do hardly anything about the famine which had afflicted northern Viet-Nam since late in 1944.

Meanwhile in South China a number of Vietnamese political groups were active, of which the Communists were by far the most effective and the only ones in touch with a solid movement within the country. Their leader in China was Ho Chi Minh, who as Nguyen Ai Quoc had played a significant part in founding the Indochinese Communist Party in 1930 and who now returned from Moscow as its Comintern-appointed leader. In June 1941 a meeting between the Chinese-based leaders and the leaders of the party still active in Tongking, at a place near the border of Viet-Nam and Guangxi (Kwangsi) decided to found the Viet-Nam Doc Lap Dong Minh Hoi (Revolutionary League for the Independence of Viet-Nam), usually known as the Viet-Minh. During the next few years the Communists sought to establish two base areas in Tongking and survived a series of French punitive campaigns against them.

In spring 1945, after a period of imprisonment at the hands of the Chinese Nationalists, Ho Chi Minh made contact with the American OSS and obtained their assistance in expanding his base areas inside Tongking. When the Japanese overthrew the French regime, the Viet-Minh were ready to take advantage of an increasingly chaotic situation, and in August they emerged as the most effective political force within the country.

When the Japanese surrendered, the Viet-Minh decided to act quickly and by August 20th were in control of Hanoi. The next few days saw their flag raised in many provinces throughout the country, and on August 24th Bao-Dai (at Hué) abdicated in their favour. The defeated Japanese acquiesced in this change, and on September 2nd, 1945, Ho Chi Minh, as president of the new provisional government, read the Declaration of Independence which marked the foundation of the Democratic Republic of Viet-Nam. In the next month, the Viet-Minh leaders carried out the first stages of what amounted to a political and social revolution. Inevitably, however, they were stronger in the North, where they had been active throughout the war. In the South they had only a loosely arranged front organization, in which their allies and rivals included the formerly pro-Japanese sects and various other small groups. Their Provisional Committee took over in Saigon but was not very firmly established in power.

The Allies had agreed at the Potsdam Conference that the Japanese surrender would be received by the Chinese in the northern half of Indochina and by the British in the south. This led to the temporary occupation of Viet-Nam by British and by Chinese nationalist forces, respectively south and north of the sixteenth parallel: the first contingents of both arrived about September 20th. In the South, Franco-British co-operation made it relatively easy for the French to recover control in Saigon and to land reinforcements there in October. By the end of the year the British zone was virtually in their hands, apart from a number of rural areas where guerrillas held out; the British themselves left early in 1946. In the North, the French had to negotiate first with the Chinese, who agreed to withdraw in March 1946, and then with the Viet-Minh government in Hanoi. The latter had survived, still under the presidency of Ho Chi Minh, despite the presence of Chinese troops and of various Vietnamese nationalist parties which had Chinese support. Elections for a National Assembly were held in the North, and some parts of the South, in January 1946. The Viet-Minh dominated the polls, although they reserved a number of seats for Nationalist members, and they had the upper hand in the coalition government formed in February 1946. The withdrawal of the Chinese troops in the next few months left the Nationalists with very little power. In the meantime, the regime attempted a number of reforms: it took firm measures to prevent a recurrence of the famine of 1944–45, and it conducted an extensive literacy campaign. The significance of the revolutionary changes in that period has probably been underestimated by Western commentators.

Negotiations between the French and the Viet-Minh permitted the return of a French army to Tongking in the spring of 1946, and culminated in a conference at Fontainebleau in July. But this failed to produce agreement, and a semi-formal *modus vivendi* broke down by the end of the year. The Haiphong incident of November 20th–27th, 1946, was followed by an attempted Viet-Minh rising in Hanoi on December 19th. By then the French had sufficient troops in the north to defeat the rising, and the Viet-Minh withdrew to the countryside to plan a more protracted guerrilla war based on the tactics which Mao Zedong (Mao Tse-tung) had begun to use so effectively in China. Their leaders narrowly escaped capture in 1947, but then began to build up their strength and by 1950 were in a position seriously to challenge the French. On their side, the French decided against the creation of a separate state of Cochinchina in 1946, and began a series of negotiations with Vietnamese anti-Communists (including Bao-Dai) which led to the establishment of the Associated State of Viet-Nam in 1949. If the French could recover firm control over the country, it was to be united under the new regime with France retaining control of defence and other key decisions. The new state had a succession of prime ministers between then and 1954, and was internationally recognized by the Western powers early in 1950. At about the same time, China and the Soviet Union recognized the Democratic Republic of Viet-Nam.

The war situation was transformed in 1950–51. Communist victories in China gave Viet-Nam a common frontier with a Communist state, and the United States responded by offering aid to the French side. The Communist Party re-emerged in 1951, renamed the Viet-Nam Workers' (Lao-Dong) Party, and held its Second National Congress that year. The conflict took on a "cold war" dimension. Despite defeats at Vinh-Yen and Dong-Trieu in early 1951, the Viet-Minh armies gained in strength and by the end of 1953 the French Government was increasingly unable to cope with the situation. The military climax came with the siege of Dien-Bien-Phu, a fortress-encampment near the Laos border, which fell to the Viet-Minh in May 1954. The extent of Viet-Minh dependence on Chinese military assistance at that time did not become known until 1979.

In the meantime the great powers had agreed on an international conference in Geneva, which began its deliberations on Indochina just as Dien-Bien-Phu fell. On July 21st, 1954, a ceasefire agreement was signed by representatives of the French and Viet-Minh high commands, and an international declaration by 14 governments set forth conditions for an eventual political settlement, including a provision for national elections in July 1956. Both the agreement and the (unsigned) declaration made clear that the partition was purely military and that politically Viet-Nam remained one country. But in effect two zones were created, to be administered by the two existing Vietnamese governments: that of the Democratic Republic in Hanoi and that of the State of Viet-Nam in Saigon, with latitude 17° North as the boundary between them. A period of 300 days was allowed for regroupment, during which between 30,000 and 100,000 people moved north whilst perhaps 800,000 people (mainly Catholics) moved to the South.

SOUTH VIET-NAM AND THE WAR

The State of Viet-Nam, originally within the French Union, made an independence agreement with France in June 1954. After the ceasefire agreements at Geneva in July, French forces withdrew, leaving the State's jurisdiction limited to the zone south of 17° N. Complete sovereignty was transferred by France in December 1954.

For a little over twenty years after the Geneva agreements, the area south of the seventeenth parallel remained a separate state with an anti-communist administration supported by the United States. A French community continued to look after its own interests there, notably the large rubber estates north of Saigon. But economically, culturally, and above all militarily, South Viet-Nam moved out of the French world into the American sphere of influence, developing much closer relations with other pro-U.S. states: the Philippines, Thailand, South Korea. It very soon became dependent for its survival on U.S. aid.

From 1954 to 1963, the politics of South Viet-Nam were dominated by Ngo Dinh Diem and his brother Nhu. Coming from a family of Catholic mandarins (a combination characteristic of the colonial period), Diem had been a minister at Hué briefly in 1933 but had since become strongly anti-French, as well as being deeply anti-communist. From the United States' point of view this made him an apparently ideal choice for leadership of a nationalist state in Viet-Nam, and he became Prime Minister at the behest of the U.S.A. in June 1954. For the next year and more his position was very insecure; but after careful political manoeuvring and several street battles, he defeated the leaders of the sects and of the Binh-Xuyen secret society that had controlled the Saigon underworld. In October 1955 he was strong enough to hold a referendum, the result of which enabled him to depose Bao-Dai and to proclaim himself President of the Republic of Viet Nam. He went on to repudiate the Geneva declaration and to reject any idea of holding the elections which it had envisaged for July 1956. During the next few years, he set about destroying the Viet-Minh (or, as he labelled it, Viet-Cong) network in the South. By 1959, the Communists and their sympathizers who had remained in the South in 1954 were under severe pressure from the Diem regime; numbers of them were imprisoned, along with many more "suspects". During 1959 the Communists, with the approval of Hanoi, decided to fight back by means of a low-level guerrilla war which would at least prevent their total annihilation. By 1960 it became clear that there would be a serious armed confrontation between the two sides, and in December of that year the Communists created the National Front for the Liberation of South Viet-Nam, to unite opposition to Diem.

American determination to prevent any communist advance in South-East Asia led President Kennedy to take a firm line during 1961–62 and by the end of 1962 there were about 8,000 United States troops serving as advisers to the South Vietnamese army. During 1963 this conflict became even more intense. But by that time United States confidence in Ngo Dinh Diem himself was beginning to decline. In May 1963 a Buddhist demonstration in Hué precipitated a conflict between the Catholic President and the Buddhist sects. The U.S.A. withdrew support from Diem, and in November 1963 he was overthrown by a military coup with their tacit approval. But a change of government in Saigon was no solution to the principal problem for the United States: how to protect the Saigon Government against a growing rural guerrilla movement. During the autumn of 1963 the communists adopted a more offensive strategy and by the end of the year the situation for Saigon was precarious. French proposals to neutralize Viet-Nam were unacceptable to the United States; and, soon after the death of U.S. President Kennedy, the next President, Lyndon Johnson, committed the U.S.A. to a policy of defending South Viet-Nam at all costs.

Nor was it easy to create a stable regime with Diem gone. A second military coup in January 1964 brought to power General Nguyen Khanh. But he retained his dominant position for barely a year, during which he was almost overthrown by the other generals in August 1964 when he tried to make himself president. In February 1965 he was forced out by a group of younger officers led by the air force commander

Nguyen Cao Ky. A nominally civilian government under Phan Huy Quat was followed, in June 1965, by a new military regime, with Lt.-Gen. Nguyen Van Thieu as Head of State and Air General Nguyen Cao Ky as Prime Minister.

By that time the U.S.A. had made up its mind to reinforce the Saigon government by sending its own combat troops to fight in Viet-Nam. An incident involving U.S. ships in the Gulf of Tongking in August 1964 enabled President Johnson to obtain virtually a free hand from Congress, and he used the power granted to him at that time to deal with the Vietnamese situation without any formal declaration of war. The number of American forces in Viet-Nam increased from 23,000 at the beginning of 1965 to over half a million by March 1968; in addition, contingents were sent from South Korea, Australia, the Philippines and Thailand. The conflict, as a result, escalated into a war of major proportions, with the Communists obliged to send regular North Vietnamese troops to the South, and to rely increasingly on aid from China and the Soviet Union. In addition to sending troops to the South, the U.S.A. also bombed the North from the air, beginning in March 1965.

Escalation of the war continued during 1966 and 1967, but those years also saw the gradual return of a measure of stability to the political scene in Saigon, where Nguyen Cao Ky defeated a Buddhist revolt during the spring of 1966. Out of the crisis, there emerged the promise of a new constitution for South Viet-Nam, and it came into effect in 1967. As a result General Nguyen Van Thieu was elected President in September 1967, with General Ky as his Vice-President; elections were also held for the upper and lower houses of a legislature based on the American model. Thieu remained the President from October 1967 until April 1975, being re-elected unopposed (after splitting with General Ky) in October 1971.

The war reached a crisis point in January-February 1968, when the Communists launched an offensive to coincide with the lunar New Year (known as *Tet*). It was on a larger scale than any previous operation, and included attacks on Saigon, Hué and many other towns. There was also heavy fighting just south of the seventeenth parallel. The *Tet* offensive, although only a partial success, forced the United States to reconsider its policy. It is now clear that Secretary of Defence Clark Clifford played a key role in the U.S. decision not to send any more troops to Viet-Nam, despite the request of General William Westmoreland, commander of the U.S. Military Assistance Command for an additional 200,000 men. At the end of March 1968 President Johnson announced a partial cessation of bombing raids over North Viet-Nam, thus opening the way to talks between American and North Vietnamese representatives which began in Paris in May 1968. The following October, Washington and Hanoi agreed to an enlargement of the talks and the United States thereupon ended completely its bombing raids against the North. Heavy bombing continued, however, to be an essential part of U.S. strategy in the South, and the talks led to no decrease in the fighting.

The transfer of power in the U.S.A. from President Johnson to President Nixon and his foreign policy adviser, Dr. Henry Kissinger, marked a turning-point not only for Viet-Nam, in the long run, but for the whole pattern of negotiations on world-wide issues between the United States and the Soviet Union. Almost immediately, on January 25th, 1969, the informal talks in Paris were transformed into a formal conference between representatives of the United States, North Viet-Nam, South Viet-Nam and the National Liberation Front. In June 1969 the NLF was supplemented by the creation of a new Provisional Revolutionary Government of South Viet-Nam. During 1969–70 the war dragged on. The most important change was that the United States began to withdraw its own troops and to pursue a policy of "Vietnamization". At the same time, fears that the North Vietnamese might take advantage of the withdrawal led to a sequence of moves by the U.S.A. which tended in fact to intensify the war. The most spectacular was the invasion of Cambodia in April 1970, following American-supported moves to overthrow the Government of Prince Sihanouk in Phnom-Penh. Equally important was the "Lam-Son" operation of February 1971 in Laos, which damaged North Vietnamese supply lines even though it ended in South Vietnamese retreat. By this time the communist war effort in the South was very largely dependent on the presence of North Vietnamese regular troops.

In March 1972, with U.S. forces reduced to about 95,000, the North Vietnamese launched a new offensive which led to some of the most intense fighting of the war. Quang-Tri, the northernmost provincial capital in the South, was totally destroyed: after falling to the Communists in May it was recaptured by the South Vietnamese army in September. There was also fierce fighting at An-Loc, north of Saigon, where the offensive was defeated only with the aid of massive U.S. air power. U.S. troops were not in the forefront of the ground fighting, but the United States reacted to the offensive by renewing its bombing of the North and by mining Haiphong and other harbours. By September it was clear that the situation had reached stalemate, whilst in the United States itself there was mounting pressure to bring the war to a speedy end. Secret meetings in Paris between Dr. Kissinger and Mr. Le Duc Tho of the Vietnamese Politburo had taken place several times since 1969. They now began to bear fruit, following Dr. Kissinger's visit to Moscow in September 1972. By November an agreement seemed to have been reached; but in December 1972, for reasons which have still to be made clear, American planes conducted the heaviest bombing raids of the war against North Viet-Nam. Only after that was the ceasefire agreement finally signed in Paris in January 1973.

The Paris Agreement provided for the complete withdrawal of all U.S. troops from Viet-Nam, together with the return of U.S. prisoners of war, by the end of March 1973. That part of the agreement was largely fulfilled, although the Communists later accused the United States of keeping some military personnel in Viet-Nam disguised as civilians. But the remaining terms of the agreement, including provisions for political freedom in the South and the creation of a national council of reconciliation and concord, were virtually ignored during the next two years. Further talks between Kissinger and Tho produced a supplementary agreement in June 1973, but the effect was only temporary. For the United States the war was over. Since 1961 they had suffered 45,941 combat deaths and over 10,000 deaths from other causes in Viet-Nam, as well as 150,000 casualties serious enough to require hospital treatment. In the same period, probably well over a million Vietnamese on both sides had been killed in the war.

For the Vietnamese, in any case, the war was not yet over. Despite protests by President Thieu, the Paris Agreement provided for a ceasefire in place, with limitations on the introduction of more arms but without any requirement that North Vietnamese forces be withdrawn from the South. Nor was there any provision for action by the U.S.A. to enforce the agreement, and in July 1973 the United States Congress made any further U.S. military action in Indochina illegal. The International Commission set up to supervise the ceasefire was not able to prevent frequent outbreaks of fighting between the two sides, whilst the North Vietnamese were now free to make preparations, in their own liberated areas, for an eventual final offensive. Towards the end of 1974, more serious fighting began and in January 1975 the entire province of Phuoc-Long was taken by the Communists. In March their capture of the highland centre of Ban Me Thuot threw the forces of President Thieu completely off balance and led him to order the virtual evacuation of all the Central Highlands. Within weeks the retreat became a rout, so that by the end of March the Communists controlled Hué and Da Nang and were advancing southwards along the coast. In April they threatened Saigon, overcoming the only significant resistance at Xuan-Loc, Thieu resigned, to be succeeded for a few days by his Vice-President and then by Gen. Duong Van Minh. By April 30th, 1975, the Americans had evacuated the last members of their embassy and other personnel and the Communists had entered Saigon. Although not yet formally reunified, Viet-Nam was now controlled entirely by the Communists and its ideological partition was at an end.

NORTH VIET-NAM

During the same twenty-year period following the Geneva Agreements, Viet-Nam north of the seventeenth parallel underwent a political and social revolution under a Communist-led regime. The first steps towards this were already being taken in the liberated areas from 1953, the date of an Agrarian Reform Law designed to revolutionize the pattern of land distribution and of agricultural production. This land reform programme was interrupted during the period immediately after the Geneva Agreement, but was resumed and completed throughout the North in 1955–56. There has been much controversy about the reform, and the Government subsequently admitted a number of excesses in its application, but its object was to eliminate as a class the landlords and rich peasants who—often through money-lending as much as through actual ownership of land—had dominated the economic life of the villages. Land was confiscated and redistributed, and in many cases the former owners were publicly disgraced. The most significant aspect of the reform was that it made possible a social revolution in the countryside. It was followed in 1959–60 by a movement for co-operativization.

In 1955 Ho Chi Minh visited the U.S.S.R. and China and signed aid agreements with both countries, in preparation for a national economic plan for 1956–57. There followed a Three-Year Plan in 1958–60, and a Five-Year Plan beginning in 1961, both of which made some progress towards developing agricultural and industrial production using a limited amount of material and technical aid from the major Communist countries. But these programmes were always accompanied by a sense of frustration that the southern half of the country, with its agricultural surplus, was separated from the North both politically and economically by the Geneva partition and by the impossibility of implementing those parts of the agreement relating to reunification.

The detailed political history of North Viet-Nam after 1954 has yet to be written, and there is still much that is unknown to outsiders. But it is clear that, within the revolutionary framework of the Lao-Dong party and its objectives, there have been several occasions of conflict within the leadership. Probably the first major crisis occurred in 1957, after it became clear that the South was not going to collapse and that the elections envisaged by the Geneva Agreements for 1956 would never be held. There was a conflict of priorities between the desire to press on with socialist revolution in the North, and the policy of "completing the revolution" in the South and bringing about national reunification. It was probably not finally settled until 1960, when the Hanoi leaders decided on a combination of support for the National Liberation Front in the South, and the simultaneous implementation of the Five-Year Plan in the North.

During 1960, indeed, the political life of the Democratic Republic of Viet-Nam took on a more settled pattern. At the beginning of that year a new Constitution came into effect, and in May elections were held for a new National Assembly to take the place of the one elected in 1946. Its first session in July endorsed a new distribution of power and responsibilities amongst the top leaders, whilst the Third National Congress of the Lao-Dong Party in September 1960 established the broad framework of policy within which the country was to develop, despite the ravages of war, over the next fifteen years. Taken together, these meetings established a balance of personalities in the top leadership which was to last for the next two decades.

The policy adopted in 1960 assumed a substantial measure of economic and military aid from the Soviet Union, which was apparently negotiated by Ho Chi Minh on a visit to Moscow that year. It meant, however, that the Vietnamese, seeking to continue good relations with both the U.S.S.R. and China, were very vulnerable in the face of a growing split between the two major Communist powers. Ho Chi Minh made every effort to avoid a split, but by 1963 it was impossible to prevent it. The Vietnamese were reluctant to take sides when the Nuclear Test Ban treaty was signed in August 1963. By deciding not to sign, they appeared to be choosing China. However, following the fall of Khrushchev in October 1964, Vietnamese-Soviet relations improved. The escalation of the war in the South in 1965 made it imperative to secure more Soviet aid, and Hanoi sought to steer a difficult middle path of friendship with both Moscow and Beijing (Peking) for the next ten years.

The North was involved in the war as the "rear area" of the NLF, following a decision in 1960 that the South Vietnamese should, in principle, achieve their own revolution, with as much support from the North as they needed. By 1973 there were 150,000 regular North Vietnamese troops in the South, but their status there continued to be denied. The war seriously disrupted life in the North during the years of American bombing, from March 1965 until November 1968, and again in 1972, from May to October and in December. The latter raids were more devastating than the earlier series, but those of December 1972 also involved serious U.S. aircraft losses. During 1965–66, to defend the economy against this aerial bombardment, the Hanoi Government devised a system of decentralized activity which may well have long-term significance for economic development. However, by 1969, when Ho Chi Minh died, it became concerned about the possibility that in a more liberal system, capitalist agriculture might again take root. During 1969–70 Troung Chinh led a movement to create higher-level co-operatives and to limit the encroachments of individualism on the collective system. However, from mid-1970, and especially after 1974, it became clear that Le Duan was the dominant leader in the Party; he placed more emphasis on economic modernization than on ideological purity. The war in the South again intensified during 1971–72 and, even after the Paris agreement of January 1973, there continued to be a strong emphasis on combining defence and production.

THE SOCIALIST REPUBLIC OF VIET-NAM

The period from the fall of Saigon in April 1975 to mid-1976 was one of transition. At first it appeared that the northern and southern parts of the country might continue to have a separate existence for several years, although it was clear that the ultimate authority in both halves was a single united Party, with its Political Bureau and Secretariat in Hanoi and a southern bureau in Saigon (now renamed Ho Chi Minh City). In May 1975 revolutionary committees were created at all levels in the South, with (for a time) a military management committee for the conurbation of Saigon-Giadinh. The much-publicized "third force" in South Vietnamese politics was not allowed a significant political role, and even the Provisional Revolutionary Government did not emerge as a real centre of decision-making. On the other hand the South was recognized as having its own distinctive problems, arising from the fact that its "national democratic" revolution had still to be completed whereas the North was already in the stage of "socialist" revolution. A first priority in the South was to bring the economy under control, and, following the closure of private banks in August, there was a full-scale attack in September 1975 on the "comprador bourgeoisie" who had dominated the Saigon economy under Nguyen Van Thieu. They were accused of hoarding commodities and their stores were confiscated; their savings (in piastres) were rendered valueless by the introduction of a new currency which could more easily be regulated. Within the new framework of state banking and the new currency, however, it was permissible for small capitalist enterprises to continue operating and even to expand their activity. At the same time the state took steps to control, if not to own, capitalist enterprises left behind by foreign investment. Foreign banks and enterprises were no longer allowed. Another aspect of this period was the programme for "re-educating" the former members of the South Vietnamese "puppet" army and civil service, who in May and June were obliged to register themselves and then to report for political study courses. Many were subsequently released and rejoined their families, but some were held for longer periods in camps where study was combined with labour.

In November 1975 a reunification conference was held in Ho Chi Minh City, presided over by Truong Chinh (representing the North) and Pham Hung (representing the South), which formally decided that reunification should take place through elections to be held throughout the country during 1976. Accordingly, a single National Assembly was elected in April, and when it met in June 1976 it declared the inauguration of the Socialist Republic of Viet-Nam, with its capital in Hanoi. The new government included a few members of the former Provisional Revolutionary Government of South Viet-Nam, but it was dominated for the most part by the leaders of the former Democratic Republic and, in effect, of the Party's Political Bureau. The Assembly also set up a committee to draft a new constitution, but it soon became clear that that would be a controversial and possibly long drawn out procedure.

Reunification had important implications for the Party and, after some hesitation, it finally held its long-awaited Fourth National Congress in December 1976. In redefining the Party line for the new stage of the revolution, the Congress took a number of decisions about its own membership and reorganization, and also about the principles of economic planning and the role of the army. It was decided that the immediate economic priorities were the development of agriculture and light industry, with heavy industry (the ultimate goal) taking second place for the time being.

External economic relations, however, remained a serious problem. One school of thought favoured strengthening Viet-Nam's position vis-à-vis the non-communist world, and to that end Viet-Nam sought (and gained) membership of the IMF and the World Bank. In spring 1977 Pham Van Dong paid visits to France and Scandinavia, seeking Western investment in Vietnamese industrial projects. During the same year there were moves towards the "normalization" of relations between Viet-Nam and the U.S.A., which abandoned its opposition to Vietnamese membership of the UN. Viet-Nam was subsequently admitted to the UN in September 1977. However, Congress had voted in May 1977 to forbid aid to Viet-Nam, thus preventing normalization, while the Vietnamese, until mid-1978, made the establishment of full diplomatic relations conditional on aid.

A trend towards increased dependence on the Soviet Union began with the Party Central Committee's third plenum (June–July 1977) and was consolidated during Le Duan's visit to Moscow in November 1977, culminating in the decision of June 1978 to make Viet-Nam a full member of the CMEA. During the same period, a new phase of economic transformation began, and led eventually to the abolition of private trading and street markets in the South and the unification of the currencies (March–April 1978). These changes were accompanied by a programme to co-operativize agriculture and to transform private industry in the south, and to step up the "redeployment" of labour from cities to the New Economic Zones.

It is now clear that the economic decisions of mid-1977 were part of a much more fundamental shift in Viet-Nam's orientation towards the Soviet Union and away from the People's Republic of China. When Pham Van Dong visited Beijing on his way home from Europe in June that year, the Chinese Vice-Premier, Li Xiannian, presented a memorandum on a number of issues; notably the question of Sino-Vietnamese borders (both on land and in the Gulf of Bac-Bo), and the problem of citizenship of Chinese residents living in Viet-Nam. The Chinese argued that satisfactory agreements on these matters had been reached in the mid-1950s, but that since 1974–75 the Vietnamese had been inclined to go back on them. Although these issues were not referred to publicly by either side, the situation between the former allies was now becoming tense. The Party plenum held shortly after Pham Van Dong's return to Hanoi made no conciliatory moves towards China; from that point on the situation grew steadily worse. A third issue was China's insistence on maintaining close relations with the Pol Pot regime in Kampuchea, which by this time was positively hostile towards Viet-Nam. Indeed, as time went on it became clear that their respective military campaigns of late 1974 and early 1975 had been undertaken in competition with one another rather than in collaboration. It was later revealed that border clashes had already occurred soon after the takeover of Saigon and Phnom-Penh. It would seem that the main difference between the Vietnamese and the Chinese over Kampuchea was that the former wanted to draw Phnom-Penh into close ties with Viet-Nam and Laos—perhaps even a virtual "Indochinese Federation"—whereas the Chinese wished to maintain direct relations with Kampuchea and Laos independently of Hanoi.

Attempts to settle the question of Kampuchea by negotiations failed during 1976–77, and from September 1977 there was a growing military confrontation between them. The fighting was publicly revealed at the end of the year, and continued throughout 1978. The Pol Pot forces, with Chinese aid, held their own against a series of Vietnamese attacks along their common border, until it became clear in late 1978 that the Chinese were unable or unwilling to escalate their own military involvement, and it was impossible for the Kampucheans to hold out indefinitely. In December 1978 the Vietnamese invaded, ostensibly in support of a Kampuchean National United Front for National Salvation, and gained control of Phnom-Penh and other major centres during the early part of 1979. They thereby enabled a pro-Vietnamese government under Heng Samrin to take over, although Pol Pot forces continued to resist in more remote areas. In February 1979 this government signed a treaty of friendship with Viet-Nam, comparable to that already signed with Laos, and was willing to accept the continuing presence of Vietnamese forces which by mid-1981 were said to number 200,000.

By that time relations with the People's Republic of China had deteriorated drastically. The socialist measures introduced in early 1978 affected especially the Chinese community in southern Viet-Nam. This fact, combined with fears among Chinese in northern Viet-Nam that sooner or later there might be a Sino-Vietnamese war, led to a major exodus of Chinese residents. Between April and July 1978 (when China closed its border), 160,000 of them had fled by land into Guangxi Zhuang, Guangdong and Yunnan; others began to leave by sea, hoping to find refuge elsewhere in South-East Asia. Until this point the Chinese had continued to give economic aid to Viet-Nam, although less than they were said to have originally promised. However, between May and July 1978 they pulled out all their technicians and abandoned all projects, leaving the Vietnamese more dependent than ever on the Soviet Union and Eastern Europe. The Chinese were especially angered by Viet-Nam's decision to join the CMEA and feared that their next move would be to grant military facilities to Soviet naval and air forces. Although they denied any intention of doing this, on November 3rd, 1978, Le Duan and Pham Van Dong signed a formal Treaty of Friendship and Co-operation with the Soviet Union in Moscow, which aligned Viet-Nam with Moscow politically if not militarily.

The Chinese reacted strongly to the situation which had emerged by early 1979: they were dissatisfied with Viet-Nam's invasion of Kampuchea, with its orientation towards Moscow, and with its treatment of Chinese residents; and by now there were also serious frontier clashes. On February 17th Chinese forces actually invaded Viet-Nam to "teach it a lesson", and fierce fighting lasted for a month. After capturing the town of Lang-Son, but also suffering heavy casualties, the Chinese withdrew on March 17th, 1979. The conflict then eased somewhat, and talks were held between the two sides in Hanoi from April 18th to May 18th. They produced no formal agreement but it was decided on May 26th to start the exchange of prisoners of war.

Strained relations with China led to increased conflict within the Vietnamese Communist Party, and in July 1979 the most "pro-Chinese" of the Party's original founders, Hoang Van Hoan, fled to China via Pakistan. His denunciation of his former colleagues led to the publication of the Vietnamese "White Book" of October 1979, whose revelations implied several periods of disagreement with the Chinese Party, going back at least to the early 1960s. Hoan was sentenced to death *in absentia* in June 1980.

Meanwhile, Vietnamese policy towards the Chinese residents (also known as "Hoa" people) had become so severe that vast numbers of them were taking to ships in the South China Sea, hoping to reach land or to be picked up by larger vessels. It was said that the Vietnamese authorities had now ceased to object to their leaving, but charged large sums in gold or dollars for exit papers. More Chinese also crossed into the People's Republic of China at this time. By mid-1979 it was estimated that there were 200,000 such refugees from Viet-Nam in China, and perhaps another 200,000 had reached other countries of South-East Asia, Hong Kong, Taiwan or Australia. Many more thousands were thought to have drowned at sea. The exodus attained the proportions of an international crisis in July, when a UN conference was convened to discuss the problem. As a result of the conference Viet-Nam agreed to halt the exodus for a temporary period to allow the UN High Commissioner for Refugees to seek more effective measures to bring the situation under control. Nevertheless, some refugees were still leaving the country during 1980–82.

Important political changes occurred during 1980–81, starting with a government reshuffle in January 1980 which replaced three prominent cabinet members. A few months later the death of President Ton Duc Thang was announced; Nguyen Huu Tho acted in his place, but was not confirmed in the appointment. In December 1980, after four years of debate, a new constitution was finally adopted, under which a newly elected National Assembly met in July 1981 and appointed both a State Council (which was to constitute a collective presidency) and a new Council of Ministers. Despite some speculation about the promotion of younger men, Truong Chinh moved up to become Chairman of the former, and therefore Head of State, while Pham Van Dong remained Prime Minister with slightly reduced powers. Le Duan, still dominant in the Party, was not included in either of the principal state organs. During 1982 Truong Chinh appeared to play an increasingly prominent role and his position was probably strenthened further by changes in the composition of the State Council in June of that year.

The Party's Fifth Congress, twice postponed, was eventually held at the end of March 1982. In the interval it became clear, from the reports of preparatory congresses at provincial level, that the Party was deeply divided and that some elements in the leadership were being blamed for the country's severe economic failures. When the Congress finally met, a number of prominent figures were dropped from the new Politburo (including Vo Nguyen Giap) and others from the Central Committee. Behind the façade of unity, which in the end was preserved at the Congress itself, there was believed to be acute rivalry between the surviving top leaders, notably Le Duan, Le Duc Tho and Truong Chinh. A number of younger men were promoted, but the generation of the 1950s had still not finally relinquished control.

Kampuchea remained a problem for the Vietnamese. The presence of 200,000 troops was reportedly reduced by 15–20,000 men in June 1982 (subsequently doubted), but still met resistance from *Khmer Rouge* forces. The resulting tension between Thailand and Viet-Nam, which became serious from June 1980, led to the greater involvement of ASEAN countries over the Kampuchean question, which resulted in a coalition-in-exile in June 1982. The Vietnamese boycotted an ASEAN-sponsored conference on the issue at the UN in July 1981, which issued a communiqué calling for the removal of Vietnamese forces from Kampuchea and for free elections. Relations with China remained tense, with more border clashes in May 1981, while the alliance with the Soviet Union became closer, not only politically but also economically and culturally. Russian became the principal foreign language taught in Vietnamese schools, an estimated 50,000 Vietnamese were working in Eastern bloc countries, and there were said to be several thousand Soviet advisers of various kinds in Indochina as a whole. The U.S.A., meanwhile, refused to restore relations with Viet-Nam so long as the Kampuchean question remained unresolved.

ECONOMIC SURVEY

Ralph Smith

(Revised since 1981 by Harvey Demaine)

BACKGROUND: REGIONAL CONTRASTS

In its present transitional stage, the Vietnamese economy reflects important contrasts between different regions of the country, which are partly the result of geography but also in part the outcome of political partition between 1954 and 1976. The two most important natural differences are those between lowland and upland areas, and between lowland areas with different densities of population. In general, the lowlands have been settled longest and are predominantly concerned with wet rice agriculture, as well as having the principal urban concentrations. Other areas, especially those often referred to by the Vietnamese as "midlands" (between the flat plains and the true hill areas), offer opportunities for new settlement and development and are now an important focal point of economic effort. However, there are also differences within the lowlands, especially between the very densely populated areas of the North and Centre (Bac-Bo and Trung-Bo, formerly Tongking and Annam) and the less densely settled areas of the South (Nam-Bo). The latter region became Vietnamese only after about 1700, and much of it came under cultivation only during the French colonial period; some areas are still available for new settlement or can be made to yield greater productivity. In the French period, it was the South which exported rice on a large scale, whereas the Centre and North were rice deficit areas. The export trade was disrupted by war after 1940, however, and during the war against the U.S.A. agricultural production in the South was so badly damaged that rice had to be imported even there.

Politically, the colonial economy was succeeded in 1954 by two utterly different regimes to the north and south of the 17th parallel. In the South, with U.S. backing both militarily and economically, the Governments of Ngo Dinh Diem (1954–63), Nguyen Khanh (1964–65), Nguyen Cao Ky (1965–67) and Nguyen Van Thieu (1967–75) sought to create a "free world" economy which would participate in international trade and investment, and would eventually aim at development along capitalist lines. The growing burden of war from 1959–60, however, made it increasingly difficult for them to achieve any significant economic objectives without massive U.S. aid. As a result, by 1975 the South had a highly artificial economy whose future was rather uncertain, even if it had remained independent. In the North, on the other hand, the Communist regime which took over from the French in 1954 was devoted to the "socialist transformation" of the economy; to be followed by "socialist construction" on the Soviet or Chinese model, with economic and technical aid from the Communist bloc. It too suffered serious disruption from the war, especially during the periods of severe U.S. bombing in 1965–68 and 1972; but it made progress towards socialist development in certain respects during the 21 years of partition.

The combination of natural regional variations and political partition tended to distort economic development throughout the 20 years from 1955 to 1975. Despite frequent requests from Hanoi from 1955–58 for "normalization" of economic relations between the zones, the Diem regime refused to permit even limited trade between North and South. Some observers suggested that the rice deficit in the North was an important factor driving the Communists to resume armed struggle at the end of 1958. In any case, it was impossible to combine the theoretical capacity of the South to export primary produce with the potential of the North for industrial development, so that, by 1975, when re-unification occurred, the economies of the two zones were not complementary as before, and were structurally so different that it was impossible to incorporate them into a single system for planning. In fact, it has become increasingly clear that, in the initial period after 1975. Viet-Nam was willing to seek a compromise between the two systems, but it was subsequently decided to speed up "socialization" of the South during 1978. Even so a number of significant differences remain.

Since reunification there have been moves to develop a new overall economic pattern, notably through the movement of population to areas of under-developed resource potential. The full census of the country in October 1979 revealed a total population of 52.7 million, rather higher than anticipated, and rising at an estimated rate of 2.8 per cent per annum. This represents an increase of some 1.5 million people per year, giving a mid-1982 population of perhaps 56.4 million. Population distribution, however, remains very uneven: an average density of 160 persons per square kilometre (1979) hides variations between very thinly populated areas of the northern hills and Central Highlands and concentrations of up to 1,500 persons per square kilometre in parts of the Red River delta (Thai Binh province as a whole has 1,120 persons per square kilometre). Moreover, the South had suffered severe dislocation in rural areas during the later stages of the war (especially from 1968) and many people had fled to the towns and cities. Saigon's population rose from 2 to 4 million, and by 1975 the unemployment problem there was severe. In order to redress some of the imbalance, in 1975–76 the Government embarked on a policy of creating New Economic Zones (NEZs), particularly in the South, and redeploying labour from the southern cities and from the densely populated northern plains. Although the objective of resettling 4 million people by 1980 has been too ambitious, it is stated that a total of 1.4 million people were moved in the course of the 1976–80 Plan, 711,000 of them to the NEZs in the south. In 1981 a further 160,000 people were settled, with a target, rather unrealistically, of 620,000. Nevertheless the magnitude of the problem may be assessed by the fact that in the meantime the number of people working in agriculture is said to have risen by a full 4 million and the population of Ho Chi Minh City (Saigon) remained at 3.4 million in 1979.

SOCIALIST TRANSFORMATION AND PLANNING

In conformity with the principles of Marxism-Leninism, as they have been applied in predominantly agrarian societies, the economic revolution in Viet-Nam involves two phases: "socialist transformation" in order to destroy the "feudal" and "capitalist" elements in the pre-revolutionary society; and "socialist construction", based on State control and planning. Since 1980, however, it may be suggested that the country has entered a third phase, characterized by a greater pragmatism in its economic system.

Because of the period of partition, the actual chronology of the economic revolution has been different between the two zones. In North Viet-Nam the first phase of "socialist transformation" began in the early 1950s, even before the French withdrawal from Hanoi. A two-stage land reform was implemented in areas already under Viet-Minh control: first mass mobilization for rent reduction, then actual confiscation and redistribution of land. The Vietnamese at this stage followed the Maoist model of creating a mass movement in the villages, putting landlords on trial and in some cases punishing them as counter-revolutionaries. Although the process began in an orderly fashion in the years 1953–55, it was speeded up after mid-1955 and led to serious "excesses" which had to be corrected during a rectification drive in 1956–57. The result of this phase was to redistribute large amounts of land and to eliminate both landlords and rich peasants as a class. In all, the land reform programme was said to have distributed some 810,000 hectares of land to approximately 2.1 million peasant families. The programme thus in no way solved the basic problem of small, scarcely-viable holdings in the northern agricultural sector and was merely a prelude to the co-operativization movement. A start was also made on creating mutual aid teams to develop a pattern of co-operative labour. The next phase came in 1958–60, with the co-operativization of most of the agriculture of the North, but by bureaucratic methods rather than by mass mobilization. Such co-operatives have remained the basis of organization of this region's agriculture up to the present.

It seems clear, however, that the co-operatives as a whole have not been outstandingly successful in ensuring the necessary increases in agricultural production. Since late 1980 there have been increasingly frank criticisms of their performance and as many as 70 per cent have been described as being in a "weak" condition. It has been admitted that the peasants have shown little general enthusiasm for working co-operative land on the basis of work points, the allocation of which has reportedly been abused. These deficiencies have led to the re-emergence of the system of "contracting-out" of co-operative land to individual families or small production teams, which in 1968 had resulted from the decentralization of the economy under the impact of the bombing. This practice had been condemned by Truong Chinh, who, as Secretary-General of the Party before 1956 and as Deputy Premier in 1958–60, had feared that it would lead to a return to rural capitalism and secured the enactment of new regulations for agricultural co-operatives (promulgated in August 1969), which forbade such contracts. It now appears that the State has accepted the system in the hope that it will relieve some of the problems in the agricultural sector, although various leaders continue to emphasise the need for strict control over the practice. In general the contracts are given for families to work the land after the initial land preparation stages of cultivation, on the basis that a certain production quota must be given to the State via the co-operative, although any excess may be sold by the peasants on the open market, in much the same way as the produce from private plots which were untouched by the earlier phrases of co-operativization. There was a move to abolish trading in agricultural produce, starting in 1968, but it proved difficult to eliminate the "black market" entirely, even in the North. Compared with agriculture, it proved relatively easy to co-operativize handicrafts and nationalize existing industry, and to ensure that all new industrial development took place under State control.

In the South the pattern of land reform based on mass campaigns against landlords and rich peasants was not repeated; instead, "socialist transformation" was conducted along bureaucratic lines. It should be noted that by 1975 the large landowners of the French period had already been eliminated by the Thieu government's "land to the tiller" law of 1970. That had abolished absentee landlordism but the maximum permitted holdings still allowed rich peasants to prosper. On the other hand, many landless people had migrated to the cities during the war against the U.S.A., without necessarily finding work. The new regime in 1975 decided to allow peasant ownership of land to continue for the time being, but began to control the market for produce. A "moderate" policy towards private participation in industry was also followed during 1975–77. In July 1977, however, it was decided to accelerate the process of "socialist transformation" in the South and, by the end of that year over 600 agricultural co-operatives had been created in the South, and 9,000 "production collectives", as well as many more thousands of "production solidarity terms". It was planned to have the transformation of agriculture complete by the end of 1980. Transformation of industry proceeded more gradually but in the sphere of commerce it was decided to abolish all private enterprise at one fell swoop on March 23rd, 1978. The measure took effect in April, and was followed by the announcement in May that henceforth the two halves of the country would have the same currency. (A new but still separate currency had been introduced in the South in September 1975.) The abolition of private trading affected about 30,000 families, many of them Chinese, in Ho Chi Minh City (formerly Saigon) and other towns. The change was an important factor in the mass exodus of Chinese from about that time, although it should be recognized that the latter also had political aspects.

"Socialist construction" required a planning system, which began to evolve in the North after 1955. It was decided in 1958 to embark on some constructive development even before the completion of "socialist transformation", and this led to the Three-Year Plan of 1958–60. It placed most emphasis on agriculture and light industry, but aimed at more than the mere restoration of pre-war levels of production. An important consequence of partition was that the North, formerly a rice deficit area, had to develop agriculture in order to feed itself. At the Third Party Congress in 1960, however, it was resolved that the first Five-Year Plan (1961–65) should give priority to heavy industry, in particular steel and engineering. This policy continued in principle until the intensification of the war in 1965; modifications were made in 1963, when agriculture experienced a major crisis. From then onwards it was accepted that, insofar as it received priority, industry must "serve agriculture". In the circumstances of war and bombing it was not feasible to start a new Five-Year Plan in

1966: indeed, much that had been built was destroyed in the years that followed. Instead, the period 1965–67 saw an important new pattern of development based on the principle of decentralization. Many economic activities were moved away from the larger cities, and new small and medium-sized enterprises were developed in the provinces and districts. Long before the U.S.A. bombed the oil depots near Hanoi in mid-1966, storage of fuel and other essential items had been decentralized and placed underground. These changes were to have long-term effects. In 1970, in an important analysis of the economy, Le Duan emphasized the value of continuing to balance the central and regional levels of the economy; during the 1970s it was decided to make the district a unit of "agro-industrial" development, and to co-ordinate the development of agriculture and industry at province level. Only certain major projects, including heavy industry, were left to be managed by central administration.

The second Five-Year Plan was designated for the years 1976–80 (corresponding to the Soviet and East European planning cycle), but its content was still being debated throughout 1976 and it was not formally approved until the Fourth Party Congress in December that year. By then the formal incorporation of the South into a united Viet-Nam meant that the Plan was broadened into what is now considered as the First National Plan. The new Plan continued to pay lip service to the concept of heavy industry, but in practice it retreated from the ambitious objectives of 1960–63. Much greater emphasis was to be placed on agriculture and light industry, which would contribute both to the improvement of material living standards within Viet-Nam and to the development of exports to earn foreign exchange. In this context, the South was to revert to its former role as the main supplier of the nation's food needs, as well as the source of agricultural exports and light industrial goods. The Plan ran into difficulties in 1977–78, however, and targets were drastically revised. While one of the reasons for this may have been the disastrous weather of these two years, it now seems that the Plan depended heavily on foreign investments, the bulk of which it was anticipated would come from the U.S.A. With the U.S.A. refusing to normalize relations, none of this aid has been forthcoming and foreign aid in general has been further reduced in reaction to Viet-Nam's action in invading Kampuchea. This and the subsequent war and general state of hostility with the People's Republic of China has drawn further resources away from the economic development effort and it is now estimated that over 40 per cent of the country's budget is being spent on defence. In such circumstances, it is hardly surprising that most of the Plan targets were subsequently revised and abandoned.

In 1980 discussions began on the Second National Plan (1981–85), also to be set within the framework of the CMEA, but this was finally revealed only at the Fifth Party Congress in March–April 1982. The delay of over a year probably relates to the failure of Viet-Nam's CMEA partners to confirm their aid commitments. Even now, the Plan remains more a statement of intentions than a detailed outline for action, but it is neverthelss clear that the new Plan will be much less ambitious than its ill-starred predecessor. Many grandiose construction projects have been suspended, while the emphasis is on small, practical projects within Viet-Nam's capabilities and, in sectoral terms, on agriculture, consumer goods industries, energy, exports and communications.

The army plays a significant role in the economy, particularly in agriculture, where it is active in the clearing of the land in advance of civilian settlement of the NEZs and state farms.

AGRICULTURE AND FOOD

Estimates by the FAO for 1979 indicated a total cultivable area of 5.9 million hectares, of which as much as 455,000 hectares may now be under permanent crops. These figures do not fully accord with recent reports of a national land survey, taken in 1979, which places the area of agricultural land at 6,954,000 hectares. The same survey notes that some 3.6 million hectares of unused land are suitable for cultivation, but this total certainly includes some of the 4.87 million hectares designated by FAO as "permanent meadows and pastures". What does seem certain is that the area cultivated is slowly expanding, mainly in the NEZs of the Mekong Delta and Central Highlands, where the main crops are rice and perennials (tea, coffee, oil palm, rubber) respectively.

By far the greatest part of the arable land is used for rice cultivation and in many areas it is possible to harvest two crops per year from the same land. Thus FAO estimates that, in 1980, the gross cultivated area was at least 7.6 million hectares, with rice occupying some 5.74 million hectares. As much as 50 per cent of the rice land is now said to be double-cropped. This is an age-old practice in most of Bac-Bo (and parts of Trung-Bo) wherever there is a double monsoon or where water can be transferred by means of irrigation works. In recent years it has been possible to grow a second crop in many more areas, including for the first time parts of the Mekong Delta. Irrigation projects had high priority in the First National Plan (1976–80) and it was initially hoped to expand the area of irrigated riceland to 3.5 million hectares by 1980, of which 2.5 million would be capable of producing two crops per year. These figures had to be modified later, particularly as a result of the serious floods of 1978, which damaged existing irrigation and drainage works.

Such irrigation improvements would have facilitated the further spread of high-yielding varieties (HYVs) of rice, the introduction of which has been a feature of the period since the early 1970s. Although first introduced in the North in 1965, they were first planted on a large scale in response to the failure of the 1971 harvests (700,000 hectares in 1972). They were also introduced into the South in the pre-unification period, but some parts of the Mekong Delta are generally unsuited to such varieties. Thus, whereas it is intended that 63 out of 67 districts in the Red River Delta will have HYVs in 1982, only

47 out of 110 districts in the Mekong Delta will be so favoured. It is planned to extend HYVs to some 33 per cent of the total planted area by 1985, particularly in the Spring crop in the north. This development could increase yields in areas adopting the HYVs by 50–60 per cent or perhaps 1 ton or more per hectare over the current yields of 1.9–2.5 metric tons per hectare.

A significant area of arable land is devoted to dry crops, both North and South, and there have been significant increases in recent years with the colonization of the uplands. The FAO estimated that in 1980 there were 480,000 hectares of maize, 400,000 hectares of sweet potatoes, 480,000 hectares of cassava and 216,000 hectares of pulses. The importance of such crops was appreciated by Communist agricultural specialists as early as 1946, when (during the rule of the original Democratic Republic in the North) they feared a repetition of the previous year's famine after another bad rice harvest, and launched an emergency campaign to cultivate dry crops as widely as possible. Such secondary food crops were also important in the North during the worst years of the war against the U.S.A. (1965–68), when it was feared that the bombing of the dykes might at any time disrupt irrigated crops. Dry crops have again been promoted in the difficult years of the late 1970s, although it may be that, because of the lack of incentive in the rice sector, expansion in some areas may have taken place at the expense of a second crop of rice. Elsewhere, however, there has been an attempt to grow a third dry crop on land that has already grown two crops of wet rice.

Expansion of agriculture has been a continuing theme in Communist planning since the mid-1960s, and this has been stressed again in the Second National Plan (1981–85). The First National Plan (1976–80) originally aimed to expand food crop production from an actual 14.5 million tons in 1975 to 21 million tons by 1980, to include 12 million tons of paddy rice in 1975 and 17.5 million tons in 1980. However, this target has proved unattainable. Adverse weather conditions contributed to bad harvests in 1977 and 1978 and in the latter year the targets for 1979–80 were re-defined. Although the revised 1980 target for all food crops was only 15 million tons (of which rice accounted for 12 million tons), typhoons in the North and drought in the Centre ensured that only 13 million tons were produced. It is now widely accepted that the country is likely to have an overall grain shortage in 1980–81 of some 4.4 million tons, unlikely to be made good by the modest supplies of food aid available from the CMEA and international agencies like the World Food Programme. In 1980 indeed food aid from the Soviet Union dropped to only 860,000 tons compared to the 1.2 million tons of the previous year and it is clear that there will be shortages of food for the Vietnamese people. Already the basic food ration has dropped to a mere 13 kilogrammes of grain per person per month and in this ration the favoured rice is increasingly substituted by cassava and sweet potato. By mid-1981 there was widespread and serious malnutrition.

It is clear that weather conditions in recent years have been particularly unfavourable, but it is debatable whether the serious shortfalls in food production in Viet-Nam can be attributed solely to such events. The FAO, indeed, regards at least 2.4 million tons of the current grain deficit as "chronic", not caused merely by losses due to bad weather. The lack of incentive for workers under the work-point system, until recently used in the co-operatives to produce over and above their own requirements, seems to have been a major factor in the poor performance. Part of the deficit in 1979–80, indeed, may be related to the Government's failure to obtain its full quota of the rice production, particularly from the peasants in the South, from where there were reports of grain's being fed to livestock rather than being offered for sale at the prevailing unattractive prices.

It is to this end that an increased procurement price has now been offered for paddy and that the system of production contracts has been promoted in the agricultural sector. Initial results of the change have been encouraging. Food output reached 15.1 million tons in 1981, of which rice contributed 12.5 million tons, a 4 per cent increase on 1980. It is too early to see this improvement as the first stage in a major upturn leading to the achievement of the 1985 target of 19–20 million tons of grain. 1981 was also a year of reasonable weather and, despite the investment in water control facilities, Viet-Nam's agriculture remains at the mercy of the elements. Even in 1981, indeed, production in the South of the country declined for this reason.

Since upland areas are increasingly required for cash crops to pay for the imports now being received from the CMEA, further increases will depend on the progress of intensification through the introduction of HYVs. Achievement of the yield potential of the HYVs will, however, depend on the availability of technical inputs, such as fertilizers, water-pumps and mechanization of land preparation. Unfortunately, the much-proclaimed policy of developing industry to serve agriculture has been less than successful. Although production of phosphate fertilizers (in terms of phosphoric acid) rose from 41,000 tons in 1973 to 130,000 tons in 1978 and there was also growth of nitrogenous fertilizers, the total output of mineral fertilizers produced in 1981 was in fact far below the original 1980 target of 1.3 million tons. It is clear that fertilizers were still in short supply in 1981, with nitrate supplies only about one-half of total requirements, and 1982 has seen Viet-Nam seeking to import chemical fertilizers from abroad, most recently through a Swedish aid agreement. The problem is not likely to be solved easily. Not only is demand likely to grow through the proposed extension of HYVs and with the realization that upland soils used for dryland cash crops like cassava are now in need of rehabilitation, but the country is also badly short of the hydrocarbon base for nitrogen fertilizers. Perhaps one answer to the problem may be the wider use of green fertilizers, and Viet-Nam already has had experience in this direction following the agricultural crisis of 1963, with the development of the nitrogenous plant *Azolla pinata* as a natural fertilizer grown on flooded paddy fields. In the same context the recent expansion of soyabean cultivation may also be instructive.

The shortage of petroleum has also been a problem in the mechanization of agriculture. This was held back by both the small size of co-operatives (and of fields) in the North, and by the availability of tractors. In 1975 North Viet-Nam had 6,850 tractors, compared with 10 in 1959; an impressive increase, but not large when compared with the size of a problem relating to shortages of draught animals and a reduced male labour force resulting from military needs. It is uncertain, moreover, just how many tractors are currently serviceable and to what extent fuel is adequate for them. Suggestions are that only about one-half of agriculture's total requirements was available in 1980 and the same problem applies to the 23,694 water pumps, 9,237 shellers and 9,058 mechanical threshing machines claimed in 1975, especially with the diversion of fuel resources into warfare and national defence since 1978. Such shortages explain partially one of the recent shifts in policy to encourage individual production teams and families to breed draught animals, previously considered a specialist enterprise. Livestock are also needed for meat, but the recent military adventures have apparently also affected livestock production on which the First National Plan also had optimistic hopes of increasing the country's meat supply, especially from pigs. The Chinese invasion of 1979 alone is said to have led to the death of 250,000 head of cattle, and the further incidence of flooding, as well as a shortage of foodstuffs, has led to outbreaks of epidemics and policies of deliberate slaughter which have almost certainly reduced livestock numbers from their 1977 levels.

The other main element in food supply is fish, from both inland waters and the South China Sea. By 1975 shellfish were one of the principal exports from the South (and one which could still be maintained), with Japan as the most important buyer. However, fish, including the ubiquitous "nuoc-mam" sauce, was also an important source of protein in Viet-Nam's own diet. The catch in South Viet-Nam in 1973 was 713,500 metric tons, while a further 300,000 tons (FAO estimate) were caught in the North, giving a total of 1.0 million tons. The original target in the First National Plan was to increase this to 1.3 million tons, but the industry has been severely hit by the reduction in the number of boats through their use by refugees, by recent fuel shortages and, once again, by the lack of incentive in the procurement system. The target for 1982 of only 600,000 tons, of which 420,000 tons is to come from marine fisheries, is indicative of how substantial a decline has taken place. Here again, production contracts have been introduced in fishing co-operatives in an attempt to remedy the situation.

FORESTRY AND PLANTATIONS

The recent land survey of the country has put the total area of forest at 13.4 million hectares, rather more than the FAO estimates of 10.38 million hectares for 1979. It is not clear, however, to what extent the contrasting figures include forest lands degraded, either through hill agriculture or through bombing and firing, and therefore to what extent it constitutes a valuable economic resource. Certainly the Government sees the forests as such, but is at the same time concerned with what it terms "irrational exploitation" of them. Recent seminars in the forestry sector have condemned the separation of agriculture and forestry and there have been numerous calls for the institution of a system of forest farming, with the replanting of over 10 million hectares, both in the hills and along the mangrove coasts. This contrasts with the aim in the First National Plan to expand timber production, from the reported level of 1.57 million cubic metres in 1976 to 3.5 million cubic metres in 1980.

Such a policy may also conflict with the desire to increase production from the plantation sector, which has involved the colonization of a substantial area of upland for cultivation of crops such as tea and coffee, mostly in state farms in such provinces as Lam Dong, Thai Binh and Dong Nai. On the other hand, the plantation sector also suffered badly in the period of warfare. Rubber production from French-owned plantations in the South continued to constitute a significant export for that zone up to the early 1970s, but increasing damage and the unwillingness to invest in the replanting of ageing stock steadily reduced their role (though figures are not available). Since unification these estates have been nationalized and Viet-Nam has sought assistance from Malaysia for their rehabilitation. Such a rehabilitation throughout the sector would clearly have an impact upon production levels, although the bulk of any expansion in output seems to be destined to offset the aid given to Viet-Nam by the CMEA and would confirm the country's role as a producer of tropical primary produce in the socialist economic system.

MINING

Interest in mineral resources was one of the factors which drew French business—and also the French army and navy—to Tongking in the late 1880s. Their exploitation was an important feature of the colonial economy, and was further developed by the Japanese during their brief control of the region in 1940–45. The Vietnamese themselves have continued this development since the 1950s with the assistance of Soviet geologists. Tin, sometimes in association with tungsten (wolfram), is found in significant quantities in the area west of Cao Bang, where there have been recent operations to expand the Tinh Tuc mine. There are large reserves of zinc in the hills to the west of Lang Son. Important deposits of iron are being exploited near Thai Nguyen, and exploitation for more iron ore and pyrite ores was under way by 1979. Other minerals being exploited in some measure are antimony, chromium, apatite, other phosphates and bauxite. Manganese is also present, but was extracted in significant quantities only in the Japanese period.

The most important mining activity arises from the presence of extensive reserves of coal, including some of anthracite, in the Quang Yen basin, the Phan Me basin and Tuyen Quang. Coal mines were developed by the French at Cam Pha and Hon Gay, initially to supply their Far East fleet but later also for export. Output expanded considerably in recent years, rising from 3 million tons in 1973 to 6.2 million tons in 1977, but since then has stagnated, with 1980 output apparently at similar levels, lower than the revised target figure of 7.0 million tons. The target for 1982 has been set at 6.3 million tons. The shortfall may be chiefly attributed to the widespread withdrawal of Chinese labourers after the deterioration of Sino-Vietnamese relations in 1978–79. Coal exports, which are among Viet-Nam's major sources of foreign exchange, declined for three years in succession from 1977 to only 600,000 tons in 1980. However, with South Korea entering the market alongside Japan, the traditional customer, there are hopes for a return to export levels of 1 million tons in 1981.

Much more tentative is the objective of developing petroleum production. Soviet experts have played a part in on-shore prospecting and are said to have had some success in southern Bac-Bo, but off-shore exploration has been entirely undertaken by Western and Japanese oil firms. In 1973 North Viet-Nam entered into an arrangement with the Italian ENI organization for exploration in the Gulf of Bac-Bo and also the training of Vietnamese technicians in Milan. At about the same time, South Viet-Nam granted off-shore concessions to Mobil Oil, to be followed by others in 1974 to the Japanese consortium Kaiyo Oil and the French firm Aquitaine. Petroleum was struck at a point 190 km. southeast of the then Saigon in February 1975, but these operations came to an end with the fall of the Thieu regime. Since then, however, the Vietnamese have created a new Oil and Gas Agency which has renewed contacts with Western companies. Exploration has been carried out off the Mekong Delta by Canadian, German and Norwegian concerns, but so far has yielded no fresh discoveries and these companies have been unwilling to risk American sanction by working in the blocks already successfully drilled by United States companies. Since 1980 Viet-Nam has turned to the Soviet bloc for further assistance in this field, almost certainly under some pressure from a Soviet Union anxious to secure any likely resources. Although there must be some doubts about Soviet expertise in off-shore drilling, an agreement for a joint enterprise for exploration and exploitation was signed in June 1981. Under this agreement, there were suggestions that the U.S.S.R. would construct a refinery at Ho Chi Minh City; such proposals have been discounted in the initial commentaries on the Second National Plan, although Soviet technicians are planning to place a production system on a former Mobil well, and limited production is expected by 1983.

MANUFACTURING

Only a limited range of industrial activity was allowed to develop during the colonial period; it was against French principles to permit their colonies to develop industries that would compete with those of the metropolitan country in supplying the needs of France overseas. Apart from mining, the only significant industries in Indochina before 1940 were those of cement at Haiphong and textiles at Nam Dinh and Hanoi. New light industries were started on a small scale in the Japanese period owing to the breakdown of communications with France, to meet local needs for goods previously imported: paper and certain chemical products, for example. After 1954 the Vietnamese set out to develop both existing and new industries. In the South there was some development of light industry in the late 1950s and early 1970s, mainly related to the production or assembly of consumer goods and a cement works was established at Ha Tien near the Kampuchean border. When the Communists took over Saigon in 1975 they were at pains to ensure continuity of production and to prevent sabotage.

The main question of "socialist construction" concerned the attempt to create a heavy industrial base for the new economy; above all, whether socialism was possible without it. On the one hand, the Soviet model as developed by Stalin required such a base and implied that great sacrifices should be made in other areas in order to develop it. On the other hand, the U.S.S.R.'s international economic thinking of the 1960s and 1970s was tending to favour an international division of labour, which would place countries like Viet-Nam once again in the role of primary producers and suppliers of light industrial products to a wider market. The advocates of heavy industry won this debate in 1960, but much that was achieved before 1965 was reduced to rubble by the U.S. bombing. Since 1968 there has been a gradual decline in the emphasis on heavy industry and, although it has not been renounced altogether, it seems clear that one of the major emphases in the Second National Plan will be towards light and consumer goods industries in an effort to relieve the shortages of basic commodities which are leading to disillusion amongst the long-suffering population. To this end, in 1979 it was decided that family enterprises with fewer than 20 employees should be allowed to produce what they like, providing that taxes are fully paid, and it was recently estimated that as many as 2,000 new small enterprises have sprung up in Ho Chi Minh City alone.

Whether such moves will prove adequate to revitalize industry is, however, a problem. Many existing consumer industries inherited from the former regime in the South require the import of raw materials and parts from the West, for which foreign exchange is not available at present. Shortfalls in the agricultural sector have also affected supplies of raw materials, while the refugee outflow of 1979–81 has left the country short of a good many skilled workers and managerial staff. Equally, if not more serious, is the power shortage in the country which condemns many plants to work at only 30–40 per cent of total capacity. The growth of electric power generating capacity was always constrained in the North by air attack and by 1975 the total output of both zones of the country was only 3,000 million kWh. The planned target for 1980 was some 5,000 million kWh., but the target for 1982 of only 4,035 million kWh. indicates a substantial shortfall. Two major Soviet-supported projects are intended to improve the situation: a 500 MW. thermal power station at Pha Lai, of which it is still hoped to complete the first stage of 200 MW. by 1983, and a vast hydro-electric project on the Black River at Hoa Binh. This latter has, however, been under way for almost a decade already; if and when it is completed, it should have a capacity of 1.5 million kW.

Nevertheless, the two Soviet-supported projects seem likely to be continuing priorities under the Second National Plan (1981–85), despite the fact that such large industrial projects will be strictly limited in number, compared with the ambitious expectations of the First Plan. Even where some increases have been achieved in capacity since 1976, with limited foreign aid, these have fallen badly short of the targets for 1980. There were hopes, for example, that the target of 130,000 tons for paper production would be reached following the completion of a large mill built with Swedish aid, but this has apparently done no more than to stop and start machinery and the target for 1982 is a mere 55,000 tons. Similarly, the Federal Republic of Germany, Italy and Belgium have combined to finance two spinning mills which could increase textile production; however, even the revised 1980 target of 370 million square metres has been downgraded to a target of 260 million in 1982. The cement industry has again been increased in capacity following the completion of the Bim Son cement works; production of some 600,000 tons in 1975 expanded to 845,000 tons in 1977, but the 1982 target of 962,000 tons is far below the original 2 million tons forecast for 1980. It must be assumed also that the production of another major building material, bricks, has not reached targets, following the major shortfall in building targets in 1978 (1.5 million square metres as opposed to 4 million) and its cutback to a 1 million square metre target in 1979.

The picture in the heavy industries of chemicals and steel is apparently no brighter. The country's chemical industry consists mainly of the production of phosphate and nitrogenous fertilizers, originally planned to rise to 1.3 million tons by 1980, but later revised to 740,000 tons. However, the diversion of raw materials supplies for the latter for the war effort does not augur well and fertilizers for agriculture are admitted to be in very short supply. The emphasis on heavy industry after 1960 led to the building of an iron and steel plant in Thai Nguyen, which was operational by 1965 but still sent its ingots to the People's Republic of China for rolling. After heavy damage during the war it was revived, together with smaller furnaces elsewhere, so that by 1975 North Viet-Nam was producing 50,000 tons of steel a year. In the South three smaller plants existed by 1971 to produce bars, tubes and wire from military scrap; annual production there was 75,000 tons. The overall target set for 1980 was 300,000 tons but, with reduced Soviet and Chinese enthusiasm for such projects, it was necessary to look elsewhere for assistance. In 1977 an agreement was negotiated for major French participation in expanding the Thai Nguyen plant, but the following year the French firm concerned withdrew from the project. One source put actual steel output for 1979 at only 100,000 tons.

TRANSPORT AND COMMUNICATIONS

One further factor in the continuing economic problems of Viet-Nam is the inadequacy of the transport network. The French endowed Viet-Nam with a railway system whose main arteries were lines between Hanoi and Saigon (now Ho Chi Minh City) and between Haiphong and Yunnan. After 1954 the Chinese helped to build a third major route between Hanoi and Guangxi via Lang Son. The system was badly damaged during the war, in both North and South Viet-Nam, and its reconstruction was a priority task after 1975. The lines to the People's Republic of China, however, were closed towards the end of 1978 and some stretches inside Viet-Nam were damaged as a result of the war of February-March 1979. Other lines are in extreme need of modernization, but it is now reported that the Soviet offer to improve the Hanoi-Ho Chi Minh City route has been dropped in favour of the much shorter line between Hanoi and Haiphong.

Road transport became increasingly important in the 1960s, although roads and bridges also suffered heavy damage during the war. In the South the U.S.A. built a new highway between Ho Chi Minh City and Bien Hoa, as well as a large number of lesser roads. However, the value of such routes depends on the availability of trucks and other vehicles. Despite some recent truck purchases, the severe shortage of fuel and spare parts means that the road transport sector is still judged to be a "weak link" in the economy.

The principal port facilities before 1975 were at Haiphong, Da Nang and Ho Chi Minh City. By 1978 moves were being made to build a completely new port at Cua Lo, as well as to modernize Haiphong to increase its capacity to 2.7 million tons per year. Until this work is completed, the latter will continue to suffer badly from congestion. In the southern-central provinces, it was decided to modernize the ports of Qui Nho and Nha Trang, to enable them to cope with timber exports.

Air traffic was also increasing inside Viet-Nam and to Laos in the late 1970s, with a new airport being opened not far from Hanoi. The one western airline serving Viet-Nam, Air France, preferred to use the more familiar airport of Tan Son Nhut near Ho Chi Minh City.

FOREIGN TRADE

The pattern of Viet-Nam's foreign trade has changed greatly since the colonial period, when (apart from 1940–45) it was dominated by France. From 1954 North Viet-Nam traded predominantly with the

People's Republic of China, the U.S.S.R. and other Communist countries, while even South Viet-Nam began to limit its economic relations with France and to develop new ties with the U.S.A. and with the American-oriented economies of Japan, Taiwan and South Korea. However, in the early 1970s Hong Kong, Japan and France remained the chief markets for South Vietnamese exports. By 1975 Singapore had also become a significant trading partner with the South. Reunification transformed the situation yet again. By 1976 Viet-Nam as a whole drew 35.4 per cent of its imports from the U.S.S.R. and 15.6 per cent from Japan, while its top four export markets were the U.S.S.R. (36.8 per cent), Japan (21.3 per cent), Singapore (11 per cent) and Hong Kong (10 per cent). Following its membership of the CMEA there has been a trend towards greater trade dependence on Eastern Europe. By 1978 the U.S.S.R. was taking almost 60 per cent of the country's exports and was supplying 66 per cent of its imports. Nevertheless, it is clear that Viet-Nam is increasingly keen to lessen this dependence. In 1981, trade with the West increased, particularly with the former colonial power, France.

Throughout the 1960s and 1970s both North and South Viet-Nam had adverse trade balances. Up to 1974 the South had by far the larger deficit; in that year, according to one source, it was about U.S. $1,180 million, compared with the North's $310 million. By 1976, the South having cut its links to the U.S.A. and having no independent source of funding, the pattern was reversed: North Viet-Nam had a deficit of $450 million and the South one of only $120 million, making $570 million in all; in 1978 this rose to $663 million and in 1979 to $778 million, with exports valued at only $420 million and imports at around $1,198 million. This continuing deficit has led to a serious shortage of foreign exchange, and particularly, given the growing domination of trade with the Soviet bloc, of convertible currencies. To remedy this, there was an attempt in 1980 to limit imports and expand exports, a policy extended into the Second National Plan, with its emphasis on the export of tropical primary produce and consumer goods. Some of these are being exported directly from the major cities, which have each established import-export corporations to serve their particular needs. Trade figures for 1980 indicate, however, that, although imports declined to $1,023 million, the export drive did not compensate for the poor showing of coal exports and total export earnings also declined, to $360 million, leaving a trade deficit of $663 million. This deficit may have been reduced, however, by the growing flow of remittances sent home by the increasing numbers of Vietnamese abroad.

FOREIGN AID AND INVESTMENT

The foreign economic relations of the two halves of Viet-Nam were distorted by the consequences of a war in which both sides had to rely massively on their respective allies for military and economic aid. Both of them received vast sums which it would be impossible for either to repay, had that been required. In 1961 the U.S.S.R. cancelled the previous debts of North Viet-Nam and embarked on a long period of giving non-refundable aid, which came to an end after 1973; the People's Republic of China also gave substantial sums. Also in 1961 the Staley Mission assessed the economic requirements of South Viet-Nam to expand its armed forces and sustain a counter-insurgency programme. U.S. aid, much of it in the form of financing imports by counterpart funding, continued to grow alongside the deployment of U.S. forces after 1964; it became especially large when the "Vietnamization" programme got under way after 1969. Total U.S. aid to South Viet-Nam between 1954 and 1974 was said to amount to at least $14,500 million.

After unification, despite Vietnamese hopes that the U.S.A. would contribute to the process of reconstruction, aid from this source was not forthcoming. Until mid-1977 the Vietnamese sought to attract Western and Japanese trade and investment in the hope of maintaining at least some measure of independence of the U.S.S.R. and the People's Republic of China. In September 1976 the new Government of the Socialist Republic of Viet-Nam was allowed to join the IMF, the World Bank and the Asian Development Bank, on the strength of South Viet-Nam's previous membership of these bodies. In January 1977 the IMF made $35.8 million available to Viet-Nam to help cover its trade deficits, and a second drawing of $27.2 million was made in 1978. Further payments of $12 million were made in both 1979 and 1980 and as much as $33.5 million in 1981, although a second request in the same year was reportedly turned down owing to doubts over the management of the country's economy. On more specifically development-oriented projects, the World Bank in 1978 provided credit worth $60 million for the Dau Tieng irrigation project in the South, but since then no further loans have been made and, under pressure from the U.S.A., a complete ban on aid to Viet-Nam was instituted in 1980. American pressure also delayed the reactivation of former loans to Viet-Nam by the Asian Development Bank until 1978, since which time a total of $44.63 million has been granted. None of this relates to new projects and as long as Japan, the major donor nation to ADB, is opposed to assistance to Viet-Nam in relation to her presence in Kampuchea, then these may not be forthcoming. Thus most multilateral development aid has come recently from the relatively limited resources of the United Nations Development Programme, which has provided $118 million for a large number of small irrigation and agricultural projects. In fact, most recently the bulk of aid from multilateral agencies has been more oriented towards humanitarian ends to offset the natural disasters and food deficit problems which have beset the country over the past few years.

Development aid from individual capitalist countries has derived mainly from France, Japan and the Scandinavian countries, especially Sweden. Total French aid in mixed credits increased to as much as

$363 million by late 1977, but not all these credits were taken up. However, a number of new projects have been started, including a cotton mill in Ho Chi Minh City and rice silos. Japan has had a programme totalling some $65 million, partly in grant aid, partly in loans, but this was finally suspended in September 1979 as the Vietnamese presence in Kampuchea grew ever more permanent. Of the Scandinavian countries, the Swedish programme is the largest, with grants of some $100 million per year being made since 1976, mainly for two hospitals in Hanoi and the large paper mill mentioned above. There was a slight reduction in 1981, perhaps as a reflection of the poor performance of the latter. Denmark has contributed some $75 million, Finland $37 million, mainly for fisheries, and Norway grants of some $52 million. Other West European countries have contributed smaller sums as Viet-Nam has tried to extend relations to more countries offering aid; recently the United Kingdom has given export credits for gas turbines for Haiphong's power plant, Belgium has contributed railway locomotives and Fiat of Italy is also now established in the country.

Nevertheless, the bulk of aid continues to come from the Communist powers. From about July 1977 the Vietnamese authorities embarked on a series of policies which tended towards the more rapid "socialization" of the southern economy and culminated in the decision to join the CMEA as a full member in June 1978. This movement, along with the alienation of the West over the invasion of Kampuchea, has tended to shift the pattern of the country's aid receipts, as with trading relationships, more towards the Soviet bloc. In fact, up to the end of 1975, it was estimated that total Communist aid to North Viet-Nam had already amounted to $4,500 million, including $1,800 million from the People's Republic of China. Much of it took the form of basic foodstuffs and other essential supplies. However, from 1974 the U.S.S.R. and Eastern European countries ceased making non-refundable grants and insisted on long-term loans. There was also increasing pressure on the Vietnamese to participate in the "international division of labour" among socialist countries. Nevertheless, it is estimated that during the second Five-Year Plan financial assistance from the CMEA countries amounted to some $6,000 million, although once again a considerable amount remains unused. The U.S.S.R. alone has allocated $3,750 million, a large part of it for large scale projects such as the Black River hydroelectric project, the Pha Lai power plant, the Bim Son cement works, the Cao Son coal mine expansion and the rehabilitation of Haiphong harbour. Czechoslovakia has contributed some $150 million on several industrial projects, Bulgaria $143 million on agricultural projects and Hungary $188 million on joint projects for spinning mills. East Germany, however, is the second most important donor, with a variety of grant and loan projects totalling over $200 million.

East Germany has also promised significant assistance for the Second National Plan, including a cotton mill, modernization of dockyards, a flat-glass mill and aid for the rebuilding of the town of Vinh, but generally it would appear that the Soviet bloc is rather less willing to finance this Plan than the previous one. The internal economic difficulties of the East European countries clearly limit their ability to offer aid, and the U.S.S.R. is reported to have made closer supervision of its aid a condition of expanded funds. Viet-Nam seems unwilling to accept such controls and the ties which come with much of the Soviet aid. It is to this end that the country is turning more to the West, but, with a massive debt service ratio in relation to hard currency borrowings, there must be limits to the amounts which can be supplied. It is in these circumstances that the Second National Plan has become more pragmatic, less ambitious and based rather upon what Viet-Nam can achieve with its own resources.

STATISTICAL SURVEY

Note: **Some of the data relating to South Viet-Nam may refer only to areas controlled by the former Republic of Viet-Nam. No figures are available for areas under the control of the former Provisional Revolutionary Government.**

AREA AND POPULATION

Area	Estimated Population (mid-year)						
	1973	1974	1975	1976	1977	1978	1979†
329,566 sq. km.*	42,700,000	43,940,000	45,211,000	46,523,000	47,872,000	49,260,000	52,741,766

* 127,246 square miles. † Census of October 1st, 1979.

ADMINISTRATIVE DIVISIONS

(October 1st, 1979)

	Area (sq. km.)	Population ('000)
Provinces:		
Lai Chau	17,408	322.1
Son La	14,656	487.8
Hoang Lien Son	14,125	778.2
Ha Tuyen	13,519	782.5
Cao Bang	} 13,781	479.8
Lang Son		484.7
Bac Thai	8,615	815.1
Quang Ninh	7,076	750.1
Vinh Phu	5,187	1,488.3
Ha Bac	4,708	1,662.7
Ha Son Binh	6,860	1,537.2
Hai Hung	2,526	2,145.7
Thai Binh	1,344	1,506.2
Ha Nam Ninh	3,522	2,781.4
Thanh Hoa	11,138	2,532.3
Nghe Tinh	22,380	3,112.0
Binh Tri Thien	19,048	1,901.7
Quang Nam-Da Nang	11,376	1,529.5
Nghia Binh	14,700	2,095.4
Gia Lai-Kon Tum	18,480	595.9
Dac Lac	18,300	490.2
Phu Khanh	9,620	1,188.6
Lam Dong	10,000	396.7
Thuan Hai	11,000	938.3
Dong Nai	12,130	1,304.8
Song Be	9,500	659.1
Tay Ninh	4,100	684.0
Long An	5,100	957.3
Dong Thap	3,120	1,182.8
Tien Giang	2,350	1,264.5
Ben Tre	2,400	1,041.8
Cuu Long	4,200	1,504.2
An Giang	4,140	1,532.4
Hau Giang	5,100	2,232.9
Kien Giang	6,000	994.7
Minh Hai	8,000	1,219.6
Vung Tau-Con Dau	n.a.	91.6
Cities:		
Hanoi	597	2,570.9
Ho Chi Minh City	1,845	3,419.9
Haiphong	1,515	1,279.1
Total	329,466	52,741.8

PRINCIPAL TOWNS

(estimated population in 1973)

Hanoi (capital)	2,570,905*
Ho Chi Minh City (formerly Saigon)	3,419,978*
Haiphong	1,279,067*
Da Nang	492,194
Nha Trang	216,227
Qui Nhon	213,757
Hué	209,043
Can Tho	182,424
Mytho	119,892
Cam Ranh	118,111
Vungtau	108,436
Dalat	105,072

* Population Census, October 1979.

Births and deaths: Average annual birth rate 40.8 per 1,000 in 1970–75, 40.1 per 1,000 in 1975–80; death rate 19.9 per 1,000 in 1970–75, 14.3 per 1,000 in 1975–80 (UN estimates).

ECONOMICALLY ACTIVE POPULATION

(ILO estimates, 'ooo persons at mid-year)

	1960			1970		
	Males	Females	Total	Males	Females	Total
Agriculture, etc.	7,167	6,606	13,773	8,152	6,193	14,346
Industry	551	277	828	798	439	1,237
Services	1,389	916	2,305	1,905	1,282	3,187
TOTAL	9,107	7,799	16,906	10,855	7,915	18,770

Source: ILO, *Labour Force Estimates and Projections, 1950–2000.*

1981 (official estimate): Total economically active 22 million.

AGRICULTURE

LAND USE, 1979

('ooo hectares)

Arable land	5,430*
Land under permanent crops	455*
Permanent meadows and pastures	4,870
Forests and woodland	10,380†
Other land	11,401
Inland water	420
TOTAL AREA	32,956

* FAO estimate. † Unofficial figure.

Source: FAO, *Production Yearbook.*

PRINCIPAL CROPS

	AREA HARVESTED ('ooo hectares)			PRODUCTION ('ooo metric tons)		
	1978	1979	1980*	1978	1979	1980*
Rice (paddy)	5,486	5,481	5,740†	10,040	10,742	10,000
Maize	401	371	410	485	475	520
Sorghum*	30	30*	30	35	35	37
Sweet potatoes	360	380*	400	2,067	2,200*	2,400
Cassava (Manioc)	417	460*	480	3,495	3,800*	4,000
Dry beans	91	86*	91	44	45*	50
Other pulses	120	122	125	60	62*	64
Soybeans	43	44*	46	24	20	25
Groundnuts (in shell)	100	102*	105	92	82	95
Cottonseed	10	10*	10	3	3*	3
Cotton (lint)				1†	2*	2
Coconuts	n.a.	n.a.	n.a.	199	211*	210
Vegetables (including melons)*	n.a.	n.a.	n.a.	2,374	2,437*	2,500
Fruit (excluding melons)*	n.a.	n.a.	n.a.	1,914	1,918*	2,038
Sugar cane	72	80*	74	2,847	3,446	3,550
Coffee (green)	17	18*	20	10*	5	9
Tea (made)	47	48*	49	19	21	22
Tobacco (leaves)	29	22	28	26	16	22
Jute and substitutes	14	14*	15	30	26	30
Natural rubber	n.a.	n.a.	n.a.	46	55*	57

* FAO estimates. † Unofficial figures.

Source: FAO, *Production Yearbook.*

LIVESTOCK

('000 head, year ending September)

	1978	1979	1980*
Horses	126	126	127
Cattle	1,648	1,600	1,450
Buffaloes	2,324	2,300	2,200
Pigs	8,823	9,359	9,354†
Sheep*	13	13	14
Goats	201	200	200
Chickens	57,200	57,300†	55,000
Ducks	30,000	30,200†	29,000

* FAO estimates. † Unofficial estimates.

Source: FAO, *Production Yearbook*.

LIVESTOCK PRODUCTS

('000 metric tons—FAO estimates)

	1978	1979	1980
Beef and veal	33	34	31
Buffalo meat	60	62	60
Pig meat	410	435	415
Poultry meat	91	92	88
Cows' milk	22	25	26
Buffaloes' milk	42	45	48
Hen eggs	117	122	122
Other poultry eggs	60.0	61.0	61.0
Cattle and buffalo hides	13.1	13.6	12.8

Source: FAO, *Production Yearbook*.

FORESTRY

ROUNDWOOD REMOVALS

('000 cubic metres, excluding bark)

	1976	1977	1978	1979	1980
Sawlogs, etc.: Coniferous*	112	112	112	112	112
Broadleaved	1,200	1,200*	1,200*	1,200*	1,200*
Other industrial wood (all broadleaved)*	1,332	1,362	1,394	1,394	1,427
Fuel wood (all broadleaved)*	56,288	57,608	58,979	60,389	61,827
TOTAL	58,932	60,282*	61,685*	63,095*	64,566*

* FAO estimates.

Source: FAO, *Yearbook of Forest Products*.

SAWNWOOD PRODUCTION

('000 cubic metres, incl. boxboards)

	North Viet-Nam					South Viet-Nam				
	1966	1967	1968	1969	1970*	1966	1967	1968	1969	1970
Coniferous	30	25	25	25	25	17	18	15	35	44
Broadleaved	270	225	225	225	225	157	119	176	273	226
TOTAL	300	250	250	250	250	174	137	191	308	270

* FAO estimates.

1971–80 ('000 cubic metres): Annual production for all Viet-Nam 520 (coniferous 69, broadleaved 451), i.e. as in 1970 (FAO estimates).

Source: FAO, *Yearbook of Forest Products*.

FISHING

('000 metric tons, live weight)

South Viet-Nam

	1970	1971	1972	1973
Inland waters . .	64.1	71.1	81.8	91.3
Pacific Ocean . .	453.3	516.4	595.9	622.2
TOTAL CATCH .	517.4	587.5	677.7	713.5

North Viet-Nam (FAO estimates, '000 metric tons, 1970–73): Annual catch 300 (Inland waters 85; Pacific Ocean 215).

1974–80 ('000 metric tons): Annual catch for all Viet-Nam 1,013.5 (Inland waters 176.3, Pacific Ocean 837.2), i.e. as in 1973 (FAO estimates).

Source: FAO, *Yearbook of Fishery Statistics.*

MINING

('000 metric tons—estimates)

	1975	1976	1977	1978	1979
Hard coal	5,200	5,600	6,200	6,000	6,000
Salt (unrefined) . . .	377	581	580	530	514
Phosphate rock* . . .	1,400	1,500	1,500	1,500	n.a.

* Estimates by International Phosphate Industry Association.

Source: UN, *Yearbook of Industrial Statistics.*

INDUSTRY

SELECTED PRODUCTS

		1975	1976	1977	1978	1979
Phosphate fertilizers* . .	'000 metric tons	100	95	126	130	30
Cement	,, ,, ,,	537	738	845	843	705
Electric energy . . .	million kWh.	2,428	2,957	3,473	3,500†	3,600†

* Estimated production in terms of phosphoric acid. † Estimate.

Source: UN, *Yearbook of Industrial Statistics.*

FINANCE

100 xu=10 hào=1 dông.

Coins: 1, 2 and 5 xu; 1 dông.

Notes: 2 and 5 xu; 1, 2 and 5 hào; 1, 2, 5, 10, 20, 30, 50 and 100 dông.

Exchange rates (June 1982): £1 sterling=16.53 dông; U.S. $1=9.54 dông.

100 dông=£6.05=$10.48.

Note: The new dông, equal to 1,000 old dông, was introduced in North Viet-Nam (the Democratic Republic of Viet-Nam) in February 1959. Since January 1961 the basic exchange rate has been linked to the Soviet rouble at a parity of 1 dông= 30.6 kopeks. Until August 1971 the basic rate was U.S. $1=2.49 dông (1 dông=34.01 U.S. cents). From December 1971 to February 1973 the rate was $1=2.71 dông. In terms of sterling, the basic rate between November 1967 and June 1972 was £1=7.056 dông. In 1961 a commercial exchange rate was established for foreign trade transactions. This was £1=10.08 dông ($1=3.60 dông) until November 1967, after which it was £1=9.00 dông, equal to $1=3.75 dông from November 1967 to August 1971 and $1=3.45 dông from December 1971 to June 1972. This commercial rate has been abolished. The non-commercial exchange rate for tourists from non-Communist countries was £1=4.20 dông until August 1971 and $1=3.87 dông from December 1971 to February 1973. A new tourist rate of $1=3.48 dông was introduced in February 1973. After the reunification of Viet-Nam in July 1976, separate currencies circulated in North and South until May 1978, when the Northern dông became established as the currency of the whole country. Consequently the Northern dông took over as Viet-Nam's currency within the IMF, with an exchange rate fixed at 2.66358 dông per Special Drawing Right (SDR) or 1 dông=0.3754 SDR. In 1981 the dông was devalued to 0.09635 SDR (1 SDR=10.37883 dông).

BUDGET
(million dông)

	1977
Receipts	9,043
Expenditure	9,179

1979: Budget to balance at 10,500 million dông.

1980 PRODUCTION TARGETS
(Second Five-Year Plan, 1976–80)

Food crops	million metric tons	21.0
Paddy rice	,, ,, ,,	17.5–18.0
Other	,, ,, ,,	3.0–4.0
Fish	,, ,, ,,	1.3–1.5
Meat	,, ,, ,,	1.0
Steel	,, ,, ,,	0.3
Cement	,, ,, ,,	2.0
Chemical fertilizer	,, ,, ,,	1.3
Textiles	million metres	450
Timber	million cubic metres	3.5

EXTERNAL TRADE
(U.S. $ million)

	1977	1978	1979
Imports	1,142	1,159	1,225
Exports	456	482	535

Source: Economist Intelligence Unit, *Annual Supplement*, 1980.

SELECTED COMMODITIES

Imports		1976	1977	1978
Agricultural machines	million dông	198	203	132
Motor lorries	'ooo	3.2	2.9	2.4
Tractors	,,	1.6	5.2	3.6
Tyres	'ooo pairs	190	209	121
Chemical fertilizers	'ooo metric tons	571	636	636
Petroleum	,, ,, ,,	225	172	171
Wool	metric tons	941	598	256
Cotton fabrics	million metres	39.8	19.0	19.5
Rice	'ooo metric tons	148	197	35
Corn and corn flour	,, ,, ,,	497	971	1,278
Maize	,, ,, ,,	89	96	105
Sugar	,, ,, ,,	116	81	89
Meat products	million dông	17.2	5.2	2.9
Milk	,, ,,	23.7	10.2	8.6

Exports		1976	1977	1978
Coal	'ooo metric tons	1,306	1,463	1,430
Chromium	,, ,, ,,	13	10	9
Floor lumber	'ooo cu. metres	15.2	53.1	60.0
Rubber	'ooo metric tons	27.8	35.7	24.8
Footwear	million dông	21.7	19.3	28.4
Embroidery, local crafts, etc.	,, ,,	28.8	42.7	70.9
Rattan bamboo and rush articles	,, ,,	49.0	29.8	75.0
Tea	million metric tons	7.9	9.7	7.8
Coffee	'ooo metric tons	8.5	2.1	3.5
Liquor	million litres	4.4	8.3	9.8
Peanuts	'ooo metric tons	15.9	10.4	12.0
Canned fruit and vegetables	,, ,, ,,	8.2	13.4	18.5
Pineapples, oranges, bananas	,, ,, ,,	27.9	31.5	34.0
Eggs	million	19.3	12.1	1.7

Source: General Statistical Office, Hanoi.

SELECTED TRADING PARTNERS*

(U.S. $ million)

	Imports			Exports		
	1974	1975	1976	1974	1975	1976
Australia	14.0	22.0	41.0	—	—	0.2
France	28.0	21.6	29.8	14.0	8.3	3.1
German Democratic Republic	50.0	63.0	n.a.	17.0	23.0	n.a.
Germany, Federal Republic	17.0	10.0	10.0	2.0	1.0	—
Hong Kong	23.0	19.2	35.2	25.7	14.8	23.8
Italy	11.0	22.5	2.9	1.0	0.6	—
Japan	125.0	81.5	167.5	61.0	41.4	49.0
Singapore	216.7	81.6	15.8	13.6	8.7	25.4
Sweden	13.0	31.5	29.0	—	0.3	—
U.S.S.R.	256.4	220.6	224.6	57.9	66.4	84.6
Others†	785.0	301.7	48.7	30.1	24.3	15.0
Total‡	1,539.1	875.2	604.5	222.3	188.8	201.1

* Based on data reported by partner countries. Figures for imports are partners' exports f.o.b.; exports are partners' imports c.i.f.

† Including the U.S.A.

‡ Excluding figures for trade with Bulgaria, the People's Republic of China, Czechoslovakia, Hungary and Poland.

Sources: IMF, *Direction of Trade*, July 1977; official statistical publications; compiled by Economics Department, Citibank, Hong Kong.

TRANSPORT

North Viet-Nam

INTERNATIONAL SEA-BORNE SHIPPING

(estimated freight traffic in '000 metric tons)

	1970	1971	1972	1973	1974	1975
Goods Loaded . . .	350	500	300	250	750	700
Goods Unloaded . . .	1,200	1,170	900	700	650	970

Source: United Nations, *Statistical Yearbook.*

South Viet-Nam

RAILWAYS

	1971	1972	1973
Passengers ('000 passenger-km.) . .	85,657	65,672	170,043
Freight ('000 ton-km.) . . .	38,208	6,617	1,214

ROAD TRAFFIC

(motor vehicles in use)

	1972	1973	1974
Passenger cars	74,600	66,120	70,000
Commercial vehicles	91,250	97,661	100,000

INTERNATIONAL SEA-BORNE SHIPPING

('000 metric tons)

	1970	1971	1972	1973	1974*	1975*
Goods Loaded	84	57	63	198	160	100
Goods Unloaded . . .	6,818	6,518	5,612	4,875	3,480	1,150

* Estimates.

Source: UN, *Statistical Yearbook.*

CIVIL AVIATION

	1971	1972	1973
INTERNATIONAL			
Flights	18,039	15,219	8,253
Passengers	746,617	528,489	236,459
Freight (metric tons) .	72,717	105,753	33,747
Mail (,, ,,) .	4,334	7,702	2,713
DOMESTIC			
Flights	85,169	89,572	64,420
Passengers	1,723,823	1,411,073	1,007,677
Freight (metric tons) .	9,116	7,622	5,277
Mail (,, ,,) .	825	1,335	1,561

EDUCATION
(1980, '000)

	Pupils
Kindergarten	1,587
General	14,289
Vocational	133
Higher	146

Source: Ministry of Education.

Sources (unless otherwise indicated): General Statistical Office of the Democratic Republic of Viet-Nam; South Viet-Nam statistics from Institut National de la Statistique, Saigon; Communist Party of Viet-Nam.

THE CONSTITUTION

In December 1980 a new constitution was adopted to replace the 1959 constitution of the Democratic Republic of Viet-Nam. It consists of a preamble and 12 chapters comprising 147 articles. A summary of the main provisions follows:

General Principles: The Socialist Republic of Viet-Nam is an independent, sovereign and united country. It is a proletarian dictatorship and the people exercise state power through the National Assembly and the People's Councils.

Economic System: The economy is run on the principles of socialism, and ensures the working people's collective ownership of the means of production. The economy is directed by unified plans.

National Assembly: elected for five years by nationwide elections. It meets regularly twice a year and also in extraordinary sessions. It elects from its deputies the Chairman, Vice-Chairmen and other members of the Council of State. The Assembly also appoints the Council of Ministers, the Chief Justice of the Supreme People's Court and the Procurator-General of the Supreme People's Organ of Control. It decides, assisted by the Standing Commissions of the National Assembly, domestic and foreign policies, economic plans and, among other functions, examines and approves the budget.

Council of State: the highest body of the National Assembly and the Collective Presidency of Viet-Nam. It is concerned with the building of socialism, national defence, the implementation of laws, and all domestic and foreign affairs. Its term of office is the same as that of the National Assembly and its Chairman is concurrently Chairman of the National Defence Council.

Council of Ministers: the Government of Viet-Nam is responsible to the National Assembly, and submits draft laws, decrees and budgets to it. Its term of office corresponds with that of the National Assembly.

Local Government: the country is divided into provinces and municipalities directly under central authority, and subdivided into districts, towns and villages. These are under the authority of locally elected People's Councils.

Judicial System: consists of the Supreme People's Court, the local People's Courts and the Military Tribunals. There are also local People's Organs of Control, under the Supreme People's Organ of Control, to ensure observance of law.

THE GOVERNMENT

COUNCIL OF STATE

President: Truong Chinh.

Vice-Presidents: Nguyen Huu Tho, Le Thanh Nghi, Chu Huy Man, Huynh Tan Phat.

General Secretary: Le Thanh Nghi.

Members of the Council: Nguyen Duc Thuan, Nguyen Thi Dinh, Ngo Duy Dong, Le Thanh Dao, Y Ngong Niek Dam, Dam Quang Trung, Vu Guang.

COUNCIL OF MINISTERS
(July 1982)

Chairman of the Council (Premier): Pham Van Dong.

Vice-Chairmen: Pham Hung, Gen. Vo Nguyen Giap, To Huu, Vu Dinh Lieu, Vo Van Kiet, Dong Si Nguyen, Tran Phuong, Do Muoi, Tran Quynh.

Minister, General Secretary and Director of the Office of the Council: Nguyen Huu Tho.

Minister of the Interior: Pham Hung.

Minister of Foreign Affairs: Nguyen Co Thach.

Minister of National Defence: Gen. Van Tien Dung.

Chairman of the State Commission for Planning: Vo Van Kiet.

Minister and Vice-Chairman of the State Commission for Planning: VU DAI.

Minister of Agriculture: NGUYEN NGOC TRIU.

Minister of Forestry: PHAN XUAN DOT.

Minister of Water Conservancy: NGUYEN CANH DINH.

Minister of Engineering and Metals: NGUYEN VAN KHA.

Minister of Power: PHAM KHAI.

Minister of Mines and Coal: NGUYEN CHAN.

Minister of Construction: PHAN NGOC TUONG.

Minister of Communications and Transport: DONG SI NGUYEN.

Minister of Light Industry: NGUYEN CHI VU.

Minister of the Food Industry: VO TUAN.

Minister of Food: LA LAM GIA.

Minister of Marine Products: NGUYEN TIEN TRINH.

Minister of Internal Trade: LE DUC THINH.

Minister of Foreign Trade: LE KHAC.

Minister of Finance: CHU TAM THUC.

Director-General of the State Bank: NGUYEN DUY GIA.

Chairman of the State Commission for Prices: DOAN TRONG TRUYEN.

Minister of Labour: DAO THIEN THI.

Minister of Supply: HOANG DUC NGHI.

Chairman of the Government Committee for Nationalities: HOANG VAN KIEU.

Chairman of the State Commission for Science and Technology: DANG HUU.

Chairman of the State Commission for Capital Construction: (vacant).

Chairman of the Government Inspectorate: BUI QUANG TAO.

Minister of Culture: NGUYEN VAN HIEU.

Minister of Higher and Secondary Vocational Education: NGUYEN DINH TU.

Minister of Justice: PHAN HIEN.

Minister of Education: Mrs. NGUYEN THI BINH.

Minister of Public Health: DANG HOI XUAN.

Minister for Disabled Soldiers and Social Affairs: SONG HAO.

NATIONAL DEFENCE COUNCIL

Chairman: TRUONG CHINH.

Vice-Chairman: PHAM VAN DONG.

Members: PHAM HUNG, Gen. VAN TIEN DUNG, TO HUU.

LEGISLATURE

QUOC HOI

The Sixth National Assembly, the first since 1946 to be based on nationwide elections, was elected on April 25th, 1976. It directed the Standing Committee to hold the next General Election at a convenient time after the promulgation of the draft constitution. The 496 members of the Seventh National Assembly were elected on April 26th, 1981. It held its first session in June–July 1981, when it elected members of the Council of State and the Council of Ministers.

Chairman: NGUYEN HUU THO.

Vice-Chairmen: XUAN THUY, NGUYEN XUAN YEM, NGUYEN XIEN, Y PEN, CAM NGOAN, HUYNH CUONG, Superior Bonze THICH THE LONG, The Rev. VO THANH TRINH, PHAN ANH.

POLITICAL PARTIES AND ORGANIZATIONS

Dang Cong san Viet-Nam (*Communist Party of Viet-Nam*): 10 Hoang Van Thu St., Hanoi; f. 1976; party of Government; formerly the Viet-Nam Workers' Party which succeeded the Communist Party of Indochina, f. 1930; 1,727,784 mems.; Gen. Sec. of Cen. Cttee. LE DUAN; publs. *Nhan Dan* (daily), *Tap Chi Cong San* (monthly).

Politburo:

13 full members.

LE DUAN, TRUONG CHINH, PHAM VAN DONG, PHAM HUNG, LE DUC THO, Gen. VAN TIEN DUNG, VO CHI CONG, CHU HUY MAN, TO HUU, VO VAN KIET, DO MUOI, LE DUC ANH, NGUYEN DUC TAM

2 alternate members.

NGUYEN CO THACH, DONG SI NGUYEN

Secretariat:

LE DUAN, LE DUC THO, VO CHI CONG, NGUYEN DUC TAM, NGUYEN LAM, LE QUANG DAO, HOANG TUNG, NGUYEN THANH BINH, TRAN KIEN, TRAN XUAN BACH

Dang dan chu (*Democratic Party*): 32 Tran Tien St., Hanoi; f. 1944; party of the middle classes and intelligentsia; Sec.-Gen. NGHIEM XUAN YEM; publ. *Doc Lap* (Independence).

Dang xa Hoi (*Socialist Party*): 53 Nguyen Du St., Hanoi; f. 1946; consists mainly of intelligentsia; Gen. Sec. NGUYEN XIEN; publ. *To Quoc* (Fatherland).

Ho Chi Minh Communist Youth Union: 60 Bà Triêu St., Hanoi; f. 1931; 4,380,000 mems.; Sec.-Gen. DANG QUOC BAO; publ. *Tien Phong* (Vanguard).

Vietnamese Women's Union: 39 Hang Chuoi St., Hanoi; f. 1930; Pres. NGUYEN THI DINH; publ. *Phu Nu Viet-Nam* (Vietnamese Women).

Viet-Nam Fatherland Front: 46 Trang Thi St., Hanoi; f. 1955; replaced the Lien-Viet (Viet-Nam National League), the successor to Viet-Nam Doc-Lap Dong Minh Hoi (Revolutionary League for the Independence of Viet-Nam) or Viet-Minh; in January 1977 the original organization agreed to merge with the National Front for the Liberation of South Viet-Nam and the Viet-Nam Alliance of National, Democratic and Peace Forces to form a single front; Pres. HOANG QUOC VIET; Gen. Sec. NGUYEN VAN TIEN.

DIPLOMATIC REPRESENTATION

EMBASSIES ACCREDITED TO VIET-NAM

(In Hanoi unless otherwise stated)

Afghanistan: Beijing, People's Republic of China.

Albania: 49 Dien Bien Phu; *Ambassador:* MAXHUN PEKA.

Algeria: 12 Phan Chu Trinh; *Chargé d'affaires:* YOUCEF MEHENNI.

Argentina: Tokyo, Japan.

Australia: 66 Ly Thuong Kiet; *Ambassador:* JOHN MCCARTHY.

Austria: Beijing, People's Republic of China.

Bangladesh: Rangoon, Burma.

Belgium: Khu Van Phuc B3; *Chargé d'affaires:* FERDINAND VAN WICHELEN.

Bulgaria: 43 Tran Phu; *Ambassador:* PHILIP V. MARKOV.

Burma: Hotel Thong Nhat, 15 Ngo Quyen; *Ambassador:* KYAW THANT.

Burundi: Beijing, People's Republic of China.

Canada: Bangkok, Thailand.

China, People's Republic: 46 Hoang Dieu; *Ambassador:* QIU LIXING.

Colombia: New Delhi, India.

Congo: Beijing, People's Republic of China.

Costa Rica: Tokyo, Japan.

Cuba: 65 Ly Thuong Kiet; *Ambassador:* FAURE CHOMON MEDIAVILLA.

Cyprus: New Delhi, India.

Czechoslovakia: 13 Chu van An; *Ambassador:* BOHUSLAV HANDL.

Denmark: Khu Van Phuc, A3; *Chargé d'affaires:* SOEREN VOSS.

Egypt: 26 Phan Boi Chau; *Ambassador:* MOSTAFA HASSAN ALORABY.

Equatorial Guinea: Beijing, People's Republic of China.

Ethiopia: Beijing, People's Republic of China.

Finland: E1 Trung Tu; *Ambassador:* UNTO KORHONEN.

France: 57 Tran Hung Dao; *Ambassador:* YVAN BASTOUIL.

German Democratic Republic: 29 Tran Phu; *Ambassador:* KLAUS ZORN.

Germany, Federal Republic: 25 Phan Boi Chau; *Ambassador:* CLAUS VOLLERS.

Greece: Beijing, People's Republic of China.

Guinea: Beijing, People's Republic of China.

Hungary: 47 Dien Bien Phu; *Ambassador:* JÓZSEF VARGA.

India: 58 Tran Hung Dao; *Ambassador:* KULDIP SAHDEV.

Indonesia: 38 Tran Hung Dao; *Ambassador:* SUDARSONO.

Iran: New Delhi, India.

Iraq: 66 Tran Hung Dao; *Ambassador:* NATIQ ABD AL-HAMID TAWFIQ AL-WADI.

Italy: 9 Le Phung Hieu; *Ambassador:* LODOVICO MASETTI.

Japan: Khu Trung Tu E3; *Ambassador:* ATSUHIKO YATABE.

Kampuchea: 71 Tran Hung Dao; *Ambassador:* SIENG SARAL.

Korea, Democratic People's Republic: 25 Cao Ba Quat; *Ambassador:* PAC KE YEN.

Laos: 22 Tran Binh Trong; *Ambassador:* KHAMPHEUANE TOUNALOM.

Madagascar: Beijing, People's Republic of China.

Malaysia: Room 207, Hotel Thong Nhat, 15 Ngo Quyen; *Ambassador:* AJIT SINGH.

Mali: Beijing, People's Republic of China.

Mauritania: Beijing, People's Republic of China.

Mongolia: 39 Tran Phu; *Ambassador:* LEGDENGIYN DAMDINJAV.

Nepal: Rangoon, Burma.

Netherlands: 53 Ly Thai To; *Chargé d'affaires:* DIRK WILLEM SCHIFF.

New Zealand: Bangkok, Thailand.

Nigeria: Beijing, People's Republic of China.

Norway: Beijing, People's Republic of China.

Philippines: El Khu Trung Tu; *Ambassador:* JUAN B. CRUZ Jr.

Poland: 3 Chua Mot Cot; *Ambassador:* JAN SLIWINSKI.

Portugal: Bangkok, Thailand.

Romania: 5 Le Hong Phong; *Ambassador:* ION MEDREA.

Rwanda: Beijing, People's Republic of China.

Senegal: Beijing, People's Republic of China.

Somalia: Beijing, People's Republic of China.

Sri Lanka: Beijing, People's Republic of China.

Sweden: So 2, Duong 358 Van Phuc; *Ambassador:* RAGNAR DROMBERG.

Switzerland: 27 Pho Quang Trung, P.O.B. 24; *Chargé d'affaires:* IVAN ETIENNE.

Syria: Beijing, People's Republic of China.

Tanzania: Beijing, People's Republic of China.

Thailand: El Khu Trung Tu; *Ambassador:* KANIT SRI CHAROEN.

Tunisia: Beijing, People's Republic of China.

Turkey: Kuala Lumpur, Malaysia.

Uganda: Beijing, People's Republic of China.

U.S.S.R.: 58 Tran Phu; *Ambassador:* BORIS NIKOLAYEVICH CHAPLIN.

United Kingdom: 16 Pho Ly Thuong Kiet; *Ambassador:* DEREK TONKIN, C.M.G.

Upper Volta: Beijing, People's Republic of China.

Yemen Arab Republic: Beijing, People's Republic of China.

Yemen, People's Democratic Republic: Beijing, People's Republic of China.

Yugoslavia: 27B Tran Hung Dao; *Ambassador:* MILORAD BOZINOVIĆ.

Zaire: Beijing, People's Republic of China.

Zambia: Beijing, People's Republic of China.

Viet-Nam also has diplomatic relations with Angola, Benin, Cameroon, Cape Verde, Chad, Chile, Ecuador, Gabon, The Gambia, Ghana, Grenada, Guinea-Bissau, Guyana, Iceland, the Ivory Coast, Jamaica, Jordan, Kuwait, Lebanon, Libya, Luxembourg, Maldives, Malta, Mexico, Mozambique, Nicaragua, Niger, Pakistan, Panama, Saint Lucia, São Tomé and Príncipe, Seychelles, Sierra Leone, Singapore, Spain, Sudan, Suriname, Togo, Vanuatu and Zimbabwe.

JUDICIAL SYSTEM

The Judicial System, based on French lines, has been thoroughly revised since 1954. The Supreme People's Court in Hanoi is the highest court and exercises civil and criminal jurisdiction over all lower courts. The Supreme Court may also conduct trials of the first instance in certain cases. There are People's Courts in each province and city which exercise jurisdiction in the first and second instance. Military courts hear cases involving members of the People's Army and cases involving national security. The observance of the law by ministries, government offices and all citizens is the concern of the People's Organs of Control, under a Supreme People's Organ of Control.

President of the People's Supreme Court: PHAM HUWNG.

President of the Supreme People's Organ of Control: TRAN LE.

RELIGION

Traditional Vietnamese religion included elements of all three Chinese religions: Mahayana Buddhism, Daoism and Confucianism. Its most widespread feature was the cult of ancestors, practised in individual households and clan temples. In addition, there were (and remain) a wide variety of Buddhist sects, the sects belonging to the "new" religions of Caodaism and Hoa Hao, and a Catholic Church. The Government has stated that there is complete freedom of religious belief in Viet-Nam.

BUDDHISM

In the north a Buddhist organization, grouping Buddhists loyal to the Democratic Republic of Viet-Nam, was formed in 1954. In the south the United Buddhist Church was formed in 1964, incorporating several disparate groups, including the "militant" An-Quang group (mainly natives of central Viet-Nam), the group of Thich Tam Chau (mainly northern emigrés in Saigon) and the southern Buddhists of the Xa-Loi temple. In 1981, at an assembly convened in Hanoi, the Buddhist sects were unified into one organization, the Viet-Nam Buddhist Church, headed by THICH TRI THU.

CAODAISM

Formally inaugurated in 1926, this is a syncretic religion based on spiritualist seances with a predominantly ethical content, but sometimes with political overtones. A number of different sects exist, of which the most politically involved (1940–75) was that of Tay-Ninh. Another sect, the Tien-Thien, has been represented in the National Liberation Front since its inception. Together the sects are said to number two million adepts. They live mostly in the south.

HOA HAO

A new manifestation of an older religion called Buu Son Ky Huong, the Hoa Hao sect was founded by Huynh Phu So in 1939, and at one time claimed 1.5 million adherents in southern Viet-Nam.

CATHOLICISM

The Vietnamese Church has existed since the 17th century, and since the 1930s has been led mainly by Vietnamese priests. Many Catholics moved from North to South Viet-Nam in 1954–55 to avoid living under Communist rule, but some remained in the north. There are about three million Catholics throughout the country.

ARCHBISHOPS

Hanoi: H.E. Cardinal TRINH VAN CAN.

Hué: Most Rev. PHILIPPE NGUYEN KIM DIEN.

Ho Chi Minh City: Most Rev. PAUL NGUYEN VAN BINH.

THE PRESS

DAILIES

HANOI

Hanoi Moi (*New Hanoi*): 44 Ave. Le Thai To; f. 1976; organ of Hanoi Committee of the Communist Party; Editor HONG LINH.

Nhan Dan (*The People*): 71 Hang Trong St.; f. 1946; official organ of the Communist Party; Editor-in-Chief HOANG TUNG; circ. 300,000.

Quan Doi Nhan Dan (*People's Army*): 7 Phan Dinh Phung St.; f. 1950; published by the Army; Editor Col. BUI TIN; circ. 200,000.

HO CHI MINH CITY

Saigon Giai Phong (*Liberated Saigon*): 432 Xo-Viet Nghe-Tinh St.; f. 1975; organ of Ho Chi Minh City Committee of the Communist Party; Editor VO NHAN LY; circ. 45,000.

PERIODICALS

Chinh Nghia (*Justice*): 59 Trang Tri St., Hanoi; organ of the Vietnamese Catholics' National Liaison Committee; weekly.

Cong Giao va Dan Toc (*Catholics and the Nation*): Ho Chi Minh City; f. 1975; Catholic; weekly; Editor NGUYEN DINH-THI.

Dai Doan Ket (*Great Union*): 66 Ba Trieu St., Hanoi; and 176 Vo Thi Sau St., Ho Chi Minh City; f. 1977; weekly; organ of the Viet-Nam Fatherland Front.

Doc Lap (*Independence*): 59 Ly Thuong Kiet St., Hanoi; weekly; organ of the Viet-Nam Democratic Party.

Khoa Hoc va Doi Song (*Science and Life*): 70 Tran Hung Dao St., Hanoi; fortnightly.

Lao Dong (*Labour*): 51 Hang Bo St., Hanoi; weekly; organ of Federation of Trade Unions; circ. 37,530.

Nguoi Giao Vien Nhan Dan (*People's Teacher*): 14 Le Truc St., Hanoi; monthly.

Phu Nu Viet-Nam (*Vietnamese Women*): 47 Hang Chuoi, Hanoi; weekly; women's magazine.

Tap Chi Cong Doan (*Trade Unions Review*): 65 Quan Su St., Hanoi; every two months.

Tap Chi Cong San (*Communist Review*): 1 Nguyen Thuong Hien St., Hanoi; f. 1955 as *Hoc Tap*; monthly; political and theoretical organ of the Communist Party; Editor-in-Chief DAO DUY TUNG; circ. 100,000.

The Duc The Thao (*Physical Culture and Sports*): 5 Trinh Hoai Duc St., Hanoi; three a month.

Thieu Nien Tien Phong (*Young Pioneers*): 15 Ho Xuan Huong St., Hanoi; weekly.

Tien Phong (*Vanguard*): 15 Ho Xuan Huong St., Hanoi; f. 1957; weekly; organ of the Youth Movement; circ. 16,000.

Tin Viet-Nam (*Viet-Nam Courier*): 46 Tran Hung Dao St., Hanoi; f. 1964; monthly; English, French and Russian editions; Chief Editor HOANG NGUYEN.

To Quoc (*Fatherland*): 53 Nguyen Du St., Hanoi; f. 1946; monthly; organ of Viet-Nam Socialist Party.

Van Nghe (*Arts and Letters*): 17 Tran Quoc Tuan St., Hanoi; f. 1949; organ of the Vietnamese Writers' Union.

Viet-Nam: 79 Ly Thuong Kiet, Hanoi; f. 1954; illustrated monthly; published by Committee for Cultural Relations with Foreign Countries; in Vietnamese, Russian, Chinese, French, Spanish and English; Dir. LE BA THUYEN; circ. 86,000.

Vietnamese Studies: 46 Tran Hung Dao, Hanoi; quarterly; English and French editions; Dir. NGUYEN KHAC VIEN.

NEWS AGENCIES

Viet-Nam News Agency (VNA): 5 Ly Thuong Kiet, Hanoi; Dir.-Gen. DÀO TÙNG.

FOREIGN BUREAUX

Agence France-Presse (AFP): 18 Phung Khac Khoan, Hanoi; Chief MICHEL BLANCHARD.

Agentstvo Pechati Novosti (APN) (*U.S.S.R.*): 15 Thuyen Quang St., Hanoi; Bureau Chief IGOR V. SAVVICHEV.

Allgemeiner Deutscher Nachrichtendienst (ADN) (*German Democratic Republic*): 7 Pho Yet Kieu, Hanoi; Correspondent HELMUT KAPFENBERGER.

Československá tisková kancelář (ČTK) (*Czechoslovakia*): 63 Hoang Dieu St., Hanoi; Bureau Chief TOMÁŠ CHUDLARSKÝ.

Polska Agencja Prasowa (PAP) (*Poland*): B17 Kim Lien Residential Quarter, Hanoi.

Prensa Latina (*Cuba*): 66 Ngo Thi Nham, Hanoi.

Telegrafnoye Agentstvo Sovietskogo Soyuza (TASS) (*U.S.S.R.*): 23 Cao Ba Quat, Hanoi.

PRESS ASSOCIATION

Viet-Nam Journalists' Association: 59 Ly Thai To St., Hanoi; f. 1945; association of editors, reporters and photographers working in the press, radio, television and news agencies; 6,000 mems.; Pres. HOANG TUNG.

PUBLISHERS

Giao Duc (*Educational*) **Publishing House:** 81 Tran Hung Dao, Hanoi; f. 1957; controlled by the Ministry of Education; school books; Man. NGUYEN SI TY.

Khoa Hoc (*Scientific*) **Publishing House:** 70 Tran Hung Dao St., Hanoi.

Khoa Hoc Xa Hoi (*Social Sciences*) **Publishing House:** 61 Phan Chu Trinh St., Hanoi.

Lao Dong (*Labour*) **Publishing House:** 91 Tran Hung Dao St., Hanoi.

Ngoai Van (*Foreign Languages*) **Publishing House:** 46 Tran Hung Dao St., Hanoi; Chief Editor NGUYEN KHAC VIEN.

Public Security Publishing House: Hanoi; f. 1981; state-controlled; cultural and artistic information, public order and security.

Quan Doi Nan Dan (*Popular Army*) **Publishing House:** 23 Ly Nam De St., Hanoi.

Su That (*Truth*) **Publishing House:** 24 Quang Trung St., Hanoi; controlled by the Communist Party; Marxist classics, political and philosophical works; Dir. PHAM THANH.

Van Hoc (*Literature*) **Publishing House:** 49 Tran Hung Dao, Hanoi; state-controlled; Dir. NHU PHONG.

Women's Publishing House: 39 Hang Chuoi, Hanoi.

Y Hoc (*Medical*) **Publishing House:** 7 Trinh Hoai Duc St., Hanoi.

RADIO AND TELEVISION

Viet-Nam Radio and Television Commission (VNRTC): 58 Quan-Su St., Hanoi; Chair. TRAN LAM.

RADIO

Voice of Viet-Nam: 58 Quan-Su St., Hanoi; controlled by VNRTC; separate programme network operating from Ho Chi Minh City; home service in Vietnamese; foreign service in English, Japanese, French, Khmer, Laotian, Spanish, Thai, Cantonese and Standard Chinese, Indonesian and Russian; Dir.-Gen. and Editor-in-Chief LE QUY.

TELEVISION

Central Television: Giang Vo St., Hanoi; controlled by VNRTC; television was introduced into South Viet-Nam in 1966 and in North Viet-Nam in 1970; in 1980 there were television stations at Hanoi, Hué, Qui Nhon, Da Nang, Nha Trang, Ho Chi Minh City and Can Tho; Editor-in-Chief LY VAN SAU.

In 1976 there were approximately two million television receivers.

FINANCE

BANKING

The State Bank of Viet-Nam is the state's sole banking system, with branches all over the country and a network of reconstruction banks, foreign trade banks, savings funds and credit co-operatives.

State Bank of Viet-Nam (Viet-bank): 7 Le-Lai St., Hanoi; f. 1951; central bank of issue; Dir.-Gen. NGUYEN DUY GIA; Deputy Dirs.-Gen. TRAN LINH SON, NGUYEN VAN TRUONG, LE HOANG, NGUYEN VAN CHUAN; 532 brs. and sub-brs.

Bank for Foreign Trade of Viet-Nam (Vietcombank): 47–49 Ly Thai To Blvd., Hanoi; f. 1963; the only bank in the country authorized to deal with foreign currencies and international payments; Chair. LE HOANG; Deputy Chairs. NGUYEN VAN GIOC, NGUYEN CAO TIEU, NGUYEN VAN DE, NGUYEN DUY LO, TRAN QUOC QUYNH; 4 brs.

Bank for Investment and Reconstruction: 10 Phan Huy Chu St., Hanoi; Dir. PHAM NGOC LAM; Deputy Dirs. VU VAN THAO, CHU VAN NGUYEN, TRUONG CONG PHU, NGUYEN THI AN, NGUYEN DOAN.

Savings Fund for Socialism: 7 Le Lai St., Hanoi; Dir. NGO QUAT; Deputy Dirs. DANG DINH NHUAN, HUYNH KY.

INSURANCE

Viet-Nam Insurance Co.: 7 Ly Thuong Kiet, Hanoi; f. 1965; state company; aircraft, marine, motor, domestic and petroleum insurance; Gen. Man. NGO THIET THACH.

TRADE AND INDUSTRY

Chamber of Commerce of the Socialist Republic of Viet-Nam (Vietcochamber): 33 Ba Trieu St., Hanoi; Pres. HOANG TRONG DAI; attached organizations are:

Vinacontrol (*The Viet-Nam Superintendence and Inspection Co.*): 96 Yet Kieu St., Hanoi; f. 1959; branches in all main Vietnamese ports; controls exports and imports and transit of goods; Dir. HO MINH KHA; Vice-Dirs. NGUYEN DANG UYEN, LE DINH HAU.

Foreign Trade Arbitration Committee: 46 Ngo Quyen St., Hanoi; settles disputes arising from foreign trade transactions between Vietnamese and foreign economic organizations.

Maritime Arbitration Committee: 46 Ngo Quyen St., Hanoi; settles and exercises jurisdiction over disputes arising from sea transportation.

Viet-Nam Exhibition and Advertising Agency (Vinexad): 33 Ba Trieu St., Hanoi; f. 1975; organizes commercial exhibitions in Viet-Nam and abroad; Pres. DO XUAN PHUONG; Dir.-Gen. NGUYEN TRONG NHUAN (acting).

All foreign trade activities are directed and controlled by the State through the intermediary of the Ministry of Foreign Trade. To this effect, several National Import-Export Corporations have been set up (*see below*).

FOREIGN TRADE CORPORATIONS

Agrexport (*Viet-Nam National Agricultural Produce and Foodstuffs Export-Import Corporation*): 6 Trang Tien St., Hanoi; imports and exports agricultural produce and foodstuffs, wine and edible oils.

Animex (*Viet-Nam National Animal Products Import and Export Co.*): 33 Ba Trieu St., Hanoi; imports and exports live animals and animal products.

Artexport (*Viet-Nam National Handicrafts and Arts Products Export-Import Corporation*): 31–33 Ngo Quyen St., Hanoi; deals in craft products and art materials.

Barotex (*Viet-Nam National Bamboo and Rattan Export Corporation*): 37 Ly Thuong Kiet St., Hanoi; specializes in export of cane, rattan and bamboo products.

Fafim (*Viet-Nam Film Export-Import and Distribution Corporation*): 73 Nguyen Trai St., Hanoi; f. 1953; export and import of films; organization of film shows and participation of Vietnamese films in international film festivals.

Generalimex (*General Import-Export Company*): 64 Truong Dinh St., Ho Chi Minh City; f. 1981 by Ministry of Foreign Trade; exports staples from various regions and products from State-run enterprises and imports goods for processing and sale.

Imex (*Import and Export Co. of Ho Chi Minh City*): imports and exports products of municipal enterprises.

Machinoimport (*Viet-Nam National Machinery Export-Import Corporation*): 8 Trang Thi St., Hanoi; imports and exports machinery and tools; Dir.-Gen. LE QUANG TUONG.

Minexport (*Viet-Nam National Minerals Export-Import Corporation*): 35 Hai Ba Trung, Hanoi; exports minerals and metals, quarry products, building materials, chemical products, pharmaceutical products; imports coal, metals, pharmaceutical and chemical products, industrial and building materials, fuels and oils, asphalt, fertilizers, gypsum and cement bags.

Naforimex (*Viet-Nam National Forest and Native Produce Export-Import Corporation*): 19 Ba Trieu St., Hanoi; imports cigarette paper, rubber, linseed oil, tallow and plywood; exports oils, forest products, coffee, tea, gum benzoin, medicinal herbs and miscellaneous products.

Technoimport (*Viet-Nam National Complete Equipment Import and Technical Exchange Corporation*): 16–18 Trang Thi St., Hanoi; imports industrial plant and secures technical service of foreign specialists.

Textimex (*Viet-Nam National Textiles Export-Import Corporation*): 25 Ba Trieu St., Hanoi; imports raw and synthetic fibres and exports garments, woven articles and laces.

Tocontap (*Viet-Nam National Sundries Export-Import Corporation*): 36 Ba Trieu St., Hanoi; imports and exports consumer goods.

Transaf (*Viet-Nam National Foreign Trade Corporation*): 46 Ngo Quyen, Hanoi; import and export transactions with foreign co-operative societies and firms in consumer goods; foodstuffs and handicrafts; re-exports; compensation trade; agents for all commercial transactions.

Unimex Hanoi (*Hanoi Import and Export Union*): 12 Hang Dieu St., Hanoi; imports and exports products of municipal enterprises; operates INTERSHOPS in Hanoi.

Unimex Haiphong (*Haiphong Import and Export Union*): 16 Cu Chinh Lan St., Haiphong; handles products of municipal enterprises; operates INTERSHOPS in Haiphong.

Vegetexco (*Viet-Nam National Vegetables and Fruit Export-Import Corporation*): 46 Ngo Quyen St., Hanoi; exports vegetables and fruit, tinned and processed vegetables and fruit, marmalade, spices and flowers; imports vegetable seeds and processing materials.

Vietfracht (*Viet-Nam Foreign Trade Transportation Corporation*): 74 Nguyen Du St., Hanoi; in charge of all activities concerning sea transport; provides regular services to and from South-East Asian ports, mainly Haiphong/Ho Chi Minh City–Hong Kong–Singapore and main Japanese ports; provides services to and from the Black Sea and western and northern Europe.

Vietrans (*Viet-Nam Foreign Trade Forwarding and Warehousing Corporation*): 13 Ly Nam De St., Hanoi; agent for foreign establishments for international trade with Viet-Nam; warehousing and inland transport services for export goods.

Xunhasaba (*Viet-Nam State Corporation for Export and Import of Books, Periodicals and other Cultural Commodities*): 32 Ha Ba Trung St., Hanoi.

All commercial and non-commercial payments to foreign countries are effected through the Bank for Foreign Trade of Viet-Nam.

TRADE UNIONS

Tong Cong Dean Viet-Nam (TCD) (*Viet-Nam Federation of Trade Unions*): 82 Tran Hung Dao, Hanoi; f. 1946; merged with the South Viet-Nam Trade Union Federation for Liberation in 1976; 2,200,000 mems.; Pres. and Gen. Sec. NGUYEN DUC THUAN, Vice-Pres. NGUYEN HO; publs. *The Vietnamese Trade Unions* (in English, French and Spanish), *Lao dong* (weekly in Vietnamese), *Cong doan* (monthly in Vietnamese).

TRANSPORT

RAILWAYS

Viet-Nam Railway Central Department: 180 Nam Bo St., Hanoi; Government-owned; total length of track (1980) 3,216 km.; lines reported to be in operation are: Hanoi–Ho Chi Minh City (1,730 km.), Hanoi–Haiphong (104 km.), Hanoi–Muc Nam Quan (162 km.), Hanoi–Thanh Hoa (167 km.), Hanoi–Lao Cai (296 km.), Dong Anh–Thai Nguyen (51 km.); Dir.-Gen. TRAU LU.

ROADS

National Automobile Transport Undertaking: Hanoi; f. 1951; operates long distance and municipal bus services.

In 1980 there were 347,243 km. of roads, of which 41,200 km. were main roads.

SHIPPING

The principal port facilities are at Haiphong, Da Nang and Ho Chi Minh City.

Viet-Nam Ocean Shipping Agency (VOSA): 25 Dien Bien St., Haiphong; in charge of performing all such facilities as may be required for the coming and going of merchant shipping, arranges repairs and surveys of ships, arranging salvage of vessels in distress and attending to settlements of salvage remuneration; booking passages and arranging embarkation and disembarkation formalities for passengers; brs. in Ho Chi Minh City, Da Nang, Hon Gay, Cam Pha, Ben Thuy, Quy Nhon, Nha Trang and Vung Tau.

Nam-Hai: 20 Nguyen Cong Tru, Ho Chi Minh City.

CIVIL AVIATION

Viet-Nam's principal airports are Gia Lam, near Hanoi, Tan Son Nhut International Airport, Ho Chi Minh City, and Thuo Do (Capital) International Airport at Noi Bai. They cater for domestic and foreign traffic. Airports at Da Nang, Hué, Nha Trang, Dalat and Can Tho handle domestic traffic.

Air Viet-Nam: Hanoi; f. 1954; former South Vietnamese airline; operates internal services to Da Nang and Phu Quoc Island.

Hang Khong Viet-Nam (*Viet-Nam Airline*): Gia Lam Airport, Hanoi; formerly the General Civil Aviation Administration of Viet-Nam; operates passenger services between Hanoi and Ho Chi Minh City, and international services to Laos and Thailand; fleet of 1 Boeing 707-320, 3 Ilyushin Il-18, 3 DC-6, 2 DC-4, 2 Tupolev Tu-134A, 2 Yak-40, 3 DC-3 and 8 Antonov An-24; Chief of Directorate of Civil Aviation KHOANG IGOK ZIEU.

FOREIGN AIRLINES

The following foreign airlines also serve Viet-Nam: Aeroflot (U.S.S.R.), Air France, Air Lao, Balkan (Bulgaria), ČSA (Czechoslovakia), Interflug (German Democratic Republic) and Thai Airways.

TOURISM

Vietnamtourism (*Viet-Nam Travel Service*): 54 Nguyen Du St., Hanoi; operates in 17 provinces throughout Viet-Nam; Dir. HO VAN PHONG.

In June 1978 it was announced that a general department for tourism would be established.

DEFENCE

Armed Forces and Equipment: (1981): Total 1,029,000, of which army 1,000,000; navy 4,000; air force 25,000 (plus paramilitary forces of 1,570,000). Equipment is largely of Soviet and Chinese origin and includes about 1,000 tanks and 485 combat aircraft, and a significant amount of U.S. arms and equipment of the former government of South Viet-Nam.

Military Service: Two years minimum between 18 and 35 years of age.

Commander-in-Chief of the Armed Forces: Sr. Gen. VAN TIEN DUNG.

Chief of General Staff, Army: Col.-Gen. LE TRONG TAN.

EDUCATION

The war in Viet-Nam destroyed more than 3,000 educational establishments but since 1975 great efforts have been made to improve the situation. There is compulsory, free education, where possible, for 10 years. In the 1979/80 school year there were 11.9 million students receiving general education, 329,000 receiving higher secondary and professional education, and 138,000 receiving technical education. At the end of 1977 there were over 40,000 nurseries and kindergartens in Viet-Nam. There is some disagreement concerning the number of teachers' colleges in Viet-Nam. In 1981 there were 36 post-graduate schools and 149 teachers' schools. There are three universities and it has been reported that two new universities are to be opened in the South, at Dalat and in the Central Highlands. A 12-year educational reform programme was introduced in 1981/82 to replace the 10-year universal educational system.

BIBLIOGRAPHY

BUTTINGER, J. Vietnam, a Political History (André Deutsch, London, 1969).

Vietnam: a Dragon Embattled (Pall Mall Press, London, 1967).

CAMERON, A. W. Viet-Nam Crisis, a Documentary History (1940–56) (Cornell University Press, Ithaca, N.Y., 1971).

CHALIAND, G. The Peasants of North Vietnam (Penguin Books, Harmondsworth, 1969).

CHEN, K. Vietnam and China 1938–54 (Princeton University Press, Princeton, N.J., 1969).

CHESNEAUX, J., BOUDAREL, G., HEMERY, D. *et al.* Tradition et Révolution au Vietnam (Editions Anthropos, Paris, 1971).

DEVILLERS, P. Histoire du Viet-Nam de 1940 à 1952 (Le Seuil, Paris, 1952).

DEVILLERS, P. and LACOUTURE, J. End of a War, Indochina 1954 (Pall Mall Press, London, 1969).

DUIKER, WILLIAM J. The Rise of Nationalism in Vietnam 1900–1941 (Cornell University Press, Ithaca, N.Y., 1976).

FALL, B. The Two Viet-Nams, a Political and Military Analysis (2nd edn., Pall Mall Press, London, 1967).

Street Without Joy: Insurgency in Indochina 1946–63 (Pall Mall Press, London, 1963).

Hell in a very Small Place: the Siege of Dien Bien Phu (Pall Mall Press, London, 1967).

GEEB, L. H., and BETTS, R. K. The Irony of Vietnam (Brookings Institution, Washington, 1979).

HALBERSTAM, D. The Best and the Brightest (Barrie and Jenkins, London, 1973).

HAMMER, E. J. The Struggle for Indochina (Stanford University Press, Stanford, Calif., 2nd edn., 1966).

HICKEY, G. C. Village in Vietnam (Yale University Press, New Haven, Conn., 1964).

HONEY, P. J. Communism in North Vietnam (MIT Press, Cambridge, Mass., 1963).

HUYNH KIM KHANH. Vietnamese Communism 1925–45 (Cornell University, Ithaca, N.Y., 1982).

KALB, M. and ABEL, E. Roots of Involvement: the U.S. in Asia 1784–1971 (Pall Mall, London, 1971).

KATTENBURG, P. M. The Vietnam Trauma in American Foreign Policy 1945–75 (Transaction Books, 1981).

LACOUTURE, J. Ho Chi Minh (Penguin Books, London, 1968).

LANCASTER, D. The Emancipation of French Indochina (Oxford University Press, London, 1961).

LANSDALE, E. G. In the Midst of Wars: an American Mission to South-east Asia (Harper & Row, New York, N.Y., 1972).

LE THANH KHOI. Le Viet-Nam, Histoire et Civilisation (Editions de Minuit, Paris, 1955).

LEWY, G. America in Vietnam (O.U.P., New York, 1978).

MCALEAVY, H. Black Flags in Vietnam (Allen and Unwin, London, 1968).

MCALISTER, J. T. Viet-Nam, the Origins of Revolution (Allen Lane, London, 1970).

MCCOY, A. W. The Politics of Heroin in South-east Asia (Harper & Row, New York, N.Y., 1972).

MARR, D. G. Vietnamese Anticolonialism, 1885–1925 (University of California, Berkeley, Calif., 1971).

Vietnamese Tradition on Trial 1920–45 (University of California, Berkeley, 1981).

NGO VINH LONG. Before the Revolution: the Vietnamese Peasants under the French (MIT Press, Cambridge, Mass., 1973).

OSBORNE, M. E. The French Presence in Cochinchina and Cambodia: Rule and Response (1859–1905) (Cornell University Press, Ithaca, N.Y., 1969).

PATTI, A. L. A. Why Vietnam? Prelude to America's Albatross (University of California, 1981).

The Pentagon Papers: the Defense Department History of U.S. Decision-making on Vietnam ("Senator Gravel Edition", 4 vols., Beacon Press, Boston, Mass., 1971).

PIKE, D. Viet Cong, the Organization and Techniques of the National Liberation Front of South Vietnam (MIT Press, Cambridge, Mass., 1966).

PORTER, G. (editor). Vietnam: the Definitive Documentation of Human Decisions, 2 vols. (Heyden, London and Philadelphia, 1979).

RACE, J. War comes to Long An: Revolutionary Conflict in a Vietnamese Province (University of California, Berkeley, Calif., 1972).

SANSOM, R. L. The Economics of Insurgency in the Mekong Delta of Vietnam (MIT Press, Cambridge, Mass., 1970).

SHAPLEN, R. The Lost Revolution in Vietnam 1945–65 (London, 1965).

SMITH, R. Viet-Nam and the West (Heinemann Educational, London, 1968).

SNEPP, F. Decent Interval, an Insider's Account of Saigon's Indecent End (Random House, New York, 1978).

TRUONG BUU LAM. Patterns of Vietnamese Response to Foreign Intervention 1858–1900 (Yale University Press, New Haven, Conn., 1967).

TRUONG CHINH. Primer for Revolt (ed. B. B. Fall, Praeger, New York, N.Y., 1963).

VAN DYKE, J. M. North Vietnam's Strategy for Survival (Palo Alto, Calif., 1972).

VO NGUYEN GIAP. People's War, People's Army (Praeger, New York, N.Y., 1962).

VO NHAN TRI. Croissance Economique de la République Démocratique du Viet-Nam (Hanoi, 1967).

WOODSIDE, A. B. Vietnam and the Chinese Model: a Comparative Study of Vietnamese and Chinese Government in the first half of the Nineteenth Century (Harvard University Press, Cambridge, Mass., 1971).

ZASLOFF, J., and BROWN, MCA. (eds.). Communism in Indochina: New Perspectives (Heath & Co., Lexington, Mass., 1975).

See also Kampuchea and Laos.

Other Reference Material

Who's Who in the Far East and Australasia	1230
Weights and Measures	1385
Calendars and Time Reckoning	1391
Research Institutes Studying the Far East and Australasia	1394
Select Bibliography (Periodicals)	1405

WHO'S WHO IN THE FAR EAST AND AUSTRALASIA

Names of biographees from the People's Republic of China have been romanized according to the Pinyin system. The spelling of the names of overseas Chinese and people from Hong Kong and Taiwan are given according to the Wade-Giles spelling. A list of Pinyin names, with their Wade-Giles equivalents, appeared in the 1979/80 and 1980/81 editions of *The Far East and Australasia.*

A

Abdul Rahman, Tunku ibni Al-Marhum Sultan Abdul Hamid Halim Shah, C.H., B.A.; Malaysian politician; b. 8 Feb. 1903; ed. St. Catharine's Coll., Cambridge, and Inner Temple, London.
Took a leading part in formation of United Malays' Nat. Org. (UMNO) 46; Chair. UMNO in Kedah 49; Pres. UMNO 51; unofficial mem. Exec. and Legislative Councils; Leader, Fed. Legislative Council; Chief Minister and Minister for Home Affairs 55; first Prime Minister and Minister of External Affairs, Federation of Malaya Aug. 57-Feb. 59, Aug. 59-Sept. 63; Prime Minister and Minister of External Affairs, Malaysia Sept. 63-Sept. 70; Minister of Information and Broadcasting 63-64; Minister of Culture, Youth and Sports 64; Sec.-Gen. UMNO 70; Sec.-Gen. of Islamic Conf. 69-72; Order of Nat. Crown of Malaysia; Kedah Order of Merit; numerous foreign honours.
Publs. *Mahsuri* (play) 41, *Raja Bersiong* 66 (dir. film version 66), *Looking Back* 77.
Jalan Tunku 1, Kuala Lumpur; and 16 Ayer Rajah Road, Penang, Malaysia.

Abdullah, Sheikh Mohammad; Indian politician; b. 5 Dec. 1905, Soura, Srinagar, Kashmir; ed. Kashmir, Lahore and Aligarh (U.P.).
Founder of Kashmir Muslim Conf., later Kashmir Nat. Conf., for representative govt. in Kashmir 38; Pres. All-India States People's Conf. 46; sentenced to 9 years' imprisonment for leading peoples of Jammu and Kashmir State in struggle against Maharajah of Kashmir for constitutional govt. and civil liberties Aug. 46 (sentence not carried out in full); Head of Interim Govt. Nov. 47; mem. Indian Del. to UN Jan. 48; Prime Minister of Jammu and Kashmir 48-53; mem. Indian Constituent Assembly 49; in detention 53-58, 58-64, 65-68; in exile 71-72; Chief Minister of Jammu and Kashmir Feb. 75-March 77, July 77-; Leader State Congress Party Feb. 75-March 77, Nat. Conference Party March 77-.
Secretariat, Srinagar; Home: 10 Maulana Azad Road, Srinagar, Kashmir.

Abdullah bin Mohd Salleh, Tan Sri, B.A.; Malaysian petroleum executive and fmr. civil servant; b. 24 June 1926, Malacca; ed. High School Malacca, Malay Coll., Kuala Kangsar, Univ. of Malaya, Singapore.
Posts in Admin. and Diplomatic Service 56-69; Registrar, Nat. Univ. of Malaysia 69; Sec.-Gen. Ministry of Agric. and Fisheries 72; Dir.-Gen. Public Service Dept. 74; Chair. of Council, Nat. Univ. of Malaysia, Chief Sec. to Govt. of Malaysia, Sec. to Cabinet, Head of the Civil Service 76-78; Chair. and Chief Exec. PETRONAS (Nat. Petroleum Co. of Malaysia) 79-.
PETRONAS, 136 Jalan Pudu, Kuala Lumpur; Home: 21 Jalan Setiajaya, Damasara Heights, Kuala Lumpur, Malaysia.

Abe, Kobo; Japanese novelist and playwright; b. 7 March 1924; ed. Tokyo Univ.
Twenty-fifth Akutagawa Prize 51, Post-War Literature Prize 49, Yomiuri Literary Prize 62, Kishida Prize for Drama 58.
Publs. *Owarishi Michino Shirubenni* (The Road Sign at the End of the Road), *Akai Mayu* (Red Cocoon) 49, *Kabe-S. Karumashi No Hanzai* (The Crimes of S. Karma, Esq.) 51, *Kiga Domei* (Hunger Union) 54, *Seifuku and other plays* (The Uniform) 55, *Doreigari* (Hunt for a Slave) 55, *Kemonotachi wa Kokyo o Mezasu* (Animals are Forwarding to Their Natives) 57, *Dai Yon Kanpyoki* (Inter Ice Age IV) 59, *Yurei wa Kokoni Iru* (Here is a Ghost) 59, *Ishi no Me* (Eyes of Stone) 60, *Suna no Onna* (The Woman in the Dunes) 62, *Tanin no Kao* (The Face of Another) 64, *Omaenimo Tsumi Ga Aru* (You are Guilty Too) 65, *Enomoto Buyo* (Buyo Enomoto) 65, *Tomodachi* (Friends) 67, *The Ruined Map* 69, *Ai no Meganewa Irogatasu* (Love's Spectacles are Coloured Glass) 73, *Midoriiro no Stocking* (Green Stocking) 74, *Hakootoko* (The Box Man) 75, *Warau Thuki* (Laughing Moon) 75, *Mikkai* (Secret Rendezvous) 77, *Kozo wa Shinda* (The Little Elephant is Dead, play) 79.
1-22-10, Wakaba Cho, Chofu City, Tokyo, Japan.

Abe, Shintaro; Japanese journalist and politician.
Member House of Reps. 58-; Private Sec. to Prime Minister Nobusuke Kishi; fmr. Deputy Sec.-Gen. Liberal-Democratic Party, fmr. Vice-Pres. LDP Diet Policy Cttee.; Minister of Agric. and Forestry 74-76; Chief Cabinet Sec. 77-78; Minister of Int. Trade and Industry Nov. 81-.
c/o Liberal-Democratic Party, 7, 2-chome, Hirakawacho, Chiyoda-ku, Tokyo, Japan.

Adams-Schneider, Lance Raymond; New Zealand politician and diplomatist; b. 1919, Wellington; ed. Mt. Albert Grammar School.
Manager, Taumarunui dept. store; served in Second World War, N.Z. Medical Corps; Vice-Chair. Nat. Party in Waitomo electorate; mem. South Auckland Div. Exec.; M.P. for Hamilton 59-69, for Waikato 69-81; Minister of Broadcasting, Minister Asst. to Minister of Customs 69; Minister of Customs, Asst. Minister of Industries and Commerce 69-72; Minister of Health and Social Welfare Feb.-Nov. 72; Opposition Spokesman on Health and Social Welfare 72-74, on Trade, Industry and Customs 74-75; Minister of Trade and Industry 75-81; Amb. to U.S.A. May 82-.
New Zealand Embassy, 37 Observatory Circle, N.W., Washington, D.C. 20008, U.S.A.

Adermann, (Albert) Evan; Australian (b. British) politician; b. 10 March 1927, Kingaroy, Queensland.
Public accountant; mem. House of Reps. 72-; opposition spokesman on customs and excise June 74, assisting spokesman on trade, resources allocation and decentralization June 74; mem. Joint Cttee. on Public Accounts 73-74; Minister for the Northern Territory 75-78; Minister assisting Minister for Nat. Resources 75-77; assisting Minister for Primary Industry 77; Minister for Veterans' Affairs, Acting Minister for Primary Industry, assisting Minister for Transport 78-80; mem. Gen. Admin. Cttee. 76-80; Nat. Country Party.
Parliament House, Canberra, A.C.T. 2600; Howard Chambers, Queen Street, Nambour, Queensland; Home: 29 Oxleigh Crescent, Nambour, Queensland, Australia.

Adiseshiah, Malcolm Sathianathan, M.A., PH.D.; Indian economist; b. 18 April 1910; ed. Madras, London and Cambridge Univs.
Professor of Econs., Calcutta and Madras Univs. 30-46; Assoc. Gen. Sec. Int. Student Service 46-48; Deputy Dir. Exchange of Persons Service, UNESCO 48-50; Dir. Dept. of Tech. Assistance, UNESCO 50-53; Asst. Dir.-Gen. UNESCO 54-63, Deputy Dir.-Gen. 63-70; Chair. Madras Inst. of Devt. Studies 78- (Dir. 71-77); Vice-Chancellor, Univ. of Madras 75-78; mem. Rajya Sabha 78.

Publs. *Demand for Money* 38, *Agricultural Economic Development* 41, *Handicraft Industries* 42, *Rural Credit* 43, *Planning Industrial Development* 44, *Restless Nations* 62, *War on Poverty* 63, *Non-political UN* 64, *Welfare and Wisdom* 65, *Economics of Indian Natural Resources* 66, *Education and National Development* 67, *International Role of the University* 68, *Unesco and the Second Development Decade* 69, *Let My Country Awake* 70, *It is Time to Begin* 71, *Techniques of Perspective Planning* 72, *Plan Implementation Problems and Perspective* 73, *Science in the Battle Against Poverty* 74, *Towards a Functional Learning Society* 75, *Mid-Term Review of the Economy* 76, *Backdrop to Learning Society* 78, *Mid-Year Review of the Economy 1979–1980* 79, *Educational Perspectives in Tamil Nadu: 1976–86* 78, *Economics of Non-formal Education* 79, *Adult Education Faces Inequalities* 81.
79 Second Main Road, Gandhinagar, Adyar, Madras 600 020, India.

Advani, Lal K.; Indian politician, fmr. journalist and social worker; b. 8 Nov. 1927, Karachi (now in Pakistan); ed. St. Patrick's High School, Karachi, D.G. Nat. Coll., Hyderabad, Sind, Govt. Law Coll., Bombay.
Joined Rashtriya Swayam Sevak Sangh (RSS, social work org.) 42, Sec. of Karachi branch 47; joined Bharatiya Jana Sangh (BJS) 51; party work in Rajasthan until 58, Sec. of Delhi State Jana Sangh 58-63, Vice-Pres. 65-67; mem. Cen. Exec. of BJS 66; mem. interim Metropolitan Council, Delhi 66, leader of Jana Sangh Group 66; Chair. of Metropolitan Council 67; mem. Rajya Sabha 70-, head of Jana Sangh parl. group 70; Pres. Bharatiya Jana Sangh 73-77 (incorp. in Janata); detained during emergency June 75-Jan. 77; Gen. Sec. Janata Party Jan.-May 77; Minister of Information and Broadcasting 77-79; after collapse of Janata Party Gen. Sec. Bharatiya Janata Party (BJP) and Leader BJP, Rajya Sabha 80-.
C 1/6 Pandara Park, New Delhi 3, India (Home).
Telephone: 384397 (Home).

Adyaa, Gelegiyn; Mongolian politician; b. 1934; ed. Trade Tech. School, Faculty of Foreign Languages and Literature, Mongolian State Univ.
Journalist on newspaper *Ünen* 57-60; journalist, Editor Information and Radio Directorate of Council of Ministers 60-64; Duty Editor and head of a dept., State Cttee. for Information and Radio 64-68; Deputy Chair. State Cttee. for Information, Radio and TV 68-71; head of Party Orgs. Dept. Mongolian People's Revolutionary Party (MPRP) Cen. Cttee. 72-79; mem. MPRP Cen. Cttee. 76-; Sec. MPRP Cen. Cttee. 79-; Deputy to People's Great Hural (Assembly) 73-.
Central Committee of the Mongolian People's Revolutionary Party, Ulan Bator, Mongolia.

Ahmed, Khandakar Moshtaque; Bangladesh lawyer and politician; b. 1918; ed. Dacca Univ.
Joined Quit India movement 42; imprisoned 46; collaborated with Sheikh Mujibur Rahman in Bengali language movement, later in Awami League; imprisoned several times by Pakistan authorities; Minister of Foreign Affairs, Law and Parl. Affairs in Govt. of Bangladesh April-Dec. 71 (in exile in India), of Law, Parl. Affairs and Land Revenue 71-72, of Power, Irrigation and Flood Control 72-74, of Trade and Commerce 74-75; Pres. of Bangladesh, also Minister of Defence and Home Affairs Aug.-Nov. 75; reported arrested, sentenced to five years' imprisonment Feb. 77, additional three years March 77; released March 80.

Ahmed, Rafeeuddin, M.A.; Pakistani diplomatist and international official; b. 2 Oct. 1932, Sukkur; ed. Forman Christian Coll., Lahore, Univ. of Punjab, Tufts Univ.
Lecturer in Political Science, Govt. Coll., Lyallpur (now Faisalabad) 53-55; Officer on Special Duty, Ministry of Foreign Affairs 55-58; Attaché Pakistani Embassy, People's Repub. of China 58-61, Egypt 61-63, High Comm. Canada 63-65; mem. Pakistan Del. to UN 65-70; Sec. UN Econ. and Social Council 70-73; Dir. Resources and Programme Planning Office UN Dept. of Econ. and Social Affairs 73-75; Chef de Cabinet UN Sec.-Gen. 75-80; Special Rep. of UN Sec.-Gen. for Humanitarian Affairs in South-East Asia 81-.
Office of the Secretary-General, United Nations, New York, N.Y. 10017; 401 East 89th Street, New York, N.Y. 10028, U.S.A. (Home).

Aitmatov, Chingiz Torekoluvich; Soviet (Kirghiz) writer; b. 1928; ed. Kirghiz Agricultural Inst.
Writer 52-; First Sec. of Cinema Union of Kirghiz S.S.R. 64-69, Chair. 69-; Candidate mem. Central Cttee. of C.P. of Kirghiz S.S.R.; Lenin Prize for *Tales of the Hills and the Steppes* 63; State Prize 68, Hero of Socialist Labour 78.
Publs. include stories: *Face to Face, Short Stories, Melody* 61, *Tales of the Hills and the Steppes* 63; novels: *Djamilya* 59, *My Poplar in a Red Kerchief* 60, *Camel's Eye, The First Teacher, Farewell Guilsari, The White Steamship, The Lament of the Migrating Bird*, co-author of *Earth and Water* 78, *Works* (3 vols.) 78, *Early Storks* 79, *Stories* 79.
Kirghiz Branch of Union of Writers of U.S.S.R., Ulitsa Pushkina 52, Frunze, Kirghiz S.S.R., U.S.S.R.

Akama, Yoshihiro; Japanese banker; b. 2 Dec. 1916, Tokyo; ed. Tokyo Univ.
Managing Dir. Mitsubishi Trust & Banking Corpn 65-69, Senior Man Dir. 69-70, Deputy Pres. 70-71, Pres. 71-78, Chair. 78-; Blue Ribbon Medal 77.
Mitsubishi Trust & Banking Corporation, 4-5, Marunouchi, 1-chome, Chiyoda-ku, Tokyo; Home: 4-15-22 Komagome Toshima-ku, Tokyo, Japan.
Telephone: 03-917-5755.

Akashi, Toshio: Japanese banker; b. 24 Aug. 1915, Fukuoka Prefecture; ed. Tokyo Univ.
Joined Sanwa Bank 42, Chief Sec. 58, Gen. Man. of Shimbashi Branch 60, of Tokyo Govt. and Municipal Business Dept. 62, of Tokyo Business Promotion Dept. 63, of Fukuoka Branch 64, of Personnel Dept. 66, Dir. 67, Man. Dir. 68, Senior Man. Dir. 72, Deputy Pres. 73, Pres. Sanwa Bank April 76-.
Sanwa Bank Ltd., 4-10, Fushimi-cho, Higashi-ku, Osaka, Japan.

Akatani, Genichi; Japanese United Nations official; b. 29 Sept. 1918, Taipei, Taiwan, China; ed. Univ. of Oxford and Sophia Univ., Tokyo.
Joined Japanese Foreign Service 45; Second Sec., Paris 54, First Sec. 55; Head, East-West Trade Div., Econ. Affairs Bureau, Ministry of Foreign Affairs 58; Counsellor, Washington, D.C. 61-66; Counsellor, Public Information Bureau, Ministry of Foreign Affairs 66-72; Asst. Sec.-Gen. UN 72-77, Under Sec.-Gen., Dept. of Public Information 78-79; del. to several sessions of UN Gen. Assembly.
United Nations Secretariat, First Avenue, New York, N.Y. 10017, U.S.A.

Akhund, Iqbal Ahmad, M.A.; Pakistani diplomatist; b. Aug. 1924, Hyderabad, Sind; ed. Bombay Univ.
Entered Pakistan Foreign Service 49, served in Canada, Spain, Netherlands, Saudi Arabia, Malaysia and Perm. Mission to UN, New York 49-56; Private Sec. to Minister of Foreign Affairs 56-58; Dir. and Dir.-Gen. Ministry of Foreign Affairs 64-66, 66-68; Amb. to Egypt 68-71, to Yugoslavia 71-72; Perm. Rep. to UN 72-78; Vice-Pres. Econ. and Social Council 74, Pres. 75; Chair. Ad Hoc Cttee. on Transnational Corpns. 74, UN Cttee. on Sanctions against Rhodesia 76; Pres. of UN Security Council Oct. 76; Chair. Group of 77 76-77; Amb. to France (also accred. to Ireland) 78-79; UN Co-ordinator of Assistance for the

Reconstruction and Devt. of Lebanon 79-; mem. Int. Cttee. on Man and Science, New York; Special Adviser Aspen Inst. for Humanistic Studies.
c/o United Nations, New York, N.Y., U.S.A.

Akilandam, Perungalur Vaithialingam (*pseudonym* Akilon); Indian Tamil writer; b. 27 June 1922; ed. Maharaja's Coll., Pudukkottai.
Writer 40-; in Indian Post & Telegraph Dept. 45-58; freelance writer 58-65; Sec. Tamil Writers' Asscn., Tiruchy 53-57; Sec. Gen. Fed. of All-India Tamil Writers 62-65; Dir. Tamil Writers' Co-op. Soc. 63-; mem. Tamil Advisory Board, Sahitya Akademi 64-; Producer, Spoken Word in Tamil, All-India Radio, Madras 65-; Pres. Tamil Writers Asscn. 67; Kalai Magal Prize for *Penn* 46, Tamil Akademi Award for *Nenjin Alaigal* 53, Sahitya Akademi Award for *Vengaiyin Maindan* 63, Tamil Nadu Govt. Award for *Kayalvizhi* 68, for *Erimalai* 73, Rajasir Annamalai Award for *Engay Pogirom* 75, Bharatiya Jnanpith Award for *Chittirappaavai* 75, Soviet Land Nehru Award 78.
Publs. include novels: *Penn* 46, *Snehithi* 50, *Nenjin Alaigal* 53, *Pavai Vilakku* 58, *Vengaiyin Maindan* 61, *Ponmalar* 64, *Kayalvizhi* 64, *Chittirappaavai* 67; short stories: *Sakthivel* 47, *Nilavinilay* 50, *Vazhi Pirandhadu* 52, *Sahodara Andro?* 63, *Nellore Arisi* 67, *Erimalai* 70.
13 Kastian Beach Street, Santhome, Madras 600004, India.
Telephone: 75173.

Ali, H. A. Mukti; Indonesian specialist in comparative religion; b. 1923, Central Java; ed. Indonesia, Karachi, Pakistan and McGill Univ., Canada.
Vice-Chancellor, IAIN "Sunan Kalijaga", Yogyakarta; Minister of Religious Affairs 71-78; mem. Supreme Advisory Council Aug. 78-; Adviser to UNESCO on Islamic Culture 79-.
Publs. *Modernization of Islamic Schools, Comparative Religion, Its Method and System, Religion and Development in Indonesia* (8 vols.), etc.
Supreme Advisory Council, Jalan Merdeka Utara 17, Jakarta; Home: Sagan Gk 1/100, Yogyakarta, Indonesia.

Ali, Sadiq, B.A.; Indian politician; b. 1910; ed. Allahabad Univ.
Associated with Indian freedom movement 30; Perm. Sec., All-India Congress Cttee. 38-49; mem. Lok Sabha 50-51, Rajya Sabha 58-70; Gen. Sec. Indian Congress Party 58-69; Pres. Opposition Congress Party 71-73; Chair. Gandhi Smarak Sangrahalaya Samiti 67-77; Chief Editor *Political and Economic Review* 60-69; Gov. of Maharashtra 77-80, of Tamil Nadu 80-; Chair. Gandhi Nat. Museum and Library, New Delhi.
Publs. *Know Your Country, Congress Ideology and Programme, Culture in India, General Elections 1957, Towards Socialist Thinking in Congress.*
Raj Bhavan, Madras 600022, Tamil Nadu, India.

Alston, Philip Henry, Jr., LL.B.; American diplomatist and former company director; b. 19 April 1911, Atlanta, Ga.; ed. Univ. of Georgia, Emory Univ., Harvard Law School.
Admitted to Georgia bar 34; practised with firm Alston, Miller & Gaines, Atlanta, Ga. 34-77; served to Lieut., U.S. Naval Reserve 42-45; Dir. Printpack, Inc., Triton, Inc., Nat. Data Corpn. until 77; Trustee Charles Loridans Foundation, Vasser Woolley Foundation until 77; U.S. Amb. to Australia 77-81, concurrently to Nauru Aug. 79-; Pres. Univ. of Georgia Alumni Soc. 63-64; mem. Board of Regents, Univ. System Georgia 70-72.
c/o State Department, 2201 C Street, Washington, D.C. 20520, U.S.A.

Altangerel, Bat-ochiryn; Mongolian politician; b. 10 Feb. 1934; ed. Higher School of Engineering, U.S.S.R.
Senior eng. Ulan Bator meat combine 58-61; Minister of Food Industry 61-63; deputy to People's Great Hural (Assembly) 60-; Chair. of People's Great Hural 63-69, 81-; mem. Presidium of People's Great Hural 69-73; mem. Cen. Cttee., Mongolian People's Revolutionary Party (MPRP) 61-; First Sec. Ulan Bator MPRP Cttee. 63-; candidate mem. Political Bureau, MPRP Cen. Cttee. 73-81, mem. 81-. Central Committee of the Mongolian People's Revolutionary Party, Ulan Bator, Mongolia.

Amir Machmud, Lt.-Gen.; Indonesian army officer and politician; b. 21 Feb. 1923, Cimahi, West Java; ed. Technical School, Army Staff Coll. (SSKAD).
Several army posts 43-65, including Deputy Chief of Staff Dwilora Command I 61, Commdr. Mil. Territory X, Lambung Mangkurat, S. Kalimantan 62-65, Commdr. Mil. Territory V/Djaja 65; promoted to rank of Lt.-Col. 57, Col. 61, Brig.-Gen. 64, Maj.-Gen. 66, Lt.-Gen. 70; Minister of Home Affairs, Pembangunan (Devt.) Cabinet 69; Chair. of govt. body for the implementation of Act of Free Choice in W. Irian (now Irian Jaya) according to New York Agreement on Irian Jaya 69; implemented general elections 71; Minister of Home Affairs 73-.
Department of Home Affairs, Jalan Veteran, Jakarta, Indonesia.

Amirthalingam, Appapillai, B.A.; Sri Lankan (Tamil) lawyer and politician; b. 26 Aug. 1927, Jaffna; ed. Univ. of Ceylon, Ceylon Law Coll.
Called to the Bar 52; mem. House of Reps. for Vaddukoddai 56-70, Nat. State Assembly for Kankesanturai July 77-; in political detention 58, 59, 61, 76; founder mem. Ilankai Tamil Arasu Kadchi (Ceylon Fed. Party) 49-, Gen. Sec. 64-72, Pres. 73-; Sec.-Gen. Tamil United Liberation Front 73-; Leader of Opposition July 77-.
Publs. (in Tamil) *Our Objective* 54, *Lessons of Bangladesh* 72, *Racial Segregation in Ceylon* 73.
Office of the Leader of the Opposition, Parliament, Colombo 1; Home: Moolai, Chulipuram, Sri Lanka.
Telephone: 31296 (Colombo); Vaddukoddai 235 (Chulipuram).

Amritanand, Rt. Rev. Joseph; Indian ecclesiastic; b. 17 Feb. 1917; ed. Forman Christian Coll., Lahore and Bishop's Coll.
Ordained Deacon 41, Priest 43; Bishop of Assam 49-62, of Lucknow 62-70, Bishop of Calcutta 70-82; first Bishop of Durgapur 72-74.
c/o Bishop's House, 51 Chowringhee Road, Calcutta 700071, West Bengal, India.
Telephone: 44-5259.

An Pingsheng; Chinese politician.
Provincial cadre in Guangdong 55, Vice-Gov. Guangdong 56-61; Sec. Guangxi CCP Cttee. 61-67, 71-75, First Sec. 75-; Vice-Chair. Guangxi Revolutionary Cttee. 68-75, Chair. 75-77; First Sec. Yunnan CCP Cttee. Feb. 77-; Chair. Yunnan Revolutionary Cttee. Feb. 77-; First Political Commissar, Yunnan Mil. District Feb. 77-; Chair. People's Congress, Yunnan; mem. 10th Cen. Cttee. 73, 11th Cen. Cttee. 77.
People's Republic of China.

Anand, Bal Krishan, M.B., B.S., M.D.; Indian physiologist; b. 19 Sept. 1917; ed. Government Coll. and K.E. Medical Coll., Lahore.
Professor of Physiology, Lady Hardinge Medical Coll., New Delhi 49-57; All-India Inst. of Medical Sciences, New Delhi 57-74, Prof. Emer. 77-; Pres. XXVI Int. Congress of Physiological Sciences, New Delhi 74; Asst. Dir. WHO (S.E. Asia) 74-77; Vice-Chancellor Banaras Hindu Univ., Varanasi 78; Pres. Indian Acad. of Medical Sciences and Nat. Bd. of Examinations 79; Rockefeller Foundation Fellow at Yale Univ. School of Medicine 50-51; Fellow, Indian Acad. of Medical Sciences, Nat. Inst. of Sciences

(F.N.I.); Indian Council of Medical Research Senior Research Award 62; Watumull Foundation Award in Medicine 61; Sir Shanti Swaroof Bhatnagar Memorial Award for Scientific Research in Medicine 63; Padma Shri 69; Medical Council of India Silver Jubilee Research Award 69.
B9/21, Vasant Vihar, New Delhi, India.

Anand, Mulk Raj, PH.D.; Indian author and critic; b. 12 Dec. 1905; ed. Punjab and London Univs.
Active in Nationalist and Gandhi movements; lecturer, London County Council; B.B.C. broadcaster; film script writer, British Ministry of Information; edited (56) various magazines, Leverhulme Fellow for Research in Hindustani literature; Editor *Marg* magazine, India; mem. India Nat. Acad. of Letters, Indian Nat. Acad. of Arts, Indian Nat. Book Trust; Tagore Prof. of Art and Literature, Panjab Univ., Chandigarh; fmr. Chair. Nat. Acad. of Art, New Delhi; Padma Bhushan 67.
Publs. Novels: *Morning Face, Private Life of an Indian Prince, Confession of a Lover, Untouchable Coolie, The Barbers' Trade Union, Seven Summers,* etc.; Essays: *Apology for Heroism, Seven Little Known Birds of the Inner Eye,* etc.
Jassim House, 25 Cuffe Parade, Colaba, Bombay 5, India. Telephone: Bombay 252576 (Marg Publs.).

Anderson, Harold David, O.B.E., A.O., B.A.; Australian diplomatist; b. 6 Sept. 1923, Adelaide; ed. St. Peter's Coll., Adelaide, Melbourne and Adelaide Univs.
Third Sec. Dept. of External Affairs, Canberra 45-46, Australian Embassy, Paris 47-49, High Comm., Karachi 49-50; Consul, New Caledonia 50-53; Second Sec. Dept. of External Affairs, Canberra 53-55; Chargé d'affaires, Phnom-Penh 55-57; First Sec., Tokyo 57-58; Asst. Sec., Canberra 61-62; attached to Imperial Defence Coll., London 63; Amb. to Repub. of Viet-Nam 64-66; Asst. Sec. and Acting First Asst. Sec., Canberra 66-68; Observer at Viet-Nam Peace Talks, Paris 68-70; First Asst. Sec. (Asia Div.), Canberra 70-73; Amb. to France and concurrently Amb. to Morocco and Perm. Del. to UNESCO 77-78, Amb. and Perm. Rep. to UN 78-.
Australian Mission to the United Nations, 1 Dag Hammarskjold Plaza, New York, N.Y. 10017; Apartment 5C, 1 Beekman Place, New York, N.Y., U.S.A. (Home).

Anderson, Dame Judith, D.B.E.; Australian actress; b. 10 Feb. 1898, Adelaide; ed. Norwood High School.
Stage debut in *A Royal Divorce*, Theatre Royal, Sydney 15; went to New York 18; stage appearances have included: *The Dove, Behold the Bridegroom, Strange Interlude, Mourning becomes Electra, Come of Age, The Old Maid, Hamlet, Macbeth, Family Portrait, Tower Beyond, Three Sisters, Medea*; films: *Rebecca, Edge of Darkness, Laura, King's Row, Spectre of the Rose, The Red House, Pursued, Tycoon, Cat on a Hot Tin Roof, Macbeth, Don't Bother to Knock, A Man Called Horse, The Chinese Prime Minister* (TV) 74.
808 San Ysidro Lane, Santa Barbara, Calif. 93103, U.S.A.

Ansell, Graham Keith, B.A.; New Zealand diplomatist; b. 2 March 1931, Lower Hutt, New Zealand; ed. Horowhenua Coll., Palmerston North Boys' School and Victoria Univ., Wellington.
Department of Industries and Commerce 48-51, of External Affairs 51-56; Second Sec., High Comm. in Canada 56-59; Asst., then Acting Head, Econ. and Social Affairs Div., Dept. of External Affairs 59-62; Deputy High Commr., Western Samoa 62-64, Australia 64-68; Head, Econ. Div., Ministry of Foreign Affairs 68-71; Minister, N.Z. Embassy, Japan 71-73; High Commr., Fiji 73-76, concurrently to Nauru 74-76; Amb. to Belgium, Denmark, Luxembourg and the EEC 77-80; Asst. Sec., Ministry of Foreign Affairs 80-81; Dir. New Zealand Planning Council May 81-.
New Zealand Planning Council, National Provident Fund Building, Wellington; Home: 57 Rimu Road, Raumati Beach, New Zealand.

Anthony, Rt. Hon. (John) Douglas, C.H.; Australian farmer and politician; b. 31 Dec. 1929; ed. Murwillumbah High School, The King's School, Paramatta, and Queensland Agricultural Coll.
Member House of Reps. 57-; Minister for the Interior 64-67, of Primary Industry 67-71; Leader of Country Party 71-; Minister for Trade, Deputy Prime Minister 71-72; Deputy Prime Minister, Minister for Overseas Trade Nov. 75-, also Minister for Minerals and Energy Nov.-Dec. 75, for National Resources 75-77, for Trade and Resources Dec. 77-; Privy Councillor 71.
Parliament House, Canberra, A.C.T., Australia.

Anwar Sani, Chaidir; Indonesian diplomatist; b. 19 Feb. 1918, Padang; ed. Univ. of Leiden.
Joined Indonesian Foreign Service 50; First Sec., Paris 50-52; Ministry of Foreign Affairs 52-55; Counsellor, Cairo 55, Beijing 55-57; Ministry of Foreign Affairs 57-60; Minister, Counsellor, New Delhi 60-64; Ministry of Foreign Affairs 64-70; Amb. to Belgium and Luxembourg and Head, Indonesian Mission to EEC 70-72; Perm. Rep. to UN 72-79; Amb. to Trinidad and Tobago 74-79, to the Bahamas 77-79; Ministry of Foreign Affairs 79-.
Ministry of Foreign Affairs, Jalan Penjambon 6, Jakarta Pusat, Indonesia.

Aquino, Benigno, Jr.; Philippine politician; b. 27 Nov. 1932.
Youngest senator at 34 yrs. old; tried under martial law Sept. 72; imprisoned Fort Bonifacio mil. camp 72-80; sentenced to death by mil. tribunal Nov. 77; released to undergo heart surgery in Dallas, U.S.A. May 80; now Fellow, Cen. for Int. Affairs, Harvard Univ., U.S.A. 80-; Leader Lakas Ng Bayan—Laban (People's Power Movement—Fight); Sec.-Gen. Liberal Party.
Harvard University, Cambridge, Mass. 02138, U.S.A.

Aramaki, Torao; Japanese business executive; b. 22 Nov. 1902; ed. Yokohama Nat. Univ.
Chairman Isuzu Motors Ltd.
Isuzu Motors Ltd., 6-22-10, Minami-Oi, Shinagawa-ku, Tokyo; Home: 2-3-7, Ikeda, Kawasaki City, Kanagawa Pref., Japan.

Aryal, Krishna Raj, M.ED., M.A.; Nepalese politician; b. Dec. 1928, Kathmandu; ed. Durbar High School, Tri-Chandra Coll., Allahabad Univ., India, Univ. of Oregon, U.S.A.
Lecturer, Nat. Teachers' Training Centre 54-56; Prof. of Educ., Coll. of Educ. 56-59; Editor *Education Quarterly* 56-59, *Nabin Shikshya* 56-59; Founder, Admin. and Principal Shri Ratna Rajya Laxmi Girls' Coll. 61-71; Asst. Minister for Educ. 71-72; Minister of State for Educ. 72-73; Minister of Educ. 73-75, concurrently Pro-Chancellor, Tribhuvan Univ. and Chair. Nat. Educ. Cttee. 73-75; Minister of Foreign Affairs 75-79; Amb. to France 80-; Chair. Asian Group, Vice-Chair. Group 77, UNESCO, Paris; mem. many social orgs. and philanthropic socs. in Nepal; Gorakha Dakhinbahu, First Class; Grand Officer of Yugoslav Star, Second Class; Grand Cordon of Yugoslav Star, First Class; Order of the Rising Sun, First Class (Japan).
Publs. *Monarchy in the Making of Nepal* (in English), *Education for Development of Nepal* (in English), *Facts of Interest* (series in Nepali), *Science of Education* (Nepali) and numerous articles.
7 rue Alberic Magnard, Paris 16e, France; Gaihiri Dhara, Kathmandu, Nepal (Home).

Asada, Shizuo; Japanese aviation official; b. 13 Oct. 1911; ed. Law Dept., Tokyo Imperial Univ.
Dir. Bureau of Shipping, Ministry of Transport 58-61;

Admin. Vice-Minister of Transport 61-63; Senior Vice-Pres. Japan Air Lines 63-69, Exec. Vice-Pres. 69-71, Pres. 71-81, Counsellor, Dir. 81-.
Japan Air Lines, 7-3, Marunouchi 2-chome, Chiyoda-ku, Tokyo 100; Home: 1-45, Tokiwadai, Hodogaya-ku, Yokohama, Kanagawa 240, Japan.

Asano, Teiji; Japanese business executive; b. 1906; ed. Tohoku Imperial Univ.
Joined shipbuilding dept., Mitsui & Co. 30; entered Tamano Shipyard Ltd. (predecessor of Mitsui Shipbuilding & Engineering Co. Ltd.) 48; Man. Dir. Mitsui Shipbuilding & Engineering Co. (now Mitsui Engineering & Shipbuilding Co., Ltd.) 58, Senior Man. Dir. 65, Vice-Pres. 68, Chair. of Board 70-, Director and Counsellor 73-76, Counsellor 76-; Pres. Showa Aircraft Industry Co. Ltd. 73-79, Chair. 79-.
Mitsui Shipbuilding & Engineering Co. Ltd., 6-4, Tsukiji 5-chome, Chuo-ku, Tokyo, Japan.
Telephone: 544-3000.

Ashihara, Yoshinobu, B.A., M.ARCH., D.ENG.; Japanese architect; b. 7 July 1918; ed. Univ. of Tokyo and Harvard Univ. Graduate School.
Worked in architectural firms, Tokyo 46-52; in Marcel Breuer's firm, New York 53; visited Europe on Rockefeller Travel Grant 54; Head, Yoshinobu Ashihara, Arch. and Assocs. 55-; Lecturer in Architecture, Hosei Univ., Tokyo 55-59, Prof. of Architecture 59-65; visited Europe and U.S.A. to study exterior space in architecture 60; Prof. of Architecture, Musashino Art Univ., Tokyo 64-70; Prof. Univ. of Tokyo 70-79; Pres. Japan Architects Asscn.; Visiting Prof., School of Architecture and Building, Univ. of New South Wales, Australia 66, Univ. of Hawaii 69; Award of Architectural Inst. of Japan for Chuo-Koron Building 60; Hon. Fellow American Inst. of Architects; Special Award of Architectural Inst. of Japan for Komazawa Olympic Gymnasium 65; Ministry of Educ. Award for Japan Pavilion *Expo 67*, Montreal; NSID Golden Triangle Award (U.S.A.) 70; Commendatore, Ordine al Merito (Italy) 70.
Works include: Chuo-Koron Building, Sony Building, Komazawa Olympic Gymnasium 65, Japanese Pavilion, Expo 67, Montreal, Fuji Film Building 69, Head Office Building Dai-Ichi Kangyo Bank 80.
Publs. *Exterior Design in Architecture* 70, *The Aesthetic Townscape* 81.
Y. Ashihara, Architects and Associates, 7th Floor, Sumitomo-seimei Shibuya Building, 31-15 Sakuragaokacho, Shibuya-ku, Tokyo; Home: 47 Nishihara-3, Shibuya-ku, Tokyo, Japan.

Asri bin Haji Muda, Datuk Haji Mohamed, S.P.M.K.; Malaysian politician; b. 10 Oct. 1923.
Former teacher; Acting Sec.-Gen. Pan-Malayan Islamic Party 49-54, Commr., Kelantan 54-61, Vice-Pres. 61-64, Pres. 64-; mem. Kelantan State Assembly 59-68, Speaker 64-68; mem. Parl. 59-68; mem. Nat. Unity Council 69-; Minister of Land Devt., Mines and Special Functions 73-76, of Land, Mines and Regional Devt. 76-77; Deputy Chair. Nat. Council for Islamic Affairs 73-.
c/o Nippon Shakaito, 1-8-1 Nagata-cho, Chiyoda-ku, Tokyo, Japan.

Asukata, Ichio; Japanese politician; b. 1915.
Mayor of Yokohama 63; Head Nat. Asscn. of progressive mayors; fmr. mem. House of Councillors; Chair. Socialist Party of Japan Dec. 77-.
c/o Nippon Shakaito, 1-8-1 Nagata-cho, Chiyoda-ku, Tokyo, Japan.

Avhia, Col.-Gen. Jarantayn; Mongolian government official and soldier; b. 14 June 1923; ed. V. I. Lenin Army Political Acad., U.S.S.R.
From Private to Battalion Commdr., Frontier and Internal Troops Directorate, Ministry of Internal Affairs 43-55; head of a section, Ministry of Army and Public Security Affairs 55-56; deputy head of a dept., State Security Directorate, Ministry of Public Security 60-61; deputy head and head of Chief Militia Directorate, First Deputy Minister of Public Security 61-69; Procurator of the MPR 69-78; First Deputy Minister of Defence April-Sept. 1978, Minister of Defence Sept. 78-; mem. Cen. Cttee. Mongolian People's Revolutionary Party 71-; Deputy to People's Great Hural (Assembly) 66-; Order of Sühbaatar, Order of Red Banner of Military Merit, Order of Military Merit, Order of the Pole Star.
Ministry of Defence, Ulan Bator, Mongolia.

Azimov, Pigam Azimovich; Soviet specialist in Turkmenian language and literature; b. 1915; ed. Ashkhabad Pedagogic Inst.
Member C.P.S.U. 39-; at Ashkhabad Pedagogic Inst. 48-50; at Turkmenian State Univ. 50-65; mem. Turkmenian Acad. of Sciences 51-; Pres. 66-78; several U.S.S.R. decorations.
c/o Presidium of the Turkmenian Academy of Sciences, 15 Gogol Street, Ashkhabad, Turkmen S.S.R., U.S.S.R.

Aziz, Ungku Abdul, D.ECONS.; Malaysian professor; b. 28 Jan. 1922, London, England; ed. Raffles Coll. and Univ. of Malaya, Singapore, Waseda Univ., Tokyo, Univ. of Pittsburgh, U.S.A.
Johore State Civil Service; Lecturer in Econs., Univ. of Malaya, Singapore until 52; Head, Dept. of Econs., Univ. of Malaya, Kuala Lumpur 52-61, Dean of Faculty 61-65, Vice-Chancellor 68-, Royal Prof. of Econs. June 78-; Pres. Nat. Co-operative Movement (ANGKASA) March 71, Asscn. of S.E. Asian Insts. of Higher Learning (ASAIHL) 73-75; Chair. Asscn. of Commonwealth Univs. 74-75, Malaysian Nat. Council for ASAIHL, Malaysian Nat. Asscn. for UNESCO; mem. Econ. Asscn. of Malaysia, Int. Asscn. of Agricultural Economists, Joint Advisory Cttee. of FAO, UNESCO and ILO; mem. UN Cttee. for Devt. Planning 78-80; mem. Council, UN Univ. 80-(86); Ordre des Arts et des Lettres, France 65, Tun Abdul Razak Foundation Award 78, Japan Foundation Award 81; Fellow, World Acad. of Arts and Sciences 65; corresp. mem. advisory board, *Modern Asian Studies* 73-75.
Office of the Vice-Chancellor, University of Malaya, Kuala Lumpur 22-11, Malaysia.
Telephone: Kuala Lumpur 568400.

B

Bahadur, Raj, B.SC., M.A., LL.B.; Indian lawyer and politician; b. 21 Aug. 1912; ed. Agra Coll. and St. John's Coll., Agra.
Member Cen. Advisory Cttee. Bharatpur State 39-42, Municipal Comm. 41-42; resigned to join "Quit India" Movement; mem. Rep. Assembly 43; Sec. Assembly Praja Parishad Party 43-48; Gen. Sec. Matsya Union Congress Cttee. 48-49; Pres. Bharatpur Bar Asscn. 48-51; mem. Indian Constituent Assembly 48-50, mem. Provisional Lok Sabha 50-51; Sec. Congress Party in Lok Sabha 50-52; Deputy Minister, later Minister of State for Communications 51-56; led Indian del. to 10th Session of Int. Civil Aviation Organization, Caracas; Minister of Communications 56-57, Minister of State for Transport and Communications 57-62, for Transport 62-64; Minister of Transport 64-66, of Information and Broadcasting 66-67; Advocate, Supreme Court of India 67; Amb. to Nepal 68-71; Minister of Parl. Affairs, Shipping and Transport 71-73, of Communications 73-74, of Tourism and Civil Aviation 74-76; Sr. Advocate, Supreme Court 77-; mem. Rajasthan State Legis. Assembly June 80-; Leader, Congress (S) opposition in Assembly; mem. Rajasthan P.C.C. and All-India Congress Cttee. 56-82; Congress Party; awarded Tamrapatra 74.
Basan Gate, Bharatpur, Rajasthan, India.

Bahuguna, Hemavati Nandan; Indian politician; b. 25 April 1919, Bughani, Garhwal; ed. D.A.V. Coll., Dehra Dun, and Allahabad Univ.
Active in Independence Movement whilst a student; participated in Quit India Movement 42; trade union organizer under Indian Nat. TUC, Allahabad; formed Mazdoor Sabha trade union org., Allahabad; mem. Uttar Pradesh Legislative Assembly 52-69; Parl. Sec. to State Minister of Labour and Social Welfare 57, later Deputy Minister of Labour and Industries; State Minister of Labour 62-67, of Finance and Transport 67-69; Gen. Sec. All-India Congress Cttee. 69-71; mem. from Allahabad, Lok Sabha 71-73; Union Minister of Communications 71-73; leader of Congress Legislative Party in Uttar Pradesh 73; Chief Minister of Uttar Pradesh 73-75, resgnd.; resgnd. from Congress Party Feb. 77, rejoined, then resgnd. 80; Gen. Sec. Congress for Democracy Feb.-May 77; Minister of Fertilizers, Petroleum and Chemicals 77-79, of Finance July-Oct. 79; mem. Janata Party 77-79; mem. Lok Sabha from Lucknow 77-81; fmr. Sec.-Gen. Indian Nat. Congress (I); founder-Pres. Democratic Socialist Party; won Garwhal-In-Up Hills parliamentary by-election May 82.
Lok Sabha, New Delhi, India.

Bai Rubing; Chinese party official; b. 1906, Shaanxi.
Director, Cen. Admin. of Handicraft Industry, State Council 54-58; Sec. CCP Shandong 58-67; Vice-Gov. of Shandong 58-63, Gov. 63-67; criticized and removed from office during Cultural Revolution 67; Vice-Chair. Shandong Revolutionary Cttee. 71; Deputy Sec. CCP Shandong 71; First Political Commissar Jinan Mil. Region, PLA 74-80; Second Sec. CCP Shandong 74, First Sec. 74-; now also Chair. Shandong Revolutionary Cttee.; mem. 10th Cen. Cttee. of CCP 73, 11th Cen. Cttee. 77.
People's Republic of China.

Bainqen Erdini Qoigyu Gyaincain (*see* Panchen Lama).

Bakht, Sikander, B.SC.; Indian politician; b. 24 Aug. 1918, Delhi; ed. Delhi Univ.
Member of Indian Nat. Congress until 69; mem. All-India Congress Cttee. (Org.), also mem. Working Cttee. and Gen. Sec. Congress Cttee. (Org.) 69-77; mem. Delhi Metropolitan Council for 5 years; detained for 18 months during emergency 75-76; mem. for Chandni Chowk, Lok Sabha March 77-; Minister of Works, Housing, Supply and Rehabilitation 77-79; mem. and Gen. Sec. Janata Party 77; Gen. Sec. Bharatiya Janata Party (BJP) 80-82.
Lok Sabha, New Delhi, India.

Ballmer, Ray Wayne, M.SC.; American mining executive; b. 6 May 1926, Santa Rita, New Mexico; ed. N.M. School of Mines, Mass. Inst. of Technology.
Held senior posts with Kennecott Copper Corpn., U.S.A., with responsibilities in Ariz. and Bingham Canyon, Utah operations; later Man. Dir. Bougainville Copper Ltd. and Dir. Bougainville Mining Ltd., responsible for design, construction and commissioning of Bougainville copper operations; later Pres. Amoco Minerals Co. and Exec. Vice-Pres. Cyprus Mines Corpn.; now Pres. and Chief Operating Officer Rio Algom Ltd.
Rio Algom Ltd., 120 Adelaide Street West, Toronto, Ontario M5H 1W5, Canada.

Bandaranaike, Felix Dias; Ceylonese politician; b. 1931.
Minister of Finance and Parl. Sec. to Minister of Defence and of External Affairs 60-62; Minister without Portfolio Nov. 62-63, of Agriculture, Food and Co-operatives 63-65; Minister of Public Admin., Local Govt. and Home Affairs 70-75, of Justice 72-77, of Finance 75-77; deprived of civic rights for 7 yrs. for misuse of power 80.
c/o Sri Lanka Freedom Party, 407 Galle Road, Colombo, Sri Lanka.

Bandaranaike, Sirimavo Ratwatte Dias; Ceylonese politician; b. 17 April 1916; ed. St. Bridget's Convent, Colombo.
Widow of the late S. W. R. D. Bandaranaike (Prime Minister of Ceylon 56-59); Pres. of Sir Lanka Freedom Party 60-; Prime Minister, Minister of Defence and External Affairs 60-65; mem. Senate until 65; mem. Parl. and Leader of Opposition 65-70; Prime Minister, Minister of Defence and External Affairs 70-77, also Minister of Planning and Econ. Affairs, and of Plan Implementation 73-77; deprived of civic rights for 7 yrs. and expelled from Parl. for misuse of power 80.
Horagolla, Nittambuwa, Sri Lanka.

Bansal, Ghamandi Lal, M.A., LL.B.; Indian commercial executive; b. 3 Dec. 1914; ed. A.V. Mission School, Ranikhet, Government Intermediate Coll., Almora, and Lucknow Univ.
Former Dir. State Bank of India; mem. Indian Parl. 52-57; Sec.-Gen. Fed. of Indian Chambers of Commerce and Industry, All-India Organization of Industrial Employers, Indian Nat. Cttee. of Int. Chamber of Commerce 54-75; Chair. Governing Body of Shri Ram Coll. of Commerce, Nat. Cttee. for the Devt. of Backward Areas; Vice-Pres. Indian Council of World Affairs; Dir.-Gen. Econ. Research Division, Birla Inst. of Scientific Research; Dir. Rohtas Industries Ltd.; Leader trade dels. to foreign countries; Trustee, Indian Council for Child Welfare.
Publ. *India and Pakistan—An Analysis of Economic, Agricultural and Mineral Resources.*
A-37, Kailash Colony, New Delhi 110048, India.

Barker, Edmund William, M.A., LL.B.; Singapore politician; b. 1920; ed. Raffles Coll., Singapore, St. Catharine's Coll., Cambridge and Inner Temple, London.
Practised law in Singapore 52-64; M.P. in constituency of Tanglin 63-; Speaker of Singapore Legislative Assembly 63-64; Minister for Law 64-; Minister for Nat. Devt. 65-75, for the Environment 75-79, for Science and Technology 79-81; Leader in Parliament and Pres. of Singapore Nat. Olympic Council.
Ministry of Law, City Hall, St. Andrew's Road, Singapore.

Barooah, Dev Kanta (*see* Borooah, Dev Kanta).

Barr, Morris Alfred, LL.D.; Australian international business executive and administrator; b. 23 Dec. 1922; ed. Scotch Coll., Melbourne Univ. and Melbourne Conservatorium of Music.
Member editorial staff Melbourne *Argus*; served with Australian Imperial Forces, mem. Far Eastern Liaison Office; Head, Melbourne Conservatorium of Music 48; with English-Speaking Union 51-; Dir. of Programmes 59-64, Dir.-Gen. 64-69; Int. Co-ordinator Winston Churchill Memorial Trust 60-65; Chair., Man. Dir. Associated Consultants Construction Ltd. 69-; Trustee, Univ. of Louisville (Humphrey Centenary Scholarship Trust); Chair. Australian Musical Asscn. 74-; Deputy Chair. Victoria Promotion Cttee. (London) 78; Trustee, Britain Australia Vocational Exchange 74-; Assoc. Consultants Ltd.
88 Baker St., London, W.1; Home: 16 Park Place Villas, London, W.2, England; 6 Walker Street, Balwyn, Melbourne, Vic., Australia.
Telephone: 01-935 4253 (London).

Barwick, Rt. Hon. Sir Garfield Edward John, P.C., A.K., G.C.M.G., B.A., LL.B.; Australian lawyer and fmr. politician; b. 22 June 1903; ed. Sydney Univ.
Admitted to N.S.W. Bar 27, Victoria Bar 45, Queensland Bar 58; Pres. N.S.W. Bar Asscn. 50-52, 55-56, Law Council of Australia 52-54; mem. Fed. House of Reps. for Parramatta 58-64; Attorney-Gen. 58-64; Acting Minister for External Affairs 59, 60, Minister 61-64; Chief Justice of Australia 64-81; Chancellor Macquarie Univ. 67-78; Pres. Australian Inst. of Int. Affairs 72-; Pres. Royal N.S.W.

Inst. for Deaf and Blind Children 76-; Hon. LL.D. (Sydney).
Mundroola, George Street, Careel Bay, Sydney, N.S.W., Australia.

Basarah, Air Chief Marshal Saleh; Indonesian air force officer and diplomatist; b. 14 Aug. 1928, Manonjaya; ed. Air Force schools.
Various posts in Air Force; Commdr. Fifth Regional Air Command 66-69; Chief of Staff, Departmental Affairs, Dept. of Defence and Security 70; Air Force Chief of Staff 73-77; Amb. to U.K. 78-81; numerous medals.
c/o Ministry of Foreign Affairs, Jakarta, Indonesia.

Ba Swe, U; Burmese politician; b. 19 April 1915, Tavoy; ed. Rangoon Univ.
Member of exec. cttee. Rangoon Univ. Students' Union (RUSU) 37-38; co-founder, People's Revolutionary Party 39; Sec.-Gen. All Burma Student Union and RUSU 39-40, Pres. RUSU 40-41; detained by British 40-41; Chief of Civil Defence, Rangoon 42-45; leader Anti-Fascist People's Freedom League (AFPFL), detained by Japanese 45; participated in resistance 45; Sec.-Gen. Socialist Party 45, AFPFL 47-51, Vice-Pres. 52; Pres. Burma TUC 48-63; mem. Chamber of Deputies for Taikkyi 52-56, for Lanmadau 56-62; Minister for Defence and Mines 52-56; Chair. Asian Socialist Conf. 52-54, 54-56, 56-58; Prime Minister 56-57; Deputy Prime Minister for Defence and Law and Order 57-58; Pres. Stable AFPFL; detained by Revolutionary Council 63-66; Yugoslav Banner, First Class, Noble Order of the White Elephant (Thailand), Star of Revolution, First Degree.
84 Innes Road, Rangoon, Burma.
Telephone: 31323.

Bateman, Leslie Clifford, C.M.G., D.SC., PH.D., F.R.S., P.S.M.; British scientist; b. 21 March 1915; ed. Univ. Coll., London, and Oriel Coll., Oxford.
Chemist, British (now Malaysian) Rubber Producers' Research Asscn., England 41-53, Dir. of Research 53-62; Controller of Rubber Research and Chair. Malayan Rubber Research and Devt. Board 62-74; Sec.-Gen. Int. Rubber Study Group 76-; Colwyn Medal 62 and Jubilee Foundation Lecturer 71, Inst. of the Rubber Industry; Hon. D.Sc. (Malaya) 68, (Aston) 72; Fellow, Univ. Coll., London 74.
Publs. Editor and contributor to *The Chemistry and Physics of Rubber-like Substances* 63; numerous publs. in *Journal of the Chem. Soc.* etc., and on the technoeconomic position of the natural rubber industry.
3 Palmerston Close, Welwyn Garden City, Herts. AL8 7DL, England.

Batmönh, Jambyn; Mongolian politician; b. 10 March 1926; ed. Mongolian State Univ. and Acad. of Social Sciences of CPSU Central Cttee., U.S.S.R.
Lecturer, Mongolian State Univ. and Pedagogical Inst. 51-52; lecturer, Vice-Rector, Higher Party School of Mongolian People's Revolutionary Party (MPRP) Cen. Cttee. 52-58; Head of Dept., Vice-Rector, Rector, Higher School of Econs. 62-67; Vice-Rector, Rector, Mongolian State Univ. 67-73; Head of Science and Educ. Dept., MPRP Cen. Cttee. 73-74; Deputy Chair. Council of Ministers May-June 74, Chair. June 74-; cand. mem. MPRP Cen. Cttee. 71-76, mem. Cen. Cttee. 76-, mem. Political Bureau, MPRP Cen. Cttee. 74-; deputy to People's Great Hural (Assembly) 73-; Order of Sühbaatar.
Government Palace, Ulan Bator, Mongolia.

Batt, Neil Leonard Charles, B.A.; Australian business executive and fmr. politician; b. 14 June 1937, Hobart, Tasmania; ed. Hobart High School, Univ. of Tasmania.
Secondary School Teacher 60-61 and 64-66; mem., House of Assembly, Tasmanian Parl. 69-80; Minister of Transport, Tasmania, and Chief Sec. 72-74, Minister for Educ. 74-77, Minister for Econ. Planning and Devt. 77-79; Deputy Premier and Treasurer 77-80, Minister for Forests 78-80, Minister for Finance 79-80; Nat. Pres., Australian Labor Party (ALP) 78-80; State Pres., Tasmanian Branch ALP 76-79; Australian Pres. Freedom from Hunger Campaign 72-75; Nat. Chair. Australian Council for Overseas Aid 75-78; UNICEF Rep., Bangladesh 80-81; Resident Dir., TNT-Ansett Group, W.A. 81-; Chair. Airlines of Western Australia 81-; Assoc. Trustee, Cttee. for Econ. Devt. of Australia (CEDA) 81-; mem. Chartered Inst. of Transport 81-; Council mem. Perth Chamber of Commerce (Chair. Educ. Cttee. and mem. Legis. Review Cttee.) 81-; Exec. Council mem. West Australian Road Transport Asscn. Inc. 81-; W.A. Council mem. Australian Road Transport Industrial Org. 81-; Fellow, Australian Inst.,of Petroleum Ltd. 81-.
Publs. *The Great Depression in Australia* 70, *The Role of the University Today* 77, *Information Power* 77, *Labor's Social Policy and Objectives* 77, *Unemployment in Tasmania during the Great Depression* 78, *Away from the Mandarin Society* 78, *Tasmanian Labor Party Conferences* 1930-35 79, *Labor Directions for the Eighties* 80.
450 Belmont Avenue, Kewdale, Western Australia 6105 (Office); 15 Neesham Street, Booragoon, Western Australia 6154, Australia (Home).
Telephone: 458 6000 (Office); 364 2502 (Home).

Beale, The Hon. Sir Howard, K.B.E., Q.C., B.A., LL.B. Australian lawyer, diplomatist and company director; b. 1898; ed. Univ. of Sydney.
Called to the Bar 25; Queen's Counsel 50; R.A.N. 42-45; Liberal mem. for Parramatta, House of Reps. 46-58; mem. Commonwealth Parl. Public Works Cttee. 47-49; Cabinet Minister in Menzies' Govt. 49-58, Minister for Information and Transport 49-50, for Supply 50-58, and of Defence Production 56-58 and Minister-in-Charge of Atomic Energy Comm. and Aluminium Production Comm. 50-58; Acting Minister for Immigration 51-52, 53, 54, for Nat. Development 52-53, for Air 52, for Defence 57; mem. Australian Defence Council, Cabinet Defence Preparations Cttee., Cabinet Cttee. on Uranium and Atomic Energy 50-58; Amb. to U.S.A. 58-64; Alternate Gov. Int. Monetary Fund 60, 62, 64; Del. to ANZUS Council 58, 59, to Colombo Plan Conf. 58, to UN 59, to SEATO Conf. 59, 60, to World Food Congress 63; Pres. Arts Council of Australia 64-68; Woodward Lecturer, Yale Univ. 60, Regents' Visiting Prof., Univ. of California 66, Marquette Univ. 67, 69; now Dir. and Adviser to various Australian, British and U.S. industrial and financial corporations; Hon. LL.D., Kent Univ., Ohio 59, Marquette Univ. 69; Hon. D. H. Lit., Nebraska 62.
Publ. *This Inch of Time* 77.
1-4 Marathon Road, Darling Point, N.S.W. 2027, Australia.

Beattie, Hon. Sir David Stuart, G.C.M.G., G.C.V.O., Q.C., LL.B.; New Zealand lawyer and administrator; b. 29 Feb. 1924, Sydney, Australia; ed. Dilworth School and Univ.
Naval Officer, Second World War; barrister and solicitor; Judge of Supreme Court 69-80; Governor-General of New Zealand Oct. 80-; Pres. Auckland District Law Soc. 64-; N.Z. Services rugby 44-45.
Government House, Private Bag, Wellington; Home: 53B Chatsworth Road, Silverstream, Wellington, New Zealand.

Bedi, Bishan Singh, B.A.; Indian cricketer; b. 25 Sept. 1946, Amritsar; ed. Punjab Univ.
Employed by State Bank of India, New Delhi; slow left-arm bowler; has played for India in 53 Tests 66-, captained India in 14 Tests; has captained Delhi in Ranji Trophy and North Zone in Duleep Trophy; played for Northamptonshire, England 72-77; Padma Shri 69; Arjuna Award 71; Hon. Life mem. MCC 81
1250-Azad Nagar, Putlighar, Amritsar, Punjab, India.
Telephone: 43133.

Beeby, Clarence Edward, C.M.G., M.A., PH.D.; New Zealand educationist and administrator; b. 16 June 1902; ed. Christchurch Boys' High School, Canterbury Coll., Univ. of New Zealand, University Coll., London, and Univ. of Manchester.
Lecturer in Philosophy and Education, Canterbury Univ. Coll., Univ. of N.Z. 23-34; Dir. NZ. Council for Educational Research 34-38; Asst. Dir. of Education, Education Dept., N.Z. 38-40; Dir. of Education 40-60 (on leave of absence 48-49); Asst. Dir.-Gen. of UNESCO 48-49; Ambassador to France 60-63; leader N.Z. Dels. to Gen. Confs. of UNESCO 46, 47, 50, 53, 54, 56, 58, 60, 63; Hon. Counsellor of UNESCO 50; mem. of UNESCO Exec. Board 60-63, Chair. 63; Research Fellow, Harvard Univ. 63-67; Chair. UNESCO Evaluation Panel for World Functional Literacy Projects 67-70; Commonwealth Visiting Prof., Univ. of London 67-68; Consultant to Australian Govt. on educ. in Papua and New Guinea 69; Educ. Consultant to Ford Foundation in Indonesia 70-77; Consultant to UNDP (Malaysia) 76; mem. Council of Consultant Fellows, Int. Inst. for Educ. Planning, Paris 72-78; Foreign Assoc., U.S. Nat. Acad. of Educ. 81; Hon. LL.D., Hon. Litt.D.; Grand Cross, Order of St. Gregory; Mackie Medal (ANZAAS) 71.
Publs. *The Intermediate Schools of New Zealand* 38, *Entrance to University* (with W. Thomas and M. H. Oram) 39, *The Quality of Education in Developing Countries* 66, *The Qualitative Aspects of Educational Planning* (ed.) 69, *Assessment of Indonesian Education: a Guide in Planning* 78.
New Zealand Council for Educational Research, P.O. Box 3237, Wellington; 73 Barnard Street, Wellington, New Zealand.

Benedicto, Roberto S., A.A., LL.M.; Philippine lawyer, banker and diplomatist; b. 17 April 1917; ed. Univ. of the Philippines, George Washington Univ., U.S.A.
Major in the Philippines Armed Forces 41-45; Acting Provincial Fiscal, Negros Occidental 45; Prof. Commercial and Labour Laws, Far Eastern Univ. 48-55; Gov. Devt. Bank of the Philippines 57-59; Exec. Vice-Pres., Treas., Philippines Commercial and Industrial Bank 62-65; Pres., Vice-Chair. Philippine Nat. Bank 66-70; Amb. to Japan 72-78; Chair. Philippine Sugar Comm.; Pres. Nat. Sugar Trading Corpn.; Chair. Repub. Planters' Bank 78-80; Vice-Chair. Kilusan ng Bagong Lipunan, Region VI 78-81; mem. Cabinet Exec. Cttee. Aug. 82-; mem. Bd. of Regents, Univ. of Philippines 82; Pres. Boy Scouts of the Philippines 81-82; mem. Monetary Bd., Cen. Bank of the Philippines; Legion of Merit, Order of the Rising Sun (First Class); Liberation Medal, World War II Victory Medal; Outstanding Citizen of Manila; Rep. Community Chest of Greater Manila.
Home: Kanlaon Towers, Roxas Boulevard, Metro Manila, Philippines.

Bentley, William, C.M.G.; British diplomatist; b. 15 Feb. 1927, Bury; ed. Bury High School, Manchester Univ., Wadham Coll., Oxford, Coll. of Europe, Bruges.
His Majesty's Forces 45-48; Foreign Office 52; Third Sec., later Second Sec., Tokyo 52; Foreign Office 58; First Sce,, Perm. Mission to UN, New York 60; Foreign Office 63. Head of Chancery, Kuala Lumpur 65; Counsellor 69; Sec.-Gen. British Pavilion, *Expo 70* 69; Counsellor, Belgrade 70; Head of Perm. Under-Sec.'s Dept., Foreign and Commonwealth Office 73, of Far Eastern Dept. 74; Amb. to Philippines 76-81; High Commissioner in Malaysia 81-.
British High Commission, Wisma Damansara, Jalan Semantan, P.O. Box 1030, Kuala Lumpur, Malaysia; Home: 6 Landsdowne Close, London, S.W.20, England.

Beresford, Bruce; Australian film director; b. 1940; ed. Univ. of Sydney.
Worked in advertising; worked for Australian Broadcasting Comm.; went to England 61; various jobs incl. teaching; film editor, Nigeria 64-66; Sec. to British Film Institute's Production Bd. 66; feature film dir. 71-; directed many short films 60-75; directed feature films: *The Adventures of Barry Mackenzie* 72, *Barry Mackenzie Holds His Own* 74, *Side by Side* 75, *Don's Party* 76, *The Getting of Wisdom* 77, *Money Movers* 79, *Breaker Morant* 80, *Puberty Blues* 81, *Fortress* 81.
c/o Australian Film Commission, West Street, Sydney, N.S.W., Australia.

Bhabha, Jamshed Jehangir, B.A.; Indian company director and patron of the Arts; b. 21 Aug. 1914, Bombay; ed. Gonville and Caius Coll., Cambridge.
Joined Tata Iron and Steel Co. Ltd. 40; Dir. Tata Sons Ltd., Indian Hotels Co. Ltd., Cen. India Spinning, Weaving and Mfg. Co. Ltd., RDI Print and Publishing Pte. Ltd., CBS Gramophone Records and Tapes (India) Ltd.; Chair. Tata Services Ltd., Stewarts and Lloyds of India Ltd., Tata Press Ltd. and Tata McGraw-Hill Publishing Co. Ltd., Marg Publications; Vice-Chair. Associated Building Co. Ltd.; Vice-Chair. and Trustee-in-Charge, Nat. Centre for the Performing Arts; Managing Trustee, Sir Dorabji Tata Trust; Trustee, the J. N. Tata Endowment for Higher Educ. of Indians, Lady Tata Memorial Trust, J. R. D. Tata Trust, Prince of Wales Museum of Western India, Homi Bhabha Fellowships Council, Homi Bhabha Memorial Trust; Chair. Governing Bd., Tata Inst. of Social Sciences, Bombay; mem. Gen. Assembly and Finance Cttee., Indian Council for Cultural Relations, Court of Govs., Admin. Staff Coll. of India, Governing Council, Nat. Inst. of Design, Council of Management, M. Visvesvaraya Industrial Research and Devt. Centre, Sangeet Natak Akademie (also mem. Exec. Bd.), Court of Indian Inst. of Science, Bangalore, Philatelic Advisory Cttee., Ministry of Communications, Indian Nat. Comm. for Co-operation with UNESCO, Discovery of India (Museum) Advisory Cttee., Nehru Centre; Pres. Soc. of Friends of Trees; Vice-Pres. Soc. for Clean Cities; mem. Admin. Council of the Int. Fund for the Promotion of Culture, UNESCO; Knight Commdr. of the Order of Merit (Italy), Cross of Commdr. of Order of Merit (Fed. Repub. of Germany), Commdr.'s Cross of the Order of the Crown (Belgium).
Bombay House, 24 Homi Mody Street, Bombay 400023; Home: 12 Little Gibbs Road, Malabar Hill, Bombay 400006, India.

Bhagat, Dhanraj: Indian sculptor; b. 20 Dec. 1917; ed. Khalsa High School and Mayo School of Arts, Lahore.
Teacher, Mayo School of Arts 39 and 44; Lecturer in Sculpture, Delhi Polytechnic Art Dept. 46-60, Sr. Lecturer 60-62, Asst. Prof. 62-68, Prof. 68-73; numerous comms. throughout India; works in stone, wood, plaster, cement, and metal-sheet; nine one-man sculpture shows in India 50-67; exhibitions abroad in London and Paris 48, East European countries 55 and 58, U.S.A. 54, Fed. Repub. of Germany 58, São Paulo 62, South Africa 65, London and Ghent 66; mem. Delhi Silpi Chakra; mem. Nat. Cttee. of the Int. Asscn. of Plastic Arts, Paris; Nat. Award, Lalit Kala Akademy 61; State Award 69.
College of Art, 22 Tilak Marg, New Delhi; and H 20, New Delhi South Extension Part 1, New Delhi, India.

Bhagavantam, Suri, M.SC.; Indian scientist and university professor; b. 1909, Gudivada, A.P.; ed. Nizam Coll., Hyderabad and Madras Univ.
Professor of Physics, Andhra Univ. until 48; Scientific Liaison Officer, British Commonwealth Scientific Offices and Scientific Adviser to Indian High Commr. in U.K., London 48-49; Prof. of Physics, Osmania Univ. 49-52, Vice-Chancellor and Dir. Physical Laboratories 52-57; Dir. Indian Inst. of Science, Bangalore 57-62; Scientific Adviser to Minister of Defence 61-69; Pres. ICSU Cttee. on Science and Tech. in Developing Countries (COSTED) 72-80; Chair. Bharat Electronics Ltd., Cttee. on Org. of Scientific

Research; Vice-Pres. Int. Union of Pure and Applied Physics; Dir. Hindustan Aeronautics India Ltd.; Hon. D.Sc., F.N.I. and F.A.Sc.
Publs. *Scattering of Light and Raman Effect* 40, *Theory of Groups and Its Application to Physical Problems* 52, *Crystal Symmetry and Physical Properties* 66.
Indian Institute of Science, Bangalore 560012, India.

Bhandari, Sunder Singh, M.A., LL.B.; Indian politician; b. 12 April 1921, Udaipur, Rajasthan; ed. Sirohi, Udaipur and Kanpur.
Advocate, Mewar High Court, Udaipur 42-43; Headmaster, Shiksha Bhawan, Udaipur 43-46; Divisional Pracharak, Rashtriya Swayamsewak Sangh, Jodhpur 46-51; Provincial Sec. Bharatiya Jana Sangh (People's Party), Rajasthan 51-57; All India Sec. Bharatiya Jana Sangh 61-65, 66-67, All India Organizing Sec. 65-66; mem. Rajya Sabha 66-72, 76-82; Leader, Jana Sangh Group in Rajya Sabha 67-68; Gen. Sec. Bharatiya Jana Sangh 67-77; mem. Nat. Exec. Janata Party 77-79; Deputy Leader, Janata Parl. Party 77-79; Treas. Bharatiya Janata Party 79-80, Vice-Pres. 80-, Deputy Leader Parliamentary Party 79-82; Convenor, Janata Parl. Party Cttee. on Foreign Collaboration; mem. Janata Party Cen. Election Panel; mem. sub-cttee. on Interests of Scheduled Castes and Tribes; mem. Del. to Inter-Parl. Council session (Lisbon, Portugal) 78; mem. Cen. P & T Advisory Council and Agricultural Prices Comm. Panel of Farmers, Govt. of India 78-79; mem. Parl. Comm. on Public Undertakings 80-81, Rajya Sabha Comm. on Subordinate Legislation 81-82.
10 Dr. Rajendra Prasad Road, New Delhi; Panchayati Nohara, Udaipur, Rajasthan, India.
Telephone: 387830 (New Delhi); 5244 (Udaipur).

Bhatt, Ravishanker, B.A., M.A.; Indian merchant banker; b. 13 Dec. 1909; ed. Samaldas Coll., Bhavnagar, Bombay School of Economics and Sociology and London School of Economics.
Secretary, Industrial Investment Trust Ltd., 36-40; Sec. Diwan's Office, Bhavnagar State, subsequently Nayab Diwan (finance and railway) 40-47; Finance Officer, Oriental Govt. Security Life Assurance Co. Ltd. 48-53; Man. Dir. Bombay State Finance Corpn. 53-57; mem. Govt. of India Tariff Comm. 57-60; Exec. Dir. Indian Investment Centre 60-64, Chair. 72-; Chair. Unit Trust of India 64-72; Adviser, Merchant Banking Div., State Bank of India; Chair. Ahmedabad Electricity Co. Ltd., Surat Electricity Co. Ltd., Rydak Syndicate Ltd., Micro-Precision Pumps and Gears Ltd.; Dir. Premier Automobiles Ltd., Atul Products Ltd., Industrial Investment Trust Ltd., Shree Vallabh Glass Works Ltd., Zaudu Pharmaceutical Works Ltd., Jardine Henderson Ltd., Synthetics and Chemicals Ltd., Indian Rayon Corpn. Ltd., Kesoram Industries and Cotton Mills Ltd., Gujerat Steel Tubes Ltd., Gaekwar Mills Ltd.; mem. State Planning Bd., Govt. of Gujerat; Leader, Indian Del. to UN Comm. on Transnat. Corpns.; Hon. Fellow, London School of Econs.
Publs. *Capital for Medium and Small-Scale Industries*; various articles on economic and financial subjects.
Ewart House, Homi Mody Street, Bombay 400023, India.
Telephone: 272543.

Bhatt, Uddhav Deo, M.A.; Nepalese diplomatist; b. 1 March 1932, Baitadi.
Section officer, Ministry of Foreign Affairs 60; First Sec. then Counsellor, New Delhi 61-67; Chief of Protocol 67-68; Deputy Perm. Rep. to UN, New York 69-72; Joint Sec. Int. Org. Div., Ministry of Foreign Affairs 72-75, Foreign Sec. 75-79; del. to confs. of Non-Aligned Heads of State and ministerial meetings 73-; Perm. Rep. to UN 79-.
Permanent Mission of Nepal to the United Nations, 711 Third Avenue, Room 1806, New York, N.Y. 10017, U.S.A.

Bhattacharyya, Birendra Kumar, B.SC., M.A.; Indian journalist and writer; b. 14 Oct. 1924; ed. Jorhat Government High School, Cotton Coll., Gauhati, Calcutta Univ. and Gauhati Univ.
Former Science Teacher, Ukrul High School, Manipur; Editor *Ramdhenu* 51-61, *Sadiniya Navayung* 63-67; Exec. mem. Samyukta Socialist Party, Assam; Sec. Archaeological Soc. of Assam.; Sahitya Akademi Award for Assamese Literature 61, Jnanapith Award 79; Hon. D.Phil. (Gauhati Univ.) 77.
Publs. novels: *Iyaruingam* (won Akademi Award). *Raipathe Ringiai* (Call of the Main Street), *Mother*, *Sataghai* (Killer), *Mrityunjay* (won Jnanapith Award), *Pratipad*, *Nastachandra*, *Ballart*, *Kabar Aru Phul*, *Ranga Megh*, *Daint*; collections of short stories: *Kolongcjioboi* (Still Flows the Kolong), *Satsari* (Necklace); *Aurobindo* (biography).
Kharghuli Development Area, Gauhati 1, Assam, India.
Telephone: 25019.

Bhaya, Hiten, M.A.; Indian business executive; b. 29 Feb. 1920, Muzaffarpur, Bihar; ed. Patna Univ.
Joined Indian Navy Armament Supply Org. and trained in Royal Naval Establishments in Ceylon and U.K.; Dir., Naval Armaments, Naval H.Q. 55-59; joined Industrial Management Pool 59, Dir. Purchase and Stores, Bhilai Steel Plant 59-61; Sec. Hindustan Steel 61-67, Gen. Man. Alloy Steels Plant, Durgapur 67-70, Dir. Hindustan Steel, in charge of Commercial Operations 70-72, Chair. Hindustan Steel Ltd. 72-77, Indian Iron and Steel Co. Ltd.; Chair. Durgapur Devt. Authority, Standing Advisory Cttee. on Govt. Corpns., West Bengal; Dir. Inst. of Management, Calcutta 77-; Dir. Indian Oil Corpn., Industrial Devt. Bank of India, Industrial Reconstruction Corpn. of India; Leader, Employers' Del. ILO Conference 76; Sir Jehangir Gandhi Medal for Industrial Peace 76.
16 New Road, Calcutta 700027, West Bengal, India.
Telephone: 456548.

Bhumibol Adulyadej; King of Thailand; b. 5 Dec. 1927, Cambridge, Mass., U.S.A.; ed. Bangkok and Lausanne, Switzerland.
Youngest son of Their Royal Highnesses Prince and Princess Mahidol of Songkhla; succeeded his brother, the late King Ananda Mahidol, June 46; married Her Majesty the present Queen Sirikit, daughter of H.H. the late Prince Chandaburi Suranath, 28 April 50; formal Coronation 5 May 50; three daughters, H.R.H. Princess Ubol Ratana, b. 51, H.R.H. Princess Maha Chakri Sirindhorn, b. 55, H.R.H. Princess Chulabhorn, b. 57; one son, H.R.H. Crown Prince Maha Vajiralongkorn, b. 52.
Chitralada Villa, Bangkok, Thailand.

Bhushan, Shanti, B.SC., LL.B.; Indian lawyer and politician; b. 11 Nov. 1925, Bijnor, Uttar Pradesh.
Set up legal practice in Allahabad High Court 48; Senior Standing Counsel 62; Advocate-Gen. of Uttar Pradesh 69; Chair. Uttar Pradesh Bar Council 69; Treas. Working Cttee. of Org. Congress 72-77; counsel for Raj Narain (*q.v.*) in Rae Bareli Constituency case; Treas. Janata Party Jan.-April 77; Minister of Law, Justice and Company Affairs 77-79; leader of several Indian Dels. to int. conferences.
A-126, Neeti Bagh, New Delhi 110001, India (Home).
Telephone: 663802 (Home).

Bhutan, King of (*see* Wangchuk, Jigme Singye).

Binh, Nguyen Thi (*see* Nguyen Thi Binh).

Birendra Bir Bikram Shah Dev; King of Nepal; b. 28 Dec. 1945, Kathmandu; ed. St. Joseph's Coll., Darjeeling, Eton Coll., England, Univ. of Tokyo and Harvard Univ.
Has travelled extensively throughout Europe, North and South America, U.S.S.R., Iran, Japan, China and several African countries; Supreme Commdr.-in-Chief, Royal Nepalese Army 72; Chief Patron Nepal Scouts; came to the throne 31 Jan. 72, crowned 24 Feb. 75; married Princess

Aishwarya Rajya Laxmi Devi Rana 70; children Crown Prince Deependra Bir Bikram Shah Dev, b. 71, Princess Shruti Rajya Laxmi Devi Shah, b. 76, Prince Nirajan Bir Bakram Shah, b. 78.
Narayanhity Royal Palace, Kathmandu, Nepal.

Birendra Singh, Rao, B.A.; Indian politician; b. 20 Feb. 1921, Rewari, Haryana; ed. Univ. of Delhi.
Served in army as commissioned officer 42-47, Territorial Army 50-52; mem. Punjab Legis. Council 54-66; Minister, Govt. of Punjab 56-61; mem. Haryana Assembly 67-71, Speaker 67; Chief Minister, SVD Govt. March-Nov. 67; f. Vishal Haryana Party 67; Leader of Opposition, Haryana Assembly 68-71; mem. Lok Sabha 71-77, 80-; Minister of Agric. and Rural Reconstruction Jan. 80-, of Irrigation 80-81, of Civil Supplies 81, Govt. of India.
Ministry of Agriculture, New Delhi, India.

Bista, Kirti Nidhi, M.A.; Nepalese politician; b. 1927; ed. Tri-Chandra Coll., Kathmandu and Lucknow Univ.
Assistant Minister for Education 61-62, Minister for Educ. 62-64, for Foreign Affairs 64; Vice-Chair. Council of Ministers and Minister for Foreign Affairs and Educ. 64-66; Vice-Chair. Council of Ministers and Minister for Foreign Affairs and Econ. Planning 66-67; Deputy Prime Minister and Minister for Foreign Affairs and Educ. 67-68; Prime Minister, Minister of Finance, Gen. Administration and Palace Affairs 69-73; Prime Minister 77-79; Leader Nepalese Dels. to UN Gen. Assemblies 64, 65, 66, to UNESCO Gen. Confs. 62, 64, 66, 68, and to various other confs.; accompanied late H.M. King Mahendra on many State visits; mem. Royal Advisory Cttee. 69-70; Order of Maha Ujjwal Kirtimaya Nepal Shreepad, Order of Jyotirmaya Subikyat Trisakti Patta, Order of Suprasidoha Prabal Gorka Dakshin Bahu, Order of Ati Subiklyat Sewa Lankar, Ordre national du Million d'Eléphants (Laos), Ordre du Parasol blanc (Laos), Grand Cross, Order of Orange-Nassau (Netherlands), Order of Merit of Fed. Repub. of Germany, Légion d'honneur.
Office: Singhdurbar, Kathmandu; Home: Gyaneshwor, Kathmandu, Nepal.

Bjelke-Petersen, Johannes; Australian politician; b. 13 Jan. 1911, Dannevirke, New Zealand.
Farmer; mem. Queensland Legislative Assembly 47-; Minister for Works and Housing, Queensland 63-68; Deputy Leader Nat. Country Party of Queensland 68; Leader Aug. 68-; Premier of Queensland 68-.
Premier's Department, Brisbane, Queensland, Australia.

Bo Yibo; Chinese government official; b. 1901, Shanxi; ed. Taiyuan Normal School and Beijing Univ.
Joined Chinese C.P. about 27; arrested for subversive activities 32; organized Sacrifice for Nat. Salvation League in Taiyuan 37; during Sino-Japanese War was Chair. S.E. Admin. Office of Shanxi Govt., Commdr. Taiyuan Mil. Area and Special Commissar in 3rd Admin. Commissar's Office 37-45; mem. Central Cttee. of C.P, 45-67; Chair. Shanxi-Hebei-Shandong-Henan Border Region Govt. 45-47, also reportedly Vice-Chair. Revolutionary Mil. and Political Acad. for Korean Cadres. Yenan; Deputy Political Commissar Central China P.L.A., Commdr. 8th Column 47-48; Political Commissar N. China Mil. Area, First Vice-Pres. N. China People's Govt., Chair. N.E. Finance and Econ. Cttee. and mem. C.P.N. China Bureau 48; mem. Preparatory Cttee. for C.P P.C.C. 49; mem. Govt. Admin. Council, Vice-Chair. Cttee. of Finance and Econs., and Minister of Finance 49-53; Political Commissar Suiyuan Mil. Area 49; mem. Board All-China Fed. of Co-operatives 50; Chair. Govt. Econ. Investigation Cttee. (led anti-corruption drive) 51; mem. State Planning Comm. 52-67, Deputy Chair. 62-67; mem. Constitution Drafting Cttee. 53; mem. N.P.C. 54-67, May 79-; Chair. State Construction Comm. 54-56; Head of Third Office, State Council 55-59; Vice-Chair. Planning Comm. for Scientific Devt. 56-67; Chair. State Econ. Comm. 58-67; Alt. Mem. Politburo of C.P. 58-69; Vice-Premier 58-67, June 79-; Deputy Dir. State Office of Industry and Communications 59-61, Dir. 61-67; criticized during Cultural Revolution 66; arrested 67; rehabilitated 79; Min. in Charge of Machine-Building Industry Comm. 79-; mem. 11th Cen. Cttee. CC..P. 79-.
People's Republic of China.

Bole, Filipe Nagera, M.A.; Fijian diplomatist; b. 23 Aug. 1936; ed. Victoria Univ. and Auckland Teachers' Coll., New Zealand.
Joined Civil Service as teacher, then Education Officer (Secondary) and Chief Educational Officer (Secondary); Deputy Sec. for Education 72-73; Perm. Sec. for Urban Devt., Housing and Social Welfare 73-74, for Education, Youth and Sport 74-80; Perm. Rep. to UN and Amb. to U.S.A. (also accred. to Canada) 80-; mem. Council, Univ. of South Pacific, Fiji 74-80; served on several Govt. cttees. on education and sport.
Embassy of Fiji, 1629 K Street, N.W., Washington, D.C. 20006, U.S.A.

Bolkiah Mu'izuddin Waddaulah, H.H. Sultan Hassanal, D.K., P.S.P.N.B., P.S.N.B., P.S.L.J., S.P.M.B., P.A.N.B.; Sultan of Brunei; b. 15 July 1946; *s.* of former Sultan Sir Muda Omar Ali Saifuddin, K.C.M.G. (*q.v.*, under Omar Ali Saifuddin); ed. privately, and Victoria Inst., Kuala Lumpur, Malaysia, and Royal Military Acad., Sandhurst.
Appointed Crown Prince and Heir Apparent 61; Ruler of State of Brunei Oct. 67-; Hon. Capt. Coldstream Guards 68; Sovereign and Chief of Royal Orders instituted by Sultans of Brunei.
Istana Darul Hana, Brunei; The Aviary, Osterley, England.

Bonynge, Richard, C.B.E.; Australian conductor; b. 29 Sept. 1930, Sydney; *m.* Joan Sutherland (*q.v.*) 1954.
Trained as a pianist; debut as conductor with Santa Cecilia Orchestra, Rome 62; conducted first opera *Faust*, Vancouver 63; has conducted in most of leading opera houses; Artistic Dir., Principal Conductor Sutherland/Williamson Int. Grand Opera Co., Australia 65; Artistic Dir. Vancouver Opera Assn. 74-78, Consultant Artistic Dir. 78-80; Musical Dir. Australian Opera 76-.
Has conducted *La Sonnambula, La Traviata, Faust, Eugene Onegin, L'Elisir d'Amore, Orfeo* (Haydn) 67, *Semiramide*, Florence 68, *Giulio Cesare, Lucia*, Hamburg, New York 69-71, *Norma* and *Orfeo* 70, *The Tales of Hoffman* 73, Sydney Opera House 74, *Esclarmonde* (Massenet), San Francisco and New York 74-76, *Werther*, New York 79.
Major recordings include *Alcina, La Sonnambula, Norma, Beatrice di Tenda, I Puritani, Faust, Semiramide, Lakmé, La Fille du Régiment, The Messiah, Don Giovanni, Les Huguenots, L'Elisir d'Amore, Lucia, Rigoletto, The Tales of Hoffmann, Thérèse, Esclarmonde* and *La Roi de Lahore* (Massenet), numerous orchestral works, ballet including *Giselle, Coppelia, Sylvia, Nutcracker*.
c/o The Australian Opera, P.O. Box R223, Royal Exchange, N.S.W. 2000, Australia; or c/o Ingpen and Williams, 14 Kensington Court, London, W.8, England.

Booth, Charles Leonard, C.M.G.; British diplomatist; b. 7 March 1925; ed. Pembroke Coll., Oxford.
H.M. Forces 43-47; Foreign Office 50; Third and Second Sec., Rangoon 51; Foreign Office 55; Private Sec. to the Parl. Under-Sec. of State 58; First Sec., Rome 60; Head of Chancery, Rangoon 63, Bangkok 64; Foreign Office 67, Counsellor 68; Deputy High Commissioner, Kampala 69; Counsellor (Admin.) and Consul-Gen., Washington 71; Counsellor, Belgrade 73; Amb. to Burma Feb. 78-.
British Embassy, 80 Strand Road (P.O. Box 638), Rangoon, Burma.
Telephone: Rangoon 75700/1, 72292, 75138, 75616, 75812.

Border, Lewis Harold, A.O., M.V.O.; Australian diplomatist; b. 16 April 1920; ed. The Armidale School, Armidale, and Univ. of Sydney.
Australian Army 41-45; entered Australian Diplomatic Service 45, served Japan, Switzerland, India and Washington, D.C. 47-59; Amb. to Burma 63-65, to Republic of Viet-Nam 66-68; Australian High Commr. in Pakistan and Amb. to Afghanistan 68-70; Deputy Sec. Dept. Foreign Affairs 71-75; Amb. to Fed. Repub. of Germany 75-77; High Commr. in New Zealand 77-80.
P.O. Mooball, N.S.W., Australia.

Borooah, Dev Kanta, LL.B.; Indian politician; b. 22 Feb. 1914, Dibrugarh (Assam); ed. Nowgong Govt. School and Banaras Hindu Univ.
Secretary, Assam P.C.C. 38-45; Editor *Dainik, Assamiya* and *Natun Asamiya* (daily newspapers); mem. Constituent Assembly 49-51, Lok Sabha 52-57; mem. Legislative Assembly of Assam 57-60, Speaker, 60; Chair. Oil Refinery 60; mem. Assam Legislative Assembly 62-66, 67; Minister of Educ. and Co-operation 62; Chair. Oil India 68; Gov. of Bihar 71-73; Union Minister of Petroleum and Chemicals 73-74; Pres. Indian Nat. Congress Party 74-77, resigned March 77; del. to Commonwealth Conf., UN Gen. Assembly and mem. several Indian dels. visiting overseas countries.
Publ. a volume of poetry in Assamese.
23 Tughlak Road, New Delhi, India.

Borrie, Wilfred David, C.B.E., M.A., F.A.C.E., F.A.S.S.A.; British (b. New Zealand) demographer; b. 2 Sept. 1913; ed. Waitaki Boys High School, Oamaru, New Zealand, Univ. of Otago, N.Z. and Cambridge Univ.
Lecturer, Social History and Econs., Sydney Univ. 44-46, Senior Lecturer 46-47; Research Fellow, Research School of Social Sciences, Australian Nat. Univ. 49-52, Reader 52-57, Prof. and Head of Dept. of Demography 57-68; Dir. of Research School 68-73; Vice-Pres. Int. Union for Scientific Study of Population 61-63; Pres. Social Science Research Council of Australia 62-64, Australian Council of Social Services 63-64; Chair. Population Comm., UN 65-69; mem. Immigration Planning Council of Australia 65-72, Australian Population and Immigration Council 72-81; Dir. Nat. Population Inquiry 70-78; Dir. Acad. of the Social Sciences in Australia 79-; Emeritus Prof. 79-; Hon. D.Litt. (Tas.) 75; Hon. D.Sc.Econ. (Sydney) 79; Hon. LL.D. (ANU) 82.
Publs. *Population Trends and Policies* 47, *Immigration* 48, *Italians and Germans in Australia* 54, *The Cultural Integration of Immigrants* (Part I and General Editor) 59, *Australia's Population Structure and Growth* (with G. Spencer) 65, *The Growth and Control of World Population* 70, *Population and Environment in Society* 73, (with others) *Population and Australia, First Report of the National Population Inquiry* 75, *Supplementary Report* 78.
29 Norman Street, Deakin, A.C.T. 2600, Australia.

Bowen, Hon. Sir Nigel Hubert, K.B.E., Q.C., B.A., LL.B.; Australian lawyer and politician; b. 26 May 1911, Summerland, British Columbia, Canada; ed. King's School, Sydney, and St. Paul's Coll., Univ. of Sydney.
Admitted to N.S.W. Bar 36, Victoria Bar 54; Q.C. 53; Editor *Australian Law Journal* 46-58; Vice-Pres. Law Council of Australia 57-60; Lecturer, Univ. of Sydney 57-58; Pres. N.S.W. Bar Council 59-61; mem. of Parl. 64-73; Attorney-Gen. 66-69; Minister of Educ. and Science 69-71; Attorney-Gen. March-Aug. 71; Minister of Foreign Affairs Aug. 71-72; Judge, N.S.W. Court of Appeal 73-76, Chief Judge in Equity 74-76; Chief Judge of Fed. Court of Australia Dec. 76-; head of del. to UN Conf. on Human Rights, Vice-Pres. 68; head of del. to UNESCO Conf. on Cultural Policies 70, to UN Gen. Assembly 71, 72; Liberal.
Publs. reports: *Legal Education in N.S.W.; Conflict of Public Duty and Private Interest.*
Chief Judge's Chambers, Federal Court of Australia, Queen's Square, Sydney, N.S.W., Australia.

Boyd, Arthur Merric Bloomfield; Australian painter; b. 24 July 1920; ed. State School, Murrumbeena, Victoria.
Learned painting and sculpture from parents and grandfather; painted and exhibited in Australia 37-59, in England 59-81, in Australia 81-; Retrospective Exhibitions: Whitechapel Gallery, London 62, Adelaide 64, Edinburgh and London 69; exhibited Australia 71, London 73, Australia 76, London 77.

Brabham, Sir Jack (John Arthur), Kt., O.B.E.; Australian professional racing driver (retd.); b. 2 April 1926, Sydney; ed. Hurstville Technical Coll., Sydney.
Served in R.A.A.F. 44-46; started own engineering business 46; Midget Speedway racing 46-52; numerous wins driving a Cooper-Bristol, Australia 53-54; went to Europe 55; won Australian Grand Prix 55, 63; World Champion, Formula II 58; Formula II Champion of France 64; World Champion Driver 59-60, 60-61, 66; first in Monaco and U.K. Grandes Epreuves 59; won Grand Prix of Netherlands, Belgium, France, U.K., Portugal, Denmark 60, Belgium 61, France 66, 67, U.K. 66; began building own cars 61; Man. Dir. Jack Brabham (Motors) Ltd., Jack Brabham (Worcester Park) Ltd., Brabham Racing Org. Ltd., Engine Devts. Ltd.; Ferodo Trophy 64, 66; RAC Gold Medal 59, 66, 67; Formula I Mfrs. Championship 66, 67.
c/o 248 Hook Road, Chessington, Surrey, England.
Telephone: 01-397 4343.

Brack, Robert William, A.O., B.A., F.A.I.M.; Australian business executive; b. 1921; ed. Telopea Park High School, Canberra and Melbourne Univs.
With Dept. of Trade and Customs 38-41; served 8th Div. A.I.F. 41-45, P.O.W. Singapore and Thailand; Aust. High Commr.'s Office, London 49-51, 56-57; Aust. Embassy, Washington 52-53; Asst. Comptroller Gen. of Customs, Canberra 59-63; Collector of Customs for N.S.W. 63-64; Commercial Man. Aust. Consolidated Industries Ltd. 64-66, Asst. Gen. Man. 66-67, Gen. Man. 67-, Dir. 74-, Man. Dir. 78-81; Chair. Australian Telecommunications Comm. 81-; Commr. Australian Nat. Airlines Comm. (TAA) 78, Vice-Chair. 79.
Communications House, 199 William Street, Melbourne, Vic. 3000, Australia.

Bradman, Sir Donald George, Kt., A.O.; Australian cricketer and company director; b. 27 Aug. 1908, Cootamundra, N.S.W.; ed. Bowral Intermediate High School.
Played cricket for N.S.W. 27-34, for S. Australia 35-39; played for Australia 28-48, Captain 36-48; in test cricket made 6,996 runs (average 99.9), in all first-class cricket 28,067 runs (average 95); scored 117 centuries in first-class matches; mem. Australian Bd. of Control for Int. Cricket 45-, Chair. 60-63, 69-72; Vice-Pres. S. Australia Cricket Asscn. 51-65, Pres. 65-73, now Trustee and mem. Ground and Finance Cttee.; fmr. Australian Test Selector; fmr. mem. Stock Exchange of Adelaide; now Dir. many public cos.; Champion Mt. Osmond Country Club (Golf) 36, 49; fmr. S. Australia Amateur Squash Champion.
Publs. *Don Bradman's Book* 30, *How to Play Cricket* 35, *My Cricketing Life* 38, *Farewell to Cricket* 50, *The Art of Cricket* 58.
2 Holden Street, Kensington Park, South Australia 5068, Australia.

Brash, Robert, C.M.G.; British diplomatist; b. 30 May 1924; ed. Trinity Coll., Cambridge.
War service 43-46; entered Foreign Service 49; Third Sec., Jakarta, Indonesia 51-55; Foreign Office 55-58 (First Sec. 56); Consul, Jerusalem 58-61; First Sec., Bonn 61-64; Head of Chancery, Bucharest 64-66; Foreign Office 66-70; Counsellor and Head East-West Contacts Dept., FCO 68; Canadian Nat. Defence Coll. 70-71; Counsellor and Consul-Gen., Saigon 71-73; Counsellor, Vienna 74-78; Consul-

Gen., Düsseldorf 78-81; Amb. to Indonesia 81-.
British Embassy, Jalan MH Thamrin 75, Jakarta, Indonesia.
Telephone: 341091-9.

Brembridge, John Henry, O.B.E., M.A.; British businessman and colonial administrator; b. 12 July 1925, South Africa; ed. Dragon School, Cheltenham, St. John's Coll., Oxford.
In Far East 50-; Chair. Swire Group U.K. 73-80; Financial Sec., Hong Kong 81-; Hon. D.Soc. (Chinese Univ. of Hong Kong) 80.
Colonial Secretariat, Central District, Hong Kong.

Brook, John Howard, LL.B.; Australian diplomatist; b. 25 Jan. 1931, Melbourne; ed. Scotch Coll., Melbourne, Univ. of Melbourne.
Joined Foreign Service 53; served in Korea, Malaya, Burma, South Africa, Ghana, Thailand, U.S.S.R.; served also in Dept. of Foreign Affairs and on secondment to Dept. of Defence and Public Service Board; Amb. to Viet-Nam 76-78, to Algeria 79-80; Supreme Court Prize 53.
c/o Department of Foreign Affairs, Canberra, Australia.

Brunei, Sultan of (*see* Bolkiah Mu'izuddin Waddaulah, H.H. Sultan Hassanal).

Bugotu, Francis, C.B.E., M.A.; Solomon Islands educationist, civil servant and diplomatist; b. 27 June 1937; ed. Ardmore Teachers' Training Coll., Auckland, Queensland Univ., Edinburgh Univ., Lancaster Univ., England.
Teacher and Insp. of Mission Schools, Melanesia 59-60; Lecturer, Solomon Islands Teachers' Coll. 64-68; Chief Educ. Officer and Perm. Sec. to Ministry of Educ. 68-75; Perm. Sec. to Chief Minister and Head of Civil Service 76-78; Sec. for Foreign Affairs and Roving Amb. July 78-; Perm. Rep. to UN 79-82; Sec.-Gen. South Pacific Comm. 82-(85); Chair. Solomon Islands Tourist Authority 70-73, Review Cttee. on Educ. 74-75, Solomon Islands Scholarship Cttee. 74-78; mem. Solomon Islands Legis. Council 60-62; Chief Commr. of Scouts for Solomon Islands 70-77; Lay Canon, Church of Melanesia. 70-.
Publs. *The Impact of Western Culture on Solomon Islands Society: A Melanesian Reaction* 69, *Politics, Economics and Social Aspects in the Developing Solomons* 70, *Recolonizing and Decolonizing: The Case of the Solomons* 75, *This Man* (play), *No Longer Thru a Glass Darkly* 82.
c/o South Pacific Commission, Post Box D5, Nouméa, New Caledonia.

Burbury, Sir Stanley Charles, K.C.V.O., K.B.E., LL.B.; Australian fmr. state governor; b. 2 Dec. 1909; ed. Univ. of Tasmania.
Barrister; Solicitor-Gen. Tasmania 52; Chief Justice of Tasmania 56-73; Gov. of Tasmania 73-82; Pres. Nat. Heart Foundation of Australia 67-73; Dir. Winston Churchill Memorial Trust 67-78, Nat. Pres. 80-; Hon. LL.D. (Tasmania).
c/o Government House, Hobart, Tasmania, Australia.

Burnet, Sir Frank Macfarlane, O.M., A.K., K.B.E., SC.D., F.R.S., F.R.C.P., F.R.A.C.P., F.A.C.P.; Australian scientist; b. 3 Sept. 1899, Traralgon, Victoria; ed. Melbourne Univ.
Resident Pathologist, Melbourne Hospital 23-25; Beit Fellow for Medical Research at Lister Inst., London 26-27; Asst. Dir. Walter and Eliza Hall Inst. for Medical Research 28-31 and 34-44, Dir. 44-65; Dunham Lecturer, Harvard Medical School 44; Croonian Lecturer, Royal Society 50; Herter Lecturer, Johns Hopkins Univ. 50, Flexner Lecturer at Vanderbilt Univ. 58; Chair. Board of Trustees, Commonwealth Foundation 66-69; Foreign mem. Royal Swedish Acad. of Science 57; Foreign Assoc. Nat. Acad. of Sciences, U.S.A. 54; Copley Medal Royal Society 59, Nobel Prize for Medicine 60; Pres. Australian Acad. of Sciences 65-69; Hon. F.R.C.S.Eng.
Publs. *Biological Aspects of Infectious Disease* 40, *Production of Antibodies* 49, *Viruses and Man* 53, *Principles of Animal Virology* 55, *Enzyme, Antigen and Virus* 56, *Clonal Selection Theory of Immunity* 59, *Integrity of the Body* 62, *Auto-Immune Diseases* (with I. R. Mackay) 63, *Changing Patterns* 68, *Cellular Immunology* 69, *Dominant Mammal* 70, *Immunological Surveillance* 70, *Genes, Dreams and Realities* 71, *Walter and Eliza Hall Institute 1915-65* 71, *Auto-Immunity and Auto-Immune Disease* 72, *Intrinsic Mutagenesis* 74, *Immunology* 76, *Immunology, Ageing and Cancer* 76, *Endurance of Life* 78, *Credo and Comment* 79.
48 Monomeath Avenue, Canterbury, Vic. 3126, Australia.

Butement, William Alan Stewart, C.B.E., D.SC., C.ENG., F.I.E.E., F.INST.P., F.A.I.P., F.I.R.E.E. (Aust.), F.T.S.; Australian scientist; b. 18 Aug. 1904; ed. Scots Coll., Sydney, Australia, Univ. Coll. School, Hampstead and London Univ.
Scientific Officer, War Office 28-39; Asst. Dir. Scientific Research, Ministry of Supply 39-47; First Chief Superintendent, Research Establishment and Rocket Range, Woomera, Australia 47-49; Chief Scientist, Australian Dept. of Supply 49-66; Dir. Plessey Pacific 67-; leading figure in early radar devt.; demonstrated a working radar 31; developed Malkara first anti-tank weapon.
Publ. *Precision Radar* 45-46.
5A Barry Street, Kew, Victoria, Australia.
Telephone: 861 8375.

C

Cadwallader, Sir John, Kt.; Australian business executive; b. 25 Aug. 1902, Melbourne; ed. Sydney Church of England Grammar School.
Managing Dir. Mungo Scott Pty. Ltd. until incorporation of Allied Mills Ltd. 19-49; Chair. and Man. Dir. Allied Mills Ltd. 49-; Dir. Bank of New South Wales 45-78, Pres. 59-78; Chair. Bushells Investments Ltd. 63-Oct. 76; Dir. Queensland Insurance Co. Ltd. 46-75.
27 Marian Street, Killara, N.S.W. 2071, Australia.
Telephone: 49-1974.

Cairns, James Ford, PH.D.; Australian politician; b. 4 Oct. 1914, Carlton, Victoria; ed. Univ. of Melbourne.
Junior Clerk, Australian Estates Co. Ltd. 32-35; with Victoria Police Detective Force 35-44; Australian Infantry Forces 44-46; Senior Lecturer of Econ. History, Univ. of Melbourne 46-55; mem. House of Reps. for Yarra 55-69, for Lalor 69-77; Minister for Overseas Trade 72-74, of Secondary Industry 72-73; Deputy Prime Minister 74-75; Fed. Treas. Dec. 74-June 75; Minister of Environment and Conservation June-July 75; mem. Fed. Parl. Labor Party Exec. 60-62, 64-75; del. to IPU Conf., Paris 71; Labor Party.
Publs. *Australia* 52, *Living with Asia* 65, *The Eagle and the Lotus* 69, *Silence Kills* 70, *Tariffs and Planning* 71, *The Quiet Revolution* 72, *Oil in Troubled Waters* 76, *Viet-nam: Scorched Earth Reborn* 76, *Theory of The Alternative* 76.
21 Wattle Road, Hawthorn, Vic. 3122, Australia.

Cakobau, Ratu Sir George Kadavulevu, G.C.M.G., G.C.V.O., O.B.E., J.P.; Fijian politician and administrator; b. 6 Nov. 1911, Suva; ed. Queen Victoria School Fiji, Newington Coll. Australia, Wanganui Tech. Coll. New Zealand.
Capt. Fiji Rugby Team touring Australia 39; Vice-Capt. Fiji Cricket Team touring N.Z. 48; Military service (Capt. Fiji Mil. Forces) 42-44; mem. Great Council of Chiefs 38-72, Legislative Council 51-70; Roko and Fijian Magistrate 40-42, 50-62; Rep. to Coronation of H.M. Queen Elizabeth II 53, to Silver Jubilee 77; Vunivalu of Bau (Paramount Chief) 60; Minister of Fijian Affairs and Local Govt. 70-71, without Portfolio 71-72; Gov.-Gen. of Fiji 73-; K.St.J.
Government House, Suva, Fiji.

Calvo, Paul McDonald, B.SC.; Guamanian politician; b. 25 July 1934, Agaña; ed. George Washington High School, Agaña, Peacock Mil. Acad., San Antonio, Texas, Univ. of Santa Clara, Calif.
Insurance exec. 58-65, 67-70, 74-78; mem. Guam Legis. 65-67, 70-74, Minority Leader 70-74; Gov. of Guam Jan. 79-(83); Chair. Guam Republican Party 67-70; mem. Board Guam Red Cross 70-73; mem. numerous civic and charitable orgs.; Republican.
Office of the Governor, P.O. Box 2950, Agaña, Guam 96910.

Cao Yu; Chinese dramatist; b. 1910; ed. Tsinghua Univ.
Chair. Chinese Dramatists' Asscn.
Plays include: *Thunderstorm* 33, *Bright Skies* 54, *Wang Zhao Jun*.
Chinese Dramatists' Association, Beijing, People's Republic of China.

Carnegie, Sir Roderick Howard, Kt., B.SC., M.A. (OXON.), M.B.A.; Australian mining executive; b. 27 Nov. 1932; ed. Trinity Coll., Melbourne Univ., New Coll., Oxford, Harvard Business School, Boston, U.S.A.
Associate McKinsey and Co., Melbourne and New York 59-64, Principal Assoc. 64-68, Dir. 68-70; Dir. Conzinc Riotinto of Australia Ltd. 70, Joint Man. Dir. 71-72, Man. Dir. 72-74, Chief Exec. 72-, Chair. 74-; Dir. Rio Tinto-Zinc Corpn. Ltd., Comalco Ltd., and several other cos. in the C.R.A group.
C.R.A. Ltd., 55 Collins Street, Melbourne, Vic. 3000, Australia.

Carrick, Sir John Leslie, K.C.M.G.; Australian politician; b. 4 Sept. 1918, Sydney; ed. Sydney Technical High School, Univ. of Sydney.
Army service 39-48; prisoner-of-war 42-45; mem. Citizen Mil. Force 48-51; Gen. Sec. N.S.W. Div. of Liberal Party of Australia 48-71; mem. Senate 71-; mem. Senate Standing Cttee. on Educ., Science and the Arts 71-75, on Foreign Affairs and Defence 71-75, Joint Cttee. on Foreign Affairs 71-72, on Foreign Affairs and Defence 73-75; opposition spokesman for federalism and intergovernment relations 75; Minister for Housing and Construction, for Urban and Regional Devt. Nov.-Dec. 75; Minister for Educ. 75-79; Minister assisting the Prime Minister in Fed. Affairs 75-78; Govt. Leader in the Senate 78-; Vice-Pres. Exec. Council Aug. 78-; Minister for Nat. Devt. & Energy 79-.
Parliament House, Canberra, A.C.T. 2600; 8 Montah Avenue, Killara, N.S.W., Australia (Home).
Telephone: 72 7078 or 73 3588 (Canberra).

Castro, Amado Alejandro, B.S., A.M., PH.D.; Philippine economist; b. 29 May 1924, Manila; ed. Univ. of the Philippines and Harvard Univ., U.S.A.
Instructor in Econs., Univ. of the Philippines 48-53, Asst. Prof. 54-56, Assoc. Prof. 56-62, Head of Econs. Dept. 56-58, Acting Dean, Coll. of Business Admin. Jan.-Sept. 58, Prof. of Econs. 62-, Dean, School of Econs. 65-73, Prof. of Monetary Econs. 72-; Gov. and Acting Chair. Devt. Bank of the Philippines 62-66; Dir. Inst. of Econ. Devt. and Research 58-66, Dir. Econ. Bureau ASEAN Secr. 77-80.
School of Economics, University of the Philippines, Quezon City, Philippines 3004; 67 Valenzuela, San Juan, Metro Manila, Philippines 3134 (Home).

Cater, Sir Jack, K.B.E.; British colonial administrator; b. 21 Feb. 1922; ed. Sir George Monoux Grammar School, Walthamstow.
War service 39-45; British Mil. Admin., Hong Kong 45; joined Colonial Administrative Service, Hong Kong 46; attended 2nd Devonshire Course, Queen's Coll., Oxford 49-50; various posts incl. Registrar of Co-operative Socs. and Dir. of Marketing, Dir. of Agric. and Fisheries, Deputy Econ. Sec.; Imperial Defence Coll. (now Royal Coll. of Defence Studies) 66; Defence Sec., Special Asst. to Gov. and Deputy Colonial Sec. (Special Duties) 67; Exec. Dir. Hong Kong Trade Devt. Council 68-70; Dir. Commerce and Industry, Hong Kong 70-72; Sec. for Information 72, for Home Affairs and Information 73; Commr., Ind. Comm. Against Corruption 74-78; Chief Sec., Hong Kong 78-81 (occasional Acting Gov.); Hong Kong Commr., London 81-; Hon. Dr. of Social Sciences (Hong Kong Univ.) 82.
Hong Kong Government Office, 6 Grafton Street, London, W.1 (Office); 19 Cowley Street, London, S.W.1, England (Home).

Chan, Rt. Hon. Sir Julius, P.C., K.B.E.; Papua New Guinea politician; b. 29 Aug. 1939, Tanga, New Ireland; ed. Marist Brothers' Coll., Ashgrove, Queensland, and Univ. of Queensland, Australia.
Co-operative Officer, Papua New Guinea Admin. 60-62; Man. Dir. Coastal Shipping Co. Pty. Ltd.; mem. House of Assembly (now Nat. Parl.) 68-, Deputy Speaker, Vice-Chair. Public Accounts Cttee. 68-72; Parl. Leader, People's Progress Party 70; Minister of Finance and Parl. Leader of Govt. Business 72-77; Deputy Prime Minister and Minister of Primary Industry 77-78; Prime Minister 80-82; Gov. for Papua New Guinea and Vice-Chair. Asian Devt. Bank 75-77; Fellowship mem. Int. Bankers' Asscn. Inc., U.S.A. 76-; Hon. D.Ec., Dankook (Repub. of Korea).
P.O. Box 381, Port Moresby, Papua New Guinea.

Chan Si; Kampuchean politician; b. 1933.
Vice-Chairman Council of Ministers, and Minister of Defence 80-81; Chair. Council of Ministers Dec. 81-.
c/o People's Revolutionary Council of Kampuchea, Phnom-Penh, Kampuchea.

Chandra, Satish, M.A., B.SC.; Indian business executive and fmr. politician; b. 1917; ed. S.M. Coll., Chandausi, Govt. Agricultural Coll., Kanpur, and Bareilly Coll., Bareilly (Agra Univ.).
Indian Nat. Congress 36-; mem. Indian Constituent Assembly 48-50, Provisional Parl. 50-52, Lok Sabha 52-62; Parl. Sec. to Prime Minister 51-52; Union Dep. Minister for Defence 52-55, for Production 55-57, for Commerce and Industry 57-62; Chair. Indian Airlines Corpn. and Dir. Air-India 63, 64; Chair. British India Corpn. Ltd., The Elgin Mills Co. Ltd., Cawnpore Textiles Ltd., Cawnpore Sugar Works Ltd., Champarun Sugar Co. Ltd., Saran Engineering Co. Ltd. 62-, also fmr. Chair. and Man. Dir. Fertilizer Corpn. of India; Dir. other cos.
Chitrakut, Parbati Bagla Road, Kanpur, U.P., India.

Chandrachud, Yeshwant Vishnu, LL.B.; Indian judge; b. 12 July, 1920, Pune; ed. Univ. of Bombay.
Practised at Bombay bar 43-61; Govt. Pleader, Bombay High Court 58-61, Judge 61-72; Judge Supreme Court 72-, Chief Justice Feb. 78-; Pres. Int. Law Asscn. (India Branch) 78-, India Law Inst. 78-.
Supreme Court, Tilak Marg, New Delhi 110001; 5 Krishna Menon Marg, New Delhi 110011, India (Home).
Telephone: 387165 (Office); 374053 and 372922 (Home).

Chandrasekhar, Bhagwat Subrahmanya, B.SC.; Indian cricketer and bank executive; b. 17 May 1945, Mysore; ed. National Education Society, Bangalore.
Right-arm leg-spin, googly bowler; bowling arm withered by attack of polio at age of 6; debut in First Class Cricket 63, Test Cricket 64; had taken 857 First Class wickets and 198 Test wickets by Aug. 78; plays for Karnataka in Ranji Trophy competition (nat. championship of India); Arjuna Award; Padma Shri 72; Hon. Life mem. MCC 81.
571 31st Cross, 4th Block, Jayanagar, Bangalore 560011, India.
Telephone: 41268.

Chandrasekhar, Sripati, M.A., M.LITT., M.SC., PH.D., Indian economist and demographer; b. 22 Nov. 1918; ed. Madras Presidency Coll., Univ. of Madras and Columbia, New York and Princeton Univs.

Visiting Lecturer, Univ. of Pa. and Asia Inst., New York 44-46; Prof. of Econs. and Head of Dept., Annamalai Univ. 47-50; Dir. Demographic Research UNESCO, Paris 47-49; Prof. of Economics and Head of Dept., Baroda Univ. 50-53; Nuffield Fellow, London School of Economics 53-55; Dir. Indian Inst. for Population Studies 56-67; mem. Rajya Sabha 64-70; Minister of State for Health and Family Planning 67-Nov. 67, for Health, Family Planning and Urban Devt. 67-70; Research Prof. of Demography, Univ. of Calif.; Fellow, Battelle Research Centre 71-72; Distinguished Visiting Prof. of Sociology, Calif. State Univ, 72-73; Visiting Prof. of Demography and Public Health. Univ. of Calif., Los Angeles 73-74, Regents Prof., Univ. of Calif., Santa Barbara 75; Vice-Chancellor, Annamalai Univ., Chidambaram 75-80; Lucy Stern Trustee Prof. of Sociology, Mills Coll., Oakland, Calif. 79-80; Visiting Prof. of Sociology, San Diego State Univ. 81-; Editor *Population Review*; Hon. D.Litt. (Univs. of Redlands, Kurukshetra), Hon. M.D. (Budapest), Hon. D.Sc. (Univ. of the Pacific), Hon. LL.D. (Punjab Univ.); Watumull Award for distinguished work in Indian demography 64; Kaufman Award 69; Margaret Sanger Gold Medal for leadership in population control 71, Honour Award of India League of America (Chicago) 75, U.S. Bicentennial Gold Medal from East-West Center, Honolulu 77.

Publs. *India's Population* 46, *Census and Statistics in India* 47, *Indian Emigration* 48, *Hungry People and Empty Lands* 52, *Population and Planned Parenthood in India* 55, *Infant Mortality in India* 59, *China's Population* 59, *Communist China Today* 61, *Red China: An Asian View* 62, *A Decade of Mao's China* (Editor) 63, *American Aid and India's Economic Development* 65, *Asia's Population Problems* 67, *Problems of Economic Development* 67, *India's Population: Fact, Problem and Policy* 68, *Infant Mortality, Population Growth and Family Planning* 72, *Abortion in a Crowded World* 74, *Population and Law in India* 76, *Ananda K. Coomaraswamy: A Critical Appreciation* 77, *The Nagarathars of South India* 80, *A Dirty, Filthy Book—The Bradlaugh-Besant Trial* 81.

8976 Cliffridge Avenue, La Jolla, Calif. 92037, U.S.A.; "Green Acres", Kodaikanal, Tamil Nadu, India.

Chandrasekharan, Komaravolu, M.A., M.SC., PH.D.; Indian mathematician; b. 21 Nov. 1920; ed. Presidency Coll., Madras, and Inst. for Advanced Study, Princeton, U.S.A.

Professor, Eidgenössische Technische Hochschule, Zürich; Sec. Int. Math. Union 61-66, Pres. 71-74; Vice-Pres. Int. Council of Scientific Unions 63-66, Sec.-Gen. 66-70; mem. Scientific Advisory Cttee. to Cabinet, Govt. of India 61-66; Visiting Lecturer, American Math. Soc. 63; Fellow, Nat. Inst. of Sciences of India, Indian Acad. of Sciences; Foreign mem. Finnish Acad. of Science and Letters 75; Padma Shri 59; Shanti Swarup Bhatnagar Memorial Award for Scientific Research 63; Ramanujan Medal 66.

Publs. *Fourier Transforms* (with S. Bochner) 49, *Typical Means* (with S. Minakshisundaram) 52, *Lectures on the Riemann Zeta-function* 53, *Analytic Number Theory* 68, *Arithmetical Functions* 70.

Eidgenössische Technische Hochschule, 8092 Zürich, Rämistrasse 101; Home: Hedwigstrasse 29, 8032 Zürich, Switzerland.

Telephone: 53-96-86.

Chandy, Kanianthra Thomas, M.A., LL.M.; Indian business executive; b. 1913; ed. London Univ.

Law practice; Hindustan Lever Ltd., Dir. 56-62; Dir. of Research Hyderabad Admin. Staff Coll. 57; Dir. Indian Inst. of Management, Calcutta 62-66; Chair. Food Corpn. of India 66-68, Hindustan Steel Ltd. 68-72, Kerala State Industrial Devt. Corpn. Ltd. 72-; Pres. Calcutta Management Assn.; Chair. Kerala State Textile Corpn. Ltd., Board of Govs. Indian Inst. of Technology (IIT), Exec. Council Nat. Metallurgical Laboratory, Jamshedpur, All-India Board of Management Studies, Nat. Productivity Council, New Delhi, Board of Apprenticeship Training, Kerala State Industrial Devt. Corpn., Nat. Productivity Council of India; Vice-Chair. Kerala State Planning Board; first Vice-Chair. Asian Productivity Org., Chair. May 76-; Dir. Int. Iron and Steel Inst., Brussels, Belgium; mem. Board of Govs. Indian Insts. of Management, Calcutta and Bangalore, Council of IITs, All India Council of Technical Educ.; fmr. mem. Univ. Grants Comm., Nat. Planning Council.

P.O. Box 105, Trivandrum 695003, Kerala, India.

Chao Yao-tung; Chinese politician; b. 1914; ed. M.I.T. Manager China Steel Corpn., Taiwan until 81; Minister of Econ. Affairs, Taiwan Nov. 81-.

Ministry of Economic Affairs, Taipei, Taiwan.

Chappell, Gregory (Greg) Stephen; M.B.E.; Australian cricketer and insurance executive; b. 7 Aug. 1948, Adelaide; ed. St. Leonard's Primary School and Plympton High School, Adelaide, and Prince Alfred Coll., Adelaide. Grandson of V. Y. Richardson (Australian Cricket Captain 35-36); brother of I. M. Chappell (Australian Cricket Captain 71-75); represented S. Australia 66-73, Somerset (England) 68-69, Queensland 73-77; Captain of Queensland 73-77, 79-, of Australia 75-77, 79-80, 81-; signed contract for World Series Cricket and became their Australian Vice-Captain 77; made century in test debut v. England, Perth 70; only captain to have scored a century in each innings of 1st test as captain (v. West Indies, Brisbane 75); holds record for most catches in a test match (7 v. England, Perth 75); holds record for most runs (aggregate) in a test match (247 not out and 133 v. New Zealand, Wellington 74); Australian Sportsman of the Year 76.

67 St. Paul's Terrace, Brisbane, Queensland (Office); 5 Delphin Street, Kenmore, Queensland, Australia (Home).

Telephone: 2295416 (Office); 378-5034 (Home).

Charusathiara, Field-Marshal Prapas; Thai army officer and politician; b. 25 Nov. 1912; ed. Chulachomklao Royal Military Acad. and National Defence Coll.

Army service 32-, rose to Gen. 60; Minister of Interior 57-71, Deputy Prime Minister 63-71, Army Deputy Commdr. and Deputy Supreme Commdr. 63-64, Supreme Commdr. 64-73; Deputy Supreme Commdr. Armed Forces Sept.-Oct. 73; Vice-Pres. and Rector Chulalongkorn Univ. 61; mem. Nat. Exec. Council 71-72; Dir. of Security Council (Defence and Interior) 71-72; Deputy Prime Minister, Minister of Interior 72-73; in exile 73-76, returned to Thailand Jan. 77; Crown of Thailand (Highest Class).

Publs. *The Role of the Ministry of the Interior in the Development of National Security, The Role of the Ministry of Interior in Maintenance of National Peace and Order.*

132-5 Suan Puttan Residence, Bangkok, Thailand.

Chattopadhyay, Kamaladevi; Indian political and social worker; b. 3 April 1903, Mangalore; ed. Mangalore, Bedford Coll. and London School of Economics, London Univ. Joined Congress; elected to A.I.C.C. 27; Organizing Sec. and Pres. All-India Women's Conf.; imprisoned 30, 32, 34 and 42; founded Indian Co-operative Union to rehabilitate refugees on a co-operative basis 48; Chair. All-India Handicrafts Board 52-; fmr. Vice-Chair. Sangeet Natak Akad., now Chair.; Chair. Council for Performing Arts, Children's Book Trust; Pres. Theatre Centre of India; helped to found World Crafts Council and is its Senior Vice-Pres.; Vice-Pres. India Int. Centre, India Council for Cultural Relations; Indian and foreign awards; Deshikotlama Award (Vishwa Bharati Univ. at Shantiniketan) 70, Watumull Foundation Award, Ramon Magsaysay Int. Award, Pres. of Czechoslovakia Gold Medal for Promoting Int. Amity and Understanding, UNESCO Award 77.

Publs. *In War-torn China, Japan: Its Weakness and*

Strength, Socialism and Society, America, the Land of Superlatives, Uncle Sam's Empire, Glory of Indian Handicrafts, Carpets and Floor Coverings of India, Handicrafts of India, Towards a National Theatre, Awakening of Indian Womanhood, At the Cross-Roads, Japan, Tribalism and Tribals in India.
Bharatiya Natya Sangh, 34 New Central Market, New Delhi; Flat No. 6, Chateau Marine, Subhas Road, Bombay, India.
Telephone: New Delhi 386408; Bombay 299676.

Chau, Dr. the Hon. Sir Sik-Nin, Kt. C.B.E., M.B., B.S., D.O.M.S., D.L.O., J.P.; Hong Kong business executive; b. 1903; ed. St. Stephen's Coll., Hong Kong, Univs. of Hong Kong, London and Vienna.
Chairman, Hong Kong Productivity Council 70-73; Pres. Fireworks Co. Ltd. (Taiwan), Hong Kong Model Housing Soc., Hong Kong Marine Food Co. Ltd., The Hong Kong Chinese Bank Ltd., State Trading Corpn. (Far East) Ltd., Kowloon Motor Bus Co., Man Lee Cheung Co. Ltd., Pioneer Trade Devt. Co. Ltd., Repulse Bay Enterprises Ltd., Far East Insurance Co. Ltd., Nin Fung Hong, Oriental Express Ltd., Sik Yuen Co. Ltd., Atherton Co. Ltd., Yin Bong Ltd., Marquise Industrial Estate Co. Ltd., Swiss Watch Case Center Ltd., H.K. and Kowloon Land and Loan Co. Ltd., Hong Kong Cttee. for Osaka World *Expo 1970*; Vice-Pres. Hong Kong Anti-Tuberculosis Asscn.; Pres.-Designate, World Council of Management 77; Dir. numerous companies, official, educational and philanthropic orgs.; Hon. LL.D. (Hong Kong Univ.), Order of Sacred Treasure (Japan) 69, Silver Jubilee Medal 77.
c/o The Hong Kong Chinese Bank Ltd., 61-65 Des Voeux Road, Hong Kong; 3547 Hatton Road, Hong Kong.
Telephone: 433695.

Chaudhuri, Nirad Chandra, B.A.; Indian writer; b. 23 Nov. 1897; ed. Calcutta Univ.
Former Asst. Editor *The Modern Review* (Calcutta); fmr. Sec. to Sarat Bose (Leader of Congress Party, Bengal); fmr. Commentator, All-India Radio; has contributed to *The Times, Encounter, New English Review, The Atlantic Monthly, Pacific Affairs;* also contributed to Indian papers *The Statesman, The Illustrated Weekly, The Hindustan Standard, The Times of India;* Duff Cooper Memorial Prize for *The Continent of Circe* 67.
Publs. *The Autobiography of an Unknown Indian* 51 (published as *Jaico*, India 64), *A Passage to England* 59, *The Continent of Circe* 65, *Woman in Bengali Life* (in Bengali) 68, *Scholar Extraordinary: The Life of Professor the Rt. Hon. Friedrich Max Müller P.C.* 74, *Clive of India* 75, *Hinduism* 79.
P. and O. Buildings, Nicholson Road, Delhi 6, India.

Chavan, Yeshwantrao Balwantrao, B.A., LL.B.; Indian politician; b 21 March 1913; ed. Rajaram Coll., Kolhapur, and Law Coll., Pune.
Practised law at Karad; directed underground movement in Satara District 42-43; arrested 43-44; Pres. District Congress Cttee., Satara; Sec. Maharashtra Provincial Congress Cttee. 48-50; mem. Bombay Legislative Assembly and Parl. Sec. 46; started a Marathi daily, *Prakash*, at Satara; Minister for Civil Supplies 52, later Minister of Local Self-Govt. and Forests; Chief Minister, Bombay State 56-60, Maharashtra State 60-62; mem. Bombay Legislative Assembly 57-60; Treas. Working Cttee. All-Indian Congress 58; Leader Congress Party in Rajya Sabha 63; mem. Lok Sabha 64-; Minister of Defence, India 62-66, of Home Affairs 66-70; Minister of Finance 70-74, of External Affairs 74-77, Deputy Prime Minister and Minister of Home Affairs 79-80; Parl. Leader, Indian Nat. Congress Party 77-81 (resgnd.); Pres. Inst. for Defence Studies and Analysis.
1 Racecourse Road, New Delhi, India.
Telephone: 376588.

Chea Sim; Kampuchean politician.
Former Regional Sec. CP of Cambodia; mem. People's Rep. Assembly 76-78, People's Revolutionary Council 79-; Vice-Pres. Cen. Cttee. Ranakse Sangkroh Cheat Kampuchea (Kampuchean Nat. United Front for Nat. Salvation) and Minister of the Interior 79-81; Chair. Nat. Assembly May 81-.
c/o National Assembly, Phnom-Penh, Kampuchea.

Chen Chu; Chinese diplomatist.
Counsellor, Chinese Embassy, Moscow 56-59; Dir. Dept. of W. Asian and N. African Affairs, Ministry of Foreign Affairs 64-65; Amb. to Ghana Jan.-Oct. 66, to Japan 73-76; Dir. Information Dept., Ministry of Foreign Affairs 71; Perm. Rep. to UN 78-80.
c/o Permanent Mission of the People's Republic of China to the United Nations, 155 West 66th Street, New York, N.Y. 10023, U.S.A.

Chen Guodong; Chinese politician.
Leading figure Baoji (Shaanxi) Mil. Control Comm. 49; Dir., Finance Dept., E. China Cttee. of Financial and Econ. Affairs 49-50; mem. Cttee. of Financial and Econ. Affairs 49-50; mem. Cttee. of Financial and Econ. Affairs, E. China Mil. and Admin. Council and concurrently Dir. of its Finance Dept. 50-52; mem. E. China Cttee. on Org. 50; Dir. E. China Cttee. for Regulating the Distribution of Goods in Storage 50; mem. E. China Cttee. for Govt. Offices Production Man. 52; Vice-Minister of Finance, Cen. People's Govt. 52-53; Vice-Minister of Food 53, Minister 79-81; Sec. Leading Party Mems.' Group of CCP Cttee. in Ministry of Food 57; head, team of leading party mems. in rectification movement conducted in Ministry 57; mem. Cen. Famine Relief Cttee. for Nat. Conf. of Reps. of Outstanding Groups and Individuals in Culture and Educ. 60, mem. Presidium of that Conf. 60; Del. as specially invited personage to 4th CPPCC 64; mem. Presidium CCP 11th Nat. Congress 77; mem. CCP 11th Cen. Cttee. 77-; Dir. All China Fed. of Supply and Marketing Co-operatives 78-79; Second Sec., Shanghai Municipal Cttee. Jan.-March 80; First Sec., Shanghai Municipal Cttee. March 80-.
People's Republic of China.

Chen Hanseng; Chinese economist; b. Wuxi, Jiangsu Province, 5 Feb. 1897; ed. Germany and U.S.A.
Former History Prof., Beijing Univ.; Head, Inst. of Social Sciences of Academia Sinica; after war became prof., Washington State Univ. until return to China 51; Vice-Pres. Chinese People's Inst. of Foreign Affairs 51-66; Vice-Pres. Sino-Indian Friendship Asscn. 52-68; Del. for Hopeh Province to the Nat. People's Congress 54, 58 and 64; Deputy Dir. of Research, Inst. of Int. Relations 56-71; Vice-Chair. of Editorial Bd. *China Reconstructs* 52-68; Chair. Chinese Soc. for Central Asian Studies 79-; Consultant, Chinese Acad. of Social Sciences 77-; Visiting Prof. Beijing Univ. 78-; mem. Chinese People's Nat. Assembly for Political Consultation 78-.
Publs. *Land and Peasant in China* 27, *Industrial Capital and Chinese Peasants* 27, *The Agrarian Regions of India and Pakistan* 59, *Historical Data for the Study of Chinese Coolies Abroad* 80; articles on agrarian problems in various Chinese and foreign periodicals.
38 Dong Ha Men Street, Beijing, People's Republic of China.

Chen Jide; Chinese soldier.
Political Commissar Hubei PLA Mil. Dist. 78-.
People's Republic of China.

Chen Muhua, Miss; Chinese government and party official.
Minister for Econ. Relations with Foreign Countries Jan. 77-80, 81-82, also a Vice-Premier March 78-; Deputy for Zhejiang 5th NPC 78; mem. Presidium NPC 78; Vice-Chair. Cen. Patriotic Sanitation Campaign Cttee. State Council; Head, Birth Planning Leading Group State

Council 78-; Minister in charge of State Family Planning Comm. 81-82; Minister of Foreign Trade and Econ. Relations March 82-, also Minister of State Foreign Investment Comm. and Import-Export Comm. March 82-; mem. 10th Cen. Cttee. of CCP 73; alt. mem. Politburo, 11th Cen. Cttee. 77.
People's Republic of China.

Chen Pixian; Chinese politician; b. 1911, Fuzhou, Fujian.
Provincial Secretary Children's Bureau CCP Cen. Cttee.; Sec. S. Jiangsu Prov. Cttee. Communist Youth League 35; Co-Commdr. Mil. Dist.; Sec. and Deputy Sec. CCP Border Dist. Special Cttee. 35; mem. CCP S. Jiangxi Dist. Special Cttee. 36; Sec. CCP Cen. Jiangsu Dist. Cttee. 37; Responsible Officer N. Jiangsu Army Corps 48; mem. Cen. Cttee. New Democratic Youth League 49-53; Sec. CCP S. Jiangsu Dist. Cttee. 49-52; Pol. Commissar PLA S. Jiangsu Mil. Dist. 49-52; mem. E. China Mil. and Admin. Cttee. 50-53; mem. S. Jiangsu Admin. Office 50-52; Chair. Financial and Econ. Cttee. S. Jiangsu Admin. Office 51-52; Fourth Sec. E. China Bureau CCP Cen. Cttee. 52-54; Fourth Sec. CCP Shanghai Municipal Cttee. 52-54; mem. E. China Admin. Cttee. 53-54; Sec. Secr. CCP Shanghai Municipal Cttee. 54-55; mem. Shanghai Municipal Fed. of Trades Unions 55; mem. Shanghai Municipal People's Council 55; Second Sec., Secr. CCP Shanghai Municipal Cttee. 55-56; Sec. Secr. CCP Shanghai Municipal Cttee. 56-65; mem. Exec. Cttee. China Welfare Inst. 56; alt. mem. CCP 8th Cen. Cttee. 56; Vice-Pres. Shanghai Branch Sino-Soviet Friendship Asscn. 57; Chair. Shanghai Municipal Cttee. CPPCC 58; Pol. Commissar PLA, Shanghai Garrison H.Q. 60; Sec. Secr. E. China Bureau CCP Cen. Cttee. 64; mem. Presidium Fourth Shanghai Peoples' Pol. Consultative Conf. 64; Chair. Fourth Shanghai Municipal Cttee. CPPCC 64; First Sec. CCP Shanghai Municipal Cttee. 65-67; mem. Presidium 5th Shanghai People's Congress 65; allegedly suppressed the Shanghai Worker's Movement 66; reportedly wrote a lengthy statement of confession 67; tried by Shanghai workers at three televised sessions Dec. 67, Mar. 68, Apr. 68; mem. Presidium CCP 11th Nat. Congress 77-; mem. CCP 11th Cen. Cttee. 77-; First Sec. Hubei CCP Prov. Cttee. 78-; Chair. Prov. Revolutionary Cttee. 78-; First Pol. Commissar, Hubei Mil. Dist. 78-; Chair. Hubei People's Congress 79-.
People's Republic of China.

Chen Weida; Chinese politician.
Member Standing Cttee. CCP Zhejiang Prov. Cttee. 57; Vice-Gov. Zhejiang 58-64; mem. Presidium First Nat. Games 59; Sec. CCP Zhejiang Prov. Cttee. 60; mem. 11th Cen. Cttee. CCP 77-; Chair. Tianjin Municipal Revolutionary Cttee. 78-79; First Sec. Tianjin CCP Cttee. 78-80.
People's Republic of China.

Chen Xilian, Gen.; Chinese army officer; b. 1913, Hungan, Hubei; ed. Red Army Acad.
Joined CCP 27; Battalion Commdr. 31-33; on Long March 34-35; Regimental Commdr. 37; Commdr. 3rd Army Corps, 2nd Field Army 49; Mayor of Chongqing 49; Commdr. of Artillery Force, People's Liberation Army 51; Gen. 55; Alt. mem. 8th Cen. Cttee. of CCP 56; Commdr. Shenyang Mil. Region, PLA 59-73; Sec. N.E. Bureau, CCP 63-67; Chair. Liaoning Revolutionary Cttee. 68; mem. Politburo, 9th Cen. Cttee. of CCP 69, 10th Cen. Cttee. 73, 11th Cen. Cttee. 77; First Sec. CCP Liaoning 71; Commdr. Beijing Mil. Region PLA 74-78; Vice-Premier, State Council 75-80; mem. Politburo, 11th Cen. Cttee. of CCP 77 (reported to have been suspended June 79), Mil. Comm. CCP Cen. Cttee. 78-80; removed from all major Party/State posts 80; Adviser to Mil. Comm. and Mil. Adviser in an unspecified Mil. Region 80-.
People's Republic of China.

Chen Yonggui; Chinese party and government official; b. 1913, Shiyang, Shanxi.
National Model Worker; Sec. CCP Dazhai Production Brigade, Shanxi 63-; Vice-Chair. Shanxi Revolutionary Cttee. 67; mem. 9th Cen. Cttee. of CCP 69; Sec. CCP Shanxi 71; mem. Politburo, 10th Cen. Cttee. of CCP 73, 11th Cen. Cttee. 77 (reported to have been suspended June 79), Vice-Premier, State Council 75-80; Deputy for Shanxi 5th NPC 78; mem. Presidium, NPC.
Publs. *We are Peasants of the New Type* 66, *Tachai Advances in the Midst of the Struggle Against China's Khrushchev* 67, *To be the Most Reliable Ally of the Working Classes* 68, *On the Study of Scientific Agrarian Methods* 75.
People's Republic of China.

Chen Yun; Chinese politician; b. 1905, Qingbu, Jiangxi.
Joined CCP 25; Trades Union activist 25-27; mem. 6th Cen. Cttee. of CCP 31; on Long March 34-35; Deputy Dir. Org. Dept., CCP 37, Dir. 43; Dir. Peasants Dept., CCP 39; mem. 7th Cen. Cttee. of CCP 45; Vice-Premier 49-75, 78-80; Minister of Heavy Industry 49-50; Sec., Secr. of Cen. Cttee., CCP 54; Vice-Chair. CCP 56-69; mem. Standing Cttee., Politburo of CCP 56-69, 78-; Minister of Commerce 56-58; Chair. State Capital Construction Comm. 58-61; mem. 9th Cen. Cttee. of CCP 69, 10th Cen. Cttee. 73, 11th Cen. Cttee. 77; Exec. Chair. Presidium; Vice-Chair. Standing Cttee. 5th Nat. People's Congress; First Sec. Cen. Cttee. for Inspecting Discipline; Cen. Cttee. 78-; Chair. Financial and Economic Cttee. State Council 79-; Vice-Chair. CCP 11th Cen. Cttee. 79-; Vice-Chair. Cen. Mil. Comm.
People's Republic of China.

Chen Zaidao; Chinese army officer; b. 1908, Macheng, Hubei.
Guerrilla leader 27; Commdr. 4th Army 34, 2nd Column, Cen. Plains Field Army 44; Commdr. Henan Mil. District, People's Liberation Army 49, Wuhan Mil. Region, PLA 54-67; Gen. 55; Leader of Wuhan Incident uprising (an anti-Maoist army revolt during Cultural Revolution, for which he was criticized and removed from office) 20 July 67; Deputy Commdr. Fuzhou Mil. Region, PLA 73-; mem. Standing Cttee. 5th Nat. People's Congress 78-; Commdr. PLA Railway Corps. 78-.
People's Republic of China.

Chiang Ching-kuo; Chinese politician; b. 18 March 1910; ed. Sun Yat-sen Univ., Moscow, and U.S.S.R. Military and Political Inst.
Eldest son of the late Gen. Chiang Kai-shek; Admin. Commr. for South Jiangsi 39-45; Foreign Affairs Commr. of Mil. and Political Admin. for N.E. China 45-47; Deputy Econ. Control Supervisor for Shanghai 48; Chair. Kuomintang Taiwan Province H.Q. 49-50; Dir., Gen. Political Dept., Ministry of Nat. Defence 50-54; mem. Central Revision Cttee. of Kuomintang 50-52; Minister without Portfolio 63; Deputy Minister of Nat. Defence 64-65, Minister 65-69; Vice-Premier 69-72, Premier 72-78; Pres. Repub. of China (Taiwan) May 78-; Deputy Sec.-Gen. Nat. Defence Council 54-67; Chair. Nat. Gen. Mobilization Cttee.; mem. Standing Cttee. of Kuomintang; Chair. Kuomintang 75-.
Office of The President, Taipei, Taiwan.

Chiang Kai-shek, Madame (Soong Mayling); Chinese sociologist; b. 1899, Shanghai; sister of late Song Qingling (Madame Sun Yat-sen); ed. Wellesley Coll., U.S.A.
Married Chiang Kai-shek 27 (died 75); first Chinese woman appointed mem. of Child Labour Comm.; inaugurated Moral Endeavour Asscn.; established schools in Nanjing for orphans of revolutionary soldiers; fmr. mem. Legislative Yuan; served as Sec.-Gen. of Chinese Comm. on Aeronautical Affairs; Dir.-Gen. New Life Movement; founded and directed Nat. Chinese Women's Asscn. for War Relief and Nat. Asscn. for Refugee Children; accompanied husband on mil. campaigns; Founder and Dir. Cheng

Hsin Rehabilitation Center for Post-Polio Crippled Children; Chair. Board of Dirs. Fujen Catholic Univ.; mem. Board of Govs. Nat. Palace Museum; Hon. Chair. American Bureau for Medical Aid to China and Cttee. for the promotion of the Welfare of the Blind; Patroness Int. Red Cross Cttee.; Hon. Chair. British United Aid to China Fund and United China Relief; First Hon. Mem. Bill of Rights Commemorative Soc.; first Chinese woman to be decorated by Nat. Govt. of China, awards include Gold Medal of Nat. Inst. of Social Sciences; L.H.D. (John B. Stetson Univ., Bryant Coll., Hobart and William Smith Colls.); LL.D. (Rutgers Univ., Goucher Coll., Wellesley Coll., Loyola Univ., Russell Sage Coll., Hahnemann Medical Coll., Univs. of Michigan and Hawaii, and Wesleyan Coll., Macon); Hon. F.R.C.S. (Eng.).
Publs. *Sian: A Coup d'Etat* 37, *China in Peace and War* 39, *China Shall Rise Again* 39, *This Is Our China* 40, *We Chinese Women* 41, *Little Sister Su* 43, *The Sure Victory* 55, *Madame Chiang Kai-shek: Selected Speeches* 58-59, *Selected Speeches* 65-66, *Album of Chinese Orchid Paintings* 71, *Album of Chinese Bamboo Paintings* 72, *Album of Chinese Landscape Paintings* 73, *Album of Chinese Floral Paintings* 74.
Long Island, N.Y., U.S.A.

Chipp, Hon. Donald Leslie, B.COM., A.A.S.A.; Australian politician; b. 21 Aug. 1925, Melbourne, Victoria; ed. Northcote High School, Melbourne Univ.
R.A.A.F. 43-45; Registrar, Commonwealth Inst. of Accountants and Australian Soc. of Accountants 50-55; Chief Exec. Officer Olympic Civic Cttee. 55-56; Councillor, City of Kew 55-61; mem. House of Reps. 60-; Minister for Navy and Minister in charge of Tourist Activities 66-68, Minister for Customs and Excise 69-72; Minister assisting Minister for Nat. Devt. 71-72; Minister for Social Security Health, Repatriation and Compensation Nov.-Dec. 75; mem. Liberal Party until March 77; Leader Australian Democrats Party 77-; Senator 78-.
Publs. *Don Chipp—The Third Man* (with J. Larkin) 78; numerous papers and articles.
Parliament House, Canberra, A.C.T. 2600, Australia.
Telephone: 62-2521 (Office).

Chiu Chuang-huan; Chinese politician; b. 25 July 1925, Changhua County; ed. School of Political Science, Nat. Chengchi Univ.
Director 3rd Dept., Ministry of Personnel, Taiwan 65-67; Dept. Dir. 5th Section, Cen. Cttee., Kuomintang 67-68; Commr. Dept. of Social Affairs, Taiwan Prov. Govt. 69-72; Dir. Dept. of Social Affairs, Cen. Cttee., Kuomintang 72-78; Minister without Portfolio 76-78; Deputy Sec.-Gen., Cen. Cttee., Kuomintang 78; Minister of the Interior 78-81; Vice-Premier Exec. Yuan, Repub. of China (Taiwan) Dec. 81-; Hon. Ph.D. (Youngnam Univ., Repub. of Korea).
Publs. *Thought Regarding Social Welfare in the Three Principles of the People, A Summary of the Chinese Social Welfare System.*
1 Chung-hsiao E. Road, Sec. 1, Taipei, Taiwan.

Cho, Kiyoko Takeda, PH.D.; Japanese historian; b. 20 June 1917, Kobe; ed. Kobe Jogakuin Coll., Olivet Coll., Michigan, Columbia Univ., Union Theological Seminary, New York, and Univ. of Tokyo.
National Sec. for Univ. and Coll. Students, Japan YWCA 47-53; Prof. Int. Christian Univ. 53-; Research Assoc. in Asian Studies, Princeton and Harvard Univs. 65-67; Dean, Coll. of Liberal Arts, Int. Christian Univ. 67-69, Prof. of Intellectual History 61-, Dean of Graduate School 70-74; Dir. Inst. of Asian Cultural Studies 71-; mem. Exec. Cttee. World Student Christian Fed.; Pres. World Council of Churches 71-75; Senior Assoc. Fellow, St. Antony's Coll., Oxford 75-76; Trustee, United Board for Christian Educ. in Asia 74-79.
Publs. *Conflict in Concept of Man in Modern Japan* 59, *The Emperor System and Educational Thought* 64, *Indigenization and Apostasy: Traditional Ethos and Christianity* 67, *The Genealogy of Apostates: the Japanese and Christianity* 73, *Between Orthodoxy and Heterodoxy* 76, *The Dual Image of the Japanese Tennō* (Emperor)—*Before and After 1945* 78; Editor: *Method and Objectives of History and Thoughts—Japan and the West* 61, *Comparative Modernization Theories* 70, *Human Rights in Modern Japan* 70, *Collection of Religious Literature of the Meiji Period* 75; has translated works of Reinhold Niebuhr into Japanese.
1-59-6 Nishigahara, Kita-ku, Tokyo 114, Japan.

Choi Kyu Hah; Korean politician; b. 16 July 1919, Wonju City, Kangwon-do; ed. Kyungg High School, Seoul; Tokyo Coll. of Educ., Japan, and Nat. Daedong Inst., Manchuria.
Professor, Coll. of Educ., Seoul Nat. Univ. 45-46; Dir. Econ. Affairs Bureau, Ministry of Foreign Affairs 51-52; Consul-Gen. Korean Mission, Japan 52-57, Minister 59; Vice-Minister of Foreign Affairs 59-60; Amb. to Malaysia 64-67; Minister of Foreign Affairs 67-71; Special Asst. to the Pres. for Foreign Affairs 71-75; Acting Prime Minister 75-76, Prime Minister 76-79; Acting Pres. Oct.-Dec. 79, Pres. Dec. 79-Aug. 80 (resgnd.); Head of Korean del. to UN Gen. Assembly 67, 68, 69; del. to numerous int. confs. 55-; Hon. Litt. Dr. (Hankook Univ. of Foreign Studies, Seoul); decorations from Ethiopia, Panama, El Salvador, Malaysia, Repub. of Viet-Nam, Tunisia and Belgium; Order of Diplomatic Service Merit.
Chong Wa Dae, Seoul, Republic of Korea.

Choudhury, Abul Barkat Ataul Ghani Khan, B.A.; Indian politician; b. 1926, Malda District, W. Bengal; ed. Inst. of Int. Studies, Geneva.
Member W. Bengal Assembly 52-; Minister for Irrigation and Power, Govt. of W. Bengal 72-77; Minister for Energy and Irrigation, Govt. of India 80-81, of Energy 81-.
Ministry of Energy, New Delhi, India.

Choudhury, Dr. A. Q. M. Badruddoza, M.B.B.S., T.D.D., F.R.C.P.E.; Bangladesh professor of medicine and politician; b. 1 Nov. 1932, Comilla; ed. Dacca Univ., Univ. of Wales, Royal Coll. of Physicians, Edinburgh.
Medical Registrar, London 61-62; Assoc. Prof. of Medicine Rajshani Medical Coll. 64-65, Sir Salimullah Medical Coll. 65-70; Prof. of Medicine Sylhet Medical Coll. 70-77; led dels. to several int. health conferences 74-79; mem. Advisory Council to Pres. of Bangladesh 77; Minister of Health and Population Control 78-79, of Health, Population Control and Family Planning 79-80; Senior Deputy Prime Minister May-Aug. 79; Deputy Leader of Parl. 79-80; Pres. Nat. Anti-Tuberculosis Asscn. of Bangladesh 74-; Sec. Gen. Bangladesh Nationalist Party (BNP) Aug. 79- (all political activity suspended March 82-); Pres. Int. Union against Tuberculosis (IUAT) Eastern Region; Vice-Pres. Bangladesh UN Asscn.; Chair. Bangladesh-Egypt Friendship Soc.; Life mem. Bangla Acad.; mem. Academic Council Jahangir Nagar Univ.; Convenor Nat. Health Movement of Bangladesh; Hon. Prof. of Medicine, Inst. of Post Graduate Medicine and Research, Dacca Medical Coll.
Shyamoli, 227 Maghbazar Outer Circular Road, Dacca 2, Bangladesh.

Chow Shu-kai; Chinese politician and diplomatist; b. 21 Aug. 1913, Hubei, China; ed. National Central Univ., Nanjing and Univ. of London.
Chinese Consul, Manchester, England 44-45; Assoc. Prof. of Int. Relations, Univ. of Nanjing 46-47; Deputy Dir. Information Dept., Ministry of Foreign Affairs 47-49; Minister, Chargé d'affaires, Manila 53-55; Deputy Minister of Foreign Affairs 56-60; Cabinet Minister and Chair. Overseas Chinese Affairs 60-62; Amb. to Spain 63-65, to

U.S.A. 65-71; Minister of Foreign Affairs 71-72, without Portfolio 72-77; Amb. to the Holy See 78-.
Embassy of the Republic of China to the Holy See, Piazza delle Muse 7, Rome 00197, Italy.

Chowdhury, Abu Sayeed, M.A., B.L.; Bangladesh lawyer, administrator and diplomatist; b. 31 Jan. 1921, Nagbari (Tangail); ed. Presidency Coll., Calcutta Univ. and Lincoln's Inn, London.
Member del. to UN Gen. Assembly 59; Advocate-Gen., E. Pakistan 60-61; mem. Constitution Comm. 60-61; Judge, Dacca High Court 61-72; Chair. Cen. Board for Devt. of Bengal 63-68; Vice-Chancellor, Univ. of Dacca 69-71; Amb.-at-Large and Head, Bangladesh Missions in London and New York April 71-Jan. 72; Pres. of Bangladesh 72-73; Special Govt. Rep. in charge of Foreign Relations and int. agencies 74-75; Minister of Foreign Affairs, Shipping and Ports Aug. 75; Leader dels. to WHO, UNESCO, IAEA, etc.; Hon. Research Fellow, Open Univ. 77; mem. UN Sub-Cttee. on Prevention of Discrimination and Protection of Minorities 78-; Hon. Deshikottama Viswabharati (Shantinikatan) 72; Hon. LL.D. (Calcutta) 72.
2 Paper Buildings, Temple, London, E.C.4, England.

Chowdhury, Abul Fazal Mohammad Ashanuddin, LL.B.; Bangladesh politician and judge; b. 1915, Mymensingh; ed. Univ. of Dacca.
Joined fmr. Bengal Civil Service (Judicial) 42; served as District Judge in several regions; elected to High Court Bench 68, Appellate Div. of Supreme Court of Bangladesh 73; retd. from judiciary Nov. 77; Pres. of Bangladesh March 82-; also in charge of Pres.'s. Secr., Cabinet Div. and Ministries of Defence and Planning March 82-.
Office of tee President, Dacca, Bangladesh.

Christiansen, Prof. Wilbur Norman, D.SC.; Australian radio astronomer; b. 9 Aug. 1913, Melbourne; ed. Caulfield Grammar School and Univ. of Melbourne.
Research laboratories, Amalgamated Wireless (Australasia) Ltd. 37-47; Radiophysics Div., CSIRO 47-60; Prof. of Electrical Engineering, Univ. of Sydney 60-78; Visiting Fellow, Australian Nat. Univ. 78-; also worked Institut d'Astrophysique 54, Leiden Univ. 60-61, 70, and Beijing Observatory 66-67; Chair. Australian Nat. Cttee. for Radio Science 60-72; Vice-Pres. Int. Astronomical Union 64-70; Vice-Pres. Int. Union for Radio Science 72-78, Pres. 78-81; Fellow Australian Acad. of Science 59-, Council 74-77, Foreign Sec. 81; medals in physics, astronomy, engineering.
Publs. *Radiotelescopes* (with J. A. Hogbom) 69 and articles in scientific journals.
"Bingera", RMB 436 Mack's Reef Road, via Bungendore, N.S.W. 2621, Australia.

Chu Huy Man, Lieut.-Gen.; Vietnamese soldier and politician; b. 1920.
Member of Cen. Cttee., Lao Dong Party; Maj.-Gen. in Viet-Nam People's Army; fmr. Political Commdr. in Western Highlands; mem. Politburo of Communist Party of Viet-Nam Dec. 76-; represents the ethnic minorities in Govt.
Central Committee of the Communist Party of Viet-Nam, No. 1-c, boulevard Hoang Van Thu, Hanoi, Viet-Nam.

Chulasapya, Air Chief Marshal Dawee; Thai air force officer and politician; b. 8 Aug. 1914, Thon Buri; ed. Mil. Acad. (now Chulachomklao), Flying Training School and Command and Gen. Staff Coll. Fort Leavenworth, U.S.A., Fighter pilot, Royal Thai Air Force 36; intelligence work and studies abroad during World War II; Dir. of Intelligence 48-55; Acting Dir. Civil Aviation 48-55; Air Marshal 55; Chief of Air Staff 55-61; Air Chief Marshal 57; Chief of Staff, Supreme Command 61-63; SEATO Mil. Adviser 61-63; rank of Gen. and Admiral 63; Special Officer, First Royal Guard Infantry 63; Deputy Minister of Defence 63-69; Minister of Communications 69-71; Chair. Thai Maritime Navigation Co. 69-74; Dir. of Nat. Devt., Agriculture and Communications in Nat. Exec. Council 71; Minister of Agriculture and Co-operatives 72-73, of Defence 73-74; fmr. Chair. Joint Chiefs of Staff of Nat. Security Command; fmr. Deputy Dir. Communist Suppression Operations Command; concurrently Deputy C.-in-C. Armed Forces and Acting Supreme Commdr. 73; retd. 74; mem. House of Reps. for Mae Hong Son April-Oct. 76; leader Social Justice Party until Oct. 76; Deputy Prime Minister 68-80, Minister of Public Health April-Oct. 76; Medal of Courage 72, numerous other awards.
Bangkok, Thailand.

Chun Doo-Hwan; Korean army officer (retd.) and politician; b. 18 Jan. 1931, Kyongsangnamdo Prov.; ed. Primary School, Taegu, Taegu Tech. High School, Mil. Acad. and Army Coll.
Joined army 51; Second Lieut. 55; U.S. Special Forces and Psychological Warfare School 59; U.S. Army Infantry School 60; Acting Planning Dir. Special Warfare Bureau, Army H.Q. 61; Domestic Affairs Sec. to Chair. Supreme Council for Nat. Reconstruction 61-62; Dir. Personnel Admin. Bureau, Korean C.I.A. 63; Exec. Officer, 1st Airborne Special Forces Group 66-67; Commdr. 30th Bn., Capital Garrison Command 67-69; Sr. Aide to Army Chief of Staff 69-70; Commdr. 29th Regt., 9th Infantry Div., Viet-Nam 70-71; Commdr. 1st Airborne Special Forces Group 71; Commanding Gen. 1st Infantry Div. 78, Defence Security Command 79 and Mil. Security Dec. 79-; Acting Dir. South Korean C.I.A. April 80; Chair. Special Cttee. for Nat. Security Measures and Internal Standing Cttee. June 80; promoted to full General Aug. 80; resgnd. from army Aug. 80; Pres. Repub. of Korea Sept. 80-; Pres. Democratic Justice Party Jan. 81-; numerous decorations.
Office of the President, Seoul; 302–3 Yonhi Dong, Sodaemun-Ku, Seoul, Republic of Korea.

Chunder, Pratap Chandra, LL.B., M.A., PH.D.; Indian lawyer and politician; b. 1 Sept. 1919, Calcutta; ed. Univ. of Calcutta.
Law practice in Calcutta 45; mem. Senate and Law Faculty of Calcutta Univ. 61-68; mem. Exec. Council of Rabindra Bharati Univ. 62-68; mem. West Bengal Legislative Assembly 62-68; Pres. West Bengal Provincial Congress Cttee. 67-76; Minister of Finance and Judiciary in State Govt. 68; mem. Working Cttee. and Cen. Parl. Board of Org. Congress 69-76; mem. Janata Party 77-; mem. Lok Sabha from Calcutta North East 77-79; Minister of Education, Social Welfare and Culture, Govt. of India 77-79; mem. Incorporated Law Soc. and Calcutta Bar Asscn.; Pres. Int. Educ. Conf. UNESCO 77-79; Hon. D.Sc. and D.Litt.; fmr. editor literary magazines; Best Playwright award, Calcutta Univ. 65; Fellow, Asiatic Soc. of Calcutta 75.
Publs. include *Kautilya on Love and Morals, The Sons of Mystery, Job Charnock and His Lady Fair.*
23 Nirmal Chunder Street, Calcutta 12, India.

Chung, Kyung-Wha; Korean violinist; b. 26 March 1948, Seoul; ed. Juilliard School of Music, U.S.A.
Studied under Ivan Galamian; started career in U.S.A.; winner of Leventritt Competition 68; European debut 70; has played under conductors such as Abbado, Barenboim, Davis, Dorati, Dutoit, Giulini, Haitink, Jochum, Kempe, Kondrashin, Leinsdorf, Levine, Maazel, Mehta, Previn, Rozhdestvensky and Solti; has played with major orchestras including all London Orchestras, Chicago, Boston and Pittsburgh Symphony Orchestras, New York, Cleveland, Philadelphia, Berlin, Israel and Vienna Philharmonics, Orchestre de Paris; has toured world; recordings for Decca; played at Salzburg Festival with London Symphony Orchestra 73.
c/o Harrison/Parrott Ltd., 12 Penzance Place, London W11 4PA, England.

Clark, Colin Grant, M.A.; Australian economist; b. 2 Nov. 1905; ed. Dragon School, Oxford, Winchester Coll., and Brasenose Coll., Oxford.
Assistant Social Surveys of London 28-29, of Merseyside 29-30; Economic Advisory Council 30-31; Lecturer, Cambridge Univ. 31-37; Visiting Lecturer, Univs. of Sydney, Melbourne and Western Australia 37-38; Under-Sec. of State for Labour and Industry, Dir. Bureau of Industry, Financial Adviser to Treasury, Queensland 38-52; Dir. Inst. for Research in Agricultural Economics, Oxford 53-69; Research Consultant, Queensland Univ.; Corresp. Fellow, British Acad.; Fellow Brasenose Coll., Oxford; Fellow Econometric Soc.; Hon. Sc.D. (Milan), D.Litt. (Oxford); Hon. D.Econ. (Tilburg).
Publs. *The National Income, The Conditions of Economic Progress, The Economics of 1960, Welfare and Taxation, British Trade in the Common Market, Economics of Irrigation, National Income of Australia* (with J. G. Crawford) 38, *Australian Hopes and Fears* 58, *Population Growth and Land Use* 67, *Starvation or Plenty* 70, *The Myth of Overpopulation* 72, *The Value of Agricultural Land* 73, *The Economics of Subsistence Agriculture* (with M. R. Haswell), *The Economics of Irrigations* (with I. Carruthers) 81, *Regional and Urban Location* 82.
Department of Economics, University of Queensland, St. Lucia, Queensland, Australia.

Coleman, Peter Tali, B.SC., LL.B.; American public administrator; b. 8 Dec. 1919; ed. St. Louis Coll., Honolulu, Georgetown Univ., Washington, D.C.
Captain U.S. Army 46; entered public service Washington, D.C. 51; Attorney-Gen. American Samoa 55-56, Gov. 55-60, 77-; District Admin., Marshall Islands 61-66, Mariana Islands 66-70; Deputy High Commissioner, Trust Territory of the Pacific Islands 69-77, Acting High Commissioner 77.
Office of the Governor, Pago Pago, Tutuila, American Samoa 96799.

Collins, Arthur John, O.B.E.; British diplomatist; b. 17 May 1931; ed. Purley Grammar School.
Served R.A.F. 49-51; Ministry of Health 51-58, Private Sec. to Perm. Sec. 60-61, to Parl. Sec. 62-63; FCO 68-69; First Sec. and Head of Chancery, Dacca 70-71; Brasília 72-74; Asst. Head of Latin America and Caribbean Dept., FCO 74-77; High Commr. in Papua New Guinea 81-.
British High Commission, United Church Building, 3rd Floor, Douglas Street, Port Moresby, Papua New Guinea.
Telephone: 212500.

Connelly, Michael Aynsley, B.COM., F.C.A., C.M.A.; New Zealand politician; b. 21 Feb. 1916; ed. Greymouth, Central Otago, and Univ. of Otago.
Served World War II in RNZAF; mem. of Parl. for Riccarton 56-69, for Wigram 69-78, for Yaldhurst 78-; served on numerous parl. cttees.; fmr. Christchurch City Councillor; first Pres. Canterbury Savings Bank; Minister of Police 72-75, of Customs 72-74; Assoc. Minister of Finance 72-74; Minister of Statistics 74-75; Minister of Works and Devt. 75; Minister in charge of Earthquake and War Damage 75; Chair. Nat. Roads Board 75; Chair. Nat. Water and Soil Conservation Authority 75; Opposition Spokesman on Defence, Works and Devt., and Police; mem. Labour Party Policy Council; mem. Public Expenditure Select Cttee.; led del. to 30th session ECAFE Conf., Sri Lanka 74; fmr. mem. Lincoln Coll. Council and Univ. of Canterbury Council; Pres. Adult Cerebral Palsy Soc.; Chair. Exec. Cttee., Canterbury Provincial Bldgs. Board; Patron N.Z. Greyhound Racing Asscn., N.Z. Fed. of Roller Skating, N.Z. Antique Arms Asscn., N.Z. Riding for the Disabled Asscn. (Christchurch group), etc.; Hon. M.A.
Parliament Buildings, Wellington; Home: Corner of Yaldhurst and Pound Roads, Yaldhurst, R.D.5, Christchurch, New Zealand.

Cooray, H.E. Cardinal Thomas B., PH.D., D.D., B.A. (LOND.); Sri Lankan ecclesiastic; b. 28 Dec. 1901; ed. Univ. Coll., Colombo and Anglicum Univ., Rome.
Ordained Roman Catholic priest 29; Titular Archbishop of Preslavo and Co-adjutor Archbishop of Colombo 45; Archbishop of Colombo and Pres. Sri Lanka Catholic Bishops' Conference 47-76; mem. Pontifical Comm. for Canon Law; created Cardinal 65.
Cardinal's Residence, Tewatta, Ragama, Sri Lanka.
Telephone: 538-208.

Cordeiro, H.E. Cardinal Joseph; Pakistani ecclesiastic; b. 19 Jan. 1918, Bombay, India.
Ordained 46; Archbishop of Karachi 58-; created Cardinal 73.
St. Patrick's Cathedral, Karachi 3, Pakistan.

Corden, Warner Max, M.COMM., M.A., PH.D.; Australian professor of economics; b. 13 Aug. 1927, Breslau, Germany (now Wrocław, Poland); ed. Melbourne Boys High School, Melbourne Univ. and London School of Economics.
Lecturer, Univ. of Melbourne 58-61; Professorial Fellow, Australian Nat. Univ. 62-67, Prof. of Econs. 76-; Nuffield Reader in Int. Econs. and Fellow of Nuffield Coll., Oxford 67-76; Visiting Prof., Univ. of California (Berkeley) 65, Univ. of Minn. 71, Princeton Univ. 73; Pres. Econ. Soc. of Australia and New Zealand 77-80.
Publs. *The Theory of Protection* 71, *Trade Policy and Economic Welfare* 74, *Inflation, Exchange Rates and the World Economy* 77.
Department of Economics, School of Pacific Studies, Australian National University, Canberra, Australia.

Corea, Gamani, D.PHIL.; Sri Lankan economist, diplomatist and international civil servant; b. 4 Nov. 1925; ed. Royal Coll., Colombo, Corpus Christi Coll., Cambridge, and Nuffield Coll., Oxford.
Director, Planning Secr. and Sec. Nat. Planning Council 56-60; Dir. of Econ. Research, Central Bank of Ceylon 60-64; Perm. Sec. to Ministry of Planning and Econ. Affairs 65-70; Deputy Gov. Central Bank of Ceylon 70-73; Chair. Expert Group on Int. Monetary Reform and Developing Countries 69; Pres., Ceylon Asscn. for Advancement of Science 71; Chair. Expert Panel on Devt. and Environment 71; Special Rep. of Sec.-Gen. UN Conf. on Human Environment 71; Chair. UN Cttee. for Devt. Planning 72-74, UN Cocoa Conf. 72, ECAFE Expert Group on Regional Performance Evaluation during 2nd Devt. Decade 71-73; Amb. to EEC and the Benelux countries 73-74; Sec.-Gen. UNCTAD 74-; Sec.-Gen. UN Conf. on Least Developed Countries 81; Chancellor Open Univ., Sri Lanka; Chair. Bd. of Govs. Marga Inst.; Research Fellow, Int. Devt. Research Centre, Canada 73; Visiting Fellow, Nuffield Coll., Oxford Univ. 74-79; mem. Bd. of Govs. Inst. of Devt. Studies, Univ. of Sussex; mem. Exec. Cttee. of Third World Forum, Int. Foundation for Devt. Alternatives, Int. Econ. Asscn., Dag Hammarskjöld Foundation; mem. Soc. for Int. Devt.; Dr. h.c. (Nice) 77; Hon. D.Litt. (Colombo).
Publs. *The Instability of an Export Economy, Need for Change: Towards the NIEO* and articles on international economic issues.
United Nations Conference on Trade and Development, Palais des Nations, 1211 Geneva 10, Switzerland; and Horton Lodge, 21 Horton Place, Colombo 7, Sri Lanka.

Corner, Frank Henry, C.M.G., M.A.; New Zealand diplomatist; b. 17 May 1920; ed. Victoria Univ. of Wellington.
First Sec., Washington, D.C. 48-51; Senior Counsellor, London 52-58; Deputy Sec. of External Affairs 58-62; Perm. Rep. to UN 62-67; Amb. to U.S.A. 67-72; Sec. of Foreign Affairs 73-80.
Ministry of Foreign Affairs, Wellington, New Zealand.

Cortazzi, Sir (Henry Arthur) Hugh, K.C.M.G.; British diplomatist; b. 2 May 1924; ed. Sedbergh School and St. Andrews and London Univs.
Royal Air Force 43-48; Foreign Office 49; Third Sec., Singapore 50; Third, later Second Sec., Tokyo 51; Foreign Office 54; First Sec., Bonn 58; Tokyo 61 (Head of Chancery 63); First Sec. (Notional Counsellor) Foreign Office 65; Counsellor (Commercial), Tokyo 66; Royal College of Defence Studies 71; Minister (Commercial), Washington 72-75; Deputy Under Sec. of State, Foreign and Commonwealth Office 75-80; Amb. to Japan 80-.
British Embassy, 1, Ichiban-cho, Chiyoda-ku, Tokyo 102, Japan.
Telephone: (03) 265-5511.

Cotton, Hon. Sir Robert Carrington, I.C.M.G., A.A.S.A.; Australian politician and diplomatist; b. 29 Nov. 1915, Broken Hill, N.S.W.; ed. St. Peter's Coll., Adelaide.
Former Fed. Vice-Pres. Liberal Party of Australia, State Pres. Liberal Party, N.S.W. 57-60, Acting Pres. 65; Senator for N.S.W. 65-78, leader del. to IPU confs., Majorca and Geneva 67; Chair. Cotton's Pty. Ltd., Broken Hill; Minister of State for Civil Aviation 69-72, Minister of Manufacturing Industry, Science and Consumer Affairs Nov.-Dec. 75, of Industry and Commerce 75-77; Consul-Gen. in New York, N.Y., U.S.A. 78-; Liberal.
The Senate, Parliament House, Canberra, A.C.T.; Carrington Park, Oberon, N.S.W. 2787, Australia.

Court, Hon. Sir Charles Walter Michael, K.C.M.G., O.B.E. (MIL.), F.C.A., F.C.I.S.; Australian retd. politician; b. 29 Sept. 1911, Crawley, Sussex, England; ed. Perth, Australia.
Founder Partner, Hendry, Rae & Court, chartered accountants 38, served Australian Imperial Forces 40-46, rank of Lt.-Col.; mem. W. Australia Legis. Assembly for Nedlands 53-82; Deputy Leader of Opposition 57-59; Minister for Railways 59-67, for Industrial Devt. and the N.W. 59-71, for Transport 65-66; Deputy Leader of Opposition 71-72, Leader 72-73; Premier, State Treas., Minister Co-ordinating Econ. and Regional Devt., W. Australia 74-82; Financial Consultant 82-; State Registrar (W. Australia) Inst. of Chartered Accountants in Australia 46-52; Senator Junior Chamber Int. 71; Hon. Col. W. Australia Univ. Regt. 69-74, S.A.S. Regt. 76-80; Hon. LL.D. W. Australia Univ. 69; Australian Mfrs. Export Council Award 70, Inst. of Production Engs. Award 71; Liberal.
Publs. many papers on industrial, economic and resource development matters.
Perpetual Trustees Building, 89 St. George's Terrace, Perth, Western Australia; Home: 46 Waratah Avenue, Dalkeith, W. Australia 6009, Australia.
Telephone: Perth 322-4387 (Office); 386-1257 (Home).

Cowen, Rt. Hon. Sir Zelman, P.C., A.K., G.C.M.G., G.C.V.O., Q.C., F.R.S.A.; Australian academic and fmr. Governor-General; b. 7 Oct. 1919, Melbourne; ed. Scotch Coll., Melbourne, Univ. of Melbourne, Univ. of Oxford.
Served in Royal Australian Naval Volunteer Reserve 40-45; Rhodes Scholar 41; legal consultant to British Occupation Army in Germany 47-51; Dominion Liaison Officer to British High Commission, Canberra 51-66; Dean of Faculty of Law, Prof. of Public Law, Univ. of Melbourne 51-66, Prof. Emer. 67-; Vice-Chancellor, Univ. of New England, N.S.W. 67-70, Univ. of Queensland 70-77; Gov.-Gen. of Australia 77-82; Provost, Oriel Coll., Oxford 82-; Fellow, Oriel Coll., Oxford 47-50; Visiting Prof., Univ. of Chicago 49, Harvard Law School 53-54, Fletcher School of Law and Diplomacy 63-64, Univ. of Utah 54, Illinois 57-58, Washington Univ., St. Louis 59, Univ. of Calcutta, India 75; Pres. Adult Education Asscn. of Australia 68-70, Australian Inst. of Urban Studies 73-77; mem. and (at various times) Chair. (Victorian) State Advisory Cttee. to Australian Broadcasting Comm.; mem. Devt. Corpn. of N.S.W. 67-70, Regional Advisory Cttee. for North-West N.S.W. 67-70, Board of Int. Asscn. for Cultural Freedom 70-75, Council of Univ. of Lesotho 76-77; Academic Gov. of Board of Govs., Hebrew Univ. of Jerusalem 69-77; a Dir. Australian Opera 69-77; mem. Club of Rome 74-77; Pres. Australian Inst. of Urban Studies 73; Chair. Board of Govs., Utah Foundation 75-77; Law Reform Commissioner, Commonwealth of Australia 76-77; Chair. Australian Vice-Chancellor's Cttee. 77; Trustee Sydney Opera House 69-70; Pres. Australian and New Zealand Asscn. for the Advancement of Science Inc. (ANZAAS) 81-82; Hon. Fellow, Acad. of Social Sciences in Australia, Australian Coll. of Educ., Australian Nat. Univ., Oriel Coll., Oxford, New Coll., Oxford, Royal Australian Inst. of Architects, Royal Australasian Coll. of Physicians, University House, A.N.U., Australian Acad. of Tech. Sciences, Australian Acad. of Humanities, Australian Soc. of Accountants, Royal Australian Coll. of Medical Administrators, Royal Australian Coll. of Obstetricians and Gynaecologists, Inst. of Chartered Accountants in Australia; Foreign Hon. mem. American Acad. of Arts and Sciences 65; Hon. Master of Bench, Gray's Inn 78; Hon. LL.D. (Hong Kong) 67, (Queensland) 72, (Melbourne) 73, (Western Australia) 81, (Turin) 81; Hon. D.Litt. (Univ. of New England, N.S.W.) 79, (Sydney) 80, (James Cook Univ., N. Queensland) 82; Hon. D.Hum.Litt. (Hebrew Union Coll.—Jewish Inst. of Religion, Cincinnati) 80; Hon. D.Univ. (Newcastle) 80, (Griffith) 81; Hon. D.Phil. (Hebrew Univ. of Jerusalem) 82; K. St. J.
Publs. include numerous books on legal and constitutional matters; chapters, articles and essays for books and journals in Australia, U.K., U.S.A., Canada, Europe.
Oriel College, Oxford, England.

Cradock, Sir Percy, K.C.M.G.; British diplomatist; b. 26 Oct. 1923.
Joined Foreign Office 54; First Sec. Kuala Lumpur, Malaya 57-61, Hong Kong 61-62, Beijing 62-63; Foreign Office 63-66; Counsellor and Head of Chancery, Beijing 66-68, Chargé d'affaires 68-69; Head of Foreign and Commonwealth Office Planning Staff 69-71; Asst. Under-Sec. of State and Head of Cabinet Office Assessments Staff 71-76; Amb. to German Democratic Repub. 76-78; Leader of U.K. Del. to Comprehensive Test Ban Talks, Geneva 77-78; Amb. to People's Repub. of China 78-.
British Embassy, 11 Guang Hua Lu, Jian Guo Men Wai, Beijing, People's Republic of China.
Telephone: 51-1961/2/3/4.

Crawford, Sir John Grenfell, Kt., A.C., C.B.E., M.EC.; Australian administrator; b. 4 April 1910; ed. Univ. of Sydney.
Director, Commonwealth Bureau of Agricultural Economics 45-50; Commonwealth Wool Adviser 49-55; Sec. Dept. of Commerce and Agriculture, Canberra 50-56, Dept. of Trade 56-60; Dir. School of Pacific Studies, Australian Nat. Univ. 60-67 and Fiscal Adviser to Univ., Vice-Chancellor of ANU 68-73; Chancellor, Univ. of Papua New Guinea 72-75; Consultant to IBRD; Vice-Chair. Commonwealth Econ. Enquiry 63-64; Gov. Canadian Int. Devt. Research Centre 70-; Chair. Tech. Advisory Cttee. advising IBRD, FAO, etc. on Int. Research in Agric. 71-78; Chair. Int. Food Policy Research Inst., Washington, D.C.; Chancellor, ANU 76-; mem. Board Int. Fertilizer Devt. Centre 77-; Walter and Eliza Hall Fellow 33-35; Commonwealth Fund Fellow, U.S.A. 38-40; Farrer Medallist (and Orator) 57; Fellow, Australian Inst. of Agricultural Science 58, Acad. of Social Sciences in Australia; Hon. Foreign Mem., American Acad. of Arts and Sciences; ANZAAS Medal 71; Order of the Sacred Treasure, First Class (Japan) 72; Independence Medal (Papua New Guinea) 78; Hon. D.Sc., Hon. D.Ec., Hon. LL.D., etc.
Publs. *Australian Trade Policy 1942-1949: A Documentary*

History 68; various articles and reports to Govt., incl. *Okita/Crawford Report on Australia, Japan and Western Pacific Relations.*
32 Melbourne Avenue, Deakin, A.C.T. 2600, Australia.

Critchley, Thomas Kingston, A.O., C.B.E.; Australian diplomatist; b. 27 Jan. 1916; ed. North Sydney Boys' High School and Sydney Univ.
Assistant Econ. Adviser, Dept. of War Organization of Industry 43-44; Head, Research Section, Far Eastern Bureau, New Delhi, British Ministry of Information 44-46; Head, Economic Relations Section, Dept. of External Affairs, Canberra 46-47; Australian Rep. UN Cttee. of Good Offices on Indonesian Question 48-49; rep. UN Comm. for Indonesia 49-50; Acting Australian Commr. Malaya 51-52; Australian rep. on UNCURK 52-54; Head. Pacific and Americas Branch, Dept. of External Affairs, Canberra 54-55; Commr. Fed. of Malaya 55-57, High Commr. 57-63, High Commr. in Malaysia 63-65; Senior External Affairs Rep., High Comm., U.K. 66-69; Amb. to Thailand and SEATO 69-74; High Commr. of Papua New Guinea 74-75; Australian High Commr. in Papua New Guinea 75-78; Amb. to Indonesia 78-81.
26 Fuller Street, Deakin, A.C.T. 2600, Australia.

Crocker, Sir Walter Russell, K.B.E.; Australian State Government official and fmr. farmer and diplomatist; b. 25 March 1902; ed. Balliol Coll., Oxford, Univ. of Adelaide, Australia, and Stanford Univ., California.
With British Colonial Service 30-34, L.N. and I.L.O. 34-40; served army 40-46; with UN 46-49; Prof. of Int. Relations, Australian Nat. Univ. 49-52, Acting Vice-Chancellor 51; High Commr. for Australia in India 52-55; Amb. to Indonesia 55-57; High Commr. in Canada 57-59; High Commr. in India 59-62 and Amb. to Nepal 60-62; Amb. to the Netherlands and Belgium 62-65; Amb. to Ethiopia and High Commr. in Kenya and in Uganda 65-67; Amb. to Italy 67-70; Lieut.-Gov. of S. Australia 73-; Croix de Guerre, Order of the Lion (Belgium), Knight Grand Cross of Italy, Grand Officer, Order of Malta.
Publs. *The Japanese Population Problem* 31, *Nigeria: Critique of Colonial Administration* 36, *On Governing Colonies* 46, *Self-Government for Colonies* 49, *Can the UN Succeed?* 51, *The Racial Factor in International Relations* 55, *Nehru* 66, *Australian Ambassador* 71, *Memoirs* 81.
Government House, Adelaide, S.A. 5000, Australia.

Cutler, Sir (Arthur) Roden, V.C., A.K., K.C.M.G., K.C.V.O., C.B.E., B.EC.; Australian public servant and diplomatist; b. 24 May 1916; ed. Sydney High School and Univ. of Sydney.
Justice Dept. N.S.W. (Public Trust Office) 35-42; army war service 40-42; State Sec. Returned Servicemen's League N.S.W. 42-43; mem. Aliens' Classification and Advisory Cttee. to advise Commonwealth Govt. 42-43; Asst. Deputy Dir. of Security Service N.S.W. 43; Commonwealth Asst. Commr. of Repatriation 43-46; High Commr. in New Zealand 46-52, in Ceylon 52-55; Minister to Egypt 55-56; Sec.-Gen. SEATO 57; Chief of Protocol, Dept. of External Affairs, Canberra 57; State Pres. Returned Servicemen's League, A.C.T. 58; High Commr. in Pakistan 59-61; rep. to independence of Somalia 60; Consul-Gen., New York 61-65; del. to UN Gen. Assembly and rep. Fifth Cttee. 62, 63, 64; Amb. to the Netherlands 65-66; Gov. N.S.W. 66-81; acted as Admin. of Commonwealth of Australia in the absence of the Gov.-Gen.; Chair. State Bank of N.S.W.; Dir. several cos.; Hon. LL.D. (Sydney Univ.), Hon. D.Sc. (Univs. of N.S.W. and of Newcastle), Hon. D.Lit. (New England Univ.); Hon. Col. Royal N.S.W. Regt., Sydney Univ. Regt.; K.St.J.
22 Ginahgulla Road, Bellevue Hill, Sydney, N.S.W. 2023, Australia.

D

Dalai Lama (Tenzin Gyatso); temporal and religious head of Tibet (Xizang); b. 6 July 1935, Taktser, Amdo District.
Born of Tibetan peasant family; enthroned as XIV Dalai Lama at Lhasa 40; rights exercised by regency 34-50; was requested to take full political power 50; fled to Chumbi in S. Tibet on Chinese invasion 50; negotiated agreement with China 51; Hon. Chair. Chinese Buddhist Asscn. 53-59; Del. to Nat. People's Congress 54-59, Vice-Chair. Standing Cttee.; mem. Nat. Cttee. Chinese People's Political Consultative Council 51-59; Chair. Preparatory Cttee. for the Xizang Autonomous Region 55-59; left Tibet for India after abortive resistance to Chinese 59; refused invitation to return May 77; Dr. of Buddhist Philosophy (Monasteries of Sera, Dangzhe, Gadansi in Lhasa) 59; Supreme Head of all Buddhist sects in Tibet (Xizang).
Publs. *My Land and People* 62, *The Opening of the Wisdom Eye* 63, *The Buddhism of Tibet and the Key to the Middle Way* 75.
Thekchen Choling, McLeod Gunj 176219, Kangra District, Himachal Pradesh, India.
Telephone: 343.

Damdin, Paavangiyn; Mongolian politician; b. 1931; ed. Financial and Econ. Tech. School, Ulan Bator and a higher school of econs. in U.S.S.R.
Accountant, Finance Section of Mongolian People's Revolutionary Party (MPRP) Cen. Cttee. 50-52; Specialist, Head of Dept. State Planning Comm. 58-60; Minister of Industry 60-68; Minister of Light and Food Industry 68-79; mem. MPRP Cen. Cttee. 61-; Sec. MPRP Cen. Cttee. 79-; Deputy to People's Great Hural (Assembly) 60-; Order of the Red Banner of Labour, Order of the Pole Star.
Central Committee of the Mongolian People's Revolutionary Party, Ulan Bator, Mongolia.

Dandavate, Madhu; Indian politician and fmr. professor of physics; b. 21 Jan. 1924, Ahmed Nagar, Maharashtra; ed. Royal Inst. of Science, Bombay.
Participated in Independence Movement, later in Quit India Movement 42; leader of passive resistance in Goa Campaign 55; took part in Samyukta Maharashtra Movement for formation of Maharashtra state; joined Praja Socialist Party (PSP) 48, Chair. Maharashtra State Unit of PSP, later Joint Sec. of All-India PSP; participated in Land Liberation Movement 69; associated with Maharashtra Citizens' Defence Cttee. during conflicts with People's Repub. of China and Pakistan; mem. Maharashtra Legislative Council 70-71; mem. Lok Sabha from Rajapur 71-; Vice-Principal and Head of Physics Dept., Siddhartha Coll. of Arts and Science, Bombay until 71; mem. Janata Party 77-; Minister of Railways 77-79.
Publs. *Gandhiji's Impact on Socialist Thinking, Three Decades of Indian Communism, Evolution of Socialist Policies, Kashmir—a Test for Secularism, Myth and Mystery of Congress Socialism, Bharatiya Swarajwad* (in Marathi).
Lok Sabha, New Delhi, India.

Dang Mingzhao; Chinese United Nations official; b. 1910, Guangdong Prov.; ed. Qinghua Univ. and Univ. of California, U.S.A.
Former mem. Council, Chinese People's Inst. on Foreign Affairs, Chinese People's Asscn. for Friendship with Foreign Countries; Deputy to Nat. Congress, People's Repub. of China; Under-Sec.-Gen. for Political Affairs, Trusteeship and Decolonization, UN 72; mem. del. to UN Gen. Assembly 71.
c/o State Council, Beijing, People's Republic of China.

Dange, Shripad Amrit; Indian trade union leader and politician; b. 10 Oct. 1899.
Took a prominent part in organizing Textile Workers'

Unions in Bombay; arrested on many occasions for trade union and political activity; sentenced to twelve years' transportation in the Meerut conspiracy trial; released 36; imprisoned 39-43; Pres. Girni Kamgar Union; Pres. All-India T.U.C. 43-45; Del. to W.F.T.U. Paris 45, Moscow 46; Vice-Pres. W.F.T.U. 48, mem. Exec. Bureau; Editor and Founder of *Socialist* 22, first Marxist paper in India; Editor and Founder of *Kranti*, first working class paper in Marathi language; mem. Legislative Assembly, Bombay 46; imprisoned 48-50; Gen. Sec. All-India TUC 56-; mem. Lok Sabha 57-62, 67-72; Chair. Nat. Council, Communist Party of India 62-77; expelled from Communist Party April 81; Order of Lenin 74.
Publs. *Gandhi versus Lenin* 21, *Hell Found* 27, *Literature and the People* 45, *India from Primitive Communism to Slavery* 49, *One Hundred Years of Our Trade Unions* 52, *Mahatma Gandhi and History* 68, *When Communists Differ* 70, etc.
c/o All-India Trade Union Congress, 24 K.M. Munshi Lane, New Delhi 110001; Ajoy Bhavan, Kotla Marg, New Delhi 110004, India.

Darmojuwono, H.E. Cardinal Justine; Indonesian ecclesiastic; b. 2 Nov. 1914.
Ordained Roman Catholic Priest 47; Archbishop of Semarang 63-; created Cardinal by Pope Paul VI 67; mem. Congregation of Sacraments and Divine Worship; mem. Secr. for Non-Christians; Bishop of Indonesian Armed Forces.
Jalan Pandanaran 13, Semarang, Java, Indonesia.

Das Gupta, Bimal; Indian artist; b. 27 Dec. 1917; ed. Krishnalth Collegiate School, Berhampore, W. Bengal, and Govt. Coll. of Arts and Crafts, Calcutta.
Originally painted landscapes in water colours; is now avant-garde painter in oils; Senior Lecturer in Painting, Coll. of Art, Delhi 63-; paintings in Nat. Gallery of Modern Art, New Delhi, Nat. Gallery of Poland, Warsaw, Berlin Museum, Pilnitz Gallery, Dresden, Hermitage Gallery, Leningrad; one-man exhbns. in Delhi, Calcutta, Bombay, Madras, Amritsar, Mysore, Berlin, Poland, London, New York, Cairo, Moscow, Belgrade and Paris; exhibited at São Paulo Biennale, and int. exhbns. in Japan, New York and U.S.S.R.
22 Tilak Marg, New Delhi, India.

Das Gupta, Prodosh Kusum, B.A.; Indian sculptor and art gallery director; b. 10 Jan. 1912; ed. Univ. of Calcutta, Government Schools of Arts and Crafts, Lucknow and Madras, Royal Acad. of Arts, London and Ecole de Grand Schaumère, Paris.
Founder, Calcutta Group (pioneer org. of modern art in India) 43, Sec. 43-51; Reader and Head, Dept. of Sculpture, Baroda Univ. 50; Prof. of Sculpture, Govt. Coll. of Arts and Crafts, Calcutta 51-57; Dir. Nat. Gallery of Modern Art, New Delhi 57-70; Pres. Third Congress, Int. Asscn. of Arts, Vienna 60; mem. Indian Artists' Dels. to U.S. and U.S.S.R.; represented India in int. sculpture competition *The Unknown Political Prisoner*, Tate Gallery, London; works in Nat. Gallery of Modern Art, New Delhi, Madras Museum, Acad. of Fine Arts Gallery, Calcutta and in private collections in India and abroad.
Publs. *My Sculpture, Temple Terracottas of Bengal, Fallen Leaves*, and numerous articles on art.
5 Jatin Das Road, Calcutta 29, W. Bengal, India.

Dash, Mangaljavyn; Mongolian politician; ed. Moscow Agricultural Acad.
Head Cen. Cttee. Agric. Dept. 63-68; Deputy to Great People's Hural (Assembly) 63-77, 81-; mem. Mongolian People's Revolutionary Party (MPRP), Cen. Cttee. 66-76, 81-, Cand. mem. 76-81, Sec. Cen. Cttee. 81-; Minister of Agric. 68-76, 80-81; Amb. to Poland and Fed. Repub. of Germany 76-79, to Syria and Afghanistan 79-80; Chair. Fed. of Agricultural Production Asscns. 68-76, 80-81.
Central Committee of the Mongolian People's Revolutionary Party, Ulan Bator, Mongolia.

Davis, Owen Lennox, O.B.E., B.A., LL.B.; Australian diplomatist; b. 12 April 1912; ed. King's School, Sydney, and Sydney Univ.
Barrister-at-Law 38-40; Australian Forces (Capt.) 40-45; joined Australian Dept. of External Affairs 46; First Sec. Washington 48-51, Karachi 52-53; Acting High Commr., Wellington, N.Z. 54-55; Senior External Affairs Rep., London 57-59; Australian High Commr. to S. Africa 59-61, Amb. 61-62; Amb. to Brazil 62-64; Asst. Sec. Ministry of External Affairs 65-66, First Asst. Sec. 67-69; Amb. to Belgium and EEC 69-72, concurrently to Luxembourg 70-72; Amb. to Mexico 72-74; Amb. and Perm. Rep. to UN, Geneva 74-77; Rep. to UN Human Rights Comm. 78-81.
c/o Mrs. Woodhead, Thakeham, Pulborough, Sussex, RH20 3EF, England.

Davis, Dr. Sir Thomas Robert Alexander Harries, K.B.E., M.D.; Cook Islands physician and politician; b. 11 June 1917, Ruatonga, Rarotonga; ed. Univ. of Otago Medical School, School of Tropical Medicine, Univ. of Sydney and Harvard School of Public Health.
Medical Officer and Surgeon Specialist, Cook Islands Medical Service 45-48; Research mem. Dept. of Nutrition, Harvard School of Public Health 52; Head of Dept. of Environmental Medicine, Arctic Aero-medical Laboratory, Fairbanks, Alaska 55-56; U.S. Army Medical Research Laboratory, Fort Knox, Ky. 56-61; Dir. of Research, U.S. Army Research Inst. of Environmental Medicine 61-63; employed by Arthur D. Little Inc. 63-71; returned to Cook Islands 71, formed Democratic Party; Premier of Cook Islands July 78-; Fellow, Royal Soc. of Tropical Medicine and Hygiene; mem. Royal Soc. of Medicine; Pres. Medical and Dental Asscn.; Silver Jubilee Medal 77; Order of Merit, Fed. Repub. of Germany 78; Pa Tute Rangi Ariki 79.
Publs. *Doctor to the Islands, Makutu.*
Prime Minister's Department, Avarua, Rarotonga, Cook Islands.

Dejid, Bugyn; Mongolian official; b. 1927; ed. Ulan Bator veterinary school and Mongolian State Univ.
Senior Veterinary Surgeon Gov'-altay Province; Deputy Chair. for Agriculture, Gov'-altay and Töv Provinces; Chair. Bayandzürh agricultural co-operative in Töv province 57-63; First Sec. Töv Province Cttee. of Mongolian People's Revolutionary Party (MPRP) 63-66; First Sec. Bayan-ölgiy Province MPRP Cttee. 66-70; First Deputy Minister of Public Security 70-71, Minister of Public Security 71-81; Cand. mem. Politburo MPRP 81-; Chair. Party Control Cttee. 81-; Maj.-Gen. 70-72; Lt.-Gen. 72; Col.-Gen. 79; Deputy to People's Great Hural (Assembly) 66-; Cand. mem. MPRP Cen. Cttee. 61-66, mem. Cen. Cttee. 66-.
Central Committee of the Mongolian People's Revolutionary Party, Ulan Bator, Mongolia.

Delacombe, Sir Rohan, K.C.M.G., K.C.V.O., K.B.E., C.B., D.S.O.; British administrator and former army officer; b. b. 25 Oct. 1906, Malta; ed. Harrow, Royal Mil. Acad., Sandhurst, and Staff Coll., Camberley.
Served in Egypt, North China, India, active service 37-39, in Palestine, France, Norway, Normandy, Italy and South-East Asia 39-45; Deputy Mil. Sec., War Office 53-55; G.O.C. 52nd Lowland Div. 55-58; Major-Gen. 56, G.O.C., Berlin 59-62; retd. 62; Gov. Victoria, Australia 63-May 74; Administrator of Australia on four occasions 71-74; Freeman City of Melbourne; Hon. LL.D. (Melbourne, Monash); K.St.J.
Shrewton Manor, Salisbury, Wilts. SP3 4DB, England.
Telephone: Shrewton (0980) 620-253 (Home).

Deng Xiaoping; Chinese politician; b. 22 Aug. 1904, Guangan, Sichuan; ed. French School, Chongqing, in France and Far Eastern Univ., Moscow.
Dean of Educ., Zhongshan Mil. Acad., Shaanxi 26; Chief of Staff Red Army 30; Dir. Propaganda Dept., Gen. Political Dept., Red Army 32; on Long March 34-36; Political Commissar during Sino-Japanese War; mem. 7th Cen. Cttee. of CCP 45; Political Commissar 2nd Field Army, People's Liberation Army 48-54; First Sec. E. China Bureau, CCP 49; Sec.-Gen. Cen. Cttee. of CCP 53-56; Minister of Finance 53; Vice-Chair. Nat. Defence Council 54-67; Vice-Premier, State Council 54-67; mem. Politburo, CCP 55-57; Sec., Secr. of Cen. Cttee., CCP 56-67; Gen. Sec. 8th Cen. Cttee. of CCP 56; criticized and removed from office during cultural revolution 67; mem. 10th Cen. Cttee., CCP 73, Vice-Chair. Jan. 75-April 76, July 77-; mem. Politburo of CCP 74-April 76, of Standing Cttee. of Politburo 75-April 76, July 77-; Vice-Chair. Mil. Affairs Cttee. of Cen. Cttee. 75, July 77-; Chief of Gen. Staff, PLA Jan. 75-April 76, 77-80; First Vice-Premier, State Council Jan. 75-April 76, 77-80; criticized for political views and removed from all posts April 76, reinstated July 77; Vice-Chair. CCP Mil. Comm. 77-81, Chair. 81-; mem. Politburo 11th Cen. Cttee. CCP 77-; Exec. Chair. Presidium 5th Nat. NPC 78-; Exec. Chair. 5th Nat. Cttee. CPPCC.
People's Republic of China.

Deng Yingchao; Chinese party official; b. 1903, Xinyang, Henan; *m.* Zhou Enlai 1925 (died 1976); ed. Tianjin No. 1 Girls Nat. School.
Arrested for involvement in May 4th Movt. 19; studied in France 20; participated in Long March 34-36; Dir. Women's Work Dept., Cen. Cttee. of CCP 37; Alt. mem. 7th Cen. Cttee. of CCP 45; Vice-Chair. Nat. Women's Federation of China 53-; mem. 8th Cen. Cttee. of CCP 56, 9th Cen. Cttee. 69, 10th Cen. Cttee. 73, 11th Cen. Cttee. CCP 77; a Vice-Chair. Standing Cttee. of Nat. People's Congress Nov. 76-, 5th Nat. People's Congress; Exec. Chair. Presidium 5th NPC 78-; mem. Politburo Cen. Cttee. CCP 78-; Second Sec. Cen. Comm. for Inspecting Discipline 78-.
People's Republic of China.

Deng Zhunjing; Chinese party official.
Member Standing Cttee. Nei Monggol Regional CCP Cttee. 78-; Pol. Commissar Nei Monggol PLA Mil. Dist. 78-, Commdr. 79-.
People's Republic of China.

Denson, John Boyd, C.M.G., O.B.E.; British diplomatist; b. 13 Aug. 1926; ed. Perse School and St. John's Coll., Cambridge.
His Majesty's Forces 44-48; Hong Kong 51; Third Sec., Tokyo 52; Third later Second Sec., Peking 53; Foreign Office 55; Second later First Sec. Helsinki 57; Washington, 60; First Sec., Consul and Head of Chancery, Vientiane 63; Foreign Office 65; Counsellor 68; Consul-Gen. and Chargé d'Affaires, Peking 69-71; Royal Coll. of Defence Studies; 72; Counsellor and Consul-Gen., Athens 73-77; Amb. to Nepal May 77-.
British Embassy, Lainchaur Kathmandu, P.O. Box 106, Kathmandu, Nepal.
Telephone: 11081, 11588/9.

DeRoburt, Hammer, O.B.E.; Nauruan politician and administrator; b. 25 Sept. 1923, Nauru; ed. Nauru Secondary School, Geelong Tech. Coll., Victoria, Australia.
Teacher 40-42, 51-57; deported by Japanese 42-46; Educ. Liaison Officer, Dept. of Nauruan Affairs 47-51; mem. Nauru Local Govt. Council 55-68, Chair. and Head Chief of Nauru 65-68; Chair. Transitional Council of State Jan.-May 68; Pres. of Nauru 68-76, May 78-; Minister of Internal Affairs, External Affairs, Island Devt., Industry, Civil Aviation and Public Service; Leader of the Opposition 76-78; Hon. LL.D. (Univ. of S. Pacific).
Office of the President, Nauru.

Desai, Hitendra Kanaiyalal, B.A., LL.B.; Indian politician; b. 9 Aug. 1915, Surat; ed. Bombay Univ.
Took part in anti-British political activities; imprisoned 30, 41, 42-43; set up private legal practice in Surat 39; elected mem. Surat Municipal Council 39-57; mem. Bombay Legislative Assembly 57-60; Minister of Educ., Bombay 57-60; Minister of Revenue, Gujarat State 60, later Home Minister; Leader of the House Gujarat Assembly 60-; Chief Minister of Gujarat 65-72; mem. Lok Sabha, re-elected March 77; Minister for Works and Housing 76-77, of Commerce and Civil Supplies 79-80; mem. Congress Party, elected to Supreme Exec. 68; Pres. Gujarat Pradesh Congress Cttee. 75-76; Treas. All India Congress Cttee. 78.
Dufnala, Shahibag, Ahmedabad 380004, Gujarat, India.

Desai, Shri Morarji Ranchhodji; Indian politician; b. 29 Feb. 1896; ed. Bulsar and Wilson Coll., Bombay.
Served in the Provincial Civil Service in the Bombay Presidency 18-30; joined Civil Disobedience Movement led by Mahatma Gandhi 30, and was convicted for it; mem. of All-India Congress Cttee. since 31; Sec. Gujarat Provincial Congress Cttee. 31-37, 39-46; Min. for Revenue and Forests 37-39; imprisoned for Quit India Movement for about five years; Home and Revenue Minister, Bombay 46-52; Chief Minister of Bombay 52-56; Union Minister for Commerce and Industry 56-58, Finance Minister 58-63; Chair. Admin. Reforms Comm. 66-67; Deputy Prime Minister and Minister of Finance 67-69; mem. Congress Party Parliamentary Board 63; Treas. of Congress 50-5°; mem. All-India Congress Cttee. until Nov. 69; Chair. Parl. Group, Org. Congress 69-77; detained June 75-Jan. 77; Chair. Janata Party 77-79; Prime Minister 77-79; mem. Lok Sabha 57-79; Chancellor, Gujarat Vidyapeeth, Ahmedabad and Jawaharlal Nehru Univs.; Pres. Lok Bharati Univ.; Hon. Fellow, Coll. of Physicians and Surgeons, Bombay; fmr. Chair. Dept. of Atomic Energy, Space and Electronics, Science and Tech.; Hon. Fellow, Coll. of Physicians and Surgeons, Bombay; Hon. LL.D. (Karnatak Univ. 57, Utkal Univ., Cuttack 62).
Publs. *A View of the Gita, In My View, A Minister and His Responsibilities, The Story of My Life, Indian Unity: From Dream to Reality*.
1 Safdarjung Road, New Delhi 110001; Oceana, Marine Drive, Bombay, India.

Devan Nair, Chandra Veetil; Singapore trades unionist and politician; b. 5 Aug. 1923, Malacca, Malaysia; ed. Victoria Secondary School, Singapore and Cambridge, England.
Teacher, St. Andrew's School, Singapore 49-51; Gen. Sec. Singapore Teachers' Union 49-51; detained 51-53; Convenor and mem. Cen. Exec. Cttee., People's Action Party (PAP) 54-56; Sec. Singapore Factory and Shopworkers' Union 54-56; detained 56-59; Political Sec. Ministry of Educ. 59-60; Chair. Prisons Inquiry Comm. 60; Chair. Adult Educ. Bd. 60-64; Sec. Nat. Trades Union Congress (NTUC) and Dir. its Research Unit, Singapore 64-65; mem. House of Reps., Malaysia 64-69; Founder and First Sec.-Gen. Democratic Action Party, Malaysia 64-69; Dir. NTUC Research Unit 69-81; Sec.-Gen. NTUC 69-79, Pres. 79-81; Pres. ICFTU Asian Regional Org. 75-81; M.P. for Anson, Singapore 79, re-elected 80; resgnd. as M.P. and Pres. NTUC Oct. 81; Pres. of Repub. of Singapore Oct. 81-; Hon. D.Litt. (Univ. of Singapore) 76; Public Service Star, Singapore 63.
The Istana, Singapore 0922, Singapore.

Devesi, Sir Baddeley, G.C.M.G.; Solomon Islands politician and administrator; b. 16 Oct. 1941; ed. St. Mary's School, Maravovo, King George VI School, Solomon Islands, Ardmore Teachers' Training Coll., Auckland.

Teacher Melanesian Mission schools, Solomon Islands 65-66; elected mem. British Solomon Is. Legis. and Exec. Councils 67-68; Lecturer, Solomon Is. Teachers' Coll. 70-72; Asst. Sec. for Social Services 72, Internal Affairs 72; District Officer, S. Malaita 73-75; Perm. Sec., Ministry of Works and Public Utilities 76, Ministry of Transport and Communications 77; Gov.-Gen. and C.-in-C. of Solomon Islands July 78-; Chancellor, Univ. of S. Pacific 80-.
Government House, Honiara, Solomon Islands.

Dey-Deva, Mukul Chandra, M.C.S.E., F.R.S.A., A.R.C.A.; Indian artist; b. 23 July 1895, Sridharkhda village, District Dacca; ed. Santiniketan School, Rabindranath Tagore, West Bengal.
Studied art in Calcutta with Abanindra Nath Tagore, in Japan with Yokoyama Taikan 16, in Chicago with James Blanding Sloan 16-17, and in London with Muirhead Bone 20-27; exhibited Indian Soc. of Oriental Art, Calcutta 13, Tokyo 16, Art Int., Chicago 16; studied Slade School of Art, London with Prof. Henry Tonks 20; scholarship Royal Coll. of Art, London 20-22; Art Teacher King Alfred School, Hampstead 20-21; Lecturer Indian Art, L.C.C. London 25-27; Royal Acad. 22-23; 1st one-man show, London 27; executed murals Wembley Exhbn., London 25; exhibited Philharmonic Hall, Berlin 26; Principal, Govt. School of Art, Calcutta; Officer-in-Charge Art Section and Keeper Govt. Art Gallery, Indian Museum, Calcutta; Trustee Indian Museum 28-43; Mahatma Gandhi Founded Mukul Dey Art Gallery at Kalika 44; Fulbright Visiting Prof. of Art in U.S.A. 53-54; Curator Nat. Gallery of Modern Art, Govt. of India, New Delhi 55-57; exhbn., Commonwealth Inst., London 60; exhbn. of books of own art in Commonwealth Inst., London 77; UNESCO grant 80; works acquired by British Museum, Metropolitan Art Museum, New York 70, Philadelphia, Boston, Prince of Wales Museum, Bombay, Lahore; Award and Cert. of Honour in Painting, Rabindra Bharati Univ., Calcutta 71-72. **Works include paintings, portraits, drypoint-etchings, engravings, copies of frescoes in Ajanta and Bagh Caves, Pollonaruwa temples, Sri Lanka, Sittanavasal caves, S. India, Rabindra Bharati Univ., Calcutta, British Museum, London, etc.**
Publs. include *12 Portraits* 17, *My Pilgrimages to Ajanta and Bagh* 25 and 51, *My Reminiscences* 38, *15 Drypoints* 39, *20 Portraits* 43, *Portraits of Mahatma Gandhi* 48, *Birbhum Terracottas* 60, *Indian Life and Legends* Vol. I 74.
Kalika Art Gallery, P.O. Santiniketan, West Bengal, India.

Dhanabalan, Suppiah; Singapore politician; b. 1937; ed. Singapore Univ.
Entered politics in his late 30s; Ministry of Finance; Econ. Devt. Bd.; Exec. Vice-Pres. Devt. Bank of Singapore; Minister of Foreign Affairs June 80-, also of Culture Jan. 81-.
Ministry of Foreign Affairs, City Hall, St. Andrew's Road, Singapore 0617.
Telephone: 3361177.

Dharia, Mohan; Indian politician; b. 14 Feb. 1925, Nate village, Kolaba; ed. Mahad, Poona, Poona Law Coll.
Took active part in Independence Movement, organized youth march to Mahad Tehsil 42; associated with several trade unions; imprisoned five times after independence; joined Congress Party 61; Gen. Sec. Maharashtra Pradesh Congress Cttee. 62-67; mem. Rajya Sabha 64-71; mem. Lok Sabha from Pune (Poona) 71-; Minister of State for Planning 71-75; left Congress Party 75; detained during emergency June 75-Jan. 77; mem. Janata Party 77-79; Minister of Commerce, Civil Supplies and Co-operation 77-79; mem. Deccan Educ. Soc., Shikshan Prasarak Mandali, Janata Educ. Soc., also several co-operative orgs.
Publ. *Fumes and the Fire* 75.
Lok Sabha, New Delhi, India.

Dharmasakti, Sanya; Thai lawyer and judge; b. 5 April 1907, Bangkok; ed. Bangkok and London.
Former Chief Justice of Thailand; fmr. Rector Thammasat Univ.; Prime Minister 73-75; Pres. Privy Council 76; fmr. Pres. Buddhist Asscn. of Thailand; Vice-Pres. World Fellowship of Buddhists.
15 Sukhumvit Road, Soi 41, Bangkok, Thailand.

Dhillon, Gurdial Singh, LL.B.; Indian politician; b. 6 Aug. 1915, Amritsar; ed. Govt. Coll., Lahore, Univ. Law Coll., Lahore.
Law practice 37-47; army service; active in Congress movement; imprisoned twice before independence in 1947; journalist and co-founder, Punjab daily *Vartman* 48-52; Chief Editor Urdu daily *Sher-e-Bharat* 48-52; Man. Dir. Nat. Sikhs Newspapers Ltd.; founder mem. Fed. of Working Journalists of India; mem. Punjab Legis. Assembly 52-67, Deputy Speaker 52-54, Speaker 54-62, Sec.-Gen. and Chief Whip Congress Legis. Party 64-67; Punjab State Minister of Transport 65-66; mem. Lok Sabha 67-77, Chair. Parl. Cttee. on Public Undertakings 68-69, Speaker 69-75; Minister of Transport and Shipping 75-77; mem. A.I.C.C., mem. Cen. Election Cttee. 77-, Invitee Working Cttee. and Parliamentary Bd. 77-; Pres. Commonwealth Speakers' Conf. 70, Chair. Standing Cttee. of Commonwealth Speakers 71-74; mem. Exec. Commonwealth Parl. Asscn. 69-, Vice-Pres. 73-74, Pres. 74-Nov. 75; Pres. IPU Conf. 69, mem. Exec. Cttee. IPU 69-72, Pres. 74-76; High Commissioner in Canada 80-; mem. Senate and Syndicate Punjab Univ. 56-, Fellow 68-69, now Dean Faculty of Law; mem. Syndicate and Fellow, Guru Nanak Univ. 70-; Chair., Dr. Zakir Husain Educational and Cultural Foundation; Pres. and Trustee, Jalleanwala Bagh Memorial Trust; several hon. degrees, honours and medals.
Indian High Commission, 10 Springfield Road, Ottawa K1M 1C9, Canada.

Diah, Burhanudin Mohamad (husband of Herawati Diah, *q.v.*); Indonesian journalist and diplomatist; b. 1917; ed. Taman Siswa High School, Medan, Sumatra and Ksatrian School for Journalism, Bandung, Java.
Assistant editor daily *Sinar Deli* 37-38; free-lance journalist 38-39; Chief of Indonesian Information Desk, British Consulate-Gen. 39-41; Editor-in-chief Indonesian monthly *Pertjaturan Dunia dan Film* 39-41; radio commentator and editorial writer daily *Asia Raya* 42-45; Editor-in-chief daily *Merdeka* 45-49, 68-; Chair. elect Indonesian Journalists Asscn.; Pres. Merdeka Press Ltd., Masa Merdeka Printing Presses; active in political movement, especially during Japanese occupation; Chair. New Youth (underground) movement and jailed by Japanese in 42 and again in 45; active in forcing proclamation of Indonesian Independence Aug. 45; mem. Provisional Nat. Cttee., Republic of Indonesia 45-49; mem. Provisional Indonesian Parl. 54-56; mem. Nat. Council 57-59; Amb. to Czechoslovakia (concurrently to Hungary) 59-62, to U.K. 62-64, to Thailand 64-66; Min. of Information 66-68; Vice-Chair. Press Council of Indonesia 70-; Gov. for Indonesia to Int. Atomic Energy Agency (IAEA), Vienna, Austria.
Office: Jalan A. M. Sangadji 11, Jakarta; Home: Jalan Diponegoro 61, Jakarta, Indonesia.
Telephone: 364858 (Office); 341565 (Home).

Diah, Herawati, B.A. (wife of Burhanudin Mohamad Diah, *q.v.*); Indonesian journalist; b. 1917; ed. Barnard Coll. (Columbia Univ.).
Announcer and feature writer, Indonesian Radio 42; Sec. to Minister of Foreign Affairs, Republic of Indonesia Sept.-Dec. 45; reporter daily *Merdeka* 46; Editor *Minggu Merdeka* Jan.-July 47 (when it was banned by Dutch authorities); reporter *Merdeka* 47-48; Editor *Madjalah Merdeka* 48-51, of *Minggu Merdeka* May 51, *Keluarga*

(Family) 53-59, of *Indonesian Observer* 55-59; Founder, Dir. Foundation for Preservation of Indonesian Art and Culture 67-; Pres. P.T. Hotel Prapatan 74; mem. Int. Fund for Cultural Devt. (UNESCO body) 77; mem. Exec. Board of Inst. for Man. and Education Devt.
Jalan Diponegoro 61, Jakarta, Indonesia.

Dias, Anthony Lancelot, B.A., B.SC.(ECON); Indian civil servant; b. 13 March 1910, Poona; ed. Deccan Coll., Poona, London School of Econs. and Magdalene Coll., Cambridge.
Entered Indian Civil Service 33; Sec. Educ. Dept. 52-55, Agricultural Dept. 55-57, Home Dept. 57-60; Chair. Bombay Port Trust 60-64; Sec. Dept. of Food, Ministry of Food and Agriculture 64-70; Lieut.-Gov. of Tripura 70-71; Gov. of West Bengal 71-77; mem. Board of Govs., Int. Devt. Research Centre, Ottawa, Canada 70-74; Chair. Indian Inst. of Man. 76-; Chair. Nat. Book Trust, India 78-; Hon. Fellow London School of Econs. 78; Padma Vibhushan 70.
National Book Trust, India, A-5 Green Park, New Delhi-110016, India.
Publ. *Feeding India's Millions.*
Telephone: 668607.

Dias Abeyesinghe, Edwin Felix, B.A.; Sri Lankan civil servant and diplomatist; b. 16 May 1918; ed. St. Thomas' College, Mount Lavinia, University College, Colombo, London School of Economics.
Administrator, Ministry of Local Govt. 44-57, Commr. of Local Govt., Chair. Local Govt. Service Comm. 57; Commr. of Elections 57-78; High Commr. in Australia, also accredited to New Zealand 78-82.
c/o Ministry of Foreign Affairs, Colombo, Sri Lanka.

Die Ying; Chinese party official.
Divisional Political Commissar, East China Field Army 48; Deputy Dir. Mil. Tirbunal, Nanjing Mil. Region, PLA 55; Sec. CCP Zhejiang 72-77; Vice-Chair. Zhejiang Revolutionary Cttee. 72-77; Political Commissar, Zhejiang Mil. District, PLA 72; Alt. mem. 10th Cen. Cttee. CCP 73; First Sec. CCP Zhejiang, and Chair. Zhejiang Revolutionary Cttee. 77-; Chair. Zhejiang People's Congress; mem. 11th Cen. Cttee. CCP 77.
People's Republic of China.

Ding Sheng; Chinese army officer; b. 1912, Jiangxi; ed. Red Army School and Mil. Coll.
Participated in Long March 34-35; Battalion Commdr. 37; Div. Commdr. 4th Field Army 49; Commdr. 54th Army, People's Liberation Army, Xizang 54-55; Deputy Commdr. Xinjiang Uygur Mil. Region, PLA 63-68; Guangzhou Mil. Region, PLA 68; mem. 9th Cen. Cttee. of CCP 69; Sec. CCP Guangdong 71; Commdr. Guangzhou Mil. Region, PLA 72-73; Chair. Guangdong Revolutionary Cttee. 72-; First Sec. CCP Guangzhou 72-73; mem. 10th Cen. Cttee. of CCP 73; Commdr. Nanjing Mil. Region, PLA 74-78.
People's Republic of China.

Do Muoi; Vietnamese politician; b. 1911, North Viet-Nam.
A Vice-Premier and Minister of Building in Democratic Repub. of Viet-Nam 74-76; in charge of building Ho Chi Minh Mausoleum; a Vice-Premier of Socialist Repub. of Viet-Nam Dec. 76-, also Minister of Construction 76-77; in charge of Capital Construction, Industry, Communications, Transport and Postal Services Nov. 77-; Chair. Econ. Affairs Board in Office of the Premier Dec. 76-; Chair Cttee. for Transformation of Private Industry and Trade 78; alt. mem. Politburo of Communist Party of Viet-Nam Dec. 76-.
Council of Ministers, Hanoi, Viet-Nam.

Dobbs, William Bernard Joseph; British diplomatist; b. 3 Sept. 1925.
Military service 43-47; Patent Office 57-61; Asst. Trade Commr., Lagos, Nigeria 62-64; Second Sec. (Commercial), Freetown, Sierra Leone 64-66; Commonwealth Office, London 66-68; First Sec. (Commercial), Rangoon, Burma 68-72; Consul (Commercial), Milan, Italy 72-76; First Sec. (Commercial), Kinshasa, Zaire 76-80; First Sec., Head of Chancery and Consul, Vientiane 80-82; Amb. to Laos 82-.
British Embassy, rue Pandit J. Nehru, P.O.B. 224, Vientiane, Laos.

Doha, Aminur Rahman Shams-Ud, B.A., B.SC.; Bangladesh soldier, journalist and diplomatist; b. 1929.
Served in Pakistan Artillery 52-67; School of Artillery and Guided Missiles, Okla. 57-58, Royal Mil. Coll., Shrivenham, Berks., U.K. 64-65; Editor, *Interwing*, Rawalpindi 68-71; Gen. Sec. Awami League 69-71; Amb. to Yugoslavia and Romania 72-74, to Iran and Turkey 74-77, High Commr. in U.K. 77-82; mem. Advisory Council (Martial Law Admin.) in charge of Ministry of Information and Broadcasting May 82-; Minister of Foreign Affairs June 82-; mem. Cen. Exec. Cttee. Bangladesh Nationalist Party; several military awards.
Publs. *The Arab-Israeli War, 1967*, *Aryans on the Indus.*
c/o Ministry of Foreign Affairs, Dacca, Bangladesh.

Doi, Shozaburo; Japanese banking executive; b. 23 Dec. 1907, Yonago City; ed. Aoyama Gakuin Univ.
Joined the Mitsui Trust & Co. Ltd. 29; Dir. The Mitsui Trust & Banking Co. Ltd. 58, Pres. 68-71, Chair. 71-76, Counsellor 76-; Dir. Mitsui Petroleum Devt. Co. Ltd. 69-77, Mitsui Ocean Devt. Co. Ltd. 70-73, Mitsui Devt. Co. 71-72; Auditor The Developer Sanshin Co. Ltd. 71-73, Mitsui Alumina Co. Ltd. 72; Insp. Japan Medical Foods Asscn. 72.
The Mitsui Trust and Banking Co. Ltd., 1-1, Nihombashi Muromachi 2-chome, Chuo-ku, Tokyo 103; and 3-7 Higashi-Tamagawa 2-chome, Setagaya-ku, Tokyo, Japan.

Dong Guogui; Chinese army official.
Commander Shandong Mil. District, PLA 67-74, Hunan Mil. District, PLA 75-; Sec. Hunan Cttee. CCP Nov. 76-.
People's Republic of China.

Dorji-Khangsarpa of Chakhung, Kazi Lhendup; Indian (Sikkimese) politician; b. Sept. 1904, Pakyong; ed. Enchey School, Gangtok and Rumtek Monastery.
Head Lama, Rumtek Monastery 22-30; founder of various Schools in W. Sikkim in collaboration with his brother the late Kazi Phag Tshering; founded Sikkim Praja Mandal 45, elected Pres. 45; Pres. Sikkim State Congress 53-58; led del. to India 54; founded Sikkim Nat. Congress 62; Exec. Councillor for Agriculture, Animal Husbandry and Transport Authority 70-72; tour of Europe 72; Pres. Joint Action Council, later Sikkim Congress (merger of Sikkim Janata Congress and Sikkim Nat. Congress) 73-; Chief Minister and Leader of Sikkim Assembly 74-79.
Publs. Various articles on the need for democratization of Sikkim, usually in *Bulletin of the Sikkim Congress.*
Chakhung House, Kalimpong, West Bengal, India.

Dorman, Richard Bostock; British diplomatist; b. 8 Aug. 1925; ed. Sedbergh School, St. John's Coll., Cambridge.
Served army 44-48; War Office 51-58; Commonwealth Relations Office 58-60; First Sec. British High Comm., Nicosia; Deputy High Commr. in Sierra Leone 64-66; Foreign Office 67-68; NATO Defence Coll., Rome 68-69; Counsellor, Embassy, Bucharest 74-77, Pretoria 77-82; High Commr. in Vanuatu 82-.
British High Commission, Melitco House, Rue Pasteur, P.O. Box 567, Port Villa, Vanuatu.

Dowiyogo, Bernard; Nauru politician; b. 14 Feb. 1946; ed. local schools and Australian Nat. Univ.
Lawyer; mem. Parl. 73; Sec. Nauru Gen. Hosp. and Gen. Man. Nauru Co-operative Soc.; Pres. of Nauru 76-78; Leader Nauru Party.
c/o Parliament House, Nauru.

Drysdale, Sir (George) Russell, Kt.; British-born Australian artist; b. 7 Feb. 1912; ed. Geelong Grammar School, Victoria, Australia.

Art studies in Melbourne, London and Paris; works in New York Metropolitan Museum of Art, Nat. Gallery, London, Tate Gallery, London, Nat. Galleries of New South Wales, Victoria, South Australia, etc.; mem. Australian Soc. of Artists; mem. Commonwealth Art Advisory Board 62-73; Dir. Pioneer Sugar Mills Ltd.
Publ. (with Jock Marshall) *Journey Among Men* 62.
Bouddi Farm, Kilcare Heights, Hardy's Bay, N.S.W., Australia.

Du Ping; Chinese soldier; b. Jiangsu.
Red Army Cadre during Long March; Deputy Dir., Pol. Dept. Chinese People's Volunteers 51; responsible for PLA Shenyang Units 53; Lt.-Gen. PLA 55; C.-in-C. PLA Shenyang Units 53; Deputy Pol. Commissar Shenyang Mil. Region 58-63; Head PLA Nanjing Units 63; Pol. Commissar PLA Nanjing Units 65-; mem. Presidium CCP 9th Nat. Congress 69 (re-elected to CCP 10th Nat. Congress 73); mem. CCP 9th Cen. Cttee. 69 (re-elected to 10th Cen. Cttee. 73); Alt. mem. CCP 11th Cen. Cttee. 77-.
People's Republic of China.

Du Yide; Chinese military official.
Vice-Commdr. PLA Navy 61; Deputy Political Commissar PLA Navy 65; purged 67; rehabilitated 72; Deputy Political Commissar PLA Navy 75; Political Commissar PLA Navy 78; mem. Presidium CCP 11th Nat. Congress 77; mem. 11th Cent. Cttee. 77; Commdr. Lanzhou Mil. Region 80-.
People's Republic of China.

Duan Junyi; Chinese politician; b. 1913, Shandong; ed. School of Tech., Jinan Univ.
Responsible for Nat. Fed. of Students and rep., Beiping (now Beijing) Fed. of Students 37; Sec. CCP Hebei-Henan Region Cttee., before 49; mem., S.W. Mil. and Admin. Cttee. 50; Dir., Industry Dept. S.W. Mil. and Admin. Cttee. 50; Vice-Chair. Financial and Econ. Cttee., S.W. Mil. and Admin. Cttee. 50-54; Vice-Minister 1st Ministry of Machine Building 52-60; Deputy for Shandong to 1st NPC 54; mem. Nat. Cttee., All China 1st Machine Building Trades Union 55; Minister, 1st Ministry of Machine Building 60; CCP Del. to Nat. Cttee., 4th CPPCC 64; mem. Presidium CCP 11th Nat. Congress 77-; mem. CCP 11th Cen. Cttee. 77-; Minister of Railways 78; First Sec. Henan Provincial CCP Cttee. 78-80; Chair. Henan CCP Provincial People's Govt. 78-79; First Pol. Commissar PLA Henan Mil. Dist. 78-81; CCP First Sec., Beijing March 81-.
People's Republic of China.

Duan, Le (*see* Le Duan).

Duckmanton, Sir Talbot Sydney, Kt., C.B.E.; Australian broadcasting executive; b. 1921; ed. Newington Coll., Stanmore, New South Wales, Sydney Univ. and Australian Administrative Staff Coll.
Australian Army and Air Force service; Australian Broadcasting Comm. 39-, Man. for Tasmania 53-57, Controller of Admin. 57-59, Asst. Gen. Man. (Admin.) 59-64, Deputy Gen. Man. 64-65, Gen. Man. 65-; Vice-Pres. Asian Broadcasting Union 70-73, Pres. 73-77; Trustee, Visnews Ltd. 65-; mem. Council Australian Admin. Staff Coll. 69-, Australian Film Devt. Corpn. 70-75, Australian Council for the Arts 73-75; Pres. Commonwealth Broadcasting Asscn. 75-.
Australian Broadcasting Commission, Broadcast House, 145-153 Elizabeth Street, Sydney, N.S.W. 2001, Australia.
Telephone: 339-02-11.

Dügersüren, Mangalyn; Mongolian diplomatist; b. 15 Feb. 1922; ed. Inst. of International Relations, Moscow.
Schoolmaster 41-44; Deputy Head, Head of a Dept., Ministry of Foreign Affairs 51-53; Sec. of Cen. Cttee. Mongolian Revolutionary Youth League 53-54; Deputy Minister of Justice 54-56; Deputy Minister of Foreign Affairs 56-58; Amb. to India 58-62; First Deputy Minister of Foreign Affairs 62-63; Minister of Foreign Affairs 63-68; Perm. Rep. to UN 68-72; Perm. Rep. to UN Office in Geneva 72-76; Minister of Foreign Affairs Aug. 76-; Deputy to People's Great Hural (Assembly) 63-69, 77-; mem. Cen. Cttee. Mongolian People's Revolutionary Party.
Ministry of Foreign Affairs, Ulan Bator, Mongolia.

Dunlop, Sir John Wallace, K.B.E.; Australian company director; b. 20 May 1910; ed. Geelong Grammar School, Univ. of Sydney.
Chairman CSR Ltd. 77, Edwards Dunlop and Co. Ltd.; Dir. Australian Industry Devt. Corpn., Australian Bank Ltd., Rothmans of Pall Mall (Australia) Ltd., Lansing Australia Pty. Ltd.; Senior Adviser on Australian Affairs, Banque de Paris et des Pays-Bas.
275 George Street, Sydney, N.S.W. 2000, Australia.
Telephone: 2-0222.

Dunstan, Donald Allan, A.C., Q.C., LL.B.; Australian lawyer and politician; b. 21 Sept. 1926, Fiji; ed. St. Peter's Coll. and Univ. of Adelaide, S. Australia.
Practised law for two years in Fiji, returned to S. Australia; mem. S. Australia House of Assembly for Norwood 53-79; mem. S. Australia Labor Party Exec. 55, Junior Vice-Pres. 58, Senior Vice-Pres. 59, Pres. S. Australian Branch of Labor Party 60; del. to Fed. Exec. of Labor Party 60-64; Attorney-Gen., Minister of Aboriginal Affairs and Social Welfare, S. Australia 65; Premier, Treasurer, Minister of Housing 67-68; Leader of Opposition 68-70; Premier, Treasurer 70-79; Minister of Devt. and Mines 70-73.
Publs. *Don Dunstan's Cookbook* 76, *Don Dunstan's Australia* 78, *Felicia* (political memoirs) 81.
15 Clara Street, Norwood, South Australia 5067, Australia (Home).

Dunstan, Lieut.-Gen. Sir Donald Beaumont, K.B.E., C.B.; Australian army officer and state governor; b. 18 Feb. 1923; ed. Prince Alfred Coll., South Australia, Royal Mil. Coll., Duntroon.
Served Second World War; served Korea 54; Instructor, Royal Mil Coll, Duntroon 55-56, 63; Staff Coll, Queenscliff 58, Camberley 59-60; Deputy Commdr 1 Task Force, Viet-Nam 68-69; Commdr 10th Task Force, Holsworthy, N S.W. 69; Imperial Defence Coll. 70; Commdr. Australian Force, Viet-Nam 71; Chief of Material 72-74; GOC Field Force Command 74-77; Deputy Chief of Gen. Staff 77, Chief of Gen. Staff 77-82; Gov. of South Australia 82-.
Government House, Adelaide, South Australia 5000, Australia.

Durack, Peter Drew, Q.C., LL.B., B.C.L.; Australian barrister and politician; b. 20 Oct. 1926, Perth; ed. Christian Brothers' Coll., Aquinas Coll., Univ. of Western Australia, Lincoln Coll., Oxford.
President Nat. Union of Univ. Students 48; Western Australia Rhodes Scholar 49; barrister, Gray's Inn, London 53; tutor in law, Oxford 52-53; legal practice, Perth 54-; mem. W.A. Legis. Assembly for Perth (Lib.) 65-68; Pres. Liberal Party (W.A.) 68-71; Senator from W.A. 71-; Minister for Repatriation (now Veterans' Affairs), Fed. Exec. Council 76-77; Attorney-Gen. 77-.
34 Melvista Avenue, Claremont, Western Australia, 6010, Australia.

Dy, Francisco Justiniano, M.D., M.P.H.; Philippine public health administrator; b. 17 Sept. 1912; ed. Univ. of Philippines and School of Hygiene and Public Health, Johns Hopkins Univ., U.S.A.
Research Asst. and Instructor, Inst. of Hygiene, Univ. of Philippines 38-41; U.S. Army 42-45; Senior Surgeon, U.S. Public Health Service 45-46; Consultant and Chief of Malaria Division, U.S. Public Health Service Rehabilitation Programme in Philippines 46-50; Prof. of Malariology

and Chair. Dept. of Parasitology, Inst. of Hygiene, Univ. of Philippines 50-52; Deputy Chief, Malaria Section, World Health Org. (WHO), Geneva 50-51; Regional Malaria Adviser, WHO, for W. Pacific Region 51-57; Dir. of Health Services, WHO Regional Office for W. Pacific 58-66, Regional Dir. of WHO for W. Pacific 66-79, Regional Dir. Emer. 79-; Prof. of Community Medicine, Univ. of Philippines June 69-; mem. Nat. Research Council of Philippines; Distinguished Service Star (Philippines); Legion of Merit, with Oak Leaf Cluster (U.S.A.), Distinguished Order of Diplomatic Service, Hueng-In Medal (Repub. of Korea), Ancient Order of Sikatuna Medal (Philippines).
Publs. on malariology and public health.
Regional Office for the Western Pacific, World Health Organization, P.O.B. 2932, Manila; Home: 901 E. de los Santos Avenue, Quezon City, Philippines.
Telephone: 59-20-41 (Office); 98-47-39 (Home).

E

Eccles, Sir John Carew, Kt., M.B., B.S., D.PHIL., F.R.A.C.P., F.R.S.N.Z., F.A.A., F.R.S.; Australian research physiologist; b. 27 Jan. 1903; ed. Melbourne Univ., Magdalen Coll., Oxford.
Rhodes Scholar 25; Junior Research Fellow, Exeter Coll., Oxford 27-32, Staines Medical Fellow 32-34; Fellow and Tutor, Magdalen Coll., Oxford, lecturer in physiology 34-37; Dir. Kanematsu Memorial Inst. of Pathology, Sydney, Australia 37-43; Prof. of Physiology, Otago Univ., New Zealand 44-51, Australian Nat. Univ., Canberra 51-66; at AMA/ERF Inst. for Biomedical Research, Chicago 66-68; at State Univ. of New York at Buffalo 68-75; Waynflete lecturer, Oxford 52; Herter lecturer. Johns Hopkins Univ., Baltimore 55; Foreign Hon. mem, American Acad. of Arts and Sciences, Accademia Nazionale dei Lincei, Deutsche Akad. der Naturforscher Leopoldina (Cothenius Medal); mem. Pontifical Acad. of Sciences, American Philosophical Soc.; Ferrier Lecturer, Royal Soc. 60; Pres. Australian Acad. of Science 57-61; Gifford Lecturer, Edinburgh Univ. 77-78; Hon. Fellow Exeter Coll. and Magdalen Coll., Oxford, Hon. Fellow New York Acad. of Sciences; Hon. Sc.D. (Cambridge, Tasmania, Univ. of British Columbia, Gustavus Adolphus Coll., Fribourg), Hon. LL.D. (Melbourne); Hon. M.D. (Charles Univ., Yeshiva Univ.); Hon. D.Sc. (Oxford); Royal Medal, Royal Soc. 62, Nobel Prize for Medicine 63.
Publs. *Reflex Activity of the Spinal Cord* (in collaboration) 32, *Neurophysiological Basis of Mind* 53, *Physiology of Nerve Cells* 57, *Physiology of Synapses* 64, *The Cerebellum as a Neuronal Machine* 67, *Inhibitory Pathways of the Central Nervous System* 69, *Facing Reality* 70, *The Understanding of the Brain* 73, *The Self and its Brain* (with K. R. Popper) 77, *The Molecular Neurobiology of the Mammalian Brain* 78, *Sherrington: His Life and Thought* (with W. C. Gibson) 79, *The Human Mystery* 79, *The Human Psyche* 80.
Ca' a la Gra', CH 6611 Contra (Ticino), Switzerland.
Telephone: 093-672931.

Efi, Taisi Tupuola Tufuga; Western Samoan politician; b. 1 March 1938; ed. St. Joseph's Coll., Apia, Western Samoa, and Victoria Univ., Wellington, N.Z.
Elected to Western Samoan Parl. 65; Minister of Works, Civil Aviation, Marine and Transport 70-73; Prime Minister March 76-.
c/o Office of the Prime Minister, Apia, Western Samoa.

Ellicott, Robert James, Q.C.; Australian lawyer and politician; b. 15 April 1927, Moree, N.S.W.; ed. Fort Street Boys' School and Univ. of Sydney.
Admitted to Bar in N.S.W. 50, Victoria 60; Q.C. 64; Commonwealth Solicitor-Gen. 69-73; mem. House of Reps. for Wentworth, N.S.W. 74-80; opposition spokesman on consumer affairs and commerce 74-75; Attorney-Gen. 75-77; Minister for Home Affairs and for the Capital Territory 77-81; Judge, Federal Courts March 81-; Liberal Party.
Parliament House, Canberra, A.C.T. 2600, Australia.

Enderby, Keppel Earl, Q.C., LL.M.; Australian lawyer and politician; b. 25 June 1926; ed. Dubbo High School, Univs. of Sydney and London.
Practising barrister 50-62, 66-70, 76-82; admitted to N.S.W. Bar 50; Lecturer, Examiner, in Commercial Law, Sydney Technical Coll. 55-62; Senior Lecturer in Law, Australian Nat. Univ. 63-65; mem. House of Reps. for A.C.T. 70-74, for Canberra 74-75; del. to Fed. Exec. of Australian Labor Party 71-74, Chair. Econs. Cttee.; Chair. House of Reps. Privileges Cttee. 73-75; Minister for A.C.T. and Northern Territory 72-73, of Secondary Industry and Supply 73-74, for Mfg. Industry 74-75; Attorney-Gen. Feb.-Nov. 75, Minister for Customs and Excise Feb.-June 75; Judge Supreme Court N.S.W. 82-.
Publs. articles in *Fed. Law Review* 64, *Australian Quarterly* 76.
2 Phoebe Street, Balmain, Sydney, N.S.W. 2041, Australia.

Ershad, Lieut.-Gen. Hossain Mohammad; Bangladesh army officer and politician; b. 1 Feb. 1930, Rangpur; ed. Univ. of Dacca, Officers' Training School, Kohat, Pakistan.
First appointment in 2nd East Bengal Regt.; several appointments in various units including Adjutant, East Bengal Regt. Centre, Chittagong 60-62; completed staff course, Quetta Staff Coll. 66; promoted Lieut.-Col. 69; Commdr. 3rd East Bengal Regt. 69-70, 7th East Bengal Regt. 71-72; Adjutant Gen. Bangladesh Army; promoted Col. 73; attended Nat. Defence Coll., New Delhi, India 75; promoted Brigadier 75, Major-Gen. 75; Deputy Chief of Army Staff 75-78, Chief of Army Staff 78-; promoted Lieut.-Gen. 79; led mil. takeover in Bangladesh March 82; Chief Martial Law Administrator 24 March 82-; also in charge of six ministries including Home Affairs; Chair. Nat. Sports Control Bd.; Pres. Bangladesh Lawn Tennis Fed.; Chief Adviser, Bangladesh Freedom Fighters' Asscn.
Office of the Chief Martial Law Administrator, Dacca, Bangladesh.

Esaki, Leo, PH.D.; Japanese scientist; b. 12 March 1925, Osaka; ed. Univ. of Tokyo.
With Sony Corpn. 56-60, conducted research on heavily-doped germanium and silicon which resulted in the discovery of tunnel diode; with IBM Corpn., U.S.A. 60-, IBM Fellow, IBM T. J. Watson Research Cen., New York 60-, Man. Device Research 62-; Dir. IBM-Japan 77-, Yamada Science Foundation 77-; Sir John Cass Sr. Visiting Research Fellow, London Polytechnic 82; major field of research is nonlinear transport and optical properties on semiconductors, junctions, thin films, etc.; currently involved on a man-made semiconductor lattice grown by a sophisticated ultra-high vacuum evaporation system: a computer-controlled molecular-beam epitaxy; mem. Japan Acad. 75; Foreign Assoc. American Nat. Acad. of Sciences 76, American Nat. Acad. of Engineering 77; Nishina Memorial Award 59, Asahi Press Award 60, Toyo Rayon Foundation Award 61, Morris N. Liebmann Memorial Prize 61, Stuart Ballantine Medal, Franklin Inst. 61, Japan Acad. Award 65; shared Nobel Prize for Physics 73; Order of Culture, Japanese Govt. 74.
Publs. numerous articles in professional journals.
IBM T. J. Watson Research Center, P.O. Box 218, Yorktown Heights, N.Y. 10598; 16 Shady Lane, Chappaqua, N.Y. 10514, U.S.A. (Home).
Telephone: (914) 945-2342 (Office); (914) 238-3329 (Home).

Espie, Sir Frank Fletcher, Kt., O.B.E.; Australian mining engineer; b. 1917, Bawdwin, Burma; ed. St. Peter's Coll., Adelaide, Adelaide Univ

Served 9th Div., AIF, N. Africa and New Guinea rising to rank of Capt. 40-45; Underground Man., then Mine Supt., Zinc Corpn.-New Broken Hill Consolidated Mines 49-57, Asst. Gen. Man. for Production 57-61; Gen. Man. Comalco Products, Yennora, Sydney 61-62, Gen. Man. Industrial Div., Conzinc Riotinto of Australia Ltd. (now CRA Ltd.) 64-65; successively Exec. Dir., Man. Dir., Chair. of Dirs., Bougainville Copper Ltd. and Bougainville Mining Ltd. 65-79; Exec. Dir. Conzinc Riotinto of Australia Ltd. 68-79, Deputy Chair. 74-79, now Dir.; Dir. CRA Ltd. 79-, Bougainville Copper Ltd., ICI Australia Ltd. 79-, Tubemakers of Australia Ltd. 80-, Bank of N.S.W. 81-, Woodside Petroleum Ltd. 81-; mem. Exec. Cttee. Australian Mining Industry Council 73-81 (Pres. 78-80); mem. Council Australasian Inst. of Mining and Metallurgy (Pres. 75), Australian Acad. of Technological Sciences; Australasian Inst. of Mining and Metallurgy Medal 80.
CRA Ltd., 55 Collins Street, Melbourne, Vic. 3001, Australia.

Everingham, Douglas Nixon, M.B., B.S., M.H.R.; Australian medical practitioner and politician; b. 25 June 1923; ed. Fort Street School, Univ. of Sydney.
Resident medical officer in gen. and mental hospitals -46-53 gen. practice 53-67; mem. House of Reps. 67-75, 77-; Minister for Health Dec. 72-Nov. 75; Opposition Spokesman on Aboriginal Affairs and N. Aust. 77-80, on Veterans' Affairs and Capital Territory 80; Vice-Pres. World Health Assembly 75.
Publs. *Chemical Shorthand for Organic Formulae* 43, *Critique of Bliss Symbols* 56, *Braud Inglish Speling* 66.
Parliament House, Canberra, A.C.T. 2600; Cinema Centre, Denham Street, Rockhampton, Queensland 4700, Australia.
Telephone: Canberra (062) 72 1211; Rockhampton (079) 276455.

F

Fairbairn, Sir David Eric, K.B.E., D.F.C., M.A.; Australian retd. grazier and politician; b. 3 March 1917; ed. Geelong Grammar School and Jesus Coll., Cambridge.
Farmer and grazier, Woomargama, nr. Albury, N.S.W. until 71; in R.A.A.F. 40-45; mem. for Farrer, House of Reps. 49-75; Chair. Immigration Planning Council 60-62; Minister for Air 62-64; Minister for Nat. Devt. 64-69, and Leader in House 66; Chair. Joint Parl. Cttee. on Foreign Affairs 70-71; Minister for Educ. and Science March-Aug. 71, for Defence 71-72; opposition spokesman on Nat. Devt. 73-74; mem. N.S.W. State Liberal Party Exec. 73-75; Amb. to the Netherlands 77-80; Liberal.
2/3 Tasmania Circle, Forrest, A.C.T. 2603, Australia.

Fan Ziyou; Chinese politician.
On Long March in Dept. of Supplies, 2nd Front Army 34-35; Champion of Swimming Contest for Generals in People's Liberation Army Units 60; Maj.-Gen., Gen. Logistics Dept., PLA 64; Minister of Commerce 71-78.
People's Republic of China.

Fang, Roland Zhong, M.A.; Chinese scholar; b.1902; ed. Qinghua Coll., Beijing, Calif. and Stanford Univs.
Professor of English Literature, Central Univ. Nanjing 28-30; Prof. of English Literature and Head of English Dept., Wuhan Univ. 31-44; Visiting Prof. Trinity Coll. Cambridge Univ. 44-46; Prof. of English and Head of Dept. of Foreign Languages, Zhejiang Univ. 47-51, Zhejiang Teachers' Coll. 51-52; Prof. Anhui Univ. 52-53, East China Teachers' Univ., Shanghai 53-54, Fudan Univ., Shanghai 54-56; Head, English Dept., Shanghai Inst. of Foreign Languages 57-80; Dir. Research Cen. Inst. of Foreign Language and Literature, Shanghai.
Publs. *Book of Modern English Prose* (2 vols.) 34, *Studies in English Prose and Poetry* 39, *A Chinese Verse Translation of Shakespeare's Richard III* 59, *Complete Works of Chaucer translated into Chinese* 62, *Chaucer's Canterbury Tales* (revised edn.) 63, *First Complete Shakespeare in Chinese* (nine plays) 78, *Gleanings from Tao Yuan-ming: His Prose and Poetry* 79.
Shanghai Institute of Foreign Languages, Shanghai, People's Republic of China.

Fang Yi; Chinese politician; b. 1909, Xiamen, Fujian.
Editor Commercial Press, Shanghai 30; on Long March 34; Sec.-Gen. N. China People's Govt. 48; Vice-Gov. of Shandong 49, of Fujian 49-52; Deputy Mayor of Shanghai 52-53; Vice-Minister of Finance 53-54; with Embassy of People's Repub. of China, Hanoi 54-61; Alt. mem. 8th Cen. Cttee. of CCP 56; Dir. of Bureau for Econ. Relations with Foreign Countries, State Council 61-64; Chair. Comm. for Econ. Relations with Foreign Countries 64-68; Alt. mem. 9th Cen. Cttee. of CCP 69; Minister of Econ. Relations with Foreign Countries 69-76, for State Scientific and Tech. Comm. Feb. 78-, also a Vice-Premier, State Council 78-82; Vice-Pres. Chinese Acad. of Sciences 77-79, Pres. 81; Deputy for Fujian 5th NPC and mem. Presidium 5th NPC 78; mem. 10th Cttee. of CCP 73, 11th Central Cttee. of CCP and its Political Bureau.
People's Republic of China.

Fateh, A. F. M. Abul, M.A.; Bangladesh diplomatist; b. 28 Feb. 1926; ed. Dacca Univ. and London School of Econs.
Carnegie Fellow in Int. Peace 62-63; Pakistan Foreign Service 49-71; Third Sec. Pakistan Embassy, France 51-53, High Comm. Calcutta, India 53-56; Second Sec. Embassy, U.S.A. 56-60; Dir. Ministry of Foreign Affairs, Karachi 61-65; First Sec., Czechoslovakia 65-66; Counsellor, New Delhi, India 66-67; Deputy High Commr., Calcutta 68-70; Amb. to Iraq 71; Adviser to Acting Pres. of Bangladesh July 71; Foreign Sec. of Bangladesh Jan. 72; Amb. to France and to Spain 72-75; Perm. Del. to UNESCO 72-76; led. Del. to Commonwealth Youth Ministers' Conf., Lusaka 73; High Commr. in U.K. 76-77; Chair. Commonwealth Human Ecology Council Symp., London 77; Amb. to Algeria 77-.
Bangladesh Embassy, 141 blvd. Salah Bouakouir, Algiers, Algeria.

Faulkner, Arthur James; New Zealand politician; b. 20 Nov. 1921; ed. Otahuhu District High School.
Member of Parl. for Roskill 57-81; undertook fact-finding missions to S. Viet-Nam, Indonesia, Malaysia, Thailand, Singapore and the Philippines 63, 67; visited U.S.A. 65; study tour of Britain to discuss EEC 69; Minister of Defence and concurrently in charge of War Pensions and Rehabilitation 72-74, of Labour and State Services 74-75; Pres. N.Z. Labour Party and Opposition Spokesman for Labour and State Services 76-79; Shadow Minister of Foreign Affairs and Defence 79-81.
1 Inverness Avenue, Mt. Roskill, Auckland 4, New Zealand.

Fenner, Frank John, C.M.G., M.B.E., M.D., F.R.A.C.P., F.R.C.P., F.A.A., F.R.S.; Australian research biologist; b. 21 Dec. 1914; ed. Thebarton Technical High School, Adelaide High School, Adelaide Univ.
Medical Officer, Hospital Pathologist, Australian Forces 40-43, Malariologist 43-46; Francis Haley Research Fellow, Walter and Eliza Hall Inst. for Medical Research, Melbourne 46-48; Travelling Fellow, Rockefeller Inst. for Medical Research 48-49; Prof. of Microbiology, Australian Nat. Univ. 49-73; Dir. John Curtin School of Medical Research, Australian Nat. Univ. 67-73, Dir. Centre for Resource and Environmental Studies 73-79, Fellow, Aust. Nat. Univ. 80-; David Syme Prize, Melbourne Univ. 49; Harvey Lecturer, Harvey Soc. of N.Y. 58; Overseas Fellow, Churchill Coll., Cambridge 61-62; Mueller Medal 64, Britannica Australia Award 67, ANZAAS Medal 80,

ANZAC Peace Award; Matthew Flinders Lecturer 67, Fogarty Scholar, Nat. Insts. of Health (U.S.A.) 71 and 74; Foreign Assoc., Nat. Acad. of Sciences (U.S.A.) 77.
Publs. about 140 scientific papers, mainly on acidfast bacilli, pox viruses and environmental problems, *The Production of Antibodies* (with F. M. Burnet) 49, *Myxomatosis* (with F. N. Ratcliffe) 65, *The Biology of Animal Viruses* (2 vols.) 68, 2nd edn. 74, *Medical Virology* (with D. O. White) 70, 2nd edn. 76, *The Classification and Nomenclature of Viruses* 76, *The Australian Academy of Science: the First Twenty-Five Years* (with A. L. G. Rees) 80.
Office: John Curtin School of Medical Research, P.O. Box 334, Canberra, A.C.T. 2601; Home: 8 Monaro Crescent, Red Hill, Canberra, A.C.T. 2603, Australia.
Telephone: 49-2526 (Office); 95-9176 (Home).

Fernandes, George; Indian trade unionist and politician; b. 3 June 1930, Mangalore, Karnataka; ed. St. Peter's Seminary, Bangalore.
Joined Socialist Party of India 49; Editor *Konkani Yuvak* (Konkani Youth) monthly in Konkani language 49, *Raithavani* weekly in Kannada language 49, *Dockman* weekly in English 52-53, also *New Society*; fmr. Chief Editor *Pratipaksha* weekly in Hindi; trade union work in South Kanara 49, 50, in Bombay and Maharashtra 50-58; founding Pres. All-India Radio Broadcasters and Telecasters Guild, Khadi Comm. Karmachari Union, All-India Univ. Employees' Confed.; Pres. All-India Railwaymen's Fed. 73-74; organized nat. railways strike 74; Treas. All-India Hind Mazdoor Sabha 58; formed Hind Mazdoor Panchayat 58, Gen. Sec. for over 10 years; Convenor, United Council of Trade Unions; fmr. mem. Gen. Council of Public Services Int. (PSI), Int. Transport Workers' Fed. (ITF); Founder Chair. Bombay Labour Co-operative Bank Ltd.; mem. Nat. Cttee. of Socialist Party of India 55-77, Treas. 64, Chair. 73-77; Gen. Sec. Samyukta Socialist Party of India 69; mem. Bombay Municipal Corpn. 61-68; mem. for Bombay City, Lok Sabha 67-77; went underground on declaration of emergency 75; arrested and charged in the Baroda Dynamite Case June 76, case withdrawn March 77; mem. Lok Sabha for Muzaffarpur, Bihar (elected while in prison) March 77-; Minister for Communications March-July 77, for Industries 77-79; mem. Janata Party 77-; resgnd. from Govt. July 79; Deputy Leader, Lok Dal 80-, mem. Nat. Exec.; Pres. Schumacher Foundation, India.
Publ. *What Ails the Socialists.*
26 Tughlak Crescent, New Delhi-11, India.

Fernando, Biyagamage Jayasena; Sri Lankan barrister and diplomatist; b. 14 Sept. 1934; ed. Univs. of Ceylon and London.
Barrister-at-law, Middle Temple, London 58; practised law in Districts Courts, Colombo; mem. Supreme Court, Bar Council of Bar Asscn. of Sri Lanka, Chair. 76; mem. Exec. Cttee. of United National Party 73-; fmr. Chair. Uni-Walkers Ltd.; fmr. Dir. several cos.; Perm. Rep. to the UN 78-80.
c/o Ministry of Foreign Affairs, Colombo, Sri Lanka.

Fernando, Most Rev. Nicholas Marcus, B.A., D.D.; Sri Lankan ecclesiastic; b. 6 Dec. 1932; ed. St. Aloysius Seminary, Colombo, Univ. de Propaganda Fide, Rome.
Ordained Roman Catholic Priest 59; Archbishop of Colombo 77-; Chair. Episcopal Comm. for Seminaries, Sri Lanka.
Archbishop's House, Gnanarthapradeepaya Mawatha, Colombo 8, Sri Lanka.
Telephone: 95471.

Fernando, Thusew Samuel, C.B.E., Q.C., LL.B.; Sri Lankan judge; b. 5 Aug. 1906; ed. Royal College, Colombo, Univ. Coll., Colombo, Univ. Coll., London, and Lincoln's Inn, London.
Crown Counsel 36-52; Solicitor-Gen., Ceylon 52-54; Attorney-Gen. 54-56; Justice, Supreme Court of Ceylon 56-68; Pres. Int. Comm. of Jurists, Geneva 66-77, Vice-Pres. 77-; mem. Int. Cttee. of Inst. on Man & Science, New York; Pres. Court of Appeal of Sri Lanka 71-73; mem. Constitutional Court 72; High Commr. in Australia and New Zealand 74-78.
3 Cosmas Avenue, Barnes Place, Colombo 7, Sri Lanka.

Fitzgerald, Dr. Stephen A.: Australian scholar and diplomatist; b. 1938, Hobart; ed. Australian Nat. Univ., Canberra.
Department of Foreign Affairs 61-66; Resident Scholar, Australian Nat. Univ. 66-69; Resident Fellow 69-71, Fellow 72-73, Prof. 77-, Head of Dept. of Far Eastern History and Head, Contemporary China Centre, Research School of Pacific Studies; Amb. to People's Repub. of China (also accred. to Democratic People's Repub. of Korea) 72-76; Ed., *Australian Journal of Chinese Affairs*; Deputy Chair. Australia-China Council 79-; council mem. and Chair. Asian Studies Asscn. of Australia; mem. Australian Acad. of Science Sub-Cttee. on Relations with China.
Publs. *China and the Overseas Chinese, Talking with China, China and the World.*
Stephen Fitzgerald and Co., P.O. Box 249, Civic Square, A.C.T. 2608, Australia.

Fleming, Sir Charles Alexander, K.B.E., F.R.S., F.R.S.N.Z., D.SC.; New Zealand naturalist and paleontologist; b. 9 Sept. 1916; ed. Kings Coll., Auckland and Auckland Univ. Coll.
Joined N.Z. Geological Survey as Asst. Geologist 40, becoming Paleontologist and later Chief Paleontologist; published research on geological and biological topics, mainly on history of life in N.Z.; has taken part in expeditions to subantarctic islands; Pres. Royal Soc. N.Z. 62-66; Chief Paleontologist, N.Z. Geological Survey (Dept. of Scientific and Ind. Res.), retd. 77; Hon. Lecturer, Victoria Univ., Wellington; Pres. Australian and N.Z. Asscn. for Advancement of Science 68-69, Ornithological Soc. of N.Z. 45; Corresp. Fellow, American Ornithologists Union; Commonwealth Fellow, Geological Soc. of London; Hon. Fellow, Zoological Soc. of London; Foreign mem. American Philosophical Soc.; fmr. mem. Nat. Parks Authority; Hector and Hutton Medals of Royal Soc. of N.Z.; Walter Burfitt Medal of Royal Soc. of N.S.W., ANZAAS Medal 72, Herbert E. Gregory Medal (Pacific Science Asscn.) 79.
Publs. *Checklist of New Zealand Birds* (editor) 53, Hochstetter's *Geology of New Zealand* (translator and editor) 59, *Stratigraphic Lexicon: New Zealand* (editor) 59, *Marwick's Illustrations of New Zealand Shells* 66, *The Geological History of New Zealand and its Life* 79, and over 200 research papers on N.Z. geology, paleontology, zoology and biogeography.
"Balivean", 42 Wadestown Road, Wellington, New Zealand.

Foots, Sir James (William), Kt.; Australian industrialist and mining engineer; b. 12 July 1916; ed. Coburg and Univ. High Schools, Melbourne and Melbourne Univ.
Mining engineer 38-45, with North Broken Hill Ltd. 38-43, Allied Works Council 43-44, Lake George Mines Ltd. 44-45, Zinc Corpn. Ltd. 46-54; Asst. Gen. Man. Zinc Corpn. and New Broken Hill Consolidated Ltd. 52-54; Gen. Man. Mount Isa Mines Ltd. 55-56, Dir. 56-, Man. Dir. 66-70, Chair. 70-81; Chief Exec. M.I.M. Holdings Ltd. 70-81, Chair. (non-exec. 81-) 70-; Dir. Bank of New South Wales 71-; mem. Senate Queensland Univ. 70-; Pres. Australian Mining Industry Council 74, 75; mem. Australasian Inst. of Mining and Metallurgy, Pres. 74; mem. Econ. Advisory Group of Fed. Govt.; Hon. D.Eng.
P.O. Box 2236, Brisbane, Queensland 4001, Australia.

Forster, Oliver Grantham, C.M.G., M.V.O.; British diplomatist; b. 2 Sept. 1925; ed. Hurstpierpoint and King's Coll., Cambridge.
His Majesty's Forces 44-48; Commonwealth Relations Office (CRO) 51; Private Sec. to Parliamentary Under-Sec. of State 53; Second Sec., Karachi 54; First Sec. CRO 56-59, Madras 59-62, Washington 62-65; Private Sec. to Sec. of State for Commonwealth Affairs 65-67; Counsellor and Head of Chancery, Manila 67-70; Counsellor (Commercial/Economic) later Minister (March 75), New Delhi 70; Asst. Under-Sec. of State and Deputy Chief Clerk, Foreign and Commonwealth Office 75-79; Amb. to Pakistan July 79-.
British Embassy, Diplomatic Enclave, Ramna 5, P.O. Box 1122, Islamabad, Pakistan.
Telephone: 22131/5.

Fou Ts'ong; Chinese pianist; b. 10 March 1934; ed. Shanghai and Warsaw.
First performance, Shanghai 53, concerts in Eastern Europe and U.S.S.R. 53-58; London debut 59, concerts in Europe, North and South America, Australia and Far East.
62 Aberdeen Park, London, N5 2BL, England.
Telephone: 01-226 9589.

Frame, Janet; New Zealand writer; b. 1924; ed. Oamaru North School, Waitaki Girls' High School, Dunedin Training Coll. and Otago Univ.
Hubert Church Award for New Zealand Prose; New Zealand Scholarship in Letters 64, Burns Fellow Otago Univ. Dunedin.
Publs. *Lagoon* 51, *Owls do Cry* 57, *Faces in the Water* 61, *The Edge of the Alphabet* 62, *Scented Gardens for the Blind* 63, *The Reservoir* (stories), *Snowman, Snowman* (fables), *The Adaptable Man* 65, *A State of Siege* 67, *The Pocket Mirror* (poetry), *The Rainbirds* 68, *Intensive Care* 71, *Daughter Buffalo* (novel) 72, *Living in the Maniototo* (novel) 79.
276 Glenfield Road, Auckland, 10 New Zealand.

Francis, Harold Huyton, M.A.; New Zealand diplomatist; b. 1 May 1928, Auckland; ed. Univ. Coll., Oxford and Auckland Univ.
Joined Dept. of External Affairs 54; Third Sec., High Commission in London 54-57, Second Sec. 57-60; Head of S. Pacific and Antarctic Div. of External Affairs Dept. 60-62; First Sec., later Counsellor, Washington, D.C. 62-65; Head, Asian Div. of Ministry of Foreign Affairs, as Counsellor then Minister 66-70; High Commr. in Singapore 70-73; Asst. Sec., Ministry of Foreign Affairs 74-78; Perm. Rep. to the UN Sept. 78-.
Permanent Mission of New Zealand to the United Nations, 1 United Nations Plaza, 25th Floor, New York, N.Y. 10017, U.S.A.

Fraser, Rt. Hon. (John) Malcolm, P.C., C.H., M.A. (OXON.); Australian politician; b. 21 May 1930; ed. Melbourne Church of England Grammar School and Magdalen Coll., Oxford.
Member of House of Reps. for Wannon, Victoria 55-; Joint Parl. Cttee. of Foreign Affairs 62-66; Chair. Govt. Members' Defence Cttee. 63-65; Sec. Govt. Members' Wool Cttee.; mem. Govt. Members' Cttees. on Housing, Food and Agriculture, Industrial Relations and Research, Science and Communications; mem. Council of Australian Nat. Univ. 64-66; Minister for the Army 66-68, for Educ. and Science 68-69, 71-72, for Defence 69-71; Parl. Leader Fed. Liberal Party March 75-; Prime Minister Nov. 75-.
Parliament House, Canberra, A.C.T. 2600, Australia.

Freeman, H.E. Cardinal Sir James Darcy, K.B.E.; Australian ecclesiastic; b. 19 Nov. 1907, Sydney; ed. Christian Brothers' High School, Sydney, St. Columba's Coll., Springwood and St. Patrick's Coll., Manly.
Ordained Priest 30; Private Sec. to H.E. Cardinal Gilroy, Archbishop of Sydney 41-46; Auxiliary Bishop of Sydney 57; Bishop of Armidale 68; Archbishop of Sydney 71-; created Cardinal March 73; Knight of the Holy Sepulchre.
St. Mary's Cathedral, Sydney, N.S.W., Australia.
Telephone: 232-3788.

Freeth, Sir Gordon, K.B.E.; Australian diplomatist, lawyer and former politician, b. 6 Aug. 1914; ed. Sydney Church of England Grammar School, Guildford Grammar School, Western Australia Univ.
Barrister and solicitor, Supreme Court of W.A. 38-; practised at Katanning, W.A. 39-49; Pilot, R.A.A.F. 42-45, Flight Lieut.; rowed for Australia in British Empire Games 38; mem. House of Reps. for Forrest, 49-69; Minister for Interior and Works 58-63; Minister Assisting the Attorney-Gen. 62-64; Minister for Shipping and Transport 63-68; Minister for Air, Minister Assisting the Treasurer 68; Minister for External Affairs Feb.-Oct. 69; Amb. to Japan 70-73; practised law in Perth, W.A. 73-77; High Commr in U.K. 77-80; Legal Consultant, Muir, Williams, Nicholson Solicitors, Perth 81-; Chair. Consolidated Minerals.
25 Owston Street, Mosman Park, W.A. 6012, Australia.

Fu Zhuanzuo; Chinese soldier.
Divisional Commdr., First Field Army 49; Deputy Commdr., Wuhan Mil. Region, PLA Air Force 54, Commdr. 72; Political Commissar, PLA Air Force 73-.
People's Republic of China.

Fujimoto, Ichiro, B.ENG.; Japanese metallurgical engineer and steel mfg. executive; b. 21 Jan. 1909; ed. Tokyo Univ.
Joined Kawasaki Dockyard Co., Ltd. 32, Man. Rolling Dept., Fukiai Works 45; Dir. Kawasaki Steel Corpn. and Asst. Gen. Supt. of Fukiai Works 53-55, Gen. Supt. of Fukiai Works 55-57; Man. Dir. Kawasaki Steel Corpn. 57-62, Sr. Man. Dir. 62-64, Exec. Vice-Pres. 64-66, Pres. 66-77, Chair. 77-; Gisuke Watanabe Award for contribution to devt. of Japanese iron and steel industry 73; First Order of the Sacred Treasure 79.
Kawasaki Steel Corporation, New Yurakucho Building, 1-12-1 Yurakucho, Chiyoda-ku, Tokyo 100, Japan.

Fujinami, Takao; Japanese politician; b. 3 Dec. 1933; ed. Waseda Univ.
Member Mie Prefectural Assembly; returned to House of Reps. 67-; Parl. Vice-Minister for Science and Tech. 72, for Educ. 73; Labour Minister Nov. 79-June 80; Chair. Educational Affairs Div. 75 and Vice-Chair. Policy Affairs Research Council 78; Liberal-Democratic Party.
c/o Liberal-Democratic Party, 7, 2-chome, Hirakawacho, Chiyoda-ku, Tokyo, Japan.

Fujioka, Masao; Japanese international banker.
Adviser Ministry of Finance, Export-Import Bank of Japan; Pres. and Chair. Asian Devt. Bank Aug. 81-.
Asian Development Bank, 2330 Roxas Boulevard, Pasay City, P.O. Box 789, Manila, Philippines.

Fujisaki, Akira, LL.B.; Japanese business executive; b. 1 May 1917, Kagoshima; ed. Tokyo Imperial Univ.
Joined Sumitomo Mining Co. Ltd. (later Sumitomo Metal Mining Co. Ltd.) 42, Controller 64, Dir. 67, Man. Dir. 70, Pres. 73-; Pres. Japan Mining Industry Asscn. 76-77, 81-82; Exec. Dir. Fed. of Econ. Orgs. 76-; Vice-Chair. Japan Cttee. for Econ. Devt. 77-.
Sumitomo Metal Mining Co. Ltd., 11-3, 5-chome, Shimbashi Minato-ku, Tokyo; Home: 2-7-14, Nishi-Kamakura, Kamakura-shi, Kanagawa Prefecture, Japan.
Telephone: 03-436-7711 (Office); 0467-32-6233 (Home).

Fujiyama, Naraichi; Japanese diplomatist; b. 17 Sept. 1915, Tokyo; ed. Univs. of Tokyo and N. Carolina.
Consul, New York 53-54; Counsellor, Vienna 59-63, Jakarta 63-65; Chief of Protocol, Ministry of Foreign Affairs 65-68, Dir.-Gen. Public Information Bureau 68-71; Amb. to Austria 71-75, to Italy 75-79, to U.K. 79-82;

Chair. Bd. of Governors, IAEA, Vienna 73-74; Press Sec to Emperor Hirohito on his State visit to U.S.A. 75.
c/o Ministry of Foreign Affairs, Tokyo, Japan.

Fukuda, Hajime; Japanese politician; b. 1902; ed. Tokyo Univ.
Reporter, Political Editor, Kyodo News Service; mem. House of Reps. for Fukui Pref. 49-; fmr. Parl. Vice-Minister of Labour; Minister of Int. Trade and Industry 62, for Home Affairs 72-73, for Home Affairs, Chair. Nat. Public Safety Comm., Dir.-Gen. Hokkaido Devt. Agency 74-Sept. 76; Minister of Justice 76-77; Speaker House of Reps. 80-; Liberal-Democratic Party.
Official Residence of the Speaker of the House of Representatives, 2-18-1, Nagata-cho, Chiyoda-ku, Tokyo, Japan.

Fukuda, Takeo; Japanese politician; b. 14 Jan. 1905; ed. Tokyo Imperial Univ.
With Ministry of Finance 29-50, Deputy Vice-Minister 45-46, Dir. of Banking Bureau 46-47, Dir. Budget Bureau 47-50; mem. House of Reps. 52-; Chair. Policy Board, Liberal-Democratic Party, Sec.-Gen. 66-68; fmr. Minister of Agriculture and Forestry; Minister of Finance 65-Dec. 66, 68-71; Minister of Foreign Affairs 71-July 72; Minister of State, Dir.-Gen. Admin. Management Agency Dec. 72-73; Minister of Finance Nov. 73-74, Deputy Prime Minister and Dir. Econ. Planning Agency 74-76, resgnd.; Prime Minister and Pres. Liberal-Democratic Party 76-78.
1-247 Nozawa-machi, Setagaya-ku, Tokyo, Japan.

Fukuhara, Nobusaku, D.SC.; Japanese business executive; b. 12 Nov. 1911, Ginza, Chuo-ku, Tokyo; ed. Yokohama Inst. of Tech. (now Yokohama Nat. Univ.) and Duke Univ. Graduate School of Arts and Sciences, U.S.A.
Shiseido Co. Ltd. 32-, Dir. 52, Man. Dir. 62, Senior Man. Dir. 73, Pres. 75-78; mem. Presidium, Int. Fed. of Socs. of Cosmetic Chemists 73-; Chair. and Pres. Soc. of Cosmetic Chemists of Japan 78-.
Office: Shiseido Company Ltd., 5-5, Ginza 7-chome, Chuo-ku, Tokyo; Home: 2-18-5 Minami-senzoku, Ohta-ku, Tokyo, Japan.
Telephone: 572-5111 (Office); 727-3902 (Home).

Fukui, Kenichi; Japanese professor of chemistry; b. 4 Oct. 1918, Nara; ed. Kyoto Imperial Univ.
Lecturer, Faculty of Eng., Kyoto Univ. 43-45; Asst. Prof. 45-51, Prof. of Physical Chemistry 51-, Dean 71-73; mem. Int. Acad. Quantum Molecular Science 70-; Foreign Assoc., Nat. Acad. of Science 81-; Order of Culture; shared Nobel Prize for Chemistry 81 with Prof. Roald Hoffmann for work on chemical reactions; Person of Cultural Merits.
23 Kitashira Rawa Hirai-cho, Sakyo-ku, Kyoto 606, Japan.
Telephone: (075) 781-5785.

Funahashi, Masao; Japanese business executive; b. 3 May 1913, Aichi Pref.; ed. Tokyo Univ.
Manager of Purchasing Dept., Furukawa Electric Co. Ltd. 59, of Finance and Accounting Dept. 61, Dir. 64, Man. Dir. 68, Exec. Dir. 71, Vice-Pres. 73, Pres. 74-.
6-1, Marunouchi 2-chome, Chiyoda-ku, Tokyo, Japan.
Telephone: (03) 286-3010 (Office).

G

Gair, George Frederick, B.A.; New Zealand politician; b. 13 Oct. 1926, Dunedin; ed. Wellington and Wairarapa Colls., Univ. of N.Z.
Public Relations Officer 53-57, Personal Asst. to Gen. Man. Air New Zealand 60-66; M.P. for North Shore constituency 66-; Minister of Customs and Assoc. Minister of Finance 72, Minister of Housing and Regional Devt. and Deputy Minister of Finance 75-77, Minister of Energy 77-78, of Health and Social Welfare 78-81, of Transport, Civil Aviation and Meteorological Services, and of Railways Dec. 81-.
c/o Parliament Buildings, Wellington; 41 Hauraki Road, Takapuna, Auckland 9, New Zealand (Home).

Gan Weihan; Chinese soldier.
Director Cadres Dept. PLA N.E. Mil. Region 53; Dir. Cadres Dept. PLA Gen. Pol. Dept. 60; mem. Nat. Cttee. 4th CPPCC 64; responsible for PLA Chengdu Units 66; Dep. Sec. CCP Cttee. PLA Chengdu Mil. Region 67; made self-examination in Beijing 67; Pol. Commissar Shenyang Mil. Region 78-.
People's Republic of China.

Gandar, Leslie Walter, D.SC., F.INST.P.; New Zealand sheep farmer, politician and diplomatist; b. 26 Jan. 1919, Wellington; ed. Wellington Coll. and Victoria Univ., Wellington.
R.N.Z.A.F. 40-44; sheep farming 45-; mem. Pohangina County Council 52-69, Chair. 59-69; mem. M'tu Catchment Bd. 56-58; mem. Massey Univ. Council 63, Chancellor 70-75; Minister of Educ., Science and Tech. 75-78; High Commr. in U.K. 79-82; Fellow, N. Z. Inst. of Agricultural Science; D.Sc. (Massey).
Moorlands, No. 6 RD, Feilding, New Zealand.

Gandhi, Indira Priyadarshini; Indian politician; b. 19 Nov. 1917, Allahabad; ed. in India, Switzerland, Visva Bharati Univ., Somerville Coll., Oxford.
Daughter of late Pandit Jawaharlal Nehru; founded Vanar Sena, a children's organization to aid Congress non-cooperation movement 29; joined Congress 38; imprisoned for thirteen months 42; hostess for her father 46-64; worked in riot areas under Mahatma Gandhi 47; Pres. Indian Nat. Congress 59-60; Minister for Information and Broadcasting, New Delhi 64-66, Prime Minister 66-March 77, Jan. 80-; Chair. Planning Comm. 66-March 77, Minister of Atomic Energy 67-March 77, 81-, of External Affairs 67-69, of Finance 69-70, of Home Affairs 70-73, of Information and Broadcasting 71-74, of Space 72-March 77, 81-, of Electronics 73-March 77, of Planning Jan. 75-March 77, of Defence Nov.-Dec. 75, 80-82, of Science and Tech. 81-; mem. Rajya Sabha 64-67, mem. Lok Sabha 67-77, Nov.-Dec. 78 (expelled, imprisoned and released Dec. 78), 80-, Leader, Congress Parl. Party 67-March 77, resigned from party Jan. 78; Leader Indian Nat. Congress (I) Jan. 78- (official Opposition party April 78-Jan. 80); Founder-Pres. Bal Sahayog, New Delhi; Pres. Training Centre for Vagrant Boys, Allahabad; Vice-Pres. Indian Council of Child Welfare; Chair. Standing Cttee. Children's Film Soc.; mem. Standing Cttee., Cen. Social Welfare Board, Children's Book Trust; mem. Working Cttee., All-India Congress Cttee., Pres. Women's Dept., mem. Cen. Electoral Board, Youth Advisory Board; Pres. All-India Congress Party 59-60; mem. UNESCO Exec. Board 60; Deputy Pres. Int. Union of Child Welfare; Howland Memorial Prize, Yale Univ. 60; Hon. D.Litt. (Agra), Hon. D.C.L. (Oxford) 71, Hon. D.Sc. (U.S.S.R. Acad. of Sciences) 76, (Sorbonne) and numerous other hon. degrees; Bharat Ratna Award 71 and several other awards.
Publs. *The Years of Challenge 1966-69*, *The Years of Endeavour 1969-72*, *India* 75, *Indira: the Speeches and Reminiscences of Indira Gandhi* 75, *Eternal India* 80.
1 Safdarjang Road, New Delhi 110011, India.

Gandhi, Rajiv; Indian airline pilot and politician; b. 1945; son of Indira Gandhi (*q.v.*); ed. Trinity Coll., Cambridge.
Trained as airline pilot, U.K.; pilot with India Airlines; entered politics 81; contested Lok Sabha by-election and won seat, Amethi, Uttar Pradesh (fmrly. held by younger brother, late Sanjay Gandhi) June 81; mem. Nat. Exec. Indian Youth Congress June 81-; Congress (I) Party.
Lok Sabha, New Delhi, India.

Ganilau, Ratu Sir Penaia Kanatabatu, K.B.E., C.M.G., C.V.O., D.S.O., E.D.; Fijian politician; b. 28 July 1918; ed. Queen Victoria School, Fiji, Devonshire Course for Admin. Officers, Wadham Coll., Oxford.
Served with Fiji Infantry Regt. 40-46, to rank of Capt.; Colonial Admin. Service 47, District Officer 48-53; mem. Comm. on Fijian Post-Primary Educ. 53; service with Fiji Mil. Forces 53-56, to rank of Temporary Lt.-Col.; Hon. Col., 2nd Bn. (Territorial) Fiji Infantry Regt. 73; seconded to post of Fijian Econ. Devt. Officer and Roko Tui Cakaudrove 56; Tour Man. and Govt. Rep., Fiji Rugby Football tour of New Zealand 57 and U.K. 70; mem. House of Reps.; Deputy Sec. for Fijian Affairs 61, Minister for Fijian Affairs and Local Govt. 65; Leader of Govt. Business and Minister for Home Affairs, Lands and Mineral Resources 70; Minister for Communications, Works and Tourism 72; Deputy Prime Minister 73-; Minister for Home Affairs 75-77, of Fijian Affairs and Rural Devt. 77-; mem. Council of Ministers; Official mem. Legislative Council; Chair. Fijian Affairs Board, Fijian Devt. Fund Board, Native Land Trust Board, Great Council of Chiefs.
Ministry for Fijian Affairs and Rural Development, Box 2100, Government Buildings, Suva, Fiji.

Gao Yang; Chinese politician; b. Liaoning.
Deputy Sec. and concurrently Dir., Org. Dept., CCP Shenyang Municipal Cttee.; Chair., Liaotung 50-52; Dir. Labour Bureau, Liaotung People's Prov. Govt. 50; Council mem. N. E. People's Govt. 51-53; Sec. CCP Liaotung Prov. Cttee. 53; Deputy 1st NPC 54, 2nd NPC 58, 3rd NPC 64; mem. Control Cttee., CCP Central Cttee. 65-Cultural Revolution; Deputy Dir. Industrial Work Dept., CCP Cen. Cttee. 58; Minister of Chemical Industry 62-Cultural Revolution; Sec., Secretariat, CCP Cen. Cttee., disappeared during Cultural Revolution; rehabilitated 78; Minister of State Farms and Land Reclamation 80-.
People's Republic of China.

Gao Yangwen; Chinese politician; b. 1917.
Assistant Minister of Metallurgical Industry 55-57, Vice-Minister 57-65, 78-80; Vice-Chair. State Econ. Comm. 65-66; Sec. Beijing Municipality CP 66; Minister of Coal Industry Feb. 80-.
Ministry of Coal Industry, State Council, Beijing, People's Republic of China.

Gapurov, Mukhamednazar; Soviet politician; b. 1922; ed. Chardzhou Pedagogic Inst.
Soviet Army 41-43; Young Communist League and Party work 43-57; mem. C.P.S.U. 44-; First Sec. Chardzhou District C.P. Turkmen S.S.R. 57-61; Chair. of Council of Ministers and Minister of Foreign Affairs of Turkmen S.S.R. 63-69; First Sec. Cen. Cttee. of C.P. Turkmen S.S.R. 69-; mem. Presidium Cen. Cttee. C.P. Turkmen S.S.R.; Deputy to Supreme Soviet of the U.S.S.R. 62-; mem. Planning and Budgetary Comm., Soviet of the Union, U.S.S.R. Parl. Group; Alternate mem. Cen. Cttee. C.P.S.U. 66-71, mem. 71-.
Central Committee of the Communist Party, Ashkhabad, Turkmen S.S.R., U.S.S.R.

Garland, Hon. Sir Victor, K.B.E., B.A., F.C.A.; Australian politician and diplomatist; b. 5 May 1934, Perth; ed. Hale School and Univ. of W. Australia.
Councillor, Claremont Town Council 63-70; Deputy Mayor of Claremont 69; Senior Vice-Pres. Liberal Party of W. Australia 65-69; mem. House of Reps. 69-81; mem. House Cttee. 69-71, Parl. Cttee. on Pharmaceutical Benefits 70; Minister for Supply 71-72; Minister assisting the Treas. 72; Acting Minister for Customs and Excise 72; Chief Opposition Whip 74-75; Minister for Posts and Telecommunications and Minister Assisting the Treas. Dec. 75-Feb. 76; Minister for Veterans' Affairs Sept. 77, Dec. 77-July 78; Minister for Special Trade Representations and Minister Assisting Minister for Trade and Resources 77-79; Acting Minister for Trade and Resources several times 78-79; Minister representing Govt. at Commonwealth Ministerial Meeting for the Common Fund, London, April 78, and at Ministerial Meeting of ESCAP Aug. 78; Minister for Business and Consumer Affairs and Minister Assisting Minister for Industry and Commerce Dec. 79-Nov. 80; High Commissioner in U.K. April 81-; Leader Del. to IPU Conf. 71 and to UNCTAD V May 79; mem. Parl. Prices Cttee. 73-, House of Reps. Privileges Cttee. 73-74, House of Reps. Standing Orders Cttee. 73-75; Parl. Adviser, Mission to UN Gen. Assembly Sept.-Dec. 73; mem. New and Permanent Parl. House Cttee. 75-, Foreign Affairs and Defence Cttee. 76-; Chair. House of Reps. Expenditure Cttee. 76-77, Govt. Members' Treasury Cttee. 77.
Australia House, Strand, London, WC2B 4LA, England; Richardson Avenue, Claremont, W.A. 6010, Australia.

Gavaskar, Sunil, B.A.; Indian cricketer and business executive; b. 10 July 1949, Bombay; ed. St. Xavier's High School, Bombay, and St. Xavier's College, Bombay University.
First-class cricket debut 67, regular 70-; Test debut 71; played for Rest of the World team in Australia 71-72; Captain of Bombay 75-; Captain, India (27 tests) 78-; played for Somerset in English County Championship 80; over 7,000 runs in Test cricket up to 82, including 26 centuries in 78 Tests; over 18,000 runs in first-class cricket -82; Arjuna Award 75, Padma Bhushan 80, both Govt. of India.
Publ. *Sunny Days—An Autobiography* 76.
Nirlon Synthetic Fibres and Chemicals Ltd., Nirlon House, 254-B, Dr. Annie Besant Road, Worli, Bombay-400025; Home: 40-A, Sir Bhalchandra Road, Dadar, Bombay-400014, India.

Gayoom, Maumoon Abdul, M.A., Maldivian diplomatist and politician; b. 29 Dec. 1937; ed. Al-Azhar Univ., Cairo, and American Univ. of Cairo.
Lecturer in Islamic Studies, Abdullahi Bayero Coll., Ahmadu Bello Univ., Nigeria 69-71; entered Govt. service, Maldives 71, Man. Shipping Dept. and later Dir. of Telephone Dept.; Special Under-Sec. in Office of Prime Minister 74; Deputy Amb. to Sri Lanka 75; Deputy Minister of Transport; Perm. Rep. to UN 76-77; Minister of Transport 77-78; Pres. of Maldives Nov. 78-, Minister responsible for Home Affairs and Public Safety 78-81, attended UN Gen. Assembly 75, Head of del. to UN Gen. Assembly 76.
Office of the President, Malé, Maldives.

Geng Biao; Chinese diplomatist, politician and fmr. army officer; b. 1909, Liling, Hunan; ed. Chinese Worker-Peasant Red Army Coll.
Major-General 46; Chief of Staff, N. China Field Army 47; Amb. to Sweden 50-56, concurrently Minister to Denmark 50-55, to Finland 51-54; Amb. to Pakistan 56-59; Vice-Minister of Foreign Affairs 60-63; Amb. to Burma 63-67, to Albania 69-71; Dir. Int. Liaison Dept., CCP 71-78; a Vice-Premier, State Council March 78-; Sec.-Gen. Mil. Comm., CCP Cen. Cttee. 80-; Minister of Defence March 81-; mem. 9th Cen. Cttee. of CCP 69, 10th Cen. Cttee. 73; mem. of Politburo 11th Cen. Cttee. CCP 77, Mil. Comm. Cen. Cttee. CCP 79-.
People's Republic of China.

George, Donald William, A.O., PH.D., F.T.S., F.I.E.E., F.I.MECH.E., F.I.E.AUST., F.A.I.P.; Australian professor of engineering; b. 22 Nov. 1926, Adelaide; ed. Canberra High School, Univ. of Sydney.
Senior Lecturer, Electrical Eng., Univ. of Sydney 60-66, Assoc. Prof. 67-69, P. N. Russell Prof. of Mech. Eng. 69-74; Vice-Chancellor and Principal, Univ. of Newcastle Jan 75-; Chair. Australian Atomic Energy Comm. May 76-; Dir. Australian-American Educ. Foundation 76-, Chair. 77-; mem. Board of Trustees Asian Inst. of Tech., Bangkok

78-, Deputy Chair. 82-; Chair. Australian Vice-Chancellors' Cttee. 80-81.
Publs. various scientific and tech. papers.
Office of the Vice-Chancellor, University of Newcastle, N.S.W. 2308; Australian Atomic Energy Commission, 45 Beach Street, Coogee, N.S.W. 2034; 48 Ridgeway Road, New Lambton, N.S.W. 2305, Australia (Home).

Ghazali bin Shafie, Tan Sri Haji Muhammad, P.M.N., S.I.M.P., P.D.K.S., LL.B.; Malaysian politician; b. 22 March 1922, Kuala Lipis, Pahang; ed. Raffles Coll., Singapore, Univ. Coll. of Wales, London School of Econs., Lincoln's Inn, Inst. of Commonwealth Studies, U.K.
Fought in the resistance against Japanese occupation in World War II; Second Asst. State Sec., Selangor 51; First State Sec., Negri Sembilan 52; High Commissioner in India 57; Sec.-Gen. Ministry of Foreign Affairs to 70; co-opted mem. of Senate 70-72; Minister with special functions 70-72; Minister of Information 71-72, 73-74, of Home Affairs 73-81, of Foreign Affairs July 81-; mem. for Kuala Lipis, House of Reps. 72-.
Ministry of Foreign Affairs, Kuala Lumpur, Malaysia.

Ghosh, Amalananda, M.A.; Indian archaeologist; b. 3 March 1910; ed. A.B. High School, Banaras (now Varanasi), Queen's Coll., Banaras, Univs. of Allahabad and London.
Assistant Supt., Archaeological Survey of India 37-44, Supt. 44-50; Deputy Dir.-Gen. for Exploration, Archaeological Survey of India 50-52; Joint Dir.-Gen. of Archaeology in India, Archaeological Survey of India 52-53, Dir.-Gen. 53-68; UNESCO Consultant on Archaeology to Govts of Qatar 68, Bahrain 68, Saudi Arabia 69, Yemen Arab Republic 70; Fellow Indian Inst. of Advanced Study 68-71; Visiting Prof. of Indian Culture, Univ. of Indonesia 73-74; Dir. Dictionary of Indian Archaeology 76-79; Indian Council of Historical Research 80-; Hon. mem. and Fellow Int. Congress for Prehistoric and Protohistoric Sciences; Vice-Pres. Royal India, Pakistan and Ceylon Soc., London; Hon. Fellow, Soc. of Antiquities of London; Fellow, Deutsches Archäologisches Inst.; Hon. Corresp., Archaeological Survey of India; Special Hon. Fellow, Asiatic Soc., Calcutta.
Bankuli, Gurgaon Road, New Delhi 110037, India.
Telephone: 39-2318.

Giap, General Vo Nguyen (*see* Vo Nguyen Giap, General).

Gibbs, Rt. Hon. Sir Harry (Talbot), P.C., G.C.M.G., K.B.E., B.A., LL.M.; Australian lawyer; b. 7 Feb. 1917; ed. Ipswich Grammar School, Queensland and Univ. of Queensland.
Admitted to Queensland Bar 39; mil. service 39-45; Judge, Supreme Court, Queensland 61, Federal Court of Bankruptcy and Supreme Court of Australian Capital Territory 67-70; Justice, High Court, Australia 70-81; Chief Justice of Australia 81-; Hon. LL.D.
Office of the Chief Justice, High Court of Australia, Sydney, N.S.W.; 27 Stanhope Road, Killara, N.S.W. 2071, Australia (Home).

Gibson, Joseph David, C.B.E., B.A.; Fijian diplomatist; b. 26 Jan. 1928; ed. Levuka Public School, Marist Brothers High School, Suva, Auckland Teachers' Coll. and Auckland Univ., N.Z.
Teacher, Fiji 52-62; Principal, Queen Victoria School 61-62; Secondary School Inspector 64-65; Asst. Dir. of Educ. 66-69, Deputy Dir. 70-71, Dir. and Perm. Sec. for Educ. 71–74; Deputy High Commr. in U.K. 74-76, High Commr. 76-81; High Commr. in New Zealand 81-.
Fiji High Commission, 2nd Floor, Robert Jones Building, P.O. Box 3940, Wellington, New Zealand.

Giri, Dr. Tulsi; Nepalese politician; b. Sept. 1926.
Deputy Minister of Foreign Affairs 59; Minister of Village Development 60; Minister without Portfolio 60; Minister of Foreign Affairs, the Interior, Public Works and Communications 61; Vice-Chair. Council of Ministers and Minister of Palace Affairs 62; Chair. Council of Ministers and Minister of Foreign Affairs 62-65; mem. Royal Advisory Cttee. 69-74; Adviser to the King 74-; Prime Minister, Minister of Palace Affairs and Defence 75-77.
Jawakpurdham, District Dhanuka, Nepal.

Glenn, Sir (Joseph Robert) Archibald, Kt., O.B.E., D.UNIV., B.C.E., F.I.E. (AUST.), M.I.CHEM.E.; Australian businessman; b. 24 May 1911, Sale, Victoria; ed. Scotch Coll., Melbourne, Melbourne and Harvard Univs.
Chief Engineer ICIANZ (now ICI Australia Ltd.) 47-49, Gen. Man. 49-53, Man. Dir. 53-73, Chair. 63-73; Dir. Imperial Chemical Industries Ltd. 70-75; Chair. Fibremakers Ltd. 63-73, IMI Australia Ltd. 73-78, IC Insurance Australia Ltd. 73-, Collins Wales Ltd. 74-, Tioxide Australia Ltd. 77-; Dir. Bank of New South Wales 67-, Alcoa Australia Ltd. 73-, Hill Samuel Australia 73-, Newmont Pty. 77-, Westralian Sands 77-; Chair. Council, Scotch Coll.; Chancellor, La Trobe Univ., Melbourne 66-72; Gov. Atlantic Inst. of Int. Affairs, Council, Pacific Inst. 70-; mem. Australia-Japan Cttee. 63-75.
Home: 3 Heyington Place, Toorak, Vic. 3142, Australia.

Goh Keng Swee, B.SC.(ECON.), PH.D.; Singapore politician; b. 6 Oct. 1918; ed. Raffles Coll., London Univ.
First Vice-Chairman People's Action Party; elected Legislative Assembly from Kreta Ayer Div. and Minister for Finance 59-65; initiated Singapore's industrialization plan, the establishment of Econ. Devt. Board; Minister of Defence 65-67; Minister of Finance 67-70; Minister of Defence 70-79, 81, of Education 79-81, 81-, First Deputy Prime Minister 72-, with responsibility for the Monetary Authority of Singapore (MAS) Jan. 81-; Hon. Fellow, London School of Econs.; Magsaysay Award for Govt. Service 72; Order of Sikatuna, Philippines.
Publs. *Urban Incomes and Housing* a report on social survey of Singapore 53, 58, *Economics of Modernization and Other Essays* 72. *The Practice of Economic Growth* 77.
Monetary Authority of Singapore, SIA Building, 77 Robinson Road, Singapore 0106.

Goh Poh Seng, M.B., B.CH., B.A.O.; Singapore author and physician; b. 19 July 1936, Kuala Lumpur; ed. Victoria Inst., Kuala Lumpur, Blackrock Coll. and Univ. Coll., Dublin.
Chairman Nat. Theatre Trust, Singapore 67-73; Vice-Pres. Singapore Arts Council 67-73; mem. Board of Govs. Nat. Youth Leadership Training Inst. 67-73, Peoples Asscn. 70-72; mem. Singapore Tourist Promotion Board 69-71, Termination of Pregnancy Advisory Board 70-74; Nat. Book Devt. Award for Fiction (for *If We Dream Too Long*) 76; has written and produced three plays.
Publs. *If We Dream Too Long* 73, *The Immolation* 76, *The Dance of Moths* (novels); *Eyewitness* 76, *Lines from Batu Ferringhi* 78, *Bird With One Wing* (ed.) 82 (poetry).
Island Group Clinic, Suites 527-529, Tanglin Shopping Centre, Singapore 10 (Office); 23 Sommerville Estate Road, Singapore 10 (Home).

Goheen, Robert F., M.A., PH.D.; American professor and diplomatist; b. 15 Aug. 1919, Vengurla, India; ed. Kodaikanal School, South India, Lawrenceville School, U.S.A., Princeton Univ.
Instructor and Asst. Prof. of Classics, Princeton Univ. 48-57; Dir. Woodrow Wilson Fellowship Program of Asscn. of American Univs. 53-56; Pres. Princeton Univ. 57-72, Pres. Emer. 72-; Prof. Princeton Univ. 57-72; Chair. Council on Foundations 72-76; Pres. Edna McConnell Clark Foundation Jan.-May 77; Amb. to India 77-80; Sr. Fellow, Woodrow Wilson School, Princeton Univ. 80-; Dir. Mellon Fellowships in the Humanities 82-; Legion of Merit; Hon. degrees from 26 Colls. and Univs.

Publs. *The Imagery of Sophocles' Antigone* 49, *The Human Nature of a University* 69.
1 Orchard Circle, Princeton, N.J. 08540, U.S.A.

Gombojav, Damdiny; Mongolian politician; b. 12 April 1919; ed. Inst. of Oriental Studies, Inst. of Foreign Trade, U.S.S.R.
Head of Import Dept., Foreign Trade Board, Deputy Trade Minister 54-56; Trade Rep. in Moscow 56-60; Minister of Foreign Trade 60-65; Deputy Chair. Council of Ministers, Chair. Comm. for CMEA Affairs 65-77; Sec. Cen. Cttee., Mongolian People's Revolutionary Party (MPRP), Alt. mem. Political Bureau MPRP, 77-81, mem. 81-; Deputy to the People's Great Hural (Assembly); Chair. Mongolian-Soviet Friendship Soc.; Order of Sühbaatar and other awards.
Central Committee of the Mongolian People's Revolutionary Party, Ulan Bator, Mongolia.

Gopal-Ayengar, Anekal Ramaswamiengar, M.SC., M.A., PH.D.; Indian biologist; b. 1 Jan. 1909; ed. Univs. of Mysore and Toronto.
Lecturer in Botany, Mysore Univ. 33-38; Vincent Massey Fellow, Univ. of Toronto 38-39; Senior Instructor, Univ. of Toronto 41-45, Kettering Research Fellow, Barnard Skin and Cancer Hospital and Research Assoc., Washington Univ., St. Louis, Mo. 45-47; Chief Research Cytologist, Tata Memorial Hospital, Bombay 47-51; Head, A.E.C. Unit on Cell Biology 48-51; Senior Int. Research Fellow, Lady Tata Trust and Research Assoc., Chester Beatty Research Inst., London and Inst. for Cell Research, Karolinska Inst., Stockholm 51-53; Chief Scientific Officer and Head, Biological and Medical Divs., Atomic Energy Establishment, Trombay (AEET) 60-62; Dir. Biology Group (AEET) 62-67; Expert, Radiation Cttee. of World Health Org. (WHO) 58-73; mem. Int. Cttee. on Experimental Studies on Human Cancer, Comm. for Experimental Oncology; Rep. for South-East Asia on Genetics Section of Int. Union of Biological Sciences (IUBS) and Int. Cell Research Org. 63-66; Chair. Nat. Cttee. for Biophysics 62-; Pres. Indian Soc. of Genetics and Plant Breeding 63-64 and Comm. on Radiation Biophysics of Int. Union for Pure and Applied Physics (IUPAP) 65-69, Sec. 69-72; Associated with Int. Soc. for Cell Biology, New York Acad. of Sciences and American Asscn. for Cancer Research; Dir. Bio-Medical Group 68-71; Emer. Dir. and Bio-Medical Adviser A.E.C. 71-; official of numerous scientific orgs.; Pres. Indian Asscn. for Radiation Protection (IARP) 69-72; Hon. Prof. of Cell Biology Madurai Univ. 69-; mem. Editorial Board *Radiation Botany and Biophysik*; Fellow, Indian Acad. of Sciences; J. H. Bhabha Prize 48; Padma Shri 67; D.Sc. h.c. (Mysore), Sc.D. h.c. (Hannover).
8B Atomic Energy Officers Apartments, Little Gibbs Road, Malabar Hill, Bombay 400006, India.
Telephone: 359346.

Gorai, Rt. Rev. Dinesh Chandra, B.A., B.D.; Indian ecclesiastic; ed. Serampore Coll.
Ordained Priest 62; Methodist Minister, Calcutta, Barrackpore 70-82; Bishop of Barrackpore 70-82, of Calcutta 82-; Moderator Church of North India 80-.
Bishop's House, 51 Chowringhee Road, Calcutta, West Bengal, India.
Telephone: 44-5259.

Gosse, Edmund Barr, M.A. (CANTAB.); Australian company director; b. 14 July 1915, Perth; ed. St. Peter's Coll., Adelaide, Trinity Hall, Cambridge.
Chairman, John Lysaght (Aust.) Ltd., 67-; Man. Lysaght's Works, Newcastle 53-63; Dir. ICI Australia Ltd., Perpetual Trustees Australia Ltd., Guest, Keen and Nettlefolds (Overseas) Ltd., Amalgamated Wireless Australasia Ltd.; mem. Metals Soc., U.K.
27 Sutherland Crescent, Darling Point, N.S.W. 2027, Australia.

Grassby, Albert Jaime; Australian politician; b. 12 July 1926, Brisbane, Queensland; ed. schools in Australia, Univ. of California.
Specialist Officer, Information Dept., CSIRO 48; Specialist Officer, Agricultural Extension Service, N.S.W. 50; Exec. Officer, Irrigation Research and Extension Org., N.S.W. 53; mem. N.S.W. Parl. for Murrumbidgee 65-69; mem. House of Reps. for Riverina 69-74; Minister of Immigration 72-74; Special Govt. Adviser on Community Relations 74-75; Commr. for Community Relations 75-; Commdr. Order of Solidarity of the Repub. of Italy 70, Knight Grand Cross of Mil. Order of St. Agatha of Paterno 69, Citation, Univ. of Santo Tomás (Philippines) 74, Grand Cross of Mil. Order, Malta 74; Hon. citizen of Sinopoli and Plati (Italy), Akrata and Platynos (Greece); Hon. D. Phil. (Munich) 79.
Publs. *Griffith of the Four Faces*, *The Morning After* and several papers on population and immigration, irrigation and agricultural devt. in Australia.
Office: Acton House, Canberra, A.C.T.; Home: 1 Wargi Place, Aranda, A.C.T. 2614, Australia.

Gresford, Guy Barton, B.SC., F.R.A.C.I.; Australian science administrator; b. 7 March 1916; ed. Hobart High School, Royal Melbourne Technical Coll., Trinity Coll., Univ. of Melbourne, and School of Administration, Harvard Univ.
Officer in Charge, Australian Scientific Liaison Office, London 42-46; Asst. Sec. (Australian) Commonwealth Scientific and Industrial Research Org. 47-52, Sec. (Physical Sciences) 52-59, Sec. 59-66; Dir. for Science and Technology, UN 66-73; Sec. UN Advisory Cttee. for Application of Science and Technology to Devt. 66-73; Senior Adviser on Science, Technology and the Environment, Australian Dept. of Foreign Affairs 73-78· Deputy Sec.-Gen. UN Conf. on Science and Technology for Devt. 78-79; Consultant 80-; Harkness Fellow Commonwealth Fund of New York 57.
2 Jacka Crescent, Canberra, A.C.T. 2601, Australia.
Telephone: (062) 478667.

Grover, Amar Nath, M.A., LL.B.; Indian judge; b. 15 Feb. 1912, Shwebo (British Upper Burma); ed. Univs. of Punjab, Lahore and Cambridge and Middle Temple, London.
Called to Bar 36; Barrister, High Court, Lahore 36-47, later at High Court of E. Punjab, Simla and Chandigarh; mem. Punjab Bar Council 54-57; Judge, High Court, Punjab 57-68; Judge, Supreme Court of India 68-73; Chair. Press Council of India 79-; Chair. Comm. of Inquiry 77-79; mem. Int. Law Asscn., Indian Law Inst.; mem. World Peace Through Law Centre.
Publs. several articles on various branches of law.
132 Sunder Nagar, New Delhi 110003, India.

Gu Mu; Chinese politician; b. 1914, Roncheng Cty., Shandong Prov.
Joined CP 32; Mayor of Jinan 50-52; Deputy Sec. CCP Shanghai 53-54; Vice-Chair. State Construction Comm. 54-56, State Econ. Comm. 56-65; Chair. State Capital Construction Comm. 65-67; criticized and removed from office during Cultural Revolution 67; Minister of State Capital Construction Comm. 73-81, of Foreign Investment Comm. 79-82, of Import-Export Comm. 79-82, also a Vice-Premier, State Council 75-; mem. 11th Cen. Cttee. CCP 77; Deputy for Shandong, 5th NPC, mem. Presidium 5th NPC 78; Sec., Secretariat, Cen. Cttee. 80-; Political Commissar, PLA Capital Construction Engineering Corps 79-.
People's Republic of China.

Guan Zhongding; Chinese army officer.
Member Standing Cttee. Zhejiang Provincial CCP Cttee. 78-; Commdr. Zhejiang Mil. Dist. 78-.
People's Republic of China.

Guha, Phulrenu, D.LITT.; Indian social and political worker; b. 13 Aug. 1911; ed. Calcutta and Paris Univs.
Participated in Freedom Movement from early days; social worker for over forty-five years; Sec. United Council for Relief and Welfare; Gen. Sec. and Vice-Pres. All-India Women's Conf.; Chair. W. Bengal State Social Welfare Advisory Board; Pres. India Council for Child Welfare; Chair. Cttee. on Status of Women in India; mem. Rajya Sabha 64-70; Union Minister of State for Social Welfare 67-70; mem. Comm. Adim-Jati Seva Sangha, All India Congress Cttee., Cottage Industries Cen. Social Welfare Board; Pres. Karmakutir, W. Bengal Asscn. for Social Health; Vice-Pres. West Bengal Pradesh Congress Cttee.; Working Chair. Indo-Soviet Cultural Soc.; Working Chair. W. Bengal Cttee. on Eradication of Illiteracy; Adviser Indian Inst. of Social Welfare and Business Management; mem. Nat. Cttee. on Women, Chair. Indo-G.D.R. Friendship Asscn. W. Bengal; Chair. Cttee. for Nat. Integration and Democratic Rights and Centre for Women's Devt. Studies; attended many seminars and confs.; Padma Bhushan 77.
Publs. include *Participation of Women in India's Economy, Rammohan to Vivekanda, Role of Voluntary Organizations in Promoting Nutrition to Pre-School Children, The Role of the Woman in India's Economy,* articles on social problems, lectures on social and political problems.
55/5 Purna Das Road, Calcutta 29, W. Bengal, India.

Guilfoyle, Dame Margaret Georgina Constance, D.B.E.; Australian accountant and politician; b. 15 May 1926, Belfast, Northern Ireland.
Chartered Sec. and Accountant 47-; Liberal mem. Senate for Victoria 71-; Minister for Educ. Nov.-Dec. 75, for Social Security 75-80, for Finance Nov. 80-; Fellow Australian Soc. of Accountants; Assoc. Chartered Inst. of Secs. and Administrators.
Parliament House, Canberra, A.C.T. 2600; 21 Howard Street, Kew, Victoria, Australia (Home).

Guise, Sir John, G.C.M.G., K.B.E.; Papua New Guinean politician; b. 29 Aug. 1914, Milne Bay; ed. Anglican School, Dogura, Milne Bay Province.
Sergeant-Major, Royal Papua New Guinea Constabulary 46-57; mem. Legis. Council 61-63, House of Assembly 64-75, Speaker 68-71; Deputy Chief Minister 72-75, Minister of the Interior, later of Agriculture 72-75; Gov.-Gen. of Papua New Guinea 75-77; mem. Nat. Parl. June 77-; independent, later United Party; Hon. LL.D.; K. St. J.
Lalaura Village, Cape Rodney, Central Province, Papua New Guinea.

Guna-Kasem, Pracha, PH.D.; Thai diplomatist; b. 29 Dec. 9134, Bangkok; ed. Dhebsirinda School, Bangkok, Marlborough Coll., England, Oxford and Yale Univs.
Ministry of Foreign Affairs 59-; Chief of Section, Political Div. of Dept. of Int. Org. 60-61, Second Sec. SEATO Div. 62-63; alt. mem. for Thailand, SEATO Perm. Working Group 62-63; Embassy in Egypt 64-65; Chief of Foreign News Analyses Div. of Information Dept., concurrently in charge of press affairs 66-69, Chief of Press Div. 70-71, Dir.-Gen. of Information Dept. 73-75; Consul-Gen. in Hong Kong 71-73; Perm. Rep. to UN 75-80; Amb. and Perm. Rep. to UN, Geneva July 80-; Special Lecturer, Thammasat Univ., Thai Nat. Defence Coll.; mem. Del. to UN Gen. Assembly 62, 68, 70, 74, to 2nd Afro-Asian conf., Algeria 65, to SEATO Council 66; Knight Grand Cross of Order of the Crown, Knight Grand Cross of Order of the White Elephant, Grand Cordon, Order of the Crown of Thailand.
Permanent Mission of Thailand to the United Nations, 28B Chemin du Petit-Saconnex, 1209 Geneva, Switzerland.

Gunaratne, Victor Thomas Herat, L.M.S., D.T.M. & H.; D.P.H., F.R.C.P.(E.); Sri Lankan international health official. b. 11 March 1912, Madampe; ed. Ceylon Medical Coll., London School of Hygiene and Tropical Medicine, and Univ. of Edinburgh Medical School.
Deputy Dir. Public Health Services, Ceylon 59-61; Deputy Dir. Ceylon Medical Services 61-64; Dir. Health Services, Govt. of Ceylon 64-68; Pres. World Health Assembly 67; Dir. WHO Regional Office for S.E. Asia 68-81; Fellow, Sri Lanka Public Health Asscn. 67; Hon. Fellow, Indian Acad. of Medical Sciences 75, Indian Soc. of Malaria and other Communicable Diseases 79, Ceylon Coll. of Physicians 76; Hon. degrees from Mahidol Univ., Thailand, Univ. of Sri Lanka, State Medical Inst., Mongolian People's Repub., Banaras Hindu Univ., India.
Publs. *A History of Medicine and Public Health in Sri Lanka, Selected Addresses, The Challenge Faced by the Medical Profession in Tropical Developing Countries, Challenges and Response, Voyage Towards Health,* and articles in professional journals.
c/o WHO Regional Office for South-East Asia, World Health House, Ring Road, Indraprastha Estate, New Delhi 11002, India.
Telephone: 270181.

Guo Weicheng, Maj.-Gen.; Chinese army officer and government official; b. 1912, Liaoning Prov.
Vice-Minister of Railways 77-78, Minister 78-81.
c/o State Council, Beijing, People's Republic of China.

H

Ha Van Lau; Vietnamese diplomatist; b. 4 Dec. 1918, Thua Thien.
Served with Viet-Nam People's Army 45-54; a del. of Democratic Repub. of Viet-Nam to Geneva Conf. on Indochina 54, Paris Conf. on Viet-Nam 68; Asst. Minister of Foreign Affairs 73; Amb. to Cuba 74-78; Perm. Rep. to UN Sept. 78-.
Permanent Mission of Viet-Nam to the United Nations, 20 Waterside Plaza, New York, N.Y. 10010, U.S.A.

Habib, Philip Charles, B.S., PH.D.; American diplomatist; b. 25 Feb. 1920, New York; ed. Univ. of Idaho, and Univ. of California (Berkeley).
Served U.S. army 42-46 (rank of Major); entered Foreign Service 49; Third Sec. U.S. Embassy, Canada 49-51; Second Sec. U.S. Embassy, New Zealand 52-54; Research specialist, Dept. of State, Washington 55-57; U.S. Consulate-Gen., Trinidad 58-60; Foreign Affairs Officer, Dept. of State 60-61; Counsellor for Political Affairs U.S. Embassy, Repub. of Korea 62-65, Repub. of Viet-Nam 65-67; rank of Minister 66-67, Amb. 69-71; Deputy Asst. Sec. of State for East Asian and Pacific Affairs 67-69; Adviser U.S. del. to meetings on Viet-Nam, Paris 68-71; Amb. to Repub. of Korea 71-74; Asst. Sec. of State for East Asian and Pacific Affairs 74-75; Under-Sec. of State for Political Affairs 76-78; Diplomat-in-Residence, Stanford Univ. 78-; U.S. Envoy in Middle East 81, 82; Rockefeller Public Service Award 69, Nat. Civil Service League Award 70.
c/o Department of Political Science, Stanford University, Stanford, Calif. 94305, U.S.A.

Haddon-Cave, Sir (Charles) Philip, K.B.E., C.M.G., M.A.; British colonial administrator; b. 6 July 1925; ed. Univ. of Tasmania, King's Coll., Cambridge Univ.
With Colonial Admin. Service 52-; successively posted in Kenya, Seychelles and Hong Kong; Financial Sec. and mem. Exec. & Legis. Council, Hong Kong 71-81, Chief Sec. 81-.
Colonial Secretariat, Central District, Hong Kong; Home: 45 Shouson Hill, Hong Kong.

Hadiwijaya, Toyib, D.AGR.SC.; Indonesian agriculturist and politician; b. 12 May 1919, Ciamis, W. Java; ed. Middelbare Landbouwschool Bogor, Faculty of Agri-

culture, Bogor, Univ. of Indonesia and special studies in U.S.A., Europe and Asia.
Assistant plant pathologist, Inst. for Plant Diseases, Dept. of Agriculture, Bogor 39-48; Student and Instr. of Plant Pathology, Faculty of Agric., Univ. of Indonesia, Bogor 48-55, Asst. Prof. 55-56, Prof. 56-78; Dean of Faculty of Agric. 57-62; mem. Regional Rep. Council, W. Java 60-62; Minister of Higher Educ. and Science 62-64; Amb. to Belgium and Luxembourg 65-66; Pres. Bogor Agric. Univ. 66-70; Minister of Plantations 67-68, of Agric. 68-78; mem. Supreme Advisory Council and Nat. Ass. 78-; mem. Trustees Int. Rice Research Inst, Los Baños, Philippines 70-74; Pres. 19th Session FAO Conf., Rome 78; Chair. and mem. of numerous advisory cttees.; chief del. to several int. confs.
Publs. Many scientific publs. and papers in Indonesian, Dutch, English and French.
c/o Supreme Advisory Council, 1751 Merdeka Utara, Jakarta Selan (Office); 9 Jl. Perdatan, Jakarta Selantan, Indonesia (Home).
Telephone: 792400, 794252 Jakarta.

Haksar, Ajit Narain, B.A., M.B.A.; Indian tobacco executive; b. 11 Jan. 1925, Gwalior, Madhya Pradesh; ed. Doon School, Dehra Dun, Allahabad Univ., Harvard Univ., U.S.A.
Training with J. Walter Thompson Co., N.Y. 45-46; joined India Tobacco Co. Ltd. (fmrly. The Imperial Tobacco Co. of India Ltd.) as Asst. Marketing Man. 48; seconded to British-American Tobacco Co. Ltd., London 48-50; Marketing Dir. Board of India Tobacco Co. (ITC) 66, Deputy Chair. 68, Chair. 69-; fmr. Chair. Local Board, Indian Leaf Tobacco Devt. Co. Ltd.; Chair. Board of Govs. Indian Inst. of Technology; Gov. Indian Inst. of Management 71-; non-exec. Chair. Webstar Ltd.; Dir. Reserve Bank of India 77-, Chair. Local Board (Eastern Area) 77-; mem. Industrial Advisory Cttee., Industrial and Commercial Dept., Govt. of Jammu and Kashmir Dec. 77-, Gen. Assembly Indian Council for Cultural Relations July 78-; Dir. Indian Airlines; Past Pres. Bengal Chamber of Commerce and Industry.
Office: Virginia House, 37 Chowringhee, Calcutta 700071; Home: 24B Raja Santosh Road, Calcutta 700027, India.
Telephone: 248141 (Office); 457696 (Home).

Halstead, Eric Henry, E.D., M.A., B.COM., F.C.A.(N.Z.), F.C.I.S.; New Zealand politician and company director; b. 26 May 1912; ed. Auckland Univ. Coll. and Teachers' Training Coll.
Major N.Z. Forces Middle East and Italy 39-45; head of Commercial and Accountancy Dept., Seddon Memorial Technical Coll. 45-49; Mem. of Parl. (mem. of National Party) 49-57; Minister of Social Security and Minister-in-Charge of Tourist and Health Resorts 54-56; Minister-Asst. to the Prime Minister 54-57, concurrently Minister of Industries and Commerce and of Customs 56-57; partner Mabee, Halstead and Co.; Pres. Auckland Savings Bank; Dir. Air New Zealand Ltd. 65-70; mem. Council Univ. of Auckland 61-70; Amb. to Thailand and Laos 70-73, to Italy, also accred. to Egypt, Iraq, Saudi Arabia (76-80) and Yugoslavia and High Commr. in Malta 76-80; rep. to SEATO 70-73, to ECAFE Confs. 71-73; mem. Board Asian Inst. of Technology 70-74, Deputy Chair. 72-74; Rep. at FAO, IFAD and Common Fund confs. 76-79; Business Consultant and Co. Dir. 74-76, 80-; Commr. New Zealand Industries Devt. Comm. 80-; Dr. (Academia Tiberina) 80.
Publs. several textbooks and contributions to econ. and professional journals.
6A Kabul Street, Wellington, New Zealand.

Hameed, A. C. S.: Sri Lankan politician.
Minister of Foreign Affairs, Govt. of Sri Lanka 77-; first man to hold separate portfolio of foreign affairs; United Nat. Party.
Ministry of Foreign Affairs, Colombo, Sri Lanka.

Hamengkubuwono IX, H.R.H. Sultan Dorodjatun; Indonesian ruler; b. 12 April 1912; ed. Univ. of Leiden.
Inaugurated Sultan of Yogyakarta 40; Mil. Gov. of Special Territory (with rank of Maj.-Gen. of the Army) 45-49; Head of Special Territory 46; Gov., Head of Special Territory 59; mem. Provisional People's Consultative Assembly Aug. 59, Titular Gen. of the Army 60; Minister of State Oct. 46-49; Minister of Defence and Co-ordinator of Domestic Security Aug.-Dec. 59; Defence Minister, Cabinet of the Repub. of the United States of Indonesia Dec. 49, 53; Deputy Prime Minister 50-April 51; Curator Univ. of Gajah Mada Dec. 51; Chair. Supervisory Comm. for the Apparatus of the State Aug. 59; Minister and Head, Body for Controlling State Finance 64; First Minister for Econ. and Financial Affairs in the Presidium and Deputy Prime Minister 66-68; State Minister for Econ. Affairs, Finance and Industry 68-73; Vice-Pres. 73-78; Chair. Indonesian Olympic Cttee. 51, Tourist Inst. 56, Asian Games Fed. 58, Indonesian Tourist Council 62-73, 82-; Chair. Session, Econ. Comm. for Asia and the Far East (ECAFE) 57, Nat. Preparatory Cttee. for New York World Fair 63; Chief Del. of Indonesia, Pacific Area Travel Asscn. (PATA); U.S. 58, UN First World Conf. of Int Travel and Tourism, Rome 63; Medal of the Guerilla, Medal of Loyalty to the Independence and the Order of the White Elephant (Thailand); Hon. titles of Maha Putra (Spes Patria) and Pramuka Agung (Supreme Boy Scout).
Jalan Prapatan 42, Jakarła Pusat, Indonesia.

Hamer, Alan William; Australian business executive; b. 27 Nov. 1917, Melbourne; ed. Oxford Univ.
Joined ICI Australia, England 41, returned to Australia 42; associated with setting up of new plants; Works Man. Yarraville plant 50-56; Controller Technical Dept. 56-59, Dir. 59-68; Chair. ICI Group of Cos., India 68-71, concurrently non-exec. Dir. ICI Australia Board; Man. Dir. and Deputy Chair. ICI Australia Ltd. 71-79; Dir. EZ Industries, Woodside Petroleum, Tubemakers of Aust., Reckitt & Coleman Aust., Grindlays Aust., E.R.A., H. C. Sleigh; Rhodes Scholar 37.
182 George Street, East Melbourne, Vic., Australia.

Hamer, Hon. Sir Rupert, K.C.M.G., E.D., LL.M.; Australian solicitor and politician; b. 29 July 1916, Kew, Vic.; ed. Melbourne and Geelong Grammar Schools, Univ. of Melbourne.
Joined Australian Imperial Forces 40; C.O. Vic. Scottish Regt., Citizen Mil. Forces 54-58; mem. Vic. Legislative Council for E. Yarra 58-71; Minister for Immigration, Vic. 62-64, for Local Govt., Vic. 64-71; mem. Vic. Legislative Assembly for Kew 71-81; Deputy Leader Parl. Liberal Party 71-72; Chief Sec., Deputy Premier Vic. 71-72, Premier 72-81, also Treas. and Minister of the Arts 72-79, Minister of State Devt., Decentralization and Tourism 79-81.
c/o Office of the Premier of Victoria, Melbourne, Victoria, Australia.

Hammond, Dame Joan Hood, D.B.E., C.M.G.; Australian singer (retd.); b. 24 May 1912, Christchurch, New Zealand; ed. Presbyterian Ladies Coll., Pymble, Sydney and Sydney Conservatorium of Music.
Former mem. Sydney Philharmonic Orchestra and sports writer, *Daily Telegraph*, Sydney; first public (singing) appearance, Sydney 29; London debut in *Messiah* 38; operatic debut, Vienna 39; has appeared as guest artist at Royal Opera House, Covent Garden, Sadlers Wells, Vienna State Opera, Bolshoi Theatre, Moscow, New York City Center, Netherlands Opera, Barcelona Liceo, etc.; world tours have included Europe, U.S.A., Canada, Australasia, India, S. Africa and U.S.S.R.; repertoire

includes: *Aïda, Madame Butterfly, Tosca, Othello, Don Carlos, La Traviata, La Bohème, Turandot, Tannhäuser, Lohengrin,* and *Die Zauberflöte*; Head of Vocal Studies, Victorian Coll. of Arts; records for HMV (fmrly. for Columbia); mem. Victorian Council for the Arts, Bd. of Dirs. Victorian State Opera; Hon.D.Mus. (Western Australia); Coronation Medal 53; Sir Charles Santley Award, Worshipful Co. of Musicians 70.
Publ. *A Voice, A Life.*
Private Bag 101, Geelong Mail Centre, Victoria 3221, Australia.

Han Xianchu; Chinese army officer; b. 1911, Hunan.
Battalion Commdr. Red 4th Front Army 31; Commdr. 73rd Div. Red 25th Army 33; Commdr. 689th Regt. 8th Route Army 38; Commdr. N.E. 4th Column 47; Commdr. 40th Army 4th Field Army 49; Vice-Commdr. PLA Hunan Mil. Dist. 49-50; Del. of 4th Field Army to 1st CPPCC 49; mem. Guangdong People's Provincial Govt. 50-54; mem. Hainan Mil. and Admin. Cttee. 50; Vice-Chair. Joint Chief of Staff Chinese and N. Korean Forces 51; Chinese Rep. in negotiations with UN regarding Armistice 52; Chief of Staff Chinese People's Volunteers 52; mem. Nat. Defence Council 54; training at Mil. Coll. 55; Alt. mem. 8th Cen. Cttee. 58; rank of Gen. 60; Chief PLA Fujian Front Units 60; Deputy Chief PLA Gen. Staff H.Q. 65; Chair. Fujian Provincial Revolutionary Cttee. 68-73; Commdr. Fujian Front Units 68; mem. CCP 9th Cen. Cttee. 69; First Sec. Fujian Provincial Cttee. 71-73; mem. CCP 10th Cen. Cttee. 73; Commdr. Fuzhou PLA Mil. Region 72; Commdr. Lanzhou Mil. Region 73-80; mem. Presidium 4th NPC 75; mem. CCP 11th Cen. Cttee. 77-; mem. Standing Cttee., Mil. Comm. 80-.
People's Republic of China.

Hara, Shiro; Japanese journalist; b. 15 Feb. 1908, Takayama, Gifu; ed. Hosei Univ.
Reporter, *Kokumin Shimbun* 34; joined *Yomiuri Shimbun* 36, Deputy Editor-in-Chief 55, Dir. 57, Exec. Dir. and Editor-in-Chief 65-, Exec. Vice-Pres. 71-; Dir. *Hochi Shimbun* 66-; Chair. Nihon Kisha Club (Japan Journalists Club) 69-.
Yomiuri Shimbun, 1-7-1, Otemachi, Chiyoda-ku, Tokyo, Japan.
Telephone: 242-1111.

Hara, Sumio; Japanese banker; b. 7 March 1911, Yokosuka, Kanagawa; ed. Faculty of Law, Tokyo Imperial Univ.
Joined Ministry of Finance 34; Deputy Dir. Budget Bureau 53-56; Dir.-Gen. of the Tax Bureau 56-60; Commr. Nat. Tax Admin. Agency 60-62; Deputy Pres. The Bank of Tokyo Ltd. 62-65, Pres. 65-73, Chair. 73-77, Exec. Adviser 77-; mem. Tobacco Cultivation Council (Japan Monopoly Corpn.) 74-, Customs Tariff Council (Ministry of Finance) 76-; Vice-Pres. Japan Tariff Asscn. 68-; Special Adviser to the Pres. Japan Chamber of Commerce and Industry 75, Tokyo Chamber of Commerce and Industry 75-; Adviser, Nat. Personnel Authority 75-; mem. Trilateral Comm. 73-, Int. Advisory Board, Sperry Corpn. N.Y. 74-; Arbitrator Int. Centre for Settlement of Investment Disputes, Washington, D.C. 80-; mem. Price Stabilization Policy Council, Econ. Planning Agency 81-; Chair. Steering Cttee., Okinawa Devt. Finance Corpn. 81-.
Bank of Tokyo Ltd., 1-6-3 Nihombashi Hongokucho, Chuo-ku, Tokyo; Home: 26-14, Tsutsujigaoka, Midori-ku, Yokohama, Kanagawa, Japan.
Telephone: 03-245-1111 (Office); 045-981-7507 (Home).

Harjono, Maj.-Gen. Piet; Indonesian industrial executive and fmr. army officer; b. 1919.
Posts in financial admin. of armed forces 52-66, Ministry of Finance 66-76; acting Pres.-Dir., then Pres.-Dir. PERTAMINA (nat. oil co.) 76-81.
c/o PERTAMINA, Jalan Perwira 2-6, Jakarta, Indonesia.

Harry, Ralph Lindsay, A.C., C.B.E.; Australian diplomatist; b. 10 March 1917, Geelong, Victoria; ed. Tasmania and Lincoln Coll., Oxford.
Department of External Affairs 40-78; Private Sec. to Minister of External Affairs; Asst. Official Sec., Canada 43-45; Second Sec., later First Sec., Washington, D.C., U.S.A. 45-49 (at UN, New York 47-48); Dept. of External Affairs, Canberra 49-53; Consul-Gen. in Switzerland 53-56; rep. in Singapore, Brunei, Sarawak and Borneo 56-57; seconded to Department of Defence 58-59; Asst. Sec. Department of External Affairs 60-65; Amb. to Belgium and the EEC 65-68, to Repub. of Viet-Nam 68-70, to Fed. Repub. of Germany 71-75, to UN 75-78; fmrly. leader dels. to UN Conf. on the Law of the Sea, Cttee. on Outer Space, Preparatory Cttee. for UN Gen. Assembly Special Session on Disarmament; Dir. Australian Inst. of Int. Affairs 79-81; mem. Nat. Australia Day Cttee. 80-81; Pres. Australian Esperanto Asscn.
8 Tennyson Crescent, Forrest, A.C.T. 2603, Australia.

Hasegawa, Norishige; Japanese industrialist; b. 8 Aug. 1907, Kumamoto City; ed. Tokyo Imperial Univ.
Joined Sumitomo Partnership Co. Ltd. 31, Sumitomo Chemical Co. Ltd. 34, Dir. 51, Man. Dir. 56, Exec. Vice-Pres. 63, Pres. 65-77, Chair. 77-; Chair. Sumitomo Aluminium Smelting Co. Ltd., Mount Pleasant Chemical Co. Ltd.; Pres. Nippon Asahan Aluminium Co. Ltd.; Dir. Nihon Oxirane Co. Ltd.; Vice-Chair. Keidanren (Fed. of Econs. Orgs.); Life Trustee Japan Cttee. for Econ. Devt.; mem. Econ. Council of Prime Minister's Office, Advisory Cttee. of Japanese Nat. Railways, Price Stabilization Policy Council of Prime Minister's Office; Chair. Japan-U.S. South-East Asscn., Japan-U.S. Mid-West Asscn.; Japan Nat. Chair., Japan-New Zealand Businessmen's Conf.; Standing Dir. Kansai Econ. Fed.; Exec. Councillor, Osaka Chamber of Commerce and Industry; mem. Exec. Cttee., Japan-U.S. Econ. Council, Japan Comm. of Trilateral Comm.; Adviser, Japan Chemical Industry Asscn.; Chair. Int. Primary Aluminium Institute; Pres. Japan-Greece Soc.; Deputy Chair. Int. Management Asscn. of Japan (IMAJ); mem. Visiting Cttee. Centre for Int. Studies, M.I.T.; Trustee, Univ. of the Sacred Heart, Kobe Kaisei Coll.; Medal for Distinguished Industrialist of Osaka Prefecture 68, Blue Ribbon Medal 69, Commdr. Order of the Phoenix (Greece) 75, First Order of the Sacred Treasure (Japan) 79.
Sumitomo Chemical Co., 15, 5-chome, Kitahama, Higashi-ku, Osaka; 12-7, Aioi-cho, Hyogo Prefecture, Japan (Home).
Telephone: (06) 220-3151 (Office); 0798-72-2400 (Home).

Hasegawa, Takashi; Japanese politician; b. 1 April 1912; ed. Waseda Univ.
Editor Kyushu daily paper; Private Sec. to Minister of State; mem. House of Reps. 53-; Deputy Minister of Education 61-62; Vice-Chair. Public Relations Cttee., Liberal-Democratic Party 63, Chair. 66; Minister of Labour 74-76; Pres. Japan Fencing Asscn. 82-.
8-903, Yonban-cho, 9-chome, Chiyoda-ku, Tokyo, Japan.

Hasluck, Rt. Hon. Sir Paul Meernaa Caedwalla, P.C., G.C.M.G., G.C.V.O., M.A.; Australian historian, diplomatist and politician; b. 1 April 1905; ed. Western Australia Univ.
Member Editorial staff *The West Australian*; Lecturer in History Western Australia Univ.; mem. staff Australian Dept. of External Affairs 41-47; Sec. Canberra Conf. Jan. 44; Adviser on Australian del. to Wellington Conf. Nov. 44; Adviser British Commonwealth Meeting London April 45; Adviser San Francisco Conf. April 45; Australian del. Exec. Cttee. of United Nations Preparatory Comm. London Aug. 45; alt. del. Preparatory Comm. Nov. 45; del. General Assembly Jan. and Sept. 46; Dir. post-hostilities Div.,

Australian Dept. of External Affairs April 45; Counsellor Australian Mission UN H.Q. March 46; Acting Rep. of Australia on Security Council and Atomic Energy Comm. July 46; Research Reader in History, Univ. of W. Australia 48; mem. Commonwealth Parl. as Liberal M.P. 49-69; Minister for Territories 51-63, of Defence Dec. 63-April 64, of External Affairs 64-69; Gov.-Gen. 69-74; Fellow, Royal Australian Historical Acad., Australian Acad. of the Humanities, Acad. of Social Sciences in Australia; K.St.J. Publs. *Into the Desert* 39, *Black Australians* 42 (2nd edn. 70), *Workshop of Security* 47, *The Government and the People, 1939-1945*, 2 vols. (Australian Official War History) 52, 69, *Native Welfare in Australia* 53, *Collected Verse* 70, *An Open Go* 72, *The Poet in Australia* 75, *A Time for Building* 76, *Australian Administration in Papua New Guinea* 76, *Mucking About, an Autobiography* 77, *Diplomatic Witness* 80, *The Office of Governor-General* 80, *Sir Robert Menzies* 80.
2 Adams Road, Dalkeith, W.A. 6009, Australia.

Hathi, Jaisukhlal; Indian lawyer and politician; b. 19 Jan. 1909, Muli, Gujarat; ed. legal training in Bombay.
District and Sessions Judge, Rajkot State; Chief Sec. to Govt. of Saurashtra State; mem. Constituent Assembly 46-47, Provisional Parl. 48-52, Rajya Sabha 52-57, 62-74, Leader 67-69, Deputy Parl. Leader of Congress Party 72-74; mem. Lok Sabha 57-62; Deputy Minister of Irrigation and Power 52-62; Minister of State for Labour 62; Minister of Supply 62-64; Minister of State in Ministry of Home Affairs 64-66; Minister of Defence Supplies 65-66; Minister of State for Defence 66-67; Minister of Labour and Rehabilitation 67-69; now Advocate, Supreme Court of India; Chair. Cttee. of Enquiry on Drugs and Pharmaceuticals, Govt. of India 72-74; Chair. Indian Drugs and Pharmaceuticals Ltd. 75-76; Gov. of Haryana 76-77, of Punjab 77-82; Chair. Nat. Lawyers' Forum; mem. Cttee. on Legal Aid, Govt. of India; Chair. Nat. Flood Comm.; Vice-Pres. Bharatiya Vidya Bhavan, Bombay; Pres. Gandharva Maha Vidyalaya; Trustee, Som Nath Temple Trust.
Publs. *Place of Indian States in Federation, Sidelights of Indian Princes.*
c/o Punjab Raj Bhavan, Chandigarh, India.
Telephone: 24461 (Office); 24400 (Home).

Hatoyama, Iichiro; Japanese politician; b. 11 Nov. 1918, Tokyo; *s.* of late Ichiro Hatoyama (Prime Minister of Japan, 1955-56); ed. Faculty of Law of Tokyo Imperial Univ.
Joined Ministry of Finance 41; served Imperial Navy 41-46; returned to Ministry of Finance 46, Deputy Dir.-Gen. of Budget Bureau 64-66; Deputy Vice-Minister for Admin., Econ. Planning Agency 66; Dir.-Gen. of Financial Bureau of Ministry of Finance 67, Dir.-Gen. of Budget Bureau 68-71, Vice-Minister of Finance 71-72; mem. House of Councillors 74-; Minister for Foreign Affairs 76-77.
7-1, Otowa 1-chome, Bunkyo-ku, Tokyo, Japan.

Hatsumara, Takiichiro; Japanese politician; b. 5 Nov. 1913, Nagasaki Pref.
Member House of Councillors 70-, Chair. Standing Cttee. on Agric., Forestry and Fisheries 73; Vice-Chair. Liberal Democratic Party Diet Policy Cttee. 76; Parl. Vice-Minister of Agric., Forestry and Fisheries 77; Minister of Labour Nov. 81-.
c/o Liberal-Democratic Party, 7, 2-chome, Hirakawacho, Chiyoda-ku, Tokyo, Japan.

Hawke, Robert (Bob) James Lee, A.C., B.A., LL.B., B.LITT.; Australian trade union executive; b. 9 Dec. 1929, Bordertown, S. Australia; ed. Univs. of Western Australia and Oxford.
Research Officer and Advocate, Australian Council of Trade Unions 58-70, Pres. 70-80; Senior Vice-Pres. Australian Labor Party 71-73, Pres. 73-78; mem. Board of Reserve Bank of Australia 73-; mem. Nat. Labour Consultative Council; mem. Governing Body ILO, Australian Population and Immigration Council 76-, Australian Manufacturing Council 77-; mem. Aust. Refugee Advisory Council 79-; mem. House of Reps. Oct. 80-.
c/o Australian Council of Trade Unions, 5th Floor, 254 La Trobe Street, Melbourne, Victoria 3000, Australia.

Hawley, Sir Donald (Frederick), K.C.M.G., M.B.E.; British diplomatist (retd.); b. 22 May 1921; ed. Radley, New College, Oxford.
H.M. Forces 41-43; Sudan Political Service and Sudan Judiciary 41-45; First Sec. Foreign Office 56; Politica Agent Trucial States in Dubai 58; Foreign Office 61; First Sec. and Head of Chancery, Cairo 62; Counsellor 65; Counsellor and Head of Chancery, Lagos 65; sabbatical year at Durham Univ. 67; Counsellor (Commercial), Baghdad 68; Consul-Gen., Muscat May 71; Amb. to Oman July 71-75; Assistant Under-Sec. of State, Foreign and Commonwealth Office 75-77; High Commissioner in Malaysia 77-81; Special Adviser Hongkong and Shanghai Banking Corpn.; Dir. Ewbank and Partners Ltd. (U.K.); Chair. Anglo-Omani Soc. 75-77, Vice-Pres. 81; mem. Council Reading Univ.
Publs. *Courtesies in the Trucial States* 65, *The Trucial States* 70, *Oman and its Renaissance* 77, *Courtesies in the Gulf Area* 78.
Little Cheverell House, nr. Devizes, Wilts., England.
Telephone: Lavington 3322.

Hayaishi, Osamu, M.D., PH.D.; Japanese biochemist; b. 8 Jan. 1920, Stockton, Calif., U.S.A.; ed. Osaka High School, Osaka Univ.
Assistant Prof., Dept. of Microbiology, Washington Univ. School of Medicine, St. Louis 52-54; Chief, Toxicology, Nat. Inst. of Arthritis and Metabolic Diseases, Nat. Insts. of Health, Bethesda 54-58; Prof. Medical Chem. Dept., Kyoto Univ. 58-, Molecular Biology Dept. of Inst. for Chem. Research 59-76; Chair. and Prof. Dept. of Biochem., School of Medicine, Osaka Univ. 61-63; Prof. Physiological Chem. and Nutrition Dept., Tokyo Univ. 70-74; Prof. Inst. of Scientific and Industrial Research, Osaka Univ. 75-76; mem. WHO Global Advisory Cttee. 78-, Scientific Council Int. Inst. of Cellular and Molecular Pathology (Belgium) 79-; Foreign Hon. mem. of American Acad. of Arts and Sciences 69; Foreign Assoc. U.S. Nat. Acad. of Arts and Sciences 72; mem. Japan Acad. of Sciences 74, Deutsche Akad. (Leopoldina) 78; Hon. mem. American Soc. of Biological Chemists 74; Fellow, New York Acad. of Sciences 76; Award of Japan Soc. of Vitaminology 64, Award of Matsunaga Science Foundation 64, Asahi Award for Science and Culture 65, Award of Japan Acad. of Sciences 67, of Fujiwara Science Foundation 75, Louis and Bert Freedman Foundation Award for Research in Biochemistry, New York Acad. of Science 76; Order of Culture 72; Bronze Medal (City of Paris) 75, CIBA Foundation Gold Medal 76, Jiménez Díaz Memorial Award (Spain) 79.
Publs. *Oxygenases* 62, *Molecular Mechanisms of Oxygen Activation* 74, *Molecular Oxygen in Biology* 74, and nearly 350 scientific reviews and articles.
Department of Medical Chemistry, Kyoto University Faculty of Medicine, Sakyo-ku, Kyoto 606; Home: 23 Kita-chanoki-cho, Shimogamo, Sakyo-ku, Kyoto, Japan.
Telephone: 075-751-2111 (Office); 075-781-1089 (Home).

Hayden, William George, B.ECONS.; Australian politician; b. 23 Jan. 1933, Brisbane, Queensland; ed. Brisbane State High School, Univ. of Queensland.
Police constable, Queensland 53-61; mem. Parl. for Oxley 61-; mem. Queensland Admin. Cttee, Australian Labor Party 65-; Parl. Spokesman on Health and Welfare 69-72; Minister of Social Security 72-75; Fed. Treas. June-Nov. 75; Parl. Spokesman on Defence and Econ. Man. 76-77;

Leader of Labor Party in Opposition Dec. 77-; mem. Select Cttee. on Pharmaceutical Benefits 70.
Parliament House, Canberra, A.C.T.; Home: 16 East Street, Ipswich, Queensland 4305, Australia.

He Changgong; Chinese politician; b. 1900, Huarong Cty., Hunan; ed. France.
Joined Chinese Youth Communist Party, France 22; mem. CCP 22-; mem. Jinggang mountains special cttee., Standing Cttee. of front cttee. 28; Party rep., 5th column 5th Army, Red Army, Pres. Red Army Academy, Commdr. Guangdong-Jiangxi Mil. Area Command 29-; on Long March; acting Minister of Heavy Industry, Vice-Minister of Geology after 49; currently Vice-Pres. Mil. Acad.; Vice-Chair. CPPCC Nat. Cttee. Sept. 80-.
People's Republic of China.

He Guangyou; Chinese army officer.
Major-General, Deputy Commdr. Guizhou Mil. District, People's Liberation Army 58, Commdr. 66-80; Vice-Chair. Guizhou Revolutionary Cttee. 67; Deputy Sec. CCP Guizhou 71; Deputy Cmmdr. PLA Lanzhou Units 80-.
People's Republic of China.

He Yixiang; Chinese army officer.
Took part in capture of Nanjing 49; mem. Presidium first Nanjing Party Congress 49; Chief of Staff, Shandong Mil. Dist. 53; Maj.-Gen. PLA Force in Zhejiang 63; Acting Dir., Nat. Defence Athletic Asscn. Zhejiang Provincial People's Council 64; Deputy Commdr. Zhejiang Mil. Dist. 65; Commdr. Shanghai Mil. Dist. 78-; Deputy Head Shanghai Group for People's Air Defence 78-.
People's Republic of China.

He Youfa; Chinese army officer.
Deputy Commdr. Jilin Mil. District, People's Liberation Army 67, Commdr. 68-; Vice-Chair. Jilin Revolutionary Cttee. 68; Sec. CCP Jilin 71.
People's Republic of China.

He Zhengwen; Chinese soldier.
Chief of Staff, Third Army Corps 49; Deputy Commdr. of Chengdu Mil. Region, PLA 55-74; Deputy Chief of Gen. Staff 74-.
People's Republic of China.

He Zhiyuan; Chinese soldier.
Political Commissar, Shandong Mil. District, PLA 74-.
People's Republic of China.

Heng Samrin; Kampuchean soldier and politician; b. 1934.
Joined CP of Cambodia 59, Battalion Commdr. and Regimental Chief in CP forces; Deputy Commdr. and Political Commissar E. Zone (Svay Rieng, Prey Veng and Kompong Cham Provs.) 77; mem. Exec. Cttee. CP of Kampuchea 77; Pres. Cen. Cttee. Ranakse Sangkroh Cheat Kampuchea (Kampuchean Nat. United Front for Nat. Salvation) and Pres. People's Revolutionary Council of Kampuchea (Head of State) Jan. 79-; Chair. State Council 81-; Sec.-Gen. People's Revolutionary Party Dec. 81-.
Office of the President, Phnom-Penh, People's Republic of Kampuchea.

Hewitt, Sir (Cyrus) Lenox (Simson), Kt., O.B.E., B.COMM., F.A.S.A., F.C.I.S., L.C.A.; Australian airline and business executive; b. 7 May 1917, St. Kilda, Vic.; ed. Scotch Coll., Melbourne, Melbourne Univ.
Worked with Broken Hill Proprietary Co. Ltd. 33-39; Asst. Sec. Commonwealth Prices Branch 39-46; Economist, Post War Construction Dept. 46-49; Official Sec. and Acting Deputy High Commr., London 50-53; Asst. Sec. Commonwealth Treasury 53-55; First Asst. Sec. (Budget and Accounting) 55-62, Deputy Sec. (Supply and Gen.) 62-66; Chair. Australian Univs. Comm. 67-68; Sec. to Prime Minister's Dept. 68-71, to Dept. of Vice-Pres. of Exec. Council 71, to Dept. of the Environment, Aborigines and the Arts 71-72, to Dept. of Minerals and Energy 72-75; Chair. Qantas Wentworth Holdings 75-80, Jetabout Ltd. 75-80, Orient Airlines Asscn. 77-78; Dir. East-Australia Pipeline Corpn. 73-75, Qantas Airways Ltd. 73-80, Chair. 75-80; Dir. Mary Kathleen Uranium 75-80; mem. Exec. Cttee. I.A.T.A. 75-80, Chair. 76-77; Chair. Pontello Constructions Pty. Ltd. 80-, Endeavour Resources Ltd. 82-; Adviser Ansett Transport Industries Ltd. 80-, Dir. 82-; Dir. Short Bros. (Australasia) Pty. Ltd. 80-, Aberfoyle Ltd. 80-, Santos Ltd. 80-82.
Ansett Transport Industries Limited, P.O. Box 33, Redfern, N.S.W. 2016; 9 Torres Street, Red Hill, A.C.T. 2603, Australia (Home).

Hibberd, Sir Donald James, Kt., O.B.E., B.ECON.; Australian company executive; b. 26 June 1916, Sydney; ed. Fort Street High School, Sydney Univ.
Commonwealth Dept. of Trade and Customs 39-46; Exec. Asst. Commonwealth Treasury 46-53; Dir. C.O.R. 49-51; mem. Australian Aluminium Producers Comm. 53-57; First Asst. Sec., Banking, Trade and Industry Branch of Commonwealth Treasury 53-57; Exec. Dir. Commonwealth Aluminium Corpn. 57-61; Man. Dir. Comalco Industries Pty. Ltd. 61-69, Chief Exec. 69-78, Chair. 69-80; Dir. G. E. Crane Holdings Ltd. 61-78, Conzinc Rio Tinto of Australia Ltd. 62-71; Vice-Chair. Queensland Alumina Ltd. 64-80; mem. Board, Reserve Bank of Australia 66-; mem. Melbourne Univ. Council 67-; Chair. New Zealand Aluminium Smelters Ltd. 69-80, Munich Reinsurance Co. of Australia 70-; Pres. Australian Mining Industry Council 72-73; Dir. Oil Co. of Aust. 79-.
193 Domain Road, South Yarra, Vic. 3141, Australia.

Hidayatullah, Mohammed, O.B.E., M.A.; Indian judge; b. 17 Dec. 1905; ed. Government High School, Raipur, Morris Coll., Nagpur, Trinity Coll., Cambridge, and Lincoln's Inn, London.
Advocate, Nagpur High Court 30-46; Advocate-Gen. C.P. and Berar 43-46; Puisne Judge 46-54; Dean of Faculty of Law, Nagpur Univ. 49-53; Chief Justice, Nagpur High Court 54-56; Chief Justice, Madhya Pradesh High Court 56-58; Judge, Supreme Court of India 58-68; Chief Justice of India 68-70; Acting Pres. of India 69, Vice-Pres. of India 79-; Chair. (formerly Speaker) Rajya Sabha; Hon. Bencher, Lincoln's Inn; Fellow, State Univ. of Buffalo, Univ. of New York; Hon. LL.D. (Univ. of the Philippines) 70, (Ravishankar Univ.) 70, (Rajasthan Univ.) 76, (Banaras Hindu Univ.) 80; Hon. D.Litt. (Bhopal Univ., Kakatiya Univ.); Silver Elephant and War Service Badge 47; Bronze Medal for Gallantry 69; Order of the Yugoslav Flags with Sash 71; Kt. of Mark Twain 75; Chief Scout for India.
Publs. *Democracy in India and the Judicial Process, The South-West Africa Case, Mulla's Mahomedan Law* (editor, 18th edn.), *A Judge's Miscellany* (two series), *U.S.A. and India* 77, *My Own Boswell* (memoirs).
Office of the Vice-President, 6 Maulana Azad Road, New Delhi; Home: 10 Janpath, New Delhi 110011, India.

Highet, Hon. (David) Allan; New Zealand businessman and politician; b. 27 May 1913, Dunedin; ed. Otago Boys' High School and Otago Univ.
Practised as chartered accountant, Wellington 42-60; Gen. Man. L. J. Fisher & Co. Ltd., Auckland 60-64; Senior Partner, Cox, Elliffe, Twomey, Highet & Co. (Chartered Accountants), Auckland 64-; Wellington City Councillor 54-59; mem. Parl. for Remuera 66-; Minister of Internal Affairs, of Local Govt., of Civil Defence and Assoc. Minister of Social Welfare 72, of Internal Affairs, of Local Govt., of Recreation and Sport, of Civil Defence, for the Arts Dec. 75-; Nat. Party.
28 Burwood Crescent, Remuera, Auckland, New Zealand.
Telephone: 549-507.

Hijikata, Takeshi; Japanese business executive; b. 18 March 1915, Ena City, Gifu Prefecture; ed. Tokyo Imperial Univ.
Joined Sumitomo Chemical Co. Ltd. 41, Dir. 71, Man. Dir. 73, Exec. Vice-Pres. 77, Pres. 77-; Chair. Mount Pleasant Chemical Co. Ltd.; Vice-Chair. Petrochemical Corpn. of Singapore (Pte.) Ltd.; Pres. Japan-Singapore Petrochemicals Co. Ltd.; Dir. Petrochemical Feedstock Importing Co. Ltd., Nihon Singapore Polyolefin Co. Ltd., Fuji Oil Co. Ltd., Seitetsu Kagaku Co. Ltd., Japan Cttee. for Econ. Devt., Japan Urea and Ammonium Sulphate Industry Asscn.; Exec. Dir. Fed. of Econ. Orgs. (*Keidanren*); Pres. Kansai Chem. Industry Asscn., Asscn. of Petrochemical Industry in Japan; Vice-Pres. Japan Chem. Industry Asscn.; Standing Dir. Kansai Econ. Fed.; Auditor Nihon Oxirane Co. Ltd.
Sumitomo Chemical Co. Ltd., 15, 5-chome, Kitahama, Higashi-ku, Osaka; 7-9, Nihonbashi 2-chome, Chuo-ku, Tokyo (Offices); 19-11, Miderigaoka 2-chome, Meguro-ku, Tokyo, Japan (Home).
Telephone: 06 (220) 3150 (Osaka office); 03 (278) 7005 (Tokyo office).

Hillary, Sir Edmund Percival, K.B.E.; New Zealand mountaineer and explorer; b. 20 July 1919; ed. Auckland Grammar School and Univ. of Auckland.
Went to Himalayas on N.Z. Garwhal expedition 51, when he and another were invited to join the British reconnaissance over Everest under Eric Shipton; took part in British expedition to Cho Oyu 52, and in British Mount Everest Expedition under Sir John Hunt 53, when he and Tenzing reached the summit on May 29th; Leader N.Z. Alpine Club Expedition to Barun Valley 54; N.Z. Antarctic Expedition 56-58, reached South Pole Dec. 57; Leader Himalayan Expeditions 61, 63, 64; Pres. Volunteer Service Abroad in New Zealand 63-64; built a hospital for Sherpa tribesmen, Nepal 66; has built 12 schools for Nepalese hillmen 60-70; Leader climbing expedition on Mount Herschel, Antarctica 67; River Ganges Expedition 77; Dir. Field Educ. Enterprises of Australasia Pty. Ltd.; Hubbard Metal 54; Polar Medal 58; R. M. Johnston Memorial Medal 59; Gurkha Right Hand (1st Class); Star of Nepal (1st Class); Hon. LL.D. Victoria Univ., British Columbia 69, Victoria Univ., Wellington 70; James Wattie Book of the Year Award (N.Z.) 75.
Publs. *High Adventure* 55, *The Crossing of Antarctica* (with Sir Vivian Fuchs) 58, *No Latitude for Error* 61, *High in the Thin Cold Air* (with Desmond Doig) 63, *Schoolhouse in the Clouds* 65, *Nothing Venture, Nothing Win* (autobiog.) 75, *From the Ocean to the Sky* 78.
278A Remuera Road, Auckland, New Zealand.

Hirahara, Tsuyoshi; Japanese diplomatist; b. 25 Oct. 1920, Kagoshima; ed. Tokyo Imperial Univ.
Military service 43-45; Attaché, Treaty Bureau, Ministry of Foreign Affairs 45-47; Sec. to Foreign Minister 47-48; Section Chief, Special Procurement Board 48-50; Sec. of Embassy, Belgium 50-52; Deputy Dir. Econ. Affairs Bureau, Ministry of Foreign Affairs 52-55, Dir. 59-61, Counsellor 61-64, Deputy Dir.-Gen. 69-70, Dir.-Gen. 70-72; Dir. Asian Section, UNESCO, Paris 55-59; Interpreter to H.I.M. the Emperor of Japan 60-64; Consul-Gen., Milan 64-66; Minister, Embassy in Belgium and Luxembourg 64-69; Amb. to Morocco 72-74, to OECD, Paris 74-80; Chair. OECD Exec. Cttee. 77-80; Amb. to U.K. 82-; Commdr., Ordre de la Couronne; Grand Officier, Ordre de Léopold II; Grand Officier, Ouissam Alaouite.
Japanese Embassy, 43 Grosvenor Street, London W1X 0BA, England.

Hiraizumi, Wataru; Japanese politician; b. 26 Nov. 1929; ed. Tokyo Univ., Univs. of Grenoble and Aix-Marseilles, Ecole Nat. de l'Admin., Paris.
Member of Foreign Service 51-64; mem. House of Councillors 65-76, House of Reps. 76-79, 80-; fmr. Parl. Vice-Minister of Science and Technology; Vice-Pres. Kajima Corpn. 70-71; State Minister, Dir.-Gen. of Science and Technology 71; mem. Exec Council, Liberal-Democratic Party 81-; Vice-Pres. Kajima Inst. for Int. Peace 65-.
Kajima Inst. for Int. Peace, Akasaka, 6-5-13, Minato, Tokyo (Office); 9-15, Harai-kata-matchi Shinjuku, Tokyo, Japan (Home).

Hirao, Teruo; Japanese economist and financial official; b. 23 Dec. 1925, Osaka; ed. Kyoto Univ.
Joined Ministry of Finance 51; IMF 67-70; Dir. Tax Bureau, Ministry of Finance 70-71; Counsellor Environmental Protection Agency 71-73; Dir. Securities Bureau 73-75; Dir.-Gen. Tohoku District Financial Bureau 75-76; Deputy Dir.-Gen. Minister's Secr. 76-77; Senior Deputy Dir.-Gen. Int. Finance Bureau 77-79; Exec. Dir. for Japan, IMF 79-.
International Monetary Fund, 700, 19th Street, N.W., Washington, D.C., 20431 U.S.A.
Telephone: (202) 477-3345.

Hirata, Kusuo; Japanese business executive; b. 7 Sept. 1909, Ooita; ed. Kwansei Gakuin Univ.
With Daicel Ltd. 33-34; joined Fuji Photo Film Co. Ltd. 34, Man. Finance Dept. 50-62, Dir. 54-64, Man. Planning Div. 62-66, Man. Dir. 64-69, Man. Sales Div. 66-71; Senior Man. Dir. 69-71, Pres. 71-80, Chair. 80-; Blue Ribbon Medal 74; Order of the Sacred Treasure 79.
Fuji Photo Film Co. Ltd. 26-30, Nishiazabu 2-chome, Minato-ku, Tokyo; Home: 48-12, Utsukushigaoka 2-chome, Midori-ku, Yokohama-shi, Kanagawa, Japan.
Telephone: 03-406-2111 (Office); 045-901-1771 (Home).

Hiratsuka, Masunori, M.A., LITT.D.; Japanese educationist; b. 1907; ed. Tokyo Imperial Univ.
Lecturer, Aoyama Gakuin Theological School 31-36, Ferris Seminary 32-36, St. Paul Univ. 36-39, Hiroshima Higher Normal School 39-40, Prof. 40-44; Prof. Faculty of Letters, Kyushu Imperial Univ. 44-49, Faculty of Educ. 49-63, leave of absence 60, Dean of Faculty of Educ. 54-56, Dir. Research Inst. of Educ. and Culture 56-63; Dir. Dept. of Educ., UNESCO, Paris 60, Prof. 56-63, Emer. 64-; Dir.-Gen. Nat. Inst. for Educational Research 63-; mem. Cen. Advisory Council on Educ., Council on Social Educ., Japan Educ. Soc. (Gov. of Board), Japan Educ. Philosophy Soc., Japan Educ. History Soc.; Chair. World Council of Comparative Educ. Socs., Japan Comparative Educ. Soc.; Gov. Board of Nat. Educ. Hall; Dir.-Gen. Nat. Inst. for Educational Research; Pres. Japanese Nat. Comm. for UNESCO 72-; Chair. Emer. Baiko Women's Univ.; Commdr. Palmes Académiques (France) 61.
Publs. *The Educational Thought of the Old Testament* 35 and 57, *History of Education in Japan* 38, *History of Modern Education in China* 44, *Future of Japan and Moral Education* 59, *Future of Japanese Education* 64.
Kokuritsu Kyoiku Kenkyusho (NIER), 6-5-22 Shimomeguro, Meguro-ku, Tokyo (Office); 1-5-44 Takanawa, Minato-ku, Tokyo, Japan (Home).
Telephone: 714-0111 (Office); 441-7630 (Home).

Hiro, Keitaro; Japanese business executive; b. 7 Dec. 1908, Hyogo; ed. Ritsumeikan Univ.
Teacher, Ohkura Commercial High School 38-43; Chief, Accounting Dept., Kubota Ltd. 46, Man. Financial Dept. 50, Dir. Financing 51, Man. Dir. 53, Senior Man. Dir. 60, Pres. 71-; Co-Chair. Kansai Cttee. for Econ. Devt. (Osaka) 79-; Dir. Japan Productivity Asscn. 61, Osaka Industrialist Asscn. 61, Kansai Management Asscn. 61; Blue Ribbon Medal.
Kubota Ltd., 2-47, Shikitsuhigashi, 1-chome, Naniwa-ku,

Osaka; Home: 15-32, Takakura-cho, Nishinomiya City, Hyogo, Japan.
Telephone: 06-648-2111 (Office); 0798-22-3191 (Home).

Hirohito, Emperor of Japan; b. 29 April 1901.
Son of Emperor Taishô, married Princess Nagako Kuni 24; Regent 21-26; succeeded 26; heir H.I.H. Crown Prince Akihito (Tsugunomiya), b. 33, married Michiko Shoda 59; Fellow Royal Soc. (U.K.) 71.
Publs. Nine books on plant and marine biology.
The Imperial Palace, Tokyo, Japan.

Hirooka, Tomoo; Japanese newspaper publishing executive; b. 24 Aug. 1907, Hyogo Prefecture; ed. Univ. of Tokyo.
Joined *Asahi Shimbun* newspaper 32, Editorial Writer 42, Econ. Editor 48, Man. Editor 54, Dir. 56, Rep. of Seibu Main Office 60, Rep. Dir., Man. Dir. 64, Pres. 67, Chair. of the Bd. 77-; Pres. of Nihon Shimbun Kyokai (Japanese Newspapers Publishers Asscn.) 75-79.
c/o The Asahi Shimbun, 3-2, Tsukiji 5-chome, Chuo-ku, Tokyo 100, Japan.
Telephone: 03 (212) 0131.

Hirose, Sinichi, B.L.; Japanese business executive; b. 25 Jan. 1927; ed. Tokyo Imperial Univ.
Joined Ministry of Transport, Vice-Minister of Transport 64; joined Nippon Express Co., Ltd., Senior Man. Dir. 68, Exec. Vice-Pres. 72-76, Pres. 76-; mem. Cttee. of Overall Nat. Land Devt. Council 75-; Dir. Japanese Fed. of Employers' Asscn. and of Fed. of Econ. Orgs. 75-; Chair. Int. Air Freight Asscn. of Japan 77.
3-12-9, Soto-Kanda, Chiyoda-ku, Tokyo (Office); 1-29-12, Amanuma, Suginami-ku, Tokyo, Japan (Home).

Hitam, Datuk Musa; Malaysian politician; b. 1934, Johore; ed. Univ. of Malaya and Univ. of Sussex, England.
Associate Sec., Int. Students Conf., Leiden, the Netherlands 57-59; Political Sec. to Minister of Transport 64; Minister of Primary Industries 71-78, of Education 78-81; Deputy Prime Minister and Minister of Home Affairs July 81-; Deputy Pres. UMNO 81-; Chair. Exec. Cttee. of Gen. Council of Commonwealth Parl. Asscn. (CPA) 76-79.
Office of the Deputy Prime Minister, Kuala Lumpur, Malaysia.

Holland, Eric Sidney Fostyn; New Zealand politician and business executive; b. 28 June 1921, Christchurch; *s.* of the late Sir Sidney Holland (fmr. Prime Minister of New Zealand); ed. Elmwood School, St. Andrew's Coll. and Canterbury Univ. Coll.
Member of Parl. 67-; Minister of Housing, Minister in Charge of State Advances Corpn. and Assoc. Minister of Labour Feb.-Nov. 72; Minister of Energy Resources, Electricity and Mines 75-77, of Housing and Minister in charge of Public Trust Office 77-78; National Party.
7 Moorpark Place, Christchurch, New Zealand.
Telephone: 749-199 (Parliament); 556-611 (Home).

Holyoake, Rt. Hon. Sir Keith (Jacka), K.G., P.C., G.C.M.G., C.H.; New Zealand politician and farmer; b. 11 Fed. 1904. Pahiatua; ed. Tauranga, Hastings, Motueka.
Nelson Provincial Pres. Farmers' Union 30-41; Pres. N.Z. Hop Marketing Cttee. 38-41; Dominion Vice-Pres. Farmers' Union 40-50; mem. Dominion Exec. Farmers' Union 40-50; mem. N.Z. Tobacco Growers' Fed. and N.Z. Fruit Exporters' Asscn.; M.P. 32-77; Deputy Leader of Opposition 47; Deputy Prime Minister and Minister of Agriculture 49-57; Prime Minister and Minister for Maori Affairs Sept.-Dec. 57; Leader of Opposition 57-60; Prime Minister 60-Feb. 72, Minister of Foreign Affairs 60-Nov. 72, of State 75-77; Gov.-Gen. Oct. 77-80; N.Z. rep. at Farmers' World Conf., London 46; Chair. Gen. Council FAO 55; Nat. Party; Hon. LL.D. (Victoria Univ., N.Z.) 66, Hon. LL.D. (Agric.) (Seoul Nat. Univ.) 68; Hon. Freeman City of London.
52 Aurora Terrace, Wellington, New Zealand.

Hon Sui Sen; Singapore politician; b. 16 April 1916, Penang; ed. St. Xavier's Inst., Penang, and Raffles Coll., Singapore (now Univ. of Singapore).
Joined Straits Settlements Civil Service 39, subsequently transferred to Singapore Admin. Service; Perm. Sec., Office of the Prime Minister and Perm. Sec., Econ. Devt. Div., Ministry of Finance 59-61; Chair. Econ. Devt. Board 61; Chair. and Pres. Devt. Bank of Singapore Ltd. 68; mem. Parl. April 70-; Minister for Finance 70-; Meritorious Service Medal 62, Malaysia Medal 64, Distinguished Service Order 67; Hon. D.Litt. (Univ. of Singapore) 69.
Ministry of Finance, 40th Floor, CPF Building, 79 Robinson Road, Singapore 0106; 35 Malcolm Road, Singapore 1130, Singapore.

Honda, Chikao; Japanese newspaper executive; b. 1899; ed. Waseda University.
Joined *Osaka Mainichi* 24, Editor-in-Chief 45-48; Pres. Mainichi Newspapers 48-; fmr. Pres. Japanese Newspaper Publishers' and Editors' Asscn. (Nihon Shimbun Kyokai).
126 Hara-machi, Bunkyo-ku, Tokyo, Japan.

Honda, Soichiro; Japanese business executive; b. 17 Nov. 1906.
Garage apprentice 23, opened own garage 28; Owner and Head, Piston Ring Production Factory 34; started producing motor cycles 48; Pres. Honda Motor Co. until 73, Dir. and Supreme Adviser 73-; Founder, Honda Foundation 77; Foreign mem. Royal Swedish Acad. of Eng. Science 80; Hon. D.Eng. (Michigan Tech. Univ.) 74; Hon. D.Hum.Litt (Ohio State Univ.) 79; Mercurio D'Oro Prize 71.
Honda Motor Company, 27-8, 6-chome, Jingumae Shibuya-ku, Tokyo 150; Wel Building, 1-13-8, Ginza Chuo-ku, Tokyo 104; 4-10-13, Nishiochiai Shinjuku-ku, Tokyo 161, Japan.

Hongskula, Air Chief Marshal Harin; Thai air force officer (retd.) and government official; b. 29 Aug. 1914, Bangkok; ed. Mil. Cadet Acad., Flying Training School, School of Air Navigation (U.K.), School of Air Navigation (U.S.A.), Mil. Staff Coll., R.A.F. Staff Coll. (U.K.), Nat. Defence Coll.
Director of Intelligence, Royal Thai Air Force; Air Attaché, Royal Thai Embassy, London; Dir.-Gen. of Educ. and Training, R.T.A.F.; Deputy C.-in-C., R.T.A.F.; mem. Constituent Assembly; mem. Senate; mem. Senate Cttee. for Foreign Affairs, Senate Cttee. for Communications; fmr. mem. and Pres. Nat. Admin. Reform Assembly 76-77; mem. and Pres. Nat. Legislative Assembly 77-79; mem. and Pres. Senate and Pres. Nat. Assembly 79-; lectured in many colls. and insts.; Hon. Command Pilot, U.S.A.F.; Hon. Pilot, Air Force of Repub. of China; Assoc., Royal Aeronautical Soc. (U.K.); Hon. Ph.D. (Political Sciences).
Publs. *Strategic Bombing, Deterrence, Limited War, General War, Parliament and National Security*, etc.
National Assembly, Parliament Building, U-Thong Nai Road, Bangkok; Home: Swangjitt House, 1B Baholyothin Road, Donmuang, Bangkok, Thailand.

Hope, Alec Derwent, A.C., O.B.E., F.A.H.A.; Australian poet; b. 21 July 1907; ed. Sydney and Oxford Univs.
Former Lecturer Sydney Teachers' Coll. and Senior Lecturer Melbourne Univ.; Prof. of English Canberra Univ. Coll. 50-60, Australian Nat. Univ. 60-68; Library Fellow, Australian Nat. Univ. 69-72 (retd.); Arts Council Prize 65, Britannica-Australia Award 66, Levinson Prize for Poetry 69, Ingram Merrill Award 69, Robert Frost Award 76; Hon. D.Litt. (Australian Nat. Univ.) 72, (Univ. of New England) 73, (Monash Univ.) 76, (Melbourne Univ.) 76.
Publs. *The Wandering Islands* 55, *Poems* 60, *The Cave and the Spring* 65, *New Poems* 69, *A Mid-summer Eve's Dream* 70, *Dunciad Minor* 70, *Collected Poems 1930–1970* 72, *Native Companions* 73, *A Late Picking* 75, *A Book of*

Answers 78, *The Pack of Autolycus* 79, *The New Cratylus* 79, *The Drifting Continent* 79, *Antechinus* 81, *The Tragical History of Dr. Faustus. . . Purged and Amended* 82; verse and criticism in numerous magazines, including *Meanjin*, *Southerly*, *M.U.M.*, *Hermes*, *Quadrant*, *The Hudson Review*, *The Southern Review* and *Australian Literary Studies*.
66 Arthur Circle, Canberra, A.C.T., Australia.
Telephone: Canberra 95-1525.

Hossain, Kemaluddin, B.A., LL.B.; Bangladeshi judge; b. 31 March 1923, Calcutta, India; ed. Ballygunge Govt. High School, Calcutta, St. Xavier's Coll. and Calcutta Univ. Law Coll.
Advocate, High Court, Dacca 50-69; Sr. Advocate Supreme Court, Pakistan 66-69; Deputy Attorney-Gen., Pakistan 68-69; Judge, High Court, Dacca 69-72; Judge, High Court, Bangladesh 72-75, Appellate Div. 75-78; Chief Justice, Bangladesh 78-; Negotiator, Indus Water Treaty 60; part-time law lecturer, City Law Coll., Dacca 56-68; Chair. Law Cttee. 78; attended several int. law confs. incl. Commonwealth Chief Justices Conf., Canberra May 80.
Chief Justice's House, 19 Hare Road, Dacca, Bangladesh.
Telephone: 243585 (Office); 404849 (Home).

Howard, John Winston, LL.B.; Australian politician; b. 26 July 1939, Earlwood, N.S.W. ed. Earlwood Primary School, Canterbury Boys' High Sch ol, Sydney Univ.
Practised as a solicitor in Sydney 61-74; mem. for Bennelong, House of Reps. May 74-; Shadow Minister for Consumer Affairs and Commerce March-Nov. 75; Minister for Business and Consumer Affairs 75-77; Minister Assisting the Prime Minister May-Nov. 77; Minister for Special Trade Negotiations July-Nov. 77; Treas. Nov. 77-.
Commonwealth Parliamentary Offices, 5 Martin Place, Sydney, N.S.W. 2000; Parliament House, Canberra, A.C.T. 2600; Home: 19 Milner Crescent, Wollstonecroft, N.S.W., Australia.

Hsiung Shih-i; Chinese author; b. 14 Oct. 1902; ed. Teachers' Coll., Nat. Univ. Beijing.
Associate Man. Zhen Guang Theatre, Beijing 22; Prof. Agricultural Coll., Nanchang 23; Editor, Commercial Press, Shanghai 26, Special Editor 28; Prof. Zhong Shan Univ., Nanchang 27; Man. Dir. Pantheon Theatres Ltd., Shanghai 29; Prof. Min Guo Univ., Beijing 30; Sec. China Soc., London 33, Hon. Sec. 35; Chinese del. to Int. PEN Congress 34, 35, 38, 39, 40, 47, to Int. Theatre Inst. Congress 48; lecturer, Cambridge Univ. 50-53; Dean, Coll. of Arts, Nanyang Univ. 54-55; Man. Dir. Pacific Films Co. Ltd., Hong Kong 55-; Chair. Board of Dirs. Standard Publishers Ltd., Hong Kong 61-; Pres. Tsing Hua Coll., Hong Kong 63-; Hon. Ph.D.
Publs. in English: *Lady Precious Stream* 34, *The Romance of Western Chamber* 35, *The Professor from Peking* 39, *The Bridge of Heaven* 43, *The Life of Chiang Kai-shek* 48, *The Gate of Peace* 49, *The Story of Lady Precious Stream* 50, *Book of Chinese Proverbs* 53, *Memoirs* (Vols. I and II) 78; trans. into Chinese of B. Franklin's *Autobiography* 23, of Barrie's and Shaw's plays, and Hardy's novels 26-33.
20 Aberdare Gardens, London, N.W.6, England; Tsing Hua College, Kowloon, Hong Kong; 101 Crespi Drive, San Francisco, Calif. 94132, U.S.A.

Hsu Ching-chung, DR.AGRIC.; Chinese politician; b. 19 July 1907, Taipei; ed. Taihoku Imperial Univ.
Professor, Nat. Taiwan Univ. 45-47; Dir. Agricultural and Forestry Admin., Taiwan Provincial Govt. 47-49; Commr. Dept. of Agriculture and Forestry, Taiwan Provincial Govt. 49-54, Commr. 54-57; mem. Cen. Planning and Evaluation Cttee., China Nationalist Party 55-61, Deputy Sec.-Gen. Cen. Cttee. 61-66, now mem. Cen. Standing Cttee. (CSC); Minister of the Interior 66-72; Vice-Premier of Exec. Yuan 72-81; mem. Standing Cttee., Taiwan Land Bank 46-67, China Farmers' Bank 67-72; Medal of Clouds and Banner.
Publs. several studies on agricultural problems in Taiwan.
30, Lane 63, Liang Ning Street, Taipei, Taiwan.
Telephone: 772957.

Hu Bingyun; Chinese army officer.
Cadre 6th Co. Red 4th Regt. 8th Route Army 35; took part in Long March 35; Maj.-Gen. PLA Units in Lanzhou 59; Vice-Commdr. PLA Lanzhou Mil. Region 60; Commdr. PLA Shaanxi Mil. Dist. 64-; Vice-Chair., Shaanxi Prov. People's Congress 79-; Sec. Shaanxi CCP Cttee.
People's Republic of China.

Hu Qiaomu; Chinese party official; b. 1912, Yancheng, Jiangsu Province.
Joined CCP 35; Secretary to Mao Zedong, Sec. of Political Bureau of Party Cen. Cttee. after 41; Dir. Xinhua News Agency 48; Dir. Press Admin. 49; Deputy Head Propaganda Dept. CCP Cen. Cttee. 50; Deputy Sec.-Gen. CCP Cen. Cttee. 54; alt. mem. Secretariat, Party Cen. Cttee. 56; helped draft Constitution of the People's Republic of China 54; co-edited *The Selected Works of Mao Zedong*; mem. Del. of CCP to the Soviet Union 56, 57, 60; Pres. Chinese Acad. of Social Sciences 77-; mem. 8th and 11th Central Cttees. of CCP.
Publ. *The 30 Years of the Communist Party of China*.
Chinese Academy of Social Sciences, 5 Jianguomen Nei Da Jie, Beijing, People's Republic of China.

Hu Shangli; Chinese politician.
Political Commissar Henan Mil. Dist. 78-, Sec. Henan Provincial CCP Cttee. 78-, Vice Chair. Henan Revolutionary Cttee. 78-.
People's Republic of China.

Hu Wei; Chinese army officer.
Deputy Commdr., Shanxi People's Liberation Army 67; Vice-Chair. Shaanxi Provincial Revolutionary Cttee. 68; Alt. mem. 9th Central Cttee. of CCP 69, 10th Cen. Cttee. of CCP 73; Deputy Chief of Gen. Staff, PLA 74.
People's Republic of China.

Hu Yaobang; Chinese party official; b. 1915, Liuyang City, Hunan.
Joined CCP 33; Head Communist Youth League's Org. Dept. 35; mem. Cen. Cttee. Communist Y.L. 36; Head Pol. Dept. 2nd Field Army 48; Vice-Chair. Taiyuan Mil. Control Comm. 49; mem. Cen. Cttee. Communist Youth League 49; mem. Exec. Board Sino-Soviet Friendship Asscn. 49-54; Head Pol. Dept. 18th Corps 2nd Field Army 49; Dir., N. Sichuan People's Admin. Office 50; Head NSPAO Finance and Econs. Cttee. 50; Pol. Commissar N. Sichuan Mil. Dist. 50; mem. S.W. Mil. and Admin. Cttee. 50-52; Head, New Dem. Youth League 52; Sec. New Dem. Youth League 53; First Sec. Communist Youth League 57; mem. Nat. Cttee. of the All-China Fed. of Dem. Youth 53-58; Vice-Chair. World Fed. of Dem. Youth 53-59; mem. Standing Cttee. 1st NPC 54-59 (re-elected 2nd NPC 59, 3rd NPC 64); mem. Exec. Cttee. All-China Fed. of Trades Unions 53-57; mem. Cen. Work Cttee. for the Popularization of Standard Spoken Chinese 56; Vice-Chair. Nat. Asscn. for the Elimination of Illiteracy 56; mem. 8th Cen. Cttee. CCP 56-67; Acting First Sec. Shaanxi CCP Cttee. 65; mem. 11th Cen. Cttee. CCP 77-; mem. Politburo CCP Cen. Cttee. 78-; Sec.-Gen. CCP Cen. Cttee. 78-81; Dir. Propaganda Dept. CCP Cen. Cttee. 78-81; 3rd Sec. Cen. Comm. for Inspecting Discipline 78-81; Sec.-Gen., Secretariat, Cen. Cttee. 80-81; Chair. 11th Cen. Cttee. June 81-.
Central Committee, Zhongguo Gongchan Dang, Beijing, People's Republic of China.

Hua Guofeng; Chinese politician; b. 1920, Shanxi.
Vice-Governor of Hunan 58-67; Sec. CCP Hunan 59; Vice-Chair. Hunan Revolutionary Cttee. 68, Chair. 70; mem. 9th Cen. Cttee. of CCP 69; First Sec. CCP Hunan 70-77;

Political Commissar Guangzhou Mil. Region, People's Liberation Army 72; First Political Commissar Hunan Mil. District, PLA 73; mem. Politburo, 10th Cen. Cttee. of CCP 73, First Vice-Chair. Cen. Cttee. April-Oct. 76, Chair. 76-81; Minister of Public Security 75-76; Vice-Premier, State Council 75-76 and 81, Acting Premier Feb.-April 76, Premier 76-81; Chair. Mil. Affairs Comm. 76-81; Chair. and mem. Politburo, 11th Cen. Cttee. CCP 77-81, Vice-Chair. 81-; Exec. Chair. Presidium, 5th NPC.
c/o State Council, Beijing, People's Republic of China.

Huang Chieh; Chinese civil servant; b. 2 Nov. 1903, Hunan Province; ed. Mil. Acad., Army War Coll. and Nat. Defence Coll.
Commandant, Cen. Training Corps 45-48; Vice-Minister of Nat. Defence 48-49; Gov. of Hunan, concurrently Commdg. Gen. 1st Army 49; Commdg. Gen. Chinese Troops stationed in Indo-China 49-53; Taipei Garrison Command 53-54; C.-in-C. Chinese Army 54-57; Personal Chief of Staff to the Pres. 57-58; C.-in-C. Taiwan Garrison Gen. H.Q. 58-62; Gov. Taiwan Province 62-69; Minister of Nat. Defence 69-72; Gen. Special Adviser to Pres. on Mil. Strategy 72-; numerous decorations from China, U.S.A., Thailand, Philippines, Spain, Iran, Iraq, Korea and Venezuela.
297 Fu Hsin South Road, Section 1, Taipei, Taiwan.

Huang Hou; Chinese army officer.
Commander Inner Mongolia Autonomous Region Mil. District 80-.
People's Republic of China.

Huang Hua; Chinese diplomatist and politician; b. 1910; ed. Yanqing Univ., Beijing.
Student leader in Beijing, active in December 9th Movt. 35; Councillor, Ministry of Foreign Affairs 53; Chief Chinese del. at Panmunjon 53; Amb. to Ghana 60-66, to Egypt 66-70, to Canada April-Nov. 71; Perm. Rep. to UN 71-76; Minister of Foreign Affairs Dec. 76-; a Vice-Premier, State Council 80-82; mem. 11th Cen. Cttee. CCP 77.
Ministry of Foreign Affairs, Beijing, People's Republic of China.

Huang Huoqing; Chinese politician; b. Hebei.
Section Chief Social Affairs Dept. and concurrently Dir., Labor Dept. CCP Cen. Cttee. 26; mem. Board of Dirs. Sino-Soviet Friendship Asscn. 49-54; mem. Tianjin Fed. of Trades Unions 49-53; mem. Standing Cttee. All-China Fed. of Trades Unions 52; Chair. Tianjin Fed. of Trades Unions 53-55; Acting Sec. CCP Tianjin Municipal Cttee. 52-53; Sec. CCP Tianjin Municipal Cttee. 53-58 (office renamed that of First Sec. 55); mem. Exec. Cttee. All-China Fed. of Trades Unions 53-57; Chair. Tianjin Municipal CPPCC Cttee. 53-58; mem. Standing Cttee. 1st NPC 54-59; Mayor of Tianjin 55-58; Alt. mem. CCP 8th Cen. Cttee. 56; First Sec. Liaoning Prov. CCP Cttee. 58-67; First Pol. Commissar N.E. Bureau Liaoning 61; Sec., Secr., N.E. Bureau CCP Cen. Cttee. 61; Chief Procurator of Supreme People's Procuratorate 78-82; Dep. Liaoning, 5th NPC 78; mem. 11th Cen. Cttee. CCP 79.
People's Republic of China.

Huang Jingkun; Chinese army officer.
Commander Jiangsu Mil. District 80-.
People's Republic of China.

Huang Jingyao; Chinese army officer.
Deputy Commdr. Heilongjiang Mil. District, People's Liberation Army 59; Commdr. Shaanxi Mil. District, PLA 67-; Vice-Chair. Shaanxi Revolutionary Cttee. 68; Sec. CCP Shaanxi 71; Commdr. Ningxia Mil. District, Deputy Cmmdr. Lanzhou Mil. Region, PLA 78; Sec. Ningxia Regional CCP Cttee. 78.
People's Republic of China.

Huang Oudong; Chinese party official; b. *circa* 1907, Pingxiang, Jiangxi.
Regimental Commdr. 129th Div. 39, Brigade Commdr. 45; Gov. of Liaoning 49-55, 58-68; Mayor of Shenyang 52-54; Sec. CCP Liaoning 54-57, First Sec. 57-58, Second Sec. 58-68; Alt. mem. 8th Cen. Cttee. of CCP 56; Sec. N.E. Bureau, CCP 62-68; criticized and removed from office during Cultural Revolution 68; Vice-Chair. Liaoning Revolutionary Cttee. 73; Sec. CCP Liaoning 73-; mem. 11th Cen. Cttee. CCP 77; Second (formerly Third) Sec., Liaoning Prov. Cttee. 80-; Second Sec., Tianyin Municipal Cttee. 80-; Chair. Liaoning People's Congress 80-.
People's Republic of China.

Huang Shao-ku; Chinese government official; b. 9 June 1901; ed. National Peiping Normal Univ.
Secretary-General of Exec. Yuan 49-54; Vice-Premier, Exec. Yuan 54-58, 66-69; Minister of Foreign Affairs 58-60; Amb. to Spain 60-62; Sec.-Gen. Nat. Security Council 67-79; Senior Adviser to the Pres. 76-; Pres. Judicial Yuan 79-.
10, Lane 85, Sungkiang Road, Taipei, Taiwan.

Huang Zhen; Chinese diplomatist and politician; b. 1909.
Deputy Dir. 18th Div., Shanxi-Hebei-Shandong Border Region Army 44; after war Deputy Political Dir. in mil. admin. areas; Amb. to People's Republic of Hungary 50-54; Amb. to Republic of Indonesia 54-61; Deputy Foreign Minister 61-64; Amb. to France 64-73; Head Liaison Office, Washington, D.C. 73-77; Minister of Culture 77-81, in charge of Comm. for Cultural Relations with Foreign Countries March 81-; Deputy Head of CCP Propaganda Dept. Dec. 77-; mem. 11th Cen. Cttee. CCP 77; Rep. for Lit. and Art Circle 5th CPPCC 78; mem. Presidium and Standing Cttee. 5th CPPCC 78-; rep. at the Afro-Asian Congress 55; Golden Eagle Medal (Philippines) 81.
People's Republic of China.

Hujio, Masayuki; Japanese politician; b. 1 Jan. 1917, Tokyo; ed. Sophia Univ., Tokyo.
With newspaper *Yomiuri Shimbun* 41; mem. House of Reps. 63-; Parliamentary Vice-Minister of Int. Trade and Industry 68-69, of Construction 71-72; Chair. House of Reps. Standing Cttee. on Cabinet 75-76, on Educ. 76-77; Vice-Chair. Liberal-Democratic Party Policy Affairs Research Council 79; Minister of Labour 80-81.
c/o Liberal-Democratic Party, 7, 2-chome, Hirakawacho, Chiyoda-ku, Tokyo, Japan.

Hun Sen; Kampuchean politician; b. 1952.
Joined army 70; Co. Commdr. 73, Regimental Commdr. 76; Minister of Foreign Affairs Jan. 79-, also Vice-Premier, mem. Cen. Cttee., People's Revolutionary Party, mem. Politburo.
Ministry of Foreign Affairs, Phnom-Penh, People's Republic of Kampuchea.

Hunt, Ralph James Dunnet; Australian politician; b. 31 March 1928, Narrabri, N.S.W.; ed. Scots Coll., Sydney.
Grazier, farmer, merino stud breeder; mem. Cen. Council of Australian Country Party (ACP) 53-, Cen. Exec. of ACP 60-, Fed. Exec. 64-; Chair. Gwydir Electorate Council, ACP 53-69; Chair. of ACP in N.S.W. 69; Fed. Chair. of ACP in N.S.W. 69; mem. for Gwydir, N.S.W., House of Reps. 69-; Minister of the Interior 71-72; mem. House of Reps. Select Cttee. on Aboriginal Affairs 72-73; Minister for Health 75-79; Minister for Transport Dec. 79-, and Construction 82-.
Parliament House, Canberra, A.C.T. 2600; Home: 1 Merindah Avenue, Moree, N.S.W. 2400, Australia.

Huo Shilian; Chinese politician; b. 1911, Shaanxi.
Vice-Gov. Zhejiang 54-68, Sec. CCP Zhejiang 57-66, First Sec. CCP Shaanxi 66-68; removed from office during Cultural Revolution 67; Sec. CCP Ningxia 73; First Sec. CCP Ningxia 77-80; Chair. Ningxia Hui Revolutionary Cttee. 77-79; mem. 11th Cen. Cttee. CCP 77; First Political Commissar, Ningxia Mil. District, PLA 78-80; Minister of

Agriculture 79-81; First Sec. CCP, Shanxi Prov. 81-; First Political Commissar, Shanxi Mil. District 81-.
c/o State Council, Beijing, People's Republic of China.

Huq, Muhammad Shamsul, M.A.; Bangladesh politician; b. 2 Dec. 1910, Comilla; ed. Univ. of Calcutta, Dacca and London.
Chairman, Cttee. on Int. Co-operation apptd. by Commonwealth Educ. Conf., New Delhi 62; Vice-Chancellor, Rajshahi Univ. 65-69; Minister for Educ., Scientific and Technological Research of former Pakistan 69-70; led Del. 25th Anniversary of ECOSOC, Geneva, and Del. Gen. Conf. of ECOSOC, Paris 70; mem. UNESCO Int. Experts Cttee. on Formulation of Policy of Training Abroad, Paris 70; Fellow Woodrow Wilson Int. Center for Scholars, Smithsonian Inst., Washington, D.C. 71-73; Vice-Chancellor Dacca Univ. 75-76; led del. to UN Gen. Assembly Conf. of Foreign Ministers of Non-Aligned Nations 77, 78, 79, 80, 81; Islamic Foreign Ministers' Conf. 77, 78, 79, 80; active in int. negotiations such as Ganges Waters Agreement with India 77; Chair. Planning Cttee. Social Science Research Council 77-; mem. Pres.'s Council of Advisers in charge of Ministry of Foreign Affairs 77-78; Minister of Foreign Affairs 78-82; mem. Advisory Council (Martial Law Admin.) in charge of Ministry of Health and Population Control April 82-; Scholar-in-Residence Inst. Advanced Projects, East-West Cen., Honolulu 63-64; B.B. Gold Medal, Univ. of Calcutta 33.
Publs. several books on education.
10 Eskatan Garden Road, Dacca 2, Bangladesh.
Telephone: 405050.

Husain, Maqbool Fida; Indian painter; b. 17 Sept. 1915.
Joined Progressive Artists Group, Bombay 48; first one-man exhbn., Bombay 50, later at Rome, Frankfurt, London, Zürich, Prague, Tokyo, New York, New Delhi, Calcutta, Kabul and Baghdad; mem. Lalit Kala Akademi, New Delhi 54; mem. Gen. Council Nat. Academy of Art, New Delhi 55; First Nat. Award for Painting 55; Int. Award, Biennale Tokyo 59.
Major works: Murals for Air India Int. at Hong Kong, Bangkok, Zürich and Prague 57, and WHO Building, New Delhi 63; Mural in Mosaic for Lever Bros. and Aligarh Univ. 64; working on High Ceramic Mural for Indian Govt. Building, New Delhi; Exhibitor "Art now in India" exhbn., London 67.
Film: *Through the Eyes of the Painter* 67 (Golden Bear Award, Berlin 67).
Publs. *Husain's Letters* 62, *Husain* 71, *Poetry to be seen* 72, *Triangles* 76.
6 Zeenat Manzil L. Jamshedji Road, Mahim, Bombay 16, India.

Hussain, Mohamed Mustafa; Maldivian politician; b. 1948; ed. Armidale Coll. of Advanced Education, Australia.
Taught Majeediyya School, Malé, Maldive Islands 74; Dir. Radio Maldives 74; Under-Sec. Dept. of Education 75; Under-Sec. Dept. of Home Affairs in charge of Atolls Div. 76; Under-Sec. in charge of Foreign Investments Div. of Dept. of External Affairs 76; Counsellor to Maldives Mission to UN 76; Deputy Perm. Rep. and Deputy to Head of the Dept. of External Affairs of the Maldives 77; Perm. Rep. of the Maldives to the United Nations 78-80; Minister of Health Nov. 78-.
c/o Ministry of Health, Malé, Maldives.

Hussein bin Onn, Datuk, S.P.M.J.; Malaysian barrister and politician; b. 12 Feb. 1922; ed. Cambridge School, Indian Mil. Acad., Dehra Dun, Lincoln's Inn, England.
Commissioned in Indian Army 42, served in Middle East and India; Mil. Gen. H.Q., New Delhi; with British Liberation Forces, Malaya 45; served Malay Admin. Service, Kuala Selangor and Klang 46-47; Nat. Youth Leader and Sec. Gen. United Malays Nat. Org. (UMNO) 47; mem. Fed. Legislative Council, Johore Council of State and State Exec. Council 48-57; qualified as Barr.-at-Law, England, legal practice 60; rejoined UMNO 68, Deputy Pres. until 76, acting Pres. 76-81; mem. of Parl. 70-; Minister of Educ. 70-73; Deputy Prime Minister 73-75, Prime Minister 76-81 (retd. owing to ill health); Minister of Trade and Industry 73-74, of Finance and Public Corpns. 74-75, of Defence 76-78 and 80-81, of Federal Territory 78-80 Seri Maharaja Mangku Negara 81.
c/o Prime Minister's Office, Kuala Lumpur 11-01; Home: 3 Jalan Kenny, Kuala Lumpur, Malaysia.

Hutasingh, Prakob, LL.B., D.JUR.; Thai jurist; b. 5 Feb. 1912; ed. Vajiravuth Coll., Univ. of Jena and Thammasat Univ., Bangkok.
Joined the judiciary 37; Asst. Judge Court of Appeal 41; Sec. Supreme Court 48; Asst. Judge Supreme Court 50; Judge, Appeal Court 53; Judge, Supreme Court 60; Pres. Supreme Court 67-72; Minister of Justice 73-74; Deputy Prime Minister June 74-75; Pres. Thai Bar and Inst. of Legal Educ., Thai Bar; mem. Thai Privy Council 75-; Hon. D.C.L.
Publs. various legal textbooks.
71 Soi Senanikom 1, Phaholyotin Road, Bangkok, Thailand.
Telephone: 5791335 or 5791934.

Huxley, Sir Leonard George Holden, K.B.E., M.A., D.PHIL., PH.D., F.A.A.; Australian public official; b. 29 May 1902; ed. The Hutchins School, Hobart, Tasmania Univ. and New Coll., Oxford.
On scientific staff, C.S.I.R., Sydney 29-30; Lecturer, Univ. Coll., Nottingham, England 30-32; Head, Physics Dept., Univ. Coll., Leicester, England 32-40; Principal Scientific Officer, Telecommunications Research Establishment M.A.P. 40-46; Reader in Electromagnetism, Birmingham Univ., England 46-49; Elder Prof. of Physics, Adelaide Univ. 49-60; Vice-Chancellor, Australian Nat. Univ. 60-67, Pres. Australian Inst. of Physics 62-65; Chair. Radio Research Board of Australia 58-63, Radio Frequency Allocation Cttee. 60-64, Australian Nat. Standards Comm. 53-65; mem. U.S. Educ. Foundation in Australia 60-64; mem. Nat. Library Council 60-72, Exec. Commonwealth Scientific and Industrial Research Org. (CSIRO) 60; Chair. Australian-American Educ. Foundation 65-69; Chair. Gen. Council Australia-Britannica Awards Scheme 64-68; mem. Council Canberra Coll. of Advanced Educ. 68-74; Trustee, Australian Humanities Research Council 68-70; Fellow, Australian Acad. of Science 54-.
Publs. *Wave Guides* (with R. W. Crompton) 49, *The Diffusion and Drift of Electrons in Gases* 74, numerous papers on gaseous electronics, electromagnetism, ionosphere and upper atmosphere.
19 Glasgow Place, Hughes, Canberra, A.C.T. 2605, Australia.
Telephone: Canberra 815560.

Huynh Tan Phat; Vietnamese politician; b. 1913.
Member Vanguard Youth 45; Editor *Thanh-nien* during anti-French struggle; remained in S. Viet-Nam after Geneva Agreement 54; Sec.-Gen. Democratic Party; mem. Cen. Cttee. Nat. Liberation Front (N.L.F.) 64-; Pres. Provisional Revolutionary Govt. of S. Viet-Nam 69-76 (in Saigon (now Ho Chi Minh City) 75-76); Vice-Premier Council of Ministers, Socialist Republic of Viet-Nam 76-82; Vice-Pres. Council of State June 82-; Chair. State Capital Construction Comm. 79-82.
Council of State, Hanoi, Viet-Nam.

Hyder, Sajjad, B.A.; Pakistani diplomatist; b. 1920; ed. Govt. High School, Jullundur, D.A.V. Coll., Jullundur, and Indian Mil. Acad., Dehra Dun.
War service; Third Sec., Indian Foreign Service, New Delhi 47, Second Sec., U.S.A. 48; Second Sec., First Sec. and Counsellor, U.K. 52; Dir. Pakistan Foreign Office, Karachi 55; Deputy High Commr., New Delhi 57-59, London 59-

61; Amb. to Iraq 61-65, to United Arab Republic 65-68; High Commr. in India 68-71; Amb. to Fed. Repub. of Germany 72-74, to U.S.S.R. (also accred. to Finland) 75-78, to Netherlands 79-81.
c/o Ministry of Foreign Affairs, Islamabad, Pakistan.

Hyuga, Hosai; Japanese industrialist; b. 1906; ed. Univ of Tokyo.
Head Office, Sumitomo Group 31-41; Govt. Service 41; Sumitomo Group 41-, Dir. Sumitomo Metal Industries Ltd. 49-, Man. Dir. 52-58, Senior Man. Dir. 58-60, Exec. Vice-Pres. 60-62, Pres. 62-74, Chair. 74-; Pres. Kansai Econ. Fed. 77-; Counsellor, Bank of Japan 77-.
Sumitomo Metal Industries Ltd., 5-15, Kitahama, Higashiku, Osaka, Japan.
Telephone: 0797-22-3249.

I

Ibe, Kyonosuke; Japanese banker; b. July 1908, Tokyo; ed. Tokyo High School, Tokyo Imperial Univ.
Joined Sumitomo Bank 33, Dir. 57-60, Man. Dir. 60-64, Senior Man. Dir. 64-71, Deputy Pres. 71-73, Pres. 73-77, Chair. 77-; Dir. Kubota Ltd. 78-, Matsushita Electric Industrial Co. Ltd., Nippon Electrical Co. Ltd. and several others 79-; Chair. Board of Trustees Kansai Cttee. for Econ. Devt. 67-69, Trustee 69-; Pres. Board of Trustees Osaka Philharmonic Soc. 77-; Trustee Japan Cttee. for Econ. Devt. 71-72, 73-; Exec. Dir. Japan Fed. of Econ. Orgs. 73-; Vice-Chair. Fed. of Bankers' Asscns. of Japan 73-74; Chair. Osaka Bankers' Asscn. 73-74, Vice-Chair. 74-77; Blue Ribbon Medal 75; First Class Order of the Sacred Treasure 81.
The Sumitomo Bank, 22, 5-chome, Kitahama, Higashi-ku, Osaka (Office); 20–41 Higashiashiya-cho, Ashiya City, Hyogo, Japan (Home).

Ibuka, Masaru; Japanese industrialist; b. 11 April 1908; ed. Waseda Senior High School and Waseda Univ.
Research Engineer, Photo-Chemical Laboratory 33-37; Man. Radio Telegraphy Dept., Japan Audio Optical Industrial Corpn. 37-40; Man. Dir. Japan Measuring Apparatus Co. Ltd. 40-45; Organizer, Tokyo Telecommunications Engineering Corpn. 46- (Sony Corpn. since 58), Pres. 50-71, Chair. 71-76, Hon. Chair. and Chair. Exec. Advisory Cttee. Jan. 76-; Chair. Exec. Cttee. Japan Cttee. for Econ. Devt.; Chair. Early Devt. Asscn.; Pres. Japan Inst. of Invention and Innovation, Japan Audio Soc.; Vice-Chair. Japan Asscn. for Int. Exposition Tsukuba 75; Fellow Inst. of Electrical and Electronics Engineers; Foreign mem. Royal Swedish Acad. of Engineering Science; Foreign Assoc. Nat. Acad. of Engineering; Hon. D.Sc. (Plano Univ.) 74, (Waseda Univ.) 79; Hon. D.Eng. (Sophia Univ., Tokyo) 76; Dir. several industrial asscns.; Blue Ribbon Medal 60; Founders Medal, IEEE 72; Order of the Sacred Treasure (First Class) 78.
Sony Corporation, 7-35 Kitashingawa 6-chome, Shinagawuku, Tokyo; and 7-1-702 Mita 2-chome, Minato-ku, Tokyo, Japan.

Ichikawa, Kon; Japanese film director; b. 1915; ed. Ichioka Commercial School, Osaka.
Films include: *Poo-San* 53, *A Billionaire* 54, *The Heart* 54, *Punishment Room* 55, *The Burmese Harp* 56, *The Men of Tohoku* 56, *Conflagration* 58, *Fires on the Plain* 59, *The Key* 59, *Bonchi* 60, *Her Brother* 60, *The Sin* 61, *Being Two Isn't Easy* 62, *The Revenge of Yuki-No-Jo* 63, *Alone on the Pacific* 63, *Tokyo Olympiad* 64, *Seishun* 70, *To Love Again* 71, *The Wanderers* 73, *Visions of Eight* (co-dir.) 73, *Wagahai wa Neko de Aru* 75, *The Inugamis* 76, *Gokumon-to* 77, *Joobachi* 78, *Byoin-zaka no Kubikukuri no Ie* 79, *Ancient City* 80.

Idham Chalid, Dr. Kyai Haji; Indonesian politician; b. 27 Aug. 1922, Amuntai, Kalimantan; ed. Islamic Teachers' Coll., Ponorogo, E. Java.
Teacher 43-47; mem. Parl. of Repub. of United States of Indonesia 48; mem. House of Reps. 50; mem. Constituent Assembly 56; Second Deputy Prime Minister 56-59; mem. Supreme Advisory Council 59; mem. Exec. Board of Nat. Front 60, Deputy Chair. 61; mem. and Deputy Chair. Provisional People's Consultative Assembly (MPRS) 60-65; First Minister of People's Welfare 67-71; Chair. People's Consultative Assembly 73-77; Speaker of the House of Reps. 73-77; Chair. Nahdlatul-'Ulama (Moslem Scholars' Party) 56- (resgnd. owing to ill health but withdrew resignation May 82); Pres. Partai Persatuan Pembangunan (Devt. Unity Party) 73-; Chair. Supreme Advisory Council 78; Leader of Muslim community in Indonesia; Star of Yugoslav Flag, Medal of Honour (Egypt), Groot kruis (Netherlands), Star of Belgium, Star of Gwan Hwa, Republic of Korea.
15 Mangunsarkoro, Jakarta, Indonesia.

Ieng Sary; Kampuchean politician; b. 1925, Vinh Bihn Province, Viet-Nam; ed. Lycée Sisowath, Phnom-Penh, Institut d'Etudes Politiques, Paris.
President Khmer Students' Union 55-56; taught at Lycée Sisowath and Lycée Kampubat 57-63; active in left-wing movements and forced to flee Phnom-Penh 63; prominent in Khmers Rouges insurgent movement 63-75; Khmers Rouges liaison officer to Royal Govt. of Nat. Union of Cambodia (GRUNC) in exile 71-75; mem. Politburo Nat. United Front of Cambodia (FUNC) 70-; Special Adviser to Deputy Prime Minister Khieu Samphan (*q.v.*) 73; Second Deputy Prime Minister of Democratic Kampuchea, with special responsibility for Foreign Affairs 75-79; sentenced to death *in absentia* Aug. 79; Deputy Prime Minister in charge of Foreign Affairs, Democratic Kampuchean Govt. in exile (Khmer Rouge) fighting Vietnamese forces Dec. 79-; mem. Finance and Economy Cttee., Kampuchea coalition govt. in exile, Thailand July 82-.

Ikeda, Daisaku; Japanese religious and fmr. political leader; b. 2 Jan. 1928, Tokyo; ed. Fuji Junior Coll.
President of Soka Gakkai 60-79, Hon. Pres. 79-; founder, Min-on Concert Asscn. 63, Komeito (Clean Govt.) Party 64, Soka Junior and Senior High Schools 68, Soka Univ. 71, Sapporo Soka Kindergarten 76, Tokyo Soka Primary School 78; Fuji Art Museum 73, Oriental Inst. of Academic Research.
Publs. (Japanese) *The Human Revolution* Vols. I-X 65-79, *Science and Religion* 65, *My Thought and Opinion* 70, *New Life* (poems) 70, *Essays on Life* 70, *Modern Civilization and Religion* 72, *Civilization, East and West—Dialogue with Richard Coudenhove Kalergi* 72, *My View on Sakyamuni* 73, *Dialogue on Life* Vols. I-III 73-74, *Essays on Women* 74, *Dialogue towards the 21st Century* (with Arnold Toynbee) 75; (English) *The Human Revolution* Vols. I-III 72-76, *Buddhism: The Living Philosophy* 74, *The Living Buddha* 76, *The Toynbee-Ikeda Dialogue—Man Himself Must Choose* 76, *Choose Life* (OUP edn. of *The Toynbee-Ikeda Dialogue*) 76, *Buddhism: The First Millenium* 77, *Songs from My Heart* (poetry) 78, *Glass Children and Other Essays* 79, *La Nuit Appelle l'Aurore* 80, *Choisis La Vie* 81, *A Lasting Peace—Collected Addresses of Daisaku Ikeda* 81, *Life: an Enigma, a Precious Jewel* 82.
c/o The Soka Gakkai, 32 Shinano-machi, Shinjuku-ku, Tokyo 160, Japan.
Telephone: 353-7111.

Ikeura, Kisaburo, LL.B.; Japanese banker; b. 21 April 1916, Wakayama Prefecture; ed. Tokyo Univ.
Industrial Bank of Japan Ltd. 39-, Dir. 64, Man. Dir. 65, Deputy Pres. 73, Pres. 75-.
3-3 Marunouchi 1-chome, Chiyoda-ku, Tokyo; Home: 22-12, 4-chome Numabukuro, Nakano-ku, Tokyo, Japan.
Telephone: 214-1111 (Office); 386-1443 (Home).

Ilangaratne, Tikiri Bandara; Sri Lankan politician, writer, playwright, novelist; b. 27 Feb. 1913; ed. St. Anthony's Coll., Kandy.
Clerical posts until 47; mem. of Parl. for Kandy 48, for Galaha 52; Gen. Sec. Sri Lanka Freedom Party 54-, Deputy Pres. 81-; mem. of Parl. for Hewaheta 56; Minister for Social Services and Housing 56-59, of Home Affairs 59, of Trade, Commerce, Food and Shipping 61-63, of Finance 63-64, of Trade and Supplies 64-65; Vice-Pres. Sri Lanka Freedom Party 66, 81-; mem. of Parl. for Kolonnawa 67, responsible for nationalizing foreign oil companies in Sri Lanka; Pres. Peace Council of Sri Lanka; Minister of Foreign and Internal Trade 70-77, of Public Admin. and Home Affairs 75-77.
Publs. (in Sinhalese): Novels: *Wilambeeta, Denuwara, Kathava, Thilaka, Lasanda, Thilaka and Thilaka, Nedeyo*; Plays: *Häramitiya, Manthri Hamuduruwo, Jataka Natyaya, Rangamandala, Handahana, Ambaryaluwo*; Short stories: *Onchillawa* etc.
Sri Lanka Freedom Party, 301 Darley Road, Colombo; Home: 302 High Level Road, Colombo 6, Sri Lanka.

Imai, Kenji; Japanese architect; b. 11 Jan. 1895, Tokyo; ed. Architectural Dept., Waseda Univ., Tokyo.
Assistant Prof. Waseda Univ. 20-37, Prof. 37-65, Hon. Prof. 65-; Prof. Kantö Gakuin Univ., Yokohama 66-; Hon. Counsellor Tama Fine Arts Univ., Tokyo 65-; studied in Europe and America 26-27; mem. Catholic Art Soc. 49-; Rep. of Japan Branch of Gaudi Friends' Circle 56, participated in 10th Anniversary of Antonio Gaudi Friends' Circle, Barcelona 63; Hon. mem. Rudolf Steiner Goetheanum 63; one-man exhbn. of European sketches 64; Prize of Architectural Inst. of Japan 59, 62; Marquis Ohkuma Academic Prize, Waseda Univ. 62; Japan Art Acad. Prize 66.
Major works include: Waseda Univ. Library 25, Waseda Univ. Museum of Drama 28, Aeroplane Monument, Tokyo 41, Ohtakimachi Town Office, Chiba Prefecture 59, Memorial Centre for Japanese 26 Martyrs 62, Chapel for Sisters of the Visitation Convent (Kamakura) 65, *Toka Gakudo*—The Empress' Memorial Music Hall, Imperial Palace 66, Marquis Ohkuma Memorial Hall, Saga Prefecture 66, Toyama Memorial, Fine Arts Museum, Kawagoe Prefecture 70.
Publs. *Gunnar Asplund* 30, *Das Vorbild der Katholischen Gattin—Architecture and Humanity* 54, *Öryo Sobyö* (Sketch of Travel through Europe) 63, *Tabiji* (Voyage) 67; collection of artistic works in commemoration of 70th birthday 68.
4-12-28, Kitazawa, Setagaya-ku, Tokyo, Japan.
Telephone: 03-468-2708.

Imai, Tadashi; Japanese film director; b. 1912, Tokyo.
Joined Toho production company with first film *Numazu Naval Academy* 39; films concerned with plight of the poor, e.g. *Rice* 75, *A Story from Echigo* 64, and oppressed minorities, e.g. *Kiku and Isamu* 59 and two-part *The River Without a Bridge* 69-70; Grand Prix, Berlin Int. Film Festival for *Bushido* 63; Gold Prize, Int. Film Festival of India for *Brother and Sister* (76) 77. Other films include: *Minshu no Teki* 46, *Blue Mountain* 49, *Till We Meet Again* 50, *And Yet We Live* 51, *School of Echo* 52, *Lily Corps, Nigorie* 53, *Here is a Fountain* 55, *Darkness at Noon* 56, *Tale of Pure Love* 57, *The Adulteress* 58, *A Woman Named Oen* 71, *My Voiceless Friends, Eternal Cause* 72, *Kobayashi Takiji* 74, *Rika* 78.
c/o Haiyuza Film Production Ltd., Minota-ku Roppongi 4-10-3, Fukuyama Bldg., Tokyo 106, Japan.

Inayama, Yoshihiro; Japanese industrialist; b. 2 Jan. 1904, Chuo-ku, Tokyo; ed. Tokyo Univ.
Yawata Iron and Steel Co. Ltd. 28-, Man. Dir. 50-60, Vice-Pres. 60-72, Pres. 62-70, also Chair. Japan Iron and Steel Federation 65-; Pres. Nippon Steel Corpn. 70-73, Chair. 73-81, Hon. Chair. 81-; Chair. Int. Iron and Steel Inst. 71-73, Vice-Chair. 73-76; Pres. Keidanren (Fed. of Econ. Orgs.) May 80-; Medal of Honor with Blue Ribbon 62, First Order of Merit with Order of the Sacred Treasure 74, First Order of Merit with Grand Cordon of the Rising Sun 82.
Nippon Steel Corporation, Shin Nittetsu Building, 6-3, Otemachi 2-chome, Chiyoda-ku, Tokyo 100 (Office); 28-8, 1-chome, Daizawa, Setagaya-ku, Tokyo, Japan (Home).
Telephone: 421-0533 (Home).

Inglés, José D.; Philippine lawyer and diplomatist; b. 24 Aug. 1910; ed. Univ. of the Philippines, Santo Tomás Univ., Manila, and Columbia Univ., New York.
Attorney 32-36; Legal Asst., Pres. of the Philippines 36-39; Asst. Solicitor-Gen. 40; Judge First Instance 41-43; Prof. Philippine Law School 45-46; Vice-Chair. Trusteeship Cttee., Paris 51, Special Political Cttee. 63-65; mem. Philippine del. to UN 46-56, 62-68, 74, Chair. Credentials Cttee.; Vice-Pres. Gen. Assembly 74; rep. to Security Council, Trusteeship Council, ECOSOC; Chair. Sub-Comm. on Prevention of Discrimination and Protection of Minorities, Comm. on Human Rights, Cttee. on Elimination of Racial Discrimination; Deputy Perm. Rep. to UN 55-56; Minister to Fed. Repub. of Germany 56-58, Amb. 58-62; Amb. to Thailand 62-66; rep. South-East Asia Treaty Org. (SEATO) 62-66, Council of Ministers 68; mem. Standing Cttee. Asscn. of South-East Asia (ASA) 63-66, Chair. Standing Cttee. ASEAN and ASPAC 70-71; Under-Sec. of Foreign Affairs 66-78, Acting Sec. of Foreign Affairs intermittently 66-78, Deputy Minister of Foreign Affairs 78-81, Acting Minister of Foreign Affairs Sept.-Dec. 78, June-July 79, April-May, May-June and Sept.-Dec. 80, May 81; Sec.-Gen. Nat. Secr. (ASEAN) 66-69; Chair. ASEAN Senior Officials Meetings 71-77; Chair. del. to ASEAN Ministerial Meeting 72 and 79; Chair. Del. to UNESCO Gen. Conf. 70; Acting Perm. Rep. to UN 74; Chair. UN Cttee. on Elimination of Racial Discrimination 82-83; Dean Coll. of Foreign Service, Lyceum of Philippines 81-; Grosskreuz des Verdientstordens der Bundesrepublik Deutschland, Most Noble Order of the Crown of Thailand, Most Exalted Order of the White Elephant, Gran Cruz del Orden de Mayo, Grand-Croix de l'Ordre de Léopold II, Nat. Order of Viet-Nam, Grand Cross Sovereign Mil. Order of Malta; Gold Grotius Medal.
Publs. numerous papers on economics and int. affairs.
1 Vinzons Street, Heroes' Hill, Quezon City, Philippines.
Telephone: 99-3808.

Inoue, Yuichi; Japanese artist; b. 1916, Tokyo.
Co-founder "Bokujin-kai" group of calligraphers 52-; rep. travelling exhbn. of Japanese Calligraphy, Europe 55, São Paulo Bienal 57, Brussels Int. Exhbn. 58, Kassel Int. Exhbn. 59, Pittsburgh Int. Exhbn. 61, São Paulo Bienal 61, one-man show at Ichibankan Gallery, Tokyo 71.
Ohkamiyashiki, 2475-2 Kurami, Samukawa-machi 253-01, Koza-gun, Kanagawa-ken, Japan.
Telephone: 0467-74-4721.

Inouye, Kaoru; Japanese banker; b. 13 May 1906, Chiba Pref.; ed. Tokyo Univ.
Joined The Dai-Ichi Bank Ltd. 29, Dir. 54, Deputy Pres. 61, Pres. 62-66, 69-71, Chair. 66-69; Chair. The Dai-Ichi Kangyo Bank 71-76, Chair. Senior Exec. Cttee. 76-; Dir. Asahi Mutual Life Insurance Co., Taisei Fire and Marine Insurance Co. Ltd., K. Hattori and Co. Ltd.; auditor, Furukawa Electric Co.; adviser, Kawasaki Heavy Industries Ltd.; Chair. Financial Group, Councillor, Tokyo Chamber of Commerce and Industry.
The Dai-Ichi Kangyo Bank, 1-5, Uchisaiwai-cho 1-chome, Chiyoda-ku, Tokyo 100, Japan.

Ishibashi, Kanichiro; Japanese business executive; b. 1 March 1920; ed. Faculty of Law, Univ. of Tokyo.
Naval service 43-45; joined Bridgestone Tire Co. Ltd. 45,

Dir 49-, Vice-Pres. 50-63, Pres. 63-73, Chair. 73-; Exec. Dir. Fed. of Econ. Orgs.; Exec. Dir. Japan Fed. of Employers' Asscns.; Adviser Mitsui LPG Co. Ltd.
Office: 10-1, Kyobashi 1-chome, Chuo-ku, Tokyo; Home: 1 Nagasaka-cho, Azabu, Minato-ku, Tokyo, Japan.
Telephone: 03-567-0111 (Office); 03-583-0150 (Home).

Ishihara, Takashi; Japanese motor industry executive; b. 3 March 1912, Tokyo; ed. Tohoku Univ.
Joined Nissan Motor Co. Ltd. 37; Gen. Man. Planning 48, Finance and Accounting 49-54; Dir. Finance and Accounting 54-57, Export and Overseas Operations 57-63; Man. Dir. Export and Overseas Operations 63-65, Domestic Sales 65-69; Exec. Man. Dir. Domestic Sales 69-73; Exec. Vice-Pres. 73-77, Pres. 77-; Pres. Nippon Motor Corpn. U.S.A. 60-65, now Chair.; Exec. Dir. Keidanren (Fed. of Econ. Orgs.); Dir. Nikkeiren (Fed. of Employers' Asscns.); Vice-Chair. Keizai Doyukai (Cttee. for Econ. Devt.); Pres. Japan Automobile Mfrs. Asscn., Inc., Japan Motor Industrial Fed., Inc.; Blue Ribbon Medal 74.
17-1, Ginza 6-chome, Chuo-ku, Tokyo, Japan.
Telephone: 03-473-3830.

Ishikawa, Shigeru, D.ECON.; Japanese economist; b. 7 April 1918; ed. Tokyo Univ. of Commerce (now Hitotsubashi Univ.).
Attached to Jiji News Agency 45-56, Hong Kong Corresp. 51-53; Asst. Prof., Inst. of Econ. Research, Hitotsubashi Univ. 56-63, Prof. 63-82, Dir. 72-74, Prof. Emer. 82-; Visiting Prof. School of Oriental and African Studies (London Univ.) 80; Prof. School of Int. Political Science and Econs., Aoyamagakuin Univ.
Publs. *National Income and Capital Formation in Mainland China* 65, *Economic Development in Asian Perspective* 67, *Agricultural Development Strategies in Asia* 70, *Labor Absorption in Asian Agriculture* 78, *Essays on Technology, Employment and Institutions in Economic Development* 81.
19-9, 4-chome Kugayama, Suginami-ku, Tokyo, Japan.
Telephone: 332 8376.

Islam, Nurul, PH.D.; Bangladesh economist; b. 1 April 1929, Chittagong; ed. Univ. of Dacca and Harvard Univ.
Professor of Econs. Dacca Univ. 60-64; Dir. Pakistan Inst. of Devt. Econs., Karachi 64-72; Visiting Prof. Econ. Devt. Inst., World Bank 67-68; Professorial Research Assoc., Yale Econ. Growth Cen. 68 and 71; Deputy Chair. Bangladesh Planning Comm. (with ministerial status) 72-75; Chair. Bangladesh Inst. of Devt. Studies, Dacca 75-77; mem. Bd. of Trustees Int. Rice Research Inst., Manila 73-, Exec. Cttee. Third World Forum 74-, Bd. of Govs. Int. Food Policy Research Inst. 75-, UN Cttee. on Devt. Planning 77; Assistant Dir.-Gen. Econ. and Social Policy Dept., Food and Agriculture Org. of UN 77-; mem. Editorial Bd. *The World Economy*, London; UNDP Consultant on Econ. Planning, Yemen Arab Republic Aug. 76; Nuffield Foundation Fellow at Univs. of London and Cambridge 58-59; Rockefeller Fellow, Netherlands School of Economics 59.
Publs. *An Econometric Analysis* 64, *Studies in Foreign Capital and Economic Development* 60, *Studies in Commercial Policy and Economic Growth* 70, *Development Planning in Bangladesh—A Study in Political Economy* 77, *Development Strategy of Bangladesh* 78, *Interdependence of Developed and Developing Countries* 78, *Foreign Trade and Economic Controls in Development: The Case of United Pakistan* 80.
Viale Piramide Cestia 1/C, Apt. 19, 00153, Rome, Italy.
Telephone; 577.9962 (Home); 5797.3001 (Office).

Ismail bin Mohamed Ali, Tan Sri Datuk, M.A.; Malaysian bank official and barrister-at-law; b. 16 Sept. 1918, Port Swettenham, Selangor; ed. Univ. of Cambridge and Middle Temple, London.
Malayan Civil Service 46-48; Asst. State Sec., Govt. of Selangor 48-50; Econ. Div. of Treasury 50-53, Econ. Officer, Penang 54-55; Controller, Trade Div., Ministry of Commerce and Industry 55-57; Minister Malaysian Embassy, Washington 57-58, Econ. Minister 58-60; Exec. Dir. IBRD, Int. Finance Corpn., Int. Devt. Asscn. 58-60; Deputy Gov. Bank Negara Malaysia (Central Bank) 60-62, Gov. 62-80; Chair. Capital Issues Cttee. 68-, Malaysian Industrial Devt. Finance Ltd. 69-; Pres. Malaysian Inst. of Management 66-68; mem. Nat. Devt. Planning Cttee. 62-, Council of Univ. of Malaya 62-72, Board of Govs., Asian Inst. of Management 70-, Urban Devt. Authority 71-75; Adviser Nat. Corpn. 71-; mem. Foreign Investment Cttee. 74-; Chair. Nat. Equity Corpn. 78-; Chair. of Council Inst. of Bankers, Malaysia 78-; Dir. Sime, Darby Berhad 80-; Order of Panglima Mangku Negara 64; Order of Panglima Negara Bintang Sarawak 76; Order of Seri Paduka Mahkota Selangor 77; Order of Seri Paduka Mahkota Johar 79; Award of Tun Abdul Razak Foundation 80; Hon. LL.D. (Univ. of Malaya) 73.
c/o Bank Negara Malaysia, P.O.B. 922, Kuala Lumpur; Home: 23 Jalan Natesa, off Cangkat Tunku, Kuala Lumpur, Malaysia.
Telephone: 987954 (Office); 940259 (Home).

Isoda, Ichiro; Japanese banker; b. 12 Jan. 1913, Kumamoto; ed. Law Dept. Kyoto Imperial Univ.
Joined Sumitomo Bank Ltd. 35, Dir. 60-63, Man. Dir. 63-68, Senior Man. Dir. 68-73, Deputy Pres. 73-77, Pres. 77-80; Counsellor Bank of Japan 78-; Vice-Chair. Fed. of Bankers' Asscn 79-; Chair. Osaka Bankers' Asscn. 79-; Standing Dir. Kansai Economic Fed.; Trustee Japan/Kansai Cttee. for Economic Devt. 79-; Blue Ribbon Medal 78.
c/o The Sumitomo Bank, 5-22 Kitahama, Higashi-ku, Osaka, Japan.

Itakura, Joji; Japanese banker; b. 3 June 1912, Tokyo; ed. Keio Univ.
Managing Dir. Mitsui Bank Ltd. 68-71, Senior Man. Dir. 71-72, Deputy Pres. 72-74, Pres. 74-78, Counsellor 78-; Chair. Tokyo Bankers' Asscn. Ltd.
The Mitsui Bank Ltd., 1-2 Yuraku-cho 1-chome, Chiyoda-ku, Tokyo 100; Home: 6-8 Shinoharakita 2-chome, Kohoku-ku, Yokohama City, Kanagawa Prefecture, Japan.
Telephone: 501-1111 (Office); 045-401-5155 (Home).

Ito, Masayoshi; Japanese politician; b. 1914, Fukushima Pref.; ed. Tokyo Univ.
Elected to House of Reps. six times; Dir.-Gen. Fisheries Agency; Vice-Minister of Agric. and Forestry; State Minister and Chief Cabinet Sec. 79-80; Acting Prime Minister June-July 80; Minister of Foreign Affairs July 80-May 81 (resgnd.); Chair. Finance Cttee., Liberal-Democratic Party (LDP); Vice-Chair. Policy Affairs Research Council, LDP.
c/o Ministry of Foreign Affairs, 2-1, Kasumigaseki 2-chome, Chiyoda-ku, Tokyo, Japan.

Ito, Shinsui; Japanese painter; b. 1898; ed. Kiyokata Art School, Tokyo.
Has exhibited many pictures of women incl. *A Mirror* (Nat. Acad. of Art Prize 46); organizer of Jitsugetsu Sha, and art league of young painters of promise; mem. Council of the Nat. Art Exhbn.; Sec. Japan Fed. of Art Socs.
Kita-Kamakura, Kanagawa Prefecture, Japan.

Itoh, Junji; Japanese business executive; b. 10 July 1922, Qingdao, China; ed. Keio Univ.
With Kanegafuchi Spinning Co. Ltd. (now Kanebo Ltd.) 48-60; Dir. Kanebo Ltd. 61, Man. Dir. 64, Exec. Dir. 66, Vice-Pres. 68, Pres. 68-; Pres. Kanebo Cosmetics Inc. 69-, Kanebo Foods Ltd. 71-74, Kanebo Pharmaceutical Co. Ltd. 72-, Kanebo Synthetic Fibres Ltd. 79-, Kanebo Synthetic Textiles Ltd. 80-; Man. Dir. Japan Fed. of Econ. Orgs. 68-, Japan Spinners' Asscn. 68-77 (Chair. 71-72),

Japan Chemical Fibres Asscn. 68-; Vice-Chair. Japan Textile Fed. 71-72; Trustee, Keio Univ. 70-78; Grão Cruz Orden Acadêmico São Francisco (Brazil) 72.
Kanebo Ltd., Osaka Ekimae Daini Building, 2-2, Umeda 1-chome, Kita-ku, Osaka 530; Home: 28-9 Denenchofu, 3-chome, Ota-ku, Tokyo 145, Japan.
Telephone: (06) 348-5002. (Office)

Itoh, Kyoichi; Japanese industrialist; b. 27 May 1914; ed. Kobe Univ.
Director Kureha Spinning Co. Ltd. 56, Man. Dir. 56-63, Exec. Dir. 63, Pres. 63-66; Dir. Nippon Lactum Co. Ltd. 63-74; Dir. Japan Fed. of Econ. Orgs. 64-66; Dir. Japan Fed. of Employers' Asscns. 64-67; Exec. Vice-Pres. Toyobo Co. Ltd. 66-73, Chair. 73-74, Counsellor 74-; Chair. Nippei Sangyo Ltd. 69-, Toyo Pulp Co. Ltd. 75-81; Hon. Consul-Gen. of El Salvador, Osaka 58-; Pres. Japan-El Salvador Soc. 67-, Japan-America Soc., Osaka 80-81; Vice-Pres. Osaka-San Francisco Sister City Asscn. 68-80, Pres. 80-81; Gov., Rotary Int. District 266 78-79.
Toyobo Co. Ltd., 2-8, Dojima Hama 2-chome, Kita-ku, Osaka 530; Home: 11-17, Sumiyoshi-Yamate 4-chome, Higashinada-ku, Kobe 658, Japan.
Telephone: 06-348-3252 (Office); 078-851-5211 (Home).

Itokawa, Hideo; Japanese aeronautics engineer; b. 1912; ed. Tokyo Univ.
Engineer, Nakajima Aircraft Co. 39-41; Asst. Prof. of Engineering at Tokyo Univ. 41-48, Prof. 48-67; Exec. Dir. Space Engineering Dept., Inst. of Industrial Science 55-; Pres. Japanese Rocket Soc. 56-58; Convenor Nat. Cttee. on Space Research, Japan Science Council 56-; mem. Nat. Space Council 60-; Dep. Dir. Inst. of Space and Aeronautical Science 64-67; Dir. Systems Research Inst. 67.
34-15, 4-chome, Matsubara, Setagaya-ku, Tokyo, Japan.

Iwama, Kazuo; Japanese electronics industry executive; b. 7 Feb. 1919, Anjo City, Aichi Prefecture; ed. Tokyo Imperial Univ.
Joined Tokyo Tsushin Kogyo K.K. 46 (name changed to Sony Corpn. 58), Senior Man. Dir. 66, Deputy Pres. and Rep. Man. Dir. 73-76, Pres. and Chief Operating Officer Jan. 76-; Chair. Board of Dirs., Sony Corpn. of America 78-.
Died 24 August 1982.

Iwasa, Yoshizane; Japanese banker; b. 6 Feb. 1906, Tokyo; ed. Tokyo Univ.
Joined Yasuda Bank, forerunner of Fuji Bank 28, Dir. 48, Vice-Chair. 48-57, Deputy Chair. 57-63, Chair. of Board and Pres. 63-71, Chair. Advisory Cttee. 71-75, Counsellor 75-81, Adviser 81-; Chair. Bd. of Councillors Fed. of Econ. Orgs. (Keidanren); Chair. Japan-California Asscn.; Vice-Chair. Japan-China Asscn.; Trustee Japanese Cttee. for Econ. Devt.
1-5-5, Otemachi, Chiyoda-ku, Tokyo 100; Home: 5-2-4, Minami-Aoyame, Minato-ku, Tokyo 107, Japan.

J

Jagvaral, Nyamyn; Mongolian politician; b. 4 May 1919; ed. Inst. of Oriental Studies, Moscow.
Chairman, Cttee. of Sciences and Higher Educ. 53-57; Minister of Agriculture 57-61; Deputy Chair. Council of Ministers 57-61, 61-69; Chair. State Rural Construction Comm. 71-; Chair. State Comm. for Winter and Spring Control of Livestock 73-; Deputy to People's Great Hural (Assembly); cand. mem. Political Bureau, Mongolian People's Revolutionary Party (MPRP) Cen. Cttee. 58-60, 81-, mem. Political Bureau 60-81; Sec. MPRP Cen. Cttee. 63-81; Deputy Chair. Hural Presidium 81-; mem. Acad. of Sciences; Order of Sühbaatar and other awards.
Central Committee of the Mongolian People's Revolutionary Party, Ulan Bator, Mongolia.

Jain, Surendra Kumar, M.A., LL.M.; Indian international official; b. 22 Dec. 1922, India; ed. High School, New Delhi, Punjab and Lucknow Univs.
Lecturer, Delhi School of Law, Delhi Univ. 46-47; Int. Labour Office, Geneva 47-, Chef de Cabinet to Dir.-Gen. 57-59, Dir. Office for Near and Middle East, Istanbul 59-62, Field Office for Asia, Colombo 62-65, Regional Dir. for Asia, Bangkok 66-75, Deputy Dir.-Gen. in charge of Technical Programmes June 75-; Gold Medal (Lucknow Univ.).
Publs. articles on labour and social problems in *International Labour Review* and other journals.
International Labour Office, 1211 Geneva 22; Residence: 32 rue Daubin, 1203 Geneva, Switzerland.
Telephone: 99-65-31 (Office); 45-80-82 (Residence).

Jaisingh, Hari, M.A.; Indian newspaper editor; b. 29 March, 1941, Karachi, Pakistan; ed. Calcutta.
With *Hindustan Standard*, Calcutta 63-67, Ed.-in-charge overseas edition; columnist *Indian Scene*; Asst. Ed. *The Tribune*, Chandigarh 67-79; Resident Ed. *Indian Express* 79-80; Ed. *National Herald* 80-; Corresp. for *Morning Telegraph*; lectured Punjab Univ., Chandigarh, Punjabi Univ., Patiala.
National Herald, Herald House, Bahadurshah Zafar Marg, New Delhi-2 (Office); C-146, Defence Colony, New Delhi, India (Home).
Telephone: 276661 (Office); 622838 (Home).

Jalan-aajav, Sampilyn; Mongolian politician; b. 18 June 1923; ed. Central Party-State School and Higher Party School of Mongolian People's Revolutionary Party (MPRP) Cen. Cttee., Ulan Bator, and law studies in U.S.S.R.
Lecturer and Vice-Rector, Higher Party School 43-51, lecturer and Dean 56-58; Head of Propaganda and Culture Dept. of MPRP Cen. Cttee. 58-59; Procurator of the Mongolian People's Repub. 59-60; Chair. Legal Cttee. of Council of Ministers 60-64; Chair. State Cttee. for Information, Broadcasting and TV 64-71; Deputy to People's Great Hural (Assembly) 66-; Deputy Chair. Parl. Group 71-77; Deputy Chair. Presidium, People's Great Hural 77-; Sec. Cen. Cttee. MPRP 71-; cand. mem. MPRP Cen. Cttee. 61-71, mem. Cen. Cttee. 71-; cand. mem. Political Bureau, MPRP Cen. Cttee. 71-73, mem. Political Bureau 73-; Order of the Red Banner of Labour.
Central Committee of the Mongolian People's Revolutionary Party, Ulan Bator, Mongolia.

Jameel, Fathulla, B.A.; Maldivian politician and diplomatist; b. 5 Sept. 1942, Malé; ed. Al-Azhar and Ain Shams Univs., Cairo.
Under-Secretary Ministry of External Affairs 73-76, Deputy to Head of Dept. 76-77; Perm. Rep. of Repub. of Maldives to UN 77-78; Minister of External Affairs March 78-.
Ministry of External Affairs, Malé; Munnaarudhoshuge, Henveiru, Malé, Maldives.

Japan, Emperor of (*see* Hirohito).

Jatti, Basappa Danappa, B.A., LL.B.; Indian politician; b. 10 Sept. 1912, Savalgi, Bijapur District; ed. Bijapur Govt. High School, Rajaram Coll., Sykes Law Coll., Kolhapur.
Practised law at Jamkhandi; State Minister, Jamkhandi, later Chief Minister; mem. Legislative Assembly, Bombay, later Mysore; Parl. Sec., Deputy Minister of Health and Labour, Bombay 52; Chair. Land Reforms Cttee.; Chief Minister, Mysore 58-62; Minister of Finance 62-65, of Food 65-67; Lt.-Gov. of Pondicherry 68; Gov. of Orissa 72-74; Vice-Pres. of India 74-79, Acting Pres. Feb.-July 77, Chair. Rajya Sabha 74-79; Vice-Pres. discharging duties of

Pres. Sept. 77; Hon. LL.D. (Karnatak Univ.) 74, (Guru Nanak Dev. Univ.) 77.
c/o Office of the Vice-President, 6 Maulana Azad Road, New Delhi, India.

Jayawardena, M. D. H., DIP.ECON., BARR.-AT-LAW; Sri Lankan lawyer and politician; b. 29 March 1915; ed. Trinity Coll., Kandy and Ceylon Univ. Coll., Colombo.
Advocate, Colombo and Avissawella 41; called to Lincoln's Inn, London 49; mem. House of Reps., Ceylon (later Nat. State Assembly, Sri Lanka) 52-56, 65-; Parl. Sec. to Minister of Finance 52-54; Minister of Finance 54-56; Joint Gen. Sec. United Nat. Party 58-; Minister of Health 65-70, of Plantation Industries 77-79 (resgnd.); fmr. Pres. Buddhist Theosophical Soc.; helped to form many cos. including Mercantile Credit Ltd., Ceylon Bulbs and Electricals Ltd. and Mahajana Credit Ltd.
c/o United National Party, 532 Galle Road, Colombo, Sri Lanka.

Jayawardene, Junius Richard; Sri Lankan lawyer and politician; b. 17 Sept. 1906, Colombo; ed. Royal Coll., Univ. Coll., and Law Coll., Colombo.
Member Colombo Municipal Council 41; mem. State Council 43; mem. House of Representatives 47-; Minister of Finance 47-53; Hon. Sec. Ceylon Nat. Congress 40-47; Hon. Treas. United Nat. Party 47-48 and Vice-Pres. 53; Leader of the House of Representatives and Minister of Agric. and Food 53-56; Minister of Finance, Information, Broadcasting, Local Govt. and Housing March-July 60; Deputy Leader of Opposition July 60-65; Minister of State, and Parl. Sec. to Minister of Defence, External Affairs and Planning 65-70; Leader of Opposition 70-77; Prime Minister, Minister of Defence, Planning and Econ. Affairs and of Plan Implementation July 77-Feb. 78, Pres. of the Democratic Socialist Repub. of Sri Lanka, Minister of Defence and Plan Implementation, Commdr.-in-Chief of the Armed Services Feb. 78-, also of Aviation Sept. 78-, of Higher Education, Janatha (People's) Estate Development and State Plantations Jan. 81-, of Power and Energy Jan. 82-; Sec. United Nat. Party 72, Leader 73-June 75, July 75-; del. to numerous confs.
Publs. *Some Sermons of the Buddha, Buddhist Essays, In Council* (speeches), *Buddhism and Marxism, Selected Speeches.*
President's House, Colombo; Home: 66 Ward Place, Colombo 7, Sri Lanka.
Telephone: Colombo 95028 and 92332.

Jejeebhoy, Sir Jamsetjee, Bt., B.A.; Indian industrialist; b. 19 April 1913; ed. St. Xavier's School and Coll., Bombay.
Chairman Board of Trustees, Sir J. J. Parsi Benevolent Institution, Sir J. J. Charity Funds, Rustomjee Jamsetjee Jejeebhoy Gujarati Schools' Funds, Bombay Panjrapole, Wadiaji's Fire Temple, Parsi Charity Org. Soc., Iran League, M. F. Cama Athornan Inst.; Trustee, Sir J. J. School of Arts, Byramjee Jejeebhoy Parsi Charitable Institution, Iranee Charity Funds and Dharamshala, Zoroastrian Building Fund, Petit Parsee Gen. Hosp., K.R. Cama Oriental Inst., Petit and Ashburner Fire Temples, A. H. Wadia Charity Trust, etc.; Dir. Enjay Estates (Pte.) Ltd., Beaulieu Investment (Pte.) Ltd.
Maneckji Wadia Building, Mahatma Gandhi Road, Fort, Bombay 400001; Home: Beaulieu, 95 Worli Seaface, Bombay 25, India.
Telephone: 273-843, 271-960 (Office); 4220955, 4228517 (Home).

Jek, Yeun-Thong; Singapore politician and diplomatist; b. 29 July 1930, Singapore; ed. Singapore Chinese High School.
Member of Parl. 63; Minister of Labour 63-68, of Culture 68-72, 72-77; High Commr. in U.K. 77-.
High Commission of the Republic of Singapore, 2 Wilton Crescent, London, SW1X 8RW, England.
Telephone: 01-235 8315.

Jeyaretnam, J. B., LL.B.; Singapore lawyer and politician; b. 5 Jan. 1926, Ceylon; ed. Muar, Johore, Malaysia, St. Andrew's School, Singapore, Univ. Coll. London.
Joined Singapore legal service 52; First District Judge until 63; legal practice 63-; Sec.-Gen. Workers' Party 71-; M.P. for Anson Oct. 81-; first opposition M.P. for 15 years.
Workers' Party, Elections Office, City Hall, Singapore 0617, Singapore.

Jha, Lakshmi Kant, M.B.E., B.A., I.C.S.; Indian economist and retd. civil servant; b. 22 Nov. 1913, Bhagalpur; ed. Banaras Hindu Univ., Varanasi and Trinity Coll., Cambridge.
Indian civil service 36-67; Under-Sec. Govt. of Bihar, Local Self-Govt. Dept. 41-42; Deputy Sec. Supply Dept., Govt. of India 42-46; del. to UN Maritime Conf.; Chief Controller of Imports and Exports 47-50; Sec. Ministry of Commerce and Industry 50-56, 57-60; Sec. Ministry of Heavy Industries 56-57; Chair. GATT 57-58, UN Cttee. on Int. Commodity Arrangements 59-61; Sec. Ministry of Finance, Dept. of Econ. Affairs 60-64; Dir. Reserve Bank of India and State Bank of India; Alt. Gov. Int. Bank for Reconstruction and Devt. 60-64; Sec. to Prime Minister 64-67, retd. 67; Gov. Reserve Bank of India 67-70, IMF 69-70; Amb. to U.S.A. 70-73; Gov., State of Jammu and Kashmir 73-81; Chair. UN Group of Eminent Persons on Multinational Corpns. 73-74, Jammu and Kashmir Devt. Review Cttee. 75-76, Indirect Taxes Enquiry Cttee. 76-77, Commonwealth Group of Industrial Specialists 76-78; mem. Independent Comm. on Int. Devt. Issues 77-79; mem. Indian Del. to Cancun Summit Oct. 81; Chair. Econ. Admin. Reforms Comm. 81-.
Publs. *India's Foreign Trade*, Parts I and II, *Price Policy in a Developing Economy, Economic Development—Ends and Means, The International Monetary Scene, The Human Factor in Economic Development, Shortages and High Prices: the Way Out and Economic Strategy for the 80s.*
10 Janpath, New Delhi, India.
Telephone: 387146.

Ji Dengkui; Chinese party official.
First Sec. CCP Loyang District, Henan 59; Alt. Sec. CCP Henan 66; Vice-Chair. Henan Revolutionary Cttee. 68; Alt. mem. Politburo, 9th Cen. Cttee. of CCP 69; mem. Politburo, 10th Cen. Cttee. of CCP 73-77, 11th Cen. Cttee. 77 (reported to have been suspended June 79); First Political Commissar, Beijing Region, PLA 74-78; a Vice-Premier, State Council 75-80; Chair. Credentials Cttee. 5th Nat. People's Congress 78; dismissed from posts 80; Deputy Dir. China Int. Travel Service 80.
People's Republic of China.

Ji Pengfei; Chinese politician; b. 1910, Yongji, Shaanxi; ed. Mil. Medical Coll.
Joined Communist Party 31; on Long March in Medical Dept., Red Army 35; Deputy Political Commissar, Army Corps, 3rd Field Army 50; Amb. to German Democratic Repub. 50-55; Vice-Minister of Foreign Affairs 55-72; Acting Minister of Foreign Affairs 68-72, Minister 72-74; Sec.-Gen. Nat. People's Congress Standing Cttee. 75-79; mem. 10th Cen. Cttee. of CCP 73, 11th Cen. Cttee. 77; Exec. Chair. Presidium 5th Nat. People's Congress 78; Vice-Premier, State Council Sept. 79-, Sec.-Gen. 80-81; Dir. CP Int. Liaison Office 81-.
People's Republic of China.

Jian Min; Chinese politician.
Minister of Fourth Ministry of Machine Building 78-79 and 80-.
People's Republic of China.

Jiang Hua; Chinese party official; b. Hubei.
Guerrilla activist with New 4th Army, CCP 40; Mayor of Hangzhou 49-51; Deputy Sec. CCP Zhejiang 52-55, First Sec. 52-68; Alt. mem. 8th Cen. Cttee. of CCP 56; First Political Commissar Zhejiang Mil. District, People's Liberation Army 56-68; Prof. of Political Theories, Zhejiang Univ. 58; Sec. E. China Bureau 65; criticized and removed from office during Cultural Revolution 68; Alt. mem. 10th Cen. Cttee. of CCP 73, mem. 11th Cen. Cttee. 77; Pres. Supreme People's Court 74-.
People's Republic of China.

Jiang Nanxiang; Chinese politician.
Former Vice-Minister of State, Scientific and Tech. Comm.; removed from office during Cultural Revolution; Minister of Educ. 79-; mem. 11th Cen. Cttee. 79-; mem. NPC Standing Cttee.
People's Republic of China.

Jiang Qing; Chinese party official; b. 1914, Zhucheng Shandong; *m.* Mao Zedong 1939 (died 1976); ed. Shandong Experimental Drama Acad., Jinan.
Librarian, Qingdao Univ. 33; film actress 34-38; joined CCP 37; Instructor Lu Xun Art Acad., Yanan 39; Head of Cen. Film Admin. Bureau, Propaganda Dept., CCP 49; with Ministry of Culture 50-54; Organizer of Reforms in Beijing Opera 63; First Deputy Head of Cen. Cultural Revolution Group 66; leading pro-Maoist activist in propaganda work during Cultural Revolution 65-69; mem. Politburo, 9th Cen. Cttee. of CCP 69, Politburo, 10th Cen. Cttee. 73-76; arrested as leader of the "Gang of Four" Oct. 76; expelled from CCP July 77; tried with "Gang of Four" and sentenced to death (suspended for two yrs.) Jan. 81.
People's Republic of China.

Jiang Weiqing; Chinese party official; b. Jiangsu.
Deputy Political Commissar, People's Liberation Army, Nanjing 49; Second Sec. CCP Jiangsu 53-55, First Sec. 56-68; Alt. mem. 8th Cen. Cttee. of CCP 56; First Political Commissar Jiangsu Mil. District, PLA 60-68; Sec. E. China Bureau, CCP 66; criticized and removed from office during Cultural Revolution 68; Alt. mem. 10th Cen. Cttee. of CCP 73; First Sec. CCP Jiangxi 75-80; Chair. Jiangxi Revolutionary Cttee. 75-79; mem. 11th Cen. Cttee. of CCP 77; Political Commissar Fuzhou PLA Mil. Region; First Political Commissar Jiangxi PLA Mil. District 78-.
People's Republic of China.

Jiao Ruoyu: Chinese politician; b. 1916, Yexian Cty., Henan Prov.
Mayor, Shenyang 54; Amb. to Dem. People's Repub. of Korea 65-67, to Peru 72-77, to Iran 77-79; Minister of Eighth Ministry of Machine Building 79-81; acting Chair. People's Govt. (Mayor) of Beijing Jan. 81-.
People's Republic of China

Johnson, Leslie Royston; Australian politician; b. 22 Nov. 1924, Sydney.
Member House of Reps. for Hughes, N.S.W. 55, 58, 61, 63, 69-; Minister of Housing 72-73, of Housing and Construction 73-75, of Aboriginal Affairs June-Nov. 75; Opposition Whip March 77-.
Parliament House, Canberra, A.C.T.; Home: 25/1 Kooroo-ma Place, Sylvania, N.S.W., Australia.

Johnson, Leslie Wilson, C.B.E., M.A.; Australian public servant; b. 2 April 1916; ed. Perth Modern School, Univ. of Western Australia.
Became teacher, then lecturer, and later Inspector, Educ. Dept. Western Australia 36-61; Dir. Educ. Papua New Guinea 62-66; mem. House of Assembly, Papua New Guinea 64-70; Asst. Admin. (Services) Papua New Guinea 66-70, Administrator 70-73, High Commr. 73-74; Dir. Australian Devt. Assistance Agency 74-76; Amb. to Greece and High Commr. in Cyprus 76-.
Australian Embassy, 15 Odos Messoghion, Athens, Greece; Home: 3 Lutana Street, Lyons, Canberra, A.C.T., Australia.

Jones, Alan Stanley, O.B.E.; Australian racing driver; b. 2 Nov. 1946, Melbourne; ed. Xavier Coll., Melbourne.
Began racing in Australia 64; raced in Britain from 70; World Champion 80, runner-up 79; CanAm Champion 78; Grand Prix wins (all for Williams-Ford except Austrian 77, Shadow-Ford): German 79, Austrian 79, Dutch 79, Canadian 79; Argentine 80, French 80, British 80, Canadian 80, U.S. 80; U.S. 81; announced retirement 81.
c/o Williams Grand Prix Engineering Ltd., Unit 10, Station Road Industrial Estate, Didcot, Oxon., England.
Telephone: Didcot 813678.

Jones, Sir Philip Frederick, Kt., A.C.A., A.A.S.A.; Australian company director; b. 14 Aug. 1912, Napier, New Zealand; ed. Barker's Coll., Hornsby, N.S.W.
General Man. The Herald & Weekly Times Ltd., 53-63, Dir. 57-, Vice-Chair. 66-70, Chair. 70-78; Chair. W. Australian Newspapers Ltd. 72-, Herald-Sun TV Pty. 73-; Dir. Australian Newsprint Mills Ltd. 57-, Vice-Chair. 60-; Dir. Tasman Pulp and Paper Co. Ltd. 63-74, Queensland Press Ltd. 70-.
The Herald and Weekly Times Group, 44 Flinders Street, Melbourne, Vic.; Home: 99 Spring Street, Melbourne, Vic. 3000, Australia.

Jung, Nawab Mir Nawaz (M. Mir Khan), B.A., LL.B., M.SC.; Pakistani financier and diplomatist; b. 1914; ed. Nizam's Coll., Hyderabad and Univs. of London, Paris and Geneva.
In service of Hyderabad State, holding posts of Cabinet Sec., Sec Railways and Civil Aviation, Sec. Finance, Official Dir. State Bank, Deccan Airways, Coal Mines Co., etc.; prior to partition was Hyderabad's Envoy in London; Minister of Pakistan to Sweden, Norway, Denmark and Finland 51-53; Amb. to the UN 54-57, Pres. Econ. and Social Council of the UN 57-58; Amb. to France and to the Vatican 57-59; Amb.-at-Large to African States 60; Regional Rep. of UN to N.W. Africa, Dakar 61-65; UN Rep., Tunis 65-68; Senior Consultant to UN Devt. Programme (UNDP); Grand Officier de la Légion d'honneur; Grand Officier Ordre National, Senegal; Ordre National, Mauritania; Grand Cordon de l'Ordre National, Tunisia.
Publs. *Federal Finance* 36, *Central Banking* 45, *Five Year Appraisals* (1960-64) *of UN and Agencies* (co-author).
UNDP, Palais des Nations, Geneva; and 137 rue de Lausanne, Geneva, Switzerland.
Telephone: 317082 (Home).

Jusuf, Lieut.-Gen. Andi Mohamad; Indonesian army officer and politician; b. 23 June 1929, Sulawesi; ed. Dutch Secondary School, and Higher Secondary School.
Former Chief of Staff of Hasanuddin and Commdr. S.E. Mil. District; Minister of Light and Basic Industry 66, of Basic Industry and Power 66, of Trade and Commerce 67, of Industry 68-78, of Defence and Security, also C.-in-C. Armed Forces 78-.
c/o Ministry of Defence, Jakarta, Indonesia.

K

Kaifu, Toshiki; Japanese politician; b. 1932.
Elected to House of Reps. six times; Parl. Vice-Minister of Labour; Chair. Steering Cttee. of House of Reps.; various posts in admin. of Takeo Miki (*q.v.*) 74-76, incl. Deputy Chief Cabinet Sec., Chair. of Diet Policy Cttee. of Liberal-Democratic Party (LDP); Minister of Educ. 76-77.
c/o Ministry of Education, Tokyo, Japan.

Kaiser, Khwaja Muhammad; Bangladesh diplomatist; b. 13 Sept. 1918, Dacca; ed. Dacca Univ.
Indian Police Service 41-50; Second Sec. Deputy High

Commr. for Pakistan, Calcutta 50; Deputy Sec. Ministry of External Affairs, Dacca 50-51; Deputy Sec. Ministry of External Affairs, Karachi 51-55; Counsellor, Beijing 55-57; Consul-Gen., New York 57-60; Minister, Washington 60-62; High Commr. in Australia and New Zealand 62-65; Dir.-Gen. Ministry of Foreign Affairs, Pakistan 65-66; Pakistan Amb. to Sweden, Norway, Denmark, Finland 66-68, to People's Repub. of China 69-72, also accred. to Mongolia; Bangladesh Amb. to Burma, also accred. to Dem. People's Repub. of Korea, Dem. Repub. of Viet-Nam, Thailand and Provisional Revolutionary Govt. of S. Viet-Nam, also High Commr. in Singapore 72-76; Perm. Rep. to U.N. 76-, mem. UN Security Council 78-; Sitara-e-Quaid-e-Azam 62.
Publ. (co-author) *Yellow Sand Hills and the Street of the Plentiful.*
821 United Nations Plaza, 8th Floor, New York, N.Y. 10016, U.S.A.

Kamath, Hari Vishnu, B.SC.; Indian politician; b. 13 July 1907; ed. Mangalore and Presidency Coll., Madras.
Joined Indian Civil Service in London 29; served I.C.S. 30-38; resigned for political reasons; joined Congress and then the Forward Bloc as Sec.-Gen.; in prison 40-41, 42-45; mem. Constituent Assembly 46-49, and mem. Nagpur Provincial Congress Cttee.; mem. Provisional Parl. 50-52; Praja Socialist Mem. of Lok Sabha 55-57, 62-67; Chair. Praja Socialist Party, Madhya Pradesh 58-60; mem. Nat. Exec. Praja Socialist Party 53-71, Nat. Cttee. Socialist Party 71-77 (party merged with others to form Janata Party May 77); Chair. Cen. Parl. Board, Praja Socialist Party 65-70; mem. Admin. Reforms Comm., Govt. of India 66-70; candidate for Vice-Pres. 69; mem. Lok Sabha 77-79; Chair. Lok Sabha Cttee. on Petitions 77-79; Alt. Leader del. to UN Gen. Assembly 77; mem. Press Council of India 79; mem. Nat. Exec. Janata Party 79-.
Publs. *Communist China colonises Tibet, invades India* 59, *Principles and Techniques of Administration* 71, *The Last Days of Jawaharlal Nehru* 77.
Western Court, New Delhi 110001 (Office); Dhantoli, Nagpur 440012, India (Home).
Telephone: 25059 (Home).

Kamei, Masao; Japanese business executive; b. 20 April 1916, Kobe City, Hyogo Pref.; ed. Tokyo Univ.
Director Sumitomo Electric Industries Ltd. 64-66, Man. Dir. 66-69, Senior Man. Dir. 69-71, Exec. Vice-Pres. 71-73, Pres. Nov. 73-; Exec. Dir. Fed. of Econ. Orgs. (Keidanren) 73-, Kansai Econs. Fed. 74-; Vice-Pres. Japan Fed. of Employers' Asscns. (Nikkeiren) May 77-; Pres. Kansai Employers' Asscn. April 77-, Japanese Electric Wire and Cable Makers' Asscn. May 77-; Blue Ribbon Medal.
7-25, 1-chome Kamikoshien, Nishinomiya City, Hyogo Prefecture, Japan.
Telephone: 0798-47-3948.

Kamil, Abdullah; Indonesian diplomatist; b. 27 Dec. 1919, Binjai.
Information Officer, Indonesian Office and then Second Sec., Bangkok; Indonesian Embassy, Bangkok 48-52; Deputy Chief, Information Directorate, Ministry of Foreign Affairs 52-56; First Sec. Indonesian Embassy, The Hague 55-56; Indonesian Consul in Kuala Lumpur 56-57; Counsellor, Indonesian Mission to UN 57-60, Indonesian Embassy, Tunis 65-66; Ministry of Foreign Affairs 60-65; Head Int. Org. Directorate 71-75; Amb. to Yugoslavia 68-71, to Austria 75-79; Perm. Rep. to UN April 79-.
Permanent Mission of Indonesia to the United Nations, 666 Third Avenue, 12th Floor, New York, N.Y. 10017, U.S.A.
Telephone: (212) 286-8910.

Kanakaratne, Neville, M.A., LL.B.; Sri Lankan diplomatist; b. 19 July 1923, Colombo; ed. Royal Coll., Colombo, Univs. of Ceylon and Cambridge, and Middle Temple.
Crown Counsel, Dept. of Attorney-Gen. 51-57; First Sec. and Legal Adviser, Perm. Mission of Ceylon at UN 57-61; Legal Adviser to Special Rep. of UN Sec.-Gen. in the Congo 61-62; Legal and Political Adviser to Commdr., UN Emergency Force, Gaza 62-64; Legal Adviser to Commdr. UN Peace Keeping Force, Cyprus and to Special Rep. of UN Sec.-Gen. 64-65; Senior Fellow, Centre for Int. Studies, New York Univ. 65-66; Minister for Econ. Affairs, Ceylon High Comm., London 67-70; Amb. to U.S.A. (also accred. to Mexico) 70-78; Adviser to UN Sec.-Gen.'s Special Rep. for Namibia 78-; Del. to numerous int. confs. and several sessions of UN Gen. Assembly; Hon. LL.D. (George Washington Univ.).
Room A-3165, UN Headquarters, New York, N.Y. 10017, U.S.A.

Kaneshige, Kankuro; Japanese educationalist; b. 5 April 1899; ed. Tokyo Imperial Univ.
Technician, Kanegafuchi Spinning Co. 23-25; Asst. Prof. of Mechanical Engineering, Tokyo Imperial Univ. 25-42; Prof. of Mechanical Engineering, Univ. of Tokyo 42-60; Dir. Inst. of Industrial Science, Univ. of Tokyo 51-54; Pres. 51-52, Hon. mem. 60- Japan Soc. of Mech. Engineers; Dir. Nat. Aeronautical Laboratory 55-57; Pres. Science Council of Japan 58-60; Prof. Emer., Univ. of Tokyo 60-; Full-time Commr. of Atomic Energy Comm. of Japan 60-65; Chair. Nat. Space Activities Council 60-67; Japanese Co-Chair., U.S.-Japan Cttee. on Scientific Co-operation 61-70; Second Vice-Pres. Int. Fed. of Automatic Control 63-66; mem. UN Advisory Cttee. on the Application of Science and Technology to Devt. 64-69; Full-time mem. Council for Science and Technology 65-74; Trustee, Asian Inst. of Technology, Bangkok 71-76; Fellow American Asscn. for the Advancement of Science 78-; Hon. mem. American Soc. of Mech. Engineers 80-; Hon. D.Tech. (Asian Inst. of Tech.) 76.
5-46-25 Asagayakita, Suginami-ku, Tokyo 166, Japan.
Telephone: 03-337-4991.

Kang Shien; Chinese government official; b. 1910, Beijing.
Assistant to Minister of Petroleum Industry 55-56; Vice-Minister of Petroleum Industry 56; criticized and removed from office during the Cultural Revolution 67; Minister of Petroleum and Chemical Industries 75-78, of Petroleum Industry March 81-, of State Econ. Comm. 78-81, also a Vice-Premier, State Council March 78-; mem. 11th Cen. Cttee. CCP 77.
c/o State Council, Beijing, People's Republic of China.

Kao Shoukun; Chinese army officer.
Commander Jinan Mil. Region PLA 80-.
People's Republic of China.

Karakeyev, Kurman Karakeyevich; Soviet historian; b. 1913, Kurmenty Village, Kirghizia; ed. Higher Party School and Acad. of Social Sciences.
Member C.P.S.U. 38-; C.P. work 39-60; mem. and Pres. Kirghiz Acad. of Sciences 60-79; Corresp. mem. U.S.S.R. Acad. of Sciences 68-; Deputy to U.S.S.R. Supreme Soviet 62-; mem. Comm. for Legislative Proposals; mem. Cen. Cttee. C.P. of Kirghizia; Orders and medals of U.S.S.R.
Publs. *The History of Kirghiz SSR* (co-author and editor) 63, 68, *The History of the Communist Organizations in Central Asia* 67, *The Great October and the Science of Kirghiztan* 77.
c/o Presidium of Kirghiz S.S.R. Academy of Sciences, Frunze 720071, Leninskii Prospect 265A, Kirghiz S.S.R., U.S.S.R. (Office).

Karmal, Babrak; Afghan politician and diplomatist; b. 1929; ed. Kabul Univ.
Detained for 5 years for political activities in 1950s; in Ministry of Planning 57-65; mem. of Parl. 65-73; f. Khalq

political party 65, Leader breakaway Parcham party 67-77; after merger in 77 of Khalq and Parcham parties (now known as People's Democratic Party of Afghanistan (PDPA)) Deputy Leader 77-78; Editor underground newspaper *Parcham;* Deputy Prime Minister and Vice-Pres. of Revolutionary Council April-July 78; Amb. to Czechoslovakia (also accred. to Hungary) 78-79; returned to Afghanistan after Soviet invasion Dec. 79; Apptd. Prime Minister of Afghanistan Dec. 79-June 81 (resgnd.); Pres. of the Revolutionary Council, Gen.-Sec. of PDPA Cen. Cttee. and mem. of Politburo Dec. 79-; C.-in-C. of the Armed Forces Dec. 79-; Order of Sun of Freedom 82.
Office of the President, Revolutionary Council, Da Khalkoo Koor, Kabul, Afghanistan.

Karunandhi, Dr. Muthuvel; Indian politician and playwright; b. 3 June 1924; ed. Thiruvarur Board High School.
Editor-in-Charge *Kudiarasu*; journalist and stage and screen playwright in Tamil, acting in his own plays staged to collect party funds; has written over 35 film-plays including the screen version of the Tamil classic *Silappadhikaram*, stage plays and short stories; started first student wing of the Dravidian movement called Tamilnadu Tamil Manavar Mandram; one of the founder mems. of Dravida Munnetra Kazhagam Legis. Party (D.M.K.) 49, Treas 61, deputy Leader 68, Leader 69-; founder-editor of the Tamil daily organ of the D.M.K. *Murasoli*; represented Kulittalai in State Assembly 57-62, Thanjavur 62-67, Saidapet 68-; led the Kallakkudi Agitation and was imprisoned for six months; fmr. Minister of Public Works; Chief Minister of Tamil Nadu (Madras) 69-76; (presidential rule imposed) Thamizha Vell (Patron of Tamil), Asscn. of Research Scholars in Tamil 71; Hon. D.Litt. (Annamalai Univ., Tamil Nadu) 71.
Dravida Munnetra Kazhagam, Arivagam, Royapuram, Madras 13, Tamil Nadu, India.

Karunaratne, Nuwarapaksa Hewayalage Asoka Mahaname; Sri Lankan politician; b. 26 Jan. 1916; ed. St. Anthony's Coll., Kandy and Nalanda Vidyalaya, Colombo.
Member of Parl. 58-; Parl. Sec. to Minister of Justice 60; Junior Minister of Justice 63, resigned from office because of critical attitude to Govt.; helped to form Sri Lanka Freedom Socialist Party 64; Minister of Social Services 65-70, July 77-.
Ministry of Social Services, Colombo, Sri Lanka.

Kashiwagi, Yusuke, LL.B.; Japanese banker; b. 17 Oct. 1917, Dairen; ed. Tokyo Imperial Univ.
Entered Ministry of Finance 41; Foreign Exchange Bureau 41, Minister's Secretariat 45, Budget Bureau 48, Senior Budget Examiner 51, Dir. Research Section of Foreign Exchange Bureau 54, Dir. Planning Section 56; Financial Sec. Embassy in Washington, D.C. 58; Financial Counsellor, Ministry of Finance 61; Financial Commr. 65; Dir.-Gen. Int. Finance Bureau 66; Vice-Minister of Finance for Int. Affairs 68; resgnd. from Ministry of Finance 71, Special Adviser to Minister of Finance 71-72; Deputy Pres. Bank of Tokyo Ltd. 73-77, Pres. 77-; Chair. Board of Dirs. Bank of Tokyo Int. Ltd. London 78-, Bank of Tokyo (Luxembourg) SA 77-, Bank of Tokyo (Holland) NV, Amsterdam 77-; Perm. Rep. of Bank of Tokyo on Board of Dirs. Banque Européenne de Tokyo SA, Paris 77-; Dir. Sony Corpn. 76-; Adviser Int. Finance Corpn., Washington, D.C. 79-; mem. Exec. Cttee. Trilateral Comm. 73-; mem. 77- and mem. Bd. of Dirs. 79-, Int. Monetary Conf.
Bank of Tokyo Ltd., 6-3, Nihombashi Hongokucho 1-chome, Chuo-ku, Tokyo 103, Japan.
Telephone: 03-245-1111 (Office).

Katayama, Nihachiro; Japanese business executive; b. 31 March 1916, Tosu City, Saga Pref.
Pres. Mitsubishi Electric Corpn.
Mitsubishi Electric Corpn., 2-2-3 Marunouchi, Chiyoda-ku, Tokyo; 683-6 Ozenji, Tama-ku, Kawasaki City, Kanagawa Prefecture, Japan (Home).
Telephone: 03-218-2111 (Office).

Kater, Sir Gregory Blaxland, Kt., M.A.; Australian banker and grazier; b. 15 May 1912, Orange, N.S.W.; ed. The King's School, Sydney and Cambridge Univ., England.
Director, Oil Search Ltd. 50, Chair. 57-79; Dir. Perm. Trustee Co. Ltd. 51, Chair. 56-; Dir. Commercial Banking Co. of Sydney Ltd. 51, Chair. 66-79; Dir. CSR Ltd. 49, Chair. 77-79; Chair. Mercantile & Gen. Reinsurance Co. of Australia Ltd. 57-79, Mercantile & Gen. Life Reassurance Co. of Australia Ltd. 57-79; Dir. H. E. Kater & Son Pty. Ltd. 48-, Vickers Australia Ltd. 65-, Vickers Cockatoo Docks Pty. Ltd. 72-, W. R. Carpenter Holdings Ltd. 70-; Vice-Pres. N.S.W. Soc. for Crippled Children 50.
56 Pitt Street, Sydney, N.S.W. 2000; Home: 106 Victoria Road, Bellevue Hill, N.S.W. 2023, Australia.
Telephone: 27-2872 (Office); 36-7295 (Home).

Kato, Ichiro, LL.D.; Japanese lawyer, professor and university administrator; b. 28 Sept. 1922, Tokyo; ed. Faculty of Law, Univ. of Tokyo.
Associate Prof. of Law, Univ. of Tokyo 48-57, Prof. of Law 57-68, 74-; Dean of Law and Acting Pres. Univ. of Tokyo 68-69, Pres. 69-73; Vice-Rector UN Univ. 75-76, Senior Adviser fo Rector of UN Univ. 76-79; mem. Admin. Board, Int. Asscn. of Univs. 70-; Pres. Nat. Univ. Asscn. (Japan) 69-73; Matsunaga Foundation Prize 66.
Publs. Several books and many treatises on law of torts, environmental law and other legal subjects (in Japanese).
University of Tokyo, Hongo, Bunkyo-ku, Tokyo; 10-30, Seijo 3-chome, Setagaya-ku, Tokyo, Japan.
Telephone: 03-416-2769.

Kaul, Triloki Nath; Indian diplomatist; b. 8 Feb. 1913; ed. Univs. of Punjab, Allahabad, London.
Joined Indian Civil Service 37; served in United Provinces as Joint Magistrate and Collector 37-47; Sec. Indian Council of Agricultural Research, New Delhi 47; First Sec. Indian Embassy, Moscow 47-49, Washington 49-50; Counsellor 50-52, and Minister 52-53, Beijing; Joint Sec. Ministry of External Affairs, New Delhi 53-57; Chair. Int. Comm. for Supervision and Control, Viet-Nam 57-58; Amb. to Iran 58-60; Deputy High Commr., U.K. 60-61, Acting High Commr. 61-62; Amb. to U.S.S.R. and Mongolia 62-66; Sec. to Govt. of India, Ministry of Foreign Affairs, New Delhi, June 66-68; Sec.-Gen. Ministry of External Affairs 68-73; Amb. to U.S.A. 73-76; Indian rep. Exec. Bd. UNESCO 80-(85); Pres. Indian Council for Cultural Relations 77 (resigned April 77); Hon. Fellow, King's Coll., London 62; Hon. Prof., Kashmir Univ. 78; Hon. Chair. Editorial Board Man. and Devt. Council for Research in Rural and Industrial Devt., Chandigarh.
Publs. *Diplomacy in Peace and War: Recollections and Reflections* 78, *India, China and Indochina* 79.
1037, Sector 21B, Chandigarh, India.
Telephone: 23136.

Kaula, Prithvi Nath, M.A., M.LIBR.SC.; Indian professor of library and information science; b. 13 March 1924, Srinagar; ed. S.P. Coll., Srinagar, Punjab Univ., Delhi Univ., Banaras Hindu Univ.
Member Council, Indian Library Asscn. 49-53, 56-62; Man. Ed. Annals, Bulletin and Granthalays of Indian Library Asscn. 49-53; Sec. Ranganathan Endowment for Library Science 51-61; Gen. Sec. Delhi Library Asscn. 53-55, 58-60; Vice-Pres. 56-58; Visiting Lecturer in Library Science, Aligarh Muslim Univ. 51-58; Expert mem. Ind. Standards Inst. 57-62, Comm. on Scientific Terminology 62-; Reader Dept. of Library Science, Univ. of Delhi 58-60; Vice-Pres. Govt. of India Libraries Asscn. 58-61; mem. Review Cttee. on Library Science, Univ. Grants Comm. 61-63; Visiting Lecturer Documentation, Research and Training Cen., Bangalore 62, 65; Ed.

Herald of Library Science 62-; Chair. Fed. of Indian Library Asscns. 66, Pres. 74-; mem. Governing Council, Nat. Library of India 66-69; UNESCO Expert, UNESCO Regional Cen. in the Western Hemisphere, Havana 67-68; Gen. Sec. Indian Asscn. of Teachers of Library Science 69, Pres. 73-; Ed. *Granthalaya Vijnana* 70-; Librarian, Banaras Hindu Univ. 71-78, Prof. and Head of Dept. of Library and Information Science 71-78; Chair. Council of Literacy and Adult Educ. 71-; Expert mem. UNESCO Advisory Group on Comparability of Higher Degrees in Library Science 73-; on Panel Library and Information Science of Univ. Grants Comm.; Dean, Faculty of Arts, Banaras Hindu Univ. 79-; Bureau for Promotion of Urdu Library Science 80-; mem. State Library Cttee., Uttar Pradesh 81-, Raja Rammohun Roy Library Foundation 81-, Bd. of Studies in Library and Information Science, 11 univs.; Ed.-in-Chief *International Information, Communication and Education* 81-; Visiting Prof. 25 Indian Univs., 7 American Univs., Univ. of Havana, Hebrew Univ., Jerusalem and Univs. in Fed. Repub. of Germany, G.D.R., Hungary, Thailand, U.K. and the U.S.S.R.; Consultant on Library Science to several int. orgs. and nat. asscns.; Organizing Sec. and Pres. numerous confs.; Kaula Endowment in Library and Information Science established 75; Kaula Gold Medal annual award through an Int. awards Cttee. 75-; Honoured by Int. Festschrift Cttee. 74; Indian Library Movement Award 74; Pro Mundi Beneficio Medal 75, Deutsche Bucherei Medal 81.
Publs. 47 publications, 43 bibliographies and over 600 technical papers and book reviews on library science, labour problems and student unrest.
Cl, Banaras Hindu University, Varanasi 221005, India.

Kaushik, Purushottam, B.A., LL.B.; Indian politician; b. 24 Sept. 1930, Mahasamund; ed. Raipur, Sagar, Nagpur Univ.
Joined Socialist Party 52; engaged in political org. of Adivasi peasants and agricultural workers in Chattisgarh; organized hunger marches 65, 74; helped to form Kisan Khetihar Mazdoor Sangh (co-operative org.) in Chattisgarh; mem. Vidhan Sabha (legislature) of Madhya Pradesh for Mahasamund 72-75; mem. Exec., Madhya Pradesh Unit of Socialist Party, also mem. Nat. Cttee.; Chair. Madhya Pradesh Socialist Party 75-77; detained during emergency 75-Feb. 77; mem. Janata Party 77-; mem. Lok Sabha from Raipur March 77-; Minister for Tourism and Civil Aviation 77-79, of Information and Broadcasting 79-80.
Lok Sabha, New Delhi, India.

Kawai, Ryoichi; Japanese business executive; b. 18 Jan. 1917; ed. Tokyo Univ.
President, Komatsu Ltd.
Komatsu Bldg., 3-6, 2-chome, Akasaka, Minato-ku, Tokyo, Japan.
Telephone: 584-7111.

Kawamata, Katsuji; Japanese business executive; b. 1 March 1905; ed. Tokyo Univ. of Commerce.
Japan Industrial Bank 29-47, Branch Man. Hiroshima 46-47; Man. Dir. Nissan Motor Co. 47-57, Pres. 57-73, Chair. 73-; Chair. Nissan Diesel, Nissan Shatai, Japan Automobile Mfrs. Asscn. 62-72; Vice-Pres. Fed. of Econ. Orgs. (Keidanren) 72; Governing Dir. Fed. of Employers' Asscn. (Nikkeiren); Auditor Tokyo Chamber of Commerce and Industry; Vice-Chair. Japan Productivity Cen.; Blue Ribbon Medal 62; Educ. Minister's Commendation 74; 1st Order of Sacred Treasure 75.
Nissan Motor Co. Ltd., 17-1, 6-chome, Ginza Chuo-ku, Tokyo 104, Japan.

Kawasaki, Kunio; Japanese business executive; b. 23 Sept. 1907; ed. Tokyo Univ.
Japan Woollen Yarn Spinning Co. Ltd. 32-42, Toyobo Co. Ltd. (after merger) 42-, Dir. 56-57, Man. Dir. 57-61, Senior Man. Dir. 61-63, Vice-Pres. 63-66, Pres. 66-74, Chair. of Board 74-78, Counsellor 78-; Auditor Japan Exlan Co. Ltd. (acrylic fibres) 66-76; Exec. Dir. Kansai Econs. Fed. 66-68, Vice-Pres. 68-; Exec. Dir. Fed. of Econ. Orgs. 66-78, Japan Fed. of Employers' Asscn. 67-76; Pres. Toyobo Petcord Co. Ltd. 69-76; Gen. Counsellor Toyo Rubber Industry Co. Ltd. 71-; Chair. Japan Spinners' Asscn. 72-73; Pres. Osaka-São Paulo Sister City Asscn. 70-74, Dir. 74-78; Exec. Dir. Japan Textile Fed. 73-78; Pres. Kansai Int. Students Inst. 74-76; Vice-Pres. Japan Overseas Enterprise Asscn. 74-80; Pres. Osaka Int. Trade Fair Comm. 74-77; Blue Ribbon Medal 69; Order of the Rising Sun (2nd Class) 79.
Toyobo Co. Ltd., 2-8, Dojima Hama 2-chome, Kita-ku, Osaka 530; Home: 1-28, 1-chome, Hibarigaoka Yamate, Takarazuka City, Hyogo Prefecture, 665, Japan.
Telephone: 06-348-3253 (Office); 0727-59-2556 (Home).

Kazi, A. G. N.; Pakistani banker and civil servant; b. Naushahro Fereze, Nawabshah District.
Joined I.C.S. 43; held various admin. posts in Bihar-Oresia Service; Collector, Thatta; Financial Sec. Sind Govt.; Econ. Minister for Pakistan, Washington, D.C. 62-65; Additional Chief Sec. Planning and Devt.; Chair. W.A.P.D.A.; Sec. Ministry of Industries and Natural Resources 69, Ministry of Finance 70; Sec.-Gen. Finance and Econ. Co-ordination 73; Adviser to C.M.L.A. for Finance and Econ. Affairs Jan. 78-; Gov. and Chair. State Bank of Pakistan July 78-.
State Bank of Pakistan, Central Directorate, I.I. Chundrigar Road, P.O. Box 4456, Karachi, Pakistan.

Ke Hua; Chinese diplomatist; b. 1915, Guangdong Province.
Director of Protocol Dept., Ministry of Foreign Affairs 55-57, Dir. W. Asia and Africa Dept. 57-60; Amb. to Guinea 60-64, to Ghana 72-74, to Philippines 75-78, to U.K. Sept. 78-; Dir. Africa Dept., Ministry of Foreign Affairs 64-Cultural Revolution, Dir. Asia Dept. April-July 75.
Embassy of the People's Republic of China, 31 Portland Place, London, W1N 3AG; (Home) 11 West Heath Avenue, London, N.W.11, England.
Telephone: 01-636 5726.

Kedah, H.R.H. the Sultan of; Tuanku Haji Abdul Halim Mu'adzam Shah Ibni Almarhum Sultan Badlishah, D.K., D.K.H., D.K.M., D.M.N., D.U.K., D.K. (Kelantan), D.K. (Pahang), D.K. (Selangor), D.K. (Perlis), D.P. (Sarawak), S.P.M.K., S.S.D.K.; Ruler of Kedah, Malaysia; b. 28 Nov. 1927, Alor Setar; ed. Sultan Abdul Hamid Coll., Alor Setar, and Wadham Coll., Oxford.
Raja Muda (Heir to Throne of Kedah) 49-58, Regent of Kedah 57-58, Sultan 58-; Timbalan Yang Di Pertuan Agong (Deputy Supreme Head of State of Malaysia) 65-70, Yang Di Pertuan Agong (Supreme Head of State of Malaysia) 70-75; Col. Commdt. Malaysian Reconnaissance Corps 66; Col.-in-Chief Royal Malay Regt.; First Class Order of the Rising Sun, Japan 70, Bintang Maha Putera, Klas Satu, Indonesia 70, Knight Grand Cross of the Bath, U.K. 72, K.St.J. 72, Most Auspicious Order of the Rajamitrathorn, Thailand 73.
Alor Setar, Kedah, Malaysia.

Kelantan, H.R.H. the Sultan of; Tuanku Ismail Petra ibni Al-Marhum Sultan Yahya Petra, D.K., D.M.N., S.P.M.K., S.J.M.K., S.P.S.K.; Ruler of Kelantan, Malaysia; b. 11 Nov. 1949; ed. Maktab Sultan Ismail Coll., Kota Bharu, Kelantan.
Tengku Mahkota Kelantan 67; Regent 74-79; Sultan of Kelantan April 79-.
Kota Bharu, Kelantan, Malaysia.

Kelly, Sir Theo (William Theodore), Kt., O.B.E., J.P., F.R.S.A., F.A.I.M.; Australian business executive (retd.); b. 27 June 1907, Chatswood, Sydney; ed. Sydney.
Served World War II, Wing Commdr. R.A.A.F. 42-44;

Chair. Canteen Services Board 44-59; Man. Dir. Woolworths Ltd. Aust. 45-70, Chair. 63-79; Chair. Woolworths (N.Z.) Ltd. and Woolworths (Properties) Ltd. -80; mem. Board, Reserve Bank of Aust. 61-75; Dir. Aust. Mutual Life Assurance Co.; Chair. Computer Sciences of Australia Ltd.; Deputy Chair. Australian Mutual Provident Soc. 67-79; Chair. Key Travel Services Pty. Ltd. 79-; Fellow, Univ. of Sydney and mem. Senate 68-75; mem. Board, Royal N. Shore Hosp. 69-77.
c/o Key Travel Services Ltd., P.O. Box KX 84, Kings Cross, N.S.W. 2011. Australia.

Keneally, Thomas Michael, F.R.S.L.; Australian author; b. 7 Oct. 1935.
Lecturer in Drama, Univ. of New England, Armidale, N.S.W. 68-70; Royal Soc. of Literature Prize.
Publs. *Bring Larks and Heroes* 67, *Three Cheers for the Paraclete* 68, *The Survivor* 69, *A Dutiful Daughter* 70, *The Chant of Jimmie Blacksmith* 72, *Blood Red, Sister Rose* 74, *Gossip from the Forest* 75, *Season in Purgatory* 76, *A Victim of the Aurora* 77, *Ned Kelly and the City of the Bees* 78, *Confederates* 79, *Schindler's Ark* 82.
c/o Tessa Sayle, 11 Jubilee Place, Chelsea, London SW3 3TE, England.

Kenilorea, Rt. Hon. Peter, P.C., DIP. ED.; Solomon Islands politician; b. 23 May 1943, Takataka, Malaita; ed. King George VI School, Wanganui Boys' Coll., New Zealand, and Ardmore Teachers' Training Coll., Auckland, New Zealand.
Schoolmaster, King George VI Secondary School 68-70; Asst. Sec. Finance 71; Admin. Officer, district admin. 71-73; Lands Officer 73-74; Deputy Sec. to Cabinet and to Chief Minister 74-75; District Commr., Eastern Solomons 75-76; mem. Legislative Assembly June 76-; Chief Minister of Solomon Islands 76-78, Prime Minister 78-81; founder mem. and Leader Solomon Islands United Party 80-.
Publs. numerous articles for political and scientific publications.
c/o Prime Minister's Office, Honiara, Guadalcanal, Solomon Islands.
Telephone: 373 (Home).

Kerr, Rt. Hon. Sir John Robert, A.K., G.C.M.G., G.C.V.O., P.C., LL.B., Q.C.; Australian lawyer and fmr. Governor-General of Australia; b. 24 Sept. 1914, Sydney; ed. Fort St. Boys' High School, Sydney Univ.
Admitted to New South Wales Bar 38; army service 42-46; Principal, Australian School of Pacific Admin. 46-48; Organizing Sec. South Pacific Comm. 46-47; Q.C. (N.S.W.) 53; mem. N.S.W. Bar Council 60-64; Vice-Pres. N.S.W. Bar Asscn. 62-63, Pres. 64; Vice-Pres. Law Council of Australia 62-64, Pres. 64-66; Pres. N.S.W. Marriage Guidance Council 61-62, Industrial Relations Soc. of Australia 64-66, Law Asscn. for Asia and Western Pacific 66-70; Deputy Pres. Trades Practices Tribunal 66-72, Copyright Tribunal 69-72; Pres. Third Commonwealth and Empire Law Conf., Sydney 65; mem. Medical Board of N.S.W. 63-66, Board of the Council on New Guinea Affairs 64-71; Judge of Commonwealth Industrial Court and Judge of Supreme Court of A.C.T. 66-72, Judge of Courts of Marine Inquiry 67-72, Judge of Supreme Court of Northern Territory 70-72; Chair. Commonwealth Cttee. on Review of Pay for Armed Services 70-72, Commonwealth Cttee. on Review of Parl. Salaries 71; Chief Justice, Supreme Court, N.S.W. 72-74; Lieut.-Gov. N.S.W. 73-74; Gov.-Gen. of Australia 74-77; Hon. Life mem. Law Soc. of England and Wales 65; Hon. mem. American Bar Asscn. 67; K.St.J. 74.
Publs. *Matters for Judgment* 78; papers and articles on industrial relations, New Guinea affairs, organization of legal profession, etc.
c/o Australia House, Strand, London, WC2B 4LA, England.

Keuneman, Pieter Gerald Bartholomeus, M.A.; Sri Lankan politician; b. 3 Oct. 1917, Colombo; ed. Royal Coll. Colombo, Univ. Coll. Colombo, Pembroke Coll. Cambridge, and Gray's Inn, London.
Worked briefly as journalist in London; Asst. Editor, *Ceylon Daily News* 40-; founder mem. and Gen. Sec. Ceylon Communist Party (now Communist Party of Sri Lanka) 43-73, Chair. 73-80; mem. Parl. for Colombo Central 47-; Minister of Housing and Construction 70-77; resigned together with all CP mems. of Govt. Feb. 77.
Publs. several books, pamphlets and articles on socialism and political and economic problems of Sri Lanka.
c/o Central Headquarters, Communist Party of Sri Lanka, 91 Cotta Road, Colombo 8; Home: 8/2 27th Lane, Colombo 3, Sri Lanka.
Telephone: 93855 (CP H.Q.); 23620 (Home).

Khan, Akbar Ali, B.A., LL.B.; Indian lawyer and fmr. state governor; b. 20 Nov. 1899, Hyderabad; ed. Jamia Millia, New Delhi; Aligarh Muslim Univ., Osmania and London Univs.
Called to the Bar, London; joined Congress 49; mem. Rajya Sabha 54-72; Senior Advocate Supreme Court; Gov. of Uttar Pradesh 72-74, of Orissa 74-76; Founder Jawaharlal Nehru Polytechnic; Pres. Abul Kalam Azad Oriental Research Inst., Osmania Univ. Graduates Asscn., Econ. Soc., All-India Exhbn. Soc., Hyderabad; Vice-Pres. Hyderabad Municipal Corpn., Cen. Co-operative Union, Food Relief Asscn.; Gen. Sec. Hyderabad Lawyers' Conf.; mem. Exec. Cttee. All-India Co-operative Unions, exec. councils of several orgs.; Pres. Village Reconstruction Org. in Andhra Pradesh, Tamil Nadu and Orissa; Pres. Andhra Pradesh Consumers' Council; Padma Bhushan 65.
Stone House, Secretariat Road, Saifabad, Hyderabad, Andhra Pradesh, India.

Khan, Ali Akbar; Indian musician; b. 14 April 1922, Shivpur (now in Bangladesh); son of late Allauddin Khan, father of Ashish Khan (*q.v.*).
Concert recitals on Sarod, in India since 36, and all over the world since 55; Founder Ali Akbar Coll. of Music, Calcutta 56, Ali Akbar Coll., San Rafael, Calif. 68; Musical Dir. of many films including award-winning *Hungry Stones* and numerous contributions on All-India Radio; Lecture recitals at univs. in U.S. and Canada; first long-playing gramophone record introduced by Yehudi Menuhin; musical collaboration with Ravi Shankar, the late Duke Ellington and others; composer of concerti, orchestral pieces and ragas, notably *Chandranandan, Gauri Manjari, Alamgiri, Medhavi*; Hon. D.Litt. (Rabindra Bharati Univ., Calcutta) 74; Pres. of India Award, 63, 66; Padmabhushan; Grand Prix du Disque 68.
74 Broadmoor Avenue, San Anselmo, Calif. 94960, U.S.A.; 159/1A Rashbehari Avenue, Calcutta 70029, India.

Khan, Ashish; Indian musician; b. 5 Dec. 1939; son of Ali Akbar Khan (*q.v.*); studied with his grandfather, Allauddin Khan, his father and with Annapurna Shankar, his aunt.
Gave first public concert playing sarod duets with grandfather, the late Allauddin Khan, and played in trio with his father and grandfather; concert tour with his father to East-West Music Encounter, Japan 62; appeared in Festival of India at Hollywood Bowl 67; concert tours in U.S.A., Canada, France, Fed. Repub. of Germany, U.K. 68-; has taught Indian music at Univ. of Washington, Seattle, Calif. State Coll., Long Beach and Ali Akbar Coll. of Music, San Rafael, Calif.; formed pop group Shanti 70, group The Third Eye to play music of various styles and traditions 78.
Compositions include *Ragmala* for string quartet, sarod and tabla 69, *Symphony in Raja* 73, music for the film *Jatugriha* and many other films; has made recordings for several companies.
74 Broadmoor Avenue, San Anselmo, Calif. 94960, U.S.A.
Telephone: (415) 456-5963.

Khan, Ghulam Ishaq; Pakistani civil servant; b. 1915; ed. Islamia Coll., Peshawar, and Punjab Univ.
North-West Frontier Province (N.W.F.P.) Civil Service (India) 40-47, Sub-Divisional Officer, Treasury Officer and Magistrate First Class 40-44, Bursar and Sec. to Council of Management of Islamia Coll., Peshawar; Sec. to Chief Minister, N.W.F.P. 47; Home Sec. Food and Dir. Civil Supplies to Govt. N.W.F.P. 48; Devt. and Admin. Sec. for Agriculture, Animal Husbandry, Forests, Industries, Co-operatives and Village Aid 49-52; Devt. Commr. and Sec. to Devt. Dept., N.W.F.P. 53-56; Sec. for Devt. and Irrigation, Govt. of W. Pakistan 56-58; mem. W. Pakistan Water and Power Devt. Authority 58-61, Chair. 61-66; mem. Land Reforms Comm. 58-59; Sec. Finance, Govt. of Pakistan 66-70; Cabinet Sec., Govt. of Pakistan 70; Gov. State Bank of Pakistan 71-75; Sec.-Gen. Ministry of Defence 75-77; Sec.-Gen.-in-Chief, Adviser for Planning and Co-ordination 77-78; Minister of Finance and Planning 78-79; Adviser to Chief Martial Law Administrator 78-; Minister for Finance and Co-ordination 78-79, for Finance, Commerce and Provincial Co-ordination and Deputy Chair. Planning Comm. April 79-; Tamgha-i-Pakistan 59; Sitara-i-Pakistan 62; Hilal-i-Quaid-i-Azam 68.
Ministry of Finance, Islamabad; 2, 52nd Street, Shalimar 6/4, Islamabad, Pakistan (Home).
Telephone: 68709; 26050 (Home).

Khan, Air Marshal Mohammad Asghar; Pakistani air force officer and politician; b. 17 Jan. 1921; ed. Imperial Defence Coll., U.K.
Staff Coll., Andover, England 49, Joint Services Staff Coll. 52; C.-in-C. Pakistan Air Force and Mil. Adviser SEATO 57-65; Pres. Pakistan Int. Airlines 65-68; entered politics Nov. 68; head and founder of Tehrik-i-Istiqlal 68; mem. Nat. Assembly March-July 77; detained March-Aug. 77; joined Pakistan People's Party 78; detained Oct. 79-.
23 Kutchery Road, Abbottabad, Pakistan.

Khan, Rana Mohammed Hanif: Pakistan politician; b. 1921, Garh Shankar, E. Punjab; ed. Govt. Coll., Ludhiana.
Pres. Pakistan Students' Fed., U.K. 54-55; called to the Bar, Lincoln's Inn, London 55; legal practice, Shahiwal 55-; Pres. District Bar Asscn., Shahiwal 62-63, 66-67; mem. Pakistan People's Party 70-; mem. Nat. Assembly 70-77; Minister of Labour, Works and Local Bodies Dec. 71-74, of Finance, Planning and Devt. 74- March 77, of Commerce and Local Govt. April-July 77; detained July 77; mem. High Court, Lahore; mem. High Court Bar Asscn., Lahore; permitted to participate in politics again; Perm. mem. Inns of Courts Students' Union, London.
153/B-VII, opposite Stadium, Civil Lines, Shahiwal, Punjab, Pakistan.

Khan, Rear-Admiral Musharraf Husain; Bangladesh naval officer and government official (retd.); ed. T.S. Dufferin, Bombay, Royal Naval Coll., Dartmouth, Greenwich, U.K., Nat. Defence Coll., Rawalpindi, Pakistan.
Navigation Officer, P.N.S. *Tippusultan* 59-60; Staff Officer, Operations, Naval HQ, Pakistan 62-64; Commdr. Patrol Craft Sqn. and C.O. of P.N.S. *Jessore* 65; Second-in-Command of Destroyers *Shahjahan* and *Jahangir* 66-67; Controller of Shipping 68-69; Exec. Officer of Cruiser *Babur* 69-70; C.O. of Destroyer *Khaiber* 70-71; Chief of Naval Staff, Bangladesh Navy 73-80; Deputy Chief Martial Law Admin. and mem. Advisory Council to the Pres. of Bangladesh in charge of Communications, Power, Water Resources and Flood Control, Ports and Shipping, Posts, Telephones and Telegraphs and Inland Water Transport 75-77; Acting Pres., People's Repub. of Bangladesh Aug. 76; leader dels. to 4 UN Confs. 76-77; signed Farakka Agreement with India Nov. 77; Chair. Nat. Oceanographic and Maritime Inst. 79-; involved in industry and social work 80-.
"The Anchorage", 100A Shahbag Avenue, Ramna, Dacca 2 (Office); "The Mooring", 243A, DOHS, Mohakhali, Dacca 12, Bangladesh (Home).

Khan, Lieut.-Gen. Sahabzada Yaqub; Pakistani politician, diplomatist and retd. army officer; b. 1920.
Served Second World War, Middle East; joined Pakistan Army, Commdr. armoured regt. 47; attended Army Staff Coll., Quetta 49, Ecole Supérieure de Guerre, Paris 53-54, later Imperial Defence Coll., London; Vice-Chief Gen. Staff, Pakistan Army 58; Commdr. armoured div.; Commandant Army Staff Coll., Quetta; Chief Gen. Staff; Corps Commdr. and Commdr., Eastern Command until 1970; Amb. to France (also accred. to Ireland and Jamaica) 72, to U.S.A. 73-79, to U.S.S.R. 79-80, to France 80-82; Minister of Foreign Affairs March 82-.
Ministry of Foreign Affairs, Islamabad, Pakistan.

Khan, Air Chief Marshal Zulfiqar Ali; Pakistani air force officer and government official; b. 10 Dec. 1930, Lahore; ed. Pakistan Air Force Acad., Risalpur and Pakistan Air Force Staff Coll., Karachi.
Commissioned in Pakistan Air Force 50; various staff and command appointments; Dir. of Operations and Plans and Asst. Chief of Air Staff (Operations) until 74; Chief of Air Staff (Operations) until 74; Chief of Air Staff 74-78; mem. Mil. Council (mil. govt. under Gen. Mohammad Zia ul-Haq, *q.v.*) 77-78.
c/o Air Headquarters, Peshawar, Pakistan.

Khanal, Yadu Nath; Nepalese politician and diplomatist; b. 13 Aug. 1913; ed. Nepal and India.
Professor, Tri-Chandra Coll., Kathmandu 43-56; Councillor, Kathmandu Municipality 48-49; mem. and Sec. Del. of Nepal to Asian-African Conf., Bandung 55; Home Sec. of Nepal 56-57; delegate to UN Gen. Assembly 59, 60, 67; Foreign Sec. 61-63; Amb. to India 63-67; mem. dels. to Non-Aligned Confs., Belgrade 61, Cairo 64; Foreign Sec. 67; Amb. to U.S.A. 73-75; Chair. Public Service Comm. 75-77; Amb. to People's Repub. of China (also accred. to Democratic People's Repub. of Korea) 78-; Harvard Fellow CIFA 70.
Publs. *Reflections on India-Nepal Relations* 64, *Stray Thoughts* 66, *Nepal: Transition from Isolationism* 77, two books in Nepali on literary subjects.
Nepalese Embassy, 12 San Li Tun Lu, Beijing, People's Republic of China.

Khanna, Charan Das, M.A., C.A.I.I.B., A.I.B.; Indian financial official; b. 22 March 1915, Kangra; ed. Punjab Univ.
Worked in various supervisory capacities in Indian and English commercial banks in India 38-48; joined Industrial Finance Corpn. of India 48, Sec. 65-66, Gen. Man. 66-70, Chair. 70-74; Dir. Industrial Reconstruction Corpn. of India 71-; Trustee, Unit Trust of India 73-; Fellow. Econ. Devt. Inst. of World Bank; Pochkanwala Prize, Indian Inst. of Bankers.
Publs. several papers on banking and industrial finance.
Industrial Finance Corporation of India, Bank of Baroda Building, 16 Parliament Street, P.O. Box 363, New Delhi 110001, India.
Telephone: 312440 (Office); 672832 (Home).

Khanna, Kanahiya Charan, B.SC.; Indian engineer and business executive; b. 17 Sept. 1924, Lucknow, Uttar Pradesh; ed. Banaras Hindu Univ.
Engineer in foundry industry 48-56, Bhilai Steel Plant 56-64; Supt. (Blast Furnace) Durgapur Steel Plant 64-67, Chief Supt. (Iron and Steel) 67-69, Asst. Gen. Supt. (Iron and Steel) 69-71; Gen. Supt. and Gen. Man. Bokaro Steel Ltd, 71-74, Man. Dir. 74-76; Chair. and Man. Dir. Kuderamukh Iron Ore Co. Ltd. 76-80; Chair. Steel Authority of India 80-81; fmr. Chair. Visvesvaraya Iron and Steel Co. Ltd.; Dir. numerous cos.; mem. Council of Scientific and Industrial Research, Public Enterprise Bd.,

Indian Inst. of Metals, All India Bd. of Man. Studies (Ministry of Education); Fellow Inst. of Dirs., London; Nat. Metallurgists Award 64.
5 Vishav Rockey Street, Lucknow, Uttar Pradesh, India (Home).
Telephone: 81348 (Home).

Kharmawan, Byanti; Indonesian international finance official; b. 1 June 1906, Tegal, Central Java; ed. School of Economics, Rotterdam.
Became civil servant 49; Econ. Adviser, Ministry of Econ. Affairs and Ministry of Finance; Chief Econ. Adviser and Deputy Gov., Central Bank of Indonesia; Exec. Dir. Asian Devt. Bank 66-68; Exec. Dir. Int. Monetary Fund (IMF) 68-.
Publs. *Willem Kloos en de Dichtkunst* and articles on literary and economic topics.
International Monetary Fund, 19th and H Streets, N.W., Washington, D.C. 20431, U.S.A.

Khatri, Maj.-Gen. Padma Bahadur, K.C.V.O.; Nepalese diplomatist; b. Feb. 1915, Kathmandu; ed. in Calcutta and Tri-Chandra Coll., Kathmandu.
Joined Nepal Army 35; war service 40-46; Military attaché Nepalese Embassy London 47-49; Observer, UN Gen. Assembly 48; Nepalese Liaison Officer to British Brig. of Gurkhas, Malaya 50; Nepalese rep. to Non-Aligned Conf., Bandung 55, Cairo 64; Sec. Coronation Cttee. 56; Chair. Nepal-China Boundary Cttee. 60-62; Minister of Defence 62-63, of Foreign Affairs 63-64, 72-75; Amb. to U.S.A., Argentina, Canada and Chile 64-68, 76-80, to Mexico and Peru 77-80; Perm. Rep. to UN 64-72; fmr. Vice-Pres. UN Gen. Assembly (twice), Pres. UN Security Council (twice); Chair. UN Special Del. to Security Council, Guinea 70; accompanied the late H.M. King Mahendra on several State visits, etc.; Orders of Gorkha Dakshin Bahu I, Nepal Sripad II, Sainik Dirgha Sewa Patta, Nepal Tara I, Trisaktipatta I, Grand Cross (Fed. Repub. of Germany), Officier, Légion d'honneur (France).
c/o Ministry of Foreign Affairs, Kathmandu, Nepal.

Khiem, Gen. Tran Thien (*see* Tran Thien Khiem, Gen.).

Khieu Samphan; Kampuchean politician; b. 1932; ed. Paris Univ.
Founded French-language journal, Cambodia; Deputy Nat. Assembly in Prince Sihanouk's party, Sangkum Reastr Nyum (Popular Socialist Community); served as Sec. of State for Commerce; left Phnom-Penh to join Khmers Rouges 67; Minister of Defence in Royal Govt. of Nat. Union of Cambodia (GRUNC) 70-75, Deputy Prime Minister 70-76 (in exile 70-75, in Phnom-Penh 75-76); Pres. of State Presidium (Head of State) of Democratic Kampuchea 76-79; mem. Politburo Nat. United Front of Cambodia (FUNC) 70-79; C.-in-C. Khmer Rouge High Command 73-79; Prime Minister of Democratic Kampuchea (Khmer Rouge) opposition Govt. fighting Vietnamese forces Dec. 79-; Vice-Pres. Coalition Govt. of Democratic Kampuchea, Thailand June 82-.

Khorana, Har Gobind, PH.D.; American (born Indian) scientist; b. 1922; ed. Punjab Univ.
Began career as organic chemist; worked with Sir Alexander Todd on nucleotides, Cambridge 50-52; later worked at Nat. Research Inst., Canada until 60; Prof. Inst. of Enzyme Chemistry, Univ. of Wisconsin 60-70; Sloan Prof. of Biology and Chemistry, Mass. Inst. of Technology 70-; mem. Nat. Acad. of Sciences; Nobel Prize for Medicine and Physiology (with Holley and Nirenberg) for their interpretation of the genetic code and its function in protein synthesis 68; Louisa Gross Horwitz Prize for Biochemistry 68, Lasker Foundation Award 68, American Chemical Soc. Award, American Acad. of Achievement Award 71; Hon. D.Sc. (Liverpool, Delhi, Chicago); Hon. LL.D. (Simon Fraser Univ.).
Department of Biology and Chemistry, Massachusetts Institute of Technology, Cambridge, Mass. 02139, U.S.A.

Kibria, Shah A.M.S., M.A.; Bangladesh United Nations official; b. 1 May 1931, Sylhet; ed. Univ. of Dacca, Fletcher School of Law and Diplomacy, Boston, Mass., U.S.A.
Joined diplomatic service of Pakistan 54; served various embassies until 71; declared allegiance to Bangladesh and joined Bangladesh mission, Washington, D.C. Aug. 71; Dir.-Gen. Political Affairs Dept., Ministry of Foreign Affairs March 72; Sec., Ministry of Foreign Affairs 72-73; High Commr. in Australia (also accred. to New Zealand and Fiji) 73-76; Perm. Rep. to UN Offices, Geneva 76-78; Chair. Preparatory Cttee., Group of 77 for UNCTAD V, Geneva 78; Foreign Sec., Ministry of Foreign Affairs 78-81; Exec. Sec. UN Econ. and Social Comm. for Asia and the Pacific (ESCAP) May 81-.
Economic and Social Commission for Asia and the Pacific, UN Building, Rajdamnern Avenue, Bangkok 2, Thailand.

Kijima, Torazo, B.ECON.; Japanese business executive; b. 18 Dec. 1901; ed. Tokyo Imperial Univ.
Director Japanese Nat. Railways 50-52; mem. House of Councillors 53-59; Pres. Hinomaru Ceramic Industry Co. Ltd. 53-, Aito Vehicles Industries Co. Ltd.; Chair. Board of Dirs. Nippon Express Co. Ltd. 68-; Second Grand Order of Sacred Treasure (Japan) 72, Commdr., Grand Order (Malagasy Republic) 73.
3-12-9, Soto-Kanda, Chiyoda-ku, Tokyo; Home: 3-42-17, Wakamiya, Nakano-ku, Tokyo, Japan.

Kiki, Sir Albert Maori, K.B.E., M.P.; Papua New Guinean fmr. politician and business executive; b. 21 Sept. 1931, Orokolo, Gulf Province; ed. Fiji School of Medicine, Papua New Guinea Admin. Coll.
Public Health Officer, Welfare Officer, Patrol Officer 54-64; founded first trade union in Papua New Guinea 62; Pres. council of Trade Unions 62-; land claims work with Koiari people; Founder mem. Pangu Pati 65, Gen. Sec. 65-72; mem. City Council, Port Moresby 71-73; mem. for Port Moresby Inland, House of Assembly 72-; Minister for Lands and Environment 72-73, for Defence, Foreign Affairs, Trade, Migration and Customs 74-77; Deputy Prime Minister and Minister for Defence, Foreign Affairs and Trade 75-77; Chair. Interim Constitutional Comm. 76; Chair. New Guinea Motors, First Finance Co.—Credit Corpn. Pty. Ltd.; part owner and Chair. Kwila Insurance Corpn. Ltd.; Hon. Dr. of Law (Kyung Hee Univ., Republic of Korea) 76.
Publs. *Ten Thousand Years in a Lifetime* (autobiography) 70; co-author *Ho Hao* (arts and culture of the Orokolo people) 72.
Granville Farm, 8 Mile, Port Moresby, Papua New Guinea.

Kikutake, Kiyonori, B.A.; Japanese architect; b. 1 April 1928, Kurume; ed. Waseda Univ.
Established Kiyonori Kikutake & Assocs. (Architects) 53, now Rep. Dir.; Prof. Dept. of Architecture, Waseda Univ. 59-; mem. Board, Architectural Inst. of Japan 62-; Visiting Prof. Univ. of Hawaii 71; del. to UNESCO Int. Conf., Zurich 70; Hon. Fellow, American Inst. of Architects 71; several awards including Ministry of Educ. Arts Award 64, Architectural Inst. of Japan Award 64, Geijutsu Sensho Prize 64, Pan Pacific Architecture Citation, Hawaii Chapter A.I.A. 64, August Perret Award 64, 78, Cultural merits of Kurume City 75, XXI Mainichi Art Awards 79; Major works include: Shimane Prefectural Museum 58, Admin. Bldg. for Izumo Shrine, Tatebayashi City Hall 63, Hotel Tokoen, Yonago-City, Miyakonojo Civic Centre, Pacific Hotel, Chigasaki 66, Iwate Prefectural Library 67, Shimane Prefectural Library, Hagi Civic Centre 68, Kurume Civic Centre 69, Expo Tower for *Expo 70*, Osaka 70, branches of Kyoto Community Bank 71-, Pasadena Heights (tiered mass housing) 74, Aquapolis (floating module for ocean) Ocean, *Expo 75* 75, Hagi City Hall 74,

redevt. of Yamaga city centre 75, Tsukuba Academic New Town, pedestrian deck network and the Symbol Tower 76, Otsu shopping centre 76, Tanabe Museum, Matsue City 79; now Exec. Dir. Tokyo YMCA Inst. of Design.
Publs. *Metabolism 1960* 60, *Taisha Kenchi ku-ron* (Metabolic Architecture) 68, *Ningen-no-Kenchiku* (Human Architecture) 70, *Ningen-no-Toshi* (A Human City) 70, *Works and Methods* 73, *Concepts and Planning* 78, *A Human Environment* 78.
1-11-15, Ohtsuka, Bunkyo-ku, Tokyo, Japan.
Telephone: 03-941-9184; 03-941-0830.

Killen, Sir (Denis) James, K.C.M.G., LL.B.; Australian lawyer and politician; b. 23 Nov. 1925, Dalby, Queensland; ed. Brisbane Grammar School and Univ. of Queensland.
Foundation Pres. Young Liberal's Movement, Queensland 49; Vice-Pres. Liberal Party Queensland Div. 53-56; mem. House of Reps. for Moreton, Queensland 55-; Minister for the Navy 69-71; opposition spokesman for educ. 73-74, for defence 75; Minister for Defence 75-82; Vice-Pres. Exec. Council and Govt. Leader, House of Reps.
Parliament House, Canberra, A.C.T. 2600; Commonwealth Parliament Offices, 295 Ann Street, Brisbane, Queensland 4000; 22 Cook Street, Yeronga, Queensland 4104, Australia.
Telephone: 733955 (Canberra); 2293975 (Brisbane); 652455 (Russell Hill).

Kim, H.E. Cardinal Stephen Sou Hwan; Korean ecclesiastic; b. 8 May 1922, Taegu; ed. Sophia Univ., Tokyo, Major Seminary, Seoul, and Sociology Dept., Univ. of Münster, Germany.
Ordained priest 51; Pastor of Andong, Archdiocese of Taegu 51-53; Sec. to Archbishop of Taegu 53-55; Pastor of Kimchon (Taegu) 55-56; Editor-in-Chief *Catholic Shibo* (weekly) 64-66; sociology studies, Univ. of Münster, Germany 56-64; Dir. Sung-Eui Schools, Kimchon 55-56; Bishop of Masan 66-68; Archbishop of Seoul 68-; cr. Cardinal 69; Dr. h.c. (Notre Dame Univ., U.S.A.) 77.
Archbishop's House, 2-Ga 1, Myong-Dong, Chung-gu, Seoul, Republic of Korea.
Telephone: 776-4083.

Kim Dong Jo; Korean diplomatist; b. 14 Aug. 1918; ed. Coll. of Commerce, Seoul, Kyushu Imperial Univ. Law School, Japan.
Secretary-General, Ministry of Communications 49-51, Dir. Political Affairs 51-52, 54-57; Counsellor, Korean Embassy, Taiwan 52-54; Vice-Minister of Foreign Affairs 57-59; Special Envoy to Repub. of China, Malaysia, Philippines, Thailand and Repub. of Viet-Nam 59; private law practice 60-63; Leader Korean Del. to Asian People's Anti-Communist League, Viet-Nam 63; Chair. Foreign Relations and Defence Cttee. 63; Pres. Korea Trade Promotion Corpn. 64; Amb. to Japan 64-65, 66-67, to U.S.A. 67-73; Amb.-at-large 65-66; Minister of Foreign Affairs 73-75; Special Asst. to the Pres. for Foreign Affairs 76-79; Leader econ. co-operation mission to South-East Asia 67; Hon. LL.D. (Illinois Coll.) 69.
c/o Office of the President, Chong Wa Dae, Seoul, Republic of Korea.

Kim Il; Korean politician.
Member, Presidium of Central Cttee. of Workers' Party of Korea; Vice-Premier, Democratic People's Repub. of Korea 56-57, First Vice-Premier 57-72; Premier of Admin. Council 72-76; First Vice-Pres April 76-; mem. Cen. People's Cttee.; Star of Romanian Socialist Repub. (first class).
Office of the First Vice-President, Pyongyang, Democratic People's Republic of Korea.

Kim Il Sung, Marshal; Korean politician; b. 15 April 1912 (as Kim Song Ju), Mangyongdae, Pyongyang; ed. Yuwen Middle School, Kirin.
Formed Down-with-Imperialism Union 26; formed Young Communist League of Korea 27; imprisoned 29-30; formed Korean Revolutionary Army 30; formed Korean People's Revolutionary Army 32; organized and led Korean People's Revolutionary Army in struggle against Japanese 32-45; founded National Restoration Asscn. 36, elected Chair. 36; founded Workers' Party of Korea, elected Chair. 45, Gen. Sec. Central Cttee. 66; founded Korean People's Army 48; Premier of the Cabinet and Head of Govt., Democratic People's Repub. of Korea 48-72, Pres. and Head of State Dec. 72-; C.-in-C. 50-53; Marshal and three times Hero of Democratic People's Repub. of Korea, Hero of Labour of Democratic People's Repub. of Korea (twice), Order of Nat. Flag (1st Class) (four times), Order of Freedom and Independence (1st Class), Order of the 20th Anniversary Commemoration of the Democratic People's Repub. of Korea and numerous foreign decorations including Order of Lenin 72, Karl Marx Order (German Democratic Repub.) 82.
Publs. *Selected Works of Kim Il Sung* (7 vols.), etc.
Office of the President, Pyongyang, Democratic People's Republic of Korea.

Kim Jong Il; Korean politician; b. 16 Feb. 1941, Mt. Paekdu, Maritime Prov. of Siberia; *s.* of Kim Il Sung (*q.v.*); ed. Kim Il Sung Univ., Pyongyang.
Trained as pilot, German Democratic Republic; Head Communist Party propaganda dept. 73; in charge of Three Major Revolutions (ideological, cultural and technological) 73; Sec. CP Cen. Cttee.; mem. Standing Cttee., Politburo, mem. Mil. Comm., Cen. Cttee. and Deputy Chair. CP Secr. Oct. 80-; mem. People's Supreme Assembly Feb. 82-; Hero of Democratic People's Repub. of Korea and other awards and decorations.
c/o Central Committee of the Communist Party, Pyongyang, Democratic People's Republic of Korea.

Kim Jong Pil, Brig.-Gen.; Korean army officer and politician; b. 7 Jan. 1926, Puyo; ed. High School, Konguj, Seoul Nat. Univ. and Korean Military Acad.
Served in Korean war; Dir. Korean Central Intelligence Agency 61-63; mem. Nat. Assembly 63-68, 71-; Chair. Democratic Republican Party 63-68; Senior Adviser to Pres. 70; Vice-Pres. Democratic Republican Party March 71, Pres. 79-80 (banned from political activity 80); Prime Minister 71-75; mem. Spanish Nat. Acad., Korean Nat. Acad.; numerous awards from Korean and foreign govts.; Hon. LL.D. (Long Island Univ., N.Y. 64, Chungang Univ. Seoul 66, Fairleigh Dickinson Univ. 68); Hon. D.Hum.Litt. (Westminster Coll., Fulton, Mo. 66); Hon. Ph.D. (Hongik Univ., Seoul) 74.
340-38, Sindang 4-dong, Sundong-ku, Seoul, Republic of Korea.

Kim Joon-sung; Korean banker and politician; b. 1924; ed. Seoul Commercial High School.
Branch Dir. Nat. Agric. Co-operatives' Fed., Pusan 58; Chair. Knitted Wear Makers' Asscn., Kvongsang Pukto 63; Vice-Chair. Korea Chamber of Commerce and Industry, Taegu Chapter 67; Pres. Taegu Bank 67, then Pres. Korea First Bank, Korea Exchange Bank, Korea Devt. Bank until 80; Gov. Bank of Korea 80-82; Deputy Prime Minister and Minister of Econ. Planning Jan. 82-.
Office of the Deputy Prime Minister, Seoul, Republic of Korea.

Kim Sang Hyup; Korean politician; b. 1920.
Former Prof. of Law; Pres. Korea Univ.; Minister of Educ. 62; Prime Minister Repub. of Korea June 82-.
Prime Minister's Residence, 106 Samchongdong Chongnoku, Seoul, Republic of Korea.

Kim Woun-gie; Korean politician and banker; b. 3 Dec. 1924, Dangjin, Chungchong Namdo; ed. Korea Univ.
Director, Fin. Management Bureau, Ministry of Finance 61; Vice-Minister of Construction 69-70; Vice-Minister of

Finance 70-72; Standing mem. Korean Olympic Cttee. 71-, Vice-Chair. 74-; Pres. Korean Devt. Bank 72-78; Vice-Chair. Seoul Bank Asscn. 75-; Minister of Finance 78-80; Deputy Prime Minister and Minister of Economic Planning June-Sept. 80; Pres. Korean Traders' Asscn. Nov. 80-.
201-17, Tonggyo-dong, Mapogu, Seoul, Republic of Korea.

Kim Yong Shik; Korean diplomatist; b. 11 Nov. 1913; ed. Chu-ou Univ., Tokyo.
Consul, Hong Kong 49; Consul-Gen., Honolulu 49; Minister, Korean Mission, Japan 51; Minister, Korean Legation, France 57; Minister, Korean Mission, Geneva 59; Perm. Vice-Minister, Ministry of Foreign Affairs 60; Amb. to U.K. (also accred. to Sweden, Denmark, and Norway) 61; Amb. to the Philippines 62; Minister of Foreign Affairs March 63; Minister without Portfolio Dec. 63; Perm. Observer of Repub. of Korea at UN, concurrently accred. as Amb. to Canada 64-70; Special Asst. to Pres. for Foreign Affairs Dec. 70; Minister of Foreign Affairs 71-73, of the Board of Nat. Unification 73-74; Amb. to U.K. 74-77, to the U.S.A. 77-81; Hon. D.Jur. (Missouri Valley Coll.).
c/o Ministry of Foreign Affairs, Seoul, Republic of Korea.

Kimura, Motoo, PH.D., D.SC.; Japanese geneticist; b. 13 Nov. 1924, Okazaki; ed. Kyoto Univ., Univ. of Wisconsin.
Assistant Kyoto Univ. 47-49; Researcher Nat. Inst. of Genetics 49-57, Laboratory Head 57-64, Head of Dept. of Population Genetics 64-; Visiting Prof. of Univ. of Pavia 63, 65, Univ. of Wisconsin 66, Princeton Univ. 69, Stanford Univ. 73; Foreign mem. Nat. Acad. of Sciences, U.S.A. 73; Foreign Hon. mem. American Acad. Arts and Sciences 78; Hon. D.Sc. (Chicago) 78; Japanese Genetics Soc. Prize, Weldon Memorial Prize, Japan Acad. Prize, Japan Soc. of Human Genetics Prize; Hon. citizen of Okazaki 77; Order of Culture (Japan) 76.
Publs. *Outline of Population Genetics* (Japanese) 60, *Diffusion Models in Population Genetics* 64, *An Introduction to Population Genetics Theory* (with J. F. Crow) 70, *Theoretical Aspects of Population Genetics* (with T. Ohta) 71, *Future of Man from the Standpoint of Genetics* (editor, Japanese) 74.
National Institute of Genetics, Yata 1, 111, Mishima 411; Home: 7-24 Kiyozumi-cho, Mishima 411, Japan.
Telephone: 0559-75-0771 (Office); 0559-75-8635 (Home).

Kinoshita, James Otoichi; Japanese author; b. 3 June, 1889; ed. Univs. of California and Southern California.
Former Corresp. Washington Disarmament Conf.; Editor *Tsingtao Leader* (English daily), Sec.-Gen. Tokyo Press Asscn. and Dir. Liberal News Agency; Exec. Dir. Japan Trade Promotion Asscn. 30, Pres. 48; Founder The Friends of the UN 48 (now The Friends of the World), Man. Dir. 52-, Vice-Pres. 62-69, Pres. 69-; Pres. Nippon Mutual Devt. Co. Ltd. 63.
Publs. *Is the World Growing Better?*, *World: A Spiritual System*, *Religion of Love* (trans.), *The Child Welfare Movement*, *Thrice Around the World*, *Rationalisation of American Industry*, *Cherry Blossom Around the World: Donation of Japanese Schoolchildren*.
2056 Izumi, Komae-Shi, Tokyo 201, Japan.
Telephone: 489-1300.

Kinoshita, Keisuke; Japanese film director; b. 1912; ed. Hamamatsu Industrial Coll.
Began his career in Shochiku Studio, Kamata; directed first film *Hanasaku Minato* 43; Henrietta Award for *Nijushi no Hitomi* 55, Golden Globe Award of Hollywood Foreign Press for *Taiyo to Bara* 57.
Films include: *Hanasaku Minato* (Port of Flowers) 43, *Yabure Daiko* (Torn Drum), *Carmen kokyo ni Kaeru* (Carmen Comes Home) 49, *Nippon no Higeki* (The Tragedy of Japan) 53, *Nijushi no Hitomi* (Twenty-Four Eyes) 54, *Nogiku no Gotoki Kimi Nariki* (My First Love Affair) 55, *Yuyakegumo* (Farewell to Dreams), *Taiyo to Bara* (The Rose of his Arm) 56, *Yorokobi-mo Kanashimimo Ikutoshitsuki* (The Lighthouse), *Fuzen no Tomoshibi* (Danger Stalks Near) 57, *Narayama-bushi Ko* (Ballad of the Narayama), *Kono ten no Niji* (The Eternal Rainbow) 58, *Kazahana* 59, *Sekishuncho*, *The River Fuefuki* 61, *Eien no Hito* (Bitter Spirit) 62.
1366 Tsujido, Fujisawa, Kanagawa Prefecture, Japan.

Kintanar, Roman, PH.D., M.A.; Philippine scientist, government official and university professor; b. 13 June 1929, Cebu City; ed. Univ. of the Philippines, Univ. of Texas.
Professor of Physics, Univ. of the Philippines 55-56, Feati Univ. 58-65; Professorial lecturer, Ateneo de Manila Univ. 66-68; Chief Geophysicist, Philippine Weather Bureau 53-58, Dir. 58-72; Admin. Philippine Atmospheric, Geophysical and Astronomical Services Admin. (PAGASA) 72-77, Dir.-Gen. 77-; Del. or invited participant to 57 Regional or Int. Scientific Confs. 59-79; Chair. or Vice-Chair. sessions WMO/ESCAP Typhoon Cttee. 67-79; Perm. Rep. to WMO 58-; Vice-Pres. Regional Asscn. V for South West Pacific (WMO-RA V) 66-74; Pres. 74-78; Vice-Pres. WMO 78-79, Pres. 79-; mem. Philippine Asscn. for the Advancement of Science, Nat. Research Council of the Philippines, Philippine Meteorological Soc., Int. Asscn. of Seismology and Physics of the Earth's Interior and many other scientific socs.; Fulbright Smidthmundt Scholarship (U.S. Educational Foundation), Office of the Pres. Ecology Award, Budiras Award for Outstanding Performance (Bureau Dirs. Asscn.), Parangal ng PAGASA Award.
Publs. *A Study of Typhoon Microseisms* 58, and many articles in scientific journals.
Philippine Atmospheric, Geophysical and Astronomical Services Administration (PAGASA), 1424 Quezon Avenue, Quezon City, Philippines.
Telephone: 98-06-61 to 70.

Kirkup, James, B.A., F.R.S.L.; British writer; b. 23 April 1918; ed. Durham Univ.
Gregory Fellow in Poetry, Leeds Univ. 50-52; Visiting Poet, Bath Acad. of Art 53-56; travelling lectureship from Swedish Ministry of Educ. 56-57; Prof. of English Language and Literature, Salamanca (Spain) 57-58; Prof. of English Literature, Tohoku Univ. 50-61; Visiting Prof. of English Literature, Japan Women's Univ., Tokyo 64-69; Visiting Prof. and Poet in Residence, Amherst Coll., Mass. 68-69; Prof. of English Literature, Univ. of Nagoya, Japan 69-72, BBC TV Open Univ. 74-75; Fellowship in Creative Writing, Univ. of Sheffield 74-75; Literary Editor *Orient-West Magazine*, Tokyo 63-65; Visiting Prof. in Int. Literature, Ohio Univ. 75-76; Playwright in Residence, Sherman Theatre, Univ. Coll., Cardiff 76-77; Prof. of English Literature, Kyoto Univ. of Foreign Studies 76-; Atlantic Award in Literature (Rockefeller Foundation) 59, First Prize, Japan P.E.N. literary contest 65, Mildred Batchelder Award, A.L.A. 68, Arts Council Award 72, Keats Prize for Poetry 75; Crowned Ollave of the Order of Bards, Ovates and Druids 74; Hon. Fellow Inst. of Psychophysical Research, Oxford 70.
Publs. *The Cosmic Shape* 47, *The Drowned Sailor* 48, *The Creation* 50, *The Submerged Village* 51, *A Correct Compassion* 52, *A Spring Journey* 54, *Upon This Rock*, *The Dark Child*, *The Triumph of Harmony* 55, *The True Mistery of the Nativity*, *Ancestral Voices*, *The Radiance of the King* 56, *The Descent into the Cave*, *The Only Child* (autobiography) 57, *The Peach Garden* (TV play), *Two Pigeons Flying High* (TV play), *Sorrows, Passions and Alarms* (autobiography) 60, *The True Mistery of the Passion*, *The Prodigal Son* (poems) 56-60, *These Horned Islands* (travel) 62, *The Love of Others* (novel) 62, *Tropic Temper* (travel) 63, *Refusal to Conform, Last and First Poems* 63, *The Heavenly Mandate* 64, *Japan Industrial*, Vols. I and II 64-65, *Tokyo* (travel) 66, *Bangkok* (travel) 67, *Michael Kohlhaas* 67, *Paper Windows: Poems from Japan*

68, *Filipinescas* (travel) 68, *One Man's Russia* (travel) 68, *Hong Kong* (travel) 69, *Japan Physical* (poems) 69, *White Shadows, Black Shadows: Poems of Peace and War* 70, *Japan Behind the Fan* (travel) 71, *The Body Servant: Poems of Exile* 71, *A Bewick Bestiary* (ill. poems) 71, *Insect Summer* (novel) 71, *Transmental Vibrations* 72, *The Magic Drum* (novel) 73, *Zen Gardens* (ill. poems) 73, *Poems of Takagi Kyozo* (trans. and editor), *Heaven, Hell and Hara-kiri* 74, *The Physicists, The Meteor, Play Strindberg* (trans.) 73, *Cyrano de Bergerac* (trans.) 74, *The Conformist* (trans.) 75, *The Magic Drum* (musical play for children), *Modern Japanese Poetry* (trans.) 78, *Scenes from Sesshu* 78, *Zen Contemplations* 78, *Enlightenment* 79, *Encounters* 79, *An Actor's Revenge* (opera) 79, *Achilles* (opera) 79, *Friends in Arms, The Tao of Water* 80, *Cold Mountain Poems* 80, *Dengonban Messages: One-line Poems* 80, *The Guardian of the Word* (trans. Camara Laye) 80, *Toki* (Japanese trans. of *The Body Servant*) 81, *Scenes from Sutcliffe* 81, *The British Lady and Gentleman, I am Count Dracula* 81, *Ecce Homo: My Pasolini* 81, *The Damask Drum* (libretto), *The Guardian of the Word* 81, *To the Unknown God* 82, *The Bush Toads* 82, *Folktales Japanesque* 82, and numerous trans. from French, German and Japanese.
c/o BM-Box 2780, London, WC1N 3XX, England.
Telephone: 01-405 0463.

Kirloskar, Shantanu Laxman, B.SC.; Indian industrialist; b. 28 May 1903; ed. Massachusetts Inst. of Technology, U.S.A.
Kirloskar Brothers 26-; Chair. and Man. Dir. Kirloskar Oil Engines Ltd., Kirloskar Brothers Ltd., Pune; Chair. Kirloskar Pneumatic Co. Ltd., Central Pulp Mills Ltd., Kirloskar Tractors Ltd., Pudumjee Pulp and Paper Mills Ltd., Poona Industrial Hotels Ltd., Kirloskar Cummins Ltd., Kirloskar Consultants Ltd., G. G. Dandekar Machine Works Ltd., Bharat Forge Co. Ltd.; Dir. numerous other cos.; fmr. Chair. Indian Inst. of Management, Ahmedabad; Past Pres. Mahratta Chamber of Commerce and Industries, Pune, Fed. of Indian Chambers of Commerce and Industry, New Delhi 65-66; First Pres. Indo-American Chamber of Commerce; Dir. Reserve Bank of India, Industrial Devt. Bank of India; mem. Exec. Cttee., Int. Chamber of Commerce 76-; Chair. Cttee. for Econ. Devt. in India; Sir Walter Puckey Prize 68; Life mem. Inst. of Engineers (India) 70; Karma Viroltama, Eng. Asscn. of India 72; Vanijya Ratna 76; Padma Bhushan 65.
Publ. *Jet Yugateel Marathi Manus* (A man from Maharashtra in the Jet Age).
Office: Kirloskar Oil Engines Ltd., Corporate Office, 11 Koregaon Road, Pune 411001; Home: "Lakaki", Shivajinagar, Pune 411016, India.

Kirpal, Prem Nath, M.A., LL.B.; Indian educationist; b. 30 April 1909, Moga, Punjab; ed. Punjab Univ. and Balliol Coll., Oxford.
Lecturer then Prof. of History and Political Science 34-45; Educ. Adviser, Indian High Comm., London 45-48; Deputy Sec. Ministry of Educ. and Sec.-Gen. Indian Nat. Comm. for UNESCO 48-52; Deputy Dir. then Dir. UNESCO Dept. of Cultural Activities 52-57; Joint Sec. Ministry of Educ. and Joint Educ. Adviser to Govt. of India 57-60; Sec. Ministry of Educ. 60-69; Senior Specialist, East-West Centre, Honolulu, Hawaii 69; Dir. Int. Study of Private Philanthropy 69-; Pres. Exec. Board UNESCO 70-72; Founder, Pres., Inst. of Cultural Relations and Devt. Studies, New Delhi 71-; Pres. Indian Council of Peace Research 72-; Pres. Int. Educational Consortium, New Delhi 79-81; Consultant, World Bank, Washington, D.C.; mem. Exec. Council, Delhi Univ.; Chair. Delhi Public Library, Delhi School of Social Work; Pres. Forum of Educ., India; Hon. LL.D. (Temple Univ.), Hon. D.Sc. (Leningrad), Hon. D.Litt. (Punjab Univ.); UNESCO Gold Medal 72; Orders of Repub. of Egypt and of U.A.R. 72; 30th Anniversary Award, UNESCO 76, and other awards.
Publs. *East India Company and Persia 1800–1801: A Study in Diplomatic Relations, Memoirs of Wollebrant de Jong 1624, Life of Dyal Singh Majithia, Main Trends in Cultural Development of India, A Decade of Indian Education 1958–68, Indian Education—Twenty-five Years of Independence, Youth Values and Established Culture, Education and Development, In Quest of Humanity, The Cosmic Sea and other Poems* 80; and over 20 articles on educ., culture and int. co-operation.
Executive Board UNESCO, place de Fontenoy, 75700 Paris, France; 63F Sujan Singh Park, New Delhi 3, India (Home).

Kishi, Nobusuke; Japanese politician; b. 1896; elder brother of the late Eisaku Sato (Prime Minister of Japan, 1964-72); ed. Tokyo Imperial Univ.
Clerk of Ministry of Agriculture and Commerce 20; Chief of Industrial Admin. Section, Industrial Affairs Bureau 32, concurrently Sec., Ministry of Foreign Affairs 33; Chief of Archives Section, Ministry of Commerce and Industry 33; Sec. of Temporary Industrial Rationalization Bureau and Dir. of Industrial Affairs Bureau 35-36; served in various admin. capacities in Govt. of Manchukuo 36-39; Vice-Minister of Commerce and Industry 39-41 and Oct.-Nov. 43; Minister of Commerce and Industry Oct. 41-April 42; elected mem. of House of Reps. 42; Minister of State without Portfolio Oct. 43-July 44; dismissed from public service Dec. 47; apptd. Chair. Board of Dirs. of Toyo Pulp Mfg. Co. Ltd. 49; re-elected mem. of House of Reps. 53 and 55; Chair. of Railway Construction Council 55; Minister of Foreign Affairs Dec. 56; Prime Minister 57-60; Pres. Liberal-Democratic Party 57-60 (re-elected 59).
c/o Liberal-Democratic Party, 7, 2-chome, Hirakawacho, Chiyoda-ku, Tokyo, Japan.

Kishtmand, Sultan Ali; Afghan politician; b. 1935; ed. univ.
Member of Hazara ethnic minority; a founder mem. People's Democratic Party of Afghanistan (PDPA) and mem. Cen. Cttee. 65; with Parcham faction when PDPA split 67; Minister of Planning April-Aug. 78; tried on charges of conspiracy and sentenced to death 78; sentence commuted by Pres. Amin. Oct. 78; Vice-Pres. of Revolutionary Council, Deputy Prime Minister and Minister of Planning after Soviet intervention Dec. 79-81; Prime Minister of Afghanistan June 81-, also Minister of Planning, Pres. Council of Ministers and Pres. State Planning Cttee.; mem. Politburo, Cen. Cttee. PDPA.
Office of the Prime Minister, Kabul, Afghanistan.

Kittikachorn, Field-Marshal Thanom; Thai army officer and politician; b. 11 Aug. 1911, Tak; ed. Wat Kokplu School (Tak) and Military Acad., Bangkok.
Entered Mil. Survey Dept. as student officer 31, assigned to Planning Section 34; Lieut. in Mil. Educ. Dept. 35, Instructor 36-38, 39-41, 44-46; Capt. 38, student officer in Infantry School, active service in Shan State 41; Major 43, Lieut.-Col. 44; Instructor Mil. Acad. technical branch 46-47; Commdr. 21st Infantry Regt. 47; Col., Commdr. 11th Infantry Regt. 48; Deputy Commdr. 1st Infantry Div. 49, Commdr. 50; Major-Gen., Deputy Commdr. 1st Army 51; Commdr. 1st Army 54; Lieut.-Gen., mem. Defence Coll. 55; Deputy Minister of Co-operatives 55; Asst. C.-in-C. of Army 57; Deputy Minister of Defence April 57, Minister Sept. 57; Prime Minister, Minister of Defence, Gen. 58; Deputy Prime Minister and Minister of Defence 59-63; Prime Minister 63-71, Dec. 72-Oct. 73, Minister of Defence and Foreign Affairs 73; Chair. Nat. Exec. Council 71-72; Special A.D.C. to King; Chair. United Thai People's Party 68-73; in U.S.A. 73-74; detained upon return to Bangkok Dec. 74; lived in Singapore 74-76, returned to Bangkok Sept. 76; served as a monk Sept. 76-Feb. 77.

Klychev, Anna Muchamed; Soviet politician; b. 1912; ed. Higher Party School.
Soviet Army 41-45; mem. C.P. of Soviet Union 47-; managerial work 47-51; party and political work 53-63; Chair. Presidium of Supreme Soviet of Turkmen S.S.R. 63-79; mem. Presidium of Cen. Cttee. of C.P. of Turkmen S.S.R.; Deputy Chair. Presidium of Supreme Soviet of U.S.S.R.; mem. Cen. Auditing Comm., C.P.S.U. 66-; Deputy to Supreme Soviet of U.S.S.R. 66- and of Turkmen S.S.R.
Presidium of Supreme Soviet of Turkmen S.S.R., Ashkhabad, Turkmen S.S.R., U.S.S.R.

Knight, Sir Harold Murray, K.B.E., D.S.C., M.COM.; Australian banker; b. 13 Aug. 1919, Melbourne; ed. Scotch Coll. Melbourne, Univ. of Melbourne.
Commonwealth Bank of Australia 36-40; A.I.F. 40-43; Royal Australian Naval Volunteer Reserve (Lieut.) 43-45; Commonwealth Bank of Australia 46-55; Statistics Div., Research and Statistics Dept. of IMF 55-59, Asst. Chief 57-59; research economist, Reserve Bank of Australia 60, Asst. Man. Investment Dept. 62-64, Man. 64-68, Deputy Gov. and Deputy Chair. of Board 68-75, Gov. and Chair. of Board 75-.
Publ. *Introducción al Análisis Monetario* 59.
65 Martin Place, Sydney, N.S.W. 2000, Australia.

Kobayashi, Koji, D.ENG.; Japanese business executive; b. 1907; ed. Tokyo Imperial Univ.
Senior Vice-Pres. and Dir. Nippon Electric Co. Ltd. 56-61, Exec. Vice-Pres. 61-62, Senior Exec. Vice-Pres. 62-64, Pres. 64-76, Chair. 76-; Chair. of Board Nippon Electric Kyushu Ltd. 78-, Nippon Avionics Co. Ltd. 69-; Pres. Industrial Research Inst., Japan, Japan Inst. of Industrial Eng. 74-; Vice-Pres. Japan Telecommunication Industrial Fed. 74-, Int. Management Asscn. of Japan; Foreign Assoc. of Nat. Acad. of Engineering; Prime Minister's Prize for Export Promotion 64; Blue Ribbon Medal 64; Frederik Philips Award 77; Grand Cross (Peru) 70, Jordan Star, Third Class 72, Order of Sacred Treasure, First Class 78, and numerous other foreign decorations.
Publs. *Carrier Transmission System* 37, *Challenge to the Computer Age* 68, *The Problem of Management in the 1970s* 71, *Quality-oriented Management* 76.
Nippon Electric Co. Ltd., 33-1, Shiba 5-chome, Minato-ku, Tokyo 108; and 15-10 Denenchofu 5-chome, Ohta-ku, Tokyo 145, Japan.

Kobayashi, Taiyu; Japanese company executive; b. 13 June 1912, Hyogo Prefecture; ed. Kyoto Univ.
Joined Fuji Electric Co. 35; joined Fujitsu Ltd. 35, Dir. 64, Man. Dir. Nov. 69, Exec. Dir. 72, Exec. Vice-Pres. 75, Pres. 76-; Pres. Communications Industries Asscn. of Japan 76-78; Chair. VLSI Tech. Research Asscn. 78-79; Pres. Japan Electronics Industries' Devt. Asscn. 79-; Chair. Engineering Research Asscn. of Opto-Electronics Applied System 81-; Purple and Blue Ribbon Awards with Medal of Honour.
Fujitsu Ltd., Furukawa Sogo Building, 6-1, Marunouchi 2-chome, Chiyoda-ku, Tokyo; Home: 674 Nitta Kannami-cho, Tagata-gun, Shizuoka, Japan.

Koga, Issac, PH.D.; Japanese radio engineer; b. 5 Dec. 1899; ed. Univ. of Tokyo.
Assistant Prof. Tokyo Inst. of Technology 29-39, Prof. 39-58; Prof. Univ. of Tokyo 44-60, Dean of Engineering 58-60; Vice-Pres. Int. Union of Radio Science, Brussels 57-63, Pres. 63-66; Pres. Inst. of Electrical Communication Engineers of Japan 47-48; Pres. Inst. of Electrical Engineers of Japan 57-58; mem. Technical Advisory Cttee. Nat. Broadcasting Corpn. 51-66; mem. Advisory Council for Nat. Language, Ministry of Educ. 61-; mem. Advisory Cttee. for Radio and Telecommunications, Ministry of Posts and Telecommunications 63-72; mem. Advisory Council for Educ. of Educators, and Central Advisory Council for Educ. (both in Ministry of Educ.) 67-72; Pres. ITU Asscn. of Japan 61-; Fellow, Inst. of Electrical and Electronics Engineers, New York 57; Hon. mem. Inst. of Electrical Communication Engineers of Japan 64, Inst. of Electrical Engineers of Japan 65; mem. Japan Acad. 76; Order of Cultural Merit 63; First Class Order of the Sacred Treasure 70; C. B. Sawyer Memorial Award 70.
Major works include: invention of crystal plates of zero frequency-temperature coefficient, investigation on piezo-electric oscillating crystal and quartz crystal circuit (Japan Acad. of Sciences Prize) 48, frequency demultiplier by means of a vacuum tube circuit.
17-5, 2-chome Aobadai, Megoruku, Tokyo 153, Japan.
Telephone: (Tokyo) 461-3395.

Koh, Tommy Thong Bee, LL.M.; Singapore law teacher and diplomatist; b. 12 Nov. 1937; ed. Univ. of Singapore and Harvard and Cambridge Univs.
Assistant Lecturer, Univ. of Singapore 62-64, Lecturer 64-; Sub-Dean, Faculty of Law, Univ. of Singapore 65-67, Vice-Dean 67-68; Visiting Lecturer, State Univ. of New York at Buffalo 67; fmr. Legal Adviser to trade unions in Singapore and fmr. Sec. Inst. of Int. Affairs, Singapore; Amb. and Perm. Rep. to UN 68-71, July 74-, concurrently High Commr. of Singapore in Canada 68-71; Pres. UN Law of the Sea Conf. 81- (Chair. Singapore del. to conf.); Assoc. Prof. of Law and Dean, Faculty of Law, Univ. of Singapore 71-74, 78-; Adrian Clarke Memorial Medal, Meritorious Service Medal, Leow Chia Heng Prize, Public Service Star.
Permanent Mission of Singapore to the United Nations, 26th Floor, 1 United Nations Plaza, New York, N.Y. 10017, U.S.A.; and Faculty of Law, University of Singapore, Bukit Timah Road, Singapore 10, Singapore.

Kojima, Kiyoshi, PH.D.; Japanese economist; b. 22 May 1920; ed. Tokyo Univ. of Commerce and Economics, Leeds Univ. (U.K.) and Princeton Univ. (U.S.A.).
Assistant Prof. of Int. Econs., Hitotsubashi Univ. 45-60, Prof. 60-; Secretariat (Dir.) for UN Conf. on Trade and Devt. 63; British Council Scholarship 52-53, Rockefeller Foundation Fellowship 53-55.
Publs. (in Japanese): *Theory of Foreign Trade* 50, *Japan's Economic Development and Trade* 58, *Japan in the World Economy* 62, *The Economics of EEC* 62, *Trade Expansion for Developing Countries* 64, *Japan and a Pacific Free Trade Area* 71, *Japan and a new World Economic Order* 77, *Direct Foreign Investment* 78; Editor (in English): *Japan and a Pacific Free Trade Area* 71, *Papers and Proceedings of a Conference on Pacific Trade and Development* 68, 69, 73; also articles in English on int. trade.
3-24-10 Maehara-cho, Koganei-shi, Tokyo, Japan.
Telephone: 0423-81-1041.

Komiyama, Jushiro; Japanese politician; b. 1928; ed. Waseda Univ.
Reporter, *Yomiuri Shimbun*; Private Sec. to the late Eisaku Sato (Prime Minister of Japan 1964-72); elected five times to House of Reps. from constituency in Saitama Prefecture; fmr. Parl. Vice-Minister of Int. Trade and Industry; fmr. Deputy Dir.-Gen. of Admin. Affairs in Office of P.M.; fmr. Chair. Judicial Affairs Cttee. of House of Reps.; fmr. Deputy Sec.-Gen. of Liberal-Democratic Party (LDP); Minister of Posts and Telecommunications 76-77.
c/o House of Representatives, Tokyo, Japan.

Komoto, Toshio; Japanese politician; b. 1911, Aioi City Hyogo Prefecture; ed. Nihon Univ.
Former Parl. Vice-Minister for Econ. Planning Agency; fmr. Chair. of Justice Cttee., House of Reps.; fmr. Chair. Cabinet Cttee., House of Reps.; Minister of Posts and Telecommunications 68-70, of Int. Trade and Industry 74-76, 77-78; Chair. Policy Research Council, Liberal-Democratic Party 74-75, 78-79; Minister of State, Dir.-

Gen. of Econ. Planning Agency 80-; fmr. Pres. Sanko Steamship Co.; Liberal-Democrat.
c/o Liberal-Democratic Party, 7, 2-chome, Hirakawacho, Chiyoda-ku, Tokyo, Japan.

Kosaka, Tokusaburo; Japanese politician; b. 20 Jan. 1916, Nagano Pref.; ed. Tokyo Univ.
Joined Asahi Newspaper Co.; Man. Shinetsu Chemical Industry Co. 49, Vice-Pres. 51, later Pres.; Lecturer, Dept. of Economics, Univ. of Tokyo 59-62, Dept. of Commercial Sciences, Keio Univ. 60-62; Dir. Japan Chemical Industry Asscn., Coal Industry Asscn., Shinano Mainichi Newspaper Co., Shinano Broadcasting Co.; mem. House of Reps. 69-; Dir.-Gen. Prime Minister's Office 73-74; Chair. Public Relations Cttee., Liberal-Democratic Party (LDP) 76-77, Econ. and Price Policy Board, LDP 77-78; Minister of State for Econ. Planning 78-79; Minister of Transport Nov. 81-.
c/o Liberal-Democratic Party, 7, 2-chome, Hirakawacho, Chiyoda ku, Tokyo, Japan.

Kothari, Dayanad Chandulal; Indian industrialist; b. 28 Feb. 1914.
Chairman and Man. Dir. Kothari (Madras) Ltd.; Vice-Chair. Kothari Sugars and Chemicals Ltd., Indian Standards Institution and numerous other cos.; Dir. Brook Bond (India) Ltd, and other cos.; mem. Bd. of Trustees and Exec. Cttee., Unit Trust of India; fmr. Pres. Confed. of Asian Chambers of Commerce and Industry; fmr. Dir. Cen. Board, Reserve Bank of India; fmr. Pres. All-India Org. of Employers.
Kothari Buildings, 114/117 Nungambakkam High Road, Madras 600034; Home: Kothari House, 29 Kothari Road, Nungambakkam, Madras 600034, India.
Telephone: 85099, 812130 (Office); 88777 (Home).

Koyama, Goro; Japanese banker; b. 25 March 1909; ed. Tokyo Imperial Univ.
Managing Dir. The Mitsui Bank Ltd. 63-65, Deputy Pres. 65-68, Pres. 68-74, Chair. 74-.
The Mitsui Bank Ltd., 1-2, Yurakucho 1-chome, Chiyoda-ku, Tokyo; Home: 3-15-10, Takaido-Higashi, Suginami-ku, Tokyo, Japan.
Telephone: 501-1111 (Office); 333-0843 (Home).

Kraivixien, Thanin, LL.B.; Thai jurist and politician; b. 5 April 1927; ed. Suan Kularp School, Thammasat Univ., Univ. of London, Gray's Inn.
Senior Judge, Civil Court 69; Senior Judge, Court of Appeal 72; Judge, Supreme Court 72-76, Senior Judge 76; mem. Nat. Assembly 73-76; Prime Minister 76-77; Chair. Investment Board of Thailand 76-77.
Publs. *Democracy, Communist Ideology and Tactics, The Language of the Thai Law, The Use of Anti-Communist Law, Constitutional Monarchy, The Reform of the Legal and Judicial Systems during the Reign of King Chulalongkorn.*
c/o Office of the Prime Minister, Government House, Bangkok, Thailand.

Kriangsak Chomanan, Gen.; Thai army officer and politician; b. 1917; ed. Thai Royal Mil. Acad. and U.S. Army Staff Coll.
Served in Second World War and Korean War; Deputy Chief of Staff, Supreme Command Headquarters to 74, Chief of Staff 74-76; Deputy Supreme Commdr. of Royal Thai Armed Forces 76-77, Supreme Commdr. 77-78; participated in mil. coups Oct. 76 and Oct. 77; Gen. Sec. Nat. Administrative Reform Council 6-22 Oct. 76; Vice-Chair. Prime Minister's Advisory Council Oct. 76-Oct. 77; Sec.-Gen. Revolutionary Council, Nat. Dir. of Peace-keeping Oct.-Nov. 77; Sec.-Gen. Nat. Policy Council Nov. 77-; Prime Minister Nov. 77-March 80, also Minister of the Interior Nov. 77-Aug. 78, of Defence Aug. 78-80; of Agric. 79-80; M.P. for Muang Roi-et Aug. 81-.
c/o Office of the Prime Minister, Government House, Bangkok, Thailand.

Krishna Rao, Gen. K.V.; Indian army officer; b. 16 July 1923; ed. Imperial Defence Coll.
Commissioned into the army Aug. 42; served Burma and North-Western Frontier, Second World War; served Jammu and Kashmir operations after India's independence; Instructor, Defence Service Staff Coll., Wellington 63-65; commanded infantry and mountain divs. 69-72; Chief of Staff Western Command 72-74; Corps Commdr., Jammu Region 74-78; Chair. Expert Cttee. on Reorganization and Modernization of Army; Deputy Chief of Army Staff 78-79; GOC (in C) Western Command 79-81; Chief of Army Staff June 81-; Chair. Chiefs of Staff Cttee. March 82-; Param Vishisht Seva Medal 71.
c/o Army Headquarters, New Delhi, India.

Krishnan, Natarajan, B.A.ECONS.; Indian diplomatist; b. 6 Oct. 1928, Mayuram, Tamil Nadu; ed. Univ. of Madrid.
Joined Indian Foreign Service 51; Third Sec., later Second Sec., Bangkok 55-56; Second Sec., Chargé d'affaires, Phnom-Penh 56-57; Under Sec. Ministry of External Affaires 57-58; First Sec., Chargé d'affaires, Buenos Aires 59-62; Deputy Sec., Dir. Ministry of External Affairs 62-67; Consul-Gen. and Perm. Rep. to UN Offices, Geneva 67-71; Joint Sec. Ministry of External Affairs 71-76; Amb. to Yugoslavia 76-79; Additional Sec. Ministry of External Affairs 79-81; Amb. and Perm. Rep. to UN April 81-.
Permanent Mission of India to the United Nations, 750 Third Avenue, 21st Floor, New York, N.Y. 10017, U.S.A.

Krishnan, Rappal Sangameswara, D.SC., PH.D.; Indian physicist; b. 1911; ed. Univ. of Madras, St. Joseph's Coll., Trichy, Indian Inst. of Science, and Trinity Coll., Cambridge.
Research Asst. Indian Inst. of Science 35-38; 1851 Exhbn. Overseas Scholar, Univ. of Cambridge 38-41; Lecturer in Physics, Inst. of Science 42-45, Asst. Prof. 45-48, Prof. and Head, Dept. of Physics 48-72, Emer. 72-73; Vice-Chancellor, Kerala Univ. 73-July 77; Prof. Emer., Indian Inst. of Science, Bangalore 77-; Visiting Prof. North Texas State Univ. 71-72; Fellow of Inst. of Physics, London, of American Physical Soc., of Indian Acad. of Sciences, and of Nat. Inst. of Sciences; Pres. Physics Section, Indian Science Congress 49; specialist in colloid optics, Raman effect in crystals, crystal physics and nuclear physics; discovered optical effect known as "Krishnan effect", a universal phenomenon of reciprocity theorem in light scattering.
Publs. *Progress in Crystal Physics*, Vol. I 58, part of *Raman Effect*, Vol. I 71, *Thermal Expansion of Crystals* 79.
Physics Department, Indian Institute of Science, Bangalore, Karnataka; Home: No. 232, 18th Cross, Palace, Upper Orchards, Sadasiv Nagar, Bangalore 560080, Karnataka, India.
Telephone: 34411 (Office); 30703 (Home).

Krishnaswamy, K. S., PH.D.; Indian economist and banker; b. 1920; ed. Univ. of Mysore and London School of Economics.
Lecturer in Econs., Univ. of Bombay 46-47; Research Officer, Planning Comm., New Delhi; Research Officer, Research Dept., Reserve Bank of India, Bombay 52-54, Deputy Dir. of Research, Research Dept. 54-56; Staff mem. Econ. Devt. Inst. (World Bank), Washington 56-59; Deputy Chief, Industrial Finance Dept., Reserve Bank of India 59-61; Chief, Econ. Policy Section, Planning Comm. 61-64; Economic Adviser, Planning Commission 64-67; Dir. Econ. Devt. Inst., Int. Bank for Reconstruction and Devt. 67-71, Principal Adviser, Reserve Bank of India 72, Exec. Dir. 73-75, Deputy Gov. 75-; Chair. Oil Prices Cttee. 74-76; Pres. Indian Econ. Asscn. 76.
Reserve Bank, Central Office, Bombay 400001, India.

Kularatnam, Karthigesapillai, M.A., PH.D., DR.SC.; Sri Lankan educationist, geographer and geologist; b. 28 May 1911.
Professor Emer. and Dean, Univ. of Sri Lanka; taught in Univs. of Edinburgh, Sheffield, Birmingham, London, Madras, New York, Kansas City and Sir George Williams (Montreal); Pres. Inst. of Environmental Sciences; Pres. Ceylon Geographical Soc., Gemmologists' Asscn. f., Ceylon, Soil Conservation Soc.; Dir. Commonwealth Geographical Bureau; Senior Consultant, Population Div., UN/ESCAP.
Publs. several essays on Sri Lanka.
61 Abdul Caffoor Mawatha, Colombo 3, Sri Lanka.

Kulatov, Turabay; Soviet politician; b. 1908; ed. Kyzyl-Kiysk Soviet-Party School and Higher Party School.
Trade union official 34; mem. Bureau of the Central Cttee. of the C.P. of Kirghizia 38; Chair. of the Council of People's Commissars of Kirghizia 38-45; Pres. of the Presidium of the Supreme Soviet of Kirghizia 45-78; Vice-Chair. of the Presidium of the Supreme Soviet of the U.S.S.R. 46-78; mem. Central Auditing Comm., C.P.S.U.; Deputy to U.S.S.R. and Kirghiz S.S.R. Supreme Soviets; mem. Cen. Cttee. C.P. Kirghiz S.S.R., and mem. Politburo; awarded Order of Lenin (four times).
c/o Supreme Soviet of Kirghizia, Frunze, U.S.S.R.

Kunayev, Askar Minliakhmedovich; Soviet metallurgist and politician; b. 1929; ed. Moscow Inst. of Steel and Alloys.
Steel founder, Kazakh Metallurgical Works, Temir-Tau, foreman, shift foreman, 51-53; laboratory asst., Inst. of Metallurgy and Ore-Dressing, Kazakh S.S.R. Acad. of Sciences 53, then junior research worker, senior research worker, head of Inst.; then Dir. Lab. of Physical Chem. of Alloying Metals; Vice-Pres. Kazakh S.S.R. Acad. of Sciences 72-74, Pres. 74-; Deputy to U.S.S.R. Supreme Soviet 74-; mem. Cttee. for Foreign Affairs, Soviet of Nationalities; mem. C.P.S.U. 71-; mem. C.P. of Khazakstan, Alma-Ata Regional Cttee.; mem. U.S.S.R. Acad. of Sciences; Kazakh S.S.R. State Prize 72; Order of the Red Banner of Labour.
Presidium of the Kazakh S.S.R. Academy of Sciences, 28 Ul. Shevchenko, Alma-Ata, Kazakh S.S.R., U.S.S.R.

Kunayev, Dinmohammed Akhmedovich; Soviet (Kazakh) politician and mining engineer; b. 1912; ed. Moscow Inst. of Non-Ferrous Metals.
Former Dir. Kounrad Mine, Kazakh S.S.R.; Vice-Chair. Council of Ministers Kazakh S.S.R. 45-52, Chair. 52-60, 62-; First Sec. Kazakh C.P. 60-62, 64-; Alt. mem. Politburo, Central Cttee. of C.P.S.U. April 66- April 71, mem. April 71-; Deputy to Supreme Soviet of the U.S.S.R. and Supreme Soviet of the Kazakh S.S.R.; mem. Presidium of Supreme Soviet of the U.S.S.R. 62-; mem. C.P.S.U. Central Cttee. 56-; mem. and fmr. Pres. Acad. of Sciences of the Kazakh S.S.R.; Hero of Socialist Labour, Order of Lenin, Hammer and Sickle Gold Medal, Order of the October Revolution 80 etc.
Central Committee of Communist Party of the Kazakh S.S.R., Alma-Ata, Kazakh S.S.R., U.S.S.R.

Kuroda, Mizuo; Japanese diplomatist; b. 1919, Osaka Pref.; ed. Tokyo Univ.
Entered diplomatic service 45; Third Sec., Washington 52-54; Treaty Bureau, Ministry of Foreign Affairs 54-58; First Sec., London 58-62; Private Sec. to Prime Minister 62-64; Dir. North East Asia Div., Asian Affairs Bureau, Ministry of Foreign Affairs 64-66; Counsellor, Washington 66-67, Manila 67-69; Consul-Gen., Manila 67-69; Minister, Manila 69; Washington 69-71; Deputy Dir.-Gen., UN Bureau, Ministry of Foreign Affairs 71-72, Dir.-Gen., Research and Planning Dept. 72, Public Information Bureau 73; Amb. to Yugoslavia 76-78, to Egypt (concurrently to Yemen P.D.R.) 78-80, to Australia 80-.
112 Empire Circuit, Yarralumla, Canberra, A.C.T. 2600 (Office); 114 Empire Circuit, Yarralumla, Canberra, A.C.T. 2600, Australia (Residence).

Kurokawa, Kisho, M.TECH.; Japanese architect; b. 8 April 1934; ed. Kyoto and Tokyo Univs.
President, Kisho Kurokawa Architect & Assocs., Urban Design Consultants Co. Ltd.; Prin. Inst. of Social Engineering; Adviser, Japan Nat. Railways, Ministry of Public Welfare, Int. Design Conf. in Aspen, Japan Broadcasting Asscn.; mem. Architectural Inst. of Japan, Japan Soc. of Futurology, City Planning Inst. of Japan, Japan Architects Asscn., Japan Fed. of Professional Architects Asscn, Cen. Council for Educ., Ministry of Educ.; Life F.R.S.A.; Hon. Fellow American Inst. of Architects; numerous exhbns. throughout the world; numerous awards incl. Takamura Kotaro Design Prize and prizes in int. competitions in Peru, France, Tanzania, Abu Dhabi and Fed. Repub. of Germany, prize for conference city, Abu Dhabi, United Arab Emirates 76.
Works include: Nitto Food Co. 63, Cen. Lodge in Nat. Children's Land 64, Hans Christian Andersen Memorial Lodge 64, Handicapped People's Town 66, Sagae City Hall 67, Odakyu Rest House 69, Sakura City Hall 69, Takara, Toshiba and Theme Pavilions, *Expo* 70, Sapporo Prince Hotel 71, Nakagin Business Capsule 71, Karuizawa Prince Hotel 73, Shirahama Prince Hotel 73, Bank of Fukuoka 74, Sony Building 74, Hotel New Ohtani, Bulgaria 75, Headquarters of Japan Red Cross Soc. 77, Ishikawa Cultural Centre 77, Museum for Kumamoto City 77, Nat. Ethnology Museum 77, Fukuoka Prefectual Governmental HQ 81, Design of Great Japan Exhbn., Royal Acad., London 81.
Publs. include: *Prefabricated House* 60, *Metabolism* 60, *Urban Design* 65, *Action Architecture* 67, *Homo-Movens* 69, *Kisho N. Kurokawa—Architecture of Metabolism* 69, *Works of Kisho N. Kurokawa* 70, *Creation of Contemporary Architecture* 71, *In the Realm of the Future* 72, *Conception of Metabolism* 72, *Introduction to Urbanology* 73, *Metabolism in Architecture* 77, *A Culture of Grays* 77, *Concept of Space* 77, *Concept of Cities* 77, *Thesis on Architecture—Towards Japanese Space* 82.
Aoyama Building 11F, 1-2-3 Kita Aoyama, Minato-ku, Tokyo, Japan.

Kurosawa, Akira; Japanese film director, b. 1910; ed. Keika Middle School.
Joined Toho Film Co. as asst. dir. 36; dir. his first film *Sugata Sanshiro* 43; First Prize, Venice Film Festival for *Rashomon*, Silver Lion for *The Seven Samurai*, American Motion Picture Acad. Award for *Rashomon*, co-winner Palme d'Or Cannes Film Festival for *Kagemusha* 80; David di Donatello Award for *Kagemusha*; Order of the Yugoslav Flag.
Films: *Sugata Sanshiro, Ichiban Utsukushiku, Torano Owofumu Otokotachi, Waga Seishun ni Kuinashi, Subarashiki Nichiyobi, Yoidore Tenshi, Shizukanaru Ketto, Norainu, Rashomon* 50, *Hakuchi, Ikiru, The Seven Samurai* 54, *Ikimono no Kiroku, Kumonosu Jio, Donzoko, Kakushi Toride no San Akunin, The Throne of Blood* 57, *The Hidden Fortress* 58, *The Bad Sleep Well* 59, *Yojimbo* 61, *Sanjuro* 62, *High and Low* 62, *Akahige, Redbeard* 64, *Dedes'ha-den, Derzu Uzala* 76, *Barkerousse* 77, *Kagemusha* 80.

Kusumaatmadja, Mochtar, LL.D.; Indonesian politician; b. Feb. 1929, Jakarta; ed. Univ. of Indonesia, Yale and Harvard Law Schools and Univ. of Chicago Law School.
Minister of Justice 74-77; Acting Foreign Minister 77-78, then Minister of Foreign Affairs March 78-; Indonesian rep. at Law of the Sea Conference, Geneva, and at Seabed Cttee. sessions, New York; involvement in numerous int. orgs.
Ministry of Foreign Affairs, Jakarta, Indonesia.

Kuwabara, Takeo, B.A.; Japanese writer; b. 10 May 1904; ed. Kyoto Univ.
Lecturer, Kyoto Univ. 31-42; Asst. Prof., Tohoku Univ. 43-48; Prof. Kyoto Univ. 48-68, Emer. Prof. 68-; Dir. Univ. Inst. of Humanistic Studies 59-63; mem. Science Council of Japan 51-72, Vice-Pres 60-72; Vice-Pres. Japan PEN Club 74-75; mem. Acad. of Arts 77-; Man of Cultural Merits 79.
Publs. *Fiction and Reality* 43, *Reflections on Contemporary Japanese Culture* 47, *Some Aspects of Contemporary French Literature* 49, *Introduction to Literature* 50, *Conquest of Mount Chogolisa* 59, *Studies on J.-J. Rousseau* 51, *Studies on the Encyclopédie* 54, *Studies on the French Revolution* 59, *Studies on Chomin Nakae* 66, *European Civilization and Japan* 74, *Selected Works* (in 10 vols.) 80-81.
421, Tonodan-Yabunosita, Kamikyo-ku, Kyoto 602, Japan. Telephone: 231-0261.

Ky, Air Vice-Marshal Nguyen Cao (*see* Nguyen Cao Ky, Air Vice-Marshal).

Kyle, Air Chief Marshal Sir Wallace (Hart), G.C.B., K.C.V.O., C.B.E., D.S.O., D.F.C.; Australian air force officer and administrator; b. 22 Jan. 1910, Kalgoorlie, W.A.; ed. Guildford Grammar School, W.A., R.A.F. Coll., Cranwell, and R A.F. Staff Coll., England.
17th Squadron 30-31, Fleet Air Arm 31-34; flying instructor 34-39; R.A.F. Bomber Command 40-45; R.A.F. Staff Coll. 45-47; Middle East 48-50; ADC to H.M. King George VI 49, to H.M. the Queen 53; Asst. Commdt. R.A.F. Coll. Cranwell 50-52; Dir. of Operational Requirements, Air Ministry 52-54; Air Officer Commanding, Malaya 55-57; Asst. Chief of Air Staff, Operational Requirements 57-59; Air Officer Commanding-in-Chief, Tech. Training Command 59-62; Vice-Chief of Air Staff 62-65; Air ADC to H.M. the Queen 66-68; Air Officer Commanding-in-Chief, Bomber Command 65-68, Strike Command 68; retd. 68; Gov. of Western Australia 75-80; Pres. Fairbridge Soc. 80-; K.St.J.; Hon. D.Tech. (W.A.I.T.) 79; Hon. LL.D. (Univ. of W. Australia) 80.
Kingswood, Tiptoe, Lymington, Hampshire, SO4 OFT; and R.A.F. Club, 128 Piccadilly, London, W.1, England

L

Laking, George Robert, C.M.G., LL.B.; New Zealand diplomatist and public servant; b. 15 Oct. 1912; ed. Auckland Grammar School, and Auckland and Victoria Univs.
Prime Minister's and External Affairs Depts. 40-49; Counsellor, New Zealand Embassy, Washington 49-54, Minister 54-56; Deputy Sec. of External Affairs, Wellington 56-58; Acting High Commr. for New Zealand in London 58-61; Amb. to European Economic Community (EEC) 60-61, to U.S.A. 61-67; Perm. Head, Prime Minister's Dept. and Sec. of Foreign Affairs 67-72; Parl. Commr. (Ombudsman) 75-77, Chief Ombudsman 77, Privacy Commr. 77-78; mem. Human Rights Comm. 78-; Chair. N.Z.-U.S.A. Educational Foundation 78-80; Pres. Inst. of Int. Affairs; mem. Public and Admin. Law Reform Cttee.
3 Wesley Road, Wellington, New Zealand.

Lal, Bansi, LL.B.; Indian politician; b. 10 Oct. 1927, Golagarh, Bhiwani District; ed. privately and Law Coll., Jullundur.
Took part in Praja Mandal Movement, Loharu State; Sec. Loharu Praja Mandal 43-44; Pres. Mandal Congress Cttee., Kural 59-60; Gen. Sec. Tosham Mandal Congress Cttee. 55; mem. Punjab PCC 59-62, Rajya Sabha 60-66, Haryana Assembly 67-75, later Lok Sabha until March 77; Chief Minister Haryana 68-75; Minister without portfolio, Govt. of India, Nov.-Dec. 75, Minister of Defence Dec. 75-March 77; expelled from Indian Nat. Congress April 77; conduct during Emergency subject to comm. of Enquiry July 77; Hon. LL.D. (Kurukshetra Univ.) 72, D.Sc. (Haryana Agric. Univ.) 72.
Chandigarh 160017, Haryana State, India.

Lall, Arthur; Indian teacher and diplomatist; b. 14 July 1911; ed. Punjab and Oxford Univs.
Appointed to Indian Civil Service and served in the Punjab and with Central Govt.; Commercial Counsellor, High Comm., London 47-51; Consul-Gen., with rank of Minister, New York 51-54; Perm. Rep. to UN 54-59; Chair. UN Mission to Samoa 59; Amb. to Austria and Gov. Int. Atomic Agency 59-63; Prof., Cornell Univ. 63-; Prof. of International Relations, Columbia Univ., New York 65-; Chair. Common Heritage Int.; Consultant, UNITAR, New York; Del. to UN Econ. and Social Council and Trusteeship Council; Del. to numerous int. confs.
Publs. *Modern International Negotiation* 66, *How Communist China Negotiates* 68, *The UN and the Middle East Crisis* 68, *The United Nations Security Council in the 1970s*, *The Emergence of Modern India* 80; numerous articles on int. affairs; short stories; novels: *The House at Adampur*, *Seasons of Jupiter*.
230 East 81st Street, New York, N.Y. 10028, U.S.A.

Latter, Edward Gale, M.B.E., E.D.; New Zealand diplomatist; b. 29 Feb. 1928; ed. Christ's College, Christchurch.
Sheep farmer; Brigadier (retd.); M.P. Marlborough Electorate 75-78, National Party; High Commissioner for New Zealand in Canada Jan. 80- (also accred. to Jamaica, Barbados, Trinidad and Tobago, Guyana).
New Zealand High Commission, Suite 801, 99 Bank Street, Ottawa, Ontario, K1P 6G3, Canada.

Lauti, Rt. Hon. Toaripi, P.C.; Tuvaluan politician; b. 28 Nov. 1928, Papua New Guinea; ed. Queen Victoria School, Fiji, Wesley Coll., Paerata, N.Z., St. Andrew's Coll., Christchurch, Christchurch Teachers' Coll.
Secondary School Teacher in the former Gilbert and Ellice Islands 53-62; Labour Relations and Training Officer for Nauru and Ocean Island Phosphate Comm. 62-74; Chief Minister and Minister of Home Affairs, Tuvalu 75-78; Prime Minister, Minister of Finance, of Foreign Affairs, Tuvalu Oct. 78-.
Office of the Prime Minister, Vaiaku, Funafuti; Tuvalu House, Vaiaku, Funafuti, Tuvalu (Residence).

Laver, Rod(ney) George, M.B.E.; Australian lawn tennis player; b. 9 Aug. 1938, Rockhampton, Queensland; ed. Rockhampton Grammar School.
Professional player since 63; Australian Champion 60, 62, 69; Wimbledon Champion 61, 62, 68, 69; U.S.A. Champion 62, 69; French Champion 62, 69; first player to win double Grand Slam 62, 69; first player to win over U.S. $1 million in total prize money 72; played Davis Cup for Australia 58, 59, 60, 61, 62 and 73 (first open Davis Cup).
Publs. *How to Play Winning Tennis* 64, *Education of a Tennis Player* 71.
International Management Group, 1 Erieview Plaza, Cleveland, Ohio 44114, U.S.A.

Law, Phillip Garth, A.O., C.B.E., M.SC., F.A.I.P., F.T.S., F.A.A.; Australian scientist, Antarctic explorer and educationist; b. 21 April 1912; ed. Ballarat Teachers' Coll., and Univ. of Melbourne.
Science master in secondary schools 33-38; Tutor in Physics, Newman Coll., Melbourne Univ. 40-47 and Lecturer in Physics 43-48; Research Physicist and Asst. Sec. Scientific Instrument and Optical Panel, Ministry of Munitions 40-45; Scientific Mission to New Guinea battle areas for the Australian Army 44; Senior Scientific Officer Australian Nat. Antarctic Research Expeditions 47-49, Leader 49-66; Dir. Antarctic Div., Dept. of External Affairs 49-66; Australian Observer Norwegian-British-Swedish Antarctic Expedition 50; led expeditions to establish first perm. Australian research station at Mawson, MacRobertson Land 54 and at Davis, Princess Elizabeth

Land 57; exploration of coast of Australian Antarctica 54-66; mem. gov. council Melbourne Univ. 59-78, La Trobe Univ. 64-74; Exec. Vice-Pres. Victoria Inst. of Colleges 66-77; Chair. Australian Nat. Cttee. on Antarctic Research 66-80; Pres. Victorian Inst. of Marine Sciences 78-80; Pres. Royal Soc. of Victoria 67-68; Trustee of Science Museum of Victoria 68-, Deputy Pres. 80-; Pres. Melbourne Univ. Graduate Union 71-77; Pres. Aust. and N.Z. Scientific Exploration Soc. 76-82; Hon. F.R.M.I.T., Hon. D.APP.Sc., Hon. D.ED.; Founders Medal (Royal Geographical Soc.) 60, also medals of Royal Geographical Soc., Australia, and Royal Soc. of Tasmania.
Publs. *ANARE* (with Bechervaise) 57, also numerous articles on antarctic exploration and research and papers on cosmic rays, thermal conductivity, optics and education.
16 Stanley Grove, Canterbury, Vic. 3126, Australia.

Laya, Jaime C., M.S., PH.D.; Philippine central banker; b. 8 Jan. 1939; ed. Univ. of the Philippines, Georgia Inst. of Tech. and Stanford Univ., U.S.A.
Former partner accounting firm Sycip, Gorres Velayo (SGV); Dean, Coll. of Business Admin., Univ. of Philippines 68-74; Cabinet mem. 75-81; Deputy Gov., Cen. Bank of the Philippines 74-78; Minister for the Budget 75-81; Chair. Appropriations Cttee., Batasang Pambansa 78-81; Gov. and Chair. Monetary Bd., Cen. Bank of the Philippines 81-; Gov. IMF, Philippines; Alt. Gov. Asian Devt. Bank, Philippines; Deputy Dir. Nat. Econ. Devt. Authority (NEDA) 74-78; Hon. D. Hum. (Mindanao State Univ.) 80; Outstanding Certified Public Accountant in Govt., Philippine Inst. of Certified Public Accountants 79.
Office of the Governor, Central Bank of the Philippines, A. Mabini corner Vito Cruz, Malate, Metro Manila, Philippines.

Le Duan; Vietnamese politician; b. 1908, Quang Tri Province, Central Viet-Nam.
Secretary with local railways, Hanoi; imprisoned for political activity 31, released 36, and again 40, released 45 when Viet Minh came to power; active mem. Communist Party of Indochina; prominent in Viet Minh resistance 46; Commr. Mil. Headquarters, S. Viet-Nam 52; Sec. Lao Dong Cen. Cttee. for Southern Region 56, Sec.-Gen. Lao Dong Party (renamed Communist Party of Viet-Nam Dec. 76) 59, First Sec. 59-76, Sec.-Gen. Dec. 76-; mem. Nat. Defence Council, Socialist Repub. of Viet-Nam July 76-81, Politburo (Sec.-Gen.), Cen. Cttee. and Secretariat of Communist Party of Viet-Nam 76-; accompanied Ho Chi Minh on official visits; led dels. to 23rd Soviet Party Congress 67, to Celebrations for 50th Anniversary of October Revolution 67, to Centenary of Lenin's birth 70; Lenin Peace Prize; Order of Lenin.
Publs. major articles in *Nhan Dan* (party organ).
Central Committee, Communist Party of Viet-Nam, 1-c boulevard Hoang Van Thu, Hanoi, Viet-Nam.

Le Duc Tho; Vietnamese politician; b. 14 Oct. 1911, Nam Ha Province, North Viet-Nam (as Phan Dinh Khai).
Founder mem. Communist Party of Indochina 30; imprisoned, escaped to China 40; founder mem. Viet Minh, returned to Hanoi 45; Viet Minh del. for S. Viet-Nam 49; Sec.-Gen. Viet Minh Exec. Cttee., S. Viet-Nam, then mem. Cen. Cttee. Lao Dong Party; mem. Politburo, Lao Dong Party 55, Dir. Party Training School 59; mem. Lao Dong Secretariat 60-76, Secretariat and Politburo of Communist Party of Viet-Nam Dec. 76-; Special Adviser to N. Vietnamese del. at Paris peace talks 68-72; led dels. to U.S.S.R. 61, France 65, 70, German Democratic Repub. 71, has attended several Communist Party congresses abroad; declined Nobel Peace Prize 73.
Central Committee, Communist Party of Viet-Nam, 1-c boulevard Hoang Van Thu, Hanoi, Viet-Nam.

Le Thanh Nghi; Vietnamese politician.
Deputy Premier of Democratic Repub. of Viet-Nam 74-76; Chair. State Planning Comm. 74-81; mem. Nat. Defence Council, Socialist Repub. of Viet-Nam 76-81; Deputy Premier, Socialist Repub. of Viet-Nam 76-81; mem. Politburo of Communist Party of Viet-Nam; Vice-Pres. Council of State 81-, Gen.-Sec. June 82-.
Dang Cong san Viet-Nam, 10 Hoang Van Thu Street, Hanoi, Viet-Nam.

Le Van Luong; Vietnamese politician; b. 1910, North Viet-Nam.
Member of Politburo, Lao Dong party 51-56; assoc. with Truong Chinh (*q.v.*); mem. Politburo, Communist Party of Viet-Nam 76-82.
Central Committee of the Communist Party of Viet-Nam, 1-c boulevard Hoang Van Thu, Hanoi, Viet-Nam.

Lealofi IV, Hon. Tupua Tamasese; Western Samoan politician and doctor; b. 8 May 1922; ed. Apia Marist Brothers School, Malifa School and Fiji School of Medicine.
Medical practitioner with Western Samoa Health Dept. 40-69; succeeded to Paramount Chief (Tama-a-Aiga) of Tupua Tamasese 65; mem. Council of Deputies 68-69; mem. Parl. 70-; Prime Minister 70-73, May 75-March 76; Minister of Internal and External District Affairs, Labour and Audit, Police and Prisons 75-March 76.
c/o Office of the Prime Minister, Apia, Western Samoa.

Lee, General Honkon; Korean army officer and diplomatist; b. 11 Dec. 1920, Kong Joo City; ed. Japanese Imperial Mil. Acad., Japanese Field Artillery, U.S. Infantry School.
Superintendent, Korean Mil. Acad. 46-48; Mil. Attaché, Washington 49; Commdg. Gen., Eighth Republic of Korea Army Division 49-50, Third Army Corps. 50-51, First Army Corps 52-54; UN Command Del. to Korean Armistice 51-52; Chair. Joint Chiefs of Staff 54-56, Chief of Staff 56-58; Nat. Pres. Korean Veterans' Asscn. 58-61; Amb. to Philippines 61-62, to U.K. 62-67 (also to Scandinavian countries, Iceland, Malta and African countries concurrently); Amb. at Large 67-69; Chair. President's Advisory Comm. on Govt. Admin. 69; Chair. Korean Anti-Communist League 76-; Chair. Korea-British Soc. 78-; 43 Korean and foreign decorations.
Publs. *Nation's Destination* 50; *Free Opinion* (monthly publication) 76-.
San 5-19, Changchung-dong, Chung-ku, Seoul (Office); 51, Daeshin-Dong, Sudaemoon-ku, Seoul, Republic of Korea (Home).
Telephone: 252-4316 (Office); 33-5233 (Home).

Lee Bum Suk; Korean diplomatist and politician; b. 1925.
Red Cross rep. during Korean war; fmr. del. to Int. Red Cross Soc., Geneva; chief negotiator with People's Republic of Korea for reuniting 10 million people separated from their families by mil. demarcation lines drawn between North and South Korea 72; Amb. to India 76-80; Minister for Nat. Unification 80-82; Chief Sec., Pres's Office Jan. 82; Minister of Foreign Affairs June 82-.
Ministry of Foreign Affairs, Seoul, Republic of Korea.

Lee Kuan Yew, M.A.; Singapore politician and barrister; b. 16 Sept. 1923, Singapore; ed. Raffles Coll., Singapore, Fitzwilliam Coll., Cambridge, and Middle Temple, London.
One of the founders of the Socialist People's Action Party 54, Sec.-Gen. 54-; mem. for Tanjong Pagar, Legis. Assembly 55-; (first) Prime Minister 59-; won five subsequent general elections 63, 68, 72, 76, 80; mem. Singapore Internal Security Council; mem. Malaysian Parl. 63-65; mem. Bureau of the Socialist Int. 67-76; Fellow, Inst. of Politics, Harvard Univ. 68; Hoyt Fellow, Berkeley Coll., Yale Univ. 70; Hon. Bencher of Middle Temple 69; Hon. Fellow, Fitzwilliam Coll., Cambridge 69, Royal Australasian Coll. of Surgeons 73, Royal Australasian Coll. of Physicians 74; Grand Cordon of Order of The

Nile 62, Grand Cross of Royal Order, Cambodia 66, First Class Order of the Rising Sun, Japan 67, Bintang Republik Indonesia Adi Pradana 73, Order of Sikatuna, The Philippines 74; Hon. Freeman, City of London 82; Hon. LL.D. (Royal Univ. of Cambodia 65, Hong Kong 70, Liverpool 71, Sheffield 71); Hon. C.H. 70; Hon. G.C.M.G. 72.
Prime Minister's Office, St. Andrew's Road, Singapore 0617.
Telephone: 3378191.

Lee San Choon; Malaysian politician; b. 1935, Pahang.
Youngest M.P. 59; Parl. Sec. 63: Minister of Tech., Research and Co-ordination of New Villages 73-75, of Labour and Manpower 75-78, of Works and Public Utilities 78-80, of Transport 80-; Pres. Malaysian Chinese Asscn. (MCA) 74-.
Malaysian Chinese Association, P.O. Box 626, 67 Jalan Ampang, Kuala Lumpur, Malaysia.

Lee Seung-yun; Korean politician and economist; b. 7 Nov. 1931, Incheon; ed. Coll. of Liberal Arts and Sciences, Seoul Nat. Univ., Adams State Coll., and Graduate School, Univ. of Missouri, U.S.A.
Associate Prof., Seoul Nat. Univ. 61-64; Prof., Coll. of Econ. and Commerce, Sogang Univ. 64-76, Dean, 70-76; mem. Monetary Bd. 71-76; mem. 9th Nat. Assembly (Yujeong-hoe) 76-; Minister of Finance 80-81.
Publ. *The Neo-Monetary and Banking Theory and Korea's Monetary System.*
c/o Ministry of Finance, Seoul, Republic of Korea.

Lee Tsung-dao, PH.D.; Chinese physicist; b. 25 Nov. 1926, Shanghai; ed. National Chekiang Univ., National Southwest Univ. (China) and Univ. of Chicago.
Research Assoc. in Astronomy, Univ. of Chicago 50; Research Assoc. and Lecturer in Physics, Univ. of Calif. 50-51; mem. Inst. for Advanced Study Princeton, N.J. 51-53; Asst. Prof. of Physics, Columbia Univ. 53-55; Assoc. Prof. 55-56 and Prof. 56-60, 63-; Prof. Princeton Inst. for Advanced Study 60-63; mem. Nat. Acad. of Sciences; shared Nobel Prize for Physics 57 with Prof. Yang Chen-ning for work on elementary particles; Albert Einstein Award in Science 57.
Publs. articles in physical journals.
Department of Physics, Columbia University, Morningside Heights, New York, N.Y., 10027; 25 Claremont Avenue, New York, N.Y., 10027, U.S.A.

Leymang, Father Gérard; Vanuatu ecclesiastic and politician; b. 9 May 1937, Port-Sandwich, Malakula; ed. Ecole Ste. Jeanne d'Arc, Port-Vila, Catholic Seminary, Paita.
Teacher, Coll. Catholique de Montmartre 62-66; attached to Mission Catholique d'Océanie, Lyon 66-69; Parish Priest, Melsissi 69-71, Walarano 71-73, Port-Vila 74-; Adviser to Union des Communautés Néo-Hébridaises (UCNH) in Rep. Assembly 75; Minister of Social Affairs and Educ. 78; Chief Minister 78-79.
c/o Office of the Chief Minister, Government Building, Port-Vila, Vanuatu.

Lho Shin Yong, M.A., LL.B.; Korean politician; b. 28 Feb. 1930; ed. Seoul Nat. Univ., Kentucky Graduate School.
Joined Foreign Service 55; First Sec., Washington, D.C. 59, Ankara 60; Dir.-Gen., Archives Bureau 62; Counsellor, Bangkok 63; Dir.-Gen. Asian Affairs Bureau 64; Consul-Gen., Los Angeles 68; Amb. to India 73; Vice-Minister of Foreign Affairs 74; Amb. to UN offices, Geneva 76; Minister of Foreign Affairs 80-82; Dir. Agency for Nat. Security Planning (fmrly. Korean CIA) June 82-; Order of Diplomatic Service Merit, Heung-In Medal 79, Gwang-Hwa Medal 80.
1 Sejong-ro, Jongro-ku, Seoul (Office); San 8-35 Hannam-dong, Yongsan-ku, Seoul, Republic of Korea (Home).

Li Baohua; Chinese party and government official; b. 1908, Luoting, Hebei.
Alternate mem. 7th Cen. Cttee. of CCP 45; Vice-Minister of Water Conservancy 49-63 and of Electric Power 58-63; mem. 8th Cen. Cttee. of CCP 56; First Sec. CCP Anhui 63-67; Third Sec. E. China Bureau, CCP 65; First Political Commissar Anhui Mil. District, People's Liberation Army 66; criticized and removed from office during Cultural Revolution 67; mem. 10th Cen. Cttee. of CCP 73, 11th Cen. Cttee. 77; Second Sec. CCP Guizhou 73; Chair. Kweichon Prov. Revolutionary Cttee. 78-80; mem. State Council and Pres. People's Bank of China March 78-; 1st Gov. IMF for China May 80-.
People's Republic of China.

Li Baoji; Chinese soldier.
Political Commissar Shanghai Mil. Dist. 78-.
People's Republic of China.

Li Choh-ming, M.A., PH.D.; American (b. Chinese) educator and university professor; b. 17 Feb. 1912; ed. Univ. of Nanjing, China, and Univ. of California.
Professor of Economics, Nankai, Southwest Associated and Nat. Central Univs., China 37-43; mem. special mission to U.S.A., Canada and U.K. 43-45; Deputy Dir.-Gen. Chinese Nat. Relief and Rehabilitation Admin. (CNRRA) 45-47; Chief Del. of Repub. of China to UN Econ. Comm. for Asia and the Far East 47-49; Chair. Board of Trustees for Rehabilitation Affairs, Nat. Govt. of China 49-50; Expert on the UN Population Comm. and Statistical Comm. 52-57; Lecturer, Assoc. Prof. and Prof. of Business Admin, sometime Dir. Centre for Chinese Studies, Univ. of Calif. (Berkeley) 51-63; Vice-Chancellor Chinese Univ. of Hong Kong 63-78; Pres. Asscn. of Southeast Asian Insts. of Higher Learning 68-70; Dir. Asian Workshop on Higher Educ. 69; mem. Editorial Boards *Asian Economic Review, Asian Survey, Modern Asian Studies, Tsing Hua Journal of Chinese Studies*; Trustee, Asian Inst. of Technology 73-; Prof. Emer. of Business Admin., Univ. of Calif. 74-; Life Fellow, Royal Econ. Soc., Royal Soc. of Arts, London; mem. American Econ. Asscn., Asscn. for Asian Studies (U.S.A.) and other socs.; Dr. of Law h.c. Chinese Univ. of Hong Kong, Univs. of Hong Kong, Michigan, Marquette, W. Ontario; D.Sc.S. (Pittsburgh); Elise and Walter A. Haas Int. Award (Univ. of Calif.) 74, Clark Kerr Award (Univ. of Calif.) 79, Soong Foundation Hall of Fame Award (U.S.A.) 80; Hon. K.B.E. (U.K.).
Publs. *Economic Development of Communist China* 59, *Statistical System of Communist China* 62; Editor: *Industrial Development in Communist China* 64, *Asian Workshop on Higher Education—Proceedings* 69, *The First Six Years 1963-69, The Emerging University* 74, *New Era Begins, 1975-78* 79, *Li's Chinese Dictionary* 80.
81 Northampton Avenue, Berkeley, Calif. 94707, U.S.A.

Li Da; Chinese army officer; b. 1905, Shaanxi; ed. Moscow Mil. Acad., U.S.S.R.
Staff Officer, Red 6th Army, on Long March 34-36; Staff Officer, 129th Div. 37-45; Chief of Staff, Cen. Plains Field Army 47, Chinese People's Volunteers in Korea 53-54; Vice-Minister of Nat. Defence 54-59; Gen. 55; Chair. Nat. Defence Sports Asscn. 58-67; criticized and removed from office during Cultural Revolution 67; Deputy Chief of Cen. Staff, People's Liberation Army 72-; Adviser, Mil. Comm., Cen. Cttee. 80-; mem. 10th Cen. Cttee. of CCP 73, 11th Cen. Cttee. 77.
People's Republic of China.

Li Desheng, Gen.; Chinese army officer; b. 1916, Hubei.
Company Commdr. Red 4th Front Army on Long March 34-36; Div. Commdr. 2nd Field Army, People's Liberation Army 49; Gen. PLA 64; Commdr. Anhui Mil. District, PLA 67; Chair. Anhui Revolutionary Cttee. 68; Alt. mem. Politburo, 9th Cen. Cttee. of CCP 69; Dir., Gen.

Political Dept., People's Liberation Army 69-74; First Sec. CCP Anhui 71-73; mem. Standing Cttee. of Politburo and Vice-Chair. 10th Cen. Cttee. of CCP 73, Politburo 11th Cen. Cttee. 77; Commdr. Shenyang Mil. Region, PLA 74-; Head, Leading Group for the Prevention and Treatment of Endemic Disease in N. China, Cen. Cttee. 79-.
People's Republic of China.

Li Jing; Chinese soldier.
Commander Gansu PLA Mil. Dist. 78-.
People's Republic of China.

Li Jingchuan; Chinese party official; b. 1905, Huichang, Jiangxi.
Political Commissar 1st Front Army 31; guerrilla leader in Sikang 34; Political Commissar Suiyan-Nei Monggol Mil. Region 37, Shanxi-Suiyuan Mil. Region 47; Dir. W. Sichuan Admin. Office 50; Gov. of Sichuan 52-55; Sec. CCP Sichuan 52-55, First Sec. 55-65; Political Commissar Sichuan Mil. District, People's Liberation Army 52, Chengdu Mil. Region, PLA 54-67; mem. 8th Cen. Cttee. of CCP 56; mem. of Politburo, CCP 58-67; First Sec. S.W. Bureau, CCP 61-67; Vice-Chair. Nat. People's Congress 65; criticized and removed from office during Cultural Revolution 67; mem. 10th Cen. Cttee. of CCP 73, 11th Cen. Cttee. 77; Exec. Chair. Presidium, Vice-Chair. Standing Cttee., 5th NPC 78-.
People's Republic of China.

Li Ka-shing; Chinese business executive; b. 1928, Chaozhou, Guangdong Prov., China; ed. Hong Kong.
Began career as salesman, plastics factory, made Man. 48; started own plastics factory 50; moved into plastic flowers market 57; bought first industrial property 58; started Cheung Kong (property devt. co.) 71; formed Dorset Land with Slater Walker Securities (Hong Kong) 73; Dorset Land absorbed into Cheung Kong; formed Canadian Eastern Finance with Canadian Imperial Bank of Commerce 74; purchased Wynncor (owner of Hong Kong Hilton) 77; joint venture with Hong Kong Electric 78, subsequently became new co. Int. City Holdings 81; joint ventures with Green Island Cement, Wheelock Marden, Realty Devt. and Hong Kong Land to develop property; Vice-Pres. Chiu On Asscn., Hong Kong; Hon. Pres. Chiu Chau Plastics Mfrs. Asscn.; Dir. Hong Kong Chiu Chow Chamber of Commerce, Hong Kong Chiu Chow Merchants Mutual Assistance Soc.
Office of the Chairman, Cheung Kong, Hong Kong.

Li Kwoh-ting, B.S.; Chinese government official; b. 28 Jan. 1910; ed. Nat. Central Univ., China, and Cambridge Univ., England.
Superintendent of Tze Yu Iron Works, Chongqing 42-45; Pres. Taiwan Shipbuilding Corpn. 51-53; mem. Industrial Devt. Comm., Econ. Stabilization Board 53-58; Sec.-Gen. Council for U.S. Aid, Convenor of Industrial Planning and Co-ordination Group of Ministry of Econ. Affairs, Head of Industrial Devt. and Investment Center 58-63; Vice-Chair. Council for Int. Econ. Co-operation and Devt. 63-73; Minister of Econ. Affairs 65-69, of Finance 69-76, without Portfolio and of State 76-; mem. Nat. Security Council 67-; Vice-Chair. Nat. Reconstruction Planning Cttee. 67-72; mem. Council for Econ. Planning and Devt. 77-; Ramon Magsaysay Award for Govt. Service 68 and decorations from Repub. of Korea, Spain, Repub. of Viet-Nam, Jordan, Madagascar, Thailand, Gabon and Paraguay.
Publs. *Symposium on Nuclear Physics, British Industries, Japanese Shipbuilding Industry, The Growth of Private Industry in Free China, Economic Policy and Economic Development, The Experience of Dynamic Economic Growth on Taiwan.*
3 Lane 2, Tai-an Street, Taipei, Taiwan.

Li Quiang; Chinese politician and telecommunications specialist.
Member 6th Exec. Cttee., Nat. Fed. of Trade Unions 48-53; Dir. Radio Bureau, Ministry of Post and Telecommunications 50; Commercial Attaché, Embassy in Moscow 52-54; mem. Scientific Planning Comm., State Council 57; Deputy Dir. Bureau for Econ. Relations with Foreign Countries, State Council 61; Vice-Chair. Comm. for Econ. Relations with Foreign Countries 65-67; Vice-Minister of Foreign Trade 68-73, Minister 73-81; Adviser to State Council 81-; mem. 9th Cen. Cttee. of CCP 69, 10th Cen. Cttee. of CCP 73, 11th Cen. Cttee. 77; Vice-Chair. Credentials Cttee. 5th Nat. People's Congress 78-.
People's Republic of China.

Li Ruishan; Chinese party official.
Secretary CCP Hunan 58-68; First Sec. CCP Changsha 59; Chair. Shaanxi Revolutionary Cttee. 68-; Political Commissar Lanzhou Mil. Region, People's Liberation Army 68; mem. 9th Cen. Cttee. of CCP 69; First Sec. CCP Shaanxi 71-78; mem. 10th Cen. Cttee. of CCP 73, 11th Cen. Cttee. 77.
People's Republic of China.

Li Shuiqing; Chinese politician.
Divisional Commdr., People's Liberation Army 49; Maj.-Gen. PLA 57; Chief of Staff Jinan Mil. Region, PLA 68; mem. 9th Cen. Cttee. of CCP 69; Minister of First Ministry of Machine Building 72-75, First Minister of Mechanical Industry 75-78; mem. 10th Cen. Cttee. of CCP 73, 11th Cen. Cttee. 77.
People's Republic of China.

Li Tze-chung; Chinese librarian; b. 1927, Jiangsu; ed. Suzhou Univ., Southern Methodist Univ., Harvard Univ., Columbia Univ., New School for Social Research.
District Judge 49-51; Section Chief, Ministry of Nat. Defence 51-56; Vice-Pres. Atlantic Fiscal Corpn., New York 62-64; Asst. Prof. of Library Science, Asst. Librarian Illinois Normal Univ. 65-66; Asst. Prof. of Political Science and Library Science Rosary Coll. 66-70, Assoc. Prof. of Library Science 70-74, Prof. 75-; Visiting Assoc. Prof. Nat. Taiwan Univ., Suzhou Univ. 69; Dir. Nat. Cen. Library 70-72, Consultant 74-76; Consultant Dr. Sun Yat-sen Memorial Library, Taipei 71; mem. Nat. Council of Culture Renaissance 70-; Chair. Graduate Inst. of Library Science, Nat. Cen. Library 71-72; mem. of Board, Center for American Studies, Academia Sinica 71-73; Exec. Ed., Journal of Library and Information Science 75-80; Pres. Chinese-American Educ. Foundation, Chicago 69-70; Chair. Cttee. on High School Library Standards, Ministry of Educ. 72; Convenor, Board of Dirs., Chinese Library Asscn. 70-71; Regional Rep. Int. Asscn. of Orientalist Librarians 71-76; Pres. Mid-West Chinese-American Librarians Asscn. 73-76; Sec.-Treas., Int. Relations Round Table, American Library Asscn. 75-77; Pres. Chinese Culture Service Inc. 75-; Chair. Chinese-American Librarians Asscn. 76-77; Exec. Dir. American Libraries Asscn. 77-; Dir. Continuing Educ., Rosary Coll. 79-; Bd. Dirs. Asian Human Service Inc., Chicago 80-81; Elsie O. and Philip D. Sang Award for Excellence in Teaching (Rosary Coll.) 71.
Publs. eleven books, and many articles.
Graduate School of Library and Information Science, Rosary College, River Forest, Ill. 60305, U.S.A.

Li Xiannian; Chinese politician; b. 1905, Huangan, Hubei.
Joined CCP 27; Political Commissar 30th Army, 4th Front Red Army 35; Commdr. 5th Column, New 4th Army 38; mem. 7th Cen. Cttee. of CCP 45; Gov. of Hubei 49; Commdr., Political Commissar Hubei Mil. District, People's Liberation Army 49; Vice-Premier, State Council 54-80; Minister of Finance 54-75; mem. Politburo, 8th Cen. Cttee. of CCP 56; Sec., Secr. of Cen. Cttee., CCP 58-66; Vice-Chair. State Planning Comm. 62; mem. Politburo, 9th Cen. Cttee. of CCP 69, Politburo, 10th Cen. Cttee. 73,

Politburo 11th Cen. Cttee. 77; Vice-Chair. CCP; Exec. Chair. Presidium 5th Nat. People's Congress 78-.
People's Republic of China.

Li Zhimin; Chinese soldier; b. 1908; Hunan.
Political Commissar First Div., Red 3rd Army Corps 31; Political Commissar 3rd Army Corps PLA, 2nd Field Army 49; mem. Shaanxi Provincial People's Govt. 49-53; mem. N.W. Mil. and Admin. Cttee. 50-53; Pol. Commissar Chinese People's Volunteers 50-57; Dir., Pol. Dept., Chinese People's Volunteers 53; Deputy for PLA 1st NPC 54; Col.-Gen. 55; Alt. mem. CCP 8th Cen. Cttee. 56; Pol. Commissar PLA Mil. Acad. in Beijing 63; purged 67; Pol. Commissar PLA Fuzhou Mil. Region 73-; mem. CCP 10th Cen. Cttee. 73; mem. Presidium 4th NPC 75; mem. Presidium CCP 11th Nat. Congress 77-; mem. CCP 11th Cen. Cttee. 77.
People's Republic of China.

Liang Lingguang; Chinese politician.
Former administrator in Fujian; Minister of Light Industry 78-81; Mayor of Canton 81-.
People's Republic of China.

Liao Chengzhi; Chinese party official; b. 1908, Tokyo, Japan; ed. Lingnan Univ., Guangzhou, Waseda Univ., Japan and Berlin and Hamburg Univs., Germany.
Joined CCP 25; studied Political Econ., Germany 28; Chair. Seaman's Union 33; participated in Long March 34-36; Dir. New China News Agency 38; prisoner of Kuomintang 42-46; Alt. mem. 7th Cen. Cttee. of CCP 45; Chair. Nat. Fed. of Democratic Youth 49; Dir. Inst. of Foreign Affairs 49-54; mem. 8th Cen. Cttee. of CCP 56; Chair. Comm. for Overseas Chinese Affairs 59-67, Hon. Chair. 79-; Pres. Overseas Chinese Univ., Fujian 61-67, China-Japan Friendship Asscn. 63-; criticized and removed from office during Cultural Revolution 67; rehabilitated and returned to previous positions 72; mem. 10th Cen. Cttee. of CCP 73, 11th Cen. Cttee. 77; Exec. Chair. Presidium, Vice-Chair. Standing Cttee. 5th Nat. People's Congress 78-; Dir. Office of Overseas Chinese Affairs 78-.
People's Republic of China.

Liao Hansheng; Chinese politician; b. 1910, Hunan.
Political Commissar 6th Div., 2nd Front Army 34; Pol. Commissar Div., 2nd Front Red Army 36; Pol. Commissar 716 Regt., 120th Div., 8th Route Army; Pol. Commissar 1st Column, N.W. Liberation Army 47; Pol. Commissar 2nd Army Group CCP Red Army 49; Chair. Qinghai Mil. and Admin. Cttee. 49; Pol. Commissar Qinghai Mil. Area 49; Vice-Chair. Qinghai People's Provincial Govt. 49-56; Deputy Commdr. Qinghai Mil. Area 50; mem. N.W. Mil. and Admin. Cttee. 50; mem. N.W. Admin. Cttee. 53; Deputy Pol. Commissar N.W. Mil. Area 54; Deputy for PLA to 1st Nat. People's Congress (NPC) 54; mem. Nat. Defence Council 54; rank of Lt.-Gen. 55; Alt. mem. CCP 8th Cen. Cttee. 56; Pres. Mil. Acad. of PLA 57; responsible for PLA Units in Nanjing 57; responsible for PLA Units in Beijing 62; Deputy for Beijing PLA Units to 3rd NPC 64; mem. Presidium 3rd NPC 64; Sec. CCP N. China Bureau 65; detained in Beijing Garrison H.Q., 67; branded a 3-Anti Element 67; resumed activities 72; Vice-Pres. Acad. of Mil. Science 74; First Pol. Commissar PLA Nanjing Mil. Region 78-80; First Pol. Commissar, PLA Shenyang Units 80-.
People's Republic of China.

Liao Zhigao; Chinese party official; b. *c.* 1908, Jianning, Sichuan; ed. Qinghua Univ., Beijing.
Director Political Dept., N. Shaanxi 47; Political Commissar Sigang Mil. District, People's Liberation Army 50-55; Gov. of Sigang Provisional Govt. 50-55; Vice-Gov. of Sichuan 55-68; Sec. CCP Sichuan 56-65; First Sec. 65-68; Alt. mem. 8th Cen. Cttee. of CCP 56; Sec. S.W. Bureau, CCP 64-68; criticized and removed from office during Cultural Revolution 68; Alt. mem. 10th Cen. Cttee. of CCP 73, mem. 11th Cen. Cttee. 77; First Sec. CCP Fujian 75-; Chair. Fujian People's Govt. (fmrly. Revolutionary Cttee.) Cttee.; First Political Commissar Fujian Mil. District 75; Chair. Fujian Prov. People's Congress 79-; First Political Commissar PLA Fuzhou Mil. Region 80-.
People's Republic of China.

Licaros, Gregorio S., LL.B., B.SC.; Philippine lawyer and banker; b. 12 March 1909; ed. Far Eastern Univ.
Chairman Board of Trustees, Govt. Service Insurance System 54-61; Chair. Board of Govs., Devt. Bank of the Philippines and mem. Central Bank Monetary Board 58-61; Chair. Board of Dirs., CCP Securities Corpn. 63-65; Gov. and Chair. Central Bank of the Philippines 70-81; concurrently Gov. Int. Monetary Fund for the Philippines; mem. Council of Central Bank Govs. of S.E. Asia, N.Z., Australia (SEANZA) 70-, Nat. Econ. Council, Financial and Fiscal Policy Council, Foreign Trade Council, Surigao Mineral Reservation Board 70-; mem. Board of Dirs., Philippine Deposit Insurance Corpn. 70-; Chair. Gold Mining Industry Assistance Bd. 70-; Hon. Dr. of Public Admin. 78; Hon. Dr. of Laws (Far East Univ.) 78, (Univ. of Philippines) 80; Outstanding CPA, Philippine Asscn. of Bd. of Examiners 58, and many other awards.
802 Harvard Street, Mandaluyong, Rizal, Philippines.

Lillee, Dennis K., M.B.E.; Australian cricketer; b. 18 July 1949.
Played for Western Australia 69-; for Haslingden, Lancashire League, England 71; 55 test matches for Australia -Feb. 82; became leading wicket-taker in test matches beating previous record of 309 on 27 Dec. 81; leading wicket-taker in England/Australia test matches with 152 in 27 tests -Aug. 81.

Lim Chong Eu, Dr., M.B., CH.B.; Malaysian politician; b. 28 May 1919, Penang; ed. Penang Free School, Edinburgh Univ.
Medical Officer (Flight Lieut.) Malayan Auxiliary Air Force 51-54; private medical practice; mem. Penang State Settlement Council 51; Radical Party 52-58; mem. Fed. Council for Penang 55-57, Alliance Chief Whip; Pres. Malayan Chinese Asscn. (M.C.A.) 58-59, resigned as Pres. 59, left M.C.A. 60; Chair. pro tem. Cttee. of United Democratic Party 62-63, Gen. Sec. 63-66, Pres. 66-68; Deputy Chair. Gerakan Rakyat Malaysia 68-71, Pres. 71-80, Chair. Tanjong Branch 69-, Hon. Adviser and mem. Cen. and Cen. Working Cttees. 80-; mem. for Kota, Penang State Assembly, mem. for Tanjong, House of Reps. 64-; Chief Minister of Penang 69-; Chair. Penang State Goodwill Cttee. 69-, State Operations Cttee. 69-; mem. Malayan Medical Council 64; Pres. Northern Branch of Malayan Medical Asscn. 68-69, fmr. mem. Exec. Council, now mem. House Cttee.; Chair. Penang Devt. Corpn. 70-; Chair. Barisan Nasional 78-; fmr. Pres. Penang Medical Practitioners' Soc., Hon. mem. 69-; Hon. LL.D. (Univ. of Science, Malaysia) 76.
Pejabat Ketua Menteri, Bangunan Tuanku Syed Putra, Peti Surat 3006, Penang, Malaysia.

Lim Kim San; Singapore politician; b. 1916, Singapore; ed. Raffles Coll., Singapore.
Director United Chinese Bank Ltd., Chair. Batu Pahat Bank Ltd., and Pacific Bank Ltd. 40-; mem., Deputy Chair. Public Service Comm., Singapore 59-63; Chair. Housing Devt. Board; Deputy Chair. Econ. Devt. Board; 61-63; Minister for Nat. Devt. 63-65, for Finance 65-67, for the Interior and Defence 67-70, for Educ. 70-72; Minister of the Environment 72-75, for Nat. Devt. and Communications 75-78, for Nat. Devt. 78-79, for the Environment 79-81; Chair. Public Utilities Board 71-78, Port of Singapore Authority 79-; Man. Dir. Monetary Authority of Singapore 81-; mem. Dewan Ra'ayat; Darjah Utama

Temasek (Order of Temasek) 62, Ramon Magsaysay Award for community leadership 65.
Port of Singapore Authority, P.O. Box 300, Singapore 9005.

Lin Chin-sheng, B.L.; Chinese politician; b. 4 Aug. 1916; ed. Law Coll., Tokyo Imperial Univ.
Magistrate, Chiayi Co. Govt. 51-54; Chair. Yunlin Co. H.Q., Kuomintang 54-57; Magistrate, Yunlin Co. Govt. 57-64; Dir. Cheng-Ching Lake Industrial Waterworks 64-67; Commr., Taiwan Provincial Govt. 66-70; Sec.-Gen. Taiwan Provincial H.Q., Kuomintang 67-68; Chair. Taipei Municipal H.Q. 69-70, Deputy Sec.-Gen. Cen. Cttee. 70-72; Minister of the Interior 72-76, of Communications 76-81, without Portfolio 81-; mem. Standing Cttee. of Kuomintang Cen. Cttee. Nov. 76-; Order of the Brilliant Star.
c/o Ministry of Communications, Taipei, Taiwan.

Lin Hujia; Chinese politician.
Director Propaganda Dept. CCP Zhejiang Provincial Cttee. 51; mem. Council Zhejiang People's Provincial Govt. 51; Deputy Sec. CCP Zhejiang Provincial Cttee. 55, Sec. 57-67; Deputy Head production inspecting del. CCP Zhejiang Provincial Cttee. 58; denounced as a rightist opportunist 67; mem. Presidium CCP 11th Cen. Nat. Congress 77-; mem. CCP 11th Cen. Cttee. 77-; First Sec. Tjanin Municipal CCP Cttee. 78; Chair. Tjanin Municipal Revolutionary Cttee. 78; First Sec. Beijing CCP Cttee. 78-80; Chair. Beijing Revolutionary Cttee. 78-80; Mayor, Beijing 78-81; Minister of Agric. March 81-.
People's Republic of China.

Ling Qing; Chinese diplomatist; b. 1923, Fujian Prov.
Former Section Chief American and Australian Dept., Ministry of Foreign Affairs; First Sec., Romania and Indonesia; Deputy Dir. Western European and American Dept., Dir. Dept. of Int. Orgs., Law and Treaty, Ministry of Foreign Affairs; Amb. to Venezuela; Perm Rep. to UN Aug. 80-; del. to 28th and 32nd sessions, UN Gen. Assembly, to 17th session UNESCO; Chair. del. to 4th session Third UN Conf. on Law of the Sea; Vice-Chair. dels. to First and Second Conf. on Law of the Sea, 10th special session UN Gen. Assembly, Conf. on Indochinese Refugees, Geneva 79, 36th session ESCAP.
Permanent Mission of the People's Republic of China to the United Nations, 155 West 66th Street, New York, N.Y. 10023, U.S.A.

Lini, Father Walter Hayde, C.B.E.; Vanuatu ecclesiastic and politician; b. 1943, Pentecost; ed. for Anglican priesthood, Solomon Islands and New Zealand.
Ordained deacon 68; ordained priest 70; Deputy Chief Minister and Minister of Social Services Jan.-Nov. 79; Chief Minister and Minister of Justice 79-80; Prime Minister of Vanuatu July 80-; Pres. Vanuaaku Pati (VP), formerly the Nat. Party.
Office of the Prime Minister, Government Building, Port Vila, Vanuatu.

Liu Bocheng, Marshal; Chinese fmr. army officer; b. 1892, Kaixian, Sichuan; ed. Chengdu Mil. School and Moscow Mil. Inst.
Joined CCP 26; Head Chief of Staff Nanchang Uprising 27; Chief of Gen. Staff, Red Army 32; on Long March 34-35; Pres. Red. Army Univ., Gansu 36; Commdr. 129th Div., 8th Route Army 37-40; mem. 7th Cen. Cttee. of CCP 45; Commdr. 2nd Field Army 49-54; Second Sec. S.W. Bureau, CCP 50; Pres. Nanjing Mil. Acad. 51-58; Vice-Chair. Nat. Defence Council 54-; Dir., Gen. Training Dept., People's Liberation Army 54-57; Marshal, PLA 55; mem. Politburo, 8th Cen. Cttee. of CCP 56; Vice-Chair. Nat. People's Congress 59-80; mem. Politburo, 9th Cen. Cttee. of CCP 69, Politburo, 10th Cen. Cttee. 73, 11th Cen. Cttee. 77; Vice-Chair. Standing Cttee. 5th Nat. People's Congress 78-80, CCP Cen. Cttee. Mil. Comm. 78-.
People's Republic of China.

Liu Chieh; Chinese diplomatist; b. 16 April 1906; ed. Oxford and Columbia Univs.
Foreign Service 31-; Chinese Del. to League of Nations 32-39; Counsellor, Chinese Embassy, London 33-40, Minister, Washington 40-45; Vice-Minister for Foreign Affairs 45-47; Amb. to Canada 47-63; Pres. UN Trusteeship Council 48; mem. Int. Law Comm. 61-66; Perm. Rep. of Repub. of China to UN 62-71; Amb. to the Philippines 72-75; Presidential Adviser 75-; Chair. Research and Planning Comm., Ministry of Foreign Affairs 75-.
c/o Ministry of Foreign Affairs, Taipei, Taiwan.

Liu Guangdao; Chinese soldier.
Divisional Political Commissar in Fourth Field Army, PLA 49; Political Commissar of Fortieth Army, PLA 61, of Heilongjiang Mil. District, PLA 69; Vice-Chair. Heilongjiang Revolutionary Cttee. 70; Deputy Political Commissar, Shenyang Mil. Region, PLA 70; Second Sec. of CCP Cttee., Heilongjiang 71; First Political Commissar of Heilongjiang Mil. District, PLA 71; Alt. mem. 10th Cen. Cttee., CCP 73, 11th Cen. Cttee. 77; First Sec. CCP Heilongjiang March-Dec. 77; Sr. Political Commissar, Heilongjiang March -Dec. 77; disappeared Dec. 77.
People's Republic of China.

Liu Jianxun; Chinese party official; b. 1907, Hebei.
Second Sec. CCP Hubei 52-54, Sec. 54-55; Political Commissar Hubei Mil. District, People's Liberation Army 52; Deputy Dir. Rural Dept., CCP 56; First Sec. CCP Guangsi 57-61; Alt. mem. 8th Cen. Cttee. of CCP 56; First Sec. CCP Henan 61-66; Political Commissar Henan Mil. District, PLA 64; Sec. Cen.-South Bureau, CCP 65-66; Sec. CCP Beijing 66; Second Sec. N. China Bureau, CCP 66; Vice-Chair. Beijing Revolutionary Cttee. 67; First Political Commissar Henan Mil. District, PLA 67; Deputy Political Commissar Wuhan Mil. Region, PLA 67, Political Commissar 71-; Chair. Henan Revolutionary Cttee. 68-; mem. 9th Cen. Cttee. of CCP 69; First Sec. CCP Henan 71-78; mem. 10th Cen. Cttee. of CCP 73, 11th Cen. Cttee. 77.
People's Republic of China.

Liu Shijian; Chinese soldier.
Political Commissar PLA Kunming Mil. Region 78-.
People's Republic of China.

Liu Wei; Chinese politician and party official.
Director 8th Bureau, Ministry of Public Security 52; Asst. to Ministry of Geology 55-57; Vice-Minister, Second Ministry of Machine-Building 61-78, Minister 78-79 and 80-; mem. 11th Cen. Cttee. CCP 77.
People's Republic of China.

Liu Xingyuan; Chinese party official; b. 1914, Hunan.
Deputy Political Commissar, Guangzhou Mil. Region, People's Liberation Army 55, Second Political Commissar 63; Lieut.-Gen. 75; mem. Nat. Defence Council 65; Chair. Guangdong Revolutionary Cttee. 69; mem. 9th Cen. Cttee. of CCP 69; First Sec. CCP Guangdong 71; Chair. Sichuan Revolutionary Cttee. 72; First Sec. CCP Sichuar. 72; First Political Commissar Chengdu Mil. Region, PLA 73-76, Commdr. 76-77; mem. 10th Cen. Cttee. of CCP 73, 11th Cen. Cttee. 77.
People's Republic of China.

Liu Xiyao; Chinese party and government official.
Deputy Sec. CCP Hubei 53-54; Vice-Chair. State Technological Comm. 57-59, State Scientific and Technological Comm. 59-67; Alt. mem. 9th Cen. Cttee. of CCP 69; Dir. Scientific and Educ. Group, State Council 72-77; Alt. mem. 10th Cen. Cttee. of CCP 73, 11th Cen. Cttee. 77; Minister, Second Ministry of Machine Bldg. 75; Minister of Educ. 77-79; Vice-Gov. Sichuan Prov.
People's Republic of China.

Liu Zhanyang; Chinese army officer.
Commander Hunan Mil. District 80-.
People's Republic of China.

Liu Zhen; Chinese soldier.
Commander Xinjiang Uygur PLA Mil. Region 77-; 2nd Sec. Xinjiang Uygur CCP Cttee. 78-; mem. Presidium CCP 11th Nat. Congress 77-; mem. 11th Cen. Cttee. 77.
People's Republic of China.

Liu Zhonggui; Chinese party official.
Military Attaché at Embassy, Dem. Repub. of Viet-Nam 60-63; Deputy Commdr., Guangxi Mil. District, PLA 65, Political Commissar 70-; Second Sec. Guangxi Regional CCP Cttee., Vice-Chair. Guangxi Revolutionary Cttee.
People's Republic of China.

Liu Zihou; Chinese party official; b. *c.* 1910, Hebei.
Joined CCP 37; Deputy Gov. of Hubei 52-54; Gov. 54-56; Second Sec. CCP Hubei 53-56; Dir. Sanmen Gorge Construction Bureau 56-58; Gov. of Hebei 58-68; Sec. CCP Hebei 58-64; Alt. mem. 8th Cen. Cttee. of CCP 56; Sec. N. China Bureau, CCP 63-68; Second Sec. CCP Hebei Revolutionary Cttee. 64-68; First Vice-Chair. Hebei Revolutionary Cttee. 68, Chair. 70-79; mem. 9th Cen. Cttee. of CCP 69; First Sec. CCP Hebei 71-80; mem. 10th Cen. Cttee. of CCP 73, 11th Cen. Cttee. 77; First Political Commissar Hebei Mil. Dist.
People's Republic of China.

Loane, Most Rev. Sir Marcus Lawrence, K.B.E., M.A., D.D.; Australian ecclesiastic; b. 14 Oct. 1911; ed. The King's School, Parramatta, Univ. of Sydney, and Moore Theological Coll., Sydney.
Resident Tutor and Chaplain, Moore Theological Coll., Sydney 35-38, Vice-Principal 39-53, Principal 54-58; Canon, St. Andrew's Cathedral 49-58; Bishop Co-adjutor, Diocese of Sydney 58-66; Archbishop of Sydney and Metropolitan of New South Wales 66-81; Primate of Australia 78-.
Publs. *Oxford and the Evangelical Succession* 51, *Cambridge and the Evangelical Succession* 52, *Masters of the English Reformation, History of Moore Theological College* 55, *Life of Archbishop Mowll* 59, *Pioneers of the Reformation in England* 63, *Makers of Our Heritage, The Hope of Glory* 68, *This Surpassing Excellence* 69, *They Were Pilgrims* 70, *By Faith We Stand* 71, *They Overcame* 71, *The King is Here* 73, *Good News to Tell* 75, *He Came to Serve, Hewn from the Rock* (*Origins and Traditions of the Church in Sydney*) 76, *This is My Son* 77, *The God Who Acts* 78.
c/o St. Andrew's House, Sydney Square, Sydney, N.S.W. 2000, Australia

Lokoloko, Sir Tore, G.C.M.G., O.B.E.; Papua New Guinean farmer and politician; b. 21 Sept. 1930, Iokea; ed. London Missionary Soc. School, Iokea, Sogeri High School, Port Moresby.
Clerk in New Guinea Co-operative Socs., later Asst. Registrar until 68; mem. House of Assembly 68-77; Deputy Spokesman Admin's. Exec. Council 68-72, Ministerial Asst. for Health; Gov.-Gen. of Papua New Guinea March 77-; K.St.J.
Government House, P.O. Box 79, Port Moresby; Iokea, Gulf Province, Papua New Guinea (Home).

Lon Nol, Marshal; Kampuchean fmr. military commander and politician; b. 13 Nov. 1913, Kampong Leav; ed. Chasseloup Laubat High School, S. Viet-Nam, and Royal Mil. Acad., Cambodia.
Government official 37-52; Gov. of Kratie province 45, later Chief of Nat. Police; Army Area Commdr. 52; Gov. of Battambang province 54; Minister of Nat. Defence and Chief of Gen. Staff 55-66; C.-in-C. of the Khmer Royal Armed Forces 60; Deputy Prime Minister of Cambodia 63, Prime Minister 66-67, First Vice-Pres. in Charge of Nat. Defence 67-69; Prime Minister and Minister of Nat. Defence 69-71; led coup to overthrow Prince Norodom Sihanouk (*q.v.*) March 70; Titular Prime Minister 71-72; Pres. of Khmer Repub. 72-75; Supreme Commdr. of Armed Forces 72-74; Chair. Supreme State Council 73-74, High Exec. Council 74-75; left the country April 75.
Fullerton, Calif. 92635, U.S.A.

Long Bingju; Chinese party official.
Regimental Commdr. 45; Maj.-Gen., Gansu Mil. District, PLA 63, Political Commissar 70-.
People's Republic of China.

López, Fernando; Philippine agriculturalist and politician; b. 13 April 1904, Jaro, Iloilo; ed. San Juan de Letrán Coll., Univ. of Santo Tomás.
Member, Philippine Bar 26; Mayor, Iloilo City 45; Senator of Philippines 47, Vice-Pres. 49, Sec. Agriculture and Natural Resources 50-71, Pres. Pro-Tempore 58, 60; Vice-Pres. of Philippines 65-69, 69-71; Sec. Agriculture and Natural Resources 70-71; Special Grand Cordon of Most Noble Order of Crown of Thailand; Officer of Nat. Order of Vietnam; Hon. LL.D., Manhattan Coll., New York City; Gran Cruz, Orden de Isabel la Católica; Mil. Order of Christ, and other awards.
6 Flame Tree Place, Forbes Park, Makati Rizal; Penthouse, Chronicle Building, Meralco Avenue Pasig, Metro Manila, Philippines.

López, Salvador P.; Philippine journalist, diplomatist and university professor; b. 27 May 1911; ed. Univ. of the Philippines.
With *Philippines Herald* 33-41; Radio Commentator 40-41; Army Service 42-46; Diplomatic Service 46-69; Adviser on Political Affairs, Philippine Mission to UN 46-48, Senior Adviser 48-49, Chargé d'Affaires a.i. 50-52, Acting Perm. Rep. to UN 53-54; Minister to France 55-56, concurrently Minister to Belgium and Netherlands 55-59, to Switzerland 57-58; Amb. to France 56-62, concurrently Perm. Rep. to UNESCO 58-62, Minister to Portugal 59-62; Under-Sec. of Foreign Affairs, Philippines 62-63; Sec. of Foreign Affairs 63-64; Perm. Rep. to UN 64-68, concurrently Amb. to U.S.A., Dominican Repub., Haiti, Cuba 68-69; Pres. Univ. of the Philippines 69-75, Prof. 75-; Adviser to Pres. of Philippines 75-; numerous decorations.
Publs. *Literature and Society* 51, *Freedom of Information* 53, *English for World Use* 54, *The United States—Philippines Colonial Relationship* 66, *Human Rights and the Constitution* 70, *The Philippines under Martial Law* 74, *New Directions in Philippine Foreign Policy* 75, *Reflections on Human Rights in the Philippines* 77.
c/o University of the Philippines, Quezon City, Philippines.

Loton, Brian Thorley, B.MET.ENG., F.A.I.M.; Australian business executive; b. 17 May 1929, Perth; ed. Hale School, Perth, Trinity Coll., Melbourne Univ.
Started as Cadet, Broken Hill Pty. Co. Ltd. 54, Tech. Asst. to Production Superintendent 59, Asst. Chief Engineer 61, Gen. Man. Planning and Devt. 69, Dir. 69-; Gen. Man. Newcastle Steelworks 70, Exec. Gen. Man. Steel Div 73, Chief Gen. Man. Dec. 77-, Man. Dir. 82; Dir. Australian Iron and Steel Ltd., Hematite Petroleum Pty. Ltd., Dampier Mining Co. Ltd., Groote Eylandt Mining Co. Pty. Ltd., Mount Newman Mining Co. Pty. Ltd., Tasmanian Electro Metallurgical Co. Pty. Ltd., Queensland Coal Mining Co. Ltd., AWI Holdings Pty. Ltd., Woodside Petroleum Ltd.; Vice-Chair. Defence Industry Cttee.; Vice-Pres. Australian Mining Industry Council; Fellow Inst. of Engineers Australia, Inst. of Dirs. Australia, Australian Inst. of Man., Australian Acad. of Tech. Sciences; Pres. and Councillor Australasian Inst. of Mining and Metallurgy; mem. Victoria State Govt. Long Range Policy Planning Cttee. 80-82, Dept. of Immigration and Ethnic Affairs Advisory Cttee., Metals Soc. (U.K.), A.I.M.E. (U.S.A.), Australian Science and Tech. Council 77-80,

Faculty of Eng., Melbourne Univ., Australian Manufacturing Council.
c/o G.P.O. Box 86A, Melbourne, Victoria 3001, Australia. Telephone: 60-0701.

Lowe, Douglas Ackley; Australian politician; b. 15 May 1942, Hobart; ed. St. Virgil's Coll.
Worked as electrical fitter, Electrolytic Co.; State Sec. Tasmanian Section, Australian Labor Party 65-69, State Pres. 74-75; mem. Tasmania House of Assembly 69-; Minister of Housing 72-74; Chief Sec. 74, Deputy Premier 75-77, Chief Sec. and Minister for Planning and Reorganization 75, Minister for Industrial Relations 76-79, for Planning and the Environment 76, for Health 76, for Manpower Planning 76-79, Minister for Economic Planning and Devt. and Minister for Energy 79-81; Premier of Tasmania 77-81, also Treas. 80-81; resgnd. from Labor Party Nov. 81, re-elected as Independent mem. of Assembly May 82; del. to Australian Constitutional Convention; Queen's Silver Jubilee Medal 77.
Parliament House, Hobart, Tasmania 7000; Home: 15 Tooma Avenue, Chigwell, Tasmania 7011, Australia.

Lu Dong; Chinese politician.
Former Minister of Metallurgical Industy; Minister Third Ministry of Machine-Building 78-81.
People's Republic of China.

Lu Zhengcao; Chinese soldier; b. 1903, Liaoning Prov.; ed. Northeast Mil. Acad.
Joined Army 21; Regimental Commdr. in Kuomintang Army 33; joined CCP 36; Commdr. Northeast Railway Protection Corps 48; Vice-Minister of Railways 49-61; Commdr. PLA Railway Corps 50; Acting Minister of Railways 61-65, Minister 65-66; criticized and removed from office during Cultural Revolution 67; Political Commissar, PLA Railway Corps 76; mem. 11th Cen. Cttee. of CCP 77.
People's Republic of China.

Lubis, Mochtar; Indonesian journalist; b. 1922.
Joined Indonesian Antara News Agency 45; Co-publisher daily *Indonesian Raya* 49-61, Editor 56-61, 66- (*Raya* banned Jan. 74); published and edited *The Times of Indonesia* 52; Dir.-Gen. Press Foundation of Asia, Manila; Vice-Chair. Jakarta Acad.; Chair. Bd. of Editors *Horison* (literary monthly); Chair. Legal Aid Foundation; Nat. Literary Award 53; Pres. Magsaysay Award for the Press 58, Golden Pen of Freedom, Int. Fed. of Publishers 67
Publs. ***Pers and Wartawan, Tak Ada Esok, Si Djamal*** **(short stories),** ***Djalan Ada Udjung, Korean Notebook, Perkenalan Di Asia Tenggara, Melawat Ke Amerika, Stories from Europe, Indonesia Dimata Dunia, Stories from China, Twilight in Djakarta, Road with No End, Tiger! Tiger!, Subversive Notes, Love and Death*** 76, *Indonesia, Land Under the Rainbow, Indonesia, Land Under the Sun, Bromocorah* (collected short stories)
Jalan Bonang 17, Jakarta Pusat, Indonesia.

Luo Yuzhuan; Chinese politician.
Minister of Forestry 79-80.
People's Republic of China.

Luvsangombo, Col.-Gen. Sonomyn; Mongolian politician; b. 19 Dec. 1924; ed. Higher Mil. School, Ulan Bator, Acad. of Mil. Eng., U.S.S.R. and Higher School of Civil Eng.
Army technician, instructor, divisional supply officer 48-56; Senior End., Ministry of Construction 56-59; Deputy and First Deputy Minister of Construction and Construction Materials Industry, Deputy Chair. State Construction Cttee. 59-71; Chair. Exec. Cttee. of Ulan Bator People's Deputies' Hural (Assembly) 71-72; Deputy Chair. Council of Ministers 72-82; Chair. Cttee. for Construction and Architecture and Tech. Control 81-82; Deputy to People's Great Hural (Assembly); Cand. mem. Mongolian People's Revolutionary Party Cen. Cttee. 66-71, mem. Cen. Ctee. 71-; Cand. mem. Politburo 82; Minister of Public Security March 82-; Order of the Pole Star, Order of the Red Banner of Labour.
Ministry of Public Security, Ulan Bator, Mongolia.

Luvsanravdan, Namsrayn; Mongolian politician; b. 6 Feb. 1923.
Schoolmaster 43-45; Head of dept. in Ministry of Educ. 45-50; Head of dept. in Ulan Bator City Cttee., Mongolian People's Revolutionary Party (MPRP) 50-53; Second Sec. Ulan Bator City Cttee.; mem. Presidium, People's Great Hural (Assembly) 63-, Deputy Chair. 63-66, 69-71, 77-81; First Sec. Ulan Bator Cttee., MPRP 60; cand. mem. Political Bureau, MPRP Cen. Cttee. 60-71, mem. Political Bureau 71-81; Chair. Party Control Cttee. of MPRP Cen. Cttee. 63-81; lost Party and State positions 81; Order of Sühbaatar.
c/o Central Committee of the Mongolian People's Revolutionary Party, Ulan Bator, Mongolia.

Lwin, U; Burmese diplomatist; b. 10 Dec. 1912.
Former officer, Burma army; Mil. Adviser, Burma Del. to UN Gen. Assembly 53; Amb. to Fed. Germany 66-71, also to Netherlands 69-71; Perm. Rep. to UN 71-72; Minister for Planning and Finance 72-75, for Information 75-March 77; Deputy Prime Minister 74-77; withdrew from Cen. Cttee. of Burma Socialist Programme Party Feb. 77.
c/o Ministry of Information, Rangoon, Burma.

Lynch, Rt. Hon. Sir Phillip Reginald, P.C., K.C.M.G., B.A., DIP.ED.; Australian politician; b. 27 July 1933, Melbourne; ed. Marist Bros. Coll., Hawthorn, Xavier Coll., Melbourne, Univ. of Melbourne.
Former school teacher; management consultant; fmr. co. dir.; fmr. Pres. Victorian Young Liberal Movement; fmr. mem. State Exec. Liberal Party, mem. Fed. Exec. and Fed. Council 73-; mem. House of Reps. 66-; Minister for the Army 68-69, for Immigration and assisting the Treasurer 69-71, for Labour and Nat. Service 71-72; Deputy Leader of the Opposition, House of Reps. 72-75; Deputy Leader of Fed. Parl. Liberal Party 72-82; Fed. Treas. 75-77; Minister for Finance 76-77, for Industry and Commerce Dec. 77-; del. to numerous confs., incl. Ministerial Council of OECD, Paris 70, 76, 82, IMF/World Bank Group annual meetings, Manila 76, Commonwealth Finance Ministers Meeting, Hong Kong 76, European Management Forum and UNIDO III 80; led del. to European Man. Forum 81, to UN Conf. on New and Renewable sources of Energy, Nairobi 81; Fellow, Inst. of Dirs., Australian Inst. of Management; Liberal.
Parliament House, Canberra, A.C.T.; Home: Mt. Eliza, Victoria 3930, Australia.

M

Ma Hui; Chinese army officer; b. 1910.
Divisional Commdr. 51; Maj.-Gen. People's Liberation Army 60; Deputy Commdr. Hebei Mil. District, PLA 64, Commdr. 65-; Vice-Chair. Hebei Revolutionary Cttee. 68; Sec. CCP Hebei 71-; mem. 11th Cen. Cttee. of CCP 77.
People's Republic of China.

Ma Wenrui; Chinese politician; b. 1909, Shaanxi.
Cadre, N.W. China Bureau, CCP 49-54; Minister of Labour 54-65; alt. mem. 8th Cen. Cttee. 56; criticized and removed from office 67; Vice-Minister of State Planning Comm. 77; mem. 11th Cen. Cttee., CCP 77; First Sec., CCP Shaanxi 79-; Chair. Shaanxi Prov. Peoples' Congress; First Political Commissar Shaanxi Mil. District 79-.
People's Republic of China.

Macapagal, Diosdado; Philippine politician; b. 28 Sept. 1910; ed. Santo Tomás Univ.
Diplomatic Service 46-49, Second Sec., Washington, D.C.

48; mem. House of Reps. 49-57; Vice-Pres. of the Philippines 57-61, Pres. 61-65; Chair. Liberal Party 57-61; Pres. Constitutional Convention 71.
92 Cambridge Circle, North Forbes Park, Makati, Rizal, Philippines.

McClelland, Douglas; Australian politician; ed. Parramatta Commercial Boys' High School, Metropolitan Business Coll.
Joined Australian Imperial Forces 44; Court Reporter 49-61; mem. N.S.W. Labor Party Exec. 57-61; mem. Senate 62-; Minister for the Media 72-75; Man. of Govt. Business in the Senate 74-75; Special Minister of State June-Nov. 75; Shadow Minister for Admin. services and Man. of Opposition Business in the Senate 76-77; Deputy Leader of Opposition in the Senate 77-; Deputy Pres. and Chair. of Cttees. 81-; mem. Senate Select Cttee. on the Encouragement of Australian Production for Television 62-63, Joint Cttee. on Broadcasting of Parl. Proceedings 65-, Joint Select Cttee. on the New and Perm. Parl. House 67-, Senate Select Cttee. on Medical and Hospital Costs 68-, Senate Standing Cttee. on Health and Welfare 70-, Senate Standing Cttee. on Finance and Govt. Relations 77-; Labor Party.
The Senate, Canberra, A.C.T.; Home: 6A Carlton Crescent, Kogarah Bay, N.S.W. 2217, Australia.

MacIntyre, Duncan, D.S.O., O.B.E., E.D.; New Zealand farmer and politician; b. 10 Nov. 1915, Hastings; ed. Larchfield School, Scotland, Christ's Coll., Christchurch.
Farming 33-39, 47-; army service 39-45; Territorial Army 49-60; Territorial mem. of N.Z. Army Board 60-; M.P. for Hastings 60-72, for Bay of Plenty 75-78, for East Cape 78-; Minister of Lands, Minister of Forests, Minister in Charge of the Valuation Dept. 66-72, of Maori and Island Affairs 69-72, of the Environment Feb.-Dec. 72, of Agriculture and Fisheries, in Charge of the Rural Banking and Finance Corpn. Dec. 75-, of Maori Affairs 75-81, Deputy Prime Minister Feb. 81-; National Party.
Parliament Buildings, Wellington, New Zealand.

Mackay, Ian Keith, C.M.G.; New Zealand broadcasting executive; b. 19 Oct. 1909; ed. Nelson Coll., New Zealand.
Broadcasting Station Man., New Zealand 39-43; Senior Exec., Commercial Div., New Zealand Broadcasting Comm. 44-50; Production Man., Macquarie Network, Australia 50-61; Dir.-Gen. Nigerian Broadcasting Corpn. 61-64, Adviser Board of Govs. 64-65; Public Relations Officer, Dept. of Information, Papua New Guinea 66-67, Broadcasts Supervisor (Management) 68-69; seconded to special admin. duties, creation of Nat. Broadcasting Comm. 69-72; Asst. to Chair. Papua New Guinea Broadcasting Comm. 73-75, Consultant 75-; mem. Royal Soc. of Literature, Soc of Authors.
Publs. *Broadcasting in New Zealand* 53, *Broadcasting in Australia* 57, *Macquarie—the Story of a Network* 60, *Broadcasting in Nigeria* 64, *Broadcasting in Papua New Guinea* 76, *Presenting Papua and New Guinea* (compiler), *Directory of Papua and New Guinea* (compiler), and other articles on broadcasting.
405A Main Road, Karori, Wellington, New Zealand.

MacKellar, Michael John Randal, B.SC.AGR., M.A.; Australian politician, b. 27 Oct. 1938; ed. Sydney Church of England Grammar School, Sydney Univ., Balliol Coll., Oxford.
New South Wales Dept. of Agriculture 61-69; mem. for Warringah, N.S.W., House of Reps. 69-; mem. Council of Australian Nat. Univ. 70-75; mem. House of Reps. Select Cttee. on Foreign Affairs 71-72, Joint Parl. Cttee. on Foreign Affairs and Defence 72-74, Joint Standing Cttee. on Public Accounts 72-74; mem. first Australian Parl. del. to People's Repub. of China 73; Parl. Sec. to Leader of Opposition 73-74; Shadow Minister for Immigration 74-75; Minister for Immigration and Ethnic Affairs 75-79 and Minister Assisting the Treas. 78-79; Minister for Health 79-82, Minister Assisting the P.M. 79-80, March 81-, Minister for Home Affairs and Environment Feb.-March 81; leader of del. to UN Habitat Conf. 76; mem. N.S.W. Advisory Cttee. for Australian Broadcasting Comm. 73-75; mem. Council Royal Blind Soc., N.S.W. 70-; Liberal Party.
Parliament House, Canberra, A.C.T. 2600; Home: 1 Lewis Street, Balgowlan Heights, N.S.W. 2093, Australia.

MacLehose, Sir (Crawford) Murray, G.B.E., K.C.M.G., K.C.V.O.; British diplomatist and administrator; b. 16 Oct. 1917, Glasgow; ed. Rugby School and Balliol Coll., Oxford, Served with R.N.V.R. 39-45; entered diplomatic service 47; Acting Consul, Hankow 47, Acting Consul-Gen. 48; Foreign Office 50; First Sec., Prague 51; seconded to Commonwealth Relations Office for service in Wellington 54; returned to Foreign Office and transferred to Paris 56; Counsellor 59; Political Adviser, Hong Kong; Counsellor, Foreign Office 63; Principal Private Sec. to Sec. of State 65-67; Amb. to Repub. of Viet-Nam 67-69, to Denmark 69-71; Gov. of Hong Kong 71-82; cr. Life Peer 82.
Beoch, Maypole, Ayrshire, Scotland.

McLennan, Sir Ian Munro, K.C.M.G., K.B.E., B.E.E.; Australian engineer; b. 30 Nov. 1909; ed. Scotch Coll., Melbourne and Melbourne Univ.
Assistant Gen. Man. Broken Hill Pty. Co. Ltd. 47-50, Gen. Man. 50-56, Dir. 53-, Senior Gen. Man. 56-59, Chief Gen. Man. 59-67, Man. Dir. 67-71, Chair. and Dir. of Admin. 71-77; Chair. Joint War Production Cttee. 56-69, Defence Industrial Cttee. 69-77; Councillor, Australian Inst. of Mining and Metallurgy (Pres. 51, 57, 72); Chair. BHP-GKN Holdings Ltd. 70-78, Tubemakers of Australia Ltd. 73-79, Interscan (Australia) Pty. Ltd. 78-; mem. Int. Council, Morgan Guaranty Trust Co. of N.Y. 73-79; Dir. ICI Australia Ltd. 76-79; Dir. Australia and New Zealand Banking Group 76-; Chair. 77-82; Pres. Australian Acad. of Tech. Sciences 76-; Chair. Elders (IXL) Ltd. 81-; mem. Deputy Chair. Immigration Planning Council 49-67; Pres. Australia/Japan Business Co-operation Cttee. 77-; Australasian Inst. of Mining and Metallurgy Medal 59, Inst. of Production Engineers' James N. Kirby Award 64, Australian Inst. of Engineers Medal 68, Charles F. Rand Memorial Gold Medal, American Inst. of Mining, Metallurgical and Petroleum Engineers 78, Bessemer Gold Medal, Metals Soc., London 81.
Office: 140 William Street, Melbourne, Vic.; Home: Apartment 3, 112 Walsh Street, South Yarra, Vic. 3141, Australia.
Telephone: 609-3880 (Office); 263651 (Home).

McMahon, Rt. Hon. William, P.C., C.H., G.C.M.G., LL.B., B.ECONS.; Australian lawyer and politician (retd.); b. 23 Feb. 1908; ed. Sydney Univ.
Practised as solicitor until 39; served 39-45 war; mem. House of Reps. for Lowe, N.S.W. 49-81; Minister for Navy and Air 51-54, for Social Services 54-56, for Primary Industry 56-58, for Labour and Nat. Service 58-66, Treas. 66-69; Acting Minister for Trade 56 (in charge C.S.I.R.O. 56), for Labour and Nat. Service 57, 66, 68, 69, for Nat. Devt. 59; Acting Attorney-Gen. 60, 61; Acting Minister for Territories 61; Vice-Pres. Executive Council 64-66; Deputy Leader Liberal Party 66-71, Leader 71-72; Minister for Foreign Affairs 69-71; Prime Minister 71-72; Leader Australian Del. Commonwealth Parl. Conf. New Delhi 57; Pres. ILO Regional Conf., Melbourne 62; Gov. Asian Devt. Bank 68-69, Chair. 68-69; Gov. IMF 66-69; led del. to ECAFE, Bangkok 70, to SEATO, Manila 70, 25th UN Gen. Assembly; Commonwealth Prime Ministers Conf., Singapore 71.
Parliament House, Canberra, A.C.T. 2600; and Westfield Tower, 100 William Street, Sydney, N.S.W. 2011, Australia.
Telephone: 731023 (Canberra); 358-1433 (Sydney).

McNeill, Sir James Charles, Kt., C.B.E., F.A.S.A., F.A.I.M.; Australian accountant and business executive; b. 29 July 1916, Hamilton, N.S.W.; ed. Newcastle High School, N.S.W.
Accountant, The Broken Hill Proprietary Co. Ltd. 47-54, Asst. Sec. 54-56, Asst. Gen. Man. (Commercial) 56-59, Gen. Man. (Commercial) 59-67, Exec. Gen. Man. 67-71, Man. Dir 71-77, Chair. and Dir. of Admin. 77-; Chair. North West Shelf Devt. Pty. Ltd., Australian Iron & Steel Pty. Ltd., AWI Holdings Pty. Ltd., BHP Nominees Pty. Ltd., Dampier Mining Co. Ltd., Groote Eylandt Mining Co. Ltd., Hematite Petroleum Pty. Ltd., Tasmanian Electro Metallurgical Co. Ltd., JLA Holding Ltd., Mount Newman Mining Co. Pty. Ltd., Tubemakers of Aust. Ltd.; Deputy Chair. Private Investment Co. for Asia, Woodside Petroleum Ltd.; Dir. Mount Newman Mining Co. Pty. Ltd., Int. Iron and Steel Inst.; mem. Mfg. Industries Advisory Council; Past Pres. and mem. Exec. Cttee. Australian Mining Industry Council; mem. Council, Chair. Finance Cttee., Monash Univ.; mem. Govt.'s Econ. Consultative Group; mem. Morgan Guaranty Trust Co. of New York Int. Council; Walter and Eliza Hall Inst. Finance Advisory Cttee.; Asian Pacific Advisory Council of AT and T Int.; Councillor Inst. of Public Affairs, Int. Councillor The Conf. Bd.
The Broken Hill Proprietary Co. Ltd., BHP House, 140 William Street, Melbourne, Vic. 3000; 104 Mont Albert Road, Canterbury, Vic. 3126, Australia.

Madan, Bal Krishna, PH.D.; Indian banker and economist; b. 13 July 1911; ed. Univ. of Punjab, Lahore.
Lecturer in Econs., Univ. of Punjab 36-37; Officer for Enquiry into Resources, Punjab Govt. 37-38; mem. Punjab Board for Econ. Enquiry 38-40, Sec. 38; Econ. Adviser to Punjab Govt. 40-41; Dir. of Research, Reserve Bank of India, Bombay 41-45, Econ. Adviser 50, Principal Adviser 57, Exec. Dir. 59, Deputy Gov. 64-67; Sec. Indian del. to Bretton Woods 44; Deputy Sec. Indian Tariff Board 45; mem. Indian Legislative Assembly and Assembly Cttee. on Bretton Woods Agreement 46; Alt. Exec. Dir. IMF 46-48, IBRD 47-48, Exec. Dir. IMF 48-50, 67-71; mem. Indian del., First Commonwealth Finance Ministers' Conf. London 49; adviser Indian del. to UN ECOSOC 49; mem. UN Cttee. on Domestic Financing of Econ. Devt. 49; mem. Finance Comm., Indian Govt. 52; mem. Taxation Enquiry Comm. 53-54; mem. Experts Group on UN Special Fund for Econ. Devt. 55; mem. Governing Body Indian Investment Centre 60-67, Board of Dirs., Industrial Finance Corpn. 62-64, Life Insurance Corpn. of India 64-66, Board of Trustees, Unit Trust of India 64-67, Nat. Council of Applied Econ. Research 74-, Risk Capital Foundation, New Delhi 75-78, Nat. Inst. of Public Finance and Policy 76-; Pres. Indian Econ. Asscn. 61; Vice-Chair. Industrial Devt. Bank of India 64-67; Chair. Bonus Review Cttee., Govt. of India 72-74; Chair. Management Devt. Inst. 73-80; Chair. Madras Petrochem Ltd. 77-, Madhya Pradesh Technical Consultancy Org. 80-.
Publs. *India and Imperial Preference—A Study in Commercial Policy* 39, *Aspects of Economic Development and Policy* 64, *Real Wages of Industrial Labour in India* 77, *Report on the Study of Debt-Equity Norms* 77.
B-100, Greater Kailash-I, New Delhi 110 048, India.
Telephone: 649006.

Madia, Chunilal Kalidas; Indian writer; b. 12 Aug. 1922; ed. Bhagwatsinjhi High School, Dhoraji, Gujarat, and H.L. Coll. of Commerce, Ahmedabad.
Writes mainly in Gujarati; Editorial Staff *Prabhat* and *Navsaurashtra* 42-44; Editor *Varta* (short story monthly) 43; Editorial Staff, Janmabhoomi Group of Newspapers, Bombay 45-50; Language Editor, U.S. Information Service, Bombay 50-62; now Editor *Ruchi* (literary and cultural magazine); Literary Editor *Sandesh* (Gujarati daily); Narmad Gold Medal for Best Play Writing 51; Ranajitram Gold Medal for Outstanding Creative Writing 57, numerous other prizes; del. Int. PEN Congress Ivory Coast 67.
Publs. (in Gujarati): novels: *Vyajano Varas, Velavelani Chhanyadi, Liludi Dharati, Kumkum Ane Ashaka;* short stories: *Ghooghavatan Pur, Padmaja, Champo Ane Kel, Tej Ane Timie, Roop-Aroop, Antasrota;* plays; *Rangada, Vishavimochan, Raktatilak, Shoonyashesh;* poems: *Sonnet* (collected sonnets); criticism: *Granthagarima, Shahamrig, Suvarnamrig;* in Malayalam: *Gujarati Kathakal.*
B-213, Chandralok, Manav Mandir Road, Malabar Hill, Bombay 6, India.
Telephone: 36-8245.

Madigan, Sir Russel Tullie, Kt., O.B.E., LL.B.; Australian business executive; b 22 Nov. 1920; ed. Univ. of Adelaide.
Joined Zinc Corpn. 46; travelling scholarship in Canada and U.S.A. 47-49, Underground Man. Zinc Corpn. Ltd., NBHC Ltd. 56-59; Gen. Man., Gen. Mining Div., Conzinc Riotinto Australia Ltd. 60-64; Dir. 68-, Dep. Chair. 78-; Man. Dir. Hamersley Iron 65-71, Chair. 71-; Chair. Blair Athol Coal Pty. Ltd. 71-80, IOL Petroleum Ltd. 72-, Hamersley Holdings, Atlas Steels (Australia) Pty. Ltd. 76-; Dir. Rio Tinto-Zinc. Corpn. Ltd. 71-, Rio Tinto-Zinc (Japan) Ltd., Commercial Union Assurance Co. 69-; Chair. Australia-Japan Foundation, Chair. Australian Nat. Cttee.; mem. Pacific Basin Econ. Council; Fellow, S. Australian School of Mines.
Hamersley Holdings, 55 Collins Street, Melbourne, Victoria; Home: 60 Broadway, East Camberwell, Victoria, Australia.

Maegraith, Brian Gilmore, C.M.G., T.D., M.B., B.S., D.PHIL., F.R.C.P.(L. & E.), F.R.A.C.P.; Australian professor of tropical medicine; b. 26 Aug. 1907; ed. St. Peter's and St. Mark's Colls., Univ. of Adelaide, Magdalen and Exeter Coll., Univ. of Oxford.
Medical Fellow and Tutor in Physiology, Exeter Coll., Oxford 34-40; Univ. Lecturer and Demonstrator in Pathology, Oxford 37-44, Dean of Medical School 38-44; Lieut.-Col. R.A.M.C., O.C. Malaria Research Unit, War Office 39-45; mem. Medical Research Council Malaria Cttee. 43-46; Tropical Medicine Research Board (Medical Research Council) 59-69, Council Royal Society of Tropical Medicine 47-51 (Vice-Pres. 49-51, 57-59, Pres. 69-71); Dean, Liverpool School of Tropical Medicine 44-75, Prof. Tropical Medicine 44-72, Emer. 72-; Hon. Consulting Physician in Tropical Medicine, Royal Liverpool Hospital; Nuffield Consultant in Tropical Medicine, West Africa 49; Consultant, Faculty of Tropical Medicine, Bangkok 59-, and S.E. Asian Int. Centre for Tropical Medicine (SEAMES) 65-72; Chair. Council of European Insts. of Tropical Medicine 69-72, Pres. and Life mem. 75-; Hon. Fellow St, Mark's Coll. Adelaide; Hon. mem. Belgian, American. German and Canadian Socs. of Tropical Medicine; Chalmers Gold Medal, Royal Soc. of Tropical Medicine 51, Le Prince Medal, American Soc. of Tropical Medicine 55, Bernhard Nocht Medal (Hamburg) 57, Mary Kingsley Medal (Liverpool School of Tropical Medicine) 73, Jubilee Medal, Swedish Acad. 80; Memorial Plaque, Mahidol Univ., Bangkok 80; Hon. D.Sc. (Bangkok), Emer M.D. (Athens) 72; Knight Order of St. Lazarus of Jerusalem 77.
Publs. *Pathological Processes in Malaria* 48, *Methods in Tropical Medicine* 62, *Exotic Diseases in Practice* 65, *Tropical Medicine for Nurses* (fifth edn.) 80, *Clinical Tropical Diseases* (seventh edn.) 80.
School of Tropical Medicine, Pembroke Place, Liverpool L3 5QA; 23 Eaton Road, Cressington Park, Liverpool 19, England.
Telephone: 051-427-1133.

Maekawa, Kunio, B.ENG.; Japanese architect; b. 14 May 1905; ed. Tokyo Imperial Univ.

Worked in Le Corbusier's office, Paris 28-30, Antonin Raymond's office, Tokyo 30-35; Pres., Kunio Maekawa Architect's Office 35-; Pres. Japan Architects Asscn. 59-62; mem. Japanese Del., Exec. Cttee. of Int. Union of Architects 59-69; numerous prizes and decorations.
Buildings include: Taiyo Bank (Nihon Sogo Bank) 52, Kanagawa Prefectural Library and Concert Hall 54, Japanese Pavilion, Brussels World Fair 58, Kyoto Cultural Centre 59, Gakushuin Univ. 60, Tokyo Metropolitan Festival Hall 61, Saitama Cultural Centre 66, Saitama Prefectural Museum 71, Museum für Ostasiatische Kunst, Cologne 77.
Office: 8 Honshio-cho, Shinjuku-ku, Tokyo; Home: Kami-Osaki 3-10-59, Shinagawa-ku, Tokyo, Japan.
Telephone: Tokyo 351-7101 (Office).

Mafatlal, Arvind N.; Indian industrialist; b. 27 Oct. 1923, Ahmedabad; ed. St. Xavier's High School and Sydenham Coll. of Commerce and Econs., Bombay.
Chairman Nat. Organic Chem. Industries Ltd., Polyolefins Industries Ltd., Mafatlal Engineering Industries Ltd.; Dir. Tata Engineering and Locomotive Co. Ltd., and others; Trustee Bharatiya Agro-Industries Foundation, Uruli Kanchan; Chair. and Man. Trustee, Shri Sadguru Seva Singh Trust; employers' del. to 43rd ILO Conf.; mem. Maharashtra and Gujarat State Advisory Councils of Industries; Durga Prasad Khaitan Memorial Gold Medal 66, Business Leadership Award (Madras Man. Asscn.) 71, Sir Jehangir Ghandy Medal for Industrial Peace (Xavier Labour Relations Inst.) 79.
Mafatlal House, Backbay Reclamation, Bombay 400020; and 10 Altamount Road, Bombay 400026, India.

Mahathir Mohamed, Datuk Seri Dr.; Malaysian politician; b. 20 Dec. 1925, Alor Star; ed. Sultan Abdul Hamid Coll. and Univ. of Malaya in Singapore.
Medical Officer, Kedah and Perlis 53-57; private practice 57-64; mem. UMNO to 69, 72-, mem. Supreme Council 72-, Pres. 81-; mem. House of Reps. for Kota Star Selatan 64-69, for Kubang Pasu 74-; mem. Senate 73; Chair. Food Industries of Malaysia Sdn. Bhd. 73; Minister of Educ. 74-77, of Trade and Industry 77-81; Deputy Prime Minister 76-81; Prime Minister and Minister of Defence July 81-.
Publ. *The Malay Dilemma* 69.
Office of the Prime Minister, Kuala Lumpur, Malaysia.

Mahindra, Keshub, B.SC.; Indian business executive; b. 9 Oct. 1923, Simla; ed. Univ. of Pennsylvania, U.S.A.
President, Asscn. of Indian Automobile Mfrs. 64-65, Bombay Chamber of Commerce and Industry 66-67, Assoc. Chamber of Commerce and Industry 69-70, Maharashtra Econ. Devt. Council 69-70; Chair. Indian Council of Trade Fairs and Exhibns. 64-69, Indian Soc. of Advertisers 68-71, Housing and Urban Devt. Corpn. Ltd. 71-75, Vickers Sperry India Ltd. 65-75; Chair. Mahindra and Mahindra Ltd., Union Carbide India Ltd., Indian Aluminium Co. Ltd., Remington Rand of India Ltd., Mahindra Spicer Ltd., Kema Services (Ind.) Private Ltd., Otis Elevator Co. (India) Ltd., Machinery Mfrs. Corpn. Ltd.; Dir. Bombay Dyeing and Mfg. Co. Ltd., WIMCO Ltd., Bombay Burmah Trading Corpn. Ltd., North Borneo Timbers Berhard (Malaysia), Indian Hotels Co. Ltd., Tata Iron and Steel Co. Ltd., Metal Box India Ltd., Mahindra Ugine Steel Co. Ltd., Tata Chemicals Ltd., Indian Dyestuff Ind. Ltd., Industrial Credit and Investment Corpn. of India Ltd., Ballarpur Industries Ltd., Atul Products Ltd.; Vice-Chair. Housing Devt. Finance Corpn. Ltd.; Chair. Board of Govs., Indian Inst. of Management, Ahmedabad: dir. several cos. Mahindra and Mahindra Ltd., Gateway Building, Apollo Bunder, Bombay 400039; Home: St. Helen's Court, Pedder Road, Bombay 400026, India.

Mahmud Husain, Syed Abul Basher; Bangladesh judge, b. 1 Feb. 1916; ed. Shaistagonj High School, M.C. Coll.; Sylhet, Dacca Univ.
Pleader, Judge's Court, Dacca 40-42; Additional Govt. Pleader, Habiganj 43-48; Advocate, Dacca High Court Bar 48-51; Attorney, Fed. Court of Pakistan 51-53, Advocate 53-58; Senior Advocate of Supreme Court of Pakistan 58-65; Asst. Govt. Pleader, High Court of East Pakistan 52-56, Senior Govt. Pleader and later acting Advocate-Gen. of East Pakistan 56-65; Judge, High Court of East Pakistan 65-72, of Bangladesh 72, of Appellate Div. of High Court 72, of Appellate Div. of Supreme Court 72-75; Chief Justice Nov. 75-Aug. 76, Chief Justice of Supreme Court 76-78; retd. from service Feb. 78; Councillor, Assam Provincial Muslim League 44-47, All-India Muslim League 45-47, All-Pakistan Muslim League 47-55; mem. Constituent Assembly of Pakistan 49-54, Commonwealth Parl. Asscn. 50-54, Interparl. Union 50-54, Pakistan Tea Board 52-54, Exec. Council of Dacca Univ. 52-54, Bar Council of Dacca High Court 58-66; 34th descendant of Prophet Mohammed.
56/1 Shah Saheb Lane, Narinda, Dacca, Bangladesh.
Telephone: 281986.

Mahtab, Harekrushna, D.LITT., LL.D.; Indian politician and journalist; b. Nov. 1899; ed. Ravenshaw Coll., Cuttack.
Joined non-co-operation movement 21; worker for Indian Nat. Congress 21-; mem. Bihar & Orissa Legislative Council 24; civil disobedience movements 30, 32; Pres. Utkal Provincial Congress Cttee. 30, 37; organized Inchudi Salt Satyagraha, imprisoned 30-31, 32, 42; mem. Congress Working Cttee. 38-46; Leader, Congress Assembly Party, Orissa; Chief Minister, Orissa State 46-50, 56-61; Minister for Commerce and Industry, Govt. of India 50-52; Sec.-Gen. Congress Parl. Party 52-55, Deputy Leader 62-63; Gov. of Bombay 55-56; mem. Lok Sabha 62-67, Orissa Legislative Assembly 67-77; detained during emergency 75-76; Editor, *Prajatantra* (also feature writer) and *Jhankar*.
Publs. *History of Orissa*; four novels, one play and essays: *Gandhi the Political Leader, Road Ahead, Beginning of the End*.
Ekrama Nivas, Bhuvaneshwar 2, Orissa, India.
Telephone: 51946.

Maki, Fumihiko, B.ARCH., M.ARCH.; Japanese architect; b. 6 Sept. 1928; ed. Univ. of Tokyo, Cranbrook School of Art, Mich. and Harvard Univ.
Associate Prof. Washington Univ. 56-62, Harvard Univ. 62-66; Lecturer, Dept. of Urban Engineering, Univ. of Tokyo 64-, Prof. of Architecture 79-; Principal Partner, Maki and Associates (architectural firm) 64-; Visiting Lecturer and Critic to various univs. and insts. in Canada and U.S. 60-; awards include Gold Medal of Japan Inst. of Architects 64; Hon. Fellow, American Inst. of Architects; major works include Steinberg Hall, Washington Univ. 60, Toyoda Memorial Hall, Nagoya Univ. 60, Lecture Hall, Chiba Univ. 64, and Rissho Univ. Campus 66-, Nat. Aquarium, Okinawa 75, Tsukuba Univ. Complex 76, Hillside Terrace Housing Complex 78, The Royal Danish Embassy, Tokyo 79.
Publs. *Investigations in Collective Form* 64, *Movement Systems in the City* 65, *Metabolism* 60, *Structure in Art and Science* (contrib.) 65.
16-22, 5-chome Higashi-Gotanda, Shinagawa-ku, Tokyo, Japan.

Makino, Koji; Japanese banker; b. 7 March 1914, Hyogo Prefecture; ed. Tokyo Univ.
Director of Sumitomo Trust & Banking Co. Ltd. 60, Man. Dir. 63, Senior Man. Dir. 69, Deputy Pres. 72, Pres. 76-81, Chair. 78-; Dir. Trust Co. Asscn. of Japan, Osaka Bankers Asscn.; Standing Dir. Kansai Econ. Fed.; Dir. Kansai

Cttee. for Econ. Devt.; Medal of Honour with Blue Ribbon.
Sumitomo Trust & Banking Co. Ltd., 15 Kitahama 5-chome, Higashi-ku, Osaka; Home: 25-407 Kasumi-cho, 3-chome, Nishinomiya City, Hyogo Prefecture, Japan.

Makita, Hisao, B.A.; Japanese business executive; b. 13 Dec. 1909, Saga Pref.; ed. Tokyo Univ. of Commerce.
Joined Nippon Kokan K.K. 34, Dir. 57, Man. Dir. 65, Senior Man. Dir. 67, Exec. Vice-Pres. 69, Pres. 71-80, Chair. of Bd. June 80-; Pres. Kokan Mining Co. (subsidiary of Nippon Kokan) Nov. 61-June 66; Chair. Japan-Canada Businessmen's Conf., Japanese Cttee.; Medal of Honour with Blue Ribbon.
Nippon Kokan K.K., 1-1-2, Marunouchi, Chiyoda-ku, Tokyo 100; Home: 2-4-1, Ohmiya, Suginami-ku, Tokyo 168, Japan.
Telephone: 03-212-7111 (Office); 03-311-0298 (Home).

Malietoa Tanumafili II, H.H., C.B.E., Western Samoan politician; b. 4 Jan. 1913; ed. Wesley Coll., Auckland, New Zealand.
Adviser, Samoan Govt. 40; mem. New Zealand del. to UN 58; fmr. mem. Council of State; Joint Head of State of Western Samoa 62-63, Sole Head of State (O le Ao o le Malo) April 63-; Fautua of Maliena.
Government House, Vailima, Apia, Western Samoa.

Malik, Adam; Indonesian politician and diplomatist; b. 22 July 1917, Pematang Siantar, N. Sumatra; ed. Dutch primary school and a religious school.
Chairman, Partai Indonesia in Pematang Siantar and Medan, N. Sumatra 34-38; founded *Antara* Press Bureau (later *Antara* News Agency), Java 37; mem. Exec. Board Gerindo Party 40-41; later mem. Persatuan Perdjoeangan (Struggle Front) (a movt. to obtain independence); a founder of Partai Rakjat (People's Party) 46; Founder and Exec. mem. Murba Party 48-56; elected to House of Reps. 56, mem. Provisional Supreme Advisory Council 59; Amb. to U.S.S.R. and Poland 59-62; mem. Exec. Board *Antara* 62; Minister of Commerce 63-65; Minister-Co-ordinator for the Implementation of Guided Economy 65; Vice-Prime Minister for Social and Political Affairs 66; Presidium Minister for Political Affairs 66; Minister of Foreign Affairs 66-77; mem. House of Reps. May 77-, Speaker 77-78; Chair. People's Consultative Assembly 77-78; Vice-Pres. of Indonesia March 78-; Pres. UN Gen. Assembly 71-72; rep. of Indonesia at various int. confs. and has led Indonesian del. to sessions of UN Gen. Assembly since 66; Dag Hammarskjöld Award for Diplomacy.
Office of the Vice-President, Medan Merdeka Selatan 6, Jakarta (Office); Jalan Diponegoro 29, Jakarta Pusat, Indonesia (Residence).
Telephone: 363443 (Office); 373390 (Residence).

Malik, Gunwantsingh Jaswantsingh, B.SC., M.A.; Indian diplomatist; b. 29 May 1921, Karachi, Pakistan; ed. Bombay and Cambridge Univs.
Physicist, British Industrial Plastics 41-42; Tech. Officer R.A.F. 43-46; Indian Foreign Service 47-79; Second Sec. Indian Embassy Belgium 48-50; in Ethiopia 50; Under-Sec. Ministry of External Affairs 50-52; First Sec. and Chargé d'affaires Argentina 52-56; in Japan 56-59; Commercial Counsellor and Asst. Commr. Singapore 59-63; Dir. Ministry of Commerce 63-64; Joint Sec. Ministry of External Affairs 64-65; Amb. to the Philippines 65-68, to Senegal, concurrently to the Ivory Coast and Upper Volta 68-70, to Chile, concurrently to Ecuador, Colombia and Peru 70-74, to Thailand 74-77, to Spain 77-79; Perm. Rep. to ESCAP 74-77; leader trade del. to S. America 64; mem. del. to ECAFE 65, to Group of 77 in Lima 71, to Gov. Body of UNDP 71, to UNCTAD III 72, to ESCAP 75, 76; Chair. Tech. and Drafting Cttee. (ESCAP) 76, Deputy Chair. Cttee. of the Whole 77.
21A Nizamuddin West, New Delhi, India.
Telephone: 619785 (New Delhi).

Mamaloni, Solomon; Solomon Islands politician; b. 1943, Arosi, San Cristobal; ed. King George VI School, Te-Aute Coll., New Zealand.
Executive Officer, Civil Service, then clerk to Legis. Council; M.P. for Makira 70-76, for West Makira 76-77; Chief Minister (British) Solomon Islands 74-76; Prime Minister of Solomon Islands Aug. 81-; f. and Leader, People's Progress Party (merged with Rural Alliance Party to form People's Alliance Party 79); Man. Dir. Patosha Co. 77.
Office of the Prime Minister, Honiara, Guadalcanal, Solomon Islands.
Telephone: 202.

Manickavasagar, Balasegaram, M.B., F.R.C.S., F.R.C.S.E., F.R.A.C.S., F.A.C.S.; Malaysian surgeon; b. 15 April 1929, Selangor; ed. King Edward VII Medical Coll., Singapore and Univ. of Malaya.
Medical Officer and later Registrar, Surgical Unit, Gen. Hosp., Kuala Lumpur 57-59, Consultant Surgeon Surgical Unit II 69-, Prof. and Head of Second Surgical Div. 72-; Consultant Surgeon, Kota Bharu, Kelantan 60-61; Consultant Surgeon and Head Dept. of Surgery, Gen. Hosp., Seremban 61-69; Kehormat Prof. of Surgery Nat. Univ. of Malaysia Sept. 79-; Senior Consultant Surgeon, Head Dept. of Surgery, Gen. Hosp., Kuala Lumpur; Senior Surgeon, Ministry of Health, Malaysia; mem. Pan Pacific Surgical Asscn., Int. Fed. of Surgical Colls., Malaysian Medical Asscn. and many other orgs.; mem. Malaysian Acad. of Medicine, Singapore Acad. of Medicine; Hon. Fellow, Polish Asscn. of Surgeons, Philippine Coll. of Surgeons; Fellow, Asscn. of Surgeons of Great Britain and Ireland, American Soc. for the Advancement of Surgery of Trauma; mem. editorial cttee. *British Journal of Surgery, Journal of Medical Progress, Journal of Modern Medicine, Journal of Int. Surgery,* Editorial Board *Asian Journal of Medicine,* Editorial Advisory Cttee. *Clinical Oncology,* Editor-in-Chief *Malaysian Journal of Surgery* 72-78; Visiting Prof. Marburg Univ., Fed. Repub. of Germany 72, Madras Univ., India 75-76, Univ. of Columbus, Ohio, Tumour Cen., Houston, Texas 80; Hunterian Prof. Royal Coll. of Surgeons (U.K.) 69; Hon. Prof. of Surgery, Nat. Univ. of Malaysia and many other univs. and colls.; Chiene Memorial Lecturer, Royal Coll. of Surgeons, Edinburgh 71, Abraham Colles Lecturer, Royal Coll. of Surgeons, Ireland 74; Hon. Fellow of numerous socs. and colls.; founder mem. Int Soc. of Disease of the Oesophagus, Asian Pacific Asscn. for the Study of the Liver; Examiner, Royal Coll. of Surgeons, Edinburgh 72-, Royal Australian Coll. of Surgeons 76-; Jacksonian Prize and Medal, Royal Coll. of Surgeons (U.K.) 70, and many other awards.
Publs. several books and more than 130 articles on the liver, pancreas, oesophagus, stomach, gall bladder, and oral, bone and joint surgery.
Department of Surgery, General Hospital, Kuala Lumpur; Home: 5 Jalan Liew Weng Chee, Off Jalan Yap Kwan Seng, Kuala Lumpur, Malaysia.
Telephone: 927617 (Office); 420632 (Home).

Mansfield, Michael Joseph, A.M.; American politician and diplomatist; b. 16 March 1903, New York; ed. Univ. of Montana.
Former mining engineer; Prof. of History and Political Science, Univ. of Montana 33-42; mem. House of Reps. 43-52; Senator from Montana 52-76; Majority Whip 57-61; Leader of Senate 61-76; Amb. to Japan 77-; Democrat.
United States Embassy, Chancery, 10-5 Akasaka 1-chome, Minato-ku, Tokyo, Japan.

Mao Zhiyong: Chinese party official.
Secretary CCP, Hunan, Chair. Hunan Revolutionary Cttee., and First Political Commissar, Hunan Mil. District,

PLA 77-80; mem. 11th Cen. Cttee. CCP 77; First Sec., Hunan Provincial Cttee. 77-.
People's Republic of China.

Mara, Rt. Hon. Ratu Sir Kamisese Kapaiwai Tuimacilai, P.C., K.B.E., M.A.; Fiji politician; b. 13 May 1920; ed. Sacred Heart Coll. and Central Medical School, Suva, Fiji, Otago Univ., Oxford Univ., and London School of Economics.
Joined British Colonial Service 50, Admin. Officer, District Officer and Commissioner, Fiji 51-61; mem. Legis. Council, Fiji 53-, Exec. Council, Fiji 59-61; founded Alliance Party 60; Minister for Natural Resources 64-66; Leader, Fiji Del. Constitutional Conf., London 65; Chief Minister 67-70; Prime Minister 70-April 77; resigned; re-appointed April 77-; Chancellor, Univ. of S. Pacific 77-80; Hon. Fellow, Wadham Coll. 71; Hon. Dr. of Laws (Guam), Hon. LL.D. (Otago, New Delhi, Univ. of S. Pacific, Univ. of Papua New Guinea), Hon. Dr. Pol. Sci. (Yousei Univ., Republic of Korea, Tokai Univ.); Grand Cross, Order of the Nat. Lion, Senegal 75; Order of Diplomatic Service Merit, Repub. of Korea 78.
The Office of the Prime Minister, Suva, Fiji.
The Office of the Prime Minister, Suva; (Home): 11 Battery Road, Suva, Fiji.

Maramis, J. B. P., D.R.S.; Indonesian United Nations official; b. 23 Jan. 1922, Limbung, Celebes Island, Indonesia; ed. Univ. of Leyden.
Served in Directorate of Econ. Affairs, Ministry of Foreign Affairs 51-54; First Sec., Teheran 54-58; Deputy Head, Directorate of UN Affairs, Ministry of Foreign Affairs 58-60; Counsellor, Indonesian Mission to UN 60-65; Head, Directorate of Int. Orgs., Ministry of Foreign Affairs 65-68; del. to UN Gen. Assembly 66-68; Deputy Perm. Rep. to UN Oct. 69-71, Acting Perm. Rep. 71-72; Vice-Pres. UN Econ. and Social Council (ECOSOC) 69, Pres. 70; Amb. to Belgium and Luxembourg, Head Indonesian Mission to EEC 72-73; Exec. Sec. UN Econ. Comm. for Asia and the Far East (ECAFE) now Econ. and Social Comm. for Asia and the Pacific (ESCAP) 73-81.
c/o Economic and Social Commission for Asia and the Pacific, UN Building, Rajdamnern Avenue, Bangkok 2, Thailand.

Marcos, Ferdinand Edralin; Philippine lawyer and politician; b. 11 Sept. 1917; ed. Univ. of the Philippines.
Lieutenant, later Major, in Philippines Army; took part in anti-Japanese resistance; Special Asst. to Pres. Manuel Roxas 46-47; mem. House of Reps. 49-59, Senate 59-66; Pres. of Senate 63-65; Pres. of Philippines 65- (re-elected 69, 81, term of office extended until 87), Prime Minister 73-81; mem. Liberal Party until 64, Nat. Party 64-78, Leader *Kilusan Bagong Lipunan* (New Society Movement) 81-; Dag Hammarskjöld Award 68; numerous war decorations.
Malacañan Palace, Manila, Philippines.

Marcos, Imelda Romualdez; Philippine politician and social leader; b. *c.* 1930; *m.* Ferdinand E. Marcos (*q.v.*).
Governor of Metro Manila Nov. 75-; Roving Amb.; visited Beijing 76; took part in negotiations in Libya over self-govt. for southern provinces 77; Leader *Kilusan Bagong Lipunan* (New Society Movement) formed from Nat. Party and Marcos Admin. supporters 78-81; mem. *Batasang Pambansa* (Interim Legislative Assembly) April 78-; Minister of Human Settlements June 78-, of Human Settlements and Ecology 79-; mem. Cabinet Exec. Cttee. Aug. 82-; Chair. Southern Philippines Devt. Authority June 80-.
Malacañan Palace, Manila, Philippines.

Marshall, David Saul, LL.B.; Singapore lawyer and fmr. politician; b. 1908, Singapore; ed. Raffles Institution, Middle Temple and Univ. of London.
Worked in Singapore as sharebroker, salesman and sec. to a shipping co. 24-32; then studied law in England; legal career in Singapore 37-78; joined Singapore Volunteer Corps 38; imprisoned by Japanese 42-45; founder Sec. War Prisoners' Asscn.; founder and Chair. Labour Front; founder and Pres. Workers' Party -62; Chief Minister of Singapore 55-56; mem. Singapore Legislative Assembly 61-63; Chair. Singapore Inst. of S.E. Asian Studies 70-74; Amb. to France 78-, also accred. to Spain and Portugal 81-; Del. to UN 23rd Gen. Assembly 68; Chevalier, Légion d'honneur 78; awarded Datuk Kurnia Johan Pahlawan by Sultan of Pahang, Malaysia.
Singapore Embassy, 12 sq. de l'avenue Foch, 75116 Paris, France.

Marshall, Rt. Hon. Sir John Ross, P.C., G.B.E., C.H., B.A., LL.M.; New Zealand lawyer and politician; b. 5 March 1912, Wellington; ed. Victoria Univ. Coll., Univ. of N.Z.
Admitted barrister and solicitor of Supreme Court of N.Z. 36; army service 41-46; M.P. 46-75; lecturer in law, Victoria Univ. Coll. 48-51; Minister Assisting the Prime Minister and Minister for State Advances Corpn., Public Trust Office and Census and Statistics 49-54; also Minister of Health 51-54, of Information and Publicity 51-57; Minister of Justice and Attorney-Gen. 54-57; Deputy Prime Minister 57, 60-72; Deputy Leader of Opposition 57-60, Leader 72-74; Minister of Industry and Commerce 60-69, and of Overseas Trade 60-72; Minister of Customs 60-61; Attorney-Gen. 69-71; Minister of Labour and Immigration 69-72; Prime Minister Feb.-Dec. 72; N.Z. rep. at Colombo Plan Conf., New Delhi 53; rep. N.Z. at GATT Ministerial Conf. 61, 63, 66, ECAFE Conf. 62, 64, 66, 68 and 70, Chair. ECAFE 65; N.Z. rep. at Commonwealth Prime Ministers' Conf. 62, Commonwealth Trade Ministers' Conf. 63, 66, Commonwealth Parl. Conf. 65; Privy Councillor 66; Chair. Nat. Devt. Council 69-72, N.Z. Comm. for *Expo 70*; Visiting Fellow, Victoria Univ. of Wellington; mem. Advisory Council, World Peace Through Law; Chair. Nat. Bank of N.Z. Ltd., Phillips Electrical Industries (N.Z.) Ltd., DRG (N.Z.) Ltd.; Hon. Bencher Gray's Inn 72; Consultant Partner Buddle, Anderson, Kent & Co., Wellington 75; Patron, World Vision in New Zealand; Chair. Cttee. on Registration of Teachers 76-77; Vice-Pres. United Bible Socs., Asia and the Pacific; Pres. Bible Soc. of N.Z. 78-80; Chair. Bible Soc. Devt. Inc.; mem. Nat. Party, Leader 72-74; Hon. LL.D.
Publs. *Law Relating to Watercourses*; *The Adventures of Dr. Duffer, Dr. Duffer and the Lost City, Dr. Duffer and the Treasure Hunt, Dr. Duffer's Outback Adventures* (children's books).
22 Fitzroy Street, Wellington 1, New Zealand.
Telephone: 736631.

Martodihardjo, Lt.-Gen. Sarbini; Indonesian army officer and politician; b. 10 June 1914; ed. elementary and secondary schools and various military schools and courses.
Former public health service employee; subsequently served as commissioned officer in Indonesian army; Minister of Veterans and Demobilization 64-66, 66-68, of Defence Feb.-Mar. 66, of Transmigration and Co-operatives 68-71; mem. Supreme Advisory Council of Indonesia 71-, now Vice-Chair.; Chair. Nat. H.Q. of Indonesian Scout Movement, Cen. Council H.Q. of Veterans Legion of Indonesia; Chair. Univ. of Islamic Devt.
Office: 17 Merdeka Utara, Jakarta; Home: Jalan Imam Bonjol 48, Jakarta, Indonesia.

Masamune, Isao, B.ECON.; Japanese banker; b. 30 March 1912, Tokyo; ed. Tokyo Univ.
Joined Industrial Bank of Japan Ltd. 33, Dir. 57, Man. Dir. 59, Deputy Pres. 64, Pres. 68, Chair. 75-.
Office: 3-3 Marunouchi 1-chome, Chiyoda-ku, Tokyo; Home: 2-21-5 Uehara, Shibuya-ku, Tokyo, Japan.
Telephone: 214-1111 (Office); 467-1843 (Home).

Masani, Minoo; Indian writer, management consultant and fmr. politician and diplomatist; b. 20 Nov. 1905; ed. Elphinstone Coll., Bombay, and London School of Economics.
Barrister of Lincoln's Inn; one of the founders of Congress Socialist Party and Sec. till 39; Mayor of Bombay 43-44; mem. Constituent Assembly and Provisional Parl. of India 47-52; Amb. to Brazil 48-49; mem. UN Sub-Comm. on Discrimination and Minorities 47-52; mem. Lok Sabha 49-52, 57-62, 63-71, Chair. Public Accounts Cttee. 67-69; Pres. Swatantra Party 70-71; Chair. Minorities Comm. Feb.-May 78.
Publs. *Our India, Socialism Reconsidered, Your Food, Picture of a Plan, Plea for the Mixed Economy, Our Growing Human Family, Communist Party of India—a Short History, Congress Misrule and the Swatantra Alternative, J.P.—Mission Partly Accomplished, Bliss Was It in That Dawn, Against the Tide.*
Breach Candy House, Bhulabhai Desai Road, Bombay 400 026, India.
Telephone: 243268 (Office); 824107 (Home).

Mason, Sir John Charles Moir, K.C.M.G.; British diplomatist; b. 13 May 1927; ed. Manchester Grammar School and Peterhouse, Cambridge.
Lieutenant 20th Lancs. Fusiliers 46-48; Capt. Royal Ulster Rifles, Korea 50-51; entered Foreign Service 52; Third Sec. Foreign Office (FO) 52-54; Second Sec. and Private Sec. to Amb., Rome 54-56; Second Sec., Warsaw 56-59; First Sec. FO 59-61; First Sec. (Commercial), Damascus 61-65; First Sec. and Asst. Head of Dept., FO 65-68; Dir. Trade Devt. and Deputy Consul-Gen., New York 68-71; Head European Integration Dept., Foreign and Commonwealth Office 71-72; seconded as Under-Sec. Export Credits Guarantee Dept. 72-75; Amb. to Israel 76-80; High Commissioner in Australia 80-.
British High Commission, Commonwealth Avenue, A.C.T. 2600, Canberra, Australia.

Matane, Paulias Nguna; Papua New Guinea diplomatist; b. 5 July 1932.
Senior positions in Dept. of Educ. 57-69; mem. Public Service Board 69; Head, Dept. of Lands, Surveys and Mines 69, of Business Devt. 70-75; Amb. to U.S.A. and Mexico Sept. 75-, Perm. Rep. to UN 75-81, concurrently High Commr. in Canada 77-.
Publs. *My Childhood in New Guinea, A New Guinean Travels through Africa, Two New Guineans Travel through South East Asia, What Good is Business* and four children's books.
c/o Ministry of Foreign Affairs, Port Moresby, Papua New Guinea.

Matheson, Sir (James Adam) Louis, K.B.E., C.M.G., PH.D., F.I.STRUCT.E., F.T.S., F.ENG.; Australian professor of engineering; b. 11 Feb. 1912; ed. Bootham School, York and Manchester Univ.
Lecturer, Birmingham Univ. 38-46; Prof. Civil Eng., Univ. of Melbourne 46-50; Beyer Prof. of Eng., Manchester Univ. 51-59; Vice-Chancellor, Monash Univ., Melbourne 59-76; Chancellor Papua New Guinea Univ. of Technology 73-75; mem. Mission on Technical Educ. to the W. Indies 57, Ramsey Cttee. on Devt. of Tertiary Educ. in Victoria 61-63, Commonwealth Scientific and Industrial Research Org. Advisory Council 62-67, Royal Comm. into Failure of Kings Bridge 62-63; Trustee Science Museum of Victoria 64-, Chair. 69-73; mem. Council, Inst. of Engineers, Australia 65-81, Pres. 75-76, Hon. Fellow 81; mem. Council, Inst. of Civil Engineers 66-68, Hon Fellow 77; Vice-Pres. Inst. of Structural Engineers 67-68; mem. Interim Council Univ. of Papua and New Guinea 65-68; Chair. Papua New Guinea Inst. of Higher Technical Educ. 66-72, Australian Vice-Chancellors Cttee. 67-68, Asscn. of Commonwealth Univs. 67-69; Chair. Australian Science and Tech. Council 75-76, mem. 77-79; mem. Cttee. on Post-Secondary Educ. in Victoria 77-78; Chair. Commonwealth Schools Comm. Bldg. Cttee. 77-81, Victorian Planning and Finance Cttee. 79-; Dir. Nauru Phosphate Co. 77-79; Hon. D.Sc. (Hong Kong), Hon. LL.D. (Manchester, Melbourne and Monash Univs.); Kernot Medal 70, Peter Nicol Russell Medal 76.
Publs. *Hyperstatic Structures* 59, *Still Learning* 80, and papers on technical and educational subjects.
26/166 West Toorak Road, South Yarra, Vic. 3141, Australia.

Matsukata, Masanobu; Japanese business executive; b. 13 Aug. 1907; ed. Keio Univ.
With Tokyo Gas, Electric and Engineering Co. Ltd. 32; Head of Gen. Affairs Dept., Tokyo Automobile Industry Co. Ltd., Hino Plant 40; Head of Sales Dept., Hino Heavy Industry Co. Ltd. 42, Head of Supply Div. 43, Dir. and Gen. Man. 45; Man. Dir. Hino Industry Co. Ltd. 46; Senior Man. Dir. Hino Diesel Industry Co. Inc. 50, Vice-Pres. 54; Pres. Hino Motors Ltd. 61-74, Chair. 74-; now also Chair. Hino Motor Sales Ltd., Sitsui Seiki Kogyo Co. Ltd., Teikoku Auto Industry Co. Ltd.; Dir. Sawafuji Electrical Co. Ltd., Auto Industry Employers' Asscn., Japan Automobile Mfrs. Asscn. Inc., Japan Ordinance Asscn., Japan Automobile Chamber of Commerce; Financial Dir. Japan Fed. of Employers' Asscns.; Blue Ribbon Medal.
Hino Motors Ltd., Hinodai 3-1-1, Hino City, Tokyo, Japan.
Telephone: 03-272-4811 (Office).

Matsumoto, Shigeharu, B.A.; Japanese writer and business executive; b. 2 Oct. 1899, Osaka; ed. Faculty of Law, Univ. of Tokyo, Yale Univ., Univs. of Wisconsin, Geneva and Vienna.
Assistant, Faculty of Law, Univ. of Tokyo 28-30; Lecturer Chuo Univ., Hosei Univ., Japan Women's Univ. 30-32; Rep. Shanghai Branch Rengo News Service 32-36, Domei (now Kyodo) News Service 36-39; Editor-in-Chief Domei News Service 39-43, and Man. Dir. 43-45; mem. U.S. Educ. Comm. (Fulbright), Tokyo 54-57; Columnist Asahi Newspaper 56; Gen. Partner Matsumoto, Kojima and Masukata (law office) 47-; Man. Dir. Int. House of Japan, Inc. 52-65, Chair. Board of Dirs. Int. House of Japan, Inc. 65-; Pres. Japanese Asscn. for American Studies 52-70, Man. Dir. 70-; Pres. Inst. of Nat. Econ. (Kokumin Keizai Kenkyu Kyokai) 51-61; Dir. Nippon Light Metal Co. 57-75, Dentsu Advertising Ltd. 61-; Vice-Pres. Nat. Comm. of Japan for UNESCO 57-63; Counsellor, Inst. of Asian Econ. Affairs 60-; mem. Board of Govs. Japan Broadcasting Corpn. 61-65; Chair. Grew Foundation 71-, Bancroft Educational Aid Fund 71-; Hon. LL.D. (Rutgers Univ.) 66, (Earham Coll.) 80, Lit.D. (Sophia Univ.) 76; First Class Order of the Sacred Treasure 69, Person of Cultural Merit 76, Japan Foundation Award 79, Ramon Magsaysay Award 80.
Publs. *Shanghai Jidai 1932-38* (My Shanghai Days); co-edited *A Documentary History of American People* 6 vols. (in Japanese) 50-58; translated: Allen Johnson's *Three Representative Americans* (with Y. Takagi) 28, Albert Thomas's *Histoire Anecdotique du Travail* 32, C. A. Beard's *The Republic* 2 vols. 48-49, *A Basic History of the United States* 2 vols. (with K. Kishimura) 54-56, *American Spirit* (with Y. Takagi) 54, *Beard's New Basic History of the United States* (with K. Kishimura and N. Homma) 64; edited: *Memoirs of Aisuke Kabayama* (in Japanese) 55, Arnold Toynbee's *Lessons of History* (lectures in Japan) 57, *A History of the World* 45-61 (in Japanese) 62, *The Mind of India* (lectures in Japan by J. Nehru and others) 62, *Lectures on Aspects of American Culture* (lectures in Japan by David Riesman) 62, *Basic Problems of U.S. Foreign Policy* (lectures in Japan by George Kennan) 65, *My Shanghai Days 1932–38* (3 vols.) 74.

The International House of Japan, Inc., 11-16, Roppongi 5-chome, Minato-ku, Tokyo, Japan.
Telephone: 03-470-4611.

Matsunaga, Masanao; Japanese international financial official; b. 1924; ed. Faculty of Law, Tokyo Univ.
Ministry of Finance 48-63; Financial Attaché, Embassy in Brussels 63-65; Financial Attaché, Paris 65-68; Dir. Second Insurance Div. of Insurance Dept., Banking Bureau in Ministry of Finance 68-70; Dir. Int. Orgs. Div. of Int. Finance Bureau 70-71, Int. Co-ordination Div. 71-73; Dir.-Gen. Nagoya Regional Tax Admin. 73-74; Deputy Dir.-Gen. Int. Finance Bureau, Ministry of Finance 74-75, with Securities Bureau 75-76; Exec. Dir. for Japan, IMF Nov. 76-79; Councillor, Ministry of Finance 79-80; Special Adviser Sumitomo Trust and Banking Co.
c/o Sumitomo Trust and Banking Co. Ltd., 2-3-1 Yaesu, Chuo-ku, Tokyo, Japan.

Matsushita, Konosuke; Japanese businessman; b. 27 Nov. 1894, Wasa Village, Kaiso-gun, Wakayama Pref.; ed. Ono Primary School, Wakayama, Kansai Commercial and Industrial School.
Founded Matsushita Electric Housewares Mfg. Works Co. 18, incorporated into Matsushita Electric Industrial Co. Ltd. 35, fmr. Pres., Chair. 61-73, Exec. Adviser, mem. of the Board 73-; Pres. Matsushita Communication Industrial Co. Ltd. 58-66, Chair. 66-70, Dir. 70-; Pres. Matsushita Real Estate Co. Ltd. 52-; Pres. Matsushita Electronics Corpn. 52-66, Chair. 66-71, Dir. 71-; Chair. Kyushu Matsushita Electric Co. Ltd. 55-74, Adviser 74-; Chair. Nakagawa Electric Co. Ltd. (now Matsushita Reiki Co. Ltd.) 53-74, Dir. 74-; Chair. Matsushita Electric Works Ltd. 51-77, Adviser 77-; Dir. Matsushita Electric Trading Co. Ltd. 52-74, Adviser 74-; Chair. Matsushita Electric Corpn. of America 59-74; Chair. Victor Co. of Japan Ltd, 62-70, Exec. Adviser 70-74, Adviser 74-; Chair. Matsushita Research Inst. Tokyo Inc.; Dir. Matsushita Kotobuki Electronics Industries Ltd.; Adviser Matsushita Graphic Communication Systems Inc., Matsushita Seiko Co. Ltd., Kansai Electric Power Co. Inc.; Exec. Dir. Fed. of Econ. Orgs. of Japan 56-73, Hon. Mem. 70-; mem. Advisory Cttee. Japan Nat. Railway 62-71; Chair. Invention Asscn. of Japan 68-71, Adviser 71-; Hon. LL.D. (Waseda, Keio and Doshisha Univs.); Blue Ribbon Medal 56; Commdr., Order of Orange Nassau (Netherlands) 58, Second Class Order of the Rising Sun 65, First Class 81; First Class Order of the Sacred Treasure 70; Commdr., Ordre de la Couronne (Belgium) 72, Panglima Mangku Negara (Malaysia) 79.
Publs. *What I do, and What I think, The Dream of My Work and the Dream of Our Life, The Words of Peace and Happiness through Prosperity, My View Towards Prosperity, My Thoughts on Man, Looking Back on the Past and Forward to Tomorrow, Reflections on Business, Reflections on Management, A Way to Look at and Think About Things, Why?, Japan at the Brink, A Plan to Give Japan More Space, 21st Century Japan.*
Matsushita Electric Industrial Co. Ltd., 1006 Kadoma, Kadoma City, Osaka 571, Japan.
Telephone: Osaka (06) 908-1121.

Matsushita, Masaharu, B.IUR.; Japanese businessman; b. 17 Sept. 1912, Tokyo; ed. Tokyo Imperial Univ.
Mitsui Bank 35-40; Matsushita Electric Industrial Co. Ltd. 40-, Auditor 44-47, Dir. 47-49, Vice-Pres. 49-61, Pres. 61-77, Chair. 77-; Dir. Matsushita Electronics Corpn. 52-72, Chair. 72-; Auditor, Matsushita Real Estate Co. Ltd. 52-68, Dir. 68-; Dir. Matsushita Communication Industrial Co. Ltd. 58-70, Chair. 70-; Dir. Matsushita Seiko Co. Ltd. 56-, Kyushu Matsushita Electric Co. Ltd. 55-, Matsushita Reiki Co. Ltd. (formerly Nakagawa Electric Inc.) 61-, Matsushita Electric Corpn. of America 59-74 (Chair. 74-); Pres. Electronics Industries Asscn. of Japan 68-70; Rep. Dir., Kansai Cttee. for Econ. Devt. 62-, Dir. 75-; mem. Standing Cttee., Osaka Chamber of Commerce 66-; Standing Dir. Kansai Econ. Fed. 70-, Vice-Pres. 77-; Blue Ribbon Medal 72; Commdr. of Order of Orange-Nassau (Netherlands); Commdr., Ordre de la Couronne (Belgium) 81.
Matsushita Electric Industrial Co. Ltd., 1006 Kadoma, Kadoma City, Osaka 571 (Office); 2-23, Natsugi-cho, Nishinomiya, Hyogo Pref., Japan.

Matsuzawa, Takuji; Japanese banker; b. 17 July 1913, Tokyo; ed. Tokyo Imperial Univ.
The Yasuda Bank Ltd. 38- (name changed to The Fuji Bank Ltd. 48), Chief Man. Planning and Co-ordination Div. 59-61, Dir. and Chief Man. Planning and Co-ordination Div. 61-63, Man. Dir. 63-71, Deputy Pres. 71-75, Chair. of Board and Pres. 75-81, Chair. The Fuji Bank Ltd. 81-; Chair. of Research and Policy Cttee., Japan Cttee. for Econ. Devt. (Keizai Doyukai) 73-75; Man. Dir. Japan Fed. of Econ. Orgs. (Keidanren) 75-; Pres. Fed. of Bankers Asscn. 78-79.
The Fuji Bank Ltd., 5-5, Otemachi 1-chome, Chiyoda-ku, Tokyo; Home: 8-7, 2-chome Shoto, Shibuya-ku, Tokyo, Japan.
Telephone: 467-8838.

Maung, Maung, LL.D., D.S.L.; Burmese jurist; b. 31 Jan. 1925, Mandalay; ed. Rangoon, Utrecht and Yale Univs., and Lincoln's Inn, London.
Served in Burma Nat. Army and Resistance during Second World War; practised law; Lecturer in Int. Law, Univ. of Rangoon; Deputy Attorney-Gen. of Burma 58-60; visiting lecturer Yale; Judge, Supreme Court 62; Chief Justice 65-72; Minister of Judicial Affairs 72-74; mem. State Council March 74-; Pres. Burma Red Cross Soc. 67-72; Chair. Burma Law Comm. 78-.
Publs. *Burma in the Family of Nations* 56, *Burma's Constitution* 59, *A Trial in Burma* 62, *Aung San of Burma* 62, *Law and Custom in Burma* 63, *Burma and General Ne Win* 69, *To a Soldier Son* 74.
State Council, Rangoon, Burma.

Maung Maung Gyee, U, B.A.; Burmese diplomatist; b. 15 Feb. 1921; ed. Univ. of Rangoon.
Officer Burma Defence Army in the Burmese independence movt.; Ministry of Foreign Affairs 48; served in embassies in Paris, Washington, D.C., Tokyo, Peking, Rome and Kathmandu as Third, Second and First Sec. and Counsellor; Dir.Gen. Int. Orgs. and Econ. Dept., Ministry of Foreign Affairs; Perm. Rep. of Burma to UN 77-81.
c/o Ministry of Foreign Affairs, Rangoon, Burma.

Maung Maung Kha, U; Burmese politician; b. 1919.
Prime Minister of Burma 77-; mem. State Council.
Office of the Prime Minister, Rangoon, Burma.

Maydar, Damdinjavyn; Mongolian politician; b. 15 Aug. 1916; ed. Moscow and Novosibirsk.
Chairman of State Planning Comm. 47-54; Deputy Chair. Council of Ministers 54-72; First Deputy Chair. Council of Ministers 72-; Chair. State Construction Cttee. 59-63, 67-68; Deputy Chair. State Cttee. for Foreign Econ. Relations 63-67; Chair. State Cttee. for Science and Tech. 71-; Chair. Soc. for Protection of Nature and the Environment 75-; Deputy Chair. State Rural Construction Comm. 71-; Deputy to People's Great Hural (Assembly); cand. mem. Political Bureau of Mongolian People's Revolutionary Party (MPRP) Cen. Cttee. 61-66, mem. Political Bureau 58-61, 66-.
Government Palace, Ulan Bator, Mongolia.

Mendis, Vernon Lorraine Benjamin, B.A., M.PHIL.; Sri Lankan diplomatist; b. 5 Dec. 1925, Colombo; ed. Prince of Wales Coll., Moratuwa, Royal Coll., Colombo, Univ. of Ceylon and School of Oriental and African Studies, London.
Entered Diplomatic Service 49; attached to High Comm.,

London; Third Sec., Washington, D.C. 51; Official Sec., Tokyo 53; Chargé d'affaires, Paris 55; First Sec., Moscow 58; Chief of Protocol, Ministry of Foreign Affairs 60, Counsellor for Foreign Relations 61; Counsellor, High Comm. in London 63-66; Deputy High Commr. New, Delhi 66-69; mem. Sri Lanka del. to UN Gen. Assembly 69, 70, 71, 74; Dir.-Gen. Ministry of Foreign Affairs 70-74; High Commr. in Canada and concurrently Amb. to Cuba 74-75; High Commr. in U.K. 75-78; Amb. to France, Switzerland and the Vatican 78-80; Perm. Rep. to UNESCO 78-80; UNESCO Rep. in Egypt Oct. 80-; Sec.-Gen. Conf. of Non-Aligned Countries, Colombo 62, Summit Conf. of Non-Aligned Countries, Colombo 76; Chair. Commonwealth Sanctions Cttee. 77, Chair. Asia Group, UNESCO 79.
Publ. *The Advent of the British to Ceylon 1760–1815; Currents of Asian History 1000–1500* 80, *Foreign Relations of Sri Lanka, Earliest Times to 1965.*
c/o UNESCO, 7 place de Fontenoy, 75700 Paris, France.

Menon, Chelat Achutha, B.A., B.L.; Indian politician; b. 27 Jan. 1913, Trichur.
District Court Pleader, Trichur; took part in congress and trade union activities; restricted for one year for anti-war speech 40; joined Communist Party and detained for communist activities 42; Sec. District Cttee. of Communist Party 43-47; underground 48-52; elected to Travancore-Cochin Legislative Assembly 52; mem. Kerala Legislative Assembly 57, later Finance Minister; mem. Rajya Sabha 68-69; Chief Minister of Kerala 69-77.
Publs. Translation of *Short History of the World* by H. G. Wells, *Soviet Nadu, A Kissan Text Book, Kerala State—Possibilities and Problems*, translation of *Man Makes Himself* by Gordon Child, *Sheafs from Memory.*
"Saketham", Trichur, India.
Telephone: 22693.

Menon, Mambillikalathil Govind Kumar, M.SC., PH.D., F.R.S.; Indian physicist; b. 28 Aug. 1928, Mangalore; ed. Jaswant Coll., Jodhpur, Royal Inst. of Science, Bombay, Univ. of Bristol.
Research Assoc., Univ. of Bristol 52-53; Senior Award of Royal Comm. for Exhbn. of 1851, Univ. of Bristol 53-55; Reader Tata Inst. of Fundamental Research, Bombay 55-58; Assoc. Prof. 58-60, Prof. and Dean of Physics Faculty 60-64, Senior Prof. and Deputy Dir. (Physics) 64-66, Dir. Tata Inst. of Fundamental Research 66-75; Chair. Electronics Comm. and Sec. to Govt. of India Dept. of Electronics 71-78; Scientific Adviser to Minister of Defence, Dir.-Gen. Defence Research and Devt. Org. and Sec. for Defence Research 74-78; mem. and Chair. for two years UN Advisory Cttee. on Application of Science and Tech. to Devt. 72-79; Chair. Preparatory Cttee. for UN Conf. on Science and Tech. for Devt. Jan.-Aug. 79; Sec. to Dept. of Science and Tech. 79-82; Dir.-Gen. Council of Scientific and Industrial Research 79-81; Chair. Comm. for Additional Sources of Energy 81-82; Chair. Science Advisory Cttee. to the Cabinet; Chair. Nat. Biotechnology Bd., Nat. Science and Technology Entrepreneurship Bd.; mem. Council of Defence Research and Devt. Org.; Foreign Hon. mem. American Acad of Arts and Sciences; Fellow Royal Soc; Fellow, Indian Acad. of Sciences (Pres. 74-76), Indian Nat. Science Acad. (Pres. 81-82); Hon. Fellow, Inst. of Electronics and Telecommunications Eng. of India; Hon. Fellow Nat. Acad. of Sciences, Allahabad; Hon. Fellow Aeronautical Soc. of India; Special Adviser, Int. Fed. of Institutes for Advanced Study, Stockholm; Shanti Swarup Bhatnagar Award 60, Padma Shri 61, Padma Bhushan 68; Khaitan Medal of Royal Asiatic Soc. 73; Hon. D.Sc. (Delhi, Jodhpur, Sardar Patel, Allahabad, Roorkee, Banaras Hindu, Jadhavpur and Sri Venkateswara Univs.).
Publs. 76 papers on cosmic ray and elementary particle physics.
Planning Comm., Room 125, Yojana Bhavan, Parliament Street, New Delhi 110001; Home: 1 Motilal, Nehom Marg, New Delhi 110011, India.
Telephone: 382148 (Office); 387784 (Home).

Menon, Vatakke Kurupath Narayana, M.A., PH.D.; Indian arts centre director; b. 27 June 1911., Trichur, Kerala; ed. Univ. of Madras and Edinburgh Univ.
Script Writer, Producer and Adviser for E. Services of B.B.C. during Second World War; returned to India 47; Dir. of Broadcasting, Baroda State 47-48; joined All-India Radio as Dir. of Staff Training 48, became Dir. of Delhi, Madras and Calcutta Stations, Dir. of External Services and Deputy Dir.-Gen.; Sec. Nat. Acad. of Music, Dance and Drama, India 63-65; Dir.-Gen. All-India Radio 65-68; Pres. Int. Music Council (UNESCO) 66-68, 76-78; mem. Faculty of Music, Delhi Univ.; Exec. Dir. Nat. Centre for the Performing Arts, Bombay 68-; Vice-Chair. Int. Inst. for Comparative Music Studies, Berlin; Hon. Exec. Dir. Homi Bhabha Fellowships Council 68-; Scholar-in-Residence, Aspen Inst. for Humanistic Studies 73; Trustee, Int. Broadcast Inst. 69-77; Hon. mem. Int. Music Council 80; Fellow Sangeet Natak Akademi 81; Padma Bhushan 69.
Publs. *Development of William Butler Yeats* 42, 60, *Kerala, a Profile* 61, *Balasaraswathi* 63, *The Communications Revolution* 76.
National Centre for the Performing Arts, Nariman Point, Bombay 400021, India.
Telephone: 233737 (Office); 231919 (Home).

Middleton, Donald King, C.B.E.; British diplomatist; b. 24 Feb. 1922.
Ministry of Health 58-61; Commonwealth Relations Office 61; First Sec. (Information), Lagos 61-65; Commonwealth Office (later FCO) 66; First Sec. and Head of Chancery, Saigon 70-72; Deputy High Commissioner, Ibadan 73-75; Chargé d'Affaires, Phnom-Penh 75; on loan to N. Ireland Office, Belfast 75; High Commissioner in Papua New Guinea 77-81.
c/o Foreign and Commonwealth Office, King Charles Street, London, S.W.1, England.

Mifune, Toshiro; Japanese actor; b. 1 April 1920, Chintago, China.
First screen appearance in *Shin Baka Jidai* (These Foolish Times) 47; played leading role in *Rashomon* 50; other films in which he has played important roles include *Yoidore Tenshi* (Drunken Angel), *Shichinin no Samurai* (The Seven Samurai), *Miyamoto Musashi* (The Legend of Musashi) 54, *Kumonosu-Jo, Muhomatsu no Issho* (The Rickshawman) 58, *Kakushitoride no San Akunin* (The Hidden Fortress) 58, *Sengoku Guntoden* (Saga of the Vagabonds) 59, *Nippon Tanjo* (The Three Treasures) 59, *Ankokugai no Taiketsu* (The Last Gunfight) 60, *Taiheiyo no Arashi* (The Storm of the Pacific), *Yosimbo, Tsubaki Sanjuro, Osakajo Monogatari* (Daredevil in the Castle), *Akahige* 65, *Grand Prix* 66, *Rebellion, Admiral Yamamoto* 68, *Hell in the Pacific* 68, *Furinkazan* 69, *Red Sun* 71, *Paper Tiger* 74, *The Battle of Midway* 75, *Shogun* 81, *The Equals* 81.
Mifune Productions Co. Ltd., 9-30-7 Seijyo, Setagaya-ku, Tokyo; Home: 6-25-18 Seijo, Setagaya-ku, Tokyo, Japan.
Telephone: 484-1111 (Office); 484-2231 (Home).

Mihara, Asao; Japanese politician; b. 1909.
Deputy Speaker of Fukuoka Prefectural Assembly; mem. House of Reps. 63-; Parl. Deputy Dir.-Gen. of Defence Agency; Parl. Deputy Chief Cabinet Sec.; Vice-Chair. of Diet Policy Cttee. of Liberal-Democratic Party (LDP); Chair. House of Reps. Cabinet Cttee.; Minister of Educ. Nov.-Dec. 74; Minister of State, Dir.-Gen. of Defence Agency 76-77; Minister of State, Dir.-Gen. of Prime

Minister's Office and of Okinawa Devt. Agency Dec. 78-Nov. 79.
c/o Liberal-Democratic Party, 7, 2-chome, Hirakawacho, Chiyoda-ku, Tokyo, Japan.

Miki, Takeo, LL.M.; Japanese politician; b. 17 March 1907, Tokushima-ken; ed. Meiji Univ., Tokyo.
Member House of Reps. 37-; Minister of Communications 47-48, of Transport 54-55; Sec.-Gen. Liberal-Democratic Party 56, 64; State Minister, Dir.-Gen. of Econ. Planning Agency 58-59, of Science and Technology, Chair. of Atomic Energy Comm. 61-62; Minister of International Trade and Industry 65-66; Minister of Foreign Affairs 66-68; Deputy Prime Minister, Minister of State, Dir.-Gen. Environment Agency 72-74, resigned; Prime Minister 74-Dec. 76; resigned; Pres. Japanese Liberal-Democratic Party 74-Dec. 76; resigned; Hon. LL.D. (Univ. of Southern Calif., Columbia Univ.).
18-20, Nanpeidaimachi, Shibuya-ku, Tokyo 180, Japan.
Telephone: (03) 463-8000.

Mills, Frank, C.M.G.; British diplomatist; b. 3 Dec. 1923; ed. King Edward VI School, Nuneaton, Emmanuel Coll., Cambridge.
Royal Air Force Volunteer Reserve 42-45; Commonwealth Relations Office (CRO) 48; Second Sec. (Admin.), Karachi 49, (Gen.) Dacca 49; CRO 51-55; Private Sec. to Parl. Under-Sec. of State 52-53; Prin. 53; First Sec. (Econ., Defence, Admin.), Cape Town/Pretoria 55; CRO 58-62; Private Sec. to Sec. of State 60-62; First Sec. (Political), Kuala Lumpur 62; Counsellor 63; Counsellor, Singapore 64; Deputy Head of Personnel Operations Dept. 66, Head (also of Personnel Dept., Gen. and Training) 69; Head of Personnel Policy Dept. 69; Royal Coll. of Defence Studies 71; Counsellor and Head of Chancery, New Delhi 72, Minister 74; High Commr. in Ghana 75-78; accred. as Amb. and Consul-Gen. (non-resident) to Togo 76; Asst. Under-Sec. of State, FCO 78; Dir. of Communications, FCO 78-81; High Commr. in Bangladesh Oct. 81-.
British High Commission, DIT Building Annex, Dilkhusha, P.O. Box 90, Dacca 2, Bangladesh.

Minowa, Noboru, M.D.; Japanese politician; b. 5 March 1924, Hokkaido; ed. Hokkaido Univ.
Member House of Reps. 67-; Parl. Vice-Minister of Defence 72-73; Chair. Standing Cttee. on Transport, House of Reps. 78-79; Deputy Sec.-Gen. Liberal-Democratic Party 80; Minister of Posts and Telecommunications Nov. 81-.
c/o Liberal-Democratic Party, 7, 2-chome, Hirakawacho, Chiyoda-ku, Tokyo, Japan.

Mintaredja, Hadji Mohamad Sjafa'at, M.LL.; Indonesian lawyer and diplomatist; b. 17 Feb. 1921, Bogor, Java; ed. Gajah Madal Univ., Leiden Univ., Netherlands, and Univ. of Indonesia, Jakarta.
Member of Board of many nat. youth movements 36-44; Judge, Court of First Instance in Bandung 44-46; Cen. Office for Elections, Yogyakarta 46-50; Inst. for Foreign Currency, Jakarta 50-55; Dir. P. T. Saudjana Corpn. Ltd., Industrial, Devt. and Trade Bank, P. T. Gedeh Ltd., P. T. Ceramics Ltd., P. T. Hazareem and various other cos. 58-67; Asst. to the Minister of Social Affairs 65-68; Chair. Board of Dirs. of two state construction cos. 66-68; Minister of State 68-71; Minister of Social Affairs 71-78; Chair. Partai Muslimin Indonesia 70-73; Exec. Chair. Partai Persatuan Pembangunan (grouping of the fmr. Islamic parties) 73-78; Amb. to Turkey 80-; Founder Islamic Indonesia Students Org. (HMI) 47, Chair. 47-50; mem. Board of Muhammadiyah Social Welfare Agency 65-71.
Publs. (in Indonesian): *A Reflection and Revision of Ideas: Islam and Politics, Islam and State in Indonesia* (also transl. in English, Dutch and Arabic) 71, *Rationalism versus Religious Belief, Family Life and the Haj Pilgrimage;* many articles in Indonesian magazines and journals.
Indonesian Embassy, Abdullah Cevdet Sok, 10 Çankaya, Ankara, Turkey.

Mishra, Brajesh Chandra; Indian diplomatist; b. 29 Sept. 1928.
Entered Indian Foreign Service 51; Third Sec., Karachi; Second Sec., Rangoon; First Sec., Brussels; Under-Sec. Ministry of Foreign Affairs 56-57, Deputy Sec. 57-60; First Sec., then Counsellor, Perm. Mission of India at UN, New York 64-69; Minister and Chargé d'affaires Beijing 69-73; Amb. and Perm. Rep. to UN 79-81, Consultant at UN April 81-; UN Commr. for Namibia April 82-.
c/o United Nations, Room 328 DC, 1 UN Plaza, New York, N.Y. 10017, U.S.A.

Mita, Katsushige, B.E.E.; Japanese business executive; b. 6 April 1924, Tokyo; ed. Univ. of Tokyo.
Joined Hitachi Ltd. 49; Gen. Man. Omika Works Aug.-Nov. 71, Kanagawa Works 71-75; Dir. 75; Man. Computer First Group 77-79; Exec. Man. Dir. 79-80; Exec. Vice-Pres. 80-81; Pres. and Rep. Dir. Hitachi Ltd. June 81-.
Hitachi Ltd., New Marunouchi Building, No. 5-1, Marunouchi 1-chome, Chiyoda-ku, Tokyo 100, Japan.

Mitra, Sombhu; Indian actor and stage director; b. 22 Aug. 1915; ed. Ballygunge Govt. High School and St. Xavier's Coll., Calcutta.
Public Stage, Bengal 39-42; Producer-Dir.-Actor, Indian People's Theatre Asscn. 43-46; Producer-Dir.-Actor Bohurupee (non-commercial theatre) 48-; Prof. and Head of Dept. of Drama, Rabindra Bharati Univ., Calcutta; Fellow Sangeet Natak Akademi, New Delhi; Grand Prix Karlovy Vary Film Festival 57; Padma Bhushan 69, Ramon Magsaysay Award 76.
Productions include: *Four Chapters* (Tagore) 51, *An Enemy of the People* (Ibsen) 52, *Red Oleanders* (Tagore) 54, *The Doll's House* (Ibsen) 58, *Sacrifice* (Tagore) 61, *The King of the Dark Chamber* (Tagore) 64, *Oedipus Rex* (Sophocles) 64, *Baki Itihas* 67, *Pagla Ghora* 71.
Publs. *Abhinay-Natak-Mancha* 57, *Putul Khela* 58, *Kanchanranga* 61, *Ghurnee* 67, *Raja Oidipous* 69, *Prasanga Natya* 73.
Bohurupee, 11A Nasiruddin Road, Park Circus, Calcutta 700017; Home: 96 Park Street, Calcutta 700017, India.

Mitsui, Shingo, DR.AGR.SC.; Japanese agricultural scientist; b. 1 Jan. 1910, Tokyo; ed. Univ. of Tokyo.
Senior Chemist, Dept. of Agricultural Chem. Nat. Agricultural Experiment Station of Ministry of Agriculture and Forestry 32-45; Dir. of Dept. of Soil and Fertilizer 45-48; Asst. Prof. (Fertilizer and Plant Nutrition) Faculty of Agriculture, Univ. of Tokyo 48-52, Prof. (Fertilizer and Plant Nutrition) 52-63, Dean of Dept. of Chemical Sciences of Graduate School 63-65, Prof. Emer. 70-; mem. Scientific Advisory Cttee. of Int. Atomic Energy Agency (IAEA) 65-; Dir. Fertilizer Research Inst. 69-; Lecturer, FAO Int. Training Centre on Fertilizer and Soil for Rice, India 52; Councillor, Japan Radio Isotope Asscn. and Scientific Expert to Atomic Energy Comm., Japan 55-; Del. to numerous int. confs. on rice cultivation and peaceful uses of atomic energy; Prize of Japan Acad. and others.
Publs. *Dynamic Studies on the Nutrients Uptake by Crop Plants* (with others) Parts 1-45, 51-64, *Inorganic Nutrition Fertilization and Soil Amelioration for Lowland Rice* 54, *Efficient Use of Urea Fertilizer in Japan* 65, *The Denitrification in Wet-Land Rice Soil—its Recognition and Impact* 78.
Higashi Fushimi 2-2-25, Hoya-shi, Tokyo, Japan.
Telephone: 0424-63-1453.

Miyadoh, Daigo; Japanese banker; b. 25 Sept. 1912, Hiroshima Prefecture; ed. Tokyo Univ.
Joined Sanwa Bank 36, Chief Sec. 55-58, Gen. Man. San Francisco Branch 58-60, Chief Rep. New York Rep.

Office 60-61, Dir. 61-, Dir. and Gen. Man. Foreign Dept. 62-63, Man. Dir. 63-68, Deputy Pres. 72-76, Chair. 76-.
4-7-3 Tezukayama-naka Sumiyoshi-ku, Osaka 558, Japan. Telephone: (06) 671-3644.

Miyake, Shigemitsu; Japanese banker; b. 27 Feb. 1911, Osaka; ed. Tokyo Imperial Univ.
Bank of Japan 33-67, Dir. 62-67, Adviser 74-; Deputy Pres. Tokai Bank Ltd. 67-68, Pres. 68-69, Chair. and Pres. 69-75, Chair. 75-; Exec. Dir. Japan Man. Orgs. 70, Japan Fed. of Econ. Orgs. 71; Pres. Nagoya Chamber of Commerce and Industry 74-81; Vice-Pres. Japan Chamber of Commerce and Industry 74-81; Blue Ribbon Medal 74.
Tokai Bank Ltd., 3-21-24, Nishiki, Naka-ku, Nagoya; Home: Tsukimigaoka Mansion C-7, 2-5 Ho-o-cho, Chikusa-ku, Nagoya, Japan.

Miyake, Shoichi; Japanese politician; b. 1900, Gifu Prefecture; ed. Waseda Univ.
Participated in peasant movement in Niigata Prefecture; a founding mem. of Japan Socialist Party (JSP); several posts in right-wing faction during party split in 50s; Head of Gen. Affairs Bureau and Educ. and Propaganda Bureau of reunified JSP 55; Vice-Chair. JSP 68, later adviser; elected to House of Reps. 14 times; third senior mem. of Diet 76; Deputy Speaker, House of Reps. Dec. 76-; disaffiliated from JSP 77.
House of Representatives, Tokyo, Japan.

Miyamori, Kazuo; Japanese oil executive; b. 17 Sept. 1902; ed. Meiji Univ.
With Yamaguchi Bank Ltd. 25-33; joined Sanwa Bank Ltd. 33, Dir. 56, Deputy Pres. 64-66; Pres. and Chief Exec. Officer Maruzen Oil Co. Ltd. 64-76, Chair. 76-; Pres. Maruzen Tanker Co. Ltd. and Maruzen Real Estate Co. 65-; Dir. Maruzen Petro-Chemical Co. Ltd. 64-, Kansai Oil Co. and Kansai and Osaka Petro-Chemical Cos. Ltd. 65-, Kanegabuchi Gosei Kagaku Kogyo Co. Ltd. 67-; Auditor, Palace Side Bldg. Co. 63-, Ogbayashi Road Construction Co. Ltd. and Japan Industrial Land Devt. Co. 64-.
Maruzen Oil Co. Ltd., Nagahoribashi-suji, Minami-ku, Osaka, Japan.

Miyamoto, Kenji; Japanese writer and politician; b. 17 Oct. 1908; ed. Tokyo Imperial Univ.
Member Japanese CP 31-, mem. Cen. Cttee. 33-; imprisoned 33-45; Gen. Sec. of Cen. Cttee. 58-, Chair. of Presidium of Cen. Cttee. 70-; mem. House of Councillors 77-.
Publs. *Twelve Years' Letters* 52, *World of Yuriko Miyamoto* 54, *Prospects of Japanese Revolution* 61, *The Path of Our Party's Struggle* 61, *Actual Tasks and the Communist Party of Japan* 66, *The Road to a New Japan* 70, *Standpoint of the Communist Party of Japan* 72, *Dialogues with Kenji Miyamoto* 72, (sequel) 77, *Kenji Miyamoto with Pressmen* 73, *Interviews with Kenji Miyamoto* 75, *Kenji Miyamoto on Our Times* 75, *The Defeated Literature* 75, *Documentation of Trials of Kenji Miyamoto* 76, *Dialogues with Kenji Miyamoto, sequel* 77, *Kenji Miyamoto on Contemporary Politics* 78, *Selections from Literary Critiques of Kenji Miyamoto* (4 vols.) 80.
Central Committee of the Japanese Communist Party, Sendagaya 4-chome 26, Shibuya-ku, Tokyo, Japan.

Miyazaki, Kagayaki; Japanese chemical executive; b. 19 April 1909, Nagasaki Prefecture; ed. Tokyo Univ.
Governing Dir. Japan Fed. of Employers' Asscns. 49-; Man. Dir. Japan Chemical Industry Asscn. 50-; with Asahi-Dow Ltd. 52; mem. Employers' Cttee. of Central Labour Relations Board 53-62; Pres. Asahi Chemical Industry Co. Ltd. 61-; Exec. Dir. Fed. of Econ. Orgs. 61-; mem. Export and Import Trading Council 69-73; Vice-Pres. Japan Textile Fed. 69-; mem. Tariff Council of Ministry of Finance 70-; Counsel, Japan Chemical Fibres Asscn. 71-77, Chair. 77-; mem. Japan External Trade Operational Council 71-, Comm. for Admin. Man. and Inspection 75-.
Asahi Chemical Industry Co. Ltd., Tokyo Kaijo Building, 2-1, Marunouchi 1-chome, Chiyoda-ku, Tokyo; 26-8 Funabashi 1-chome, Setagaya-ku, Tokyo, Japan.
Telephone: 429-2027.

Miyazawa, Kiichi; Japanese politician; b. 8 Oct. 1919; ed. Tokyo Univ.
Ministry of Finance 41-49; Private Sec. to Minister of Finance 49-51, to Minister of Int. Trade and Industry 51-52; mem. House of Councillors 53-65, Chair. Steering Cttee. 61-62; Minister of State in charge of Econ. Planning Agency 62-64, 66-68; mem. House of Reps. 67-; Minister of Int. Trade and Industry (in charge of *Expo 70*) 70-71, of Foreign Affairs 74-Sept. 76; Minister of State and Dir.-Gen. Econ. Planning Agency 77-78; Minister of State and Chief Cabinet Sec. July 80-.
c/o Liberal-Democratic Party, 7, 2-chome, Hirakawacho, Chiyoda-ku, Tokyo; 1-34, 6-chome, Jingumae, Shibuya-ku, Tokyo, Japan.

Mizushima, Sanichiro, D.SC.; Japanese physical chemist; b. 21 March 1899, Tokyo; ed. Univ. of Tokyo.
Professor of Physical Chem., Univ. of Tokyo 38-59, Prof. Emer. 59-; mem. Japan Science Council 50-62; Dir. Fundamental Research Laboratories of Nippon Steel Corpn. 59-69, Hon. Dir. 69-73, Adviser 73-; Counsellor, Inst. of Physical and Chemical Research; mem. Japan Acad.; Bureau mem. Int. Union of Pure and Applied Chem. 55-67; mem. Pontifical Acad. of Sciences, Nat. Acad. of Sciences (U.S.A.); Hon. mem. Royal Spanish Soc. of Physics and Chem., Higher Science Council of Spain, Indian Acad. of Sciences, American Acad. of Arts and Sciences, Chemical Soc. of Japan (Pres. 60-61); Chemical Soc. Prize 29, Imperial Acad. Prize 38, Decoration of Emperor for Cultural Merits 61, Decoration of Emperor of the First Class 70.
Publs. *Quantum Chemistry* 40, *Electric Waves and Matter* 46, *Structure of Molecules and Internal Rotation* 54, *Raman Effect* 58, *Collection of Scientific Papers* 59, *A History of Physical Chemistry in Japan* 72, *Ancient Tokaido Roads* 73, *Cultural and Social Background of the Rapid Modernization of Japan* 79.
2-10-6, Tamagawa-Denenchofu, Setagayaku, Tokyo 158, Japan.
Telephone: Tokyo 721-4045.

Mo Wenhua; Chinese soldier; b. 1915, Nanning, Jiangxi province; ed. China Workers' and Peasants' Red Army Coll.
Participated in Guangzhou uprising 27; Mayor of Nanning 50; Dir. of Political Dept., PLA Northeast Region 53; Pres. of PLA Political Coll. 58; Political Commissar, PLA Armoured Corps 75.
People's Republic of China.

Mody, Piloo, M.A.; Indian architect and politician; b. 14 Nov. 1926, Bombay; ed. Doon School, Dehra Dun, Sir J.J. School of Art, Bombay, and Univ. of California.
Worked with Le Corbusier on Chandigarh project 51-53; practising architect 53-; mem. Lok Sabha for Godhra, Gujarat 67-77; mem. Rajya Sabha for Gujarat 78-; Pres. Swatantra Party 72-74, now Exec. Vice-Pres.; Sec.-Gen. Bharatiya Lok Dal 74-76; detained June 75-Oct. 76; Pres. Panchmahals Community Chest, Bombay 68-; Chair. Art Purchasers' Cttee. Nat. Gallery of Modern Art 77-; Vice-Pres. Indian Inst. of Architects 60-67; mem. Cttee. of All India Bd. of Technical Education on Architecture and Regional Planning 65-67; Editor *March of the Nation* 62-75.
Publs. *Zulfi my Friend* 73.

Mody and Colgan, Stadium House, 81-83 Vir Nariman Road, Bombay 20; Home: 20C Prithviraj Road, New Delhi, India.

Moertono, Maj.-Gen. Amir; Indonesian politician and retd. army officer; ed. Mil. School of Law, Jakarta.
Staff Officer with Dept. of Defence during 50s; attended intelligence course with Lightning Div. of U.S. Army 59; worked with Sekber Golkar (now Golongan Karya) (Secretariat of Functional Groups forming a political front) 64-; Brig.-Gen. 69; Asst. for Socio-Political Affairs, Hankam (Ministry of Defence and Security) 69; Maj.-Gen. 71; Chair. Golkar 72, Gen. Chair. 73-; retd. from Army 72.
Golongan Karya, Jakarta, Indonesia.

Moertopo, Lieut.-Gen. Ali; Indonesian army officer; b. 23 Sept. 1924, Blora, Java; ed. Dutch Secondary School, Army Staff Command Coll.
Several army posts as 2nd Lieut., active in guerrilla war for nat. independence, 1st Lieut., Capt. active in putting down rebellion in West Sumatra 58, Maj. with Special Operational Command for the liberation of West Irian and Mandala Operational Command "Trikora" (People's Threefold Command) 61; promoted Lieut.-Col.; Asst. for Intelligence for army operations in West Irian 63, in confrontation with Malaysia and Singapore 64, later as Strategic Intelligence Officer of Special Operations prominent in settlement with Malaysia and Singapore; promoted Col.; Head Foreign Intelligence, Dept. of Chair. of Cabinet Presidium 67, Personal Asst. to the Pres. for Special Affairs 69; promoted Brig.-Gen. 69, Maj.-Gen. 71; Third Deputy Chief State Intelligence Co-ordinating Agency 70-76, Deputy Chief 76-78; Minister of Information March 78-; mem. People's Consultative Assembly 72-; several awards for distinguished army service including War for Independence Medal I, II, Medal of Loyalty, Medal of Defender.
Publs. *The Acceleration of Modernization during 25 Years of Development* 72, *Indonesia in Regional and International Co-operation* 73, *National Political Strategy* 74, *Cultural Strategy* 78.
9 Jalan Medan Merdeka, Jakarta (Office); 18 Jalan Matraman Raya, Jarkarta Timur, Indonesia (Home).

Mohammed Zahir Shah; ex-King of Afghanistan; b. 15 Oct. 1914; ed. Habibia High School, Istiqlal Coll. (both in Kabul), Lycée Janson-de-Sailly and Univ. of Montpellier, France.
Graduated with highest honours; attended Infantry Officers' School, Kabul 32; married Lady Homira, November 4th 1931; children, Princess Bilqis, Prince Ahmad Shah Khan, Princess Maryam, Prince Mohammed Nadir Khan, Prince Shah Mahmoud Khan, Prince Mohammed Daoud Jan, Prince Mirvis Jan; Asst. Minister in Ministry of National Defence 32-33; acting Minister of Education 33; crowned King 8 Nov. 33, deposed 17 July 73, abdicated 24 Aug. 73.

Molom, Tsendiyn; Mongolian politician; b. 1932; ed. Financial and Econ. Tech. School, Ulan Bator and a higher school of econs. in U.S.S.R.
Teacher, Dir. Financial and Econ. Tech. School, Ulan Bator; Head of a Dept., Ministry of Finance 58-60; Deputy Minister of Finance 61-63; Perm. Mongolian Rep. on Board of Int. Bank for Econ. Co-operation 63-65; Trade Rep. in U.S.S.R. 65-68; First Deputy Minister of Finance 68-69; Minister of Finance 69-79; Deputy Chair. Council of Ministers 79-; Chair. People's Control Cttee. 79-; Alt. mem. Cen. Cttee. Mongolian People's Revolutionary Party (MPRP) 71-76, mem. 76-; Deputy to People's Great Hural (Assembly) 69-.
Government Palace, Ulan Bator, Mongolia.

Molomjamts, Demchigiyn; Mongolian politician; b. 24 Nov. 1920; ed. Inst. of Finance and Econs., U.S.S.R.
Minister of Finance 54-57; Second Deputy Chair. Council of Ministers 57-59; Chair. State Planning Comm. 59-60; Chair. State Cttee. for Foreign Econ. Relations 63-65; Perm. Rep. to CMEA (Comecon) 63-65; Deputy to People's Great Hural (Assembly); cand. mem. Political Bureau of Mongolian People's Revolutionary Party (MPRP) Cen. Cttee. 58-59, mem. Political Bureau 59-; Sec. MPRP Cen. Cttee. 64-.
Central Committee of the Mongolian People's Revolutionary Party, Ulan Bator, Mongolia.

Momin, Abdul; Bangladesh diplomatist; b. 1 March 1921; ed. Presidency Coll., Calcutta, Calcutta Univ.
Administrative Service, Pakistan 46-50; Officer on Special Duty, Ministry of Foreign Affairs, Karachi 50-51; Third Sec., Rangoon 51-53; Vice-Consul, Akyab (Sittwe, Burma) 53-54; Second Sec., Washington, D.C. 54-57; Political Sec., Baghdad Pact Secretariat, Iraq 57; Under-Sec., Ministry of Foreign Affairs 57-58; Asst. High Commr., Shillong, India 58-61; First Sec., Brussels 62-63; Chargé d'affaires, Lisbon 64-67; Dir. Ministry of Foreign Affairs 67-70; Amb. to Argentina 70-71; Sec. Ministry of Foreign Affairs, Bangladesh 72; High Commr. in Canada 72-76; Amb. to People's Repub. of China 76-79, concurrently to Democratic People's Repub. of Korea 77-79, to France (also accred. to Spain) 80- (also accred. to Portugal 81-); Perm. del. to UN Aug. 80-; Amb. Designate to Morocco.
Embassy of Bangladesh, 5 Square Petrarque, Paris 16e, France.

Moorehead, Alan, C.B.E.; Australian writer; b. 22 July 1910, Melbourne; ed. Scotch Coll. and Melbourne Univ.
Sunday Times Gold Medal 56; Duff Cooper Award (for *Gallipoli*) 56; Order of Australia.
Publs. *Mediterranean Front* 41, *A Year of Battle* 43, *The End in Africa* 43, *African Trilogy* 44, *Eclipse* 45, *Montgomery* 46, *The Rage of the Vulture* 48, *The Villa Diana* 51, *The Traitors* 52, *Rum Jungle* 53, *A Summer Night* 54, *Gallipoli* 56, *The Russian Revolution* 58, *No Room in the Ark* 59, *The White Nile* 60, *The Blue Nile* 62, *Coopers Creek* (Royal Soc. of Literature Award) 63, *The Desert War* 65, *The Fatal Impact* 66, *Darwin and the Beagle* 69, *A Late Education* 70.
10 Egbert Street, London, N.W.1, England.

Moorthy, Arambamoorthy Thedchana, B.A.; Sri Lankan diplomatist; b. 10 Aug. 1928; ed. Univ., Sri Lanka, and Gray's Inn, London.
Joined foreign service 53; Chargé d'Affaires a.i. and Perm. Rep. to ESCAP 69-70; Chargé d'Affaires, Baghdad 70-74; Amb. to Pakistan 78-80, concurrently to Iran 80; High Commissioner in U.K. Jan. 81-.
Sri Lanka High Commission, 13 Hyde Park Gardens, London, W2 2LU; 35 Avenue Road, London, N.W.8, England (Residence).
Telephone: 01-262 1841 (Office); 01-722 0617 (Residence).

Moraes, Dominic; Indian writer and poet; b. 19 July 1938; ed. St. Mary's High School, Bombay, and Jesus Coll., Oxford.
Consultant UN Fund for Population Activities 73; Man. Editor *The Asia Magazine*, Hong Kong 72; Hawthornden Prize for *A Beginning* 57.
Publs. include: *A Beginning* 57, *Gone Away* 60, *My Son's Father* (autobiog.) 68, *The Tempest Within* 72-73, *The People Time Forgot* 72, *A Matter of People* 74, *Voices for Life* (essays) 75, *Mrs. Gandhi* 80; books of poems and travel books on India.
c/o United Nations Fund for Population Activities, 485 Lexington Avenue, 20th Floor, New York, N.Y. 10017, U.S.A.

Morgan, John Albert Leigh, C.M.G.; British diplomatist; b. 21 June 1929; ed. London School of Economics.
Served in Army 47-49; entered Foreign Service 51; Foreign Office (FO) 51-53; Third Sec. and Private Sec. to Amb., Moscow 53-56; Second Sec., Beijing 56-58; FO 58-63;

First Sec. 60; Head of Chancery and First Sec. (Commercial), Rio de Janeiro 63-64; FO 64-65; First Sec., Moscow 65-67; Foreign and Commonwealth Office (FCO) 68; Counsellor 70; Head Far Eastern Dept., FCO 70-72; Head Cultural Relations, FCO 72-80; Amb. to Repub. of Korea 80-; Gov. L.S.E. 71-; Fellow, Royal Asiatic Soc.
British Embassy, 4 Chung-dong, Chung-ku, Seoul, Republic of Korea; 41 Hugh Street, London, SW1V 1QJ, England.
Telephone: 75-7341 or 73-7689 (Embassy); 01-821 1037 (England).

Morgan, Michael Hugh, C.M.G.; British diplomatist; b. 18 April 1925; ed. Shrewsbury School, Downing Coll., Cambridge, School of Oriental and African Studies, London Univ.
War service 43-46; His Majesty's Overseas Civil Service, Malaya 46-56; Foreign Office 56-57; First Sec., Beijing 57-60; Belgrade 60-64; attached to industry 64; First Sec. FCO 64-68; Counsellor and Head of Chancery, Cape Town/Pretoria 68-72; Counsellor, Beijing 72-75; Insp. FCO 75-77; High Commissioner in Sierra Leone 77-81; Amb. to the Philippines 81-.
British Embassy, Electra House, 115-117 Esteban Street, Legaspi Village, Makati, Metro Manila, Philippines.

Mori, Haruki; Japanese diplomatist; b. 1911; ed. Univ. of Tokyo.
Ministry of Foreign Affairs, served U.S.A. and Philippines 35-41; Head of Econ. Section Dept. of Political Affairs 50-53; Counsellor Rome 53-55; Counsellor Asian Affairs Bureau, Tokyo 55-56; Private Sec. to Prime Minister 56-57; Counsellor Int. Co-operation 57; Dir.-Gen. of American Affairs Bureau 57-60; Minister to U.K. 60-63, to France 63-64; Perm. Rep. to OECD 64-67; Deputy Vice-Minister at Ministry of Foreign Affairs 67-70, Vice-Minister 70-72; Amb. to U.K. 72-75; Adviser to Ministry of Foreign Affairs 75-.
c/o Ministry of Foreign Affairs, Tokyo, Japan.

Morishima, Michio, M.A.; Japanese professor of economics; b. 18 July 1923, Osaka; ed. Univ. of Kyoto.
Assistant Prof. Univ. of Kyoto 50-51; Asst. Prof. and Prof. Univ. of Osaka 51-69; Prof. Univ. of Essex 68-70; Prof. of Econs. L.S.E. 70-.
Publs. *Equilibrium, Stability and Growth* 64, *Theory of Economic Growth* 69, *The Working of Econometric Models* 72, *The Theory of Demand: Real and Monetary* 73, *Marx's Economics* 77, *Value, Exploitation and Growth* 78.
International Centre for Economics and Related Disciplines, London School of Economics and Political Science, 10 Portugal Street, London, WC2 2HD (Office); Ker, Hutton Mount, Brentwood, Essex, England (Home).
Telephone: 01-242 3388 (Office); 0277 219956 (Home).

Morita, Akio; Japanese business executive; b. 26 Jan. 1921, Nagoya; ed. Osaka Imperial Univ.
Co-founder SONY Corpn., Tokyo 46, Exec. Man. Dir. 58-59, Exec. Vice-Pres. 59-71, Pres. 71-76, Chair. of Board and Chief Exec. Officer 76-; Pres. SONY Corpn., U.S.A. 60-66, Chair. of Board 66-72, also Pres. 68-71, Chair. Exec. Cttee. 74-77, Finance Cttee. 77-; Dir. IBM World Trade Americas/Far East Corpn. 72-77, Pan American World Airways Inc. 80-; Chair. Cttee. on Int. Investment and Tech. Exchange (IITEC), Keidanren (Fed. of Econ. Orgs.) 81-; mem. Int. Council, Morgan Guaranty Trust Co.; Edwardo Rihan Award for Int. Marketing 69, Albert Medal, Royal Soc. of Arts 82.
Publs. *Gakureki Muyouron* 66, *Shin Zitsuryoku Shugi* 69.
SONY Corporation, 7-35, Kitashinagawa 6-chome, Shinagawa-ku, Tokyo, Japan.

Moriya, Gakuji; Japanese business executive; b. 1 June 1907, Okayama Prefecture; ed. Tokyo Imperial Univ.
Worked for Mitsubishi Aircraft Co. Ltd. 30-34, Mitsubishi Heavy Industries Ltd. 34-50, Central Japan Heavy Industries Ltd. 50-52, Shin Mitsubishi Heavy Industries Ltd. 52-64, Dir. 62-63, Man. Dir. 63-64; Man. Dir. Mitsubishi Heavy Industries Ltd. 64-69, Exec. Vice-Pres. 69-73, Pres. 73-77, Chair. 77-81, Counsellor 81-; First Order of the Sacred Treasure 77; Blue Ribbon Medal 71.
5-1, Marunouchi, 2-chome, Chiyoda-ku, Tokyo; Home: 7-1, 2-chome, Kamiosaki, Shinagawa-ku, Tokyo, Japan.
Telephone: 03-212-3111 (Office); 03-442-3871 (Home).

Morrison, William Lawrence, B.ECONS.; Australian politician; b. 3 Nov. 1928; ed. North Sydney Technical High School, Univ. of Sydney, London School of Slavonic and East European Studies.
Joined Australian Diplomatic Service 50; Australian Embassy, Moscow 52-54; Econ. Relations Branch, Dept. of External Affairs 54-57; Australian Embassy, Bangkok, concurrently Liaison Officer UN Econ. Comm. for Asia; Chair. SEATO Cttee. on Soviet Econ. Penetration in Asia and Far East 57-59; Australian Embassy, Washington 59-61, Moscow 61-63; Head Information and Cultural Relations Branch, Dept. of External Affairs 63-66; Deputy High Commr. to Malaysia 67-68; mem. Parl. for St. George, N.S.W. 69-75, 80-; Deputy Chair. Joint Parl. Foreign Affairs Cttee. 69-72; Minister for Science 72-75, and External Territories 72-73; Asst. Minister for Foreign Affairs, with special responsibility for Papua New Guinea 73-75, Asst. Minister for Defence 74-75, Minister for Defence June-Nov. 75; Deputy Chair. Defence Sub-Cttee., Joint Parliamentary Foreign Affairs and Defence Cttee.; Labor Party.
20A Gipps Street, Arncliffe, N.S.W. 2205, Australia.

Moses, Sir Charles Joseph Alfred, Kt., C.B.E.; Australian broadcasting official; b. 21 Jan. 1900, Little Hulton, Lancashire, England; ed. Oswestry Grammar School, and Royal Mil. Coll., Sandhurst.
Lieutenant in 2nd Border Regt. (British Regular Army) 18-22; fruit-grower, Bendigo, Australia 23-24; motor salesman and sales man. 24-30; announcer, Nat. Broadcasting Service 30-32; N.S.W. Sporting and Talks Editor, Australian Broadcasting Comm. 33-34; Fed. Talks Controller, A.B.C. 35; Gen. Man. A.B.C. 35-65; Sec.-Gen. Asian Broadcasting Union 65-77, Hon. Councillor 77-; joined A.I.F. 40; rose to rank of Lt.-Col. 42; served in Malaya Feb. 41-Feb. 42, New Guinea Sept. 42-Feb. 43; mentioned in despatches Sept. 43; Trustee and mem. Exec. Cttee., Australian Elizabethan Theatre Trust; Chair. Marionette Theatre of Australia; Vice-Pres. Royal Agricultural Soc. of N.S.W.; Pres. Austrian-Australian Cultural Soc.; Vice-Chair. Asian Mass Communications Information and Research Centre, Singapore; Vice-Pres. Council of Royal Inst. for Deaf/Blind Children (N.S.W.); fmr. mem. Australian-American Asscn.; fmr. mem. Int. Advisory Cttee. of Prix Jeunesse Foundation (Munich); Hon. Dir. Post-graduate Medical Foundation of Australia; Commdr., Order of Merit (Austria).
Publs. *Diverse Unity—A History of the ABU 57-77* and numerous articles on broadcasting.
Suite 43, 203 Castlereagh Street, Sydney, N.S.W.; Home: 78 New Beach Road, Darling Point, Sydney, N.S.W., Australia.
Telephone: 617406 (Office); 324224 (Home).

Muhammad, Valiyaveettil Abdulaziz Seyid, PH.D.; Indian diplomatist and lawyer; b. 29 May 1923, Kerala State; ed. Aligarh Muslim Univ., Univ. of London.
Imprisoned as mem. Quit India Movt.; called to Bar, London 53; lawyer and Advocate Gen., Kerala State 65-67; Sr. Standing Counsel for Kerala and Union of India Supreme Court 67-75; Sr. Adviser, Indian Del. to UN 71, Alt. del., Indian Del., UN Gen. Assembly 75; mem. Rajya Sabha 73-77, Lok Sabha 77-80; Minister of State for Law, Justice and Co. Affairs 75; High Commr. in U.K. Sept. 80-; Leader Indian Haj Goodwill Del. to Saudi

Arabia 76; Chair. High-Power Panel on Minorities, Scheduled Castes, Scheduled Tribes and Weaker Sections 80; awarded Tamarapatra by Pres. of India.
Publs. *Indian Advocate* (Jt. Editor), *Our Constitution—for Haves and Have-nots, Legal Framework of World Trade.*
India House, Aldwych, London, WC2 4NA (Office); 9 Kensington Palace Gardens, London, W.8, England (Residence).
Telephone: 01-836 8484 (Office); 01-229 7241 (Residence).

Muhammadullah; Bangladesh lawyer and politician; b. 21 Nov. 1921, Saicha; ed. Dacca and Calcutta Univs.
Joined Dacca Bar 50; Lawyer, High Court 64; mem. Awami League 50-; Sec. E. Pakistan Awami League 52-72; mem. E. Pakistan Provincial Assembly 70; Political Adviser to Acting Pres. Syed Nazrul Islam 71; Deputy Speaker Bangladesh Constituent Assembly April-Nov. 72, Speaker 72-73; Speaker Bangladesh Parl. 73-74; Acting Pres. of Bangladesh Dec. 73-Jan. 74, Pres. 74-75; Minister of Land Admin. and Land Reforms Jan.-Aug. 75; Vice-Pres. of Bangladesh Aug.-Nov. 75.

Muir, Sir David John, Kt., C.M.G., F.C.I.S., F.A.S.A., F.A.I.M., A.A.U.Q., J.P.; Australian civil servant; b. 20 June 1916, Brisbane; ed. Commercial High School, Brisbane.
Clerk, Lands Dept. 33; Private Sec. to Queensland Premier 39; Investigations Officer, Sugar Cane Prices Board 43; Official Sec. to Premier 46; Permanent Under-Sec., Premier and Chief Sec.'s Dept., and Clerk, Exec. Council of Queensland 48; Agent-Gen. for Queensland in London 51-64; Dir. of Industrial Development, Queensland, and Chair. Industries Assistance Board 64-77; Chair. Public Service Board 77-79; Parl. Commr. for Admin. Investigations (Ombudsman) 79-81; Australian rep. on Int. Sugar Council 51-64 (Chair. 58); Pres. Chartered Inst. of Secs. 64; Chair. Queensland Cultural Centre Trust 76-; James N. Kirby Medal of Inst of. Production Engineers 69.
Home: 28 Buena Vista Avenue, Coorparoo, Brisbane, Queensland; Office: Queensland Cultural Centre Trust. Brisbane, Queensland, Australia.
Telephone: 398-3012 (Home); 240-7202 (Office).

Mukherjee, J. N., C.B.E., D.SC., F.N.I.; Indian chemist and soil scientist; b. 1893, Mahadebpur, Rajshahi; ed. Univs. of Calcutta and London.
Assistant to Palit Prof. of Chemistry, Calcutta Univ. 15-19; Guruprasad Prof. of Chemistry 21-37, Ghose Prof. of Chemistry 37-45; fmr. Dir. Indian Agricultural Research Inst., New Delhi and Cen. Building Research Inst. Roorkee; fmr. Chair. sub-cttee. Nat. Planning Cttee. of Indian Nat. Congress; leader Indian del. 3rd Int. Congress of Soil Science 35; Convener and Pres. Indian Soc. of Soil Science 35; mem. India Scientific Mission to U.K. and U.S.A. 45; mem. Royal Society Empire Scientific Conf. and British Commonwealth Official Scientific Conf. 46; Leader, Indian Del. to Conf. on Tropical and Sub-Tropical Soil, U.K. 48; mem. UN Scientific Conf. on Conservation and Utilisation of Resources and Pres. of its Land Section Meeting U.S.A. 49; mem. Gen. Assembly Int. Council of Scientific Unions, London 46, Copenhagen 49; mem. Exec. Cttee. and Board Int. Council of Scientific Unions 47-52; Vice-Pres. Int. Soil Science Congress, Netherlands 50; Foreign Sec. Nat. Inst. of Sciences of India 52; Pres. Indian Science Congress Asscn. 52; Pres. Trustees, Surendraneth Teaching Insts. 52-; mem. Central Tea Board 54; Scientific Adviser, Dept. of Agriculture and Forests, West Bengal 52-56; Administrator, Board of Secondary Education, West Bengal 55-56; mem. Union Public Service Comm. 56-58; Chair. Land Utilization Board, West Bengal 59-66; Padma Bhushan 64; Hon. D.Sc. (Calcutta and Burdwan Univs.) 76.
Publs. Over 250 papers on physical chemistry, electrochemistry, colloids, soil science, etc.
10 Puran Chand Nahar Avenue, Calcutta 13, India.
Telephone: 24-3845.

Mukherjee, Pranab, M.A., LL.B.; Indian politician; b. 11 Dec. 1935, Birbhum District, W. Bengal; ed. Univ. of Calcutta.
Started career as lecturer; Ed. *Palli-O-Panchauat Sambad* (Bengali monthly); Founder-Ed. *Desher Dak* (Bengali weekly) 67-71; mem. Rajya Sabha; Deputy Minister of Industrial Devt., Govt. of India 73; Deputy Minister for Shipping and Transport 74; Minister of State, Ministry of Finance 74; Minister for Revenue and Banking 75-77; Minister of Commerce 80-82, Steel and Mines 80-82, of Finance Jan. 82-.
Publs. *Bangla Congress: An Aspect of Constitutional Problems in Bengal* 67, *Mid-term Election* 69.
Ministry of Commerce, New Delhi, India.

Muldoon, Rt. Hon. Robert David, C.H., P.C., M.P., F.C.A.N.Z., C.M.A.N.Z., F.C.W.A., F.C.I.S., A.I.N.Z.; New Zealand politician and public accountant; b. 21 Sept. 1921, Auckland; ed. Mount Albert Grammar School.
Senior Partner, Kendon Mills Muldoon and Browne, Auckland; Lecturer in Auditing 48-54; Pres. New Zealand Inst. of Cost Accountants 56, Auckland Horticultural Council 59-60; M.P. for Tamaki 60-; Parl. Under-Sec. to Minister of Finance 63-66; Minister of Tourism and Publicity 67, of Finance 67-72; Deputy Prime Minister Feb.-Dec. 72; Dominion Councillor, New Zealand Nat. Party 60-, Deputy Parl. Leader 72-74, Leader of Opposition 74-75; Prime Minister and Minister of Finance Dec. 75-, also Minister in charge of Audit Dept., Legislative Department and Security Intelligence Service; Chair Board of Govs. IMF and World Bank 78-79; mem· Select Cttees., on Fishing Industry 63, Road Safety 65, Parl. Procedure 67; mem. Public Expenditure Cttee. 61-66, Chair. 63-66; Lever Hulme Prize, Inst. of Cost and Works Accountants 47, Maxwell Award, New Zealand Inst. of Cost Accountants 56.
Publs. *Rise and Fall of a Young Turk* 74, *Muldoon* 77, *My Way* 81.
Vogel House, 75 Woburn Road, Lower Hutt, New Zealand.
Telephone: 696-084.

Munekata, Eiji, DR.ENG.SC.; Japanese industrialist; b. 24 Jan. 1908, Tokyo; ed. Tokyo Imperial Univ.
Section Chief, Nippon Bemberg Silk Co. 31; Chief Engineer, Chosen Artificial Petroleum Manufacturing Co. 39; Head of Dept., Nippon Chisso Fertilizer Co. 44; Dir., subsequently Man. Dir. Asahi Chemical Industry Co. 47; Dir. Japan Atomic Energy Research Inst. 62, Pres. 68-78.
Publs. *Separation* 50, *Man-made Fibre* 55, *Researches on Chemistry and Industrialization* 65.
31 1-chome, Zenpukuji-machi, Suginami-ku, Tokyo, Japan.
Telephone: 03-390-6364.

Munro, Sir Robert Lindsay, Kt., C.B.E., LL.B.; Fijian lawyer; b. 2 April 1907, Auckland, New Zealand; ed. Auckland Grammar School and Auckland Univ.
In private practice as barrister, Fiji 34; mem. Legis. Council 45-46; Chair. Fiji Broadcasting Comm. 53-61; Norwegian Consul for Fiji, Gilbert and Ellice Islands (now Tuvalu and Kiribati) and Tonga 48-; Pres. Fiji Law Society 60-62, 67-69, Family Planning Asscn. of Fiji 63-; Pres. Fiji Senate 70-; mem. Governing Body, Int. Planned Parenthood Fed. 73-; Order of St. Olav (Norway).
6 Milne Road, Suva, Fiji.

Muramota, Shuzo; Japanese banker; b. 8 Feb. 1915, Hiroshima Prefecture; ed. Tokyo Imperial Univ.
Joined Dai-Ichi Bank Ltd. 37, Dir. 65, Man. Dir. 69, Sr. Man. Dir. 69, Deputy Pres. 70; Deputy Pres. Dai-Ichi Kangyo Bank Ltd., formed by merger with Nippon

Kangyo Bank Ltd.; Pres. Dai-Ichi Kangyo Bank Ltd. Dec. 76-; Dir. Nippon Light Metal Co. Ltd. May 73-.
510, 14-6, Komagome 4-chome, Toshima-ku, Tokyo 170, Japan.
Telephone: 03-918-1007.

Murata, Masachika; Japanese architect; b. 6 Sept. 1906, Yokkaichi Mie Pref.; ed. Tokyo Acad. of Fine Arts.
Designer, Shinichiro Okada Architect Office, Tokyo 29-30, Building Dept. of Ministry of Imperial Household, Tokyo 31-36; Researcher of facilities of Museums of Europe and America at request of Ministry of Educ. 37-39; Architect, Kameki Tuchiura Architect Office 40-46; Vice-Chief of Architectural Div., Conf. of Devt. of Kainan-tow (Hainan Island, China) 43; Pres. Masachika Murata Architect Office 46-; Dir. Board, Japan Architects' Asscn. 54-79; Dir. Sports and Recreation Facilities, Union of Int. Architects 59-77; Prize of Ministry of Construction 70; Nat. Medal for Merit 73; Architecture Prize, Middle Area of Japan 73.
Works include: Yokohama building of Yokohama Trading Building Co. Ltd. (Kanagawa Prefecture Architectural Prize) 51; Tokyo Metropolitan Indoor Pool, Tokyo 57; Exhbn. Halls of Tokyo Int. Trading Center, Tokyo 59; Tokyo Olympic Komazawa Stadium (Special Prize of Architectural Inst. of Japan and Building Contractors' Soc. of Japan) 62; Italian Embassy, Tokyo 63, 80; IBM Educ. Centre, Izu 67; Mount Tateyama Hotel, Toyama 68; Matsuzakaya Dept. Store, Shizuoko 70; Club House of Mitsubishi Bank, Tokyo 72; Tokyo Metropolitan Sewage Treatment Plant 60, 71, 73; Shinjuku Ward Recreation Center, Hakone 73; Kanebo Cosmetics Inc. Buildings 75; Nagano Athletic Stadium 75; Dentsu Kobe Building 75, Dentsu Headquarters Building 76; Shinjuku Cultural Center, Tokyo 78; Gymnasium, Indoor Pool 71 and Youth Cen., Itabashi Ward, Fujimi Plateau 80, Athletic Field Tamagawa Univ. 79.
Office: Jingugaien Building, 2-7-25 Kita Aoyama, Minato-ku, Tokyo 107; Home: 2-14-4 Moto-Azubu, Minato-ku, Tokyo 106, Japan.
Telephone: 403-1451 (Office); 451-1672 (Home).

Murayama, Tatsuo; Japanese politician.
Served in Finance Ministry; Chief Accounts Bureau, Liberal-Democratic Party; mem. House of Reps. for Niigata Prefecture; Minister of Finance 77-78, of Health and Welfare 78-81.
c/o Liberal-Democratic Party, 7, 2-chome, Hirakawacho, Chiyoda-ku, Tokyo, Japan.

Murdoch, (Keith) Rupert; Australian newspaper publisher; b. 11 March 1931, Melbourne, Victoria; ed. Geelong Grammar School, Victoria and Worcester Coll., Oxford, U.K.
Chief Executive and Man. Dir., News Limited Group and associated cos. (Group includes Mirror Newspapers Ltd., Nationwide News Pty. Ltd., *Daily Mirror, The Australian, Daily Telegraph, Sunday Telegraph, Sunday* (Sydney), *Sunday Sun* (Brisbane), *The News and Sunday Mail* (Adelaide), *The Sunday Times* (Perth), Southern Television Corpn. Ltd., Southdown Press Ltd., Cumberland Newspapers Ltd.; Chair. News America Publishing Inc. (*The Star, San Antonio Express & News*) U.S.A.; Chair. City Post Publishing Corpn. (*New York Post, New York Magazine, New West* magazine and *The Village Voice*), U.S.A.; Chair. News International Ltd. Group (London *Sun, News of the World*, Berrows Newspapers, Worcestershire, C. Townsend Hook Ltd., Convoys Ltd., Eric Bemrose Ltd.), U.K.; Chief Exec. Ansett Transport Industries Dec. 79-; acquired Times Newspapers Ltd. Feb. 81, group includes *The Times, The Sunday Times, The Times Literary Supplement, The Times Educational Supplement, The Times Higher Education Supplement*; Vice-Pres. Times Newspaper Holdings Ltd. 81-, Chair. Jan. 82-.
210 South Street, New York, N.Y. 10002, U.S.A.

Murphy, Lionel Keith, LL.B., B.SC.; Australian judge; b. 31 Aug. 1922, Sydney; ed. Sydney High School and Univ. of Sydney.
Admitted to N.S.W. Bar 47, Victoria 58; Q.C., N.S.W. 60-, Victoria 61-; mem. Senate 62-75, Leader of Opposition in the Senate 67-72; Attorney-Gen., Minister for Customs and Excise and Leader of Govt. in Senate 72-75; Judge, Australian High Court 75-; mem. Exec. Int. Comm. of Jurists Australian Section 63-79; del. to UN Conf. on Human Rights, Teheran 68; mem. Exec. Council of Australian Nat. Univ. 69-73; represented Australia at Int. Court of Justice in Nuclear Tests Case 73-74; initiated reforms in fields of family law, human rights, anti-trust, consumer protection.
High Court of Australia, Canberra, A.C.T. 2600, Australia.

Murray, Rear-Admiral Sir Brian Stewart, K.C.M.G., A.O.; Australian retd. naval officer and state governor; b. 26 Dec. 1921; ed. Hampton High School, Royal Naval Coll., Dartmouth, England.
Served Royal Australian Navy 39-; Commdr. 55, Capt. 61; Commanding Officer H.M.A.S. *Condamine* 54-55, *Queensborough* 61-62, *Parramatta* 63, *Supply* 67, *Sydney* 70-71; Dir. of Plans, Navy Office 64-65; Imperial Defence Coll. 66; Australian Services Attaché, Tokyo 68-70; Dir. Joint Operations and Plans, Dept. of Defence 71; Dir. Joint Policy, Dept. of Defence 72-73; Naval Officer in Charge, Victoria 74-75; fmr. Deputy Chief of Naval Staff; Gov. of Victoria 81-; Hon. A.D.C. to H.M. The Queen 71-72.
Government House, Melbourne, Victoria 3004, Australia.
Telephone: 63-9971.

Mustapha bin Datu Harun, Tun Datu Haji, O.B.E., K.V.O.; Sabah (Malaysian) administrator; b. 31 Aug. 1918.
Member Legislative Council of North Borneo 54-63; mem. Exec. Council 56-63; Chair. Sabah (North Borneo) Nat. Council; f. United Sabah Nat. Org. (USNO) 61, Chair. and Leader USNO until Aug. 76, Pres. 81-; Yang Di Pertuan Negara (Head of State) of Sabah 63-67, Chief Minister 67-76; served on Malaysia Solidarity Consultative Cttee. and Inter-Govt. Cttee. on Malaysia; Life mem. Commonwealth Parl. Asscn.; mem. Royal Commonwealth Soc., London; mem. Nat. Unity Council.
United Sabah National Organization, Kota Kinabalu, Sabah, Malaysia.

Myint Maung, U.; Burmese diplomatist; b. 10 March 1921, Magwe; ed. Univ. of Rangoon.
Joined Army 42; has held the following positions: Head of Co-operative Dept.; Chief of Admin. Div. of Burma Socialist Programme Party, also mem. Party Inspection Cttee.; mem. Pyithu Hluttaw (People's Congress) for Magwe Constituency; mem. Board of Dirs. of People's Bank of the Union of Burma, Exec. Cttee. of Burma Sports and Physical Fitness Cttee., Cen. Cttee. of Burma Red Cross Soc.; Chair. Resettlement Cttee. of Cen. Security and Admin. Cttee., Independence Award Cttee.; Perm. Rep. to UN 75-77; Minister for Foreign Affairs 77-79.
c/o Ministry of Foreign Affairs, Rangoon, Burma.

N

Nadao, Hirokichi; Japanese politician; b. 1899; ed. Tokyo Univ.
Entered Home Ministry 24; Gov. Oita Prefecture 41; Chief, Livelihood Bureau and Sanitation Bureau, Home Ministry 44; Vice-Minister of Home Affairs 45; mem. House of Reps. 45-; Minister of Educ. 56-57, 58-59, 63-64, Nov. 67-68; fmr. mem. House of Reps. Standing Cttees. for the Budget and Local Education; fmr. Vice-Chair. Political Affairs Investigation Cttee. of Liberal-Democratic Party, Chair Exec. Council 74-76; Speaker, House of Reps. 79-80; Pres. Nat. Social Welfare Council; mem. Local Admin.

System Research Council; Dir. Paper Bag Mfg. Co.; Independent; Order of the Rising Sun.
c/o Official Residence of the Speaker of the House of Representatives, 2-18-1, Nagata-cho, Chiyoda-ku, Tokyo, Japan.

Nagano, Shigeo; Japanese business executive; b. 15 July 1900; ed. Tokyo Imperial Univ.
General Man. Fuji Steel Works, Japan Iron Steel Co. Ltd. 34-40; Gen. Man. Japan Iron and Steel Co. Ltd. 40-46; Man. Dir. Japan Iron and Steel Co. Ltd. 46-47, 48-50; First Deputy Dir. Japan Govt Econ. Restabilization Board 47-48; Pres. Fuji Iron and Steel Co. Ltd. 50-70; Chair. Nippon Steel Corpn. 70-73, Dir. and Hon. Chair. 73-; Pres. Japan Chamber of Commerce and Industry 69-; Pres. Tokyo Chamber of Commerce and Industry 69-; Hon. Pres. Japan Iron and Steel Fed. 65-; Counsellor, Ministry of Foreign Affairs 62-; Vice-Pres. Pacific Basin Econ. Council 70-; Chair. Japan-Australia Business Co-operation Cttee. 61-; Japan-India Business Co-operation Cttee. 66-; Adviser, Fed. of Employers' Asscns. 70-, Fed. of Econ. Orgs. 70-; Counsellor, Bank of Japan 70-; Chair. Prime Minister's Council for Foreign Econ. Co-operation 69-; Order of Sacred Treasure, First Class 70; Hon. K.B.E.
Nippon Steel Corporation, 6-3, Otemachi 2-chome, Chiyoda-ku, Tokyo; Home: 34-4, Matsubara 4-chome, Setagaya-ku, Tokyo, Japan.
Telephone: 242-4111 (Office); 321-0141 (Home).

Nagata, Takao; Japanese shipbuilding executive; b. 1 Sept. 1911; ed. Nagasaki Univ.
Osaka Iron Works (later became Hitachi Shipbuilding and Engineering and Hitachi Zosen 82) 34-, Dir. 51-60, Vice-Pres. 60-62, Pres. 62-82, Chair. 79-; Adviser Japan Fed. of Employers' Asscn.; Pres. Japan Overseas Enterprises Asscn.; Exec. Dir. Fed. of Econ. Orgs.; Commdr.'s Cross, Order of Dannebrog (Denmark) 67.
c/o Hitachi Zosen Corporation, 6-14 Edobori 1-chome, Nishi-ku, Osaka 550, Japan.

Nagata, Takesi; Japanese geophysicist; b. 24 June 1913, Tokyo.
Director Nat. Inst. of Polar Research; Prof. Emer. Tokyo Univ.; recipient of lunar samples from U.S. *Apollo* missions; Foreign mem. Nat. Acad. of Sciences (U.S.A.).
National Institute of Polar Research, 9-10, Kaga-1, Itabashi-ku, Tokyo 173, Japan.

Nair, C. V. Devan (*see* Devan Nair, C. V.).

Nair, Raman Narayan, C.B.E., M.V.O., J.P.; Fijian diplomatist; b. 17 June 1922.
Clerk, Fiji Civil Service 40-62, District Officer 62-68; District Commr. 68-70; High Commr. in Australia 70-76 and Papua New Guinea 75-76; Consul-Gen. for Fiji in Australia 79-.
9 Beagle Street, Red Hill, A.C.T. 2603, Australia.

Nakagawa, Ichiro; Japanese politician.
Member House of Reps. for Hokkaido; fmr. Private Sec. to late Banboku Ohno; fmr. Parl. Finance Vice-Minister; fmr. Head, Liberal-Democratic Party's Nat. Movement Promotion H.Q.; fmr. Chief of Secr. for Party Reform Plans Implementation H.Q.; mem. Seirankai Group; Minister of Agriculture and Forestry 77-78; mem. Exec. Council Liberal-Democratic Party Dec. 77-; Minister of State, Dir.-Gen. Science and Tech. Agency and Chair. Atomic Energy Comm. 80-.
Director-General's Secretariat, Science and Technology Agency, 2-2-1 Kasumigaseki, Chiyoda-ku, Tokyo 100, Japan.

Nakamura, Toshio; Japanese banker; b. 7 Jan. 1910, Ibaragi Pref.; ed. Law Dept., Tokyo Univ.
Joined the Mitsubishi Bank Ltd. 32, Dir. 60-, Man. Dir. 63-65, Deputy Pres. 65-70, Pres. 70-78, Chair. 78-; Dir. Mitsubishi Warehouse and Transportation Co. Ltd., Tokyo Marine and Fire Insurance Co., Honda Motor Co. Ltd.; Auditor, Mitsubishi Heavy Industries Ltd. and Mitsubishi Petrochemical Co. Ltd.; Exec. Dir. Japan Fed. of Employees' Asscn.; Dir. Japan Foreign Trade Council, Keizai Doyukai; Trustee Tokyo Univ. Alumni Asscn.; Medal of Honour with Blue Ribbon 71.
Office: 7-1, Marunouchi 2-chome, Chiyoda-ku, Tokyo; Home: 17-8, Mejirodai 1-chome, Bunkyo-ku, Tokyo, Japan.

Nakasone, Yasuhiro; Japanese politician; b. 27 May 1918; ed. Tokyo Imperial Univ.
Member House of Reps.; fmr. Minister of State, Dir.-Gen. of Science & Technology Agency; Chair. Nat. Org. Liberal-Democratic Party, Joint Cttee. on Atomic Energy, Special Cttee. on Scientific Technology; fmr. Pres. Takushoku Univ.; Minister of Transport Nov 67- Dec. 68; Minister of State, Dir.-Gen. Defence Agency Jan. 70-71; Chair. Exec. Council Liberal-Democratic Party 71-72, Sec.-Gen. 74-Sept. 76, Chair. 77-80; Minister of Int. Trade and Industry 72-74; Minister of State and Dir.-Gen. of the Admin. Man. Agency July 80-.
Publs. *Ideal of Youth, South Pole—Human & Science, Frontier in Japan.*
3-22-7 Kamikitazawa, Setagaya-ku, Tokyo, Japan.
Telephone: (03) 263-0001 (Office); 304-7000 (Home).

Nakayama, Sohei, M.COM.; Japanese banker; b. 5 March 1906, Tokyo; ed. Tokyo Coll. of Commerce.
Nippon Kogyo Ginko (Industrial Bank of Japan Ltd.) 29-, Dir. 47-50, Man. Dir. 50-51; Dir. Japan Devt. Bank 51-54; Deputy Pres. Industrial Bank of Japan 54-61, Pres. 61-68, Chair. 68-70, Counsellor 70-; mem. Exec. Cttee. Japan Cttee. for Econ. Devt. 59-; Exec. Dir. Fed. of Econ. Orgs. 62-; Pres. Overseas Technical Co-operation Agency 68-; Dir. Matsushita Electric Industrial Co. Ltd. 71-; Chair. Cttee. for Energy Policy Promotion 73-.
3-3, Marunouchi 1-chome, Chiyoda-ku, Tokyo 100; Home: No. 10, 10, 6-chome, Zushi, Zushi-City, Kanagawa Prefecture, Japan.

Nam Duk-Woo, PH.D.; Korean economist and politician; b. 10 Oct. 1924; ed. Kook Min Coll., Seoul, Seoul Nat. Univ., Okla. State and Stanford Univs.
With Bank of Korea 52-54; Asst. Prof., Assoc. Prof., Prof., Dean of Econ. Dept., Kook Min Coll. 54-64; Prof. Sogang Univ. and Dir. Research Inst. for Econ. and Business 64-69; Minister of Finance 69; Gov. for Korea, IMF, IBRD, ADB 69-72; Chair. Board of Govs. ADB 70; Deputy Prime Minister and Minister of Econ. Planning 74-78; Special Asst. for Econ. Affairs to the Pres. 79; Prime Minister Sept. 80-Jan. 82; mem. Advisory Cttee. on Evaluation of Econ. Devt. Plan, Nat. Mobilization Board 64-69; Adviser to Korea Devt. Bank 64-69; Assoc. mem. Econ. and Scientific Council 67-69.
Publs. *History of Economic Theory* 58, *Price Theory* 65, *History of Economic Theory* (co-author) 62, *The Determinants of Money Supply and Monetary Policy: in the case of Korea 1954-64* 66, *Social Science Research and Population Policy* (jt. author) 80, *Changes in the Pattern of Trade and Trade Policy in a Pacific Basin Community* 80.
363-23 Seokyo-Dong, Mapo-Ku, Seoul, Republic of Korea.
Telephone: 323-6767 (Home).

Narain, Raj, LL.B.; Indian politician; b. 1917, Motikot village, Varanasi (Banaras) district, Uttar Pradesh; ed. Banaras Hindu Univ.
Member of Nat. Cttee. of All-India Students' Fed. 39-44; took part in sabotage in Quit India Movement 42; detained 42-45; detained frequently after independence; associated with Congress Socialist Party until 48; fmr. mem. Nat. Exec., Praja Socialist Party; Gen. Sec. All-India Samyukta Socialist Party 65-66; mem. Uttar Pradesh Legislative Assembly and unofficial leader of Opposition 52-62; mem. Rajya Sabha 66-72, 74-77; cand. for Lok Sabha in Rae Bareli Constituency, Uttar Pradesh 71, defeated by Indira Gandhi (*q.v.*); filed petition contesting election result;

petition upheld in High Court 75; detained during emergency June 75-Feb. 77; mem. Janata Party 77-; mem. Lok Sabha for Rae Bareli March 77-; Minister for Health and Family Welfare March 77-78 (resigned June 78); fmr. Publisher, *Kesari* (Hindi weekly); fmr. mem. Editorial Board *Jan* (Hindi monthly).
Nirman Bhavan, New Delhi 110011, India.

Narasimha Rao, P.V., B.SC., LL.B.; Indian politician; b. 28 June 1921, Karimnagar; ed. Osmania, Bombay and Nagpur Univs.
Chair. Telugu Acad., Andhra Pradesh 68-74; Vice-Pres. Dakshin Bharat Hindi Prachar Sabha 72; mem. Andhra Pradesh Legis. Assembly 57-77; Minister, Govt. of Andhra Pradesh 62-71, Chief Minister 71-73; Minister of External Affairs, Govt. of India Jan. 80-.
Publs. translations into Telugu and Hindi of several famous works; many articles in journals on political matters and allied subjects.
Ministry of External Affairs, New Delhi, India.

Narayan, Rasipuram Krishnaswamy; Indian writer; b. 10 Oct. 1906.
Honorary mem. American Acad. and Inst. of Arts and Letters 82.
Publs. (all in English), novels: *Swami and Friends* 35, *The Bachelor of Arts, The Dark Room, The English Teacher, Mr. Sampath, The Financial Expert, Waiting for the Mahatma, The Guide* 58, *The Man-Eater of Malgudi* 61, *Gods, Demons and Others* 64, *The Sweet-Vendor* 67; short stories: *An Astrologer's Day, The Lawley Road, A Horse and Two Goats, The Painter of Signs*; non-fiction: *The Ramayana*, (prose trans.) 72, *My Days* (autobiog.) 74.
Yadavagiri, Mysore 2, India; c/o Wallace and Shiel Agency Inc., 118 East 61st Street, New York, N.Y. 10021, U.S.A.; c/o Anthony Shiel Associates, 2 Morwell Street, London WC1B 3AR, England.

Narayanan, Kocheril Raman; Indian diplomatist; b. 4 Feb. 1921, Ozhavoor, Kerala; ed. Travancore Univ. and London School of Econs., Univ. of London.
Worked in Editorial Dept. of *Hindu* newspaper, Madras 44-45; Reporter, *Times of India* 45; London correspondent of *Social Welfare* weekly, Bombay 45-48; entered Foreign Service 49; served Rangoon, Tokyo, London and in Ministry of External Affairs 49-60; Joint Dir. of Orientation Course for Foreign Technicians, Delhi School of Econs., lecturer in Public Admin. 54-55; Acting High Commr. in Australia 61-62; Consul-Gen., Hanoi 62-63; Dir. of China Div., Ministry of External Affairs 63-67; Amb. to Thailand 67-69; Joint Sec. for Policy Planning in Ministry 69-70; Amb. to Turkey 73-75; Additional Sec. for Policy Planning, Asia and Africa Div. of Ministry 75-76; Sec. for the East and Policy Planning, Ministry of External Affairs April-May 76; Amb. to People's Repub. of China 76-78, to U.S.A. 80-; mem. Indian Del. to UN General Assembly 79; Co-Chair. Indo-U.S. sub-comm. on Educ. and Culture 80; mem. Indian Council for Social Science Research, New Delhi; mem. Bd. of Govs. IIT, Delhi, Nat. Book Trust of India, Indian Inst. of Management; Hon. Prof., Jawaharlal Nehru Univ. 70-72, Vice-Chancellor 79-80; Jawaharlal Nehru Fellow 70-72; Hon. Fellow, London School of Econs. 72-.
Publs. various on int. relations, Indian politics, literary subjects.
Embassy of India, 2107 Massachusetts, N.W., Washington, D.C. 20008; 2700 Macomb Street, N.W., Washington, D.C. 20008, U.S.A.; Kocheril House, Ozhavoor P.O., Kerala, India (Home).

Narayanan, Palayil Pathazapurayil; Malaysian trade unionist; b. 15 Feb. 1923, India; ed. Tech. Coll., Kuala Lumpur.
Member, Fed. Legislative Council and Finance Cttee. 48-53, 55-59; mem. ILO Plantation Cttee. 50, Del. to ILO Conf. 57, 65, 72, (Adviser) 74, 79, ILO Advisory Cttee. on Rural Devt. 73-; mem. Exec. Council of Malayan (later Malaysian) TUC (MTUC) 49-; Pres. MTUC 50-52, 54-55, 74-, now also Chair. Bldg., Educ. and Int. Cttees.; Gen. Sec. Nat. Union of Plantation Workers 54-; Pres. ICFTU Asian Regional Org. (ICFTU-ARO) 60-66, 69-76, Chair. ICFTU-ARO Educ. Cttee. 60-75; Chair. World Econ. Cttee. of ICFTU 68-, Pres. ICFTU 75-; mem. Court, Univ. of Malaya 72-75; now Vice-Pres. Int. Fed. of Plantation, Agric. and Allied Workers; Pres. Sree Sathya Sai Samithi P. Jaya; mem. Nat. Joint Advisory Council, Nat. Electricity Board; Life mem. Commonwealth Parl. Asscn., Tamil Journalists Union, Sri Aurobindo Soc.; Fellow Malaysian Inst. of Man.; Gold Medal, MTUC 51, Ramon Magsaysay Award for Community Service 62, Gold Medal of Railways' Union of Malaya 66, Golden Key and Freedom of City of Osaka, Japan 72, Hon. LL.D. (Penang) 74.
Publs. short story collections: *The Interview, Light in Darkness*; various trade union publs., articles in trade union journals; poems in Malayalam.
National Union of Plantation Workers, 2 Jalan Templer, Petaling Jaya, Selangor, Malaysia.
Telephone: Kuala Lumpur 59909, 59791.

Narlikar, Jayant Vishnu, M.A., PH.D., SC.D., F.R.A.S.; Indian physicist; b. 19 July 1938, Kolhapur; ed. Banaras Hindu Univ. and Fitzwilliam Coll., Cambridge.
Berry Ramsey Fellow, King's Coll. Cambridge 63-69; Graduate Staff Mem., Inst. of Theoretical Astronomy, Cambridge 66-72; Senior Research Fellow, King's Coll. 69-72; Prof. Tata Inst. of Fundamental Research 72-; Jawaharlal Nehru Fellow 73-75; Fellow, Indian Acad. of Sciences, Indian Nat. Science Acad.; Padma Bhushan 65, S.S. Bhatnagah Award 78.
Publs. Articles on cosmology, general relativity and gravitation, quantum theory, astrophysics, etc., in the *Proceedings of the Royal Society, The Monthly Notices of the Royal Astronomical Society, The Astrophysical Journal, Nature, Observatory, The Annals of Physics*, and scientific articles in various magazines; (with Sir F. Hoyle): *Action at a Distance in Physics and Cosmology* 74, *The Structure of the Universe* 77, *General Relativity and Cosmology* 78, *The Physics Astronomy Frontier* (with Sir Fred Hoyle) 80. *Violent Phenomena in the Universe* 82.
Tata Institute of Fundamental Research, Bombay 400005; Home: Flat 701, Colaba Housing Colony, Homi Bhabha Road, Bombay, India.

Nasir, Amir Ibrahim; Maldivian politician; b. 2 Sept. 1926, Malé; ed. Ceylon (now Sri Lanka).
Under-Secretary of State to Minister of Finance and to Minister of Public Safety 54; Minister of Public Safety 56, of Home Affairs 57; Prime Minister 57-59, Prime Minister and Minister of Home Affairs, Finance, Educ., Trade, External Affairs and Public Safety 59-64, Prime Minister, Minister of Finance, Educ., External Affairs and Public Safety 64-68; Pres. of the Maldives 68-78 (retd.); Awards of Nishaan Gazee ge Izaiteri Veriya, Ranna Bandeiri Kilegefaanu; Hon. K.C.M.G.
c/o Office of the President, Malé, Maldives.

Nasution, Gen. Abdul Haris; Indonesian retd. army officer; b. 3 Dec. 1918, Kotanopan, N. Sumatra; ed. Netherlands Military Acad., Bandung.
Sub-Lieut. Netherlands Indies Army 41; Col. 45; Commanding Gen. First Siliwangi Div. West Java; commanded guerilla warfare in West Java against Dutch Military Action 46-48; Dep. C.-in-C. of Armed Forces of Indonesia 48; Commanding Gen. Java Military and Territorial Command in defence of Java against Dutch second Military Action 48-49; suppressed Indonesian Communist Party's rebellion (Madiun revolt) 48; Army Chief of Staff 50-52, re-appointed 55-62; mem. Constituent Assembly 55; Chair. of Joint Chiefs of Staff and mem. Nat. Council 57; Lieut.-Gen. 58;

planned campaign against rebellion in Sumatra and Sulawesi 58; Minister of Defence and People's Security 59-66; Chair. People's Consultative Congress 66-72; rank of Gen. 60; Deputy C.-in-C. West Irian (W. New Guinea) Liberation Command 62; retd. 62; numerous Indonesian and foreign awards.
Publs. *Principles of Guerilla Warfare, The Indonesian National Army, Notes on the Army Policy of the Republic of Indonesia, Truth and Justice, Dual Function of the Indonesian National Army, Towards a People's Army, To Safeguard the Banner of the Revolution, War for Freedom, Rethinking New Order, Students and National Policies, From the 1965 Coup to the Congress Session in 1967, Leadership, Towards Harmony Among Religious Communities, To Bridge the Gap between Rich and Poor, Indonesian Struggle for Independence* (11 vols). 79.
40 Teuku Umar, Jakarta, Indonesia.

Nayar, Sushila, M.B., B.S., M.D., DR.P.H.; Indian physician; b. 26 Dec. 1914, Kunjah District, Gujrat, Pakistan; ed. Lahore Coll. for Women, Lady Hardinge Medical Coll., Delhi, Johns Hopkins Univ., U.S.A.
Medical attendant to Mahatma Gandhi and his Ashram; medical work at Sevagram and Noakhali, W. Punjab and Delhi; Chief Medical Officer Faridabad; Sec. Medical Board of Kasturba Trust; Sec. Leprosy Board of Gandhi Memorial Trust; participated in independence movement, imprisoned 42-44; mem. Lok Sabha 57-71; fmr. Minister of Health, Rehabilitation and Transport, Delhi State; Speaker Delhi Legislative Assembly 52-56; Minister of Health, Govt. of India 62-67; Pres. S.P.C.A. 52-62; Chair. Indian Red Cross; Pres. All-India Inst. of Medical Sciences, Tuberculosis Asscn. of India 64-67; Pres. Kasturba Health Soc. 64-; Dir. M.G. Inst. of Medical Sciences, Prof. of Preventive and Social Medicine 69-.
Publs. *Kasturba, Karavas ki Kahani*, etc.
Kasturba Hospital, Sevagram, Wardha A.2. Soami Napar, New Delhi 17, India.

Ne Win, U (Maung Shu Maung); Burmese fmr. army officer and politician; b. 24 May 1911; ed. Govt. High School, Prome and Rangoon Univ.
Joined Allied Forces 45; Vice-Chief of Gen. Staff and Major-Gen. 48; Deputy Prime Minister 49-50; Gen. 56; Prime Minister and Minister of Defence Oct. 58-60; Chief of Gen. Staff 62-72; led coup to depose govt. of U Nu (*q.v.*) March 62; Prime Minister, Minister of Defence, Finance and Revenue, Nat. Planning and Justice 62-63; Prime Minister, Minister of Nat. Planning and Defence 63; Prime Minister and Minister of Defence, also Chair. of Revolutionary Council 65-74; Chair. Exec. Cttee. Burma Socialist Prog. Party 73-; Pres. of Burma 74-81, also Chair. Council of State 74-81; Legion of Merit (U.S.A.), State Medal of Honour 1st class (Burma).
c/o Office of the President, Rangoon, Burma.

Needham, Joseph, SC.D., F.R.S., F.B.A.; British biochemist, historian of science and orientalist; b. 1900, London; ed. Oundle School and Cambridge Univ.
Fellow Caius Coll., Cambridge 24-, Pres. 59-66, Master 66-76; Head of Sino-British Science Co-operation Office and Counsellor British Embassy, Chongqing 42-46; Head of Div. of Natural Sciences UNESCO 46-48; now Hon. Counsellor to UNESCO; Dir. East Asian History of Science Library, Cambridge 76-; Hon. Prof. of History of Science, Academia Sinica, Beijing 80; Radhakrishnan Lecturer, Oxford Univ. 81; numerous visiting professorships, etc. latest at Northwestern Univ., U.S.A. 78; foreign mem. Nat. Acad. of China, Royal Danish Acad.; mem. Int. Acads. of the History of Science, of the Philosophy of Science and the History of Medicine; Order of Brilliant Star (China); Hon. D.Sc. (Brussels, E. Anglia, London), Hon. LL.D. (Toronto), Hon. D.Litt. (Hong Kong, Salford, Hull, Newcastle, Cambridge); Phil. Dr.h.c. (Uppsala); Sir William Jones Medal, Asiatic Soc. of Bengal, George Sarton Medal, History of Science Soc., Leonardo da Vinci Medal, History of Technology Soc.; Dexter Plaque, American Chem. Soc.
Publs. *Chemical Embryology* (3 vols.) 31, *Biochemistry and Morphogenesis* 42, *Science and Civilisation in China* (7 vols. in 20 parts) 54-, *Heavenly Clockwork* 60, *Development of Iron and Steel Technology in China* 64, *Within the Four Seas* 69, *The Grand Titration* 69, *Clerks and Craftsmen in China and the West* 70, *Moulds of Experience, a pattern of Natural Philosophy* 76, *Celestial Lancets, a History and Rationale of Acupuncture and Moxa* 80.
East Asian History of Science Library, 16 Brooklands Avenue at Clarendon Road, Cambridge, England.

Nehru, Braj Kumar, B.SC., B.SC.(ECON.); Indian civil servant and Barrister-at-Law; b. 4 Sept. 1909, Allahabad; ed. Allahabad Univ., London School of Economics, Balliol Coll., Oxford, Inner Temple, London.
Joined Indian Civil Service 34; Asst. Commr. 34-39; mem. Indian Legis. Assembly 39; Under-Sec., Dept. of Educ., Health and Lands, Govt. of India 39; Officer on special duty, Reserve Bank of India, Under-Sec., Finance Dept., Govt. of India 40, Joint Sec. 47; Exec. Dir. World Bank 49-54, 58-62; Minister, Indian Embassy, U.S.A. 49-54; Joint Sec., Dept. of Econ. Affairs 54-57, Sec. 57-58, Commr.-Gen. for Econ. Affairs 58-61; Amb. to U.S.A. 61-68; Gov. of Assam and Nagaland 68-73, of Meghalaya, Manipur and Tripura 72-73; High Commr. in U.K. 73-77; Gov. of Jammu and Kashmir 81-; rep. Reparations Conf. 45, Commonwealth Finance Ministers Conf., UN Gen. Assembly 49-52, 60, FAO Confs. 49-50, Sterling Balances Confs. 47-49, Bandung Conf. 55; deputed to enquire into Australian Fed. Finance 46; mem. UN Advisory Cttee. on Admin. and Budgetary Questions 51-53; financial adviser to Sudan 55; mem. UN Investment Cttee. 61-, Chair. 77-; Fellow, London School of Econs.; Hon. LL.D. (Missouri Valley Coll.), Hon. Litt.D. (Jacksonville Univ.).
Publs. *Speaking of India, Australian Federal Finance.*
Raj Bhavan, Srinagar, India.

Neilson, Hon. William Arthur, A.C.; fmr. Australian politician; b. 27 Aug. 1925, Tasmania; ed. Ogilvie Commercial High School.
Elected to Tasmanian House of Assembly 46; Labor Party Whip 46-55; Tasmania State Minister for Tourism, Immigration and Forests 56-58; Attorney-Gen. 58; Treasurer 59; Minister of Educ. 58, 59, 59-69, 72-74; Attorney-Gen. 74-75; Deputy Premier, Minister for the Environment, administering Police Dept. and the Licensing Act 74-75; Premier and Treasurer 75-77, Premier, Treasurer and Minister of Planning and Devt. 76-77; Agent-Gen. for Tasmania in London 78-81; Pres. Tasmanian Section of Australian Labor Party 68-69.
31 Rose Bay, Hobart, Tasmania 7000.

Nepal, King of (*see* Birendra Bir Bikram Shah Dev).

Newcombe, John David, O.B.E.; Australian professional tennis player; b. 23 May 1944, Sydney; ed. Sydney Church of England Grammar School.
Winner of Wimbledon Singles Championship 67, 70, 71, U.S.A. Singles Championship 67, 73, Australian Singles Championship 73-75, World Championship Tennis Crown 74, Wimbledon Doubles Championship 65-66, 68-70, 74; played with Australian Davis Cup Team 63-67, 73-76; Pres. Asscn. of Tennis Professionals 76-; Pres. Program Tennis Services, Texas Co.; Chair. Custom Credit Operation Tennis Australia, Nat. Australia Day Cttee.
Pubs. *The Family Tennis Book*, 75, *The Young Tennis Player* 81.
P.O.Box 1200 Crows Nest, 2065 N.S.W., Australia.

Newsom, David Dunlop, A.B., M.S.; American diplomatist. b. 6 Jan. 1918; ed. Richmond Union High School and Calif; and Columbia Univs.

Reporter, *San Francisco Chronicle* 40-41; U.S. Navy 41-45; Newspaper publisher 45-47; Information Officer, U.S. Embassy, Karachi 47-50; Consul, Oslo 50-51; Public Affairs Officer, U.S. Embassy, Baghdad 51-55; Dept. of State 55-59; U.S. Nat. War Coll. 59-60; First Sec. U.S. Embassy, London 60-62; Dir. Office of Northern African Affairs, State Dept. 62-65; Amb. to Libya 65-69; Asst. Sec. of State for African Affairs 69-74; Amb. to Indonesia 74-77, to the Philippines 77-78; Under-Sec. of State for Political Affairs 78-81, Dir. Georgetown Univ. School of Foreign Service Inst. for the Study of Diplomacy 81-; Dept. of State Meritorious Service Award 58; Nat. Civil Service League Career Service Award 71; Rockefeller Public Service Award 72; Dept. of State Distinguished Honour Award 81.
Georgetown University School of Foreign Service Institute for the Study of Diplomacy, Washington, D.C. 20057 (Office); 3308 Woodley Road, N.W., Washington, D.C. 20008, U.S.A.

Ngapoi Ngawang Jigme; Tibetan leader; b. 1909.
Leader Tibetan Army resisting Chinese invasion 50; First Deputy Commdr. Xizang Mil. Region, People's Liberation Army 52; mem. Nat. Defence Council 54-Cultural Revolution; Vice-Chair. Preparatory Cttee. for Xizang Autonomous Region 59-65; Vice-Chair. Standing Cttee., Nat. People's Congress 65-; Chair. Xizang Autonomous Region People's Govt. 65-68; Vice-Chair. Xizang Revolutionary Cttee. 68; Exec. Chair. Nat. People's Congress 78; Chair. Xizang Autonomous Region People's Congress 79-81; Gov. People's Govt., Xizang Autonomous Region 81-.
Publ. *Tibet* (with others).
People's Republic of China.

Nguyen Cao Ky, Air Vice-Marshal; Vietnamese air force officer and politician; b. 8 Sept. 1930; ed. High School, Hanoi, and Officers' Training School, Hanoi.
Flight Training, Marrakech until 54; commanded Transport Squadron 54, later commdr. Tan Son Nhât Air Force Base, Repub. of Viet-Nam; spent six months at U.S. Air Command and Staff Coll., Maxwell Field, Alabama, U.S.A.; later, Commdr. Air Force, Repub. of Viet-Nam; Prime Minister 65-67; Vice-Pres. Repub. of Viet-Nam 67-71; went to U.S.A. April 75; owns liquor store.
Publ. *Twenty Years and Twenty Days* 77.
Huntington Beach, Los Angeles, Calif., U.S.A.

Nguyen Co Thach; Vietnamese politician.
Served Embassy, Delhi 56-60; took part peace talks, Geneva 62; Chair. Cttee. to Investigate U.S. War Crimes 66; Minister of Foreign Affairs Feb. 80-; Alt. mem. Politburo 82-.
Ministry of Foreign Affairs, Hanoi, Viet-Nam.

Nguyen Duy Trinh; Vietnamese politician.
Member of Secretariat and Politburo, Communist Party of Viet-Nam; Vice-Premier and Minister of Foreign Affairs, Democratic Repub. of Viet-Nam to July 76, Socialist Repub. of Viet-Nam 76-80; mem. Politburo and Sec. CPV Cen. Cttee.
Council of Ministers, Hanoi, Viet-Nam.

Nguyen Huu Tho; Vietnamese politician; b. 10 July 1910, Cholon.
Participated in liberation war against French colonialists; organized mass demonstration, Saigon-Cholon area March 50 against U.S. interference; imprisoned 50-52; opposed 1954 Geneva agreements on Indo-China; founded Saigon-Cholon Peace Movement; subsequently arrested, escaped 61; Chair. of Cen. Cttee. of Nat. Liberation Front (NLF) 62-, of NLF Presidium 64-, of Consultative Council, Provisional Revolutionary Govt. of Repub. of South Viet-Nam 69-76 (in Saigon (now Ho Chi Minh City) 75-76); Vice-Pres. Socialist Repub. of Viet-Nam 76-80, Acting Pres., Council of State 80-81, Vice-Pres., Council of State 81-; Chair. Standing Cttee., Nat. Assembly 81-.
Council of State, Hanoi, Viet-Nam.

Nguyen Thi Binh, Madame; Vietnamese politician; b. 1927; ed. Saigon.
Student political leader in Saigon; organized (with Nguyen Huu Tho, *q.v.*) first anti-U.S. demonstration 50; imprisoned by French authorities 51-54; Vice-Pres. South Vietnamese Cttee. for Solidarity with the American People; Council mem. Union of Women for the Liberation of South Viet-Nam; mem. Cen. Cttee. Nat. Liberation Front (NLF); appointed NLF spokesman to peace talks, Paris, Nov. 68; Minister of Foreign Affairs in Provisional Revolutionary Govt. of S. Viet-Nam 69-76 (in Saigon (now Ho Chi Minh City) 75-76); Minister of Educ., Socialist Repub. of Viet-Nam June 76-; mem. Council of State 81-; Gen.-Sec. Vietnamese Nat. Cttee. for Int. Year of the Child 78; Pres. Vietnamese Women's Union, Hanoi.
Ministry of Education, 21 Le Thanh Tong, Hanoi, Viet-Nam.

Nguyen Van Binh, Most Rev. Paul, LIC.TH.; Vietnamese ecclesiastic; b. 1 Sept. 1910; ed. Seminary of Saigon and Propaganda Fide Univ., Rome.
Ordained 37; Parish Priest, Duc-Hoa and Can-Dat; Prof., Major Seminary of Saigon 37-55; Bishop 55; Apostolic Vicar of Can-Tho 55-61; Archbishop of Saigon (now Ho Chi Minh City) 61-; fmr. Pres. Episcopal Conf. of Viet-Nam.
Archevêché de Ho Chi Minh-Ville, 180 rue Nguyen Dinh Chieu, Ho Chi Minh City, Viet-Nam.

Nguyen Van Linh; Vietnamese politician; b. 1913, North Viet-Nam.
Member of Cen. Cttee. of Lao Dong Party for many years; fmr. Sec. Saigon (now Ho Chi Minh City) Cttee. of Lao Dong Party, second in command to Pham Hung (*q.v.*); now a party leader in Ho Chi Minh City; mem. Secretariat and Politburo, CP of Viet-Nam 76-82; Pres. Viet-Nam Gen. Fed. of Trade Unions 78-80.
Ho Chi Minh City Committee of the Communist Party of Viet-Nam, Ho Chi Minh City, Viet-Nam.

Nguyen Van Thieu, Lt.-Gen.; Vietnamese army officer and politician; b. 5 April 1923; ed. Catholic Pellerin School, Hué, and Nat. Military Acad., Hué.
Viet-Nam Nat. Army 48-54; Republic of Viet-Nam Army 54-75; Commdr. First Infantry Div. 60-62, Fifth Infantry Div. 62-64; Deputy Premier and Minister of Defence 64-65; Chair. Nat. Leadership Cttee. and Head of State 65-67; Pres. of Republic of Viet-Nam 67-April 75; founded Dan Chu Party 73; went to Taiwan April 75 and later to the U.K.
The White House, Coombe Park, Kingston-upon-Thames, Surrey, England.

Ni Zhifu; Chinese engineer and party official.
Engineering worker; invented Ni Qiafu drillhead 53; Eng. Beijing No. 1 Machine Tool Plant 64; mem. 9th Cen. Cttee. of CCP 69; active in Labour Union's activities 70-; alt. mem. Politburo, 10th Cen. Cttee. of CCP 73, mem. Politburo, 11th Cen. Cttee. of CCP 77 (reported to have been suspended June 79); Second Sec., CCP Shanghai 77; Chair. All-China Fed. of Trade Unions 78-.
People's Republic of China.

Niazi, Maulana Kausar; Pakistani journalist and politician; b. 21 April 1934; ed. Punjab Univ.
Former editor *Tasneem* (daily), Lahore and later *Kausar*; founded *Shahab* (weekly) 60; mem. Pakistan People's Party 70-; political imprisonment 70; Minister of Information and Broadcasting 72-74, of Religious Affairs 74, also of Minority Affairs and Overseas Pakistanis 76-77; arrested July 77.
Publs. several books on religious and literary topics.
Islamabad, Pakistan.

Nicholas, Sir John William, K.C.V.O., C.M.G., B.A.; British diplomatist; b. 13 Dec. 1924, Worcester; ed. Birmingham Univ.

Served in 7th Rajput Regt., Indian Army 44-47; War Office 49-57; Commonwealth Relations Office 57-; First Sec. British High Comm., Malaysia 57-61; Econ. Div., Commonwealth Relations Office 61-63; Deputy High Commr., Malawi 64-66, Sri Lanka 70-71, Calcutta 74-76; Diplomatic Service Insp. 67-69; Dir. Establishments and Finance Div., Commonwealth Secr. 71-73; Head of Pacific Dependent Territories Office, Foreign and Commonwealth Office 73-74; Consul-Gen., Melbourne 76-79; British High Commr. in Sri Lanka and Amb. (non-resident) to Repub. of Maldives 79-.
British High Commission, Galle Road, Kollupitiya, (P.O. Box 1433), Colombo 3, Sri Lanka.
Telephone: 27611-17.

Nie Fengzhi; Chinese army officer.
Commander 27th Corps, East China Field Army 48; Educational Dir., East China Mil. Acad. 49; Commdr. Air Force units, Nanjing Mil. Region, PLA 54-68; Deputy Commdr. Nanjing Mil. Region, PLA 75, Commdr. 77-; mem. 11th Cen. Cttee. CCP 77.
People's Republic of China.

Nie Rongzhen, Marshal; Chinese politician and fmr. army officer; b. 1889, Jiangqin, Sichuan; ed. Univ. de Travail, France, Far Eastern and Red Army Univs., Moscow.
Joined CCP 23; Pol. Instructor, Huangpu Mil. Acad. 25; participated in Nanchang and Guangzhou Uprisings 27; Pol. Commissar 10th Army Corps 31-36; Commdr. Shanxi-Zhaha-Hebei Field Army 37-48; mem. 7th Cen. Cttee. of CCP 45; Mayor of Beijing 49-51; Vice-Chair. Nat. Defence Council 54-; Marshal 55; mem. 8th Cen. Cttee. of CCP 56; Vice-Premier, State Council 56-74; Chair. Scientific and Technological Comm. 58-; mem. 9th Cen. Cttee. of CCP 69, 10th Cen. Cttee. 73, Politburo, 11th Cen. Cttee. 77; Exec. Chair. Presidium 5th Nat. People's Congress 78; Vice-Chair. Standing Cttee. 5th Nat. People's Congress 78-; Vice-Chair. Mil. Cttee. CCP Cen. Cttee. 78-.
People's Republic of China.

Nihal Singh, Surendra, B.A.; Indian journalist; b. 30 April 1929, Rawalpindi (now in Pakistan); ed. Delhi Univ.
Sub-editor with *The Times of India*, Delhi 51-53; Staff Reporter, Parl. Corresp., *The Statesman*, Calcutta 54-61, Special Corresp. for S.E. Asia and Far East, Singapore 62-67, Pakistan 67, for Soviet Union and Eastern Europe, Moscow 68-69, Political Corresp., Delhi 69-71, Special Corresp. London 71-74, Resident Editor Delhi 74-75, Editor, Calcutta and Delhi 75-80; Editor-in-Chief *Indian Express* 81-; Int. Editor of the Year Award (Atlas Press Service, N.Y.) 78.
Publs. *Malaysia—A Commentary* 71, *From the Jhelum to the Volga* 72, *Indira's India* 78, *The Gang and 900 Million* 79, *My India* 81.
Indian Express, Bahadur Shah Zafar Marg, New Delhi 2, India.
Telephone: 276094 (Office).

Nishikawa, Shojiro, B.ECON.; Japanese banker; b. 23 Sept. 1913, Tokyo; ed. Tokyo Imperial Univ.
Joined Nippon Kangyo Bank Ltd. 36, Branch Man. Tsurumi Branch 54-60, Gen. Man. Planning Div. 60-61, Dir. and Branch Man., Nagoya Branch 61-62, Dir. Osaka Branch 62-63; Gen. Man. Osaka Branch 62-65, Man. Dir. Osaka Branch 63-65, Man. Dir., Gen. Man. Securities Div. 65-68, Dir., Administrative Gen. Man., Branch Admin. and Business Devt. Group 68-79, Deputy Pres. 69-71, Deputy Pres. Dai-Ichi Kangyo Bank 71-76, Chair. Dec. 76-; Medal with Blue Ribbon 78.
Dai-Ichi Kangyo Bank Ltd., 1-5, Uchisaiwai-cho 1-chome, Chiyoda-ku, Tokyo; Home: 48-16 Shakujii-cho 8-chome, Nerima-ku, Tokyo, Japan.
Telephone: 03-216-1111.

Nisibori, Masahiro; Japanese diplomatist; b. 14 Nov. 1918, Hakodate; ed. Hitotsubashi Univ., Tokyo, Brown Univ. and Harvard Univ., U.S.A.
Entered Foreign Service 41; Deputy Vice-Minister of Foreign Affairs for Admin. Affairs 65; Consul-Gen., Geneva and concurrently Minister of Del. to Int. Orgs. 66-69; Dir.-Gen. UN Bureau in Ministry of Foreign Affairs 70-71; Amb. to Disarmament Cttee. in Geneva 72-75, to Belgium, Luxembourg and EEC 76-78, to UN 79-.
Japanese Ambassador's Residence, 740 Park Avenue, New York, N.Y. 10021; Permanent Mission of Japan to the United Nations, 866 United Nations Plaza, New York, N.Y. 10017, U.S.A.
Telephone: 744-2523 (Res.).

Nitisastro, Widjojo, PH.D.; Indonesian politician; b. 23 Sept. 1927, Malang, East Java; ed. Univ. of Indonesia and Univ. of Calif., Berkeley, U.S.A.
Dean, Faculty of Econs., Univ. of Indonesia 65-67; seconded to UN as expert engaged in drawing up plan for 2nd UN Econ. Devt. Decade and mem. Gov. Council, UN Asian Inst. of Devt. and Planning 67-71; Minister of State for National Planning and Construction Sept. 71-74, for Economic Financial and Industrial Affairs 73-78; Minister-Co-ordinator for Economic, Financial and Industrial Affairs, also Chair. Nat. Planning Board March 78-.
Publs. include: *Population Trends in Indonesia, The Relevance of Growth Models for Less Developed Economies, The Role of Research in a University, Public Policies, Land Tenure and Population Movements, Population Problems and Indonesia's Economic Development.*
Ministry for Economic, Financial and Industrial Affairs, Jakarta, Indonesia.

Niwano, Nikkyō; Japanese religious leader; b. 15 Nov. 1906, Niigata Pref.; ed. Oike Primary School, Suganuma.
President Rissho Kosei-kai (org. of Buddhist laymen with 5.4 million mems.) 38-; Chair. Union of the New Religious Orgs. in Japan (UNROJ) 65-, Japanese Cttee. for World Conf. on Religion and Peace 72-; Pres. Int. Asscn. for Religious Freedom 78-81; Pres. Niwano Peace Foundation Conf. on Religion and Peace 72-; Vice-Pres. Int. Asscn. for Religious Freedom 78-; Pres. Niwano Peace Foundation 78-; Chair. Asian Conf. on Religion and Peace 79-; Hon. Pres. World Conf. on Religion and Peace 79-; Trustee Japan Religions League 67-; Hon. LL.D. (Meadville/Lombard Theol. School); Imperial Household Agency Medal of Honour with Dark Navy Blue Ribbon 58, Templeton Foundation Prize for Progress in Religion 79.
Publs. in English: *Buddhism for Today: a Modern Interpretation of the Threefold Lotus Sutra* 76, *A Buddhist Approach to Peace* 77, *Lifetime Beginner* (autobiog.) 78; in Japanese: *Buddhism for Today* (5 vols.) 59-60, *A New Interpretation of the Threefold Lotus Sutra* (10 vols.) 64-68, *A Guide to the Threefold Lotus Sutra* 75.
Rissho Kosei-kai, 2-11 Wada 1-chome, Suginami-ku, Tokyo 166, Japan.
Telephone: (03) 383-1111.

Nixon, Peter James; Australian politician and farmer; b. 22 March 1928, Orbost, Victoria; ed. Wesley Coll. Melbourne.
Member, House of Representatives 61-; mem. Joint Cttee. Public Accounts 64; mem. Joint Cttee. Foreign Affairs 67; Minister for the Interior 67-71, for Shipping and Transport 71-72, for Transport 75-79; Postmaster Gen. Nov.-Dec. 75; Minister for Primary Industry Sept. 79-; Nat. Country Party.
Parliament House, Canberra, A.C.T. 2600, Australia.
Telephone: Canberra 726661.

Nolan, Sir Sidney Robert, Kt., C.B.E.; Australian artist; b. 22 April 1917; ed. Melbourne State and Technical schools, Melbourne Nat. Gallery.
One-Man Shows Paris, London, New York, Rome, Venice,

Zurich and capital cities of Australia; Arts Council Travelling Exhbns., Great Britain; also exhibited at Pittsburgh Int. Exhbn. 53, 54, 55, 64, 67, 71, New Delhi Int. Exhbn. 53, Pacific Loan Exhbn. Australia and U.S.A. 56, Brussels Int. Exhbn. 58, Documenta II, Kassel 59, Dunn Int. Exhbn. London 63, Edinburgh Festival 64, Retrospective Exhbn. 1937-67 Sydney, Melbourne 67, Perth 68, Aldeburgh Festival 64, 68, 71, Beijing 75; retrospective exhbn. Darmstadt 71, Dublin 73, Stockholm 76; set designs for *Icare*, Sydney 49, *The Guide*, Oxford 61, the *Rite of Spring*, Covent Garden 62, *The Display*, Adelaide Festival 64, Canberra 65, *Samson and Delilah*, Covent Garden 81; Commr. for Australia and del. for Australian documentary films, Venice Biennale 54; Italian Govt. Scholarship 56; Commonwealth Fund Fellowship for travel in U.S.A. 59-61; Nat. Univ., Canberra Fellowship 65; made a number of films including *Toehold in History* 65, *Kelly Country, The Paintings of Sidney Nolan* 70; Fellow Bavarian Acad. 71; Hon. Fellow York Univ. 71; Hon. LL.D. (Australian Nat. Univ., Canberra) 71; Hon. D.Litt. (London) 74.
Principal works in Tate Gallery (London), Museum of Modern Art (New York), Nat. Galleries of Australia, Tom Collins Memorial (Perth Univ.), Contemporary Art Soc. and Arts Council of Great Britain (London), Power Bequest, Sydney Univ.
Publs. *Ned Kelly* 63, *Sidney Nolan: Myth and Imagery* 67, *Open Negative* 67, *Paradise Gardens* 71; (illustrated) *Hear the Ocean* (Robert Lowell) 68, *Children's Crusade* (Bertolt Brecht, Benjamin Britten) 73.

Noma, Shoichi, B.A.; Japanese publisher; b. 9 April 1911, Shizuoka; ed. Univ. of Tokyo.
South Manchuria Railway Co. 34-41; Dir. Kodansha Ltd. 41-48, Pres. 49-81, Hon. Chair. 81-; Man. Dir. Noma Hokokai 48-81; Chair. King Records 61-; Dir. Toppan Printing Co. Ltd. 64-; Controller Asahi Nat. Broadcasting Co. Ltd. 68-79; Dir. Tokyo Broadcasting Co. 75-; Man. Dir. Japan Magazine Publishers' Asscn. 56-68; Pres. Japan Book Publishers' Asscn. 60-; Pres. Publishers' Asscn. for Cultural Exchange 61-, Editological Soc. of Japan 67-73 (Hon. Chair. 74), Magazine Advertising Asscn. of Japan 67-; mem. Japanese Nat. Cttee. for UNESCO 67-77; Adviser, Japan Cultural Asscn. with Foreign Countries 68-; mem. Int. Cttee. of Int. Publishers' Asscn. (IPA) 68, Exec. Cttee. of IPA 70, Vice-Pres. IPA 72-76; Dir.-Gen. Tokyo Book Devt. Centre 71-72; Vice-Pres. Asian Cultural Centre for UNESCO 73-; Printers' Cultural Prize, Japan Printers' Asscn. 67; Int. Book Award of Int. Book Cttee. 74; Dr. h.c. (Moscow) 76.
c/o Kodansha Ltd., 2-12-21 Otowa, Bunkyo-ku, Tokyo 112; Home: 2-11-30 Sekiguchi, Bunkyo-ku, Tokyo 112, Japan.
Telephone: 03-945-1111 (Office); 03-941-0880 (Home).

Norodom Sihanouk, Prince Samdech Preah; fmr. Head of State of Cambodia (now Kampuchea); b. 31 Oct. 1922; ed. in Saigon (now Ho Chi Minh City) and Saumur, France (mil. training).
Elected King April 41; abdicated March 55; founder-Pres. Popular Socialist Community 55-70; Prime Minister and Minister of Foreign Affairs Oct. 55, March 56, Sept. 56, April 57; Perm. Rep. to UN Feb.-Sept. 56; elected Head of State after death of his father 60, deposed March 70; lived in Beijing 70-75; founded Royal Govt. of Nat. Union of Cambodia (GRUNC) May 70; restored as Head of State when GRUNC forces overthrew Khmer Republic April 75, resgnd. April 76; Special Envoy of Khmer Rouge to UN; mem. People's Rep. Assembly 76-79; left country 79; f. Nat. United Front for an Independent, Neutral, Peaceful, Co-operative Kampuchea 81; Pres. Coalition Govt. of Democratic Kampuchea, Thailand June 82-; journalist, musician, producer of film *Le Petit Prince*.
Publs. *L'Indochine vu de Pékin* (with Jean Lacouture) 72, *My War with the C.I.A.* (with Wilfred Burchett) 73, *War and Hope: The Case for Cambodia* 80, *Bitter-Sweet Memories* (autobiog.) 81, *Souvenirs doux étamers* 81.
Bangkok, Thailand.

Nosaka, Sanzo; Japanese politician; b. 1892, Hagi, Yamaguchi Pref.; ed. Keio Univ.
Secretary Brotherhood Asscn. (later called Japanese Fed. of Labour) 17-25; joined CP of Great Britain, expelled from U.K., visited U.S.S.R. via France and Germany 19-20; mem. Japanese Communist Party 22; Dir. Industry Labour Research Inst. 24-31; imprisoned 23, 26, 28-30; mem. Cen. Cttee. Japanese Communist Party 31; exiled to U.S.S.R. 31; mem. Presidium Exec. Cttee. Communist Int. 35-43; directed Japanese Communist Party from U.S.A. 34-35, 36-38; anti-war activities in Yenan (China) 40-45; returned to Japan and elected mem. Cen. Cttee. and Politburo Japanese Communist Party 46; mem. House of Reps. and Chair. Communist Group in Diet 46-50; underground activity after being banned from political activity 50-55; Chair. Cen. Cttee. Japanese Communist Party 58-; mem. House of Councillors 56-77.
Publs. *Selected Works*, 2 vols., *My Stormy Path* (autobiography, 6 vols. not yet concluded).
26, 4-chome, Sendagaya, Shibuya-ku, Tokyo, Japan.
Telephone: 03-403-6111.

Nu, U (formerly **Thakin Nu**), B.A.; Burmese politician and writer; b. 1907; ed. Rangoon Univ.
For some years headmaster Nat. High School, Pantanaw; joined Dobhama Asiayone (Our Burma) Organization; detained by British 40, released after Japanese occupation 43, worked for Dobhama Asiayone; Minister of Foreign Affairs 43-44; Minister for Publicity and Propaganda 44-45; Vice-Pres. Anti-Fascist People's Freedom League (AFPFL) after Allied re-occupation; elected Speaker Constituent Assembly 47; Deputy Chair. Gov.'s Exec. Council 47; signatory Anglo-Burmese Treaty, London; Prime Minister 48-56, 57-58, worked on AFPFL re-organization 56-57; Prime Minister, Minister of Home Affairs, Relief and Resettlement, Democratization of Local Administration, Information, Transport, Posts and Telegraphs, Shipping and Aviation, Housing and Rehabilitation 60-62 (deposed by military coup); in custody 62-Oct. 66; left Burma to organize opposition 69; in Thailand 69-70; returned to Burma to lead revolutionary movement against Gen. Ne Win Oct. 70; in exile 11 years; returned to Burma after general amnesty July 80; State Medal 1st Class (Burma) 81.
Publs. Plays and stories.

Nur Khan, Air Marshal M.; Pakistani airline executive; b. 1923, Tamman; ed. Col. Brown's Cambridge School and Prince of Wales Royal Indian Mil. Coll.
Commissioned Royal Indian Air Force 41; Man. Dir. Pakistan Int. Airlines (PIA) 59-65; C.-in-C. Pakistan Air Force 65-68; Gov. W. Pakistan 69; Chair. PIA 73-79; Head PIA Investments Ltd. 81-; Pres. Pakistan Hockey Federation 67-69, 77-; Hilal-e-Jurat 65.
c/o Pakistan International Airlines Corporation, PIA Building, Karachi Airport, Pakistan.
Telephone: 412011-96, Ext. 2666.

Nurjadin, Air Chief Marshal Roesmin; Indonesian diplomatist and politician; b. 31 May 1930, Malang; ed. Gajah Mada Univ., R.A.F. Flight Instructor School, England, D.C. Staff Coll., Wellington, India.
Squadron Commdr. 53-62; Deputy C.-in-C. Operational Command, later C.-in-C. Air Defence Command 62-64; Air Attaché, Bangkok and Moscow 64-65; Minister, C.-in-C., Chief of Staff, Air Force 66-70; Amb. to U.K. 70-74, to U.S.A. 74-77; Minister of Transport, Communications and Tourism 78-; various mil. and foreign decorations.
Ministry of Communications, Jakarta, Indonesia.

O

Ochiai, Eiichi, B.SC.; Japanese trade unionist; b. 15 Jan. 1916; ed. Yokohama Nat. Univ.
Mitsui Metal Mine Co. Ltd. 36-41, Toshiba Electric Co. 43-46; Adviser, Japan Asscn. of Science and Technology 44-47; Pres. All-Japan Electric Industry Workers Unions 46-48; mem. Exec. Board Congress of Industrial Labour Union 46-49; Gen. Sec. Nat. Fed. of Industrial Orgs. 49-64; mem. Labour Problems Cttee. 61-64, Small and Medium Enterprise Retirement Countermeasure Cttee. 60-64; Dir. Tokyo Office, Int. Confederation of Free Trade Unions (ICFTU) and Special Rep. in Japan 64-77; Trustee, Japan ILO Asscn. 62-.
Publs. *Import of Foreign Capital and Production Struggle* 49, *Directory of Trade Union Administration* 49, *Earth of North America and Blood of Great Britain* 59.
38-302 Keyakidai, 4-chome, Nishimachi, Kokubunji-Shi, Tokyo, Japan (Home).
Telephone: 36-8306 (Home).

O'Connor, Raymond James, M.L.A.; Australian politician; b. 6 March 1926, Perth; ed. York, Narrogin and Perth.
Joined the army 43; served Bougainville and New Britain; discharged 46; in motor trade; mem. Western Australia Legis. Assembly 59-; Hon. Minister assisting Minister for Railways and Transport 65, later Minister for Transport (cabinet post); Minister for Transport and Railways 67-71; Minister for Transport, Traffic and Police 74, subsequently of Works, Water Supplies and Housing; Minister of Labour and Industry, Consumer Affairs, Immigration, Fisheries and Wildlife and Conservation and the Environment 78; Deputy Leader Parl. Liberal Party 80; Deputy Premier 80-82; Premier of Western Australia Jan. 82-; also Treas. and Minister Co-ordinating Econ. and Regional Devt.
Premier's Department, 32 St. George's Terrace, Perth, Western Australia 6000, Australia.
Telephone: Perth 32-3749.

Oda, Shigeru, LL.D., J.S.D.; Japanese lawyer; b. 22 Oct. 1924; ed. Univ. of Tokyo, Yale Univ.
Research Fellow, Univ. of Tokyo 47-49; lecturer, Univ. of Tôhoku 50-53, Asst. Prof. 53-59, Prof. 59-76; Tech. Adviser, Atomic Energy Comm. 61-64; Special Asst. to Minister of Foreign Affairs 73-76; mem. Science Council of Ministry of Educ. 69-76, of Council for Ocean Devt. in Prime Minister's Office 71-76, Advisory Cttee. for Co-operation with UN Univ. 71-76; Judge, Int. Court of Justice Feb. 76-; del. to UN Confs. on Law of the Sea 58, 60, 73-75; Rep. at 6th Gen. Conf. of Inter-Governmental Oceanographic Comm. 69; consultative positions with bodies concerned with marine questions; Counsel for Fed. Repub. of Germany before Int. Court of Justice 68; Editor-in-Chief, *Japanese Annual of International Law* 73-; Assoc. Inst. de Droit Int. 69, mem. 79; Hon. mem. American Soc. of Int. Law 75; Hon. D.Jur. (Bhopal Univ.) 80, (New York Law School) 81.
Publs. in Japanese: *International Law of the Sea* 56-69, *International Law and Marine Resources* 71-75; in English: *International Control of Sea Resources* 62, *The International Law of Ocean Development* 72-77, *The Law of the Sea in Our Time* 77, *International Law of the Resources of the Sea* 79, *The Practice of Japan in International Law:* 1961-70; various articles.
International Court of Justice, Peace Palace, The Hague 2517 KJ, The Netherlands (Office); 11-1002 Kawauchi-jutaku, Kawauchi, Sendai 980, Japan (Home).
Telephone: 070-92.44.41 (Office); 0222-64.30.68 (Home.)

Oë, Kenzaburo; Japanese author; b. 1935.
First stories published 57; Akutagawa prize for novella *The Catch* 58; first full-length novel *Pluck The Flowers, Gun The Kids* 58; represented young Japanese writers at Beijing 60; travelled to Russia and Western Europe writing a series of essays on Youth in the West 61; Shinchosha Literary Prize 64; Tanizaki Prize 67.
Publs. *The Catch* 58, *Pluck The Flowers, Gun The Kids* 58, *Our Age* 59, *Screams* 62, *The Perverts* 63, *Hiroshima Notes* 63, *Adventures in Daily Life* 64, *A Personal Matter* 64, (English 69), *Football in The First Year of Mannen* 67.
585 Seijo-machi, Setagaya-Ku, Tokyo, Japan.
Telephone: 482-7192.

Oemar-Senoadji; Indonesian lawyer and politician; b. 5 Dec. 1915; Surukarta, Central Java; ed. Rechts Hoge School, Gajah Mada Univ., Yogyakarta.
Worked for Ministry of Justice 45-50; Judge, Yogyakarta Regional Court 50; Chief Public Prosecutor, Regional Court of Justice, Semarang 50-53; Public Prosecutor, Jakarta 53-55; Head, Investigation Section, Attorney-Gen.'s Office 55-59; Deputy Attorney-Gen. of Supreme Court 59-60; Prof. Faculty of Law and Social Sciences, Univ. of Indonesia 60-, Dean 66; Minister of Justice 66-74; Chair., Supreme Court 74-; mem. working cttee.
Inst. for Devt. of Nat. Law 62; various awards.
Supreme Court of Indonesia, Jakarta, Indonesia.

Ogawa, Heiji; Japanese politician; b. 1910, Nagano Prefecture.
Elected 10 times to House of Reps. 52-; fmr. Deputy Cabinet Sec.; Minister of Labour 67-68; Vice-Chair. Policy Affairs Research Council of Liberal-Democratic Party (LDP), also Chair. LDP Research Comm. on the Tax System; assoc. of late Masayoshi Ohira; Minister of Home Affairs, Chair. Nat. Public Safety Comm., Dir.-Gen. of Hokkaido Devt. Agency 76-77; Minister of Educ. Nov. 81-.
c/o Liberal-Democratic Party, 7, 2-chome, Hirakawacho, Chiyoda-ku, Tokyo, Japan.

Ogawa, Heishiro, B.A.; Japanese diplomatist; b. 17 March 1916; ed. Tokyo Univ. Law Dept.
Joined Ministry of Foreign Affairs 38; Consul, Hong Kong 52; Chief, China Div., Ministry of Foreign Affairs 54-57; Counsellor, Japanese Embassy, Washington 57-60; Consul-Gen., Hong Kong 60-63; Dir.-Gen. Asian Affairs Bureau 66-68; Amb. to Denmark 68-72; Pres. Foreign Service Inst. 72-73; Amb. to People's Republic of China 73-77; Fellow Woodrow Wilson Center, Washington, D.C. 77-78; Adviser Sumitomo Corpn., Tokyo 78-; Vice-Pres. Japan China Asscn. 80-.
Publs. *Four Years in Peking, China Revisited.*
Sumitomo Corpn., 1-2-2, Hitotsubashi, Chiyoda-ku, Tokyo, Japan.

Ogawa, Masaru, M.A.; Japanese journalist; b. 22 March 1915; ed. Univ. of California at Los Angeles, Tokyo Imperial and Columbia Univs.
Domei News Agency 41-46; Kyodo News Service 46-48; *The Japan Times* 48-, Chief, political section 49, Asst. Man. Editor 50, Chief Writer 52, Man. Editor 58-64, Dir. 59-, Exec. Editor 64-68, Senior Editor 68-71, Chief Editorial Writer 69-71, Editor 71-77, Adviser 77-; mem. Yoshida Int. Educ. Foundation 68-, Exec. Dir. 72-; mem, Japan Broadcasting Corpn. Overseas Programme Consultative Council 74-, Editorial Board *Media* Magazine. Hong Kong 74; Chair. Bd. *Asia-Pacific* Magazine, Manila 81-; Dir. American Studies Foundation 80-, Yoshida Shigeru Memorial Foundation 80-; Exec. Dir. America-Japan Soc. 81-; Life Mem. Foreign Corresp. Club of Japan 73-; Pres. Pacific News Agency 73-; Lecturer, Tokyo Univ. 54-58; Hon. D.Litt. (Lewis and Clark Coll., Portland, Oregon) 79.
2, 14-banchi, 5-chome, Mejiro, Toshima-ku, Tokyo, Japan.
Telephone: 952-8822.

Ogura, Takekazu; Japanese agriculturalist; b. 2 Oct. 1910, Fukui Prefecture; ed. Tokyo Imperial Univ.
Posts with Ministry of Agriculture and Forestry 34-56; Lecturer, Faculty of Agriculture, Univ. of Tokyo 47-61;

Dir.-Gen. Food Agency 56-58; Vice-Minister of Agriculture and Forestry 60-61; Chair. Agriculture, Forestry and Fisheries Research Council 63-75; Commr. Tax Comm., Prime Minister's Office 63-69, Chair. 69-71, 74-; Dir. Research Inst. of Mechanization of Agric. 65-77; Pres. Inst. of Developing Economies 67-72, Chair. 72-75, Chair. Agric. Policy Research Center 67-; Chair. Advisory Council to Prime Minister on Tax 74-; Chair. Japan FAO Asscn. 75-80; mem. Policy Board of Bank of Japan 75-.
Publs. *Agricultural Policy of Japan* 65 (in Japanese), *Agricultural Development in Modern Japan* 66, *Agrarian Problems and Agricultural Policy in Japan* 67 (in English), *The Food Problem and Agricultural Structure in Japan* 77 (in English), *Can Japanese Agriculture Survive?* 79 (in English); articles in English and Japanese.
The Bank of Japan, 2-1 Nihonbashi-Hongoku-cho 2-chome, Chuo-ku, Tokyo 103; Home: 3-1-1006 Otsuka 2-chome, Bunkyo-ku, Tokyo 112, Japan.
Telephone: Tokyo 945-1805 (Home).

Ohara, Eiichi; Japanese business executive; b. 2 Dec. 1912, Hiroshima; ed. Tokyo Univ.
With the Industrial Bank of Japan 36-63; Exec. Vice-Pres. Fuji Heavy Industries Ltd. 63-70, Pres. 70-78, Chair. 78-; Chair. Fuji Robin Industries Ltd.; Pres. Transport Machine Industries Ltd.; mem. Japan Fed. of Econ. Orgs., Aircraft Industry Council; Dir. Japan Automobile Mfrs. Asscn.; Trustee, Japan Cttee. for Econ. Devt.
Fuji Heavy Industries Ltd., Subaru Buildings, 7, 1-chome, Nishishinjuku, Shinjuku-ku, Tokyo, Japan.

Ohtani, Ichiji; Japanese textile executive; b. 31 Aug. 1912, Kobe; ed. Kobe Univ.
Director Toyobo Co. Ltd. 64-68, Man. Dir. 68-72, Senior Man. Dir. 72-74, Deputy Pres. 74, Pres. 74-78, Chair. 78-; Dir. Toyobo Petcord Co. Ltd. 69-; Vice-Pres. Industrias Unidas, S.A. 73-; Chair. Japan Spinners' Asscn. 76-79, Adviser 79-; Vice-Pres. International Textile Mfrs. Fed. 78-80, Pres. 80-; Exec. Dir. Japan Fed. of Econ. Orgs. 76-; Chair. Diafibres Co. 77-; Blue Ribbon Medal 79.
Toyobo Co. Ltd., 2-8 Dojima Hama 2-chome, Kita-ku, Osaka 530; Home: 7-18 Yamate-cho, Ashiya-shi 659, Japan.
Telephone: (06) 348-3251 (Office); (0797) 32-2107 (Home).

Okauchi, Hideo; Japanese business executive; b. 19 Nov. 1908, Ayauta-gun, Kagawa-ken; ed. Takamatsu Commercial High School (now Kagawa Univ.).
Joined Shiseido Co. Ltd. 29, Dir. 47, Man. Dir. 60, Senior Man. Dir. 66, Pres. 67-75, Chair. 75-78; Dir. Fed. of Econ. Orgs. 67-75, Chair. 75-; Exec. Counsellor, Tokyo Chamber of Commerce and Industry 67-; Rep. Dir. Tokyo Cosmetic Industry Asscn. 72-, Cosmetic Fair Trade Council 72-; Dir. Japan Cosmetic Industry Asscn. 72-, Japan Cosmetic Asscn. 71-, Japan Man. Asscn. 67-.
5-16-7 Nishikoiwa, Edogawa-ku, Tokyo, Japan.
Telephone: 657-0958 (Home).

Okawara, Yoshio, LL.B.; Japanese diplomatist; b. 5 Feb. 1919, Gunma; ed. Tokyo Univ.
First Sec., Washington, D.C. 62, Counsellor 63-65; Dir. Personnel Div., Ministry of Foreign Affairs 65-67, Deputy Dir.-Gen. of American Affairs Bureau 67-71, Dir.-Gen. 72-74; Minister, Washington, D.C. 71-72; Deputy Vice-Minister for Admin., Ministry of Foreign Affairs 74-76; Amb. to Australia (also accred. to Nauru) 76-80, to U.S.A. 80-; Fellow, Center for Int. Affairs, Harvard Univ. 62.
Embassy of Japan, 2520 Massachusetts Avenue, N.W., Washington, D.C. 20008, U.S.A.

Okita, Saburo; Japanese economist; b. 3 Nov. 1914, Dairen; ed. Engineering Faculty, Tokyo Univ.
Served in Ministry of Posts 37-39, Ministry of Greater East Asia 39-45, Ministry of Foreign Affairs 45-47, Econ. Stablization Board, Chief Research Div. 47; UN Econ. Comm. for Asia and the Far East 52; Chief, Econ. Co-op. Unit Econ. Planning Agency 53, Dir.-Gen. Planning Bureau 57, Devt. Bureau 62-63; Pres. Japan Econ. Research Center 63-73, Chair. of the Board 73-79; Pres. Overseas Econ. Co-operation Fund 73-77; Special Adviser, Int. Devt. Centre of Japan 73-79; Minister for Foreign Affairs Nov. 79-July 80; Govt. Rep. for External Econ. Relations 80-81; Chair. Inst for Domestic and Int Policy Studies 81-; Pres. Int Univ. of Japan April 82-; mem. UN Devt. Planning Cttee. 66-80; mem. Pearson Comm. on Int. Devt. of World Bank 69; mem. OECD High Level Expert Group on Science Policy for the 1970s 70-71; mem. Board of Govs. of NHK (Japan Broadcasting Corpn). 75-77; Chair. Japan India Study Cttee. 75-77, Japan Australia Study Cttee. 76-; Ramon Magsaysay Award for Int. Understanding 71; Hon. D.Econ. (Ministry of Educ.) 67, Hon. LL.D. (Univ. of Mich.) 77, (ANU).
Publs. *The Future of Japan's Economy* 60, *Japan's Post-War Economic Policy* 61, *Economic Planning* 62, *Japanese Economy in the Asian Setting* 66, *Role of the Economist* 73, *The position of Japan, a Country of Poor Resources, in the World Economy* 75, *Japan and the World Economy* (English) 76, *Autobiography* 77, *Economic Strategy for Vulnerability* 78, *The Developing Economies and Japan* (English) 80, *252 Days of an Economist Foreign Minister* 80, *Hurried Missions in Various Directions* (autobiog.) 81.
5-13-12 Koishikawa, Bunkyo-ku, Tokyo, Japan.
Telephone: 03-811-0742.

Okuk, Iambakey Palma; Papua New Guinean politician, b. 1943, Pari, Chimbu Prov.; ed. Nat. High School; Sogeri.
Member Papua New Guinea Nat. Parl. 72-; Minister for Agric. 72-73, for Transport 73-75, for Educ. 75; Leader of the Opposition 78-80; Deputy Prime Minister and Minister for Transport and Civil Aviation 80-82.
c/o Office of the Deputy Prime Minister, Post Office, Wards Strip, Waigani, Papua New Guinea.

Okuno, Seisuke; Japanese politician; b. 12 July 1913, Nara Pref.; ed. First High School, Univ. of Yokyo.
Chief, Gen. Affairs Section, Yamanashi Pref. Govt. and Kagoshima Pref. Govt. 38; Officer Dept. of Local Govt., Ministry of Home Affairs 43; Head of Police Dept., Kochi Pref. Govt. 47; Head, Finance and Research Divs., Local Autonomy Agency 49; Dir. Bureau of Taxation, Ministry of Autonomy 53, Bureau of Finance 58; Perm. Vice-Minister, Ministry of Autonomy 63; mem. House of Reps. 63-; Minister of Educ. 72-74; Minister of Justice 80-81; Liberal-Democratic Party.
c/o Office of the Deputy Prime Minister, Post Office, Wards 5-7-10 Jingumae, Shibuya-ku, Tokyo, Japan.
Telephone: 03-407-3535 (Home).

Omar Ali Saifuddin, Sa'adul Khairi Waddin, H. H. Sultan, D.K., P.S.P.N.B., P.S.N.B., S.P.M.B., D.M.N., D.K. (Kelantan), D.K. (Johore), D.K. (Selangor), K.C.M.G.; former ruler of Brunei; b. 1916; ed. Malay Coll., Kuala Kangsar, Perak, Malaya.
Served as a Govt. official in various depts. in Brunei; Grand Vizier (First Minister), mem. State Council 57-60; Sultan of Brunei 50-67; abdicated Oct. 67; visited U.K. and Europe 52, 53, 57, 59, 63, U.K. and America 65, U.K. 68; pilgrimage to Mecca 53 and 62, travelled round the world 65.
Istana Darul Hana, Brunei.

Omura, Joji; Japanese politician; b. 30 March 1919, Okayama Pref.; ed. Tokyo Univ.
Member House of Reps. 67-; Parl. Vice-Minister of Finance 72-73; Deputy Chief Cabinet Sec. 73; Vice-Chair. Liberal-Democratic Party (LDP) Policy Affairs Research Council 76, Chair. Standing Cttee. on Finance 78, LDP Deputy Sec.-Gen. 80; Minister of State and Dir.-Gen. Defence Agency 80-81.

Publs. *Chiho Jichi to Yosan* (*Local Government and Budget*), *Kokoro no Kane* (collection of poems).
c/o Liberal-Democratic Party, 7, 2-chome, Hirakawacho, Chiyoda-ku, Tokyo, Japan.

Ong, Tan Sri Haji Omar Yoke-Lin, P.M.N.; Malaysian politician, diplomatist, banker, industrialist and company director; b. 23 July 1917, Kuala Lumpur.
Member Kuala Lumpur Municipal Council 52-; co-founder Alliance Party; mem. Fed. Legislative Council 54-; Malayan Minister of Posts and Telecommunications 55-56, of Transport 56-57, of Labour and Social Welfare 57-59, of Health and Social Welfare 59-64; M.P. 59-62; Vice-Pres. Commonwealth Parl. Asscn. 61; Amb. to U.S.A. and UN 62-64; Amb. to U.S.A. 64-72; Minister without Portfolio, Malaysia 64-73; Pres. of Senate 73-80; Chair. Asian Int. Merchant Bankers Bhd., Maju Jaya Industries Sdn. Bhd., Omariff Holdings Sdn. Bhd., Syarikat Ong Yoke-Lin Sdn. Bhd., OYL Industries Sdn. Bhd., Raza Sdn. Bhd., Malaysian Oxygen Bhd. and other cos.; Dir. Esso Malaysia Berhad, Hume Industries (Malaysia) Berhad, Malayan Flour Mills, Unite Chemical Industries, Socoil Corpn.; Chair. Malaysian Red Cross Soc. 59-62; Hon. Order of the Crown of Selangor, First and Second Class, Most Illustrious Order of Kinabalu, First Class.
Parliament House, Kuala Lumpur (Office); 44 Pesiaran Duta, Kuala Lumpur, Malaysia (Home).

Onn, Datuk Hussein bin (*see* Hussein bin Onn, Datuk).

Ooka, Shohei; Japanese writer; b. 1909; ed. Univ. of Kyoto.
Translator of French literature, especially Stendhal; soldier and prisoner of war in the Philippines 44-45; novelist and critic 48-; Teacher at Meiji Univ. 52-55; visited U.S.A., England and France as Creative Fellow, Rockefeller Foundation 53-54; Yokomitsu Prize 49, Yomiuru Prize 52, Mainichi Shincho Prize 61, Mainichi Geijitsu Prize 72, Noma Prize 74, Asahi Prize 76, Mystery Writers' Union Prize 78.
Publs. Translated Alain's *Stendhal* 40, Stendhal's *Chartreuse de Parme* 49, etc.; novels: *Furyoki* (Memories of a Prisoner of War) 49, *Musashino Fujin* (A Woman of Musashino Plain) 50, *Nobi* (Fires of the Plain) 51, *Sanso* (Oxygen) 53, *Hamlet Nikki* (Diary of Hamlet) 55, *Kaei* (Under the Shadow of Cherry-blossom) 61, *Reite Senki* (Battle on Leyte) 71 *Nakahara Chuya* (biography) 74, *Shonen* (A Boy) 75, *Jiken* (A Trial) 77, *Nagai Tabi* (A Long Journey) 82.
7-15-12 Seijo, Setagaya-ku, Tokyo, Japan.

Ople, Blas F.; Philippine politician; b. 3 Feb. 1927, Hagonoy, Bulacan; ed. Philippine public and private schools, Far Eastern Univ. and Manuel L. Quezon Univ., Manila.
Copy editor and columnist *The Daily Mirror*, Manila 50-53; Asst. to Pres. Ramon Magsaysay on labour and agrarian affairs 54-57; writer and labour leader 58-64; Head, Propaganda Div., Ferdinand E. Marcos' presidential campaign 65; Special Asst. to Pres. Marcos (*q.v.*) and Commr., Social Security System 66; Sec. of Labour 67-78, Minister 78-; Chair. Nat. Manpower and Youth Council, 67-71; mem. Board of Trustees, Land Bank 68-; Chair. Govt. Group, Int. Labour Conf. 69-, Pres. 75-76; Chair. Asian Labour Ministers' Conf. 67; various govt. and civic awards.
61 Visayas Avenue, Project 6, Quezon City, Philippines.
Telephone: 99-67-56; 98-20-56.

Oshima, Nagisa; Japanese film director; b. 1932, Kyoto; ed. Kyoto Univ.
With Shochiku Co. 54-59; formed own film company 61; has also directed television films.
Films: *Ai To Kibo No Machi* (A Town of Love and Hope) 59, *Seishun Zankoku Monogatari* (Cruel Story of Youth) 60, *Taiyo No Hakaba* (The Sun's Burial) 60, *Nihon No Yoru To Kiri* (Night and Fog in Japan) 60, *Shiiku* (The Catch) 61, *Amakusa Shiro Tokisada* (The Rebel) 62, *Etsuraku* (The Pleasures of the Flesh) 65, *Yunbogi No Nikki* (The Diary of Yunbogi) 65, *Hakuchu No Torima* (Violence at Noon) 66, *Ninja Bugeicho* (Band of Ninja) 67, *Nihon Shunka-ko* (A Treatise on Japanese Bawdy Songs) 67, *Muri Shinju Nihon No Natsu* (Japanese Summer: Double Suicide) 67, *Koshikei* (Death By Hanging) 68, *Kaettekita Yopparai* (Three Resurrected Drunkards) 68, *Shinjuku Dorobo Nikki* (Diary of a Shinjuku Thief) 68, *Shonen* (Boy) 69, *Tokyo Senso Sengo Hiwa* (He Died after the War) 70, *Gishiki* (The Ceremony) 71, *Natsu No Imooto* (Dear Summer Sister) 72, *Ai no Corrida* (In the Realm of the Senses) 76, *Ai no Borei* (Empire of Passion) 78.
Oshima Productions, 2-15-7 Akasaka, Minato-ku, Tokyo, Japan.

Osmany, Gen. Muhammad Ataul Ghani, M.A.; Bangladesh politician and retired soldier; b. 1 Sept. 1918, Sunamganj; ed. Aligarh Muslim Univ., Indian Mil. Acad., Dehra Dun and Staff Coll. Quetta.
Lieutenant, British Indian Army 40, rank of Lt.-Col. 47; active service Burma 42-45; various commands in Punjab and E. Bengal Regts. 47-55; Dir. Mil. Operations and mem. Pakistan Air Defence Cttee. 56-66; attained rank of Brig. 57; Defence Rep. Pakistan Cttee. reviewing participation in Pacts 61; Pres. Pakistan Army Sports Control Board 65-66; retired from army 67; mem. Awami League 70-75; elected to Pakistan Nat. Assembly 70; recalled to mil. duty 71, Gen. and C.-in-C. Bangladesh Armed Forces 71-72; mem. Bangladesh Parl. 72-75; Minister of Shipping, Inland Water Transport and Aviation 72-74, also of Posts and Telecommunications 73; resgnd. from Cabinet 74, Parl. Jan. 75; Defence Adviser to Pres. Aug.-Nov. 75; formed Jatiyo Janata Party 76; Convenor 76-; seven-party opposition nominee, Presidential election 78; contested Presidential election 81; Pres. Bangladesh Wildlife Preservation Soc. 73-77.
c/o Jonota Bhaban, 47A Toynbee, Circular Road Dacca-3; Nur Manzil, Naiyorpool, Sylhet, Bangladesh.

Otani, Sachio, B.ARCH.; Japanese architect; b. 20 Feb. 1924; ed. Univ. of Tokyo.
Architectural designer under Dr. Kenzo Tange 46-60; Lecturer in Architecture, Univ. of Tokyo 55-64, Assoc. Prof. of Urban Engineering 64-73, Prof. 73-; works include Kojimachi area (of Tokyo) redevelopment plan 60-64, Tokyo children's cultural centre 61-63 and Kyoto Int. Conf. Hall 63-66.
Department of Urban Engineering, Faculty of Engineering, University of Tokyo, 1-3-7 Hongo, Bunkyo-ku, Tokyo; Home: 15-22-3 Shoan, Suginami-ku, Tokyo, Japan.
Telephone: 333-6708.

Othman bin Wok; Singapore politician and diplomatist; b. 8 Oct. 1924; ed. Telok Saga Malay School, Raffles Inst. and London School of Journalism.
Worked on *Utusan Melayu* as reporter and Deputy Editor 46-63; mem. People's Action Party 54-; mem. Parl. for Pasir Panjang Constituency 63-81; Minister for Social Affairs 63-65; Minister for Culture and Social Affairs, 65-68; Minister of Social Affairs 68-77; Amb. to Indonesia (also accred to Papua New Guinea) 77-81; Chair. Multiplex Overseas Construction 81-; mem. Singapore Tourist Promotion Bd. 81-(83); Maj. in People's Defence Force.
Embassy of Singapore, Jalan Proklamasi 23, Jakarta, Indonesia.

Ozawa, Seiji; Japanese conductor; b. 1 Sept. 1935, Shenyang; ed. Toho School of Music, Tokyo (under Prof. Hideo Saito), Tanglewood, U.S.A. and in Berlin under Herbert von Karajan.
Early engagements with Radio Orchestra (N.H.K.) and

Japan Philharmonic; Asst. Conductor (under Leonard Bernstein), New York Philharmonic 61-62 (including tour of Japan 61); guest conductor, San Francisco Symphony, Detroit Symphony, Montreal, Minneapolis, Toronto and London Symphony Orchestras 61-65; Music Dir. Ravinia Festival, Chicago 64; Music Dir. Toronto Symphony Orchestra 65-70; toured Europe conducting many of the major orchestras 66-67; Salzburg Festival 69; Music Dir. San Francisco Symphony Orchestra 70-76; Music Dir. Boston Symphony 73-; now makes frequent guest appearances with most of the leading orchestras of America, Europe and Japan; First Prize, Int. Competition of Orchestra Conductors, France 59, Koussevitsky Memorial Scholarship 60; recordings for RCA, CBS, Polydor and EMI.
c/o Ronald A. Wilford (Columbia Artists Management Inc., Conductors Division), 165 West 57th Street, New York, N.Y. U.S.A.; c/o Harold Holt Ltd., 31 Sinclair Road, London, W.14, England.

P

Pachariyangkun, Upadit, D.ECON. ET POL.; Thai diplomatist; b. 10 Dec. 1920; ed. Univs. of Berlin and Berne.
Entered Foreign Service at Legation in Berlin 42; Chief of Div., UN Dept. 54; First Sec., Legation in Buenos Aires 57; Dir.-Gen. of Econ. Dept., Foreign Ministry 63; Amb. and Acting Perm. Rep. to UN 64; Amb. to Nigeria and concurrently to Ivory Coast and Liberia 66; Dir.-Gen. Econ. Dept., ASEAN Sec.-Gen. for Thailand, ASPAC Sec.-Gen. for Thailand 70; Amb. to Switzerland, Perm. Rep. to UN Office at Geneva and concurrently Amb. to Yugoslavia and Vatican City 72; Amb. to Fed. Repub. of Germany 73, to U.S.A. 76; Minister of Foreign Affairs 76-80; Paramabhorn (Special Grand Cordon), Order of the White Elephant; Knight Grand Order of Most Exalted Order of Crown of Thailand.
c/o Ministry of Foreign Affairs, Saranrom Palace, Bangkok; Home: 1097 Nakorn Chaisri Road, Amphur Dusit, Bangkok, Thailand.
Telephone: 585-9164 (Home).

Packer, Kerry Francis Bullmore; Australian business executive; b. 17 Dec. 1937, Sydney; ed. Cranbrook School, Geelong Church of England Grammar School.
Chairman and Man. Dir. Consolidated Press Holdings Ltd., Publishing and Broadcasting Ltd. 74; Chair. Australian Consolidated Press Ltd. 74-; promoted World Series Cricket Australia 78-79; came to agreement with Australian Cricket Bd. in organizing and televising Test series, Australia 79-80.
Australian Consolidated Press Ltd., 54 Park Street, Sydney, N.S.W. 2000, Australia.

Padamasankh, Padung, LL.B., M.A.; Thai diplomatist; b. 24 May 1923, Bangkok; ed. Thammasat Univ. and New York Univ.
Entered Foreign Service 46; attached to Protocol Div. 46-50; Chief Legal and Judicial Section, Gen. Affairs Div., UN Dept. 50; Attaché then Third Sec., Perm. Mission to UN 53-58; First Sec. Office of the Under Sec. of State 60, The Hague 61; Chief Social Div., Dept. of Int. Org. 66-71; Chief Personnel and Training Div., Office of Under Sec. of State 71; Counsellor and Chargé d'Affaires a.i., Belgrade 72; Amb. to Belgium concurrently Amb. and Perm. Rep. Australia 80-, concurrently to Fiji 81-; Prathamabhorn (Knight Grand Cross, Order of the White Elephant), Mahavajira (Knight Grand Cordon, Order of the Crown of Thailand), Grand Cross, Order of the Crown, Belgium, Officer, Order of Orange Nassau, Netherlands; Chakrabarti Mâlâ Medal.
Embassy of Thailand, 111 Empire Circuit, Yarralumla, A.C.T. 2600, Australia.

Pahang, H.R.H. the Sultan of; Sultan Haji Ahmad Shah Al-Mustain Billah ibni Al-Marhum Sultan Sir Abu Bakar Ri'ayatuddin Al-Mu'adzam Shah, D.K., S.P.C.M., S.P.M.J.; Malaysian ruler; b. Oct. 1930, Pekan; ed. Malay Coll., Clifford School, Worcester Coll., Oxford.
Secretariat, Kuala Lipis, mem. State Council and Chair. Council of Supporters until 55; married H.R.H. the Tengku Ampuan, then Tengku Hajjah Afzan binti Tengku Muhammad 54; Captain in Royal Malay Regt. 54, Commdr. then Lieut.-Col.; appointed Regent during his Father's absence 56, 59, 65; succeeded his late father as Ruler of Pahang 74; Timbalan Yang di-Pertuan Agong (Deputy Supreme Head of State of Malaysia) 75-79, elected 7th Yang di-Pertuan Agong (Supreme Head of State of Malaysia) April 79-(84).
Pekan Lama, Kuantan, Pahang, Malaysia.

Pai, Ei Whan, B.S., M.B.A.; Korean diplomatist and economist; b. 1907; ed. in Korea and business admin. colls. in U.S.A.
With Brokerage Co., U.S.A. 38-42; Department of Justice, U.S.A. 42; Far Eastern Div., Office of Censorship, Washington, D.C. 43; Far Eastern Div., Foreign Econ. Admin., Washington, D.C. 44; Financial Adviser to Mil. Govt. Coll., Virginia; Asst. Dir. Dept. of Finance, Mil. Govt., Korea 46-49, Pres. of Fed. of Financial Asscns., Korea, Financial Adviser to Nat. Econ. Board, Mil. Govt. Korea; Pres. of Korean Chamber of Commerce, Hawaii, and Pres. of Far Eastern Trading Co., Hawaii 50; Gov. of Bank of Korea 60; Amb. to Japan 61, to Argentina, Chile, Paraguay, Uruguay and Bolivia 65, to U.K. 67-71; Amb.-at-Large 71-73; Pres. Overseas Econ. Research Inst. 73-, Korean-British Soc.; mem. Pres. Council of Econ. and Scientific Advisers 73-; Conciliator of Int. Centre for Settlement of Investment Disputes 80-; Hon. Ph.D.
Overseas Economic Research Institute, C.P.O. Box 5864, Seoul, Republic of Korea.

Paik, General Sun Yup; Korean army officer and diplomatist; b. 1920; ed. Pyongyang Normal School and Mukden Mil. Acad., Manchuria.
Korean Constabulary 46-48; Repub. of Korea Army 48-60, Chief of Staff 52-54, 57-59, Gen. 53, Chair. Joint Chiefs of Staff 59-60; Amb. to Repub. of China 60-61, to France 61-65, to Canada 65-69; Minister of Transportation 69-70; Pres. Korea Gen. Chemical Corpn. 71-; decorations from Korea, France, U.S.A. and many other countries.
68 Kyunchi-dong, Chongro-ku, Seoul; Home: 258-97 Itaewon-dong, Yongsan-ku, Seoul, Republic of Korea.

Pal, Benjamin Peary, M.SC., PH.D., F.R.S : Indian agricultural scientist; b. 26 May 1906, Mukandpur, Punjab; ed. Rangoon and Cambridge Univs.
Second Econ. Botanist, Imperial Agricultural Research Inst., 33-37, Imperial Econ. Botanist 37-50; Head of Botany Div., Indian Agricultural Research Inst., then Dir. 50-65; Dir.-Gen. Indian Council of Agricultural Research 65-71, Scientist Emer. 72-; fmr. Pres. of Botany and Agriculture sections, Indian Science Congress, Dir.-Gen. 70-71; fmr. Chair. Special Advisory Cttee. on Food and Agriculture, Dept. of Atomic Energy; Chair. Nat. Cttee. on Environmental Planning and Co-ordination 77-; has served on govt. educ. comm., heading task force on agricultural educ.; Vice-Pres. All-India Fine Arts and Crafts Soc.; helped to establish Postgraduate School at Indian Agric. Research Inst.; research in wheat breeding and genetics; revision work on Int. Code of Nomenclature of Agricultural and Horticultural Plants; Fellow, Indian Nat. Science Acad., Pres. 75-76; Royal Nat. Rose Soc., Indian Botanical Soc., Royal Horticultural Soc. of London; foreign mem. All Union Lenin Acad. of Agricultural Sciences 67-; Hon. mem. Japan Acad., Acad. d'Agriculture de France; Awards include Padma Shri 58, Rafi Ahmed Kidwai Memorial Prize of the Indian Council of Agricultural Research 57, Birbal Sahni

Medal, Indian Botanical Soc. 62, Srinivasa Ramanujan Medal, Nat. Inst. of Sciences of India 64, Gold Medal, Rose Soc. of India 68; Padma Bhushan 68; Hon. D.Sc. (Punjab, Sardar Patel, Uttar Pradesh, Orissa and Haryana Univs.), Aryabhata Medal, Indian Nat. Science Acad. 80.
Publs. *Beautiful Climbers of India, Charophyta, The Rose in India, Wheat, Flowering Shrubs* 68, *Bougainvilleas* 74; over 160 scientific papers.
P-11 Hauz Khas Enclave, New Delhi 16, India.
Telephone: 660245.

Panchen Lama (Bainqen Erdini Qoigyu Gyaincain); Tibetan religious and political leader; b. 1938 in Qinghai, China.
Installed as Panchen Lama at Tashilumpo Monastery 44, not accepted in Xizang, installed as Panchen Lama in new ceremony at Kumbun Monastery, Qinghai 49; first visited Xizang 52, in charge of Shigatse sub-region; Vice-Chair. Chinese People's Political Consultative Council (CPPCC) 54-64; mem. Nat. People's Congress (NPC) 54-64, mem. Standing Cttee. 61-64; Vice-Chair. Preparatory Cttee. for Xizang Autonomous Region 56-59, Provisional Chair. after flight of Dalai Lama to India 59-65; Hon. Chair. Chinese Buddhist Asscn. 53-; mem. Sino-Soviet Friendship Asscn. 54; Chair. Tashilumpo Monastery Democratic Admin. Cttee. 61; denounced as reactionary by Chou En-Lai 64; Vice-Chair. Standing Cttee. 5th CPPCC 78; Vice-Chair. Standing Cttee. NPC 80-.
Standing Committee, National People's Congress, Beijing, People's Republic of China.

Pandit, Vijaya Lakshmi; Indian politician and diplomatist; b. 18 Aug. 1900; sister of late Jawaharlal Nehru; ed. privately.
Joined Non-Co-operation Movement, imprisoned for one year 31; mem. Allahabad Municipal Board 36, Chair. Education Cttee. Municipal Board; Minister of Local Self-Govt. and Public Health, Uttar Pradesh Govt. 37-39, 46-47 (1st woman minister); mem. Congress Party; sentenced to three terms of imprisonment 32, 41 and 42; detained under Defence Regulations 42-43; leader of Indian del. to UN 46-51, 63; Amb. to U.S.S.R. 47-49, to U.S.A. 49-51; Pres. UN Gen. Assembly 53-54; High Commr. in U.K. and Amb. to Ireland 55-61, concurrently Amb. to Spain 58-61; Gov. of Maharashtra 62-64; mem. Lok Sabha 52-54, 64-68; left Indian Nat. Congress to join Congress for Democracy Feb. 77, which merged with Janata Party May 77; mem. Janata Party 77-; Indian Rep. Human Rights Comm. 78; Hon. D.C.L. (Oxford).
Publ. *The Scope of Happiness* (memoirs) 79.
181-B Rajpur Road, Dehra Dun, Uttar Pradesh, India.

Panggabean, Gen. Maraden Saur Halomoan; Indonesian politician and army officer; b. Tarutung, North Sumatra, June 1922.
Studied military affairs in various mil. acads. including the Advanced Infantry Officer Course, U.S.; mil. posts include: Commdr. of the Army 68, Vice-Commdr. of the Armed Forces 69; mem. People's Consultative Assembly March 72-; Acting Minister of Home Affairs then appointed to Second Devt. Cabinet 73; Minister of Defence and Security (Second Devt. Cabinet); Co-ordinating Minister for Defence and Political Affairs (Third Devt. Cabinet) March 78-.
c/o Ministry for Defence and Political Affairs, Jakarta, Indonesia.

Pant, Apasaheb Balasaheb, M.A.; Indian politician and diplomatist; b. 11 Sept. 1912; ed. Univs. of Bombay and Oxford, and Lincoln's Inn, London.
Former Minister of Educ., Aundh State, Prime Minister 38-44, Minister 44-48; mem. All-India Congress Cttee. 48; Commr. for Govt. of India, British East Africa 48-54, concurrently Consul-Gen. in Belgian Congo and Ruanda-Urundi 48-54, concurrently Commr. in Central Africa and Nyasaland 50-54; Ministry of External Affairs, New Delhi 54-55; Political Officer, Sikkim and Bhutan 55-61; Amb. to Indonesia 61-64, to Norway 64-66, to U.A.R. 66, also accred. to Libya and Yemen; High Commr. in U.K. 69-72; Amb. to Italy 72-76, concurrently High Commr. in Malta 72-76; Del. to UN Gen. Assembly 51, 52, 65; Padma Shri 54.
Publs. *Yoga* 68, *Surya Namaskar* 69, *Aggression and Violence: Gandhian Experiments to Fight Them* 68, *A Moment in Time, Mandala—An Awakening* 76, *Survival of the Individual* 78, *Surya Namaskar* (in Danish) 78.
Pant Niwas Bhandarkar Inst. Road, Deccan Gymkhana, Pune 4, India.
Telephone: 58615.

Pant, Krishna Chandra, M.SC.; Indian politician; b. 10 Aug. 1931, Bhowali, Nainital Dist.; ed. St. Joseph's Coll., Nainital, Univ. of Lucknow.
Member of Lok Sabha for Nainital 62-77, 78-; Minister of Finance 67-69, of Steel and Heavy Engineering 69-70, of Home Affairs and Head Depts. of Electronics, Atomic Energy, Science and Technology 70-73; Minister of Irrigation and Power 73-74; Minister of State for Energy, Parl. Asst. to Prime Minister for Depts. of Atomic Energy, Electronics and Space 74-March 77; Sec.-Gen. Indian Nat. Congress, mem. Congress Working Cttee. May 77; elected mem. Rajya Sabha from Uttar Pradesh April 78-; Minister of Energy 79-80; First Vice-Pres. Human Rights Comm. 66; leader del. to Int. Conf. on Human Rights, Teheran 68; del. to various other int. confs.; Hon. Fellow Inst. of Engineers; Hon. D.Sc. (Udaipur Univ.).
22 Dakshineshwar Building, 10 Hailey Road, New Delhi 110001, India.

Pant, Sumitranandan; Indian writer; b. 1900.
Member Sahitya Acad.; Padma Bhushan 61; Sahitya Akademi Award; Bhartiya Jnanpith Award 69.
Publs. *Pallav* 26, *Vina-Gramthi* 30, *Birth of Poetry, Jyotsna* (drama) 34, *Panch Kahaniyan* (short stories) 36, *Uppara* (poetry) 49, *Gradya-Path* (essays) 53, *Chidambara* (poetry) 58, *Kala Aur Boodhachand* 59, *Lokayatan* (epic, Soviet Nehru Award), etc.
18-B7 K. G. Marg, Allahabad, Uttar Pradesh, India.
Telephone: Allahabad 3540.

Panyarachun, Anand; Thai diplomatist; b. 9 Aug. 1932; ed. Bangkok Christian Coll., Dulwich Coll., London and Univ. of Cambridge.
Joined Ministry of Foreign Affairs 55; Sec. to Foreign Minister 58; First Sec. Perm. Mission to UN 64, Counsellor 66, Acting Perm. Rep. 67-72, concurrently Amb. to Canada; Perm. Rep. to UN 72-75, also Amb. to U.S.A. 72-75; Perm. Under-Sec. of State for Foreign Affairs Sept. 75-Oct. 76, Amb.-at-Large 77, Amb. to Fed. Repub. of Germany 79-80; Chair. Group of 77 on Law of the Sea 73; Rep. to UN ECOSOC 74-75; Chair., Thai Del. to 7th Special Session of UN Gen. Assembly, Vice-Chair. of ad hoc cttee. Sept. 75; Chair. Textport Int. Corpn. Ltd.; Vice-Chair. Saha-Union Corpn. Ltd. 79-; mem. Govt. Council to Nat. Inst of. Devt. Admin. 79; Vice-Pres. Asscn. of Thai Industries 80; Vice-Chair. ASEAN-U.S. Business Council 80; Pres. ASEAN Chamber of Commerce and Industry 82.
26 Sukhumvit 53, Bangkok 11, Thailand

Pao, Sir Yue-Kong, Kt., C.B.E., LL.D., J.P.; Chinese shipowner; b. 1918, Zhejiang; ed. Shanghai.
Banking 39-49; Chair. World Wide-Shipping Group; Chair. World Finance Int. Ltd., IBJ Finance (H.K.) Ltd., Intertanko; Chair. The Hongkong & Kowloon Wharf and Godown Co. Ltd.; Deputy Chair. Hongkong and Shanghai Banking Corpn.; Dir. Mass Transit Railway Corpn., Hong Kong, Hang Seng Bank Ltd., Cathay Pacific Airways, Inchcape Far East Ltd., South China Morning Post Ltd.; Adviser Industrial Bank of Japan Ltd.; founder World-Wide Sea Training School; Hon. Chair. Nippon Kaiji

Kyokai of Japan; mem. and Council mem. of Int. Gen. Cttee., Bureau Veritas of France; mem. Asia/Pacific Advisory Council, American Telephone and Telegraph Int.; life mem. Court, Univ. of Hong Kong; Hon. Vice-Pres. Maritime Trust of U.K.; mem. Gen. Cttee. Lloyds' Register of Shipping (Chair. East Asia Cttee.), Board of Managers of American Bureau of Shipping, Int. Advisory Cttee., Chase Manhattan Bank; Hon. mem. Intertanko.
World-Wide Shipping Agency Ltd., 15th-17th Floors, Berwick House, 7 Canton Road, Kowloon, Hong Kong.
Telephone: 3-7327333 (Office).

Parbo, Sir Arvi Hillar, Kt., B.ENG.; Australian mining engineer; b. 10 Feb. 1926, Tallinn, Estonia (now in the U.S.S.R.); ed. Estonia, Germany and Univ. of Adelaide.
Western Mining Corpn. Ltd. 56-, mining eng. 56, Underground Man. Nevoria Mine 58, Technical Asst. to Man. Dir. Western Mining Corpn. 60, Deputy Gen. Supt. W. Australia 64, Gen. Man. Western Mining Corpn. Ltd. 68, Deputy Man. Dir. 70, Man. Dir. 71-, Vice-Chair. 73, Chair. 74-.
Western Mining Corporation Ltd., 360 Collins Street, Melbourne, Vic. 3001; Home: Longwood, Highbury Road, Vermont South, Vic. 3133, Australia.
Telephone: 602-0300 (Office); 232-8264 (Home).

Parecattil, H.E. Cardinal Joseph; Indian ecclesiastic; b. 1 April 1912, Kidangoor; ed. Papal Seminary, Kandy, Sri Lanka.
Ordained 39; Titular Bishop of Aretusa (Syria) 53; Archbishop of Ernakulam 56-; mem. Pontifical Comm.; Vice-Pres. Catholic Bishops' Conf. on India 66, Pres. 72, 74; mem. Sacred Congregation for the Oriental Churches; cr. Cardinal 69; mem. Secr., Christian Unity, Rome 70, Secr. for non-Christians 74-; Pres. Pontifical Comm. for revision of Oriental Canon Law 72; Pres. Syro-Malabar Bishops' Conf., Kerala Catholic Bishops' Conf. 71-77; Chancellor, Pontifical Inst. of Philosophy and Theology in Alwaye 73-77, Chancellor, Dharmaram Inst. of Theology and Philosophy, Bangalore.
Archbishop's House, Post Bag 1209, Cochin 682031, Kerala, India.
Telephone: Cochin 32629.

Parekh, Hasmukh, B.A., B.SC.; Indian investment broker; b. 10 March 1911, Surat; ed. Bombay Univ., London School of Econs.
Worked as stockbroker with leading Bombay firm 36-56; Deputy Gen. Man. Industrial Credit and Investment Corpn. of India 58-68, Deputy Chair. and Man. Dir. 68-71, Chair. and Man. Dir. 72-73, Exec. Chair. 73-78; Chair. Housing Devt. Finance Corpn. Oct. 77-.
Publs. *The Bombay Money Market* 53, *The Future of Joint Stock Enterprise in India* 58, *India and Regional Development* 69, *Management of Industry in India, Regional Cooperation in South Asia* 81.
Housing Development Finance Corporation, 169 Backbay Reclamation, Bombay 400020; Home: Kastur Nivas No. 1, French Road, Chowpatty, Bombay 400007, India.
Telephone: 223725 (Office); 35949 (Home).

Park Choong-hoon; Korean politician; b. 19 Jan. 1919, Cheju-do; ed. Doshisha Commercial Coll., Japan.
Trade Affairs Dir. of Minister of Commerce and Industry 48; retired as Air Force Maj.-Gen. 61; Vice-Minister of Commerce and Industry 61, Minister of Commerce and Industry 63; Deputy Prime Minister and Minister of Econ. Planning 67-69; Standing mem. Econ. and Scientific Council 70-71; Chair. AIRC 71-73, Korean Traders' Asscn., *Naeoe Business Journal* (daily), and Pres. Trade Press 73-80; Acting Prime Minister May-Sept. 80; Acting Pres. Aug.-Sept. 80; Chair. Korea Industrial Devt. Research Inst.
1-36, Seongbuk-dong, Seongbuk-ku, Seoul, Republic of Korea.

Park Tong-jin; Korean diplomatist and politician; b. 11 Oct. 1922, North Kyeonsang Prov.; ed. Chuo Univ., Japan.
Counsellor, Korean Embassy, U.K. 59; Vice-Minister of Foreign Affairs 61; Amb. to Viet-Nam 61, to Brazil 62, to UN, Geneva 68, to UN, New York 73-75; Minister of Foreign Affairs 75-80; mem. Nat. Assembly 81-.
c/o Ministry of Foreign Affairs, Seoul, Republic of Korea.

Parthasarathi, Gopalaswami, B.A., M.A.; Indian diplomatist; b. 7 July 1912; ed. Univ. of Madras and Oxford Univ.
Assistant Editor *The Hindu* 36-49; Chief Rep. Press Trust of India, London 49-52, Chief Ed. Press Trust of India 51-53; Chair. Int. Comm. for Cambodia 54-55; Int. Supervisory Comm. for Viet-Nam 55-56; Amb. to Indonesia 57-58, to People's Republic of China 58-61; Chair. Int. Comm. for Supervision and Control, Viet-Nam 61-62; High Commr. in Pakistan 62-65, Perm. Rep. of India to UN Aug. 65-69; Chair. Policy Planning Cttee., Ministry of Foreign Affairs 75-77; Vice-Chancellor of Jawaharlal Nehru Univ. 69-74; mem. Board of Trustees, UN Inst. for Training and Research 70-81; Chair. Indian Inst. of Mass Communication 81-, Indian Council of Social Research 81-.
49 Lodi Estate, New Delhi 110 003, India.
Telephone: 693107.

Patel, Babhubai Jashbhai, LL.B.; Indian politician; b. 9 Feb. 1911, Nadiad, Kaira District, Gujarat; ed. Govt. High School, Nadiad; Baroda Coll. and Ferguson Coll., Poona; Wilson Coll. and St. Xaviers Coll., Bombay; Govt. Law Coll., Bombay.
Took part in Independence Movement, detained six times 30-41; took part in Quit India Movement 42; mem. Bombay Legislative Assembly 37-67; Parl. Sec. to Chief Minister of Bombay 49-52; Deputy Minister, Public Works Dept. and Transport 52-56; Minister for Planning, Devt., Electricity and Housing, Bombay Govt. 56-57; joined Govt. of Gujarat 67; Minister for Public Works Dept., Electricity and Civil Supplies and later for Finance in Gujarat Govt. 67-71; Chief Minister of Gujarat June 75-March 76, April 77-80; del. to Commonwealth Park Conf., Ottawa, Canada Sept. 77; fmr. Vice-Chancellor Sardar Patel Univ.; fmr. Pres. Gujerat Pradesh Congress and Pradesh Janata Party; Chair. Sardar Vallebhbhai Patel Memorial Soc., Nadrad and Ahmedabad; Fellow, Bombay Univ. and Gujarat Univ. 46-52; Janata Party.
Publ. *Three Years of State Transport, Bombay State, State Transport X-rayed, Tenancy Reform, Sales Tax Law*, etc.
Sector 19, Plot 26, nr. Gymkhana, Gandhinagar 382019, Gujerat, India (Home).
Telephone: 2020.

Patel, Baburao; Indian writer, editor, film producer and politician; b. 4 April 1904.
Began free-lance journalism 22; wrote, directed and produced motion pictures, founder and Editor *Filmindia* 35-; lectured in U.S. and Europe on India's ancient culture and civilization; set up a production code and fought for revision of film censorship; Ed. *Mother India*; Man. Dir. Sumati Publications Pvt. Ltd. 58; mem. Parl. for Shajapur 67-; Founder and Chair. Mother India Pharmaceuticals Ltd.
Publs. *Grey Dust, Burning Words, The Sermon of the Lord, Prayer Book, Rosary and the Lamp, Homœopathic Lifesavers for Home and Community;* Films: (wrote and produced) *Kismet, Mahananda, Bala Joban, My Darling, Maharanee, Draupadi, Gvalan.*
Girnar, Pali Hill, Bombay 50, India.
Telephone: 257037 (Office); 533414 (Home).

Patel, Hirubhai M., C.I.E., B.A., B.COM.; Indian politician; b. 26 Aug. 1904, Bombay; ed. Oxford and London Univs.
Separation Officer, Sing 35; Finance Dept., Bombay 36; Sec. to Stock Exchange Cttee. 36-37; Trade Commr., for

N. Europe, Hamburg 37-39; Deputy Trade Commr., London 39-40; Deputy Sec. Eastern Group Supply Council 41-42; Deputy Dir.-Gen. Supply Dept. 42-43; Joint Sec. and Sec. Industries and Civil Supplies Dept. 43-46, Cabinet Secr. 46-47; Defence and Partition Sec. 47-53; Sec. Food and Agriculture 53-54, Dept. of Econ. Affairs, Ministry of Finance 57; Principal Finance Sec. 57-59; Chair. Life Insurance Corpn. of India 56-57; Chair. Gujarat Electricity Board 60-66; mem. Gujarat Legislative Assembly 67-71; Chair. Charutar Vidyamandal, Vallal Vidyanagar 59-; Pres. Gujarat Swatantra Party 67-72, All-India Swatantra Party 71-72; Chair. Charutar Arogyamandal 72; mem. Lok Sabha from Dhanduka, Gujarat 71-77, from Sabarkantha, Gujarat 77-80; mem. Cttee. of Janata Party Jan. 77-; Minister of Finance, Revenue and Banking 77-79, of Home Affairs 79; Gov. IMF 77-79; Hon. LL.D. (Sardar Patel Univ.); Albert Schweitzer Medal of Animal Welfare Inst. (U.S.A.) 80.
Charutar Vidyamandal, Vallabh Vidyanagar, 388 120 Gujarat, India (Home).

Patel, Indraprasad Gordhanbhai, B.A., PH.D.; Indian economist; b. 1924; ed. Baroda Coll., Bombay Univ., King's Coll., Cambridge and Harvard Univ.
Professor of Econs., Maharaja Sayajirao Univ., Baroda (now Vadodara) 49-50; Economist and Asst. Chief, Financial Problems and Policies Div., IMF 50-54; Deputy Econ. Adviser, Indian Ministry of Finance 54-58; Alt. Exec. Dir. for India, IMF 58-61; Chief Econ. Adviser, Ministry of Finance, India 61-63, 65-67, Special Sec., Min. of Finance 68-69, Sec. 70-72; Deputy Admin. UN Devt. Programme 72-77; Gov. Reserve Bank of India Dec. 77-; Reserve Bank of India, Central Office, Bombay 400001; 5 Carmichael Road, Bombay 400 026, India.
Telephone: 295868 (Office); 361634 (Home).

Patel, Jeram; Indian painter and graphic designer; b. 20 June 1930; ed. Sir J. J. School of Art, Bombay, Central School of Arts and Crafts, London.
Reader in Applied Arts, M.S. Univ., Baroda (now Vadodara) 60-61, 66-; Reader in Visual Design, School of Architecture, Ahmedabad 61-62; Deputy Dir. All India Handloom Board 63-66; mem. *Group 1890* (avant-garde group of Indian artists), Lalit Kala Akademi; one man exhbns. in London 59, New Delhi 60, 62-65, in Calcutta 66; in Tokyo Biennale 57-63, São Paulo Biennale 63; represented in Nat. Gallery of Modern Art, New Delhi, Art Soc. of India, Bombay, Sir J. J. Inst. of Applied Arts, Bombay, and in private collections in U.S.A., London, Paris and Tokyo; Lalit Kala Akademi Nat. Awards 57, 64; Bombay State Award 57; Silver Medal, Bombay Art Soc. 61, Gold Medal Rajkot Exhbn.
Faculty of Fine Arts, M.S. University, Vadodara 2, India.

Paterson, James Rupert; British diplomatist; b. 7 Aug. 1932.
First Sec. FCO 70-72; Islambad 72-75; Deputy High Commr. in Trinidad and Tobago 74-78; First Sec. FCO 78-81; Amb. to Mongolia 82-.
British Embassy, 30 Enh Tayvny Gudamj, G.P.O. Box 703, Ulan Bator, Mongolia.

Patil, Veerendra, B.A., LL.B.; Indian politician and lawyer; b. 28 Feb. 1924, Chincholi, Gulbarga District; ed. Osmania Univ., Hyderabad.
Practised law 47, 50-55; mem. Hyderabad State Assembly 55-56, 62-; Deputy Minister for Home and Industries, Mysore till 58; Minister for Excise and Rural Industries 61-62, for Public Works 62; Chief Minister of Mysore 68-72; Pres. Karnataka Pradesh Congress (Org.) Cttee. 71-77, Janata Party in Karnataka 77-; Minister of Petroleum and Chemicals (Govt. of India) Jan.-Oct. 80, of Shipping and Transport Oct. 80-; mem. Rajya Sahba 72-78; mem. del. to U.S.S.R. 65, Japan and S.-E. Asia 70, Australia 72, U.K. and Europe 73.
174-49, 9th Main Road, 2 Cross, Raja Mahal Vilas Extension, Bangalore 560006, India.
Telephone: 30998.

Patnaik, Bijoyananda (Biju); Indian politician b.; 5 March 1916, Cuttack; ed. Ravenshaw Coll., Cuttack.
Joined Indian Nat. Airways; founded Kalinga Airways; participated in Quit India Movement 42; elected to Orissa Legislative Assembly 52, leader Pragati Party legislative group until 73; Chief Minister of Orissa 61-63; resigned to work in party org.; mem. Rajya Sabha 72; Chair. Orissa Planning Board 63-67, 72; founded Kalinga Foundation Trust awarding Kalinga Prize for promotion and popularization of Science; mem. Janata Party 77-; mem. Lok Sabha March 77-; Minister for Steel and Mines March 77-80.
Lok Sabha, New Delhi, India.

Patnaik, Janaki Ballav, M.A.; Indian politician; b. 3 Jan. 1927, Rameswar, Puri District, Orissa; ed. Banaras Univ. Sub-Ed. for *Eastern Times* 49, Jt. Ed. 50, Ed. (also for *Prajatantra*) 52-67; Ed. *Paurusha*; led tenant's agitation in Madhupur, Cuttack District 53; mem. Sahitya Akademi, Orissa 56-57, Lok Sabha 71-77; Minister of State for Defence, Govt. of India 73-77; Minister of Tourism, Civil Aviation and Labour Jan.-Dec. 80.
c/o Ministry of Tourism and Civil Aviation, New Delhi India.

Peacock, Andrew Sharp, LL.B.; Australian politician; b. 13 Feb. 1939, Melbourne; ed. Scotch Coll., Univ. of Melbourne.
President, Victorian Liberal Party 65-66; mem. House of Reps. for Kooyong, Vic. 66-; partner Rigby & Fielding, solicitors; Chair. Peacock & Smith Pty. Ltd., engineers 62-69; Minister for the Army 69-72; Assisting the Prime Minister 69-71, Assisting the Treasurer 71-72; Minister for External Territories Feb.-Dec. 72; mem. Opposition Exec. 73-75, Spokesman on Foreign Affairs 73-75; Minister for Foreign Affairs 75-80, for the Environment Nov.-Dec. 75, for Industrial Relations Nov. 80-April 81 (resgnd.).
400 Flinders Street, Melbourne, Vic. 3000; Home: 30 Monomeath Avenue, Canterbury, Vic. 3126, Australia.

Peljee, Myatavyn; Mongolian politician; b. 1927; ed. Mongolian State Univ. and Acad. of Social Sciences of CPSU Central Cttee., Moscow.
Official of the Mongolian People's Revolutionary Party (MPRP) Cen. Cttee. 50-56; Head of a Dept. of MPRP Cen. Cttee. 60-66; Minister of Geology 66-68, of Fuel, Power and Geology 68-76, of Geology and Mining Industry April-June 76; Deputy Chair. Council of Ministers 76-; Chair. Comm. for CMEA (Comecon) Affairs 77-; mem. MPRP Cen. Cttee. 61-; Deputy to People's Great Hural (Assembly) 63-; Order of the Red Banner of Labour, Order of the Pole Star.
Government Palace, Ulan Bator, Mongolia.

Pen Sovan; Kampuchean soldier and politician; b. 1936, Takeo Province.
Joined armed unit of CP of Cambodia 50; served in various units in eastern region, becoming Deputy to Div. Commdr. 70; mem. Editorial Board Kampuchean United Front Radio 70-75; C.-in-C. Kampuchean Armed Forces Jan. 79-; Vice-Pres. of People's Revolutionary Council of Kampuchea and Minister of Nat. Defence 79-81; Sec.-Gen. People's Revolutionary Party of Kampuchea May-Dec. 81; mem. Politburo and Secr., Cen. Cttee. May 81-.
c/o People's Revolutionary Council of Kampuchea, Phnom-Penh, Kampuchea.

Peng Chong; Chinese party official; b. Fujian.
Mayor, Nanjing 55-59; Deputy Sec., CCP Jiangsu 60-65, Sec. 65-68; Vice-Chair. Jiangsu Provincial Revolutionary Cttee. 68; Alt. mem. 9th Cen. Cttee. of CCP 69; Deputy Sec., CCP Jiangsu 71; Alt. mem. 10th Cen. Cttee. of CCP

73; First Sec., CCP Jiangsu 74-76; Third Sec., CCP Shanghai 76-79, First Sec. 79-80; Chair. Shanghai People's Govt. (fmrly. Revolutionary Cttee.) 79-80; mem. Politburo, 11th Cen. Cttee. of CCP 77; Exec. Chair. Nat. Cttee. CCP, Vice-Chair. 78; Mayor, Shanghai; Sec. Secretariat Cen. Cttee. CCP 80-; a Vice-Chair. Standing Cttee. of Nat. People's Congress Sept. 80-.
People's Republic of China.

Peng Zhen; Chinese politician; b. 1902, Shanxi.
Joined CCP 35; mem. 7th Cen. Cttee. CCP 45; Chair. People's Govt. (Mayor) of Beijing 49-66; First Sec. CCP 49-66; mem. 8th Cen. Cttee. CCP 56; Sec., Secr. Cen. Cttee. CCP 56-66; mem. Politburo CCP 56-66; criticized and removed from office during Cultural Revolution 66; mem. 11th Cen. Cttee. CCP 79; mem. Politburo CCP 79; Chair. Legal Cttee. NPC 79; Vice-Chair. Standing Cttee. NPC 79-.
People's Republic of China.

Penjor, Lyonpo Sangye; Bhutan diplomatist; b. 13 Feb. 1928, Bamthang; ed. local school.
Entered govt. service 45; Officer-in-charge of Royal Household of Tashichholing; Chief District Officer, Bumthang District, Deputy Chief Sec. 60; Minister for Communications 70-71; Perm. Rep. to UN Sept. 71-75; Amb. to India 75-81 (also accred. to Bangladesh).
c/o Ministry of Foreign Affairs, Thimphu, Bhutan.

Penn Nouth, Samdech; Kampuchean politician; b. 1906; ed. Cambodian School of Admin.
Ministry of Colonies, Paris 38; Assistant to Minister of Palace 40; Acting Minister of Finance 45; Gov. of Phnom-Penh 46-48; Minister of State 46; Minister of State without Portfolio 47; Prime Minister Sept. 48-Jan. 49, 52-55, 58; Amb. to France 58-60; Prime Minister, Minister of the Interior and Minister of Religious Affairs Jan.-Nov. 61; Prime Minister and Minister of Religious Affairs 61-62; Adviser to the Govt. 67; Prime Minister 68-69; Prime Minister of Royal Govt. of Nat. Union of Cambodia (GRUNC) 70-76 (in Phnom-Penh 75-76); High Counsellor, State Presidium 76-79; numerous decorations.

Perak, H.R.H. the Sultan of; Sultan Idris Al-Mutawakil Allahi Shah ibni Al-Mahrum Sultan Iskandar Shah Kaddasallah, D.K., D.M.N., S.P.M.P., D.K. (Johore), S.P.G.M., S.P.M.P., P.J.K., C.M.G.; Malaysian ruler; b. 17 Aug. 1924, Kuala Kangsar; ed. Malay School, Clifford School, Malay Coll., Kuala Kangsar, Univ. of London.
Raja Muda of Perak 48; served as Regent of Perak 48; Chair. Council of Regency 56; succeeded cousin as Sultan of Perak 63; Maj. Federated Malay States Volunteer Forces 52; Hon. Col.-in-Chief Malaysian Engineers; Patron Nat. Silat Gayong Asscn. (Malay martial art of self-defence).
Ipoh, Perak, Malaysia.

Perera, Liyanagé Henry Horace, B.A.; Sri Lankan international official; b. 9 May 1915; ed. St. Benedict's Coll., Colombo, Univ. Coll. London, Univ. of Ceylon.
Senior Master in Govt. and History, Ceylon 36-59; Asst. Registrar, Aquinas Univ. Coll., Colombo 60-61; Educ. Dir. World Fed. of UN Asscns. 61-63, Deputy Sec.-Gen. and Educ. Dir. 63-66, Sec.-Gen. 66-76; Special Asst. for the Asian and South Pacific Region, World Confed. of Orgs. of the Teaching Profession 76-; mem. Int. Cttee. on Adult Educ. (UNESCO) 63; Pres. Conf. of Int. Non-Governmental Orgs. in Consultative Status with UN ECOSOC 69-72; Pres. Non-Governmental Orgs. Special Cttee. on Devt. 75-; Hon. Pres. World Fed. of UN Asscns.; Consultant to Pontifical Comm. on Peace and Justice; WCOTP Co-ordinator for Int. Year of the Child; William Russel Award 74; Award of Int. Asscn. of Educ. for World Peace 74; Gold Medal, Czechoslovak Soc. for Int. Relations.
Publs. *Ceylon and Indian History (Early Times to 1500)*, *Ceylon Under Western Rule (1500-1948)*, *Groundwork of Ceylon and World History (Early Times to 1500)*.
World Confederation of Organizations of the Teaching Profession, 5 avenue du Moulin, 1110 Morges; Home: 22 avenue Luserna, 1203 Geneva, Switzerland.
Telephone: (021) 71-74-67 (Office); (022) 44-07-37 (Home).

Perlis, H.R.H. the Raja of; Tuanku Syed Putra ibni Al-Marhum Syed Hassan Jamalullial, D.K., S.P.M.P., D.K. (Malaysia, Selangor, Kelantan, Kedah, Pahang den Brunei), D.M.N., S.M.N., S.P.D.K.(SABAH), K.C.M.G.; ruler of Perlis, Malaysia.
Appointed Bakal Raja (Heir-Presumptive) of Perlis April 38; attached to Courts in Kangar 40; worked for a year in the Land Office, Kuala Lumpur, and for a year in the Magistrates' Court, Kuala Lumpur; in private business during Japanese occupation; Timbalan Yang di-Pertuan Agong (Deputy Supreme Head of State) of Malaya April-Sept. 60, Yang di-Pertuan Agong (Supreme Head of State) Sept. 60-Sept. 63, of Malaysia 63-65.
Istana Arau, Perlis; Home: Istana Kerangan Indah, Repoh, Perlis, Malaysia.
Telephone: 752212; 751142.

Pham Hung; Vietnamese politician; b. 1912, Vinh Long Province.
Joined Revolutionary Youth League under Ho Chi Minh in 1920s; founding mem. Indochinese Communist Party 30, later mem. of Lao Dong Party; imprisoned for 15 years by French and sentenced to death, later reprieved; mem. Cen. Cttee. Lao Dong Party (party renamed Communist Party of Viet-Nam Dec. 76) 51-, also mem. Politburo; Deputy Sec. Cen. Office of South Viet-Nam (COSVN) with responsibility for mil. operations in S. Viet-Nam 51-57; Minister at Office of Premier, Hanoi 57-67 (acting Premier during 61); Sec. of COSVN (in S. Viet-Nam) and Political Commissar of People's Liberation Armed Forces 67-June 76; Vice-Premier, Council of Ministers, Socialist Repub. of Viet-Nam July 76-, Minister with Responsibility for the Interior Feb. 80-; mem. Nat. Defence Council July 76-.
Communist Party of Viet-Nam, 1-C Blvd. Hoang van Thu, Hanoi, Viet-Nam.

Pham Van Dong; Vietnamese politician; b. 1 March 1906, Quang Nam Province (S. Viet-Nam).
Close collaborator of Ho Chi Minh; underground communist worker since 25; imprisoned by French authorities for seven years; upon release in 36, resumed revolutionary activities; a founder of the Revolutionary League for the Independence of Viet-Nam (the Viet-Minh) 41; mem. Lao Dong (now Communist) Party 51-, also mem. Politburo; Minister for Foreign Affairs, Democratic Repub. of Viet-Nam 54-61, Prime Minister 55-76; Prime Minister, Socialist Repub. of Viet-Nam 76-80; Vice-Chair. Nat. Defence Council July 76-; Chair. Council of Ministers 81-; Order of Lenin 82.
Office of the Chairman of the Council of Ministers, Hanoi, Viet-Nam.

Pham Van Ky; Vietnamese writer; b. 1916; ed. Secondary School, Hanoi, and Univ. of Paris.
Went to France 39; prepared thesis on religion for the Institut des Hautes Etudes Chinoises; Grand Prix du Roman, Académie Française 61.
Publs. *Fleurs de jade* (poems), *L'homme de nulle part* (short stories) 46, *Frères de sang* (novel) 47, *Celui qui régnera* (novel) 54, *Les yeux courroucés* (novel) 58, *Les contemporains* (novel) 59, *Perdre la demeure* (novel) 61, *Poème sur Soie* (poems) 61, *Des Femmes Assises Çà et Là* (novel) 64, *Mémoires d'un Eunuque* (novel) 66, *Le Rideau de Pluie* (play) 74.
62/2 avenue du Général de Gaulle, Maisons-Alfort 94700, France.
Telephone: 368-22-94.

Phat, Huynh Tan (*see* Huynh Tan Phat).

Phomvihane, Kaysone; Laotian politician; b. 13 Dec. 1920, Savannakhet Province; ed. Univ. of Hanoi.
Helped anti-French forces in Viet-Nam after 45; joined Neo Lao Issara (Free Lao Front) nationalist movement in exile in Bangkok 45; attended first resistance congress; Minister of Defence in Free Lao Front resistance Govt. 50; C.-in-C. of Pathet Lao forces 54-57; mem. People's Party of Laos 55; mem. Neo Lao Hak Sat (Lao Patriotic Front) 56, Vice-Chair. 59, Vice-Chair. of Cen. Cttee. 64; Prime Minister of Laos Dec. 75-; Sec.-Gen. Cen. Cttee. Lao People's Revolutionary Party; Order of the Gold Star; Order of Lenin (U.S.S.R.).
Office of the Prime Minister, Vientiane, Laos.

Phoumsavanh, Nouhak; Laotian politician; ed. primary school.
Leader of Pathet Lao del. to Conf. of Asian and Pacific Region in Beijing 52; rep. of Pathet Lao at Geneva Conf. on Indochina 54; Minister of Foreign Affairs in Neo Lao Issara (Free Lao Front) resistance Govt.; Deputy for Sam Neua to Nat. Assembly 57; arrested 59, escaped 60; led Neo Lao Hak Sat (Lao Patriotic Front) del. to Ban Namone peace talks 61; mem. People's Party of Laos 55; mem. Lao Patriotic Front, mem. Standing Cttee. 64, now Deputy Sec.-Gen. Cen. Cttee. Lao People's Revolutionary Party; Vice-Prime Minister and Minister of Finance Dec. 75-.
Ministry of Finance, Vientiane, Laos.

Phung Van Cung; Vietnamese physician and politician, b. 1908, Vinh Long Province; ed. Faculty of Medicine; Hanoi Univ.
Director of public health service in Rach Gia Province, later in Chau Doc Province; physician, Fujian Hosp., Cholon; joined army and rose to rank of Col. under Pres. Diem; joined resistance 60; Vice-Pres. Cen. Cttee. Nat. Liberation Front (NLF); Pres. South Vietnamese Peace Cttee., NLF Red Cross Soc.; Vice-Pres. Provisional Revolutionary Govt. of South Viet-Nam, Minister of the Interior 69-76 (in Saigon (now Ho Chi Minh City) 75-76).
c/o Communist Party of Viet-Nam, 1c boulevard Hoang van Thu, Hanoi, Viet-Nam.

Pirzada, Abdul Hafiz; Pakistani lawyer and politician; b. 24 Feb. 1935, Sukkur; ed. D. J. Sindh Govt. Science Coll. and in U.K.
Called to the Bar, Lincoln's Inn, London 57; commenced legal practice in High Court of W. Pakistan, Karachi 57, joined Chambers of Zulfiqar Ali Bhutto (fmr. Prime Minister of Pakistan) 57-58; Advocate, W. Pakistan High Court and Supreme Court of Pakistan; mem. Cen. Cttee. Pakistan People's Party; mem. Nat. Assembly 70-July 77; Minister of Law and Parl. Affairs, Educ. and Provincial Co-ordination 71-74, of Educ. and Science, Technology and Provincial Co-ordination 74-76, of Educ. and Provincial Co-ordination Feb. 76-March 77, of Finance April-July 77.
Sukkur, Sind, Pakistan.

Pirzada, Sharifuddin, LL.B.; Pakistani lawyer and politician; b. 12 June 1923; ed. Univ. of Bombay.
Secretary Muslim Students' Fed. 43-45; Sec. Provincial Muslim League 46; Man. Editor *Morning Herald* 46; Prof., Sind Muslim Law Coll., Karachi 47-55; Adviser to Constitution Comm. of Pakistan 60; Chair. Pakistan Company Law Comm. and mem. Int. Rivers Cttee. 60; Pres. Pakistan Branch Int. Law Asscn. and Pres. Legal Aid Soc.; Pres. Karachi Bar Asscn.; Senior Advocate, Supreme Court of Pakistan; Attorney-Gen. of Pakistan 64-66, 68-71, July 77-; Minister of Foreign Affairs 66-68, of Law and Parliamentary Affairs 79-81; led Pakistan del. to Law of the Sea Confs. 78-79; on panel of Pakistan Perm. Court of Arbitration, of Arbitrators maintained by the Council of Int. Civil Aviation, of Arbitrators maintained by the Int. Court of Settlement of Investment Disputes, Washington; mem. UN Int. Law Comm. 81-; Sitara-e-Pakistan.
Publs. include: *Evolution of Pakistan, Fundamental Rights and Constitutional Remedies in Pakistan, Foundations of Pakistan* Vol. I 69, Vol. II 70.
C-37, K.D.A. Scheme No. 1, Habib Ibrahim Rahimtoola Road, Karachi, Pakistan.
Telephone: 436977.

Plimsoll, Sir James, A.C., C.B.E.; Australian diplomatist; b. 25 April 1917; ed. Sydney High School and Univ. of Sydney.
With Econ. Dept., Bank of New South Wales, Sydney 38-42; served in Australian Army 42-47; mem. Australian Del., Far Eastern Comm. 45-48; Rep. UN Comm. for Unification and Rehabilitation of Korea 50-52; Asst. Sec., Dept. of External Affairs 53-59; Perm. Rep. to UN 59-63; High Commr. in India and Amb. to Nepal 63-65; Sec. Dept. of External Affairs 65-70; Amb. to U.S.A. 70-74, to U.S.S.R. and Mongolia 74-77, to Belgium, Luxembourg and the European Communities 77-80; High Commissioner in the U.K. 80-81; Amb. to Japan 81-82; Gov. of Tasmania 82-; K. St. J. 82.
Government House, Hobart, Tasmania 7000, Australia.

Poddar, Prof. Ramendra Kumar, M.SC., PH.D.; Indian university administrator; b. Nov. 1930.
Biophysicist, Univ. of California, Berkeley 58-60; Research Fellow, Purdue Univ., U.S.A. 60-61; Scientific Adviser, Int. Atomic Energy Authority, UN, Bamako, Mali, West Africa 63; Assoc. Prof., Saha Inst. of Nuclear Physics 68-73; Research Fellow, California Inst. of Tech. 70; Prof. of Biophysics, Calcutta Univ. 73-77, Pro-Vice-Chancellor for Academic Affairs 77-79, Vice-Chancellor June 79-; research into molecular genetics, radiation and photo-biology; mem. Nat. Cttee. on Biophysics, Indian Nat. Science Acad. 72-78, Indian Biophysical Soc., State Advisory Cttee. of Vice-Chancellors, West Bengal; Vice-Chair. Bd. of Trustees, Indian Museum, Calcutta.
Publs. over 25 articles in various scientific journals.
Senate House, University of Calcutta, College Street, Calcutta, India.

Pol Pot; Kampuchean politician (widely identified with Saloth Sar, fmr. military commdr. of FUNC); b. 1925, Kompong Thom Province; ed. Phnom-Penh Technical School, École Française de Radio-Électricité.
Member Indo-Chinese Communist Party until 46, Pracheachon (Cambodian Communist Party) 46-; Editor *Solidarity* 54-55; arrested 55, lecturer in private school 55-63; declined invitation to join Prince Norodom Sihanouk's Govt. 63 and joined Maquis against French rule; reported to have been elected to Cen. Cttee. Pracheachon as standing mem. 60, Deputy Sec. 61, Acting Sec. 62, Sec. 63; signatory to FUNC's appeal to Lon Nol 74; Chair. Military Cttee. Pracheachon 70-75; elected Sec. Pracheachon 71, 76; visited People's Repub. of China 75; mem. People's Representative Assembly 76-79; Prime Minister of Democratic Kampuchea 76-79; withdrew from office because of ill-health 76-77; resumed duties Sept. 77; overthrown after Vietnamese invasion of Kampuchea and left country Jan. 79; sentenced to death *in absentia* Aug. 79; Commdr. of guerrilla army after invasion 79-; medical treatment in Thailand 82.

Ponce Enrile, Juan, LL.M.; Philippine lawyer and professor of taxation; b. 14 Feb. 1924, Gonzaga, Cagayan; ed. Univ. of the Philippines and Harvard Law School.
Under-Secretary of Finance 66-68; Acting Sec. of Finance; Acting Insurance Commr.; Acting Commr. of Customs; Sec. of Justice 68-70, of Nat. Defence 70-71 (resgnd.), 72-78, Minister 78-; mem. Batasang Pambansa; mem. several Govt. cttees.; mem. Exec. Cttee.; practising corpn. lawyer and Prof. of Taxation, Graduate School Coll. of Law, Far Eastern Univ.; Chair. Bd. of Dirs., United Coconut Plan-

ters Bank; Chair. Exec. Cttee. of Nat. Security Council, Nat. Disaster Control Center; Dir. Philippine Communication Satellite Corpn.; Trustee, Young Artists' Foundation of the Philippines; mem. Nat. Energy and Devt. Authority, Energy Devt. Bd., Nat. Environmental Protection Council, Philippine Crop Insurance Corpn., numerous law and commercial asscns.; Hon. Dr. of Laws (Manila Law Coll., Southwestern Univ., Cebu City, Univ. of Manila); Hon. Hum.D. (St. Paul's Univ., Cagayan Valley); Mahaputra Adipranada Medal (Indonesia); Commdr., Philippine Legion of Honour.
Publs. *A Proposal on Capital Gains Tax* 60, *Income Tax Treatment of Corporate Merger and Consolidation Revisited* 62, *Tax Treatment of Real Estate Transactions* 64; various articles on law, the military and govt.
Ministry of National Defence, Camp General Emilio Aguinaldo, Quezon City; Home: Dasmariñas Village, Makati, Metro Manila, Philippines.
Telephone: 78-97-26 or 79-03-90.

Poonacha, Cheppudira Muthana; Indian politician; b. 1910, Attur, Coorg, Karnataka State; ed. St. Aloysius Coll., Mangalore.
Joined Satyagraha Movement for imprisoned 30, Satyagraha activities; Sec. District Congress Cttee., Coorg 33; mem. Exec. Cttees., Karnatak and All India Congress Cttees. and Coorg District Board 38, Pres., Coorg District Board 41; mem. Exec. Cttee. Coorg Legislative Council and Leader, Congress Legislative Party in the Council 45-46; mem. Constitutent Assembly and Provisional Parl. 47-51; Chief Minister of Coorg 52-56; Minister for Industries and Commerce 57, and later for Home and Industries at Mysore; Chair. State Trading Corpn. of India 59-63; Leader of Trade Dels. to various countries 61, 63; mem. Rajya Sabha 64; Minister for Revenue and Expenditure Jan. 66; Minister of State in Ministry of Transport and Aviation 66-67; Minister of Railways 67-69, of Steel and Heavy Eng. Feb.-Dec. 69; Chair. Malabar Chemicals and Fertilizers Ltd. 70-71; Gov. of Madhya Pradesh 78-80, Orissa May 80-.
Home Estate, Athur Post via Pollibetta, Coorg, Karnataka State, India.
Telephone: Gonicopal 85.

Porritt, Baron (Life Peer), cr. 73, of Wanganui in New Zealand and of Hampstead in Greater London; **Arthur Porritt,** Bt., G.C.M.G., G.C.V.O., C.B.E.; British (b. New Zealand) surgeon and administrator; b. 10 Aug. 1900, Wanganui; ed. Wanganui Collegiate School and Otago Univ., New Zealand, Oxford Univ. and St. Mary's Hosp. Medical School, London.
St. Mary's Hospital Surgical Staff 36-65; War service with R.A.M.C. Second World War; mem. Royal medical Household 36-67; Surgeon to Duke of York 36, to Household 37-46, to King George VI 46-52, Sergeant-Surgeon to Queen Elizabeth 53-67; Consulting Surgeon to the Army; Pres. Royal Coll. of Surgeons of England 60-63; Pres. B.M.A. 60-61; mem. Int. Olympic Cttee. 34- (now Hon. mem.); Chair. British Empire and Commonwealth Games 48-67, Vice-Pres. 68-; Pres. Royal Soc. of Medicine 66-67; Gov.-Gen. of New Zealand 67-72; Pres. Medical Comm. on Accident Prevention; fmr. Pres. Co. of Veteran Motorists, British Asscn. of Sport and Medicine; Pres. Arthritis and Rheumatism Council 74-, Royal Australian Coll. of Radiologists; Vice-Pres. Royal Commonwealth Soc.; mem. Chapter, Gen. Order of St. John and Knight of Justice; Dir. Sterling Winthrop Pharmaceuticals Ltd., Sterling Europa; Hon. Fellow, Royal Coll. of Surgeons of Edinburgh, Glasgow, Ireland, Australasia and Canada, and American and South African Colls. of Surgeons; Hon. Fellow, Royal Coll. of Physicians (London), Royal Australian Coll. of Physicians, Royal Coll. of Obstetricians and Gynaecologists; Hon. LL.D. (St. Andrews, Birmingham, Otago and New Zealand), Hon. D.Sc. (Oxford), Hon. M.D. (Bristol); Gold Medal B.M.A.; bronze medal, 100 metres, Olympic Games 24.
Publs. *Athletics* (with D. G. A. Lowe) 29, *Essentials of Modern Surgery* (with R. M. Handfield-Jones) 39, and numerous articles in medical journals.
57 Hamilton Terrace, London, N.W.8, England.

Porter, Hal; Australian author and playwright; b. 16 Feb. 1911, Albert Park, Vic.; ed. Kensington and Bairnsdale State Schools, Bairnsdale High School.
Schoolmaster, Educ. Dept. of Victoria State 27-37, Queen's Coll., Adelaide 38-41, Prince Alfred Coll., Adelaide 42-45, Hutchins School, Hobart 46-47, Knox Grammar School, Sydney 47-48, Ballarat Coll., Ballarat 48-49, Nijimura School, Japan 49-51; Regional Librarian for Gippsland and North Central Vic. 52-60; full-time author 61-; Commonwealth Literary Fellowships 56, 60, 64, 68, 72, 74-76, 77-79, 80; Britannica Literary Award 76, Fellow Emer. 81.
Publs. *Short Stories* 42, *The Hexagon* 56, *A Handful of Pennies* 58, *The Tilted Cross* 61, *A Bachelor's Children* 62, *The Tower* 63, *The Watcher on the Cast-Iron Balcony* 63, *The Cats of Venice* 65, *Stars of the Australian Stage and Screen* 65, *The Paper Chase* 66, *The Professor* 66, *The Actors: an Image of the New Japan* 68, *Elijah's Ravens* 68, *Eden House* 69, *Mr. Butterfry* 70, *Selected Stories* 71, *The Right Thing* 71, *It Could be You* 72, *Fredo Fuss Love Life* 74, *In an Australian Country Graveyard* 74, *The Extra* 75, *Bairnsdale: Portrait of an Australian Country Town* 77, *Seven Cities* 78, *A Portable Hal Porter* 80, *Parker* 81, *The Clairvoyant Goat* 81.
Weeroona, 504 Nicholson Street, Ballarat, Vic. 3350, Australia.
Telephone: (053) 306631.

Prabhjot Kaur; Indian poet and politician; b. 6 July 1927; ed. Khalsa Coll. for Women, Lahore and Punjab Univ.
First collected poems published 43; rep. India at numerous int. literary confs.; mem. Legislative Council, Punjab 66-; mem. Cen. Comm. of UNESCO; Editor *Vikendrit*; Assoc. Editor *Byword*; Sahitya Sharomani 64; Padma Shri 67; title of Rajya Kavi (Poet Laureate) by Punjab Govt. 64; mem. Sahitya Akademi (Nat. Acad. of Letters) (mem. Exec. Bd. 78); Sahitya Akademi Award 65; Grand Prix de la Rose de France 68; Most Distinguished Order of Poetry, World Poetry Society Intercontinental, U.S.A. 74; Woman of the Year, U.P.L.I., Philippines 75; Sewa Sifti Award 80; NIF Cultural Award 81; Josh Kenya Award 82.
Publs. 35 books, including: Poems: *Supne Sadran* 49, *Do Rang* 51, *Pankheru* 56, *Lala* (in Persian) 58, *Benkapani* 58, *Pabbi* 62, *Plateau* (English) 66, *Khari* 67, *Wad-Darshi Sheesha* 72, *Madhiantr* 74, *Chandra Yug* 78, *Dreams Die Young* 79; Short stories: *Kinke* 52, *Aman de Na* 56, *Zindgi de Kujh Pal* 82.
D-203, Defence Colony, New Delhi 24, India.

Pramoedya Ananta Toer; Indonesian novelist; b. 26 Feb. 1925, Blora, East Java.
Worked with *Domei*, Japanese news agency to 45; studied as stenographer; wrote first book *Sepulah Kepala Nika* (Ten Chiefs of Nika), Jakarta 45; manuscript lost before printing; 2nd Lieut., Indonesian revolution, Bekasi, east of Jakarta; with Voice of Free Indonesia producing Indonesian language magazine; arrested by Dutch July 47; wrote first major works, Bukit Duri gaol; editor, Indonesian Library of Congress after release to 51; arrested on order of Gen. A. H. Nasution (*q.v.*) in connection with book on overseas Chinese 60; released 61; aligned with communist-sponsored cultural groups; leading figure in Lekkra, Indonesian Communist Party cultural asscn.; arrested Nov. 66; with first political prisoners on Buni island; released Jan. 80; 7 novels (2 published so far), one drama

and 2 minor works composed in prison, Buni 66-80; novels banned May 81.
Novels incl. *Keluarga Guerilya*, *Bumi Manusia* (The World of Man) 73, *Anak Semua Bangsa* (A Child of All Nations), *Jajak Langkah* (Strides Forward), *Bumah Kaca* The Greenhouse).

Pramoj, Mom Rachawongse Kukrit; Thai politician; b. 20 April 1911; brother of M. R. Seni Pramoj (*q.v.*); ed. Suan Kularb Coll., Trent Coll., Queen's Coll., Oxford.
With Revenue Dept., Ministry of Finance; Siam Commercial Bank; Head of Gov.'s Office, Bank of Thailand, later Head of Issue Dept.; mem. Parl. 46-76, Nat. Legis. Assembly 77-; Deputy Minister of Finance 47-48, later of Commerce; Founded *Siam Rath* newspaper 50; Leader Social Action Party; Speaker Nat. Assembly 73-74; Prime Minister March 75-April 76, also Minister of the Interior Jan.-April 76; mem. Cttee. to draft new Constitution 77-78; Dir. of Thai Studies, Thammasat Univ.; Pres. Exec. Cttee., Foundation for the Assistance of Needy Schoolchildren; appeared in film *The Ugly American* 63.
National Legislative Assembly, Bangkok, Thailand.

Pramoj, Mom Rachawongse Seni, B.A.; Thai lawyer and politician; b. 26 May 1905, Nakhon Sawan Province; brother of M. R. Kukrit Pramoj (*q.v.*); ed. Trent Coll. and Worcester Coll., Oxford.
Called to English Bar and later to Thai Bar; Judge, Appeal Court, Bangkok; Minister, Thai Legation Washington, D.C.; Prime Minister 45-46; law practice 46-; successively Minister of Foreign Affairs, of Justice, of Educ., of Defence 46-47; lectured at Thamasat and Chulalongkorn Univs. 47; Deputy Leader Prachatipat Party (Democratic Party), Leader 68-; mem. Nat. Assembly 69-71; Prime Minister Feb.-March 75, April-Oct. 76; Minister of the Interior April-Oct. 76; resgnd. for one day in Sept.; formed new cabinet; deposed by mil. coup Oct. 76; mem. Cttee. to draft new Constitution 77-78.
Publs. several law books and English translations of Thai poetry.
219 Egamai Road, Bangkok, Thailand.
Telephone: 3911632.

Prapas Charusathiara, Field-Marshal (*see* Charusathiara, Field-Marshal Prapas).

Prawiro, Radius, M.A.; Indonesian economist and banker; b. 29 June 1928, Yogyakarta; ed. Senior High School, Yogyakarta, Nederlandsche Economische Hoogeschool, Rotterdam, Econ. Univ. of Indonesia.
Secretary Defence Cttee., Yogyakarta during revolution 45; with Army High Command, Yogyakarta 46-47; Angauta Tentara Pelajar (Army) 48-51; Officer in Govt. Audit Office, Ministry of Finance 53-65; Vice-Minister, Deputy Supreme Auditor, mem. Supreme Audit Office 65-66; Gov. Bank Indonesia 66-73; Gov. for Indonesia, IMF 67-71; Chair. Board of Govs., IBRD, IDA, IFC 71-72; Alt. Gov. Asian Devt. Bank 67-72; Minister of Trade 73-78, of Trade and Co-operatives 78-; Chair. Special Co-ordinating Cttee. ASEAN 73-78; Chair. Indonesian Assen. of Accountants 65-; mem. Econ. Council of the Pres. 68-, Nat. Econ. Stabilization Council 68-, Indonesian Monetary Council, Gov. Board Christian Univ. of Indonesia, Supervisory Board Trisakti Univ.
Ministry of Trade and Co-operatives, Jalan Abdul Muis 87, Jakarta; Home: Taman Dharmawangsa 11, Jakarta Selatan, Indonesia.

Prem Chand, Lieut.-Gen. D.; Indian army officer (retd.) and United Nations official; b. 1916, Muzaffargarh (now in Pakistan); ed. Govt. Coll., Lahore and Staff Coll., Quetta.
Commissioned Indian Army 37; served in Gen. Staff Army HQ, New Delhi 47, later apptd. Mil. Asst. to Chief of Army Staff; commanded Regimental Cen. of First Gurkha Rifles; Instructor, Defence Services Staff Coll., Wellington; subsequently apptd. Deputy Dir. of Mil. Training, Dir. of Personnel Services, Dir. of Mil. Intelligence, New Delhi; Chief of Staff, HQ Western Command, Simla 61, Commanded Brigade and Div. in Western Command; Gen.-Officer, Katanga Area, UN Operation in the Congo 62-63; Commanded Div. in Eastern Command, Chief of Staff, HQ Eastern Command, Calcutta; Dir.-Gen. Nat. Cadet Corps; retd. 67 then held admin. post in industrial concern; Commdr. UN Force, Cyprus (UNFICYP) 69-76; UN Sec.-Gen.'s Rep. for Rhodesia 77; Commdr. (designate) UN Group for Namibia 80-; rank of Lieut.-Gen. 74; Param Vishisht Seva Medal.
c/o UN Information Centre, 55 Lodi Estate, New Delhi, India.

Prem Tinsulanond, Gen. (*see* Tinsulanond, Gen. Prem).

Premadasa, Ranasinghe; Sri Lankan politician and local government official; b. 23 June 1924; ed. Lorenz Coll., St. Joseph Coll., Colombo.
Began political career as member of Ceylon Labour Party and elected to Municipal Council, Colombo 50, Deputy Mayor 55; joined United Nat. Party (U.N.P.) 56; Third Mem. Colombo Cen. Constituency, House of Reps. 60-65, Second Mem. 65-70, First Mem. 70-77; First Mem. Colombo Cen. Constituency, Nat. State Assembly 77-; Parl. Sec. to Minister of Local Govt. 65, Chief Whip of Govt. Parl. Group 65, Parl. Sec. to Minister of Information and Broadcasting, and to Minister of Local Govt. 66; Minister of Local Govt. 68-70; Chief Whip of Opposition Parl. Group, House of Reps. (later Nat. State Assembly) 70-77; Deputy Leader U.N.P. 76-; Minister of Local Govt., Housing and Construction, and Leader of Nat. State Assembly July 77-, Prime Minister of Sri Lanka Feb. 78-, also Minister of Highways 80-; Del. to Buddha Sangayana, Burma 55, to China and Soviet Union 59, to Commonwealth Parl. Conf., Canberra, Australia 70; successful negotiations with Friedrich Ebert Foundation (Fed. Repub. of Germany) to set up Sri Lanka Inst. in Sri Lanka 65.
Publs. numerous books in Sinhala.
Office of the Prime Minister, Colombo, Sri Lanka.

Price, Sir (James) Robert, K.B.E., D.PHIL., D.SC., F.A.A., Australian organic chemist; b. 25 March 1912, Kadina; S. Australia; ed. St. Peter's Coll., Adelaide and Univs. of Adelaide and Oxford.
Head, Chemistry Section, John Innes Horticultural Inst., U.K. 37; Ministry of Supply (U.K.) 39; Council for Scientific and Industrial Research (C.S.I.R.) Div. of Industrial Chem., Australia 45; Officer in charge, Organic Chem. Section, Commonwealth Scientific and Industrial Research Org. (CSIRO) 60, subsequently Chief Organic Chem. Div.; mem. Exec. CSIRO 66; Chair. CSIRO 70-77; retd.; Chair. Nat. Cttee. for Chem. 66-69; Pres. Royal Australian Chem. Inst. (R.A.C.I.) 63-64; mem. Council Monash Univ. 79-; H. G. Smith Memorial Medal (R.A.C.I.) 56, Leighton Memorial Medal (R.A.C.I.) 69.
Publs. Numerous scientific papers and articles.
"Yangoora", 2 Ocean View Avenue, Red Hill South, East R.S.D., Dromana, Vic. 3936, Australia.

Pringle, John Martin Douglas, M.A.; British journalist; b. 28 June 1912; ed. Shrewsbury School, and Lincoln Coll., Oxford.
Member staff of *Manchester Guardian* 34-39; served in Army 40-44; Asst. Editor *Manchester Guardian* 44; joined staff *The Times* 48; Editor *Sydney Morning Herald* 52-57, 65-70; Deputy Editor *The Observer* 58-63; Man. Editor *Canberra Times* 64-65.
Publs. *China Struggles for Unity* 38, *Australian Accent* 58, *Australian Painting Today* 63, *On Second Thoughts* 71, *Have pen: will travel* 73; *The Last Shenachie* 76.
103 Riverview Road, Avalon Beach, N.S.W. 2107, Australia.

Q

Qi Tian; Chinese politician.
Minister of the First Ministry of Machine-Building 79-80.
People's Republic of China.

Qian Changzhao; Chinese politician; b. 1899, Changshu City, Jiangsu; ed. London School of Economics and Oxford Univ.
Secretary in Foreign Affairs Ministry, Kuomintang (KMT) Govt., Sec. of Nat. Govt., Perm. Vice-Minister of Educ. 28-30; then successively Deputy Sec.-Gen., Deputy Dir. and Chair. Nat. Resources Comm., Kuomintang Govt. 32-47; attended first session CPPCC and elected mem. Nat. Cttee. June 49; later mem. Financial and Econ. Comm. under Govt. Admin. Council and Deputy Dir. Planning Bureau; currently mem. Comm. Legis. Affairs, NPC Standing Cttee., and Vice-Chair. Cen. Cttee. of Revolutionary Cttee. of Chinese KMT; Vice-Chair. CPPCC Nat. Cttee. Sept. 80-.
People's Republic of China.

Qian Zhengying, Miss; Chinese government official; b. 1922; ed. Dadong Univ., Shanghai.
Vice-Minister of Water Conservancy 52-58, of Water Conservancy and Electrical Power 58; Minister of Water Conservancy and Power 75-79, of Water Conservancy 79-; also of Power March 82-; Adviser to State Council 81-82, mem. 82-; mem. 11th Cen. Cttee. of CCP 77.
People's Republic of China.

Qian Zhiguang; Chinese party official; b. 1901.
Vice-Minister of Textile Industry 49; Minister of Light Industry 75-78, of Textile Industry 78-81; Adviser to State Council 81-; mem. 11th Cen. Cttee. of CCP 77.
c/o State Council, Beijing, People's Republic of China.

Qiao Guanhua; Chinese politician; b. 1908, Yancheng, Jiangsu; ed. Qinghua Univ., Beijing and Univ. of Tübingen, Fed. Repub. of Germany.
Director S. China Branch, New China News Agency 46-49; Deputy Dir., Gen. Office, Cen. People's Govt. 49-54; Asst. to Minister of Foreign Affairs 54-64; Vice-Minister of Foreign Affairs 64-74, Minister 74-Dec. 76; Head of Chinese del. to Sino-Soviet Border talks 69; Leader of del. to UN Gen. Assembly 71; mem. 10th Cen. Cttee. of CCP 73.
People's Republic of China.

Qiao Xiaoguang; Chinese party official.
Deputy Sec. CCP Guangxi 53, Sec. 61-66, 73-76, First Sec. 77-; Vice-Chair. Guangxi Revolutionary Cttee. 68-76, Chair. 77-; First Sec. CCP Guangxi and Chair., Guangxi Revolutionary Cttee. 77; First Political Commissar, Guangxi Mil. District PLA 77-79; mem. 11th Cen. Cttee. of CCP 77.
People's Republic of China.

Qin Jiwei; Chinese army officer; b. Hongan, Hubei.
Company Commdr. Red Army 31; Deputy Commdr. Yunnan Mil. District, People's Liberation Army 54; Deputy Commdr. Kunming Mil. Region, PLA 55, Commdr. 58; Lieut.-Gen. PLA 55; Sec. CCP Yunnan 66-68; Commdr. Chengdu Mil. Region, PLA 73-76; Second Political Commissar, Beijing Mil. Region 76-78, First Political Commissar 78-; Cmmdr. Beijing Mil. Region 80; mem. 10th Cen. Cttee. of CCP 73, 11th Cen. Cttee. 77.
People's Republic of China.

Quiazon, Troadio T., LL.B.; Philippine government official; b. 13 June 1921, Manila; ed. Univ. of the Philippines.
Member of the Philippine Bar 48; Professorial Lecturer in Public Law, Univ. of the Philippines 58-70; Legal Counsel and Chief of Legal Staff, Joint Legislative Executive Tax Comm. 60-68, Tax Consultant 67-70; Officer-in-charge, Board of Industries 62-70, Securities and Exchange Comm. 70; Chair. Board of Travel and Tourist Industry 71-73; Under-Sec. of Industry 70-71, Sec. of Commerce and Industry 71-72, of Trade and Tourism 72-73, of Trade 73-78; Minister of Trade 78-79; Chair. Metric System Board, Philippine Shippers Council, Philippine Int. Trading Corpn., Fair Trade Board, Price Stabilization Council, Design Centre Philippines and 8 other orgs. concerned with trade or nat. econ.; mem. 33 other bodies, incl. Nat. Econ. and Devt. Authority, Philippine Export Council, Philippine Port Authority, Maritime Industry Authority, Cement Industry Authority; Vice-Chair. ECAFE Session, Bangkok 72; Chair. or Head of Philippine dels. to int. confs. concerning trade incl. UNCTAD, ECAFE, ESCAP, ASEAN.
Publs. co-author: *Philippine Law on Income, Estate Inheritance and Gift Taxation.*
c/o Ministry of Trade, Filcapital Building, Ayala Avenue, Makati, Metro Manila, Philippines.

Qureshi, Anwar Iqbal, M.A., M.SC., PH.D.; Pakistani economist; b. 10 April 1910; ed. Forman Christian Coll., Lahore, London School of Economics, Trinity Coll., Dublin.
Professor, Head Econs. Dept., Osmania Univ. 37-47; Econ. Adviser, Govt. of Hyderabad 44-47; Deputy Econ. Adviser Govt. of Pakistan 47-51; Adviser, IMF 51-55; Financial and Econ. Adviser, Saudi Arabia 55-59; Econ. Adviser and Sec. Govt. of Pakistan 61-68, Additional Sec. 68-70, retd.; Chief Economist, Sabasun Tech. Services, Lahore 74-; mem. Council for Econ. Advisory Affairs 75-; Econ. Adviser, Engineering and Technical Consultants, Lahore 78-, Lahore Chambers of Commerce and Industry; Pres. Pakistan Econ. Asscn.; Sitara-i-Quaid-i-Azam 65.
Publs. *The Farmer and His Debt* 34, *Agricultural Credit* 36, *The State and Economic Life* 37, *State Banks for India* 39, *Islam and the Theory of Interest* 46, *The Future of Co-operative Movement in India* 47, *Economic Development of Hyderabad* 48, *Development in Pakistan's Economy since the Revolution* 60, *Pakistan's March on Road to Prosperity* 65, *Mr. Mujib's Six Points: An Economic Appraisal* 70, *Economic Problems Facing Pakistan* 71, *The Economy of Pakistan from January 1972 to June 1977: an Economic Appraisal, The Economic History of Pakistan, The Fiscal System of Islam, The Economic and Social System of Islam.*
Al-Haniyah, 295/3 Sarwar Road, Lahore Cantt., Pakistan.
Telephone: 70431.

Qureshi, Ishtiaq Husain, M.A., PH.D.; Pakistani scholar and politician; b. 20 Nov. 1903, Patiali; ed. St. Stephen's Coll. (Univ. of Delhi), and Sidney Sussex Coll., Cambridge.
Lecturer in History, St. Stephen's Coll. 28; Reader in History Univ. of Delhi 40, Prof. and Head of Dept. of History 44, Dean of Faculty of Arts 45; mem. for Bengal, Constituent Assembly of Pakistan 47; Prof. of History and Head of Dept. of History, Punjab Univ. 48; Deputy Minister of the Interior, Information and Broadcasting, Refugees and Rehabilitation, Govt. of Pakistan 49, Minister of State 50, Minister for Refugees and Rehabilitation, Information and Broadcasting 51-53; Minister of Educ. 53-55; mem. Advisory Council of Islamic Ideology 62-63, Nat. Comm. on Educ. and Manpower 68-69; mem. Tehrik-i-Istiqlal Party (Vice-Pres. 76-); Visiting Prof. Columbia Univ., New York 55-60; Dir. Central Inst. of Islamic Research, Karachi 60-62; Vice-Chancellor Univ. of Karachi 61-71; Pres. Pakistan Acad. of Letters 79; Chair. Nat. Language Authority, Karachi 79; Star of Pakistan 64.
Publs. *The Administration of the Sultanate of Delhi* 41, *The Pakistani Way of Life* 56, *The Muslim Community in the Indo-Pakistan Sub-Continent* 62, *The Struggle for Pakistan* 65, *The Administration of the Moghul Empire* 67, *Ulema in Politics* 72, *Education in Pakistan* 75, *Akbar* 78, *Perspectives of Islam and Pakistan* 79.

3-B 4th Central Lane, Defence Housing Society, Karachi; Zeba Manzar, 1 Sharafabad, Shahid-i-Millat Road, Karachi 5, Pakistan.
Telephone: 541211; 411339.

Qureshi, Moeen Ahmad, M.A., PH.D.; Pakistani economist and international official; b. 26 June 1930, Lahore; ed. Islamia Coll. and Govt. Coll., Univ. of Punjab and Indiana Univ., U.S.A.
Social Science Consultant, Ford Foundation, Pakistan 53; Hon. Lecturer, Univ. of Karachi 53-54; Asst. Chief, Planning Comm., Govt. of Pakistan 54-56, Deputy Chief 56-58; Economist, IMF 58-61, Div. Chief 61-65, Adviser Africa Dept. 65-66, Resident Rep., Ghana 66-68, Senior Adviser 68-70; Econ. Adviser IFC 70-74, Vice-Pres. 74-77, Exec. Vice-Pres. 77-80; Vice-Pres. Finance, World Bank 79-80, Sr. Vice-Pres. Finance Aug. 80-.
Publs. various articles in economic journals.
c/o International Finance Corporation, 1818 H Street, N.W., Washington, D.C. 20433; 11108 Gilcrist Court, Potomac Falls, Potomac, Md. 20854, U.S.A. (Home).
Telephone: (202) 477-2281 (IFC); (301) 299-9542 (Home).

R

Rabukawaqa, Sir Josua Rasilau, K.B.E., M.V.O.; Fijian diplomatist; b. 2 Dec. 1917; ed. Queen Victoria School, Fiji, Teachers' Training Coll., Auckland, N.Z.
Teacher, Fiji 38-52; Platoon Officer 1st Battalion Fiji Infantry Regt. Malayan Campaign 54-55; Adjutant Fiji Mil. Forces 55-56; Co-operatives Inspector 53-57; Asst. Econ. Devt. Officer 57-61; Asst. Roko 59-62; District Officer, Overseas Colonial Service 62-68; Clerk to Council; First Protocol Officer in Fiji; Commr. Central 69-70; High Commr. in U.K. 70-76, Perm. Rep. to EEC 70-76; Amb.-at-Large 77-80; Special Rep. and High Commissioner to South Pacific Forum states 78-80; Head of Protocol 78-80; Man. Fiji Cricket Team in World Cup Competition, England 79.
6 Vunivini Hill, Nausori, Fiji.

Ragchaa, Tümenbayaryn; Mongolian politician; b. 21 Jan. 1917; ed. Central School for Party and State Cadres, Ulan Bator, higher co-operative courses, U.S.S.R. and Mongolian State Univ.
Clerk in Uvs Province admin. office, primary school teacher 30-32; official of various provincial co-operative orgs. 36-54; Head of a Dept., then Deputy Chair. Cen. Co-operative Union, then Chief Book-keeper, then Dir. of Finance Dept. of Ministry of Foreign Trade 54-58; lecturer at Mongolian State Univ. 58-59; First Deputy Chair. State Planning Comm. 59-60; Deputy Chair. Council of Ministers 60-72, First Deputy Chair. 72-; Deputy Chair. State Rural Construction Comm. 71-; mem. Mongolian People's Revolutionary Party (MPRP) Cen. Cttee. 61-; cand. mem. Political Bureau of MPRP Cen. Cttee. 72-74, mem. Political Bureau 74-; Deputy to People's Great Hural (Assembly) 60-; Order of Sühbaatar (twice).
Government Palace, Ulan Bator, Mongolia.

Raghavan, Venkatarama, M.A., PH.D.; Indian Sanskrit scholar; b. 22 Aug. 1908; ed. Tiruvarur High School and Madras Univ.
Superintendent Sarasvati Mahal Manuscript Library, Tanjore 30; successively Research Scholar, Research Asst., Lecturer, Reader, Prof. and Head of Dept., Madras Univ. Dept. of Sanskrit 31-69; Editor *Journal of Oriental Research, Madras Music Academy Journal, Sanskrita-Pratibha, Sanskrit Ranga Annual, Malayamaruta*; mem. Govt. of India Sanskrit Comm. and Cen. Sanskrit Board, Indian Acad. of Letters; Fellow, Acad. of Music, Dance and Drama; Hon. corresp. mem. Ecole Française d'Extrême Orient, Austrian Acad. of Sciences; Pres. All-India Oriental Conf., Int. Asscn. of Sanskrit Studies; Kane Gold Medal (Bombay Asiatic Soc.) 53; awarded titles of Kavikokila and Sakalakala-Kalapa by Sankaracharya 53; Padma Bhushan by Govt. of India 63; Indian Acad. of Letters, Award for best book on Sanskrit research 66; Jawaharlal Nehru Fellowship 69; Gold Medal and Membership of Noble Order of St. Martin (Austria) 67; Kalidas Award (Uttar Pradesh) 74, (Madhya Pradesh) 75; Hon. D.Litt. (Sanskrit Univ., Varanasi).
Publs. include: English: *Some Concepts of Alankara Sastra* 42, 73, *New Catalogus Catalogorum* 49-68, *The Indian Heritage, Sanskrit and Allied Indological Studies in Europe, Yantras or Mechanical Contrivances in Ancient India* 56, *Concept of Culture* 71, *Seasons in Sanskrit Literature* 72; Tamil: *Varalakshmivratam* (short stories) 50, *Bharata Natya* 59, *Kadaikkadal* 59, *Nataka Lakshanaratnakosa* 61, *Bhoja's Sringara Prakasa* 63; Patel Lectures: *The Great Integrators—Saint-Singers of India* 66, *Nrttaratnavali* 68, *The Greater Ramayana* 73, *Sanskrit in Allied Indian Studies in S.* 75, *Ramayana in Greater India* 75, *Festivals and Pastimes of India* 77; Sanskrit: *Rasalila, Kamasuddhi, Manunitichola, Davabandi Varadaraia, Prekshanakatrayi, Vimukti, Valmiki pratibha, Natirpuja, Vidyanathavidambana, Anarkali* 74 (poems and plays).

Rahma Brahmam, Muluktla, B.E., F.I.E.; Indian oil executive; b. 24 Aug. 1912, Paddapuram, Andhra; ed. Madras Univ.
Superintendent Engineer and Engineer-in-Charge, Kandla Port Trust 50-59; Chief Engineer and Gen. Man., Gauhati Refinery, Assam 59-65; Man. Dir. Madras Refineries Ltd. 65-69, Chair. and Man. Dir. 69-71; Chair. Indian Oil Corpn. Ltd. 71-73, Madras Refineries Ltd. 72-78, Bongaigaon Refinery and Petrochemicals Ltd. 75-78; Man. Dir. Madras Petrochemicals Ltd. 78-; Fellow, Inst. of Engineers (India); Padma Bhushan 70.
Publs. technical papers in engineering journals in India and abroad.
c/o Madras Petrochemicals Ltd., Manali, Madras 600068; Home: AB-51 Anna Nagar, Madras 600040, India.
Telephone: 553395 (Office); 613958 (Home).

Rahman, Shah Azizur; Bangladesh politician and lawyer; b. 23 Nov. 1925, Kushtia.
General Sec. All-India Muslim Students Fed., All-Bengal Muslim Students League 45-47; Chair. East Pakistan Combined Opposition Party 64; Leader Awami League Parl. Party and Deputy Leader of Opposition, Nat. Assembly of Pakistan 65-69; Senior Advocate Supreme Court of Bangladesh; mem. Bangladesh Parl. for Daulatpore, Kushtia constituency; Leader of the House; Minister for Labour and Industrial Welfare 78-79; Prime Minister and Minister of Educ. 79-82, Minister of Law and Parl. Affairs, Local Govt., Rural Devt. and Co-operatives, and Religious Affairs Feb.-March 82; mem. Bangladesh Bar Council.
c/o Office of the Prime Minister, Dacca, Bangladesh.

Rais Abin, Maj.-Gen.; Indonesian army officer; b. 15 Aug. 1926; ed. Army Staff Coll., Queenscliffe, Australia, Nat. Defence Coll., Indonesia, Defence Management Inst., Indonesia.
Senior Asst. Planning of Army Logistics, Indonesian Army 69-72; Deputy Commdr., Army Staff and Command Coll., Indonesia 73-75; Chief of Staff, UN Emergency Force (in Egypt) Jan.-Nov. 76, Acting Force Commdr. Dec. 76, Force Commdr. 77-.
United Nations Emergency Force, P.O. Box 138, Ismailia, Egypt; 50 Cik Ditiro, Jakarta, Indonesia.

Raisani, Sardar Ghaus Bakhsh; Pakistani politician; b. 6 Sept. 1924, Kanak, Baluchistan; ed. Col. Brown Cambridge School, Dehra Dun.
Commissioned, Indian Army 45, served 45-48; Tribal Chief, Baluchistan 49-; active in politics 49-; Convener,

Baluchistan State Muslim League; mem. W. Pakistan Assembly 56; founder and Convener, Baluchistan United Front 70; mem. Baluchistan Assembly 70-77, Leader of the Opposition 72-74; Gov. of Baluchistan 71-72; Fed. Minister of Food and Agriculture 72-74; Senior Minister Baluchistan Prov. Cabinet 74-76; Pres. Pakistan People's Party Baluchistan 74-77.
Shara-e-Nawab Raisani, Raisani House, Quetta, Pakistan. Telephone: 70661.

Raja Haji Ahmad, Raja Tan Sri Aznam, P.S.M., B.A.; Malaysian diplomatist; b. 21 Jan. 1928, Taiping; ed. King Edward VII Coll., Taiping, Malay Coll. Kuala Kangsar, Univ. of Malaya in Singapore.
Joined Malayan Civil Service 53, Foreign Service 56; Second Sec., Bangkok 57, First Sec., Cairo 60-62; Principal Asst. Sec. Ministry of Foreign Affairs 62-65; Deputy Perm. Rep. to UN 65-68; High Commr. in India 68-71; Amb. to Japan 71-74, to U.S.S.R., Bulgaria, Hungary, Mongolia, Poland and Romania 74-77, to France, Morocco, Portugal and Spain 77-79; High Commr. in U.K. July 79-.
Malaysian High Commission, 45 Belgrave Square, London, SW1X 8QT, England.
Telephone: 01-235 8033.

Rajaratnam, Sinnathamby; Singapore politician; b. 23 Feb. 1915, Ceylon (now Sri Lanka); ed. Raffles Inst., Singapore, King's Coll., London.
Associate Ed. *Singapore Standard* 50-54; Editorial Staff *Straits Times* 54-59; co-founder, also fmr. Pres. Singapore Union of Journalists; mem. Malayanization Cttee. 55; mem. Minimum Standards of Livelihood Cttee. 56; a Convenor and Founder-mem. of People's Action Party 54, later mem. Cen. Exec. Cttee. and Dir. of Political Bureau; mem. Legislative Assembly for Kampong Glam constituency 59-; mem. Fed. Malaysian Parl. 63-65; Minister for Culture 59-65, for Foreign Affairs 65-80, concurrently for Labour 68-71; Second Deputy Prime Minister (Foreign Affairs) June 80-.
Office of the Second Deputy Prime Minister, Singapore 6.

Ram, Dr. Bharat, B.A.; Indian industrialist, b. 5 Oct. 1914; ed. privately and at St. Stephen's Coll., Delhi. Joined Delhi Cloth and General Mills Co. 35, Joint Man. Dir. 48, Chair. Board of Dirs. 58-; also Chair. Bengal Potteries, Shriram Bearings; Chair. Coromandel Fertilisers 67-; Chair. Indian Airlines 67-69; Chair. Indian Cotton Mills Federation 61-63; Pres. Fed. of Indian Chambers of Commerce & Industry 63-64; Pres. Int. Chamber of Commerce 69-71, World Council of Management 76-80; mem. Bd. of Govs., Delhi and Pilani Insts. of Technology; Dir. New India Assurance Co., Escorts, Bajaj Electricals.
25 Sarder Patel Road, New Delhi, India.

Ram, Jagjivan, B.SC.; Indian politician; b. 5 April 1908, Arrah, Bihar; ed. Patna Univ., Banaras Hindu Univ. and Calcutta Univ.
Joined Indian Nat. Congress 32; Gen. Sec. All-India Depressed Classes League until 36; Pres. 36-46; mem. Legislative Council, Bihar 36, Parl. Sec. 37-39; formed Bihar section of Khet Mazdoor Sabha (Agricultural Labourers' Org.) 37; Sec. Bihar Provincial Congress Cttee. 40-46; Vice-Pres. Bihar Branch All-India T.U.C. 40-46; imprisoned 40, 42, released 43; Chair. Preparatory Conf. of ILO Asian Region 47, leader del. to ILO Conf., Chair. Conf. 50; Minister for Labour 46-52 (Interim Govt. and first Fed. Govt.), for Communications 52-56, 62-63, for Railways and Transport 56-57, for Railways 57-62, resgnd. to work in admin. of Congress 63-66; Minister for Labour and Employment and Rehabilitation 66-67, for Food, Agriculture, Community Devt. and Co-operation 67-70, for Defence 70-74, for Agriculture and Irrigation 74-Feb. 77, resgnd.; mem. numerous cttees. and Cen. Parl. Bd. of All-India Congress Cttee. 48-77; Pres. All-India Congress Cttee. 69-71, 81-; resgnd. from Congress to set up Congress for Democracy Feb. 77, which merged with Janata Party May 77; mem. Janata Party Exec. Cttee., Chair. 79-80; Minister for Defence 77-79, Deputy Prime Minister June-July 79; mem. Lok Sabha for Sarasararn, Bihar March 77-; resgnd. from Janata Party 80; mem. opposition Congress Party 80-81; mem. Indian Nat. Congress Aug. 81-; leader of dels. to FAO conf. 67, 70, 74, 75, 76; Chair. Indian Inst. of Public Admin. 74-; numerous hon. degrees and awards.
6 Krishna Menon Marg, New Delhi 110011, India (Home). Telephone: 376555 (Home).

Ramachandran, Gopalasamudram Narayana, D.SC., PH.D., F.R.S., F.R.S.A.; Indian scientist and university professor; b. 8 Oct. 1922; ed. Maharaja's Coll., Ernakulam (Cochin), Indian Inst. of Science, Univs. of Madras and Cambridge.
Lecturer in Physics, Indian Inst. of Science 46-49, Asst. Prof. 49-52; 1851 Exhbn. Scholar, Univ. of Cambridge 47-49; Prof. and Head of Dept. Univ. of Madras 52-70, Dean of Faculty 63-70; Prof. of Biophysics, Indian Inst. of Science 70-, of Math. Philosophy 78-81; Fogarty Scholar, Nat. Insts. of Health, Washington, D.C. 76-77; ed. *Current Science* 49-56, *Journal of the Indian Inst. of Science* 73-76; mem. 6 editorial Boards; Fellow, Indian Acad. of Sciences 50 (Vice-Pres. 62-66); mem. Nat. Cttee. for Biophysics 61-; Fellow Indian Nat. Science Acad. 63-; part-time Prof., Univ. of Chicago 67-; Hon. Fellow Nat. Acad. of Sciences 77-; Hon. mem. American Soc. of Biological Chemists 65-; Hon. Foreign mem. American Acad. of Arts and Sciences 70-; Hon. D.Sc. (Roorkee Univ.) 78; Bhatnagar Memorial Prize 68, Ramanujam Medal 72, Meghnad Saha Medal 71, J.C. Bose Award (U.G.C.) 74, Gold Medal and Prize (Bose Inst.) 75, Fogarty Medal 78, Rotary Award 80, Kerala Award 80.
Publs. contributions to books and journals, ed. four books on optics, crystal physics, X-ray crystallography, biophysics and collagen.
CCMB, Regional Research Laboratory Campus, Hyderabad 500009; Home: 5, 10A Main, Malleswaram West, Bangalore 560055, India.
Telephone: 71874 (Office); 30362 (Home).

Ramachandran, Parthasarathy, M.A.; Indian politician; b. 15 July 1921, Korkai village in Cheyyar, Tamil Nadu; ed. Voorhese Coll., Vellore, Pachiayappa's Coll., Madras, Madras Univ.
Member of Indian Nat. Congress (later Org. Congress) 40-77; mem. Students Congress 40-45; Convener of Youth Congress in Madras 53-55; lecturer, P.S.G. Arts Coll. in Coimbatore mem. Tamil Nadu Legislative Assembly for Cheyyar 57-62, for Peranamallur 62-67, Chief Whip of Congress Party in Assembly 57-67, Chair. Estimates Cttee. 65-67, Vice-Chair. Co-ordinating Cttees. for planning forums set up in various colls. in Tamil Nadu; Sec. Tamil Nadu Org. Congress 69-72, Pres. 72-77; Pres. Janata Party in Tamil Nadu May 77-; mem. Lok Sabha from Madras Cen. March 77-; Minister for Energy 77-79.
Lok Sabha, New Delhi; Home: 55-B 7th Cross Street, Shastri Nagar, Madras 600020, India.

Ramalingaswami, Vulimiri, M.D., D.SC., F.R.C.P.; Indian medical scientist; b. 8 Aug. 1921, Srikakulum, Andhra Pradesh; ed. Univ. of Oxford.
Pathologist for Indian Council of Medical Research at Nutrition Research Laboratories, Coonor 47-54; Asst. Sec. and Deputy Dir. Indian Council of Medical Research 54-57; Prof. of Pathology and Head of Dept., All-India Inst. of Medical Sciences 57-69, Dir. and Prof. of Pathology 69-79; Dir.-Gen. Indian Council of Medical Research 79; Pres. Indian Asscn. for Advancement of Medical Educ. 74-; Fellow Indian Acad. of Medical Science 61-, Indian Nat. Science Acad. 71 (Pres. 79-80); Hon. Fellow, American Coll. of Physicians 70-; Foreign Assoc., Nat. Acad. of

Sciences, U.S.A. 73-; Dr. Sc. h.c. (Andhra Univ.) 67, Hon. Dr. Med. (Karolinska Inst.) 74; Silver Jubilee Research Award, Medical Council of India 74; Padma Bhushan 71; Bernard Prize, WHO 76; J.C. Bose Medal, Indian Nat. Science Acad. 77; R.D. Birla Award 80.
Publs. author and co-author of many papers, articles, lectures, monographs and books.
Indian Council of Medical Research, Ansari Nagar, New Delhi 110029, India.
Telephone: 667204 (Office); 373848 (Home).

Ramanujam, G.; Indian trade unionist; b. 2 Feb. 1916.
Pres. Tamil Nadu Indian Nat. Trade Union Congress; Pres. Indian Nat. Plantation Workers Fed. 60-75; Pres. Indian Nat. Trade Union Congress 58, 59, Gen. Sec. 65-; Man. Editor *Indian Worker* 65-78; Dir. Industrial Finance Corpn. of India 68-72, Indian Telephone Industries Bangalore 70-77; Chair. Cotton Corpn. of India, Bombay 74, Cen. Bd. for Workers Educ. 81-.
Publs. *From the Babul Tree, Industrial Relations—A Point of View, The Payment of Bonus Act, Payment of Gratuity Act, The Third Party.*
c/o Indian National Trade Union Congress, 1-B, Maulana Azad Road, New Delhi, India.

Ramkumar, Ramkumar, M.A.; Indian artist; b. 23 Sept. 1924; ed. Delhi Univ., Académie André Lhote, Paris, and Acad. Montmartre, Paris (with Fernand Léger).
Worked in bank for one year; French Govt. scholarship, Paris 50-52; returned to India 52; exhbns. in Europe 55, 58; travelled in Europe, Afghanistan, Ceylon, Turkey and Egypt; mem. Lalit Kala Akademi, Sahitya Akademi; Nat. Award, Nat. Art Exhbn., India 56, 58; one-man exhbns. in Delhi, Bombay, Calcutta, Paris, Prague, Warsaw, Colombo 50-65; Group exhbns. with other Indian artists in London, New York, Tokyo, etc.; exhibited at Int. exhbns., Venice, São Paulo (Hon. mention 59), Tokyo.
Publs. two novels, two story collections and a travel book.
14 A/20 W.E. Area, New Delhi 5, India.

Ramsay, Commodore Sir James Maxwell, K.C.M.G., C.B.E., D.S.C.; Australian naval officer and state governor; b. 27 Aug. 1916; ed. Hutchins School, Hobart, Tasmania.
Royal Australian Naval Coll., Jervis Bay 30, Midshipman 34, Lieut. 38, H.M.A. (Australian) and H.M. ships *Hobart, King George V, Danae, Bungaree, Warramunga, Napier, Australia* 39-45; Royal Navy Staff Course 45, Lieut.-Commdr. 46-, Fleet Navigator H.M.A.S. *Sydney* 48-50, Commdr. 50; Commanding Officer (C.O.) H.M.A.S. *Warramunga*, Korea 52, C.O. H.M.A.S. *Arunta* 53; Admiralty 53-55; U.S. Armed Forces Staff Coll. 55-56; Captain 56; Dir. of Plans 56-58; A.D.C. Gov.-Gen. 57-60; C.O. R.A.N. Coll. Jervis Bay 59-60; C.O. H.M.A.S. *Vendetta* 61-62; Imperial Defence Coll. 63; Aust. Naval Rep., U.K., as Commodore 64-65, A.D.C. to H.M. the Queen 64-66; Naval Officer Commdg. W. Australia Area and C.O. H.M.A.S. *Leeuwin* 68-72; Lieut.-Gov. W. Australia 74-77; Gov. Queensland 77-; U.S. Legion of Merit; K.St.J. 77.
Government House, Brisbane, Queensland 4001, Australia.

Rao, Calyampudi Radhakrishna, M.A., SC.D., F.N.A., F.R.S.; Indian statistician; b. 10 Sept. 1920; ed. Andhra and Calcutta Univs.
Research at Indian Statistical Inst. 43-46, Cambridge Univ. 46-48; Prof. and Head of Div. of Theoretical Research and Training 49-64; Dir. Research and Training School, Indian Statistical Inst. 64-72, Sec. and Dir. 72-76, Jawaharlal Nehru Prof. 76-; Fellow Inst. of Math. Statistics Pres.-elect 75-76, Pres. 76-77; Fellow American Statistical Asscn., Econometric Soc., Indian Acad. of Sciences; Hon. Fellow, King's Coll. Cambridge, Royal Statistical Soc.; Hon. Foreign mem. American Acad. of Arts and Science; Treas. Int. Statistical Inst. 61-65, Pres.-elect 75-77, Pres. 77-79; Pres. Biometric Soc. 74-76; Editor of *Sankhya* (Indian Journal of Statistics); Bhatnagar Memorial Award for Scientific Research; Padma Bhushan; Guy Silver Medal, Royal Statistical Soc.; Meghnad Saha Gold Medal, Indian Nat. Science Acad.; J. C. Bose Gold Medal; Hon. D.Sc. (Andhra, Leningrad, Athens, Osmania, Ohio State), D.Litt. (Delhi).
Publs. include: *Advanced Statistical Methods in Biometric Research, Linear Statistical Inference and its Application, Generalized Inverse of Matrices and its Applications, Characterization Problems of Mathematical Statistics*; over 200 research papers in mathematical statistics.
Indian Statistical Institute, 7 S.J.S. Sansanwal Marg, New Delhi 110029, India.

Rao, Chandra Rajeswar; Indian politician; b. 6 June 1914; ed. Hindu High School, Masulipatam, and Banaras Hindu Univ.
At Vizagapatam Medical Coll. 36-37; joined Communist Party, Andhra 36; mem. Cen. Cttee. Communist Party of India 48, Gen. Sec. 50-51, 64-; Order of Lenin, U.S.S.R. 74.
c/o Communist Party of India, Ajoy Bhavan, Kotla Marg, New Delhi, India.
Telephone: New Delhi 273618.

Rao, Chintamani Nagesa Ramachandra, M.SC., D.SC., PH.D., F.R.S.C., F.A.SC., F.N.A., F.R.S.; Indian chemist; b. 30 June 1934, Bangalore; ed. Mysore, Banaras, Purdue and California Univs.
Lecturer, Indian Inst. of Science, Bangalore 59-63; Prof., later Sr. Prof., Indian Inst. of Technology, Kanpur 63-77; Dean of Research and Devt. 69-72; Visiting Prof. Purdue Univ., U.S.A. 67-68, Oxford Univ. 74-75; mem. IUPAC Bureau and Chair. IUPAC Cttee. on Teaching of Chem.; mem. Nat. Cttee. on Science and Tech. 70-74, Exec. Cttee. CODATA/I.C.S.U., editorial boards of fifteen int. journals; mem. Scientific Advisory Cttee. to Cabinet 81-; Fellow, Indian Acad. of Sciences, Indian Nat. Science Acad., St. Catherine's Coll., Oxford 74-75; Jawaharlal Nehru Fellow, Indian Inst. of Tech. 73-75; Foreign mem. Acad. of Science, Yugoslavia; Hon. D.Sc. (Purdue Univ.) 82; Marlow Medal, Faraday Soc. 67; Centennial Foreign Fellowship, American Chem. Soc. 76; Bhatnagar Award 68; Padma Shri 74, FICCI Award 77, Sir C. V. Raman Award 78; S. N. Bose Medal 80; Royal Soc. of Chem. Medal 81.
Publs. *Ultraviolet Visible Spectroscopy* 60, *Chemical Applications of Infra-red Spectroscopy* 63, *Spectroscopy in Inorganic Chemistry* 70, *Modern Aspects of Solid State Chemistry* 70, *Solid State Chemistry* 74, *Phase Transitions in Solids* 78, *Preparation and Characterization of Materials* 81; nearly 400 original research papers.
Solid State and Structural Chemistry Unit, Indian Institute of Science, Bangalore 560012 (Office); Amba, 57 8th Main Road, Malleswaram, Bangalore 560055, India (Home).
Telephone: 34411 (Office); 35910 (Home).

Rao, K. N., M.B., B.S., M.D.; Indian medical official and administrator; b. 31 Jan. 1907; ed. Univ. of Madras.
Entered Indian Medical Service 35; Prof. of Medical Jurisprudence, Christian Medical Coll., Vellore 48-49; Tuberculosis Adviser to Govt. of Madras 51-54; Dir. of Medical Services, Andhra Pradesh 54-63; Dir.-Gen. of Health Services, Govt. of India 64-68; Chair. Exec. Board, WHO 67-68; Pres. World Fed. of Public Health Asscns. 67-68; Pan American Health Org. and WHO Consultant on Medical Educ. in Latin America 68; WHO Visiting Prof. of Int. Health, School of Hygiene, Toronto Univ. 68; Exec. Dir., Indian Asscn. for Advancement of Medical Educ. 68-70; WHO Consultant, Medical Educ. in Africa 70; Sec.-Gen. Population Council of India 70-73; Visiting Prof. of Medicine, Sri Venkateswara Univ. 70-71; Editor-in-Chief *Journal of Medical Education* 70-74; Exec. Dir.

Nat. Acad. of Medical Sciences 75-80; consultant, Pan American Health Org. and WHO on Health and Population Dynamics 73-74; Sec. Nat. Board of Examinations 75-80; Chair. Health Asscn. India 68-81; Pres (and Fellow) Int Medical Sciences Acad. 81-; official on numerous Indian and int. health orgs.; Fellow, Indian Acad. of Medical Sciences, Nat. Coll. of Chest Physicians; Hon. Fellow, American Public Health Asscn.; Hon. LL.D.; numerous awards.
Publs. *Recent Development in the Field of Health and Medical Education* 66, *India and World Health* 68, *Philosophy of Medicine* 68; Gen. Ed. *Text Book of Tuberculosis* 72.
Home: D-57 Naraina, New Delhi 110028, India.
Telephone: 538778 (Home).

Rao, P. V. Narasimha (*see* Narasimha Rao, P. V.).

Rao, Raja; Indian writer; b. 21 Nov. 1909; ed. Nizam Coll., Hyderabad, Univs. of Montpellier and Paris.
Former Prof. of Philosophy, now Prof. Emer., Univ. of Texas; Sahitya Akademi Award 66; Padma Bhushan 69.
Publs. *Kanthapura, Cow of the Barricades, The Serpent and the Rope, The Policeman and the Rose*, short stories in French and English, *The Cat and Shakespeare, Comrade Kirillov*, novels.
c/o Department of Philosophy, College of Humanities, University of Texas at Austin, Austin, Tex. 78712, U.S.A.

Rao, Vijayendra Kasturi Ranga Varadaraja, M.A., PH.D.; Indian economist and educationist; b. 8 July 1908; ed. Wilson Coll., Bombay, and Gonville and Caius Coll., Cambridge.
Principal and Prof. of Econs., L.D. Arts Coll., Ahmedabad 37-42; Prof. and Head of Dept. of Econs., Delhi Univ. 42-57; Dir. of Statistics, Govt. of India 44-45; Planning Adviser, Govt. of India 45-46; Food and Econ. Adviser, Embassy of India, Washington 46-47; Founder and Dir. Delhi School of Econs., Delhi Univ. 49-57, Vice-Chancellor. 57-60, Prof. emer. 66-; Founder and Dir. Inst. of Econ. Growth 60-63; mem. Indian Planning Comm. 63-66; Chair, UN Sub-Comm. on Econ. Devt. 47-50; mem. Lok Sabha 37-; Union Minister for Transport and Shipping 67-69, for Education and Youth Services 69-71; founder and Dir. Inst. for Social and Econ. Change, Bangalore 72-77; Nat. Fellow ICSSR; Hon. D.C.L. (Oxford) 69; Hon. Fellow Gonville and Caius Coll., Cambridge 71; Padma Vibhushan Award 74.
Publs. *Taxation of Income in India* 31, *An Essay on India's National Income, 1925-29* 39, *The National Income of British India, 1931-32* 40, *War and Indian Economy* 43, *India and International Currency Plans* 46, *Post-war Rupee* 48, *Foreign Aid and India's Economic Development* 62, *Essays on Economic Development* 63, *Greater Delhi—A Study in Urbanisation 1947-57* 65, *Education and Human Resource Development* 66, *Gandhian Alternative to Western Socialism* 70, *The Nehru Legacy* 71, *Values and Economic Development, The Indian Challenge* 71, *Growth with Justice in Asian Agriculture, Inflation and India's Economic Crisis* (co-author) 73, *Iran's Fifth Plan—An Attempted Economic Leap* 75, *Vivekananda—Prophet of Vedantic Socialism* 79, *Many Languages and One Nation—The Problem of Integration* 79.
Dayanidi, 1170-A, 26-A Main Road, 4th "T" block Jayanagar, Bangalore 560011, India.
Telephone: 41515.

Rashid, Sheikh Mohammad, B.A., LL.B.; Pakistani lawyer and politician; b. 24 May 1915, Kalawala, Sheikhupura District.
Joined Muslim League 40; imprisoned for political activities 47; Sec.-Gen. Pakistan Muslim League Council 48-50; Pres. Pakistan Kisan Cttee. (Organization of Peasants) 50-77; organized Azad Pakistan Party (later re-named Nat. Awami Party), Sec.-Gen. 52; launched Kisan Morcha Movt. Lahore 56; founder mem. Pakistan People's Party; Advocate, Supreme Court of Pakistan; mem. Nat. Assembly; Minister of Social Welfare, Health and Family Planning 71-74, of Food, Agriculture, Co-operatives, Underdeveloped Areas and Land Reforms 74-77, concurrently of Works 74-76; Minister of Agriculture, Co-operatives and Land Reforms March-July 77; imprisoned 77-79.

Rashidov, Sharaf Rashidovich; Soviet politician; b. 6 Nov. 1917; ed. Zhizak Teachers' Training Coll., Uzbek State Univ.
Teacher 36-37; Sec. and Asst. Ed. 38-41, Ed. of the newspaper *Lenin-Yuly* 41, 43; School Dir. 42; cadres Sec. of the Samarkand Regional Cttee. of the Party 44-47; Chief Ed. of the republican newspaper *Kzyl Uzbekistan*, Pres. of the Presidium of the Uzbek Union of Soviet Writers 47-50; Pres. of the Presidium of the Supreme Soviet of Uzbekistan, Vice-Pres. of the Presidium of the Supreme Soviet of the U.S.S.R. 50-59, mem. 70-; one of the chief organizers of the Afro-Asian Solidarity Cttee., Cairo 57; 1st Sec. Uzbek Communist Party 59-; Candidate mem. Presidium of Cen. Cttee. of CPSU 61-66, Alt. mem. Politburo 66-; awarded Order of Lenin (six times), Order of the Red Banner of Labour, Order of the Red Star, Badge of Honour, Order of the October Revolution, Hero of Socialist Labour and other decorations.
Publs. *My Rage* (poetry) 45, *Victors* 51, *Kashmir Song* 56, *Stronger than the Storm* 58, *Peaceful Wave* 64, etc.
Central Committee of Communist Party of Uzbekistan, Tashkent, Uzbek S.S.R., U.S.S.R.

Rau, Chalapathi M., M.A., B.L.; Indian newspaper editor.
Assistant Editor *National Herald*, Lucknow 38-42; Asst. Editor *Hindustan Times*, New Delhi 43-45; Asst. Editor *National Herald* 45-46, Editor 46-77, Chair. 77-81; Alt. rep. UNESCO Gen. Conf. New Delhi 56, Paris 60; Rep. UN Gen. Assembly 58; Vice-Pres. UNESCO Conf. on Journalism Training 56; Rep. UN Gen. Assembly 58; Pres. Indian Fed. of Working Journalists; mem. Indian Press Comm. 52-54, Exec. Cttee. Jawaharlal Nehru Memorial Trust, Exec. Council Nehru University, Cttee. on Broadcasting and Information Media; Chair. Nehru Fund, Nehru Memorial Museum and Library; Nehru Award; Hon. D.Litt. (Agra, Andhra Univs.) Hon. LL.D. (Sri Venkateswara Univ.).
Publs. *Fragments of a Revolution, Gandhi and Nehru* 67, *The Press in India* 68, *All in All* 72, *Jawaharlal Nehru* 73.
13 Shahjahan Road, New Delhi, India.
Telephone: 383855 (Home).

Rau, Santha Rama; Indian writer; b. 24 Jan. 1923; ed. St. Paul's Girls' School, London, and Wellesley Coll.. U.S.A.
Numerous journeys in Europe, India, America, South-East Asia, Japan and Russia; fmr. teacher Hani Freedom School, Tokyo; English teacher at Sarah Lawrence Coll. 71-74; Hon. doctorates from Bates, Brandeis and Roosevelt Colls.
Publs. *Home to India, East of Home, Remember the House, View to the South-East, My Russian Journey, The Cooking of India* 69, *The Adventuress* 71; dramatized version of E. M. Forster's *A Passage to India*; *Gifts of Passage* (autobiog.), *A Princess Remembers* 76, *An Inheritance* 79.
425 East 58th Street, Apartment 21C, New York, N.Y. 10022; Amenia, N.Y. 12501, U.S.A.

Ray, Ajit Nath, M.A.; Indian judge; b. 29 Jan. 1912, Calcutta; ed. Presidency Coll., Calcutta, Oriel Coll., Oxford and Gray's Inn, London.
Formerly practised as a barrister, Calcutta High Court; Judge, Calcutta High Court 57; Judge, Supreme Court of India 69-73, Chief Justice 73-77; Hon. Fellow, Oriel Coll. Oxford; Pres. Int. Law Asscn. 74-76, Vice-Pres. 77-; mem. Int. Court of Arbitration 76-.
15 Panditia Place, Calcutta 29, India.
Telephone: 47-5213.

Ray, Satyajit; Indian film director; b. 2 May 1921; ed. Ballygunge Govt. School, Presidency Coll., Calcutta. Commercial artist in Calcutta before beginning his career in films; directed *Pather Panchali* 54 (Cannes Int. Film Festival Award for "the most human document" 56, Golden Laurel Award, Edinburgh Film Festival 57), *Aparajito* 56 (sequel to *Pather Panchali*, Grand Prix, Venice Film Festival 57), *The Philosopher's Stone, Jalsaghar* (The Music Room), *Apur Sansar* (The World of Apu), *The Goddess* 61, *Three Daughters* 61, *Abhijan* 62, *Kanchanjangha* 62, *Mahanagar* 64, *Charulata* 65, *Kapurush-o-Mahapurush* 65, *Nayak* 66, *Chiriakhana* 68, *The Adventures of Goopy and Bagha* 69, *Days and Nights in the Forest* 69, *Seemabaddha* (Company Limited) 70, *Pratidwandi* (The Adversary) 71, *Distant Thunder* 73 (Golden Bear Award, Berlin Film Festival 73), *Golden Fortress* 74, *The Middle Man* 75, *The Chessplayers* 77, *Elephant God, Hirak Rajar Deshe* (The Kingdom of Diamonds) 81; composed the music for all his films since *Three Daughters*; Editor *Sandesh*, children's magazine; Magsaysay Award for Journalism and Literature 67; Order of the Yugoslav Flag 71; Hon. D.Litt. (Royal Coll. of Art, London) 74, (Oxford) 78.
Publ. *Our Films, Their Films* 77.
Flat No. 8, 1/1 Bishop Lefroy Road, Calcutta 20, India.
Telephone: 44-8747.

Razaleigh Hamzah, Tengku Tan Sri Datuk, P.S.M., S.P.M.K.; Malaysian politician and fmr. company executive; b. *c.* 1936; ed. Queen's Univ., Belfast and Lincoln's Inn, London.
Chairman of Kelantan Div. of United Malays' Nat. Org. (UMNO) in early 60s; mem. Kelantan State Assembly for some years; Man. Dir. Bank Bumiputra 70; Exec. Dir. PERNAS 71-74; Chair. Malaysian Nat. Insurance; led trade mission to Beijing 71; a Vice-Pres. UMNO 75-; Pres. Assoc. Malay Chambers of Commerce until Oct. 76; Chair. PETRONAS (Nat. Oil Co.) 74-76; Minister of Finance Oct. 76-; Chair. Islamic Devt. Bank 77, Asram Devt. Bank 77-, IMF Meetings 78-.
Ministry of Finance, State Secretariat Building, Kuala Lumpur, Malaysia.

Reddy, Kasu Brahmananda, B.A., B.L.; Indian politician; b. 1909.
President Guntur District Board 36; mem. Madras Assembly 46-52; Gen. Sec. Andhra Pradesh Congress Cttee. 55; Minister of Finance and Planning, Andhra Pradesh 60-62, of Finance and Co-operation 62-64, Chief Minister 64-71; Union Minister of Communications Jan.-Oct. 74; Minister of Home Affairs 74-77, of Industry 79-80; Pres. Indian Nat. Congress May 77-Feb. 78 (resigned); mem. Lok Sabha for Narasaraopet.
c/o Ministry of Industry, New Delhi, India.

Reddy, Marri Channa, M.B., B.S.; Indian agriculturalist and politician; b. 13 Jan. 1919, Sirpur Village, Vikarabad Taluk, District of Hyderabad; ed. Chadarghat High School and Osmania Univ.
Left medical practice to devote himself to politics in Hyderabad; Gen. Sec. Andhra Mahasabha 42; held organizational posts in Indian Nat. Congress Party; Editor *Hyderabad* 48; leader in Hyderabad Congress; mem. Provisional Parl. 50-51; Minister of Agriculture, Food, Planning and Rehabilitation, Hyderabad 52-56, of Planning and Panchayati Raj, Andhra Pradesh 62-64, for Finance and Medium and Small Scale Industry, Andhra Pradesh 64-67; Union Minister of Steel, Mines and Metals 67-68; mem. Rajya Sabha 67-68; participated in division of Indian Nat. Congress 69; Head of movement for a separate state of Telangana 71-72; Gov. Uttar Pradesh 74-77; Chief Minister of Andhra Pradesh 78-80; Gov. Punjab April 82-.
Punjab Raj Bhavan, Chandigarh, India.
Telephone: 24461.

Reddy, (Neelam) Sanjiva; Indian Politician; b. 19 May 1913, Illuru village, Anantapur District, Andhra Pradesh; ed. Theosophical High School, Adyar and Arts Coll., Anantapur.
Secretary, Andhra Pradesh Congress Cttee. 36-46; active in Satyagraha movement; mem. and Sec. Madras Legislative Assembly 46; mem. Indian Constituent Assembly 47; Minister for Prohibition, Housing and Forests, Madras Govt. 49-51; Pres. Andhra Pradesh Congress Cttee. 51-52; mem. Rajya Sabha 52-53, Andhra Pradesh Legislative Assembly 53-64; Deputy Chief Minister, Andhra Pradesh 53-56, Chief Minister 56-57; Leader of Andhra Congress Legislature Party 53-64; Pres. Indian Nat. Congress 60-62; Chief Minister of Andhra Pradesh 62-64; Union Minister of Steel and Mines 64-65, of Transport, Aviation, Shipping and Tourism 66-67; mem. Lok Sabha from Hindupur, Andhra Pradesh and Speaker of Lok Sabha 67-69; cand. in presidential election 69; engaged in agriculture 69-77; mem. Lok Sabha 77-; mem. Cttee. of Janata Party Jan. 77; Speaker of Lok Sabha March-July 77; Pres. of India 77-82.
c/o Rashtrapati Bhavan, New Delhi 110004, India.

Reddy, Pingle Jaganmohan, B.A., B.COM., LL.B.; Indian judge; b. 23 Jan. 1910, Hyderabad; ed. Univs. of Leeds and Cambridge.
Legal practice as barrister 37-46; Legal dept. Govt. of Hyderabad 46-48; District and Sessions Judge, Secunderabad 50-52; Puisne Judge, High Court, Hyderabad 48, 52-56; Judge, High Court, Andhra Pradesh 56-66, Chief Justice 66-69; Judge, Supreme Court of India 69-75; Chair. Comm. of Inquiry into allegations against Bansi Lal and the Nagarwala case 77-78; mem. Syndicate and Dean, Faculty of Law, Osmania Univ. 52-59, Vice-Chancellor, Osmania Univ. 75-77; Chair. Andhra Pradesh State Film Award Cttee. 76-77; mem. Court of Govs. of Administrative Staff Coll. of India; Chair. Inst. of Public Enterprise; Hon. LL.D. (Andhra Univ.) 75, Hon. D.Litt. (Sri Venkateshwara Univ.) 76.
Publs. *The Hyderabad Excess Profits Tax Act, Quest o, Justice, Perspectives in Education and Culture, Social Justice and the Constitution, Minorities and the Constitution, Liberty, Equality, Property and the Constitution, We have a Republic—Can we keep it?*
Plot No. 1, 7-1-22/16 Begumpet P.O., Hyderabad 500016, India.

Rees, Albert Lloyd George, C.B.E., D.SC., PH.D., D.I.C., F.R.A.C.I., F.A.A.; Australian scientist; b. 15 Jan. 1916, Melbourne; ed. Univs. of Melbourne and London.
Lecturer in Chem., Univ. of W. Australia 39, Beit Scientific Research Fellow, Imperial Coll., London 39-41; Extra-Mural Research in Chem. Defence, Ministry of Supply, U.K., 39-41; Research and Devt. Philips Electrical Industries, U.K. 41-44; with Commonwealth Scientific and Industrial Research Org. (CSIRO) 44-78, Chief Div. of Chemical Physics 58-78; Chair. Chem. Research Labs. 61-70; Chair. External Review of Defence Science and Technology Org. 79-80; mem. Bureau and Exec. Cttee., Int. Union of Pure and Applied Chem. 63-73, Vice-Pres. 67-69, Pres. 69-71; mem. Exec. Cttee. ICSU 69-72, Gen. Cttee. 72-76; mem. Bd. of Studies, Victoria Inst. of Colls. 68-80, Council 78-80; Pres. Royal Australian Chem. Inst. (R.A.C.I.) 67-68; mem. Council Australian Acad. of Science 63-68, 69-73; Liversidge Lecturer, Royal Soc. of N.S.W. 52; Einstein Memorial Lecturer, Australian Inst. of Physics 70; Rennie Medal 46, H. G. Smith Medal (R.A.C.I.) 51, Leighton Memorial Medal (R.A.C.I.) 70; Hon. Dr. of Applied Science (Victoria Inst. of Colls.) 70.
Publs. *Chemistry of the Defect Solid State* 54, and many articles in learned journals.
9 Ajana Street, North Balwyn, Victoria 3104, Australia (Home).
Telephone: 857-9358.

Refshauge, Major-Gen. Sir William Dudley, A.C., C.B.E., E.D., M.B., B.S., F.R.C.O.G., F.R.A.C.S., F.R.A.C.P., F.R.A.C.M.A., F.R.A.C.O.G.; Australian medical administrator; b. 3 April 1913, Melbourne; ed. Hampton High School and Scotch Coll., Melbourne and Melbourne Univ.
Resident Medical Officer, Alfred Hosp., Melbourne 39, Women's Hosp. Melbourne 46; Registrar, Women's Hosp. 46-47, Medical Supt. 48-51; Deputy Dir.-Gen. Army Medical Services 51-55, Dir.-Gen. 55-60; Commonwealth of Australia Dir.-Gen. of Health 60-73; Chair. Nat. Health and Medical Research Council 60-73, Commonwealth Council for Nat. Fitness 60-73, Commonwealth Health Insurance Council 60-73, etc.; mem. Exec. Board, WHO 67-70, Chair. 69-70; Pres. World Health Assembly 71; Sec.-Gen. World Medical Asscn. 73-76; mem. Board, Walter and Eliza Hall Inst. of Medical Research 77-, Canberra Girls' Grammar School 77-78; Hon. Consultant Aust. Foundation on Alcohol and Drugs of Dependence 79-; Chair. A.C.T. Cttee. and mem. Nat. Cttee. of Sir Robert Menzies Foundation for Health, Physical Fitness and Personal Achievement 79-; Pres. 1st Pan-Pacific Conf. on Drugs and Alcohol 80; Chair. A.C.T. Blood Transfusion Cttee., Australian Red Cross Soc. 80-81; Nat. Trustee, Returned Services League 62-73, 77-; Fellow, Royal Soc. of Medicine; Hon. Life mem. Australian Dental Asscn.; Hon. Fellow, Royal Soc. of Health; Patron Australian Sports Medicine Asscn.
Publs. various publications in *Medical Journal of Australia* and *New Zealand Medical Journal*.
26 Birdwood Street, Hughes, A.C.T. 2605, Australia.
Telephone: (062) 473939 (Office); 810943 (Home).

Ren Rong; Chinese party official.
Member Chinese People's Volunteers Korean Truce Comm., N. Korea 60; Deputy Political Commissar Xizang Mil. Region, People's Liberation Army 65, First Political Commissar 71-80; Vice-Chair. Xizang Revolutionary Cttee. 68, Acting Chair. 71-79; First Sec. Xizang Autonomous Region 71-80; First Sec. CCP Xizang 71-79; Alt. mem. 10th Cen. Cttee. of CCP 73; mem. 11th Cen. Cttee. of CCP 77.
People's Republic of China.

Ren Zhongyi; Chinese politician; b. 1 Aug. 1914, Wei County, Hebei Province.
Member CCP 36-; mem. Lushan-Dalian Dist. People's Govt. 51; Sec. Lushan-Dalian Municipal Work Cttee. New Dem. Youth League 51; Deputy for Harbin to 1st NPC; 2nd Sec. CCP Harbin Municipal Cttee. 55-56; Sec. CCP Heilongjiang Provincial Cttee. 57; First Sec. CCP Harbin Municipal Cttee. 57-67; Deputy for Heilongjiang 2nd NPC 58; Chair. Harbin Municipal Cttee. CPPCC 57; mem. Standing Cttee. CCP Heilongjiang Provincial Cttee. 59; Alt. Sec. CCP Heilongjiang Provincial Cttee. 60; Pol. Commissar Harbin Militia 60; Sec. CCP Heilongjiang Provincial Cttee. 61-67; First Sec. Liaoning Provincial CCP Cttee. 78-; Chair. Liaoning People's Govt. (fmrly. Revolutionary Cttee.) 78-80; First Political Commissar, Liaoning Provincial PLA, Deputy to 11th Nat. Congress, CCP and 5th NPC 78; First Sec. Guangdong Provincial CCP Cttee. 81.
People's Republic of China.

Renshaw, John Brophy, A.C.; Australian politician; b. 8 Aug. 1909, Wellington, N.S.W.; ed. Binnaway School and Holy Cross Coll., Ryde, Sydney.
Farmer; mem. Binnaway-Coonabarabran Shire Council 37-41; Shire Press 39-40; mem. New South Wales legislature 41-; Sec. for Lands, N.S.W. Govt. 50-52, for Public Works 52-56, for Public Works and Local Govt. 52-53, Minister 53-59, Minister for Highways 56-59, Deputy Premier and Treas. 59-62, Minister for Lands 60-61, for Agric. 61-62, for Industrial Devt. and Decentralization 62-64, Premier, Treas., Minister for Industrial Devt. and Decentralization 64-65, Treas. 76-80; N.S.W. Agent-Gen., London 80-; Leader of Opposition in Legislative Assembly 65-68; Labor Party.
New South Wales House, 66 Strand, London, W.C.2, England.

Reyes, Narciso G., A.B.; Philippine journalist and diplomatist; b. 6 Feb. 1914; ed. Univ. of Santo Tomás.
Associate Editor *Philippines Commonweal*, Manila 35-41; mem. Nat. Language Faculty, Ateneo de Manila 39-41; Assoc. Editor *Manila Post* 45-47; Assoc. News Editor *Evening News*, Manila 47-48; Man. Dir. Philippine Newspaper Guild's organ 47-48; Adviser to Philippine Mission to UN and Rep. of the Philippines to numerous ECOSOC sessions and UN Gen. Assemblies, and many other UN activities 48-54; Philippine Amb. to Burma 58-62, to Indonesia 62-67, to U.K. 67-70; Perm. Rep. to UN 70-77; Amb. to People's Repub. of China 77-80; Chair. 19th Session UN Social Development Comm. 68, Social Panel, Int. Non-Governmental Organizations Conf. on Human Rights 68, 26th UN Gen. Assembly Econ. and Financial Cttee., UNICEF Exec. Board 72-74; Pres. UNDP Governing Council 74-; mem. UN Group of Experts on Disarmament and Devt. 78-(81); Hon. LL.D.
c/o Ministry of Foreign Affairs, Manila, Philippines.

Rha Woong-Bae, PH.D.; Korean politician; b. 24 July 1934, Taejoen; ed. Seoul Nat. Univ., Stanford Univ. Business School, Univ. of Calif., Berkeley.
Economist, Research Dept., Bank of Korea 57-62; Prof. Coll. of Commerce, Seoul Nat. Univ. 62-73; Pres. Hai-Tai Confectionery Co. Ltd. 73-79; Hankook Tire Mfg. Co. Ltd. 80-81; mem. Nat. Assembly 81-; Minister of Finance Jan.-June 82.
Publs. *Managerial Strategies in the 70s, An Application of Mathematical Programming to the Choice of Investment, Econometric Analysis for Business.*
c/o Ministry of Finance, 82 Sejongro, Chongroku, Seoul 120; 74-6 Yunhidong, Seodaemoonku, Seoul 120, Republic of Korea (Home).

Rinchin, Lodongiyn; Mongolian agronomist politician and diplomatist; b. 25 July 1929; ed. Higher School of Agriculture, U.S.S.R.
Agronomist, Dir. of Dept., Chief Agronomist at Ministry of Animal Husbandry 55-60; First Deputy Minister of Agriculture 60-67; Chair. Supreme Council, Fed. of Agricultural Co-operatives 67-70; Dir. Dept. of Agriculture, Trade and Transport of Mongolian People's Revolutionary Party (MPRP) Cen. Cttee. 70; Minister of Foreign Affairs 70-76, of Agriculture 76-80; mem. MPRP Cen. Cttee. 61-80; Deputy to People's Great Hural (Assembly) 69-80; Amb. to Yugoslavia 81-.
Mongolian Embassy, Generala Vasića 5, Belgrade, Yugoslavia.

Ritchie, Robert James, C.B.E.; Australian business executive; b. 5 Nov. 1915; ed. Cleveland Street High School, Sydney.
Joined Amalgamated Wireless Australia Ltd. 29, later flew with Kingsford Smith Aerial Services Ltd., Sydney, and Mandated Airlines Ltd., New Guinea; Pilot, W. R. Carpenter & Co. 38; First Officer, Qantas Empire Airways Ltd. 43, Captain 44, Flight Captain 46; Flight Captain (Constellations) 47-48; Flight Superintendent, Kangaroo Service 47-49; Asst. Operations Man. Qantas 49-55, Tech. Man. 55-59, Dir. of Tech. Services 59-61, Deputy Chief Exec. and Deputy Gen. Man. 61-67, Gen. Man. 67-76, Dir. 70-76; Vice-Chair. Air Niugini 73-76; Dir. Qantas Wentworth Holdings Ltd. 67-76; Vice-Chair. Australian Tourist Comm. 76-77, Chair. 77-; Dir. various holding companies 76-; Trustee, Mitsui Australia Educ. Trust 75-; Dir. Royal N.S.W. Inst. for Deaf and Blind Children 75-.
12 Graham Avenue, Pymble, New South Wales 2073, Australia.

Rithaudeen al-Haj bin Tengku Ismail, Y.M. Tengku Ahmad; Malaysian barrister and politician; b. 24 Jan. 1932; mem. of Royal family of Kelantan; ed. Nottingham Univ. and Lincoln's Inn, U.K.
Circuit Magistrate in Ipoh 56-58, Pres. of Sessions Court 58-60; Deputy Public Prosecutor and Fed. Counsel 60-62; mem. Council of Advisers to Ruler of State of Kelantan (MPR), resigned to enter private practice; Chair. East Coast Bar Cttee. of Malaya; Chair. Sri Nilam Co-operative Soc., Malaysia; mem. Malayan Council 67, 68, 69, 70; Sponsor, Adabi Foundation; Sponsor, Kelantan Youth; Adviser, Kesatria; Minister with Special Functions Assisting Prime Minister on Foreign Affairs 73-75; mem. Supreme Council, United Malays' Nat. Org. June 75-; Minister for Foreign Affairs 75-81, for Trade and Industry July 81–.
Ministry of Trade and Industry, Kuala Lumpur, Malaysia.

Roberts, Sir Denys Tudor Emil, K.B.E., Q.C., M.A., B.C.L.; British administrator and judge; b. 19 Jan. 1923, London; ed. Aldenham School, Wadham Coll., Oxford and Lincoln's Inn.
Royal Artillery (Captain) 43-46; English Bar 50-53; Crown Counsel, Nyasaland (now Malawi) 53-59; Attorney-Gen. Gibraltar 60-62; Solicitor-Gen. Hong Kong 62-66, Attorney-Gen. 66-73; Colonial Sec. Hong Kong 73-76, Chief Sec. Hong Kong 76-78; Chief Justice Hong Kong and Brunei 79-.
Publs. five novels 55-65.
Chief Justice's Chambers, Supreme Court, Hong Kong; Home: Chief Justice's House, Gough Hill Road, Hong Kong.

Robertson, Sir Rutherford Ness, A.C., Kt., C.M.G., D.SC., PH.D., F.R.S.; Australian botanist; b. 29 Sept. 1913; ed. St. Andrew's Coll., Christchurch, New Zealand, Sydney Univ., and St. John's Coll., Cambridge.
Assistant Lecturer, later Lecturer in Botany, Sydney Univ. 39-46; Senior Research Officer, later Chief Research Officer, Commonwealth Scientific and Industrial Research Org. (C.S.I.R.O.), Div. of Food Preservation 46-59, mem. Exec. of C.S.I.R.O. 59-62; Visiting Prof. Univ. of California 58-59; Prof. of Botany, Univ. of Adelaide 62-69; Chair. Australian Research Grants Cttee. 65-69, Australian Nat. Univ.; Master, Univ. House 70-72; Dir. Research School Biological Sciences, Australian Nat. Univ. 73-78; Deputy Chair. Australian Science and Technology Council 77-81; Fellow, Australian Acad. of Science 54, Pres. 70-74; Foreign Assoc. U.S. Acad. of Sciences 62; Pres. Australian and New Zealand Asscn. for the Advancement of Science 65; Foreign mem. American Philosophical Soc. 71; Hon. mem. Royal Soc. of New Zealand 71; Foreign Hon. mem. American Acad. of Arts and Sciences 72; Hon. Fellow St. John's Coll., Cambridge 73-; Hon. Visitor, Sydney Univ. 79-; Clarke Memorial Medal, Royal Soc. of New South Wales 54, Farrer Memorial Medal 63, A.N.Z.A.A.S. Medal 68, Mueller Medal 70, Burnet Medal 75.
Publs. *Electrolytes in Plant Cells* (co-author) 61, *Protons, Electrons, Phosphorylation and Active Transport* 68.
School of Biological Science, University of Sydney, Sydney, N.S.W. 2000, Australia.
Telephone: 692-2385.

Romualdez, Eduardo Z.; Philippine banker and diplomatist; b. 22 Nov. 1909, Tolosa, Leyte; ed. Univs. of the Philippines and Santo Tomás, and Georgetown Univ., Washington, D.C.
President, Bankers' Asscn. of the Philippines 50-53; Dir. Chamber of Commerce of the Philippines 50-52; Regional Vice-Pres. American Bankers' Asscn. 51-65; Chair of Board of Dirs., Philippine Air Lines (PAL) 54-62, Pres. 61-62; mem. Monetary Board, Central Bank of the Philippines 54-61, Pres. 66-70; Gov. IMF 56-61, IBRD 56-61, 66-70, IFC 57-61; Chair. Rehabilitation Finance Corpn., 54-57, Nat. Econ. Devt. Council 56-58, 68-69, Devt. Bank of the Philippines 58, Tax Comm. 59-61, 66-70, Board of Industries 66-70; Pres. Philippine Trust Co, 47-54, 62-65, Fidelity and Surety Co. of the Philippines Inc. 47-54, 62-65; Philippines Nat. Bank 59-61; Sec. of Finance, Repub. of the Philippines 66-70; Chair. Asian Devt. Bank 66-68; Amb. to U.S.A., also accred. to Dominican Repub. 71-, the Bahamas 79-, and to Jamaica 80-; Chair. Philippine Air Lines May 82-; mem. numerous cttees., etc., and del. to many int. confs.
Philippine Air Lines, Makati, Metro Manila, Philippines.

Romulo, Brig.-Gen. Carlos Peña; Philippine writer, educator and diplomatist; b. 14 Jan. 1899; ed. Univ. of the Philippines and Columbia Univ.
Associate Prof. of English, Univ. of the Philippines 26-30, mem. Board of Regents 31-41; Editor-in-Chief TVT Publications 31, Publisher DMHM Newspapers 37-41; Staff of Gen. MacArthur and Sec. of Information and Public Relations, Philippine War Cabinet in U.S.A. 43-44, Brigadier-Gen. 44; Acting-Sec. of Public Instruction 44-45, Chief Del. to UN 45-55, Pres. 49-50, Security Council 57; Sec. of Foreign Affairs 50-52; Amb. to the U.S.A. 52-53, 55-62, Special Envoy 54-55, concurrently Minister to Cuba 59; Pres. Univ. of the Philippines 62-68, Philippine Acad. of Sciences and Humanities; Presidential Adviser on Foreign Affairs; Sec. Dept. of Educ. 66-68; Sec. for Foreign Affairs 68-78, Minister 78-; numerous decorations, honours, hon. degrees and awards, incl. Pulitzer Prize 42, Nat. Artist in Literature (Philippines) 82.
Publs. *I saw the Fall of the Philippines* 42, *Mother America* 43, *My Brother Americans* 45, *Crusade in Asia* 55, *The Meaning of Bandung* 56, *The Magsaysay Story* 56, *Friend to Friend* 58, *I Walked with Heroes* (*An Autobiography*) 61, *Contemporary Nationalism and World Order* 64, *Mission to Asia* 64, *Identity and Change* 65, *Evasions and Response* 66, *Clarifying The Asian Mystique* 69.
Ministry of Foreign Affairs, Padre Faura, Manila; and 74 McKinley Road, Forbes Park, Makati, Rizal, Philippines.

Rong Yiren; Chinese industrial and government official; b. 1916, Wuhsi City, Jiangsu Province; ed. St. John's Univ., Shanghai.
First job managing one of father's flour mills; inherited 24 textile, dyeing, flour and machinery factories in 8 cities; after founding of People's Repub., appointed Deputy Mayor of Shanghai and Vice-Minister of Textile Industries; Vice-Chair. Fifth Nat. Cttee. of CPPCC and mem. of Standing Cttee. of Fifth Nat. People's Congress 78–; Chair. and Pres. China Int. Trust and Investment Corpn. (CITIC) Oct. 79-.
c/o State Council, Beijing, People's Republic of China.

Rosales, H.E. Cardinal Julio; Philippine ecclesiastic; b. 18 Sept. 1906.
Ordained 29; Bishop of Tagbiliran 46-49; Archbishop of Cebu 49-81; cr. Cardinal 69; Pres. Catholic Bishops' Conf. of the Philippines 61-65, 74-76; mem. Sacred Congregation of the Clergy, Rome, Sacred Congregation of Catholic Educ., Rome, Secr. for Non-Christians, Rome; Grand Cross, Order of St. Raymundo de Pennafort, Knight Order of Corpus Christi in Toledo; Gran Cruz de Isabel la Católica, Spain; LL.D. (Univ. of San Carlos, Univ. of Visayas, Adamson Univ.); D.H. (De La Salle Coll., Divine Word Univ.).
c/o Archbishop's Residence, P.O.B. 52, Cebú City, Philippines.

Ross, Lewis Nathan, C.M.G., F.C.A.; New Zealand chartered accountant and company director; b. 7 March 1911, Auckland; ed. Auckland Grammar School, Univ. of Auckland.
Commenced practice as a chartered accountant in Auckland 32; Pres. Asscn. of Chamber of Commerce of N.Z. 56-57, N.Z. Soc. of Accountants 72-73; Chair. Govt.

Cttee. to Review Taxation in N.Z. 66-67; mem. Nat. Devt. Council 69-74; Chair. Bank of N.Z., Rex Consolidated Ltd., N.Z. Sugar Co. Ltd., N.Z. Forest Products Ltd., Bank of Western Samoa; Dir. James Hardie-Impey Ltd., Revertex Industries Ltd., Mainzeal Corpn. Ltd., Andas Group Ltd., UEB Industries Ltd., Sanford Ltd.
Publs. *Taxation: principles, purpose and incidence* 72; one research lecture, several booklets and articles on finance and taxation.
Achilles House, Customs Street, Auckland, P.O. Box 881 (Office); 11 Rewiti Street, Orakei, Auckland, New Zealand (Home).
Telephone: 798-665 (Office); 547-449 (Home).

Rowland, Air Marshal Sir James Anthony, K.B.E., D.F.C., A.F.C., B.E., C.ENG., F.R.AE.S., F.I.E.(AUST.); Australian air force officer (retd.) and state governor; b. 1 Nov. 1922, Armidale, N.S.W.; ed. Univ. of Sydney.
Master Bomber, Pathfinder, Bomber Command R.A.F. 44; with R.A.A.F.: Chief Test Pilot, Aircraft Research and Devt. Unit 51-54; Chief Tech. Officer, No. 82 Wing 57; O.C. Research and Devt. 58, C.O. 59-60; Mirage Mission, Paris 61-64; Commanding No. 3 Aircraft Depot, Amberley 67-68; Senior Tech. Staff Officer, H.Q. Operational Command 69-70; with Dept. of Air: Dir.-Gen. of Aircraft Eng. 72, Air. Mem. for Tech. Services 73-74; Chief of Air Staff, R.A.A.F. 75-79; Councillor, Royal Aeronautical Soc., Australian Branch 73-75; Gov. of New South Wales 81-; K. St. J.
Publs. official reports, contributions to journals.
Government House, Sydney, N.S.W., Australia.
Telephone: 233-2233.

Rowland, John Russell; Australian diplomatist; b. 10 Feb. 1925; ed. Cranbrook School, Sydney, and Univ. of Sydney.
Department of External Affairs 44-, served Moscow 46-48, Saigon 52, 54-55, Washington 55-56, London 57-59; Asst. Sec., Dept. of External Affairs 61-65; Amb. to U.S.S.R. 65-68; First Asst. Sec. Dept. of External Affairs 69; High Commr. in Malaysia 69-72; Amb. to Austria 73-74, concurrently accred. to Czechoslovakia, Hungary and Switzerland; Deputy Sec., Dept. of Foreign Affairs 75-78; Amb. to France (also accred. to Morocco) 78-.
Publs. *The Feast of Ancestors, Snow, Times and Places, The Clock Inside* (poetry).
Australian Embassy, 4 rue Jean Rey, 75724 Paris, France.

Rowling, Wallace Edward, M.A.; New Zealand politician; b. 15 Nov. 1927; ed. Nelson Coll. and Canterbury Univ.
Former Educ. Officer, New Zealand Army; mem. Parl. for Buller 62-72, Tasman 72-; Pres. Labour Party 70-73; Minister of Finance, in charge of Dept. of Statistics, Friendly Socs. 72-74; Prime Minister 74-Nov. 75; also Minister of Foreign Affairs and Minister in Charge of Audit Dept., Legislative Dept. and N.Z. Security Intelligence Service 74-Nov. 75; Leader of the Opposition Dec. 75-.
Office of the Leader of the Opposition, Parliament Buildings, Wellington, New Zealand.

Roxas, Sixto K., M.A.; Philippine investment banker; b. 6 Aug. 1927, Los Baños, Laguna; ed. Ateneo de Manila and Fordham Univ., U.S.A.
Director-General, Program Implementation Agency, Office of the Pres. of the Philippines 62-63; Chair. Nat. Econ. Council 63-64; now Pres. Bancom Devt. Corpn. and Bancom Philippine Holdings Inc., Bancom Int. Holdings Ltd.; Chair. G. A. Machineries Inc., distributors of tractors and agricultural equipment; Co-Chair. Asian Inst. of Management; Dir. Sime Darby Holdings Ltd., American Express Int. Banking Corpn., Bacnotan Consolidated Industries Inc. and other cos.; Chair. Asian Finance Publications; Vice-Chair. Philippine Business for Social Progress org. and Dir. other civic orgs.; Presidential Award for Merit 64; Hon. D.Sc. (Xavier Univ.) 69, Hon. D.Hum.Litt. (Ateneo de Manila) 75, Hon. D.B.A. (P.W.U. Conrado Benitez Inst. of Business Admin.) 76.
Publs. *Southeast Asian Financial Markets: the Present and the Future* 75, *Money and Capital Markets in an Asian Setting* 76, *Managing Asian Financial Development* 76.
Bancom Development Corpn., Bancom I Building, Pasay Road, Makati, Manila; Home: 7 Second Street, Villamar Court, Parañaque, Rizal, Philippines.

Roy, Bhabesh Chandra, D.I.C., M.SC., DR.ING.; Indian geologist; b. 1 Aug. 1907; ed. Imperial Coll., London, Univ. of Nancy, and Univ. of Freiberg, Germany.
Joined Geological Survey of India 37, Dir. 58-61, Dir.-Gen. 61-65; UN Fellow in U.S.A. and Canada 57; mem. Oil and Natural Gas Comm. 64; Del. to ECAFE Mineral Confs. in Tokyo 55, Kuala Lumpur 58, U.S.S.R., U.K., France and Germany 55, Rome and Bandung 63, Vienna 64, Antwerp 66, Mexico City 67, New Zealand 70; Leader Del. Int. Geological Congress, Copenhagen 60; and numerous other int. geological meetings; Pres. Geological, Mining and Metallurgical Inst. of India 58-59, Indian Asscn. of Geohydrologists 70-71; Co-ordinator Geological Map for Asia and Far East 58-68; Vice-Pres. Int. Union of Geological Sciences 61-68; Sec.-Gen. Int. Geol. Congress, New Delhi 64; Chair. Dept. of Geology, Univ. of Nigeria 66-67, U.G.C. Prof., Presidency Coll., Calcutta 68-71; Editor *Journal of Mines, Metals and Fuels* 68-; Vice-Pres. IGC Comm., History of Geol. Sciences 68-76; Adviser Int. Devt. Confs., Hong Kong and Calcutta; Fellow, Nat. Inst. of Sciences of India; Medal of Czechoslovak Acad. of Sciences 69.
Publs. include: *Mineral Resources of Bombay* 51, *Economic Geology and Mineral Resources of Saurashtra* 53, *The Nellore Mica Belt* 56, *The Economic Geology and Mineral Resources of Rajasthan and Ajmer* 57; numerous articles on Geology and Mineral Resources.
37/3, Southend Park, Calcutta 29, W. Bengal, India.
Telephone: 46-3189.

Rukmini, Devi; Indian dancer and arts patron; b. 1904, Madurai.
Started dancing under Anna Pavlova; extensive tours throughout India and Europe with dance recitals and lectures; lecture visits to U.S.A.; also lectures and writes on Theosophy, Religion, Art, Culture, Educ., etc.; Dir. Arundale Training Centre, Madras, Int. Soc. for the Prevention of Cruelty to Animals, London for India, Dr. V. Swaminatha Iyer Tamil Library; Head Int. Theosophical Centre, Huizen, Holland; Pres. The Bharata Samaj, Indian Vegetarian Congress, Kalakshetra (Int. Art Centre), Besant Centenary Trust, Young Men's Indian Asscn.; Chair. Animal Welfare Board and mem. various int. animal welfare orgs.; fmr. mem. Rajya Sabha; Padma Bhushan 56, Sangit Natak Akademi Award 57, Queen Victoria Silver Medal of R.S.P.C.A. 58, Prani Mitra (Animal Welfare Board) 68; Hon. D.H. (Wayne Univ.) 60; Fellowship, Sangit Natak Akademi 68; D.h.c. (Rabindra Bharathi Univ.), Calcutta 70; Desikothama, Viswabharati Univ., Shantiniketan 72.
Productions: *The Light of Asia, Incidents from the Life of Bishma, Karaikal Ammayar* (Tamil), *Rukmini Swayamwaram* (Kathakali), *Kutrala Kuravanji* (temple drama), *Kumara Sambhavam, Usha Parinayam* (Telegu), *Sita Swayamwaram, Rama Vanagamanam, Paduka Pattabhishekham, Sabari Moksham, Choodamani Pradanam, Maha Pattabhishekkam, Gita Govinham, Andal Charitram, Kannapar Kuravanji, Rukmini Kalyanam, Dhruva Charitram, Krishnamari Kuravanji, Shakuntalam, Shyama, Kuchelopakhyanam.*
Publs. *Yoga: Art or Science, Message of Beauty to Civilisation, Women as Artists, Dance and Music, The Creative Spirit, Art and Education.*

Animal Welfare Board of India, Gandhinagar, Madras 20; Kalakshetra, Madras 41, India.
Telephone: 74307 (Office); 74836 (Home).

Ryan, Peter Allen, B.A., M.M.; Australian publisher; b. 4 Sept. 1923; ed. Malvern Grammar School, Melbourne and Univ. of Melbourne.
Military Service 42-45; Dir. United Service Publicity Pty. Ltd. 53-57; Public Relations Manager, Imperial Chemical Industries of Australia and New Zealand Ltd. 57-61; Asst. to Vice-Chancellor, Univ. of Melbourne 62; Dir. Melbourne Univ. Press 62-.
Publs. *Fear Drive My Feet* 59, *The Preparation of Manuscripts* 66, *The Encyclopaedia of Papua and New Guinea* (Gen. Editor) 72, *Redmond Barry* 72.
932 Swanston Street, Carlton, Vic. 3053, Australia.
Telephone: 347-3455.

S

Saba, Shoichi, B.A., F.I.E.E.E.; Japanese business executive; b. 28 Feb. 1919; ed. Tokyo Imperial Univ.
Director Japan Electric Machinery Asscn. 80-, Dir. and Vice-Chair. Japan Electronics Industry Promotion Asscn. 80-; Pres. Toshiba Corpn. 80-; Dir. numerous other bodies; Progress Prize (Japan Inst. of Electric and Electronics Engineers) 58; Blue Ribbon Medal (Govt. of Japan) 80.
8-26-38, Kinuta, Setagaya-ku, Tokyo 157, Japan.
Telephone: 03-416-4315.

Sadli, Mohammad, M.SC., PH.D.; Indonesian politician; b. 10 June 1922; ed. Univs. of Gajah Mada and Indonesia, Mass. Inst. of Technology, Univ. of Calif. (Berkeley) and Harvard Univ.
Lecturer, Univ. of Indonesia 57, Army Staff Coll. 58, Navy Staff Coll. 58; Dir. Inst. of Econ. and Social Research, Faculty of Econs., Univ. of Indonesia 57-63; Asst. to Pres., Univ. of Indonesia 63-64; mem. Gov. Council, UN Asian Inst. of Devt. and Planning 63-64; Fellow, Harvard Univ. Centre for Int. Affairs 63-64; Chair. Indonesian Economists Asscn. 66-67; Chair. Technical Cttee. for Foreign Investment 67-73; Minister of Manpower 71-73, of Mining Affairs 73-78; Chair. Bd. of Govt. Commrs., PERTAMINA State Oil Corpn. 73-78; Prof. of Econs., Univ. of Indonesia 78-; Adviser Bapindo (State Devt. Bank) 78-; Assoc. Faculty, Lemhamas (Nat. Defence Inst.) 78-; Chair. Bd. P.T. Aneka Tambang (state mining co.) 79-; Assoc. P.T. Indoconsult 79-; mem. UN Group on Multinational Cos. 73-74; mem. Advisory Group on Planning in the 80s, ADB, Manila 81-82.
Brawijaya IV, 24 Kebayoran Baru, Jakarta Selatan, Indonesia.
Telephone: 772599.

Sadykov, Abid Sadykovich; Soviet chemist; b. 1913; ed. Central Asia State Univ.
Teacher, Uzbek State Univ. 39-41, Central Asia State Univ. 41-46; Dir. Inst. of Chemistry, Uzbek Acad. of Sciences 46-50; Rector, Tashkent State Univ. 58-66; mem. Uzbek Acad. of Sciences 47-, Pres. 66-; Corresp. mem. U.S.S.R. Acad. of Sciences 66-73, mem. 73-; mem. C.P.S.U. 46-; orders and medals of U.S.S.R.
Publs. *The Chemistry of Alkaloids, Cotton Leaves as Valuable Chemical Raw Material, Chemistry of Central Asian Flora* 73, *Synthesis of Organic Preparations of the Pyridine Type* 74.
Presidium of Uzbek Academy of Sciences, Ul. Kuibysheva 15, Tashkent, Uzbek S.S.R., U.S.S.R.

Saheki, Isamu, LL.B.; Japanese business and transport executive; b. 25 March 1903; ed. Tokyo Imperial Univ.
Kinki Nippon Railway Co. 25-, Sr. Man. Dir. 47-51, Pres. 51-73, Chair. 73-; Chair. Kintetsu Business Group; Pres. Osaka Chamber of Commerce and Industry; Vice-Pres. Fed. of Econ. Orgs.; Adviser Japan Air Lines; Founder Yamato Bunka-kan Museum, History Class on Nara; Exec. of many orgs. and asscns.; Blue Ribbon Medal.
2-1-4 Tomigaoka, Nara City, Japan (Home).
Telephone: 0742 (45) 4550.

Sahgal, Mrs. Nayantara; Indian writer; b. 10 May 1927, Allahabad; ed. Wellesley Coll., U.S.A.
Scholar-in-residence, holding creative writing seminar, Southern Methodist Univ. Dallas, Texas 73, 77; adviser English Language Board, Sahitya Akademi (Nat. Acad. of Letters), New Delhi; Fellow, Radcliffe Inst. (Harvard Univ. 76; mem. Indian del. to UN Gen. Assembly 78; Fellow, Wilson Int. Center for Scholars, Washington, D.C.
Publs. *Prison and Chocolate Cake* 54, *A Time to be Happy* 58, *From Fear Set Free* 62, *This Time of Morning* 65, *Storm in Chandigarh* 69, *The Freedom Movement in India* 70, *The Day in Shadow* 71, *A Situation in New Delhi* 77, *A Voice for Freedom* 77, *Indira Gandhi's Emergence and Style* 78, *Indira Gandhi: The Road to Power* 81.
10 Massey Hall Jai Singh Road, New Delhi 110001, India.
Telephone: 312656.

Saigol, Mohammed Rafique; Pakistani business executive; b. 1933, Calcutta; ed. Aitchison Coll., Lahore and Clemson Coll., S.C., U.S.A.
Formerly Man. Dir. Kohinoor Textile Mills, Lyallpur and Chair. Cen. Board of Management of the Saigol Group; Chair. Lyallpur Improvement Trust 58; mem. Nat. Assembly, Parl. Sec. to Govt. of Pakistan 65-69; Chair. All Pakistan Textile Mills Asscn. 67-68; Pres. Lahore Chamber of Commerce and Industry 68-69, Lahore Stock Exchange Ltd. 71; Man. Dir. Progressive Papers Ltd. 71, Pakistan Int. Airlines Corpn. 72-73; Chair. Saigol Brothers Ltd., Nat. Construction Co. (Pakistan) Ltd.; Man. Trustee Saigol Foundation; Dir. State Bank of Pakistan, Sui Northern Gas Pipelines Ltd.; mem. Advisory Council on Econ. Affairs, and other advisory bodies.
176 Shadman II, Lahore; Home: 91-E-1 Gulberg 3, Lahore, Pakistan.

Saito, Eiichi; Japanese newspaper executive; b. 3 Dec. 1910, Osaka; ed. Osaka Higher Commercial School.
Reporter, *Mainichi Shimbun*, Osaka 31; Overseas correspondent London 41; Asst. City News Editor, Osaka 42; Chief, Kyoto Branch Office 45; City News Editor, Osaka 47; Editorial Writer 50; overseas correspondent, U.S.A. 51; Asst. Man. Editor 54; Chief, London Office 56; Gen. Man., European Office 57; Man. Editor, Osaka 61, Tokyo 63; mem. Board of Dirs. 64; Man. Dir. and Exec. Editor 68-.
Mainichi Shimbun, 1-1-1, Hitotsubashi, Chiyoda-ku, Tokyo, Japan.

Saito, Eishiro; Japanese steel industry executive; b. 22 Nov. 1911, Niigata City; ed. Tokyo Imperial Univ.
Joined Japan Iron and Steel Co. Ltd. 41; Dir. Yawata Iron and Steel Co. Ltd. 61, Man. Dir. 62, Sr. Man. Dir. 68; Sr. Man. Dir. Nippon Steel Corpn. 70, Exec. Vice-Pres. 73, Rep. Dir. and Pres. 77-81, Chair. 81-; Vice-Chair. Japan Cttee. of Econ. Devt.; Chair. Japan Iron and Steel Fed., Kozai (Steel Materials) Club; Chair. Japan Iron and Steel Exporters Asscn.; Sr. Dir. Japan Fed. of Econ. Orgs.; Chair. Int. Iron and Steel Inst. 77-79, Vice-Chair. 79-; Blue Ribbon Medal 67.
Nippon Steel Corporation, 6-3, Otemachi 2-chome, Chiyoda-ku, Tokyo 100, Japan.
Telephone: (03) 242-4111.

Saito, Kiyoshi; Japanese wood print artist; b. 1907, Fukushima Pref.
First specialized in oil painting and held many exhbns. in Japan; later turned to wood printing, often using Haniwa (Ancient Clay Image) as material; one-man exhbn. Corcoran Gallery of Art, Washington, D.C. 57; numerous exhbns. throughout U.S.A. 57-59; took part in Asia and

Africa Art exhbn. sponsored by Egyptian Govt. and won prize 57; one-man exhbns. at Nordness Gallery, New York 62, Sydney and Melbourne 65, Fine Arts Gallery of San Diego 69; two-man exhbn. Hawaii Museum 64; awarded the Int. Biennial Exhbn. of Prints in Yugoslavia; awarded Prize for Japanese Artists at Int. Arts Exhbn., Brazil.

Saito, Nobufusa, D.SC.; Japanese atomic scientist; b. 28 Sept. 1916; ed. Tokyo Imperial Univ.
Former Asst. Prof., Kyushu and Seoul Univs., Prof. of Inorganic Chem., Tokyo Univ. 56-65; fmr. Consultant to Int. Atomic Energy Agency (I.A.E.A.), Dir. of Isotopes Div. 63-65; Prof. Inorganic and Nuclear Chem., Tokyo Univ. 65-77, Dir. Radioisotope Centre 70-77; Prof. Inorganic and Analytical Chemistry, Toho Univ. 78-, Dean, Faculty of Science 79-; Vice-Pres. Chemical Soc. of Japan 76-78, Pres. 81-82; Dir. Japan Radioisotopes Asscn. 67-; Tech. Adviser, Japan Atomic Energy Research Inst. 66-; mem. American Chemical Soc., Atomic Energy Soc. of Japan, Japan Soc. for Analytical Chem., Pres. 79-80; Co-Editor *Int. Journal of Applied Radiation & Isotopes*; Chem. Soc. of Japan Award 74; Purple Ribbon Medal 79.
Department of Chemistry, Faculty of Science, Toho University, 2-2-1, Miyama, Funabashi 274; and 5-12-9, Koshigoe, Kamakura 248, Japan.
Telephone: 0467-31-3178.

Saito, Shigeyoshi; Japanese politician; b. 9 Aug. 1918, Shizuoka Pref.; ed. Waseda Univ.
Vice-President Daishowa Paper Mfg. Co. 61-64; Mayor, Yoshihara City, Shizuoka Pref. 64-66, Fuji City, Shizuoka Pref. 66-69; mem. House of Reps. 69-; Parl. Vice-Minister of Labour 76; Minister of Construction 80-81.
c/o Liberal-Democratic Party, 7, 2-chome, Hirakawacho, Chiyoda-ku, Tokyo, Japan.

Saito, Shizuo; Japanese diplomatist; b. 1914; ed. Tokyo Imperial Univ.
Counsellor, London 59-62; Minister in Bangkok 62-63; Dir. UN Bureau 63-64; Amb. to Indonesia 64-66; Deputy Vice-Minister for Admin., Ministry of Foreign Affairs 66-69; Amb. to Australia 70-74, concurrently to Fiji, Nauru 72-74; Perm. Rep. to UN 74-76; Pres. Foreign Press Centre of Japan, Asia Pacific Asscn., Australia-Japan Soc.; Lecturer, Keio Univ.; Adviser to Prince Hitachi 77-; Prof. Aoyamagakuin Univ.; Council mem. UN Univ., Tokyo.
Publs. *Through the Window of the UN* 76, *On the UN* 77, *Private Papers on Japanese Occupation of Indonesia* 77, *New Trend in UN* 78, *The United Nations System*, *The Diplomatic Lessons of Japanese History* 81.
2-1 Ichiban-cho Park Mansion, Ichiban-cho, Chiyoda-ku, Tokyo, Japan.

Saito, Shoichi; Japanese business executive; b. June 1908, Nagoya; ed. Tohoku Univ.
With Toyoda Automatic Loom Works 35-37; joined Toyota Motor Co. 37, mem. Board of Dirs. 46-50, Man. Dir. 50-60, Senior Man. Dir. 60-67, Exec. Vice-Pres. 67-72, Chair. 72-; Dir. Toyota Motor Sales U.S.A. Inc. 67-; Dir. Toyota Cen. Research and Devt. Laboratories Inc. 68-77; Pres. Soc. of Automotive Engineers of Japan 68-72; Auditor Aisin Seiki Co. Ltd. 65-, Towa Real Estate Co. Ltd. 71-, Toyoda Gosei Co. Ltd. 72-, Toyota Automatic Looms Works Ltd. 73-; Hon. Blue Ribbon Medal 70.
Publs. *The Earth is Round, America: the Country of Automobiles.*
Toyota Motor Co. Ltd., 1 Toyota-cho, Toyota-shi, Aichi-ken 471; Home: 26 Takamine-cho, Showa-ku, Nagoya-shi, Aichi-ken 466, Japan.
Telephone: 0565-28-2121 (Office).

Sakamoto, Isamu; Japanese business executive; b. 23 Oct. 1911; ed. Kyoto Univ.
Director and Man. Engineering Div. and Research and Devt. Labs., Sumitomo Electric Industries Ltd. (SEI) 58; Man. Dir. SEI 61, Exec. Vice-Pres. 69, Pres. 69-73, Chair. of Board Nov. 73-; Dir. Meidensha Ltd., Sumitomo-3M Co. Ltd.; Pres. Sumitomo Atomic Energy Co. Ltd.; fmr. Pres. Japan-U.S. Soc. of Osaka; fmr. Chair. Int. Wrought Copper Council.
5-3, 2-chome, Fujishirodai, Suita City, Osaka, Japan.
Telephone: 06-872-2837.

Sakamoto, Tomokazu, B.A.; Japanese broadcasting executive; b. 28 March 1917, Kanda, Tokyo; ed. Waseda Univ.
Joined Nippon Hoso Kyokai (Japanese Broadcasting Corpn.) 39, Head Scripts Section 49, Man. Literary Arts Div., Radio Dept. 56, Man. Radio and TV Programming 57, Deputy Dir. Entertainment 60, Dir. 65, Deputy Dir-Gen. Broadcasting 68-71, Man. Dir. and Dir.-Gen. 71-73, Exec. Vice-Pres. 76, Pres. July 76-; Grosses Silbernes Ehrenzeichen (Austria) 76; Aguila Azteca (Mexico) 81.
Nippon Hoso Kyokai, 2-2-1, Jinnan, Shibuya-ku, Tokyo; 1805-10, Kamiasoo, Tama-ku, Kawasaki-shi, Japan (Home).

Sakata, Michita; Japanese politician; b. 1916; ed. Tokyo Imperial Univ.
Former Private Sec. to Minister of Commerce and Industry; fmr. Parl. Vice-Minister for Transport; fmr. Minister of Health and Welfare; Minister of Education 68-71; Minister of State, Dir.-Gen. of Defence Agency 74-76; Minister of Justice Nov. 81-; mem. House of Reps.; Liberal-Democrat.
Dai-ichi Gi-in-kaikan, 2-2-1, Nagato-cho, Chiyoda-ku, Tokyo, Japan.
Telephone: Tokyo 581-4877.

Sakurada, Takeshi; Japanese industrialist; b. 17 March 1904; ed. Tokyo Univ.
Nisshin Spinning Co. Ltd. 43-, Man. Dir. 44-45, Pres. 45-64, Chair. of Board 64-70, Adviser 70-; Dir. The Industry Club of Japan 49-; Adviser to Board, Japan Radio Co. Ltd. 56, New Japan Radio Co. Ltd. 59; Pres. Japan Fed. of Employers' Asscns. 60, Hon. Pres. 79-; Auditor Fuji Television Broadcasting Co. Ltd. 67-; Chair. Toho Rayon Co. Ltd. 66-; Promoter and Auditor Arabian Oil Co. Ltd. 58-; mem. Public Security Comm. 64-; Deputy Chair. Fiscal System Council 65-75, Chair. 75-.
8, 22-Kamiyamacho, Shibuya-ku, Tokyo, Japan.

Sakurauchi, Yoshio; Japanese politician; b. 1912.
Elected to House of Reps. 13 times, House of Councillors once; Parl. Vice-Minister of Justice; Minister of Int. Trade and Industry 64-65; Chair. House of Reps. Foreign Affairs Cttee. 71; Minister of Agric. and Forestry 72-73; Chair. Policy Research Council, Liberal-Democratic Party (LDP) Sept.-Dec. 76; Minister of Construction and Dir.-Gen. Nat. Land Agency 77-78; Sec.-Gen. LDP 79-81; Minister of Foreign Affairs Nov. 81-.
Ministry of Foreign Affairs, 2-1, Kasumigaseki 2-chome, Chiyoda-ku, Tokyo, Japan.

Salam, Abdus, M.A., PH.D., D.SC., F.R.S.; Pakistani physicist; b. 29 Jan. 1926; ed. St. John's Coll., Cambridge and Government Coll., Lahore.
Professor of Mathematics, Govt. Coll., Lahore 51-54; Head, Mathematics Dept., Panjab Univ., Lahore 52-54; Lecturer, Univ. of Cambridge 54-56; Prof. of Theoretical Physics, Imperial Coll. of Science and Technology, Univ. of London 57-; mem. Pakistan Atomic Energy Comm. 58-74; Pakistan Science Council 63-75; Chief Scientific Adviser to Pres. 61-74; Gov., Int. Atomic Energy Agency 62-63; Dir. Int. Centre for Theoretical Physics 64-; mem. UN Advisory Cttee. on Science and Technology 64-75, Chair. 71; mem. scientific Council Stockholm Int. Peace Research Inst. (SIPRI) 70; Vice-Pres. Int. Union of Pure and Applied Physics 72-78; mem. London and American Physical Socs.; Fellow, Royal Swedish Acad. of Sciences; Foreign mem. U.S.S.R. Acad. of Sciences, American Acad. of Arts and Sciences; Hon. D.Sc. (Maiduguri, Nigeria) 82; Oppen-

heimer Prize and Medal; Atoms for Peace Award 68; joint winner Nobel Prize for Physics 79; many other awards.
Publs. about 200 articles.
Department of Physics, Imperial College of Science and Technology, London, S.W.7, England; and International Centre for Theoretical Physics, Miramare, Trieste, Italy. Telephone: 01-589 5111, ext. 2513; Trieste 22 42 81/6.

Salas, Rafael M.; Philippine United Nations official; b. 7 Aug. 1928, Bago, Negros Occidental; ed. Univ. of the Philippines and Harvard Univ. Littauer Centre for Public Admin.
Chair. Pres. Consultative Council of Students 54; Asst. to Exec. Sec., Office of the Pres. 54-55; Technical Adviser to the Pres. 56-57; Supervising Economist, Nat. Econ. Council 57-60, Exec. Dir. with Cabinet rank 60-61, Acting Chair. 66, 68; Special Asst. to Sec. of Agriculture and Natural Resources 61, to the Pres. for Local Govts. 61; Lecturer in Political Science and Econ., Univ. of the Philippines 55-59, in Econs., Graduate School of Far Eastern Univ. 60-61, in Law, Univ. of Philippines 63-66, mem. Board of Regents 66-69, Asst. to Vice-Pres. 62-63; Gen. Man. *Manila Chronicle* 63-65; Chair. of Board Govt. Service Insurance System 66; Action Officer, Nat. Rice and Corn Sufficiency Programme 66-69; Overall Co-ordinator and Action Officer for Nat. Projects 66-69; Chair. Govt. Re-org. Comm. 68-69; Exec. Sec. of the Philippines 66-69; del. UNESCO conf. on Media and Youth 52; Exec.-Sec. UNESCO Nat. Comm. for the Philippines 57; Asst. Sec.-Gen. 2nd Asian Productivity Conf. 60; mem. del. to ECAFE 61, adviser 62, 68; Amb. to Indonesia on Merdeka Day 67; Vice-Pres. UN Int. Conf. on Human Rights 68, mem. del. UN Gen. Assembly 68; Vice-Pres. Pledging Cttee. UNDP 68; Exec. Dir. UN Fund for Population Activities 69-; Asst. Sec.-Gen. of UN 71-72, Under-Sec.-Gen. 73-; UN Official in charge of World Population Year 74; Ph.D. (h.c.), D.P.A. (h.c.), LL.D. (h.c.).
Publs. *People: an International Choice* 76, *International Population Assistance: The First Decade* 79; fmr. Editor *Philippine Law Journal*; articles in Philippine magazines and newspapers.
United Nations Fund for Population Activities, United Nations, New York, N.Y. 10017, U.S.A.

Salato, Esika Macu, C.B.E.; Fijian civil servant and international official; b. 1 May 1915; ed. Queen Victoria School and Central Medical School.
Medical practice 35-74; Fiji Royal Naval Reserve Force 43-46; Deputy Dir. Medical Services 65-68, Dir. 68-74; Mayor of Suva 70; Acting High Commr. in U.K. and Rep. to EEC 74; Sec.-Gen. South Pacific Comm. 75-79.
Suva, Fiji.

Saleh, Rachmat, DRS.EC.; Indonesian banker; b. 1 May 1930, Surabaya; ed. Univ. of Indonesia.
Joined Bank Indonesia 56, Acting Rep. New York 58. Sec. to Board of Dirs. Amsterdam Branch 58, Man. Research Dept. 59, Gen. Man. 61, Man. Dir. 64-73, Gov. 73-; Chair. Man. Board Foreign Exchange Inst. 68, Supervisory Board Indonesia Devt. Bank 73-, Indonesia Overseas Bank, Amsterdam 73-; Gov. for Indonesia IBRD 73-; Alt. Gov. for Indonesia ADB 73-, Islamic Devt. Bank 77-; mem. Indonesia Monetary Board 73-; Chair. Trustees Inst. for Banking Devt. in Indonesia; Mahaputra Decoration.
Bank Indonesia, Jalan M.H. Thamrin 2, Jakarta; Jalan Senopati 8, Kebayoran Baru, Jakarta, Indonesia (Home).

Sami, Abdus, M.A., F.I.B.; Pakistani banker; b. 13 Dec. 1927.
Entered banking 48; United Bank 62-74; Bank of Credit and Commerce Int., London 74-78; Pres. Muslim Commercial Bank Ltd. 78-80; Pres. United Bank Ltd. 80-; Man. Dir. Union Bank of the Middle East, A. W. Galadari Holdings (Pvt.) Ltd., Dubai; Dir. Investment Corpn. of Pakistan, Nat. Investment Trust, Pakistan, Bankers Equity Ltd., Pakistan, Commercial Bank of Oman, United Bank AG (Zürich), Switzerland, United Bank of Lebanon and Pakistan, SAL, Lebanon.
United Bank Ltd., State Life Building No. 1, I. I. Chundrigar Road, Karachi, Pakistan.

Samphan, Khieu (*see* Khieu Samphan).

San Yu, Brig.-Gen. U; Burmese army officer and politician; b. 1919, Prome; ed. Univ. of Rangoon and an American military coll.
Commissioned 42, served in Second World War; Mil. Sec. to Chief of Gen. Staff 56-59; Officer commanding the North and North-West mil. areas; mem. Revolutionary Council, Deputy Chief of Gen. Staff, Commdr. of Land Forces and Minister of Finance and Revenue 63; Gen. Sec. Cen. Organizing Cttee., Burma Socialist Programme Party 65-73; Gen. Sec. Burma Socialist Prog. Party 73-; Minister of Nat. Planning, Finance and Revenue 69-72; Deputy Prime Minister 71-74; Minister of Defence 72-74; Chief of Gen. Staff April 72-74; Sec. Council of State 74-81; Chair. Council of State and Pres. of Burma Nov. 81-; Vice-Chair. Socialist Econ. Planning Cttee.
Office of the President, Rangoon, Burma.

Sananikone, Phoui; Laotian politician; b. 1903.
Head of Province 41-46; Pres. Chamber of Deputies 48-50, 60-74 (Nat. Assembly dissolved); Prime Minister and Pres. of the Council of Ministers Feb. 50-Nov. 51, 58-Dec. 59; Minister of Foreign Affairs 53-54, 54-56, 57-58, 59; Vice-Pres. Council of Ministers 53-56; numerous other cabinet posts; fmr. Pres. Nat. Assembly; Pres. Nationalist group and Speaker, Rassemblement du Peuple Lao 62-74; sentenced to death *in absentia* Sept. 75; Grand Croix Ordre Royal du Million d'Eléphants et du Parasol Blanc; Commdr., Légion d'honneur; Croix de guerre avec palme.

Sandberg, Michael Graham Ruddock, O.B.E.; British banker; b. 31 May 1927; ed. St. Edward's School, Oxford. Served 6th Lancers (Indian Army) and 1st King's Dragoon Guards 45; joined The Hongkong and Shanghai Banking Corpn. 49; service in Hong Kong, Japan and Singapore; Gen. Man. 71, Exec. Dir. 72, Deputy Chair. 73-77, Chair. 77-; Chair. British Bank of the Middle East 80-, Mercantile Bank Ltd. 77-; Treas. Univ. of Hong Kong 77-; Chair. Bd. of Stewards, Royal Hong Kong Jockey Club 81; mem. (unofficial) Exec. Council, Hong Kong 78-; Pres. Community Chest of Hong Kong 81; Vice-Chair. Hong Kong Arts Festival Soc. 79.
c/o The Hongkong and Shanghai Banking Corporation, 1 Queen's Road Central, Hong Kong.

Sanford, Francis Ariioehau; French Polynesian politician; b. 11 May 1912; ed. Papeete Central School.
Teacher 29-32; Asst. to Admin., Tuamotu Group 32-39; Admin., Gambier Islands 39-41; Liaison Officer with American Forces, Borobora 42-46; Director of Educ. 50-65; Mayor of Faza, Tahiti, 65; elected Deputy to France 67; Vice-Pres. French Polynesia Council of Govt. 78-79; Légion d'honneur; Medal of Freedom (U.S.A.).
c/o Office of the Vice-President, Council of Government, Papeete, Tahiti, French Polynesia.

Sary, Ieng (*see* Ieng Sary).

Sasaki, Kunihiko; Japanese banker; b. 20 Dec. 1908; ed. Tokyo Univ.
Manager, Planning and Co-ordination Dept. of Head Office Business Div., Yasuda Bank 47-48; Man. Planning and Co-ordination Dept. of Head Office Business Div., Fuji Bank 48-49, Man. Credit Dept. 49-50, Deputy Man. Osaka Branch 50-51, Chief Man. Foreign Div. 51-54, Dir. 54-57, Man. Dir. 57-63, Deputy Pres. 63-71, Chair. of the Board and Pres. 71-75, Dir. and Hon. Chair. 75-81; Counsellor 81-.

The Fuji Bank Ltd., 5 5, 1-chome, Ohtemachi, Chiyoda-ku, Tokyo; 18-10, 6-chome, Matsubara, Setogayaku, Tokyo Japan (Home).

Sasaki, Takanobu; Japanese business executive; b. 1912; ed. Kyoto Univ.
President and Rep. Dir. Nippon Mining Co. Ltd. 78-.
Nippon Mining Co. Ltd., 10-1 Toranomon 2-chome, Minato-ku, Tokyo (Office); 5-24-26 Higashi-cho, Koganei-shi, Tokyo, Japan (Home).
Telephone: (03) 582-2111.

Sasaki, Yoshitake; Japanese politician.
Director, Atomic Energy Comm. 56; mem. Liberal-Democratic Party, fmr. Head of LDP Cttee. on Science and Technology; mem. House of Reps. (five times); Dir. Science and Technology Agency 74-76; Minister of Int. Trade and Industry Nov. 79-June 80.
c/o Liberal-Democratic Party, 7, 2-chome, Hirakawacho, Chiyoda-ku, Tokyo, Japan.

Sathe, Vasant P., B.A., LL.B.; Indian politician; b. 5 March 1925, Nasik, Maharashtra.
Took part in Quit India Movt., imprisoned 42; associated with Socialist Party and PSP until 64; Pres. Madhya Pradesh Textile Workers' Fed. 56-60, Vidarbha Textile Workers' Fed. 60-65; mem. Lok Sabha 72-; Minister of Information and Broadcasting, Govt. of India Jan. 80-; Sr. adviser, Indian del. to 25th UN Gen. Assembly; mem. inter-parl. del. to Tokyo 64.
Ministry of Information and Broadcasting, New Delhi, India.

Satpathy, Nandini; Indian politician and social worker; b. 9 June 1931, Cuttack; ed. Ravenshaw Coll., Cuttack.
Leader of the student movements in Orissa and Sec. Girls Students' Asscn. 48-49; took part in many welfare activities, organized and became Sec. of the Orissa Women's Relief Cttee.; organized Orissa branch, Asscn. of Social and Moral Hygiene in India 58; associated with numerous nat. welfare, literary and other orgs.; mem. Rajya Sabha (Upper House) 62-71; Deputy Minister for Information and Broadcasting 66-69; Deputy Minister attached to Prime Minister 69-70; Minister of State for Information and Broadcasting 70-72; Leader Indian film del. to Moscow 66, 68 and Tashkent 72; del. Gen. Conf. UNESCO, Paris 72; mem. Indian del. to Commemorative Session UN, N.Y.C. 70; Chief Minister of Orissa 72-73, 74-Dec. 76, resigned; Pres. Orissa Pradesh Congress Cttee. 73-76; mem. Working Cttee. of the All-India Congress Cttee.; resigned from Congress Party to join Congress for Democracy Feb. 77, which merged with Janata Party May 77; Chair. Orissa Flood and Cyclone Relief Cttee.; mem. Board of Dirs. Int. Centre of Films for Children and Young People, Paris 68-; Editor *Dharitri* (Mother Earth) and *Kalana* (Assessment), monthly magazines; received many literary prizes; popular short story writer.
Publs. *Ketoti Katha*, collection of short stories.
107 Surya Nagar, Bhubaneswar, Orissa, India.
Telephone: 53200, 50784 (Bhubaneswar); 618253 (New Delhi).

Sattar, Abdul; Maldivian politician; b. 18 June 1936, Malé; ed. Saniyya-Majeediyya School, Malé, St. Peter's Coll., Colombo.
Under-Secretary Dept. of External Affairs 58-59, Deputy to Head of Dept. 59-60; Deputy Minister of Educ. 59-60; Maldivian Govt. Rep. in Ceylon 60-66; Amb. to Ceylon (now Sri Lanka) 66-67, to U.S.A. and concurrently Perm. Rep. to UN 67-70; Minister of Finance 70-75; Vice-Pres. in charge of Dept. of Finance 75-77; Minister of Educ. 77-78, of Fisheries 78-.
Ministry of Fisheries, Faamuladheyri Building, Malé; G. Helengeli, Malé, Maldives (Home).
Telephone: 2620 (Office); 2700 (Home).

Sattar, Abdus, M.A., B.L.; Bangladesh politician and judge; b. 1 March 1906, Birbhum, India; ed. Calcutta.
Councillor Calcutta City Corpn. 39; Assessor Calcutta Improvement Tribunal 40-42; Advocate Calcutta High Court 41, Dacca High Court 50; Chief Exec. Officer Calcutta City Corpn. 45; mem. Second Constitutent Assembly Pakistan 54; Minister for Interior and Educ. 56; Judge E. Pakistan High Court 57, Supreme Court of Pakistan 68; Chief Election Commr. Pakistan 69; Chair. Board Bangladesh Life Insurance Corpn. 73, Bangladesh Journalists Wage Board 74; Special Asst. to Pres. of Bangladesh 75-81; Minister of Law and Parl. Affairs 75-77, 80-82; Vice-Pres. of Bangladesh 77-81, Acting Pres., Minister of Defence and of Science and Tech. June 81-Jan. 82, Pres Jan.-March 82; Chair. Nat. Party Jan.-March 82; Pres. Bangladesh Inst. of Law and Int. Affairs.
c/o Martial Law Administration, Dacca, Bangladesh.

Savetsila, Air Chief Marshal Siddhi; Thai air force officer and politician.
Minister for Foreign Affairs Feb. 80-.
Ministry for Foreign Affairs, Saranrom Palace, Bangkok, Thailand.

Saxena, Surrendra Kumar, M.A., M.SOC.SC., PH.D.; Indian International Co-operative official; b. 3 April 1926; ed. Univ. of Agra, Inst. of Social Studies, The Hague, Municipal Univ., Amsterdam.
Assistant Prof., Dept. of Econs., Birla Coll., Pilani 49-52; Research Fellow, Inst. of Social Studies, The Hague 55-56; with ICA Regional Office and Educ. Centre for S.E. Asia 59-61, Regional Officer 61-68; Chair. India Devt. Group, London; Dir. Int. Co-operative Alliance (ICA) 68-81; Sr. Consultant to Swedish Co-operative Centre, Stockholm 81-; Vice-Pres. Union of Int. Asscns., Brussels; life mem. Inst. of Public Admin., New Delhi; Dr. h.c. (Univ. of Sherbrooke, Canada); Severin Jørgensen Prize (Danish Co-operative Movement) 78, Indian Co-operative Movement Medal 79, Highest Medal of Yugoslavia Co-operative Union 80.
Publs. *Nationalisation and Industrial Conflict: Example of British Coal Mining* 55, *Agricultural Co-operation in S.E. Asia* 61, *Role of Foreign Aid in Development of Co-operative Processing* 65, *Activities and Role of the International Co-operative Alliance in S.E. Asia* 66, *The International Co-operative Alliance and Co-operative Trade* 67, etc.
72 Wellington Street West, Ste 204, Martham, Ont. L3P 1A8 (Office); 56 Ramerville Drive, Markham, Ont. L3P 1J5, Canada.

Sayem, Abusadat Mohammad, B.A., B.L.; Bangladesh politician and judge (retd.); b. 1 March 1916; ed. Rangpur Zilla School, Presidency Coll., Calcutta, Carmichael Coll., Rangpur, Univ. Law Coll., Calcutta.
Advocate, Calcutta High Court 44; joined Dacca High Court Bar 47; Examiner in Law, Dacca Univ.; mem. Local Board, State Bank of Pakistan until 56; Sponsor, Gen. Sec. and Vice-Pres. East Pakistan Lawyers Asscn.; fmr. Sec. and Vice-Pres. High Court Bar Asscn.; Advocate, Fed. Court of Pakistan 51-59; Senior Advocate, Supreme Court of Pakistan 59-62; mem. Bar Council until 62; Judge High Court, Dacca 62; mem. of various legal comms. of inquiry; mem. Pakistan Election Comm. for nat. and provincial assemblies 70-71; first Chief Justice, High Court of Bangladesh 72; Chief Justice, Supreme Court 72-75; Chief Martial Law Admin. Nov. 75-Nov. 76; Pres. of Bangladesh, Minister of Defence, of Law, of Parl. Affairs and Justice, of Foreign Affairs and of Agric. 75-77; resigned because of ill health.
105 Azimpur Road, Dacca 5, Bangladesh.

Scott, Hon. Douglas Barr; Australian politician; b. May 1920, Grenfell, N.S.W.; ed. Scotch Coll., Adelaide, St. Andrew's Coll., Sydney Univ.
Royal Australian Navy 41-46; entered Parl. as Senator

Aug.-Nov. 70; re-elected Nat. Country Party Senator for N.S.W. 74, 75; Deputy Leader Nat. Country Party Feb. 76; mem. Senate Standing Cttee. on Foreign Affairs and Defence 76-, Standing Orders and Privileges Cttees., Deputy Pres. and Chair. Govt. Cttees. 78-, including Industrial Relations Cttee.; Leader Parl. Del. to Commonwealth Parl. Asscn. Conf. in Mauritius 76, to S.E. Asia and Republic of Korea 79; Minister for Special Trade Representations and Assisting Minister for Trade and Resources 79-; mem. Livestock and Grain Producers' Asscn.; Nat. Country Party.
Department of Special Trade Representations, Edmund Barton Building, Kings Avenue, Barton, A.C.T. 2600, Australia.

Scott, John Vivian, LL.B.; New Zealand diplomatist; b. 19 Nov. 1920; ed. Victoria Univ., Wellington.
Joined New Zealand Dept. of External Affairs 47; has served in Canberra, New York and London; mem. New Zealand Perm. Mission at UN 51-55; Amb. to Japan 65-69; Perm. Rep. to UN 69-73; Deputy Sec. of Foreign Affairs, Wellington 73-79; Amb. to France, also accred. to Spain, Portugal, Vatican City and concurrently Perm. Rep. to OECD 79-.
New Zealand Embassy, rue Léonard de Vinci 7, 75116 Paris, France.

Sculthorpe, Peter Joshua, M.B.E.; Australian composer; b. 29 April 1929; ed. Launceston Grammar School, Univ. of Melbourne and Wadham Coll., Oxford.
Senior Lecturer in Music, Univ. of Sydney 63-; Reader in Music, University of Sydney 68-; Visiting Fellow, Yale Univ. 65-67; Visiting Prof. Univ. of Sussex 71-72; commissions from Australian Broadcasting Comm., Birmingham Chamber Music Soc., Australian Elizabethan Theatre Trust, Australian Ballet and others; Australian Council Composer's Award 75-78.
Compositions published include: *The Loneliness of Bunjil* 54, *Sonatina* 54, *Variations* 54, *Irkanda I* 55, *Sonata for Viola and Percussion* 60, *Irkanda IV* 61, *The Fifth Continent* 63, *String Quartet No. 6* 65, *Sun Music I* 65, *Canto 1520* 66, *Night Piece* 66, *Red Landscape* 66, *Morning Song* 66, *Sun Music III* 67, *Three Haiku* 67, *Sun Music IV* 67, *Tabuh Tabuhan* 68, *Autumn Song* 68, *Sun Music II* 68, *Interlude* 68, *Sun Music Ballet* 68, *From Tabuh Tabuhan* 68, *Sea Chant* 68, *Ketjak* 69, *String Quartet Music* 69, *Love 200* 70, *The Stars Turn* 70, *Music for Japan* 70, *Rain* 70, *Overture for a Happy Occasion* 70, *Dream* 70, *Night* 71, *Snow, Moon and Flowers* 71, *Stars* 71, *Landscape* 71, *How the Stars were Made* 71, *Ketjak* 72, *Koto Music* 72, *Rites of Passage* 73, *Music of Early Morning* 74, documentary and feature film scores, music for theatre, radio and television.
147B Queen Street, Woollahra, Sydney, N.S.W. 2025, Australia.
Telephone: 32-4 701.

Seaman, Rev. Sir Keith Douglas, K.C.V.O., O.B.E., B.A., LL.B.; Australian state governor and Methodist minister; b. 11 June 1920; ed. Unley High School and Univ. of Adelaide.
South Australia (S.A.) Public Service 37-54; entered Methodist ministry 54; Minister, Renmark 54-58; Cen. Methodist Mission 58-77; Dir. 5KA, 5AU, 5RM Broadcasting Cos. 60-77 (Chair. 71-77); Sec. Christian TV Asscn. S.A. 59-73; mem. Exec. World Asscn. of Christian Broadcasting 63-70; R.A.A.F. Overseas HQ, London 41-45, Flt. Lt.; Supt. Adelaide Cen. Methodist Mission 71-77; mem. Aust. Govt. Social Welfare Comm. 73-76; Gov. of South Australia 77-82; K.St.J.
Victor Harbor, Adelaide, South Australia 5011, Australia.

Sehgal, Amar Nath, B.SC., M.A.; Indian sculptor; b. 5 Feb. 1922, Campbellpur, West Pakistan; ed. Punjab Univ., Govt. Coll., Lahore, and New York Univ.
One-man exhbns. New York 50-51, Paris 52, East Africa and India; Hon. Art Consultant to Ministry of Community Devt., Govt. of India 55-66; organized sculpture exhbn., Belgrade 64, Musée d'Art Moderne, Paris 65, Paulskirche, Frankfurt 65, Haus am Lutzoplatz Berlin 66, Musées Royaux D'Art et Histoire, Brussels 66, Musée de l'Etat, Luxembourg 66, Wiener Secession, Vienna 66, Flemish Acad. Arts 67, 25th Independence Celebration, Retrospective exhbn. (1947–72), Nat. Gallery, New Delhi 72, 10th Tokyo Int. Fair 73, City Hall Ottawa 75, Aerogolf Luxembourg 75, New India House, New York 76, Rathaus, Fransheim, Konstanz, Flughafen Frankfurt, all Fed. Repub. of Germany 77, Neustadt, Fed. Repub. of Germany 78, Baden Baden Fed. Repub. of Germany 79, Luxembourg 80; exhbns. Dubai, Abu Dhabi 80, Jeddah 81; organized Int. Art Workshop for UNESCO, Paris 79; participated in Sculpture Biennale, Musée Rodin, Paris 66 and UNESCO Conf. on role of art in contemporary soc. 74; Sculpture Award, Lalit Kala Akademy 57; President's Award, Lalit Kala Akademy 58 (donated to Prime Minister Nehru during Chinese invasion).
Major works: *Voice of Africa* (Ghana) 59, *A Cricketer* 61, Mahatma Gandhi, Amritsar, *To Space Unknown* (bronze, Moscow) 63; commissioned to decorate Vigyan Bhawan (India's Int. Conferences Building) with bronze sculptural mural depicting rural life of India; bronze work *Conquest of the Moon* in White House Collection 69; bronze work *Rising Tide*, Ford Foundation Collection 69; bronze work *Anguished Cries*, West Berlin 71; Gandhi Monument, Luxembourg 72; Monument to Aviation, New Delhi Airport 72; bronze work *Rising Spirit*, President Carter Collection 78; bronze work *Victor and Vanquished*, Sheikh Rashid (Prime Minister U.A.E. and Ruler of Dubai) collection 80; works in Jerusalem, Vienna, Paris, West Berlin, Wiesbaden, Antwerp, New Delhi, Luxembourg, Kaiserslautern (Fed. Repub. of Germany), Connecticut.
Publs. *Arts and Aesthetics*, *Organising Exhibitions in Rural Areas*, *Der Innere Rhythmus* (poems).
J-23 Jangpura Extension, New Delhi 110014, India.
Telephone: 79206.

Seidler, Harry, O.B.E., M.ARCH.; Australian (b. Austrian) architect; b. 25 June 1923; ed. Wasagymnasium, Vienna, Austria, Cambridge Technical School, U.K., Univ. of Manitoba, Canada, Harvard Univ., U.S.A., and Black Mountain Coll., U.S.A.
Postgraduate work under Walter Gropius, Harvard Univ. 46; study with painter Joseph Albers, Black Mountain Coll. 46; Chief Asst. with Marcel Breuer New York 46-48; Principal Architect Harry Seidler and Assocs., Sydney, Australia 48-; Visiting Prof. Harvard Univ. 76-77, Univ. of Virginia 78, Univ. of N.S.W. 80; Hon. F.A.I.A., F.R.A.I.A., Wilkinson Award 65, 66, 67; American Inst. of Architects Pan Pacific Citation 68; Sir John Sulman Medal 51, 67; Architecture and Arts Building of the Year Award 60, Civic Design Award 67; R.A.I.A. Gold Medal 79.
Major works: city centre redevelopment "Australia Square", Sydney 62-66; office complex, Dept. of Trade, Canberra 70; M.L.C. Center, Martin Place, Sydney 72-75; Australian Embassy, France 74-77; mem. Hong Kong Club 80-, Garden Islands Weapons Workshop 80-.
Publs. *Houses, Interiors and Projects 1949-1954*, *Harry Seidler 1955-63*, *Australia Square, Sydney* 69, *Architecture in the New World* 74, *Australian Embassy, Paris* 79, *Two Towers, Sydney* 80.
Office: 2 Glen Street, Milsons Point, N.S.W. 2061; Home: 13 Kalang Avenue, Killara, N.S.W. 2071, Australia.
Telephone: 922 1388 (Office); 4985986 (Home).

Selangor, H.R.H. the Sultan of; Sultan Salahuddin Abdul Aziz Shah Ibni Al-Marhum Sultan Hisamuddin Alam Shah Alhaj, D.K., D.M.N., S.P.M.S., S.P.D.K., D.P.; Malaysian ruler; b. 8 March 1926; ed. Sekolah Melayu Pengkalan Batu, Kelang, Malay Coll., Kuala Kangsar, London Univ.

Tengku Laksamana Selangor 46; Regent of Selangor during father's absence 60; succeeded his late father as Ruler of Selangor Sept. 60; Maj. Royal Malay Regt.; Colonel-in-Chief Royal Malaysia Air Force.
Shah Alam, Selangor, Malaysia.

Sen, Amartya Kumar, M.A., PH.D.; Indian economist; b. 3 Nov. 1933, Santiniketan, Bengal; ed. Presidency Coll., Calcutta and Trinity Coll., Cambridge.
Professor of Econs., Jadavpur Univ., Calcutta 56-58; Fellow, Trinity Coll., Cambridge 57-63; Prof. of Econs., Univ. of Delhi 63-71, Chair. Dept. of Econs. 66-68; Hon. Dir. Agricultural Econs. Research Centre, Delhi 66-68, 69-71; Prof. of Econs. London School of Econs. 71-77, Oxford Univ. 77-80; Drummond Prof. of Political Economy, Oxford Univ. 80-; Visiting Prof., Univ. of Calif., Berkeley 64-65, Harvard Univ. 68-69; Andrew D. White Prof.-at-Large, Cornell Univ.; Foreign Hon. mem., American Acad. of Arts and Sciences; Fellow, Econometric Soc., British Acad.; Hon. D.Litt.
Publs. *Choice of Techniques: An Aspect of Planned Economic Development* 60, *Growth Economics* 70, *Collective Choice and Social Welfare* 70, *On Economic Inequality* 73, *Employment, Technology and Development* 75, *Poverty and Famines: An Essay on Entitlement and Deprivation* 81, *Utilitarianism and Beyond* 82; articles in various journals in economics, philosophy and political science.
All Souls College, Oxford, England.
Telephone: Oxford 722251.

Sen, Mrinal; Indian film director; b. Calcutta.
Started making films 56; directed 17 feature films; films include: *The Dawn* 56, *Bhuvan Shome* 68, Calcutta trilogy—*The Interview, Calcutta 71* and *Guerrilla, Royal Hunt, The Outsiders, Man with an Axe, In Search of Famine* 80, *And Quiet Rolls the Dawn* 80.

Sen, S. R., PH.D.; Indian economist; b. 29 June 1916; ed. Calcutta Presidency Coll., Univ. of Dacca and London School of Econs.
Active in Indian freedom movt. 32 and 42; taught economics, Univ. of Dacca 40-48; Deputy Econ. Adviser, Govt. of India 48-51; Econ. and Statistical Adviser, Govt. of India 51-58; Joint Sec. (Plan Co-ordination), Planning Comm. 59-63; Adviser (Programme Admin.) and Additional Sec., Govt. of India 63-69; Vice-Chair. Irrigation Comm., Govt. of India 69-70; Exec. Dir. IBRD, IFC and IDA 70-78; Chair. Govt. of India Comm. on Cost of Production 79; Chair. Int. Food Policy Research Inst., Washington, D.C. 79-; has taken part in and led numerous Indian and int. agric. and devt. comms. and delegations; Pres. Int. Asscn. of Agric. Economists 70-76; First Prize, Asia, World Essay Competition 37.
Publs. *Strategy for Agricultural Development, Economics of Sir James Steuart, Population and Food Supply, Planning Machinery in India, Growth and Instability in Indian Agriculture, Politics of Indian Economy, India's Defence Development and Administration, International Monetary System and Financial Institutions.*
41 Poorvi Marg, Vasant Vihar, New Delhi 57, India.

Senanayake, E. L., B.SC.; Sri Lankan politician; b. Aug. 1920; ed. Trinity Coll., Kandy.
Member of Kandy Municipal Council 43-; Mayor of Kandy; M.P. for Kandy 52-; represented Ceylon in Econ. Cttee. at 20th Gen. Session of UN 65; mem. Exec. Cttee. Inter-Parl. Asscn.; represented Ceylon at Inter-Parl. Confs., Belgrade 63, Dublin 65, Canberra 66; represented Ceylon at World Mayors' Conf., Bangkok and Paris 67; Founder mem. United Nat. Party; Minister of Health 68-70, of Agricultural Devt. and Research 77-82, of Health 4-12 May 82 (resgnd.).
c/o Ministry of Health, Colombo, Sri Lanka.

Senanayeke, Maithripala; Sri Lankan politician; b. 1916; ed. St. Joseph's Coll., Anuradhapura, St. John's Coll., Jaffna, and Nalanda Vidyalaya, Colombo.
Joined Govt. Service 40, Cultivation Officer 40-47; mem. Parl. 47-; Deputy Minister of Home Affairs 52; Minister of Transport and Works 56-Dec. 59; Minister of Industries, Home Affairs and Cultural Affairs July 60-July 63; Minister of Commerce and Industries July 63-June 64, of Rural and Industrial Devt. 64-65; Minister of Irrigation, Power and Highways 70-July 77; Leader, House of Reps. (later Nat. State Assembly) 70-77; Pres. Sri Lanka Freedom Party Sept.-Dec. 81; M.P.
61 Jawathe Road, Colombo 5, Sri Lanka.

Sengoku, Jo, LL.B.; Japanese business executive; b. 26 Jan. 1904, Osaka; ed. Tokyo Univ.
Director, Kuraray Co. Ltd. 42, Man. Dir. 45, Senior Man. Dir. 48, Vice-Pres. 61, Pres. 68-75, Chair. 75-; Pres. Kyowa Gas Chemical Industry Co. 61-78, Counsellor 78-; Dir. Keihanshin Real Estate Co. 52-, Kurashiki Cen. Hosp. 68, Sanyo Broadcasting Co., Hotel Plaza 69; Blue Ribbon Medal; Second Order of Merit, Order of Sacred Treasure.
Kuraray Co. Ltd., 1-12-39 Umeda, Kita-ku, Osaka City; Home 1-37, Kumoicho, Nishinomiya, Hyogo Pref., Japan.

Serisawa, Kojiro; Japanese author; b. 1897; ed. Tokyo and Paris Univs.
Administrative Official, Ministry of Agriculture 22-25; Prof. at Chuo Univ. 30-32; Pres. Japanese PEN Club 48-; mem. Japanese Acad.; awarded Prix des Amitiés Françaises 59, Prize of Japanese Govt. 70, of Japanese Acad. 72; Commdr. de l'Ordre des Arts et des Lettres 74.
Publs. *Death in Paris* 40, *One World* 54, *Mrs. Aida* 57, *Under the Shadow of Love and Death* 53, *House on the Hill* 59, *Parting* 61, *Love, Intelligence and Sadness* 62, *Fate of Man* (14 vols.) 62-71, *La Porte Etroite, Porte de la Mort* 78, *Les Ombres de L'Amour* 81.
5-8-3 Higashinakano, Nagano-ku, Tokyo, Japan.

Sethi, Prakash Chandra, B.A., LL.B.; Indian politician, b. 19 Oct. 1920, Jhalrapatan, Rajasthan; ed. Madhav Coll.; Ujjain and Holkar Coll., Indore.
President Madhav Nagar Ward Congress 47, Ujjain District Congress 51, 54, 57, Textile Clerks Asscn. 48-49; Vice-Pres. Madhya Bharat Employees Asscn. 42, 49, 52; Treas. Madhya Bharat Congress 54-55; mem. Ujjain District and Madhya Bharat Congress Cttee. Exec. 53-57; Dir. Ujjain District Co-operative Bank 57-59; A.I.C.C. Zonal Rep. for Karnatak, Maharashtra, Bombay and Gujarat 55-56; observer for Bihar 66; mem. Rajya Sabha 61-67, Lok Sabha 67-; Deputy Minister for Steel, Heavy Industries and Mines, Cen. Govt. 62-67, Minister of State 67-69; Minister of Revenue and Expenditure 69-70, of Defence Production 70-71, of Petroleum and Chemicals 71-72; Chief Minister Madhya Pradesh 72-75; Minister of Fertilizers and Chemicals Dec. 75-77; arrested Oct. 77; Minister of Works and Housing Jan.-Oct. 80, of Petroleum, Chemicals and Fertilizers Oct. 80-Jan. 81, of Railways Jan. 82-; rep. of Govt. of India at Commonwealth Finance Ministers' Conf., Barbados 69; leader del. to Colombo Plan Conf., Victoria 69; Gov. for India, Asian Devt. Bank, Manila, and IBRD 69.
Ministry of Railways, New Delhi, India.

Sethna, Homi Nusserwanji, B.SC., M.S.E., D.SC.; Indian engineer; b. 24 Aug. 1923; ed. St. Xavier's School and Coll., Bombay, Univ. of Bombay, and Michigan Univ.
Works Man. Indian Rare Earths Ltd. (Govt. Co.) 49-50; joined Atomic Energy Establishment, Trombay (now Bhabha Atomic Research Centre) 59, Dir. 66; constructed Monazite Plant, Alwaye, Kerala, Thorium and Uranium Metal Plants and Plutonium Plant, Trombay, and Uranium Mill, Jadugoda, Bihar; Deputy Sec.-Gen. of UN Conf. on Peaceful Uses of Atomic Energy, Geneva 58; Chair. Fertilizer Corpn. of India Ltd. until 73, Madras and

Rajasthan Atomic Power Project Boards; mem. Scientific Advisory Cttee. to Cabinet 61, 80-; mem. Int. Atomic Energy Agency (IAEA) 66, UN Cttee. of Specialists on Nuclear Technology and the developing countries; mem. for Research and Devt., Atomic Energy Comm. 66-, Dir. 66; Chair. Atomic Energy Comm. 72, Bd. of Govs. Indian Inst. of Tech. 71-74; Prin. Sec. to Govt. of India, Dept. Atomic Energy; mem. Cttee. on Scientific Research, Planning Comm.; Dir. Andhra Valley Power Supply Co. Ltd., Bombay 75-; Chancellor North-Eastern Hill Univ.; first Pres. Maharashtra Acad. of Sciences 76-79; mem. Bd. of Govs. Tata Memorial Centre, Indian Rare Earths Ltd., Electronics Corpn. of India Ltd.; mem. Gov. Council Tata Inst. of Fundamental Research; mem. Scientific study team, Govt. of India; mem. UN Scientific Advisory Cttee., IAEE; mem. Indian Inst. of Chemical Engineers, Inst. of Engineers; Life mem. Indian Acad. of Science; mem. Royal Swedish Acad. of Engineering Sciences; Fellow, Indian Nat. Science Acad.; Dr. h.c. (Marathwada Univ.) 73; Hon. LL.D. (Bombay) 74; Hon. Dr. Tech. (Jawaharlal Nehru Tech. Univ.) 74; Hon. D.Sc. (Roorkee and Karnataka Univs. and Indian Inst. of Tech., Bombay) 75, (Orissa and Mysore Univs.) 76, (Utkal Univ.) 77; Padma Shri Award 59, Shanti Swarup Bhatnagar Memorial Award 60, Padma Bhushan 66, Sesquicentennial Award, Univ. of Michigan 67, Sir Walter Puckey Award 71, Sir William Jones Memorial Medal 74, Padma Vibhushan 75, Sir Devprasad Sarbadhikari Gold Medal 75.
12th Floor, Dept. of Atomic Energy Officers' Apartments, Little Gibbs Road No. 2, Malabar Hill, Bombay 400 006; Old Yacht Club, Chatrapati Shiraji Maharaj Marg, Bombay 400 039, India (Home).

Seyid Muhammad, V. A. (*see* Muhammad, V. A. S.).

Seypidin, Gen.; Chinese (Uygur) politician; b. 1916, Atushi, Xinjiang Uygur; ed. Cen. Asia Univ., Moscow.
Leader of Uygur Uprisings 33, 44; Minister of Educ., E. Turkestan Repub. 45; Deputy Chair. Xinjiang Uygur People's Govt. 49-54, Chair. 55-68; Deputy Commdr. Xinjiang Uygur Mil. Region, People's Liberation Army 49, 55-; Second Sec. CCP Xinjiang Uygur 56-58; Alt. mem. 8th Cen. Cttee. of CCP 56; Pres. Xinjiang Uygur Univ. 64; Vice-Chair. Xinjiang Uygur Revolutionary Cttee. 68, Chair. 72-78; mem. 9th Cen. Cttee. of CCP 69; Second Sec. CCP Xinjiang Uygur 71, First Sec. 73-78; Alt. mem. Politburo 10th Cen. Cttee. of CCP 73, 75-78; First Political Commissar Xinjiang Uygur Mil. Region, PLA 74-78; Chair. Presidium Nat. People's Congress 75; alt. mem. Politburo, 11th Cen. Cttee. CCP 76; Exec. Chair. Presidium 5th Nat. People's Congress; Vice-Chair. Cttee. 5th Nat. People's Congress 78-.
People's Republic of China.

Shafie, Tan Sri Haji Muhammad Ghazali bin (*see* Ghazali bin Shafie, Tan Sri Haji Muhammad).

Shafiq, Mohammad Musa, M.A.; Afghan politician; b. 1924, Kabul; ed. Ghazi High School, Al Azhar Univ., Cairo and Columbia Univ., U.S.A.
Joined Ministry of Justice 57, later became Dir. Legislative Dept.; also taught at Faculty of Law and Political Science, Kabul Univ.; Partner, private law firm, Kabul 61; Deputy Minister of Justice 63-66; Adviser, Ministry of Foreign Affairs 66-68; Amb. to Egypt (also accred. to Lebanon, Sudan and Ghana) 68-71; Minister of Foreign Affairs 71-73, Prime Minister 72-73 (deposed by mil. coup); in detention 73-75; arrested April 78.

Shaha, Rishikesh; Nepalese politician, diplomatist and professor of politics; b. 1925; ed. Patna and Allahabad Univs., India.
Lecturer in English and Nepali Literature, Tri-Chandra Coll. 45-48; Leader of Opposition in first Advisory Assembly 52; Gen. Sec. of Nepali Congress 53-55; Amb. and Perm. Rep. to UN 56-61; Amb. to U.S.A. 58-61; Minister of Finance, Planning and Econ. Affairs 61-62, of Foreign Affairs July-Sept. 62; Amb.-at-Large 62-63; Visiting Prof. East-West Center, Hawaii 65-66; mem. Nat. Panchayat (Assembly) 67-70; solitary confinement 69-70; Visiting Prof., School of Int. Studies of Jawaharlal Nehru Univ. 71; Regent's Prof., Univ. of Calif. at Berkeley 71-72; returned to Nepal; arrested Dec. 74; Fellow, Woodrow Wilson Int. Center for Scholars, Washington, D.C. 76-77; returned to Nepal; arrested May 77.
Publs. *Nepal and the World* 54, *Heroes and Builders of Nepal* (in U.K.) 65, *An Introduction to Nepal* 76, *Nepali Politics—Retrospect and Prospect* (in U.K.) 76.
Shri Nivas, Kamal Pokhari, Kathmandu, Nepal.
Telephone: 11766.

Shahi, Agha, M.A., LL.B.; Pakistani diplomatist; b. 25 Aug. 1920, Bangalore; ed. Madras Univ. and Allahabad Univ.
Indian Civil Service 43; Pakistan Foreign Service 51-; Deputy Sec., Ministry of Foreign Affairs, in charge of UN and Int. Confs. Branch 51-55; First Counsellor and Minister, Wash. 55-58; Deputy Perm. Rep. to UN 58-61; Dir.-Gen. in charge Divs. of UN and Int. Conf. Affairs, Soviet, Chinese and Arab Affairs, Ministry of Foreign Affairs 61-64; Additional Foreign Sec. 64-67; Perm. Rep. to UN 67-72; Pakistan Rep. to Security Council 68-69; Pres. UN Security Council Jan. 68; Chair. Pakistan Del. to Conf. of Non-Nuclear Weapons States 68; Pres. Governing Council for UN Devt. Programme 69; Pakistan Rep. to Conf. of the Cttee. on Disarmament 69; Amb. to People's Repub. of China 72-73; Foreign Sec. 73-77; Chair. Pakistan Del. UN Gen. Assembly 73-77; Sec.-Gen. Foreign Affairs 77-78; Minister of State, Adviser to Pres. on Foreign Affairs 78-82; Chair. UN Advisory Bd. on Disarmament Studies Nov. 78-; Chair. of Extraordinary Session of the Conf. of Foreign Ministers of Islamic Countries Jan. 80.
c/o Ministry of Foreign Affairs, Islamabad, Pakistan.

Shahi, K. B.; Nepalese politician.
Minister for Communications 79-80; Minister for Foreign Affairs. 79-81.
c/o Ministry of Foreign Affairs, Kathmandu, Nepal.

Shahidi, Burhan; Chinese (Uighur) politician; b. 1894; Wensu City, Xinjiang.
Studied Berlin Univ. 29; Vice-Chair. three regions, revolutionary coalition, Xinjiang 46; Chair. Prov. Govt. and mem. Standing Cttee., Sub-bureau CCPCC, Xinjiang, mem. Mil. and Pol. Comm., North-West China after 49; Dir. Nationalities Inst. of Chinese Acad., Vice-Pres. Pol. Science and Law Asscn. of China, Vice-Chair. China Peace Cttee. after 56; Vice-Chair. CPPCC Nat. Cttee. Sept. 80-.
People's Republic of China.

Shankar (Shankar Pillai, K.); Indian newspaper cartoonist; b. 31 July 1902.
Former cartoonist for *Hindustan Times*, New Delhi; founded *Indian News Chronicle*, Delhi 47; Founder and Editor *Shankar's Weekly* 48-; initiated Shankar's Int. Children's Art Competition 49; founded Children's Book Trust 57 of which he is now Exec. Trustee; Dir. Int. Dolls Museum 65; Founder and Editor *Children's World Magazine* 68; founder and Dir. Children's Library and Reading Room; Padma Shri 55, Padma Bhushan 66, Padma Vibushan 76, Order of Smile (Poland) 77, UN Asscn. (Hamilton Branch) Award 79, and several other awards and medals.
Children's Book Trust, Nehru House 4, B.S.Z. Marg, New Delhi 110002 (Office); 9 Purana Kila Road, New Delhi 1, India (Home).
Telephone: 271921-5, 273568 (Office); 386306 (Home).

Shankar, Ravi; Indian sitar player and composer; b. 7 April 1920; ed. under Ustad Allauddin Khan of Maihar.
Trained in the *Guru-Shishya* tradition; pupil of Ustad Allauddin Khan 38; solo sitar player; fmr. Dir. of Music All-India Radio and founder of the Nat. Orchestra; Founder-Dir. Kinnara School of Music, Bombay 62-, Kinnara School of Music, Los Angeles 67; organized Research Inst. for Music and Performing Arts (RIMPA), Varanasi; many recordings of traditional and experimental variety in India, U.K. and the U.S.A.; Concert tours in Europe, U.S.A. and the East; Visiting Lecturer Univ. of Calif. 65; appeared in film *Raga* 74; Fellow, Sangeet Natak Akademi 76; Hon. D.Litt. (Banaras Hindu Univ.); Silver Bear of Berlin; Award of Indian Nat. Acad. for Music, Dance and Drama 62; award of Padma Bhushan 67, Int. Music Council UNESCO Award 75, Padma Vibhushan 81.
Film Scores: *Pather Panchali, The Flute and the Arrow, Nava Rasa Ranga, Charly, Gandhi,* etc. and many musical compositions including *Concerto for Sitar* 71, *Raga Jogeshwari* 81, *Raga for Mahatma Gandhi* 81, *Concerto for Sitar No. 2* 81.
Publ. *My Music, My Life* 69, *Rag Anurag* (Bengali).
Hemangana, S. 13/131 Tarana Bazar, Shivpur, Varanasi, India.

Shankaranand, B., B.A., LL.B.; Indian politician; b. 19 Oct. 1925, Chikodi, Belgaum District, Karnataka; ed. Govt. Law Coll., Bombay and R. L. Law Coll., Belgaum.
Formerly associated with Republican Party of India and PSP; mem. Lok Sabha; Gen. Sec. Congress Party and Chair. its Exec. Cttee. 69-71; Deputy Minister, Dept. of Parliamentary Affairs, Govt. of India 71-77; Minister of Educ., Health and Social Welfare Jan.-Oct. 80, of Health and Social Welfare Oct. 80-; del. to UNCTAD 68, UN Gen. Assembly 69.
c/o Ministry of Education, New Delhi, India.

Shann, Sir Keith Charles Owen, Kt., C.B.E., B.A.; Australian diplomatist; b. 22 Nov. 1917; ed. Trinity Grammar School, Kew, and Trinity Coll., Melbourne Univ., Australia.
United Nations Div., Dept. of External Affairs 46-49; Australian Mission to UN, New York 49-52; Head, UN Branch, Dept. of External Affairs 52-55; Australian Minister to the Philippines 55-56; Amb. 56-59; Australian External Affairs Officer, London 59-62; Amb. to Indonesia 62-66; First Asst. Sec. Dept. of External Affairs 66-70, Deputy Sec. 70-74; Amb. to Japan 74-77; Chair. Australian Public Service Board 77-78; Dir. Mount Isa Mines Holdings 78-; mem. Australia-Japan Foundation 78-.
11 Grey Street, Deakin, Canberra, A.C.T. 2600, Australia (Home).
Telephone: 73-1390 (Home).

Shantaram, V(ankudre); Indian film director, producer and actor; b. 18 Nov. 1901; ed. Kolhapur High School.
Worked in film industry 20-; Founder mem. Prabhat Film Co., Poona; fmr. Chief Producer Govt. of India Films Div., mem. Censor Board, Film Advisory Board, Film Enquiry Cttee.; Chair. Children's Film Soc.; has directed and produced over 60 films 26-, including *King of Ayodhya, Chandrasena, Duniya-na-mane, Shakuntala* (first Indian film released in U.S.A.), *Ramjoshi, Amar Bhoopali, Jhanak Jhanak Payal Baaje* and *Do Ankhen Barah Haath* (11 awards incl. Berlin Gold Bear, Int. Catholic Award and Hollywood Foreign Press Award).
Rajkamal Kalamandir Private Ltd. Parel, Bombay 12, India.

Shen Hong; Chinese politician; b. Shanghai.
Engineer, Dept. of Enterprises, N. China People's Govt. 48-49; mechanical engineer, Bureau of Industry, Shansi-Chahar-Hopei Border Govt. 48; mem. Exec. Cttee. All-China Fed. of Labour 48-53; del. 1st CPCC 49; Chief, Heavy Industry Div., Planning Bureau, Financial and Econ. Comm., GAC 50-52; asst. to Minister, 3rd Ministry of Machine-Building 55-56; Vice-Minister of Electrical Equipment Industry 57; Vice-Minister of Coal Industry 57-59; Vice-Minister of Agricultural Machine Industry 59-61; Vice-Minister, 1st Ministry of Machine-Building 61-; deputy to 3rd NPC 64-75; mem. Standing Cttee. 5th NPC 78-; Vice-Minister in Charge of Machine-Building Comm., State Council 80-; Vice-Premier, State Council 80.
People's Republic of China.

Shi Lin; Chinese politician.
Vice-Minister for Economic Relations with Foreign Countries 73-80; Deputy 5th NPC 78; Minister for Economic Relations with Foreign Countries 80.
People's Republic of China.

Shi Xinan; Chinese party official.
Deputy Political Commissar, Guizhou Mil. District, PLA 58, Political Commissar 64-.
People's Republic of China.

Shieh Tung-min; Chinese politician; b. 25 Jan. 1907, Taiwan; ed. Nat. Sun Yat-sen Univ.
Magistrate, Kaohsiung County; Deputy Dir. Civil Affairs Dept.; Vice-Commr. of Educ.; Pres. Taiwan Province Teachers' Coll.; Chair. Taiwan Co-op. Bank; Commr. and Sec.-Gen. Taiwan Provincial Govt.; Speaker, Taiwan Provincial Assembly; Gov. of Taiwan 72-78; Vice-Pres. Repub. of China (Taiwan) May 78-.
Office of the Vice-President, Taipei, Taiwan.

Shiga, Yoshio; Japanese journalist; b. 8 Jan. 1901; ed. Imperial Univ., Tokyo.
Joined Communist Party 23, becoming editor of *Marxism;* elected mem. of Central Cttee. of Communist Party 27; imprisoned for political reasons 28-45; re-elected mem. of Central Cttee. 45; mem. of House of Representatives 46-47 and 49-50; removed from public office by Gen. MacArthur, June 50; underground activity 50-54; re-elected mem. House of Reps. 55-; mem. Presidium Central Cttee. Japanese Communist Party, expelled from Party 64; founded the Voice of Japan Soc.; edited internationalist newspaper *Nihon-no-Koe* 64, *Heiwa to Shakaishugi* 77.
Publs. *Eighteen Years of Imprisonment* 46, *On the State* 49, *Japanese Revolutionaries* 56, *On Japan* 60, *My Appeal against Atomic Bomb* 64, *Kuril and Security in Asia* 71, *World Currency Crisis and Labour* 72, *The Japanese Imperialism* 72, *Collective Security of Asia and Kuril Problem* 74, *Problems of the Communist Movement in Japan* 74, *Kuril Problems* (2 vols.) 75, *Notes on the History of the Communist Party of Japan* 79, *Rice Riot in Japan* 80.
Minamicho 3-26-15, Kichijoji, Musashino City, Tokyo 180, Japan.
Telephone: 0422-43-8374.

Shimoda, Takeso; Japanese diplomatist; b. 3 April 1907; ed. Tokyo Imperial Univ.
Entered Japanese Diplomatic Service 31, served Nanking, Moscow, The Hague; Dir. Treaties Bureau Ministry of Foreign Affairs 52-57; Minister to U.S.A. 57-60; Adviser to Minister of Foreign Affairs 60-61; Amb. to Belgium and Chief of Japanese Del. to European Communities 60-63; Amb. to U.S.S.R. 63-65; Vice-Minister of Foreign Affairs 65-67; Amb. to U.S.A. 67-70; Justice of the Supreme Court 70-77; Judge, Perm. Court of Arbitration 72-; Adviser to Minister of Foreign Affairs 77-; Pres. Honda Foundation 77-; Commr. of Professional Baseball 79-; Dir. Japanese Asscn. of Int. Law, Japanese Asscn. of Maritime Law; Hon. mem. American Bar Asscn.; Hon. LL.D. (Univ. of Nebraska); Grand Cross of Order Rising Sun; numerous foreign decorations.
1-4-16, Nishikata, Bunkyo-ku, Tokyo, Japan.

Shinde, Annasaheb, P., B.A., LL.B.; Indian politician, lawyer and agriculturist; b. 21 Jan. 1922, Padali, Maharashtra Province; ed. Wildon Coll., Bombay, Baroda Coll., Law Colls., Poona and Ahmedabad.

Practised law before political imprisonment 44; organized landowning farmers who had leased land to private sugar factories for nominal rents and became heavily involved in educational and agricultural projects; fmr. Chair. Maharashtra State Co-operative Sugar Factories Fed.; organizer of numerous co-operative insts. in fields of agric., finance and educ.; now Pres. Nat. Fed. of Co-operative Sugar Factories Ltd., New Delhi; mem. 3rd Lok Sabha 62-67; Parl. Sec. to Minister of Food and Agric. 62-63, to Minister for Community Devt. and Co-operation 64-65; Union Deputy Minister for Food, Agric., Community Devt. and Co-operation 66-67; Minister of State, Ministry of Food, Agric., Community Devt. and Co-operation 67-74, Ministry of Agric. and Irrigation 74-77; Alt. Chair. Indian del. 2nd World Food Congress, The Hague 70; del. Int. Sugar Conf., Geneva 77.
Publs. *Problems of Indian Agriculture and Food, The Indo-Pakistan Conflict.*
338 Gurdwara Rakabganj Road, New Delhi, India.

Shindo, Sadakazu; Japanese business executive; b. 4 March 1910; ed. Kyushu Univ.
Chairman, Mitsubishi Electric Corpn. 80-.
Mitsubishi Electric Corpn., 2-2-3 Marunouchi, Chiyoda-ku, Tokyo; 3-36-8-101 Yoyogi, Shibuya-ku, Tokyo, Japan.
Telephone: 03-374-0777 (Home).

Shinto, Hisashi, D.ENG.; Japanese industrial executive; b. 2 July 1910, Fukuoka Prefecture; ed. Saga Senior High School and Kyushu Imperial Univ.
Entered Harima Shipbuilding & Eng. Co. Ltd. 34; entered Nat. Bulk Carriers Corpn., Kure Yard 51; Man. Dir. Ishikawajima-Harima Heavy Industries Ltd. (IHI), Div. Man. of Shipbuilding Div. 60, Exec. Vice-Pres. IHI 64, Pres. IHI 72-79, Counsellor 79-80; Dir. Tokyo Shibaura Electric Co. Ltd. (Toshiba) 66-79; Exec. Dir. Fed. of Econ. Orgs. (Keidanren) 69-79; Dir. Nippon Atomic Industry Group Corpn. 75-80; mem. Japan Cttee. for Econ. Devt. 75-80; Pres. Japan Shipbuilders' Asscn. 77-79; Dir. Japan Line Ltd. 77-80; Counsellor Transportation Technics, Ministry of Transportation 79-81; Man. Dir. Japan Ship Exporters' Asscn. 79-80; Pres. and Commr. Man. Cttee. Nippon Telegraph and Telephone Public Corpn. (NTT) Jan. 81-; Medal of Honour with Blue Ribbon 70; Légion d'honneur 77.
NTT, Head Office, 1-6, Uchisaiwai-cho 1-chome, Chiyoda-ku, Tokyo 100; Home: 9-15, Zenpukuji 1-chome, Suginami-ku, Tokyo 167, Japan.
Telephone: 03-509-5111 (Office); 03-390-0219 (Home).

Shirayanagi, Mgr. Peter Seiichi; Japanese ecclesiastic; b. 17 June 1928, Tokyo; ed. Faculty of Theology, Sophia Univ., Tokyo and Urban Coll., Rome.
Ordained Priest 54, subsequently at Tokyo Chancery Office; Procurator, Archdiocese of Tokyo 60; Auxiliary Bishop of Tokyo 66; Coadjutor-Archbishop with right of succession 69-70; Archbishop of Tokyo Feb. 70-; Pres. Episcopal Comm. for Social Action 75-; Vice-Pres. Bishops' Conf. of Japan 75-.
Archbishop's House, 16-15 Sekiguchi, 3-chome, Bunkyo-ku, Tokyo 112, Japan.
Telephone: 03-943-2301.

Shirendev, Badzaryn, DR.HIST.; Mongolian historian and politician; b. 14 May 1912; ed. School of Agriculture at Tsetserleg, Mongolian Workers' Faculty at Ulan-Ude, U.S.S.R., State Pedagogical Inst., Irkutsk, Inst. of Oriental Studies, Moscow.
Chairman of an agricultural co-operative 30-31; army service on special duty with Marshal Choybalsan 41-43; Rector of Mongolian State Univ. 44-51; Minister of Educ. 51-54; Chair. Mongolian Peace Cttee. 49-59; First Deputy Chair. Council of Ministers 54-57; Pres. Acad. of Sciences 61-82; Chair. Nat. Council Intercosmos Studies 66-; Chair. Perm. Cttee. of Int. Congress of Mongolists 70-; Chair. Mongolian Asscn. of Graduates from Soviet Educ. Insts. 72-; Deputy Chair. of People's Great Hural (Assembly) 81-; Deputy to People's Great Hural; mem. World Peace Cttee. 57-; mem. Political Bureau of Mongolian People's Revolutionary Party (MPRP) Cen. Cttee. 53-58; mem. MPRP Cen. Cttee. 44-; Hon. mem. Acad. of Sciences of Bulgaria, Czechoslovakia, German Democratic Repub., Hungary, Poland; Hon. Dr. Litt. (Leeds); awards from Bulgaria and Democratic People's Repub. of Korea; Order of Sühbaatar.
Publs. numerous books on Mongolian history.
c/o Academy of Sciences, Ulan Bator, Mongolia.

Shishido, Fukushige, B.COM.; Japanese business executive; b. 27 Sept. 1913, Fukushima prefecture; ed. Kobe Univ. of Commerce.
With Dai-ichi Kangyo Bank Ltd. 37-63; Dir. Fuji Electric Co. Ltd. 63-65, Man. Dir. 65-70, Exec. Dir. 70-72, Vice-Pres. 72-74, Pres. 74-; Auditor, Fujitsu Ltd. 65-.
3-25 Chihaya-cho, Toshima-ku, 171 Tokyo, Japan.
Telephone: (03) 957-5044.

Shrimali, Kalu Lal, M.A., PH.D.; Indian educationist and politician; b. 30 Dec. 1909; ed. Banaras Hindu Univ., Calcutta Univ. and Columbia Univ., New York.
Life mem. Vidya Bhavan Soc. 31-; Parl. Sec. Ministry of Educ. New Delhi 53-55, Deputy Minister for Educ. 55-57, Minister of State in Ministry of Educ. and Scientific Research 57-58, Minister of Education 58-63; Vice-Chancellor Univ. of Mysore 64-69; Vice-Chancellor Banaras Hindu Univ. 69-77; Chair. Asscn. of Commonwealth Univs. 69-70, Inter-Univ. Board of India 72-73; Pres. All-India Fed. of Educ. Asscns.; mem. Admin. Board, Int. Asscn. of Univs. 70-74, Vice-Pres. 75-80; Hon. D.Litt. (Banaras Hindu, Mysore and Agra Univs.), Hon. LL.D. (Vikram Univ.), Hon. D.Sc. (Kiev, U.S.S.R.); Padma Vibhushan 76.
Publs. *Bachon Ki Kuch Samasyayen* (Hindi), *Shiksha aur Bhartiya Loktantra* (Hindi), *The Wardha Scheme, Adventures in Education, Problems of Education in India, Education in Changing India, The Prospects of Democracy in India, A Search for Values in Indian Education.*
310 Fatehpura, Udaipur, Rajasthan, India.

Shukla, Shyama Charan; Indian politician; b. 27 Feb. 1925, Raipur; ed. Raipur, Banaras and Nagpur.
Member, Vidhan Sabha (legislature of Madhya Pradesh) 57-; Minister for Irrigation 67; Chief Minister, Madhya Pradesh 69-72, Dec. 75-77; Chief Editor, Founder *Mahakoshal.*
c/o Vidhan Sabha, Bhopal, Madhya Pradesh, India.

Shukla, Vidya Charan, B.A.; Indian politician; b. 2 Aug. 1929, Raipur; ed. Morris Coll., and Univ. Coll. of Law, Nagpur.
Member, Lok Sabha 57-62, 62-67, 67-70, 71-77; Deputy Minister, Communications and Parl. Affairs Jan.-Feb. 66; Deputy Minister for Home Affairs 66-67; Minister of State in Ministry of Home Affairs 67-70; Minister of Revenue and Expenditure in Ministry of Finance 70-71, Minister of Defence Production 71-74, Minister of State for Planning 74-75, for Information and Broadcasting 75-77; Minister of Civil Supplies 77-80; convicted of destroying film Feb. 80.
146 Sundernagar, New Delhi 110003, India.

Sicat, Gerardo P., M.A., PH.D.; Philippine professor of economics and government official; b. 7 Oct. 1935; ed. Univ. of the Philippines and Massachusetts Inst. of Technology.
Professor of Economics, Univ. of the Philippines 69-, Regent 72-; Chair. Nat. Econ. Council and Cen. Planning Agency, Govt. of the Philippines 70-72; Dir.-Gen. Nat. Econ. and Devt. Authority (Sec. for Econ. Planning) 72-78; Minister of Nat. Econ. Planning 74-; mem. *Batasang Pambansa* (Interim Legislative Assembly) 78-; Chair.

Philippines Inst. of Devt. Studies 78-, Population Comm. 78-; mem. Monetary Bd. of the Philippines.
Publs. *Regional Economic Development in the Philippines* 70, *Philippine Development and Economic Policy* 72, *Taxation and Progress* 72, *New Economic Directions in the Philippines* 74, and several other works.
National Economic and Development Authority, Padre Faura Street, Manila, Philippines.
Telephone: 58-56-14, 59-48-75, 50-39-71.

Siddiqi, M. Raziuddin, M.A., PH.D., D.SC.; Pakistani educationist; b. 7 April 1905; ed. Osmania, Cambridge, Berlin, Göttingen, Leipzig, Paris Univs.
Professor of Mathematics, Dir. of Research and Vice-Chancellor, Osmania Univ. 31-50; Dir. of Research and Vice-Chancellor, Peshawar Univ. 50-58; Vice-Chancellor, Univ. of Sind 59-64; Pres. Pakistan Acad. of Sciences 61-67, Sec. 53-61, 69-, Sec.-Gen. 78-; Vice-Chancellor, Univ. of Islamabad 65-73; Joint Sec. (in charge) Scientific and Technological Research Div., President's Secretariat; Sec.-Gen. Pakistan Acad. of Sciences 78-; Star of Order of Merit (Pakistan) 60; Grand Cross of Order of Merit (Fed. Repub. of Germany) 62; Hilal-i-Imtiaz 82.
Publs. *Lectures on Quantum Mechanics* 37, *Boundary Problems in Non-linear Partial Differential Equations* 38, *Theory of Relativity* 40, *Problems of Education* 43, *Iqbal's Concept of Time and Space* 73, *Establishing a New University: Policies and Procedures.*
Telephone: 23541; 27789.
Pakistan Academy of Sciences, Constitution Avenue, Islamabad, Pakistan.

Siddiqui, Salimuzzaman, M.B.E., D.PHIL., F.R.S.; Pakistani scientist; b. 19 Oct. 1897, Subeha, U.P., India; ed. Muslim Univ., Aligarh, India, Univ. Coll. London and Univ. of Frankfurt-am-Main.
Director Research Inst., Ayurvedic and Unani Tibbi Coll., Delhi 28-40; Organic Chemist, Council of Scientific and Industrial Research (India) 40-44, Acting Dir. 44-47; Dir. Nat. Chemical Lab. (India) 47-51; Dir. Dept. Scientific and Industrial Research (Pakistan) 51-66; Dir. and Chair. Pakistan Council of Scientific and Industrial Research 53-66; Chair. Nat. Science Council 61-66; Dir. H.E.J. Research Inst. of Chem. Univ. of Karachi, Pakistan 66-; Pres. Pakistan Acad. of Sciences 67; mem. Vatican Acad. of Sciences and Pontifical Acad.; Gold Medal, U.S.S.R. Acad. of Sciences; President's Pride of Performance Medal (Pakistan) 66; Hon. D.Sc. (Karachi and Leeds); D.Med. h.c. (Frankfurt); Hilal-e-Imtiaz.
Publs. Over 130 research papers and memoirs on chemical studies relating to alkaloids, triterpenoids, flavonoids and natural resins; correlation of chemical structure and physiological activity. Granted over 50 patents to processes concerned with utilization of natural products.
H.E.J. Research Institute of Chemistry, University of Karachi, Karachi; 8 A, Karachi University Campus, Country Club Road, Karachi 32, Pakistan.
Telephone: 46314 (Office); 464698 (Home).

Sihanouk, Prince Samdech Preah Norodom (*see* Norodom Sihanouk, Prince Samdech Preah).

Sikivou, Semesa Koroikilai, C.B.E., M.A.; Fijian diplomatist and politician; b. 13 Feb. 1917, Vutia, Rewa; ed. Rewa Central School, Suva Methodist Boys' School and Teachers' Training Inst., Davuilevu, Auckland Univ. Coll. and Inst. of Educ., Univ. of London.
Served as Asst. Master Suva Methodist Boys' School 35-42; war service as Lieut., Fiji Military Forces 42-46; Asst. Master Queen Victoria School 49, 51-59; mem. Fiji Legis. Council 56-66; Educ. Officer 60-62; Asst. Dir. of Educ. 63-66, Deputy Dir. 66-70; Perm. Rep. of Fiji to UN 70-76, concurrently High Commr. in Canada 71-76; Amb. to U.S.A. 71-76; M.P. 77-; Minister for Educ. 77-, also of Sport 78-; Vice-Pres. of 28th Session of UN Gen. Assembly 73; mem. Fiji Broadcasting Comm. 55-62, 66-70; mem. Fijian Affairs Board 55-66, 69-70, Fijian Devt. Fund Board 56-66, Native Land Trust Board 65-70; mem. Advisory Council on Educ. 54-70; mem. Council of Chiefs 52-70, 77-.
Ministry of Education, Selborne Street, Suva (Office); P.O. Box 2311, Suva, Fiji (Home).

Simatupang, Lt.-Gen. Tahi Bonar; Indonesian international church official and army officer (retd.); b. 28 Jan. 1920, Sidikalang; ed. Mil. Acad.
Director of Org., Gen. Staff of Indonesian Nat. Army 45-48; Deputy Chief of Staff, Armed Forces 48-49, Acting Chief of Staff 49-51, Chief of Staff 51-54; Mil. Adviser to Govt. 54-59; retd. from mil. service 59; Pres. Council of Churches in Indonesia 67-, Christian Conf. in Asia 73-77; mem. Presidium, World Council of Churches 75-; mem. Supreme Advisory Council Repub. of Indonesia 73-78; D.Hum.Litt. (Tulsa Univ.) 69.
Publs. *Pioneer in War, Pioneer in Peace* (Role of the Armed Forces in Indonesia) 54, *Report from Banaran—Experiences during the People's War* 59, *Christian Task in Revolution* 66.
Jalan Diponegoro 55, Jakarta, Indonesia.

Sin, H.E. Cardinal Jaime L., B.SC.ED., D.D.; Philippine ecclesiastic; b. 31 Aug. 1928, New Washington, Aklan; ed. New Washington Elementary School, St. Vincent Ferrer Seminary.
Ordained Roman Catholic Priest 54; Missionary Priest 54-57; First Rector, St. Pius X Seminary, Roxas City 57-67; Domestic Prelate to Pope John XXIII 60; Auxiliary Bishop of Jaro, Iloilo 67; Archbishop of Jaro 72, of Manila 74-; cr. Cardinal 76; Chair. Comm. on Seminaries and Priestly Vocations 69-73, Comm. on Clergy 74-77; mem. Pontifical Comm. on Social Communications 75-, Pontifical Comm. on the Evangelization of Peoples 78, Pontifical Comm. for Social Communications 78; Perm. mem. of the Synod of Bishops in Rome 77-; mem. Admin. Council, Catholic Bishops' Conf. of the Philippines (CBCP) 68-72, Vice-Pres. CBCP 70-74, Pres. 77-; Hon. LL.D. 75, Hon. D.H.L. 75, Hon. D.S.T. 77, Hon. LL.D. (Angeles Univ.) 78, Hon. D.H. 80, Hon. D.Phil. Hum. Litt. (Fu Jen Catholic Univ., Taipei, Taiwan) 80; over 200 citations and numerous awards.
Publs. *Ratio Fundamentalis for Philippine Seminaries* 72, *The Revolution of Love* 72, *The Church Above Political Systems* 73, *A Song of Salvation* 74, *Unity in Diversity* 74, *La Iglesia Renueva sus Medios de Evangelicación y adapta a la Idiosincracia de los Pueblos* 78, *The Future of Catholicism in Asia* 78, *Christian Basis of Human Rights* 78, *Separation, Not Isolation* 78, *Slaughter of the Innocents '79* 79, *Discipline, Discipleship and Discerning Service, The Making of "Men for Others"* 80, over 200 papers, articles in periodicals.
Villa San Miguel, Shaw Boulevard, Mandaluyong, Metro Manila, Philippines.
Telephone: 79-26-71.

Sinclair, Ernest Keith, C.M.G., O.B.E., D.F.C.; Australian journalist; b. 13 Nov. 1914, Hawthorn, Victoria; ed. Melbourne High School.
Served R.A.F., Second World War; C.O. 97 Pathfinder Sqn. 44-45; Foreign Corresp., Europe 38, 46; Editor *The Age* 59-66; Chair. Australian Assoc. Press 65-66; Dir.-Gen. Television Corpn. 59-66; Consultant to Prime Minister Dept. of Prime Minister and Cabinet 67-74, 77-79; Dir. Australian Paper Manufacturers 66-, Hecla-Rowe Ltd. 66-80; Deputy Chair. Australian Tourist Comm. 69-75; Vice-Pres. Library Council of Victoria 73-78; mem. Australia-Japan Business Co-operation Cttee. and Pacific Basin Econ. Council 73-75; Assoc. Commr. Industries Comm. 74-80; Commr. Australian Heritage Comm. 76-81.
138 Toorak Road West, South Yarra, Victoria 3141, Australia.
Telephone: 267-1405 (Melbourne).

Sinclair, Rt. Hon. Ian McCahon, P.C., B.A., LL.B.; Australian barrister, grazier and politician; b. 10 June 1929, Sydney; ed. Knox Grammar School, Wahroonga and Sydney Univ.
Barrister 52-; mem. Legislative Council of N.S.W. 61-63; mem. House of Representatives for New England 63-; Minister of State for Social Services, Canberra 65-68; Minister assisting Minister for Trade and Industry 66-71; Minister of State for Shipping and Transport 68-71; Minister for Primary Industry 71-72, mem. Cabinet 67-72; Deputy Leader Country Party 71-; Chair. Defence, Foreign Affairs and Security Cttee. of Country Party 72-75; Leader of House for the Opposition 74-75; opposition spokesman on agric. 74-75; Minister for N. Australia Nov.-Dec. 75; Minister for Primary Industry and Leader of the House 75-79; Minister for Special Trade Representations Aug.-Nov. 80; Minister for Communications and Leader of the House 80-82; Minister of Defence May 82-; Grazier and Man. Dir. Sinclair Pastoral Co. 53-; Dir. Farmers and Graziers' Co-operative Co. Ltd. 62-65; mem. Legislative Council, N.S.W. 61-63; National Country Party.
Glenclair, Bendemeer, N.S.W., Australia.

Singh, Birendra Bahadur, M.A.; Indian public official; b. 1 March 1928; ed. Allahabad Univ.
Indian Defence Accounts Service 53; Controller of Accounts, Int. Comm. for Supervision and Control for Viet-Nam, Laos and Cambodia 60-62; Asst. Financial Adviser, Ministry of Irrigation and Power 62-63; Deputy Sec. Ministry of Finance 63-66, Deputy Sec. Ministry of Finance on deputation to Harvard Univ. as Public Service Fellow 66-67; Deputy Financial Adviser, Ministry of Food and Agric., Dept. of Food 67-68; Financial Adviser and Chief Accounts Officer Hindustan Copper Ltd. (Govt. of India undertaking) 68-70, Acting Chair. and Managing Dir. 69-70; Financial Adviser, Indian Farmers Fertilizers Co-operative Ltd. 70-72, Finance Dir. 72-75; Chair. and Managing Dir. Nat. Fertilisers Ltd., New Delhi 75-79; Chair. Industrial Finance Corpn. of India Oct. 79-; currently Dir. on Bd. of Dirs. Industrial Devt. Bank of India, Industrial Reconstruction Corpn. of India Ltd., Rajasthan Consultancy Org. Ltd., Jaipur and Delhi Stock Exchange Asscn. Ltd.; mem. of Gen. Council Nat. Co-operative Devt. Corpn.; mem. of Bd. of Govs. of Management Devt. Inst., Bd. of Trustees of Risk Capital Foundation and Unit Trust of India; mem. Exec. Bd. Standing Conf. of Public Enterprises; Fellow Kennedy School of Govt., Harvard Univ.
Industrial Finance Corporation of India, Bank of Baroda Building, 16 Sansad Marg, P.O. Box 363, New Delhi-110001, India.
Telephone: 312440 and 311994 (Office); 650613 and 650763 (Home).

Singh, (Chaudhuri) Charan, B.SC., M.A., LL.B.; Indian politician; b. 1902, Noorpur, Meerut district; ed. Agra Univ.
Started legal practice in Ghaziabad, moved to Meerut 39; participated in Independence Movement; mem. from Chhaprauli, Uttar Pradesh Legislative Assembly 37; Parl. Sec. in various depts. of Uttar Pradesh State Govt. 46-51; State Minister for Justice and Information 51-52, for Revenue and Agric. 52, later for Revenue and Transport until 59, resigned; State Minister for Home Affairs and Agric. 60, for Agric. and Forests 62-65, for Local Self-Govt. 66-67; leader of Samyukta Vidhayak Dal (political party) 67; Chief Minister of Uttar Pradesh 67-68, Feb.-Oct. 70; founder and Pres. Bharatiya Kranti Dal 69-77; Deputy Chair. Janata Party 77-79; Minister for Home Affairs 77-78 (resigned); Joint Deputy Prime Minister and Minister of Finance Jan.-July 70; Prime Minister 79-80; Chair. Lok Dal (political party) Sept. 79-.
Publs. books and pamphlets incl. *Abolition of Zamindari, Co-operative Farming X-rayed, India's Poverty and its Solution, Peasant Proprietorship or Land to the Workers, Prevention of Division of Holdings below a Certain Minimum, India's Economic Policy—a Ghandian Blueprint, Economic Nightmare of India: Its Cause and Cure* 81.
Lok Sabha, New Delhi, India.

Singh, Giani Zail (*see* Zail Singh, Giani).

Singh, Karan, M.A., PH.D.; Indian politician; b. 9 March 1931, Cannes, France; ed. Doon School, Univ. of Jammu and Kashmir and Delhi Univ.
Appointed Regent of Jammu and Kashmir 49; elected Sadar-i-Riyasat (Head of State) by Jammu and Kashmir Legislative Assembly Nov. 52; recognized by Pres. of India and assumed office 17 Nov. 1952, re-elected 57 and 62, Gov. 65-67; Union Minister for Tourism and Civil Aviation 67-73, for Health and Family Planning 73-75, 76-March 77; re-elected to Parl. 77; Minister of Educ. July-Sept. 79, of Educ., Soc. Welfare and Culture Sept. 79-Jan. 80; mem. Lok Sabha 80-; Vice-Pres. Indian Council for Cultural Relations; Vice-Pres. World Health Assembly 75-76; Life Trustee India Int. Centre; fmr. Chancellor Jammu and Kashmir Univ. and Banaras Hindu Univ.; Pres. Delhi Music Soc., Authors' Guild of India, Sansadiya Sanskrit Parishad; associated with other cultural and scholarly orgs.; Hon. Maj.-Gen. Indian Army; Hon. Col. Jammu and Kashmir Regt.; Hon. doctorate (Aligarh Muslim Univ.) 63.
Publs. *The Political Thought of Sri Aurobindo Ghosh*; 10 works on political science; travelogues, folksong translations, essays, poems.
3 Nyaya Marg, Chanakyapuri, New Delhi, India.
Telephone: 371744.

Singh, Kewal; Indian diplomatist; b. 1 June 1915; ed. Forman Christian Coll., Lahore, Law Coll., Lahore, and Balliol Coll., Oxford.
Joined Indian Civil Service 38; Indian Civil Service appointments 40-48; First Sec. Indian Embassy, Ankara 48-49; Indian Military Mission, Berlin 49-51; Chargé d'affaires, Lisbon 51-53; Consul-General, Pondicherry 53-54; Chief Commr., State of Pondicherry, Karaikal, Mahe and Yanan 55-57; Amb. to Cambodia 57-58, to Sweden, concurrently accred. to Denmark and Finland 59-62; Deputy High Commr. in U.K. 62-65; High Commr. in Pakistan 65-66; Amb. to U.S.S.R. and Mongolia 66-69; Sec. in Ministry of External Affairs 68-70; Amb. to Fed. Repub. of Germany 70-72; Foreign Sec. 72-76; Amb. to U.S.A. 76-77; Distinguished Visiting Prof., Calif. State Univs. of Northridge, Los Angeles, San Francisco, Foulerton and Domingez Hill 78-79; Visiting Prof., Univ. of Kentucky Jan.-June 79; Distinguished Visiting Prof., Univ. of Kentucky, Lexington Jan. 79-Dec. 79; Regent Lectureship, Univ. of Calif., Los Angeles May 80-; awarded Padma Shri for distinguished services leading to merger of French Possessions with India.
c/o Ministry of External Affairs, New Delhi 110011, India.

Singh, Khushwant, LL.B.; Indian author; b. 1915; ed. Government Coll., Lahore, King's Coll. and Inner Temple, London.
Practised, High Court, Lahore 39-47; joined Indian Ministry of External Affairs 47; Press Attaché, Canada and then Public Relations Officer, London 48-51; Ministry of Information and Broadcasting; edited *Yojana* 56-58; Dept. of Mass Communication, UNESCO 54-56; commissioned by Rockefeller Foundation and Muslim Univ., Aligarh to write a history of the Sikhs 58; Visiting Lecturer at various U.S. univs. and numerous TV and radio appearances; Ed. *The Illustrated Weekly of India* 69-78, Ed.-in-Chief *National Herald*, New Delhi 78-79, Chief Ed. *New Delhi Magazine* 79-80, Ed. *The Hindustan Times*, New Delhi 80-; mem. Rajya Sabha; Grove Press Award 54; Padma Bhushan 74.
Publs. *Mark of Vishnu* 49, *The Sikhs* 51, *Train to Pakistan* 54, *Sacred Writings of the Sikhs* 60, *I shall not hear the*

Nightingale 61, *Umrao Jan Ada—Courtesan of Lucknow* (trans.) 61, *History of the Sikhs (1769-1839)* Vol. I 62, *Ranjit Singh: Maharaja of the Punjab* 62, *Fall of the Sikh Kingdom* 62, *The Skeleton* (trans.) 63, *Land of the Five Rivers* (trans.) 64, *History of the Sikhs (1839-Present Day)* 65, *Khushwant Singh's India* 69, *Shikwah and Jawah-e-Shikwah, Iqbal's Dialogue with Allah*.
c/o The Hindustan Times, 18-20 Kasturba Gandhi Marg, New Delhi; 49E Sujansingh Park, New Delhi, India.
Telephone: 387707.

Singh, Lallan Prasad, M.A.; Indian administrator and diplomatist; b. 1 July 1912; ed. Allahabad Univ.
Chief Sec. Govt. of Bihar 48-56; Dir. Dept. of Manpower, Ministry of Home Affairs, also Sec. Second Pay Comm. 56-59; Special Sec. Ministry of Home Affairs 60-64; Home Sec. 64-70; Amb. to Nepal 71-73; Gov. Assam, Manipur, Meghalaya, Nagaland and Tripura and Chair. N.E. Council 73-82; Fellow, Centre for Int. Affairs, Harvard Univ. 59-60; fmr. Gov. Indian Inst. of Public Admin., Indian Inst. of Man., Ahmedabad, Indian Inst. of Manpower Research, Indian Council of Social Science Research.
c/o Raj Bhavan, Shillong 793001, Meghalaya, India.
Telephone: 3001.

Singh, Nagendra, M.A., LL.D., D.LITT., D.PHIL., D.SC., D.C.L.; Indian civil servant and international lawyer; b. 18 March 1914, Dungarpur, Rajasthan; ed. Agra and Cambridge Univs. and Gray's Inn, London.
Entered Indian Civil Service 38; recent posts include: Special Sec. Ministry of Information and Broadcasting 64, Ministry of Transport Aug. 64; Sec. Ministry of Transport and Dir.-Gen. of Shipping 66; Sec. to Pres. of India 66-72; Constitutional Adviser to Govt. of Bhutan 70-72; Chief Election Comm., Govt. of India 72; Chair. Govt. Shipping Corpn. 62, The Mogul Line Ltd. 60-61, 63-67, The Hindustan Shipyard Ltd. 62-67 (Dir. 56-67); mem. Indian Constituent Assembly 47-48; Justice of the Peace, Bombay 48-; Nehru Prof. of Int. Law and Co-operation, Graduate Inst. of Int. Studies, Univ. of Geneva; Prof. of Human Rights and Int. Co-operation, Univ. of Tribhuban, Nepal; Prof. of Int. Law and Maritime Law, Univ. of Madras; mem. Perm. Court of Arbitration, The Hague 67; mem. Int. Law Comm. 66-, Vice-Chair. 69; Vice-Chair. UN Comm. on Int. Trade Law 69, Chair. 71; Judge Int. Court of Justice 73-, Vice-Pres. 76-79; founder mem. Int. Council for Environmental Law 69; Pres. Indian Soc. of Int. Law, Maritime Law Asscn. of India, Indian Acad. of Environmental Law, Conservation and Research; Vice-Pres. Legal Cttee. of IUCN; mem. Indian Inst. of Public Admin., India Int. Centre, Inst. de Droit Int.; Visiting Prof., Univs. of Delhi and Bombay; Pres. IMCO Assembly 63-65; Pres. ILO Maritime Session 70; Pres. Afro-Asian Legal Consultative Cttee. 73; Master Bencher Gray's Inn 73; Fellow, St. John's Coll., Cambridge 74; Hon. LL.D. (Jodpur, Kurukshetra, Punjab and Guru Nanak Univs.) 75-77; Padma Vibhushan Award 73.
Publs. *Termination of Membership of International Organizations* 58, *Nuclear Weapons and International Law, Defence Mechanism of the Modern State* 63, *The Concept of Force and Organization of Defence in the Constitutional History of India* 69, *Achievements of UNCTAD I and II in the field of Invisibles* 69, *India and International Law* 69, *Bhutan* 71, *Maritime Flag and International Law* 78, *Juristic Concepts of Ancient India* 80, *Human Rights and the Future of Mankind* 81; several vols. of lectures and numerous articles on questions of int. law, etc.
International Court of Justice, Peace Palace, The Hague 2012, Netherlands; 6 Akbar Road, New Delhi, India.

Singh, Raja Roy; Indian educationist; b. 5 April 1918; ed. Univ. of Allahabad.
Entered Indian Admin. Service 43; fmr. Dir. of Educ., Uttar Pradesh; fmr. Joint Sec., Fed. Ministry of Educ., New Delhi; fmr. Joint Dir. Indian Council of Educational Research and Training, Nat. Inst. of Educ.; at Office of Educational Planning, UNESCO Headquarters, Paris 64-65; Dir. UNESCO Regional Office for Eudc. in Asia 65-; Asst. Dir.-Gen. UNESCO.
Publ. *Education in the Soviet Union*.
UNESCO Regional Office for Education in Asia, Darakarn Building, 920 Sukhumvit Road, Bangkok, Thailand.
Telephone: 391-8474.

Singh, Sher, M.A.; Indian agriculturalist and politician; b. 18 Sept. 1917; ed. Delhi Univ.
Former Lecturer, M.S.J. Coll., Bharatpur, and Lecturer in Mathematics, Jat Coll., Rohtak; elected to Punjab Legislative Assembly 46, 52, 57, Punjab Legislative Council 62; Parl. Sec., Punjab 48-51; Deputy Leader of Congress Legislative Party in Punjab 56-57; Minister of Irrigation and Power, Punjab 56-57; mem. Lok Sabha; Minister of State in Ministry of Educ. 67-69; Minister of State for Communications 69-71; Minister of State, Ministry of Agriculture 71-74, Ministry of Communications 74-77; Chancellor of Gurukul (system of teaching based on ancient Indian culture), Jhajjar; mem. Syndicate of Gurukul, Kangri Univ.; fmr. Founder-Pres. Haryana Lok Samiti; del. to several int. confs.
c/o Lok Sabha, New Delhi, India.

Singh, Swaran, M.SC., LL.B.; Indian politician; b. 19 Aug. 1907; ed. Govt. Coll., Lahore, and Lahore Law Coll.
Elected Punjab Legislative Assembly 46; Minister of Development, Food, Civil Supplies 46-47; mem. Gov.'s Security Council, then Partition Cttee. 47; Minister of Home, Gen. Admin., Revenue, Irrigation and Electricity in first Punjab Congress Ministry 47-49; resigned to resume legal practice; Minister of Capital Projects and Electricity 52; Minister for Works, Housing and Supply (Central Govt.) 52-57; fmr. mem. Rajya Sabha, initiated Subsidized Industrial Housing Scheme; led Indian del. to ECOSOC in 54 and 55; mem. Lok Sabha 57-March 77; Minister for Steel, Mines and Fuel 57-62; Minister for Railways 62-63, of Food and Agric. 63-64, of Industry, Engineering and Tech. Devt. June-July 64, of External Affairs 64-66, 70-74, of Defence 66-70, 74-75; Pres. Indian Nat. Congress March-May 77, 78-79; Pres. Indian Council of World Affairs; led Indian Del. to UN Gen. Assembly 64-66, 70-73, ECOSOC 54, 55; Rep. to Commonwealth Prime Ministers' Conf. 71, 73.
c/o Indian National Congress, 5 Dr. Rajendra Prasad Road, New Delhi, India.

Singh, Tarlok, B.A., B.SC.; Indian economist; b. 26 Feb. 1913; ed. St. Vincent's School and Deccan Coll., Pune, Gujarat Coll., Ahmedabad and London School of Economics.
Indian Civil Service 37-62; Colonization Officer, Nili Bar Colony, Punjab 43; Finance Dept. Govt. of India 44-46; Private Sec. to Vice-Pres. Interim Govt. and to Prime Minister 46-47; Dir.-Gen. of Rehabilitation 47-49; with Planning Comm. 50-67, Additional Sec. 58-62, mem. 62-67; Hon. Fellow, London School of Econs.; Fellow, Inst. for Int. Econ. Studies, Univ. of Stockholm 67, 69-70; Visiting Senior Research Economist, Woodrow Wilson School, Princeton Univ. 68; Deputy Exec. Dir. (Planning) UNICEF 70-74; Chair. Indian Asscn. of Social Science Insts. 79-; Co-ordinator Indian Studies on Co-operation for Devt. in S. Asia 79-; Hon. Fellow, London School of Econs.; Hon. D. Litt. (Punjabi Univ.) 79; Padma Shri 54, Padma Bhushan 62; Söderström Medal, Swedish Royal Acad. of Sciences 70.
Publs. *Poverty and Social Change* 45, 69, *Resettlement Manual for Displaced Persons* 52, *Towards an Integrated Society* 69, *India's Development Experience* 74.
74 Paschimi Marg, New Delhi 57; and Indian Council on World Affairs, 110 Sundar Nagar, New Delhi, India.
Telephone: 67-13-42.

Singh, Zail (*see* Zail Singh, Giani).

Sivasithamparam, M.; Sri Lankan (Tamil) lawyer and politician; b. 20 July 1923, Jaffna; ed. Vigresmara Coll., St. Joseph's Coll., Univ. Coll., Law Coll.
Secretary of Union Soc., Univ. Coll. 47-48; Pres. Law Students' Union Law Coll. 49-50; mem. House of Reps. for Udduppiddi 60-70; mem. Nat. State Assembly (now Parl.) for Nallur 77-; Gen. Sec. All Ceylon Tamil Congress 66-77, Pres. 77-; Joint Sec.-Gen. Fed. Party, Tamil United Liberation Front (TULF) 76-78, Pres. 78-; mem. Parliamentary Del. to U.S.S.R.
Tamil United Liberation Front, 238 Main St., Jaffna; 100 Norris Canal Road, Colombo 10, Sri Lanka (Home). Telephone: 7176 (Office); 91017 (Home).

Slater, Gordon James Augustus; British diplomatist; b. 8 July 1922; ed. Sydney, Australia.
Commonwealth Relations Office 58; First Sec. (Information), Karachi, Dacca 58, Vancouver 61, Kuala Lumpur 64; First Sec. and Head of Information Section, Lagos 67; Foreign and Commonwealth Office 70; Consul, First Sec. and Deputy High Commr., Port Moresby 73; Seconded to Dept. of Industry 75; Deputy Gov. Falkland Is. 76; High Commr. in Solomon Is. 78-82.
c/o Foreign and Commonwealth Office, King Charles Street, London S.W.1., England.

Smith, Bruce Henderson, LL.B., B.COM.; New Zealand diplomatist and fmr. banker and company director; b. 28 Aug. 1918, Auckland; ed. Mount Albert Grammar School, Auckland Univ. and Canterbury Univ.
Joined Bank of New Zealand 35, Man. Int. Div. 56, Deputy General Man. 67-73, Gen. Man. and Chief Exec. Officer 73-80; Pres. Bankers Inst. of N.Z. 77-79; Dir. Bank of Western Samoa 73-79, Bank of Tonga 73-79, B.N.Z. Finance Co. Ltd. 75-79, Petroleum Corpn. of N.Z. (Exploration) Ltd. 78-79, Bradbury Wilkinson and Co. (N.Z.) Ltd.; mem. N.Z. Wool Comm. 68-70, Nat. Devt. Council 70-74, Trade Promotion Council 77-79, 1978 Export Year Cttee. 78-79, Bd. of Trustees Massey Univ. Research Foundation 78-79; Assoc. Bankers Inst. of Australasia; Consul-Gen. in New York 80-; mem. Bar Asscn., New York.
New Zealand Consulate General, 630 Fifth Avenue, Suite 530, New York, N.Y. 10111, U.S.A.

Snedden, Rt. Hon. Sir Billy Mackie, K.C.M.G., Q.C., M.P.; Australian lawyer and politician; b. 31 Dec. 1926.
Admitted to Supreme Court, W.A. 51, Victoria 55, Victorian Bar 55; Migration Officer Italy, England 52-54; mem. House of Reps. Bruce, Victoria 55-; Commonwealth Attorney-Gen. 63-66; appointed Q.C. 64; Chair. First Commonwealth Law Ministers Conf., Canberra 65; Australian Rep. Second Commonwealth Law Ministers Conf. London 66; Fed. Minister of Immigration Dec. 66-69, of Labour and Nat. Service 69-71; Treasurer 71-72; Leader House of Reps. 66-71; Deputy Leader of the Liberal Party 71-72, Party Leader and Leader of Opposition 72-75; Speaker of House of Reps. Feb. 76-.
Office of the Speaker, 4 Treasury Place, Melbourne, Victoria; Home: 22 Pine Crescent, Ringwood, Victoria, Australia.

Sodnom, Dumaagiyn; Mongolian politician; b. 1933; ed. School of Finance and Econs., Ulan Bator, Higher School of Finance and Econs., U.S.S.R.
Worked in Ministry of Finance 50-54, Dir. of Dept. in Ministry 58-63; Minister of Finance 63-69; First Deputy Chair. State Planning Comm. with rank of Minister 69-72, Chair. State Planning Comm. 72-; Vice-Chair. Council of Ministers 74-; mem. Cen. Cttee. Mongolian People's Revolutionary Party (MPRP) 66-; Deputy to People's Great Hural (Assembly) 66-.
Government Palace, Ulan Bator, Mongolia.

Soedjatmoko; Indonesian social scientist and public official; b. 10 Jan. 1922, Sawahlunto, Sumatra; ed. Medical Coll., Jakarta and Littauer Graduate School of Public Admin., Harvard Univ.
Deputy Head of Foreign Press Dept., Ministry of Information 45; Chief Ed. *Het Inzicht*, Ministry of Information 46; Deputy Chief Ed. *Siasat* magazine 47; Del., later Alt. Perm. Rep. to UN 47-51; mem. Indonesian Constituent Assembly 56-59; Assoc. Ed. *Pedoman* (daily) 52-60; Dir. P.T. Pembangunan (publishing co.) 53-61; Vice-Chair. Del. to 21st UN Gen. Assembly 66; Personal Adviser to Minister of Foreign Affairs 67-77; Amb. to U.S.A. 68-71; Special Adviser on Social and Cultural Affairs to Chair. Nat. Devt. Planning Agency 71-80; Rector UN Univ., Tokyo 80-; Magsaysay Award for Int. Understanding 78; Hon. doctorates from Yale Univ., Williams Coll., Mass. and Cedar Crest Coll., Pa., U.S.A., Asian Inst. of Tech., Bangkok, Thailand.
Publs. *An Introduction to Indonesian Historiography* (co-editor) 65, *The Re-emergence of Southeast Asia: An Indonesian Perspective, Southeast Asia in World Politics* (published jointly as *Southeast Asia Today and Tomorrow* 69), *Development and Freedom* 80, also articles in periodicals and reviews.
United Nations University, 29th Floor, Toho Seimei Building 15-1, Shibuya 2-chome, Shibuya-ku, Tokyo 150 (Office); Apt. 204, Aobadai Homes 4-7, Aobadai 1-chome, Meguro-ku, Tokyo 153, Japan (Home).

Somare, Rt. Hon. Michael Thomas, P.C., C.H., M.P.; Papua New Guinea politician; b. 9 April 1936; ed. Sogeri Secondary School, Admin. Staff Coll.
Teacher 56-62; Asst. Area Educ. Officer, Madang 62-63; Broadcasts Officer, Dept. of Information and Extension Services, Wewak 63-66, journalist 66-68; mem. House of Assembly for E. Sepik Region 68-72, 72-75; mem. Second Select Cttee., on Constitutional Devt. 68-72, Advisory Cttee. of Australian Broadcasting Comm.; Parl. Leader of Pangu Pati 69-72; Deputy Chair. Admin.'s Exec. Council 72-73, Chair. Exec. Council (Cabinet) 73-75; Chief Minister, First Nat. Coalition Govt. 72-75; Minister of Information and Extension Services 74-75; Prime Minister 75-80, 82-, also Minister for Police 77-78, for Justice 79-80; Leader of the Opposition 80-82; Sana (Chief) of Saet clan, Murik Lakes area 74-; Pres. Bd. of Trustees, P.N.G. Museum; Hon. Dr. of Laws (Australian Nat. Univ.) 79, Hon. LL.D. (Univ. of S. Pacific) 80; Order of Sikatuna, Philippines 77.
Officer of the Prime Minister, Waigani; Karan, Murik Lakes, East Sepik, Papua New Guinea.

Son Sann; Kampuchean financial administrator and politician; b. 1911, Phnom-Penh; ed. Ecole des Hautes Etudes Commerciales de Paris.
Deputy Gov. Provinces of Battambang and Prey-Veng 35-39; Head of Yuvan Kampuchearath (Youth Movement); Minister of Finance 46-47; Vice-Pres. Council of Ministers 49; Minister of Foreign Affairs 50; M.P. for Phnom-Penh and Pres. Cambodian Nat. Assembly 51-52; Gov. of Nat. Bank of Cambodia 54-68; Minister of State (Finance and Nat. Economy) 61-62; Vice-Pres. in charge of Economy, Finance and Planning 65-67, Pres. Council of Ministers May-Dec. 67; First Vice-Pres. in charge of Econ. and Financial Affairs 68; Leader Khmer People's Nat. Front; involved in help for Khmer refugees 79; involved in anti-Vietnamese guerrilla war 79-; Prime Minister, Coalition Govt. of Democratic Kampuchea, Thailand June 82-; Grand Croix de l'Ordre Royal du Cambodge, Séna yayasedth, Commdr. du Sowathara (Mérite économique), Grand Officier, Légion d'honneur, Commdr. du Monisaraphon, Médaille d'or du Règne, Grand Officier du Million d'Eléphants (Laos).

Son Sen; Kampuchean politician; b. *c.* 1930, Tra Vinh Province, Viet-Nam; ed. Ecole Normale, Phnom-Penh, Univ. in France.
Former Dir. Nat. Pedagogical Inst.; exile in Hanoi 63; mem. Cen. Cttee. Pracheachon (Cambodian Communist Party); liaison officer between Khmer Rouge and exiled Royal Govt. of Nat. Union in Beijing 70; Chief of Gen. Staff, Khmer Rouge armed forces 71-79; Third Deputy Prime Minister, Minister of Defence 75-79; mem. Standing Cttee., Cen. Cttee. Pracheachon 75-77, alt. mem. 78-79; Deputy Premier in charge of Nat. Defence, Govt. of Democratic Kampuchea, in exile after Vietnamese invasion 79-; mem. Defence Cttee., Coalition Govt. of Democratic Kampuchea, Thailand July 82-.

Song Beizhang; Chinese party official.
Deputy Political Commissar, Anhui Mil. District, People's Liberation Army 68; Vice-Chair. Anhui Revolutionary Cttee. 68, Chair. 75-77; Sec. CCP Anhui 71, First Sec. 75-June 77; criticized for being associated with the "Gang of Four" and removed from office.
People's Republic of China.

Song Ping; Chinese party official.
Vice-Minister, Labour 53; Vice-Chair. State Planning Comm. 57-63; Sec. CCP Gansu, and Vice-Chair. Gansu Revolutionary Cttee. 72, First Sec. CCP Gansu, Chair. Gansu Revolutionary Cttee., and First Political Commissar Gansu Mil. District, PLA 77-81; Second Police Commissar PLA Lanzhou Mil. Region 78-81; mem. 11th Cen. Cttee. CCP 77; First Vice-Chair, State Planning Comm. 81-.
State Planning Commission, Beijing, People's Republic of China.

Song Renqiong; Chinese party official; b. 1909, Liuyang County, Hunan Prov.
Joined CCP 26; Political Commissar 28th army of Red Army 36; First Deputy Sec. South-West China Bureau of Cen. Cttee. and Deputy Political Commissar South-West China Mil. Command 52; Deputy Sec.-Gen. Party Cen. Cttee., Minister, Second Ministry of Machine-building, First Sec. North-East China Bureau of Cen. Cttee. 54-; Minister, Seventh Ministry of Machine-building, Head Org. Dept., Party Cen. Cttee. 77-79; Vice-Chair. 4th and 5th Nat. Cttees., CPPCCC to 80; alt. mem. 7th Cen. Cttee., mem. 8th Cen. Cttee.; mem. Secretariat, Political Bureau CCP Cen. Cttee. March 80-.
People's Republic of China.

Song Yangchu; Chinese politician.
Vice-Chairman of State Planning Comm. 59-64; Vice-Chair. Economy Comm. 64-66; Minister of Building Materials 79-82.
People's Republic of China.

Song Zhenming; Chinese politician.
Secretary of CCP, Daqing Oilfield 76-; Vice-Minister of Petroleum and Chemical Industry 76-78; Minister of Petroleum Industry 78-80.
People's Republic of China.

Song Zhiguang; Chinese diplomatist; b. April 1916, Guangdong Province; ed. univ.
Counsellor, embassy in German Democratic Repub.; Deputy Dir. Dept. of W. European Affairs, Ministry of Foreign Affairs; Counsellor, embassy in France; Amb. to German Democratic Repub. 70-72, to U.K. 72-77, to Japan 82-; Asst. to Minister of Foreign Affairs 77-81.
Embassy of the People's Republic of China, 4-5-30, Minami Azabu, Minato-ku, Tokyo, Japan.

Sonoda, Sunao; Japanese politician.
Kamikaze paratroop commdr. during World War II; mem. House of Reps. for Kumatomo Prefecture; Minister of Health and Welfare 67-70; Chief Cabinet Sec. 76-77; Minister for Foreign Affairs 77-79, May Nov.-81, for Health and Welfare Sept. 80-May 81; Liberal-Democratic Party.
c/o Ministry of Foreign Affairs, 2-1, Kasumigaseki 2-chome, Chiyoda-ku, Tokyo, Japan.

Soong Mayling (*see* Chiang Kai-shek, Madame).

Souphanouvong; Laotian politician; b. 1902; half-brother of Prince Souvanna Phouma (*q.v.*); ed. Lycée Saint-Louis (Paris), Ecole Nationale des Ponts et Chaussées.
Studied engineering in France; returned to Laos 38 and became active in the Nationalist Movement; joined Pathet Lao and fought against the French; formed nationalist party (Neo Lao Haksat) in Bangkok 50; Leader of the Patriotic Front; Minister of Planning, Reconstruction and Urbanism 58; arrested 59, escaped May 60 and rejoined Pathet Lao Forces; Pathet Lao del. Geneva Conf. on Laos 61-62; Vice-Premier and Minister of Econ. Planning 62-74; Chair. Joint Nat. Political Council 74-75, Pres. of Lao People's Democratic Repub. Dec. 75-, also Pres. Supreme People's Assembly; Chair. Cen. Cttee. Lao Front for Nat. Reconstruction 79-; Order of the October Revolution (U.S.S.R.) 79.
Office of the President, Vientiane, Laos.

Sourinho, Vithaya, D.IUR.; Laotian diplomatist; b. 5 Feb. 1937, Phiafay; ed. Univ. of Montpellier, France.
Attaché, Cabinet of Ministry of Foreign Affairs 68; Dir. Inst. of Law and Admin. 69; Dir.-Gen. Civil Service 70-72; Head of Mission to Presidency of the Council of Ministers 70-72; Counsellor to Lao Perm. Mission to UN 72-77, Acting Chargé d'Affaires, Minister-Counsellor and Deputy Perm. Rep. 77-79, Perm. Rep. July 79-.
Permanent Mission of the Lao People's Democratic Republic to the United Nations, 321 East 45th Street, Apt. 7G, New York, N.Y. 10017, U.S.A.
Telephone: 986-0227.

Souvanna Phouma, Prince; Laotian engineer and politician; b. 7 Oct. 1901, Luang Prabang; half-brother of Souphanouvong (*q.v.*); ed. Coll. Paul Bert and Lycée Albert Sarraut, Hanoi, Univs. of Paris and Grenoble.
Entered Public Works Service of Indo-China 31; Engineer at Phoukhoun 40-41, at Luang Prabang 41-44; Chief Engineer, Bureau technique à la Circonscription Territoriale des Travaux Publics du Laos 44-45; Principal Engineer (1st Class) of the Public Works Service of Indochina; Minister of Public Works in Lao Issara 45-49; exiled in Bangkok 46-49; returned to Laos 49; Minister of Public Works 50-51; Prime Minister, Pres. of the Council, Minister of Public Works and of Planning 51-54; Vice-Pres. of the Council and Minister of Nat. Defence and Ex-Servicemen 54-56; Prime Minister, Pres. of the Council, Minister of Nat. Defence and Ex-Servicemen, of Foreign Affairs and of Information 56-57, Prime Minister 57-58; Amb. to France 58-59; Pres. National Assembly 60; Prime Minister, Minister of Defence and Foreign Affairs Aug-Dec. 60; Leader of Neutralist Govt. 60-62; Prime Minister 62-75; Minister of Defence and Veterans and Social Affairs 62-74, of Foreign Affairs 64-74, of Rural Devt. 71-74; Counsellor to the Govt. Dec. 75-; Grand Cross Order of Million Elephants, Grand Officier Légion d'honneur, etc.
c/o Office of the Prime Minister, Vientiane, Laos.

Souza, Francis Newton; Indian painter; b. 12 April 1924, ed. St. Xavier's Coll. and Sir J. J. School of Art, Bombay, Central School of Art, London, Ecole des Beaux Arts; Paris.
In London 49-; one-man exhbns. London and major English cities, Paris, Stockholm, Frankfurt, Stuttgart, Bombay, New Delhi, Karachi, Copenhagen, Geneva, Johannesburg and in U.S.A. and United Arab Emirates; represented in Baroda Museum, Nat. Gallery, New Delhi, Tate Gallery, London, Wakefield Gallery, Haifa Museum,

Nat. Gallery, Melbourne, Museum of Modern Art, N.Y., Musée d'Art Moderne, Paris, '*Expo 67*, Montreal, Artists of Fame exhbn., Commonwealth Inst., London 77 etc.; retrospective exhbns. in London 51, New Delhi 65, Leicester 67, Detroit 68, Minneapolis Int. Art Festival 72, Indian Silver Jubilee Exhbn. 73, London 77; Guest Lecturer, Cooper Union, Asia Soc., N.Y.; represented in hundreds of private collections throughout the world; several awards.
Publs. *Nirvana of a Maggot in Encounter*, *Words and Lines* (autobiography) 59, *Statements* 77.
148 W. 67th Street, New York, N.Y. 10023, U.S.A.
Telephone: (212) 874-2181.

Srivastava, Chandrika Prasad, LL.B., M.A.; Indian international civil servant; b. 8 July 1920, Unnao; ed. Univ. of Lucknow.
Deputy Dir.-Gen. of Shipping, Govt. of India 54-57; Joint Sec. to Prime Minister 64-66; Chair. State Shipping Corpn. of India 66-73; Pres. Indian Nat. Shipowners' Asscn. 71-73; Dir. Reserve Bank of India 72-73; Pres. UN Conf. on a Code of Conduct for Liner Confs. 73-74; Sec.-Gen. Int. Maritime Org. (IMO) Jan. 74-; Gold Medals for English Literature and Political Science (Univ. of Lucknow); Padma Bhushan 72.
Publs. contributions to maritime journals.
International Maritime Organization, 101-104 Piccadilly, London, W1V 0AE; 48 Brompton Square, London, S.W.3, England.

Stansfield, George Norman, O.B.E.; British diplomatist; b. 28 Feb. 1926; ed. Wallasey.
Royal Air Force 44-47; Civil Service 47-61; Commonwealth Relations Office 61; Second Sec., Calcutta 62, Port of Spain 66; First Sec. FCO 68; First Sec., Singapore 71; Consul, Durban, South Africa 74; Head of Overseas Estates Dept. FCO 78; High Commr. in Solomon Islands 82-.
British High Commission, P.O. Box 676, Soltel House, Mendana Avenue, Honiara, Solomon Islands.
Telephone: 705, 706.

Staples, Hubert Anthony Justin, C.M.G.; British diplomatist; b. 14 Nov. 1929; ed. Downside and Oriel Coll., Oxford.
Served in R.A.F. 52-54; entered Foreign Service 54; 3rd Sec., Bangkok 55-59; Foreign Office 59-62; 1st Sec. (Deputy Political Adviser), Berlin 62-65; Vientiane 65-68, acting Chargé d'affaires 66 and 67; transferred to Foreign Office and seconded to Cabinet Office 68; Counsellor U.K. Del. to NATO, Brussels 71-74; Counsellor and Consul-Gen., Bangkok 74-78, acting Chargé d'affaires 75 and 77; Counsellor, Dublin 78-81; Amb. to Thailand 81-.
British Embassy, Wireless Road, Bangkok, Thailand.
Telephone: 2527161/9.

Stead, Christina Ellen; Australian writer; b. 17 July 1902, Banksia, Rockdale, N.S.W.; ed. Sydney Girls' High School, Sydney Teachers' Coll., Business Coll.
Began career as a schoolteacher; Demonstrator in Psychology, Teachers' Coll., Sydney; went to London 28; lived for some years in London and Paris, working as a clerk for mercantile and banking houses and travelling in Europe; visited U.S.A. 35, then lived in Spain, Belgium and England; lived in U.S.A. 37-45, then in Belgium and England, in Australia 74-; Fellow in the Creative Arts, Australian Nat. Univ. 69-80, Emer. Fellow 80-81; Patrick White Award (first recipient) 74.
Publs. fiction: *The Salzburg Tales* 34, *Seven Poor Men of Sydney* 34, *The Beauties and Furies* 36, *House of All Nations* 38, *The Man Who Loved Children* 40, *For Love Alone* 44, *Letty Fox—Her Luck* 46, *A Little Tea, A Little Chat* 48, *The People with the Dogs* 52, *Cotter's England* 66, *Puzzleheaded Girl* 68, *Little Hotel* 74, *Miss Herbert* 76.
68 Bent Street, Lindfield, N.S.W. 2070, Australia.

Stephen, Rt. Hon. Sir Ninian Martin, K.B.E., P.C.; Australian lawyer and administrator; b. 15 June 1923; ed. Edinburgh Acad., St. Paul's School, London, Scotch Coll., Melbourne, Melbourne Univ.
Served Second World War, Australian Army; admitted as barrister and solicitor, Victoria 49; Q.C. 66; Judge, Supreme Court, Victoria 70; Justice, High Court, Australia 72-82; Gov.-Gen. of Australia July 82-.
Government House, Canberra, A.C.T. 2600, Australia.

Stewart, D. S., O.B.E.; Australian mechanical and electrical engineer; b. 18 Dec. 1919, Brisbane; ed. Queensland Univ.
Former Man. Britannia Production and Devt., Bristol Aircraft Co.; Dir., Gen. Man. Hestair Group; Dir. of Eng., Clyde Eng. Pty. Ltd., Chief Exec., Hadfields-Goodwin-Scotts Group; Man. Dir. Hamersley Holdings Ltd. and Hamersley Iron Pty. Ltd.; Deputy Chair., Chief Exec. Peko-Wallsend Ltd.; Fellow, Inst. of Engs., Australia; mem. Royal Aeronautical Soc.
Peko-Wallsend Ltd., 47 Macquarie Street, Sydney, N.S.W. 2000, Australia.

Stone, John O., B.A., B.SC.; Australian financial executive; b. 31 Jan. 1929; ed. Univ. of Western Australia and New Coll., Oxford.
Assistant to Australian Treasury Rep. in London 54-56, Australian Treasury Rep. in London 58-61; in Research and Information Branch, Gen. Financial and Econ. Policy Div., Dept. of Treasury, Canberra 56-57, in Home Finance Branch 61-62, Asst. Sec. Econ. and Financial Surveys Branch 62-66; Exec. Dir. for Australia, New Zealand and South Africa, IMF, IBRD 67-70; First Asst. Sec., Revenue, Loans and Investment Div., Dept. of Treasury, Canberra 71; Sec. Australian Loan Council and Nat. Debt Comm. 71; Deputy Sec. (Econ.), Dept. of Treasury 71-76, Deputy Sec., Dept. of Treasury 76-79, Sec. to the Treasury 79-; mem. Australian dels. to GATT, IMF and IBRD annual meetings, OECD, etc.
Department of the Treasury, Canberra, A.C.T. 2600, Australia.
Telephone: Canberra 63 2650.

Stratton, Richard James, C.M.G., M.A.; British diplomatist; b. 16 July 1924, London; ed. The King's School, Rochester, Merton Coll., Oxford.
Joined Foreign Service 47; Private Sec. to Minister without Portfolio, Foreign Office 63-64, to Minister of State for Foreign Affairs 64-66; Counsellor and Head of Chancery, British High Comm., Rawalpindi, Pakistan 66-69; Imperial Defence Coll. 70; Head UN (Political) Dept., Foreign and Commonwealth Office (FCO) 71-72; Political Adviser to the Gov. of Hong Kong 72-74; Amb. to Zaire and Congo 74-77, to Burundi 75-77, to Rwanda 77; Asst. Under-Sec. of State FCO 77-80; High Commr. in New Zealand (also accred. to Western Samoa) 80-.
British High Commission, Reserve Bank Building, 9th Floor, 2 The Terrace, P.O. Box 1812, Wellington, New Zealand; 18 Clareville Court, Clareville Grove, London, SW7 5AT, England (Home).
Telephone: 726-049 (Office); 01-373 2764 (Home).

Street, Anthony Austin; Australian politician; b. 8 Feb. 1926, Victoria; ed. Melbourne Grammar School.
Royal Australian Navy; primary producer; mem. House of Rep. for Corangamite 66; Sec. Govt. Mems. Defence and Woos Cttees 76-71; mem. Joint Parl. Cttee. on Foreign Affairs 69; Chair. Fed. Rural Cttee. of Liberal Party 70-74; mem. Fed. Exec. Council 71; Asst. Minister of Labour and Nat. Service 72; mem. Liberal Party shadow cabinet for social security, health and welfare 73, for primary industry, shipping and transport 73, for science and tech. and A.C.T. 74, for labour 75; Minister for Labour and Immigration Nov.-Dec. 75; Minister Assisting the Prime Minister in Public Service Matters 75-77, Minister for Employment

and Industrial Relations 75-78, for Industrial Relations 79-80, for Foreign Affairs Nov. 80-; Liberal.
Ministry of Foreign Affairs, Canberra, A.C.T.; Home: Eildon, Lismore, Victoria, Australia.

Su Kezhi; Chinese army officer.
Political Commissar, Guangdong Mil. District 71-; Commdr. Guangdong Mil. District 80-.
People's Republic of China.

Su Yu; Chinese politician and army officer; b. 1909, Fujian; ed. Hunan Prov. No. 2 Normal School, Changte.
Commander Training Battalion, Red Army Coll. 31; Deputy Commdr. N. Jiangsu Command, New 4th Army 39; Alt. mem. 7th Cen. Cttee. of CCP 45; Deputy Commdr. 3rd Field Army 48; Acting Mayor of Nanjing 49; Chief of Staff People's Liberation Army 54-58; Gen. 55; mem. 8th Cen. Cttee. of CCP 56; Vice-Minister of Nat. Defence 59-; mem. 9th Cen. Cttee. of CCP 69, 10th Cen. Cttee. 73, 11th Cen. Cttee. 77, Standing Cttee. 5th Nat. People's Congress 78-; Leading mem. Mil. Comm. CCP Cen. Cttee. 78-; First Political Commissar, Acad. of Mil. Science 78-; a Vice-Chair. Standing Cttee., Nat. People's Congress Sept. 80-.
Quanguo Renmin Daibiao Dahui, Beijing, People's Republic of China.

Subandrio, Dr.; Indonesian politician, diplomatist and surgeon; b. 1914; ed. Medical Univ., Jakarta.
Active in Nat. Movement as student and gen. practitioner; worked with underground anti-Japanese Forces during Second World War; forced to leave post at Jakarta Cen. Hosp. and then established a private practice at Semarang; following Declaration of Independence abandoned practice to become Sec.-Gen., Ministry of Information and was later sent by Indonesian Govt. as special envoy to Europe; established Information Office, London 47; Chargé d'affaires, London 49, Amb. to U.K. 50-54, to U.S.S.R. 54-56; Foreign Minister 57-66; Second Deputy First Minister 60-66, concurrently Minister for Foreign Econ. Relations 62-66; convicted of complicity in attempted communist coup and sentenced to death Oct. 66; sentence commuted to life imprisonment April 70.
Jakarta, Indonesia.

Subbulakshmi, Madurai Shanmugavadivu; Indian classical musician; b. 16 Sept. 1916; ed. privately.
Recitals with her mother and Guru Veena Shanmugavadivu 28-32; gave solo performances and became a leading musician before age 18; acted title role in Hindi film *Meera*; numerous benefit performances; donated royalties from many of her records to social and religious causes; rep. Karnatic music at Edinburgh Festival 63; concerts in London, Frankfurt, Geneva, Cairo; 7-week tour of U.S.A. 66; performed in Tokyo, Bangkok, Hong Kong, Manila, Singapore, Malaysia; Pres. Madras Music Acad. Conf. 68; Padma Bhushan 54; President's Award for Karnatic Music 56; Ramon Magsaysay Award for Public Service (Philippines) 74; Sangeet Natak Acad. Fellowship 74; Padma Vibhushan 75; honorific title Sangeetha Khalanidhi; honorific title Sapthagiri Sangeetha Vidwanmani 75; Hon. D. Litt. (Rabindra Bharati Univ.) 67, (Shri Venkateswara Univ.) 71, (Delhi Univ.) 73.
c/o T. Sadasivam, 4 Tank Road, Nungambakkam, Madras 600034, India.

Subramaniam, Chidambaram, B.A., B.L.; Indian politician; b. 30 Jan. 1910; ed. Madras Univ.
Joined Satyagraha Movement and imprisoned 32; started law practice in Coimbatore 36, imprisoned 41, 43; Pres. Coimbatore District Congress, mem. All-India Congress Cttee.; mem. Constituent Assembly of India 46-51, Madras Legislative Assembly 52-62; Minister of Finance, Educ. and Law, Madras State 52-62; mem. Lok Sabha 62-67; Minister of Steel and Heavy Industry, Cen. Govt. 62-63, of Steel, Mines and Heavy Eng. 63-64, of Food and Agriculture 64-67, Aug.-Oct. 74, also of Community Devt. and Co-operation 66-67; Pres. Tamil Nadu Congress Cttee. 68-69; Chair. Cttee. on Aeronautics, Govt. of India 67-68; mem. Nat. Exec. Indian Nat. Congress 68-; Minister of Planning, Science and Tech. 71-72, of Industrial Devt., Science and Tech. 72-74, of Finance 74-77, of Defence 79-80; Chair. Nat. Comm. on Agriculture 70; Deputy Chair. Nat. Planning Comm. 71; Chair. Rajaji Int. Inst. of Public Affairs and Admin.; mem. Governing Council of Int. Wheat and Maize Improvement Centre, Mexico; mem. Bd. of Govs. Int. Rice Research Inst., Manila; Pres. All-India Tennis Asscn.
Publs. Travelogues in Tamil: *Countries I Visited, Around the World, India of My Dreams, War on Poverty, New Agricultural Strategy*.
River View, Guindy, Madras 25; 26 Tughlak Crescent, New Delhi, India.

Subroto, M.A., PH.D.; Indonesian politician; b. 19 Sept. 1928, Surakarta; ed. Univ. of Indonesia, McGill, Stanford and Harvard Univs.
Former Dir.-Gen. of Research and Devt., Ministry of Trade; Prof. in Int. Econs., Univ. of Indonesia; Minister of Manpower, Transmigration and Co-operatives Sept. 71-78, of Mining and Energy 78-.
Publs. numerous books on economic topics.
Ministry of Mining and Energy, Jakarta, Indonesia.

Sucharitkul, Sompong, M.A., D.PHIL., D.D., LL.M.; Thai diplomatist and international lawyer; b. 4 Dec. 1931, Bangkok; ed. Univs. of Oxford and Paris, Harvard Law School, Middle Temple, London and Int. Law Acad., The Hague.
Lecturer in Int. Law and Relations, Chulalongkorn Univ. 56, also lecturer in Int. Econ. Law, Thammasat Univ.; mem. Nat. Research Council 59-70; joined Ministry of Foreign Affairs 59, Sec. to Minister 64-67, Dir.-Gen. Econ. Dept. 68-70; Amb. to Netherlands (also accred. to Belgium and Luxembourg), Head of Mission to EEC April 70-73, to Japan 74-77, to France and Portugal 77-78, to Italy and Greece 80-; Thai Rep., UN Comm. on Int. Trade Law (UNCITRAL) 67; Perm. Del. to UNESCO 77-78, mem. UN Int. Law Comm. 77-; Dir.-Gen. Treaty and Legal Dept. Ministry of Foreign Affairs; Assoc. L'Inst. de Droit Int. 73, mem. 79; mem. Civil Aviation Board of Thailand.
Publs. various books and articles on int. law and int. trade law.
Royal Thai Embassy, Villa Thai, Via Nomentana 130-132, Rome 00 162, Italy.

Sueyoshi, Toshio, B.A.(ECON.); Japanese business executive; b. 13 Feb. 1907, Tokyo; ed. Tokyo Univ. of Commerce.
Mitsui Mining Co. 30-31; Miike Nitrogen Industries Co. 31-37; Toyo Koatsu Industries Inc. 37-68, Dir. 47-55; Man. Dir. 55-57, Vice-Pres. 57-68; Vice-Pres. Mitsui Toatsu Chemicals Inc. 68-70, Pres. 70-; Pres. Japan Phosphatic and Compound Fertilizers Mfrs. Asscn. 71; Blue Ribbon Medal 68.
Mitsui Toatsu Chemicals Inc., 2-5, Kasumigaseki 3-chome, Chiyoda-ku, Tokyo; Home: 45-7, Kitasenzoku 2-chome, Ohta-ku, Tokyo, Japan.
Telephone: 581-6111 (Office); 729-2270 (Home).

Sugitani, Takeo, B.L.; Japanese banker; b. 7 Aug. 1903, Miyagi Pref.; ed. Tokyo Imperial Univ.
Joined the Mitsui Trust Co. Ltd. 26; Dir. The Mitsui Trust & Banking Co. Ltd. 48; Man. Dir. The Mitsui Trust & Banking Co. Ltd. 57, Pres. 60-68, Chair. 68-71, Counsellor 71-; Auditor, Mitsui Petrochemical Industries Ltd. 67-; Counsellor, Mitsui Real Estate Co. Ltd. 61-, Mitsui Mining Co. Ltd. 64-; Counsellor and Auditor, Japan Women's Univ. 73-.

The Mitsui Trust & Banking Co. Ltd., 1-1 Nihonbashi Muromachi 2-chome, Chuo-ku, Tokyo; 14-5 Meguro 3-chome, Meguro-ku, Tokyo, Japan.
Telephone: 03-712-1600.

Sugiura, Binsuke; Japanese banker; b. 13 Nov. 1911, Tokyo; ed. Tokyo Univ.
Director, Long-Term Credit Bank of Japan Ltd. 58-61, Man. Dir. 61-68, Senior Man. Dir. 68-69, Deputy Pres. 69-71, Pres. 71-78, Chair. 78-; Blue Ribbon Medal; First Class Order of the Sacred Treasure.
The Long-Term Credit Bank of Japan Ltd., 2-4, Otemachi 1-chome, Chiyoda-ku, Tokyo 100; Home: 31-5, Kami-Meguro 3-chome, Meguro-ku, Tokyo 153, Japan.
Telephone: 211-5111 (Office); 719-5505 (Home).

Suharto, Gen., T.N.I.; Indonesian army officer and politician; b. 8 June 1921; ed. Indonesian Army Staff and Command Coll.
Officer in Japanese-sponsored Indonesian Army 43; Battalion, later Regimental, Commdr. Yogjakarta 45-50; Regimental Commdr., Central Java 53; Brig.-Gen. 60; Deputy Chief of Army Staff 60-65; Maj.-Gen. 62; Commdr. Strategy of the Army 63; Commdr. for Restoration of Security and Order 65; Chief of Army Staff 65-68, Supreme Commdr. 68-73; Minister of Army 65; Lieut.-Gen. 66; Deputy Prime Minister for Defence and Security 66; Chair. of Presidium of Cabinet, in charge of Defence and Security, also Minister of Army 66-67; Full Gen. 66; Acting Pres. of Indonesia 67-68; Minister for Defence and Security 67-73; Pres. of Indonesia March 68-.
Office of the President, 15 Jalan Merdeka Utara, Jakarta; Home: 8 Jalan Cendana, Jakarta, Indonesia.

Sukhedev; Indian film maker; b. 1933; ed. Bombay.
Has directed, produced, edited and acted in films since 60; has produced documentaries and short films; Padma Shri 68.
Works: *And Miles to Go, After the Eclipse, An Indian Day* (fmrly. *India '67*), *Thoughts on a Museum, Khilonewalla, Nine Months to Freedom* 72.
c/o Film Niryat, 6/33-37, Tardeo AC Market Building, P.O. Box 7928, Tardeo Road, Bombay 34, India.

Suma, Michiaki; Japanese diplomatist; b. 25 Jan. 1918, Tokyo; ed. Univ. of Tokyo.
Director, Third Div., Asian Affairs Bureau, Ministry of Foreign Affairs 57; Dir. S.E. Asian Div., Asian Affairs Bureau, Ministry of Foreign Affairs 58; Dir., American Affairs Div., Econ. Affairs Bureau 58; Consul, Consulate-Gen., New York 61; Counsellor Embassy in The Netherlands 64; Deputy Dir.-Gen., Econ. Affairs Bureau 66; Amb. to Tanzania 69-72; Consul-Gen., Hong Kong 72-74; Amb. to Malaysia 74-76; Dir.-Gen. Osaka Liaison Office, Ministry of Foreign Affairs 76-78; Amb. to Canada 78-81.
c/o Ministry of Foreign Affairs, 2-1, Kasumigaseki 2-chome, Chiyoda-ku, Tokyo, Japan.

Sun Daguang; Chinese politician.
Dir. N.E. General Bureau of Navigation 49; Dir. Planning Dept., Ministry of Communications 53-54; Pres. N.E. Navigation Coll. 54-; Asst. to Minister of Communications 55-58; Vice-Minister of Communications 58-64; mem. Cttee. for Receiving and Resettling Returned Overseas Chinese, State Council 60; Minister of Communications 64; Deputy to 3rd NPC 64; mem. Nat. Defence Council 65-Cultural Revolution; disappeared during Cultural Revolution; rehabilitated 74; Dir. Nat. Geological Bureau, State Council 78; deputy to 5th NPC 78; Minister of Geology 80-.
People's Republic of China.

Sun Jian; Chinese government official.
Vice-Premier, State Council 75-78.
People's Republic of China.

Sun Jingwen; Chinese politician; b. Hebei.
Director of Propaganda CCP Chahar Provincial Cttee. 49; Mayor of Zhangjiakou 50; mem. Zahar Provincial People's Govt. 50; 2nd Sec. CCP Zhahar Provincial Cttee. 50; Vice-Chair. Zhahar People's Provincial Govt. 52; Dir. Urban Construction Bureau, Ministry of Building 54-55; mem. State Construction Comm., State Council 54-58; Deputy Dir., Urban Construction Bureau, State Council, 55-56; Vice Minister Urban Construction 57-58; Vice-Minister of Building 58-59; Vice-Minister of Petroleum 59; Vice-Chair. State Capital Construction Comm., State Council 65; Minister of Chemical Industry 78-82.
People's Republic of China.

Sun Yefang; Chinese economist.
Economic theorist; joined CCP 24; studied in U.S.S.R. 25; engaged in CCP cultural and united front work Shanghai 37-39; Deputy Dir., Dept. of Heavy Industry, E. China Mil. and Admin. Cttee. 49; mem. Financial and Econ. Cttee., E. China Mil. and Admin. Cttee. 49-54; Deputy Minister of Industry, E. China Mil. and Admin. Cttee. 50-53; Pres. Shanghai Coll. of Finance and Econs. 50-53; Dir., State Statistics Bureau Del. to U.S.S.R. 56; Deputy Dir. State Statistics Bureau, State Council 55-61; Acting Dir. Inst. of Econs., Chinese Acad. of Science 57; revisited U.S.S.R. 59, 61; Dir., Inst. of Econs., Chinese Acad. of Science 66; purged 66; rehabilitated after downfall of "Gang of Four" 78; Consultant of Econ. Research Inst., Chinese Acad. of Social Sciences 77; mem. 5th Nat. Congress, Chinese Nat. Assembly for Political Consultation 78; visited Yugoslavia and Romania 78; Chinese Acad. of Social Sciences, concurrently Visiting Prof. at Beijing Univ.
Publs. Co-editor *National Salvation Handbook* 38, trans. *Concise Dictionary of Philosophy* (M. Rozentale and P. Uena) 40; *Some Theoretical Problems of Socialist Economy* 79.
Suite No. 11, Entrance No. 2, No. 22 Building Fuxing Men Wai Street, Beijing, People's Republic of China.
Telephone: 362520.

Sun Yiran; Chinese party official.
Member CCP 11th Cen. Cttee. 77-; Sec. Shandong Prov. CCP Cttee. 78-; Vice-Chair. Shandong Provincial Revolutionary Cttee. 78-; First Pol. Commissar Shandong Mil. Dist. 78-.
People's Republic of China.

Sun Yun-suan, B.S.; Chinese engineer and politician; b. 11 Nov. 1913, Shandong; ed. Harbin Polytech. Inst.
Electrical engineer 34; with Nat. Resources Comm. 37-40; Supt. Tianzhui Electric Power Plant 40-43; Head Engineer Electric and Mechanical Dept. Taiwan Power Co. 46-50; Chief Engineer Taiwan Power Co. 50-52; Vice-Pres. and Chief Engineer 53-62, Pres. 62-64; Chief Exec. and Gen. Man. Electricity Corpn. of Nigeria 65-67; Minister of Communications 67-69, of Econ. Affairs 69-78; Prime Minister Repub. of China (Taiwan) May 78-; Cravat of the Order of Brilliant Star 52; Engineering Award of the Chinese Inst. of Engineers 54.
1 Chung Hsaio E. Road, Sec. 1, Taipei 100, Taiwan.
Telephone: 3915231.

Sunderland, Sir Sydney, Kt., C.M.G., D.SC., M.D., B.S., F.R.A.C.P., F.R.A.C.S., F.A.A.; Australian anatomist; b. 31 Dec. 1910, Brisbane; ed. Melbourne Univ.
Senior Lecturer in Anatomy, Melbourne Univ. 36-37; Asst. Neurologist Alfred Hosp. Melbourne 36-37; Demonstrator Dept. of Human Anatomy Oxford 38-39; Prof. of Anatomy and Histology Melbourne Univ. 39-61, of Experimental Neurology 61-75, Dean Medical Faculty 53-71, Prof. Emer. 76-; Visiting Specialist, injuries of the peripheral nervous system, Australian Gen. Mil. Hosp. 41-45; Visiting Prof. of Anatomy, Johns Hopkins Univ. 53-54; mem. Nat. Health and Medical Research Council of

Australia 53-69; Foundation Fellow and Sec. for Biological Sciences, Australian Acad. of Sciences 55-58; Trustee, Nat. Museum of Victoria 54-, Van Cleef Foundation 71; Fellow and Founders Lecturer American Soc. for Surgery of the Hand 79; mem. Zool. Board of Victoria 44-65; Deputy Chair. Advisory Cttee. of Victorian Mental Hygiene Authority 52-63; rep. Pacific Science Council 57-69; mem. Defence Research and Devt. Policy Cttee. 57-75, Medical Services Cttee. 57-78, Commonwealth Dept. of Defence; Nat. Radiation Advisory Cttee. 57-64, Chair. 59-69; Chair Safety Review Cttee. 61-74, Australian Atomic Energy Comm.; Medical Research Advisory Cttee. of Nat. Health and Medical Council 53-69, Chair. 64-69; Chair. Protective Chemistry Research Advisory Cttee., Dept. of Supply 64-73; Vice-Pres. Int. Asscn. for Study of Pain 75-78; mem. Scientific Advisory Cttee. Australian Atomic Energy Comm. 62-63, Australian Univs. Comm. 62-, 76, Cttee. of Management Royal Melbourne Hosp. 63-71; Victorian Medical Advisory Cttee. 62-71, Advisory Medical Council of Australia 70-71; Foreign mem. Soc. Française de Neurologie; Hon. mem. American Neurological Asscn., Australian Asscn. of Neurologists, Neurosurgical Soc. of Australasia; Fogarty Scholar-in-Residence, Nat. Insts. of Health, Bethesda, U.S.A. 72, Sterling Bunnell Lecturer and Visiting Prof. of Orthopaedic Surgery, Univ. of Calif. 77; Gov. Ian Potter Foundation 64-; mem. Board Walter and Eliza Hall Inst. 68-75; Hon. M.D. (Tasmania) 70, (Queensland) 75; Hon. LL.D. (Melbourne) 75, (Monash) 77.

Publ. *Nerves and Nerve Injuries* 68.

Department of Experimental Neurology, University of Melbourne, Parkville 3052, Victoria, Australia.

Telephone: 203431.

Süren, Choynoryn; Mongolian politician; b. 1932; ed. Teacher Training School, Higher School of Eng. and Econs., U.S.S.R.

Teacher in various provinces 49-52; technician in State Construction Directorate 55-56; expert of State Construction Cttee., Deputy Chair. State Construction Comm. 59-61; Deputy Minister of Construction and Construction Materials Industry 61-64; lecturer at Mongolian State Univ., Dir. of Dept. at Construction Research Inst. 64-67; Deputy Chair. and later Chair. of Exec. Cttee. of Darhan City People's Deputies' Hural (Assembly) 67-72; Counsellor, Embassy in Moscow 72-74; Deputy Chair. Council of Ministers 74-; Chair. State Cttee. for Construction, Architecture and Tech. Control 82-; mem. Central Cttee. Mongolian People's Revolutionary Party (MPRP) 76-; Deputy to People's Great Hural (Assembly) 77-.

Suthayakhom, Wichet; Thai diplomatist; b. 21 Sept, 1923, Surathani, South Thailand; ed. School of Laws. Thammasat Univ., Bangkok and George Washington Univ., Washington, D.C., U.S.A.

First Sec., Embassy in Kuala Lumpur 60-65; Consul-Gen. Kota Bharu, Kelantan, Malaysia 65-67; Chief of Protocol Div., Ministry of Foreign Affairs 67-70; Deputy Dir.-Gen. of Protocol Dept. 70-71, Dir.-Gen. 71-73; Amb. to Pakistan and Iraq 73-76, to Australia 76-80 and concurrently Amb. to Fiji until Jan. 78; Knight Grand Cross of the Most Exalted Order of the Crown, Knight Grand Cross of the Most Exalted Order of the White Elephant; P.S.M. (Malaysia); C.M.G. (U.K.).

c/o Ministry of Foreign Affairs, Saranrom Palace, Bangkok, Thailand.

Sutherland, Dame Joan, A.C., D.B.E., F.R.C.M.; Australian opera singer; b. 7 Nov. 1926, Sydney; *m.* Richard Bonynge (*q.v.*) 1954; ed. St. Catherine's School, Waverley, Sydney. Début as Dido in Purcell's *Dido and Aeneas*, Sydney 47; Royal Opera Co., Covent Garden, London 52-; has sung leading soprano roles at the Vienna State Opera, La Scala, Milan, Teatro Fenice, Venice, the Paris Opera, Glyndebourne, San Francisco and Chicago Operas, The Metropolitan, New York, etc.; Hon. life mem. Australia Opera Co. 74; Companion Order of Australia 75.

c/o Ingpen and Williams Ltd., 14 Kensington Court, London, W.8, England; c/o The Australian Opera, P.O. Box R223, Royal Exchange, N.S.W. 2000, Australia.

Sutowo, Lieut.-Gen. Dr. Ibnu; Indonesian industrialist. President-Director, PERTAMINA March 76; under house arrest since April 77 until completion of investigations.

Suzuki, Gengo; Japanese financial executive; b. 11 Feb. 1904; ed. Government College of Commerce, Taihoku and Univ. of Wisconsin.

Lecturer and Professor in Econ. Govt. Coll. of Commerce, Taihoku, Taiwan 31-49, concurrently Civil Administration Official, Govt.-Gen. Taiwan 44-45, Prof. of Econs., Taiwan Province School of Law and Commerce 45-47, Prof. of Econ. Nat. Univ. of Taiwan 47-48; Deputy Financial Commr., Ministry of Finance, Japanese Govt. 49-51, Financial Commr. 51-57; Financial Minister, Embassy in U.S.A. 57-60; Special Asst. to Minister for Foreign Affairs, and to Minister of Finance 60-66; Auditor, Bank of Japan, Tokyo 66-70; Exec. Dir. for Burma, Japan, Nepal, Sri Lanka and Thailand, IMF, IBRD 60-66; mem. Advisory Board, Cttee. for Co-ordination of Investigations of the Lower Mekong Basin 68-; mem. World Bank's Investment Dispute Conciliation Panel 68-74; Chair. Board Assoc. Japanese Bank (Int.) Ltd., London 70-79, Bd. Counsellors 79-; Publisher Int. Devt. Journal 70-; Gov. and steering cttee. mem., Atlantic Inst. for Int. Affairs (Paris) 71-; mem. European Atlantic Group 71-; mem. Council of Int. Chamber of Commerce (ICC) 74-, ICC Comm. on Unethical Practices 76-77.

29-30 Cornhill, London, E.C.3.; Home: Flat 38, London House, 7-9 Avenue Road, London, N.W.8, England; 2-5-13 Nukuikitamachi, Koganei shi, Tokyo, Japan; and 717 The Olympus, 6301 Stevenson Avenue, Alexandria, Virginia, U.S.A.

Telephone: 01-623 5661 (London Office); 01-586 2721 (London Home); 0423-83-5751 (Tokyo Home); 703-370-8649 (Virginia Home).

Suzuki, Haruo, LL.B.; Japanese business executive; b. 31 March 1913, Hayama, Kanagawa Pref.; ed. Tokyo Univ.

With Nomura Securities Co. Ltd. 36-39; joined Showa-Denko K.K. 39, Exec. Vice-Pres. 59-71, Pres. 71-, Chair. 81-; Chair. Showa Neoprene K.K. 75-80, Showa Aluminium Industries K.K. 76-, Showa Unox K.K. 75-80, Tokuyama Petrochem. Co. 77-; Chair. Cttee. of Gen. Dirs., Japan Cttee. for Econ. Devt. 71-; Man. Dir. Japan Fed. of Econ. Orgs. 72-; Chair. Council on Basic Material Industries 78-; Pres. Econ. Policy Cttee., Japan Chamber of Commerce 82-; mem. Industrial Structure Council, Electric Utility Industry Council of Ministry of Int. Trade and Industry 72-, Comité de Reflexion sur l'avenir des relations franco-japonais, Ministry of Foreign Affairs 82-; Special mem. Securities Exchange Council, Ministry of Finance 82-; Hon. D. Econ. (Humboldt Univ., Berlin) 75.

Publ. *Chemical Industry* 68, *What the Classics have Taught Me* 69.

Showa Denko K.K., 13-9, Shiba Daimon 1-chome, Minato-ku, Tokyo; Home: 7-1-810 Mita 2-chome, Minato-ku, Tokyo, Japan.

Telephone: 432-5111 (Office).

Suzuki, Jitsujiro; Japanese business executive; b. 29 Nov. 1913, Fujieda, Shizuoka; ed. Hamamatsu Technical School. With Suzuki Motor Co. Ltd. 40-, Dir. 48-, Man. Dir. 61-67, Senior Man. Dir. 67-73, Pres. 73-77, Chair. 77-; Ranjyu Hosho (Japan Nat. Prize) 74.

Suzuki Motor Co. Ltd., P.O. Box 116, Hamamatsu 430, Japan.

Telephone: 0534-52-0579.

Suzuki, Kyoji, M.A.; Japanese business executive; b. 18 March 1909, Kyoto; ed. Tokyo Imperial Univ.
With Dai-Ichi Bank Ltd. 31-48; Dir. Ajinomoto Co. Inc. 48, Exec. Vice-Pres. 59, Exec. Dir. Ajinomoto-Insud S.p.A., Rome 63; Pres. Ajinomoto Inc. 65-73, Chair. 73-75, Auditor May 75-; Chair. Knorr Food Products (Japan) Ltd.; Blue Ribbon Medal.
Ajinomoto Co. Inc., 1-6 Kyobashi, Chuo-ku; Home: 3-8-2 chome Shoto, Shibuya-ku, Tokyo, Japan.
Telephone: 03-272-1111.

Suzuki, Zenko; Japanese politician; b. 11 Jan. 1911, Iwate Pref.; ed. Fishery Training Inst. of Ministry of Agric. and Forestry.
Elected to Parlt. as a Socialist 47; joined Liberal-Democratic Party 49; elected 13 times to House of Reps. for constituency in Iwate prefecture; Minister of Postal Services July-Dec. 60; Chief Cabinet Sec. July-Nov. 64; Minister of Health and Welfare 65-67; various posts in Liberal-Democratic Party (LDP) incl. Chair. of Exec. Council; assoc. of Masayoshi Ohira; Minister of Agriculture and Forestry 76-77; Prime Minister July 80-.
Prime Minister's Office, 1-6-1, Nagata-cho, Chiyoda-ku, Tokyo, Japan.
Telephone: 01-581-2361.

Swaminathan, Jagdish; Indian painter; b. 21 June 1928, Simla; ed. Delhi Polytechnic and Acad. of Fine Arts, Warsaw.
Early career of freedom fighter, trade unionist, journalist, and writer of children's books; mem. Delhi State Cttee. of Congress Socialist Party and Editor of its weekly organ, *Mazdoor Awaz;* Senior Art Teacher, Cambridge School, New Delhi; Founder-mem. *Group 1890* (avant-garde group of Indian artists); mem. Nat. Cttee., Int. Assc. of the Arts 67-, Exec. Cttee. Delhi Slipi Chakra 67, also Founder-Editor monthly journal, *Contra 66* and full-time painter; one-man exhbns. in New Delhi 62, 63, 64, 65, 66, in Bombay 66; in group shows Warsaw 61, Saigon 63, Tokyo Biennale 65, *Art Now in India*, London, Newcastle and Brussels 65-66, *Seven Indian Painters*, London 67; mem. Int. Jury, São Paulo Bienal 69; Jawaharlal Nehru Fellow for thesis *The Significance of the Traditional Numen to Contemporary Art* 69; represented in various public and private collections in India and abroad.
c/o Gallery Chemould, Jahangir Art Gallery, Mahatma Gandhi Road, Bombay 1; and 6/17 W.E.A. New Delhi 5, India.

Swaminathan, Monkombu Sambasivan, PH.D.; Indian agriculturalist, botanist and cytogeneticist; b. 7 Aug. 1925, Kumbakonam, Tamil Nadu; ed. Univ. of Cambridge, England.
Assistant Botanist, Cen. Rice Research Inst., Cuttack 54; Asst. Cytogeneticist, Indian Agricultural Research Inst. (IARI) 54-56, Cytogeneticist 56-61, Head Botany Div. 61-66; Dir. IARI 66-72; Independent Chair. UN Food and Agric. Org. Council; Vice-Pres. Protein Group, UN; Sec. of Agricultural and Rural Devt., Govt. of India 79-80; Dir.-Gen. Int. Rice Research Inst. (IRRI) 82-; introduced dwarf wheat into India and initiated high-yielding varieties programme; Pres. Indian Science Congress Asscn. 76; Fellow Royal Soc., U.S. Nat. Acad. of Sciences, Swedish Seed Asscn., Indian Nat. Science Acad., Indian Acad. of Sciences; Foreign mem. Lenin Acad. of Agricultural Sciences; Shanti Swarup Bhatnagar Award 61, Mendel Memorial Award 65, Birbal Sahni Medal 65, Ramon Magsaysay Award for Community Leadership 71, Indian Nat. Science Acad. Silver Jubilee Award, Barclay Medal of Asiatic Soc.
International Rice Research Institute, P.O. Box 933, Manila, Philippines.

Swe, Ba (*see* Ba Swe, U).

Syed Putra ibni Syed Hassan Jamalullial (*see* Perlis).

Syme, Sir Colin York, A.K., Kt., LL.B.; Australian businessman; b. 22 April 1903; ed. Perth and Melbourne Univs.
Partner firm of Hedderwick, Fookes and Alston 28-66; Dir. Broken Hill Pty. Co. Ltd. 37-, Chair. 52-71, Dir. of Admin. 66-71; Chair. Tubemakers of Australia Ltd. 66-73; Pres. Walter and Eliza Hall Inst. of Medical Research 61-78, Hon. Gov. 79; Dir. Australian Industry Devt. Corpn. 71-77; Chair. inquiry into hospital and health services in Victoria 73-75, Victorian Health Planning 75-78; Hon. Consultant Health Comm. of Victoria 78-; Adviser to The Private Investment Co. of Asia 79-; Hon. D.Sc., Hon. LL.D.
22 Stonnington Place, Toorak, Victoria 3142, Australia.
Telephone: 20-5254.

T

Tabai, Hon. Ieremia T., C.M.G.; Kiribati (Gilbertese) politician; b. 1950, Nonouti; ed. King George V School, Tarawa, St. Andrew's Coll., Christchurch, Victoria Univ., Wellington.
Member Gilbert Islands House of Assembly 74-79; Chief Minister 78-79; Pres. Republic of Kiribati July 79-, also Minister of Foreign Affairs.
Office of the President, Tarawa, Kiribati.

Takeda, Chobei; Japanese business executive; b. 29 April 1905; ed. Keio Gijuku Univ.
President, Takeda Chemical Industries Ltd. until 74, Chair. 74.
Takeda Chemical Industries Ltd., 27 Doshomachi 2-chome, Higashi-ku, Osaka, Japan.

Takeiri, Yoshikatsu; Japanese politician; b. 10 Jan. 1926, Nagano Prefecture; ed. Inst. of Politics (Seiji Daigakko).
With Japan Nat. Railwavs 48-59; Bunkyo Ward Ass. Tokyo 59; Tokyo Metropolitan Ass. 63-67; Vice Sec.-Gen. Komeito (Clean Govt.) Party Nov. 64-67, Chair. 67-; mem. House of Reps. 67-.
17 Minamimoto-machi, Shinjuku-ku, Tokyo 160, Japan.
Telephone: 353-0111.

Takemi, Taro: Japanese physician; b. 7 March 1904, Kyoto; ed. Keio Univ. School of Medicine.
Pioneer in study of medical application of nuclear physics; mem. team measuring radioactivity of atomic bomb, Hiroshima 45; built the first portable electro-cardiograph 37; invented the vectorcardiograph 39; also patented the method of extracting chlorophyll and the mfg. process for pentose nucleotide; Asst., Keio Univ. Hosp. 30-37; Inst. of Physical and Chem. Research 38-50; Takemi Clinic 39-; now also Visiting Prof. at Keio, Kitasato and Tokai Univs.; Vice-Pres. Japan Medical Asscn. 50, Pres. 57-82; Pres. World Medical Asscn. 75-76; also of Japan-Latin America Medical Asscn. and Japan-Italy Medical Asscn.; Vice-Pres. Japan-WHO Asscn.; Adviser, Nat. Cancer Centre; Trustee, Japan Cancer Soc., Princess Takamatsu Cancer Research Fund; Auditor, Nishina Memorial Foundation, Waksman Foundation; Pres. Keio Univ. Medical School Alumni Asscn., Commdr., Italian Order of Merit 63, Grand Cross Honour of Fed. German Order of Merit 74, Order of Rising Sun-First Class 75, Special Cravat of Order of Brilliant Star (Taiwan) 76, Nat. Order of Southern Cross (Brazil) 76, Hon. K.B.E. 77, Grande Ufficiale nell' Ordine (Italy), Civil Merit Mu Gung Hua Medal (Repub. of Korea), The Golden Heart Presidential Award (Philippines).
Publs. *An Epigram on Medical Affairs, My Memoirs,* numerous papers.
c/o Seisho-kan, 2, Ginza 4-chome, Chuo-ku, Tokyo 106; Home: 8-48 Moto-azabu 3-chome, Minato-ku, Tokyo 104, Japan.
Telephone: 03-401 2439 (Home).

Takeshita, Noboru; Japanese politician; b. 26 Feb. 1924; ed. Waseda Univ.
Junior High School teacher; Prefectural Assemblyman, Shimane Pref.; mem. House of Reps. 58-, Parl. Vice-Minister for Int. Trade and Industry 58; Deputy Cabinet Sec. 64, Chief Cabinet Sec. 71-76; Construction Minister 76; Finance Minister Nov. 79-June 80; Chair. Diet Policy Cttee., Nat. Org. Cttee. of Liberal-Democratic Party, Standing Cttee. on Budget, House of Reps. 80.
Publ. *Waga Michi o Iku (Going My Way)* 79.
c/o Liberal-Democratic Party, 7, 2-chome, Hirakawacho, Chiyoda-ku, Tokyo, Japan.

Talboys, Rt. Hon. Brian Edward, C.H., P.C.; New Zealand farmer and politician; b. 7 June 1921, Wanganui; ed. Wanganui Collegiate School, and Victoria Univ., Wellington.
R.N.Z.A.F. 39-45; joined *New Zealand Dairy Exporter* 50, later Asst. Editor; M.P. 57-, Parl. Under-Sec. 60-62; Minister of Agriculture 62-69, of Educ. 69-72, of Science 64-72, of Industries and Commerce and of Overseas Trade 72; Deputy Prime Minister, Minister of Foreign Affairs and of Overseas Trade 75-81, also Minister of Nat. Devt. 75-77; not seeking re-election to Parl. 81; mem. National Party, Deputy Leader 74-81; Chair. Indosuez New Zealand Ltd. 82; Hon. D.Sc. (Massey Univ.) 08; Order of Merit (Fed. Repub. of Germany) 81; Hon. Companion, Order of Australia 82.
Parliament House, Wellington; and 1 Hamilton Avenue, Winton, Southland, New Zealand.
Telephone: 533 (Home).

Taleyarkhan, Homi J. H., B.A.; Indian state governor; b. 9 Feb. 1917, Bombay; ed. Bombay Univ., King's Coll., Univ. of London, and Lincoln's Inn.
Member Bombay Municipal Corpn. and Chair. Works Cttee. 48-52; mem. Maharashtra State Legis. Assembly 52-71; Gen. Sec. Congress Legislature Party, Chief Whip, Parl. Sec. and Cabinet Minister (successively Minister of Health, Family Planning, Food, Civil Supplies, Housing, Tourism, Nat. Savings, Fisheries and Printing Presses); Amb. to Libya 71-77; Chair. Maharashtra State Financial Corpn. 77-81; Gov. of Sikkim Jan. 81-; Del. to UNCTAD II, Delhi; mem. first UNCTAD Group on Food and fifth Cttee. on Trade and Devt.; mem. numerous other dels.; Chair. Nat. Savings Reorganization Cttee., Land Reorganization Cttee., Govt. of India; mem. Small Family Norms Cttee., All India Congress Cttee.; Vice-Pres. Maharashtra State Congress Cttee.; Dir. Shipping Corpn. of India; Vice-Pres. Indian Council of Foreign Trade and mem. Working Cttee., All India Mfrs. Org.; mem. Exec. Cttee., Asscn. of Industries, Engineering Asscn., Nat. Productivity Council; Founder Pres. Int. Tourism Council; Vice-Pres. Anti-TB Asscn., Maharashtra; Chair. World Assembly of Small and Medium Enterprises, Maharashtra Branch.
Publs. *I have it from Gandhiji, They told me so, Hyderabad and Her Destiny, United India in Australia, In the Land of the Blue Hills, Three Graces of Kashmir, Roads to Beauty Around Bombay, Village Welfare on the Way, Community Projects in India, Escape from the City, Splendour of Sikkim,* numerous pamphlets and papers.
Raj Bhavan, Gangtok 737 101, Sikkim, India.
Telephone: 400 (Office); 577 and 450 (Home).

Talwar, Raj Kumar, M.A., C.A.I.I.B.; Indian banker; b. 3 June 1922, Gujrat (West Punjab).
Joined State Bank of India 43, Sec. and Treas. Hyderabad Circle 65-66, Bombay Circle 66-68, Man. Dir. 68-69, Chair. 69-75; *ex-officio* Chair. seven subsidiary banks; Vice-Pres. Indian Inst. of Bankers 69-; Dir. Industrial Reconstruction Corpn. of India Ltd., Calcutta; mem. Small Scale Industries Board, Gov. Board of Nat. Inst. of Bank Management, Board of Govs. Indian Inst. of Management.
Dunedin, 5 J. M. Mehta Road, Bombay 400006, India.

Tan, Juan Cañizares, A.A., LL.B.; Philippine trade unionist; b. 10 Oct. 1922, Manila; ed. Ateneo de Manila Univ., Philippine Law School.
Executive Sec. Inst. of Social Order 46-50; Pres. Fed. of Free Workers (FFW) 50-; Prof. of Labor-Man. Relations, Feati Univ. Graduate School 58-60; Sec.-Gen. Brotherhood of Asian Trade Unionists (BATU), Regional Org. of World Confed. of Labour (WCL) in Asia 63-74, Pres. 74-; mem. Confederal Bd. WCL 69-81, Vice-Pres. for Asia 75-81, Pres. 81-; mem. numerous dels. to int. labour confs. 62-; mem., representing labour, Nat. Manpower and Youth Council, Ministry of Labour and Employment 71-; mem. Bd. of Trustees, World Health Foundation of Philippines 74-; mem. Ramon Magsaysay Memorial Soc. 56-; Vice-Chair. for Labor, Philippine-U.S.S.R. Friendship Soc. 76; Philippine Labor Day Award, Medal of Honor 69; Ozanam Award, Ateneo de Manila Univ. 71.
c/o Federation of Free Workers, 4th Floor, Cuevas Buildings, cnr. Pedro Gil and Taft Avenue, P.O. Box 163, Manila, Philippines.

Tan Chee Khoon, Tan Sri, L.M.S.; Malaysian politician and medical practitioner; b. 4 March 1919; ed. High School, Kajang, Victoria Inst., King Edward VII Coll. of Medicine, Singapore.
Served at Gen. Hospital, Kuala Lumpur 50-51; private practice 52-; Chair. Kuala Lumpur Branch, Labour Party of Malaya 56-68, Selangor Div. 59-61; Nat. Vice-Chair. Labour Party 59-62; Nat. Treas. Labour Party of Malaya 63-68; mem. Dewan Raayat for the constituency of Batu 64, Selangor State Assembly, constituency of Kepong 64-; Sec.-Gen. Parti Gerakan Rakyat 64-71; Pres. Malayan Medical Asscn. 67; mem. Malayan Medical Council 61-; mem. Nik Kamil Cabinet Cttee. to make recommendations on medical legislation in Malaysia; mem. Singapore Medical Council, Vice-Chair. 67, Chair. 71; mem. Council, Univ. of Malaya 59-76, Board of Management, Univ. Hosp. 68-76, Higher Educ. Council 73-76, Tariff Advisory Board 66-68, 68-70; now Chair. PEKEMAS; Hon. L.L.D. (Univ. of Malaya) 71.
Sentosa Clinic, 316 Jalan Tuanku Abdul Rahman, Kuala Lumpur, Malaysia.

Tan Chin Tuan, Tan Sri, P.S.M., C.B.E., J.P.; Singapore banker and company director; b. 21 Nov. 1908, Singapore; ed. Anglo-Chinese School.
Member Singapore Municipal Comm. 39-41; Deputy Pres. Singapore Legislative Council 51-55; mem. Singapore Exec. Council 48-55; Chair. Kinta Kellas Tin Dredging Ltd. 69-74, Oversea-Chinese Banking Corpn. Ltd. 66-, Fraser & Neave Ltd. 57-, Great Eastern Life Insurance Co., Ltd. 69-, Malayan Breweries Ltd. 57-, Wearne Bros. Ltd. 73-, Overseas Assurance Corpn. Ltd. 69-81, Robinson & Co. Ltd. 57-76, Sime Darby Holdings Ltd. 73-75, The Straits Trading Co. Ltd. 65-; Dir. Gopeng Consolidated Ltd. 67-82, Petaling Tin Berhad 67-78, Tronoh Mines Ltd. 67-78, United Malacca Rubber Estates Berhad 69-78, Tanjong Tin Dredging Ltd. 69-75, Int. Bank of Singapore 74-77; Pres. Raffles Hotel Ltd. 69-; Fellow, Inst. of Bankers (London) 65, Australian Inst. of Man. 62.
Oversea-Chinese Banking Corporation Ltd., OCBC Centre, Chulia Street, Singapore; Home: 42 Cairnhill Road, Singapore 0922, Singapore.

Tan Qilong; Chinese politician; b. 1912, Jiangxi.
Director Political Dept., Hunan-Hubei-Jiangxi Border Region 37; Political Commissar, Guerrilla Force 43, People's Liberation Army 44-49; Deputy Sec. CCP Zhejiang 49-52, Sec. 52-55; Political Commissar Zhejiang Mil. District, PLA 52-55; Gov. of Zhejiang 52-55; acting Gov. of Shandong 54; Alt. mem. 8th Cen. Cttee. of CCP 56; Sec. CCP Shandong 55-56, Second Sec. 56-61, First Sec. 61-67; Gov. of Shandong 58-63; First Political Commissar Jinan Mil. Region, PLA 63; Sec. E. China Bureau, CCP

65-67; criticized and removed from office during Cultural Revolution 67; Alt. mem. 9th Cen. Cttee. of CCP 69; Vice-Chair. Fujian Revolutionary Cttee. 70; Sec. CCP Fujian 71; Sec. CCP Zhejiang 72, First Sec. 73-77; Vice-Chair. Zhejiang Revolutionary Cttee. 73, later Chair. until 77; Chair. Qinghai Revolutionary Cttee. 77-79; First Sec. CCP Qinghai 77; First Political Commissar Qinghai Mil. District; First Sec. CCP Sichuan March 80-; mem. 10th Cen. Cttee. CCP 73, 11th Cen. Cttee. 77.
People's Republic of China.

Tan Siew Sin, Tun, S.S.M., J.P.; Malaysian businessman and politician; b. 1916; ed. Malacca and Raffles Coll. Singapore.
Malacca Municipal Commr. 46-49; mem. Fed. Legislative Council 48-74, mem. Standing Cttee. on Finance 49-55; mem. Rubber Producers' Council 51-57, Vice-Chair. 57; mem. Rubber Industry Replanting Board 52-57, Vice-Chair. 57; Pres. Malayan Estate Owners' Asscn. 56, 57; mem. Malacca Chinese Advisory Board 50-55; Hon. Sec. Malacca Branch, Malayan Chinese Asscn. 49-57, Chair. Malacca Branch 57-61; Vice-Pres. Malayan Chinese Asscn. 57-61, Pres. 61-74; Fed. Minister of Commerce and Industry 57-59, Minister of Finance, Malaya 59-63, Malaysia 63-69; Minister with Special Functions 69-70; Minister of Finance 70-74; Pro-Chancellor Malaysia Nat. Univ. 71-; mem. IMF Cttee. of Twenty 73-74; Treas.-Gen. Alliance Party 58-65, Vice-Chair. 65-74; Chair. Commonwealth Parl. Asscn. 70-71, Electoral Review Comm. for Seychelles 75; Chair. United Malacca Rubber Estates Bhd. 74-, Sime Darby Bhd. 76-, Pacific Bank 76-, Malayan Trustees Bhd. 76-, Consolidated Plantations Bhd. 77-, Kempas (Malaya) Bhd. 80-, and dir. of numerous other cos.; Financial Consultant to Govt. of Malaysia 74-; Pres. Science and Tech. Foundation of Malaysia 78-; Pres. Nat. Shooting Asscn. of Malaysia 65-; Vice-Pres. Asian Taekwondo Union 68-; Hon. LL.D. (Univ. of Malaya) 65; several decorations including Seri Setia Mahkota 67; Order of Sikatum (Class Duta) of the Philippines 68; Bintang Mahaputera Kelas Dua of Indonesia 70.
8 Jalan Clifford, Kuala Lumpur 10-02, Malaysia.
Telephone: 926313.

Tan Zhenlin; Chinese politician; b. 1902, Youxien, Hunan; ed. Ruichen Red Army Univ. and Moscow Red Army Univ.
Joined CCP 26; participated in Autumn Harvest Uprising 27; Political Commissar in Red Army during Civil and Sino-Japanese Wars; mem. 7th Cen. Cttee. of CCP 45; Gov. of Zhejiang 49-50; Sec. CCP Zhejiang 49-52; Gov. of Jiangsu 52-55; mem. Sec. of Secr., Deputy Sec.-Gen. 8th Cen. Cttee. of CCP 56; mem. Politburo, CCP 58-67; Vice-Premier, State Council 59; Dir. Office of Agriculture and Forestry, State Council 62-67; Vice-Chair. State Planning Comm. 62-67; criticized and removed from office during Cultural Revolution 68; mem. 10th Cen. Cttee. of CCP 73; a Vice-Chair. Standing Cttee. of Nat. People's Congress (NPC) 75-, Perm. Chair. Presidium of NPC 75-; mem. 11th Cen. Cttee. CCP 77.
People's Republic of China.

Tanabe, Bunichiro; Japanese business executive; b. 5 Sept. 1907, Kanagawa; ed. Tokyo Univ. of Commerce.
Joined Mitsubishi Corpn. 30; Dir. 60-, Man. Dir. 62-69, Senior Man. Dir. 69-71, Exec. Vice-Pres. 71-74, Pres. 74-; Blue Ribbon Medal, Commdr. de l'Ordre de la Côte d'Ivoire.
Mitsubishi Corporation, 6-3, Marunouchi 2-chome, Chiyoda-ku, Tokyo; 7-10, Tokiwa-cho, Chigasaki-shi, Kanagawa-ken, Japan (Home).

Tanaka, Hideho, B.A.; Japanese diplomatist; b. 17 May 1919, Sapporo; ed. Tokyo Univ. of Commerce.
Director of Information Div., Ministry of Foreign Affairs 61; Counsellor, Embassy in Nigeria 63; Consul-Gen., Houston, U.S.A. 64; Dir.-Gen. of Gen. Affairs Dept., Overseas Tech. Co-operation Agency 68; Deputy Dir.-Gen. Middle Eastern and African Affairs Bureau in Ministry 70, Dir.-Gen. 72-74; Amb. to New Zealand 74-77, to Nigeria 77-79, to Philippines 79.
Publs. *Texas Fudoki* (Topography of Texas), *Mekong no Konjaku* (The Mekong River, Past and Present); transl. into Japanese: *Palestine or Israel* (Jon Kimche).
c/o Ministry of Foreign Affairs, 2-1, Kasumigaseki 2-chome, Chiyoda-ku, Tokyo, Japan.

Tanaka, Kakuei; Japanese politician; b. 4 May 1918, Niigata Prefecture; ed. Chuo Technical School.
Member, House of Reps. 47-; Minister of Posts and Telecommunications (Kishi Cabinet) 57; Chair. Policy Board of Liberal-Dem. Party 61-65, Sec.-Gen. Liberal-Dem. Party 65-66, 68-70, Pres. 72-July 76; Minister of Finance 62-65, of Int. Trade and Industry 71-72; Prime Minister 72-74; Chair. Board of Dirs., Echigo Traffic Co. Ltd. 60; charged with corruption July 76, resigned from party leadership July 76; on trial for corruption.
Publ. *Building a New Japan* 72.
12-19-12, Mezirodai, Bunkyo-ku, Tokyo, Japan.
Telephone: 03-943-0111.

Tanaka, Rokusuke; Japanese politician and journalist; b. 23 Jan. 1922, Fukuoka Pref.; ed. Waseda Univ.
Journalist with *Nihon Keizai Shimbun* 49-60, Chief Corresp., London 56-58; mem. House of Reps. 63-; Parl. Vice-Minister for Foreign Affairs 68-70, for Finance 71-72; Chair. Standing Cttee. on Finance 76-78; Minister of State and Chief Cabinet Sec. 78-79; Minister of Int. Trade and Industry 80-82; Chair. Liberal-Democratic Party (LDP) Research Bureau 74-75, Deputy Sec.-Gen. LDP 79-80, Policy Chair.
c/o Liberal-Democratic Party, 7, 2-chome, Hirakawacho, Chiyoda-ku, Tokyo, Japan.

Tanaka, Tatsuo; Japanese politician; b. 1911; *s.* of late Gen. Giichi Tanaka, fmr. Prime Minister.
Worked with Manchuria Railway Co.; elected Gov. of Yamaguchi after World War II; mem. House of Reps. 53-; worked on problems related to small businesses; various posts in admin. of late Eisaku Sato 64-72, incl. Dir.-Gen. of Admin. Affairs in Office of PM, Parl. Vice-Minister of Econ. Planning Agency, Deputy Chief Cabinet Sec.; assoc. of Takeo Fukuda (*q.v.*); Minister of Int. Trade and Industry 76-77; Minister of Educ. 80-81; Chair. LDP Research Council on Petroleum 77-80; Liberal-Democratic Party (LDP).
Publs. *Yearning South America* 54, *A Historical View of the Relationships between Japan and Korea* 63.
Ministry of Education, 3-2-2 Kasumigaseki, Chiyoda-ku, Tokyo, Japan.
Telephone: 03-581-4211.

Tanco, Arturo R., Jr., D.B.A., M.I.L.R.; Philippine government executive; b. 22 Aug. 1933, Manila; ed. De la Salle Coll., Manila, Ateneo de Manila Univ., Union Coll. of New York, Cornell and Harvard Univs.
General Man. and mem. Board, Philippines Investment Management Inc. (PHINMA) 56; Pres. and Gen. Man., Management and Investment Devt. Associates Inc., (MID-A) 64; Vice-Chair. Asian Vegetable Research and Devt. Centre (Taipei), Int. Rice Research Inst. (Manila); Under Sec. for Agriculture and Natural Resources 71-74; Sec. of Agriculture 74-78, Minister 78-; Chair. largest Philippine fertilizer co. 74-; Pres. UN World Food Council 77-81; mem. Bd. Philippine Nat. Bank 81-; Hon. LL.D. (Univ. of the Philippines), Hon. D.Hum. (Central Luzon State Univ.).
Publs. articles in magazines and newspapers including the *Financial Times* (London) and *The Sunday Times Magazine* (London), *Far Eastern Economic Review*.

Department of Agriculture, Diliman, Quezon City; Home: No. 3 Second Street, Villamar Court, Parañaque, Rizal, Philippines.
Telephone: 99-89-46, 99-87-41 (Office).

Tang, Bishop Dominic; Chinese ecclesiastic; b. 1908, Hong Kong.
Apostolic Administrator, Canton 51-57; imprisoned China 57; released 80; apptd. Archbishop of Canton by Pope John Paul II June 81; appointment rejected by Chinese Catholics.

Tang Ke; Chinese politician; b. 1918.
Vice-Minister, Petroleum Industry 65-67; criticized and removed from office during Cultural Revolution 67; Vice-Minister of Fuel and Chemical Industries 71-76; Vice-Minister of Metallurgical Industry 76-77, Minister 77-; mem. 11th Cen. Cttee. and Presidium 11th Nat. Congress CCP 77.
People's Republic of China.

Tange, Kenzo, DR. ENG.; Japanese architect; b. 4 Sept. 1913; ed. Tokyo Univ.
Professor, Univ. of Tokyo 46-74, Emer. 74-; Visiting Prof. M.I.T. 59-60, Harvard Univ. 72; Prof. Honorario Universidad Nacional Federico Villareal, Peru 77; mem. Japanese Architects Asscn.; Hon. mem. American Acad. of Arts and Letters. Akad. der Künste, West Berlin; Hon. Fellow American Inst. of Architects; Royal Gold Medal, Royal Inst. of British Architects 65; A.I.A. Gold Medal, American Inst. of Architects 66, Orden pour le Mérite (Fed. Repub. of Germany) 76, Commdr. Ordre Nat. du Mérite (France) 77; Commendatore nell' Ordine "Al Merito della Repubblica Italiana", 79; Person of Merit in Japanese Cultural Achievement, 79; Hon. Dr. Fine Arts, Univ. of Buffalo, N.Y.; Hon. Dr.-Ing., Technische Hochschule, Stuttgart; Hon. Dr. Arch., Politecnico di Milano, Italy; Hon. Dr. Arts, Harvard Univ.; Hon. D.Sc. (Hong Kong Univ.); Hon. D.Litt. (Sheffield); Hon. Dr. of Univ. of Buenos Aires; Grande Médaille d'Or, French Acad. of Architecture 73.
Buildings include: Peace Memorial Park and Buildings, Hiroshima, Tokyo City Hall, Tokyo, Kurashiki City Hall, Kurashiki, Kagawa Prefectural Govt. Office, Takamatsu, Roman Catholic Cathedral, Tokyo, Nat. Gymnasiums for 1964 Olympic Games, Tokyo, Kuwait Int. Air Terminal, Skopje City Centre Reconstruction Project, Skopje, Yugoslavia, Yamanashi Press and Broadcasting Centre, Yamanashi, Master Plan for Flushing Meadows Sports Park, Master Plan for *Expo* 70, Osaka, Fiera District Centre, Bologna, Italy, Univ. Hosp. and Dormitory, Oran, Algeria, Baltimore Inner Harbour Project; Supervising Designer, Federal Capital of Nigeria.
Publs. include: *Katsura, Tradition and Creation in Japanese Architecture* 60, *Japan in the Future, Formation of Tokaido Megalopolis* (in Japanese) 66, *Man and Architecture* (in Japanese) 70, *Architecture and City* (in Japanese) 70, *Japan in 21st Century* (with Study Team, in Japanese) 71, *Architecture and Urban Design* (in Japanese) 75.
Office: 7-2-21 Akasaka, Minato-ku, Tokyo 107; Home: 1702, 2-3-34 Mita, Minato-ku, Tokyo 108, Japan.
Telephone: 408-7121/4 (Office); 455-2787 (Home).

Tanigaki, Senichi; Japanese politician; b. 18 Jan. 1912, Fukuchiyama, Kyoto Pref.; ed. Law Faculty, Tokyo Univ.
Entered Agric. and Forestry Ministry 36, Chief Sec. to Minister 55, Dir.-Gen. Livestock Industry Bureau 56-58; mem. House of Reps. 60-; Parl. Vice-Minister for Construction 65-66, for Health and Welfare 67-68; Deputy Sec.-Gen. Liberal-Democratic Party 76; Minister of Educ. Nov. 79-June 80; Chair. Standing Cttee. on Local Admin., House of Reps. 72.
c/o Liberal-Democratic Party, 7, 2-chome, Hirakawacho, Chiyoda-ku, Tokyo, Japan.

Taniguchi, Toyosaburo; Japanese textile executive; b. 29 July 1901; ed. Tokyo Univ.
Director Osaka Godo Spinning Co. Ltd. 29-31; Dir. Toyobo Co. Ltd. 31-42, Exec. Vice-Pres. 51-59, Pres. 59-66, Chair. of Board 66-72, Gen. Adviser 72-77, Hon. Adviser 77-; Auditor Japan Exlan Co. Ltd. 56-66; Rep. Dir. Kansai Cttee. for Econ. Devt. 59-60; Pres. Toyobo-Howa Textile Eng. Co. Ltd. 61-; Junior Vice-Pres. IFCATI 64-66, Senior Vice-Pres. 66-68, Pres. 68-70; Chair. Japan Spinners' Asscns. 66-68; Vice-Pres. Japan Tax Asscn. 67-; Vice-Chair. Board of Councillors, Fed. of Econ. Orgs. 68-; Pres. Expo Textile Asscn. 67-71, Japan Textile Color Design Center 68-72; Pres. Japan Textile Fed. 70-71, Supreme Adviser 71-; Blue Ribbon Medal 65, First Class Order of the Sacred Treasure 73.
Toyobo Co. Ltd., 2-8 Dojima Hama 2-chome, Kita-ku, Osaka 530; Home: 283 Gunge Kakiuchi, Mikage-cho, Higashinada-ku, Kobe 658, Japan.
Telephone: 06-348-3251 (Office); 078-851-2327 (Home).

Tanimura, Hiroshi, B.A.; Japanese financial official; b. 26 May 1916, Tokyo; ed. Tokyo Imperial Univ.
Ministry of Finance 38-68, Chief Sec. to Minister 63-65, Dir. of Budget Bureau 65-67, Vice-Minister 67-68; Chair. Fair Trade Comm. 69-72; Pres. Tokyo Stock Exchange 74-.
Publs. two essays 70, 74.
c/o Tokyo Stock Exchange, 1-6 Kabuto-cho, Nihonbashi, Tokyo, Japan.
Telephone: Tokyo 666-0141.

Tapase, Shri Ganpatrao Devaji, B.A., LL.B.; Indian politician; b. 30 Oct. 1908; ed. Forgusson Coll., Law Coll., Pune.
Practised law 38-40; elected to Satara City Municipality 38, Chair. Standing Cttee. and School Board; Pres. Satara City Congress Cttee. 38-46, Sec. 39-46; mem. Maharashtra PCC Exec. 39-46; took part in Quit India Movement, detained 40-41, 42-43; represented Satara in Bombay Legis. Assembly 46-52, Bombay 52-57; Bombay State Govt. Minister (several portfolios) 46-57; mem. All-India Congress Cttee. until 57; mem. Rajya Sabha 62-68; Chair. Railway Service Comm., Bombay 68-71; Gov. Uttar Pradesh 77-80; Gov. Haryana Feb. 80-; Del. to Human Rights Conference, Teheran 68.
Raj Bhavan, Chandigarh 160019, Haryana (Office); Jahangir Building, 71/2 Dr. Patkar Marg, Bombay 400007, India (Home).

Tashiro, Kikuo; Japanese newspaper executive; b. 22 April 1917; ed. Waseda Univ.
Joined *Asahi Shimbun* 40; City Editor 59, Man. Editor 66; Exec. Dir. in charge of Editorial Affairs 69-.
Asahi Shimbun, 3-2, Tsukiji 5-chome, Chuo-ku, Tokyo Japan.

Tata, Jehangir Ratanji Dadabhoy; Indian industrialist; b. 29 July 1904.
Joined Tata Sons Ltd. 26; Chair. Tata Sons Ltd., The Tata Iron and Steel Co. Ltd., The Tata Oil Mills Co. Ltd., Tata Chemicals Ltd., Tata Ltd., London, Tata Inc., New York, Tata A.G., Switzerland, Tata International A.G., Switzerland, Tata Inst. of Fundamental Research, Indian Hotels Co. Ltd., Tata Burroughs Ltd., Sir Dorabji Tata Trust, Lady Tata Memorial Trust, J. N. Tata Endowment, Managing Council, Nat. Centre for the Performing Arts, Homi Bhabha Fellowships Council, Family Planning Foundations, Tata Energy Research Inst., Air India 53-78; Pres. Court of Indian Inst. of Science, Bangalore; Dir. Tata Engineering and Locomotive Co. Ltd., Air India; mem. Atomic Energy Comm.; Hon. Patron mem. Indo-French Chamber of Commerce and Industry; Trustee Gandhi Smarak Nidhi, Kasturba Gandhi Nat. Memorial Trust, Jawaharlal Nehru Memorial Fund; first pilot to qualify in India 29, solo flights to U.K. 30; founded Tata Airlines 32; Hon. Air Vice Marshal, Indian

Air Force; Hon. D.Sc. (Allahabad) 47; Hon. LL.D. (Bombay) 81; Officer, Légion d'honneur 54, Padma Bhushan 55, Knight Commdr., Order of Merit (Fed. Repub. of Germany) 78; Tony Jannus Award 79; numerous citations and awards.
Bombay House, Homi Mody Street, Bombay 400 023; Home: The Cairn, Altamount Road, Bombay 400026, India.

Taufa'ahau Tupou IV, HON. G.C.M.G., HON. G.C.V.O., HON. K.B.E., B.A., LL.B.; H.M. King of Tonga; b. 4 July 1918; eldest son of the late Queen Salote Tupou III of Tonga and the late Hon. Uiliami Tungi, C.B.E., Premier of Tonga; brother of Prince Fatafehi Tu'ipelahake (*q.v.*); ed. Tupou Coll., Tonga, Newington Coll. and Sydney Univ., N.S.W.; married H.R.H. Princess Mata'aho 47; four children, of whom the eldest, H.R.H. Crown Prince Tupoutoa, is heir to the throne.
Premier of Tonga 49-65; King of Tonga 65-; Chancellor of the University of the South Pacific 70-73; Hon. LL.D.; Kt. Commdr., Order of Merit (Fed. Repub. of Germany) 78; numerous citations and awards.
The Palace, Nuku'alofa, Tonga.

Te Kanawa, Dame Kiri, D.B.E.; New Zealand opera singer (soprano); b. 6 March 1944, Gisborne; ed. St. Mary's Coll., Auckland, London Opera Centre.
First appearance at Royal Opera, Covent Garden, London 70, Santa Fe Opera, U.S.A. 71, Lyons Opera, France 72, Metropolitan Opera, New York, U.S.A. 74; appeared at Australian Opera, Royal Opera House, Covent Garden, Paris Opera, Houston Opera, U.S.A., San Francisco 73, Glyndebourne Festival Opera 76, Munich Opera 78, Cologne Opera 79, Vienna State Opera 80, Hamburg Opera 80; debut La Scala, Milan 78, Salzburg Festival 79; sang at various festivals including Helsinki and Edinburgh; sang at wedding of Prince of Wales and Lady Diana Spencer, St. Paul's Cathedral, London 29 July 81; Hon. LL.D. (Dundee) 82; Dr. h.c. (Durham Univ.) 82.
Leading roles in *Boris Godunov* 70-71, *Parsifal* 71, *The Marriage of Figaro* 71, 72, 73, 76, *Otello* 72, 73, 74, *Simone Boccanegra* 73, 74, 75, 76, 77, *Carmen* 73, *Don Giovanni* 74, 75, 76, 81, *Faust* 74, *The Magic Flute* 75, *La Bohème* 75, 76, 77, 79, *Eugene Onegin* 75, 76, *Così fan tutte* 76, 80, 81, *Arabella* 77, 80, 81, *Die Fledermaus* 77, *La Traviata* 78, 80, *Der Rosenkavalier* 81, *Tosca* 82; *Don Giovanni* (film) 79; numerous recordings.
c/o Basil Horsfield, L'Estoril (B), rue Princesse Grace 31, Monte Carlo, Monaco.

Tebbit, Sir Donald Claude, G.C.M.G., M.A.; British diplomatist (retd.); b. 4 May 1920, Cambridge; ed. Perse School, Cambridge, Trinity Hall, Cambridge Univ.
Served with Royal Navy 41-46; Foreign Office 46-48; Second Sec., British Embassy, U.S.A. 48-51; Foreign Office 51-54; First Sec. (Commercial), Federal Repub. of Germany 54-58; Private Sec. to Minister of State, Foreign Office 58-61, Counsellor 62, Sec. Cttee. on Representational Services Overseas 62-64; Counsellor and Head of Chancery, Denmark 64-67; Head of W. and Gen. Africa Dept. Commonwealth Office 67; Asst. Under-Sec. of State, FCO 68; Commercial Minister, U.S.A. 70-71, Minister 71-72; Deputy Under-Sec. of State, FCO 73-76; High Commr. in Australia 76-80; Dir. Rio Tinto Zinc Corpn. 80-; Dir.-Gen. British Property Fed. 80-; Pres. (U.K.) Australia/Britain Trade Asscn. 80-; Chair. Diplomatic Service Appeals Bd. 80-; mem. Appeals Bd., Council of Europe 80-, Council Australia/Britain Soc., Fairbridge Soc., Nuffield Nursing Homes Trust 80-; Pres. Old Persean Soc. 81-.
Priory Cottage, Toft, Cambridge; 35 Buckingham Gate, London, S.W.1, England.

Templeton, Malcolm J. C.; New Zealand diplomatist; b. 12 May 1924, Dunedin; ed. Otago Univ.
Joined Ministry of Foreign Affairs 46; held diplomatic posts in U.S.A. 51-57; Head UN Div., later Defence Div., Ministry of Foreign Affairs 57; Counsellor, London 62, Minister 64-67; Imperial Defence Coll., London 63; Asst. Sec. of Foreign Affairs 67-72; seconded to Prime Minister's Dept. as Deputy Perm. Head 72; Acting Deputy Sec. of Foreign Affairs Jan.-May 73; Perm. Rep. to UN 73-78; rep. to several int. confs., including meeting of Colombo Plan, SEATO Council, Commonwealth Prime Ministers, UN Gen. Assemblies, Third UN Conf. on Law of the Sea, and other UN confs.; Deputy Sec. of Foreign Affairs Aug. 78-.
Ministry of Foreign Affairs, Private Bag, Wellington, New Zealand.

Tenzing Norgay, G.M.; Nepalese climber; b. *c.* 1914 in eastern Nepal, migrated to Bengal 32.
Took part (as porter) in expedition under Shipton 35, Ruttledge 36 and Tilman 38; joined small expedition to Karakoram 50, and French expedition to Nanda Devi 51, when he and one Frenchman climbed the east peak; Sirdar to both Swiss expeditions 52, joining assault parties and reaching about 28,000 feet; Sirdar to British Everest expedition 53, when he and Hillary reached the summit on 29 May; Dir. of Field Training, Himalayan Mountaineering Inst., Darjeeling 54-76, Adviser 76-, also adviser to Himalayan Mountaineering Inst.; Coronation Medal 53, Star of Nepal 53, numerous medals and awards.
Publ. *After Everest* (autobiog). 77.
1 Tonga Road, Ghang-La, Darjeeling, West Bengal, India.
Telephone: 2161.

Teresa, Mother (Agnes Gonxha Bojaxhiu); Albanian-born Roman Catholic missionary; b. 27 Aug. 1910, Skopje (now Yugoslavia).
Joined Sisters of Loretto 28; worked at Loretto insts. in Ireland and India; Principal St. Mary's High School, Calcutta; founded the Missionaries of Charity to help destitute, the Missionary Brothers of Charity, the Int. Co-Workers, the Int. Sick and Suffering Co-Workers; through the Missionaries of Charity has set up over 50 schools, orphanages and houses for the poor in India and other countries; opened Nirmal Hriday (Pure Heart) Home for Dying Destitutes 52; started a leper colony in West Bengal 64; Pope John XXIII Peace Prize 71, Templeton Foundation Prize 73, Nobel Peace Prize 79, Bharat Ratna (Star of India) 80; Hon. D.D. (Cambridge) 79; Hon. Dr. Med. (Catholic Univ. of Sacred Heart, Rome) 81.
Missionaries of Charity, 5A Lower Circular Road, Calcutta, India.
Telephone: 24 7115.

Tetsuo, Yamanaka; Japanese banker; b. 24 May 1921, Nagasaki; ed. Tokyo Imperial Univ.
Chief Rep., Bank of Japan, New York 67; Adviser to Gov. Bank of Japan on Foreign Affairs 70; Man., Management Service and Computer Dept. 70, Personnel Dept. 71, Foreign Dept. 74, Exec. Div. 75; Sr. Adviser to Gov. 79; Deputy Pres., Kyowa Bank 79, Pres. 80-.
The Kyowa Bank Ltd., 1-2 Otemachi 1-chome, Chiyoda-ku, Tokyo; 2-21-6-1301 Himonya, Meguro-ku, Tokyo, Japan (Home).
Telephone: (03) 716-2614 (Home).

Thailand, King of (*see* Bhumibol Adulyadej).

Thajeb, Sjarif, M.D.; Indonesian diplomatist; b. 7 Aug. 1920, Peureula, Aceh; ed. Jakarta Medical Coll., Harvard Medical School, Temple Univ. School of Medicine, Philadelphia, Pa. and Army Staff and Command School, Jakarta.
Former army doctor; Lecturer, Children's Div., Dept. of Medicine, Univ. of Indonesia; Pres. Univ. of Indonesia; Minister of Higher Educ. and Sciences; Vice-Chair. of Parl.; Amb. to U.S.A. 71-74; Minister of Educ. and Culture

74-77; Acting Minister of Foreign Affairs 77-78; mem. Exec. Board of UNESCO Oct. 76-; participant in several int. paediatric confs.; Hon. doctorate, Univ. of Mindanao (Philippines); several medals and decorations.
Publs. papers and articles on various subjects published in numerous paediatric magazines and journals.
c/o Ministry of Foreign Affairs, Jakarta, Indonesia.

Thammasak, Sanya (*see* Dharmasakti, Sanya).

Thanin Kraivichien (*see* Kraivixien, Thanin).

Thanom Kittikachorn (*see* Kittikachorn, Thanom).

Thapa, Surya Bahadur; Nepalese politician; b. 20 March 1928, Muga, East Nepal; ed. Allahabad Univ., India.
House Speaker, Advisory Assembly to King of Nepal 58; mem. Upper House of Parl. 59; Minister of Forests, Agriculture, Commerce and Industry 60; Minister of Finance and Econ. Affairs 62; Vice-Chair. Council of Ministers, Minister of Finance, Econ. Planning, Law and Justice 63; Vice-Chair. Council of Ministers, Minister of Finance, Law and Gen. Admin. 64-65; Chair. Council of Ministers, Minister of Palace Affairs, Gen. Admin. and Panchayat Affairs 65-69; mem. Royal Advisory Cttee. 69-72; arrested 72-75; Minister of Finance 79-80; Prime Minister and Minister of Palace Affairs June 79-; Minister of Defence 80-81, of Foreign Affairs 82-; Sri-Shakti-Patta 63, Gorkha Dakshinbahu I 65, Om Rama Patta 80; several Nepalese and foreign awards.
Naxal, Kathmandu, Nepal.

Thi Binh, Nguyen (*see* Nguyen Thi Binh).

Thieu, Lt.-Gen. Nguyen Van (*see* Nguyen Van Thieu, Lt.-Gen.).

Thin, U Tun, PH.D.; Burmese economist; ed. Rangoon, Michigan and Harvard Univs.
Chairman Econ. Dept., Univ. of Rangoon; Dir. Cen. Statistics and Econs. Dept., Ministry of Planning, Burma; Alt. Exec. Dir. IMF for Burma, Ceylon, Japan and Thailand; Asst. Dir. IMF Asian Dept. 59-66, Deputy Dir. 66-72, Dir. 72-.
Publ. *Theory of Markets* 70.
Asian Department, International Monetary Fund, 700 19th Street, N.W., Washington, D.C. 20431, U.S.A.
Telephone: 202-477-2911.

Tho, Le Duc (*see* Le Duc Tho).

Thomson, David Spence, M.C., E.D.; New Zealand dairy farmer and politician; b. 14 Nov. 1915; ed. Stratford Primary and High School.
Territorial Army 31-59, served Middle East 39-45, Prisoner of war 42, Brigadier (Reserve of Officers); Chair. Fed. Farmers Sub-provincial Exec. 59-63; M.P. for Stratford 63-; Minister of Defence, Minister of Tourism and Publicity 66-69; Minister of Defence, Minister in charge of War Pensions and Rehabilitation 67-72, also of Police 69-72; Assoc. Minister in charge of Labour and Immigration 71-72, Minister Feb.-Dec. 72; Minister of Justice 75-78, Minister of State, Minister of State Services and Leader of the House of Reps. Nov. 78-, Minister of Defence 80-81, Minister in charge of War Pensions and Rehabilitation Aug. 80-; National Party..
Parliament Buildings, Wellington; Home: Bird Road, Stratford, New Zealand.

Thomson, Sir John Adam, K.C.M.G., M.A.; British diplomatist; b. 27 April 1927, Bieldside; ed. Philip's Exeter Acad., U.S.A., Univ. of Aberdeen, Trinity Coll., Cambridge Univ.
Joined Foreign Service 50; Third Sec. Jeddah 51-54, Damascus 54-55; Foreign Office, London 55-60, Private Sec. to Perm. Under-Sec. 58-60; First Sec. Washington, D.C. 60-64; Foreign Office, London 64-71, Acting Head of Planning Staff 67-68, seconded to Cabinet Office as Chief of Assessments Staff 68-71; Minister and Deputy Perm. Rep. to N. Atlantic Council 72-73; Head of U.K. Del. to M.B.F.R. Exploratory Talks, Vienna 73; Asst. Under-Sec. Foreign Office 73-76; High Commr. in India 77-82; Perm. Rep. of U.K. to UN and U.K. Rep. on Security Council 82-.
Publ. *Crusader Castles* (with R. Fedden).
Permanent Mission of the United Kingdom to the United Nations, 845 Third Avenue, New York, N.Y. 10022, U.S.A.; Lochpatrick Mill, Kirkpatrick Durham, Castle Douglas, Kirkcudbrightshire, Scotland (Home).
Telephone: (212) 752-8586.

Thomson, Peter William, C.B.E.; Australian professional golfer (retd.); b. 23 Aug. 1929, Melbourne.
Winner British Open Championship 54, 55, 56, 58 and 65, Australian Open 51, 67 and 72; winner New Zealand Open (9 times) and Hong Kong, Philippines, India, Italy, Spain and Germany Opens and many professional events; Pres. Professional Golfers' Asscn. of Australia; Chair. James McGrath Foundation, Vic.; mem. Australia-Japan Foundation.
Malvern, Victoria 3141, Australia.

Thondaman, Savumiamoorthy; Sri Lankan (Tamil) agriculturist; b. 30 Aug. 1913; ed. St. Andrew's Coll., Gampola.
Member Ceylon Parl. 47-51, 60-70; mem. ILO Asian Advisory Cttee.; Substitute Deputy mem. Governing Body of ILO; mem. Exec. Board ICFTU; Vice-Pres. ICFTU-ARO; Pres. Ceylon Worker's Congress; Leader of movement for political and econ. rights of Tamil community in Sri Lanka.
Wavendon Group, Tawalantenne Estate, Ramboda, Sri Lanka.

Tikaram, Sir Moti, K.B.E., LL.B.; Fijian judge and public official; b. 18 March, 1925; ed. Marist Brothers' High School, Suva and Victoria Univ., Wellington, New Zealand.
Law practice, Fiji 54; Stipendiary Magistrate 60-68; Puisne Judge 68-72; acting Chief Justice 71; Ombudsman 72-.
45 Domain Road, Suva, Fiji.

Tinsulanond, Gen. Prem.; Thai army officer and politician; b. 26 Aug. 1926, Songkhla Province; ed. Suan Kularb High School, Bangkok and Chulachomklao Royal Mil. Acad.
Started mil. career as Sub-lieut. 41; attended company and battalion commdr. courses, U.S. Army Calvary School, Fort Knox, Kentucky; Commdr. Cavalry H.Q. 68; Royal ADC 69 and 75; Deputy C.-in-C. then C.-in-C. 2nd Army 73-77; Asst. Army C.-in-C. 77, C.-in-C. Sept. 78-; Deputy Minister of the Interior Nov. 77-May 79; Prime Minister and Minister of Defence March 80-; Chair. Petroleum Authority of Thailand 81-; awarded Ramathipbodi Order by King of Thailand.
Office of the Prime Minister, Government House, Luke Luang Road, Bangkok 2, Thailand.

Tirikatene-Sullivan, Tini Whetu Marama, B.A.; New Zealand politician; b. 1932; ed. Rangiora High School, Victoria Univ. of Wellington, Nat. Univ. of Australia.
Secretary, Royal Tour Staff for visit of H.M. Queen Elizabeth II and H.R.H. The Duke of Edinburgh 53-54; fmr. Social Worker, Depts. of Maori Affairs, Social Security and Child Welfare; mem. for Southern Maori Electorate, N.Z. House of Reps. 67-; Minister of Tourism 72-75, Minister for the Environment 74-75; Dipl. Social Sciences.
Parliament Buildings, Wellington; Home: Main North Road, Kaiapoi, North Canterbury, New Zealand.

Tizard, Robert James, M.A.; New Zealand teacher and politician; b. 7 June 1924; ed. Auckland Grammar School, Auckland Univ.

Served in R.N.Z.A.F., Canada, U.K. 42-46; Junior Lecturer in History, Auckland Univ. 49-53, teaching posts 55-57, 61-62; mem. Parl. 57-60, 63-; Minister of Health and State Services 72-74, in charge of State Advances Corpn. 72-73; Deputy Prime Minister, Minister of Finance, Minister in Charge of Friendly Socs. 74-75; Chair. Board of Govs. Asian Devt. Bank 74-75; Deputy Leader of the Opposition 75-80.
Parliament Buildings, Wellington; Flat 3, 69 Alfred Street, Onehunga, Auckland 6, New Zealand (Home).

To Huu; Vietnamese poet and politician; b. 1920, Central Viet-Nam.
Poet and leading intellectual; in charge of propaganda and ideological training in Lao Dong Party (now Communist Party of Viet-Nam); alt. mem. Politburo, Communist Party of Viet-Nam Dec. 76-, also mem. Secr.; Vice-Premier, Council of Ministers 80-; mem. Nat. Defence Council 81-.
Central Committee of the Communist Party of Viet-Nam, No. 1-C, rue Hoang Van Thu, Hanoi, Viet-Nam.

Toh Chin Chye, PH.D.; Singapore physiologist and politician; b. 10 Dec. 1921; ed. Raffles Coll., Singapore, Univ. Coll., London Univ., and National Inst. for Medical Research, London.
Founder mem. People's Action Party, Chair. 54-81; Reader in Physiology, Univ. of Singapore 58-64; mem. Parl. 59-; Deputy Prime Minister 59-68; Minister for Science and Technology 68-75, for Health 75-80; Chair., Board of Govs., Singapore Polytechnic 59-75; Vice-Chancellor, Univ. of Singapore 68-75; Chair. Board of Regional Inst. for Higher Educ. and Devt. 70-75; Hon. LL.D. (Singapore) 76.
23 Greenview Crescent, Singapore 11, Singapore (Home).

Toma, Maiava Iulai; Western Samoan diplomatist; b. 5 July 1940; ed. Marist Brothers School, Apia, Scots Coll. Wellington, N.Z., Victoria Univ., Wellington.
Joined W. Samoan Public Service, Prime Minister's Dept. 64; Senior Commr. to S. Pacific Comm. 74-77; Sec. to Govt. of W. Samoa 75-77; Perm. Rep. to UN and concurrently Amb. to U.S.A. and High Commr. in Canada 77-.
Permanent Mission of Western Samoa to the United Nations, 820 Second Avenue, New York, N.Y. 10017; 300 East 56th Street, New York, N.Y. 10022, U.S.A.

Tomonaga, Sin-itiro, D.SC.; Japanese physicist; b. 31 March 1906; ed. Third High School, Kyoto, and Kyoto Imperial Univ.
Research student, Inst. of Physical and Chemical Research 32-39; studies, Univ. of Leipzig 37-39; Asst., Inst. of Physical and Chemical Research 39-40; Lecturer, Tokyo Bunrika Univ. (absorbed into Tokyo Univ. of Educ. 49) 40, Prof. of Physics 41-69; Dir. of Inst. of Optical Research, Kyoiku Univ. (Tokyo Univ. of Educ.) 63-69; Pres. Tokyo Univ. of Educ. 56-62; Pres. Science Council of Japan 63-69; Japan Academy Prize 48, Order of Culture 52, Lomonosov Medal (U.S.S.R.) 64; Nobel Prize for Physics 65.
Publs. *On the photo-electric production of positive and negative electrons* 34, *Innere Reibung und Wärmeleitfähigkeit der Kernmaterie* 38, *On a Relativistically Invariant Formulation of the Quantum Theory of Wave Fields* 46, *On the Effect of the Field Reactions on the Interaction of Mesotrons and Nuclear Particles I, II, III, IV* 46-47, *A Self-Consistent Subtraction Method in Quantum Field Theory I, II* 48, *Remarks on Bloch's Method of Sound Waves to Many-Fermion Problems* 50.
3-17-12, Kyonan-cho, Musashino City, Tokyo, Japan.
Telephone: 0422-32-2410.

Tonga, H.M. King of (*see* Taufa'ahau Tupou IV).

Tonkin, Derek, M.A.; British diplomatist; b. 30 Dec. 1929; ed. High Pavement Grammar School, Nottingham and Oxford Univ.
Forces service 48-49; Foreign Office 52; Warsaw 55; Second Sec. (Inf.) Bangkok 57, Phnom-Penh 61; Foreign Office 63; First Sec. 64; First Sec. and Head of Chancery, Warsaw 66; First Sec. and later Head of Chancery, Wellington 68; Foreign and Commonwealth Office 72; Deputy Head of Permanent Under-Secretary's Dept. 73; Counsellor (Commercial), East Berlin 76-80; Amb. to Viet-Nam 80-.
British Embassy, 16 Pho Ly Thuong Kiet, Hanoi, Viet-Nam; Heathfields, Berry Lane, Worplesdon, Surrey England.
Telephone: 52349, 52510 (Embassy); Worplesdon 232955.

Tope, Trimbak Krishna, M.A., LL.D.; Indian lawyer and teacher; b. 28 Feb. 1914, Yeola, Nasik District; ed. Bombay Univ.
Professor of Sanskrit, Ramnarain Ruia Coll. 39-47; Advocate, Bombay High Court 46; Prof. of Law, Govt. Law Coll. 47, Principal and Perry Prof. of Jurisprudence 58-; Vice-Chancellor, Univ. of Bombay 71-78; Hon. Prof. K.C. Law Coll., Bombay; Pres. Maharashtra Samajik Parishad; Hon. LL.D. (Andhra Univ.) 77.
Publs. *Why Hindu Code?, Indian Constitution, A Modern Sage.*
c/o K.C. Law College, Bombay 20, India.
Telephone: 291750 (Home).

Toshima, Kenkichi, B.S.; Japanese metallurgical engineer and business executive; b. 30 June 1902; ed. Kyoto Univ.
Kobe Steel Ltd., Kobe 32-, Dir. 49-53, Man. Dir. 53-56, Senior Man. Dir. 56-58, Pres. 58-72, Chair. 72-74, Adviser 74-; Blue Ribbon Medal, Kien Itto Zuihosho, First Class Order of the Sacred Treasure; Chevalier, Légion d'honneur.
Office: Kobe Steel Ltd., 3-18, 1-chome, Wakinohama-cho, Fukiai-ku, Kobe; Home: 15-16 Rokurokuso-cho, Ashiya City, Hyogo Prefecture, Japan.
Telephone: Kobe 251-1551 (Office); Ashiya 22-4561 (Home).

Toyoda, Eiji; Japanese motor executive; b. 12 Sept. 1913, Kinjo, Nishi Kasugai-gun, Aichi-ken; ed. Tokyo Univ.
President, Toyota Motor Co. Ltd. 67-; Dir. Aishin Seiki Co. Ltd. 65-, Toyota Automatic Loom Works Ltd. 69, Aichi Steel Works Ltd. 61-, Toyota Machine Works Co. Ltd. 64-, Toyota Central Research and Devt. Laboratories Inc. 60, Toyota Motor Sales Co. Ltd. 71-, Towa Real Estate Co. Ltd. 53-, Toyota Motor Sales U.S.A. Inc. 57-, Chiyoda Fire and Marine Insurance Co. Ltd. 73-; Chair. Japan Automobile Mfrs. Asscn. 72-, Japan Motor Industrial Fed. 72-; Exec. Dir. Japan Fed. of Employers' Asscns. 67, Fed. of Econ. Orgs. 67; Blue Ribbon Medal 71.
Office: Toyota Motor Co. Ltd., 1 Toyota-cho, Toyota-shi, Aichi-ken; Home: 12 Yagen, Takemachi, Toyota-shi, Aichi-ken, Japan.
Telephone: 0565-28-2121 (Office); 0565-52-7535 (Home).

Tran Nam Trung (*see* Tran Van Tra, Gen.).

Tran Thien Khiem, Gen.; Vietnamese army officer and politician; b. 15 Dec. 1925.
Army Service 47-75; held off attempted coup against President Diem 60, took part in coup against him 63; with Gen. Nguyen Khan led coup removing Gen. Duong Van Minh 64; Defence Minister and C.-in-C. 64; Amb. to U.S. Oct. 64-Oct. 65, to Taiwan Oct. 65-May 68; Minister of the Interior 68-73, Deputy Prime Minister March-Aug. 69, Prime Minister 69-75, Minister of Defence 72-75; flew to Taiwan April 75.

Tran Van Huong; Vietnamese politician; b. 1 Dec. 1903.
Former school-teacher; participated in Viet-Minh resistance against French; Mayor of Saigon 54; political imprisonment 60, Prime Minister, Repub. of Viet-Nam 64-65, 68-69; Vice-Pres. 71-75, Pres. 21-28 April 75; Hon. Corporal Repub. of Viet-Nam Armed Forces 74.

Tran Van Tra, Gen. (also known as Tu Chi and Tran Nam Trung); Vietnamese army officer and politician; b. 1918, Quang Ngai Province, S. Viet-Nam.
Alternate mem. Cen. Cttee. Lao Dong party; Deputy Chief of Staff, N. Vietnamese Army; Chair. Mil. Affairs Cttee., Cen. Office of S. Viet-Nam (COSVN) 64-76; Minister of Defence, Provisional Revolutionary Govt. of S. Viet-Nam 69-76 (in Saigon 75-76); rose to rank of General May 75; head of mil. cttee. controlling Saigon and district May 75-Jan. 76; Chair. Inspectorate, Council of Ministers, Socialist Repub. of Viet-Nam 76-81.
Council of Ministers, Hanoi, Viet-Nam.

Trengganu, H.H. the Sultan of; Tuanku Ismail Nasiruddin Shah ibni Al-Marhum Sultan Zainal Abidin, D.K., D.K.(M), D.M.N., S.P.M.T., D.K. (Kelantan), D.K. (Selangor), K.C.M.G.; Ruler of Trengganu, Malaysia; b. 24 Jan. 1907.
Joined Trengganu Civil Service 29, later served as High Court Registrar and Chief Magistrate; acceded to throne of Trengganu 45, installed 49; Timbalan Yang Di-Pertuan Agong (Deputy Head of State) of Malaya, later Malaysia 60-66, Yang Di-Pertuan Agong (Head of State) 66-70.
Istana Badariah, Kuala Trengganu, Trengganu, West Malaysia.

Tripathi, Kamalapati; Indian politician.
Member, Legislative Assembly of Uttar Pradesh 36-; Minister for Irrigation and Information and later for Home Affairs, Educ. and Information, U.P.; Deputy Chief Minister of Uttar Pradesh 69-71, Chief Minister 71-73; Minister of Shipping and Transport 73-75, of Railways Feb. 75-March 77; mem. Rajya Sabha 73-, re-elected March 77; Minister of Railways Jan.-Nov. 80 (resgnd.).
9 Akbar Road, New Delhi 100011, India.

Tripp, (John) Peter, C.M.G.; British diplomatist (retd.); b. 27 March 1921; ed. Sutton Valence School, Institut de Touraine.
Royal Marines 41-46; Sudan Political Service 46-54; with Foreign Service (later Diplomatic Service) 54-81; Amb. to Libya 70-74; High Commr. in Singapore 74-78; Amb. to Thailand 78-81; political adviser to Inchcape Group and Chair. Private Investment Co. Asia (U.K.) Ltd.; Dir. Gray Mackenzie and Co. Ltd.
c/o PICA (U.K.) Ltd., 6 Derby Street, London, W.1, England.

Trowbridge, Rear-Admiral Sir Richard (John), K.C.V.O.; British naval officer and administrator; b. 21 Jan. 1920; ed. Andover Grammar School.
Joined Royal Navy as boy seaman 35; commissioned as Sub-Lieut. Dec. 40; mentioned in despatches Aug. 45; Commdr. 53; Commdr. Destroyer *Carysfort* 56-58; Exec. Officer HMS *Bermuda* 58-59, HMS *Excellent* 59-60; Captain 60; Commdr. Fishery Protection Squadron 62-64; completed course Imperial Defence College 66; Commdr. HMS *Hampshire* 67-69; Rear-Admiral 70; Extra Equerry to the Queen 70-; Flag Officer Royal Yachts 70-75; Younger Brother of Trinity House 72; Governor of Western Australia Nov. 80-.
Old Idsworth Garden, Finchdean, Portsmouth; Government House, Perth, W.A., Australia.

Truong Chinh (fmrly. known as Dang Xuan Khu); Vietnamese politician.
Secretary-General, Communist Party of Indo-China, later of Lao Dong party 41-56; Chair. Standing Cttee. of Nat. Assembly of Democratic Repub. of Viet-Nam 60-76; Chair. Standing Cttee. of Nat. Assembly of Socialist Repub. of Viet-Nam 76-81; Pres. and Chair. Council of State 81-; Chair. Nat. Defence Council; mem. Politburo of Communist Party of Viet-Nam; Chair. Cttee. for drafting Constitution of Socialist Repub. of Viet-Nam 75-76; Order of Lenin 82.
Quoc Hoi, Hanoi, Viet-Nam.

Tsedenbal, Marshal Yumjaagiyn; Mongolian politician; b. 17 Sept. 1916; ed. Inst. of Finance and Econs. in U.S.S.R.
Teacher at Ulan Bator Financial Coll.; Deputy Minister, then Minister of Finance 39-40; Deputy C.-in-C. Mongolian People's Army, Dir. of Political Directorate 41-45; Chair. State Planning Comm. 45-48; Deputy Chair. Council of Ministers 48-52, Chair. 52-74; Deputy to People's Great Hural (Assembly) 40-, Chair. of Presidium of People's Great Hural (Head of State) June 74-; Chair. Defence Council Aug. 79-; mem. Cen. Cttee. of Mongolian People's Revolutionary Party (MPRP) 40-, mem. Presidium and Gen. Sec. of Cen. Cttee. 40-54, First Sec. of Cen. Cttee. 58-81, Gen. Sec. 81-; Hon. mem. Acad. of Sciences; Order of Sühbaatar, Hero of the Mongolian People's Repub., Order of Lenin.
Government Palace, Ulan Bator, Mongolia.

Tsevegmid, Dondogiyn; Mongolian biologist and politician; b. 26 March 1915; ed. Teacher Training School, Ulan Bator and Moscow Univ.
Teacher 30-45; Rector, Mongolian State Univ., Chair. Cttee. of Sciences 59-60; Deputy Minister of Foreign Affairs 60-62; Amb. to China 62-67; Rector, Mongolian State Univ. 67-72; Deputy to People's Great Hural (Assembly), Chair. 69-72; Deputy Chair. Councilof Ministers 72-; Minister of Culture 80-; Chair. Exec. Cttee. of Parl. Group; Chair. Atomic Energy Comm.; Chair. Cttee. for Higher and Special Secondary, Technical-Vocational Educ. 73-; cand. mem. Mongolian People's Revolutionary Party Cen. Cttee. 58-66, mem. Cen. Cttee. 66-; Deputy to People's Great Hural (Assembly); corresp. mem. Acad. of Sciences; Dr. h.c. (Lomonosov Univ., Moscow, Humboldt Univ., Berlin).
Publs. *The Ecological and Morphological Analysis of the Duplicidentate* 50, *Fauna of the Transaltai* 63, *Selected Works* 46, 56, 74.
Government Palace, Ulan Bator, Mongolia.

Tsiang Yien-si, PH.D.; Chinese politician; b. 27 Feb. 1915, Zhejiang; ed. Univ. of Minnesota, U.S.A.
Instructor, Univ. of Minnesota 42-45; Advisor Chinese Del. to FAO 46; Prof. Nanjing Univ. 47; Chief, Dept. of Miscellaneous and Special Crops, Nat. Agric. Research Bureau 48; Exec. Officer Joint Comm. on Rural Reconstruction 48-52, Sec.-Gen. 52-61, Commr. 61-; Vice-Chair. Cttee. for Scientific Devt., Nat. Science Council 66-; Sec.-Gen. Exec. Yuan 67-72; Minister of Educ. 72-77, of Foreign Affairs 78-80; mem. Council Acad. Sinica 63-, Nat. Science Devt. Comm. 63-, Chair. 66-; mem. Atomic Energy Council 66-; Pres. Agric. Asscn. of China 61-63; Eisenhower Fellow, Univ. of Minnesota 62.
c/o Ministry of Foreign Affairs, Taipei; 6-A, Lane 35, Jenai Road, Section 4, Taepei 106, Taiwan (Home).

Tu Chi (*see* Tran Van Tra, Gen.).

Tuchinda, Prakorb, M.D.; Thai government official; b. 3 Jan. 1922, Nakhonpathom; ed. Univ. of Medical Sciences, Bangkok, New York State Laboratory, Nat. Inst. of Health, Tokyo and Lister Inst. of Preventive Medicine, U.K.
Medical Officer, Dept. of Medical Sciences, Ministry of Public Health 44-52; Chief, Div. of Medical Research, Dept. of Medical Sciences 53-63, Dir. Virus Research Inst. 63-66, Deputy Dir.-Gen., Dept. of Medical Sciences 67-69, Dir.-Gen. 70-73; Dir.-Gen. Dept. of Medical Services, Ministry of Public Health 74-75, Under-Sec. of State for Public Health 75-; Pres. 32nd Assembly, WHO; Hon. D.Sc.
Publs. About 25 scientific papers in medical and scientific journals.
Ministry of Public Health, Devavesm Palace, Samsen

Road, Bangkok 2 (Office); 66/1 Soi Lang Suan, Ploenchitr Road, Bangkok, Thailand (Home).
Telephone: 2819473 (Office); 2518944 (Home).

Tu'ipelehake, H.R.H. Prince Fatafehi, HON. K.B.E.; Tongan politician; b. 7 Jan. 1922, second son of the late Queen Salote Tupou III of Tonga and the late Hon. Uiliami Tungi, C.B.E., Premier of Tonga; brother of H.M. King Taufa'ahau Tupou IV (*q.v.*); ed. Newington Coll., Sydney, N.S.W., and Gatton Agricultural Coll., Queensland; married H.R.H. Princess Melenaite Tupoumoheofo 47; six children.
Governor of Vava'u 49, later held other ministerial posts as Gov. of Ha'apai and Minister of Lands; Prime Minister of Tonga 65-, also Minister for Agric.; fmr. Minister for Foreign Affairs, Tourism, Telegraphs and Telephones; Chair. Tonga Commodities Bd.; 'Uluafi Medal 82.
Office of the Prime Minister, Nuku'alofa, Tonga.

Tuita, Baron Siosaia Aleamotu'a Laufilitonga, C.B.E.; Tongan civil servant and government official; b. 29 Aug. 1920, Lapaha, Tongatapu; ed. Tupou Coll., Wesley Coll., Auckland, New Zealand, Oxford, England.
Lieutenant Officer, Tonga Defence Service 42-43; Court Interpreter and Registrar, Supreme Court 50; Asst. Sec., Prime Minister's Office 54; Registrar of Supreme Court 54; Acting Gov. of Vava'u 56, Gov. 57-65; Acting Minister of Lands 62; Acting Minister of Police 64-65; Chair. Niuafo'ou evacuation 65; Minister of Lands and Survey and Minister of Health 65-74; assumed title of Tuita 72; Deputy Prime Minister and Minister of Lands 74-; Acting Prime Minister 81; mem. H.M.'s Cabinet and Privy Council; M.P.; Chair. Town Planning Cttee.; Baron of 'Utungake 80.
Office of the Deputy Prime Minister, Nuku'alofa; Mahinafekite, Nuku'alofa, Tonga (Home).
Telephone: 22-451.

Tupou IV, Taufa'ahau (*see* Taufa'ahau Tupou IV).

U

Ulanhu, Gen.; Chinese (Mongolian) politician; b. 1906, Suiyuan; ed. Far Eastern Univ., Moscow.
Joined CCP 25; Alt. mem. 7th Cen. Cttee. of CCP 45; Chair. Nei Monggol People's Govt. 47-67; Commdr., Political Commissar Nei Monggol Mil. Region, People's Liberation Army 47-67; Vice-Premier, State Council 54-67; Chair. Nationalities Comm. 54-67; First Sec. CCP Nei Monggol 54-67; Gen. 55; Alt. mem. Politburo, CCP 56-67; criticized and removed from office during Cultural Revolution 67; mem. 10th Cen. Cttee. of CCP 73, 11th Cen. Cttee. 77, mem. Politburo 77-; Vice-Chair. Standing Cttee., Nat. People's Congress 78-; Dir. United Front Work Dept., Cen. Cttee. CCP 78-.
People's Republic of China.

Umeda, Zenji; Japanese shipbuilder; b. 13 Sept. 1913, Wakayama; ed. Kyoto Univ.
Joined Kawasaki Dockyard Co. Ltd. (now Kawasaki Heavy Industries) 39, Dir. 64, Man. Dir. 69, Sr. Man. Dir. 75, Exec. Vice-Pres. and Dir. 76, Pres. and Dir. 77-81, Chair. June 81-; Vice-Pres. Shipbuilders' Asscn. of Japan 78; Pres. Japan Ship Exporters' Asscn. 79; Blue Ribbon Medal 71; Award of Minister of Int. Trade and Industry 74.
3-25-8 Kami Meguro, Meguro-ku, Tokyo, Japan.
Telephone: (03) 713 0220.

Unger, Leonard, A.B.; American diplomatist; b. 17 Dec. 1917, San Diego, Calif.; ed. Harvard Univ.
National Resources Planning Board 39-41; Dept. of State 41-, served Trieste, Naples; Officer in Charge of Politico-Military Affairs, European Regional Affairs Div., State Dept. 53-57; Deputy Chief of Mission, American Embassy, Bangkok, Thailand 58-62; Amb. to Laos 62-64; Deputy Asst. Sec. of State for Far Eastern Affairs 65-67; Amb. to Thailand 67-74, to Taiwan 74-79; Professor of Diplomacy, Fletcher School of Law and Diplomacy, Medford, Massachusetts 79-; Distinguished Honor Award, Dept. of State; Order of the White Elephant, Thailand.
Publs. articles in *Foreign Policy* magazine Autumn 79, *Harvard Political Review* Spring 80, *Geographical Review*.
12701 Circle Drive, Rockville, Md. 20850, U.S.A. (Home).

Uno, Osamu, B.L.; Japanese business executive; b. 29 May 1917, Kyoto; ed. Tokyo Univ.
Director Toyobo Co. Ltd. 71, Man. Dir. 74-76, Sr. Man. Dir. 76-77, Deputy Pres. 77-78, Pres. 78-; Vice-Pres. Japan Chemical Fibres Asscn. 80-81, Pres. 81-82; Vice-Pres. Japan Spinners' Asscn. 82-; Blue Ribbon Medal 82.
2-8 Dojima Hama 2-chome, Kita-ku, Osaka 530 (Office); 1-46 Showa-cho, Hamadera Sakai 592, Japan (Home).
Telephone: (06) 348-3252 (Office).

Uno, Sosuke; Japanese politician; b. 1922.
Elected six times to House of Reps.; Parl. Vice-Minister of Int. Trade and Industry; Deputy Sec.-Gen. of Liberal Democratic Party (LDP); Minister of State, Dir.-Gen. of Defence Agency Nov.-Dec. 74; Chair. Diet Policy Cttee. of LDP 74-76; assoc. of Yasuhiro Nakasone (*q.v.*); Minister of State, Dir.-Gen. of Science and Technology Agency, Chair. Atomic Energy Comm. 76-77; Minister of State, Dir.-Gen. of Admin. Man. Agency 79-80.
c/o Administrative Management Agency, Tokyo, Japan.

Upadhyay, Shailendra Kumar; Nepalese diplomatist; b. 13 Sept. 1929; ed. Banaras Hindu Univ.
Founder member, Communist Party of Nepal 50, mem. Cen. Cttee. and Political Bureau 50-56; Founder, Progressive Communist Party of Nepal 58; Minister for Forest and Food and Agriculture 62-64; Minister in charge of Panchayat 64-65; mem. Rashtriya Panchayat 62-71; Vice-Chair. Nat. Planning Comm. 68-70; Minister for Home and Panchayat and Minister for Land Reforms and Information 70-71; Perm. Rep. to UN 72-78; also Amb. to Argentina, Chile, Peru and Brazil 77-78; leader of del. to meeting of Bd. of Govs. of IBRD 65, UN Law of the Sea Conf. (1st-7th sessions), and other UN confs.; f. Common Heritage Int. 78; Pres. Nepal Research Foundation 81.
5/108 Jawala Khel, Lalitpur, Kathmandu, Nepal.
Telephone: 21587.

Upadit Pachariyangkun, (*see* Pachariyangkun, Upadit).

Uquaili, Nabi Baksh Mohammed Sidiq, F.C.A.; Pakistani accountant and banker; b. 11 Aug. 1913, Karachi.
Experience of banking and finance over 35 years; Minister of Finance 66-69; has represented Pakistan on many int. confs. on banking and finance; now Chair. Board of Dirs., Pakistan Industrial Credit and Investment Corpn. Ltd., also of various financial and industrial cos. in Pakistan 77-80; awards from Pakistan and Fed. Repub. of Germany.
22F Dawood Colony, Stadium Road, Karachi 5, Pakistan.
Telephone: 225626 (Office); 411013 (Home).

Urabe, Shizutaro; Japanese architect; b. 31 March 1909; ed. Kyoto Univ.
Kurashiki Rayon Co. Ltd. 34-64; Lecturer (part-time) in Architecture, Osaka Univ. Technical Course 54-55; Lecturer (part-time) in Architecture, Kyoto Univ. Technical Course 62-66; Pres. K.K., S. Urabe & Assoc. Architects 62-; Prize of *Mainichi Shuppan Bunka Sho* (publication) 61; Osaka Prefecture Architectural Contest Prize 62; *Annual of Architecture* Prize 63; Architectural Inst. of Japan Prize 64; Osaka Prefecture Order of Merit 65.
Buildings include: Ohara Museum (Annex) 61, Suita Service Area 63 and other offices of Japan Road Corpn. 65, Kurashiki Int. Hotel 63, Aizenbashi Hospital and Nursery School, etc. 65, Asahi Broadcasting Co. Ltd. (consultant) 66, Tokyo Zokei Univ. 66, Tokyo Women's Christian Coll., Research Inst. 67.

Offices: S. Urabe and Assoc. Architects, 7th Floor, New Hankyu Building, 8, Umeda, Kita-ku, Osaka; Z-4 Muromachi Nihonbashi, Chuo-ku, Tokyo; Home: 1-181, Kotoen, Nishinomiya Hyogo, Japan.

Uren, Thomas; Australian politician; b. 28 May 1921, Balmain, Sydney.
Army service 39-45; mem. Parl. for Reid 58-; mem. Fed. Parl. Labor Party Exec. 69-72, Deputy Leader Jan. 76-Dec. 77; First Minister of Urban and Regional Devt. 72-75; Acting Minister for Services and Property June-July 73; House of Reps. Standing Cttee. on Printing 62-66, on Standing Orders 76-77; Opposition Spokesman on Urban and Regional Affairs, Decentralization, Local govt., Housing and Construction; Nat. Estate Deputy Leader 54th Conf., IPU, Ottawa 65 and 56th Conf., Canberra 66; del. to Australian Area Conf. of Commonwealth Parl. Asscn., Darwin 68, to Australian Parl. Mission to Europe 68, to Commonwealth Parl. Asscn. Conf., Canberra 70; Labor Party.
Parliament House, Canberra, A.C.T. 2600, Australia.

Ushiba, Nobuhiko, B.L.; Japanese diplomatist; b. 16 Nov. 1909, Kobe; ed. Tokyo Imperial Univ.
Chief, 1st Section, 4th Div., Cen. Liaison Office 45-49; Dir. Secr. Foreign Exchange Cen. Cttee., Office of the Prime Minister 49-51; Dir.-Gen. Int. Trade Bureau, Ministry of Int. Trade and Industry 51-54; Councillor of Embassy, Burma 54-56; Councillor, Planning Council, Ministry of Foreign Affairs 56-57, Dir.-Gen. Econ. Affairs Bureau 57-61; Amb. to Canada 61-64; Deputy Vice-Minister of Foreign Affairs 64-67, Vice-Minister 67-70; Amb. to U.S.A. 70-73, Minister of State for External Economic Affairs 77-78; Adviser to Ministry of Foreign Affairs 73-; Rep. to Multilateral Trade Negotiations 78-79; Chair. (Japan) Japan-U.S. Econ. Relations Group 79-81; numerous decorations from Fed. Repub. of Germany, Iran, Mexico, Peru, Philippines, Korea, Afghanistan, Japan, Austria, Yugoslavia.
c/o Ministry of Foreign Affairs, 2-2-1 Kasumigaseki, Chiyoda-ku, Tokyo, Japan.

Usmankhodjayev, Inamdjon Buzrukovich; Soviet (Uzbek) architect and politician; b. 1930, Bagdad Village, Bagdad District, Ferghana Region; ed. Higher Tashkent Polytechnic Inst.
Worked as engineer and Section Chief, Ferghanavodstroi Trust, then Chief Architect, Margelan 55-60; Instructor, Ferghana Regional Party Cttee. and Head Ferghana Regional Collective Farm Construction Bd. 60; Chair. Exec. Cttee. Ferghana City Council 62-65; nominated Sec. Syr Darya Regional Party Cttee. 65; Instructor, Central Cttee. of C.P.S.U. 69-72; Chair. Namangan Regional Exec. Cttee. 72-74; First Sec. Andidjan Regional Party Cttee. 75; Chair. of Presidium of Supreme Soviet, Uzbek S.S.R. Dec. 79-; Order of Lenin, Order of the Red Banner of Labour (twice), Badge of Honour and medals.
Presidium of Supreme Soviet of Uzbek S.S.R., Tashkent, U.S.S.R.

V

Vaea of Houma, Baron; Tongan diplomatist; b. 1921; ed. Wesley Coll., Auckland, N.Z.
Served R.N.Z.A.F. 42-44; Tonga Civil Service 45-53; A.D.C. to Queen Salote of Tonga 53-58; Gov. of Ha'apai 59-67; Acting Minister of Police 68-69; Commr., Consul in the U.K. 69-70, High Commr. 70-72; Minister of Commerce, Labour and Industry 73-, Deputy Minister of Finance 73; Minister of Tourism and Co-op. Soc. 73; mem. Privy Council of Tonga 59-.
Ministry of Commerce, Labour and Industry, P.O. Box 110, Nuku'alofa (Office); P.O. Box 262, Nuku'alofa, Tonga (Home).

Vajpayee, Atal Bihari, M.A.; Indian politician; b. 25 Dec. 1926, Gwalior; ed. Victoria Coll., Gwalior, D.A.V. Coll., Kanpur.
Vice-President of Union, Victoria Coll.; edited Hindi newspapers *Rashtradharma, Panchajanya, Veer Arjun*; mem. Rashtriya Swayamsewak Sangh 41, Indian Nat. Congress 42-46; mem. Lok Sabha 57-62, 67- (for New Delhi March 77-), Rajya Sabha 62-67; founder mem. Bharatiya Jana Sangh, Pres. 68-74, Parl. Leader 74-77; detained during emergency 75-77; mem. Cttee. of Janata Party Jan. 77-; Minister of External Affairs 77-79; mem. Nat. Integration Council 62, IPU Conf., Tokyo 75, Railway Convention Cttee. 71-72.
Publs. *Amar Balidan, Mrityuya Hatya, Jana Sangh Our Musalman.*
7 Safdaring Road, New Delhi 110011, India.
Telephone: 375141.

Van Praagh, Dame Margaret (Peggy), D.B.E.; British ballet director; b. 1 Sept. 1910; ed. King Alfred School, London.
Dancer with Dame Marie Rambert 33; examiner for Cecchetti Soc. 35-; dancer, Sadler's Wells Ballet 41-46, ballet mistress Sadler's Wells Theatre Ballet 46-51; Asst. Dir. to Dame Ninette de Valois 51-56; Artistic Dir., Borovansky Ballet, Australia 60-61; Artistic Dir., The Australian Ballet 62-74, 78-79; mem. Victoria Council of the Arts; Hon. D.Litt. (Univ. of New England) 74; Hon. Dr. Laws (Melbourne Univ).
Publs. *How I became a Ballet Dancer, The Choreographic Art* (with Peter Brisnon).
5248 The Avenue, Parkville, Vic. 3052, Australia.
Telephone: 38-5773.

Varma, Ravindra; Indian politician; b. 18 April 1925, Mavelikkara, Kerala; ed. Maharaja's Coll. of Arts, Trivandrum, Christian Coll., Madras.
Member, Madras State United Nat. Students' Org. 44; took active part in State Congress movement for responsible govt. in Travancore and Mysore states; mem. Quit India Movement; Pres. All-India Students' Congress 46-49; mem. Int. Exec. of Int. Students' Service—World Univ. Service 49; Sec. and later Pres., Indian Youth congress; Sec. Indian Cttee. of World Assembly of Youth 58, Int. Pres. 58-62; mem. UNESCO Int. Perm. Cttee. for Educ.; mem. third Lok Sabha 62-67; mem. Janata Party 77-; mem. Lok Sabha from Ranchi March 77-; Minister of Parl. Affairs and Labour 77-79; Pres. ILO 79-80.
c/o Ministry of Foreign Affairs, New Delhi, India.

Venkataraman, R., M.A., B.L.; Indian politician; b. 4 Dec. 1910; ed. Madras Univ.
Advocate, Madras High Court and Supreme Court; detained during Quit India Movt. 42-44; mem. Prov. Parl. 50; mem. Lok Sabha 52-57, 77-; Minister for Industry and Labour, Govt. of Madras 57-67, mem. Planning Comm. 67-71; Chair. Nat. Research and Devt. Corpn.; Man. Ed. *Labour Law Journal* 71-; Minister of Finance and Industry 80-82, of Defence Jan 82-; del to ILO 58, UN Gen. Assembly 53-61
Ministry of Defence, New Delhi, India.

Verma, Brij Lal, LL.B.; Indian politician; b. 1916, Vallari village, Raipur district; ed. Nagpur Univ.
Participated in Quit India Movement whilst a student; legal practice in Baloda Bazar, Raipur district; provided free legal aid to poorer sections of society; elected to Vidhan Sabha (legislature) of Madhya Pradesh 52; fmr. mem. Socialist Party; mem. Indian Nat. Congress 65-67; Minister of Irrigation, Land, Planning and Devt. in State Govt. 67-69; mem. Jana Sangh Party 70-77, Pres. Madhya Pradesh Branch 74-77; detained during emergency June 75; mem. Janata Party Jan. 77-; mem. Lok Sabha from Mahasamund, Madhya Pradesh 77-; Minister for Indus-

tries March-July 77, for Communications 77-79; associated with many Kisan and co-operative orgs.; Chair. Janpad Sabhas in Raipur.
Lok Sabha, New Delhi, India.

Vernon, Sir James, A.C., C.B.E., PH.D.; Australian business executive; b. 13 June 1910, Tamworth; ed. Sydney Univ., Univ. Coll. London.
Chief Chemist, Colonial Sugar Refining Co. Ltd. (C.S.R.) 38-51, Senior Exec. Officer 51-56, Asst. Gen. Man. 56-57, Gen. Man. 58-72, Dir. 58-, Chair. 78-80; Dir. MLC Ltd., Commercial Banking Co. of Sydney Ltd., Westham Dredging Australia Pty. Ltd.; Chair. Martin Corpn. Ltd., Volvo Australia Pty. Ltd., Commonwealth Cttee. of Econ. Inquiry 63-65; Pres. Australian-Japan Business Co-op. Cttee. 72-77; Pres. Australian Cttee. of the Pacific Basin Econ. Council 72-78, Int. Pres. 80-; Chair. Australian Post Office Cttee. of Inquiry 73-74; mem. Chase Manhattan Bank Int. Advisory Cttee., Wells Fargo Bank Int. Advisory Cttee.; Hon. D.Sc. (Sydney and Newcastle); A. E. Leighton Memorial Medal, Royal Australian Chemical Inst. 65, John Storey Medal, Australian Inst. of Management.
16 O'Connell Street, Sydney, N.S.W. 2000; Home: 27 Manning Road, Double Bay, N.S.W. 2028, Australia.

Villa, José Garcia, A.B.; Philippine poet and critic; b. 5 Aug. 1914, Manila; ed. Univs. of the Philippines and New Mexico and Columbia Univ.
Associate Editor New Directions Books 49; Cultural Attaché Philippine Mission to UN 53-63; Dir. N.Y. City Coll. Poetry Workshop 52-63, Prof. of Poetry, New School for Social Research 64-74; Philippines Presidential Adviser on Cultural Affairs 68-; Guggenheim Fellowship 43, Bollingen Fellowship 51, Rockefeller Grant 64; American Acad. of Arts and Letters Award 42, Shelley Memorial Award 59, Pro Patria Award 61, Philippines Cultural Heritage Award 62; Nat. Artist in Literature 73; Hon. D.Litt. (Far Eastern Univ.) 59, L.H.D. (Univ. of the Philippines) 73.
Publs. *Footnote to Youth* (stories) 33, *Many Voices* 39, *Poems by Doveglion* 41, *Have Come, Am Here* 42, *Volume Two* 49, *Selected Poems and New* 58, *Poems Fifty-five* 62, *Poems in Praise of Love* 62, *Selected Stories* 62, *The Portable Villa* 63, *The Essential Villa* 65, *Appassionata* 79; Editor: *E. E. Cummings, Marianne Moore, A Celebration for Edith Sitwell* 48, *A Doveglion Book of Philippine Poetry* 75, *Bravo: the Poet's Magazine* 81.
780 Greenwich Street, New York, N.Y. 10014, U.S.A.

Viner, Robert Ian, LL.B.; Australian politician; b. 21 Jan. 1933, Claremont, W.A.; ed. Bunbury High School, Univ. of Western Australia.
Member for Stirling, House of Reps. 72-; Minister for Aboriginal Affairs Dec. 75-Nov. 76; Minister for Aboriginal Affairs 76-79, also Minister Assisting the Treasurer 76-77, Minister Assisting the Prime Minister 77-79, 80-82, Minister for Employment and Youth Affairs 78-81; Leader of the House 79-80; Minister for Industrial Relations 81-82, for Defence Support May 82-, also Minister Assisting Minister for Defence May 82-
Room L121, Parliament House, Canberra, A.C.T. 2600; and Shop 2, Karrinyup Shopping Centre, Karrinyup, Perth, W.A., Australia.

Vines, Sir William Joshua, Kt., C.M.G.; Australian business executive and grazier; b. 27 May 1916; ed. Haileybury Coll., Victoria.
Army service, Middle East, New Guinea and Borneo 39-45; Sec. Alexander Fergusson Pty. Ltd. 38-40, 45-47; Dir. Goodlass Wall and Co. Pty. Ltd. 47-49, Lewis Berger and Sons (Australia) Pty. Ltd. and Sherwin Williams Co. (Aust.) Pty. Ltd. 52-55; Man. Dir. Lewis Berger and Sons (Victoria) Pty. Ltd. 49-55; Man. Dir. Lewis Berger & Sons Ltd. 55-60; Man. Dir. Berger, Jenson & Nicholson Ltd. 60-61; Man. Dir. Int. Wool Secretariat 61-69, mem. Board 69-79; Chair. Dalgety Australia Ltd. 69-80, Dir. 80-; Chair. Carbonless Papers (Wiggins Teape) 70-78, Assoc. Pulp and Paper Mills Ltd 78-; Chair. ANZ Banking Group Ltd.; Deputy Chair. Tubemakers of Australia Ltd.; Dir. Conzinc Riotinto of Australia Ltd. 69-80; Chair. of Council, Hawkesbury Agricultural Coll.; Chair. Sir Robert Menzies Memorial Trust.
73 Yarranabbe Road, Darling Point, N.S.W. 2027; "Cliffdale", Currabubula, N.S.W. 2342; "Tandara", Breeza, N.S.W. 2342, Australia.
Telephone: 328-7970, Southwood 351.

Vinicchayakul, Serm, D.en. D.; Thai politician and lawyer; b. 2 June 1908; ed. Assumption Coll. and Faculté de Droit, Univ. of Paris.
Appointed Sec.-Gen. of Judicial Council 46; Gov. Bank of Thailand 46-47, 52-54; Prof. of Law Thammasat Univ. 54; Under-Sec. for Finance 54-65; Gov. IBRD, IFC and IDA 65; Minister of Finance 65-71, 72-73; Chair. Exec. Board of Econ. and Social Devt. Council 72; mem. Senate 74-76; Pres. Royal Inst. of Thailand 76-; Knight Grand Cross (1st Class), Order of Chula Chom Klao; Knight Grand Cordon (Special Class), Order of the White Elephant; Knight Grand Cordon, Order of the Crown of Thailand.
159 Asoke Road, Bangkok, Thailand.

Virata, Cesar Enrique, B.S.B.A., B.S.M.E., M.B.A.; Philippine financial executive and politician; b. 12 Dec. 1930; ed. Univs. of the Philippines and Pennsylvania.
Instructor and lecturer, Graduate School, Univ. of the Philippines 53-61, Dean Coll. of Business Admin. 61-69; Principal and Head, Management Services Div., Sycip, Gorres, Velayo & Co. (accountants) 56-67; Chair. Board of Investments 67-70; Deputy Dir.-Gen. Presidential Econ. Staff 67-68; Under-Sec. of Industry, Dept. of Commerce and Industry 67-69; Chair. and Dir. Philippine Nat. Bank 67-69; Minister of Finance and mem., Monetary Board, Cen. Bank of the Philippines 70-81; Chair. Land Bank of the Philippines 73-, Philippine Guarantee and Export Credit Corpn.; Vice-Chair. Nat. Econ. and Devt. Authority 72-; Chair. Devt. Cttee. of IBRD and IMF 76-80, Bd. of Govs. Asian Devt. Bank 79-80, Chair. Group of 24 81-82; Prime Minister of the Philippines July 81-; Chair. Exec. Cttee., Philippine Govt. 81-; Diploma of Merit, Univ. of the Philippines 69; Hon. LL.D. 76, Hon. D.H.L. (Ateneo Univ.) 74, Hon. D.P.A. (St. Louis) 75.
Publs. Articles in work simplification, industrial engineering, business policy, monetary and fiscal policies.
Executive House, Manila; Home: 63 East Maya Drive, Quezon City, Philippines.
Telephone: 405533 (Manila).

Viswanathan, Kambanthodath Kunhan, B.A., B.L.; Indian administrator; b. 4 Nov. 1914, Mattancheri, Kerala.
Law practice in Cochin 38; mem. Cochin Assembly, later mem. Travancore-Cochin Assembly 48-50; mem. Kerala Assembly 57, re-elected 60; Sec. Congress Legislature Party 57-59, 60-64; Gen. Sec. Kerala Pradesh Congress Cttee. 66-69, Convenor ad hoc 69, Pres. 70-73; editor *The Republic*, Malayalam weekly 67-69; Gov. of Gujarat 73-78.
c/o Raj Bhavan, Shahibag, Ahmedabad-380004, Gujarat, India.
Telephone: 66477.

Vo Chi Cong; Vietnamese politician; b. 1914, Central Viet-Nam.
Former mem. Vietcong forces; frm. Sec. Southern People's Party, a main element in Nat. Liberation Front (NLF); mem. Cen. Cttee. of Lao Dong party for many years; Minister for Fisheries, Socialist Repub. of Viet-Nam 76-77; Vice-Premier, Council of Ministers 76-82; Minister for

Agric. 77-78; mem. Politburo of CP of Viet-Nam Dec. 76-. c/o Communist Party of Viet-Nam, 10 Hoang Van Thu Street, Hanoi, Viet-Nam.

Vo Nguyen Giap, General; Vietnamese army officer; b. 1912; ed. French lycée in Hue, and law studies at Univ. of Hanoi.
History teacher, Thang Long School, Hanoi; joined Viet-Nam C.P. in early 1930s; fled to China 39; helped organize Viet-Minh Front, Viet-Nam 41; Minister of Interior 45, became Commdr.-in-Chief of Viet-Minh Army 46; defeated French at Dien-Bien-Phu 54; Deputy Prime Minister, Minister of Defence and Commdr.-in-Chief, Democratic Repub. of Viet-Nam until 76; Commander-in-Chief Armed Forces and Minister of Nat. Defence, Socialist Repub. of Viet-Nam 76-80; Vice-Premier, Council of Ministers 76-; mem. Politburo Lao-Dong Party until Dec. 76, CP of Viet-Nam 76-82.
Publs. *People's War, People's Army, Big Victory, Great Task* 68.
Dang Cong san Viet-Nam, 1C Bd. Hoang Van Thu, Ho Chi Minh City, Viet-Nam.

Vo Van Kiet; Vietnamese politician; b. 1922, South Viet-Nam.
Joined Communist Party of Indo-China in 30s; mem. Lao Dong Party (renamed Communist Party of Viet-Nam Dec. 76), mem. Cen. Cttee. 58-; mem. Cen. Office for South Viet-Nam during war; alt. mem. Politburo, CP of Viet-Nam Dec. 76-; Chair. party Cttee. in Ho Chi Minh City; Vice-Premier and Chair. State Planning Comm.
c/o Ho Chi Minh City Committee of the Communist Party of Viet-Nam, Ho Chi Minh City, Viet-Nam.

Vu Van Mau, LL.B., LL.D.; Vietnamese lawyer, diplomatist and politician; b. 25 July 1914; ed. Univ. of Hanoi and Univ. of Paris.
Lawyer, Hanoi 49; Dean, Faculty of Law, Univ. of Saigon 55-58; First Pres. Vietnamese Supreme Court of Appeal 55; Min. of Foreign Affairs, Repub. of Viet-Nam 55; Sec. of State for Foreign Affairs 56-63 (resgnd.); Pres. Vietnamese Nat. Asscn. of Comparative Law; Amb. to United Kingdom, Belgium and Netherlands 64-65; Prof. of Law, Univ. of Saigon 65-75; Senator 70-75; Pres. Forces for Nat. Reconciliation Sept. 74-April 75; Prime Minister 28-30 April 75; detained April-Nov. 75.
Publs. legal works in French and Vietnamese.
132 Suong Nguyet Anh, Ho Chi Minh City, Viet-Nam.

Vunibobo, Berenado, C.B.E., B.AGR.SC.; Fijian agronomist and government official; b. 24 Sept. 1932, Nukutubu, Rewa; ed. St. Joseph's Catholic Mission School, Rewa, Marist Brothers High School, Suva, Queensland State Agric. Coll., Queensland Univ., Imperial Coll. of Tropical Agric., Trinidad.
Government Service 51-, District Agric. Officer 62-67, Senior Agric. Officer and later Chief Agric. Officer 68-69; Deputy Dir. of Agric. 69-70, Dir. of Agric. 70-71; Perm. Sec. for Agric., Fisheries and Forests 71-72, for Works 73-76; Perm. Rep. to UN, Amb. to U.S.A., High Commr. in Canada 76-80; Perm. Sec. for Transport and Civil Aviation 80-81; Chair. Civil Aviation Authority 80-81; Resident Rep. UN Devt. Programme, Seoul, Republic of Korea 81-; Chair. Coconut Pests and Diseases Bd., Banana Marketing Bd., Nat. Marketing Authority 70-72; mem. Bd., Fiji Devt. Bank 70-72; mem. Native Lands Trust Bd. 68-75, Fijian Affairs Bd. 68-76, Great Council of Chiefs 68-76, Cen. Whitley Council 70-76, Joint Industrial Council 70-76, Fiji Electricity Authority 75-76, Bd. of Ports Authority, Air Pacific Ltd., Fiji Air Ltd. 80-81.
c/o UNDP, P.O. Box 143, Seoul, Republic of Korea.

Vuong Van Bac; Vietnamese diplomatist; b. 1927, Bac Ninh, N. Viet-Nam; ed. Hanoi Univ., Michigan State Univ., Vanderbilt Univ., U.S.A.
Admitted to Hanoi Bar Asscn. 52, Saigon Bar Asscn. 54; Prof. of Constitutional and Political Science, Nat. Inst. of Admin. 55; Chair. Dalat Univ. 65; Sec.-Gen. Viet-Nam Lawyer's Fed. 61; mem. Council of Lawyers, Saigon High Court 62-68, Board of Dirs., Viet-Nam Council on Foreign Relations 68; Legal Adviser to Repub. of Viet-Nam Liaison and Observation Del. at Paris talks 68; Amb. to U.K. 72-73; Minister of Foreign Affairs 73-75; has attended numerous int. confs. on legal and econ. affairs.

W

Wadati, Dr. Kiyoo: Japanese meteorologist; b. 8 Sept 1902, Nagoya; ed. Tokyo Univ.
Entered Meteorological Observatory; has conducted research into earthquakes, tidal waves, etc.; fmr. Dir. of Gen. Meteorological Observatory; fmr. Pres. Science Council of Japan; Pres. Saitama Univ. 66-74; Pres. Japan Acad. 74-80.
Publs. *Earthquakes, Meteorological Glossary, Oceanographic Glossary.*
Japan Academy, 7-32, Ueno Park, Taito-ku, Tokyo 110; Home: 1-8 Naitomachi, Shinjuku-ku, Tokyo 160, Japan.
Telephone: 03-341-3503.

Wade-Gery, Robert Lucian, C.M.G.; British diplomatist; b. 22 April 1929; ed. Winchester, New Coll., Oxford.
Joined Foreign Service 51; Econ. Relations Dept., Foreign Office (FO) 51-54; Third, later Second Sec., Bonn 54-57; Private Sec. to Perm. Under-Sec., later Southern Dept., FO 57-60; First Sec., Tel Aviv 60-64; Planning Staff, FO 64-67; Head of Chancery, Saigon 67-68; Sec. to Duncan Cttee., Cabinet Office 68-69; Counsellor 69; on loan to Bank of England 69; Head of Financial Policy and Aid Dept., FCO 69-70; on loan to Cabinet Office (Cen. Policy Review Staff) 71-73; Minister, Madrid 73-77, Moscow 77-79; Deputy Sec. of Cabinet 79-82; High Commr. in India 82-.
British High Commission, Shanti Path, Chanakyapuri, New Delhi 110021, India.

Wadia, Sophia; Indian editor; b. 13 Sept. 1901; ed. Lycée Molière, Paris, Columbia Univ., New York, School of Oriental and African Studies, London.
Lecturer; founder-organizer P.E.N. All-India Centre; Pres. Indian Inst. of World Culture, Bangalore, Asian Book Trust Bombay; Assoc. United Lodge of Theosophists; Editor *Aryan Path* 29- and *The Indian P.E.N.* 34-, Bombay; Vice-Pres. Bombay City Council for Child Welfare; also worker in women's social educational and cultural movements.
Publs. *The Brotherhood of Religions, Preparation for Citizenship.*
Theosophy Hall, 40 New Marine Lines, Bombay 400-020, India.
Telephone: 292173.

Wahi, Prem Nath, M.D., F.R.C.P.; Indian physician; b. 10 April 1908; ed. K.G. Medical Coll., Lucknow, London Hospital Medical School, London, and New England Deaconess Hospital, Boston, U.S.A.
Professor of Pathology, S.N. Medical Coll., Agra 41-; Principal, S.N. Medical Coll., Agra 60-; Dean, Faculty of Medicine, Agra Univ. 61-64; Dir. WHO Int. Reference Centre and Cancer Registry 63-; mem. Expert Panel of WHO on Cancer, Lyon, France 65-; has attended numerous int. conferences on cancer; Lady Brahamachari Readership, Calcutta Univ. 65; Fellow, Nat. Inst. of Sciences, India; Founder Fellow, Coll. of Pathologists, London 63; Founder Fellow, Indian Acad. of Medical Sciences 64.
S.N. Medical College, Agra, Uttar Pradesh, India.

Walker, Sir (Charles) Michael, G.C.M.G.; British diplomatist; b. 22 Nov. 1916, Simla, India; ed. Charterhouse, and New Coll., Oxford.

Army service 39-45; Dominions Office 47-49; First Sec. British Embassy, Washington 49-51; Office of High Commr., Calcutta and New Delhi 52-55; Establishment Officer Commonwealth Relations Office 55-58; Imperial Defence Coll. 58-59; Asst. Under-Sec. of State and Dir. of Establishments and Org., Commonwealth Relations Office 59-62; High Commr. in Ceylon 62-65, in Malaysia 66-71; Sec. to Overseas Devt. Admin., Foreign and Commonwealth Office 71-73; High Commr. in India 73-76; Chair. Commonwealth Scholarship Comm. 77-, Festival of India Trust 79-; Hon. D.C.L. (City Univ.) 80.
40 Bourne Street, London, S.W.1, England.

Walker, Sir Michael (*see* Walker, Sir Charles Michael).

Walsh, Sir Alan, Kt., M.SC.TECH., D.SC., F.INST.P., F.A.I.P., F.A.A., F.R.S.; British physicist; b. 19 Dec. 1918, Darwen, Lancs.; ed. Darwen Grammar School and Manchester Univ.
At British Non-Ferrous Metals Research Asscn. 39-46; seconded to Ministry of Aircraft Production 43; with Commonwealth Scientific and Industrial Research Org. (C.S.I.R.O.), Australia 46, Asst. Chief of Div. of Chemical Physics, C.S.I.R.O. 61-76; Consultant Perkin-Elmer Corpn., Norwalk, U.S.A. 77; Pres. Australian Inst. of Physics 67-68; Hon. Fellow Chemical Soc. of London 72; Hon. Research Fellow, Monash Univ.; Hon. Fellow, Australian Inst. of Physics 79; Hon. mem. Soc. for Analytical Chemistry, Royal Soc. of New Zealand 75; foreign mem. Royal Acad. of Sciences, Stockholm; Hon. D.Sc. Monash Univ.; Britannica Australia Science Award 66, Royal Soc. of Victoria Medal 69, Talanta Gold Medal 69, Maurice Hasler Award of Soc. of Applied Spectroscopy, U.S.A. 72, James Cook Medal, Royal Soc. of New South Wales 76, Torbern Bergman Medal (Swedish Chemical Soc.) 76, Royal Medal of Royal Soc. 76, John Scott Award (City of Philadelphia) 78, Matthew Flinders Medal, Australian Acad. of Science 80, Robert Boyle Medal, Royal Soc. of Chem. 83.
Publs. numerous papers in scientific journals.
11 Dendy Street, Brighton, Vic. 3186, Australia (Home).
Telephone: 03-592-4897 (Home).

Wan Li; Chinese government official; b. Sichuan.
Vice-Minister of Building Construction 52-56; Minister of Urban Construction 56-58; Sec. CCP, Beijing 58-66; Vice-Mayor of Beijing 58-66; criticized and removed from office during Cultural Revolution 67; Minister of Railways 75-Sept. 76, criticized and removed from office during Tienanmen incident, reinstated Oct. 76-Feb. 77; Vice-Minister of Light Industry 76; First Sec. CCP Anhui June 77-80; Sec. Secretariat, Cen. Cttee. 80-; a Vice-Premier, State Council April 80-; Minister in Charge of the State Agric. Comm. 80, 81-82; mem. 11th Cen. Cttee. CCP 77.
People's Republic of China.

Wang Bicheng; Chinese army officer; b. 1912, Hunan.
Deputy Commdr. Zhejiang Mil. District, People's Liberation Army 49, Commdr. 51; Maj.-Gen. PLA 55; Commdr. Shanghai Garrison District, PLA 55-61; Deputy Commdr. Nanjing Mil. Region, PLA 61; Deputy Commdr. Kunming Mil. Region, PLA 69, Commdr. 72-79; Commdr. Wuhan Mil. Region 79-; Second Sec. CCP Yunnan 71; First Vice-Chair. Yunnan Revolutionary Cttee. 72; mem. 10th Cen. Cttee. of CCP 73, 11th Cen. Cttee. 77.
People's Republic of China.

Wang Bingqian; Chinese politician.
Deputy Minister of Finance 73-80; Minister of Finance 80-.
State Council, Beijing, People's Republic of China.

Wang Dongxing; Chinese party official.
Bodyguard of Mao Zedong 47; Capt. of Guards of Cen. Cttee., CCP 47-49; Capt. of Guards, Gen. Admin. Council 49-54; Vice-Minister of Public Security 55-58, 62-80; Vice-Gov. of Jiangxi 58-60; Sec. CCP Jiangxi 58-60; mem. Cen. Cultural Revolution Group 67; Dir. Admin. Office of Cen. Cttee., CCP 69; Alt. mem. Politburo, 9th Cen. Cttee. of CCP 69; mem. Politburo, 10th Cen. Cttee. of CCP 73; mem. Standing Cttee. 77; Vice-Chair. CCP 77; Exec. Chair. Presidium 5th Nat. People's Congress 78; dismissed from all posts 80; deputy administrator in Jiangxi Prov. 80-.
People's Republic of China.

Wang Feng; Chinese politician; b. Shaanxi.
Commander Security Force Shaanxi-Gansu-Ningxia Border Region and concurrently Commdr. Lushan Mil. Region; Pol. Commissar 38th Army PLA 46; Dir. United Front Dept. N.W. Bureau CCP Cen. Cttee. 49-52; Chair. Nationalities Affairs Cttee. N.W. Mil. and Admin. Cttee. 50-52; mem. Land Reform Cttee. N.W. Mil. and Admin. Cttee. 51; Pres. N.W. Nationalities Coll. 52; mem. Pol. and Legal Cttee. N.W. Mil. and Admin. Cttee. 52; Vice-Chair. Nat. Affairs Cttee. Govt. Admin. Council 52-54; Vice-Chair. Nat. Affairs Cttee., State Council 54; mem. N.W. Admin. Cttee. 53-54; Deputy for Qinghai 1st NPC 54; Deputy Dir., United Front Dept. CCP Cen. Cttee. 55; mem. Standing Cttee. 1st NPC 58-59; Alt. mem. CCP 8th Cen. Cttee. 58; First Sec. CCP Ningxia Provincial Cttee. 58-61; mem. Nationalities Cttee. 2nd NPC 59-64; First Sec. CCP Gansu Prov. Cttee. 61-66; mem. Standing Cttee. 3rd NPC 65; Sec. CCP N.W. Bureau 65-68; mem. Presidium 11th Nat. Congress CCP 77-; mem. CCP 11th Cen. Cttee. 77-; First Sec. Xinjiang Provincial CCP Cttee. 78-80; Chair. Xinjiang CCP Revolutionary Cttee. 78-80; First Pol. Commissar PLA Xinjiang Mil. Region 78-80.
People's Republic of China.

Wang Guozhuan; Chinese diplomatist; b. 1911.
Ambassador to German Democratic Republic 57-64, to Poland 64-69; Pres. Chinese People's Asscn. for Friendship with Foreign Countries June 72-; Amb. to Australia 73-76.
c/o Ministry of Foreign Affairs, Beijing, People's Republic of China.

Wang Hongwen; Chinese fmr. party official; b. 1937.
Worker Shanghai No. 17 Cotton Textile Mill; founded Shanghai Workers Revolutionary Rebel Gen. H.Q. during Cultural Revolution 67; Vice-Chair. Shanghai Revolutionary Cttee. 68; Sec. CCP Shanghai 71; Political Commissar Shanghai Garrison District, PLA 72; First Vice-Chair. CCP 73-76, Vice-Chair. April-Nov. 76; mem. Standing Cttee. of Politburo, CCP 73-Nov. 76; Vice-Chair. Mil. Affairs Comm. 75-Nov. 76; arrested as a mem. of the "Gang of Four" Oct. 76; expelled from CCP July 77; tried with others in "Gang of Four" Nov. 80-Jan. 81; sentenced to life imprisonment Jan. 81.
People's Republic of China.

Wang Lei; Chinese politician.
Cadre in S.W. China 50; Vice-Minister of Commerce 53; Vice-Minister of First Ministry of Commerce 58; Deputy Sec.-Gen. Beijing Revolutionary Cttee. 73; Minister of Commerce 77-78, 79-82.
People's Republic of China.

Wang Ling, M.A., PH.D.; Chinese historian; b. 23 Dec. 1918, Nangdong, Jiangsu Province; ed. National Central Univ., China and Trinity Coll., Cambridge.
Junior Research Fellow, Inst. of History and Philology, Academia Sinica 41-44; Senior Lecturer, Nat. Futan Univ. 44-45, Assoc. Prof. 45-46; Collaborator to J. Needham (*q.v.*), Cambridge Univ. 46-57; Visiting Lecturer, Cambridge Univ. 53, Canberra Univ. Coll., Melbourne Univ. 57-59; Assoc. Fellow, Nat. Acad. of Science, Academia Sinica 55-57; Senior Lecturer Univ. Coll., Australian Nat. Univ., Canberra 60-61, Assoc. Prof. 61-63; Professorial Fellow, Inst. of Advanced Studies, Australian Nat. Univ. 63-; Visiting Prof. of Chinese Literature, Cornell Univ. 66; Visiting Prof. of Chinese Classics, Wisconsin Univ. 66; mem. Comm. for History of the Social Relations of Science

of Int. Union for the History of Science 48-56; corresp. mem. Int. Acad. of History of Science, Paris 64-.
Publs. *Science and Civilisation in China* (assisted Dr. J. Needham, F.R.S.) Vol. I 54, Vol. II 56, Vol. III 59, Vol. IVa 62, Vol. IVb 64, Vol. IVc 71, *Heavenly Clockwork* (assisted Dr. J. Needham, F.R.S.) 60, *A Study on the Chiu Chang Suan Shu* 62.
Institute of Advanced Studies, Australian National University, Canberra, A.C.T. 2600, Australia.
Telephone: Canberra 493171.

Wang Liusheng; Chinese party official.
Major-General People's Liberation Army, Shanghai 64; Deputy Political Commissar Nanjing Mil. Region, PLA 66; Alt. mem. 9th Cen. Cttee. of CCP 69; First Political Commissar Wuhan Mil. Region, PLA 72; Second Sec. CCP Hupeh 72; Alt. mem. 10th Cen. Cttee. of CCP 73, 11th Cen. Cttee. 77; Political Commissar, PLA Eng. Corps 76.
People's Republic of China.

Wang Meng; Chinese politician.
Minister of Physical Culture and Sports 71-74, 77-81; mem. 11th Cen. Cttee. CCP 77.
People's Republic of China.

Wang Ping; Chinese politician; b. 1911, Jiangxi.
Director Pol. Dept. 3rd Red Army Corps 35; Chair. Mobilization Cttee. N. China Bureau, 37; Acting Chief, 29th Group CCP Section, Mil. Mediation Dept. 46; Chair. Tadong Mil. Control Comm. 49; Vice-Chair. Zhahar, 49-52; Deputy Chief, Shanxi-Zhahar Sub-Del. to visit bases in N. China 51; Dir., Cadres Dept., N. China Mil. Region 53; Gen. 55; Deputy Pol. Commissar, Chinese People's Volunteers 57; Pol. Commissar Chinese People's Volunteers 57-58; Deputy for PLA to 2nd NPC 59, (re-elected to 3rd NPC 64); Pol. Commissar Nanjing Mil. Region 59; mem. Nat. Defence Council 59 (re-appointed 65); mem. Presidium CCP 11th Cen. Cttee. 77-; mem. CCP 11th Cen. Cttee. 77-; Pol. Commissar PLA Gen. Logistics Dept. 78-; mem. Standing Cttee. Mil. Comm., Cen. Cttee. 80-.
People's Republic of China.

Wang Qian; Chinese party official.
Deputy Sec.-Gen. Rural Work Dept., CCP Cen. Cttee. 55; visited Eastern Europe 55; Sec. CCP Shanxi 57, Second Sec. 66-67, Sec. 73, First Sec. 75-; Gov. of Shanxi 65-67; alt. mem. 10th Cen. Cttee. CCP 73; Vice-Chair. Shanxi Revolutionary Cttee. 73, Chair. 75-; mem. 11th Cen. Cttee. 77.
People's Republic of China.

Wang Renzhong; Chinese government official; b. 1906, Hebei.
Chair. S. Hebei Admin. 41; Dir. S. Hebei Party Cttee. Propaganda Dept.; Head Jinan Admin. Office 48; Vice-Mayor Wuhan 52-54; Vice-Chair. Hubei Finance and Econs. Cttee. 50; mem. Cen. S. Mil. and Admin. Cttee., Finance and Econs. Cttee. 50-54, mem. Standing Cttee. Hubei CCP Cttee. 52; First Sec. Wuhan Cttee. 53-54; First Sec. Hubei CCP Prov. Cttee. 54-66; Deputy for Wuhan to 1st NPC 54; mem. Hubei Prov. People's Council 55-; First Pol. Commissar Wuhan Mil. Region 55-67; Alt. mem. 8th CCP Cen. Cttee. 58-68; Second Sec. Cen. S. Bureau 61-66, First Sec. 66-67; purged 68; First Sec. Shaanxi CCP Prov. Cttee. 78-79; a Vice-Premier, State Council 78-80; mem. 11th CCP Cen. Cttee. 78-; Minister in Charge of the State Agric. Comm. 79-80; Dir. of CCP Propaganda March 80; Sec. Secretariat, Cen. Cttee. 80-.
People's Republic of China.

Wang Shangrong; Chinese army officer; b. 1906, Shanxi; ed. Sun Yat-sen Univ., Moscow.
On Long March 34; Div. Commdr., Red Army 36; Commdr. Qinghai Mil. District 49; Lt.-Gen. 55; Alt. mem. 8th Cen. Cttee. of CCP 58; Dir. Combat Dept., People's Liberation Army Gen. Staff H.Q. 59-66; criticized and removed from office during Cultural Revolution 67; Deputy Chief of Gen. Staff, PLA 74, 78-; Alt. mem. 11th Cen. Cttee. of CCP 77-.
People's Republic of China.

Wang Yi; Chinese army officer.
Major-General People's Liberation Army 64; Commdr. Tianjin Garrison District, PLA 69-; Vice-Chair. Tianjin Revolutionary Cttee. 70; Sec. CCP Tianjin 71; mem. Nat. Cttee. 5th Nat. People's Congress 78.
People's Republic of China.

Wang Zhen; Chinese party and government official; b. 1909, Liuyang, Hunan.
Regimental Political Commissar 30; Alt. mem. 7th Cen. Cttee. of CCP 45; Commdr. of 1st Army Corps, 1st Field Army, People's Liberation Army 49; Commdr. Xinjiang Uygur Mil. Region, PLA 50; Minister of State Farms and Land Reclamation 56; mem. 8th Cen. Cttee. of CCP 56, 9th Cen. Cttee. 69, 10t h Cen. Cttee. 73; a Vice-Premier of State Council 75-80; mem. 11th Cen. Cttee. CCP 77, Politburo Cen. Cttee. of CCP78-; Deputy for Shensi 5th NPC 78; mem. Presidium NPC 78-; Dir. Cen. Cttee. of CCP Party School 82-.
People's Republic of China.

Wang Zigang; Chinese politician.
Director of Bureau of Telecommunications, Ministry of Posts and Telecommunications 49-51; Vice Minister of Posts and Telecommunications 52-Cultural Revolution, Minister 78-79; Chair. Electronics Soc. 64-Cultural Revolution 76-79; Vice-Minister, Fourth Ministry of Machine Building 77-78.
People's Republic of China.

Wangchuk, Jigme Singye; Druk Gyalpo (King) of Bhutan; b. 11 Nov. 1955; ed. North Point, Darjeeling, Ugyuen Wangchuk Acad., Paro, also in England.
Crown Prince March 72; succeeded to throne 24 July 72, crowned 2 June 74; Chair. Planning Comm. of Bhutan March 72-; Commdr.-in-Chief of Armed Forces.
Royal Palace, Thimphu, Bhutan.

Wardhana, Ali, M.A., PH.D.; Indonesian economist and politician; b. 6 May 1928, Surakarta, Central Java; ed. Univ. of Indonesia, Jakarta and Univ. of California (Berkeley), U.S.A.
Director Research Inst. of Econ. and Social Studies 62-67; Prof. of Econs. and Dean, Faculty of Econs., Univ. of Indonesia 67-78; Econ. Adviser to Gov. of Cen. Bank 64-68; mem. team of experts of Presidential Staff 66-68; Minister of Finance 68-; Chair. Board of Govs. Cttee. on Reform of the Int. Monetary System and Related Issues, IMF 72-74; Grand Cross Order of Léopold II (Belgium) 70, Order of Orange Nassau (Netherlands) 71; Mahaputra Adipradana II Award (Indonesia) 73.
Ministry of Finance, Jakarta; 5 Jalan Brawijaya III, Kebayoran Baru, Jakarta, Indonesia.

Wark, Sir Ian (William), Kt., C.M.G., C.B.E., D.SC., PH.D.; Australian physical chemist; b. 8 May 1899; ed. Scotch Coll., Melbourne, and Univs. of Melbourne, London and Calif. (Berkeley).
Exhibition of 1851 Science Research Scholarship 21-24; Lecturer in Chemistry, Univ. of Sydney 25; Research Chemist, Electrolytic Zinc Co. of Australasia Ltd. 26-39; Commonwealth Scientific and Industrial Research Organization, Chief, Div. of Industrial Chemistry 40-58, Dir. Chemical Research Laboratories 58-60, mem. of Exec. 61-65, Consultant, CSIRO Minerals Research Laboratories 71-; Gov. Ian Potter Foundation 64-; Chair. Commonwealth Advisory Cttee. on Advanced Educ. 65-71; Gen. Pres. Royal Australian Chemical Inst. 57-58; Fellow, Australian Acad. of Science 54, Treas. 59-63; hon. mem. Australasian Inst. Mining and Metallurgy 60-; Fellow Univ. Coll.

London 65, Australian Acad. of Technological Sciences; Hon. Dr. Applied Science (Melbourne) 77, Hon. Dr. Arts and Sciences (Victoria Inst. of Colls.) 79; Australia and New Zealand Asscn. for the Advancement of Science Medal 73.
Publs. *Principles of Flotation* (monograph) 38, (revised with K. L. Sutherland 55), *Why Research?* 68.
31 Linum Street, Blackburn, Vic. 3130, Australia.
Telephone: Melbourne 877-2878.

Watanabe, Bunzo, B.A.; Japanese company executive; b. 20 May 1907, Tokyo; ed. Hitotsubashi Univ.
Vice-President, Ajinomoto Co. Inc. 65, Pres. 73-; Chair. Board, Knorr Foods Co. Ltd., Japan 73-; mem. Board, Morishita Pharmaceutical Co. Ltd. 63-, Ajinomoto Gen. Foods Inc. 73-, Eurolysine S.A., France 74-, Ajinomoto U.S.A. Inc. 74-, Union Chemicals Inc., Philippines 75-; mem. Board, Japan Cttee. for Industrial Devt. (Keizai Doyukai) 72-, Fed. of Econ. Orgs. (Keidanren) 73-; Trustee, Int. Christian Univ., Tokyo 73-; Blue Ribbon Medal 75.
Ajinomoto Co. Inc., 5-8, Kyobashi 1-chome, Chuo-ku, Tokyo 104, Japan.
Telephone: 03-272-1111.

Watanabe, Eiichi; Japanese politician; b. 11 Oct. 1918; ed. Nagoya Univ.
Mayor, Minokamo, Gifu Pref. for 17 years; mem. House of Reps. 63-; Parl. Vice-Minister for Construction 68-70, for Educ. 71-72; Minister for Construction 79-80; Chair. Standing Cttee. on Construction, House of Reps. 76; Vice-Sec.-Gen. of Liberal-Democratic Party (LDP) 74-76, 77-78; Dir. Accounting Bureau, LDP 78-79.
Publ. *Obei no Sugao* 63.
Liberal-Democratic Party, 7, 2-chome, Hirakawacho, Chiyoda-ku, Tokyo, Japan.

Watanabe, Michio; Japanese politician; b. 1924, Tochigi Prefecture; ed. Tokyo Commercial Coll. (now Hitotsubashi Univ.).
Military service; engaged as salesman 45-50; practice as tax lawyer; mem. Prefectural Legislature of Tochigi; mem. House of Reps. 63-; Deputy Sec.-Gen. of Liberal-Democratic Party (LDP); Chair. of Cabinet Cttee. of House of Reps.; Minister of Health and Welfare 76-77; Parl. Deputy Minister of Agric. and Forestry; Minister of Agric., Forestry and Fisheries 78-80; Minister of Finance July 80-; mem. of Seirankai (conservative group) in LDP.
Ministry of Finance, 3-1-1 Kasumigaseki, Chiyoda-ku, Tokyo, Japan.
Telephone: 03-581-4161.

Watanabe, Takeshi; Japanese banker and financial consultant; b. 15 Feb. 1906; ed. Law School of Tokyo Imperial Univ.
Ministry of Finance, Japan 30, serving as Chief Liaison Officer, Chief of the Minister's Secr. and Financial Commr.; Minister, Japanese Embassy in Washington 52-56; Exec. Dir. IBRD and IMF for Japan 56-60; int. financial consultant 60-65; Adviser to Minister of Finance, Japan 65; Pres. Asian Devt. Bank, Manila 66-72; Adviser to Pres. Bank of Tokyo 73-79; Japanese Chair. Trilateral Comm. 73-; Chair. Revlon K.K. 77-; Chair. Japan Silver Volunteers Inc. 79, Asia Community Trust 79-, AFS Japan 80-; Order of the Sacred Treasure, First Class.
Publs. *Japanese Finance in Early Post-War Years* 66, *Diary of ADB President* (in Japanese), *Towards a New Asia* (in English) 77.
Japan Center for International Exchange, 9-17 Minami Azabu, 4-chome, Minato-ku, Tokyo; Home: 35-19 Oyamacho, Shibuyaku, Tokyo, Japan.

Webster, James Joseph, A.A.S.A.; Australian politician and diplomatist; b. 14 June 1925, Flinders Island, Tasmania; ed. Caulfield Grammar School, Royal Melbourne Tech. Coll.
Member of Senate 64-79, Deputy Pres. and Chair. of Cttees. 74-75; Deputy leader of Nat. Country Party in Senate 74-75, leader 76-79; Minister for Science 75-79, of Environment 78-79; mem. Senate Off-shore Petroleum Resources Cttee.; High Commr. in New Zealand Feb. 80-; first Australian Minister to visit the South Pole.
Australian High Commission, 72-78 Hobson Street, Thorndon 1, P.O. Box 12145, Wellington, New Zealand.

Wei Guoqing, Gen.; Chinese party and government official; b. 1914, Donglan, Guangxi.
Regimental Commdr. 33; on Long March 34-35; Deputy Political Commissar 10th Army Corps, 3rd Field Army, People's Liberation Army 49; Mayor of Fuzhou 49; Gov. of Guangxi 55-58; Alt. mem. 8th Cen. Cttee. of CCP 56; Sec. CCP Guangxi 57-61, First Sec. 61-68; Chair. Guangxi People's Govt. 58-68; First Political Commissar Guangxi Mil. District, PLA 64-73; Sec. Cen.-South Bureau, CCP 66; Political Commissar Guangzhou Mil. Region, PLA 67-; Chair. Guangxi Revolutionary Cttee. 68; mem. 9th Cen. Cttee. of CCP 69; First Sec. CCP Guangxi 71-75; First Sec. Guangdong CCP Cttee. 75-78; Chair. Guangdong Revolutionary Cttee. 75-78; mem. Politburo, 10th Cen. Cttee. of CCP 73, Politburo 11th Cen. Cttee. CCP 77; Dir.-Gen. Political Dept. PLA 77-; Exec. Chair. Presidium and Nat. Cttee. and Vice-Chair. Nat. Cttee. 5th Nat. People's Congress 78-80; Del. to CCP, 5th CPPCC; Vice-Chair. Standing Cttee. 78-; Dir.-Gen. Political Dept. PLA 78-; mem. Standing Cttee. NPC.
People's Republic of China.

Wei Wenbo; Chinese politician; b. 1905.
Vice-Minister of Justice 52-56; Sec. Shanghai Municipality CP 56-67 and Dir. its Rural Work Dept. 59-67; Sec. East China Bureau, CCP Cen. Cttee. 66-67; Deputy Sec. CCP Cen. Cttee.'s Comm. for the Inspection of Discipline 78; Minister of Justice 79-82.
People's Republic of China.

Weir, Peter Lindsay; Australian film director; b. 21 June 1944, Sydney; ed. Scots Coll., Sydney, Vaucluse Boys' High School, Sydney Univ.
Worked in real estate until 65; worked as stagehand in television, Sydney 67-; directed film sequences in variety show 68; directed amateur reviews, university and Indie 67-69; dir. for Film Australia 69-73; made own short films 69-73; independent feature-film dir. and writer 73-; various film awards.
Films: *Cars That Ate Paris* 73, *Picnic at Hanging Rock* 75, *The Last Wave* 77, *The Plumber* (television) 78, *Gallipoli* 80, *The Year of Living Dangerously* 82.
c/o Australian Film Commission, West Street, Sydney, N.S.W., Australia.

West, Morris (Langlo); Australian author; b. 26 April 1916, Melbourne; ed. Univ. of Melbourne.
Teacher of Modern Languages and Mathematics, New South Wales and Tasmania 33-39; Army service 39-43; Sec. to William Morris Hughes, fmr. Prime Minister of Australia 43; Nat. Brotherhood Award, Nat. Council of Christians and Jews 60, James Tait Black Memorial Prize 60, William Heinemann Award, Royal Soc. of Literature 60 (all prizes for *The Devil's Advocate*); Fellow, Royal Soc. of Literature, World Acad. of Arts and Sciences; Hon. D.Litt. (Santa Clara Univ., Calif.) 69; Int. Dag Hammarskjöld Prize (Grand Collar of Merit) 78.
Publs. *Gallows on the Sand* 55, *Kundu* 56, *Children of the Sun* 57, *The Crooked Road* (English title *The Big Story*) 57, *The Concubine* 58, *Backlash* (English title *Second Victory*) 58, *The Devil's Advocate* 59 (filmed 77), *The Naked Country* 60, *Daughter of Silence* 61, *Daughter of Silence* (play) 61, *The Shoes of the Fisherman* 63, *The Ambassador* 65, *The Tower of Babel* 68, *The Heretic* (play) 70, *Scandal in the Assembly* (with Robert Francis) 70, *Summer of the*

Red Wolf 71, *The Salamander* 73, *Harlequin* 74, *The Navigator* 76, *Proteus* 79, *The Clowns of God* 81.
c/o Greenbaum, Wolff and Ernst, 437 Madison Avenue, New York, N.Y. 10022, U.S.A.

White, Patrick, B.A.; Australian writer; b. 28 May 1912, London, England; ed. Cheltenham Coll., and King's Coll., Cambridge.
Intelligence officer, R.A.F., World War II; W. H. Smith & Son Award 59; Nobel Prize for Literature 73; Australian of the Year 74; awarded A.C. 75, resigned from Order 76.
Publs. Novels: *Happy Valley* 39, *The Living and the Dead* 41, *The Aunt's Story* 48, *The Tree of Man* 55, *Voss* 57, *Riders in the Chariot* 61, *The Burnt Ones* 64, *The Solid Mandala* 66, *The Vivisector* 70, *The Eye of The Storm* 73, *The Cockatoos* 74, *A Fringe of Leaves* 76, *The Twyborn Affair* 79; Plays: *The Ham Funeral* 61, *Night on Bald Mountain* 62, *Big Toys* 77, *The Night, The Prowler* (screenplay) 77, *Flaws in the Glass* (autobiog.) 81, *Signal Driver* (play) 81.
20 Martin Road, Centennial Park, Sydney, N.S.W., Australia.

Whitlam, (Edward) Gough, A.C., Q.C., B.A., LL.B.; Australian barrister and politician; b. 11 July 1916; ed. Knox Grammar School, Sydney, Canberra High School, Canberra Grammar School and Univ. of Sydney.
Royal Australian Air Force 41-45; admitted to New South Wales Bar 47; mem. House of Representatives 52-78; mem. Parl. Cttee. on Constitutional Review 56-59; mem. Fed. Parl. Exec. of Australian Labor Party 59-77; Deputy Leader of Australian Labor Party in Fed. Parl. 60-67, Leader 67-77; Prime Minister 72-75, concurrently Minister of Foreign Affairs 72-73; mem. Australian Constitutional Convention 73-76; Pres. Int. Comm. of Jurists (Australia) 82-; Visiting Fellow, Australian Nat. Univ. 78-79, first Nat. Fellow 80-81; Fellow, Sydney Univ. Senate 81-; Visiting Prof. of Australian Studies, Harvard Univ. 79; Hon. LL.D. (Philippines) 74; Hon. D.Litt. (Sydney Univ.) 81.
Publs. *The Constitution v. Labor* 57, *Australian Foreign Policy* 63, *Socialist Policies within the Constitution* 65, *Australia—Base or Bridge* 66, *Beyond Viet-Nam—Australia's Regional Responsibility* 68, *Australia: An Urban Nation* 70, *The New Federalism* 71, *Australia and her Region* 72, *Labor in Power* 73, *Australian Public Administration and the Labor Government* 73, *Australia's Foreign Policy, New Directions, New Definitions* 73, *Road to Reform: Labor in Government* 75, *Government of the People by the People for the People's House* 75, *The Labor Government and the Constitution* 76, *On Australia's Constitution* (articles and lectures 1957-77) 77, *Reform During Recession* 78, *The Truth of the Matter* 79, *Labor Essays* 80, *The Italian Inspiration in English Literature* 80, *A Pacific Community* (Harvard Lectures) 81, *The Cost of Federalism* 82.
c/o 100 William Street, Sydney, N.S.W. 2011, Australia.
Telephone: (02) 358 2022.

Wild, John Paul, C.B.E., M.A., SC.D., F.T.S., F.R.S., F.A.A.; Australian radio astronomer; b. 1923, Sheffield, England; ed. Whitgift School, Croydon, England and Peterhouse, Cambridge.
Radar Officer, Royal Navy 43-47; Researcher in Radio Astronomy, especially of the Sun, Radiophysics Div. of Commonwealth Scientific and Industrial Research Org. (C.S.I.R.O.), N.S.W., Australia 47-77, Dir. C.S.I.R.O. Solar Radio Observatory, Culgoora, N.S.W. 66-, Chief of Radiophysics Div. 71-77; Pres. Radio Astronomy Comm. of Int. Astronomical Union 67-70; Assoc. mem. CSIRO Exec. 77-78, Chair. CSIRO 78-; Foreign mem. American Philosophical Soc.; Foreign Hon. mem. American Acad. of Arts and Sciences; Corresp. mem. Royal Soc. of Sciences, Liège; Edgeworth David Medal, Hendryk Arctowski Gold Medal of Nat. Acad. of Sciences, U.S., Balthasar van der Pol Gold Medal of Int. Union of Radio Science, Herschel Medal of Royal Astronomical Soc., Thomas Rankin Lyle Medal of Australian Acad. of Science.
Publs. various papers on radio astronomy in scientific journals.
CSIRO, P.O. Box 225, Dickson, A.C.T. 2602; RMB 338, Sutton Road, via Queanbeyan, N.S.W. 2620, Australia (Home).
Telephone: (062) 484621.

Willesee, Donald Robert; Australian politician; b. 14 April 1916, Derby, W. Australia; ed. State schools.
Member of Senate 49-75, Leader of Opposition in Senate 66-67, Deputy Leader 69-72; Special Minister of State 72; Minister Assisting the Prime Minister 72-73, for Foreign Affairs 73-75; Vice-Pres. Exec. Council 72-75; mem. Joint Cttee. on Foreign Affairs 67-, Privileges Cttee. 69-; mem. several Parl. dels. abroad; Labor.
95 Walton Place, Quinns Rocks, Western Australia 6030, Australia.

Wilson, Ralph Frederick, O.B.E., M.COM.; British (New Zealand) economist and politician (retd.); b. 21 Sept. 1912; ed. Otago Boys' High School and Univ. of Otago.
Assistant Sec. Bureau of Industry 38; Private Sec. Minister of Supply and Industries and Commerce 41-47; Sec. N.Z. Board of Trade 50-54; Sec. N.Z. Retailers' Fed. 54-59; Gen. Dir. N.Z. Nat. Party 59-73; Economist M. Y. Walls and Assocs. 73-78; mem. Decimal Coinage Cttee. 58; mem. Representation Comm. 71-72; mem. State Insurance Investment Bd. 77-.
1 Aotea Road, Ruamati Beach, Wellington, New Zealand.

Wimalasena, Nanediri; Sri Lankan politician and diplomatist; b. 22 March 1914; ed. Univ. Coll. of Sri Lanka, Law Coll., Sri Lanka.
Member Kandy Municipal Council 46-47, Mayor of Kandy 63; M.P. for Senkadagala 60, 65, 70-77; Deputy Minister of Finance 65-70; Gov. for Sri Lanka, Asian Devt. Bank 65-70, Pres. Board of Govs. 68; High Commr. in U.K. Nov. 77-80; mem. Sri Lanka Branch, Exec. Cttee. IPU 65-77.
c/o Ministry of Foreign Affairs, Colombo, Sri Lanka.

Win Maung, U, B.A.; Burmese politician; b. 1916; ed. Judson Coll., Rangoon.
Joined Burmah Oil Co. after leaving coll.; then entered govt. dept.; joined Army as 2nd Lieut. 40; during Second World War took active part in resistance movement of Anti-Fascist Organization; went to India, where he received training in tactics of military and guerrilla warfare at Mil. Coll., Calcutta and Mil. Camp, Colombo 44; rejoined guerrilla forces in Burma 45; Vice-Pres. Karen Youth Organization and Ed. *Taing Yin Tha* 45; mem. Constituent Assembly 47; Minister for Industry and Labour 47, of Transport and Communications 49; later Minister for Port, Marine, Civil Aviation and Coastal Shipping; mem. Burmese Parl. for Maubin South (Karen) 51-55 and 56-57; Pres. of Burma 57-62; detained after mil. coup 62-67.
Rangoon, Burma.

Winneke, Sir Henry Arthur, A.C., K.C.M.G., K.C.V.O., O.B.E., Q.C.; Australian state governor; b. 29 Oct. 1908, Melbourne; ed. Ballarat Grammar School, Melbourne and Melbourne Univ.
Admitted to Bar 31; war service in R.A.A.F., Group Captain, Dir. Personnel Services 39-46; returned to bar 46; mem. Victorian Bar Council 48-50; Appointed King's Counsel for Victoria 49; Senior Counsel to Attorney-Gen., Victoria and Crown Prosecutor 49-51; Solicitor-Gen. Victoria 51-64; Chief Justice of Supreme Court of Victoria 64-74; Lieut.-Gov. of Victoria 72-74, Gov. 74-82; K. St. J.
4A The Pines, Kew, Victoria 3101, Australia.
Telephone: 80-4600.

Withers, Reginald Greive, LL.B.; Australian politician; b. 26 Oct. 1924, Bunbury, W.A.; ed. Bunbury and Univ. of Western Australia.
Royal Australian Navy 42-46; mem. Bunbury Municipal Council 54-56, Bunbury Diocesan Council 58-59, Treas. 61-68; State Vice-Pres., Liberal and Country League of W.A. 58-61, State Pres. 61-65; mem. Fed. Exec. of Liberal Party 61-65, Fed. Vice-Pres. 62-65; mem. Senate for W.A. Feb.-Nov. 66, Nov. 67-, Govt. Whip in Senate 69-71, Leader of Opposition in Senate 72-75; Special Minister of State, Minister for A.C.T., Minister for the Media and Minister for Tourism and Recreation Nov.-Dec. 75, Leader of Govt. in Senate and Minister for Admin. Services Dec. 75-78; Vice-Pres. Exec. Council 75-78; fmr. Chair. Joint Cttee. on A.C.T., Select Cttee. on Foreign Ownership and Control of Australian Resources, Senate Standing Cttee. on Constitutional and Legal Affairs; mem. del. to Conf. of Commonwealth Parl. Asscn., Trinidad 69; Liberal.
Parliament House, Canberra, A.C.T. 2600; and Commonwealth Parliament Offices, City Centre, 44 St. George's Terrace, Perth, W.A. 6000, Australia.
Telephone: (09) 3214608.

Woodcock, Leonard; American diplomatist and former labour union leader; b. 15 Feb. 1911, Providence, R.I.; ed. St. Wilfrid's Coll., U.K., Northampton Town and Country School, U.K., Wayne Univ., Detroit, Mich., U.S.A.
Served Int. Union, United Automobile, Aerospace and Agricultural Implement Workers of America (UAW) 40-, Staff Rep. 40-46, Admin. Asst. to Pres. 46-47, Regional Dir. 47-55, Vice-Pres. 55-70, Pres. 70-77, Pres. Emer. 77-; Chief of Mission, U.S. Liaison Office, People's Repub. of China 77-79; Amb. 79-81; Adjunct Prof., Univ. of Michigan; Hon. degrees from 17 univs. and colls. in U.S.A.
2404 Vinewood Boulevard, Ann Arbor, Mich. 48104, U.S.A. (home address).

Woolcott, Richard, B.A.; Australian diplomatist; b. 11 June 1928; ed. Frankston High School, Geelong Grammar School, Univ. of Melbourne and London Univ. School of Slavonic and East European Studies.
Joined Australian Foreign Service 51; served in Australian missions in London, Moscow (twice), S. Africa, Malaysia, Singapore and Accra; attended UN Gen. Assembly 62; Acting High Commr. to Singapore 63-64; First Public Information Officer, Dept. of Foreign Affairs 64-67; High Commr. in Ghana 67-70; Asst. Sec. Policy Research Branch, Dept. of Foreign Affairs 70-72; accompanied Prime Ministers Menzies 65, Holt 66, McMahon 71, 72 and Whitlam 73, 74 on visits to Asia, Europe, the Americas and the Pacific; Head, South Asia Div., Dept. of Foreign Affairs 73; Deputy Sec., Dept. of Foreign Affairs 74; Amb. to Indonesia 75-78, to Philippines 78-; has attended several int. confs.
Publs. *The Australian Press and Foreign News* 67, *Australian Foreign Policy* 73.
Australian Embassy, Makati, Metro Manila, Philippines.

Wriedt, Kenneth Shaw; Australian politician; b. 11 July 1927; ed. Univ. High School, Melbourne.
Served in the Merchant Navy 44-58; State Insurance Office, Tasmania 58-68; mem. Senate 68-, Leader of Govt. in Senate Feb.-Nov. 75; Minister of Primary Industry Dec. 72-73, for Agriculture 74-75, for Minerals and Energy Oct.-Nov. 75; Leader of Opposition in the Senate 76-82; Opposition spokesman on Educ. 76-77, on Foreign Affairs 77-; Labor Party.
Parliament House, Canberra, A.C.T. 2600; Marine Board Building, Hobart, Tasmania 7000; Home: 25 Corinth Street, Howrah, Hobart, Tasmania 7018, Australia.

Wright, Judith Arundell; Australian writer; b. 31 May 1915, Armidale, N.S.W.; ed. New England Girls' School, Armidale, N.S.W., and Sydney Univ.
Commonwealth Literary Fund Scholarship 49, 62; Lecturer in Australian literature at various Australian univs.; Senior Writers' Fellowship, Australia Council 77-79; Encyclopedia Britannica Writers' Award 64; Hon. D.Litt. (Univs. of Queensland, Sydney, Monash, New England and Australian Nat. Univ.); F.A.H.A. 71, Robert Frost Memorial Medal 76, Alice Award (Women Writers) 80.
Publs. Poetry: *The Moving Image* 46, *Woman to Man* 49, *The Gateway* 53, *The Two Fires* 55, *A Book of Birds* 62, *Five Senses* 63, *The Other Half* 66, *Collected Poems* 71, *Alive* 73, *Fourth Quarter* 76, *The Double Tree* 78; criticism: *Charles Harpur* 63, *Preoccupations in Australian Poetry* 64; anthologies: *A Book of Australian Verse* 56, *New Land, New Language* 57; biography: *The Generations of Man* 58; short stories: *The Nature of Love* 66; Prose: *Because I Was Invited* 75, *The Coral Battleground* 77, *The Cry for the Dead* 81.
Edge, Half Moon Wildlife District, Mongarlowe, N.S.W. 2622, Australia.

Wu Bo; Chinese politician.
Deputy Dir. Finance Dept., N. China People's Govt. 48; Dir.-Gen. Office of Ministry of Finance 49-54; Vice-Minister of Finance 52-60, 61-63, Minister 79-80.
People's Republic of China.

Wu Dao; Chinese army officer and party official; b. 1915.
Military official 30-67; Deputy Political Commissar, Nei Monggol Mil. Region, PLA 60, Political Commissar 67-; Vice-Chair. Nei Monggol Revolutionary Cttee. 67-71; Sec. CCP Nei Monggol 71-; Deputy Political Commissar, Beijing Mil. Region 76-; mem. 9th Cen. Cttee. CCP 69, 10th Cen. Cttee. 73.
People's Republic of China.

Wu Dasheng; Chinese party official.
Vice-Chair. Jiangsu Revolutionary Cttee. 68; Political Commissar Jiangsu Mil. District PLA 69, Sec. CCP Jiangsu Province 70-; mem. 9th Cen. Cttee. CCP 69, 10th Cen. Cttee. 73.
People's Republic of China.

Wu De; Chinese party official; b. 1914, Fengrun, Hebei; ed. China Univ., Beijing.
Workers' leader in Tangshan 35; Regimental Political Commissar 42; Vice-Minister of Fuel Industry 49-50; Sec. CCP Pingyuan 50-52; Deputy Sec. CCP Tianjin 52-55; Deputy Mayor of Tianjin 52-53, Mayor 53-55; Pres. Tianjin Univ. 52-57; Alt. mem. 8th Cen. Cttee. of CCP 56; First Sec. CCP Jilin 56-66; Political Commissar Jilin Mil. District, People's Liberation Army 58; Sec. N.E. Bureau, CCP 61; Second Sec. CCP Beijing 66; Acting Mayor of Beijing 66-78; Vice-Chair. Beijing Revolutionary Cttee. 67-72, Chair. (Mayor) 72-78; mem. 9th Cen. Cttee. of CCP 69; Head of Cultural Group, State Council 71; Second Sec. CCP Beijing 71, First Sec. 72-78; mem. Politburo 10th Cen. Cttee. of CCP 73, Politburo 11th Cen. Cttee. 77; Second Political Commissar, Beijing Mil. Region, PLA; Exec. Chair. Presidium 5th Nat. People's Congress; a Vice-Chair. Standing Cttee. of Nat. People's Congress (reported to have been suspended June 79); dismissed from Politburo and all other posts 80; Deputy Dir. Acad. of Social Sciences 80.
People's Republic of China.

Wu Gehua; Chinese party official.
Commander PLA Railway Corps. 73; Commdr. Chengdu Mil. Region, PLA 77-79, Xinjiang Uygur Mil. Unit 79-80; Urumqi Units 79-80; Guangzhou Mil. Unit 80-; Alt. mem. 11th Cen. Cttee. CCP 77.
People's Republic of China.

Wu Guixian; Chinese party official; b. 1935.
Woman worker in textile mill at N.W. State Cotton Mill No. 1, Xian; mem. Shaanxi Revolutionary Cttee. 68; mem. 9th Cen. Cttee. of CCP 69; Deputy Sec. CCP Shaanxi 71;

Alt. mem. Politburo, CCP 73-77; a Vice-Premier, State Council 75-78; mem. 11th Cen. Cttee. CCP 77.
People's Republic of China.

Wu Lie; Chinese soldier.
Political Commissar Beijing Units 78-80; Second Political Commissar, Beijing Garrison 80-.
People's Republic of China.

Wu Qinying; Chinese army officer.
Commander Guizhon Mil. District 80-.
People's Republic of China.

Wu Shengrong; Chinese soldier.
Secretary CCP Henan Prov. Cttee. 78-; Commdr. Qinghai Provincial Mil. Dist. 78-.
People's Republic of China.

Wu Xiuzhuan; Chinese politician; b. 1903, Hubei; ed. Middle School, Wuhan, Moscow.
Professor of Politics, Fudan Univ., Shanghai 31; Instructor, Red Army School, Jiangxi 32; Dir. Foreign Affairs Dept. CCP 36; Dir. Dept. of Soviet Union and East European Countries, Ministry of Foreign Affairs 49-52, Vice-Minister of Foreign Affairs 51-55; Amb. to Yugoslavia 55-58; head Dept. Int. Relations 59-67; criticized and removed from office during Cultural Revolution 67; joined CCP 25, Deputy Dir. Int. Liaison Dept. CCP 64, mem. 8th Cen. Cttee. CCP 56; Deputy Chief of Gen. Staff, PLA 75-.
People's Republic of China.

Wu Zhong; Chinese army officer.
On Long March 34; Company Commdr. 37, Div. Commdr. 49; Sec. CCP Beijing 71; Commdr. Beijing Garrison District PLA 73-; Alt. mem. 9th Cen. Cttee. CCP 69, 10th Cen. Cttee. 73, 11th Cen. Cttee. 77.
People's Republic of China.

X

Xi Jinwu; Chinese soldier; b. 1913, Fuping County, Shaanxi Prov.
Commander, Xizang Mil. District, PLA 75; Sec. Xizang Regional CCP Cttee. 78-.
People's Republic of China.

Xi Zhongxun; Chinese soldier and party official.
Leading mem. in Shaanxi-Gansu border area before 49; Sec., special Party Cttee., Guanchong Pref. 36-48; mem., N.W. China Bureau CCP Cen. Cttee. 45; sent to reinforce leadership of Field Army led by Wang Zhen 46; First Sec. Guangdong Provincial CCP Cttee. 78-; Commdr. Henan Mil. District 78-; Vice-Chair. Standing Cttee., NPC Sept. 80-; mem. NPC Legis. Affairs Comm. 81-.
People's Republic of China.

Xiang Zhonghua; Chinese army officer.
Deputy Political Commissar, People's Liberation Army Armoured Force 53, Political Commissar 58; Lieut.-Gen. 55; Deputy Chief of Staff PLA 72-77; Alt. mem. 10th Cen. Cttee. of CCP 73; Political Commissar, Guangzhou Mil. Region, PLA 77.
People's Republic of China.

Xiao Han; Chinese government and party official.
Vice-Minister of the Coal Industry 75, Minister 77-80; Deputy Minister State Econ. Comm. Jan. 80-; Alt. mem. 11th Cen. Cttee. of CCP 77.
People's Republic of China.

Xiao Jingguang; Chinese army officer; b. 1904, Changsha, Hunan; ed. Hunan Provincial Normal School, Sun Yat-sen Univ. and Red Army Coll., Moscow, U.S.S.R.
Joined Communist Youth League and CCP 20; Instructor Huangpu Mil. Acad. 24; Political Commissar 5th Army Corps 31; on Long March 34-35; Commdr. Cavalry, Red Army 38; Alt. mem. 7th Cen. Cttee. of CCP 45; Commdr. Hunan Mil. District, People's Liberation Army 49; Commdr. PLA Navy 60-79; Vice-Minister of Nat. Defence 54-; Vice-Chair. Standing Cttee. NPC July 79-; mem. 8th Cen. Cttee. of CCP 56, 9th Cen. Cttee. 69, 10th Cen. Cttee. 73, 11th Cen. Cttee. 77.
People's Republic of China.

Xiao Ke; Chinese politician; b. 1908, Jiahe Cty., Hunan.
Joined CCP 27; on Long March; then Deputy Commdr. Second Front Army, Commdr. 31st army of Fourth Front Army, Commdr. Hebei-Rhe-Chahar advance army (successively); Dir. mil. training dept. under Mil. Comm. CCP Cen. Cttee. and Vice-Minister Nat. Defence after 49; Pres. Mil. and Political Acad. 72; currently Vice-Minister Nat. Defence and Pres. and First Pol. Commissar Mil. Acad.; Vice-Chair. CPPCC Nat. Cttee. Sept. 80-.
People's Republic of China.

Xiao Wangdong; Chinese soldier; b. Jiangxi.
Leader Guerrilla Detachment New 4th Army 38; mem. E. China Mil. and Admin. Cttee. 49-53; Sec. CCP N. Jiangsu Dist. Cttee. 49; mem. N. Admin. Council 50-52; mem. Jiangsu People's Provincial Govt. 52; mem. E. China Admin. Cttee. 53; Dep. Pol. Commissar PLA Nanjing Mil. Region 57; Deputy Sec. CCP Cttee. PLA Nanjing Units 58; Lt.-Gen. PLA 58; Deputy for Nanjing Units to 2nd NPC 58, re-elected 3rd NPC 64; mem. Nat. Defence Council 65-67; Vice-Minister of Culture 65-67; Sec. Cultural Dept. CCP Cen. Cttee. 66; Acting Dir. Cultural Dept. CCP Cen. Cttee. 66; denounced as a capitalist roader and a counter-revolutionary revisionist July 67; Pol. Commissar Jinan PLA Mil. Region 78-, First Pol. Commissar 80-.
People's Republic of China.

Xie Xuegong; Chinese party official.
Shanxi Provincial People's Govt. 50-52; Vice-Minister of Foreign Trade 52-58; Pres. Beijing Foreign Trade Coll. 54-58; Sec. CCP Hebei 58-68; Sec. N. China Bureau 63-68; Chair. Tianjin Revolutionary Cttee. 67-; mem. 9th Cen. Cttee. of CCP 69; First Sec. CCP Tianjin 71-; mem. 10th Cen. Cttee. of CCP 73, 11th Cen. Cttee. 77.
People's Republic of China.

Xie Zhengrong; Chinese soldier.
Commander of Jilin Garrison District, PLA 58-69; Sec. of CCP Cttee., Sichuan 71; Commdr. Sichuan Mil. District, PLA 73; Vice Chair. Sichuan Revolutionary Cttee. 73; Alt. mem. 11th Cen. Cttee. of CCP 77.
People's Republic of China.

Xin Junjie; Chinese army officer.
Commander Hubei Mil. District, People's Liberation Army 70-72; Vice-Chair. Hubei Revolutionary Cttee. 71; Commdr. Jiangxi Mil. Dist. 78-; mem. Standing Cttee. Jiangxi CCP Cttee. 78-.
People's Republic of China.

Xu Deheng; Chinese politician; b. 1894, Jiangxi Prov.
Member People's Political Council under Nationalist govt. 47; mem. Nat. Cttee. 1st CPPCC 49; Chief of Political and Legal Section, CPPCC 49-54; mem. Political and Legal Cttee. Jiu San Soc. (JSS); mem. Cttee. for Checking up on Austerity Programme, GAC 51; mem. CPPCC Standing Cttee. 53; mem. Bills Cttee., 1st NPC 54; mem. Standing Cttee., 1st NPC 54-56; mem. Standing Cttee., 2nd CPPCC 54; Chief of Educ. Section, CPPCC 54; Vice-Chair. Study Cttee., CPPCC 56; Minister of Aquatic Products 56-69; Chair. 2nd Cen. Cttee., JSS 58; mem. Standing Cttee., 3rd CPPCC 59; Vice-Chair. Standing Cttee., 4th CPPCC 65-78, 5th CPPCC 78, 4th NPC 75-78, 5th NPC 78; Chair. JSS Cen. Cttee. 79; Vice-Chair. Standing Cttee., NPC 80-.
People's Republic of China.

Xu Dixin; Chinese economist; b. Oct. 1906, Mian Hu Jieyang Co., Guangdon Province.
Participated in Left-Wing Culture Movt., Shanghai in 30s; Admin. Union of Chinese Social Scientists Asscns. (U.S.S.A.), Gen. Union of Left-Wing Culture (G.U.L.C.) 33-35; Ed. and mem. Ed. Cttee. Wuhan and Chongqing *Xinghua Ribao* (New China Daily) 37-46, Joint Ed. *Masses* magazine in Hong Kong 46-49; Vice-Chair. E. China Financial and Econ. Cttee., Shanghai Municipal, Financial and Econ. Cttee. 49-52; Head Shanghai Municipal Admin. Bureau of Industry and Commerce, United Front Dept. Shanghai Municipal Party Cttee., Sec.-Gen. Shanghai Municipal People's Govt. 49-52; Head 6th Office Cen. Financial and Econ. Comm. of State Council, Deputy Head 8th Office 52-58; Head Cen. Admin. Bureau of Industry and Commerce 52-69; Deputy Head United Front Dept. of Party Cen. Cttee. 55-75; Rep. 3rd Nat. People's Congress 64-75, mem. Standing Cttee. of 5th Nat. People's Congress 78-82; Adviser, Research Inst. of Econs. of State Planning Comm. 75-77; Dir. Inst. of Econs., Chinese Acad. of Social Sciences 77-, Vice-Pres. 77-; Fellow, Dept. of Philosophy and Social Sciences, Chinese Acad. of Science.
Institute of Economics, Chinese Academy of Social Sciences, 2 Yuetan Bei Xiao Jie, Beijing, People's Republic of China.
Telephone: 89 5322.

Xu Jiatun; Chinese politician.
Member of CCP, Deputy Sec., Sec., Fuzhou Municipal Cttee. in Fujian Province 50; Sec. Nanjing Municipal Cttee. CCP in Jiangsu Province 54; mem. Secr. Jiangsu Provincial Cttee. CCP and Vice-Gov. 56; mem. Standing Cttee. and Vice-Chair. Jiangsu Provincial Revolutionary Cttee. 70, 74; Sec. then First Sec. Jiangsu Provincial Cttee. CCP; Chair. Jiangsu Provincial Revolutionary Cttee.; Chair. Standing Cttee. of Fifth People's Congress of Jiangsu Province; First Political Commissar of PLA of Jiangsu Provincial Mil. Area, First Sec. of Party Cttee.; mem. 11th Cen. Cttee. of CCP 77-.
Nanjing, People's Republic of China.

Xu Shiyou, Gen.; Chinese army officer; b. 1906, Henan.
Commander 9th Army 33; Chief Commdr. of Cavalry 35; Brigade Commdr. 40; Commdr. Jingluo Mil. District 42, Ponai Mil. District 44; Commdr. 11th Army Corps, 3rd Field Army 48; Commdr. Shandong Mil. District, People's Liberation Army 50; Deputy Commdr. 3rd Field Army, PLA 54; mem. Nat. Defence Council 54-; Col.-Gen. 55; Alt. mem. 8th Cen. Cttee. of CCP 56; Commdr. Nanjing Mil. Region, PLA 57-73; Vice-Minister of Nat. Defence 59; Sec. E. China Bureau, CCP 66; Chair. Jiangsu Revolutionary Cttee. 68-73; mem. Politburo, 9th Cen. Cttee. of CCP 69; First Sec. CCP Jiangsu 71; fmr. Chair. Jiangsu Revolutionary Cttee.; mem. Politburo, 10th Cen. Cttee. of CCP 73, 75, 11th Cen. Cttee. 77-; Commdr. Guangzhou Mil. Region PLA 74-77; Vice-Minister of Nat. Defence 78-; Deputy for PLA 5th NPC 78-.
People's Republic of China.

Xu Xiangqian, Marshal; Chinese politician and fmr. army officer; b. 1902, Wutai, Shanxi; ed. Taiyuan Normal School, Huangpu Mil. Acad.
Director Political Dept., Student Army 26; joined CCP 27; Workers' Leader in Guangzhou Uprising 27; Commdr.-in-Chief 4th Front Army 31; Deputy Commdr. 129th Div. 39; mem. 7th Cen. Cttee. of CCP 45; Commdr., Political Commissar 1st Army Corps 48; Deputy Commdr. N. China Region, People's Liberation Army 49-54; Chief of Staff PLA 49-54; Vice-Chair. Nat. Defence Council 54-; Marshal PLA 55; mem. 8th Cen. Cttee. of CCP 56, 9th Cen. Cttee. 69, 10th Cen. Cttee. 73; mem. Politburo, 11th Cen. Cttee. 77; Vice-Chair. Standing Cttee., Nat. People's Congress 65-81; a Vice-Premier 78-80, Minister of Nat. Defence 78-81; Vice-Chair. Mil. Affairs Cttee., CCP Cen. Cttee. 75-; Deputy for PLA, 5th NPC 78; mem. Presidium, NPC 78.
People's Republic of China.

Xuan Thuy; Vietnamese politician; b. 2 Sept. 1912.
In numerous nat. liberation movements until 45; later Editor *Cuu Quoc* (National Salvation—organ of the Viet-Minh); Pres. Asscn. of Journalists of Democratic Repub. of Viet-Nam; Deputy Vice-Speaker and Sec.-Gen. of Nat. Assembly, Democratic Repub. of Viet-Nam; mem. Presidium Fatherland Front Cen. Cttee.; Deputy Chair. Democratic Repub. of Viet-Nam Del. to Geneva Conf. on Laos 61; Minister of Foreign Affairs 63-65; Minister without Portfolio to head Democratic Repub. of Viet-Nam's delegation, Paris 68-73; Vice-Chair. Standing Cttee. of Nat. Assembly of Socialist Repub. of Viet-Nam July 76-; Vice-Pres. and Gen. Sec. Council of State 81-82; mem. Secretariat of Cen. Cttee. Lao Dong Party until 76, of Communist Party of Viet-Nam 76-82.
National Assembly, Hanoi, Viet-Nam.

Xue Muqiao; Chinese economist and politician; b. 25 Oct. 1904, Wuxi County, Jiangsu Province; largely self-taught, ed. later high school.
Worked in Inst. of Social Sciences attached to Cen. Research Acad. conducting surveys of rural economy 20s; Prof. of Rural Econs., normal school, Guangxi Prov. 33; with other organized Soc. for Research in China's Rural Economy and Ed. *Rural China* monthly, Shanghai; 1st Dir. of Dept. of Training, Anti-Japanese Mil. and Political Acad. of Cen. China, Sec.-Gen. Anti-Japanese Democratic Govt. of Shandong Univ., war with Japan 37-45; successively Sec.-Gen. of Financial and Econ. Comm. of Govt. Admin. Council, Vice-Minister in Charge of State Planning Comm., Dir. of State Statistical Bureau, Dir. Nat. Price Comm., mem. Council of Social Sciences, Academia Sinica; del. to First, Second and Third Nat. People's Congresses; mem. Nat. Cttee. Fifth Chinese People's Political Consultative Conf.; now adviser to State Planning Comm., Dir. its Econ. Inst., Prof., Peking Univ., Pres. Nat. Statistical Soc., Deputy Dir. and mem. Academic Cttees. of the Econ. Inst. and Inst. of the World Economy, Chinese Acad. of Social Sciences.
Publs. *The Elementary Knowledge of China's Rural Economy, The ABC of Rural Economy, The Socialist Transformation of China's National Economy* (English, Japanese, French and Russian translations available), *Some Theoretical Problems Concerning the Socialist Economy, Research on Problems Concerning China's Socialist Economy* (English, Japanese, French and Spanish trans. available).
State Planning Commission, Beijing, People's Republic of China.

Y

Yamada, Hisamari; Japanese politician.
Member, House of Reps. 67-; fmr. Admin. Deputy Foreign Minister; fmr. Amb. to Moscow; Dir.-Gen. Environment Agency 77-78.
c/o Liberal-Democratic Party, 7, 2-chome, Hirakawacho, Chiyoda-ku, Tokyo, Japan.

Yamagata, Shiro, B.ENG.; Japanese business executive; b. 26 Dec. 1902, Iwakuni City; ed. Tokyo Univ.
Osaka Refinery, Mitsubishi Metal Corpn. 27-, Man. Osaka Refinery 47-48, Dir. 50-, Man. Dir. 56-60, Pres. 60-67, Chair. 67-71; Pres. Mitsubishi Nuclear Fuel Co. Ltd. 71-; Cordon of the Rising Sun, Second Class 73.
Mitsubishi Nuclear Fuel Company Limited, Tokyo, Japan.

Yamanaka, Seiichiro; Japanese banker; b. 13 Oct. 1916; ed. Keio Univ.
Joined Mitsui Trust and Banking Co. Ltd. 39, Dir. and

Man. Security Dept. 64, Dir. and Man. 68, Senior Man. Dir. 71, Deputy Pres. 76, Pres. 79-82, Chair. 82-; Trustee and mem. Research and Policy Cttee. Japan Cttee., for Econ. Devt. 79; Standing Cttee. Fed. of Econ. Orgs. and Standing Cttee. of Finance Div. Tokyo Chamber of Commerce and Industry 79.
Mitsui Trust and Banking Co. Ltd., 1-1, Nihonbashi-Muromachi 2-chome, Chuo-ku, Tokyo 103, Japan.

Yamanouchi, Ichiro; Japanese politician; b. 15 Feb. 1913, Fukui Pref.; ed. Tokyo Univ.
Joined Home Affairs Ministry 36; Vice-Minister of Construction 63-65; mem. House of Councillors 65-; Chair. Standing Cttee. on Local Admin., House of Councillors 70-71; Parl. Vice-Minister of Nat. Land Agency 74-76; Vice-Chair. Liberal Democratic Party Policy Affairs Research Council 77; Chair. Standing Cttee. on Budget, House of Councillors 79-80; Minister of Posts and Telecommunications 80-81.
Publs. *Mitekita Soren, Chukinto* 67 etc.
c/o Liberal-Democratic Party, 7, 2-chome, Hirakawacho, Chiyoda-ku, Tokyo, Japan.

Yamashita, Isamu; Japanese business executive; b. 15 Feb. 1911; ed. Tokyo Imperial Univ.
Joined shipbuilding dept., Mitsui & Co. 33; entered Tama Shipyard Ltd. (predecessor of Mitsui Shipbuilding & Engineering Co. Ltd.) 37; Man. Dir. Mitsui Shipbuilding & Engineering Co. Ltd. (now Mitsui Engineering and Shipbuilding Co. Ltd.) 62, Senior Man. Dir. 66, Vice-Pres. 68, Pres. 70-, Chair. 79-.
Mitsui Engineering & Shipbuilding Co. Ltd., 6-4, Tsukiji 5-chome, Chuo-ku, Tokyo, Japan.
Telephone: 544-3001.

Yamashita, Toshihiko; Japanese business executive; b. 18 July 1919; Osaka; ed. Osaka Municipal Izuo Tech. School.
Joined Matsushita Electric Industrial Co. Ltd. 38, Asst. Gen. Man. Electron Tube Div. and Plant Man. Electronic Component Factory 56; Man. Dir. West Electric Co. Ltd. 62-65; Gen. Man. Air Conditioner Dept., Matsushita Electric Industrial Co. Ltd. 65, mem. Advisory Council 71-, Dir. 74-, Pres. 77-; Pres. Electronic Industries Asscn. of Japan 78-80; Dir. Japan Electrical Mfrs. Asscn. 77-; Chevalier de l'Ordre National (Malagasy Democratic Repub.) 79.
Matsushita Electric Industrial Co. Ltd., Kadoma City, Osaka Prefecture (Office); 4-11-10 Aoyama-dai, Suita City, Osaka, Japan (Home).

Yang Dayi; Chinese army officer.
Regimental Commdr. 49; Deputy Commdr. Hunan Mil. District PLA 67, Commdr. 69-75; Commdr. Liaoning Mil. District, PLA 76-; Vice-Chair. Hunan Revolutionary Cttee. 68; Deputy Sec. CCP Hunan 70, Sec. 73; Alt. mem. 10th Cen. Cttee. CCP 73, 11th Cen. Cttee. 77.
People's Republic of China.

Yang Dezhi, Gen.; Chinese army officer; b. 1910, Liling, Hunan; ed. Red. Army Acad. and Nanjing Mil. Acad.
Joined CCP 27; on Long March 34-35; Regimental Commdr., Red Army 35; Commdr. Ningxia Mil. Region, People's Liberation Army 49; Chief of Staff Chinese People's Volunteers in Korea 51, Deputy Commdr. Chinese People's Volunteers 53-54, Commdr. 54-55; mem. Nat. Defence Council 54; Gen. 55; Alt. mem. 8th Cen. Cttee. of CCP 56; Commdr. Jinan Mil. Region, PLA 58-73; First Vice-Chair. Shandong Revolutionary Cttee. 67, Chair. 71-76; mem. 9th Cen. Cttee. of CCP 69; First Sec. CCP Shandong 71-76; Vice-Chair. Liaoning Revolutionary Cttee. 72; mem. 10th Cen. Cttee. of CCP 73, 11th Cen. Cttee. 77; Commdr. Wuhan Mil. Region, PLA 72-79; First Sec. CCP Cttee. Units, Commdr. PLA Kunming Mil. Region 79-80; Vice-Minister of Nat. Defence 80-; Chief of Gen. Staff, PLA Feb. 80-; Sec., Secretariat, Cen. Cttee. 80-.
People's Republic of China.

Yang Jingren; Chinese politician; b. 1905, Gansu.
Former High Imam of Islam; First Sec., Ningxia Hui CCP 61-67; criticized and removed from office during Cultural Revolution 67; mem. 11th Cen. Cttee. 77; Minister in charge of State Nationalities Affairs Comm. March 78-; Exec. Chair. 5th Nat. Cttee. of CPPCC 78, Vice-Chair. 78-80; Vice-Chair. Standing Cttee. of Nat. People's Congress 78; a Vice-Premier, State Council Sept. 80-.
State Council, Beijing, People's Republic of China.

Yang-Kang Lin (alias Chih-Hung); Chinese politician; b. 10 June 1927, Nantou Co., Taiwan Province; ed. Dept. of Political Science, Nat. Taiwan Univ.
Chief, Admin. Section, Civil Affairs Bureau, Nantou Co. Govt. 53; Magistrate, Nantou Co. 67; Sec. Taiwan Prov. Govt. 64, Commr., Dept. of Reconstruction 72; Gov. of Taiwan 79-81; Minister of the Interior 81-82; Gov. Taiwan Prov. 82-; Mayor Taipei Special Municipality 76; Order of Diplomatic Service Merit, Korea 77.
Taiwan Provincial Government, Chung Hsin New Village, Nantou County, Taiwan, Republic of China.

Yang Ligong; Chinese politician.
Minister of Agric. 78-79, of Forestry 78-79, of Agricultural Machinery 79-82.
People's Republic of China.

Yang Shankun; Chinese politician; b. 1907, Tongnan Cty., Sichuan Prov.; ed. Sun Yat-sen Univ., Moscow.
Joined Communist Youth League 25, Chinese Communist Party (CCP) 26; Sec. Party Fraction All-China Fed. of Trade Unions and Head Propaganda Dept. CCPCC 31; Dir. Political Dept. First Front Army and Deputy Dir. Gen. Political Dept. Red Army; on Long March 34-35; Sec. North China Bureau CCPCC 37; Sec.-Gen. Mil. Comm. CCPCC 45; Dir. Gen. Office and Deputy Sec.-Gen. CCPCC after founding of People's Repub.; Second Sec. Guangdong Prov. Party Cttee., Vice-Chair. GP Rev. Cttee., Vice-Gov. Guangdong Prov., First Sec. Guangzhou (Canton) City Party Cttee. and Chair. Guangzhou Rev. Cttee. 78; Vice-Chair. NPC Standing Cttee. 80; Sec.-Gen. CCP Mil. Comm. June 81-; mem. 8th Cen. Cttee. of CCP 56, 11th Cen. Cttee. 77; mem. 1st, 2nd, 3rd and 5th Nat. Cttees. CPPCC and Standing Cttees. People's Republic of China.

Yang Xiufeng; Chinese politician; b. 1897, Qianan Cty., Hebei.
Studied in France 29; joined CCP 30; deported from France 31; studied in Soviet Union 32; party work, Germany and U.K.; Commdr. Western Hebei guerrilla detachment in Sino-Japanese war; Chair. Shanxi-Hebei-Shandong-Henan border region govt. and Sec.-Gen. Preparatory Cttee. of People's Rep. Conf. after war; Vice-Chair. North China People's Govt. during Civil War; after 49 successively Chair. Hebei Prov. Govt., Minister of Higher Educ., Minister of Educ. and Pres. Supreme People's Court; Vice-Chair. CPPCC Nat. Cttee. Sept. 80-.
People's Republic of China.

Yang Yichen; Chinese party official.
First Sec. Heilongjiang Provincial CCP Cttee. 77-; mem. 11th Cen. Cttee., CCP 77; First Political Commissar, PLA Heilongjiang Mil. District 79-.
c/o People's Government of Heilongjiang Province, People's Republic of China.

Yang Yong; Chinese army officer; b. 1906, Liuyang, Hunan; ed. Red Army Coll.
Joined CCP 26; Regimental Deputy Commdr., Red Army 37; Commdr. 5th Army Group, 2nd Field Army, People's

Liberation Army 48; Deputy Commdr. 2nd Field Army, PLA 49; Gov. of Guizhou 49-55; Deputy Commdr. Chinese People's Volunteers, Korea 54, Commdr. Chinese People's Volunteers 55-58; Alt. mem. 8th Cen. Cttee. CCP 56; Commdr. Beijing Mil. Region, PLA 60-67; criticized and removed from office during Cultural Revolution 67; Commdr. Xinjiang Uygur Mil. Region, PLA 73-77; Vice-Chair. Xinjiang Uygur Revolutionary Cttee. 73; Second Sec. CCP. Xinjiang Uygur 73-77; mem. 11th Cen. Cttee. of CCP 77; Deputy Chair. PLA Gen. Staff 77-; mem. Standing Cttee., Mil. Comm., Cen. Cttee. 80-.
People's Republic of China.

Yang Zhongsheng; Chinese party official.
On "Long March" 34; Regt. Commdr. 45, Div. Commdr. 49, Commdr. 16th Army, Jilin 63; Vice-Chair. Beijing Revolutionary Cttee. 69; Sec. CCP Beijing 71; Political Commissar, Beijing Garrison District PLA 73-; Alt. mem. 9th Cen. Cttee. CCP 69, 10th Cen. Cttee. 73, 11th Cen. Cttee. 77.
People's Republic of China.

Yango, Alejandro D., LL.B.; Philippine diplomatist; ed. Coll. of Law, Univ. of the Philippines and Acad. of American and Int. Law, S. Methodist Univ., Dallas, Texas.
Member Philippine Bar 46; joined Philippine Foreign Service; Vice-Consul, Sydney 48-51, Jakarta 51-53, Hong Kong 53-55, Agana 55-56; Consul, Tokyo 56-60; Consul-Gen., Honolulu 62-66; Asst. Sec. for UN Affairs and Int. Confs. Dept. of Foreign Affairs, Manila 72-74; Minister, Philippine Mission to UN 66, Amb. 71-72, Dep. Perm. Rep. 74-77, Acting Perm. Rep. 77-79, Perm. Rep. June 79-; Rep. to UN Security Council 80-81; attended Conf. on Non-Nuclear Weapons States, Geneva 68, INTELSAT Conf., Washington 69, Conf. on the Law of the Sea 74-79, UN World Conf. for Action against Apartheid, Lagos 77, UN Conf. on the Succession of States with Respect to Treaties, Vienna 78; mem. Expert Advisory Panel on Disarmament Studies to UN Sec.-Gen.
Permanent Mission of the Republic of the Philippines to the United Nations, 556 Fifth Avenue, 5th Floor, New York, N.Y. 10036, U.S.A.
Telephone: 764-1309.

Yano, Junya; Japanese politician; b. 27 April 1932, Osaka; ed. Kyoto Univ.
With Ohbayashi-gumi Ltd. 56-; mem. Osaka Prefectural Assembly 63; mem. House of Reps. 67-; Sec.-Gen. Komeito (Clean Govt.) Party 67-; mem. Forum to Consider a New Japan Nov. 76.
Komeito Party, 17 Minamimoto-machi, Shinjuku-ku, Tokyo; 536 Mikuriya, Higashi-Osaka-shi, Osaka, Japan.

Yao Wenyuan; Chinese journalist; b. 1924.
Journalist and youth activist before Cultural Revolution; leading pro-Maoist journalist during Cultural Revolution 65-68; Editor *Wen Hui Bao* 66, *Liberation Daily* 66; mem. Cen. Cultural Revolution Group, CCP 66; Vice-Chair. Shanghai Revolutionary Cttee. 67-76; Editor *People's Daily* 67-76; mem. Politburo, CCP 69; Second Sec. CCP Shanghai 71; mem. Politburo, 10th Cen. Cttee. of CCP 73-76; arrested as a mem. of the "Gang of Four" Oct. 76; expelled from CCP July 77; tried with "Gang of Four" Nov. 80-Jan. 81; sentenced twenty yrs. imprisonment Jan. 81.
People's Republic of China.

Yao Yilin; Chinese politician; b. 1915, Jiangxi.
Organized anti-Japanese demonstrations in Beijing 35; Sec.-Gen. North China Bureau Cen. Cttee. CCP during Sino-Japanese War 37-46; mem. Cttee. on Finance and Trade, Head of Trade Dept. People's Govt. of North China Jan. 49; Deputy Minister of Trade 49-62, Minister 62-67; criticized and removed from office during Cultural Revolution 67; Deputy Minister of Foreign Affairs 73-78; a Vice-Premier 78-; Minister of Commerce 78-79, of Fourth Ministry of Machine Building 79-80; Sec., Secretariat and Deputy Sec.-Gen. Cen. Cttee. 80-; Minister in Charge of the State Planning Comm. Aug. 80-; Alt. mem. 11th Cen. Cttee. of CCP 77.
People's Republic of China.

Yasui, Kaoru, LL.D.; Japanese jurist and poet; b. 25 April 1907, Osaka; ed. Tokyo Univ.
Assistant Prof. Tokyo Univ. 32-42, Prof. 42-48; Prof. Hosei Univ. 52-, Dean Faculty of Jurisprudence 57-63, Dir. 63-66, Prof. Emer. 78-; Leader (Chair. etc.) Japan Council Against Atomic and Hydrogen Bombs 54-65; Pres. Japanese Inst. for World Peace 65-; Pres. Maruki Gallery for Hiroshima Panels 68-; Chair. Japan-Korea (Democratic People's Repub.) Solidarity Cttee. of Social Scientists 72-; Dir.-Gen. Int. Inst. of the Juche Idea 78-; Hon. mem. Japanese Asscn. of Int. Law 76-; Lenin Peace Prize 58; Peace Medal (Fed. Repub. of Germany) 60; Gold Medal (Czechoslovakia) 65; Hon. Dr. Law (San Gabriel Coll. U.S.A.).
Publs. *Outline of International Law* 39, *Banning Weapons of Mass Destruction* 55, *People and Peace* 55, *Collection of Treaties* 60, *My Way* 67, *The Dialectical Method and the Science of International Law* 70, *A Piece of Eternity* (poems) 77.
Minami-Ogikubo 3-13-11, Suginami-ku, Tokyo, Japan.
Telephone: 03-332-3580.

Yasui, Kizo; Japanese business executive; b. 2 Dec. 1899, Shiga; ed. Tokyo Univ. of Commerce.
Joined the Mitsui Bank Ltd. 26, Dir. 51, Man. Dir. 54, Senior Man. Dir. 57, Deputy Pres. 59; President Mitsui Petrochemicals Co., Ltd. 61; Exec. Vice-Pres. Toray Industries Inc. 63, Chair. 71-78, Senior Adviser 78-; Pres. Japan Chemical Fibres Asscn. 73-76; Vice-Pres. Japan Fed. of Econ. Orgs. (Keidanren) 74-80, Counsellor 80-; Chair. Inquiry and Audit Board Japanese Nat. Railways 74-; Order of the Rising Sun 70, Order of the Sacred Treasure (First Class) 79.
Toray Industries Inc., Toray Building, 2 Nihonbashi, Muromachi, 2-chome, Chuo-ku, Tokyo; No. 5-36, 4-chome Minamiazabu, Minato-ku, Tokyo 106, Japan.
Telephone: 03-473-0520.

Ye Fei; Chinese party official; b. 1909, Fuan, Fujian.
Guerrilla leader in Fujian 26-29; joined CCP 27; Div. Commdr. New 4th Army 41; Corps Commdr. 3rd Field Army 49; Vice-Gov. of Fujian 49-54, Gov. 55-59; Mayor of Xiamen 49; First Sec. CCP Fujian 55-68; Gen. 55; Alt. mem. 8th Cen. Cttee. of CCP 56; Political Commissar Fuzhou Mil. Region, People's Liberation Army 57-67; Sec. E. China Bureau, CCP 63-68; criticized and removed from office during Cultural Revolution 67; Alt. mem. 10th Cen. Cttee. of CCP 73; Minister of Communications 75-79; mem. 11th Cen. Cttee. CCP 77; First Political Commissar PLA Naval Units 79-; Cmmdr. Navy 80-.
People's Republic of China.

Ye Jianying, Marshal; Chinese party leader and fmr. army officer; b. 14 May 1897, Meixien, Guangdong; ed. Yunnan Mil. Inst., Sun Yat-sen Univ., Moscow, in France and Germany.
Instructor Huangpu Mil. Acad. 24; joined CCP 24; participated in Nanchang Uprising 27, Guangzhou Uprising 27; Principal Red Army Coll. 31; Deputy Chief of Staff on Long March 34-36; mem. 7th Cen. Cttee. of CCP 45; Mayor of Beijing 49; First Political Commissar Guangzhou Mil. District, People's Liberation Army 49; Gov. of Guangdong 49-55; Vice-Chair. Nat. Defence Council 54-; Dir. Inspectorate of Armed Forces, PLA 54-58; Marshal PLA 55; mem. 8th Cen. Cttee. of CCP 56; Pres. PLA Mil. Acad. 58; Sec., Secr. of Cen. Cttee., CCP 66; Vice-Chair. Mil. Affairs Comm., Cen. Cttee. 67-; presumed Acting Minister of Nat. Defence 71-75, Minister 75-78; Vice-Chair. CCP 73;

mem. Standing Cttee. of Politburo, 10th Cen. Cttee. of CCP 73; mem. Politburo 11th Cen. Cttee. CCP 77; Vice-Chair. CCP 77-; Chair. Nat. People's Congress Standing Cttee. March 78-; Exec. Chair. Presidium 5th Nat. People's Congress 78.
People's Republic of China.

Ye Junjian (Chun-chan Yeh); Chinese writer and translator; b. 1915, Hupei Province.
Founder *Chinese Literature* (monthly, English and French); mem. China PEN Centre Council.
Publs. (in English) *The Mountain Village, They Fly South, The Ignorant and the Forgotten, Three Seasons and Other Stories*; (in Chinese) *New Schoolmates, The Emperor Real and False, Sketches of Two Capitals, Pioneers of the Virgin Soil, On the Steppe, Flames, Freedom, Dawn*, etc. Trans.: *Complete Hans Andersen, Agamemnon*, etc.
c/o China PEN Centre, Shatan Beijie 2, Beijing, People's Republic of China.

Yen Chia-kan, Dr., B.SC.; Chinese politician; b. 23 Oct. 1905, Suzhou, Jiangsu; ed. St. John's Univ., Shanghai.
Various government posts including Commr. of Reconstruction, Fujian Provincial Govt. 38-39, Finance Commr. Fujian Province, Chair. Fujian Provincial Bank 39-45; Dir. of Procurement, War Production Board 45; Communications Commr., Taiwan Provincial Govt. 45-46, Finance Commr. 46-49; Chair. Bank of Taiwan 46-49; Minister of Econ. Affairs, Republic of China (Taiwan) 50, of Finance 50-54, 58-63; Vice-Chair. Council for U.S. Aid 50, 63; Gov. of Taiwan 54-57; Minister without Portfolio 57-58; Chair. Council for U.S. Aid 57-58; Pres. Exec. Yuan (Prime Minister) 63-72; Chair. Council for Int. Econ. Co-operation and Devt. 63-69; Vice-Pres. Repub. of China (Taiwan) 66-75, Pres. 75-78; Hon. LL.D. (Seoul Nat. Univ., Korea) 64, Hon. D.Pol. (Chulalongkorn Univ., Thailand) 68, Hon. D.Lit. (Soochow Univ.) 80; numerous awards.
4 Section II, Chungking South Road, Taipei, Taiwan.

Yendo, Masayoshi, B.ENG.; Japanese architect; b. 30 Nov. 1920, Yokohama; ed. Waseda Univ.
Murano architect office 45-49; Pres. M. Yendo Associated Architects and Engineers 52-; Dir. Board, Japan Architects Asscn. 82-; Geijutsu Sensyo (Art Commendation Award) 65; Architectural Inst. of Japan Award 65.
Buildings include: 77th Bank Head Office 57, Hieizan Int. Sightseers' Hotel 59, Keio Terminal and Dept. Store Building 60, Resort Hotel Kasyoen 62, Yamaguchi Bank Head Office 62, 77th Building (77th Bank, Tokyo Branch) 63, Japan Coca-Cola Concentrating Plant 64, Coca-Cola (Japan) Head Office 68, Yakult Co. Ltd. Head Office 70, Tokyo American Club 71, Heibon-sha Co. Ltd. Head Office 72, Taiyo Fishery Co. Ltd. Head Office 73, Seiyu Store Kasugai Shopping Centre 75.
M. Yendo Associated Architects and Engineers, 5-6, 8-chome, Ginza, Chuo-ku, Tokyo, Japan.
Telephone: 572-8321 (Tokyo).

Yogyakarta, Sultan of (*see* Hamengkubuwono IX, H.R.H. Sultan Dorodjatun).

Yokota, Takashi; Japanese banker; b. 31 Jan. 1909, Tokyo; ed. Keio Univ.
Joined The Nippon Kangyo Bank Ltd. 33, Dir. 58, Deputy Pres. 66, Pres. 69; Pres. The Dai-Ichi Kangyo Bank Ltd. 71-76, Chair. Senior Exec. Cttee. 76-; Dir. Fukoku Mutual Life Insurance Co.; Commr. of Management Cttee. Nippon Telegraph and Telephone Public Corpn. Tokyo; Chair. Board of Councillors Keio Univ.; Order of the Sacred Treasure (1st Class) 79.
The Dai-Ichi Kangyo Bank Ltd., 1-5, Uchisaiwai-cho 1-chome, Chiyoda-ku, Tokyo; 1-30-12, Fukazawa, Setagaya-ku, Tokyo, Japan.
Telephone: 03-596-1111 (Office); 03-405-0510 (Home).

Yokoyama, Soichi; Japanese banker; b. 30 Nov. 1914, Tokyo; ed. Hitotsubashi Univ.
Yokohama Specie Bank 38-47; Bank of Tokyo Ltd. 47-, Dir., Agent of New York Agency 63, Resident Dir. for Europe, London 65, Man. Dir. 65, Senior Man. Dir. 69, Deputy Pres. 72, Pres. 73-, Chair. 77; Chair. Bank of Tokyo (Switzerland) Ltd. 78-; Dir. UBAN—Arab Japanese Finance Ltd., Hong Kong 74-; Chair. Cttee. on Int. Finance, Fed. of Econ. Org. 74-.
Bank of Tokyo Ltd., 1-6-3, Hongoku-cho, Nihombashi, Chuo-ku, Tokyo 103; Home 14-25, Sugamo 3-chome, Toshima-ku, Tokyo 170, Japan.
Telephone: 03-245-1111 (Office); 03-918-1894 (Home).

Yoshida, Taroichi; Japanese international banker; ed. Tokyo Imperial Univ.
Ministry of Finance 44-56 and 60-70; mem. staff, IMF, Washington 56; Deputy Vice-Minister, Econ. Planning Agency 71-72; Dir.-Gen. Banking Bureau 72-74; Vice-Minister of Finance for Int. Affairs 74-76; Special Adviser to Minister of Finance 76; Chair. and Pres. Asian Devt. Bank 76-81.
c/o Asian Development Bank, 2330 Roxas Boulevard, Pasay City, P.O.B. 789, Manila, Philippines.

Yoshiki, Masao, DR. ENG.; Japanese engineer; b. 20 Jan. 1908, Nagasaki; ed. Univ. of Tokyo.
Lecturer, School of Engineering, Univ. of Tokyo 30-32; Asst. Prof., Univ. of Tokyo 32-44, Prof. of Naval Architecture 44-68; Pres. Soc. of Naval Architects of Japan 61-63; Dean, School of Engineering, Univ. of Tokyo 62-64; Chair. Int. Ships Structures Congress 67-70; Chief Dir., Japan Soc. for the Promotion of Science 68-76; Prof. Emer. Univ. of Tokyo; Commr. Space Activities Comm. 68-74, 76-; Chair. Science Council, Ministry of Educ. 74-; Pres. Japan Fed. of Eng. Socs. 77-; Vice-Chair. Japanese Nat. Comm. for UNESCO 76; Vice-Pres. Science Council of Japan 69-71; mem. Council for Science and Technology 74-77; Prize of Japan Acad. 66, Purple Ribbon Decoration 68, Fujiwara Prize 68, Chevalier Légion d'honneur 77, Order of the Sacred Treasure (1st Class).
Publs. Articles in journals.
c/o Science and Technology Agency, 2-2 Kasumigaseki 3-chome, Chiyoda-ku, Tokyo; Home: 43-14, Izumi 2-chome, Suginami-ku, Tokyo, Japan.
Telephone: 03-581-1559 (Office); 03-328-0210 (Home).

Yoshikuni, Ichiro; Japanese civil servant; b. 2 Sept. 1916, Yokohama; ed. Tokyo Imperial Univ.
With Ministry of Commerce and Industry 40-47; mem. Board of Trade 47-48; Attorney-Gen.'s Office, Legislative Bureau 48-52; Cabinet Legislative Bureau 52-76, Dir. of Third Div. 59-64, Dir. First Div. 64, Asst. Dir.-Gen. 64-72, Dir.-Gen. 72-76; Pres. Japan Regional Devt. Corpn 76-; Chair. Man. Cttee. N.T.T.; Hon. K.B.E. 75.
Publs. (co-author) *Manual on the Drafting, Application and Interpretation of Law* 49, *Legislative Drafting* 52, *Dictionary of Public Finance and Accounting* 74.
5-35-17 Jingumae, Shibuya-ku, Tokyo, Japan.
Telephone: 03-501-5211 (Office); 03-499-4492 (Home).

Yoshimura, Junzo; Japanese architect; b. 7 Sept. 1908; ed. Tokyo Acad. of Fine Arts.
At architectural office of Antonin Raymond 31-42; own architectural practice 43-; Asst. Prof. in Architecture, Tokyo Univ. of Arts 44-61, Prof. 62-70, Emer. Prof. 70-; mem. Architectural Inst. of Japan, Japan Architects' Asscn.; Hon. Fellow, American Insts. of Architects 75; Architectural Inst. Prize 56, Parsons Medal (New York) 56; Award from Japanese Acad. of Arts 75.
Works include: Int. House of Japan, Tokyo 55, Public Kambara Hospital 56, The Motel on the Mountain, New York 56, Hotel Kowakien, Hakone, 59, Mountain House for Yawata Iron and Steel Co., Kujyu 60, N.C.R. H.Q., Tokyo 62, Americana Building, Osaka 65, Prefectural

Aichi Univ. of Arts, Aichi 65-70, Hotel Fujita, Kyoto 70, Japan House, New York 71, Nara Nat. Museum 73, Norwegian Embassy, Tokyo 78, and many residences.
8-6, Mejiro 3-chome, Toshima-ku, Tokyo; Home: 5-30-24 Minamidai, Nakano-ku, Tokyo, Japan.
Telephone: 954-0991 (Office) and 381-1282 (Home).

Yoshino, Bunroku; Japanese diplomatist; b. 8 Aug. 1918, Matsumoto.
Entered Foreign Ministry 41; Attaché, Berlin 41; Sec., Washington, D.C. 53; Econ. Dept. of Ministry 56; Counsellor, Bonn 61; Deputy Dir.-Gen. Econ. Co-operation Dept. of Ministry 64; Head of Mission, Washington, D.C. 68; Dir.-Gen. U.S. Dept. of Ministry 71; Amb. to OECD, Paris 72-75; Sec. of State, Ministry of Foreign Affairs 75-78; Amb. to Fed. Repub. of Germany 78-82.
c/o Ministry of Foreign Affairs, 2-1, Kasumigaseki 2-chome, Chiyoda-ku, Tokyo, Japan.

Yoshiyama, Hirokichi; Japanese business executive; b. 1 Dec. 1911; ed. Faculty of Engineering, Univ. of Tokyo.
Joined Hitachi, Ltd 35, Dir. 61, Exec. Man. Dir. 64, Senior Exec. Man. Dir. 68, Exec. Vice-Pres. 39, Pres. 71-81.
c/o Hitachi, Ltd., New Marunouchi Building, No. 5-1, Marunouchi 1-chome, Chiyoda-ku, Tokyo 100, Japan.
Telephone: 03-212-1111.

Yosizaka, Takamasa; Japanese architect and town planner; b. 13 Feb. 1917; ed. Waseda Univ., Tokyo.
Lecturer, Japan Women's Coll. 42-50, Tokyo Agricultural School 45-48, Yamanasi Univ. 56-57, Tucumán Nat. Univ., Argentina 61-62; Asst. Prof. Waseda Univ. 50, Prof. 59, Head of Dept. of Architecture 64-66, Dean of School of Science and Engineering, Waseda Univ. 69-72; Manager Waseda Univ. Expedition to Equatorial Africa 58, and Leader of its MacKinley Alaska Expedition 60; Vice-Pres. Architectural Inst. of Japan 66-68, Pres. 73-74; Pres. Japan Inst. of Study of Living 74-; Dir. Japanese Asscn. of Architects 66-68, Capital Region Comprehensive Planning Inst. 74-; Pres. Waseda Univ. Coll. 78-; G.S.D. (Harvard Univ.) 78.
Principal works: Japanese Pavilion, Venice Biennale 56, Maison Franco-Japonaise 59, Athénée Française 62, Gotu City Hall 62, Univ. Seminar House 65; Projects: Redevelopment Plans for Takada-no Baba District and Izu, Oosima; Space Museum 69; Future of Sendai City 73.
Publs. *Form and Environment* 55, *Primitive Country to Civilized Country* 61, *Study on Dwelling* 65, *A Study for 21st Century Japan* 70, *Directives* 73; trans. into Japanese *Le Modulor, Modulor II, Vers une Architecture* (Le Corbusier), *Erreurs Monumentales* (M. Ragon), *Moi, j'aime pas la mer* (Xénakis), *Le Corbusier Oeuvres complètes* (8 vols., trans. into Japanese 77-79), *Primitive Architecture*, Enrico Guidoni (trans. into Japanese) 80.
2-17-24 Hyakunintyo, Sinziku-ku, Tokyo 160, Japan.
Telephone: 03-361-1083.

Yotsumoto, Kiyoshi; Japanese business executive, b. 29 Sept. 1908; ed. Kyoto Univ.
Chairman, Kawasaki Heavy Industries Ltd. -81.
c/o Kawasaki Heavy Industries Ltd., Nissei-Kawasaki Building, 16-1, Nakamachi-dori 2-chome, Ikuta-ku, Kobe, P.O. Box 1140, Kobe Central; Home: 4-14-14, Takanawa, Minato-ku, Tokyo, Japan.

Youde, Sir Edward, K.C.M.G., M.B.E.; British diplomatist and administrator; b. 19 June 1924, Penarth, Glamorgan, Wales; ed. School of Oriental and African Studies, Univ. of London.
Served in various diplomatic posts in China, U.S.A. and U.K. 47-65; Counsellor, Perm. Mission to UN 65-69; Private Sec. to Prime Minister 69-70; Imperial Defence Coll. 70-71; Head of Personnel Services Dept., F.C.O. 71-73; Asst. Under-Sec. of State, F.C.O. 73-74; Amb. to People's Repub. of China 74-78; Deputy Under-Sec. of State (Chief Clerk), F.C.O. 78-82, Deputy to Perm. Under-Sec. of State 80-82; Gov. of Hong Kong May 82-.
Government House, Hong Kong.

Young, William Lambert; New Zealand politician and diplomatist; b. 13 Dec. 1913, Kawa Kawa; ed. Wellington Coll.
With Murray Roberts Co. Ltd. 30-46, Russell Import Co. Ltd. 46-56; Man. Radio Corpn. of New Zealand 56-62; M.P. 66-81; Minister of Works and Devt. 75-81; High Commr. in U.K. 82-.
New Zealand High Commission, New Zealand House, Haymarket, London, SW1Y 4TQ, England.
Telephone: 01-930 8422.

Yu Daizhong; Chinese party official.
Commander People's Liberation Army Unit 6410, Jiangsu 68; Alt. mem. 9th Cen. Cttee. of CCP 69; Chair. Nei Monggol Revolutionary Cttee. 70-; First Sec. CCP Nei Monggol 71-78; mem. 10th Cen. Cttee. of CCP 73, 11th Cen. Cttee. 77; Commdr. Nei Monggol Mil. District, PLA; Deputy Commdr. Beijing PLA Mil. Unit. 78-; Commdr. Chengdu Units 80-.
People's Republic of China.

Yu Guangmao; Chinese army officer.
Commdr. Anhui Mil. District, PLA; mem. Standing Cttee. Anhui CCP Cttee.
People's Republic of China.

Yu Kuo-hwa; Chinese banker; b. 1914; ed. Tsinghua Univ., Harvard Univ. Graduate School, U.S.A., London School of Econs.
Secretary to Pres. of Nat. Mil. Council 36-44; Alt. Exec. Dir. Int. Bank for Reconstruction and Devt. 47-50; Alt. Exec. Dir. IMF 50-55; Pres. Cen. Trust of China 55-61; Man. Dir. China Devt. Corpn. 59-67; Chair. Board of Dirs., Bank of China 61-67, China Insurance Co. Ltd. 61-67; Alt. Gov. IBRD 64-67, Gov. for Repub. of China 67-69; Minister of Finance 67-69; Gov. Cen. Bank of China 69-; Minister without Portfolio 69-; Gov. Int. Monetary Fund 69-, Asian Devt. Bank 69-; Chair. Council for Econ. Planning and Devt. 77-; Dr. h.c. (St. John's Univ., Jamaica, N.Y.).
Central Bank of China, 2 Roosevelt Road, 1st Section, Taipei, Taiwan.

Yu Qiuli; Chinese party official; b. 1914, Sichuan.
Political Commissar of Detachment, 120th Div. 34; Deputy Political Commissar Qinghai Mil. District, People's Liberation Army 49; Lieut.-Gen. PLA 55; Dir. Finance Dept., PLA 56-57; Political Commissar Gen. Logistics Dept., PLA 57-58; Minister of Petroleum Industry 58; Vice-Chair. State Planning Comm. 65, Chair. 72-80; Minister in Charge 80; Minister in Charge of the State Energy Comm. Aug. 80-; mem. 9th Cen. Cttee. of CCP 69, 10th Cen. Cttee. 73; Vice-Premier, State Council Jan. 75-; mem. Politburo, 11th Cen. Cttee. CCP 77; Deputy for Kiangsu, 5th NPC 78; mem. Presidium 5th NPC 78; Sec. Secretariat, Cen. Cttee. 80-81.
People's Republic of China.

Yukawa, Morio; Japanese diplomatist (retd.) and government official; b. 23 Feb. 1908; ed. Tokyo Univ.
Entered Foreign Service 33; served U.K., Geneva; Dir. Econ. Stabilization Board, Cabinet 50-51; Dir. Econ. Affairs Bureau, Foreign Office 51-52; Minister-Counsellor to France 52-54; Dir. Int. Co-operation Bureau, Foreign Office 54-55; Dir. Econ. Affairs Bureau, Foreign Office 55-57; Amb. to Philippines 57-61; Deputy Vice-Minister, Foreign Office 61-63; Amb. to Belgium, Luxembourg and European Econ. Community 63-68, to U.K. 68-72; Grand Master of Ceremonies, Imperial Household 73-79.
Hilltop, 5-10 Sanbancho, Chiyoda-ku, Tokyo 102, Japan.

Z

Zafrulla Khan, Sir Muhammad, K.C.S.I., B.A., LL.B.; Pakistani politician; b. 6 Feb. 1893; ed. Govt. Coll., Lahore, and King's Coll., London.
Barrister-at-Law (Lincoln's Inn); Advocate, Sialkot, Punjab 14-16; practised Lahore High Court 16-35; mem. Punjab Legislative Council 26-35; del. Indian Round Table Confs. 30, 31, 32; del. Joint Select Cttee. of Parl. on Indian Reforms 33; Pres. All-India Muslim League 31; mem. Gov.-Gen.'s Exec. Council 35-41; leader Indian del. to Assembly of LN 39; Agent-Gen. of Govt. of India in China 42; Judge, Fed. Court of India 41-47; Constitutional Adviser to H.H. Ruler of Bhopal June-Dec. 47; Leader Pakistan Del. to Annual Session of UN Gen. Assembly Sept.-Nov. 47; Minister of Foreign Affairs and Commonwealth Relations, Govt. of Pakistan Dec. 47; Leader Pakistan Del. to UN Security Council on India-Pakistan dispute 48-54, and to sessions of UN Gen. Assembly 47-54; Leader Pakistan del. to San Francisco Conf. on Japanese Peace Treaty 51; Leader Pakistan Del. to SEATO Conf. Manila 54; Judge at the Int. Court of Justice, The Hague 54-61, 64-73, Vice-Pres. 58-61, Pres. 70-73; Perm. Rep. of Pakistan to UN 61-64; Pres. 17th session UN Gen. Assembly 62-63; Hon. LL.D. (Cambridge); Hon. Bencher Lincoln's Inn; Hon. Fellow L.S.E.
Publ. *Islam: Its Meaning for Modern Man* 62, *The Quran* (trans.) 70.
16 Gressenhall Road, London, S.W.18, England.
Telephone: 01-874 6298.

Zahir, Abdul; Afghan politician; b. 3 May 1910, Lagham; ed. Habibia High School, Kabul and Columbia and Johns Hopkins Univs., U.S.A.
Practised medicine in U.S.A. before returning to Kabul 43; Chief Doctor, Municipal Hospitals, Kabul 43-50; Deputy Minister of Health 50-55, Minister 55-58; Amb. to Pakistan 58-61; Chair. House of the People 61-64, 65-69; Deputy Prime Minister and Minister of Health 64-65; Amb. to Italy 69-71; Prime Minister June 71-Dec. 72.

Zahiruddin bin Syed Hassan, Tun Syed, G.C.V.O., S.M.N., D.U.N.M., P.S.M., S.P.M.P., J.M.N., P.J.K.; Malaysian state governor; b. 11 Oct. 1918, Perak; ed. Raffles Coll., Singapore.
Malay Officer 45-47; Deputy Asst. District Officer, Krian 48, Asst. District Officer 51; Asst. District Officer, Tanjong Malim 53, Ipoh 54; Second Asst. State Sec., Perak 55, Registrar of Titles and Asst. State Sec. (Lands) 56; District Officer, Batang Padang, Tapah 57; Deputy Sec. Public Services Comm. 58; Principal Asst. Sec., Federation Establishment Office 60; State Sec. Perak 61; Perm. Sec. Ministry of Agric. and Co-operatives 63, Ministry of Educ. 66; Dir.-Gen. Public Services Comm. 69; Chair. Railway Services Comm. 72-; High Commr. to United Kingdom 74-75; Gov. of Malacca 75-; mem. Special Cttee. on Superannuation, Board of Govs. Malay Coll., Interim Council of Nat. Inst. of Tech., Cen. Board; Vice-Pres. Subang Nat. Golf Club.
Office of the Governor, Malacca, Malaysia.

Zail Singh, Giani; Indian politician; b. 5 May 1916, Sandhwan, Faridket district, Punjab.
Took leading part in movt. against autocratic rule in Punjab states; arrested at Faridket 38; f. Faridket State Congress and launched Nat. Flag Movt. 46; formed parallel Govt. in Faridket State 48; Pres. State Praja Sandal 46-48; Revenue Minister, Govt. 48-49, Minister for Public Works and Agric. 51-52; Pres. PEPSU PCC 55-56; mem. Rajya Sabha 56-62, Punjab Assembly 62; Minister of State and Pres. Punjab PCC 66-72; Chief Minister of Punjab 72-77; Pres. Punjab Co-operative Union; Minister of Home Affairs, Govt. of India 80-82; Pres. of India July 82-.
Office of the President, Rashtrapati Bhavan, New Delhi, India.

Zain Azraai, Datuk; Malaysian diplomatist; b. 1936; ed. Univ. of Oxford and London School of Econs.
Asst. Sec., Political Div., Ministry of Foreign Affairs 59-62; engaged in work connected with formation of Malaysia, High Comm., London 62; Perm. Mission to UN 62-66; Principal Asst. Sec., later Under-Sec. Political Affairs, Ministry of Foreign Affairs 66-70; Principal Pte. Sec. to Tun Abdul Razak, Prime Minister of Malaysia 71-76; Amb. to U.S.A., also accred. to Brazil and Mexico 76-; Exec. Dir. IBRD 78-; del. to numerous int. confs. including Non-Aligned Summit, Algiers 73, ASEAN Summit, Bali 76; fmr. Chair. Bd. of Trustees, Malaysian Nat. Art Gallery.
Embassy of Malaysia, 2401 Massachusetts Avenue, N.W., Washington, D.C. 20008, U.S.A.
Telephone: 202-328-2700.

Zaiton Ibrahim, Tan Sri, B.A.; Malaysian diplomatist; b. 26 May 1921; ed. High School, Klang, Malay Coll., Kuala Kangsar, Raffles Coll., Singapore, Univ. of Wales, Cardiff, London School of Econs., U.K.
Malayan Civil Service 52, Foreign Service 54-; Principal Asst. Sec., Ministry of External Affairs 57, Deputy Perm. Sec. 59-62; Amb. to the Philippines 62-63; High Commr. in India and Ceylon, Amb. to Nepal 64-67; Amb. to Japan 67-68, to U.S.S.R. 68-70; Sec.-Gen. Ministry of Foreign Affairs 70-76; Perm. Rep. to UN 76-80; Chair. Malaysian Del. to UN 72; Panglima Setia Negara, Hon. K.C.M.G.
c/o Ministry of Foreign Affairs, Kuala Lumpur, Malaysia.

Zakaria, Datuk Haji Mohamed Ali, P.S.D., J.M.N., A.M.N.; Malaysian diplomatist; b. 8 Oct. 1929, Kuala Lumpur; ed. Univ. of Malaya, Singapore, and London School of Econs.
Served in various capacities in Malaysian Civil Service; entered foreign service 56; Second Sec., later Information Officer, London 57-59; First Sec., later Counsellor, Perm. Mission of Malaya at UN 59-65; Deputy Sec. (Gen. Affairs), Ministry of Foreign Affairs 65-67; Deputy High Commr. in U.K. 67-69; High Commr. in Canada and concurrently Perm. Rep. to UN 70-74; Sec.-Gen. Ministry of Foreign Affairs 76-; Panglima Selia Di Raja, Johan Mangku Negara, Ahli Mangku Negara.
Ministry of Foreign Affairs, Kuala Lumpur, Malaysia.

Zaki, Ahmed; Maldivian diplomatist; b 16 April 1931; ed. Sri Lanka.
Joined govt. service as officer in Ministry of Communications 53; Dept of External Affairs 53; Govt Rep , Ceylon (now Sri Lanka) 56; Deputy Minister of Public Endowment 59, then of Trade and Food; Chair People's Majlis (Parl.) 60; Minister of Trade and Food, and of Justice; Minister of External Affairs 68-72; Prime Minister of Maldives 72-75; Perm. Rep. of Maldives to the United Nations 79-.
Permanent Mission of Maldives to the United Nations, 212 East 47th Street, Apartment 15B, New York, N.Y. 10017, U.S.A.

Zeidler, Sir David R., Kt., C.B.E. M.SC., F.R.A.I.C., M.I.CHEM.E., F.A.I.M.; Australian business executive; b. 18 March 1918; ed. Scotch Coll., Univ. of Melbourne.
With CSIRO 42-52; joined ICI Australia Research Dept. 52, Research Man. 53-59, Devt. Man. 59-62, Controller Dyes and Fabrics Group 62-63, Dir. 63-71, Man. Dir. 71-72, Deputy Chair. 72-73; Chair. ICI Australia Ltd. 73-80, Metal Mfrs. Ltd. April 81-; Dir. Commercial Bank of Australia Ltd., Broken Hill Proprietary Co., Amatil Ltd., CBA Ltd., Queen's Silver Jubilee Trust; Chair. Defence Industry Cttee.; Vice-Pres. Walter and Eliza Hall Inst., Australian Acad. of Technological Sciences.
360 Collins Street, Melbourne, Vic.; Home: 45/238 The Avenue, Parkville, Vic. 3052, Australia.

Zeng Mei; Chinese party official.
Military sub-district Commdr. 43; Chief of Staff, Beijing-Tianjin Garrison H.Q. 54; Political Commissar Hebei Mil.

District, PLA 66; Vice-Chair. Hebei Revolutionary Cttee., PLA 68-.
People's Republic of China.

Zeng Shaoshan; Chinese party official; b. 1910, Hunan. On Long March 34-35; Regimental Commdr. 38; Brigade Commdr. 41; Deputy Commdr. E. Sichuan Mil. District, People's Liberation Army 50-52; Lieut.-Gen. PLA 57; Commdr. Jinan Mil. Region, PLA 57; Political Commissar Shenyang Mil. Region, PLA 60; mem. 9th Cen. Cttee. of CCP 69; Second Sec. CCP Liaoning 71, First Sec. 75-; Vice-Chair. Liaoning Revolutionary Cttee. 73, Chair. 75-78; mem. 10th Cen. Cttee. of CCP 73, 11th Cen. Cttee. 77.
People's Republic of China.

Zeng Siyu; Chinese army officer; b. 1907.
Staff Officer Red 1st Front Army 35; Commdr. 4th Column, N. China PLA 48; Lieut.-Gen. Shenyang Mil. Region, PLA 60, Deputy Commdr. 65-67; Commdr. Wuhan Mil. Region, PLA 67-73; mem. 9th Cen. Cttee. of CCP 69; First Sec. CCP Hubei 71; mem. 10th Cen. Cttee. of CCP 73, 11th Cen. Cttee. 77; Commdr. Jinan Mil. Region, PLA 74-80.
People's Republic of China.

Zhai Shufan; Chinese politician; b. 1905, Hubei.
Minister of Sixth Ministry of Machine-Building 78-81.
c/o State Council, Beijing, People's Republic of China.

Zhang Aiping, Gen.; Chinese army officer and politician; b. 1908, Sichuan.
Joined CCP 26; veteran army and party cadre; mil. cadre in East China 49-54; Deputy Chief of Gen. Staff PLA 54-67; alt. mem. 8th Cen. Cttee. CCP 58; criticized and removed from office during Cultural Revolution 67; Chair. Science and Tech. Comm. for Nat. Defence 75-77; Deputy Chief of Gen. Staff PLA 77; mem. 11th Cen. Cttee. CCP 77; a Vice-Premier, State Council 80-82.
State Council, Beijing, People's Republic of China.

Zhang Caiqian; Chinese army officer.
Guerrilla leader in Hubei, Henan, Anhui and Hunan 46; Chief of Staff Hubei Mil. District, People's Liberation Army 50; Lieut.-Gen. PLA 58; Deputy Commdr. Nanjing Mil. Region, PLA 58-70; mem. 9th Cen. Cttee. of CCP 69, 10th Cen. Cttee. 73, 11th Cen. Cttee. 77; Deputy Chief of Staff PLA 71-; Commdr. PLA Wuhan Units 80-.
People's Republic of China.

Zhang Chiming; Chinese army officer.
Political Commissar, 4th Field Army, People's Liberation Army 50; Political Commissar in Gen. Logistics Dept., Cen.-South Mil. District, PLA 54; re-assigned to Cen. Mil. Org. 54; Lieut.-Gen. PLA 55; Pres. Logistics Inst., PLA 60; Deputy Dir., Gen. Logistics Dept., PLA 65, Political Commissar 67-.
People's Republic of China.

Zhang Chunqiao; Chinese politician; b. *c.* 1911.
Director East China Gen. Branch, New China News Agency 50; Dir. *Liberation Daily*, Shanghai 54; Alt. Sec. CCP Shanghai 64, Sec. 65; Chair. Shanghai Revolutionary Cttee. 67; Deputy Head Cen. Cultural Revolution Group 67; First Political Commissar Nanjing Mil. Region, People's Liberation Army 67-; mem. Politburo, 9th Cen. Cttee. CCP 69; First Sec. CCP, Shanghai 71-76; mem. Standing Cttee. of Politburo, 10th Cen. Cttee. of CCP 73, 75-Nov. 76; Vice-Premier, State Council Jan. 75-Nov. 76; Dir.-Gen. Political Dept., PLA 75-Nov. 76; arrested as a mem. of the "Gang of Four" Oct. 76; expelled from CCP July 77; tried with others in "Gang of Four" Nov. 80-Jan. 81; sentenced to death Jan. 81 (sentence suspended).
People's Republic of China.

Zhang Dazhi; Chinese soldier; b. 1911, Shaanxi Prov.; ed. China Workers' and Peasants' Red Army Univ., Yanan.
Director, Public Security Dept. of North-West Mil. and Admin. Cttee. 52; Commdr. Lanzhou Mil. Region, PLA 54-72; Alt. mem. 8th Cen. Cttee. of CCP 56, mem. 9th Cen. Cttee.; Commdr. PLA Artillery Corps 72-.
People's Republic of China.

Zhang Dingfa, Gen.; Chinese air force officer and party official.
Deputy Chief of Staff, PLA Air Force 58, Deputy Commdr. 64; criticized and removed from office during Cultural Revolution 67; Deputy Commdr. Air Force 73; Political Commissar 76; mem. Politburo, 11th Cen. Cttee. of CCP 77-; Commdr. PLA Air Force 78-.
People's Republic of China.

Zhang Haitang; Chinese army officer.
Deputy Chief of Staff Liaoning Mil. District, PLA 59, Deputy Commdr. 60, Commdr. 72-75; Commdr. Yunnan Mil. District, PLA 75-; Maj.-Gen. PLA 59; fmr. Vice-Chair. Liaoning Revolutionary Cttee. 72; Vice-Chair. Yunnan Revolutionary Cttee.; mem. Standing Cttee. Yunnan CCP Cttee.; Chair. Sichuan Revolutionary Cttee. 75-80; First Political Commissar Chengdu Mil. Dist., PLA 78; mem. Standing Cttee. of Politburo 80.
People's Republic of China.

Zhang Jingfu; Chinese politician; b. 1901, Beijing.
Member CCP 34-; fmr. Vice-Minister of Local Industry and Vice-Pres. Scientific and Tech. Comm.; alt. mem. 8th Cen. Cttee. of CCP 56; Vice-Minister of Forestry 56-58; criticized and removed from office during Cultural Revolution 67; Minister of Finance 75-79; Gov. and First Sec., Anhui Prov. Cttee. 80-81; First Political Commissar Anhui Mil. Div. 80-82; State Counsellor 82-; Minister in Charge of State Econ. Comm. 82-; mem. State Finance and Econ. Comm.
People's Republic of China.

Zhang Jingyao; Chinese army officer.
Commander Guangdong Mil. District, People's Liberation Army 73-80.
People's Republic of China.

Zhang Lixiong; Chinese party official.
Political Commissar Jiangxi Mil. Dist. 78-.
People's Republic of China.

Zhang Pinghua; Chinese politician; b. 1903, Hunan.
Political Commissar in 120th Div. 47; Sec. CCP Wuhan 49-52; Third Sec. CCP Hubei 55-56, Second Sec. 56, Sec. 57-59; Alt. mem. 8th Cen. Cttee. of CCP 56; First Sec. CCP Hunan 59-67; First Political Commissar Hunan Mil. District, People's Liberation Army 60; Sec. Cen.-South Bureau, CCP 66-67; Deputy Dir. Propaganda Dept., CCP 66, Dir. 77-; criticized and removed from office during Cultural Revolution 67; Vice-Chair. Shanxi Revolutionary Cttee. 71; Sec. CCP Shanxi 71; Sec. CCP Hunan 73, Second Sec. 74-76, Acting First Sec. 76-; mem. 10th Cen. Cttee. of CCP 73, 11th Cen. Cttee. 77; Acting Chair. Hunan Revolutionary Cttee. 76; mem. Standing Cttee. 5th NPC 78; Dir. CCP Cen. Cttee. Propaganda Dept. 78-.
People's Republic of China.

Zhang Renxia, M.A.; Chinese artist, poet and art historian; b. 31 Jan. 1904; ed. Nat. Central Univ., Nanjing, Imperial Univ., Tokyo.
Has lectured at Int. Univ. of Santiniketan, India, at Central Univ., Chongqing and at Coll. of Oriental Studies, Kunming; Prof. of History of Art, Central Acad. of Fine Arts.
Publs. *Forget-Me-Not* 32, *Harvest* 40, *Mongolian Love Songs* 44, *The Relationship in Art Between China and India* 55, *The Classical Art of China* 56, *A Study of Hanchao Paintings* 55, *The Art of the Ajunta Caves* 56, *Oriental Art* 56, *An Art History of India and South East Asia* 64, *The Relationship in Art Between China and Japan* 64, *Culture and Art from Silk Road to China and Japan* 79.

Central Academy of Fine Arts, Beijing; Home: Dong Dan, Xi-Zong-Bu Hu Dong No. 51, Beijing, People's Republic of China.

Zhang Xiulong; Chinese soldier.
Deputy Commdr. Zhejiang Mil. District, PLA 66-72; Commdr. Hubei Mil. District, PLA 72-.
People's Republic of China.

Zhang Xudeng; Chinese army officer.
Commander Guangxi Mil. District 80-.
People's Republic of China.

Zhang Zhen; Chinese politician.
Minister of the Fifth Ministry of Machine-Building 78-82; Head PLA Gen. Logistics Dept. 78-80; Deputy Chief of Staff PLA 80-; alt. mem. 11th Cen. Cttee. CCP 77.
People's Republic of China.

Zhang Zhixiu; Chinese army officer.
Head (Maj.-Gen.) PLA Yentai Units, Shandong 57; Dep. Cmmdr. Jinan Mil. Region, post-Cultural Revolution; Sec., CCP Shandong Prov. Cttee. and Vice-Chair. Shandong Revolutionary Cttee. pre-75; Dep. Commdr. Kunming Mil. Region 76-80; Sec. CCP Yunnan Prov. Cttee. 77; Vice-Chair. Yunnan Prov. Revolutionary Cttee. 77; mem. Presidium CCP 11th NPC; mem. 11th Cen. Cttee. 77-; Commdr. Kunming Mil. Region 80-.
People' Republic of China.

Zhang Zhong; Chinese army officer.
Commander Gansu Mil. District, PLA 67-78; Vice-Chair. Gansu Revolutionary Cttee. 68; Sec. CCP Gansu 72; Commdr. Guizhai Mil. District 76; Exec. Chair. 5th Nat. Cttee. CPPCC, Vice-Chair. 78-.
People's Republic of China.

Zhang Zicun, PH.D.; Chinese economist; b. 5 April 1918; ed. Qinghua Univ., Beijing, Univ. of Cambridge, England.
Instructor, Dept. of Econs., Qinghua Univ. 40-43; Economist, Statistics Div., Research Dept., IMF 47-48; Sr. Econ. Affairs Officer, Econ. Stability Section, UN 48, Chief, Developing Areas Section 55, Deputy Dir. Centre for Devt. Planning, Projections and Policies 63, Dir. Div. of Public Admin. and Finance 73, Sr. Adviser, Dept. of Tech. Co-operation for Devt. 80; Deputy Dir. Financial Research Inst., People's Bank of China 80; Exec. Dir. for China, IMF 80-.
Publs. *Cyclical Movements in the Balance of Payments* 49 and articles in various professional journals.
36 Kilmer Road, Larchmont, N.Y. 10538; Apt. W-801, 3003 Van Ness Street, N.W., Washington, D.C. 20008, U.S.A.
Telephone: (914) 834-7257; (202) 363-0417.

Zhang Zongxun; Chinese army officer; b. 1898, Shaanxi; ed. Huangpu Mil. Acad.
Graduated 1925; Div. Commdr. Red Army 29; Chief of Staff, 4th Front Army on "Long March" 34; Brigade Commdr. 37; Alt. mem. 7th Cen. Cttee. 45; Deputy Commdr. First Field Army, PLA 49-54, Deputy Chief of Gen. Staff 54-75; Alt. mem. 8th Cen. Cttee., CCP 56; visited Eastern Europe 59; Dir.-Gen. and Head Armaments Dept., Logistics Dept., PLA 75-78.
People's Republic of China.

Zhao Cangbi; Chinese government official.
Cadre in S.W. China in early 50s, Vice-Gov. Sichuan 58, Sec. CCP Sichuan 60, 76; removed from office during Cultural Revolution 67; mem. 11th Cen. Cttee. CCP 77; Minister of Public Security 77-.
People's Republic of China.

Zhao Feng; Chinese soldier.
Leader PLA unit 6011, 67; Alt. mem. CCP 9th Cen. Cttee. 69; Alt. mem. CCP 10th Cen. Cttee. 73; Commdr. Shandong Mil. Dist. 78-.
People's Republic of China.

Zhao Wenjin; Chinese army officer.
Vice-Commander 9th Regt. Pingxi Advance Army, 8th Route Army 38; Vice-Commdr. PLA Tibet (Xizang) Mil. Region 62-80; Deputy for PLA, 5th NPC 78; Deputy Commdr. PLA Chengdu Units 78-; Commdr. Sichuan Mil. Dist. PLA 80-.
People's Republic of China.

Zhao Xianshun; Chinese soldier.
Commander, Heilongjiang Mil. District, PLA 76-.
People's Republic of China.

Zhao Xinju; Chinese party official.
Secretary, CCP Hubei 57-65; Vice-Gov. Hubei 58-64; Vice-Minister of Culture 65; criticized and removed from office during Cultural Revolution 66; rehabilitated as a "leading cadre" in Nei Monggol A.R. 72; Vice-Chair. Provincial Revolutionary Cttee. and Sec. CCP, Hubei 73, Chair. Revolutionary Cttee. and First Sec., Hubei 75-; mem. 11th Cen. Cttee. of CCP 77-; Minister of Food 80-82.
People's Republic of China.

Zhao Ziyang; Chinese politician; b. 1919, Huaxian County, Henan Prov.
Secretary-General S. China Sub-Bureau, CCP 50-54, Third Sec. 54-55; Third Deputy Sec. CCP Guangdong 55, Sec. 62, First Sec. 65-67; Political Commissar Guangdong Mil. District, People's Liberation Army 64; Sec. Cen.-South Bureau, CCP 65-67; criticized and removed from office during Cultural Revolution 67; Vice-Chair. Nei Monggol Revolutionary Cttee. 71; Sec. CCP Nei Monggol 71, CCP Guangdong 72; Vice-Chair. Guangdong Revolutionary Cttee. 72; mem. 10th Cen. Cttee. of CCP 73; First Sec. CCP Guangdong 74; Chair. Guangdong Revolutionary Cttee. 74; Chair. Sichuan Revolutionary Cttee. 75-80; First Sec. CCP Cttee., Sichuan 75-80; First Political Commissar, Chengdu Units 76-80; alt. mem. Politburo 11th Cen. Cttee. CCP 77-79, mem. Sept. 79-, mem. Standing Cttee. of Politburo Feb. 80-, Vice-Chair. Cen. Cttee. 81-; a Vice-Premier, State Council April-Sept. 80, Premier Sept. 80-; Exec. Chair. 5th CPPCC Nat. Cttee.; Vice-Chair. 5th CPPCC Nat. Cttee. 78-80; First Political Commissar Chengdu Mil. District PLA 78; Minister of State Comm. for Econ. Reconstruction May 82-.
Office of the Premier, State Council, Beijing, People's Republic of China.

Zhen Hejiao; Chinese soldier.
Political Commissar, Second Artillery Corps., PLA 76-82.
People's Republic of China.

Zheng Sheng; Chinese politician; b. 1911.
Minister of Communications 79-81; Adviser to State Council 81-.
People's Republic of China.

Zheng Tianxiang; Chinese politician.
Minister Seventh Ministry of Machine-Building 79-82.
People's Republic of China.

Zheng Zihua; Chinese politician; b. 1905, Xiexian Cty., Shanxi.
Joined CCP 26; served second revolutionary war, Commdr. and Pol. Commissar 25th army, Red Army; on Long March 35; Sec. Hebei-Chahar-Rehe-Liaoning Sub-bureau of CCP Cen. Cttee., Commdr. and Pol. Commissar Hebei-Chahar-Rehe-Liaoning Mil. Area Command and Commdr. 13th army corps, Fourth Field Army in rev.; after 49 successively Sec. Shanxi Prov. CCP Cttee., Chair. Shanxi Prov. Govt., Dir. All-China Fed. of Supply and Marketing Co-operatives, Min. of Commerce, Vice-Minister in charge State Capital Construction Comm., Vice-Minister State Planning Comm. and Sec. South-West China Bureau, CCP Cen. Cttee.; Minister of Civil Affairs March 78-; mem. 11th Cen. Cttee. CCP 77; Deputy for Shanxi, 5th NPC 78; mem.

Presidium, NPC 78; Vice-Chair. CPPCC Nat. Cttee. Sept. 80-.
People's Republic of China.

Zhi Haodian; Chinese army officer.
Deputy Chief of Gen. Staff PLA 78-.
People's Republic of China.

Zhou Feng; Chinese army officer.
Commander Shandong Mil. District 80-.
People's Republic of China.

Zhou Hui; Chinese politician.
Member Hunan Provincial People's Council 55; Deputy Sec. CCP Hunan Provincial Cttee. 56; Sec. CCP Hunan Provincial Cttee. 57; Head 2nd sub-group, del. to inspect Hunan's Campaign for Increasing Production and Practising Austerity 59; First Sec. Nei Monggol CCP Cttee. 78-; mem. 11th Cen. Cttee. 78-.
People's Republic of China.

Zhou Peiyuan; Chinese scientist and politician; b. 1902, Yixing Cty., Jiangsu; ed. Qinghua Univ.
Research on theoretical physics, U.S.A., Germany and Switzerland; Dean and Prof. of Physics, Qinghua Univ. 47-52; Chair. Physics Soc. 48-58; mem. Council, Fed. of Scientific Socs. 50, Dir. Org. Dept. 52; mem. Cen. Cttee. Jiusan (3 Sept.) Soc. 53-, Vice-Chair. 58-; on staff of Beijing Univ. 53-, Vice-Chair. Revolutionary Cttee. 70, Pres. Beijing Univ. 78-; Deputy to NPC 54-, mem. Standing Cttee. 78; mem. World Peace Council 57-65; Sec. Scientific and Tech. Asscn. 58, Vice-Chair. 63-77, Chair. 77-; joined CCP 59; mem. Standing Cttee., CPPCC 59-78, Vice-Chair. Nat. Cttee. Sept. 80-; Deputy Dir. Inst. of Foreign Affairs 72-; Vice-Pres. Acad. of Sciences 78-; Pres. Physics Soc. 78-.
Office of the President, Beijing University, Beijing, People's Republic of China.

Zhou Zhunlin; Chinese soldier.
Commander, Shanghai Garrison District, PLA 70; Vice-Chair. Shanghai Revolutionary Cttee. 70; Sec. Shanghai Party Cttee., CCP 71; Deputy Commdr. Nanjing Mil. Region, PLA 72-; mem. 10th Cen. Cttee. CCP 73, 11th Cen. Cttee. 77.
People's Republic of China.

Zhou Zijian; Chinese politician.
Chief, Secretariat, United Front Work Dept., CCP Cen. Cttee. 49; Dep. Chief, Secretariat, GAC and concurrently Chief Gen. Office (GAC) 49-50; Dep. Dir. Govt. Offices Bureau, 51-54; Asst. to Minister, First Ministry of Machine-Building 56-59; Dir. Third Bureau, First Ministry of Machine-Building 59; Vice-Minister, First Ministry of Machine-Building 60-73; Minister, First Ministry of Machine-Building 73-79; mem. Presidium CCP 11th Nat. Congress 77; alt. mem. 11th Cen. Cttee. 77-; Minister, First Ministry of Machine-Building 80-81, of Machine-Building Industry May 82-; Gov. and First Sec. Anhui Prov. Cttee. 81.
People's Republic of China.

Zhu Yaoha; Chinese army officer.
Major-General PLA Fujian Front 64; Vice-Chair. Fujian Revolutionary Cttee. 68; Commdr. Fujian Mil. District, PLA 68; Deputy Commdr. Fuzhou Mil. Region, PLA 73.
People's Republic of China.

Zia ul-Haq, Gen. Mohammad; Pakistani army officer; b. 1924, Jullundar; ed. Command and Staff Coll., Quetta.
Active service in Burma, Malaya, Indonesia during World War II; commissioned 45; 19 years in various instructional, staff and command appointments; attended two courses for staff officers in U.S.A. 59, 63; Lieut.-Col. 64; Instructor, Command and Staff Coll., Quetta 64; in command of a Cavalry Regt. 66-68; Col. in command of an armoured div. 68; Brig. in command of an armoured brigade 69; Maj.-Gen. in command of an armoured div. 72; Lieut.-Gen. and a Corps Commdr. April 75; Gen. and Chief of Army Staff March 76-; led coup deposing Zulfiqar Ali Bhutto July 77; Chief Martial Law Admin. and Chief of Mil. Council July 77-, also responsible for Cabinet Division, Chief Martial Law Administrator's Secretariat, Defence, Foreign Affairs, Information and Broadcasting, Science and Tech. and Atomic Energy Comm. July-Aug. 77, for Cabinet Division, Chief Martial Law Administrator's Secretariat Aug. 77-, Defence, Production and Foreign Affairs 77-78, for States and Frontier Affairs, Health and Population, Science and Tech. April 79-; Chair. Planning Comm. April 79-; Pres. of Pakistan Sept. 78-; Hon. LL.D. (Lahore) 77; Al-Kawkab Medal (Jordan), Al-Istiqlal Medal (Jordan) for services with the Jordanian army; Order of Yugoslav Flag 82.
Office of the President, Islamabad, Pakistan.

Zui Dianmin; Chinese party official.
CCP activist in Shaanxi province in late 1920s; Deputy Political Commissar, PLA Railway Corps 50, Political Commissar 73-; mem. Nat. Defence Council 65.
People's Republic of China.

Weights and Measures

Principal weights and units of measurement in common use as alternatives to the Metric and Imperial Systems

WEIGHT

Unit	Country	Imperial Equivalent	Metric Equivalent
Acheintaya	Burma	360.1 lb.	163.33 kg.
Arroba	Philippines	25.35 lb.	11.5 kg.
Baht, Bat, Kyat or Tical	Burma, Thailand (Old Chinese System)	0.266 oz.	7.56 gm.
	Siamese system	0.529 oz.	14.11 gm.
Beittha or Viss	Burma	3.601 lb.	1.63 kg.
Candareen or Fen	China (Old system)	0.0133 oz.	0.378 gm.
	China (New system)	0.010 oz.	0.283 gm.
	Hong Kong	0.0133 oz.	0.378 gm.
Candy	Sri Lanka	560 lb.	254 kg.
	India—Bombay	560 lb.	254 kg.
	India—Madras	500 lb.	226.8 kg.
	Burma	80 tons	81 metric tons
Catty, Gin, Jin, Kan, Kati, Katti, Kin, Kon or Zhang	China (Old system)	1.333 lb.	0.603 kg.
	China (New system)	1.102 lb.	0.5 kg.
	Hong Kong	1.333 lb.	0.603 kg.
	Indonesia	1.362 lb.	0.617 kg.
	Japan	1.323 lb.	0.6 kg.
	Malaysia and Singapore	1.333 lb.	0.603 kg.
	Thailand (Old Chinese system)	1.333 lb.	0.603 kg.
	Siamese	1.333 lb.	0.603 kg.
Charak	Afghanistan	3.894 lb.	1.7278 kg.
Chittack	India	2.057 oz.	57.5 gm.
Dan	China (Old system)	133.3 lb.	60.48 kg.
	China (New system)	110.23 lb.	50 kg.
Fan	China (Old system)	0.0133 oz.	0.378 gm.
	China (New system)	0.011 oz.	0.311 gm.
	Hong Kong	0.0133 oz.	0.378 gm.
Hyaku-mé	Japan	13.226 oz.	374.85 gm.
Kharwar	Afghanistan	1,246.2 lb.	564.528 kg.
Khord	Afghanistan	3.89 oz.	110.28 gm.
Koyan	Malaysia and Singapore	5,333.3 lb.	2,419 kg.
Kwan or Kan	Japan	8.267 lb.	3.749 kg.
Liang or Tael	China (Old system)	1.333 oz.	37.8 gm.
	China (New system)	1.102 oz.	31.18 gm.
	Hong Kong	1.333 oz.	37.8 gm.
Mace	China (Old system)	0.133 oz.	3.78 gm.
	China (New system)	0.110 oz.	3.11 gm.
	Hong Kong	0.133 oz.	3.78 gm.
Maund	Bangladesh	82.28 lb.	37.29 kg.
	India—Government	82.28 lb.	37.29 kg.
	India—Bombay	28 lb.	12.7 kg.
	India—Madras	25 lb.	11.34 kg.
	Pakistan	82.28 lb.	37.29 kg.
Me	Japan	0.133 oz.	3.78 gm.
Momme	Japan	0.133 oz.	3.78 gm.
Neal	Kampuchea	1.323 lb.	0.6 kg.
Ngamus	Burma	0.288 oz.	8.2 gm.
Nijo	Japan	0.529 oz.	15.02 gm.

[*continued*

WEIGHT—*continued*]

Unit	Country	Imperial Equivalent	Metric Equivalent
Pa	India	8.288 oz.	235 gm.
Picul, Pikul, Picol, Taam or Tam	China (Old system)	133.33 lb.	60.48 kg.
	China (New System)	110.23 lb.	50 kg.
	Hong Kong	133.33 lb.	60.48 kg.
	India	133.33 lb.	60.48 kg.
	Indochina (Old Chinese system)	133.33 lb.	60.48 kg.
	Indochina (Siamese system)	132.277 lb.	60 kg.
	Indonesia	136.16 lb.	61.76 kg.
	Japan	132.276 lb.	60 kg.
	Malaysia and Singapore	133.33 lb.	60.48 kg.
	Sabah and Sarawak	135.64 lb.	61.53 kg.
	Philippines	139.44 lb.	63.25 kg.
	Thailand (Old Chinese system)	133.33 lb.	60.48 kg.
	Thailand (Siamese system)	135.5 lb.	60.55 kg.
Pood or Poud	U.S.S.R.	36.133 lb.	16.38 kg.
Pyi	Burma	4.69 lb.	2.13 kg.
Quintal	Indonesia	220.462 lb.	100 kg.
	Philippines	101.4 lb.	46 kg.
Seer	Afghanistan	15.58 lb.	7.07 kg.
	India—Government	2.057 lb.	0.93 kg.
	India—Madras	0.617 lb.	0.28 kg.
	India—Bombay	0.72 lb.	0.33 kg.
	Pakistan	2.057 lb.	0.93 kg.
Tahil	Malaysia and Singapore	1.33 oz.	37.8 gm.
Tola	India and Pakistan	180 grains	11.66 gm.
Visham	India	3 lb.	1.36 kg.
Viss	Burma	3.601 lb.	1.63 kg.

LENGTH

Unit	Country	Imperial Equivalent	Metric Equivalent
Archinne	U.S.S.R.	27.996 in.	71.1 cm.
Ch am am	Kampuchea	9.84 in.	24.9 cm.
Ch'ek or Foot	Hong Kong—by statute	14.625 in.	37.16 cm.
	Hong Kong—in practice	14.14 in.	35.82 cm.
Cheung	Hong Kong	4.063 yd.	3.698 m.
Chi	China (Old system)	35.814 in.	91 cm.
	China (New System)	13.123 in.	33.27 cm.
Cho	Japan (length)	119.302 yd.	109.12 cm.
Chung	South Korea	119.302 yd.	109.12 cm.
Coss	India—Bengal, Pakistan and Bangladesh	2,000 yd.	1,920.2 m.
Cubit	Burma	18 in.	45.72 cm.
Cun	China (Old system)	1.41 in.	3.58 cm.
	China (New system)	1.312 in.	3.33 cm.
	Hong Kong	1.41 in.	3.58 cm.
Danda	India, Pakistan and Bangladesh	2 yd.	1.83 m.
El, Ell or Ella	Indonesia	27.08 in.	68.8 cm.
	Malaysia and Singapore	1 yd.	0.914 m.
	Sabah	1 yd.	0.914 m.

[*continued*

LENGTH—*continued*]

UNIT	COUNTRY	IMPERIAL EQUIVALENT	METRIC EQUIVALENT
Fen	China	0.13 in.	0.33 cm.
Garwode	Burma	12.727 miles	20.44 km.
Gereh-gaz-sha	Afghanistan	2.6 in.	6.6 cm.
Girah	Pakistan	2.25 in.	5.7 cm.
Gudge, Gueza, Guz or Ver	India—Bengal	36 in.	91.44 cm.
	India—Bombay	27 in.	68.58 cm.
	India—Madras	33 in.	83.82 cm.
	Pakistan and Bangladesh	36 in.	91.44 cm.
Hat	Kampuchea	19.68 in.	50 cm.
Hath	India, Pakistan and Bangladesh	18 in.	45.72 cm.
Hiro	Japan	1.657 yd.	1.516 m.
Jareeb	Pakistan—Punjab	22 yd.	20.117 m.
Jo	Japan	3.314 yd.	3.032 m.
Kawtha	Burma	3.182 miles	5.116 km.
Ken	Japan South Korea	1.988 yd.	1.82 m.
Keup	Thailand	9.07 in.	23.04 cm.
Koss	India—Bengal	2,000 yd.	1,828.8 m.
Lan	Burma	2 yd.	1.83 m.
Li or Lei	China (Old system)	706–745 yd.	645–681 m.
	China (New system)	546.8 yd.	500 m.
	Hong Kong	706–745 yd.	645–681 m.
	South Korea	2.44 miles	3.926 km.
Niew	Thailand	0.820 in.	2.09 cm.
Oke thapa	Burma	70 yd.	64 m.
Paal	Java	1,647 yd.	1,506 m.
	Sumatra	2,025 yd.	1,851.7 m.
Palgate	Burma	1 in.	2.54 cm.
Pulgada	Philippines	0.914 in.	2.31 cm.
Ri	Japan—length	2.44 miles	3.926 km.
	Japan—marine measure	1 nautical mile	1.85 km.
Sawk	Burma	19.8 in.	50.29 cm.
Sen	Thailand	43.74 yd.	40 m.
Shaku	Japan	11.93 in.	30.3 cm.
Sun	Japan	1.193 in.	3.02 cm.
Taing	Burma	2.43 miles	3.911 km.
Tar	Burma	3.5 yd.	3.2 m.
Taung	Burma	18 in.	45.72 cm.
Tjengkal	Indonesia	4 yd.	3.66 m.
Ungul	India, Pakistan and Bangladesh	0.75 in.	1.9 cm.
Verst or Versta	U.S.S.R.	0.6629 miles	1.067 km.
Wah	Thailand	2.19 yd.	2 m.
Yote	Thailand	9.942 miles	16 km.
Yuzamar	Burma	47.121 miles	75.83 km.
Zhang	China	3.45 yd.	3.34 m.

CAPACITY

Unit	Country	Imperial Equivalent	Metric Equivalent
Bag	Burma	27 galls.	122.75 lit.
Bottle	Sri Lanka	0.16 galls.	0.73 lit.
Cavan	Philippines	16.5 galls.	75 lit.
Chupa	Philippines	0.0825 galls.	0.37 lit.
Chupak	Malaysia and Singapore	0.25 galls.	1.14 lit.
Ganta	Philippines	0.660 galls.	3 lit.
Gantang	Malaysia and Singapore	1 gall.	4.55 lit.
	Indonesia (used mainly for rice)	1.887 galls.	8.58 lit.
Go	Japan	1.27 gills	0.17 lit.
Gwe	Burma	4.5 galls.	20.45 lit.
Koku	Japan	39.682 galls.	180.38 lit.
Kwe	Burma	4.5 galls.	20.45 lit.
Kwien	Thailand	439.95 galls.	2,000 lit.
Pau	Singapore	0.5 pints	0.28 lit.
Pyi	Burma	0.56 galls.	2.56 lit.
Sale	Burma	0.14 galls.	0.64 lit.
Sat	Thailand	4.40 galls.	20 lit.
Sayut	Burma	1.12 galls.	5.12 lit.
Seik	Burma	2.250 galls.	10.24 lit.
Ser	India	1.76 pints	1 lit.
Shaku	Japan	0.127 gill	0.017 lit.
Sho	Japan	0.397 galls.	1.8 lit.
Suk	South Korea	38.682 galls.	175.8 lit.
Tanan	Thailand	0.22 galls.	1 lit.
Tin, Tunn, Tin-han or **basket**	Burma (Thamardi)	9 galls.	40.91 lit.
Tinaja	Philippines	10.56 galls.	48 lit.
To	Japan	3.97 galls.	17.76 lit.

AREA

Unit	Country	Imperial Equivalent	Metric Equivalent
Bahoe or Bouw	Indonesia	1.7536 acres	0.709 ha.
Bigha	India	0.625 acres	0.253 ha.
	Pakistan—Punjab	1,620 sq. yds.	1354.5 m.²
	Bangladesh	1,600 sq. yds.	1337.8 m.²
Bu	Japan	3.95 sq. yds.	3.3 m.²
Cawny or Cawnie	India—Madras	1.322 acres	0.534 ha.
Chattak	Bangladesh	5 sq. yds.	4.18 m.²
Cho	Japan (square measure)	2.45 acres	1 ha.
Chungbo or Jongbo	Korea	2.45 acres	1 ha.
Cottah	Bangladesh	80 sq. yds.	66.89 m.²
Jemba	Malaysia and Singapore	16 sq. yds.	13.38 m.²
Marabba	Pakistan	25 acres	10.12 ha.
Morabba	Pakistan—Punjab	25 acres	10.12 ha.
Mu	China	0.165 acres	0.065 ha.
Ngan	Thailand	478.4 sq. yds.	400 m.²
Paal	Indonesia	561.16 acres	227.08 ha.
Qing	China (New system)	16.47 acres	6.66 ha.
Rai	Thailand	0.395 acres	0.16 ha.
Se	Japan	118.61 sq. yds.	99.17 m.²
Square	Sri Lanka	100 sq. yds.	83.61 m.²
Tan	Japan	0.245 acres	0.1 ha.
Tsubo	Japan	3.95 sq. yds.	3.3 m.²

DEPTH

Unit	Country	Imperial Equivalent	Metric Equivalent
Sazhene	U.S.S.R.	1 fathom	1.83 m.

QUANTITY

Unit	Country	Quantity
Crore	India, Pakistan, Bangladesh	10,000,000 (1,00,00,000)
Lakh	India, Pakistan, Bangladesh	100,000 (1,00,000)

METRIC TO IMPERIAL CONVERSIONS

Metric Units	Imperial Units	To Convert Metric into Imperial Units Multiply by:	To Convert Imperial into Metric Units Multiply by:
Weight			
Gramme (gm.)	Ounce (Avoirdupois)	0.035274	28.3495
Kilogramme (kg.)	Pound (lb.)	2.204622	0.453592
Metric ton ('000 kg.)	Short ton (2,000 lb.)	1.102311	0.907185
	Long ton (2,240 lb.)	0.984207	1.016047
	(The short ton is in general use in the U.S.A., while the long ton is normally used in the U.K. and the Commonwealth.)		
Length			
Centimetre (cm.)	Inch	0.393701	2.54
Metre (m.)	Yard (=3 feet)	1.09361	0.9144
Kilometre (km.)	Mile	0.62137	1.609344
Capacity			
Litre (lit.)	Gallon (=8 pints)	0.219969	4.54609
	Gallon (U.S.)	0.264172	3.78541
Area			
Square metre (m.²)	Square yard	1.19599	0.836127
Hectare (ha.)	Acre	2.47105	0.404686
Square kilometre (km.²)	Square mile	0.386102	2.589988

SYSTEMS OF MEASUREMENT

WEIGHT

Afghanistan	Kharwar = 80 Seer
	Seer = 4 Charak
	Charak = 16 Khord
Burma	Candy = 500 Acheintaya
	Acheintaya = 10 Beittha or Viss
	Beittha or Viss = 200 Ngamus
China	Picul = 100 Catty
	Catty = 16 Liang
	Liang = 10 Mace
	Mace = 10 Fan or Candareen
India, Pakistan and Bangladesh	Maund = 40 Seer
	Seer = 16 Chittack
	Pa = 20 Tola
Japan	Picul = 16 Kwan (Kan)
	Kwan = 16 Hyaku-mé
	Hyaku-mé = 20 Nijo
	Nijo = 5 Me or Mommé
Malaysia	Koyan = 40 Picul
Philippines	Quintal = 4 Arroba
Thailand	Picul = 100 Catty or Kon
	Catty = 40 Baht or Kyat

LENGTH

Burma	Garwoke = 4 Kawtha
	Oke thapa = 20 Tar
	Tar = 7 Cubit or Taung
	Lan = 4 Cubit or Taung
	Cubit = 18 Palgate
China	Li = 1,500 Chi
	Chi = 10 Cun
	Cun = 10 Fen
Hong Kong	Cheung = 10 Chek
	Chek = Chi (see China)
India, Pakistan and Bangladesh	Coss = 1,000 Danda
	Danda = 2 Gudge
	Gudge = 2 Hath
	Hath = 24 Ungul
Japan	Jo = 2 Hiro
	Hiro = 5 Shaku
	Shaku = 10 Sun
Kampuchea	Hat = 2 Chamam
Thailand	Sen = 20 Wah
	Wah = 8 Keup

CAPACITY

Burma	Bag = 3 Tin
	Tin = 2 Kwe
	Kwe = 2 Seik
	Seik = 2 Sayut
	Sayut = 2 Pyi
Japan	To = 10 Sho
	Sho = 10 Go
	Go = 10 Shaku
Philippines	Cavan = 25 Ganta
	Tinaja = 15 Ganta
	Ganta = 8 Chupa
Thailand	Kwien = 100 Sat
	Sat = 20 Tanan

AREA

China	Qing = 100 Mu
Indonesia	Paal = 320 Bahoe or Bouw
Japan	Cho = 10 Bu or Tan
	Bu = 2 Se
	Se = 30 Tsubo
Pakistan	Bigha = 20 Cottah
	Cottah = 16 Chattah
Thailand	Ngan = 2½ Rai

Calendars and Time Reckoning

THE MUSLIM CALENDAR

The Muslim era dates from July 16th, A.D. 622, which was the beginning of the Arab year in which the *Hijra*, Muhammad's flight from Mecca to Medina, took place. The Muslim or Hijra Calendar is lunar, each year having 354 or 355 days, the extra day being intercalated eleven times every thirty years. Accordingly the beginning of the Hijra year occurs earlier in the Gregorian Calendar by a few days each year. The Muslim year 1403 A.H. begins on October 19th, 1982.

The year is divided into the following months:

1. Muharram	30 days		7. Rajab	30 days	
2. Safar	29 ,,		8. Shaaban	29 ,,	
3. Rabia I	30 ,,		9. Ramadan	30 ,,	
4. Rabia II	29 ,,		10. Shawwal	29 ,,	
5. Jumada I	30 ,,		11. Dhu'l-Qa'da	30 ,,	
6. Jumada II	29 ,,		12. Dhu'l-Hijja	29 or 30 days	

The Hijra Calendar is used for religious purposes throughout the Islamic world and is the official calendar in Saudi Arabia and the Yemen Arab Republic. In most Arab countries it is used side by side with the Gregorian Calendar for official purposes, but in Indonesia, Malaysia and Pakistan the Gregorian Calendar has replaced it.

PRINCIPAL MUSLIM FESTIVALS

New Year: 1st Muharram. The first ten days of the year are regarded as holy, especially the tenth.

Ashoura: 10th Muharram. Celebrates the first meeting of Adam and Eve after leaving Paradise, also the ending of the Flood and the death of Hussain, grandson of Muhammad. The feast is celebrated with fairs and processions.

Mouloud (*Birth of Muhammad*): 12th Rabia I.

Leilat al Meiraj (*Ascension of Muhammad*): 27th Rajab.

Ramadan (*Month of Fasting*).

Id ul Fitr or **Id ul Saghir** or **Küçük Bayram** (*The Small Feast*): Three days beginning 1st Shawwal. This celebration follows the constraint of the Ramadan fast.

Id ul Adha or **Id al Kabir** or **Büyük Bayram** (*The Great Feast, Feast of the Sacrifice*): Four days beginning on 10th Dhu'l-Hijja. The principal Muslim festival, commemorating Abraham's sacrifice and coinciding with the pilgrimage to Mecca. Celebrated by the sacrifice of a sheep, by feasting and by donations to the poor.

Hijra Year	1401		1402		1403	
New Year	Nov. 9th,	1980	Oct. 30th,	1981	Oct. 19th,	1982
Ashoura	Nov. 18th,	,,	Nov. 8th,	,,	Oct. 28th,	,,
Mouloud	Jan. 18th,	1981	Jan. 8th,	1982	Dec. 28th,	,,
Leilat al Meiraj	May 31st,	,,	May 21st,	,,	May 10th,	1983
Ramadan begins	July 3rd,	,,	June 23rd,	,,	June 12th,	,,
Id ul Fitr	Aug. 2nd,	,,	July 23rd,	,,	July 12th,	,,
Id ul Adha	Oct. 9th,	,,	Sept. 29th,	,,	Sept. 18th,	,,

Note: Local determinations may vary by one day from those given here.

HINDU CALENDARS

In India there are two principal Hindu calendars, the Vikrama and the Saka.

The Vikrama or Samvat era is dated from a victory of King Vikramaditya in 58 B.C. The year 1982 of the Christian era therefore corresponds to 2039 in the Vikrama era. The New Year begins in March or April in eastern India, but in October or November in the western States.

The Saka era, beginning in A.D. 78, is attributed to the Saka King Kanishka. 1982 of the Christian era corresponds with 1904 of the Saka era.

The Official Calendar in India, adopted in 1957, is based on the Saka year but has been fixed in relation to the Gregorian calendar so that New Year (Chaitra 1) falls always on March 22nd, except in Leap Years when it falls on March 21st. This calendar is used for dating official documents, for All-India Radio broadcasts, and other official purposes; however, the Gregorian calendar is still widely used in India.

FESTIVALS

Holi: Spring Festival in honour of Krishna, usually held in March.

Mahendra Jatra: Nepalese festival to ensure the monsoon rains; June.

Dussera: Ten-day festival of Durga; early October.

Diwali: Festival of lights, dedicated to Lakshmi; late October.

There is also a large number of local agricultural and commemorative festivals.

BUDDHIST AND THE SOUTH INDIAN CALENDARS

The Buddhist era is attributed to the death of Buddha, historically dated at about 483 B.C. The era in use in fact dates from 544 B.C., making the year 1982 of the Christian era equal to 2525 of the Buddhist era. The Jain era, based on the death of Mahavira, starts in 528 B.C., making A.D. 1982 equal to 2509.

In south and south-east Asia there is widespread use of a lunar year of 354 days, with months of alternately 29 or 30 days, and with extra (intercalary) months approximately every third year. Under this system New Year may fall in either April or March. In Burma, New Year is regularly on April 13th. The Burmese era, the *Khaccapancha*, is ascribed to the ruler Popa Sawrahan, and begins in A.D. 638. 1982 of the Gregorian calendar is equivalent to 1344 B.E.

Sri Lanka adopted the Buddhist calendar as its official and commercial calendar in 1966. Sunday is treated as a normal working day, while the lunar quarter days (Poya days) are public holidays; some of these are two-day holidays. New Year is on April 13th or 14th.

Thailand used the Burmese calendar until 1889, when a new civil era was introduced commemorating the centenary of the first king of Bangkok. Since 1909 a calendar based on the year 543 B.C. (traditionally the year of Gautama Buddha's attainment of nirvana) has been in official use. The months have been adapted to correspond with those of the Gregorian calendar, but New Year is on April 1st every year. In this calendar, the *Pra Putta Sakarat*, A.D. 1982 is equivalent to 2524.

FESTIVALS

The principal festivals in the Buddhist calendars are the New Year and the spring and autumn equinox, and local festivals connected with important pagodas.

THE CHINESE CALENDAR

China has both lunar and solar systems of dividing the year. The lunar calendar contains twelve months of 29 or 30 days, and in each period of 19 years 7 intercalary months are inserted at appropriate intervals. In order not to disturb the twelve-month cycle these extra months bear the same title as that which has preceded them. The intercalary months may not be introduced after the first, eleventh or twelfth month of any year.

The solar year used by the peasant community of China begins regularly on February 5th of the Gregorian calendar, and is divided into 24 sections of 14, 15 or 16 days. This calendar is not upset by the discrepant cycle of the moon, and is therefore suitable for the regulation of agriculture.

Until the Revolution of 1911 years were named according to a sixty-year cycle, made up of ten stems (*Ban*) and twelve branches (*Ji*). Each year of the cycle has a composite name composed of a different combination of stem and branch. Similar sixty-year cycles of year-names have been in use in Thailand and Japan at various times and are still in use in Hong Kong, Malaysia and Singapore.

Since 1911 years have been dated from the Revolution as Years of the Republic; A.D. 1982 is the 71st year of the Republican era. In the People's Republic of China the Gregorian system is used.

Japan has used the Gregorian system since 1873, but a National Calendar has also been introduced, derived from the traditional date of accession of the first Emperor, Zinmu, in 660 B.C. The year A.D. 1982 corresponds to 2641 of this era.

STANDARD TIME

The following table gives the standard time adopted in the various countries and territories covered in this book, in relation to Greenwich Mean Time (G.M.T.). For the U.S.S.R., figures refer to Zone time, one hour behind Standard time.

+4
U.S.S.R. (Ashkhabad)

+4½
Afghanistan

+5
Maldives
Pakistan
U.S.S.R. (Alma Ata, Karaganda, Frunze)

+5½
Bhutan
India
Nepal
Sri Lanka

+6
Bangladesh
China (Xizang A.R.)
U.S.S.R. (Novosibirsk, Krasnoyarsk)

+6½
Burma
Cocos (Keeling) Is.

+7
China (Chongqing, Lanzhou)
Indonesia (Sumatra, Java, Bali, Madura)
Kampuchea
Laos
Mongolia (Western)
Thailand
U.S.S.R. (Irkutsk)
Viet-Nam

+8
Australia (W. Australia)
Brunei
China (Beijing, Shanghai)
Hong Kong
Indonesia (Kalimantan, Timor, Celebes)
Macau
Malaysia
Mongolia (Eastern)
Philippines
Singapore
Taiwan
U.S.S.R. (Yakutsk)

+8½
China (Harbin)

+9
Indonesia (Moluccas, Irian Jaya)
Japan
Korea
U.S.S.R. (Khabarovsk, Vladivostok)

+9½
Australia (Northern Territory, South Australia)

+10
Australia (Vic., N.S.W., Qld., Tas.)
Caroline Is.
Guam
Northern Mariana Is.
Papua New Guinea (excl. Solomon Is.)
U.S.S.R. (Magadan, Sakhalin)

+11
New Caledonia
Solomon Is.
Truk Is.
U.S.S.R. (Petropavlovsk, Kamchatskii)
Vanuatu

+11½
Nauru
Norfolk Is.

+12
Fiji
Kiribati
Marshall Is.
New Zealand (Chatham Is.+12¾)
Tuvalu
U.S.S.R. (Anadyr)
Wallis and Futuna Is.

+13
Tonga

−11
American Samoa
Niue
Tokelau
Western Samoa

−10½
Cook Is.

−10
French Polynesia
Hawaii

−9
Pitcairn Is.

Research Institutes

Associations and institutions studying the Far East and Australasia

(*See also* Part Two, Regional Organizations—Education.)

AFGHANISTAN

Anjumani Tarikh (*Historical Society*): Kabul; f. 1931; to study and promote international knowledge of the history of Afghanistan; Head Dr. M. Yakub Wahidi; publs. *Aryana* (quarterly, in Pashtu and Dari) and *Afghanistan* (English and French, quarterly).

British Institute of Afghan Studies: P.O.B. 3052, Kabul; f. 1972; supports research relating to history, antiquities, archaeology, languages, literature, art, culture, customs and natural history of Afghanistan.

AUSTRALIA

Australian Institute of International Affairs: Box E 181, Post Office, Canberra, A.C.T.; f. 1932; 2,177 mems.; brs. in all States; Pres. Rt. Hon. Sir Garfield Barwick, A.K., G.C.M.G.; Dir. D. P. McElligott, M.B.E.; publs. *The Australian Outlook* (3 times yearly), *World Review* (4 times yearly), *Dyason House Papers* (4 times yearly).

Centre of Southeast Asian Studies: Monash University, Clayton, Vic. 3168; f. 1964; Dir. Assoc. Prof. David P. Chandler; publs. papers on South-East Asia and working papers.

Department of Oriental Studies: University of Sydney, Sydney, N.S.W. 2006.

Faculty of Asian Studies: Australian National University, P.O. Box 4, Canberra, A.C.T. 2600; Dean Dr. J. T. F. Jordens.

Research School of Pacific Studies: Australian National University, P.O. Box 4, Canberra, A.C.T. 2600; Dir. Prof. R. G. Ward; publs. *Australian Journal of Chinese Affairs, Bulletin of Indonesian Economic Studies, Canberra Anthropology, Canberra Papers on Strategy and Defence, Canberra Studies on World Affairs, Contemporary China Papers*, etc.

AUSTRIA

Afro-Asiatisches Institut in Wien: 1090 Vienna, Türkenstrasse 3; f. 1959; cultural and other exchanges between Austria and African and Asian countries, lectures, economic and social research, seminars; Pres. Bishop Dr. A. Wagner; Gen. Sec. G. Bittner; publ. *Treffpunkte* (quarterly).

Ludwig Boltzmann Institute for China and South-East Asia: Vienna; f. 1978; Pres. Dr. Gerd Kaminski.

Institut für Japanologie der Universität Wien: A 1010 Vienna, Universitätsstrasse 7; f. 1965; Japanese Studies: Dir. Sepp Linhart; publ. *Beiträge zur Japanologie* (irregular).

Institut für Sinologie der Universität Wien: 1010 Vienna, Rathausstrasse 19/9; Dir. Prof. Dr. Otto Ladstätter.

BANGLADESH

Bangladesh Economic Association: c/o Economics Dept., Dacca University, Dacca; f. 1958 to promote economic research; Pres. Dr. Mazharul Huq; Sec. Dr. S. R. Bose.

Bangladesh Institute of Development Studies: Adamjee Court, Motijheel Commercial Area, Dacca 2; f. 1957; to function as an agency for undertaking and promoting study, research and dissemination of knowledge in the field of development economics, demography and other social sciences relating to planning for national development and social welfare; to collect information, conduct investigations and undertake research projects for purposes of assistance, planning, and formulation of policy, and implementation of plans and policies; to provide facilities for training in economics, demography and other social sciences: and to provide information and offer advice on modern research techniques and methodology in economics, demography and other social sciences; library of 61,000 books and bound periodicals, 42,000 documents (including 20,500 microfiches) and 750 periodicals; Chair. Dr. Monowar Hossain (acting); publs. *Bangladesh Development Studies* (quarterly), series and monographs.

Bangladesh Institute of International and Strategic Studies: 1/46 Elephant Rd., Dacca; f. 1978; Dir.-Gen. Brig. A. H. M. Abdul Momen.

Institute of Bangladesh Studies: University of Rajshahi, Rajshahi; Dir. S. A. Akanda.

Varendra Research Museum: Rajshahi; f. 1910, under control of University of Rajshahi since 1964; investigation and encouragement of history, archaeology, anthropology, literature, and art; collection and preservation of archaeological and other relics, ancient MSS., etc., and publication of original works on these subjects; library of about 10,000 vols.; 7,570 items in museum, including 4,500 ancient MSS.; Dir. Dr. M. Rahman, M.A., PH.D., F.R.A.S.; publ. *Journal* (annually).

BELGIUM

Institut Orientaliste: Faculté de Philosophie et Lettres de l'Université Catholique de Louvain, Collège Erasme, B-1348 Louvain-la-Neuve; f. 1936; Pres. Prof. J. Ryckmans; publs. *Le Muséon* (periodical), *Bibliothèque du Muséon, Publications de l'Institut Orientaliste de Louvain* (*P.I.O.L.*).

BURMA

Burma Research Society: Universities' Central Library, University Post Office, Rangoon; f. 1910 to promote cultural and scientific studies and research relating to Burma and neighbouring countries; 1,040 mems.; 855 vols.; Pres. U Tha Myat; Hon. Sec. Dr. Shein; publ. *Journal* (twice yearly).

Department of Religious Affairs: Kaba-aye Pagoda Compound, Rangoon; a government-supported centre for research and studies in Buddhist and allied subjects; library of 17,000 vols., 7,000 periodicals, 7,650 palm leaf MSS., 1,022 parabaiks (folding parchments) and Kammaraca (brass plate MSS.); Dir.-Gen. U Kyi Nyunt.

CANADA

Canada-Mongolian Society/Association Canada-Mongolie: P.O. Box 9210, Saskatoon S7K 3X5; Exec. Dir. Robert I. Binnick; publ. *The Canada-Mongolia Review/La Revue Canada-Mongolie* (irregular).

Department of Asian Studies, University of British Columbia: Vancouver V6T 1W5, British Columbia; f. 1962; instruction and research in East, South and South-East Asia; Head Prof. A. N. Aklujkar.

PEOPLE'S REPUBLIC OF CHINA

Chinese Academy of Social Sciences: Beijing; f. 1977; Pres. Hu Qiaomu; comprises the following relevant research institutes; **Archaeology Institute,** Dir. Xia Nai; **History (Ancient) Institute,** Deputy Dir. Yin Da, publ. *Lishi yenjiu* (Historical Researches) series; **History (Modern) Institute,** Deputy Dirs. Li Shu, Li Xin, Liu Danlan; **Linguistics and Philology Institute,** Dir. Lu Shuxiang; **Literature Institute,** Deputy Dir. You Guanying, publ. *Wenxue pinglun* (Discourses on Literature) series; **Nationalities Institute,** Dir. Yun Beifung; **National Minorities Languages Institute.**

CZECHOSLOVAKIA

Oriental Institute: Slovak Academy of Sciences, Klemensova 19, 88416 Bratislava; f. 1960; 12 mems.; Pres. Dr. I. Doležal; Vice-Pres. Dr. V. Krupa; publ. *Asian and African Studies* (annual).

Oriental Institute: Czechoslovak Academy of Sciences, Lázeňská 4, 118 37 Prague 1; f. 1922; Chinese library of 62,000 vols., general library of 178,843 vols.; publs. *Archiv orientální* (quarterly), *Nový Orient* (monthly).

DENMARK

Orientalsk Samfund: Kejsergade 2, 1155 Copenhagen; f. 1915 to undertake the study and further the understanding of Oriental cultures and civilizations; 75 mems.; Pres. Prof. Søren Egerod; Sec. Prof. J. P. Asmussen; publ. *Acta Orientalia* (annually).

FIJI

The Fiji Society: Box 1205, Suva; f. 1936; concerned with subjects of historic and scientific interest to Fiji and other islands of the Pacific; Pres. Ivan Williams; publ. *Transactions* (irregular).

FINLAND

Suomen Itämainen Seura (*Finnish Oriental Society*): c/o Department of Asian and African Studies, University of Helsinki, 00100 Helsinki 10; f. 1917; 150 mems.; Pres. J. Aro; Sec. T. Harviainen; publ. *Studia Orientalia.*

FRANCE

Association pour une meilleure connaissance de l'Asie (A.M.C.A.): B.P. No. 1, 37220 L'Ile-Bouchard; Dir. François Joyaux; publ. *Mondes Asiatiques* (quarterly).

Centre d'Etudes de l'Orient Contemporain: 13 rue de Santeuil, 75231 Paris Cedex 05; f. 1945; Dir. H. Mammeri; publs. *Maghreb-Machrek* (in conjunction with La Documentation Française).

Centre de Hautes Etudes sur l'Afrique et l'Asie Modernes: 13 rue du Four, 75006 Paris; f. 1936; library of 14,000 vols.; Dir. G. R. Malécot; publs. *L'Afrique et L'Asie Modernes* (quarterly), *Cahiers de l'Afrique et l'Asie* (irregular), *Langues et Dialectes d'Outre-Mer* (irregular), *Recherches et Documents du CHEAM* (irregular), *Cahiers du CHEAM* (irregular).

Ecole des Langues Orientales Anciennes: Institut Catholique de Paris, U.E.R. de Théologie et de Sciences Religieuses, 21 Rue d'Assas, 75270 Paris Cedex 06; f. 1887; study of and research into Ancient Oriental languages; Dir. Joseph Trinquet.

Institut National des Langues et Civilisations Orientales: 2 rue de Lille, 75007 Paris; f. 1795; courses in 82 languages; research; information centre; organizes international exchanges; Pres. Henri de La Bastide; publs. encyclopedias, textbooks, translations, etc.

Musée Cernuschi: 7 ave. Velasquez, 75008 Paris; f. 1896; ancient art and contemporary painting of China; Dir. Vadime Elisseeff; publs. catalogues.

Musée Guimet (*Asiatic Dept. of National Museums*): 6 Place d'Iéna, 75116 Paris; f. 1889; library of 100,000 vols.; art, archaeology, religions, history, literature and music of India, Central Asia, Tibet, Pakistan, Vietnam, China, Korea, Japan, Kampuchea, Thailand, Laos, Burma and Indonesia; Curator A. Le Bonheur; Librarian F. Macouin; publs. *Annales du Musée Guimet, Arts Asiatiques.*

Société Asiatique: 3 rue Mazarine, 75006 Paris; f. 1822; library of 80,000 vols.; 650 mems.; Pres. C. Cahen; Vice-Pres. J. Filliozat, A. Caquot; publs. *Journal Asiatique* (quarterly), *Cahiers.*

Unité d'Enseignement et de Recherche (U.E.R.) Asie Orientale: Université Paris VII, 2 place Jussieu, 75221 Paris Cedex 05; f. 1971; Principal Officers Mrs. J. Pigeot (Japanese studies), Yves Hervouet (Chinese studies), Li Ogg (Korean studies), Nguyen Phu Phong (Vietnamese studies).

U.E.R. Etudes Slaves, Orientales et Asiatiques: 2 rue de la Liberté, 93526 St. Denis Cedex 02; Dir. Y. Hervouet.

U.E.R. Langues et Civilisations de l'Orient et de l'Afrique du Nord: Université de Paris III, 17 rue de la Sorbonne, 75230 Paris Cedex 05.

GERMAN DEMOCRATIC REPUBLIC

Akademie der Wissenschaften der DDR-Wissenschaftsbereich Allgemeine Geschichte: 108 Berlin, Clara-Zetkin-Str. 26; Dir. Dr. Martin Robbe; publ. *Asien, Afrika, Lateinamerika* (bi-monthly).

Ostasiatische Sammlung des Staatliche Museen zu Berlin: Berlin 102, Bodestrasse 1/3; f. 1907; Dir. Bruno Voigt; publ. *Abhandlungen für Forschungen und Berichte.*

Vorderasiatisches Museum: 1020 Berlin, Bodestrasse 1-3; Dir. Dr. Liane Jakob-Rost.

FEDERAL REPUBLIC OF GERMANY

China-Institut: Johann Wolfgang von Goethe-Universität, 6 Frankfurt/Main, Dantestr. 4-6; Dir. Prof. Dr. Tsung-Tung Chang.

Deutsch-Indische Gesellschaft e.V.: 7000 Stuttgart 1, Charlottenplatz 17; publ. *Indo-Asia* (quarterly).

Deutsche Gesellschaft für Asienkunde e.V. (*German Association for Asian Studies*): 2 Hamburg 13, Rothenbaumchaussee 32; f. 1967; promotion and co-ordination of contemporary Asian research; 650 mems.; Pres. Günter Diehl; Sec. Monika Schädler; publ. *ASIEN. Deutsche Zeitschrift für Politik, Wirtschaft und Kultur* (quarterly).

Deutsche Morgenländische Gesellschaft e.V. (*German Oriental Society*): Postfach 1407, 1000 Berlin 30; f. 1845; sponsors research and holds meetings and lectures in the field of Oriental studies; 650 mems.; Chair. Prof. Dr. Hans R. Roemer; Sec. Dr. D. George; publs. *Zeitschrift, Abhandlungen für die Kunde des Morgenlandes, Beiruter Texte und Studien, Bibliotheca Islamica, Verzeichnis der Orientalischen Handschriften in Deutschland, Nepal Research Centre Publications.*

Deutsche Orient-Gesellschaft: Museum für Vor- und Frühgeschichte, 1 Berlin 19, Schloss Charlottenburg, Langhansbau; f. 1898; 580 mems.; Pres. Prof. Dr. Barthel Hrouda; Sec. Prof. Dr. Volkmar Fritz; publs. *Mitteilungen, Wissenschaftliche Veröffentlichungen, Abhandlungen.*

Institut für Asienkunde (*Institute of Asian Affairs*): 2000 Hamburg 13, Rothenbaumchaussee 32; f. 1956; research and documentation into all aspects of contemporary South, South-East and East-Asia; Pres. Dr. Dr. W. Röhl; Dir. Dr. W. Draguhn.

Museum für Indische Kunst (*Museum of Indian Art*): Staatliche Museen Preussischer Kulturbesitz, 1 Berlin 33 Takustrasse 40; Dir. Prof. Dr. Herbert Härtel; publs. catalogues, handbooks and series *Veröffentlichungen des Museums für Indische Kunst.*

Museum für Islamische Kunst (*Islamic Art and Antiquities*): Staatliche Museen Preussischer Kulturbesitz, 1 Berlin 33, Takustrasse 40; f. 1904; Dir. Prof. Dr. Klaus Brisch.

Museum für Ostasiatische Kunst (*Museum of Far Eastern Art*): Staatliche Museen Preussischer Kulturbesitz, 1 Berlin 33, Takustrasse 40; Dir. Prof. Dr. B. von Ragué.

Seminar für Sprache und Kultur Japans der Universität Hamburg: Von-Melle-Park 6, 2000 Hamburg 13; f. 1919; research into Japanese studies; 30,000 vols.; Dir. Prof. Dr. O. Benl; publ. *Oriens Extremus.*

Südasien-Institut der Universität Heidelberg: Heidelberg, Im Neuenheimer Feld 330; f. 1962; Dir. Prof. Dr. D. Rothermund; publs. *Schriftenreihe des Südasien—Instituts, Beiträge zür Südasienforschung, South Asian Digest of Regional Writing, South Asian Studies, Bulletin.*

HONG KONG

Centre of Asian Studies: University of Hong Kong; f. 1967; traditional and contemporary China, Hong Kong, East and South-East Asia; Dir. Dr. Edward K. Y. Chen; Research Officers Steve S. K. Chin, Patrick Fung, Billie Lo; publs. monographs and occasional paper series, research guides and bibliographies, *Journal of Oriental Studies.*

Institute of Chinese Studies: The Chinese University of Hong Kong, Shatin, New Territories; f. 1967; Hon. Dir. Cheng Te-k'un, ph.d.

HUNGARY

Magyar Tudományos Akadémia Orientalisztikai Munkaközössége (*Orientalist Research Centre of the Hungarian Academy of Sciences*): 1014 Budapest 1, Országház u. 30; f. 1979; Head Prof. Ferenc Tőkei.

INDIA

Abul Kalam Azad Oriental Research Institute: Public Gardens, Hyderabad 500004, A.P.; f. 1959; research in history, philosophy, culture and languages; library of 15,000 vols.; Pres. Mir Akbar Ali Khan, m.p.; Chair. M. A. Abbasi; Hon. Gen. Sec. and Dir. Khwaja Muhammad Ahmad.

All-India Oriental Conference: Bhandarkar Oriental Research Institute, Pune 411004; f. 1919; 1,200 mems.; Pres. Prof. Gawrinath Sastri; Sec. Prof. R. N. Dandekar; publs. *Proceedings of its Sessions, Index of Papers* (in 3 vols.).

Anjuman-i-Islam Urdu Research Institute: 92 Dr. Dadabhoy Nowroji Rd., Bombay 400001; f. 1947; postgraduate degree courses and research in Urdu language and literature; library of 20,000 vols.; also embraces Kitabat School of arts which provides instruction in Jamia Urdu, Adib, Adib-e-Maher and Adib-e-Kamil; Dir. Prof. N. S. Gorekar; publs. *Nawa-e-Adab* (biannual) and research books in Urdu.

Asiatic Society of Bengal: 1 Park St., Calcutta; f. 1784; 696 mems.; Pres. Prof. S. K. Saraswati, m.a., f.a.s.; Gen. Sec. Dr. Bireswar Banerjee, m.a., d.lit.; publs. *Journal* (4 issues a year), *Year Book, Bibliotheca Indica, Monographs,* etc.

Asiatic Society of Bombay: Town Hall, Shahid Bhagatsingh Rd., Bombay 400 023; f. 1804 as Bombay Literary Society; to investigate and encourage sciences, arts and literature in relation to Asia, and India in particular; to promote research and publish research works; 1,470 mems.; maintains the Central Library for the State of Maharashtra (depository library), 207,416 vols. (491,308 in Central Library), 2,300 MSS., 5,000 old coins; Pres. Shri Soli J. Sorabjee; Hon. Sec. Mrs. Bansari K. Sheth; publs. *Journals, Monographs, Reports.*

Bhandarkar Oriental Research Institute: Pune 411004; f. 1917; Sec. Dr. R. N. Dandekar, m.a., ph.d.; Curator Dr. V. G. Rahurkar, m.a., ph.d.; Dir. Dr. G. B. Palsule, m.a., ph.d., d.litt.; 600 mems.; library of 50,000 vols., 30,000 MSS.; publs. *Annals of the Bhandarkar Oriental Research Institute* (Parts I-IV published annually), *Bhandarkar Oriental Series, Bombay Sanskrit and Prakrit Series, Government Oriental Series* (almost 270 titles), Research Unit Publications, Critical Editions of the *Mahabharata* and *Harivamsa.*

K. R. Cama Oriental Institute and Library: 136 Bombay Samachar Marg, Fort, Bombay 400023; f. 1916; 100 mems.; library of 16,000 vols., 1,800 MSS., 4,500 journals; Pres. Adi N. Chinoy; Secs. H. J. M. Desai, N. D. Minochehr-Homji, H. N. Modi; Librarian J. G. Panji; publ. *Journal* (annually).

G. N. Jha Kendriya Sanskrit Vidyapeetha (*fmrly. Ganganatha Jha Research Institute*): M. L. Nehru Park, Allahabad 211002, U.P.; f. 1943; research into Sanskrit and other branches of Indology; library of 30,000 vols., 25,000 Sanskrit MSS.; Principal Dr. Gaya Charan Tripathi, m.a., ph.d., dr.phil.; publs. *Quarterly Research Journal, Annual Bibliography of Indology, Catalogues of MSS.,* many Sanskrit texts and independent research works.

Gujarat Research Society: Sanshodhan Sadan, South Ave., Khar, Bombay 400052; f. 1936; to organize and coordinate research in social and cultural activities; library of 8,000 vols.; Pres. Dr. M. R. Shah; publ. *Journal of the Gujarat Research Society* (quarterly).

Heras Institute of Indian History and Culture: St. Xavier's College, Bombay 400001; f. 1926; Dir. J. Correia-Afonso; publ. *Indica* (twice yearly).

Indian Council for Cultural Relations: Azad Bhavan, Indraprastha Estate, New Delhi 110002; f. 1950 to establish and strengthen cultural relations between India and other countries, and to project Indian cultural image abroad; br. offices in Bangalore, Bombay, Calcutta, Chandigarh, Madras and Varanasi; cultural centres in Suva (Fiji), Georgetown (Guyana) and Paramaribo (Suriname); activities include exchange visits between scholars, artists and men of eminence in the field of art and culture, exchange of exhibitions; international conferences and seminars, lectures by renowned scholars including the Azad Memorial Lecture; establishment of chairs and centres of Indian studies abroad and welfare of overseas students in India; administration of Jawaharlal Nehru Award for International Understanding; library of over 25,000 vols. on India and other countries; publs. interpretations of Indian Art and Culture and translations of Indian works into foreign languages; Pres. Minister for External Affairs; Sec. Mrs. Manorama Bhalla; publs. *Indian Horizons* (in English, quarterly), *Cultural News from India* (in English, quarterly), *Thaqafatul-Hind* (in Arabic, quarterly), *Papeles de la India* (in Spanish, quarterly), *Rencontre avec l'Inde* (in French, quarterly), *ICCR Newsletter* (English quarterly for foreign students), *Africa Quarterly* (in English, quarterly on African affairs) and *Gaganachal* (in Hindi, quarterly).

Indian Council of World Affairs: Sapru House, Barakhamba Rd., New Delhi 110001; f. 1943; non-governmental institution for the study of Indian and international questions; 1,500 mems.; library of 102,500 vols., 1,050 periodicals, 10,717 microfilms and microfiches, over 13 million press-cuttings and all UN publs.; Pres. SARDAR SWARAN SINGH; Sec.-Gen. S. C. PARASHER; publs. *India Quarterly*, *Foreign Affairs Reports* (monthly).

Indian Economic Association: Delhi School of Economics, Delhi 9; f. 1918; Pres. Prof. V. M. DANDEKAR; Hon. Sec. Prof. K. A. NAQVI; publ. *Indian Economic Journal*.

Indian Society of Oriental Art (Calcutta): 17 Park St., Calcutta 700016; f. 1907; 350 mems.; to promote and research all aspects of ancient and contemporary art; Hon. Sec. INDIRA NAG CHAUDHURI; publ. *Journal* (annual).

Institute of Economic Growth and Research Centre on Social and Economic Development in Asia: University Enclave, Delhi 110007; f. 1967; research into the problems of social and economic development of South and South East Asia; specialized library and documentation services; Dir. of Institute Prof. C. H. HANUMANTHA RAO; Head of Centre Dr. T. N. MADAN; publs. *Asian Social Science*, *Bibliography* (annual), *Contributions to Indian Sociology: New Series* (annual), *Studies in Asian Social Development* (occasional).

International Academy of Indian Culture: J 22 Hauz Khas Enclave, New Delhi 110016; f. 1935; to study India's artistic and historic relations with other Asian countries; library of 45,000 vols., 40,000 MSS.; Hon. Dir. Dr. LOKESH CHANDRA; Hon. Sec. Dr. SHARADA RANI; publs. *Satapitaka Series* (irregular).

Islamic Research Association: 8 Shepherd Rd., Bombay 400008; f. 1933; Pres. Prof. S. S. DESNAVI; publs. 12 vols. of research work on *Islamic Studies*.

Ismaili Society: P.O.B. 6052, Bombay 5; f. 1946; Pres. G. H. BUNDALLY; Hon. Editor W. IVANOW; publ. translations and texts of Ismaili works, monographs on Ismailism.

K. M. Institute of Hindi Studies and Linguistics: Agra Univ., Agra 282004, U.P.; Dir. Dr. VIDYA NIWAS MISRA.

Kuppuswami Sastri Research Institute: 84 Royapettah High Road, (Sanskrit College Campus), Mylapore, Madras 600004; f. 1944; promotion of Oriental learning; 300 mems.; library of 20,000 vols. (including palm-leaf MSS.); Pres. Dr. S. RADHAKRISHNA; Sec. and Dir. Miss S. S. JANAKI; publs. *Journal of Oriental Research* and numerous research publs.

Maha Bodhi Society: 4A Bankim Chatterjee St., Calcutta 700073; f. 1891; 23 brs. in other cities and countries; 1,800 mems.; Gen. Sec. Ven. Dr. N. JINARATANA NAYAKA THERA; publs. *Mahabodhi Journal* (English monthly), books on Buddhism.

Mumbai Marathi Granth Sangrahalaya: Dadar, Bombay 400014; f. 1898; research in Marathi language and literature; library of 185,020 vols.; Pres. S. K. PATIL.

Nava Nalanda Pali Institute: P.O. Nalanda, Bihar 80311; f. 1951; postgraduate studies and research in Pali, Buddhist studies, ancient Indian and Asian history and philosophy; library of 32,000 vols.; Dir. Dr. C. S. UPASAK; publ. *Nava Nalanda Mahavihara Research* (annual), *Pali Tipitaka*, Pali commentaries and research publs.

Oriental Institute: Maharaja Sayajirao University of Baroda, Lokmanya Tilak Rd., Vadodara 390002, Gujarat; f. 1915; library of 40,382 vols. on Indology and Sanskrit, MSS. library of 26,395 MSS.; 21 mems.; Dir. Prof. Dr. S. G. KANTAWALA; Deputy Dir. Dr. B. N. BHATT; publs. *Gaekwad's Oriental Series*, *M.S. Lecture Series*, *M.S. University Oriental Series*, *Critical Edition of Visnupurāna*, *Svadhyāya* (Gujarati research quarterly), *Journal of the Oriental Institute* (English quarterly).

Oriental Research Institute: Mysore; library of 25,000 vols.; collection of 60,000 ancient MSS.; Dir. G. MARULASIDDAIAH, M.A., PH.D.

Sikkim Research Institute of Tibetology (fmrly. the *Namgyal Institute of Tibetology*): Gangtok, Sikkim; f. 1958; research centre for study of Mahayana (Northern Buddhism); library of Tibetan literature (canonical of all sects and secular) in MSS. and xylographs; museum of icons and art objects; Dir. Prof. RAM RAHUL; publs. in Tibetan, Sanskrit and English, including *Bulletin of Tibetology* (3 times a year).

Sri Venkateswara University Oriental Research Institute: Tirupati, Andhra Pradesh 517502; f. 1939; research in language and literature, philosophy and religion, arts and archaeology, history and social sciences; library of 27,000 vols., 14,000 MSS; publs. *Institute Journal* and other treatises.

Tamil Nadu Tamil Development and Research Council: Directorate of Tamil Development "Kuralagam", Madras 600001; f. 1959; development of Tamil in all its aspects, especially as a modern language; Chair. Chief Minister; Vice-Chair. Minister for Education; Sec. Dir. of Tamil Development; publ. *Tamil Nadu Tamil Bibliography*, *History of Tamil Nadu*, translations of world classics into Tamil and Tamil classics into other world languages.

Vishveshvaranand Vishva Bandhu Institute of Sanskrit and Indological Studies: Panjab University, Sadhu Ashram P.O. Hoshiarpur; f. 1965; postgraduate teaching, research and study in Indology and Sanskrit, including language, literature and religion; library of 100,000 vols.; Dir. S. BHASKARAN NAIR; publs. *Panjab University Indological Series*, *Vishveshvaranand Indological Journal* (two a year).

INDONESIA

Centre for Strategic and International Studies (CSIS): Jalan Tanah Abang III/27, Jakarta; f. 1971; undertakes policy-oriented studies in international and domestic-matters in collaboration with the industrial, commercial, political, legal and journalist communities of Indonesia; inter-disciplinary research projects concerning the area; Chair. DAOED JOESOEF; publs. *The Indonesia Quarterly*, *Analisa* (monthly), books.

LEKNAS-LIPI (*National Institute of Economic and Social Research—Indonesian Institute of Sciences*): Jalan Gondangdia Lama 39, Jakarta Pusat, P.O. Box 310; f. 1962; government organization which can receive research work from government institutions and/or international organizations on a contractual basis; it has four research centres: economic research, political development, social research and population studies; and has 26 research staff; its objectives are to undertake social and economic research, to evaluate the results of government socio-economic programmes (not including family planning), to co-operate with other institutes and agencies both in Indonesia and abroad, and to provide library services; Dir. SUHARSO.

National Institute for Cultural Studies: Indonesian Institute of Sciences, Jalan Pejambon 3, P.O. Box 165, Jakarta.

Perpustakaan Nasional, Direktorat Jenderal Kebudayaan, Depostemen Pendidikan dan Kebudayaan (*The National Library of Indonesia*): Jalan Iman Bonjol 1, Jakarta; f. 1980; 540,000 vols., 72,000 maps; Dir. Miss MASTINI HARDJO PRAKOSO; publs. National Bibliography, subject catalogues, subject indexes.

Pusat Pembinaan dan Pengembangan Bahasa (*National Centre for Language Development*): Jalan Diponegoro 82, P.O. Box 2625, Jakarta: f. 1975; attached to the Ministry of Education and Culture; language policy and planning, research on language and foreign language teaching; library of 35,000 vols.; Dir. Prof. Dr. AMRAN HALIM; Librarian Ms IPON PURAWIJAYA; publs. *Bahasa dan Sastra* (bi-monthly), *Pengajaran Bahasa dan Sastra* (bi-monthly), *Informasi Mutakhir* (bi-monthly).

IRAN

Asia Institute: University of Shiraz, Shiraz; Dir. Dr. Y. M. NAVABI; publs. *Bulletin, Monographs.*

ISRAEL

Harry S. Truman Research Institute for the Advancement of Peace: The Hebrew University of Jerusalem, Mt. Scopus, Jerusalem 91905; f. 1966; conducts and sponsors social science and historical research, organizes conferences and publishes works on many regions including Asia; Academic Dir. Prof. HAROLD Z. SCHIFFRIN.

Institute of Asian and African Studies: The Hebrew University of Jerusalem, Givat-Ram, Jerusalem; provides degree courses, covering history, social sciences and languages, in Chinese and Japanese studies; Chair. of Inst. Prof. SHAUL SHAKED; Chair. Dept. of East Asia Dr. BENAMI SHILLONY.

Israel Association for Asian Studies: c/o Institute for Asian and African Studies, The Hebrew University of Jerusalem, Givat-Ram, Jerusalem; f. 1972 to promote teaching and research on the cultures and societies of Asia and to foster understanding of Asian affairs; Pres. Prof. HAROLD Z. SCHIFFRIN.

Israel Oriental Society: The Hebrew University of Jerusalem, Givat-Ram, Jerusalem; f. 1949; aims to produce interest in and knowledge of history, politics, economics and culture in the Middle East, Asia and Africa; arranges lectures and symposia; Pres. A. EBAN; publs. *Hamizrah Hehadash* (*The New East*) (Hebrew quarterly), *Oriental Notes and Studies, Asian and African Studies* (three times a year).

ITALY

Istituto Italiano Per il Medio ed Estremo Oriente (ISMEO): Palazzo Brancaccio, via Merulana 248, Rome; f. 1933; a library and museum of oriental art are attached to the Institute; Hon. Pres. Prof. GIUSEPPE TUCCI; Pres. Prof. GHERARDO GNOLI; Vice-Pres. Prof. LIONELLO LANCIOTTI; publs. *East and West* (quarterly), *Rome Oriental Series, Nuovo Ramusio, Archaeological Reports, Restorations.*

Istituto Universitario Orientale (*Oriental University Institute*): Piazza San Giovanni Maggiore 30, 80134 Naples; f. 1732; library of 100,000 vols.; Dir. Prof. M. TADDEI; publ. *Annal* and various series of books.

JAPAN

Ajia Keizai Kenkyusho (*Institute of Developing Economies*): 42 Ichigaya-Hommura-cho, Shinjuku-ku, Tokyo 162; f. 1958; research on economic and related subjects in Asia and other developing areas; 270 mems.; Chair. MIYOHEI SHINOHARA; Pres. HISATOSHI MORISAKI; library of 160,000 vols.; publs. *Ajia Keizai* (monthly in Japanese), *The Developing Economies* (quarterly in English), *Library Bulletin* (monthly in Japanese); Occasional Papers Series (irregular, in English), etc.

Ajia Seikei Gakukai (*Society for Asian Political and Economic Studies*): Institute of Oriental Culture, University of Tokyo, 3-1 Hongo 7, Bunkyo-ku, Tokyo; f. 1953; 600 mems.; Pres. S. ETO; publ. *Aziya kenkyū* (quarterly).

Center for Modern Chinese Studies: c/o Tōyō Bunko, 28-21, Honkomagome 2-chome, Bunkyo-ku, Tokyo; f. 1962; collection on modern China deposited in the Tōyō Bunko; publ. *Kindai Chūgoku Kenkyū Ihō* (annual).

Center for Southeast Asian Studies: 46 Shimoadachi-cho, Yoshida, Sakyo-ku, Kyoto 606; attached to Kyoto University; Dir. Prof. T. WATABE; publs. *Southeast Asian Studies* (quarterly), *Monographs* (English and Japanese, irregular), *Discussion Papers, Reprint Series.*

Centre for East Asian Cultural Studies: c/o The Tōyō Bunko, Honkomagome 2-chome, 28-21, Bunkyo-ku, Tokyo 113; f. 1961; Dir. MASAO MORI; publs. *East Asian Cultural Studies*, Directories, East Asian Cultural Studies Series, Bibliographies, Translations of historical documents.

Chūgoku Kenkyūjo (*Chinese Research Institute*): 4-1-34 Kudan-kita, Chiyoda-ku, Tokyo; f. 1947; Dir. T. ITO; publs. *China Research Monthly, Asia Economic Bulletin* (36 issues yearly) and *New China Year Book.*

Gakushuin Tōyō Bunka Kenkyūjo (*Gakushuin University Research Institute for Oriental Studies*): 1-5-1, Majiro, Toshima-ku, Tokyo; f. 1953; Dir. H. KATO.

Institute for Asian Studies (*Ajia Daigaku*): Asia University, 5-24-10 Sakai, Musashino-shi, Tokyo 180; f. 1973; Dir. N. KAJIMURA; publs. *Journal* (annually), *Bulletin of Institute for Asian Studies* (quarterly).

Institute for the Study of Languages and Cultures of Asia and Africa: Tokyo University of Foreign Studies, 4-51-21 Nishigahara, Kita-ku, Tokyo 114; f. 1964; 38 researchers, 34 administrators, 34,046 vols.; Dir. Prof. HAJIME KITAMURA; publs. *Journal of Asian and African Studies* (twice a year), *Newsletter* (three times a year).

Kyōto Daigaku Jimbunkagaku Kenkyūsho (*Research Institute of Humanistic Studies of Kyoto University*): Ushinomiyacho, Yoshida, Sakyo-ku, Kyoto; f. 1939; Dir. Prof. SHUMPEI UEYAMA; publs. *Jimbun gakuhō, Tōhō gakuhō, Toyogaku Bunken Ruimoku, Zinbun.*

Nihon-Indogaku-Bukkyōgakkai (*Japanese Association of Indian and Buddhist Studies*): c/o Department of Indian Philosophy and Sanskrit Philology, Faculty of Letters, University of Tokyo, Bunkyo-ku, Tokyo; f. 1951; 2,121 mems.; Pres. SHOSON MIYAMOTO; publ. *Journal of Indian and Buddhist Studies* (Indogaku Bukkyōgaku Kenkyū).

Nihon Keizai Kenkyu (*Japan Economic Research Centre*): Nikkei Building, 9–5, Otemachi, 1-chome, Chiyoda-ku, Tokyo 100; f. 1964; 290 corporate mems. and 390 individual mems.; library of 33,700 vols. and 2,100 titles; Chair. (vacant); Pres. HISAO KANAMORI; publs. *Nihon Keizai Kenkyu Kaiho* (semi-monthly), *The Journal of Research on the Japanese Economy* (annual), *Economic Forecast Series, International Conference Series, English Reprint Series.*

Nippon Kokusai Mondai Kenkyūjo (*Japan Institute of International Affairs*): c/o Ministry of Foreign Affairs, 2-2-1, Kasumigaseki, Chiyoda-ku, Tokyo; f. 1960; massive documentation on the history of the People's Republic of China and the Chinese Communist Party.

Tōyō Bunko (*Oriental Library*): Honkomagome 2-chome, 28–21, Bunkyo-ku, Tokyo 113; f. 1917; 512,168 vols.; major centre of academic research on China and adjacent areas; Librarian NAOSHIRO TSUJI; publs. *Tōyō Gakuhō* (quarterly), *Memoirs of the Research Department*, Monographs Series A, Miscellaneous Series C.

Tōhō Gakkai (*Institute of Eastern Culture*): 4-1, 2-chome, Nishi Kanda, Chiyoda-ku, Tokyo; f. 1947; 1,000 mems.; Chair. Prof. TATSURO YAMAMOTO; publs. *Acta Asiatica, Tōhōgaku.*

Tōkyō Daigaku Tōyō Bunka Kenkyūjo (*Institute of Oriental Culture, the University of Tokyo*): 7-3-1, Hongo, Bunkyo-ku, Tokyo; f. 1941; Dir. Prof. Miss

Chie Nakane; publ. *Tōyō bunka kenkyūjo kiyo* (annual).

Toyoshi Kenkyukai (*The Society of Oriental Researches*): Kyoto University, Kyoto City; f. 1935; 1,350 mems.; Pres. I. Miyazaki; publ. *Journal of Oriental Researches* (quarterly).

KAMPUCHEA

Institut Bouddhique: Phnom-Penh; f. 1930; Buddhist studies and the Khmer culture; publs. *Dictionnaire Cambodgien* and numerous bulletins; Dir. Leang Hap An.

REPUBLIC OF KOREA

Asiatic Research Center: Korea University, Anam-Dong, Seoul; Dir. Prof. Jun-Yop Kim; publ. *Journal of Asiatic Studies*.

Center for Far Eastern Studies: Jeonbug University, 664–14 Deogjin Dong 1-ka, Jeonju, Jeonbug; Dir. Choo-Whang Park.

Institute of Korean Studies: Yonsei University, Sudaemun-ku, Seoul; f. 1949; Dir. Chong-Young Lee; publ. *Dong Bang Hak Chi* (*Journal of Far Eastern Studies*) (quarterly).

Korean Association of Sinology: c/o Asiatic Research Center, Korea University, Anam-dong, Seoul; f. 1955; 100 mems.; Chair. Jun-Yop Kim; publ. *Journal of Chinese Studies*.

Oriental Studies Center: Yeungnam University, Gyongsan 632; Dir. Prof. Kyu Seol Cho.

Research Institute of Oriental Culture: Sung Kyun Kwan University, 53, 3-ka, Myung Ryun-dong, Chongro-ku, Seoul; Dir. Woo-Sung Lee.

MALAYSIA

Language and Literature Planning and Development Agency of Malaysia (*Dewan Bahasa dan Pustaka*): P.O.B. 803, Kuala Lumpur; f. 1956; to develop and enrich the Malay language; to develop literary talent particularly in Malay; to print, publish or assist in the printing or publication of publications in Malay and other languages; to standardize spelling and pronunciation and devise appropriate technical terms in Malay; library of 65,000 vols., in Malay, English, Indonesian, Arabic and others; Chair. Tan Sri Haji Hamdan bin Sheikh Tahir; Dir.-Gen. Datuk Haji Hassan bin Ahmad; publs. *Dewan Bahasa, Dewan Budaya, Dewan Masyarakat, Dewan Pelajar, Dewan Perintis, Dewan Sastera* (monthly), *Dewan Siswa, Tenggara*, textbooks and general books.

Royal Asiatic Society: c/o Ibu Pejabat Pendaftaran Negara, Jalan Persiaran Barat, Petaling Jaya, Selangor; Pres. Tun Mohamed Suffian bin Hashim; publs. *Journal* (semi-annual), monographs and reprints.

MEXICO

Centre for Asian and African Studies: El Colegio de México, Camino al Ajusco 20, Pedregal Sta. Teresa, México 20, D.F.; publ. *Estudios de Asia y Africa* (quarterly); Dir. Prof. Manuel Ruiz Figueroa.

MONGOLIA

Institute of Oriental Studies: Academy of Sciences, Ulan Bator; Dir. Sh. Sandag.

NEPAL

Research Centre for Nepal and Asian Studies: Tribhuvan University, Tripureswor, Kathmandu.

NETHERLANDS

Koninklijk Instituut voor Taal-, Land- en Volkenkunde: Stationsplein 10, P.O. Box 95 07, 2300 RA Leiden; f. 1851 to promote the study of linguistics, geography, anthropology and history of South-East Asia (especially Indonesia), the South Pacific area and the Caribbean region (in particular Suriname and the Netherlands Antilles); 1,248 mems.; library of over 90,000 vols.; Pres. Dr. A. J. Piekaar; Gen. Sec. Dr. J. Noorduyn; publs. *Bijdragen* (quarterly), *F Verhandelingen, Bibliotheca Indonesica*, F Bibliographical series, Translation series.

NEW CALEDONIA

Société des Etudes Mélanésiennes: Nouméa.

NEW ZEALAND

New Zealand Geographical Society: Department of Geography, University of Canterbury, Christchurch; f. 1944 to promote and stimulate the study of geography; branches in Auckland, Christchurch, Dunedin, Hamilton, Palmerston North and Wellington; 800 mems. in New Zealand, 630 overseas mems.; Pres. A. E. McQueen, m.a., m.cit.; Sec. I. F. Owens, m.a., ph.d.; publs. *New Zealand Geographer* (twice yearly) and the *New Zealand Journal of Geography* (twice yearly), *Proceedings of the New Zealand Geography Conference*.

New Zealand Institute of Economic Research: P.O.B. 3479, Wellington; f. 1958; research into New Zealand economic development; quarterly analysis and forecast of economic conditions; quarterly survey of business opinion; economic investigations on contract basis; Dir. B. H. Easton; Chair. John Mowbray; Sec. S. M. Usher.

New Zealand Institute of International Affairs: 88 Fairlie Terrace, Kelburn, Wellington 5; P.O. Box 19–102, Aro Street, Wellington 2; f. 1934; to promote understanding of international questions particularly as far as they may relate to New Zealand, the Commonwealth, South-East Asia and the Pacific; Pres. G. R. Laking, c.m.g.; Vice-Pres. N. B. Beach; Dir. C. C. Aikman; publ. *New Zealand International Review* (bi-monthly).

Polynesian Society: f. 1892; to promote the study of the anthropology, ethnology, philology, history and antiquities of the Polynesians and other related peoples; library; 1,500 mems.; Pres. Prof. B. Biggs; Hon. Sec. P. Ranby, Anthropology Dept., Univ. of Auckland, Private Bag, Auckland 1; publs. *Memoirs, Journal* (quarterly), *Maori Monographs, Maori Texts*.

PAKISTAN

Anjuman Taraqqi-e-Urdu Pakistan: Baba-e-Urdu Rd., Karachi 1; f. 1902; for promotion of Urdu language and literature; general library of 12,000 vols., research library of 50,000 vols. and MSS.; Pres. Akhtar Hussain, c.s.p.; Sec. Jamil Uddin A'Li; publs. *Urdu* (quarterly), *Qami Zaban* (monthly).

Institute of Islamic Culture: Club Rd., Lahore; f. 1950; about 200 publications on Islamic subjects in English and Urdu; Dir. Prof. M. Saeed Sheikh; Hon. Publs. Adviser and Sec. M. Ashraf Darr; publ. *Al-Ma'arif* (Urdu, monthly).

Islamic Research Institute: P.O.B. 1035, Islamabad; f. 1960; to conduct and co-ordinate research in Islamic studies; library of 25,271 vols., 473 microfilms, 114 MSS.; Dir. Dr. A. J. Halepota; publs. *Islamic Studies* (English, quarterly), *Al-Dirasat al-Islamiyya* (Arabic, quarterly), *Fikr-o-Nazar* (Urdu, monthly).

Pakistan Economic Research Institute (P.E.R.I.): 9 Jan Mohammad Rd., Anarkali, Lahore; f. 1955 to undertake socio-economic investigations and co-ordinate research in economic problems of Pakistan; to collect, compile and interpret statistical data; to publish the results and findings of investigations; Dir. A. Aziz Anwar; Sec. A. R. Arshad; publs. Research Papers, Reports.

Pakistan Historical Society: 30 New Karachi Co-operative Housing Society, Karachi 5; f. 1950; historical studies and research; particularly history of Islam and the Indo-Pakistan sub-continent; library of 7,709 vols.; Pres. HAKIM MUHAMMAD SAID; Gen. Sec. Dr. S. MOINUL HAQ; publs. *Journal* (quarterly), Monographs, Research Studies.

Pakistan Institute of Development Economics: P.O. Box 1091, Islamabad; f. 1956; library of 18,500 vols., 295 current periodicals; carries out basic research studies on the economic problems of development in Pakistan and other Asian countries and trains post-graduate scholars on methods of economic research, planning and administration; Dir. Prof. SYED NAWAB HAIDER NAQVI; Deputy Sec. M. A. HAFEEZ; publ. *Pakistan Development Review* (quarterly).

Pakistan Institute of International Affairs: Aiwan-i-Sadar Rd., Karachi 1; f. 1947 to study international affairs and to promote the scientific study of international politics, economics and jurisprudence; library of over 20,000 vols; over 600 mems.; Administrator Justice QADEERUDDIN AHMAD (Retd.); Sec. RAUF AHMAD SIDDIQUI; publs. *Pakistan Horizon* (quarterly), books and monographs.

Quaid-i-Azam Academy: 297 M. A. Jinnah Rd., P.O.B. 894, Karachi; f. 1976; research on Quaid-i-Azam Mohammed Ali Jinnah, the historical background of the Pakistan Movement (including its cultural, religious, literary, linguistic, social, economic and political implications) and various aspects of Pakistan; Chair. President of the Islamic Republic of Pakistan; Dir. SHARIF AL MUJAHID; publs. bibliographies, research studies and monographs.

Research Society of Pakistan: University of the Punjab, 2 Narsingdas Garden, Club Rd., Lahore; f. 1963; conducts research into the origins of the modern state of Pakistan and into the culture, politics, literature, linguistics, economics, history, topography and archaeology of Pakistan; Dir. Dr. A. SHAKOOR AHSAN; publ. *Journal of the Research Society of Pakistan* (quarterly).

PAPUA NEW GUINEA

Institute of Papua New Guinea Studies: Box. 1432, Boroko; f. 1973; study and documentation of Papua New Guinea cultures; expanding collection of ethnographic films; field research in music, art, folklore, oral history, dance; Dir. JOHN KOLIA; publs. *Bikmaus* (quarterly), *Oral History* (bi-monthly).

PHILIPPINES

Asian Center: University of the Philippines, Diliman, Quezon City 3004; publs. *Asian Studies Journal* (twice a year), *Occasional Papers*, *Monographs* series, *Bibliography* series; Dean Dr. JOSEFA M. SANIEL.

Cultural Center of the Philippines: Roxas Blvd., Metro Manila; f. 1966 by Imelda Romualdez Marcos to promote Philippine culture and to encourage the organization of cultural groups, associations or societies and the holding of cultural exhibitions, performances etc.; Pres. LUCRECIA R. KASILAG.

Institute of Philippine Culture: Ateneo de Manila University, Loyola Heights, Quezon City, P.O.B. 154, Manila 2801; f. 1960; social science research organization to study aspects of rural and urban poverty; social and cultural change to include development programmes on social service delivery, agrarian reform, population resettlement, family planning, social forestry and ethnic communities; basic research on culture and social structure with emphasis on social class, kinship and alliance networks, rural organizations, collectivities and demographic processes; management of community resources; evaluation of action programmes; and research methodology; Visiting Research Associate programme; Dir. Dr. PERLA Q. MAKIL; publs. (irregular) *IPC Papers*, *IPC Monographs*, *IPC Reprints*, textbooks and final reports of IPC projects (mimeo).

Research Institute for Mindanao Culture: Xavier University, Ateneo de Cagayan, Cagayan de Oro City 305; f. 1957; to study and assist the development of north Mindanao and its peoples; Dir. FRANCIS C. MADIGAN, PH.D.; publs. *Xavier University Studies* (irregular), *Bulletin of APRIAS—Asian Population and Information Society* (quarterly).

POLAND

Komitet Nauk Orientalistycznych PAN (*The Committee for Oriental Studies of the Polish Academy of Sciences*): Grójecka 17 pok. 111 02-021 Warsaw; Pres. Prof. Dr. TADEUSZ LEWICKI; publs. *Rocznik Orientalistyczny*, series *Prace orientalistyczne*, *Historyczno—socjologiczne monografie Krajów Afryki*.

Polskie Towarzystwo Orientalistyczne (*Polish Oriental Society*): Warsaw, ul. Śniadeckich 8; f. 1922; Pres. STANISŁAW KAŁUŻYŃSKI; Sec. LESZEK CYRZYK; publ. *Przegląd Orientalistyczny* (quarterly).

SINGAPORE

The China Society: 190 Keng Lee Rd., Singapore 11; f. 1948 to promote Chinese culture and to introduce Chinese culture to the non-Chinese; 250 mems.; Pres. LEE SIOW MONG; publ. *Annual of China Society*.

Economic Research Centre: National University of Singapore, Kent Ridge, Singapore 0511; f. 1965; carries out policy-oriented economic and social studies for the public sector in Singapore; also undertakes projects for international organizations and private firms; Dir. Dr. PANG ENG FONG; publs. *ERC Occasional Papers*, *Research Monographs and Malayan Economic Review* (in conjunction with the Dept. of Economics, Nat. Univ. of Singapore, and Econ. Soc. of Singapore.

Institute of Southeast Asian Studies: Heng Mui Keng Terrace, Singapore 0511; f. 1968 for the promotion of research on South-East Asia; research focused on the problems of development, modernization and political and social change; library of 42,000 vols., 87,000 microforms; Dir. Prof. KERNIAL SINGH SANDHU; Exec. Sec. V. R. GROSSE; Librarian P. LIM PUI HUEN; publs. *Southeast Asian Affairs* (annual), *Contemporary Southeast Asia* (quarterly).

Singapore Indian Fine Arts Society: P.O.B. 2812, 29 Branksome Rd., Singapore 15; f. 1949; Pres. M. KARTHIGESU; Hon. Gen. Sec. I. S. MENON.

SOLOMON ISLANDS

Solomon Islands National Museum and Cultural Centre: P.O.B. 313, Honiara; run in conjunction with the Cultural Association of the Solomon Islands; collection began in 1950s, permanent site 1969; research into all aspects of Solomons culture; Curator HENRY ISA; publs. *Journal*, *Custom Stories*.

SPAIN

Asociación Española de Orientalistas: Juan XXIII No. 5, Madrid 3; publs. *Boletín* (annual and other publications).

SRI LANKA

Buddhist Academy of Sri Lanka: 109 Rosmead Place, Colombo.

Maha Bodhi Society of Sri Lanka: 130 Maligakande Road, Maradana, Colombo 10; f. 1891 for propagation of Buddhism throughout the world; 12,000 mems.; Pres. HEMA H. BASNAYAKA, Q.C.; Hon. Sec. LALITH HEWAVIRARANE; publs. *Sinhala Bauddhaya* (weekly), *Sinhala Bauddhaya* (Wesak number; annual).

Postgraduate Institute of Pali and Buddhist Studies: University of Kelaniya, Kelaniya; Dir. Dr. L. P. N. PERERA; publ. *Journal of the Postgraduate Institute of Pali and Buddhist Studies* (bi-annual).

Royal Asiatic Society: 1st Floor, Grandstand Bldg., Reid Ave., Colombo 7; f. 1845 and incorporated with the Royal Asiatic Society of Great Britain and Ireland; institutes and promotes inquiries into the history, religions, languages, literature, arts, sciences and social conditions of the present and former inhabitants of Ceylon and connected cultures; Pres. Prof. M. B. ARIYAPALA, P.HD.; Hon. Secs. G. P. S. H. DE SILVA, WILFRED M. GUNASEKERA; library contains one of the largest existing collections of books on Ceylon, and others on Indian and Eastern culture in general; publ. *Journal*.

SWITZERLAND

Schweizerische Gesellschaft für Asienkunde—Société suisse d'études asiatiques: Sekretariat, Ostasiatisches Seminar, Universität, Mühlegasse 21, 8001 Zürich; f. 1947; 200 mems.; Pres. R. P. KRAMERS; publ. *Schweizer Asiatische Studien/Etudes Asiatiques Suisses* (series).

TAIWAN

Academia Historica: 225 Sec. 3, Pei Yi Road, Hsintien, Taipei; contains national archives, library, documents; engaged in preparing history of China since the establishment of the Republic of China; Pres. HUANG CHI-LU.

Chia Hsin Foundation: 96 Chang Shan Rd., N., Section 2, Taipei; f. 1963 for the promotion of culture in Taiwan; operates nationally in the fields of the arts, social studies, science and medicine, law and education, through research projects, courses, conferences etc.; Chair. Dr. CHEN-HSING YEN; Sec. WU-HSIONG TSENG.

China Academy: P.O. Box 12, Yang Ming Shan, Taipei; f. 1966; private institution for advanced sinological research; Pres. Dr. CHANG CHI-YUN; publ. *Chinese Culture* (quarterly), *Sino-American* (quarterly), *World Sinological Quarterly*.

The China Society: Taipei; f. 1960; society with monthly lectures on Chinese culture; about 100 mems.; Pres. Dr. ALBERT R. O'HARA, S.J.; Vice-Pres. Dr. MA HAN-PAO; publ. *Journal of the China Society* (annual).

Chinese Culture University: Hwa Kang, Yang Ming Shan, 113 Taipei; f. 1962; Founder Dr. CHI-YUN CHANG; Pres. PAN WEI-HO; 1,724 teachers; 16,554 students; library of 427,970 vols.

THAILAND

Buddhist Research Centre: Wat Benchamabopitr, Bangkok; f. 1961; sponsored by Department of Religious Affairs, Ministry of Education; publ. *Pali-Thai-English Dictionary*, vol. 1.

The Siam Society: G.P.O. Box 65, Bangkok; f. 1904 to promote interest and research in art, science and cultural affairs of Thailand and neighbouring countries; Kamthieng House exhbn. of northern Thai artefacts; library of 14,000 vols.; Pres. H. S. H. Prince SUBHADRADIS DISKUL; Hon. Sec. Ms NONGYAO NARUMIT; publs. *Journal of the Siam Society* (semi-annual).

U.S.S.R.

Institute of Oriental Studies of the Department of History, U.S.S.R. Academy of Sciences: Armyansky per. 2, Moscow; Dir. Acad. B. G. GAFUROV; publ. *Asia and Africa Today* (monthly).

Institute of Far Eastern Studies: U.S.S.R. Academy of Sciences, Krasikova 27, Moscow 117218; f. 1967; Dir. M. I. SLADKOVSKY; publ. *Far Eastern Affairs*.

Institute of Oriental Languages of the Academy of Sciences of the Armenian S.S.R.: Ul. Abovyana 15, Erevan 1; Dir. G. K. SARKISYAN.

Institute of Oriental Studies of the Academy of Sciences of the Georgian S.S.R.: Ul. Tskhakaya 10, Tbilisi; Dir. G. V. TSERETELI.

Scientific Council on the History of Siberia: V. Siberian Dept., Academy of Sciences of the U.S.S.R., Prospekt Nauky 21, Novosibirsk; Chair. Acad. A. P. OKLADNIKOV.

Scientific Council on Oriental Studies: Department of History, U.S.S.R. Academy of Sciences, Ul. D. Ulyanova 19, Moscow; Chair. Acad. B. G. GAFUROV.

Section of Oriental Studies and Ancient Scriptures of the Academy of Sciences of the Tajik S.S.R.: Parvin Ul. 8, Dushanbe; Dir. A. M. MIRZOEV.

UNITED KINGDOM

British Association for Chinese Studies: c/o Dept. of Oriental Manuscripts and Printed Books, Store St., London W.C.1; f. 1975; provides forum for academics etc. in the field; holds annual conference; Pres. RAYMOND DAWSON; Sec. BETH MCKILLOP; publ. *Bulletin* (4 a year).

Central Asian Research Centre: 8 Wakley St., London, EC1V 7LT; f. 1953; Dir. DAVID L. MORISON; research on Soviet Central Asia and Soviet policies in Asia and Africa; publ. *U.S.S.R. and Third World*.

Centre for South-East Asian Studies: The University of Hull, Cottingham Rd., Hull, HU6 7RX; Dir. Dr. D.K. BASSETT; publs. *Hull Monographs on South-East Asia, Occasional Papers Series*.

Centre of Japanese Studies: University of Sheffield, Sheffield S10 2TN; Dir. G. H. HEALEY (acting).

Centre of South Asian Studies: University of Cambridge, Laundress Lane, Cambridge, CB2 1SD; Dir. B. H. FARMER, M.A.

China Society: 31B Torrington Square, London, W.C.1; f. 1906 to encourage the study of the Chinese language, literature, history, folk-lore, art, etc.; *c.* 150 mems.; Pres. Col. KENNETH CANTLIE; Chair. R. BURRELL, D.F.C.; Sec. Vice-Adm. Sir JOHN GRAY, K.B.E., C.B.

Contemporary China Institute: School of Oriental and African Studies, Malet Street, London, WC1E 7HP; f. 1968; Head Dr. H. D. R. BAKER; publs. *The China Quarterly, Research Notes and Studies* (short monographs) and C.C.I./Cambridge University Press series.

Department of Chinese Studies: University of Leeds, Leeds, LS2 9JT; Head of Dept. DON RIMMINGTON

Department of South East Asian Studies: University of Kent, Canterbury, Kent CT2 7NS; Chair. Dr. D. J. DUNCANSON.

European Association for Japanese Studies: c/o The Hon. Sec. Prof. O. LIDIN, East Asian Institute, University of Copenhagen, Kesjergade 2, Copenhagen K, Denmark; f. 1973; Hon. Pres. Prof. C. J. DUNN; publs. *Bulletin of the European Association for Japanese Studies* (twice yearly).

Far Eastern Department, Victoria and Albert Museum: South Kensington, London SW7 2RL; f. 1970; permanent displays and exhbns. of Far Eastern art; lectures and research; national art reference library; Dir. Sir ROY STRONG; Keeper JOHN AYERS.

India Office Library (British Library): 197 Blackfriars Rd., London, SE1 8NG; f. 1801; about 346,000 European and Oriental printed books, 28,000 oriental MSS., 14,000 British paintings and drawings relating principally to India and the East, 11,000 oriental drawings and miniatures, 2,300 prints and 180,000 photographs; Dir. B. C. BLOOMFIELD, M.A., F.L.A.; publs. *Annual Report, Guide* and catalogues of the collections.

India Office Records (British Library): 197 Blackfriars Rd., London SE1 8NG; official archives of the London administration (175,000 vols., files and boxes), official publications (70,000 vols.); 30,000 maps and private papers (10,500 vols. and boxes) relating to pre-Independence India (1600–1947); some post-1947 private papers; Dir. B. C. BLOOMFIELD, M.A., F.L.A.; publs. *Annual Report*, Catalogues, Lists and Guides.

Institute of Development Studies at The University of Sussex: Brighton, Sussex, BN1 9RE; f. 1966; teaching and research concerned with Third World development and the unequal relationships between rich and poor countries; Dir. MIKE FABER; publs. *IDS Bulletin* (quarterly), *IDS Discussion Papers, Annual Report, Development Studies, Register of Research in the U.K.* (biennial), *Development Research Digest* (semi-annual), final research reports, books, occasional guides and publications catalogue.

Oriental Ceramic Society: 31B Torrington Square, London, W.C.1; f. 1921 to increase knowledge and appreciation of Eastern ceramic and other arts; Pres. Prof. WILLIAM WATSON; Sec. Vice-Adm. Sir JOHN GRAY, K.B.E., C.B.; Hon. Sec. Miss MARGARET MEDLEY.

Oriental Institute: University of Oxford, Pusey Lane, Oxford OX1 2LE; f. 1960; Sec. Mrs. A. M. LONSDALE.

Percival David Foundation of Chinese Art: 53 Gordon Square, London, W.C.1; f. 1951; outstanding collection of Chinese pottery and porcelain formed for study and research by those interested in Chinese art and archaeology; annual colloquies on art and archeaology in Asia; library of 4,000 vols.; Head Prof. WILLIAM WATSON; Curator Miss MARGARET MEDLEY; publs. monographs, catalogues and colloquy reports.

Royal Asiatic Society of Great Britain and Ireland: 56 Queen Anne St., London, W1M 9LA; f. 1823 for the study of the history, sociology, institutions, customs, languages and art of Asia; approx. 900 mems.; approx. 800 subscribing libraries; branches in various Eastern cities; Sec. Miss E. V. GIBSON; publs. *Journal* and monographs on Oriental subjects; library of 100,000 vols. and 1,500 MSS.

Royal Society for Asian Affairs: 42 Devonshire Street, London, W.1; f. 1901; 1,500 mems. with knowledge of, and interest in, Central Asia, Middle and Far East; library of about 5,000 vols.; Pres. The Lord GREENHILL of HARROW, G.C.M.G., O.B.E.; Chair. Sir ARTHUR DE LA MARE, K.C.M.G., K.C.V.O.; Sec. Miss M. FITZSIMONS; publ. *Journal* (3 issues per annum).

St. Antony's College: Oxford, OX2 6JF; f. 1950; Far East Centre devoted to the study of the modern Far East; Warden A. R. M. CARR, M.A.

School of African and Asian Studies: University of Sussex, Falmer, Brighton, BN1 9QN; Dean P. K. CHAUDHURI, B.A., M.SC.

School of Oriental and African Studies: University of London, Malet St., London, WC1E 7HP; f. 1916; includes Centre of South Asian Studies, Centre of South East Asian Studies (Chair. R. H. TAYLOR), Japan Research Centre (Head Prof. W. G. BEASLEY); library of over 500,000 vols., 2,500 MSS., 31,000 printed maps, 5,500 microfilms and 35,000 microfiches; Dir. Prof. C. D. COWAN, M.A., PH.D.; publs. *The Bulletin, Calendar, Annual Report.*

Society for Anglo-Chinese Understanding: 152 Camden High Street, London, NW1 0NE; f. 1965; gives lectures, films and exhbns. on contemporary China; organizes tours, cultural exchanges; 1,500 mems.; library of 1,800 vols. and newspaper cuttings; Chair. PETER THIELE; Pres. JOSEPH NEEDHAM; publ. *China Now.*

UNITED STATES OF AMERICA

American Asiatic Association: India House, 1 Hanover Square, New York, N.Y. 10004; f. 1898; 46 mems.; Pres. M. ZUCKERMAN; Sec. D. G. ALLEN, c/o Manufacturers Hanover Trust Co., 44 Wall St., New York, N.Y. 10004.

American Oriental Society: 329 Sterling Memorial Library, Yale Station, New Haven, Conn.; f. 1842; 1,650 mems.; library of 19,560 vols.; Pres. WILLIAM J. GEDNEY; Sec. STANLEY INSLER; publ. *Journal of the American Oriental Society* (quarterly).

The Asia Foundation: P.O.B. 3223, San Francisco, Calif. 94119 (Main Office); offices in Washington and 10 Asian countries (Bangladesh, Indonesia, Japan, Republic of Korea, Malaysia, Pakistan, Philippines, Sri Lanka, Taiwan and Thailand); programmes in China, Hong Kong, Maldives, Nepal, the Pacific Islands and Singapore; f. 1954; 3,370 vols. on current Asian and world affairs; works with Asian organizations, institutions and individuals dedicated to furthering social and economic progress within their societies by providing small-grant assistance in the fields of rural and community health, law and justice, communication, books and libraries, management, employment and economic development, and exchange for Asian-American understanding; Chair. Board of Trustees RUDOLPH A. PETERSON; Pres. HAYDN WILLIAMS; Sec. TURNER H. MCBAINE; publs. *President's Review and Annual Report* (annual), *The Asia Foundation News* (bi-monthly).

Asian Art Museum of San Francisco, the Avery Brundage Collection: Golden Gate Park, San Francisco, Calif. 94118; f. 1969; museum and centre of research and publication on outstanding collections of Chinese, Japanese, Korean, Indian, South-East Asian, Lamaist and Islamic art; library of 14,000 vols.; Dir. and Chief Curator RENÉ-YVON LEFEBVRE D'ARGENCÉ.

Association for Asian Studies Inc.: One Lane Hall, University of Michigan, Ann Arbor, Mich. 48109; f. 1941; Sec.-Treas. RHOADS MURPHEY; publs. *Asian Studies Newsletter, Bibliography of Asian Studies, Journal of Asian Studies* (quarterly).

Boston Museum of Fine Arts: Boston, Mass. 02115; a private corporation; incorp. 1870; department of Asiatic art with outstanding collection of Chinese and Japanese sculpture, painting, and ceramics; Indian and Islamic art; library of 105,000 books and periodicals; 60,000 pamphlets; Dir. JAN FONTEIN; publs. *Calendar of Events* (monthly), *Bulletin* (annual), catalogues, handbooks.

Center for Asian and Pacific Studies: University of Hawaii, Moore Hall 315, 1890 East-West Road, Honolulu, Hawaii 96822; presides over the East Asia Language and Area Centre; Dir. STEPHEN UHALLEY, Jr. (acting).

Columbia University East Asian Institute: 507 Kent Hall, New York, N.Y. 10027; library of 230,000 vols.; Dir. GERALD L. CURTIS.

Columbia University Southern Asian Institute: c/o Columbia University, Morningside Heights, New York, N.Y. 10027; Dir. AINSLIE T. EMBREE.

Cornell University China-Japan Program: Ithaca, N.Y. 14853; f. 1950 for the development of instruction and research on China and Japan; library of 300,000 vols.; 75 graduate students; Dir. Dr. T. J. PEMPEL; publ. *Cornell East Asia Papers*.

Cornell University South Asia Program: 130A Uris Hall, Ithaca, N.Y. 14853; Dir. Prof. GERALD KELLEY.

Cornell University Southeast Asia Language and Area Center: Ithaca, N.Y. 14853; f. 1950 for the development of instruction and research on South-East Asia; library of 159,934 vols., 14,626 periodicals and 789 newspapers; 70 graduate students; Dir. Prof. STANLEY J. O'CONNOR.

East-West Center—Center for Cultural and Technical Interchange between East and West: 1777 East- West Rd., Honolulu, Hawaii 96848; f. 1960; to promote better relations and understanding among the nations and peoples of Asia, the Pacific and the United States through co-operative study, training and research. Five institutes: Communication, Culture Learning, Environment and Policy, Population and Resource Systems; also Open Grants. Provides awards to scholars, authorities, research workers, graduate students, and managers to study central problems of public policy facing the Pacific region; Pres. VICTOR LI.

Foundation for the Peoples of the South Pacific: 158 West 57th St., New York, N.Y. 10019; f. 1965 to carry out development research and evaluation and to stimulate a programme of development in the South Pacific based on the felt needs of the indigenous people and the belief that the response to those needs should be a form of self-help; operates in the fields of education, social welfare, health, industry, agriculture, housing and community development; Pres. ELIZABETH SILVERSTEIN; Exec. Dir. Rev. STANLEY W. HOSIE.

Freer Gallery of Art: 12th St. and Jefferson Drive, S.W., Washington, D.C. 20560; established 1906; opened 1923; devoted to research on the outstanding collections of Oriental and American art, gift of the late Charles L. Freer, of Detroit; art collection of 12,000 objects; library of 30,000 vols., 60,000 slides, 8,000 study photographs; Dir. THOMAS LAWTON, PH.D.; Curator, Islamic Art ESIN ATIL, PH.D.; Curator, Chinese Art SHEN FU, PH.D.; Curators, Japanese Art YOSHIAKI SHIMIZU, PH.D., ANN YONEMURA; Head Cons. WILLIAM THOMAS CHASE, M.F.A.; publs. *Occasional Papers, Oriental Studies, Ars Orientalis*, etc.

George Washington University, Institute for Sino-Soviet Studies: 2130 H Street, N.W., Suite 601, Washington, D.C. 20052; f. 1962; Dir. Dr. GASTON J. SIGUR.

Harvard-Yenching Institute: 2 Divinity Ave., Cambridge, Mass. 02138; f. 1928 to promote the growth and advancement of higher education in eastern and southern Asia, especially with regard to the history and culture of that area; publs. *Harvard Journal of Asiatic Studies, Harvard-Yenching Institute Monographs, Harvard-Yenching Institute Studies, Scripta Mongolica;* Dir. ALBERT M. CRAIG.

Indiana University Research Institute for Inner Asian Studies: Goodbody Hall, Bloomington, Ind. 47405; research into social sciences and humanities of Inner Asia; Dir. STEPHEN A. HALKOVIC.

Institute for Medieval Japanese Studies: 847 Williams Hall, University of Pennsylvania, Philadelphia, Pa. 19104; Dir. Dr. BARBARA RUCH.

JDR 3rd Fund: Room 5432, 30 Rockefeller Plaza, New York, N.Y. 10020; f. 1963 by John D. Rockefeller 3rd; organizes an Asian Cultural Programme and supports cultural exchange activities in the visual and performing arts between the U.S.A. and Asian countries; Dir. RICHARD S. LANIER.

John King Fairbank Center for East Asian Research (Harvard University): 1737 Cambridge Street, Cambridge, Mass. 02138; Dir. PHILIP A. KUHN; publs. *Harvard East Asian Monographs, Harvard East Asian Series* (Harvard Univ. Press.)

The Mongolia Society: P.O. Box 606, Bloomington, Ind. 47402; f. 1961; to promote and further the study of Mongolia, its history, language and culture; Pres. OWEN LATTIMORE; publs. *Mongolian Studies: Journal of the Mongolia Society*, occasional and special papers.

Princeton University Department of East Asian Studies: Princeton, N.J. 08544; Chair. MARION J. LEVY, Jr.

Research Institute on International Change: School of International Affairs Building, 420 West 118th St., New York, N.Y. 10027; Dir. Prof. SEWERYN BIALER; publs. *Global Political Assessment* (semi-annual), monographs.

St. John's University Center of Asian Studies: Grand Central and Utopia Parkways, Jamaica, N.Y. 11439; Exec. Officer BARBARA MORRIS.

Seton Hall University Institute of Far Eastern Studies: South Orange, N.J. 07079; library of 40,000 vols.; Dir. JOHN YOUNG.

Stanford University—University of California, Berkeley, Joint East Asia Language and Area Center: 200 Lou Henry Hoover Bldg., Stanford University, and 460 Stephens Hall, University of California, Berkeley; f. 1973; Co-Dirs. Prof. ALBERT E. DIEN (Stanford), Prof. JAMES BOSSON (Berkeley); publs. periodic newsletter, Bay Area directory of East Asian scholars.

University of Arizona Department of Oriental Studies: Tucson, Ariz.; Head Dr. ROBERT M. GIMELLO.

University of California Center for South and Southeast Asia Studies: Berkeley, Calif. 94720; Chair. GEORGE F. DALES.

University of California Department of Oriental Languages: 104 Durant Hall, Berkeley, Calif. 94720; Head of Dept. Prof. CYRIL BIRCH.

University of California Department of South and Southeast Asia Studies: Berkeley, Calif. 94720.

University of Illinois Center for Asian Studies: 1208 West California, Urbana, Ill. 61801; f. 1965; Dir. PETER SCHRAN; publs. Illinois Papers on Asian Studies.

University of Iowa Department of Asian Languages and Literature: University of Iowa, Iowa City, Iowa 52242; Chair. Prof. W. SOUTH COBLIN.

University of Kansas Center for East Asian Studies: Lawrence, Kansas; Dirs. CHAE JIN LEE, CAMERON HURST.

University of Michigan Center for Chinese Studies: 104 Lane Hall, Ann Arbor, Mich. 48109; f. 1961; library of 214,827 vols, reels of microfilm and sheets of microfiches; Dir. ALBERT FEUERWERKER; publs. *Michigan Papers in Chinese Studies, Michigan Abstracts of Chinese and Japanese Works on Chinese History, Science, Medicine and Technology in East Asia, Ars Orientalis, CCS News* circ. 1,000).

University of Michigan Center for Japanese Studies: 108 Lane Hall, Ann Arbor, Mich. 48109; f. 1947; library of 167,801 vols., reels of microfilm, sheets of microfiche (Asia Library Japanese collection); Dir. Dr. JOHN C. CAMPBELL; publs. *Michigan Papers in Japanese Studies.*

University of Michigan Center for South and Southeast Asian Studies: 130 Lane Hall, Ann Arbor, Mich. 48109; Dirs. ARAM A. YENGOYAN, MADHAV DESHPANDE; publs. *Michigan Papers on South and Southeast Asia, The Michigan Series in South and Southeast Asian Languages and Linguistics* (occasional papers).

University of Minnesota Department of East Asian Languages: Minneapolis, Minn. 55455.

University of Minnesota Department of South Asian Studies: Minneapolis, Minn. 55455.

University of Pennsylvania, Department of South Asia Regional Studies: 820 Williams Hall, Philadelphia, Pa. 19104; library of 300,000 vols.; Librarian KANTA BHATIA.

University of Pittsburgh Department of East Asian Languages and Literatures: Pittsburgh, Pa. 15260; Chair. Dir. Dr. GORDON M. BERGER; publs. occasional papers.

University of Southern California East Asian Studies Center: University Park, Los Angeles, Calif. 90007; f. 1962; Dir. GORDON M. BERGER; publs. occasional papers.

University of Southern California Research Institute on Communist Strategy and Propaganda: University Park, Los Angeles, Calif. 90007; library of 50,000 vols.; Librarian Mrs. I. O. HABERLY.

University of Southern California-University of California at Los Angeles Joint East Asia Language and Area Center: VKC 213, University Park, Los Angeles, Calif. 90007; f. 1979; Dir. Dr. GORDON M. BERGER; publ. *Newsletter.*

University of Wisconsin East Asian Studies Program: 1440 Van Hise Hall, Madison, Wis. 53706; Co-Chairs. WILLIAM NIENHAUSER and JAMES O'BRIEN.

Wake Forest University Asian Studies Program: P.O.B. 7547, Reynolda Station, Winston-Salem, N.C. 27109; library of 25,000 vols.; Dir. Dr. B. G. GOKHALE; publ. *Asian Studies*, Vols. I–II.

Yale University Southeast Asia Studies: Yale University, Box 13A, New Haven, Conn. 06520; library of 260,000 vols.

VATICAN

Pontificium Institutum Orientale (*Pontifical Oriental Institute*: 7 Piazza Santa Maria Maggiore, 00185 Rome; f. 1917; library of 130,000 vols.; Pres. Rev. PETER HANS KOLVENBACH, S.J.; Sec. Rev. J. ŘEZÁČ, S.J.; publs. *Orientalia Christiana Periodica, Orientalia Christiana Analecta, Concilium Florentinum* (*Documenta et Scriptores*), *Anaphorae Syriacae.*

VIET-NAM

Hoi Phat Hoc Nam Viet (*Association for Buddhist Studies*): Xa-Loi Pagoda, 89 Ba Huyen Thanh Quan, Ho Chi Minh City; f. 1950; study and practice of Buddhism; 30,000 mems.; 5,000 vols.; meditation room; Pres. Dr. CAO VAN TRI; publ. *Tu Quang, Le Ngoc Diep.*

SELECT BIBLIOGRAPHY (PERIODICALS)

ACTA ASIATICA. Bulletin of the Institute of Eastern Culture (The Tōhō Gakkai), 4-1, 2-chōme, Nishi-Kanda, Chiyoda-ku, Tokyo, Japan; f. 1960; semi-annual; in English.

ACTA ORIENTALIA. Publ. Munksgaard, Nørre Søgade 35, 1370 Copenhagen K, Denmark, by the Oriental Societies of Denmark, Finland, Norway and Sweden; history and language of the Near and Far East; annual; Editor Prof. SØREN EGEROD; Editorial Sec. LISE SODE-MOGENSEN, Scandinavian Institute of Asian Studies, Kejsergade 2, 1155 Copenhagen K, Denmark.

ACTA ORIENTALIA ACADEMIAE SCIENTIARUM HUNGARICAE. Magyar Tudományos Akadémia Orientalisztikai Közleményei, P.B. 24, Budapest 1363, Hungary; papers on oriental philology and culture in English, German, French and Russian; three times a year.

AFGHANISTAN JOURNAL. Akademische Druck- und Verlagsanstalt, Graz, Austria; f. 1974; quarterly; in German, English and French; Editor Dr. K. GRATZL, Auersperggasse 12, 8010 Graz, Austria.

L'AFRIQUE ET L'ASIE MODERNES. Centre de Hautes Etudes sur l'Afrique et l'Asie Modernes, 13 rue du Four, 75006 Paris, France; f. 1948; quarterly; Dir. GEORGES R. MALÉCOT.

ANNALS OF THE BHANDARKAR ORIENTAL RESEARCH INSTITUTE. Bhandarkar Oriental Research Institute, Pune 411004, India; annual; Editor R. N. DANDEKAR.

ANNALS OF ORIENTAL RESEARCH. University of Madras, Madras 600005, India; f. 1936; irregular; Editor Dr. K. KUNJUNNI RAJA.

ANNUAL BIBLIOGRAPHY OF ORIENTAL STUDIES (*see* Tōyōgaku Bunken Mokuroku).

ARCHAEOLOGY IN OCEANIA. Mackie Bldg., The University, Sydney, N.S.W. 2006, Australia; f. 1966; 3 issues a year; Editor J. P. WHITE.

ARCHÍV ORIENTÁLNÍ. Quarterly Journal of African, Asian and Latin American Studies of the Oriental Institute of the Czechoslovak Academy of Sciences. Academia Publishing House, Lázeňska 4, 118 37 Prague 1, Czechoslovakia; contributions in English or French, German, Russian and Spanish with English résumé; f. 1929; book reviews and notes; quarterly; Editor Dr. MILOSLAV KRÁSA.

ARTIBUS ASIAE. Publ. by Artibus Asiae Publishers, 6612 Ascona, Switzerland for the Institute of Fine Arts, New York University, 1 East 78th Street, New York, N.Y. 10021, U.S.A.; f. 1925; Asian art and archaeology; illustrated; quarterly and annual volume; Editor-in-Chief ALEXANDER C. SOPER.

ARTS OF ASIA. 1309 Kowloon Centre, 29–39 Ashley Rd., Kowloon, Hong Kong; f. 1971; six times a year; Publr. and Editor TUYET NGUYET.

ARTS ASIATIQUES. Annales du Musée Guimet et du Musée Cernuschi. L'Ecole Française d'Extrême-Orient, 22 ave. du Président-Wilson, 75016 Paris, France; f. 1954; annual; Editor-in-Chief JEANNINE AUBOYER.

ASEAN BUSINESS QUARTERLY. Asia Research Pte. Ltd., P.O.B. 91, Alexandra Post Office, Singapore 9115; f. 1977; quarterly; Editor J. DRYSDALE.

ASIA AND AFRICA TODAY. Institute of Oriental Studies, Dept. of History, U.S.S.R. Academy of Sciences, Armyansky per 2, Moscow, U.S.S.R.; scientific, social and political; monthly in Russian, bi-monthly in English and French.

ASIA PACIFIC COMMUNITY. The Asian Club, P.O.B. 71, Trade Center, Tokyo 105, Japan; f. 1974; political, economic, social, cultural etc.; quarterly; Editor HIDEO UENO; Man. Editor JOHEI TACHIBANA.

ASIA RESEARCH BULLETIN. Asia Research Pte. Ltd., Alexandra, P.O.B. 91, Singapore 9115; f. 1971; political and economic monthly reports.

ASIAN AFFAIRS. Journal of the Royal Society for Asian Affairs, 42 Devonshire St., London, W.1, England; covers economic, cultural and political problems affecting the Near East, Far East and the Orient; three times yearly; Editor P. ROBERTSON.

ASIAN AND AFRICAN STUDIES. Israel Oriental Society, The Institute of Middle Eastern Studies, University of Haifa, Israel; f. 1965; three times a year; Editor GABRIEL R. WARBURG.

ASIAN AND AFRICAN STUDIES. Department of Oriental Studies of the Slovak Academy of Sciences, Klemensova 19, 884 16 Bratislava, Czechoslovakia; Veda, publishing house of the Slovak Academy of Sciences, Bratislava; Curzon Press, London and Dublin; f. 1965; annual; Chief Editor IVAN DOLEŽAL.

ASIAN ALMANAC. Publr. and Editor VEDAGIRI T. SAMBANDAN, 2003A International Plaza, Anson Rd., Singapore 0207, P.O.B. 2737, Singapore 9047 and P.O.B. 712 Johor Bahru, Malaysia; f. 1963; weekly abstracts of Asian affairs.

ASIAN NEWSLETTER. Asian and Pacific Development Institute, Sri Ayudhya Rd., Bangkok, Thailand.

ASIAN PROFILE. Asian Research Service, P.O. Box 2232, G.P.O., Hong Kong; f. 1973; six a year; multidisciplinary study of Asian affairs.

ASIAN RECORDER. C-2 Gulmohar Park, P.O.B. 595, New Delhi 110049, India; f. 1955; record of Asian events; weekly; Editor M. S. R. KHEMCHAND.

ASIAN STUDIES JOURNAL. Asian Center, University of the Philippines, Diliman, Quezon City 3004, Philippines; annual; no permanent editor.

ASIAN SURVEY. Periodicals Dept., University of California Press, 2223 Fulton St., Berkeley, Calif. 94720, U.S.A.; f. 1961; monthly; Editors ROBERT A. SCALAPINO and LEO E. ROSE; circ. 3,500.

ASIAN THOUGHT AND SOCIETY: AN INTERNATIONAL REVIEW. Dept. of Political Science, State University of New York, Oneonta, N.Y. 13820; f. 1976; analysis of social structures and changes in Pacific and South Asian countries with special reference to socialist and communist theories; three a year; Editor-in-Chief I. J. H. TS'AO.

ASIATIC STUDIES (*see* Aziya Kenkyu).

ASIATISCHE FORSCHUNGEN. Monographienreihe zur Geschichte, Kultur und Sprache der Völker Ost- und Zentralasiens. Verlag Otto Harrassowitz, D-6200 Wiesbaden 1, Taunusstrasse 6, Federal Republic of Germany; f. 1959; in German, French and English; irregular; Editor WALTHER HEISSIG, Seminar für Sprach- und Kulturwissenschaft Zentralasiens, D5300 Bonn, Regina Pacis-Weg 7, Federal Republic of Germany.

ASIATISCHE STUDIEN/ETUDES ASIATIQUES. Verlag Peter Lang, Auslieferung, Jupiterstr. 15, 3015 Berne, Switzerland; for the Swiss Society for Asian Studies; Editors CH. BÜRGEL, R. KRAMERS, J. MAY, C. OUWE-

HAND, H. ZIMMERMANN, Ostasiatiches Seminar der Universtät Zürich, Muhlegasse 21, 8001, Zurich, Switzerland; semi-annual.

L'ASIE NOUVELLE. Chambre de Commerce Franco-Asiatique, 94 rue St. Lazare, 75009 Paris, France; f. 1952; weekly; Dir. ANDRÉ ROUX.

ASIE DU SUD-EST ET MONDE INSULINDIEN (ASEMI). Publ. by le Centre de Documentation et de Recherches sur l'Asie du Sud-Est et le Monde Insulindien with l'Ecole des Hautes Etudes en Sciences Sociales and le Centre National de la Recherche Scientifique, ASEMI-Bureau 714, 54 Boulevard Raspail, 75006 Paris, France; f. 1971; quarterly; Dir. GEORGES CONDOMINAS.

ASIEN, AFRIKA, LATEINAMERIKA. Zeitschrift des Zentralen Rates für Asien-, Afrika- und Lateinamerikawissenschaften in der DDR. 1034 Berlin, Frankfurter Tor 8a, German Democratic Republic; scientific journal; bi-monthly.

ASIEN-BIBLIOGRAPHIE. Asien Bücherei, 3590 Bad Wildungen, Federal Republic of Germany; quarterly.

AUSTRALIAN GEOGRAPHER. Geographical Society of New South Wales, P.O.B. 328 North Ryde, N.S.W. 2113, Australia; f. 1928; Editor Dr. PHILIP TILLEY; Assoc. Editor Prof. B. J. GARNER.

AUSTRALIAN JOURNAL OF CHINESE AFFAIRS. Contemporary China Centre, RSPacS, Australian National University, P.O.B. 4, Canberra, A.C.T. 2600, Australia; f. 1979; Editor STEPHEN FITZGERALD.

AUSTRALIAN JOURNAL OF POLITICS AND HISTORY. University of Queensland Press, P.O. Box 42, St. Lucia, Qld. 4067, Australia; f. 1955; emphasis on Australia, Pacific Countries, North America and Europe; 3 a year; Editor GORDON GREENWOOD.

AUSTRALIAN OUTLOOK. Australian Institute of International Affairs, Box E 181, Post Office, Canberra, A.C.T., Australia; 3 times a year; Editor Dr. IAN CLARK.

AUSTRALIAN QUARTERLY. Australian Institute of Political Science, 2nd Floor, 32 Market St., Sydney, N.S.W. 2000, Australia; f. 1929; quarterly; Editors ELAINE THOMPSON and HUGH PRITCHARD.

AZIYA KENKYU. (Asiatic Studies) Ajia Seikei Gakukai, Institute of Oriental Culture, University of Tokyo, 3-1 Hongo 7-chome, Bunkyo-ku, Tokyo, Japan; quarterly; in Japanese.

BANGLADESH DEVELOPMENT STUDIES. Quarterly journal of the Bangladesh Institute of Development Studies, Adamjee Court, Motijheel Commercial Area, Dacca 2, Bangladesh; f. 1974; Exec. Editor Dr. S. R. OSMANI.

BEIJING REVIEW. 24 Baiwanzhuang Rd., Beijing, People's Republic of China; weekly; current affairs; English, French, Spanish, Japanese, German and Arabic editions.

BEITRÄGE ZUR JAPANOLOGIE. Institut für Japanologie, Universität Wien, Universitätsstrasse 7/4, 1010 Vienna, Austria; irregular; Editors A. SLAWIK and S. LINHART.

BOLETÍN DE LA ASOCIACIÓN ESPAÑOLA DE ORIENTALISTAS. Juan XXIII (antes Limite) no. 5, Madrid 3, Spain.

BULLETIN DE L'ECOLE FRANÇAISE D'EXTRÊME-ORIENT. Ecole Française d'Extrême-Orient, 22 avenue Président-Wilson, 75016 Paris, France; f. 1901; annual.

BULLETIN OF INDONESIAN ECONOMIC STUDIES. Dept. of Economics, Research School of Pacific Studies, Australian National University, P.O. Box 4, Canberra, A.C.T. 2600, Australia; 3 times yearly; Editor H. W. ARNDT.

BULLETIN OF THE INSTITUTE OF TRADITIONAL CULTURES, MADRAS. University of Madras, Madras 600005, India; semi-annual; Director K. K. PILLAY.

BULLETIN OF THE SCHOOL OF ORIENTAL AND AFRICAN STUDIES. School of Oriental and African Studies, University of London, Malet St., London, WC1E 7HP, England; f. 1917; 3 issues annually.

CENTRAL ASIATIC JOURNAL. International Journal for the languages, literature, history and archaeology of Central Asia, Verlag Otto Harrassowitz, D-6200 Wiesbaden 1, Taunusstrasse 6, Federal Republic of Germany; English language; quarterly; Editor-in-Chief K. JAHN, Müllnergasse 3/31, A 1090 Vienna, Austria.

CEYLON JOURNAL OF HISTORICAL AND SOCIAL STUDIES. University of Peradeniya, Peradeniya, Sri Lanka; f. 1958; semi-annual; Editor KINGSLEY M. DE SILVA.

CHANOYU QUARTERLY: TEA AND THE ARTS OF JAPAN. Urasenke Foundation, Ogawa Teranouchi agaru, Kamikyo-ku, Kyoto 602, Japan, and the Urasenke Foundation of Hawaii, 245 Saratoga Road, Honolulu, Hawaii 96815, U.S.A.; f. 1970; Editor PETER DUPPENTHALER; Assoc. Editors LINDA CRAWFORD and GAYLE YOSIDA.

CHINA GEOGRAPHER. Westview Press, 5500 Central Ave., Boulder, Col. 80301, U.S.A.; annual; Editor CLIFTON PANNELL; Co-Editor C. L. SALTER.

CHINA QUARTERLY. Contemporary China Institute, School of Oriental and African Studies, Malet St., London, WC1E 7HP, England; f. 1959; all aspects of 20th century China, including Taiwan and the overseas Chinese; quarterly; Editor BRIAN HOOK.

CHINA REPORT. Centre for the Study of Developing Societies, 29 Rajpur Rd., Delhi 110054, India; f. 1964; topical notes and research articles, book reviews, and documentation; bi-monthly; Editor C. R. M. RAO.

CHINESE CULTURE. Institute for Advanced Chinese Studies, China Academy, Box 12, Yang Ming Shan, Taiwan; f. 1957; English language; quarterly; Editor Dr. SHEE SUNG.

CHINESE ECONOMIC STUDIES. M. E. Sharpe Inc., 80 Business Park Drive, Armonk, N.Y. 10504, U.S.A.; f. 1967; quarterly; translations from Chinese sources; Editor G. C. WANG.

CHINESE LAW AND GOVERNMENT. M. E. Sharpe Inc., 80 Business Park Drive, Armonk, N.Y. 10504, U.S.A.; f. 1968; quarterly; translations of scholarly works and policy documents in the field of politics and government published originally in the People's Republic of China; Editor M. Y. M. KAU.

CHINESE SOCIOLOGY AND ANTHROPOLOGY. M. E. Sharpe Inc., 80 Business Park Drive, Armonk, N.Y. 10504, U.S.A.; f. 1968; quarterly; translations of empirical and analytical studies of cultural phenomena such as marriage and the family, the role of ideology, social change and problems of youth and education in contemporary China; Editor S. L. GREENBLATT.

CHINESE STUDIES IN HISTORY. M. E. Sharpe Inc., 80 Business Park Drive, Armonk, N.Y. 10504, U.S.A.; f. 1967; quarterly; translations of articles from original sources in the People's Republic of China; Editor LI YU-NING.

CHINESE STUDIES IN PHILOSOPHY. M. E. Sharpe Inc., 80 Business Park Drive, Armonk, N.Y. 10504, U.S.A.; f. 1969; quarterly; translations of articles from original sources in the People's Republic of China; Editor CHUNG-YING CHENG.

CHINOPERL PAPERS. The Conference on Chinese Oral and Performing Literature, c/o China-Japan Program, Cornell University, 140 Uris Hall, Ithaca, N.Y. 14853, U.S.A.; f. 1969; annual; Chinese oral and performing literature; Editor HAROLD SHADICK.

CINA. Centro di Ricerche Sinologiche, Istituto Italiano per il Medio ed Estremo Oriente, Via Merulana 248, 00185 Rome, Italy; f. 1956; annual; Editors Prof. LIONELLO LANCIOTTI and Prof. MARIO SABATTINI.

CONTRIBUTIONS TO ASIAN STUDIES. Sponsored by the Canadian Association for South Asian Studies; publ. by E. J. Brill, Leiden, Netherlands; f. 1971; irregular; Editor K. ISHWARAN.

THE DEVELOPING ECONOMIES. The Institute of Developing Economies, 42 Ichigaya-Hommura-cho, Shinjuku-ku, Tokyo 162, Japan; f. 1962; English language; quarterly.

DEVELOPMENT STUDIES CENTRE MONOGRAPH SERIES. Australian National University, P.O.B. 4, Canberra, A.C.T. 2600, Australia; approx. 5 a year.

DONG BANG HAK CHI. (Journal of Far Eastern Studies) Institute of Korean Studies, Yonsei University, Sudaemun-ku, Seoul, Republic of Korea; f. 1954; quarterly; in Korean.

EAST AND WEST. Istituto Italiano per il Medio ed Estremo Oriente (ISMEO), Palazzo Brancaccio, via Merulana 248, 00185 Rome, Italy; f. 1950; quarterly; Gen. Editor GIUSEPPE TUCCI.

EAST ASIAN CULTURAL STUDIES. Centre for East Asian Cultural Studies, c/o The Toyo Bunko, Honkomagome 2-chome, 28-21, Bunkyo-ku, Tokyo 113, Japan; f. 1961; quarterly; Editor Prof. M. MORI.

EAST ASIAN REVIEW. Institute for East Asian Studies, C.P.O. Box 6856, Seoul, Republic of Korea; f. 1974; quarterly; Editor KIM YU-NAM.

EASTERN ECONOMIST. United Commercial Bank Building, Parliament St., New Delhi 110001, India; f. 1943; economic and financial weekly in English; Editor V. BALASUBRAMANIAN; printer and publisher R. P. AGARWALA.

ECONOMIC AND POLITICAL WEEKLY. Skylark, 284 Frere Road, Bombay 400038, India; f. 1966; weekly; Editor KRISHNA RAJ.

ESTUDIOS DE ASIA Y AFRICA. Centre for Asian and African Studies, El Colegio de México, Camino al Ajusco 20, Pedregal Santa Teresa, México 01000 D.F., Mexico; quarterly.

FAR EASTERN ECONOMIC REVIEW. 6/F, Centre Point, 181 Gloucester Rd., Hong Kong; f. 1946; weekly; Editor DEREK DAVIES.

FOLIA ORIENTALIA. Polska Akademia Nauk, Oddział w Krakowie, Komisja Orientalistyczna, ul. Sławkowska 17, 31-016 Kraków, Poland; f. 1959; annual; in French, English and German; Editor T. LEWICKI.

GEOGRAPHICAL REVIEW OF INDIA. Geographical Society of India, 35 Ballygunge Circular Road, Calcutta 700019, India; quarterly; Editor Dr. S. C. CHAKRAVORTY.

HARVARD JOURNAL OF ASIATIC STUDIES. Harvard-Yenching Institute, 2 Divinity Ave., Cambridge, Mass. 02138, U.S.A.; f. 1936; twice yearly; Editor DONALD SHIVELY.

HITOTSUBASHI JOURNAL OF ARTS AND SCIENCES. Hitotsubashi Academy, Hitotsubashi University, Kunitachi, Tokyo, Japan; f. 1960; annual; Editor Assoc. Prof. YOSHIO INOUE.

HITOTSUBASHI JOURNAL OF ECONOMICS. Hitotsubashi Academy, Hitotsubashi University, Kunitachi, Tokyo, Japan; f. 1960; semi-annual; Editors Prof. YUICHI SHIONOYA and Assoc. Prof. JURO TERANISHI.

HONG KONG ECONOMIC PAPERS. Publ. by United Publishers Services (Hong Kong) Ltd., Stanhope House, 734 King's Road, Hong Kong, for the Hong Kong Economic Association, P.O. Box 4004, Hong Kong; f. 1961; annual; Chair. A. J. YOUNGSON.

HONG KONG LAW JOURNAL. 1030 Prince's Building, Hong Kong; f. 1971; three a year; Editor-in-Chief HENRY LITTON, Q.C.

INDIA QUARTERLY. Indian Council of World Affairs, Sapru House, Barakhamba Road, New Delhi 110001, India; f. 1953; journal of the Indian Council of World Affairs; English language; quarterly.

INDIAN ADVOCATE. Bar Association of India, Chamber No. 93, Supreme Court Building, New Delhi 110001, India; quarterly; Editor Shri C. K. DAPHTARY.

INDIAN ECONOMIC DIARY. P.O. Box No. 702, New Delhi 110001, India; weekly; Editor HARI SHARAN CHHABRA.

INDIAN ECONOMIC JOURNAL. Department of Economics, University of Bombay, Kalina Campus, Santa Cruz, Bombay 400029, India; English language; quarterly.

INDIAN ECONOMIC REVIEW. Vikas Publishing House Pvt. Ltd., 5 Ansari Road, New Delhi 110002, India; f. 1952; semi-annual; Man. Editor S. D. TENDULKAR, Delhi School of Economics, University Enclave, Delhi 110007, India.

INDIAN ECONOMIC AND SOCIAL HISTORY REVIEW. Vikas Publishing House Pvt. Ltd., 5 Ansari Road, New Delhi 110002, India; f. 1963; quarterly; Editor DHARMA KUMAR, Delhi School of Economics, University Enclave, Delhi 110007, India.

INDIAN AND FOREIGN REVIEW. India Ministry of Information and Broadcasting, Publications Division, Government of India, Patalia House, A Block, New Delhi 110001, India; semi-monthly; Editor I. RAMAMOHAN-RAO.

INDIAN JOURNAL OF INTERNATIONAL LAW. Indian Society of International Law, 7-8 Scindia House, Kasturba Gandhi Marg, New Delhi 110001, India; f. 1961; quarterly; Editor-in-Chief NAGENDRA SINGH, Exec. Editors M. K. NAWAZ, K. NARAYANA RAO and Prof. RAHMATULLAH KHAN.

INDIAN LITERATURE. Sahitya Akademi, Rabindra Bhavan, 35 Ferozeshah Rd., New Delhi, India; English language; bi-monthly; Editor KESHAV MALIK.

INDIAN POLITICAL SCIENCE REVIEW. c/o Dept. of Political Science, University of Delhi, Delhi 110007, India; semi-annual; Editor HARNAM SINGH.

INDIAN STUDIES: PAST AND PRESENT. 3 Sambhunath Pandit St., Calcutta 20, India; f. 1959; English language; quarterly; Editor DEBIPRASAD CHATTOPADHYAHYA.

INDICA. Heras Institute of Indian History and Culture, St. Xavier's College, Bombay 400001, India; f. 1964; English language; twice yearly; Editor J. VELINKAR.

INDO-ASIA. Deutsch-Indische Gesellschaft, 7000 Stuttgart 1, Charlottenplatz 17, Federal Republic of Germany; political, cultural and economic studies; German language; quarterly; Editor Dr. GISELA BONN.

THE INDONESIAN QUARTERLY. Centre for Strategic & International Studies, Jalan Tanah Abang III/27, Jakarta Pusat, Indonesia; f. 1972; Man. Editor R. S. ROOSMAN.

INTERNATIONAL STUDIES. Publ. by Vikas Publishing House Pvt. Ltd., 5 Ansari Rd., New Delhi 110002, India; for the School of International Studies, Jawaharlal Nehru University, New Delhi 110037, India; English language; quarterly; Editor K. P. MISRA.

INTERNATIONALES ASIENFORUM. Weltforum Verlag, Tintorettostrasse 1, 8000 Munich 19, Federal Republic of Germany; f. 1970; international quarterly for Asian studies.

ISLAMIC CULTURE. Islamic Culture Board, Post Box 171, opp. Osmania University Post Office, Hyderabad 7, India; f. 1927; quarterly.

JAPAN INTERPRETER: A JOURNAL OF SOCIAL AND POLITICAL IDEAS. Center for Japanese Social and Political Studies 2-8-8 Nishinogawa, Komae-shi, Tokyo 201, Japan; f. 1963; Editor KANO TSUTOMU.

JAPAN QUARTERLY. Asahi Shimbun, Tsukiyi, Chuo-ku, Tokyo, Japan; f. 1954; English language; quarterly; Exec. Editor YASUO AKIYAMA.

JAPANESE ANNUAL OF INTERNATIONAL LAW. Publ. by the International Law Association of Japan, Kenkyushitsu, Faculty of Law, University of Tokyo, 3-1, Hongo 7-chome, Bunkyo-ku, Tokyo 113, Japan; f. 1957; Editor-in-Chief Prof. SOJI YAMAMOTO.

JERNAL UNDANG-UNDANG/JOURNAL OF MALAYSIAN AND COMPARATIVE LAW. c/o Faculty of Law, University of Malaya, Kuala Lumpur, Malaysia; f. 1974; semi-annual; in English and Malay; Editor-in-Chief Prof. AHMAD IBRAHIM.

JOURNAL OF THE AMERICAN ORIENTAL SOCIETY. American Oriental Society, 329 Sterling Memorial Library, Yale Station, New Haven, Conn. 06520, U.S.A.; f. 1842; Biblical studies, Ancient Near East, South Asia and Far East; quarterly; Editor E. BENDER, 820 Williams Hall, University of Pennsylvania, Philadelphia, Pa. 19174, U.S.A.

JOURNAL OF ASIAN AND AFRICAN STUDIES. Department of Sociology, York University, Downsview M3J IP3, Canada; published by E. J. Brill, Leiden, Netherlands.

JOURNAL OF ASIAN HISTORY. Verlag Otto Harrassowitz, D6200 Wiesbaden 1, Taunusstrasse 6, Federal Republic of Germany; f. 1967; bi-annual; Editor DENIS SINOR, Goodbody Hall, Indiana Univ., Bloomington, Ind. 47405, U.S.A.

JOURNAL OF ASIAN STUDIES. Association for Asian Studies, One Lane Hall, Univ of Michigan, Ann Arbor, Mich. 48109, U.S.A.; f. 1941, formerly *Far Eastern Quarterly;* English language; quarterly.

JOURNAL OF THE ASIATIC SOCIETY OF BANGLADESH (HUMANITIES). Asiatic Society of Bangladesh, Dacca Museum Bldgs., Dacca 2; f. 1971; three a year.

JOURNAL OF THE ASIATIC SOCIETY OF BANGLADESH (SCIENCE). Asiatic Society of Bangladesh, Dacca Museum Bldgs., Dacca 2; semi-annual.

JOURNAL OF ASIATIC STUDIES. Asiatic Research Center, Korea University, Anam-Dong, Seoul, Republic of Korea; f. 1958; twice yearly; Editor LEE IL-SUN.

JOURNAL ASIATIQUE. La Société Asiatique, 3 rue Mazarine, 75006 Paris, France; f. 1822; covers all phases of Oriental research; quarterly.

JOURNAL OF THE BURMA RESEARCH SOCIETY. c/o University Library, University of Arts and Science, Rangoon, Burma; f. 1911; bi-annual.

JOURNAL OF CHINESE PHILOSOPHY. Dialogue Publishing Co., P.O. Box 11071, Honolulu, Hawaii 96826, U.S.A.; f. 1974; quarterly; Editor CHUNG-YING CHENG, Dept. of Philosophy, University of Hawaii, Honolulu, Hawaii 96822, U.S.A.

JOURNAL OF CONTEMPORARY ASIA. P.O. Box 49010, Stockholm 49, Sweden; Editors PETER LIMQUECO, BRUCE MCFARLANE; f. 1970; English language; quarterly.

JOURNAL OF THE ECONOMIC AND SOCIAL HISTORY OF THE ORIENT. Publ. E. J. Brill, Oude Rijn 33a, Leiden, Netherlands; f. 1957; annual (containing 3 issues); English, French and German text; Editors C. CAHEN and W. F. LEEMANS.

JOURNAL OF FAR EASTERN STUDIES (*see* Dong Bang Hak Chi).

JOURNAL OF THE HONG KONG BRANCH OF THE ROYAL ASIATIC SOCIETY. P.O. Box 3864, Hong Kong; f. 1960; annual; Editor D. FAURE.

JOURNAL OF INDIAN HISTORY. Dept. of History, University of Kerala, Karyavattam P.O., Trivandrum 695518, India; f. 1921; three a year; Editor T. K. RAVINDRAN.

JOURNAL OF THE INDIAN LAW INSTITUTE. Bhagwandas Road, New Delhi 110001, India; f. 1958; quarterly; Editor S. N. JAIN.

JOURNAL OF INDIAN PHILOSOPHY. D. Reidel Publishing Co., P.O. Box 17, 3300AA Dordrecht, Netherlands; f. 1970; quarterly; Editor BIMAL K. MATILAL, All Souls' College, Oxford University, Oxford, England.

JOURNAL OF THE INSTITUTE OF BANGLADESH STUDIES. Institute of Bangladesh Studies, Rajshahi University, Rajshahi, Bangladesh; f. 1976; irregular; Editor S. A. AKANDA.

JOURNAL OF JAPANESE STUDIES. Society for Japanese Studies, Thomson Hall, DR-05, University of Washington, Seattle, Washington 98195, U.S.A.; f. 1974; twice yearly; Man. Editor SUSAN B. HANLEY.

JOURNAL OF THE MALAYSIAN BRANCH OF THE ROYAL ASIATIC SOCIETY. c/o Ibu Pejabat Pendaftaran Negara Malaysia, Jalan Persiaran Barat, Petaling Jaya, Malaysia; f. 1888; Pres. Tun MOHAMED SUFFIAN BIN HASHIM; Hon. Sec. and Editor Tan Sri MUBIN SHEPPARD; twice yearly.

JOURNAL OF THE ORIENTAL INSTITUTE. Oriental Institute, M.S. University of Baroda, Tilak Road, Opp. Sayaji Gunj Tower, Vadodara 390002, Gujarat, India; f. 1951; quarterly; Editor Prof. Dr. S. G. KANTAWALA.

JOURNAL OF ORIENTAL RESEARCH. c/o Kuppaswami Sastri Research Institute, 84 Royapettah High Rd., Mylapore, Madras 600004, India; quarterly; Editor Miss S. S. JANAKI.

JOURNAL OF THE ORIENTAL SOCIETY OF AUSTRALIA. Dept. of Oriental Studies, University of Sydney, Sydney, N.S.W. 2006, Australia; f. 1961; annual; Editor Prof. A. R. DAVIS.

JOURNAL OF ORIENTAL STUDIES. Centre of Asian Studies, University of Hong Kong, Hong Kong; semi-annual; Editors Dr. L. Y. CHIU, Dr. C. K. LEUNG.

JOURNAL OF ORIENTAL STUDIES. Research Institute for Humanistic Studies, Kyoto University, Ushinomiyacho, Yoshida, Sakyo-ku, Kyoto, Japan; annual.

JOURNAL OF PACIFIC HISTORY. Australian National University, Box 4, G.P.O., Canberra, A.C.T. 2600, Australia; f. 1966; twice yearly; Editors W. N. GUNSON and D. SCARR.

JOURNAL OF THE PAKISTAN HISTORICAL SOCIETY. Pakistan Historical Society, 30 New Karachi Housing Society, Karachi 5; f. 1953; quarterly; Editor Dr. S. MOINUL HUQ.

JOURNAL OF THE POLYNESIAN SOCIETY. f. 1892; quarterly study of the peoples of the Pacific area; Editors GEOFFREY IRWIN and ROGER OPPENHEIM, Anthropology Dept., University of Auckland, Private Bag, Auckland, New Zealand.

JOURNAL OF THE ROYAL ASIATIC SOCIETY OF GREAT BRITAIN AND IRELAND. 56 Queen Anne St., London, W1M 9LA, England; f. 1834; covers all phases of Oriental research; semi-annual.

JOURNAL OF THE SIAM SOCIETY. G.P.O. Box 65, Bangkok, Thailand; f. 1905; English language; semi-annual; Hon. Editor Dr. TEJ BUNNAG.

JOURNAL OF SOUTH ASIAN LITERATURE. Asian Studies Center, Center for International Programs, Michigan State University, East Lansing, Mich. 48824, U.S.A.; semi-annual; Editor C. COPPOLA, Dept. of Modern Languages, Oakland Univ., Rochester, Mich. 48063, U.S.A.

JOURNAL OF SOUTHEAST ASIAN STUDIES. Department of History, National University of Singapore, Kent Ridge, Singapore 0511; f. 1970; published and distributed by Singapore University Press Pte. Ltd.; Editor YONG MUN CHEONG; twice yearly.

JOURNAL OF THE SRI LANKA BRANCH OF THE ROYAL ASIATIC SOCIETY. 22 Deal Place, Colombo 3, Sri Lanka; f. 1845; annual; Hon. Secs. P. R. SITTAMPALAM and K. M. W. KURUPPU.

KANSAI UNIVERSITY REVIEW OF ECONOMICS AND BUSINESS. Kansai University, Suita, Osaka, Japan; semi-annual; Editor KOICHI SHIGETA.

KEIO ECONOMIC STUDIES. Keio Economic Society, 2-15-45 Mita, Minato-ku, Tokyo 108, Japan; f. 1963; semi-annual; Editor Prof. HIROAKI OSANA.

KOREA OBSERVER. Academy of Korean Studies, C.P.O. Box 3410, Seoul 100, Republic of Korea; f. 1968; quarterly; Editor EUN HO LEE.

KYOTO UNIVERSITY ECONOMIC REVIEW. Faculty of Economics, Kyoto University, Sakyo-ku, Kyoto, Japan; f. 1926; semi-annual.

LAWASIA. New South Wales Institute of Technology, P.O. Box 123, Broadway, N.S.W. 2007, Australia; f. 1969; annual; Editor G. W. BARTHOLOMEW.

AL MA'ARIF. Institute of Islamic Culture, Club Rd., Lahore, Pakistan; f. 1968; monthly; Urdu; Editor M. ISHAQ BHATTI; Dir. Prof. M. SAEED SHEIKH; Hon. Publs. Adviser and Sec. M. ASHRAF DARR.

MALAYA LAW REVIEW. Faculty of Law, National University of Singapore, Kent Ridge, Singapore 0511; f. 1959; semi-annual; Editor TAN KENG FENG.

MĀRG. Marg Publications, Army and Navy Building, 148 Mahatma Gandhi Road, Bombay 400023, India; f. 1947; quarterly magazine of the arts; Editor Dr. (Mrs.) SARYU DOSHI.

MARGA. Marga Institute, 61 Isipathana Mawatha, Colombo 5, Sri Lanka; quarterly; Editor GODFREY GUNATILLEKE.

MELANESIAN LAW JOURNAL. Faculty of Law, University of Papua New Guinea, P.O. Box 4817, University, Papua New Guinea; f. 1970; semi-annual; Editor C. E. P. HAYNES.

MODERN ASIA. P.O.B. 9765, Hong Kong; f. 1967; business monthly (11 a year); Editor DAVID CREFFIELD.

MODERN ASIAN STUDIES. Cambridge University Press, The Edinburgh Bldg., Shaftesbury Rd., Cambridge CB2 2RU, England; f. 1967; quarterly; Editor Dr. GORDON JOHNSON.

MODERN CEYLON STUDIES. University of Peradeniya, Peradeniya, Sri Lanka; semi-annual journal of the social sciences; Editors Dr. S. PATHMANATHAN and Prof. W. A. WARNAPALA.

MODERN CHINA. Sage Publications Inc., 275 S. Beverly Drive, Beverly Hills, Calif. 90212, U.S.A.; f. 1975; international quarterly of history and social sciences; Editor-in-Chief PHILIP C. C. HUANG.

MONDES ASIATIQUES. B.P. No. 1, 37220 L'Ile Bouchard, France; quarterly; Editor FRANÇOIS JOYAUX.

MONGOLIAN STUDIES. Journal of the Mongolia Society. P.O.B. 606, Bloomington, Ind. 47401, U.S.A.; f. 1962; annual; Orientalist periodical emphasizing Mongolia and Inner Asia of all periods; Gen. Editor JOHN R. KRUEGER.

MONUMENTA NIPPONICA. Sophia University, 7-Kioi-chō, Chiyoda-ku, Tokyo 102, Japan; f. 1938; quarterly; studies in Japanese culture; Editor MICHAEL COOPER.

MONUMENTA SERICA. Arnold-Janssen-Strasse 20, 5025 St. Augustin 1, Federal Republic of Germany; f. 1935; annual journal of oriental studies; Editor HEINRICH BUSCH.

LE MUSÉON. Institut Orientaliste, Université Catholique de Louvain, B.P.41, Louvain, Belgium; f. 1882; review of Oriental studies; two double vols. a year; Editor Prof. G. GARITTE, Beukenlaan 9, Héverlé-Louvain.

NARODY ASII I AFRIKI (Istoriya, Ekonomika, Kultura). Akademi Nauk S.S.S.R., Institut Vostokovedeniya, Institut Afriki, 103045 Moscow, K-45, ul. Zhdanova 12, U.S.S.R.; f. 1955; bi-monthly; Editor-in-Chief Prof. A. A. KUTSENKOV.

OCEANIA. Mackie Bldg., The University, Sydney, N.S.W. 2006, Australia; f. 1930; anthropology; quarterly; Editor P. LAWRENCE.

ORIENS EXTREMUS. Zeitschrift für Sprache, Kunst und Kultur des Fernen Ostens. Verlag Otto Harrassowitz, D-6200 Wiesbaden 1, Taunusstrasse 6, Federal Republic of Germany; f. 1954; in German and English; semi-annual; Editors O. BENL, T. GRIMM, K. WENK (Seminar für Sprache und Kultur Japans, Von-Melle-Park 6, D2000 Hamburg 13, Federal Republic of Germany.

ORIENTAL ART. 12 Ennerdale Road, Richmond, Surrey, England; f. 1949; quarterly; Editor EDMUND CAPON, 89 Thurleigh Rd., London SW12 8TY, England.

ORIENTAL ECONOMIST. Hongoku-cho, Nihonbashi, Chuo-ku, Tokyo, Japan; f. 1934; economics, business and politics; monthly; Editor A. TSURUOKA.

ORIENTAL GEOGRAPHER. Bangladesh Geographical Society, Dept. of Geography, University of Dacca, Dacca 2, Bangladesh; semi-annual; Editor LUTFUL HAQ.

PACIFIC AFFAIRS. Publ. by University of British Columbia, 2021 West Mall, Vancover, B.C., Canada, V6T 1W5; f. 1928; covers political, economic, social and diplomatic problems of eastern and southern Asia and Australasia; research articles, book reviews; quarterly; Editor H. B. CHAMBERLAIN.

PACIFIC COMMUNITY. Pacific Institute, P.O.B. 2043S, Melbourne, Vic. 3001, Australia; f. 1969; quarterly; Asian and Pacific affairs; Published by Hawthorn Press; Editor CHRISTOPHER CLARK.

PACIFIC HISTORICAL REVIEW. Pacific Coast Branch, American Historical Asscn., c/o University of California, Los Angeles, Calif. 90024, U.S.A.; f. 1932; quarterly; Editor NORRIS HUNDLEY.

PACIFIC ISLANDS MONTHLY. Pacific Publications (Aust.) Pty. Ltd., 76 Clarence St., Sydney 2000, N.S.W., Australia; f. 1930; news magazine of the South Pacific; monthly; Editor ANGUS SMALES.

PACIFIC VIEWPOINT. Victoria University, Private Bag, Wellington, New Zealand; f. 1960; semi-annual; Editor Prof. R. F. WATTERS.

PAKISTAN DEVELOPMENT REVIEW. Pakistan Institute of Development Economics, P.O. Box 1091, Islamabad, Pakistan; f. 1956, fmrly. *The Economic Digest*; quarterly; Editor Prof. SYED NAWAB HAIDER NAQVI.

PAKISTAN ECONOMIC AND SOCIAL REVIEW. Dept. of Economics, University of the Punjab, New Campus, Lahore 20, Pakistan; quarterly; Editor RAFIQ AHMAD.

PAKISTAN HORIZON. Pakistan Institute of International Affairs, Aiwan-e-Sadar Road, Karachi 1, Pakistan; f. 1948; English language; quarterly; Editor KHALIDA QURESHI.

PHILIPPINE ECONOMIC JOURNAL. Philippine Economic Society, P.O. Box 1964, Manila, the Philippines; f. 1962; quarterly; Editor MAHAR MANGAHAS.

PHILIPPINE STUDIES. Ateneo de Manila University Press, P.O. Box 154, Manila 2801, the Philippines; f. 1953; quarterly; Editor JOSEPH L. ROCHE.

PRZEGLĄD ORIENTALISTYCZNY. Polskie Towarzystwo Orientalistyczne, 00-656 Warsaw, ul. Sniadeckich 8, Poland; quarterly; Editor STANISLAW KALUŻYŃSKI.

QUARTERLY REVIEW OF HISTORICAL STUDIES. Institute of Historical Studies, 35 Theatre Road, Calcutta 700017, India; f. 1961; quarterly; Editor Prof. N. R. RAY.

REVIEW OF INDONESIAN AND MALAYAN AFFAIRS (RIMA). Dept. of Indonesian and Malayan Studies, The University of Sydney, N.S.W. 2006, Australia; produced in co-operation with the Royal Institute for Anthropology and Linguistics, Leiden, Netherlands; f. 1967; bi-annual; Editors MICHAEL VAN LANGENBERG (Australia) and CEES VAN DIJK (Netherlands).

RIVISTA DEGLI STUDI ORIENTALI. Scuola Orientale, Città Universitaria, Rome, Italy; f. 1907; quarterly.

ROCZNIK ORIENTALISTYCZNY. 02-021 Warsaw, Gròjecka 17 pok. 112, Poland; f. 1915; Editor-in-Chief EDWARD TRYJARSKI, Sec. JANUSZ DANECKI; semi-annual.

SINGAPORE JOURNAL OF TROPICAL GEOGRAPHY. Department of Geography, National University of Singapore, Singapore; f. 1953; bi-annual; Editor OOI JIN-BEE.

SOUTH ASIA: JOURNAL OF SOUTH ASIAN STUDIES. University of Western Australia, for the South Asian Studies Association, with the South Asia Institute, University of Heidelberg; f. 1971; annual; Editor H. F. OWEN, Centre for South and Southeast Asian Studies, University of Western Australia, Nedlands, W.A. 6009, Australia.

SOUTH ASIAN ANTHROPOLOGIST. 18 Church Rd., Ranchi, Bihar, India; f. 1980; bi-annual; Man. Editor P. DASH SHARMA.

SOUTHEAST ASIAN JOURNAL OF SOCIAL SCIENCE. Chopmen Enterprises, 428–429 Katong Shopping Centre, Singapore 15; f. 1973; semi-annual; Editor PETER S. J. CHEN, Dept. of Sociology, University of Singapore, Singapore 10.

SOUTHEAST ASIAN STUDIES (*see* Tonan Ajia Kenkyu).

SOUTH PACIFIC BULLETIN. South Pacific Commission, Box N324, Grosvenor St., P.O. Sydney, N.S.W., Australia 2000; f. 1951; quarterly; English and French editions; Editor KEVIN EARL.

SRI LANKA JOURNAL OF THE HUMANITIES. University of Peradeniya, Peradeniya Campus, Sri Lanka; f. 1975; twice a year; Man. Editor P. B. MEEGASKUMBURA, Dept. of Sinhala, University of Sri Lanka.

STATESMAN. 4 Chowringhee Square, Calcutta, India; f. 1875; overseas weekly; English language; Editor AMALENDU DAS GUPTA.

STUDIA ORIENTALIA. Suomen Itämainen Seura (Finnish Oriental Society), c/o Department of Asian and African Studies, University of Helsinki, 00100 Helsinki 10, Finland; f. 1917; Editorial Board J. ARO, S. PARPOLA, T. HARVIAINEN, H. HALÉN.

SVADHYAYA. Oriental Institute, M.S. University of Baroda, Tilak Rd., Opp. Sayaji Gunj Tower, Vadodara 390002, India; f. 1962; quarterly; Gujarati; Editor A. N. JANI.

TIBET JOURNAL. Library of Tibetan Works and Archives, Dharamsala, Kangra, Himachal Pradesh, India; f. 1975; quarterly; Man. Editor K. DHONDUP.

TONAN AJIA KENKYU. (Southeast Asian Studies.) The Center for Southeast Asian Studies of Kyoto University, 46 Shimoadachi-cho, Yoshida, Sakyo-ku, Kyoto 606, Japan; quarterly.

T'OUNG PAO. Publ. E. J. Brill, Oude Rijn 33a, Leiden, Netherlands, for the Centre National Français de la Recherche Scientifique and The Netherlands Organization for the Advancement of Pure Research, The Hague; f. 1890; annually (containing 5 issues); a leading journal of Chinese studies; Editors JACQUES GERNET, E. ZÜRCHER.

TŌYŌGAKU BUNKEN RUIMOKU. (Annual Bibliography of Oriental Studies.) Research Institute for Humanistic Studies, Kyoto University, Ushinomiyacho, Yoshida, Sakyo-ku, Kyoto, Japan; annual; in Japanese and European languages.

TRANSACTIONS OF THE KOREA BRANCH OF THE ROYAL ASIATIC SOCIETY. P.O. Box 255, Seoul 100, Republic of Korea; f. 1900; annual; Pres. Dr. JAMES HOYT.

TRANSLATIONS ON THE PEOPLE'S REPUBLIC OF CHINA, U.S. Joint Publications Research Service, NTIS. Springfield, Va. 22151, U.S.A.; f. 1964; *c.* 40 issues a year.

TRIBUNE: CEYLON NEWS REVIEW, 43 Dawson St., Colombo 2, Sri Lanka; f. 1954; weekly; Editor S. P. AMARASINGAM.

VIEWPOINT. Publ. by Ahmad Azeez Zia, P.O. Box No. 540, Lahore, Pakistan; f. 1975; weekly; Editor MAZHAR ALI KHAN.

WALKABOUT. Leisure Magazines, P.O. Box 319, Avalon, N.S.W. 2107, Australia; f. 1934; magazine of the Australian way of life; monthly; Editor P. WEBSTER.

WIENER ZEITSCHRIFT FÜR DIE KUNDE DES MORGENLANDES. Institut für Orientalistik der Universität Wien, 1010 Vienna 1, Universitätsstrasse 7/V, Austria; f. 1887; annual; Editor ANDREAS TIETZE.

WIENER ZEITSCHRIFT FÜR DIE KUNDE SÜDASIENS UND ARCHIV FÜR INDISCHE PHILOSOPHIE. E. J. Brill, Leiden, Netherlands, Gerold & Co., Vienna, Austria, Motilal Banarsidass, Delhi, India for Institut für Indologie, Universität Wien; f. 1957; annual; Editor G. OBERHAMMER, Institut für Indologie, Universität Wien, 101 Vienna, Universitätsstrasse 7, Austria.

ZENTRALASIATISCHE STUDIEN DES SEMINARS FÜR SPRACH- UND KULTURWISSENSCHAFT ZENTRALASIENS DER UNIVERSITÄT BONN. Verlag Otto Harrassowitz, D-6200 Wiesbaden 1, Taunusstrasse 6, Federal Republic of Germany; f. 1967; annual; Editor W. HEISSIG, D-5300 Germany.